2400

The New
CENTURY DICTIONARY

The New

CENTURY DICTIONARY
[Reg. U. S. Pat. Off.]

OF THE

ENGLISH LANGUAGE

*Based on matter selected from the original Century Dictionary
and entirely rewritten, with the addition of a great amount
of new material, and containing the great mass of words
and phrases in ordinary use. 12,000 quotations.
4,000 pictorial illustrations.*

EDITED BY

H. G. Emery and K. G. Brewster

Revision Editor, Charles H. Fitch

**With supplements of synonyms and antonyms,
foreign words and phrases, biographical
names, geographical names, etc.**

VOLUME TWO

pock-mark—zymurgy

ALSO

SUPPLEMENTS

Distributed, by arrangement with D. Appleton-Century Company, by

P. F. COLLIER & SON CORPORATION

NEW YORK

CONTENTS OF VOLUME I

LIST OF COLOR-PLATES

CONTENTS OF VOLUME II

LIST OF COLOR-PLATES

pock=mark (pok′märk), *n.* A mark or pit left by a pustule in smallpox or the like.—**pock′=marked**, *a.*

po-co-cu-ran-te (pō″kō-kō-rän′tā). [It. *poco curante*, 'little caring.'] **I.** *a.* Caring little; careless or indifferent; nonchalant. **II.** *n.* A careless or indifferent person; one who shows little interest.—**po″co-cu-ran′tism,** *n.*

po-co-sin (pō-kō′sin), *n.* [N. Amer. Ind.] A tract of swampy land; a dismal. [Southern U. S.]

pod[1] (pod), *n.* [Origin uncertain.] A more or less elongated, two-valved seed-vessel, as that of the pea or bean; a dehiscent fruit or pericarp with several seeds; also, the straight groove or channel in the body of certain augers or bits.—**pod**[1], *v. i.*; *podded, podding*. To produce pods; also, to swell out like a pod.

pod[2] (pod), *n.* [Origin unknown.] A small herd or school, esp. of seals or whales; a small flock of birds.

-pod. A termination from Gr. πούς (ποδ-), foot, serving to form adjectives and nouns, as *arthropod, cephalopod, tetrapod, uropod.*

Different kinds of Pod.— 1. legume of common vetch (*Vicia sativa*); 2. follicle of peony (*Pæonia officinalis*); 3. silique of a cress (*Cardamine hirsuta*); 4, silicle of a cress (*Thlaspi arvense*).

po-dag-ra (pō-dag′rä), *n.* [L., < Gr. ποδάγρα, < πούς (ποδ-), foot, + ἄγρα, a catching.] Gout in the foot; also, gout generally.—**po-dag′ric,** *a.*

pod-ded (pod′ed), *a.* Bearing pods; leguminous; also, inclosed within a pod; also, swollen like a pod.

po-des-tà (pō-des-tä′), *n.* [It., < L. *potestas*, power, magistrate, < *potis*, able: see *potent*.] Any of certain magistrates in Italy, as a chief magistrate in medieval towns and republics or a subordinate municipal judge in modern cities.

podg-y (poj′i), *a.* Same as *pudgy.*

po-di-a-trist (pō-dī′a-trist), *n.* [Gr. πούς (ποδ-), foot, + ἰατρός, physician.] One who treats disorders of the human foot. Cf. *chiropodist*.—**po-di′a-try** (-tri), *n.*

po-dit-ti (pō-dit′i), *n.* [Australian.] An Australian kingfisher, *Syma flavirostris.*

po-di-um (pō′di-um), *n.*; pl. *-dia* (-di-ä). [L., elevated place, balcony, < Gr. πόδιον, dim. of πούς (ποδ-), foot: cf. *pew*.] In *arch.*, a continuous projecting base or pedestal; a stylobate; also, a raised platform surrounding the arena of an ancient amphitheater; also, a continuous bench around a room; in *zoöl.* and *anat.*, a foot; a structure serving as a foot or leg; in *bot.*, a footstalk or the like.

Poditti.

pod-o-phyl-lin (pod-ō-fil′in), *n.* [See *podophyllum.*] A resin obtained from podophyllum: used as a cathartic.

pod-o-phyl-lum (pod-ō-fil′um), *n.* [NL. *Podophyllum*, < Gr. πούς (ποδ-), foot, + φύλλον, leaf.] The dried rhizome of the May-apple, *Podophyllum peltatum*, used as a cathartic.

po-em (pō′em), *n.* [F. *poème*, < L. *poema*, < Gr. ποίημα, something made, a poem, < ποιεῖν: see *poet*.] A composition in verse, esp. one characterized by artistic construction and imaginative or elevated thought (as, a lyric *poem*, a pastoral *poem*); also, a composition which, though not in verse, is characterized by great beauty of language or thought (as, a prose *poem*); fig., something having qualities suggestive of or likened to those of poetry (as, "The Celts . . .

gave to the seas and mountains names which are *poems*, and imitate the pure voices of nature," Emerson's "English Traits," iv.; a life, or a face, which is a *poem*).

pœ-nol-o-gy (pē-nol′ō-ji), etc. See *penology*, etc.

po-e-sy (pō′e-si), *n.*; pl. *-sies* (-siz). [OF. *poesie* (F. *poésie*), < L. *poesis*, < Gr. ποίησις, a making, poetic composition, poetry, < ποιεῖν: see *poet*.] The work or the art of poetic composition (archaic); also, poetry or verse (archaic); also, a poem†; also, a verse of poetry or the like used as a motto† (see *posy*).

po-et (pō′et), *n.* [OF. *poete* (F. *poète*), < L. *poeta*, < Gr. ποιητής, maker, poet, < ποιεῖν, make, produce, compose, write poetry.] One who composes poetry; one having the gift of poetic thought, imagination, and creation, together with eloquence of expression.—**poet laureate,** formerly, a title given to any eminent poet; in modern use, in Great Britain, the title given to a poet who is appointed a salaried officer of the royal household to write odes, etc., in celebration of court and national events; in certain States of the U. S., a title officially conferred upon some native or resident poet of the State.

po-et-as-ter (pō′e-tas-tėr or pō-e-tas′tėr), *n.* [NL.: see *-aster*.] A petty or inferior poet; a writer of indifferent verse.

po-et-ess (pō′et-es), *n.* A female poet.

po-et-ic, po-et-i-cal (pō-et′ik, -i-kal), *a.* [F. *poétique*, < L. *poeticus*, < Gr. ποιητικός.] Of or pertaining to a poet or poets; characteristic of or befitting a poet (as, *poetic* feeling); also, endowed with the faculty or feeling of a poet, as a person; having or showing the sensibility of a poet; also, of or pertaining to poetry (as, *poetic* justice, *poetic* license: see phrases below); of the nature of poetry (as, a *poetic* composition); possessing the qualities or the charm of poetry (as, *poetic* prose; *poetic* descriptions of nature); also, celebrated in poetry, as a place; such as affords a subject for poetry.—**poetic justice,** an ideal distribution of rewards and punishments such as is common in poetry and works of fiction.—**poetic license,** license or liberty taken by a poet in deviating from rule, conventional form, or fact, in order to produce a desired effect.—**po-et′ic,** *n.* Poetics.—**po-et′i-cal-ly,** *adv.*—**po-et′i-cal-ness,** *n.*—**po-et′i-cism** (-sizm), *n.* Poetic character or practice.—**po-et′ics,** *n.* That part of literary criticism which treats of the nature and laws of poetry; also, a treatise on poetry (as, the "Poetics" of Aristotle).

po-et-i-cule (pō-et′i-kūl), *n.* [Dim. < L. *poeta*, poet.] A petty or insignificant poet.

po-et-ize (pō′et-īz), *v.*; *-ized, -izing*. **I.** *intr.* To compose poetry. **II.** *tr.* To write about in poetry; express in poetic form; make poetic (as, "All the activities of newspaper production were poetized by her fervour": Arnold Bennett's "Hilda Lessways," i. 13).

po-et-ry (pō′et-ri), *n.* [OF. *poetrie*, < ML. *poetria*.] The art of metrical composition; the art of exciting pleasure by means of beautiful, imaginative, or elevated thought expressed in appropriate words, usually in metrical form; also, literary work in metrical form; verse; prose with poetic qualities; also, poetic quality; poetic spirit or feeling; something suggestive of or likened to poetry.

pog-a-mog-gan (pog-a-mog′an), *n.* [N. Amer. Ind.] A kind of war-club having a slender handle and a heavy knobbed head, used by some American Indian tribes.

po-go-ni-a (pō-gō′ni-ä), *n.* [NL., < Gr. πώγων, beard (with reference to the frequently fringed lip).] A plant of the genus *Pogonia*, comprising terrestrial orchids of North America.

Flowering Plant and Leaf of Pogonia (*P. ophioglossoides*).

po-go (pō′gō) **stick.** [Said to be named from a village in Transylvania, where such sticks were found in use for crossing a stream.] A kind of stick containing a spring, with which children and others jump about for amusement or exercise, placing the feet on foot-rests near the bottom and holding the upper end in the hands.

po-grom (pō-grom′), *n.* [Russ., devastation, destruction.] In Russia, an organized massacre, esp. of Jews.

po-gy (pō′gi), *n.*; pl. *-gies* (-giz). [From N. Amer. Ind. name.] The menhaden (fish), *Brevoortia tyrannus*.

poh (pō), *interj.* Same as *pooh*.

po-i (pō′i or poi), *n.* [Hawaiian.] A Hawaiian dish made of the root of the taro baked, pounded, moistened, and fermented.

poign-ant (poi′nant), *a.* [OF. F. *poignant*, ppr. of *poindre*, < L. *pungere*, prick, pierce: cf. *pungent*.] Piercing or sharp-pointed, as a weapon†; hence, pungent to the taste or smell (as, *poignant* sauces; *poignant* perfumes); also, sharp or acutely distressing to the physical feelings (as, *poignant* suffering; *poignant* thirst); also, keenly distressing to the mind (as, *poignant* regret; "a matter of *poignant* anxiety," George Eliot's "Adam Bede," xxxix.; "*Poignant* grief cannot endure for ever," W. H. Hudson's "Purple Land," xvi.); stinging or severe, as speech, sarcasm, etc.; also, keen or strong in mental appeal (as, a subject of *poignant* interest; "That figure beside him . . . gave him perhaps the most *poignant* glimpse of mystery that he had ever had," Galsworthy's "Patrician," ii. 10); sometimes, agreeably keen or intense (as, *poignant* delight); highly piquant. —**poign′an-cy**, *n.*—**poign′ant-ly**, *adv.*

poi-lu (pwo-lü), *n.*; pl. *poilus* (F. -lü). [F., lit. 'hairy,' < *poil*, < L. *pilus*, hair: cf. F. *homme à poil*, 'man with hair,' one who is virile and energetic.] A French common soldier. [Colloq.]

poin-ci-a-na (poin-si-ā′na), *n.* [NL.; from M. de *Poinci*, governor of the French West Indies in the 17th century.] A plant of the cæsalpiniaceous genus *Poinciana*, of the warmer parts of the world, comprising trees or shrubs with showy orange or scarlet flowers; also, a cæsalpiniaceous tree, *Delonix regia* ('royal poinciana'), native in Madagascar but now widely cultivated, remarkable for its showy scarlet flowers and extremely long woody pods (this tree also being referred by some authorities to the genus *Poinciana*).

poin-set-ti-a (poin-set′i-ä), *n.* [NL.; from J. R. *Poinsett*, U. S. minister to Mexico, who discovered the plant there in 1828.] Any of the euphorbiaceous herbs constituting the genus *Poinsettia*, esp. *P. pulcherrima*, a cultivated species with crowded cymes of small yellowish flowers surrounded by large scarlet floral leaves.

point (point), *n.* [OF. F. *point*, masc., *pointe*, fem., respectively < L. *punctum*, prick, dot, spot, small portion, instant, and ML. *puncta*, sharp or tapering end, being prop. the pp. neut. and fem. of L. *pungere*, prick, pierce: cf. *pungent*. A few senses are from *point*, *v.*] A prick† or puncture†; hence, a mark made as with the sharp end of something; a dot; a mark of punctuation, esp. the period; a diacritical mark, as in Hebrew; a decimal point; one of the embossed dots used in certain systems of writing and printing for the blind (see *point system*, below); also, a single or separate article or item, as in an extended whole; an individual part or element of something (as, "There were many good, nay, noble *points* in her character": H. Kingsley's "Geoffry Hamlyn," xxxviii.); a detail or particular; a particular respect (as, "His wife was a lady in every *point*": Galt's "Annals of the Parish," xlix.); also, a jot† or bit†; also, a short musical strain, esp. one sounded on an instrument as a signal (archaic: as, a *point* of war); also, a single unit, as in counting; a unit of count in the score of a game; a unit of price quotation, as, in the U. S., one dollar in stock transactions, one hundredth of a cent in cotton and coffee, or one cent in oil, grain, pork, etc.; a unit of measurement for type-bodies, being .0138 of an inch in the U. S. system (see *point system*, below); also, something that has position but not extension, as the intersection of two lines (specif. in *math.*); in general, a place of which the position alone is considered; a spot; hence, any definite position, as in a scale, course, etc.; a degree or stage (as, "to carry callousness to the *point* of insult": Arnold Bennett's "Hilda Lessways," vi. 6); a particular instant of time; often, the critical position in a course of affairs; a decisive state of circumstances (as, "Here then the matter is brought to a *point*": J. Butler's "Analogy of

Religion," i. 6); the precise moment for action; also, state† or condition† (as, "He was a lord ful fat and in good *point*": Chaucer's "Prologue to the Canterbury Tales," 200); also, a distinguishing mark or quality; a characteristic, peculiarity, or trait; often, a physical characteristic or feature in an animal (as, "The good *points* in a cow aren't necessarily features of beauty": W. Churchill's "Modern Chronicle," i. 9); also, the precise matter in discussion (as, "Please . . . do try and keep to the *point*": Mallock's "New Republic," i. 3); the important or essential thing (as, the *point* of the matter); an essential or indispensable thing (as, to make a *point* of a thing); also, a particular aim, end, or purpose (as, "Cato resisted them, and carried his *point*": Froude's "Cæsar," xii.); also, an end or conclusion (obs. or rare); also, point-lace; also, a sharp or tapering end, as of a dagger or a pen; a projecting part of anything; a tapering extremity, as a cape or a mountain-peak; *pl.*, the extremities of a horse; also, *sing.*, something having a sharp or tapering end; a pointed tool or instrument, as an etching-needle; a pointed weapon, as a dagger; a vaccine-point; a branch of a deer's antler; a tapering movable rail, as in a railroad-switch; one of the narrow tapering spaces marked on a backgammon-board; also, each of the 32 positions indicating direction marked at the circumference of the card of a compass, or the interval of 11° 15′ between any two adjacent positions; also, a tagged lace or cord, formerly much used in dress, as for tying or fastening parts (archaic); sometimes (in nautical use), a reef-point; also, the salient feature of a story, epigram, joke, etc.; force or effectiveness, as in speech, writing, or action (as, a remark lacking *point*; "She . . . criticised the appointments of the studio with freedom and some *point*," Kipling's "Light That Failed," ix.); also, the position of one of the players in various games, as in cricket, that of the fielder who stands a short distance in front

Points in Costume.

and to the off side of the batsman, or, in lacrosse, that of the player who stands a short distance in front of the goal-keeper; the player himself; also, the act of pointing; often, a hint or suggestion (as, to give one *points* about a matter).—**in point,** apposite to the matter in hand; pertinent: as, a case *in point*.—**in point of,** in the matter of; with respect to; as regards: as, *in point of* fact (that is, as a matter of fact; in fact).—**on the point of,** on the verge of; just about: as, "He was *on the point of* leaving England" (Peacock's "Nightmare Abbey," xi.).—**point of order,** in deliberative bodies, a question raised as to whether proceedings are in order, or in conformity with parliamentary law and the special rules of the particular body.—**point of view,** a point from which things are viewed; often, fig., a mental position from which subjects are considered and ideas and opinions formed; a viewpoint.—**point system,** any of certain systems of writing and printing for the blind which employ symbols formed of embossed or raised points to represent letters, numerals, punctuation-marks, musical notation, etc. (cf. *braille*); also, in *printing*, a system for grading the sizes of type-bodies, leads, etc., which employs the point as a unit of measurement, the point in the U. S. system being the twelfth part of a pica, and equivalent to .0138, or nearly one seventy-second, of an inch.—**to the point,** apposite to the matter in hand; pertinent: as, "What was more *to the point*, he advised Kim as to the care of his own body" (Kipling's "Kim," x.). —**point,** *v.* **I.** *tr.* To prick† or puncture†; also, to mark with one or more points, dots, or the like; punctuate, as writing; separate by points or dots, as figures; also, to furnish with a point or points; sharpen (as, "to *point* a lead-pencil": M. Hewlett's "Open Country," xiv.); also, to give point or force to (speech, action, etc.); also, to fill the joints of (brickwork, etc.) with mortar or cement, smoothed with the point of the trowel; also, to indicate the presence

4 POINT	
5 POINT.	
6 POINT.	
7 POINT.	
8 POINT.	
9 POINT.	
10 POINT.	
11 POINT.	
12 POINT.	

Sizes of Type according to the Point System.

or position of, as with the finger (now usually with *out*); direct attention to (with *out*); of a hound, to indicate (game) by standing rigid with the muzzle directed toward it; also, to direct (the finger, a weapon, the attention, etc.) at, to, or upon something. **II.** *intr.* To indicate position or direction, or direct attention, with or as with the finger; direct the mind or thought in some direction (as, everything *points* to his guilt); of a hound, to point game; also, to aim; fig., to have a tendency, as toward something; also, to have a specified direction; face in a particular direction, as a building; also, of an abscess, to come to a head; also, *naut.*, to sail close to the wind.

point=blank (point′blangk′). [Cf. *blank*, white spot in the center of a target.] **I.** *adv.* With a direct aim; directly; straight; fig., without deviation or circumlocution (as, "He asked Mr. Hughes *point blank* why it was that he disapproved of his idea": S. Butler's "Way of All Flesh," lxvi.); also, without deliberation or forethought. **II.** *a.* Aimed or fired straight at the mark; direct; fig., straightforward, plain, or explicit (as, "To use the concise, *point-blank* phrase of the sailors, I had made up my mind to 'run away'": H. Melville's "Typee," iii.).

point=de-vice (point′dē-vīs′). [ME. *at point devys* (cf. OF. *devis*, devised, arranged).] **I.** *adv.* Completely; perfectly; exactly. [Archaic.] **II.** *a.* Perfect; precise; scrupulously nice or neat. [Archaic.]

point-ed (poin′ted), *a.* Having a point or points (as, a *pointed* arch, one with a pointed crown, characteristic of the 'pointed' or Gothic style of architecture; fig., sharp or piercing (as, *pointed* wit); having point or force (as, *pointed* comment); also, directed or aimed; fig., directed particularly, as at a person; directly applicable; marked or emphasized (as, "Only ten days ago had he elated her by his *pointed* regard": Jane Austen's "Northanger Abbey," xxix.).— **point′ed-ly**, *adv.*— **point′ed-ness**, *n.*

point-er (poin′ter), *n.* One who or that which points (sharpens, points out or indicates, or directs or aims); a long, tapering stick used by teachers, lecturers, etc., in pointing things out on a map, blackboard, or the like; a hint or suggestion (colloq.); one of a breed of short-haired hunting-dogs trained to point game; *pl.* [*cap.*], in *astron.*, the two outer stars in the bowl of the Dipper in Ursa Major, the line joining which points toward the pole-star.

poin-til-lism (pwan′ti-lizm), *n.* [F. *pointillisme*, < *pointiller*, cover with little points or dots, < *point*, E. *point*.] A method of painting, introduced by French impressionists, in which luminosity is produced by laying on the colors in points or dots of unmixed color, which are blended by the eye.— **poin′til-list**, *n.*— **poin-til-lis′tic**, *a.*

point=lace (point′lās′), *n.* Lace made with a needle rather than with bobbins; needle-point.

Pointed Style. — Typical scheme of a fully developed French cathedral of the 13th century.

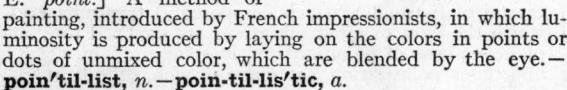

Pointer.

point-less (point′les), *a.* Without a point; blunt, as an instrument; without force, as a remark; without a point scored, as a competitor in a game.— **point′less-ly**, *adv.*— **point′less-ness**, *n.*

poise (poiz), *n.* [OF. *pois* (F. *poids*), earlier *peis*, < L. *pensum*, weight, prop. pp. neut. of *pendere*, weigh.] Weight† or heaviness†; fig., gravity†, moment†, or importance† (as, "Occasions . . . of some *poise*, Wherein we must have use of your advice": Shakspere's "King Lear," ii. 1. 122); also, a weight, as of a clock, or as one used in a balance or weighing apparatus†; also, a state of balance or equilibrium, as from equality or equal distribution of weight; equipoise; fig., mental balance, composure, or self-possession (as, "Cynthia's impassiveness, her complete *poise*, had fascinated Miss Duncan": W. Churchill's "Coniston," ii. 11). also, steadiness or stability; also, a state of being balanced or of hanging between alternatives; hence, suspense or indecision; also, the way of being poised, held, or carried (as, "the gladiatorlike *poise* of his small round head on his big neck and shoulders": Du Maurier's "Trilby," vii.); also, a state or position of poising or hovering (as, the *poise* of a bird in the air).—

poise, *v.*; poised, poising. [OF. F. *peser* (OF. 3d pers. sing. pres. ind. *peise*, later *poise*, F. *pèse*), < L. *pensare*, freq. of *pendere*.] **I.** *tr.* To weigh†; fig., to ponder or consider (obs. or rare); also, to balance evenly, or adjust or hold in equilibrium (as, "This magnet is sustained by a very strong axle . . . and is *poised* so exactly that the weakest hand can turn it": Swift's "Gulliver's Travels," iii. 3); hold or carry in equilibrium, or evenly or steadily; hold supported or raised, as in position for casting, using, etc. (as, to *poise* a spear or a harpoon; to *poise* one's pen over paper); hold or carry in a particular manner or posture (as, "Her head was *poised* so that the sunlight framed her face": Galsworthy's "Saint's Progress," i. 2). **II.** *intr.* To be balanced, or rest in equilibrium; hang supported or suspended; hover, as a bird in the air.— **pois′er**, *n.*

poi-son (poi′zn), *n.* [OF. *poison*, potion, draft, poison (F. *poison*, poison), < L. *potio(n-)*, E. *potion*.] A potion†, esp. a deadly potion†; hence, any deadly or highly dangerous drug, or anything that acts like such a drug (as, one man's meat is another man's *poison*); specif., any substance (liquid, solid, or gaseous) which by reason of an inherent deleterious property tends to destroy life or impair health when taken into the system (as into the stomach, blood, or lungs); more generally, any toxic substance, whether introduced from without or formed within the living body; fig., anything morally fatal, baneful, or highly pernicious, as to character, happiness, or well-being (as, the *poison* of slander, suspicion, or evil example; "Avoid hatreds — they are *poison!*" Galsworthy's "Saint's Progress," iii. 2).— **poi′son**, *v. t.* [OF. *poisonner*.] To administer poison to (a person or animal); kill or injure with poison, or as poison does; also, to put poison into or upon, or impregnate with poison (as, to *poison* food; to *poison* arrows; to *poison* the water or air); also, fig., to affect banefully or perniciously, ruin, vitiate, or corrupt (as, to *poison* the mind or the happiness; "Whispering tongues can *poison* truth," Coleridge's "Christabel," ii.).— **poi′son=dog′wood**, **poi′son=el′der**, *n.* Same as *poison-sumac*.— **poi′son-er**, *n.*— **poi′son=gas′**, *n.* A poisonous gas; esp., any of various deadly gases used in warfare, as chlorine, phosgene, etc.— **poi′son=hem′lock**, *n.* The common hemlock, *Conium maculatum*.— **poi′son=i′vy**, *n.* Any of

Branch of Poison-ivy (*Rhus radicans*), with male flowers.— *a*, male flower; *b*, fruits.

several North American shrubs of the genus *Rhus* (sumac), poisonous to the touch, with trifoliolate leaves, green flowers, and whitish berries; esp., a climbing species, *R. radicans*, growing on fences, rocks, trees, etc. See cut on preceding page.—**poi′son=oak′**, *n.* A poison-ivy, as *Rhus radicans.* —**poi′son-ous**, *a.* Full of or containing poison; having the properties or effects of a poison; venomous; fig., baneful; highly pernicious; malignant. —**poi′son-ous-ly**, *adv.*—**poi′son-ous-ness**, *n.*—**poi′son=su′mac**, *n.* A highly poisonous shrub or small tree, *Rhus vernix*, a species of sumac with pinnate leaves and whitish berries, growing in swamps.

po-kal (pō-käl′), *n.* [G.] An ornamental drinking-cup or goblet, of silver, glass, or other material, esp. one of German make.

poke[1] (pōk), *n.* [N. Amer. Ind.] Pokeweed.

poke[2] (pōk), *n.* [ME. *poke*: cf. OF. *poke, poque, poche,* Icel. *poki,* AS. *pohha,* bag, also E. *pocket* and *pouch.*] A bag or sack (now chiefly prov., or as in the phrase 'a pig in a poke,' fig., something bought or accepted without being seen or without the actual value or character being known); also, the pocket (archaic: as, "not a penny in *poke*," Browning's "Ring and the Book," v.).

Pokal of Rock-crystal.

poke[3] (pōk), *v.; poked, poking.* [ME. *poken* = MLG. and D. *poken,* poke: cf. *poach*[2].] **I.** *tr.* To thrust against or into (something) with the finger or arm, the end of a stick, or the like (as, to *poke* a person in the ribs; to *poke* the fire with a poker); prod; also, to make (a hole, the way, etc.) by or as by thrusting; also, to thrust or push (as, "*poking* his stick through a hole in the carpet": W. Churchill's "Coniston," ii. 7); often, to thrust obtrusively (lit. or fig.: as, to *poke* one's finger or nose into what does not concern one); also, to force or drive (*away, in, out,* etc.) by or as by thrusting or pushing (as, "She always *poked* me out of bed before it was light": Mrs. Stowe's "Oldtown Folks," xiv.); shut (*up*) in some small, dull, or 'poky' place (colloq.); also, to direct (fun), esp. covertly or slyly, at a person or thing. **II.** *intr.* To make a thrust or thrusts with the finger, a stick, or the like; also, to thrust itself or stick (*out:* as, "The grass *poked* out through their [trucks'] wheels," H. G. Wells's "Italy, France, and Britain at War," iii. 1); also, to thrust one's self obtrusively, as into a matter; pry; search curiously; go prying or looking about a place; also, to go or proceed in a slow, dawdling, or aimless way (as, "They . . . dig out a canoe from a cotton-wood tree, and in this *poke* along shore silently," Irving's "Captain Bonneville," xliv.; "I never tried to do anything, but just *poked* along low-spirited," Mark Twain's "Huckleberry Finn," iv.); potter. —**poke**[3], *n.* A poking; a thrust or push; also, a projecting brim at the front of a woman's bonnet or hat (as, "The close *poke* of her little black bonnet hid her face from him": George Eliot's "Adam Bede," l.); a bonnet or hat with such a brim; also, a slow or dawdling person (colloq.).

poke-ber-ry (pōk′ber″i), *n.; pl. -berries* (-iz). The berry of the pokeweed; also, the plant.

poke=bon-net (pōk′bon′et), *n.* A woman's bonnet with a poke or projecting brim.

pok-er[1] (pō′ker), *n.* One who or that which pokes; a metal rod for poking or stirring a fire.

po-ker[2] (pō′ker), *n.* [Origin uncertain: cf. F. *poque,* old game of cards.] A card-game played by two or more persons, in which the players bet on the value of their hands, the winner taking the pool.

po-ker[3] (pō′ker), *n.* [Cf. Sw. *pocker,* Dan. *pokker,* the devil, the deuce, and E. *puck.*] A hobgoblin or demon; a bugbear. [Obs. or archaic.]—**po′ker-ish**, *a.* Mysteriously fearsome; eerie; uncanny. [Colloq., U. S.]

pok-er=work (pō′ker-werk), *n.* Ornamental work executed by burning designs on wood, etc., with a hot instrument, orig. a poker; pyrography.

poke-weed (pōk′wēd), *n.* [See *poke*[1].] A tall herb, *Phytolacca decandra,* of North America, whose juicy purple berries and poisonous root are used in medicine, and whose young shoots are sometimes cooked and eaten like asparagus.

pok-y (pō′ki), *a.; compar: pokier,* superl. *pokiest.* Poking or pottering, as a person; slow; dull; of a place, small and dull, petty, or mean (as, "Do you suppose I gave up my position at school in order to live in a *poky* little hole at eighteen pounds a year?" Arnold Bennett's "Helen with the High Hand," xvi.); of dress, etc., dowdy. [Colloq.]—**pok′i-ness**, *n.*

po-lac-ca[1] (pō-lak′ä), *n.* [It.] A polonaise (dance or music).

po-lac-ca[2], **po-la-cre** (pō-lak′ä, pō-lä′ker), *n.* [It. *polacca,* F. *polacre.*] A merchant vessel with two or three masts, used on the Mediterranean.

Po-lack (pō′lak), *n.* [Pol. *Polak.*] A Pole.

po-lar (pō′lär), *a.* [ML. *polaris.*] Of or pertaining to a pole, as of the earth, a magnet, an electric battery, etc.; being at or near, proceeding from, or connected with a pole; also, having magnetic polarity; in fig. use, likened to a pole of the earth in position; central; also, analogous to the pole-star as a guide; guiding; also, opposite in character or action, like the poles of a magnet.—**polar bear,** a large white bear, *Ursus maritimus,* of the arctic regions.—**polar body,** in *biol.,* one of the minute cells arising by a very unequal mitotic division of the ovum at or near the time of fertilization.—

Polar Bear.

polar circle, either of two circles of the earth parallel to the equator, one of which is everywhere distant 23° 28′ from the north pole and the other equally distant from the south pole; the arctic or the antarctic circle.—**polar lights,** the aurora borealis or the aurora australis. See *aurora.*

po-la-rim-e-ter (pō-la-rim′e-ter), *n.* [ML. *polaris,* polar: see *-meter.*] An instrument for measuring the amount of polarized light in the light received from a given source; also, an instrument (a form of polariscope) for measuring the angular rotation of the plane of polarization.

po-lar-i-scope (pō-lar′i-skōp), *n.* [ML. *polaris,* polar: see *-scope.*] An instrument for exhibiting the polarization of light, or for examining substances in polarized light.

po-lar-i-ty (pō-lar′i-ti), *n.* The power or tendency of a magnetized bar, etc., to point with its ends toward the magnetic poles of the earth; the quality of possessing magnetic poles; hence, in general, the possession of an axis with reference to which certain physical properties are determined; the possession of two poles or parts having opposite properties; also, positive or negative polar condition, as in electricity; in fig. use, tendency, as of thought or feeling, in a particular direction; also, the possession or exhibition of two opposite or contrasted principles or tendencies.

po-lar-i-za-tion (pō″lär-i-zā′shon), *n.* [F. *polarisation.*] The production or acquisition of polarity; in *elect.,* the process by which gases produced during electrolysis are deposited on the electrodes of a cell, giving rise to a reverse electromotive force; in *optics,* a state, or the production of a state, in which rays of light exhibit different properties in different directions, as when they are passed through a crystal of tourmalin, which (supposedly) transmits rays in which the light or ether vibrations are confined to a single plane.—**plane of polarization,** in *optics,* in light which has undergone polarization, the plane in which the light vibrations are confined, or, according to some authorities, to which they are at right angles.

po-lar-ize (pō′lär-īz), *v. t.*; *-ized*, *-izing*. [F. *polariser*.] To give polarity to; cause polarization in.—**po′lar-iz-er** (-ī-zėr), *n.*

pol-der (pōl′dėr), *n.* [D.] A tract of low land, esp. in the Netherlands, reclaimed from the sea or other body of water and protected by dikes.

pole[1] (pōl), *n.* [AS. *pāl*, < L. *palus*, stake, E. *pale*[1].] A long, slender, usually more or less cylindrical piece of wood or other material; specif., the long tapering piece of wood extending from the front of a vehicle, between the animals drawing it; a ship's mast (as, "We were scudding before a heavy gale, under bare *poles*": Marryat's "Peter Simple," xxxviii.); also, a rod used in measuring; hence, a measure of length or surface, a rod (5½ yards or 16½ feet), or a square rod (30¼ square yards).—**pole**[1], *v.*; *poled*, *poling*. **I.** *tr.* To furnish with poles; also, to push, strike, etc., with a pole; propel with a pole, as a boat or raft (as, "Barges . . . floated and sailed from the upper rivers to New Orleans . . . and were tediously . . . *poled* back by hand": Mark Twain's "Life on the Mississippi," iii.). **II.** *intr.* To propel a boat, etc., with a pole.

pole[2] (pōl), *n.* [L. *polus*, < Gr. πόλος, pivot, axis, pole, < πέλειν, move.] Each of the two points in which the axis of the earth produced cuts the celestial sphere, about which the stars seem to revolve ('celestial pole'); also, each of the extremities of the axis of the earth or of any more or less spherical body; also, the firmament or sky (poetic and archaic: as, "Stars unnumber'd gild the glowing *pole*," Pope's tr. Homer's "Iliad," viii.); in *physics*, each of the two regions or parts of a magnet, electric battery, etc., at which certain opposite forces are manifested or appear to be concentrated; in *anat.*, the point in a nerve-cell where a process forming an axis-cylinder begins; in *biol.*, either end of an ideal axis in a nucleus, cell, or ovum, about which parts are more or less symmetrically arranged; also, either end of a spindle-shaped figure formed in a cell previous to division into two new cells during mitosis.—**magnetic pole.** See under *magnetic*.

Pole[3] (pōl), *n.* A native or inhabitant of Poland; esp., a member of the principal Slavic people of Poland, belonging to the western group of the Slavic peoples, and speaking their native (Polish) tongue.

pole-ax, pole-axe (pōl′aks), *n.* [Earlier *pollax*: see *poll*[1].] A kind of battle-ax; a halberd; a hatchet-like weapon formerly used in the navy; a kind of ax used in felling or stunning animals.—**pole′ax, pole′axe**, *v. t.* To fell with a poleax: as, "He went over as if he had been *pole-axed*" (Conan Doyle's "Exploits of Brigadier Gerard," iv.).

pole-cat (pōl′kat), *n.* [Cf. F. *poule*, hen.] Any of various animals of the genus *Putorius*, of the weasel family, esp. *P. fœtidus* of Europe, a small, dark-brown, carnivorous animal with a fetid odor (cf. *ferret*[2]); any of various similar animals, as the North American skunk.

Polecat (*Putorius fœtidus*).

po-lem-ic (pō-lem′ik). [Gr. πολεμικός, of or for war, < πόλεμος, war.] **I.** *a.* Of or pertaining to disputation or controversy; controversial: as, "My father's little library consisted chiefly of books in *polemic* divinity" (B. Franklin's "Autobiography," i.). **II.** *n.* A controversial argument; argumentation against some opinion, doctrine, etc.; also, one who argues in opposition to another; a controversialist, esp. in theology.—**po-lem′i-cal**, *a.* Polemic.—**po-lem′i-cal-ly**, *adv.*—**po-lem′ics**, *n.* The art or practice of disputation or controversy, esp. of conducting theological controversy.

pol-e-mist (pol′ė-mist), *n.* [Gr. πολεμιστής, warrior, < πολεμίζειν: see *polemize*.] One engaged or versed in polemics; a controversialist: as, "Jesuit *polemists*" (Morley's "Oliver Cromwell," ii. 3).

pol-e-mize (pol′ė-mīz), *v. i.*; *-mized*, *-mizing*. [Gr. πολεμίζειν, wage war, < πόλεμος, war.] To engage in polemics; carry on a controversy.

pol-e-mo-ni-a-ceous (pol-ė-mō-ni-ā′shius), *a.* [NL. *Polemonium*, the typical genus, < Gr. πολεμώνιον, kind of plant.] Belonging to the *Polemoniaceæ*, a family of plants including the Jacob's-ladder, phlox, etc.

po-len-ta (pō-len′tä), *n.* [It., < L. *polenta*, peeled barley.] A thick porridge made of maize-meal, much used in Italy.

pole=plate (pōl′plāt), *n.* In *building*, a timber or piece resting on the tie-beams of a roof, and supporting the lower ends of the rafters.

pol-er (pō′lėr), *n.* One who or that which poles; also, a horse or other draft-animal harnessed to the pole of a vehicle; a wheeler.

pole=star (pōl′stär), *n.* A star of the second magnitude (also called *Polaris*) situated in the constellation Ursa Minor, close to the north pole of the heavens, formerly much used as a guide in navigation; the north star; hence, that which serves as a guide; a lodestar; a guiding principle; also, a center of attraction; a cynosure.

pole=strap (pōl′strap), *n.* A heavy strap for connecting the pole of a vehicle with the collar of a horse.

pole=vault (pōl′vält), *n.* A vault or leap, generally over a horizontal bar, performed with the aid of a long pole.—**pole′=vault″ing**, *n.*

po-lice (pō-lēs′), *n.* [F. *police*, government, civil administration, police, < L. *politia*: see *polity*, and cf. *policy*[1].] The regulation and control of a community, esp. with reference to the maintenance of public order, safety, health, morals, etc.; also, the department of the government concerned with this, esp. with the maintenance of order; also, an organized civil force for maintaining order, preventing and detecting crime, and enforcing the laws; the members of such a force (construed as *pl.*); hence, any body of men officially maintained or employed to keep order, enforce regulations, etc.; also, *milit.*, in the U. S. army, the cleaning and keeping clean of a camp, garrison, etc.; the condition of a camp, garrison, etc., with reference to cleanliness; the soldiers detailed to clean and keep clean a camp, garrison, etc.—**kitchen police.** See under *kitchen*, *n.*—**po-lice′**, *a.* Of or pertaining to the police; belonging to or connected with the police.—**police court**, an inferior court with summary jurisdiction for the trial of persons accused of any of certain minor offenses, and with power to hold those charged with more serious offenses for trial in a superior court or for the action of the grand jury.—**police dog**, a dog of any of various kinds used or trained to assist the police; specif., one of a type of sheep-dogs of wolf-like appearance, developed in Germany, etc., by selective breeding and by training, and used in police work and otherwise.—**police justice** or **magistrate**, a justice who presides at a police court.—**police officer**, an officer in a police force; also, commonly, a policeman.—**po-lice′**, *v. t.*; *-liced*, *-licing*. To regulate, control, or keep in order by or as by police, or as police do; *milit.*, to clean and keep clean (a camp, garrison, etc.).—**po-lice′man** (-man), *n.*; pl. *-men*. A member of a body or force of police.—**po-lice′wom″an**, *n.*; pl. *-women* (-wim″en).

pol-i-clin-ic (pol-i-klin′ik), *n.* [G. *poliklinik*, < Gr. πόλις, city, + G. *klinik*, clinic.] Orig., a clinic held at private houses in a city; also, a department of a hospital at which out-patients are treated. Cf. *polyclinic*.

pol-i-cy[1] (pol′i-si), *n.*; pl. *-cies* (-siz). [OF. *policie*, government, civil administration, < L. *politia*: see *polity*, and cf. *police*.] Government†; a form or system of government†, or polity†; also, political sagacity or skill, or statecraft (as, "The *policy* of the Catholic monarch was at all times equal to his piety": Irving's "Conquest of Granada," lxxxi.); hence, sagacity, shrewdness, or shrewdly prudent procedure in any affairs (as, "That which was only *policy* in the father became black dissimulation in the son": Stevenson's "Master of Ballantrae," i.); prudence, practical wisdom, or expediency; action or procedure conforming to, or considered with reference to, prudence or expediency (as, it was *policy*, or good *policy*, to consent; "I could not very well tell the old man that he was lying to me — that would have been bad *policy*," W. H. Hudson's "Green Mansions," viii.); also, a course dictated by prudence or expediency (as, honesty is the best *policy*; "Their true *policy* was to rely on themselves," Prescott's "Conquest of Mexico," iii. 6); hence, a definite course of action adopted as expedient or from other considerations (as, a business *policy*; a *policy* of economy or of liberality; to change one's *policy*); specif., a course or line of action adopted and pursued by a government, ruler, political party, or the like (as, the foreign, commercial, or naval *policy* of a country; "Alexander Hamilton, whose genius was responsible for the establishment of our financial system, early committed this Government to a *policy* of debt payment and keeping expenditures within income," A. W. Mellon's "Taxation," ii.); also, in Scotland, the grounds about a country-seat or rural mansion (as, "The laird . . . was advised to let the *policy* out as a farm": Galt's "Annals of the Parish," vii.).

pol-i-cy[2] (pol′i-si), *n.*; pl. *-cies* (-siz). [F. *police*, prob. through Pr. and L. < Gr. ἀπόδειξις, a showing or setting forth, < ἀποδεικνύναι, show, demonstrate: see *apodictic.*] A document embodying a contract of insurance; also, a method of gambling in which bets are made on numbers to be drawn by lottery (U. S.).—**pol′i-cy=hold″er**, *n.* One who holds a policy or contract of insurance.—**pol′i-cy=shop**, *n.* A place where bets are made in policy gambling. [U. S.]

pol-i-o-my-e-li-tis (pol″i-ō-mī-ẹ-lī′tis), *n.* [NL., < Gr. πολιός, gray, + μυελός, marrow.] In *pathol.*, inflammation of the gray matter of the spinal cord, esp. an infectious form chiefly affecting young children and causing motor paralysis. Cf. *infantile paralysis.*

Pol-ish[1] (pō′lish). **I.** *a.* Of or pertaining to the Poles or Poland. **II.** *n.* The language of the Poles, belonging to the Slavic group.

pol-ish[2] (pol′ish), *v.* [OF. F. *polir* (*poliss-*), < L. *polire* (pp. *politus*), polish, smooth, improve, embellish.] **I.** *tr.* To make smooth and glossy, esp. by friction (as, to *polish* metal, marble, or wood; to *polish* a gem); fig., to free from roughness, rudeness, or crudeness (as, to *polish* the mind, manners, or literary style; to *polish* a literary work); refine; render finished, cultured, or elegant; also, to take or bring (*away, off, out*, etc.) by smoothing or refining (as, to *polish* away superficial imperfections); also, with *off*, to finish, or dispose of, quickly or summarily (slang, orig. pugilistic: as, "He stood up to the Banbury man . . . and *polished* him *off* in four rounds easy," Thackeray's "Vanity Fair," xxxiv.; to *polish off* a dinner). **II.** *intr.* To become smooth and glossy; take on a polish; fig., to become refined or elegant. —**pol′ish**[2], *n.* The act or an act of polishing, the state of being polished; smoothness and gloss of surface such as is produced by polishing; fig., superior or elegant finish imparted (as, social *polish*; the *polish* of literary style); refinement; elegance; also, a substance used to give smoothness or gloss (as, furniture-*polish*; shoe-*polish*; stove-*polish*). —**pol′ished**, *p. a.* Made smooth and glossy, esp. by friction; hence, naturally smooth and glossy (as, "birds that have a *polished* plumage": W. H. Hudson's "Green Mansions," xiv.); fig., finished, refined, or elegant (as, "He looked the *polished* man of the world": F. M. Crawford's "Mr. Isaacs," vii.).—**pol′ish-er**, *n.*

po-lite (pō-līt′), *a.*; compar. *politer*, superl. *politest.* [L. *politus*, pp. of *polire*: see *polish*[2].] Polished or smooth, as of surface†; fig., refined or cultured (as, *polite* society; "the rich and *polite* Constantinople," Macaulay's "Hist. of Eng.," i.); of a refined or elegant kind (as, *polite* learning or literature; "rustic phrases which . . . did not suit the *polite* style of a court," Swift's "Gulliver's Travels," ii. 3); polished, refined, or well-bred, as persons or their manners, behavior, speech, etc.; hence, showing good manners toward others, as in action or speech; courteous or civil, esp. according to conventional standards (as, to be *polite* to a person; *polite* officials; a *polite* refusal).—**po-lite′ly**, *adv.*—**po-lite′ness**, *n.* The quality of being polite; polite or courteous manner or behavior toward others; courtesy or civility.

pol-i-tesse (pol-i-tes′, F. po-lē-tes), *n.* [F.] Politeness: as, "The frank address, and *politesse*, Are all finesse in Rob Mossgiel" (Burns's "O Leave Novels"). [Now chiefly as French.]

pol-i-tic (pol′i-tik), *a.* [OF. F. *politique*, < L. *politicus*, < Gr. πολιτικός, pertaining to citizens or to the state or its

administration, civic, political, < πολίτης, citizen, < πόλις, city, state.] Political (now chiefly in 'body politic,' which see under *body, n.*); also, characterized by policy, sagacious, or prudent (as, "He was too *politic* to quarrel with so important a personage": Motley's "Dutch Republic," ii. 4); shrewd; artful; also, in keeping with policy, expedient, or judicious (as, "To secure his good wishes was . . . *politic*": Scott's "Castle Dangerous," xviii.).—**po-lit-i-cal** (pō-lit′i-kạl), *a.* Of or pertaining to citizens (as, *political* status or capacity; *political* rights); also, of or pertaining to the state or its government (as, *political* affairs; *political* power; *political* measures); affecting or involving the state or government (as, a *political* offense or offender; a case with a *political* aspect); engaged in or connected with civil administration (as, *political* officials or office); also, having a definite polity or system of government (as, a *political* community); also, exercising or seeking power in the governmental or public affairs of a state, municipality, or the like (as, a *political* party or faction; a *political* leader, candidate, or boss); pertaining to or connected with a political party, or its principles, aims, activities, etc. (as, a *political* platform, campaign, or orator; a *political* badge or procession); partizan; also, pertaining to or dealing with the science or art of politics (as, *political* writers; a *political* treatise); also, politic† or sagacious†, or expedient† or judicious†.—**political economist**, one versed in political economy.—**political economy**, economics.—**political geography**, a branch of geography treating of the political divisions or states of the earth, their boundaries, possessions, centers of population, etc.—**political liberty.** See *liberty.*—**political science**, the science of politics, or of the principles and conduct of government.—**po-lit′i-cal-ly**, *adv.*

po-lit-i-cas-ter (pō-lit′i-kas-tẽr), *n.* [See *-aster*.] A petty politician.

pol-i-ti-cian (pol-i-tish′ạn), *n.* One versed in or concerned with the science of politics or the subject of political government (now rare: as, "Thus these *politicians* proceed, whilst little notice is taken of their doctrines," Burke's "Revolution in France," 18); also, one skilled in political government or administration; a statesman; more commonly, now, one who holds a political office, or is occupied with political affairs (as, "the shallow *politicians* who now labour at the helm of administration," Smollett's "Humphry Clinker," June 5; "We still teach diplomats to lie and *politicians* to cadge for votes like the street-boys for coppers," M. Hewlett's "Open Country," xiv.); often, one who is active in party politics, or who makes a trade of politics for party ends or personal gain.

pol-i-tic-ly (pol′i-tik-li), *adv.* In a politic manner.

po-lit-i-co- (pō-lit′i-kō-). Form of Gr. πολιτικός, political, or of E. *political*, used in combination, as in *politico-military* (political and military), *politico-religious*, *politico-social.*

pol-i-tics (pol′i-tiks), *n.* [From *politic.*] The science or art of political government; also, the practice or profession of conducting political affairs (as, "*Politics* became a trade, and a very base trade," H. G. Wells's "Outline of History," xxxvii. § 6; to enter or to withdraw from *politics*); political affairs (as, to discuss *politics*); political methods or maneuvers; political principles or opinions (construed as *pl.*: as, what are your *politics*?); also, fig., the conduct of private affairs (as, "Truth might be heroic, but it was not within the range of practical domestic *politics*": S. Butler's "Way of All Flesh," xxxix.); the use in private affairs of methods analogous to those used by politicians.

pol-i-ty (pol′i-ti), *n.*; pl. *-ties* (-tiz). [L. *politia*, < Gr. πολιτεία, citizenship, government, form of government, commonwealth, < πολίτης, citizen, < πόλις, city, state.] The condition of being constituted as a state or other organized community or body (as, races without *polity*; civil *polity*; ecclesiastical *polity*); also, government or administrative regulation (as, various forms or systems of *polity*; to direct the internal *polity* of a colony); also, a particular form or system of government (civil, ecclesiastical, or other: as, "that the true historical *polity* of the Netherlands was a representative, constitutional government," Motley's "Dutch Republic," v. 1; the papal *polity*; the episcopal, the presbyterian, or the congregational *polity*); also, a state or other organized community or body (as, "that . . . the Jewish *polity* was utterly destroyed, and the nation dispersed over the face of the earth": J. Butler's "Analogy of Religion," ii. 7); also, policy†.

pol-ka (pōl′kä), *n.* [Cf. Pol. *Polka*, fem. of *Polak*, a Polack or Pole.] A lively round dance of Bohemian origin, with music in duple time; also, a piece of music for such a dance or in its rhythm.—**polka mazurka**, a modification of a mazurka to the movement of a polka, with music in triple time; also, a piece of music for this dance or in its rhythm.—**pol′ka**, *v. i.*; -kaed, -kaing. To dance the polka.—**pol′ka=dot′**, *n.* A dot or round spot (printed, woven, or embroidered) repeated to form a pattern on a textile fabric; also, a pattern of or a fabric with such dots.—**pol′ka=dot′ted**, *a.*

poll[1] (pōl), *n.* [ME. *polle* = MD. and LG. *polle*.] The head, esp. the part of it on which the hair grows; also, the nape of the neck; also, a person or individual in a number or list; also, an enumeration or a list of individuals, as for purposes of taxing or voting; also, the registering of votes, as at an election; the voting at an election; the number of votes cast, or the numerical result of the voting (as, a heavy *poll*; "He was returned at the head of the *poll*," Froude's "Cæsar," xi.); the place where votes are taken (usually in *pl.*); also, a poll-tax.—**poll**[1], *v.* **I.** *tr.* To cut off or cut short the hair, etc., of (a person, etc.); crop; clip; shear; cut off or cut short (hair, etc.); now, esp., to cut off the top of (a tree, etc.); pollard; also, to cut off or cut short the horns of (cattle); also, fig., to plunder or despoil (archaic); also, to enroll in a list or register, as for purposes of taxing or voting; also, to take or register the votes of, as persons; also, to bring to the polls, as voters; receive at the polls, as votes; also, to deposit or cast at the polls, as a vote. **II.** *intr.* To vote at the polls; give one's vote: as, "They went every man of them and *polled* for an independent candidate" (Maria Edgeworth's "Belinda," iv.).

poll[2] (pol), *n.* [Cf. Gr. οἱ πολλοί, 'the many': see *hoi polloi*.] At Cambridge University, England, those students who read for or obtain a 'pass' degree, that is, a degree without honors.

Poll[3] (pol), *n.* [Var. of *Moll*, for *Mary*, woman's name.] A common name for a parrot.

pol-lack, pol-lock (pol′ak, -ok), *n.*; pl. *pollacks, pollocks*, or (esp. collectively) *pollack, pollock*. [Origin uncertain.] A food-fish of the gadoid genus *Pollachius*, which contains the 'true pollack,' *P. pollachius*, of European waters, and the 'green pollack' or coalfish, *P. carbonarius*, of the northern Atlantic; also, a food-fish of the gadoid genus *Theragra*, as *T. chalcogramma* ('Alaska pollack') of the northern Pacific.

Pollack (*Theragra chalcogramma*).

pol-lard (pol′ärd), *n.* [From *poll*[1], *v.*] An animal, as a stag, ox, or sheep, without horns; also, a tree cut back nearly to the trunk, so as to produce a dense mass of young branches; also, bran sifted from flour.—**pol′lard**, *v. t.* To convert into a pollard, as a tree.

pol-len (pol′en), *n.* [L., fine flour, dust.] The fertilizing element of flowering plants, consisting of fine, powdery yellowish grains or spores, sometimes compacted into masses. See cut in next column.

poll-er (pō′lėr), *n.* One who polls.

poll=e-vil (pōl′ē″vl), *n.* [See *poll*[1].] In *vet. science*, a suppurating swelling on the poll, or back of the head, of a horse, due to bruising followed by infection.

pol-lex (pol′eks), *n.*; pl. *pollices* (-i-sēz). [L., thumb.] The innermost digit of the fore limb; the thumb. Cf. *hallux*.—**pol-li-cal** (pol′i-kal), *a.*

pol-li-nate (pol′i-nāt), *v. t.*; -nated, -nating. [L. *pollen* (*pollin-*), E. *pollen*.] In *bot.*, to convey pollen for fertilization to; shed pollen upon.—**pol-li-na′tion** (-nā′shon), *n.*—**pol-lin-ic** (po-lin′ik), *a.* Of or pertaining to pollen.—**pol-li-nif′er-ous** (-nif′e-rus), *a.* [See *-ferous*.] Producing or bearing pollen.—**pol-lin′i-um** (-i-um), *n.*; pl. *-ia* (-i-ä). [NL.] In *bot.*, an agglutinated mass or body of pollen-

grains, characteristic of orchidaceous and asclepiadaceous plants.

pol-li-wog (pol′i-wog), *n.* [Earlier *polliwig*, *polwigge*, ME. *polwygle*, = E. *poll*[1] + *wiggle*.] A tadpole.

pol-lock (pol′ok), *n.* See *pollack*.

poll=par-rot (pol′par′ot), *n.* [See *Poll*[3].] A parrot.

poll=tax (pōl′taks), *n.* [See *poll*[1].] A tax of so much per head or person; a tax levied on every person, or every person of a specified class; a capitation-tax.

pol-lute (po-lūt′), *v. t.*; -luted, -luting. [L. *pollutus*, pp. of *polluere*, < *por-* (= *pro*, before) + *luere*, wash.] To make physically foul or unclean (as, "Three weeks long did these unburied bodies *pollute* the streets": Motley's "Dutch Republic," iii. 8); dirty, stain, or befoul; also, to render morally unclean or impure, or defile; often, to render ceremonially impure, or desecrate (as, "an ancient temple . . . which having been *polluted* some years before by an unnatural murder, was . . . looked upon as profane": Swift's "Gulliver's Travels," i. 1).—**pol-lut′er** (-lū′tér), *n.*—**pol-lu′tion** (-lū′shon), *n.* [LL. *pollutio(n-)*.] The act of polluting, or the state of being polluted; defilement; uncleanness.

Pol-ly (pol′i), *n.* Same as *Poll*[3].

pol-ly-wog (pol′i-wog), *n.* See *polliwog.*

po-lo (pō′lō), *n.* [Native (Tibetan) name in northern India.] A game resembling hockey, played on horseback with long-handled mallets and a wooden ball; also, some game more or less resembling this, as water-polo.—**po′lo-ist**, *n.*

po-lo-naise (pō-lō-nāz′), *n.* [F., fem. of *polonais*, Polish.] A slow dance of Polish origin, in triple rhythm, consisting chiefly of a march or promenade in couples; a piece of music for, or in the rhythm of, such a dance; also, a woman's overdress combining a bodice and an overskirt.

po-lo-ni-um (pō-lō′ni-um), *n.* [NL., < ML. *Polonia*, Poland.] A substance with radioactive properties (supposed to be a new metallic element) discovered in pitchblende by M. and Mme. Curie in 1898.

pol-ter-geist (pol′tėr-gīst), *n.* [G.] A ghost or spirit which manifests its presence by noises, knockings, etc.

pol-troon (pol-trön′), *n.* [F. *poltron*, < It. *poltrone*, < *poltro*, lazy, sluggish.] A spiritless, cowardly person; a wretched coward; a craven: as, "What a miserable little *poltroon* had fear . . . made of me!" (C. Brontë's "Jane Eyre," iv.).—**pol-troon′er-y**, *n.* The behavior of a poltroon; cowardice.—**pol-troon′ish**, *a.*

poly-. [Gr. πολυ-, repr. πολύς, much, many (compar. πλείων, superl. πλεῖστος), neut. πολύ (used as adv.); akin to L. *plus*, more (see *plus*), and ult. to E. *full*[1].] A combining-form or prefix, meaning 'much,' 'many,' first occurring in words from the Greek, but now used freely as a general formative, esp. in scientific or technical words. See *mono-*.—**pol-y-a-cid** (pol-i-as′id), *a.* In *chem.*, equivalent in combining capacity to an acid radical of valence greater than unity, as a base.—**pol″y-a-del′phous** (-a-del′fus), *a.* [+ *-adelphous*.] In *bot.*, having the stamens united in more than two bundles or groups.—**pol″y-æs-the′sia** (-es-thē′zi-ä), *n.* [NL.: see *æsthesia*.] In *pathol.*, a morbid condition of the sense of touch, as in locomotor ataxia, in which a single stimulus, as the prick of a pin, is felt at two or more places.

pol-y-an-drous (pol-i-an′drus), *a.* [Gr. πολύανδρος, < πολύς, much, many, + ἀνήρ (ἀνδρ-), man.] Having more than one husband at one time; characterized by plurality of husbands for one wife; in *bot.*, having the stamens indefinitely numerous; specif., having twenty or more free stamens.—**pol-y-an′dry** (-dri), *n.* The practice or the condition of having more than one husband at one time; marriage with several husbands; in *bot.*, the fact of being polyandrous.

Grains of Pollen of (*a*) evening primrose (*Onagra biennis*), (*b*) chicory (*Cichorium intybus*), (*c*) hibiscus (*Hibiscus moscheutos*), (*d*) passion-flower (*Passifloracærulea*), and (*e*) Scotch pine (*Pinus sylvestris*).

Stamens of Polyadelphous Plant.

pol-y-an-thus (pol-i-an'thus), n. [NL., < Gr. πολύανθος, having many flowers, < πολύς, much, many, + ἄνθος, flower.] The oxlip, *Primula elatior*; also, a narcissus, *Narcissus tazetta*, in many varieties, bearing clusters of small white or yellow flowers.

pol-y-ar-chy (pol'i-är-ki), n. [Gr. πολυαρχία, < πολύς, much, many, + ἄρχειν, rule.] Government by many.

pol-y-a-tom-ic (pol"i-a-tom'ik), a. [See *poly-*.] In chem., having many atoms in the molecule; also, containing more than one replaceable atom or group.

pol-y-ax-i-al (pol-i-ak'si-al), a. [See *poly-*.] Having many or several axes.

pol-y-ba-sic (pol-i-bā'sik), a. [See *poly-*.] In chem., of an acid, having three or more atoms of replaceable hydrogen.

po-lyb-a-site (pō-lib'a-sīt or pol-i-bā'sīt), n. [G. *polybasit*, < Gr. πολύς, much, + βάσις, base.] A blackish mineral with a metallic luster, consisting essentially of silver, sulphur, and antimony: a valuable silver ore.

pol-y-car-pel-la-ry (pol-i-kär'pe-lä-ri), a. [See *poly-*.] In *bot.*, consisting of many or several carpels. Also **pol-y-car'pous.**

pol-y-chæte (pol'i-kēt). [NL. *Polychæta*, pl., < Gr. πολυχαίτης, having much hair, < πολύς, much, + χαίτη, hair.] In *zoöl.*: **I.** n. Any of the *Polychæta*, a group or division of chætopods having unsegmented rudimentary limbs with many chætæ or bristles, and including most of the common marine worms. **II.** a. Pertaining to the polychætes; belonging to the *Polychæta*.—**pol-y-chæ'tous** (-kē'tus), a.

pol-y-cha-si-um (pol-i-kā'zi-um), n.; pl. *-sia* (-zi-ä). [NL., < Gr. πολύς, much, + χάσις, separation.] In *bot.*, a form of cymose inflorescence in which each axis produces more than two lateral axes.—**pol-y-cha'si-al**, a.

pol-y-chro-mat-ic (pol"i-krō-mat'ik), a. [See *poly-* and *chromatic*.] Having many colors; exhibiting a variety of colors.

pol-y-chrome (pol'i-krōm), a. [Gr. πολύχρωμος, < πολύς, much, many, + χρῶμα, color.] Being of many or various colors; decorated or executed in many colors, as a statue, a vase, a mural painting, a printed work, etc. Also **pol-y-chro'mic** (-krō'mik).—**pol'y-chro-my** (-mi), n. Polychrome coloring; decoration or execution in many colors.

Pol-y-cle-tan (pol-i-klē'tan), a. Same as *Polyclitan*.

pol-y-clin-ic (pol-i-klin'ik), n. [See *poly-*.] A clinic or a hospital dealing with various diseases. Cf. *policlinic*.

Pol-y-cli-tan (pol-i-klī'tan), a. [L. *Polyclitus*, also *Polycletus*, < Gr. Πολύκλειτος, Polyclitus.] Of or pertaining to Polyclitus, or Polycletus, of Argos, a celebrated Greek sculptor who flourished about 450—420 B.C., and whose statue of the Doryphorus (spear-bearer) long served as a canon or standard of the perfect human proportions; pertaining to or observing the principles of art laid down by Polyclitus.

pol-y-con-ic (pol-i-kon'ik), a. [See *poly-*.] Pertaining to or based upon many cones.

pol-y-dac-tyl (pol-i-dak'til). [Gr. πολυδάκτυλος, < πολύς, much, many, + δάκτυλος, finger or toe.] **I.** a. Having many or several digits; esp., having more than the normal number of fingers or toes (see cut in next column). **II.** n. A polydactyl animal.—**pol-y-dac'tyl-ism**, n.

pol-y-foil (pol'i-foil). [See *poly-* and *foil[1]*.] In *arch.*: **I.** a. Having many, esp. more than five, foils: as, a *polyfoil* window; a *polyfoil*

Polyclitan Canon. — Copy of the Doryphorus of Polyclitus; Museo Nazionale, Naples.

arch (see cut below). **II.** n. A polyfoil ornament or decorative feature; a multifoil.

po-lyg-a-la (pō-lig'a-lä), n. [L., < Gr. πολύγαλον, milkwort, < πολύς, much, + γάλα, milk.] Any of the herbs and shrubs, commonly known as milkworts, which constitute the genus *Polygala*, as *P. paucifolia* ('fringed polygala') of North America.—**pol-y-ga-la-ceous** (pol"i-ga-lā'shius), a.

po-lyg-a-mist (pō-lig'a-mist), n. One who practises or favors polygamy.

Polydactyl Hand.

po-lyg-a-mous (pō-lig'a-mus), a. [Gr. πολύγαμος, < πολύς, much, many, + γάμος, marriage.] Having many or several wives or husbands at the same time; practising polygamy; of, pertaining to, or characterized by polygamy; in *bot.*, bearing both unisexual and hermaphrodite flowers on the same or on different plants.—**po-lyg'a-mous-ly**, adv.—**po-lyg'a-my** (-mi), n. [Gr. πολυγαμία.] The practice or condition of having many or several spouses, esp. wives, at one time; marriage with several, or more than one, at once; in *zoöl.*, the habit of mating with several, or more than one, of the opposite sex.

pol-y-gen-e-sis (pol-i-jen'e-sis), n. [See *poly-* and *genesis*.] In *biol.*, the descent of a species or race from several separate and independent germs or ancestors.—**pol"y-ge-net'ic** (-jē-net'ik), a.

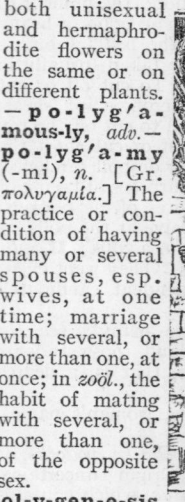
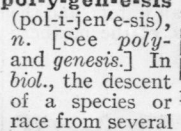

Polyfoil Arch.— Main portal of Lichfield Cathedral, England.

po-lyg-e-ny (pō-lij'e-ni), n. [See *poly-* and *-geny*.] The theoretical origination of mankind or a human race from several separate and independent pairs of ancestors.—**pol-y-gen-ic** (pol-i-jen'ik), a.

pol-y-glot (pol'i-glot). [Gr. πολύγλωττος, < πολύς, much, many, + γλῶττα, γλῶσσα, tongue.] **I.** a. Versed in or using many or several languages, as a person; also, containing, made up of, or in several languages (as, a *polyglot* Bible). **II.** n. One who understands or uses several languages; also, a book or writing, esp. a Bible, containing the same text in several languages (as, "commentaries and *polyglots*": Scott's "Guy Mannering," xx.); also, a mixture or confusion of languages.—**pol-y-glot'tal**, **pol-y-glot'tic**, a.

pol-y-gon (pol'i-gon), n. [LL. *polygonum*, < Gr. πολύγωνος, many-angled, < πολύς, much, many, + γωνία, angle.] A figure, esp. a plane figure, having many (more than four) angles and sides.

pol-y-go-na-ceous (pol"i-gō-nā'shius), a. [See *polygonum*.] Belonging to the *Polygonaceæ*, or buckwheat family of plants, including the knot-grass, jointweed, dock, etc.

po-lyg-o-nal (pō-lig'ō-nal), a. Having the form of a polygon.—**po-lyg'o-nal-ly**, adv.

po-lyg-o-num (pō-lig'ō-num), n. [NL., < Gr. πολύγονον, knot-grass, < πολύς, much, many, + γόνυ, knee, joint.] Any plant of the genus *Polygonum*, which consists chiefly of herbs, often with knotty, jointed stems, and which includes the knot-grass, bistort, smartweed, etc.

pol-y-graph (pol'i-gråf), n. [Gr. πολυγράφος, writing much, < πολύς, much, + γράφειν, write.] An apparatus for multiplying copies of a drawing or writing; also, a prolific or versatile author.—**pol-y-graph'ic** (-graf'ik), a.

po-lyg-y-nous (pō-lij'i-nus), a. [Gr. πολύς, much, many, + γυνή, woman.] Having more than one wife at one time; characterized by plurality of wives for one husband; in bot., having many pistils or styles.—**po-lyg'y-ny** (-ni), n. The practice or the condition of having more than one wife at one time; marriage with several wives; in bot., the fact of being polygynous.

pol-y-hal-ite (pol-i-hal'īt), n. [G. polyhalit, < Gr. πολύς, much, + ἅλς, salt.] A mineral consisting essentially of a hydrous sulphate of calcium, magnesium, and potassium, occurring usually in fibrous masses, and of a brick-red color due to the presence of iron.

pol-y-he-dron (pol-i-hē'dron), n.; pl. -drons or -dra (-drä). [Gr. πολύεδρον, neut. of πολύεδρος, having many bases, < πολύς, much, many, + ἕδρα, seat, base.] A solid figure having many faces.—**pol-y-he'dral**, a.

pol-y-his-tor (pol-i-his'tor), n. [L., < Gr. πολυΐστωρ, very learned, < πολύς, much, + ἵστωρ, knowing, learned: see history.] A person of great or varied learning.—**pol"y-his-tor'ic** (-tor'ik), a.—**pol-y-his'to-ry** (-tō-ri), n. Great or varied learning.

Pol-y-hym-ni-a (pol-i-him'ni-ä), n. [L., < Gr. Πολύμνια, < πολύς, much, many, + ὕμνος, E. hymn.] The Muse of sublime hymns or serious sacred songs.

pol-y-lith (pol'i-lith), n. [Gr. πολύς, much, many, + λίθος, stone.] A structure, as a monument or column, built up of many or several stones: opposed to monolith.—**pol-y-lith'ic**, a.

pol-y-math (pol'i-math), n. [Gr. πολυμαθής, having learned much, < πολύς, much, + μανθάνειν, learn.] A person of great or varied learning.—**pol-y-math'ic**, a.—**po-lym-a-thy** (pō-lim'a-thi), n. [Gr. πολυμαθία.] Great learning.

pol-y-mer (pol'i-mėr), n. [Gr. πολυμερής, of many parts, < πολύς, much, many, + μέρος, part.] In chem., any of two or more polymeric compounds; specif., a compound polymeric with and regarded as derived from another of lower molecular weight.—**pol-y-mer'ic** (-mer'ik), a. In chem., of compounds, or of one compound in relation to another, having the same elements combined in the same proportions by weight, but differing in molecular weight.—**po-lym-er-ism** (pō-lim'e-rizm), n. In chem., polymeric state; in biol. and bot., polymerous state.—**pol"y-mer-i-za'tion** (-i-zā'shon), n. In chem., the act or process of forming a polymer or polymeric compound; the union of two or more molecules of a compound to form a more complex compound with a higher molecular weight; the conversion of one compound into another by such a process (as, the polymerization of acetylene to benzene).—**pol'y-mer-ize** (-īz), v. t. or i.; -ized, -izing. To combine so as to form a polymer; subject to or undergo polymerization.—**po-lym'er-ous**, a. In biol., composed of many parts; in bot., of flowers, having numerous members in each whorl.

pol-y-morph (pol'i-môrf), n. [Gr. πολύμορφος, multiform, < πολύς, much, many, + μορφή, form.] A polymorphous organism or substance, or one of its various forms, etc.—**pol-y-mor'phic** (-môr'fik), a. Polymorphous.—**pol-y-mor'phism**, n. Polymorphous state or condition.—**pol-y-mor'phous**, a. Having, assuming, or passing through many or various forms, stages, or the like.

Pol-y-ne-sian (pol-i-nē'shian or -zhian). [From Polynesia, < Gr. πολύς, much, many, + νῆσος, island.] **I.** a. Of or pertaining to Polynesia (a geographical division comprising the numerous small islands in the Pacific Ocean east of Australia and the Malay Archipelago, or, more strictly, east of Melanesia and Micronesia), its inhabitants, or their languages. **II.** n. A member of any of the brown races inhabiting Polynesia; also, any of the languages or dialects spoken in Polynesia (exclusive of Melanesia and Micronesia).

pol-y-no-mi-al (pol-i-nō'mi-al). [From poly- + -nomial as in binomial.] **I.** a. Consisting of or characterized by many or several names or terms. **II.** n. A polynomial name or the like; in zoöl. and bot., a polynomial scientific name; esp., a species name containing more than two terms; in alg., an expression consisting of two or more terms, as $a + b + c - d$.

pol-y-nu-cle-ar (pol-i-nū'klē-ạr), a. [See poly-.] Same as multinuclear.

pol-yp (pol'ip), n. [F. polype, < L. polypus, < Gr. πολύπους, octopus, also polypus in the nose, prop. adj., many-footed, < πολύς, much, many, + πούς, foot.] In zoöl., an octopus†; also, any of various coelenterate animals, soft or hard, free or fixed, simple or compound, as the hydra and other hydrozoa, and the sea-anemones, corals, and other actinozoa or anthozoa; also, any of various other aquatic organisms, as a polyzoön, a crinoid, a rotifer, or a sponge; also, an individual zoöid of a compound or colonial organism.—**pol'y-pa-ry** (-i-pā-ri), n. The common supporting structure of a colony of polyps, as corals.

pol-y-pet-a-lous (pol-i-pet'a-lus), a. [See poly-.] In bot., having many or (commonly) separate petals.

pol-y-pha-gi-a (pol-i-fā'ji-ä), n. [NL., < Gr. πολυφαγία, < πολύς, much, + φαγεῖν, eat.] In pathol., excessive desire of eating; in zoöl., the habit of subsisting on many different kinds of food.—**po-lyph-a-gous** (pō-lif'a-gus), a.

pol-y-phase (pol'i-fāz), a. [See poly-.] In elect., having different phases; noting or pertaining to a system combining two or more alternating currents which differ from one another in phase.

pol-y-phone (pol'i-fōn), n. [Gr. πολύφωνος, having many tones, < πολύς, much, many, + φωνή, sound.] In phonetics, a letter or other symbol having more than one phonetic value.—**pol-y-phon'ic** (-fon'ik), a. Consisting of or having many voices or sounds; in music, having two or more voices or parts, each with an independent melody, but all harmonizing (opposed to homophonic); contrapuntal; pertaining to music of this kind; also, of a musical instrument, capable of producing more than one tone at a time, as an organ or a harp; in phonetics, having more than one phonetic value, as a letter. Also **po-lyph-o-nous** (pō-lif'ō-nus).—**po-lyph'o-ny** (-ni), n. [Gr. πολυφωνία.] The quality of being polyphonic; in music, polyphonic composition; counterpoint; in phonetics, representation of different sounds by the same letter or symbol.

pol-y-phote (pol'i-fōt), n. [Gr. πολύς, much, many, + φῶς (φωτ-), light.] In elect., noting or pertaining to an arc-lamp designed to be run in series with similar lamps.

pol-y-phy-let-ic (pol"i-fi-let'ik), a. [Gr. πολύς, much, many, + φυλή, tribe.] Of or pertaining to several tribes or stocks; developed from more than one ancestral type, as a group of animals.

pol-y-phyl-lous (pol-i-fil'us), a. [Gr. πολύφυλλος, < πολύς, much, many, + φύλλον, leaf.] In bot., having many leaves; having distinct or separate leaves.

pol-y-pi (pol'i-pī), n. Plural of polypus.

po-lyp-i-dom (pō-lip'i-dom or pol'i-pi-), n. [L. polypus, E. polyp, + domus, house.] Same as polypary.

pol-y-pite (pol'i-pīt), n. An individual zoöid of a compound polyp.

pol-y-po-di-a-ceous (pol"i-pō-di-ā'shius), a. [See polypody.] Belonging to the Polypodiaceæ, the chief family of ferns, including the polypody, spleenwort, walking-fern, maidenhair, brake, certain tree-ferns, etc.

pol-y-po-dy (pol'i-pō-di), n.; pl. -dies (-diz). [L. polypodium, < Gr. πολυπόδιον, < πολύπους, many-footed: see polyp.] Any fern of the genus Polypodium, as P. vulgare, a common species with creeping rootstocks, deeply pinnatifid evergreen fronds, and round, naked sori.

Polypody (Polypodium vulgare). — a, pinna with sori; b, a sporangium.

pol-y-poid (pol'i-poid), a. [See -oid.] Resembling a polyp; in pathol., resembling a polypus.

pol-y-prag-mat-ic (pol"i-prag-mat'ik), a. [Gr. πολυπράγματος, < πολύς, much, many, + πρᾶγμα, affair: see pragmatic.] Busy about many affairs; officious; meddlesome.—**pol-y-prag'ma-tism** (-ma-tizm), n. Officiousness.

pol-yp-tych (pol′ip-tik), *n.* [Gr. πολύπτυχος, of many folds; < πολύς, much, many, + πτυχή, a fold.] A combination of more than three panels or frames bearing pictures, carvings, or the like. Cf. *diptych* and *triptych*.

pol-y-pus (pol′i-pus), *n.*; pl. *-pi* (-pī). [L.: see *polyp*.] A polyp; in *pathol.*, a tumor, usually pedunculate, arising from a mucous surface, as in the nose.

pol-y-sep-a-lous (pol-i-sep′a-lus), *a.* [See *poly-*.] In *bot.*, having many or (commonly) separate sepals.

pol-y-sper-mous (pol-i-spér′mus), *a.* [Gr. πολύσπερμος, < πολύς, much, many, + σπέρμα, seed.] In *bot.*, containing or producing many seeds.

pol-y-syl-lab-ic (pol″i-si-lab′ik), *a.* [Gr. πολυσύλλαβος, of many syllables, < πολύς, much, many, + συλλαβή: see *syllable*.] Consisting of many, or more than three, syllables, as a word; characterized by such words, as language, etc. —**pol″y-syl-lab′i-cal-ly**, *adv.* —**pol-y-syl′la-ble** (-sil′a-bl), *n.* A polysyllabic word.

pol-y-syn-de-ton (pol-i-sin′de-ton), *n.* [NL., < Gr. πολύς, much, many, + σύνδετος, bound together: see *asyndeton*.] In *rhet.*, the use of a number of conjunctions in close succession, as in Rom. viii. 38, 39. Cf. *asyndeton*.

pol-y-syn-the-sis (pol-i-sin′the-sis), *n.* [See *poly-*.] Synthesis of many elements; specif., the combination of several words of a sentence into one word, as in the languages of the North American Indians. —**pol″y-syn-thet′ic**, *a.*

pol-y-tech-nic (pol-i-tek′nik). [F. *polytechnique*, < Gr. πολύτεχνος, < πολύς, much, many, + τέχνη, art.] **I.** *a.* Pertaining to or dealing with various arts: as, a *polytechnic* school (one in which instruction in various technical subjects is given). **II.** *n.* A polytechnic institution or school.

pol-y-the-ism (pol′i-thē-izm), *n.* [F. *polythéisme*, < Gr. πολύθεος, of many gods, < πολύς, much, many, + θεός, god.] The doctrine of, or belief in, many gods or more gods than one. —**pol′y-the-ist**, *n.* One who believes in or maintains polytheism. —**pol″y-the-is′tic**, *a.* Pertaining to or characterized by polytheism. —**pol″y-the-is′ti-cal-ly**, *adv.*

pol-y-typ-ic (pol-i-tip′ik), *a.* [See *poly-*.] Having or involving many or several types. Also **pol-y-typ′i-cal**.

pol-y-u-ri-a (pol-i-ū′ri-ä), *n.* [NL., < Gr. πολύς, much, + οὖρον, urine.] In *pathol.*, the passing of an excessive quantity of urine, as in diabetes, certain nervous diseases, etc. —**pol-y-u′ric**, *a.*

pol-y-va-lent (pol-i-vā′lent or pō-liv′a-), *a.* [See *poly-* and *-valent*.] In *chem.*, multivalent. —**pol-y-va′lence**, *n.*

pol-y-zo-an (pol-i-zō′an). **I.** *a.* Belonging or pertaining to the *Polyzoa*. See *polyzoön*. **II.** *n.* Any member of the *Polyzoa*; a polyzoön.

pol-y-zo-a-ri-um (pol″i-zō-ā′ri-um), *n.*; pl. *-ria* (-ri-ä). [NL., < *polyzoön*.] In *zoöl.*, a colony of polyzoa, or its supporting skeleton. —**pol″y-zo-a′ri-al**, *a.*

pol-y-zo-ic (pol-i-zō′ik), *a.* Pertaining to or of the nature of the *Polyzoa* (see *polyzoön*); composed of a number of zoöids existing in the form of a colony.

pol-y-zo-ön (pol-i-zō′on), *n.*; pl. *-zoa* (-zō′ä). [NL., < Gr. πολύς, much, many, + ζῷον, animal.] Any member of the *Polyzoa*, a class of small aquatic animals usually forming colonies or compound masses often moss-like or coral-like in appearance, and found attached to objects under water; a bryozoön or sea-moss.

Portion of the Polyzoarium of *Plumatella repens*, one of the Polyzoa.

pom-ace (pum′ās), *n.* [L. *pomum*, fruit, ML. apple.] The substance of apples or similar fruit crushed to a pulpy mass, as in making cider; hence, any crushed or ground pulpy substance.

po-ma-ceous (pō-mā′shius), *a.* [ML. *pomum*, apple.] Belonging to the *Pomaceæ* or *Malaceæ*, the apple family of plants; malaceous.

po-made (pō-mād′), *n.* [F. *pommade*, < It. *pomata* (so called because orig. made with apples), < ML. *pomum*, apple: cf. *pomatum*.] A scented ointment, esp. one used for the scalp and in dressing the hair. —**po-made′**, *v. t.*; *-maded, -mading*. To anoint or dress with pomade.

po-man-der (pō-man′dèr or pō′man-), *n.* [OF. *pome* (< ML. *pomum*), apple, + *ambre*, ambergris, E. *amber*.] A mixture of aromatic substances, often in the form of a ball, formerly carried on the person for perfume or as a guard against infection; also, the case or hollow ball, as of gold, silver, etc., in which this was carried.

po-ma-tum (pō-mā′tum), *n.* [NL.] Pomade. —**po-ma′tum**, *v. t.* To anoint or dress with pomatum: as, "his hair well curled and *pomatumed*" (Du Maurier's "Trilby," ii.).

pome (pōm), *n.* [OF. *pome* (F. *pomme*), < ML. *pomum*, apple, L. fruit.] An apple; in *bot.*, the characteristic fruit of the apple family, as an apple, pear, quince, etc.

pome-gran-ate (pom′gran-āt, pom-gran′āt, or pum′-), *n.* [OF. *pome grenate*: *pome*, apple, fruit (see *pome*); *grenate*, < L. *granata*, fem. of *granatus*, having grains or seeds, < *granum*, E. *grain²*.] The fruit of the tree *Punica granatum*, orange-like in size, having a hard reddish-yellow rind, and containing many seeds and a pleasantly acid, juicy red pulp; also, the tree, native in southwestern Asia but widely cultivated in warm regions.

pom-e-lo (pom′e-lō), *n.*; pl. *-los* or *-loes* (-lōz). [Origin uncertain.] The grape-fruit.

Pom-e-ra-ni-an (pom-e-rā′ni-an). **I.** *a.* Of or pertaining to Pomerania, on the south coast of the Baltic Sea: as, a *Pomeranian* dog (one of a breed of medium-sized or small dogs with sharp nose, pointed ears, and long, thick silky hair: cf. *spitz*). **II.** *n.* A native or inhabitant of Pomerania; also, a Pomeranian dog.

Branch of Pomegranate with Flowers. — *a*, the fruit ; *b*, the fruit, transverse section ; *c*, flower, longitudinal section, the petals removed.

po-mi-cul-ture (pō′mi-kul-tūr), *n.* [L. *pomum*, fruit, + *cultura*, culture.] The cultivation or growing of fruit. —**po-mi-cul′tur-ist**, *n.*

po-mif-er-ous (pō-mif′e-rus), *a.* [L. *pomifer*, < *pomum*, fruit, + *ferre*, bear.] In *bot.*, bearing pomes or pome-like fruits.

pom-mel (pum′el), *n.* [OF. *pomel* (F. *pommeau*), dim. < ML. *pomum*, apple, E. *pome*.] A knob, as on the hilt of a sword, dagger, etc.; also, the protuberant part at the front and top of a saddle. —**pom′mel**, *v. t.*; *-meled* or *-melled, -meling* or *-melling*. To strike or beat with or as with the pommel of a sword; beat with the fists: as, "My cousin defied me to . . . fight him . . . I agreed, for I felt the strength of a giant in me, and I longed to *pommel* him soundly" (Irving's "Tales of a Traveler," ii. 9). —**pom′mel-er**, *n.*

po-mol-o-gy (pō-mol′ō-ji), *n.* [L. *pomum*, fruit: see *-logy*.] The branch of science that deals with fruits and fruit-growing. —**po-mo-log-i-cal** (pō-mō-loj′i-kal), *a.* —**po-mol′o-gist**, *n.*

pomp (pomp), *n.* [OF. F. *pompe*, < L. *pompa*, < Gr. πομπή, solemn procession, parade, pomp, orig. a sending, < πέμπειν, send.] A stately or splendid procession, or pageant (obs. or archaic: as, "The heavens . . . rung . . . While the bright *pomp* ascended jubilant," Milton's "Paradise Lost," vii. 564); also, stately or splendid show or display, splendor, or magnificence (as, festal, ceremonial, or funeral *pomp*; "Farewell . . . Pride, *pomp* and circumstance of glorious war!" Shakspere's "Othello," iii. 3. 354); sometimes, ostentatious or vain display, or parade; parade of dignity or importance (as, "Nae mair the Council waddles down the street, In all the *pomp* of ignorant conceit": Burns's "Brigs of Ayr," 185); *pl.*, pompous displays or things (as, "that I should renounce . . . the *pomps* and vanity of this wicked world": Book of Common Prayer, Catechism).

Pom-pa-dour (pom′pa-dör). **I.** *a.* Pertaining to or named after the Marquise de *Pompadour* (1721–64), mistress of

Louis XV. of France: as, *Pompadour* pattern (a pattern of colored flowers on silks, ribbons, etc.); *Pompadour* ribbons. **II.** *n.* [*l. c.*] A shade of rose-color or pink; also, an arrangement of a woman's hair in which it is raised above the forehead, often over a pad; also, an arrangement of a man's hair, brushed up from the forehead.

pom-pa-no (pom′pạ-nō), *n.*; pl. *-nos* (-nōz). [Sp. *pámpano*.] A food-fish of the carangoid genus *Trachynotus*, esp. *T. carolinus* of the West Indies and the neighboring coasts of North America; also, any of certain other food-fishes, as *Palometa simillima* of the coast of California.

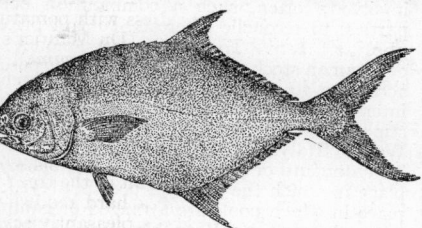

Common Pompano (*Trachynotus carolinus*).

Pom-pe-ian (pom-pē′ạn), *a.* Of or pertaining to Pompeii, a city of Italy, which was buried by an eruption of Mount Vesuvius, A.D. 79, and whose ruins have been partly laid bare by excavation.—**Pompeian red,** a dull red color of the shade found on the walls of many houses in Pompeii.

pom-pion (pum′piọn), *n.* See *pumpion*.

pom-pom (pom′pom), *n.* [Imit.] A colloquial name for a machine-gun of large caliber.

pom-pon (pom′pon, F. pôṅ-pôṅ), *n.* [F., perhaps < *pompe*, E. *pomp*.] An ornamental tuft or ball of feathers, silk, or the like, used in millinery, etc.; a tuft of wool or the like worn on a shako, a sailor's cap, etc.

pom-pos-i-ty (pom-pos′i-ti), *n.* The quality of being pompous; pompous parade of dignity or importance; ostentatious loftiness of language or style (as, "a certain sententiousness and *pomposity* of speech": W. De Morgan's "Alice-for-Short," i.).

pom-pous (pom′pus), *a.* [OF. *pompeus* (F. *pompeux*), < LL. *pomposus*, < L. *pompa*, E. *pomp*.] Characterized by pomp, stately splendor, or magnificence (as, "It was a glorious spectacle . . . to behold this *pompous* pageant issuing forth . . . the pennons and devices . . . fluttering above a sea of crests and plumes": Irving's "Conquest of Granada," xxxvi.); also, characterized by a parade of dignity or importance (as, "In his general deportment he was *pompous* and important, affecting a species of florid elocution," Scott's "Guy Mannering," xlii.; a *pompous* bow, pronouncement, or manner); ostentatiously dignified; consequential; of language, style, etc., ostentatiously lofty.—**pom′pous-ly,** *adv.*—**pom′pous-ness,** *n.*

Pomp-tine (pomp′tin), *a.* See *Pontine*.

ponce-let (pons′let), *n.* [From J. V. *Poncelet* (1788–1867), French mathematician and engineer.] In *physics*, a unit of power equivalent to 100 kilogrammeters per second.

pon-cho (pon′chō), *n.*; pl. *-chos* (-chōz). [S. Amer. Sp.] A kind of cloak worn in South America and elsewhere, resembling a blanket with a slit in the middle for the head; also, a similar garment, esp. one of waterproof material, worn elsewhere, as by soldiers, sportsmen, etc.

pond (pond), *n.* [= *pound*[1].] A body of still water smaller than a lake, esp. one artificially formed, as by damming up a stream; in fig. or humorous use, the sea, esp. the Atlantic Ocean.—**pond,** *v. t.* To form or dam into or as into a pond.—**pond′age** (-ạj), *n.* The ponding of water; also, the capacity of a pond.

pon-der (pon′dèr), *v.* [OF. *ponderer* (F. *pondérer*), < L. *ponderare*, weigh, ponder, < *pondus* (*ponder-*), weight, < *pendere*, weigh.] **I.** *tr.* To weigh†; also, fig., to weigh carefully in the mind, or consider carefully (as, "The modest queen a while . . . *Ponder'd* the speech; then briefly thus replies": Dryden's tr. Virgil's "Æneid," i. 789). **II.** *intr.* To consider deeply; meditate: as, "The Doctor had been *pondering*, and had made up his mind to a certain course" (H. Kingsley's "Geoffry Hamlyn," xxxv.).—**pon′der-a-ble,** *a.* [LL. *ponderabilis*.] Capable of being weighed; having appreciable weight; appreciable.—**pon-der-a′tion**

(-ā′shọn), *n.* [L. *ponderatio*(*n-*).] The act of weighing (lit. or fig.).—**pon′der-er,** *n.*—**pon′der-ing-ly,** *adv.*

pon-der-ous (pon′dèr-us), *a.* [OF. *pondereux*, < L. *ponderosus*, < *pondus* (*ponder-*), weight: see *ponder*.] Of great weight, or heavy (as, a *ponderous* mass of iron); massive (as, "a *ponderous* gateway under a heavy stone arch": Trollope's "Warden," i.); esp., heavy to the point of being clumsy or unwieldy (as, *ponderous* armor or weapons; "a *ponderous* folio volume," Hawthorne's "Twice-Told Tales," Dr. Heidegger's Experiment); fig., heavy, dull, or without graceful lightness or ease (as, a *ponderous* dissertation; a *ponderous* joke or compliment; a *ponderous* way of speaking); also, weighty† or important†.—**pon-der-os′i-ty** (-os′i-ti), **pon′der-ous-ness,** *n.*—**pon′der-ous-ly,** *adv.*

pond=fish (pond′fish), *n.* Any of various fishes found in ponds, esp. any of numerous small American fresh-water sunfishes.

pond=lil-y (pond′lil″i), *n.*; pl. *-lilies* (-iz). A water-lily, esp. one of the genus *Nymphæa* ('yellow pond-lily').

pond-weed (pond′wēd), *n.* Any of the aquatic plants constituting the genus *Potamogeton*, most of which grow in ponds and quiet streams; also, any of various allied or similar plants.

pone (pōn), *n.* [N. Amer. Ind.] Bread or cake, esp. of a plain or simple kind, made of Indian meal; also, a loaf or cake of it. [Southern U. S.]

po-nent (pō′nent). [= It. *ponente*, < ML. *ponens* (*ponent-*), the west, lit. 'setting (sun),' prop. ppr. of L. *ponere*, place, put, set down.] **I.**† *n.* The west. **II.** *a.* Western; west: as, "Forth rush the Levant and the *Ponent* winds" (Milton's "Paradise Lost," x. 704). [Archaic.]

pon-gee (pon-jē′), *n.* [Chinese.] A soft, plain-woven, unbleached or dyed silk fabric made in China and elsewhere.

pon-iard (pon′yärd), *n.* [F. *poignard*, < *poing*, < L. *pugnus*, fist.] A short weapon for stabbing; a dagger.—**pon′iard,** *v. t.* To stab with a poniard.

pons (ponz), *n.*; pl. *pontes* (pon′tēz). [L.] A bridge; in *anat.*, a connecting part; esp. ('pons Varolii': see below), a band of nerve-fibers in the brain connecting the lobes of the cerebellum, as well as the medulla and cerebrum.—**pons asinorum** (as-i-nō′rum). [L., 'bridge of asses.'] The geometrical proposition (Euclid, i. 5) that if a triangle has two of its sides equal, the angles opposite these sides are also equal: so named from the difficulty experienced by beginners in mastering it.—**pons Varolii** (vạ-rō′li-ī). [NL., 'bridge of Varoli': named from Costanzo Varoli (1543?–75), Italian anatomist.] See *pons*, above.

Fruit-bearing Plant of Pond-weed (*Potamogeton natans*).— *a*, a flower.

Poniard, entirely of steel; 17th century.

Pon-tic (pon′tik), *a.* [L. *Ponticus*, < Gr. Ποντικός, < Πόντος, the Black Sea, also Pontus, particular use of πόντος, sea.] Pertaining to the Pontus, or Black Sea, or to Pontus, an ancient country south of it.

pon-ti-fex (pon′ti-feks), *n.*; pl. *pontifices* (pon-tif′i-sēz). [L., usually explained as < *pons* (*pont-*), bridge, + *facere*, make; but the first element is uncertain.] A member of the principal college of priests in ancient Rome, whose head was the *Pontifex Maximus*, or chief priest; *eccles.*, a pontiff or bishop, specif. the Pope.

pon-tiff (pon′tif), *n.* [F. *pontife*, < L. *pontifex*: see *pontifex*.] An ancient Roman pontifex; in general, a high or chief priest; *eccles.*, a bishop; specif., the bishop of Rome (the Pope).—**pon-tif′i-cal** (-tif′i-ḳal). [L. *pontificalis*, < *pontifex*.] **I.** *a.* Of, pertaining to, or characteristic of a

pontiff (as, *pontifical* mass, a mass celebrated by a bishop); specif., pertaining to the Pope; papal. **II.** *n.* In the Western Church, a book containing the forms for the sacraments and other rites and ceremonies to be performed by bishops; also, *pl.*, the vestments and other insignia of a pontiff, esp. a bishop, or, loosely, of a priest.—**pon-tif'i-cal-ly,** *adv.*—**pon-tif'i-cate** (-kāt), *n.* [L. *pontificatus*, n.] The office, or term of office, of a pontiff.—**pon-tif'i-cate,** *v. i.; -cated, -cating.* [ML. *pontificatus*, pp. of *pontificare,* < L. *pontifex.*] To perform the functions of a pontiff; officiate at pontifical mass; hence, to assume the airs of a pontiff.

pon-til (pon'til), *n.* [F.] Same as *punty*.

Pon-tine, Pomp-tine (pon'tin, pomp'tin), *a.* [L. *Pontinus, Pomptinus,* < *Pometia,* ancient town in Latium.] Noting or pertaining to an extensive marshy district southeast of Rome.

pont-lev-is (pont-lev'is), *n.* [F.] A drawbridge.

pon-to-nier (pon-tọ̄-nēr'), *n.* [F. *pontonnier.*] *Milit.*, an officer or soldier in charge of the bridge equipment or the construction of pontoon-bridges.

pon-toon (pon-tön'), *n.* [F. *ponton,* < L. *ponto*(n-), < *pons* (*pont-*), bridge.] A low flat-bottomed boat used as a lighter, etc.; specif., as in military use, such a boat, or some other floating structure, used as one of the supports for a temporary bridge over a river; also, in *engin.*, a water-tight structure used in raising a submerged vessel, etc.—**pon-toon',** *v. t.* To bridge or to cross by means of pontoons.—**pon-toon'=bridge,** *n.* A bridge supported by pontoons.—**pon-toon'=train,** *n.* *Milit.*, a train of vehicles carrying pontoons and other bridge equipment.

Pontoon-bridge.

po-ny (pō'ni), *n.; pl. -nies* (-niz). [Prob. < OF. *poulenet,* dim. of *poulain,* colt, < L. *pullus,* young animal: see *foal.*] A horse of a small breed, specif. one not over 14 hands high; also, the sum of £25 (slang, Eng.); also, a crib, or translation or other illicit aid (school and college slang, U. S.); also, something small of its kind; a small glass for liquor, or the amount of liquor it will hold; a girl of small stature, as in the chorus of a musical comedy or the like (slang).—**po'ny,** *v. t. or i.; -nied, -nying.* To prepare (lessons) by means of a pony or crib; also, to pay (money), as in settling an account (with *up*). [Slang.]

pood (pöd), *n.* [Russ. *pud.*] A Russian weight equal to about 36 pounds avoirdupois.

poo-dle (pö'dl), *n.* [G. *pudel.*] One of a breed of intelligent pet dogs, of numerous varieties, with thick curly hair.

pooh (pö or pụ̈). **I.** *interj.* An exclamation of disdain or contempt: often repeated, *pooh! pooh!*—as, "'Pooh! pooh!' cries the squire; 'all stuff and nonsense'" (Fielding's "Tom Jones," vi. 7). **II.** *n.* An exclamation of 'pooh!'—**pooh,** *v.* **I.** *intr.* To say 'pooh': as, "Legree *poohed* and pished, but read, turning page after page" (Mrs. Stowe's "Uncle Tom's Cabin," xxxix.). **II.** *tr.* To say 'pooh' at or to.—**pooh=pooh** (pö-pö'), *v. t.* To express disdain or contempt for; make light of; dismiss as unworthy of consideration: as, "He *pooh-poohed* the notion" (Mrs. H. Ward's "Robert Elsmere," x.).

Poodle.

pool¹ (pöl), *n.* [AS. *pōl* = MLG. *pōl* = D. *poel.*] A small body of standing or still water; a small pond; sometimes, a puddle; any small collection of liquid standing on a surface (as, a *pool* of blood); also, a still, deep place in a stream; also, a tank or large basin of water to swim or bathe in.

pool² (pöl), *n.* [F. *poule,* lit. 'hen': see *pullet.*] The stakes in certain games; also, a game played by two or more persons on a billiard-table with six pockets, the object of the players being to pocket balls of ivory or other material by means of cues; also, the total amount staked by a combination of betters, as on a race, to be awarded to the successful better or betters; the combination of such betters; also, a combination of interests, funds, etc., for common advantage; the combined interests or fund; the persons or parties involved; often, such a combination between competing parties, to reconcile interests, control prices, or the like.—**pool²,** *v.* **I.** *tr.* To put (interests, money, etc.) into a pool, or common stock or fund, as for the purpose of a distribution according to agreement; form a pool of; make a common interest of: as, "the current proposal to *pool* all clerical stipends for the common purposes of the church" (H. G. Wells's "Italy, France, and Britain at War," iv. 3). **II.** *intr.* To enter into or form a pool.—**pool'=room,** *n.* A room or place in which the game of pool is played; also, a room or place in which pools are arranged or gambling is carried on on races, etc.—**pool'=ta"ble,** *n.* A billiard-table with six pockets, on which pool is played.

poon (pön), *n.* [E. Ind. (Dravidian).] Any of several East Indian trees of the clusiaceous genus *Calophyllum,* which yield a light, hard wood used for masts, spars, etc.; also, the wood.

poop (pöp), *n.* [OF. F. *poupe,* < L. *puppis.*] The aftermost part, or stern, of a ship; also, a deck above the ordinary deck in that part, often forming the roof of a cabin.—**poop,** *v. t.* Of a wave, to break over the stern of (a ship): as, "The frigate was *pooped* by a tremendous sea" (Marryat's

Ship of War with High Poop; 17th century.

"Mr. Midshipman Easy," xxv.).—**pooped,** *a.* Having a poop: as, high-*pooped.*

poor (pör). [OF. *povre* (F. *pauvre*), < L. *pauper,* poor: cf. *pauper.*] **I.** *a.* Having little or nothing in the way of wealth, goods, or means of subsistence (as, "The *poor* man had nothing, save one little ewe lamb," 2 Sam. xii. 3; "*Poor* men . . . Must be content to sit by little fires," Tennyson's "Holy Grail," 612); lacking means to procure the comforts or the necessaries of life; specif., esp. in legal use, dependent upon charity; of a country, institution, etc., meagerly supplied or endowed with resources or funds; of the circumstances, life, home, dress, etc., characterized by or showing poverty; also, deficient or lacking in something specified (as, a region *poor* in mineral deposits; a mind *poor* in ideas; works *poor* in merit); also, deficient in desirable ingredients, qualities, or the like (as, *poor* soil, ore, or coal; *poor* milk; *poor* paper; a *poor* novel); lean or emaciated, as cattle; in general, of an inferior, inadequate, or unsatisfactory kind, or not good (as, a *poor* substitute; *poor* service; a *poor* excuse; *poor* health or eyesight); often, deficient in aptitude or ability (as, a *poor* head for figures; a *poor* judge of distance; a *poor* reasoner; a *poor* cook); also, deficient in moral excellence; esp., spiritless, cowardly, abject, or mean; also, scanty, meager, or paltry in amount or number (as, a *poor* pittance; "Upon this discovery the treasure-seekers, already reduced to a *poor* half dozen . . . fled outright," Stevenson's "Master of Ballantrae," xi.); also, trifling or unimportant (as, "What were thy lips the worse for one *poor* kiss?" Shakspere's "Venus and Adonis," 207); humble or insignificant (often used to lend modesty to speech: as, deign to visit our *poor* house; in my *poor* opinion); also, unfortunate or hapless (much used to express pity: as, the *poor* mother was in despair; "Why then is . . . this *poor* innocent fellow treated as a malefactor?" Smollett's "Humphry Clinker," June 11); hence, an epithet of regret often used in speaking of a deceased person (as, "when I . . . was married to my *poor* husband": Thackeray's "Newcomes," xxiii.). **II.** *n.* A poor person†; also, poor persons collectively (as *pl.*, and commonly with *the*: as, "The destruction of the *poor* is their poverty," Prov. x. 15).—**poor'=box,** *n.* A box, esp. in a church, for receiving contributions for the poor.—**poor′house**, *n.* A house in which paupers are maintained at the public expense.—**poor′ish**, *a.* Rather poor.—**poor′=law**, *n.* A law or system of laws providing for the relief or support of the poor at the public expense. —**poor′ly**, *a.* In poor health; somewhat ill; unwell. [Chiefly colloq.]—**poor′ly**, *adv.*—**poor′ness**, *n.*—**poor′= spir′it-ed**, *a.* Having or showing a poor, cowardly, or abject spirit.

poor=will (pör′wil), *n.* [Imit. of its note: cf. *whippoorwill.*] A goatsucker, *Phalænoptilus nuttalli*, of western North America, resembling a whippoorwill but smaller.

pop[1] (pop). [Abbr. of *popular*.] **I.** *a.* Popular: as, a pop concert. [Colloq.] **II.** *n.* A popular concert. [Colloq.]

pop[2] (pop), *v. i.*; *popped*, *popping*. [Imit.] To make a short, quick, explosive sound or report (as, pistols were *popping*; "The loud *popping* of a cork roused him," Galsworthy's "Saint's Progress," iii. 7); burst open with such a sound, as chestnuts or corn in roasting; also, to shoot with a firearm (as, to *pop* at a mark); also to come or go quickly, suddenly, or unexpectedly (*in, into, out, off, up,* etc.: see phrases below); also, to 'pop the question,' or propose marriage (colloq.).—**to pop in,** to come in unexpectedly or without ceremony, as for a short visit; drop in: as, "Well, father, we just *popped in* to see how you were" (Arnold Bennett's "Clayhanger," iii. 2). [Colloq.]—**to pop off,** to die, esp. suddenly: as, "I might *pop off* any minute" (Arnold Bennett's "Helen with the High Hand," xvii.). [Colloq.]—**pop**[2], *v. t.* To cause to make a sudden, explosive sound; cause to burst open with such a sound; fire (a gun, etc.); shoot (*down,* etc.); also, to put or thrust quickly, suddenly, or unexpectedly (*in, into, out, up,* etc.: as, to *pop* a cherry into the mouth; "The little attorney *popped* up his head and whispered to me," Kingsley's "Alton Locke," xxix.); also, to pawn (slang, Eng.: as, "Let's hurry up and find a pawnbroker's, and I'll *pop* my watch!" L. Merrick's "Position of Peggy Harper," i. 3).—**to pop corn,** to parch or roast the kernels of certain varieties of maize until they burst open.—**to pop the question,** to propose marriage. [Colloq.]—**pop**[2], *n.* A popping; a short, quick, explosive sound (as, " 'Done!' quoth my grandmother, with a *pop* like a roasted chestnut bursting out of the fire": Mrs. Stowe's "Oldtown Folks," xx.); a shot with a firearm; also, an effervescent beverage, esp. an unintoxicating one.—**pop**[2], *adv.* With a pop or explosive sound (as, "*Pop* cracked the guns!" Holmes's "Comet"); also, quickly, suddenly, or unexpectedly.

pop[3] (pop), *n.* Shortened form of *papa*[1], father: often applied to any elderly or old man. [Colloq., U. S.]

pop-corn (pop′kôrn′), *n.* Any of several varieties of maize or Indian corn whose kernels burst open and puff out when subjected to dry heat; also, popped corn (as, "wooden stands filled with common people eating peanuts and *popcorn*": W. Churchill's "Modern Chronicle," i. 5).

pope (pōp), *n.* [AS. *pāpa*, < ML. *papa,* pope, LL. bishop, < Gr. πάππας, father, orig. in childish use, later, also πάπας, παπᾶς, as an eccles. title (cf. *papa*[2]); in the last sense, through Slav. (Russ. *pop*) < Gr. παπᾶς.] The bishop of Rome as head of the Roman Catholic Church (*cap.* or *l. c.*: as, the *Pope*; the last three *popes*); hence, one considered as having or assuming a similar position or authority; in the *Gr. Ch.*, a parish priest.—**pope′dom** (-dom), *n.* The office or dignity of a pope; the tenure of office of a pope; also, the papal government; a system resembling the papacy. —**pop-er-y** (pō′pe̱-ri), *n.* The doctrines, customs, and ceremonies associated with the Pope as head of the Roman Catholic· Church; the papal system; the Roman Catholic religion: used in disparagement.—**pope′s′=nose′**, *n.* The uropygium of a bird. [Colloq.]

pop=eyes (pop′īz), *n. pl.* Bulging or prominent eyes.— **pop′=eyed**, *a.*

pop=gun (pop′gun), *n.* A child's toy consisting of a short tube or imitation gun from the mouth of which a pellet is shot with a popping sound by compression of air.

pop-in-jay (pop′in-jā), *n.* [OF. F. *papegai*, parrot; appar. of African or Asiatic origin.] A parrot (obs. or archaic); also, a figure of a parrot formerly used as a target (as, "He had . . . on several occasions, carried off the prize from the Duke in shooting at the *popinjay*": Motley's "Dutch

Republic," iii. 2); also, a vain, chattering person; a cox-comb; a fop; also, a woodpecker, esp. the green woodpecker, *Gecinus viridis*, of Europe.

Popinjay, or Green Woodpecker (*Gecinus viridis*).

pop-ish (pō′pish), *a.* Of or pertaining to popery or the Roman Catholic Church: used in disparagement.— **pop′ish-ly**, *adv.*

pop-lar (pop′lär), *n.* [OF. *poplier* (F. *peuplier*), < L. *populus*, poplar.] Any of various rapidly growing trees constituting the salicaceous genus *Populus*, yielding a useful, light, soft wood, as *P. nigra italica* ('Lombardy poplar'), a tall tree of striking columnar or spire-shaped outline due to the fastigiate habit of its branches; the wood itself; also, any of various trees resembling these in some respect, as the tulip-tree, *Liriodendron tulipifera* ('yellow poplar'); the wood of any such tree.

pop-lin (pop′lin), *n.* [F. *popeline*, < It. *papalina*, fem. of *papalino*, papal; so called from being made at the papal city of Avignon.] A corded fabric with a silk warp and a woolen weft, or a similar fabric of wool and cotton or linen: used for women's dresses, etc.

pop-lit-e-al (pop-lit′ē̱-al or pop-li-tē′al), *a.* [NL. *popliteus*, < L. *poples* (*poplit-*), the ham.] In *anat.*, of or pertaining to the ham, or part of the leg back of the knee.

pop-o-ver (pop′ō′′vér), *n.* A kind of muffin so light as to overflow its pan in cooking.

pop-per (pop′ér), *n.* One who or that which pops; a utensil for popping corn.

pop-pet (pop′et), *n.* [Earlier form of *puppet.*] A puppet† or doll†; a marionette†; a term of endearment for a girl or child (now prov. Eng.: as, "'Little *poppet!*' she murmured to herself, maternally reflecting upon Florence's tender youth," Arnold Bennett's "Hilda Lessways," i. 5); in *mach.*, a poppet-head; also, a valve which in opening is lifted bodily from its seat instead of being hinged at one side. —**pop′pet=head**, *n.* The tail-stock of a lathe.

pop-pied (pop′id), *a.* Covered or adorned with poppies; also, affected by or as by poppy-juice or opium; listless.

pop-ple (pop′l), *v. i.*; *-pled*, *-pling*. [ME. *poplen*; prob. imit.] To move in a tumbling, irregular manner, as boiling water; bob up and down, or move to and fro, as a floating object.—**pop′ple**, *n.* A poppling motion.

pop-py (pop′i), *n.*; pl. *poppies* (-iz). [AS. *popig, popæg,* ult. < L. *papaver*, poppy.] Any plant of the genus *Papaver*, comprising herbs with showy flowers of various colors, esp. *P. somniferum*, which is the source of opium, and which yields a valuable oil; an extract, as opium, from such a plant; also, any of various other papaveraceous plants, as the eschscholtzia, *Eschscholtzia californica* ('California poppy'), or the plant *Argemone mexicana*, with prickly stems, leaves, and capsules ('prickly poppy'); also, a bright red color.

pop-py-cock (pop′i-kok), *n.* [Origin obscure.] Nonsense; bosh: as, "All this profit-sharing and welfare work and insurance . . . is simply *poppycock*" (Sinclair Lewis's "Main Street," iv.). [Colloq.]

pop-py=head (pop′i-hed), *n.* In *arch.*, a finial or other ornament, often richly carved, as at the top of the upright end of a bench or pew. See cut on following page.

Poppy (*Papaver somniferum*).— *a,* the upper part of the stem with the flower; *b,* the lower part of the plant; *c,* the fruit.

pop-u-lace (pop′ū-lās), *n.* [F. *populace*, < It. *popolaccio*, pejorative of *po-polo*, < L. *populus*, E. *people*.] The common people of a community, as distinguished from the higher classes: orig. and still often used with a disparaging force, or in speaking of popular discontent or disorder: as, "The *populace*, who hated Pompey, threw flowers upon the tribune [Curio] as he passed" (Froude's "Cæsar," xx.); "Then the *populace* flowed in like an angry sea" (Motley's "Dutch Republic," ii. 7).

pop-u-lar (pop′ū-lär), *a.* [L. *popularis*, < *populus*,

Poppy-head. — Choir-stalls of Lincoln Cathedral, England.

E. *people*.] Of, pertaining to, or representing the people or general body of citizens, or the common people, rather than a ruling or other special class (as, the *popular* voice; *popular* discontent; "If a *popular* chief raised his standard in a *popular* cause, an irregular army could be assembled in a day," Macaulay's "Hist. of Eng.," i.); participated in or carried on by the people (as, *popular* government); also, prevailing among the people generally (as, a *popular* notion; *popular* errors); also, regarded with favor or approval by the people or public generally (as, a *popular* preacher; "Peace would be *popular* everywhere, upon whatever terms it might be concluded," Motley's "Dutch Republic," i. 3); enjoying general favor or liking, as with associates, acquaintances, etc. (as, "At school he was not actively disliked . . . but he was too dull and deficient in animal spirits to be *popular*": S. Butler's "Way of All Flesh," vii.); also, suited to or intended for ordinary people; adapted to the ordinary intelligence (as, *popular* lectures or books on science); adapted to the ordinary taste (as, *popular* music; a *popular* program); suited to the means of ordinary people (as, *popular* prices; *popular* concerts; a *popular* edition of an expensive book); also, plebeian† or vulgar† (as, "Art thou officer? Or art thou base, common and *popular?*" Shakspere's "Henry V.," iv. 1. 38).—**pop-u-lar′i-ty** (-lar′i-ti), *n.* The quality or fact of being popular; esp., favor enjoyed with the people, the public generally, or a particular circle or set of people (as, "The *popularity* . . . with which the young Sovereign had begun her reign, had entirely disappeared": Lytton Strachey's "Queen Victoria," iii.).—**pop′u-lar-ize** (-lär-īz), *v. t.*; *-ized, -izing.* To make popular.—**pop″u-lar-i-za′tion** (-i-zā′shon), *n.*—**pop′u-lar-iz-er** (-ī-zėr), *n.* —**pop′u-lar-ly,** *adv.*

pop-u-late (pop′ū-lāt), *v. t.*; *-lated, -lating.* [ML. *populatus*, pp. of *populare*, < L. *populus*, E. *people*.] To inhabit; also, to furnish with inhabitants, as by colonization; people. —**pop-u-la′tion** (-lā′shon), *n.* The act or process of populating; also, the state of a locality with reference to the number of its inhabitants; hence, the total number of persons inhabiting a country, city, or any district or area; the body of inhabitants of a place; sometimes, the number or body of inhabitants of a particular race or class in a place (as, the Jewish *population* of New York; "Besides our Indian *population*, we had also a few negroes," Mrs. Stowe's "Oldtown Folks," v.).—**pop′u-la-tor,** *n.*

Pop-u-lism (pop′ū-lizm), *n.* [L. *populus*, people.] The principles and policies of the so-called People's party. See *Populist.*—**Pop′u-list,** *n.* In *U. S. politics,* a member of the People's party, a political organization formed in 1891, advocating expansion of the currency, state control of rail-roads, the placing of restrictions upon the ownership of land, etc.—**Pop-u-lis′tic,** *a.*

pop-u-lous (pop′ū-lus), *a.* [L. *populosus*, < *populus*, E. *people*.] Full of people or inhabitants, as a region or place (as, "the Pays de Caux, the most fertile and *populous* region in all France": J. F. Kirk's "Charles the Bold," iii. 2); well populated; also, comprising many people†, or multitudinous†.—**pop′u-lous-ly,** *adv.*—**pop′u-lous-ness,** *n.*

por-bea-gle (pôr′bē″gl), *n.* [Cornish name; origin uncertain.] A shark of the genus *Lamna,* esp. *L. cornubica,* a voracious species which attains a length of from ten to twelve feet.

porce-lain (pôrs′lān or pôr′sẹ-lān), *n.*

Porbeagle (*Lamna cornubica*).

[F. *porcelaine,* < It. *porcellana,* porcelain, orig. a kind of shell, appar. ult. < L. *porcus,* hog, pig.] A fine, more or less translucent kind of ceramic material or ware made from kaolin, etc.; china; also, a vessel or object made of this material.—**artificial soft=paste porcelain,** a soft-paste porcelain more or less resembling glass in composition.—**hard=paste** (or **natural**) **porcelain,** true porcelain, the principal ingredients used in its manufacture being kaolin and feldspar.—**natural soft=paste porcelain,** a soft-paste porcelain which has clay for its basis.—**soft=paste** (or **artificial**) **porcelain,** a product made originally to imitate hard-paste porcelain, and prepared from various materials, such as sand, soda, gypsum, etc., or clay, calcined bone, etc.—**por-cel-la-ne-ous** (pôr-sẹ-lā″nẹ-us), *a.* Resembling porcelain.—**por′cel-la-nite** (-lạ-nīt), *n.* A clay hardened by natural calcination, somewhat resembling porcelain or jasper.

porch (pôrch), *n.* [OF. F. *porche,* < L. *porticus,* porch, portico, < *porta,* gate, door: cf. *portico.*] An exterior appendage to a building, forming a covered approach or vestibule to a doorway; also, a veranda (U. S.); also, a portico or covered walk; [*cap.*] with *the,* a public ambulatory in ancient Athens to which the Stoic philosopher Zeno of Citium (about 336—about 264 B.C.) and his followers resorted (also called the *Painted Porch*); hence, the Stoic school. — **porch′climb″er,** *n.* A thief who secures entrance to a house by climbing a porch or veranda. [Colloq.]

por-cine (pôr′sin or -sīn), *a.* [L. *porcinus,* < *por-*

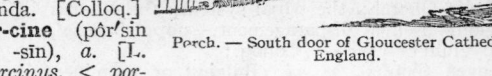

Porch. — South door of Gloucester Cathedral, England.

cus, hog, pig.] Pertaining to, of the nature of, or resembling swine; often, suggesting a swine or something characteristic of a swine (as, "The *porcine* head of the church-warden was not on his shoulders by accident": G. Mac-Donald's "Annals of a Quiet Neighbourhood," xvii.); swinish, hoggish, or piggish.

por-cu-pine (pôr′kū-pīn), *n.* [OF. *porc espin,* < L. *porcus,* hog, pig, + *spina,* thorn, spine.] Any of various rodents (family *Hystricidæ*) having the body covered with stout

erectile spines, as *Hystrix cristata* ('European porcupine')
with long spines,
or *Erethizon dor-
satus* ('Canada
porcupine') with
short spines.—
**porcupine
ant=eater,** an
echidna.

European Porcupine (*Hystrix cristata*).

pore[1] (pōr), *v. i.*;
pored, poring.
[ME. *pouren,
puren;* origin
uncertain.] To
gaze earnestly
or steadily; read or study with steady attention or application (as, "Have you ever *pored* . . . over the pages
of Snorro?" Borrow's "Lavengro," ii.); also, to meditate
or ponder intently: usually with *over, on,* or *upon.*

pore[2] (pōr), *n.* [OF. F. *pore,* < L. *porus,* < Gr. πόρος,
passage, way: see *fare.*] A minute opening or orifice, as in
the skin or a leaf; also, one of the minute interstices or spaces
between the particles or molecules of matter.

por-er (pōr′ėr), *n.* One who pores, as over a book.

por-gy (pôr′gi), *n.*; pl. *-gies* (-giz). [Origin uncertain;
prob. from several sources.] Any of numerous fishes, esp. a
sea-bream, *Pagrus pagrus,* of Mediterranean and Atlantic
waters ('red porgy'),
or a related fish, the
scup, of the eastern
U. S. coast.

po-rif-er-ous (pō-rif′-
ẹ-rus), *a.* [L. *porus,*
pore, + *ferre,* bear.]
Bearing or having
pores.

Red Porgy (*Pagrus pagrus*).

po-rism (pō′rizm), *n.* [Gr. πόρισμα, < πορίζειν, bring,
deduce, < πόρος, passage, way, E. *pore*[2].] A form of mathematical proposition among the Greeks which has been
variously defined, esp. as an extra proposition or corollary
inserted by Euclid's commentators, or as a proposition
affirming the possibility of finding such conditions as will
render a certain problem indeterminate, or capable of
innumerable solutions.

pork (pôrk), *n.* [OF. F. *porc,* < L. *porcus,* hog, pig: see
farrow[1].] A swine†; also, the flesh of swine used as food;
also, profit accruing from appropriations voted by Congress,
a State legislature, or the like, for political reasons rather
than because of public necessity, as for public buildings,
river and harbor improvements, etc., in localities whose
needs or relative importance would not establish a just
claim to them (political slang, U. S.).—**pork=bar″rel,** *n.*
An imaginary barrel colloquially spoken of as the source of
political pork. [Political slang, U. S.]—**pork′er,** *n.* A
swine, esp. one fatted for killing: as, "Sleek unwieldy *pork-
ers* were grunting in the repose and abundance of their
pens" (Irving's "Sketch-Book," Sleepy Hollow).—**pork′-
fish,** *n.* A sparoid fish, *Anisotremus virginicus,* of the
Atlantic coast
from Florida
to Brazil.—
pork′y, *a.*
Pork-like; fat.

por-nog-ra-phy
(pôr-nog′ra-fi),
n. [LGr. πορ-
νογράφος, writ-
ing of prosti-
tutes, < Gr.
πόρνη, prosti-
tute, + γράφειν,
write.] The

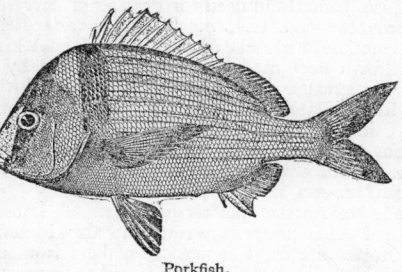

Porkfish.

description of prostitutes or prostitution; hence, obscene
literature or art.—**por-nog′ra-pher,** *n.*—**por-no-graph′ic**
(-nō-graf′ik), *a.*

po-rous (pō′rus), *a.* Full of pores; permeable by water, air,
or the like.—**po-ros-i-ty** (pō-ros′i-ti), **po′rous-ness,** *n.*—
po′rous-ly, *adv.*

por-phy-rit-ic (pôr-fi-rit′ik), *a.* Of, pertaining to, containing, or resembling porphyry; noting, pertaining to, or
resembling the texture or struc-
ture characteristic of porphyry.—
por-phy-rit′i-cal-ly, *adv.*

por-phy-roid (pôr′fi-roid), *n.* [See
-oid.] A rock resembling porphyry; esp., a sedimentary rock
which has been altered by some
metamorphic agency so as to take
on a slaty and more or less perfectly developed porphyritic structure.

Porphyritic Structure.

por-phy-ry (pôr′fi-ri), *n.*; pl. *-ries*
(-riz). [OF. *porfire* (F. *porphyre*), < Gr. πορφύρεος, purple:
cf. L. *porphyrites,* porphyry, < Gr. πορφυρίτης, like purple.]
Orig., a very hard rock, anciently quarried in Egypt, having a dark purplish-red ground-mass containing small crystals
of feldspar; now, any rock of similar texture, esp. one with a
fine-grained or microcrystalline ground-mass through which
are disseminated distinctly recognizable crystals of some mineral; sometimes, any of various igneous rocks without this texture.

por-poise (pôr′pus), *n.* [OF. *porpois, porpeis,* < L. *porcus,*
hog, + *piscis,* fish.] Any of the gregarious cetaceans
constituting the genus *Phocæna* (family *Delphinidæ*), five
to eight feet
long, usually
b l a c k i s h
above and
paler be-
neath, and
having a
blunt, round-
ed snout;

Common Porpoise (*Phocæna communis* or *phocæna*).

also, any of several other small cetaceans, as the common
dolphin, *Delphinus delphis.*

por-ra-ceous (po-rā′shius), *a.* [L. *porraceus,* < *porrum,*
leek.] Leek-green.

por-ridge (por′ij), *n.* [Altered form of *pottage.*] Pottage†;
also, a food made of oatmeal or some other meal or cereal
boiled to a thick consistence in water or milk (as, "an English breakfast—*porridge,* chops, marmalade": Galsworthy's
"Dark Flower," i. 11).

por-rin-ger (por′in-jėr), *n.* [Altered form of earlier *potager,*
< OF. *potager,* < *potage,* F. *pottage.*] A dish, deeper than
a plate or saucer, from which soup, broth, porridge, etc.,
may be eaten.

port[1] (pōrt), *n.* [AS. *port,* < L. *portus,* harbor, haven:
see *fare,* and cf. *port*[2].] A recess, as of the sea or a lake,
where vessels may take refuge from storms; a harbor; a
haven; also, a town or place to which vessels resort to load
or unload; specif., any place where persons and merchandise
are allowed to pass (by water or land) into and out of a
country and where customs officers are stationed to inspect
or appraise imported goods.

port[2] (pōrt), *n.* [OF. F. *porte,* < L. *porta,* gate, door, akin
to *portus,* harbor, haven: see *port*[1] and *fare.*] A gate or
portal, as of a town or fortress (now chiefly Sc.); *naut.,* an
opening in the side of a ship, as for pointing cannon through
or for the admission of light and air (as, "He peeped through
the *ports,* which were open, and looked down into the deep
blue wave": Marryat's "Mr. Midshipman Easy," x.); a
port-hole; also, the covering or shutter for a port-hole;
in *mech.,* an aperture for the passage of steam, air, water, etc.

port[3] (pōrt). [Origin uncertain.] *Naut.*: **I.** *n.* The left
side of a ship, looking from stern to bow: opposed to *starboard,* and sometimes supplanted by *left.* Cf. *larboard.*
II. *a.* Pertaining to the port; being on the left side of a
vessel: as, "the *port* side of the main deck" (J. Conrad's
"Rescue," i. 1).—**port**[3], *v. t.* or *i. Naut.,* to turn or shift
to the port or left side: as, to *port* the helm.

port[4] (pōrt), *n.* [From *Oporto* (Pg. *o porto,* 'the port'), in
Portugal.] Any of a class of wines, mostly dark-red, orig.
from Portugal.

port[5] (pōrt), *v. t.* [OF. F. *porter,* < L. *portare,* carry: see
fare.] To carry†; *milit.,* to carry (a rifle, etc.), with both
hands, in a slanting direction across the front of the body,

with the barrel or like part near the left shoulder.—**port**[5], *n.* [OF. F. *port.*] Manner of bearing one's self, carriage, or bearing (as, "She dressed well, and had a presence and *port* calculated to set off handsome attire": C. Brontë's "Jane Eyre," iv.); also, style of living, esp. grand style (obs. or archaic: as, "The duke himself, and the magnificoes Of greatest *port*," Shakspere's "Merchant of Venice," iii. 2. 283); *milit.*, the position of a rifle or other weapon when ported.

por-ta-ble (pōr′ta̤-bl), *a.* [LL. *portabilis*, < L. *portare*, carry, E. *port*[5].] Capable of being carried in the hand or on the person: that may be moved from place to place; easily carried or conveyed; also, bearable† or endurable† (as, "How light and *portable* my pain seems now!" Shakspere's "King Lear," iii. 6. 115).—**por-ta-bil′i-ty** (-bil′i-ti), *n.*

por-tage (pōr′tāj), *n.* [OF. F. *portage*, < *porter*, carry, E. *port*[5].] The act of carrying; carriage; esp., the carrying of boats, goods, etc., overland from one navigable water to another; a place or course over which this must be done (as, "As we were carrying the canoe upon a rocky *portage*, she fell, and was entirely bilged": Stevenson's "Master of Ballantrae," iii.); also, cost of carriage.—**por′tage**, *v. t.* or *i.*; *-taged*, *-taging*. To carry (boats, etc.) over a portage.

por-tal[1] (pōr′tal̤), *a.* [NL. *porta*, the transverse fissure of the liver, L. gate, door, E. *port*[2].] In *anat.*, noting or pertaining to the transverse fissure of the liver (as, the *portal* vein, the large vein conveying blood to the liver from the veins of the stomach, intestine, and spleen); also, pertaining to the portal vein.

por-tal[2] (pōr′ta̤l), *n.* [OF. *portal*, < ML. *portale*, < L. *porta*, gate, door, E. *port*[2].] A door, gate, or entrance, esp. one of imposing appearance, as in a cathedral. Also fig.

Portal. — West front of Peterborough Cathedral, England.

por-ta-men-to (pōr-tä-men′tō), *n.* [It., < *portare*, < L. *portare*, carry, E. *port*[5].] In *music*, a passing or gliding from one pitch or tone to another without break or perceptible step.

por-tance (pōr′tạns), *n.* [Obs. F. *portance*, < *porter*, carry, E. *port*[5].] Carriage; bearing; port; behavior. [Archaic.]

por-ta-tive (pōr′ta̤-tiv), *a.* [OF. F. *portatif*, < L. *portare* (pp. *portatus*), carry, E. *port*[5].] Easily carried; portable; also, having or pertaining to the power or function of carrying.

port=cray-on (pōrt′krā′ọn), *n.* [F. *portecrayon*, 'carry-crayon.'] A holder or handle for a drawing-crayon.

port-cul-lis (pōrt-kul′is), *n.* [OF. *porte coleice*: *porte*, gate, door, E. *port*[2]; *coleice*, fem. of *coleis*, flowing, gliding, sliding, < L. *colare*, strain.] In *fort.*, a strong grating, as of iron, made to slide in vertical grooves at the sides of the gateway of a fortified place, and let down to prevent entrance: as, "Up drawbridge, grooms — what, Warder, ho! Let the *portcullis* fall" (Scott's "Marmion," vi. 14). See cut in next column.—**port-cul′lised**, *a.*

Porte (pōrt), *n.* [F. (see *port*[2]), for *Sublime Porte*, lit. 'High Gate,' tr. the Turkish official title, having reference to the palace gate at which justice was anciently administered.] The Ottoman court; the Turkish government.

porte=co-chère (pōrt′kọ-shār′), *n.* [F., 'gate for coaches.'] A carriage-entrance leading into a courtyard; also, a porch at the door of a building for sheltering persons entering and leaving carriages (as, "They alighted under a *porte-cochère* with a glass roof": W. Churchill's "Inside of the Cup," iii.).

porte=mon-naie (pōrt′mọ-nā′), *n.* [F., 'carry-money.'] A purse or pocket-book.

por-tend (pôr-tend′), *v. t.* [L. *portendere* (pp. *portentus*), point out, indicate, portend, < *por-* (= *pro*), before, + *tendere*, stretch, E. *tend*[1].] To indicate beforehand, or presage, as an omen does (as, "Had it not been written . . . that his sign in the high heavens *portended* war and armed men?" Kipling's "Kim," v.); betoken as impending; foreshadow; also, to forecast or foretell (rare).

por-tent (pôr′tent), *n.* [L. *portentum*, prop. neut. of *portentus*, pp. of *portendere*, E. *portend*.] An indication or omen of something about to happen, esp. something momentous or calamitous (as, "My loss, by dire *portents*, the gods foretold": Dryden's tr. Virgil's "Pastorals," i. 22); a sign, esp. of coming evil; an ominous occurrence; also, ominous significance (as, an occurrence of dire *portent*); also, a prodigy or marvel (as, "There have been great captains . . . But Frederic was not one of these brilliant *portents*": Macaulay's "Essays," Frederic the Great).—**por-ten′tous** (-ten′tus), *a.* [L. *portentosus*.] Of the nature of a portent (as, "direful omens and *portentous* sights and sounds in the air": Irving's "Sketch-Book," Sleepy Hollow); ominous; of ominous significance; ominously indicative (*of*: as, "big flakes . . . which melt as they touch the ground, and are *portentous* of a soaking rain," Hawthorne's "Twice-Told Tales," Snow-Flakes); also, awe-inspiring, marvelous, or amazing (as, "What must have been the sensations of the Aztecs themselves, as they looked on the *portentous* pageant!" Prescott's "Conquest of Mexico," iii. 9); extraordinary; prodigious, or prodigiously great (often humorously: as, "Mr. Bumble . . . shook his head with *portentous* solemnity," Dickens's "Oliver Twist," xvii.; "There were priests in *portentous* hats," Thackeray's "Newcomes," xxxv.).—**por-ten′tous-ly**, *adv.*—**por-ten′tous-ness**, *n.*

por-ter[1] (pōr′tẻr), *n.* [OF. F. *portier*, < LL. *portarius*, < L. *porta*, gate, door, E. *port*[2].] One who has charge of a door or gate; a doorkeeper; a janitor.

por-ter[2] (pōr′tẻr), *n.* [OF. *porteor* (F. *porteur*), < ML. *portator*, < L. *portare*, carry, E. *port*[5].] One employed to carry burdens or baggage, as at a railroad-station or a hotel; also, an attendant in a parlor-car or sleeping-car (U. S.); also, something used for bearing or carrying.

por-ter[3] (pōr′tẻr), *n.* [Orig. *porter's ale*, or *porter's beer*; commonly associated with *porter*[2].] A kind of heavy dark-brown beer made with malt browned by drying at a high temperature: as, "The only genuine and wholesome beverage in England is London *porter*" (Smollett's "Humphry Clinker," April 28).

por-ter-age (pōr′tẻr-ạj), *n.* The work of a porter or carrier; also, the charge for such work.

por′ter-ess, *n.* See *portress*.

por-ter-house (pōr′tẻr-hous), *n.* A house at which porter and other liquors are retailed; also, a chop-house.—**porter-house steak**, a choice cut of beef from between the prime or best ribs and the sirloin: said to be so called from a porter-house in New York, where it was served.

port-fo-lio (pōrt-fō′liō), *n.*; pl. *-lios* (-liōz). [It. *portafoglio*, *portafogli*, < *portare* (< L. *portare*), carry, + *foglio* (< L. *folium*), leaf, sheet.] A portable receptacle or case for detached papers, prints, etc. (as, "adding to the many notes and tentative essays which had already accumulated

Portcullis.

in his *portfolios*": S. Butler's "Way of All Flesh," lxxxi.); specif., such a receptacle for documents of a state department; hence, the office or post of a minister of state or member of a cabinet.

port=hole (pōrt′hōl), *n.* An aperture in a ship's side, as for discharging cannon through or for admitting light and air; also, an opening in a wall, door, etc., as one through which to shoot; also, a port or aperture for the passage of steam, air, etc.

por-ti-co (pōr′ti-kō), *n.*; pl. *-coes* or *-cos* (-kōz). [It., < L. *porticus*, porch, portico: see *porch*.] A structure consisting of a roof supported by columns, usually attached to a building as a porch, but sometimes detached as an ambulatory, etc.; also [*cap.*], with *the*, the Porch. —**por′ti-coed** (-kōd), *a.*

por-tière (pōr′tiār, F. pôr-tyār), *n.* [F., < *porte*, door: see *port²*.] A curtain hung at a doorway, either to replace the door or merely for decoration.

por-tion (pōr′shọn), *n.* [OF. F. *portion*, < L. *portio(n-)*, share, part, akin to *pars*, E. *part*.] The part of a whole allotted or belonging to one person or group of persons (as, "Father, give me the *portion* of goods that falleth to me": Luke, xv. 12); a share; an allotment or allowance; specif., a quantity of food served for one person; also, the part of an estate that goes to an heir; also, the money, goods, or estate which a woman brings to her husband at marriage, or a dowry (as, "I married Mrs. Mary Burton . . . with whom I received four hundred pounds for a *portion*": Swift's "Gulliver's Travels," i. 1); fig., that which is allotted to a person by God or fate, or one's lot or fate (as, "This is the *portion* of a wicked man from God," Job, xx. 29; "Otherwise delirium or death would have been my *portion*," Mrs. Shelley's "Frankenstein," xxiv.); also, a part of any whole, whether actually separated from it or not (as, *portions* of the wall had fallen, "a *portion* of the manuscript is illegible"). —**por′tion,** *v. t.* To divide into or distribute in portions or shares; parcel (*out*: as, "The country was *portioned* out among the captains of the invaders," Macaulay's "Hist. of Eng.," i.); also, to furnish with a portion, inheritance, or dowry; fig., to provide with a lot or fate (as, "What words are these? That one, long *portion'd* with his doom of death, Should change his lot!" M. Arnold's "Balder Dead," i.). —**por′tion-er,** *n.* —**por′tion-less,** *a.* Having no portion; esp., having no dowry.

Port-land (pōrt′lạnd) **ce-ment′.** A kind of hydraulic cement usually made by burning a mixture of limestone and clay in a kiln: so called because its color resembles that of Portland stone, a limestone quarried in the Isle of Portland, a peninsula of southern England, in the English Channel.

port-ly (pōrt′li), *a.* [See *port⁵*, *n.*] Stately, dignified, or imposing in bearing or appearance, as a person; now, usually, large in person, stout, or corpulent (as, "a *portly*, rubicund man of middle age," W. Churchill's "Coniston," i. 13; "a . . . man of rather *portly* figure, whose round, rosy, good-humoured face had a look of sober goodness," Galsworthy's "Saint's Progress," iii. 6); also, sometimes, of things, stately or magnificent. —**port′li-ness,** *n.*

port-man-teau (pōrt-man′tō), *n.*; pl. *-teaus* or *-teaux* (-tōz). [F. *portemanteau*, 'carry-mantle.'] A bag or case to carry clothing, etc., in when traveling, orig. one of flexible make and nearly cylindrical form for carrying on horseback, now one of stiff make and oblong form with two compartments hinged together and opening like a book.

por-trait (pōr′trāt), *n.* [F. *portrait*, orig. pp. of *portraire*, E. *portray*.] A pictorial representation of some object (as, "the most ancient extant *portrait* anyways purporting to be the whale's": H. Melville's "Moby-Dick," lv.); now, usually, a picture of a person, esp. of the face, made from life; fig., a verbal picture, or graphic representation in words, now usually of a person (as, "Imaginary *Portraits*," title of a book, published in 1887, by Walter Pater; "That character . . . is almost the only exact *portrait* in the whole book," Kingsley's "Yeast," ii.). —**por′trait-ist,** *n.* A maker of portraits; esp., one who paints portraits.

por-trai-ture (pōr′trā-ṭūr), *n.* [OF. F. *portraiture*, < *portraire*, E. *portray*.] The act or art of portraying; sometimes, the art of making portraits; also, a pictorial representation; a portrait; fig., a verbal picture.

por-tray (pōr-trā′), *v. t.* [Also formerly *pourtray*; OF. F.

portraire, < ML. *protrahere*, depict, portray, L. draw forth, draw out: see *protract*.] To represent by a drawing, painting, carving, or the like (as, "She saw men *pourtrayed* upon the wall, the images of the Chaldeans *pourtrayed* with vermilion," Ezek. xxiii. 14; to *portray* a historical scene); depict, picture, or delineate; fig., to picture to one's self mentally†; also, to represent dramatically, as on the stage; also, to depict in words, or describe graphically (as, a lecture or a book *portraying* life in colonial days); also, to adorn with pictures†. —**por-tray′a-ble,** *a.* That may be portrayed. —**por-tray′al,** *n.* The act of portraying; also, a representation portraying something. —**por-tray′er,** *n.*

por-tress, **por-ter-ess** (pōr′tres, pōr′tėr-es), *n.* A female porter or doorkeeper.

Por-tu-guese (pōr′ṭū-gēz or pōr-ṭū-gēz′), *a.* Of or pertaining to Portugal, its people, or their language. —**Portuguese man=of=war,** any of several large oceanic hydrozoans of the genus *Physalia*, having a large, crested, bladder-like structure by which they are buoyed up and from which depend numerous processes: remarkable for brilliant coloring and great power of stinging. —**Por′tu-guese,** *n.*; pl. *-guese.* A native of Portugal; also, the language of Portugal, belonging to the Romance group.

Portuguese Man-of-war (*Physalia pelagica*).

por-tu-la-ca (pōr-ṭū-lā′kạ or -lak′ạ), *n.* [L., purslane.] Any plant of the genus *Portulaca*, which comprises herbs with thick, succulent leaves and variously colored flowers, as *P. grandiflora*, cultivated in gardens, and *P. oleracea*, the common purslane. —**por″tu-la-ca′ceous** (-lạ-kā′shius), *a.* Belonging to the *Portulaceæ*, or portulaca family of plants.

po-sa-da (pō-sä′dạ), *n.* [Sp.] An inn.

pose¹ (pōz), *v.*; posed, posing. [OF. F. *poser*, put, < ML. *pausare*, lay down (a sense due to confusion with L. *ponere*, place, put: see *position*), L. halt, cease, < L. *pausa*, E. *pause.* Compounds of OF. F. *poser*, E. *pose¹* (see *compose*, *dispose*, etc.), are regularly associated with derivatives actually belonging to L. *ponere* (see *composite*, *composition*, *disposition*, etc.).] **I.** *tr.* To put or place (archaic, as in *her.*: as, interchangeably *posed*, see under *interchangeably*); also, to lay down in words, assert, state, or propound (as, "The great unanswerable questions . . . are there *posed* with the severest and most appalling distinctness": Mrs. Stowe's "Oldtown Folks," iii.); also, to place in a suitable position or attitude for a picture, tableau, or the like (as, an artist *poses* his models; to *pose* a group for a photograph, or for a stage effect). **II.** *intr.* To assume or hold a position or attitude for some artistic purpose (as, "Jane Map, as Enid Anstruther, was *posing* on the model's throne": Arnold Bennett's "Great Man," xxvii.); hence, to assume a studied attitude for mere effect; attitudinize; fig., to affect a particular character as with a view to the impression made on others (as, "Don't be an idiot. You can't *pose* with us here": Kipling's "Light That Failed," viii.); present one's self before others (*as*: as, "He soon began to *pose* as a judge of literature," S. Butler's "Way of All Flesh," ii.). —**pose¹,** *n.* The act or period of posing, as for a picture (as, "She used to sit at Carrel's, and during the *pose* she would sing": Du Maurier's "Trilby," ii.); also, a position or attitude assumed in posing, or exhibited by a figure in a picture, sculptural work, tableau, or the like; in general, attitude or posture of body (as, "She too got up . . . Her pose had a kind of defiance in it": Mrs. H. Ward's "Robert Elsmere," xx.); often, a studied attitude assumed for mere effect; fig., attitude assumed in thought or conduct; a studied show or mere affectation, as of some character, quality, sentiment, or course (as, his liberality is all a *pose*; "She had said to herself that his happy temper, his eternal gayety, was an affectation, a *pose*," H. James's "Europeans," x.).

pose² (pōz), *v. t.*; posed, posing. [For obs. *appose*, for *oppose*, in an obs. sense.] To examine by putting questions†; also, to embarrass by a difficult question or problem (as, "Kolory himself would be effectually *posed* were he called upon to draw up the articles of his faith": H. Melville's "Typee," xxiii.); puzzle completely; nonplus.

Po-sei-don (pō-sī′dǫn), *n.* [Gr. Ποσειδῶν.] The Greek god of the sea, identified by the Romans with Neptune.

pos-er[1] (pō′zèr), *n.* One who poses or attitudinizes; a poseur.

pos-er[2] (pō′zèr), *n.* One who examines by questions (archaic); also, a question, problem, or matter that poses, or puzzles completely.

Poseidon, with his Trident, overwhelming the giant Polybotes, for whom Gæa makes intercession. (From a Greek red-figured vase of the 4th century B.C.)

po-seur (pō-zèr′), *n.* [F.] One given to posing; one who affects a particular pose of mind or character, line of conduct, etc., as with a view to the impression made on others: as, "I was . . . a little of a prig and *poseur* in those days" (H. G. Wells's "Tono-Bungay," ii. 1. § 2).—**po-seuse** (-zèz), *n.* [F.] Fem. of *poseur.*

po-sied (pō′zid), *a.* Inscribed with a posy or motto (archaic); also, furnished with posies or nosegays.

pos-it (poz′it), *v. t.* [L. *positus*, pp. of *ponere*: see *position*.] To place, put, or set; also, to lay down or assume as a fact or principle; affirm; postulate.

po-si-tion (pǫ-zish′ǫn), *n.* [OF. F. *position*, < L. *positio(n-)*, < *ponere* (pp. *positus*), place, put, set down: cf. *ponent*, *posit*, and *pose*[1].] The act of placing or putting†; also, condition with reference to place (as, the hill offered advantages of *position*); location or situation; hence, a place occupied or to be occupied, or a situation or site (as, a house in a sheltered *position*; a fortified *position*; to select *positions* for military purposes); proper or appropriate place (as, to be in *position*, or out of *position*); fig., situation or condition, or a situation, with relation to circumstances (as, to realize the gravity of one's *position*; to be in an awkward *position*); status or standing, esp. high standing, as in society (as, "People should live up to their *position*," G. Meredith's "Diana of the Crossways," vi.; "I couldn't bear him to feel I wanted *position* or money from him," Galsworthy's "Saint's Progress," ii. 4); a post of employment (as, a *position* in a bank); also, manner of being placed, disposed, or arranged (as, the relative *position* of the hands of a clock; the *position* of draperies; the oriented *position* of a church); posture or attitude of body (as, to stand in an ungraceful *position*); fig., mental attitude, or way of viewing a matter (as, to define one's *position* on a public question); sometimes, posture or condition (of affairs, etc.); also, the act of positing as a fact or principle; affirmation; that which is posited; a statement or assertion; also, in *anc. pros.*, the situation of a short vowel before two or more consonants or their equivalent, by reason of which the syllable is metrically long.—**po-si′tion**, *v. t.* To put in a particular or appropriate position; place; also, to determine the position of; locate.—**po-si′tion-al**, *a.*

pos-i-tive (poz′i-tiv). [OF. F. *positif*, < L. *positivus*, < *ponere*: see *position*.] **I.** *a.* Arbitrarily laid down; determined by enactment or convention (opposed to *natural*: as, *positive* law); also, explicitly laid down or expressed (as, a *positive* declaration; admitting of no question (as, *positive* proof); stated; express; definite; emphatic; also, confident in opinion or assertion, as a person; fully assured; hence, overconfident or dogmatic (as, "Where men of judgment creep and feel their way, The *positive* pronounce without dismay": Cowper's "Conversation," 146); also, without relation to or comparison with other things (opposed to *relative* and *comparative*); absolute; hence, downright or out-and-out (colloq.: as, "Most of the luxuries . . .

are . . . *positive* hinderances to the elevation of mankind," Thoreau's "Walden," i.; "You are a *positive* enigma," Bulwer-Lytton's "My Novel," x. 10); also, concerned with or based on matters of experience (as, the *positive* philosophy: see *positivism*); practical; not speculative or theoretical; also, consisting in or characterized by the presence or possession, as opposed to the absence or want, of distinguishing or marked qualities or features (opposed to *negative*: as, light is *positive*, darkness negative; *positive* coloring; *positive* pleasure); denoting the presence of such qualities, as a term; in specif. use, denoting a quantity greater than zero; involving or denoting addition, or plus (as, the *positive* or plus sign); also, measured or proceeding in a direction assumed as that of increase, progress, or onward motion; in *elect.*, noting or pertaining to the kind of electricity developed on glass when rubbed with silk, or the kind of electricity present at that pole ('positive pole') connected with the carbon or least attacked plate of a voltaic cell; noting the zinc or most attacked plate or element of a voltaic cell; in *chem.*, of an element or radical, basic; in *photog.*, showing the lights and shades as seen in the original, not reversed; also, in *gram.*, denoting a quality or manner absolutely or without qualification (as, the *positive* degree of comparison of adjectives or adverbs; a *positive* adjective, an adjective in its simple form, as *low*, in contradistinction to its comparative *lower* and its superlative *lowest*; a *positive* adverb, an adverb in its simple form, as *well*, in contradistinction to its comparative *better* and its superlative *best*). **II.** *n.* Something positive; a positive (rather than negative) quality or characteristic; also, specif., a positive quantity or symbol; in *elect.*, the positive plate or element in a voltaic cell; in *photog.*, a positive picture; also, in *gram.*, the positive degree, or that form of an adjective or adverb expressing it.—**pos′i-tive-ly**, *adv.*—**pos′i-tive-ness**, *n.*

pos-i-tiv-ism (poz′i-tiv-izm), *n.* [F. *positivisme*.] The state or quality of being positive; definiteness; assurance; dogmatism; also, a philosophical system founded by Auguste Comte (1798—1857), which concerns itself only with positive facts and phenomena, excluding speculation upon ultimate causes or origins.—**pos′i-tiv-ist**, *n.* An adherent of positivism.—**pos″i-tiv-is′tic**, *a.*

pos-i-tiv-i-ty (poz-i-tiv′i-ti), *n.* The state or character of being positive.

pos-net (pos′net), *n.* [OF. *poçonnet*, dim. of *poçon*, pot, vessel.] A metal pot or vessel for use in cooking. [Archaic or prov. Eng.]

po-sol-o-gy (pǫ-sol′ǫ-ji), *n.* [Gr. πόσος, how much: see *-logy*.] That part of medical science which is concerned with the quantities or doses in which medicines should be administered.

pos-se (pos′ē), *n.* [ML., power, force, noun use of L. *posse*, inf., be able, have power: see *potent*.] Possibility; also, a posse comitatus; also, a body or force armed with legal authority (as, "a strong *posse* of peace-officers": Scott's "Guy Mannering," viii.); hence, a band, company, or assemblage (as, "A *posse* of children came down for the summer holidays": L. Merrick's "Conrad in Quest of His Youth," v.).—**posse comitatus** (kom-i-tā′tus). [ML., 'power of the county.'] The body of men that the sheriff is empowered to call into service in case of riot or the like; a body of men so called into service; sometimes, a posse, band, or company.

pos-sess (pǫ-zes′), *v. t.* [OF. *possesser*, < L. *possidere* (pp. *possessus*), possess, own, < *pos-* (cf. L. *por-* for *pro*, before) + *sedere*, sit.] To have as property; have belonging to one; own; sometimes, to hold or occupy, or have in possession, in distinction from owning; also, to have as a faculty, quality, attribute, or the like (as, to *possess* courage; to *possess* knowledge); sometimes, to have knowledge of, or be conversant with (as, "He wrote and spoke equally well in French, German, or Flemish; and he *possessed*, besides, Spanish, Italian, Latin": Motley's "Dutch Republic," vi. 7); also, to seize or take (archaic); gain or win (archaic); also, to keep or maintain (one's self, one's mind, etc.) in a certain state, as of peace, patience, etc.; maintain control over, or keep calm (one's self, one's mind, etc.: as, "uneasy persons, who cannot *possess* their own minds," Steele, in "Spectator," 137); also, of a spirit, esp. an evil one, to occupy and control, or dominate from within, as a person; hence, of a feeling, idea, etc., to dominate or actuate after the manner of such a spirit (as, "a naturally taciturn man *possessed* by an idea": J. Conrad's "Lord Jim," xvii.); also, to put (a person) in possession; make (one) the owner, holder, or master, as of property, information, etc.; also, to cause to be dominated or influenced, as by a feeling, idea, etc.; imbue (*with*).—**possessed'**, *p. a.* Dominated by an evil spirit or influence; demoniac; demented; mad: as, "He upset the table . . . and rushed through the coffee-room like one *possessed*" (Lever's "Harry Lorrequer," xxi.).

pos-ses-sion (po̧-zesh'on), *n.* [OF. F. *possession*, < L. *possessio(n-).*] The act or fact of possessing, or the state of being possessed; ownership; often, actual holding or occupancy, as distinct from ownership; also, a thing possessed; *pl.*, property or wealth; also, *sing.*, a territory subject to a ruler or state; a foreign dominion of a country (as, "the loss to Spain of all her American *possessions*": W. H. Hudson's "Purple Land," Appendix); also, control over one's self, one's mind, etc., or self-possession (rare); also, control or domination by an evil spirit within one (cf. *obsession*); domination or actuation by a feeling, idea, etc.; hence, the feeling or idea itself.

pos-ses-sive (po̧-zes'iv), *a.* [L. *possessivus.*] Of or pertaining to possession or ownership; in *gram.*, denoting a possessor (as, a *possessive* pronoun or adjective); noting the case in declension in English that expresses possession, etc. (see phrase below); being in or pertaining to this case.— **possessive case**, in *Eng. gram.*, the case which expresses possession and kindred and derived relations: regularly formed in singular nouns by the addition of *'s* (see *apostrophe²*), as in *the boy's book*, *James's money*, *Socrates's wife* (the *s* being sometimes omitted, as in *for conscience' sake*, *Socrates' wife*, *Moses' mandates*, either by a natural contraction of two sibilant sounds into one or in order to avoid an unpleasant sequence of sibilants), and in plural nouns ending in *s* by the addition of the apostrophe alone, as in *the boys' books*, and in other plural nouns by the addition of *'s*, as in *men's wear.*—**pos-ses'sive**, *n.* In *gram.*, a possessive pronoun or adjective; the possessive case, or a word in that case.—**pos-ses'sive-ly**, *adv.*

pos-ses-sor (po̧-zes'or), *n.* [L.] One who possesses; the owner or holder of property; one who has a thing as his own or in his keeping and control.—**pos-ses'sor-ship**, *n.*— **pos-ses'so-ry** (-zes'ō-ri), *a.* [L. *possessorius.*] Pertaining to a possessor, or to possession; arising from possession (as, a *possessory* interest); also, having possession.

pos-set (pos'et), *n.* [ME. *possyt*, *poshet*; origin obscure.] A drink made of hot milk curdled with ale, wine, or other liquor, and often sweetened and spiced: formerly much in favor as a delicacy and for the health.—**pos'set**, *v. t.*; *-seted*, *-seting* (sometimes *-setted*, *-setting*). To give or administer a posset to (as, "As she laid him in bed and *possetted* him, how frail and fragile he looked!" Arnold Bennett's "Old Wives' Tale," ii. 5); also, to curdle like a posset† (see Shakspere's "Hamlet," i. 5. 68).—**pos'set=cup**, *n.* A cup, often with two or more handles, used in drinking posset.

Posset-cup.

pos-si-bil-i-ty (pos-i-bil'i-ti), *n.*; pl. *-ties* (-tiz). The state or fact of being possible (as, to doubt the *possibility* of a thing; to preclude the *possibility* of error); also, a possible thing or person (as, "to . . . renounce the romantic *possibilities* of an unknown future," G. B. Shaw's "Man and Superman," iv.; "To her he was that divine *possibility* which every young man is to every young maiden," Howells's "Chance Acquaintance," i.).

pos-si-ble (pos'i-bl), *a.* [OF. F. *possible*, < L. *possibilis*, < *posse*, be able: see *potent*.] That may or can be, exist, happen, be done, be used, etc. (as, the best of all *possible* worlds; no *possible* cure; come if *possible*; the only means or way *possible*); also, that may be true or a fact, or may

perhaps be the case, as something concerning which one has no knowledge to the contrary (as, it is *possible* that he went; that is a *possible* reason for the act; these and other *possible* outbreaks may have hastened the end).—**pos'si-bly**, *adv.* In a possible manner; by any possibility (as, I cannot *possibly* go); also, perhaps or maybe (as, *possibly* you have not seen him; five or *possibly* ten minutes).

pos-sum (pos'um), *n.* Shortened form of *opossum*. [Colloq.] —**to play possum**, to feign; dissemble: in allusion to the opossum's habit of feigning death when attacked or caught. [Colloq.]

post¹ (pōst), *n.* [AS. *post*, < L. *postis*, post.] A stout piece of timber, metal, or the like, set upright as a support, a point of attachment, a place for displaying notices, etc.: as, the *posts* of a door, gate, or bed; a hitching-*post*; a sign-*post*; a whipping-*post*.—**post¹**, *v. t.* To affix (a notice, etc.) to a post, wall, or the like; also, to bring to public notice by or as by a placard (as, to *post* a person for nomination; to *post* a reward); denounce by a public notice or declaration (as, to *post* a person as a coward); enter the name of in a published list; publish the name of (a ship) as missing or lost; also, to placard (a wall, etc.) with notices or bills.

post² (pōst), *n.* [F. *poste*, < It. *posto*, < L. *positum*, pp. neut. of *ponere*, place, put: cf. *position* and *post³*.] The station, or the round or beat, of a soldier, sentry, or other person on guard or watch; hence, in general, a place assigned or occupied (as, "Men like soldiers may not quit the *post* Allotted by the Gods," Tennyson's "Lucretius," 148; the nurse's *post* in the sick-room); a position of duty, employment, or trust to which one is assigned or appointed (as, the *post* of secretary; a diplomatic *post*; "The opening of all *posts* to talent had brought an extraordinary amount of ability to the forefront," Lecky's "Hist. of Eng. in the 18th Century," i.); a situation or office; also, a military position or station, or the body of troops occupying a military station; hence, a local subdivision of the Grand Army of the Republic (see under *grand*); also, a trading-post (as, "Fort Laramie is one of the *posts* established by the American fur company . . . Here . . . the arm of the United States has little force": Parkman's "Oregon Trail," ix.); also, *milit.*, in the British army, either of two bugle-calls ('first post' and 'last post') giving notice of the hour for retiring, as for the night. —**post²**, *v. t.* To station at a post or place as a sentry or for some other purpose (as, "locking up the town-gates and *posting* the guard at nightfall," Besant's "Coligny," i.; "Kim felt sure that the boy had been *posted* to guide him," Kipling's "Kim," ix.); place (troops, etc.) at a particular point (as, "He *posted* his army at Gravelines": Motley's "Dutch Republic," i. 2); also, *milit.* and *naval*, to appoint to a post of command.

post³ (pōst), *n.* [F. *poste*, < It. *posta*, < L. *posita*, pp. fem. of *ponere*, place, put: cf. *post².*] One of a series of fixed stations along a route, for furnishing relays of men and horses for carrying letters, etc., and supplying service for travelers by post-horse, post-chaise, or the like (now chiefly hist.); hence, one of the men with horses in readiness at such stations to relay letters, etc.†; also, one who travels express, esp. over a fixed route, with letters, etc.; a courier; hence, a postman; sometimes, a vehicle or a vessel used to carry mail; formerly, a post-horse†; also, a single despatch or delivery of mail, or the mail itself; the letters, etc., coming to a single person or recipient (as, "A few mornings later, in his *post* . . . Henry found a letter from Mark Snyder": Arnold Bennett's "Great Man," xiv.); also, an established service or system for the conveyance of letters, etc., esp. under governmental authority; also, a post-office or a postal letter-box (Great Britain); also, haste† or speed†; also, a size of paper, about 16 by 20 inches (said to have been watermarked orig. with a figure of a postman's horn).—**post³**, *v.* **I.** *intr.* To travel with post-horses, or by post-chaise or carriage (as, "His father and mother were with him, having *posted* from home in their own carriage": S. Butler's "Way of All Flesh," xxviii.); hence, to travel with speed; go or pass rapidly; hasten (as, "He *posted* upstairs, taking three steps at once": Scott's "Guy Mannering," lviii.). **II.** *tr.* To send posting, or traveling with speed; also, to convey in the manner of a post, or post-haste† (as, "The swiftest harts have *posted* you by land": Shakspere's "Cymbeline," ii. 4. 27); also, to

---

(variable) d̦ as d or j, s̨ as s or sh, t̨ as t or ch, z̨ as z or zh; *o*, F. *cloche*; ü, F. *menu*; ċh, Sc. *loch*; ṅ, F. *bonbon*; ', primary accent; ", secondary accent; †, obsolete; <, from; +, and; =, equals. See also lists at beginning of book.

place in a post-office or a letter-box for transmission; mail; in *bookkeeping*, to transfer (an entry or item), as from the journal to the ledger; enter (an item) in due place and form; make all the requisite entries in (the ledger, etc.: often with *up*); hence, in general use, to supply with information up to date, or inform (commonly in the passive, and sometimes with *up*: as, to be well *posted* on current events; "Robert . . . had been *posted* up in many things concerning the neighbourhood," Mrs. H. Ward's "Robert Elsmere," xvii.). —**post**[3], *adv.* With post-horses, or by posting (as, to ride or travel *post*); by post or courier (as, to send despatches *post*); hence, with speed or haste, or post-haste.

post-. [L. *post-*, repr. *post*, adv. and prep.] A prefix meaning 'behind,' 'after,' occurring orig. in words from the Latin, but now freely used as an English formative, as in *post-Elizabethan*, *postfix*, *postgraduate*. Cf. *ante-* and *pre-*.

post-age (pōs′tāj), *n.* Posting†, or traveling with post-horses†; also, the conveying of letters, etc., by post (obs. or rare); also, a postal service†; now, usually, the charge for the conveyance of a letter or other matter sent by post or mail (ordinarily prepaid by means of a stamp or stamps: see *postage-stamp*).—**postage currency**, a fractional paper currency issued by the U. S. in 1862–63, during the Civil War, imitating in style the postage-stamps that had previously replaced coins.—**post′age=stamp**, *n.* An official stamp in the form of a design on an envelop, etc., or a printed adhesive label to be affixed to a letter, etc., as evidence of prepayment of a designated postage.

pos-tal (pōs′tạl), *a.* [F. *postal*, < *poste*, E. *post*[3].] Of or pertaining to the post or mail service: as, *postal* regulations. —**postal card**, a card with a printed governmental stamp, for correspondence at a rate lower than that for letters; also, an unofficial post-card.—**postal currency**, postage currency.—**postal note**, a receipt-bearing note issued by a post-office for amounts up to $10, payable to the payee at any post-office, the names being filled in by the purchaser. —**pos′tal**, *n.* A postal card.

post-bee-tle (pōst′bē″tl), *n.* Any of various beetles, as species of *Lyctus* (family *Ptinidæ*), whose larvæ bore into posts and other timber.

post bel-lum (pōst bel′um). [L.] After the war: a phrase sometimes used adjectively (as, *post-bellum* conditions).

Post-beetle (*Lyctus planicollis*). — *a*, larva; *b*, adult; *c*, pupa; *d*, leg of larva; *a*, *b*, *c*, much enlarged, *d*, more enlarged.

post-boy (pōst′boi), *n.* A boy or man who rides post or carries mail; also, a postilion.

post=ca-non-i-cal (pōst-kạ-non′i-kạl), *a.* [See *post-*.] Of later date than the canon; written later than the canon of Scripture.

post=card (pōst′kärd), *n.* A postal card with a printed governmental stamp (the usual term in Great Britain); also, an unofficial card, often pictorial, mailable when bearing an adhesive postage-stamp.

post=chaise (pōst′shāz), *n.* A chaise or carriage for hire, for posting or traveling: used in the 18th and early in the 19th century.

post=char-i-ot (pōst′char″i-ọt), *n.* A carriage for posting or traveling: used esp. in the 18th century.

post-clas-sic, post-clas-si-cal (pōst-klas′ik, -i-kạl), *a.* [See *post-*.] Existing or occurring after the classic or classical period, esp. of Greek and Latin literature or art.

post-date (pōst-dāt′), *v. t.*; -dated, -dating. [See *post-*.] To give a later date to than the true date; also, to follow in time.

post-di-lu-vi-an (pōst-di-lū′vi-ạn), *a.* [L. *post*, after, + *diluvium*, deluge.] **I.** *a.* Existing or occurring after the Flood. Cf. *antediluvian*. **II.** *n.* One who has lived since the Flood.

post-ed (pōs′ted), *a.* Having posts: as, a four-*posted* bed.

post-er[1] (pōs′tẹr), *n.* One who posts bills, etc.; also, a placard or bill posted or for posting in some public place

(as, "He . . . noted . . . the glare of the recruiting *posters* on every vacant piece of wall," H. G. Wells's "Soul of a Bishop," iv.; to make a collection of artistic *posters*).

post-er[2] (pōs′tẹr), *n.* One who travels post (now rare); also, a post-horse; also, one who posts a letter or the like.

poste res-tante (post res-tänt). [F., 'post remaining.'] A direction written on mail which is to remain at the post-office until called for; hence, a post-office department in charge of such mail.

pos-te-ri-or (pos-tē′ri-ọr). [L., compar. of *posterus*, coming after, < *post*, behind, after.] **I.** *a.* Situated behind, or hinder (opposed to *anterior*); also, coming after in order, as in a series; also, coming after in time (opposed to *prior*); later; subsequent (sometimes followed by *to*). **II.** *n.* *Pl.*, the hinder parts of the body; the buttocks.—**pos-te-ri-or′i-ty** (-or′i-ti), *n.* Posterior position or date.—**pos-te′ri-or-ly**, *adv.*

pos-ter-i-ty (pos-ter′i-ti), *n.* [OF. *posterite* (F. *postérité*), < L. *posteritas*, < *posterus*: see *posterior*.] Descendants collectively (as, "that the inheritance of the king should be to his *posterity* alone": Ecclus. xlv. 25); also, succeeding generations collectively (as, "Methinks the truth should live from age to age, As 'twere retail'd to all *posterity*": Shakspere's "Richard III.," iii. 1. 77).

pos-tern (pōs′tẹrn). [OF. *posterne* (F. *poterne*), for *posterle*, < LL. *posterula*, < L. *posterus*: see *posterior*.] **I.** *n.* A back door or gate, or any lesser or private entrance: as, "We slipped out of the side *postern* into a night of darkness" (Stevenson's "Master of Ballantrae," viii.). Also fig. **II.** *a.* Of the nature of or pertaining to a postern: as, a *postern* door or gate; "entering the castle of Ellangowan by a *postern* doorway" (Scott's "Guy Mannering," xli.).

postero-. Form of L. *posterus*, coming after, used in combination. Cf. *antero-*.—**pos-te-ro-lat-er-al** (pos″tẹ-rō-lat′ẹ-rạl), *a.* At the back, at one side; both posterior and lateral.

post=ex-il-i-an (pōst-eg-zil′i-ạn), *a.* [See *post-*.] Subsequent to the Babylonian exile or captivity of the Jews. Also **post=ex-il′ic**.

post-fix (pōst-fiks′), *v. t.* [From *post-* + *-fix* as in *prefix*.] To affix at the end of something; append; suffix.—**post′-fix**, *n.* Something postfixed; in *gram.*, a suffix.

post=gla-cial (pōst-glā′shiạl), *a.* [See *post-*.] In *geol.*, existing or occurring subsequently to the glacial period; recent.

post-grad-u-ate (pōst-grad′ū-āt). [See *post-*.] **I.** *a.* Pertaining to or prosecuting a course of study after graduation. **II.** *n.* A postgraduate student.

post=haste (pōst′hāst′). **I.** *n.* Haste or speed like that of a post or courier; great haste: as, "Norfolk and myself, In haste, *post-haste*, are come to join with you" (Shakspere's "3 Henry VI.," ii. 1. 139). [Archaic.] **II.** *adv.* With the haste of a post; with all possible speed or expedition: as, to ride or go *post-haste*; "This . . . brought Mr. Beaulieu Plummer *post-haste* from the estate office up to the house" (H. G. Wells's "Bealby," v.).

post=horse (pōst′hôrs), *n.* A horse kept, as at a station on a post-road, for the use of persons riding post or for hire by travelers.

post-hu-mous (pos′tụ-mus), *a.* [L. *posthumus*, erron. (by association with *humus*, earth, ground, as if referring to burial) for *postumus*, last, posthumous, superl. adj. < *post*, behind, after.] Born after the death of the father (as, a *posthumous* son); also, published after the death of the author (as, a *posthumous* book); also, arising, existing, or continuing after one's death (as, "Martyrdom . . . would ensure them a glorious future in the next world, and at any rate *posthumous* renown in this": S. Butler's "Way of All Flesh," xii.).—**post′hu-mous-ly**, *adv.*

pos-tiche (pos-tēsh′). [F., < It. *posticcio*, for *apposticcio*, *appositizio*, put on, superadded, factitious, false, < L. *appositus*: see *apposite*.] **I.** *a.* Superadded, esp. inappropriately, as a sculptural or architectural ornament; also, artificial, counterfeit, or false. **II.** *n.* An imitation or substitute; also, pretense.

pos-ti-cous (pos-tī′kus), *a.* [L. *posticus*, < *post*, behind.] In *bot.*, hinder; posterior; also, extrorse.

---

pos=til=ion, pos=til=lion (pŏs-til'yǫn), *n.* [F. *postillon*, < It. *postiglione*, < *posta*, E. *post*[3].] A post† or courier†; also, one who rides the near horse of the leaders when four or more horses are used to draw a carriage or post-chaise, or who rides the near horse when one pair only is used and there is no driver on the box.

post=im=pres=sion=ism (pōst-im-presh'ǫn-izm), *n.* [See *post-*.] The doctrines and methods of certain modern artists, who first attracted wide attention about 1910, although already active in Europe for some years, opposing the objective realism and scientific methods of the later impressionists (cf. *neo-impressionism*), and maintaining the theory that art must be absolutely individual, spontaneous, and untrammeled by reality or tradition. Cf. *cubism* and *futurism*.—**post=im=pres'sion=ist**, *n.*

post=lim=i=ny (pōst-lim'i-ni), *n.* [L. *postliminium*, < *post*, behind, + *limen* (*limin-*), threshold.] In *Rom. law*, the right of a person to resume his former condition and privileges on his return home from banishment or captivity; in *international law*, the right by which persons and things taken in war are restored to their former status when coming again under the power of the nation to which they belonged.—**post=lim'i=na=ry** (-nạ-ri), *a.*

post=lude (pōst'lūd), *n.* [From *post-* + *-lude* as in *prelude*.] In *music*, a concluding piece or movement; esp., a voluntary at the end of a church service.

post=man (pōst'mạn), *n.*; pl. *-men.* A post† or courier†; also, a postal employee whose work it is to carry and deliver letters and other mail.

post=mark (pōst'märk), *n.* An official mark stamped on a letter or other mail, to cancel the postage-stamp, indicate the place and date of sending or of receipt, etc.—**post'=mark**, *v. t.* To stamp with a postmark.

post=mas=ter (pōst'mȧs″tẽr), *n.* An official in charge of posts or couriers†; also, the master of a station on a post route, charged with transmitting letters, etc.†; hence, the official in charge of a post-office; also, the master of a station for furnishing post-horses for travelers.—**post'mas″ter=gen'er=al**, *n.*; pl. *postmasters-.* The executive head of the postal system of a country.

post=me=rid=i=an (pōst-mē-rid'i-ạn), *a.* [L. *postmeridianus*, < *post*, after, + *meridies*, midday.] Occurring after noon; of or pertaining to the afternoon. Cf. *antemeridian.*

post me=rid=i=em (pōst mē-rid'i-em). [L.] After noon: used in specifying the hour of the day, usually in the abbreviated form *P.M.*, as, 10 P.M. (or P.M.).

post=mil=le=na=ri=an (pōst″mil-e-nā'ri-ạn), *n.* [See *post-* and *millenarian*.] A believer in postmillennialism; a postmillennialist.—**post″mil=le=na'ri=an=ism**, *n.*

post=mil=len=ni=al (pōst-mil-en'i-ạl), *a.* [See *post-*.] Of or pertaining to the period following the millennium.—**post=mil=len'ni=al=ism**, *n.* The doctrine or belief that the second coming of Christ will follow the millennium.—**post=mil=len'ni=al=ist**, *n.*

post=mis=tress (pōst'mis″tres), *n.* A woman who has charge of a post-office.

post=mor=tem (pōst-môr'tem). [L. *post mortem*, after death.] **I.** *a.* Subsequent to death, as an examination of the body. Cf. *ante-mortem.* **II.** *n.* A post-mortem examination; an autopsy.

post=na=tal (pōst-nā'tạl), *a.* [L. *post*, after, + *natus*, born.] Subsequent to birth: as, "I . . . had . . . hopes, therefore, that his son's blunders might be due to *postnatal*, rather than congenital misfortunes" (S. Butler's "Way of All Flesh," lxiii.).

post=nup=tial (pōst-nup'shạl), *a.* [L. *post*, after, + *nuptiæ*, marriage.] After marriage: as, a *postnuptial* settlement on a wife.

post=o=bit (pōst-ō'bit or -ob'it). [L. *post*, after, + *obitus*, death.] **I.** *a.* Effective after a particular person's death: as, a *post-obit* bond. **II.** *n.* A bond securing to a lender a sum of money on the death of some specified person from whom the borrower has expectations.

post=of=fice (pōst'of″is), *n.* The governmental department charged with the conveyance of letters, etc., by post; also, an office or station of a governmental postal system, for receiving, distributing, and transmitting mail, selling postage-stamps, and other service.

post=paid (pōst'pād'), *a.* With the postage prepaid.

post=plane (pōst'plān), *n.* An aëroplane employed in the postal service.

post=pon=a=ble (pōst-pō'nạ-bl), *a.* That may be postponed.

post=pone (pōst-pōn'), *v. t.*; *-poned, -poning.* [L. *postponere* (pp. *postpositus*), < *post*, behind, after, + *ponere*, put.] To put off to a future or later time, or defer (as, "He *postponed* his departure until after supper": H. G. Wells's "Mr. Britling," i. 5. § 9); also, to place after in order of importance or estimation, or subordinate (as, to *postpone* private considerations to the public interest; "To headless Phœbe his fair bride *postpone*, Honour a Syrian prince above his own," Pope's "Dunciad," iv. 367).—**post=pone'ment**, *n.* The act of postponing, or the state of being postponed.—**post=pon'er** (-pō'nẽr), *n.*

post=po=si=tion (pōst-pǫ-zish'ǫn), *n.* [L. *post*, behind, after, + *positio(n-)*, a placing: cf. *preposition*.] The act of placing after, or the state of being so placed; in *gram.*, a word or particle placed after, or at the end of, a word, usually as an enclitic.—**post=pos'i=tive** (-poz'i-tiv). **I.** *a.* Characterized by postposition; placed after; enclitic. **II.** *n.* A postpositive word or particle.

post=pran=di=al (pōst-pran'di-ạl), *a.* [L. *post*, after, + *prandium*, luncheon, meal.] After-dinner: as, a *postprandial* speech.

post=rid=er (pōst'rī″dẽr), *n.* One who rides post; a mounted mail-carrier.

post=road (pōst'rōd), *n.* A road with stations for furnishing horses for post-riders, mail-coaches, or travelers; a road or route over which mail is carried.

post=script (pōst'skript), *n.* [L. *postscriptum*, pp. neut. of *postscribere*, write after, < *post*, after, + *scribere*, write.] A paragraph added to a letter which has already been concluded and signed by the writer (as, "Sir Gervaise, like a woman, had written his mind in his *postscript*," Cooper's "Two Admirals," xi.: abbreviated *P. S.*); in general, a supplementary part appended to any composition or literary work (as, the "*Postscript*" of Godwin's "Caleb Williams").—**post'script=al**, *a.*

pos=tu=lant (pos'tụ-lạnt), *n.* [F. *postulant*, < L. *postulans* (*-ant-*), ppr. of *postulare*: see *postulate*.] One who asks or applies for something; a petitioner; an applicant; a candidate, esp. for admission into a religious order.

pos=tu=late (pos'tụ-lāt), *v. t.*; *-lated, -lating.* [L. *postulatus*, pp. of *postulare*, ask, demand, prob. < *poscere*, ask.] To ask, demand, or claim; also, to claim or assume the existence or truth of, esp. as a basis for reasoning; assume without proof, or as self-evident; take for granted; *eccles.*, to ask legitimate ecclesiastical authority to admit (a nominee) by dispensation, when a canonical impediment is supposed to exist; hence, to nominate or elect, subject to superior sanction.—**pos'tu=late** (-lạt), *n.* [L. *postulatum*, prop. pp. neut.] A demand or claim (now rare); also, something postulated or assumed without proof as a basis for reasoning or as self-evident; hence, a fundamental principle; a necessary condition; a prerequisite; in *geom.*, etc., a self-evident proposition to the effect that something is possible.—**pos=tu=la'tion** (-lā'shǫn), *n.* [L. *postulatio(n-).*] The act of postulating; also, that which is postulated.—**pos=tu=la'tion=al**, *a.*

pos=tur=al (pos'tụr-ạl), *a.* Of or pertaining to posture.

pos=ture (pos'tụr), *n.* [F. *posture* = It. *postura*, < L. *positura*, < *ponere*, place, put: cf. *position*.] The relative disposition of the various parts of anything, esp. the position of the body and limbs as a whole (as, a change of *posture*; "He . . . did his best so to arrange his *posture* that he might suffer least from his long lying," J. H. Newman's "Callista," xiii.); attitude, or an attitude (as, a sitting *posture*); sometimes, an affected or unnatural attitude, or a contortion of the body (as, "He would . . . dance about him, and make a thousand antic *postures* and gestures": Defoe's "Robinson Crusoe," ii. 2); fig., mental or spiritual attitude; also, position, condition, or state, esp. of affairs (as, "to deliver a religious and political exhortation on the present *posture* of public affairs": Galt's "Annals of the Parish," xliv.); a condition suited for something (as, to put a town in a *posture* of defense; "I arranged briefly my affairs, put them in a *posture* to be easily at my command from a distance,"

Irving's "Tales of a Traveler," i. 9).—**pos′ture**, v.; *-tured, -turing.* **I.** *tr.* To place in a particular posture or attitude, or dispose in postures: as, "Alice had been playing with the mirror's reflections — *posturing* her arms . . . clasping her hands behind her neck" (Tarkington's "Alice Adams," ii.). **II.** *intr.* To assume a particular posture; esp., to assume affected or unnatural postures; bend or contort the body in various ways, specif. in public performing; hence, to act in an affected or artificial way, as if for show; pose for effect; also, to assume artificial mental attitudes or poses.—**pos′ture=mas″ter**, n. A contortionist or acrobat (as, "throwing himself into all the attitudes of a *posture-master*": H. Melville's "Typee," x.); also, a teacher of postures. [Archaic.]—**pos′tur-er, pos′tur-ist**, n.—**pos′tur-ize**, v. i.; *-ized, -izing.* To posture; pose.

post=war (pōst′wâr′), a. [See *post-.*] After the war: as, *post-war* economic conditions. Cf. *pre-war.*

post-wom-an (pōst′wŭm″ạn), n.; pl. *-women* (-wim″en). A female letter-carrier.

po-sy (pō′zi), n.; pl. *posies* (-ziz). [Contr. of *poesy.*] A brief motto or the like, such as is inscribed within a ring (archaic); also, a flower; a nosegay or bouquet.

pot¹ (pot), n. [AS. *pott* = D. and LG. *pot* = OF. F. *pot,* pot.] An earthen, metallic, or other vessel, usually of cylindrical or other rounded form and deep rather than broad, used for holding various materials for domestic or other purposes; such a vessel, as of metal, to cook in; such a vessel, as of metal or earthenware, to hold liquor or to drink liquor from; such a vessel, as of unglazed earthenware, for holding a growing plant; also, such a vessel with its contents; hence, the quantity it will hold; a potful; often, a potful of liquor (as, "He carries her into a public-house, to give her a *pot* and a cake": Defoe's "Captain Singleton," i.); hence, liquor or drink; drinking; also, a wicker vessel for trapping fish or crustaceans; also, a chimney-pot; also, a large sum of money (slang); also, the aggregate of bets at stake at one time, as in card-playing; also, a person of importance (slang, Eng.: as, "one of the principal men out there — a big *pot*," J. Conrad's "Lord Jim," xxiii.); also, a pot-shot.—**to go to pot**, fig., to go to destruction or ruin: as, "We went by sea . . . and, coming back, had like to have *gone to pot* in a storm" (Smollett's "Humphry Clinker," Sept. 7); business is all *going to pot.*—**pot**¹, v.; *potted, potting.* **I.** *tr.* To put into a pot; put up and preserve (food) in a pot; cook in a pot, or stew; plant in a flower-pot; also, to shoot or kill (game) for the pot, or for cooking; hence, in general, to bring down or kill by a pot-shot or by shooting (as, "We had got to within sixty yards' range . . . and were just about to sit down comfortably to '*pot*' them [two lions], when they suddenly surprised us by . . . bolting off": J. H. Patterson's "Man-Eaters of Tsavo," xxiv.); also, to capture, secure, or win (colloq.). **II.** *intr.* To drink from a pot (archaic); also, to take a pot-shot; shoot.

pot² (pot), n. [ME. *pot,* hole, pit: cf. Sw. dial. *pott, putt.*] A deep hole; a pit; a pot-hole. [Sc. and prov. Eng.]

po-ta-ble (pō′tạ-bl). [F. *potable,* < LL. *potabilis,* < L. *potare,* drink.] **I.** *a.* Fit or suitable for drinking: as, "huge packs of provisions edible and *potable*" (F. M. Crawford's "Mr. Isaacs," ix.). **II.** *n.* Anything drinkable: usually in *pl.*—**po-ta-bil′i-ty** (-bil′i-ti), n.

po-tage (po-täzh′), n. [F.: see *pottage.*] Soup.

po-tam-ic (pō-tam′ik), a. [Gr. ποταμός, river.] Pertaining to rivers.

pot-a-mol-o-gy (pot-ạ-mol′ọ-ji), n. [Gr. ποταμός, river: see *-logy.*] The scientific study of rivers.—**pot″a-mo-log′i-cal** (-mọ-loj′i-kạl), a.—**pot-a-mol′o-gist**, n.

pot-ash (pot′-ash), n. [Orig. in *pot-ashes,* pl., = D. *potasch-en.*] Potassium carbonate, esp. the crude impure form obtained from wood-ashes; also, potassium hy-

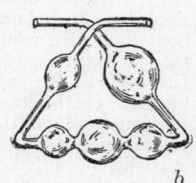

Potash-bulbs. — *a*, Geissler's form; *b*, Liebig's form.

droxide ('caustic potash'); also, the oxide of potassium; also, potassium (in phrases, as 'carbonate of potash').—**pot′ash=bulbs**, n. pl. A combination of glass bulbs for holding a solution of caustic potash, used in chemical analysis of organic substances. See cut in preceding column.

po-tas-sic (pō-tas′ik), a. In *chem.,* of, pertaining to, or containing potassium.

po-tas-si-um (pō-tas′i-um), n. [NL.; named from *potass* (< F. *potasse*), a former equivalent of *potash.*] Chem. sym., K (see *kalium*); at. wt., 39.10; sp. gr., 0.87. A silvery-white metallic element, which oxidizes rapidly in the air.—**potassium bicarbonate**, a crystalline compound, $KHCO_3$, used in medicine, etc.—**potassium carbonate**, a white solid, K_2CO_3, used in the manufacture of glass, etc.—**potassium dichromate**, an orange-red crystalline compound, $K_2Cr_2O_7$, used in dyeing, photography, etc.—**potassium hydroxide**, a white caustic solid, KOH, used in making soft soap, etc.—**potassium permanganate**, a nearly black crystalline compound, $KMnO_4$, forming red-purple solutions in water: used as an oxidizing agent, disinfectant, etc.

po-ta-tion (po-tā′shọn), n. [OF. *potacion,* < L. *potatio(n-),* < *potare,* drink.] The act of drinking, or a drink or draft, esp. of alcoholic liquor (as, "Jucundus . . . paid the not uncommon penalty of his *potations,* for the wine mounted to his head": J. H. Newman's "Callista," vi.); also, a liquid or liquor for drinking, or a beverage (as, "The emperor took no other beverage than . . . a *potation* of chocolate, flavored with vanilla": Prescott's "Conquest of Mexico," iv. 1).

po-ta-to (pō-tā′tō), n.; pl. *-toes* (-tōz). [Sp. *patata,* white potato, *batata,* sweet potato; from Haitian.] The sweetish edible (spindle-shaped) root of a cultivated vine, *Batatas* (or *Ipomœa*) *batatas,* or the vine itself ('sweet potato'); also, the edible tuber of a cultivated plant, *Solanum tuberosum,* or the plant itself ('white potato' or 'Irish potato').—**po-ta′to=bee″tle, po-ta′to=bug**, n. A beetle, *Leptinotarsa decem-lineata,* with black and yellow stripes, which causes much damage to potato-plants. Also called *Colorado beetle.*—**po-ta′to=race**, n. A race in which each runner picks up and carries to a receptacle, one at a time, potatoes placed at intervals along the course.—**po-ta′to=ring**, n. A ring or circular band, esp. of silver

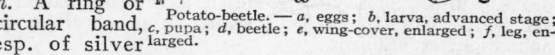

Potato-beetle. — *a,* eggs; *b,* larva, advanced stage; *c,* pupa; *d,* beetle; *e,* wing-cover, enlarged; *f,* leg, enlarged.

and often highly decorated, used in Ireland in the 18th century as a stand for a bowl or the like: so called from the erroneous supposition that it was used for keeping potatoes together on the table.

po-ta-to-ry (pō′tạ-tọ-ri), a. [L. *potatorius,* < *potare,* drink.] Of, pertaining to, or given to drinking; also, potable (rare): as, "I helped myself to the *potatory* food," Bulwer-Lytton's "Pelham," xxxix.].

po-ta-to=vine (pō-tā′tō-vīn), n. The potato-plant, esp. the part above ground; also, a convolvulaceous vine, *Ipomœa pandurata,* of North America, having large white or purplish funnel-shaped flowers and a large root ('wild potato-vine') (see cut at *man-of-the-earth*).

pot=bel-ly (pot′bel″i), n. A distended or protuberant belly.—**pot′=bel″lied**, a.

pot=boil-er (pot′boi″lẽr), n. A work of literature or art produced merely 'to keep the pot boiling,' that is, to provide the necessaries of life. [Colloq.]

pot=bound (pot′bound), *a.* Of plants or plant-roots, limited in growth by the inclosing pot.

pot=boy (pot′boi), *n.* A boy or man who carries pots of beer, ale, etc., to customers; an assistant in a tavern, etc.

pot=com-pan-ion (pot′kọm-pan″yọn), *n.* A companion in drinking; a boon companion.

po-teen (po-tēn′), *n.* [Ir. *poitín*, small pot.] In Ireland, illicitly distilled whisky.

po-tence (pō′tẹns), *n.* Potency, power, or strength.

po-ten-cy (pō′tẹn-si), *n.*; pl. *-cies* (-siz). [L. *potentia*, < *potens*: see *potent*.] The quality of being potent; power or authority; powerfulness or effectiveness; strength or efficacy, as of a drug; sometimes, a person or thing exerting power or influence; also, capability of development, or potentiality (as, "Books . . . do contain a *potency* of life in them to be as active as that soul was whose progeny they are": Milton's "Areopagitica"); in *homeopathy*, the power of a drug as developed by attenuation.

po-tent (pō′tẹnt), *a.* [L. *potens* (*potent-*), able, powerful, ppr. of *posse*, be able, have power, < *potis*, able, + *esse*, be: cf. Skt. *pati*, master, lord, husband, Gr. πόσις, husband, δεσπότης, master, lord, E. *despot*.] Possessed of great power or authority (as, "His haughty demeanor touched the pride of his more *potent* vassals": Prescott's "Conquest of Mexico," iv. 1); fig., exercising great moral influence (as, "if bravery be the most *potent* charm to win the favor of the fair": Parkman's "Oregon Trail," xii.); powerful; mighty; cogent or effective, as reasons, motives, etc.; also, producing powerful physical or chemical effects, as a drug; also, possessing sexual power.

po-ten-tate (pō′tẹn-tāt), *n.* [LL. *potentatus*, potentate, L. power, dominion, < L. *potens*: see *potent*.] One who possesses great power or sway; a sovereign, monarch, or ruler (as, "a king of Denmark, a margrave of Brandenburg, or some other rising *potentate* of Northern Europe": J. F. Kirk's "Charles the Bold," iv. 1); also, a powerful city, state, or the like.

po-ten-tial (pō-ten′shạl). [ML. *potentialis*, < L. *potentia*, E. *potency*.] **I.** *a.* Potent (now rare); also, possible as opposed to actual; capable of being or becoming; latent; in *gram.*, expressing possibility; noting or pertaining to that mode of the verb which expresses possibility and related ideas, by the use of the auxiliaries *may, might, can, could,* etc.; in *physics*, noting energy which is due to position or the like and not to motion, as that possessed by a raised weight. **II.** *n.* A possibility or potentiality; in *gram.*, the potential mode, or a verb-form belonging to it; in *elect.*, an attribute of a point near or within an electrified body, represented by the work necessary to bring a unit of positive electricity from an infinite distance to that point.—**po-ten-ti-al′i-ty** (-shi-al′i-ti), *n.*; pl. *-ties* (-tiz). Potential state or quality; power or powerfulness; esp., possibility, as opposed to actuality; capability of development; latent power or capacity (as, "the sense of his mission in the world . . . and his *potentiality* for good": Arnold Bennett's "Great Man," xxvi.); also, something potential; a possibility; something not yet actualized, but which may be developed into actuality.—**po-ten′-tial-ize**, *v. t.*; *-ized, -izing.* To make po tential; give poten tiality to.—**po-ten′-tial-ly**, *adv.*

po-ten-til-la (pō-tẹn-til′ạ), *n.* [NL., dim. < L. *potens*: see *potent*.] Any plant of the rosaceous genus *Potentilla*, comprising herbs and

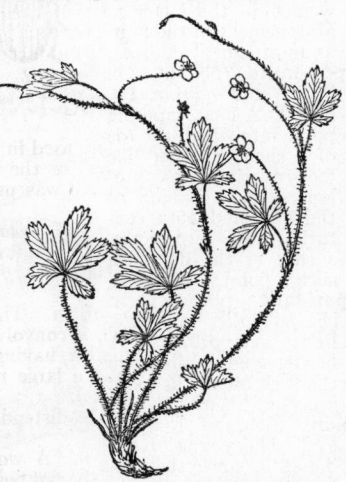

Potentilla, or Wild Strawberry (*Potentilla canadensis*).

shrubs with mainly alternate pinnate or palmate leaves, as the European cinquefoil, *P. reptans*, or a North American species, *P. canadensis* (often called *wild strawberry*: see cut in preceding column).

po-ten-ti-om-e-ter (pō-ten-shi-om′e-tėr), *n.* [From *potential*, *n.*, + *-meter*.] In *elect.*, any of various instruments for measuring electromotive force or difference in potential; specif., in *wireless teleg.* and *teleph.*, a device for varying or adjusting potential.

po-tent-ize (pō′tẹn-tīz), *v. t.*; *-ized, -izing.* To render potent; in *homeopathy*, to develop the power of (a drug) by attenuation.—**po″tent-i-za′tion** (-tẹn-ti-zā′shọn), *n.*

po-tent-ly (pō′tẹnt-li), *adv.* In a potent manner; powerfully; effectively.

pot-ful (pot′fùl), *n.*; pl. *-fuls.* As much as a pot will hold.

po-theen (po-thēn′), *n.* Same as *poteen*.

poth-er (pọᴛʜ′ėr), *n.* [Origin uncertain.] A choking or suffocating cloud, as of smoke or dust; also, commotion; uproar; a disturbance or fuss (as, "the feudal system, about which the writers of this age have made such a *pother*": Smollett's "Humphry Clinker," Sept. 6); also, mental perturbation; trouble.—**poth′er**, *v.* **I.** *tr.* To harass and perplex; bother; worry. **II.** *intr.* To worry; fuss.

pot-herb (pot′ėrb), *n.* Any herb prepared as food by cooking in a pot, as spinach, or added as seasoning in cookery, as thyme.

pot-hole (pot′hōl), *n.* A deep hole; a pit; esp., a more or less cylindrical hole formed in rock by the grinding action of the detrital material in an eddying current of water.

pot-hook (pot′hùk), *n.* A hook for suspending a pot or kettle over an open fire; also, an iron rod, usually curved, with a hook at the end, used to lift hot pots, irons, stove-lids, etc.; also, an S-shaped stroke in writing, esp. as made by children in learning to write (cf. *hanger*); a crooked stroke in writing.

pot-house (pot′hous), *n.* A place where pots of ale, beer, etc., are retailed; an ale-house.

pot-hunt-er (pot′hun″tėr), *n.* One who hunts merely to fill the pot or for profit, or shoots anything he comes upon, regardless of the rules of sport (as, "flocks [of birds] that have escaped the murderous gun of the *pot-hunter*": G. W. Cable's "Bonaventure," iii. 6); also, one who takes part in contests merely to win prizes.—**pot′=hunt″ing**, *n.* and *a.*

po-tiche (po-tēsh′), *n.* [F., < *pot*, pot.] A vase or jar, as of porcelain, of Chinese or Japanese style, with rounded or polygonal body narrowing at the top.

po-tion (pō′shọn), *n.* [OF. *pocion* (F. *potion*), < L. *potio(n-)*, drinking, draft, potion, < *potare*, drink: cf. *poison*.] A drink or draft, esp. one of a medicinal, poisonous, or magical kind (as, "a pitch-like *potion* of gin and molasses . . . a sovereign cure for all colds and catarrhs," H. Melville's "Moby-Dick," iii.; "You promised me that your charms and *potions* would secure me her acceptance," Wiseman's "Fabiola," i. 9); also, a kind of drink, or beverage (rare: as, "As to the intoxicating *potion* sold for wine, it is a vile, unpalatable, and pernicious sophistication," Smollett's "Humphry Clinker," June 8).

Potiche.

pot-latch (pot′lach), *n.* [N. Amer. Ind.] Among some American Indians of the northern Pacific coast, a gift or present (as, "They [Indians] . . . expressed the friendliest sentiments, perhaps with a view to a liberal '*potlatch*' of trinkets": T. Winthrop's "Canoe and the Saddle," iv.); also, a ceremonial festival at which gifts are bestowed on the guests.

pot-luck (pot′luk′), *n.* One's luck as to what may chance to be in the pot or provided for a meal: as, to take *pot-luck* with a friend; "Lapham's idea of hospitality was still to bring a heavy-buying customer home to *pot-luck*" (Howells's "Rise of Silas Lapham," ii.).

pot-mar-i-gold (pot′mar′i-gōld), *n.* The common marigold, *Calendula officinalis*, the flower-heads of which are sometimes used in cookery for seasoning.

pot-pie (pot′pī), *n.* A baked meat-pie; also, a stew, as of chicken or veal, with dumplings.

pot-pour-ri (pō-pö-rē′), *n.* [F. *pot pourri*, 'rotten pot,' tr. Sp. *olla podrida*: see under *olla*.] A stew of various kinds of meat cooked together†; also, a mixture of dried petals of roses or other flowers with spices, etc., kept in a jar for the fragrance; also, a musical medley; also, a literary medley; a collection of miscellaneous literary extracts.—**pot-pour-ri′=jar,** *n.* A covered jar for holding potpourri (of rose-petals, etc.).

pot-sherd (pot′shėrd), *n.* [Cf. *sherd* for *shard*.] A fragment or broken piece of earthenware.

pot=shot (pot′shot), *n.* A shot fired at game merely to fill the pot, with little regard to skill or the rules of sport; hence, a shot at an animal or person within easy reach, as from ambush.

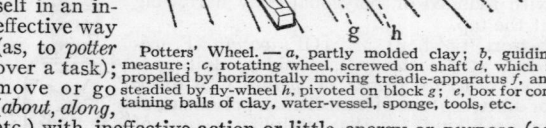

Potpourri-jar.

pot-stone (pot′stōn), *n.* A kind of soapstone, sometimes used for making pots and other household utensils.

pot-tage (pot′āj), *n.* [OF. F. *potage*, < *pot*, pot.] A thick soup made of vegetables, without or with meat.

pot-ter[1] (pot′ėr), *n.* One who makes earthen pots or vessels. —**potters' clay,** clay used by potters; any clay which is free or nearly free from iron and is thus suitable for making pottery.—**potter's field,** a piece of ground reserved as a burial-place for strangers and the friendless poor. See Mat. xxvii. 7.—**potters' wheel,** a device with a rotating horizontal disk upon which clay is molded into vessels, etc., of rounded form, by a potter.

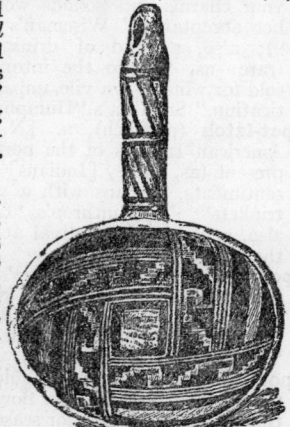

Potters' Wheel.—*a*, partly molded clay; *b*, guiding measure; *c*, rotating wheel, screwed on shaft *d*, which is propelled by horizontally moving treadle-apparatus *f*, and steadied by fly-wheel *h*, pivoted on block *g*; *e*, box for containing balls of clay, water-vessel, sponge, tools, etc.

pot-ter[2] (pot′ėr), *v. i.* [Appar. freq. of obs. or prov. *pote*, push, poke, < AS. *potian*, push, thrust.] To busy or occupy one's self in an ineffective way (as, to *potter* over a task); move or go (about, along, etc.) with ineffective action or little energy or purpose (as, "Wang . . . began to *potter* mysteriously about some plants at the foot of the veranda": J. Conrad's "Victory," iii. 3); move or go slowly or aimlessly, dawdle, or loiter (as, "Past the old church, and down the footpath, *pottered* the old man and the child hand in hand": Hughes's "Tom Brown's School Days," i. 2).—**pot′ter**[2], *n.* Pottering or ineffective action; dawdling.—**pot′ter-er,** *n.*—**pot′ter-ing-ly,** *adv.*

pot-ter-y (pot′ėr-i), *n.*; pl. *-ies* (-iz). [OF. F. *poterie*, < *potier*, potter, < *pot*, pot.] A place where earthen pots or vessels are made; also, the art or business of a potter; ceramics; also, ware or vessels fashioned from clay or other earthy material and hardened by heat (sometimes used esp. of the coarser, cruder, or primitive kinds: as, native Mexican *pottery*; Pueblo Indian *pottery*: cf.

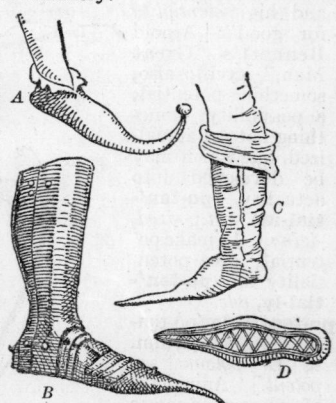

Pueblo Indian Pottery.—Dipper, from ancient ruins in Arizona. (Pennsylvania Museum, Philadelphia.)

porcelain).—**the Potteries,** a name popularly applied to a district in northern Staffordshire, England, the principal seat of the pottery industry in England.

pot-tle (pot′l), *n.* [OF. *potel*, dim. of *pot*, pot.] A former liquid measure equal to two quarts; a pot or tankard of this capacity; the wine, etc., contained in it; hence, liquor; also, a small wicker basket, as for fruit (as, "a *pottle* of fine strawberries": Smollett's "Humphry Clinker," June 2).

pot-to (pot′ō), *n.*; pl. *pottos* (-ōz). [W. Afr.] A small West African mammal, *Perodicticus potto*, of the lemur kind; also, the kinkajou.

Pott's (pots) **dis-ease′.** [From Percival *Pott* (1714–88), English surgeon, who described it.] In *pathol.*, caries of the bodies of the vertebræ, often resulting in marked curvature of the spine.

pot-val-iant (pot′val″yant), *a.* Courageous through drink: as, "a man who has drunk himself *pot-valiant*" (Smollett's "Humphry Clinker," May 29).

pot-wal-lop-er (pot′wol″op-ėr), *n.* [Earlier *pot-waller*, one who boils a pot (obs. or prov. *wall*, < AS. *weallan*, boil).] Formerly, in some English boroughs, a man qualified for a parliamentary vote as a householder (as distinguished from a man merely a member or inmate of a householder's family): the test being the possession of a separate fireplace over which food for himself and his family was cooked.

pouch (pouch), *n.* [OF. *pouche*, var. of *poche*, also *poque*, *poke*, bag: cf. *poke*[2].] A bag, sack, or similar receptacle, esp. one for small articles; a small money-bag (as, "a poor devil without penny in *pouch*": Irving's "Tales of a Traveler," ii. 4); a pocket in a garment (chiefly Sc.); a bag or case for ammunition (as, "a great leather *pouch* which held about a pound and a half of powder . . . and another with shot": Defoe's "Robinson Crusoe," i. 2); a cartridge-box; a bag for carrying mail; also, something shaped like or resembling a bag or pocket; a baggy fold of flesh under the eye (as, "His lips were parted and pale, and there were deep *pouches* under the eyes": Kipling's "Light That Failed," iii.); in *anat.*, *zoöl.*, etc., a bag-like or pocket-like part; a sac or cyst; the gular sac beneath the bill of pelicans, etc.; the sac-like dilatation of the cheek of gophers, etc.; a marsupium; in *bot.*, a bag-like cavity; a silicle.—**pouch,** *v.* **I.** *tr.* To put into or inclose in a pouch, bag, or pocket; pocket; fig., to submit to without protest (as, "I will *pouch* up no such affront": Scott's "Ivanhoe," xxxiii.); sometimes, of a fish or bird, to swallow; also, to arrange (something) in pouch-like form; also, to supply the purse or pocket of, provide with money, or give a present of money to (colloq.: as, "Coningsby . . . had been *pouched* in a manner worthy of a Marquess," Disraeli's "Coningsby," i. 8). **II.** *intr.* To form a pouch or a pouch-like cavity.—**pouched,** *a.* Having a pouch, as the pelicans, gophers, and marsupials. —**pouched rat.** See *gopher*.

pouf (pöf), *n.* [F.: cf. *puff*.] A kind of head-dress worn by women in the latter part of the 18th century; also, an arrangement of the hair over a pad; also, a puff of material as an ornament in dress or millinery.

pou-laine (pö-lān′), *n.* [OF., < *Poulaine*, Poland.] A long, tapering point into which the toe of a shoe or other like foot-covering was prolonged, in a fashion of the 14th and 15th centuries; also, a shoe or the like with such a point.

pou-lard (pö-lärd′), *n.* [F. *poularde*, < *poule*, hen: see *pullet*.] A hen spayed to improve the flesh for use as food; a fattened hen.

poult (pōlt), *n.* [= *pullet*.] The young of the domestic fowl, the turkey, the pheasant, or a similar bird.

Poulaines, close of 14th century.—*A*, slipper; *B*, jambe and solleret with poulaine; *C*, riding-boot; *D*, sole of clog for wearing with either *A* or *C*.

fat, fāte, fär, fåll, åsk, fāre; net, mē, hėr; pin, pīne; not, nōte, mŏve, nôr; up, lūte, půll; oi, oil; ou, out; (lightened) aviặry, ẽlect, agŏny, intọ, ūnite; (obscured) errặnt, operặ, ardẹnt, actọr, natụre; ch, chip; g, go; th, thin; ᵺ, then; y, you;

poult=de=soie (pö-dĕ-swo′), n. [F., also *pou-de-soie*, *pout-de-soie*, OF. *pout de soye*, *poul de soie*, lit. 'pout(?) of silk'; first element unexplained.] A soft, rich silk fabric of the grosgrain type. Cf. *peau-de-soie*.

poul-ter (pōl′tẽr), n. [OF. *pouletier*, < *poulet*: see *pullet*.] A dealer in poultry. [Obs. or hist.]

poul-ter-er (pōl′tẽr-ẽr), n. [Extended form of *poulter*.] A dealer in poultry.

poul-tice (pōl′tis), n. [First recorded as *pultes*, appar. orig. the plural of L. *puls* (*pult-*), thick pap: cf. *pulse*[1].] A soft, moist mass of bread, meal, herbs, etc., applied as a medicament to the body.—**poul′tice**, v. t.; *-ticed*, *-ticing*. To apply a poultice to.

poul-try (pōl′tri), n. [OF. *pouletrie*, < *pouletier*, E. *poulter*.] Domestic fowls collectively, as chickens, turkeys, guinea-fowls, ducks, and geese.

pounce[1] (pouns), n. [ME. *pownce*; prob. akin to *punch*[1], *puncheon*[1].] The claw or talon of a bird of prey; also, a pouncing or sudden swoop, as on prey; also, a hole or cut made by punching, pinking, or the like, for ornamental purposes, as in cloth or a garment†.—**pounce**[1], v.; *pounced*, *pouncing*. **I.** tr. To seize with the pounces or talons, or swoop down upon and seize suddenly, as a bird of prey does (as, "As if an eagle . . . Stoop'd from his highest pitch to *pounce* a wren": Cowper's "Table Talk," 553); also, to emboss (metal) by hammering on an instrument applied on the reverse side (obs. or hist.); also, to ornament (cloth, etc.) by punching holes, etc., or pinking (obs. or hist.). **II.** intr. To swoop down suddenly and lay hold, as a bird does on its prey (lit. or fig.: as, "His mother would *pounce* . . . on his remarks as a barn-owl *pounces* upon a mouse," S. Butler's "Way of All Flesh," xlviii.); make a pounce; hence, to spring, dash, or come suddenly (as, to *pounce* into a room).

pounce[2] (pouns), n. [F. *ponce* < L. *pumex* (*pumic-*), E. *pumice*.] A fine powder, as of cuttlebone, formerly used to prevent ink from spreading in writing, as over an erasure or on unsized paper, or to prepare parchment for writing; also, a fine powder used for transferring a design through a perforated pattern.—**pounce**[2], v. t.; *pounced*, *pouncing*. To sprinkle, smooth, or prepare with pounce; also, to trace (a design), or trace a design upon (a surface), with pounce rubbed through perforations; also, to finish the surface of (hats) by rubbing with sandpaper or the like.—**pounce′=box**, n. A box for holding pounce, as for use in writing.

poun-cet=box (poun′set-boks), n. [Perhaps for *pounced box*: see *pounce*[1], v. t.] A small box with a perforated lid, used for holding perfume (as, "He was perfumed like a milliner; And . . . held A *pouncet-box*, which ever and anon He gave his nose and took 't away again": Shakspere's "1 Henry IV.," i. 3. 38); also, erroneously, a pounce-box. [Archaic.]

pound[1] (pound), n. [AS., recorded in *pundfald* (see *pinfold*); origin unknown.] An inclosure maintained by authority for confining trespassing or stray cattle, dogs, etc., or for keeping goods seized by distress; in general, an inclosure for sheltering, keeping, confining, or trapping animals; an inclosure or trap for fish (cf. *pound-net*); in fig. use, a place of confinement or imprisonment (cf. *Lob's pound*); a position from which escape is difficult (specif. in *hunting*); also, a pond, or accumulation of water (now prov. Eng.); hence, in a canal, a reach above a lock or between locks.—**pound**[1], v. t. To shut up in or as in a pound; impound; confine within limits; imprison.

pound[2] (pound), v. [AS. *punian*, akin to D. *puin*, rubbish.] **I.** tr. To crush by beating, as with an instrument (as, to *pound* drugs with a pestle in a mortar); bray, pulverize, or triturate; also, to strike repeatedly and with great force, as with an instrument, the fist, heavy missiles, etc. (as, "It was an energetic discourse, and the pulpit cushion was well *pounded*," H. Melville's "Omoo," xl.; "The Germans suddenly got the range . . . and begun to *pound* us with high explosive," H. G. Wells's "Mr. Britling," ii. 4. § 14); thump, pommel, or batter; also, to produce (sound) by striking or thumping, or with an effect of thumping (often with *out*: as, to *pound* out a tune on a piano; the piano *pounded* out a tune); force (a way) by battering (as, "The German phalanx of guns *pounds* its way through the Russian hosts": H. G. Wells's "Soul of a Bishop," vii.); also, to make

(ground, etc.) solid or firm by beating. **II.** intr. To strike heavy blows repeatedly, thump, hammer, or batter (as, to *pound* on a door; guns *pounding* at a fortification); hence, to strike heavily against the waves, as a boat; beat or throb violently, as the heart; give forth a sound of or as of thumps (as, the drums *pounded* loudly; the *pounding* of a radiator); also, to walk or go with heavy steps; ride heavily; move along with force or vigor.—**pound**[2], n. The act of pounding; a heavy or forcible blow, or the sound of it; a thump.

pound[3] (pound), n. [AS. *pund*, < L. *pondo*, a pound, prop. adv., 'in weight' (*libra pondo*, 'a pound in weight'), connected with *pondus*, weight: see *ponder*.] A unit of weight, varying greatly in different periods and countries; esp., in the British Empire and the U. S., either of two legally fixed units, the 'pound avoirdupois' (of 7,000 grains, divided into 16 ounces) used for ordinary commodities, or the 'pound troy' (of 5,760 grains, divided into 12 ounces) used for gold, silver, etc., and also serving as the basis of apothecaries' weight; also, a British money of account ('pound sterling') of the value of 20 shillings, or 240 pence, and equivalent to about $4.86⅔ (denoted by the symbol £ before the numeral or sometimes *l.* after it, and orig. equivalent to a pound of silver); also, a former Scottish money of account ('pound Scots'), orig. the equivalent of the pound sterling, but at the union of the crowns of England and Scotland in 1603 worth only one twelfth of the pound sterling; also, a gold coin and monetary unit of Egypt, Peru, and Turkey (see *lira*), approximately equal to the pound sterling; also, in the New Testament, a mina (see Luke, xix.).—**pound-age** (poun′dāj), n. A tax, commission, rate, etc., of so much per pound sterling or per pound weight.—**pound-al** (poun′dạl), n. In *physics*, a unit of force: equivalent to the force which, acting for one second on a mass of one pound, gives it a velocity of one foot per second.—**pound′=cake**, n. A kind of rich, sweet cake in which the butter, sugar, and flour are used pound for pound.

pound-er[1] (poun′dẽr), n. One who or that which pounds, pulverizes, or beats.

pound-er[2] (poun′dẽr), n. A person or thing having, or associated with, a weight or value of a pound or a specified number of pounds; a gun that discharges a missile of a specified weight in pounds (as, "fine cannon, eighteen-*pounders*, with their carriages": B. Franklin's "Autobiography," viii.); a person possessing, receiving an income of, or paying a specified number of pounds.

pound=fool-ish (pound′fōl′ish), a. Foolish or careless in regard to large sums. Cf. *penny-wise*.

pound=net (pound′net), n. A kind of weir or fish-trap of netting having a pound or inclosure with a contracted opening.

pour (pōr), v. [ME. *pouren*; origin uncertain.] **I.** tr. To send (a liquid or fluid, or anything in loose particles) flowing or falling, as from a vessel or into, over, or on something (as, to *pour* milk from a pitcher into a cup; to *pour* sauce over food; to *pour* forth smoke; to *pour* coal on the fire); emit or discharge (a liquid, etc.) in a stream, as a vessel, a tube or spout, or the like does; send down (rain, etc.) in a streaming or heavy fall; of a stream, to send (itself, its waters, etc.) rolling along or flowing into something; also, to send forth or discharge as in a stream, or continuously and rapidly, or in profusion (as, "We *poured* our broadside into the headmost frigate," Marryat's "Peter Simple," xvi.; "Behold . . . How London doth *pour* out her citizens!" Shakspere's "Henry V.," v., Prologue, 24); shed or expend freely (with *out* or *forth*: as, to *pour* out one's blood or fortune for a cause); send forth (words, etc.) as in a stream or flood (as, "He *poured* a thousand blessings on her head," Jane Porter's "Scottish Chiefs," vii.; to *pour* forth cries, entreaties, or thanks); express, or make known by utterance or expression, freely or without reserve (often with *out* or *forth*: as, "I could *pour* out to her all my little worries," S. Butler's "Way of All Flesh," lxxxvi.; to *pour*

Pound-net.— *b*, pound inclosed by wall-net with wings *c, c*; *a*, up-right net for guiding fish into pound.

forth one's feelings in song or verse). **II.** *intr.* To flow forth or along, as a liquid, a stream, etc. (as, "The torrent brooks . . . From craggy hollows *pouring*," Tennyson's "Dream of Fair Women," 182; lava and ashes *pour* from a volcano); fall heavily, as rain, or rain hard (as, the rain *poured* down in torrents; it *poured* all day); also, to issue, move, or proceed as in a stream, or in great quantity or number (as, "The cold blasts *poured* down from the mountains," Cooper's "Spy," xv.; the mob *poured* into the palace); stream; come or go in profusion.—**pour,** *n.* A pouring; an abundant or continuous flow or stream; often, a heavy fall of rain; also, a great quantity or number (chiefly Sc.: as, "The coal-heughs . . . brought a *pour* of money among us," Galt's "Annals of the Parish," viii.).

pour-boire (pör-bwor), *n.* [F., lit. 'for to drink.'] A gratuity to be spent on drink; hence, in general, a fee; a tip.

pour-er (pōr′ėr), *n.* One who or that which pours.

pour-par-ler (pör-pär-lā), *n.* [F., orig. inf., OF. *pourparler*, discuss, < *pour*- (< L. *pro*, before) + *parler*, speak, E. *parl.*] An informal preliminary conference: as, "If his conditions were not fulfilled, a breach between the two Powers would follow without further *pourparlers*" (Buchan's "Hist. of the Great War," liv.).

pour-point (pör′point), *n.* [OF. F. *pourpoint*, orig. pp. of *pourpoindre*, quilt, < *pour*-, for *par*- (< L. *per*), through, + *poindre*, < L. *pungere*, prick, pierce.] A stuffed and quilted doublet worn by men in the 14th and 15th centuries.

pour-tray′†, *v. t.* See *portray.*

pousse=ca-fé (pös-ká-fā), *n.* [F., lit. 'push-coffee.'] A small glass of liqueur served after coffee; specif., a glass of various liqueurs arranged in layers.

pous-sette (pö-set′), *n.* [F., dim. < *pousser*, E. *push.*] A dancing round and round with hands joined, as of a couple in a country-dance.—**pous-sette′,** *v. i.*; *-setted, -setting.* To perform a poussette, as a couple in a country-dance: as, "The turf-cutter seized old Olly Dowden, and . . . *poussetted* with her" (Hardy's "Return of the Native," i. 3).

pou sto (pö stō). [Gr. ποῦ στῶ, 'where I may stand': from the alleged saying of Archimedes, "Give me where I may stand, and I will move the earth."] A place to stand on; a basis of operations: as, "She . . . Who learns the one *pou sto* whence other-hands May move the world" (Tennyson's "Princess," iii. 246).

pout[1] (pout), *n.* [AS. *pūta*, recorded in *ǣlepūta*, eel-pout.] A marine food-fish, *Gadus luscus*, of northern waters; also, any of certain large-headed fresh-water catfishes (esp. *Amiurus nebulosus*) with conspicuous barbels ('horn-pout').

pout[2] (pout), *v.* [ME. *pouten*; origin uncertain.] **I.** *intr.* To thrust out or protrude the lips, esp. in displeasure or sullenness; hence, to look sullen; also, to swell out or protrude, as lips. **II.** *tr.* To protrude (lips, etc.); also, to utter or say with a pout (as, " 'That's the reason!' *pouted* Louisa": Dickens's "Hard

Horn-pout (*Amiurus nebulosus*).

Times," i. 4).—**pout**[2], *n.* A protrusion of the lips, as in pouting; hence, a fit of sullenness (as, "There ensued a puerile tussle that put me in a precious *pout*, that I should be kept waiting by such things": G. W. Cable's "Cavalier," xxxvii.).—**pout′er,** *n.* One who pouts; also, one of a breed of long-legged domestic pigeons which have a habit of puffing out the breast, sometimes to surprising size (see cut in next column).—**pout′ing-ly,** *adv.*

pov-er-ty (pov′ėr-ti), *n.* [OF. *poverte* (F. *pauvreté*), < L. *paupertas*, < *pauper*, poor: cf. *poor* and *pauper.*] The condition of being poor with respect to money, goods, or means of subsistence (as, comparative or genteel *poverty*; utter or dire *poverty*; "No signs of care or *poverty* were

visible in the attire or countenance of the buxom widow," Thackeray's "Newcomes," lxxiii.); poor circumstances; indigence; also, deficiency or lack of something specified (as, *poverty* of ideas or invention); also, deficiency of desirable ingredients, qualities, etc. (as, *poverty* of soil); leanness, as of cattle; inadequacy or unsatisfactoriness (as, "You see the *poverty* of all these explanations": G. W. Cable's "Bonaven-

English Pouter.

ture," iii. 12); also, scantiness, or scanty amount (as, the *poverty* of the available supply of workers); also, poor persons†, or the poor†; also, poor or paltry matter† (as, "Alack. what *poverty* my Muse brings forth!" Shakspere's "Sonnets," ciii.).—**pov′er-ty=strick″en,** *a.* Suffering from poverty; wretchedly poor: as, "The *poverty-stricken* exiles contributed far more, in proportion . . . than the wealthy merchants" (Motley's "Dutch Republic," iii. 4).

pow (pō or pou), *n.* Sc. and north. Eng. form of *poll*[1].

pow-der[1] (pou′dėr), *v. i.* [Origin uncertain.] To rush; hurry with impetuous speed. [Colloq.]

pow-der[2] (pou′dėr), *n.* [OF. F. *poudre*, < L. *pulvis* (*pulver-*), dust, powder.] Any solid substance in the state of fine, loose particles, as produced by crushing, grinding, or disintegration; dust; also, a preparation in this form for some special purpose; such a preparation for medicinal use, or a dose of it; such a preparation for toilet purposes (as, face-*powder*; "The color of her hair was lost in the profusion of *powder* with which it was covered," Cooper's "Spy," xiii.); also, gunpowder, or any similar explosive.—**pow′der**[2], *v.* [OF. F. *poudrer.*] **I.** *tr.* To sprinkle or cover with powder; apply powder to (the face, skin, etc.) as a cosmetic; hence, to sprinkle or strew as with powder; ornament with small objects scattered over a surface (as, "a canopy of gaudy feather-work, *powdered* with jewels": Prescott's "Conquest of Mexico," iii. 9); also, to sprinkle or scatter like powder; also, to reduce to powder; pulverize. **II.** *intr.* To use powder as a cosmetic (as, "She saw herself going down the years, *powdering* a little more, painting a little more": Galsworthy's "Saint's Progress," iii. 12); also, to become pulverized.—**pow′der=down,** *n.* Certain modified down-feathers which grow indefinitely and continually break down at their ends into a kind of powdery or scurfy exfoliation: found esp. in the herons.—**pow′der=flask,** *n.* A flask or case, as of horn, leather, or metal, for carrying gunpowder.—**pow′der=horn,** *n.* A powder-flask made of horn, usually the horn of an ox or cow having the larger end fitted with a wooden or metal bottom and the small end with a movable stopper or the like. See cut on following page.—**pow′der=mill,** *n.* A mill in which gunpowder is made.—**pow′der=mon″key,** *n.* A boy formerly employed on war-ships, etc., to carry powder (as, "Ellangowan had him placed as cabin-boy or *powder-monkey* on board an armed sloop or yacht belonging to the revenue": Scott's "Guy Mannering," lii.); also, a man in charge of explosives in any operation requiring their use. [Humorous.]—**pow′der=post,** *n.* Wood decayed to powder, or eaten by worms which burrow through it and convert it into powder.—**pow′der=puff,** *n.* A soft, feathery ball or pad, as of down, for applying powder to the skin.—**pow′der-y,** *a.* Of the nature of, or consisting of, powder; also, easily reduced to powder; also, sprinkled or covered with pow-der.

pow-er (pou′ĕr), *n.* [OF. *poeir* (F. *pouvoir*), power, prop. inf., be able, < ML. *potere*, for L. *posse*, be able: see *potent.*] Ability to do or act; capability of doing or effecting something (as, "I shall be happy to give you any information in my *power*": Marryat's "King's Own," xliii.); also, a particular faculty of body or mind (chiefly in *pl.*: as, "an amiable . . . lad, blessed with fine digestive *powers*," Aldrich's "Story of a Bad Boy," i.; "O what a glorious animal were Man,

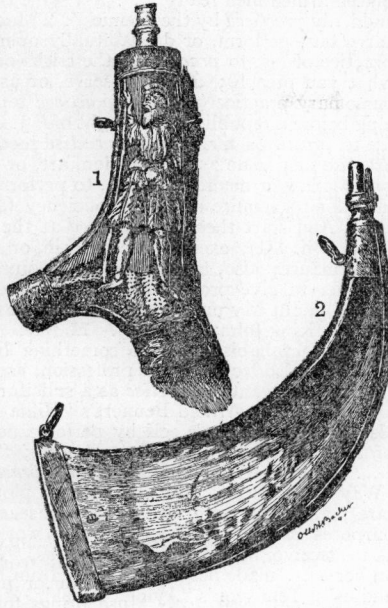

Powder-horns.— 1, of stag's horn, 17th or 18th century; 2, of cow's horn.

Knew he but his own *powers*," Southey's "Thalaba," iv. 293); also, great or marked ability to do or act; strength; might; force; often, political or national strength (as, the balance of *power* in Europe); also, the possession of control or command over others; dominion; authority; ascendancy or influence; political ascendancy or control in the government of a country, etc. (as, the party in *power*); also, legal ability, capacity, or authority; delegated authority; authority vested in a person or persons in a particular capacity; also, a written statement, or a document, conferring legal authority; also, one who or that which possesses or exercises authority or influence; a state or nation having international authority or influence (as, the great *powers* of the world); also, a deity or divinity (often in *pl.*: as, "Then adore the woodland *pow'rs* with pray'r," Dryden's tr. Virgil's "Georgics," iv. 783; by all the *powers!*); *pl.*, an order of angels (see *angel*: see also Milton's "Paradise Lost," v. 601); also, *sing.*, a military or naval force (archaic: as, "Brutus and Cassius Are levying *powers*," Shakspere's "Julius Cæsar," iv. 1. 42); hence, a large number or amount (now colloq.: as, "I've heard a *power* of queer things of yourself," Synge's "Well of the Saints," ii.); in *mech.*, energy or force available for application to work; mechanical energy as distinguished from hand-labor; a particular form of mechanical energy; capacity for exerting mechanical force, as measured by the rate at which it is exerted or at which the work is done (cf. *horse-power*); also, a simple machine (see *machine*, *n.*); in *optics*, the magnifying capacity of a microscope, telescope, etc.; in *math.*, the product obtained by multiplying a quantity by itself one or more times (as, 4 is the second, 8 the third, 16 the fourth, *power* of 2: cf. *root*). —**power politics**, international politics, esp. when associated with a certain amount of coercion.

pow-er=boat (pou′ĕr-bōt), *n.* A boat propelled by an engine on board; specif., a boat having an internal-combustion engine to furnish the driving power; a motor-boat.

pow-ered (pou′ĕrd), *a.* Having power: as, high-*powered*.

pow-er-ful (pou′ĕr-ful). **I.** *a.* Having or exerting great power or force; strong physically, as a person; producing great physical effects, as a machine or a blow; potent, as a drug; having or showing great intellectual force, as the mind; having great moral influence, as a speech or speaker, a description, etc.; cogent or effective, as reasons or motives; often, having great power, dominion, authority, or influence, as a nation; mighty; also, great in amount or number (prov.

or colloq.: as, "a *powerful* deal o' trouble," Mrs. Stowe's "Uncle Tom's Cabin," xxxiii.). **II.** *adv.* In a great degree; very; extremely: as, *powerful* weary. [Prov.]—**pow′er-ful-ly**, *adv.*—**pow′er-ful-ness**, *n.*

pow-er=house (pou′ĕr-hous), *n.* A building containing the necessary apparatus (as boilers, engines, dynamos) for the generation of power for operating an industrial plant, an electric lighting system, or the like.

pow-er-less (pou′ĕr-les), *a.* Lacking power or ability; unable to produce any effect; impotent; helpless: as, "a *powerless* hand" (Shakspere's "King John," ii. 1. 15); "I now felt *powerless* to escape" (W. H. Hudson's "Green Mansions," iii.).—**pow′er-less-ly**, *adv.*—**pow′er-less-ness**, *n.*

pow-er=plant (pou′ĕr-plant), *n.* A plant (including engines, dynamos, etc., with the building or buildings) for the generation of power; a power-station; also, the apparatus for supplying power for a particular mechanical process or operation (as, the *power-plant* of an automobile).

pow-er=sta-tion (pou′ĕr-stā″shọn), *n.* A building or a group of buildings where power is generated, as for an electric railway or lighting system; a power-house.

pow-wow (pou′wou), *n.* [Algonquian.] Among the North American Indians, a priest or medicine-man; also, a ceremony, esp. one accompanied by magic, feasting, and dancing, performed for the cure of disease, success in a hunt, etc.; also, a council or conference of or with Indians; hence, any conference or meeting compared to an Indian powwow (colloq.: as, "I'll be back early, for a last *pow-wow* on the terrace," Mrs. Wharton's "Son at the Front," viii.).—**pow′wow**, *v. i.* To hold a powwow; hence, to confer (colloq.: as, "We would go to the cave and *powwow* over what we had done," Mark Twain's "Huckleberry Finn," iii.).

pox (poks), *n.* [For *pocks*, pl. of *pock*.] Any of certain diseases characterized by eruptive pustules; often, formerly, smallpox; now, usually, syphilis ('great pox' or 'French pox').

poz-zo (pot′sō), *n.*; pl. *pozzi* (-sē). [It., < L. *puteus*, well: cf. *pit¹*.] In Italian use, a well; in Venice, a cistern, sometimes with elaborately ornamented curb.

poz-zuo-la-na, poz-zo-la-na (pot-swọ-lä′nä, pot-sō-), *n.* [It.] A volcanic rock or ash, first found at Pozzuoli, Italy, used in making hydraulic cement.

Pozzo, in Venice.

praam (präm), *n.* See *pram¹.*

prac-tic (prak′tik), *a.* Same as *practical.* [Obs. or archaic.]

prac-ti-ca-bil-i-ty (prak″ti-ka-bil′i-ti), *n.*; pl. *-ties* (-tiz). The quality of being practicable; capability of being done, effected, or used; feasibility; *pl.*, things practicable or feasible.

prac-ti-ca-ble (prak′ti-ka̧-bl), *a.* [F. *praticable*, < *pratiquer*: see *practise*.] Capable of being put into practice, done, or effected, esp. with the available means or with reason or prudence (as, to seek a *practicable* method; "As soon as it was *practicable*, he would wind up his business with Jonathan Burge," George Eliot's "Adam Bede," xlviii.); feasible; also, capable of being used or traversed, or admitting of passage (as, a *practicable* road; "The moat had been rendered *practicable* in many places by the heaps of rubbish," Motley's "Dutch Republic," vi. 2); in theatrical use, admitting of actual use, in distinction from being merely simulated (as, "I bowed my way back to the '*practicable*' door, through which I made my exit," Lever's "Harry Lorrequer," xlix.; a *practicable* bridge or window).—**prac′-ti-ca-ble-ness**, *n.*—**prac′ti-ca-bly**, *adv.*

prac-ti-cal (prak'ti-kạl), *a.* [F. (obs.) *practique*, now *pratique*, < LL. *practicus*, < Gr. πρακτικός, active, practical, < πράσσειν, do.] Pertaining or relating to practice or action (as, *practical* agriculture; *practical* philosophy; *practical* principles or standards: opposed to *theoretical*, *speculative*, or *ideal*); consisting of, involving, or resulting from practice or action (as, a *practical* demonstration of one's power; a *practical* application of a rule; a *practical* joke, see phrase below; "Though I was not a stranger to books, I had no *practical* acquaintance with men," Godwin's "Caleb Williams," i.); pertaining to or connected with the ordinary activities, business, or work of the world (as, *practical* affairs; *practical* pursuits; *practical* life); also, suitable for being applied or used in practice, or adapted for actual use (as, a *practical* method or device; a *practical* style of dress; "My scheme . . . was so much more *practical* . . . than the one hatched by those three simple-minded conspirators," W. H. Hudson's "Purple Land," xxv.); also, engaged or experienced in actual practice or work (as, a *practical* politician; a *practical* printer); inclined toward or fitted for actual practice or work or useful activities (as, a *practical* man; a *practical* mind); interested in actualities; sometimes, mindful of the results, usefulness, advantages or disadvantages, etc., of action or procedure (as, to be *practical* in one's methods, choice, or ideas); seeking material results; also, matter-of-fact or prosaic (as, "A common-place, *practical* reply . . . was, I was sure, the best": C. Brontë's "Jane Eyre," xxxvii.); also, being such in practice or effect, or virtual (as, a victory may be a *practical* defeat; a *practical* certainty).—**practical joke**, a joke or jest carried out in action; a trick played upon a person.—**prac-ti-cal'i-ty** (-kal'i-ti), *n.*; pl. *-ties* (-tiz). The quality of being practical; practical usefulness; practical habit of mind; also, a practical matter.—**prac'ti-cal-ly**, *adv.* In a practical manner; in relation to practice; from a practical point of view; also, in effect, or virtually; to all intents and purposes.—**prac'ti-cal-ness**, *n.*

prac-tice (prak'tis), *v.* See *practise*.

prac-tice (prak'tis), *n.* [From *practice*, *practise*, *v.*] The action or process of performing or doing something (opposed to *theory* or *speculation*); performance; operation; esp., habitual or customary performance (as, "to live in the conscientious *practice* of all that is good": J. Butler's "Analogy of Religion," i. 7); a habitual performance, or a habit or custom (as, "a time when a doubt in the existence of witches was interpreted as equivalent to a justification of their infernal *practices*": Scott's "Guy Mannering," xlvi.); also, the exercise of a profession or occupation, esp. law or medicine; the business of a professional man (as, a lawyer with a large *practice*); also, repeated performance or systematic exercise for the purpose of acquiring skill or proficiency (as, *practice* makes perfect); a process of practising for exercise (as, "He got the keys of St. Michael's church and went to have a farewell *practice* upon the organ": S. Butler's "Way of All Flesh," xliv.); the condition of ability and readiness to do something resulting from frequent and recent performance or exercise (as, to be in *practice*, or out of *practice*, at playing a game or speaking a foreign language); skill gained by experience or exercise (as, "What *practice* howsoe'er expert . . . Hath power to give thee as thou wert?" Tennyson's "In Memoriam," lxxv.); also, plotting, intriguing, or trickery; a plot or intrigue; a stratagem or maneuver; also, dealings or negotiations, esp. of a secret or underhand kind (now rare); also, a practising or working on a person, etc., to deceive or beguile (now rare); in *law*, the established method of conducting legal proceedings.

prac-ti-cian (prak-tish'ạn), *n.* [OF. *practicien* (F. *praticien*), < ML. *practica*, practice, prop. fem. of LL. *practicus*: see *practical*.] One engaged in practice; one concerned with practice rather than theory.

prac-ti-cum (prak'ti-kum), *n.*; pl. *-cums*, L. *-ca* (-kä). [= G. *praktikum*, < NL. (*collegium*) *practicum*, 'practical (course).'] In colleges and schools, a course in practical work or in independent research, or an exercise of a practical nature as in laboratory or field work.

prac-tise, prac-tice (prak'tis), *v.*; *-tised*, *-ticed*, *-tising*, *-ticing*. [OF. *practiser*, *pratiser*, for *pratiquer* (F. *pratiquer*), < ML. *practicare*, perform, practise, < LL. *practicus*: see *practical*.]

I. *tr.* To carry out in action, perform, or do (as, "Judas placed armed men ready . . . lest some treachery should be suddenly *practised* by the enemies": 2 Mac. xiv. 22); esp., to carry out, perform, or do habitually or usually, or make a practice of (as, to *practise* all the tricks of a trade; *practise* what you preach); follow, observe, or use habitually or in customary practice (as, "We *practised* republican principles long before a republic was thought of," J. Conrad's "Rover," i.; to *practise* a method; to *practise* moderation); also, to exercise or pursue as a profession, art, or occupation (as, to *practise* law or medicine); also, to perform or do repeatedly in order to acquire skill or proficiency (as, "Attitude, and stare, And start theatric, *practised* at the glass": Cowper's "Task," ii. 431); exercise one's self in, or study, by repeated performance; also, to exercise (a person, etc.) in something in order to give proficiency; train or drill; also, to plot† (as, "I doubt My uncle *practises* more harm to me": Shakspere's "King John," iv. 1. 20). **II.** *intr.* To act or operate; esp., to act habitually; do something habitually or as a practice; also, to pursue a profession, esp. law or medicine (as, "If you want to *practise* as a solicitor you have to pass examinations": Arnold Bennett's "Hilda Lessways," iii. 2); also, to exercise one's self by performance tending to give proficiency (as, to *practise* at shooting; "in the old church . . . when his friend the organist was *practising*," S. Butler's "Way of All Flesh," xxxvii.); also, to plot or conspire (now rare); also, to treat or negotiate, esp. secretly or with secret purposes (*with*: now rare); also, to work (*on* or *upon*) so as to deceive, beguile, or persuade (as, "You have *practised* on her . . . made her . . . Swerve from her duty to herself and us": Tennyson's "Aylmer's Field," 302).—**prac'tise**, *n.* See *practice*, *n.*—**prac'tised, prac'ticed**, *p. a.* Experienced; skilled; expert; proficient; also, acquired or perfected through practice.—**prac'tis-er, prac'ti-cer** (-ti-sèr), *n.*

prac-ti-tion-er (prak-tish'ọn-ėr), *n.* [From *practician*.] One engaged in the practice of a profession or the like (as, a legal or a medical *practitioner*); a professional or experienced worker; also, one who practises, or adheres to the practice of, something specified (as, "To these simple *practitioners* of the open-air life the settled populations seemed corrupt, crowded, vicious": H. G. Wells's "Outline of History," xxxiv. § 5 D).

pra-do (prä'dō), *n.* [Sp., < L. *pratum*, meadow, plain.] [*cap.*] A celebrated boulevard or fashionable promenade in Madrid, Spain; [*l. c.*] a similar boulevard or promenade elsewhere; also [*cap.*], the famous national art-gallery (Museo del Prado) on the Prado in Madrid.

præ-di-al (prē'di-ạl), **præ-fect** (prē'fekt), etc. See *predial*, *prefect*, etc.

præ-mu-ni-re (prē-mū-nī'rē), *n.* [ML. *præmunire* (a word used in the writ), for L. *præmonere*, forewarn, admonish: see *premonish*.] In *Eng. law*, a writ of summons on the charge of resorting to a foreign court or authority, as that of the Pope, and thus disregarding the supremacy of the sovereign; also, the offense, or the penalty of forfeiture, imprisonment, outlawry, etc., incurred.

præ-no-men (prē-nō'men), *n.*; pl. *-nomina* (-nom'i-nä). [L., < *præ*, before, + *nomen*, name.] The first or personal name of a Roman citizen, as in 'Caius Julius Cæsar.' Cf. *nomen*, *cognomen*, *agnomen*.

præ-pos-i-tor (prę-poz'i-tọr), *n.* See *prepositor* and *præpostor*.

præ-pos-tor, pre-pos-tor (prę-pos'tọr), *n.* [For *præpositor*, *prepositor*, < L. *præpositus*: see *provost*.] At various English public schools, any of certain senior pupils to whom authority is delegated for the government of the students: as, "Tom [at Rugby] at the very bottom of the second table, next to the *præpostor* (who sat at the end to keep order there)" (Hughes's "Tom Brown's School Days," i. 5).

præter-, etc. See *preter-*, etc.

præ-tex-ta (prę-teks'tä), *n.*; pl. *-tæ* (-tē). [L., lit. 'bordered (toga),' prop. fem. of *prætextus*, pp. of *prætexere*, weave before, border: see *pretext*.] In *Rom. antiq.*, a white robe with a purple border, worn orig. by magistrates and some of the priests, and later also by children (by boys until their assumption of the toga virilis and by girls until their marriage): as, "the usual youth's garment, the short *prætexta*, reaching below the knee" (Wiseman's "Fabiola," i. 2).

præ-tor (prē'tor), etc. See *pretor*, etc.

prag-mat-ic (prag-mat'ik). [L. *pragmaticus*, < Gr. πραγματικός, active, businesslike, versed in state affairs, < πρᾶγμα, a thing done, deed, affair, < πράσσειν, do.] **I.** *a.* Pertaining to the affairs of a state or community (as, *pragmatic* sanction, a name given to various imperial decrees issued as fundamental law); also, busy or active; esp., officiously busy; meddlesome; also, conceited; opinionated; dogmatic; also, practical; matter-of-fact; also, treating historical phenomena with special reference to their causes, antecedent conditions, and results (as, *pragmatic* history); in *philos.*, of or pertaining to pragmatism; concerned with practical consequences or values. **II.** *n.* A pragmatic sanction; also, a busybody; also, a conceited person.— **prag-mat'i-cal,** *a.* Pragmatic.—**prag-mat'i-cal-ly,** *adv.* —**prag-mat'i-cal-ness,** *n.*

prag-ma-tism (prag'ma-tizm), *n.* [Gr. πρᾶγμα (πραγματ-): see *pragmatic*.] Pragmatic character or conduct; officiousness; dogmatism; practicality; in *philos.*, a tendency, movement, or more or less definite system of thought in which stress is placed upon practical consequences and practical values as standards for explicating philosophic conceptions, and as tests for determining their value and esp. their truth.—**prag'ma-tist,** *n.* A busybody; also, an adherent of philosophical pragmatism.—**prag-ma-tis'tic,** *a.*

prag-ma-tize (prag'ma-tīz), *v. t.*; *-tized, -tizing.* [Gr. πρᾶγμα (πραγματ-): see *pragmatic*.] To represent (something subjective or imaginary) as real or actual.—**prag'ma-tiz-er** (-tī-zėr), *n.*

Prai-ri-al (prā-ryäl), *n.* [F. *prairial*, < *prairie*: see *prairie*.] In the calendar of the first French republic, the ninth month of the year, extending from May 20 to June 18.

prai-rie (prā'ri or prär'i), *n.* [F. *prairie*, meadow, < ML. *prataria*, < L. *pratum*, meadow.] A meadow; a tract of grassland; esp., an extensive level or slightly undulating treeless tract of land in the Mississippi valley, characterized by a highly fertile soil and covered with a coarse grass (as, "We saw the green, oceanlike expanse of *prairie*, stretching swell over swell to the horizon": Parkman's "Oregon Trail," ii.); also, a small open space in a forest (local, U. S.).— **prai'rie-chick"en,** *n.* The prairie-hen.—**prai'rie-clo"ver,** *n.* Any plant of the fabaceous genus *Petalostemon*, comprising chiefly perennial herbs with small pink, purple, or white flowers in dense heads or spikes.—**prai'ried,** *a.* Abounding in or bordered by prairies.—**prai'rie-dog,** *n.* Any of certain gregarious burrowing rodents (genus *Cynomys*) of American prairies, which utter a bark-like cry.— **prai'rie-hen,** *n.* A species of grouse, *Tympanuchus americanus*, of the American prairies, valued as a game-bird; also, the sharp-tailed grouse, *Pediœcetes phasianellus*, a bird with a slightly crested head, of the northwestern U. S. and Canada.— **prai'rie-schoon"er,** *n.* A large covered wagon used by emigrants in crossing the prairies and plains of North America before the construction of railroads.— **prai'rie-squir"rel,** *n.* Any of various burrowing rodents (genus *Citellus*, or *Spermophilus*) of western North America. Also called *gopher.*—**prai'rie-wolf,** *n.* The coyote.

Prairie-dogs (*Cynomys ludovicianus*).

Prairie-hen (*Tympanuchus americanus*).

praise (prāz), *v. t.*; *praised, praising.* [OF. *preisier*, value, prize, < LL. *pretiare*, prize, < L. *pretium*, price: cf. *prize*².] To set or estimate the value of (obs. or prov.); also, to value highly† or prize†; also, to express approbation or admiration of (as, "She was enthusiastically *praising* the beauties of Gothic architecture": F. M. Crawford's "Mr. Isaacs," vii.); commend; extol; also, to offer grateful homage to (God or a deity), as in words or song (as, "*Praise* God, from whom all blessings flow": Thomas Ken's Doxology, last stanza of hymn "Awake, my soul, and with the sun"); glorify.— **praise,** *n.* The act of praising, or the state of being praised; commendation; laudation; also, the offering of grateful homage in words or song, as an act of worship; often, the musical part of worship; also, a ground for praise, or a merit (archaic: as, "A restless crowd . . . Whose highest *praise* is that they live in vain," Cowper's "Retirement," 23); an object of praise†.—**praise'ful,** *a.* Praiseworthy†; also, giving praise.—**prais'er,** *n.*—**praise'wor"thy,** *a.* Worthy or deserving of praise; commendable; laudable.—**praise'wor"thi-ly,** *adv.*—**praise'wor"thi-ness,** *n.*

Pra-krit (prä'krit), *n.* [Skt. *prākrita*, natural, common, vulgar: cf. *Sanskrit*.] A collective name for the vernacular languages or dialects of northern and central India, esp. those of the ancient and medieval periods, as distinguished from the Sanskrit; also, any of these languages or dialects.— **Pra-krit'ic,** *a.*

pra-line (prä'lēn), *n.* [F.; from Marshal du Plessis-*Praslin* (1598—1675), whose cook invented the sweetmeat.] Any of various confections of almonds or other nut-kernels cooked in a syrup.

prall-tril-ler (präl'tril"ėr), *n.*; pl. *-triller.* [G.] In *music*, a melodic embellishment consisting of a rapid alternation of a principal tone with a supplementary tone one degree above it. Also called *inverted mordent.*

pram¹, praam (präm), *n.* [D. *praam* = LG. and Dan. *pram*.] A flat-bottomed boat or lighter, used in the Netherlands and the Baltic ports for loading and unloading merchant vessels; also, *milit.*, a barge or lighter with mounted guns, used as a floating battery (as, "One of the *praams* mounted ten guns": Marryat's "Peter Simple," lviii.).

pram² (pram), *n.* Shortened form of *perambulator*: as, "The baby, interested in the shadow falling across its *pram*, ceased crying" (Galsworthy's "Saint's Progress," iv. 2). [Colloq., Eng.]

prance (präns), *v.*; *pranced, prancing.* [ME. *prancen, prauncen*; origin obscure.] **I.** *intr.* To spring, or move by springing, from the hind legs, as a horse (as, "Proudly at morning the war-steed was *prancing*": Holmes's "Lexington"); also, to ride on a horse doing this (as, "The insulting tyrant, *prancing* o'er the field . . . His horse's hoofs wet with patrician blood": Addison's "Cato," i. 1); ride gaily, proudly, or insolently, in general, to move or go in an elated manner; move or go arrogantly or insolently; swagger; also, to caper or dance. **II.** *tr.* To cause to prance.— **prance,** *n.* The act of prancing; a prancing movement. —**pran'cer** (prän'sėr), *n.*—**pran'cing-ly,** *adv.*

pran-di-al (pran'di-al), *a.* [L. *prandium*, luncheon, meal.] Of or pertaining to a meal, esp. dinner.—**pran'di-al-ly,** *adv.*

prank¹ (prangk), *v.* [Cf. D. *pronken*, MLG. and G. *prunken*, Dan. *prunke*, make a show, also E. *prink*.] **I.** *tr.* To dress or deck in a showy manner; adorn: as, "all the burghers of New-Amsterdam with their wives and daughters, *pranked* out in their best attire" (Irving's "Knickerbocker's New York," vii. 2); "when violets *pranked* the turf with blue" (Holmes's "Old-Year Song"). **II.** *intr.* To make an ostentatious show or display: as, "White houses *prank* where once were huts" (M. Arnold's "Obermann Once More").

prank² (prangk), *v. i.* [Cf. *prance*, also *prank¹*.] To prance; caper; dance. [Archaic or prov.]—**prank²,** *n.* A trick of a malicious nature (esp. formerly: as, "If she discovered I knew or suspected her guilt, she would be playing off some of her malignant *pranks* on me," C. Brontë's "Jane Eyre," xvi.); now, commonly, a trick of a frolicsome nature (as, "They . . . played all manner of mischievous *pranks*": H. Melville's "Typee," xxvi.); a frolic.—**prank'er,** *n.*—**prank'ish,** *a.* Of the nature of a prank; full of pranks. Also **prank'some** (-sum).

prase (prāz), *n.* [F. *prase*, < L. *prasius*, a leek-green stone, < Gr. πράσιος, leek-green, < πράσον, leek.] A leek-green cryptocrystalline variety of quartz.

pra-se-o-dym-i-um (prā″sē-ọ̄-dim′i-um), *n.* [NL., < Gr. πράσιος, leek-green, + NL. (*di*)*dymium*: see *didymium.*] Chem. sym., Pr; at. wt., 140.9. A rare metallic element: so named from its green salts.

prate (prāt), *v.*; *prated, prating.* [ME. *praten* = D. and LG. *praten.*] **I.** *intr.* To talk much or long and to little purpose; talk or discourse in an empty or windy, foolish way: as, "The boy was very pert and impudent, and *prated* without ceasing" (Smollett's "Humphry Clinker," Sept. 30); "He opposed himself to the demagogue who was *prating* daily of Greece, Rome, and Geneva" (Motley's "Dutch Republic," vi. 2). **II.** *tr.* To utter in empty or foolish talk.—**prate,** *n.* The act of prating; empty or foolish talk: as, "Hold your *prate*" (Lover's "Handy Andy," xviii.). —**prat-er** (prā′tėr), *n.*

prat-in-cole (prat′ing-kōl), *n.* [NL. *pratincola,* < L. *pratum,* meadow, + *incola,* inhabitant.] Any of the limicoline birds of the eastern hemisphere which constitute the genus *Glareola,* allied to the plovers but resembling the swallows, esp. *G. pratincola,* the common European species.

prat-ique (prat′ik, F. prä-tēk′), *n.* [F., lit. 'practice,' < ML. *practica:* see *practician.*] In *com.,* license or permission to hold intercourse with a port, given to a ship after quarantine or on showing a clean bill of health.

Common Pratincole (*Glareola pratincola*).

prat-tle (prat′l), *v.*; *-tled, -tling.* [Freq. and dim. of *prate.*] **I.** *intr.* To talk or chatter in a simple-minded or foolish way (as, "What great ones do the less will *prattle* of": Shakspere's "Twelfth Night," i. 2. 33); babble; now, esp., to talk freely and artlessly, as a child does or like children (said of children and, more or less tolerantly, of older persons: as, "Clive and Rosey *prattled* together," Thackeray's "Newcomes," xliv.); fig., of running water, rustling leaves, etc., to make a light sound suggestive of childish talk. **II.** *tr.* To utter by chattering or babbling (as, "*prattling* scandal as he goes": Cowper's "Task," ii. 382); now, esp., to utter in a childish way; also, to drive or bring by prattle (see Shakspere's "All's Well," iv. 1. 46).—**prat′tle,** *n.* The act of prattling; chatter; babble; esp., childish or artless talk (as, "The boy had plenty of *prattle* in him when he was not snubbed": S. Butler's "Way of All Flesh," xxxii.); fig., a sound suggestive of childish talk, as the noise of running water (as, "the *prattle* of a hidden river": Mrs. Stowe's "Oldtown Folks," xiv.).—**prat′tle-ment,** *n.* Prattling; prattle.—**prat′tler,** *n.*

pra-u (prä′ö or prou), *n.* See *proa.*

prav-i-ty (prav′i-ti), *n.*; pl. *-ties* (-tiz). [L. *pravitas,* < *pravus,* crooked, bad.] Bad or corrupt state; esp., moral perversion or corruption; depravity.

prawn (prân), *n.* [ME. *prane*; origin uncertain.] Any of various shrimp-like decapod crustaceans of the genera *Palæmon, Penæus,* etc. (suborder *Macrura*), certain of which are used as food.

prax-is (prak′sis), *n.* [ML., < Gr. πρᾶξις, < πράσσειν, do.] Practice, esp. as distinguished from theory; also, use or custom; also, an example or collection of examples for practice.

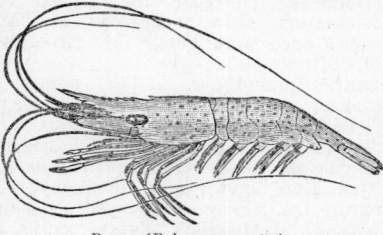

Prawn (*Palæmon serratus*).

pray (prā), *v.* [OF. *preier* (F. *prier*), < L. *precari,* ask, beg, pray; akin to Skt. *prach-,* AS. *friegan,* and G. *fragen,* ask.] **I.** *intr.* To make earnest request or petition; make entreaty or supplication, as to a person or for a thing; esp., in religious usage, to make devout petition to God or to an object of worship; hence, to enter into spiritual communion with God or an object of worship through prayer. *Pray* (representing the earlier *I pray, I pray you, pray you,* etc.) is often used conventionally to emphasize or supplement a request, question, or the like: as, "*Pray, pray,* for my sake, John, give it up" (Trollope's "Warden," vi.); "What the dickens do you want to be educating yourself for, *pray?*" (Kingsley's "Alton Locke," iv.). Cf. *prithee.* **II.** *tr.* To entreat or beseech (a person, etc.) for something; make earnest petition to (a person, etc.), as to do something, or that something may be; esp., in religious use, to make devout petition to (God or an object of worship); also, to make petition or entreaty for (as, "I know not how to *pray* your patience": Shakspere's "Much Ado about Nothing," v. 1. 280); crave; also, to offer (a prayer: as, "I'll *pray* a thousand prayers for thy death," Shakspere's "Measure for Measure," iii. 1. 146); also, to bring, put, etc., by praying (as, to *pray* souls out of purgatory).—**to pray in aid,** to make petition for, or call in, the aid or assistance of some one: as, "The tenant may *pray in aid,* or call for assistance of another, to help him to plead" (Blackstone's "Commentaries," III. 300).

pray-a (prī′ä), *n.* [Pg. *praya, praia,* shore, < L. *plaga,* region, tract: cf. *playa.*] An embankment forming a promenade and carriageway along a water-front, as in India; a bund.

pray-er[1] (prā′ér), *n.* One who prays.

prayer[2] (prār), *n.* [OF. *preiere* (F. *prière*), < ML. *precaria,* orig. neut. pl. of L. *precarius,* obtained by entreaty, < *prex* (*prec-*), entreaty, prayer, connected with *precari,* ask, pray: see *pray,* and cf. *precarious.*] The act of praying; petition; supplication; a petition or entreaty; esp., the action or practice of praying to God or an object of worship; spiritual communion with God or an object of worship, as in supplication, thanksgiving, adoration, or confession; a devout petition to, or any form of spiritual communion with, God or an object of worship; also, a form of words used in or appointed for praying (as, the Lord's *Prayer:* see under *lord, n.*); also, a religious observance, either public or private, consisting wholly or mainly of prayer (as, morning *prayer*; evening *prayer*; family *prayers*); also, that which is prayed for.—**prayer′=book,** *n.* A book of forms of prayer; specif. [usually *cap.*], the Book of Common Prayer (see under *book, n.*).—**prayer′ful,** *a.* Given to, characterized by, or expressive of prayer; devout.—**prayer′ful-ly,** *adv.*—**prayer′ful-ness,** *n.*—**prayer′less,** *a.* Without prayer or the habit of praying; not having the blessing or protection of prayer.—**prayer′less-ly,** *adv.*—**prayer′less-ness,** *n.*—**prayer′=meet″ing,** *n.* A meeting for prayer and other religious exercises.—**prayer′=rug,** *n.* A rug to kneel on at prayer: used esp. by Mohammedans. —**prayer′= wheel,** *n.* A wheel or cylinder rotating on a spindle and inscribed with or containing prayers, used by the Buddhists of Tibet and other parts of the East as a mechanical aid to or a substitute for prayer, each revolu-

Prayer-wheel in Buddhist Temple at Asakusa, Tokyo, Japan.

tion of the wheel or cylinder counting as an uttered prayer.

pre-. [L. *præ-*, also (chiefly ML.) *pre-*, repr. *præ*, adv. and prep., before; akin to Skt. *pra*, before, L. *pro*, Gr. πρό, before, for, and E. *fore* and *for*: see *pro-* and *fore*.] A prefix meaning 'before,' in place, time, order, or rank, occurring orig. in words from the Latin, but now freely used as an English formative, as in *pre-Christian*, *pre-Hellenic*, *premolar*, *preordain*, *prepay*. Cf. *ante-* and *post-*.

preach (prēch), *v.* [OF. *preechier* (F. *prêcher*), < L. *prædicare*, declare publicly, proclaim, assert, LL. preach: see *predicate*.] **I.** *intr.* To pronounce a public discourse upon a religious subject; deliver a sermon; also, to give earnest advice, as on religious or moral subjects; often, to do this in an obtrusive or tedious way. **II.** *tr.* To proclaim or make known by public discourse (the gospel, good tidings, etc.); also, to set forth in the way of exhortation; advocate or inculcate (religious or moral truth, right conduct, etc.) in speech or writing (as, "I have *preached* righteousness in the great congregation," Ps. xl. 9; "She had formed a habit of *preaching* moderation to Gerald," Arnold Bennett's "Old Wives' Tale," iii. 2); also, to deliver (a sermon or the like); also, to bring, put, etc., by preaching (as, "These hundred doctors try To *preach* thee to their school": M. Arnold's "Empedocles on Etna," i. 2).—**to preach down,** to decry by preaching; discourse against; also, to put down or silence by preaching.—**to preach up,** to commend by preaching; discourse in favor of: as, "Philosophy and Christianity both *preach up* forgiveness of injuries" (Fielding's "Tom Jones," ix. 2).—**preach,** *n.* A sermon; a preachment. [Now colloq.]—**preach′er,** *n.* One who preaches; esp., one whose occupation or function it is to preach the gospel; specif., one duly authorized to preach; also [*cap.*], with *the*, the author of, or the speaker in, the book of Ecclesiastes, in the Old Testament (see *ecclesiast* and *Ecclesiastes*); hence, the book itself.—**preach′er-ship,** *n.* —**preach-i-fy** (prē′chi-fī), *v. i.*; *-fied, -fying.* [See *-fy.*] To preach (used in disparagement); moralize in an obtrusive or tedious way. [Colloq.]—**preach′ing,** *n.* The act or practice of one who preaches; the art of delivering sermons; also, that which is preached; a sermon; also, a public religious service with a sermon.—**preach′ing=cross,** *n.* A cross formerly erected to mark a place for open-air preaching, as by monks. —**preach′-ment,** *n.* The act of preaching; also, a sermon or other moralizing discourse, esp. when obtrusive or tedious. —**preach′y,** *a.* Inclined to or suggestive of preaching. [Colloq.]

Preaching-cross at Inveraray, Argyllshire, Scotland.

pre-a-dam-ic (prē-a-dam′ik), *a.* [See *pre-.*] Prior to Adam.—**pre-ad-a-mite** (prē-ad′a-mīt). **I.** *n.* One believed to have lived before Adam; also, one who holds that there were men in existence before Adam. **II.** *a.* That existed before Adam (as, "detached broken fossils of *preadamite* whales": H. Melville's "Moby-Dick," civ.); also, pertaining to the preadamites.—**pre-ad-a-mit′ic** (-mit′ik), *a.* **pre-am-ble** (prē′am-bl), *n.* [= F. *préambule*, < ML. *præambulum*, prop. neut. of LL. *præambulus*, walking before, < L. *præ*, before, + *ambulare*, walk.] A preliminary statement; an introductory paragraph or division of a discourse or writing; a preface; an introduction; esp., the introductory part of a statute, deed, or the like, stating the

reasons and intent of what follows; also, a preliminary or introductory fact or circumstance; esp., a presage.

pre-ap-point (prē-a-point′), *v. t.* [See *pre-.*] To appoint beforehand.—**pre-ap-point′ment,** *n.*

pre-ar-range (prē-a-rānj′), *v. t.* [See *pre-.*] To arrange beforehand.—**pre-ar-range′ment,** *n.*

preb-end (preb′end), *n.* [OF. *prebende* (F. *prébende*), < ML. *præbenda*, prebend, LL. allowance from the state to a private person, prop. neut. pl. gerundive of L. *præbere*, *præhibere*, offer, furnish, < *præ*, before, + *habere*, have, hold: cf. *provender*.] A stipend allotted from the revenues of a cathedral or a collegiate church to a canon or member of the chapter; also, the separate portion of land yielding such a stipend; also, a prebendary.—**pre-ben-dal** (prē-ben′dal), *a.* Pertaining to a prebend or a prebendary.— **preb′en-da-ry** (-en-dā-ri), *n.*; pl. *-ries* (-riz). One who holds a prebend.

Pre=Cam-bri-an (prē-kam′bri-an). [See *pre-.*] In *geol.*: **I.** *a.* Noting, pertaining to, or consisting of rocks older than the Cambrian; specif., according to some authorities, noting or pertaining to a geological period or a system of rocks embracing the whole time or all the rocks previous to the Cambrian. **II.** *n.* Pre-Cambrian rocks or strata; specif., the Pre-Cambrian period or system.

pre-ca-ri-ous (prē-kā′ri-us), *a.* [L. *precarius*, obtained by entreaty or by mere favor, uncertain, precarious: see *prayer*[2].] Dependent on the will or pleasure of another; liable to be withdrawn or lost at the will of another (as, *precarious* tenure); hence, dependent on circumstances beyond one's control; uncertain, unstable, or insecure (as, "His power was more *precarious* than . . . he was willing to admit": Scott's "Quentin Durward," xviii.); liable to adverse changes (as, "For eighteen days he lay in a most *precarious* state": Motley's "Dutch Republic," vi. 5); exposed to or involving danger, dangerous, perilous, or risky (as, "the life of a sea-rover . . . a simple, venturesome, *precarious* life, full of risks and leaving no time for introspection": J. Conrad's "Rover," xi.); also, having insufficient, little, or no foundation, as an opinion, inference, or ostensible proof.—**pre-ca′ri-ous-ly,** *adv.*—**pre-ca′ri-ous-ness,** *n.*

prec-a-tive (prek′a-tiv), *a.* [LL. *precativus*, < L. *precari*: see *pray*.] Expressing entreaty or desire; supplicatory.

prec-a-to-ry (prek′a-tō-ri), *a.* [LL. *precatorius*, < L. *precari*: see *pray*.] Pertaining to, of the nature of, or expressing entreaty or supplication.

pre-cau-tion (prē-kâ′shon), *n.* [F. *précaution*, < LL. *præcautio(n-)*, < L. *præcavere*, guard against beforehand, < *præ*, before, + *cavere*, be on one's guard.] Caution employed beforehand; prudent foresight; also, a measure taken beforehand to ward off possible evil or secure good results (as, "Their vigilant general took all possible *precautions* for their safety": Prescott's "Conquest of Mexico," iii. 6).—**pre-cau′tion-al,** *a.* Precautionary.—**pre-cau′tion-a-ry** (-a-ri), *a.* Pertaining to or of the nature of precaution or a precaution (as, "the *precautionary* measures which had been taken," Motley's "Dutch Republic," vi. 6; "throwing a *precautionary* glance around, as if to assure himself that we were alone," Lever's "Harry Lorrequer," xvii.); also, expressing or advising precaution.—**pre-cau′tious** (-shus), *a.* Using or displaying precaution.

pre-cede (prē-sēd′), *v.*; *-ceded, -ceding.* [OF. *preceder* (F. *précéder*), < L. *præcedere* (pp. *præcessus*), < *præ*, before, + *cedere*, go.] **I.** *tr.* To go before, as in place, order, rank, importance, or time; also, to introduce by something preliminary; preface. **II.** *intr.* To go or come before.— **pre-ced′ence** (-sē′dens), *n.* The act or fact of preceding; priority in order, rank, importance, etc.; priority in time, or previous existence or occurrence; specif., the right to precede others in ceremonies or social formalities; ceremonial priority; social superiority; also, the order to be observed ceremonially by persons of different ranks; also, something that precedes†. Also **pre-ced′en-cy.**—**pre-ced′ent** (-sē′dent), *a.* Preceding; prior; previous.— **pre-ce-dent** (pres′ē-dent), *n.* Something preceding†; a sign†, token†, or indication†; an original from which a copy is made†; also, a preceding instance or case which may serve as an example for or a justification in subsequent cases;

---

specif., a legal decision or form of proceeding serving as an authoritative rule or pattern in future similar or analogous cases.—**pre-ce-dent-ed** (pres'ẹ-den-ted), *a.* Justified by precedent.—**pre-ce-den-tial** (pres-ẹ-den'shạl), *a.* Of the nature of or constituting a precedent; also, having precedence; preceding; preliminary; also, pertaining to social precedence.—**pre-ced-ent-ly** (prẹ-sē'dẹnt-li), *adv.*—**pre-ced'ing** (-sē'ding), *p. a.* That precedes; going or coming before; previous.

pre-cent (prẹ-sent'), *v. i.* [Back-formation from *precentor.*] To act as precentor.

pre-cen-tor (prẹ-sen'tọr), *n.* [L. *præcentor,* < *præcinere,* sing before, < *præ,* before, + *canere,* sing.] One who leads a church choir or congregation in singing.—**pre-cen-to-ri-al** (prē-sen-tō'ri-ạl), *a.*—**pre-cen'tor-ship,** *n.*

pre-cept (prē'sept), *n.* [L. *præceptum,* prop. neut. of *præceptus,* pp. of *præcipere,* take beforehand, admonish, direct, instruct, < *præ,* before, + *capere,* take.] A commandment or direction given as a rule of action or conduct; esp., an injunction as to moral conduct; a maxim; also, a rule, as for the performance of some technical operation; in *law,* a writ or warrant; a written order issued pursuant to law, as a sheriff's order for an election.—**pre-cep-tive** (prẹ-sep'tiv), *a.* [L. *præceptivus.*] Of the nature of or expressing a precept; mandatory; giving instructions; instructive.

pre-cep-tor (prẹ-sep'tọr), *n.* [L. *præceptor,* < *præcipere,* instruct: see *precept.*] An instructor; a teacher; a tutor; also, the head of a preceptory.—**pre-cep-to-ri-al** (prē-sep-tō'ri-ạl), *a.*—**pre-cep'tor-ship,** *n.*—**pre-cep'to-ry** (-tọ-ri), *n.;* pl. *-ries* (-riz). [ML. *præceptoria.*] A subordinate house or community of the Knights Templars.—**pre-cep'-tress,** *n.* A female preceptor.

pre-ces-sion (prẹ-sesh'ọn), *n.* [LL. *præcessio(n-),* < L. *præcedere,* E. *precede.*] The act or fact of preceding; precedence; in *astron.,* the precession of the equinoxes (see phrase below); hence, in *physics,* etc., any motion analogous to that of the axis of the earth in the precession of the equinoxes; the slow, steady motion in which the axis of a rapidly spinning top or the like describes a right circular cone about the vertical.—**precession of the equinoxes,** in *astron.,* the earlier occurrence of the equinoxes in each successive sidereal year because of a slow retrograde motion of the equinoctial points along the ecliptic, this being due to a gradual change in the direction of the earth's axis caused by the combined action of the sun, moon, etc., on the mass of matter accumulated about the earth's equator; hence, this motion of the equinoctial points, or this change in direction of the earth's axis. Cf. *zodiac.*—**pre-ces'sion-al,** *a.*

pré-cieuse (prā-syèz'), *n.;* pl. *-cieuses* (-syèz'). [F., fem. of *précieux,* E. *precious.*] A woman who affects extreme or excessive refinement of language or taste.

pre-cinct (prē'singkt), *n.* [ML. *præcinctum,* prop. neut. of L. *præcinctus,* pp. of *præcingere,* gird about, surround, < *præ,* before, + *cingere,* gird.] A walled or otherwise bounded or limited space within which a building or place is situated; esp., the ground immediately surrounding a church, temple, or the like (as, the *precinct* of a cathedral; "They reached the *precinct* of the God, And on the hallowed turf their feet now trod," W. Morris's "Jason," ix. 1); *pl.,* the parts or regions immediately about any place, or the environs (as, to approach the *precincts* of a town); also, *sing.,* a space or place of definite or understood limits (as, "She made the House . . . like a home to him, and the garden a familiar *precinct,*" Hawthorne's "House of the Seven Gables," xii.; "The slightest invasion of the *precincts* which had been assigned to another tribe produced desperate skirmishes," Scott's "Guy Mannering," vii.); specif., a district within certain boundaries, for governmental, administrative, or other purposes (as, a police *precinct*; an election *precinct*); also, an inclosing boundary or limit (often in *pl.*: as, "The whole population of the valley seemed to be gathered within the *precincts* of the grove," H. Melville's "Typee," xxii.).

pre-ci-os-i-ty (presh-i-os'i-ti), *n.;* pl. *-ties* (-tiz). [OF. *preciosite* (F. *préciosité*), < L. *pretiositas.*] The quality of being precious; now, esp., fastidious or carefully affected refinement, as in language, style, or taste; hence, the body of persons exhibiting such refinement (as, "All London had

indeed been present . . . The entire *preciosity* of the metropolis!" Arnold Bennett's "The Old Adam," vii.); also, *pl.,* precious things, or articles of value (now rare: as, "five invaluable trunks, full of *preciosities,*" Arnold Bennett's "Helen with the High Hand," xix.).

pre-cious (presh'us). [OF. *precios* (F. *précieux*), < L. *pretiosus,* < *pretium,* E. *price.*] **I.** *a.* Of great price or value, valuable, or costly (as, *precious* merchandise; *precious* metals, such as gold and silver; *precious* stones, such as the diamond, ruby, sapphire, etc.); also, of great worth, or deserving to be highly valued or esteemed (as, *precious* remains of ancient art; the *precious* light of day; "O sovran, virtuous, *precious* of all trees In Paradise!" Milton's "Paradise Lost," ix. 795); often, of great moral or spiritual worth (as, the *precious* heritage of an honorable name; "the *precious* blood of Christ," 1 Pet. i. 19); worth much, or of great importance (*to*: as, "They were folk to whom sleep was *precious,*" Galsworthy's "Dark Flower," i. 11); dear or beloved (as, my *precious* child); also, choice, fine, or 'pretty' (used ironically, to imply the opposite: as, he's a *precious* specimen; "Did you ever see such a *precious* set of villains?" Marryat's "Mr. Midshipman Easy," xxx.); egregious, arrant, or gross (as, "Here, Mr. Speaker, is a *precious* mockery," Burke's "American Taxation"); very great (colloq.: as, "It's hard enough to see one's way, a *precious* sight harder than I thought last night," Hughes's "Tom Brown's School Days," ii. 7); also, exhibiting or affecting a refined delicacy of style or taste, as language, artistic work, etc., or persons (from a French use: cf. *précieuse*); often, affectedly or excessively refined or nice. **II.** *n.* Precious one; darling: a term of endearment.—**pre'cious,** *adv.* Extremely; very: as, "I'll take *precious* good care never to sing in a theatre again!" (Du Maurier's "Trilby," vii.). [Colloq.]—**pre'cious-ly,** *adv.*—**pre'-cious-ness,** *n.*

pre-ci-pice (pres'i-pis), *n.* [F. *précipice,* < L. *præcipitium,* < *præceps* (*præcipit-*), headlong: see *precipitate.*] A headlong fall†; also, a lofty bank or mass of rock, etc., from the edge of which one falling would plunge directly downward (as, "A few steps more, and I was standing on the very edge of a bank, a *precipice* not less than fifty feet deep": W. H. Hudson's "Green Mansions," vi.); a cliff with a vertical, or nearly vertical, or overhanging face; fig., a situation of great peril; a critical position.

pre-cip-i-ta-ble (prẹ-sip'i-tạ-bl), *a.* That may be precipitated, as from solution.—**pre-cip″i-ta-bil'i-ty** (-bil'i-ti), *n.*

pre-cip-i-tance (prẹ-sip'i-tạns), *n.* Precipitant action or character; headlong haste; precipitancy: as, "The youth expects to force his way by genius, vigour, and *precipitance*" (Johnson's "Rasselas," xxvi.).—**pre-cip'i-tan-cy** (-tạn-si), *n.;* pl. *-cies* (-siz). The quality or fact of being precipitant (as, "hurried on by the *precipitancy* of youth": Swift's "Gulliver's Travels," i. 7); headlong or rash haste; also, *pl.,* hasty or rash acts.

pre-cip-i-tant (prẹ-sip'i-tạnt). [L. *præcipitans* (*-ant-*), ppr. of *præcipitare:* see *precipitate.*] **I.** *a.* Falling headlong; descending or directed straight downward (as, "He . . . Downright into the world's first region throws His flight *precipitant*": Milton's "Paradise Lost," iii. 563); also, rushing headlong, rapidly, or hastily onward; proceeding with headlong haste; acting or done with precipitation; hasty; rash; unduly sudden or abrupt. **II.** *n.* In *chem.,* anything that causes precipitation.—**pre-cip'i-tant-ly,** *adv.*

pre-cip-i-tate (prẹ-sip'i-tāt), *v.;* *-tated, -tating.* [L. *præcipitatus,* pp. of *præcipitare,* cast or fall headlong, < *præceps* (*præcipit-*), headlong, lit. 'head first,' < *præ,* before, + *caput,* head.] **I.** *tr.* To cast down headlong; fling or hurl down; hence, to cast, plunge, or send violently or abruptly (as, to *precipitate* one's self into a struggle or upon an adversary); also, to cause to move or proceed rapidly; urge on; hasten; often, to hasten the occurrence of (as, "Doubtless the mere mention of Mr. Alexander . . . *precipitated* that which had so long impended": Stevenson's "Master of Ballantrae," x.); bring about in haste or suddenly (as, to *precipitate* a quarrel or a catastrophe); in *chem.,* to separate (a substance) out in solid form from a solution, as by means of a reagent; in *physics,* to condense (moisture) from a state of vapor in the form of rain, dew, etc. **II.** *intr.* To fall headlong†; also, to rush headlong, or proceed rapidly or with haste (obs. or rare); in *chem.*, to separate from a solution as a precipitate; in *physics*, to be condensed as rain, dew, etc.—**pre-cip'i-tate** (-tāt), *a.* Cast down or falling headlong; headlong; also, rushing headlong or rapidly onward (as, "Through the Sweet-water Valley *precipitate* leaps the Nebraska": Longfellow's "Evangeline," ii. 4); proceeding rapidly or with great haste (as, a *precipitate* retreat); greatly hurried; exceedingly sudden or abrupt; also, acting, or done or made, in sudden haste or without due deliberation (as, "Some of the fickle populace began to doubt whether they had not been rather *precipitate* in deposing his brother," Irving's "Conquest of Granada," xxxv.; "Any *precipitate* speech, or hasty action, would be a crime," Mrs. H. Ward's "Robert Elsmere," xxvi.); overhasty; rash.—**pre-cip'i-tate** (-tāt), *n.* In *chem.*, a substance precipitated from a solution; in *physics*, moisture condensed in the form of rain, dew, etc.—**pre-cip'i-tate-ly** (-tāt-li), *adv.*—**pre-cip'i-tate-ness**, *n.*

pre-cip-i-ta-tion (prē-sip-i-tā'shon), *n.* [L. *præcipitatio(n-).*] The act of precipitating, or the state of being precipitated; a casting down or falling headlong; a hastening or hurrying in movement, procedure, or action; hence, sudden or precipitate haste; unwise or rash rapidity; in *chem.* and *physics*, the precipitating of a substance from a solution, or of moisture in the form of rain, dew, etc.; also, that which is precipitated, as a chemical precipitate, or as rain or dew.—**pre-cip'i-ta-tor**, *n.*

pre-cip-i-tin (prē-sip'i-tin), *n.* [From *precipitate.*] Any of a group of substances developed in certain blood-serums, capable of precipitating albuminoid substances, etc.

pre-cip-i-tous (prē-sip'i-tus), *a.* [Obs. F. *precipiteux*, < L. *præceps* (*præcipit-*), headlong: see *precipitate.*] Rushing headlong or with great rapidity (now rare: as, "The sweep Of some *precipitous* rivulet to the wave," Tennyson's "Enoch Arden," 583); also, precipitate†, hasty†, or rash†; also, of the nature of a precipice, or characterized by precipices (as, a *precipitous* wall of rock; "hills as steep as they could be without being *precipitous*," Scott's "Guy Mannering," xxv.); extremely or impassably steep.—**pre-cip'i-tous-ly**, *adv.*—**pre-cip'i-tous-ness**, *n.*

pré-cis (prā-sē'), *n.*; pl. *précis* (-sē). [F., noun use of *précis*, adj.: see *precise.*] An abstract or summary.

pre-cise (prē-sīs'), *a.* [OF. *precis* (F. *précis*), < L. *præcisus*, cut short, brief, pp. of *præcidere*, cut off, cut short, abridge, < *præ*, before, + *cædere*, cut.] Definitely or strictly stated, defined, or fixed; or definite or exact (as, *precise* directions or stipulations; a more *precise* limitation of powers); definite or distinct in the mind, as ideas, etc.; also, exactly identified, or identical, particular, or very (as, the *precise* point in question; that is the *precise* reason for the change); being just that, and not some other; also, being exactly that, and neither more nor less (as, the *precise* amount or weight: opposed to *approximate*); also, definite or exact in statement, as a person (as, please be more *precise* on this point); carefully distinct, as the voice or utterance; also, exact in measuring, recording, etc., as an instrument; also, strict in observance of rules, usages, or forms; punctilious, scrupulous, or particular; sometimes, excessively or rigidly particular; puritanical; in general, exact, studied, careful, or particular (as, a *precise* arrangement of furniture in a room; *precise* handwriting; *precise* dress).—**pre-cise'ly**, *adv.*—**pre-cise'ness**, *n.*

pre-ci-sian (prē-sizh'an), *n.* [From *precise.*] One who adheres punctiliously to the observance of rules or forms, esp. in matters of religion; specif., one of the English Puritans of the 16th and 17th centuries (as, "Some *precisians* had scruples about teaching the Latin grammar, because the names of Mars, Bacchus, and Apollo occurred in it": Macaulay's "Hist. of Eng.," i.).—**pre-ci'sian-ism**, *n.*

pre-ci-sion (prē-sizh'on), *n.* [F. *précision*, < L. *præcisio(n-)*, < *præcidere*: see *precise.*] The quality or state of being precise, definite, or exact as to statement (as, *precision* of expression; to speak with *precision*); also, exactness or accuracy, often mathematical or mechanical exactness (as, "The Spaniards had occasion . . . to admire the mechanical science of the Aztecs, in the geometrical *precision* with which the work was executed": Prescott's "Conquest of Mexico,"

iii. 9); also, punctiliousness, particularity, or careful exactness (as, "dressed with his usual *precision* and neatness": Marryat's "King's Own," xvii.).—**pre-ci'sion-ist**, *n.* One who insists on or affects precision, esp. in expression or language; a purist.

pre-clude (prē-klöd'), *v. t.*; *-cluded, -cluding.* [L. *præcludere* (pp. *præclusus*), < *præ*, before, + *cludere, claudere*, shut, close.] To close (a passage, etc.) so as to prevent access or use (obs. or archaic); also, to shut out or exclude (chiefly fig.); prevent the presence, existence, or occurrence of (as, "To have greatly dreamed *precludes* low ends," Lowell's "Columbus," 143; "a tranquillity which . . . his wife's presence would have *precluded*," J. H. Newman's "Callista," ii.); render impossible; also, to shut out, debar, or prevent (a person, etc.) from something (as, to be *precluded* from enjoying a privilege).—**pre-clu'sion** (-klö'zhon), *n.* [L. *præclusio(n-).*] The act of precluding, or the state of being precluded.—**pre-clu'sive** (-siv), *a.* Tending or serving to preclude; preventive (*of*).—**pre-clu'sive-ly**, *adv.*

pre-co-cious (prē-kō'shus), *a.* [L. *præcox* (*præcoc-*), early ripe, precocious, < *præcoquere*, cook beforehand, ripen early, < *præ*, before, + *coquere*, cook: cf. *apricot.*] Flowering, fruiting, or ripening early, as plants, fruit, etc.; fig., forward in development, esp. mental development, as a child or young person; prematurely developed, as the mind, faculties, etc.; pertaining to or showing premature development (as, "Her imperfect articulation was the least *precocious* thing she had about her," C. Brontë's "Villette," iii.; a *precocious* remark); in general, of early development, or occurring before the natural time (as, "In the Italian States, as in many natural bodies, untimely decrepitude was the penalty of *precocious* maturity": Macaulay's "Essays," Machiavelli); in *bot.*, bearing blossoms before leaves, as plants; appearing before the leaves, as flowers.—**pre-co'cious-ly**, *adv.*—**pre-co'cious-ness**, *n.*—**pre-co'ci-ty** (-kos'i-ti), *n.*; pl. *-ties* (-tiz). The quality of being precocious; early maturity; forwardness in development (as, "Although scarcely yet fifteen years old, she was a grown woman . . . It was uncanny — the *precocity* of the children of the poor!" Arnold Bennett's "Hilda Lessways," i. 12); esp., premature advancement or ripeness of the mental powers, as of a child; also, a precocious child.

pre-cog-ni-tion (prē-kog-nish'on), *n.* [LL. *præcognitio(n-)*, < L. *præcognoscere*, foreknow, < *præ*, before, + *cognoscere*, come to know: see *cognition.*] Previous cognition or knowledge; foreknowledge; in *Sc. law*, a preliminary examination, as of witnesses; the evidence taken at it.

pre-con-ceive (prē-kon-sēv'), *v. t.* [See *pre-.*] To conceive beforehand; form an idea of in advance.—**pre-con-cep'tion** (-sep'shon), *n.* The act of preconceiving; also, a conception or opinion formed in advance of actual knowledge (as, "the incapacity of actual objects for satisfying our *preconceptions* of them": Lamb's "Old Margate Hoy").

pre-con-cert (prē-kon-sèrt'), *v. t.* [See *pre-.*] To concert or arrange beforehand: as, "The rebellion was *preconcerted* and simultaneous" (Froude's "Cæsar," vii.); "acting in concert by the aid of *preconcerted* signals" (Irving's "Conquest of Granada," iv.).—**pre-con'cert** (-kon'sèrt), *n.* A previous concert or arrangement; preconcerted agreement or action: as, "We arose, as if by *preconcert*, to make examination of our treasure" (Poe's "Gold-Bug").—**pre-con-cert'ed-ly**, *adv.*

pre-con-demn (prē-kon-dem'), *v. t.* [See *pre-.*] To condemn beforehand.—**pre-con-dem-na'tion** (-kon-dem-nā'shon), *n.*

pre-con-di-tion (prē-kon-dish'on), *n.* [See *pre-.*] An antecedent or preliminary condition; a prerequisite.

pre-co-nize (prē'kō-nīz), *v. t.*; *-nized, -nizing.* [ML. *præconizare*, < L. *præco(n-)*, crier, herald.] To proclaim; publish; commend publicly; also, to summon publicly; in the *Rom. Cath. Ch.*, of the Pope, to ratify in a public consistory the appointment of (a bishop, etc.).—**pre''co-ni-za'tion** (-ni-zā'shon), *n.*

pre-con-scious (prē-kon'shus), *a.* [See *pre-.*] Antecedent to consciousness.

pre-con-sid-er (prē-kon-sid'ėr), *v. t.* [See *pre-.*] To consider beforehand.—**pre-con-sid-er-a'tion** (-ė-rā'shon), *n.*

pre-con-tract (prē-kon-trakt′), *v. t.* or *i.* [See *pre-*.] To contract beforehand.—**pre-con′tract** (-kon′trakt), *n.* A previous contract; esp., a preëxisting contract of marriage.

pre-curse (prē-kėrs′), *v. t.*; *-cursed, -cursing.* [L. *præcursus,* pp. of *præcurrere,* < *præ,* before, + *currere,* run.] To run or go before; forerun; precede and indicate the approach of.—**pre-curse′**†, *n.* A forerunning.—**pre-cur′sive** (-kėr′siv), *a.* Precursory.—**pre-cur′sor,** *n.* [L. *præcursor.*] One who or that which runs or goes before; a forerunner; a predecessor; esp., one who or that which precedes and indicates the approach of another or something else.—**pre-cur′so-ry** (-sọ-ri), *a.* Of the nature of a precursor; introductory; indicative of something to follow.

pre-da-cious (prē-dā′shus), *a.* [L. *prædari,* take booty, E. *prey, v.*] Living by prey; disposed to prey or plunder; predatory.—**pre-da′cious-ness, pre-da′ci-ty** (-das′i-ti), *n.*

pre-date (prē-dāt′), *v. t.* [See *pre-*.] To date before the actual time; also, to precede in date.

pred-a-to-ry (pred′a-tọ-ri), *a.* [L. *prædatorius,* < *prædari,* take booty, E. *prey, v.*] Of, pertaining to, or characterized by plundering, pillaging, or robbery (as, "the ruthless *predatory* instinct of certain bold and unscrupulous persons," F. M. Crawford's "Mr. Isaacs," i.; "a *predatory* war," Macaulay's "Hist. of Eng.," i.); also, addicted to or living by plundering or robbery (as, a *predatory* race; *predatory* bands); in *zoöl.,* habitually preying upon other animals.—**pred′a-to-ri-ly,** *adv.*—**pred′a-to-ri-ness,** *n.*

pre-de-cease (prē-dē-sēs′), *v. t.* [See *pre-*.] To die before (a person or an event).—**pre-de-cease′,** *n.* Prior decease.

pre-de-ces-sor (prē-dē-ses′or or pred-ē-), *n.* [OF. *predecesseur* (F. prédécesseur), < LL. *prædecessor,* < L. *præ,* before, + *decessor,* one retiring from office, < *decedere,* depart: see *decedent.*] One who precedes another in an office, position, etc.; also, anything to which something else has succeeded (as, "The features of this Ann. Dom. partook of the character of its *predecessor*": Galt's "Annals of the Parish," xxxi.); also, an ancestor or forefather.

pre-del-la (prē-del′ä), *n.* [It.] The platform on which an altar is placed; also, a raised shelf at the back of an altar; also, a painting or sculpture on the front of this, often forming an appendage to an altarpiece; hence, any painting forming an appendage to another painting.

pre-des-ig-nate (prē-dez′ig-nāt), *v. t.* [See *pre-*.] To designate beforehand; in *logic,* to designate by prefixing a sign or word of logical quantity.—**pre-des-ig-na′tion** (-nā′shọn), *n.*

pre-des-ti-na-ri-an (prē-des-ti-nā′ri-an). [From *predestine.*] **I.** *a.* Of or pertaining to predestination; believing in the doctrine of predestination. **II.** *n.* One who holds the doctrine of predestination.—**pre-des-ti-na′ri-an-ism,** *n.*

pre-des-ti-nate (prē-des′ti-nāt), *v. t.*; *-nated, -nating.* [L. *prædestinatus,* pp. of *prædestinare,* < *præ,* before, + *destinare,* E. *destine.*] To foreordain; predetermine; in *theol.,* to foreordain by divine decree or purpose.—**pre-des′ti-nate,** *a.* Predestinated; foreordained. [Archaic.]—**pre-des-ti-na′tion** (-nā′shọn), *n.* [LL. *prædestinatio(n-).*] The act of predestinating or predestining, or the resulting state; fate or destiny; in *theol.,* the action of God in foreordaining from eternity whatever comes to pass; the decree of God by which men are foreordained to everlasting happiness or misery, esp. to everlasting happiness (election).—**pre-des′ti-na-tor,** *n.*

pre-des-tine (prē-des′tin), *v. t.*; *-tined, -tining.* [OF. *predestiner* (F. prédestiner), < L. *prædestinare:* see *predestinate.*] To destine beforehand; foreordain; predetermine; predestinate.

pre-ter-mine (prē-dē-tėr′min), *v. t.*; *-mined, -mining.* [LL. *prædeterminare,* < L. *præ,* before, + *determinare,* E. *determine.*] To determine or decide beforehand; ordain beforehand, or predestine; also, to direct or impel beforehand to something.—**pre-de-ter′mi-na-ble** (-mi-na-bl), *a.*—**pre-de-ter-mi-na′tion** (-nā′shọn), *n.*

pre-di-al (prē′di-al), *a.* [ML. *prædialis,* < L. *prædium,* farm, estate.] Pertaining to or consisting of land or farms (as, *predial* estates); real; landed; also, arising from or consequent upon the occupation of farms or land (as, *predial* tithes); also, attached to farms or land (as, *predial* serfs); owing service as tenanting land.

pred-i-ca-ble (pred′i-ka-bl). [ML. *prædicabilis.*] **I.** *a.* That may be predicated or affirmed; assertable. **II.** *n.* That which may be predicated; an attribute; specif., in *logic,* any one of the various kinds of predicate (in the Aristotelian logic, genus, species, difference, property, and accident) that may be used of a subject.

pre-dic-a-ment (prē-dik′a-ment), *n.* [LL. *prædicamentum.*] That which is predicated or asserted; specif., one of the classes or categories of logical predications; also, a class or kind about which a statement is made; also, a particular state, condition, or situation; esp., an unpleasant, trying, or dangerous situation.—**pre-dic-a-men′tal** (-men′tal), *a.*

pred-i-cant (pred′i-kant). [LL. *prædicans (-ant-),* ppr. of *prædicare,* preach: see *predicate* and *preach.*] **I.** *a.* Preaching. **II.** *n.* A preacher.

pred-i-cate (pred′i-kāt), *v.*; *-cated, -cating.* [L. *prædicatus,* pp. of *prædicare,* declare publicly, proclaim, assert, LL. preach, < L. *præ,* before, + *dicare,* declare: cf. *preach.*] **I.** *tr.* To proclaim or declare; affirm or assert; esp., to affirm as an attribute or quality of something (as, "the schoolmen . . . deeming it necessary to *predicate* metaphysical infinity of all the divine attributes": Hallam's "Literature of Europe," iv. 4. § 33); specif., to affirm or assert (something) of the subject of a logical proposition; make (a term) the predicate of such a proposition; also, to connote or imply; also, to found or base (a statement, action, etc.) on something (U. S.). **II.** *intr.* To make an affirmation or assertion.—**pred′i-cate** (-kat). **I.** *a.* Predicated; in *gram.,* belonging to the predicate; made, through the instrumentality of a verb, to qualify its subject, or sometimes its direct object, as the adjective *ill* in 'he is ill' and 'it made him ill,' and the noun *captain* in 'he is captain' and 'they elected him captain.' **II.** *n.* In *logic,* that which is predicated or said of the subject in a proposition; in *gram.,* the word or words expressing what is affirmed or denied of a subject, being a finite verb alone or a finite verb with object, complement, etc.—**pred-i-ca′tion** (-kā′shọn), *n.* [L. *prædicatio(n-).*] The act of predicating; affirmation; assertion; specif., in *logic,* the assertion of something about a subject.—**pred′i-ca-tive** (-ka-tiv), *a.* [L. *prædicativus.*] Predicating; expressing predication.—**pred′i-ca-tive-ly,** *adv.* As a predicate; in the predicate.—**pred′i-ca-to-ry** (-ka-tọ-ri), *a.* Pertaining to preaching.

pre-dict (prē-dikt′), *v.* [L. *prædictus,* pp. of *prædicere,* < *præ,* before, + *dicere,* say.] **I.** *tr.* To foretell; prophesy. **II.** *intr.* To foretell the future; prophesy.—**pre-dict′a-ble,** *a.* That may be predicted.—**pre-dic′tion** (-dik′shọn), *n.* [L. *prædictio(n-).*] The act of predicting; also, an instance of this; a prophecy.—**pre-dic′tive,** *a.* Prophetic.—**pre-dic′tive-ly,** *adv.*—**pre-dic′tor,** *n.*

pre-di-gest (prē-di-jest′ or prē-dī-), *v. t.* [See *pre-*.] To digest beforehand; specif., to treat (food), before introduction into the body, by an artificial process similar to digestion, in order to make it more easily digestible.—**pre-di-ges′tion** (-jes′chọn), *n.*

pre-di-lec-tion (prē-di-lek′shọn or pred-i-), *n.* [F. *prédilection,* < ML. *prædiligere,* prefer, < L. *præ,* before, + *diligere,* choose, like: see *diligent.*] A prepossession of the mind in favor of something; a partiality: as, "In spite of her *predilection* for my powerful rival, she liked to flirt with me" (Irving's "Tales of a Traveler," ii. 7).

pre-dis-pose (prē-dis-pōz′), *v. t.* [See *pre-*.] To dispose beforehand; give a previous inclination or tendency to (as, "The early study of Larochefoucauld and his school had not *predisposed* me to an unlimited belief in the disinterestedness of mankind": F. M. Crawford's "Mr. Isaacs," ii.); render subject or liable (as, "Semi-starvation and neglected colds had *predisposed* most of the pupils to receive infection": C. Brontë's "Jane Eyre," ix.); also, to dispose of beforehand.—**pre-dis-po-si′tion** (-pọ-zish′ọn), *n.* The condition of being predisposed; previous inclination or tendency; susceptibility or liability; specif., in *pathol.,* a condition of the body in which a slight exciting cause may produce a disease.

pre-dom-i-nant (prē-dom′i-nant), *a.* Predominating; having ascendancy, power, authority, or influence over others; superior; ascendant; also, prevailing or prevalent (as, "the *predominant* opinion of man . . . upon sudden death":

De Quincey's "English Mail-Coach," ii.).—**pre-dom′i-nance**, *n.*—**pre-dom′i-nant-ly**, *adv.*
pre-dom-i-nate (prē-dom′i-nāt), *v.*; *-nated, -nating.* [L. *præ*, before, + *dominari* (pp. *dominatus*), bear rule: see *dominate*.] **I.** *intr.* To have or exert controlling power (often with *over*: as, "Knowledge will always *predominate* over ignorance, as man governs the other animals," Johnson's "Rasselas," xi.); surpass others in authority or influence; be superior; also, to be the stronger or leading element (as, "In this character of the Americans, a love of freedom is the *predominating* feature": Burke's "Conciliation with the Colonies"); preponderate; prevail; also, to occupy a dominating position, or tower (*over*: as, "The tall gables and elms of the rectory *predominate* over the tiny white-washed church," George Eliot's "Adam Bede," v.). **II.** *tr.* To dominate over; prevail over: as, "Let your close fire *predominate* his smoke" (Shakspere's "Timon of Athens," iv. 3. 142).—**pre-dom′i-nat-ing-ly** (-nā-ting-li), *adv.*—**pre-dom-i-na′tion** (-nā′shon), *n.* The act or fact of predominating; superior influence; ascendancy.
pre-doom (prē-döm′), *v. t.* [See *pre-*.] To doom beforehand.
pree (prē), *v. t.* [For *preve, prieve*, old var. of *prove*.] To make proof of; try; taste. [Sc. and north. Eng.]
pre-ë-lect (prē-ē-lekt′), *v. t.* [See *pre-*.] To elect or choose beforehand.—**pre-ë-lec′tion** (-lek′shon), *n.*
pre-ëm-i-nent (prē-em′i-nent), *a.* [L. *præeminens* (-ent-), ppr. of *præeminere*, < *præ*, before, + *eminere*, stand out: see *eminent*.] Eminent before or above others; superior to or surpassing others; distinguished beyond others.—**pre-ëm′i-nence**, *n.*—**pre-ëm′i-nent-ly**, *adv.*
pre-ëmpt (prē-empt′), *v.* [Back-formation from *preëmption*.] **I.** *tr.* To secure, as land, by preëmption; hence, to occupy (land) in order to establish a preëmptive title; fig., to acquire or appropriate beforehand. **II.** *intr.* To preëmpt land.
pre-ëmp-tion (prē-emp′shon), *n.* [L. *præ*, before, + *emere* (pp. *emptus*), buy.] The act or right of purchasing before or in preference to others.—**pre-ëmp′tive**, *a.* Pertaining to or of the nature of preëmption.—**pre-ëmp′tor**, *n.* [LL. *præemptor*.] One who preëmpts; esp., one who takes up land with the privilege of preëmption.—**pre-ëmp′to-ry** (-tō-ri), *a.* Preëmptive.
preen[1] (prēn), *n.* [AS. *prēon*.] A pin. [Sc. and north. Eng.]
preen[2] (prēn), *v. t.* [Prob. var. of *prune*[2].] To trim or dress (the feathers, etc.) with the beak, as a bird does (as, "Past the Ryemeadow's lonely woodland nook Where many a stubble gray-goose *preens* her wing": Masefield's "Daffodil Fields," i.); hence, to prepare, dress, or array (one's self) carefully in making the toilet.
pre-ën-gage (prē-en-gāj′), *v. t.* or *i.* [See *pre-*.] To engage beforehand.—**pre-ën-gage′ment**, *n.*
pre-ës-tab-lish (prē-es-tab′lish), *v. t.* [See *pre-*.] To establish beforehand.—**pre-ës-tab′lish-ment**, *n.*
pre-ëx-il-i-an (prē-eg-zil′i-an), *a.* [See *pre-*.] Previous to the Babylonian exile or captivity of the Jews. Also **pre-ëx-il′ic**.
pre-ëx-ist (prē-eg-zist′), *v. i.* [See *pre-*.] To exist beforehand, or before something else; exist in a previous state.—**pre-ëx-ist′ence** (-eg-zis′tens), *n.* Previous existence, as of the soul before union with the body.—**pre-ëx-ist′ent**, *a.*
pre-fab-ri-cate (prē-fab′ri-kāt), *v. t.* [See *pre-*.] To fabricate or construct beforehand; specif., to manufacture (houses, etc.) in standardized parts or sections ready for rapid assembling and erection where wanted.—**pre-fab-ri-ca′tion** (-kā′shon), *n.*
pref-ace (pref′ās), *n.* [OF. *preface* (F. *préface*), < L. *præfatio*, < *præfari* (pp. *præfatus*), say beforehand, < *præ*, before, + *fari*, speak, say.] A statement, as by the author or editor, prefixed to a literary work, and differing from an introduction in being more or less personal in character; hence, an introductory part, as of a speech; preliminary remarks or explanation; also, fig., something preliminary or introductory; *eccles.*, the introduction to the canon of the mass, ending with the Sanctus.—**pref′ace**, *v.*; *-aced, -acing.* **I.** *intr.* To make a prefatory statement. **II.** *tr.* To provide with or introduce by a preface; also, to

serve as a preface to (as, "A depressing and difficult passage has *prefaced* every new page I have turned in life": C. Brontë's "Villette," xxx.); also, to set forth by way of preface (as, "It is necessary to *preface*, that she is the only child of a decrepit father": Steele, in "Spectator," 449).—**pref′a-cer** (-ā-sėr), *n.*
pref-a-to-ry (pref′a-tō-ri), *a.* [L. *præfari* (pp. *præfatus*): see *preface*.] Of the nature of a preface; preliminary.—**pref′a-to-ri-ly**, *adv.*
pre-fect (prē′fekt), *n.* [= F. *préfet*, < L. *præfectus*, overseer, director, prop. pp. of *præficere*, set over, < *præ*, before, + *facere*, do, make.] A person appointed to any of various positions of command, authority, or superintendence, as a chief magistrate in ancient Rome, or the chief administrative official of a department of France.—**pre-fec-to-ral, pre-fec-to-ri-al** (prē-fek′tō-ral, prē-fek-tō′ri-al), *a.*—**pre′fec-ture** (-tūr), *n.* [L. *præfectura*.] The office, jurisdiction, territory, or official residence of a prefect.—**pre-fec′tur-al**, *a.*
pre-fer (prē-fėr′), *v.*; *-ferred, -ferring.* [OF. *preferer* (F. *préférer*), < L. *præferre*, bear before, set before, prefer, < *præ*, before, + *ferre*, bear.] **I.** *tr.* To put forward or advance, as in rank or office (as, "He never *preferred* a man who has not proved remarkably serviceable to his country": Steele, in "Tatler," 4); also, to put forward for acceptance, proffer, or offer (archaic); recommend (archaic: as, "I *preferred* Mr. Philips (nephew of Milton) to the service of my Lord Chamberlaine," Evelyn's "Diary," Sept. 18, 1677); also, to put forward or present (a statement, suit, charge, etc.) for consideration or sanction (as, "He gave audience to those of his subjects who had petitions to *prefer*": Prescott's "Conquest of Mexico," iv. 4); also, to set or hold before or above other persons or things in estimation (as, to *prefer* one writer to another; to *prefer* to go alone; to *prefer* working unaided); like better; choose rather; in *law*, to give preference or priority to, as a creditor. **II.** *intr.* To have a preference, as for one thing over another; like: as, I will come later, if you *prefer*.
pref-er-a-ble (pref′e-ra-bl), *a.* Worthy to be preferred; more desirable.—**pref′er-a-ble-ness**, *n.*—**pref′er-a-bly**, *adv.*
pref-er-ence (pref′e-rens), *n.* [F. *préférence*, < ML. *præferentia*.] The act of preferring, or the state of being preferred; estimation of one thing above another; prior favor or choice; also, that which is preferred; the object of prior favor or choice; also, a prior right or claim, as to payment; also, the practical favoring of one above others, as in business relations; the favoring of one country or group of countries by granting special advantages over others in international trade; a practical advantage given to one over others.—**preference stock.** See *preferred stock*, under *preferred*.—**pref-er-en′tial** (-e-ren′shal), *a.* Pertaining to or of the nature of preference; showing or giving preference; receiving or enjoying preference.—**pref-er-en′tial-ly**, *adv.*
pre-fer-ment (prē-fėr′ment), *n.* The act of preferring, or the state of being preferred; preference; sometimes, priority of right or claim, as to payment (now rare); commonly, advancement or promotion, as in rank or position (as, "their hunger for lands and office and *preferment*": Froude's "Cæsar," xxii.); also, a position or office giving social or pecuniary advancement, esp. one in the church.
pre-ferred (prē-fėrd′), *p. a.* Having obtained preferment, advancement, or promotion; also, liked better; chosen in preference to another or others; also, having a prior right or claim, as to payment; privileged.—**preferred stock,** stock on which dividends are payable before those on common or ordinary stock. Also called *preference stock*.
pre-fer-rer (prē-fėr′ėr), *n.* One who prefers.
pre-fig-u-ra-tion (prē-fig-ū-rā′shon), *n.* [LL. *præfiguratio(n-)*.] The act of prefiguring; representation beforehand by a figure or type; also, that in which something is prefigured; a prototype.—**pre-fig′u-ra-tive** (-ra-tiv), *a.*
pre-fig-ure (prē-fig′ūr), *v. t.*; *-ured, -uring.* [LL. *præfigurare*, < L. *præ*, before, + *figurare*, E. *figure, v.*] To represent beforehand by a figure or type (as, "At her call, a waking dream *Prefigured* to his sense the Egyptian Lady": Wordsworth's "Egyptian Maid," 306); foreshow; foreshadow;

also, to figure or represent to one's self beforehand (as, "My first sensations . . . were far from being so flattering as I had *prefigured* them": Sterne's "Sentimental Journey," Paris).—**pre-fig'ure-ment**, *n*.

pre-fix (prē-fiks'), *v. t.* [L. *præfixus*, pp. of *præfigere*, fix before, < *præ*, before, + *figere*, fix.] To fix or put before or in front; affix at the beginning of something (as, to *prefix* a syllable to a word); also, to fix, settle, or appoint beforehand (as, "The hour draws on *Prefix'd* by Angelo": Shakspere's "Measure for Measure," iv. 3. 83).—**pre-fix** (prē'-fiks), *n.* [NL. *præfixum*, prop. neut. of L. *præfixus*, pp.] Something prefixed, as a title before a person's name; esp., in *gram.*, a word, a syllable, or a number of syllables affixed to the beginning of a word to qualify its meaning, as *super-* in *superfine*.—**pre-fix'al**, *a.*—**pre-fix'ion** (-fik'shon), *n.* The act of prefixing; esp., the placing of a prefix at the beginning of a word.

pre-form (prē-fôrm'), *v. t.* [L. *præformare*, < *præ*, before, + *formare*, E. *form*, *v.*] To form beforehand; determine beforehand the form or shape of.—**pre-for-ma'tion** (-fôr-mā'shon), *n.* Previous formation; in *biol.*, a theoretical process of formation in which the individual, having all its parts, preëxists in the germ, with growth from microscopic to normal proportions subsequent to fertilization (opposed to *epigenesis*).—**pre-for-ma'tion-ist**, *n.* One who accepts the theory of preformation.—**pre-for'ma-tive** (-fôr'ma-tiv), *a.* Preforming; determining form beforehand.

preg-na-ble (preg'na-bl), *a.* [OF. F. *prenable*, < *prendre*, < L. *prendere*, *prehendere*, seize, take.] Capable of being taken or won by force, as a fortress; fig., open to attack; assailable.—**preg-na-bil'i-ty** (-bil'i-ti), *n.*

preg-nan-cy (preg'nan-si), *n.* The condition or quality of being pregnant; specif., the condition, fact, or period of being pregnant with child or young; gestation.

preg-nant (preg'nant), *a.* [L. *prægnans* (*prægnant-*), also *prægnas*, < *præ*, before, + *gna-*, occurring also in *gnasci*, *nasci*, be born: see *native*.] Being with child or young, as a woman or a female animal; gravid; enceinte; fig., charged or fraught with something likely to be produced or to result (followed by *with*: as, a policy or situation *pregnant* with danger; "a nervous timidity which may . . . be *pregnant* with serious consequences to yourself," S. Butler's "Way of All Flesh," viii.); hence, in general, fraught, filled, or abounding (*with*: as, words *pregnant* with meaning; "This whole eighth book is *pregnant* with profound and original thinking," Hallam's "Literature of Europe," iii. 3. § 56); fertile or rich (*in*: as, a mind *pregnant* in ideas; "Mr. Falkland, wise as he is, and *pregnant* in resources," Godwin's "Caleb Williams," xxxix.); also, full of possibilities, involving important issues or results, or momentous (as, "to state . . . the real condition of the Christian Church under the various circumstances of that most *pregnant* portion of her history": Wiseman's "Fabiola," i. 11); also, full of meaning, highly significant, or suggestive (as, a *pregnant* utterance; "After throwing out this *pregnant* hint, Mr. Poyser recurred to his pipe," George Eliot's "Adam Bede," xxxi.); implying a meaning beyond the strict or obvious one (as, a *pregnant* use of a word; to use a word in a *pregnant* sense — as, for instance, to use *temperament* to imply certain peculiarities of feeling, temper, action, etc., not strictly expressed by the word); also, teeming with ideas, or quick of invention or intelligence (archaic: as, to have a *pregnant* wit; "The Oxford scholar poor, Of *pregnant* parts and quick inventive brain," M. Arnold's "Scholar-Gipsy"); also, ready†, disposed†, or willing† (see Shakspere's "Hamlet," iii. 2. 66); also, weighty, cogent, or convincing, as an argument, proof, etc. (obs. or archaic: as, "One of the constables, besides the *pregnant* proof already produced, offers to make oath," Scott's "Guy Mannering," xliii.); hence, clear† or obvious†. —**preg'nant-ly**, *adv.*

pre-heat (prē-hēt'), *v. t.* [See *pre-*.] To heat before using or before submitting to some process: as, to *preheat* the air used in the blast of a blast-furnace.—**pre-heat'er**, *n.* A furnace, hot chamber, or the like, in which something is placed, or through which something is passed, in order to be preheated.

pre-hen-sile (prē-hen'sil), *a.* [F. *préhensile*, < L. *pre-hendere* (pp. *prehensus*), seize.] Adapted for seizing, grasping, or laying hold of anything; esp., fitted for grasping by folding or wrapping round an object (as, the *prehensile* tail of a spider-monkey or an opossum).
—**pre-hen-sil-i-ty** (prē-hen-sil'i-ti), *n.*
pre-hen-sion (prē-hen'shon), *n.* [L. *prehensio(n-)*, < *pre-hendere*, seize.] The act of seizing, grasping, or taking hold (chiefly in *zoöl.*); also, mental apprehension.
—**pre-hen'sive**, **pre-hen'so-ry** (-siv, -sō-ri), *a.*
pre-his-tor-ic (prē-his-tor'ik), *a.* [See *pre-*.] Of or belonging to a period prior to that of recorded history.—**pre-his-tor'i-cal-ly**, *adv.*

Prehensile Tail. — Spider-monkey (*Ateles paniscus*).

prehn-ite (prān'īt), *n.* [G. *prehnit*; from Colonel *Prehn*, who brought it from Cape Colony in the 18th century.] A mineral consisting of a hydrous silicate of aluminium and calcium, occurring in crystalline aggregates, and usually of a pale-green color.

pre-ig-ni-tion (prē-ig-nish'on), *n.* [See *pre-*.] An ignition of the combustible charge in an internal-combustion engine before the piston is in a position to commence its working stroke.

pre-judge (prē-juj'), *v. t.* [See *pre-*.] To judge beforehand; hence, to pass judgment on prematurely or in advance of due investigation.—**pre-judg'ment**, **pre-judge'ment**, *n.*—**pre-judg'er**, *n.*

prej-u-dice (prej'ŏ-dis), *n.* [OF. *prejudice* (F. *préjudice*), < L. *præjudicium*, a preceding judgment, disadvantage, prejudice, < *præ*, before, + *judicium*, judgment, < *judex*, judge.] A judgment passed beforehand, esp. in advance of due examination†; hence, a preconceived opinion or feeling, favorable or unfavorable (as, "I am . . . a bundle of *prejudices* — made up of likings and dislikings," Lamb's "Imperfect Sympathies"; "Belinda . . . had imbibed some of Mrs. Stanhope's *prejudices* in favour of rank and fashion," Maria Edgeworth's "Belinda," i.); mental bias, favorable or unfavorable (as, a mind free from *prejudice*; to consider a matter without *prejudice*); esp., an unfavorable opinion or feeling conceived beforehand or independently of experience or reason (as, "a Boston of mysterious *prejudices* and lofty reservations; a Boston of high and difficult tastes": Howells's "Chance Acquaintance," vii.); unfavorable mental bias (as, to object from mere *prejudice*); also, disadvantage resulting from some judgment or action of another; resulting injury or detriment (as, "The measures . . . were evidently intended to serve the proprietary interest, with great *prejudice* to that of the people": B. Franklin's "Autobiography," xiii.); in general, damage† or harm†.—**prej'u-dice**, *v. t.*; *-diced*, *-dicing*. To affect with a prejudice, favorable or unfavorable (as, these facts had *prejudiced* us in his favor; "They suspected the Cardinal of *prejudicing* the mind of their sovereign against them," Motley's "Dutch Republic," ii. 3); bias, often unfavorably; also, to affect disadvantageously or detrimentally; result unfavorably for (as, "His bravado carried him too far and *prejudiced* his case. At least . . . opinion settled finally against him": Stevenson's "Master of Ballantrae," xi.).—**prej'u-diced**, *p. a.* Swayed by prejudice, or biased (as, "Montmorency, now old, was *prejudiced* and obstinate": Besant's "Coligny," vii.); colored by or showing prejudice (as, a *prejudiced* view or statement).—**prej-u-di'cial** (-dish'al), *a.* Prejudiced† or biased†; also, causing prejudice or disadvantage, or detrimental (as, "A violent collision must be *prejudicial* even to the victor": Prescott's "Conquest of Mexico," iv. 6).—**prej-u-di'cial-ly**, *adv.*

prel-a-cy (prel'ạ-si), *n.*; pl. *-cies* (-siz). The office or dignity of a prelate; also, the order of prelates; the body of prelates collectively; also, the system of church government by prelates (often opprobrious).

prel-ate (prel'ạt), *n.* [OF. *prelat* (F. *prélat*), < ML. *prælatus*, prop. pp. of L. *præferre*, set before, prefer: see *prefer*.] An ecclesiastic of a higher order, as an archbishop, bishop, etc.; a church dignitary.—**prel'ate-ship**, *n.* The office or dignity of a prelate.—**pre-lat-ic**, **pre-lat-i-cal** (prę-lat'ik, -i-kạl), *a.* Of or pertaining to a prelate; of the nature of a prelate; also, adhering to prelacy, or episcopal (often opprobrious).—**prel'at-ism** (-ạt-izm), *n.* Prelacy or episcopacy; adherence to prelacy or episcopacy. [Often opprobrious.]—**prel'at-ist**, *n.* An adherent of prelacy. [Often opprobrious.]—**prel'at-ize**, *v. t.*; *-ized, -izing.* To make prelatical; bring under the influence and power of prelacy.—**prel'a-ture** (-ạ-ṭūr), *n.* [F. *prélature*, < ML. *prælatura*.] The office or dignity of a prelate; also, the order of prelates; prelates collectively.

pre-lect (prę-lekt'), *v. i.* [L. *prælectus*, pp. of *prælegere*, < *præ*, before, + *legere*, read.] To read a lecture or discourse in public; discourse publicly; lecture.—**pre-lec'tion** (-lek'shọn), *n.* [L. *prælectio(n-)*.] A public lecture or discourse. —**pre-lec'tor**, *n.* [L. *prælector*.] A public reader of lectures or discourses; a lecturer, as in a university.

pre-li-ba-tion (prē-li-bā'shọn), *n.* [LL. *prælibatio(n-)*, < L. *prælibare*, taste beforehand, < *præ*, before, + *libare*, taste.] A tasting beforehand or by anticipation; a foretaste; also, an offering of the first-fruit, or of the first taste, of anything.

pre-lim-i-na-ry (prę-lim'i-nạ-ri). [NL. *præliminaris*, < L. *præ*, before, + *limen* (*limin-*), threshold.] **I.** *a.* Preceding and leading up to the main matter or business; introductory; preparatory. **II.** *n.*; pl. *-ries* (-riz). Something preliminary; an introductory or preparatory step, measure, or the like: as, "a serpent, which, as a *preliminary* to fascination, is said to fill the air with his peculiar odor" (Hawthorne's "House of the Seven Gables," viii.). **III.** *adv.* As a preliminary (*to*).—**pre-lim'i-na-ri-ly**, *adv.*

pre-lude (prē'lūd or prel'ūd), *n.* [F. *prélude*, < ML. *præludium*, < L. *præludere*, play beforehand, < *præ*, before, + *ludere*, play.] An introductory performance; a preliminary to an action, event, condition, or work of broader scope and higher importance (as, "There were fiery spirits who . . . saw in the Roman alliance a *prelude* to annexation," Froude's "Cæsar," xiv.; "Maybe wildest dreams Are but the needful *preludes* of the truth," Tennyson's "Princess," Conclusion, 74); a preface; an introduction; preliminary action, remarks, etc. (as, "Then the question . . . was put quite suddenly, without preparation or *prelude*": H. G. Wells's "Soul of a Bishop," i.); in *music*, a prefatory or introductory piece, movement, strain, or the like.—**pre-lude** (prę-lūd' or prel'ūd), *v.*; *-luded, -luding.* **I.** *tr.* To serve as a prelude or introduction to (as, "When the gray Of morn *preludes* the splendour of the day": Dryden's tr. Ovid's "Metamorphoses," xv. 283); also, to introduce by a prelude (as, "He *preluded* his address by a sonorous blast of the nose": Irving's "Knickerbocker's New York," iv. 2); in *music*, to introduce with a prelude; also, to play as a prelude. **II.** *intr.* To serve as a prelude; also, to give a prelude; in *music*, to play a prelude.—**pre-lud'er** (-lū'dėr), *n.*

pre-lu-sion (prę-lū'zhọn), *n.* [L. *prælusio(n-)*, < *præ-ludere*: see *prelude*.] A prelude.—**pre-lu'sive, pre-lu'so-ry** (-lū'siv, -sọ-ri), *a.* Serving as a prelude; introductory.

pre-ma-ture (prē-mạ-tūr'), *a.* [L. *præmaturus*, < *præ*, before, + *maturus*, E. *mature*.] Mature or ripe before the proper time; hence, coming into existence or occurring too soon (as, "He was already decrepit with *premature* old age": Motley's "Dutch Republic," i. 1); overhasty or precipitate, as in action (as, "I had been a little too *premature* in coming to this conclusion": H. Melville's "Typee," xvi.).—**pre-ma-ture'ly**, *adv.*—**pre-ma-ture'ness, pre-ma-tu'ri-ty** (-tū'ri-ti), *n.*

pre-max-il-la (prē-mak-sil'ạ), *n.*; pl. *premaxillæ* (-ē). [See *pre-*.] In *anat.* and *zoöl.*, one of a pair of bones of the upper jaw of vertebrates, situated in front of and between the maxillary bones.—**pre-max'il-la-ry** (-mak'si-lạ-ri). In *anat.* and *zoöl.*: **I.** *a.* Situated in front of the maxillary bones; noting or pertaining to the premaxillæ. **II.** *n.*; pl. *-ries* (-riz). A premaxilla.

pre-med-i-tate (prę-med'i-tāt), *v. t.* or *i.*; *-tated, -tating.* [L. *præmeditatus*, pp. of *præmeditari*, < *præ*, before, + *meditari*, meditate.] To meditate, consider, or plan beforehand.—**pre-med'i-tat-ed** (-tā-ted), *p. a.* Meditated or planned beforehand.—**pre-med'i-tat-ed-ly**, *adv.*—**pre-med-i-ta'tion** (-tā'shọn), *n.* [L. *præmeditatio(n-)*.] The act of premeditating; previous deliberation; planning. —**pre-med'i-ta-tive** (-tạ-tiv), *a.* Characterized by premeditation.

pre-mi-er (prē'mi-ėr or prem'iėr). [OF. F. *premier*, first, < L. *primarius*: see *primary*.] **I.** *a.* First in rank or importance; chief; leading; also, first in time; earliest. **II.** *n.* A chief officer; esp., the first minister of state; the prime minister, as of France, Great Britain, or one of the British dominions.—**pre-mière** (prę-myãr), *n.* [F., fem. of *premier*.] The leading woman, as in a drama; also, a first public performance of a play, etc.—**pre'mi-er-ship**, *n.*

pre-mil-le-na-ri-an (prē'mil-e-nā'ri-ạn), *n.* [See *pre-* and *millenarian*.] A believer in premillennialism; a premillennialist.—**pre'mil-le-na'ri-an-ism**, *n.*

pre-mil-len-ni-al (prē-mi-len'i-ạl), *a.* [See *pre-*.] Of or pertaining to the period preceding the millennium.—**pre-mil-len'ni-al-ism**, *n.* The doctrine or belief that the second coming of Christ will precede the millennium.—**pre-mil-len'ni-al-ist**, *n.*

prem-ise (prem'is), *n.* [Earlier *premiss*, < OF. *premisse* (F. *prémisse*), < ML. *præmissa*, prop. fem. of L. *præmissus*, pp. of *præmittere*, send before, < *præ*, before, + *mittere*, send.] An antecedent statement or proposition from which an inference or conclusion is drawn; specif., either of the first two propositions of a logical syllogism; also, *pl.*, esp. in *law*, things stated or mentioned previously; specif., a certain part in the beginning of a deed or other legal document, as that part of a conveyance giving the names of the parties concerned, the description of the property conveyed, the consideration, etc.; also, the property forming the subject of a conveyance; hence, a piece of real estate; a house or building with the grounds, etc., belonging to it.—**pre-misc** (prę-mīz'), *v. t.*; *-mised, -mising.* To set forth beforehand, as by way of introduction or explanation: as, "Having *premised* these circumstances, I will now let the nervous gentleman proceed with his stories" (Irving's "Tales of a Traveler," i. 1).

prem-iss (prem'is), *n.* [See *premise*.] A premise in reasoning.

pre-mi-um (prē'mi-um), *n.*; pl. *-ums.* [L. *præmium*, profit, reward, < *præ*, before, + *emere*, take, buy.] A reward given for a particular action or as an incentive; a prize to be won in a competition; a fee paid for instruction in a trade or profession; a bonus, or sum additional to price, wages, interest, or the like; formerly, interest paid for the loan of money; also, the amount paid or agreed to be paid in one sum or periodically as the consideration for a contract of insurance; also, the excess value of one form of money over another of the same nominal value; also, a sum above the nominal or par value of a thing; an increase of value, above the nominal value, attaching to something in demand (as, "The Federal Government could certainly reduce and probably destroy the present *premium* on tax-exempt securities by changing its own tax system": A. W. Mellon's "Taxation," viii.).—**at a premium**, above par; hence, in high esteem; in demand.

pre-mo-lar (prē-mō'lạr). [See *pre-*.] **I.** *a.* Noting or pertaining to certain of the permanent teeth in mammals (in man, usually called bicuspid teeth) in front of the molars; also, sometimes, noting or pertaining to the molars of the milk-teeth. **II.** *n.* A premolar tooth.

pre-mon-ish (prę-mon'ish), *v.* [L. *præmonere* (pp. *præmonitus*), < *præ*, before, + *monere*, remind, advise.] **I.** *tr.* To advise or caution beforehand; forewarn: as, "We enter'd by the draw-bridge, which has an invention to let one fall, if not *premonished*" (Evelyn's "Diary," May 2, 1644). **II.** *intr.* To give warning beforehand.—**pre-mo-ni-tion** (prē-mọ̄-nish'ọn), *n.* [LL. *præmonitio(n-)*.] The act of premonishing; a forewarning; also, a presentiment (as, "I had slept heavily, and awakened with a *premonition* of some evil to befall": Stevenson's "Master of Ballantrae," viii.).—**pre-mon′i-to-ry** (-i-tọ-ri), *a.* Giving premonition; serving to warn beforehand.—**pre-mon′i-to-ri-ly**, *adv.*

Pre-mon-strant (prẹ-mon′strạnt), *n.* and *a.* Same as *Premonstratensian.*

Pre-mon-stra-ten-sian (prẹ-mon-strạ-ten′shiạn). [ML. *Premonstratensis*, of Prémontré.] **I.** *a.* Noting or pertaining to a Roman Catholic religious order founded by St. Norbert at Prémontré, near Laon, France, in 1120. **II.** *n.* A member of the Premonstratensian order; a white canon.

pre-morse (prẹ-môrs′), *a.* [L. *præmorsus*, pp. of *præmordere*, bite in front, < *præ*, before, + *mordere*, bite.] Having the end irregularly truncate, as if bitten or broken off: as, a *premorse* root.

pre-mun-dane (prē-mun′dān), *a.* [L. *præ*, before, + *mundus*, world.] Existing or occurring before the creation of the world; antemundane.

pre-mu-ni-re (prē-mụ-nī′rē), *n.* See *præmunire.*

pre-na-tal (prē-nā′tạl), *a.* [L. *præ*, before, + *natus*, born.] Previous to birth; antenatal.—**pre-na′tal-ly**, *adv.*

pre-no-men (prē-nō′men), *n.* See *prænomen.*

pre-nom-i-nate† (prẹ-nom′i-nāt), *v. t.* [LL. *prænominatus*, pp. of *prænominare*, < L. *præ*, before, + *nominare*, name.] To name beforehand; mention or specify in advance.— **pre-nom′i-nate†**, *a.* Named beforehand; forementioned.

pre-no-tion (prē-nō′shọn), *n.* [L. *prænotio(n-)*, < *prænoscere*, foreknow, < *præ*, before, + *noscere*, know.] An anticipatory knowledge or perception of a thing; also, a preconceived notion or idea; a preconception.

pren-tice (pren′tis). **I.** *n.* An apprentice. [Archaic.] **II.** *a.* Pertaining to or suggestive of an apprentice, as in inexperience or lack of skill: as, "that purposeless indecision of touch which often characterizes the *prentice* hand" (Du Maurier's "Trilby," ii.). [Archaic.]

pre-oc-cu-pan-cy (prẹ-ok′ụ-pạn-si), *n.* Previous occupancy or occupation; also, the state of being preoccupied or engaged.

pre-oc-cu-pa-tion (prẹ-ok-ụ-pā′shọn), *n.* The act of preoccupying, or the state of being preoccupied; occupation or appropriation in advance; mental absorption or engrossment (as, "our partner's *preoccupation* with the uncommercial aspects of life": H. G. Wells's "Tono-Bungay," iii. 1. § 2); also, prepossession or bias; also, an occupation that takes precedence of all others.

pre-oc-cu-py (prẹ-ok′ụ-pī), *v. t.* [See *pre-*.] To occupy, take possession of, or appropriate beforehand or before others (as, "A . . . body of these light cavalry had . . . *preoccupied* the pass by some hours": De Quincey's "Revolt of the Tartars"); also, to engage beforehand, or engross to the exclusion of other things, as the mind or attention (as, "His mind was *preoccupied* with grave and heavy matters": Arnold Bennett's "Clayhanger," i. 1); absorb or engross the mind or attention of (as, "He seemed *preoccupied*, and heedless of the salutations he received": W. Churchill's "Coniston," ii. 4).

pre-o-ral (prē-ō′rạl), *a.* [L. *præ*, before, + *os (or-)*, mouth.] In *zoöl.*, situated in front of or before the mouth.—**pre-o′ral-ly**, *adv.*

pre-or-dain (prē-ôr-dān′), *v.t.* [See *pre-*.] To ordain beforehand; foreordain.—**pre-or-dain′ment**, *n.*

pre-or-di-nance† (prē-ôr′di-nạns), *n.* [See *pre-*.] An ordinance previously established. See Shakspere's "Julius Cæsar," iii. 1. 38.

prep (prep). **I.** *a.* Colloq. form of *preparatory*: as, a *prep* school. [U. S.] **II.** *n.* A preparatory school. [Colloq., U. S.]

prep-a-ra-tion (prep-ạ-rā′shọn), *n.* [OF. *preparacion* (F. *préparation*), < L. *præparatio(n-)*.] The act of preparing, or the state of being prepared; also, a proceeding, measure, or provision by which one prepares for something (as, to make *preparations* for a journey); any proceeding, experience, or the like considered as a mode of preparing for the future (as, his early life was a poor *preparation* for facing the world); also, something prepared, manufactured, or compounded (as, a medicinal *preparation*; a food *preparation*); also, a specimen, as an animal body, prepared for scientific examination, dissection, etc.; formerly, a force or fleet equipped for war† (as, "The Turkish *preparation* makes for Rhodes": Shakspere's "Othello," i. 3. 14); also, in the New Testament, the day before the Sabbath or some other feast-day (as, "It was the *preparation*, that is, the day before the *sabbath*," Mark, xv. 42; "It was the *preparation* of the passover, and about the sixth hour," John, xix. 14); in *music*, the preparing of a discord, as by introducing the dissonant tone as a consonant tone in the preceding chord; also, the tone so introduced.

pre-par-a-tive (prẹ-par′ạ-tiv). [OF. *preparatif* (F. *préparatif*), < ML. *præparativus*.] **I.** *a.* Serving or tending to prepare; preparatory. **II.** *n.* A preparative agency; something that serves to prepare: as, "if discontent and misery are *preparatives* for liberty" (Kingsley's "Alton Locke," xxviii.).—**pre-par′a-tive-ly**, *adv.*

pre-par-a-tor (prẹ-par′ạ-tọr), *n.* [= F. *préparateur*, < LL. *præparator*.] One who prepares; a preparer; specif., one who prepares specimens, etc., as for scientific purposes.

pre-par-a-to-ry (prẹ-par′ạ-tọ-ri). [LL. *præparatorius*.] **I.** *a.* Serving or designed to prepare or make ready (as, *preparatory* measures or arrangements; *preparatory* training or study; a *preparatory* school or department, in which students are prepared to enter college); hence, preliminary or introductory (as, " 'Sophia,' he addressed her, and made *preparatory* noises in his throat while she waited": Arnold Bennett's "Old Wives' Tale," i. 3); also, undergoing preparation for entering college, as a student in a special (preparatory) school. **II.** *adv.* As a preparatory measure (to some action, etc.); preliminary (*to*).—**pre-par′a-to-ri-ly**, *adv.*

pre-pare (prẹ-pār′), *v.*; -pared, -paring. [OF. *preparer* (F. *préparer*), < L. *præparare*, make ready beforehand, < *præ*, before, + *parare*, make ready: see *pare*.] **I.** *tr.* To make ready, or put in due condition, for something (as, to *prepare* a chicken for roasting; to *prepare* a manuscript for printing; "He had *prepared* for him a great chamber, where aforetime they laid the meat offerings," Neh. xiii. 5); fit out or equip (as, troops or vessels *prepared* for foreign service); fit (a person, etc.) by training or instruction for some work or post, or for college, an examination, or the like; often, to render mentally ready for something unexpected (as, to *prepare* a person for bad news; "I was not *prepared* for the extreme calm of voice and manner that marked his first words," F. M. Crawford's "Mr. Isaacs," xiv.); render ready, willing, or disposed (as, "The Belgians of the north were not *prepared* to part so easily with their liberty": Froude's "Cæsar," xiv.); also, to make or get ready, as something provided, arranged, or made in due manner (as, "My servants shall be with thy servants . . . to *prepare* me timber in abundance," 2 Chron. ii. 9; to *prepare* a sling for an injured arm); get ready for eating, as a meal, a dish of food, etc., by due assembling, dressing, or cooking; get ready for recitation, as a lesson by study; also, to put into a desired or finished condition by some special or technical process of dressing or working (as, to *prepare* raw materials; to *prepare* skins or feathers); also, to make, produce, or form by due process (as, "He seeketh . . . a cunning workman to *prepare* a graven image," Isa. xl. 20; to *prepare* ink or medicine; to *prepare* a letter); manufacture, compound, or compose; in *music*, to lead up to (a discord, an embellishment, etc.) by means of some preliminary tone or tones. **II.** *intr.* To put things or one's self in readiness; make preparations; get ready: as, to *prepare* for war; "The thunderbolt Hangs silent; but *prepare*. I speak, it falls" (Tennyson's "Princess," ii. 206).—**pre-par′ed-ly** (-pār′ed-li), *adv.*—**pre-par′ed-ness**, *n.* The state of being prepared; readiness, as for action or for any emergency; esp., the state of being prepared, by the possession of an adequate army and navy, to meet threats or outbreaks of war.—**pre-par′er**, *n.*

pre-pay (prē-pā′), *v. t.*; -paid, -paying. [See *pre-*.] To pay beforehand; also, to pay the charge upon in advance.— **pre-pay′a-ble**, *a.* That may be or is to be prepaid.— **pre-pay′ment**, *n.*

pre-pense (prẹ-pens′), *a.* [Earlier *prepensed*, for *purpensed*, repr. OF. *purpensé*, pp. of *purpenser*, premeditate, < *pur-* (< L. *pro*), before, + *penser*, think: see *pensive*.] Considered and planned beforehand; premeditated: chiefly in the phrase 'malice prepense.'—**pre-pense′ly**, *adv.*

pre-pon-der-ance (prē-pon′dėr-ạns), n. The quality or fact of being preponderant; superiority in weight, power, influence, number, etc.

pre-pon-der-ant (prē-pon′dėr-ạnt), a. Preponderating; superior in weight, force, influence, number, etc.; predominant.—**pre-pon′der-ant-ly**, adv.

pre-pon-der-ate (prē-pon′dėr-āt), v. i.; -ated, -ating. [L. præponderatus, pp. of præponderare, < præ, before, + ponderare, weigh: see ponder.] To exceed something else in weight; be the heavier; hence, to incline downward or descend, as one scale or end of a balance, because of greater weight; be weighed down; in fig. use, to be superior in power, force, influence, number, amount, etc. (as, "The good in this state of existence preponderates over the bad": Dickens's "Nicholas Nickleby," vi.); predominate.—**pre-pon′der-at-ing-ly** (-ā-ting-li), adv.—**pre-pon-der-a′tion** (-ā′shọn), n. [LL. præponderatio(n-).] The act or fact of preponderating; superiority in weight, force, number, etc.

prep-o-si-tion (prep-ọ-zish′ọn), n. [L. præpositio(n-), < præponere, place before, < præ, before, + ponere, place, put.] In gram., an indeclinable part of speech, as by, in, to, for, from, etc., governing (and usually placed before) a noun or its equivalent, and showing the relation to some other word.—**prep-o-si′tion-al**, a.—**prep-o-si′tion-al-ly**, adv.

pre-pos-i-tive (prē-poz′i-tiv). [LL. præpositivus, < L. præponere: see preposition.] I. a. Put before; prefixed. II. n. A prepositive word or particle.—**pre-pos′i-tive-ly**, adv.

pre-pos-i-tor, præ-pos-i-tor (prē-poz′i-tọr), n. Same as præpostor.

pre-pos-sess (prē-pọ-zes′), v. t. [See pre-.] To take possession of beforehand or before others (now rare); also, to possess or dominate mentally beforehand, as a prejudice does; render possessed with a feeling or opinion, favorable or unfavorable, in advance (as, "The teacher . . . did not prepossess me in favour of his pursuits": Mrs. Shelley's "Frankenstein," iii.); prejudice or bias, esp. favorably; impress favorably beforehand or at the outset (as, "Leslie was much prepossessed by her frank manner, and by her charming voice," Mallock's "New Republic," i. 2: cf. prepossessing).—**pre-pos-sess′ing**, p. a. That prepossesses, esp. favorably; making a favorable first impression; pleasing: as, "a maid of about sixteen . . . not ugly, nor yet prepossessing" (W. H. Hudson's "Green Mansions," v.); "His countenance was frank and handsome; and his demeanour easy and prepossessing" (Dickens's "Oliver Twist," xxxiv.).—**pre-pos-sess′ing-ly**, adv.—**pre-pos-sess′ing-ness**, n.—**pre-pos-ses′sion** (-zesh′ọn), n. Prior possession (now rare); also, the state of being mentally prepossessed; antecedent mental bias, favorable or (now less frequently) unfavorable; a prejudice, esp. in favor of a person or thing (as, "It is your business to create in those who hear you a prepossession in your favour": Godwin's "Caleb Williams," xxii.); a favorable feeling or opinion conceived in advance.

pre-pos-ter-ous (prē-pos′tẹ-rus), a. [L. præposterus, with the hinder part foremost, < præ, before, + posterus, coming after.] Having that first which should be last, or reversed in order or position (now rare); hence, directly contrary to nature, reason, or common sense (as, "It would be preposterous to take so grave a step on the advice of an enemy": Froude's "Cæsar," xvii.); absurd, senseless, or utterly foolish; amusingly absurd, or ridiculous (as, "the most preposterous little fat man in the world": H. G. Wells's "Tono-Bungay," iii. 2. § 9).—**pre-pos′ter-ous-ly**, adv.—**pre-pos′ter-ous-ness**, n.

pre-pos-tor (prē-pos′tọr), n. See præpostor.

pre-po-tent (prē-pō′tẹnt), a. [L. præpotens (-ent-), ppr. of præposse, < præ, before, + posse, have power: see potent.] Preëminent in power, authority, or influence (as, "An ambiguous, prepotent figure had come to disturb the . . . jealously guarded balance of the English Constitution": Lytton Strachey's "Queen Victoria," v.); predominant; in biol., noting or pertaining to a preponderating tendency or power of one germ-cell, one parent, one ancestor, or the like, to fix the character of descendants; having such a tendency or power.—**pre-po′tence, pre-po′ten-cy**, n.

pre-puce (prē′pūs), n. [OF. prepuce (F. prépuce), < L. præputium.] The foreskin.—**pre-pu′tial** (prē-pū′shạl), a.

Pre=Raph-a-el-ite (prē-raf′ạ-el-īt). [See pre-.] I. n. One of a group of English artists (the 'Pre-Raphaelite Brotherhood,' formed in 1848, and including Holman Hunt, Millais, and Dante Gabriel Rossetti) who endeavored to revive the style and spirit of the Italian artists before the time of Raphael, and laid stress upon delicacy of color and finish and fidelity to nature; sometimes, any modern artist of like aims or methods; also, one of the Italian painters who preceded Raphael. II. a. Of, pertaining to, or characteristic of the Pre-Raphaelites; also, existing before the time of Raphael.—**Pre=Raph′a-el-it-ism** (-īt-izm), n.

pre-re-qui-site (prē-rek′wi-zit). [See pre-.] I. a. Required beforehand; requisite as an antecedent condition. II. n. Something prerequisite.

pre-rog-a-tive (prē-rog′ạ-tiv). [OF. prerogative (F. prérogative), < L. prærogativa, prerogative, prop. fem. of prærogativus, voting first, < prærogare, ask first, < præ, before, + rogare, ask.] I. n. A prior, peculiar, or exclusive right or privilege; esp., such a right attaching to an office or position, as that of a sovereign; also, precedence†. II. a. Having or exercising a prerogative; pertaining to, characteristic of, or existing by virtue of, a prerogative; also, pertaining to a prerogative court.—**prerogative court**, in England and Ireland, a former ecclesiastical court for the trial of certain testamentary cases; in the State of New Jersey, the court of probate.—**pre-rog′a-tived**, a. Endowed with a prerogative.

pre-sa (prä′sä), n.; pl. prese (-sā). [It., a taking, < prendere, < L. prendere, prehendere, take.] In music, a mark, as :S:, +, or ✕, used in a canon, fugue, etc., to indicate where the successive voice-parts are to take up the theme.

pres-age (pres′ạj or prē′sāj), n. [OF. presage (F. présage), < L. præsagium, presentiment, foreboding, < præsagire, perceive beforehand, < præ, before, + sagire, perceive acutely: see sagacious.] A presentiment or foreboding, or a prophetic impression (as, "She could not sleep at night and was haunted by a presage of disaster": S. Butler's "Way of All Flesh," lxxx.); also, something that portends or foreshadows a future event; an omen, prognostic, or warning indication (as, "a low, constant . . . murmur of dissatisfaction . . . a warning presage of the coming storm": Motley's "Dutch Republic," i. 3); also, prophetic significance, or augury (as, an occurrence of dire presage); also, a forecast or prediction.—**pre-sage** (prē-sāj′), v.; -saged, -saging. [F. présager, < présage.] I. tr. To have a presentiment of; also, to portend, foreshow, or foreshadow (as, "The yellow and vapory sunset . . . had presaged change": Hardy's "Return of the Native," iii. 6); also, to forecast or predict. II. intr. To have a presentiment; also, to make a prediction.—**pre-sage′ful**, a. Full of presage; foreboding; also, ominous.—**pre-sa′ger** (-sā′jėr), n.—**pre-sa′ging-ly**, adv.

pres-by-o-pi-a (pres-bi-ō′pi-ạ or prez-), n. [NL., < Gr. πρέσβυς, old man, + ὤψ, eye.] In pathol., a defect of vision incident to advancing age, in which near objects are seen with difficulty.—**pres-by-op′ic** (-op′ik), a.

pres-by-ter (pres′bi-tėr or prez′-), n. [LL. presbyter, < Gr. πρεσβύτερος, an elder, prop. adj., older, compar. < πρέσβυς, old man: cf. priest.] In the early Christian church, an elder; in hierarchical churches, a priest; in Presbyterian churches, a member of a presbytery.—**pres-byt-er-al** (pres-bit′ẹr-ạl or prez-), a. Of or pertaining to presbyters.—**pres-byt′er-ate** (-āt), n. [LL. presbyteratus.] The office of presbyter; also, a body of presbyters.—**pres-by-te′ri-al** (-tē′ri-ạl), a. Of or pertaining to a presbytery; also, presbyterian.—**pres-by-te′ri-an. I.** a. Pertaining to or based on the principle of ecclesiastical government by presbyters or presbyteries; [cap.] designating or pertaining to various churches having this form of government and holding more or less modified forms of Calvinism. II. n. [cap.] A member or adherent of a Presbyterian church. —**Pres-by-te′ri-an-ism**, n. The system of church government by presbyters or elders, characterized by equality of all elders and absence of ecclesiastical ranks; also, the doctrines of Presbyterian churches.—**pres′by-te-ry** (-te-ri), n.; pl. -ries (-riz). [LL. presbyterium, < Gr. πρεσβυτέριον.] A body of presbyters or elders; in Presbyterian churches, a judicatory consisting of all the ministers (teaching elders) and certain of the lay or ruling elders within a district; also, the district under the jurisdiction of a presbytery; also [*cap.*], Presbyterianism (as, "Englishmen who doubted of Episcopacy . . . made no secret of their distaste for *Presbytery* in France, Geneva . . . or in Scotland," Morley's "Oliver Cromwell," ii. 1: now rare); also [*l. c.*], the part of a church appropriated to the clergy; also, a clergyman's or priest's house (now only in Roman Catholic use).

Choir and Presbytery of Gloucester Cathedral, England, looking east.

pre-science (prē′shiẹns or presh′iẹns), *n.* [OF. F. *prescience*, < LL. *præscientia*, < L. *præsciens*: see *prescient*.] Knowledge of things before they exist or happen; foreknowledge; foresight: as, "Perhaps he knew already, by the *prescience* of a general, the hopelessness of the struggle" (Besant's "Coligny," viii.).

pre-scient (prē′shiẹnt or presh′iẹnt), *a.* [F. *prescient*, < L. *præsciens* (*præscient-*), ppr. of *præscire*, foreknow, < *præ*, before, + *scire*, know.] Having foreknowledge, as of things to come (as, a *prescient* mind); foreseeing; characterized by or showing foreknowledge (as, a *prescient* moment; "the sharks . . . following them in the same *prescient* way that vultures hover over the banners of marching regiments," H. Melville's "Moby-Dick," cxxxv.).—**pre′scient-ly,** *adv.*

pre-scind (prē-sind′), *v.* [L. *præscindere*, cut off in front, < *præ*, before, + *scindere*, cut.] **I.** *tr.* To cut off or away; remove; also, to separate in thought; abstract. **II.** *intr.* To withdraw the attention (*from*); turn aside in thought.

pre-scribe (prē-skrīb′), *v.*; -scribed, -scribing. [L. *præscribere* (pp. *præscriptus*), < *præ*, before, + *scribere*, write.] **I.** *tr.* To lay down, in writing or otherwise, as a rule or a course to be followed; appoint, ordain, or enjoin (bounds, duties, actions, methods, etc.); in *med.*, to designate or order for use, as a remedy or treatment; in *law*, to render invalid or outlawed by negative prescription. **II.** *intr.* To lay down rules, direct, or dictate (as, to do as the law *prescribes*); in *med.*, to designate remedies or treatment to be used; in *law*, to claim a right or title by prescription, or by virtue of long use and enjoyment (esp. with *for* or *to*); also, to become invalid or outlawed by negative prescription, or through lapse of time, as a claim or action.—**pre-scrib′er** (-skrī′bėr), *n.*

pre-script (prē-skript′), *a.* [L. *præscriptus*, pp.: see *prescribe.*] Prescribed; laid down as a rule; appointed, ordained, or enjoined. [Now rare.]—**pre-script** (prē′skript), *n.* [L. *præscriptum*, prop. neut. of *præscriptus*, pp.] That which is prescribed; a rule; a regulation or ordinance; a direction or injunction; also, a medical prescription (now rare).

pre-scrip-ti-ble (prē-skrip′ti-bl), *a.* Subject to (legal) prescription; depending on or derived from prescription, as a claim or right.

pre-scrip-tion (prē-skrip′shọn), *n.* [L. *præscriptio(n-)*.] The act of prescribing; also, that which is prescribed; in *med.*, a direction (usually written) for the preparation and use of a medicine or remedy; also, the medicine prescribed; in *law*, the operation of long or immemorial possession or use of a thing to give a right or title to it (as, to claim a right by *prescription*; to acquire a thing by *prescription*: often used figuratively or by transference in general language); right or title acquired by virtue of long and uninterrupted use and enjoyment; also, limitation of the time within which a claim may be made or an action brought ('negative prescription').

pre-scrip-tive (prē-skrip′tiv), *a.* That prescribes; giving directions or injunctions; also, depending on or arising from legal prescription, as a right or title; hence, in general, arising from or established by long use, custom, or existence (as, "the *prescriptive* respectability of a family with a mural monument and venerable tankards": George Eliot's "Silas Marner," x.); long recognized or sanctioned.—**pre-scrip′tive-ly,** *adv.*—**pre-scrip′tive-ness,** *n.*

pres-ence (prez′ẹns), *n.* [OF. *presence* (F. *présence*), < L. *præsentia*.] The state or fact of being present, as with others or in a place (as, "I was ignorant of his *presence* here. I thought him in Paris": G. Meredith's "Lord Ormont and His Aminta," xviii.); attendance or company (as, to request one's *presence* at a gathering; to relieve others of one's *presence,* as by departing); immediate vicinity or close proximity (as, an act done in the *presence* of witnesses; chemical changes taking place in the *presence* of a catalytic agent; coolness in the *presence* of danger); esp., the immediate personal vicinity of a great personage giving audience or reception or permitting attendance (as, to be admitted to the royal *presence*); hence, a presence-chamber†; also, a company or assembly of persons present† (as, "Here is like to be a good *presence* of Worthies": Shakspere's "Love's Labour's Lost," v. 2. 536); also, one's person or self as actually present (as, "Her ample *presence* fills up all the place": Pope's "Dunciad," i. 261); personal appearance or bearing, esp. of a dignified or imposing kind (as, a man of fine *presence*; "The maidens gather'd strength and grace And *presence*, lordlier than before," Tennyson's "In Memoriam," ciii.); a person, esp. of dignified or fine appearance, or an imposing personage (as, "Slowly passed that august *Presence* Down the thronged and shouting street": Whittier's "Sycamores"); in general, something present, esp. a divine or spiritual being or any incorporeal agency (as, "She really felt drawn to worship him, as if he were the shrine . . . of that *Presence* to which he bore such solemn witness," J. H. Newman's "Callista," xxvii.; "It [a secret] haunted all the chambers of their souls as an invisible *presence*," Longfellow's "Kavanagh," xxiii.).—**presence of mind,** alert and collected state of mind in emergencies; self-possession enabling one to act promptly and suitably under unexpected or trying circumstances: as, "He . . . nearly lost his *presence of mind.* He was utterly unaccustomed to such crises" (Arnold Bennett's "Helen with the High Hand," v.).—**pres′ence=cham″ber,** *n.* The room in which a great personage, as a sovereign, receives guests or those entitled to come before him: as, "The Spanish sovereigns fixed their throne in the *presence-chamber* of the palace" (Irving's "Conquest of Granada," c.).—**pres′ence=room,** *n.* Same as *presence-chamber.*

pres-ent[1] (prez′ẹnt), *a.* [OF. *present* (F. *présent*), < L. *præsens* (*præsent-*), lit. 'being before (one),' ppr. of *præesse*, < *præ*, before, + *esse*, be.] Being before or with one or others, or in a company or place specified or understood (as, "Assemble me the men of Judah . . . and be thou here *present*," 2 Sam. xx. 4; to be *present* at a wedding; no one was *present* when this happened: opposed to *absent*); being here or there, rather than elsewhere; hence, existing in a place, thing, combination, or the like (as, traces of gold were *present* in this locality; rudimentary wings are *present* in some species; carbon is *present* in many minerals); fig., being before the mind (as, "Let this great truth be *present* night and day": Pope's "Essay on Man," iii. 5); being actually or here under consideration (as, "I might open the *present* chapter . . . by a description of a November afternoon": Thackeray's "Newcomes," li.); also, having the mind attentive to what is about one, or being mentally alert and collected in emergencies (obs. or rare: cf. *presence of mind,* under *presence*); also, being at hand or ready at need, as with aid (archaic: as, "God is our refuge and strength, a very *present* help in trouble," Ps. xlvi. 1); also, being, existing, or occurring at this time or now (as, the *present* ruler; *present* conditions; the *present* hour; the *present* outbreaks: opposed to *past* and *future*); for the time being (as, articles for *present* use; "The log-hut, for *present* shelter meant, Not future comfort," Whittier's "Panorama"); also, immediate† or instant† (as, "a horrid place . . . in which we saw nothing but *present* death": Defoe's "Captain Singleton," vi.); in *gram.*, denoting action now going on or a state now existing (as, the *present* tense).—**present value,** or **present worth,**

of a sum payable at a given future date, an amount which, plus the interest upon it for the time from the actual date to the given future date, will equal the sum then due: as, the *present value* of $1,060 due one year from date, interest being allowed at 6%, is $1,000.—**pres'ent**[1], *n.* That which is present or before one†; the matter in hand†; also, the present time (as, "To judge rightly of the *present*, we must oppose it to the past": Johnson's "Rasselas," xxx.); *pl.*, in *law*, the present writings, or this document (used in a deed of conveyance, a lease, or other document, to denote the document itself, as in the phrase 'Know all men by these *presents*'); *sing.*, in *gram.*, the present tense, or a verb-form in the present tense.—**at present**, at the present time; now. **pre-sent**[2] (prẹ-zent'), *v. t.* [OF. *presenter* (F. *présenter*), < L. *præsentare* (pp. *præsentatus*), place before, show, present, < *præsens*: see *present*[1].] To bring (a person, etc.) before, or into the presence of, another, esp. a superior; introduce ceremoniously or formally (as, to be *presented* at court, or to society; "*Presented* to Melusine, he bowed, smiled, and said, 'Greatly charmed,' " M. Hewlett's "Open Country," xi.); bring before or introduce to the public (as, a theatrical manager *presents* an actor or a company in a play); come to show (one's self) before a person, in or at a place, etc. (as, "Call Joshua, and *present* yourselves in the tabernacle": Deut. xxxi. 14); also, to offer to view or notice, or show or exhibit (as, the picture *presents* him in his prime; to *present* a fine appearance, or signs of decay); bring before the mind, or offer for consideration (as, "Hear what to my mind first thoughts *present*": Milton's "Paradise Lost," ix. 213); set forth in words (as, to *present* facts, reasons, or arguments); represent, personate, or act, as on the stage; also, to direct, point, or turn to something or in a particular way (as, to *present* one's face to the foe); level or aim (a weapon, esp. a firearm); also, to hold out or offer for taking, hand over, or deliver, esp. with formality (as, to *present* one's card to a person); hand or send in, as a bill or a check for payment; tender, render, or convey (as, to *present* one's compliments, respects, or thanks to a person; to *present* a message); often, to bring or deliver for acceptance, as an offering or gift (as, to *present* a sacrifice on an altar; "They *presented* unto him gifts; gold, and frankincense, and myrrh," Mat. ii. 11); give, esp. in a formal or ceremonious way; fig., to afford or furnish (an opportunity, possibility, etc.); also, to approach or furnish (a person, etc.) with something offered (as, "A footman entered, and *presented* Mrs. Holt with some mail on a silver tray," W. Churchill's "Modern Chronicle," i. 7; to *present* a person with a bill for services rendered); often, to furnish or endow with a gift or the like, esp. by formal act (as, to *present* a man with a gold watch; to *present* a college with a new building); *eccles.*, to offer or recommend (a clergyman) to the bishop for institution to a benefice; in *law*, to bring formally to the notice of the proper authority, as an offense; bring a formal charge against, as a person.— **to present arms**, *milit.*, to bring a rifle (or other weapon) to a perpendicular position in front of the body, as in saluting a superior officer.—**pre-sent'**[2], *v. i.* To level or aim a weapon (as, "Drawing a large horse-pistol, he *presented*": Smollett's "Humphry Clinker," May 17); also, to point, face, or project in a particular direction; *eccles.*, to present a clergyman for institution to a benefice.—**pres-ent**[2] (prez'ent), *n.* [OF. *present* (F. *présent*).] The presenting of a thing as a gift, or a presentation or gift of something (as, "I can make no marriage *present*; Little can I give my wife": Tennyson's "Lord of Burleigh," 13); also, a thing presented as a gift (as, to accept a thing as a *present*; Christmas *presents*); a gift.

pre-sent-a-ble (prẹ-zen'tạ-bl), *a.* That may be presented; esp., suitable, as in appearance, dress, manners, etc., for being introduced into society or company (as, "In Mrs. Percival's phrase, 'She may meet anybody there.' The child must be *presentable*": M. Hewlett's "Open Country," i.); hence, of sufficiently good appearance, or fit to be seen (as, "My very shoes and stockings were purified and rendered *presentable*": C. Brontë's "Jane Eyre," xxix.).—**pre-sent-a-bil'i-ty** (-bil'i-ti), *n.*—**pre-sent'a-bly**, *adv.*

pres-en-ta-tion (prez-en-tā'shọn), *n.* [OF. *presentacion* (F. *présentation*), < LL. *præsentatio(n-)*.] The act of presenting, or the state of being presented; introduction,

as of a person at court; exhibition or representation, as of a play; offering or delivering, as of something to be taken; bestowal, as of a gift; also, that which is presented, as a gift (obs. or rare); *eccles.*, the act or the right of presenting a clergyman to the bishop for institution to a benefice; in *com.*, the presentment of a bill, note, or the like; in *obstet.*, the appearance of a particular part of the fetus at the os uteri during labor; in *psychol.*, a cognitive modification of consciousness; an idea; a perceptual cognition.—**pres-en-ta'tion-al**, *a.*—**pres-en-ta'tion-ism**, *n.* The doctrine that perception is an immediate cognition.—**pres-en-ta'tion-ist**, *n.*

pre-sen-ta-tive (prẹ-zen'tạ-tiv), *a.* *Eccles.*, admitting of or pertaining to presentation; in *psychol.*, of, pertaining to, or of the nature of a presentation.

pres-en-tee (prez-en-tē'), *n.* One to whom something is presented; also, one who is presented; *eccles.*, one presented for institution to a benefice.

pre-sent-er (prẹ-zen'tẻr), *n.* One who presents.

pre-sen-tient (prē-sen'shi̯ent), *a.* [L. *præsentiens (-ent-)*, ppr. of *præsentire*, feel beforehand, < *præ*, before, + *sentire*, feel.] Feeling or perceiving beforehand; having a presentiment.

pre-sen-ti-ment (prẹ-sen'ti-mẹnt or prẹ-zen'-), *n.* [F. *presentiment*, now *pressentiment*, < L. *præsentire*: see *presentient*.] A feeling or impression of something about to happen, esp. something evil; a vague sense of impending misfortune or trouble; a foreboding: as, "A *presentiment* told me there was trouble in the wind" (F. M. Crawford's "Mr. Isaacs," xi.); "A *presentiment* of evil hung over him" (Kingsley's "Yeast," xiii.).—**pre-sen-ti-men'tal** (-men'-tạl), *a.*

pre-sen-tive (prẹ-zen'tiv). [From *present*[2], *v.*] In *gram.*: **I.** *a.* Of words, presenting an object or conception directly to the mind: opposed to *symbolic*. **II.** *n.* A presentive word.—**pre-sen'tive-ly**, *adv.*—**pre-sen'tive-ness**, *n.*

pres-ent-ly (prez'ẹnt-li), *adv.* At present (now prov.); also, immediately (now prov.); now, usually, in a little while, or soon (as, "The reports grew *presently* to have a more serious tone": Howells's "Chance Acquaintance," vii.).

pre-sent-ment (prẹ-zent'mẹnt), *n.* [OF. *presentement*, < *presenter*, E. *present*[2], *v.*] The act of presenting, or the state of being presented; presentation; representation; also, a representation, picture, or likeness (as, "Look here, upon this picture, and on this, The counterfeit *presentment* of two brothers": Shakspere's "Hamlet," iii. 4. 54); in *com.*, the presenting of a bill, note, or the like, as for acceptance or payment; in *law*, the statement by a grand jury of an offense from their own knowledge or observation, without any indictment laid before them.

pres-en-toir (prez-en-twor'), *n.* [Cf. F. *présentoir*, broadbladed knife formerly used at table for presenting food to persons.] A shallow bowl or cup with a tall supporting stem, for holding fruit or flowers (obs. or hist.); also, a tray or salver on which things are presented; also, a kind of stand or holder for a bowl, cup, or the like.

pres-ent=per-fect (prez'ẹnt-pẻr'fekt), *a.* and *n.* In *gram.*, same as *perfect*.

pre-serv-a-ble (prẹ-zẻr'vạ-bl), *a.* Capable of being preserved.

pres-er-va-tion (prez-ẻr-vā'shọn), *n.* [OF. *preservation* (F. *préservation*).] The act of preserving, or the state of being preserved.

Presentoir of Japanese Lacquer-ware, with Bowl.

pre-ser-va-tive (prẹ-zẻr'vạ-tiv). [OF. *preservatif* (F. *préservatif*).] **I.** *a.* Tending to preserve. **II.** *n.* Something that preserves or tends to preserve; a medicine that preserves health or prevents disease; a chemical substance or preparation used to preserve foods, etc., from decomposition or fermentation.

pre-ser-va-to-ry (prẹ-zẽr'vạ-tō-ri). **I.** *a.* Preservative. **II.** *n.*; pl. *-ries* (-riz). A preservative; also, an apparatus for preserving substances for food; also, a place where the preserving of food-products is carried on.

pre-serve (prẹ-zẽrv'), *v.*; *-served*, *-serving*. [OF. *preserver* (F. *préserver*), < LL. *præservare*, < L. *præ*, before, + *servare*, keep.] **I.** *tr.* To keep safe from harm or injury; save; also, to keep alive or in existence, or make lasting (as, "those who wish to preserve the present order of society": Kingsley's "Yeast," xiv.); keep up, or maintain (as, "Mr. Travers *preserved* an immobility which struck d'Alcacer as obviously affected": J. Conrad's "Rescue," v. 6); keep possession of, or retain (as, to *preserve* one's composure); also, to prepare (food or any perishable substance) so as to resist decomposition or fermentation (as, "a way how to *preserve* our beef without cask or pickle": Defoe's "Captain Singleton," ii.); esp., to prepare (fruit, etc.) by cooking with sugar; also, to keep (game, etc.) undisturbed for personal use in hunting or fishing. **II.** *intr.* To preserve fruit, etc.; make preserves.—**pre-serve'**, *n.* Something that preserves; also, that which is preserved; esp., fruit, etc., prepared by cooking with sugar (usually in *pl.*); also, a place set apart for the protection and propagation of game or fish for sport, etc.—**pre-serv'er**, *n.*

pre-side (prẹ-zīd'), *v. i.*; *-sided*, *-siding*. [F. *présider*, < L. *præsidere*, sit before, guard, preside over, < *præ*, before, + *sedere*, sit.] To occupy the place of authority or control, as in an assembly; act as chairman or president; also, to exercise superintendence or control (as, "the dining-room . . . *presided* over by the decorous butler and his assistants": W. Churchill's "Modern Chronicle," i. 7).

pres-i-dence (prez'i-dẹns), *n.* The action or function of presiding; also, the office of president (now rare).

pres-i-den-cy (prez'i-dẹn-si), *n.*; pl. *-cies* (-siz). The office, function, or term of office of a president; specif., the office of President of the United States (often *cap.*); also, in British India, one of two (formerly three) great administrative divisions, orig. governed by presidents (Madras and Bombay, and formerly Bengal).

pres-i-dent (prez'i-dẹnt), *n.* [OF. *president* (F. *président*), < L. *præsidens* (-ent-), ppr. of *præsidere*, E. *preside*.] One who presides; the appointed governor of a province or the like†; an officer appointed or elected to preside over an organized body of persons; the chief officer of a college, university, society, corporation, etc.; [often *cap.*] the highest executive officer of a modern republic.—**pres-i-den'tial** (-den'shạl), *a.* Of or pertaining to a president or presidency; also, of the nature of a president; presiding.—**pres-i-den'tial-ly**, *adv.*—**pres'i-dent-ship**, *n.* The office, function, or term of office of a president.

pre-sid-er (prẹ-zī'dẽr), *n.* One who presides.

pre-sid-i-o (prẹ-sid'i-ō), *n.*; pl. *-os* (-ōz). [Sp., < L. *præsidium*, guard, garrison, post, < *præsidere*: see *preside*.] In Spanish use, a garrisoned fort; a military post; also, a penal settlement.—**pre-sid'i-al**, *a.*

pre-sig-ni-fy (prē-sig'ni-fī), *v. t.*; *-fied*, *-fying*. [L. *præsignificare*, < *præ*, before, + *significare*, E. *signify*.] To signify or indicate beforehand; foreshow.—**pre-sig″ni-fi-ca'tion** (-fi-kā'shọn), *n.*

press¹ (pres), *v.* [OF. F. *presser*, < L. *pressare*, freq. of *premere* (pp. *pressus*), press.] **I.** *tr.* To act upon with weight or force; weigh heavily upon; bear upon; subject to pressure; sometimes, to clasp (the hand of another); hold closely in an embrace; also, to move by weight or force in a certain direction or into a certain position; push, drive, or thrust; also, to compress or squeeze, as to alter in shape or size, to smooth, etc.; iron (clothes, etc.); extract juice, etc., from by pressure; also, to squeeze out or express, as juice; also, to beset or harass (as, "that longing for the country which had always come on him when he was hard *pressed*": Galsworthy's "Saint's Progress," iii. 7); oppress or trouble; put to straits, as by want of something (as, "They were *pressed* for time to reach a certain spot before the snow should fall": Stevenson's "Master of Ballantrae," xi.); also, to urge or impel, as to a particular course (as, "Why should he stay, whom love doth *press* to go?" Shakspere's

"Midsummer Night's Dream," iii. 2. 184); constrain or compel (as, "The two gentlemen . . . were *pressed* by their private affairs to return in three days": Swift's "Gulliver's Travels," iii. 8); urge onward, hurry, or hasten; also, to urge (a person, etc.) by words (as, "Isaacs hesitated long, but as every one *pressed* him in turn, he yielded at last": F. M. Crawford's "Mr. Isaacs," vii.); importune, beseech, or entreat, as to do something (as, "He warmly *pressed* me to stay to breakfast": W. H. Hudson's "Purple Land," ix.); also, to urge, or insist on; make earnest request for (as, to *press* the payment of a debt); insist on the admission or acceptance of (as, to *press* one's opinions or theories); lay stress on, or emphasize (as, to *press* the importance of education); plead with insistence (as, to *press* a claim); also, to urge for acceptance (as, "She did not *press* on him the post of umpire": G. Meredith's "Lord Ormont and His Aminta," viii.); in general, to push forward (as, to *press* matters to extremities); also, to crowd upon or throng (archaic). **II.** *intr.* To exert weight, force, or pressure; also, to iron clothes, etc.; also, fig., to bear heavily, as upon the mind; also, to compel haste (as, "Time *presses*, and we must come to the point": Conan Doyle's "Exploits of Brigadier Gerard," v.); demand immediate attention (as, "For the present other matters *press*": H. Melville's "Moby-Dick," lxxiii.); also, to use urgent entreaty (as, to *press* for an answer); also, to push forward with force, eagerness, or haste (as, "The head of the column had reached the shore, and came *pressing* up the bank": Irving's "Captain Bonneville," xli.); crowd or throng (as, "the nations of Germany, who perpetually *pressed* on the frontiers of the empire": Gibbon's "Decline and Fall of the Roman Empire," xii.); also, to obtrude one's self (archaic).—**press¹**, *n.* [OF. F. *presse*.] The act or an act of pressing; pressure; also, pressed state; a crease caused by pressing; also, pressure or urgency, as of affairs or business (as, "that *press* of engagements which was his excuse so many times": Thoreau's "Walden," ii.); also, a pressing or pushing forward; also, a pressing together in a crowd, or a crowding or thronging; the crush or collision of battle (as, "He . . . fought sword in hand, in the thickest *press*": Macaulay's "Hist. of Eng.," vii.); a crowd, throng, or multitude (as, "The hot and crowded bazars blazed with light as they made their way through the *press* of all the races in Upper India": Kipling's "Kim," i.); also, any of various instruments or machines for exerting pressure (as, a cotton-*press*; a letter-*press*; a stamping-*press*); esp., a printing-press, or machine used for printing; an establishment for printing books, etc.; the process or art of printing; printed publications collectively, esp. newspapers and periodicals; the body or class of persons engaged in writing for or editing newspapers or periodicals; the critical comment of newspapers, etc., on some matter of current public interest (colloq., and orig. British: as, to be given a good *press*; "No other book of mine ever had such a bad *press*," Arnold Bennett's "Truth about an Author," Preface); also, an upright case, or piece of furniture, for holding clothes, books, etc.—

press of sail, or **press of canvas**, *naut.*, as much sail as the state of the wind, etc., will permit a ship to carry: as, "a frigate under a *press of sail*" (Marryat's "King's Own," xiii.); "The British Fleet was just out of sight with the exception of one or two stragglers, under a *press of canvas*" (J. Conrad's "Rover," xvi.).

Press of Walnut-wood. (German, 15th century.)

press² (pres), *v. t.* [Altered form of *prest¹*, *v.*, by association with *press¹*.] To force into service, esp. naval or military service; impress.—**press²**, *n.* Impressment into service, esp. naval or military service; also, an order or commission for such impressment.

press=a-gent (pres'ā″jẹnt), *n.* A person employed to attend to the advertising of a theatre, play, etc., through advertisements and other notices in the press.—**press'=a″gent,** *v. t.* To give publicity to or advertise, as a press-agent does, or through a press-agent.

press=board (pres'bōrd), *n.* A kind of millboard or pasteboard.

press-er (pres'ėr), *n.* One who or that which presses, or applies pressure.

press=gang (pres'gang), *n.* A body of men under the command of an officer, employed to impress other men for service, esp. in the navy or army: as, "A *pressgang,* that was in need of men for a man-of-war, came on board, and pressed poor Charles" (Galt's "Annals of the Parish," ix.).

press-ing (pres'ing), *p. a.* Urgent, or demanding immediate attention (as, "The danger now became too *pressing* to admit of longer delay": Cooper's "Spy," v.); also, urgent or persistent in solicitation (as, "He was very *pressing* with Brown to send the 'order'": J. Conrad's "Lord Jim," xxxix.); importunate; expressed with earnest desire for compliance, as a request or summons.—**press'ing-ly,** *adv.*—**press'ing-ness,** *n.*

pres-sion (presh'ọn), *n.* [L. *pressio(n-).*] Pressure.

press-man (pres'man), *n.;* pl. *-men.* A man who operates or has charge of a printing-press; also, a writer or reporter for the press (colloq.).

press=mark (pres'märk), *n.* In libraries, a mark put upon a volume to indicate its location in the library.

press=mon-ey (pres'mun″i), *n.* [Earlier *prest-money:* see *prest*[1].] Money paid to a soldier or sailor on enlistment. [Now only hist.]

pres-sor (pres'ọr), *a.* [NL.: cf. *depressor.*] In *physiol.,* that presses; increasing pressure; stimulating: as, a *pressor* nerve (a nerve whose stimulation causes an increase of blood-pressure).

press=room (pres'röm), *n.* A room or apartment containing a press or presses; esp., the room in a printing establishment in which the presses are kept and operated.

pres-sure (presh'ụr), *n.* [OF. *pressure,* < L. *pressura,* < *premere:* see *press*[1].] The act of pressing, or the state of being pressed; the exertion of force upon a body by another body in contact with it; compression; fig., harassment; oppression; a state of trouble or embarrassment; a constraining or compelling force or influence; urgency, as of affairs or business; also, that which is impressed†; impression† or stamp†; in *mech.,* an equilibrated force; a force per unit area exerted over a surface; stress; in *elect.,* electromotive force.—**pres'sur-al,** *a.*—**pres'sure=gage,** *n.* An apparatus for measuring the pressure of gases or liquids, as an attachment for indicating the pressure of steam in a boiler; in *gun.,* an instrument used to determine the pressure in the bore or chamber of a gun when the charge explodes.

press-work (pres'wėrk), *n.* The working or management of a printing-press, or the work turned out by it.

prest[1]† (prest), *n.* [OF. *prest* (F. *prêt*), a loan, < *prester* (F. *prêter*), lend, < L. *præstare,* perform, pay, furnish, < *præ,* before, + *stare,* stand.] A loan; an advance payment, as to a soldier or sailor at enlistment.—**prest**[1]†, *v. t.* [Cf. *press*[2].] To engage with an advance payment; enlist; press into service.

prest[2]† (prest), *a.* [OF. *prest* (F. *prêt*), < LL. *præstus,* ready, < L. *præsto,* adv., at hand, appar. < *præ,* before, + *situs,* pp., put, placed: see *site.*] Ready.

pres-ta-tion (pres-tā'shọn), *n.* [OF. F. *prestation,* < L. *præstatio(n-),* < *præstare:* see *prest*[1].] A payment made or exacted, as in money or service, by way of feudal or customary duty.

pres-ter (pres'tėr), *n.* [OF. *prestre* (F. *prêtre*): see *priest.*] Priest: used in the name of a supposed Christian potentate ('Prester John') of the middle ages, said to have a kingdom in some part of Asia or Africa.

pres-ti-dig-i-ta-tion (pres-ti-dij-i-tā'shọn), *n.* [F. *prestidigitation,* < It. *presto,* quick (see *presto*), + L. *digitus,* finger: cf. *prestigiation.*] Sleight of hand; legerdemain; jugglery.—**pres-ti-dig'i-ta-tor,** *n.* [F. *prestidigitateur.*] One who practises sleight of hand; a conjurer; a juggler.

pres-tige (pres-tēzh' or pres'tij), *n.* [F., illusion, glamour, prestige, < LL. *præstigium,* illusion, L. *præstigiæ,* pl., illusions, jugglers' tricks.] An illusion†; hence, distinction or reputation (illusory or well-founded) attaching to a

person or thing and dominating the mind of others or of the public (as, "A certain seclusion, a certain aloofness, would add greatly to the *prestige* of the god": H. G. Wells's "Outline of History," xix. § 2); often, reputation or influence arising from success, achievement, rank, or other circumstances (as, "After Napoleon's first battles, *prestige* did half his work for him": G. Meredith's "Lord Ormont and His Aminta," ix.).

pres-tig-i-a-tion (pres-tij-i-ā'shọn), *n.* [LL. *præstigiare,* deceive by jugglery, < L. *præstigiæ:* see *prestige.*] The practice of magic or jugglery; conjuring; juggling; prestidigitation. [Now rare.]—**pres-tig'i-a-tor,** *n.*

pres-ti-gious (pres-tij'us), *a.* [L. *præstigiosus,* < *præstigiæ:* see *prestige.*] Practising or involving magic or jugglery; illusory; deceptive. [Now rare.]

pres-tis-si-mo (pres-tēs'sē-mō), *a.* or *adv.* [It., superl. of *presto:* see *presto.*] In *music,* in the most rapid tempo.

pres-to (pres'tō). [It., adj. and adv., < LL. *præstus,* adj., ready, L. *præsto,* adv., at hand: see *prest*[2].] **I.** *a.* Ready or at hand; quick or rapid; also, of the nature of jugglery; juggling; in *music,* in quick tempo. **II.** *adv.* Quickly, rapidly, or immediately (used by jugglers or conjurers in various phrases of command); in *music,* in quick tempo. **III.** *n.* The utterance 'presto'; in *music,* a movement or piece in quick tempo.

pre-sum-a-ble (prẹ-zū'ma-bl), *a.* Capable of being presumed, or taken for granted; probable; likely.—**pre-sum'a-bly,** *adv.* As may be presumed; probably.

pre-sume (prẹ-zūm'), *v.;* *-sumed,* *-suming.* [OF. *presumer* (F. *présumer*), < L. *præsumere* (pp. *præsumptus*), take beforehand, anticipate, assume, venture, < *præ,* before, + *sumere,* take.] **I.** *tr.* To take upon one's self, or undertake, with unwarrantable boldness (as, "Bold deed thou hast *presumed,* adventurous Eve": Milton's "Paradise Lost," ix. 921); esp., to undertake or venture (to do something) as by taking a liberty (as, to *presume* to speak for another; "the plan which I shall *presume* to suggest," Burke's "Conciliation with the Colonies"); also, to take for granted, assume, or suppose (as, "You have an . . . undeniable right, sir, to enter the house . . . always *presuming* you to be called there by the duty of your office," Scott's "Guy Mannering," xlvii.; "I *presume* you're tired after the long ride," Mrs. Wharton's "Ethan Frome," vii.); in *law,* to assume as being true or a fact in the absence of proof to the contrary (as, to *presume* the death of one missing beyond a fixed term of years). **II.** *intr.* To act or proceed with unwarrantable or impertinent boldness; take liberties; rely (*on* or *upon*) in acting unwarrantably or taking liberties (as, "Nor was that King wise who *presumed* far on the forbearance of the English people," Macaulay's "Hist. of Eng.," i.; to *presume* upon one's position as a guest); aspire, venture, or go presumptuously (now rare: as, "Into the heaven of heavens I have *presumed,* An earthly guest," Milton's "Paradise Lost," vii. 13); also, to take something for granted; suppose.—**pre-sum'ed-ly** (-zū'med-li), *adv.* As is or may be presumed or supposed.—**pre-sum'er,** *n.*—**pre-sum'ing,** *p. a.* That presumes; presumptuous; unduly bold.—**pre-sum'ing-ly,** *adv.*

pre-sump-tion (prẹ-zump'shọn), *n.* [OF. *presumpcion* (F. *présomption*), < L. *præsumptio(n-).*] The act of presuming, or taking upon one's self more than right or propriety warrants (as, "This is a matter that concerns myself only, and it is *presumption* on his part to interfere in it": W. H. Hudson's "Purple Land," xvii.); unwarrantable, unbecoming, or impertinent boldness in conduct or thought; also, the act of presuming, taking for granted, or assuming; assumption of something as true; belief on reasonable grounds or probable evidence; hence, that which is presumed, or taken for granted; an assumption (as, "Whatever he was doing at one moment, the *presumption* was a sure one that he would not be doing it the next": Parkman's "Oregon Trail," xx.); also, a ground or reason for presuming or believing, or a presumptive evidence (as, "The more he disliked a thing the greater the *presumption* that it was right," S. Butler's "Way of All Flesh," xxxi.; "The next thing . . . is, to consider the supposed *presumptions* against revelation," J. Butler's "Analogy of

Religion," ii. 2); in *law*, an inference as to the existence of one fact from the known existence of other facts; an inference in accordance with the common experience of mankind and the established principles of logic, or with the prescribed policy of the law.

pre-sump-tive (prḝ-zump′tiv), *a.* [F. *présomptif*, < LL. *præsumptivus*.] Presumptuous†; also, presumed, or regarded as such by presumption (as, an heir *presumptive*, see under *heir*, *n.*; *presumptive* murder); based on presumption (as, a *presumptive* title); also, affording ground for presumption, or warranting a belief or inference (as, "The blush of virtuous indignation was construed into *presumptive* evidence of guilt": Marryat's "King's Own," i.). —**pre-sump′tive-ly**, *adv.*

pre-sump-tu-ous (prḝ-zump′tū-us), *a.* [OF. *presumptueux* (F. *présomptueux*), < LL. *præsumptuosus*.] Full of, characterized by, or showing presumption, or readiness to presume in conduct or thought; unwarrantably or impertinently bold; forward; presuming: as, "with the undoubting self-reliance of a *presumptuous* novice, ready to advance fixed opinions and plans of action" (Bancroft's "Hist. of the U. S.," Amer. Revolution, i. 2); "a *presumptuous* mockery of the Creator" (Hawthorne's "Twice-Told Tales," The Prophetic Pictures).—**pre-sump′tu-ous-ly**, *adv.*—**pre-sump′tu-ous-ness**, *n.*

pre-sup-pose (prḝ-su-pōz′), *v. t.*; -posed, -posing. [OF. *presupposer* (F. *présupposer*), < *pre-* (< L. *præ*), before, + *supposer*, E. *suppose*.] To suppose or assume beforehand; take for granted in advance; also, of a thing, to require or imply as an antecedent condition (as, an effect *presupposes* a cause).—**pre-sup-po-si′tion** (-sup-ǫ-zish′ǫn), *n.*

pre-sur-mise (prḝ-sėr-mīz′), *n.* [See *pre-*.] A surmise previously formed.

pre-tence′, *n.* See *pretense*.

pre-tend (prḝ-tend′), *v.* [OF. *pretendre* (F. *prétendre*), < L. *prætendere* (pp. *prætentus*, LL. *prætensus*), stretch forth, put forward, pretend, < *præ*, before, + *tendere*, stretch, E. *tend¹*.] **I.** *tr.* To stretch forth†, present†, or offer†; also, to spread before or over something as a protection†; also, to put forward as a pretext or excuse†; also, to allege or assert (as, "even admitting the evidence of religion to be as doubtful as is *pretended*": J. Butler's "Analogy of Religion," ii. 6); esp., to allege or profess insincerely or falsely; hence, to feign (as, to *pretend* illness; "My bedmate *pretended* to be asleep," G. W. Cable's "Cavalier," xxvii.); also, to lay claim to†; also, to take upon one's self, venture, or attempt (to do something: as, "Whether my bullets did any execution or not I cannot *pretend* to say," W. H. Hudson's "Purple Land," xviii.); also, to intend† or plan†. **II.** *intr.* To reach forward†; also, to tend†; also, to make believe; also, to lay claim (*to*); fig., to make pretentions (*to*: as, "a square white house *pretending* neither to beauty nor state," Mrs. H. Ward's "Robert Elsmere," xi.); also, to aspire (*to*), as a suitor or candidate (as, "A . . . fellow . . . might *pretend* surely to his kinswoman's hand": Thackeray's "Newcomes," xxiv.). —**pre-tend′ant**, *n.* [F. *prétendant*, prop. ppr. of *prétendre*.] A pretender; a claimant; also, a suitor or wooer.—**pre-tend′ed**, *p. a.* Alleged or asserted; reputed; insincerely or falsely professed; also, feigned, fictitious, or counterfeit (as, "The *pretended* elk, throwing off his hide and his horn, started forth an Indian warrior": Irving's "Captain Bonneville," xxiv.).—**pre-tend′ed-ly**, *adv.*—**pre-tend′er**, *n.* One who pretends; one who makes false professions; a claimant; an aspirant or candidate; specif., a claimant to a throne (as, the Old *Pretender* and the Young *Pretender*, James Francis Edward Stuart and Charles Edward Stuart, son and grandson of James II. of England).—**pre-tend′ing-ly**, *adv.*

pre-tense, pre-tence (prḝ-tens′), *n.* [= AF. *pretense*, < LL. *prætensa*, fem. of *prætensus*, pp.: see *pretend*.] The act of pretending or alleging, now esp. falsely; insincere or false profession; also, pretending or feigning, or make-believe (as, "My sleepiness was all *pretence*": W. H. Hudson's "Purple Land," xvii.); a false show of something (as, a *pretense* of friendship); a piece of make-believe (as, "It is part of the decent and useful *pretences* of our world that children . . . know nothing of love": H. G. Wells's "Tono-Bungay," i. 1. § 8); also, an alleged or pretended reason or excuse, or a pretext (as, "The man, under *pretence* of going a journey, took lodgings in the next street": Hawthorne's "Twice-Told Tales," Wakefield); also, the putting forth of a claim, or the claim itself; fig., pretension (*to*: as, destitute of any *pretense* to wit); esp., pretension to dignity, importance, or the like; pretentiousness; also, an intention† or purpose†.

pre-ten-sion (prḝ-ten′shǫn), *n.* [F. *prétention*, sometimes formerly *pretension*, < ML. *prætentio(n-)*, *prætensio(n-)*, < L. *prætendere*, E. *pretend*.] The act of pretending or alleging, or an allegation; also, a pretext; also, a laying claim to something, or a claim made; hence, a claim or title to something (as, "a prince with considerable *pretensions* to the throne": De Quincey's "Revolt of the Tartars"); fig., claim made, esp. indirectly or by implication, to some quality, merit, or the like (often in *pl.*: as, to make no *pretensions* to superior judgment); also, claim or right to be considered as possessing something (with *to*, and often in *pl.*: as, to have no *pretensions* to beauty); esp., claim to dignity, importance, or merit (in *sing.* or *pl.*: as, "The front door . . . rested on Corinthian pillars of some architectural *pretension*," Mrs. Stowe's "Oldtown Folks," xv.; "These were not commonplace young ladies, but had *pretensions* quite above the ordinary run," Irving's "Tales of a Traveler," ii. 7); pretentiousness or ostentation.

pre-ten-tious (prḝ-ten′shus), *a.* [F. *prétentieux*, < *prétention*, E. *pretension*.] Full of pretension; characterized by assumption of dignity or importance; making an exaggerated outward show; ostentatious.—**pre-ten′tious-ly**, *adv.*—**pre-ten′tious-ness**, *n.*

preter-. [L. *præter-*, repr. *præter*, adv. and prep., past, by, beyond, besides, < *præ*, before: see *pre-*.] A prefix meaning 'past,' 'beyond,' 'more than,' occurring orig. in words from the Latin, but now used also as an English formative.

pre-ter-hu-man (prē-tėr-hū′man), *a.* [See *preter-*.] Beyond what is human.

pret-er-it, pret-er-ite (pret′ḝ-rit). [L. *præteritus*, pp. of *præterire*, go by, < *præter*, past, by, + *ire*, go.] **I.** *a.* Bygone; past; in *gram.*, expressing past time; esp., denoting past action or state simply, without implication as to continuance (as, the *preterit* tense). **II.** *n.* In *gram.*, the preterit tense; a verb-form in this tense, as '(I) loved.'

pret-er-i-tion (pret-ḝ-rish′ǫn), *n.* [LL. *præteritio(n-)*, < L. *præterire*: see *preterit*.] The act of passing by or over, or the state of being passed by or over; omission; neglect; in *Calvinistic theol.*, the passing over by God of those not elected to salvation or eternal life; in *law*, the passing over by a testator of an heir otherwise entitled to a portion.

pre-ter-i-tive (prḝ-ter′i-tiv), *a.* [L. *præteritus*, pp.: see *preterit*.] In *gram.*, expressing past time; also, of certain verbs, limited to past tenses.

pret-er-it=pres-ent, pret-er-ite=pres-ent (pret′ḝ-rit-prez′-ent). In *gram.*: **I.** *a.* Combining preterit form with present meaning: applied specif. to certain Teutonic verbs. **II.** *n.* A preterit-present verb or verb-form.

pre-ter-mit (prē-tėr-mit′), *v. t.*; -mitted, -mitting. [L. *prætermittere* (pp. *prætermissus*), < *præter*, past, + *mittere*, send.] To let pass without notice or mention; disregard; overlook; leave out or omit; leave undone; forbear or neglect to perform.—**pre-ter-mis′sion** (-mish′ǫn), *n.*

pre-ter-nat-u-ral (prē-tėr-nat′ū-ral), *a.* [See *preter-*.] Beyond what is natural (as, "*preternatural* keenness of sight": W. H. Hudson's "Green Mansions," xix.); abnormal; also, out of the ordinary course of nature (as, "A stillness almost *preternatural* spread over the sea": H. Melville's "Moby-Dick," lix.); sometimes, supernatural (as, "Eglintoun Wood — a place well noted from ancient times for *preternatural* appearances": Galt's "Ayrshire Legatees," iv.).—**pre-ter-nat′u-ral-ism**, *n.* Preternatural character or condition; also, recognition of the preternatural.—**pre-ter-nat′u-ral-ly**, *adv.*—**pre-ter-nat′u-ral-ness**, *n.*

pre-ter-nor-mal (prē-tėr-nôr′mal), *a.* [See *preter-*.] Beyond what is normal.

pre-text (prē′tekst), *n.* [L. *prætextus*, outward show, pretext, < *prætexere*, weave before, put forward as a pretext, < *præ*, before, + *texere*, weave.] That which is put forward to conceal a true purpose or object; an ostensible reason; an excuse; a pretense: as, "Under the *pretext* of making lawful reprisals . . . he had sent an armed fleet against the ports of Normandy" (J. F. Kirk's "Charles the Bold," iii. 1).— **pre-text** (prē-tekst′), *v. t.* To use as a pretext; pretend.

pre-tor, præ-tor (prē′tọr), *n.* [L. *prætor,* < *præire,* go before, < *præ,* before, + *ire,* go.] In *Rom. hist.,* orig., the title of a consul as leader of the army; later, one of a number of elected magistrates, engaged chiefly in the administration of justice.—**pre-to-ri-al, præ-to-ri-al** (prē-tō′ri-ạl), *a.* [L. *prætorius.*] Of or pertaining to a pretor. —**pre-to′ri-an, præ-to′ri-an.** [L. *prætorianus.*] **I.** *a.* Of or pertaining to a pretor; [often *cap.*] designating or pertaining to the body-guard of a Roman military commander or emperor. **II.** *n.* A man of pretorian rank; [often *cap.*] a soldier of the pretorian guard.—**pre-to′ri-um, præ-to′ri-um** (-um), *n.;* pl. *-ria* (-ri-ạ). [L. *prætorium.*] The commander's headquarters in an ancient Roman camp; also, the official residence of the governor of an ancient Roman province.—**pre′tor-ship, præ′tor-ship,** *n.* The office, dignity, or term of office of a pretor.

pret-ti-fy (prit′i-fī), *v. t.;* -fied, -fying. [See -*fy.*] To make pretty: often used with a disparaging force: as, to *prettify* a stately mansion or a work of art.

pret-ti-ly (prit′i-li), *adv.* In a pretty manner; pleasingly; gracefully; nicely.—**pret′ti-ness,** *n.*

pret-ty (prit′i), *a.;* compar. *prettier,* superl. *prettiest.* [AS. *prættig,* cunning, wily, < *prætt,* wile, trick; akin to D. *part,* trick, prank, Icel. *prettr,* trick, *prettugr,* tricky.] Cunning† or wily†; hence, clever or ingenious (obs. or archaic: as, a *pretty* stratagem; "We have . . . *pretty* traps to catch the petty thieves," Shakspere's "Henry V.," i. 2. 177); neatly effective (as, a *pretty* wit); also, brave, stout, or hardy (archaic or Sc.: as, "He . . . observed they [recruits] were *pretty* men, meaning, not handsome, but stout warlike fellows," Scott's "Waverley," xvii.); also, smart, fine, or elegant (archaic: as, "The *pretty* gentleman must have his airs," Steele, in "Guardian," 38); also, good-looking, handsome, or comely, as a person (when applied seriously to a man, now prov.); fair or attractive to the eye in a feminine or childish way (as, a *pretty* woman, girl, or baby; a *pretty* face); having a delicate, simple, or graceful beauty (often implying a slight or trivial type); of things, places, etc., pleasing to the eye, esp. without stateliness or grandeur (as, a *pretty* bird; a *pretty* flower; a *pretty* cottage or scene); pleasing to the ear (as, a *pretty* tune); pleasing to the mind or esthetic taste (as, "some *pretty,* graceful, little story which should be full of whatever people knew and liked best": S. Butler's "Way of All Flesh," lxxiii.); in general, fine, nice, pleasant, or excellent (common in prov. expressions, as, a *pretty* smell or taste, *pretty* weather, and also much used ironically, as, a *pretty* state of affairs); also, considerable, or fairly great (now chiefly colloq. or prov.: as, "We've got a *pretty* bit o' building on hand now," George Eliot's "Adam Bede," xlix.).—**a pretty penny.** See *penny.*—**pret′ty,** *n.;* pl. *pretties* (-iz). A pretty one (used esp. in address: as, "Back to back, my *pretties,*" Goldsmith's "She Stoops to Conquer," ii.); also, a pretty thing, as a knickknack, trinket, or ornamental article of dress (commonly in *pl.:* cf. *pretty-pretty, n.*).—**pret′ty,** *adv.* Prettily or nicely (chiefly prov.: as, to behave or talk *pretty*); also, fairly, moderately, or tolerably (expressing a degree less than *very:* as, "The wind blew *pretty* hard," Defoe's "Robinson Crusoe," i. 16; "not such a very bad, but a *pretty* bad boy," Aldrich's "Story of a Bad Boy," i.).—**pret′ty=pret′ty. I.** *a.* Pretty in an overdone or mawkish way: as, *pretty-pretty* pictures or verse; the *pretty-pretty* style in art. **II.** *n.;* pl. *-pretties* (-iz). A pretty thing; a pretty: commonly in *pl.*

pre-typ-i-fy (prē-tip′i-fī), *v. t.;* -fied, -fying. [See pre-.] To typify beforehand; prefigure.

pret-zel (pret′sẹl), *n.* [G. *pretzel, prezel,* var. of *bretzel, brezel.*] A little biscuit, usually in the form of a knot, salted on the outside.

pre-vail (prē-vāl′), *v. i.* [L. *prævalere,* < *præ,* before, + *valere,* be strong.] To be or prove superior in strength, power, or influence (as, to *prevail* in a struggle; "the assumption that truth would *prevail* against humbug," H. Kingsley's "Geoffry Hamlyn," xvii.; "The disquiets of my mind *prevailed* over my weariness, and kept me awake," Swift's "Gulliver's Travels," iii. 1); also, to operate effectually,

or be efficacious (as, no arguments or inducements *prevailed;* "But why *Prevail'd* not thy pure prayers?" Tennyson's "Supposed Confessions," 89); use persuasion or inducement successfully (*on, upon,* or *with:* as, "He had *prevailed* upon the king to spare them," Defoe's "Captain Singleton," xiv.; "The governor *prevailed* with me to take charge of our Northwestern frontier," B. Franklin's "Autobiography," xii.); also, to appear or occur as the more important or frequent feature or element, or predominate (as, green tints *prevail* in the picture); hence, to exist widely, or be widespread; be current, or in general use or practice; exist everywhere or generally (as, "For some time a dead silence *prevailed*": De Quincey's "Revolt of the Tartars").—**pre-vail′ing,** *p. a.* That prevails; having superior power or influence; effectual; predominant; generally current.— **pre-vail′ing-ly,** *adv.*

prev-a-lent (prev′ạ-lẹnt), *a.* [L. *prævalens* (-ent-), ppr. of *prævalere:* see *prevail.*] That prevails; having the superiority or ascendancy (now rare); effectual or efficacious (now rare); now, esp., widespread; of wide extent or occurrence; in general use or acceptance.—**prev′a-lence,** *n.*—**prev′a-lent-ly,** *adv.*

pre-var-i-cate (prē-var′i-kāt), *v. i.;* -cated, -cating. [L. *prævaricatus,* pp. of *prævaricari,* walk crookedly, < *præ,* before, + *varicare,* straddle, < *varus,* bent.] To swerve from the proper course†; also, to deviate from straightforwardness; act or speak evasively; equivocate; quibble. —**pre-var-i-ca′tion** (-kā′shọn), *n.* [L. *prævaricatio*(n-).] The act of prevaricating; deviation from straightforwardness or truth; evasion; equivocation; quibbling.—**pre-var′i-ca-tor,** *n.*

pre-ve-nient (prē-vē′niẹnt), *a.* [L. *præveniens* (-ent-), ppr. of *prævenire:* see *prevent.*] Coming before; antecedent; also, anticipatory.—**pre-ve′nience,** *n.*—**pre-ve′nient-ly,** *adv.*

pre-vent (prē-vent′), *v.* [L. *præventus,* pp. of *prævenire,* come before, anticipate, prevent, < *præ,* before, + *venire,* come.] **I.** *tr.* To come or go before, or precede (archaic); act in anticipation of (archaic: as, "Mine eyes *prevent* the night watches, that I might meditate in thy word," Ps. cxix. 148; "Bertram . . . from the towers, *preventing* day, With Wilfrid took his early way," Scott's "Rokeby," ii. 4); anticipate (a person, etc.) in action (archaic); also, to cut off beforehand or debar (a person, etc.), as from something (now rare); hinder (a person, etc.), as from doing something (as, there is nothing to *prevent* us from going); also, to keep from occurring; hinder. **II.** *intr.* To interpose a hindrance; hinder: as, he will come if nothing *prevents.*—**pre-vent′a-ble, pre-vent′i-ble,** *a.* That may be prevented.—**pre-ven′ta-tive** (-ven′tạ-tiv), *a.* and *n.* Same as *preventive.*—**pre-vent′er,** *n.*—**pre-ven′tion** (-shọn), *n.* [LL. *præventio*(n-).] The act of preventing; effectual hindrance; also, that which prevents; a preventive.—**pre-ven′tive. I.** *a.* Serving to prevent or hinder; in *med.,* warding off disease. **II.** *n.* A preventive agent or measure; in *med.,* a drug, etc., for preventing disease.—**pre-ven′tive-ly,** *adv.*—**pre-ven-to-ri-um** (prē-ven-tō′ri-um), *n.;* pl. *-riums* or *-ria* (-ri-ạ). [NL.] An institution for preventing the spread of a disease, esp. tuberculosis, as by the treatment of persons in an incipient stage of the disease or in danger of the disease.

pre-view (prē′vū), *n.* [See pre-.] A previous view; a view in advance, as of a moving picture.—**pre-view** (prē-vū′), *v. t.* To view beforehand or in advance.

pre-vi-ous (prē′vi-us), *a.* [L. *prævius,* < *præ,* before, + *via,* way.] Coming or occurring before something else (as, the *previous* day, or the day *previous;* "A *previous* blast foretells the rising storm," Young's "Night Thoughts," iii. 218); prior; also, done, occurring, acting, etc., before the proper time, or premature (usually preceded by *too:* colloq.).— **previous question,** in parliamentary procedure, the question whether a vote shall be taken on a main question, moved before the main question is put: in the U. S., resorted to in order to cut off debate and bring the main question to an immediate vote.—**pre′vi-ous,** *adv.* At a time previous: often with *to:* as, he did this *previous* to his departure. —**pre′vi-ous-ly,** *adv.*—**pre′vi-ous-ness,** *n.*

pre-vise (prē-vīz′), *v. t.;* -vised, -vising. [L. *prævisus,* pp. of *prævidere,* foresee, < *præ,* before, + *videre,* see.] To fore-

---

see; also, to forewarn.—**pre-vi′sion** (-vizh′ǫn), *n.* Foresight, foreknowledge, or prescience (as, "She knew by *prevision* what most women learn only by experience": Hardy's "Return of the Native," i. 7); also, an instance of this; an anticipatory vision or perception (as, "Was it some *prevision* of the end?" Stevenson's "Master of Ballantrae," ix.).

pre-vo-ca-tion-al (prē-vǫ-kā′shǫn-ạl), *a.* [See *pre-*.] Consisting of or pertaining to a preliminary or elementary type of vocational training.

pre-voy-ance (prē-voi′ạns), *n.* [F. *prévoyance*, < *prévoir*, < L. *prævidere*: see *previse*.] Foresight; forethought.

pre=war (prē′wâr′), *a.* [See *pre-*.] Before the war: as, *pre-war* conditions. Cf. *post-war*.

prex-y, prex (prek′si, preks), *n.* [For *president*.] A president, as of a college. [Students' slang, U. S.]

prey (prā), *n.* [OF. *preie* (F. *proie*), < L. *præda*, booty, spoil, prey.] Spoil, booty, or plunder (now rare); also, an animal hunted or seized for food, esp. by a carnivorous animal; hence, a person or thing that falls a victim to an enemy, a sharper, a disease, or any adverse agency (as, "the easy *prey* of the first adventurer who comes across him," S. Butler's "Way of All Flesh," lxxviii.; "Ill fares the land, to hastening ills a *prey*, Where wealth accumulates, and men decay," Goldsmith's "Deserted Village," 51); also, the action or habit of preying (now esp. in 'beast of prey,' 'bird of prey,' etc.).—**prey,** *v. i.* [OF. *preier*, < L. *prædari*, take booty.] To take booty or plunder; also, to seek for and seize prey, as an animal does; hence, to make profit by operations on a victim (as, "You are *preyed* on by idle mendicants": Smollett's "Humphry Clinker," June 8); exert a baneful or destructive influence (as, "The anxieties of my mind . . . *preyed* upon my health": Godwin's "Caleb Williams," xxxvi.).—**prey′er,** *n.*

pri-a-can-thid (prī-ạ-kan′thid). [NL. *Priacanthidæ*, pl., < Gr. πρῖων, a saw, + ἄκανθα, thorn, spine.] **I.** *n.* Any of the small, carnivorous acanthopterygian fishes constituting the family *Priacanthidæ*, of tropical seas, as *Priacanthus cruentatus*, of the West Indies, occasionally found on the coast of the U. S. **II.** *a.* Belonging or pertaining to the *Priacanthidæ*.

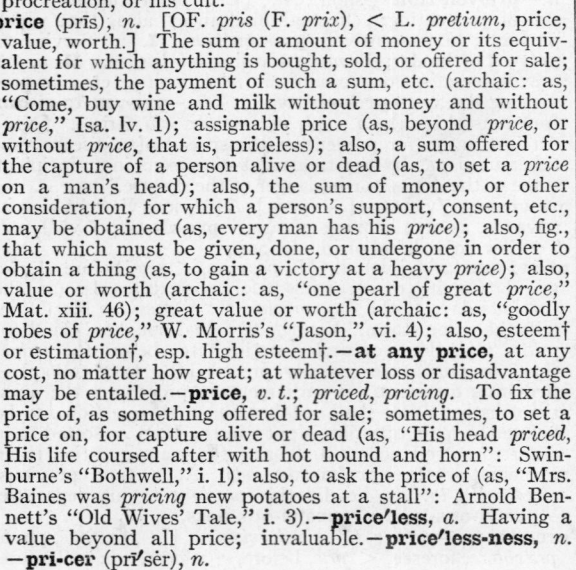

Priacanthid (*Priacanthus cruentatus*).

Pri-ap-ic (prī-ap′ik), *a.* Of or pertaining to Priapus, the Greek and Roman god of procreation, or his cult.

price (prīs), *n.* [OF. *pris* (F. *prix*), < L. *pretium*, price, value, worth.] The sum or amount of money or its equivalent for which anything is bought, sold, or offered for sale; sometimes, the payment of such a sum, etc. (archaic: as, "Come, buy wine and milk without money and without *price*," Isa. lv. 1); assignable price (as, beyond *price*, or without *price*, that is, priceless); also, a sum offered for the capture of a person alive or dead (as, to set a *price* on a man's head); also, the sum of money, or other consideration, for which a person's support, consent, etc., may be obtained (as, every man has his *price*); also, fig., that which must be given, done, or undergone in order to obtain a thing (as, to gain a victory at a heavy *price*); also, value or worth (archaic: as, "one pearl of great *price*," Mat. xiii. 46); great value or worth (archaic: as, "goodly robes of *price*," W. Morris's "Jason," vi. 4); also, esteem† or estimation†, esp. high esteem†.—**at any price,** at any cost, no matter how great; at whatever loss or disadvantage may be entailed.—**price,** *v. t.*; priced, pricing. To fix the price of, as something offered for sale; sometimes, to set a price on, for capture alive or dead (as, "His head *priced*, His life coursed after with hot hound and horn": Swinburne's "Bothwell," i. 1); also, to ask the price of (as, "Mrs. Baines was *pricing* new potatoes at a stall": Arnold Bennett's "Old Wives' Tale," i. 3).—**price′less,** *a.* Having a value beyond all price; invaluable.—**price′less-ness,** *n.* —**pri-cer** (prī′sėr), *n.*

prick (prik), *n.* [AS. *prica*, puncture, point, dot, = MLG. *pricke*, sharp point or implement, = D. *prik*, puncture, point, = Icel. *prik*, dot, little stick.] A puncture made by a needle, thorn, or the like; the print on the ground of the foot of a hare; also, a small or minute mark, a dot, or a point (now rare); also, the spot in the center of a target†, or the target itself†; also, a minute particle or quantity†; also, a sharp projecting part or organ, or a prickle (obs. or rare); a goad for oxen (archaic: as, to kick against the *pricks* see under *kick, v. i.*); a skewer†; any pointed instrument or weapon†; also, the act or an act of pricking (as, the *prick* of a needle); the state or sensation of being pricked.—**prick,** *v.* [AS. *prician* = MLG. *pricken* = D. *prikken* = Icel. *prika*, prick.] **I.** *tr.* To pierce with a sharp point; puncture; also, to affect with sharp pain, as from piercing; esp., to cause sharp mental pain to (as, "His conscience *pricked* him suddenly": Galsworthy's "Saint's Progress," iii. 7); sting, as with remorse or sorrow; torment; also, to urge on with a goad or spur; impel or incite as with a spur (as, "My duty *pricks* me on to cause that Which else no worldly good should draw from me": Shakspere's "Two Gentlemen of Verona," iii. 1. 8); also, to mark (a surface) with pricks or dots in tracing something; mark or trace (something) on a surface by pricks or dots; set down by means of pricks or marks, as music (archaic); mark or indicate by or as by a prick, puncture, or dot, as a name in a list; pick out or choose by or as by such marking; also, to thrust (a pointed object) into something†; stud or dot (something) as with objects thrust in (obs. or rare); also, to cause to stand erect or point upward (as, to *prick* up, or *prick*, the ears, of an animal, to raise the ears in listening—hence often fig. of persons). **II.** *intr.* To perform the action of piercing or puncturing something; cause a sensation of sharp pain as by piercing; also, to have a sensation of being pricked (as, "When the blood creeps, and the nerves *prick* And tingle": Tennyson's "In Memoriam," l.); also, to spur or urge a horse on, ride rapidly, or advance on horseback (archaic: as, "Still at the gallop *prick'd* the Knight," Scott's "Lady of the Lake," v. 18; "The man *pricked* up to the fence to come over it, but his horse was of another mind," G. W. Cable's "Cavalier," xxvi.); also (with *up*), to rise erect or point upward, as the ears of an animal.—**prick′=eared,** *a.* Having the ears erect, as an animal; also, having the hair cut short and the ears standing out prominently (applied opprobriously to the English Roundheads or Puritans).—**prick′er,** *n.* One who or that which pricks; a horseman (archaic); any of various sharp-pointed instruments.

prick-et (prik′et), *n.* [From *prick, n.*] A sharp metal point on which to stick a candle; a candlestick with one or more such points; also, a buck in his second year, with straight, unbranched horns.

prick-le (prik′l), *n.* [AS. *pricel, pricels*, from the stem of *prician*, E. *prick, v.*] A sharp point or pointed projection; esp., a small, pointed process growing from the bark of a plant; also, a pricking sensation (now colloq.). —**prick′le,** *v.*; -led, -ling. **I.** *tr.* To prick; also, to cause a pricking sensation in. **II.** *intr.* To be affected with a pricking sensation, or tingle as if pricked (as, "The skin of her face *prickled*": Arnold Bennett's "Hilda Lessways," ii. 6); also, to rise or stand erect like prickles (as, "The . . . sound . . . made the hair on my old grey head to *prickle* up": Galt's "Annals of the Parish," xliv.).—**prick′li-ness,** *n.* The quality or state of being prickly.—**prick′ly,** *a.* Full of or armed with prickles; fig., full of troublesome points, or difficult to deal with (as, "One never knew when she would . . . put some *prickly* question": Weir Mitchell's "Hugh Wynne," xiv.); also, having the sensation of being pricked; smarting. —**prickly heat,** in *pathol.*, a cutaneous eruption accompanied by a prickling and itching sensation, due to an inflammation of the sweat-glands.—**prick′ly=pear′,** *n.* The pear-shaped or ovoid, often prickly and sometimes edible, fruit of any of certain species of cactus (genus *Opuntia*); also, the plant itself (see *opuntia*).

prick-song (prik′sông), *n.* Written music; also, descant or counterpoint. [Obs. or archaic.]

Pricket.

prick=spur (prik′spėr), *n.* An early form of horseman's spur with a single pricking point: in general use before the 14th century, when it was superseded by the spur with a rowel.

pride (prīd), *n.* [AS. *prȳte*, < *prūt*, E. *proud*.] The state or feeling of being proud; high or inordinate opinion of one's own dignity, importance, merit, or superiority, whether as cherished in the mind or as displayed in bearing, conduct, etc. (as, "My *pride* fell with my fortunes," Shakspere's "As You Like It," i. 2. 264; "The little

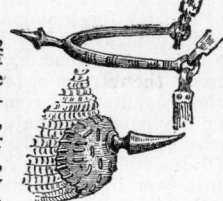

Prick-spurs of the 13th century.

rascal's *pride* and arrogance were perfectly insufferable," Thackeray's "Newcomes," xxi.); becoming or dignified sense of what is due to one's self or one's position or character, or self-respect or self-esteem (as, "What is a woman's *pride* but the staff and banner of her soul?" G. Meredith's "Lord Ormont and His Aminta," vii.; to strengthen a person's resolution by appealing to his *pride*); pleasure or satisfaction taken in something done by or belonging to one's self or conceived as reflecting credit upon one's self (as, to take a just *pride* in an achievement; a father's *pride* in his children; patriotic or civic *pride*); also, that of which a person or a body of persons is proud (as, he was the *pride* of the family; "Glasgow is the *pride* of Scotland," Smollett's "Humphry Clinker," Sept. 3); also, the best or most admired part of anything; the most flourishing state or period, or the prime (as, in the *pride* of manhood; "The bees humming round the gay roses Proclaim it the *pride* of the year," Burns's "Where Are the Joys"); also, splendor, magnificence, or pomp (archaic: as, "The chapel's silver bell . . . That summons you to all the *pride* of prayer," Pope's "Moral Essays," iv. 142); ornament or adornment (archaic); also, mettle in a horse; also, sexual desire†.—**pride,** *v. t.* To indulge (one's self) in a feeling of pride; plume (one's self): esp. with *on* or *upon*: as, "that rich culture on which the present age so justly *prides* itself" (Mallock's "New Republic," iii. 3). —**pride′ful** (-fúl), *a.* Full of pride; proud.—**pride′ful-ly,** *adv.*—**pride′less,** *a.* Without pride.—**pride′=of=Chi′na,** **pride′=of=In′di-a,** *n.* The azedarach or china-tree.

prie=dieu (prē-dyė), *n.* [F., 'pray God.'] A piece of furniture for kneeling on during prayer, having a rest above, as for a book: as, "a dark-red *prie-dieu*, furnished duly with rich missal and ebon rosary" (C. Brontë's "Villette," xxxiv.).

pri-er (prī′ėr), *n.* [See *pry²*, *v.*] One who pries or looks or searches curiously or inquisitively into something.

priest (prēst), *n.* [AS. *prēost*, ult. < LL. *presbyter*, elder, whence also OF. *prester*, F. *prêtre*, priest: see *presbyter*, and cf. *prester*.] One whose office it is to perform religious rites, and esp. to make sacrificial offerings (as, "The *priest* shall burn all on the altar, to be a burnt sacrifice . . . of a sweet savour unto the Lord": Lev. i. 9); a minister of any religion; in Christian use, one ordained to the sacerdotal or pastoral office; a clergyman; a minister; in hierarchical churches, a clergyman of the order next below that of bishop, authorized to administer the sacraments and pronounce absolution.—**priest,** *v. t.* To ordain as a priest.—**priest′craft,** *n.* Priestly craft or arts: as, "It is better that men should be governed by *priestcraft* than by brute violence" (Macaulay's "Hist. of Eng.," i.).—**priest′ess,** *n.* A woman who officiates in sacred rites.—**priest′=fish,** *n.* A rockfish, *Sebastodes mystinus* (family *Scorpænidæ*), of a slaty-black color, abundant along the Pacific coast of the U. S.—**priest′hood** (-húd), *n.* [AS. *prēost-hād*.] The condition or office of a

Priest-fish.

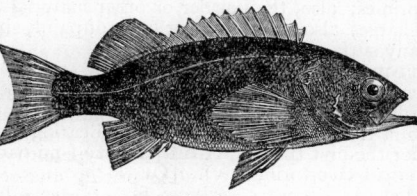

priest; also, priests collectively (as, "The profanation of their temples touched a deeper feeling, of which the *priesthood*

were not slow to take advantage": Prescott's "Conquest of Mexico," iv. 5).—**priest′ly,** *a.* Of or pertaining to a priest; sacerdotal; characteristic of or befitting a priest.—**priest′li-ness,** *n.*—**priest′=rid″den,** *a.* Managed or governed by priests; dominated by priestly influence.

prig¹ (prig), *v.*; *prigged*, *prigging.* [Origin obscure; orig. thieves' slang.] **I.** *tr.* To pilfer or steal: as, "I think we'd find that Mr. Beeton has been *prigging* little things out of the rooms here and there" (Kipling's "Light That Failed," xiv.). [Slang.] **II.** *intr.* To haggle about the price of anything (Sc. and north. Eng.); also, to make entreaty (Sc.).—**prig¹,** *n.* A thief. [Slang.]

prig² (prig), *n.* [Origin obscure; recorded later than *prig¹*.] A coxcomb† (as, "Marlow is a coxcombical *prig* . . . I do hate a Frenchified fop": Godwin's "Caleb Williams," ix.); also, a precisian in religion†, or a puritanical person†; hence, one who is precise to an extreme in attention to principle or duty (as, "The school was kept by a conscientious *prig* of the ancient system," Irving's "Tales of a Traveler," ii. 7; "You can't expect men . . . to keep bucked up to a high pitch of efficiency for any length of time . . . They hate being *prigs*," H. G. Wells's "Mr. Britling," ii. 4. § 15); one who affects great superiority in principles, views, or standards, esp. in a self-righteous way (as, "Who but a *prig* would set himself high aims, or make high resolves at all?" S. Butler's "Way of All Flesh," lxxx.); a person obnoxious in his pretension to principles and ideals above the level of other persons.—**prig′ger-y,** *n.* The conduct or character of a prig.—**prig′gish,** *a.* Having the character of a prig; characteristic of or befitting a prig; excessively precise; affectedly superior or high-minded; oppressively virtuous. —**prig′gish-ly,** *adv.*—**prig′gish-ness,** *n.*—**prig′gism,** *n.* Priggish character or ideas: as, "intellectual *priggism*" (Hughes's "Tom Brown's School Days," i. 2).

prim (prim), *v.*; *primmed*, *primming.* [Origin uncertain; perhaps intended to suggest the drawing up of the lips or mouth in pronouncing *prim*.] **I.** *intr.* To draw up the mouth in an affectedly nice or precise way. **II.** *tr.* To form (the mouth, etc.) into an expression of affected niceness or preciseness; also, to make prim, as in appearance.—**prim,** *a.*; compar. *primmer*, superl. *primmest.* Affectedly precise or proper, as persons, demeanor, behavior, etc. (as, "friends . . . staid and *prim*, of evangelical tendencies," S. Butler's "Way of All Flesh," xii.; "She was about to take her *prim* leave," Arnold Bennett's "Hilda Lessways," ii. 6); also, stiffly precise or neat in appearance (as, "her *prim* little curls," Mrs. Gaskell's "Cranford," ii.; "*Prim* is her gown and quakerlike her shawl," Henley's "In Hospital," xx.); stiffly formal or regular, as a garden.

pri-ma-cy (prī′mạ-si), *n.*; pl. -cies (-siz). [OF. *primacie* (F. *primatie*), < ML. *primatia*, < L. *primas*: see *primate*.] The state of being first in order, rank, importance, etc.; preëminence; superiority; *eccles.*, the office, rank, or dignity of a primate.

pri-ma don-na (prē′mạ don′ạ); pl. *prima donnas*, It. *prime donne* (prē′mä don′nā). [It., 'first lady.'] A first or principal female singer, as in an operatic company.

pri-ma fa-ci-e (prī′mạ fā′shi-ē). [L.] At first appearance; at first view, before investigation: a phrase sometimes used adjectively (as, *prima facie* evidence, in *law*, evidence sufficient to establish a fact, or to raise a presumption of fact, unless rebutted).

pri-mage (prī′māj), *n.* [= AL. *primagium*: cf. *prime²*.] A small allowance formerly paid by a shipper to the master and crew of a vessel for the loading and care of the goods: now charged with the freight and retained by the ship-owner.

pri-mal (prī′mạl), *a.* [ML. *primalis*, < L. *primus*, first, E. *prime¹*.] Of the first age or period, original, or primeval (as, "God first created space, the basis of existence, the *primal* substance," Hallam's "Literature of Europe," iii. 3. § 9; "It hath the *primal* eldest curse upon 't, A brother's murder," Shakspere's "Hamlet," iii. 3. 37); also, of the first rank or importance; fundamental.—**pri′mal-ly,** *adv.*

pri-ma-ri-ly (prī′mạ-ri-li), *adv.* In the primary or first instance; at first; originally; also, in the first place; chiefly; principally.—**pri′ma-ri-ness,** *n.*

pri-ma-ry (prī'mạ-ri), *a.* [L. *primarius,* < *primus,* first, E. *prime*[1]: cf. *premier.*] First in time; earliest; primitive; also, first in order in any series, sequence, etc.; constituting, or belonging to, the first stage in any process; of the nature of the ultimate or simpler constituents of which something complex is made up; original, not derived or subordinate; fundamental, basic, or radical; immediate or direct, or not involving intermediate agency; also, first or highest in rank or importance; chief; principal; in *ornith.,* noting or pertaining to any of a set of flight-feathers situated on the distal segment (that corresponding to the hand in higher vertebrates) of a bird's wing; in *elect.,* noting or pertaining to the inducing circuit, coil, or current in an induction-coil or the like.—**primary colors.** See under *color, n.*—**primary planets.** See under *planet.*—**primary school,** a school for elementary instruction; esp., in the U. S., a school covering the first part, usually the first four years, of the public school course.—**pri'ma-ry,** *n.;* pl. *-ries* (-riz). That which is first in order, rank, or importance; also, a meeting or gathering of the voters of a political party in an election district for the purpose of nominating candidates for office, choosing delegates for a convention, etc. (U. S.); in *ornith.,* a primary feather; in *elect.,* a primary circuit or coil; in *astron.,* a body in relation to a smaller body or smaller bodies revolving around it, as a planet in relation to its satellites.

pri-mate (prī'māt), *n.* [OF. F. *primat,* < LL. *primas* (*primat-*), chief, head, ML. eccles. primate, noun use of L. *primas,* adj., of the first rank, < *primus,* first, E. *prime*[1].] A chief or leader (now rare); *eccles.,* an archbishop or bishop ranking first among the bishops of a province, country, etc.; in *zoöl.,* any of the *Primates,* the highest order of mammals, including man, monkeys, and lemurs.—**pri'mate-ship,** *n.*—**pri-ma'tial** (-mā'shạl), *a.*

prime[1] (prīm), *a.* [OF. F. *prime,* adj. and n., < L. *primus,* adj., first, superl. of *prior,* former (see *prior*); as n., in part through OF. < L. *prima,* fem. of *primus,* in *prima hora,* first hour.] First in order of time; earliest; primitive; also, first in order of existence or development; original; fundamental; also, first or highest in rank, dignity, or authority (as, the *prime* minister: see phrase below); chief; first in importance, excellence, or value; principal; main; first in comparison with others (as, "My mother was a *prime* favourite with this masterful lady": Weir Mitchell's "Hugh Wynne," iii.); of the first grade or best quality (as, *prime* ribs of beef; *prime* oysters); also, ruttish†; in *math.,* not divisible without remainder by any number except itself and unity (as, 5 is a *prime* number); also, having no common divisor except unity (as, 2 is *prime* to 9).—**prime meridian,** a meridian from which longitude east and west is reckoned, as that of Greenwich, England.—**prime minister,** the principal minister of a government; the chief of the cabinet or ministry: as, the British *prime minister.*—**prime mover,** in *mech.,* the initial agent which puts a machine in motion, as wind, electricity, etc.; also, a machine, as a water-wheel or steam-engine, which receives and modifies energy as supplied by some natural source.—**prime**[1], *n.* The first hour or period of the day, after sunrise (as, "Awake; the morning shines, And the fresh field Calls us; we lose the *prime*": Milton's "Paradise Lost," v. 21); also, the beginning or earliest stage of any period; the spring of the year (as, "And brought him presents, flowers if it were *prime,* Or mellow fruit if it were harvest time": Spenser's "Astrophel," 47); the time of early manhood or womanhood (as, "They were now in the happy *prime* of youth," Hawthorne's "Twice-Told Tales," Dr. Heidegger's Experiment; "They had by this time passed their *prime,* and got on the wrong side of thirty," Steele, in "Spectator," 282); also, the period or state of greatest perfection or vigor of human life, before strength begins to decline (as, "He was still in the *prime* of life, not more than four and forty," George Eliot's "Romola," xxxix.; "a man in strong middle *prime* of age," F. M. Crawford's "Mr. Isaacs," x.); in general, the most flourishing stage or state (as, " 'Twas in the *prime* of summer time," Hood's "Dream of Eugene Aram," 1; "The clusters of grapes were just now in their *prime,* very ripe and rich," Defoe's "Robinson Crusoe," i. 7); also, the choicest or best part of anything; also, one of the equal parts into which a unit is primarily divided, esp. one of the sixty parts (minutes) in a degree; the

mark (/) indicating such a division (also variously used as a distinguishing mark); *eccles.,* the second of the seven canonical hours, or the service for it, orig. fixed for the first hour of the day (beginning at 6 A.M.); in *fencing,* the first in a series of eight parries; in *math.,* a prime number; in *music,* a tone on the same degree of the scale or staff with a given tone; the relation of pitch existing between two such tones; their simultaneous combination; also, in a scale, the tonic or key-note.—**prime**[1], *adv.* In prime or first-rate order; excellently: as, "My barmie noddle's working *prime*" (Burns's "To James Smith," 20); "They made a heap of fuss over him, and fixed him up *prime*" (Mark Twain's "Huckleberry Finn," xliii.). [Colloq.]

prime[2] (prīm), *v.;* primed, priming. [Origin uncertain; commonly associated with *prime*[1], as if expressing a first or preliminary action.] **I.** *tr.* To load, charge, or fill (obs. or rare in general use); now, esp., to supply (a firearm) with powder for communicating fire to a charge (as, "Our two combatants had taken the ground, and were *priming* their pistols": Smollett's "Humphry Clinker," April 17); hence, to lay a train of powder to (any charge, a mine, etc.); also, to prepare or make ready for a particular purpose or operation; pour water into (a pump) so as to swell the sucker and make it work effectively; cover (a surface) with a preparatory coat or color, as in painting; also, fig., to supply or equip with information, words, etc., for use (as, "I, too, *primed* with topics innumerable to discuss . . . could not say a word": Lever's "Harry Lorrequer," xxxviii.). **II.** *intr.* To prime a firearm; also, of a boiler or steam-engine, to operate so that water is carried over into the cylinder with the steam.

prime-ly (prīm'li), *adv.* [See *prime*[1], *a.*] At first†, or originally†; chiefly† or principally†; in the highest degree†; exceedingly well, or excellently (colloq.).—**prime'ness,** *n.*

prim-er[1] (prī'mér), *n.* [See *prime*[2].] One who or that which primes; esp., a cap, cylinder, or other device, containing a compound which may be exploded by percussion or other means, used for firing a charge of powder.

prim-er[2] (prim'ér), *n.* [ME. *prymer,* < ML. *primarium,* prop. neut. of L. *primarius,* E. *primary.*] An elementary book for teaching children to read; hence, any small book of elementary principles (as, a *primer* of physiology; a *primer* of phonetics); *eccles.,* formerly, a devotional manual for the laity.—**great primer,** a printing-type (18 point). See *type.*—**long primer,** a printing-type (10 point) of a size between bourgeois and small pica. See *type.*

pri-me-ro (pri-mā'rō), *n.* [Sp. *primera,* fem. of *primero,* first, < L. *primarius,* E. *primary.*] A certain game of cards, fashionable in England in the 16th and 17th centuries.

pri-me-val (prī-mē'vạl), *a.* [L. *primævus,* < *primus,* first, + *ævum,* age.] Of or pertaining to the first age or ages, esp. of the world (as, "a *primeval* God": Keats's "Hyperion," i.); dating from the first ages or earliest times (as, "the remains of *primeval* forests": J. H. Newman's "Callista," i.); characteristic of the first ages or of early times, or primitive (as, "the *primeval* simplicity of manners": Goldsmith's "Vicar of Wakefield," iv.).—**pri-me'val-ly,** *adv.*

pri-mi-ge-ni-al (prī-mi-jē'ni-ạl), *a.* [L. *primigenius,* < *primus,* first, + *gen-,* beget, produce: see *genius.*] First generated or produced†; primary† or original†; also, of a primitive type (as, the *primigenial* elephant).

pri-mine (prī'min), *n.* [L. *primus,* first, E. *prime*[1].] In *bot.,* the outer integument of an ovule. Cf. *secundine.*

prim-ing (prī'ming), *n.* The act of one who or that which primes; also, the powder or other material used to ignite a charge; also, a first coat or layer of paint, size, etc., given to any surface as a ground.

pri-mip-a-ra (prī-mip'ạ-rä), *n.;* pl. *-ræ* (-rē) [L., < *primus,* first, + *parere,* bring forth.] In *obstet.,* a woman who has borne but one child, or who is parturient for the first time.—**pri-mip'a-rous,** *a.* Bearing a child (or young) for the first time.—**pri-mi-par'i-ty** (-mi-par'i-ti), *n.*

prim-i-tive (prim'i-tiv). [OF. F. *primitif,* < L. *primitivus,* first of its kind, < *primus,* first, E. *prime*[1].] **I.** *a.* Being the first or earliest of the kind or in existence, esp. in an early age of the world (as, "our *primitive* great sire [Adam]," Milton's "Paradise Lost," v. 350; *primitive* forms of life;

---

primitive man); early in the history of the world or of mankind (as, "Like a picture it seemed of the *primitive*, pastoral ages, Fresh with the youth of the world": Longfellow's "Courtship of Miles Standish," ix.); characteristic of early ages or of an early stage of human development (as, *primitive* customs or institutions; *primitive* art); unaffected or little affected by civilizing influences (as, "To visit this *primitive* wilderness had been a cherished dream," W. H. Hudson's "Green Mansions," i.; "to live a *primitive* and frontier life, though in the midst of an outward civilization," Thoreau's "Walden," i.); rude, or rudely simple (as, "benches of the simplest and most *primitive* form": Mrs. Stowe's "Oldtown Folks," v.); old-fashioned; also, being in its or the earliest period, or early (as, the *primitive* church; the *primitive* Christians); also, original or radical (as opposed to *derivative*: as, a *primitive* word); primary (as opposed to *secondary*) in *biol.*, rudimentary, as an organ; sometimes, of early formation and temporary, as a part that subsequently disappears; primordial. **II.** *n.* Something primitive; a word from which another is derived; in *math.*, a geometrical or algebraic form or expression from which another is derived; in *art*, an artist, esp. a painter, belonging to an early period, esp. that preceding the Renaissance; a work of art by such an artist.—**prim′i·tive·ly,** *adv.*—**prim′i·tive·ness, prim·i·tiv′i·ty** (-tiv′i-ti), *n.*

prim·ly (prim′li), *adv.* In a prim manner.—**prim′ness,** *n.*

pri·mo (prē′mō), *n.* [It., first, < L. *primus*, E. *prime*[1].] In *music*, the first or principal part, as in a duet; also, its performer.

pri·mo·gen·i·tor (prī-mō-jen′i-tọr), *n.* [L. *primo*, at first, + *genitor*, male parent: see *genitor*.] A first parent or earliest ancestor; a forefather or ancestor.

pri·mo·gen·i·ture (prī-mō-jen′i-tūr), *n.* [ML. *primogenitura*, < L. *primogenitus*, first-born, < *primo*, at first, + *genitus*, pp. of *gignere*, beget, bear.] The state or fact of being the first-born among the children of the same parents; also, the right or principle of inheritance or succession by the first-born, specif. the eldest son.

pri·mor·di·al (prī-môr′di-ạl), *a.* [LL. *primordialis*, < L. *primordium*, the beginning, < *primus*, first, + *ordiri*, begin to weave, begin.] Pertaining to or existing at or from the very beginning (as, *primordial* matter; "*Primordial* man could have had little or no tradition before the development of speech," H. G. Wells's "Outline of History," xii. § 1; *primordial* instincts); of earliest origin; primitive; also, constituting a beginning, or giving origin to something derived or developed; original; elementary; in *biol.*, primitive.—**pri·mor′di·al·ism,** *n.* Continuance of or adherence to what is primordial or primitive.—**pri·mor′di·al·ly,** *adv.*

primp (primp), *v.* [Cf. *prim* and *prink*.] **I.** *tr.* To dress or deck with nicety. [Prov. or colloq.] **II.** *intr.* To primp one's self; prink. [Prov. or colloq.]

prim·rose (prim′rōz). [ME. *primerose*, appar. an altered form of *primerole*, < OF. *primerole*, primrose, dim. < *prime*, first: see *prime*[1], and cf. *primula*.] **I.** *n.* Any plant of the genus *Primula* (family *Primulaceæ*), comprising perennial herbs with variously colored flowers, as *P. vulgaris*, a common yellow-flowered European species cultivated in many varieties, or *P. sinensis*, with flowers of various colors, a native of China but much cultivated elsewhere (see also *auricula, cowslip,* and *oxlip*); also, a plant, *Onagra*

Primrose (*Primula sinensis*).

biennis (family *Onagraceæ*), with yellow flowers that open at nightfall, or any of various related plants ('evening primrose'); also, a pale-yellow color. **II.** *a.* Pertaining to the primrose; abounding in primroses; hence, pleasant, or being that of pleasure (as, "the *primrose* path of dalliance": Shakspere's "Hamlet," i. 3. 50); also, of a pale-yellow color.

prim·u·la (prim′ū·lạ), *n.* [ML., prop. fem. of L. *primulus*, dim. of *primus*, first, E. *prime*[1].] Any plant of the genus *Primula*; a primrose.—**prim·u·la′ceous** (-lā′shius), *a.* Belonging to the *Primulaceæ*, a family of plants of which the primula or primrose is the type.

pri·mum mo·bi·le (prī′mum mō′bi-lē or mob′i-). [ML., 'first movable.'] In the Ptolemaic system of astronomy, the outermost of the revolving concentric spheres of the universe, which was supposed to give motion to the others.

prim·y (prī′mi), *a.* At the prime or best stage: as, "a violet in the youth of *primy* nature" (Shakspere's "Hamlet," i. 3. 7).

prince (prins), *n.* [OF. F. *prince*, < L. *princeps* (*princip-*), first or principal person, prince, prop. adj., first, principal, chief, < *primus*, first, + *capere*, take.] A sovereign or monarch; a king or, formerly, a queen; also, a chief† or leader†; also, one who or that which is chief or preëminent in any class, group, etc. (as, "that *prince* of pioneers [Daniel Boone]," Parkman's "Oregon Trail," x.; a merchant *prince*); in specific use, the ruler of a small state, as one actually or nominally subordinate to a suzerain; also, a non-regnant male member of a royal family, esp., in Great Britain, a son, or a grandson (if the child of a son), of a king or queen; also, the English equivalent of certain titles of nobility of varying importance or rank in certain continental European (or other) countries, as in *Prince* von Bismarck (German: cf. *fürst*) and in *Prince* Kropotkin (Russian); a holder of such a title.—**Prince Albert coat,** a double-breasted frock-coat. —**prince consort,** a prince who is the husband of a reigning female sovereign: used esp. of Prince Albert of Saxe-Coburg-Gotha, husband of Queen Victoria.—**prince imperial,** the eldest son of an emperor or empress.—**prince of darkness,** the devil; Satan.—**Prince of Peace,** Christ. See Isa. ix. 6. —**prince of the blood,** a prince of the royal family.— **Prince of Wales,** a title conferred on the eldest son, or heir apparent, of the British sovereign.—**prince regent,** a prince who is regent of a country, as during the minority, absence, or disability of the sovereign.—**prince royal,** the eldest son of a king or queen.—**prince′dom** (-dọm), *n.* The position, rank, or dignity of a prince; also, a principality (territory); also, *pl.,* the principalities (angels).—**prince′kin, prince′let, prince′ling,** *n.* A little or petty prince: as, "the younger son of a German *princeling*" (Lytton Strachey's "Queen Victoria," i.).—**prince′ly,** *a.* Of, like, or befitting a prince; royal; noble; magnificent.—**prince′li·ness,** *n.*— **prince′ly,** *adv.*

prin·cess (prin′ses), *n.* [OF. F. *princesse*, fem. of *prince*, E. *prince*.] A female sovereign; in specific use, the consort of a prince; also, a non-regnant female member of a royal family, esp., in Great Britain, a daughter, or a granddaughter (if the child of a son), of a king or queen.—**princess dress,** a woman's close-fitting dress cut in continuous length from top to bottom, thus combining bodice and skirt.— **princess of the blood,** a princess of the royal family.— **princess royal,** the eldest daughter of a king or queen.

prin·ci·pal (prin′si-pạl), *a.* [OF. F. *principal*, < L. *principalis*, first, chief, < *princeps*, first: see *prince*.] First or highest in rank, importance, value, etc.; chief; foremost; hence, of the first order; prominent; also, of the nature of principal, or a capital sum.—**principal parts,** in *gram.*, certain leading parts of a verb-system (as, in English, regularly, the present infinitive or present tense, the preterit, and the past participle) from which, when given, the rest can be derived: as, *smite, smote, smitten; go, went, gone.*— **prin′ci·pal,** *n.* A chief or head; specif., a governing or presiding officer, as of a school or (esp. in British use) a college; also, one who takes a leading part; a chief actor or doer; specif., the person for whom and by whose authority another acts (as, "Louis, having thus completed his negotiations with the agent, addressed a long and earnest letter to the royal *principal*": Motley's "Dutch Republic," iii. 9);

the person from whom an agent's authority is derived; also, each of the combatants in a duel, as distinguished from the seconds; also, something of principal or chief importance; a principal rafter (see *rafter²*, *n.*); in *law*, a person directly responsible for a crime, either as actual perpetrator or as abetter present at its commission (cf. *accessory*); also, a person primarily liable for an obligation, for whom another becomes surety; also, the main body of an estate, etc., as distinguished from income; in *com.*, a capital sum, as distinguished from interest or profit; in *music*, an organ-stop whose tones are of the same quality as those of the open diapason, but an octave higher in pitch.—**prin-ci-pal'i-ty** (-pal'i-ti), *n.*; pl. *-ties* (-tiz). Principal rank or place†, or preëminence†; also, the position or authority of a prince or chief ruler; sovereignty; supreme power; also, the rule of a prince of a small or subordinate state; also, a territory ruled by, or a country giving title to, a prince (as, "In that province [Normandy] they founded a mighty state, which gradually extended its influence over the neighbouring *principalities* of Brittany and Maine," Macaulay's "Hist. of Eng.," i.; the *principality* of Wales); also, *pl.*, an order of angels (see *angel*).—**prin'ci-pal-ly**, *adv.* In the principal or chief place; chiefly; mainly; for the most part.—**prin'ci-pal-ship**, *n.* The position or office of a principal, as of a school.

prin-ci-pate (prin'si-pāt), *n.* [L. *principatus*, < *princeps*, first: see *prince*.] Chief place or authority; also, a principality (territory).

prin-cip-i-a (prin-sip'i-ä), *n. pl.* [L., pl. of *principium*: see *principle*.] First principles; elements.

prin-ci-ple (prin'si-pl), *n.* [OF. F. *principe*, < L. *principium*, a beginning, < *princeps*, first: see *prince*.] Beginning† or commencement†; also, an originating or actuating agency or force (as, the *principle* of life, or of motion; "In this corporeal mass, God called to being two workmen . . . heat and cold, the active *principles* diffused through all things," Hallam's "Literature of Europe," iii. 3. § 9); an actuating agency in the mind or character, as an instinct, faculty, or natural tendency (as, "Two *principles* in human nature reign; Self-love, to urge, and Reason, to restrain": Pope's "Essay on Man," ii. 53); also, a determining characteristic of something; essential quality or character; also, a fundamental, primary, or general truth, on which other truths depend (as, the *principles* of morality or government; the *principles* of a science); also, a fundamental doctrine or tenet, or a distinctive ruling opinion (as, the *principles* of the Stoics; religious or political *principles*; socialistic *principles*); also, an accepted or professed rule of action or conduct (as, to make it a *principle* never to borrow; to live up to one's *principles*; a man of good or bad *principles*); esp., *pl.*, right rules of conduct; *sing.*, guiding sense of the requirements and obligations of right conduct (as, a man of *principle*; men of ability but wholly destitute of *principle*); also, fixed rule or adopted method as to action (as, "In all things he acted more from impulse than from fixed *principle*," Longfellow's "Hyperion," iii.; on *principle*, see phrase below); also, a rule or law exemplified in natural phenomena, in the construction or operation of a machine, the working of a system, or the like (as, the *principle* of capillary attraction; the *principle* of the pulley or the aëroplane); the method of formation, operation, or procedure exhibited in a given case (as, a toy built on the *principle* of an automaton; a company organized on the *principle* of one great family); in *chem.*, a constituent of a substance, esp. one giving to it some distinctive quality or effect.—**on principle**, according to fixed rule, method, or practice (as, to agree *on principle* to reasonable requests); often, according to the personal rule for right conduct, or as a matter of moral principle (as, to refrain *on principle* from unfair acts).—**prin'ci-pled**, *a.* Imbued with or having principles: as, high-*principled*.

prin-cock†, **prin-cox**† (prin'kok, -koks), *n.* [Origin obscure.] A pert or conceited young fellow.

prink (pringk), *v.* [Appar. akin to *prank¹*.] **I.** *tr.* To deck or dress for show. **II.** *intr.* To deck one's self out; make a careful toilet, esp. before the looking-glass; study one's toilet or appearance in the looking-glass.—**prink**, *n.* A process of prinking.—**prink'er**, *n.*

print (print), *n.* [OF. *preinte*, impression, print, < *preindre*,

press, stamp, < L. *premere*, press: cf. *press¹*.] An indentation, mark, etc., made by the pressure of one body or thing on another (as, "The planks . . . bore the *print* of many feet": Stevenson's "Treasure Island," xxv.); also, something with which an impression is made; a stamp or die; also, something that has been subjected to impression, as a cake of butter; printed cotton cloth (as, "Her dress . . . was a cotton *print* so faded that the pattern was quite undistinguishable," W. H. Hudson's "Purple Land," vii.: often used attributively, as in 'a *print* gown'); also, the state of being printed (as, in *print*, out of *print*: see phrases below); also, printed lettering, esp. with reference to character, style, or size; printed matter; a printed publication, as a newspaper (as, "the story they had read . . . in the public *prints*": Tarkington's "Gentleman from Indiana," xv.); a picture, design, or the like, printed from an engraved or otherwise prepared block, plate, etc. (as, "*prints* of race-horses": Galsworthy's "Dark Flower," iii. 2); also, news-print; in *photog.*, a picture made from a negative.—**in print**, in printed form; published; also, of a book, etc., still available for purchase from the publisher.—**out of print**, of a book, etc., no longer available for purchase from the publisher; sold out by the publisher.—**print**, *v.* **I.** *tr.* To indent or mark (a surface, etc.) by pressing something into or on it; also, to produce or fix (an indentation, mark, etc.) as by pressure (as, "heavy footmarks *printed* off distinctly in the snow": Whyte-Melville's "Katerfelto," xxx.); fig., to impress on the mind, memory, etc.; also, to apply (a thing) with pressure so as to leave an indentation, mark, etc.; in specif. use, to produce (a book, picture, etc.) by applying inked types, plates, blocks, or the like, with direct pressure to paper or other material; cause (a manuscript, etc.) to be reproduced in print; also, to write in letters like those commonly used in print; also, to mark (cotton cloth, oil-cloth, etc.) with a pattern or design in color, transferred by pressure, as by machinery; in *photog.*, to make a positive picture from (a negative); also, to produce as a positive from a negative by the transmission of light. **II.** *intr.* To take impressions from type, etc., as in a press; produce books, etc., by means of a press; follow the vocation of a printer; also, to give an impression on paper, etc., as types, plates, etc.; also, to write in characters such as are used in print.—**print'a-ble**, *a.* Capable of being printed; fit to be printed; also, capable of being printed from.—**print'er**, *n.* One who or that which prints; esp., one who carries on or is engaged in the business of typographic printing, or of printing books, etc.; specif., a compositor.—**printer's devil.** See *devil*, *n.*—**print'er-y**, *n.*; pl. *-ies* (-iz). An establishment for the printing of calico or the like; also, an establishment for typographic printing.—**print'ing**, *n.* The act or an act of one who or that which prints; esp., the art, process, or business of producing books, newspapers, etc., by impression from movable types, plates, etc.; typography; also, words, etc., in printed form; printed matter; also, the whole number of copies of a book, etc., printed at one time; also, writing in which the letters are like those commonly used in print.—**printing out**, in *photog.*, the act of printing an image on a kind of sensitized paper ('printing-out paper') so that it is visible and complete in detail, and need not be brought out by developing.—**print'ing=ink**, *n.* Ink used in typographic printing.—**print'ing=press**, *n.* A machine for printing on paper or the

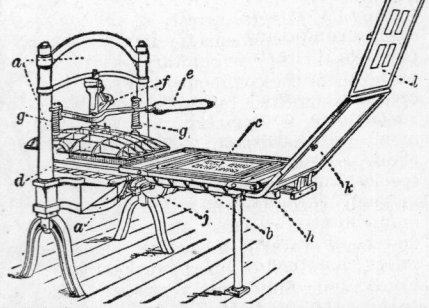

Printing-press (Hand-press).— *a*, *a*, frame; *b*, bed, containing a four-page form, *c*; *d*, platen; *e*, bar that moves compound lever; *f*, compound lever; *g*, *g*, platen-springs; *h*, one of two ribs on which the bed slides on its way to the platen; *j*, rounce, with handle, attached to girths that pull the bed to and from the platen; *k*, tympan; *l*, frisket.

like from types, plates, etc.—**print'less**, *a.* Making, retaining, or showing no print or impression.—**print'=pa"-per**, *n.* Paper of a kind or class used for printing on.—**print'=sell'er**, *n.* One who sells prints or engravings.—**print'=shop**, *n.* A shop where prints or engravings are sold; also, a shop for typographic printing.—**print'=works**, *n. pl.* or *sing.* An establishment for printing calico or the like.

pri-or (prī'ǫr). [L. *prior*, former, superior, a compar. form associated with *primus*, first, as superl.: see *prime*[1].] **I.** *a.* Preceding in time, or in order; earlier or former; anterior or antecedent (often with *to*): as, the *prior* year; a *prior* agreement; "His course can be the fac-simile of no *prior* one" (Carlyle's "Sartor Resartus," ii. 4); "The thought is always *prior* to the fact" (Emerson's "Essays," History). **II.** *adv.* Previous (*to*): as, this happened *prior* to the year 1900.—**pri'or**, *n.* [OF. *prior* (F. *prieur*), < ML. *prior*, < L. *prior*.] A superior officer in a monastic order or religious house, sometimes next in rank below an abbot; also, formerly, a chief magistrate, as in the medieval republic of Florence.—**pri'or-ate** (-ạt), *n.* [ML. *prioratus*.] The office, rank, or term of office of a prior; also, a priory.—**pri'or-ess**, *n.* [OF. *prioresse*.] A woman holding a position corresponding to that of a prior, sometimes ranking next below an abbess.—**pri-or'i-ty** (-or'i-ti), *n.* The state of being earlier in time, or of preceding something else; also, precedence in order, rank, etc.; the having of certain rights before another.—**pri'or-ship**, *n.* The office or dignity of a prior.—**pri'or-y**, *n.*; pl. -*ies* (-iz). [OF. *priorie*.] A religious house governed by a prior or prioress, often dependent upon an abbey.

pris-can (pris'kạn), *a.* [L. *priscus*.] Primitive.

Pris-cian (prish'iạn), *n.* [LL. *Priscianus*.] The name of a celebrated Latin grammarian who flourished about A.D. 500: often used in the phrase 'to break Priscian's head' (to violate the rules of grammar).

prise (prīz), *n.* and *v.* See *prize*[3].

prism (prizm), *n.* [LL. *prisma*, < Gr. πρίσμα, lit. 'something sawed,' < πρίζειν, saw.] A solid whose bases or ends are any similar, equivalent, and parallel polygons, and whose sides are parallelograms; in *optics*, a body of this form (esp. with triangular bases) made of glass or other transparent substance, used esp. for decomposing light into its spectrum; in *crystal.*, a form consisting of faces which are parallel to the vertical axis (in distinction from *dome*); also, loosely, a dome ('horizontal prism').—**pris-mat-ic** (priz-mat'ik), *a.* Of, pertaining to, or like a prism; also, formed by or as if by a transparent prism; varied in color; brilliant.—**prismatic colors**, the colors into which ordinary white light is decomposed by a prism, comprising an infinite number of lines ranging from red to violet, but commonly regarded as the seven colors, red, orange, yellow, green, blue, indigo, and violet.—**pris-mat'i-cal-ly**, *adv.*—**pris'moid**, *n.* [See -*oid*.] A body whose form approaches that of a prism.—**pris-moi'dal**, *a.*—**pris'my**, *a.* Prismatic: as, "They saw the *prismy* hues in thin spray showers" (Whittier's "Tent on the Beach").

Triangular Prism.

pris-on (priz'n), *n.* [OF. F. *prison*, < L. *prensio*(n-), *prehensio*(n-), seizure, arrest, < *prendere*, *prehendere*, seize.] Captivity or confinement; imprisonment; hence, a place of confinement or involuntary restraint; specif., a public building for the confinement or safe custody of criminals and others committed by process of law.—**state prison.** See under *state*, *a.*—**pris'on**, *v. t.* To imprison: now chiefly fig.—**pris'on=breach, pris'on=break"ing**, *n.* In *law*, a breaking and going out of prison by one lawfully confined therein.—**pris'on-er**, *n.* [OF. *prisonier* (F. *prisonnier*).] One who is confined in prison or kept in custody, esp. as the result of legal process; also, one taken by an enemy in war ('prisoner of war'); a captive; hence, one who or something that is deprived of liberty or kept in restraint (as, "An untimely ague Stay'd me a *prisoner* in my chamber": Shakspere's "Henry VIII.," i. 1. 5).—**prisoners' base**, an old game variously played, esp. by boys, consisting essentially in an attempt to touch or tag players as they run out from their base or home.

pris-sy (pris'i), *a.* [Cf. *precise*.] Precise; prim; affectedly nice: used disparagingly. [Prov. or colloq., U. S.]

pris-tine (pris'tin or -tīn), *a.* [L. *pristinus*, akin to *prior*, former: see *prior*.] Of or pertaining to the earliest period or state; original; primitive: as, "Many noble monuments which have since been destroyed or defaced still retained their *pristine* magnificence" (Macaulay's "Hist. of Eng.," i.).

prith-ee (priᴛн'ē). Corruption of (I) *pray thee*: as, "*Prithee*, young one, who art thou?" (Hawthorne's "Scarlet Letter," viii.). [Archaic.]

prit-tle=prat-tle (prit'l-prat'l), *n.* [Varied redupl. of *prattle*.] Empty or idle talk; trifling loquacity; chatter. [Archaic or prov.]

pri-va-cy (prī'vạ-si), *n.*; pl. -*cies* (-siz). The state of being private; absence of publicity (as, "In other nations having income tax laws, *privacy* of returns is respected": A. W. Mellon's "Taxation," iii.); secrecy; retirement or seclusion; also, a private matter (now rare: as, "So few of the new generation seemed aware that there were any *privacies* left to respect!" Mrs. Wharton's "Son at the Front," xii.); also, a private or retired place (now rare).

pri-vat-do-cent (prē-vät'dō-tsent'), *n.* [G., 'private instructor.'] In German and certain other universities, a private teacher or lecturer recognized by the university but receiving no compensation from it, being remunerated by fees.

pri-vate (prī'vạt), *a.* [L. *privatus*, private, not public, pp. of *privare*, separate, deprive, < *privus*, single, individual, private, deprived.] Not holding public office or employment, as a person (as, "Any *private* person . . . that is present when any felony is committed is bound by the law to arrest the felon": Blackstone's "Commentaries," IV. 292); hence, not having a public character, or not having relations with or being known to the public generally; also, without rank, or common or ordinary (as, a *private* soldier); also, of or pertaining to a person in a non-official or a non-public character (as, the *private* correspondence of a king; the *private* life of a public man); not of an official or public character (as, to retire to *private* life); also, removed from or out of public view or knowledge, or secret (as, "Placing the purse . . . in a *private* pocket, our traveller strode gallantly on through the wood": Scott's "Guy Mannering," xxviii.); also, not open or accessible to people in general (as, a *private* road or way; "I met him at a *private* party," Marryat's "Peter Simple," lxiv.); restricted for the use or enjoyment of particular persons; also, belonging to some particular person or persons (as, *private* property); belonging to one's self, or being one's own; also, pertaining to or affecting a particular person or a small group of persons (as, "For your *private* satisfaction . . . I will let you know," Shakspere's "Julius Cæsar," ii. 2. 73; "Dante, who avenged, in vindictive melodies, all his *private* wrongs," Emerson's "Representative Men," iii.); individual; personal; also, confined to or intended only for the person or persons immediately concerned (as, a *private* communication; to have *private* conversation with a person); confidential; also, without the presence of others, or alone (as, "I left him *private*, Full of sad thoughts and troubles": Shakspere's "Henry VIII.," ii. 2. 15); also, retiring or secluded, as a person; also, retired or secluded, as a place.—**private law**, that branch of the law which deals with the rights and duties of persons in their relations with one another as private individuals.—**pri'vate**, *n.* A person not in public office or position†; also, a private soldier; also, privacy (now only in 'in private': as, "her opinion, founded on observation of him *in* public and *private*," G. Meredith's "Ordeal of Richard Feverel," i.); also, *pl.*, the external organs of sex.

pri-va-teer (prī-vạ-tēr'), *n.* [Earlier called *private man-of-war*; from *private*, *a.*] An armed vessel owned by private persons, holding a government commission to act against an enemy's shipping; also, the commander, or one of the crew, of such a vessel.—**pri-va-teer'**, *v. i.* To cruise as a privateer: chiefly in *privateering*, *n.*—**pri-va-teers'man** (-tērz'man), *n.*; pl. -*men.* An officer or seaman of a privateer.

pri-vate-ly (prī'vạt-li), *adv.* In a private manner or capacity; not officially; not publicly; secretly; individually or personally.—**pri'vate-ness**, *n.*

(variable) d̦ as d or j, ş as s or sh, ț as t or ch, z̦ as z or zh; o, F. cloche; ü, F. menu; ċh, Sc. loch; ṅ, F. bonbon; ', primary accent; ", secondary accent; †, obsolete; <, from; +, and; =, equals. See also lists at beginning of book.

pri-va-tion (prī-vā'shǫn), *n.* [L. *privatio(n-)*, < *privare*, deprive: see *private*.] A depriving, or the state of being deprived (now rare: as, "Maggie's sense of loneliness, and utter *privation* of joy," George Eliot's "Mill on the Floss," iv. 3); also, want of the usual comforts or necessaries of life, or an instance of this (as, to lead a life of *privation*; "I was spent with my long journey and the many *privations* I had suffered," W. H. Hudson's "Green Mansions," xviii.); destitution; in *logic*, the condition of being deprived of or without something formerly or properly present; loosely, negation.

priv-a-tive (priv'ạ-tiv). [L. *privativus*, < *privare*, deprive: see *private*.] **I.** *a.* Having the quality of depriving; serving to take away; also, consisting in or charactèrized by the taking away of something, or the loss or want of something properly present; loosely, negative; in *gram.*, expressing privation or negation (as, a *privative* prefix). **II.** *n.* That which is privative; in *gram.*, a privative word-element.— **priv'a-tive-ly**, *adv.*

priv-et (priv'et), *n.* [Origin uncertain.] A European oleaceous shrub, *Ligustrum vulgare*, with evergreen leaves and small white flowers, much used for hedges; any of various other species of the genus *Ligustrum*; also, any of certain other plants, as *Adelia* (or *Forestiera*) *acuminata* ('swamp-privet'), an oleaceous shrub or small tree of the southern U. S., or *Lawsonia inermis* ('Egyptian privet,' or henna), a lythraceous shrub or small tree of Asia and the Levant.

priv-i-lege (priv'i-lej), *n.* [OF. *privilege* (F. *privilège*), < L. *privilegium*, privilege, orig. a law in favor of or against an individual, < *privus*, private, + *lex* (*leg-*), law.] A right or immunity enjoyed by a person or persons beyond the common advantages of others; a special advantage; also, a special right or immunity granted to persons in authority or office; a prerogative; also, a grant to an individual, a corporation, etc., of a special right or immunity, sometimes in derogation of the common right; a franchise; a patent; also, the principle or condition of enjoying special rights or immunities; also, any of the more sacred and vital rights common to all citizens under a modern constitutional government; in the stock-exchange, etc., a speculative contract covering a call, put, spread, or straddle.— **priv'i-lege**, *v. t.*; *-leged*, *-leging*. To grant a privilege to; invest with some special right or immunity; also, to give (a person, etc.) immunity, or exempt (*from*); also, to authorize or license (something otherwise forbidden).

priv-i-ly (priv'i-li), *adv.* In a privy manner; secretly.

priv-i-ty (priv'i-ti), *n.*; pl. *-ties* (-tiz). [OF. *privite*, *privete*, < L. *privus*, private: see *private*.] Privacy†; also, participation in the knowledge of something private or secret, esp. as implying concurrence or consent (as, "There had been five distinct attempts to assassinate the Prince, all of them with the *privity* of the Spanish government": Motley's "Dutch Republic," vi. 7); private knowledge; in *law*, the relation between privies.

priv-y (priv'i), *a.* [OF. *prive* (F. *privé*), adj. and n., < L. *privatus*: see *private*.] Private, or belonging or pertaining to some particular person or persons (now esp. with reference to a sovereign: see phrases below); also, removed from or out of public sight or knowledge, or secret, concealed, hidden, or secluded (archaic); acting or done in secret or by stealth (archaic); also, participating in the knowledge of something private or secret (usually followed by *to*: as, "Many persons were *privy* to the plot," Motley's "Dutch Republic," v. 3); also, intimate† or familiar†.— **privy chamber**, a room reserved for the private or exclusive use of some particular person or persons (archaic); specif., a private apartment in a royal residence, as in Great Britain.— **privy council**, a board or select body of personal advisers, as of a sovereign; specif., in Great Britain, a body of advisers, some selected by the sovereign and others serving by usage, whose function of advising the crown in matters of state is now for the most part discharged by the cabinet (see *order in council*, under *order*, n.); also, any similar body, as one appointed to assist the governor of a British dominion.— **privy counselor** or **privy councilor**, a private adviser, as of a sovereign; a member of a privy council.— **privy purse**, an allowance for the private expenses of the British sovereign.— **privy seal**, in Great Britain, the seal affixed to grants, etc., which are afterwards to pass the great seal, and to documents of minor importance which do not require the great seal.— **priv'y**, *n.*; pl. *-ies* (-iz). A place of retirement for defecation; in *law*, one who has a legally recognized interest or responsibility in an estate, transaction, etc. (often distinguished from a *party*).

prize[1] (prīz). [OF. F. *prise*, a taking, < *prendre*, < L. *prendere*, *prehendere*, seize, take; some uses being due to ME. *pris*, *prise*, price, reward, prize, E. *price*.] **I.** *n.* A taking† or capturing†; also, something seized or captured, esp. an enemy's ship with the property in it taken at sea by the rights of war; also, a reward of victory or superiority, as in a contest or competition; that which is won in a lottery or the like; fig., anything striven for, worth striving for, or much valued (as, "The beautiful Miss Mannering, of high family, with an Indian fortune, was a *prize* worth looking after": Scott's "Guy Mannering," xx.); an advantage or privilege (as, "It is war's *prize* to take all vantages": Shakspere's "3 Henry VI.," i. 4. 59); also, a contest† or match† (as, "Like one of two contending in a *prize*, That thinks he hath done well in people's eyes": Shakspere's "Merchant of Venice," iii. 2. 142). **II.** *a.* That has gained a prize; worthy of a prize; also, given or awarded as a prize.— **prize**[1], *v. t.*; *prized*, *prizing*. To seize as a prize, as a ship.

prize[2] (prīz), *v. t.*; *prized*, *prizing*. [OF. *prisier* (F. *priser*), var. of *preisier*, value, prize: see *praise*.] To set or estimate the value of†; also, to value or esteem highly.— **prize**[2]†, *n.* Valuation; appraisement.

prize[3] (prīz), *n.* [OF. F. *prise*, a taking, grasp, hold: see *prize*[1].] A lever (now prov.); also, leverage.— **prize**[3], *v. t.*; *prized*, *prizing*. To raise, move, or force with a lever; force or press with or as with a lever.

prize=court (prīz'kōrt), *n.* A court whose function it is to adjudicate on prizes taken in war.

prize=fight (prīz'fīt), *n.* An exhibition contest between pugilists or boxers for a prize or stake.— **prize′=fight″er**, *n.* —**prize′=fight″ing**, *n.*

prize-man (prīz'mạn), *n.*; pl. *-men*. A man who wins a prize, esp. in a college or school (as in Great Britain).

prize=mon-ey (prīz'mun″i), *n.* A portion of the money realized by the sale of a prize, esp. an enemy's vessel, distributed among the captors; also, a sum of money distributed by a government among those who had part in the destruction of an enemy's vessel or vessels.

priz-er (prī'zèr), *n.* [See *prize*[1], *n.*] One who engages in a contest; one who competes for a prize, as a prize-fighter. [Archaic.]

prize=ring (prīz'ring), *n.* A ring or inclosed square area for prize-fighting.

pro[1] (prō), *adv.* [L. *pro*, prep., before, for: see *pro-*.] In favor of a proposition, opinion, etc.: opposed to *con* (L. *contra*), and often used as a noun, as in *pros and cons* (arguments, considerations, votes, etc., for and against something): as, "the manufacturer meditating the *pros and cons* of an adulteration" (H. G. Wells's "Outline of History," xxxviii. § 6).

pro[2] (prō). [Short for *professional*.] **I.** *a.* Professional (rather than amateur): as, a *pro* golfer. [Colloq.] **II.** *n.*; pl. *pros* (prōz). A professional: as, "Circumstances made me go into the business [on the stage], but I was never a *pro*, I mean to say a 'professional,' by nature" (L. Merrick's "Conrad in Quest of His Youth," xiii.). [Colloq.]

pro-. [L. *pro-*, repr. *pro*, prep., before, for; also Gr. προ-, repr. πρό (= L. *pro*), prep., before, occasionally for: see *pre-* and *fore*.] A prefix meaning 'before,' 'forward,' 'forth,' also 'for,' 'in place of,' 'in behalf of,' occurring orig. in words from the Latin and Greek, but now used freely as a general formative, as in *procathedral*, *proleg*, *prothorax*, and esp., in the sense of 'in favor of,' 'on the side of,' in such words as *pro-British*, *pro-German*, *pro-slavery*, and many others, largely self-explanatory, and often opposed to compounds in *anti-* (cf. *anti-*).

pro-a (prō'ä), *n.* [Also *prau*: Malay *prāū*.] A swift Malay sailing-boat built with the lee side flat and balanced by an outrigger: as, "the piratical *proas* of the Malays, lurking among the low shaded coves and islets of Sumatra" (H. Melville's "Moby-Dick," lxxxvii.). See cut on following page.

---

fat, fāte, fär, fȧll, ȧsk, fâre; net, mē, hėr; pin, pīne; not, nōte, mȯve, nȯr; up, lūte, pull; oi, oil; ou, out; (lightened) aviạry, ẹlect, agǫny, intȯ, ụnite; (obscured) errạnt, operạ, ardẹnt, actǫr, natụre; ch, chip; g, go; th, thin; ᴛʜ, then; y, you;

prob-a-bil-ism (prob′ạ-bil-izm), *n.* [L. *probabilis*: see *probable*.] In *Rom. Cath. theol.*, the doctrine that in cases of doubt as to the lawfulness or unlawfulness of an action, it is permissible to follow a soundly probable opinion favoring its lawfulness; in *philos.*, the doctrine that certainty is impossible, and that probability suffices to govern faith and practice.—**prob′a-bil-ist**, *n.*

Proa, with Outrigger.

prob-a-bil-i-ty (prob-ạ-bil′i-ti), *n.*; pl. *-ties* (-tiz). The quality or fact of being probable; likelihood; a likelihood or chance of something (as, there is a *probability* of his coming); also, a probable event, circumstance, etc. (as, to regard a thing as a *probability*); something likely to occur, be true, etc.; *pl.*, probable weather conditions, as in the U. S. official daily forecast (the chief of the Weather Bureau being humorously referred to as 'Old Probabilities'); in *math.*, the likelihood of an event happening, as measured by the relative frequency of events of the kind in the course of experience.

prob-a-ble (prob′ạ-bl), *a.* [L. *probabilis*, < *probare*, E. *prove*.] Capable of being proved (obs. or rare); also, plausible†; specious†; also, having more evidence for than against, or evidence which inclines the mind to belief but leaves some room for doubt; likely to occur or prove true (as, the *probable* consequences of an action; the *probable* reasons that led to a decision); also, affording ground for belief (as, *probable* evidence).—**prob′a-bly**, *adv.* In a probable manner; with probability; in all likelihood.

pro-bang (prō′bang), *n.* [Earlier *provang*; origin unknown.] In *surg.*, a long, slender, elastic rod with a sponge, ball, or the like, at the end, to be introduced into the esophagus, etc., as for removing foreign bodies.

pro-bate (prō′bāt). [L. *probatus*, pp. of *probare*, E. *prove*.] **I.** *n.* In *law*, the official proving of a will as authentic or genuine; also, an officially certified copy of a will so proved. **II.** *a.* Of or pertaining to probate or a court of probate.—**pro′bate**, *v. t.*; *-bated, -bating.* To establish the authenticity of (a will).

pro-ba-tion (prō-bā′shọn), *n.* [OF. F. *probation*, < L. *probatio(n)-*, < *probare*, E. *prove*.] The act of testing, or putting to the proof; now, esp., the testing or trial of a person's conduct, character, qualifications, or the like, or the state or period of such testing or trial; the testing or trial of a candidate for membership in a religious body or order, for holy orders, etc.; moral trial, or testing of moral character (as, "the general doctrine of religion, that our present life is a state of *probation* for a future one": J. Butler's "Analogy of Religion," i. 4); also, a method of dealing with offenders, esp. young persons guilty of minor crimes or first offenses, by allowing them to go at large conditionally under supervision, as that of a person ('probation officer') appointed for such duty; also, proof or demonstration (now rare: as, "It was clear, even to *probation*, the pamphlets had some share in this revolution," Stevenson's "Master of Ballantrae," x.). —**pro-ba′tion-al**, *a.*—**pro-ba′tion-a-ry** (-ạ-ri), *a.* Of or pertaining to probation; undergoing probation.—**pro-ba′tion-er**, *n.* One undergoing probation or trial; one who is on probation: as, "In progress of time, Abel Sampson, *probationer* of divinity, was admitted to the privileges of a preacher" (Scott's "Guy Mannering," ii.).

pro-ba-tive (prō′bạ-tiv), *a.* [L. *probativus*, < *probare*, E. *prove*.] Serving or designed for testing or trial; also, affording proof or evidence. Also **pro′ba-to-ry** (-tọ-ri).

probe (prōb), *n.* [ML. *proba*, test, LL. proof: see *proof*.] A slender surgical instrument for exploring the depth or direction of a wound, sinus, or the like; also, the act or an act of probing.—**probe**, *v.*; *probed, probing.* **I.** *tr.* To examine or explore with or as with a probe; fig., to search into or examine thoroughly; question closely. **II.** *intr.* To penetrate with or as with a probe: as, "He was trying to *probe* into her secret" (Mrs. Wharton's "Age of Innocence," xii.).— **prob-er** (prō′bẻr), *n.*—**prob′ing-ly**, *adv.*

prob-i-ty (prob′i-ti), *n.* [L. *probitas*, < *probus*, good, upright, honest.] Tried virtue or integrity; uprightness; honesty; high principle: as, "a man of . . . unquestioned *probity*" (Smollett's "Humphry Clinker," May 10).

prob-lem (prob′lem), *n.* [OF. *probleme* (F. *problème*), < L. *problema*, < Gr. πρόβλημα, < προβάλλειν, throw before, propose, < πρό, before, + βάλλειν, throw.] A question proposed for solution or discussion; hence, any doubtful or difficult question; a matter involving doubt, uncertainty, or difficulty (as, "The Nor' West Passage, so long a *problem* to man, was never a *problem* to the whale," H. Melville's "Moby-Dick," xli.; "the officer, who had the *problem* of keeping his men together and getting them somewhere," Buchan's "Hist. of the Great War," liii.); in *geom.*, a proposition requiring something to be done.—**prob-lem-at′ic**, **prob-lem-at′i-cal** (-le-mat′ik, -i-kạl), *a.* [Gr. προβληματικός.] Of the nature of a problem; doubtful; uncertain; questionable.—**prob-lem-at′i-cal-ly**, *adv.*

pro-bos-cid-e-an (prō-bo-sid′ē-ạn). [NL. *Proboscidea*, pl., < L. *proboscis*: see *proboscis*.] **I.** *a.* Pertaining to or resembling a proboscis; also, having a proboscis; also, belonging or pertaining to the *Proboscidea*, an order of mammals consisting of the elephants and their extinct allies. **II.** *n.* One of the *Proboscidea.* Also **pro-bos-cid′i-an**, *a.* and *n.*

pro-bos-cis (prō-bos′is), *n.*; pl. *proboscises*, L. *proboscides* (-i-dēz). [L. *proboscis* (*proboscid-*), < Gr. προβοσκίς (προβοσκιδ-), < πρό, before, + βόσκειν, feed.] An elephant's trunk; a long flexible snout, as of the tapir; a part or organ projecting in front of an animal, as the tubular sucking organ of certain insects; also, humorously, the human nose.—**pro-bos′cis-mon″key**, *n.* A large, long-tailed monkey, *Nasalis larvatus*, of Borneo, having a long nose.

pro-ca-cious (prō-kā′shus), *a.* [L. *procax* (*procac-*), < *procare*, ask.] Bold; forward; pert. [Now rare.]—**pro-ca′ci-ty** (-kas′i-ti), *n.*

pro-cam-bi-um (prō-kam′bi-um), *n.* [NL.: see *pro-* and *cambium*.] In *bot.*, the meristem from which the vascular bundles are developed.—**pro-cam′bi-al**, *a.*

Proboscis-monkey.

pro-ca-the-dral (prō-kạ-thē′drạl), *n.* [See *pro-*.] A church used temporarily as a cathedral.

pro-ce-den-do (prō-sẹ-den′dō), *n.* [L., abl. gerund of *procedere*, E. *proceed*.] In *law*, a writ issuing out of a superior court commanding a subordinate court to proceed to judgment, as when the subordinate court has wrongfully delayed judgment, or when it appears that the action has been removed to the superior court on insufficient grounds.

pro-ce-dure (prō-sē′dụr), *n.* [F. *procédure*, < *procéder*, E. *proceed*.] The act or manner of proceeding in any action or process; conduct; a particular course or mode of action; esp., mode of conducting legal, parliamentary, or other business, specif. litigation and judicial proceedings.

pro-ceed (prō-sēd′), *v. i.* [OF. *proceder* (F. *procéder*), < L. *procedere* (pp. *processus*), < *pro*, before, + *cedere*, go.] To move or go forward or onward, esp. after stopping (as, "On the first day, they *proceeded* about eight miles to the southeast," Irving's "Captain Bonneville," vi.; the vessel stopped at Gibraltar and then *proceeded* on her voyage); also, to go on with or carry on any action or process; go on or act according to a particular method; deal (*with*: as, "I will not hide My judgments; how with mankind I *proceed*," Milton's "Paradise Lost," xi. 69); specif., to begin and carry on a legal action; take legal proceedings (*against*: as, "Though rebellion is declared, it is not *proceeded* against as such," Burke's "Conciliation with the Colonies"); also, to go on with or continue some action or process; go further; continue one's discourse; go on (to do something: as, "This pledge the Duke *proceeded* to violate almost as soon as made," Motley's "Dutch Republic," vi. 6); go or pass on to the next point or to something else; also, to advance to a higher status, as from the academic degree of bachelor to that of master or doctor (as, to *proceed* master of arts); also, to be carried on, as an action, process, etc.; take effect; be advanced or carried on further; also, to go or come forth, or issue (as, "I believe in the Holy Ghost, The Lord, and Giver of Life, Who *proceedeth* from the Father and the Son": Book of Common Prayer, Communion): arise, originate, or result (as, an error *proceeding* from excessive haste).—**pro-ceed** (prō'sēd), *n.* That which proceeds, results, or accrues, as from some possession or transaction; the sum derived from a sale or other transaction: now usually in *pl.*—**pro-ceed'er**, *n.*—**pro-ceed'ing**, *n.* The act of one who or that which proceeds; onward movement; action, course of action, or conduct; a particular action or course of action; *pl.*, records of the doings of a society (sometimes restricted to a record of business done, as distinguished from *transactions*, which then consist of a report of addresses delivered, etc.); also, *sing.*, in *law*, the instituting or carrying on of an action at law; a legal step or measure (as, to institute *proceedings* against a person).

pro-ce-leus-mat-ic (pros''e-lūs-mat'ik). [LL. *proceleusmaticus*, < Gr. προκελευσματικός, < προκελεύειν, rouse to action beforehand, < πρό, before, + κελεύειν, urge.] **I.** *a.* Inciting, animating, or inspiriting (as, a *proceleusmatic* song); in *pros.*, noting a metrical foot of four short syllables; pertaining to or consisting of feet of this kind. **II.** *n.* In *pros.*, a proceleusmatic foot.

pro-cel-la-ri-an (pros-e-lā'ri-an), *a.* [NL. *Procellaria*, genus of petrels, < L. *procella*, storm.] Of or pertaining to the petrel family of sea-birds.

pro-ce-phal-ic (prō-se-fal'ik), *a.* [Gr. πρό, before, + κεφαλή, head.] In *zoöl.*, pertaining to or forming the fore part of the head.

pro-cess (pros'es or prō'ses), *n.* [OF. *proces* (F. *procès*), < L. *processus*, < *procedere*, E. *proceed*.] The action of going forward or on, or the condition of being carried on, or progress or course (as, "Saturnian Juno now, with double care, Attends the fatal *process* of the war," Dryden's tr. Virgil's "Æneid," vii. 790: now chiefly in the phrase 'in process,' as, "The place seemed in *process* of being dismantled," Arnold Bennett's "Hilda Lessways," iii. 1); also, course or lapse, as of time (as, "In *process* of time he began to build": Peacock's "Headlong Hall," v.); also, a course of activity or proceeding; a continuous action or operation, or a series of actions or changes, taking place in a definite manner (as, the *processes* of growth; the *process* of decomposition); a systematic series of actions directed to some end (as, the *process* of making butter); a particular method of operation, as in manufacture; specif., photomechanical or photo-engraving methods collectively (often attributively: as, *process* pictures); also, a narration†, relation†, or story†; also, the act of proceeding, coming forth, or issuing from a source (obs. or rare); also, a projection from a main body; esp., a natural outgrowth, projection, or appendage (as, a *process* of a bone); a prominence or protuberance; also, in *law*, the whole course of the proceedings in an action at law; also, the summons, mandate, or writ by which a defendant or thing is brought before court for litigation.—**pro'cess**, *v. t.* To institute a legal process against; serve a process or summons on; also, to treat or prepare by some particular process; specif., to convert (an agricultural commodity) into marketable form by some special process.

pro-ces-sion (prō-sesh'on), *n.* [OF. F. *procession*, < L. *processio(n-)*, < *procedere*, E. *proceed*.] The proceeding or

moving along in orderly succession, in a formal or ceremonious manner, of a line or body of persons, animals, vehicles, or other things; also, the line or body of persons or things moving along; also, an office, litany, etc., said or sung in a religious procession; also, the act of proceeding forth from a source.—**pro-ces'sion-al. I.** *a.* Of or pertaining to a procession; of the nature of a procession; characterized by processions; sung or recited in procession, as a hymn. **II.** *n.* An office-book containing hymns, litanies, etc., for use in religious processions; also, a processional hymn.—**pro-ces'sion-al-ly**, *adv.*

pro-ces-sor (pros'es''or), *n.* One who processes; specif., one engaged in converting an agricultural commodity into marketable form.

pro-cès=ver-bal (pro-se-ver-bàl), *n.*; pl. *procès-verbaux* (-bō). [F.] A report of proceedings, as of an assembly; in *French law*, an authenticated written account of facts in connection with a criminal or other charge.

pro-cho-ös (prō'kǫ-os), *n.*; pl. *prochoöi* (-kǫ-oi). [Gr. πρόχοος, < προχεῖν, pour forth, < πρό, before, + χεῖν, pour.] In *Gr. antiq.*, a pitcher-like vessel, resembling the oinochoë but usually more slender, used for pouring out wine and for pouring water on the hands before a meal.

pro-chro-nism (prō'krǫ-nizm), *n.* [Gr. πρό, before, + χρόνος, time: cf. *anachronism*.] The assigning of an event, etc., to a period earlier than its actual date.

pro-claim (prō-klām'), *v.* [L. *proclamare* (pp. *proclamatus*), < *pro*, before, + *clamare*, cry out: cf. *claim*.] **I.** *tr.* To make announcement of by public cry or declaration (as, "Stand in the gate of the Lord's house, and *proclaim* there this word": Jer. vii. 2);

Greek Prochoös, with black-figured decoration.

announce or declare publicly and officially (as, to *proclaim* war); declare officially to be (with a complement: as, to *proclaim* a man king; to *proclaim* one an outlaw); hence, elliptically, to declare to be king or ruler (as, "He [Monmouth] was *proclaimed* in the market place of Taunton": Macaulay's "Hist. of Eng.," v.); declare to be an outlaw, evil-doer, or the like (as, "I heard myself *proclaim'd*; And by the happy hollow of a tree Escaped the hunt": Shakspere's "King Lear," ii. 3. 1); denounce or prohibit publicly; declare (a district, etc.) subject to particular legal restrictions; also, in general, to announce or declare publicly or openly (as, to *proclaim* one's opinions; to *proclaim* one's self a supporter of a cause); of things, to give intimation or indication of, or make known (as, "Screams and tumultuous shouts *proclaimed* the progress of the massacre," De Quincey's "Revolt of the Tartars"; "six vessels, whose black hulls, and bristling broadsides, *proclaimed* their warlike character," H. Melville's "Typee," ii.). **II.** *intr.* To make proclamation.—**pro-claim'**, *n.* A proclaiming; proclamation. [Obs. or rare.]—**pro-claim'er**, *n.* —**proc-la-ma-tion** (prok-la-mā'shon), *n.* [L. *proclamatio(n-)*.] The act of proclaiming; also, that which is proclaimed; a public and official announcement.—**pro-clam'a-to-ry** (-klam'a-tǫ-ri), *a.* Making proclamation.

pro-clit-ic (prō-klit'ik). [NL. *procliticus*, < Gr. προκλίνειν, lean forward, < πρό, before, + κλίνειν, incline: cf. *enclitic*.] In *gram.*: **I.** *a.* Of a word, so closely connected with a following word as to have no independent accent. Cf. *enclitic*. **II.** *n.* A proclitic word.—**pro-clit'i-cal-ly**, *adv.*

pro-cliv-i-ty (prō-kliv'i-ti), *n.*; pl. *-ties* (-tiz). [L. *proclivitas*, < *proclivis*, sloping forward, inclined, prone, < *pro*, before, + *clivus*, slope.] Natural or habitual inclination or tendency (often to, toward, or to do something objectionable); propensity; predisposition; proneness: as, a *proclivity* to faultfinding, or to grumble; to guard against one's unfortunate *proclivities*; "a painter of bohemian *proclivities*" (Watts-Dunton's "Aylwin," iv. 2).

proc-ni-as (prok′ni-as), *n.* [NL., < L. *Procne*, < Gr. Πρόκνη, the mythical Procne (sister of Philomela), who was turned into a swallow.] A tropical American bird, *Procnias tersa*, of the tanager family.

Procnias.

pro-con-sul (prō-kon′sul), *n.* [L., < *pro*, for, + *consul*, consul.] Among the ancient Romans, a governor or military commander of a province with duties and powers similar to those of a consul. — **pro-con′-su-lar** (-sū-lär), *a.* Of, pertaining to, or governed by a proconsul: as, "In no province of the vast Roman empire . . . did Nature wear a richer . . . garb than she displayed in *Proconsular* Africa" (J. H. Newman's "Callista," i.). — **pro-con′su-late** (-lāt), **pro-con′sul-ship**, *n.*

pro-cras-ti-nate (prō-kras′ti-nāt), *v.*; *-nated*, *-nating.* [L. *procrastinatus*, pp. of *procrastinare*, < *pro-*, forward, + *crastinus*, of to-morrow, < *cras*, to-morrow.] **I.** *tr.* To put off till another day or time, or from day to day; defer; delay: as, "my prospects, yet unsettled; my departure, continually *procrastinated*" (C. Brontë's "Jane Eyre," xxxii.). **II.** *intr.* To defer action; delay; be dilatory: as, to *procrastinate* until an opportunity is lost. — **pro-cras-ti-na′tion** (-nā′shon), *n.* [L. *procrastinatio(n-).*] The act or the habit of procrastinating; dilatoriness. — **pro-cras′ti-na-tive, pro-cras′ti-na-to-ry** (-nā-tiv, -nā-tō-ri), *a.* Procrastinating; dilatory. — **pro-cras′ti-na-tor** (-nā-tor), *r.*

pro-cre-ant (prō′krē-ant), *a.* Procreating; generating; pertaining to procreation.

pro-cre-ate (prō′krē-āt), *v. t.*; *-ated*, *-ating.* [L. *procreatus*, pp. of *procreare*, < *pro*, before, + *creare*, bring into being, create.] To beget or generate (offspring); hence, fig., to produce; engender; bring into being. — **pro-cre-a′tion** (-ā′shon), *n.* [L. *procreatio(n-).*] The act of procreating; generation of offspring; fig., production or origination. — **pro′cre-a-tive** (-ā-tiv), *a.* Having the power of procreating; concerned with or pertaining to procreation — **pro′cre-a-tor** (-ā-tor), *n.*

proc-ris (prok′ris), *n.* [NL., < L. *Procris*, < Gr. Πρόκρις, Procris, daughter of Erechtheus, a mythical king of Athens.] Any moth of the genus *Procris* (family *Zygænidæ*), as *P. americana*, an American species whose larvæ feed on the leaves of the grape.

Procris. — Larvæ of *P. americana* feeding.

Pro-crus-te-an (prō-krus′tē-an), *a.* Pertaining to or suggestive of Procrustes, a fabled robber of ancient Greece who stretched or mutilated his victims to make them conform to the length of his bed; hence, tending to produce conformity by violent or arbitrary means.

proc-tor (prok′tor), *n.* [Contr. of *procurator*.] One employed to manage the affairs of another; a procurator; specif., a person employed to manage another's cause in a court of civil or ecclesiastical law; also, in a university or college, an official charged with various duties, esp. with the maintenance of good order. — **proc-to′ri-al** (-tō′ri-al), *a.* Of or pertaining to a proctor. — **proc′tor-ship**, *n.*

pro-cum-bent (prō-kum′bent), *a.* [L. *procumbens* (-ent-), ppr. of *procumbere*, fall forward, < *pro*, before, + *-cumbere*, lie.] Lying on the face; prone; prostrate; in *bot.*, of a plant or stem, lying along the ground, but without putting forth roots.

pro-cur-a-ble (prō-kūr′a-bl), *a.* That may be procured.

proc-u-ra-cy (prok′ū-ra-si), *n.*; pl. *-cies* (-siz). [ML. *procuratia*, for L. *procuratio(n-)*, E. *procuration*: cf. *proxy*.] The office or service of a procurator; management of an affair for another.

proc-u-ra-tion (prok-ū-rā′shon), *n.* [L. *procuratio(n-)*, < *procurare*: see *procure*.] Care† or management†; also, management for another; procuracy; agency; also, the appointment of a procurator, agent, or attorney, or the authority given, or a document whereby the authority is given (as, "He was then directed to send his *procuration* to certain persons . . . whom he might wish to appear in his behalf": Motley's "Dutch Republic," iii. 5); also, the act of procuring, obtaining, or getting.

proc-u-ra-tor (prok′ū-rā-tor), *n.* [L., < *procurare*: see *procure*.] One employed to manage the affairs of another, or authorized to act for another; an agent, deputy, or attorney; also, among the ancient Romans, any of various imperial officers with fiscal or administrative powers. — **proc″u-ra-to′ri-al** (-rā-tō′ri-al), *a.* Of or pertaining to a procurator or a proctor; proctorial. — **proc′u-ra-tor-ship** (-rā-tor-ship), *n.* — **proc′u-ra-to-ry** (-rā-tō-ri), *a.* Pertaining to a procurator or to procuration.

pro-cure (prō-kūr′), *v.*; *-cured*, *-curing.* [OF. F. *procurer*, < L. *procurare*, take care of, look after, manage, < *pro*, before, for, + *curare*, care for, E. *cure*, *v.*] **I.** *tr.* To bring about or effect by care, contrivance, or special agency (as, to *procure* a person's death; "Montezuma was desired to *procure* a further mitigation of the punishment," Prescott's "Conquest of Mexico," iv. 4); hence, in general, to bring about, produce, or cause (obs. or archaic: as, "Thus might we *procure* great evil against our souls," Jer. xxvi. 19); also, to obtain or get by care, effort, or the use of special agencies or means (as, to *procure* evidence or facts; to *procure* an invitation; to *procure* a horse or a guide; "What need of weapons, then, except to *procure* food?" W. H. Hudson's "Green Mansions," xiv.); also, to obtain (women) for the gratification of lust. **II.** *intr.* To act as a procurer (pander) or procuress. — **pro-cure′ment**, *n.* The act of procuring; effecting or contrivance (as, "He and Teach were of a mind; and by their joint *procurement* . . . the whole crew went off": Stevenson's "Master of Ballantrae," iii.); obtaining or getting (as, "It doth not appear . . . how any one virtue is required towards the *procurement* of any one station among you": Swift's "Gulliver's Travels," ii. 6). — **pro-cur′er** (-kūr′ėr), *n.* One who procures; specif., a pander or pimp; also, a procurator†. — **pro-cur′ess**, *n.* A female procurer; a bawd.

pro-cu-reur (pro-kü-rėr′), *n.* [F., < L. *procurator*: see *procurator*.] A procurator; an attorney or legal representative; a public prosecutor.

prod (prod), *v. t.*; *prodded*, *prodding.* [Origin uncertain.] To poke or jab with something pointed (as, to *prod* an animal with a stick; to *prod* a person with the finger; "The bull . . . *prodded* me with his horns," W. H. Hudson's "Purple Land," xii.); fig., to seek to rouse or incite as if by poking (as, to *prod* a lazy or reluctant person; "She reverted to her resolution to change the town — awaken it, *prod* it, 'reform' it," Sinclair Lewis's "Main Street," x.); urge or goad, as into action; harass or irritate, as by comments; also, to make by poking (as, "The lady has *prodded* little spirting holes in the damp sand . . . with her **parasol"**: Dickens's "Our Mutual Friend," i. 10).—**prod,** *n.* An act of prodding; a poke or jab; also, any of various pointed instruments, as a goad.—**prod′der,** *n.*

pro-de-ni-a (prō̞-dē′ni-ạ), *n.* [NL.] Any of the noctuid moths of the widespread genus *Prodenia,* as *P. eudiopta,* common in the U. S., whose larvæ feed on various succulent vegetables.

Prodenia (*P. eudiopta*).— *a,* larva; *b,* wings of moth.

prod-i-gal (prod′i-gal). [OF. *prodigal,* < L. *prodigus,* wasteful, < *prodigere,* drive forth, get rid of, < *prod-,* for *pro-,* forth, + *agere,* drive.] **I.** *a.* Wastefully or recklessly extravagant in spending money or resources (as, to be liberal but not *prodigal;* a *prodigal* administration; the parable of the *prodigal* son, see Luke, xv. 11–32); characterized by or involving reckless extravagance (as, *prodigal* expenditure; *prodigal* living; *prodigal* munificence); also, giving or yielding lavishly or profusely (as, "The chariest maid is *prodigal* enough, If she unmask her beauty to the moon," Shakspere's "Hamlet," i. 3. 36; a *prodigal* soil); lavish (*of:* as, "a most reckless . . . young flirt . . . *prodigal* of smiles," Thackeray's "Newcomes," xxxiii.; "orchards . . . in blossom and . . . *prodigal* of odors," C. B. Brown's "Wieland," v.); profuse, or lavishly abundant (as, "Justice is degraded by the *prodigal* use of bills of attainder": Green's "Short Hist. of the Eng. People," vi. 3). **II.** *n.* One who spends, or has spent, his money or substance with wasteful extravagance; a spendthrift.—**prod-i-gal′i-ty** (-gal′i-ti), *n.;* pl. *-ties* (-tiz). The quality or fact of being prodigal; wasteful or reckless extravagance in spending, or an instance of it; lavishness; profuseness; lavish abundance.—**prod′i-gal-ly,** *adv.*

pro-di-gious (prō̞-dij′us), *a.* [L. *prodigiosus,* < *prodigium,* E. *prodigy.*] Of the nature of a prodigy or portent†; ominous†; also, out of the ordinary course of nature, abnormal, or monstrous (as, "Nature breeds, Perverse, all monstrous, all *prodigious* things": Milton's "Paradise Lost," ii. 625); also, wonderful or marvelous (as, a *prodigious* feat; "*Prodigious* this! the frail one of our play From her own sex should mercy find to-day!" Pope's "Epilogue to Mr. Rowe's Jane Shore," 1); extraordinary in size, amount, extent, degree, force, etc., or very great (as, a *prodigious* mass, sum, or length; a *prodigious* noise; *prodigious* haste or efforts; "an event of *prodigious* importance," Thackeray's "Newcomes," ii.). —**pro-di′gious-ly,** *adv.*—**pro-di′gious-ness,** *n.*

prod-i-gy (prod′i-ji), *n.;* pl. *-gies* (-jiz). [L. *prodigium,* prophetic sign, portent, prodigy.] Something extraordinary regarded as of prophetic significance, or a portent (as, "The old men paid careful attention to omens and *prodigies,* and especially to their dreams": Parkman's "Oregon Trail," xv.); also, something out of the ordinary course of nature; something abnormal or monstrous; also, something wonderful or marvelous, or a wonder or marvel (as, "Lilliput, whose inhabitants looked upon me as the greatest *prodigy* that ever appeared in the world": Swift's "Gulliver's Travels," ii. 1); a marvelous example (*of:* as, "that *prodigy* of learning, the noble and illustrious Joseph Scaliger," Evelyn's "Diary," Aug. 19, 1641; "The warriors . . . were performing *prodigies* of valor," H. Melville's "Typee," xvi.); a person endowed with extraordinary gifts or powers (as, a musical *prodigy;* an infant *prodigy*).

pro-drome (prō̞′drōm), *n.* [F. *prodrome,* < Gr. πρόδρομος, running before, < πρό, before, + δραμεῖν, run.] A forerunner† or precursor†; hence, a preliminary treatise; in *pathol.,* a premonitory symptom.—**prod-ro-mal** (prod′rō̞-mạl), **pro-drom-ic** (prō̞-drom′ik), *a.*

pro-duce (prō̞-dūs′), *v.;* *-duced, -ducing.* [L. *producere* (pp. *productus*), lead or bring forward, extend, prolong, bring forth, produce, < *pro,* before, + *ducere,* lead.] **I.** *tr.* To bring forward; present to view or notice; exhibit; specif., to bring (a play, etc.) before the public; also, to extend or prolong, as a line; also, to bring forth, bear, or yield, as young or natural products; give forth, furnish, or supply (as, a mine *producing* silver); yield, or cause to accrue (as,

money *producing* interest); bring into existence, give rise to, cause, or make (as, to *produce* steam, heat, a result, or a noise); bring into being by mental or physical labor, as a work of literature or art; make by working upon raw material, or manufacture; in *polit. econ.,* to create (something having an exchangeable value). **II.** *intr.* To bring forth or yield appropriate offspring, products, etc.; in *polit. econ.,* to create value; bring crops, goods, etc., into a state in which they will command a price.—**prod-uce** (prod′ūs), *n.* That which is produced; yield; product; specif., agricultural or natural products collectively.—**pro-du′cer** (-dū′-sėr), *n.* One who or that which produces; in *polit. econ.,* one who creates value, or produces articles of consumption (opposed to *consumer*).—**pro-du′ci-ble,** *a.* [LL. *producibilis.*] Capable of being produced.

prod-uct (prod′ukt), *n.* [L. *productus,* pp. of *producere:* see *produce.*] Something produced; a thing produced by nature or by a natural process (as, "They beheld the rich *products* of various climes growing side by side, fields of towering maize, the juicy aloe . . . and large plantations of the cactus": Prescott's "Conquest of Mexico," iii. 6); a thing produced by any action or operation, or by labor; an effect or result; in *chem.,* a substance obtained from another substance through chemical change (as distinguished from an *educt*); in *math.,* the result obtained by multiplying two or more quantities together.

pro-duc-tion (prō̞-duk′shọn), *n.* [L. *productio(n-).*] The act of producing, or the state of being produced; presentation or exhibition; extension or prolongation; creation; manufacture; also, that which is produced; a product; a work of literature or art; in *polit. econ.,* the creation of value; the producing of articles having an exchangeable value.

pro-duc-tive (prō̞-duk′tiv), *a.* Having the power of producing; generative; creative; causative; also, producing readily or abundantly; fertile; prolific; in *polit. econ.,* producing or tending to produce exchangeable value.—**pro-duc′tive-ly,** *adv.*—**pro-duc′tive-ness, pro-duc-tiv-i-ty** (prō̞-duk-tiv′i-ti), *n.*

pro-em (prō̞′em), *n.* [OF. *proeme* (F. *proème*), < L. *proœmium,* < Gr. προοίμιον, < πρό, before, + οἶμος, way, course, strain of song.] An introductory discourse; an introduction; a preface; a preamble.—**pro-e-mi-al** (prō̞-ē′mi-ạl), *a.*

pro-face† (prō̞-fās′), *interj.* [OF. *prou fasse: prou,* profit (see *improve*); *fasse,* 3d pers. sing. pres. subj. of *faire,* < L. *facere,* do.] May it do you good! — a courteous expression used at a dinner or other meal. See Shakspere's "2 Henry IV.," v. 3. 30.

prof-a-na-tion (prof-ạ-nā′shọn), *n.* [LL. *profanatio(n-).*] The act of profaning; desecration; defilement; debasement. —**pro-fan-a-to-ry** (prō̞-fan′ạ-tō̞-ri), *a.*

pro-fane (prō̞-fān′), *a.* [OF. *prophane* (F. *profane*), < L. *profanus,* lit. 'before (outside of) the temple,' < *pro,* before, + *fanum,* temple, E. *fane.*] Not sacred, or not devoted to sacred purposes; unconsecrated; secular (as, *profane* history or literature); sometimes, unholy; heathen or pagan; also, characterized by irreverence or contempt for God or sacred things; irreverent; irreligious; esp., speaking or spoken in manifest or implied contempt for sacred things; taking God's name in vain; blasphemous; also, not initiated into religious rites or mysteries, as persons; in general, uninitiated; common or vulgar.—**pro-fane′,** *v. t.;* *-faned, -faning.* [L. *profanare,* < *profanus.*] To treat (anything sacred) with irreverence or contempt (as, "They *profaned* my holy name," Ezek. xxxvi. 20; "the temple and its holy rites *profan'd,*" Cowper's "Expostulation," 145); desecrate; hence, to misuse (anything that should be held in reverence or respect); defile; debase; employ basely or unworthily (as, "I feel me much to blame, So idly to *profane* the precious time": Shakspere's "2 Henry IV.," ii. 4. 391).—**pro-fane′ly,** *adv.*—**pro-fane′ness,** *n.*—**pro-fan′er** (-fā′nėr), *n.*—**pro-fan′i-ty** (-fan′i-ti), *n.;* pl. *-ties* (-tiz). The quality of being profane; irreverence; also, profane conduct or language; a profane act or utterance.

pro-fert (prō̞′fėrt), *n.* [L., 'he brings forward.'] In *law,* an exhibition of a record or paper in open court, or a formal allegation that it is so exhibited.

pro-fess (prọ-fes'), v. [L. professus, pp. of profiteri, declare publicly, < pro, before, + fateri, acknowledge.] **I.** tr. To declare openly (as, to profess one's satisfaction, or one's antagonism; to profess faith in a person; "We profess Ourselves to be the slaves of chance," Shakspere's "Winter's Tale," iv. 4. 550); announce or affirm; avow or acknowledge; also, to lay claim to (a feeling, etc.), often insincerely (as, "For the present . . . Alençon professed the most friendly sentiments towards the Prince," Motley's "Dutch Republic," v. 5; "Every one was amused or professed to be," F. M. Crawford's "Mr. Isaacs," vii.); make protestation of; pretend to; also, to affirm faith in or allegiance to (a religion, God, etc.: as, "He did not profess any particular religion," B. Franklin's "Autobiography," ii.); also, to declare one's self skilled or versed in; claim to have knowledge of; make (a thing) one's profession or business; also, to teach (a subject) as a professor; also, to receive or admit into a religious order. **II.** intr. To make profession; also, to take the vows of a religious order; also, to act as a professor.—**pro-fessed'**, p. a. Avowed or acknowledged; sometimes, alleged or pretended; also, that professes to be qualified; professional (rather than amateur); also, having taken the vows of, or been received into, a religious order.—**pro-fess'ed-ly**, adv.

pro-fes-sion (prọ-fesh'ọn), n. [L. professio(n-), < profiteri: see profess.] The act of professing; declaration; avowal; a declaration, whether true or false (as, "professions of love," Jane Austen's "Pride and Prejudice," xxv.; "professions of regret," Lamb's "Oxford in the Vacation"); specif., the declaration of belief in or acceptance of religion or a faith (as, "the public profession and external practice of Christianity": J. Butler's "Analogy of Religion," ii. 1); hence, a religion or faith professed; also, the declaration or vow made on entering a religious order; also, a professed occupation or calling; a vocation; esp., one of the three vocations of theology, law, and medicine (formerly known specifically as 'the professions,' also 'the learned professions'), or some other vocation requiring knowledge of some department of learning or science, or in which such knowledge is used in the practice of an art (as, "My acquaintances went . . . into trade or the professions," Thoreau's "Walden," i.; the profession of teaching, or of dentistry); also, the body of persons engaged in an occupation or calling (as, to be at the head of one's profession).—**pro-fes'sion-al.** **I.** a. Pertaining to, connected with, or appropriate to a profession or calling (as, professional studies; "Mr. Mortcloke the undertaker . . . with a visage of professional length and most grievous solemnity," Scott's "Guy Mannering," xxxvii.); also, engaged in one of the learned or skilled professions (as, a professional man; the professional class); also, following an occupation as a means of livelihood or for gain (as, a professional soldier); specif., following as a business an occupation ordinarily engaged in as a pastime (as, a professional golfer); sometimes, in disparagement, making a business or trade of something not properly to be regarded as a business (as, a professional politician; a professional beauty); also, undertaken or engaged in as a means of livelihood or for gain, or by professionals rather than amateurs (as, professional baseball). **II.** n. One belonging to one of the learned or skilled professions; also, one who makes a profession or business of an occupation, etc., esp. of an art or sport in which amateurs are accustomed to engage for amusement or recreation.—**pro-fes'sion-al-ism**, n. Professional character, spirit, or methods; also, the standing, practice, or methods of a professional as distinguished from an amateur.—**pro-fes'sion-al-ize**, v. t. or i.; -ized, -izing. To make or become professional.—**pro-fes'sion-al-ly**, adv.

pro-fes-sor (prọ-fes'ọr), n. [L., < profiteri: see profess.] One who professes, or makes open declaration of his sentiments, beliefs, allegiance, etc.; specif., one who makes open profession of religion (as, "Then the name of a professor was odious; now . . . religion is counted honourable": Bunyan's "Pilgrim's Progress," ii.); also, a teacher of the highest rank in a particular branch of learning in a university, college, etc.; in general, a title for a teacher, as of drawing or music, and sometimes for an instructor in some popular art, as boxing.—**pro-fes'sor-ate** (-ạt), n. The office or the

period of service of a professor or teacher; also, a body of professors.—**pro-fes-so-ri-al** (prọ-fe-sọ'ri-ạl), a. Of, pertaining to, or characteristic of a professor.—**pro-fes-so'ri-al-ly**, adv.—**pro-fes-so'ri-ate** (-ạt), n. A body of professors.—**pro-fes'sor-ship**, n. The office or post of a professor.

prof-fer (prof'ẹr), v. t. [AF. profrer, for OF. porofrir, < por- (< L. pro, before) + ofrir, < L. offerre, E. offer.] To put before a person for acceptance, or offer or tender (as, "I felt rather dubious of their accepting them [tracts] had I proffered them with my own hand," Borrow's "Bible in Spain," iii.; "Mr. van der Luyden . . . proffered to Newland low-voiced congratulations," Mrs. Wharton's "Age of Innocence," vii.); also, to offer or propose (to do something: archaic).—**prof'fer**, n. The act of proffering; an offer or tender (as, "proffers of assistance": Bret Harte's "Tennessee's Partner"); also, an essay†, attempt†, or endeavor†. —**prof'fer-er**, n.

pro-fi-cien-cy (prọ-fish'ẹn-si), n. The state of being proficient: as, "Don Geronimo had been educated in England . . . which . . . accounted for his proficiency in the English language" (Borrow's "Bible in Spain," ii.).

pro-fi-cient (prọ-fish'ẹnt). [L. proficiens (-ent-), ppr. of proficere, make progress: see profit.] **I.** a. Well advanced or versed in any art, science, or subject; skilled; adept; expert. **II.** n. One who is proficient; an adept or expert: as, "She was a proficient in music" (Peacock's "Nightmare Abbey," iii.).—**pro-fi'cient-ly**, adv.

pro-file (prọ'fẹl or -fil), n. [It. profilo, < profilare, draw in outline, < L. pro, before, + filum, thread.] The outline or contour of anything, as the human face, esp. as seen from the side; also, an outline drawing or picture of anything as seen from the side; in arch., engin., etc., a drawing of a section, esp. a vertical section, through something.—**pro'file**, v. t.; -filed, -filing. To draw a profile of; outline, esp. in vertical section; also, to shape as to profile.—**pro'fil-ist** (-fẹl-ist or -fil-ist), n. One who makes profile portraits, esp. silhouettes.

prof-it (prof'it), n. [OF. F. profit, < L. profectus, progress, profit, < proficere, make progress, derive advantage, be advantageous, < pro, before, + facere, do, make.] Advantage, benefit, or gain (as, "This I speak for your own profit": 1 Cor. vii. 35); also, returns, proceeds, or revenue, as from property or investments (often in pl.); also, pecuniary gain resulting from the employment of capital in any transaction (often in pl.: as, gross profits; net profits: see gross, a., and net², a.); also, the ratio of such pecuniary gain to the amount of capital invested; in polit. econ., the surplus left in the hands of the producer or employer after deducting wages, rent, cost of raw materials, etc., and now, usually, such additional charges as interest on capital, insurance, etc. (usually in pl.).—**profit and loss**, an inclusive expression for the gain and loss arising from commercial or other transactions: applied esp. to an account in bookkeeping showing gains and losses in business.—**prof'it**, v. [OF. F. profiter, < profit.] **I.** intr. To be of advantage or benefit (as, "Riches profit not in the day of wrath": Prov. xi. 4); also, to gain advantage or benefit (as, "He at once saw his advantage, and determined to profit by it": Cooper's "Spy," vii.); take advantage (as, "I profited of this time to rest for a few hours": Mrs. Shelley's "Frankenstein," letter iv.); make profit. **II.** tr. To be of advantage or profit to: as, "For what shall it profit a man, if he shall gain the whole world, and lose his own soul?" (Mark, viii. 36).—**prof'it-a-ble**, a. [OF. F. profitable.] Yielding profit; beneficial or useful; lucrative or remunerative.—**prof″it-a-bil'i-ty** (-bil'-i-ti), **prof'it-a-ble-ness**, n.—**prof'it-a-bly**, adv.—**prof-it-eer'** (-i-tēr'), n. One who seeks or exacts exorbitant profits, as by taking advantage of public necessity.—**prof-it-eer'**, v. i. To act as a profiteer; seek or exact exorbitant profits: chiefly in profiteering, n. and p. a.: as, "There were harsh laws against 'profiteering' in France in 1793" (H. G. Wells's "Outline of History," xxxvii. § 11).—**prof'it-er**, n.—**prof'it-less**, a. Void of profit; unprofitable.—**prof'it-less-ly**, adv.—**prof″it=shar″ing. I.** n. The sharing of profits, as between employer and employee, esp. according to a method by which the laborer receives, in addition to his wages, a share in the profits of the business. **II.** a. Pertaining to, characterized by, or involving profit-sharing.

---

prof-li-ga-cy (prof′li-gā-si), *n.* Profligate character or conduct; shameless dissoluteness; reckless prodigality.

prof-li-gate (prof′li-gāt). [L. *profligatus*, pp. of *profligare*, overthrow, ruin, < *pro-*, forward, + *-fligare*, for *fligere*, strike.] **I.** *a.* Overthrown or routed, as a contending force†; also, given over utterly and shamelessly to vice or immorality (as, "a *profligate* wretch without any sense of principle, morality, or religion": Smollett's "Humphry Clinker," May 17); thoroughly abandoned or dissolute, as in life, habits, or character; shamelessly immoral or vicious, as the life, habits, etc.; also, recklessly prodigal or extravagant. **II.** *n.* A profligate person.—**prof′li-gate-ly**, *adv.*—**prof′li-gate-ness**, *n.*

prof-lu-ent (prof′lö-ent), *a.* [L. *profluens* (-*ent*-), ppr. of *profluere*, < *pro*, before, + *fluere*, flow.] Flowing forth or along: as, "the *profluent* stream" (Milton's "Paradise Lost," xii. 442).

pro for-ma (prō fôr′mä). [L., 'for form.'] For the sake of form; as a matter of form: a phrase sometimes used adjectively (as, a *pro forma* invoice, a statement in the form of an invoice drawn up to show the price or value of goods specified, as one for a prospective purchaser, or one sent in advance to an importer for goods ordered and shipped and enabling him to comply with some legal requirement).

pro-found (prō-found′). [OF. F. *profond*, < L. *profundus*, < *pro*, before, + *fundus*, bottom.] **I.** *a.* Deep, or of great depth (as, "a succession of steep and isolated hills, with *profound* valleys": Irving's "Captain Bonneville," xxxii.); extending, situated, or originating far down, or far beneath the surface (as, a *profound* incision; a *profound*, or deep-seated, artery; a *profound* sigh); carried far down, or low (as, a *profound* bow); also, fig., being or going far beneath what is superficial, external, or obvious (as, to make a *profound* impression on the mind; *profound* meaning; *profound* insight); of deep meaning (as, a *profound* remark; "The man ... exchanged a *profound* look with the old Malay," J. Conrad's "Rescue," vi. 8); recondite or abstruse (as, a *profound* subject; "She had read much, and especially in *profounder* books," Wiseman's "Fabiola," i. 4); penetrating or entering deeply into subjects of thought or knowledge (as, a *profound* student, thinker, or philosopher; *profound* learning or scholarship); characterized by or showing deep learning; also, deep, intense, or extreme (as, *profound* sleep, silence, or peace; *profound* darkness; *profound* ignorance); very great; thorough. **II.** *n.* That which is profound; the deep, or deep sea, or ocean; any place or space of profound depth (also fig.); an abyss. [Chiefly poetic.]—**pro-found′ly**, *adv.*—**pro-found′ness**, *n.*

pro-fun-di-ty (prō-fun′di-ti), *n.*; pl. *-ties* (-tiz). [LL. *profunditas.*] The quality of being profound; depth (lit. or fig.); profoundness; also, a profoundly deep place or space; an abyss (as, "through the vast *profundity* obscure": Milton's "Paradise Lost," vii. 229); also, *pl.*, profound or deep matters.

pro-fuse (prō-fūs′), *a.* [L. *profusus*, pp. of *profundere*, pour forth, < *pro*, before, + *fundere*, pour.] Spending or giving freely and in large amount, often to excess (as, "Lothair was *profuse*, but he was not prodigal," Disraeli's "Lothair," vii.; "He was fond of splendor, *profuse*, and in debt," Bancroft's "Hist. of the U. S.," Amer. Revolution, i. 2); lavish, excessively liberal, or extravagant; characterized by lavishness or extravagance (as, *profuse* expenditure; "His *profuse* magnificence insulted the general poverty," Gibbon's "Decline and Fall of the Roman Empire," x.); also, in general, giving, yielding, using, or uttering something freely and in great abundance (with *of* or *in*: as, "Patriots ... Profuse of blood," Byron's "Siege of Corinth," xii.; "a green shady bank, *profuse* of flowers," Milton's "Paradise Lost," viii. 286; to be *profuse* of words, or *profuse* in apologies); made or done freely and abundantly (as, a *profuse* use of ornament; "a *profuse* interchange of courtesy," Motley's "Dutch Republic," iii. 9); abundant, copious, or in great amount (as, *profuse* ornament; *profuse* perspiration; *profuse* thanks).—**pro-fuse′ly**, *adv.*—**pro-fuse′ness**, *n.*

pro-fu-sion (prō-fū′zhon), *n.* [L. *profusio*(*n*-), < *profundere*: see *profuse*.] A pouring forth† or shedding†; also, profuse spending or giving; lavishness or extravagance; also, abundance, or abundant quantity (as, "a certain fruit which grew in *profusion* there": J. Conrad's "Rescue," v. 2); a great quantity or amount (*of*: as, "He wore a *profusion* of ribbons on his garment," Hawthorne's "Scarlet Letter," xxi.; "He ... overwhelmed her with a *profusion* of compliment," Smollett's "Humphry Clinker," May 6).

prog (prog), *v. i.*; *progged, progging.* [Origin uncertain.] To search or prowl about, as for plunder or food; forage; also, to go about begging. [Now prov.]—**prog**, *n.* Food or victuals; often, provisions for a journey or excursion. [Now prov. or slang.]

pro-gen-i-tive (prō-jen′i-tiv), *a.* [L. *progenitus*, pp. of *progignere*: see *progenitor*.] Producing offspring; reproductive.

pro-gen-i-tor (prō-jen′i-tor), *n.* [L., < *progignere* (pp. *progenitus*), beget, produce, < *pro*, before, + *gignere*, beget, bear.] An ancestor in the direct line; a forefather.—**pro-gen-i-to′ri-al** (-tō′ri-al), *a.*—**pro-gen′i-tor-ship**, *n.*—**pro-gen′i-tress**, *n.* A female progenitor.

prog-e-ny (proj′e-ni), *n.* [OF. *progenie*, < L. *progenies*, < *progignere*: see *progenitor*.] Offspring; issue; more broadly, descendants; fig., that which is produced by or originates from something (as, "Around this fort a *progeny* of little Dutch-built houses ... soon sprang up": Irving's "Knickerbocker's New York," ii. 8); also, a race†, stock†, or family†; also, descent† or lineage†.

pro-glot-tis (prō-glot′is), *n.*; pl. *proglottides* (-i-dēz). [NL., < Gr. πρό, before, + γλῶττα, γλῶσσα, tongue.] In *zoöl.*, one of the segments or joints of a tapeworm, containing both male and female sexual organs.—**pro-glot′tic**, *a.*

prog-nath-ic (prog-nath′ik), *a.* Prognathous.

prog-na-thous (prog′na-thus), *a.* [Gr. πρό, before, + γνάθος, jaw.] Of a skull or a person, having protrusive jaws; of a jaw, protruding.—**prog′na-thism**, **prog′na-thy** (-thi), *n.*

prog-no-sis (prog-nō′sis), *n.* [LL., < Gr. πρόγνωσις, < προγιγνώσκειν, know beforehand, < πρό, before, + γιγνώσκειν, know.] Prognostication; in *med.*, forecasting of the probable course and termination of cases of disease, or a particular forecast made.

prog-nos-tic (prog-nos′tik). [Gr. προγνωστικός, foreknowing (as n., L. *prognosticon*, < Gr. προγνωστικόν, neut., a prognostic), < προγιγνώσκειν, know beforehand: see *prognosis*.] **I.** *a.* Indicating something in the future (as, *prognostic* signs); foreshowing; in *med.*, of or pertaining to prognosis. **II.** *n.* An indication, sign, or omen of what is to come (as, "The behaviour of this ... old man ... was a dreadful *prognostic* for all my future life": Godwin's "Caleb Williams," xxxiii.); often, a sign of coming weather (as, "They knew, by sure *prognostics* seen on high, The future tone and temper of the sky": Cowper's "Expostulation," 157); also, a forecast or prediction (as, "Philosophers ... awaited in anxious impatience the fulfilment of their *prognostics*": Irving's "Knickerbocker's New York," i. 1); in *med.*, a sign or symptom on which prognosis is based.

prog-nos-ti-ca-ble (prog-nos′ti-ka-bl), *a.* That may be prognosticated.

prog-nos-ti-cate (prog-nos′ti-kāt), *v.*; *-cated, -cating.* [ML. *prognosticatus*, pp. of *prognosticare*, < L. *prognosticon*: see *prognostic*.] **I.** *tr.* To forecast or predict (something future) from present indications or signs; foretell or prophesy (as, "He did *prognosticate* ... that on the eighteenth of April a storm should burst over this land": Jane Porter's "Scottish Chiefs," xlviii.); also, to indicate beforehand as a sign does, presage, or portend (as, "The looks of her medical attendants *prognosticated* the worst event": Mrs. Shelley's "Frankenstein," iii.). **II.** *intr.* To make a forecast or prediction; prophesy.—**prog-nos-ti-ca′tion** (-kā′shon), *n.* The act of prognosticating; a forecast or prediction (as, "The Doctor's *prognostication* in reference to the weather was speedily verified": Dickens's "Martin Chuzzlewit," xlii.); sometimes, a presentiment; also, a prognostic, sign, or omen, as of something to come (now rare).—**prog-nos′ti-ca-tor**, *n.*

pro-gram, pro-gramme (prō′gram), *n.* [= F. *programme*, < LL. *programma*, < Gr. πρόγραμμα, public notice in writing, < προγράφειν, write publicly, < πρό, before, + γράφειν, write.] A public notice†; also, a list of items, pieces, performers, etc., in a musical, theatrical, or other entertainment; an entertainment with reference to its pieces or numbers;

also, a prospectus or syllabus; in general, a plan to be followed (as, "His nurses relieved each other according to the contingencies of the moment rather than by a set *programme* of hours": Arnold Bennett's "Old Wives' Tale," i. 3). —**program music,** music intended to convey an impression of a definite series of images, scenes, or events.—**pro′gram, pro′gramme,** *v. t.*; *-grammed, -gramming.* To arrange or enter in a program; draw up a program for.—**pro-gram-mat′ic** (-grạ-mat′ik), *a.* Pertaining to or of the nature of a program; of the nature of program music.

prog-ress (prog′res or prō′gres), *n.* [L. *progressus,* < *progredi,* go forward, < *pro,* before, + *gradi,* walk, go.] A going or traveling forward or onward, or a march or journey (as, "The Pilgrim's *Progress* from This World to That Which Is to Come," the title of a famous work by John Bunyan); specif., a journey of state, as of a sovereign (as, a royal *progress;* "I attended the King and Queen in their *progresses,*" Swift's "Gulliver's Travels," ii. 4); also, onward movement in space, or course (as, "A thousand rills their mazy *progress* take": Gray's "Progress of Poesy," i. 1); hence, course of action, of events, of time, etc. (as, "a stage . . . early in the *progress* of the disease": Arnold Bennett's "Hilda Lessways," i. 4); also, forward movement in space, rather than rest or backward movement; advance (as, "The folded gates would bar my *progress*": Cowper's "Task," i. 330); hence, fig., a proceeding to a further or higher stage, or through such stages successively (as, the *progress* of a scholar in his studies); advance or advancement in general; growth or development; continuous improvement.—**in progress,** proceeding; taking place; happening: as, "Preparations were *in progress* for a dance" (G. W. Cable's "Cavalier," xii.).—**pro-gress** (prō-gres′), *v. i.* To go forward or onward; proceed; also, to make progress; advance; improve.

pro-gres-sion (prō-gresh′ọn), *n.* [L. *progressio(n-),* < *progredi:* see *progress.*] The act of progressing; forward or onward movement; a passing successively from one member of a series to the next, or succession; advance; development; in *math.,* a succession of quantities in which there is a constant relation between each member and the one succeeding it (as, an arithmetical *progression,* in which the members increase or decrease by a constant difference; a geometrical *progression,* in which each member is derived from the preceding one by multiplication by a constant factor); in *music,* motion; also, a sequence.—**pro-gres′sion-al,** *a.*—**pro-gres′sion-ist,** *n.* One who believes in or advocates progress, as in politics; also, one who holds that organic existence is characterized by progression from simpler to more complex forms.

prog-ress-ist (prog′res-ist), *n.* One favoring progress, as in politics; a progressive.

pro-gres-sive (prō-gres′iv). [F. *progressif,* < L. *progressus,* pp. of *progredi:* see *progress.*] **I.** *a.* Characterized by progressing, or going forward or onward; also, passing on successively from one member of a series to the next; proceeding step by step; marked by succession; specif., noting a form of certain games, as euchre and whist, played simultaneously by several sets of players at a number of tables, under rules providing for the advancement, after each game or round, of certain players from one table to the next; also, noting or pertaining to a form of taxation in which the rate increases with certain increases in the amount taxed; also, progressing or advancing; making progress toward higher or better conditions, more enlightened or liberal ideas, the use of new and advantageous methods, etc. (as, a *progressive* nation or community; a *progressive* business house); characterized by such progress, or by continuous improvement; also, of a disease, continuously increasing in extent or severity; also, favoring or advocating progress, improvement, or reform, esp. in political matters; specif. [*cap.*], in *U. S. politics,* noting or pertaining to a party formed in 1912 under the leadership of Theodore Roosevelt, advocating popular control of government, direct primaries, the initiative, the referendum, the recall, woman suffrage, etc. **II.** *n.* One who is progressive, or who favors progress or reform, esp. in political matters; specif. [*cap.*], a member of the Progressive party.—**pro-gres′sive-ly,** *adv.*—**pro-gres′sive-ness,** *n.*—**pro-gres′siv-ism,** *n.* The principles and practices of progressives.

pro-gres-sor (prō-gres′ọr), *n.* [LL.] One who progresses.

pro-hib-it (prō-hib′it), *v. t.* [L. *prohibitus,* pp. of *prohibere,* hold back, restrain, forbid, < *pro,* before, + *habere,* have, hold.] To forbid (a thing) by authority, or interdict (as, "Cortés had *prohibited* all wanton injuries to the natives": Prescott's "Conquest of Mexico," iii. 7); forbid (a person) from doing something (as, a rule *prohibiting* employees from accepting fees); also, to prevent, preclude, or debar (an action, etc.: as, "Gates of burning adamant Barr′d over us *prohibit* all egress," Milton's "Paradise Lost," ii. 437).

pro-hi-bi-tion (prō-hi-bish′ọn), *n.* [L. *prohibitio(n-).*] The act of prohibiting; an edict or decree forbidding or debarring; specif., the interdiction by law of the manufacture and sale of alcoholic drinks for common consumption.—**Prohibition party,** in *U. S. politics,* a national party organized in 1869, advocating the legislative prohibition of the manufacture and sale of alcoholic drinks.—**pro-hi-bi′tion-ism,** *n.* The principles and practices of prohibitionists.—**pro-hi-bi′tion-ist,** *n.* One who favors or advocates prohibition, specif. of the manufacture and sale of alcoholic drinks; [*cap.*] a member of the Prohibition party.

pro-hib-i-tive (prō-hib′i-tiv), *a.* That prohibits or forbids something; also, such as serves to prevent the use, purchase, etc., of something (as, a *prohibitive* tax or duty; "The cost of the four-color process was at that time *prohibitive,*" Bok's "Americanization of Edward Bok," xxi.).—**pro-hib′i-tive-ly,** *adv.*—**pro-hib′i-tive-ness,** *n.*

pro-hib-i-tor (prō-hib′i-tọr), *n.* [L.] One who prohibits. —**pro-hib′i-to-ry** (-tọ-ri), *a.* Prohibitive.

pro-ject (prō-jekt′), *v.* [L. *projectus,* pp. of *projicere, proicere,* < *pro,* before, + *jacere,* throw.] **I.** *tr.* To throw, cast, or impel forward or onward; also, to throw or cause to fall upon a surface or into space, as a ray of light, a shadow, etc. (as, "Across the bright plains . . . the vast pyramidal shadow of Mount Etna is definitely and visibly *projected*": Motley's "Dutch Republic," ii. 3); cause (a figure or image) to appear as on a background; also, fig., to visualize and regard (an idea, etc.) as an objective reality; also, to cause to jut out or protrude; also, to propose, contemplate, or plan, as something to be carried out (as, "I had *projected* an excursion to the Highlands": Smollett's "Humphry Clinker," Sept. 6); form a project of; plan (to do something: as, "He indited an excellent ballad . . . which he *projects* to publish," Galt's "Annals of the Parish," xlviii.); in *geom.,* etc., to carry forward (a point, etc.) in a given direction; throw forward (a figure, etc.) by straight lines or rays (parallel or from a center) which pass through all points of it and reproduce it on a surface; delineate by any system of correspondence between points. **II.** *intr.* To extend or protrude beyond something else; jut out (as, "The booths where goods were exposed to sale *projected* far into the streets": Macaulay's "Hist. of Eng.," iii.); also, to make plans or experiments, esp. in an ineffective way, potter about, or play tricks (prov. or slang, U. S.).—**proj-ect** (proj′ekt), *n.* [= F. *projet,* < L. *projectum,* neut. of *projectus,* pp.] Something projected, contemplated, or planned; a plan; a scheme: as, "No enterprise was too difficult, no *project* too vast, for his ambition" (Amelia B. Edwards's "Thousand Miles up the Nile," xv.); "a *project* for extracting sun-beams out of cucumbers" (Swift's "Gulliver's Travels," iii. 5).

pro-jec-tile (prō-jek′til). [NL. *prōjectilis,* < L. *projectus,* pp.: see *project, v.*] **I.** *a.* Impelling or driving forward, as a force; also, caused by impulse, as motion; also, capable of being projected or impelled forward, as a missile; in *zoöl.,* protrusile, as the jaws of a fish. **II.** *n.* A body projected or impelled forward, as through the air; specif., a missile for a cannon.

pro-jec-tion (prō-jek′shọn), *n.* [L. *projectio(n-),* < *projicere:* see *project, v.*] The act of projecting, or the state of being projected; a casting forward or onward, or impulsion; the act of visualizing and regarding an idea or the like as an objective reality, or that which is so visualized and regarded; a causing to jut out or protrude, the state or fact of jutting out or protruding, or a projecting or protruding part; the act of planning or scheming; in *alchemy,* the casting of the powder of the philosophers' stone upon metal in fusion in order to transmute it into gold or silver (as, "Had he not had *projection,* think you? Saw you no ingots in the crucibles?" Scott's "Kenilworth," xli.); hence, fig., change from one thing into another; transmutation; in *geom.*, etc., the act, process, or result of projecting; the projecting of a figure, etc., upon a surface, or the representation or picture formed.

One kind of Map-projection.

pro-jec-tive (prọ-jek′-tiv), *a.* Of or pertaining to projection; produced, or capable of being produced, by projection.—**pro-jec′-tive-ly**, *adv.*—**pro-jec-tiv′-i-ty** (prō-jek-tiv′i-ti), *n.*

pro-jec-tor (prọ-jek′tọr), *n.* One who or that which projects or throws forward; a device for projecting a beam of light, as a lens; an apparatus for throwing an image on a screen, as a magic lantern, etc.; also, one who forms projects or plans; a schemer.

pro-jet (pro-zhā′), *n.* [F.: see *project, n.*] A project; a plan; a draft of a proposed treaty.

pro-lapse (prọ-laps′), *v. i.*; -*lapsed, -lapsing.* [L. *prolapsus,* pp. of *prolabi,* < *pro,* before, + *labi,* fall, slide.] To fall or slip down or out of place: chiefly in *pathol.*—**pro-lapse′**, *n.* [LL. *prolapsus,* n., < L. *prolabi.*] In *pathol.,* a falling down of an organ or part, as the uterus, from its normal position. Also **pro-lap′sus** (-lap′sus).

pro-late (prō′lāt), *a.* [L. *prolatus,* pp. of *proferre,* bring forward, extend, < *pro,* before, + *ferre,* bear.] Elongated in the direction of the polar diameter, as a spheroid generated by the revolution of an ellipse about its longer axis: opposed to *oblate.*

pro-leg (prō′leg), *n.* [See *pro-.*] One of the abdominal ambulatory processes of caterpillars and other larvæ, as distinct from the true or thoracic legs.

Larva of Butterfly (*Anosia plexippus*), showing Prolegs (to the right).

pro-le-gom-e-non (prō-le-gom′e-non), *n.*; pl. -*na* (-nä). [NL., < Gr. προλεγόμενον, neut. ppr. pass. of προλέγειν, say beforehand: see *prologue.*] A preliminary observation, as on the subject of a book: usually in *pl.,* as applied to an introductory discourse prefixed to a book or treatise.—**pro-le-gom′e-na-ry** (-nä-ri), **pro-le-gom′e-nous,** *a.*

pro-lep-sis (prọ-lep′sis), *n.* [L., < Gr. πρόληψις, < προλαμβάνειν, anticipate, < *pro,* before, + λαμβάνειν, take.] Anticipation; also, a prochronism; in *rhet.,* an anticipation of objections in order to answer them in advance; also, the use of an epithet in anticipation of its becoming applicable.—**pro-lep′tic,** *a.* Anticipative (as, "A *proleptic* instinct made him look forward": Eden Phillpotts's "Grey Room," ii.); in *rhet.,* characterized by or involving prolepsis.

pro-lé-taire (pro-lā-tār′), *n.* [F.] A proletarian.

pro-le-ta-ri-an (prō-le-tā′ri-an), **I.** *a.* Of or belonging to the proletary class or proletariat. **II.** *n.* A member of the proletariat: as, "The *proletarians* had not come from their factories at this hour" (Tarkington's "Alice Adams," xiv.).—**pro-le-ta′ri-an-ism,** *n.*

pro-le-ta-ri-at, pro-le-ta-ri-ate (prō-le-tā′ri-at, -āt), *n.* [F. *prolétariat.*] The proletary class; that class of the community which is dependent for support on daily or casual employment; loosely, the laboring class, or wage-earners in general.

pro-le-ta-ry (prō′le-tä-ri). [L. *proletarius,* < *proles,* offspring, progeny.] **I.** *a.* Belonging to the lowest or poorest class of the people, orig. those in ancient Rome regarded as contributing nothing but offspring to the state; proletarian. **II.** *n.*; pl. -*ries* (-riz). A member of the proletary class.

pro-li-cide (prō′li-sīd), *n.* [L. *proles,* offspring: see *-cide.*] The crime of destroying one's offspring either before or soon after birth.

pro-lif-er-ate (prọ-lif′e-rāt), *v. i.* or *t.*; -*ated, -ating.* [See *proliferous.*] To grow or produce by multiplication of parts, as in budding or cell-division.—**pro-lif-er-a′tion** (-e-rā′shọn), *n.*

pro-lif-er-ous (prọ-lif′e-rus), *a.* [L. *proles,* offspring, + *ferre,* bear.] Proliferating; in *bot.,* producing new individuals by budding or the like; also, producing an organ or shoot from an organ which is itself normally ultimate, as a shoot or a new flower from the midst of a flower; in *zoöl.,* reproducing by budding or the like; esp., bearing generative zoöids.

pro-lif-ic (prọ-lif′ik), *a.* [F. *prolifique,* < L. *proles,* offspring, + *facere,* make.] Producing offspring or young, esp. abundantly (as, *prolific* animals; a *prolific* female); also, bearing or yielding fruit, esp. abundantly, as plants, soil, etc.; fruitful; in general, producing much or abundantly (as, a *prolific* imagination; a *prolific* writer; a *prolific* source of misunderstanding); also, abundantly productive of or fruitful in something specified (as, an age *prolific* of great men; a mind *prolific* in expedients); also, characterized by, involving, or causing abundant production (as, a *prolific* season for fruit; a *prolific* harvest; the *prolific* Nile).—**pro-lif′i-cal-ly, pro-lif′ic-ly,** *adv.*—**pro-lif′ic-ness,** *n.*

pro-lig-er-ous (prọ-lij′e-rus), *a.* [L. *proles,* offspring, + *gerere,* bear.] Producing progeny; generative; germinative; in *bot.,* proliferous.

pro-lix (prō′liks or prọ-liks′), *a.* [L. *prolixus,* extended, long, prolix.] Long in spatial extent (obs. or rare: as, "with wig *prolix,* down-flowing to his waist," Cowper's "Tirocinium," 361); also, of long duration†; also, of speech or writing, extended to great, unnecessary, or tedious length; lengthy; long and wordy; of persons, speaking or writing at great or tedious length; long-winded.—**pro-lix-i-ty** (prọ-lik′si-ti), *n.* The state or quality of being prolix; esp., great or tedious lengthiness of speech or writing; tediously lengthy discourse (as, "listening to the insufferable *prolixity* of the most prolix of hosts": Lever's "Harry Lorrequer," xi.).—**pro′lix-ly,** *adv.* —**pro′lix-ness,** *n.*

pro-loc-u-tor (prọ-lok′ū-tọr, prō′lọ-kū-tọr, or prol′ọ-), *n.* [L., < *proloqui,* speak out, < *pro,* before, + *loqui,* speak.] One who speaks for another or others (now rare); also, a presiding officer of an assembly; a chairman.—**pro-loc′u-tor-ship,** *n.*

pro-log-ize (prō′log-īz or prō′lọ-jīz), *v. i.* Same as *prologuize.*

pro-logue (prō′log), *n.* [OF. F. *prologue,* < L. *prologus,* < Gr. πρόλογος, < προλέγειν, ¦say beforehand, < πρό, before, + λέγειν, speak.] A preliminary discourse; a preface or introductory part of a discourse, poem, novel, etc.; a speech, usually in verse, addressed to the audience by an actor at the beginning of a play; the actor who delivers the speech; an introductory act of a dramatic performance; fig., any introductory proceeding, event, etc.—**pro′logue,** *v. t.*; -*logued, -loguing.* To introduce with or as with a prologue. —**pro′lo-guize** (-log-īz), *v. i.*; -*guized, -guizing.* To compose or deliver a prologue.

pro-long (prọ-lông′), *v. t.* [OF. *prolonguer, prolongier* (F. *prolonger*), < LL. *prolongare* (pp. *prolongatus*), < L. *pro,* before, + *longus,* long.] To lengthen out in time, or extend the duration of (as, to *prolong* one's life: "It was useless to *prolong* the discussion," Mrs. Wharton's "Age of Innocence," xiv.); cause to continue longer; keep up or draw out (sound); also, to make longer in spatial extent (as, to *prolong* a line; to *prolong* a railroad to the coast); also, to put off in time†, or postpone† (as, "This wedding-day Perhaps is but *prolong'd*: have patience": Shakspere's "Much Ado about Nothing," iv. 1. 256).—**pro-long′a-ble,** *a.* Capable of being prolonged.—**pro-lon-gate** (prọ-lông′gāt or prō′lông-), *v. t.*; -*gated, -gating.* [LL. *prolongatus,* pp.] To prolong. [Now rare.]—**pro-lon-ga-tion** (prō-lông-gā′shọn), *n.* The act of prolonging, or the state of being prolonged; lengthening in time or duration or in spatial extent; extension; also, a prolonged or extended form of something (as, "the sofas resembling a *prolongation* of uneasy chairs": George Eliot's "Middlemarch," xvii.); also, an added part by which something is prolonged (as, mountains forming a *prolongation* of a range); an extension.

pro-longe (prō-lonj′, F. pro-lôṅzh), *n.* [F., < *prolonger*: see *prolong*.] *Milit.*, a rope having a hook at one end and a toggle at the other: used for various purposes, as to draw a gun-carriage without the limber.

pro-longed (prō-lôngd′), *p. a.* Lengthened in time or space; extended or long-continued (as, "the last guest who had made a *prolonged* stay in his hotel": J. Conrad's "Victory," ii. 4); long in form beyond the ordinary (as, "a lean, lank, dark young man with . . . irregular, rather *prolonged* features": H. G. Wells's "Soul of a Bishop," v.).

pro-long-er (prō-lông′ėr), *n.* One who or that which prolongs.

pro-long-ment (prō-lông′ment), *n.* The act of prolonging, or the state of being prolonged; prolongation.

pro-lu-sion (prō-lū′zhọn), *n.* [L. *prolusio*(n-), < *proludere*, play beforehand, < *pro*, before, + *ludere*, play.] Preliminary exercise or a preliminary performance before a game, entertainment, or the like (as, "But why such long *prolusion* and display, Such turning and adjustment of the harp?" Browning's "Transcendentalism," 6); hence, in general, preliminary action, speech, or matter (as, "All this tiresome *prolusion* is only to enable you to understand": W. H. Hudson's "Green Mansions," i.); esp., a preliminary written article; an essay preliminary to a more profound work, or of an introductory or slight nature.—**pro-lu′so-ry** (-sō-ri), *a.* Serving for prolusion; of the nature of a prolusion.

prom-a-chos (prom′ạ-kos), *n.* [Gr. πρόμαχος, < πρό, before, + μάχεσθαι, fight.] In *Gr. antiq.*, one who fights before or for others; a champion or defender: applied esp. to deities, as Athene.

prom-e-nade (prom-e-näd′), *n.* [F., < *promener*, lead out, take for a walk or airing, < L. *prominare*, drive forward, < *pro*, before, + *minare*, drive.] A walk, esp. in a public place, as for pleasure or display (as, "The avenue is . . . as pretty a place for a morning *promenade* as any lounger could wish": H. Melville's "Omoo," lxxv.); a ride, drive, or airing; sometimes, an excursion in a boat (as, "What do you think of a little *promenade* at sea?" J. Conrad's "Rover," xv.); also, a place for walking or promenading; a public walk, as at a seaside resort (as, "She saw the broad and boundless *promenade* [at Brighton] alive with all its processions of pleasure": Arnold Bennett's "Hilda Lessways," iii. 3); also, a space on an upper deck of a passenger-vessel for the use of passengers (as, "On the forward *promenade* of the Saguenay boat . . . Miss Kitty Ellison sat tranquilly": Howells's "Chance Acquaintance," i.); also, an entertainment at which present walk about; in American colleges, a ball or dance.—**prom-e-nade′**, *v.*; -naded, -nading. **I.** *intr.* To take a promenade. **II.** *tr.* To take a promenade through or about; also, to take or conduct on or as on a promenade; parade.—**prom-e-nad′er** (-nä′dėr), *n.*

prom-er-ops (prom′ẹ-rops), *n.* [NL., < Gr. πρό, before, + μέροψ, bee-eater (bird).] Either of two South African birds of the genus *Promerops*

Promachos.— Athene the Defender. (Marble from Herculaneum, in the Museo Nazionale, Naples.)

Cape Promerops.

(referred by some to the *Meliphagidæ*, or honey-eaters), with a slender, curved bill and a very long tail, as *P. cafer* (the 'Cape promerops': see cut in preceding column); also, any of various other slender-billed birds.

Pro-me-the-an (prō-mē′thẹ-ạn), *a.* Of, pertaining to, or suggestive of Prometheus, a Greek demigod fabled to have made men out of clay, to have stolen fire for them from Olympus, and to have taught them various arts, in punishment for which he was chained to a rock in the Caucasus, where his liver was daily preyed upon by a vulture: as, *Promethean* fire.

prom-i-nence (prom′i-nens), *n.* The state of being prominent; conspicuousness; also, that which is prominent; a projection or protuberance. Also **prom′i-nen-cy.**

prom-i-nent (prom′i-nent), *a.* [L. *prominens* (-ent-), ppr. of *prominere*, jut out, < *pro*, before, + -*minere*, project: see *eminent*.] Standing out beyond the adjacent surface or line; projecting; also, standing out so as to be easily seen, or conspicuous (as, "the ancient church . . . the most *prominent* object, not only of the town but of the province, visible over leagues of sea": Motley's "Dutch Republic," iii. 8); fig., especially noticeable (as, a *prominent* feature of a case); of note, important, or leading (as, a *prominent* citizen or family; a *prominent* politician).—**prom′i-nent-ly,** *adv.*

pro-mis-cu-i-ty (prō-mis-kū′i-ti), *n.*; pl. *-ties* (-tiz). The state of being promiscuous; promiscuous mixture; indiscriminate mingling, or an instance of it (as, "In the informal *promiscuities* which followed the prize distribution, Cyril joined his father and mother": Arnold Bennett's "Old Wives' Tale," ii. 4); specif., promiscuous sexual union, as among some races.

pro-mis-cu-ous (prō-mis′kū-us), *a.* [L. *promiscuus*, < *pro*, before, for, + *miscere*, mix.] Consisting of parts, elements, or individuals of different kinds brought together without order (as, a *promiscuous* mass of rubbish; a *promiscuous* crowd); mingled indiscriminately, as parts or individuals of different kinds (as, "a wild, where weeds and flowers *promiscuous* shoot": Pope's "Essay on Man," i. 7); also, characterized by or involving indiscriminate mingling or association (as, *promiscuous* confusion; "The ideas of democracy, of equality, and above all of *promiscuous* fraternity have certainly never really entered into the English mind," H. G. Wells's "Tono-Bungay," i. 1. § 3; *promiscuous* sexual union); indiscriminate, or without discrimination (as, "Pryer had done well to warn Ernest against *promiscuous* house to house visitation": S. Butler's "Way of All Flesh," lxi.); making no distinctions, as a person (as, to be *promiscuous* in one's friendships); also, casual, accidental, or without particular plan or reason (colloq.).—**pro-mis′cu-ous-ly,** *adv.*—**pro-mis′cu-ous-ness,** *n.*

prom-ise (prom′is), *n.* [L. *promissum*, a promise, prop. neut. of *promissus*, pp. of *promittere*, send forth, say beforehand, promise, < *pro*, before, + *mittere*, send.] A declaration made, as to another person, with respect to the future, giving assurance that one will do or not do, or will give, something, or that something shall or shall not be done; an express assurance on which expectation is to be based; an engagement; assurance or promising (as, "words of *promise*": Tennyson's "Day-Dream," 123); also, fig., something that has the effect of an express assurance, or gives ground for expectation, of what is to come (as, "Tropical birds flew out . . . glittering in the sun, the gorgeous *promises* of the new country": G. W. Curtis's "Prue and I," ii.); indication of what may be expected (as, the clouds give *promise* of rain; a case affording *promise* of startling disclosures; "He hath borne himself beyond the *promise* of his age," Shakspere's "Much Ado about Nothing," i. 1. 14); often, indication of future excellence (as, a writer or a book that shows *promise*); apparent capacity for future achievement or distinction (as, "a young man of striking talent and *promise*": Froude's "Cæsar," iv.); also, that which is promised (as, "He to his own a Comforter will send, The *promise* of the Father": Milton's "Paradise Lost," xii. 487).—**Land of Promise.** See under *land, n.* —**prom′ise,** *v.*; -ised, -ising. **I.** *tr.* To make a promise of (as, to *promise* all that is asked; to *promise* help); engage or undertake by promise (with an infinitive or a clause: as, to *promise* to help, or not to interfere; to *promise* that no one

---

(variable) ḍ as d or j, ṣ as s or sh, ṭ as t or ch, ẓ as z or zh; *o*, F. cloche; ü, F. menu; ċh, Sc. loch; ṅ, F. bonbon; ′, primary accent; ″, secondary accent; †, obsolete; <, from; +, and; =, equals. See also lists at beginning of book.

shall interfere); often, to make a promise of (something) to (a person, etc., this latter being properly the indirect object, but in passive constructions sometimes appearing as the subject: as, "I was *promised* them [ribbons] against the feast," Shakspere's "Winter's Tale," iv. 4. 237); also, to engage to give in marriage, or betroth; also, fig., to give indication of, as something to be expected (as, the clouds *promise* rain; "The occasion seemed to *promise* the greatest facetiousness," Bret Harte's "Luck of Roaring Camp"); afford ground for expecting; also, to assure (used in emphatic declarations: colloq.: as, "I *promise* you, I went the more heartily about the preparations," Stevenson's "Master of Ballantrae," viii.). **II.** *intr.* To make a promise; also, fig., to afford ground for expectation (often with *well* or *fair*: as, "He thought that voyage *promised* very fair, and that there was a great prospect of advantage," Defoe's "Robinson Crusoe," ii. 13).—**prom′ised,** *p. a.* Of which promise has been made.—**Promised Land.** Same as *Land of Promise,* under *land, n.*—**prom-is-ee′** (-i-sē′), *n.* One to whom a promise is made: as, "Promises . . . where God was considered as the *promisee* . . . were strictly to be fulfilled" (Hallam's "Literature of Europe," iii. 4. § 8).—**prom′is-er,** (in *law*) **prom′is-or,** *n.* One who makes a promise.—**prom′is-ing,** *p. a.* Giving promise, esp. of good; likely to turn out well; hopeful: as, a *promising* prospect; a *promising* boy.—**prom′is-ing-ly,** *adv.*

prom-is-so-ry (prom′i-sō-ri), *a.* [ML. *promissorius,* < L. *promittere* (pp. *promissus*): see *promise.*] Containing or implying a promise; of the nature of a promise.—**promissory note,** a written promise to pay a specified sum of money to a person designated or to his order, or to the bearer, at a fixed time or on demand.

prom-on-to-ry (prom′on-tō-ri), *n.*; pl. *-ries* (-riz). [ML. *promontorium,* for L. *promunturium,* perhaps < *prominere,* jut out: see *prominent.*] A high point of land or rock projecting into the sea or other water beyond the line of coast (as, "that bold green *promontory,* known to seamen as Java Head": H. Melville's "Moby-Dick," lxxxvii.); a headland; in *anat.,* a prominent or protuberant part.

pro-mor-phol-o-gy (prō-môr-fol′ō-ji), *n.* [G. *promorphologie:* see *pro-* and *morphology.*] In *biol.,* that branch of morphology which deals with organic forms from the point of view of geometry or mathematical law.—**pro-mor-pho-log-i-cal** (prō-môr-fō-loj′i-kal), *a.*—**pro-mor-phol′o-gist,** *n.*

pro-mote (prō-mōt′), *v. t.; -moted, -moting.* [L. *promotus,* pp. of *promovere,* move forward, advance, < *pro,* before, + *movere,* E. *move.*] To advance in rank, dignity, etc.; raise to a higher post or position (as, "There were two young Gauls with Cæsar whom he had *promoted* to important positions," Froude's "Cæsar," xxii.; "the girl who had been suddenly *promoted* to the leading part," L. Merrick's "Conrad in Quest of His Youth," xiv.); also, to further the growth, development, progress, etc., of (as, "They thought nothing blameworthy which *promoted* its [their country's] glory, its power, or its welfare": Bancroft's "Hist. of the U. S.," Amer. Revolution, ii. 1); advance; further; encourage; specif., to aid in organizing (financial undertakings: as, "Sir Paul was *promoting* a strictly private syndicate," Arnold Bennett's "Mr. Prohack," ix.).—**pro-mot′er** (-mō′tėr), *n.* One who or that which promotes; specif., one who aids in organizing financial undertakings; one who makes it his business to assist in the organization and capitalization of corporations.—**pro-mo′tion** (-mō′shon), *n.* [L. *promotio(n-).*] The act of promoting, or the state of being promoted; advancement in rank or position; furtherance or encouragement.—**pro-mo′tive,** *a.* Tending to promote.

prompt (prompt), *a.* [OF. F. *prompt,* < L. *promptus,* visible, at hand, ready, prompt, pp. of *promere,* take out, bring to light, < *pro,* before, + *emere,* take.] Ready in action (as, "*prompt* at Duty's call": Whittier's "Snow-Bound"); quick to act as occasion demands; ready and willing; also, done, performed, delivered, etc., at once or without delay (as, a *prompt* reply).—**prompt,** *v. t.* To move or incite to action (as, "His heart had *prompted* him . . . to take the little outcast home": Hawthorne's "Twice-Told Tales," The Gentle Boy); also, to assist (a person speaking) by suggesting something to be said; esp., to assist (an actor or reciter) by supplying the words next in order

(cf. *prompter*); also, to suggest or induce (action, etc.); inspire or occasion (as, "The invitation . . . was mainly *prompted* by Mr. Travers' desire to have somebody to talk to": J. Conrad's "Rescue," iii. 1).—**prompt,** *n.* An act of prompting; something that prompts; in *com.,* a limit of time given for payment for merchandise purchased, the limit being stated on a note of reminder called a *prompt-note.*—**prompt′er,** *n.* One who or that which prompts; specif., a person stationed out of view of the audience of a theater to prompt the actors.—**promp-ti-tude** (promp′ti-tūd), **prompt′ness,** *n.*—**prompt′ly,** *adv.*—**promp′ture** (-tūr), *n.* Prompting; suggestion; instigation: as, "Though he hath fall'n by *prompture* of the blood, Yet hath he in him . . . a mind of honour" (Shakspere's "Measure for Measure," ii. 4. 178). [Archaic.]

pro-mul-gate (prō-mul′gāt or prō′mul-), *v. t.; -gated, -gating.* [L. *promulgatus,* pp. of *promulgare,* make publicly known, publish; origin uncertain.] To make known by open declaration; publish; proclaim formally (a law or decree); set forth or teach publicly (a creed, doctrine, etc.).—**pro-mul-ga-tion** (prō-mul-gā′shon), *n.* [L. *promulgatio(n-).*] The act of promulgating, or the fact of being promulgated; open declaration; publication; specif., the official publication of a new law, decree, etc.—**pro′mul-ga-tor,** *n.*

pro-mulge (prō-mulj′), *v. t.; -mulged, -mulging.* [L. *promulgare:* see *promulgate.*] To promulgate. [Archaic.]

pro-na-os (prō-nā′os), *n.* [L., < Gr. πρόναος, < πρό, before, + ναός, temple.] In *arch.,* the porch or vestibule in front of the naos or cella of a temple.

Temple with Pronaos, adjoining the baths at Assos, in the Troad (in northwestern Asia Minor). (Restoration.)

pro-nate (prō′nāt), *v. t.; -nated, -nating.* [LL. *pronatus,* pp. of *pronare,* < L. *pronus,* E. *prone.*] To render prone; rotate or place (the hand or fore limb) so that the palmar surface is downward when the limb is stretched forward horizontally. Cf. *supinate.*—**pro-na-tion** (prō-nā′shon), *n.*—**pro-na′tor,** *n.*

prone (prōn), *a.* [L. *pronus,* turned or leaning forward, inclined downward, disposed, prone, akin to *pro* and *præ,* before: see *pre-.*] Bending forward and downward; having the front or ventral part downward; lying face downward or on the belly; also, having the palm downward, as the hand; also, lying flat, or prostrate (as, "Ancient tow'rs . . . Fall *prone*": Cowper's "Task," ii. 125); also, having a downward direction or slope (as, "The sun . . . was hasting now with *prone* career To the ocean isles," Milton's "Paradise Lost," iv. 353; "down the *prone* vale," Shelley's "Witch of Atlas," xli.); fig., abject; base; also, having a natural inclination or tendency to something, disposed, or liable (as, "We are all *prone* to evil," Galt's "Ayrshire Legatees," vii.; "He knew how *prone* he was to be led," Trollope's "Warden," xviii.).—**prone′ly,** *adv.*—**prone′ness,** *n.*

pro-neph-ros (prō-nef′ros), *n.* [NL., < Gr. πρό, before, + νεφρός, kidney.] In *embryol.,* the most anterior part of the primitive renal organ or kidney of a vertebrate embryo. Cf. *mesonephros.*—**pro-neph′ric,** *a.*

prong (prông), *n.* [Also formerly *prang;* origin obscure.] A fork or forked instrument (now chiefly prov. Eng.); also, one of the pointed divisions or tines of a fork; also, any pointed projecting part, as of an antler.—**prong,** *v. t.* To pierce or stab with a prong; also, to supply with prongs.—**pronged,** *a.* Having prongs: as, two-*pronged.*—**prong′-**

horn, *n.* A fleet antelope-like ruminant, *Antilocapra americana*, of the plains of western North America.

pro-nom-i-nal (prō-nom'i-nal), *a.* [LL. *pronominalis*, < L. *pronomen*: see *pronoun*.] Of, pertaining to, or of the nature of a pronoun.—**pronom'i-nal-ly**, *adv.*

pro-non-cé (pro-nôn-sā), *a.* [F.] Pronounced.

pro-noun (prō'noun), *n.* [Altered (after *noun*) < F. *pronom*, < L. *pronomen*, pronoun, < *pro*, for, + *nomen*, name, E. *noun*.]

Pronghorn.

In *gram.*, a word used in place of a noun (or its equivalent) in order to designate, without naming, a person or thing: as, personal *pronouns* (I, you, he, we, they, etc.); possessive *pronouns* (my, your, his, our, their, etc.); interrogative *pronouns* (who, which, what, etc.); relative *pronouns* (who, that, which, what, etc.).

pro-nounce (prō-nouns'), *v.*; -nounced, -nouncing. [OF. *prononcier* (F. *prononcer*), < L. *pronuntiare*, proclaim, announce, recite, utter, < *pro*, before, + *nuntiare*, announce, < *nuntius*, messenger.] **I.** *tr.* To utter or deliver formally or solemnly; announce authoritatively or officially; also, to declare (a person or thing) to be as specified (as, "The gentlemen *pronounced* him to be a fine figure of a man," Jane Austen's "Pride and Prejudice," iii.; "George Laird passed the crisis . . . and . . . was *pronounced* out of danger," Galsworthy's "Saint's Progress," i. 4); also, to enunciate or articulate (words, etc.: as, "Language of man *pronounced* By tongue of brute," Milton's "Paradise Lost," ix. 553; "My surname no native can *pronounce*," W. H. Hudson's "Purple Land," xxi.); utter or sound in a particular manner in speaking (as, to *pronounce* a word as French). **II.** *intr.* To make a statement or assertion, esp. an authoritative statement; give an opinion or decision (as, "No one can *pronounce* on what this life has been to him until he has passed entirely through it": Mrs. Stowe's "Oldtown Folks," xli.); also, to pronounce words, etc. (as, "In speaking, they *pronounce* through the nose and throat": Swift's "Gulliver's Travels," iv. 3).—**pro-nounce'a-ble**, *a.* That may be pronounced.—**pro-nounced'**, *p. a.* Clearly expressed or indicated; strongly marked or defined; decided: as, "a moderate High Churchman of no very *pronounced* views" (S. Butler's "Way of All Flesh," li.).—**pro-noun'ced-ly** (-noun'sed-li), *adv.*—**pro-nounce'ment**, *n.* The act of pronouncing; a formal or authoritative statement; an opinion or decision.—**pro-noun'cer** (-sėr), *n.*

pron-to (pron'tō), *adv.* [Sp., adj. and adv., < L. *promptus*, E. *prompt*.] Promptly; quickly.

pro-nun-ci-a-men-to (prō-nun"si-a-men'tō), *n.*; pl. *-tos* (-tōz). [Sp. *pronunciamiento*, 'pronouncement.'] A formal announcement; a proclamation; a manifesto. Also (Sp.)

pro-nun-cia-mien-to (prō-nön"thyä-myen'tō).

pro-nun-ci-a-tion (prō-nun-si-ā'shon), *n.* [L. *pronuntiatio(n-)*.] The act or manner of pronouncing words, etc.

pro-œ-mi-on, pro-œ-mi-um (prō-ē'mi-on, -um), *n.*; pl. *-mia* (-mi-ä). Same as *proem*.

proof (prööf). [OF. *prueve* (F. *preuve*), < LL. *proba*, proof, < L. *probare*, E. *prove*.] **I.** *n.* The act or an act of testing or making trial of anything (as, to make *proof* of a person's trustworthiness; to put a thing to the *proof*); test; a trial; specif., an arithmetical operation serving to check the correctness of a calculation; also, the state of having been tested and approved; proved strength, as of armor; specif., the standard strength, as of alcoholic liquors (see *proof-spirit*); strength with reference to this standard; also, the establish-

ment of the truth of anything (as, to offer evidence in *proof* of an assertion); demonstration; the effect of evidence in convincing the mind; also, evidence sufficient to establish a thing as true, or to produce belief in its truth; anything serving as such evidence; in *printing*, a trial impression, as of composed type, taken so that errors may be corrected and alterations made; in *engraving*, etc., an impression taken from a plate or the like to show its state during the progress of execution; also, one of a number of early and superior impressions taken before the printing of the ordinary issue; in *photog.*, a trial print from a negative. **II.** *a.* Of tested or proved strength or quality (as, *proof* armor: much used in composition, as in *air-proof*, *bomb-proof*, etc., that is, of tested power of resistance to air, bombs, etc.); impenetrable, impervious, or invulnerable (lit. or fig.: as, *proof* against temptation); also, of standard strength, as an alcoholic liquor; also, used for testing or proving; serving as proof.—**proof**, *v. t.* To render proof against something; render impervious; specif., to render (a fabric, etc.) impervious to water; waterproof.—**proof'less**, *a.* Lacking proof.—**proof'=read**, *v. t.* or *i.* To read (printers' proofs, etc.) in order to detect and mark errors to be corrected.—**proof'=read"er**, *n.* One whose business it is to read printers' proofs for correction.—**proof'=read"ing**, *n.*—**proof'=sheet**, *n.* A printers' proof.—**proof'=spir'it**, *n.* An alcoholic liquor, or mixture of alcohol and water, containing a standard amount of alcohol: in the U. S., one with a specific gravity of .93353 (containing one half of its volume of alcohol of a specific gravity of .7939 at 60° Fahrenheit), and in Great Britain, one with a specific gravity of .91984.

prop (prop), *n.* [ME. *proppe* = MD. *proppe*, prop, support.] A stick, rod, pole, beam, or other rigid support for sustaining an incumbent weight, esp. when not forming a part of the object supported (as, a *prop* for vines; a *prop* for an old wall); that on or against which something rests for support; fig., a person or thing serving as a support or stay (as, "Stifford had become a great and wonderful man, and Edwin's constant fear was that he might lose this indispensable *prop* to his business," Arnold Bennett's "Clayhanger," iv. 3; "They lost the independence of their state, the greatest *prop* of national spirit," Smollett's "Humphry Clinker," Sept. 20).—**prop**, *v. t.*; propped, propping. To support, or prevent from falling, with or as with a prop (as, to *prop* a roof or a wall; "They found the giant *propped* up in bed with pillows," Kingsley's "Yeast," iv.); rest (a thing) against something which serves as a support (as, "I picked him up and *propped* his head against the dead tiger": F. M. Crawford's "Mr. Isaacs," x.); also, to serve as a prop for (as, "She sat silent, her head still *propped* by the arm that rested on the back of the sofa": Mrs. Wharton's "Age of Innocence," xii.); also, fig., to support or sustain (as, to *prop* a failing cause).

pro-pæ-deu-tic (prō-pē-dū'tik). [Gr. προπαιδεύειν, teach beforehand, < πρό, before, + παιδεύειν, bring up, teach, < παῖς (παιδ-), child.] **I.** *a.* Of, pertaining to, or of the nature of preliminary instruction; introductory to some art or science. **II.** *n.* A propædeutic subject or study.—**pro-pæ-deu'ti-cal**, *a.*—**pro-pæ-deu'tics**, *n.* The preliminary body of knowledge and rules necessary for the study of some art or science.

prop-a-ga-ble (prop'a-ga-bl), *a.* Capable of being propagated.—**prop''a-ga-bil'i-ty** (-bil'i-ti), *n.*

prop-a-gan-da (prop-a-gan'dä), *n.* [Short for NL. *congregatio de propaganda fide*, 'congregation for propagating the faith': *propaganda*, abl. fem. gerundive of L. *propagare*: see *propagate*.] [*cap.*] A committee of cardinals, established in 1622 by Pope Gregory XV., having supervision of the foreign missions of the Roman Catholic Church; [*l. c.*] any organization or concerted movement for propagating particular doctrines or principles; also, the doctrines or principles propagated.—**prop-a-gan'dism**, *n.* The practice or spirit of a propaganda; zealous propagation of particular doctrines or principles.—**prop-a-gan'dist**, *n.* A member or agent of a propaganda; one devoted to the propagation of particular doctrines or principles: as, "The monks . . . were the chief *propagandists* of Christianity in Palestine" (Kinglake's "Eothen," x.).—**prop''a-gan-dis'tic**, *a.*—**prop-a-gan'dize**, *v.*; -dized, -dizing. **I.** *tr.* To propagate or spread (principles, etc.) by a propaganda. **II.** *intr.* To carry on a propaganda.

prop-a-gate (prop′a-gāt), *v.*; *-gated, -gating.* [L. *propagatus*, pp. of *propagare*, propagate (orig. plants by layers or slips), < *pro*, before, + *pag-*, stem of *pangere*, make fast: see *pact*.] **I.** *tr.* To cause (plants, animals, etc.) to multiply by any process of natural reproduction from the parent stock; reproduce (itself, its kind, etc.), as a plant or an animal does; produce or generate (new plants, or offspring); transmit (traits, etc.) in reproduction, or through offspring; also, fig., to cause to increase in number or amount (as, to *propagate* causes of discontent; to *propagate* vice); cause to extend to a greater distance, or transmit through space or a medium (as, to *propagate* light or sound; to *propagate* motion); often, to spread (a report, doctrine, practice, etc.) from person to person or from place to place (as, "His adversary had *propagated* a rumor injurious to his character," C. B. Brown's "Wieland," xxvii.; an organization for *propagating* communistic principles); disseminate; diffuse. **II.** *intr.* To multiply by any process of natural reproduction, as plants or animals; breed; fig., to increase; spread.—**prop-a-ga′tion** (-gā′shon), *n.* [L. *propagatio(n-).*] The act of propagating, or the fact of being propagated; multiplication, as of plants or animals, by natural reproduction; reproduction; generation; fig., increase; extension or transmission; spreading or dissemination.—**prop′a-ga-tive** (-gā-tiv), *a.* Serving or tending to propagate.—**prop′a-ga-tor** (-gā-tor), *n.*

pro-pane (prō′pān), *n.* [From *propyl.*] In *chem.*, a gaseous hydrocarbon, C_3H_8, of the methane series, found in petroleum.

pro-par-ox-y-tone (prō-par-ok′si-tōn). [Gr. προπαροξύτονος, < πρό, before, + παροξύτονος, E. *paroxytone.*] In *gram.*: **I.** *a.* Having an acute accent on the antepenult. **II.** *n.* A proparoxytone word.

pro-pel (prō-pel′), *v. t.*; *-pelled, -pelling.* [L. *propellere* (pp. *propulsus*), < *pro*, before, + *pellere*, drive.] To drive, or cause to move, forward or onward (as, a boat *propelled* by oars, by wind and sails, or by a motor); fig., to impel or urge onward.—**pro-pel′la-ble**, *a.* Capable of being propelled.—**pro-pel′lant**, *n.* A propelling agent; specif., an explosive used in a gun or the like to propel a projectile, as distinguished from the more violent explosives used in blasting, in exploding shells, etc.—**pro-pel′lent.** [L. *propellens* (-ent-), ppr.] **I.** *a.* Propelling; driving forward. **II.** *n.* A propelling agent.—**pro-pel′ler**, *n.* One who or that which propels; esp., a device consisting of a revolving hub with radiating blades operating on the principle of a screw, for propelling a steamship, airship, etc. ('screw-propeller'); also, a ship with such a device.

pro-pend (prō-pend′), *v. i.* [L. *propendere* (pp. *propensus*), hang forward, be inclined, < *pro*, before, + *pendere*, hang.] To hang or lean forward or downward†; fig., to incline or tend (obs. or archaic: as, "My thinking all *propended* to the ancient world of herdsmen and warriors," Kinglake's "Eothen," xii.].

pro-pense (prō-pens′), *a.* [L. *propensus*, pp. of *propendere*: see *propend*.] Inclined, disposed, or prone, as to something or to do something (now rare: as, "Feeble hearts, *propense* enough before To waver," Milton's "Samson Agonistes," 455); also, favorable or partial, as to a person or thing†.—**pro-pense′ly**, *adv.*—**pro-pense′ness**, *n.*

pro-pen-sion (prō-pen′shon), *n.* [L. *propensio(n-)*, < *propendere*: see *propend*.] Inclination or tendency (as, "There seemed to be something fatal in that *propension* of nature tending directly to the life of misery which was to befall me": Defoe's "Robinson Crusoe," i. 1); also, favorable inclination. [Now rare.]

pro-pen-si-ty (prō-pen′si-ti), *n.*; pl. *-ties* (-tiz). [From *propense*.] Natural or habitual inclination or tendency (as, to indulge one's *propensity* to, or for, exaggeration; "the natural *propensity* to find fault," Cooper's "Two Admirals," xi.; selfish *propensities*); proclivity; also, favorable disposition†, or partiality† (as, "an idiot boy . . . who . . . showed a strong *propensity* to bees": G. White's "Nat. Hist. of Selborne," ii. 27).

pro-pe-nyl (prō′pe-nil), *n.* [From *propyl.*] In *chem.*, any of certain hydrocarbon radicals of the formula C_3H_5, esp. the trivalent radical $CH_2.CH.CH_2$.

prop-er (prop′ėr). [OF. F. *propre*, < L. *proprius*, one's own.] **I.** *a.* Belonging to one's self or itself, or own (now archaic in general use: as, "to shroud me from my *proper* scorn," Tennyson's "In Memoriam," xxvi.); also, belonging or pertaining exclusively or distinctively to a person or thing, or peculiar (as, "I can discover within me no power of perception which is not glutted with its *proper* pleasure," Johnson's "Rasselas," ii.; qualities *proper* to a substance); also, strictly belonging or applicable (as, to use a word in its *proper* sense; the *proper* pronunciation of a name); strict; accurate; also, strictly so called, or in the strict sense of the word (now usually following the noun: as, shell-fish do not belong to the fishes *proper*); normal or regular (as, a *proper* fraction, one in which the numerator is less than the denominator); complete or thorough (now prov. or colloq.: as, a *proper* thrashing); excellent, capital, or fine (as, "a *proper* jest, and never heard before," Shakspere's "2 Henry VI.," i. 1. 132: often ironical, and now archaic or prov.); good-looking or handsome (archaic or prov.: as, "By St. Anne! but he is a *proper* youth," Scott's "Quentin Durward," ii.); also, adapted or appropriate to the purpose or circumstances (as, the *proper* tool for an operation; the *proper* time to plant a crop); fit; suitable; fitting; right; also, in conformity to established standards of behavior or manners, or seemly, decorous, or decent (as, "It was not thought *proper* then for a young woman to go on pillion behind a young man": Weir Mitchell's "Hugh Wynne," xi.); of persons, conforming to such standards; correct or decorous in behavior (as, "He would be very old and terribly good and *proper*, by now!" Galsworthy's "Saint's Progress," i. 8); also, of good character, honest, or respectable (now rare); in *gram.*, of a name or noun, designating a particular person or thing, and written with an initial capital letter, as *John, Chicago, Monday* (cf. *common, a.*); having the force or function of a proper name (as, a *proper* adjective); in *her.*, of an object used as a bearing, represented in its natural color or colors (as, an eagle *proper*). **II.** *adv.* Properly; completely; thoroughly: as, "Down the stair they came, habited, booted, hatted, and gloved *proper*" (M. Hewlett's "Open Country," vii.); "Had 'em that time — had 'em *proper!*" (Conan Doyle's "Tragedy of the Korosko," ix.). [Prov. or colloq.]

pro-per-i-spom-e-non (prō″per-i-spom′e-non), *n.*; pl. *-na* (-nä). [Gr. προπερισπώμενον, neut. ppr. pass. of προπερισπᾶν, < πρό, before, + περισπᾶν, mark with a circumflex: see *perispomenon*.] In *Gr. gram.*, a word having a circumflex accent on the next to the last syllable.

prop-er-ly (prop′ėr-li), *adv.* In a proper manner; particularly or distinctively; strictly or accurately; appropriately; suitably, or fittingly; decorously, or with propriety; completely, thoroughly, or exceedingly (now prov. or colloq.); excellently or admirably (archaic or prov.).—**prop′er-ness**, *n.*

prop-er-tied (prop′ėr-tid), *a.* Owning property.

prop-er-ty (prop′ėr-ti), *n.*; pl. *-ties* (-tiz). [OF. *proprete*, *propriete* (F. *propriété*), < L. *proprietas*, < *proprius*, one's own, E. *proper*: cf. *propriety*.] The condition or fact of belonging to a particular owner (obs. or rare); hence, ownership, or right of possession, enjoyment, or disposal of anything, esp. of something tangible (as, to have *property* in land; "deer . . . running wild, which they scruple not to kill as venison, without being at much pains to ascertain the *property*," Smollett's "Humphry Clinker," Sept. 3); also, that which one owns; the possession or possessions of a particular owner; goods, lands, etc., owned (as, a man of *property*; landed *property*); often, a piece of land or real estate (as, a *property* on Main street); fig., something at the disposal of a person, a group of persons, or the community or public (as, advantages that are the *property* of every citizen; the secret became common *property*; "This episode was town *property*," Arnold Bennett's "Old Wives' Tale," i. 3); also, any portable object, as a chair, rug, etc., used in producing a play or the like (chiefly in *pl.*: as, "I will draw a bill of *properties*, such as our play needs," Shakspere's "Midsummer Night's Dream," i. 2. 108: also fig.); also, an instrument†, tool†, or means to an end† (as, "Do not talk of him, But as a *property*": Shakspere's "Julius Cæsar," iv. 1. 40); also, an essential or distinctive attribute

---

or quality of a thing or (formerly) a person; in general, any quality or characteristic; also, propriety†, suitability†, or fitness†.—**prop'er-ty**, *v. t.*; *-tied, -tying*. To make one's own property, or appropriate (rare); also, to make a property or tool of†; also, to invest with a property or quality†.—**prop'er-ty=man** (-man), *n.*; pl. *-men*. A man employed in a theater to look after the stage properties.

proph-e-cy (prof'e-si), *n.*; pl. *-cies* (-siz). [OF. *prophecie* (F. *prophétie*), < LL. *prophetia*, < Gr. προφητεία, prophecy, < προφητεύειν, prophesy, < προφήτης, E. *prophet*.] The action, function, or faculty of a prophet (as, "the gift of *prophecy*," 1 Cor. xiii. 2; "If aught of *prophecy* be mine, Thou wilt not live in vain," Tennyson's "To ——," Clear-headed friend, i.); divinely inspired utterance or revelation; foretelling or prediction (orig. by divine inspiration) of what is to come; also, that which is declared by a prophet or in prophesying (as, "*Prophecy* is nothing but the history of events before they come to pass," J. Butler's "Analogy of Religion," ii. 7; "Happiness . . . is always like *prophecy*, it is only fulfilled in the future," Mallock's "New Republic," i. 4); a divinely inspired prophetic utterance, discourse, or writing (as, "In them is fulfilled the *prophecy* of Esaias," Mat. xiii. 14; "Blessed is he that readeth . . . the words of this *prophecy*," Rev. i. 3); in general, a prediction (as, "the dreamer Merlin and his *prophecies*": Shakspere's "1 Henry IV.," iii. 1. 150); fig., a foreshadowing indication of something to come (as, "A laughing face . . . where scarce appeared The uncertain *prophecy* of beard": Whittier's "Snow-Bound"); also, interpretation or exposition of the Scriptures†.

proph-e-sy (prof'e-sī), *v.*; *-sied, -sying*. [OF. *prophecier*, < *prophecie*, E. *prophecy*.] **I.** *intr*. To utter prophecy; speak as a prophet, in the name of a deity or by divine inspiration (as, "The Lord said unto me, Go, *prophesy* unto my people Israel": Amos, vii. 15); make inspired declarations of what is to come; hence, in general, to make predictions; also, to interpret or expound the Scriptures†. **II.** *tr*. To utter in prophecy or as a prophet (as, "The Lord perform thy words which thou hast *prophesied*," Jer. xxviii. 6; "The prophets *prophesy* lies in my name," Jer. xiv. 14); declare or foretell by or as by divine inspiration (as, Isaiah *prophesied* the birth of Immanuel); in general, to foretell or predict (as, to *prophesy* a storm; "I *prophesied* . . . that this proposal would be made," Marryat's "King's Own," xxxvi.); fig., to indicate beforehand (as, "Methought thy very gait did *prophesy* A royal nobleness": Shakspere's "King Lear," v. 3. 175).—**proph'e-si-er** (-sī-ėr), *n.*

proph-et (prof'et), *n.* [OF. *prophete* (F. *prophète*), < L. *propheta*, < Gr. προφήτης, spokesman, interpreter, prophet, < προφάναι, say before, < πρό, before, + φάναι, say.] One who speaks for God or a deity, or by divine inspiration (in popular use implying esp. the foretelling of future events); one of a class of persons in the early church, next in order after the apostles, recognized as inspired to utter special revelations and predictions (see 1 Cor. xii. 28); [*cap.*] with *the*, Mohammed, the founder of Islam (see *Koran*); [*l. c.*] in general, one regarded as, or claiming to be, an inspired teacher or leader; a spokesman or proclaimer of some doctrine, cause, or the like (as, "Nothing could have been further from Roosevelt's intentions than to set up as his *prophet* of some great Reformation": Charnwood's "Theodore Roosevelt," v.); also, one who foretells or predicts what is to come (as, a weather-*prophet*; "Jesters do oft prove *prophets*," Shakspere's "King Lear," v. 3. 71); fig., something that indicates or foreshadows what is to come (as, "Like the mystic fire on a mast-head, *Prophet* of storm": Tennyson's "Princess," iv. 256); also, pl. [*cap.* or *l. c.*], the books which form the second of the three Jewish divisions of the Old Testament, comprising (1) Joshua, Judges, 1 and 2 Samuel, and 1 and 2 Kings, (2) Isaiah, Jeremiah, and Ezekiel ('Major Prophets'), and (3) Hosea, Joel, Amos, Obadiah, Jonah, Micah, Nahum, Habakkuk, Zephaniah, Haggai, Zechariah, and Malachi ('Minor Prophets'), the first group (1) being called 'Former Prophets,' and the second and third groups together 'Latter Prophets' (cf. *law* and *Hagiographa*).—**proph'et-ess**, *n.* A female prophet.—**proph'et-hood** (-hụd), *n.* The character or office of a prophet.

pro-phet-ic (prọ-fet'ik), *a.* [F. *prophétique*, < LL. *pro-*

pheticus, < Gr. προφητικός.] Of or pertaining to a prophet (as, the *prophetic* function; *prophetic* inspiration or powers); having the function or powers of a prophet, as a person; of the nature of or containing prophecy (as, *prophetic* utterances or declarations; *prophetic* writings); in general, giving warning or indication of what is to come (sometimes with *of*: as, "The presage with which I was visited was *prophetic*," Godwin's "Caleb Williams," xli.; "It seem'd to those within the wall A cry *prophetic* of their fall," Byron's "Siege of Corinth," xi.); predictive; presageful; ominous. Also **prophet'i-cal.—pro-phet'i-cal-ly**, *adv.*

proph-et-ship (prof'et-ship), *n.* Prophethood.

proph-y-lac-tic (prof-i-lak'tik or prō-fi-). [Gr. προφυλακτικός, < προφυλάσσειν, take precautions against, < πρό, before, + φυλάσσειν, guard.] **I.** *a.* Defending or protecting from disease, as a drug; preventive; preservative; protective. **II.** *n.* A prophylactic medicine or measure; a precaution (as, "To keep the mind engrossed was the great *prophylactic* against fear": Buchan's "Hist. of the Great War," liii.).—**proph-y-lac'ti-cal-ly**, *adv.*

proph-y-lax-is (prof-i-lak'sis or prō-fi-), *n.* [NL., < Gr. προφυλάσσειν: see *prophylactic*.] The preventing of disease; prophylactic treatment.

pro-pine (prọ-pīn'), *v. t.*; *-pined, -pining*. [L. *propinare*, < Gr. προπίνειν, drink before or to, give to drink, < πρό, before, + πίνειν, drink.] To offer or present (something) to one to drink; wish (health, etc.) to one in drinking; also, to offer for acceptance; present as a gift; also, to present (a person, etc.) with something. [Obs. or Sc.]—**pro-pine'**, *n.* A present or gift. [Obs. or Sc.]

pro-pin-qui-ty (prọ-ping'kwi-ti), *n.* [OF. *propinquite*, < L. *propinquitas*, < *propinquus*, near, < *prope*, adv., near.] Nearness in place, or proximity; esp., personal nearness, as in company or association (as, a case of love arising from *propinquity*); fig., nearness or closeness of relation; nearness of blood or kinship (as, "Here I disclaim all my paternal care, *Propinquity* and property of blood": Shakspere's "King Lear," i. 1. 116); affinity of nature, or similarity; also, nearness in time.

pro-pi-ol-ic (prō-pi-ol'ik), *a.* [From *propionic*.] In *chem.*, noting or pertaining to a liquid organic acid, $CH\!:\!C.CO_2H$, with an odor resembling that of acetic acid.

pro-pi-on-ic (prō-pi-on'ik), *a.* [Gr. πρῶ(τος), first, + πίων, fat.] In *chem.*, noting or pertaining to a liquid organic acid, $CH_3.CH_2.CO_2H$, with a pungent odor, found in perspiration, etc.—**pro-pi-o-nyl** (prō'pi-ọ-nil), *n.* [See *-yl*.] In *chem.*, a univalent radical, $CH_3.CH_2.CO$, contained in propionic acid, etc.

pro-pi-ti-ate (prọ-pish'i-āt), *v. t.*; *-ated, -ating*. [L. *propitiatus*, pp. of *propitiare*, < *propitius*, E. *propitious*.] To render favorably inclined; appease; conciliate: as, "Let fierce Achilles . . . The god *propitiate*, and the pest assuage" (Pope's tr. Homer's "Iliad," i.).—**pro-pi'ti-at-ing-ly** (-ā-ting-li), *adv.*—**pro-pi-ti-a'tion** (-ā'shọn), *n.* [LL. *propitiatio(n-)*.] The act of propitiating; conciliation; also, that which propitiates.—**pro-pi'ti-a-tor**, *n.*—**pro-pi'ti-a-to-ry** (-ạ-tọ-ri). [LL. *propitiatorius*, adj. (as n., *propitiatorium*).] **I.** *a.* Serving or intended to propitiate; making propitiation; conciliatory: as, "Christ offered himself a *propitiatory* sacrifice" (J. Butler's "Analogy of Religion," ii. 5); "He was anxious to be *propitiatory*, for he had a plan to further" (Arnold Bennett's "The Old Adam," viii.). **II.** *n.* In *Jewish antiq.*, the mercy-seat.

pro-pi-tious (prọ-pish'us), *a.* [OF. *propicius*, < L. *propitius*, favorable, propitious.] Favorably inclined (as, "My Maker, be *propitious* while I speak": Milton's "Paradise Lost," viii. 380); disposed to be gracious; ready to bestow favors or to forgive; also, indicative of favor, or that is of favorable import (as, to receive a *propitious* reception; *propitious* omens); also, presenting favorable conditions, or favorable or advantageous (as, "Although it was already late in the autumn, the weather was *propitious*": Motley's "Dutch Republic," iii. 8).—**pro-pi'tious-ly**, *adv.*—**pro-pi'tious-ness**, *n.*

prop-o-lis (prop'ọ-lis), *n.* [L., < Gr. πρόπολις, < πρό, before, + πόλις, city.] A reddish resinous substance collected by bees from the buds of trees, used to stop up crevices in the hives, strengthen the cells, etc.

---

pro-pone (prō-pōn′), *v. t.*; -poned, -poning. [L. *proponere* (pp. *propositus*), place before, set forth, propose, < *pro*, before, + *ponere*, place, put: cf. *propound*.] To put forward for consideration, adoption, etc.; propose; propound. [Now only Sc.]—**pro-po′nent** (-pō′nent), *n.* One who puts forward a proposition or makes a proposal; a proposer.

pro-por-tion (prō-pôr′shon), *n.* [OF. F. *proportion*, < L. *proportio(n-)*, < *pro*, for, according to, + *portio(n-)*, share, E. *portion*.] Comparative relation between things or magnitudes as to size, quantity, number, etc. (as, a house tall in *proportion* to its width; the *proportion* of births to deaths in a community during a given period); ratio; in general, relation, comparison, or analogy (as, "Oaths . . . hold with deeds *proportion*, so As shadows to a substance do": Butler's "Hudibras," ii. 2); also, proper relation between things or parts (as, "The commerce of your colonies is out of all *proportion* beyond the numbers of the people," Burke's "Conciliation with the Colonies"; a man whose reputation never bore any *proportion* to his merits); symmetry; harmony; agreement; also, relative size or extent; now, *pl.*, dimensions (as, a mass of rock of gigantic *proportions*); also, *sing.*, form† or shape†; also, a portion or part in its relation to the whole (as, a large or a small *proportion* of a total amount or number); sometimes, in general, a portion or part; in *math.*, the equality of ratios; a relation of four quantities such that the first divided by the second is equal to the third divided by the fourth; also, the method of finding the fourth quantity of such a series when three quantities are known; the rule of three.—**pro-por′tion**, *v. t.* [OF. F. *proportionner*, < ML. *proportionare*, < L. *proportio(n-)*.] To adjust in proper proportion or relation, as to size, quantity, number, etc. (as, to *proportion* the thickness of a thing to its length; "eating with a voracity *proportioned* to previous starvation," Irving's "Captain Bonneville," xv.); also, to adjust the proportions of; also, to bear a due proportion to†; also, to divide into or distribute in proportionate parts†; assign to one as his portion†.—**pro-por′tion-a-ble**, *a.* Being in due proportion; corresponding; proportional: as, "For us to levy power *Proportionable* to the enemy Is all impossible" (Shakspere's "Richard II.," ii. 2. 125).—**pro-por′tion-a-bly**, *adv.*—**pro-por′tion-al.** [L. *proportionalis*.] **I.** *a.* Of or pertaining to proportion; relative; also, being in or characterized by proportion; having due proportion; corresponding; in *math.*, having the same or a constant ratio or relation. **II.** *n.* In *math.*, one of the quantities of a proportion.—**pro-por-tion-al′i-ty** (-al′i-ti), *n.*—**pro-por′tion-al-ly**, *adv.*—**pro-por′tion-ate** (-āt), *a.* [LL. *proportionatus.*] Proportioned; being in due proportion; proportional: as, "He stood six feet four and a half inches in height, and his girth was *proportionate*" (Arnold Bennett's "Clayhanger," i. 9); "I toiled hard, and my success was *proportionate* to my efforts" (C. Brontë's "Jane Eyre," viii.).—**pro-por′tion-ate** (-āt), *v. t.*; -ated, -ating. To make proportionate.—**pro-por′tion-ate-ly**, *adv.* —**pro-por′tion-ate-ness**, *n.*—**pro-por′tion-er**, *n.*—**pro-por′tion-ment**, *n.* The act of proportioning, or the state of being proportioned.

pro-po-sal (prō-pō′zal), *n.* The act or an act of proposing; a putting forward or suggesting of something for acceptance, adoption, or performance; an offer, specif. of marriage; also, a plan or scheme proposed.

pro-pose (prō-pōz′), *v.*; -posed, -posing. [OF. F. *proposer*, < *pro-* (< L. *pro*), before, + *poser*, put (see *pose*[1]), but associated with derivatives of L. *proponere*: see *proposition*.] **I.** *tr.* To put forward (a matter, subject, case, etc.) for consideration, discussion, or disposal; propound (a question, riddle, etc.), as for solution; present to the mind or attention (as, "Men must be taught as if you taught them not, And things unknown *proposed* as things forgot": Pope's "Essay on Criticism," 575); state; also, to put forward for acceptance, adoption, or favorable action (as, to *propose* terms of agreement; to *propose* a plan, method, or name; to *propose* marriage; to *propose* a toast or hearth); present (a person) for acceptance for some position or office, membership, candidacy, or the like; put forward or suggest as something to be done (often with a clause or infinitive as object: as, he *proposed* the sending of a messenger, or that a messenger

should be sent; it was *proposed* to send a messenger); also, to put before one's self as something to be done, or purpose, design, or intend (as, I am *proposing* a short journey; "We do not *propose* to stay long at Harrowgate," Smollett's "Humphry Clinker," June 23). **II.** *intr.* To make a proposal, specif. of marriage; also, to form or entertain a purpose or design (as, man *proposes*, but God disposes — a medieval proverb); also, to converse† (see Shakspere's "Much Ado about Nothing," iii. 1. 3).—**pro-pose′**†, *n.* A proposal; also, purpose; also, conversation or talk.—**pro-pos′er** (-pō′zẽr), *n.*

prop-o-si-tion (prop-ō-zish′on), *n.* [OF. F. *proposition*, < L. *propositio(n-)*, a setting forth, < *proponere*, set forth, propose: see *propone* and *propound*, and cf. *propose*.] The act of putting forward or propounding something for consideration, discussion, etc.; a statement wherein something is propounded; an assertion; also, the act of proposing, or a proposal of, something to be accepted, adopted, or done (as, "I have a *proposition* to make; or, if your lordship prefers, a favour to ask": Stevenson's "Master of Ballantrae," x.); an offer of terms for a transaction, as in business; a plan or scheme proposed (as, "To this rational *proposition* no objection could be raised": Cooper's "Spy," xxiii.); a thing presented for purchase, or considered with reference to its value to the purchaser or owner (as, the land is a good, or a poor, *proposition*; the enterprise proved to be a paying *proposition*); in general, a thing, matter, or person considered as something dealt with or encountered in experience (slang, U. S.: as, this lock is a troublesome *proposition*; the expense is a serious *proposition*; the boy is a tough *proposition*); in *logic*, a statement in which something is affirmed or denied of a subject; in *math.*, a formal statement of either a truth to be demonstrated or an operation to be performed; a theorem or a problem.—**prop-o-si′tion-al**, *a.* Pertaining to or constituting a proposition; considered as a proposition. —**prop-o-si′tion-al-ly**, *adv.*

pro-pound (prō-pound′), *v. t.* [Later form of *propone*: cf. *compound* and *expound*.] To put forward or propose for consideration, discussion, acceptance, or adoption (as, "Telesio . . . and others had been *propounding* theories of their own": Hallam's "Literature of Europe," iii. 3. § 6); often, to put forward (a question, riddle, etc.) for answering or solution (as, "She asked me many questions and *propounded* many problems": Kipling's "Kim," iv.).—**pro-pound′er**, *n.*

pro-pre-tor, **pro-præ-tor** (prō-prē′tor), *n.* [L. *propraetor*, < *pro*, for, + *praetor*, pretor.] In *Rom. hist.*, an officer who, after having served as pretor in Rome, was sent to govern a province with pretorial authority: as, "In 92 Sylla went as *proprætor* to Asia" (Froude's "Cæsar," vi.).

pro-pri-e-ta-ry (prō-prī′ẹ-tā-ri). [LL. *proprietarius*, < L. *proprietas*, E. *property*.] **I.** *a.* Belonging or controlled as property (as, a *proprietary* medicine, one whose manufacture and sale are restricted by patent or otherwise to some particular person or persons; a *proprietary* colony, see *proprietary*, *n.*); belonging to a proprietor or proprietors; also, holding property (as, the *proprietary* class); being a proprietor or proprietors; also, pertaining to property or ownership (as, *proprietary* rights). **II.** *n.*; pl. -ries (-riz). An owner or proprietor; specif., in American colonial history, the grantee or owner, or one of the grantees or owners, of certain North American colonies granted by the British crown to particular persons (as, "A diminution of the privileges of its [Maryland's] *proprietary* was the condition on which alone it was willing to give aid": Bancroft's "Hist. of the U. S.," Amer. Revolution, i. 5); also, a body of proprietors (as, "The *proprietary* desired certain modifications in the existing policy": Arnold Bennett's "Truth about an Author," x.); also, the holding of property; ownership; also, something owned or held as property; specif., a proprietary medicine.

pro-pri-e-tor (prō-prī′ẹ-tor), *n.* [For earlier *proprietary*: cf. F. *propriétaire*, owner, landlord.] One who has the exclusive right or title to something; an owner, as of landed property; the owner or the acting head of a business establishment, a hotel business, etc.—**pro-pri-e-to′ri-al** (-tō′ri-al), *a.*—**pro-pri′e-tor-ship**, *n.*—**pro-pri′e-tress**, *n.* A female proprietor.

---

pro-pri-e-ty (prō̍-prī′ẹ-ti), *n.*; pl. *-ties* (-tiz). [OF. *pro-priete* (F. *propriété*): see *property*.] Property† or owner-ship†; also, something owned†, or a possession†; a landed estate†; also, proper or peculiar character (now rare: as, "Silence that dreadful bell: it frights the isle from her *propriety*," Shakspere's "Othello," ii. 3. 176); also, a prop-erty, peculiarity, or characteristic of something†; also, appropriateness to the purpose or circumstances; fitness or suitability; rightness or justness; also, conformity to established standards of behavior or manners (as, "He was afraid that, from some obscure motive of *propriety* . . . she would bring Janet with her": Arnold Bennett's "Clay-hanger," ii. 18); seemliness; decorousness; decency; *pl.*, with *the*, the conventional standards or requirements of proper behavior.

props (props), *n. pl.* [Short for *properties*, pl. of *property*.] Theatrical or stage properties (also fig.); also, as *sing.*, a property-man. [Slang.]

pro-pug-nac-u-lum (prō̍-pug-nak′ū-lum), *n.*; pl. *-la* (-lä). [L., < *propugnare*, defend, < *pro*, before, + *pugnare*, fight.] A bulwark; a defense.

pro-pul-sion (prō̍-pul′shọn), *n.* [F. *propulsion*, < L. *propellere*, E. *propel*.] The act of propelling or driving forward or onward, or the state of being propelled; pro-pulsive force; impulse given.—**pro-pul′sive** (-siv), **pro-pul′-so-ry** (-sọ-ri), *a.* Serving to propel.

pro-pyl (prō̍′pil), *n.* [From *prop(ionic)* + *-yl*.] In *chem.*, the univalent radical, C_3H_7, of propane.

prop-y-læ-um (prop-i-lē′um), *n.*; pl. *-læa* (-lē′ä). [L., < Gr. προπύλαιον, neut. of προπύλαιος, before the gate, < πρό, before, + πύλη, gate.] A vestibule or entrance to a temple or other inclosure, esp. when elaborate or of archi-tectural importance.

pro-pyl-ic (prō̍-pil′ik), *a.* In *chem.*, of, pertaining to, or containing propyl.

prop-y-lite (prop′i-līt), *n.* [So named because supposed to open the Tertiary volcanic epoch, < Gr. πρόπυλον, gateway: see *propylon*.] An altered form of andesite or some allied rock.—**prop-y-lit′ic** (-lit′ik), *a.*

prop-y-lon (prop′i-lon), *n.*; pl. *-lons* or *-la* (-lä). [L., < Gr. πρόπυλον, < πρό, before, + πύλη, gate.] In *anc. Egypt. arch.*, a monumen-tal gateway standing be-fore the ac-tual entrance, or pylon, of a temple, etc.

pro ra-ta (prō rā′tä). [ML., ac-cording to rate.] In due propor-tion; accord-ing to the share, inter-est, etc., of each; propor-tionally.

pro=rat-a-ble (prō̍-rā′tạ-bl), *a.* That may be pro-rated.

pro=rate (prō̍-rāt′), *v.*; *-rated, -rat-*

Propylon at Karnak (Thebes), Egypt.

ing. [From *pro rata.*] **I.** *tr.* To divide pro rata; distrib-ute or assess proportionally: as, "He is perfectly willing to *pro rate* the special assessment" (Sinclair Lewis's "Babbitt," iii.). **II.** *intr.* To make an arrangement on a basis of proportional distribution.

prore (prōr), *n.* [OF. *prore*, < L. *prora*: see *prow¹*.] The prow or fore part of a ship or boat: as, "The tall ship, whose lofty *prore* Shall never stem the billows more" (Scott's "Lady of the Lake," vi. 13). [Now poetic.]

pro-ro-ga-tion (prō̍-rọ-gā′shọn), *n.* [L. *prorogatio(n-).*]

The act of proroguing, or the state of being prorogued; dis-continuance of the meetings of a parliament, as of the British Parliament by command of the sovereign, without dis-solution.

pro-rogue (prō̍-rōg′), *v. t.*; *-rogued, -roguing.* [OF. *pro-roguer* (F. *proroger*), < L. *prorogare*, prolong, protract, defer, < *pro*, before, + *rogare*, ask.] To protract†; also, to defer†; postpone†; also, to discontinue the meetings of (the British Parliament or a similar body) for a definite or indefinite time, without dissolving it.

pro-sa-ic (prō̍-zā′ik), *a.* [LL. *prosaicus*, < L. *prosa*, E. *prose*.] Of, pertaining to, or consisting of prose (now rare); also, having the character or spirit of prose as opposed to poetry, as verse or writing; hence, in general, common-place or dull (as, to lead a *prosaic* life); of persons, etc., matter-of-fact or unimaginative (as, the *prosaic* type of mind).—**pro-sa′i-cal-ly**, *adv.*—**pro-sa′ic-ness**, *n.*

pro-sa-ism (prō̍′zạ-izm), *n.* [= F. *prosaïsme*, < L. *prosa*, E. *prose*.] Prosaic character; also, a prosaic expression.—

pro′sa-ist, *n.* A writer of prose; also, a prosaic person.

pro-sa-teur (pro-zä-tér′), *n.* [F.] A writer of prose.

pro-sce-ni-um (prō̍-sē′ni-um), *n.*; pl. *-nia* (-ni-ä). [L., < Gr. προσκήνιον, < πρό, before, + σκηνή, tent, stage, E. *scene*.] In the ancient theater, the stage; in the modern theater, that part of the stage in front of the curtain or drop-scene, often including the curtain and the framework which holds it.

pro-scribe (prō̍-skrīb′), *v. t.*; *-scribed, -scribing.* [L. *pro-scribere* (pp. *proscriptus*), write before, publish, proscribe, < *pro*, before, + *scribere*, write.] To publish the name of (a person) as condemned to death and confiscation of property; put out of the protection of the law, or outlaw; banish or exile; also, to denounce or condemn (a thing) as dangerous; interdict; prohibit.—**pro-scrib′er** (-skrī′bèr), *n.*

pro-script (prō̍′skript), *n.* [L. *proscriptus*, pp.: see *pro-scribe*.] A proscribed person: as, "As each *proscript* rose and stood From kneeling in the ashen dust" (Rossetti's "Dante at Verona").

pro-scrip-tion (prō̍-skrip′shọn), *n.* [L. *proscriptio(n-).*] The act or an act of proscribing, or the state of being pro-scribed; outlawry; interdiction.

pro-scrip-tive (prō̍-skrip′tiv), *a.* Characterized by pro-scribing or proscription; tending to proscribe.—**pro-scrip′-tive-ly**, *adv.*

prose (prōz). [OF. F. *prose*, < L. *prosa*, prop. fem. (*prosa oratio*, prose speech) of *prosus*, *prorsus*, straightforward, in prose, for *proversus*, pp. of *provertere*, turn forward, < *pro*, before, + *vertere*, turn.] **I.** *n.* The ordinary form of spoken or written language, without metrical struc-ture (opposed to *poetry* or *verse*); hence, matter-of-fact, commonplace, or dull expression, quality, etc.; also, a prosy discourse. **II.** *a.* Consisting of or pertaining to prose; hence, prosaic; matter-of-fact; commonplace.—**prose**, *v.*; *prosed, prosing.* **I.** *tr.* To compose or express in prose; turn into prose. **II.** *intr.* To compose prose; also, to write or discourse in a dull or prosy manner.

pro-sec-tor (prō̍-sek′tọr), *n.* [LL., < L. *prosecare*, < *pro*, before, + *secare*, cut.] One who dissects cadavers for the illustration of anatomical lectures or the like.

pros-e-cute (pros′ẹ-kūt), *v.*; *-cuted, -cuting.* [L. *prosecutus*, pp. of *prosequi*, follow, pursue, continue, < *pro*, before, + *sequi*, follow: cf. *pursue*.] **I.** *tr.* To follow up or out, go on with, or pursue (something undertaken or begun: as, "We *prosecuted* our journey to Dumfries," Smollett's "Humphry Clinker," Sept. 12; to *prosecute* an inquiry; to *prosecute* one's studies); also, to carry on or practise (as, "Those polar fisheries could only be *prosecuted* in the short summer of that climate": H. Melville's "Moby-Dick," ci.); also, to follow out in detail, or enter into the particulars of, as a subject; in *law*, to pursue, as an action; seek to enforce or obtain by legal process, as a claim or a right; also, to institute legal proceedings against (a person, etc.); arraign before a court of justice for some crime or wrong. **II.** *intr.* In *law*, to institute and carry on a legal prosecution; act as prosecutor.—**pros′e-cut-a-ble** (-kū-tạ-bl), *a.*—**pros-e-cu′-tion** (-kū′shọn), *n.* [LL. *prosecutio(n-).*] The act or process of prosecuting; the following up of any matter in hand (as, "the *prosecution* of my task": Mrs. Shelley's

"Frankenstein," xviii.); the carrying on of a pursuit, etc.; specif., in *law*, the institution and carrying on of legal proceedings against a person; hence, the party by whom such proceedings are instituted and carried on.—**pros'e-cu-tor**, *n.* [LL.] One who prosecutes; specif., in *law*, one who institutes and carries on legal proceedings in a court of justice, esp. in a criminal court; also, an officer charged with the conduct of criminal prosecutions in the interest of the public ('public prosecutor').—**pros-e-cu'trix** (-triks), *n.* A female prosecutor.

pros-e-lyte (pros'ē-līt), *n.* [LL. *proselytus*, < Gr. προσή-λυτος, new-comer, proselyte, < πρός, to, + ἐλυθ-, stem of parts of ἔρχεσθαι, come.] One who has come over or changed from one opinion, religious belief, sect, or the like to another; a convert.—**pros'e-lyte**, *v. t.* or *i.*; -*lyted*, -*lyting.* To proselytize.—**pros'e-lyt-ism** (-li-tizm or -lī-tizm), *n.* The state or condition of a proselyte; also, the practice of making proselytes.—**pros'e-lyt-ist**, *n.*—**pros'e-lyt-ize** (-li-tīz or -lī-tīz), *v.*; -*ized*, -*izing.* **I.** *tr.* To make a proselyte of; convert. **II.** *intr.* To make proselytes.—**pros'e-lyt-iz-er** (-li-tī-zėr or -lī-tī-zėr), *n.*

pros-en-ceph-a-lon (pros-en-sef'a-lon), *n.*; pl. -*la* (-lä). [NL., < Gr. πρός, before, + NL. *encephalon.*] In *anat.*, the anterior segment of the brain, consisting of the cerebral hemispheres (or their equivalent) and certain adjacent parts; the forebrain.—**pros''en-ce-phal'ic** (-se-fal'ik), *a.*

pros-en-chy-ma (pros-eng'ki-mä), *n.* [NL., < Gr. πρός, toward, to, + -*enchyma* as in *parenchyma.*] In *bot.*, the tissue characteristic of the woody and bast portions of plants, consisting typically of long, narrow cells with pointed ends.—**pros-en-chym'a-tous** (-kim'a-tus), *a.*

pros-er (prō'zėr), *n.* One who proses; a prose-writer; one who writes or discourses in a dull or prosy manner.

pros-i-ly (prō'zi-li), *adv.* In a prosy manner; prosaically; tediously.—**pros'i-ness**, *n.*

pro-sit (prō'zit). [L.] 'May it do good!' — an expression of good wishes used among Germans in drinking health and otherwise.

pro=slav-er-y (prō-slā'vėr-i), *a.* [See *pro-.*] Favoring slavery; in *U. S. hist.*, favoring the continuance of the institution of negro slavery, or opposed to interference with it.

pro-so (prō'sō), *n.*; pl. -*sos* (-sōz). [Russ., millet.] Any of certain varieties of millet, *Panicum miliaceum*, introduced into America from Russia, the grain of which is used for feeding hogs, poultry, etc. Also called *hog-millet.*

pro-sod-ic (pro-sod'ik), *a.* Pertaining to prosody.—**pro-sod'i-cal-ly**, *adv.*

pros-o-dist (pros'ō-dist), *n.* One versed in prosody.

pros-o-dy (pros'ō-di), *n.* [L. *prosodia*, < Gr. προσῳδία, tone or accent, modulation of voice, song sung to music, < πρός, to, + ἀείδειν, sing.] The science of poetic meters and versification.

pros-o-po-pe-ia, pros-o-po-pœ-ia (pros''ō-pō-pē'iä), *n.* [L. *prosopopœia*, < Gr. προσωποποιία, < πρόσωπον, face, person, + ποιεῖν, make.] In *rhet.*, personification, as of inanimate things; also, representation of an imaginary or absent person as speaking or acting.

pros-pect (pros'pekt), *n.* [L. *prospectus*, outlook, view, prospect, < *prospicere*, look forward, < *pro*, before, + *specere*, look at.] Outlook or view, as over a region or in a particular direction (as, "The freedom of *prospect*, the proximity to the horses, the elevation of seat — these were what we required," De Quincey's "English Mail-Coach," i.; "the gate whose *prospect* is toward the east," Ezek. xlii. 15); also, sight, view, or range of vision (archaic: as, "Eden, and all the coast, in *prospect* lay," Milton's "Paradise Lost," x. 89); also, a view or scene presented to the eye, esp. a more or less wide expanse of natural or outdoor scenery (as, "Far beyond stretched a wide *prospect* of fields and waving woods": Prescott's "Conquest of Mexico," iv. 2); a wide, long, straight street or avenue (in Russian use); sometimes, formerly, a place affording a view†; also, in fig. use, a mental view or survey, as of a subject or situation, or that which is presented to the mental vision (as, "I had a dismal *prospect* of my condition": Defoe's "Robinson Crusoe," i. 4); also, a mental looking forward, or contemplation of something future or expected; expectation (as, advantages present or

in *prospect*); a view presented to the mind of something as future or to be expected (as, "She hated the *prospect* of Mr. Critchlow as a landlord": Arnold Bennett's "Old Wives' Tale," ii. 7); the outlook for the future, or that which appears as an indication of what may be expected (as, the business *prospect* for the coming season; a gloomy or an encouraging *prospect*); an indication of something as to be expected, or a ground of expectation (as, "They . . . were anxious to know the *prospect* of killing buffalo," Parkman's "Oregon Trail," xxvi.; is there any *prospect* of a change?); *pl.*, apparent probabilities of advancement, success, profit, etc. (as, a young man's *prospects* in life; "With the death of Francis, the *prospects* of the Huguenots brightened," Besant's "Coligny," viii.; "a letter on the *prospects* of the English iron trade," Mallock's "New Republic," v. 1); also, *sing.*, something in view as a source of profit (as, "I had another *prospect*, which I promised myself would yield equal profit . . . and this was . . . the Red Sea": Defoe's "Captain Singleton," xii.); specif., a prospective customer, as in business (as, "the fortnightly form-letter, to be mimeographed and sent out to a thousand '*prospects*' ": Sinclair Lewis's "Babbitt," iii.); in *mining*, an apparent indication of metal, etc., or a spot giving such indications.—**pros'pect**, *v.* **I.** *intr.* To explore a region for gold or the like. Also fig. **II.** *tr.* To explore (a region), as for gold; also, to work (a mine or claim) experimentally in order to test its value.—**pro-spec-tion** (prō-spek'shon), *n.* A looking forward; foresight; also, a prospecting, as for gold.—**pro-spec'tive**, *a.* Looking forward in time; having reference to the future; also, being in prospect or expectation, expected, or future (as, *prospective* advantages to be gained; "I won't have a prospective guest discussed," W. Churchill's "Modern Chronicle," i. 7).—**pro-spec'tive-ly**, *adv.*—**pros-pec-tor**, **pros-pect-er** (pros'pek-tor, -tėr, or prō-spek'-), *n.* One who prospects, as for gold.

pro-spec-tus (prō-spek'tus), *n.*; pl. -*tuses*, L. -*tus* (-tus). [L.: see *prospect.*] A printed statement distributed to describe and advertise a forthcoming literary work, a proposed or new enterprise, or the like: as, "He wanted his son to learn how little confidence was to be placed in glowing *prospectuses* and flaming articles" (S. Butler's "Way of All Flesh," lxxviii.).

pros-per (pros'pėr), *v.* [OF. *prosperer* (F. *prospérer*), < L. *prosperare*, make prosperous, < *prosper*: see *prosperous.*] **I.** *tr.* To make prosperous or successful; cause to succeed, flourish, or thrive: as, "Let every one of you lay by him in store, as God hath *prospered* him" (1 Cor. xvi. 2). **II.** *intr.* To be prosperous or successful; succeed, flourish, or thrive: as, "Well may you *prosper!*" (Shakspere's "King Lear," i. 1. 285); "Whatsoever he doeth shall *prosper*" (Ps. i. 3).—**pros'per-er**, *n.*—**pros'per-ing-ly**, *adv.*

pros-per-i-ty (pros-per'i-ti), *n.*; pl. -*ties* (-tiz). Prosperous, flourishing, or thriving condition; good fortune; success; *pl.*, prosperous circumstances (as, "the comforts and *prosperities* of his middle age": H. G. Wells's "Mr. Britling," i. 2. § 2).

pros-per-ous (pros'pėr-us), *a.* [OF. *prospereus*, for *prospere* (F. *prospère*), < L. *prosper*, *prosperus*, favorable, fortunate, perhaps < *pro*, for, according to, + *sper-* as in *sperare*, hope: cf. *despair.*] Favorable or propitious (as, "We had a very *prosperous* gale till we arrived at the Cape of Good Hope": Swift's "Gulliver's Travels," ii. 1); also, attended with or characterized by good fortune (as, a *prosperous* journey; a *prosperous* reign; "My father was a merchant in *prosperous* circumstances," F. M. Crawford's "Mr. Isaacs," i.); having continued good fortune, flourishing, or thriving (as, a *prosperous* merchant; a *prosperous* city; a *prosperous* school); fortunate or successful; well-to-do or well off (as, "the period when every *prosperous* family with children kept a Newfoundland dog": Tarkington's "Magnificent Ambersons," i.).—**pros'per-ous-ly**, *adv.*—**pros'per-ous-ness**, *n.*

pros-tate (pros'tāt). [ML. *prostata*, the prostate, < Gr. προστάτης, one standing before, < προϊστάναι, < πρό, before, + ἱστάναι, cause to stand.] In *anat.*: **I.** *n.* A large gland surrounding the commencement of the male urethra in front of the mouth of the bladder. **II.** *a.* Designating or pertaining to the prostate.—**pro-stat-ic** (prō-stat'ik), *a.*

---

fat, fāte, fär, fåll, åsk, fāre; net, mē, hèr; pin, pīne; not, nōte, mŏve, nôr; up, lūte, púll; oi, oil; ou, out; (lightened) aviāry, ēlect, agŏny, intŏ, ūnite; (obscured) errant, operä, ardent, actor, natūre; ch, chip; g, go; th, thin; ᴛн, then; y, you;

pros-the-sis (pros'the-sis), *n.* [LL., < Gr. πρόσθεσις, a putting to, addition, < προστιθέναι, < πρός, to, + τιθέναι, set, put.] In *gram.*, the addition of a letter or syllable to a word, esp. at the beginning; in *surg.*, the addition of an artificial part to supply a defect of the body.—**pros-thet'ic** (-thet'ik), *a.* In *gram.*, pertaining to prosthesis; added, esp. prefixed, as a letter or syllable; in *surg.*, pertaining to or of the nature of prosthesis (as, *prosthetic* dentistry: see *operative, a.*).

pros-ti-tute (pros'ti-tūt), *v. t.*; *-tuted, -tuting.* [L. *prostitutus*, pp. of *prostituere*, place before, expose publicly, prostitute, < *pro*, before, + *statuere*, set: see *statute.*] To submit to unlawful, esp. indiscriminate, sexual intercourse for gain or hire (with reference to a woman, and commonly reflexively); hence, to surrender to any vile or infamous purpose for gain; put to any base or unworthy use (as, "the soup — alas! that I should so far *prostitute* the word": Lever's "Harry Lorrequer," xiii.).—**pros'ti-tute. I.** *a.* Prostituted; openly devoted to lewdness for gain; licentious; hence, surrendered to any vile purpose for gain (as, "I found how the world had been misled by *prostitute* writers": Swift's "Gulliver's Travels," iii. 8); basely venal; corrupt. **II.** *n.* A woman given to unlawful, esp. indiscriminate, sexual intercourse for gain or hire; a harlot; hence, a base hireling; an abandoned person.—**pros-ti-tu'tion** (-tū'shon), *n.* [LL. *prostitutio(n-).*] The act or practice of prostituting; the offering of the body by a woman to indiscriminate sexual intercourse for hire; hence, devotion to any infamous or base use.—**pros'ti-tu-tor**, *n.*

pros-trate (pros'trāt), *v. t.*; *-trated, -trating.* [L. *prostratus*, pp. of *prosternere*, < *pro*, before, + *sternere*, spread out: see *stratum.*] To lay flat, as on the ground; throw down level with the ground; also, to cast (one's self) down in humility or adoration; also, fig., to overthrow, overcome, or reduce to helplessness (as, "In *prostrating* one enemy, he had mortified a hundred": Scott's "Talisman," xv.); also, to reduce to physical weakness or exhaustion (as, to be *prostrated* by disease, fatigue, or grief).—**pros'trate**, *a.* Lying flat or at full length, as on the ground (as, "the *prostrate* trunk of a cocoa-nut tree": H. Melville's "Typee," xviii.); also, lying with the face to the ground, as in token of submission or humility (as, a *prostrate* foe; "Heselrigge, as he lay *prostrate* . . . implored for life," Jane Porter's "Scottish Chiefs," iii.); lying or bowed low, as in adoration or worship; also, fig., submissive (as, "She took all Mr. Rossiter's snubs . . . with the most *prostrate* humility": Mrs. Stowe's "Oldtown Folks," xxxiii.); overthrown, overcome, or helpless (as, a *prostrate* country or industry); also, in a state of physical weakness or exhaustion; in *bot.*, of a plant or stem, lying along the ground.—**pros-tra'tion** (-trā'shon), *n.* [LL. *prostratio(n-).*] The act of prostrating, or the state of being prostrated; a laying or lying flat or prostrate; a casting or bowing down, as in adoration or worship; abject submission; humiliation or abasement; reduction to a powerless or helpless condition; extreme mental depression or dejection; extreme physical weakness or exhaustion (as, nervous *prostration*).—**pros'tra-tor**, *n.*

pro-style (prō'stīl). [L. *prostylos*, < Gr. πρόστυλος, < πρό, before, + στῦλος, pillar, column.] In *arch.*: **I.** *a.* Having a portico in front, standing out from the walls of the building, as a temple. **II.** *n.* A prostyle building.

pros-y (prō'zi), *a.*; compar. *prosier*, superl. *prosiest.* Of the nature of, or resembling, prose; hence, prosaic; commonplace; dull and wearisome (as, "an argument that was so *prosy* that many a head by and by began to nod": Mark Twain's "Tom Sawyer," v.); given to discoursing in a commonplace, dull, or wearisome manner (as, "this excellent but somewhat *prosy* old gentleman": Hawthorne's "Twice-Told Tales," Edward Randolph's Portrait).

pro-ta-gon (prō'tạ-gon), *n.* [G., < Gr. πρῶτος, first, + ἄγων, ppr. of ἄγειν, lead.] In *chem.*, a crystalline substance (composed of carbon, hydrogen, nitrogen, phosphorus, and oxygen) occurring in nerve-tissue, etc.

Plan of Prostyle Temple.

pro-tag-o-nist (prō-tag'ọ-nist), *n.* [Gr. πρωταγωνιστής, < πρῶτος, first, + ἀγωνιστής, contender, actor, E. *agonist.*] The leading character in a play; hence, any leading character or personage.

pro-tan-dry (prō-tan'dri), etc. [See *proto-.*] Same as *proterandry*, etc.

prot-a-sis (prot'ạ-sis), *n.* [L., < Gr. πρότασις, < προτείνειν, stretch before, < πρό, before, + τείνειν, stretch.] In the ancient drama, the first part of the play, in which the characters are introduced and the subject is proposed and entered upon (cf. *epitasis*); in *gram.*, the clause expressing the condition in a conditional sentence (opposed to *apodosis*).

Pro-te-an (prō'tẹ-ạn), *a.* Of, like, or suggestive of Proteus (see *Proteus*); hence [*l. c.*], readily assuming different forms or characters; exceedingly variable.

pro-tect (prō-tekt'), *v. t.* [L. *protectus*, pp. of *protegere*, < *pro*, before, + *tegere*, cover.] To cover or shield from injury or danger; defend or guard from attack, invasion, annoyance, insult, etc.; preserve in safety; extend patronage to; also, to act as official or legal protector or guardian of; in *polit. econ.*, to guard against the competition of foreign productions by means of import duties on the latter (as, to *protect* home industries); in *com.*, to provide funds for the payment of (a draft, etc.).—**protected cruiser.** See under *cruiser.*—**pro-tect'ing-ly**, *adv.*

pro-tec-tion (prō-tek'shon), *n.* [LL. *protectio(n-).*] The act of protecting, or the state of being protected; preservation from injury or harm; patronage; also, something that protects; a shelter; a defense; also, a writing or document that guarantees protection; a safe-conduct, passport, or other writing which secures from molestation the person specified in it; in the U. S., a certificate of nationality issued to seamen who are citizens (as, "the outward-bound sailor in quest of a *protection*": Hawthorne's "Scarlet Letter," The Custom House); in *polit. econ.*, the system or theory of fostering or developing home industries by protecting them from foreign competition through duties imposed on importations from foreign countries (cf. *free trade*, under *free, a.*).—**pro-tec'tion-al**, *a.* Pertaining to, or characterized or fostered by, protection: as, "the *protectional* expansion of national commerce" (Morley's "Oliver Cromwell," iv. 1).—**pro-tec'tion-ism**, *n.* The economic system or theory of protection.—**pro-tec'tion-ist**, *n.* An advocate of economic protection.

pro-tec-tive (prō-tek'tiv). **I.** *a.* Having the quality of protecting; tending to protect; also, of or pertaining to economic protection; designed to protect economically (as, a *protective* tariff). **II.** *n.* Something that protects.—**pro-tec'tive-ly**, *adv.*—**pro-tec'tive-ness**, *n.*

pro-tec-tor (prō-tek'tọr), *n.* [LL.] One who or that which protects; a defender; a guardian; a patron; in *Eng. hist.*, one in charge of the kingdom during the sovereign's minority, incapacity, or absence; also [*cap.*], the title (more fully *Lord Protector*) of the head of the executive during part of the period of the Commonwealth (held by Oliver Cromwell 1653–58, and by Richard Cromwell 1658–59).—**pro-tec'tor-ate** (-ạt), *n.* The government of a protector; the office or position, or the term of office, of a protector; specif. [*cap.*], the period (1653–59) in English history during which Oliver and Richard Cromwell held the title of Lord Protector; also, the relation of a strong state toward a weaker one which it protects and partly controls; the relation of a superior power to a territory inhabited by native tribes and not ranking as a state, to which it gives its protection; hence, a state or territory so protected.—**pro-tec'tor-ship**, *n.*—**pro-tec'to-ry** (-tọ-ri), *n.*; pl. *-ries* (-riz). An institution for the shelter and training of destitute or delinquent children.—**pro-tec'tress**, *n.* A female protector.

pro-té-gé (prō'tạ-zhā, F. pro-tā-zhā), *n.*; pl. *-gés* (-zhāz, F. -zhā). [F., pp. of *protéger*, < L. *protegere*, E. *protect.*] One who is under the protection or friendly patronage of another, esp. of a person of superior standing or influence.—**pro-té-gée** (prō'tạ-zhā, F. pro-tā-zhā), *n.*; pl. *-gées* (-zhāz, F. -zhā). [F.] Fem. of *protégé.*

pro-te-id (prō'tẹ-id). [From *protein.*] **I.** *n.* Any of the various complex nitrogenous substances which form an essential part of animal and vegetable cells, and which are the most important constituents of food: called *protein* by some authorities. **II.** *a.* Of the nature of a proteid; belonging or pertaining to the proteids.

pro-te-in (prō′tē-in), *n.* [F. *protéine* = G. *protein*, < Gr. πρῶτος, first.] Formerly, a substance thought to be the essential nitrogenous component of all organic bodies; now, a proteid; collectively, the nitrogenous constituents of animal and vegetable substances.

pro-tend (prō-tend′), *v. t.* [L. *protendere* (pp. *protensus*), < *pro*, before, + *tendere*, stretch.] To stretch forth; hold out before one's self; also, to extend lengthwise or in one dimension; also, to extend in duration; protract; prolong.— **pro-ten′sion** (-ten′shon), *n.*—**pro-ten′sive** (-siv), *a.* Extended lengthwise or in one dimension; relating to linear extension; also, extended in time; lasting; enduring.

pro-te-ol-y-sis (prō-tē-ol′i-sis), *n.* [From *proteid* + *-lysis*.] The hydrolysis or breaking down of proteids into simpler compounds, as in digestion.—**pro″te-o-lyt′ic** (-ō-lit′ik), *a.* Pertaining to proteolysis; effecting proteolysis (as, a *proteolytic* enzyme).

pro-te-ose (prō′tē-ōs), *n.* [From *proteid* + *-ose²*.] In *physiol. chem.*, any of a class of soluble compounds derived from proteids by the action of gastric juice, etc.

prot-er-an-dry (prot-ẹ-ran′dri), *n.* [Gr. πρότερος, being before, former (compar. < πρό, before: see *protist*), + ἀνήρ (ἀνδρ-), man, male.] In *bot.*, the maturation of the anthers and the discharge of the pollen in a monoclinous flower before the stigmas of that flower are receptive of pollen. Cf. *proterogyny.*—**prot-er-an′drous**, *a.*

prot-er-og-y-ny (prot-ẹ-roj′i-ni), *n.* [Gr. πρότερος, being before (see *proterandry*), + γυνή, woman, female.] In *bot.*, the maturation of the stigmas in a monoclinous flower before the anthers of that flower are ready to discharge pollen. Cf. *proterandry.*—**prot-er-og′y-nous**, *a.*

Prot-er-o-zo-ic (prot″ẹ-rō-zō′ik). [Gr. πρότερος, being before (see *proterandry*), + ζωή, life.] **I.** *a.* Noting or pertaining to a geological era or a group of rocks preceding the Paleozoic and equivalent to the Algonkian. **II.** *n.* The Proterozoic era or group.

pro-ter-vi-ty (prō-tėr′vi-ti), *n.*; pl. *-ties* (-tiz). [OF. *protervite*, < L. *protervitas*, < *protervus*, violent, wanton, bold, pert.] Wantonness; waywardness; petulance; also, an instance or exhibition of this. [Now rare.]

pro-test (prō-test′), *v.* [OF. F. *protester*, < L. *protestari*, declare publicly, < *pro*, before, + *testari*, bear witness, < *testis*, a witness.] **I.** *tr.* To declare solemnly or formally (as, he *protested* that he had taken every precaution; "Pat . . . *protested* his intention to hold out to the last," H. Melville's "Omoo," xxxvi.; "I die *protesting* my innocence! " Godwin's "Caleb Williams," xli.); affirm; assert; also, to make a formal declaration of the non-acceptance or non-payment of (a bill of exchange or note); also, to make a protest or remonstrance against; object to as disqualified, as a player on an opposing football team; also, to say in protest or remonstrance (as, " 'Oh no, you didn't! ' she *protested*, firmly": Arnold Bennett's "Helen with the High Hand," iv.); also, to make known† (as, "Do me right, or I will *protest* your cowardice": Shakspere's "Much Ado about Nothing," v. 1. 149); also, to promise solemnly† (as, "On Diana's altar to *protest* For aye austerity and single life": Shakspere's "Midsummer Night's Dream," i. 1. 89); also, to call to witness†. **II.** *intr.* To make solemn declaration (as, "The man did solemnly *protest* unto us, saying . . . ," Gen. xliii. 3; "The lady doth *protest* too much, methinks," Shakspere's "Hamlet," iii. 2. 240); also, to give formal expression to objection or disapproval (as, "They *protested* to milliners and dressmakers if they were kept waiting": W. Churchill's "Modern Chronicle," ii. 3); remonstrate.—**pro-test** (prō′test), *n.* An act of protesting or affirming; a solemn declaration; also, the action taken to fix the liability for a dishonored bill of exchange or note; specif., a formal declaration, as by a notary, of the non-acceptance or non-payment of a bill of exchange or note; also, a written and attested declaration made by the master of a ship stating the circumstances under which some injury has happened to the ship or cargo, or other circumstances involving the liability of the officers, crew, etc.; also, the formal expression of objection or disapproval, often in opposition to something

which one is powerless to prevent or avoid (as, a statement of *protest*; a meeting in *protest*; to submit under *protest*); a statement or declaration of objection, or a remonstrance.

prot-es-tant (prot′es-tạnt). [G. or F. *protestant*, < L. *protestans* (-*ant*-), ppr. of *protestari*: see *protest*.] **I.** *a.* Protesting (also pron. prō-tes′tạnt); also [*cap.*], belonging or pertaining to Protestants or their religion. **II.** *n.* One who protests (also pron. prō-tes′tạnt); specif. [*cap.*], orig., any of the Lutherans who protested against the decision of the Diet of Spires in 1529, which had denounced the Reformation; later, an adherent of any of those Christian bodies which separated from the Church of Rome at the Reformation, or of any religious body descended from them; any Western Christian not an adherent of the Roman Catholic Church.—**Prot′es-tant-ism**, *n.* The religion of Protestants; adherence to Protestant principles; also, Protestants, or the Protestant churches, collectively.—**Prot′es-tant-ize** (-īz), *v. t.*; *-ized*, *-izing.* To render Protestant; convert to Protestantism.—**Prot′es-tant-iz-er** (-ī-zėr), *n.*

prot-es-ta-tion (prot-es-tā′shọn), *n.* [OF. F. *protestation*, < LL. *protestatio(n-).*] The act of protesting or affirming (as, to make *protestation* of one's innocence); a solemn declaration or affirmation (as, "The Duke was . . . vehement . . . in his *protestations* of loyalty": Motley's "Dutch Republic," vi. 6); also, the formal expression of objection or disapproval; a protest, or formal statement of objection. —**pro-tes-ta-to-ry** (prō-tes′tạ-tọ-ri), *a.* Making protestation; expressing or conveying a protest.

pro-test-er, pro-test-or (prō-tes′tėr, -tọr), *n.* One who protests.

pro-test-ing (prō-tes′ting), *p. a.* That protests; making a protest.—**pro-test′ing-ly**, *adv.*

Pro-teus (prō′tūs, also -tẹ-us), *n.* [L., < Gr. Πρωτεύς.] A sea-god of classical mythology who had the power of assuming different forms; hence, a person or thing capable of taking on various aspects or characters; also [*l. c.*], a blind, tailed amphibian, *Proteus anguinus*, inhabiting the subterranean waters of limestone caves in Europe, to the eastward of the Adriatic Sea (related to the menobranch, of North America).

Proteus (*P. anguinus*).

pro-te-van-gel (prō-tẹ-van′jẹl), *n.* Same as *protevangelium.*

pro-te-van-gel-i-um (prō″tẹ-van-jel′i-um), *n.* [NL., < Gr. πρῶτος, first, + LL. *evangelium*, E. *evangel.*] The promise concerning the seed of the woman, contained in Gen. iii. 15, regarded as the earliest announcement of the gospel.

pro-tha-la-mi-on, pro-tha-la-mi-um (prō-thạ-lā′mi-on, -um), *n.*; pl. *-mia* (-mi-ạ). [NL., < Gr. πρό, before, + θάλαμος, bridal chamber.] A song or poem written to celebrate a marriage: as, "Prothalamion; or, A Spousall Verse," the title of a poem by Edmund Spenser.

pro-thal-li-um (prō-thal′i-um), *n.*; pl. *prothallia* (-ạ). [NL., < Gr. πρό, before, + θαλλίον, dim. of θαλλός, young shoot.] In *bot.*, the gametophyte of ferns, etc.; the analogous rudimentary gametophyte of seed-bearing plants.— **pro-thal′li-al**, *a.*

pro-thal-lus (prō-thal′us), *n.*; pl. *prothalli* (-ī). [NL.] Same as *prothallium.*

proth-e-sis (proth′e-sis), *n.* [LL., < Gr. πρόθεσις, a putting before, < προτιθέναι, < πρό, before, + τιθέναι, set, put.] In the *Gr. Ch.*, the preparation and preliminary oblation of the eucharistic elements; the table on which this is done; the part of the bema or sanctuary where this table stands; in *gram.*, the addition of a letter or syllable at the beginning of a word.—**pro-thet-ic** (prō-thet′ik), *a.*

pro-thon-o-ta-ry, pro-ton-o-ta-ry (prō-thon′ō-tạ-ri, prō-ton′-), *n.*; pl. *-ries* (-riz). [LL. *protonotarius*, ML. also *prothonotarius*, < Gr. πρῶτος, first, + L. *notarius*, E. *notary.*] A chief clerk or secretary; a registrar; esp., a chief clerk or registrar of a court; in the *Rom. Cath. Ch.*, one of a college of ecclesiastics of superior rank charged with the registry of pontifical acts, canonizations, etc.; also, any of certain prelates of similar rank; in the *Gr. Ch.*, the chief secretary of the patriarch of Constantinople.—**prothonotary warbler,** a beautiful warbler, *Protonotaria citrea*, of the southern U. S., of a rich yellow color passing by degrees through olivaceous to bluish tints on the wings, rump, and tail.—**prothon-o-ta'ri-al** (-tā'ri-a̤l), *a.*— **pro-thon'o-ta-ry-ship,** *n.*

Prothonotary Warbler.

pro-tho-rax (prō-thō'raks), *n.* [NL.: see *pro-* and *thorax*.] The anterior division of an insect's thorax, bearing the first pair of legs. See cuts at *mesothorax* and *metathorax*.—**pro-tho-ra-cic** (prō-thō-ras'ik), *a.*

pro-tist (prō'tist), *n.* [NL. *Protista*, pl., < Gr. πρώτιστος, the very first, superl. of πρῶτος, first, itself a superl. (with compar. πρότερος) < πρό, before: see *pro-*, *proterandry*, and *proto-*.] In *biol.*, any of a group of organisms (the *Protista*: a term proposed by Haeckel) including all the unicellular animals and plants.—**pro-tis-tan** (prō-tis'ta̤n), *a.* and *n.*— **pro-tis'tic,** *a.*

proto-, prot-. Forms of Gr. πρῶτος, first, primary, original, used in combination: in *chem.*, indicating the first of a series of compounds, or the one containing the minimum amount of an element, as in *protoxide*. Cf. *proto-element*.

pro-to-cal-ci-um (prō'tō-kal'si-um), *n.* See *proto-element*.

pro-to-ca-non-i-cal (prō'tō-ka̤-non'i-ka̤l), *a.* [See *proto-*.] Of, pertaining to, or forming a first or original canon: as, *protocanonical* books (the books of the Bible whose canonicity has always been universally acknowledged in the church). Cf. *deuterocanonical*.

pro-to-ce-ras (prō-tos'e̤-ras), *n.* [NL., < Gr. πρῶτος, first, + κέρας, horn.] An extinct ungulate mammal of North America, about the size of a sheep and distantly related to the existing chevrotains, with two, or possibly three, pairs of horns on the head of the male.

Protoceras. — From a skeleton in the Princeton Museum.

pro-to-col (prō'tō-kol), *n.* [F. *protocole*, < ML. *protocollum*, < LGr. πρωτόκολλον, orig. a first leaf glued to the front of a manuscript and bearing notes as to contents, < Gr. πρῶτος, first, + κόλλα, glue.] An original draft, minute, or record from which a document, esp. a treaty, is prepared.—**pro'to-col,** *v.*; *-colled*, *-colling.* **I.** *intr.* To draw up protocols. **II.** *tr.* To embody in a protocol.

pro-to-el-e-ment (prō'tō-el'e̤-ment), *n.* [See *proto-*.] In *chem.*, a primitive form or prototype of an element (also called a *protometal*, or, when a particular one is meant, *protocalcium*, *protomagnesium*, etc.) supposed, from spectroscopic observations, to exist at high temperatures, as in the hottest stars.

pro-to-gine (prō'tō-jin), *n.* [F., < Gr. πρῶτος, first, + γίνεσθαι, γίγνεσθαι, be born or produced.] A fine-grained variety of granite, occurring chiefly in the Alps.

pro-tog-y-ny (prō-toj'i-ni), etc. [See *proto-*.] Same as *proterogyny*, etc.

pro-to-lith-ic (prō-tō-lith'ik), *a.* [Gr. πρῶτος, first, + λίθος, stone.] In *anthropol.*, noting or pertaining to stone implements selected according to fitness of form and gradually shaped by wear, without definite shaping on the part of the operator. Cf. *technolithic*.

pro-to-mag-ne-sium (prō'tō-mag-nē'shium or -zhium), *n.* See *proto-element*.

pro-to-mar-tyr (prō-tō-mär'ter), *n.* [ML., < LGr. πρωτό-μαρτυρ, < Gr. πρῶτος, first, + μάρτυρ, E. *martyr*.] The first martyr in any cause; specif., the first Christian martyr (Stephen).

pro-to-met-al (prō'tō-met''al), *n.* See *proto-element*.

pro-ton (prō'ton), *n.* [Gr. πρῶτον, neut. of πρῶτος, first.] In *biol.*, the first rudiment of a structure or organ in the embryo; in *physics* and *chem.*, the fundamental unit of atomic structure, being electropositive, and composing with electrons (electronegative) the atoms of all elements.

pro-to-ne-ma (prō-tō-nē'mä), *n.*; pl. *-mata* (-ma̤-tä). [NL., < Gr. πρῶτος, first, + νῆμα, thread.] In *bot.*, a primary, usually filamentous structure which is produced by the germination of the spore in mosses and certain related plants, and upon which the leafy plant which bears the sexual organs arises as a lateral or terminal shoot.—**pro-to-ne'mal,** *a.*

pro-ton'o-ta-ry, *n.* See *prothonotary*.

pro-to-plasm (prō'tō-plazm), *n.* [NL. *protoplasma*, < Gr. πρῶτος, first, + πλάσμα, something formed, E. *plasma*.] In *biol.*, a complex substance (typically colorless and of viscid semifluid consistence) regarded as the physical basis of life, having the power of spontaneous motion, reproduction, etc., and forming the living matter of all vegetable and animal cells and tissues.—**pro-to-plas'mic** (-plaz'mik), *a.*

pro-to-plast (prō'tō-plast), *n.* [LL. *protoplastus*, the first man, < Gr. πρωτόπλαστος, formed first, < πρῶτος, first, + πλαστός, adj. < πλάσσειν, form, mold.] One who or that which is first formed; the original; esp., the hypothetical first individual or one of the supposed first pair of a species or the like.—**pro-to-plas'tic,** *a.*

pro-to-pope (prō'tō-pōp), *n.* [See *proto-* and *pope*.] In the *Gr. Ch.*, a priest of superior rank; a chief priest.

pro-to-ste-le (prō'tō-stē''lē), *n.* [NL.: see *proto-* and *stele*.] In *bot.*, the solid stele of most roots, and of the first-formed portion of the stem.

pro-to-type (prō'tō-tīp), *n.* [F. *prototype*, < Gr. πρωτότυπον, prototype, prop. neut. of πρωτότυπος, prototype, primitive, < πρῶτος, first, + τύπος, E. *type*.] The first or primary type of anything; the original or model after which anything is formed.—**pro'to-ty-pal** (-tī-pa̤l), **pro-to-typ'ic** (-tip'-ik), *a.*

pro-tox-ide (prō-tok'sīd or -sid), *n.* [See *proto-*.] In *chem.*, that member of a series of oxides which has the smallest proportion of oxygen.

Pro-to-zo-a (prō-tō-zō'ä), *n. pl.* [NL., pl. of *protozoön*, < Gr. πρῶτος, first, + ζῷον, animal.] A large zoölogical division, or a phylum, comprising organisms which consist of a single cell and are mostly microscopic. Cf. *Metazoa*.— **pro-to-zo'an.** **I.** *a.* Belonging or pertaining to the *Protozoa*. **II.** *n.* One of the *Protozoa*.—**pro-to-zo'ic,** *a.* Protozoan.

pro-to-zo-öl-o-gy (prō''tō-zō-ol'ō-ji), *n.* [See *Protozoa* and *-logy*.] The science or study of the *Protozoa*, esp. of disease-producing protozoans.—**pro''to-zo-öl'o-gist,** *n.*

pro-to-zo-ön (prō-tō-zō'on), *n.*; pl. *-zoa* (-zō'ä). [See *Protozoa*.] One of the *Protozoa*.

pro-tract (prō-trakt'), *v. t.* [L. *protractus*, pp. of *protrahere*, draw forth, draw out, < *pro*, before, + *trahere*, draw: cf. *portray*.] To draw out or lengthen in time, or extend the duration of (as, "The dance . . . was *protracted* to a late hour," Motley's "Dutch Republic," v. 3; "this most arduous and *protracted* war," Irving's "Conquest of Granada," lxxvii.); also, to extend in space (as, "Their shaded walks And long *protracted* bow'rs": Cowper's "Task," i. 257); also, to put off in time, or postpone (as, "He attempted . . . to prevent, or at least to *protract*, his ruin": Gibbon's "Decline and Fall of the Roman Empire," v.); in *surv.*, etc., to plot; draw by means of a scale and protractor; in *anat.*, etc., to extend or protrude.—**pro-trac'tile** (-trak'til), *a.* Capable of being protracted or lengthened out, or of being protruded or thrust forth.—**pro-trac'tion** (-shon), *n.* [LL.

protractio(n-).] The act of protracting; extension in time or duration; extension in space; in *anc. pros.*, the treating as metrically long of a syllable usually taken as short; in *surv.*, etc., the act of protracting or plotting, as on paper; also, that which is protracted or plotted; a plot.—**pro-trac′tive** (-tiv), *a.* Protracting; prolonging.—**pro-trac′tor,** *n.* One who or that which protracts; in *surv.*, etc., an instrument for laying down and measuring angles on paper; in *anat.*, a muscle which extends a part.

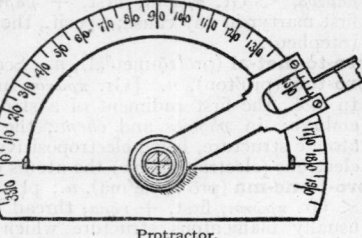

Protractor.

pro-trud-a-ble (prọ-trö′dạ-bl), *a.* Protrusible.

pro-trude (prọ-tröd′), *v.*; *-truded, -truding.* [L. *protrudere* (pp. *protrusus*), < *pro,* before, + *trudere,* thrust.] **I.** *tr.* To thrust or push forward or forth; cause to project: as, "*protruding* his head beyond the corner of the house" (J. Conrad's "Rover," viii.). **II.** *intr.* To stick out; project: as, "the window, whence the flag-post *protruded*" (Barrie's "Sentimental Tommy," xxi.).—**pro-tru′si-ble** (-trö′si-bl), *a.* Capable of being protruded or thrust forth.—**pro-tru′sile** (-sil), *a.* Capable of being thrust forth or extended, as a limb, etc.—**pro-tru′sion** (-zhọn), *n.* The act of protruding, or the state of being protruded; also, that which protrudes or projects.—**pro-tru′sive** (-siv), *a.* Thrusting forward or forth; also, obtrusive; also, projecting.

pro-tu-ber-ance (prọ-tū′bẹ-rạns), *n.* Protuberant state or form; also, a protuberant part; a rounded projection. Also **pro-tu′ber-an-cy.**

pro-tu-ber-ant (prọ-tū′bẹ-rạnt), *a.* [LL. *protuberans* (-ant-), ppr. of *protuberare:* see *protuberate.*] Bulging out beyond the surrounding surface; prominent.—**pro-tu′ber-ant-ly,** *adv.*

pro-tu-ber-ate (prọ-tū′bẹ-rāt), *v. i.* or *t.*; *-ated, -ating.* [LL. *protuberatus,* pp. of *protuberare,* < L. *pro,* before, + *tuber,* hump, swelling: cf. *tuber.*] To bulge out; project or cause to project in rounded form. [Now rare.]

pro-tyle (prō′til or -tīl), *n.* [Gr. πρῶτος, first, + ὕλη, matter.] The hypothetical undifferentiated matter or parent substance from which, according to some, all the chemical elements may have been derived.

proud (proud), *a.* [Late AS. *prūt, prūd,* proud, = Icel. *prūdhr,* magnificent, stately, gallant: cf. OF. *prod, prud, prou,* valiant, gallant, E. *prow²*.] Having or cherishing, or proceeding from or showing, a high, esp. an inordinately high, opinion of one's own dignity, importance, or superiority (as, "this *proud* fellow . . . who scorns us all," Tennyson's "Lancelot and Elaine," 1058; *proud* disdain; *proud* looks); haughty; supercilious; arrogant; also, having, or proceeding from, a becoming or dignified sense of what is due to one's self or one's position or character (as, to be too *proud* to lie; too *proud* to fight; *proud* self-restraint); having or showing self-respect or self-esteem; also, feeling pleasure or satisfaction over something conceived as highly honorable or creditable to one's self (often with *of,* an infinitive, or a clause: as, "a woman for a man to be *proud* of," W. H. Hudson's "Purple Land," xxi.; to be *proud* to receive an invitation; to be *proud* that one's son should win a prize); also, such as to give occasion for pride; of lofty dignity or distinction (as, a *proud* name or rank); highly honorable or creditable (as, *proud* trophies; a *proud* achievement); highly gratifying to the feelings or self-esteem (as, "This was a *proud* moment for Tommy": Barrie's "Sentimental Tommy," vii.); also, of persons, of exalted rank or station (as, *proud* nobles); of lofty pretensions (as, "Nature . . . wisely curb'd *proud* man's pretending wit," Pope's "Essay on Criticism," 53; the *proud* world); of things, stately, majestic, or magnificent (as, *proud* temples; *proud* ships; *proud* cities); also, full of vigor, spirit, or mettle, as an animal (chiefly poetic); also, high or swollen, as a stream, etc.; swollen by growth, or overgrown, as plants, tissues, etc. (now chiefly prov. Eng.); also, sexually excited (now prov. Eng.).—**proud flesh,** in

pathol., a growth due to an excessive formation of granulations in a wound or sore.—**proud′ly,** *adv.*—**proud′ness,** *n.*

proust-ite (pröst′īt), *n.* [F.; from J. L. *Proust* (1754–1826), French chemist.] A mineral consisting of a sulphide of arsenic and silver, occurring in crystals or masses of a red color.

prov-a-ble (prö′vạ-bl), *a.* Capable of being proved.—**prov′a-ble-ness,** *n.*—**prov′a-bly,** *adv.*

prov-and (prov′ạnd), *n.* [OF. *provende:* see *provender.*] Provender; provisions; esp., food and fodder for an army. [Archaic.] Also **prov′ant** (-ạnt).

prove (pröv), *v.*; *proved* (pp. sometimes, esp. in law, *proven*), *proving.* [OF. *prover* (F. *prouver*), < L. *probare,* try, test, prove, approve, < *probus,* good: cf. *probity.*] **I.** *tr.* To make trial of, or put to the test (as, "*Prove* all things; hold fast that which is good," 1 Thes. v. 21; "the chastening by which God *proves* the soul He loves," Mrs. H. Ward's "Robert Elsmere," xxv.); try or test; subject to some testing process; also, to have experience of, or experience (archaic); also, to establish as true, or demonstrate the truth of, as by evidence or argument (as, to *prove* one's contention; to *prove* that a charge is false; "He was not so anxious to *prove* himself right, as to be so," Trollope's "Warden," iii.); also, to give demonstration of by action (as, "Ev'ry knight is proud to *prove* his worth": Dryden's tr. Virgil's "Georgics," iv. 105); also, to establish the genuineness or validity of; specif., to establish the authenticity of (a will); probate; in *printing,* etc., to take a trial impression of (type, etc.); in *math.,* to test or verify the correctness of (a calculation). **II.** *intr.* To make trial†; also, to be found by trial or experience, or in the event, to be (as, "Have I *proved* a traitor?" Wiseman's "Fabiola," ii. 24; "The way *proved* longer than he had anticipated," Scott's "Guy Mannering," xxiii.); turn out (as, the report *proved* to be false; he *proved* to have considerable ability); also, to become (archaic: as, "Then her countenance all over Pale again as death did *prove,*" Tennyson's "Lord of Burleigh," 66); also, to turn out well†, succeed†, or prosper†.

pro-vec-tion (prọ-vek′shọn), *n.* [LL. *provectio*(n-), advancement, < L. *provehere,* carry forward, < *pro,* before, + *vehere,* carry.] In *philol.,* the carrying of a terminal letter of a word to the beginning of the succeeding word, as in *a newt* for *an ewt.*

pro-ved-i-tor (prọ-ved′i-tọr), *n.* [It. *proveditore* (now *provveditore*), < *provedere,* < L. *providere,* E. *provide.*] A purveyor; a steward; also, an overseer. [Obs. or rare.]

prov-en (prö′vn). Occasional past participle of *prove.* [Orig. in Sc. law.]

prov-e-nance (prov′ẹ-nạns), *n.* [F., < *provenir,* < L. *provenire,* come forth: see *provenience.*] The fact of coming from a particular place or source; origin; provenience.

Pro-ven-çal (pro-voṅ-säl′). [F., < *Provence,* < L. *provincia,* E. *province.*] **I.** *a.* Of or pertaining to Provence, anciently a Roman province, in southeastern France, or its people, or their language. **II.** *n.* A native or inhabitant of Provence; also, the Romance tongue spoken in Provence.

prov-en-der (prov′ẹn-dėr), *n.* [OF. *provendre,* var. of *provende,* prebend, provender, < ML. *præbenda:* see *prebend.*] Food or provisions (of food for human beings, now humorous); esp., dry food for beasts, as hay; fodder.—**prov′en-der,** *v. t.* To provide (horses, etc.) with provender.

pro-ve-nience (prọ-vē′niẹns), *n.* [L. *proveniens* (-ent-), ppr. of *provenire,* come forth, < *pro,* before, + *venire,* come.] Provenance; origin.

prov-er (prö′vėr), *n.* One who or that which proves.

prov-erb (prov′ėrb), *n.* [OF. F. *proverbe,* < L. *proverbium,* < *pro,* before, + *verbum,* word.] A short, pithy, popular saying, long current, embodying some familiar truth, practical precept, or useful thought in expressive and often picturesque language (as, "Fast bind, fast find; A *proverb* never stale in thrifty mind," Shakspere's "Merchant of Venice," ii. 5. 55; "You may have heard a military *proverb,* that it is a good thing to make a bridge of gold to a flying enemy?" Stevenson's "Master of Ballantrae," iv.); an adage; a saw; hence, a person or thing that has become proverbial or an object of common mention or reference (as, "He has become a *proverb* for fidelity, honesty, and courage": Besant's "Coligny," xi.); esp., an object of contemptuous common mention, or a byword (as, "This house . . . will I cast out of my sight; and Israel shall be a *proverb* and a byword among all people": 1 Kings, ix. 7); also, in general, a wise saying or precept, or a didactic sentence (as, "He [Solomon] was wiser than all men . . . And he spake three thousand *proverbs*," 1 Kings, iv. 32; the *proverbs* of King Alfred); sometimes, in Biblical use, a dark saying, or an oracular utterance requiring interpretation (see Prov. i. 6; John, xvi. 25); *pl.* [*cap.*], a book of the Old Testament consisting of wise sayings ascribed to Solomon and others; also [*sing.*], a play whose plot is founded upon a proverbial saying (a French use).—**to a proverb,** to the point of becoming proverbial; notoriously: as, "Salisbury was foolish *to a proverb* . . . He was represented in popular lampoons as a man made to be duped" (Macaulay's "Hist. of Eng.," vii.).—**prov′erb,** *v. t.* To utter in the form of a proverb; make (something) the subject of a proverb; hence, to make a byword of (as, "Am I not sung and *proverb′d* for a fool In every street?" Milton's "Samson Agonistes," 203); also, to provide with a proverb†.—**pro-ver-bi-al** (prō-vėr′bi-ạl), *a.* [L. *proverbialis.*] Of, pertaining to, or characteristic of a proverb (as, *proverbial* brevity; a *proverbial* mode of expression); expressed in a proverb or proverbs (as, *proverbial* wisdom); of the nature of or resembling a proverb (as, *proverbial* sayings or expressions); also, having been made the subject of a proverb (as, the *proverbial* rolling stone that gathers no moss); hence, having become an object of common mention or reference (as, "His [a savage's] inconstancy and treachery are *proverbial*": H. Melville's "Typee," x.); recognized by common mention; notorious.—**pro-ver′-bi-al-ist,** *n.* One who originates, collects, or uses proverbs.—**pro-ver′bi-al-ly,** *adv.*

pro-vide (prō-vīd′), *v.; -vided, -viding.* [L. *providere* (pp. *provisus*), foresee, look after, provide for, < *pro*, before, + *videre*, see.] **I.** *tr.* To foresee†; also, to bring about or ensure by foresight (as, "O, 'tis an accident that heaven *provides!*" Shakspere's "Measure for Measure," iv. 3. 81); arrange for or stipulate beforehand, as by a provision or proviso (commonly with a clause: as, the contract *provides* that specified materials shall be used); also, to get ready, prepare, or procure beforehand (as, "The wise ant her wintry store *provides*": Dryden's tr. Virgil's "Georgics," i. 271); also, to furnish or supply (something), as for a person or thing, for a purpose, etc. (as, to *provide* food or clothing for the needy; to *provide* materials or workers for carrying on an enterprise); afford or yield (as, "Such cooling fruit As the kind hospitable woods *provide*": Milton's "Comus," 187); also, to furnish or supply (a person or thing, etc.) with something (as, to *provide* one's self with necessaries or information; to *provide* an army with munitions; to *provide* a building with fire-escapes); also, to prepare, equip, or supply in a suitable manner† (as, "My lord, I cannot be so soon *provided*": Shakspere's "Two Gentlemen of Verona," i. 3. 72). **II.** *intr.* To take measures with due foresight (*for* or *against*: as, to *provide* for one's comfort; to *provide* for the sending of messengers; to *provide* against accident); make arrangements for supplying means of support, money, etc. (*for*: as, to *provide* for a person in one's will); supply means of support, etc. (often with *for*: as, the Lord will *provide*; to *provide* liberally for one's family).—**pro-vid′ed** (-vī′ded), *conj.* [Orig. pp.] It being stipulated or understood (that); on the condition or supposition (that): as, to consent, *provided*, or *provided* that, all the others agree.

prov-i-dence (prov′i-dẹns), *n.* [OF. F. *providence,* < L. *providentia,* < *providere:* see *provide.*] Foresight, forethought, or provident care (as, "This bloody deed . . . will be laid to us, whose *providence* Should have . . . restrain'd . . . This mad young man": Shakspere's "Hamlet," iv. 1. 17); provident or prudent management of resources, or economy; specif., the foreseeing care and guardianship of God over his creatures (as, "Men are naturally liable to diseases; for which God, in his good *providence*, has provided natural remedies": J. Butler's "Analogy of Religion," ii. 3); hence [*cap.*], God (as, "Vigilant over all that he has made, Kind *Providence* attends with gracious aid": Cowper's "Table Talk," 249); fig., one who exercises a providential care over others; also [*l. c.*], a manifestation of the divine care or direction (as, "There's a special *providence* in the

fall of a sparrow": Shakspere's "Hamlet," v. 2. 231); an occurrence or circumstance regarded as specially ordained by God (as, "I sincerely gave thanks to God for opening my eyes, by whatever afflicting *providences*, to see the former condition of my life": Defoe's "Robinson Crusoe," i. 8).—**prov′i-dent,** *a.* [L. *providens* (-*ent*-), ppr. of *providere.*] Having or showing foresight, or careful in providing for the future (as, "He had been *provident* enough to take with him some of his best working tools": J. H. Newman's "Callista," xxix.); mindful (*of*), as in making provision (as, "The parsimonious emmet, *provident* Of future": Milton's "Paradise Lost," vii. 485); characterized by or proceeding from foresight (as, *provident* care or management); also, economical or frugal.—**prov-i-den′tial** (-den′shạl), *a.* Provident†; also of, pertaining to, or proceeding from divine providence (as, *providential* care; "a *providential* appointment of every day's experience," J. Butler's "Analogy of Religion," ii. 5); hence, opportune, fortunate, or lucky (as, a *providential* occurrence; "Well, 'twas *providential* we took Colonel Devenport 'long with us," Mrs. Stowe's "Oldtown Folks," xxviii.).—**prov-i-den′tial-ly,** *adv.*—**prov′i-dent-ly,** *adv.* **pro-vid-er** (prō-vī′dėr), *n.* One who or that which provides.—**lion's provider.** See under *lion.*
pro-vid-ing (prō-vī′ding), *conj.* [Orig. ppr. of *provide.*] Making the proviso or stipulation that; with the understanding that; provided.

prov-ince (prov′ins), *n.* [OF. F. *province,* < L. *provincia,* province, official charge; origin uncertain.] A country or territory outside of Italy, brought under the ancient Roman dominion, and administered by a governor sent from Rome; also, an administrative division or unit of a country (as, the *provinces* of Spain or of Canada); also, formerly, the name applied to those North American colonies of Great Britain now forming provinces of Canada, and also to certain of those which after the Revolutionary War united to form the United States (as, "William Penn, in 1697, had proposed an annual congress of all the *provinces* on the continent of America": Bancroft's "Hist. of the U. S.," Amer. Revolution, i. 5); also, an ecclesiastical territorial division, as that within which an archbishop or a metropolitan exercises jurisdiction; also, in general, a country, territory, district, or region (as, "Over many a tract Of heaven they march'd, and many a *province* wide": Milton's "Paradise Lost," vi. 77); also, *pl.,* with *the,* the parts of a country outside of the capital or the largest cities, as, in England, all parts of the country outside of London; also, *sing.,* a department or branch of learning or activity (as, the *province* of mathematics; the *province* of politics); a division of any subject; also, the sphere or field of action of a person, etc.; one's office, function, or business. —**pro-vin-cial** (prō-vin′shạl). [L. *provincialis.*] **I.** *a.* Of or pertaining to an ancient Roman province, a province or administrative division of a modern country, or an ecclesiastical province; formerly, of or pertaining to any of the American provinces of Great Britain; also, belonging or peculiar to some particular province or provinces rather than to the whole country (as, *provincial* customs; *provincial* idioms; *provincial* English); local; sometimes, of or pertaining to the provinces rather than the capital or the largest cities (as, the *provincial* press; "a second-rate *provincial* actress," L. Merrick's "Conrad in Quest of His Youth," xiii.); hence, having or showing the manners characteristic of inhabitants of a province or the provinces; exhibiting the narrowness of interests or view attributed to inhabitants of the provinces; narrow or illiberal; lacking the refinement or polish characteristic of the capital or the largest cities; countrified or rustic. **II.** *n.* A native or inhabitant of an ancient Roman province, or of a province of a modern country; formerly, an inhabitant of one of the American provinces of Great Britain; also, one who lives in or comes from the provinces rather than the capital or the largest cities (as, "Ask ten well-informed *provincials* which is the first hotel in London, and nine of them would certainly reply, the Grand Babylon": Arnold Bennett's "The Old Adam," iii.); a provincial or countrified person; *eccles.,* the head of an ecclesiastical province; a member of a religious order presiding over his order in a given district or province. —**pro-vin′cial-ism,** *n.* Provincial character or peculiarity; manners, habit of thought, etc., characteristic of a province

(variable) d̦ as d or j, ș as s or sh, ț as t or ch, z̦ as z or zh; o, F. *cloche;* ü, F. *menu;* c̆h, Sc. *loch;* n̦, F. *bonbon;* ′, primary accent; ″, secondary accent; †, obsolete; <, from; +, and; =, equals. See also lists at beginning of book.

or the provinces; narrowness of interests or view; lack of enlightenment or polish; also, a peculiarity confined to a province or district; esp., a word, expression, or mode of pronunciation peculiar to a province or district of a country; also, sometimes, devotion to one's own province and its interests before the country or nation as a whole.—**pro-vin-ci-al′i-ty** (-shi-al′i-ti), *n.*; pl. *-ties* (-tiz). Provincial character; a provincial characteristic or trait.—**pro-vin′cial-ly**, *adv.*

pro-vi-sion (prṓ-vizh′ọn), *n.* [OF. F. *provision*, < L. *provisio*(n-), < *providere*, E. *provide*.] Foresight†; also, the act of providing; arrangement or preparation beforehand, as for the doing of something, the meeting of needs, the supplying of means, etc. (as, to make *provision* for the carrying out of a plan; to make *provision* for the support of one's family); the providing or supplying of something, as of necessaries or food; also, something provided; a measure or other means for meeting a need; a supply or stock of something provided; esp., *pl.*, supplies of food (as, a dealer in *provisions*; *provisions* for a ship; "I have warriors, *provisions*, and ammunition in plenty to defend it [a post] three years," Bancroft's "Hist. of the U. S.," Amer. Revolution, ii. 4); also, *sing.*, a condition providing for something, as in a contract; a stipulation; a proviso; a clause in a legal instrument, a law, etc., providing for a particular matter; *eccles.*, appointment to an ecclesiastical office, esp. appointment by the Pope to a see or benefice not yet vacant.—**pro-vi′sion**, *v. t.* To supply with provisions, or stores of food: as, "a grant of two ships, *provisioned*, armed, and fully manned" (Besant's "Coligny," iv.); "The cave was well *provisioned*; they had bread, oil, figs, dried grapes, and wine" (J. H. Newman's "Callista," xxx.).—**pro-vi′sion-al**, *a.* Pertaining to or of the nature of a temporary provision or arrangement (as, *provisional* measures; a *provisional* agreement); provided for present need or for the time being (as, a *provisional* government or governor); temporarily established; temporary.—**pro-vi′sion-al-ly**, *adv.*—**pro-vi′sion-a-ry** (-ạ-ri), *a.* Provisional; also, pertaining to or of the nature of a provision or stipulation.—**pro-vi′sion-er**, *n.* One who furnishes, or deals in, provisions.

pro-vi-so (prṓ-vī′zō), *n.*; pl. *-sos* or *-soes* (-zōz). [L., abl. neut. of *provisus*, pp. of *providere*, E. *provide*.] A clause in a statute, contract, or the like, by which a condition is introduced; in general, a stipulation or condition.

pro-vi-sor (prṓ-vī′zọr), *n.* [AF. *provisour*, OF. F. *proviseur*, < L. *provisor*, one who provides, < *providere*, E. *provide*.] One who provides†; a purveyor†; also, a supervisor†; *eccles.*, the holder of a papal provision.

pro-vi-so-ry (prṓ-vī′zọ-ri), *a.* [F. *provisoire*, < L. *providere*, E. *provide*.] Provisional; also, containing a proviso or condition; conditional.—**pro-vi′so-ri-ly**, *adv.*

prov-o-ca-tion (prov-ọ-kā′shọn), *n.* [L. *provocatio*(n-).] The action of provoking; esp., incitement to action; instigation; something that incites or instigates (as, "This daring outrage on law, faith, and honour was a *provocation* to civil war": Morley's "Oliver Cromwell," i. 7); also, incitement to anger or irritation (as, to remain calm under severe *provocation*); a cause of anger or irritation.

pro-voc-a-tive (prṓ-vok′ạ-tiv). [LL. *provocativus*.] **I.** *a.* Tending or serving to provoke; inciting or stimulating to action, thought, etc.; irritating or vexing; calling forth or giving rise to something (with *of*: as, "a Falstaff, almost as *provocative* of laughter as his prototype," Hawthorne's "Twice-Told Tales," Howe's Masquerade). **II.** *n.* Something provocative; something that calls forth or gives rise to something else (as, "To joke him about some suitable widow . . . was a *provocative* of mirth ever fresh and ever young": Mrs. Stowe's "Oldtown Folks," xxxiv.); specif., something that excites appetite or lust.—**pro-voc′a-tive-ly**, *adv.*—**pro-voc′a-tive-ness**, *n.*

pro-voc-a-to-ry (prṓ-vok′ạ-tọ-ri), *a.* Same as *provocative*.

pro-voke (prṓ-vōk′), *v. t.*; *-voked*, *-voking*. [OF. F. *provoquer*, < L. *provocare* (pp. *provocatus*), call forth, challenge, provoke, < *pro*, before, + *vocare*, call.] To call forth†; summon†; also, to challenge†; defy†; also, to incite or stimulate (a person, etc.) to action (as, "Beauty *provoketh* thieves sooner than gold," Shakspere's "As You Like It," i. 3. 112); "Mine [shadow], spindling into longitude immense . . .

Provokes me to a smile," Cowper's "Task," v. 14); excite; rouse; also, to excite to anger or displeasure (as, "Charity . . . is not easily *provoked*," 1 Cor. xiii. 5; "Sometimes this attitude of hers *provoked* him," Howells's "Foregone Conclusion," v.); enrage; exasperate; vex; also, to stir up, arouse, or call forth (as, "Let my presumption not *provoke* thy wrath," Shakspere's "1 Henry VI.," ii. 3. 70; "a situation which in the country would have *provoked* meetings more or less public," Galsworthy's "Saint's Progress," iii. 6); give rise to, induce, or bring about (as, a drug which *provokes* a rise of temperature).—**pro-vok′er** (-vō′kẻr), *n.*—**pro-vok′ing**, *p. a.* That provokes; esp., exciting anger or irritation (as, "There's positively nothing to eat. It really is too *provoking*": Marryat's "King's Own," xlviii.).—**pro-vok′ing-ly**, *adv.*

prov-ost (prov′ọst), *n.* [Partly < AS. *profost*, also *prafost*, partly < OF. *provost*, for *prevost* (F. *prévôt*), by change of prefix (L. *pro* for *præ*), < L. *præpositus*, president, head, prop. pp. of *præponere*, place before: see *preposition*.] One appointed to superintend or preside, as the head of certain colleges or churches, the chief magistrate in Scottish burghs, etc.—**provost marshal**, in the army, an officer acting as head of police in a camp or district, and charged with the maintenance of order, etc.; in the navy, an officer charged with the safe-keeping of a prisoner pending trial by court-martial. [Often pron. prō′vō mär′shạl, in partial imitation of F. *prévôt*.]—**prov′ost-ship**, *n.*

prow¹ (prou), *n.* [OF. F. *proue*, < L. *prora*, < Gr. πρῷρα, prow, < πρό, before.] The fore part of a ship or boat; the bow; also, some thing or part resembling this, as the front end of an airship; also, a ship (poetic).

prow² (prou), *a.* [OF. *prou*, *pro* (F. *preux*), earlier *prud*, *prod*, valiant, gallant, good, perhaps connected with L. *prodesse*, be of use or profit: cf. *improve*, *proud*, *prude*, *prud'homme*, also *prowess*.] Valiant; brave; gallant. [Archaic.]

Prow of French Ship of War of about 1680.

prow-ess (prou′es), *n.* [OF. *proece* (F. *prouesse*), < *pro*: see *prow²*.] Valor; bravery; martial daring and skill; valorous achievement; also, a valiant or daring deed.—**prow′ess-ful** (-fúl), *a.*

prowl (proul), *v.* [ME. *prollen*; origin uncertain.] **I.** *intr.* To rove or go about stealthily in search of what may be found, as prey or plunder (as, "vagabond Indian dogs, *prowling* about in quest of food": Irving's "Captain Bonneville," iv.); hence, in general, to wander about stealthily, curiously, or idly (as, "He got up and *prowled* about his room, blundering against chairs and tables in the darkness": H. G. Wells's "Mr. Britling," ii. 4. § 8). **II.** *tr.* To rove over or through in search of what may be found; traverse stealthily, curiously, or idly.—**prowl**, *n.* The action or an act of prowling, as for prey or plunder: as, on the *prowl* (that is, prowling about); "some wild animal in its nightly *prowl*" (Jane Porter's "Scottish Chiefs," lxiv.).—**prowl′er**, *n.*—**prowl′ing-ly**, *adv.*

prox-i-mad (prok′si-mad), *adv.* [See *proximal* and *-ad*.] In *anat.*, toward the point of origin, or proximal part.

prox-i-mal (prok′si-mạl), *a.* [L. *proximus*, nearest, next, superl. adj. < *prope*, near.] Situated toward the point of origin or attachment, as of a limb or bone: opposed to *distal*.—**prox′i-mal-ly**, *adv.*

prox-i-mate (prok′si-mạt), *a.* [L. *proximatus*, pp. of *proximare*, come near, < *proximus*: see *proximal*.] Next; nearest; closely adjacent; also, coming next or very near in time; also, coming next in a chain of relation (as, a *proximate* cause); also, nearly or fairly accurate; approximate.—**proximate analysis**, in *chem.*, a form of analysis in which the constituent compounds of a complex mixture are determined. Cf. *ultimate analysis*.—**prox′i-mate-ly**, *adv.*—**prox′i-mate-ness**, *n.*

prox-im-i-ty (prok-sim′i-ti), *n.* [F. *proximité*, < L. *proximitas*, < *proximus*: see *proximal*.] The state of being proximate, near, or close by; nearness in place, time, or relation.

prox-i-mo (prok′si-mō), *adv.* [L., 'in the next (month),' abl. of *proximus*: see *proximal*.] In or of the next or coming month: as, on the 1st *proximo.* Abbreviated *prox.* **Cf.** *ultimo.*

prox-y (prok'si), *n.;* pl. *proxies* (-siz). [Contr. of *procuracy.*] The agency of a person deputed to act for another (as, "a person who did every thing by *proxy*": Godwin's "Caleb Williams," xxxv.); the action of a deputy or substitute; also, the person so deputed; an agent; a substitute; also, a writing authorizing the person or persons named to act, esp. to vote, for another; hence, a vote so given.

prude (pröd), *n.* [F. *prude,* a prude, as adj. prudish, from (or as in) OF. *preudefeme, prodefeme,* good or discreet woman, fem. corresponding to *prodome:* see *prud'homme.*] A woman (or sometimes a man) who affects extreme modesty or propriety.

pru-dence (prö'dẹns), *n.* [OF. F. *prudence,* < L. *prudentia,* < *prudens,* E. *prudent.*] The quality or fact of being prudent; cautious practical wisdom; good judgment; discretion; regard for one's own interests; provident care in management; economy or frugality; also, wisdom†; knowledge†.

pru-dent (prö'dẹnt), *a.* [OF. F. *prudent,* < L. *prudens* (*prudent-*), foreseeing, knowing, sagacious, judicious, contr. of *providens,* E. *provident.*] Wise, judicious, or wisely cautious in practical affairs, as persons; sagacious or judicious; discreet or circumspect; careful of one's own interests; provident, or careful in providing for the future; also, characterized by or proceeding from prudence, as conduct, action, etc. (as, "I thought it *prudent* not to exacerbate the growing moodiness of his temper by any comment": Poe's "Gold-Bug"); also, in general, wise†.

pru-den-tial (prö-den'shạl), *a.* Of, pertaining to, or characterized by prudence (as, *prudential* considerations or motives; a *prudential* policy); also, of persons, exercising prudence (as, "a numerous class of more thinking and *prudential* persons, who never-forsook them [the Puritans] till they became unfortunate": Scott's "Peveril of the Peak," iv.); also, having discretionary charge of certain matters (as, a *prudential* committee).—**pru-den'tial-ly,** *adv.*

pru-dent-ly (prö'dẹnt-li), *adv.* In a prudent manner.

prud-er-y (prö'dẻr-i), *n.;* pl. *-ies* (-iz). [F. *pruderie.*] Prudish quality; extreme modesty or propriety; *pl.,* prudish actions or speeches.

prud'-homme (prü-dom), *n.* [F. *prud'homme,* OF. *preud-home, prodome,* good or discreet man, < *prod,* good (see *prow²*), + *ome,* home (F. *homme*), < L. *homo* (*homin-*), man: cf. *prude.*] A member of a French tribunal appointed to arbitrate labor disputes.

prud-ish (prö'dish), *a.* Having the character of a prude; extremely proper; characteristic of a prude, as actions, etc.; also, fig., excessively formal or precise (as, "The trees are planted in *prudish* rows": Smollett's "Humphry Clinker," Aug. 8).—**prud'ish-ly,** *adv.*—**prud'ish-ness,** *n.*

pru-i-nose (prö'i-nōs), *a.* [L. *pruinosus,* < *pruina,* hoarfrost.] Covered with a frost-like bloom or powdery secretion, as a plant-surface.

prune¹ (prön), *n.* [OF. F. *prune,* < ML. *pruna,* for L. *prunum,* plum (*prunus,* plum-tree), < Gr. προῦνον, προύμνον, plum.] A plum†; now, a dried plum used for eating, cooked or uncooked; also, a variety of plum used for drying.—**prunes and prism** (or **prisms**), a mincing or affectedly nice manner of speaking or behaving: derived from the use of the phrase in Dickens's "Little Dorrit," ii. 5 ("Papa, potatoes, poultry, prunes, and prism, are all very good words for the lips: especially prunes and prism").

prune² (prön), *v. t.;* *pruned, pruning.* [ME. *pruynen, proynen;* origin uncertain: cf. *preen²* and *prune³.*] Of birds, to preen or dress (the feathers, etc.) with the beak; of persons, to arrange or dress carefully, as in making the toilet. [Archaic.]

prune³ (prön), *v. t.;* *pruned, pruning.* [ME. *prouynen,* < OF. *proognier, proignier,* prune (vines); origin uncertain: cf. *prune².*] To cut or lop superfluous twigs or branches from (a vine, bush, tree, etc.); trim; hence, to rid or clear of anything superfluous or undesirable (as, "an essay . . . *pruned* of its redundancies": S. Butler's "Way of All Flesh," xlvi.); also, to cut or lop off (twigs or branches); hence, to remove (superfluities, etc.).

pru-nel-la (prö-nel'ä), *n.* [= F. *prunelle,* supposed to be

named for its dark color from *prunelle,* sloe, dim. of *prune,* E. *prune¹.*] A strong, smooth, closely woven woolen fabric, commonly black, used esp. for the uppers of shoes.

pru-nelle (prö-nel'), *n.* [Cf. F. *prunelle,* sloe (see *prunella*), also obs. It. *prunella,* small plum.] A small yellow plum dried for the market, both skin and stone being removed.

prun-er (prö'nẻr), *n.* One who prunes.

prun-ing=hook (prö'ning-húk), *n.* An implement with a hooked blade, used for pruning vines, etc.

prunt (prunt), *n.* [Origin uncertain: cf. *print.*] An ornamental stud or shaped piece of glass fixed on a glass vessel; also, a tool with which such pieces are formed.—**prunt'ed,** *a.* Ornamented with prunts.

pru-ri-ent (prö'ri-ẹnt), *a.* [L. *pruriens* (*prurient-*), ppr. of *prurire,* itch.] Itching (rare: as, "In filthy sloughs they [swine] roll a *prurient* skin," Tennyson's "Palace of Art," 201); fig., morbidly uneasy, as desire or longing (as, "the reading public . . . in its usual *prurient* longing after anything like personal gossip or scandalous anecdote": Kingsley's "Alton Locke," xiv.); also, inclined to or characterized by lascivious thought; also, excessive in growth, as parts of a plant.—**pru'ri-ence, pru'ri-en-cy,** *n.*—**pru'ri-ent-ly,** *adv.*

pru-ri-go (prö-rī'gō), *n.* [L., < *prurire:* see *prurient.*] In *pathol.,* a skin affection characterized by itching papules.—**pru-rig'i-nous** (-rij'i-nus), *a.*

pru-ri-tus (prö-rī'tus), *n.* [L., < *prurire:* see *prurient.*] In *pathol.,* itching, esp. when without visible eruption.—**pru-rit'ic** (-rit'ik), *a.*

Prus-sian (prush'ạn), *a.* Of or pertaining to Prussia or its inhabitants.—**Prussian blue,** a deep-blue pigment, essentially a cyanogen compound of iron.—**Prus'sian,** *n.* A native or inhabitant of Prussia; orig., one of a Lettic people formerly inhabiting territory along and near the coast at the southeastern corner of the Baltic Sea; now, one of the people of modern Prussia, which is chiefly Germanic; also, the Lettic language spoken by the early Prussians ('Old Prussian'), extinct since the 16th or 17th century; also, the dialect of German spoken in modern Prussia.—**Prus'sian-ism,** *n.* The spirit, system, policy, or methods of the Prussians.—**Prus'sian-ize** (-īz), *v. t.;* *-ized, -izing.* To make Prussian; subject to Prussian domination or influence.—**Prus″sian-i-za'tion** (-i-zā'shọn), *n.*—**Prus'sian-iz-er** (-ī-zẻr), *n.*

prus-si-ate (prus'i-āt), *n.* In *chem.,* a salt of prussic acid.

prus-sic (prus'ik), *a.* [F. *prussique,* < *Prusse,* Prussia, in *bleu de Prusse,* Prussian blue.] In *chem.,* pertaining to or derived from Prussian blue: as, *prussic* acid (hydrocyanic acid).

pry¹ (prī), *n.;* pl. *pries* (prīz). [Reduced form of *prize³.*] Any instrument for raising or moving a thing by force of leverage, as a crowbar. [U. S. and prov. Eng.]—**pry¹,** *v. t.;* *pried, prying.* To raise, move, or force with a pry, or by force of leverage: as, "Run . . . and fetch something to *pry* open the door" (H. Melville's "Moby-Dick," xvii.). [U. S. and prov. Eng.]

pry² (prī), *v.;* *pried, prying.* [ME. *pryen, prien;* origin uncertain.] **I.** *intr.* To look closely or curiously, peer, or peep (as, "O eye of eyes, Why *pry'st* thou through my window? leave thy peeping": Shakspere's "Lucrece," 1089); hence, to search or inquire curiously or inquisitively into something (as, to *pry* into the affairs of others; "Let us not *pry* further into her secrets," Hawthorne's "Blithedale Romance," iv.). **II.** *tr.* To ferret or find (*out*) by curious searching or inquiry: as, "that inquisitive and busybody John Fry, who would *pry* out almost anything for the pleasure of telling his wife" (Blackmore's "Lorna Doone," xv.).—**pry²,** *n.;* pl. *pries* (prīz). The act of prying; a prying glance; also, an inquisitive person.—**pry'er,** *n.* See *prier.*—**pry'ing,** *p. a.* That pries; looking or searching curiously; unduly curious; inquisitive.—**pry'ing-ly,** *adv.*

pryt-a-ne-um (prit-ạ-nē'um), *n.;* pl. *-nea* (-nē'ä). [L., < Gr. πρυτανεῖον, < πρύτανις: see *prytanis.*] In ancient Greek states and cities, a public hall housing the official hearth of the community; esp., that of Athens, in which the hospitality of the city was extended to honored citizens, ambassadors, etc.

pryt-a-nis (prit'ạ-nis), *n.;* pl. *-nes* (-nēz). [L., < Gr. πρύτανις, prob. < πρό, before.] In certain ancient Greek

---

(variable) ḏ as d or j, ş as s or sh, ṭ as t or ch, ẓ as z or zh; *o,* F. *cloche;* ü, F. *menu;* ċh, Sc. *loch;* ṅ, F. *bonbon;* ′, primary accent; ″, secondary accent; †, obsolete; <, from; +, and; =, equals. See also lists at beginning of book.

states, a chief magistrate; in ancient Athens, a member of any of the ten sections of the council or senate during the presidency of that section, each section presiding for a period of five weeks.—**pryt′a-ny** (-ni), *n.*; pl. -*nies* (-niz). [Gr. πρυτανεία.] The office or dignity of a prytanis; also, each of the ten sections of the ancient Athenian council or senate during the presidency of that section; also, the period of five weeks during which each section presided.

psalm (säm), *n.* [AS. *sealm*, < LL. *psalmus*, < Gr. ψαλμός, song sung to the harp, orig. a plucking, as of strings, < ψάλλειν, pluck, twitch, play on a stringed instrument, sing to the harp.] A sacred or solemn song, or hymn (as, "Hymns devout and holy *psalms* Singing everlastingly," Milton's "At a Solemn Musick," 15; "crooning a strange *psalm* of victory," F. M. Crawford's "Mr. Isaacs," x.); hence, a poem of like character (as, "A *Psalm* of Life," the title of a poem by Longfellow); specif. [also *cap.*], any of the 150 sacred songs or hymns which together form a certain book of the Old Testament ("Book of Psalms"); a metrical version or paraphrase of any of these; pl. [*cap.*], the Book of Psalms; the Psalter.—**psalm**, *v. t.* To celebrate in psalms; hymn.—**psalm′ist**, *n.* The author of a psalm or psalms; [*cap.*] with *the*, David, the traditional author of the Psalms; also [*l. c.*], *eccles.*, one of a class of official singers in the church service, in early times, regarded in some branches of the church as constituting a minor order; a cantor or precentor.

psal-mo-dy (sal′mō-di or sä′mō-di), *n.*; pl. -*dies* (-diz). [LL. *psalmodia*, < Gr. ψαλμῳδία, < ψαλμός, psalm, + ἀείδειν, sing.] The act, practice, or art of singing psalms or hymns (as, "All of them joined in the *psalmody* with strong marks of devotion," Smollett's "Humphry Clinker," June 10; "He was also an expert in *psalmody*, having in his youth been the pride of the village singing-school," Mrs. Stowe's "Oldtown Folks," iv.); also, the arrangement of psalms for singing; also, psalms or hymns collectively.—**psal-mod-ic** (sal-mod′ik), *a.*—**psal′mo-dist**, *n.*

Psal-ter (sâl′tėr), *n.* [AS. *saltere*, also OF. *saltier* (F. *psautier*), < LL. *psalterium*, the Psalter, L. a psaltery: see *psaltery*.] The Book of Psalms, in the Old Testament; also [sometimes *l. c.*], a particular version of it, as for liturgical or devotional use, or a copy of such a version.—**psal-te′ri-an** (-tē′ri-an), *a.*

psal-te-ri-on (sal-tē′ri-on), *n.* Same as *psaltery*.

psal-te-ri-um (sal-tē′ri-um), *n.*; pl. -*ria* (-ri-ä). [LL., the Psalter (the folds of the omasum being likened to the leaves of a book).] The omasum, or manyplies.

psal-ter-y (sâl′tėr-i), *n.*; pl. -*ies* (-iz). [OF. *psalterie*, < L. *psalterium*, psaltery, LL. the Psalter, < Gr. ψαλτήριον, psaltery, later the Psalter, < ψάλλειν, pluck: see *psalm*.] An ancient musical instrument of the zither type, played by plucking the strings with the fingers or a plectrum.—**psal′tress**, *n.* A woman who plays on the psaltery.

psam-mite (sam′īt or psam′-), *n.* [F. *psammite*, < Gr. ψάμμος, sand.] In *geol.*, any sandstone: contrasted with *psephite*.—**psam-mit-ic** (sa-mit′ik or psa-), *a.*

pschent (psċhent), *n.* [Egypt.] In *archæol.*, the sovereign crown of all Egypt, composed of the white crown or tall, pointed miter of southern Egypt combined with the red crown, square in front and rising to a point behind, of northern Egypt: as, "Rameses, wearing the red and white *pschent*" (Amelia B. Edwards's "Thousand Miles up the Nile," xviii.). See cut in next column.

Psaltery of the 12th century.

pse-phite (sē′fīt or psē′-), *n.* [F. *pséphite*, < Gr. ψῆφος, pebble.] In *geol.*, any coarse fragmental rock, as breccia: contrasted with *psammite*.—**pse-phit-ic** (sē-fit′ik or psē-), *a.*

pseu-dax-is (sū-dak′sis or psū-), *n.* [See *pseudo-* and *axis*.] In *bot.*, same as *sympodium*.

pseu-de-pig-ra-pha (sū-de-pig′ra-fä or psū-), *n. pl.* [NL., < Gr. ψευδεπίγραφα, neut. pl. of ψευδεπίγραφος, falsely inscribed, bearing a false title, < ψευδής, false, + ἐπιγράφειν, inscribe: see *epigram*.] Writings or books inscribed

with a false title, or falsely ascribed to some one other than the true author; specif., certain writings (other than the canonical books and the Apocrypha) professing to be Biblical in character, but not considered canonical or inspired, or worthy of a place in religious use. —**pseu-de-pig′ra-phal, pseu-de-pig′ra-phous,** *a.* Having the character of pseudepigrapha; of or pertaining to pseudepigrapha. Also **pseu″dep-i-graph′ic** (-dep-i-graf′ik).

Pschent. — From reliefs of the temple-court of Edfu, Egypt.

pseudo-, pseud-. Forms of Gr. ψευδής, false, used in combination, as in *pseudo-apostle, pseudo-Christ, pseudo-Gothic.* Hence, **pseu′do** (sū′dō or psū′-), *a.* False; counterfeit; spurious; sham; pretended: as, "One played the part of the lion . . . another bolted . . . with the *pseudo* lion roaring after him" (J. H. Patterson's "Man-Eaters of Tsavo," xxii.).

pseu-do=ar-cha-ic (sū″dō-är-kā′ik or psū″-), *a.* [See *pseudo-*.] Professedly but not genuinely archaic.

pseu-do-carp (sū′dō-kärp or psū′-), *n.* [See *pseudo-* and -*carp*.] In *bot.*, a fruit which includes other parts in addition to the mature ovary and its contents, as the apple, pineapple, etc.—**pseu-do-car′pous** (-kär′pus), *a.*

pseu-do=clas-si-cism (sū″dō-klas′i-sizm or psū″-), *n.* [See *pseudo-*.] False, spurious, or sham classicism.

pseu-dol-o-gy (sū-dol′ō-ji or psū-), *n.* [Gr. ψευδολογία, < ψευδολόγος, speaking falsely, < ψευδής, false, + λέγειν, speak.] False speaking; lying; esp., lying considered as an art or a subject of study (humorous).—**pseu-do-log-i-cal** (sū-dō-loj′i-kal or psū-), *a.*—**pseu-dol′o-gist**, *n.*

pseu-do-morph (sū′dō-môrf or psū′-), *n.* [See *pseudo-* and -*morph*.] A false or deceptive form; in *mineral.*, a mineral having the form proper, not to its own substance, but to some other substance which has wholly or partially disappeared, as in consequence of chemical change. Cf. *paramorph.*—**pseu-do-mor′phic** (-môr′fik), *a.*—**pseu-do-mor′phism** (-fizm), *n.* The state of being a pseudomorph, or the process by which this is brought about.—**pseu-do-mor′phous** (-fus), *a.* Having a false form, or a form proper to something else; characterized by or pertaining to pseudomorphism.

pseu-do-nu-cle-in (sū-dō-nū′klē-in or psū-), *n.* [See *pseudo-*.] Same as *paranuclein*.

pseu-do-nym (sū′dō-nim or psū′-), *n.* [F. *pseudonyme*, < Gr. ψευδώνυμος, under a false name, < ψευδής, false, + ὄνυμα, name.] A false or fictitious name, esp. one assumed by an author in publishing his work.—**pseu-do-nym′i-ty** (-i-ti), *n.* Pseudonymous character; the use of a pseudonym or assumed name.—**pseu-don-y-mous** (sū-don′i-mus or psū-), *a.* [Gr. ψευδώνυμος.] Bearing a false name; esp., writing or written under an assumed or fictitious name, as an author or a book.—**pseu-don′y-mous-ly**, *adv.*

pseu-do-pod, pseu-do-pode (sū′dō-pod, -pōd, or psū′-), *n.* Same as *pseudopodium*.

pseu-do-po-di-um (sū-dō-pō′di-um or psū-), *n.*; pl. -*dia* (-di-ä). [NL., < Gr. ψευδής, false, + πούς (ποδ-), foot.] In *zoöl.*, a temporary protrusion of the protoplasm of a protozoan, serving as an organ of locomotion, prehension, etc.; also, the posterior extremity of a rotifer, serving as a swimming-organ, etc.—**pseu-do-po′di-al**, *a.*

pseu-do-scope (sū′dō-skōp or psū′-), *n.* [See *pseudo-* and -*scope*.] An optical instrument which makes concave objects appear convex, and convex objects concave.—**pseu-do-scop′ic** (-skop′ik), *a.*

pshaw (shâ or pshâ). **I.** *interj.* An exclamation expressing impatience, contempt, etc.: as, "Oh, *pshaw!* it doesn't sound a bit funny as I tell it" (G. W. Cable's "Cavalier," xxviii.). **II.** *n.* An exclamation of 'pshaw!' as, "My obtuseness provoked him into a contemptuous '*Pshaw!*'" (J. Conrad's "Lord Jim," viii.).—**pshaw**, *v.* **I.** *intr.* To say 'pshaw': as, "He fretted, pished and *pshawed*" (C. Brontë's "Jane Eyre," xxiv.). **II.** *tr.* To say 'pshaw' at or to.

psi (sī or psē), *n.* [Gr. ψῖ.] The twenty-third letter (Ψ, ψ, = English ps) of the Greek alphabet.

psi-lan-thro-pism (sī-lan'thrọ-pizm or psī-), *n.* [Gr. ψιλάνθρωπος, merely human, < ψιλός, bare, mere, + ἄνθρωπος, man.] The doctrine or belief that Jesus Christ was a mere man. Also **psi-lan'thro-py** (-pi).—**psi-lan'-thro-pist,** *n.*

psi-lom-e-lane (sī-lom'e-lān or psī-), *n.* [Gr. ψιλός, bare, mere, + μέλας (μελαν-), black.] A mineral consisting of a hydrous oxide of manganese, and occurring in smooth, black to steel-gray, botryoidal or stalactitic forms and in amorphous masses.

psi-lo-sis (sī-lō'sis or psī-), *n.* [NL., < Gr. ψίλωσις, < ψιλοῦν, strip bare, < ψιλός, bare.] In *pathol.*, the falling out of the hair; alopecia; also, a chronic disease, occurring chiefly in the tropics, characterized by diarrhea, ulceration of the mucous membrane of the digestive tract, and a smooth, shining appearance of the tongue.

psit-ta-cine (sit'ạ-sin or psit'-), *a.* [L. *psittacinus*, < *psittacus*, < Gr. ψιττακός, parrot.] Parrot-like; of the parrot kind.

pso-as (sō'as or psō'-), *n.* [NL., < Gr. ψόα.] In *anat.*, either of two muscles of the loin, one a large muscle ('psoas magnus') arising from the spinal column and inserted into the femur, and the other a small muscle ('psoas parvus'), frequently absent in man, arising from the spinal column and inserted into the brim of the pelvis.—**pso-ad-ic** (sō-ad'ik or psō-), *a.*

pso-ra (sō'rạ or psō'-), *n.* [L., < Gr. ψώρα, the itch.] In *pathol.*, the itch, esp. that due to the itch-mite.

pso-ra-le-a (sō-rā'lẹ-ạ or psō-), *n.* [NL., < Gr. ψωραλέος, scabby, < ψώρα, the itch; from the glandular dots sprinkled over the plant.] Any plant of the widely distributed fabaceous genus *Psoralea*, which comprises herbs and shrubs bearing compound leaves and spikes or racemes of purple, blue, red, or white flowers.

pso-ri-a-sis (sō-rī'ạ-sis or psō-), *n.* [NL., < Gr. ψωρίασις, < ψωριᾶν, have the itch, < ψώρα, the itch.] In *pathol.*, a chronic skin-disease characterized by the formation of scaly patches.—**pso-ri-at-ic** (sō-ri-at'ik or psō-), *a.*

psy-chal (sī'kạl or psī'-), *a.* [Gr. ψυχή, soul.] Of or pertaining to the soul; spiritual; psychic.

psy-cha-nal-y-sis (sī-kạ-nal'i-sis or psī-), etc. Same as *psychoanalysis.*

psy-chas-the-ni-a (sī-kạs-thē'ni-ạ or psī-), *n.* [NL., < Gr. ψυχή. soul, mind, + ἀσθένεια, weakness: see *asthenia*.] In *pathol.*, mental weakness or exhaustion.—**psy-chas-then'ic** (-then'ik), *a.*

Psy-che (sī'kẹ or psī'-), *n.* [L., < Gr. Ψυχή, personification of ψυχή, breath, spirit, soul, mind, < ψύχειν, breathe, blow.] In *class. myth.*, the soul or spirit personified, usually represented in art as a fair maiden, often with the wings of a butterfly, and fabled to have been beloved of Eros, or Cupid; also [*l. c.*], the human soul, spirit, or mind.— **Psyche knot,** a knot or knotted arrangement of a woman's hair projecting from the back of the head, such as is seen in various representations of Psyche in art.

psy-chi-a-ter (sī-kī'ạ-tẻr or psī-), *n.* [Gr. ψυχή, soul, mind, + ἰατήρ, ἰατρός, physician, < ἰᾶσθαι, heal.] One who treats mental diseases; an alienist; a psychiatrist.

—**psy-chi-at'ric, psy-chi-at'ri-cal** (-ki-at'rik, -ri-kạl), *a.* Of or pertaining to psychiatry. — **psy-chi'a-trist** (-kī'ạ-trist), *n.* One who is versed in or practises psychiatry; a psychiater.—**psy-chi'a-try** (-tri), *n.* [Gr. ψυχή +

Cupid (Eros) and Psyche. — Capitoline Museum, Rome.

ἰατρεία, healing.] The practice or the science of treating mental diseases.

psy-chic (sī'kik or psī'-). [Gr. ψυχικός, < ψυχή, soul, mind: see *Psyche*.] **I.** *a.* Of or pertaining to the human soul or mind; mental (as opposed to *physical*); due to mental influence or affection, as diseases; also, of or pertaining to the animal soul, as distinguished from the spiritual or higher soul; natural or animal; also, exerted by or proceeding from the mind or some spiritual or non-physical agency (as, *psychic* force, a supposed non-physical force or power assumed to operate in various obscure phenomena, as those of telepathy, clairvoyance, spiritualism, etc.; *psychic* influences); of the nature of such an agency; associated with or attributed to such agencies, as phenomena, etc.; of or pertaining to the class of phenomena associated with such agencies (as. *psychic* investigation or research); of persons, the mind, etc., specially susceptible to psychic influences. **II.** *n.* A person specially susceptible to psychic influences; a medium —**psy'chi-cal,** *a.* Psychic.—**psy'chi-cal-ly,** *adv.*—**psy'chics,** *n.* Psychology; also, the study of psychic phenomena

psycho-, psych-. Forms of Gr. ψυχή, breath, spirit, soul, mind, used in combination.

psy-cho-a-nal-y-sis (sī"kọ-ạ-nal'i-sis or psī"-), *n.* [See *psycho-*.] Psychic analysis; minute examination of the mind, as of a patient, with a view to ascertaining underlying mental causes producing certain disordered states (psychoses or neuroses).—**psy-cho-an'a-lyst** (-an'ạ-list), *n.* One who is versed in or practises psychoanalysis.—**psy"cho-an-a-lyt'ic** (-lit'ik), *a.* Pertaining to or of the nature of psychoanalysis.—**psy"cho-an-a-lyt'i-cal-ly,** *adv.*—**psy-cho-an'a-lyze** (-līz), *v. t.*; -lyzed, -lyzing. To examine by psychoanalysis, as a patient.

psy-cho-gen-e-sis (sī-kọ-jen'e-sis or psī-), *n.* [See *psycho-*.] The genesis or origin and development of the soul or mind; also, in *animal evolution*, origin or development due to psychic or mental activity.—**psy"cho-ge-net'ic** (-jẹ-net'ik), *a.*

psy-cho-gen-ic (sī-kọ-jen'ik or psī-), *a.* [See *psycho-* and *-genic*.] Of psychic origin, or dependent on psychic conditions or processes, as a mental disorder.

psy-chog-o-ny (sī-kog'ọ-ni or psī-), *n.* [See *psycho-* and *-gony*.] The genesis and development of the soul or mind.— **psy-cho-gon'ic** (-kọ-gon'ik), *a.*

psy-chog-ra-phy (sī-kog'rạ-fi or psī-), *n.* [See *psycho-* and *-graphy*.] Descriptive psychology; also, writing supposed to be due to a disembodied spirit.

psy-cho-log-ic, psy-cho-log-i-cal (sī-kọ-loj'ik, -i-kạl, or psī-), *a.* [See *psychology*.] Of or pertaining to psychology; hence, pertaining to the mind or to mental phenomena as the subject-matter of psychology; mental, psychic, or subjective (as, a condition of affairs that is purely *psychological*).— **psychological moment,** the most appropriate moment for effect on the mind; hence, the fitting or proper moment; the critical moment.—**psy-cho-log'i-cal-ly,** *adv.*—**psy-chol'o-gist** (-kol'ọ-jist), *n.* One versed in psychology.— **psy-chol'o-gize** (-jīz), *v.*; -gized, -gizing. **I.** *intr.* To make psychological investigations or speculations. **II.** *tr.* To study or investigate psychologically: as, "A man about town does not *psychologise* himself, he accepts his condition with touching simplicity" (Galsworthy's "Country House," i. 1).

psy-cho-logue (sī'kọ-log or psī'-), *n.* [F.] A psychologist.

psy-chol-o-gy (sī-kol'ọ-ji or psī-), *n.*; pl. -gies (-jiz). [NL. *psychologia*, < Gr. ψυχή, soul, mind, + -λογία, < λέγειν, speak.] The science of mind, or of mental states and processes; the science which treats of the analysis, laws of connection, and conditions of mental phenomena; also, a treatise, or a system of teaching, on this science; also, popularly, analysis of the mental states and processes of a person or of a number of persons, esp. as determining action; the mental states and processes of a person or of a number of persons, esp. as determining action (as, "The *psychology* of the fighting man in war had never as yet been made the subject of a professorial treatise": Buchan's "Hist. of the Great War," liii.).

psy-cho-man-cy (sī'kọ-man-si or psī'-), *n.* [Gr. ψυχόμαντις, a necromancer, < ψυχή, spirit, soul, + μάντις, a diviner.] Necromancy†; also, occult communication between souls or with spirits.—**psy-cho-man'tic,** *a.*

psy-chom-e-ter (sī-kom′e-tẽr or psī-), n. [See *psycho-* and *-meter.*] One supposed to possess the faculty of psychometry; in *psychol.,* an instrument used in psychometry.—**psy-cho-met′ric, psy-cho-met′ri-cal** (-kō̇-met′rik, -ri-kạl), a. Pertaining to or of the nature of psychometry.—**psy-chom′e-trist,** n. One supposed to possess the faculty of psychometry; in *psychol.,* one skilled in psychometry.—**psy-chom′e-trize** (-trīz), v. t.; *-trized, -trizing.* To practise the art of psychometry upon (an object).—**psy-chom′e-try** (-tri), n. [See *-metry.*] The alleged art or faculty of divining the properties of an object, or matters associated with it, through contact with or proximity to it; also, in *psychol.,* the measurement of the duration and relations of mental states and processes.

psy-cho-mo-tor (sī-kō̇-mō′tọr or psī-), a. [See *psycho-* and *motor.*] Inducing movement by mental action, or pertaining to such movement.

psy-cho-neu-ro-sis (sī″kō̇-nū-rō′sis or psī″-), n.; pl. *-roses* (-rō′sēz). [NL.: see *psycho-* and *neurosis.*] In *pathol.,* a mental disease or diseased condition without organic lesion. —**psy″cho-neu-rot′ic** (-rot′ik), a.

psy-cho-path (sī′kō̇-path or psī′-), n. [See *psychopathy.*] One affected with psychopathy.—**psy-cho-path′ic,** a. Pertaining to, affected with, or engaged in treating psychopathy.—**psy-chop′a-thist** (-kop′ạ-thist), n.

psy-cho-pa-thol-o-gy (sī″kō̇-pạ-thol′ō̇-ji or psī″-), n. [See *psycho-.*] Mental pathology.—**psy″cho-pa-thol′o-gist,** n.

psy-chop-a-thy (sī-kop′ạ-thi or psī-), n. [See *psycho-* and *-pathy.*] Mental disease or disorder; also, the treatment of disease by mental or psychic influence.

psy-cho-phys-ics (sī-kō̇-fiz′iks or psī-), n. [See *psycho-.*] That department of psychology which deals with the physical aspects of mental phenomena.—**psy-cho-phys′i-cal,** a.—**psy-cho-phys′i-cist** (-sist), n.

psy-cho-phys-i-ol-o-gy (sī″kō̇-fiz-i-ol′ō̇-ji or psī″-), n. [See *psycho-.*] That department of physiology which deals with mental phenomena.—**psy″cho-phys-i-ol′o-gist,** n.

psy-cho-pomp (sī′kō̇-pomp or psī′-), n. [Gr. ψυχοπομπός, < ψυχή, spirit, soul, + πέμπειν, send.] One who conducts spirits or souls to the other world, as Hermes or Charon.

psy-cho-sis (sī-kō′sis or psī-), n.; pl. *-choses* (-kō′sēz). [NL., < Gr. ψυχή, mind.] In *pathol.,* any form of mental affection or disease; in *psychol.,* a psychic or mental process, esp. as corresponding to a nerve-action, or neurosis; also, the state of consciousness at any given time.

psy-cho-so-mat-ic (sī″kō̇-sō̇-mat′ik), a. [See *psycho-* and *somatic.*] Having bodily symptoms of a mental origin.

psy-cho-ther-a-peu-tics (sī″kō̇-ther-ạ-pū′tiks or psī″-), n. [See *psycho-.*] The branch of therapeutics concerned with the treatment of disease by psychic influence, as by mental suggestion.—**psy″cho-ther-a-peu′tic,** a.—**psy″cho-ther-a-peu′tist,** n.—**psy-cho-ther′a-py** (-pi), n. Treatment of disease by psychic influence.

psy-chot-ic (sī-kot′ik or psī-), a. Of or pertaining to a psychosis.

psy-chrom-e-ter (sī-krom′e-tẽr or psī-), n. [Gr. ψυχρός, cold: see *-meter.*] A kind of hygrometer, consisting of two thermometers, one having its bulb covered with wet cloth.

ptar-mi-gan (tär′mi-gạn), n.; pl. *ptarmigans* or (esp. collectively) *ptarmigan.* [Appar. < Gael. *tarmachan.*] Any of various species of grouse of the genus *Lagopus,* characterized by feathered feet, and found in mountainous and cold regions. See cut in next column.

pter-i-dol-o-gy (ter-i-dol′ō̇-ji or pter-), n. [Gr. πτερίς (πτεριδ-), fern: see *-logy.*] The branch of botany that treats of ferns.—**pter″i-do-log′i-cal** (-dō̇-loj′i-kạl), a.—**pter-i-dol′o-gist,** n.

pter-i-do-phyte (ter′i-dō̇-fīt or pter′-), n. [NL. *Pteridophyta,*

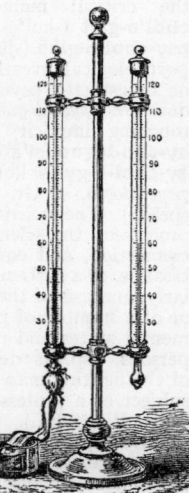

Psychrometer.

pl., < Gr. πτερίς (πτεριδ-), fern, + φυτόν, plant.] Any of the *Pteridophyta,* a primary division of the vegetable kingdom comprising plants (as the ferns and allied plants) which are without seeds, have vascular tissue, and are differentiated into root, stem, and leaf.—**pter″i-do-phyt′ic** (-fit′ik), a.

Rock Ptarmigan (*Lagopus rupestris*), in winter plumage.

pter-o-dac-tyl (ter-ō̇-dak′til or pter-), n. [NL. *Pterodactylus* (genus-name), < Gr. πτερόν, wing, + δάκτυλος, finger or toe.] Any member of the *Pterosauria,* an order of extinct flying reptiles (sometimes measuring 20 feet between the wing-tips) having one digit of the fore limb

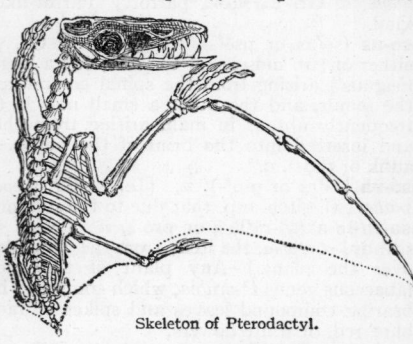

Skeleton of Pterodactyl.

greatly elongated and supporting a wing-membrane.

pter-o-pod (ter′ō̇-pod or pter′-). [NL. *Pteropoda,* pl., < Gr. πτερόπους (-ποδ-), wing-footed, < πτερόν, wing, + πούς (ποδ-), foot.] **I.** n. Any of the *Pteropoda,* a group of mollusks which have the lateral portions of the foot expanded into wing-like lobes. **II.** a. Belonging or pertaining to the *Pteropoda.*—**pte-rop-o-dan** (te-rop′ō̇-dạn or pte-), a. and n.—**pte-rop′o-dous,** a.

pter-o-saur (ter′ō̇-sâr or pter′-), n. [NL. *Pterosauria,* pl., < Gr. πτερόν, wing, + σαῦρος, lizard.] A flying reptile of the order *Pterosauria;* a pterodactyl.—**pter-o-sau′ri-an,** a. and n.

-pterous. [Gr. -πτερος, < πτερόν, feather, wing.] An adjective termination meaning 'winged,' as in *brachypterous, dipterous, micropterous, tetrapterous.*

Pteropod (*Clione borealis*).

pter-y-goid (ter′i-goid or pter′-), a. [Gr. πτερυγοειδής, wing-like, < πτέρυξ (πτερυγ-), wing, + εἶδος, form.] Wing-like; in *anat.,* noting or pertaining to a certain process ('pterygoid process': see below) of the sphenoid bone.—**pterygoid process,** in *anat.,* either of two processes descending, one on each side, from the point where the body of the sphenoid bone unites with an alisphenoid bone, each process consisting of two plates ('external pterygoid plate' and 'internal pterygoid plate') separated by a notch; also, either of these two plates.—**pter′y-goid,** n. In *anat.,* a pterygoid process, muscle, etc.

pter-y-la (ter′i-lạ or pter′-), n.; pl. *-læ* (-lē). [NL., < Gr. πτερόν, feather, + ὕλη, wood, forest.] In *ornith.,* one of the definite tracts or areas on the skin of a bird, on which feathers grow.—**pter-y-log′ra-phy** (-log′rạ-fi), n. [See *-graphy.*] The description of pterylæ; a treatise on pterylosis.—**pter-y-lo′sis** (-lō′sis), n. [NL.] In *ornith.,* the arrangement or disposition of the feathers of a bird in definite tracts, or pterylæ.

ptis-an (tiz′ạn), n. [OF. F. *tisane,* < L. *ptisana,* < Gr. πτισάνη, peeled barley, barley-water, < πτίσσειν, peel.]

A nourishing decoction, often having a slight medicinal quality, orig. one made from barley.

Ptol-e-ma-ic (tol-ẹ-mā'ik), *a.* Of or pertaining to Ptolemy, an astronomer who lived at Alexandria in the 2d century A.D.: as, the *Ptolemaic* system of astronomy (a system elaborated by Ptolemy and subsequently modified by others, according to which the earth was the fixed center of the universe, with the heavenly bodies, which were thought to be set in a series of concentric revolving heavens or transparent spherical shells, moving about it). Also, of or pertaining to the Ptolemies, a dynasty of Macedonians who ruled in Egypt from 323 to 30 B.C.—**Ptol-e-ma'ist**, *n.* A believer in the Ptolemaic system of astronomy.

pto-ma-ine, pto-ma-in (tō'mạ-in or ptō'-, commonly tō'mān), *n.* [It. *ptomaina*, < Gr. πτῶμα, dead body, < πίπτειν, fall.] In *chem.*, any of a class of basic organic compounds, some of them very poisonous, produced in animal and vegetable matter during putrefaction.

pto-sis (tō'sis or ptō'-), *n.* [NL., < Gr. πτῶσις, a falling, < πίπτειν, fall.] In *pathol.*, a falling or drooping of the upper eyelid, due to paralysis of its levator muscle.—**pto'tic**, *a.*

pty-a-lin (tī'ạ-lin or ptī'-), *n.* [Gr. πτύαλον, spittle, saliva, < πτύειν, spit.] In *physiol. chem.*, an enzyme contained in the saliva of man and certain of the lower animals, possessing the property of converting starch into dextrin and maltose.

pty-a-lism (tī'ạ-lizm or ptī'-), *n.* [Gr. πτυαλισμός, < πτυαλίζειν, expectorate, < πτύαλον: see *ptyalin*.] Excessive secretion of saliva; salivation.

pub (pub), *n.* [Abbr. of *public*.] A public house; a tavern: as, "A man might have gone to a *pub*, and got decently drunk" (Kipling's "Light That Failed," iv.). [Slang, British.]

pu-ber-ty (pū'bėr-ti), *n.* [L. *pubertas*, < *puber*, *pubes*, adult.] Sexual maturity; the earliest age at which a person is capable of procreating offspring (in common law presumed to be 14 years in the male and 12 years in the female).

pu-bes (pū'bēz), *n.* [L., < *pubes*, adult.] The hair appearing on the lower part of the abdomen at the age of puberty; hence, the lower part of the hypogastrium; also, in *bot.*, pubescence.

pu-bes-cence (pū-bes'ẹns), *n.* The state or fact of being pubescent; in *bot.* and *zoöl.*, a soft, downy growth occurring on certain parts of various plants and animals; also, the fact of having such a growth.

pu-bes-cent (pū-bes'ẹnt), *a.* [L. *pubescens* (*-ent-*), ppr. of *pubescere*, reach puberty, become hairy or downy, < *pubes*, adult.] Arriving or arrived at puberty; in *bot.* and *zoöl.*, covered with down or fine short hair.

pu-bic (pū'bik), *a.* Pertaining to the pubes or pubis.

pu-bis (pū'bis), *n.*; pl. *-bes* (-bēz). [For NL. *os pubis*, bone of the pubes.] In *anat.*, that part of either innominate bone which, with the corresponding part of the other, forms the front of the pelvis.

pub-lic (pub'lik), *a.* [Formerly *publick*; OF. F. *public*, < L. *publicus*, earlier *poplicus*, < *populus*, E. *people*.] Of, pertaining to, or affecting the people as a whole, or the community, state, or nation (as, *public* opinion; *public* buildings; *public* affairs; "To the *publick* good Private respects must yield," Milton's "Samson Agonistes," 867); done, made, acting, etc., for the people or community as a whole (as, *public* relief of the poor; a *public* prosecutor); also, open to all the people (as, a *public* meeting); not restricted to any person or persons, or any particular class of the community; that may be used, enjoyed, shared, or competed for by all, or by all properly qualified; often, maintained at the public expense, under public control, and open to the public generally (as, a *public* library); also, open to the view or knowledge of all (as, "not willing to make her a *publick* example," Mat. i. 19; "The fact became *public*," Arnold Bennett's "Helen with the High Hand," ii.); existing, done, etc., in public; also, pertaining to or engaged in the affairs or service of the community or nation (as, *public* office or employment; a *public* official); also, holding a position of general influence in the community, or having relations with or being known to the public generally (as, a *public* man; a *public* character); pertaining to a person regarded as a public character or considered in his relations or intercourse with the public generally (as, a statesman speaking in his *public* capacity; the *public* life or actions of a man); also, devoted or directed to the interests of the community (as, *public* spirit); also, international (as, *public* law).—**public house**, an inn or hostelry; esp., in British use, a tavern.—**public school**, in England, orig., a grammar-school founded or endowed for the benefit of the public and carried on under some form of public control; now, any of certain large endowed boarding-schools, patronized esp. by the wealthy classes, which prepare pupils mainly for the universities or for the public service; in the U. S., a school maintained at the public expense for the education of the youth of a community or district, as part of a system of public (and usually free) education (commonly forming one of a series of graded schools including *primary schools*, comprising the first four grades or years of the standard course, *grammar-schools*, the second four grades or years, and *high schools*, the last four years, the primary schools and grammar-schools together being known as *elementary* or *common schools*, the high schools, as distinguished from these, as *secondary schools*: see also *high school*, under *high*, *a.*).—**public=service corporation**, a corporation formed or chartered to render service to the general public, as in operating a street-railway, furnishing gas or electric light, or the like.—**pub'lic**, *n.* The people constituting a community, state, or nation; also, a particular section of the people (as, the novel-reading *public*); also, public view or access (in 'in public'); also, a public house (colloq., British).

pub-li-can (pub'li-kạn), *n.* [L. *publicanus*, < *publicum*, public revenue, prop. neut. of *publicus*, E. *public*.] In ancient Rome, one who farmed the public revenues; a tax-gatherer; hence, any collector of toll, tribute, or the like; also, the keeper of a public house (British: as, "The *publican* took the opportunity to present my hero with a bill . . . for bottles of spirits supplied to his wife," S. Butler's "Way of All Flesh," lxxv.).

pub-li-ca-tion (pub-li-kā'shọn), *n.* [OF. F. *publication*, < L. *publicatio(n-)*, < *publicare*: see *publish*.] The act of publishing, or the state or fact of being published; public announcement; the publishing of a book, periodical, map, piece of music, engraving, or the like; also, that which is published, as a book, periodical, or the like.

pub-li-cist (pub'li-sist), *n.* [F. *publiciste*, < *public*, E. *public*.] One versed in public or international law; also, one who is versed in or writes on current public or political affairs.

pub-li-ci-ty (pub-lis'i-ti), *n.* [F. *publicité*, < *public*, E. *public*.] The state of being public, or open to general observation or knowledge; in recent use, esp., the state of being brought to public notice by announcements or advertisements, mention in the press, or any means serving to effect the purpose; public notice as the result of advertising or other special measures; hence, the measures, process, or business of securing public notice (as, "a campaign of *publicity* announcing the most popular attractions offered by any magazine of the day," Bok's "Americanization of Edward Bok," xviii.: often attrib., as, *publicity* work, a *publicity* agent).

pub-li-cize (pub'li-sīz), *v. t.*; *-cized*, *-cizing*. To give publicity to; bring to public notice; advertise.

pub-lic-ly (pub'lik-li), *adv.* In a public or open manner; without reserve or privacy; openly; also, by the public or community; in the name of the community; by public or common action or consent.—**pub'lic-ness**, *n.*

pub-lic=spir-it-ed (pub'lik-spir'i-ted), *a.* Having or showing an unselfish desire for the public good.

pub-lish (pub'lish), *v. t.* [OF. F. *publier*, < L. *publicare*, make public property, make publicly known, publish, < *publicus*, E. *public*.] To make publicly or generally known (as, "*Publish* it that she is dead," Shakspere's "Much Ado about Nothing," iv. 1. 206; "Far from desiring to *publish* the connection, he became as anxious to conceal it as myself," C. Brontë's "Jane Eyre," xxvii.); declare or announce openly; specif., in legal use, to communicate or exhibit, as a libel or a will, to a limited number of persons regarded as representing the public; also, to announce formally or officially (as, "The Charter was *published* throughout the whole country": Green's "Short Hist. of the Eng. People,"

iii. 3); proclaim; promulgate; also, to proclaim as being something specified†; sometimes, to denounce†; also, to issue, or cause to be issued, in copies made by printing or other process, for sale or distribution to the public, as a book, periodical, map, piece of music, engraving, or the like.— **pub′lish-a-ble**, *a.* That may be published.— **pub′lish-er**, *n.* One who publishes; esp., one whose business is the publishing of books, periodicals, engravings, or the like.— **pub′lish-ment**, *n.* Publication.

puc-coon (pu-kön′), *n.* [N. Amer. Ind.] Any of certain plants which yield a red dye, as the bloodroot (*Sanguinaria canadensis*) and certain herbs of the boraginaceous genus *Lithospermum.*

puce (pūs). [F., lit. 'flea,' < L. *pulex* (*pulic-*), flea.] **I.** *a.* Purplish-brown. **II.** *n.* A purplish-brown color.

puck (puk), *n.* [AS. *pūca* (also *pūcel*) = Icel. *pūki*, a mischievous demon: cf. *poker*[3].] A malicious or mischievous demon or spirit; a goblin; [*cap.*] a particular mischievous or tricksy sprite or fairy, also called *Hobgoblin* and *Robin Goodfellow*, who appears as a character in Shakspere's "Midsummer Night's Dream"; also [*l. c.*], a rubber disk used in place of a ball in hockey.

puck-a (puk′ạ), *a.* [Hind. *pakkā*, cooked, ripe, mature.] Solid; substantial; permanent; reliable; good. [Anglo-Ind.]

puck-er (puk′ėr), *v. t.* or *i.* [Appar. a freq. form connected with *poke*[2] (bag).] To draw or gather into wrinkles or irregular folds.— **puck′er**, *n.* A wrinkle; an irregular fold; a puckered part, as of cloth tightly or crookedly sewed; also, a state of agitation or perturbation (colloq.).— **puck′er-y**, *a.* Puckered; puckering; tending to pucker.

puck-ish (puk′ish), *a.* [Also *cap.*] Resembling, or characteristic of, the fairy Puck; mischievous; impish.— **puck′-ish-ness**, *n.*

puc-ras, puk-ras (puk′rạs), *n.* [Native name.] Any pheasant of the genus *Pucrasia*, of the Himalaya region and parts of India and China, distinguished by the long crests and ear-tufts of the males.

pud-ding (pud′ing), *n.* [ME. *puddyng, poding*; origin uncertain.] A piece of intestine of an animal, stuffed with seasoned minced meat, etc., and cooked by boiling; also, a dish made in many forms and of various materials, as flour (or rice, tapioca, or the like), milk, and eggs, with fruit or other ingredients or seasoning, and commonly sweetened. — **pud′ding= head**, *n.* A pudding-headed or stupid person. [Colloq.]— **pud′ding=**

Pucras (*Pucrasia macrolopha*).

head″ed, *a.* Stupid: as, "a *pudding-headed* fellow" (S. Butler's "Way of All Flesh," i.). [Colloq.]— **pud′ding=stone**, *n.* In *geol.*, a conglomerate.

pud-dle (pud′l), *n.* [ME. *puddel, podel*, appar. dim. < AS. *pudd*, ditch.] A small pool of water, esp. dirty water, as in a road after rain; sometimes, a small pool of any liquid; also, clay, or a similar material, which has been mixed with water and tempered, used as a water-tight lining, etc.— **pud′dle**, *v.*; -*dled, -dling.* **I.** *tr.* To mark or fill with puddles; wet with dirty water, etc.; also, to make (water) muddy or dirty; also, in fig. use, to muddle or confuse; sully; also, to make (clay, etc.) into puddle; also, to cover with, or render water-tight by the use of, pasty clay or puddle; also, to subject (pig-iron) to the process of puddling. **II.** *intr.* To dabble about in water, mud, etc.; fig., to busy one's self in an untidy or disorderly manner.— **pud′dler**, *n.*— **pud′-dling**, *n.* The act of one who puddles; esp., the process of converting pig-iron into wrought-iron by heating and stirring the molten metal in a reverberatory furnace, in the presence of an oxidizing agent; also, puddle (pasty clay, etc.).— **pud′dly**, *a.* Full of puddles; puddle-like.

pu-den-cy (pū′dẹn-si), *n.* [LL. *pudentia*, < L. *pudens* (*pudent-*), ppr. of *pudere*, feel shame.] Shamefacedness; modesty.

pu-den-dum (pū-den′dum), *n.*; pl. -*da* (-dạ). [L., neut. of *pudendus*, that one should be ashamed of, gerundive of *pudere*, feel shame.] In *anat.*, the external genital organs, esp. those of the female: commonly in *pl.*—**pu-den′dal**, *a.*

pudg-y (puj′i), *a.*; compar. *pudgier*, superl. *pudgiest.* [Origin obscure.] Short and fat or thick: as, "Mr. Isaac Worthington . . . sitting next to the Rev. Mr. Sweet, who is rather *pudgy* by contrast" (W. Churchill's "Coniston," i. 11); "A *pudgy* hand was laid on his shoulder" (Thackeray's "Vanity Fair," xxii.).— **pudg′i-ness**, *n.*

pu-di-bund (pū′di-bund), *a.* [L. *pudibundus*, < *pudere*, feel shame.] Shamefaced; modest; prudish.

pu-di-ci-ty (pū-dis′i-ti), *n.* [F. *pudicité*, < L. *pudicus*, modest, < *pudere*, feel shame.] Modesty; chastity.

pueb-lo (pweb′lō), *n.*; pl. -*los* (-lōz). [Sp., people, town, village, < L. *populus*, E. *people.*] In Spanish America, a town or village; in New Mexico and adjoining regions, a village of certain partly civilized Indians, built of adobe or stone in the form of a communal house or group of houses; also [*cap.*], one of these Indians; also [*l. c.*], in the Philippine Islands, a town or a township.

pu-er-ile (pū′ẹ-ril), *a.* [L. *puerilis*, < *puer*, child, boy.] Of or pertaining to a child or boy; childish or juvenile; now, usually, merely childish; childishly foolish, irrational, trifling, or trivial (as, *puerile* excuses; "Such ravings, invented by the pen of fiction, would seem *puerile* caricature," Motley's "Dutch Republic," iii. 9).— **pu′er-ile-ly**, *adv.*— **pu-er-il′i-ty** (-ẹ-ril′i-ti), *n.*; pl. -*ties* (-tiz). The quality of being puerile; childish foolishness or triviality; also, something puerile; a puerile act, idea, remark, etc.

pu-er-pe-ra (pū-ėr′pẹ-rạ), *n.* [L., < *puer*, child, + *parere*, bring forth.] In *obstet.*, a woman in childbed, or in the period immediately following parturition.— **pu-er′pe-ral**, *a.* Of or pertaining to a woman in childbed; pertaining to or consequent on childbirth.— **pu-er-pe-ri-um** (pū-ėr-pē′ri-um), *n.* [L.] In *obstet.*, the state of a woman at and immediately following childbirth.

puff (puf), *v.* [ME. *puffen*, puff, blow; of imit. origin.] **I.** *intr.* To blow with short, quick blasts, as the wind; be emitted in a puff or puffs; also, to emit a puff or puffs; breathe quick and hard, as after violent exertion (as, "The grave was deep, and Mr. Trigg assisted in filling it, *puffing* very much over the task": W. H. Hudson's "Far Away and Long Ago," iii.); go with puffing or panting (as, "as she *puffed*, with her stoutness, up the stairs": Arnold Bennett's "Old Wives' Tale," ii. 5); emit puffs or whiffs of vapor or smoke (as, "The ship lay in the stream; busy little boats and *puffing* steamers darted about it": G. W. Curtis's "Prue and I," iii.); move with such puffs (as, "The engines of the Truro Railroad are now *puffing* in and out of the yards": W. Churchill's "Coniston," ii. 2); take puffs or whiffs at a cigar, etc. (as, "Agg . . . was *puffing* violently at a cigarette": Arnold Bennett's "Roll-Call," vii.); also, to blow abruptly from the lips to express scorn or contempt† (as, "As for all his enemies, he *puffeth* at them": Ps. x. 5); also, to become inflated or distended (usually with *up*). **II.** *tr.* To send forth (air, vapor, etc.) in short, quick blasts (as, "The old man *puffed* a prodigious cloud of smoke": G. W. Curtis's "Prue and I," v.); drive or impel by puffing, or with a short, quick blast (as, "A radical in thought, he *puffed* away With shrewd contempt the dust of usage gray": Lowell's "Fitz Adam's Story," 29); blow or put (*out*) by a puff (as, to *puff* out a light); puff at or smoke (a cigar, cigarette, etc.: as, "He *puffed* his Caporal . . . and found that he had lost his relish for French tobacco," L. Merrick's "Conrad in Quest of His Youth," i.); also, to inflate or distend with breath or air (as, "Shaw *puffed* his cheeks and frowned": J. Conrad's "Rescue," iv. 4); distend in any way, as by stuffing, bunching up, etc.; arrange in puffs, as the hair; fig., to inflate with pride, vanity, conceit, etc. (often with *up*: as, "The heart is *puffed* with pride," W. B. Yeats's "Land of Heart's Desire"; "Alf was not a nice child, being *puffed* up with many school-board certificates for good conduct," Kipling's "Light That Failed," xiv.); elate; also, to commend or praise in inflated or exaggerated language; give exaggerated praise to, often from interested motives; advertise with exaggerated or undue commendation; also, to apply (powder) with a powder-puff; apply powder to (the face, etc.) with a powder-puff.— **puff,** *n.* An act of puffing; a short, quick blast, as of wind or breath (as, "*Puffs* of wind blew about her head": J. Conrad's "Rescue," iv. 4); an abrupt emission of air, vapor, etc.; a whiff, as at a pipe; the sound of an abrupt emission of air, etc.; a small quantity of vapor, smoke, etc., emitted at one blast (as, "There came a *puff* of smoke, and then a report, and a shot plunged in the waves": Stevenson's "Master of Ballantrae," iii.); also, breath (prov. or slang: as, out of *puff*); also, an inflated or distended part or thing; a swelling; a protuberance; a portion of material gathered and held down at the edges but left full in the middle, as in dress, etc.; a cylindrical roll of hair; a form of light pastry with a filling of cream, jam, or the like; a powder-puff (as, "She produced a little bag and gazed at herself in a little mirror, and patted her chin with a little *puff*": Arnold Bennett's "Great Man," xxiv.); also, a puffball (prov.); also, inflated or exaggerated praise, esp. as uttered or written from interested motives; a commendation, esp. an exaggerated one, of a book, an actor's performance, etc.; also, a braggart or boaster (archaic).

puff=ad-der (puf′ad″ėr), *n.* A large, venomous African serpent, *Bitis* (or *Clotho*) *arietans*, which puffs up its body when irritated.

puff-ball (puf′bâl), *n.* Any of various fungi of the genus *Lycoperdon* and allied genera, characterized by a ball-like spore-case which gives off a cloud of spores when broken.

Puffball (*Lycoperdon*).

puff=bird (puf′bėrd), *n.* Any of the usually plain-colored, chiefly South American birds constituting the subfamily *Bucconinæ* (family *Galbulidæ*): so called from their habit of puffing out their feathers.

puff-er (puf′ėr), *n.* One who or that which puffs; esp., any of various fishes capable of inflating the body, as a globe-fish; also, a porpoise.— **puff′-er-y** (-i), *n.*; pl. *-ies* (-iz). The act or practice of puffing, or praising unduly; exaggerated commendation; a piece of puffing.

Puff-bird (*Malacoptila fusca*).

puf-fin (puf′in), *n.* [Origin uncertain.] Any of various sea-birds (genera *Fratercula* and *Lunda*) of the auk family, with a curious bill, as *F. arctica*, the common species, which abounds on both coasts of the northern Atlantic, nesting in holes in the ground.

puff-i-ness (puf′i-nes), *n.* Puffy condition.

puff-ing=ad-der (puf′ing-ad″ėr), *n.* Same as *hognose*.

puff=paste (puf′pāst′), *n.* A very light, flaky, rich paste for pies, tarts, etc.

Common Puffin (*Fratercula arctica*).

puff-y (puf′i), *a.*; compar. *puffier*, superl. *puffiest*. Coming in or characterized by puffs, as the wind; gusty; also, short-winded, as persons; also, inflated or distended with air, etc.; puffed out or swollen (as, "having . . . omitted to brush their hair out of their *puffy* eyes": Arnold Bennett's "Old Wives' Tale," iii. 7); fat or corpulent (as, "a very stout, *puffy* man": Thackeray's "Vanity Fair," iii.); fig., puffed up, vain, or conceited; turgid or bombastic.

pug[1] (pug), *n.* [Var. of *puck*.] An imp†; a goblin†; also, a monkey†; also, a name for the fox (as, "the sight of poor wearied *pug*, his once gracefully-floating brush all draggled and drooping": Kingsley's "Yeast," i.); also, one of a breed of dogs, slightly resembling the bulldog, but smaller; also, a pug-nose.

pug[2] (pug), *v. t.*; pugged, pugging. [Origin uncertain: cf. *poke*[3].] To knead (clay, etc.) with water to make it plastic, as in brickmaking; also, to stop or fill in with clay or the like; pack or cover with mortar, etc., to deaden sound.— **pug**[2], *n.* Pugged or plastic clay or the like.

pug[3] (pug), *n.* [Hind. *pag*.] A footprint, as of an animal. [Anglo-Ind.]— **pug**[3], *v. t.* or *i.*; pugged, pugging. To track (game, etc.) by footprints. [Anglo-Ind.]

pug[4] (pug), *n.* Shortened form of *pugilist*. [Slang.]

pug=dog (pug′dog′), *n.* See *pug*[1].

pug-gree, pug-ga-ree (pug′rē, pug′a̱-rē), *n.* Same as *pugree*.

pugh (pö or pụh), *interj.* [Cf. *pooh*.] An exclamation of contempt or disgust.

pu-gi-lism (pū′ji-lizm), *n.* [L. *pugil*, boxer, akin to *pugnus*, fist, and *pugnare*, fight.] The art or practice of fighting with the fists; boxing.— **pu′gi-list,** *n.* One who fights with the fists; a boxer.— **pu-gi-lis′tic,** *a.*— **pu-gi-lis′ti-cal-ly,** *adv.*

pug=mill (pug′mil), *n.* [See *pug*[2].] A machine for pugging or tempering clay or the like.

pug-na-cious (pug-nā′shus), *a.* [L. *pugnax* (pugnac-), < *pugnare*, fight: cf. *pugilist*.] Disposed to fight; given to fighting; quarrelsome: as, "a young cuckoo . . . very fierce and *pugnacious* . . . sparring and buffeting with its wings like a game-cock" (G. White's "Nat. Hist. of Selborne," ii. 7); "A firm mouth and square chin gave her a *pugnacious* appearance" (Besant's "All Sorts and Conditions of Men," viii.).— **pug-na′cious-ly,** *adv.*— **pug-na′-cious-ness, pug-na′ci-ty** (-nas′i-ti), *n.*

pug=nose (pug′nōz′), *n.* A short nose turning abruptly up at the tip, like that of the pug-dog.— **pug′=nosed,** *a.*

pug-ree (pug′rē), *n.* [Hind. *pagrī*, turban.] A light turban worn by natives in India (as, "The old maharajah . . . wore a plain white *pugree* with a large jewel set on one side": F. M. Crawford's "Mr. Isaacs," v.); also, a scarf of silk or cotton wound round a hat or helmet and falling down behind, as a protection against the sun.

puis-ne (pū′ni). [Archaic form of *puny*.] In *law*: **I.** *a.* Younger; inferior in rank; junior, as in appointment; also, later. **II.** *n.* A puisne or junior judge.

pu-is-sance (pū′i-sans or pū-is′ans), *n.* [OF. F., < *puissant*, E. *puissant*.] Power, might, or force (archaic); also, an armed force†.

pu-is-sant (pū′i-sant or pū-is′ant), *a.* [OF. F. *puissant*, < L. *posse*, be able, have power: see *potent*.] Powerful; mighty; potent; of dominating authority or influence: as, "the subservient language that was natural toward so *puissant* and successful a ruler as Elizabeth" (Morley's "Oliver Cromwell," i. 2). [Archaic.]— **pu′is-sant-ly,** *adv.*

puke (pūk), *v. i.* or *t.*; puked, puking. [Origin uncertain.] To vomit. See Shakspere's "As You Like It," ii. 7. 144. [Now prov. or vulgar.]

puk-ka (puk′a̱), *a.* See *pucka*.

puk-ras (puk′ras), *n.* See *pucras*.

pul-chri-tude (pul′kri-tūd), *n.* [L. *pulchritudo*, < *pulcher*, beautiful.] Beauty; comeliness. [Archaic or humorous.] — **pul-chri-tu′di-nous** (-tū′di-nus), *a.*

pule (pūl), *v. i.*; puled, puling. [Cf. F. *piauler*, cheep, peep, whine; imit.] To cry in a thin voice, as a child; whimper; whine; also, to peep plaintively, as a chicken.— **pul-er** (pū′lėr), *n.*— **pul′ing-ly,** *adv.*

pulk, pul-ka (pulk, pul′ka̱), *n.* [Lapp.] A boat-like traveling-sledge drawn by a single reindeer, used in Lapland.

Pulk.

pull (pụl), *v. t.* [AS. *pullian*, pull, pluck: cf. MLG. *pulen*, strip of husks, pick.] To draw or tug at with force (as, to

pull a person's hair); draw or haul toward one's self or itself, or in a particular direction, or into a particular position (as, to *pull* a trigger; to *pull* a sled up a hill; to *pull* one's hat down over one's eyes); draw, rend, or tear (*apart, to pieces,* etc.); also, to draw or pluck away from a place of growth, attachment, etc. (as, to *pull* a tooth); pluck (fruit, flowers, etc.: now chiefly prov.); also, to strip of feathers, hair, etc., as a bird, a hide, etc.; also, to draw out for use, as a knife or a pistol (slang); also, to put or carry through (something attempted: slang: cf. *to pull off,* below); also, to propel by rowing, as a boat; convey in a boat by rowing (as, "We *pulled* the agent ashore": Dana's "Two Years before the Mast," xiv.); also, to be provided with, or rowed with (a certain number of oars, as a boat (as, "She *pulled* fifty oars, but had only thirty-six manned": Marryat's "Mr. Midshipman Easy," xxx.); also, to arrest (a person) or raid (a place) (slang); in *printing,* to take (an impression or proof) from type, etc.; in *horse-racing,* to hold in or check (a horse), esp. so as to keep it from winning; in *cricket,* to hit (a ball pitched on the wicket or on the off side) to the on side; in *golf,* to play (the ball) with a curve to the left (or, if a left-handed player, to the right).—**to pull a face,** to draw one's face into a grimace; make a face or grimace.—**to pull down,** to demolish by separating the parts, as a building; reduce to ruins; also, to destroy, as an institution; put an end to; also, to depose, as a sovereign; overthrow, as a government; also, to humble; humiliate; also, to lower, reduce, or depress in value, strength, spirits, etc.—**to pull off,** to put through successfully, as something attempted; succeed in carrying out: as, "I thought it would be a pretty close thing, but felt confident that Brock . . . would manage to *pull* it *off*" (J. H. Patterson's "Man-Eaters of Tsavo," xxii.). [Slang.]—**to pull one's leg,** to impose upon, take in, or hoax a person; play upon one's credulity. [Slang.]—**to pull one's self together,** to gather together one's faculties, energies, etc., with an effort; recover one's self: as, "Gecko . . . pondered . . . Then he *pulled himself together* with an effort" (Du Maurier's "Trilby," viii.).—**to pull the strings** or **wires,** to pull the strings or wires that cause the movements of a puppet or marionette; fig., to set in operation secret means of directing the action of others who are ostensibly acting by their own impulse.—**to pull through,** to bring or get (a person, etc.) through a difficult or dangerous situation or condition (as, "It was I who *pulled* him *through* the last famine": F. M. Crawford's "Mr. Isaacs," v.); bring (a thing) to a successful issue.—**to pull up,** to pluck or tear up, as out of the ground; hence, to remove utterly; extirpate; also, to bring (a horse) to a stand by pulling on the reins; bring (anything) to a standstill; check in any course of action; also, to arrest and take before a magistrate (colloq.); also, to reprimand or reprove (colloq.).—**pull,** *v. i.* To exert a drawing, tugging, or hauling force (often with *at*); often, to pull an oar or oars so as to move a boat (as, "Our boat's crew . . . *pulled* with all their strength": Marryat's "Peter Simple," xxxiii.); row; proceed by rowing (as, "Hiring a skiff, he *pulled* up stream": Galsworthy's "Dark Flower," ii. 19); be propelled by rowing (as, "The other boats . . . had *pulled* alongside": Marryat's "King's Own," xlvi.); in general, to make the way or get (*in,* etc.) as by a pull or effort (as, to *pull* out; to *pull* through: see phrases below); also, to become or come as specified, by pulling (as, a stitch *pulls* out; a rope *pulls* apart).—**to pull for,** to row toward (as, to *pull for* the shore); also, to employ one's efforts, resources, or influence for the benefit of (a person, etc.: slang).—**to pull out,** to draw or move out from a position occupied, as a train from a station; hence, to take one's departure (colloq.); withdraw, as from an undertaking (colloq.).—**to pull through,** to get through a difficult or dangerous situation or condition.—**to pull together,** to work in harmony; get on together.—**to pull up,** to bring a horse or vehicle to a stop; come to a standstill, as a horse or vehicle does; in general, to come to a stop (as, "Michel projected himself outside headlong, but after a stumble or two *pulled up*": J. Conrad's "Rover," xiv.); also, to move toward the front in a race or other contest.—**pull,** *n.* An act of pulling or drawing; a tug; the action of pulling or drawing; force expended in pulling; pulling power; specif., a pulling at an oar, or a spell at rowing; a pulling of the ball

in cricket or golf (see *pull, v. t.*); a drawing of a draft of liquid into the mouth, or a drink (colloq.: as, "Take a *pull* at my flask," Weir Mitchell's "Hugh Wynne," xvi.); also, an advantage possessed by one person, etc., over another or others (slang: as, "that they may know what their chances are, and who naturally has the *pull* over them," Thackeray's "Newcomes," xli.); also, influence, as with persons able to grant favors (slang: as, "They used their . . . '*pull*' in Italian banking to favour German enterprises," H. G. Wells's "Italy, France, and Britain at War," ii. 3); also, an impression or proof pulled from type, etc.; also, a part or thing to be pulled, as a handle or the like; an instrument or device for pulling something.—**pull'=back,** *n.* A retarding influence; a check; a drawback. [Now colloq.]—**pull'er,** *n.*

pul-let (pùl′et), *n.* [OF. F. *poulet,* chicken, also *poulette,* young hen, dim. < *poule,* hen, < ML. *pulla,* fem. of L. *pullus,* young animal, chicken: cf. *foal.*] A young hen.

pul-ley (pùl′i), *n.*; pl. *pulleys* (-iz). [OF. F. *poulie*; origin uncertain.] A wheel with a grooved rim for carrying a line, turning in a frame or block and serving to change the direction of or transmit power, as in pulling at one end of the line to raise a weight suspended at the other end; a combination of such wheels in a block, or of such wheels or blocks in a tackle, serving to increase the power applied; also, a wheel driven by or driving a belt or the like, as in the transmission of power.—**idle pulley.** See under *idle, a.*

Pull-man (pùl′man), *n.* [From George M. *Pullman* (1831–97), the originator.] A railroad parlor-car or sleeping-car, strictly one made by the Pullman Company.

pul-lu-late (pul′ū-lāt), *v. i.*; *-lated, -lating.* [L. *pullulatus,* pp. of *pullulare,* < *pullulus,* sprout, orig. young animal, dim. of *pullus*: see *pullet.*] To come forth in growth; sprout; be produced as offspring; spring up abundantly; also, to send forth sprouts, buds, etc.; breed; multiply; teem.—**pul-lu-la′tion** (-lā′shon), *n.*

pul-mom-e-ter (pul-mom′e-tėr), *n.* [L. *pulmo,* lung: see *-meter.*] An instrument for measuring the capacity of the lungs; a spirometer.—**pul-mom′e-try** (-tri), *n.*

pul-mo-na-ry (pul′mō-nā-ri), *a.* [L. *pulmonarius,* < *pulmo(n-),* lung, akin to Gr. πλεύμων, later πνεύμων, lung: see *pneumonic.*] Of or pertaining to the lungs; of the nature of a lung, or lung-like; affecting the lungs; pertaining to or affected with disease of the lungs; also, having lungs or lung-like organs.—**pulmonary artery,** an artery conveying (venous) blood directly from the heart to the lungs.—**pulmonary vein,** a vein conveying (arterial) blood directly from the lungs to the heart.

pul-mo-nate (pul′mō-nāt). [NL. *pulmonatus,* < L. *pulmo(n-),* lung: see *pulmonary.*] **I.** *a.* Having lungs or lung-like organs; specif., belonging to the *Pulmonata,* an order or group of gastropod mollusks usually breathing by means of a lung-like sac, and including most of the terrestrial snails and the slugs and certain aquatic snails. **II.** *n.* A pulmonate gastropod.

pul-mon-ic (pul-mon′ik), *a.* [F. *pulmonique,* < L. *pulmo(n-),* lung: see *pulmonary.*] **I.** *a.* Of, pertaining to, or affecting the lungs. **II.** *n.* A medicine for disease of the lungs; also, a person who is affected with disease of the lungs.

pul-mo-tor (pul-mō′tor), *n.* [L. *pulmo,* lung, + *motor,* E. *motor.*] A mechanical device for inducing artificial respiration where respiration has ceased entirely or in part through asphyxiation, drowning, etc. [Proprietary name.]

pulp (pulp), *n.* [L. *pulpa,* fleshy substance, pulp.] A soft or fleshy part of an animal body; the inner substance of a tooth; the succulent part of a fruit; the pith of the stem of a plant; also, any soft, moist, slightly cohering mass, as that into which linen, wood, etc., are converted in the making of paper; in *mining,* ore pulverized and mixed with water; slimes; also, dry crushed ore.—**pulp,** *v.* **I.** *tr.* To reduce to pulp; also, to remove the pulp from. **II.** *intr.* To become reduced to pulp.—**pulp′er,** *n.* A machine for reducing fruit, wood, etc., to pulp.

pulp-i-fy (pul′pi-fī), *v. t.*; *-fied, fying.* [See *-fy.*] To reduce to pulp.—**pulp″i-fi-ca′tion** (-fi-kā′shon), *n.*—**pulp′-i-fi-er** (-fī-ėr), *n.*

pulp-i-ness (pul′pi-nes), *n.* Pulpy state or consistence.

pul-pit (pul′pit), *n.* [L. *pulpitum,* stage, platform, ML.

fat, fāte, fär, fȧll, ȧsk, fāre; net, mē, hėr; pin, pīne; not, nōte, mŏve, nôr; up, lūte, pùll; oi, oil; ou, out; (lightened) aviȧry, ēlect, agŏny, intŏ, ŭnite; (obscured) errȧnt, operȧ, ardẹnt, actọr, natụre; ch, chip; g, go; th, thin; ᵺ, then; y, you;

pulpit in a church.] A stage or rostrum, as for public speaking (archaic); also, a platform or raised structure in a church, from which the clergyman delivers the sermon or conducts the service; also, with *the*, preachers collectively, or the Christian ministry. —**pul-pit-eer′** (-pĭ-tēr′), *n.* A preacher by profession: usually contemptuous. Also **pul′pit-er.**

pul-pous (pul′pus), *a.* [L. *pulposus*.] Pulpy.

pulp-y (pul′pi), *a.* Of the nature of or resembling pulp; fleshy; soft.

pul-que (pul′kā), *n.* [Mex. Sp.] A fermented drink made from the juice of certain species of agave.

Pulpit of Niccolò Pisano, in the Baptistery at Pisa, Italy.

pul-sate (pul′sāt), *v. i.*; *-sated, -sating.* [L. *pulsatus*, pp. of *pulsare*, push, strike, beat, freq. of *pellere*: see *pulse*[2].] To expand and contract rhythmically, as the heart; beat; throb; in general, to vibrate; quiver.—**pul′sa-tile** (-sạ-til), *a.* Pulsating; throbbing; also, played by striking, as a musical instrument.

pul-sa-til-la (pul-sạ-til′ä), *n.* [ML., < L. *pulsare* (in allusion to the beating about of the flower in the wind): see *pulsate*.] Any of the perennial herbs with white or purplish flowers constituting the ranunculaceous genus *Pulsatilla*, certain species of which are medicinal; a pasque-flower; also, an extract or the like obtained from such a plant.

pul-sa-tion (pul-sā′shọn), *n.* [L. *pulsatio(n-)*, < *pulsare*: see *pulsate*.] The act or an act of pulsating; beating or throbbing; a beat or throb, as of the pulse; vibration or undulation; a single vibration.—**pul′sa-tive** (-sạ-tiv), **pul′sa-to-ry** (-tọ-ri), *a.* Pulsating; pulsatile.—**pul-sa′tor** (-sā′tọr), *n.* [L., striker, beater.] Something that pulsates, beats, or strikes; specif., a pulsometer (pump); also, a device for separating diamonds from earthy material after mining.

pulse[1] (puls), *n.* [OF. *pols, pouls*, < L. *puls* (*pult-*), thick pap made of meal, pulse, etc.: cf. *poultice*.] The esculent seeds of certain leguminous plants, as peas, beans, lentils, etc.; also, a plant, or the plants, producing such seeds.

pulse[2] (puls), *n.* [OF. *pous* (F. *pouls*), < L. *pulsus*, a pushing, beating, pulse, < *pellere*, drive, push, strike, beat.] The regular throbbing of the arteries caused by the successive contractions of the heart, esp. as felt in an artery at the wrist, and usually with reference to the frequency or character of the throbs as indicating the state of health; also, a single beat or throb of the arteries or the heart; also, in fig. use, life or vitality; feeling, sentiment, or tendency; a throb of life, emotion, etc.; also, the rhythmic recurrence of strokes, vibrations, or undulations (as, "the measured *pulse* of racing oars": Tennyson's "In Memoriam," lxxxvii.); a single stroke, vibration, or undulation (as, "the last faint *pulse* of quivering light": Keble's "Christian Year," ii.).—**pulse**[2], *v.*; *pulsed, pulsing.* **I.** *intr.* To beat or throb, as an artery or the heart; pulsate; in general, to beat, vibrate, or undulate. **II.** *tr.* To drive or send out as by pulses or rhythmic beats.—**pulse′less**, *a.* Having no pulse or pulsation; lifeless; without feeling; motionless.—**pulse′=warm″er**, *n.* A covering for the wrist to protect against cold; a wristlet.—**pulse′=wave**, *n.* The wave of raised tension and arterial expansion which starts from the aorta with each ventricular systole and travels to the capillaries.

pul-sim-e-ter (pul-sim′e-tẻr), *n.* [L. *pulsus*, pulse: see *-meter*.] An instrument for measuring the strength or quickness of the pulse.

pul-sion (pul′shọn), *n.* [LL. *pulsio(n-)*, < L. *pellere*: see *pulse*[2].] The act of driving or pushing forward.

pul-som-e-ter (pul-som′e-tẻr), *n.* [L. *pulsus*, pulse: see *-meter*.] An instrument for measuring the strength or quickness of the pulse; also, a pump for raising water, operating by steam but having no piston.

pul-ta-ceous (pul-tā′shius), *a.* [L. *puls* (*pult-*), thick pap: see *pulse*[1].] Resembling pap; semifluid; pulpy.

pul-ver-a-ble (pul′ve-rạ-bl), *a.* [L. *pulverare*, reduce to dust, < *pulvis* (*pulver-*), dust.] Capable of being reduced to dust or powder. Also **pul′ver-iz-a-ble** (-ve-rī-zạ-bl).

pul-ver-ize (pul′ve-rīz), *v. t.* or *i.*; *-ized, -izing.* [F. *pulvériser*, < LL. *pulverizare*, < L. *pulvis* (*pulver-*), dust.] To reduce or become reduced to dust or powder, as by pounding, grinding, etc.—**pul″ver-i-za′tion** (-ve-ri-zā′shọn), *n.*—**pul′ver-iz-er** (-ve-rī-zẻr), *n.*

pul-ver-u-lent (pul-ver′ọ-lẹnt), *a.* [L. *pulverulentus*, < *pulvis* (*pulver-*), dust.] Consisting of dust or fine powder; also, crumbling to dust; also, covered with dust or powder.—**pul-ver′u-lence**, *n.*

pul-vil-lus (pul-vil′us), *n.*; pl. *pulvilli* (-ī). [L., dim. of *pulvinus*, cushion.] In *entom.*, a cushion-like pad or process on an insect's foot.

pul-vi-nate (pul′vi-nāt), *a.* [L. *pulvinatus*, < *pulvinus*, cushion.] Cushion-like; cushion-shaped. Also **pul′vi-nat-ed** (-nā-ted).

pul-vi-nus (pul-vī′nus), *n.*; pl. *-ni* (-nī). [L., cushion.] In *bot.*, a cushion-like swelling at the base of a leaf or leaflet, at the point of junction with the axis.

pu-ma (pū′mä), *n.* [Peruvian.] The cougar.

pum-ice (pum′is), *n.* [OF. *pomis*, < L. *pumex* (*pumic-*): cf. *pounce*[2].] A porous or spongy form of lava, used, esp. when powdered, as an abrasive, etc.—**pum′ice**, *v. t.*; *-iced, -icing.* To rub, smooth, clean, etc., with pumice.—**pu-mi-ceous** (pū-mish′ius), *a.* [L. *pumiceus.*] Consisting of or resembling pumice.—**pum′ice-stone**, *n.* Pumice.

pum-mel (pum′ẹl), etc. See *pommel*, etc.

pum-me-lo (pum′e-lō), *n.* Same as *pomelo*.

pump[1] (pump), *n.* [Origin uncertain.] A light, low slipper-like shoe worn by men and women, orig. for dancing.

pump[2] (pump), *n.* [ME. *pumpe* = D. *pomp* = MLG. and G. *pumpe*, pump.] An apparatus or machine for raising, driving, exhausting, or compressing fluids, as by means of a piston or plunger.—**pump**[2], *v.* **I.** *intr.* To work a pump; raise or move water, etc., with a pump; also, to operate as a pump does; also, to exert one's self in a manner likened to pumping (as, to *pump* for words); seek to elicit information from a person; also, to move up and down like a pump-handle; perform some operation by action like that on a pump-handle. **II.** *tr.* To raise, drive, drive, etc., with a pump (as, "They *pumped* the sea into the conduits": Froude's "Cæsar," xxiii.); also, to free from water, etc., by means of a pump (as, "They were *pumping* the ship . . . and lo! no inconsiderable oil came up with the water": H. Melville's "Moby-Dick," cix.); also, to inflate (a pneumatic tire, etc.) by pumping (often with *up*); also, to drive, force, etc., as if from a pump (as, to *pump* bullets at a foe); also, to subject to a process likened to pumping, in order to extract something (as, to *pump* one's brains for ideas); seek to elicit information from, as by artful questioning (as, "His aunt drew from him . . . details of his home and school life . . . but he had no idea that he was being *pumped*": S. Butler's "Way of All Flesh," xxxii.); also, to extract or bring forth by a process likened to pumping (as, "The prize was delivered to Tom with as much effusion as the superintendent could *pump* up": Mark Twain's "Tom Sawyer," iv.); elicit (information) by questioning; also, to operate by action like that on a pump-handle; supply with air, as an organ, by means of a pump-like device; also, to put out of breath (colloq.).—**pump′er**, *n.*

Cast-iron House-pump. — *a*, lever; *b*, plunger or piston; *c*, fulcrum; *d*, cylinder or barrel; *e*, lower valve, or foot-valve; *f*, base, supporting all other parts.

pum-per-nick-el (pum′pẽr-nik″ĕl, G. pům′-), n. [G.] A coarse, slightly sour bread made of unbolted rye.

pum-pion (pum′pion), n. [OF. *pompon, popon,* < L. *pepo(n-),* melon, pumpkin: see *pepo.*] A pumpkin. [Obs. or rare.]

pump-kin (pump′kin), n. [Altered form of *pumpion.*] A large orange-yellow fruit borne by a coarse, decumbent cucurbitaceous vine, *Cucurbita pepo,* much used for making pies and as food for cattle; also, the vine; sometimes, any of certain varieties of squash.—**some pumpkins.** See under *some, a.*—**pump′kin=seed,** n. The seed of the pumpkin; also, any of various fresh-water sunfishes, esp. *Eupomotis gibbosus* of eastern North America.

pump=room (pump′rŏm), n. A room or building where a pump is worked; esp., a room or place at a spa or mineral spring where the water is dispensed for drinking, etc. (as, "I was yesterday at the *pump-room,* and drank about a pint of the water": Smollett's "Humphry Clinker," April 23).

pump=well (pump′wel), n. A well having a pump; also, a compartment containing the pumps of a ship.

pun[1] (pun), v. t.; punned, punning. [Var. of *pound*[2].] To pound; reduce to powder by beating; beat. [Obs. or prov. Eng.]

pun[2] (pun), n. [Origin obscure.] The use of a word in such a manner as to bring out different meanings or applications, or of words alike or nearly alike in sound but different in meaning, for the purpose of producing a humorous effect; a play on a word or words. Examples of pun are the B. Franklin quotation at *to hang together,* under *hang, v. i.,* and "They went and *told* the sexton, and The sexton *toll'd* the bell," from Hood's ballad of "Faithless Sally Brown."—**pun**[2], v. i.; punned, punning. To make puns; play on words.

pu-na (pö′nä), n. [Peruvian.] A high, arid plateau, as in the Peruvian Andes.

punch[1] (punch), v. t. [Appar. < *puncheon*[1].] To pierce or perforate with a pointed or cutting instrument; cut, stamp, etc., with a punch; force or drive with a punch; make with a pointed or other instrument, or a punch, as a hole; also, to poke or prod, as with a stick (as, "With a goad he *punched* each furious dame": Chapman's tr. Homer's "Iliad," vi.); drive (cattle: western U. S.: as, "Steve and I started *punching* cattle together at the Bordeaux outfit, north of Cheyenne," Wister's "Virginian," xxxi.); also, to give a sharp thrust or blow to, esp. with the fist (as, "I felt like *punching* his head": W. Churchill's "Coniston," ii. 8). —**punch**[1], n. A tool or apparatus for piercing, perforating, or stamping materials, impressing a design, forcing nails beneath a surface, driving bolts out of holes, and the like; also, a thrusting blow, esp. with the fist; hence, fig., a vigorous, telling effect or force (slang: as, an editorial with a *punch*); vigorous effectiveness (slang: as, a story or a play that lacks *punch*; "Why can't Stan Graff . . . write a letter like that? With *punch!* With a kick!": Sinclair Lewis's "Babbitt," iii.).

Punch. — *a,* piece to be punched; *p,* punch; *h,* handle; *s,* support for *a; t,* tongs. The punch is operated by striking with a hammer or sledge at *m.* The tongs are usually held in the left hand of the smith, and the handle of the punch in his right hand, his assistant delivering the blows.

Punch[2] (punch), n. [Abbr. of *Punchinello.*] The chief character in the puppet-show called "Punch and Judy," represented as a grotesque, hook-nosed, humpbacked figure who strangles his child, beats his wife (Judy) to death, etc.—**as pleased as Punch,** very much pleased: as, "I rode away *as pleased as Punch*" (Rolf Boldrewood's "Sydney-Side Saxon," ii.).

punch[3] (punch), n. [Hind. *panch,* five (meaning five ingredients), < Skt. *pañca,* five: see *five.*] A beverage consisting of wine or spirits mixed with water, milk, etc., and flavored with sugar, lemon, spices, etc.—**Roman punch.** See under *Roman, a.*—**punch′=bowl,** n. A bowl in which the ingredients of punch are mixed, and from which it is served by means of a ladle.

pun-cheon[1] (pun′chon), n. [OF. *ponchon, poinchon* (F. *poinçon),* ult. < L. *pungere* (pp. *punctus),* prick, pierce: cf. *pungent.*] Any of various pointed instruments; a punch;

a stamping-tool; also, a short upright timber in a framing; also, a slab of timber, or a piece of a split log, with the face roughly dressed, used for flooring, etc. (as, "The floors were made of rived *puncheons,* hewn smooth on one surface": Roosevelt's "Winning of the West," i. 7).

pun-cheon[2] (pun′chon), n. [OF. *poinchon* (F. *poinçon);* origin uncertain: cf. *puncheon*[1].] A large cask of varying capacity, or its volume as a measure. [Now chiefly hist.]

punch-er (pun′chẽr), n. One who or that which punches; specif., a cow-puncher (western U. S.: as, "Judge Henry gave me charge of him and some other *punchers* taking cattle," Wister's "Virginian," xxxv.).

Pun-chi-nel-lo (pun-chi-nel′ō), n.; pl. -los or -loes (-lōz). [It. *Pulcinella,* prob. orig. dim. < *pulcino,* chicken, < L. *pullus:* see *pullet.*] The chief character in a puppet-show of Italian origin, being the prototype of Punch; hence [cap. or l. c.], any similar grotesque or absurd person or thing.

punch-ing=bag (pun′ching-bag), n. A bag or ball, usually inflated but sometimes stuffed, which is suspended from above or supported on a flexible rod, and punched with the fists as an exercise.

punc-tate (pungk′tāt), a. [NL. *punctatus,* < L. *punctum,* E. *point.*] Marked or studded with points or dots; having minute spots or depressions scattered over the surface. Also **punc′tat-ed** (-tā-ted).—**punc-ta′tion** (-tā′shon), n. Punctate condition or marking; one of the marks, or minute spots or depressions.

punc-til-io (pungk-til′iō), n.; pl. -ios (-iōz). [It. *puntiglio* and Sp. *puntillo,* dim. < L. *punctum,* E. *point.*] A small point†; a point of time†; also, a nice point, particular, or detail, as of conduct, ceremony, or procedure (as, "The personal honour of knighthood rendered those who possessed it jealous of every *punctilio*": Scott's "Castle Dangerous," viii.); also, strictness or exactness in the observance of forms (as, "I had no leisure to heed the niceties of *punctilio*": C. B. Brown's "Wieland," xii.).—**punc-til′ious** (-ius), a. Attentive to punctilios; strict or exact in the observance of forms in conduct or action: as, "From being reserved and *punctilious,* he is become easy and obliging" (Smollett's "Humphry Clinker," Nov. 8); "precise and *punctilious* etiquette" (Prescott's "Conquest of Mexico," iv. 4).—**punc-til′ious-ly,** adv.—**punc-til′ious-ness,** n.

punc-tu-al (pungk′tū-al), a. [ML. *punctualis,* < L. *punctus,* a pricking, a point, < *pungere,* prick, pierce: cf. *pungent.*] Of or pertaining to a point (as, *punctual* coördinates, the coördinates of a point); of the nature of or resembling a point† (as, "this opacous earth, this *punctual* spot": Milton's "Paradise Lost," viii. 23); also, to the point†, apposite†, or apt†; express or explicit (archaic); also, exact or precise (archaic); also, punctilious (archaic); now, commonly, strictly observant of an appointed or regular time, in good time, or not late (as, "Miss Peniston was late. In all her life she was never *punctual,*" Weir Mitchell's "Hugh Wynne," xxii.; "This bird is most *punctual* in beginning its song exactly at the close of day," G. White's "Nat. Hist. of Selborne," i. 22); prompt, as an action (as, *punctual* payment).—**punc-tu-al′i-ty** (-al′i-ti), n. The quality or state of being punctual; esp., strict observance of an appointed or regular time, as in keeping engagements, meeting obligations, etc. (as, "*Punctuality* at meals was rigidly enforced at Gateshead Hall": C. Brontë's "Jane Eyre," iii.); promptness.—**punc′tu-al-ly,** adv. In a punctual manner; esp., strictly, scrupulously, or punctiliously (now archaic or rare: as, "The Commodore's arrangement had been *punctually* complied with," Marryat's "King's Own," vii.); now, commonly, with strict observance of an appointed or regular time (as, "The man pays *punctually*": G. Meredith's "Lord Ormont and His Aminta," x.).

punc-tu-ate (pungk′tū-āt), v.; -ated, -ating. [ML. *punctuatus,* pp. of *punctuare,* < L. *punctus,* a point: see *punctual.*] **I.** tr. To mark with points, dots, or minute depressions (in scientific use); also, to mark or divide with points or stops, as a sentence, etc., in order to make the meaning clear; insert marks of punctuation in; fig., to interrupt at intervals, as a speech by cheers; intersperse (a thing) with something else; also, to give point or emphasis to (as, he *punctuated* his remarks with gestures). **II.** intr. To insert or use marks of punctuation.—**punc-tu-a′tion**

(-ā′shọn), *n.* [ML. *punctuatio*(*n*-).] The act of punctuating; esp., the practice, art, or system of inserting marks or points in writing or printing, in order to make the meaning clear; the punctuating of written or printed matter with commas, semicolons, colons, periods, etc. (*punctuation-marks*).—**punc′tu-a-tive** (-ā-tiv), *a.* Serving to punctuate.—**punc′tu-a-tor** (-ā-tọr), *n.*

punc-tu-late (pungk′tụ-lāt), *a.* [NL. *punctulatus*, < L. *punctulum*, dim. of *punctum*, E. *point*.] Marked or studded with minute points, dots, or depressions; minutely punctate. Also **punc′tu-lat-ed** (-lā-ted).—**punc-tu-la′tion** (-lā′-shọn), *n.* Punctulate condition or marking.

punc-ture (pungk′tụr), *n.* [L. *punctura*, < *pungere*, prick, pierce: cf. *pungent*.] The action or an act of pricking or perforating, as with a pointed instrument or object; also, a mark or hole so made; in *zoöl.*, a small point-like depression.—**punc′ture**, *v. t.*; *-tured, -turing.* To subject to puncture; prick, pierce, or perforate (as, to *puncture* the skin with a pin; "If the nails fail, *puncture* their tires with a bullet," G. B. Shaw's "Man and Superman," iii.); also, to make (a hole, etc.) by pricking or perforating.

pun-dit (pun′dit), *n.* [Hind. *pandit*, < Skt. *pandita*, learned man, as adj. learned.] A Hindu scholar or learned man; in general, a learned man (as, "Perhaps some clever *pundit* will be able to tell me what these words mean": W. H. Hudson's "Far Away and Long Ago," i.).

pung (pung), *n.* [Of N. Amer. Ind. origin, and related to *toboggan*.] A rude sleigh consisting of an oblong box on runners; any sleigh with a box-like body. [New Eng.]

pung=chow (pung′chou′), *n.* [A combination of two words used separately to announce each a particular play in the game.] Same as *mah-jongg*. [Proprietary name.]

pun-gent (pun′jẹnt), *a.* [L. *pungens* (*pungent-*), ppr. of *pungere*, prick, pierce: cf. *poignant*, *point*, *puncheon*[1], *punctual*, *puncture*, also *compunction*, *expunge*, and *bung*.] Piercing or sharp-pointed, as (in *bot.*) the lobes of a holly-leaf, or (in *entom.*) an ovipositor; hence, sharply affecting the organs of taste or smell, as if by a penetrating power (as, *pungent* condiments; a *pungent* fragrance; "clouds of sulphurous *pungent* smoke," W. Morris's "Jason," viii. 117); biting; acrid; also, acutely distressing to the feelings or mind, or poignant (as, "The general affliction . . . was doubly *pungent* upon the present occasion": Godwin's "Caleb Williams," v.); caustic, biting, or sharply expressive, as speech, etc.; also, mentally stimulating; appealing keenly and agreeably to the mind, interest, etc. (as, "We fell into conversation, and I found him *pungent*, ready, impressive, and most entertaining": F. M. Crawford's "Mr. Isaacs," i.). —**pun′gen-cy** (-jẹn-si), *n.*—**pun′gent-ly**, *adv.*

Pu-nic (pū′nik), *a.* [L. *Punicus*, earlier *Pœnicus*, < *Pœnus*, a Carthaginian, akin to *Phœnix*, Gr. Φοῖνιξ, a Phenician: cf. *Phenician*.] **I.** *a.* Of or pertaining to the ancient Carthaginians (as, the *Punic* Wars, the three wars waged by Rome against Carthage, 264–241, 218–201, and 149–146 B.C., resulting in the overthrow of Carthage and its annexation to Rome); also (in allusion to the Roman view of the Carthaginian character), treacherous or perfidious. **II.** *n.* The language of the ancient Carthaginians, an offshoot of Phenician.

pu-ni-ness (pū′ni-nes), *n.* The state of being puny.

pun-ish (pun′ish), *v.* [OF. F. *punir* (*puniss-*), < L. *punire* (pp. *punitus*), earlier *pœnire*, < *pœna*, penalty, punishment: see *pain*.] **I.** *tr.* To inflict a penalty on (a person, etc.), as for an offense (real or imputed: as, to *punish* mutineers; to *punish* a disobedient child; "To *punish* the just is not good," Prov. xvii. 26); subject to pain, loss, confinement, death, or other penalty for some transgression or fault; also, to inflict a penalty for (an offense, fault, etc.: as, to *punish* theft; "Prisons . . . were built To bind the lawless, and to *punish* guilt," Cowper's "Charity," 281); also, to handle severely or roughly, as in a fight or struggle (colloq.); put to painful exertion, as a horse in racing or hard driving (colloq.); make a heavy inroad on, as a supply of something (colloq.: as, "He *punished* my champagne," Thackeray's "Vanity Fair," liii.). **II.** *intr.* To inflict punishment.—**pun′ish-a-ble**, *a.* Liable to or deserving of punishment.—**pun′ish-er**, *n.*—**pun′ish-ment**, *n.* The act of punishing, or the fact of being punished, as for an offense or fault;

that which is inflicted as a penalty in punishing (as, "Cain said . . . My *punishment* is greater than I can bear": Gen. iv. 13); also, severe handling or treatment (colloq.).

pu-ni-tive (pū′ni-tiv), *a.* [F. *punitif*, < L. *punire* (pp. *punitus*): see *punish*.] Serving for, concerned with, or inflicting punishment: as, *punitive* measures or laws; a *punitive* military expedition. Also **pu′ni-to-ry** (-tọ-ri).

Pun-ja-bi (pun-jä′bē), *n.* See *Panjabi*.

punk[1] (pungk), *n.* [Origin unknown.] A prostitute. [Obs. or archaic.]

punk[2] (pungk). [Cf. *spunk*.] **I.** *n.* Decayed wood used as tinder; also, amadou; also, a preparation that will smolder, used in the form of sticks, as for lighting fireworks. **II.** *a.* Poor or bad in quality; wretched. [Slang, U. S.]

pun-ka, pun-kah (pung′kä), *n.* [Hind. *pankhā*, a fan.] In the East Indies, a fan, esp. a large, swinging, screen-like fan hung from the ceiling and kept in motion by a servant or by machinery: as, "patient coolies who pulled the *punkahs* in the sleeping-rooms" (Kipling's "Kim," vii.); "The court-room was sombre . . . High up . . . the *punkahs* were swaying short to and fro" (J. Conrad's "Lord Jim," xiv.).

pun-ky, pun-kie (pung′ki), *n.*; pl. *-kies* (-kiz). [From N. Amer. Ind.] Any of certain minute flies or midges, common in wooded regions and on sandy beaches of the northeastern U. S., which bite severely; esp., *Ceratopogon nocivum*, or some related species.

pun-ster (pun′stẹr), *n.* [See *-ster*.] One given to making puns.

punt[1] (punt), *n.* [AS. *punt*, < L. *ponto*, punt, also pontoon: see *pontoon*. The football sense is from *punt*[1], *v.*] A shallow, flat-bottomed, square-ended boat, usually propelled by thrusting with a pole against the bottom of the river, etc.; in *football*, a kick given to the ball dropped from the hands, before it touches the ground.—**punt**[1], *v.* **I.** *tr.* To propel (a punt or other boat) by thrusting with a pole against the river-bottom, etc.; convey (a person, etc.) in or as in a punt; in *football*, to kick (the ball) after dropping it from the hands, before it touches the ground. **II.** *intr.* To propel a punt, or propel some other boat in the manner of a punt; also, to punt a football.

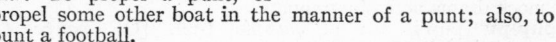

Punt.

punt[2] (punt), *n.* [F. *ponte*, < Sp. *punto*, point, < L. *punctum*, E. *point*.] A point in certain card-games; also, a punter.—**punt**[2], *v. i.* [F. *ponter*.] To lay a stake against the bank, as at faro.

punt-er[1] (pun′tẹr), *n.* One who punts a boat or a football.

punt-er[2] (pun′tẹr), *n.* One who punts at faro, etc.

pun-to† (pun′tō), *n.* [It., < L. *punctum*, E. *point*.] A thrust or pass in fencing.

pun-ty (pun′ti), *n.*; pl. *-ties* (-tiz). [F. *pontis*, *pontil*.] An iron rod used in glass-making for handling the hot glass.

pu-ny (pū′ni), *a.*; compar. *punier*, superl. *puniest*. [OF. *puisne* (F. *puiné*), < *puis*, afterward (< L. *post*, after), + *ne* (F. *né*), born: see *née*.] Puisne†, younger†, or junior†; also, inexperienced†; also, of less than normal size and strength, or undersized and weakly (as, "My uncle was a thin, *puny* little man," Irving's "Tales of a Traveler," i. 4; "The child was *puny*, white and sickly," S. Butler's "Way of All Flesh," xxi.); also, insignificantly small (as, "Tho' the *puny* wound appear, Short while it grieves": Burns's "To James Smith," 95); petty or insignificant (as, "this blood-stained rubbish of the ancient world, these *puny* kings and tawdry emperors": H. G. Wells's "Mr. Britling," iii. 2. § 11); weak, feeble, or futile (as, "a glance of hopeless and *puny* despair": G. W. Curtis's "Prue and I," v.).

pup (pup), *n.* [Abbr. of *puppy*.] A young dog; a puppy; also, a young seal.—**pup**, *v. i.*; *pupped, pupping.* To bring forth pups.

pu-pa (pū′pä), *n.*; pl. *pupæ* (-pē). [NL. use of L. *pupa*, girl, doll, puppet: cf. *pupil* and *puppet*.] In *zoöl.*, an insect in the form which it has, during metamorphosis, in the intermediate and usually quiescent stage between that of the larva and that of the imago (cf. *chrysalis* and *nymph*); also, some other invertebrate animal in an immature form or an intermediate stage of development.—**pu'pal**, *a.* Of, pertaining to, or in the form of a pupa.—**pu'pate** (-pāt), *v. i.*; *-pated, -pating.* To become a pupa.—**pu-pa'tion** (pū-pā'shọn), *n.* —**pu'pi-form** (pū'pi-fôrm), *a.* Having the form of a pupa.

pu-pil (pū'pil), *n.* [OF. F. *pupille*, < L. *pupillus*, masc., *pupilla*, fem., orphan, ward (*pupilla*, also, pupil of the eye), dim. of *pupus*, boy, *pupa*, girl.] A young person (in *civil law*, one below the age of puberty) under the care of a guardian; a ward; also, one who is under an instructor or teacher; a scholar; in *anat.*, the expanding and contracting opening in the iris of the eye, through which light passes to the retina.—**pu'pil-age, pu'pil-lage** (-pi-lāj), *n.* The state or period of being a pupil or ward, or of being a pupil or scholar.—**pu-pil-lar'i-ty** (-lar'i-ti), *n.* In *civil* and *Sc. law*, the period between birth and puberty.—**pu'pil-la-ry** (-lā-ri), *a.* [L. *pupillaris.*] Pertaining to a pupil or ward, or to a pupil or scholar; also, pertaining to the pupil of the eye.—**pu-pil-lom'e-ter** (-lom'e-tèr), *n.* [See *-meter.*] An instrument for measuring the size of the pupil of the eye.

pu-pip-a-rous (pū-pip'ạ-rus), *a.* [NL. *pupa*, pupa, + L. *parere*, bring forth.] Bringing forth pupæ; of or belonging to the *Pupipara*, a division of dipterous insects, including the horse-tick, sheep-tick, bird-tick, etc. (see *tick*[1]), in which the young are born ready to become pupæ.

pup-pet (pup'et), *n.* [Earlier *poppet*, prob. through OF. (cf. 16th century F. *poupette*, doll) < L. *pupa*, girl, doll, puppet: cf. *pupa*.] A figure representing a human being; a doll; also, a similar figure with jointed limbs, moved by wires, etc., as on a mimic stage; a marionette; hence, a person whose actions are prompted and controlled by another or others (as, "She had in general acted but as a *puppet* in the hands of others": Maria Edgeworth's "Belinda," i.). —**pup'pet-ry** (-ri), *n.*; pl. *-ries* (-riz). The action of puppets; artificial action, like that of puppets; mummery; mere show; also, puppets collectively; a set of puppets.— **pup'pet=show**, *n.* A show or exhibition of puppets; a mock drama acted by puppets.

pup-py (pup'i), *n.*; pl. *puppies* (-iz). [OF. *poupee* (F. *poupée*), doll, toy puppet, < L. *pupa*: see *puppet.*] A toy dog†; also, a young dog; a whelp; hence, the young of certain other animals, as of the shark; also, as a term of contempt, an insufferable young man, or a presuming, conceited, or empty-headed fellow (as, " 'You are an insolent *puppy*,' Sir George stated," Arnold Bennett's "Great Man," xix.; "They all chuckled at this *puppy's* silly joke," Lever's "Harry Lorrequer," xxxiv.).—**pup'py-hood** (-hùd), *n.* The state or period of being a puppy.—**pup'py-ism**, *n.* The character or conduct of a puppy.

pur (pėr), *v.* and *n.* See *purr.*

pu-ra-na (pọ̆-rä'nặ), *n.* [Skt., prop. adj., former, belonging to old times, < *purā*, formerly.] [Often *cap.*] In *Sanskrit lit.*, one of a class of sacred writings, of relatively late date, composed almost entirely in the epic couplet, and consisting of partly legendary and partly speculative histories of the universe, together with the genealogy and deeds of gods and heroes, etc. There are 18 principal puranas.— **pu-ran'ic** (-ran'ik), *a.*

pur-blind (pėr'blīnd), *a.* [ME. *pur blind*: cf. *pure, adv.*] Quite or totally blind†; also, nearly blind; partially blind; dim-sighted; fig., dull of discernment or understanding (as, "O *purblind* race of miserable men": Tennyson's "Geraint and Enid," 1).—**pur'blind**, *v. t.* To make purblind: as, "Were he [man] not . . . *purblinded* by enchantment, you had but to bid him open his eyes and look" (Carlyle's "Sartor Resartus," iii. 3).—**pur'blind-ly**, *adv.*— **pur'blind-ness**, *n.*

pur-chas-a-ble (pėr'chạ-sạ-bl), *a.* Capable of being purchased or bought; hence, that may be won over by money or other consideration, or venal (as, "If Curio was pur-

chasable, Cæsar would not have hesitated to buy him": Froude's "Cæsar," xx.).

pur-chase (pėr'chạs), *v. t.*; *-chased, -chasing.* [OF. *porchacier*, seek for, seek to obtain, procure (F. *pourchasser*, pursue), < *por-* (< L. *pro*, for) + *chacier*, E. *chase*[1].] To seek to procure or bring about†; also, to bring about†, cause†, or effect†; also, to procure†, acquire†, or obtain†; specif. (in *law*), to acquire, as an estate in lands, otherwise than by inheritance or descent; also, to acquire by the payment of money or its equivalent; buy; hence, fig., to acquire or procure by any kind of an equivalent (as, to *purchase* favor by subservience); also, to win over by money or other consideration; bribe; also, of things, to be sufficient to buy, or serve as an equivalent in procuring (as, "Would that my life could *purchase* thine!" Shelley's "Cenci," v. 1. 71); also (orig. *naut.*), to haul, draw, or raise, esp. by the aid of a mechanical power (as, "other ships . . . whose guns were trained ready to pour in a destructive fire on the least sign of an attempt to *purchase* their anchor": Marryat's "King's Own," ii.); get a purchase on; apply a purchase to.—**pur'-chase**, *n.* [OF. *porchas* (F. *pourchas*).] A seeking to procure or bring about something†, or the actual bringing about of it†; also, the action of procuring, acquiring, or obtaining something†; specif. (in *law*), the acquisition of an estate in lands, etc., otherwise than by inheritance or descent; also, acquisition by the payment of money or its equivalent; buying, or a single act of buying (as, "Grizel had completed her *purchases* by five o'clock": Barrie's "Sentimental Tommy," xviii.); hence, fig., acquisition by means of any kind of equivalent, as effort, labor, etc.; also, that which is acquired or obtained†; gain† or advantage†; booty† or plunder† (as, "We [pirates] met with little *purchase* upon this coast, except two small vessels of Golconda": Defoe's "Captain Singleton," xiii.); also, the annual return or rent from land (as, to buy an estate at ten years' *purchase*, that is, at a price equal to the return or rent from it for ten years); hence, value or worth (as, not worth an hour's *purchase*, not likely to last an hour); also, something which is purchased or bought; sometimes, a (good, bad, etc.) bargain; also, firm or advantageous hold by which power may be applied or exerted, as in moving or raising heavy bodies (as, "He took her by the hand, and braced his foot in the stirrup to afford a *purchase* for her ascent": Whyte-Melville's "Katerfelto," ix.); mechanical advantage; also, a contrivance for obtaining such hold or advantage, as a lever or a tackle; fig., a means of increasing power or influence.—**pur'chas-er**, *n.*

pur-dah (pėr'dä), *n.* [Hind. and Pers. *parda.*] In India, etc., a curtain, esp. one serving to screen women secluded from the sight of men or strangers; also, the system of such seclusion for women.

pure (pūr). [OF. F. *pur*, < L. *purus*, clean, unmixed, plain, pure: cf. *purge.*] **I.** *a.*; compar. *purer*, superl. *purest.* Free from extraneous matter, or from mixture with anything of a different, inferior, or contaminating kind (as, *pure* alcohol; *pure* gold; *pure* water or air); unmodified by any admixture (as, a *pure* color); simple or homogeneous; unmixed, as blood or descent, or of unmixed descent (as, "I saw that he was not a *pure* Indian, for . . . he wore a beard and moustache": W. H. Hudson's "Green Mansions," vii.); unqualified, absolute, utter, or sheer (as, *pure* ignorance; *pure* nonsense); being that and nothing else, or mere (as, a *pure* accident; a case of misunderstanding, *pure* and simple); also, free from foreign or inappropriate elements or characteristics, perfect, or correct (as, *pure* Attic Greek; the *purest* examples of the Doric architectural order); without discordant quality, or clear and true, as musical tones, etc.; also, clean, spotless, or unsullied (lit. or fig.: as, *pure* robes; "*pure* hands," Tennyson's "In Memoriam," xviii.); ceremonially clean; untainted with evil, innocent, blameless, or chaste (as, to be *pure* in heart, thought, or life; *pure* motives; "*pure* and vestal modesty," Shakspere's "Romeo and Juliet," iii. 3. 38); free or without guilt (*from*) or guiltless (*of*: as, "I am *pure* from the blood of all men," Acts, xx. 26; "Ambrose Wille, *pure* of all participation in the crime, stood up . . . to rebuke the outrages," Motley's "Dutch Republic," ii. 7); also, abstract or theoretical (opposed to *applied*: as, *pure* mathematics, see under *mathematics*); independent of sense or experience (as,

Pupa of a Beetle
(*Prionus laticollis*)

pure knowledge or intuition; *pure* reason). **II.** *n.* That which is pure; purity. [Poetic.]—**pure**, *adv.* [ME. *pur, pure.*] Absolutely; quite; thoroughly; very. [Now prov. Eng.]

pu-rée (pü-rā́), *n.* [F.; origin uncertain.] A soup or other food-preparation made by boiling vegetables, meat, etc., to a pulp and straining; any preparation of similar consistence.

pure-ly (pūr′li), *adv.* In a pure manner; without admixture; exclusively; merely; entirely; cleanly; innocently; chastely.—**pure′ness,** *n.*

pur-fle (pėr′fl), *v. t.*; *-fled, -fling.* [OF. *porfiler, pourfiler,* < L. *pro,* before, + *filum,* thread: cf. *profile.*] To finish (a garment, etc.) with an ornamental border, as of needlework, precious stones, beads, or fur (archaic); in general, to adorn or decorate; specif., to decorate (a violin, etc.) with a border of inlaid work along the edges of the body. —**pur′fle,** *n.* [OF. *porfil, pourfil.*] An ornamental border on a garment or the like (archaic); also, a purfling on a violin or similar instrument.—**pur′fling,** *n.* The ornamenting of the edge of something; also, ornamental bordering on something; specif., an inlaid border along the edges of a violin or similar instrument.

pur-ga-tion (pėr-gā′shọn), *n.* [OF. F. *purgation,* < L. *purgatio(n-).*] The act of purging or cleansing (lit. or fig.: as, "a thorough *purgation* of the mind," Hallam's "Literature of Europe," iii. 3. § 33); specif., evacuation of the bowels, esp. by means of a purgative; also, the action of purging or clearing of imputed guilt.

pur-ga-tive (pėr′ga-tiv), *n.* [OF. F. *purgatif,* < LL. *purgativus.*] **I.** *a.* Purging; cleansing; specif., causing evacuation of the bowels (as, a *purgative* medicine; a plant with *purgative* properties); cathartic. **II.** *n.* A purgative medicine or agent.—**pur′ga-tive-ly,** *adv.*

pur-ga-to-ri-al (pėr-ga-tō′ri-ạl), *a.* Of, pertaining to, or suggestive of purgatory: as, "to enter into the *purgatorial* state of matrimony" (W. H. Hudson's "Green Mansions," v.).

pur-ga-to-ry (pėr′ga-tō-ri). [LL. *purgatorius,* adj. (as n., ML. *purgatorium*).] **I.** *a.* Serving to purge, cleanse, or purify; expiatory. **II.** *n.*; pl. *-ries* (-riz). In the belief of Roman Catholics and others, a condition or place in which the souls of those dying penitent are purified from venial sins, or undergo the temporal punishment which, after the guilt of mortal sin has been remitted, still remains to be endured by the sinner; hence, any condition, situation, or place of temporary suffering, expiation, or the like (as, "She . . . wondered how long this *purgatory* was to last," Hardy's "Return of the Native," ii. 6; "I shuddered at the thought of spending another night in such a *purgatory,*" W. H. Hudson's "Purple Land," iii.).

purge (pėrj), *v.*; *purged, purging.* [OF. *purgier* (F. *purger*), < L. *purgare* (pp. *purgatus*), cleanse, clear, purge, < *purus,* pure, + *agere,* drive, do.] **I.** *tr.* To cleanse (lit. or fig.); rid of whatever is impure or undesirable, or purify; rid or clear (*of*) or free (*from*: as, "He insisted that the Senate must be *purged* of its corrupt members," Froude's "Cæsar," vii.; "My heart is *purged* from grudging hate," Shakspere's "Richard III.," ii. 1. 9); remove by some cleansing or purifying process (often with *away, off,* or *out*: as, "*Purge* away our sins, for thy name's sake," Ps. lxxix. 9); specif., to clear or empty (the bowels, etc.) by causing evacuation; cause evacuation of the bowels of (a person), as by means of a purgative or cathartic, or as a purgative does; also, to clear (a person, etc.) of imputed guilt; esp., to clear from an accusation of crime by making oath, with the aid of compurgators, or by ordeal; clear away or wipe out legally (an offense, contempt, etc.) by atonement or other suitable action. **II.** *intr.* To become cleansed or purified; also, to undergo or cause purging of the bowels.—**purge,** *n.* The act or a process of purging; also, something that purges; esp., a purgative medicine or dose.—**pur-ger** (pėr′jėr), *n.* —**pur′ging,** *n.* A cleansing or purifying; specif., purgation of the bowels, as by means of a purgative; sometimes, diarrhea.—**pur′ging=flax,** *n.* An old-world species of flax, *Linum catharticum,* a decoction of which is used as a cathartic and diuretic.

pu-ri-fi-ca-tion (pū″ri-fi-kā′shọn), *n.* [OF. F. *purification,* < L. *purificatio(n-).*] The act of purifying; specif., ceremonial purifying, as that enjoined by Jewish law upon a woman after childbirth (as, "When the days of her [Mary's] *purification* according to the law of Moses were accomplished, they brought him [the child Jesus] to Jerusalem": Luke, ii. 22); hence [*cap.*], with *the,* a Christian festival, observed on Feb. 2, in commemoration of the purifying of the Virgin Mary after the birth of Christ (also called 'the Purification of the Virgin Mary' or 'of the Blessed Virgin,' and 'Candlemas').—**pu′ri-fi-ca-tor,** *n.* [Cf. F. *purificatoire,* < ML. *purificatorium.*] *Eccles.,* a cloth used at communion for wiping the chalice, etc.—**pu′ri-fi-ca-to-ry** (-kā-tọ-ri), *a.* [LL. *purificatorius.*] Serving to purify.

pu-ri-fi-er (pū′ri-fī-ėr), *n.* One who or that which purifies.

pu-ri-form (pū′ri-fôrm), *a.* [L. *pus* (*pur-*), pus, + *forma,* form.] Having the form of pus; pus-like.

pu-ri-fy (pū′ri-fī), *v.*; *-fied, -fying.* [OF. F. *purifier,* < L. *purificare,* < *purus,* pure, + *facere,* make.] **I.** *tr.* To make pure; free from extraneous matter, or from anything that debases, pollutes, or contaminates (as, to *purify* metals; to *purify* the air; to *purify* the blood); cleanse; fig., to free from foreign and objectionable elements or characteristics (as, to *purify* a language); make ceremonially clean (as, "The Jews' passover was nigh at hand: and many went . . . up to Jerusalem . . . to *purify* themselves": John, xi. 55); free from whatever is evil, sinful, or base (as, to *purify* the heart or life; to *purify* politics); clear or purge (*of* or *from*: as, "Circe the wise . . . at whose hands Of late-wrought guilt shall ye be *purified,*" W. Morris's "Jason," x. 63). **II.** *intr.* To become pure.

Pu-rim (pū′rim), *n.* [Heb.] An annual Jewish festival (observed in February or in March) in commemoration of the deliverance of the Jews from the massacre planned by Haman. See Esther, ix.

pu-rin, pu-rine (pū′rin), *n.* [G. *purin,* < L. *purus,* pure, + NL. *uricus,* uric.] In *chem.,* a white crystalline compound, $C_5H_4N_4$, regarded as the parent substance of a group of compounds which includes uric acid, xanthine, caffeine, theobromine, etc.; also, any of these compounds.

pur-ism (pūr′izm), *n.* [F. *purisme,* < *pur,* E. *pure.*] Scrupulous or excessive observance of or insistence on purity in language, style, etc.—**pur′ist,** *n.* [F. *puriste.*] One who aims at or insists on scrupulous or excessive purity in language, style, etc.—**pur-is-tic** (pū-ris′tik), *a.*

pu-ri-tan (pū′ri-tạn), *n.* [LL. *puritas,* E. *purity.*] **I.** *n.* One who affects great purity or strictness of life and religious principles; [*cap.*] one of a class of Protestants that arose in the 16th century within the Church of England, demanding further reforms in doctrine and worship, with greater strictness in religious discipline, and during part of the 17th century constituted a powerful political party. **II.** *a.* [*cap.* or *l. c.*] Of or pertaining to the Puritans.—**pu-ri-tan′ic, pu-ri-tan′i-cal** (-tan′ik, -i-kạl), *a.* Of, pertaining to, or characteristic of puritans or the Puritans; having the character of a puritan; excessively strict, rigid, or austere. —**pu-ri-tan′i-cal-ly,** *adv.*—**pu′ri-tan-ism,** *n.* Strictness in matters of conduct or religion; puritanical austerity; [*cap.*] the principles and practices of the Puritans.—**pu′ri-tan-ize,** *v.*; *-ized, -izing.* **I.** *intr.* To affect or practise puritanism. **II.** *tr.* To make puritan; imbue with puritanism.

pu-ri-ty (pū′ri-ti), *n.* [OF. *purete* (F. *pureté*), < LL. *puritas,* < L. *purus,* E. *pure.*] The condition or quality of being pure; freedom from extraneous matter, or from anything that debases or contaminates (as, the *purity* of drugs, or of drinking-water); freedom from any admixture or modifying addition (as, *purity* of blood or race); freedom from foreign or inappropriate elements or characteristics, or careful correctness (as, *purity* of language or diction; *purity* of style); cleanness or spotlessness, as of garments; ceremonial cleanness; freedom from evil or guilt; innocence; blamelessness; chastity.

purl[1] (pėrl), *v. i.* [Cf. Sw. *porla,* purl, ripple, gurgle.] To flow with curling or rippling motions, as a shallow stream among or over stones or other obstructions; flow with a murmuring sound, as such a stream does; hence, to pass in a manner or with a sound likened to this (as, "The words . . . *purled* out of Miss Foster's mouth like a bright spring out of moss": Arnold Bennett's "Great Man," xii.).—**purl**[1], *n.* The action or sound of purling.

purl[2] (pėrl), n. [Origin uncertain: cf. obs. or prov. *pirl*, twist (threads, etc.) into a cord.] Thread made of twisted gold or silver wire; also, one of a series of small loops along the edge of lace, braid, etc.; also, a border of or an edging with such loops; in *knitting*, an inversion of the stitches, producing a particular appearance of surface.—**purl**[2], v. t. To embroider with gold or silver thread†; also, to finish with loops or a looped edging; also, to knit with inversion of the stitch.

Edge, with Purl (*a*).

purl[3] (pėrl), n. [Origin uncertain.] A medicated or spiced malt liquor; in later use, a mixture of hot beer with gin and sometimes also sugar and ginger.

pur-lieu (pėr′lū), n. [Altered form (simulating F. *lieu*, place) of AF. *puralee*, purlieu of forest, orig. official perambulation, < OF. *poraler*, traverse, < *por-* (< L. *pro*, before) + *aler* (F. *aller*), go.] A piece of land on the border of a forest, orig. a piece which, after having been included in a (royal) forest, was disafforested and restored to private ownership, though still subject, in some respects, to the operation of the forest laws; also, a place where one may range at large; one's haunt or resort; one's bounds; also, any bordering, neighboring, or outlying region or district; *pl.*, outskirts, neighboring parts, or neighborhood, sometimes of a poorer or squalid character (as, "The two Amazons . . . did not come from the *purlieus* of Puddledock, but from the courtly neighbourhood of Saint James's palace": Smollett's "Humphry Clinker," April 30).

pur-lin (pėr′lin), n. [ME. *purlyn, purlyon*; origin obscure.] A timber or piece laid horizontally on the principal rafters of a roof to support the common rafters. Cf. *rafter*[2], n.

pur-loin (pėr-loin′, also pėr′loin), v. [OF. *porloignier*, put off, remove, < *por-* (< L. *pro*, before) + *loin*, far off (< L. *longe*, long, far): cf. *prolong*.] **I.** *tr.* To put away†; do away with†; also, to take dishonestly, steal, or filch (as, "A certain document of the last importance has been *purloined* from the royal apartments," Poe's "Purloined Letter"; "A watch, of trifling value, had been *purloined* from the purser's cabin," Marryat's "King's Own," i.). **II.** *intr.* To commit theft.—**pur-loin′er**, n.

pur-ple (pėr′pl). [AS. (Northumbrian) *purple*, for *purpre*, < L. *purpura* < Gr. πορφύρα, shell-fish yielding purple dye, hence the dye, or something purple.] **I.** n. A color, formerly some shade of crimson (see *murex*) or red, but now formed by the mixture of varying proportions of red and blue; also, cloth or clothing of this hue, esp. as formerly worn distinctively by persons of imperial, royal, or other high rank; hence, imperial or lofty rank or position; also, the rank or office of a cardinal, in allusion to his scarlet official dress; also, any of the gastropods of the genus *Purpura*, which have a gland that secretes a purplish fluid, as *P. lapillus*, a species common on both shores of the Atlantic. **II.** a. Of the color of purple; hence, imperial or regal; also, brilliant or gorgeous.—**purple avens.** See *avens*.—**purple medic**, lucerne, or alfalfa.—**purple patch**, an ornate or striking passage in a literary composition: translating L. *purpureus pannus* (Horace's "Ars Poetica," 15).—**pur′ple**, v. t. or i.; *-pled, -pling.* To make or become purple.—**pur′plish**, a. Somewhat purple; tending to purple. Also **pur′ply** (-pli).

pur-point (pėr′point), n. Same as *pourpoint*.

Purple (*Purpura lapillus*).

pur-port (pėr′pōrt or pėr-pōrt′), v. t. [AF. *purporter*, convey, OF. *porporter*, carry, bring, < *por-* (< L. *pro*, before) + *porter* (< L. *portare*), carry.] To convey to the mind as the meaning or thing intended (as, a statement *purporting* certain facts); express; imply; also, to profess or claim, as by the tenor (as, a document *purporting* to be official); also, to intend or purpose (rare: as, "Even in the extremity of guilt No guilt he *purported*," Southey's "Roderick," x. 348).—**pur′port**, n. [AF. *purport*.] Tenor, import, or meaning (as, "Such is the general *purport* of this legendary

superstition," Irving's "Sketch-Book," Sleepy Hollow; "the direct *purport* of the words," Hawthorne's "Scarlet Letter," iii.); also, intention or purpose (now rare).—**pur′port-less**, a. Without purport or meaning.

pur-pose (pėr′pos), v. t.; *-posed, -posing.* [OF. *purposer*, var. of *proposer*, E. *propose*.] To put before one's self as something to be done or accomplished, or propose (as, to *purpose* a visit to a friend; "I *purposed* writing a little comment on each virtue," B. Franklin's "Autobiography," v.; "my next experiment . . . which I *purpose* to describe more at length," Thoreau's "Walden," ii.); determine on the performance of; design; intend; hence, in the passive (*to be purposed*), to be imbued with a purpose or intention, or be resolved (as, "I am *purposed* instantly to return": Scott's "Fair Maid of Perth," x.).—**pur′pose**, n. [OF. *purpos.*] That which one puts before one's self as something to be done or accomplished, or an object in view (as, "His *purpose* was to discover how long these guests intended to stay": J. Conrad's "Victory," ii. 5); also, intention or determination (as, "I have it in *purpose* to commit to paper . . . various thoughts of my own," J. H. Newman's "Office and Work of Universities," i.; "infirm of *purpose*," Shakspere's "Macbeth," ii. 2. 52); also, the object for which anything is done, made, used, etc., or for which it exists (as, "The *purpose* of government he conceived to be the execution of justice," Froude's "Cæsar," xxviii.; "The narrow room over the bathroom . . . served the *purpose* of a kitchen," Arnold Bennett's "Riceyman Steps," ii. 6); an intended or desired result; end or aim; the subject or matter in hand, or the point at issue (as, "Come, you are a tedious fool: to the *purpose*," Shakspere's "Measure for Measure," ii. 1. 120; from the *purpose*, that is, away from the point: now chiefly in 'to the purpose,' in the sense of 'to the point' or 'with pertinence,' as, "I'll tell you a story to the *purpose*," Defoe's "Robinson Crusoe," ii. 3); also, practical result, effect, or advantage (in phrases: as, to the *purpose*, or to *purpose*, that is, so as to secure the result or effect desired, or effectively; to good *purpose*, with good effect; to little or no *purpose*, with little or no useful effect); also, a proportion†; a riddle†; discourse† or conversation†; also, purport†, import†, or meaning†.—**of (set) purpose**, on purpose, or intentionally. [Archaic.]—**on purpose**, by design, purposely, or intentionally (as, "It was merely a mistake: — but her ladyship was convinced that it was done *on purpose*": Maria Edgeworth's "Belinda," xiv.); also, with the particular purpose specified (as, "How still the evening is, As hush'd *on purpose* to grace harmony!" Shakspere's "Much Ado about Nothing," ii. 3. 41).—**to all intents and purposes.** See under *intent*[2].—**pur′pose-ful**, a. Having a purpose, or an object in view, as a person; also, indicating purpose, intention, or plan; having a purpose or object (as, "It has been my natural disposition to see this war as something *purposeful*": H. G. Wells's "Italy, France, and Britain at War," i.).—**pur′pose-less**, a. Lacking purpose, aim, or design.—**pur′pose-less-ness**, n.—**pur′pose-ly**, adv. On purpose, by design, or intentionally (as, to do a thing *purposely*); with the particular purpose specified, or expressly (as, "As if it were the Moor Come hither *purposely* to poison me": Shakspere's "Titus Andronicus," iii. 2. 73).—**pur′pos-er** (-pos-ėr), n.—**pur′pos-ive**, a. Acting with, characterized by, or showing a purpose, intention, or design; adapted to a purpose or end, or serving some purpose; also, characterized by purpose, determination, or resolution, as persons; also, pertaining to or of the nature of purpose.—**pur′pos-ive-ly**, adv.—**pur′pos-ive-ness**, n.

pur-pres-ture (pėr-pres′tūr), n. [OF. *porpresture*, *porprendre*, seize, occupy, < *por-* (< L. *pro*, before, for) + *prendre* (< L. *prehendere*), take.] In *law*, an illegal inclosure of or encroachment upon property that belongs to the public or, formerly, to another person, as the shutting up or obstruction of a highway or of navigable waters.

pur-pu-ra (pėr′pū-rä), n. [NL. use of L. *purpura*, E. *purple*.] In *pathol.*, a disease characterized by purple or livid spots on the skin or mucous membrane, caused by the extravasation of blood.

pur-pu-rate (pėr′pū-rāt), n. In *chem.*, a salt of purpuric acid.

pur-pure (pėr′pūr), n. [OF. purpure, < L. purpura, E. purple.] In her., the color purple.

pur-pu-re-al (pėr-pū′rē-al), a. [L. purpureus.] Purple: as, "fields invested with purpureal gleams" (Wordsworth's "Laodamia," 106). [Chiefly poetic.]

pur-pu-ric (pėr-pū′rik), a. [L. purpura, E. purple.] In pathol., pertaining to or of the nature of purpura; in chem., noting or pertaining to a nitrogen-containing organic acid not occurring in the free state, but known only in compounds, esp. its ammonium salt, which forms purple-red solutions.

pur-pu-rin (pėr′pū-rin), n. [L. purpura, E. purple.] A red or orange crystalline organic compound, orig. obtained from madder, but now also prepared from alizarin: used in dyeing.

purr, pur (pėr), v.; purred, purring. [Imit.] I. intr. To utter a low, continuous murmuring sound expressive of satisfaction or pleasure, as the cat and certain other animals do (as, "It [a young leopard] was exceeding tame, and purred like a cat when we stroked it with our hands": Defoe's "Captain Singleton," vi.); hence, of persons, to show satisfaction as if by purring; talk in a manner suggestive of the purring of a cat; of things, to make a sound suggestive of the purring of a cat (as, "Unquiet ripples . . . purr," Masefield's "Christmas Eve at Sea"; "He . . . was presently running quietly with his engine purring almost inaudibly along the level road," H. G. Wells's "Mr. Britling," i. 5. § 14). II. tr. To express by or as if by purring: as, "I mentioned my consent . . . the dean purred content thereat" (Kingsley's "Alton Locke," xviii.).—
purr, pur, n. The act of purring; the sound of purring, or any similar sound.

purse (pėrs), n. [AS. purs, < ML. bursa, bag, purse: see bursa.] A small bag, pouch, or case for carrying money on the person (as, "Put money in thy purse": Shakspere's "Othello," i. 3. 345); also, a purse with its contents (as, "Who steals my purse steals trash": Shakspere's "Othello," iii. 3. 157); money, resources, or wealth (as, "He . . . had no resources save the purse of his stepfather," Arnold Bennett's "Roll-Call," i.; the nation's purse); also, a sum of money collected as a present or the like; a sum of money offered as a prize; also, a bag-like receptacle; any of various natural receptacles resembling a bag or pocket.

Belt-purse, 17th century.

—**privy purse.** See under privy, a.—**purse**, v. t.; pursed, pursing. To put into a purse (now rare); also, to contract into folds or wrinkles (as if drawing together the mouth of a purse or bag: as, "His mother merely pursed her lips," Mrs. Wharton's "Age of Innocence," v.); also, to draw into the shape of a purse or bag, as a purse-seine.—**purse′=net**, n. A net the mouth of which can be drawn close with cords.—**purse′=proud**, a. Proud of one's wealth; puffed up with the possession of riches.—**purs′er**, n. An officer, esp. on board a ship, charged with keeping accounts, etc.—**purse′=seine**, n. A seine which may be pursed or drawn into the shape of a bag.

pur-si-ness (pėr′si-nes), n. Pursy condition.

purs-lane (pėrs′lān), n. [OF. porcelaine, appar. by corruption < L. porcilaca, for portulaca, purslane.] A widely distributed, yellow-flowered species of portulaca, Portulaca oleracea, sometimes used as a salad-plant and pot-herb; also, any of various allied or similar plants.

Purse-seine. — a, boat; b and c, blocks; d, gunwale of boat; e, e′, line for drawing seine into shape of bag; f, f′, corks or floats; g, sheave; h, blocks used in hauling in line.

pur-su-a-ble (pėr-sū′a-bl), a. That may be pursued.
pur-su-al (pėr-sū′al), n. The act of pursuing; pursuit.
pur-su-ance (pėr-sū′ans), n. The act of pursuing or follow-ing; pursuit; now, usually, the following or carrying out of some plan, course, injunction, or the like (chiefly in the phrase 'in pursuance of': as, "In pursuance of this resolve, he took up his residence in the Puritan town," Hawthorne's "Scarlet Letter," ix.; "Captain M——, in pursuance of the orders which he had received, weighed his anchor," Marryat's "King's Own," xxx.).

pur-su-ant (pėr-sū′ant). I. a. Pursuing; engaged in pursuit, as of something; proceeding conformably (to: as, "My master, pursuant to the advice of his friend, carried me . . . to the neighbouring town," Swift's "Gulliver's Travels," ii. 2). II. adv. In a manner conformable (to); according (to): as, "An equal portion was reserved for the general, pursuant to the tenor of his commission" (Prescott's "Conquest of Mexico," iv. 5).—**pur-su′ant-ly**, adv.

pur-sue (pėr-sū′), v.; -sued, -suing. [OF. porsuir, porsivre, poursuivre (F. poursuivre), < L. prosequi, follow, pursue, continue: see prosecute.] I. tr. To follow (a person, animal, vehicle, vessel, etc.) with the view of overtaking, capturing, killing, etc.; chase; also, to follow with hostility, harass persistently, or persecute (as, "When I was alone with him, he pursued me with sneers": Stevenson's "Master of Ballantrae," iv.); also, to follow close upon, go with, or attend (as, "Envy will merit, as its shade, pursue," Pope's "Essay on Criticism," 466; "Fortune pursue thee!" Shakspere's "Antony and Cleopatra," iii. 12. 25); also, to follow the course of (something) with the sight, in thought, etc.; also, to follow or come after in order, succession, or time (obs. or rare); also, to seek after, or strive to gain (as, "Seek peace, and pursue it," Ps. xxxiv. 14; to pursue pleasure or fame); seek to attain or accomplish (an end, object, purpose, etc.); also, to follow (a path, etc.: as, "I . . . pursued the beaten road, hoping it might direct me to the cabin of some Indian," Swift's "Gulliver's Travels," iv. 1); continue on (one's way, course, etc.: as, "We pursued our way till we were within a quarter of a league of the huts," Borrow's "Bible in Spain," iv.); go on with or continue (a journey, etc.: as, "I . . . quitted Vagabonds' Rest to pursue my adventures elsewhere," W. H. Hudson's "Purple Land," iv.); in fig. use, to proceed in accordance with, or carry out (a method, plan, etc.); carry on (a course of action, train of thought, etc.); prosecute (inquiries, studies, etc.); practise (an occupation, profession, pastime, etc.); keep on with, or continue to discuss (a subject, topic, etc.); in law, to prosecute (chiefly Sc.). II. intr. To follow in pursuit (as, "The wicked flee when no man pursueth": Prov. xxviii. 1); also, to go on, proceed, or continue, as in speaking; in law, to prosecute (chiefly Sc.).—**pur-su′er**, n.—**pur-su′ing-ly**, adv.

pur-suit (pėr-sūt′), n. [OF. F. poursuite, < poursuivre: see pursue.] The act of pursuing or following for the purpose of overtaking, capturing, killing, etc. (as, cavalry in pursuit of a fleeing enemy; "The pursuit of whales is always under great . . . difficulties," H. Melville's "Moby-Dick," l.); a course of pursuing; a chase; also, the pursuing of, or seeking or striving after, something to be gained or attained (as, the pursuit of wealth or happiness; the pursuit of selfish ends); also, the pursuing, carrying on, or practising of something (as, while engaged in the pursuit of one's profession); any form of occupation, employment, pastime, or the like, regularly or customarily pursued (as, literary pursuits; "My father . . . had no pleasure in the pursuits of most of the young men of his age," Marryat's "Mr. Midshipman Easy," xx.); a subject of occupation or study (as, "History is, of all pursuits, the most cheering": Bancroft's "Hist. of the U. S.," Amer. Revolution, i. 1).

pur-sui-vant (pėr′swi-vant), n. [OF. F. poursuivant, prop. ppr. of poursuivre: see pursue.] Orig., in heraldic use, an official attendant on heralds; later, a heraldic officer of the third and lowest class, ranking below a herald (see Heralds' College, under herald, n.); also, a state messenger who executed warrants†; also, in general, a follower or attendant (as, "captain of a body of armed pursuivants, picked out for their savageness and hatred of Christians," Wiseman's "Fabiola," ii. 6: also fig.); a herald or messenger (chiefly fig. and poetic: as, "these grey locks, the pursuivants of death," Shakspere's "1 Henry VI.," ii. 5. 5).

pur-sy (pėr′si), a. [For earlier pursive, < OF. F. poussif, < pousser, push, heave: see push.] Short-winded or puffy;

now, usually, short-winded from corpulence or fatness; hence, corpulent or fat (as, "figures of little *pursy* Cupids": Irving's "Knickerbocker's New York," vi. 4).

pur-te-nance (pėr'tẹ-nạns), *n.* [Cf. *appurtenance*.] An appurtenance†; also, the pluck of an animal (archaic: see Ex. xii. 9).

pu-ru-lent (pū'rọ-lẹnt), *a.* [L. *purulentus*, < *pus* (*pur-*), pus.] Full of, containing, forming, or discharging pus (as, a *purulent* sore); suppurating; attended with suppuration (as, *purulent* inflammation; *purulent* appendicitis); also, of the nature of or resembling pus (as, *purulent* matter).— **pu'ru-lence, pu'ru-len-cy,** *n.*—**pu'ru-lent-ly,** *adv.*

pur-vey (pėr-vā'), *v.* [OF. *porveeir* (F. *pourvoir*), < L. *providere*, foresee, look after, provide for: see *provide*.] **I.** *tr.* To provide, furnish, or supply (something, now esp. food or provisions: as, "*Purvey* thee a better horse," Scott's "Ivanhoe," xliii.; to *purvey* provisions for a household or a fleet); also, to provide (a person, etc.) with something (archaic; furnish provisions or supplies for (also fig.: as, "He first became busy *purveying* the guillotine when they were purifying the town from all aristocrats," J. Conrad's "Rover," ii.). **II.** *intr.* To furnish provisions; act as purveyor.— **pur-vey'ance,** *n.* The act of purveying; also, that which is purveyed, as provisions; in *Eng. law*, a prerogative of the crown, abolished in 1660, of taking at an appraised value provisions or supplies for the sovereign or the royal household, and also of exacting the use of horses and vehicles and enforcing personal service.—**pur-vey'or,** *n.* One who purveys, provides, or supplies; one who supplies necessaries, esp. food or provisions, officially or as a business; fig., one who supplies something as by catering to appetites or tastes (as, a *purveyor* of gossip or scandal; "He . . . considered 'fellows who wrote' as the mere paid *purveyors* of rich men's pleasures," Mrs. Wharton's "Age of Innocence," xii.); formerly, in England, an officer who provided or exacted provisions, etc., under the prerogative of purveyance.

pur-view (pėr'vū), *n.* [OF. *porveu* (F. *pourvu*), provided, pp. of *porveeir*: see *purvey*.] That which is provided or enacted in a statute, as distinguished from the preamble; hence, the full scope or compass of a statute or law, or of any document, statement, book, subject, etc.; range of operation, activity, concern, etc. (as, matters within the *purview* of the government; a period within the *purview* of history); sometimes, range of vision, or view.

pus (pus), *n.* [L., akin to Gr. πύον, pus: see *pyin* and *foul*.] A yellowish-white, more or less viscid substance produced by suppuration and found in abscesses, sores, etc., consisting of a liquid plasma in which leucocytes, etc., are suspended; matter.

Pu-sey-ism (pū'zi-izm), *n.* The principles and teachings of Edward Bouverie Pusey (1800–82) and those associated with him in the Oxford movement; Tractarianism.—**Pu'sey-ist, Pu'sey-ite** (-īt), *n.*

push (pûsh), *v.* [OF. F. *pousser*, < L. *pulsare*, push, strike, beat: see *pulsate*.] **I.** *tr.* To exert force upon or against (a thing) in order to move it away; move (*away, off,* etc.) by exerting force thus; shove; thrust; drive; also, to butt or gore (as, "if the ox shall *push* a manservant or a maidservant," Ex. xxi. 32: now prov.); also, to make by thrusting obstacles aside (as, "Hawker *pushed* his way in among the crowd": H. Kingsley's "Geoffry Hamlyn," xiii.); also, to press or urge (a person, etc.) to some action or course; urge or impel (a horse, etc.) to greater speed; also, to press (an action, etc.) with energy and insistence; extend (operations) vigorously to a more distant place; carry (an action or thing) further, to a conclusion or extreme, too far, etc. (as, to *push* an undertaking through; "I think they have *pushed* this matter a little too far," Addison, in "Guardian," 137); also, to advance or promote; press the adoption, use, sale, etc., of (a thing); urge the advancement, etc., of (a person); press (anything) upon a person for acceptance, adoption, etc.; also, to press or bear hard upon (a person, etc.), as in dealings (as, "Excuse me . . . if I appear to *push* you; but it is really desirable that I should penetrate your intentions": Stevenson's "Master of Ballantrae," viii.); put to straits (used in the passive, and often with *for*: as, to be *pushed* for time or money; "When I am *pushed* for a bit of information I'll come to you," J. Conrad's "Res-

cue," ii. 4). **II.** *intr.* To exert a thrusting force upon something (as, "The gates . . . creaked as Audrey *pushed* against them": Arnold Bennett's "Lion's Share," xxvii.); use steady force in moving a thing away; shove; also, to move from the shore, etc., as the result of a push (often with *off*: as, "They *pushed* into the waters wan, And . . . Drew off from that unlucky fateful shore," W. Morris's "Jason," v. 126; "Getting into my canoe, I *pushed* off from shore," Swift's "Gulliver's Travels," iv. 10); also, to sit abaft an oar and propel a boat by forward strokes (as, to *push* down a stream); also, to thrust with a pointed weapon, a stick, etc. (archaic: as, "Let the green In years . . . *Push* with the lance," Cowper's tr. Homer's "Iliad," iv. 383); thrust or butt with the horns, as an animal does (now prov.); also, to stick out, or project (as, "a large promontory or cape of land, *pushing* out a long way into the sea": Defoe's "Captain Singleton," iii.); also, to make one's way with effort or persistence, as against difficulty or opposition (as, "Gathering my feeble remains of strength, I *pushed* on," C. Brontë's "Jane Eyre," xxviii.; "They *pushed* through the bustle of the enormous ship," Arnold Bennett's "The Old Adam," x.); also, to put forth vigorous or persistent efforts; work strenuously or seek actively for something. —**push,** *n.* The act or an act of pushing; a shove or thrust; sometimes, a thrust of a weapon, or the like, or of the horns of an animal; also, a vigorous onset or effort; a determined pushing forward or advance (as, "Argyle resolved to make a bold *push* for Glasgow": Macaulay's "Hist. of Eng.," v.); also, the pressure of circumstances; a case or time of pressure or stress; an emergency; also, persevering energy, or enterprise (colloq.); also, a crowd, company, or set of persons (slang); also, a contrivance or part to be pushed in order to operate a mechanism; a push-button.

push=ball (pûsh'bâl), *n.* A game played with a large, heavy ball, usually about 6 feet in diameter, which two sides of players endeavor to push toward opposite goals; also, the ball used in this game.

push=but-ton (pûsh'but''n), *n.* A small button or knob pushed to complete or break an electric circuit, as for ringing a bell or for lighting or putting out an electric light.

push=cart (pûsh'kärt), *n.* A light cart to be pushed by hand, used by street-venders, etc.

push-er (pûsh'ėr), *n.* One who or that which pushes; specif., in *aëronautics*, an aëroplane which has its propeller behind the main supporting planes.

push-ful (pûsh'fûl), *a.* Perseveringly energetic; aggressively enterprising. [Colloq.]—**push'ful-ly,** *adv.*—**push'ful-ness,** *n.*

push-ing (pûsh'ing), *p. a.* That pushes; esp., fig., energetic or enterprising (as, "We . . . are pleased with his *pushing* and persevering spirit": Irving's "Captain Bonneville," xl.); also, intrusively forward or presuming (as, "the cocksureness of *pushing* vulgarity and self-conceit": S. Butler's "Way of All Flesh," lxxxiii.).—**push'ing-ly,** *adv.*

push=pin (pûsh'pin), *n.* A children's game played with pins; fig., child's play; triviality.

Push-tu (pûsh'tö), *n.* The Afghan language.

pu-sil-lan-i-mous (pū-si-lan'i-mus), *a.* [L. *pusillanimis*, < *pusillus*, very small, petty, + *animus*, mind, spirit.] Lacking strength of mind or courage; faint-hearted; mean-spirited; cowardly; also, proceeding from or indicating a cowardly spirit (as, "One cannot contemplate this *pusillanimous* conduct of Montezuma without mingled feelings of pity and contempt": Prescott's "Conquest of Mexico," iii. 7).—**pu''sil-la-nim'i-ty** (-lạ-nim'i-ti), **pu-sil-lan'i-mous-ness,** *n.*—**pu-sil-lan'i-mous-ly,** *adv.*

pus-ley (pus'li), *n.* A corruption of *purslane*.

puss (pûs), *n.* [Cf. D. *poes*, G. *pus*, Sw. dial. *pus*.] A common name for the cat; hence, a cat; also, a name for certain other animals, esp. the hare; sometimes, a hare; also, a playful term (sometimes slightly disparaging) for a girl or woman (as, "The little *puss* seems already to have airs enough to make a husband . . . miserable," George Eliot's "Adam Bede," ix.; "What do you know about it, you inquisitive little *puss?*" Arnold Bennett's "Hilda Lessways," i. 10).—**puss'y** (-i), *n.*: pl. *-ies* (-iz). Same as *puss*; also, a silky catkin, as of a willow; also, the game of tip-cat, or the 'cat' used in it.—**puss'y=cat,** *n.*—**puss'y=**

foot, *n.*; pl. *-foots.* A person with a cat-like, or soft and stealthy, tread; in general, one who pussyfoots. [Colloq.] —**puss′y-foot,** *v. i.* To go with a soft, stealthy tread like that of a cat; proceed or act cautiously or timidly, as if afraid to commit one's self on a point at issue. [Colloq.] —**puss′y-foot″er,** *n.*—**puss′y=wil′low,** *n.* A small American willow, *Salix discolor,* with silky catkins; also, any of various similar willows.

pus-tu-lant (pus′tū-lạnt). [LL. *pustulans* (*-ant-*), ppr. of *pustulare:* see *pustulate.*] **I.** *a.* Causing the formation of pustules. **II.** *n.* A pustulant medicine or agent.

pus-tu-lar (pus′tū-lär), *a.* Of, pertaining to, or of the nature of pustules; characterized by pustules.

pus-tu-late (pus′tū-lāt), *v. i.; -lated, -lating.* [LL. *pustulatus,* pp. of *pustulare,* < L. *pustula,* E. *pustule.*] To form pustules.—**pus′tu-late, pus′tu-lat-ed** (-lā-ted), *a.* Having pustules.—**pus-tu-la′tion** (-lā′shọn), *n.*

pus-tule (pus′tūl), *n.* [L. *pustula,* blister, pimple, pustule.] A small elevation of the cuticle, or a pimple, containing pus; also, any pimple-like or blister-like swelling or elevation.—**pus′tu-lous** (-tū-lus), *a.*

put¹ (pùt), *v. t.; put, putting.* [ME. *putten, puten,* push, thrust, put: cf. AS. *putung,* an impelling, inciting, *potian,* push, thrust, also Dan. *putte,* put, put in.] To push, thrust, or shove (now prov. or rare); also, to butt (now prov.); also, to throw or cast, esp. with a forward motion of the hand when raised close to the shoulder (as, to *put* the shot, to cast a heavy ball of metal as far as possible in this manner as an exercise or competitive sport); also, to move (anything) so as to get it into or out of some place or position; cause to come into or be in a place or position expressed or implied; place, set, lay, or deposit; also, to place in or bring into, or cause to be in, some relation, state, etc. (with numerous special applications: see senses following); place in the hands or power of a person, etc., to be dealt with (as, to *put* one's self under a doctor's care); set at a particular place, point, amount, etc., in a scale of estimation (as, he *puts* the distance at five miles); render or translate, as into another language; express or state (as, to *put* a thing in writing; "My mother's way of *putting* things may have been inconsequent, but then, one never had the slightest doubt of what she meant," W. De Morgan's "Joseph Vance," i.); assign or attribute (as, to *put* a certain construction upon an action); apply, as to a use or purpose; set, give, or make (as, to *put* an end to a practice); propose or submit for answer, consideration, deliberation, etc. (as, to *put* a question); impose as a burden, charge, or the like (as, to *put* a tax on an article); lay the blame of (*on, to,* etc.: as, to *put* a mishap to a person's carelessness); place in, bring into, or reduce to a condition specified (as, to *put* a plan into execution; to *put* things to rights); subject to the endurance or suffering of something (as, to *put* a person to trouble, or to death); set to a duty, task, action, etc. (as, to *put* one to work; "I rode at him again, *putting* my pony to a trot," W. H. Hudson's "Far Away and Long Ago," vi.); force or drive to some course or action (as, to *put* an army to flight). —**to put across.** Same as *to put over,* below. [Slang.]— **to put by,** to thrust aside, or reject; turn aside, as a blow, a question, etc.; put or lay aside, as for the present; lay by, as for future use (as, "The old gentleman had *put by* a little money": Dickens's "Old Curiosity Shop," xx.).—**to put in,** to pass or spend (time), as in a manner specified. [Colloq.] —**to put in mind.** See under *mind²,* *n.*—**to put in one's oar.** See under *oar, n.*—**to put off,** to lay aside; also, to postpone (as, "La Svengali's first appearance . . . had to be *put off* for a week": Du Maurier's "Trilby," vii.); bid or cause to wait until a later time (as, "John and I quite expected to be *put off*": Drinkwater's "Robert E. Lee," iii.); get rid of (a person, demand, etc.) by delay or evasive shifts (as, "Hastings, who wanted money and not excuses, was not to be *put off* by the ordinary artifices of Eastern negotiation": Macaulay's "Essays," Warren Hastings).— **to put on,** to take upon one's self, or assume (as, to *put on* airs); also, to assume insincerely or falsely (as, his sorrow is only *put on*).—**to put one's house in order.** See under *house²,* *n.*—**to put one's nose out of joint.** See under *nose, n.*—**to put out,** to extinguish (fire, etc.); also, to confuse or embarrass; distract, disturb, or interrupt, as in

the course of an action, speech, or calculation; incommode, or subject to inconvenience; annoy, irritate, or vex.—**to put over,** to do or handle (something) so as to make a success of it; carry out successfully; also, to succeed in imposing or foisting (something) adroitly or slyly on a person, a number of persons, or the public generally. [Slang.] —**to put through,** to carry to completion; carry out successfully.—**to put to it,** to force to a course; esp., to force to do one's utmost, drive to extremities, or put to straits (chiefly in the passive: as, "Many indeed actually died of starvation, and all were hard *put to it,*" S. Butler's "Way of All Flesh," lxxx.).—**to put up,** to present in action (colloq.: as, to *put up* a good fight, or a good game); also, to lay aside, as for the present (as, *put up* your work); put (a thing) into its ordinary place when not in use, as a sword into its scabbard; also, to pack up; place in receptacles or vessels for keeping; prepare (fruit, etc.) for keeping by cooking or preserving and inclosing in suitable jars or containers; also, to accommodate with lodging or entertainment; also, to render (a person) aware of or acquainted with something (with *to:* colloq.: as, to *put* a person *up* to the ways of the place); also, to incite (a person) to something (colloq.: as, to *put* one *up* to mischief); also, to plan beforehand or deliberately, in a secret or crafty manner (colloq.: as, to *put up* a job on a person).—**put¹,** *v. i.* To push or thrust (obs. or prov.); also, to butt (now prov.); also, to cast a stone, etc., esp. with a forward motion of the hand raised close to the shoulder; also, to go, move, or proceed (chiefly in nautical use, and mostly in certain phrases: as, to *put* to sea; to *put* about, to *put* back, to *put* in, to *put* off, to *put* out, which see below); make off (colloq.: as, to *put* for home); also, to shoot out or grow, or send forth shoots or sprouts (now prov.: cf. *to put forth,* below).—**to put about,** *naut.,* to change direction, as on a course; in general, to change or reverse one's course.—**to put back,** *naut.,* to reverse one's course; return to the port left; in general, to go back.—**to put forth,** to shoot or sprout forth; send forth buds, leaves, etc.; also, to set out, or start, esp. to sea.— **to put in,** *naut.,* to enter a port or harbor, esp. in turning aside from the regular course for shelter, repairs, provisions, etc.; in general, to enter a place for safety, entertainment, etc.—**to put off,** *naut.,* to leave the land; start out, as on a voyage; also, to leave a ship, as a boat does.—**to put out,** *naut.,* to go out to sea (as, "Many a light fishing-bark *put out* to pry along the coast": Macaulay's "Armada"); start on a voyage; in general, to set out; depart.—**to put up,** to sheathe one's sword, or stop fighting (archaic: as, "*Put up,* Jack, *put up* . . . how came you in a duel, sir?" Sheridan's "Rivals," v. 3); also, to pay down or stake money (slang); also, to take lodgings; lodge.—**to put upon,** to impose upon; victimize: usually in the passive: as, "The latter . . . advised him not to carry the jest too far, for he would not endure being *put upon*" (Fielding's "Joseph Andrews," iii. 7).—**to put up with,** to bear with patience or submission; tolerate: as, "I told him . . . that I had no notion to *put up with* his pretensions" (H. Melville's "Omoo," lx.).—**put¹,** *n.* A push or thrust (obs. or prov.); also, a throw or cast, esp. from the hand raised close to the shoulder; also, in the stock-exchange, etc., the privilege of delivering a certain amount of stock, etc., at a specified price, within a specified time.

put² (put), *n.* [Origin obscure.] A stupid or silly fellow; a bumpkin. [Archaic or prov.]

put³ (put), *v.* and *n.* See *putt.*

pu-ta-men (pū-tā′men), *n.; pl. putamina* (pū-tam′i-nä). [L., that which is removed in pruning or trimming, < *putare:* see *putative.*] In *bot.,* a hard or stony endocarp, as the stone of a peach.

pu-ta-tive (pū′tạ-tiv), *a.* [LL. *putativus,* < L. *putare,* cleanse, prune, trim, settle (accounts), reckon, consider, < *putus,* clean, clear.] Commonly regarded as such; reputed; supposed: as, the *putative* father of a child; a *putative* marriage; "every professed or *putative* ruffian in the West" (Roosevelt's "Ranch Life and the Hunting-Trail," viii.). —**pu′ta-tive-ly,** *adv.*

put-log (pùt′log or put′-), *n.* [Origin uncertain.] One of the short horizontal timbers that support the floor of a scaffolding. See cut on following page.

(variable) ḑ as d or j, ş as s or sh, ţ as t or ch, ż as z or zh; *o,* F. cloche; ü, F. menu; ch, Sc. loch; ṅ, F. bonbon; ′, primary accent; ″, secondary accent; †, obsolete; <, from; +, and; =, equals. See also lists at beginning of book.

put=off (pùt'ôf), *n.* A putting off or postponing; a postponement; also, a getting rid of by evasion or the like (as, "I would have asked farther, but Alan gave me the *put-off*": Stevenson's "Kidnapped," xxii.); an evasion.

a, Putlog; b, b, Putlog-holes; c, Ledger.

put=out (pùt'out), *n.* In *baseball*, etc., an act of putting a player out. See *out*, *adv.*

pu-tre-fa-cient (pū-trẹ-fā'shẹnt), *a.* [L. *putrefaciens* (*-ent-*), ppr.] Putrefying; putrefactive.

pu-tre-fac-tion (pū-trẹ-fak'shọn), *n.* [LL. *putrefactio(n-).*] The act or process of putrefying; rotting; decomposition; also, decomposed or putrid matter.—**pu-tre-fac'tive** (-tiv), *a.* Causing putrefaction; also, characterized by or pertaining to putrefaction.

pu-tre-fi-a-ble (pū'trẹ-fī-ạ-bl), *a.* Liable to become putrefied.

pu-tre-fy (pū'trẹ-fī), *v.*; *-fied*, *-fying.* [OF. *putrefier* (F. *putréfier*), < L. *putrefacere* (passive *putrefieri*), < *putrere*, be rotten, + *facere*, make.] **I.** *tr.* To render putrid; cause to rot or decay with an offensive odor. **II.** *intr.* To become putrid; rot; sometimes, to become gangrenous.—**pu'tre-fi-er** (-fī-ėr), *n.*

pu-tresce (pū-tres'), *v. i.*; *-tresced*, *-trescing.* [L. *putrescere*, < *putrere*, be rotten: see *putrid.*] To begin to putrefy; become putrid.—**pu-tres'cence** (-tres'ẹns), *n.* Putrescent condition; also, putrescent matter.—**pu-tres'cent**, *a.* [L. *putrescens* (*-ent-*), ppr.] Becoming putrid; in process of putrefaction; also, pertaining to putrefaction.—**pu-tres'ci-ble** (-tres'i-bl). **I.** *a.* Liable to become putrid; subject to putrefaction. **II.** *n.* A putrescible substance.

pu-trid (pū'trid), *a.* [L. *putridus*, < *putrere*, be rotten, < *puter*, *putris*, rotten, < *putere*, stink: see *foul.*] In a state of foul decay or decomposition, as animal or vegetable matter; rotten; foul or fetid from or as if from rottenness or putrefaction; attended with or pertaining to putrefaction; sometimes, gangrenous (as, *putrid* sore throat); also, fig., thoroughly corrupt, depraved, or bad (as, "He trifles with vice! His mind is in a *putrid* state!" G. Meredith's "Ordeal of Richard Feverel," xvii.); as a term of strong disfavor, offensively or disgustingly objectionable or bad.—**pu-trid-i-ty** (pū-trid'i-ti), **pu'trid-ness**, *n.*—**pu'trid-ly**, *adv.*

pu-tri-fy (pū'tri-fī), etc. See *putrefy*, etc.

putsch (pùch), *n.* [G.] An uprising or insurrection.

putt (put), *v. t.* or *i.* [Var. of *put*[1].] In *golf*, to strike (the ball) gently and carefully so as to make it roll along the putting-green into the hole.—**putt**, *n.* In *golf*, an act of putting; a stroke made in putting.

put-tee (put'ē), *n.* [Hind. *pattī*, strip, band, bandage.] A long strip of cloth wound spirally round the leg from ankle to knee, worn by sportsmen, soldiers, etc., as a protection or support; also, a kind of gaiter or legging of leather or other material, worn by soldiers, riders, etc.

put-ter[1] (pùt'ėr), *n.* [See *put*[1].] One who or that which puts.

putt-er[2] (put'ėr), *n.* [See *putt*.] In *golf*, a club with a relatively short, stiff shaft and a wooden or iron head, used in putting; also, one who putts.

put-ter[3] (put'ėr), *v. i.* Same as *potter*[2].

put-ti-er (put'i-ėr), *n.* One who putties, as a glazier.

putt-ing=green (put'ing-grēn), *n.* [See *putt*.] In *golf*, that part of the course within 20 yards of a hole, excepting hazards.

put-tock (put'ọk), *n.* [ME. *puttok*; origin uncertain.] Any of certain birds of prey, esp. a kite or a buzzard. [Obs. or prov.]

put-ty[1] (put'i), *n.*; pl. *putties* (-iz). See *puttee.*

put-ty[2] (put'i), *n.* [F. *potée*, < *pot*, pot.] A kind of cement, of dough-like consistence, made of whiting and linseed-oil and used for securing panes of glass, stopping up holes in woodwork, etc.; any of various more or less similar preparations, prepared from other ingredients and used for the same or other purposes; also, the color of the whiting and linseed-oil putty, a light brownish gray; in *plastering*, etc., a very fine cement made of lime only. Also, putty-powder.—**put'ty**[2], *v. t.*; *-tied*, *-tying.* To secure, stop up, cover, etc., with putty.—**put'ty=col"or**, *n.* A light brownish gray.—**put'ty=col"ored**, *a.*—**put'ty=pow"der**, *n.* A powder for polishing glass or metal, usually consisting of an oxide of tin.—**put'ty-root**, *n.* An American orchidaceous plant, *Aplectrum spicatum*, having a slender naked rootstock which produces each year a corm filled with an extremely glutinous matter, this corm sending up late in the summer a single large leaf which lasts through the winter, and in the succeeding spring a scape with a loose raceme of brownish flowers.

put=up (pùt'up), *a.* Planned beforehand or deliberately, in a secret or crafty manner: as, a *put-up* job (see *job*[2], *n.*). [Colloq.]

puy (pwē), *n.* [F., hill, < L. *podium*, elevated place: see *podium*.] A small volcanic cone of a type common in Auvergne, central France.

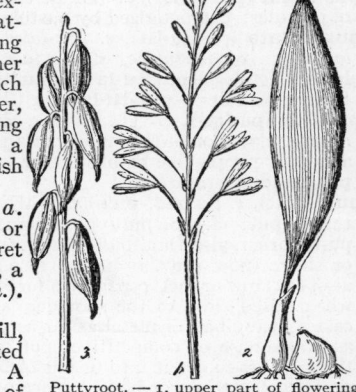

Puttyroot.— 1, upper part of flowering scape; 2, a leaf from a corm of the season, showing attachment to corm of preceding season; 3, fruiting scape.

puz-zle (puz'l), *v.*; *-zled*, *-zling.* [Origin uncertain.] **I.** *tr.* To embarrass or render helpless with confusion or uncertainty†, or bewilder† (as, "There is no darkness but ignorance; in which thou art more *puzzled* than the Egyptians in their fog": Shakspere's "Twelfth Night," iv. 2. 48); hence, to render at a loss what to do or say (as, "The poor creature *puzzled* me once in such a manner by a question merely natural and innocent, that I scarce knew what to say to him": Defoe's "Robinson Crusoe," i. 15); now, esp., to render at a loss what to think or understand (as, a problem that *puzzles* the philosophers; the long silence *puzzled* him; "that inscrutable face, which . . . even *puzzled* the ladies while he was making love to them," Barrie's "Sentimental Tommy," i.); perplex; exercise (one's self, one's brain, etc.) over some difficult problem or matter; also, to make (*out*), as something obscure, by careful study or effort (as, to *puzzle* out the meaning of a sentence); also, to render confused, intricate, involved, or complicated (as, "The ways of heaven are dark and intricate, *Puzzled* in mazes," Addison's "Cato," i. 1: now rare). **II.** *intr.* To be in perplexity; ponder or study over some perplexing problem or matter.—**puz'zle**, *n.* Puzzled or perplexed condition; a state of perplexity (as, to be in a *puzzle* over a matter); also, something puzzling; a puzzling question, matter, or person (as, "How they obtained her address was a *puzzle*," G. Meredith's "Diana of the Crossways," xiv.; "By Jove, but you're a *puzzle!*" Tarkington's "Magnificent Ambersons," xix.); specif., a toy or other contrivance designed to amuse by presenting difficulties to be solved by ingenuity or patient effort.—**puz'zle-head**, *n.* A puzzle-headed person; a person of confused ideas: as, "Most men are *puzzleheads*" (Mrs. H. Ward's "Robert Elsmere," xli.).—**puz'zle=head"ed**, *a.* Having or showing a puzzled head or confused ideas.—**puz'zle-ment**, *n.* Puzzled state; perplexity (as, "He was just talking in a tone of sheer hopeless . . . *puzzlement* — bafflement": A. S. M. Hutchinson's "If Winter Comes," iv. 2); also, something puzzling.

Puzzle-mug.— Pennsylvania-German pottery, dated 1809. (Pennsylvania Museum, Philadelphia.)

–puz′zle=mug, *n.* A drinking-vessel of pottery with perforated sides, several small spouts, and an inner tube through which the liquid contents may be drawn up to the mouth when a particular hole is closed with the finger. See cut on preceding page.—**puz′zler,** *n.*—**puz′zling-ly,** *adv.*

py-æ′mi-a, etc. See *pyemia,* etc.

pyc-nid-i-um (pik-nid′i-um), *n.;* pl. *-ia* (-i-ą). [NL., dim. < Gr. πυκνός, close, thick, dense.] In *bot.,* in certain ascomycetous fungi, a receptacle or cavity containing conidia. Also **pyc′ni-um** (-ni-um); pl. *-nia* (-ni-ą).

pyc-nom-e-ter (pik-nom′e-tėr), *n.* [Gr. πυκνός, dense: see *-meter.*] A flask or the like holding a definite volume of liquid, used in determining relative density or specific gravity.

pyc-no-style (pik′-nọ-stīl). [L. *pyc-nostylus,* < Gr. πυκνόστυλος, < πυκνός, close, + στῦλος, pillar, column.] In *arch.:* **I.** *a.* Noting or pertaining to an arrangement of columns in which the intercolumniation measures one and a half diameters. **II.** *n.* A pycnostyle colonnade.

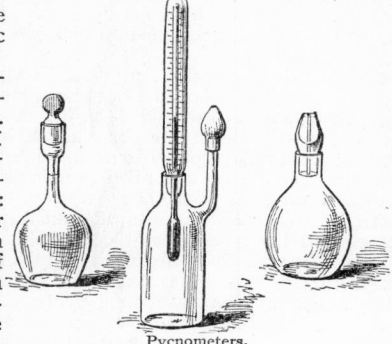

Pycnometers.

pye (pī), *n.* See *pie⁴.*

py-e-li-tis (pī-e-li′tis), *n.* [NL., < Gr. πύελος, trough: cf. L. *pelvis,* basin, E. *pelvis.*] In *pathol.,* inflammation of the pelvis of the kidney.

pyelo-. Form of Gr. πύελος, trough (see *pyelitis*), used in combination in the sense of 'pelvis.'—**py-e-lo-graph** (pī′ẹ-lọ-gráf), *n.* [+ *-graph.*] A photograph produced by pyelography. Also **py′e-lo-gram** (-gram).—**py-e-log′ra-phy** (-log′rą-fi), *n.* [+ *-graphy.*] The art of making photographs of the kidneys, etc., by means of the Röntgen rays, after the injection of an opaque solution.—**py-e-los′co-py** (-los′kọ-pi), *n.* [+ *-scopy.*] Observation of the kidneys, etc., by means of the Röntgen rays, after the injection of an opaque solution.—**py″e-lo-scop′ic** (-skop′ik), *a.*

py-e-mi-a, py-æ-mi-a (pī-ē′mi-ą), *n.* [NL., < Gr. πύον, pus, + αἷμα, blood.] In *pathol.,* a form of blood-poisoning caused by pyogenic bacteria: formerly supposed to be due to the absorption of pus by the blood.—**py-e′mic, py-æ′mic,** *a.*

py-et (pī′ẹt), *n.* See *piet.*

py-garg (pī′gärg), *n.* [L. *pygargus,* < Gr. πύγαργος, < πυγή, rump, + ἀργός, white.] A kind of antelope, perhaps the addax. Deut. xiv. 5.

py-gid-i-um (pī-jid′i-um), *n.;* pl. *-ia* (-i-ą). [NL., dim. < Gr. πυγή, rump.] In *zoöl.,* a caudal part or terminal segment of the body in many invertebrates, as insects, crustaceans, etc.—**py-gid′i-al,** *a.*

pyg-my, pig-my (pig′mi). [L. *Pygmæi,* pl., < Gr. Πυγμαῖοι, the Pygmies, prop. pl. of πυγμαῖος, dwarfish, < πυγμή, a measure of length, being the distance from elbow to knuckles, orig. the fist.] **I.** *n.;* pl. *-mies* (-miz). [*cap.*] One of a race of dwarfs in ancient history and tradition; also, a member of any of various negroid races of small stature, of Africa and of southeastern Asia, the Philippine Islands, etc.; [*l. c.*] a small or dwarfish person; anything very small of its kind; fig., one who is of small importance, or who has some quality, etc., in very small measure (as, an intellectual *pygmy*). **II.** *a.* [*cap.*] Of or pertaining to the Pygmies; [*l. c.*] of very small stature or size; diminutive or tiny; fig., of very small capacity, power, etc. (as, "a *pigmy* intellect": C. Brontë's "Jane Eyre," xxvii.).—**pyg-me′an, pig-me′an** (-mē′an), *a.*

py-in (pī′in), *n.* [Gr. πύον, pus: see *pus.*] An albuminous constituent of pus.

py-ja-mas (pī-jä′mäz), etc. See *pajamas,* etc.

py-lon (pī′lon), *n.;* pl. *-lons.* [NL., < Gr. πυλών, gateway, < πύλη, gate.] A gateway; specif., a monumental gateway to an Egyptian temple or edifice; also, a marking-post or tower for guiding aviators.

Pylon.—Temple of Edfu, Egypt.

py-lo-rus (pī-lō′rus or pi-), *n.* [LL., < Gr. πυλωρός, gate-keeper, < πύλη, gate, + οὖρος, keeper.] In *anat.,* the opening between the stomach and the intestine.—**py-lor′ic** (-lor′ik), *a.*

pyo-. Form of Gr. πύον, pus, used in combination.

py-o-gen-e-sis (pī-ọ-jen′e-sis), *n.* [See *pyo-* and *genesis.*] In *pathol.,* the generation of pus; the process of the formation of pus.—**py″o-ge-net′ic** (-jē-net′ik), *a.*

py-o-gen-ic (pī-ọ-jen′ik), *a.* [See *pyo-* and *-genic.*] In *pathol.,* producing or generating pus; attended with or pertaining to the formation of pus.

py-or-rhe-a, py-or-rhœ-a (pī-ọ-rē′ą), *n.* [NL.: see *pyo-* and *-rhea.*] In *pathol.,* discharge of pus; also, a diseased condition (in full *pyorrhea alveolaris*) characterized by the formation of pockets of pus about the alveoli, with shrinking of the gums and loosening of the teeth; Riggs's disease.

py-o-sis (pī-ō′sis), *n.* [NL., < Gr. πύωσις, < πυοῦν, cause to suppurate, < πύον, pus.] In *pathol.,* the formation of pus; suppuration.

pyr (pėr), *n.* [F., < Gr. πῦρ, fire: see *fire.*] In *photometry,* a unit of intensity of light, being somewhat less than the ordinary candle-power.

pyr-a-lid (pir′ą-lid). [NL. *Pyralidæ,* pl., < L. *pyralis,* < Gr. πυραλίς, winged insect supposed to live in fire, < πῦρ, fire.] **I.** *n.* Any of the *Pyralidæ,* a family of moths comprising numerous small or medium-sized, plain-colored species with a slender body. **II.** *a.* Pertaining to the pyralids; belonging to the *Pyralidæ.*—**py-ral-i-dine** (pi-ral′i-din), *a.* and *n.*

pyr-a-lin (pī′rą-lin), *n.* [From *pyroxylin.*] A substance composed essentially of pyroxylin and camphor, variously colored, as to imitate ivory, amber, tortoise-shell, ebony, etc., and used in the manufacture of combs and other toilet articles, knife-handles, paper-cutters, boxes, trays, counters for games, piano-keys, and numerous other articles, accessories, etc. [Proprietary name.]

pyr-a-mid (pir′ą-mid), *n.* [L. *pyramis* (pl. *pyramides*), < Gr. πυραμίς (pl. πυραμίδες); of Egyptian origin.] A massive structure built of stone, with square (or polygonal) base, and sloping sides meeting at an apex, esp. one of the class built by the ancient Egyptians to serve as royal tombs; also, a geometrical solid having a triangular, square, or polygonal base, and triangular sides which meet in a point; also,

The Pyramids of Gizeh, Egypt.

anything of such form (as, "a vivid *pyramid* of the most brilliant light": Scott's "Guy Mannering," liv.); a number of things heaped up or arranged in this form (as, "*Pyramids* of skulls were his particular architectural fancy," H. G. Wells's "Outline of History," xxxiv. § 5p; "Muskets were stacked in small *pyramids,*" J. Conrad's "Lord Jim," xliv.);

a tree pruned, or trained to grow, in this form; a pyramidal pinnacle or similar architectural feature; in *anat.* and *zoöl.*, any of various parts or structures of pyramidal form. Also, in speculation, the series of transactions involved in pyramiding.—**pyr'a·mid**, *v.* **I.** *intr.* To be disposed in the form or shape of a pyramid; also, to raise or increase something, as costs, etc., by gradual additions; specif., in speculating on margin, to enlarge one's operations in a series of transactions, as on a continued rise or decline in price, by using profits in transactions not yet closed, and consequently not yet in hand, as margin for additional buying or selling in the next transaction. **II.** *tr.* To arrange in the form of a pyramid; fig., to raise or increase (costs, wages, etc.) by gradual additions, as if building up a pyramid; specif., in speculating on margin, to operate in, or employ, in pyramiding.—**py·ram·i·dal** (pi-ram'i-dạl), *a.* [= F. *pyramidal*, < ML. *pyramidalis*.] Of or pertaining to a pyramid (as, "the *pyramidal* form": Johnson's "Rasselas," xxxi.); of the nature of a pyramid (as, "the *pyramidal* structures of ancient Egypt": Prescott's "Conquest of Mexico," iii. 6); pyramid-like; also, fig., colossal, huge, or extraordinarily great (a French use: as, a *pyramidal* success; *pyramidal* impudence).—**py·ram'i·dal·ly**, *adv.*—**pyr·a·mid'ic**, **pyr·a·mid'i·cal**, *a.* Pyramidal.—**pyr·a·mid'i·cal·ly**, *adv.*—**pyr·a·mid'i·on** (-i-on), *n.*; pl. *-ia* (-i-ạ). [NL., dim. < Gr. πυραμίς.] A small pyramid; in *arch.*, the apex in the shape of a small pyramid which often terminates the top of an obelisk.—**pyr'a·mid·ist**, *n.* One who makes a special study of the pyramids of Egypt, or is versed in their structure and history.

py·rar·gy·rite (pī-rär'ji-rīt), *n.* [G. *pyrargyrit*, < Gr. πῦρ, fire, + ἄργυρος, silver.] A dark-colored mineral consisting of a sulphide of silver and antimony, and showing (when transparent) a deep ruby-red color by transmitted light.

pyr·a·zine (pir'ạ-zin), *n.* [From *pyr*(idine) + *az*(ote) + *-ine*[2].] In *chem.*, a feebly basic, crystalline organic compound, with an odor like heliotrope; also, any of various compounds derived from it.

pyre (pīr), *n.* [L. *pyra*, < Gr. πυρά, pyre, < πῦρ, fire.] A pile or heap of wood or other combustible material (as, "Into a little *pyre* The twigs she built, and swiftly kindling fire, Set it alight": W. Morris's "Jason," vii. 161); esp., such a pile for burning a dead body (as, "Poor wretch . . . whose corpse they burnt with fire Upon a purple-covered spice-strewn *pyre*": W. Morris's "Jason," vi. 228); a funeral pile.

py·rene[1] (pī'rēn), *n.* [NL. *pyrena*, < Gr. πυρήν, fruit-stone.] In *bot.*, a putamen or stone, esp. when there are several in a single fruit; also, a nutlet.

py·rene[2] (pī'rēn), *n.* [Gr. πῦρ, fire.] In *chem.*, a solid hydrocarbon, $C_{16}H_{10}$, obtained from coal-tar, etc.

Pyr·e·ne·an (pir-ẹ-nē'ạn), *a.* Of or pertaining to the Pyrenees, a range of mountains between France and Spain.

py·ret·ic (pī-ret'ik), *a.* [Gr. πυρετός, fever, < πῦρ, fire.] Of, pertaining to, or producing fever.

pyr·e·tol·o·gy (pir-e-tol'ō-ji), *n.* [Gr. πυρετός, fever: see *-logy*.] The branch of medicine that treats of fevers.

py·rex·i·a (pī-rek'si-ạ), *n.* [NL., < Gr. πυρέσσειν, be feverish, < πυρετός, fever: cf. *apyrexia*.] In *pathol.*, fever.—**py·rex'i·al**, **py·rex'ic**, *a.*

pyr·ge·om·e·ter (pėr-jẹ-om'e-tėr), *n.* [Gr. πῦρ, fire, + γῆ, earth, + μέτρον, measure.] An instrument for measuring the heat radiated outward into space from the earth's surface.

pyr·he·li·om·e·ter (pėr-hē-li-om'e-tėr), *n.* [Gr. πῦρ, fire, + ἥλιος, sun, + μέτρον, measure.] An instrument for measuring the intensity of the sun's heat.—**pyr·he·li·om'e·try** (-tri), *n.*

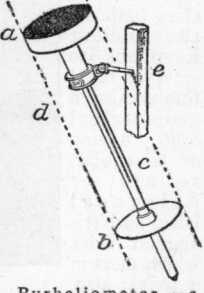

Pyrheliometer.—*a*, blackened disk exposed to sun's rays, the direction of which is indicated by dotted lines, as *db*; *c*, column of delicate thermometer whose bulb is inserted in the vessel (containing water or mercury) beneath *a*; *e*, place of support.

pyr·i·dine (pir'i-din), *n.* [Gr. πῦρ, fire.] In *chem.*, a liquid organic base, C_5H_5N, with a pungent odor, occurring in coal-tar, etc., and serving as the parent substance of many compounds: used as an antiseptic and

germicide, a remedy for asthma, etc.—**py·rid'ic** (pi-rid'ik), *a.*

pyr·i·form (pir'i-fôrm), *a.* [L. *pyrum*, prop. *pirum*, pear, + *forma*, form.] Having the shape of a pear; pear-shaped.

py·rite (pī'rīt), *n.* [L. *pyrites*: see *pyrites*.] A mineral, a native iron disulphide, FeS_2, with a brass-yellow color and a metallic luster, crystallizing in the isometric system.

py·ri·tes (pi-rī'tēz), *n.* [L., < Gr. πυρίτης, flint, pyrites, orig. adj. < πῦρ, fire.] Pyrite (usually called *iron pyrites*); also, marcasite ('white iron pyrites'); also, any of various other sulphides, as of copper, nickel, etc.—**py·rit'ic** (-rit'ik), *a.*

pyro-. Form of Gr. πῦρ, fire, used in combination: esp. used in scientific terms, as in *geol.*, *mineral.*, *physics*, and *chem.*, to imply the action of heat.

py·ro (pī'rō), *n.* Shortened form of *pyrogallic acid* or *pyrogallol*. [Colloq.]

py·ro·a·cid (pī-rō-as'id), *n.* [See *pyro-*.] In *chem.*, any of various acids obtained by subjecting other acids to heat.

py·ro·cat·e·chin (pī-rō-kat'ẹ-chin), *n.* [See *pyro-*.] In *chem.*, a white crystalline benzene derivative occurring in plants, etc., and prepared from phenol, by the distillation of catechin, etc.: used as a photographic developing agent.

py·ro·chem·i·cal (pī-rō-kem'i-kạl), *a.* [See *pyro-*.] Pertaining to or producing chemical change at high temperatures.

py·ro·clas·tic (pī-rō-klas'tik), *a.* [See *pyro-* and *clastic*.] In *geol.*, composed chiefly of fragments of volcanic origin, as agglomerate, tuff, and certain other rocks.

py·ro·crys·tal·line (pī-rō-kris'tạ-lin), *a.* [See *pyro-*.] In *petrog.*, crystallized from a molten magma or highly heated solution.

py·ro·e·lec·tri·ci·ty (pī''rō-ē-lek-tris'i-ti), *n.* [See *pyro-*.] The electrified state, or electric polarity, produced in certain crystals by a change in temperature; the science dealing with such phenomena.—**py''ro·e·lec'tric** (-ē-lek'trik), *a.* and *n.*

py·ro·gal·late (pī-rō-gal'āt), *n.* In *chem.*, a salt of pyrogallic acid: a compound more properly classed as an ether of pyrogallol.

py·ro·gal·lic (pī-rō-gal'ik), *a.* [See *pyro-*.] In *chem.*, obtained from gallic acid by the action of heat: as, *pyrogallic* acid (pyrogallol).—**py·ro·gal'lol** (-gal'ol or -ōl), *n.* In *chem.*, a white crystalline compound, $C_6H_3(OH)_3$, obtained by heating gallic acid, and used as a photographic developing agent: classed as a phenol, but often regarded as a weak acid.

py·ro·gen·ic (pī-rō-jen'ik), *a.* [See *pyro-* and *-genic*.] Producing heat or fever; also, produced by fire, as igneous rocks. Also **py·rog'e·nous** (-roj'e-nus).

py·rog·ra·phy (pī-rog'rạ-fi), *n.* [See *pyro-* and *-graphy*.] The art of burning designs on wood, leather, etc.; poker-work.—**py·ro·graph'ic** (-rō-graf'ik), *a.*

py·ro·gra·vure (pī''rō-grạ-vūr' or pī-rō-grā'vụr), *n.* [F.: see *pyro-* and *gravure*.] Pyrography.

py·rol·a·try (pī-rol'ạ-tri), *n.* [See *pyro-* and *-latry*.] The worship of fire; fire-worship.—**py·rol'a·ter**, *n.*

py·ro·lig·ne·ous (pī-rō-lig'nẹ-us), *a.* [F. *pyroligneux*, < Gr. πῦρ, fire, + L. *lignum*, wood.] Produced by the distillation of wood: as, *pyroligneous* acid (a crude acetic acid); *pyroligneous* alcohol (methyl alcohol). Also **py·ro·lig'nic**.

py·rol·o·gy (pī-rol'ō-ji), *n.* [See *pyro-* and *-logy*.] The science of heat; also, chemical analysis by means of fire or the blowpipe.—**py·rol'o·gist**, *n.*

py·ro·lu·site (pī-rō-lū'sīt), *n.* [G. *pyrolusit*, < Gr. πῦρ, fire, + λοῦσις, washing.] Native manganese dioxide: used in various manufactures, and added to molten glass to remove the brown or green tints.

py·rol·y·sis (pī-rol'i-sis), *n.* [See *pyro-* and *-lysis*.] In *chem.*, chemical decomposition produced by exposure to a high temperature.—**py·ro·lyt'ic** (-rō-lit'ik), *a.*

py·ro·mag·net·ic (pī''rō-mag-net'ik), *a.* [See *pyro-*.] Relating to magnetism as modified by heat; pertaining to or depending upon the combined action of heat and magnetism.

py·ro·man·cy (pī'rō-man-si), *n.* [ML. *pyromantia*, < Gr. πυρομαντεία, < πῦρ, fire, + μαντεία, divination.] Divination by fire, or by forms appearing in fire.

py·ro·ma·ni·a (pī-rō-mā'ni-ạ), *n.* [See *pyro-*.] A form of insanity marked by a mania for setting things on fire.—**py·ro·ma'ni·ac** (-ak), *n.*

---

py-rom-e-ter (pī-rom′e-tėr), *n.* [See *pyro-* and *-meter.*] Orig., an instrument for measuring the expansion of solids by heat; now, any of various instruments for measuring high temperatures.—**py-ro-met′ric, py-ro-met′ri-cal** (-rō-met′rik, -ri-kạl), *a.* Of or pertaining to pyrometry or the pyrometer.—**py-ro-met′ri-cal-ly,** *adv.*—**py-rom′e-try** (-tri), *n.* [See *-metry.*] The measurement of high temperatures, as with a pyrometer, or the science dealing with such measurement.

py-ro-mor-phite (pī-rō-môr′fīt), *n.* [G. *pyromorphit,* < Gr. πῦρ, fire, + μορφή, form.] A mineral consisting of a chloride and phosphate of lead, occurring in crystals and massive, and of a green, yellow, or brown color.

py-rone (pī′rōn), *n.* [Gr. πῦρ, fire: cf. *pyro-.*] In *chem.,* either of two isomeric organic compounds, $C_5H_4O_2$, having important derivatives.

py-rope (pī′rōp), *n.* [G. *pyrop,* < Gr. πυρωπός, fiery-eyed, fiery, < πῦρ, fire, + ὤψ, eye, face.] A deep-red variety of garnet, frequently used as a gem.

py-ro-pho-tom-e-ter (pī″rō-fō-tom′e-tėr), *n.* [See *pyro-.*] A form of pyrometer which measures temperature by optical means.

py-ro-phyl-lite (pī-rō-fil′īt), *n.* [G. *pyrophyllit,* so called from its exfoliating when heated, < Gr. πῦρ, fire, + φύλλον, leaf.] A mineral consisting of a hydrous silicate of aluminium, usually having a white or greenish color, and occurring in foliated masses and compact, the latter variety being used for making slate-pencils, etc.

py-ro-sal (pī′rō-sal), *n.* [From (*anti*)*pyr*(*ine*) + *sal*(*icylic*).] A colorless crystalline compound derived from antipyrine and salicylic acid, and used in medicine as an antipyretic and analgesic.

py-ro-sis (pī-rō′sis), *n.* [NL., < Gr. πύρωσις, a burning, < πυροῦν, burn, < πῦρ, fire.] In *pathol.,* an affection characterized by a burning sensation in the stomach, often extending to the esophagus, and the eructation of a watery, often acrid fluid; water-brash; heartburn.

py-ro-stat (pī′rō-stat), *n.* [See *pyro-* and *-stat.*] A thermostat; specif., a thermostat for high temperatures.

py-ro-sul-phu-ric (pī″rō-sul-fū′rik), *a.* [See *pyro-.*] In *chem.,* disulphuric.—**py-ro-sul′phate** (-fāt), *n.*

py-ro-tech-nic (pī-rō-tek′nik), *a.* [See *pyrotechny.*] Of or pertaining to pyrotechny or pyrotechnics; pertaining to, resembling, or suggesting fireworks. Also **py-ro-tech′ni-cal.**—**py-ro-tech′ni-cal-ly,** *adv.*—**py-ro-tech′nics,** *n.* The art of making fireworks; the making and use of fireworks for display, military purposes, etc.; also (often construed as *pl.*), a display of fireworks; a display of something resembling fireworks, as lightning; fig., a brilliant or sensational display, as of rhetoric, etc.—**py-ro-tech′nist,** *n.* One skilled in pyrotechny.

py-ro-tech-ny (pī′rō-tek-ni), *n.* [F. *pyrotechnie,* < Gr. πῦρ, fire, + τέχνη, art.] The art of using fire, as in mechanical operations†; also, the art of making and using fireworks; pyrotechnics.

py-ro-tox-in (pī-rō-tok′sin), *n.* [See *pyro-.*] In *chem.,* a toxin which is capable of producing elevation of temperature in the animal body.

py-rox-ene (pī′rok-sēn), *n.* [F. *pyroxène,* < Gr. πῦρ, fire, + ξένος, stranger; because orig. supposed to be a foreign substance when found in igneous rocks.] A common mineral with many varieties, usually consisting chiefly of a calcium and magnesium silicate.—**py-rox-en′ic** (-rok-sen′ik), *a.*—**py-rox′e-nite** (-rok′sē-nīt), *n.* Any rock composed essentially, or in large part, of pyroxene of any kind.

py-rox-y-lin, py-rox-y-line (pī-rok′si-lin), *n.* [F. *pyroxyline,* < Gr. πῦρ, fire, + ξύλον, wood.] Any of various substances (cellulose nitrates) made by nitrating certain forms of cellulose; guncotton or a similar substance; now, specif., any of the soluble cellulose nitrates used in making celluloid, collodion, etc.

pyr-rhic[1] (pir′ik). [L. *pyrrhicha,* < Gr. πυρρίχη, the dance; said to be named from Pyrrhichus, Gr. Πύρριχος, the inventor.] **I.** *n.* An ancient Grecian warlike dance in which the motions of actual warfare were imitated. **II.** *a.* Of or pertaining to this dance.

pyr-rhic[2] (pir′ik). [L. *pyrrhichius,* < Gr. πυρρίχιος, < πυρρίχη: see *pyrrhic*[1].] In *pros.:* **I.** *a.* Consisting of two short syllables; composed of or pertaining to pyrrhics. **II.** *n.* A pyrrhic foot.

Pyr-rhic[3] (pir′ik), *a.* Of or pertaining to Pyrrhus, king of Epirus: as, a *Pyrrhic* victory (one gained at too great a cost: in allusion to that of Pyrrhus over the Romans at Asculum, in 279 B.C., after which he is reputed to have said, "Another such victory and we are lost!").

Pyr-rho-nism (pir′ō-nizm), *n.* The doctrines or system of the Greek Skeptic philosopher Pyrrho (about 365—about 275 B.C.) and his followers; absolute or universal skepticism; hence, in general, skepticism (as, "The *Pyrrhonism* of my opinions has at all times rendered me notorious": Poe's "MS. Found in a Bottle").—**Pyr′rho-nist,** *n.*

pyr-rho-tite (pir′ō-tīt), *n.* [For earlier *pyrrhotine,* < Gr. πυρρότης, redness, < πυρρός, red, < πῦρ, fire.] A native sulphide of iron occurring in crystals and massive, of a bronze color and metallic luster, and often containing nickel, and generally slightly magnetic.

pyr-rol (pir′ol or -ōl), *n.* [Gr. πυρρός, red, + L. *oleum,* oil.] In *chem.,* a colorless, liquid organic compound, C_4H_5N, with an odor like chloroform, found in coal-tar, etc., and having the property of imparting a fiery red color to a pine shaving moistened with hydrochloric acid.

Py-thag-o-re-an (pi-thag-ō-rē′ạn). **I.** *a.* Pertaining to Pythagoras (6th century B.C.), a Greek philosopher, religious teacher, and mathematician, to whom the doctrine of metempsychosis is attributed, or to his teachings or school. **II.** *n.* A follower of Pythagoras.—**Py-thag-o-re′an-ism,** *n.*

Pyth-i-a (pith′i-ä), *n.*; pl. *-ias,* L. *-iæ* (-i-ē). [L., < Gr. Πυθία, prop. fem. of Πύθιος: see *Pythian.*] In *Gr. antiq.,* the priestess of Apollo at Delphi, who delivered the oracles.

Pyth-i-ad (pith′i-ad), *n.* [Gr. Πυθιάς (Πυθιαδ-), celebration of the Pythian games.] The period of four years intervening between two successive celebrations of the Pythian games.

Pyth-i-an (pith′i-ạn), *a.* [L. *Pythius,* < Gr. Πύθιος, < Πυθώ, Pytho, older name of Delphi.] Of or pertaining to Delphi, in ancient Greece (as, the *Pythian* games, one of the great national festivals of ancient Greece, held every four years in honor of Apollo); pertaining to the oracle or priestess of Apollo at Delphi. Also **Pyth′-ic.**

The Pythia seated on the Oracular Tripod. (From a Greek red-figured vase.)

py-tho-gen-ic (pī-thō-jen′ik), *a.* [Gr. πύθειν, rot: see *-genic.*] Produced by putrefaction or filth.

Py-thon (pī′thon), *n.* [L. *Python,* the serpent, in LL. *pytho*(*n*-), a soothsaying spirit, < Gr. Πύθων (in both senses): cf. *Pythian.*] In Greek legend, a huge serpent or monster fabled to have been slain by Apollo near

Python (*Python molurus*).

Delphi (as, "The laurel boughs That crown'd young Phœbus for the *Python* slain": Akenside's "Pleasures of the Imagination," remodeled version, i. 322); [*l. c.*] any of various large, non-venomous, old-world tropical snakes (genus *Python*), which kill by constriction (see cut on preceding page); any of various related or similar snakes, as a boa; also, a possessing spirit or demon, or one who is possessed by a spirit and prophesies by its aid.—**pyth-o-ness** (pith'ō-nes), *n.* [LL. *pythonissa*.] A woman supposed to be possessed by a soothsaying spirit, as the priestess of Apollo at Delphi; a woman with power of divination; a witch.—**py-thon-ic** (pī-thon'ik or pi-), *a.* Pertaining to the Python of Greek legend, or to pythons; python-like; also, pertaining to divination; oracular.

py-u-ri-a (pī-ū'ri-ą), *n.* [NL., < Gr. πύον, pus, + οὖρον, urine.] In *pathol.*, the presence of pus in the urine.

pyx (piks), *n.* [L. *pyxis*, < Gr. πυξίς, a box, orig. of boxwood, < πύξος, box-tree: cf. *box*[1] and *box*[2].] A box (now rare); specif., a box or chest, at a mint, in which specimen coins are deposited and reserved for trial by weight and assay ('trial of the pyx'); *eccles.*, the box or vessel in which the reserved eucharist or host is kept.

pyx-id-i-um (pik-sid'i-um), *n.*; pl. *-ia* (-i-ą). [NL., < Gr. πυξίδιον, dim. of πυξίς, box: see *pyx*.] In *bot.*, a seed-vessel which dehisces transversely, the top part acting as a lid, as in the purslane.

pyx-ie (pik'si), *n.* [Appar. < *Pyxidanthera*: see def.] A trailing, shrubby, evergreen plant, *Pyxidanthera barbulata*, of the eastern U. S., bearing numerous small, star-like blossoms.

pyx-is (pik'sis), *n.*; pl. *pyxides* (-si-dēz). [L.: see *pyx*.] A small box or box-like vase; a casket.

Pyx for holding the Consecrated Host, 12th century.

Q

Q, q (kū); pl. *Q's, q's* (kūz). A consonant, the 17th letter of the English alphabet.—**Q boat, Q ship,** a boat or ship having the appearance of some ordinary, non-combatant vessel, as a collier or any cargo-boat, but fitted up with concealed guns and arrangements for prompt action when attacked, used in the British Navy during the World War to decoy and fight enemy vessels, esp. submarines. Also called *mystery ship*.

qua (kwä or kwā), *conj.* [L., orig. abl. fem. of *qui*, who.] As; as being; in the character or capacity of: as, "*Qua* publisher's reader, I am a sad man" (Arnold Bennett's "Truth about an Author," xiv.).

quack[1] (kwak), *v. i.* [Imit.] To utter the characteristic cry of a duck, or a sound resembling it.—**quack**[1], *n.* The cry of a duck, or some similar sound.

quack[2] (kwak). [Abbr. of *quacksalver*.] **I.** *n.* An ignorant or fraudulent pretender to medical skill (as, "He who has once been under the hands of a *quack*, is for ever after prone to dabble in drugs": Irving's "Knickerbocker's New York," iv. 5); hence, one who pretends professionally or publicly to skill, knowledge, or qualifications which he does not possess (as, "In painting . . . Fortunato . . . was a *quack*," Poe's "Cask of Amontillado"; "If you are a *quack* in sanctity and devotion, you will find it an easy matter to impose on silly women," Smollett's "Humphry Clinker," June 10); a charlatan. **II.** *a.* Being a quack (as, a *quack* doctor); pertaining to or befitting a quack, or involving quackery (as, *quack* methods or medicines; "The doctors of medicine . . . offered me *quack* cures for imaginary diseases," G. B. Shaw's "Man and Superman," iii.).—**quack**[2], *v.* **I.** *intr.* To play the quack; practise quackery. **II.** *tr.* To advertise or urge, as a quack does his remedies; also, to treat by quack methods or remedies.—**quack'er-y** (-ėr-i), *n.*; pl. *-ies* (-iz). The practices or methods of a quack; an instance or example of these.—**quack'ish,** *a.* Like or befitting a quack; of the nature of quackery.

quack-sal-ver (kwak'sal-vėr), *n.* [D. *quacksalver*, now *kwakzalver*: cf. *quack*[1] and *salve*[1].] A quack in medicine; hence, in general, a charlatan. [Archaic.]

quad[1] (kwod), *n.* A quadrangle, or quadrangular court, orig. of a college: as, "Sounds of mirth come from some undergraduates' room on the opposite side of *quad*" (Hughes's "Tom Brown at Oxford," xlv.); "the *quad* of the hospital" (Trollope's "Warden," v.). [Colloq.]

quad[2] (kwod), *n.* In *printing*, a quadrat.

quad-ra (kwod'rą), *n.*; pl. *-ræ* (-rē). [L., a square, plinth, fillet: cf. *quadri-*.] A square frame or border inclosing a bas-relief, panel, or the like; hence, any frame or border. See cut in next column.

quad-ra-ble (kwod'rą-bl), *a.* [L. *quadrare*: see *quadrate*.] In *math.*, capable of being squared.

Quad-ra-ges-i-ma (kwod-rą-jes'i-mą), *n.* [LL., prop. fem. of L. *quadragesimus*, fortieth, < *quadraginta*, forty: cf. *quadri-*.] The forty days of Lent†; also, the first Sunday in Lent (more fully, 'Quadragesima Sunday').—**quad-ra-ges'i-mal,** *a.* Lasting forty days, as the fast of Lent; also [*cap.* or *l. c.*], pertaining to or suitable for Lent.

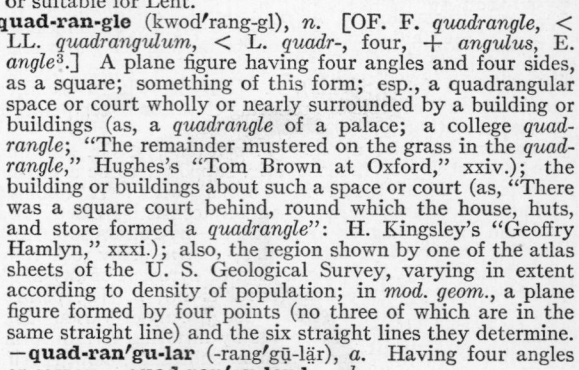
Quadra. — "Annunciation," by Luca della Robbia, in the Borgo San Jacopo, Florence.

quad-ran-gle (kwod'rang-gl), *n.* [OF. F. *quadrangle*, < LL. *quadrangulum*, < L. *quadr-*, four, + *angulus*, E. *angle*[3].] A plane figure having four angles and four sides, as a square; something of this form; esp., a quadrangular space or court wholly or nearly surrounded by a building or buildings (as, a *quadrangle* of a palace; a college *quadrangle*; "The remainder mustered on the grass in the *quadrangle*," Hughes's "Tom Brown at Oxford," xxiv.); the building or buildings about such a space or court (as, "There was a square court behind, round which the house, huts, and store formed a *quadrangle*": H. Kingsley's "Geoffry Hamlyn," xxxi.); also, the region shown by one of the atlas sheets of the U. S. Geological Survey, varying in extent according to density of population; in *mod. geom.*, a plane figure formed by four points (no three of which are in the same straight line) and the six straight lines they determine. —**quad-ran'gu-lar** (-rang'gū-lär), *a.* Having four angles or corners.—**quad-ran'gu-lar-ly,** *adv.*

quad-rant[1] (kwod'rant), *a.* [L. *quadrans* (quadrant-), ppr. of *quadrare*: see *quadrate*.] Square; of an approximately or generally square form: as, a cross nowy *quadrant* (see cut at *cross, n.*). [Obs. or archaic.]

quad-rant[2] (kwod'rant), *n.* [L. *quadrans* (quadrant-), fourth part: cf. *quadri-*.] A fourth part†; specif., the quarter of a circle; an arc of 90°, or the area included between such an arc and two radii drawn one to each extremity;

something shaped like a quarter of a circle, as a part of a machine; an instrument, usually containing a graduated arc of 90°, used in astronomy, navigation, etc., for measuring altitudes; also, in *geom.*, one of the four parts into which a plane is divided by a vertical and a horizontal line.—**quad-ran-tal** (kwod-ran′ṭạl or kwod′rạn-), *a.*

quad-rat (kwod′rạt), *n.* [Var. of *quadrate, n.*] In *printing*, a piece of type-metal of less than the height of the lettered types, serving to cause a blank in printed matter: used for spacing, etc. Commonly shortened to quad. en quad. em quad. 2-em quad. 3-em quad.

quad-rate (kwod′rāt), *v.*; *-rated, -rating.* [L. *quadratus*, pp. of *quadrare*, make or be square, < *quadra*, a square: cf. *quadri-*.] **I.** *tr.* To square (obs. or rare); also, to conform; adapt. **II.** *intr.* To agree; conform.—**quad′rate.** [L. *quadratus*, pp.] **I.** *a.* Square; rectangular. **II.** *n.* A square; something square or rectangular.

quad-rat-ic (kwod-rat′ik), *a.* [L. *quadratus*, pp.: see *quadrate*.] **I.** *a.* Square; in *alg.*, involving the square and no higher power of the unknown quantity (as, a *quadratic* equation); of the second degree. **II.** *n.* In *alg.*, a quadratic equation.—**quad-rat′i-cal-ly**, *adv.*—**quad-rat′ics**, *n.* The branch of algebra that treats of quadratic equations.

quad-ra-trix (kwod-rā′triks), *n.* [NL., < L. *quadrare*: see *quadrate*.] In *math.*, a curve used for finding a square equivalent in area to the figure bounded by a given curve, or for finding a straight line equal to a circle, arc, or the like.

quad-ra-ture (kwod′rạ-ṭūr), *n.* [L. *quadratura*, < *quadrare*: see *quadrate*.] The act of squaring; specif., the act or process of finding a square equal in area to a given surface, esp. a surface bounded by a curve (as, the *quadrature* of the circle, the insoluble problem of finding a square equal in area to a given circle); also, squared form†, or squareness†; a square space†; in *astron.*, the situation of two heavenly bodies when their longitudes differ by 90°; also, either of the two points in the orbit of a body, as the moon, midway between the syzygies.

quad-ren-ni-al (kwod-ren′i-ạl). [Earlier *quadriennial*, < L. *quadriennis*, < *quadri-*, four, + *annus*, year.] **I.** *a.* Of or for four years; also, occurring every four years. **II.** *n.* Something that occurs every four years; also, a fourth anniversary.—**quad-ren′ni-al-ly**, *adv.*—**quad-ren′ni-um** (-um), *n.*; pl. *-niums* or *-nia* (-ạ). [NL., for L. *quadriennium*, < *quadriennis*.] A period of four years.

quadri-. [L., also *quadr-, quadru-*: cf. L. *quattuor*, four.] A combining-form or prefix meaning 'four.'

quad-ric (kwod′rik). [L. *quadra*, a square: cf. *quadrate*.] In *math.*: **I.** *a.* Of the second degree: said esp. of functions with more than two variables. **II.** *n.* A quantic of the second degree.

quad-ri-cen-ten-ni-al (kwod″ri-sen-ten′i-ạl). [See *quadri-*.] **I.** *a.* Of, pertaining to, or marking the completion of, a period of four hundred years. **II.** *n.* A quadricentennial anniversary, or its celebration.

quad-ri-ceps (kwod′ri-seps), *n.* [NL., < L. *quadri-*, four, + *caput*, head.] In *anat.*, the great muscle of the front of the thigh, which extends the leg and is considered as having four heads or origins.

quad-ri-corn (kwod′-ri-kôrn), *a.* [NL. *quadricornis*, < L. *quadri-*, four, + *cornu*, horn.] Having four horns or horn-like parts, as an animal. Also **quad-ri-cor′nous.**

quad-ri-cy-cle (kwod′-ri-sī-kl), *n.* [See *quadri-*.] A vehicle similar to the bicycle and tricycle but having four wheels.

Quadricorn Sheep (*Ovis aries*, var. *quadricornis*).

quad-ri-fa-ri-ous (kwod-ri-fā′ri-us), *a.* [LL. *quadrifarius*: see *quadri-* and *-farious.*] Fourfold; in four rows.

quad-ri-fid (kwod′ri-fid), *a.* [L. *quadrifidus*: see *quadri-* and *-fid.*] Cleft into four parts or lobes.

quad-ri-fo-li-ate (kwod-ri-fō′li-āt), *a.* [L. *quadri-*, four, + *folium*, leaf.] In *bot.*, having four leaves; having leaves in whorls of four.

quad-ri-form (kwod′ri-fôrm), *a.* [LL. *quadriformis*: see *quadri-* and *-form.*] Having or combining four forms.

Quadrifoliate Stem of Four-leaved Milkweed (*Asclepias quadrifolia*).

quad-ri-ga (kwod-rī′gä), *n.*; pl. *-gæ* (-jē). [L., earlier pl., *quadrigæ*, contr. of *quadrijugæ*, < *quadri-*, four, + *jugum*, yoke.] In *class. antiq.*, a two-wheeled chariot drawn by four horses harnessed abreast.

Quadriga.—"The Rape of Proserpine by Pluto," from a Greek red-figured vase.

quad-ri-lat-er-al (kwod-ri-lat′e-rạl). [L. *quadrilaterus*, < *quadri-*, four, + *latus* (*later-*), side.] **I.** *a.* Having four sides. **II.** *n.* A plane figure having four sides and four angles; something of this form; the space inclosed between and defended by four fortresses; in *mod. geom.*, a figure formed by four straight lines which have six points of intersection ('complete quadrilateral').

quad-ri-lin-gual (kwod-ri-ling′gwạl), *a.* [L. *quadri-*, four, + *lingua*, tongue.] Using or involving four languages.

Complete Quadrilateral.

quad-ri-lit-er-al (kwod-ri-lit′e-rạl), *a.* [L. *quadri-*, four, + *litera*, letter.] Consisting of four letters, or (as certain Semitic roots) of four consonants.

quad-rille (kwod-ril′), *n.* [F. *quadrille*, < Sp. *cuadrilla*, company, troop (dim. < L. *quadra*, a square), also Sp. *cuatrillo*, the card-game, < *cuatro*, < L. *quattuor*, four.] A square dance for four couples, consisting regularly of five parts or movements, each complete in itself; some similar square dance; the music for any such dance; also, a game at cards played by four persons with forty cards, the eights, nines, and tens being discarded.

quad-ril-lion (kwod-ril′yọn), *n.* [F. *quadrillion*, < L. *quadr-*, four, + F. (*m*)*illion*, million.] In Great Britain, the fourth power of a million, represented by 1 followed by 24 ciphers; in France and the U. S., a thousand trillions, represented by 1 followed by 15 ciphers.—**quad-ril′lionth**, *a.* and *n.*

quad-ri-no-mi-al (kwod-ri-nō′mi-ạl). [From *quadri-* + *-nomial* as in *binomial.*] In *alg.*: **I.** *a.* Consisting of four terms. **II.** *n.* A quadrinomial expression.

quad-ri-par-tite (kwod-ri-pär′tīt), *a.* [L. *quadripartitus*, < *quadri-*, four, + *partitus*, pp. of *partire*, divide.] Divided into or consisting of four parts: as, a *quadripartite* vault.—**quad″ri-par-ti′tion** (-pär-tish′ọn), *n.*

quad-ri-syl-la-ble (kwod-ri-sil′ạ-bl), *n.* [See *quadri-*.] A word of four syllables.—**quad″ri-syl-lab′ic** (-si-lab′ik), *a.*

quad-ri-va-lent (kwod-ri-vā′lẹnt or kwod-riv′ạ-), *a.* [See *quadri-*

Quadripartite Vault.—Nave of Amiens Cathedral, France.

and -*valent*.] In *chem.*, having a valence of four.—**quad-ri-va′lence**, *n.*

quad-riv-i-al (kwod-riv′i-al). [L. *quadrivium*: see *quadrivium*.] **I.** *a.* Having four ways or roads meeting in a point; of ways or roads, leading in four directions; also, belonging to the quadrivium. **II.** *n.* One of the four arts constituting the quadrivium.

quad-riv-i-um (kwod-riv′i-um), *n.* [LL. use of L. *quadrivium*, place where four ways meet, < *quadri-*, four, + *via*, way.] During the middle ages, the more advanced division of the seven liberal arts, comprising arithmetic, geometry, astronomy, and music. Cf. *trivium*.

quad-roon (kwod-rön′), *n.* [Sp. *cuarterón*, < *cuarto*, < L. *quartus*, fourth: see *quart¹*.] A person having one fourth negro blood; the offspring of a mulatto and a white.

quadru-. Same as *quadri-*.

quad-ru-mane (kwod′rö-mān), *n.* A quadrumanous animal.

quad-ru-ma-nous (kwod-rö′ma-nus), *a.* [NL. *quadrumanus*, < L. *quadru-*, four, + *manus*, hand.] Four-handed; having all four feet adapted for use as hands, as animals of the monkey kind; of or pertaining to the *Quadrumana*, an old order including the monkeys, apes, lemurs, etc.

quad-ru-ped (kwod′rö-ped). [L. *quadrupes* (*quadruped-*), < *quadru-*, four, + *pes* (*ped-*), foot.] **I.** *a.* Four-footed. **II.** *n.* An animal (esp. a mammal) having four feet.—**quad-ru-ped-al** (kwod′rö-ped-al or kwod-rö′pē-dal), *a.*

quad-ru-plane (kwod′rö-plān), *n.* [From *quadru-*, for *quadri-*, + *plane²*.] An aëroplane with four supporting planes, one above another.

quad-ru-ple (kwod′rö-pl). [F. *quadruple*, < L. *quadruplus*, < *quadru-*, four, + *-plus*: see *double*.] **I.** *a.* Fourfold; consisting of four parts; four times as great. **II.** *n.* A number, amount, etc., four times as great as another.—**quad′ru-ple**, *v.*; -*pled*, -*pling*. **I.** *tr.* To make four times as great. **II.** *intr.* To become four times as great: as, "The mail *quadrupled* in size" (Bok's "Americanization of Edward Bok," xxxi.).—**quad′ru-plet** (-plet), *n.* Any group or combination of four; also, one of four children born at a birth.

quad-ru-plex (kwod′rö-pleks), *a.* [L. *quadruplex*, < *quadru-*, four, + *-plex*: see *duplex*.] Fourfold; quadruple; specif., noting or pertaining to a system of telegraphy by which four messages may be transmitted simultaneously over one wire.

quad-ru-pli-cate (kwod-rö′pli-kāt), *v. t.*; -*cated*, -*cating*. [L. *quadruplicatus*, pp. of *quadruplicare*, < *quadruplex*: see *quadruplex*.] To make fourfold; quadruple.—**quad-ru′pli-cate** (-kāt). **I.** *a.* Fourfold; quadruple. **II.** *n.* One of four things, esp. four copies of a document, exactly alike in every respect.—**in quadruplicate**, in four copies, exactly alike.—**quad-ru-pli-ca′tion** (-kā′shon), *n.* [LL. *quadruplicatio(n-)*.] The act of quadruplicating or making fourfold, or the resulting state; also, something quadruplicated or fourfold.

quad-ru-ply (kwod′rö-pli), *adv.* In a quadruple manner, measure, or degree.

quæ-re (kwē′rē). [L., impv. of *quærere*, seek, ask: cf. *query*.] **I.** A word used to introduce or suggest a question: as, *quære*, is this point fully proved? *quære*, whether the contrary is not more probable. **II.** *n.* A query or question.

quæs-tor (kwes′tor), *n.* [L., < *quærere*, seek, ask.] In ancient Rome, a public prosecutor in certain criminal cases; later, one of the officials in charge of the public funds.—**quæs′tor-ship**, *n.*

quaff (kwȧf), *v.* [Origin uncertain.] **I.** *intr.* To drink wine or the like in large drafts, as with hearty enjoyment (as, "That *quaffing* and drinking will undo you": Shakspere's "Twelfth Night," i. 3. 14); hence, to drink anything freely and with enjoyment; in general, to drink. [Now chiefly literary.] **II.** *tr.* To drink (wine, etc.) copiously and heartily (as, "They . . . poured out the sacramental wine into golden chalices, *quaffing* huge draughts to the beggars' health": Motley's "Dutch Republic," ii. 7); hence, to drink (anything) freely and with enjoyment (lit. or fig.: as, "Felicity . . . is *quaffed* out of a golden cup in every latitude," J. Conrad's "Lord Jim," xvi.); in general, to drink; also, to drink the contents of (as, "Your cup, filled with right

good wine, I have just now *quaffed* off": Scott's "Castle Dangerous," vii.). [Now chiefly literary.]—**quaff**, *n.* A quaffing, or that which is quaffed; a draft. [Now chiefly literary.]—**quaff′er**, *n.*

quag (kwag), *v. i.*; *quagged*, *quagging*. [Cf. *quake*.] To shake, as boggy ground or soft, flabby flesh. [Now prov. Eng.]—**quag**, *n.* A piece of soft, boggy ground with a surface apparently solid but shaking or yielding under the tread; a quagmire: as, "Let me get off the bridge . . . That firm bit by the *quag* will do" (Masefield's "Daffodil Fields," vii.). [British.]

quag-ga (kwag′ä), *n.* [S. Afr.] A South African quadruped, *Equus quagga*, now extinct, related to the ass and the zebra; sometimes, Burchell's zebra (see *dauw* and *zebra*).

quag-gy (kwag′i), *a.* Of the nature of or resembling a quag or quagmire (as, "Some dismal rood Of *quaggy* land about the river's edge": W. Morris's "Jason," x. 237); boggy; also, soft and flabby, as flesh, the body, etc. [Chiefly British.]

quag-mire (kwag′mīr), *n.* [Appar. < *quag* + *mire*.] A piece of miry or boggy ground whose surface shakes or yields under the tread; a bog; fig., a situation from which extrication is difficult.

qua-hog, qua-haug (kwä′hog, -hȧg, or kwa-hog′, -hȧg′), *n.* [N. Amer. Ind.] A roundish, edible American clam, *Venus mercenaria*, the 'round clam' or 'hard clam' of the Atlantic coast.

quaich, quaigh (kwäch), *n.* [Gael. *cuach*, cup.] A kind of shallow drinking-cup, commonly made of wooden staves and having two ears or handles. [Sc.]

Quahog.

quail¹ (kwāl), *v.* [ME. *quayle*, *quaile*; origin uncertain.] **I.** *intr.* To decline in strength or vigor, wither, or fade, as living beings, plants, etc. (now prov. Eng.); fig., to fail, become faint or feeble, or give way, as the courage; sink in discouragement, as the heart, etc. (as, "They . . . felt their hearts *quailing* under their multiplied hardships": Irving's "Captain Bonneville," xxx.); lose heart or courage, in difficulty or danger, as a person, etc.; shrink with fear, or as if afraid or cowed (as, "She made Barnes *quail* before her by the shafts of contempt which she flashed at him," Thackeray's "Newcomes," xxxii.; "looking at me with a rigidity of aspect under which I absolutely *quailed*," H. Melville's "Typee," ix.). **II.** *tr.* To affect injuriously†, impair†, or spoil†; fig., to cause to fail, give way, or sink, as the courage, heart, etc.; daunt or cow (a person, etc.).

quail² (kwāl), *n.*; *pl. quails* or (esp. collectively) *quail*. [OF. *quaille* (F. *caille*); from Teut.: cf. D. *kwakkel*, quail, of imit. origin.] A small, old-world gallinaceous game-bird, *Coturnix communis*; also, any of various allied or similar birds; specif., any of various American gallinaceous birds of the genus *Colinus* and allied genera, esp. *C. virginianus*, the bob-white, a well-known game-bird about ten inches long; also, a prostitute† (see Shakspere's "Troilus and Cressida," v. 1. 57).

quaint (kwānt), *a.* [OF. *cointe*, *queinte*, wise, clever, pretty, pleasing, fine, < L. *cognitus*, pp. of *cognoscere*, come to know: see *cognition*, and cf. *acquaint*.] Wise†, skilled†, or clever† (as, "to show how *quaint* an orator you are": Shakspere's "2 Henry VI.," iii. 2. 274); artful† or cunning†; also, devised or made with skill or art†, elegant†, pretty†, or fine† (as, "I never saw a better-fashion'd gown, More *quaint*, more

Common Quail of America (*Colinus virginianus*).

pleasing": Shakspere's "Taming of the Shrew," iv. 3. 102); hence, fine in dress or appearance, as persons†; also, of language, expressions, etc., elegant† or refined†; clever† or smart†; affected†; also, strange, singular, or odd (as, "In his wizard habit strange, Came forth,—a *quaint* and fearful sight," Scott's "Marmion," iii. 20: obs. except as in the following); strange or odd in an interesting, pleasing, or amusing way (as, "the *quaint* streets of New Orleans, that most foreign of American cities," W. Churchill's "Modern Chronicle," ii. 1; *quaint* carvings, imagery, or fancies; "Don Anastacio Buenavida of the corkscrew curls and *quaint* taste in pigs," W. H. Hudson's "Far Away and Long Ago," xiii.); oddly picturesque, esp. after an antique fashion (as, "the heralds in their *quaint* costume": Motley's "Dutch Republic," vi. 5); having an old-fashioned attractiveness or charm (as, a *quaint* old house or garden; a *quaint* little maiden).—**quaint′ly,** *adv.*—**quaint′ness,** *n.*

quake (kwāk), *v. i.*; quaked, quaking. [AS. *cwacian,* shake, tremble.] Of things, to shake or tremble, as from shock, internal convulsion, or instability (as, "boughs that *quaked* at every breath," Scott's "Lady of the Lake," i. 12; "the *quaking* mud," Pope's "Dunciad," ii. 292); also, of persons, to shake from cold, weakness, fear, anger, or the like (as, "*Quake* in the present winter's state and wish That warmer days would come," Shakspere's "Cymbeline," ii. 4. 5; "So terrible was the sight, that Moses said, I exceedingly fear and *quake*," Heb. xii. 21); shiver; shudder.—**quake,** *n.* A trembling or tremulous agitation; esp., an earthquake.

quak-er (kwā′kẻr), *n.* One who or that which quakes; [*cap.*] a member of the Society of Friends (see *friend*).— **Quaker gun,** a dummy gun, as in a ship or fort: so named in allusion to the Quakers' opposition to all war.—**Quak′er-ess,** *n.* A female Quaker.—**Quak′er-ish,** *a.* Like or befitting the Quakers.—**Quak′er-ism,** *n.* The principles and customs of the Quakers.—**quak′er=la′dies,** *n. pl.* The flowers of the common houstonia, or innocence.—**Quak′-er-ly,** *a.* Quaker-like.

quak-ing (kwā′king), *p. a.* That quakes; shaking; trembling.—**quak′ing-ly,** *adv.*

quak-y (kwā′ki), *a.* Inclined to quake; quaking.

qual-i-fi-a-ble (kwol′i-fī-a-bl), *a.* That may be qualified.

qual-i-fi-ca-tion (kwol″i-fi-kā′shon), *n.* [ML. *qualificatio(n-).*] The act of qualifying, or the state of being qualified; esp., modification, limitation, or restriction, or an instance of this (as, to assert a thing without any *qualification*); also, a quality† or attribute†; an accomplishment†; sometimes, character† or nature†; also, a quality, accomplishment, etc., such as qualifies or fits for some function (as, "My father, with all his high military *qualifications*, never became emperor, field-marshal, or even general": Borrow's "Lavengro," i.); a required circumstance or condition for acquiring or exercising a right, holding an office, or the like (as, a property *qualification* for the right of suffrage).—**qual′i-fi-ca-tive** (-kā-tiv). **I.** *a.* Serving to qualify. **II.** *n.* Something serving to qualify; a qualifying term, expression, or the like.

qual-i-fied (kwol′i-fīd), *p. a.* Furnished with qualities†; also, possessed of qualities or accomplishments which fit one for some function or office; having qualifications required by law or custom; also, modified, limited, or restricted in some way (as, a *qualified* statement).—**qual′i-fied-ly,** *adv.*—**qual′i-fied-ness,** *n.*

qual-i-fi-er (kwol′i-fī-ẻr), *n.* One who or that which qualifies; in *gram.,* a word, as an adjective or adverb, that qualifies another word.

qual-i-fy (kwol′i-fī), *v.*; -fied, -fying. [F. *qualifier,* < ML. *qualificare,* < L. *qualis,* of what kind, + *facere,* make.] **I.** *tr.* To attribute some quality or qualities to; characterize, call, or name (as, "The 'Devil's drawing-room,' As some have *qualified* that wondrous place": Byron's "Don Juan," x. 81); also, to furnish with a certain quality†; also, to invest with proper or necessary qualities; make competent (as, "He *qualified* himself for the business of scrivener": B. Franklin's "Autobiography," i.); specif., to furnish with legal power or capacity (as, "No one but a landholder was *qualified* to be elected into that body": Bancroft's "Hist. of the U. S.," Amer. Revolution, ii. 1); sometimes, to make legally capable by the administration of an oath; also, to

modify in some way; limit by a restriction or reservation, or make less strong or positive (as, to *qualify* a statement or an expression); make less violent, severe, or intense, or moderate or mitigate (as, to *qualify* the rigor of a statute); lessen the unpleasant effect of (as, "I had flashed a considerable quantity of gunpowder, to *qualify* the foul air within": Smollett's "Humphry Clinker," Oct. 11); modify or alter the strength or flavor of (as, to *qualify* liquors; "He . . . *qualified* his mug of water with a plentiful infusion of the liquor," Dickens's "Barnaby Rudge," xlv.); in *gram.,* to express some quality as belonging to, or limit or modify the meaning of (as, an adjective *qualifying* a noun; an adverb *qualifying* a verb). **II.** *intr.* To make one's self competent for something; obtain competent power or capacity, as by fulfilling necessary conditions or taking an oath; show one's self or be competent for something; also, to make oath to any fact (U. S.).—**qual′i-fy-ing-ly,** *adv.*

qual-i-ta-tive (kwol′i-tā-tiv), *a.* [LL. *qualitativus.*] Pertaining to or concerned with quality or qualities.—**qualitative analysis,** in *chem.,* the analysis of a substance in order to ascertain the nature of its constituents.—**qual′i-ta-tive-ly,** *adv.*

qual-i-tied (kwol′i-tid), *a.* Endowed with qualities.

qual-i-ty (kwol′i-ti), *n.*; pl. *-ties* (-tiz). [OF. *qualite* (F. *qualité*), < L. *qualitas,* < *qualis,* of what kind, such, having some quality, akin to *qui, quis,* who, and ult. to E. *who.*] Character or nature, as belonging to or distinguishing a thing (as, the *quality* of a sound; "The spring of water . . . entirely lost the deliciousness of its pristine *quality*," Hawthorne's "House of the Seven Gables," i.; "Give her what comforts The *quality* of her passion shall require," Shakspere's "Antony and Cleopatra," v. 1. 63); also, a characteristic, property, or attribute (as, the *qualities* of a metal; useful *qualities*; mental or moral *qualities*); also, character with respect to excellence, fineness, etc., or grade of excellence (as, food of poor *quality*; the finest *quality* of cloth; to consider the *quality* rather than the quantity of a thing); high grade, or superior excellence (as, goods of *quality*); also, native character, nature, or disposition, as of a person or animal (as, "You know the fiery *quality* of the duke": Shakspere's "King Lear," ii. 4. 93); mettle or temper (as, "This skeleton in the family cupboard was . . . a test of the *quality* of the man she had married": Galsworthy's "Saint's Progress," ii. 6); ability or capacity; native excellence or superiority; an accomplishment or attainment (as, "A just deportment, manners grac'd with ease, Elegant phrase . . . Are *qualities* that . . . ": Cowper's "Progress of Error," 423); also, social status or position (archaic: as, "The house . . . is frequented by gentry of the best *quality*," Fielding's "Tom Jones," ix. 4); good or high social position (as, a man of *quality*; persons of *quality*); the superiority or distinction associated with high social position (as, "There was *quality* and breeding in every movement of his body": Mrs. Stowe's "Oldtown Folks," xxiv.); persons of high social position (archaic, prov., or vulgar: as, "her ladyship . . . having in her youth been a great toast among the *quality*," Galt's "Annals of the Parish," ix.; "It was 'baker's bread' — what the *quality* eat; none of your low-down corn-pone," Mark Twain's "Huckleberry Finn," viii.); also, character or capacity (as, "The cripple . . . in his capacity of Peyrol's friend . . . had become a member of the Escampobar community": J. Conrad's "Rover," xvi.); also, profession† or occupation†; in *logic,* the character of a proposition as affirmative or negative.

qualm (kwäm), *n.* [Origin uncertain: cf. G. *qualm,* smoke, vapor, prov. swoon.] A sudden sensation of faintness or illness, now esp. of nausea; hence, a sudden sickening or disturbing feeling of some mental kind (as, "sudden *qualms* of apprehension and terror," Godwin's "Caleb Williams," iii.; "a *qualm* of home-sickness for the compact little gardener's cottage at Shonts," H. G. Wells's "Bealby," vii.); a sudden misgiving, or feeling of apprehensive uneasiness (as, "She had no *qualms,* no foreboding, no dubious sensation of weakness": Arnold Bennett's "Hilda Lessways," iii. 1); an uneasy scruple or a pang of compunction as to conduct (as, "an ignorant ruffianly gaucho, who . . . would . . . fight, steal, and do other naughty things without a *qualm*": W. H. Hudson's "Far Away and Long Ago," xii.); also, a sudden access or fit of anything (as, "Now he sure will die, By his strange *qualme* of liberality," J. Hall's "Satires," vi.; "Immediately after one of these fits of extravagance he will be taken with violent *qualms* of economy," Irving's "Sketch-Book," John Bull).—**qualm′ish**, *a.* Inclined to have, or having, qualms, esp. of nausea (as, "I am *qualmish* at the smell of leek": Shakspere's "Henry V.," v. 1. 22); characterized by qualms; of the nature of a qualm; also, apt to cause qualms.—**qualm′ish-ly**, *adv.*—**qualm′ish-ness**, *n.*—**qualm′y**, *a.* Qualmish.

quam-ash (kwom′ash or kwą-mash′), *n.* Same as *camass.*

quam-o-clit (kwam′ō-klit), *n.* [Mex.] Any of certain showy-flowered climbing plants which constitute the convolvulaceous genus *Quamoclit* (sometimes classed as a section of the genus *Ipomœa*), native in tropical or warm regions; esp., the cypress-vine, *Q. quamoclit.*

quan-da-ry (kwon′dą-ri, Brit. also kwon-dā′ri), *n.*; pl. *-ries* (-riz). [Origin unknown.] A state of embarrassing perplexity or uncertainty, esp. as to what to do; a dilemma: as, "Poor Mr. Biggs was in a sad *quandary*" (Marryat's "Mr. Midshipman Easy," xi.); "Having captured our men, we were in a *quandary* how to keep them" (Roosevelt's "Ranch Life and the Hunting-Trail," viii.).

quan-dong (kwon′dong), *n.* [Also *quandang*; native Australian.] A santalaceous tree, *Fusanus acuminatus*, of Australia, yielding an edible drupaceous fruit (called 'native peach') whose seed ('quandong-nut') has an edible kernel; also, the fruit, or the seed or nut.

quan-ta (kwon′tą), *n.* Plural of *quantum.*

quan-tic (kwon′tik), *n.* [L. *quantus*, how great: see *quantum.*] In *math.*, a rational, integral, homogeneous function of two or more variables.

quan-ti-fy (kwon′ti-fī), *v. t.*; *-fied*, *-fying.* [ML. *quantificare*, < L. *quantus*, how great, + *facere*, make.] To determine the quantity of; measure; in *logic*, to make explicit the quantity of.—**quan′ti-fi-a-ble** (-fī-ą-bl), *a.*—**quan″ti-fi-ca′tion** (-fi-kā′shọn), *n.*

quan-ti-ta-tive (kwon′ti-tą-tiv), *a.* [ML. *quantitativus.*] Pertaining to or concerned with quantity or its measurement; also, that is or may be estimated by quantity.—**quantitative analysis**, in *chem.*, the analysis of a substance in order to determine the amounts and proportions of its constituents.—**quan′ti-ta-tive-ly**, *adv.*

quan-ti-ty (kwon′ti-ti), *n.*; pl. *-ties* (-tiz). [OF. *quantite* (F. *quantité*), < L. *quantitas*, < *quantus*, how great: see *quantum.*] The being so much in relation to a possible more or less, esp. as the subject of mathematics; magnitude, size, volume, area, or length (obs. except in *math.*); amount or measure (as, food or flowers in great *quantity*; "I love thee . . . How much the *quantity*, the weight as much, As I do love my father," Shakspere's "Cymbeline," iv. 2. 17); length or duration in time (now only in legal use, with reference to the time during which the right of enjoyment of an estate is to continue, and as in *pros.* and *phonetics*, also *music*, below); also, proportion†; also, considerable or great amount (as, to extract ore in *quantity*); also, a particular, indefinite, or considerable amount of something (as, a certain, large, or small *quantity* of water; a *quantity* of waste matter; "her brown hair — of which she had *quantities*," M. Hewlett's "Open Country," iii.); a particular, indefinite, or considerable number of things or persons (as, a small *quantity* of books; a *quantity* of people; "*quantities* of collars, bracelets, wands, fans, and other trinkets," Prescott's "Conquest of Mexico," iv. 5); in *math.*, something having magnitude, or size, extent, amount, or the like; also, specif., in *pros.* and *phonetics*, of sounds (chiefly vowel sounds) or syllables, character as to being long or short, with reference to the time required in uttering them; in *music*, the length or duration of a note; in *logic*, the character of a proposition as universal or particular or sometimes as singular; also, the extension or the intension of a term or concept.

quan-tum (kwon′tum), *n.*; pl. *-ta* (-tą). [L., neut. of *quantus*, how great, how much, akin to *quam*, how, *qui*, *quis*, who: cf. *quality.*] Quantity or amount; a particular amount; a share or portion (as, "Every member pressing forward to throw on his *quantum* of wisdom, the subject was quickly buried under a mountain of words": Irving's "Knickerbocker's New York," vii. 8); in *physics*, according to a certain theory, a hypothetical particle or cell composed of the smallest amount of energy capable of existing independently, or this amount of energy regarded as a unit.

qua-qua-ver-sal (kwä-kwä-vėr′sąl or kwä-), *a.* [L. *quaqua*, whithersoever, + *versus*, pp. of *vertere*, turn.] Turned, pointing, or dipping in all directions: chiefly in *geol.*—**qua-qua-ver′sal-ly**, *adv.*

quar-an-tine (kwor′ąn-tēn), *n.* [It. *quarantina*, < *quaranta*, < L. *quadraginta*, forty.] A period of forty days (in specific uses); also, a period, orig. of forty days, of detention or isolation imposed upon ships, persons, etc., on arrival at a port or place, when liable or suspected to be bringing some infectious or contagious disease; hence, the stay required of ships or persons under such circumstances (as, "He had received orders to send back all persons coming from Egypt and force them to perform *quarantine* at El Arish": Kinglake's "Eothen," xxiii.); the detention or isolation enforced, or any strict isolation designed to prevent the spread of disease (as, a ship detained in *quarantine*; a house in *quarantine* for scarlet fever); temporary restraint or confinement for preventive sanitary purposes; also, a system of measures (detention, observation, disinfection, etc.) maintained by governmental or public authority at ports, on frontiers, etc., for preventing the spread of disease; the branch of the public service concerned with such measures; also, a place or station at which such measures are carried out.—**quar′an-tine**, *v. t.*; *-tined*, *-tining.* To put in or subject to quarantine.

quar-rel[1] (kwor′el), *n.* [OF. *quarrel* (F. *carreau*), < ML. *quadrellus*, dim. < L. *quadrus*, square.] A square-headed bolt or arrow, formerly used with a crossbow; also, any of certain tools, as a stone-masons' chisel; also, a small square or diamond-shaped pane of glass, as used in latticed windows.

quar-rel[2] (kwor′el), *n.* [OF. *querele* (F. *querelle*), < L. *querela*, *querella*, complaint, < *queri*, complain: cf. *querulous.*] A complaint†; also, an accusation† or charge†; also, a cause or occasion of complaint or hostile feeling against a person, etc., or the hostility resulting from this (as, "Herodias had a *quarrel* against him": Mark, vi. 19); one's cause or side in a dispute or contention (as, "Thrice is he armed that hath his *quarrel* just": Shakspere's "2 Henry VI.," iii. 2. 233); also, a cause†, reason† or ground† (as, "A man may have a *quarrel* to marry, when he will": Bacon's "Essays," Of Marriage and Single Life); also, an angry dispute or altercation (as, "If, upon a sudden *quarrel*, two persons fight, and one of them kills the other, this is manslaughter": Blackstone's "Commentaries," IV. 191); a disagreement marked by angry feeling or rupture of friendly relations (as, "Love *quarrels* are easily made up, but of money *quarrels* there is no end": Maria Edgeworth's "Belinda," iii.); also, quarrelsomeness†.—**quar′rel**[2], *v. i.*; *-reled* or *-relled*, *-reling* or *-relling.* To raise a complaint, or find fault (as, "All are prone to *quarrel* With Fate": Locker-Lampson's "Jester's Moral"); also, to dispute angrily, or wrangle (as, "Thro' wine they *quarrell′d*, and thro' wine were slain": Dryden's tr. Virgil's "Georgics," ii. 638); disagree angrily, squabble, or fall out (as, "The sisters *quarrelled* among themselves as all sisters will": W. Churchill's "Coniston," ii. 8).—**to quarrel with one's bread and butter**, to find fault with one's means of subsistence; indulge one's feelings by acting in opposition to one's material interests: as, "They are his [a clergyman's] bread and butter, these beliefs — and a man mustn't *quarrel with his bread and butter*" (Du Maurier's "Trilby," v.).—**quar′rel**[2], *v. t.* To dispute†, call in question†, or object to†; also, to find fault with, or reprove (a person: obs. or Sc.); also, to force or bring by quarreling. —**quar′rel-er, quar′rel-ler,** *n.*—**quar′rel-some** (-sum), *a.* Inclined to quarrel; given to quarreling: as, "On our idle days they were mutinous and *quarrelsome*, finding fault with their pork, the bread, etc., and in continual ill humor" (B. Franklin's "Autobiography," xii.).—**quar′rel-some-ly**, *adv.*—**quar′rel-some-ness**, *n.*

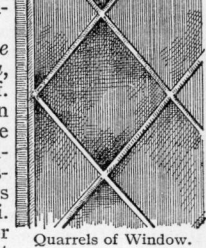

Quarrels of Window.

quar-ri-er (kwor′i-ėr), *n.* One who quarries stone.

quar-ry[1] (kwor′i), *n.*; pl. *quarries* (-iz). [For *quarrel*[1].] A quarrel, or small square or diamond-shaped pane of glass; also, a square stone or tile.

quar-ry[2] (kwor′i), *n.*; pl. *quarries* (-iz). [OF. *cuiree* (F. *curée*), < *cuir*, < L. *corium*, skin, hide.] Parts of an animal slain in the chase, given in the skin to the hounds†; also, a heap of game killed in the chase†; also, a beast or bird hunted or pursued; game, esp. game hunted with hounds or hawks; hence, any object of pursuit or attack.

quar-ry[3] (kwor′i), *n.*; pl. *quarries* (-iz). [ME. *quarey*, for earlier *quarere*, < OF. *quarriere* (F. *carrière*), < ML. *quadraria*, quarry (where stones are squared), < L. *quadrare*, make square: see *quadrate*.] An excavation or pit, usually open to the air, from which building-stone, slate, or the like is obtained by cutting, blasting, etc.—**quar′ry**[3], *v. t.*; *-ried*, *-rying*. To obtain (stone, etc.) from or as from a quarry; also, to make a quarry in.—**quar′ry=faced**, *a.* Having the face left rough as when taken from the quarry, as building-stone; built of such stone, as masonry.—**quar′ry-man** (-man), *n.*; pl. *-men.* A man employed in quarrying.

Quarry-faced Masonry.

quart[1] (kwârt), *n.* [OF. F. *quarte*, < ML. *quarta*, prop. fem. of L. *quartus*, fourth, < *quattuor*, four: see *four*.] A liquid and also dry measure of capacity, equal to one fourth of a gallon or one eighth of a peck (of varying content in different systems, places, and times); also, a vessel or measure holding a quart. See *liquid measure*, under *liquid*, *a.*, and *dry measure*, under *dry*, *a.*

quart[2] (kärt), *n.* [F. *quarte*, fem. of *quart*, fourth, < L. *quartus*: see *quart*[1].] In *card-playing*, a sequence of four cards (as, *quart* major, the sequence of the highest four cards in any suit); in *fencing*, the quarte or carte.

quar-tan (kwâr′tan). [OF. F. *quartaine*, < L. *quartana* (in *febris quartana*, quartan fever), fem. of *quartanus*, of the fourth, < *quartus*: see *quart*[1].] **I.** *a.* Of a fever, ague, etc., characterized by paroxysms which recur every fourth day, both days of consecutive occurrence being counted. **II.** *n.* A quartan fever or ague.

quarte (kärt), *n.* [F.: see *quart*[2].] In *fencing*, the fourth in a series of eight parries; carte.

quar-ter (kwâr′tėr), *n.* [OF. F. *quartier*, < L. *quartarius*, fourth part, < *quartus*: see *quart*[1].] One of the four equal or equivalent parts into which anything is or may be divided (as, to cut an apple into *quarters*; a *quarter* of a circle; a *quarter* of an hour); specif., the fourth part of a yard, or 9 inches; the fourth part of a hundredweight, or 25 pounds or 28 pounds; an old British measure of capacity for grain, etc., equal to 8 bushels, or, locally, to more or less than this; also, the fourth part of a year (cf. *quarter-day*); in schools, the fourth part of that period of the year during which instruction is given, generally 10 or 11 weeks (as, "He had withdrawn Miss Mannering from the school at the end of the first *quarter*": Scott's "Guy Mannering," xvii.); also, the fourth part of an hour (15 minutes), or the moment marking this period; also, one fourth of a dollar (25 cents), or a silver coin of this value; also, the fourth part of the distance between any two adjacent points of the 32 marked on a compass, being 2° 48′ 45″; also, one of the four parts, each including a leg, of the body or carcass of a quadruped (as, "The cattle were so small that a stout native could walk off with an entire *quarter*": H. Melville's "Omoo," lvii.); sometimes, a haunch (hind quarter), as of a horse; sometimes, one of the four parts, each including a limb, of a human body, esp. as formerly divided in the case of persons executed for treason, etc.; also, the region of any of the four principal points of the compass or divisions of the horizon, or such a point or division (as, "An aged warrior lighted the great pipe . . . and blew the smoke towards the four *quarters* of the heavens": Cooper's "Prairie," xxvii.); any point or direction of the compass (as, "Winds from all *quarters* agitate the air": Cowper's "Task," i. 373); a region, district, or place (as, "It was the opinion of Mark Lescarbot . . . that the immediate descendants of Noah peopled this *quarter* of the globe": Irving's "Knickerbocker's New York,"

i. 3); a certain part or member of the community, etc., without reference to locality (as, his information comes from a high *quarter*); a particular district of a city or town, esp. one appropriated to or occupied by a particular class or race of people (as, "the almost unmapped *quarter* inhabited by artists, musicians and 'people who wrote,' " Mrs. Wharton's "Age of Innocence," xii.; "He lived in the native *quarter*, with a native woman," J. Conrad's "Rescue," ii. 4); a place of stay, residence, or lodgment (now usually in *pl.*: as, the winter *quarters* of an army; "Colonel Despienne had *quarters* at the 'Sign of the Pheasant,' " Conan Doyle's "Exploits of Brigadier Gerard," viii.); the cabins inhabited by the negroes on a plantation (now in *pl.*: southern U. S.); appointed or appropriate position or station, as of officers or men of a war-ship in action, drill, etc. (now usually in *pl.*: as, "Call the drummer . . . and let him beat to *quarters*," Marryat's "Mr. Midshipman Easy," xxv.); also, relations with another† (as, "I knew two that were competitors . . . and yet kept good *quarter* between themselves": Bacon's "Essays," Of Cunning); treatment† or terms† (as, "They will give thee fair *quarter*": Scott's "Woodstock," xxxiii.); also, mercy or indulgence shown to a vanquished enemy in sparing his life and accepting his surrender (as, to cry *quarter*, to call for such indulgence; "those Christians . . . who . . . put whole troops of men to the sword, without giving *quarter*," Defoe's "Robinson Crusoe," i. 12); in general, mercy or indulgence; in *her.*, one of the four (or more) parts into which a shield is divided by horizontal and vertical lines; also, a charge occupying one fourth of the shield, placed in chief; also, a quartering, or one of various coats of arms marshaled upon one shield (as, "a baron of sixteen *quarters*": Scott's "Antiquary," xxiv.); in *arch.*, an upright post in partitions, to which the laths are nailed; in *vet. science*, either side of a horse's hoof, between heel and toe; in *shoemaking*, the part of a boot or shoe above the heel (and below the top), on either side of the foot, from the middle of the back to the vamp; *naut.*, the after part of a ship's side, usually from about the aftermost mast to the stern (as, "She [a ship] had the shore on her larboard *quarter*": Defoe's "Captain Singleton," xiii.); also, the part of a yard between the slings and the yard-arm; in *astron.*, a fourth of the moon's period or monthly revolution, being that portion of its period or orbital course between a quadrature and a syzygy; also, either quadrature of the moon; also, the phase of the moon at a quadrature. Cf. *phase*[2] and *moon*.—**first quarter**, in *astron.*, that fourth of the moon's period coming between the new moon and the first half-moon; also, the quadrature next after the syzygy at which the new moon occurs; also, the phase of the moon represented by the first half-moon after new moon.—**last quarter**, in *astron.*, that fourth of the moon's period coming between the second half-moon and the new moon; also, the quadrature next after the syzygy at which the full moon occurs; also, the phase of the moon represented by the half-moon after full moon.—**quar′ter**, *a.* Being one of the four equal (or approximately equal) parts into which anything is or may be divided; being equal to only about one fourth of the full measure.—**quar′ter**, *v.* **I.** *tr.* To divide into quarters, or four equal or equivalent parts; reduce to a quarter; specif., to cut the body of (a person) into quarters, esp. in executing for treason or the like; also, to divide into parts fewer or more than four; also, to put into or furnish with quarters for occupying, as soldiers or others (as, "the Scotch Greys, who were then *quartered* at Ayr," Galt's "Annals of the Parish," ii.; "Coligny . . . *quartered* all the women in the cathedral and other churches," Motley's "Dutch Republic," i. 2); station or lodge in a particular place; sometimes, to impose (soldiers) on persons, etc., to be lodged and fed (as, "Soldiers were *quartered* on recalcitrant boroughs": Green's "Short Hist. of the Eng. People," viii. 3); also, to assign to a particular position for action, etc., as on a ship; also, to range or traverse (the ground, etc.) in every direction, as dogs in search of game (as, "You could see the owls abroad . . . before sunset, in quest of prey, *quartering* the ground like harriers": W. H. Hudson's "Far Away and Long Ago," xiv.); in *her.*, to divide (a shield) into four (or more) parts by

Quarter.

horizontal and vertical lines; also, to place or bear quarterly upon a shield, as different coats of arms; add (another coat of arms) thus to one's own (as, "Might not he *quarter* a countess's coat on his brougham along with the Jones' arms?" Thackeray's "Newcomes," xxxi.); in *mach.*, to make holes in, fix, etc., a quarter of a circle apart. **II.** *intr.* To take up or be in quarters; lodge (as, "the village . . . where he proposed to *quarter* for the night": Scott's "Guy Mannering," i.); also, to range to and fro, as dogs in search of game; move about, or shift position repeatedly (as, "They *quarter* over the ground again and again, Tom always on the defensive": Hughes's "Tom Brown's School Days," ii. 5); move in a slanting direction (as, "When he had pulled a mile above the village, he started *quartering* across and bent himself stoutly to his work": Mark Twain's "Tom Sawyer," xv.); also, to drive to one side, as to avoid ruts or to let another vehicle pass (Eng.); *naut.*, to sail with the wind on the quarter; of the wind, to blow on a ship's quarter (as, "She [a ship] came down upon us with the wind *quartering*": Defoe's "Captain Singleton," xi.).

quar-ter-age (kwâr′tèr-āj), *n.* A quarterly payment, charge, or allowance; also, the quartering of troops, etc.; quarters or lodging.

quar-ter=back (kwâr′tèr-bak), *n.* In *football*, a certain player behind the forward line. See *back*[2], *n.*

quar-ter=boat (kwâr′tèr-bōt), *n. Naut.*, any boat hung on davits over a ship's quarter: as, "We . . . lowered away the *quarter-boats*, and went ashore" (Dana's "Two Years before the Mast," xxiv.).

quar-ter=crack (kwâr′tèr-krak), *n.* A sand-crack on the quarter of a horse's hoof. See *sand-crack.*

quar-ter=day (kwâr′tèr-dā), *n.* In British use, one of the four days (in England, Lady Day, Midsummer Day, Michaelmas, and Christmas; in Scotland, Candlemas, Whitsunday, Lammas, and Martinmas) regarded as marking off the quarters of the year, on which tenancies begin and end, quarterly payments fall due, etc.

quar-ter=deck (kwâr′tèr-dek), *n. Naut.*, that part of the upper deck between the mainmast and the poop or stern.

quar-tered (kwâr′tèrd), *p. a.* Divided into quarters; reduced to a quarter (as, "yon cloudless, *quartered* moon": Holmes's "For the Burns Centennial Celebration"); specif., of oak, etc., prepared by sawing the log lengthwise into quarters and then cutting into boards, in order to show the grain to advantage and prevent warping; also, furnished with quarters or lodging; also, having quarters as specified (as, a short-*quartered* horse; low-*quartered* shoes); in *her.*, divided or arranged quarterly; of a cross, having a square piece missing in the center.

A Cross Quartered.

quar-ter-ing (kwâr′tèr-ing), *n.* The act of one who or that which quarters; in *her.*, the division of a shield into (four or more) quarters; also, the marshaling of various coats of arms upon one shield, as to indicate family alliances; one of the coats so marshaled (chiefly in *pl.*: as, "a fat duchess, with fourteen *quarterings*," Lever's "Harry Lorrequer," liv.). —**quar′ter-ing**, *p. a.* That quarters; *naut.*, of a wind, blowing on a ship's quarter.

quar-ter-ly (kwâr′tèr-li). **I.** *a.* Pertaining to or consisting of a quarter; esp., pertaining to or covering a quarter of a year; occurring, done, etc., at the end of every quarter of a year. **II.** *n.*; pl. *-lies* (-liz). A periodical issued once every quarter of a year. —**quar′ter-ly**, *adv.* In or by quarters; also, once in a quarter of a year; in *her.*, with division into quarters; also, in the quarters of a shield.

Quartering. — First and fourth quarters are of one ancestor, A; second quarter is of another, B; third of another, C.

quar-ter-mas-ter (kwâr′tèr-màs″tèr), *n. Naut.*, a petty officer on a merchant vessel or the like, who has charge of the steering of the ship, the compasses, the signals, etc.; *naval*, a petty officer having charge of signals, navigating apparatus, etc.; also, *milit.*, an officer charged with providing quarters, clothing, fuel, transportation, etc., for a body of troops.—

quar′ter-mas″ter=gen′er-al, *n.*; pl. *-als. Milit.*, a staff-officer in charge of the department which provides for the quarters, equipment, transportation, etc., of troops.

quar-tern (kwâr′tèrn), *n.* [OF. F. *quarteron*, < *quart*, fourth: see *quart*[2].] A quarter, or fourth part, esp. of certain weights and measures, as of a pound, ounce, peck, or pint; also, a loaf of bread weighing about four pounds (in full, *quartern-loaf*).

quar-ter=note (kwâr′tèr-nōt), *n.* In *music*, a note equivalent to one fourth of a whole-note; a crotchet.

quar-ter=phase (kwâr′tèr-fāz), *a.* In *elect.*, noting or pertaining to a circuit made up of a combination of two alternating currents which differ in phase by one quarter of a cycle.

quar-ter=saw (kwâr′tèr-sâ), *v. t.* To saw into quarters; esp., to saw (a log) lengthwise into quarters and then into boards, as in making quartered oak, etc.

quar-ter=ses-sions (kwâr′tèr-sesh′ọnz), *n. pl.* In law, an English court of limited criminal jurisdiction combined with certain other powers, held quarterly; also, any of various other courts held quarterly.

quar-ter=staff (kwâr′tèr-stàf), *n.*; pl. *-staves* (-stāvz). An old English weapon consisting of a stout pole 6 to 8 feet long tipped with iron; exercise or fighting with this weapon (as, "He was famous throughout the province for strength of arm and skill at *quarter-staff*": Irving's "Knickerbocker's New York," iv. 6).

quar-tet, quar-tette (kwâr-tet′), *n.* [F. *quartette*, < It. *quartetto*, < *quarto*, fourth, < L. *quartus*: see *quart*[1].] A musical composition for four voices or instruments; also, a company of four singers or players; also, any group of four persons or things.

quar-tile (kwâr′til). [= F. *quartil*, < L. *quartus*, fourth: see *quart*[1].] **I.** *a.* Noting a point in a statistical series or the like, such that the number of cases above it or below it is equal to one fourth the total number of cases; in *astrol.*, noting or pertaining to the aspect of two heavenly bodies when their longitudes differ by 90°. **II.** *n.* A quartile point; in *astrol.*, a quartile aspect.

quar-to (kwâr′tō). [NL. *in quarto*, 'in fourth.']' **I.** *n.*; pl. *-tos* (-tōz). The page size of a book in which each leaf is one fourth of a whole sheet of paper; a volume of this size. Abbreviated 4*to* or 4°. **II.** *a.* In quarto.

quartz (kwârts), *n.* [G. *quarz*; origin uncertain.] A common mineral composed of silicon dioxide, having many varieties which differ in color, luster, etc. Cf. *agate*[2], *amethyst*, *bloodstone*, *chalcedony*, *jasper*, etc.—**clear fused quartz**, a clear vitreous solid, or glass, produced by fusion of a very pure form of silica, or quartz, or rock-crystal, and said to be the clearest solid known: remarkably transparent to the infra-red, visible, and ultra-violet radiations, and particularly valuable for use in transmission of ultra-violet rays (to which ordinary glass is opaque), whereby these rays, which are highly germicidal, can be carried to diseased parts of the body.—**quartz-if-er-ous** (kwârt-sif′e-rus), *a.* [See *-ferous*.] Containing quartz; consisting of quartz.—**quartz-ite** (kwârt′-sīt), *n.* A granular rock consisting essentially of quartz.—**quartz-ose** (kwârt′sōs), *a.* Consisting mainly or wholly of quartz; quartz-like.

quash[1] (kwosh), *v. t.* [OF. *quasser* (F. *casser*), < L. *quassare*, shake, break, freq. of *quatere*, shake.] To break to pieces†; crush†; fig., to put down or suppress completely; subdue; quell.

quash[2] (kwosh), *v. t.* [OF. *quasser* (F. *casser*), < LL. *cassare*, annul, < L. *cassus*, empty, void.] To make void, annul, or set aside (a law, indictment, decision, etc.): as, "A . . . lawyer . . . having examined the documents in the case, was hopeful of getting the conviction *quashed*" (Arnold Bennett's "The Old Adam," ix.).

qua-si (kwā′sī), *conj.* or *adv.* [L.] As if; as if it were; as it were. Often used as a prefix (with hyphen), less often separately as if an adjective or adverb, before a word which is not strictly applicable in the particular case: as, a *quasi*-noun (a word having the semblance or function of a noun, though not actually such); "a certain boisterous and rather coarse *quasi*-humour which passed for wit with many" (S. Butler's "Way of All Flesh," vii.); a *quasi*-official announcement.

quas-sia (kwas′iạ or kwosh′iạ), n. [NL.; named from *Quassi*, a Surinam negro who (about 1730) used the bark as a remedy for fever.] A plant of the simarubaceous genus *Quassia*, esp. *Q. amara*, a tree of tropical America; also, the bitter wood of this tree and certain other trees, or a medicinal preparation made from it. — **quas-sin** (kwas′in or kwos′-), n. In *chem.*, the bitter principle of quassia, obtained as a white crystalline substance.

Branch of Quassia (*Q. amara*), with inflorescence. — *a*, a flower; *b*, the fruit.

qua-ter-cen-te-na-ry (kwä-tẽr-sen′te-nā-ri). [L. *quater*, four times, + E. *centenary*.] **I.** *a.* Pertaining to four hundred or a period of four hundred years; marking the completion of four hundred years. **II.** *n.*; pl. *-ries* (-riz). A four-hundredth anniversary, or its celebration.

qua-ter-na-ry (kwạ-tẽr′nạ-ri). [L. *quaternarius*, < *quaterni*, four each, distributive of *quattuor*, four.] **I.** *a.* Consisting of four; arranged in fours; [cap.] in *geol.*, noting or pertaining to the most recent geological period or system of rocks, that succeeding the Tertiary and constituting the later principal division of the Cenozoic. **II.** *n.*; pl. *-ries* (-riz). A group of four; also, the number four; also [cap.], in *geol.*, the Quaternary period or system.

qua-ter-nate (kwạ-tẽr′nāt), a. [NL. *quaternatus*, < L. *quaterni*: see *quaternary*.] Consisting of four; arranged in fours; in *bot.*, consisting of four leaflets, as a compound leaf.

qua-ter-ni-on (kwạ-tẽr′ni-ọn), n. [LL. *quaternio*(n-), the number four, a group of four, < L. *quaterni*: see *quaternary*.] A group or set of four persons or things (as, "four *quaternions* of soldiers," Acts, xii. 4; "the four inside people . . . the illustrious *quaternion*," De Quincey's "English Mail-Coach," i.); in *math.*, the quotient of two vectors considered as depending on four geometrical elements and as expressible by an algebraic quadrinomial; *pl.*, the calculus of such quantities.

qua-ter-ni-ty (kwạ-tẽr′ni-ti), n.; pl. *-ties* (-tiz). [LL. *quaternitas*, < L. *quaterni*: see *quaternary*.] A group or set of four persons or things; esp., a union of four persons in the Godhead. Cf. *trinity*.

qua-tor-zain (kạ-tôr′zān or kat′ọr-), n. [F. *quatorzaine*, a set of fourteen, < *quatorze*, < L. *quattuordecim*, fourteen, < *quattuor*, four, + *decem*, ten.] A poem or stanza of fourteen lines; esp., a poem of fourteen lines resembling a sonnet but without adherence to strict sonnet forms.

quat-rain (kwot′rān), n. [F. *quatrain*, < *quatre*, four: see *quatre*.] A stanza or poem of four lines, usually with alternate rimes.

qua-tre (kä′tẽr, F. kȧtr), n. [OF. F., < L. *quattuor*, four: see *four*.] Four; the four at cards, dice, or the like.

quat-re-foil (kat′ẽr-foil), n. [OF. *quatre*, four, + *foil*, leaf: see *quatre* and *foil*¹.] A leaf composed of four leaflets, as sometimes a leaf of clover; in *arch.*, an ornament or decorative feature having four foils or lobes.

Architectural Quatrefoils.

quat-tro-cen-to (kwät-trō-chen′tō), n. [It., four hundred, short for *mille quattrocento*, one thousand four hundred.] The 15th century, with reference to Italy, and esp. to the Italian art or literature of that period. — **quat-tro-cen′tist**, n.

qua-ver (kwā′vẽr), v. [ME., freq. of *quaven*, earlier *cwavien*, shake: cf. *quiver*².] **I.** *intr.* To shake tremulously, quiver, or tremble (now said usually of the voice); sound, speak, or sing tremulously; also, to perform quavers, shakes, or trills in singing or on a musical instrument. **II.** *tr.* To utter, say, or sing with a quavering or tremulous voice; also, to sing with quavers or shakes. — **qua′ver**, n. A quavering or tremulous shake, esp. in the voice (as, "His voice . . . had nothing of the tremulous *quaver* and cackle of an old man's utterance": Hawthorne's "Scarlet Letter," The Custom House); a quavering tone or utterance; in *music*, a shake or trill, esp. in singing; also, an eighth-note. — **qua′ver-er**, n. — **qua′ver-ing-ly**, adv.

quay (kē), n. [Later spelling (after F. *quai*) of earlier *kay*, also *key* (whence the modern pronunciation of *quay*), < OF. *kay*, *cay* (F. *quai*), quay, akin to Sp. *cayo*, shoal: see *cay* and *key*².] An artificial landing-place, as of masonry, built along navigable water, for the use of vessels arriving, unloading or loading cargo, etc.: as, "to assign proper wharfs and *quays* in each port, for the exclusive landing and loading of merchandise" (Blackstone's "Commentaries," I. 264). — **quay**, v. t. To furnish with a quay or quays. — **quay′age** (-ạj), n. [F.] A charge for the use of a quay; also, quays collectively; space appropriated to quays.

quean (kwēn), n. [AS. *cwene* = OS. and OHG. *quena* = Icel. *kvenna* = Goth. *qinō*, woman; akin to Gr. γυνή, Skt. *jani*, woman, wife: cf. *queen*.] A woman, or female person (obs. or prov. in the general sense); a girl or young woman (Sc. or prov. Eng.: as, "*Queans*, A′ plump and strapping in their teens," Burns's "Tam o′ Shanter," 151); also, in various disparaging uses (now chiefly archaic or prov.), a bold, ill-behaved, or otherwise reprehensible woman; a hussy or jade; a shrew (as, "This martial scold, This modern Amazon and queen of *queans*": Byron's "Don Juan," vi. 96); a slut (as, "to call an honest woman slut and *quean*, if there be but a speck of soot upon his band-collar": Scott's "Abbot," iv.); sometimes, a harlot or strumpet.

quea-sy (kwē′zi), a. [ME. *qwesye*, *quasy*, *coysy*; origin uncertain.] Unsettled, uncertain, or ticklish, as times, matters, etc.†; also, tending to unsettle the stomach or cause nausea, as articles of food; inclined to nausea, as the stomach, a person, etc.; fig., sickened or disgusted (as, "*queasy* with his insolence," Shakspere's "Antony and Cleopatra," iii. 6. 20; "a cynic of a boy, said to be *queasy* with excess of sisters," G. Meredith's "Lord Ormont and His Aminta," i.); uneasy or uncomfortable, as feelings, the conscience, etc.; squeamish, or excessively delicate or fastidious. — **quea′si-ly**, adv. — **quea′si-ness**, n.

que-bra-cho (kā-brä′chō), n. [Sp., < *quebrar*, break, + *hacha*, ax.] Any of several hard-wooded South American trees, esp. the anacardiaceous tree *Quebrachia lorentzii* (′red quebracho′), the wood and bark of which are important in tanning and dyeing, or the apocynaceous tree *Macaglia quebracho* (′white quebracho′), which is best known for its medicinal bark; also, the wood or bark of any of these trees; specif., in *phar.*, the bark of the white quebracho.

queen (kwēn), n. [AS. *cwēn*, wife, queen, = OS. *quān*, Icel. *kvān*, wife, = Goth. *qens*, woman, wife; akin to AS. *cwene*, etc.: see *quean*.] The wife or consort of a king; also, a female sovereign or monarch; hence, a woman, or something personified as a woman, that is chief or preëminent in any respect (as, *queen* of the May; a *queen* of society; Cuba, the *queen* of the Antilles); also, the perfect or fully developed female of bees or ants, serving to propagate the species; also, a playing-card bearing a picture of a queen; in *chess*, the piece which has the greatest freedom of movement, and hence is the most powerful. — **Queen Anne style**, in *arch.*, a style which obtained in England in the early part of the 18th century, producing many commodious and dignified buildings, particularly in domestic architecture. — **queen consort**, the wife of a king. — **queen dowager**, the widow of a king. — **queen mother**, a queen dowager who is also mother of a reigning sovereign. — **queen regent**, a queen who reigns as regent; also, a queen regnant. — **queen regnant**, a queen who reigns in her own right. — **queen's English**. See under *English*, n. — **queen's evidence**. See *evidence*, n. — **queen**, v. **I.** *intr.* To reign as queen (lit. or fig.); play the queen; have queenly preëminence: usually with indefinite *it*: as, "She's a fine girl . . . fit to *queen* it in any drawing-room" (G. Meredith's "Diana of the Crossways," xxi.). **II.** *tr.* To make a queen of.

queen-dom (kwēn′dọm), *n.* The position or dignity of a queen; also, the realm of a queen.

queen-fish (kwēn′fish), *n.* A sciænoid food-fish, *Seriphus politus,* found on the coast of southern California.

Queenfish.

queen-hood (kwēn′hụd), *n.* The dignity or rank of a queen: as, "She [Queen Guinevere] . . . with all grace Of womanhood and *queenhood,* answer'd him" (Tennyson's "Marriage of Geraint," 176).

queen-ing (kwē′ning), *n.* [Appar. < *queen.*] Any of several varieties of apple.

queen-less (kwēn′les), *a.* Without a queen.

queen-let (kwēn′let), *n.* A petty queen.

queen-ly (kwēn′li), *a.;* compar. *queenlier,* superl. *queenliest.* Belonging or proper to a queen (as, *queenly* rank or majesty); also, befitting, or suggestive of, a queen (as, a *queenly* bearing or presence; *queenly* dignity or graciousness); also, like a queen (as, "You are a *queenly* creature, not to be treated as any puny trollop of a handmaid": G. Meredith's "Lord Ormont and His Aminta," vi.).—**queen′li-ness,** *n.*—**queen′ly,** *adv.* In a queenly manner; like a queen.

queen=post (kwēn′pōst), *n.* One of a pair of timbers or posts extending vertically upward from the tie-beam of a roof-truss or the like, one on each side of the center.

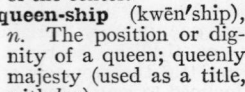

queen-ship (kwēn′ship), *n.* The position or dignity of a queen; queenly majesty (used as a title, with *her*).

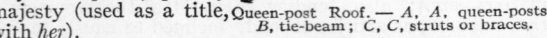

Queen-post Roof.— *A, A,* queen-posts; *B,* tie-beam; *C, C,* struts or braces.

queen's=root, queen=root (kwēnz′röt, kwēn′-), *n.* A euphorbiaceous herb, *Stillingia sylvatica,* of the southern U. S., having a thick, woody root with alterative, emetic, and purgative properties.

queer (kwēr), *a.* [Origin obscure: cf. G. *quer,* oblique, cross, adverse.] Strange, singular, or odd (as, a *queer* company; a *queer* performance, remark, or notion; "a *queer* mixture of French liveliness and savage stolidity," Howells's "Chance Acquaintance," xiii.); singular in a quaint, droll, or freakish way, or amusingly odd, in appearance, character, ways, etc. (as, a *queer* little house; "The old three-cornered hat, And the breeches, and all that, Are so *queer!*" Holmes's "Last Leaf"; "What are *queer* old women for, if young folks may not have a good laugh out of them now and then?" Mrs. Stowe's "Oldtown Folks," vi.); fantastic or bizarre (as, "some *queer* pagod": Pope's "Satires of Donne," iv. 239); peculiar or eccentric, as persons (as, "Let me be known all at once for a *queer* fellow, and avoided": Steele, in "Spectator," 474); strange or odd from a conventional point of view (as, "I don't mind your *queer* opinions one little bit," G. B. Shaw's "Man and Superman," i.; "I dare say you think it's very *queer* of me,' she added," Arnold Bennett's "Hilda Lessways," iii. 6); also, of questionable character, suspicious, or 'shady' (colloq.); also, out of the normal state of feeling physically, or giddy, faint, or qualmish (as, "They had given him brandy, rather a lot — that perhaps was the reason he felt so *queer*": Galsworthy's "Dark Flower," i. 8); mentally unbalanced or deranged (as, "She was quite satisfied that I was not going *queer* in my head, for that was what she had been fearing," W. H. Hudson's "Far Away and Long Ago," vii.; "He . . . wondered if Zeena were also turning '*queer,*'" Mrs. Wharton's "Ethan Frome," iv.); also, ill-humored or ill-tempered (prov. Eng.); also, bad, worthless, or counterfeit (slang).—**Queer Street,** an imaginary street in which persons in financial or other difficulties, or 'shady' characters generally, are supposed to have their abode: as, "Look out, fellow-Christians, particularly you that lodge in *Queer Street!*" (Dickens's "Our Mutual Friend," iii. 1).—**queer,** *n.* Counterfeit money. [Slang.]

queer, *v. t.* To quiz, or make sport of (as, "Come now,

Jeanie, ye are but *queering* us": Scott's "Heart of Midlothian," xxvi.); also, to puzzle or confuse; also, to impose on or cheat; also, to bring to confusion, or spoil (a performance, affair, etc.: as, "He cursed the blunderer. 'Lighting his fool fire *queered* the whole deal,' he added," Wister's "Virginian," xxx.); ruin (one's chances, etc.); put (a person) in a hopeless situation as to success, favor, etc. [Slang or prov.]—**queer′er,** *n.*—**queer′ish,** *a.* Rather queer: as, "a *queerish* sensation" (G. Meredith's "Diana of the Crossways," viii.).—**queer′ly,** *adv.*—**queer′ness,** *n.*

quell (kwel), *v. t.* [AS. *cwellan,* kill, causative of *cwelan,* die; akin to D. *kwellen,* G. *quälen,* Icel. *kvelja,* torment.] To kill† or slay†; fig., to put an end to, or extinguish (as, "Her sudden quips, The least whereof would *quell* a lover's hope," Shakspere's "Two Gentlemen of Verona," iv. 2. 13; "That great national sentiment surmounts and *quells* all sense of ordinary distinctions," De Quincey's "English Mail-Coach," i.); put down or suppress (disorder, mutiny, etc.: as, "The tumult . . . was not *quelled* until several had fallen on both sides," Parkman's "Oregon Trail," xi.); quiet or allay (feelings, etc.: as, "His own agitation was *quelled* by a certain awe," George Eliot's "Adam Bede," xxxix.; "Time *quells* the longings of vengeance, and hushes the promptings of rage," C. Brontë's "Jane Eyre," xxi.); also, to vanquish, subdue, or reduce to submission (as, "Young Pompey *quell'd* The Pontick king," Milton's "Paradise Regained," iii. 35; "The nation . . . rallied round the sovereign, and enabled him to *quell* the disaffected minority," Macaulay's "Hist. of Eng.," i.).—**quell,** *n.* Killing† or slaying† (see Shakspere's "Macbeth," i. 7. 72); also, power or means of quelling (poetic: as, "A sovereign *quell* is in his waving hands," Keats's "Endymion," ii.).—**quell′er,** *n.*

quench (kwench), *v.* [AS. *cwencan* (recorded in the compound *ācwencan,* extinguish), causative of *cwincan* (recorded in *ācwincan,* be extinguished) = OFries. *kwinka,* be put out.] **I.** *tr.* To put out or extinguish (fire, light, etc., lit. or fig.: as, "Not all its snow Could *quench* our hearth-fire's ruddy glow," Whittier's "Snow-Bound"; "Age had withered his form without *quenching* the fire of his spirit," Irving's "Conquest of Granada," iv.); put out the fire or flame of (something burning, giving light, etc.: as, "With odorous wine They *quenched* the ashes," W. Morris's "Jason," v. 121); sometimes, to extinguish (heat or warmth); cool suddenly, as by plunging into water, as steel in hardening or tempering it; also, fig., to suppress or stifle (as, "Hope seemed almost *quenched* in utter gloom," W. H. Hudson's "Green Mansions," xxii.; "to *quench* memory," G. Meredith's "Lord Ormont and His Aminta," vi.); put an end to; often, to slake (thirst: as, "to *quench* her thirst at the next brooke," Spenser's "Amoretti," lxvii.); sometimes, to kill (now rare). **II.** *intr.* To become quenched or extinguished. —**quench′a-ble,** *a.* That may be quenched.—**quench′er,** *n.*—**quench′less,** *a.* That cannot be quenched; inextinguishable.

que-nelle (kẹ-nel′), *n.* [F.] In *cookery,* a forcemeat ball made of chicken, veal, or the like reduced to a paste.

quer-ce-tin (kwėr′sẹ-tin), *n.* [See *quercitron.*] A yellow crystalline powder obtained from the bark of the quercitron and from other vegetable substances: used as a yellow dye. —**quer-cet′ic** (-set′ik), *a.*

quer-cine (kwėr′sin), *a.* [LL. *quercinus,* < L. *quercus,* oak.] Of or pertaining to the oak.

quer-cit-ron (kwėr′sit-rọn), *n.* [L. *quercus,* oak, + E. *citron.*] A species of oak, *Quercus velutina,* of eastern North America, whose inner bark yields a yellow dye; also, the bark itself.

quer-i-mo-ny (kwer′i-mọ-ni), *n.;* pl. *-nies* (-niz). [L. *querimonia,* < *queri,* complain.] Complaining; a complaint. —**quer-i-mo′ni-ous** (-mō′ni-us), *a.*

que-rist (kwē′rist), *n.* One who puts a query.

quern (kwėrn), *n.* [AS. *cweorn, cwyrn,* = OHG. *quirn* = Icel. *kvern* = Goth. *-qairnus,* mill.] A primitive hand-mill for grinding grain, consisting commonly of two circular stones. See cut on following page.

quer-u-lous (kwer′ọ̈-lus), *a.* [LL. *querulosus,* for L. *querulus,* < *queri,* complain.] Full of complaints, or complaining, as persons (as, "Mrs. Henry was that day ailing and *querulous*": Stevenson's "Master of Ballantrae," iv.); characterized by or uttered in complaining (as, "a *querulous* tone," Godwin's "Caleb Williams," xxii.; "a *querulous* retort," G. Meredith's "Ordeal of Richard Feverel," ii.); fretful; peevish; fig., producing sounds as of complaining, or sounding as if uttered in complaint (as, "The brown-clad maidens . . . Dance to the *querulous*

Stone Querns for Grinding. — Dublin Museum.

pipe and shrill," W. Morris's "Jason," xiv. 337; "the *querulous* pipings of a flock of young black-headed siskins," W. H. Hudson's "Purple Land," xix.).—**quer′u-lous-ly,** *adv.*—**quer′u-lous-ness,** *n.*

que-ry (kwē′ri). [For *quære*: see *quære.*] **I.** Quære (as used to introduce a question). **II.** *n.*; pl. **-ries** (-riz). A question; an inquiry; often, a question or an interrogation-point added on a manuscript, proof-sheet, or the like, with reference to some point in the text.—**que′ry,** *v.*; **-ried,** **-rying.** **I.** *tr.* To ask or inquire (as, " 'Shall we remove Mr. Butler,' *queried* the assistant": Scott's "Heart of Midlothian," xiii.); also, to interrogate (a person: rare); also, to question (a statement, etc.) as doubtful or obscure. **II.** *intr.* To put a query or queries; ask questions: as, "prompt to *query,* answer, and debate" (Pope's "Dunciad," ii. 381).

quest (kwest), *n.* [OF. *queste* (F. *quête*), < L. *quærere* (pp. *quæsitus*), seek, ask.] An inquest, or a jury of inquest (now rare); in general, an inquiry or investigation; also, a search or pursuit made in order to find or obtain something (as, a *quest* for gold; "Now, all the folk [Argonauts] who went upon this *quest* [of the golden fleece] I cannot name," W. Morris's "Jason," iii. 13; "It was decided that Hunter and I should go ashore . . . in *quest* of information," Stevenson's "Treasure Island," xvi.); in medieval romance, a knightly expedition undertaken to secure or achieve something (as, the *quest* of the Holy Grail, see *Grail*; "There sat Arthur on the dais-throne, And those that had gone out upon the *quest,* Wasted and worn . . . stood before the King," Tennyson's "Holy Grail," 719); those engaged in such an expedition; sometimes, a seeking for or collecting alms or donations, as for religious purposes; in *hunting* (now chiefly prov. Eng.), the search for game made by hounds; also, the baying of hounds in pursuit of game; the barking of hounds when in sight of game.—**quest,** *v.* [OF. *quester* (F. *quêter*).] **I.** *intr.* To search; seek; go on a quest; sometimes, to seek or collect alms or donations, esp. for religious purposes; in *hunting* (now chiefly prov. Eng.), of hounds, etc., to search for game; also, to bay or give tongue in pursuit of game, or bark when in sight of game (as, "Who cry out for him yet as hounds that *quest,* And roar as on their quarry": Swinburne's "Bothwell," iii. 13). **II.** *tr.* To search or seek for; pursue.—**quest′er,** *n.*

ques-tion (kwes′chọn), *n.* [OF. F. *question,* < L. *quæstio(n-),* < *quærere,* seek, ask.] The act of asking or inquiring, or interrogation; also, talk† or conversation† (as, "I met the duke yesterday and had much *question* with him": Shakspere's "As You Like It," iii. 4. 39); also, judicial examination or trial (obs. or rare); specif., formerly, the application of torture to prisoners under judicial examination; also, inquiry into or discussion of some problem or doubtful matter; also, dispute or controversy (as, to let a statement pass without *question*); also, a sentence in interrogative form, addressed to some one in order to elicit information (as, "Answer me Directly unto this *question* that I ask": Shakspere's "1 Henry IV.," ii. 3. 89); an interrogation, inquiry, or query; also, a matter for investigation or discussion; a problem for discussion or under discussion; a matter or point of uncertainty or difficulty (as, "To be, or not to be: that is the *question*": Shakspere's "Hamlet," iii. 1. 56); a matter or case (*of:* as, "He could neither buy nor sell as well as his father. It was not a *question* of brains; it was a *question* of individuality," Arnold Bennett's "Clayhanger," iii. 9); specif., a proposal to be debated or voted on, as in a meeting or a deliberative assembly; also, a subject of dispute or controversy (as, "since the first sword was drawn about this *question*": Shakspere's "Troilus and Cressida," ii. 2. 18).—**beyond (all) question,** beyond dispute; indisputably; unquestionably: as, this is, *beyond question,* his best book.—**in question,** under judicial examination†; also, under consideration or discussion (as, "She . . . was almost blind when it was a curate's virtues which were *in question*": Mrs. H. Ward's "Robert Elsmere," iv.); also, in dispute or controversy.—**leading question.** See under *leading*[1], *p. a.*—**out of the question,** orig., foreign to the question or matter in hand; hence, not to be considered or thought of (as, "Sleep during this interval was *out of the question*": Peacock's "Headlong Hall," xi.). —**previous question.** See under *previous, a.*—**to beg the question.** See *beg, v. t.*—**to call in question,** to subject to judicial interrogation†; hence, to call to account†; also, to dispute, question, or challenge (something); cast doubt upon (as, "a person who was jealous lest his courage should be *called in question*": Swift's "Gulliver's Travels," ii. 5).—**to pop the question.** See under *pop*[2], *v. t.*— **ques′tion,** *v.* [OF. F. *questionner.*] **I.** *tr.* To ask a question or questions of, or interrogate (a person, etc.); sometimes, to examine judicially, or call to account (now rare); also, to ask or inquire (as, " 'Tis safer to Avoid what's grown than *question* how 'tis born": Shakspere's "Winter's Tale," i. 2. 433); also, to make a question of, hold as uncertain, or doubt (as, "I yet *question* whether I could have had the assurance to behold him": Fielding's "Tom Jones," viii. 12); also, to call in question, or dispute (as, "The best English lawyers *questioned* . . . the legality of a government by royal instructions": Bancroft's "Hist. of the U. S.," Amer. Revolution, i. 7); also, to ask or inquire about† (as, "Lest that our king Come here himself to *question* our delay": Shakspere's "Henry V.," ii. 4. 142). **II.** *intr.* To ask a question or questions (as, "He that *questioneth* much shall learn much": Bacon's "Essays," Of Discourse); also, to talk or converse (*with*)†; debate or dispute (*with*)†.

ques-tion-a-ble (kwes′chọn-ạ-bl), *a.* That may be questioned or interrogated† (as, "Thou comest in such a *questionable* shape That I will speak to thee": Shakspere's "Hamlet," i. 4. 43); also, liable to be called to account†; also, that may be called in question, or open to question or dispute (as, whether this is true is *questionable*; "facts . . . *questionable* in point of authenticity," Irving's "Knickerbocker's New York," iii. 1); doubtful or uncertain (as, "It was *questionable* whether . . . he should be there in time even for the roast-beef": George Eliot's "Adam Bede," liii.); sometimes, open to question as to being such (as, a *questionable* privilege; a move of *questionable* expediency); sometimes, of doubtful propriety, honesty, morality, respectability, etc. (as, *questionable* dealings; *questionable* associates).—**ques′tion-a-ble-ness,** *n.*—**ques′tion-a-bly,** *adv.*

ques-tion-a-ry (kwes′chọn-ạ-ri). [LL. *quæstionarius.*] **I.** *a.* Questioning; interrogatory. **II.** *n.*; pl. **-ries** (-riz). A list of questions, esp. one for submission to a number of persons, as to procure information for statistical purposes; a questionnaire.

ques-tion-er (kwes′chọn-ėr), *n.* One who questions.

ques-tion-ing (kwes′chọn-ing), *p. a.* That questions; conveying a question; interrogative.—**ques′tion-ing-ly,** *adv.*

ques-tion-ist (kwes′chọn-ist), *n.* One who asks questions; a questioner; an inquirer.

ques-tion-less (kwes′chọn-les). **I.** *a.* Unquestionable; indubitable; also, unquestioning. **II.** *adv.* Without question; beyond doubt: as, "a young man . . . who can *questionless* write a good hand and keep books" (George Eliot's "Felix Holt," v.).

ques-tion=mark (kwes'chọn-märk), *n.* An interrogation-point.

ques-tion-naire (kwes-chọn-âr', F. kes-tyo-när'), *n.* [F.: cf. *questionary*.] A list of questions; a questionary, as for statistical purposes, or for governmental use (as in carrying out a selective draft), or to obtain opinions on some subject under discussion.

ques-tor (kwes'tọr), etc. See *quæstor*, etc.

quet-zal (ket'sạl or ket-säl'), *n.* [Sp.; from Mex.] A Central American trogon (bird), *Pharomacrus mocinno*, having a brilliant golden-green and scarlet plumage, and, in the male, long flowing upper tail-coverts.

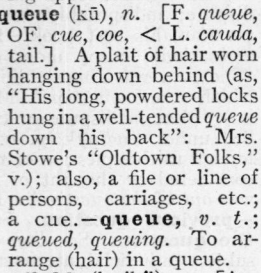

Quetzal.

queue (kū), *n.* [F. *queue*, OF. *cue*, *coe*, < L. *cauda*, tail.] A plait of hair worn hanging down behind (as, "His long, powdered locks hung in a well-tended *queue* down his back": Mrs. Stowe's "Oldtown Folks," v.); also, a file or line of persons, carriages, etc.; a cue.—**queue**, *v. t.*; *queued*, *queuing*. To arrange (hair) in a queue.

quib-ble (kwib'l), *n.* [Appar. dim. of obs. *quib*, a quibble, perhaps < L. *quibus* (dat. or abl. pl. of *qui*, who, which) as used in legal documents.] A play on words (as, "It was very natural . . . that the common people, by a *quibble* . . . should call the proposed 'Moderation' the 'Murderation'": Motley's "Dutch Republic," ii. 6); also, a use of ambiguous, prevaricating, or irrelevant language or argument to evade a point at issue, or an evasive, empty argument (as, "The fairest court of justice is a naval court-martial — no brow-beating of witnesses . . . and no legal *quibbles* attended to": Marryat's "Peter Simple," lxii.); the use of such arguments, or quibbling.—**quib'ble**, *v. i.*; *-bled*, *-bling*. To play on words (obs. or rare); also, to use a quibble or quibbles in speaking or arguing; evade the point or the truth by a quibble (as, "Oh, Miss Lucretia, who pride yourself on your plain speaking, that you should be caught *quibbling!*" W. Churchill's "Coniston," ii. 11).— **quib'bler**, *n.*—**quib'bling-ly**, *adv.*

quick (kwik), *a.* [AS. *cwic*, *cwicu*, living, = OS. *quik* = OHG. *quec* (G. *queck*, *keck*) = Icel. *kvikr*, akin to Goth. *qius*, living, also to L. *vivus*, living, *vivere*, live, Gr. βίος, life, and Skt. *jīv-*, live.] Endowed with life, or not inanimate (archaic or prov.); in a live state, or living, as persons or animals (archaic or prov.); alive or growing, as plants, etc., or consisting of living plants (as, "a *quick* or living hedge": Defoe's "Robinson Crusoe," i. 8); also, pregnant, as with child, esp. in the stage when the motion of the fetus is felt (archaic or prov.); also, having some quality suggestive of a living thing; running or flowing, as water (now rare: as, "The living stream lies *quick* below, And flows, and cannot cease to flow," Byron's "Parisina," xx.); soft and moist, so as to yield under pressure, as sand, etc. (as, "The Solway sands . . . are exceedingly dangerous, because, as the tide makes, they become *quick* in different places," Smollett's "Humphry Clinker," Sept. 12: now chiefly prov.: cf. *quicksand*); brisk, as fire, flames, heat, etc.; lively or keen, as feelings (as, "a *quick* relish of the exquisite pleasure of doing good": Steele, in "Tatler," 196); fresh or bracing, as air (rare: as, "The air is *quick* there, And it pierces and sharpens the stomach," Shakspere's "Pericles," iv. 1. 28); also, having a high degree of vigor, energy, or activity (as, "Quiet to *quick* bosoms is a hell":

Byron's "Childe Harold," iii. 42); prompt in action, or acting with swiftness or rapidity (as, "slow to resolve, but in performance *quick*," Dryden's "Hind and the Panther," iii. 921; "Isaacs was very *quick* about his toilet," F. M. Crawford's "Mr. Isaacs," xi.); prompt or swift (to do something: as, *quick* to act, see, believe, respond, etc.); prompt to perceive (as, "Some stubborn dissonance of things combin'd, Strikes on the *quick* observer," Akenside's "Pleasures of Imagination," iii. 252; a *quick* eye or ear); prompt to understand, learn, etc., or of ready intelligence (as, "I would teach them [women] all that men are taught; We are twice as *quick!*" Tennyson's "Princess," Prologue, 137; a *quick* mind); sometimes, hasty, impatient, or passionate (as, "You must not be so *quick*," Shakspere's "Love's Labour's Lost," ii. 1. 118; a *quick* temper); also, moving with speed (as, "The most terrible and nimble stroke Of *quick*, cross lightning," Shakspere's "King Lear," iv. 7. 35; "*quick* of foot," Dickens's "Barnaby Rudge," x.); swift or rapid, as motion (as, "So *quick* the run, We felt the good ship shake and reel": Tennyson's "Voyage," ii.); also, done, proceeding, or occurring with promptness or rapidity, as an action, process, etc. (as, a *quick* response; a *quick* change); prompt or immediate; that is over or completed within a short space of time; also, sharp, as a curve or turn; in *mining*, containing ore, or productive, as veins; in *finance*, yielding profit or interest, as stocks, etc.; also, readily convertible into cash, or liquid, as assets.—**quick time**, a quick rate of marching; in the U. S. army, a rate of marching in which 120 paces, each of 2½ feet, are taken in a minute.—**quick**, *n.* Living persons (without or with *the*: as, "the Judge of *quick* and dead," Acts, x. 42; "The *quick* have their sleep-walkers, so have the dead," Campbell's "Death-Boat of Heligoland"); sometimes, a living person or creature (now prov.); also, living plants (esp. of hawthorn) as set to form a hedge, or quickset (as, "The workes . . . are curiously hedg'd with *quick*": Evelyn's "Diary," Sept. 22, 1641); the hedge itself; a single such plant; also, the tender, sensitive flesh of the living body, esp. that under the nails (with *the*: as, "He had small, nervous, veiny hands with nails bitten down to the *quick*," Du Maurier's "Trilby," i.; to be cut, stung, or touched to the *quick*, fig., to suffer a sharp mental wound, or be keenly hurt or irritated in mind); also, the vital or most important part (with *the*); also, life (now chiefly prov. Eng.).—**quick**, *adv.* Quickly.

quick-en (kwik'n), *v.* **I.** *intr.* To become quick or living, or receive life (as, "Summer flies . . . That *quicken* even with blowing": Shakspere's "Othello," iv. 2. 67); specif., of a child in the womb, to begin to manifest signs of life; of the mother, to enter that stage of pregnancy in which the child gives indications of life; also, fig., to come into a state comparable to life; come into activity; become more active, sensitive, etc.; sometimes, to grow bright or brighter (as, "The river, the mountain, the *quickening* east, swam before his eyes": Bret Harte's "How Santa Claus Came to Simpson's Bar"); also, to become more rapid. **II.** *tr.* To make quick or alive; restore life to; fig., to give or restore vigor or activity to; stir up, rouse, or stimulate; reinvigorate or revive; sometimes, to kindle (fire, etc.); also, to make more rapid, or accelerate (as, "She *quickened* her pace": Marryat's "King's Own," xxxix.); hasten (an event, etc.: as, to *quicken* one's departure).—**quick'en-er**, *n.*

quick-ish (kwik'ish), *a.* Rather quick: as, "They went . . . at a *quickish* trot" (Stevenson's "Master of Ballantrae," iii.).

quick-lime (kwik'līm), *n.* Lime which has not been slaked. See *lime*[3], *n.*

quick-ly (kwik'li), *adv.* In a quick manner; with speed; rapidly; without delay.—**quick'ness**, *n.*

quick-sand (kwik'sand), *n.* An area of soft or loose, wet sand of considerable depth, on a coast or inland, yielding under weight and hence apt to engulf persons, animals, etc., coming upon it (as, "Getting his steed mired or caught in a *quicksand* is one of the commonest of the accidents that beset a horseman in the far West": Roosevelt's "Ranch Life and the Hunting-Trail," iii.); fig., something that insnares or involves inextricably, or overwhelms (as, "It is my duty . . . to see that he is properly mated, — not wrecked upon the *quicksands* of marriage": G. Meredith's "Ordeal of Richard Feverel," xiii.).

---

quick-set (kwik′set). **I.** *n.* A plant or cutting (esp. of hawthorn) set to grow, as in a hedge; also, such plants collectively; also, a hedge of such plants. **II.** *a.* Formed of quickset, or of growing plants: as, a *quickset* hedge.

quick=sight-ed (kwik′sī′ted), *a.* Having quick sight; quick to see or discern: as, "a wonderfully active and *quick-sighted* person . . . able to see what is going on all round" (W. H. Hudson's "Far Away and Long Ago," iii.).—**quick′=sight′ed-ness,** *n.*

quick-sil-ver (kwik′sil″vėr), *n.* [AS. *cwicseolfor*, 'living silver.'] The metal mercury.

quick-step (kwik′step), *n.* A lively step used in marching in quick time; a march in quick time; also, music adapted to such a march, or in a brisk march rhythm; also, a lively dance-step.

quick=tem-pered (kwik′tem′pėrd), *a.* Having a quick or hasty temper; easily moved to anger.

quick=wit-ted (kwik′wit′ed), *a.* Having a quick wit or intelligence; quick or ready of perception.—**quick′=wit′ted-ness,** *n.*

quid[1] (kwid), *n.* [Var. of *cud.*] A portion of something, esp. tobacco, for holding in the mouth and chewing: as, "A large roll of tobacco was presented . . . and every individual took a comfortable *quid*" (Smollett's "Humphry Clinker," Sept. 3); "He had a *quid* of tobacco in his cheek" (Marryat's "Peter Simple," xiv.).

quid[2] (kwid), *n.*; pl. *quid*, occasionally *quids.* [Origin obscure.] A sovereign (£1): as, "Some of you ought to be in London, getting your . . . forty *quid* a week!" (L. Merrick's "Conrad in Quest of His Youth," xiv.). [Slang, Eng.]

quid-dit (kwid′it), *n.* [For *quiddity.*] A quiddity, or trifling nicety, as in argument. [Archaic.]

quid-di-ty (kwid′i-ti), *n.*; pl. *-ties* (-tiz). [ML. *quidditas,* < L. *quid,* what.] That which makes a thing what it is, or the essential nature (as, "He did not think our faculties competent to solve the whole problem of *quiddity,* as the logicians called it, or the real nature of any thing, at least, objectively without us": Hallam's "Literature of Europe," iii. 3. § 28); also, a trifling nicety or subtle distinction, as in argument (as, "the solemn saws of the State Council and the *quiddities* from Louvain being likely to prove but slender bulwarks against the returning tide of tyranny": Motley's "Dutch Republic," v. 1).

quid-dle (kwid′l), *v. i.*; *-dled, -dling.* [Origin obscure.] To trifle, as in discourse or action; occupy one's self in a trifling way; fiddle; fuss: as, "I should like to know who's a going to stop to *quiddle* with young uns?" (Mrs. Stowe's "Oldtown Folks," xx.). [Now chiefly prov. or colloq.]—**quid′dle,** *n.* A person given to fussing: as, "The Englishman is . . . a *quiddle* about his toast and his chop" (Emerson's "English Traits," vi.). [Prov. or colloq.]

quid-nunc (kwid′nungk), *n.* [L. *quid nunc,* 'what now?'] One who is curious to know everything that passes; a newsmonger: as, "She feared the crowd of village idlers, *quidnuncs,* tattlers, and newsmongers who all day gazed . . . at the wonder-yacht" (Arnold Bennett's "Lion's Share," xxxiii.).

qui-esce (kwī-es′), *v. i.*; *-esced, -escing.* [L. *quiescere* (pp. *quietus*), be at rest, < *quies,* rest, E. *quiet*[1], *n.*] To become quiet; subside; in *philol.,* of a letter, to become silent (said specif. of consonants under certain conditions in Hebrew).—**qui-es′cence** (-es′ens), *n.* The state or fact of being quiescent. Also **qui-es′cen-cy.**—**qui-es′cent** (-es′ent), *a.* [L. *quiescens* (-ent-), ppr.] Being at rest, quiet, or still (as, "For a time, he [a whale] lay *quiescent*": H. Melville's "Moby-Dick," cxxxv.); inactive or motionless; dormant; quietly passive (as, "How for nine years you could be patient and *quiescent* under any treatment . . . I can never comprehend": C. Brontë's "Jane Eyre," xxi.); also, silent (specif. in *philol.,* as of a letter, esp. in Hebrew).—**qui-es′cent-ly,** *adv.*

qui-et[1] (kwī′et), *n.* [L. *quies* (*quiet-*), rest, repose, quiet: see *while.*] Rest or repose (as, "By day my limbs, by night my mind, For thee and for myself no *quiet* find": Shakspere's "Sonnets," xxvii.); hence, reposeful or peaceful inactivity (as, "*Quiet* to quick bosoms is a hell": Byron's "Childe Harold," iii. 42); also, freedom from disturbance or tumult, or tranquillity (as, to live in *quiet*; "Gentle lady, may thy grave Peace and *quiet* ever have," Milton's "Epitaph on the Marchioness of Winchester," 48); peace, or peaceful condition of affairs, in a place or country (as, "The city was in *quiet,*" 2 Kings, xi. 20; "His small force would be large enough to overawe them in times of *quiet,*" Prescott's "Conquest of Mexico," iv. 6); mental peace or calm (as, "Be passionate hopes not ill resign'd For *quiet,* and a fearless mind": M. Arnold's "Resignation"); also, absence of motion, or motionlessness (as, "A smooth spot Of glassy *quiet* mid those battling tides": Shelley's "Alastor," 393); also, absence of noise, or silence (as, "The people were hushed into a *quiet* that might be felt": Ian Maclaren's "Beside the Bonnie Brier Bush," ii. 1).

qui-et[2] (kwī′et), *a.* [L. *quietus,* pp. of *quiescere*: see *quiesce.*] Being at rest (as, "Why died I not . . . ? . . . For now should I have lain still and been *quiet,* I should have slept": Job, iii. 13); also, refraining or free from activity, esp. busy or vigorous activity (as, ill health obliges him to keep *quiet*; to spend a *quiet* evening at home; *quiet* games); also, making no disturbance or trouble (as, "that ye study to be *quiet,* and to do your own business": 1 Thes. iv. 11); not turbulent; peaceable; also, free from disturbance or tumult, tranquil, or peaceful (as, a *quiet* night's sleep; anything for a *quiet* life! "All had been *quiet* since the news of the capitulation at Lerida," Froude's "Cæsar," xxii.); free from disturbing emotions, etc., or mentally peaceful or calm, as the mind, heart, conscience, etc., or a person; also, motionless or still, or moving imperceptibly or gently (as, *quiet* waters; a *quiet* current); also, making no noise or sound, esp. no disturbing sound (as, *quiet* neighbors; *quiet* footsteps); free, or comparatively free, from noise (as, a *quiet* house or street); silent; also, restrained in speech, manner, etc., saying little, or not talkative or self-assertive (as, "During dinner . . . we were unusually *quiet,* even to gravity," W. H. Hudson's "Green Mansions," Prologue; a *quiet* young fellow); said, expressed, done, etc., in a restrained or unobtrusive way (as, "Mary gave him a *quiet* good evening," H. Kingsley's "Geoffry Hamlyn," iv.; *quiet* approval; a *quiet* smile or hint); also, of an unobtrusive or inconspicuous kind (as, *quiet* manners or elegance; *quiet* dress or colors); not ostentatious or showy; subdued.—**qui′et**[2], *v.* [LL. *quietare,* < L. *quietus,* pp.] **I.** *tr.* To make quiet, or reduce to quietness; make tranquil or peaceful; pacify (as, "In trying to *quiet* one set of malecontents, he had created another": Macaulay's "Hist. of Eng.," xii.); calm mentally, as a person; allay, or cause to subside, as tumult, dissension, doubt, fear, etc.; still; silence. **II.** *intr.* To become quiet.

qui-et-en (kwī′et-n), *v.* **I.** *tr.* To make quiet: as, "At last . . . to *quieten* them, I promised to try to write a short story" (Arnold Bennett's "Truth about an Author," v.). **II.** *intr.* To become quiet; quiet: often with *down*: as, "Her heart had *quietened* down while she rested" (J. Conrad's "Rover," xi.).

qui-et-er (kwī′et-ėr), *n.* One who or that which quiets.

Qui-et-ism (kwī′et-izm), *n.* [It. *quietismo,* < *quiete,* < L. *quies,* E. *quiet*[1], *n.*] A form of religious mysticism taught by Molinos, a Spanish priest, in the latter part of the 17th century, requiring extinction of the will, withdrawal from worldly interests, and passive meditation on God and divine things; hence [chiefly *l. c.*], some similar form of religious mysticism; also [*l. c.*], quietness of mind or life; inactivity. —**Qui′et-ist,** *n.* One who believes in or practises Quietism or [chiefly *l. c.*] some similar form of religious mysticism; also [*l. c.*], one who seeks quietness; one who pursues or advocates a policy of quietness or inactivity, as in politics.—**qui-et-is′tic,** *a.*

qui-et-ly (kwī′et-li), *adv.* In a quiet manner; without disturbance or tumult; peacefully; calmly; without motion; without noise; silently; unobtrusively.—**qui′et-ness,** *n.*

qui-e-tude (kwī′e-tūd), *n.* [F. *quiétude,* < LL. *quietudo,* < L. *quietus,* E. *quiet*[2], *a.*] The state of being quiet; tranquillity; calmness; stillness; quiet.

qui-e-tus (kwī-ē′tus), *n.* [ML., quit (in *quietus est,* he is quit: a formula of acquittance), L. quiet, at rest: see *quiet*[2], *a.,* and cf. *quit*[1], *a.*] Acquittance or discharge from a debt or obligation, or a document certifying this; a quittance; hence, fig., discharge or release from life, or something that

effects this (as, "When he himself might his *quietus* make
With a bare bodkin," Shakspere's "Hamlet," iii. 1. 75; "if
an unlucky bullet should carry a *quietus* with it," Sheridan's
"Rivals," v. 3); in general, a finishing stroke, or anything
that effectually ends or settles (as, to give a *quietus* to a
rumor, hope, or project; the bill received its *quietus* in the
Senate); also, sometimes, something that quiets (as, "The
nurse ran to give its accustomed *quietus* to the little screaming infant": Thackeray's "Newcomes," lxxi.).

quill (kwil), *n.* [ME. *quil*: cf. LG. *quiele*, G. *kiel*, quill.]
A hollow stem, as of a reed†; also, a piece of reed, or other
hollow stem, on which yarn is wound; in general, a bobbin
or spool; also, a musical pipe, as of reed; also, a roll of bark,
as of cinnamon, as formed in drying; also, the hard tube-like
part of a feather, nearest the body; also, one of the large
feathers of the wing or tail of a bird; also, a feather, as of a
goose, formed into a pen for writing (as, "What needes me
care for anie bookish skill, To blot white papers with my
restlesse *quill?*" J. Hall's "Satires," ii. 2); a plectrum made
from the quill of a feather; a toothpick made of the quill of
a feather; also, one of the hollow spines on a porcupine or
hedgehog.—**quill**, *v. t.* To flute or pleat (silk, lace, etc.) in
small, regular folds.

quil-lai (ki-lī′), *n.* [S. Amer.] A rosaceous tree, *Quillaia
saponaria*, of Chile, the inner bark of which is used as a
substitute for soap; also, the bark. Cf. *soap-bark*.

quill=driv-er (kwil′driⁿ′vėr), *n.*
One who works with a quill or
pen; a writer; a clerk. [Hu-
morous or contemptuous.]—
quill′=driv″ing, *n.* and *a.*

quil-let (kwil′et), *n.* [Per-
haps a corruption of *quiddit.*]
A nicety or subtlety; a quibble.

quill=feath-er (kwil′feᴛн″ėr),
n. One of the large feathers
of the wing or tail of a bird.

quill-ing (kwil′ing), *n.* A
quilled strip of silk, lace, etc.;
a fluted or pleated edging.

quil-lon (kē-yôṅ′), *n.* [F., <
quille, pin in ninepins.] Either
arm of a transverse piece
forming a guard for the hand
between the hilt and the blade
of a sword.

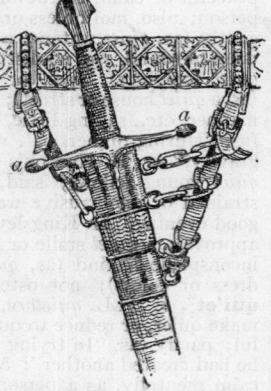
Sword-hilt. — *a, a*, quillons.

quill-wort (kwil′wėrt), *n.* Any of the aquatic and palustrine
pteridophytic plants con-
stituting the genus *Isoëtes*,
characterized by quill-like
leaves.

quilt (kwilt), *n.* [OF. *cuilte*
(F. *couette*), < L. *culcita*,
mattress, cushion.] A kind
of mattress†; also, a coverlet for a bed, made by
stitching together two thicknesses of fabric with some
soft substance, as wool, between them; in general, a
bedspread or counterpane;
also, anything quilted or resembling a quilt.—**quilt**, *v.*
I. *tr.* To stitch together, as
two pieces of cloth with a
soft interlining, in the manner of a quilt; also, to make
by this process; also, to pad
or line with some material;
also, to sew up between
pieces of material. **II.** *intr.*
To make quilts or quilted
work.—**quilt′er**, *n.*—**quilt′-
ing**, *n.* The act of one who

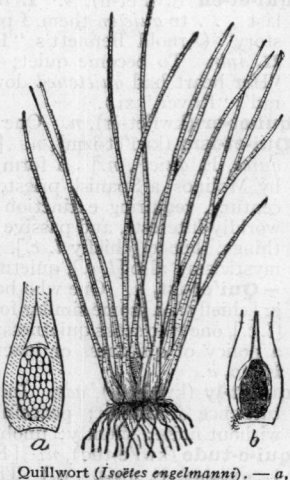
Quillwort (*Isoëtes engelmanni*). — *a*,
sporangium cut longitudinally, showing the megaspores; *b*, sporangium
cut longitudinally, showing the micro-
spores.

quilts; also, quilted work; material for making quilts; a stout
cotton or linen fabric so woven as to appear quilted; also,
a quilting-bee.—**quilt′ing=bee**, *n.* An old-time friendly

gathering of persons to make a quilt: as, " '*quilting bees*' and
'husking bees,' and other rural assemblages" (Irving's
"Knickerbocker's New York," vii. 2). [U. S.]

qui-na (kē′nä or kwi′nä), *n.* [Sp. and NL., < Peruvian
kina, bark: cf. *china*[2] and *quinine*.] Cinchona bark;
also, quinine.

qui-nal-dine (kwi-nal′din), *n.* [From *quin*(oline) +
ald(*ehyde*) + (*anil*)*ine*.] In *chem.*, a colorless liquid compound occurring in coal-tar and also obtained by synthetic
methods: used in the preparation of certain dyes.

qui-na-ry (kwi′nā-ri), *a.* [L. *quinarius*, < *quini*, five each,
distributive of *quinque*, five.] **I.** *a.* Pertaining to or consisting of five; arranged in fives; based on the number five.
II. *n.*; pl. *-ries* (-riz). A group of five.

qui-nate (kwi′nāt), *a.* [NL. *quinatus*, < L. *quini*: see
quinary.] In *bot.*, consisting of five parts or leaflets, as a
compound leaf.

quince (kwins), *n.* [Appar. orig. pl., taken as sing., of ME.
quynse, *coyn*, < OF. *cooin* (F. *coing*), < L. *cotoneum*, for
Cydonium, < Gr. Κυδώνιον, quince, lit. '(apple) of Cydonia'
(ancient city of Crete).] The hard, yellowish acid fruit of a
small, hardy malaceous tree, *Cydonia cydonia*; also, the
tree itself; also, any of
various other plants of
the genus *Cydonia*, as *C.
japonica* ('Japanese
quince'), a shrub with
ornamental flowers vary-
ing in color from creamy
white to deep red, used
for hedges, etc.

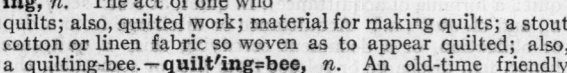
Branch with Fruit of Quince (*Cydonia
cydonia*).

quin-cen-te-na-ry (kwin-
sen′te-nä-ri). [From
quin(*que*) + *centenary*.]
I. *a.* Pertaining to five
hundred or a period of
five hundred years; mark-
ing the completion of five
hundred years. **II.** *n.*;
pl. *-ries* (-riz). A five-hundredth anniversary, or its celebration.

quin-cen-ten-ni-al (kwin-sen-ten′i-al), *a.* and *n.* Same as
quincentenary.

quin-cun-cial (kwin-kun′shal), *a.* [L. *quincuncialis*.] Of,
pertaining to, or consisting of a quincunx; in *bot.*, noting or
pertaining to the imbricated arrangement of petals or leaves
known as a quincunx; also, noting a five-ranked arrangement of leaves.—**quin-cun′cial-ly**, *adv.*

quin-cunx (kwin′kungks), *n.* [L., quincunx, orig. five
twelfths (a Roman coin worth five twelfths of the as being
marked with a quincunx of spots), < *quinque*, five, + *uncia*,
twelfth part, E. *ounce*[1].] An arrangement of five objects (as
trees) in a square or rectangle, one at each corner and one in
the middle; in *bot.*, an imbricated arrangement of five petals
or leaves, in which two are interior, two are exterior, and one
is partly interior and partly exterior.

quin-dec-a-gon (kwin-dek′a-gon), *n.* [Irreg. (after *decagon*)
< L. *quindecim*, fifteen, + Gr. γωνία, angle.] In *geom.*, a
plane figure with fifteen angles and fifteen sides.

quin-de-cem-vir (kwin-dē-sem′vėr), *n.*; pl. *-viri* (-vi-rī) or
virs. [Altered (after *decemvir*) < L. *quindecimvir*, sing.
of *quindecimviri*, pl., < *quindecim*, fifteen, + *viri*, pl. of *vir*,
man.] In *Rom. antiq.*, one of a body of fifteen men; esp.,
one of a body of fifteen priests who, at the close of the
republic, had charge of the Sibylline Books.

quin-gen-te-na-ry (kwin-jen′te-nä-ri), *a.* and *n.* [L. *quin-
genti*, five hundred.] Same as *quincentenary*.

quin-i-a (kwin′i-ä), *n.* [NL., < *quina*.] Quinine.

quin-ic (kwin′ik), *a.* [From *quina*.] In *chem.*, pertaining
to or derived from cinchona bark: as, *quinic* acid (a white
crystalline organic acid obtained from cinchona bark, coffee-
beans, etc.).

quin-i-dine (kwin′i-din), *n.* [From *quinine*.] In *chem.*, an
alkaloid isomeric with quinine, and occurring associated
with it in certain species of cinchona.

quin-in (kwin′in), *n.* Same as *quinine*.

qui-nine (kwi′nīn or kwi-nēn′), *n.* [From *quina*.] A
bitter crystalline alkaloid obtained from cinchona bark,

used, esp. in the form of a salt, as a remedy for malaria, etc.; a salt of this alkaloid, esp. the sulphate. — **qui-nin-ism** (kwī'nīn-izm or kwi-nēn'-), *n.* In *pathol.*, an abnormal condition characterized by ringing in the ears, impaired vision, etc., due to excessive use of quinine.

quin-nat (kwin'at), *n.* [N. Amer. Ind.] A large salmon, *Oncorhynchus tschawytscha*, valuable as a food-fish.

qui-noi-dine (kwi-noi'din), *n.* [From *quina* + -*oid* + -*ine*[2].] In *phar.*, a brownish-black resinous substance consisting of a mixture of alkaloids: obtained as a by-product in the manufacture of quinine, and used as a cheap substitute for it.

quin-ol (kwin'ol or -ōl), *n.* [From *quinone*.] Same as *hydroquinone*.

quin-o-line (kwin'ō-lin), *n.* [G. *chinolin*, < *china* (= E. *china*[2], *quina*) + L. *oleum*, oil.] In *chem.*, a nitrogenous organic base, a colorless liquid with a pungent odor, occurring in coal-tar, etc., and obtained in the distillation of quinine: used as an antiseptic and in the preparation of other compounds.

quin-one (kwin'ōn), *n.* [G. *chinon*, < *china*: see *quinoline*.] In *chem.*, a yellowish crystalline compound, $C_6H_4O_2$, formed by the oxidation of aniline, and regarded as benzene with two hydrogen atoms replaced by two oxygen atoms; hence, any of a class of compounds of which this is the type.

quin-qua-ge-na-ri-an (kwin"kwa-je-nā'ri-an), *a.* [L. *quinquagenarius*, < *quinquageni*, fifty each, distributive of *quinquaginta*, fifty, related to *quinque*, five.] **I.** *a.* Of the age of 50 years; between 50 and 60 years old. **II.** *n.* A quinquagenarian person.

Quin-qua-ges-i-ma (kwin-kwa-jes'i-mä), *n.* [ML., prop. fem. of L. *quinquagesimus*, fiftieth, < *quinquaginta*: see *quinquagenarian*.] The Sunday before Lent (more fully, 'Quinquagesima Sunday'), being the fiftieth day before Easter (reckoning inclusively); Shrove Sunday.

quin-quan-gu-lar (kwin-kwang'gū-lär), *a.* [LL. *quinquangulus*, < L. *quinque*, five, + *angulus*, E. *angle*[3].] Having five angles.

quinque-. Form of L. *quinque*, five, used in combination. — **quin-que-fa-ri-ous** (kwin-kwē-fā'ri-us), *a.* [+ -*farious*.] Fivefold; in five rows. — **quin'que-fid** (-fid), *a.* [+ -*fid*.] Cleft into five parts or lobes. — **quin-que-fo'li-ate** (-fō'li-āt), *a.* [+ L. *folium*, leaf.] In *bot.*, having five leaves or leaflets.

quin-quen-ni-ad (kwin-kwen'i-ad), *n.* A quinquennium.

quin-quen-ni-al (kwin-kwen'i-al). [L. *quinquennis*, < *quinque*, five, + *annus*, year.] **I.** *a.* Of or for five years; also, occurring every five years. **II.** *n.* Something that occurs every five years; also, a fifth anniversary. — **quin-quen'ni-al-ly**, *adv.* — **quin-quen'ni-um** (-um), *n.*; pl. -*niums* or -*nia* (-ä). [L., < *quinquennis*.] A period of five years.

quin-que-par-tite (kwin-kwē-pär'tīt), *a.* [L. *quinquepartitus*, < *quinque*, five, + *partitus*, pp. of *partire*, divide.] Divided into or consisting of five parts.

quin-que-va-lent (kwin-kwē-vā'lent or -kwev'a-lent), *a.* [See *quinque-* and -*valent*.] In *chem.*, pentavalent. Also **quin-qui-va'lent.**

quin-sy (kwin'zi), *n.*; pl. -*sies* (-ziz). [OF. *quinancie* (F. *esquinancie*), < LL. *cynanche*, < Gr. κυνάγχη, sore throat, < κύων, dog, + ἄγχειν, press tight, strangle.] In *pathol.*, a suppurative inflammation of the tonsils; suppurative tonsillitis.

quin-tain (kwin'tān), *n.* [OF. F. *quintaine*, < ML. *quintana*, quintain, L. street in a camp, prop. fem. of L. *quintanus*: see *quintan*.] During the middle ages and later, a post, or an object mounted on a post, for tilting at as a knightly or other exercise; also, such exercise or sport.

Movable Quintain, 14th century.

quin-tal (kwin'tal), *n.* [OF. F. *quintal*, < ML. *quintale*, < Ar. *qintār*, weight of a hundred pounds, prob. ult. < L.

centum, hundred: cf. *kantar*.] A hundredweight; in the *metric system*, a unit of weight equal to 100,000 grams (100 kilograms), or 220.46 pounds avoirdupois.

quin-tan (kwin'tan). [L. *quintanus*, belonging to the fifth, < *quintus*, fifth: see *quinte*.] **I.** *a.* Of a fever, ague, etc., characterized by paroxysms which recur every fifth day, both days of consecutive occurrence being counted. **II.** *n.* A quintan fever or ague.

quinte (kaṅt), *n.* [F., fem. of *quint*, < L. *quintus*, fifth, < *quinque*, five: see *five*.] In *fencing*, the fifth in a series of eight parries.

quin-tes-sence (kwin-tes'ens), *n.* [OF. *quinte essence* (F. *quintessence*), < ML. *quinta essentia*, fifth essence.] The fifth essence or element of ancient and medieval philosophy (in addition to earth, water, air, and fire), supposed to constitute the heavenly bodies, to permeate the material world, and to be capable of extraction; also, an extract from anything, containing its virtues or most essential part in concentrated form; the pure and concentrated essence of a substance; hence, the purest form or most perfect embodiment of something immaterial (as, "a blue-patterned tea-wrap with bows that seemed to me the *quintessence* of fashion": H. G. Wells's "Tono-Bungay," ii. 2. § 6); the most perfect example of something (as, he is the *quintessence* of a pedant). — **quin-tes-sen'tial** (-te-sen'shal), *a.* Of the nature of a quintessence; of the purest or most perfect kind. — **quin-tes-sen'tial-ly**, *adv.*

quin-tet, quin-tette (kwin-tet'), *n.* [F. *quintette*, < It. *quintetto*, < *quinto*, fifth, < L. *quintus*: see *quinte*.] A musical composition for five voices or instruments; also, a set of five singers or players; also, any set or group of five persons or things.

quin-tile (kwin'til). [= F. *quintil*, < L. *quintus*, fifth: see *quinte*.] **I.** *a.* In *astrol.*, noting the aspect of two heavenly bodies when they are distant from each other the fifth part of the zodiac, or 72°. **II.** *n.* A quintile aspect.

quin-til-lion (kwin-til'yon), *n.* [L. *quintus*, fifth, + E. (m)*illion*.] In Great Britain, the fifth power of a million, represented by 1 followed by 30 ciphers; in France and the U. S., a thousand quadrillions, represented by 1 followed by 18 ciphers. — **quin-til'lionth**, *a.* and *n.*

quin-troon (kwin-trön'), *n.* [Sp. *quinterón*, < *quinto*, fifth, < L. *quintus*: see *quintroon*.] A person having one sixteenth negro blood; the offspring of an octoroon and a white.

quin-tu-ple (kwin'tū-pl). [F. *quintuple*, < L. *quintus*, fifth, + -*plus*: see *double*, and cf. *quadruple*.] **I.** *a.* Fivefold; consisting of five parts; five times as great. **II.** *n.* A number, amount, etc., five times as great as another. — **quin'tu-ple**, *v.*; -*pled*, -*pling.* **I.** *tr.* To make five times as great: as, "He had *quintupled* a fortune already considerable" (H. James's "Europeans," vi.). **II.** *intr.* To become five times as great. — **quin'tu-plet** (-plet), *n.* Any group or combination of five; also, one of five children born at a birth.

quinze (kwinz, F. kaṅz), *n.* [F., < L. *quindecim*, fifteen, < *quinque*, five, + *decem*, ten.] A game of cards somewhat similar to vingt et un, in which the object is to count fifteen, or as near as possible to that number without exceeding it.

quip (kwip), *n.* [Perhaps < L. *quippe*, indeed, forsooth, as used sarcastically.] A sharp, sarcastic remark; a cutting jest; later, a clever or witty saying; also, a quibble; also, an odd or fantastic action or thing. — **quip**, *v. i.* or *t.*; *quipped*, *quipping.* To use, or assail with, quips. — **quip'ster** (-stèr), *n.* One given to quips.

qui-pu (kē'pö or kwip'ö), *n.*; pl. -*pus* (-pöz). [Peruvian, lit. 'knot.'] Among the ancient Peruvians, a device consisting of a cord with knotted strings of various colors attached, for recording events, keeping accounts, etc.

quire[1] (kwīr), *n.* and *v.* Same as *choir*. [Archaic.]

quire[2] (kwīr), *n.* [OF. *quaer*, *quayer* (F. *cahier*), < ML. *quaternum*, set of four sheets, < L. *quaterni*, four each: see *quaternary*, and cf. *cahier*.] A set of four sheets folded to form eight leaves, a common unit in medieval book-making; any similar set of sheets; also, a collection of 24 (or 25) sheets of paper of the same size and quality. — **in quires**, in sheets and not bound, as a book. — **quire**[2], *v. t.*; *quired*, *quiring.* To arrange in quires.

Quir-i-nal (kwir′i-nạl). [L. *Quirinalis*, < *Quirinus*, an ancient Italian war-god identified by the Romans with Romulus, appar. < *quiris*: see *Quirites*.] **I.** *a.* Of or pertaining to Quirinus (see etym.); noting or pertaining to one of the seven hills of Rome; pertaining to the Quirinal (palace or court). **II.** *n.* The Quirinal Hill at Rome; also, a palace built upon this hill, now used as the residence of the reigning house of Italy; hence, the Italian royal court or government, as distinguished from the Vatican (representing the papacy).

Qui-ri-tes (kwi-rī′tēz), *n. pl.* [L., pl. of *Quiris*, appar. < *quiris*, for Sabine *curis*, spear: cf. *Quirinal*.] The citizens of ancient Rome considered in their civil capacity.

quirk (kwėrk), *n.* [Origin obscure.] A sudden twist, turn, or curve; a flourish, as in writing; also, a piece taken from or added to a regular ground-plot or the like, as for a yard or court; also, an acute angle or a channel, as one separating a convex part of a molding from a fillet; also, a shift or evasion; a quibble; also, a clever or witty conceit, or a quip (as, "your rhymes and your rebusses, your *quirks* and your conundrums": Godwin's "Caleb Williams," iv.); also, a sudden turn or flourish in a musical air (as, "light *quirks* of music, broken and uneven": Pope's "Moral Essays," iv. 143); also, a trick or peculiarity (as, "Every man had his own *quirks* and twists": Mrs. Stowe's "Old-town Folks," v.). — **quirked**, *a.* Formed with a quirk or channel, as a molding. — **quirk′y**, *a.* Full of quirks, twists, or shifts.

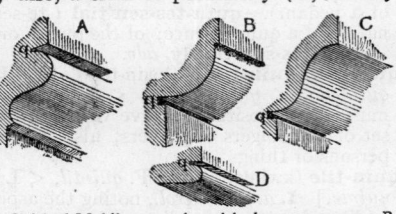

Quirked Moldings. — *A*, quirked cyma reversa; *B*, quirked ovolo; *C*, quirked cyma recta; *D*, quirked bead. *q. q. q. q.* quirks.

quirt (kwėrt), *n.* [Cf. *cuarta*.] A riding-whip consisting of a short, stout stock and a lash of braided leather. — **quirt**, *v. t.* To strike with a quirt.

Quis-ling (kwiz′ling), *n.* [Also *l. c.*] A person who undermines his own country from within; a fifth columnist: from Vidkun Quisling, a Nazi leader in Norway.

quit[1] (kwit), *a.* [OF. *quitte*, *quite* (F. *quitte*), < ML. *quietus*, quit, released, L. quiet, at rest: see *quiet*[2], *a.*, and cf. *quietus*.] Released from obligation, penalty, etc.; free, clear, or rid (*of*: as, "when I am *quit* of destiny," Eden Phillpotts's "Cherry-Stones," My Cherry Tree; "I desire simply to be *quit* of you," Stevenson's "Master of Ballantrae," xii.); also, quits†; also, clean† or complete† (cf. *quite*). — **quit**[1], *v.*; *quit* or *quitted*, *quitting*. [OF. *quitter*, *quiter* (F. *quitter*), < ML. *quietare*, release, discharge, LL. make quiet, E. *quiet*[2], *v.*] **I.** *tr.* To set free†, release†, or deliver†; free, clear, or rid of something (now rare); also, to clear of a charge, etc.†; acquit†; also, to bear, conduct, or acquit (one's self: archaic: as, "*Quit* yourselves like men, and fight," 1 Sam. iv. 9; "Can he teach others how to *quit* themselves?" Browning's "Ring and the Book," x.); also, to give up, let go, or relinquish (as, to *quit* an opinion; "The fellows immediately *quitted* their hold," Fielding's "Tom Jones," viii. 10); let go one's hold of (something grasped: as, "Nor, when he *quits* your bridle, need you wait for any other signal," Scott's "Castle Dangerous," xiv.); cease or discontinue (as, "They followed on his trail, nor *quit* hovering about him . . . until they had stolen a number of his best horses": Irving's "Captain Bonneville," xxvii.); also, to depart from, or leave (as, "He *quitted* London on the second day after his arrival," J. F. Kirk's "Charles the Bold," iii. 2; "I was about *quitting* my desk to go home," Lamb's "Superannuated Man"; "Don John scarcely *quitting* his fair guest for a moment," Motley's "Dutch Republic," v. 3); withdraw from (as, "those who *quitted* the old religion": Macaulay's "Hist. of Eng.," i.); also, to repay or requite (a person: obs. or prov.); make repayment or return for (something done); also, to pay off (a debt, etc.: as, "A thousand marks . . . To *quit* the penalty and to ransom him," Shakspere's "Comedy of Errors," i. 1. 23). **II.** *intr.* To cease from doing something; stop; also, to depart or

leave (as, "They had received notice to *quit*, as the house was coming down": W. De Morgan's "Alice-for-Short," ix.).

quit[2] (kwit), *n.* [Appar. imit.] Any of various small passerine birds of the West Indies, etc.

quitch (kwich), *n.* [AS. *cwice*: cf. AS. *cwic*, living, E. *quick*.] Couch-grass. Also **quitch′=grass**.

quit-claim (kwit′klām), *v. t.* [OF. *quite clamer*, declare quit: see *quit*[1], *a.*, and *claim*.] To quit or give up claim to (a possession, etc.). — **quit′claim**, *n.* A relinquishment of a claim, or the instrument embodying such a relinquishment.

quite (kwīt), *adv.* [ME. *quite*, < *quite*, free, clear, E. *quit*[1], *a.*] Completely, wholly, or entirely (as, "Thy memory, thy pain . . . Possess me *quite*," M. Arnold's "Southern Night"; a style *quite* out of fashion; "He was standing *quite* alone," W. Churchill's "Coniston," ii. 6; a *quite* contrary conclusion; *quite* a different matter; *quite* the reverse; *quite* another thing); also, actually, really, or truly (as, "I would not kill me, unless I came *quite* in its way," C. Brontë's "Villette," iii.; it happened *quite* suddenly; a *quite* sudden change; *quite* a sudden change; *quite* the best; "far from a lynx, and not a giant *quite*," Pope's "Satires and Epistles of Horace Imitated," Epistles, i. 1. 50; *quite* the thing); also, loosely, to a considerable extent or degree (as, *quite* pretty; *quite*, though hardly very, good; a *quite* recent occurrence; at *quite* a recent date; *quite* a number of persons; "She was *quite* a scholar," Dickens's "Hard Times," i. 9).

quit=rent (kwit′rent), *n.* [See *quit*[1], *a.*] Rent paid by a freeholder or copyholder in lieu of certain services which might be required of him.

quits (kwits), *a.* [Cf. *quit*[1], *a.*] Even, or on equal terms, by repayment or retaliation: as, "Simply knock him off his horse, and then you will be *quits*" (W. H. Hudson's "Far Away and Long Ago," xx.).

quit-tance (kwit′ạns), *n.* [OF. F. *quittance*, < *quitter*, E. *quit*[1], *v.*] Discharge from debt or obligation; also, a document certifying this (as, "He then folded the *quittance*, and put it under his cap": Scott's "Ivanhoe," x.); a receipt; also, recompense or requital.

quit-ter (kwit′ėr), *n.* One who quits, shirks, or easily gives up. [Colloq.]

quiv-er[1] (kwiv′ėr), *a.* [Cf. AS. *cwiferlīce*, actively, zealously.] Nimble; active; spry: as, "a little *quiver* fellow" (Shakspere's "2 Henry IV.," iii. 2. 301). [Now only prov. Eng.]

quiv-er[2] (kwiv′ėr), *v.* [Cf. *quaver*, also *quiver*[1].] **I.** *intr.* To shake with a slight but rapid motion; vibrate tremulously; tremble: as, "Her lip *quivered* like that of a child about to cry" (Tarkington's "Magnificent Ambersons," xvii.); "the beams of the moon *quivering* on the water" (Johnson's "Rasselas," xlv.); "His voice *quivered* with agitation" (Thackeray's "Newcomes," lxvi.). **II.** *tr.* To cause to quiver: as, "Impotent as a bird with both wings broken, it still *quivered* its shattered pinions" (C. Brontë's "Jane Eyre," xxviii.). — **quiv**[2], *n.* The act or state of quivering; a tremble; a tremor: as, "Heaven was cloudless, and grand with the *quiver* of its living fires" (C. Brontë's "Villette," xiv.); "Her face was whiter even than his, though not a *quiver* of mouth or eyelash betrayed emotion" (F. M. Crawford's "Mr. Isaacs," viii.).

quiv-er[3] (kwiv′ėr), *n.* [OF. *quivre*, *cuevre*; prob. from Teut.] A case for holding arrows (as, "a *quiver* of dogskin at his back, and a . . . bow in his hand": Parkman's "Oregon Trail," viii.); also, the contents of such a case; a quiverful. — **quiv′ered**, *a.* Furnished with a quiver; also, held

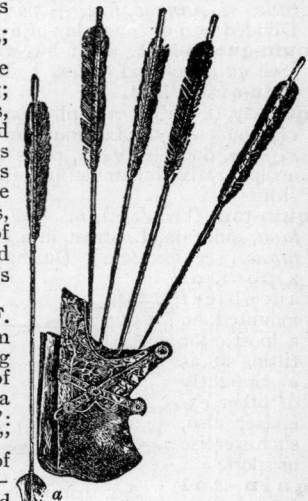

Mongol Quiver. — *a*, separate arrow.

in, or as in, a quiver.—**quiv′er-ful** (-fúl), *n.*; pl. *-fuls.* As many as a quiver holds.

qui vive (kē vēv). [F., 'live who?' — as if calling for the reply 'Vive le roi.' ('Long live the king'), or the like.] The challenge of French sentries to persons approaching: hence used as a noun in the phrase *on the qui vive* (on the alert), as, "She was . . . not so handsome as to keep perpetually *on the qui vive* a husband's jealousy" (Bulwer-Lytton's "Kenelm Chillingly," i. 1).

quix-ot-ic (kwik-sot′ik), *a.* [Sometimes *cap.*] Resembling or befitting Don Quixote, the hero of Cervantes's romance of that name, who was inspired by lofty and chivalrous but impracticable ideals; extravagantly chivalrous or romantic; visionary; impracticable: as, "This family training . . . makes them eminently *quixotic.* They can't let anything alone which they think going wrong" (Hughes's "Tom Brown's School Days," i. 1); "those *Quixotic* exaggerated notions of honour" (Bulwer-Lytton's "Caxtons," viii. 2). Also **quix-ot′i-cal.—quix-ot′i-cal-ly,** *adv.*—**quix-ot-ism** (kwik′sot-izm), *n.* [Sometimes *cap.*] Quixotic character or practice (as, "They must . . . not grumble if they find lofty *Quixotism* an expensive luxury": S. Butler's "Way of All Flesh," xix.); a quixotic idea or action (as, "There might be other *quixotisms* afoot on Mr. Charles's part": W. De Morgan's "Alice-for-Short," v.). Also **quix′ot-ry** (-ri).

quiz (kwiz), *n.*; pl. *quizzes* (kwiz′ez). [Origin uncertain.] An odd or queer person, in character or appearance (now rare: as, "Young ladies have a remarkable way of letting you know that they think you a '*quiz,*' without actually saying the words," C. Brontë's "Jane Eyre," xxi.); a queer or ridiculous thing (rare: as, "Where did you get that *quiz* of a hat?" Jane Austen's "Northanger Abbey," vii.); also, one who quizzes, ridicules, or chaffs (as, "If that divil, Tom Durfy, sees me, he'll tell it all over the country, he's such a *quiz*": Lover's "Handy Andy," viii.); also, banter; a piece of banter or ridicule; a witticism; a practical joke; a hoax; also, a questioning; an informal examination or test of a student or class.—**quiz,** *v. t.*; *quizzed, quizzing.* To make sport or fun of (as, "*Quiz* the doctor, Clary . . . he's an author — so fair game": Maria Edgeworth's "Belinda," vii.); ridicule; chaff; also, to question, or make prying inquiries of; examine informally or coach (a student or class) by questions.—**quiz′zer,** *n.*—**quiz′zi-cal,** *a.* Odd, queer, or comical (as, "I believe you have taken . . . a fancy to the old *quizzical* fellow": Maria Edgeworth's "Belinda," ix.); also, indulging in, characterized by, or suggestive of quizzing, ridiculing, or chaffing (as, "Osmond Orgreave entered the room, *quizzical,* and at once began to tease Clayhanger," Arnold Bennett's "Hilda Lessways," vi. 2; a *quizzical* smile; "a little *quizzical* wrinkle of the brow that suggested a faintly amused attempt to follow my uncle's mental operations," H. G. Wells's "Tono-Bungay," i. 2. § 4).—**quiz-zi-cal′i-ty** (-kal′i-ti), *n.* Quizzical quality or expression: as, "There was a touch of *quizzicality* in one of her lifted eyebrows" (Galsworthy's "Country House," i. 2).—**quiz′zi-cal-ly,** *adv.*

quo-ad (kwō′ad), *prep.* [L.] So far as; as to.

quod (kwod), *n.* [Origin uncertain.] Prison; jail: as, "a vagrant oft in *quod*" (Kipling's "Holy War"). [Slang.]

quod-li-bet (kwod′li-bet), *n.* [L. *quod libet,* 'what it pleases,' what you please.] A theological or scholastic question proposed for exercise in argument, or the debate or argument on such a question (now only hist.); in *music,* a fanciful harmonic combination of two or more melodies; also, a medley.

quoin (koin), *n.* [Variant spelling of *coin.*] An external solid angle of a wall or the like; also, one of the stones forming it; a corner-stone; also, a wedge-shaped piece of wood, stone, or other material, used for any of various purposes; in *printing,* a wedge of wood or metal for securing types in a chase, etc.—**quoin,** *v. t.* To provide with quoins, as a corner of a wall; also, to secure or raise with a quoin or wedge.

quoit (kwoit or, esp. Brit., koit), *n.* [ME. *coyte*; origin uncertain.] Orig., a discus; now, a flattish iron or other ring thrown

Quoit. — *a,* central opening; *b,* marginal edge, which, when the quoit is skilfully pitched, cuts into the earth; *c,* thumb-notch, by which the thrower is enabled to give the quoit a spinning motion.

in play to encircle a peg stuck in the ground or to come as close to it as possible; *pl.* (construed as *sing.*), the game so played.—**quoit,** *v. t.* To throw as or like a quoit: as, "Hundreds of tarred and burning hoops were skilfully *quoited* around the necks of the soldiers" (Motley's "Dutch Republic," iii. 9).—**quoit′er,** *n.*

quo-mo-do (kwō′mō-dō or kwō-mō′dō), *n.* [L. *quo modo,* 'in what manner.'] The manner, way, or means: as, "Mr. Northerton was desirous of departing that evening, and nothing remained for him but to contrive the *quomodo*" (Fielding's "Tom Jones," vii. 15).

quon-dam (kwon′dam), *a.* [L., adv., formerly.] That formerly was or existed; sometime; former: as, "Vivian established his *quondam* associate in the service of Trevanion" (Bulwer-Lytton's "Caxtons," xvi. 7).

Quon-set hut (kwon′set hut), a compact and serviceable metal shelter or hut resembling a more or less semicircular arch in cross-section: named from Quonset, R. I.

quo-rum (kwō′rum), *n.* [L., 'of whom': from a use of the word in commissions written in Latin.] Orig., certain justices of the peace in England whose presence was necessary to constitute a bench, but later all justices collectively; hence, such a number of the members of any constituted body as must be present for the legal or valid transaction of business.

quo-ta (kwō′tä), *n.*; pl. *-tas* (-täz). [ML., prop. fem. of L. *quotus,* of what number, < *quot,* how many, akin to *qui,* who: cf. *quality.*] The proportional part or share of a total which is due from, or is due or belongs to, a particular district, state, person, etc.: as, "The states could with difficulty extort anything like the assessed *quotas* from the different provinces" (Motley's "Dutch Republic," v. 5); "She [a city] has the usual Upper-River *quota* of factories, newspapers, and institutions of learning" (Mark Twain's "Life on the Mississippi," lviii.).

quot-a-ble (kwō′tä-bl), *a.* Capable of or suitable for being quoted.—**quot-a-bil′i-ty** (-bil′i-ti), **quot′a-ble-ness,** *n.*

quo-ta-tion (kwō-tā′shon), *n.* The act or practice of quoting; also, that which is quoted; a passage quoted from a book, speech, etc.; in *com.,* the stating of the current price of a stock, commodity, etc., or the price so stated; also, in *printing,* a large, commonly hollow quadrat for filling up the larger blanks in printed matter.—**quo-ta′tion=mark,** *n.* One of the marks used to indicate the beginning and end of a quotation: in English usually consisting of two inverted commas (") at the beginning and two apostrophes (") at the end, or, for a quotation within a quotation, of single marks of this kind, as in "He said, 'I will go,' " though frequently, esp. in Great Britain, single marks are used instead of double, the latter being then used for a quotation within a quotation.

quote (kwōt), *v.*; *quoted, quoting.* [ML. *quotare,* divide into chapters and verses, < L. *quot,* how many: see *quota.*] **I.** *tr.* To divide (a book) into chapters, etc.†; also, to specify the page, chapter, etc., of (a passage)†; also, to repeat (a passage, etc.) from a book, speech, etc., as the words of another, as by way of authority, illustration, etc. (as, "He *quoted* line after line, lingering over the cadences": Mrs. H. Ward's "Robert Elsmere," vii.); repeat words from (a book, author, etc.: as, "Why, George, you of all people *quoting* the Bible!" W. Churchill's "Inside of the Cup," i.; to *quote* Shakspere); also, to inclose (words) within quotation-marks; also, to set down in writing†; make note of†; also, to notice† or observe† (as, "What care I What curious eye doth *quote* deformities?" Shakspere's "Romeo and Juliet," i. 4. 31); also, to set down for something specified† (as, "He's *quoted* for a most perfidious slave": Shakspere's "All's Well," v. 3. 205); bring forward, adduce, or cite (as, "The Spaniard . . . *quoted* the example of Cortés," Prescott's "Conquest of Mexico," iv. 6; "He *quoted* the father of Honora's schoolmate . . . as authority for this prophecy," W. Churchill's "Modern Chronicle," i. 8); also, in *com.,* to state (a price); also, to state the current price of. **II.** *intr.* To make a quotation or quotations, as from a book or author.—**quote,** *n.* A quotation; also, a quotation-mark.—**quot-er** (kwō′tėr), *n.*—**quote′wor″thy,** *a.* Worthy to be quoted.

quoth (kwōth), *v. t. pret.* [Pret. of *quethe* (otherwise obs.), < AS. *cwethan,* say: cf. *bequeath.*] Said: used with nouns, and with pronouns of the first and third persons, and always placed before the subject (as, " 'I say it's a shame,' *quoth* my grandmother," Mrs. Stowe's "Oldtown Folks," xvi.; " 'I say,' *quoth* he, 'by heaven the man's to blame,' " Pope's "January and May," 222). [Archaic or prov.]

quoth-a (kwō'thä), *interj.* [For *quoth a,* 'quoth he.'] Forsooth! indeed! — used ironically or contemptuously in repeating the words of another (as, " 'Poetry is an agreeable and elegant amusement.' 'Elegant, *quotha!* . . . do you think he would write poetry if he could do any thing better?' " Godwin's "Caleb Williams," iv.). [Archaic or prov.]

quo-tid-i-an (kwō-tid'i-an). [OF. *cotidian* (F. *quotidien*), < L. *cottidianus, quotidianus,* < *cottidie, quotidie,* daily, < *quot,* how many, + *dies,* day.] **I.** *a.* Daily (as, "five

cats, that had risen simultaneously . . . to receive their *quotidian* morning's meal": Longfellow's "Kavanagh," xi.); also, everyday; ordinary; in *pathol.,* of a fever, ague, etc., characterized by paroxysms which recur daily. **II.** *n.* Something recurring daily; esp., a quotidian fever or ague.

quo-tient (kwō'shent), *n.* [L. *quotiens, quoties,* how many times, < *quot,* how many: see *quota.*] In *math.,* the result of division; the number of times one quantity is contained in another.

quo war-ran-to (kwō wo-ran'tō). [ML.,; 'by what warrant.'] In *law,* a writ calling upon a person to show by what warrant he exercises an office, privilege, franchise, or liberty: employed as a remedy against usurpation of office or of corporate franchises, etc.

R

R, r (är); pl. *R's, r's* (ärz). A consonant, the 18th letter of the English alphabet. — **the three R's.** See under *three, a.*

Ra, Re (rä, rā), *n.* [Egypt.] The great sun-god of the Egyptians, the sovereign god of historical Egypt, in art typically represented as a hawk-headed man bearing on his head the solar disk and the royal uræus.

ra-bat (rä-bä), *n.* [F.: see *rabbet.*] A piece or arrangement of linen, lace, or the like, worn falling from the neck over the breast, esp. in the form of two flat bands (as in ecclesiastical dress) or in a plaited or gathered form.

rab-bet (rab'et), *n.* [Prob. < OF. *rabat,* a beating down (F. a rabat), < *rabatre,* beat or put down: see *rebate*[2].] A cut, groove, or recess made on the edge or surface of a board or the like, as to receive the end or edge of another board or the like similarly or otherwise appropriately shaped; also, a joint so made. — **rab'bet,** *v.* **I.** *tr.* To cut or form a rabbet in; also, to join by a rabbet or rabbets. **II.** *intr.* To join by a rabbet. — **rab'bet=joint,** *n.* A joint formed by a rabbet or rabbets.

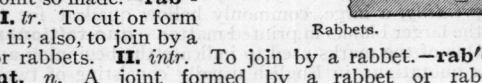

Rabbets.

rab-bi (rab'ī or rab'i), *n.;* pl. *rabbis* (rab'īz or -iz). [Heb. *rabbī,* 'my master.'] Master or lord, a Jewish title for a doctor or expounder of the law; hence, a Jewish doctor or teacher of the law, esp. one authorized by ordination to decide legal and ritualistic questions, and to perform certain functions in the synagogue, etc. — **rab-bin** (rab'in), *n.* [F.] A rabbi. — **rab'bin-ate** (-āt), *n.* The office or dignity of a rabbi; also, rabbis collectively. — **rab-bin-ic** (ra-bin'ik). **I.** *a.* Rabbinical. **II.** *n.* [*cap.*] The Hebrew language as used by the rabbis in their writings; the later Hebrew. — **rab-bin'i-cal,** *a.* Of or pertaining to the rabbis or their learning, writings, etc. — **rab-bin'i-cal-ly,** *adv.* — **rab'bin-ism,** *n.* A rabbinical expression or phrase; also, the teachings or traditions of the rabbis. — **rab'bin-ist,** *n.* Among the Jews, one who adheres to the Talmud and the traditions of the rabbis. — **rab-bin-is'tic,** *a.*

rab-bit (rab'it), *n.* [ME. *rabet:* cf. Walloon *robett,* rabbit.] A small long-eared burrowing rodent, *Lepus cuniculus,* of the hare family; also, any of various other hares, as the cottontail. Cf. *hare.* — **Welsh rabbit.** See under *Welsh*[1], *a.* — **rab'bit,** *v. i.* To hunt or catch rabbits. — **rab'bit-er,** *n.* — **rab'bit-ry** (-ri), *n.;* pl. *-ries* (-riz). A place in which rabbits are kept; also, a collection of rabbits. —

Rabbit (white lop-eared variety).

rab'bit=wood, *n.* A North American santalaceous shrub,

Pyrularia pubera, with oblong leaves, greenish-white flowers, and drupaceous fruit. Also called *buffalo-nut* and *oil-nut.* See cut at *oil-nut.*

rab-ble[1] (rab'l), *n.* [F. *râble,* earlier *rouable,* < L. *rutabulum,* instrument for raking or stirring, < *ruere,* turn up, rake up.] An iron bar sharply bent at one end, used for stirring, skimming, or gathering molten iron in puddling; also, any device used for the same purpose. — **rab'ble**[1], *v. t.;* -bled, -bling. To stir, skim, or gather with a rabble.

rab-ble[2] (rab'l), *v. t.* or *i.;* -bled, -bling. [ME. *rablen* = D. *rabbelen.*] To utter, read, or speak in a rapid, confused manner; also, to do (something) in a hurried, careless way. [Now prov. Eng. and Sc.]

rab-ble[3] (rab'l). [ME. *rabel,* pack (of hounds): cf. *rabble*[2].] **I.** *n.* A disorderly crowd or assemblage of persons, esp. of a low, rough, or turbulent kind (as, "Clergymen . . . were frequently exposed to the outrages of a fanatical *rabble*": Macaulay's "Hist. of Eng.," ii.); a mob; also, contemptuously, the rude lower class of persons (with *the:* as, "It has often been commented on how much better gentlemen of birth endure fatigue than persons of the *rabble,*" Stevenson's "Master of Ballantrae," iii.); persons of a low class (as, "In place of such lewd *rabble,* he introduced a train of holy friars to inspirit his people": Irving's "Conquest of Granada," xxvi.); also, a confused or disorderly assemblage of anything. **II.** *a.* Being or resembling a rabble; characteristic of a rabble or the rabble; disorderly; rude; low. — **rab'ble**[3], *v. t.;* -bled, -bling. To beset or assail as a rabble does; mob: as, "Those parishes of which the pastors had been *rabbled,* were declared vacant" (Macaulay's "Hist. of Eng.," xvi.). — **rab'ble-ment,** *n.* A rabble (now prov. Eng. and Sc.); also, disorder or tumult (obs. or archaic).

rab-bo-ni (ra-bō'nī or -ni), *n.* [Heb.: cf. *rabbi.*] Master: a Jewish title of especial honor. See John, xx. 16.

Rab-e-lai-si-an (rab-ẹ-lā'zi-an), *a.* Of, pertaining to, or suggesting François Rabelais (about 1490—1553), a French writer whose work is characterized by broad, coarse humor and keen satire. — **Rab-e-lai'si-an-ism,** *n.*

rab-id (rab'id), *a.* [L. *rabidus,* raving, furious, mad, < *rabere,* rave, be mad.] Furious or raging, as a person or animal, the temper, passions, etc.; violently intense or severe, as hunger, disease, etc.; irrationally extreme in opinion or practice (as, a *rabid* free-trader; "You know that by temper we are *rabid* idealists," Gissing's "New Grub Street," x.); also, specif., affected with or pertaining to rabies; mad; hydrophobic. — **rab'id-ly,** *adv.* — **rab'id-ness,** *n.*

ra-bi-es (rā'bi-ēz), *n.* [L., madness, rage, < *rabere:* see *rabid,* and cf. *rage.*] A fatal infectious disease of certain animals, as the dog, communicated to man through inoculation, as by a dog-bite; hydrophobia. — **ra-bi-et'ic** (-et'ik), *a.*

ra-ca (rä'kä or rā'-), *a.* [LL., < Gr. ῥακά, < Aram. *rēkā.*] Worthless: an ancient Jewish expression of contempt. See Mat. v. 22.

rac-coon', etc. See *racoon,* etc.

race[1] (rās), *n.* [OF. *rais, raiz,* < L. *radix* (radic-), root.] A root, as of ginger.

---

race² (rās), *n.* [F. *race*, < It. *razza*, race, breed, lineage; origin uncertain.] A group of persons connected by common descent or origin; a family; a tribe or people; a group of tribes or peoples forming an ethnic stock (as, the Teutonic *race*); a great division of mankind having certain physical peculiarities in common (as, the Caucasian or white *race*; the Mongolian or yellow *race*); also, a breed, stock, or strain of animals; a particular variety of an animal species; also, a variety or group of plants which reproduces itself with considerable certainty by seed; also, a natural kind of living creatures (as, "the human *race*," Thoreau's "Walden," iii.; "the *race* of fishes," Shelley's tr. Euripides's "Cyclops," 244; "the *race* of cows," Shelley's tr. Homer's "Hymn to Mercury," lii.); a kind of beings other than men or animals (as, "the Fauns and Satyrs, a lascivious *race*," Cowper's "Anti-Thelyphthora," 199; "the *race* of mermaids," Hawthorne's "Twice-Told Tales," The Village Uncle); often, the human race or family, or mankind (as, "That ev'ry tribe . . . Might feel themselves allied to all the *race*": Cowper's "Charity," 22); also, any group, class, or kind; esp., a class of persons (as, "the *race* of seamen": Defoe's "Captain Singleton," iv.); also, the condition of belonging to a particular people or stock, or the qualities, etc., due to this (as, "*Race* is a controlling influence in the Jew . . . *Race* in the negro is of appalling importance": Emerson's "English Traits," iv.); sometimes, lofty or noble extraction or lineage (as, "Lady Queenie obviously had what is called '*race*.' The renown of her family went back far, far beyond its special Victorian vogue," Arnold Bennett's "Pretty Lady," xiv.; "The look of *race*, which had been hers since childhood, was at nineteen more accentuated," W. Churchill's "Modern Chronicle," i. 7); sometimes, natural or inherited disposition† (see Shakspere's "Measure for Measure," ii. 4. 160); also, the characteristic taste or flavor of wine; fig., of speech, writing, etc., characteristic quality, esp. lively or piquant quality (as, "There perhaps never were two speakers whose eloquence had more of what may be called the *race*, more of the flavour imparted by moral qualities, than Fox and Pitt": Macaulay's "Essays," William Pitt).—**race suicide**, the extinction of a race or people which tends to result when, through the unwillingness or forbearance of its members to have children, the birth-rate falls below the death-rate.

race³ (rās), *n.* [ME. *rase, ras*, from Scand.: cf. Icel. *rás*, a running, race, rush or flow of liquid, course, channel, = AS. *rǽs*, a running, rush.] The act of running, or a run (now Sc.: as, "The noble stag . . . Held westward with unwearied *race*," Scott's "Lady of the Lake," i. 5); also, onward movement, or an onward or regular course (as, "The *race* Of the undeviating and punctual sun": Cowper's "Task," vi. 126); the course of time (as, "Fly, envious Time, till thou run out thy *race*": Milton's "On Time," 1); the course of life, or of a part of life (as, "At length, Their ministry perform'd, and *race* well run . . . They die": Milton's "Paradise Lost," xii. 505); also, a contest of speed, as in running, riding, driving, sailing, etc.; often, *pl.*, a series of horse-races run at a set time over a regular course (as, "We're going on to the *races*": Dickens's "Old Curiosity Shop," xvii.); also, *sing.*, a strong or rapid current of water, as in the sea or a river (as, "A little space, Through which now rushed in headlong, foaming *race*, The huddled waters of the flowing tide": W. Morris's "Jason," xii. 126); the channel or bed of such a current, or of any stream; often, a channel, esp. an artificial one, leading water to or from a place where its energy is utilized (cf. *headrace, tailrace, millrace*); the current of water in such a channel; also, a channel or path in which something moves; in *mach.*, a channel, groove, or the like, for a sliding or rolling part, as for ballbearings.—**race³**, *v.*; raced, racing. **I.** *intr.* To run, move, or go swiftly (as, "A boy . . . *raced* down to the water's edge," M. Hewlett's "Open Country," iii.; "like streamlet . . . in a torrent *racing* forth," Scott's "Marmion," iii., Introd.); specif., of an engine, wheel, etc., to run with undue or uncontrolled speed when the load or resistance is diminished without corresponding diminution of steam, power, etc. (as, "The motor engine *raced* before it was shut off": Sinclair Lewis's "Main Street," xv.); also, to engage in a contest of speed; run a race; also, to run horses in races; engage in or practise horse-racing. **II.** *tr.* To cause to run, move, or go swiftly; also, to cause to run in a race or races; also, to run a race with; try to beat in a contest of speed.—

race′a-bout″, *n.* A type of racing yacht with a short bowsprit and a rig like that of a sloop; also, a type of racing automobile.—

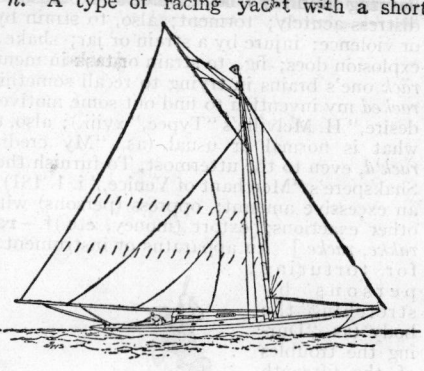

Raceabout.

race=course, *n.* A plot of ground laid out for horse-racing; the course for any race; also, a mill-race or the like.—

race′ = horse, *n.* A horse bred or kept for racing.

race=knife (rās′nīf), *n.*; pl. *-knives* (-nīvz). [Cf. *rase.*] A cutting tool with a bent-over lip for scribing, marking, numbering, etc.

ra-ceme (ra-sēm′), *n.* [L. *racemus*, cluster of grapes or berries: cf. *raisin.*] In *bot.*, a simple indeterminate inflorescence in which the flowers are borne on short pedicels lying along a common axis, as in the lily-of-the-valley (see cut at *inflorescence*); also, a compound inflorescence in which the short pedicels with single flowers of the simple raceme are replaced by racemes ('compound raceme').—**ra-cemed′** (-sēmd′), *a.* Disposed in racemes.

ra-cem-ic (ra-sem′ik or -sē′mik), *a.* [L. *racemus*: see *raceme.*] In *chem.*, noting or pertaining to an isomeric modification of tartaric acid, which is sometimes found in the juice of grapes in conjunction with the common dextrorotatory form, and which is optically inactive, but can be separated into the two usual isomeric forms, dextrorotatory and levorotatory; also, noting or pertaining to any of various organic compounds with analogous optical properties, that is, in which racemism occurs.—**ra-ce-mism** (ras′ē-mizm), *n.* In *chem.*, the character of an optically inactive substance (as racemic acid) which is separable into two other substances, each of which has the same chemical composition as the original substance, but one of which is dextrorotatory and the other levorotatory.

ra-ce-mose (ras′ē-mōs), *a.* [L. *racemosus*, clustering, < *racemus*, E. *raceme.*] Having the form of a raceme; raceme-like; also, arranged in racemes.

ra-cer (rā′sėr), *n.* One who or that which races, or takes part in a race, as a race-horse, or a bicycle, yacht, etc., used for racing; also, anything having great speed; specif., an American black-snake, *Zamenis constrictor.*

race=track (rās′trak), *n.* A race-course.

race-way (rās′wā), *n.* A passage or channel for water, as a mill-race.

ra-chis (rā′kis), *n.*; pl. *-chises*, L. *-chides* (-ki-dēz). [NL., for *rhachis*, < Gr. ῥάχις, spine, ridge.] Any of various axial structures; specif., the axis of an inflorescence when somewhat elongated, as in a raceme; also, the spinal column; also, the shaft of a feather, esp. the part bearing the web, as distinguished from the *quill.*

ra-chi-tis (ra-kī′tis), *n.* [NL., for *rhachitis*, < Gr. ῥαχῖτις, disease of the spine, < ῥάχις, spine.] In *pathol.*, rickets.—**ra-chit′ic** (-kit′ik), *a.*

ra-cial (rā′shạl), *a.* Pertaining to or characteristic of race or extraction, or a race or races.—**ra′cial-ly**, *adv.*

ra-ci-ly (rā′si-li), *adv.* In a racy manner or style. —**ra′ci-ness**, *n.*

Rye-grass. *a*, rachis.

rack¹ (rak), *v. t.* [ME. *rakken*; prob. from D. or LG.] To stretch the joints of (a person) in torture or punishment, esp. by means of a special apparatus (see *rack¹, n.*); hence, in general, to torture with suffering of body or mind (as,

"Stockmar, *racked* by dyspepsia . . . was a constitutionally melancholy man," Lytton Strachey's "Queen Victoria," iii.; "Terrible thoughts *racked* my imagination about their having found my boat," Defoe's "Robinson Crusoe," i. 11); distress acutely; torment; also, to strain by physical force or violence; injure by a strain or jar; shake violently, as an explosion does; fig., to strain or task in mental effort (as, to *rack* one's brains in trying to recall something; "In vain I *racked* my invention to find out some motive for the strange desire," H. Melville's "Typee," xviii.); also, to strain beyond what is normal or usual (as, "My credit . . . shall be *rack'd*, even to the uttermost, To furnish thee to Belmont": Shakspere's "Merchant of Venice," i. 1. 181); raise (rent) to an excessive amount; oppress (persons) with high rents or other exactions; extort (money, etc.)†.—**rack**[1], *n*. [ME. *rakke*, *racke*.] An apparatus or instrument formerly in use for torturing persons by stretching the body (as, "During the troubles of the fifteenth century, a *rack* was introduced into the Tower, and was occasionally used": Macaulay's "Hist. of Eng.,"

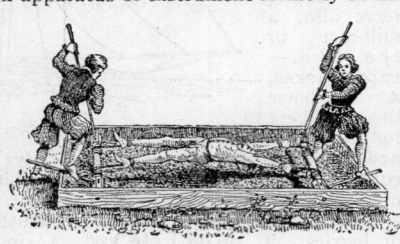

Rack.

i.); fig., a cause, or a situation or state, of intense suffering of body or mind (as, "Little knew they the *rack* of pain which had driven Lucy almost into fever": C. Brontë's "Villette," xxxviii.); torment; anguish; also, racking strain, as of storms; also, a framework of various kinds and for various purposes, as for holding things (as, a hat-*rack*; a pen-*rack*; a plate-*rack*); a framework, as in a stable or elsewhere, for holding fodder for horses or cattle; a spreading framework set on a wagon for carrying hay, straw, or the like in large loads; a framework or receptacle attached overhead to the wall in a railroad-car, for holding the passengers' bags, bundles, etc. (as, "There was no parlour car. Men and women . . . with bundles were already appropriating the seats and *racks*": W. Churchill's "Modern Chronicle," ii. 2); also, in *mach.*, a bar with teeth on one of its sides, adapted to engage with the teeth of a pinion or the like, as for converting circular into rectilinear motion or vice versa.— **on the rack,** in a state of torturing pain or distress; in painful anxiety or suspense; also, under the strain of great or special effort (as, "Martin's ingenuity was . . . *on the rack* to supply himself with a light": Hughes's "Tom Brown's School Days," ii. 3).

Rack.— Rack and pinion (at left).— Rack and worm (at right); *a*, worm; *b*, rack; *c*, wheel holding *b* against *a*.

rack[2] (rak), *n*. [Origin uncertain.] The neck portion of mutton, pork, or veal.

rack[3] (rak), *n*. [ME. *rak*, *rakke*; prob. from Scand.] Flying, broken clouds; a mass of clouds driven by the wind: as, "Across the sky the driving *rack* of the rain-cloud Grows for a moment thin" (Longfellow's "Courtship of Miles Standish," ix.).—**rack**[3], *v. i.* To drive or move, as clouds before the wind: as, "I looked up . . . and saw the clouds *rack* at an unusual rate" (Bunyan's "Pilgrim's Progress," i.).

rack[4] (rak), *n*. [= *wrack*[1], *wreck*.] Wreck; destruction: used chiefly in 'rack and ruin': as, "The houses will all go to *rack* and ruin" (Arnold Bennett's "Hilda Lessways," i. 2).

rack[5] (rak), *v. i.* [Origin obscure.] Of a horse, to go with a gait, similar to a pace, in which the legs move in lateral pairs but not quite simultaneously; single-foot; also, to pace.—**rack**[5], *n*. The gait of a horse in which the legs move in lateral pairs but not quite simultaneously; the single-foot; also, the pace.

rack[6] (rak), *v. t.* [Cf. obs. F. *raqué*, of wine, pressed from

the marc of grapes, Pr. *arracar*, to rack, *raca*, dregs.] To draw off (wine, cider, etc.) from the lees.

rack[7] (rak), *n*. Same as *arrack*.

rack-er[1] (rak′ėr), *n*. [See *rack*[1].] One who or that which racks, or tortures, strains, etc.

rack-er[2] (rak′ėr), *n*. [See *rack*[5].] A racking horse.

rack-er[3] (rak′ėr), *n*. [See *rack*[6].] One who racks wine or the like, or draws it off from the lees; also, a device for racking.

rack-et[1] (rak′et), *n*. [F. *raquette*, perhaps < Ar. *rāhat*, palm of the hand.] A light bat having a network of cord or catgut stretched in a more or less elliptical frame, used in tennis, etc.; *pl.* (construed as *sing.*), a game of ball, played in a walled court, in which such bats are used; also, *sing.*, a snow-shoe made in the manner of such a bat.

rack-et[2] (rak′et), *n*. [Prob. imit.] Loud noise, or a loud noise, esp. of a disturbing or confusing kind (as, "Imagine the thunderous *racket* made by . . .

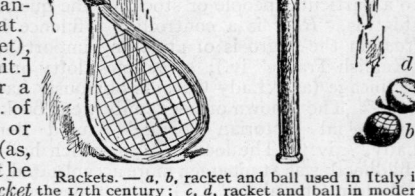

Rackets.— *a*, *b*, racket and ball used in Italy in the 17th century; *c*, *d*, racket and ball in modern use.

these carts . . . returning empty": W. H. Hudson's "Far Away and Long Ago," vii.); din; uproar; clamor or noisy fuss; a noisy disturbance or affair; also, social excitement, gaiety, or dissipation; a gay social gathering or affair; sometimes, a spree (slang); also, a scheme, trick, dodge, or special way of proceeding (slang: as, he can't work that *racket* here); a particular line of business or profit-seeking, esp. an improper or dishonest line, often an organized illegal activity such as bootlegging or as one concerned with extorting money by threat or violence from those engaged in some legitimate business (slang, U. S.); also, the adverse effects or consequences of something (in 'to stand the racket': slang).—**rack′et**[2], *v.* **I.** *intr.* To make a racket or noise; also, to indulge in social gaiety or dissipation; go (*about*, etc.) indulging in pleasure or dissipation (as, "He *racketed* round 'mong them nabobs": Mrs. Stowe's "Oldtown Folks," xlvi.). **II.** *tr.* To disturb with racket; also, to waste or destroy by racketing. [Rare.] —**rack-et-eer′** (-e-tēr′), *n*. One engaged in some (dishonest or illegal) racket. [Slang, U. S.]—**rack-et-eer′**, *v. i.* To act as a racketeer; engage in some racket. [Slang, U. S.]— **rack′et-er,** *n*.

rack-et-tail (rak′et-tāl), *n*. Any of several humming-birds which have two feathers of the tail very long, with the ends shaped like rackets.—**rack′et=tailed,** *a*.

rack-et-y (rak′et-i), *a*. Given to making racket or noise; characterized by noise; noisy; also, fond of or characterized by racketing, excitement, or dissipation.

rack-ing (rak′ing), *p. a.* That racks; torturing; causing intense suffering of body or mind; acutely distressing or disturbing: as, a *racking* headache; *racking* grief; "*racking* thoughts" (Scott's "Guy Mannering," xxxiii.).—**rack′-ing-ly,** *adv*.

rack=rail (rak′rāl), *n*. In an inclined-plane railway, a rail having cogs or teeth with which a cog-wheel on the locomotive engages.—**rack″=rail″way,** *n*.

rack=rent (rak′rent), *n*. Excessively or unreasonably high rent; a rent for land equal or nearly equal to the full annual value of the land: as, "Agriculture cannot be expected to flourish where . . . the husbandman begins on a *rackrent*" (Smollett's "Humphry Clinker," Aug. 28).—**rack′=rent,** *v. t.* To exact rack-rent from (a tenant); also, to exact rack-rent for (a farm, etc.).—**rack′=rent″er,** *n*. One who exacts rack-rent; also, one subjected to rack-rent.

rack-work (rak′wėrk), *n*. Mechanism in which a rack is used; a rack and pinion or the like.

---

ra-con-teur (rȧ-kôn-tėr), *n.* [F., < *raconter*, relate: cf. *recount²*.] A relater of anecdotes, etc.; a narrator: as, "He was a professional anecdote-monger of extraordinary brilliancy, a *raconteur* of the very first order" (Watts-Dunton's "Aylwin," v. 1). **—ra-con-teuse** (-tėz), *n.* [F.] Fem. of *raconteur*.

ra-coon, rac-coon (rȧ-kön'), *n.* [Algonquian.] A small nocturnal carnivorous animal, *Procyon lotor*, of North America, arboreal in habit, and having a sharp snout and a bushy tail; also, any other animal of the same genus. **—ra-coon'=dog,** *n.*

Common Racoon (*Procyon lotor*).

A small, short-eared canine animal, *Nyctereutes procyonoides*, of Japan and China, resembling a racoon.

Racoon-dog.

rac-quet (rak'et), *n.* See *racket¹*.

ra-cy (rā'si), *a.*; compar. *racier*, superl. *raciest*. [See *race²*.] Having an agreeably peculiar taste or flavor supposed to be due to the soil, as wine, fruits, etc.; hence, in general, having a strong distinctive and agreeable quality; having or showing a native vigor or liveliness (as, "Yorkshire has such families here and there . . . peculiar, *racy*, vigorous; of good blood and strong brain," C. Brontë's "Shirley," ix.); characterized by a pungent vigor or force, as language, etc.; sprightly or piquant (as, a *racy* style); peculiarly keen, as pleasure or enjoyment; also, showing excellent breed, as animals or their appearance, etc.

Ra-dar (rā'där), *n.* [From *ra*(dio) + *d*(etecting) + *a*(nd) + *r*(anging).] A device for determining the presence, location (direction), distance away, etc., of an enemy plane or ship obscured by darkness, fog, or the like: based on the outward projection of a beam of ultra high-frequency radio waves, which in turn are reflected back from the invisible object.

rad-dle¹ (rad'l), *n.* [Origin uncertain.] One of a number of long, slender sticks or rods fastened to or interwoven between upright stakes to form a fence, hedge, etc., or, when plastered over, a wall; such sticks collectively; a fence, etc., made with them. [Now prov. Eng.] **—rad'dle¹,** *v. t.*; *-dled, -dling*. To interweave like raddles; wattle. [Now prov. Eng.]

rad-dle² (rad'l), *n.* [Var. of *ruddle*.] Ruddle. **—rad'dle²,** *v. t.*; *-dled, -dling*. To paint or mark with or as with ruddle; color coarsely, as with rouge: as, "the second hussy being *raddled* with red paint" (Whyte-Melville's "Katerfelto," xiii.).

ra-di-al (rā'di-al), *a.* [LL. *radialis*, < L. *radius*: see *radius*.] Of or pertaining to a radius or a ray; of the nature or appearance of a radius or a ray; arranged like radii or rays; having spokes, bars, lines, etc., arranged like radii, as a machine; specif., noting or pertaining to an internal-combustion engine for an aëroplane, having radially arranged cylinders which revolve about a stationary crank-shaft; in *anat.*, of or pertaining to the radius. **—ra'di-al-ly,** *adv.*

ra-di-an (rā'di-an), *n.* [From *radius*.] In *math.*, an angle at the center of a circle, which subtends an arc of the circle equal in length to the radius: equal to 57.2958 degrees.

ra-di-ance (rā'di-ans), *n.* Radiant brightness or light (as, "the fierce *radiance* of a tropical sun," Prescott's "Conquest of Mexico," iii. 8; "A gas-jet . . . threw a strong *radiance* on her face and hair," Arnold Bennett's "Roll-Call," i.); brightness or brilliance, as of color; brightness of the face, expression, etc. (as, "A tender *radiance* lit her face like a

smile": W. H. Hudson's "Green Mansions," vi.); radiant beauty; also, radiation. Also **ra'di-an-cy.**

ra-di-ant (rā'di-ant), *a.* [L. *radians* (*radiant-*), ppr. of *radiare*: see *radiate*.] Emitting rays of light, or shining (as, the *radiant* sun; "this gloom of night . . . with all her *radiant* worlds," Young's "Night Thoughts," iv. 373); issuing in rays, or shining forth (as, "gleams of *radiant* light": Marryat's "King's Own," xv.); bright with light (as, "The new house was *radiant* with light," Arnold Bennett's "Clayhanger," ii. 4; "Her face Was *radiant* with the sunshine," Longfellow's "Masque of Pandora," i.); also, bright or brilliant in hue or appearance (as, "The piers . . . were loaded with excited humanity and *radiant* colour," Arnold Bennett's "Hilda Lessways," iv. 2; the *radiant* glow of health); bright with joy, hope, etc. (as, a face *radiant* with smiles; "She bends forward with a *radiant* look to meet the welcome visitor," Wiseman's "Fabiola," i. 1); strikingly fine, or splendid, as looks, beauty, etc., or the person (as, "He delighted in the *radiant* good looks of his betrothed," Mrs. Wharton's "Age of Innocence," vi.; "She was a tall and *radiant* woman of about thirty," Arnold Bennett's "Clayhanger," iii. 14); also, moving, operating, or extending in the manner of rays; characterized by a radial arrangement; in *physics*, emitted in rays, or by radiation (see phrases below); also, in *her.*, edged with rays, or long alternate pointed projections and depressions whose sides are formed by wavy lines. **—radiant energy,** in *physics*, that form of energy which consists of heat, light, or electricity being propagated through space: regarded as vibrations of the luminiferous ether, or, according to other theories, as electrons in motion. **—radiant heat,** in *physics*, that form of radiant energy producing heat effects. **—ra'di-ant,** *n.* A point or object from which rays proceed; in *astron.*, the point in the heavens from which a shower of meteors appears to radiate. **—ra'di-ant-ly,** *adv.*

A Chief Radiant.

ra-di-ate (rā'di-āt), *v.*; *-ated, -ating*. [L. *radiatus*, pp. of *radiare*, furnish with spokes or rays, emit rays, beam, < *radius*: see *radius*.] **I.** *intr.* To emit rays, as of light or heat; shine; also, to issue or proceed in rays; also, to spread or move like rays or radii from a center (as, "the gifts which *radiate* from Athens": J. H. Newman's "Idea of a University," ii. 1); specif., in *wireless teleg.* and *teleph.*, of a radio receiving set, to send out into the surrounding air waves or energy of its own due to oscillations set up in the vacuum-tube, thus causing interference and squeals in neighboring receiving sets (cf. *reradiate*). **II.** *tr.* To emit in rays; disseminate as from a center; specif., in *wireless teleg.* and *teleph.*, of a radio receiving set, to send out into the surrounding air (waves or energy). **—ra'di-ate. I.** *a.* Having rays, or ray-like or radial parts; represented with rays proceeding from it, as a head on a coin, in art, etc.; also, radiating from a center; in *zoöl.*, of or pertaining to the *Radiata*, an old zoölogical group including animals with radial structure, as the echinoderms. **II.** *n.* A ray;

Radiate Head of the Sun-god Helios. (Metope from New Ilium in the Troad.)

in *zoöl.*, a radiate animal. **—ra'di-at-ed** (-ā-ted), *a.* Radiate; radial. **—ra'di-ate-ly,** *adv.* **—ra-di-a'tion** (-ā'shon), *n.* [L. *radiatio*(*n*-).] The act of radiating, or the state of being radiated; also, that which is radiated; a ray or rays; also, radial arrangement of parts; one of a set of radially arranged things or parts; in *physics*, the emission and diffusion of rays of heat, light, or electricity; hence, the thing radiated (radiant energy or a particular form of it); also, the giving off of one or more rays by a radioactive substance; hence, the ray or rays given off.—**ra′di-a-tive** (-ā̯-tiv), *a.* Radiating; pertaining to radiation.—**ra′di-a-tor** (-ā-tor), *n.* One who or that which radiates; any of various heating devices, as a series or coil of pipes through which steam or hot water passes; a device for cooling circulating water, as on an automobile; in *wireless teleg.*, a form of oscillator.

rad-i-cal (rad′i-kal). [LL. *radicalis*, < L. *radix*, root.] **I.** *a.* Of or pertaining to a root or roots; hence, existing inherently in a thing or person (as, a *radical* error; *radical* defects of character); also, forming the basis or foundation, or primary (as, "the *radical* principle of happiness": Johnson's "Rasselas," xxxv.); also, going to the root or origin, or touching what is fundamental (as, a *radical* cure; a *radical* change); thorough; hence, thoroughgoing or extreme, esp. in the way of reform (as, *radical* opinions or principles); [often *cap.*] belonging or pertaining to radicals in politics, etc.; specif. [*l. c.*], in *bot.*, of or arising from the root or the base of the stem; in *math.*, pertaining to or forming a root; noting or pertaining to the sign √ (a modified *r*, the initial of Latin *radix*, root), placed before a quantity to indicate that its root is to be extracted; in *philol.*, pertaining to or of the nature of a root. **II.** *n.* A root; a basis; a fundamental; also, one who holds or follows radical or extreme principles; an extremist; [often *cap.*] an extremist in politics; an extreme liberal; often, one who advocates fundamental political reforms or changes by direct and uncompromising methods; [*cap.*] in British politics, a member of the extreme section of the Liberal party; specif.[*l.c.*], in *math.*, a quantity expressed as a root of another quantity; also, the radical sign; in *chem.*, an atom or group of atoms which is regarded as an important constituent of the molecule of a given compound, and which remains unchanged during certain reactions; in *philol.*, a radical word or part of a word; a radical letter.—**rad′i-cal-ism**, *n.* The principles or practices of radicals; the holding or following of radical or extreme views or principles.—**rad′i-cal-ize** (-īz), *v. t.* or *i.; -ized, -izing.* To make or become radical.—**rad″i-cal-i-za′tion** (-i-zā′shọn), *n.*—**rad′i-cal-ly**, *adv.*—**rad′i-cal-ness**, *n.*

rad-i-cant (rad′i-kant), *a.* [L. *radicans* (-ant-), ppr. of *radicare*: see *radicate*.] In *bot.*, producing roots: applied esp. to stems and leaves.

rad-i-cate (rad′i-kāt), *v.; -cated, -cating.* [L. *radicatus*, pp. of *radicare*, take root, < *radix*, root.] **I.** *intr.* To take root; produce roots. **II.** *tr.* To cause to take root; plant firmly.—**rad′i-cate**, *a.* In *bot.* and *zoöl.*, rooted; attached by or as by roots.—**rad-i-ca′tion** (-kā′shọn), *n.* Rooting; manner of rooting; fixation as by roots.

rad-i-cel (rad′i-sel), *n.* [NL. *radicella*, dim. of L. *radix*, root.] In *bot.*, a minute root; a rootlet.

ra-di-ces (rā′di-sēz), *n.* Plural of *radix.*

rad-i-cle (rad′i-kl), *n.* [L. *radicula*, dim. of *radix*, root.] In *bot.*, the lower part of the axis of an embryo; a rudimentary root; also, a radicel or rootlet; in *anat.*, a small rootlike part, as the beginning of a nerve-fiber; in *chem.*, a radical; in *philol.*, a radical.

ra-di-i (rā′di-ī), *n.* Plural of *radius.*

radio-. Form of L. *radius*, rod, spoke, radius, ray (see *radius*), also of NL. and E. *radium*, used in combination.

ra-di-o (rā′di-ō). [Short for *radiotelegraph*, etc., *radiotelephone*, etc.] **I.** *n.; pl. -dios* (-di-ōz). A wireless telegraph (radiotelegraph), telephone (radiotelephone), apparatus, station, or the like, for transmitting messages, etc., by means of the radiated energy of Hertzian waves, and for receiving these, or for either transmitting or receiving; often, as in popular use, a receiving apparatus of this kind, as for receiving broadcasted speeches, music, etc.; also, a wireless message, as by radiotelegraphy; also, wireless telegraphy or telephony (as, to receive a message by *radio*; speeches broadcasted by *radio*; to be interested in *radio*). **II.** *a.* Of, pertaining to, used in, or sent by radiotelegraphy or radiotelephony; wireless; often, as in popular use, pertaining to, used in, or sent by radiotelephony (as, a *radio* transmitting apparatus; a *radio* receiving set, or *radio* outfit; *radio* speeches, music, etc.).—**radio frequency.** See under *frequency.*—**ra′di-o**, *v.; -dioed, -dioing.* **I.** *tr.*

To transmit (a message, etc.) by radio; also, to send a message to (a person) by radio. **II.** *intr.* To transmit a message, etc., by radio.

ra-di-o-ac-tive (rā″di-ō-ak′tiv), *a.* [See *radio-.*] Having the property of emitting alpha rays, beta rays, or gamma rays, as is the case with radium, uranium, thorium, etc., which undergo spontaneous atomic disintegration; also, pertaining to this property.—**ra″di-o-ac-tiv′i-ty** (-tiv′i-ti), *n.* The property of being radioactive.

ra-di-o-bea-con (rā″di-ō-bē′kọn), *n.* A radio station for sending a characteristic signal out to sea, as to enable ships to determine their position or bearing by a radiocompass.

ra-di-o-broad-cast (rā″di-ō-brôd′kȧst), *v. t.* or *i.; -casted* or *-cast, -casting.* To broadcast by radio.—**ra″di-o-broad′-cast**, *n.* The broadcasting of radio messages, etc.—**ra″di-o-broad′cast″er**, *n.*

ra-di-o-cast (rā′di-ō-kȧst), *v. t.* or *i.; -casted* or *-cast, -casting.* To broadcast (messages, speeches, music, etc.) by radio.—**ra′di-o-cast-er**, *n.*

ra-di-o-chem-is-try (rā″di-ō-kem′is-tri), *n.* [See *radio-.*] The branch of chemistry that deals with radioactive substances and radioactivity.

ra-di-o-com-pass (rā″di-ō-kum′pȧs), *n.* An apparatus for finding the direction from which radio messages are received: used to determine position, as of a ship or an aircraft at sea.

ra-di-o-con-duc-tor (rā″di-ō-kọn-duk′tọr), *n.* [See *radio-.*] A device by which electric waves are detected, as the coherer in a wireless telegraph apparatus.

ra-di-o-go-ni-om-e-ter (rā″di-ō-gō-ni-om′e-tėr), *n.* [See *radio, a.*, and *goniometer*.] A device for finding the direction from which radio or wireless signals are coming: used to determine position, as of a ship or an aircraft at sea.—**ra″di-o-go-ni-om′e-try**, *n.* The use of the radiogoniometer.—**ra″di-o-go″ni-o-met′ric, ra″di-o-go″ni-o-met′-ri-cal** (-ō-met′rik, -ri-kal), *a.*

ra-di-o-gram (rā′di-ō-gram), *n.* [See *radio-* and *-gram.*] A radiograph; also, a message transmitted by radiotelegraphy; a radiotelegram.—**ra′di-o-graph** (-grȧf), *n.* [See *-graph.*] An image or picture produced by the action of Röntgen or other rays (as from radioactive substances) on a photographic plate. See *Röntgen rays*, under *Röntgen.*—**ra′di-o-graph**, *v. t.* To make a radiograph of; also, to telegraph by radio. —**ra-di-og′ra-pher** (-og′ra-fėr), *n.*—**ra″di-o-graph′ic, ra″di-o-graph′i-cal** (-graf′ik, -i-kal), *a.* Of or pertaining to radiography. —**ra″di-o-graph′i-cal-ly**, *adv.*—**ra-di-og′ra-phy** (-fi), *n.* [See *-graphy.*] The production of radiographs.

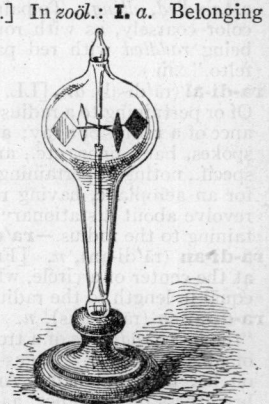

A Radiolarian (*Heliosphæra pectinata*), 160 times natural size.

ra-di-o-la-ri-an (rā″di-ō-lā′ri-ạn). [NL. *Radiolaria*, pl., < L. *radiolus*, dim. of *radius*, ray.] In *zoöl.:* **I.** *a.* Belonging or pertaining to the *Radiolaria*, an extensive group or order of minute marine protozoans, having an amœbiform body with fine radiating pseudopods. **II.** *n.* A radiolarian protozoan.

ra-di-o-lo-ca-tor (rā″di-ō-lō′kā-tọr), *n.* [See *radio-.*] A device for locating invading planes in darkness, etc.

ra-di-ol-o-gy (rā-di-ol′ọ-ji), *n.* [See *radio-* and *-logy.*] The science dealing with Röntgen rays or rays from radioactive substances, esp. for medical uses; also, examining or photographing organs, etc., with such rays.—**ra″di-o-log′ic, ra″di-o-log′i-cal** (-ō-loj′ik, -i-kal), *a.*—**ra-di-ol′o-gist**, *n.*

Crookes's Radiometer.

ra-di-om-e-ter (rā-di-om′e-tèr), n. [See *radio-* and *-meter*.] An instrument for indicating the transformation of radiant energy into mechanical work, consisting of an exhausted glass vessel containing vanes which revolve about an axis when exposed to light, etc. (see cut on preceding page); also, an instrument based on the same principle, but used for detecting and measuring small amounts of radiant energy.—**ra″di-o-met′ric** (-ō-met′rik), a. Pertaining to the radiometer or to radiometry.—**ra″di-o-met′ri-cal-ly**, adv. —**ra-di-om′e-try** (-tri), n. [See *-metry*.] The detection and measurement of radiant energy by means of the radiometer.

ra-di-o-mi-crom-e-ter (rā″di-ō-mī-krom′e-tèr), n. [See *radio-*.] A thermo-electric device for measuring minute changes in temperature.

ra-di-o-phare (rā′di-ō-fār), n. [See *radio-* and *phare, pharos* (lighthouse).] A radio or wireless station for determining the position of ships at sea.

ra-di-o-phone (rā′di-ō-fōn), n. [See *radio-* and *-phone*.] Any of various devices for producing sound by the action of radiant energy; specif., a photophone; also, a radiotelephone.—**ra″di-o-phon′ic** (-fon′ik), a. Pertaining to the radiophone or to radiophony.—**ra-di-oph′o-ny** (-of′ō-ni), n. The science or process of producing sound by the action of radiant energy.

ra-di-o-pho-to-graph (rā″di-ō-fō′tō-gràf), n. [See *radio-*.] A photograph or picture transmitted by a special radio process. Also **ra″di-o-pho′to** (-tō).—**ra″di-o-pho-to-graph′ic** (-graf′ik), a.—**ra″di-o-pho-tog′ra-phy** (-fō-tog′ra-fi), n.

ra-di-o-scope (rā′di-ō-skōp), n. [See *radio-* and *-scope*.] An instrument for studying and applying Röntgen rays; also, a form of spinthariscope.—**ra″di-o-scop′ic, ra″di-o-scop′i-cal** (-skop′ik, -i-kạl), a. Pertaining to the radioscope or to radioscopy.—**ra″di-os′co-py** (-os′kō-pi), n. [See *-scopy*.] The examination of opaque objects by means of the Röntgen rays or those emitted by radioactive substances.

ra-di-o-tel-e-gram (rā″di-ō-tel′ē-gram), n. [See *radio-*.] A message transmitted by radiotelegraphy; a wireless telegram.—**ra″di-o-tel′e-graph** (-gràf), n. A wireless telegraph. Cf. *radiotelegraphy*.—**ra″di-o-tel′e-graph**, v. t. or i. To telegraph by radiotelegraphy.—**ra″di-o-tel-e-graph′ic** (-graf′ik), a.—**ra″di-o-te-leg′ra-phy** (-tē-leg′ra-fi), n. Wireless telegraphy, in which messages are transmitted through space by means of the radiated energy of Hertzian waves.

ra-di-o-tel-e-phone (rā″di-ō-tel′ē-fōn), n. [See *radio-*.] A wireless telephone.—**ra″di-o-tel′e-phone**, v. t. or i.; *-phoned, -phoning*. To telephone by radiotelephony. —**ra″di-o-te-leph′o-ny** (-tē-lef′ō-ni), n. Wireless telephony. See *wireless*, a., and cf. *radiotelegraphy*.

ra-di-o-ther-a-peu-tics (rā″di-ō-ther-a-pū′tiks), n. [See *radio-*.] That branch of therapeutics which deals with the curative use of the Röntgen rays or of radioactive agencies. —**ra″di-o-ther′a-py** (-pi), n. Treatment of disease by means of the Röntgen rays or of radioactive agencies.— **ra″di-o-ther′a-pist**, n.

ra-di-o-tho-ri-um (rā″di-ō-thō′ri-um), n. [NL.: see *radio-* and *thorium*.] In *chem.*, a disintegration product of thorium.

ra-di-o-ul-nar (rā″di-ō-ul′nạr), a. [See *radio-*.] In *anat.*, of or pertaining to the radius and the ulna.

rad-ish (rad′ish), n. [F. *radis*, < It. *radice*, < L. *radix* (*radic-*), root, radish.] The crisp, pungent, edible root of a brassicaceous plant, *Raphanus sativus*; also, the plant.

ra-di-um (rā′di-um), n. [NL., < L. *radius*, ray: see *radius*.] Chem. sym., Ra (or Rd); at. wt., 226.4. A radioactive metallic element which undergoes spontaneous atomic disintegration, the first products formed being the element niton ('radium emanation') and alpha rays (which are regarded as positively charged particles of helium): discovered by M. and Mme. Curie in 1898. The disintegration of radium is understood to be a process by which an atom of radium breaks down into an atom of helium (the material of alpha rays) and an atom of niton (the material of the radium emanation), and by which an atom of niton loses an atom of helium and becomes radium A, and by which subsequent products are formed. See *radioactive, radium emanation, radium A,* and *radium B,* and *alpha rays, beta rays, gamma rays* (under *ray³, n.*).—**radium A,** a substance which is formed from the radium emanation by disintegration, and which in turn gives rise to the product called radium B.—**radium B,** a substance which is formed from radium A by disintegration, and which in turn gives rise to the product called radium C, from which radium D, radium E, and radium F are subsequently derived.—**radium emanation,** the element niton, a gaseous substance which is formed from radium by spontaneous atomic disintegration, and which in turn gives rise to the product called radium A. —**ra′di-um-ize** (-īz), v. t.; *-ized, -izing*. To treat with radium or the radium emanation; subject to the rays emitted by radium or its compounds or products.—**ra″di-um-i-za′tion** (-i-zā′shon), n.—**ra″di-um-ther′a-py** (-ther′a-pi), n. Treatment of disease by means of radium.

ra-di-us (rā′di-us), n.; pl. *-dii* (-di-ī) or *-diuses*. [L., staff, rod, spoke of a wheel, radius of a circle, radius of the arm, also ray or beam of light: cf. *ray³*.] A straight line extending from the center of a circle or sphere to the circumference or surface; also, any radial line, as of a curve; also, any radial or radiating part; also, a circular area of an extent indicated by the length of the radius of its circumscribing circle (as, "every house within a *radius* of forty or fifty miles": W. H. Hudson's "Far Away and Long Ago," i.); hence, field or range of operation or influence; also, extent of possible operation, travel, etc., as under a single supply of fuel (as, the flying *radius* of an aëroplane); in *anat.*, in man, that one of the two bones of the forearm which is on the thumb side; a corresponding bone in the fore limb of other vertebrates.—**ra′di-us vec′tor** (vek′tọr); pl. *radii vectores* (vek-tō′rēz) or *radius vectors*. [NL.: see *vector*.] In *math.*, a straight line (or its length) joining a fixed point or origin and a variable point; specif., in *astron.*, such a line (or distance) with the sun or other central body taken as the fixed point or origin, and a planet or the like as the variable point.

CA, CD, CB, CE, Radii of Circle.

ra-dix (rā′diks), n.; pl. *-dices* (-di-sēz) or *-dixes*. [L. *radix* (*radic-*), root.] A root; a radical; the source or origin; in *math.*, a number taken as the base of a system of numbers, logarithms, or the like.

rad-u-la (rad′ū-lä), n.; pl. *-læ* (-lē). [L., a scraper, < *radere*, scrape.] In *zoöl.*, a chitinous band in the mouth of most mollusks, set with numerous minute horny teeth, and drawn backward and forward over the odontophore in the process of breaking up food.—**rad′u-lar** (-lär), a.

ra-fale (rà-fál′), n. [F., lit. 'squall'; origin uncertain.] *Milit.*, a sudden, brief, violent burst of artillery fire, repeated at intervals.

raff¹ (raf), n. [ME. *raf*: see *riffraff*.] Trash, refuse, or rubbish (now prov. Eng. and Sc.); fig., the refuse of society, or of a community or a body of persons (as, "jostling with . . . coal-whippers, brazen women, ragged children, and the *raff* and refuse of the river": Dickens's "Oliver Twist," l.); the riffraff; the rabble; worthless or low persons; a worthless or low fellow.

raff² (raf), n. [Origin obscure: cf. *raft²*.] A great quantity or number; abundance; also, a heap or jumble. [Sc. and prov. Eng.]

raf-fi-a (raf′i-ä), n. [Malagasy.] A species of palm, *Raphia ruffia*, of Madagascar, bearing long, plume-like pinnate leaves, the leafstalks of which yield an important fiber; also, the fiber, much used for tying plants, cut flowers, small packages, etc., and for making matting, baskets, hats, and the like; also, some other palm of the same genus, or its fiber.

raf-fi-nose (raf′i-nōs), n. [F. *raffiner*, refine: see *-ose²*.] In *chem.*, a colorless crystalline sugar, $C_{18}H_{32}O_{16}$, with little or no sweetness, occurring in the sugar-beet, cotton-seed, etc.

raff-ish (raf′ish), a. Like the raff or rabble; low; vulgar.— **raff′ish-ly**, adv.—**raff′ish-ness**, n.

raf-fle¹ (raf′l), n. [Cf. *raff¹*.] Rubbish; *naut.*, a tangle, as of ropes, canvas, etc. (as, "The top-men clear the *raffle* with their clasp-knives in their teeth": Kipling's "Galley-Slave").

raf-fle² (raf′l), n. [OF. *raffle* (F. *rafle*), kind of play or game at dice; origin uncertain.] A game with dice†; also, a form of lottery in which something put up as a prize goes to

(variable) ḓ as d or j, ş as s or sh, ţ as t or ch, z̧ as z or zh; o, F. *cloche*; ü, F. *menu*; ċh, Sc. *loch*; ṅ, F. *bonbon*; ′, primary accent; ″, secondary accent; †, obsolete; <, from; +, and; =, equals. See also lists at beginning of book.

some one among a number of persons buying chances to win it.—**raf′fle**[2], *v.*; *-fled, -fling.* **I.** *intr.* To hold a raffle; take chances in a raffle. **II.** *tr.* To dispose of by a raffle: often with *off*: as, to *raffle*, or *raffle off*, a watch.—**raf′fler,** *n.*

Raf-fles (raf′lz), *n.* [From A. J. *Raffles*, chief character in "The Amateur Cracksman" (1899) and other books by E. W. Hornung (1866–1921).] A gentleman burglar.

raf-fle-si-a (ra-flē′zi-ạ̈), *n.* [NL.; named from Sir T. S. *Raffles* (1781–1826), English governor in Sumatra.] Any plant of the Malaysian genus *Rafflesia*, comprising species that consist mainly of a single flower having no leaves or proper stem and growing as a parasite on the stem or root of species of *Cissus*, as *R. arnoldi*, whose flower is sometimes 3 feet in diameter. —**raf-fle-si-a′-ceous** (-zi-ā′shius), *a.*

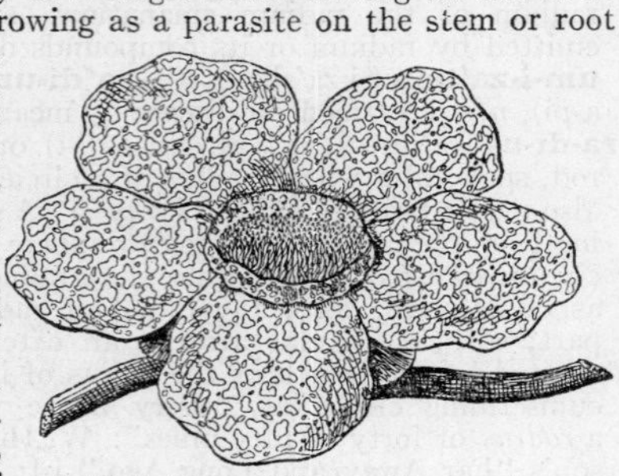

Rafflesia (*R. arnoldi*), parasitic on a stem.

raft[1] (råft), *n.* [ME. *rafte*, from Scand.: cf. Icel. *raptr*, Sw. and Dan. *raft*, rafter, also E. *rafter*[2].] A beam, spar, or rafter (archaic or prov. Eng.); also, a collection of logs, planks, casks, etc., fastened together for transportation by floating on water; also, a flat structure made of logs, planks, spars, or other material, for floating on water and carrying persons or things; also, any large floating mass, as of driftwood or ice (as, "The descending ice . . . formed a great undulating *raft*, filling up the whole river": Mrs. Stowe's "Uncle Tom's Cabin," vii.).—**raft**[1], *v.* **I.** *tr.* To form (logs, casks, etc.) into a raft; cause to float in the form or manner of a raft; also, to transport on a raft (as, "We crossed it [a river] . . . *rafting* over our horses and equipage": Parkman's "Oregon Trail," ii.); also, to travel upon or cross by means of a raft. **II.** *intr.* To use a raft; go or travel on a raft (as, "The vagabonds will have to swim for it, or *raft* off": Cooper's "Deerslayer," viii.).

raft[2] (råft), *n.* [Var. of *raff*[2].] A great quantity or number; a lot: as, a *raft* of things; a whole *raft* of children; "making such a *raft* of trouble" (Mark Twain's "Huckleberry Finn," xlii.); "They say there's a whole *raft* of stuff being smuggled across at Detroit" (Sinclair Lewis's "Babbitt," viii.). [Colloq.]

raft-er[1] (råf′tėr), *n.* One who rafts timber.

raf-ter[2] (råf′tėr), *n.* [AS. *ræfter*, akin to Icel. *raptr*, rafter: see *raft*[1].] One of the sloping timbers or members of a roof, as those ('principal rafters') which are framed into the tie-beams and support the purlins, or those ('common rafters') which are supported by the purlins and sustain the covering. —**raf′ter**[2], *v. t.* To furnish or build with rafters.—**raf′-tered,** *p. a.* Built with rafters, esp. with rafters left exposed to sight in a ceiling.

rafts-man (råfts′mạn), *n.*; pl. *-men.* A man who manages, or is employed on, a raft.

rag[1] (rag). [ME. *ragge*: cf. Icel. *rögg*, tuft or strip of fur.] **I.** *n.* A comparatively worthless fragment of cloth, esp. one resulting from tearing or wear (as, clothes torn or worn to *rags*); any shred, scrap, or waste bit of a textile fabric (as, to tie a *rag* about a bleeding finger; to use *rags* for cleaning; paper made from linen *rags*); old or waste cloth of any kind (as, a piece of *rag*); *pl.*, ragged or tattered clothing (as, "the lazar, in his *rags*": Tennyson's "In Memoriam," cxxvii.); *sing.*, any scrap or bit of cloth or clothing (chiefly in negative expressions: as, masts without a *rag* of canvas or sail; "I ha'n't a shirt . . . that I can call my own, nor a *rag* of clothes," Smollett's "Humphry Clinker," May 24); also, in general, a shred, scrap, or fragmentary bit of anything (as, a *rag* of flesh or skin; a *rag* of cloud; he hasn't a *rag* of reputation left); a rough projection or jag, as on a surface or edge; also, a piece of cloth for a particular use or purpose (as, a wash-*rag*; a dish-*rag*); often, a contemptuous or humorous term for some article of cloth, paper, or the like, such as a handkerchief, a flag, a theater curtain, or a piece of paper money; specif., a newspaper (slang: as, "When the *Rag* he wrote for praised his plucky game, Boanerges Blitzen felt that this was Fame," Kipling's "Man Who Could Write"); also, a beggarly, worthless, or wretched person (contemptuous: as, "thy father, that poor *rag*," Shakspere's "Timon of Athens," iv. 3. 271); also, a song or a piece of instrumental music in rag-time (colloq.). **II.** *a.* Made of or from rags (as, a *rag* doll; a *rag* carpet; *rag* pulp for paper-making); resembling rags, or no better than rags (as, *rag* money, a contemptuous name for paper money); pertaining to or concerned with rags (as, the *rag* trade).—**rag**[1], *v.*; *ragged, ragging.* **I.** *tr.* To make ragged; give a ragged surface, edge, or appearance to; also, to render or perform in rag-time (colloq.). **II.** *intr.* To become ragged; also, to dress or deck one's self in good or fine clothes (with *out* or *up*: slang, U. S.); also, to use rag-time (colloq.).

rag[2] (rag), *n.* [ME. *ragghe, ragge*; origin obscure.] Any of various kinds of rock used for building, etc. [Eng.]

rag[3] (rag), *v.*; *ragged, ragging.* [Origin uncertain: cf. *bully-rag.*] **I.** *tr.* To scold (as, "Boultbee was always *ragging* us because we didn't wipe our shoes": L. Merrick's "Conrad in Quest of His Youth," iii.); also, to tease, plague, or torment; esp., to harass in a boisterous or disorderly way (said esp. of students). [Chiefly British, slang or prov.] **II.** *intr.* To wrangle or dispute. [British.]—**rag**[3], *n.* An act or performance of ragging; esp., a boisterous public merry-making or demonstration by students or others, as in honor of some occasion or person. [British.]

rag-a-muf-fin (rag′ạ-muf-in), *n.* [ME. *Ragamoffyn*, name of a demon: cf. *rag*[1].] A ragged, disreputable fellow (as, "These armies were . . . a handful of hen-stealing, bottle-bruising *ragamuffins*": Irving's "Knickerbocker's New York," v. 9); a tatterdemalion; now, often, a ragged boy or child (as, "a little *ragamuffin* eight years old": W. De Morgan's "Joseph Vance," x.).—**rag′a-muf-fin-ly,** *a.*

rag=bag (rag′bag), *n.* A bag for holding rags.

rag=bolt (rag′bōlt), *n.* A bolt having the shank barbed so as to resist withdrawal.—**rag′=bolt,** *v. t.* To secure with rag-bolts.

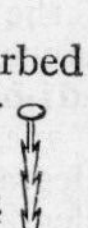

Rag-bolts.

rage (rāj), *n.* [OF. F. *rage*, < LL. *rabia*, for L. *rabies*, madness, rage: see *rabies*.] Madness, or a fit of madness (obs. or archaic); also, fury, furious spirit, or fierce violence (as, "So he came . . . having the fury of a cruel tyrant, and the *rage* of a savage beast": 2 Mac. iv. 25); esp., angry fury, or violent anger (as, "It was against the Chancellor that the *rage* of the populace was chiefly directed. His windows were broken . . . a gibbet was set up before his door," Macaulay's "Hist. of Eng.," ii.; a voice quivering with *rage*); a fit of violent anger (as, to fall into or be in a *rage*; "Naaman . . . turned and went away in a *rage*," 2 Kings, v. 12); also, fury or raging violence of inanimate things, as of wind, waves, fire, disease, etc., or an instance of it (as, "Fear no more the heat o' the sun, Nor the furious winter's *rages*": Shakspere's "Cymbeline," iv. 2. 259); also, violence of feeling, desire, or appetite (as, "Dinmont . . . said little . . . till the *rage* of thirst and hunger was appeased": Scott's "Guy Mannering," xlv.); a violent desire or passion (as, a *rage* for notoriety; a *rage* to kill); ardor, fervor, or enthusiasm (as, "Chill penury repress'd their noble *rage*," Gray's "Elegy," xiii.; poetic *rage*); also, with *the*, the object of a widespread passion or enthusiasm (as, the game soon became all the *rage*; "Every one goes to him [a lecturer]. He is the *rage*," J. H. Newman's "Callista," viii.).—**rage,** *v. i.*; *raged, raging.* [OF. *ragier* (F. *rager*).] To be or go mad†; also, to act with fury, as persons or wild beasts; rave or storm with furious utterance; manifest or feel violent anger; also, of inanimate things, to move, rush, dash, or surge furiously (as, "The chariots shall *rage* in the streets," Nahum, ii. 4; "The wind blew very boisterous, and the sea *raged* extremely," Stevenson's "Master of Ballantrae," iii.); proceed, continue, or prevail with great violence (as, "A heavy gulf thunderstorm was *raging*," J. Conrad's "Rescue," ii. 3; war, a battle, or an epidemic *rages*); of feelings, passions, etc., to hold sway with unabated violence.—**rage′ful,** *a.* Full of rage: as, "Nor thou be *rage-ful*, like a handled bee" (Tennyson's "Ancient Sage," 269). —**rage′ful-ly,** *adv.*

rag-ged (rag'ed), *a.* Torn or worn to rags, or tattered (as, *ragged* clothing; a *ragged* carpet); clothed in rags or tattered garments, as persons; characterized by rags or tatters, as the appearance, condition, etc.; in general, having, or characterized by, loose or hanging shreds or fragmentary bits (as, *ragged* meat; a *ragged* wound; *ragged* clouds); having irregular projecting or straggling parts (as, a *ragged* bush; "His hair was neglected, *ragged*, and floating," Godwin's "Caleb Williams," xxxviii.); shaggy, as an animal, its coat, etc.; rough with projections or breaks, as a surface or edge; full of rough or sharp projections, or jagged, as rocks, stone ruins, etc.; in a roughly wild, neglected, or ruinous state (as, *ragged* roadsides; a *ragged* garden; "the dreary, *ragged* cabins on the hillsides," Bret Harte's "Fool of Five Forks"); also, rough, imperfect, or faulty (as, *ragged* rimes; a *ragged* piece of work); harsh, as sound, the voice, etc.—**rag'-ged-ly**, *adv.*—**rag'ged-ness**, *n.*—**rag'ged-rob'in**, *n.* A silenaceous plant, *Lychnis flos-cuculi*, bearing pink or white flowers with dissected petals.
—**rag'ged-y** (-i), *a.* Ragged; of ragged appearance. [Colloq. or prov.]

rag'gee, *n.* See *ragi*.

rag-gy (rag'i), *a.* Ragged: as, "if it's *raggy* and dirty you are" (Synge's "Well of the Saints," i.). [Now chiefly prov.]

ra-gi, rag-gee (rä'gē, rag'ē), *n.* [Hind. *rāgī*.] A cereal grass, *Eleusine coracana*, cultivated in Asia, etc., for its grain.

ra-ging (rā'jing), *p. a.* That rages; furious; violent, as a tempest, or as disease or pain; aching violently, as a tooth.—**ra'ging-ly**, *adv.*

rag-lan (rag'lan), *n.* [From Lord *Raglan*, British commander in the Crimean War.] A loose overcoat the sleeves of which are cut so as to continue up to the collar.

Ragged-robin.— 1, upper part of stem with inflorescence; 2, lower part of stem with rhizome; *a*, a fruit.

rag-man (rag'man or -man), *n.*; pl. *-men.* A man who gathers, or deals in, rags.

ra-gout (ra-gö'), *n.* [F. *ragoût*, < *ragoûter*, restore the appetite of, < *re-* (< L. *re-*), back, + *à* (< L. *ad*), to, + *goût* (< L. *gustus*), taste.] A highly seasoned stew of meat and vegetables.—**ra-gout'**, *v. t.*; *-gouted* (-göd'), *-gouting* (-gö'ing). To make into a ragout.

rag-pick-er (rag'pik''ér), *n.* One who goes about picking up or gathering rags and other waste material from the streets, refuse-heaps, etc., for a livelihood.

rag-stone (rag'stōn), *n.* Same as *rag*[2], *n.* [Eng.]

rag=tag (rag'tag), *n.* [Cf. *tag*[1].] Ragged, inferior people; the riffraff or rabble; also, a person of this class.—**rag=tag and bobtail**, ragged, inferior persons and low nondescripts of all kinds; the riffraff generally; also, the whole pack or lot of persons.

rag=time (rag'tīm), *n.* In *music*, rhythm marked by frequent syncopation, such as is common in negro melodies; also, music in this rhythm. [Colloq.]

rag-weed (rag'wēd), *n.* Any of the composite herbs constituting the genus *Ambrosia*, as *A. artemisiæfolia*, a weed whose pollen is supposed to cause hay-fever (U. S.); also, the ragwort (Eng.).

rag-wort (rag'wèrt), *n.* Any of various composite plants of the genus

Golden Ragwort.— 1, the upper part of the stem with the heads; 2, the rhizome with the lower part of the stem and the leaves; *a*, the achene.

Senecio, as *S. jacobæa*, a yellow-flowered old-world herb with irregularly lobed leaves, or a North American species, *S. aureus* ('golden ragwort'), also bearing yellow flowers (see cut in preceding column).

raid (rād), *n.* [ME. *rade*, northern (Sc.) form of *rode*, < AS. *rād*, a riding, raid: see *road*.] A hostile or predatory incursion, orig. of mounted men; a foray; also, a sudden military assault, as for doing harm or taking prisoners; a sudden attack on the enemy, as by airships; also, in general, a sudden onset or descent, as upon something to be seized or suppressed (as, a police *raid* upon a gambling-house).—**raid**, *v.* **I.** *intr.* To engage in a raid. **II.** *tr.* To make a raid on: as, "Austrian sea-planes, which come *raiding* the Italian coast country at night" (H. G. Wells's "Italy, France, and Britain at War," ii. 1).—**raid'er**, *n.*

rail[1] (rāl), *n.* [OF. *reille*, < L. *regula*, rule, straight stick, bar: see *rule*.] A bar of wood or metal fixed horizontally for any of various purposes, as for support, or as a guard or barrier; such a bar fixed upon upright supports as part of a railing or fence; a continuous series of such bars, as in a railing or a fence; a railing or a fence constructed of such bars and supports or otherwise; also, one of the bars, as of steel, of various shapes, forming the support and guide for the wheels of locomotives, cars, etc.; a single continuous line of such bars, commonly one of a pair of lines laid in place for a track; also, the railroad as a means of transportation (as, to travel by *rail*); *pl.*, stocks, bonds, etc., of railroads; also, *sing.*, *naut.*, any of several bars, timbers, etc., serving for support or inclosure; the upper part of the bulwarks of a ship; a fence-like structure in various parts of a ship; in *joinery*, a horizontal timber or piece in a framework or in paneling.

Section of Rail.—*a*, head; *b*, web; *c*, base; *d*, inner side of head, made to correspond with the car-wheel.

—**rail**[1], *v.* **I.** *tr.* To furnish with a rail or rails; inclose with or separate by rails or a railing (as, "a space that had been *railed* off on the grass": S. Butler's "Way of All Flesh," lxxvi.); also, to lay rails on; also, to transport by railroad (as, "*Rail* me then, on my decease, To the Hills for old sake's sake!" Kipling's "Ballad of Burial"). **II.** *intr.* To travel by railroad.

rail[2] (rāl), *n.* [AS. *hrægl*.] A garment; a cloak; a kerchief: now only as in *nightrail*.

rail[3] (rāl), *n.* [OF. *raale* (F. *râle*); origin uncertain.] Any of numerous small birds constituting the subfamily *Rallinæ* (family *Rallidæ*), characterized by short wings, a narrow body, strong legs, long toes, and a harsh cry, and abounding in marshes and swamps in most parts of the world, as *Rallus aquaticus* (the common European rail), *R. virginianus* ('Virginia rail'), or *Porzana carolina* ('Carolina rail,' or sora); also, any bird of the family *Rallidæ*.

rail[4] (rāl), *v.* [OF. F. *railler*, deride, jeer, rally; origin uncertain: cf. *rally*[2].] **I.** *intr.* To utter bitter complaint or vehement denunciation: often with *at* or *against*: as, "Why *rail* at fate? The mischief is your own" (Whittier's "Panorama"). **II.** *tr.* To bring, force, etc., by railing.

Virginia Rail (*Rallus virginianus*).

rail=bird (rāl'bèrd), *n.* A rail, esp. the Carolina rail. [U. S.]

rail-er (rā'lér), *n.* One who rails, or utters bitter complaint.

rail-head (rāl'hed), *n.* The upper portion of a steel rail, with which the wheels of the vehicles of a railroad come in contact; also, the farthest point to which the rails of a railroad have been laid (as, "Each day *railhead* crept a mile or so further across the Plains": J. H. Patterson's "Man-Eaters of Tsavo," xx.).

rail-ing (rā'ling), *n.* A barrier made of rails, rails and supports, or the like (often in *pl.*, in same sense: as, "a low stone wall that was surmounted by spiked *railings*," Mallock's "New Republic," ii. 3); also, rails collectively; material for rails.

rail-ler-y (rāl'ér-i or ral'-), *n.*; pl. *-ies* (-iz). [F. *raillerie*, < *railler*: see *rail*[4], *rally*[2].] Good-humored ridicule; banter; also, a bantering remark.

rail-road (rāl'rōd), *n.* A road or way laid with rails, on which the wheels of wagons, etc., are made to run to facilitate and guide the movement of the vehicles; the runway or track thus formed; specif., a permanent road or way, laid or provided with rails, commonly in one or more pairs of continuous lines forming a track or tracks, on which cars, etc., are run for the transportation of passengers, freight, etc.; such a road together with its rolling-stock, buildings, etc.; the company of persons owning or operating it. In the U. S., *railroad* is the more common term for such roads, although *railway* is also used (esp. with reference to street-car lines); in British use, *railway* is the usual term.—**rail'-road,** *v.* **I.** *tr.* To supply with railroads; also, to transport by means of a railroad; also, to send or push forward with great or undue speed (colloq., U. S.: as, to *railroad* a bill through a legislature). **II.** *intr.* To work on a railroad; be employed in the railroad business; also, to travel by rail. —**rail'road-er,** *n.*—**rail'road-ing,** *n.* The construction or operation of railroads.

rail=tongs (rāl'tôngz), *n. pl.* or *sing.* Track-layers' tongs for lifting rails.

rail-way (rāl'wā), *n.* A railroad (see *rail-road*); also, any line or lines of rails forming a runway, as for a wheeled apparatus.—

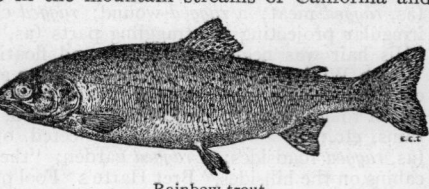
Rail-tongs.

rail'wayed, *a.* Having railways: as, "not foreseeing restless and *railwayed* generations" (A. S. M. Hutchinson's "If Winter Comes," i. 2).

rai-ment (rā'ment), *n.* [For *arrayment*.] Clothing; apparel; attire: as, "The same John had his *raiment* of camel's hair" (Mat. iii. 4). "She in goodly *raiment*, furred, was clad" (W. Morris's "Jason," iv. 407). [Archaic.]—**rai'ment,** *v. t.* To clothe. [Archaic.]

rain (rān), *n.* [AS. *regn*, *rēn*, = D. and G. *regen* = Icel. Sw., and Dan. *regn* = Goth. *rign*, rain.] Water in drops falling from the sky to the earth, being condensed from the aqueous vapor in the atmosphere, esp. as seen in the form of clouds (as, "Aquarius . . . from each ample fold Of the clouds about him rolled Scattering everywhere The showery *rain*": Longfellow's "Rain in Summer," 68); the descent of such watery drops (as, "the tender grass springing out of the earth by clear shining after *rain*": 2 Sam. xxiii. 4); a rainfall, rain-storm, or shower; specif., *pl.*, the seasonal rainfalls, or the rainy season, in some regions, as India; also, *sing.*, a quantity of anything falling in the manner of atmospheric rain, or a falling or descent of something in this manner (as, a *rain* of tears; a *rain* of flowers or of bullets; to invoke a *rain* of blessings upon a person).—**rain,** *v.* [AS. *regnian*.] **I.** *intr.* To send down or let fall rain (said of God, the sky, the clouds, etc.); of rain, to fall (also, more commonly, with impersonal *it* as subject: as, it *rained* all night; it is *raining* hard); also, to fall like rain (as, tears *rain* from the eyes; "Perfume and flowers fall in showers, That lightly *rain* from ladies' hands," Tennyson's "Sir Galahad," 12). **II.** *tr.* To send down (rain, etc.: as, "I will *rain* upon him . . . an overflowing rain, and great hailstones," Ezek. xxxviii. 22); also, to send down or cause to fall like rain (as, "I will *rain* bread from heaven for you," Ex. xvi. 4; to *rain* compliments, favors, or blows upon a person); shower down.

rain-band (rān'band), *n.* In *physics*, a dark band in the solar spectrum, due to the aqueous vapor in the atmosphere.

rain-bow (rān'bō). [AS. *rēnboga*.] **I.** *n.* A bow or arc of prismatic colors appearing in the heavens opposite the sun, due to the refraction and reflection of the sun's rays in drops of rain; also, a similar bow appearing in the spray of cata-

racts, etc.; in general, a bow of colors. **II.** *a.* Pertaining to, resembling, or suggesting a rainbow: as, "the endless parrot-tribe with their *rainbow* hues" (Prescott's "Conquest of Mexico," iv. 1).—**rain'bow=trout',** *n.* A trout, *Salmo irideus*, native in the mountain streams of California and Oregon and introduced elsewhere: named from its coloring.

Rainbow-trout.

rain=check (rān'chek), *n.* A check or ticket given for future use to spectators at a baseball game or other outdoor performance which is stopped by rain.

rain=cloud (rān'kloud), *n.* A cloud from which rain falls; a nimbus.

rain=coat (rān'kōt), *n.* A coat, as of some waterproof material, for wearing as a protection from rain.

rain-drop (rān'drop), *n.* [AS. *regndropa*.] A drop of rain.

rain-fall (rān'fâl), *n.* A fall or shower of rain; also, the amount of water falling in rain, snow, etc., within a given time and area.

rain=gage (rān'gāj), *n.* An instrument for measuring rainfall.

rain-i-ness (rā'ni-nes), *n.* The state or fact of being rainy.

rain-less (rān'les), *a.* Without rain: as, a *rainless* region or season.—**rain'less-ness,** *n.*

rain=mak-er (rān'mā"kér), *n.* One who professes or seeks to produce rain, as by supernatural means or by mechanical or physical processes.—**rain'=mak"ing,** *n.* and *a.*

rain=proof (rān'pröf), *a.* Proof against the entrance of rain; impervious to rain.

rain=storm (rān'stôrm), *n.* A storm of rain.

rain=wa-ter (rān'wâ"tér), *n.* Water fallen as rain.

rain-y (rā'ni), *a.*; compar. *rainier*, superl. *rainiest*. Characterized by rain (as, *rainy* weather; a *rainy* evening; " Much rain also in these days . . . but, it seems, this was the *rainy* season," Defoe's "Robinson Crusoe," i. 5); subject to rain, or much rain (as, "our *rainy* isles": Tennyson's "Edwin Morris," 103); wet with rain (as, *rainy* streets); also, bringing or threatening rain (as, "grey, *rainy* clouds," W. H. Hudson's "Green Mansions," i.; a *rainy* sky); also, of the nature of or resembling rain (as, *rainy* moisture; a *rainy* shower); also, of the eyes, wet with or shedding tears.—**a rainy day,** fig., a time of clouded fortunes or of want, as a possibility of the future to be provided against in the present: as, "the amount which Theobald liked to put by out of his income against, as he said, a *rainy day*" (S. Butler's "Way of All Flesh," xx.).

rais-a-ble (rā'za-bl), *a.* Capable of being raised.

raise (rāz), *v. t.*; *raised*, *raising*. [ME. *raisen*, *reisen*, from Scand.: cf. Icel. *reisa* = Sw. *resa* = Dan. *reise* = Goth. *-raisjan* = AS. *rǣran*, raise, causative of the Teut. verb (AS. *rīsan*, etc.) represented by E. *rise*: cf. *rear*[1].] To set upright, as something which has fallen over or been overturned; set erect; lift (a person, etc.) to a standing posture; also, to restore to life (as, to *raise* the dead); reanimate or revivify; also, to cause to rise or stand up, as from lying or sleeping; rouse from a retreat, as an animal; rouse for common action, as in attack or defense (as, "The great hatred that everybody has to pirates . . . would certainly *raise* the country in our pursuit": Stevenson's "Master of Ballantrae," iii.); stir up, as to do something; excite or agitate (chiefly Sc.); give vigor to, or animate, as the spirits, etc. (as, "His spirits being a little *raised* with the dram I had given him, he was very cheerful": Defoe's "Robinson Crusoe," i. 16); also, to build up, erect, or construct (as, to *raise* a palace, a monument, or a mound); set up the framework of (a house, etc.: as, "My house was framed and ready for the *raising*," Thoreau's "Walden," i.); cause (a blister, etc.) to rise or form (as, "Spoil a grace, Or *raise* a pimple on a beauteous face": Pope's "Rape of the Lock," iv. 68); also, to produce or beget (offspring); breed (animals); also, to bring up, or rear, as a person or an animal; cause or promote the growth of, as plants or flowers; also, to cause to come into being or appear, as a person (as, "The Lord thy God will *raise up* unto thee a Prophet from the midst of thee": Deut. xviii. 15); bring into existence or action, as a thing (as, to *raise* a tempest or a storm); begin or institute, as a suit at law; put forward, as an objection or a claim; bring up, as a question, etc.; in general, to cause, give rise to, or bring about (as, to *raise* a controversy, a rumor, a prejudice, a smile, or a demand); also, to move to a higher position, lift up, or elevate (as, to *raise* one's hand; to *raise* ore from a mine); lift (the hat) from the head in salutation (as, "Two middle-aged men . . . *raised* their hats to Janet": Arnold Bennett's "Hilda Lessways," ii. 3); turn upward, as the eyes (as, "He *raised* his eyes from a letter at which he had been glancing": Howells's "Chance Acquaintance," iv.); fig., to advance in rank, dignity, etc. (as, to *raise* a man to the peerage); elevate intellectually or morally, as persons; make higher or nobler, as the thoughts (as, "What in me is dark Illumine, what is low *raise* and support": Milton's "Paradise Lost," i. 23); also, to cause to rise up or ascend (as, "The herd of four or five hundred cattle trotting home-wards . . . *raising* a great cloud of dust with their hoofs": W. H. Hudson's "Far Away and Long Ago," i.); cause to appear, as by means of incantations, as a spirit (as, "grisly spectres, which the fiend had *raised*": Milton's "Paradise Regained," iv. 430); also, to bring or get together, as to procure, as money (as, "Taxation . . . is . . . a means . . . of *raising* necessary revenues for the Government," A. W. Mellon's "Taxation," iv.; "I must . . . *raise* a new loan," Stevenson's "Master of Ballantrae," iv.); gather together, collect, or muster, as an army or troops (as, "Roosevelt . . . *raised* a regiment of Rough Riders in the West": Charn-wood's "Theodore Roosevelt," iii.); also, to remove (a prohibition, etc.); end (a siege, etc.) by withdrawing the investing forces; sometimes, to end (a siege, etc.) by com-pelling the investing forces to withdraw (as, "William had still some faint hope that it might be possible to *raise* the siege": Macaulay's "Hist. of Eng.," xvii.); also, to break up and remove, as a camp (as, "Captain Bonneville and his confederate Indians *raised* their camp": Irving's "Captain Bonneville," xiv.); also, to increase in height (as, to *raise* a road-bed); cause (dough or bread) to rise by expansion and become light, as by the use of yeast; also, to increase in amount, as rent, prices, etc.; sometimes, to increase the amount specified in (a check or the like), by fraudulent alteration; sometimes, to increase the value, price, etc., of, as a commodity; specif., in games, as poker, to wager more than (another player's bet, or another player); also, to increase in degree, intensity, or force, as temperature, color, pain, etc.; make louder or of higher pitch, as the voice, etc. (as, "*Raise* your voice as you answer the questions which I am going to put to you": Scott's "Guy Mannering," xliii.); also, to utter (a cry, etc.) in a loud voice; also, to cause (the voice) to be heard (as, "Many voices were boldly *raised* in menace and accusation": Macaulay's "Hist. of Eng.," vi.); also, *naut.*, to cause (something) to rise above the visible horizon by approaching nearer to it; hence, to come in sight of (land, a whale, etc.).—**to raise Cain, the devil, the mischief,** to make a disturbance; create uproar or confusion. [Slang.]—**to raise the wind,** fig., to raise or procure money, as for one's purposes. [Colloq.]—**raise,** *n.* A raising, lifting, etc.; also, a raised place; a rising place, passage, road, etc.; sometimes, a getting together or pro-curing, by special effort, as of money (colloq.); often, an increase in amount, as of prices, wages, etc.; the amount of such an increase.—**rais′er,** *n.*

rai-sin (rā′zn), *n.* [OF. *raizin* (F. *raisin*), grapes, a grape, a raisin, < L. *racemus*, cluster of grapes: cf. *raceme*.] A cluster of grapes†, or a grape†; also, a grape of some sweet variety, suitable for the purpose, dried in the sun or arti-ficially, and used in cookery, etc.

rai-son-né (rā-zo-nā′), *a.* [F., pp. of *raisonner*, E. *reason, v.*] Reasoned out; logical; systematic. See *catalogue raisonné*, under *catalogue.*

raj (räj), *n.* [Hind. *rāj*, < Skt. *rāj-*, rule: cf. *raja*.] Rule; dominion: as, the British *raj*. [India.]

ra-ja, ra-jah (rä′jä), *n.* [Hind. *rājā*, < Skt. *rājan*, king, prince, < *rāj-*, rule: cf. *raj* and *rani*.] In India, a king or prince; also, a chief or dignitary; also, an honorary title conferred on Hindus in India (cf. *nawab*); also, a title of rulers, princes, or chiefs in Java, Borneo, etc. (as, "For his [Sir James Brooke's] services the title of *raja* of Sarawak was conferred on him by Muda Hassim": Encyc. Brit., 11th ed., IV. 645).—**ra′ja-ship, ra′jah-ship,** *n.*

Raj-put (räj′pöt), *n.* [Hind. *rājpūt*, < Skt. *rājaputra*, king's son, prince: cf. *raja*.] A member of a Hindu race claiming descent from the ancient Kshatriya or warrior caste and noted for their military spirit.

rake¹ (rāk), *n.* [AS. *raca, racu*, a rake (implement); later senses being from *rake¹, v.*] An implement with teeth or tines for gathering together hay or the like, breaking and smoothing the surface of ground, etc.; in a simple form, a hand-implement with a long handle having at the end a crosspiece set with a row of teeth turned downward in use; also, any of various implements of a similar form but having a blade, notched or plain, instead of teeth, as a croupier's implement for gathering in money on a gaming-table; also, the raking of a ship with shot; fig., a long, forcible sweep or onset (as, "The fleet was . . . far to the west-ward, where the Channel received the winds and waves from the whole *rake* of the Atlantic": Cooper's "Two Admirals," xxii.). —**rake¹,** *v.*; raked, raking. **I.** *tr.* To gather together, draw, or remove with a rake (as, to *rake* hay into heaps; to *rake* dead leaves from a lawn); also, to clear, smooth, or prepare with a rake (as, to *rake* a hay-field or a grass-plot; to *rake* a garden bed); clear (a fire, etc.) by stirring with a poker or the like; also, to cover with or bury under some-thing drawn over with a rake or the like (as, "Here, in the sands, Thee I'll *rake* up," Shakspere's "King Lear," iv. 6. 281: obs. except as in the following use); cover (a fire) with ashes etc., so as to keep it burning slowly, as through the night, (now prov.: often with *up*); also, fig., to gather (*together*) as with a rake, or with effort or difficulty (as, "I . . . sold out everything, and put all I could *rake* and scrape together into paint," Howells's "Rise of Silas Lapham," i.; "Some thousands of needy ineffectual men had been *raked* together," H. G. Wells's "Tono-Bungay," iii. 1. § 6); gather or take (*in*), as winnings or gains (as, "A daring gambler. He cor-nered cotton once, and *raked* in over a million": W. Church-ill's "Modern Chronicle," ii. 3); bring (*up*) out of oblivion or obscurity, as something forgotten or unknown (as, to *rake* up an old scandal; "Their past history was *raked* up," Mark Twain's "Tom Sawyer," xxxv.); also, to search indus-triously or thoroughly through, as if with a rake (as, to *rake* the town for votes or subscriptions; to *rake* all history to find a parallel); also, to scrape, scratch, or graze (as, "Every mast, as it passed, Seemed to *rake* the passing clouds": Longfellow's "Sir Humphrey Gilbert"); also, to sweep with shot lengthwise, as a place, troops, etc.; enfilade; fire upon (a ship) so that the shot will pass from stem to stern; fig., to sweep with the eye or glance; have a view along or over, or command. **II.** *intr.* To use a rake, as in a field, a garden, etc.; search with or as with a rake; also, to scrape or sweep (*against, over*, etc.: as, the sea *rakes* against the shore).

rake² (rāk), *v. i.*; raked, raking. [AS. *racian*, go, proceed.] To go or proceed (now prov.); in *hunting*, of a hawk, to fly along after the game, or to fly wide of it; of a dog, to hunt with the nose close to the ground.

rake³ (rāk), *v.*; raked, raking. [Origin uncertain.] **I.** *intr.* To incline from the perpendicular (as a mast) or from the horizontal. **II.** *tr.* To cause to incline or slope.—**rake³,** *n.* Inclination or slope away from the perpendicular or the horizontal.

rake⁴ (rāk), *n.* [Abbr. of *rakehell*.] A profligate or dis-solute person; one given over to loose pleasures; often, an idle, dissipated man (or woman) of fashion (as, "gambling half the day with the *rakes* and dandies of the fashionable club": Mrs. Wharton's "Age of Innocence," xx.).

rake-hell (rāk′hel), *n.* [From *rake¹, v.,* + *hell*; meaning lit. one such as to be found only by raking hell.] A profligate or abandoned person; a dissolute fellow; a rake. [Archaic.] —**rake′hell-y,** *a.* Profligate; abandoned; dissipated: as, "some idle squire, debauched page, or *rakehelly* archer from foreign parts" (Scott's "Quentin Durward," xxiii.). [Ar-chaic.]

rake=off (rāk′ôf), *n.* A share or portion, as of a sum in-volved or of profits; often, a share or amount taken or

rak-er (rā′kėr), *n.* One who rakes; also, an implement for raking.

ra-ki (rä-kē′ or rak′ē), *n.* [Turk. *rāqī*.] A spirituous liquor distilled from grain, or from grapes, plums, etc., in south-eastern Europe and the Levant.

rak-ing (rā′king), *p. a.* That rakes; specif., of gun-fire, shot, etc., sweeping lengthwise or from end to end of the place or mark aimed at (as, "A *raking* shot . . . in its passage along the main-deck, added ten men to his list of killed and wounded": Marryat's "King's Own," xvi.); enfilading.

rak-ish (rā′kish), *a.* [See *rake*4, also *rake*3, perhaps here involved.] Like or befitting a fashionable rake; 'fast'; also, smart; jaunty; dashing; of ships, having an appearance suggestive of speed and dash (sometimes associated with the rake of the masts).—**rak′ish-ly**, *adv.*—**rak′ish-ness**, *n.*

ṛâle (räl), *n.* [F., < *râler*, make a rattling sound in breathing.] In *pathol.*, an abnormal sound accompanying the normal respiratory murmur, as in pulmonary diseases.

ral-len-tan-do (räl-len-tän′dō), *a.* [It.] In *music*, slackening; becoming slower.

ral-li-er (ral′i-ėr), *n.* One who rallies.

ral-li-form (ral′i-fôrm), *a.* [NL. *Rallus* (see *ralline*) + L. *forma*, form.] Rail-like; of the rail type of birds.

ral-line (ral′in), *a.* [NL. *Rallus*, typical genus of rails.] Belonging or pertaining to the rail family of birds.

ral-ly1 (ral′i), *v.*; *-lied, -lying.* [F. *rallier*, < *re-* (< L. *re-*), back, again, + *allier*, unite, E. *ally*.] **I.** *tr.* To bring together or into order again, as an army or company which has been scattered; also, to draw or call (persons) together, as to give assistance or for common action (as, "to *rally* round the monarchy those classes which had been . . . : firm allies . . . during the troubles of the preceding generation": Macaulay's "Hist. of Eng.," ii.); also, to concentrate or revive, as one's strength, spirits, etc. (as, "The shock seemed to *rally* my faculties": H. Melville's "Typee," xii.); pull together, revive, or rouse, as a person (as, "He . . . *rallied* himself to make the best of it": Lever's "Harry Lorrequer," xlvii.). **II.** *intr.* To come together or into order again, as to renew a conflict (as, "The Englishmen were beaten back to the shealing, where they *rallied*, and continued to stand at bay": Marryat's "King's Own," lvi.); also, to come together in a body, for common action, as persons; of persons or a single person, to come to the assistance or support of a person, party, or cause (as, "Some had *rallied* to the government, some were in exile": Motley's "Dutch Republic," ii. 10); also, to acquire fresh strength or vigor; revive or recover (as, "The shares fell, sir, in consequence of the panic. I hope they will *rally*": Thackeray's "Newcomes," lxiv.); recover partially from illness (as, "She never *rallied* . . . after the first fatal seizure": Thackeray's "Newcomes," liv.); in *lawn-tennis*, etc., to engage in a rally.—**ral′ly**1, *n.*; pl. *rallies* (-iz). An act of rallying; a recovery from dispersion or disorder, as of troops (as, "Leslie's chase of the broken forces of Rupert, making a *rally* impossible": Morley's "Oliver Cromwell," ii. 2); the signal for this; a drawing or coming together of persons, as for common action, as in a political or other mass-meeting; a renewal or recovery of strength, activity, etc.; a partial recovery of strength during illness; also, a general scramble, chase, or mêlée of the characters in a pantomime; also, in *lawn-tennis*, etc., the return of the ball by both sides a number of times consecutively; in *boxing*, an exchange of blows.

ral-ly2 (ral′i), *v. t.*; *-lied, -lying.* [F. *railler*, deride, rally: see *rail*4.] To ridicule good-humoredly; banter: as, "Twopenny would often *rally* him upon his leanness, and hail him as Brother Lusty" (Lamb's "Old Benchers of the Inner Temple").—**ral′ly**2, *n.*; pl. *rallies* (-iz). A piece of rallying or banter.—**ral′ly-ing-ly**, *adv.*

ram (ram), *n.* [AS. *ramm* = D. and LG. *ram* = G. *ramm*, ram, male sheep.] A male sheep (see cut in next column); [*cap.*] the zodiacal constellation or sign Aries; also [*l. c.*], any of various devices for battering, crushing, driving, or forcing something; a battering-ram (as, "The walls . . . were forty feet in thickness, and could neither be burnt nor driven in with the *ram*": Froude's "Cæsar," xix.); a heavy

beak or spur projecting from the bow of a war-vessel, for penetrating an enemy's ship; a vessel so equipped; the heavy weight which strikes the blow in a pile-driver or the like; a piston, as on a hydraulic press; a hydraulic ram (see under *hydraulic, a.*).—**ram's horn.** See *shophar.*—**ram**, *v. t.*; *rammed, ramming.* To drive or force by heavy blows (as, to *ram* piles into the earth);

Fighting Ram, a variety of *Ovis aries.*

force (a charge) into a firearm, as with a ramrod; cram or stuff (a thing) into something; push or thrust with force (as, "He *rammed* a soft cap on to his venerable locks recklessly": J. Conrad's "Rover," xv.); also, to compact by pounding or blows; also, to strike against with great force; dash violently against; of a war-vessel, to strike (another vessel) with the ram; also, to drive (a thing) with force against something else; also, to force in the contents or charge of (a firearm, etc.); cram or stuff with something driven in forcibly; stuff or block (*up*) with something.

Ram-a-dan (ram-a-dän′), *n.* [Ar.] The ninth month of the Mohammedan year, during which fasting is rigidly practised daily from dawn until sunset. Also **Ram-a-zan′** (-zän′).

ra-mal (rā′mạl), *a.* [L. *ramus*, branch.] In *bot., anat.*, etc., of, pertaining to, or of the nature of a branch or ramus.

ram-ble (ram′bl), *v. i.*; *-bled, -bling.* [Appar. related to *roam*.] To wander about in a leisurely manner, without definite aim or direction (as, "They would go off together, *rambling* along the river, or up the park": Galsworthy's "Dark Flower," i. 11); also, to take a wandering or irregular course, as with turns or windings, as a growing plant, or a stream or a path; also, to talk or write discursively or without sequence of ideas, as a person; proceed irregularly from one subject to another, as discourse (as, "a . . . talk that *rambled* through all the universe": H. G. Wells's "Tono-Bungay," ii. 1. § 3).—**ram′ble**, *n.* The act or an act of rambling; esp. a walk or excursion without definite aim or direction, taken merely for recreation or pleasure (as, "One day . . . being on my *rambles*, I entered a green lane which I had never seen before": Borrow's "Lavengro," v.).—**ram′bler**, *n.* One who or that which rambles (as, "a *rambler* in the wood": Thoreau's "Walden," i.); esp., any of various climbing roses (as, the crimson *rambler*, an ornamental hybrid with bright crimson flowers).—**ram′bling**, *p. a.* That rambles; wandering about aimlessly from place to place; taking an irregular course, or straggling, as a growing plant or a stream; extending irregularly in various directions, or without orderly arrangement, as a building (as, "His house, a *rambling* West Indian mansion, was surrounded with deep, spacious piazzas": G. W. Curtis's "Prue and I," iv.); given to wandering in discourse or thought, as persons; straying from one subject to another, as discourse or thoughts (as, "He made a long *rambling* statement": W. H. Hudson's "Green Mansions," xii.).—**ram′bling-ly**, *adv.*

ram-bunc-tious (ram-bungk′shus), *a.* [Var. of *rumbustious* for *robustious*.] Boisterous, turbulent, or obstreperous; perversely unruly, or cantankerous (as, "Ever since she got out of college she's been too *rambunctious* to live with": Sinclair Lewis's "Babbitt," i.). [Colloq.]

ram-bu-tan (ram-bö′tạn), *n.* [Malay *rambūtan*.] The bright-red oval fruit of a Malayan sapindaceous tree, *Nephelium lappaceum*, covered with soft spines or hairs, and containing a pulp of pleasant subacid taste; also, the tree.

ram-e-kin, ram-e-quin (ram′e-kin), *n.* [F. *ramequin*; from Teut.] A small, separately cooked portion of some cheese preparation, esp. one made of grated cheese, breadcrumbs, eggs, etc., and baked in a small dish; hence, a dish suitable for such use.

ram-ie (ram'ę), n. [Malay *rāmī*.] An Asiatic urticaceous shrub, *Bœhmeria nivea*, yielding a fiber used in making textiles, etc.; also, the fiber itself.

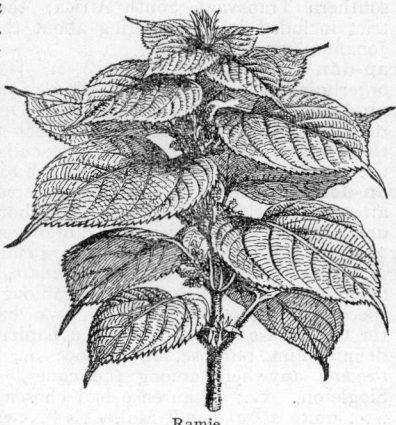

Ramie.

ram-i-fi-ca-tion (ram″i-fi-kā′shon), n. [F. *ramification*.] The act, process, or manner of ramifying; branching; also, a branching part; a branch (as, the *ramifications* of a river, or of a nerve); a division or subdivision springing or derived from a main stem or source (as, to pursue a subject in all its *ramifications*).

ram-i-form (ram′i-fôrm), a. [L. *ramus*, branch, + *forma*, form.] Having the form of a branch; branch-like; also, branched.

ram-i-fy (ram′i-fī), v. t. or i.; -fied, -fying. [F. *ramifier*, < ML. *ramificare*, < L. *ramus*, branch, + *facere*, make.] To divide or spread out into branches or branch-like parts.

Ram-il-lie (ram′i-li), n. [From *Ramillies*, in Belgium, where Marlborough won in battle against the French in 1706.] A kind of wig having a long plait or tail behind tied with a large bow at the top and a smaller one at the bottom; also, the plait or tail; also, a form of cocked hat.

ram-mer (ram′ėr), n. One who or that which rams; a device for driving or compacting something.

ram-mish (ram′ish), a. Like or characteristic of a ram (male sheep); esp., rank in smell or taste. Also **ram′my.**

ra-mose (rā′mōs or rạ-mōs′), a. [L. *ramosus*, < *ramus*, branch.] Having many branches; branching. Also **ra′mous.**

ramp[1] (ramp), v. i. [OF. *ramper*, climb (F. creep); origin uncertain: cf. *romp*.] To climb (obs. or prov.); also, to rise or stand on the hind legs, as a quadruped, esp. a lion (often one represented in heraldry or sculpture: as, "I . . . stood by her garden-gate. A lion *ramps* at the top," Tennyson's "Maud," i. 14. 1); rear as if to spring; also, to leap or dash (*about*, etc.) with fury (as, "It is one thing to hear a lion in captivity . . . quite another to listen to him when he is *ramping* around in the vicinity of one's fragile tent": J. H. Patterson's "Man-Eaters of Tsavo," xxiv.); act violently, rage, or storm, as a person; also, to go about in a wild or excited way; rampage.—**ramp**[1], n. The act of ramping; a ramping posture or movement: as, "The bold Ascalonite Fled from his lion *ramp*" (Milton's "Samson Agonistes," 139).

ramp[2] (ramp), n. [F. *rampe*, < OF. *ramper*, climb: see *ramp*[1].] A slope or ascent (as, "Under the great *ramp* to Mussoorie he drew himself together as an old hunter faces a well-remembered bank": Kipling's "Kim," xiii.); specif., a sloping way or passage connecting two different levels of a fortification or the like; any sloping or inclined plane or member; a short concave slope or bend, as one connecting the higher and lower parts of a staircase railing at a landing. —**ramp**[2], v. t. To furnish with a ramp or ramps.

ram-page (ram-pāj′ or ram′pāj), v. i.; -paged, -paging. [Orig. Sc.; appar. < *ramp*[1].] To rush, move, or act furi-

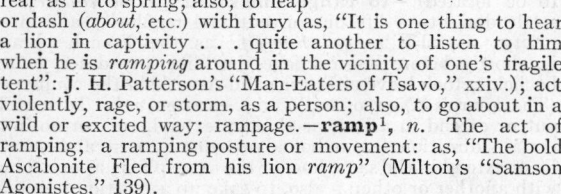

Rammers. — *a*, wooden rammer, with iron band or hoop; *b, c*, paving-rammers.

ously or violently (as, "He could not lie still, but got up and raged and *rampaged* up and down his hot, narrow, stuffy bedroom": Du Maurier's "Trilby," vi.); rage; storm; also, to run or go about in a wild or excited way (as, "They *rampaged* about wi' their grooms": Tennyson's "Village Wife," vii.); also, to romp or frolic boisterously (as, "Tom . . . had, as a boy of seven, *rampaged* on that identical Turkey hearth-rug": Arnold Bennett's "Hilda Lessways," ii. 4).—**ram-page** (ram′pāj or ram-pāj′), n. The act of rampaging, or rushing about or behaving in a furious manner (as, to be on the *rampage*); a fit of rampaging, or violent behavior; any wild outbreak or procedure; a spree.—**ram-pa′geous** (-pā′jus), a. Violent; unruly; boisterous. [Colloq.]—**ram-pa′geous-ly**, adv.—**ram-pa′geous-ness**, n.

ram-pant (ram′pant), a. [OF. *rampant*, ppr. of *ramper*, climb, E. *ramp*[1].] Ramping, or standing on the hind legs; of a lion, bear, etc., as depicted in heraldry, standing with the fore legs elevated, one higher than the other, and, unless otherwise specified, with the head in profile; also, raging or furious (as, "She had set out *rampant* from the Rue Crécy; it was necessary to tame her": C. Brontë's "Villette," xxvii.); violent in action, spirit, opinion, etc.; also, overleaping restraint or usual limits, running riot, or prevailing unbridled (as, "Anarchy and stiff-necked opposition reigned *rampant*": Irving's "Knickerbocker's New York," v. 1); of plants, etc., growing with excessive exuberance; in *arch.*, of an arch or vault, springing at one side from one level of support and resting at the other side on a higher level.—**ram′pan-cy**, n.—**ram′pant-ly**, adv.

Heraldic Lion Rampant.

ram-part (ram′pärt), n. [F. *rempart*, < *remparer*, fortify, < *re-* (< L. *re-*), again, + OF. *emparer*, fortify, through Pr. < L. *ante*, before, + *parare*, make ready.] A broad elevation or mound of earth raised as a fortification about a place, and usually having a stone parapet built upon it; also, such an elevation together with the parapet; also, anything serving as a bulwark or defense (as, "populous No . . . whose *rampart* was the sea": Nahum, iii. 8).—**ram′part**, v. t. To furnish with or as with a rampart.

Rampant Arches. — *a*, in staircase; *b*, in arcade.

ram-pi-on (ram′pi-on), n. [Cf. F. *raiponce*, It. *ramponzolo, raperonzolo*.] A European campanula, *Campanula rapunculus*, having an edible white tuberous root which is used for salad; also, any of the plants of the campanulaceous genus *Phyteuma*, bearing heads or spikes of blue flowers.

ram-pire (ram′pīr), n. and v. t. Same as *rampart*. [Archaic.]

ram-rod (ram′rod), n. A rod for ramming down the charge of a muzzle-loading firearm.

ram-shack-le (ram′shak-l), a. [Origin uncertain.] Loosely made or held together, as a vehicle, a house, furniture, etc.; rickety, shaky, or crazy; also, unsteady, thoughtless, wild, or dissipated (prov. Eng. and Sc.).—**ram′shack-ly**, a. Ramshackle or rickety: as, "decayed, *ramshackly*, superannuated old steamboats" (Mark Twain's "Life on the Mississippi," xlviii.).

ram-son (ram′zon), n. [Orig. pl. taken as sing.: AS. *hramsan*, pl. of *hramsa*, kind of garlic.] A species of garlic, *Allium ursinum*, with broad leaves; also, its bulbous root, used as a relish: usually in *pl*.

ram-stam (ram′stam). [Cf. *ram*, v.] **I.** a. Headlong; precipitate; impetuous; reckless: as, "The hairum-scairum, *ram-stam* boys, The rattlin' squad" (Burns's "To James Smith," 165). [Sc., Ir., and prov. Eng.] **II.** adv. Headlong; precipitately: as, "The least we'll get, if we gang *ramstam* in on them, will be a broken head" (Scott's "Rob Roy," xxviii.). [Sc., Ir., and prov. Eng.]

ram-til (ram'til), *n.* [Bengali *rāmtil.*] An African asteraceous plant, *Guizotia abyssinica,* cultivated in many parts of India for its oil-producing seeds.

ram-u-lose (ram'ū-lōs), *a.* [L. *ramulosus,* < *ramulus,* dim. of *ramus,* branch.] In *bot.* and *zoöl.,* having many small branches. Also **ram'u-lous.**

ra-mus (rā'mus), *n.;* pl. *-mi* (-mī). [L.] In *bot., anat.,* etc., a branch, as of a plant, a vein, a bone, etc.

ran (ran). Preterit of *run.*

rance (räns), *n.* [F.] Same as *Belgian marble* (see under *Belgian, a.*).

ranch (ranch), *n.* [Sp. *rancho,* mess, set of persons who eat together, hence as in Amer. uses: see *rancho,* def.] In the western U. S., etc., an establishment with its lands for raising cattle, horses, etc. (as, "the great fenceless *ranches,* where the cattle and their mounted herdsmen wandered unchecked over hundreds of thousands of acres": Roosevelt's "Hunting Trips of a Ranchman," i.); a stock-farm; also, the company of persons employed or living on it; loosely, any farm or farming establishment.**—ranch,** *v. i.* To conduct, or work on, a ranch: usually in *ranching, ppr.* and *n.:* as, "His full attention was given to *ranching* in real earnest" (Charnwood's "Theodore Roosevelt," ii.).**—ranch'er,** *n.* One engaged in ranching.**—ran-che-ri-a** (rän-che-rē'ä), *n.* [Sp. *ranchería.*] In Spanish America and the southwestern U. S., a collection of ranchos or rude huts, esp. of Indians; the dwelling-place of a ranchero or rancheros.**—ran-che'ro** (-chā'rō), *n.;* pl. *-ros* (-rōz). [Sp.] In Spanish America and the southwestern U. S., a rancher.—

ranch-man (ranch'man), *n.;* pl. *-men.* One who owns, conducts, or works on, a ranch.— **ran-cho** (rän'chō), *n.;* pl. *-chos* (-chōz). [Sp.] In Spanish America and the southwestern U. S., a rude hut or collection of huts for herdsmen, laborers, or travelers (as, "I put up for the night at the solitary mud *rancho* of

Ranchero.

an old herdsman [in Uruguay]": W. H. Hudson's "Purple Land," ii.); also, a ranch.

ran-cid (ran'sid), *a.* [L. *rancidus,* < *rancere,* stink, be rank.] Having the rank, unpleasant smell or taste of oil, fat, etc., when stale or spoiling (as, *rancid* butter; *rancid* bacon); rank in this manner, as a smell or taste; fig., offensive or odious (as, a *rancid* play).**—ran-cid'i-ty** (-i-ti), **ran'cid-ness,** *n.***—ran'cid-ly,** *adv.*

ran-cor (rang'kor), *n.* [OF. *rancor, rancour,* rancor, < LL. *rancor,* rank smell or taste, rancor, < L. *rancere:* see *rancid.*] Rank or rancid smell or taste†; also, bitter, rankling resentment or ill-will, or venomous animosity (as, "*Rancour* will out: proud prelate, in thy face I see thy fury," Shakspere's "2 Henry VI.," i. 1. 142; "This silly affair . . . greatly increased his *rancor* against me," B. Franklin's "Autobiography," xii.); malignant hatred or spite.**—ran'cor-ous,** *a.* Full of, characterized by, or proceeding from rancor; venomous; malignant.**—ran'cor-ous-ly,** *adv.***—ran'cor-ous-ness,** *n.*

ran'cour, *n.* British preferred form of *rancor.*

rand (rand), *n.* [AS. *rand, rond,* = D. and G. *rand,* border, margin.] A border or margin (now chiefly prov.); also, a slice of meat (now prov.); in *shoemaking,* a strip of leather, set in a shoe at the heel before the lifts are attached.**—the Rand,** an abbreviated form of

Witwatersrand, an elevated gold-bearing ridge in the southern Transvaal, South Africa; the gold-mining district included in or centering about this ridge, including Johannesburg.

ran-dan¹ (ran'dan or ran-dan'), *n.* [Cf. *random.*] Disorderly behavior; a spree. [Colloq. or prov., Eng. and Sc.]

ran-dan² (ran'dan or ran-dan'), *n.* [Origin uncertain: cf. *randan¹.*] A style of rowing in which the middle one of three rowers in a boat uses a pair of sculls and the other two use one oar each; also, a boat for such rowing.

ran-dem (ran'dem). [Appar. an altered form of *tandem,* after *random.*] **I.** *adv.* With three horses harnessed tandem. **II.** *n.* A carriage or a team driven randem.

ran-dom (ran'dom). [OF. *randon,* rushing movement, impetuosity, disorder, confusion, < *randir,* rush, gallop: prob. from Teut.] **I.** Rushing or headlong course†; headlong speed or impetuosity†; also, aimless or haphazard procedure (in the phrase 'at random,' in a haphazard way, without definite aim, purpose, or method: as, "Ten . . . fired *at random* anywhere among the canes," Defoe's "Captain Singleton," xv.; "Laurence had chosen these illustrations . . . quite *at random,*" Mallock's "New Republic," iii. 2). **II.** *a.* Going, proceeding, made, occurring, etc., at random; without definite aim, purpose, or reason; casual: as, struck by a *random* shot; *random* remarks; "lulling *random* squabbles when they rise" (Tennyson's "Holy Grail," 557). **—ran'dom-ly,** *adv.* **—ran'dom-ness,** *n.*

ran-dy (ran'di). [Origin uncertain.] **I.** *a.* Rude-mannered; coarse; abusive; disorderly. [Sc. and prov. Eng.] **II.** *n.;* pl. *-dies* (-diz). A rude-mannered beggar or vagrant; also, a virago. [Sc. and prov. Eng.]

ra-nee (rä'nē), *n.* See *rani.*

rang (rang). Preterit of *ring¹.*

range (rānj), *v. t.;* ranged, ranging. [OF. *rangier* (F. *ranger*), var. of *rengier,* arrange in line, < *reng, renc,* row, line: see *rank².*] To draw up or dispose (persons or things) in a row or line, or in rows or lines (as, "The glass cases containing the collection of butterflies were *ranged* in three long rows": J. Conrad's "Lord Jim," xx.); place (a person or persons, or a thing or things) in a row or line with others, or in a particular position, company, or group; also, to dispose systematically, set in order, or arrange; divide into classes, place in a particular class, or classify; also, to make straight, level, or even, as lines of type; in nautical use, to lay out (the cable of an anchor) so that the anchor may descend smoothly; also, to provide with things arranged in a row or rows (as, roads *ranged* with trees); also, to pass over or through (an area or region) in all directions, often in exploring or searching (as, "They . . . belonged to a large hunting party known to be *ranging* the prairie in the vicinity," Parkman's "Oregon Trail," vi.; "The king despatch'd his heralds with commands To *range* the camp," Pope's tr. Homer's "Iliad," ii.); go along or about (as, to *range* a coast in a boat); also, to pasture (cattle) on a range; also, to determine the proper elevation for, or give the proper elevation to (a gun), for a certain range; train, as a telescope, upon an object; also, to obtain the range of (something aimed at or to be located).**—to range one's self** [F. *se ranger*], to settle down to a life of conventional regularity and propriety: as, "He '*ranged himself,*' as the French phrase is, shortly before his marriage, just like any other young bachelor; took leave of Phryne and Aspasie in the coulisses" (Thackeray's "Newcomes," xxxi.).**—range,** *v. i.* To stretch out or extend in a line, as things; extend, run, or go in a certain direction (as, a boundary *ranging* east and west); lie or extend in the same line, or the same plane, as one thing with another or others; also, to take up a position in a line or in order; take up or occupy a particular place or position (as, "The Aspasia *ranged* up on the weather quarter of her antagonist," Marryat's "King's Own," xvi.; "'Tis better to be lowly born, And *range* with humble livers in content," Shakspere's "Henry VIII.," ii. 3. 20); also, to move about over or through a region in all directions, as persons, animals, etc. (as, "He spends most of his time in *ranging* through the woods": Smollett's "Humphry Clinker," Sept. 6); rove, roam, or wander (lit. or fig.: as, "The talk *ranged* over literary and publishing matters of mutual interest," Bok's "Americanization of Edward Bok," xxviii.); of the eye, to move about over a field of vision (as, "The eye *ranged* over an immense extent of wilderness": Irving's "Captain Bonneville," v.); also, to move about over an area in searching, as a dog seeking for game; also, to extend, be found, or occur over an area or throughout a period, as animals, plants, etc. (as, a plant which *ranges* from Canada to Mexico); vary within certain limits (as, at prices *ranging* from $5 to $10); also, to have range of operation; have a particular range, as a gun or a projectile; also, to find the range, as of something aimed at or to be located (cf. *sound-ranging*). —**range,** *n.* [OF. *range*.] A row, line, or series, as of persons or things (as, "We then walked down stairs through a double *range* of lackeys," Smollett's "Humphry Clinker," Sept. 28; "long *ranges* of buildings," Prescott's "Conquest of Mexico," iv. 2); specif., a chain of mountains; a mountain-range; also, in U. S. surveys of public land, one of a series of divisions numbered east or west from the prime meridian of the survey, and consisting of a row of townships, each six miles square, which are numbered north or south from a base-line (cf. *township*); sometimes, a rank, class, or order (as, "The cohesion of the nation was greatest in the lowest *ranges*": Stubbs's "Constitutional Hist. of Eng.," vii. § 81); also, a line of direction; also, the act or an act of ranging, or moving about, as over an area or region; opportunity for ranging, or liberty to range (as, "Their swine had the *range* of the forest": Bancroft's "Hist. of the U. S.," Amer. Revolution, i. 6); also, an area or tract that is or may be ranged over; an extensive stretch of grazing-ground (as, "The steers came fat off his unenclosed *range* and fattened still more in his large pasture": Wister's "Virginian," vi.); also, the region over which something is distributed, is found, or occurs (as, the *range* of an animal or a plant; the *range* of earthquakes); the period throughout which something is found or occurs; also, the extent to which, or the limits between which, variation is possible (as, the *range* of prices for a commodity); also, the extent covered by the full amount or number of something (as, the *range* of one's knowledge; "His *range* of ideas is limited," Howells's "Rise of Silas Lapham," v.); compass; scope; often, the extent or scope of the operation or action of something (as, "within *range* of vision": Tarkington's "Magnificent Ambersons," v.); the compass of a musical instrument or a voice; also, the horizontal distance to which a gun or the like is capable of sending a projectile; the distance to which a projectile is or may be sent by a gun, etc.; also, the distance from a gun, etc., of an object aimed at; the distance from some point of operation of something to be located, as in sound-ranging; also, the position of a gun in firing; also, a place with targets for practice in shooting (as, a rifle-*range*); also, a form of apparatus or stove for cooking, now esp. one having an oven or ovens, and openings on the top for carrying on several operations at once, and either built into a fireplace or portable.

range=find-er (rānj′fīn″dèr), *n.* Any of various instruments for determining the range or distance of an object, as in order that a gun may be accurately sighted when firing at it.

ran-ger (rān′jèr), *n.* One who or that which ranges; a rover or wanderer; a keeper of a royal forest or park (Eng.); a warden employed to patrol a tract of forest; one of a body of armed men employed in ranging over a region. —**ran′ger-ship,** *n.*

ran-gy (rān′ji), *a.* [Also *rangey*.] Given to or fitted for ranging or moving about, as animals (as, "The ponies . . . used for the circle-riding in the morning have need . . . to be strong and *rangey*": Roosevelt's "Hunting Trips of a Ranchman," i.); slender and long-limbed, as animals or persons; specif., having a long, slender body, as cattle or sheep; also, permitting ranging, as a place; spacious; also, having a mountain-range, or mountainous (Australia).

ra-ni, ra-nee (rä′nē), *n.* [Hind. *rānī*, < Skt. *rājñī*, fem. of *rājan*, king: see *raja*.] In India, etc., the wife of a raja, king, or prince; a reigning queen or princess.

rank[1] (rangk), *a.* [AS. *ranc*, proud, bold, showy, = Icel. *rakkr*, straight, slender, bold, = D. and LG. *rank*, slender.] Proud† or haughty†; also, strong or powerful (obs. or prov.); vigorous or violent (obs. or prov.); also, vigorous or luxuriant in growth (as, "Seven ears of corn came up upon one stalk, *rank* and good": Gen. xli. 5); now, growing with excessive luxuriance, or immoderately thick or large and coarse in growth, as vegetation, etc. (as, "great clumps of tall *rank* grass": Parkman's "Oregon Trail," iv.); also, excessively large or great†; swollen†; puffed up†; excessive in amount (chiefly in *law*); also, abundant† or copious†; also, crowded together, dense, thick, or numerous (obs. or prov.); also, projecting to an unusual extent, as the iron or blade of a plane when adjusted to cut deeply; also, producing luxuriantly, esp. too luxuriantly, or producing an excessive and coarse growth, as land; covered with a luxuriant and coarse growth, as land; also, having an offensively strong smell or taste (as, "a *rank* cigar of the sort that they sell to students": Kipling's "Kim," i.); offensively strong, as smell or taste (as, "This meat . . . had a *rank* taste and smell": W. H. Hudson's "Green Mansions," ix.); also, in general, highly offensive; disgusting; often, grossly coarse or indecent; also, of a strongly marked type, or unmitigated (as, "*rank* treachery," H. James's "Portrait of a Lady," xlv.; "This is all *rank* nonsense," Eden Phillpotts's "Grey Room," ii.); hence, utter or absolute (as, "a *rank* outsider": M. Hewlett's "Open Country," xxii.); also, lustful†; ruttish†.

rank[2] (rangk), *n.* [F. (obs.) *ranc*, now *rang*, OF. *renc*, *reng*, prob. < OHG. *hring*, ring: see *ring*[2].] A row, line, or series of things or persons (as, "a *rank* of sickly pines," Howells's "Chance Acquaintance," i.: now chiefly in specific uses); specif., a line of persons, esp. soldiers, standing abreast (as, "The Tuscan army . . . *Rank* behind *rank*," Macaulay's "Horatius," xxxv.: distinguished from *file*); *pl.*, the lines or body of an army or other force or organization; also, *pl.*, the common soldiers as distinguished from the officers (as, to rise from the *ranks*); the general body of any party, society, or organization apart from the officers or leaders; also, *sing.*, orderly arrangement, or array (as, "fifty thousand, which could keep *rank*": 1 Chron. xii. 33); also, a number of persons forming a separate class in the social scale or in any graded body (as, "He was a favourite among all *ranks*": Arnold Bennett's "Old Wives' Tale," ii. 2); hence, position or standing in the social scale or in any graded body (as, high or low *rank*; the *rank* of marquis; the *rank* of colonel; the *rank* of ambassador; "His ambition was glutted at last with the *rank* of cardinal," Green's "Short Hist. of the Eng. People," vi. 5); also, high position or station in the social or some similar scale (as, pride of *rank*; "some prisoner of *rank*," De Quincey's "Revolt of the Tartars"); also, in general, a class in any scale of comparison (as, "A station . . . Not i' the worst *rank* of manhood," Shakspere's "Macbeth," iii. 1. 103; "Oxford stood in the first *rank* among English towns," Green's "Short Hist. of the Eng. People," iii. 4); relative position or standing (as, a writer or a book of the highest *rank*); in *chess*, one of the lines of squares running from side to side on a chessboard, in distinction from a *file*, which runs from player to player. —**rank and file,** the lines of soldiers from side to side and from front to rear; also, the general body of soldiers, or of any party or organization, apart from officers or leaders (as, "the peasantry, from whom the *rank and file* of the legions had been recruited": Froude's "Cæsar," iv.). —**rank**[2], *v.* **I.** *tr.* To arrange in a rank or row, or in ranks, as things or persons; draw up (persons, esp. soldiers) in a rank or in ranks; hence, to dispose in suitable order; arrange; classify; also, to assign to a particular position, station, class, etc. (as, "How shall we *rank* thee upon Glory's page? Thou more than soldier and just less than sage!" T. Moore's "To Thomas Hume"); class; also, to outrank, or take precedence of (U. S.). **II.** *intr.* To form a rank or ranks; stand in rank; also, to take up or occupy a place in a particular rank, class, etc.; have rank or standing (as, "After the Member's house *ranked* such historic residences as those of Osmond Orgreave, the architect . . . and Fearns, the . . . lawyer": Arnold Bennett's "These Twain," i.); also, to move or march in rank. —**ranked,** *a.* Having or forming ranks: as, two-*ranked*. —**rank′er,** *n.* One who ranks; also, a person, esp. a soldier, in the ranks; also, a commissioned officer promoted from the ranks. —**rank′ing,** *p. a.* That outranks others; holding the foremost rank or standing: as, the *ranking* officer in a military force; *ranking* players in a sport.

ran-kle (rang′kl), v.; -kled, -kling. [OF. rancler, < rancle, raoncle, draoncle, < ML. dracunculus, ulcer, dim. of L. draco, serpent, E. dragon.] **I.** intr. To fester, or be painfully inflamed (as, "his limbs swelled with the rankling of his two wounds," Defoe's "Robinson Crusoe," i. 20: now chiefly fig.); also, to cause festering or painful inflammation, as a poisoned weapon, the bite of an animal, etc. (now chiefly fig.); now, usually, of unpleasant feelings, thoughts, experiences, facts, etc., to keep up within the mind keen irritation or bitter resentment (as, "insults and injuries that must have rankled in the least sensitive nature," Lecky's "Hist. of Eng. in the 18th Century," viii.; "while these grievances were rankling all over Ireland," Morley's "Oliver Cromwell," i. 6). **II.** tr. To cause (wounds, etc.) to fester; also, to irritate or embitter mentally (as, "You will say . . . I am rankled by the spleen": Smollett's "Humphry Clinker," May 19). [Archaic.]

rank-ly (rangk′li), adv. In a rank manner.—**rank′ness**, n.

ran-sack (ran′sak), v. t. [ME. ransaken, from Scand.: cf. Icel. rannsaka, < rann, house, + -saka, akin to sækja, seek (see seek).] To search thoroughly or vigorously through (a house, place, receptacle, etc.), looking into all parts or rummaging through contents (as, "We might do what we pleased; ransack her desk and her workbox, and turn her drawers inside out": C. Brontë's "Jane Eyre," xvii.); in general, to search, hunt, or look through (anything) in a thoroughgoing manner (as, "The air service ransacks the army for men with technical training," H. G. Wells's "Italy, France, and Britain at War," iii. 3; "I will ransack botany, and find a new food for man," Emerson's "Representative Men," v.); examine thoroughly; also, to search (a place, etc.) for plunder, or plunder, pillage, or rob (as, "They [a mob] pour in . . . the house is ransacked": J. H. Newman's "Callista," xvi.); also, to get or take in a search, as for plunder (now rare).—**ran′sack**, n. The act of ransacking; a rummage; a search.—**ran′sack-er**, n.

ran-som (ran′som), n. [OF. F. rançon, < L. redemptio(n-): see redemption.] The redemption of a prisoner, a slave, captured goods, etc., for a price; also, the sum or price paid or demanded (as, "After a captivity of five years she recovered her freedom on the payment of a heavy ransom": J. F. Kirk's "Charles the Bold," iii. 2); fig., a means of delivering or rescuing, esp., in religious use, from sin and its consequences (as, "Even the Son of man came . . . to give his life a ransom for many": Mark, x. 45); also, a means of atonement or expiation† (as, "Lowly words were ransom for their fault": Shakspere's "2 Henry VI.," iii. 1. 127).—**ran′som**, v. t. [OF. F. rançonner.] To redeem from captivity, bondage, detention, etc., by paying a price demanded; obtain the release or restoration of by making payment; fig., to deliver or rescue as if by paying a ransom; esp., in religious use, to deliver or redeem from sin and its consequences (as, "Poor sick people, richer in His eyes Who ransom'd us . . . than I": Tennyson's "Guinevere," 679); also, to atone for or expiate, as fault or wrong-doing†; also, to release or restore on receipt of a ransom; also, to hold for ransom, or demand a ransom for.—**ran′som-er**, n.—**ran′som-less**, a. Without ransom.

rant (rant), v. [MD. ranten, dote, rave.] **I.** intr. To speak or declaim extravagantly or violently (as, a ranting actor or preacher; "Macconochie . . . would rant against the Master by the hour," Stevenson's "Master of Ballantrae," ii.); talk in a wild or vehement way; indulge in extravagant bombast; also, to behave or make merry in a noisy or boisterous manner (Sc. and prov. Eng.: as, "Wi' quaffing and laughing, They ranted and they sang," Burns's "Jolly Beggars," 12). **II.** tr. To utter or declaim in the manner of one ranting.—**rant**, n. Ranting speech, or extravagant or violent declamation (as, "Madly enough he preached . . . with imperfect utterance, amid much frothy rant": Carlyle's "Sartor Resartus," ii. 8); a ranting utterance (as, "He sometimes . . . in his rants, talked with Norman haughtiness of the Celtic barbarians": Macaulay's "Hist. of Eng.," vi.); also, a noisy or wild frolic, or a lively merrymaking (Sc. and prov. Eng.).—**rant′er**, n.—**rant′ing-ly**, adv.

rant-i-pole (ran′ti-pōl). [Appar. < ranty + poll¹.] **I.** n. A rude, romping boy or girl; a boisterous, wild fellow; also, a termagant. [Chiefly prov. Eng.] **II.** a. Boisterous;

riotous; wild: as, "This rantipole hero had . . . singled out the blooming Katrina for the object of his uncouth gallantries" (Irving's "Sketch-Book," Sleepy Hollow). [Chiefly prov. Eng.]—**rant′i-pole**, v. i.; -poled, -poling. To behave as a rantipole; romp rudely; act in a boisterous, wild fashion: used esp. in rantipoling, ppr. or p. a. [Chiefly prov. Eng.]

rant-y (ran′ti), a. [From rant.] Raving or wild with passion, anger, pain, etc.; also, lively, boisterous, or riotous. [Prov. Eng. and Sc.]

ra-nun-cu-la-ceous (ra-nung-kū-lā′shius), a. [See ranunculus.] Belonging to the Ranunculaceæ, the crowfoot or buttercup family of plants, which includes also the marsh-marigold, aconite, black hellebore, anemone, hepatica, clematis, meadow-rue, columbine, larkspur, peony, etc.

ra-nun-cu-lus (ra-nung′kū-lus), n.; pl. -luses, L. -li (-lī). [L., kind of medicinal plant, perhaps crowfoot, orig. little frog, tadpole, dim. of rana, frog.] Any plant of the large and widely distributed genus Ranunculus, comprising herbs with leaves mostly divided and flowers, commonly yellow, with five petals; a crowfoot; a buttercup.

ranz des vaches (räns, or rän, dā vàsh). [Swiss F., 'ranz (of uncertain origin and meaning) of the cows.'] A Swiss herdsmen's melody played on the horn or sung.

rap¹ (rap), v.; rapped, rapping. [Prob. imit.] **I.** tr. To strike, now esp. with a quick and smart or light blow (as, "She rapped him over the knuckles with her fan": Smollett's "Humphry Clinker," May 6); give a rap or raps on; also, to knock or drive (out, etc.) by rapping; produce or announce by raps (with out, and used esp. of communications ascribed to spirits: cf. rap¹, n.); also, to utter sharply or vigorously (usually with out: as, "He rapped out an oath," Conan Doyle's "Exploits of Brigadier Gerard," ii.); also, to deliver a quick, smart blow with; drive, bring down, etc., with a rap. **II.** intr. To knock smartly or lightly, esp. so as to make a noise: as, to rap on a door for admittance; "Mr. Kinney, presiding . . . rapped loudly for order" (Tarkington's "Magnificent Ambersons," iii.).—**rap¹**, n. A quick and smart or light blow (as, "I shall give you a rap over the knuckles in a minute": Arnold Bennett's "Clayhanger," iv. 1); an audible knock, as on a door, for the purpose of attracting attention; in modern spiritualism, a sound as of knocking, ascribed to the agency of disembodied spirits.

rap² (rap), v. t.; rapped, also rapt, rapping. [Appar. a var. of rape¹, in later use associated with rapt².] To seize, snatch, or steal (archaic or prov.); also, to take up and carry off, or transport (archaic); also, to transport with emotion, or affect with rapture (obs. or archaic).

rap³ (rap), n. [Origin obscure.] A counterfeit coin, worth about half a farthing, which formerly passed current in Ireland for a halfpenny; hence, a coin of the smallest value, or the smallest amount of money (as, "Here is my hand to you with all my heart; but of money, not one rap": Stevenson's "Master of Ballantrae," x.); fig., the least bit (as, " 'There's no girl in Boston that I care a rap for,' he said": W. Churchill's "Coniston," ii. 8).

ra-pa-cious (ra-pā′shus), a. [L. rapax (rapac-), grasping, < rapere, seize.] Given to seizing for plunder or the satisfaction of greed (as, rapacious marauders; "Rapacious adventurers set busily to work . . . to find out flaws in men's title to individual estates," Morley's "Oliver Cromwell," i. 6; a rapacious usurer); predatory; extortionate; inordinately greedy; characterized by or showing grasping or greed (as, a rapacious disposition; "His provinces were attracting a rapacious gaze," J. F. Kirk's "Charles the Bold," iv. 2; rapacious demands); also, specif., of animals, subsisting by the capture of living prey; raptorial.—**ra-pa′cious-ly**, adv.—**ra-pa′cious-ness**, n.—**ra-pa′ci-ty** (-pas′i-ti), n. The quality or fact of being rapacious; rapacious spirit, action, or practice: as, "the rapacity of the great claimants of lands who held seats in the council" (Bancroft's "Hist. of the U. S.," Amer. Revolution, i. 6).

rap-a-ree (rap-a-rē′), n. See rapparee.

rape¹ (rāp), v.; raped, raping. [ME. rapen, prob. < L. rapere (pp. raptus), seize, snatch, carry off: cf. rap², rapid, rapine, raptorial, rapture, and ravish.] **I.** tr. To seize, take, or carry off by force; sometimes, to plunder (a place); also, to enrapture (now rare); also, to commit the crime of rape on (a woman). **II.** *intr.* To commit the crime of rape.—**rape**[1], *n.* The act of seizing and carrying off by force either a thing or a person, but esp. a woman (as, "The *Rape* of the Lock," title of a poem by Alexander Pope; the *rape* of the Sabine women, in Roman history; the *rape* of Proserpine by Pluto, in mythology); also, the crime of violating, or having unlawful carnal knowledge of, a woman forcibly and against her will.

rape[2] (rāp), *n.* [ME. *rape*; origin unknown.] One of the six divisions of the county of Sussex, England, intermediate between a hundred and the shire.

rape[3] (rāp), *n.* [F. *râpe*, < ML. *raspa*.] The refuse of grapes after the must has been expressed, used as a filter in making vinegar.

rape[4] (rāp), *n.* [L. *rapum*, *rapa*, turnip.] A brassicaceous plant, *Brassica napus*, whose leaves are used as a food for sheep, etc., and whose seeds yield rape-oil.—**rape'=oil'**, *n.* A brownish-yellow oil obtained from rape-seed: used as a lubricant, etc.—**rape'=seed**, *n.* The seed of the rape; also, the plant itself.

ra-phe (rā'fē), *n.*; pl. *-phæ* (-fē). [NL., for *rhaphe*, < Gr. ῥαφή, seam, suture, < ῥάπτειν, sew.] A seam-like union between two parts or halves of an organ or the like; in *bot.*, in certain ovules, a cord connecting the hilum with the chalaza; also, a median line or rib on a valve of a diatom.

ra-phi-a (rā'fi-ä), *n.* [NL.: cf. *raffia*.] Any of the palms of the genus *Raphia*, of tropical Africa and America, as *R. ruffia*, of Madagascar, which yields raffia fiber, and *R. vinifera*, of western Africa, which yields a kind of wine or toddy.

ra-phis (rā'fis), *n.*; pl. *raph-ides* (raf'i-dēz). [NL., for *rhaphis*, < Gr. ῥαφίς (pl. ῥαφίδες), needle, < ῥάπτειν, sew.] In *bot.*, one of the minute needle-shaped crystals of calcium oxalate which occur in the cells of many plants.

Raphia (*R. vinifera*).

rap-id (rap'id). [L. *rapidus*, < *rapere*, seize, carry off, hurry away: cf. *rape*[1].] **I.** *a.* Moving with great speed, or swift in movement (as, "*rapid* feet," Cowper's tr. Homer's "Iliad," xvii. 847; "*rapid* wheels," Milton's "Paradise Lost," ii. 532); acting with speed, or quick in performance (as, a *rapid* worker or speaker); also, characterized by speed, as motion; done or executed with speed, as action or performance; occurring with speed, or coming about within a short time (as, *rapid* growth; *rapid* development); also, of a slope, descending at a marked angle (as, "the *rapid* slopes of the valley": Stevenson's "Travels with a Donkey," v. 3). **II.** *n.* A part of a river where the current runs very swiftly, as over a steep slope in the bed: usually in *pl.*—**rap'id=fire'**, *a.* *Milit.*, etc., firing shots in rapid succession; in *ordnance*, noting or pertaining to any of various mounted guns of moderate caliber which can be fired rapidly. Also fig., characterized by or delivered or occurring in rapid procedure, esp. in speech (as, a *rapid-fire* humorist; *rapid-fire* wit; *rapid-fire* questions and replies; *rapid-fire* conversation).—**rap'id=fir'er**, *n.* In *ordnance*, a rapid-fire gun.—**rap'id=fir'ing**, *a.* *Milit.*, etc., same as *rapid-fire*.—**ra-pid-i-ty** (ra-pid'i-ti), **rap'id-ness**, *n.*—**rap'id-ly**, *adv.*

ra-pier (rā'piėr), *n.* [F. *rapière*; origin uncertain.] Orig., a long, narrow, two-edged sword, used chiefly for thrusting; later, a light sword used only for thrusting.

rap-ine (rap'in), *n.* [OF. F. *rapine*, < L. *rapina*, < *rapere*, seize, carry off: cf. *rape*[1].] The violent seizure and carrying off of property of others; plunder; robbery: as, "the incursions of barbarians whose unskilfulness in arts made it easier for them to supply their wants by *rapine* than by industry" (Johnson's "Rasselas," xxxii.).

rap-loch (rap'loċh). [Origin obscure.] **I.** *n.* Coarse woolen cloth, homespun and undyed. [Sc.] **II.** *a.* Coarse; rough; homely: as, "Tho' rough an' *raploch* be her [Muse's] measure, She's seldom lazy" (Burns's "Second Epistle to Davie," 41). [Sc.]

rap-pa-ree (rap-a-rē'), *n.* [Ir. *rapaire*.] An armed Irish freebooter or plunderer, esp. of the 17th century; in general, a freebooter or robber.

rap-pee (ra-pē'), *n.* [F. *râpé*, 'grated,' pp. of *râper*: see *rasp*.] A strong snuff made from the darker and ranker kinds of tobacco-leaves.

rap-pel (ra-pel'), *n.* [F., < *rappeler*, recall: see *repeal*.] The roll or beat of the drum to call soldiers to arms.

rap-per (rap'ėr), *n.* One who or that which raps or knocks; the knocker of a door.

rap-port (ra-pōrt', F. rȧ-pôr), *n.* [F., < *rapporter*, bring back, refer, < *re-* (< L. *re-*), back, + *apporter*, < L. *apportare*, bring to, < *ad*, to, + *portare*, carry.] Relation; connection; esp., harmonious or sympathetic relation, or accord (as, "She may . . . have taken note of a sort of *rapport* . . . between Mr. Charles and all the family except his sister": W. De Morgan's "Alice-for-Short," vi.).

rap-proche-ment (rä-prosh-moṅ'), *n.* [F., < *re-* (< L. *re-*), back, + *approcher*, E. *approach*.] A coming or bringing together or into accord; an establishment of harmonious relations.

rap-scal-lion (rap-skal'yọn), *n.* [For *rascallion*.] A rascal; a rogue; a scamp.

rapt[1] (rapt). Preterit and past participle of *rap*[2].

rapt[2] (rapt), *a.* [First used as pp., ME. *rapt*, < L. *raptus*, pp. of *rapere*, seize, carry off, transport, captivate: cf. *rapture* and *rape*[1], also *rap*[2].] Carried off or transported from one place, or sphere of existence, to another (as, "*rapt* in a chariot drawn by fiery steeds," Milton's "Paradise Lost," iii. 522; *rapt* up into heaven); carried away in spirit (as, "*Rapt* into future times, the bard begun": Pope's "Messiah," 7); also, transported with emotion, or enraptured (as, "*rapt* with joy," Addison's "Cato," iv. 3; "the *rapt* seraph that adores and burns," Pope's "Essay on Man," i. 278); also, deeply engrossed or absorbed, as in thought, a feeling, etc. (as, "The husband is . . . *rapt* in speculation": Swift's "Gulliver's Travels," iii. 2); intent upon something (as, "Ida spoke not, *rapt* upon the child": Tennyson's "Princess," vi. 203); also, indicative of, proceeding from, or characterized by a state of rapture (as, "A Brandenburg concerto by Bach . . . was encored. Pierson did not applaud, he was too far gone in pleasure, and sat with a *rapt* smile on his face": Galsworthy's "Saint's Progress," ii. 2); indicative of, proceeding from, or characterized by deep engrossment or absorption (as, "listening with a *rapt* attention," W. Churchill's "Modern Chronicle," i. 3; "She was walking, with her customary air of haughty and *rapt* leisure, across the market-place," Arnold Bennett's "Leonora," i.).—**rapt'ly**, *adv.*—**rapt'ness**, *n.*

rap-to-ri-al (rap-tō'ri-al), *a.* [NL. *Raptores*, pl. of L. *raptor*, robber, plunderer, < *rapere*, seize, carry off: cf. *rape*[1].] Belonging or pertaining to the *Raptores*, an order consisting of the birds of prey, as the eagles, hawks, etc.; in general, preying upon other animals; predatory; also, adapted for seizing prey, as the beak or claws of a bird.

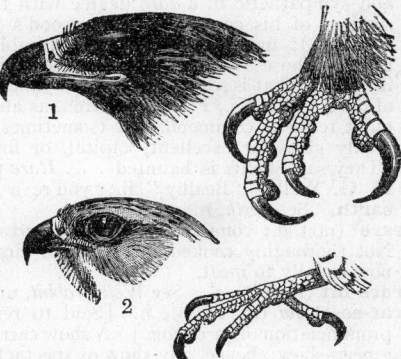

Head and Foot of Raptorial Bird. — 1, of golden eagle (*Aquila chrysaëtus*); 2, of gerfalcon (*Falco gyrfalco*).

rap-ture (rap'tūr), *n.* [L. *rapere* (pp. *raptus*), seize, carry off, transport, captivate: cf. *rape*[1].] The act of seizing and carrying off†; also, carrying or driving action or force (obs. or archaic: as, "Wave rolling after wave, where way they found, If steep, with torrent *rapture*," Milton's "Paradise Lost," vii. 299); also, the carrying or transporting of a person from one place, or sphere of existence, to another (as, the *rapture* of the prophet Elijah into heaven, see 2 Kings, ii. 11); also, mental transport or exaltation from strong pleasurable emotion, or joyful ecstasy (as, "I discovered a kind of *rapture* in his face while he spoke . . . his eyes sparkled like fire, his face glowed . . . he was fired with the joy of being embarked in such a work," Defoe's "Robinson Crusoe," ii. 6; "My reveries and imaginings all elevated me to *rapture*," Irving's "Tales of a Traveler," i. 9); hence, ecstatic joy or delight (as, "delight and wonder, rising to *rapture*": W. H. Hudson's "Far Away and Long Ago," xxii.); a state or fit of ecstatic delight (as, "Oliver would sit . . . listening to the sweet music, in a perfect *rapture*," Dickens's "Oliver Twist," xxxii.; to go into *raptures* over something; "My uncle is in *raptures* with Glasgow," Smollett's "Humphry Clinker," Sept. 3); an utterance or expression of ecstatic delight (often in *pl.*: as, "Her letters to King Leopold are sprinkled thick with *raptures*": Lytton Strachey's "Queen Victoria," iv.); also, a fit of violent excitement or passion (obs. or prov.: as, "Your prattling nurse Into a *rapture* lets her baby cry," Shakspere's "Coriolanus," ii. 1. 223).—**rap′ture,** *v. t.*; *-tured, -turing.* To move to rapture; enrapture.—**rap′tur-ous** (-tūr-us), *a.* Pertaining to or characterized by rapture or mental transport or exaltation; also, full of, feeling, or manifesting rapture or ecstatic joy or delight (as, "Observers . . . were *rapturous* in praise of the likeness": Hawthorne's "Twice-Told Tales," The Prophetic Pictures); characterized by, attended with, or expressive of such rapture (as, *rapturous* surprise; a *rapturous* moment; "Earth rolls the *rapturous* hosanna round," Cowper's "Task," vi. 797); partaking of rapture, as joy or delight.—**rap′tur-ous-ly,** *adv.*—**rap′tur-ous-ness,** *n.*

rare[1] (rār), *a.*; compar. *rarer*, superl. *rarest.* [L. *rarus*, thin, not dense, scattered, infrequent.] Having the component parts not closely compacted together (now used chiefly of air, gases, etc.: opposed to *dense*); thin; tenuous; also, thinly distributed over an area, or few and widely separated (as, "*rare* lighthouses dotting the great highway to the east": J. Conrad's "Rescue," ii. 5); also, coming or occurring far apart in time, or few and at long intervals (as, on *rare* occasions; "His gains were sure, His givings *rare*, save farthings to the poor," Pope's "Moral Essays," iii. 348); also, seldom seen or occurring, as a single thing, instance, etc. (as, "Her eyes would lighten up and the *rare* smile come more frequently to her lips," W. H. Hudson's "Purple Land," xxiv.; "By some *rare* accident, the mail was not even yet ready to start," De Quincey's "English Mail-Coach," ii.); hence, of a kind seldom seen, met with, or occurring, or unusual, uncommon, or exceptional (as, a *rare* plant or mineral; a *rare* disease; "the three-o′-clock in the morning courage, which Bonaparte thought was the *rarest*," Thoreau's "Walden," iv.); unusually great (as, "Roosevelt . . . a man conversant and sympathetic in a *rare* degree with the many different sections of his country": Charnwood's "Theodore Roosevelt," iv.); unusually excellent, admirable, or fine (as, *rare* tact; "Those *rare* souls, Poets," Tennyson's "Princess," ii. 163; "What is so *rare* as a day in June?" Lowell's "Vision of Sir Launfal," i., Prelude); often, as an ordinary or colloquial term of commendation (sometimes ironical), uncommonly good, or excellent, capital, or fine (as, *rare* sport; "They say Shonts is haunted . . . *Rare* place for a ghost," H. G. Wells's "Bealby," ii.; you're a *rare* one!).—**rare earth.** See *earth, n.*

rare[2] (rār), *a.*; compar. *rarer*, superl. *rarest.* [Var. of *rear*[2].] Not thoroughly cooked; underdone: first applied to eggs, now usually to meat.

rare-bit (rār′bit), *n.* See *Welsh rabbit*, under *Welsh*[1], *a.*

rar-ee=show (rār′ē-shō), *n.* [Said to represent foreigners' pronunciation of *rare show*.] A show carried about in a box; a peep-show; hence, any show or spectacle.

rar-e-fac-tion (rar-ē-fak′shọn or rār-), *n.* [F. *raréfaction*.] The act or process of rarefying, or the state of being rarefied. —**rar-e-fac′tive** (-tiv), *a.* Causing, attended with, or characterized by rarefaction.

rar-e-fi-ca-tion (rar″ē-fi-kā′shọn or rār″-), *n.* Rarefaction.

rar-e-fy (rar′ē-fī or rār′-), *v.*; *-fied, -fying.* [OF. *rarefier* (F. *raréfier*), < L. *rarefacere* (passive *rarefieri*), < *rarus*, rare, + *facere*, make.] **I.** *tr.* To make rare or more rare, or less dense; fig., to make less gross, or refine. **II.** *intr.* To become rare or less dense; become thinned.

rare-ly (rār′li), *adv.* As a rare thing, on rare occasions, or seldom (as, a sight *rarely* seen; he is *rarely* late); also, unusually, uncommonly, or exceptionally (as, a *rarely* exact imitation); unusually or remarkably well, or finely (as, "You can write *rarely* now, after all your schooling, I should think": George Eliot's "Mill on the Floss," iii. 3).—**rare′ness,** *n.*

rare-ripe (rār′rīp). [For *rathripe*.] **I.** *a.* Early ripe. **II.** *n.* A fruit or vegetable that is ripe early, esp. a kind of peach.

rar-i-ty (rar′i-ti or rār′-), *n.*; pl. *-ties* (-tiz). [L. *raritas*, < *rarus*, E. *rare*[1].] The state of being rare; thinness or tenuity, as of air or a gas; rare occurrence, or infrequency (as, "Alas! for the *rarity* Of Christian charity!" Hood's "Bridge of Sighs," 43); rare or unusual excellence; also, something rare, unusual, or uncommon (as, "Prompt obedience is a *rarity*": J. H. Newman's "Callista," xxv.); often, something esteemed or interesting as being rare, uncommon, or curious (as, "shelves of French *rarities*, ranging from Du Bellay's 'Visions,' with his autograph, down to the copy of 'Les Mémoires d'Outre-Tombe' presented by Chateaubriand to Madame Récamier," Mrs. H. Ward's "Robert Elsmere," xiv.; "I . . . showed him the small collection of *rarities* I made in the country," Swift's "Gulliver's Travels," ii. 8); a curiosity.

ras (ras), *n.* [Ar. *rās*, head.] A headland, promontory, or cape (used in many place-names on the Arabian and African coasts, etc.); also, in Abyssinia, a prince, governor, or chief.

ras-cal (ras′kạl). [OF. *rascaille* (F. *racaille*), rabble; origin uncertain.] **I.** *n.* The rabble†; also, a person belonging to the rabble†; a low, mean, or wretched fellow†; also, a base, dishonest fellow, a knave, or a rogue (as, "They are *rascals*; men fit to send to the hulks," Thackeray's "Vanity Fair," lxvii.; "a couple of *rascals*, who got their living by whatever the Devil sent them," Hawthorne's "Twice-Told Tales," David Swan); often, a playful epithet for any person, or sometimes for an animal (as, he's a lucky young *rascal*; come here, you little *rascal*; also, the lean or inferior deer of a herd†, or a single one of them† (see Shakspere's "As You Like It," iii. 3. 58). **II.** *a.* Belonging to or being the rabble†; low†, mean†, or wretched†; also, rascally, knavish, or dishonest (as, "bellow like a *rascal* trooper strung up for the cat," G. Meredith's "Diana of the Crossways," xxvi.; "my days spent in *rascal* enterprise and rubbish-selling," H. G. Wells's "Tono-Bungay," ii. 4. § 5).—**ras-cal′i-ty** (-kal′i-ti), *n.*; pl. *-ties* (-tiz). The rabble (obs. or archaic); also, rascally or knavish character or conduct; a rascally act or practice (as, "I don't want to be told about any of his *rascalities*": J. Conrad's "Rescue," v. 1); also, rascals or knaves collectively (as, "The rest were the dregs of colonial *rascality*": Stevenson's "Master of Ballantrae," xi.).—**ras-cal′lion** (-kal′yọn), *n.* A rascal; a rapscallion: as, "a set of tempestuous *rascallions*" (Irving's "Tales of a Traveler," ii. 10).—**ras′cal-ly,** *a.* Being, characteristic of, or befitting a rascal or knave (as, a *rascally* fellow; a *rascally* trick or performance); knavish; dishonest; sometimes, of places, etc., villainous, or wretchedly bad or unpleasant. —**ras′cal-ly,** *adv.* In a rascally manner.

rase (rāz), *v. t.*; *rased, rasing.* [OF. F. *raser*, < ML. *rasare*, freq. of L. *radere* (pp. *rasus*), scrape, scratch, shave: cf. *raze*.] To scrape† or scratch†; make (a mark, etc.) by incising; also, to scrape off, erase, or obliterate (now rare); also, to tear down, demolish, or level with the ground (as, "cities *rased* to the ground," Macaulay's "Hist. of Eng.," i.: now usually *raze*).

rash[1] (rash), *a.* [ME. *rasch* = OHG. *rasc*, G. *rasch*, quick, brisk, = Icel. *röskr*, vigorous, brave.] Active, brisk, or quick (now Sc. and prov. Eng.); also, acting with undue haste or without due consideration (as, "Be not *rash* with thy mouth," Eccl. v. 2; "You are recklessly *rash* about your own health," C. Brontë's "Jane Eyre," xxxiii.); overhasty; reckless; also, characterized by or showing undue haste or want of consideration (as, "*rash* adventures," Scott's "Lady of the Lake," iv. 28; "*rash* words or promises," Steele, in "Tatler," 78); also, of things, quick and strong in action† (as, "*rash* gunpowder": Shakspere's "2 Henry IV.," iv. 4. 48).

rash² (rash), *n.* [Cf. F. *rache*, earlier *rasche*, eruption on the head.] An eruption or efflorescence on the skin.

rash-er (rash′ėr), *n.* [Origin uncertain.] In *cookery*, a thin slice of bacon or ham for frying or broiling: as, "great *rashers* of broiled ham . . . done to a turn, and smoking hot" (Dickens's "Barnaby Rudge," xxi.).

rash-ly (rash′li), *adv.* In a rash manner; too hastily; recklessly.—**rash′ness,** *n.*

Ras-kol-nik (ras-kol′nik), *n.* [Russ., schismatic, dissenter.] In Russia, a dissenter from the Orthodox Church.

ra-so-ri-al (rā̇-sō′ri-al), *a.* [NL. *Rasores*, pl., lit. 'scratchers,' < L. *radere*, scrape, scratch.] Belonging or pertaining to the *Rasores*, an old order of birds comprising those given to scratching the ground for food, as poultry; gallinaceous.

rasp (rȧsp), *v.* [OF. *rasper* (F. *râper*), scrape, grate; prob. from Teut.] **I.** *tr.* To scrape or abrade with a rough instrument; scrape or rub roughly; fig., to grate upon or irritate (the nerves, feelings, etc.); also, to remove by scraping; scrape (*off*, etc.); also, to utter with a grating sound (as, " 'No harm?' *rasped* out Balaam": Wister's "Virginian," xxv.). **II.** *intr.* To scrape or grate; also, to make a grating sound (as, "wide fields whose multitudinous, tiny life *rasped* and buzzed under the vibrant heat": G. W. Cable's "John March, Southerner," xxiii.).—**rasp,** *n.* A coarse form of file, having separate point-like teeth; hence, any instrument for rasping; also, the act of rasping; a rasping or grating sound (as, "The breeze comes shrill with the call of the cricket, Grasshoppers' *rasp*, and rustle of sheaf," R. W. Gilder's "Song of Early Autumn"; "An astonishing *rasp* came into Twyning's voice," A. S. M. Hutchinson's "If Winter Comes," iii. 6).

Foot of Rasorial Bird. — 1, of domestic cock; 2, of red grouse (*Lagopus scoticus*).

rasp-ber-ry (rȧz′ber″i), *n.*; pl. *-berries* (-iz). [From archaic or prov. *rasp*, raspberry (fruit or plant), earlier *raspis*; origin uncertain.] The fruit of several shrubs of the rosaceous genus *Rubus*, consisting of small juicy drupelets, red, black, or pale-yellow, forming a detachable cap about a convex receptacle (being thus distinguished from the blackberry); also, a plant bearing such fruit; also, a dull pinkish or purplish red color. Also (slang), with *the*, severe censure or criticism; derision: as, to get *the raspberry*; to give a person *the raspberry* (cf. *razz*).

rasp-er (rȧs′pėr), *n.* One who or that which rasps, as a machine for rasping sugar-cane.

rasp-y (rȧs′pi), *a.* Grating; harsh; rough; also, irritable.

ras-se (ras′e or ras), *n.* [Javanese.] A small civet-cat, *Viverricula malaccensis*, widely distributed from the Malay Archipelago and Peninsula, China, India, etc., to Madagascar, and often kept in captivity for the civet which it yields.

Rasse.

ra-sure (rā′zhūr), *n.* [L. *rasura*, < *radere*: see *rase*.] The act of scraping†, or a scratch† or mark†; also, erasure, or an erasure (now rare); effacement or obliteration (now rare).

rat (rat), *n.* [AS. *ræt* = D. *rat* = G. *ratz, ratte,* rat: cf. F. *rat,* Sp. and Pg. *rato,* It. *ratto,* ML. *ratus, rattus,* rat.] Any of certain long-tailed rodents of the genus *Mus* and allied genera (family *Muridæ*), distinguished from the mouse by being larger; broadly, any rodent of the same family, or any of various similar animals (as, the spiny *rats*, hystricomorphic rodents of the South American genus *Echimys,* etc.); also, one who abandons his party or associates, esp. in time of trouble (in allusion to the belief that rats leave a house about to fall or a ship about to sink); also, a scab (workman); also, a roll of hair or other material used as a pad by women to puff out the hair; also, *pl.,* an exclamation used to indicate scornful incredulity or impatience (slang: as, " 'We are alone at last,' repeated Miss Vavasour . . . 'Oh rapture!' 'Oh *rats!*' said the manager of the theatre," L. Merrick's "Conrad in Quest of His Youth," xiv.).—**Pharaoh's rat.** See *ichneumon.*—**pouched rat.** See *gopher.*—**to smell a rat.** See under *smell, v. t.*—**rat,** *v. i.; ratted, ratting.* To hunt or catch rats; also, to desert one's party or associates, esp. in time of trouble; also, to act as a rat or scab.

rat-a-ble (rā′tȧ-bl), *a.* Capable of being rated or appraised; also, proportional; also, in British use, liable to rates or local taxes.—**rat-a-bil′i-ty** (-bil′i-ti), **rat′a-ble-ness,** *n.*—**rat′a-bly,** *adv.*

rat-a-fi-a (rat-a-fē′ä), *n.* [F.; origin uncertain.] A cordial or liqueur flavored with fruit-kernels, fruit, or the like; also, a kind of fancy cake or biscuit.

ra-tal (rā′tal), *n.* In British use, the amount on which rates or taxes are assessed.

ra-tan, rat-tan (ra-tan′), *n.* [Malay *rōtan.*] Any of various climbing palms of the genus *Calamus;* any of certain low palms ('ground-ratans') of the genus *Rhapis;* also, the tough stems of such palms, used for wickerwork, canes, etc.; also, a stick or switch of this material (as, "the boatswain's mate . . . seizing the poor little culprits . . . and using a *ratan* without mercy": H. Melville's "Omoo," xxviii.).

rat-a-plan (rat-a-plan′), *n.* [F.; imit.] A sound of or as of the beating of a drum; a rubadub.—**rat-a-plan′,** *v. t.* or *i.; -planned, -planning.* To play by or play a rataplan.

rat=a=tat (rat′a-tat′), *n.* Same as *rat-tat.*

rat=catch-er (rat′kach″ėr), *n.* A catcher of rats; esp., one whose business it is to catch rats.—**rat′=catch″ing,** *n.*

ratch¹ (rach), *v. i.* [Var. of *reach.*] *Naut.,* to reach.

ratch² (rach), *n.* [Cf. *ratchet.*] A toothed bar or wheel with which a pawl engages; a ratchet.

ratch-et (rach′et), *n.* [F. *rochet,* ratchet, bobbin; from Teut.] A toothed bar with which a pawl engages; also, a ratchet-wheel; also, the pawl used with such a device; also, a mechanism consisting of such a bar or wheel together with the pawl.—**ratch′et=brace,** *n.* A carpenters' brace in which, by means of a ratchet, a reciprocating motion of the handle is converted into a rotary motion of the bit.—**ratch′et=drill,** *n.* A drill rotated by a ratchet-wheel which is moved by a pawl and lever.—**ratch′et=wheel,** *n.* A wheel with (angular) teeth on the edge, into which a pawl drops or catches, as to prevent reversal of motion or to convert reciprocating into rotatory motion.

Ratchet-wheel. — *a,* the wheel; *b,* reciprocating lever; *c,* pawl conveying motion to wheel; *f,* spring; *d,* pawl preventing reversal of motion.

rate¹ (rāt), *v. t.* or *i.; rated, rating.* [ME. *raten;* origin uncertain.] To chide vehemently; scold.

rate² (rāt), *n.* [OF. *rate,* < ML. *rata,* fixed amount or portion, rate, prop.

fem. of L. *ratus*, fixed by calculation, determined, pp. of *reri*, reckon, calculate, think, judge: see *reason*, and cf. *ratio*.] Fixed or assigned amount or number† (as, "I judge their number Upon or near the *rate* of thirty thousand": Shakspere's "2 Henry IV.," iv. 1. 22); also, estimated value or worth (as, to value a person's abilities at a low *rate*); also, estimation† (as, "My son is lost and, in my *rate*, she too": Shakspere's "Tempest," ii. 1. 109); also, price (as, "To purchase heaven for repenting Is no hard *rate*," Herbert's "Temple," 2 Vanitie, 10; cut *rates*); also, a certain quantity or amount of one thing considered in relation to a unit of another thing and used as a standard or measure (as, at the *rate* of 10 miles an hour); also, the amount of a charge or payment with reference to some basis of calculation (as, the *rate* of interest, or of wages; "an annual rent of from twenty-five to a hundred dollars, these are the country *rates*," Thoreau's "Walden," i.); a fixed charge per unit of quantity (as, a *rate* of 10 cents a pound, or of 3 cents a mile); also, a tax on property for some local purpose (usually in *pl.*: as, poor-*rates*; church-*rates*: British); also, degree of speed, progress, etc. (as, to walk, or to work, at a rapid *rate*); degree or comparative extent of action or procedure (as, the *rate* of increase, or of change); also, relative condition or quality; grade, class, or sort (as, "She was . . . a most sensible girl, and her understanding was of the first *rate*," Fielding's "Tom Jones," vii. 3; "the common *rate* of country gentlemen," Steele, in "Spectator," 151); assigned position in any of a series of graded classes, or rating; also, manner†, method†, or way†.—at any rate, under any circumstances; in any case; at all events; at least: as, "We must not dare to offend our Harry *at any rate*" (H. Brooke's "Fool of Quality," xviii.); "Commercially the arrangement was not a success, *at any rate* for the firm" (J. Conrad's "Lord Jim," xxi.).—at that rate, or at this rate, at that, or this, rate of procedure; under such circumstances; in that, or this, case.—rate², *v.*; rated, rating. I. *tr.* To fix or assign the amount of†; also, to divide or allot proportionally†; also, to reckon or calculate (as, "To *rate* What millions died—that Cæsar might be great," Campbell's "Pleasures of Hope," ii.: now rare); also, to estimate the value or worth of; appraise; value or appraise at a certain sum, degree, etc. (as, "Plenty of people around him *rated* him extravagantly," Charnwood's "Theodore Roosevelt," iii.; "the thought that posterity might *rate* Pompey above himself [Cicero]," Froude's "Cæsar," xxvii.); also, to esteem, consider, or account (as, "He was *rated* one of the rich men of the city": W. Churchill's "Inside of the Cup," v.); also, to value for purposes of taxation, etc.; make subject to the payment of a certain rate or tax; also, to fix at a certain rate, as of charge or payment; arrange for the conveyance of (goods) at a certain rate; also, to design, as a machine, for a certain rate of speed, etc.; also, to ascertain the rate (as of speed) of; also, to place in a certain class, etc., as a ship or a seaman; give a certain rating to (as, "I should be *rated* ship's boy": Stevenson's "Treasure Island," viii.). II. *intr.* To have value, standing, etc.; also, to have position in a certain class; have rating.—rate′a·ble, etc. See *ratable*, etc.

ra·tel (rā′tẹl), *n.* [S. Afr. D.] Either of two badger-like quadrupeds, *Mellivora ratel* of South Africa and *M. indica* of India.

rate-pay·er (rāt′pā″ẽr), *n.* In British use, a payer of rates or local taxes.

rat·er (rā′tẽr), *n.* One who rates.

rath¹ (ráth), *n.* [Ir.] In *Ir. antiq.*, a wall of raised earth inclosing the residence of the chief of a tribe.

Ratel (*Mellivora ratel*).

rath², rathe (ráth, rāᴛʜ), *a.* [AS. *hræth*, also *hræd*, *hrad*, = OHG. *hrad* = Icel. *hradhr*, quick, swift.] Quick†; also, early, or coming, occurring, etc., before the usual time (as,

"laying his head in a *rath* grave": Scott's "Antiquary," xxxix.); esp., growing, blooming, or ripening early in the year or season (as, "the *rathe* primrose," Milton's "Lycidas," 142; "The *rathe* wheat rustles, the landscape gleams," Henley's "Ballade of Midsummer Days and Nights"); also, early in the day or the morning; early in any period, as in life (as, "men of *rathe* and riper years": Tennyson's "In Memoriam," cx.). [Now archaic or prov.]—rath², rathe, *adv.* [AS. *hræthe*, *hræthe*: cf. *rather*.] Quickly†; also, early (archaic or prov.: as, "The face . . . held her from her sleep, Till *rathe* she rose," Tennyson's "Lancelot and Elaine," 338).

rat-haus (rät′hous), *n.* [G., 'council house.'] A town hall.

rath-er (ráᴛʜ′ẽr or rä′ᴛʜẽr), *adv.* [AS. *hrathor*, compar. of *hrathe*, E. *rath²*, *adv.*] More quickly†; also, earlier or sooner (obs. or prov.); hence, sooner or more readily or willingly (with or without *than* introducing an alternative: as, to die *rather* than yield; I would *rather* go to-day); in preference; as a preferred or accepted alternative; also, more properly or justly, or with better reason (as, the contrary is *rather* to be supposed: "Is that not . . . perhaps *rather* a matter for her decision?" Galsworthy's "Dark Flower," ii. 15); also, more properly or correctly speaking, or more truly (as, "The fatted calf was made ready, or *rather* was already so, as if in anticipation of our coming": Lamb's "Mackery End"); also, on the contrary (as, "Suppose ye that I am come to give peace on earth? . . . Nay; but *rather* division": Luke, xii. 51); also, more than not, in a measure, to a certain extent, or somewhat (as, *rather* uncertain; *rather* good; *rather* too much; "Mr. Gradgrind seemed *rather* at a loss to understand the last four words," Dickens's "Hard Times," i. 15); with verbs, in some degree (used either literally, to modify a statement, as, he *rather* felt that this was unwise, or ironically, in colloquial use, to lend emphasis, as, "I tell you, I *rather* guess She was a wonder and nothing less!" Holmes's "Deacon's Masterpiece"); as a response, a colloquial equivalent of an emphatic affirmative (as, " 'Is Bonsecours worth going to?' '*Rather!*' " L. Merrick's "Conrad in Quest of His Youth," ix.).—had rather, would rather; would more willingly. See *had*.—the rather, the more so, as for some reason given; all the more: as, "You are come to me in happy time; *The rather* for I have some sport in hand" (Shakspere's "Taming of the Shrew," Induction, i. 91).

rath-ripe, rathe-ripe (ráth′rīp, rāᴛʜ′rīp). [See *rath²*, *adv.*] I. *a.* Early ripe. [Archaic or prov.] II. *n.* A fruit or vegetable that is ripe early. [Archaic or prov.]

raths-kel-ler (räts′kel-ẽr), *n.* [G., also *ratskeller*: cf. *rathaus*.] In Germany, the cellar of a town hall, often used as a beer-hall or restaurant; hence, any saloon or restaurant of the German type in a cellar or basement.

rat-i-fi-ca-tion (rat″i-fi-kā′shọn), *n.* [OF. F. *ratification*, < ML. *ratificatio(n-)*.] The act of ratifying, or the state of being ratified; confirmation; sanction.

rat-i-fy (rat′i-fī), *v. t.*; -fied, -fying. [OF. F. *ratifier*, < ML. *ratificare*, < L. *ratus*, fixed, determined (see *rate²*), + *facere*, make.] To confirm by expressing consent, approval, or formal sanction (as, "Upon his knees . . . he *ratified* the vow which he had made internally": Scott's "Quentin Durward," xvii.); esp., to confirm (something done or arranged by an agent or by representatives) by such action (as, "Between England and France peace existed under *ratified* treaties": Bancroft's "Hist. of the U. S.," Amer. Revolution, i. 8); also, to confirm as true or correct†.—rat′i-fi-er (-fī-ẽr), *n.*

ra-tine (ra-tēn′), *n.* [F.; origin unknown.] Any of various fabrics, of wool or cotton, with a curled or tufted nap or a looped or rough surface.

rat-ing (rā′ting), *n.* The action of one who rates (see *rate²*, *v.*); an amount fixed as a rate; esp., classification according to grade or rank; class or grade; assigned position in a particular class or grade, or relative standing, as of a ship or a seaman; *pl.*, *naut.*, men of certain ratings.

ra-tio (rā′shio or -shō), *n.*; pl. -tios (-shioz or -shōz). [L., reckoning, account, relation, reason, < *reri* (pp. *ratus*), reckon, calculate, think, judge: see *reason*, and cf. *rate²* and *ration*.] The relation between two similar magnitudes in respect to the number of times the first contains the second, integrally or fractionally (as, the *ratio* of 5 to 2, which may be written 5 : 2, or $\frac{5}{2}$); hence, proportional relation; rate; also, a ration† or allowance†.—**arithmetical ratio**, the difference between two numbers.—**geometrical ratio**, ordinary ratio.

ra-ti-o-ci-nate (rash-i-os′i-nāt), *v. i.; -nated, -nating.* [L. *ratiocinatus*, pp. of *ratiocinari*, < *ratio(n-)*: see *ratio* and *reason*.] To reason; carry on a process of reasoning.— **ra-ti-o-ci-na′tion** (-nā′shon), *n.* [L. *ratiocinatio(n-)*.] Reasoning, or a process of reasoning: as, "having by a masterly process of *ratiocination* reached this conclusion" (Arnold Bennett's "Lion's Share," xxviii.); "subtle definitions, or intricate *ratiocinations*" (Johnson's "Rasselas," xxii.).—**ra-ti-o′ci-na-tive** (-os′i-nā-tiv), *a.* Pertaining to or characterized by reasoning.—**ra-ti-o′ci-na-tor** (-nā-tor), *n.*

ra-tion (rā′shon or rash′on), *n.* [F. *ration*, < ML. *ratio(n-)*, allowance of provisions, ration, L. reckoning, account: see *ratio*.] A fixed allowance of provisions or food, esp. the daily allowance assigned to a soldier or sailor; the daily allowance of food assigned for a horse or other animal; an amount of food fixed with reference to the nature and proportion of its constituent elements (protein, fat, carbohydrates, etc.) as sufficient and suitable for daily or other regular consumption by an animal or a person (as, a scientific *ration*; a balanced or complete *ration*); in general, an allowance or portion of anything dealt out for consumption or use (as, *rations* of sugar or of coal).—**iron ration.** See under *iron, a.*—**ra′tion,** *v. t.* To supply with rations, as of food (as, to *ration* an army); also, to put on rations, or restrict to a fixed ration or allowance (as, to *ration* citizens or purchasers during a shortage of some commodity); also, to apportion or distribute as rations or by some method of allowance (as, to *ration* food or water among persons adrift at sea; to *ration,* or *ration out,* food or fuel to the public in time of war).

ra-tion-al (rash′on-al), *a.* [L. *rationalis,* < *ratio(n-)*: see *reason*.] Of or pertaining to reason (as, the *rational* faculty); proceeding or derived from reason, or based on reasoning (as, *rational* certainty; phenomena admitting of a *rational* explanation; *rational* views on religious matters); also, endowed with the faculty of reason (as, man is a *rational* animal); also, being in or characterized by full possession of one's reason, sane, or lucid (as, the patient appeared perfectly *rational*; a *rational* interval between periods of delirium or insanity); also, having or exercising reason, sound judgment, or good sense (as, "all the quiet and *rational* people in the provinces": Burke's "American Taxation"); agreeable to reason, reasonable, or sensible (as, "This, though it would require a great deal of time and labour, I thought was the most *rational* design," Defoe's "Robinson Crusoe," i. 11; *rational* expenditures; *rational* modes of dress); in *math.,* expressible in finite terms; involving no root which cannot be extracted.—**ra-tion-a-le** (rash-o-nā′lē), *n.* [L., neut. of *rationalis.*] A statement of reasons; a reasoned exposition of principles; also, the fundamental reasons serving to account for something (as, "We must examine the *rationale* of the rule": Poe's "Mystery of Marie Rogêt").—**ra′tion-al-ism,** *n.* The principle or habit of accepting reason as the supreme authority in matters of opinion, belief, or conduct; in *theol.,* the principle of using reason as a criterion in questions of doctrine, Scriptural interpretation, etc.; specif., the doctrine that human reason, unaided by divine revelation, is an adequate or the sole guide to all attainable religious truth; in *philos.,* the theory that reason is in itself a source of knowledge, independent of the senses.—**ra′tion-al-ist. I.** *n.* An adherent of rationalism. **II.** *a.* Rationalistic: as, "a liberal and *rationalist* reaction against Calvinist rigour" (Morley's "Oliver Cromwell," i. 3). —**ra″tion-al-is′tic,** *a.* Of or pertaining to rationalists or rationalism; characterized by rationalism.—**ra″tion-al-is′ti-cal-ly,** *adv.*—**ra-tion-al-i-ty** (rash-o-nal′i-ti), *n.;* pl. *-ties* (-tiz). The quality of being rational; the possession of reason; reasonableness; also, the exercise of reason; also, a rational or reasonable view, practice, etc.—**ra′tion-al-ize** (-īz), *v.; -ized, -izing.* **I.** *tr.* To make rational or conformable to reason; also, to treat or explain in a rational or rationalistic manner. **II.** *intr.* To employ reason; think in a rational or rationalistic manner.—**ra″tion-al-i-za′tion** (-i-zā′shon), *n.*—**ra′tion-al-ly,** *adv.*—**ra′tion-al-ness,** *n.*

ra-tite (rā′tīt or rat′īt), *a.* [L. *ratis,* raft.] Having a flat breast-bone with no keel, as an ostrich; without a carina, as a breast-bone; of or pertaining to the *Ratitæ,* a division of flightless birds containing the ostrich, emu, etc.

rat=kan-ga-roo (rat′-kang-ga-rö″), *n.* Any of certain small marsupials (genera *Potorous, Bettongia,* etc.) of the kangaroo family, found in Australia, etc.

Rat-kangaroo (*Potorous tridactylus*).

rat-line, rat-lin (rat′lin), *n.* [Origin uncertain.] *Naut.,* any of the small ropes or lines which traverse the shrouds horizontally, serving as steps for going aloft; also, the kind of rope or line from which these are made.

ra-toon (ra-tön′), *n.* [Sp. *retoño.*] A sprout or shoot springing up from the root of a plant (esp. a sugar-cane) after it has been cropped.—**ra-toon′,** *v. i.* or *t.* To put forth or cause to put forth ratoons.

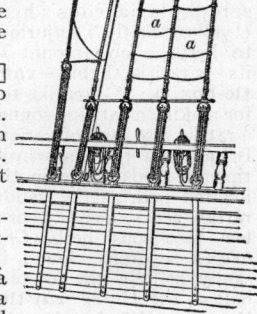

Ratlines (*a, a*).

rats-bane (rats′bān), *n.* Rat-poison, esp. the trioxide of arsenic.

rat=tail (rat′tāl), *a.* Having a tail like that of a rat; having a long and slender tail, or a tail with little or no hair; also, resembling a rat's tail, as in shape.—**rat′=tailed,** *a.*

rat-tan′, *n.* See *ratan.*

rat=tat (rat′tat′), *n.* [Imit.] A sound as of rapping: as, "Then came a sharp *rat-tat* at the door" (Gissing's "New Grub Street," vi.).

rat-teen (ra-tēn′), *n.* See *ratine.*

rat-ten (rat′n), *v. t.* or *i.* [Cf. *rat.*] To molest (a workman or an employer) by removing tools, spoiling materials, etc., as for the purpose of coercion or intimidation.

rat-ter (rat′ėr), *n.* One who or that which catches rats, as a terrier; also, one who deserts his party or associates.

rat-tish (rat′ish), *a.* Of, pertaining to, characteristic of, or resembling a rat; also, infested with rats.

rat-tle[1] (rat′l), *v. t.; -tled, -tling.* [From *rattling,* corruption of *ratline.*] *Naut.,* to furnish with ratlines: usually with *down:* as, "The men were ordered to *rattle* the rigging down" (Marryat's "Frank Mildmay," xvii.).

rat-tle[2] (rat′l), *v.; -tled, -tling.* [ME. *ratelen* = D. *ratelen* = G. *rasseln,* rattle; prob. imit.] **I.** *intr.* To give out a rapid succession of short, sharp sounds, as in consequence of agitation and repeated concussions (as, "Continuous lightning appeared to be . . . all round us, and crash quickly followed crash, making the doors and windows *rattle* in their frames": W. H. Hudson's "Far Away and Long Ago," viii.); cause such sounds, as by knocking on something or by causing things to strike together (as, "She *rattled* away with her needles": Mrs. Stowe's "Uncle Tom's Cabin," xvi.); be filled with such sounds, as a place; also, to move or go, esp. rapidly, with such sounds (as, "The coach *rattled* away": Dickens's "Oliver Twist," xii.); also, to talk rapidly, or chatter (as, "They . . . *rattled* on in a free, wild, racy talk": Howells's "Chance Acquaintance," ii.). **II.** *tr.* To cause to rattle (as, "The door did not yield . . . he *rattled* the handle violently": Mrs. Wharton's "Ethan Frome," iv.); drive, send, bring, etc., esp. rapidly, with rattling (as, "a sportive volley which the Indians *rattled* after him": Irving's "Captain Bonneville," xxiv.); also, to utter or perform in a rapid or lively manner (as, "I . . . could *rattle* off my catechism that fast, as you couldn't tell one word from another," Stevenson's "Treasure Island," xv.; "He sat down to the piano, and *rattled* a lively piece of music," Mrs. Stowe's "Uncle Tom's Cabin," xvi.); also, to scold, or rail at, noisily†; also, to stir up or rouse; also, to disconcert or confuse (a person: slang).—**rat′tle**[2], *n.* A rapid succession of short, sharp sounds, as from the collision of hard bodies (as, "There was a continuous *rattle* of picks, resembling a muffled shower of hail": Arnold Bennett's "Old Wives' Tale," i. 6); a rattling sound in the throat, as the death-rattle; sometimes, racket or uproar; also, rapid, noisy talk; trivial chatter (as, "People took her *rattle* for wit": G. Meredith's "Diana of the Crossways," xxi.); also, one who talks constantly in a lively or thoughtless manner; a constant chatterer; also, an instrument contrived to make a rattling sound, as a child's toy, or a device formerly used by watchmen to give an alarm; also, the series of horny pieces or rings at the end of a rattlesnake's tail, with which it produces a rattling sound; also, any of certain plants whose ripe seeds rattle in their cases, as *Rhinanthus crista-galli*, an old-world scrophulariaceous herb ('yellow rattle') injurious to herbage on account of its parasitic habit.—**rat′-tle-box**, *n.* A box-like toy for making a rattling sound; a rattle; also, any of various fabaceous plants whose ripened seeds rattle in the inflated pod, as the yellow rattle (see *rattle*[2], *n.*), or a low fabaceous herb, *Crotalaria sagittalis*, found in sandy soil in the eastern half of the U. S.—**rat′tle-brain, rat′tle-head, rat′-tle-pate**, *n.* A giddy, thoughtless person; an empty-headed chatterer.—**rat′tle=brained, rat′tle=head″ed, rat′tle=pat″ed**, *a.*—**rat′tler**, *n.* One who or that which rattles; esp., a rattlesnake.

Plant, with Flowers and Pods, of Rattlebox (*Crotalaria sagittalis*).

rat-tle-snake (rat′l-snāk), *n.* Any of various venomous American serpents of the genera *Crotalus* and *Sistrurus*, having several loosely articulated horny pieces or rings at the end of the tail, which produce a rattling or whirring sound when shaken.— **rat′tle-snake=plan′tain**, *n.* Any of several low terrestrial orchids of the genus *Peramium*, as *P. repens* of northern temperate regions.— **rat′tle-snake=root**, *n.* Any of certain plants of the cichoriaceous genus *Nabalus*, whose roots or tubers have been regarded as a remedy for snake-bites, as *N. serpentarius* or *N. albus*; also, the root or tuber; also, the Seneca snakeroot, *Polygala senega*, or its root.—**rat′tle-snake=weed**, *n.* A hawkweed, *Hieracium venosum*, of eastern North America, whose leaves and root are thought to possess medicinal virtue (see cut in next column); also, any of certain other plants, as the apiaceous plant *Eryngium aquaticum*.

— Hinder Part of a Rattlesnake, showing the rattle, with seven "rings" and a "button."

rat-tle-trap (rat′l-trap), *n.* A shaky, rattling object, as a rickety vehicle; *pl.*, knickknacks; odds and ends.

rat-tling (rat′ling). **I.** *p. a.* That rattles (as, "a *rattling* tray of tea-things": Arnold Bennett's "Old Wives' Tale," i. 2); characterized by rapidity and liveliness, as talk; lively in speech or manners (as, "a fine young man, *rattling*, light-hearted, and just a cordial of gladness": Galt's "Annals of the Parish," xvii.); remarkably fast, brisk, fine, great, etc. (colloq.: as, a *rattling* pace; a *rattling* game; "He . . .

preached a . . . sermon . . . that gave him a *rattling* reputation," Mark Twain's "Huckleberry Finn," xlii.). **II.** *adv.* Remarkably or extremely: as, "*rattling* good stuff" (H. G. Wells's "Tono-Bungay," iii. 3. § 2); "a *rattling* big distance off" (Mark Twain's "Huckleberry Finn," xxix.). [Colloq.]

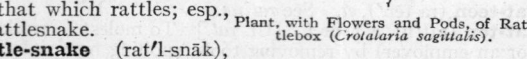

rat-tly (rat′li), *a.* Apt to rattle; making or having a rattling sound.

rat-toon (ra-tön′), *n.* and *v.* See *ratoon*.

rat-ty (rat′i), *a.* Pertaining to or characteristic of a rat; also, full of rats; also, mean, wretched, or poor (slang: as, "an old *ratty* deck of cards," Mark Twain's "Huckleberry Finn," xx.).

Lower Portion and Panicle of Rattlesnake-weed (*Hieracium venosum*).— *a*, flower; *b*, fruit.

rau-cous (râ′kus), *a.* [L. *raucus*.] Hoarse; harsh of voice or sound: as, "the harsh, *raucous* note like the caw of the carrion crow" (W. H. Hudson's "Far Away and Long Ago," vii.).—**rau′ci-ty** (-si-ti), *n.*—**rau′cous-ly**, *adv.*

rav-age (rav′āj), *n.* [F. *ravage*, < *ravir*: see *ravish*.] Devastating or destructive action, as of men or beasts, fire, tempest, pestilence, consuming passion, etc., or the result (as, "Peace . . . bid wild War his *ravage* end," Burns's "On the Seas and Far Away," 30; "It is not the *ravage* of a barbarian wolf-flock, as under Generic," Ruskin's "Crown of Wild Olive," iii.); havoc; ruinous damage; often, *pl.*, devastating, wasting, or ruinous depredations or effects (whether of physical or of moral agencies: as, the *ravages* of war, of devouring insects, or of time; the *ravages* of grief).—**rav′age**, *v.*; *-aged*, *-aging*. **I.** *tr.* To subject to ravage; devastate, or lay waste (as, "*ravaging* at pleasure other exposed portions of his rival's territory": J. F. Kirk's "Charles the Bold," iii. 1); work havoc upon; damage or mar by ravages (as, a face *ravaged* by time or grief). **II.** *intr.* To commit ravages; work havoc; do ruinous damage.—**rav′ag-er** (-ā-jėr), *n.*

rave[1] (rāv), *v.*; *raved*, *raving*. [Prob. < OF. *raver*, *resver*, wander, be delirious (F. *rêver*, dream); origin uncertain.] **I.** *intr.* To talk wildly in delirium or madness; hence, to talk as if mad; declaim in a frenzied manner; rage with furious utterance, as from anger; talk with wild or extravagant enthusiasm (as, to *rave* about a person, a place, or a book); talk extravagantly and foolishly (as, nonsense! you're *raving*); also, fig., of wind, water, storms, etc., to make a wild or furious sound, or rage, rush, dash, etc., with noisy fury (as, "The wind is *raving* in turret and tree," Tennyson's "Sisters"; "Let winter round me *rave*," Burns's "Lament of Mary Queen of Scots," 54). **II.** *tr.* To utter as if in madness, or in a frenzied or wild manner: as, "Pride, like the Delphic priestess . . . *Rav'd* nonsense" (Young's "Night Thoughts," vii. 596).—**rave**[1], *n.* The act or state of raving (as, "after our little hour of strut and *rave*": Lowell's "Commemoration Ode," iv.); a frenzy.

rave[2] (rāv), *n.* [Var. of obs. or prov. *rathe*; origin obscure.] One of the side pieces in the body of a wagon, sleigh, etc.

rav-el (rav′l), *v.*; *-eled* or *-elled*, *-eling* or *-elling*. [MD. *ravelen*, entangle, D. *rafelen*, unravel.] **I.** *tr.* To tangle or entangle; hence, to involve; confuse; perplex; also, to disengage the threads or fibers of (a woven or knitted fabric, a rope, etc.: often with *out*); draw (*out*) by unweaving or the like, as threads; hence, to disentangle, or make plain or clear (often with *out*). **II.** *intr.* To become tangled; hence, to become confused or perplexed; also, to become disjoined thread by thread or fiber by fiber; unravel; fray (*out*).— **rav′el**, *n.* A tangle or complication; also, an unraveled thread or fiber.—**rav′el-er, rav′el-ler**, *n.*

rave-lin (rav′lin), *n.* [F. *ravelin*, < It. *ravellino*, now *rivellino*; origin unknown.] A triangular outwork in a fortification, situated outside of the main ditch, and having two embankments forming a projecting angle.

rav-el-ing, rav-el-ling (rav′l-ing), *n.* Something raveled out, as a thread drawn from a woven fabric.

rav-el-ment (rav′l-ment), *n.* Entanglement; confusion.

ra-ven[1] (rā′vn). [AS. *hræfn* = OHG. *hraban* = Icel. *hrafn*, raven.] **I.** *n.* Any of certain large birds of the crow kind (genus *Corvus*), with lustrous black plumage and

Ravelin (*BB*).—*A*, its redoubt; *CC*, its ditch; *DD*, main ditch of fortress; *E*, passage giving access from fortress to ravelin.

raucous voice, esp. *Corvus corax* of Europe and Asia with two subspecies or varieties in North America (being easily tamed and sometimes taught to imitate speech, and from time immemorial regarded as portending evil or death); [*cap.*] in *astron.*, the southern constellation Corvus. **II.** *a.* Of a lustrous black: as, *raven* locks.

Raven (*Corvus corax*).

rav-en[2], **rav-in** (rav′n, -in), *n.* [OF. *ravine*, *rapine*, < L. *rapina*: see *rapine*, and cf. *ravine*.] Rapine; plunder; robbery; also, the seizing and devouring of prey (as, beasts of *raven*); also, plunder or spoil; prey (as, "The lion . . . filled . . . his dens with *ravin*": Nahum, ii. 12).— **rav-en**[2], *v.* [Also *ravin*: OF. *raviner*.] **I.** *tr.* To seize as spoil or prey; also, to devour voraciously (as, "a roaring lion *ravening* the prey": Ezek. xxii. 25). **II.** *intr.* To seek plunder or prey; also, to eat or feed voraciously or greedily; have a ravenous appetite (as, "The more they fed, they *ravened* still for more": Dryden's "Hind and the Panther," iii. 964). —**rav′en-ing**, *p. a.* That ravens; rapacious; voracious.— **rav′en-ous**, *a.* [OF. *ravinos*.] Given to plundering; extremely rapacious; also, given to seizing prey in order to devour it, as animals; voracious or gluttonous; also, extremely hungry (as, "I . . . had a second fit of violent hunger; I got up *ravenous*": Defoe's "Robinson Crusoe," ii. 8); also, greedily or intensely eager for gratification (as, appetite, desire, etc.—**rav′en-ous-ly**, *adv.*—**rav′en-ous-ness**, *n.*

ra-vi-gote (rȧ-vē-got′), *n.* [F., < *ravigoter*, revive, prob. var. of obs. *ravigorer*, reinvigorate.] A mixture of tarragon, chervil, parsley, chives, and other herbs, used in cookery as a seasoning.

rav′in, *n.* and *v.* See *raven*[2].

ra-vine (rȧ-vēn′), *n.* [F. *ravine*, torrent of water, ravine, OF. *rapine*: see *raven*[2].] A long, deep, narrow hollow or gorge, esp. one worn by water: as, "The valley between is nothing but a narrow *ravine*" (J. Conrad's "Lord Jim," xxi.). —**ra-vine′=deer**, *n.* An East Indian antelope, *Tetraceros quadricornis*, the male of which has a second pair of horns (small) on the forehead in front of the principal pair. See cut in next column.

rav-ing (rā′ving), *p. a.* That raves; delirious; frenzied; raging; also, extraordinary or remarkable (colloq.: as, "The child will be a *raving* beauty," W. Churchill's "Modern Chronicle," i. 4).—**rav′ing-ly**, *adv.*

ra-vi-o-li (rä-vyō′lē), *n. pl.* [It. *ravioli*, *raviuoli*.] Small squares or otherwise shaped pieces of paste inclosing forcemeat, cooked, and served in soup or otherwise.

rav-ish (rav′ish), *v. t.* [OF. F. *ravir* (*raviss-*), < L. *rapere*, seize, carry off, transport, captivate: cf. *rape*[1] and *rapture*.] To seize and carry off by force (as, "Is he one whom

Ravine-deer.

the wilderness folk have *ravished* from some Christian mother?" Hawthorne's "Twice-Told Tales," The Gentle Boy); esp., to carry off (a woman) by force; also, to commit the crime of rape on (a woman); also, to plunder or despoil (as, "the ease with which the Spaniards had *ravished* the city": Motley's "Dutch Republic," vi. 6); also, to carry off or transport from one place, or sphere of existence, to another, as from earth to heaven; carry away in spirit; also, to transport with strong emotion, esp. joy; affect with rapture; fill with ecstatic delight.—**rav′ish-er**, *n.*—**rav′ish-ing**, *p. a.* That ravishes; exciting rapture; entrancing; enchanting. —**rav′ish-ing-ly**, *adv.*—**rav′ish-ment**, *n.* The act of ravishing, or the state of being ravished; violent removal; the forcible abduction of a woman; the violation of a woman; transport, rapture, or ecstasy.

ra-vis-sant (rȧ-vē-sän′), *a.* [F.] Ravishing; enchanting.— **ra-vis-sante** (-sänt′), *a.* [F.] Fem. of *ravissant*.

raw (rȧ). [AS. *hrēaw*, *hrēw*, = D. *rauw* = G. *roh* = Icel. *hrár*, raw.] **I.** *a.* Uncooked, or not having undergone cooking, as articles of food (as, *raw* meat, oysters, or eggs; *raw* cabbage; most fruits are eaten *raw*); not having undergone burning, baking, or other treatment with heat in making or preparation, as bricks, pottery, glazes, pigments, etc.; in general, not having undergone processes of preparing, dressing, finishing, refining, or manufacture, as materials (as, *raw* silk or cotton; *raw* hides; *raw* sugar; *raw* clay or marble); crude, undressed, or unwrought; not finished off to prevent raveling, as the edge of textile material; not diluted, as spirits; fig., crude in quality or character; not tempered or refined by art or taste (as, *raw* coloring; a *raw* piece of work); ignorant, inexperienced, or untrained (as, a *raw* lad; a *raw* recruit or army); uncivilized or primitively barbarous (as, "Then the man; Tattoo'd or woaded . . . *Raw* from the prime": Tennyson's "Princess," ii. 106); also, unsoftened, rough, or rude (as, *raw* force; "speaking with the *raw* anger of a man with a new-born grievance," Arnold Bennett's "Leonora," i.); brutally or grossly frank (as, a *raw* portrayal of human passions); brutally harsh or unfair (slang: as, a *raw* deal); also, disagreeably damp and chilly, as the weather, air, etc. (as, "The morning was *raw*, and a dense fog was over everything": H. Kingsley's "Geoffry Hamlyn," xxiv.); also, unnaturally or painfully exposed, as flesh, etc., by removal of the skin or natural integument; painfully open, as a sore, wound, etc.; sore from loss or abrasion of skin, as a person or animal, a spot on the body, etc.; sometimes, raw-boned. **II.** *n.* Something raw, as an uncooked oyster, unrefined sugar, etc.; an inexperienced person; a raw, abraded, or sore spot on the body (also fig.: as, "By degrees a sore place, or in Hibernian parlance a *raw*, had been established in the irritable soul of the little governor," Irving's "Knickerbocker's New York," iv. 10); the raw, sore flesh (as, to touch one on the *raw*: often fig.). —**raw**, *v. t.* To make raw, as by removing or abrading the skin.—**raw′=boned**, *a.* Having little flesh on the bones; gaunt: as, "lean *raw-boned* rascals" (Shakspere's "1 Henry VI.," i. 2. 35).—**raw′head**, *n.* [Often *cap.*] A bogy of

---

ghastly appearance, of which children are told: usually called *rawhead and bloody-bones*. Also fig.—**raw'hide** (-hīd), *n.* The untanned skin of cattle; also, a rope or whip made of this.—**raw'hide**, *v. t.*; *-hided, -hiding*. To whip with a rawhide: as, "Some raftsmen would *rawhide* you till you were black and blue" (Mark Twain's "Life on the Mississippi," iii.).—**raw'ish**, *a.* Somewhat raw.—**raw'ly**, *adv.*—**raw'ness**, *n.*

rax (raks), *v.* [AS. *raxan*.] **I.** *intr.* To stretch one's self, as on waking; also, to become stretched to greater length; also, to extend the hand, or reach out, as to take something. [Sc. and north. Eng.] **II.** *tr.* To stretch or strain (one's self); also, to stretch (a thing) to greater length; also, to stretch or reach out (the hand, etc.); reach or hand (something) to a person. [Sc. and north. Eng.]

ray[1] (rā), *v. t.* [For *array*.] To array; dress; deck; also, to soil or defile. [Now prov. Eng.]

ray[2] (rā), *n.* [OF. F. *raie*, < L. *raia*.] Any of the elasmobranchiate fishes which constitute the genus *Raia* and which are characterized by a broad body with flat upper and under surfaces; any fish of the same group (*Batoidei*), as one belonging to the family *Narcobatidæ* ('electric rays'), the members of which possess a peculiar organ that enables them to stun their prey with an electric shock.

ray[3] (rā), *n.* [OF. *rai* (F. *rais*), < L. *radius*, rod, spoke, ray, beam: cf. *radius*.] Any of the lines or streams in which light appears to issue from a luminous object; a narrow beam of light; specif., in various scientific uses, the smallest portion of light or radiant energy that can be propagated alone; the straight line perpendicular to the wave-front in the propagation of radiant energy; any of certain lines or streams supposed to be produced by pulses in the luminiferous ether (cf. *Röntgen rays*); a stream of ma-

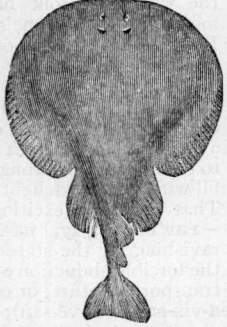

Electric Ray (*Narcobatis occidentalis*).

terial particles moving in the same line (cf. *alpha rays*, below); a stream of electrons or the like moving in the same line (cf. *beta rays*, below); a particular kind of light (as, the violet *ray*); also, a ray-like line or stretch of something (as, "silk of a blood-red, relieved by *rays* of white": Bulwer-Lytton's "Rienzi," v. 1); fig., a gleam, or slight manifestation, of intelligence, comfort, etc. (as, "He . . . gave none of us a *ray* of hope": Wister's "Virginian," xxi.); a trace of something; also, light or radiance (chiefly poetic: as, "lamps, that shed at eve a cheerful *ray*," Gray's "Alliance of Education and Government"); also, a glance of the eye (chiefly poetic: as, "All eyes direct their *rays* On him," Pope's "Dunciad," ii. 7); a line of sight; also, any of a system of parts radially arranged; in *zoöl.*, one of the branches or arms of a starfish; also, one of the hard and spinous, or the soft, jointed, and sometimes branched, processes which support and serve to extend the fin of a fish, esp. one of the latter, as distinguished from the former (which are called specifically *spines*); in *bot.*, in certain composite plants, the marginal part of the flower-head; also, a ray-flower; also, one of the branches of an umbel; also, a medullary ray (see under *medullary*); in *math.*, one of a system of straight lines passing through a point; also, an unlimited straight line considered as an element of a plane.—**alpha rays**, rays emitted by radium and other radioactive substances, supposed to consist of positively charged particles of helium.—**Becquerel rays**, rays emitted by radioactive substances, consisting of a mixture of alpha, beta, and gamma rays: first found in uranium compounds by the French physicist Antoine Henri Becquerel (1852–1908).—**beta rays**, rays emitted by radium and other radioactive substances, re-

Rays.— *a, b, c,* spines (followed by soft rays) of the dorsal, ventral, and anal fins of an acanthopterygian fish: *a,* ten spines; *b,* one spine; *c,* three spines.

sembling the cathode rays and consisting of electrons.—**canal rays,** the rays (consisting of positively charged ions) which pass through a hole in the cathode, in a direction away from the anode, when an electric discharge takes place in a vacuum-tube.—**cathode rays,** the rays generated at the cathode during an electric discharge in a vacuum-tube: used as a source of Röntgen rays.—**gamma rays,** penetrating rays emitted by radium and other radioactive substances, resembling the Röntgen rays and supposed to consist of pulses in the ether.—**hard rays,** Röntgen rays of great penetrating power, such as are obtained from tubes of high vacuum. Cf. *soft rays*, below.—**Hittorf rays.** See entry *Hittorf rays*.—**Lenard rays.** See entry *Lenard rays*.—**Röntgen rays.** See under *Röntgen*.—**soft rays,** Röntgen rays of slight penetrating power, such as are obtained from tubes of low vacuum. Cf. *hard rays*, above.—**X-rays.** See entry *X-ray*, also *Röntgen rays*, under *Röntgen*.—**ray**[3], *v.* **I.** *intr.* To emit rays; also, to issue in rays; also, to spread like rays or radii; radiate. **II.** *tr.* To send forth in rays; also, to furnish with rays or radiating lines; also, to throw rays upon; irradiate; also, to subject to the action of rays; make a radiograph of; treat with rays, as in radiotherapy.

rayed (rād), *a.* Having rays: as *five-rayed*.

ray=flow-er (rā'flou″ėr), *n.* In *bot.*, one of the marginal florets surrounding the disk of tubular florets in the flower-heads of certain composite plants.

ray=fun-gus (rā'fung″gus), *n.* Same as *actinomyces*.

ray-less (rā'les), *a.* Without rays; sending out no rays; unillumined, dark, or gloomy.

ray-on (rā'on, F. re-yôṅ), *n.* [F., ray, beam, gleam, < OF. *rai*, E. *ray*[3].] Artificial silk.

ray-on-nant (rā'o-nant, F. re-yo-näṅ), *a.* [F., ppr. of *rayonner*, send out rays, < *rayon*: see *rayon*.] Sending out rays; radiating; characterized by radiating lines, as architectural or other decoration.

raze (rāz), *v. t.*; *razed, razing.* [= *rase*.] To scrape or graze (now rare); also, to scrape off or erase (now rare); also, to tear down, demolish, or level with the ground (as, "His house was *razed* by order of the government": Borrow's "Bible in Spain," ii.); remove completely (as, "to *raze* what was left of the city from the surface of the earth": Motley's "Dutch Republic," iii. 8).

ra-zee (ra-zē'), *n.* [F. *rasé*, pp. of *raser*, rase, raze: see *rase*.] A ship, esp. a war-vessel, reduced in height by the removal of the upper deck.—**ra-zee'**, *v. t.*; *-zeed, -zeeing.* To cut down (a ship) by removing the upper deck; hence, in general, to abridge by cutting down or by cutting out parts.

ra-zor (rā'zor), *n.* [OF. *rasor*, < *raser*, scrape, shave: see *rase*.] A sharp-edged instrument used esp. for shaving the face.—**ra'zor**, *v. t.* To shave us with a razor.—**ra'zor-a-ble**, *a.* Fit to be shaved.—**ra'zor-back**, *n.* A finback or rorqual; also, one of a breed of half-wild hogs with a ridge-like back, common in the southern U. S.—**ra'zor=backed**, *a.* Having a sharp, ridge-like back.—**ra'zor-bill**, *n.* An auk, *Alca torda*, with a sharp, compressed bill.—**ra'zor= billed**, *a.* Having a razor-like bill.—**ra'zor=clam, ra'zor=fish**, *n.* Any of various bivalve mollusks of the family *Solenidæ*, with a long, narrow shell.—**ra'zor=shell**, *n.* The shell of a razor-clam, or the mollusk itself.

Razorbill, in winter plumage.

Razor-clam.

razz (raz), *n.* [Cf. *raspberry*, in same sense.] With *the*, the 'raspberry'; severe censure or criticism; derision: as, to get, or give, *the razz*; "The Red Swede got *the* grand *razz* handed to him" (Sinclair Lewis's "Main Street," xxiii.). [Slang.]—**razz**, *v. t.* To censure or criticize severely; deride. [Slang.]

raz-zi-a (raz′i-ä), *n.* [F.; from Ar.] A military incursion; a foray; a raid.

raz-zle=daz-zle (raz′l-daz′l), *n.* [Varied redupl. of *dazzle*.] A state of confusion or bewilderment, or of intoxication (slang); also, a ring-like raised platform revolving with an irregular motion about a central support from which it is hung, and on which persons ride for amusement, as at a pleasure-resort.

re¹ (rā), *n.* In *music*, the syllable used for the second tone of the scale (D, in the major scale of C), and sometimes for the tone D. See *sol-fa*.

re² (rē), *prep.* [L., abl. of *res*, thing, matter.] In the matter or case of (what is specified); with reference to: specif. in legal and business use.

Re³ (rä), *n.* See *Ra*.

re-. [L. *re-*, also *red-*.] A prefix meaning 'back,' 'again,' occurring orig. in words from the Latin, but used freely as an English formative, esp. in the sense of 'again,' 'anew,' as in *reabsorb*, *readjust*, *reappear*, *rebind*, *rebirth*, *recall*, *reëcho*, *reheat*, *reopen*, *reset*, *revamp*, and many other words, mostly self-explanatory: usually without a hyphen, except occasionally in order to distinguish one word from another of similar form but different sense (as *re-cover* from *recover*, *re-lease* from *release*), or to bring out clearly the force of the prefix (as in 'to build and *re-build*'), or to show clearly the elements of a word coined to serve the need of a particular occasion.

re-ab-sorb (rē-ab-sôrb′), *v. t.* [See *re-*.] To absorb again or anew.—**re-ab-sorp′tion** (-sôrp′shon), *n.*

reach (rēch), *v.* [AS. *ræcan* = D. *reiken* = G. *reichen*, reach.] **I.** *tr.* To stretch or hold out, or extend (as, "*Reach* hither thy hand, and thrust it into my side," John, xx. 27; a tree *reaches* out its branches); hold out to be taken, or give or pass by extending or handing (now chiefly colloq. or prov.: as, "*Reaching* the packet to Gloucester, he commanded him to read," Jane Porter's "Scottish Chiefs," lx.); also, to succeed in touching or seizing with the outstretched hand or anything extended or cast (as, to *reach* a book on a high shelf; to *reach* a bough with a pole; to *reach* bottom with a sounding-line); take or bring by a stretching effort with the hand or the like (as, "The Colonel was *reaching* down her handbag": Galsworthy's "Dark Flower," ii. 8); also, to succeed in striking or hitting, as with a weapon or missile; hence, to get at effectively in attack or retribution (as, "Atterbury . . . could be *reached* only by a bill of pains and penalties," Macaulay's "Essays," Francis Atterbury; to seek to *reach* the instigators of a crime); succeed in exerting influence upon, or in influencing, impressing, interesting, convincing, etc. (as, to *reach* a person through his vanity; to *reach* a desired class of customers; to *reach* one's audience); penetrate to and affect (the mind, heart, etc.: as, "He knew how to *reach* both the mind and the heart of his hearers," Motley's "Dutch Republic," vi. 7; "Even the savage heart of the Blackfoot chief was *reached* by this noble deed," Irving's "Captain Bonneville," xi.); also, to stretch or extend so as to touch or meet (as, the bookcase almost *reaches* the ceiling); also, to get to, or get as far as, in moving, going, traveling, etc. (as, the boat *reached* the shore; to *reach* the top of a hill; to *reach* a shelter from rain; to *reach* New York); in general, to come to (as, a letter *reaches* one; sound *reaches* the ear; a fact *reaches* one's knowledge); come to or arrive at in some course of progress or procedure (as, to *reach* the end of a book, or of a piece of work); to *reach* a conclusion by reasoning; the parties have *reached* an agreement); attain (as, to *reach* an age, rank, or condition; to *reach* perfection; to *reach* a particular degree of heat or of speed; "That night the storm *reached* its greatest fury," Bret Harte's "Outcasts of Poker Flat"); amount to, as in the sum or total (as, the cost will *reach* millions; the deaths will *reach* a hundred); carry to (a point, etc.), as the eye, a gun, etc.; also, to succeed in understanding†. **II.** *intr.* To make a stretch, as with the hand or arm, or become outstretched, as the hand or arm; make a movement or effort as if to touch or seize something (as, to *reach* toward or after a thing; to

reach for a weapon; to *reach* at a life-line: also fig.); also, to make a stretch of a certain length with the hand, arm, or something else, or as the hand or other thing does (as, he can *reach* easily to the top of the wall; I cannot *reach* as far as that); also, to extend in operation or effect (as, "His sword . . . *reaches* far, and where 'twill not extend, Thither he darts it," Shakspere's "Henry VIII.," i. 1. 111; power or influences *reaching* throughout the land; far-*reaching* consequences); also, to stretch in space, or extend in direction, length, distance, etc. (as, hills *reaching* away into the distance; a coat *reaching* to the knee; a country *reaching* from ocean to ocean); project (as, a roof *reaching* beyond the house-walls; a rock *reaching* up out of the sea); sometimes, to extend or continue in time (as, Elizabeth's reign *reaches* into the 17th century); also, to get or come to a specified place, person, point, etc. (often with *to*: as, "They could not *reach* back to the boat before it was dark," Defoe's "Robinson Crusoe," i. 18; "A prayer out of a poor man's mouth *reacheth* to the ears of God," Ecclus. xxi. 5); attain (*to*: as, "An example to mankind, Which few can *reach* to," Tennyson's "St. Simeon Stylites," 186); amount (*to*: as, sums *reaching* to a considerable total); carry, as the eye, a gun, etc.; *naut.*, to sail on a leg or reach; sail close-hauled; sail on a course with the wind forward of the beam.—

reach, *n.* The act or an act of reaching (as, to make a *reach* for a weapon); also, the extent or distance of reaching (as, the *reach* of the arm; grapes above one's *reach*, or out of *reach*; advantages within the *reach* of all; to get beyond the *reach* of the law; within *reach* of one's voice); range of effective action, or of power or capacity; sometimes, mental range, or capacity of thought or understanding (as, "philosophical *reach* of mind": J. H. Newman's "Idea of a University," i. 7); also, a continuous stretch or extent of something (as, a *reach* of woodland; a long *reach* of wharves; "Or through the long vacation's *reach* In lonely lowland districts teach," Whittier's "Snow-Bound"); specif., a portion of a river between bends (as, "A '*reach*' is a piece of straight river . . . the current drives through such a place in a pretty lively way": Mark Twain's "Life on the Mississippi," xvi.); a portion of a canal, of uniform level, between locks; an arm of the sea extending into the land, or a point of land extending into the water (now prov. or local); also, the pole connecting the hind gear of a vehicle with the forward gear; *naut.*, a leg; a course with the wind forward of the beam.—**reach′a-ble**, *a.* Capable of being reached; within reach.—**reach′er**, *n.*—**reach′less**, *a.* Beyond reach; unattainable.

re-act (rē-akt′), *v. t.* [See *re-*.] To act or perform anew. Also written *re-act*.—**re-act** (rē-akt′), *v. i.* To act in return on an agent or influence (as, "His deed was *reacting* upon him": George Eliot's "Adam Bede," xxviii.); act reciprocally upon each other, as two things; also, to act in response, as to a stimulus; hence, in recent use, to respond mentally in a particular manner, as to something presented to the attention or encountered in experience; also, to act in opposition, as against some force; also, to act in a reverse direction or manner; return toward a previous state.—**re-act′ance** (-ak′tạns), *n.* In *elect.*, that part of the impedance of an alternating-current circuit which is due to self-induction and capacity.—**re-ac′tion** (-ak′shon), *n.* Action in return, as on an agent; reciprocal action; the reciprocal action of chemical agents upon each other; a chemical change, or its result; also, action in response, as of the system, or of a nerve, muscle, etc., to a stimulus; hence, in recent use, mental response, as to something presented to the attention or encountered in experience (as, "his . . . mental *reaction* before a new experience": J. Conrad's "Rover," iii.); also, action in opposition, as to a force; specif., a force called into existence along with another force, being equal and opposite to it; also, action in a reverse direction or manner; a return to the opposite physical condition, as after shock, exhaustion, or chill; a reverse movement or tendency, as toward a previous state of affairs, esp. in politics (as, "A *reaction* was to be attempted in favor of Don John and of Catholicism": Motley's "Dutch Republic," v. 4).—**re-ac′tion-a-ry** (-ą-ri). **I.** *a.* Of, pertaining to, marked by, or favoring reaction, as in politics. **II.** *n.*; pl. *-ries* (-riz). One who favors or inclines to reaction; esp., one who seeks to reverse political action or progress.—**re-ac'tion-ist**, *n.* A reactionary.—**re-ac'tive**, *a.* Tending to react; pertaining to or characterized by reaction.—**re-ac-tiv-i-ty** (rē-ak-tiv'i-ti), *n.*

read (rēd), *v. t.; read* (red), *reading.* [ME. *reden*, < AS. *rǣdan*, counsel, advise, deliberate, consider, interpret, read, = OS. *rādan* = OHG. *rātan* (G. *raten*) = Icel. *rādha* = Goth. *-rēdan*, all used orig. of taking or giving counsel: cf. *rede*.] To counsel† or advise†: also, to guess†, make out†, or tell†; discover or explain the meaning of (a riddle, a dream, etc.); foresee, foretell, or predict (as, to *read* a person's fortune); also, to inspect or observe, and apprehend the indication or meaning of (signs, symbols, etc.); esp., to observe, and apprehend the meaning of (something written, printed, etc.); peruse (a letter, book, etc.); sometimes, to peruse books, etc., written in (a particular language), or have such knowledge of (a language) as to be able to understand things written in it; of the blind, to apprehend the meaning of (signs, characters, etc.) otherwise than with the eyes, as by means of the fingers; hence, in general, to make out the significance of, by scrutiny or observation (as, to *read* the sky; to *read* the signs of the times); make out the character, etc., of (a person, etc.), as by the interpretation of outward signs (as, "She had not *read* him right": H. James's "Portrait of a Lady," xlii.); also, to understand or take (something read or observed) in a particular way; also, to introduce (something not expressed or directly indicated) into what is read or considered, by one's manner of understanding or interpreting it; also, to adopt or give as a reading in a particular passage (as, for 'fail,' a misprint, *read* 'fall'; for 'one thousand' another version *reads* 'ten thousand'); also, to register or indicate, as a thermometer or other instrument does; also, to study, or make a study of, as by perusing books (as, to *read* law); also, to learn by perusal (as, "I have *read* the cause of his effects in Galen": Shakspere's "2 Henry IV.," i. 2. 133); learn or discern as if by perusal (as, "They . . . felt themselves in the presence of beings who seemed to have the power of *reading* the thoughts scarcely formed in their bosoms," Prescott's "Conquest of Mexico," iii. 7; "He *read* treachery in the very outline of this scheme, as stated by the Khan," De Quincey's "Revolt of the Tartars"); also, to peruse, and utter aloud; render in speech (something written, printed, etc.: as, to *read* a proposed measure before a legislative body in formally submitting it; "The company assembled at the theatre to hear Royce Oliphant *read* his play," L. Merrick's "Actor-Manager," v.); also, to impart or teach by or as by reading aloud†; also, to relate† or tell†; also, to bring, put, etc., by reading (as, to *read* one's self to sleep). See *rede, v.*—**to read one a lecture** or **a lesson**, fig., to give one a lecture or lesson by way of admonition or rebuke.—**to read one's self in,** in the Church of England, to enter upon office as incumbent of a benefice by reading publicly the Thirty-nine Articles and repeating the Declaration of Assent.—**to read out of,** to expel from (a party, organization, etc.), orig. by public declaration.—**read**, *v. i.* To inspect, and apprehend the meaning of, written or other signs or characters; read or peruse writing, printing, etc., or papers, books, etc.; occupy one's self seriously with reading, or study (as, "He . . . was . . . set to *read* with the best private tutors that could be found": S. Butler's "Way of All Flesh," viii.); also, to obtain knowledge or learn of something by reading, or in the course of reading (as, "Who hath *read* or heard Of any kindred action like to this?" Shakspere's "King John," iii. 4. 13); also, to admit of being read, esp. properly or well; produce a certain impression on being read (as, "The gallant sailor's harangue *reads* as if it had been dressed up for him either before or after delivery": Besant's "Coligny," vii.); have a certain wording, or be in effect when read (as, the passage *reads* thus); admit of being read or interpreted (as stated: as, a rule that *reads* two different ways); also, to utter aloud, or render in speech, written or printed words that one is perusing (as, to *read* to a person); give a public reading or recital; also, to give instruction by reading something aloud†.—**to read between the lines**, to discover a meaning, implication, purpose, etc., not explicitly expressed, in or as in something read.—**read** (red), *p. a.* Having knowledge gained by reading; well-informed

through reading, either on various or many subjects or in a particular field: as, "He was a young man, finely *read*" (Mrs. Stowe's "Oldtown Folks," xxx.); "He was deeply *read* in the ancients" (Fielding's "Tom Jones," iii. 3). See *well-read.*—**read** (rēd), *n.* An act of reading or perusal; a spell of reading. [Colloq.]

read-a-ble (rē'da-bl), *a.* Capable of being read; legible; also, easy or interesting to read (as, a *readable* narrative; "*readable* extracts from new books," Arnold Bennett's "Clayhanger," i. 14).—**read-a-bil'i-ty** (-bil'i-ti), **read'a-ble-ness,** *n.*

read-er (rē'dėr), *n.* One who reads; one employed to read critically manuscripts, etc., offered for publication, in order to report on their merits (as, "The ideal publisher's *reader* should have two perfections — perfect taste and perfect knowledge of what the various kinds of other people deem to be taste": Arnold Bennett's "Truth about an Author," xiv.); one employed to read printers' proofs for correction, or a proof-reader; one authorized to read the lessons, etc., in a church service (cf. *lector*); a lecturer or instructor, as in certain universities; one who reads or recites before an audience, or an elocutionist; also, a school-book for instruction and practice in reading.—**read'er-ship,** *n.*

read-i-ly (red'i-li), *adv.* In a ready manner; willingly; promptly; quickly; easily.—**read'i-ness,** *n.*

read-ing (rē'ding), *n.* The action or practice of one who reads, or a single act or course of this; the extent to which one has read, or literary knowledge; ability to read; the utterance or recital of recorded words; a public recital; the form or version of a given passage in a particular text (as, the various *readings* of a passage in Shakspere); matter read or for reading, esp. with reference to its quality (as, "several books that had been excellent *reading* in their day": Hawthorne's "House of the Seven Gables," ix.); the indication of a graduated instrument; an interpretation given to anything (as, "She gave him her *reading* of the matter": Reade's "Cloister and the Hearth," lvi.); the rendering given to a dramatic part, musical composition, etc., by a particular person.—**read'ing=desk,** *n.* A desk adapted for use in reading, esp. by a person standing; in a church, a lectern.—**read'ing=room,** *n.* A room appropriated to reading, as in a library or a club.

re-ad-just (rē-a-just'), *v. t.* [See *re-.*] To adjust again or anew; rearrange.—**re-ad-just'er,** *n.*—**re-ad-just'ment,** *n.*

re-ad-mis-sion (rē-ad-mish'ǫn), *n.* [See *re-.*] Admission again or anew.

re-ad-mit (rē-ad-mit'), *v. t.; -mitted, -mitting.* [See *re-.*] To admit again.—**re-ad-mit'tance,** *n.*

read-y (red'i). [ME. *redi, rædig*, < AS. *rǣde, gerǣde*, akin to D. *ree, gereed*, G. *bereit*, Icel. *greidhr*, ready, Goth. *raidjan*, establish, order, appoint: cf. *graith* and *array.*] **I.** *a.*; compar. *readier*, superl. *readiest.* Completely prepared or in due condition for immediate action or use (as, troops or ships *ready* for battle; to make *ready* to start; clothes *ready* to be worn; dinner is *ready*; the report will be *ready* to-morrow); duly equipped, completed, adjusted, or arranged, as for the occasion or purpose; also, mentally prepared (as, to be *ready* for school examinations; *ready* for college); morally or spiritually prepared (as, not yet *ready* to die); willing (as, *ready* to forgive; "The spirit truly is *ready*, but the flesh is weak," Mark, xiv. 38); inclined, disposed, or apt (as, too *ready* to criticize others); in a mood (to do something hasty or violent: as, "Snarling . . . *Ready* to catch each other by the throat," Shakspere's "Richard III.," i. 3. 189); also, in such a condition as to be about, or likely or liable at any moment (to do something: as, to feel *ready* to faint; a tree *ready* to fall; a spark *ready* to burst into flame); also, prompt or quick in action, performance, manifestation, etc. (as, "Rome's *readiest* champions," Shakspere's "Titus Andronicus," i. 1. 151; *ready* assistance or sympathy; "relieving us of our rifles with *ready* politeness," Parkman's "Oregon Trail," viii.); prompt or quick in perceiving, comprehending, speaking, writing, etc., or proceeding from or showing such quickness (as, a *ready* intelligence; a *ready* tongue or speaker; a *ready* versifier; a *ready* retort; "endowed with *ready* eloquence," Motley's "Dutch Republic," ii. 6); also, immediately available for use (as, a *ready* resource; *ready* money, that is, cash, or some equivalent, as bank deposits, etc.); present or convenient (to hand, to the hand, etc.: as, "the creative powers that lie *ready* to man's hand," H. G. Wells's "Soul of a Bishop," ix.); of a way, path, etc., easy, short, or direct (as, "What *readiest* way would bring me to that place?" Milton's "Comus," 305: now usually or only fig.). **II.** *n.* Ready money (colloq.); also, the condition or position of being ready (as, to bring a rifle to the *ready*).—**read′y**, *v. t.*; readied, readying. To make ready; prepare.—**read′y=made′**, *a.* Made so as to be ready for immediate use; specif., made in readiness for sale to any purchaser, rather than made specially to order (as, *ready-made* garments or shoes; to buy a coat *ready-made*; hence, made, kept, or standing in readiness for any use or occasion (as, *ready-made* excuses; "They were . . . spies and agents *ready-made* for either party," Stevenson's "Master of Ballantrae," iii.).—**read′y=wit′ted**, *a.* Having a ready or quick wit or intelligence.

re-af-firm (rē-a̯-fėrm′), *v. t.* [See re-.] To affirm again or anew: as, "He . . . *reaffirmed* his original proposition" (Arnold Bennett's "Hilda Lessways," ii. 6).—**re-af-firm′-ance, re-af-fir-ma-tion** (rē-af-ėr-mā′shọn), *n.*—**re-af-firm′er**, *n.*

re-af-for-est (rē-a-for′est), *v. t.* [See re-.] To afforest anew; cover again with forest; reforest.—**re-af-for-es-ta′tion** (-es-tā′shọn), *n.*

re-a-gent (rē-ā′jẹnt), *n.* [See re-.] One who or that which reacts; specif., a substance which, on account of the chemical reactions it causes, is used in chemical analysis; a chemical agent.

re-al[1] (rē′a̯l), *a.* [OF. *real*, *reel* (F. *réel*), < ML. *realis*, < L. *res*, thing, object, matter, fact.] Being an actual thing, with objective existence (rather than merely imaginary or phantasmal: as, "Is 't real that I see?" Shakspere's "All's Well," v. 3. 307); existing independently of the mind or thought; also, existing or occurring as fact, or actual (rather than imaginary, ideal, or fictitious: as, *real* conditions; a *real* case, or a case taken from *real* life; a *real* event; a *real* experience); also, being actually such (rather than merely so called: as, the *real* summit of a mountain; a *real* victory; *real* help); literal (rather than figurative: as, "A kingdom they portend thee; but what kingdom, *Real* or allegorick, I discern not," Milton's "Paradise Regained," iv. 390); genuine, or not counterfeit or spurious (as, a *real* antique); not artificial (as, a *real* diamond); not imitation (as, *real* sealskin; *real* lace, hand-made lace); unfeigned or sincere (as, *real* interest or sympathy; "The general, in a well-feigned or *real* ecstasy, embraced him," Prescott's "Conquest of Mexico," iv. 3); true (rather than merely ostensible, nominal, or apparent: as, the *real* reason for an act; the *real* worth of an article; the *real* head of a house; the *real* situation of affairs); also, free from artificiality, affectation, or pretense (as, "They hated banter, wish'd for something *real*, A gallant fight, a noble princess": Tennyson's "Princess," Conclusion, 18); genuine in character, as persons; also, pertaining to or concerned with things; in *math.*, either rational or irrational; not imaginary; in *optics*, noting an image formed by the actual convergence of rays, as the image produced in a camera (opposed to *virtual*); in *law*, noting or pertaining to immovable property, as lands and tenements (opposed to *personal*: see phrase *real estate*, below).—**real estate**, land and whatever by nature or artificial annexation pertains to it as a part of it or as the means of its enjoyment, as minerals on or in the earth, standing or running water, growing trees, permanent buildings, and fences; also, ownership or property in lands, etc.—**re′al**[1], *n.* Something which is real or has a real existence; also, with *the*, that which is real or actually exists.—**re′al**[1], *adv.* Really; truly; quite; very: as, *real* good; *real* well; *real* soon; *real* glad. [Colloq. or prov.]

re-al[2] (rē′a̯l, Sp. rā-äl′), *n.*; pl. *reals*, Sp. *reales* (rā-ä′les). [Sp., lit. 'royal,' < L. *regalis*, E. *regal*.] A former Spanish silver coin and money of account, current also in Spanish-American countries, equal to one eighth of a peso, or about 12½ U. S.

Obverse. Reverse.
Silver Real of Isabella II., of Spain, 1864. — British Museum.

cents; also, a former Spanish monetary unit equal to one quarter of a peseta, or about 5 U. S. cents.

re-al-gar (rē-al′gär), *n.* [ME. *realgar*, through OF. or ML. < Ar. *rahj al-ghār*, 'powder of the mine.'] Arsenic disulphide, As_2S_2, found native as an orange-red mineral and also prepared artificially: used in pyrotechnics.

re-al-ism (rē′a̯l-izm), *n.* The philosophical doctrine that universals have a real, objective existence (cf. *nominalism* and *conceptualism*); also, the doctrine that objects of sense-perception have an objective existence independent of the consciousness to which they are presented (cf. *idealism*); also, the tendency to view or represent things as they really are; specif., the treatment of subjects in literature or art with fidelity to nature or to real life (as opposed to *idealism*: cf. *naturalism*); close resemblance in literature or art to what is real; also, attention to or concern with what is real (as, "With the inexorable *realism* of her sex she easily dismissed . . . theories, and accommodated herself to the fact": Arnold Bennett's "Hilda Lessways," iv. 2).—**re′al-ist**, *n.* An adherent of philosophical realism as distinguished from nominalism and conceptualism, or from idealism; also, one addicted to realism or the tendency to view or represent things as they really are; a writer or artist who treats subjects with fidelity to nature; also, one interested in or concerned with what is real rather than what is imaginary or theoretical.—**re-al-is′tic**, *a.* Of or pertaining to realists or realism in philosophy; also, pertaining to, characterized by, or given to the representation of things as they really are, or realism in literature or art (as, "The *realistic* novel, which was created by Defoe under George I., was already foreshadowed in the admirable character sketches of Addison," Lecky's "Hist. of Eng. in the 18th Century," i.; *realistic* painting; *realistic* writers); representing reality or life in a faithful, detailed, and often unsparing manner, as a description or a picture; also, interested in or concerned with what is real or practical.—**re-al-is′ti-cal-ly**, *adv.*

re-al-i-ty (rē-al′i-ti), *n.*; pl. *-ties* (-tiz). [ML. *realitas*.] The state or fact of being real, having actual existence, or having actually occurred (as, "Christianity . . . was actually received . . . upon the professed belief of the *reality* of these miracles": J. Butler's "Analogy of Religion," ii. 7); also, resemblance to what is real (as, "In the English plays alone is to be found . . . the *reality* of painting": Macaulay's "Essays," John Dryden); also, that which is real (as, "Like sweet *reality* among Dim visionary woes": Shelley's "Revolt of Islam," vii. 16); a real thing or fact (as, "to exchange chimeras of boundless grandeur for *realities* of little worth," Mrs. Shelley's "Frankenstein," iii.; "The bright ideas of to-day are the *realities* of to-morrow," H. G. Wells's "Italy, France, and Britain at War," iv. 1); also, the real nature of something (as, "From the look on her face rather than from her words, the full *reality* of her meaning came to Leila": Galsworthy's "Saint's Progress," ii. 5); the real state of affairs; also, that which constitutes the real or actual thing, as distinguished from that which is merely apparent (as, "Clive . . . applied . . . for a formal grant of the powers of which he already possessed the *reality*": Macaulay's "Essays," Lord Clive).—**in reality**, really; actually; in fact or truth: as, "a middle-aged gentleman dressed like Lord Lechford's stockbroker, but who was *in reality* his butler" (Arnold Bennett's "Pretty Lady," xxvi.).

re-al-iz-a-ble (rē′a̯l-ī-za̯-bl), *a.* Capable of being realized.

re-al-i-za-tion (rē′a̯l-i-zā′shọn), *n.* The act of realizing, or the state of being realized; the making or being made real of something imagined, planned, etc., or the result of such a process (as, the *realization* of a project); the act of forming a clear conception of the reality of something, or of grasping or understanding it clearly, or the conception formed; the conversion into cash or money of securities, assets, etc.; the obtaining or acquiring of money, a fortune, etc.

re-al-ize (rē′a̯l-īz), *v.*; *-ized*, *-izing*. [= F. *réaliser*.] **I.** *tr.* To make real, or give reality to (a fancy, dream, hope, fear, plan, etc.); sometimes, to be the reality answering to (a fancy, hope, etc.); also, to make realistic or lifelike, as a description or a picture; also, to present to the mind as if real, or bring vividly before the mind (as, "People's poring affectionately upon the past conversation of their deceased friends so *realizes* it to them, that they are capable of fancying . . . that they see them, talk to them, and are answered by them": Defoe's "Robinson Crusoe," ii. 1); also, to conceive or comprehend as real (as, to be unable to *realize* a friend's death); grasp or understand clearly (as, "Richard Baxter . . . labours to make his readers *realize* the condition of the eternally damned": W. H. Hudson's "Far Away and Long Ago," xxiii.); also, to convert into cash or money (as, to *realize* securities; to *realize* assets); also, to obtain or gain for one's self by trade, effort, etc. (as, "I bought him cheap . . . so I *realized* six hundred on him," Mrs. Stowe's "Uncle Tom's Cabin," i.; "any man who could by diligence and thrift *realise* a good estate," Macaulay's "Hist. of Eng.," i.); also, to bring a return, as upon sale or investment (as, the goods *realized* $1,000; the money *realizes* 6%; "The prices *realised* were disappointing to the executors," S. Butler's "Way of All Flesh," xxviii.). **II.** *intr.* To convert property into cash or money (as, "He *realised* with great prudence while this mine was still at its full vogue": Thackeray's "Pendennis," i. 2); also, to realize a profit (as, "I've . . . *realized* well on 'em": Mrs. Stowe's "Uncle Tom's Cabin," i.); bring a return, as upon sale (as, the property *realized* well).—**re'al-iz-er** (-ī-zėr), *n.*—**re'al-iz-ing**, *p. a.* That realizes; clear in apprehending or understanding (as, to have a *realizing* sense of one's danger).—**re'al-iz-ing-ly**, *adv.*

re-al-ly (rē'al-i), *adv.* In reality, or actually (as, to see things as they *really* are; that could not *really* happen; "a law, nominally for the removal of all religious disabilities, but *really* for the excluding of all Protestants from all offices," Macaulay's "Essays," Sir James Mackintosh); also, genuinely or truly (as, a *really* honest man; a *really* good thing; that is *really* extraordinary); often, as a parenthetic or independent word, indeed (used for slight emphasis, in surprise or protest, interrogatively, etc.: as, "You will do 't, sir, *really*," Shakspere's "Hamlet," v. 2. 132; well, *really*, this is going too far; "Nina lives at Regent's Park," he replied . . . 'Oh, *really?*" L. Merrick's "Conrad in Quest of His Youth," vi.).

realm (relm), *n.* [OF. *reialme* (F. *royaume*), through ML. < L. *regalis*, E. *regal*.] A royal domain, or kingdom (as, the *realm* of England; "thou, great Anna! whom three *realms* obey," Pope's "Rape of the Lock," iii. 7); hence, fig., the region, sphere, or domain within which anything rules or prevails (as, the *realm* of death, or of the dead; the *realm* of sleep or dreams; "the happy *realms* of light," Milton's "Paradise Lost," i. 85); the special province or field of something (as, the *realm* of botany or of physics); in general, a region (as, "In this bleak *realm* of upper air, nothing breathed, nothing grew": Hawthorne's "Twice-Told Tales," The Great Carbuncle); in *zoögeog.*, a prime division of the earth's surface, containing one or more regions; a zoölogical region of the first order.—**realm'less**, *a.* Without a realm.

re-al-ness (rē'al-nes), *n.* The state of being real; reality.

re-al-po-li-tik (rā-äl'pō-lē-tēk″), *n.* [G.] Political realism; the political policy of considering actual circumstances and needs rather than abstract doctrines.

re-al-schu-le (rā-äl'shö″lė), *n.; pl. -len* (-len). [G., 'real (practical) school.'] In Germany, a secondary school corresponding in grade to a gymnasium, and laying special stress upon scientific subjects and modern languages.

re-al-tor (rē'al-tor), *n.* [From *realty*; coined by C. N. Chadbourn, of Minneapolis, a member of the National Association of Real Estate Boards, and formally adopted by the Association in 1916.] In the U. S., etc., a real estate broker who is an active member of a real estate board affiliated with the National Association of Real Estate Boards, and as such is an affiliated member of the National Association, subject to its rules and regulations, and officially licensed to apply the term (realtor) to himself.

re-al-ty (rē'al-ti), *n.* [From *real¹*.] Reality†; also, sincerity† or honesty† (as, "That such resemblance of the Highest Should yet remain, where faith and *realty* Remain not": Milton's "Paradise Lost," vi. 115); also, real property or real estate.

ream¹ (rēm), *n.* [OF. *rayme* (F. *rame*), through Sp. < Ar. *rizmah*, bundle.] A quantity of paper, consisting of 20 quires or 480 (often 500) sheets, or, in the case of printing-paper, of 21½ quires or 516 sheets.

ream² (rēm), *n.* [AS. *rēam* = D. *room* = G. *rahm*, cream.] Cream; also, froth; foam. [Now Sc. and prov. Eng.]—**ream²**, *v. i.* To cream; froth; foam: as, "O sweetly then thou *reams* the horn in!" (Burns's "Scotch Drink," 50). [Now Sc. and prov. Eng.]

ream³ (rēm), *v. t.* [Cf. AS. *rȳman*, make room in, enlarge, < *rūm*, E. *room*.] To enlarge (a hole or opening) by means of an instrument, esp. a rotating cutting tool; subject to or remove by the action of a reamer.—**ream'er**, *n.* One who or that which reams; a tool for reaming.

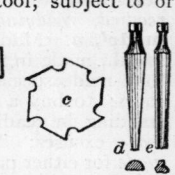

Reamers.— *a* and *b*, machinists' reamers; *c*, section of fluted reamer; *d* and *e*, flat-sided reamers, or broaches.

re-an-i-mate (rē-an'i-māt), *v. t.* [See *re-.*] To animate anew; restore to life, or resuscitate (as, "The Indian laboured to *reanimate* his master's body": Stevenson's "Master of Ballantrae," xii.); give fresh vigor, spirit, or courage to (as, to *reanimate* weary faculties; to *reanimate* disheartened troops); stimulate to renewed activity (as, to *reanimate* industries or trade).—**re-an-i-ma'tion** (-mā'shon), *n.*

re-an-nex (rē-a-neks'), *v. t.* [See *re-.*] To annex again, as territory that has been disjoined: as, "Saint Quentin, which . . . had been a Flemish town, was to be *re-annexed*" (Motley's "Dutch Republic," i. 2).—**re-an-nex-a-tion** (rē-an-ek-sā'shon), *n.*

reap (rēp), *v.* [AS. *rīpan.*] **I.** *tr.* To cut (grain, etc.) with a sickle or other implement or a machine, as in harvest (as, "With his sickle keen, He *reaps* the bearded grain": Longfellow's "Reaper and the Flowers"); hence, to gather or take (a crop, harvest, etc.); fig., to get as a return, recompense, or result (as, to *reap* large profits; "a piece of virtue of which he was now *reaping* the reward," S. Butler's "Way of All Flesh," xvi.; "Suing For peace, *reap* nothing but repulse and hate," Milton's "Samson Agonistes," 966); also, to gather the crop or yield from (as, to *reap* a field; "We'll *reap* the teeming waters As at home they *reap* the plain!" Whittier's "Fishermen"). **II.** *intr.* To reap grain, etc.; gather a harvest; fig., to get or receive the return for what one has done (as, "Let us not be weary in well doing: for in due season we shall *reap*, if we faint not": Gal. vi. 9).—**reap'a-ble**, *a.* That may be reaped.—**reap'er**, *n.* One who reaps; also, a machine for cutting standing grain; a reaping-machine.—**reap'ing-ma-chine″**, *n.* Any of various machines for reaping grain, often fitted with a device for automatically throwing out the cut grain at regular intervals.

re-ap-par-el (rē-a-par'el), *v. t.; -eled* or *-elled, -eling* or *-elling.* [See *re-.*] To apparel or clothe again or anew.

re-ap-pa-ri-tion (rē-ap-a-rish'on), *n.* [See *re-.*] An appearing again; reappearance.

re-ap-pear (rē-a-pēr'), *v. i.* [See *re-.*] To appear again, as after disappearance or absence: as, "See! the dull stars roll round and *reappear*" (Pope's "Dunciad," iii. 322).—**re-ap-pear'ance**, *n.*

re-ap-ply (rē-a-plī'), *v. t. or i.; -plied, -plying.* [See *re-.*] To apply again.—**re-ap-pli-ca-tion** (rē-ap-li-kā'shon), *n.*

re-ap-point (rē-a-point'), *v. t.* [See *re-.*] To appoint again or anew.—**re-ap-point'ment**, *n.*

re-ap-por-tion (rē-a-pôr'shon), *v. t.* [See *re-.*] To apportion again or anew.—**re-ap-por'tion-ment**, *n.*

re-ap-proach (rē-a-prōch'), *v. i. or t.* [See *re-.*] To approach again.

re-ap-pro-pri-ate (rē-a-prō'pri-āt), *v. t.; -ated, -ating.* [See *re-.*] To appropriate again.—**re-ap-pro-pri-a'tion** (-ā'-shon), *n.*

rear¹ (rēr), *v.* [AS. *rǣran*, raise: see *raise.*] **I.** *tr.* To raise to an upright position, or set upright (as, to *rear* a ladder or a flag-pole); raise (a person) to an erect or standing posture (as, "Gently *rear'd* By the angel, on thy feet thou stood'st at last," Milton's "Paradise Lost," xi. 758: now prov. Eng.); raise (itself) on the hind legs, as an animal; also, to raise by building, erect, or build (as, to *rear* a temple, a tower, or an altar; "They *reared* the marble-pillared wall That fenced the mansion round," Holmes's "Agnes," i.);

raise by heaping or casting up (as, to *rear* a cairn; "Heiliger-Lee was a wooded eminence, artificially *reared* by Premonstrant monks," Motley's "Dutch Republic," iii. 2; "that bold barrier of porphyritic rock which nature has *reared* around the Valley of Mexico," Prescott's "Conquest of Mexico," iii. 6); *fig.*, to set up or form as if by building, or found (as, to *rear* a system of philosophy; "What were the grounds on which I had *reared* this supposition?" C. B. Brown's "Wieland," xiv.); raise up, or cause to arise, as into being (as, "From their ashes shall be *rear'd* A phœnix": Shakspere's "1 Henry VI.," iv. 7. 92); set going or in action† (as, to *rear* war); also, to bring up (young) to maturity with fostering care and support (as, "The child was taken by some wretched cottagers, who *reared* it as their own," Dickens's "Oliver Twist," li.; to *rear* a young animal as a pet); nurture or educate (a person); care for the breeding and growth of, or breed or raise (animals); promote the growth of (plants) by careful tending; also, to lift or hold up, elevate, or raise (as, a serpent *rears* its head; "the cabin . . . that *reared* its adobe chimney above the umbrage," Bret Harte's "Fool of Five Forks"); direct upward, as the eyes, steps, etc. (poetic); lift up (the voice, etc.: poetic: as, "How loudly his sweet voice he *rears!*" Coleridge's "Ancient Mariner," vii.). **II.** *intr.* To rise to an upright position; rise up; esp., to rise on the hind legs, as a horse or other animal (as, "The leopard . . . *reared* up on her two hind-legs, bolt upright": Defoe's "Captain Singleton," v.); hence, of persons, to start up in angry excitement, hot resentment, or the like (commonly with *up*); also, to rise high or tower aloft, as a building.

rear² (rēr), *a.* [AS. *hrēr*: cf. *rare²*.] Not thoroughly cooked; underdone; rare: said orig. of eggs, later also of meat, etc. [Now prov. Eng.]

rear³ (rēr), *n.* [For *arrear, n.*] The hindmost portion of an army, fleet, etc., or that part which moves or is placed last in order; the hindmost or back part of anything (lit. or fig.: as, "the very *rear* of civilisation," H. G. Wells's "Mr. Britling," i. 3. § 1); the back of anything, as opposed to the front; the space or position behind, or at the back of, anything (as, "The soldiers . . . fired upon them from the *rear*," Bancroft's "Hist. of the U. S.," Amer. Revolution, i. 8; "eagerness to place that perilous passage in their *rear*," H. Melville's "Moby-Dick," lxxxvii.).—**to bring up the rear,** to move onward as the hindmost or rear portion; form the rear part; come last in order.—**to hang on** (or **upon**) **one's rear,** to follow one closely, as in order to attack when opportunity offers.—**rear³,** *a.* Situated at or pertaining to the rear: as, the *rear* ranks; "At the *rear* door of the car there was no platform" (Tarkington's "Magnificent Ambersons," i.).—**rear'=ad'mi-ral,** *n.* A naval officer next in rank below a vice-admiral.—**rear'=end',** *a.* At the rear end: said of collisions between trains, etc., as where the rear of one train is struck by the head of another.

rear-er (rēr'ėr), *n.* One who or that which rears.

rear=guard (rēr'gärd), *n.* A part of an army detached from the main body to bring up and guard the rear, esp. in a retreat.

re-ar-gue (rē-är'gū), *v. t.*; *-gued, -guing.* [See *re-*.] To argue over again.—**re-ar'gu-ment,** *n.*

rear-horse (rēr'hôrs), *n.* [See *rear¹, v. i.*] A mantis (insect).

rear-arm (rē-ärm'), *v. t.* [See *re-*.] To arm again; esp., to furnish with new or better weapons.—**re-ar'ma-ment** (-är'ma-ment), *n.*

rear-most (rēr'mōst), *a. superl.* Farthest in the rear; last of all.

rear-mouse (rēr'mous), *n.* See *reremouse.*

re-ar-range (rē-a-rānj'), *v. t.* [See *re-*.] To arrange anew: as, "No one should lay a hand on it to *rearrange* what he had once arranged" (Arnold Bennett's "Clayhanger," i. 6). —**re-ar-range'ment,** *n.*

rear-ward¹ (rēr'wȧrd), *n.* [ME. *rerewarde*: cf. *ward, n.*] The part of an army or fleet which is stationed at the rear; the rear. [Archaic.]

rear-ward² (rēr'wȧrd), *adv.* and *a.* [See *-ward*.] Toward or in the rear.

re-as-cend (rē-a-send'), *v. i.* or *t.* [See *re-*.] To ascend again.—**re-as-cen'sion** (-sen'shon), *n.* The act of re-

ascending.—**re-as-cent'** (-sent'), *n.* The act of reascending; also, a rise, as of ground, following a descent.

rea-son (rē'zn), *n.* [OF. F. *raison*, < L. *ratio(n-)*, reckoning, account, relation, respect, ground or motive, reason, reasoning, reasonableness, < *reri* (pp. *ratus*), reckon, calculate, think, judge: cf. *rate²* and *ratio*.] A ground or motive for a belief, course of action, or the like (as, I have my own *reasons* for thinking or doing this; "He made a voyage to Grand Cairo for no other *reason*, but to take the measure of a pyramid," Addison, in "Spectator," 101); a statement in justification or explanation of belief or action (as, "I have no other but a woman's *reason*; I think him so because I think him so": Shakspere's "Two Gentlemen of Verona," i. 2. 23); hence, a statement†, speech†, or remark†; also, a ground or cause, as for a fact, procedure, event, etc. (as, the *reasons* for a person's success; "There was no *reason* why they should not jog along, even if they hated each other," Galsworthy's "Man of Property," xix.; the *reason* for an accident); also, the intellectual faculty; that kind and degree of intelligence which distinguishes man from the brutes; the mental powers concerned with drawing conclusions or inferences, or with reasoning; in the use of Kant, the faculty by which we attain the knowledge of first principles, as distinguished from *understanding*; also, normal or sound powers of mind, or sanity (as, "a broken old man, bereft of *reason*": W. H. Hudson's "Purple Land," xxix.); sane or sensible mental attitude, as with reference to a matter (as, to bring a person to *reason*); sound judgment or good sense (as, "I wish you'd write to her and put some *reason* into her": Arnold Bennett's "Hilda Lessways," iii. 1); sensible, rational, or reasonable action or procedure (as, "It is not *reason* that we should leave the word of God": Acts, vi. 2); sensible speech or advice (as, to be willing to listen to *reason*); also, reasonable or proper treatment†, or justice†; also, the quality or fact of being sensible or reasonable (as, "Methinks there is much *reason* in his sayings": Shakspere's "Julius Cæsar," iii. 2. 113); in *logic*, a premise of an argument, esp. the minor premise when placed after the conclusion.—**by reason of,** on account of; because of: as, "I cannot go so fast as I would, *by reason of* this burden that is on my back" (Bunyan's "Pilgrim's Progress," i.).—**in reason,** in accordance with reason; justly or properly (as, "to show how, *in reason*, they ought to behave": J. Butler's "Analogy of Religion," ii. 8); within the limits prescribed by reason (as, I will do anything *in reason*; to be willing to pay any sum *in reason*).—**reason of state,** a political motive for some action or measure on the part of a ruler, government, or public officer, esp. a motive that it is not expedient to set forth publicly.—**to stand to reason.** See under *stand, v. i.*—**rea'son,** *v.* [OF. *raisoner* (F. *raisonner*), < ML. *rationare*, reason, argue, discourse, < L. *ratio(n-)*.] **I.** *intr.* To present reasons warranting or explaining belief or action (as, "They *reasoned* among themselves, saying, It is because we have taken no bread": Mat. xvi. 7); often, to urge reasons which should determine belief or action, as in discussing matters or in remonstrating with a person; also, to hold discourse†, or talk† (as, "I *reason'd* with a Frenchman yesterday, Who told me . . .": Shakspere's "Merchant of Venice," ii. 8. 27); also, to exercise the faculty or powers of reason; draw conclusions or inferences from facts or premises; think or argue in a logical manner. **II.** *tr.* To reason about or discuss (*what, why,* etc.: as, "I will not *reason* what is meant hereby," Shakspere's "Richard III.," i. 4. 94); consider or treat argumentatively (as, to *reason* a point); also, to think out (something) logically (often with *out*: as, to *reason out* a problem); also, to support with reasons, or by reasoning or argument; also, to conclude or infer (*that*); also, to bring, persuade, etc., by reasoning or argument (as, "Don't fancy that men *reason* themselves into convictions": Kingsley's "Yeast," x.).

rea-son-a-ble (rē'zn-a-bl), *a.* [OF. F. *raisonnable*.] Endowed with reason, or rational (as, "a *reasonable* creature": Shakspere's "Much Ado about Nothing," i. 1. 71); also, having or exercising sound judgment, or sensible (as, "No objections against any of these parts can be insisted upon by *reasonable* men": J. Butler's "Analogy of Religion," i. 7); amenable to reason, or sensibly restrained or temperate (as,

"He'll calm down and get more *reasonable* in time," A. S. M. Hutchinson's "If Winter Comes," iv. 3; "if you'll only be *reasonable* a moment, Lily," W. Churchill's "Modern Chronicle," ii. 8); sometimes, not extravagant or excessive in demands; not asking too much; also, agreeable to reason or sound judgment, or not irrational or absurd (as, a *reasonable* supposition; a *reasonable* choice); also, not exceeding the limit prescribed by reason, or not excessive (as, one's *reasonable* wants; *reasonable* terms; fair or just (as, "All . . . forage . . . is to be taken for the use of the army, and a *reasonable* price paid for the same": B. Franklin's "Autobiography," xi.); moderate, as charges or prices, or moderate in price, as goods, etc.—**rea′son-a-ble-ness**, *n.*—**rea′son-a-bly**, *adv.*

rea-son-er (rē′zn-ėr), *n.* One who reasons.

rea-son-ing (rē′zn-ing), *n.* The act or process of one who reasons; esp., the process of drawing conclusions or inferences from facts or premises.

rea-son-less (rē′zn-les), *a.* Not endowed with reason, or not rational (as, *reasonless* creatures); also, lacking reason, sound judgment, or good sense; also, not agreeable to reason; without reason.—**rea′son-less-ly**, *adv.*—**rea′son-less-ness**, *n.*

re-as-sem-ble (rē-a̱-sem′bl), *v. t.* or *i.* [See *re*-.] To assemble again.—**re-as-sem′blage** (-blāj), *n.*

re-as-sert (rē-a̱-sėrt′), *v. t.* [See *re*-.] To assert again.—**re-as-ser′tion** (-sėr′shǫn), *n.*

re-as-sign (rē-a̱-sīn′), *v. t.* [See *re*-.] To assign anew.—**re-as-sign′ment**, *n.*

re-as-sume (rē-a̱-sūm′), *v. t.* [See *re*-.] To assume or take again or anew; resume.—**re-as-sump′tion** (-sump′shǫn), *n.*

re-as-sure (rē-a̱-shör′), *v. t.* [See *re*-.] To assure again or anew; esp., to restore (a person, etc.) to assurance or confidence (as, "His confidence *reassured* me": W. H. Hudson's "Green Mansions," xviii.); also, to reinsure.—**re-as-sur′ance** (-shör′a̱ns), *n.*—**re-as-sur′ing-ly**, *adv.*

re-a-ta (rē-ä′tä), *n.* [Also *riata*; < Sp. *reata*, rope.] A lariat.

Ré-au-mur (rā-ō-mür′), *a.* Designating, or in accordance with, the thermometric scale introduced by René Antoine Ferchault de Réaumur (1683–1757), a French physicist, in which the freezing-point of water is at 0°, and the boiling-point at 80°. Abbreviated R.

reave (rēv), *v. t.*; *reaved* or *reft*, *reaving*. [AS. *reáfian* = D. *rooven* = G. *rauben* = Goth. *-raubōn*, rob: cf. *rob*.] To deprive forcibly, strip, or rob (as, "to *reave* the orphan of his patrimony": Shakspere's "2 Henry VI.," v. 1. 187); also, to take forcible possession of; take or carry away by force; take away or remove. [Archaic.]—**reav′er**, *n.*

reb (reb), *n.* Shortened form of *rebel*. [Colloq.]

re-bab (rē̱-bäb′), *n.* [Pers. and Ar. *rabāb*.] An ancient stringed musical instrument of Oriental origin, having typically either a pear-shaped or a long, narrow body with a vaulted back and without a distinct neck, played at first with the fingers and later with a bow; also, in modern times, any of various stringed instruments played with a bow, in use among the Mohammedans of northern Africa. Cf. *rebec*.

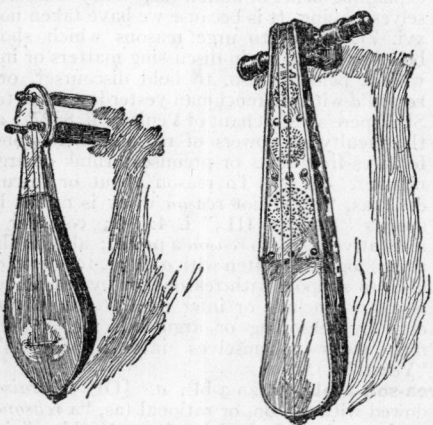

Forms of Rebab. — Originals in the Stearns Collection, University of Michigan.

re-bap-tize (rē-bap-tīz′), *v. t.* [See *re*-.] To baptize again

or anew; also, to baptize by a new name; rename.—**re-bap′tism**, *n.*

re-bate¹ (rē̱-bāt′), *n.* [Var. of *rabbet*.] A rabbet (cut, groove, or recess).—**re-bate′¹**, *v. t.* or *i.*; *-bated*, *-bating.* To rabbet.

re-bate² (rē̱-bāt′), *v. t.*; *-bated*, *-bating.* [OF. *rabatre* (F. *rabattre*), beat or put down, < *re-* (< L. *re-*), back, + *abatre*, E. *abate.*] To reduce, diminish, or lessen (now rare); also, to deduct (a certain amount), as from a total; allow as a discount or drawback; also, to make dull or blunt (as, "The broad belt . . . The point *rebated*, and repell'd the wound," Pope's tr. Homer's "Iliad," xi.: now rare).—**re-bate²** (rē̱-bāt′ or rē′bāt), *n.* Deduction or a discount, as from a sum to be paid; also, repayment, as of a part of charges; a drawback.—**re-bat′er** (-bā′tėr), *n.*

re-bec, **re-beck** (rē′bek), *n.* [F. *rebec*; from Ar.] A medieval musical instrument, derived from the Oriental rebab, having commonly a pear-shaped body and three strings, and played with a bow.

reb-el (reb′ḝl), *n.* [OF. F. *rebelle*, < L. *rebellis*, < *re-*, again, + *bellum*, war.] **I.** *a.* Resisting authority or law; rebellious; also, of or pertaining to rebels. **II.** *n.* One who refuses allegiance to, resists, or rises in arms against, the established or rightful government or ruler; hence, in general, one who or that which resists authority or control (as, "a *rebel* to her father and her God": Shelley's "Cenci," iv. 1. 90).—**re-bel** (rē̱-bel′), *v. i.*; *-belled*, *-belling.* [OF. F. *rebeller*, < L. *rebellare*, wage war again (as conquered people), < *re-*, again, + *bellare*, wage war, < *bellum*, war.] To rise in arms or active resistance against one's government or ruler; hence, to offer resistance against any authority; fig., to manifest or feel utter repugnance (as, "Her very soul *rebelled* at the thought": W. Churchill's "Modern Chronicle," ii. 8).—**re-bel′dom** (-dǫm), *n.* A region held or controlled by rebels; also, rebels collectively; also, rebellious conduct.—**re-bel′ler**, *n.*

re-bel-lion (rē̱-bel′yǫn), *n.* [L. *rebellio(n)-*, < *rebellis*: see *rebel*.] The act or an act of rebelling; open, organized, and armed resistance to one's government or ruler; an insurrection or revolt; resistance against or defiance of any authority or controlling power (as, "sullen *rebellion* against fate": Kipling's "Light That Failed," xii.).—**re-bel′lious** (-yus), *a.* Defying lawful authority; insubordinate; disposed to rebel; also, pertaining to or characteristic of rebels or rebellion; also, of things, resisting treatment; refractory.—**re-bel′lious-ly**, *adv.*—**re-bel′lious-ness**, *n.*

re-bind (rē-bīnd′), *v. t.*; pret. and pp. *-bound.* [See *re*-.] To bind (a book, etc.) again or anew.

re-birth (rē-bėrth′), *n.* [See *re*-.] Birth anew.

reb-o-ant (reb′ō-a̱nt), *a.* [L. *reboans* (-*ant*-), ppr. of *reboare*, < *re-*, back, + *boare*, bellow, roar.] Bellowing in return; resounding loudly: as, "The echoing dance Of *reboant* whirlwinds" (Tennyson's "Supposed Confessions of a Second-Rate Sensitive Mind," 97). [Poetic.]

re-boise-ment (rē-boiz′ment), *n.* [F., < *reboiser*, reforest, < *re-* (< L. *re-*), again, + *boiser*, plant with trees, < *bois*, wood: see *bush*¹.] The replanting of an area with trees; conversion into woodland; reforestation.

re-born (rē-bôrn′), *a.* [See *re*-.] Born anew.

re-bound (rē̱-bound′), *v.* [OF. F. *rebondir*, < *re-* (< L. *re-*), back, + *bondir*, E. *bound*².] **I.** *intr.* To bound or spring back from force of impact; also, to echo back, as sounds do (now rare); be filled with or emit echoes, or resound, as a place, etc. (now rare); also, to make repeated bounds or leaps (as, "Along the court the fiery steeds *rebound*": Pope's tr. Homer's "Odyssey," xv.). **II.** *tr.* To cause to bound back; cast back; also, to echo back (a sound: now rare).—**re-bound′**, *n.* The act of rebounding; recoil.

re-bo-zo (rā-bō′sō), *n.* [Sp.] A shawl or long scarf worn by Spanish-American women as a covering for the head and shoulders. See cut on following page.

re-breathe (rē-brēᴛʜ′), *v. t.* [See *re*-.] To breathe again.

re-broad-cast (rē-brôd′kȧst), *v. t.* or *i.* [See *re*-.] To broadcast again or anew; relay by broadcast (messages, speeches, etc., received from a broadcasting station).

re-buff (rē̱-buf′), *n.* [Obs. F. *rebuffe*, < It. *ributto*, < *ri-* (< L. *re-*), back, + *buffo*, a puff, blast.] A blunt or abrupt

---

che**k**, as to one making advances; a peremptory refusal of a request, offer, etc.; a snub; hence, a check to action or progress; also, a repelling blast (rare: see Milton's "Paradise Lost," ii. 936).—**re-buff'**, *v. t.* To give a rebuff to; check; repel: as, "He had . . . forgotten himself, had gone too far in his advances, and had been *rebuffed*" (Stevenson's "Master of Ballantrae," v.).

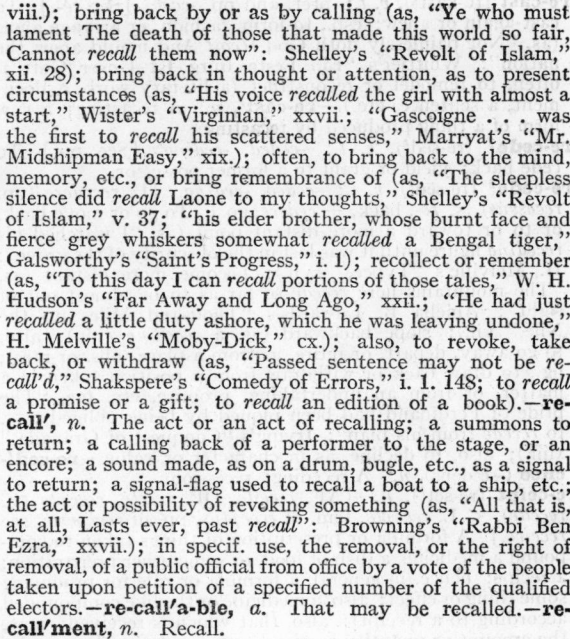

Rebozo.

re-build (rē-bild'), *v. t.*; pret. and pp. *-built.* [See *re-*.] To build again or anew; reconstruct.—**re-build'er**, *n.*

re-buk-a-ble (rē-bū'ka-bl), *a.* Deserving of rebuke.

re-buke (rē-būk'), *v.t.;-buked,-buking.* [OF. *rebuker, rebuchier,* repel, < *re-* (< L. *re-*), back, + *buchier, buschier,* strike.] To beat or force back†; repulse†; repress† or check†; also, to reprove or reprimand (as, "The men-at-arms . . . attempted to roam in quest of booty; but he called them back, and *rebuked* them severely": Irving's "Conquest of Granada," xii.); deliver reproof for, or censure (an action, etc.: as, "I must *rebuke* This drunkenness of triumph," Shelley's "Hellas," 928); fig., of things, to convey a reproof to (a person) or for (an action, etc.).—**re-buke'**, *n.* Reproof; a reprimand.—**re-buke'ful**, *a.* Full of rebuke; of a rebuking character, as words.—**re-buk'er** (-bū'kėr), *n.* —**re-buk'ing-ly**, *adv.*

re-bus (rē'bus), *n.*; pl. *rebuses.* [L., abl. pl. of *res,* thing; the original application of the word being in dispute.] An enigmatical representation of a word or phrase by means of pictures, symbols, etc., suggesting the word-elements or words: as, "For example, two gates and a head is a *rebus* for Gateshead" (H. G. Wells's "Outline of History," xviii. § 2).

Rebus of Bishop Oldham ("owldom"), Exeter Cathedral, England.

re-but (rē-but'), *v.*; *-butted, -butting.* [OF. F. *rebouter,* < *re-* (< L. *re-*), back, + *bouter,* E. *butt*[1].] **I.** *tr.* To drive back†; repel†; also, to give a check to; also, in *law,* to repel or refute by evidence or argument; oppose by contrary proof or by argument; hence, in general use, to refute or disprove (as, "Subsequent events have *rebutted* the calumny": H. Melville's "Omoo," lxxx.). **II.** *intr.* To draw back†; in *law,* to make an answer, as to a plaintiff's sur-rejoinder (as, "The plaintiff may answer the rejoinder by a sur-rejoinder; upon which the defendant may *rebut*": Blackstone's "Commentaries," III. 310).—**re-but'tal**, *n.* The act of rebutting, esp. in law.—**re-but'ter**[1], *n.* One who or that which rebuts.—**re-but'ter**[2], *n.* [OF. *rebouter,* inf., used as noun.] In *law,* an answer such as a defendant makes to a plaintiff's surrejoinder.

re-cal-ci-trant (rē-kal'si-trant), *a.* [L. *recalcitrans* (*-ant-*), ppr. of *recalcitrare:* see *recalcitrate.*] Making resistance to authority or control; not obedient or compliant; refractory: as, "to suspend the more *recalcitrant* ministers" (Green's "Short Hist. of the Eng. People," vii. 3); "his attempt to close a *recalcitrant* skylight" (W. Churchill's "Modern Chronicle," i. 12).—**re-cal'ci-trance**, *n.*

re-cal-ci-trate (rē-kal'si-trāt), *v. i.*; *-trated, -trating.* [L. *recalcitratus,* pp. of *recalcitrare,* lit. 'kick back,' < *re-,* back, + *calcitrare,* kick, < *calx,* heel.] To make resistance or opposition; be disobedient or refractory; show strong objection or repugnance.—**re-cal-ci-tra'tion** (-trā'shon), *n.*

re-ca-lesce (rē-ka-les'), *v. i.*; *-lesced, -lescing.* [L. *recalescere,* < *re-,* again, + *calescere,* grow hot, < *calere,* be hot.] To become hot again: said esp. of cooling iron, which glows with increased brilliancy upon passing certain temperatures.—**re-ca-les'cence** (-les'ens), *n.* The fact of recalescing.—**re-ca-les'cent**, *a.*

re-call (rē-kâl'), *v. t.* [See *re-*.] To call back, or summon to return (as, "He had given orders that the smaller fortresses should be dismantled and their garrisons *recalled,*" J. F. Kirk's "Charles the Bold," iii. 2; "The German Ambassador was *recalled,*" Mrs. Wharton's "Son at the Front,"

viii.); bring back by or as by calling (as, "Ye who must lament The death of those that made this world so fair, Cannot *recall* them now": Shelley's "Revolt of Islam," xii. 28); bring back in thought or attention, as to present circumstances (as, "His voice *recalled* the girl with almost a start," Wister's "Virginian," xxvii.; "Gascoigne . . . was the first to *recall* his scattered senses," Marryat's "Mr. Midshipman Easy," xix.); often, to bring back to the mind, memory, etc., or bring remembrance of (as, "The sleepless silence did *recall* Laone to my thoughts," Shelley's "Revolt of Islam," v. 37; "his elder brother, whose burnt face and fierce grey whiskers somewhat *recalled* a Bengal tiger," Galsworthy's "Saint's Progress," i. 1); recollect or remember (as, "To this day I can *recall* portions of those tales," W. H. Hudson's "Far Away and Long Ago," xxii.; "He had just *recalled* a little duty ashore, which he was leaving undone," H. Melville's "Moby-Dick," cx.); also, to revoke, take back, or withdraw (as, "Passed sentence may not be *recall'd,*" Shakspere's "Comedy of Errors," i. 1. 148; to *recall* a promise or a gift; to *recall* an edition of a book).—**re-call'**, *n.* The act or an act of recalling; a summons to return; a calling back of a performer to the stage, or an encore; a sound made, as on a drum, bugle, etc., as a signal to return; a signal-flag used to recall a boat to a ship, etc.; the act or possibility of revoking something (as, "All that is, at all, Lasts ever, past *recall*": Browning's "Rabbi Ben Ezra," xxvii.); in specif. use, the removal, or the right of removal, of a public official from office by a vote of the people taken upon petition of a specified number of the qualified electors.—**re-call'a-ble**, *a.* That may be recalled.—**re-call'ment**, *n.* Recall.

re-cant (rē-kant'), *v.* [L. *recantare* (pp. *recantatus*), < *re-,* back, + *cantare,* sing.] **I.** *tr.* To withdraw or disavow (a statement, etc.), esp. formally; retract; sometimes, to withdraw (a promise, etc.); renounce (a purpose, etc.). **II.** *intr.* To disavow an opinion, etc., esp. formally.—**re-can-ta-tion** (rē-kan-tā'shon), *n.* The act or an act of recanting; public renunciation.—**re-cant'er**, *n.*

re-cap (rē-kap'), *v. t.* [*re-* + *cap.*] To recondition (a worn automobile tire) by cementing on a strip of prepared rubber or camel back and subjecting to heat and pressure in a mold: usually applied to partial reconditionings—*top recapping* (top of tread only), *full recapping* (more complete). See *retreading.*

re-ca-pit-u-late (rē-ka-pit'ū-lāt), *v.*; *-lated, -lating.* [LL. *recapitulatus,* pp. of *recapitulare,* < L. *re-,* again, + *capitulum,* dim. of *caput,* head.] **I.** *tr.* To repeat or recite the heads, main points, or gist of (something already stated: as, to *recapitulate* an argument or a report); recite (heads, main points, etc.: as, "The heads of the previous conversation were *recapitulated* by Mr. Micklewham," Galt's "Ayrshire Legatees," v.; "His Majesty . . . was at the pains to *recapitulate* the sum of all I had spoken," Swift's "Gulliver's Travels," ii. 6); also, to recite or tell the main facts or particulars of, or recount concisely or briefly (actions, performances, experiences, occurrences, etc.: as, "The governors present, *recapitulating* their strifes with their assemblies, made answer," Bancroft's "Hist. of the U. S.," Amer. Revolution, i. 7); recite (main facts, particulars, etc.: as, "He began to *recapitulate* items in the catalogue of his escapades," H. G. Wells's "Mr. Britling," i. 4. § 5); in *biol.,* of a young animal, to repeat (ancestral evolutionary stages) in its development. **II.** *intr.* To recapitulate statements or matters; recount briefly something already said or done; in *biol.,* to repeat ancestral evolutionary stages.—**re-ca-pit-u-la'tion** (-lā'shon), *n.* [LL. *recapitulatio(n-).*] The act of recapitulating; a summary or brief recital; in *biol.,* the repetition of ancestral evolutionary stages in the development of a young animal.—**re-ca-pit'u-la-tive** (-lā-tiv), **re-ca-pit'u-la-to-ry** (-la-tō-ri), *a.* Pertaining to or characterized by recapitulation.—**re-ca-pit'u-la-tor** (-lā-tor), *n.*

re-cap-ture (rē-kap'tūr), *n.* [See *re-*.] The act of taking, or the fact of being taken, a second time; recovery or retaking by capture; specif., the taking by the government of a fixed part of all earnings in excess of a certain percentage of property value, as in the case of a railroad; also, something recaptured.—**re-cap'ture**, *v. t.* To capture again; recover by capture; specif., of the government, to take by recapture.

re-cast (rē-kȧst′), *v. t.*; pret. and pp. *-cast*. [See *re-*.] To cast again or anew; esp., to form, fashion, or arrange anew (as, "Not painlessly doth God *recast* And mould anew the nation": Whittier's "Ein Feste Burg Ist Unser Gott"); often, to remodel or reconstruct (a literary work, a document, a sentence, etc.).—**re-cast′**, *n.* A recasting; a new form of a thing produced by recasting.

re-cede¹ (rē-sēd′), *v. t.*; *-ceded, -ceding*. [See *re-*.] To cede back; yield or grant to a former possessor.

re-cede² (rē̇-sēd′), *v. i.*; *-ceded, -ceding*. [L. *recedere* (pp. *recessus*), < *re-*, back, + *cedere*, go.] To go or move back, or to or toward a more distant point (as, "I watched his *receding* figure until it was lost in the obscurity of the grove": H. Melville's "Typee," xvii.); become more distant (as, "The mountains here *recede* so far as to be almost out of sight": Amelia B. Edwards's "Thousand Miles up the Nile," vii.); slope backward (as, a *receding* chin); also, to go away, depart, or retire, as from a place (obs. or rare); fig., to draw back or withdraw from a position taken in a matter, or from an undertaking, promise, etc. (as, "The pride of Ferdinand had been piqued by being obliged . . . to *recede* from his plan": Irving's "Conquest of Granada," xliii.); also, to decline, as in character or value.—**re-ced′ence** (-sē′dens), *n.* A receding; recession.

re-ceipt (rē̇-sēt′), *n.* [AF. *receite*, OF. *recete, recepte* (F. *recette*), < L. *recepta*, fem. of *receptus*, pp. of *recipere*: see *receive*.] A formula or prescription of things taken to compound a medicine, a dish of food, or some other preparation; a recipe; hence, in general, a formula or rule for producing some thing or effect; also, a medicine or the like compounded according to a receipt†; also, that which is received; now, the amount or quantity received (commonly in *pl.*: as, "by authorizations to divert Government *receipts* before they ever reach the Treasury," A. W. Mellon's "Taxation," ii.); also, the act of receiving, or the state of being received; now, esp., the receiving of something into one's possession or custody (as, the *receipt* of money or goods; "the *receipt* of Benson's letter," G. Meredith's "Ordeal of Richard Feverel," xxi.); also, a written acknowledgment of having received money, goods, etc., specified; also, a place for receiving something, esp. money (obs. or hist.); also, capability of receiving, accommodating, or containing something†; capacity†.—**re-ceipt′**, *v.* **I.** *tr.* To give a receipt for (money, goods, etc.); also, to acknowledge in writing the payment of (a bill). **II.** *intr.* To give a receipt, as for money or goods.—**re-ceipt′or**, *n.* One who receipts; in *law*, a person to whom attached property is bailed.

re-ceiv-a-ble (rē̇-sē′va̤-bl), *a.* Capable of being received; fit for acceptance; specif., that is to be received as legal tender, as paper money; also, awaiting receipt of payment (as, bills *receivable*).

re-ceiv-al (rē̇-sē′val), *n.* The act of receiving.

re-ceive (rē̇-sēv′), *v.*; *-ceived, -ceiving*. [OF. *receveir* (F. *recevoir*), < L. *recipere* (pp. *receptus*), take back, take to one's self, receive, < *re-*, back, + *capere*, take.] **I.** *tr.* To take into one's hand or one's possession (something offered or delivered); take from another by hearing or listening (as, "A priest . . . *received* his confession": Green's "Short Hist. of the Eng. People," ix. 6); also, to take with acquiescence, or accept (something offered or presented); also, to permit one's self to be subjected to (as, "This is a nation that obeyeth not the voice of the Lord their God, nor *receiveth* correction": Jer. vii. 28); submit to; endure; also, to take by yielding to or being affected by something impressed, applied, or transmitted (as, "His tenderer cheek *receives* her soft hand's print," Shakspere's "Venus and Adonis," 353; a device for *receiving* a record); also, to become the support of, or sustain (as, "Make broad thy shoulders to *receive* my weight": Tennyson's "Passing of Arthur," 332); catch or intercept, or stand the force of (something falling or thrown, a blow, etc.); also, to take in or admit, as a receptacle; afford space or accommodation for; hold or contain; also, to take into the mind, or apprehend mentally; also, to admit (a person) to a place; give accommodation or shelter to (as, "Take heed what guests you *receive*": Shakspere's "2 Henry IV.," ii. 4. 101); also, to admit to personal relations, or to familiar or friendly intercourse; grant an audience to (a person); be at home to

(visitors); greet or welcome (guests, etc.) upon arriving (as, "George, white-gloved . . . stood with his mother and the Major . . . to '*receive*' the guests": Tarkington's "Magnificent Ambersons," iv.); also, to admit to a state or condition, a privilege, membership, etc.; accept in some capacity (as, "Why then Didst thou at first *receive* me for thy husband?" Milton's "Samson Agonistes," 883); also, to take, accept, regard, etc., in a particular manner (as, "How hath she *Received* his love?" Shakspere's "Hamlet," ii. 2. 129; "I did not *receive* all his assertions as gospel," Smollett's "Humphry Clinker," Sept. 20); also, to accept as authoritative, valid, true, or approved (as, a principle universally *received*; a *received* opinion or method); also, to have given to one's self, or get (as, to *receive* rent for a property); have delivered or brought to one's self (as, to *receive* a letter); get or learn by communication from others (as, to *receive* notice; to *receive* news); also, to have (something) bestowed, conferred, etc. (as, to *receive* power to do something; to *receive* a name); meet with, or experience (as, to *receive* attention); suffer or undergo (as, to *receive* an affront); have inflicted upon one (as, to *receive* a blow, a wound, or a broken arm); have imposed upon one (as, to *receive* sentence). **II.** *intr.* To receive (or take, accept, admit, get, etc.) something (as, "Every one . . . shall *receive* according to his deserts": J. Butler's "Analogy of Religion," i. 7); be or become a receiver or recipient; specif., to receive the eucharist; also, to receive visitors or guests (as, "The van der Luydens . . . are the most powerful influence in New York society . . . they *receive* very seldom": Mrs. Wharton's "Age of Innocence," ix.); hold a reception.—**re-ceiv′er**, *n.* One who receives; esp., one who receives something on behalf of others; one appointed to receive money due; specif., a person appointed by a court to take charge of the property of others, as pending litigation; also, one who, for purposes of profit or concealment, knowingly receives stolen goods; also, that which receives; a receptacle; a device or apparatus for receiving or holding something; a vessel for collecting and containing a gas, a distillate, or the like; the glass vessel from which the air is exhausted in an air-pump; a device which receives electrical signals, waves, or the like, and renders them perceptible to the senses, as the part of a telephone held to the ear.—**re-ceiv′er-ship**, *n.* The office of a receiver; also, the condition of being in the hands of a receiver.—**re-ceiv′ing=ship**, *n.* A vessel stationed in a harbor to receive and provide for recruits to the navy until they can be transferred to regular service.

re-cen-cy (rē′sen-si), *n.* The state of being recent.

re-cense (rē̇-sens′), *v. t.*; *-censed, -censing*. [L. *recensere*, < *re-*, again, + *censere*, tax, rate, estimate.] To review; revise; now, esp., to revise (a text).—**re-cen′sion** (-sen′shon), *n.* [L. *recensio(n-)*, < *recensere*.] A review or survey (now rare); esp., the critical or methodical revision of a text; a version of a text resulting from such revision. —**re-cen′sion-ist, re-cen′sor**, *n.*

re-cent (rē′sent), *a.* [L. *recens* (*recent-*), recent.] Of late occurrence, appearance, or origin, or lately happening, done, made, etc. (as, *recent* events; a *recent* book; a *recent* theory; a *recent* wound); still fresh or unchanged by time (as, *recent*, or newly gathered, plants or specimens); lately or newly come (poetic: as, "With disorder'd charms, All heaven beholds me *recent* from thy arms," Pope's tr. Homer's "Iliad," xiv.); also, not long past, as a period, or belonging to such a period, as a race; not remote or primitive; [*cap.*] in *geol.*, noting or pertaining to the later division of the Quaternary period or system, succeeding the Pleistocene, and regarded as the present or existing geological division. —**re′cent-ly**, *adv.*—**re′cent-ness**, *n.*

re-cept (rē′sept), *n.* [L. *receptum*, neut. of *receptus*, pp. of *recipere*: see *receive*.] In *psychol.*, an idea formed by the repetition of similar percepts, as successive percepts of the same object.

re-cep-ta-cle (rē̇-sep′ta̤-kl), *n.* [L. *receptaculum*, < *recipere*: see *receive*.] That which serves to receive or hold something; a repository; a container; specif., in *bot.*, the modified or expanded portion of an axis, which bears the organs of a single flower or the florets of a flower-head (see cut on following page).— **re-cep-tac-u-lar** (rē-sep-tak′ū-lär), *a.*

re-cep-ti-ble (rē-sep′ti-bl), a. [LL. *receptibilis*.] That may be received; receivable; also, capable of receiving.

re-cep-tion (rē-sep′shǫn), n. [OF. F. *reception*, < L. *receptio(n-)*, < *recipere*: see **receive**.] The act of receiving, or the fact of being received; a taking or getting by delivery or transfer; a taking by sustaining or intercepting; a taking in, admitting, holding, or containing;

Various forms of Receptacle (*r*). — *a*, dandelion (*Taraxacum taraxacum*); *b*, strawberry (*Fragaria elatior* or *moschata*) (longitudinal section); *c*, cleome (*Cleome serrulata*) (longitudinal section); *d*, geranium (*Geranium maculatum*); *e*, sweetbrier (*Rosa rubiginosa*) (longitudinal section).

admission to the mind; acceptance; as authoritative, valid, true, or approved; esp., the receiving of persons, etc., into a place, state, or company; the receiving of persons formally or ceremoniously, as a court, social, or other function; a function or occasion when persons are formally received (as, to hold a *reception*); also, a receiving or being received in a particular manner, or kind of reception (as, a book meets with a favorable *reception*); also, capacity for receiving†.—**re-cep′tion-ist**, n. A person employed to receive callers, as in an office.—**re-cep′tion-room**, n. A room for the reception of visitors.

re-cep-tive (rē-sep′tiv), a. [ML. *receptivus*.] Having the quality of receiving, taking in, or admitting; pertaining to or of the nature of reception; esp., able or quick to receive ideas, etc. (as, a *receptive* mind); sometimes, having, or characterized by, a disposition to receive a suggestion, offer, or the like with favor (as, we did not find him *receptive*, or in a *receptive* frame of mind).—**re-cep′tive-ly**, adv.—**re-cep′tive-ness, re-cep-tiv-i-ty** (rē-sep-tiv′i-ti), n.

re-cep-tor (rē-sep′tǫr), n. [L., a receiver.] A receiver; specif., a telephone receiver; the receiving apparatus of a wireless telegraph.

re-cess (rē-ses′, also rē′ses), n. [L. *recessus*, < *recedere*: see *recede*[2].] The act of receding, going back, or retreating (as, the access and *recess* of the tide); also, departure, as from a place†; retirement† or seclusion†; also, withdrawal or cessation for a time from the usual occupation, work, or activity, or a period of such withdrawal (as, "In every *recess* from the occupations of the field . . . he found himself solitary and forlorn": Godwin's "Caleb Williams," vi.); specif., an interval of cessation from duty of a legislative body, a jury, or the like (as, "Before the Revolution the sessions of Parliament were short and the *recesses* long": Macaulay's "Essays," Sir William Temple); in schools, a short intermission for recreation during the course of the day (as, "During that interval known as *recess*, she [a teacher] became aware . . . that they were playing a new game outside": Wister's "Virginian," xxxiii.); also, a receding part or space; an indentation in a line or extent of coast, hills, forest, etc. (as, "We . . . faced . . . across the clear pool to where its upper end . . . lay in a deep *recess* of the woods": G. W. Cable's "Cavalier," xxxiii.); a bay or alcove in a room or any walled place (as, "He sat him down in one of the deep *recesses* formed by a window which lighted the great Gothic hall": Scott's "Quentin Durward," xix.); a niche or hollow in a wall or the like (as, "his dwelling a

recess in some rude rock": Cowper's "Truth," 79); also, a place of retirement or seclusion, or a retreat (obs. or archaic: as, "Departure from this happy place, our sweet *Recess*," Milton's "Paradise Lost," xi. 304); a retired or inner place or part (now commonly in *pl.*, and often fig.: as, "In the *recesses* of the palace her mysterious figure was at once invisible and omnipresent," Lytton Strachey's "Queen Victoria," iii.; "eyes that seemed willing to penetrate the *recesses* of his most secret thoughts," Cooper's "Prairie," xxvi.).—**re-cess′**, v. **I.** *tr.* To place or set in a recess (as, "The sight of the hotel flower-stall *recessed* on the left reminded G. J. of Christine's desire": Arnold Bennett's "Pretty Lady," xiii.); also, to set or form as or like a recess (as, "Beside Fairway's dwelling was an open space *recessed* from the road": Hardy's "Return of the Native," vi. 1); also, to make a recess or recesses in (as, to *recess* a wall). **II.** *intr.* To take a recess, as a legislative body or the like; adjourn for a time.

re-ces-sion[1] (rē-sesh′ǫn), n. [See *re-*.] Cession or ceding back, as to a former possessor.

re-ces-sion[2] (rē-sesh′ǫn), n. [L. *recessio(n-)*, < *recedere*: see *recede*[2].] The act of receding; a going back or becoming more distant (as, "The young man watched [from a departing boat] the spectacular *recession* of the city": Howells's "Rise of Silas Lapham," vi.); departure or retirement; withdrawal.—**re-ces′sion-al. I.** a. Of or pertaining to recession (as, a *recessional* hymn, a hymn sung at the close of a church service while the clergy and choir retire from the chancel to the vestry); also, of or pertaining to a recess, as of a legislative body. **II.** n. A recessional hymn.

re-ces-sive (rē-ses′iv), a. [L. *recedere* (pp. *recessus*): see *recede*[2].] Tending to recede; receding; of accent, showing a tendency to recede from the end toward the beginning of a word; in Mendelian phraseology, pertaining to or exhibiting a recessive, as opposed to a dominant, character (see *recessive character*, below).—**recessive character**, in Mendelian phraseology, that one of any pair of antagonistic or mutually incompatible characters, as tallness and dwarfishness, occurring one in each of two parent animals or plants of pure breed, which is not visibly manifested in the first generation of hybrids but is latently present, and which occurs, visibly or latently, in a certain definite proportion of individuals in each succeeding generation.—**re-ces′sive**, n. In Mendelian phraseology, a recessive character, or an individual exhibiting it.—**re-ces′sive-ly**, adv.

Rech-a-bite (rek′a-bīt), n. [From the Jewish *Rechabites*, descendants of *Rechab*, mentioned in Jer. xxxv.] A total abstainer from strong drink.

re-change (rē-chānj′), v. t. or i. [See *re-*.] To change again or anew.—**re-change′**, n. A second or further change.

re-charge (rē-chärj′), v. t. or i. [See *re-*.] To charge again or anew; reload.—**re-charge′**, n. A second or additional charge.

re-char-ter (rē-chär′tèr), v. t. [See *re-*.] To charter again or anew.—**re-char′ter**, n. A rechartering; also, a second or additional charter.

ré-chauf-fé (rā-shō-fā′), n.; pl. *-fés* (-fāz, F. -fā). [F., prop. pp. of *réchauffer*, warm again, < *ré-* (< L. *re-*), again, + *chauffer*, E. *chafe*.] A warmed-up dish of food; hence, anything old or stale brought out anew, as a rehash of literary matter.

re-cheat (rē-chēt′), n. [OF. *racheter*, *rachater*, reassemble, rally.] In *hunting*, the calling together of the hounds; also, a strain on the horn sounded for this purpose, as at the beginning or the end of the chase (as, "The chase was declared to be ended . . . when the *recheat* should be blown": Scott's "Castle Dangerous," vi.). [Archaic.]

re-cher-ché (rē-sher-shā′), a. [F., pp. of *rechercher*: see *research*, v.] Sought out with care; hence, rare or choice; of studied refinement or elegance.

re-chris-ten (rē-kris′n), v. t. [See *re-*.] To christen again or anew; rename.

re-cid-i-vism (rē-sid′i-vizm), n. [See *recidivous*.] Repeated or habitual relapse into crime.—**re-cid′i-vist**, n. One who repeatedly or habitually relapses into crime; a habitual criminal.—**re-cid-i-vis′tic**, a.

re-cid-i-vous (rē-sid′i-vus), a. [L. *recidivus*, falling back, returning, < *recidere*, fall back, < *re-*, back, + *cadere*, fall.]

(variable) ḏ as d or j, ş as s or sh, ṭ as t or ch, ẓ as z or zh; o, F. cloche; ü, F. menu; c̓h, Sc. loch; ṅ, F. bonbon; ′, primary accent; ″, secondary accent; †, obsolete; <, from; +, and; =, equals. See also lists at beginning of book.

Liable to fall back or relapse, esp. into crime; habitually relapsing into crime.—**re-ci-div-i-ty** (res-i-div′i-ti), *n.*

re-ci-pe (res′i-pē), *n.* [L., 'take' (impv. of *recipere*: see *receive*), as used at the head of prescriptions.] A medical prescription; also, any receipt or formula, esp. one for preparing a dish in cookery.

re-cip-i-ent (rē-sip′i-ent). [L. *recipiens* (-ent-), ppr. of *recipere*: see *receive*.] **I.** *a.* Receiving, or capable of receiving. **II.** *n.* One who or that which receives; a receiver.—**re-cip′i-ence, re-cip′i-en-cy,** *n.*

re-cip-ro-cal (rē-sip′rō-kal). [L. *reciprocus*, returning, reciprocal, perhaps < *re-*, back, + *pro-*, forward.] **I.** *a.* Moving alternately backward and forward† (as, "Obedient to the moon, he spent his date In course *reciprocal*, and had his fate Link'd to the mutual flowing of the seas": Milton's "Second Epitaph on Hobson the Carrier," 30); also, given, performed, felt, etc., in return (as, "He contented himself with sending profuse acknowledgments of the assistance he had received . . . coupled with vague promises of *reciprocal* aid," J. F. Kirk's "Charles the Bold," iii. 2; "He was convinced of the hatred and scorn of his mistress: and this had produced . . . *reciprocal* hatred and scorn in him," Fielding's "Tom Jones," vii. 6); also, given, felt, etc., by each to or toward each, or mutual (as, *reciprocal* protection; *reciprocal* affection); mutually responsive, answering, or corresponding (as, "Their comradeship had lasted a lifetime, and no year passed without *reciprocal* visits," Eden Phillpotts's "Grey Room," i.; *reciprocal* privileges or obligations); also, inversely corresponding; inverse; in *gram.*, expressing mutual relation, as certain pronouns (see *each other*, under *each*, *pron.*, and *one another*, under *one*, *pron.*); also, reflexive. **II.** *n.* A thing that is reciprocal to something else; a return; an equivalent; a counterpart; a complement; in *math.*, that by which a given quantity is multiplied to produce unity.—**re-cip-ro-cal′i-ty** (-kal′i-ti), *n.*—**re-cip′-ro-cal-ly,** *adv.*

re-cip-ro-cate (rē-sip′rō-kāt), *v.*; -cated, -cating. [L. *reciprocatus*, pp. of *reciprocare*, < *reciprocus*: see *reciprocal*.] **I.** *tr.* To cause to move alternately backward and forward; also, to give, feel, etc., in return (as, "I verily believe he *reciprocated* the sentiment with all his heart": Irving's "Sketch-Book," Rip Van Winkle); also, to give and receive reciprocally (as, to *reciprocate* favors); interchange; also, to make correspondent. **II.** *intr.* To move alternately backward and forward; also, to make return, as for something given; also, to make interchange; also, to be correspondent.—**re-cip′ro-cat-ing** (-kā-ting), *p. a.* That reciprocates; moving alternately backward and forward, or having a part or parts so moving; esp., noting or pertaining to a steam-engine in which the piston and piston-rod move back and forth in a straight line (cf. *rotary*); also, noting or pertaining to that type of internal-combustion engine for an aëroplane, whose cylinders remain stationary and do not revolve about a crank-shaft (cf. *rotary*).—**re-cip-ro-ca′tion** (-kā′shon), *n.* [L. *reciprocatio(n-).*] The act or fact of reciprocating; motion backward and forward; a making return for something; a mutual giving and receiving; the state of being reciprocal or corresponding.—**re-cip′ro-ca-tive** (-kā-tiv), **re-cip′ro-ca-to-ry** (-tō-ri), *a.* Characterized by or pertaining to reciprocation.—**re-cip′ro-ca-tor** (-kā-tor), *n.*

re-ci-pro-ci-ty (res-i-pros′i-ti), *n.* [F. *réciprocité*, < L. *reciprocus*: see *reciprocal*.] Reciprocal state or relation; reciprocation; specif., that relation or policy with respect to commercial dealings between countries by which corresponding advantages or privileges are granted by each country to the citizens of the other.

re-cir-cu-late (rē-sèr′kū-lāt), *v. t.* [See *re-*.] To circulate again or anew.—**re-cir-cu-la′tion** (-lā′shon), *n.*

re-ci-tal (rē-sī′tal), *n.* The act of reciting; recitation; esp., the relating of facts or particulars; narration or description; detailed statement; also, an account, narrative, or description (as, "Some men . . . give us, in *recitals* of disease, A doctor's trouble, but without the fees": Cowper's "Conversation," 313); also, a musical entertainment given usually by a single performer, or consisting of selections from a single composer.—**re-ci′tal-ist,** *n.* One who gives musical recitals.

re-ci-ta-tion (res-i-tā′shon), *n.* [L. *recitatio(n-).*] The act of reciting, or an instance of it; esp., a reciting or repeating of something from memory, esp. formally or publicly; a reciting of a prepared lesson by pupils before a teacher; an elocutionary delivery of a piece of poetry or prose, without the text, before an audience, or a piece so delivered or for such delivery.—**re-ci-ta′tion-ist,** *n.* One who gives recitations of poetry or prose as a form of entertainment.

re-ci-ta-tive[1] (res′i-tạ-tiv), *a.* [See *recite.*] Pertaining to or of the nature of recital, as of facts or particulars.

re-ci-ta-tive[2] (res″i-tạ-tēv′). [It. *recitativo*, < L. *recitare*, E. *recite.*] In *music:* **I.** *a.* Of the nature of or resembling recitation or declamation; in the style of recitative. **II.** *n.* A style of vocal music intermediate between speaking and singing; a passage, part, or piece in this style.

re-ci-ta-ti-vo (res″i-tạ-tē′vō, It. rā-chē-tä-tē′vō), *n.*; pl. -vos (-vōz), It. -vi (-vē). [It.] In *music*, same as *recitative*[2], *n.*

re-cite (rē-sīt′), *v.*; -cited, -citing. [L. *recitare* (pp. *recitatus*), < *re-*, again, + *citare*, call, E. *cite.*] **I.** *tr.* To say over or repeat the words of, as from memory, esp. in a formal manner (as, to *recite* a prayer; to *recite* a lesson); specif., to repeat (a piece of poetry or prose) before an audience, as for entertainment; also, to relate the facts or particulars of, or give an account of (as, to *recite* one's adventures); declare or tell (as, "The thoughts of gods let Granville's verse *recite*": Pope's "Windsor Forest," 425); tell one by one, recount, or enumerate (as, to *recite* the names of persons present; to *recite* the items in a list). **II.** *intr.* To recite or repeat something from memory (as, "One walk'd *reciting* by herself, and one . . . held a volume as to read": Tennyson's "Princess," ii. 430); of pupils, to recite a lesson, or some part of a lesson called for, before a teacher.—**re-cit′er** (-sī′tèr), *n.*

reck (rek), *v.* [AS. *reccan* = OHG. *ruohhan* = Icel. *rækja*, reck.] **I.** *intr.* To have care, concern, or regard (often with *of*, and commonly with a negative, or *little*, or the like: as, "Of God, or hell, or worse, He [Moloch] *reck'd* not," Milton's "Paradise Lost," ii. 50; "My asperity brought . . . enmity . . . of which I *recked* very little," Stevenson's "Master of Ballantrae," iv.); care or mind (as, "I *reck* not though I end my life to-day": Shakspere's "Troilus and Cressida," v. 6. 26); take heed, or think (as, "Constance and Sophia, busy with the intense preoccupations of youth, *recked* not of such matters": Arnold Bennett's "Old Wives' Tale," i. 1); also, with impersonal subject, to be of concern or importance, or matter (as, it *recks* not; what *recks* it?). [Archaic.] **II.** *tr.* To have regard for, mind, or heed (as, "May ye better *reck* the rede Than ever did th' adviser!" Burns's "Epistle to a Young Friend," 87); also, with impersonal subject, to be of concern to, or matter to (as, "Of night, or loneliness, it *recks* me not": Milton's "Comus," 404). [Archaic.]

reck-less (rek′les), *a.* [AS. *rēcelēas*, akin to *reccan*, E. *reck.*] Careless, regardless, or heedless (*of*: as, "He gave way to an exasperation that made him *reckless* of Brighton-Pomfrey's opinion," H. G. Wells's "Soul of a Bishop," ix.; "*reckless* of consequences," H. Melville's "Typee," xxxiii.); not caring or minding (with a clause: as, "I am *reckless* what I do to spite the world," Shakspere's "Macbeth," iii. 1. 110); esp., utterly careless of the consequences of action, or boldly indifferent to or defiant of considerations of caution or prudence (as, "A *reckless* and irreverent knight was he," Tennyson's "Holy Grail," 853; "James . . . became the fiercest and most *reckless* of partisans," Macaulay's "Hist. of Eng.," vi.); characterized by or proceeding from such carelessness (as, a *reckless* spirit or mood; *reckless* extravagance; *reckless* accusations); also, not taking care†, or negligent†.—**reck′less-ly,** *adv.*—**reck′less-ness,** *n.*

reck-ling (rek′ling), *n.* [Origin uncertain.] The smallest and weakest one in a litter of animals or a family of children: as, "There lay the *reckling*, one But one hour old!" (Tennyson's "Merlin and Vivien," 707). [Chiefly prov. Eng.]

reck-on (rek′n), *v.* [AS. *(ge)recenian* = D. *rekenen* = G. *rechnen*, reckon.] **I.** *tr.* To count, compute, or calculate as to number or amount (as, to *reckon* the days to Christmas; to *reckon* sums spent; to *reckon* the cost of a year of travel); also, to include in a count, number, or class (as, "The people shall dwell alone, and shall not be *reckoned* among the nations": Num. xxiii. 9); also, to estimate or judge from counting or calculating (with a complement: as, to *reckon* the total number to be 5,000; to *reckon* the distance about 20 miles); in general, to esteem or consider (as stated: as, to *reckon* a person to be fortunate; to be *reckoned* a wit; "I cannot *reckon* you as an admirer," Hawthorne's "Blithedale Romance," vi.); also, to think or suppose (as, "I *reckon* this always, that a man is never undone till he be hanged," Shakspere's "Two Gentlemen of Verona," ii. 5. 4; "What d'you *reckon* brought Ned Ferry here?" G. W. Cable's "Cavalier," ii.: now prov. or colloq.); also, to credit, account, or impute (*to*: as, "Faith was *reckoned* to Abraham for righteousness," Rom. iv. 9). **II.** *intr.* To count; make a computation or calculation; also, to render an account, as for things received or done (see *reckoning*); also, to settle accounts, as with a person (lit. or fig.: as, "The lord of those servants cometh, and *reckoneth* with them," Mat. xxv. 19; to *reckon* with men according to their deserts); deal (*with*), as with something to be taken into account or entering into a case (as, "a kind of disclaimer of inheritance as a factor to be *reckoned* with," W. De Morgan's "Somehow Good," xxiv.; "Who was this Senhouse? He might have to be *reckoned* with at a pinch," M. Hewlett's "Open Country," xiii.); also, to count, depend, or rely (*on*), as in expectation (as, "He *reckons* on finding a woman as big a fool as himself!" G. Meredith's "Lord Ormont and His Aminta," xi.).—**to reckon without one's host,** to count up the cost of one's entertainment without consulting the host or landlord; hence, to make calculations or form plans or expectations without taking into account some important circumstance (as, "She had in one important point *reckoned without her host* . . . The two fellows, whom she went out to withstand, knew neither her nor the Latin tongue": J. H. Newman's "Callista," xxv.).—**reck′on-er,** *n.*—**reck′on-ing,** *n.* The act of one who reckons; count, computation, or calculation; estimation (as, "Half-an-hour, by the judge's *reckoning*, was to suffice for that": Hawthorne's "House of the Seven Gables," xviii.); the rendering of an account, or an accounting, as for things received or done (as, a day of *reckoning*; to give a *reckoning*; to call one to a *reckoning*); the settlement of accounts, as between parties; also, a statement of an amount due, or a bill, esp. at an inn or tavern (as, "The company having now pretty well satisfied their thirst, nothing remained but to pay the *reckoning*": Fielding's "Tom Jones," vii. 11); *naut.*, the calculation of the position of a ship; also, the position as calculated.

re-claim (rē-klām′), *v.* [OF. *reclaimer*, *reclamer* (F. *réclamer*), < L. *reclamare*, < *re-*, back, + *clamare*, cry out.] **I.** *intr.* To cry out in protest, or protest (now rare); also, to reform†. **II.** *tr.* To cry out or protest against†; also, to call back†; also, to bring back to right courses, living, principles, ideas, etc. (as, "To *reclaim* me from this course of life was the sole cause of his journey to London," Fielding's "Tom Jones," viii. 13; "Though now *reclaim'd* By modern lights from an erroneous taste," Cowper's "Task," iv. 723); bring back from wrong-doing or error, or reform (as, to *reclaim* a criminal); correct or amend (faults, errors, etc.); also, to bring out of the wild or unimproved natural state; tame or domesticate (animals); bring into a civilized condition (as, to *reclaim* a people from savagery or barbarism); bring (wild, waste, or marshy land) into a condition for cultivation or other use; often, to gain or recover (land, etc., *from*: as, to *reclaim* a tract from the desert or the sea; "The foundations of the capital were gradually *reclaimed* from the watery element," Prescott's "Conquest of Mexico," iv. 1); also, to recover (substances) in a pure or usable form from refuse matter, articles, etc. (as, to *reclaim* rubber or metals); also, to claim or demand the return or restoration of (as, "He also *reclaimed* the prisoners who still remained in the city," Motley's "Dutch Republic," vi. 6; "Pharnaces at once *reclaimed* his father's kingdom," Froude's "Cæsar," xxiii.).—**re-claim′,** *n.* Reclaiming; reclamation. —**re-claim′a-ble,** *a.* That may be reclaimed.—**re-claim′-er,** *n.*—**rec-la-ma-tion** (rek-la-mā′shon), *n.* [L. *reclamatio(n-)*.] The act or process of reclaiming, or the state of being reclaimed; specif., the reclaiming of waste, desert, marshy, or submerged land for cultivation or other use.

ré-clame (rā-kläm), *n.* [F., < *réclamer*, E. *reclaim*.] Advertisement; notoriety: as, "The idea . . . of his going into battle in hopes of electioneering *réclame*, is senseless" (Charnwood's "Theodore Roosevelt," iii.).

rec-li-nate (rek′li-nāt), *a.* [L. *reclinatus*, pp. of *reclinare*, E. *recline*.] In *bot.*, bending downward.

re-cline (rē-klīn′), *v.*; -*clined*, -*clining*. [L. *reclinare*, < *re-*, back, + *clinare*, bend, incline.] **I.** *tr.* To cause to lean back on something; place in a recumbent position. **II.** *intr.* To lean or lie back; rest in a recumbent position; as, "Ladies sat, while men *reclined* on couches during the repast" (Wiseman's "Fabiola," i. 6).—**re-clin′er** (-klī′nėr), *n.*

re-clothe (rē-klōᵀH′), *v. t.* [See *re-*.] To clothe again.

re-cluse (rē-klös′). [OF. F. *reclus* (fem. *recluse*), < LL. *reclusus*, pp. of *recludere*, shut up, L. unclose, < L. *re-*, back, again, + *cludere*, *claudere*, shut, close.] **I.** *a.* Shut up or apart from the world, or living in seclusion, as for religious or personal reasons (as, "I have liv'd *recluse* in rural shades": Cowper's "Conversation," 801); characterized by seclusion (as, a *recluse* life; "His mode of living was in the utmost degree *recluse* and solitary," Godwin's "Caleb Williams," i.); also, of places, secluded or sequestered (obs. or rare). **II.** *n.* One who lives shut up or withdrawn from the world for the purpose of religious meditation; specif., a religious voluntarily immured or remaining for life within a cell; in general, a person who lives in seclusion or apart from society (as, "a bachelor and something of a *recluse* in his private house, where he lived alone": W. H. Hudson's "Far Away and Long Ago," xvii.); also, a place of seclusion†. —**re-cluse′ly,** *adv.*—**re-cluse′ness,** *n.*—**re-clu′sion** (-klö′-zhon), *n.* [ML. *reclusio(n-)*.] A shutting or a being shut up in seclusion; the condition or life of a recluse.—**re-clu′sive** (-siv), *a.* Characterized by seclusion; recluse.

re-coal (rē-kōl′), *v.* [See *re-*.] **I.** *tr.* To supply afresh with coal: as, to *recoal* a steamship. **II.** *intr.* To take on a fresh supply of coal.

rec-og-ni-tion (rek-og-nish′on), *n.* [L. *recognitio(n-)*, < *recognoscere*: see *recognize*.] The act of recognizing, or the state of being recognized; the perception of something as identical with something previously known or in the mind; the perception of something as existing or true, or realization; the acknowledgment of something as valid or as entitled to consideration; formal acknowledgment conveying approval or sanction; the acknowledgment of kindness, service, merit, etc., or the expression of this by some token of appreciation.—**re-cog-ni-tive, re-cog-ni-to-ry** (rē-kog′ni-tiv, -tō-ri), *a.* Pertaining to recognition.

rec-og-niz-a-ble (rek′og-nī-za-bl), *a.* Capable of being recognized.—**rec′og-niz-a-bly,** *adv.*

re-cog-ni-zance (rē-kog′ni-zans or rē-kon′i-), *n.* [OF. *reconissance*, *reconoisance* (F. *reconnaissance*), < *reconoistre*: see *recognize*, and cf. *reconnaissance*.] The act of recognizing; recognition; also, a badge or token (archaic); also, in *law*, a bond or obligation of record entered into before a court of record or a magistrate, binding a person to do a particular act; also, the sum pledged as surety on such a bond.

re-cog-ni-zant (rē-kog′ni-zant), *a.* Recognizing; showing recognition: as, "They were people whom chance had brought . . . under a singular obligation to the Lapham ladies, and they were gratefully *recognisant* of it" (Howells's "Rise of Silas Lapham," ii.).

rec-og-nize (rek′og-nīz), *v.*; -*nized*, -*nizing*. [OF. *reconoistre* (*recognoiss*-, *reconuiss*-) (F. *reconnaître*), < L. *recognoscere* (pp. *recognitus*), know again, recognize, inspect, < *re-*, again, + *cognoscere*, come to know: see *cognition*, and cf. *reconnoiter*.] **I.** *tr.* To know again, or perceive to be identical with something previously known (as, "The tragic veteran could scarcely *recognize* him, or believe that he was really his quondam associate," Irving's "Tales of a Traveler," ii. 10; "I began to *recognise* familiar ground, the old trees under which I had walked or sat," W. H. Hudson's "Green Mansions," xviii.); identify from knowledge of appearance or character (as, to *recognize* a thief from published descriptions of him); also, to perceive as existing or true, or realize (as, to *recognize* unsuspected possibilities in a thing; to be the first to *recognize* a fact); also, to avow knowledge of, with approval or sanction, or acknowledge or treat as valid

---

(variable) d̦ as d or j, ș as s or sh, ț as t or ch, z̦ as z or zh; o, F. cloche; ü, F. menu; ch̦, Sc. loch; ṅ, F. bonbon; ′, primary accent; ″, secondary accent; †, obsolete; <, from; +, and; =, equals. See also lists at beginning of book.

(as, to *recognize* a person's authority in a matter; "I'll . . . try to get her to *recognize* your claim," Mrs. Wharton's "Son at the Front," xiv.); acknowledge formally as existing or as entitled to consideration (as, one government *recognizes* another; "In the winter of 1652 the Commonwealth was duly *recognized* by the government of Louis XIV," Morley's "Oliver Cromwell," iv. 5); acknowledge or accept formally as being something stated (as, to *recognize* a government as a belligerent; to *recognize* one as ambassador); concede or receive as being what is specified (as, "thankfully *recognising* those ages as a part of the great existence in which we share": Bancroft's "Hist. of the U. S.," Amer. Revolution, i. 1); specif., to acknowledge as the person entitled to speak at the particular time, or give the floor to, as in a legislative assembly; also, to acknowledge or admit as resting upon one's self (as, to *recognize* an obligation; to *recognize* one's responsibility); also, to acknowledge acquaintance with (a person, etc.), as by a salute; also, to show appreciation of (kindness, service, merit, etc.), as by some reward or tribute. **II.** *intr.* In *law,* to enter into a recognizance.—**rec′og-nized**, *p. a.* Acknowledged; admitted; approved; received: as, "every newspaper and periodical of *recognized* standing" (Bok's "Americanization of Edward Bok," xxx.); a *recognized* method of procedure.—**re-cog-ni-zee** (rḛ-kog-ni-zē′ or rḛ-kon-i-), *n.* In *law,* the person to whom one is bound in a recognizance.—**rec′og-niz-er** (-nī-zȇr), *n.* One who recognizes.—**re-cog-ni-zor** (rḛ-kog-ni-zôr′ or rḛ-kon-i-), *n.* In *law,* the person who enters into a recognizance.

re-coil (rḛ-koil′), *v. i.* [OF. F. *reculer,* < L. *re-,* back, + *culus,* the posteriors.] To draw back, retreat, or retire (as, "The . . . British had *recoiled* five and twenty miles": H. G. Wells's "Mr. Britling," ii. 1. § 16); also, to start or shrink back, as in alarm, horror, or disgust (lit. or fig.: as, "Those who had felt his strength *recoiled* from his presence," Scott's "Guy Mannering," xli.; "With a sudden revulsion his heart *recoiled* from its purpose," Longfellow's "Courtship of Miles Standish," v.); also, to spring or fly back, as in consequence of force of impact; spring back from the force of the discharge, as a firearm (as, "My pistol was overcharged: when I fired, it *recoiled,* and I received a blow on my breast": Maria Edgeworth's "Belinda," iv.); fig., to spring or come back (*on* or *upon*: as, "The imprudence of our thoughts *recoils* upon our heads," J. Conrad's "Lord Jim," xxxvi.); also, to fall back or off†, or degenerate† (see Shakspere's "Cymbeline," i. 6. 128); also, to go back, as in memory† (see Shakspere's "Winter's Tale," i. 2. 154).—**re-coil′**, *n.* The act of recoiling; a drawing back, retreating, or retiring; a starting or shrinking back, as in alarm, horror, or disgust; a springing or flying back, as from impact or by elasticity; the springing back of a firearm, etc., when discharged.—**re-coil′er,** *n.*

re-coin (rḛ-koin′), *v. t.* [See *re-.*] To coin over again.—**re-coin′age** (-āj), *n.* The process or the product of recoining.—**re-coin′er,** *n.*

re-col-lect[1] (rē-ko-lekt′), *v. t.* [Orig. < L. *recollectus,* pp. of *recolligere,* collect again (< *re-,* again, + *colligere:* see *collect*), but later taken as < *re-* + *collect,* and pronounced accordingly: cf. *recollect*[2].] To collect, gather together, or assemble again (what is scattered or dispersed); fig., to rally (one's faculties, powers, spirits, etc.); summon up (strength, courage, etc.); recover or compose (one's self: as, "Now, if Joseph would make one of his long speeches, I might *recollect* myself a little," Sheridan's "School for Scandal," v. 3). Also written *re-collect.*

rec-ol-lect[2] (rek-o-lekt′), *v.* [From the same source (L. *recollectus,* pp.) as *recollect*[1], but distinguished in sense and pronunciation.] **I.** *tr.* To recall to mind, or recover knowledge of by an act or effort of memory (as, "I know why I began the Memoir. It was as an experiment to see how much I could really *recollect* if I once began to try": W. De Morgan's "Joseph Vance," x.); remember; also, to recall (one's self) to something temporarily forgotten; bethink (one's self); also, to concentrate (the mind, etc.) in meditation or religious contemplation. **II.** *intr.* To have a recollection; remember.

Rec-ol-lect[3] (rek′o-lekt), *n.* [= F. *récollet,* < L. *recollectus,* 'recollected' (see *recollect*[2]), with reference to religious

contemplation.] In the *Rom. Cath. Ch.,* a member of a division of the Observant Franciscans following an especially strict rule.

re-col-lec-tion[1] (rē-ko-lek′shon), *n.* [See *recollect*[1].] The act of recollecting, or gathering together again, or the state of being recollected. Also written *re-collection.*

rec-ol-lec-tion[2] (rek-o-lek′shon), *n.* [See *recollect*[2].] The act or power of recollecting, or recalling to mind; remembrance; that which is recollected; also, concentration of thought as in meditation, esp. on spiritual themes; religious contemplation.—**rec-ol-lec′tive,** *a.* Pertaining to, characterized by, or concerned with recollection or remembrance; having recollection.—**rec-ol-lec′tive-ly,** *adv.*

Rec-ol-let (rek′o-let, F. rā-ko-lā), *n.* [F. *récollet:* see *Recollect*[3].] Same as *Recollect*[3].

re-com-bine (rē-kom-bīn′), *v. t.* or *i.* [See *re-.*] To combine again or anew.—**re-com-bi-na′tion** (-kom-bi-nā′-shon), *n.*

re-com-fort (rḛ-kum′fort), *v. t.* [OF. *reconforter* (F. *réconforter*).] To comfort again; cheer; console; refresh. [Archaic.]

re-com-mence (rē-ko-mens′), *v. t.* or *i.* [OF. F. *recommencer.*] To commence again or anew.—**re-com-mence′-ment,** *n.*—**re-com-men′cer** (-men′sȇr), *n.*

rec-om-mend (rek-o-mend′), *v. t.* [ML. *recommendare,* < L. *re-,* again, + *commendare,* E. *commend.*] To commend or commit, as in trust or charge (as, "I . . . devoutly *recommended* my spirit to its Maker": Stevenson's "Treasure Island," xxiii.); also, to commend by favorable representations, or present as worthy of confidence, acceptance, use, etc. (as, to *recommend* a man for a post; to *recommend* goods to a customer; to *recommend* a book, a hotel, or a dish of food); represent or urge as advisable or expedient (as, to *recommend* a method of procedure; to *recommend* caution or haste; "Cæsar . . . *recommended* that the estates of the conspirators should be confiscated," Froude's "Cæsar," xi.); also, to advise (a person, etc., to do something: as, to *recommend* one to wait; to *recommend* travelers to visit a place); advise to go, or refer by favorable representations (as, "The landlord of the Spouter-Inn had *recommended* us to his cousin Hosea Hussey of the Try Pots": H. Melville's "Moby-Dick," xv.); also, to make acceptable or pleasing (as, "I am a plain, rough man . . . with very little to *recommend* me": Dickens's "Cricket on the Hearth," iii.); render or show (one's self or itself) acceptable or satisfactory (as, to *recommend* one's self by one's merits; "This place *recommended* itself to my observation as I was wandering in quest of an abode," Godwin's "Caleb Williams," xxxix.).—**rec-om-mend′,** *n.* A recommendation: as, "I can show *recommends* from his master and others" (Mrs. Stowe's "Uncle Tom's Cabin," xiv.). [Colloq. or prov.]—**rec-om-mend′a-ble,** *a.* Suitable or worthy to be recommended.—**rec″om-men-da′tion** (-men-dā′shon), *n.* [ML. *recommendatio*(n-).] The act of recommending; representation in favor of a person or thing (as, "The other two were taken into my service, upon their captain's *recommendation*": Defoe's "Robinson Crusoe," i. 18); also, a letter or the like recommending a person or thing; also, anything that serves to recommend a person or thing or induce acceptance or favor (as, "persons whose *recommendations* for command were birth or fortune": Froude's "Cæsar," v.).—**rec-om-men′da-to-ry** (-da-tō-ri), *a.* Serving to recommend: as, "I was to take with me letters *recommendatory* to a number of his friends" (B. Franklin's "Autobiography," ii.).—**rec-om-mend′er,** *n.*

re-com-mit (rē-ko-mit′), *v. t.*; *-mitted, -mitting.* [See *re-.*] To commit again; specif., to refer again to a committee.—**re-com-mit′ment, re-com-mit′tal,** *n.*

rec-om-pense (rek′om-pens), *v. t.*; *-pensed, -pensing.* [Also formerly *recompence*; OF. *recompenser* (F. *récompenser*), < ML. *recompensare,* < L. *re-,* back, + *compensare:* see *compensate.*] To make compensation to (a person, etc.); repay, remunerate, reward, or requite for service, aid, etc. (as, to *recompense* a person for his labor or trouble; "Thou shalt be *recompensed* at the resurrection of the just," Luke, xiv. 14); make up to by payment or otherwise for loss, injury, suffering, etc. (as, to *recompense* a person for expense incurred or sacrifices made); also, to make compensation for; make a return or requital for (as, "Liberally *recompensing* their services . . . he took leave of his faithful followers": Prescott's "Conquest of Mexico," iii. 7); make up for (loss, injury, suffering, etc.); make amends or atonement for (wrong-doing, etc.: obs. or archaic: as, "Though late, yet in some part to *recompense* My rash . . . misdeed," Milton's "Samson Agonistes," 746); also, to serve as compensation to or for (as, the final success *recompensed* them for their toil and hardships; "A brighter prize than that he meant Shall *recompense* his mere intent," Cowper's "Moralizer Corrected," 56); also, to give in return or requital (obs. or archaic: as, "*Recompense* to no man evil for evil," Rom. xii. 17).—**rec′om-pense,** *n.* [Also formerly *recompence.*] Compensation made, as for service, loss, injury, or wrong (as, to make *recompense*; "That then, in *recompense* of all thy cares, Thy child shall show respect to thy gray hairs," Cowper's "Tirocinium," 879); repayment or requital; reparation or atonement; also, something given or serving to compensate; remuneration or a reward (as, "A good man's prayers are golden *recompense*," Hawthorne's "Scarlet Letter," xx.; "Do good to the godly man, and thou shalt find a *recompence*," Ecclus. xii. 2); means of reparation, or amends (as, "Some *recompense* To comfort those that mourn": Burns's "Man Was Made to Mourn," 79).

re-com-pose (rē-kọm-pōz′), *v. t.* [See *re-.*] To compose again or anew; reconstitute; rearrange; restore to composure or calmness.—**re-com-po-si′tion** (-kom-pọ-zish′ọn), *n.*

re-con-cen-tra-do (rä-kōn-sen-trä′dō), *n.*; pl. *-dos* (Sp. -dōs). [Sp., 'reconcentrated.'] One of a rural population forced to concentrate in towns, as during the Cuban rebellion of 1895 — 98 against Spain.

re-con-cen-trate (rē-kon′sẹn-trāt), *v. t.* [See *re-.*] To concentrate again; specif., to concentrate (troops, inhabitants, etc.), as for military or administrative purposes.—**re-con-cen-tra′tion** (-trā′shọn), *n.*

rec-on-cil-a-ble (rek′ọn-sī-lạ-bl), *a.* Capable of being reconciled.—**rec′on-cil-a-bil′i-ty** (-bil′i-ti), **rec′on-cil-a-ble-ness,** *n.*—**rec′on-cil-a-bly,** *adv.*

rec-on-cile (rek′ọn-sīl), *v. t.*; *-ciled, -ciling.* [OF. *reconcilier* (F. *réconcilier*) < L. *reconciliare*, < *re-*, again, + *conciliare*, bring together: see *conciliate.*] To bring again to friendly relations after estrangement or variance (as, to *reconcile* one person to, or with, another; "being all now good friends, for common danger . . . had effectually *reconciled* them," Defoe's "Robinson Crusoe," ii. 3; "to *reconcile* two nations after a long war," J. F. Kirk's "Charles the Bold," iii. 1); also, to win over to friendliness, conciliate, or placate (as, to *reconcile* a hostile person; "The Gods are hard to *reconcile*," Tennyson's "Choric Song," vi.); also, to compose or settle (a quarrel, difference, etc.); also, to render no longer opposed, or bring to acquiescence or content (with *to*: as, "The lady seemed to be *reconciled* to her lot," Barrie's "Sentimental Tommy," iii.; "But time partially *reconciles* us to anything," Lamb's "Superannuated Man"); also, to bring into agreement or harmony, or make compatible or consistent (as, "They . . . have contrived . . . to *reconcile* orthodox Christianity with unflinching democratic opinions": Kingsley's "Alton Locke," xxx.); show to be, or explain as being, compatible or consistent (as, to *reconcile* differing statements; "How, he demanded, did I *reconcile* these ancient fabulous notions with the doctrine of evolution?" W. H. Hudson's "Far Away and Long Ago," xxiv.); accept or regard as compatible or consistent (as, "Such welcome and unwelcome things at once 'Tis hard to *reconcile*": Shakspere's "Macbeth," iv. 3. 139); also, to purify ceremonially (as, "The priest shall . . . put it [blood] upon the posts of the house . . . so shall ye *reconcile* the house": Ezek. xlv. 20); specif., to purify (a church, cemetery, etc.) by special ceremonies after profanation (as, "The places of old assembly . . . were cleansed, or repaired, refitted and *reconciled*, and opened to public . . . worship": Wiseman's "Fabiola," iii. 1).—**rec′on-cile-ment,** *n.* Reconciliation.—**rec′on-cil-er** (-sī-lėr), *n.*—**rec′on-cil-i-a′tion** (-sil-i-ā′shọn), *n.* [L. *reconciliatio(n-)*.] The act of reconciling, or the state of being reconciled.—**rec-on-cil′i-a-to-ry** (-ạ-tọ-ri), *a.* Tending to reconcile.

rec-on-dite (rek′ọn-dīt), *a.* [L. *reconditus*, pp. of *recondere*, put away, hide, < *re-*, back, + *condere*, put together, lay up: see *condiment.*] Hidden from view, or concealed (now chiefly in *bot.* and *entom.*); hence, removed from ordinary knowledge or understanding, abstruse, or profound (as, *recondite* causes; *recondite* principles or truths; "oracles of the highest authority, and of the most *recondite* meaning," Macaulay's "Essays," John Dryden); dealing with abstruse or profound matters (as, *recondite* studies; a *recondite* treatise); little known, or obscure, as writers or writings.—**rec′on-dite-ly,** *adv.*—**rec′on-dite-ness,** *n.*

re-con-di-tion (rē-kọn-dish′ọn), *v. t.* [See *re-.*] To restore to a good or satisfactory condition; put in due condition again by repairing, making over, or other processes.

re-con-nais-sance (rẹ-kon′ạ-sạns), *n.* [F.: see *recognizance.*] The act of reconnoitering, or a process or operation of reconnoitering, as for military or other purposes; a preliminary examination or survey.—**reconnaissance in force,** *milit.*, a demonstration or attack by a considerable force of troops for the purpose of discovering the position and strength of an enemy.

re-con-nois-sance (rē-kon′i-sạns, also rek-ọ-noi′sạns), *n.* Same as *reconnaissance.*

rec-on-noi-ter, rec-on-noi-tre (rek-ọ-noi′tėr), *v.*; *-tered, -tred, -tering, -tring.* [F. *reconnoître*, earlier form of *reconnaître*, recognize, reconnoiter: see *recognize.*] **I.** *tr.* To recognize†; also, to inspect, observe, or survey (the enemy, the enemy's strength or position, a region, etc.) in order to gain information for military purposes (as, "Their leader . . . *reconnoitred* the works, with the view of reporting on the fittest disposition of the troops and the quarters and distances from which the siege might best be opened": J. F. Kirk's "Charles the Bold," iv. 4); hence, in general, to examine with the eye, inspect, or observe, in order to learn something (as, "Wyeth . . . *reconnoitered* them with a spy-glass, and soon perceived they were Indians": Irving's "Captain Bonneville," vi.); esp., to examine or survey (a region, etc.) for engineering, geological, or other purposes. **II.** *intr.* To make a reconnaissance.—**rec-on-noi′ter-er, rec-on-noi′trer,** *n.*

re-con-quer (rē-kong′kẻr), *v. t.* [See *re-.*] To conquer again; recover by conquest.—**re-con′quest** (-kwest), *n.* The act of reconquering; recovery by conquest: as, "He was most anxious . . . to effect the *reconquest* of some portion of Zeland" (Motley's "Dutch Republic," iv. 3).

re-con-sid-er (rē-kọn-sid′ẻr), *v.* [See *re-.*] **I.** *tr.* To consider again (as, "I implore you . . . to *reconsider* what it is we are being urged towards": H. G. Wells's "Men Like Gods," ii. 2); esp., to consider again with a view to a change of decision or action (as, to *reconsider* a choice made or a refusal given); specif., in parliamentary use, to take up for consideration a second time, as a motion or a vote, as with the view of reversing or modifying action taken; also, to bethink (one's self) with a view to doing differently. **II.** *intr.* To reconsider a matter: specif. in parliamentary use.—**re-con-sid-er-a′tion** (-ā′shọn), *n.*

re-con-sti-tute (rē-kon′sti-tūt), *v. t.* [See *re-.*] To constitute anew; reconstruct; recompose.—**reconstituted milk,** liquid milk produced from powdered or liquid skim-milk and butter by a mixing and emulsifying process; also, a mixture of powdered milk and water.—**re-con-sti-tu′tion** (-tū′shọn), *n.*

re-con-struct (rē-kọn-strukt′), *v. t.* [See *re-.*] To construct again or anew; rebuild; make over.—**re-con-struc′tion** (-struk′shọn), *n.* The act of reconstructing; in *U. S. hist.*, the process by which the States which had seceded were reorganized as a part of the Union after the Civil War, according to the acts of Congress of March 2 and 23, 1867 ('Reconstruction Acts').—**re-con-struc′tive,** *a.* Tending to reconstruct.—**re-con-struc′tor,** *n.*

re-con-vene (rē-kọn-vēn′), *v. i.* or *t.* [See *re-.*] To convene again.

re-con-vert (rē-kọn-vėrt′), *v. t.* [See *re-.*] To convert back to a previous state; also, to convert again or anew.—**re-con-ver′sion** (-vėr′shọn), *n.*

re-con-vey (rē-kọn-vā′), *v. t.* [See *re-.*] To convey again or back.—**re-con-vey′ance,** *n.*

re-cop-y (rē-kop′i), *v. t.* [See *re-.*] To copy again.

re-cord (rẹ-kôrd′), *v.* [OF. F. *recorder*, < L. *recordari*, call to mind, remember, < *re-*, back, again, + *cor* (*cord-*), heart, mind.] **I.** *tr.* To call to mind†, recall†, or remember†; also, to relate† or tell†; also, to set down in writing or the like, as for the purpose of preserving evidence (as, "And I *recorded* what I heard — A lesson for mankind," Cowper's "Doves," 39; "The first public act *recorded* of Cæsar was his refusal to divorce his wife at Sylla's bidding," Froude's "Cæsar," xxviii.); serve to relate or to tell of, as a written statement does (as, "A long inscription . . . *records* how Amenhotep . . . slew seven kings with his own hand": Amelia B. Edwards's "Thousand Miles up the Nile," xiv.); also, to set down or register in some permanent form, as instruments do; specif., to set down, register, or fix by characteristic marks, incisions, etc., for the purpose of reproduction, as speech or music on a cylinder or disk for reproduction by a phonograph; also, to cause to be set down or registered (as, to *record* one's vote); also, to attest† or confirm†; also, to recite† or repeat†; practise or sing (a tune, etc.: now only of birds). **II.** *intr.* To record something; set down or make a record; also, to practise or sing a tune, as in an undertone (now only specif. of birds).—
rec-ord (rek′ọrd). [OF. *record*.] **I.** *n.* The act of recording, or the state or fact of being recorded, as in writing; information or knowledge preserved in writing or the like (as, "Every action that hath gone before, Whereof we have *record*": Shakspere's "Troilus and Cressida," i. 3. 14); specif., the commitment to writing, as authentic evidence, of something having legal importance, esp. as evidence of the proceedings or verdict of a court, or evidence preserved in this manner (as, a court of *record*, one whose proceedings are formally enrolled and are valid as evidence); also, an account in writing or the like preserving the memory or knowledge of facts or events; a document, etc., containing such an account; specif., an official writing recording facts or events; an authentic or official written report of proceedings of a court of justice; an authentic or official copy of a writing; also, any thing or person serving as a memorial; also, the tracing, marking, or the like made by a recording instrument; a cylinder, disk, or other device having characteristic markings or the like for reproducing sound, as in a phonograph; also, a report, list, or aggregate of actions or achievements, as in the case of a person, an organization, a horse, a ship, etc. (as, to have a good, or a bad, *record*); also, a notable recorded degree of achievement or attainment; esp., the highest or furthest recorded degree attained; the best rate, amount, etc., attained, as in some form of sport (as, to break the *record* in the high jump); also, testimony or witness (obs. or archaic); also, memory† or remembrance† (see Shakspere's "Twelfth Night," v. 1. 253). **II.** *a.* Making or affording a record; notable in the degree of attainment; being the foremost or utmost in the degree of attainment: as, a *record* output; a *record* year for sales; the *record* time for the mile run.
rec-or-da-tion (rek-ọr-dā′shọn), *n.* [L. *recordatio*(*n-*), < *recordari*: see *record*.] Remembrance†; also, the act of recording, or committing to writing or the like.
re-cord-er (rẹ-kôr′dėr), *n.* A judge having criminal and civil jurisdiction in a city or borough; also, one who records, or sets down facts or events in writing, esp. as an official duty; also, a recording or registering apparatus or device; also, a witness†; also, an obsolete musical instrument of the flageolet kind (as, "flutes and soft *recorders*": Milton's "Paradise Lost," i. 551).—**re-cord′er-ship**, *n.*
re-count¹ (rẹ-kount′), *v. t.* [See *re-*.] To count again. Also written *re-count*.—**re-count¹** (rẹ-kount′ or rē′kount), *n.* A recounting; a second or additional count, as of votes in an election. Also written *re-count*.
re-count² (rẹ-kount′), *v. t.* [OF. F. *reconter*, repeat, relate, < *re-* (< L. *re-*), again, + *conter*, tell, E. *count²*.] To relate or narrate, tell in detail, or give the facts or particulars of (as, "I *recounted* to him all that had passed . . . without garbling the facts in any particular": Malkin's tr. Le Sage's "Gil Blas," vii. 2); narrate in order (as, "They used to *recount* . . . the exploits of their youth": G. White's "Nat. Hist. of Selborne," i. 7); tell one by one, or enumerate (as, to *recount* the items in a list).—**re-count′al**, **re-count′ment**†, *n.*

re-coup (rẹ-köp′), *v. t.* [F. *recouper*, cut again, < *re-* (< L. *re-*), again, + *couper*, cut: see *coupé*.] To keep back as a set-off or discount, or deduct (as, to *recoup* from wages losses due to negligence); also, to reimburse or indemnify (as, to *recoup* a person for expenses); also, to provide or be an equivalent for, or compensate for (as, to *recoup* one's losses); also, to yield in return, or return an amount equal to (as, to obtain dividends that in a few years *recoup* one's whole capital).—**re-coup′**, *n.* The act of recouping. —**re-coup′er**, *n.*—**re-coup′ment**, *n.*
re-course (rẹ-kōrs′), *n.* [OF. F. *recours*, < L. *recursus*, a running back, < *recurrere*: see *recur*.] A running, flowing, or coming back†; also, movement or course in a particular direction or to a particular place†; also, resort or application to a person or thing for help or protection, as when in difficulty (as, "The King in this extremity had *recourse* to Sir William Temple," Macaulay's "Hist. of Eng.," ii.; "They might have *recourse* to barbarity as an expedient," Macaulay's "Essays," Machiavelli); also, the right to resort to a person for pecuniary compensation (as, an indorsement without *recourse*, one by which a payee or holder of a negotiable instrument, by writing 'without recourse' with his name, merely transfers the instrument without assuming any liability upon it); also, a person or thing resorted to for help or protection; also, habitual or customary going to a place†, or resort†; also, access† or admittance† (as, "That no manner of person At any time have *recourse* unto the princes": Shakspere's "Richard III.," iii. 5. 109).
re-cov-er¹ (rē-kuv′ėr), *v. t.* [See *re-*.] To cover again. Also written *re-cover*.
re-cov-er² (rẹ-kuv′ėr), *v.* [OF. F. *recouvrer*, < L. *recuperare*: see *recuperate*.] **I.** *tr.* To get again, or regain (something lost or taken away: as, to *recover* lost property; to *recover* conquered territory; "In a few days Mr. Barnstaple had *recovered* strength of body and mind," H. G. Wells's "Men Like Gods," iii. 2; "He . . . stood in the porch a minute to *recover* his composure," Galsworthy's "Saint's Progress," iv. 3); sometimes, to win back or reconcile (a person: as, "There are ways to *recover* the general again," Shakspere's "Othello," ii. 3. 273); specif., to regain (a substance) in usable form, as from refuse material or from a waste product or by-product of manufacture; reclaim; in legal use, to obtain by judgment in a court of law or by legal proceedings (as, to *recover* damages for a wrong); also, in general, to get† or obtain†; also, to get to or reach (obs. or archaic); also, to bring back or restore (a thing), as to a person, place, etc. (as, "So had the glory of prowess been *recover'd* to Palestine": Milton's "Samson Agonistes," 1098); specif., in military use, to bring back (a weapon) to a certain position, as after use; also, to restore (a person, etc.) to life or consciousness, to health or strength, or to composure (as, "Our men in the pinnace . . . took up three men; one of which was just drowning, and it was a good while before we could *recover* him," Defoe's "Robinson Crusoe," ii. 11; "He . . . *recovered* her from an imminent and painful disease," Marryat's "Japhet," lxi.; "Partridge, whom the sound of a human voice had *recovered* from his fright," Fielding's "Tom Jones," viii. 10); restore (anything) to good or proper condition†; also, to rescue† or deliver†; reclaim from a bad state, practice, etc. (as, "till I have *recovered* them out of that desperate state of vice and folly, into which the age is fallen": Addison, in "Spectator," 10); also, to get over (sickness, misfortune, etc.: as, "Some distant, rural scene . . . where . . . I might . . . *recover* the wounds my mind had received," Godwin's "Caleb Williams," xxxix.); make up for or make good (loss, damage, etc., to one's self); remedy or rectify (fault, mischief, etc.); also, to regain the strength, composure, balance, etc., of (one's self: as, "He gave the man a few moments to *recover* himself," Mrs. H. Ward's "Robert Elsmere," xxx.). **II.** *intr.* To regain health after sickness, a wound, etc. (often followed by *of* or, now more commonly, *from*: as, "The man *recovered* of the bite — The dog it was that died," Goldsmith's "Vicar of Wakefield," xvii.; to *recover* from an illness); also, in general, to regain a former (and better) state or condition (as, "The city had not yet *recovered* from the effects of the late revolution": W. H. Hudson's "Purple Land," i.); regain consciousness; regain one's composure, balance,

etc.; also, **to return or come**, as to a place†; specif., in *fencing* and *rowing*, to make a recovery; in *law*, to obtain a favorable judgment in a suit for something.—**re-cov′er**[2], *n.* Recovery, esp. of a former position.—**re-cov′er-a-ble**, *a.* Capable of being recovered.—**re-cov′er-er**, *n.*—**re-cov′er-y** (-i), *n.*; pl. *-ies* (-iz). The act of recovering; the regaining of something lost or taken away, or the possibility of this (as, "The *recovery* of Bagdad was impossible unless the British were driven back to the Sinai desert," Buchan's "Hist. of the Great War," lxxxvii.; "The game of open resistance was lost beyond *recovery*," Froude's "Cæsar," xxv.); the regaining of substances in usable form, as from refuse material or waste products; the obtaining of right to something by verdict or judgment of a court of law; restoration or return to health from sickness; restoration or return to a former (and better) state or condition; return to a former position or attitude, as, in fencing, to that of guard after a lunge, or, in rowing, to that for making the next stroke after completing a stroke.

rec-re-ant (rek′rē-ant). [OF. *recreant*, a. and n., < *recreire*, *recroire*, yield in a contest, < ML. *recredere*, surrender, < L. *re-*, back, + *credere*, trust.] **I.** *a.* Yielding in combat, or acknowledging defeat (obs. or archaic: as, to yield one's self *recreant*); hence, cowardly or craven (as, "He blotted was with blame, And counted but a *recreant* Knight with endles shame": Spenser's "Faerie Queene," v. 11. 46); also, unfaithful, disloyal, or false (as, "Man . . . Who . . . Turn'd *recreant* to God, ingrate and false," Milton's "Paradise Regained," iii. 138; "while her [Holland's] sister provinces had proved *recreant* to him [William of Orange]," Motley's "Dutch Republic," iii. 8). **II.** *n.* A coward or craven in combat or war (as, "*Reig.* Shall we give over Orleans, or no? *Puc.* Why, no, I say, distrustful *recreants!* Fight till the last gasp": Shakspere's "1 Henry VI.," i. 2. 126); a pusillanimous person; also, one who proves unfaithful or false; an apostate; a traitor.—**rec′re-ance**, **rec′re-an-cy**, *n.*—**rec′re-ant-ly**, *adv.*

re-cre-ate[1] (rē-krē-āt′), *v. t.* [See *re-*.] To create anew. Also written **re-create**.—**re-cre-a′tion**[1] (-ā′shon), *n.*

rec-re-ate[2] (rek′rē-āt), *v.*; *-ated, -ating.* [L. *recreatus*, pp. of *recreare*, create anew, restore, < *re-*, again, + *creare*, create.] **I.** *tr.* To restore to a good condition of body or mind, or refresh physically or mentally; now, usually, to refresh with some pastime, diversion, agreeable exercise, or other means of relaxation and enjoyment, as after toil or exertion (as, "to walk abroad, and *recreate* yourselves": Shakspere's "Julius Cæsar," iii. 2. 256). **II.** *intr.* To take recreation.—**rec-re-a′tion**[2] (-ā′shon), *n.* [L. *recreatio(n-)*.] The act of recreating, or the state of being recreated; refreshment by means of some pastime, agreeable exercise, or the like; a particular form or means of such refreshment, or a pastime, diversion, exercise, or other resource affording relaxation and enjoyment (as, "Next to his flowers, walking was Uncle Tom's chief *recreation*": W. Churchill's "Modern Chronicle," i. 2); also, refreshment with food and drink†.—**rec-re-a′tion-al**, *a.* Of or pertaining to recreation: as, "the increasing *recreational* variety of life" (A. S. M. Hutchinson's "If Winter Comes," ii. 1).—**rec′re-a-tive** (-ā-tiv), *a.* Tending to recreate.

rec-re-ment (rek′rē-ment), *n.* [L. *recrementum*, < *re-*, back, + *cernere*, separate.] The useless portion of a substance; dross; in *physiol.*, a secretion which, after having been separated from the blood, is returned to it, as the saliva.—**rec″re-men-ti′tious** (-men-tish′us), *a.* Consisting of or of the nature of recrement.

re-crim-i-nate (rē-krim′i-nāt), *v.*; *-nated, -nating.* [ML. *recriminatus*, pp. of *recriminari*, < L. *re-*, back, + *criminari*: see *criminate*.] **I.** *intr.* To bring a charge in return against an accuser. **II.** *tr.* To accuse in return.—**re-crim-i-na′tion** (-nā′shon), *n.* [ML. *recriminatio(n-)*.] The act of recriminating (as, "Injudicious . . . as the conduct of England may be in this system of aspersion, *recrimination* on our part would be equally ill-judged": Irving's "Sketch-Book," English Writers on America); also, an accusation brought in return by an accused person against the accuser.—**re-crim′i-na-tive** (-nā-tiv), **re-crim′i-na-to-ry** (-tō-ri), *a.* Of the nature of or involving recrimination.

re-cross (rē-krôs′), *v. t.* or *i.* [See *re-*.] To cross again in returning (as, "He knew that time, weather, and scarcity of supplies must wear Cromwell out and compel him to *recross* the border": Morley's "Oliver Cromwell," iv. 3); also, to cross a second time or anew.

re-cru-desce (rē-krö-des′), *v. i.*; *-desced, -descing.* [L. *recrudescere*, < *re-*, again, + *crudescere*, lit. 'grow raw,' < *crudus*, raw, E. *crude*.] To break out afresh, as a sore or a disease, or anything that has been quiescent; come into renewed activity.—**re-cru-des′cence** (-des′ens), *n.* A breaking out afresh, or into renewed activity; a revival or reappearance in active existence: as, the *recrudescence* of an epidemic; a *recrudescence* of hostilities; "Conditions . . . had long prevented any *recrudescence* of gang slavery" (H. G. Wells's "Outline of History," xxxvii. § 6). Also **re-cru-des′cen-cy.**—**re-cru-des′cent**, *a.* Recrudescing; breaking out afresh; coming into renewed activity.

re-cruit (rē-kröt′), *v.* [F. *recruter*, < *recrue*, a new growth, accession to troops, < *recroître*, grow again, < *re-* (< L. *re-*), again, + *croître*, grow: see *crew*[1].] **I.** *tr.* To strengthen or supply (an army, etc.) with new men; enlist (men) for military or naval service; raise (a force) by enlistment; also, more generally, to add to or maintain the number of (any body, class, etc.: as, to *recruit* a colonial population with new settlers); furnish or replenish with a fresh supply or stock (as, "The contributions . . . did little to *recruit* the Exchequer": Green's "Short Hist. of the Eng. People," viii. 5); renew (supplies, etc.: as, "having . . . fully *recruited* our stores of all things necessary," Defoe's "Captain Singleton," vi.); increase or maintain (anything deficient or failing) by some suitable means or process; often, to renew or restore (the health, strength, etc.); refresh or revive (the spirits, etc.); reinvigorate or refresh (a person, etc.: as, "when he was *recruited* with a dram," Smollett's "Humphry Clinker," Sept. 6; "The rest and the refreshment of the fruit . . . *recruited* him, and he moved on languidly," J. H. Newman's "Callista," xii.). **II.** *intr.* To enlist or raise men for military or naval service (as, "The country's first act would be to *recruit* for the navy": Bok's "Americanization of Edward Bok," xxxiv.); also, to gain new supplies of anything lost or wasted; esp., to recover health, strength, or vigor.—**re-cruit′**, *n.* The act or process of recruiting; also, that which is secured or added by recruiting; formerly, a fresh supply of troops for military service†; now, a newly enlisted soldier or sailor; a newly secured member of any body or class (as, "Mr. E. H. Machin ('that most enterprising and enlightened *recruit* to the ranks of theatrical managers')": Arnold Bennett's "The Old Adam," viii.); a fresh supply of anything (now rare).—**re-cruit′er**, *n.*—**re-cruit′ment**, *n.*

re-crys-tal-lize (rē-kris′ta-līz), *v. t.* or *i.* [See *re-*.] To crystallize again.—**re-crys″tal-li-za′tion** (-li-zā′shon), *n.*

rec-tal (rek′tal), *a.* Of or pertaining to the rectum.

rec-tan-gle (rek′tang-gl), *n.* [F. *rectangle*, < L. *rectus*, straight, right, + *angulus*, angle.] A parallelogram with all its angles right angles.—**rec′tan-gled**, *a.* Right-angled; in *her.*, formed with right angles or a right angle.—**rec-tan′gu-lar** (-tang′gū-lar), *a.* Shaped like a rectangle; having right angles or a right angle; having the base or section in the form of a rectangle; placed at right angles; having parts at right angles to each other.—**rec-tan-gu-lar′i-ty** (-lar′i-ti), *n.*—**rec-tan′gu-lar-ly**, *adv.*

Rectangle.

A Chief Rectangled.

rec-ti-fi-a-ble (rek′ti-fī-a-bl), *a.* Capable of being rectified.

rec-ti-fi-ca-tion (rek″ti-fi-kā′shon), *n.* [OF. F. *rectification*, < LL. *rectificatio(n-)*.] The act or operation of rectifying.—**rec′ti-fi-ca-tive** (-kā-tiv), **rec′ti-fi-ca-to-ry** (-kā-tō-ri), *a.* Rectifying; corrective.

rec-ti-fy (rek′ti-fī), *v. t.*; *-fied, -fying.* [OF. F. *rectifier*, < LL. *rectificare*, < L. *rectus*, right, + *facere*, make.] To make, put, or set right; remedy (what is bad or faulty); correct (what is erroneous); put (a thing) into a good or the proper condition, as by removing defects or errors; put right by adjustment or calculation, as an instrument or a course at sea; specif., to purify or refine; purify (a spirit or liquor) by repeated distillation, raising it to a required strength, and sometimes adding flavoring material during the process; also, to make straight†, or bring into line†; in *geom.*, to equate (a curve) with a straight line, or determine the length of (the curve); in *elect.*, to change (an alternating current) into a direct current, without an intermediate transformation of energy.—**to rectify the globe,** in *astron.* and *geog.*, to adjust a globe for the solution of any proposed problem.—**rec′ti-fi-er** (-fī-ėr), *n.*

rec-ti-lin-e-al (rek-ti-lin′ē-al), *a.* Rectilinear.

rec-ti-lin-e-ar (rek-ti-lin′ē-är), *a.* [L. *rectus*, straight, + *linea*, line.] Moving in or forming a straight line; formed or characterized by straight lines.—**rec-ti-lin′e-ar-ly,** *adv.*

rec-ti-tude (rek′ti-tūd), *n.* [OF. F. *rectitude*, < L. *rectitudo*, < *rectus*, straight, right, pp. of *regere*, keep straight, direct, rule: see *regent* and *right*.] Straightness, or direction in a straight line; also, rightness of principle or practice, uprightness, integrity, or virtue (as, "The name of Brutus would be a guaranty to the people of *rectitude* of intention," Froude's "Cæsar," xxvi.; "the simple, proud *rectitude* of her life," Arnold Bennett's "Book of Carlotta," i. 4); also, correctness (as, *rectitude* of judgment; "Whatever he said was . . . uttered with *rectitude* of articulation," C. B. Brown's "Wieland," viii.).

rec-to (rek′tō), *n.*; pl. *-tos* (-tōz). [L., abl. of *rectus*, right: see *rectitude*.] In *printing*, the right-hand page of an open book; the front of a leaf: opposed to *verso*.

rec-tor (rek′tọr), *n.* [L., < *regere*, direct, rule: see *rectitude*.] A ruler†; one exercising directing control (now rare); specif., the permanent head in certain universities, colleges, and schools; the chief elective officer of a university, as in Scotland; in the *Rom. Cath. Ch.*, an ecclesiastic in charge of a college, religious house, or congregation; in the *Ch. of Eng.*, a clergyman who has the charge of a parish with full possession of all its rights, tithes, etc.; in the U. S., a clergyman in charge of a parish in the Protestant Episcopal Church.—**rec′tor-ate** (-āt), *n.* The office, dignity, or term of a rector.—**rec-to′ri-al** (-tō′ri-al), *a.* Pertaining to a rector or a rectory.—**rec′tor-ship,** *n.*—**rec′tor-y** (-i), *n.*; pl. *-ies* (-iz). A benefice held by a rector; also, a rector's house; a parsonage.

rec-tum (rek′tum), *n.*; pl. *-ta* (-tä). [NL., 'straight (intestine),' prop. neut. of L. *rectus*, straight: see *rectitude*.] In *anat.*, the comparatively straight, terminal section of the intestine, ending in the anus.

rec-tus (rek′tus), *n.*; pl. *-ti* (-tī). [NL., 'straight (muscle),' < L. *rectus*, straight: see *rectitude*.] In *anat.*, any of several muscles, as of the abdomen, thigh, eye, etc.: so called from the straightness of their course.

re-cueil (rė-kė-y′), *n.* [F., < *recueillir*, < L. *recolligere*: see *recollect*[1].] A collection of writings.

re-cum-bent (rē-kum′bent), *a.* [L. *recumbens* (-ent-), ppr. of *recumbere*, recline, < *re-*, back, + *-cumbere*, lie.] Lying down; reclining; leaning.—**re-cum′ben-cy,** *n.*—**re-cum′-bent-ly,** *adv.*

re-cu-per-ate (rē-kū′pė-rāt), *v.*; *-ated, -ating.* [L. *recuperatus*, pp. of *recuperare, reciperare*, regain, recover: cf. L. *recipere*, take back (see *receive*), also E. *recover*[2].] **I.** *tr.* To recover or regain (obs. or rare: as, to *recuperate* one's health or spirits); also, to restore to health, vigor, etc. (as, "We had paused to *recuperate* our animals": G. W. Cable's "Cavalier," i.); also, to make up for (loss, etc.: rare); recoup (one's self), as for expense or loss (rare: as, "He paid a fixed sum to the clergyman, and *recuperated* himself by a grinding tyranny of the tenants," Lecky's "Hist. of Eng. in the 18th Century," xvi.). **II.** *intr.* To recover from sickness or exhaustion; regain health or strength; also, to return to a normal condition; recover from pecuniary loss.—**re-cu-per-a′tion** (-pė-rā′shọn), *n.* [L. *recuperatio*(n-).] Recovery, as of something lost (obs. or rare); now, commonly, recovery from sickness, exhaustion, etc.—**re-cu′per-a-tive** (-pė-rā-tiv), *a.* That recuperates; having the power of recuperating; also, pertaining to recuperation or recovery from sickness, exhaustion, etc. (as, "Youth . . . has its *recuperative* powers": W. Churchill's "Modern Chronicle," i. 6).

re-cur (rē-kėr′), *v. i.*; *-curred, -curring.* [L. *recurrere*, run back, recur, < *re-*, back, + *currere*, run.] To go back, as to a place (now rare); fig., to return in action, conduct, belief, etc. (as, to *recur* to former principles); return in thought, discourse, etc. (as, to *recur* to a subject); also, to resort for assistance, or have recourse (as, to *recur* to an expedient); also, to return to the mind, thoughts, or memory, as a subject, idea, etc. (as, "Oft does my heart indulge the rising thought, Which still *recurs*": Byron's "Childish Recollections"); come up again for consideration, as a question; also, to occur again, sometimes repeatedly, as an event, an experience, an anniversary, etc.—**recurring decimal.** See under *decimal, n.*

re-cure† (rē-kūr′), *v. t.* or *i.* [L. *recurare*, < *re-*, again, + *curare*, E. *cure, v.*] To cure or become cured; heal.

re-cur-rence (rē-kur′ens), *n.* The act or fact of recurring; return, as to a place (rare: as, "those poor victims to monotony, who from day to day pace along the beach, in endless progress and *recurrence*," Lamb's "Old Margate Hoy"); fig., return to a state, habit, etc. (as, "*recurrence* to image-worship": Borrow's "Romany Rye," iii.); return in thought or discourse, as to a subject; resort or recourse to something; the return of a thought, etc., to the mind (as, "an indistinct *recurrence* of impressions": George Eliot's "Romola," lix.); the fresh or repeated occurrence of an event, experience, etc.

re-cur-rent (rē-kur′ent). [L. *recurrens* (-ent-), ppr.] **I.** *a.* That recurs; occurring or appearing again, esp. repeatedly or periodically (as, "A book he browsed over with a *recurrent* pleasure was Waterton's Wanderings in South America," H. G. Wells's "Mr. Polly," vii.; the *recurrent* attacks of a disease); also, in *anat.*, etc., turned back so as to run in a reverse direction, as a nerve, artery, branch, etc. **II.** *n.* In *anat.*, a recurrent nerve or artery.—**re-cur′rent-ly,** *adv.*

re-cur-vate (rē-kėr′vāt), *a.* [L. *recurvatus*, pp.] Recurved.

re-curve (rē-kėrv′), *v. t.* or *i.*; *-curved, -curving.* [L. *recurvare* (pp. *recurvatus*), < *re-*, back, + *curvare*, E. *curve, v.*] To curve or bend back or backward.—**re-cur-va-tion** (rē-kėr-vā′shọn), *n.*

rec-u-sant (rek′ụ-zant or rē-kū′-). [L. *recusans* (-ant-), ppr. of *recusare*: see *recuse*.] **I.** *a.* Refusing to submit, comply, etc.; obstinate in refusal; in *Eng. hist.*, refusing to attend services of the Church of England, or to acknowledge the ecclesiastical supremacy of the crown. **II.** *n.* One who is recusant; in *Eng. hist.*, a person, esp. a Roman Catholic, who refused to attend the services of the Church of England (as, "They would not promise his Majesty their consent to the repeal of the Test and penal Statutes against Popish *Recusants*": Evelyn's "Diary," March 10, 1687).—**rec′u-sance, rec′u-san-cy,** *n.*

re-cuse (rē-kūz′), *v. t.*; *-cused, -cusing.* [L. *recusare*, object to, reject, < *re-*, back, + *causa*, cause.] To reject; in *law*, to reject or challenge (a judge or juror) as disqualified to act. [Now rare.]

re-cut (rē-kut′), *v. t.*; *-cut, -cutting.* [See *re-*.] To cut again.

red[1] (red), *a.*; compar. *redder*, superl. *reddest.* [AS. *read* = D. *rood* = G. *rot* = Icel. *raudhr* = Goth. *rauths*, red; akin to L. *rufus, ruber*, Gr. ἐρυθρός, Skt. *rudhira*, red.] Of a bright, warm color like that of blood; also, having red hair, clothing, etc.; also, noting, belonging to, or pertaining to the American (Indian) race, which has a reddish or brownish skin (as, a *red* man, an American Indian: see *American, a.*); also, characterized by blood or fire, or by violence (as, "*Red* Battle stamps his foot, and nations feel the shock," Byron's "Childe Harold," i. 38; "Justice . . . Drops the *red* vengeance from his willing hand," Cowper's "Truth," 278); also, revolutionary or anarchistic (the red flag being a revolutionary emblem); ultraradical politically; also, noting or pertaining to the north pole of a magnet.—**red algæ,** the red or purplish seaweeds forming the class *Rhodophyceæ.* See *rhodophyceous.*—**red arsenic.** Same as *realgar.*—**red astrachan** (as′trạ-kạn), an early variety of apple having a yellowish skin spotted and streaked with red, and a crisp, juicy pulp of rich, acid flavor.—**red cent,** in the U. S., a cent (coin): used esp. in negative expressions: as, not worth a *red cent.* [Colloq.]—**red clover,** the common clover, *Trifolium pratense*, with red flowers: widely cultivated as a forage-plant.—**red cross,** a red Greek cross on a white ground, adopted as the badge of the Red Cross

Society, an international philanthropic organization formed, in consequence of the Geneva Convention of 1864, to care for the sick and wounded in war, and secure the neutrality of nurses, hospitals, etc., and active also in relieving suffering occasioned by pestilence, floods, fire, and other calamities; [*caps.*] the Red Cross Society, or a branch of it (as, the American *Red Cross*, incorporated in 1905).—**red deer**, a species of deer, *Cervus elaphus*, native in the forests of Europe and Asia, and formerly very abundant in England, where it served as an object of the chase; also, the common American deer, *Cariacus virginianus*, in its summer coat. —**red fir.** Same as *Douglas spruce*.—**red fire**, any of various combustible preparations (as one containing strontium nitrate) which burn with a vivid red light: used in pyrotechnic displays, signaling, etc.—**red gods,** the gods of the red men or of wild nature generally, presiding over life and pursuits in the wilds or the open (a phrase made familiar by its use in Kipling's poem, "The Feet of the Young Men," as in the lines following: "Now the Four-way Lodge is opened, now the Hunting Winds are loose . . . Now the *Red Gods* make their medicine again! . . . the *Red Gods* call us out and we must go!"); also, sometimes, the gods of war, or of slaughter or bloodshed.—**red grouse.** See *grouse*[1], *n.*—**red hat,** the official hat, or the office or dignity, of a cardinal; sometimes, a cardinal.—**red lane**, the throat. [Colloq.]—**red lattice**, a lattice painted red, formerly much used as a sign or mark of an ale-house or inn; hence (archaic), an ale-house; a tavern.—**red lead.** See under *lead*[2], *n.*— **red osier.** See *osier*, *n.*—**red pepper.** See *pepper*, *n.*— **red republican,** an extreme or radical republican; [*caps.*] in *Fr. hist.*, one of a group of more violent republicans at the time of the French Revolution and of the Commune of 1871 (orig. so called with reference to the red liberty-cap adopted as a badge).—**red tape**, tape of a red color, much used for tying up official papers; hence, excessive attention to formality and routine.—**red**[1], *n.* A red color; also, a red pigment or dye; also, something red; a red man, or American Indian; a member of a company, party, army, etc., wearing or having red as its distinctive color; [often *cap.*] an ultraradical in politics; an anarchist.—**the red,** red ink as used in bookkeeping and accounting practice for recording losses and deficits in financial statements; hence, in general, loss or deficit: as, to be in *the red*; to be out of *the red*.

red[2], **redd** (red), *v. t.*; *red* or *redd, redding*. [=MLG. and D. *redden*.] To clear; clear out; clean up; put in order; tidy; disentangle; settle (a quarrel, etc.); separate (combatants). [Sc. and prov. Eng.]

re-dact (rē-dakt'), *v. t.* [L. *redactus*, pp. of *redigere*, bring back, reduce, < *red-*, for *re-*, back, + *agere*, drive.] To bring or reduce to a certain form or state†; now, to bring (written matter) into a presentable literary form; prepare for publication; revise; edit; also, to draw up or frame (a statement, announcement, etc.).—**re-dac'tion** (-dak'-shon), *n.* The act or process of redacting; revision or editing; also, a work thus prepared; a form or version of a work as prepared by revision or editing.—**re-dac'tor,** *n.* One who redacts; an editor.

re-dan (rē-dan'), *n.* [F. *redan*, for *redent*, < L. *re-*, back, + *dens* (*dent*-), tooth.] In *fort.*, a simple work consisting of two parapets forming a salient angle.

red-ar-gue (re-där'gū), *v. t.; -gued, -guing.* [L. *redarguere* (pp. *redargutus*), < *red-*, for *re-*, back, + *arguere*, show, prove.] To confute (a person) by argument; also, to refute or disprove (a statement, argument, etc.). [Chiefly Sc.] —**red-ar-gu-tion** (red-är-gū'shon), *n.*

Redans.

red=blood-ed (red'blud'ed), *a.* Having red blood, as most vertebrates and certain worms; also, popularly, of healthy strength or vigor; vigorous; virile.

red-breast (red'brest), *n.* Either the European or the American robin; also, a wading bird, the knot, *Tringa canutus*; also, a fresh-water sunfish, *Lepomis auritus*, of the eastern U. S.—**red=breast''ed,** *a.*

red-bud (red'bud), *n.* The American Judas-tree, *Cercis*

canadensis, bearing small, bud-like, pink flowers; also, any of various related trees.

red-cap (red'kap), *n.* One who wears a red cap; also, a specter or goblin popularly supposed to haunt old castles in Scotland; also, the European goldfinch, *Carduelis elegans* (local, Eng.).—**red'=capped,** *a.*

red-coat (red'kōt), *n.* One who wears a red coat; esp., a British soldier (as, "The *red-coats* are abroad . . . these English must be looked to": Cooper's "Spy," xii.).—**red''=coat''ed,** *a.*

redd, *v. t.* See *red*[2].

red-den (red'n), *v. t. or i.* To make or become red.

red-den-dum (re-den'dum), *n.*; pl. *-da* (-dä). [L., neut. gerundive of *reddere*, give back: see *render*[2].] In *law*, a reservation in a deed whereby the grantor creates or reserves some new thing to himself out of what he had granted before.

red-dish (red'ish), *a.* Somewhat red; tending to red.— **red'dish-ness,** *n.*

red-dle (red'l), *n.* and *v.* Same as *ruddle*.

red=dog (red'dog), *n.* The lowest grade of flour produced in milling.

red=drum (red'drum'), *n.* A large drumfish, *Sciænops ocellata*, an important food-fish of the Atlantic coast of the U.S.

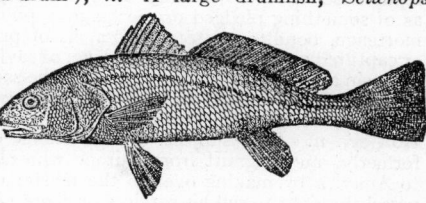

Red-drum.

rede (rēd), *v. t.* [An older spelling of *read*.] To counsel or advise (as, "I *rede* thee not to go": W. Morris's "Jason," i. 361); also, to explain or interpret (as, "a riddle that he cannot *rede*": Carlyle's "Sartor Resartus," i. 8); also, to relate or tell. See *read, v.* [Archaic or prov.]—**rede,** *n.* Counsel or advice; also, a plan, design, or scheme; also, a tale, story, or narrative. [Archaic or prov.]

re-dec-o-rate (rē-dek'ō-rāt), *v. t.* [See *re-*.] To decorate again or anew.—**re-dec-o-ra'tion** (-rā'shon), *n.*

re-deem (rē-dēm'), *v. t.* [OF. *redimer* (F. *rédimer*), < L. *redimere* (pp. *redemptus*), buy back, redeem, < *red-*, for *re-*, back, + *emere*, buy.] To buy back (as, "If a man sell a dwelling house . . . he may *redeem* it within a whole year after it is sold": Lev. xxv. 29); recover (something pledged or mortgaged) by payment or other satisfaction; buy or pay off, or clear off by payment (as, to *redeem* a mortgage; to *redeem* bonds or preferred stock; "Massachusetts had . . . voted that its public notes should be *redeemed* with the expected remittances from the royal exchequer," Bancroft's "Hist. of the U. S.," Amer. Revolution, i. 2); discharge or fulfil (a pledge, promise, etc.); also, to obtain the release or restoration of, as from captivity, bondage, detention, etc., by paying a price or ransom (as, to *redeem* prisoners or slaves; to *redeem* captured goods); ransom; hence, in general, to deliver, rescue, or save (as, "*Redeem* Israel, O God, out of all his troubles," Ps. xxv. 22; "Like some merchant who, in storm, Throws the freight over to *redeem* the ship," Browning's "Balaustion's Adventure"); specif., in religious use, to deliver from sin and its consequences by means of a sacrifice offered for the sinner (as, "Christ hath *redeemed* us from the curse of the law, being made a curse for us": Gal. iii. 13); also, to serve as a means of saving (as, "Thy ransom paid, which man from death *redeems*, His death for man," Milton's "Paradise Lost," xii. 424; "Perhaps some modern touches here and there *Redeem'd* it [a poem] from the charge of nothingness," Tennyson's "Morte d'Arthur," 279); also, to make atonement or amends for (as, "Which of you will be mortal to *redeem* Man's mortal crime?" Milton's "Paradise Lost," iii. 214; "I expect you will *redeem* past errors," Scott's "Guy Mannering," li.); serve as amends for, or make up for (as, "His want of virtue was not *redeemed* by any superior talents": Gibbon's "Decline and Fall of the Roman Empire," xlviii.); also, to save (time) from being lost (as by making use of it: as, "See then that ye walk circumspectly . . . *Redeeming* the time, because the days are evil," Eph. v. 16); also, to reclaim (land: as, a tract *redeemed* from the sea; "a plot of land *redeemed* from the heath," Hardy's "Return of the Native," i. 4).—**re-deem′a-ble**, *a.* Capable of being redeemed; esp., capable of being bought back or paid off; also, that is to be redeemed (as, bonds *redeemable* in 1938).—**re-deem′a-ble-ness**, *n.*—**re-deem′a-bly**, *adv.*—**re-deem′-er**, *n.* One who redeems; specif. [*cap.*], the Saviour of the world, Jesus Christ.—**re-deem′ing**, *p. a.* That redeems; saving; atoning; serving as amends, or compensating (as, a *redeeming* quality or feature).

re-de-liv-er (rē-dē-liv′ėr), *v. t.* [See *re-.*] To deliver back, or return; also, to deliver again or anew; also, to make report off† (see Shakspere's "Hamlet," v. 2. 186).—**re-de-liv′er-y**, *n.*

re-de-mand (rē-dē-månd′), *v. t.* [See *re-.*] To demand back; demand the return of; also, to demand again.—**re-de-mand′**, *n.* A demanding back or again.—**re-de-mand′a-ble**, *a.*

re-demp-tion (rē-demp′shon), *n.* [OF. *redemption* (F. *rédemption*), < L. *redemptio(n-)*, < *redimere*, E. *redeem*.] The act of redeeming, or the state of being redeemed; repurchase, as of something sold; recovery by payment, as of something pledged or mortgaged; paying off, as of a mortgage, bond, or note; ransom, as of prisoners, slaves, or captured goods; deliverance, rescue, or saving; deliverance from sin and its consequences through the sacrifice or atonement of Jesus Christ, or salvation; atonement (as, "the *redemption* of the transgressions": Heb. ix. 15).—**re-demp′-tion-er**, *n.* One subject to conditions of redemption; formerly, an emigrant from Europe who obtained passage to America by making over to the master or owner of the vessel the right to sell his services or claim his earnings for a term sufficient to repay all expenses.—**re-demp′tive**, *a.* Serving to redeem.

re-demp-tor (rē-demp′tor), *n.* [L., < *redimere*, E. *redeem*.] A redeemer.

Re-demp-tor-ist (rē-demp′tor-ist), *n.* [F. *rédemptoriste*, < L. *redemptor*, E. *redemptor*.] A member of the Congregation of the Most Holy Redeemer, a Roman Catholic order founded by Alfonso Maria de' Liguori of Naples in 1732 for missionary work among the poor.

re-demp-to-ry (rē-demp′tō-ri), *a.* Redemptive.

re-de-ploy (rē-dē-ploi′), *v. t.* [*re-* + *deploy*.] *Milit.*, to transfer (troops) to another theater of war, a distant location, etc.

re-de-pos-it (rē-dē-poz′it), *v. t.* [See *re-.*] To deposit again.—**re-de-pos′it**, *n.*

re-de-vel-op (rē-dē-vel′op), *v.* [See *re-.*] **I.** *tr.* To develop again; in *photog.*, to intensify by a second developing process. **II.** *intr.* To develop again.—**re-de-vel′op-er**, *n.*—**re-de-vel′op-ment**, *n.*

red-field-i-a (red-fēl′di-ä), *n.* [NL.; named from J. H. *Redfield* (1815–95), American botanist.] A tall grass, *Redfieldia flexuosa*, with a diffusely spreading panicle, found in sandy parts of Nebraska, Kansas, and other western States. Also called *Redfield's grass*.

red-fin (red′fin), *n.* Any of various small, chiefly cyprinoid, fresh-water fishes with reddish fins, as a shiner, *Notropis cornutus*, of eastern and central North America.

Redfieldia. — *a*, spikelet; *b*, flower; *c*, glumes.

red=gum[1] (red′gum), *n.* Any of several trees of the genus *Eucalyptus*, so named from the red gum which they exude. See *eucalyptus*.

red=gum[2] (red′gum), *n.* [ME. *red-gownd*: cf. AS. *gund*,

pus, matter.] A reddish eruption affecting infants (see *strophulus*); also, a rust affecting grain.

red=hand-ed (red′han′ded), *a.* Having the hands red with blood, or having the evidences of crime still on the person; in the very act of crime: as, "to be taken *red-handed* . . . from the slaughter of an adversary" (Whyte-Melville's "Katerfelto," i.); to be caught *red-handed* in robbery.

red-head (red′hed), *n.* A person having red hair; also, the old-world pochard, *Æthyia (Aythya) ferina*, or a related American duck, *Æ. americana*, both having the head of a chestnut-red color.—**red′=head″ed**, *a.*

red=hot (red′hot′), *a.* Red with heat; very hot; hence, fig., of persons, greatly excited; very enthusiastic; extreme in views, etc. (as, "He was a *red-hot* Orangeman": Lever's "Harry Lorrequer," vi.); of things, violent or furious (as, "The spirit of intestine faction was *redhot*": Morley's "Oliver Cromwell," iv. 3).

red-in-gote (red′ing-gōt), *n.* [F., < E. *riding-coat*.] A man's outer coat with long skirts that overlap in front; also, a similar garment for women, sometimes forming part of the indoor dress.

re-din-te-grate (rē-din′tē-grāt), *v.*; -grated, -grating. [L. *redintegratus*, pp. of *redintegrare*, make whole again, < *red-*, for *re-*, again, + *integrare*: see *integrate*.] **I.** *tr.* To make whole again; restore to a perfect state; renew; reëstablish. **II.** *intr.* To become whole again or renewed.—**re-din-te-gra′tion** (-grā′shon), *n.* [L. *redintegratio(n-)*.] The act or process of redintegrating; restoration to a perfect state, renewal, or reëstablishment (as, "A *redintegration* of love began to take place between the Colonel and his relatives in Park Lane": Thackeray's "Newcomes," xxiv.); in *psychol.*, the tendency of elements once combined as parts of a single mental state subsequently to recall or suggest one another.

re-di-rect (rē-di-rekt′), *v. t.* [See *re-.*] To direct again or anew.—**re-di-rect′**, *a.* In *law*, noting or pertaining to the examination of a witness by the party calling him, after cross-examination.—**re-di-rec′tion** (-rek′shon), *n.*

re-dis-count (rē-dis′kount), *v. t.* [See *re-.*] To discount again.—**re-dis′count**, *n.* A rediscounting.

re-dis-cov-er (rē-dis-kuv′ėr), *v. t.* [See *re-.*] To discover again or anew.—**re-dis-cov′er-er**, *n.*—**re-dis-cov′er-y**, *n.*

re-dis-trib-ute (rē-dis-trib′ūt), *v. t.* [See *re-.*] To distribute again or anew.—**re-dis-tri-bu′tion** (-bū′shon), *n.*

re-dis-trict (rē-dis′trikt), *v. t.* [See *re-.*] To divide anew into districts, as for administrative purposes.

red-i-vi-vus (red-i-vī′vus), *a.* [L., < *redi-*, for *re-*, again, + *vivus*, living.] Alive again; returned to life.

red=let-ter (red′let″ėr), *a.* Marked or indicated by red letters, as especially important festival days in the church calendar; hence, memorable, or especially happy (as, a *red-letter* day in one's life).

red=light (red′līt′), *a.* Having red lights; esp., using red lights as the sign of disorderly resorts or houses of ill fame; characterized by or pertaining to such resorts (as, *red-light* districts; *red-light* conditions).

red-ly (red′li), *adv.* With a red color or glow: as, "The blaze was *redly* reflected in the waters of the strait" (Borrow's "Bible in Spain," liv.).—**red′ness**, *n.*

red-o-lent (red′ō-lent), *a.* [L. *redolens* (-ent-), ppr. of *redolere*, < *red-*, for *re-*, back, + *olere*, emit a smell.] Having or diffusing a pleasant odor; fragrant; often, odorous or smelling (*of*: as, "the inn parlour, *redolent* of aromatic black tea, eggs, and hot toast," Lever's "Harry Lorrequer," xliv.); fig., suggestive or reminiscent (*of*: as, "The very sound of it [a name] is *redolent* of the twelfth century": Du Maurier's "Trilby," vi.).—**red′o-lence**, *n.*—**red′o-lent-ly**, *adv.*

re-doub-le (rē-dub′l), *v.*; -led, -ling. [OF. F. *redoubler*.] **I.** *tr.* To double, or make twice as great (as, to *redouble* one's efforts; "The wind now *redoubled* its fury," Marryat's "King's Own," lii.); also, to repeat; do, say, etc., again; sometimes, to repeat (sound); echo or reëcho (as, "Their moans The vales *redoubled* to the hills, and they To Heaven": Milton's "Sonnets," On the Late Massacre in Piemont); sometimes, to duplicate by reflection, as in water. **II.** *intr.* To be doubled, or become twice as great (as, "The musketry fire *redoubled*": Kipling's "Light That Failed," ii.); some-

fat, fāte, fär, fåll, åsk, fåre; net, mē, hėr; pin, pīne; not, nōte, mŏve, nôr; up, lūte, pull; oi, oil; ou, out; (lightened) aviąry, ēlect, agōny, intŏ, ūnite; (obscured) errąnt, operä, ardęnt, actǫr, natūre; ch, chip; g, go; th, thin; ᴛʜ, then; y, you;

times, to be echoed, or resound (as, "Loud shrieks the virgin train, And the loud shriek *redoubles* from the main": Pope's tr. Homer's "Odyssey," vi.).—**re-doub′le-ment**, *n*.

re-doubt¹ (rę̄-dout′), *n*. [F. *redoute*, < It. *ridotto*, < ML. *reductus*, a retreat, < L. *reducere*, withdraw: see *reduce*.] In *fort*., an isolated work forming a complete inclosure without reëntrant angles; also, a réduit.

re-doubt² (rę̄-dout′), *v. t*. [OF. F. *redouter*, < *re-* (< L. *re-*), back, + *douter*, E. *doubt*.] To fear; dread; be in awe of: now chiefly as in *redoubted*, *p. a*.—**re-doubt′a-ble**, *a*. [OF. F. *redoutable*.] That is to be feared or dreaded; formidable; commanding respect: often in burlesque or irony.—**re-doubt′ed**, *p. a*. Dreaded; formidable; respected; renowned: as, "The main body was led on by Edward himself, supported by a train of his most *redoubted* generals" (Jane Porter's "Scottish Chiefs," lxxxix.).

re-dound (rę̄-dound′), *v. i*. [OF. F. *redonder*, < L. *redundare*, overflow, redound, < *red-*, for *re-*, back, + *undare*, rise in waves, < *unda*, a wave.] To surge up or overflow, as water†; be in excess or superabundant†; be plentiful†, or abound†; also, to overflow with or abound in something†; also, to flow back†, or go or come back†; bound or come back†, or recoil†; echo back†; now, to come back in effect, or have effect or result, as to the advantage or disadvantage, or the credit or discredit, of a person or thing (as, "where a doubtful procedure *redounds* to the advantage of the person who adopts it," G. P. R. James's "Hist. of Charlemagne," ii.; "I did not omit . . . any . . . particular which I thought might *redound* to the honour of my country," Swift's "Gulliver's Travels," ii. 6); result or accrue, as to a person (as, "the mischief that *redounded* to our unfortunate patron from the transactions of that day": Godwin's "Caleb Williams," xii.); come back or recoil, as upon a person (as, disgrace *redounds* upon one for a discreditable action); sometimes, to proceed, issue, or arise (as, "the anxiety of spirit which *redoundeth* from knowledge": Bacon's "Advancement of Learning," i. 1. 3).—**re-dound′**, *n*. The fact of redounding or resulting: as, "Not without *redound* Of use and glory to yourselves ye come" (Tennyson's "Princess," ii. 28).

re-dout (rę̄-dout′), *n*. See *redoubt¹*.

red-o-wa (red′ō-wä or -vä), *n*. [G., < Bohem. *rejdovák*.] A Bohemian dance in two forms, one, the more common, resembling the waltz or the mazurka, the other resembling the polka; also, a piece of music for such a dance.

red-poll (red′pōl), *n*. Any of various small fringilline birds of the genus *Acanthis*, the males of which usually have a crimson poll or head; also, the common old-world linnet.—**red′=polled** (-pōld), *a*.

re-draft (rē-draft′), *n*. [See *re-*.] A second draft or drawing; in *com*., a draft on the drawer or indorsers of a protested bill of exchange for the amount of the bill plus the costs and charges.—**re-draft′**, *v. t*. To draft or draw again or anew.

Redpoll (*Acanthis linaria*).

re-draw (rē-drä′), *v. t*.; pret. *-drew*, pp. *-drawn*. [See *re-*.] To draw again or anew; make a redraft of.—**re-draw′er**, *n*.

re-dress¹ (rē-dres′), *v. t*. [See *re-*.] To dress again. Also written *re-dress*.

re-dress² (rē-dres′), *v. t*. [OF. F. *redresser*, < *re-* (< L. *re-*), again, + *dresser*, E. *dress*.] To set upright again, as something fallen or out of the perpendicular†; hence, to restore†, amend†, or mend† (as, "Broken glass no cement can *redress*": Shakspere's "Passionate Pilgrim," xiii.); also, to adjust evenly again, as a balance (usually fig.: as, "unless the balance had been *redressed* by a great transfer of power from the crown to the parliament," Macaulay's "Hist. of Eng.," i.); also, to set right (anything wrong or distressing); right, remedy, or repair (wrongs, injuries, injustice, etc.); deal with (grievances, etc.) so as to give

relief; correct or reform (abuses, evils, etc.); remedy or relieve (suffering, want, misfortune, etc.); relieve, heal, or cure (a wound, disease, etc.: as, "The frenzy of the brain may be *redress'd* By med'cine well applied," Cowper's "Task," vi. 521); also, to give relief, reparation, or redress to (as, "Hereditary bondsmen! . . . Will Gaul or Muscovite *redress* ye?" Byron's "Childe Harold," ii. 76).—**re-dress′²**, *n*. [AF. *redresse*.] The act of redressing, or the setting right of what is wrong or distressing (as, the *redress* of wrongs, grievances, or abuses); also, relief from wrong or injury, whether afforded by putting an end to it, by compensation in damages, by punishing the wrongdoer, or otherwise (as, "The people, whose privileges he has invaded, call aloud for *redress*": Jane Porter's "Scottish Chiefs," xxxvi.); also, means of redressing wrong or injury, or remedy (as, "There was no *redress* against the lawless violence to which they were perpetually exposed": Motley's "Dutch Republic," Introd., vi.).—**re-dress′a-ble**, *a*. Capable of being redressed.—**re-dress′al**, **re-dress′ment**, *n*. The act of redressing; redress.—**re-dress′er**, *n*.

red-root (red′rōt), *n*. A North American plant, *Gyrotheca tinctoria*, having sword-shaped leaves, woolly flowers, and a red root which has been used in dyeing; also, any of various other plants with red roots, as the alkanet, *Alkanna tinctoria*, and a pigweed, *Amarantus retroflexus*.

red-shank (red′-shangk), *n*. An old-world limicoline bird, *Totanus calidris*, of the snipe family (*Scolopacidæ*), or the related *T. fuscus* (the 'spotted redshank'): so called from the red legs.

Redshank (*Totanus calidris*).

red=short (red′-shôrt), *a*. In *metal*., brittle when at a red heat, as iron or steel containing too much sulphur.—**red′=short″ness**, *n*.

red-skin (red′skin), *n*. A North American Indian: as, "We have had more difficulty with white desperadoes than with the *redskins*" (Roosevelt's "Ranch Life and the Hunting-Trail," viii.).

red-start (red′stärt), *n*. [See *start¹*.] A small European bird, *Ruticilla phœnicura*, with a reddish tail; also, a fly-catching warbler, *Setophaga ruticilla*, of America (see cut below).

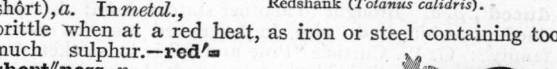

European Redstart (*Ruticilla phœnicura*).

red-top (red′top), *n*. A grass, *Agrostis alba*, certain forms of which have a reddish panicle.

re-duce (rę̄-dūs′), *v*.; *-duced*, *-ducing*. [L. *reducere* (pp. *reductus*), lead back, withdraw, restore, reduce, < *re-* back, + *ducere*, lead.] **I.** *tr*. To lead or bring back†; restore (a condition, etc.: obs. or rare: as, "while childhood, and while dreams, *reducing* childhood, shall be left," Lamb's "Old Benchers of the Inner Temple"); bring back

American Redstart (*Setophaga ruticilla*).

from error to correct conduct or belief†; bring back to a former state or condition†; also, to bring to a certain state or condition, arrangement or classification, or form or character (as, to *reduce* affairs to order; to *reduce* a theory to practice; to *reduce* a language to rules; to *reduce* things under a number of heads; to *reduce* a statement to writing; to *reduce* glass to powder); also, to adjust or correct by making allowances, as an astronomical observation; also, to bring by constraint or compulsion, as to obedience, reason, etc. (as, "The King hath two methods of *reducing* them to obedience," Swift's "Gulliver's Travels," iii. 3; "He . . . had . . . means of *reducing* her to reason," Mrs. Wharton's "Son at the Front," xiv.); bring under control or authority (as, "To Brittany Cæsar went in person to *reduce* the rebellious Veneti": Froude's "Cæsar," xvi.); bring into subjection, as a country; compel to surrender, as a town or fortress (as, "He stormed Caen, received the surrender of Bayeux, *reduced* Alençon and Falaise": Green's "Short Hist. of the Eng. People," v. 6); also, to bring down to a bad or unpleasant condition, as to poverty or to physical debility; impair in fortune; weaken physically; compel by necessity to do something (as, "A deserter . . . says the garrison is brought to the utmost necessity . . . that they were *reduced* to eat horse-flesh": Steele, in "Tatler," 59); also, to bring down to a lower rank, dignity, etc.; degrade; also, to bring down to a smaller extent, size, amount, number, etc.; lower in degree, intensity, etc. (as, to *reduce* speed); diminish or lessen; sometimes, to lower in price; specif., to make a smaller copy, as of a figure or a design, without changing the form or proportion; in *surg.*, to restore to the normal place or condition, as a dislocated organ; in *math.*, to change the denomination or form of; in *chem.* and *metal.*, to bring into the metallic state by separating from non-metallic constituents; smelt; hence, to deoxidize; add hydrogen to; specif., in *chem.*, to change (a compound) so that the valence of the positive element is lower; in *photog.*, to treat so as to make less dense, as a negative; in *Sc. law*, to rescind, revoke, or annul. **II.** *intr.* To become reduced; undergo reduction in extent, size, amount, degree, etc.; become less.—**re·duced'**, *p. a.* Brought to another state or form; also, subdued or subjugated; also, impoverished (as, "a *reduced* family": G. W. Curtis's "Prue and I," iv.); weakened or impaired; also, diminished or lessened; lowered in price; made on a smaller scale.—**re·du'cer** (-dū'sẽr), *n.* One who or that which reduces; in *mech.*, a threaded cylindrical piece for connecting one pipe with another of smaller or larger diameter; in *photog.*, a chemical substance used to reduce a negative in density; also, that ingredient of a photographic developer which causes the silver in the emulsion on the plate or print to become reduced to metallic silver.—**re·du'ci·ble**, *a.* That

a, Reducer, connecting the pipe of larger diameter *b* with the pipe of smaller diameter *c*.

may be reduced; convertible, as to a particular state, arrangement, or form; that may be diminished or lessened. —**re·du'cing=valve**, *n.* In *mech.*, an automatic valve for reducing the pressure of steam, air, or the like, as one for maintaining a lower pressure in a steam-heating apparatus than that in the boiler.

re·duc·tion (rẽ-duk'shọn), *n.* [L. *reductio*(n-).] The act of reducing, or the state of being reduced; conversion, subjugation, lowering in rank, diminution, etc. (see *reduce, v.*); also, a form of something produced by reducing; a copy of something on a smaller scale; also, the amount by which something is reduced or diminished (as, a *reduction* of 25% on a tax).—**re·duc'tive**, *a.* Serving or tending to reduce.

ré·duit (rā-dwē'), *n.* [F., < ML. *reductus*, a retreat: see *redoubt*[1].] In *fort.*, a central or retired work constructed within another.

re·dun·dance (rẽ-dun'dạns), *n.* Redundancy.

re·dun·dan·cy (rẽ-dun'dạn-si), *n.*; pl. *-dancies* (-dạn-siz). The state of being redundant; superabundance; superfluity; also, a redundant thing, part, or amount; a superfluity.

re·dun·dant (rẽ-dun'dạnt), *a.* [L. *redundans* (-ant-), ppr. of *redundare*, overflow: see *redound*.] Superabundant, or exceeding what is usual or natural (as, "These *redundant*

locks, Robustious to no purpose, clustering down, Vain monument of strength," Milton's "Samson Agonistes," 568; "foliage of such dark *redundant* growth," Cowper's "Task," i. 226); having some unusual, extra, or superfluous part or feature (as, a *redundant* interval, in *music*, an augmented interval); also, being an excess, or superfluous (as, a *redundant* part; a *redundant* word in a sentence); also, characterized by superabundance or superfluity; esp., characterized by or using too many words to express the ideas (as, *redundant* language; a *redundant* style; "Again the *redundant* Maas responded, asserting . . . the uniform satisfaction of the provinces," Motley's "Dutch Republic," i. 1).—**re·dun'dant·ly**, *adv.*

re·du·pli·cate (rẽ-dū'pli-kāt), *v.*; *-cated, -cating.* [ML. *reduplicatus*, pp. of *reduplicare*, < L. *re-*, again, + *duplicare*, double: see *duplicate*.] **I.** *tr.* To double; repeat; in *philol.*, to repeat, as a syllable or the initial part of a syllable; form by so repeating, as a word-form. **II.** *intr.* To become doubled; undergo reduplication.—**re·du'pli·cate** (-kạt), *a.* Reduplicated; in *bot.*, valvate, with the edges folded back so as to project outward (said of petals and sepals in one form of estivation, or of the estivation).—**re·du·pli·ca'tion** (-kā'shọn), *n.* [LL. *reduplicatio*(n-).] The act of reduplicating, or the state of being reduplicated; doubling; repetition; also, something resulting from reduplicating; a counterpart; also, a doubling or folding; a double or fold; in *philol.*, repetition, as of a syllable or the initial part of a syllable; also, a syllable so formed, or a word-form containing such a syllable.—**re·du'pli·ca·tive** (-kạ-tiv), *a.* Tending to reduplicate; pertaining to or marked by reduplication; in *bot.*, reduplicate.

re·dux (rē'duks), *a.* [L., leading back, also led back, < *reducere*: see *reduce*.] Brought back or returned, as from a distance, from exile, or the like: as, "Astræa *Redux*" (a poem by Dryden celebrating the restoration of Charles II. as if a return of the goddess of justice to earth); "Phineas *Redux*" (a novel by Anthony Trollope, a sequel to his "Phineas Finn").

red-ware (red'wār), *n.* [See *ware*[1].] A large brown seaweed, *Laminaria digitata*, common off the coasts of the northern Atlantic.

red-wa·ter (red'wâ"tẽr), *n.* A disease of cattle, in which the urine is colored red by hemoglobin.

red·wing (red'wing), *n.* A European thrush, *Turdus iliacus*, with the inner wing-coverts reddish; also, an American blackbird, *Agelæus phœniceus*, the male of which has a scarlet patch on the wing.

Redwing (*Turdus iliacus*).

red·wood (red'wụd), *n.* A red-colored wood; also, any of various trees with a reddish wood; esp., a pinaceous tree, *Sequoia sempervirens*, of California, remarkable for its height (commonly from 200 to 300 feet, sometimes more), or its valuable brownish-red timber.

re·ĕch·o (rẽ-ek'ō), *v.* [See *re-*.] **I.** *intr.* To echo back, as a sound (as, "The thunder of the avalanche *Re-echoes* far

Branch with Cones of Redwood (*Sequoia sempervirens*).— *a*, a cone; *b*, a seed.

behind": Southey's "Thalaba," xi. 19); also, to give back an echo, be filled with echoes, or resound, as a place (as, "A charge of snuff the wily virgin threw . . . And the high dome *re-echoes* to his nose": Pope's "Rape of the Lock," v. 86). **II.** *tr.* To echo back (sound: as, "The consecrated roof *Re-echoing* pious anthems," Cowper's "Task," i. 343); hence, to repeat like an echo (as, "The King . . . re-echoed the affectionate protestations of his niece": Lytton Strachey's "Queen Victoria," iii.).—**re-ëch'o**, *n.*; pl. *-oes* (-ōz). A reëchoing sound; an echo; also, a repeated echo.

reech-y (rē'chi), *a.* [= *reeky.*] Smoky; dirty; also, rancid. [Obs. or prov. Eng.]

reed (rēd), *n.* [AS. *hrēod* = D. *riet* = G. *ried*, reed.] The straight stalk of any of various tall grasses (esp. of the genera *Trichoön* and *Arundo*) growing in marshy places; the plant itself; such stalks or plants collectively; also, any of various things made from such a stalk or from something similar, as a dart or arrow, or a measuring-rod; hence, an old Jewish measure of length, equal to six cubits; also, a pastoral or rustic musical pipe made from a reed or from the hollow stalk of some other plant; also, in musical instruments, a thin plate or tongue of wood or metal, producing sound when vibrated by a current of air; an instrument with such a device, as the clarinet; also, in a loom, the series of parallel strips or wires which force the weft up to the web and separate the threads of the warp; in *arch., carp.*, etc., a small convex molding; a reeding.—

Common Reed (*Trichoön phragmites*).— 1, flowering plant; 2, the panicle; *a*, a spikelet.

reed, *v. t.* To thatch with or as with reed; also, to decorate with reeding.—**reed'=bird**, *n.* The bobolink, which frequents reedy marshes in the fall.—**reed'buck**, *n.* Same as *rietbok.*—**reed'=bun''ting**, *n.* A common European bunting, *Emberiza schœniclus*, frequenting reedy places.

re-ëd-i-fy (rē-ed'i-fī), *v. t.*; -fied, -fying. [OF. *reedifier* (F. *réédifier*), < LL. *ræedificare*, < L. *re-*, again, + *ædificare*, E. *edify*.] To rebuild (as, "Return'd from Babylon . . . the house of God They first *re-edify*": Milton's "Paradise Lost," xii. 350); fig., to restore; reëstablish.—**re-ëd''i-fi-ca'tion** (-fi-kā'shon), *n.*

reed-i-ness (rē'di-nes), *n.* Reedy state or quality.

reed-ing (rē'ding), *n.* A small convex or semicylindrical molding, resembling a reed; a set of such moldings, as on a column; ornamentation consisting of such moldings.

re-ëd-it (rē-ed'it), *v. t.* [See *re-*.] To edit again.

reed-ling (rēd'ling), *n.* A small European bird, *Panurus biarmicus*, frequenting reedy places, and characterized in the male by a tuft of black feathers on each side of the chin.

reed=mace (rēd'mās), *n.* The cat-tail (plant).

reed=or-gan (rēd'ôr''gan), *n.* A musical instrument resembling the pipe-organ in certain ways, but having the tones produced by small metal reeds: occurring in two principal forms, the typical *harmonium* (common in Europe), in which the air is forced outward through the reeds, and the *American organ*, in which the air is sucked inward.

re-ëd-u-cate (rē-ed'ū-kāt), *v. t.* [See *re-*.] To educate again or anew.—**re-ëd-u-ca'tion** (-kā'shon), *n.* The act of reëducating, or the state of being reëducated; esp., the process of fitting persons crippled or otherwise disabled, as in war, to resume normal activities, by means of special training designed to develop the powers or to habituate to the use of artificial substitutes for lost bodily parts.— **re-ëd-u-ca'tion-al**, *a.*

reed=war-bler (rēd'wâr''blėr), *n.* Any of several small old-world warblers of the genus *Acrocephalus*, esp. *A. streperus*, frequenting reedy places.

reed-y (rē'di), *a.* Abounding with or full of reeds (as, "the broad, *reedy* fen": Stevenson's "Treasure Island," xiv.); consisting or made of a reed or reeds (as, a *reedy* pipe); resembling or suggesting a reed or reeds (as, *reedy* grass); also, noting or having a tone like that produced by a musical reed or a reed-instrument (as, "the *reedy* notes of the accordion," Bret Harte's "Outcasts of Poker Flat"; a *reedy* voice).

reef[1] (rēf), *n.* [Prob. < D. *rif* = MLG. *rif* = Icel. *rif*, reef: cf. Icel. *rif*, rib, also E. *reef*[2].] A narrow ridge of rocks or sand, often of coral debris, at or near the surface of the water (as, "orders . . . directing him to survey a dangerous *reef* of rocks to the northward of Porto Rico," Marryat's "King's Own," xxiv.; a coral *reef*); also, in *mining*, a lode or vein (Australian: as, a *reef* of gold-bearing quartz).

reef[2] (rēf), *n.* [ME. *riff* = D. *reef* = Icel. *rif*, reef in a sail: cf. *reef*[1].] *Naut.*, a part of a sail which may be or is rolled or folded up, in order to diminish the extent of canvas exposed to the wind (as, to take in a *reef*, or take a *reef*, in a sail; "They shook a *reef* out of the topsails," Marryat's "Mr. Midshipman Easy," xiv.); also, the act of reefing; also, a particular method of reefing.—**reef**[2], *v. t. Naut.*, to reduce the size of (a sail) by rolling or folding up a part; also, to reduce the length of (a topmast, a bowsprit, etc.), as by lowering, sliding inboard, or the like.—**reef'=a-ble**, *a.* Capable of being reefed.—**reef'=band**, *n. Naut.*, a band of canvas sewed across a sail to strengthen it for the strain of the cords (reef-points) used in reefing.—**reef'er**, *n.* One who reefs; hence, a midshipman (colloq.: as, "Oakes and Bluewater were *reefers* together . . . in the Mermaid," Cooper's "Two Admirals," iii.); also, a short coat or jacket of thick cloth, worn esp. by sailors and fishermen; a short jacket for women or children; also, a long scarf or muffler, as of wool or silk, esp. for men's wear.—**reef'=knot**, *n.* A square knot (see under *square*, *a.*): so called because used in tying reef-points.—**reef'=point**, *n. Naut.*, one of a row of short cords or ropes on a reef-band of a sail, used to tie up the rolled or folded portion of the sail in reefing.

reek (rēk), *v.* [AS. *rēocan* = D. *rieken* = G. *riechen* = Icel. *rjūka*, reek.] **I.** *intr.* To emit smoke, as something burning, a chimney, etc.; emit vapor or steam (as, "many a steaming lake and *reeking* bog": Cowper's "Anti-Thelyphthora," 93); sweat, or be wet with sweat, as from heat or exertion (as, "their horses *reeking* with the speed at which they had ridden," Scott's "Guy Mannering," xxx.; to *reek* with sweat); be wet with blood, or be wet as blood on something (as, "Altars . . . *reek'd* with gore," Pope's "Essay on Man," iii. 264; "Till gallant Cessford's heart-blood dear *Reek'd* on dark Elliot's Border spear," Scott's "Lay of the Last Minstrel," i. 30); also, to emit a strong and unpleasant odor, or smell strongly and unpleasantly (as, to *reek* of garlic or of cheap perfume; "The heated air *reeked* with the smell of stale cooking," W. Churchill's "Inside of the Cup," x.); fig., to be strongly pervaded with something unpleasant or offensive (as, "The place *reeked* with pedantry," Motley's "Dutch Republic," Introd., xiv.; a community *reeking* with vice); also, of smoke, vapor, perfumes, etc., to be emitted or exhaled, issue, or rise (as, "My breath *reeked* into the frosty air," Conan Doyle's "Exploits of Brigadier Gerard," i.; "mingled and conflicting perfumes, *reeking* up from strange convolute censers," Poe's "Assignation"). **II.** *tr.* To expose to or treat with smoke; also, to emit (smoke, fumes, etc.: also fig.).—**reek**, *n.* [AS. *rēc*.] Smoke (now chiefly prov.); vapor or steam; an exhalation; also, a strong, unpleasant smell (as, "the pungent *reek* of camels," Kipling's "Light That Failed," xv.; "a perpetual *reek* of vegetable decay," H. G. Wells's "Tono-Bungay," iii. 1. § 4); also, a reeking state (as, "Here we are all just ready to drop down, and the critters all in a *reek* of sweat": Mrs. Stowe's "Uncle Tom's Cabin," vi.).—**reek'y**, *a.* Reeking; smoky, misty, or steamy; dim or dark with reek.

reel[1] (rēl), *n.* [AS. *hrēol*.] A cylinder, frame, or other device, turning on an axis, for winding something on, as thread, yarn, rope, wire, a continuous band of something, etc.; a spool; a roller; a drum; a rotatory device attached to a fishing-rod at the butt, for winding up or letting out the line; also, a quantity of something wound on a reel; specif., a roll of celluloid (orig. and normally 1,000 feet in length) bearing a series of photographs to be exhibited with a moving-picture machine.—**off the reel,** with uninterrupted procedure, or in unbroken succession, as if in the unwinding of something from a reel: as, to recite a list right *off the reel*; to win three games *off the reel.* [Colloq.]—**reel=and=bead molding,** an ornamental molding in which flattened, disklike parts alternate with elongated, rounded bodies.—

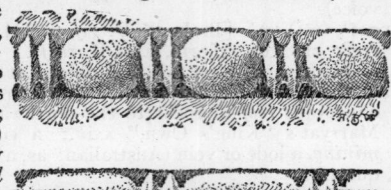

Reel-and-bead Molding.—above, Greek (Erechtheum, Athens); below, Renaissance (Venice).

reel[1], *v. t.* To wind on a reel, as thread, yarn, etc.; draw (*off, in,* etc.) with a reel, or by winding (as, to *reel* off silk from the cocoons); to *reel* in a fish-line or a fish); let (*out*) by unwinding, as a line; fig., to say, write, or produce in an easy, continuous way (as, "I incontinently *reeled* off half a page of statistics, more or less accurate": F. M. Crawford's "Mr. Isaacs," vi.); rattle (*off*).

reel[2], *v.* [ME. *relen*; origin uncertain: cf. *reel*[1].] **I.** *intr.* To turn round and round, or whirl; also, to have a sensation of whirling (as, "His eye still *reeled* under the influence of the strong potation," Scott's "Guy Mannering," xxxiii.; "My brain *reels* — and yet my foot is firm," Byron's "Manfred," i. 2); also, to sway, swing, or rock under a blow, shock, or any great stress (as, to *reel* under a heavy stroke; buildings *reel* in an earthquake; "So quick the run, We felt the good ship shake and *reel,*" Tennyson's "Voyage," ii.: also fig.); sway about unsteadily in standing or walking, as from dizziness, intoxication, faintness, etc.; stagger; totter; also, to go with swaying or staggering movements (as, a drunkard *reeling* toward home; "I became pale with terror . . . I *reeled* out of the room," Godwin's "Caleb Williams," xxxix.). **II.** *tr.* To cause to reel; also, to reel along (as, "to *reel* the streets at noon": Shakspere's "Antony and Cleopatra," i. 4. 20).—**reel**[2], *n.* The act of reeling; a reeling or staggering movement (as, "Thou mightst have tracked every *reel* and totter of my footsteps by the blood that followed": Hawthorne's "Twice-Told Tales," The Gentle Boy).

reel[3] (rēl), *n.* [Cf. *reel*[2].] A lively dance popular in Scotland, or the music for it; also, an American country-dance ('Virginia reel').—**reel**[3], *v. i.* To dance a reel.

re-ē-lect (rē-ē-lekt'), *v. t.* [See *re-.*] To elect again.—**re-ē-lec'tion** (-lek'shǫn), *n.*

reel-er (rē'lėr), *n.* One who reels, or winds on a reel; specif., one who reels silk from the cocoons.

re-ēl-i-gi-ble (rē-el'i-ji-bl), *a.* [See *re-.*] Capable of being elected again to the same office: as, "a bill to make the tribunes legally *reëligible*" (Froude's "Cæsar," iii.).—**re-ēl'i-gi-bil'i-ty** (-bil'i-ti), *n.*

reel=tow-el (rēl'tou''ęl), *n.* A roller-towel.

re-ēm-bark (rē-em-bärk'), *v. t.* or *i.* [See *re-.*] To embark again.—**re''ēm-bar-ka'tion** (-bär-kā'shǫn), *n.*

re-ē-merge (rē-ē-mėrj'), *v. i.* [See *re-.*] To emerge again.—**re-ē-mer'gence** (-mėr'jens), *n.* The act of reëmerging.—**re-ē-mer'gent,** *a.* Reëmerging.

re-ēn-act (rē-e-nakt'), *v. t.* [See *re-.*] To enact again.—**re-ēn-act'ment,** *n.*

re-ēn-coun-ter (rē-en-koun'tėr), *v. t.* or *i.* [See *re-.*] To encounter or meet again.—**re-ēn-coun'ter,** *n.* A further or subsequent encounter; a meeting again, as after separation or absence: as, "She had said it on that occasion of their first *reëncounter*" (A. S. M. Hutchinson's "If Winter Comes," ii. 7).

re-ēn-force', etc. See *reinforce*, etc.

re-ēn-gage (rē-en-gāj'), *v. t.* or *i.* [See *re-.*] To engage again.—**re-ēn-gage'ment,** *n.*

re-ēn-grave (rē-en-grāv'), *v. t.* [See *re-.*] To engrave again.

re-ēn-list (rē-en-list'), *v. t.* or *i.* [See *re-.*] To enlist again: as, "The Roman general was eager . . . to *re-enlist* so brave a soldier in the service of the empire" (Motley's "Dutch Republic," Introd., iv.).—**re-ēn-list'ment,** *n.*

re-ēn-slave (rē-en-slāv'), *v. t.* [See *re-.*] To enslave again.—**re-ēn-slave'ment,** *n.*

re-ēn-ter (rē-en'tėr), *v.* [See *re-.*] **I.** *tr.* To enter again; come or go into again (as, to *reënter* a room; to *reënter* public life); record again, as in a list or account; in *engraving*, to cut (lines) deeper, as in a plate. **II.** *intr.* To enter again; come or go in again (common in stage directions: as, "Enter Ghost . . . Exit Ghost . . . *Re-enter* Ghost," Shakspere's "Hamlet," i. 1); also, to go or turn back inward (see *reëntering, p. a.*).—**re-ēn'ter-ing,** *p. a.* That reënters; specif., of an angle, bend, or part in an outline, an inclosing wall, or the like, turning or directed back inward, as into the space inclosed, rather than extending outward; reëntrant; of a polygon, having one or more than one such angle.—**re-ēn'trance** (-trans), *n.* Entrance again, as into a place; a repeated entrance.—**re-ēn'trant. I.** *a.* Reëntering: specif., of an angle or part. **II.** *n.* A reëntering angle or part.—**re-ēn'try** (-tri), *n.*; pl. *-tries* (-triz). The act of reëntering; a new or fresh entry; in *law*, a retaking possession.

Reëntering Angle.

re-ēs-tab-lish (rē-es-tab'lish), *v. t.* [See *re-.*] To establish again; restore.—**re-ēs-tab'lish-ment,** *n.*

reeve[1] (rēv), *n.* [AS. *gerēfa.*] An administrative officer of a town or district, formerly, in England, one of high rank representing the crown; a bailiff, steward, or overseer. [Now chiefly local.]

reeve[2] (rēv), *v. t.; reeved* or *rove, reeving.* [Origin uncertain: cf. D. *reven*, to reef (sails).] *Naut.*, to pass (a rope, etc.) through a hole, ring, or the like; fasten by placing through or around something; also, to pass a rope through (a block, etc.).

reeve[3] (rēv), *n.* [Origin uncertain.] The female of the ruff (sandpiper).

re-ēx-am-ine (rē-eg-zam'in), *v. t.* [See *re-.*] To examine again; in *law*, to examine (a witness) again after cross-examination.—**re-ēx-am'in-a-ble,** *a.*—**re-ēx-am-i-na'tion** (-i-nā'shǫn), *n.*

re-ēx-change (rē-eks-chānj'), *v. t.* [See *re-.*] To exchange again or anew.—**re-ēx-change',** *n.* A second or new exchange; in *com.*, the operation by which the holder of a dishonored foreign bill of exchange recovers, in addition to the amount of the bill, the expense occasioned by its having been dishonored; the draft by which this is effected; the expense as included in it.

re-ēx-port (rē-eks-pōrt'), *v. t.* [See *re-.*] To export again, as imported goods.—**re-ēx'port,** *n.* A reëxporting; also, that which is reëxported; a reëxported commodity.—**re''ēx-por-ta'tion** (-pōr-tā'shǫn), *n.*

re-face (rē-fās'), *v. t.* [See *re-.*] To renew, restore, or repair the face or surface of (buildings, stone, etc.); also, to provide (a garment, etc.) with a new facing.

re-fash-ion (rē-fash'ǫn), *v. t.* [See *re-.*] To fashion anew: as, "the nineteenth century historian, who *refashions* the past on the lines of his own mind" (Mrs. H. Ward's "Robert Elsmere," xx.).—**re-fash'ion-er,** *n.*—**re-fash'ion-ment,** *n.*

re-fect (rē-fekt'), *v. t.* [L. *refectus*, pp. of *reficere, < re-,* again, + *facere*, make.] To restore after hunger or fatigue; refresh, esp. with food or drink. [Archaic.]

re-fec-tion (rē-fek'shǫn), *n.* [OF. *refection* (F. *réfection*), < L. *refectio(n-), < reficere:* see *refect.*] Refreshment, esp. with food or drink (as, "a pâté from the pastrycook's for my especial *refection*": Thackeray's "Newcomes," lxxii.); also, a portion of food or drink for refreshment, or a repast (as, "They sat on Meredith's big porch . . . and ate a substantial *refection*": Tarkington's "Gentleman from Indiana," xv.).—**re-fec'tion-er,** *n.* In a religious house, one who has charge of the refectory and of supplies of food: as, "two most important officers of the convent, the kitchener and *refectioner*" (Scott's "Monastery," xv.).

re-fec-to-ry (rē-fek'tǫ-ri), *n.*; pl. *-ries* (-riz). [ML. *refectorium, < L. reficere:* see *refect.*] A room for refreshment; esp., a dining-hall in a religious house, a college, or other institution (see cut on following page) (as, "In the *refectory* [of an abbey], piles of gold and silver plate were displayed on a buffet," J. F. Kirk's "Charles the Bold," iv. 1; "School was dismissed, and all were gone into the *refectory* to tea," C. Brontë's "Jane Eyre," viii.).

re-fer (rẹ-fėr'), v.; -ferred, -ferring. [OF. referer (F. ré-férer), < L. referre, bear back, return, report, relate, < re-, back, + ferre, bear: cf. relate.] **I.** tr. To bear or bring back†; also, to trace back or attribute, as to an origin, source, or cause (as, to refer a doctrine back to the ancient Greeks; to refer prevailing evils to the late war);

Refectory of the Abbey of Mont St. Michel, Normandy; 13th century.

also, to assign to a class, place, period, or the like (as, to refer bacteria to the vegetable kingdom; to refer a manuscript to a particular district or date); ascribe or regard as belonging or related; also, to hand over, commit, or submit for consideration, decision, or action (as, to refer a legislative bill to a committee; to refer a cause to arbitration; "She treated me with a certain consideration, and often referred questions to me," F. M. Crawford's "Mr. Isaacs," x.); also, to commit, commend, or betake (one's self) for support or aid (as, "I do refer me to the oracle: Apollo be my judge!" Shakspere's "Winter's Tale," iii. 2. 116); also, to direct the attention or thoughts of (as, the asterisk refers the reader to a foot-note; "These weird sisters . . . referred me to the coming on of time, with 'Hail, king that shalt be!'" Shakspere's "Macbeth," i. 5. 9); direct for information or for anything required (as, to refer students to books on a subject; to refer inquirers to the proper authorities; "A postboy . . . after hearing what he wanted, referred him to the ostler," Dickens's "Oliver Twist," xxxiii.); also, to put off, or defer (now rare: as, "You had better . . . refer what matters you have to urge . . . to some other opportunity," Fielding's "Tom Jones," vi. 9). **II.** intr. To have relation, or relate (as, letters referring to a transaction); apply in bearing or significance, or convey a reference or allusion (as, the word 'royalty' here refers to the French king); also, to direct a remark or mention, or make reference or allusion, as a speaker or writer does (as, to avoid referring to a sore subject; to refer to a person in favorable terms; to refer to a proceeding as a piece of stupidity); also, to have recourse, resort, or turn, as for aid or information (as, to refer to one's notes, or to one's watch; "She found it necessary to refer to the invaluable Larousse," Gissing's "New Grub Street," vii.); also, to direct the attention to something, as a reference-mark does; direct any one for information, esp. about one's character, abilities, etc., as to a person able to give testimony (as, to refer to a former employer).

ref-er-a-ble (ref'ẹ-rạ-bl), a. Capable of being referred.

ref-er-ee (ref-ẹ-rē'), n. [From refer + -ee.] One to whom something is referred, esp. for decision or settlement; an arbitrator; an umpire; a judge of play in certain games and sports, sometimes in addition to an umpire, each then having functions fixed by the rules; in law, a person selected by the court to try a case in place of the court, or to examine and report on a question in aid of the court.—**ref-er-ee'**, v.; -eed, -eeing. **I.** tr. To preside over as referee; act as referee in. **II.** intr. To act as referee.

ref-er-ence (ref'ẹ-rẹns), n. [= F. référence.] The act or fact of referring; attribution or assignment, as to a source, class, etc.; commitment, as to a person or body, for consideration, decision, or action; direction of the attention (as, marks of reference, see reference-mark); direction or a direction to some source of information, esp. a direction in a book or writing to some book, passage, or the like, or a note indicating this (as, the author should verify all his references; to look up a reference: cf. cross-reference); recourse or use for purposes of information (as, a library for public reference; books of reference, books such as dictionaries, encyclopedias, and other works for consultation when information is required); the fact of referring or relating, or relation, regard, or respect (as, matters having no reference to this case; to plan with, or in, reference to the future; all persons, without reference to age or sex); referring or alluding in speech or writing, or a mention or allusion made (as, to recall a matter by casual reference; the usual references were made to absent friends); also, a person to whom one refers for testimony as to one's character, abilities, etc.; also, a written testimonial as to character, abilities, etc.—**ref'er-ence=mark**, n. Any of certain characters (as *, †, ‡, etc.), or a figure or letter, used to refer a reader from one place to another, as from the text to a foot-note.

ref-er-en-da-ry¹ (ref-ẹ-ren'dạ-ri), n. [ML. referendarius, < L. referendus: see referendum.] Any of various court or state officials in medieval and later times to whom petitions or other particular matters were referred; also, one to whom some matter is referred for decision, or a referee (now rare).

ref-er-en-da-ry² (ref-ẹ-ren'dạ-ri), a. Pertaining to or of the nature of a referendum.

ref-er-en-dum (ref-ẹ-ren'dum), n.; pl. -dums or -da (-dạ). [NL., prop. neut. of L. referendus, gerundive of referre, E. refer.] The principle or procedure of referring or submitting measures already passed on by the legislative body to the vote of the electorate for approval or rejection; an instance of this procedure; a submitting of a matter already passed on by the legislative body for decision by a popular vote; hence, a submitting of any matter for decision by a popular or general vote.

ref-er-en-tial (ref-ẹ-ren'shạl), a. Pertaining to, having, or making reference.—**ref-er-en'tial-ly**, adv.

re-fer-rer (rẹ-fėr'ėr), n. One who refers.

re-fer-ri-ble (rẹ-fėr'i-bl), a. Same as referable.

re-fill (rẹ-fil'), v. t. or i. [See re-.] To fill again or anew.—**re-fill'**, n. Something for putting in to refill a thing.—**re-fill'a-ble**, a. That may be refilled.

re-fine (rẹ-fīn'), v.; -fined, -fining. [See re-.] **I.** tr. To bring to a fine or a pure state, or free from impurities (as, to refine metal, sugar, or petroleum); fig., to purify from what is gross, coarse, crude, vulgar, or debasing (as, to refine the mind, taste, manners, or speech; "Love refines The thoughts," Milton's "Paradise Lost," viii. 589); imbue with fine, delicate, or nice feeling, taste, etc.; make elegant, polished, or cultured; bring or exalt by purifying, as to a finer state or form; also, to make more fine, nice, subtle, or minutely precise (see refined); bring, change, or take by subtilizing (as, to refine argument into mere wiredrawing; to refine away differences). **II.** intr. To become pure; fig., to become more fine, nice, elegant, or polished (as, "But let a lord once own the happy lines, How the wit brightens! how the style refines!" Pope's "Essay on Criticism," 421); also, to employ nicety or subtlety of thought or language; make fine distinctions; reason or discourse with subtlety (on or upon); also, to improve (on or upon) by superior fineness, excellence, elegance, achievement, etc.—**re-fined'**, p. a. Freed from impurities (as, "refined gold," 1 Chron. xxviii. 18; refined sugar); fig., freed or free from grossness, coarseness, crudeness, vulgarity, or the like (as, refined tastes; the refined judgment of the connoisseur; "that refined and delicate style which especially characterises the bas-relief work of Goornah," Amelia B. Edwards's "Thousand Miles up the Nile," xv.); imbued with or showing nice feeling, taste, etc. (as, "conscientiously refined and low-voiced people reeking with proud bashfulness," H. G. Wells's "Tono-Bungay," iii. 2. § 4; a refined face, tone, or manner); well-bred; elegant; polite (as, refined satire); also, fine, nice, or subtle (as, refined distinctions); minutely precise (as, the most refined estimations of longitude).—**re-fin'ed-ly** (-fī'ned-li), adv.—**re-fine'ment**, n. The act of refining, or the state of being refined; fineness of feeling, taste, etc.; elegance of manners or language; polish; culture; any instance or manifestation of refined feeling, taste, manners, etc. (as, "little refinements of taste and sentiment," G. Meredith's "Ordeal of Richard Feverel," i.;

"little *refinements* of conversation," H. James's "Portrait of a Lady," xlviii.); also, nice or subtle reasoning or discourse (as, "He professed . . . to . . . despise all mystery, *refinement*, and intrigue": Swift's "Gulliver's Travels," ii. 7); an instance of this, or a fine point, subtle distinction, or the like (as, "It is vain . . . to suppose that the Conquerors troubled themselves with the *refinements* of casuistry": Prescott's "Conquest of Mexico," iv. 3); also, improvement on something else, as in excellence or achievement (as, *refinement* on the methods or work of an earlier day); an instance or result of this, or an improved, higher, or extreme form of something (as, "such *refinements* of cruelty as were practised by Caligula," W. Churchill's "Coniston," i. 10; "one . . . who regarded this career of horror as the last *refinement* of virtue," C. B. Brown's "Wieland," xxi.); in *arch.*, an intentional deviation from mechanical exactness or regularity in structural lines, as a slight curvature of lines apparently straight or a slight deviation from the strict vertical or horizontal. — **re-fin′er**, *n*.— **re-fin′er-y** (-i), *n.*; pl. *-ies* (-iz). An establishment for refining or purifying something, as metal, sugar, or petroleum.

re-fit (rẹ-fit′), *v.*; *-fitted, -fitting.* [See *re-*.] **I.** *tr.* To fit, prepare, or equip again; fit out afresh; restore after damage or decay; *naut.*, to restore (ships) to good condition by renewals and repairs. **II.** *intr.* To renew supplies or equipment; *naut.*, to get refitted (as, "His ship put into Portsmouth to *refit*": Lytton Strachey's "Queen Victoria," iv.).— **re-fit′**, **re-fit′ment**, *n.* The act or an act of refitting.

re-flect (rẹ-flekt′), *v.* [L. *reflectere* (pp. *reflexus*), bend or turn back, < *re-*, back, + *flectere*, bend.] **I.** *tr.* To bend or turn back; throw or cast back, or cause to return or rebound; specif., to cast back (light, heat, sound, etc.) after impact (as, "That globe, whose hither side With light from hence, though but *reflected*, shines": Milton's "Paradise Lost," iii. 723); also, to give back or show an image of, or mirror (as, "The vast bosom of the Hudson was like an unruffled mirror, *reflecting* the golden splendor of the heavens": Irving's "Knickerbocker's New York," vi. 4); fig., to reproduce or show, like a mirror (as, the followers *reflect* the views of the leaders; "the reality which the stage *reflected*," Arnold Bennett's "Pretty Lady," i.; "The Ferns . . . had had taste, and the new house *reflected* it," W. Churchill's "Modern Chronicle," ii. 5); also, to throw or cast, as upon a person or thing (as, "Do you *reflect* that guilt upon me, which should lie buried in your bosom?" Congreve's "Way of the World," ii.); of actions, etc., to serve to cast or bring (discredit, credit, etc.) upon a person or thing; also, to ponder or meditate on (*what, how*, etc.: as, to *reflect* what one ought to do; "He was *reflecting* how to turn the tables on them," H. Kingsley's "Geoffry Hamlyn," vi.); think (as, "He *reflected* grimly that his seven years with Zeena seemed to Starkfield 'not so long,' " Mrs. Wharton's "Ethan Frome," iv.; "He . . . *reflected*: 'Nobody else . . . could have done what I am doing,' " Arnold Bennett's "The Old Adam," vii.). **II.** *intr.* To be reflected, or turned or cast back, as light after striking on a surface; be reflected or mirrored (as, "A silver lamp, whose phosphor glow *Reflected* in the slabbed steps below": Keats's "La-

mia," i.); also, to cast back light, heat, etc.; give back or show an image of something; also, to bend or fix the thoughts on something (as, "Content| if hence . . . The learn'd *reflect* on what before they knew": Pope's "Essay on Criticism," 740); ponder or meditate; often, to consider or think carefully (as, "I could have wished that you both had taken longer to *reflect*, but I hope . . . that you will be happy": W. Churchill's "Modern Chronicle," i. 12); also, to cast some imputation or reproach upon a person or thing (as, "The clergy were strictly charged not to *reflect* on the Roman Catholic religion in their discourses": Macaulay's "Hist. of Eng.," vi.); of actions, etc., to serve or tend to bring reproach or discredit (as, "Perhaps the Romans were of opinion, that ill language and brutal manners *reflected* only on those who were guilty of them": Steele, in "Tatler," 39); sometimes, to serve to bestow a particular aspect (as, the circumstances *reflect* favorably upon the character of those concerned).— **re-flect′er**, *n.*— **re-flect′i-ble**, *a.* That may be reflected.

re-flec-tion, **re-flex-ion** (rẹ-flek′shọn), *n.* [L. *reflexio(n-).*] The act of reflecting, or the state of being reflected; the bending or folding back of a thing upon itself (esp. in *anat.*); a reflected part, or a fold; a throwing or casting back, as after impact, esp. the casting back, or the change of direction, of light, heat, sound, etc., after striking a surface; something so reflected, as heat or, esp., light; the casting of color from one thing upon another as an effect of light, or the color or tint cast; a play or change of color due to varying light (specif. in *zoöl.*); the exhibition by a mirror or the like of the image or counterpart of an object; an image or counterpart so exhibited (as, "She saw in a mirror the *reflection* of her father's dark figure": Galsworthy's "Saint's Progress," iii. 1); fig., a reproduction as if in a mirror (as, his views are a *reflection* of those of his chief); also, the bending or fixing of the thoughts on something; meditation; careful consideration; a thought occurring in meditation (as, "I fell into these *reflections* from comparing in my own mind my former experiences . . . with those of that day": G. MacDonald's "Annals of a Quiet Neighbourhood," vii.); such a thought expressed in words (as, "He made very wise *reflections* and observations upon all I said": Swift's "Gulliver's Travels," ii. 3); also, the casting of some imputation or reproach upon a person or thing; a remark or observation reflecting unfavorably upon a person or thing; an imputation; anything having the force of an imputation.— **angle of reflection**, the angle which a ray of light, or the like, reflected from a surface, makes with a perpendicular to that surface at the point of reflection. See cut at *angle of incidence*, under *incidence.*

re-flec-tive (rẹ-flek′tiv), *a.* That reflects, or reflecting; casting back something, esp. light, after it strikes upon the surface; giving back or showing an image or reproduction of an object, as a mirror; also, cast by reflection, or reflected, as light; also, given to or characterized by reflection or meditation (as, "Cromwell was of the active, not the *reflective* temper": Morley's "Oliver Cromwell," iv. 1); concerned with reflection (as, the *reflective* faculties); in *gram.*, reflexive. — **re-flec′tive-ly**, *adv.*— **re-flec′tive-ness**, *n.*

re-flec-tom-e-ter (rẹ-flek-tom′e-tèr), *n.* [See *-meter*.] An instrument for measuring the power of reflection of bodies or surfaces.

re-flec-tor (rẹ-flek′tọr), *n.* One who or that which reflects; a body, surface, or device that reflects light, heat, sound, or the like; a reflecting telescope (see *telescope*).

re-flet (rẹ-flā), *n.* [F., < It. *riflesso*, reflection, < L. *reflexus*, pp.: see *reflect*.] A reflection of light or color; an effect of luster, color, or iridescence on an object (as a piece of pottery) due to reflection of light.

re-flex (rẹ-fleks′), *v. t.* [L. *reflexus*, pp. of *reflectere*: see *reflect*.] To bend, turn, or fold back; also, to reflect (light, etc.)†; throw or cast (beams) on something†; also, in *wireless teleph.*, to subject to a reflex process (see *reflex, a.*); arrange in a reflex system.— **re-flex** (rẹ′fleks or rẹ-fleks′), *a.* [L. *reflexus*, pp.] Bent or turned back (as, "At the disk, with blunted point *Reflex*, his ineffectual weapon stay'd": Cowper's tr. Homer's "Iliad," iii. 413); also, cast back or reflected, as light, etc.; also, directed back upon the mind itself or its operations, as a mental act; pertaining to or

Architectural Refinement from Church of St. Quentin, France.

derived from such mental acts; also, occurring in reaction, or responsive; specif., in *physiol.*, noting or pertaining to an action or movement of an involuntary nature, in which a stimulus is transmitted along an afferent nerve to a nerve-center, and from there reflected along an efferent nerve to call into play muscular or other activity; also, in *wireless teleph.*, designating a radio receiving apparatus or set in which the amplifier tubes are made to function as both radio-frequency and audio-frequency amplifiers simultaneously (proprietary name); pertaining to such an apparatus or set. **—re′flex**, *n.* [L. *reflexus*, n., < *reflectere*.] Reflection, as of light; reflected light, or light or color resulting from reflection; the light reflected or cast from an illuminated surface to one in shade; also, the reflection or image of an object, as exhibited by a mirror or the like; fig., a reproduction as if in a mirror; a copy or adaptation; in *physiol.*, a reflex action or movement; in *wireless teleph.*, a reflex radio receiving apparatus or set (see *reflex, a.*).**—re-flexed′**, *p. a.* Bent, turned, or folded back; specif., in *bot.*, bent abruptly backward, as petals, sepals, etc.**—re-flex′i-ble**, *a.* Capable of being reflected.**—re-flex-i-bil′i-ty** (-bil′i-ti), *n.*— **re-flex′ion**, *n.* See *reflection*.**—re-flex′ive. I.** *a.* Capable of reflecting, or of turning or casting back (rare); also, directed back upon the mind itself, as a mental act†; also, given to or characterized by reflection or meditation†; also, of a reflex character; occurring by reaction; in *gram.*, noting or implying action which turns back upon the agent or subject, as the verb *forswore* or the pronoun *himself* in 'the witness forswore himself.' **II.** *n.* In *gram.*, a reflexive verb or pronoun.**—re-flex′ive-ly**, *adv.*—**re-flex′ly** (rē′fleks-li or rẹ-fleks′li), *adv.*

ref-lu-ent (ref′lọ-ẹnt), *a.* [L. *refluens* (-ent-), ppr. of *refluere*, flow back, < *re-*, back, + *fluere*, flow.] Flowing back; ebbing, as the waters of a tide.**—ref′lu-ence**, *n.*

re-flux (rē′fluks), *n.* [From *re-* + *flux.*] A flowing back; the flowing out of the waters of a tide.

re-for-est (rē-for′est), *v. t.* [See *re-*.] To replant with forest-trees.**—re-for-es-ta′tion** (-es-tā′shọn), *n.*

re-form¹ (rē-fôrm′), *v. t.* or *i.* [See *re-*.] To form again or anew. Also written *re-form*.

re-form² (rẹ-fôrm′), *v.* [OF. *reformer* (F. *réformer*), < L. *reformare* (pp. *reformatus*), < *re-*, back, again, + *formare*, E. *form, v.*] **I.** *tr.* To change to another and better form; improve by some alteration of form, arrangement, etc. (as, to *reform* the calendar); hence, to change from worse to better; amend by removal of faults, abuses, etc. (as, to *reform* the administration of justice; "There hath arisen a sect in England, which . . . seeketh to *reform* even the French reformation," Hooker's "Ecclesiastical Polity," iv. 8. 4; to *reform* politics); also, to cause (a person) to abandon wrong or evil ways of life or conduct, and to adopt right ones; bring about amendment in (a person, or his manner of life, conduct, etc.); also, to put an end to (abuses, disorders, etc.); correct (errors, etc.). **II.** *intr.* To abandon evil or error; amend one's life, conduct, etc.: as, "those who have gone on for some time in the ways of vice, and have afterwards *reformed*" (J. Butler's "Analogy of Religion," i. 3).**—re-form′²**, *n.* [F. *réforme.*] Improvement by alteration of arrangement, etc.; the amendment of what is faulty, wrong, corrupt, etc., or an instance of this (as, political *reform*; social *reforms*); the amendment of the manner of life, conduct, etc.**—reform school**, a reformatory.**—re-form′a-ble**, *a.* Capable of being reformed.

re-for-ma-tion¹ (rē-fôr-mā′shọn), *n.* [See *reform¹*.] The act of reforming, or forming anew, or the state of being reformed; formation over again. Also written *re-formation*.

ref-or-ma-tion² (ref-ôr-mā′shọn), *n.* [OF. *reformation* (F. *réformation*), < L. *reformatio(n-)*, < *reformare*, E. *reform².*] The act of reforming, or the state of being reformed; improvement in form, arrangement, composition, etc. (as, the *reformation* of the calendar); amendment by removal of faults, abuses, etc., as of an existing order of things, an institution, or the like; specif. [*cap.*], the great religious movement in the 16th century which had for its object the reform of the Church of Rome, and which led to the establishment of the Protestant churches; [*l. c.*] amendment of or improvement in the manner of life, conduct, etc. **—ref-or-ma′tion-al**, *a.*

re-for-ma-tive¹ (rē-fôr′ma-tiv), *a.* Having the power of forming anew. Also written *re-formative*.

re-for-ma-tive² (rẹ-fôr′ma-tiv), *a.* Tending toward or inducing reform or reformation.**—re-for′ma-tive-ly**, *adv.*

re-for-ma-to-ry (rẹ-fôr′ma-tọ-ri). **I.** *a.* Serving or designed to reform, or effect reformation; reformative. **II.** *n.*; pl. *-ries* (-riz). A penal institution for the reformation of young offenders.

re-formed (rē-fôrmd′), *p. a.* Improved in form, arrangement, etc.; amended by removal of faults, abuses, etc.; specif. [*cap.*], noting or pertaining to the Protestant churches, esp. the Calvinistic as distinguished from the Lutheran; also, a distinctive epithet in the titles of various Protestant churches; [*l. c.*], improved in conduct, morals, etc. (as, a *reformed* profligate).

re-form-er (rẹ-fôr′mẻr), *n.* One who reforms; one who effects a reform in some state of affairs, practice, etc.; [often *cap.*] one of the leaders in the Reformation in the 16th century; [*l. c.*] an advocate or supporter of reform, as in politics, social affairs, etc.

re-form-ist (rẹ-fôr′mist), *n.* An advocate of reform.

re-fract (rē-frakt′), *v. t.* [L. *refractus*, pp. of *refringere*, break up, break off, < *re-*, back, + *frangere*, break.] To bend (a ray of light, etc.) from a straight course; subject to refraction; also, in optical practice, to determine the refractive condition of (the eye), as for the purpose of correcting errors of vision by means of glasses.**—re-frac′tion** (-frak′shọn), *n.* [LL. *refractio(n-)*.] The act of refracting, or the resulting state; the change of direction of a ray of light, heat, or the like in passing obliquely from one medium into another of different density (as, in 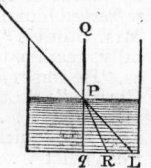 the cut, of the ray of light *SP*, incident upon the surface of the water in the vessel at *P*, which in passing into the water is bent from its original direction *SPL* toward the perpendicular to the surface of the water *Qq* in the line *SPR*, which shows the ray refracted); also, in optical practice, the refractive condition of the eye, or its condition with respect to ability to refract the light which enters it so as to form an image on the retina; also, the determining of the refractive condition of the eye, as in order to correct errors of vision by means of glasses.**—double refraction**, in *physics*, the separation of a ray of light into two unequally refracted rays, as in passing through certain crystals.**—re-frac′tion-ist**, *n.* One skilled in determining the refractive condition of the eye, as for the purpose of correcting errors of vision by means of glasses. **—re-frac′tive**, *a.* Refracting; having power to refract; of or pertaining to refraction.**—re-frac′tive-ness, re-frac-tiv-i-ty** (rē-frak-tiv′i-ti), *n.*—**re-frac-tom′e-ter** (-tom′e-tẻr), *n.* [See *-meter*.] An instrument for measuring refraction; in optical practice, an instrument for determining the refractive condition of the eye.**—re-frac′tor**, *n.* Something that refracts; a refracting telescope (see *telescope*).

Refraction.

re-frac-to-ry (rē-frak′tọ-ri), *a.* [For earlier *refractary*, < L. *refractarius*, < *refringere*: see *refract*.] Stubborn in resistance or opposition to authority or control (as, a *refractory* child; "a *refractory* donkey," Miss Mulock's "John Halifax," x.; "That force would soon break the *refractory* spirit of the nation," Macaulay's "Hist. of Eng.," i.); perverse, contumacious, or rebellious; also, resisting ordinary methods of treatment; difficult to fuse, reduce, or work, as an ore or metal; in *med.*, not yielding readily to treatment, as a disease or wound; not susceptible to morbid agencies, as a person or animal.**—re-frac′to-ri-ly**, *adv.*—**re-frac′to-ri-ness**, *n.*

re-frain¹ (rẹ-frān′), *v.* [OF. *refrener* (F. *refréner*), < L. *refrenare*, < *re-*, back, + *frenum*, bridle.] **I.** *tr.* To curb, hold back, or put restraint upon (one's self or another, feelings, actions, etc.: archaic: as, "He . . . *refrained* himself as long as he could, that his wife . . . should not perceive his distress," Bunyan's "Pilgrim's Progress," i.); withhold or restrain (*from*: archaic: as, "I have *refrained* my feet from every evil way," Ps. cxix. 101; "Stand awhile and gaze With thankful heart, and lips *refrained* from praise," H. Newbolt's "For a Trafalgar Cenotaph"); also, to keep or abstain from† (as, "Allworthy could scarce *refrain* laughter at this": Fielding's "Tom Jones," vi. 10). **II.** *intr.* To hold back, forbear, or abstain (instead of doing something: as, "*Refrain* to-night, And that shall lend a kind of easiness To the next abstinence," Shakspere's "Hamlet," iii. 4. 165); keep or abstain (*from*: as, to *refrain* from comment or interference; "I have hitherto *refrained* from appealing to you," G. B. Shaw's "You Never Can Tell," iii.).

re-frain[2] (rẹ-frān′), *n.* [OF. F. *refrain*, for OF. *refrait*, < L. *refractus*, pp.: see *refract*.] A phrase or verse recurring at intervals in a song or poem, esp. at the end of each stanza; a burden; a chorus; also, a musical setting for this.

re-frame (rē-frām′), *v. t.* [See *re-*.] To frame anew.

re-fran-gi-bil-i-ty (rẹ-fran-ji-bil′i-ti), *n.*; pl. *-ties* (-tiz). The property of being refrangible; the degree in which this property is present.

re-fran-gi-ble (rē-fran′ji-bl), *a.* [L. *re-*, back, + *frangere*, break: cf. *refract*.] Capable of being refracted, as rays of light; admitting of refraction.

re-fresh (rẹ-fresh′), *v.* [OF. *refreschier*, < *re-* (< L. *re-*), again, + *fres*, *fresche*, E. *fresh*.] **I.** *tr.* To make fresh again; restore freshness to (the earth, air, etc.), as dew, rain, cool breezes, etc., do; freshen in appearance, color, etc., by some restorative or renovating process (as, "washed gauze, and ribands three times *refreshed*": Smollett's "Humphry Clinker," July 18); make (a person or animal, the body, etc.) fresh, vigorous, or comfortable again after fatigue, exhaustion, privation, heat, etc., as rest, sleep, food, drink, and other beneficial agencies do (as, "I rose early, and going to a wide stream . . . took a plunge which greatly *refreshed* me": W. H. Hudson's "Purple Land," iii.); reinvigorate or recruit by means of rest, food, etc. (often reflexive: as, "He . . . *refreshed* himself by long and hearty pulls at the cider-mug," Mrs. Stowe's "Oldtown Folks," xviii.); reinvigorate mentally, reanimate, or cheer (a person, the mind, spirits, etc.: as, "He was *refreshed* in courage by an incredulous look from Glossin," Scott's "Guy Mannering," xliii.; "A faithful messenger . . . *refresheth* the soul of his masters," Prov. xxv. 13); quicken (the memory: as, "The Regent issued a fresh edict . . . to *refresh* the memories of those who might have forgotten previous statutes," Motley's "Dutch Republic," ii. 10); recreate agreeably (as, "I . . . *refresh* myself with a distant prospect of my estates," G. W. Curtis's "Prue and I," ii.; to *refresh* the eyes or sight); renew or replenish with anything serving to maintain activity or effectiveness (as, to *refresh* an electric battery). **II.** *intr.* To refresh one's self, as with rest, food, etc.; take refreshment, esp. food or drink.—**re-fresh′er**, *n.*—**re-fresh′ing**, *p. a.* That refreshes; restoring freshness; restoring to a fresh, vigorous, or comfortable state (as, a *refreshing* sleep; a *refreshing* drink; "handkerchiefs . . . exceeding *refreshing* to wipe my face in a hot day," Defoe's "Robinson Crusoe," i. 13); reinvigorating, physically or mentally; recreating the mind; hence, grateful or welcome to a jaded mind, or pleasing or diverting in a fresh or novel way (as, "One good action in the midst of crimes Is 'quite *refreshing*,' in the affected phrase Of these ambrosial, Pharisaic times," Byron's "Don Juan," viii. 90; *refreshing* candor or impudence).—**re-fresh′ing-ly**, *adv.*—**re-fresh′ing-ness**, *n.*—**re-fresh′ment**, *n.* The act of refreshing, or the state of being refreshed; restoration to freshness; reinvigoration, as with rest, food, etc. (as, "the *refreshment* I had received by their victuals and drink": Swift's "Gulliver's Travels," i. 1); also, that which refreshes, esp. food or drink (as, "Here comes the muscadel and the breakfast; wilt thou take some *refreshment?*" Scott's "Castle Dangerous," xiii.; "Mr. Voules wooed her to swallow a little drop of liquid *refreshment*," H. G. Wells's "Mr. Polly," vi.); *pl.*, articles or portions of food or drink, esp. such as serve for a light repast (as, a pavilion where *refreshments* are sold; to serve *refreshments* at an entertainment; "The Police came . . . and had *refreshments* in the kitchen," W. De Morgan's "Joseph Vance," x.).

re-frig-er-ant (rē-frij′ẹ-rant). **I.** *a.* Refrigerating; cooling; reducing bodily heat or fever. **II.** *n.* A refrigerant agent.

re-frig-er-ate (rē-frij′ẹ-rāt), *v. t.* or *i.*; *-ated*, *-ating*. [L. *refrigeratus*, pp. of *refrigerare*, < *re-*, again, + *frigerare*, make cool, < *frigus*, cold, coolness.] To make or keep, or to become, cold or cool.—**re-frig-er-a′tion** (-ẹ-rā′shọn), *n.* [L. *refrigeratio(n-).*] The act or process of refrigerating,

or the resulting state.—**re-frig′er-a-tive** (-ẹ-rā-tiv), *a.* Refrigerating.—**re-frig′er-a-tor** (-ẹ-rā-tọr), *n.* Something that refrigerates; specif., a box, chamber, or apparatus in which food, drink, etc., are kept cool, as by means of ice.—**re-frig′er-a-to-ry** (-ẹ-rā-tō-ri). [L. *refrigeratorius*.] **I.** *a.* Tending to cool; cooling. **II.** *n.*; pl. *-ries* (-riz). Something refrigerating, as a refrigerant or a refrigerator.

re-frin-gent (rẹ-frin′jent), *a.* [L. *refringens* (-ent-), ppr. of *refringere*: see *refract*.] Refracting; refractive.—**re-frin′gen-cy**, *n.*

reft (reft). Preterit and past participle of *reave*.

re-fu-el (rē-fū′ẹl), *v.*; *-eled* or *-elled*, *-eling* or *-elling*. [See *re-*.] **I.** *tr.* To supply afresh with fuel: as, to *refuel* an oil-burning ship; to *refuel* an aëroplane. **II.** *intr.* To take on a fresh supply of fuel.

ref-uge (ref′ūj), *n.* [OF. F. *refuge*, < L. *refugium*, < *re-*, back, + *fugere*, flee.] Shelter or protection from danger or trouble (as, to give or afford *refuge* to fugitives; to find or take *refuge* in a place; a place of *refuge*; "six cities for *refuge*, which ye shall appoint for the manslayer, that he may flee thither," Num. xxxv. 6); hence, protection or relief from annoyance, embarrassment, discomfort, etc. (as, to take *refuge* in silence, or in a book); also, a place of resort for shelter, protection, or safety (as, "The court of Pavia became a general *refuge* for the fugitives from Gaul," G. P. R. James's "Hist. of Charlemagne," ii.; "vagrants and criminals, who make this wild country a *refuge* from justice," Scott's "Guy Mannering," xxiii.); a sheltering or safe retreat; an asylum; also, one resorted to for protection, aid, or comfort, as in danger or trouble (as, "'Allah is our *refuge*,' he murmured," J. Conrad's "Rescue," v. 2; "He had become her reliance and her *refuge*," W. Churchill's "Coniston," i. 16); anything to which one has recourse for aid or relief (as, "Sleep seems their only *refuge*," Cowper's "Task," iv. 396); a resort, shift, or expedient in straits or difficulties or in any emergency (as, "Patriotism is the last *refuge* of a scoundrel," Johnson, in Boswell's "Johnson," April 7, 1775; "I consider proverbs as the *refuge* of weak minds," H. Kingsley's "Geoffry Hamlyn," xxxi.).—**ref′uge**, *v.*; *-uged*, *-uging*. **I.** *tr.* To give or afford refuge to; shelter: as, "Himself I *refug'd*, and his train reliev'd" (Dryden's tr. Virgil's "Æneid," iv. 779). [Archaic.] **II.** *intr.* To take refuge. [Archaic.]—**ref-u-gee′** (-ū-jē′), *n.* [F. *réfugié*.] One who flees for refuge or safety, esp. to a foreign country, as in time of persecution, political commotion, or war: as, the *refugees* from France after the revocation of the Edict of Nantes (see under *edict*), or during the French Revolution (see *émigré*); "the great drive of the Germans towards Antwerp . . . which swept before it multitudes of Flemish *refugees*" (H. G. Wells's "Mr. Britling," ii. 2. § 8).—**ref-u-gee′ism**, *n.*

re-ful-gence (rē-ful′jẹns), *n.* The state of being refulgent; refulgent brightness; splendor.

re-ful-gent (rẹ-ful′jent), *a.* [L. *refulgens* (-ent-), ppr. of *refulgere*, < *re-*, back, + *fulgere*, flash, shine.] Reflecting the light brilliantly, or shining (as, "In arms they stood Of golden panoply, *refulgent* host": Milton's "Paradise Lost," vi. 527); resplendent; radiant, as light; splendidly bright (as, "the *refulgent* dawn of the tropics": C. Brontë's "Jane Eyre," xxvii.).—**re-ful′gent-ly**, *adv.*

re-fund[1] (rē-fund′), *v. t.* [See *re-*.] To fund anew: as, "These maturing obligations will either be redeemed . . . or will be *refunded* into other obligations" (A. W. Mellon's "Taxation," viii.). Also written *re-fund*.

Refrigerator. — *a*, body of refrigerator; *b*, sheathing; *e*, shelf for supporting ice *i*; *f*, drip-pipe; *g*, air-trap; *h*, drip-pan; *j*, *j′*, lids covering ice-chamber; *k*, door of compartment containing shelves *l* on which are supported the articles to be preserved by refrigeration; *z*, zinc lining.

---

fat, fãte, fär, fȧll, ȧsk, fãre; net, mē, hėr; pin, pīne; not, nōte, mȯve, nọr; up, lūte, pũll; oi, oil; ou, out; (lightened) aviȧry, ẹlect, agọny, intọ, ūnite; (obscured) errȧnt, operȧ, ardẹnt, actọr, natūre; ch, chip; g, go; th, thin; ŦH, then; y, you;

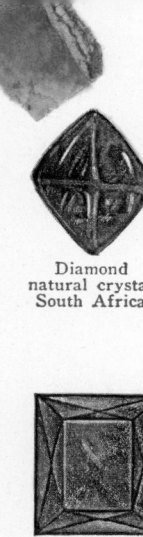

Diamond
natural crystal
South Africa

Diamond, emerald cut
South Africa

Emerald
Colombia

Ruby, carved
Burma

Ruby
Burma

Sapphire
Kashmir

Aquamarine
Brazil

Aquamarine, green
Brazil

Morganite (rose beryl)
Madagascar

Kunzite (var. of spodumene)
California

Cat's-eye
(chrysoberyl)
Ceylon

Alexandrite
Ceylon

Alexandrite
by artificial light
Ural Mountains

Star sapphire
Ceylon

Starlite (blue zircon)
Siam

Zircon, brown
Ceylon

Zircon, green
Ceylon

Peridot (olivine chrysolite)
Egypt

Garnet
India

Hyacinth hessonite
(variety of garnet)
Ceylon

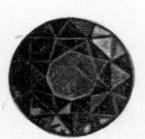

Tourmalin, green
Paris, Maine

Tourmalin, red
(rubellite)
California

Topaz, wine-yellow
Brazil

Topaz, pink
Brazil

Topaz, white
Brazil

Topaz, quartz variety
Brazil

Amethyst
Uruguay

Jade
(jadeite variety)
Burma

Opal, black
Queensland

Opal, precious
New South Wales

Fire-opal
Mexico

Moonstone
Ceylon

Turquoise
Persia

GEMS AND PRECIOUS STONES

This plate was made under the supervision of Dr. George F. Kunz, research curator of precious stones for the American Museum of Natural History, and gem expert for Messrs. Tiffany & Co. Drawn from the actual gems.

re-fund² (rē-fund′), v. [L. refundere (pp. refusus), pour back, < re-, back, + fundere, pour.] **I.** tr. To pour back†; hence, to give back or restore (esp. money); repay; pay back the amount of (as, "Perhaps I might have borrowed money . . . but that loan must have been refunded," Smollett's "Humphry Clinker," July 10; "We shall be glad to refund the unfulfilled part of their subscriptions," Bok's "Americanization of Edward Bok," xxx.); sometimes, to make repayment to, or reimburse (a person). **II.** intr. To make repayment.—**re-fund′²**, n. A refunding; repayment.—**re-fund′er**, n.—**re-fund′ment**, n.

re-fur-bish (rē-fėr′bish), v. t. [See re-.] To furbish anew: as, "Ellery Davenport was refurbishing and refurnishing the old country house" (Mrs. Stowe's "Oldtown Folks," xliv.).—**re-fur′bish-ment**, n.

re-fur-nish (rē-fėr′nish), v. t. [See re-.] To furnish anew.— **re-fur′nish-ment**, n.

re-fus-a-ble (rē-fū′za̱-bl), a. That may be refused.

re-fus-al (rē-fū′za̱l), n. The act or an act of refusing; also, the right to refuse (or to take) a thing before it is offered to others (as, "The syndicate stated that they would like to have the refusal of another serial from my pen": Arnold Bennett's "Truth about an Author," xii.).

re-fuse¹ (rē-fūz′), v.; -fused, -fusing. [OF. F. refuser, < L. refundere (pp. refusus), pour back: see refund².] **I.** tr. To decline to accept (something offered: as, to refuse an office; "The picture had been refused by the Royal Academy," Arnold Bennett's "Buried Alive," i.); reject (something available: as, "The stone which the builders refused is become the head stone of the corner," Ps. cxviii. 22); also, to decline to accept in a certain capacity (as, "Moses, whom they refused, saying, Who made thee a ruler and a judge?" Acts, vii. 35); decline to take as a wife or, now usually, a husband (as, "I, Anthony Lumpkin, Esquire . . . refuse you, Constantia Neville, spinster," Goldsmith's "She Stoops to Conquer," v.; to refuse a suitor); also, to decline to submit to (as, "To subdue By force, who reason for their law refuse": Milton's "Paradise Lost," vi. 41); sometimes, to fail to receive, or resist or repel (as, an acid which causes stone to refuse printing-ink); of a horse, to decline to leap over, or stop short at (a fence, water, etc.); also, to decline to give or grant (as, "if you refuse your aid," Shakspere's "Coriolanus," v. 1. 33; "refusing speech to any," Weir Mitchell's "Hugh Wynne," ii.); deny (a request, demand, etc.); formerly, to refrain from yielding (one's self) to something†; sometimes, to decline to grant access to (one's self), as to callers; also (with double object), to decline to give or grant (something) to (a person or thing) (as, "He . . . had refused her the canoe": J. Conrad's "Rescue," vi. 3); hence, to decline to grant something to (a person who asks: as, he asked for help, but they refused him); also, to decline, or express a determination not (to do something: as, "The commander . . . refused to discuss questions of right," Bancroft's "Hist. of the U. S.," Amer. Revolution, i. 5); also, to renounce†, give up†, or abandon† (as, "Deny thy father and refuse thy name": Shakspere's "Romeo and Juliet," ii. 2. 34); milit., to hold (troops) back, or move (troops) back from the regular alinement, when about to engage the enemy. **II.** intr. To decline acceptance, consent, or compliance.

ref-use² (ref′ūs). [Appar. < OF. refus, refusal, rejection, or refusé, pp., refused, < refuser, E. refuse¹.] **I.** a. Rejected as worthless or of little value; discarded: as, "Every thing that was vile and refuse, that they destroyed utterly" (1 Sam. xv. 9); refuse matter. **II.** n. That which is discarded as worthless or useless; refuse matter; rubbish; fig., the outcast or worthless portion of mankind, society, etc. (as, "He thought it very hard that a gentleman . . . should be driven by necessity to spend his old age among the refuse of mankind": Smollett's "Humphry Clinker," Sept. 12).

re-fus-er (rē-fū′zėr), n. One who refuses.

re-fut-a-ble (rē-fū′ta̱-bl or ref′ū-), a. [LL. refutabilis.] That may be refuted.—**re-fut-a-bil′i-ty** (-bil′i-ti), n.— **re-fut′a-bly**, adv.

re-fu-tal (rē-fū′ta̱l), n. The act of refuting; refutation.

ref-u-ta-tion (ref-ū-tā′shon), n. [L. refutatio(n-).] The act of refuting a statement, charge, etc.; disproof; confutation.—**re-fu-ta-tive** (rē-fū′ta̱-tiv), **re-fu′ta-to-ry** (-tō-ri), a. Serving to refute.

re-fute (rē-fūt′), v. t.; -futed, -futing. [L. refutare (pp. refutatus), repel, refute, < re-, back, + -futare as in confutare, E. confute.] To prove to be false or erroneous, as a statement, opinion, charge, etc. (as, "And he says much that many men dispute And cavil at with ease, but none refute": Cowper's "Truth," 360); also, to prove (a person) to be in error (as, to refute a disputant); confute.—**re-fut′er** (-fū′tėr), n.

re-gain (rē-gān′), v. t. [See re-.] To gain or get anew, or recover (as, "Hopeful to regain Thy love," Milton's "Paradise Lost," x. 972; "From day to day I regained strength," W. H. Hudson's "Far Away and Long Ago," xxii.); also, to succeed in reaching again, or get back to (as, "They had now regained the shores of the lake": Peacock's "Headlong Hall," vii.).—**re-gain′a-ble**, a. That may be regained.—**re-gain′er**, n.—**re-gain′ment**, n.

re-gal (rē′ga̱l), a. [L. regalis, < rex (reg-), king.] Belonging or pertaining to a king, or royal (as, "Charles Martel left to his sons the regal power": G. P. R. James's "Hist. of Charlemagne," i.); also, befitting a king, or kingly (as, regal pomp); resembling a king, or king-like; hence, stately, splendid, or magnificent.—**re′gal**, n. [F. régale = It. regale, appar. < L. regalis.] A kind of small, portable organ much used in the 16th and 17th centuries, having a set, or sometimes two sets, of reed-pipes, keys played with one hand, and a small bellows worked with the other hand.

Regal. — From an old painting.

re-gale (rē-gāl′), n. [Obs. F. régale (now rêgal), < It. regalo, a present, gift, < regalare, to present, regale; origin uncertain.] A choice repast, or feast (as, "They indulged in a regale, relishing their buffalo beef with inspiring alcohol": Irving's "Captain Bonneville," xli.); fig., something highly enjoyable; a treat; also, a choice article of food or drink; a dainty; also, regalement or refreshment.—**re-gale′**, v.; -galed, -galing. [F. régaler, < régale.] **I.** tr. To entertain with a choice repast; refresh with some choice or pleasing food or drink (as, "the donkey . . . wondering . . . whether he was destined to be regaled with a cabbage-stalk or two," Dickens's "Oliver Twist," iii.; "The Highlanders . . . regale themselves with whiskey," Smollett's "Humphry Clinker," Sept. 3); serve as choice refreshment for (a person), as an article of food or drink; fig., to entertain agreeably (as, "The Captain . . . regaled the company with a dashing sea-song," Aldrich's "Story of a Bad Boy," xvi.; "They would . . . regale them with grotesque feats of horsemanship," Irving's "Captain Bonneville," ii.); delight with something pleasing or as something pleasing does. **II.** intr. To feast: as, "This blooming young person was regaling on dewberries" (G. Meredith's "Ordeal of Richard Feverel," xiv.). —**re-gale′ment**, n.—**re-gal′er** (-gā′lėr), n.

re-ga-lia¹ (rē-gā′li̯ä), n. pl. [ML., prop. neut. pl. of L. regalis, E. regal.] The rights and privileges of a king; also, the ensigns or emblems of royalty, as the crown, scepter, etc.; hence, the decorations or insignia of any office or order (as, "Tom joined the new order of Cadets of Temperance, being attracted by the showy character of their 'regalia'": Mark Twain's "Tom Sawyer," xxii.).

re-ga-lia² (rē-gā′li̯ä), n.; pl. -lias. [Sp. regalia, lit. 'royal privilege.'] A kind of cigar of large size and superior quality.

re-gal-i-ty (rē-gal′i-ti), n.; pl. -ties (-tiz). [OF. regalite, < ML. regalitas, < L. regalis, E. regal.] Royalty, sovereignty, or kingship; also, a right or privilege pertaining to a king; also, a kingdom; also, in Scotland, territorial jurisdiction of a royal nature formerly conferred by the king; a territory subject to such jurisdiction (as, "The cultivators of each barony or regality, temporal or spiritual, in Scotland, were obliged to bring their corn to be grinded at the mill of the territory": Scott's "Monastery," xiii.).

re-gal-ly (rē′ga̱l-i), adv. In a regal manner.

re-gard (rē-gärd′), v. [OF. F. regarder, < re- (< L. re-), back, again, + garder, E. guard: cf. reward.] **I.** tr. Το look at, contemplate, or observe (as, "He *regarded* me with a fixed and serious eye": H. Melville's "Typee," xxxiii.); also, to take notice of, pay attention to, or heed (as, "Many past, but none *regarded* her": Tennyson's "Geraint and Enid," 520); be mindful of, or consider (as, "*Regard* thy danger": Shakspere's "Two Gentlemen of Verona," iii. 1. 256); take into consideration or account (as, "In every work *regard* the writer's end": Pope's "Essay on Criticism," 255); have or show consideration, respect, or concern for (as, "a judge, which feared not God, neither *regarded* man," Luke, xviii. 2; to *regard* the rights or feelings of others); also, to esteem, think highly of, or care for (as, "She does not *regard* you enough to appear, if you awaked her," Sheridan's "Duenna," i. 1; "Prue and her sex *regard* sentiment more than action," G. W. Curtis's "Prue and I," iv.); look upon or think of with a particular feeling (as, to *regard* a person or a proposal with favor; to *regard* a situation with anxiety); also, to contemplate or view mentally, or consider (as, to *regard* a matter from every point of view); view or consider (*as*: as, "The principal Yorkist nobles . . . still *regarded* Edward as their monarch," J. F. Kirk's "Charles the Bold," iii. 1); also, to respect, relate to, or concern (as, "The present contest . . . entirely *regards* the injustice done . . . to my own natural rights," Scott's "Castle Dangerous," xvii.; "His chronicle is less mischievous as *regards* Mrs. Warwick," G. Meredith's "Diana of the Crossways," i.). **II.** *intr.* To look or gaze; also, to pay attention; heed.—**re·gard′,** *n.* [OF. F. *regard.*] Look or gaze (as, "Claude turned and met the stranger's *regard* with a faint smile": G. W. Cable's "Bonaventure," iii. 4); also, aspect† or appearance†; also, a view or prospect seen† (as, "an indistinct *regard*": Shakspere's "Othello," ii. 1. 40); also, notice, attention, or heed (as, "Of thee these forty days none hath *regard*": Milton's "Paradise Regained," ii. 315); mindfulness, consideration, or thought of something (as, "With no *regard* Of highest favours past": Milton's "Samson Agonistes," 684); attention in practice, as to some principle, duty, etc. (as, "A constant *regard* to veracity, justice, and charity, may form distinct habits of these particular virtues": J. Butler's "Analogy of Religion," i. 5); consideration, thought, concern, or care (as, "Too capital an interest . . . was now at stake, to allow of any *regard* to minor interests," De Quincey's "Revolt of the Tartars"; to have *regard* for a person's feelings); respect or deference (as, to pay due *regard* to authority); also, esteem, kindly feeling, liking, or affection (as, respectful, friendly, or loving *regard*; a token of *regard*; "I once thought you had a kind of *regard* for her," Borrow's "Romany Rye," xi.); *pl.*, sentiments of esteem or affection as conveyed in polite messages (as, "Give her my respectful *regards*," Arnold Bennett's "Mr. Prohack," v.; to send a person one's warmest *regards*); also, *sing.*, mental view†, estimation†, or opinion† (as, in my *regard*); account or importance in the estimation of others† (as, matters of small *regard*; "I am a bard of no *regard* Wi' gentlefolks, and a' that," Burns's "Jolly Beggars," 246); also, something regarded or considered, or a consideration; also, respect, reference, or relation (as, to err in *regard* to facts; with *regard* to that you are probably right); a respect, point, or particular (as, quite satisfactory in this *regard*).

re·gard·a·ble (rẹ-gär′dạ-bl), *a.* That may be or is to be regarded.

re·gard·ant (rẹ-gär′dạnt), *a.* [OF. F., ppr. of *regarder*, E. *regard*, *v.*] Regarding; observant; in *her.*, looking backward (as, a lion *regardant*).

re·gard·er (rẹ-gär′dẻr), *n.* One who or that which regards.

re·gard·ful (rẹ-gärd′fúl), *a.* Full of regard; observant or watchful (as, "a quick *regardful* eyeing of him by all the congregation": H. Melville's "Moby-Dick," viii.); attentive, heedful, or mindful (often with *of*: as, *regardful* of appearances); considerate or thoughtful; respectful.—**re·gard′ful·ly,** *adv.*—**re·gard′ful·ness,** *n.*

A Lion Regardant.

re·gard·ing (rẹ-gär′ding), *prep.* [Orig. ppr.] With regard to; respecting; concerning: as, "*Regarding* personalities . . . I have not the same clear showing" (George Eliot's "Felix Holt," xxiv.).

re·gard·less (rẹ-gärd′les). **I.** *a.* Having or showing no regard, heedless, unmindful, or careless (often with *of*: as, "With a book he was *regardless* of time," Jane Austen's "Pride and Prejudice," iii.); also, unregarded or unheeded (as, "Frequent tears Falling *regardless* from his friendless eyes": Hood's "Midsummer Fairies," lxxxii.); also, not regarded or esteemed; despised; mean, paltry, or trivial. **II.** *adv.* Without regard, or with complete disregard (*of*: as, "Every injunction he had given was attended to, *regardless* of expense," Mrs. Gaskell's "Cranford," ii.); hence, elliptically, with complete disregard of expense or consequences (colloq.: as, to be got up *regardless*, as in fine clothes; to plunge in *regardless*).—**re·gard′less·ly,** *adv.*—**re·gard′less·ness,** *n.*

re·gath·er (rẹ-gaᴛн′ẻr), *v. t.* or *i.* [See *re-.*] To gather again or anew.

re·gat·ta (rẹ-gat′ä), *n.*; pl. *regattas* (-äz). [It. (Venetian).] Orig., a gondola-race in Venice; hence, in general, a boat-race, as of rowboats, yachts, or other vessels, or an organized series of such races.

re·ge·late (rē′jẹ-lāt), *v. i.*; *-lated*, *-lating.* [L. *re-*, again, + *gelare* (pp. *gelatus*), freeze.] To freeze together, as two pieces of thawing ice brought into contact.—**re·ge·la′tion** (-lā′shọn), *n.*

re·gen·cy (rē′jẹn-si). [ML. *regentia*.] **I.** *n.*; pl. *-cies* (-siz). The office or function of a regent; esp., the office, jurisdiction, or control of a regent or body of regents exercising the ruling power during the minority, absence, or disability of a sovereign; also, a body of regents, or a government consisting of regents; also, a territory under the control of a regent or regents; also, the term of office of a regent; specif. [usually *cap.*], in *Fr. hist.*, the period (1715–23) during which Philip, Duke of Orleans, was regent, in the minority of Louis XV.; in *Eng. hist.*, the period (1811–20) during which George, Prince of Wales (afterward George IV.), was regent, owing to the mental incapacity of George III. **II.** *a.* Pertaining to a regency, esp. [usually *cap.*] that in French history (1715–23) or that in English history (1811-20): as, the *Regency* style in decoration, etc., in France.

re·gen·er·a·cy (rẹ-jen′ẹ-rạ-si), *n.* Regenerate state.

re·gen·er·ate (rẹ-jen′ẹ-rāt), *v.*; *-ated*, *-ating.* [L. *regeneratus*, pp. of *regenerare*, < *re-*, again, + *generare*: see *generate*.] **I.** *tr.* To generate or produce anew; bring into existence again; fig., to

French Regency Style. — From Hôtel Soubise, Paris.

recreate, reconstitute, or make over, esp. in a better form or condition; often, to effect a complete moral reform in (as, "a band of Christian warriors, coming to purify and *regenerate* the land": Irving's "Conquest of Granada," xliii.); in *theol.*, to cause to be born again spiritually (as, "The doctrine of the Church is, that children are *regenerated* in holy baptism": Kingsley's "Alton Locke," xxiv.). **II.** *intr.* To come into existence or be formed again; also, to reform; become regenerate.—**re·gen′er·ate** (-ẹ-rạt), *a.* Formed again or anew; also, reconstituted or made over in a better form; also, reformed; in *theol.*, born again spiritually.—**re·gen·er·a′tion** (-ẹ-rā′shọn), *n.* [LL. *regeneratio(n-).*] The act of regenerating, or the state of being regenerated; production or formation anew; reconstitution, esp. in a better form or condition; reformation; in *theol.*, spiritual rebirth; also, in *wireless teleg.* and *teleph.*, a process by which some of the energy of the plate circuit of a vacuum-tube is transferred back to the grid circuit by means of induction or the like, thus reinforcing the current of the grid and hence causing larger variations in the current of the plates with a corresponding increase in the volume of the signals.—**re-gen′er-a-tive** (-ẹ-rā̇-tiv), *a.* Tending to regenerate; pertaining to regeneration; in *mech.*, noting or pertaining to a furnace, etc., in which the waste heat of the outgoing gases is utilized to heat the air or fuel-gas entering, as by a chamber containing fire-bricks through which both the outgoing gases and the incoming air or fuel-gas pass alternately; in *wireless teleg.* and *teleph.*, of or pertaining to regeneration.—**re-gen′er-a-tive-ly**, *adv.*—**re-gen′er-a-tor** (-ẹ-rā̇-tọr), *n.* One who or that which regenerates; in *mech.*, in a regenerative furnace, etc., the device for heating the incoming air or fuel-gas.

re-gent (rē′jẹnt). [L. *regens* (*regent-*), ppr. of *regere*, keep straight, direct, rule: see *rex* and *right*.] **I.** *a.* Ruling or governing (now rare); also, exercising vicarious ruling authority (as, a prince *regent*; a queen *regent*); acting as regent of a country; also, holding the position of a regent in a university (now only hist.). **II.** *n.* A ruler or governor (now rare); also, one who exercises the ruling power in a kingdom during the minority, absence, or disability of the sovereign; also, in old universities, a member of certain governing and teaching bodies (now chiefly hist.); in the U. S., a member of the governing board of certain universities and other institutions; at Harvard University, an officer who exercises a general supervision over the conduct and welfare of the students.—**re′gent=bird**, *n.* [So called in compliment to the Prince Regent, afterward George IV.: see *regency*, *n.*, def.] An Australian bower-bird, *Sericulus chrysocephalus* (or *melinus*), the male of which has a plumage of velvety black diversified with golden yellow.—**re′gent-ship**, *n.*

reg-i-cide (rej′i-sīd), *n.* [L. *rex* (*reg-*), king: see *-cide*.] One who kills a king; one responsible for the death of a king (esp. applied to the judges who condemned Charles I. of England to death);

Regent-bird.

also, the killing of a king.—**reg′i-ci-dal** (-sī-dạl), *a.*

ré-gie (rā-zhē′), *n.* [F., < *régir*, < L. *regere*, rule: see *regent*.] In France and elsewhere, an excise or revenue service or department.

re-gild (rē-gild′), *v. t.* [See *re-*.] To gild anew.

ré-gime (rā-zhēm′), *n.* [F., < L. *regimen*: see *regimen*.] A mode or system of rule or government; in general, a ruling or prevailing system; in *med.*, same as *regimen*.—**ancien régime** (äṅ-syaṅ′ rā-zhēm′). [F.] The ancient or old system of government; esp., the political and social system of France before the Revolution of 1789.

reg-i-men (rej′i-men), *n.* [L. *regimen* (*regimin-*), guidance, direction, rule, < *regere*: see *regent*.] Rule or government; also, a particular form or system of government; in general, a prevailing system; in *med.*, a regulated course of diet, exercise, or manner of living, intended to preserve or restore health or to attain some result (sometimes fig.); in *gram.*, government.

reg-i-ment (rej′i-mẹnt), *n.* [OF. *regiment*, rule, F. *régiment*, regiment of troops, < LL. *regimentum*, rule, government, < L. *regere*: see *regent*.] Rule, government, or regimen (now rare); also, a regiment† or régime†; also, a medical regimen†; also, a territory under a particular rule†; also, *milit.*, a unit of organization in an army, being next below a brigade and usually commanded by a colonel (as, a *regiment* of infantry, usually consisting of three battalions; a *regiment* of cavalry; a *regiment* of field artillery); hence, in general, a large body or number (as, "He was living in that magnificent house all alone, with a whole *regiment* of servants":

Arnold Bennett's "The Old Adam," v.).—**reg′i-ment** (-ment), *v. t.* To form into a regiment or regiments; hence, to form into an organized body or group; organize or systematize; also, to assign to a regiment or group.—**reg-i-men′tal** (-men′tạl). **I.** *a.* Of or pertaining to a regiment. **II.** *n. Pl.*, the uniform of a regiment; military clothing: as, "Colonel Forster . . . in his *regimentals*" (Jane Austen's "Pride and Prejudice," vii.).—**reg-i-men′tal-ly**, *adv.*—**reg″i-men-ta′tion** (-tā′shọn), *n.* Formation into regiments; organization.

re-gim-i-nal (rē-jim′i-nạl), *a.* Of, pertaining to, or of the nature of regimen.

re-gi-na (rē-jī′nạ), *n.* [L., fem. of *rex*, king.] Queen: abbreviated *R.*, as, Victoria *R.*—**re-gi′nal**, *a.* Queenly.

re-gion (rē′jọn), *n.* [OF. *regiun* (F. *région*), < L. *regio*(*n-*), direction, quarter, region, < *regere*, direct: see *regent*.] Any more or less extensive, continuous part of a surface or space: esp., a part of the earth's surface (land or sea) of considerable and usually indefinite extent (as, the north polar *region*; tropical *regions*); a tract or district without respect to boundaries or extent; a locality; specif., an administrative division of a city or territory (as, "He [Constantine] divided Constantinople into fourteen *regions* or quarters": Gibbon's "Decline and Fall' of the Roman Empire," xvii.); in general, an area or part of a surface; also, a part or division of the universe, the heavens, the interior of the earth, etc. (as, "In what far-distant *region* of the sky, Hushed in deep silence, sleep you when 'tis calm?" Thomson's "Seasons," Winter, 116); any of the successive divisions into which the atmosphere is considered as divided according to height, or the sea according to depth; in general, a part of a space or a body; also, fig., a domain, realm, or sphere (as, the *region* of art or of science); specif., in *zoögeog.*, a large faunal area of the earth's surface, sometimes one regarded as a division of a larger area or realm; in *anat.*, a place in, or a division of, the body or a part of the body (as, the abdominal *region* or *regions*).—**re′gion-al**, *a.* Of or pertaining to a particular region, district, area, or part; sectional; local; sometimes, of or pertaining to a region of considerable natural extent; not merely local.—**re′gion-al-ly**, *adv.*

reg-is-ter[1] (rej′is-tẹr), *n.* [OF. F. *registre*, < ML. *registrum*, *regestrum*, *regestum*, a register, < L. *regerere* (pp. *regestus*), carry back, transcribe, record, < *re-*, back, + *gerere*, bear.] A book in which entries of acts, occurrences, names, or the like are made for record; also, any list of such entries; a record of acts, occurrences, etc.; a roll; a list; also, an entry in such a book, record, or list; also, registration or registry; also, a device for registering something; a mechanical contrivance by which certain data are automatically recorded; also, a contrivance for regulating the passage of heat, air, or the like, esp. a closable perforated plate in a tube of a heating or ventilating system; in *com.*, an official document issued to a ship as evidence of its nationality, etc.; in *music*, the compass or range of a voice or an instrument; also, a particular series of tones, esp. of the human voice, produced in the same way and having the same quality (as, the head-*register* and the chest-*register* of the human voice, comprising tones calling the cavities of the head and the chest respectively into decided sympathetic vibration); also, in an organ, a stop (set of pipes, or a knob or handle as for controlling them); in *printing*, etc., precise adjustment or correspondence, as of lines, columns, etc., esp. on the two sides of a leaf; correct relation or exact superimposition, as of colors in color-printing.—**reg′is-ter**[1], *v.* [OF. F. *registrer*, < ML. *registrare*, < *registrum*.] **I.** *tr.* To enter formally in a register; cause to be so entered by a person charged with making such entries (as, "You will have to go to the registrar's and *register* the death": Arnold Bennett's "Buried Alive," i.); specif., to cause to be taken record of for purposes of safety (as mail matter at a post-office, for security in transmission, by payment of a special fee); in general, to set down in writing or the like; record; also, to indicate by a record, as instruments do; indicate or show, as on a scale (as, the thermometer *registers* 90°); also, to serve as or afford a record of, as a writing or something else does (as, "The wall-sculpture of Amada . . . belongs to the period of Egyptian Renaissance . . . Amada . . . *registers* an epoch in the history of the art": Amelia B. Edwards's "Thousand

Miles up the Nile," xiv.); in *moving pictures*, to show (surprise, joy, anger, etc.), as by facial expression or by actions; in *printing*, etc., to adjust so as to secure exact correspondence; cause to be in register. **II.** *intr.* To enter one's name, or cause it to be entered, in a register; also, to indicate something as by a record or on a scale, as instruments do; also, to register surprise, joy, etc., in acting for moving pictures; also, to be or become registered or indicated; in *printing*, etc., to be in register.

reg-is-ter[2] (rej'is-tėr), *n.* [For *registrer, registrar*.] A registrar.

reg-is-tra-ble (rej'is-trạ-bl), *a.* That may be registered.

reg-is-trant (rej'is-trạnt), *n.* One who registers: as, the *registrant* of a patent.

reg-is-trar (rej'is-trär), *n.* [Earlier *registrer*.] One whose business it is to keep a register; an official recorder: as, "I married her before the *registrar* at Letchbury" (S. Butler's "Way of All Flesh," lxxvi.).

reg-is-tra-tion (rej-is-trā'shon), *n.* [ML. *registratio(n-)*.] The act of registering or recording; registry; enrolment; an instance of this; an entry in a register; in *printing*, etc., register. — **reg-is-tra'tion-al**, *a.*

reg-is-trer (rej'is-trėr), *n.* Earlier form of *registrar*.

reg-is-try (rej'is-tri), *n.*; pl. *-tries* (-triz). The act of registering; registration; also, a place where a register is kept; an office of registration; also, a register, or an entry in a register.

re-gi-us (rē'ji-us), *a.* [L., < *rex* (*reg*-), king.] Royal: applied to professors in British universities who hold chairs founded by the sovereign.

ré-glage (rā-gläzh'), *n.* [F., < *régler*, regulate, < LL. *regulare*: see *regulate*.] Regulation; adjustment; specif., *milit.*, the regulation of artillery fire, as by means of aëroplanes which observe the spot where the projectiles fall and send back the necessary corrections by wireless or otherwise.

reg-let (reg'let), *n.* [F. *réglet*, dim. of *règle*, < L. *regula*, E. *rule*, *n.*] In *arch.*, a narrow, flat molding; in *printing*, a thin strip, usually of wood, less than type-high, used to produce a blank in or about a page of type; also, such strips collectively, or material for making them.

re-glow (rē-glō'), *v. i.* [See *re*-.] To glow again; recalesce. — **re-glow'**, *n.* A glowing again; recalescence.

reg-ma (reg'mạ), *n.*; pl. *-mata* (-mạ-tạ). [NL., < Gr. ῥῆγμα, fracture, < ῥηγνύναι, break.] In *bot.*, a dry fruit consisting of three or more carpels which separate from the axis at maturity.

reg-nal (reg'nạl), *a.* [ML. *regnalis*, < L. *regnum*, E. *reign*, *n.*] Of or pertaining to reigning, sovereignty, or a reign: as, a *regnal* year (a particular year of a sovereign's reign, as the first, second, third, etc., counting from the moment of accession).

reg-nant (reg'nạnt), *a.* [L. *regnans* (*regnant*-), ppr. of *regnare*, E. *reign*, *v.*] Reigning or ruling (as, a queen *regnant*); hence, exercising sway or influence; predominant; also, prevalent or widespread. — **reg'nan-cy** (-nạn-si), *n.*

re-gorge (rē-gôrj'), *v. t.*; *-gorged, -gorging*. [F. *regorger*, < *re*- (< L. *re*-), back, + *gorge*, throat, E. *gorge*.] To disgorge; cast up again; also, to swallow again.

re-grant (rē-grȧnt'), *v. t.* [See *re*-.] To grant again or anew. — **re-grant'**, *n.* A granting again; the renewal of a grant.

re-grate (rẹ-grāt'), *v. t.*; *-grated, -grating*. [OF. *regrater* (F. *regratter*); origin uncertain.] To buy up (grain, provisions, etc.) in order to sell again at a profit in or near the same market (formerly regarded as a criminal offense); also, to sell again (commodities so bought); retail. — **re-grat'er**, **re-grat'or** (-grā'tėr, -tọr), *n.*

re-greet (rē-grēt'), *v. t.* [See *re*-.] To greet in return; also, to greet anew; also, to greet or salute. [Obs. or rare.] — **re-greet'†**, *n.* A return or exchange of salutation; a greeting.

re-gress (rẹ-gres'), *v. i.* [L. *regressus*, pp. of *regredi*, < *re*-, back, + *gradi*, walk, go.] To go back; return; also, to move in a backward direction; retrograde. — **re-gress** (rē'gres), *n.* [L. *regressus*, *n.*] The act of going back; passage back; return; also, the right or liberty of returning; also, the means or way of returning (as, "This gave me . . . egress and *regress*, as it were a back way to my tent and to

my storehouse": Defoe's "Robinson Crusoe," i. 4); also, backward movement or course; retrogression. — **re-gres-sion** (rẹ-gresh'ọn), *n.* [L. *regressio(n-)*.] The act of going back or returning; return; also, backward movement or course; retrogradation or retrogression; specif., reversion to an earlier or less advanced state or form or to the common or general type. — **re-gres'sive** (-gres'iv), *a.* Characterized by regression or going back or backward; retrogressive; backward in course, tendency, or action. — **re-gres'sive-ly**, *adv.* — **re-gres'sive-ness**, *n.*

re-gret (rẹ-gret'), *v. t.*; *-gretted, -gretting*. [OF. *regreter* (F. *regretter*), appar. < *re*- (< L. *re*-), back, + *-greter*, from Teut., and akin to AS. *grǣtan*, weep, E. *greet*[1].] To think of with a more or less deep sense of loss, as a person or thing that is gone (as, "Mr. Pendexter had departed. Only a few old . . . people *regretted* him," Longfellow's "Kavanagh," xii.; to *regret* one's vanished youth); feel sorrow or be sorry for the loss of; also, to feel sorry about (loss, deprivation, or anything disappointing or unpleasant: as, "He . . . *regretted* the loss of the reward," Godwin's "Caleb Williams," xxxvii.; "He *regretted* her departure extremely," Arnold Bennett's "Roll-Call," i.; to *regret* an unfortunate occurrence); often, to feel sorry for, as some fault or error of one's own, doing or not doing something, etc. (as, to *regret* one's haste, harshness, or folly; "I've never *regretted* being a soldier," Drinkwater's "Robert E. Lee," iii.; I *regret* that I did not take your advice). — **re-gret'**, *n.* [F. *regret*.] The feeling of one who regrets; sorrow, or sense of loss, over a person or thing that is gone; sorrowful feeling, disappointment, or dissatisfaction over anything that one wishes might have been otherwise (as, "I missed him by twenty-four hours . . . It was a matter of very great *regret* to me": H. G. Wells's "Mr. Britling," i. 1. § 9); the feeling of being sorry for some fault, act, omission, etc., of one's own (as, to have or express *regret* for one's injustice to another; "More pointed still we make ourselves Regret, remorse, and shame," Burns's "Man Was Made to Mourn," 52); *pl.*, feelings of sorrow over what is lost, gone, done, or past recall (as, "The women were divided between *regrets* for the homes they had left and apprehension of the deserts . . . before them," Parkman's "Oregon Trail," vi.; "Without wasting the moments in useless *regrets*, he proceeded . . . to business," Cooper's "Spy," xxiv.); also, *pl.* or *sing.*, a polite written expression of regretful feeling, as at inability to accept an invitation (as, to send *regrets*, or a *regret*). — **re-gret'ful**, *a.* Full of regret; sorrowful because of what is lost, gone, done, etc. — **re-gret'ful-ly**, *adv.* — **re-gret'ful-ness**, *n.* — **re-gret'ta-ble**, *a.* That is to be regretted; calling for regret: as, "a fortunate delivery from a *regrettable* embarrassment" (W. De Morgan's "Alice-for-Short," xxvi.). — **re-gret'ta-bly**, *adv.* — **re-gret'ter**, *n.*

re-group (rē-gröp'), *v. t.* [See *re*-.] To group anew.

re-grow (rē-grō'), *v. i.* [See *re*-.] To grow again. — **re-growth'**, *n.*

reg-u-la (reg'ū-lạ), *n.*; pl. *-læ* (-lē). [L., rule, ruler: see *rule*, *n.*] In *arch.*, a band or fillet; esp., one of a series below the tænia of the Doric entablature, bearing guttæ on the lower side.

reg-u-la-ble (reg'ū-lạ-bl), *a.* Regulatable.

reg-u-lar (reg'ū-lär), *a.* [OF. *reguler* (F. *régulier*), < L. *regularis*, < *regula*, rule: see *rule*, *n.*] **I.** *a.* Conforming to some rule or principle of form or arrangement (as, "Mazes intricate, Eccentric, intervolved, yet *regular* Then most, when most irregular they seem," Milton's "Paradise Lost," v. 623; *regular* features; *regular* teeth); methodically formed or arranged; symmetrical; also, characterized by the operation of a fixed principle, or by uniform procedure, occurrence, etc. (as, "the *regular* line of promotion," Cooper's "Two Admirals," ii.; *regular* movements; *regular* breathing); recurring at fixed times (as, "He had been . . . going . . . without his *regular* meals": H. Melville's "Moby-Dick," xvii.); uniformly maintained (as, to receive a *regular* salary; *regular* employment); customary (as, "We'll put you into your *regular* bed-room to-morrow," Dickens's "Nicholas Nickleby," vii.; his *regular* hour of rising); also, observing a fixed or uniform principle, or adhering to rule (as, to be *regular* in one's diet); performing certain recurring actions or duties without failure, or observing fixed

---

times for the performance of these (as, to be *regular* in attendance at church; to be *regular* in one's hours); performing some action habitually or more or less frequently (as, a *regular* attendant; a *regular* customer; a *regular* contributor); sometimes, orderly or well-ordered (as, to lead a *regular* life); also, conforming to some accepted rule or standard; carried out in accordance with an accepted principle; formally correct or proper; normal or usual; properly qualified for an occupation or profession, or habitually employed in it (as, "I have a great ambition to be a *regular* journalist": Arnold Bennett's "Great Man," xii.); hence, complete, thorough, or out-and-out (colloq.: as, a *regular* landslide; a *regular* humbug; a *regular* brick); in *bot.*, uniform; of a flower, having the members of each of its floral circles or whorls normally alike in form and size; in *math.*, governed by one law throughout (as, a *regular* polygon, one having all its angles equal and all its sides equal); in *gram.*, conforming to a usual and uniform method of inflection; *milit.*, noting or belonging to the permanently organized body constituting the standing army of a state; also, sometimes, noting soldiers recognized as legitimate combatants in warfare; in *U. S. politics*, of, pertaining to, or selected by the recognized agents of a political party (as, the *regular* nomination, ticket, or candidate); conforming to the requirements or discipline of a party or its recognized agents, as a person; *eccles.*, subject to a religious rule, or belonging to a religious or monastic order (as, *regular* clergy: opposed to *secular*). **II.** *n.* One who or that which is regular; *milit.*, a member of the regular troops or standing army; a regular soldier; *eccles.*, a member of a duly constituted religious order under a rule.—**reg-u-lar′i-ty** (-lar′i-ti), *n.* The state or character of being regular (see the various senses of *regular*, *a.*).—**reg′u-lar-ize**, *v. t.*; -ized, -izing. To make regular.—**reg′u-lar-ly**, *adv.*

reg-u-lat-a-ble (reg′ū-lā-ta-bl), *a.* Capable of being regulated; regulable.

reg-u-late (reg′ū-lāt), *v. t.*; -lated, -lating. [LL. *regulatus*, pp. of *regulare*, < L. *regula*, rule: see *rule*, *n.*, and cf. *rule*, *v.*] To control or direct by rule or by some governing principle or method (as, "The life of the young ladies . . . was *regulated* on the strictest principles": W. Churchill's "Modern Chronicle," i. 6); order according to some approved principle or system (as, "If we think to *regulate* printing, thereby to rectify manners, we must *regulate* all recreations and pastimes," Milton's "Areopagitica"; "Such things have happened before . . . in the best *regulated* families," Thackeray's "Newcomes," lxxviii.); also, to adjust with reference to some standard or requirement (as, "He was able to *regulate* the temperature with hot steam": Eden Phillpotts's "Grey Room," vi.); adjust so as to ensure accuracy of operation (as, to *regulate* a clock or a watch); in general, to put in good order (as, to *regulate* the digestion).—**reg-u-la′tion** (-lā′shon). **I.** *n.* The act of regulating, or the state of being regulated; also, a rule or order, as for conduct, prescribed by authority; a governing direction or law. **II.** *a.* Prescribed by or in accord with a regulation; standard; hence, usual; ordinary.—**reg′u-la-tive** (-la̱-tiv), *a.* Serving to regulate.—**reg′u-la-tor** (-lā-to̱r), *n.* One who or that which regulates; specif., any of various devices for regulating or controlling motion, power, etc.; a device in a clock or a watch for causing it to go faster or slower; also, a timepiece used as a standard.—**reg′u-la-to-ry** (-la̱-tō̱-ri), *a.* Regulative.

reg-u-lus (reg′ū-lus), *n.*; pl. -luses or -*li* (-lī). [L., dim. of *rex* (*reg*-), king.] In *metal.*, the metallic mass which forms beneath the slag at the bottom of the crucible or furnace in smelting ores; also, an impure intermediate product obtained in smelting ores; [*cap.*] in *astron.*, a star of the first magnitude in the constellation Leo.—**reg′u-line** (-lin), *a.*

re-gur-gi-tate (rē-gėr′ji-tāt), *v.*; -tated, -tating. [ML. *regurgitatus*, pp. of *regurgitare*, < L. *re*-, back, + *gurges*, whirlpool, gulf.] **I.** *intr.* To surge or rush back or in the reverse direction, as liquids, gases, undigested food, etc. **II.** *tr.* To cause to surge or rush back; cast up or out again, as food from the stomach.—**re-gur-gi-ta′tion** (-tā′shon), *n.*

re-ha-bil-i-tate (rē-ha̱-bil′i-tāt), *v. t.*; -tated, -tating. [ML. *rehabilitatus*, pp. of *rehabilitare*, < *re*-, again, + *habilitare*:

see *habilitate*.] To restore formally to a former capacity or standing, or to rank, rights, or privileges lost or forfeited; also, to reëstablish in good repute or accepted respectability, as a person or the character, name, etc., after disrepute; also, to restore to a good condition, regenerate, or make over in an improved form (as, to *rehabilitate* human nature; to *rehabilitate* one's ideas or methods; to *rehabilitate* a house).—**re-ha-bil-i-ta′tion** (-tā′shon), *n.*

re-hash (rē-hash′), *v. t.* [See *re*-.] To hash anew; fig., to work up (old material) in a new form.—**re-hash′**, *n.* A rehashing; also, something rehashed; something old put forth again in a new form.

re-hear (rē-hēr′), *v. t.*; pret. and pp. -heard. [See *re*-.] To hear again.

re-hears-al (rē-hėr′sa̱l), *n.* The act of rehearsing; a repeating, reciting, relating, or recounting; esp., the act of going through a dramatic, musical, or other performance in private, for practice, before going through it publicly or on some formal occasion; a performance beforehand by way of practice or drill (as, a series of *rehearsals* of a play or opera).

re-hearse (rē-hėrs′), *v.*; -hearsed, -hearsing. [OF. *rehercier*, appar. < *re*- (< L. *re*-), again, + *hercier*, to harrow, < *herce*, a harrow: see *hearse*.] **I.** *tr.* To repeat, as something previously said, heard, or written (as, "*Rehearse* not unto another that which is told unto thee": Ecclus. xix. 7); also, to repeat in a formal manner, or recite (as, "Like the cavaliers . . . in the Romance Of silver-tongued Boccaccio . . . we *rehearsed* our rhymes To their fair auditor": Whittier's "Bridal of Pennacook," Prologue); also, to relate the facts or particulars of, narrate, or describe (as, "Peter *rehearsed* the matter from the beginning, and expounded it by order unto them," Acts, xi. 4; "He appeared to be *rehearsing* to his auditors events which had recently occurred," H. Melville's "Typee," xvii.); also, to tell one by one, recount, or enumerate (as, to *rehearse* the names of the leaders; "An act of the English parliament *rehearsed* the dangers to be apprehended," Bancroft's "Hist. of the U. S.," Amer. Revolution, ii. 2); also, to recite or act (a play, part, etc.) in private, by way of practice, before a public performance; go through (any performance) in private beforehand, for practice (as, to *rehearse* a symphony; to *rehearse* a wedding ceremony); drill or train (a person, etc.) by rehearsal, as for some performance or part (as, "He ought to have been carefully coached and prepared and *rehearsed* before he was put before the Lord Chancellor": H. G. Wells's "Bealby," viii.). **II.** *intr.* To recite; now, usually, to rehearse a play, part, or the like (as, "You look as if you were *rehearsing* for a villain in a play": Tarkington's "Magnificent Ambersons," viii.).—**re-hears′er**, *n.*

re-heat (rē-hēt′), *v. t.* [See *re*-.] To heat again.—**re-heat′er**, *n.* Something that reheats, as a heater for raising the temperature of steam which has been used once and is to be used again.

rei (rā), *n.* A form sometimes used as the singular of *reis*[1].

reich (rīch), *n.* [G.] In German use, a realm, kingdom, or empire; a state; a commonwealth (as [*cap.*] the German Republic).

reichs-land (rīchs′länt), *n.*; pl. -*lande* (-län-dė). [G., 'empire's land.'] In German use, a territory belonging to the empire or state: a name formerly applied, in *sing.* and also *pl.*, to Alsace-Lorraine.

reichs-mark (rīchs′märk), *n.* [G., 'state's mark.'] The reconstituted German mark introduced in November, 1924, having a gold value of 23.8 U. S. cents, and equivalent to 1,000,000,000,000 paper marks as previously issued. Cf. *rentenmark*.

Reichs-rat, Reichs-rath (rīchs′rät), *n.* [G., 'empire's, or state's, council.'] The legislature or parliament in the Cisleithan (Austrian) division of the former Austro-Hungarian Empire; also, the national council (Council of the Reich) of the German Republic, composed of members appointed to represent the component states, and corresponding to some extent to the former Bundesrat (cf. *Reichstag*).

Reichs-tag (rīchs′täch), *n.* [G., 'empire's, or state's, diet.'] The elective legislative assembly of the former German Empire, which was chosen by the people, and exercised power in combination with the Bundesrat; also, the elective legisla-

---

(variable) ḑ as d or j, ş as s or sh, ṭ as t or ch, ẕ as z or zh; o, F. cloche; ü, F. menu; ċh, Sc. loch; ṅ, F. bonbon; ′, primary accent; ″, secondary accent; †, obsolete; <, from; +, and; =, equals. See also lists at beginning of book.

tive assembly of the German Republic, chosen by popular suffrage (cf. *Reichsrat*).

re-i-fy (rē'i-fī), *v. t.*; -fied, -fying. [L. *res*, thing: see -*fy*.] To convert into or regard as a thing: as, to *reify* an abstract concept.—**re"i-fi-ca'tion** (-fi-kā'shọn), *n.*

reign (rān), *n.* [OF. *regne* (F. *règne*), < L. *regnum*, < *regere*, rule: see *regent*.] Royal rule or sway, or sovereignty (as, "Britain's isle, beneath a George's *reign*": Cowper's "Heroism," 90); fig., domination, or dominating power or influence (as, the *reign* of law; "grim care's *reign*," Shakspere's "Lucrece," 1451); also, the period or term of ruling, as of a sovereign (as, "in the fourth year of Solomon's *reign* over Israel," 1 Kings, vi. 1; the war continued through three successive *reigns*: also fig.); also, a kingdom†, realm†, or domain† (as, "Then stretch thy sight o'er all her rising *reign*," Pope's "Dunciad," iii. 65: also fig.).—**Reign of Terror**, in *Fr. hist.*, a period of the Revolution, from about March, 1793, to July, 1794, during which persons of both sexes and all ages and conditions who were considered obnoxious by the ruling faction were ruthlessly executed.—**reign**, *v. i.* [OF. *regner* (F. *régner*), < L. *regnare*, < *regnum*.] To possess or exercise sovereign power or authority, as a ruler (as, "Solomon *reigned* in Jerusalem over all Israel forty years": 2 Chron. ix. 30); sometimes, to hold the position and name of sovereign without exercising the ruling power; in general, to hold sway, or rule (as, "The laws *reigned*, and not men": Bancroft's "Hist. of the U. S.," Amer. Revolution, ii. 1); fig., to have dominion or ascendancy, or be dominant (as, "Happy star *reign* now!" Shakspere's "Winter's Tale," i. 2. 363; "Over the whole of Victoria's private life the Baroness *reigned* supreme," Lytton Strachey's "Queen Victoria," iv.); predominate by powers, superiority, etc. (as, "In the Forum and in the Curia he [Cicero] knew that he could *reign* supreme": Froude's "Cæsar," xi.); be in force, vogue, operation, or existence everywhere or generally, or prevail (as, "kinder skies, where gentler manners *reign*," Goldsmith's "Traveller," 239; order, confusion, or silence *reigns*; "A fog *reigned*," Arnold Bennett's "Old Wives' Tale," iii. 7).

re-im-burse (rē-im-bèrs'), *v. t.* [See *re*-.] To pay back or refund (money expended or lost: as, "a dead loss of two million florins, not a stiver of which was ever *reimbursed* to the sufferers by the Spanish government," Motley's "Dutch Republic," iii. 5); make repayment for (expenditure, costs, etc.: as, "satisfied that the expenses already incurred were likely to be *reimbursed*," Galt's "Ayrshire Legatees," iii.); also, to make repayment to or imburse (persons, etc.) for expense or loss incurred (as, "You have been put to some foolish expense . . . on my account; allow me to *reimburse* you": H. Mackenzie's "Man of Feeling," xxviii.).—**re-im-burse'ment**, *n.* The act of reimbursing; repayment, as for expense or loss incurred: as, "The *reimbursement* of Massachusetts for taking Louisburg was now condemned" (Bancroft's "Hist. of the U. S.," Amer. Revolution, i. 7).—**re-im-burs'er**, *n.*

re-im-port (rē-im-pōrt'), *v. t.* [See *re*-.] To bring back; specif., to import back into the country of exportation.—**re-im-por-ta'tion** (-pọr-tā'shọn), *n.*

re-im-pose (rē-im-pōz'), *v. t.* [See *re*-.] To impose again or anew.—**re-im-po-si'tion** (-pọ-zish'ọn), *n.*

re-im-pres-sion (rē-im-presh'ọn), *n.* [See *re*-.] A second or repeated impression; specif., a reprinting or a reprint.

rein (rān), *n.* [OF. *resne*, *redne* (F. *rêne*), appar. < L. *retinere*, hold back, E. *retain*.] A long, narrow strap or thong, fastened to the bridle or bit, by which a rider or driver restrains and guides a horse or other animal (often in *pl.*); any similar device used for the same purpose; also, any of certain other straps or thongs forming part of a harness, as a check-rein; fig., any means of curbing or of giving license, or of controlling and directing (often in *pl.*: as, "Approves him or restrains, As reason, or as passion, takes the *reins*," Cowper's "Progress of Error," 36; to assume the *reins* of government or power); restraint or check (as, "The men . . . let their eyes Rove without *rein*": Milton's "Paradise Lost," xi. 586).—**to give (the) rein** or **reins**, or **free rein** or **reins, to,** fig., to give complete license or free scope to: as, "Ere I *give the reins to* grief, say first, How died he" (Milton's "Samson Agonistes," 1578); "I *gave free reins to* fancy" (W. H. Hudson's "Green Mansions," xi.).—**rein**, *v.* **I.** *tr.*

To furnish with a rein or reins, as a horse; also, to check (a horse, etc.) by pulling at the reins (as, "The coachman *reins* his smoking bays Beneath the elm-tree's shade": Holmes's "Agnes," ii.); hold under control, manage, or guide by means of reins (as, "The horses set off, tightly *reined* by Rainscourt," Marryat's "King's Own," xlvii.; "She was mounted on a milk-white horse, which she *reined* with peculiar grace and dignity," Scott's "Kenilworth," xxx.); bring, turn, draw, or pull (as specified) by means of reins (as, "Shouting frantically, he *reined* his mare outwards," Galsworthy's "Dark Flower," iii. 11; to *rein* in a horse, to bring it to a slower pace or to a stand by pulling in the reins; to *rein* up a horse, to pull it up, or bring it to a stand); fig., to curb, restrain, or check (as, "*Rein* thy tongue": Shakspere's "Love's Labour's Lost," v. 2. 662); control and direct, as in action. **II.** *intr.* To obey the reins (as, "He [a horse] . . . *reins* well": Shakspere's "Twelfth Night," iii. 4. 358); also, to rein a horse (*in* or *up*: as, "another rider, meeting him and *reining* in," G. W. Cable's "Cavalier," xliii.; "The Doctor *reined* up alongside him," H. Kingsley's "Geoffry Hamlyn," xxiv.).

re-in-car-nate (rē-in-kär'nāt), *v. t.* [See *re*-.] To incarnate again or anew.—**re-in-car-na'tion** (-nā'shọn), *n.* Incarnation anew; rebirth of the soul in a new body; also, a new incarnation or embodiment, as of a person.—**re-in-car-na'tion-ist**, *n.* A believer in reincarnation.

re-in-cor-po-rate (rē-in-kôr'pọ-rāt), *v. t.* [See *re*-.] To incorporate anew.—**re-in-cor-pọ-ra'tion** (-rā'shọn), *n.*

rein-deer (rān'dēr), *n.*; pl. *-deer*, occasionally *-deers*. [ME. *raynedere*: cf. Icel. *hreinn*, reindeer.] Any of various species of deer of the genus *Rangifer*, with branched antlers, found in northern or arctic regions, and often domesticated. Cf. *caribou*.

re-in-force, re-ën-force (rē-in-fōrs', rē-en-fōrs'), *v. t.*; -forced, -forcing. [From *re-* + *inforce* (obs. var. of *enforce*), *enforce*.] To strengthen with additional men or ships for military or naval purposes (as, to *reinforce* a garrison, an army, or a fleet); also, to strengthen with some added piece,

Reindeer (*Rangifer tarandus*).

support, or material (as, to *reinforce* a part of a garment with an extra thickness of cloth; to *reinforce* a wall or a bridge; *reinforced* concrete, see *concrete*, *n.*); in general, to strengthen, or make stronger or more forcible or effective (as, to *reinforce* memory, influence, or efforts; to *reinforce* an effect); supplement the force of (an entreaty, plea, argument, etc.: as, "I now beg leave to *re-enforce* her solicitation," Smollett's "Humphry Clinker," Oct. 14; "He quoted an old, old Chinese text, backed it with another, and *reinforced* these with a third," Kipling's "Kim," v.); supplement (*with*: as, "partaking of a cup of tea . . . *reinforced* with various slices from a huge round of beef," Scott's "Guy Mannering," lii.); augment or increase (as, to *reinforce* sound; to *reinforce* a stock or supply).—**re-in-force', re-ën-force'**, *n.* Something serving to reinforce or strengthen a thing; also, a thicker and stronger part, or one of two such parts, of the body of a cannon, next to the breech.—**re-in-force'ment, re-ën-force'ment**, *n.* The act of reinforcing, or the state of being reinforced; also, something that reinforces; an additional supply of men or of ships for strengthening a military or naval force (as, "The Confederate authorities . . . sent every available *reinforcement* to Bragg," Charnwood's "Abraham Lincoln," xi.: often in *pl.*); any strengthening or effective addition (as, "We have received another still more agreeable *re-enforcement* to our company": Smollett's "Humphry Clinker," Nov. 8).—**re-in-for'cer, re-ën-for'cer**, *n.*

---

fat, fāte, fär, fȧll, ȧsk, fāre; net, mē, hėr; pin, pīne; not, nōte, mȯve, nȯr; up, lūte, pull; oi, oil; ou, out; (lightened) aviȧry, ẹlect, agọny, intọ, ūnite; (obscured) errạnt, operȧ, ardẹnt, actọr, natūre; ch, chip; g, go; th, thin; ᴛʜ, then; y, you;

re-in-form (rē-in-fôrm′), *v. t.* [See *re-*.] To inform anew.

re-in-fuse (rē-in-fūz′), *v. t.* [See *re-*.] To infuse anew.

re-in-hab-it (rē-in-hab′it), *v. t.* [See *re-*.] To inhabit again.

rein-less (rān′les), *a.* Without a rein, as a horse; fig., unrestrained or unbridled.

reins (rānz), *n. pl.* [OF. F. *reins*, < L. *renes*, pl. of *ren*, kidney.] The kidneys; also, the region of the kidneys, or the lower part of the back; also, the seat of the feelings or affections, formerly identified with the kidneys (esp. in Biblical use: as, "The righteous God trieth the hearts and *reins*," Ps. vii. 9). [Archaic.]

re-in-sert (rē-in-sèrt′), *v. t.* [See *re-*.] To insert again.—**re-in-ser′tion** (-sèr′shon), *n.*

reins-man (rānz′man), *n.*; pl. *-men.* One who uses or manages the reins, as in driving: as, a skilful *reinsman.*

re-in-spire (rē-in-spīr′), *v. t.* [See *re-*.] To inspire again or anew.

re-in-stall (rē-in-stâl′), *v. t.* [See *re-*.] To install again.—**re-in-stal′ment, re-in-stall′ment,** *n.*

re-in-state (rē-in-stāt′), *v. t.* [See *re-*.] To instate again, as in a former position; put back or establish again (*in*: as, "I would not now go back, though the Czar . . . should . . . *reinstate* me in all my former grandeur," Defoe's "Robinson Crusoe," ii. 16; "He completely *reinstated* himself in favor," Motley's "Dutch Republic," iii. 2); also, to restore to a proper state; repair or replace (damaged property, etc.: as, "All the ceilings had been whitewashed . . . the broken glass hacked out and *reinstated*," S. Butler's "Way of All Flesh," lxxii.).—**re-in-state′ment,** *n.*

re-in-sur-ance (rē-in-shōr′ans), *n.* [See *re-*.] Insurance again or anew; specif., insurance by which a first insurer relieves himself from the risk and devolves it upon another insurer; also, the amount covered by such insurance.—**re-in-sure′,** *v. t.* To insure again; specif., to insure under a contract by which a first insurer relieves himself from the risk and devolves it upon another insurer.—**re-in-sur′er,** *n.*

re-in-te-grate (rē-in′tē-grāt), *v. t.* [See *re-*.] To integrate anew; redintegrate.—**re-in-te-gra′tion** (-grā′shon), *n.*

re-in-ter (rē-in-tèr′), *v. t.*; *-terred, -terring.* [See *re-*.] To inter again.—**re-in-ter′ment,** *n.*

re-in-trench (rē-in-trench′), *v. t.* [See *re-*.] To intrench again.

re-in-tro-duce (rē-in-trō-dūs′), *v. t.* [See *re-*.] To introduce again.—**re-in-tro-duc′tion** (-duk′shon), *n.*

re-in-vest (rē-in-vest′), *v. t. or i.* [See *re-*.] To invest again or anew.—**re-in-vest′ment,** *n.*

re-in-vig-or-ate (rē-in-vig′or-āt), *v. t.* [See *re-*.] To invigorate anew; give fresh vigor to: as, "Spain . . . was in some degree *reinvigorated* by the infusion of a foreign element into her government" (Lecky's "Hist. of Eng. in the 18th Century," i.).—**re-in-vig-or-a′tion** (-ā′shon), *n.*

reis[1] (rās), *n. pl.* [Pg. *reis*, pl. of *real*, lit. 'royal,' = Sp. *real*: see *real*[2].] A former Portuguese and a Brazilian money of account, being a multiple (varying according to the particular case) of an amount equivalent in the respective cases to about ⅕ and ¹⁄₁₈ of a U. S. cent. Cf. *milreis.*

reis[2] (rīs), *n.* [Ar. *raīs*, chief.] In Egypt, etc., the master or captain of a boat.

re-is-sue (rē-ish′ŏ), *v. i. or t.* [See *re-*.] To issue again.—**re-is′sue,** *n.* A second or repeated issue.

rei-ter (rī′tèr), *n.*; pl. *reiters,* G. *reiter.* [G., lit. 'rider,' < *reiten,* ride: see *ride,* and cf. *ritter.*] A German mounted soldier, esp. in the wars of the 16th and 17th centuries: as, "Coligny engaged Germans, through Jean Casimir . . . who brought him an army of *reiters*" (Besant's "Coligny," ix.).

re-it-er-ate (rē-it′ē-rāt), *v. t.*; *-ated, -ating.* [L. *reiteratus,* pp. of *reiterare,* < *re-,* again, + *iterare:* see *iterate.*] To repeat (an action), or do (something) again or repeatedly (as, "He *reiterated* his visits to the flagon so often that at length his senses were overpowered": Irving's "Sketch-Book," Rip Van Winkle); also, to repeat (an utterance, declaration, demand, etc.), or say (something) again or repeatedly (as, "Radney replied . . . unconditionally *reiterating* his command," H. Melville's "Moby-Dick," liv.; "'I shall buy no Wilbraham Hall,' he *reiterated,*" Arnold Bennett's "Helen with the High Hand," xvi.); assert or declare again or repeatedly (as, to *reiterate* one's innocence or one's disbelief).—**re-it-er-a′tion** (-ē-rā′shon), *n.* The act of reiterating; also, that which is reiterated.—**re-it′er-a-tive** (-ē-rā-tiv), *a.* Characterized by reiteration.—**re-it′er-a-tive-ly,** *adv.*

reive (rēv), etc. See *reave,* etc.

re-ject (rē-jekt′), *v. t.* [L. *rejectus,* pp. of *rejicere, reicere,* < *re-,* back, + *jacere,* throw.] To throw or cast back (obs. or rare); also, to cast out or eject, as matter from the mouth or stomach; also, to cast out or off, as a person (obs. or archaic: as, "*Reject* me not from among thy children," Wisdom of Solomon, ix. 4; "He is despised and *rejected* of men," Isa. liii. 3); also, to throw away, discard, or refuse as useless or unsatisfactory (as, to *reject* all imperfect specimens; "The stone which the builders *rejected* is become the head of the corner," Mark, xii. 10); refuse to have or take (something available or offered); refuse to accept (an offer, bid, proposal, etc.); refuse to grant (a demand, etc.); also, to refuse acceptance or recognition to, or disallow (as, to *reject* a law, doctrine, or method; to *reject* portions of a text); also, to refuse to accept (a person offering himself or making application: as, "He again offered himself for enlistment and was again *rejected,*" A. S. M. Hutchinson's "If Winter Comes," iii. 5); often, of a woman, to refuse (a man) as a lover or husband (as, "I should like to see a girl *reject* him. The minx!" W. De Morgan's "Alice-for-Short," xii.); repulse or rebuff (any person asking, appealing, etc.: as, "Not to *reject* The penitent, but ever to forgive," Milton's "Samson Agonistes," 760).—**re-ject′,** *n.* Something rejected, as an imperfect article.—**re-ject′a-ble,** *a.* That may or should be rejected.—**re-jec-ta-men′ta** (-jek-ta-men′tä), *n. pl.* [NL.] Things or matter rejected as useless or worthless; refuse; waste; excrement.—**re-ject′er,** *n.*—**re-ject′ing-ly,** *adv.*—**re-jec′tion** (-shon), *n.* [L. *rejectio(n-).*] The act of rejecting, or the state of being rejected; also, that which is rejected.

re-joice (rē-jois′), *v.*; *-joiced, -joicing.* [OF. *resjoir* (*resjoiss-*) (F. *réjouir*), < *re-* (< L. *re-*), again, + *joir,* E. *joy, v.*] **I.** *tr.* To make joyful, or gladden (as, good news *rejoices* the heart; "It was one of those clear statements which would have *rejoiced* the House of Commons," H. G. Wells's "Men Like Gods," i. 3: often in the passive, as, I am *rejoiced* to see you); reflexively, to delight (one's self), as with something pleasurable (archaic); also, to be joyful at† (as, "Ne'er mother *Rejoiced* deliverance more": Shakspere's "Cymbeline," v. 5. 370). **II.** *intr.* To be joyful or glad (as, to *rejoice* at, or over, good fortune; "I should *rejoice* to see you married to a good man," Galsworthy's "Saint's Progress," iv. 1); have joy or take delight (*in*: as, "My heart shall *rejoice* in thy salvation," Ps. xiii. 5; "Clive always *rejoiced* in F. B.'s society," Thackeray's "Newcomes," xliv.); hence, to be happy or blessed (*in*), as the fortunate possessor (chiefly humorous: as, "Brabant . . . that province which *rejoiced* in the liberal constitution known by the cheerful title of the 'joyful entrance,'" Motley's "Dutch Republic," i. 1; a mule *rejoicing* in the name of Pearl); also, to express or manifest joy or gladness, as by speech, music, or festivities (as, "The noise of them that *rejoice* endeth, the joy of the harp ceaseth," Isa. xxiv. 8; "As when a mighty people *rejoice* With shawms, and with cymbals," Tennyson's "Dying Swan," iii.).—**re-joi′cer** (-joi′sér), *n.*—**re-joi′cing,** *n.* The act of one who rejoices; the feeling or the expression of joy; a proceeding or festivity expressing joy (often in *pl.*: as, public *rejoicings*); also, a cause of joy or gladness† (as, "Thy word was unto me the joy and *rejoicing* of mine heart": Jer. xv. 16).—**re-joi′cing-ly,** *adv.*

re-join (rē-join′), *v.* [OF. F. *rejoindre,* < *re-* (< L. *re-*), again, + *joindre,* E. *join.*] **I.** *tr.* To join together again, or reunite; also, to join again, or come again into the company of (as, to *rejoin* a friend or a party after a brief absence; a summons to *rejoin* one's regiment); also, to say in answer to a reply or to any remark made (as, "It will be replied that . . . but I *rejoin* that a translator has no such right": Dryden's Preface, in tr. Ovid's "Epistles"). **II.** *intr.* To become joined together again; also, in legal use, to answer the plaintiff's replication; hence, in general use, to make answer to a reply or to any remark made (as, "Nevertheless I responded; and he *rejoined*; and I *rejoined* again": G. W. Cable's "Cavalier," vii.).—**re-join′der** (-dèr), *n.* [OF.

rejoindre, inf., used as noun.] In legal use, the defendant's answer to the plaintiff's replication (cf. *replication* and *surrejoinder*); hence, in general use, an answer to a reply or to any remark made (as, "When one . . . makes a remark . . . you rap out a round *rejoinder*": C. Brontë's "Jane Eyre," xiv.); response or reply (as, to say a thing in *rejoinder*).

re-judge (rē-juj'), *v. t.* [See *re-.*] To judge again; pass judgment anew upon: as, "He *rejudged* the characters of all the principal authors" (Smollett's "Humphry Clinker," June 2).

re-ju-ve-nate (rē-jö'vẹ-nāt), *v. t.*; *-nated, -nating.* [L. *re-,* again, + *juvenis,* young.] To make young again; restore to youthful vigor, as persons or animals (specif. by special surgical or other processes); restore to youthful freshness, as the appearance, complexion, etc.; fig., to restore to the vigorous or flourishing condition of the early period, as an institution; in *physical geog.,* to renew the activity, erosive power, etc., of (a stream) by the uplifting of the region it drains; also, to impress again the characters of youthful topography on (a region) by the action of rejuvenated streams.—**re-ju-ve-na'tion** (-nā'shọn), *n.* The act of rejuvenating, or the state of being rejuvenated; specif., restoration to youthful vigor, or to the vigor characteristic of a more youthful period of life, by special surgical or other processes.—**re-ju've-na-tor,** *n.*

re-ju-ve-nesce (rē-jö-ve-nes'), *v.*; *-nesced, -nescing.* [ML. *rejuvenescere,* < L. *re-,* again, + *juvenescere:* see *juvenescent.*] **I.** *intr.* To become young again; become rejuvenated; in *biol.,* to accomplish or undergo rejuvenescence. **II.** *tr.* To make young again; rejuvenate; in *biol.,* to produce rejuvenescence in.—**re-ju-ve-nes'cence** (-nes'ẹns), *n.* A renewal of youth or youthful vigor; in *biol.,* the renewal of vitality, which has been exhausted through repeated cell-division, by the conjugation or fusion of two distinct cells; also, a process by which the contents of a cell escape and form a new cell with a new wall.—**re-ju-ve-nes'cent,** *a.* Becoming young again, or renewing youthful vigor; also, making young again, or rejuvenating (as, "Though utter sceptics as to its [a liquid's] *rejuvenescent* power, they were inclined to swallow it at once": Hawthorne's "Twice-Told Tales," Dr. Heidegger's Experiment).

re-ju-ve-nize (rē-jö've-nīz), *v. t.* To rejuvenate.

re-kin-dle (rē-kin'dl), *v. t.* or *i.* [See *re-.*] To kindle again or anew.—**re-kin'dle-ment,** *n.*

re-laid (rē-lād'). Pret. and pp. of *relay*[1].

re-lapse (rē-laps'), *v. i.*; *-lapsed, -lapsing.* [L. *relapsus,* pp. of *relabi,* < *re-,* back, + *labi,* fall, slide.] To fall or slip back into a former state, practice, etc. (as, "After which brief reply, John *relapsed* into taciturnity," Miss Mulock's "John Halifax," x.; "Cassock [a horse] . . . *relapsed* into a trot," Whyte-Melville's "Katerfelto," xxiv.); esp., to fall back into wrong-doing or error; backslide; also, to fall back into illness after convalescence or recovery (as, "The next day the doctors were back; Tom had *relapsed*": Mark Twain's "Tom Sawyer," xxii.).—**re-lapse',** *n.* A falling or slipping back, as into a former state (as, "his . . . *relapse* into silence": Mrs. Wharton's "Ethan Frome," Introd.); esp., a falling back into wrong-doing or error; backsliding; also, a falling back into illness, as after convalescence; a return of a disease or illness after partial recovery (as, "That night the Judge suffered a *relapse* and died": Mark Twain's "Tom Sawyer," xxii.).—**re-laps'er,** *n.*

re-late (rē-lāt'), *v.*; *-lated, -lating.* [L. *relatus,* pp. of *referre,* bear back, return, report, relate: see *refer.*] **I.** *tr.* To bring back†; also, to recount, narrate, or tell (as, "the events which I propose to *relate,*" Macaulay's "Hist. of Eng.," i.; "the history of a great revolution *related* by the principal actor in it," Froude's "Cæsar," xxviii.); also, to bring into or link in association, connection, or relation (with *to*: as, "There has been anguish enough in the prisons of the Ducal Palace, but we know little of it by name, and cannot confidently *relate* it to any great historic presence," Howells's "Venetian Life," i.); establish a connection or relation between (as, to *relate* two groups of phenomena); in the passive, to be connected or allied by nature, circumstances, origin, kinship, marriage, etc. (often with *to*: as, the two plants are not *related*; these occurrences appear to be *related,* or to be *related* to the general movement; he is *related* to my

father). **II.** *intr.* To give an account of something (as, "Adam *relating,* she sole auditress": Milton's "Paradise Lost," viii. 51); also, to have reference or respect, or refer (*to*: as, "This challenge that the gallant Hector sends . . . *Relates* in purpose only to Achilles," Shakspere's "Troilus and Cressida," i. 3. 323); also, to be related, or have some relation (*to*: as, "The critic eye . . . examines bit by bit: How parts *relate* to parts, or they to whole," Pope's "Dunciad," iv. 235).—**re-lat'ed** (-lā'ted), *p. a.* Recounted or narrated; also, associated; connected; allied by nature, origin, kinship, marriage, etc. (as, *related* subjects; *related* events; *related* families); in *music,* relative.—**re-lat'ed-ness,** *n.*—**re-lat'er,** *n.*

re-la-tion (rē-lā'shọn), *n.* [OF. F. *relation,* < L. *relatio(n-),* < *relatus:* see *relate.*] The action of relating, narrating, or telling; narration; a narrative or account (as, "He had been curious to hear the whole story of our travels, and was exceedingly delighted with the *relation*": Defoe's "Captain Singleton," ix.); also, the state or fact of being related or connected in some way; a particular way of being related or connected, or some connection existing, or conceived as existing (as, what *relation* has his presence to the occurrences? to assume a *relation* between obscure phenomena; "facts, which . . . have countless *relations* of every kind, one towards another," J. H. Newman's "Idea of a University," i. 3); the mode or kind of connection between one person and another, between man and God, etc. (as, "the *relation* of ruler and subject," Macaulay's "Hist. of Eng.," i.; "The *relation* which we stand in to God . . . is made known to us by reason," J. Butler's "Analogy of Religion," ii. 1); *pl.,* the various connections in which persons are brought together, as by intercourse or common interests; the various connections between peoples, countries, etc., brought into contact (as, commercial *relations*; a minister of foreign *relations*; public *relations,* the principles, problems, etc., concerned with the reactions between a business and its public, between one government and other governments or peoples, etc.—an advisor being called a "counsel on public relations"); *sing.,* connection between persons by blood or marriage; a kinsman or kinswoman, or a relative; also, reference, regard, or respect (as, to plan with, or in, *relation* to the future); in *law,* the statement or complaint of a relator at whose instance an action or special proceeding is brought; also, reference or application back to an earlier date; the giving force to an act or proceeding taking place at one time as if it had taken place at a previous time.—**re-la'tion-al,** *a.*—**re-la'tion-ship,** *n.* The state of being related; connection, or a particular connection (as, "At no point does the employé come into a clear *relationship* of mutual obligation with the state": H. G. Wells's "Italy, France, and Britain at War," iv. 2); connection or alliance by blood or marriage.

rel-a-tive (rel'ạ-tiv). [LL. *relativus.*] **I.** *a.* Having relation or connection (as, *relative* phenomena); also, having relation to the matter in hand; relevant; pertinent; also, having, or standing in, a certain relation; correspondent or proportionate (as, value is *relative* to demand); also, considered in relation to each other or one another or to something else, or comparative (as, "the *relative* merits of monarchy, aristocracy, and democracy," Morley's "Oliver Cromwell," iii. 4; "to compare the *relative* happiness or unhappiness of different times of one's life," S. Butler's "Way of All Flesh," xlv.; the *relative* importance of a discovery); existing or being such only by relation to something else, or not absolute or independent; specif., of worship, offered indirectly by means of an image; also, of a term, name, etc., depending for significance upon a relation to something else, or expressing or involving a relation (as, 'father,' 'better,' and 'west' are *relative* terms; "Tennessee's Partner, whom we never knew by any other than this *relative* title," Bret Harte's "Tennessee's Partner"); also, having reference or regard (*to*: as, "Everything *relative* to their return was arranged," Jane Austen's "Sense and Sensibility," xxxix.; "some inquiries *relative* to the character and usages of the remote Indian nations," Parkman's "Oregon Trail," ii.); in *gram.,* relating to an antecedent (as, a *relative* pronoun); in *music,* having a close melodic or harmonic relation. **II.** *n.* Something having, or standing in, some relation to something else; also, a relative term; also, one who is connected with another or others by blood or marriage, esp. by blood; a relation; in *gram.*, a relative word, esp. a relative pronoun. **III.** *adv.* Relatively or in proportion (*to*: as, a state whose population is large *relative* to its size); also, with relation or reference (*to*: as, to confer *relative* to a decision).—**rel′a-tive-ly,** *adv.* In a relative manner; in relation to something else; comparatively (as, a *relatively* small difference); also, in relation, or with reference (*to*: as, the value of one thing *relatively* to other things); in proportion (*to*: as, a subject little understood *relatively* to its importance).—**rel′a-tive-ness,** *n.*—**rel′a-tiv-ism** (-tiv-izm), *n.* The doctrine of the relativity of knowledge or of the merely relative truth or certainty of what is arrived at by the human mind.—**rel′a-tiv-ist,** *n.* One who adheres to the doctrine of relativism.—**rel″a-tiv-is′tic,** *a.*—**rel-a-tiv′i-ty** (-i-ti), *n.* The state or fact of being relative; relativeness; specif., in *philos.*, existence only in relation to a thinking mind; in *physics*, the character of being relative rather than absolute as ascribed to motion or velocity; hence, the principle of relativity (see phrase following).—**principle of relativity,** the principle that there is no absolute motion, or motion with respect to absolute space filled with ether, but that all motion observable is relative, being that of one portion or manifestation of matter with respect to another portion of matter — a principle which is confirmed by the fact that the velocity of light is constant and is independent of the motion of the source. Among the conclusions resulting from this principle are: that there can be no greater velocity than that of light; that the mass of a moving body is influenced by its velocity, and depends upon its content of internal energy; that time, like motion, is relative and not absolute, so that we cannot speak of the absolute simultaneity of events which occur in different places; that time and space are dependent on each other, time forming with the three dimensions of space a single four-dimensional manifold; that the presence of matter in space is associated with a 'warping' of the manifold in its neighborhood, so that a freely moving body describes, not a straight line, but a curve — this effect being what is known as gravitation; and that rays of light will be deflected, or curved, when passing through a gravitational field. When all the motions considered are very slow compared with the velocity of light, the results of this theory are practically indistinguishable from those of previously accepted principles. For velocities like those of the planets, the differences are just perceptible. For velocities approaching that of light, they are very great. The theory was developed by Albert Einstein, German-Swiss physicist, in his 'special theory of relativity,' put forth in 1905, dealing with uniform motion, and his 'general theory of relativity,' put forth in 1915, dealing with gravitation.—**relativity of knowledge,** in *philos.*, the doctrine that all human knowledge is relative to the human mind, or that the mind can know concerning things only the effects which they produce upon it and not what the things themselves are; in *psychol.*, the doctrine that we can become conscious of objects only in their relations to one another.

re-la-tor (rḛ-lā′tọr), *n.* [L.] One who relates or narrates; in *law*, a private person on whose suggestion or complaint an action or special proceeding in the name of the state is brought, to try a question involving both public and private right.

re-lax (rḛ-laks′), *v.* [L. *relaxare* (pp. *relaxatus*), < *re-*, back, + *laxare*, loosen, < *laxus*, E. *lax*.] **I.** *tr.* To make lax, or less tense, rigid, or firm (as, "I felt great numbers of people on my left side *relaxing* the cords," Swift's "Gulliver's Travels," i. 1; to *relax* the muscles); make loose or slack; diminish the force of, as a spring; loosen, as the grasp; also, to make less retentive, as the bowels; also, to make less compact or dense†; also, to make less strict or severe, as rules, discipline, etc.; mitigate or modify (as, to *relax* one's austerity; "Gloria . . . slowly *relaxes* her threatening attitude," G. B. Shaw's "You Never Can Tell," iii.); also, to slacken, remit, or abate, as effort, attention, etc. (as, "to *relax* the vigilance of the kingdom," Galt's "Annals of the Parish," xliv.; "It might be proper to *relax* a part of my precaution," Godwin's "Caleb Williams," xxvii.); also, to relieve from effort or close application, as the mind. **II.** *intr.*

To become less tense, rigid, or firm (as, "The compressed lips had *relaxed* a little and seemed ready to part": W. H. Hudson's "Green Mansions," xvii.); become loose or slack; also, to become less strict or severe; grow milder; soften, as into a less severe, austere, or unfriendly manner, as persons (as, "Alick . . . never *relaxed* into the frivolity of unnecessary speech": George Eliot's "Adam Bede," liii.); also, to abate in force or intensity (as, "The waves *relaxed* in their force until they did little more than play upon the side of the wreck": Marryat's "King's Own," lv.); slacken in effort, pains, or application (as, "So far . . . from *relaxing* in their attention . . . their politeness visibly increased": Borrow's "Bible in Spain," v.); take relaxation after effort or application.—**re-lax-a-tion** (rē-lak-sā′shọn), *n.* [L. *relaxatio*(n-).] The act of relaxing, or the state of being relaxed; loosening or slackening; diminution or remission of strictness or severity; slackening of force or intensity; abatement of effort, attention, or application (as, "Cortés punished any . . . *relaxation* of vigilance, in these sentinels, with the utmost severity": Prescott's "Conquest of Mexico," iv. 3); often, relief from bodily or mental effort or application, or recreation (as, "to note down whatever crosses one's mind . . . during study or *relaxation*": S. Butler's "Way of All Flesh," xlvi.); something affording such relief (as, "at table, the pleasures of which . . . were his only *relaxation*": Motley's "Dutch Republic," vi. 7).—**re-lax-a-tive** (rḛ-lak′sạ-tiv), *a.* Tending to relax; of the nature of relaxation. —**re-lax′er,** *n.*

re-lay¹ (rē-lā′), *v. t.*; pret. and pp. *-laid.* [See *re-*.] To lay again or anew. Also written *re-lay.*

re-lay² (rḛ-lā′ or rē′lā), *n.* [OF. F. *relais*, orig. reserves of dogs posted along the line of a hunt: cf. OF. *relais*, what is left or remains (< *relaissier*: see *release²*), also *relaier*, put (a dog) in a relay.] A fresh set of dogs or horses posted in readiness for use in a hunt; hence, a fresh set of horses or other animals, or of men, ready or obtained at some point on a route of travel (as, "The distances at which we got *relays* of horses varied greatly," Kinglake's "Eothen," ii.; "Day and night they travelled, stopping only to obtain fresh *relays* of carriers," Prescott's "Conquest of Mexico," iv. 6); also, a set of persons relieving others or taking turns in any service or performance (as, "There was no hearse . . . and we carried our dead by *relays* of four": Ian Maclaren's "Beside the Bonnie Brier Bush," i. 4); a shift of workers; also, a fresh supply of anything (as, *relays* of food for hungry persons; "O ye . . . who call aloud . . . For change of follies, and *relays* of joy," Young's "Night Thoughts," ii. 250); also, a device that extends or reinforces the action or effect of an apparatus; in *mach.*, a servo-motor; in *elect.*, a device by which telegraphic or telephonic messages are sent to a greater distance or strengthened, esp. by transference to a stronger circuit by means of an electromagnet.—**re-lay′²,** *v.*; *-layed, -laying.* **I.** *tr.* To station in relays, as along a route; also, to provide with or replace by fresh relays; also, to carry or forward by or as by relays; in *elect.*, to transmit by means of a telegraphic or telephonic relay, or as such a relay does. **II.** *intr.* To take a fresh relay, as of horses in traveling; in *elect.*, to relay a message.—**re′lay=race,** *n.* A race of two or more teams of contestants, each contestant running but part of the distance and being relieved by a teammate.

re-leap (rē-lēp′), *v. t.* [See *re-*.] To leap back or again over: as, "I resolved to pluck up courage and *releap* the dangerous abyss" (Bulwer-Lytton's "Caxtons," v. 1).

re-lease¹ (rē-lēs′), *v. t.*; *-leased, -leasing.* [See *re-*.] To lease again. Also written *re-lease.*

re-lease² (rḛ-lēs′), *v. t.*; *-leased, -leasing.* [OF. *relesser, relaissier*, let go, remit, relinquish, leave, < L. *relaxare*, E. *relax*.] To remit (a debt, tax, etc.: as, "Every creditor that lendeth ought unto his neighbour shall *release* it," Deut. xv. 2: now only in legal use); give up, relinquish, or surrender (a right, claim, etc.: now legal); make over (land, etc.), as to another (as, "that the duchy of Anjou . . . shall be *released* and delivered to the king her father," Shakspere's "2 Henry VI.," i. 1. 51: now legal); also, to free by remission, as from debt, taxes, obligations, or penalties (as, "For your sake I *release* all the Jews, from tributes . . . and from crown taxes," 1 Mac. x. 29; to *release* a person from the con-

sequences of wrong-doing); free from something imposing or involving obligation (as, to *release* a person from a promise, vow, or contract; to be *released* from duty or attendance); free or relieve from anything oppressive or grievous, or from pain, trouble, or other evil (as, "*Release* me from this life, From this intolerable agony!" Southey's "Thalaba," ii. 21); often, to set free from prison, confinement, or servitude, or from bonds (as, "Pilate, willing to content the people, *released* Barabbas unto them," Mark, xv. 15; to *release* a prisoner, captive, or slave); free from anything that restrains, detains, holds, or fastens (as, to *release* a dog from the hand or from a leash; to *release* clothing caught in a door; to *release* hair from pins; to *release* a spring); let go (one's hold, etc.); also, to allow to go forth or be issued, exhibited, or sold to the public, as on due removal of restrictions (as, to *release* an article for publication; to *release* a photoplay or a phonograph record).—**re-lease′²**, *n.* [OF. *reles, relais.*] A remission, as of a debt, tax, or tribute (obs. or legal: as, "The king . . . made a *release* to the provinces, and gave gifts," Esther, ii. 18); also, a releasing or freeing, as of a person, from obligations or penalties, or from a promise, duty, requirement, or the like; deliverance or relief from anything oppressive or distressing (as, *release* from pain, care, or toil; "I think it can't be long before I find *release*," Tennyson's "May Queen," Conclusion, 11); liberation from prison, confinement, bondage, or bonds (as, to procure the *release* of a captive); liberation from anything that restrains, holds, or fastens, or some device for effecting such liberation; the releasing of something for publication or public exhibition or sale, or something so released, as a written article, a photoplay, etc.; also, a certificate or document for releasing; a written discharge from obligation or liability (as, "I . . . caused him to draw up a general *release* or discharge for the 470 moidores which . . . he owed me": Defoe's "Robinson Crusoe," i. 19); a warrant of deliverance from a penalty (as, "The Sheriff knows him: it is Arthur Donnithorne, carrying in his hand a hard-won *release* from death": George Eliot's "Adam Bede," xlvii.); a document giving discharge from custody; in *law*, the surrender of a right or the like to another, or a document embodying such surrender; in *engin.*, in a steam-engine, the opening of the exhaust-port of the cylinder at or near the end of the working stroke of the piston. —**re-lease′ment**, *n.*—**re-leas′er**, *n.*
rel-e-ga-ble (rel′ē-gạ-bl), *a.* That may be relegated.
rel-e-gate (rel′ē-gāt), *v. t.*; *-gated, -gating.* [L. *relegatus*, pp. of *relegare*, < *re-*, back, + *legare*, send.] To send into exile, or banish, esp., in ancient Roman use, to a certain place or distance and for a certain time; also, to send, as if banishing, to some out-of-the-way or obscure place (as, "Uncle Tom, *relegated* to a corner, pretended to read his newspaper," W. Churchill's "Modern Chronicle," i. 3; "We have not *relegated* religion (like something we were ashamed to shew) to obscure municipalities or rustic villages," Burke's "Revolution in France," 153; to *relegate* old furniture to the lumber-room); consign to some obscure position or condition, or to some region, sphere, or time remote from general notice or knowledge (as, to *relegate* a candidate to the lowest place on a list; to *relegate* a book or a theory to the limbo of oblivion; "a tone that *relegated* their morning's interview to the age of fable," Howells's "Foregone Conclusion," ix.); also, to assign or refer (something) to a particular class or kind; also, to consign or commit (a matter, task, etc.), as to a person; also, to refer (a person), as for information (*to*).—**rel-e-ga′tion** (-gā′shọn), *n.* [L. *relegatio(n-).*] The act of relegating, or the state of being relegated; banishment; consignment; assignment.
re-lent (rē-lent′), *v.* [ME. *relente*, < L. *re-*, again, + *lentus*, pliant, flexible, viscous, slow.] **I.** *intr.* To melt† or dissolve†; also, to soften in feeling or temper, or become more mild, gentle, compassionate, or forgiving (as, "His heart *relented* Towards her": Milton's "Paradise Lost," x. 940); often, to soften in determination, or recede from a harsh determination (as, "Stern Proserpine *relented*, And gave him back the fair," Pope's "Ode on St. Cecilia's Day," v.; "The captain at last *relented*, and told him he might make himself at home," H. Melville's "Moby-Dick," xii.); also, to slacken† or abate†. **II.**† *tr.* To melt or dissolve (a substance); also, to soften in feeling, or cause to relent (as,

"Were Fortune lovely Peggy's foe, Such sweetness would *relent* her": Burns's "Young Peggy," 18); also, to slacken (as, "But nothing might *relent* her hasty flight": Spenser's "Faerie Queene," iii. 4. 49).—**re-lent′ing-ly**, *adv.*—**re-lent′less**, *a.* That does not relent, or unrelenting (as, a *relentless* enemy); characterized by or showing a complete absence of relenting (as, *relentless* determination; "There was a concentrated look in his face, *relentless* and hard," F. M. Crawford's "Mr. Isaacs," v.).—**re-lent′less-ly**, *adv.*—**re-lent′less-ness**, *n.*
re-let (rē-let′), *v. t.*; *-let, -letting.* [See *re-.*] To let (a house, etc.) anew.
rel-e-vant (rel′ē-vạnt), *a.* [ML. *relevans (-ant-)*, prop. ppr. of L. *relevare*, lift up: see *relieve.*] Bearing upon or connected with the matter in hand; to the purpose; pertinent: as, the testimony is not *relevant* to the case; a *relevant* remark.—**rel′e-vance, rel′e-van-cy**, *n.*—**rel′e-vant-ly**, *adv.*
re-li-a-ble (rē-lī′ạ-bl), *a.* That may be relied on; worthy of reliance; trustworthy: as, a *reliable* man; *reliable* sources of information; *reliable* goods.—**re-li-a-bil′i-ty** (-bil′i-ti), **re-li′a-ble-ness**, *n.*—**re-li′a-bly**, *adv.*
re-li-ance (rē-lī′ạns), *n.* The act or feeling of relying; confident or trustful dependence (as, "What *reliance* could they place on the protection of a prince so recently their enemy?" Prescott's "Conquest of Mexico," iv. 3); confidence; also, something relied on.
re-li-ant (rē-lī′ạnt), *a.* Having reliance, or confidently or trustfully dependent (as, "Dinah was too entirely *reliant* on the Supreme guidance to attempt to achieve any end by a deceptive concealment": George Eliot's "Adam Bede," lii.); characterized by or showing reliance; also, self-reliant.
rel-ic (rel′ik), *n.* [OF. F. *relique*, < L. *reliquiæ*, pl., remains, relics, < *relinquere*, leave behind: see *relinquish.*] Something that remains after the destruction, consumption, or passing away of the rest; esp., in *pl.*, remains, remaining parts or fragments, or remnants (as, "if there had been light to consult the *relics* of a finger-post which stood there," Scott's "Guy Mannering," i.; "After a bloody conflict of eight years . . . the *relics* of the nation submitted," Gibbon's "Decline and Fall of the Roman Empire," xlix.); often, formerly, the remains of food or of a meal (now rare: as, "He found him . . . making a supper of the *relics* of the roast beef," Scott's "Castle Dangerous," ii.); also, the remains of a deceased person; also, *sing.*, a surviving trace of something (as, a custom which is a *relic* of paganism); a surviving memorial of something past (as, "this *relic* of early settler days [an old man]": Tarkington's "Magnificent Ambersons," iv.); also, an object having interest by reason of its age or its association with the past (as, a museum of historic *relics*); something associated with some person, place, or thing, of which it is kept as a remembrance; *eccles.*, esp. in the Roman Catholic and Greek churches, the body, a part of the body, or some personal memorial, of a saint, martyr, or other sacred person, preserved as worthy of veneration.
rel-ict (rel′ikt), *n.* [L. *relictus*, masc., *relicta*, fem., pp. of *relinquere*, leave behind: see *relinquish.*] A widow: as, "Mr. Sparsit, deceased, of whom she was the *relict*" (Dickens's "Hard Times," i. 7).
re-lief (rē-lēf′), *n.* [OF. F. *relief*, < *relever*: see *relieve*, and cf. *rilievo.*] The act of relieving, or the state of being relieved; deliverance or ease through the removal, in whole or in part, of any pain, distress, difficulty, want, oppression, burden, etc.; alleviation of pain, distress, anxiety, want, pressure, monotony, etc.; also, a means of relieving; something that relieves pain, distress, anxiety, etc.; succor or aid; help or assistance given, as to those in poverty or want; something affording a pleasing change, as from monotony (as, "He has . . . interspersed several speeches, reflections, similitudes, and the like *reliefs* to diversify his narration": Addison, in "Spectator," 333); also, specif., deliverance from some hardship, burden, or grievance, as by legal means; legal remedy or redress; also, the deliverance of a besieged town, etc., from an attacking force (as, "Stilicho . . . advanced, with his united force, to the *relief* of the faithful city": Gibbon's "Decline and Fall of the Roman Empire," xxx.); also, release from a post of duty, as by the coming of a substitute; the person or persons thus bringing release;

also, the projection of a figure or part from the ground or plane on which it is formed, in sculpture or similar work, or a piece or work in such projection (as, high, middle, and low *relief*: see *alto-rilievo*, *mezzo-rilievo*, and *bas-relief*); a similar apparent projection of parts in a painting, drawing, etc.; hence, prominence or distinctness, as with reference to a back-ground (as, "a

A Relief (Assyrian Sculpture) in the British Museum.—King Asurbanipal pouring a libation. About 625 B.C.

church with its dark spire in strong *relief* against the clear, cold sky": Irving's "Sketch-Book," Christmas Day); fig., distinctness or vividness due to contrast, often as brought out in literary presentation; in *phys. geog.*, the form of a part of the earth's surface considered with respect to differences of elevation; also, in *feudal law*, a fine or composition which the heir of a feudal tenant paid to the lord for the privilege of succeeding to the estate.

re-li-er (rē-lī′ėr), *n.* [See *rely*.] One who relies, or has reliance.

re-liev-a-ble (rē-lē′vạ-bl), *a.* That may be relieved.

re-lieve (rē-lēv′), *v. t.*; -lieved, -lieving. [OF. F. *relever*, < L. *relevare*, lift up, relieve, alleviate, < *re-*, again, + *levare*, lift: see *lever*.] To raise up again†; also, to restore to physical ease or comfort (as, a medicine to *relieve* an aching head); free from distress of mind, anxiety, fear, or other disturbing feeling (as, "She . . . was a little alarmed . . . Ernest *relieved* her mind": S. Butler's "Way of All Flesh," lxxxiii.); deliver from straits, difficulties, or want (as, "This youth . . . I snatch'd one half out of the jaws of death, *Relieved* him with such sanctity of love," Shakspere's "Twelfth Night," iii. 4. 395; to *relieve* the poor and needy); ease (a person) of any burden, wrong, or oppression, as by legal means; specif., to bring efficient aid to (a besieged town, etc.: as, "Lieutenant-Colonel Henry Bouquet . . . was making his way to *relieve* Fort Pitt, with about five hundred men," Bancroft's "Hist. of the U. S.," Amer. Revolution, ii. 4); free from siege; in general, to give ease to, or ease; set free or deliver (*from*: as, "Our [male] sex . . . has been generally *relieved* from the imputation of curiosity," Bret Harte's "Miggles"); ease or rid (*of*: as, "This *relieved* Ernest of a good deal of trouble," S. Butler's "Way of All Flesh," lv.; "Uncle Pentstemon had refused to be *relieved* of his hat," H. G. Wells's "Mr. Polly," iv.); also, to release (one on duty) by coming as or providing a substitute; also, to ease or alleviate (pain, distress, anxiety, want, etc.: as, "that misery which he strives in vain to *relieve*," Thoreau's "Walden," i.; "The counsellor *relieved* her fears on this head," Scott's "Guy Mannering," xxxix.); make less tedious or unpleasant (as, to *relieve* the monotony or tedium of one's life); break or vary the sameness of appearance of (as, "The walls were of the usual dull red, *relieved* by plaster casts of arms and legs and hands and feet": Du Maurier's "Trilby," i.); also, to bring into relief or prominence (as, "The colossi come in a light-coloured vein of the rock, and so sit *relieved* against a darker background": Amelia B. Edwards's "Thousand Miles up the Nile," xvi.); heighten the effect of, as by contrast.—**re-liev′er**, *n.*

re-lie-vo (rē-lē′vō), *n.*; pl. *-vos* (-vōz). Same as *rilievo*.

re-light (rē-līt′), *v. t.* or *i.*; pret. and pp. *-lighted* or *-lit*. [See *re-*.] To light again or anew.

re-li-gieuse (rè-lē-zhyėz′), *n.*; pl. *-gieuses* (-zhyėz). [F., fem. of *religieux*: see *religious*.] A woman belonging to a religious order, community, etc.; a nun.

re-li-gion (rē-lij′ọn), *n.* [OF. F. *religion*, < L. *religio*(n-), origin uncertain.] Recognition on the part of man of a controlling superhuman power entitled to obedience, reverence, and worship; the feeling or the spiritual attitude of those recognizing such a controlling power; also, the manifestation of such feeling in conduct or life (as, "Pure *religion* and undefiled . . . is this, To visit the fatherless and widows in their affliction, and to keep himself unspotted from the world": Jas. i. 27); the practice of sacred rites or observances†; *pl.*, religious rites†; also, *sing.*, a particular system of faith in and worship of a Supreme Being or a god or gods (as, the Christian *religion*; the Mohammedan *religion*; the Buddhist *religion*; polytheistic *religions*); sometimes [usually *cap.*], with *the* (after the French use), the Reformed religion, or Protestantism (now hist.: as, "Let it be remembered that the Admiral had tried every means to protect those of *the Religion*," Besant's "Coligny," viii.); also, the state of life of the members of a monastic order (as, to enter *religion*); also, a particular monastic order (now rare); also, devotion to principle†, or conscientiousness† (as, "*Ros.* Keep your promise. *Orl.* With no less *religion* than if thou wert indeed my Rosalind": Shakspere's "As You Like It," iv. 1. 201); a point or matter of conscience (as, to make a *religion* of doing something).—**to experience**, or **get**, **religion.** See *to experience religion*, under *experience, v. t.*—**re-li′gion-a-ry** (-ạ-ri), *a.* Pertaining to religion: as, *religionary* intolerance. [Now rare.] — **re-li′gion-ism**, *n.* Excessive inclination toward or exaggerated zeal in religion.—**re-li′gion-ist**, *n.* One adhering or devoted to religion; sometimes, a religious zealot or bigot.

re-li-gi-os-i-ty (rē-lij-i-os′i-ti), *n.* The quality of being religious; religious feeling or sentiment; piety; devoutness; sometimes, excessive devotion to religion, or affectation of religious sentiment.

re-li-gious (rē-lij′us). [OF. *religius* (F. *religieux*), < L. *religiosus*, < *religio*(n-), E. *religion*.] **I.** *a.* Imbued with or exhibiting religion, pious, devout, or godly (as, "a girl intensely *religious*," Arnold Bennett's "Clayhanger," ii. 9; "That sober race of men, whose lives *Religious* titled them the sons of God," Milton's "Paradise Lost," xi. 622); also, of or pertaining to, or concerned or connected with, religion (as, a *religious* society or sect; a *religious* order; *religious* rites; *religious* liberty; *religious* teachers or books; *religious* differences); appropriate to religion or to sacred rites or observances (as, "Storied windows richly dight, Casting a dim *religious* light," Milton's "Il Penseroso," 160; "The work began in *religious* silence," Du Maurier's "Trilby," iii.); sometimes, sacred (poetic: as, "thy shrine in some *religious* wood," Wm. Collins's "Ode to Liberty," 91); also, bound by monastic vows, or belonging to a religious order, as persons; pertaining to or connected with a monastic or religious order (as, "Cloister thee in some *religious* house," Shakspere's "Richard II.," v. 1. 23; "a shaven head, and a *religious* habit," Addison, in "Spectator," 164); also, scrupulously faithful, or conscientious (as, "a coward, a most devout coward, *religious* in it," Shakspere's "Twelfth Night," iii. 4. 424; *religious* exactness or care). **II.** *n.* A member of a religious order, congregation, etc.; a monk or friar; a nun; also, as *pl.*, such persons collectively (as, "The letters . . . are yet extant in the nunnery where she resided; and are often read to the young *religious*, in order to inspire them with good resolutions": Addison, in "Spectator," 164).—**re-li′gious-ly**, *adv.*—**re-li′gious-ness**, *n.*

re-lin-quish (rē-ling′kwish), *v. t.* [OF. F. *relinquir* (*relinquiss-*), < L. *relinquere* (pp. *relictus*), leave behind, leave, < *re-*, back, + *linquere*, leave: see *loan²*.] To leave†, withdraw from†, or abandon† (a person or place: as, "Most of them *relinquished* Spain, as a country where they could no longer live in security . . . and departed . . . for Africa," Irving's "Conquest of Granada," lxxxix.); hence, to give up, abandon, put aside, or desist from (as, to *relinquish* a hope, plan, or undertaking; "The Tirpitz policy of ruthlessness must be *relinquished* in theory and practice, or America would join the belligerent Allies," Buchan's "Hist. of the Great War," liv.); resign, renounce, or surrender (a possession, right, etc.); give over (*to*: as, "I *relinquish* to them the pursuit," Thoreau's "Walden," i.); let go (something held, the hold, etc.: as, "At length they *relinquished* their hold of me," H. Melville's "Typee," xvii.).—**re-lin′quish-er**, *n.*—**re-lin′quish-ment**, *n.*

---

rel-i-qua-ry (rel'i-kwā-ri), *n.*; pl. *-ries* (-riz). [F. *reliquaire*, < L. *reliquiæ*: see *relic*.] A repository or receptacle for a relic or relics.

rel-ique (rel'ik), *n.* Archaic spelling of *relic*.

re-li-qui-æ (rē-lik'wi-ē), *n. pl.* [L.: see *relic*.] Remains, as those of fossil organisms.

rel-ish (rel'ish), *n.* [ME. *reles*, taste, flavor, aftertaste, appar. < OF. *reles, relais*, what is left or remains: see *relay²*.] A taste or flavor (as, "the salt *relish* of the drift which was pelted against his face": Scott's "Pirate," iv.); fig., a smack, trace, or touch of something (as, "Some act That has no

Reliquary in the Cathedral of Florence, containing part of the skull of St. Zenobius.

relish of salvation in 't": Shakspere's "Hamlet," iii. 3. 92); also, a pleasing or appetizing flavor (as, "Her hunger gave a *relish* to her meat": Dryden's "Cock and the Fox," 22); fig., a pleasing or enjoyable quality (as, "The cheerfulness of the children added a *relish* to his existence": Jane Austen's "Sense and Sensibility," i.); also, something appetizing or savory added to a meal, as pickles, olives, caviar, cheese, or any small, highly seasoned dish or the like (as, "This [salmon] he was resolved to consume . . . with vinegar and salt and pepper as a *relish* to his supper": H. G. Wells's "Mr. Polly," vii.); also, liking for the taste of something, or enjoyment of something eaten (as, to have no *relish* for sweets; "He ate with great *relish*, for he was very hungry," Du Maurier's "Trilby," i.); fig., pleasurable appreciation of anything, or liking (as, "A woman . . . has no keen *relish* for such jokes," Gissing's "New Grub Street," x.; "She indeed could not enjoy the present with that *relish* which he wished," J. H. Newman's "Callista," xxix.); keen enjoyment; zest.—

rel'ish, *v.* **I.** *tr.* To give a relish to, or make pleasing to the taste, as food (also fig.); also, to like the taste or flavor of, or enjoy (food, etc.: as, "The Indians *relish* wild honey as highly as do the white men," Irving's "Captain Bonneville," ii.; "How you'll *relish* your grub by-and-by!" Marryat's "Peter Simple," xx.); fig., to take pleasure in, like, or enjoy (as, "His [Petrarch's] fine taste taught him to *relish* the beauties of Virgil and Cicero," Hallam's "Literature of Europe," i. 1. § 92; "This doctrine . . . was not much *relished* by a great part of the audience," R. Graves's "Spiritual Quixote," ii. 15). **II.** *intr.* To have a taste, flavor, or smack of something (lit. or fig.: as, "Virtue cannot so inoculate our old stock but we shall *relish* of it," Shakspere's "Hamlet," iii. 1. 120); also, to taste in a particular way (lit. or fig.: as, "It [dried meat] *relished* so well, that we never gave ourselves the trouble to boil it," Defoe's "Captain Singleton," ii.; "Was it that spectacles of sadder plights, Should make our blisses *relish* the more high?" Hood's "Hero and Leander," ii.); taste well, or be appetizing or agreeable.—**rel'ish-a-ble**, *a.* Capable of being relished.—**rel'ish-er**, *n.*—**rel'ish-ing-ly**, *adv.*

re-live (rē-liv'), *v.* [See *re-*.] **I.** *intr.* To live again or anew. **II.** *tr.* To live over or through again: as, "She *relived* the scene of their good-bye" (L. Merrick's "Worldlings," xxv.).

re-load (rē-lōd'), *v. t.* or *i.* [See *re-*.] To load again.

re-lo-cate (rē-lō'kāt), *v. t.* or *i.* [See *re-*.] To locate again or anew.—**re-lo-ca'tion** (-lō-kā'shon), *n.*

re-lu-cent (rē-lū'sent), *a.* [L. *relucens* (*-ent-*), ppr. of *relucere*, < *re-*, back, + *lucere*, shine.] Casting back light; shining; bright. [Now rare.]

re-luct (rē-lukt'), *v. i.* [L. *reluctari* (pp. *reluctatus*), < *re-*, back, + *luctari*, wrestle, struggle.] To struggle against something; offer resistance or opposition; object; show reluctance.

re-luc-tance (rē-luk'tans), *n.* [From *reluctant*.] A struggling in opposition, or resistance (as, "*Reluctance* against

God and his just yoke Laid on our necks," Milton's "Paradise Lost," x. 1045: now rare); also, unwillingness or disinclination (as, to consent, but with *reluctance*; *reluctance* to speak); in *elect.*, the resistance offered to the passage of magnetic lines of force, being numerically equal to the magnetomotive force divided by the magnetic flux ('magnetic reluctance').

re-luc-tant (rē-luk'tant), *a.* [L. *reluctans* (*-ant-*), ppr. of *reluctari*: see *reluct*.] Struggling in opposition, or making resistance (as, "Down he [Satan] fell A monstrous serpent on his belly prone, *Reluctant*, but in vain," Milton's "Paradise Lost," x. 515: now rare); hence, unwilling, loath, or disinclined (as, a *reluctant* giver; "I cannot go . . . My feet *reluctant* linger at the gate," Longfellow's "Morituri Salutamus," 139; "Bartley had found an agreeable seat . . . which he was *reluctant* to leave," Howells's "Rise of Silas Lapham," i.); characterized by or showing unwillingness (as, *reluctant* obedience; a *reluctant* consent; "He put the flimsy paper down with a slow, *reluctant* movement," H. G. Wells's "Tono-Bungay," iii. 4. § 1).—**re-luc'tant-ly**, *adv.*

re-luc-tate (rē-luk'tāt), *v. i.*; *-tated, -tating.* [L. *reluctatus*, pp. of *reluctari*: see *reluct*.] To struggle against something; make resistance; show reluctance. [Now rare.]—**re-luc-ta-tion** (rē-luk-tā'shon), *n.* Resistance; opposition.

re-luc-tiv-i-ty (rē-luk-tiv'i-ti), *n.* In *elect.*, specific reluctance, or the magnetic reluctance of a material compared with that of air ('magnetic reluctivity').

re-lume (rē-lūm'), *v. t.*; *-lumed, -luming.* [From *re-* + *-lume* as in *illume*.] To relight (a light, lamp, flame, etc.); rekindle; also, to light up or illuminate (a place, etc.) again. Also **re-lu'mine** (-lū'min).

re-ly (rē-lī'), *v. i.*; *-lied, -lying.* [OF. F. *relier*, bind fast, attach, < L. *religare*, < *re-*, back, again, + *ligare*, bind.] To rest or lean in faith or confidence, as on a person or thing trusted (with *on* or *upon*: as, "He . . . Bade me *rely* on him as on my father," Shakspere's "Richard III.," ii. 2. 25; to *rely* on, or upon, one's own powers, or on promises or information received); depend confidently; sometimes, to depend or count, as on a person, with confident expectation (with an infinitive: as, we *rely* on you to keep us informed; "You are the only woman I can *rely* on to be interested in her," Galsworthy's "Country House," i. 7).

re-main (rē-mān'), *v. i.* [OF. *remanoir*, also *remaindre*, < L. *remanere*, remain behind, remain, < *re-*, back, + *manere*, remain.] To be left after the removal, loss, or departure of the rest or the others or other (as, "Gather up the fragments that *remain*, that nothing be lost," John, vi. 12; traces of the former beauty *remain*; the years of life *remaining* to one; on the death of the *remaining* parent); also, to be left as something further or still to be encountered, dealt with, done, told, etc. (as, "Thus bad begins and worse *remains* behind," Shakspere's "Hamlet," iii. 4. 179; "I plainly perceive some objections *remain*, which I ought . . . to remove," Burke's "Conciliation with the Colonies"; little *remains* to be said); be reserved or in store (as, "Norfolk, for thee *remains* a heavier doom": Shakspere's "Richard II.," i. 3. 148); be left (*to*) or rest (*with*) in the issue or result (as, "War arose . . . wherein *remain'd* . . . to our Almighty Foe Clear victory," Milton's "Paradise Lost," ii. 768; the advantage *remained* with the opposite party); also, to continue in a place, or stay (as, to *remain* in the city, at home, or in one's seat; "At church . . . fools, who came to scoff, *remain'd* to pray," Goldsmith's "Deserted Village," 180); also, to continue in the same state; continue to be (as specified: as, to *remain* at peace, in doubt, or under control; to *remain* in possession of property; to *remain* satisfied; to *remain* a widow); also, to continue to exist, or endure (as, "They shall perish; but thou *remainest*": Heb. i. 11); last; persist (as, "There I woke, but still the wish *remain'd*": Tennyson's "Lancelot and Elaine," 1041).—**re-main'**, *n.* That which remains or is left (as *sing.*, obs. or rare); a remaining part or fragment, or a remnant, relic, or survival of something (as *sing.*, now rare); *pl.*, parts, fragments, things, or articles remaining or left (as, "a few broken pillars . . . some *remains* of a flight of stone steps," Amelia B. Edwards's "Thousand Miles up the Nile," xvii.; "She cleared away the *remains* of lunch," W. De Morgan's "Joseph Vance," xvi.); parts or substances remaining from animal or plant life, occurring in the earth's crust or strata (as, fossil *remains*;

organic *remains*); that which remains of a person after death, or the dead body (as, "My grandmother's *remains* were consigned to an old family vault": Marryat's "King's Own," xxxvii.); miscellaneous, fragmentary, or other writings collected after the author's death; surviving members, as of a family or other body of persons (as, "You may remember the inquiries I made among the *remains* of my relations when you were with me in England": B. Franklin's "Autobiography," i.); remnants or traces of some quality, condition, or the like (as, the *remains* of former beauty or glory); also, *sing.*, stay, as in a place† (as, "since my here-*remain* in England": Shakspere's "Macbeth," iv. 3. 148).

re-main-der (rē-mān′dėr). [OF. *remaindre*, inf., remain, used as noun: see *remain*.] **I.** *n.* That which remains or is left; the residue or rest (as, to use part and give away the *remainder*; the *remainder* of the band surrendered; "the *remainder* of the day," Hawthorne's "Blithedale Romance," xix.); a remaining part, or a remnant (often in *pl.*: as, "the last *remainders* of unhappy Troy," Dryden's tr. Virgil's "Æneid," v. 877); specif., the copies of a book remaining in the publisher's stock when the sale has practically ceased, which are frequently sold out at a reduced price; in *arith.*, the quantity that remains after subtraction, or that is in excess after division; in *law*, a future estate so created as to take effect after another estate, as a life-interest, has determined. **II.** *a.* Remaining; left: as, "Their memories are dimm'd and torn, Like the *remainder* tatters of a dream" (Hood's "Midsummer Fairies," xxiv.). **—re-main′der**, *v. t.* To dispose of or sell as a publisher's remainder: as, "In due season the publishers . . . *'remaindered'* the poor red-and-green volume" (Arnold Bennett's "Truth about an Author," Preface). **—re-main′der-man** (-man), *n.*; pl. *-men.* In *law*, one to whom a remainder is devised.

re-make (rē-māk′), *v. t.*; *-made, -making.* [See *re-*.] To make anew; make over.

re-man (rē-man′), *v. t.*; *-manned, -manning.* [See *re-*.] To man again or anew; furnish with a fresh supply of men; also, to restore the manliness or courage of.

re-mand (rē-mand′), *v. t.* [OF. F. *remander*, < LL. *remandare*, < L. *re-*, back, + *mandare*, commit, command.] To send back, remit, or consign again (as, "the project of teaching secular knowledge in the University Lecture Room, and *remanding* religious knowledge to the parish priest": J. H. Newman's "Idea of a University," i. 3); order (a person, etc.) to go back; specif., of a court or magistrate, to send back (a prisoner or accused person) into custody, as to await further proceedings; also, to call or summon back (obs. or rare); recall, revoke, or countermand (obs. or rare: as, "I will *remand* the order I despatched to my banker," C. Brontë's "Jane Eyre," xxiv.). **—re-mand′**, *n.* The act of remanding, or the state of being remanded; specif., a sending back of an accused person into custody, as by a court. **—re-mand′ment**, *n.*

rem-a-nent (rem′a-nent), *a.* [L. *remanens* (-ent-), ppr. of *remanere*, E. *remain*.] Remaining, or left behind (now rare); also, additional or other (chiefly Sc.).

re-mark[1] (rē-märk′), *v. t.* [See *re-*.] To mark again. Also written *re-mark.*

re-mark[2] (rē-märk′), *v.* [F. *remarquer*, < *re-* (< L. *re-*), again, + *marquer*, mark (from Teut., and akin to E. *mark*[2].)] **I.** *tr.* To mark distinctly†, or indicate† (as, "His manacles *remark* him; there he sits": Milton's "Samson Agonistes," 1309); also, to mark, observe, or note (as, "Their assemblies afforded me daily opportunities of *remarking* characters and manners": Johnson's "Rasselas," ix.); notice or perceive (as, "She had *remarked* Sam and Alice come riding over the paddock": H. Kingsley's "Geoffry Hamlyn," xxix.); also, to observe or say, as in making a comment or casually expressing a thought or opinion (as, "My father . . . would *remark* that Mrs. Rollick was of a querulous nature," Bulwer-Lytton's "Caxtons," xii. 4; "'Another of mother's menagerie,' *remarked* Robert," W. Churchill's "Modern Chronicle," i. 7). **II.** *intr.* To make a remark or observation; comment: with *on* or *upon*. **—re-mark′**[2], *n.* [F. *remarque*, < *remarquer*.] The act of remarking; observation or notice (as, "The cause . . . may yet elude Conjecture and *remark*, however shrewd": Cowper's "Table Talk," 205); comment (as, to let a thing

pass without *remark*; an action likely to occasion *remark*); a comment, observation, or casual or brief expression of thought or opinion (as, a caustic or a humorous *remark*; after a few *remarks* from the chairman the meeting closed); in *engraving*, a remarque. **—re-mark′a-ble**, *a.* [F. *remarquable*.] Worthy of remark or notice (as, "The odds is gone, And there is nothing left *remarkable* Beneath the visiting moon": Shakspere's "Antony and Cleopatra," iv. 15. 67); hence, notably or conspicuously unusual, or extraordinary (as, a *remarkable* man, plant, book, or performance; a *remarkable* change; *remarkable* success; "This story of Mongolian conquests is surely the most *remarkable* in all history," H. G. Wells's "Outline of History," xxxiv. § 3). **—re-mark′a-ble-ness**, *n.* **—re-mark′a-bly**, *adv.*

re-marque (rē-märk′), *n.* [F.: see *remark*[2], *n.*] In *engraving*, a distinguishing mark or peculiarity indicating a particular stage of a plate; esp., a small sketch engraved on the margin of a plate, and usually removed after a fixed number of early proofs have been taken; also, a proof or print having such a distinguishing feature.

re-mar-ry (rē-mar′i), *v. t.* or *i.* [See *re-*.] To marry again. **—re-mar′riage** (-mar′āj), *n.*

Rem-brandt-esque (rem-bran-tesk′), *a.* [See *-esque*.] In the manner or style of Rembrandt (1606 – 69), the great Dutch painter and etcher, notable for striking effects due to studied contrast of high lights and deep shadows; resembling or suggesting a picture by Rembrandt (as, "One goes through a vast *Rembrandtesque* shed opening upon a great sunny field": H. G. Wells's "Italy, France, and Britain at War," iii. 3).

re-me-di-a-ble (rē-mē′di-a-bl), *a.* [L. *remediabilis*.] Capable of being remedied. **—re-me′di-a-bly**, *adv.*

re-me-di-al (rē-mē′di-al), *a.* [LL. *remedialis*.] Affording remedy; tending to remedy something. **—re-me′di-al-ly**, *adv.*

re-me-di-ate† (rē-mē′di-āt), *a.* Remedial. See Shakspere's "King Lear," iv. 4. 17.

rem-e-di-less (rem′e-di-les), *a.* Not possessing a remedy, or destitute of remedy, as a person (now rare); also, not admitting of remedy, as disease, trouble, damage, wrong, etc.; incurable; irreparable.

rem-e-dy (rem′e-di), *n.*; pl. *-dies* (-diz). [L. *remedium*, < *re-*, again, + *mederi*, heal: cf. *medic*[1].] Something that cures or relieves a disease or bodily disorder; a healing medicine, application, or treatment; also, something that corrects or removes an evil of any kind (as, "Things without all *remedy* Should be without regard," Shakspere's "Macbeth," iii. 2. 11; "Religion, and not atheism, is the true *remedy* for superstition," Burke's "Conciliation with the Colonies"); a corrective; relief; reparation; specif., in *law*, legal redress; the legal means of enforcing a right or redressing a wrong; in *coinage*, a certain allowance at the mint for deviation from the standard weight and fineness of coins. **—rem′e-dy**, *v.t.*; *-died, -dying.* [L. *remediare*, < *remedium*.] To cure or heal (a disease, etc.); sometimes, to cure or heal (a person, bodily part, etc.: now rare); also, to put right, or restore to the natural or proper condition (as, to *remedy* a matter); counteract or remove (as, to *remedy* an evil; "The defects of the structure . . . could be *remedied* or concealed only by fresh additions and supports," J. F. Kirk's "Charles the Bold," iv. 1).

re-melt (rē-melt′), *v. t.* or *i.* [See *re-*.] To melt again.

re-mem-ber (rē-mem′bėr), *v. t.* [OF. *remembrer*, < LL. *rememorari*, < L. *re-*, again, + *memorare*, bring to remembrance, < *memor*, mindful: see *memory*.] To have (something) come into the mind again (as, he had just *remembered* a task that he had left undone); recall to the mind by an act or effort of memory, or recollect (as, I could not *remember* his name, or where I had seen him before); also, to retain in the memory, or preserve in the mind unforgotten (as, "*Re-membering* no more of that other day Than the hot noon *remembereth* of the night": W. Morris's "Earthly Paradise," August, Ogier the Dane); also, to bear in mind, be mindful of, or take care not to forget (as, "*Remember* whom thou hast aboard," Shakspere's "Tempest," i. 1. 20; "But still re-*member*, if you mean to please, To press your point with modesty and ease," Cowper's "Conversation," 103); keep in mind with some feeling, as gratitude (as, "That they may have their wages duly paid 'em, And something over to *remember* me by": Shakspere's "Henry VIII.," iv. 2. 151); bear (a person) in mind as deserving a gift, reward, or fee (as, to *remember* a person in making one's will; "He then asked me to *remember* the coachman, which . . . implied that I was not to forget to give him a shilling," Marryat's "Peter Simple," iii.); hence, to reward, fee, or tip (a person); also, to bethink or recollect (one's self: now rare); also, to recall (something) to the mind of another†; mention† (as, "that phenomenon in the face of the former, which we have above *remembered*": Fielding's "Tom Jones," iii. 4); mention (a person) to another as sending kindly greetings (as, he wished to be *remembered* to you); also, to remind (a person) of something, to do something, etc. (archaic or prov.). —**it remembers me** (**you**, etc.), impersonally, I (you, etc.) remember or recall: as, "*It* may *remember you* that I undertook . . . to temporize a little with the Scots" (Scott's "Castle Dangerous," i.). [Archaic.]—**to be remembered**, to remember or recall: as, "*Are you remembered* how you crossed me in my conference with the Emperor?" (Marlowe's "Doctor Faustus," x.). [Obs. or prov. Eng.]—**to remember one's courtesy**†, to put on one's hat.—**re-mem′ber**, *v. i.* To have something return to the mind; recall something to the mind; retain something in the memory; also, to possess or exercise the faculty of memory; also, to have memory or recollection (*of*: as, "I *remember* Of such a time," Shakspere's "Henry VIII.," i. 2. 190: now rare).— **re-mem′ber-a-ble**, *a.* Capable or worthy of being remembered.—**re-mem′ber-er**, *n.*

re-mem-brance (rę̄-mem′brạns), *n.* [OF. *remembrance*.] The act or fact of remembering; recollection; memory; the power or faculty of remembering; the length of time over which recollection or memory extends (as, there has been no such case within my *remembrance*); a mental impression retained, or a recollection (as, "How sharp the point of this *remembrance* is!" Shakspere's "Tempest," v. 1. 138); also, the state of being remembered; the state of being held honorably, gratefully, affectionately, etc., in memory (as, "The righteous shall be in everlasting *remembrance*": Ps. cxii. 6); the surviving memory of a person, etc. (as, "I will utterly put out the *remembrance* of Amalek from under heaven": Ex. xvii. 14); also, memory or commemoration (as, "In *remembrance* of so brave a deed, A tomb and fun'ral honours I decreed": Dryden's tr. Virgil's "Æneïd," vi. 680); also, something that serves to bring to or keep in mind; a memento, token, or souvenir; a record or memorial of something or person (now rare); also, mention† or notice†; also, the act of reminding or putting in mind† (as, "It serveth . . . for a sign of *remembrance* to put us in mind of our duty": Hooker's "Ecclesiastical Polity," v. 65. 4); a reminder given (obs. or rare); also, *pl.*, greetings reminding the recipient of the sender (as, give him my *remembrances*).—**re-mem′brancer** (-brạn-sėr), *n.* One who reminds another of something, esp., formerly, one engaged to do this; also, something that reminds one; a reminder; sometimes, a memento or souvenir; also [usually *cap.*], in England, any of certain officials of the Court of Exchequer, of whom only one, known as the *King's* (or *Queen's*) *Remembrancer* and charged with the collection of debts due to the sovereign, still survives, now as an officer of the Supreme Court; also, an officer of the corporation of the City of London.

re-mex (rē′meks), *n.*; pl. *remiges* (rem′i-jēz). [NL. use of L. *remex* (remig-), oarsman, < *remus*, oar.] In *ornith.*, a flight-feather.—**re-mig-i-al** (rę̄-mij′i-ạl), *a.*

re-mind (rę̄-mīnd′), *v. t.* [See *re-*.] To put (one) in mind of something; cause (one) to remember: as, "a place where everything *reminded* her of former delight" (Jane Austen's "Sense and Sensibility," ii.); "Your looks *remind* me to proceed" (Mrs. Shelley's "Frankenstein," iv.); "laughingly *reminding* her that I was proof against all perils" (W. H. Hudson's "Green Mansions," x.).—**re-mind′er**, *n.* One who or that which reminds one; something intended to remind one; a mention made for the purpose of reminding one.—**re-mind′ful**, *a.* Reviving memory of something; reminiscent; also, retaining memory of something; mindful.

rem-i-nisce (rem-i-nis′), *v. i.*; *-nisced, -niscing.* [Back-formation from *reminiscence*.] To indulge in reminiscence; recall past experiences. [Colloq.]

rem-i-nis-cence (rem-i-nis′ęns), *n.* [F. *réminiscence*, < LL. *reminiscentia*, < L. *reminiscens*, ppr.: see *reminiscent*.] The act or process of remembering or recollecting; the recalling to the mind of past incidents, events, etc., within one's personal knowledge; also, a mental impression retained and revived, or a recollection (as, "Her mind seemed wholly taken up with *reminiscences* of past gayety": C. Brontë's "Jane Eyre," xxi.); often, a recollection narrated or told; an account of some incident, event, or circumstance within one's knowledge or experience, as given from memory (often in *pl.*: as, to listen to an old man's *reminiscences*; the published *reminiscences* of a statesman); also, something that recalls, awakens memories of, or strongly suggests something else.

rem-i-nis-cent (rem-i-nis′ęnt), *a.* [L. *reminiscens* (-ent-), ppr. of *reminisci*, remember, < *re-*, again, + *min-*, as in *meminisse*, remember: see *mind*[2].] Having remembrance or recollection of something; indulging in or given to reminiscence, as a person; also, of or pertaining to reminiscence; characterized by or of the nature of reminiscence or reminiscences (as, *reminiscent* talk; "Bok asked him to write a *reminiscent* article on his famous master," Bok's "Americanization of Edward Bok," xxxii.); also, awakening memories of something else; suggestive (*of*: as, "She was dressed in a way and moved across the room in a way that was . . . *reminiscent* of Botticelli's Spring," H. G. Wells's "Soul of a Bishop," vi.).—**rem-i-nis′cent-ly**, *adv.*

rem-i-nis-cen-tial (rem″i-ni-sen′shạl), *a.* Of or pertaining to reminiscence.—**rem″i-nis-cen′tial-ly**, *adv.*

re-mise[1] (rę̄-mīz′), *v. t.*; *-mised, -mising.* [OF. F. *remis*, pp. of *remettre*, put back, give up, deliver, < L. *remittere*: see *remit*.] In *law*, to give up a claim to; surrender by deed.

re-mise[2] (rê-mēz′), *n.* [F., < *remettre*: see *remise*[1].] A house or shelter for a carriage; also, a carriage hired from a livery-stable.

re-miss (rę̄-mis′), *a.* [L. *remissus*, pp. of *remittere*: see *remit*.] Not diligent, careful, or prompt in the performance of duty, business, engagements, etc., as persons (as, "The prince must think me tardy and *remiss*": Shakspere's "Troilus and Cressida," iv. 4. 143); negligent; slack; careless; dilatory; characterized by negligence or carelessness, as conduct; also, lax, as discipline (obs. or rare); also, lacking force or energy, without vehemence, or mild; languid or sluggish, as motion.

re-mis-si-ble (rę̄-mis′i-bl), *a.* [LL. *remissibilis*.] That may be remitted.—**re-mis-si-bil′i-ty** (-bil′i-ti), *n.*

re-mis-sion (rę̄-mish′ọn), *n.* [OF. *remission* (F. *rémission*), < L. *remissio(n-)*.] The act of remitting, or the state of being remitted; esp., pardon or forgiveness, as of sins or offenses; also, the relinquishment of a payment, obligation, etc.; the remitting of a punishment, penalty, etc.; also, abatement, as of diligence, labor, intensity, etc.; a temporary decrease or subsidence, as of the violence of a disease or of pain.—**re-mis′sive** (-mis′iv), *a.* Inclined to or productive of remission or pardon (now rare); also, characterized by remission or abatement.

re-miss-ly (rę̄-mis′li), *adv.* In a remiss manner; negligently; slackly.—**re-miss′ness**, *n.*

re-mit (rę̄-mit′), *v.*; *-mitted, -mitting.* [L. *remittere* (pp. *remissus*), send back, let go, relax, abate, remit, < *re-*, back, + *mittere*, send.] **I.** *tr.* To send back†; send back to prison or custody, as a person (now rare); put back into a previous position or condition (as, "Nor only dost degrade them, or remit To life obscured," Milton's "Samson Agonistes," 687; to *remit* a people to slavery); also, to refer (a matter) for consideration, decision, action, etc., to a person or a body of persons; specif., in legal use, to send back (a case) to an inferior court for further action; also, to refer (a person) to another person, a book, etc. (obs. or rare); also, to assign or make over (something), as to a person or thing; also, to transmit or send (money, etc.) to a person or place (as, "He had recently *remitted* a great part of his fortune to Europe," Macaulay's "Essays," Lord Clive; "I *remit* you a Post Office order for your fare," S. Butler's "Way of All Flesh," lxxxii.); also, to put off, defer, or postpone; also, to pardon or forgive (a sin, offense, etc.: as, "She had lately *remitted* the trespass of a stage-coachman, who had overturned her postchaise into a ditch," Fielding's "Tom Jones," vii. 9); also, to refrain from exacting, as a payment or service; refrain from inflicting or enforcing, as a punishment, sentence, etc.; also, to give up, resign, or surrender, as a possession or right† (as, "*Prin*. Will you have me, or your pearl again? *Biron*. Neither of either; I *remit* both twain": Shakspere's "Love's Labour's Lost," v. 2. 459); also, to set free, release, or liberate, as a person†; also, to give over or abandon, as a pursuit, etc.; slacken or abate, as diligence, attention, etc. (as, "They might . . . *remit* in some degree their watchfulness over my movements": H. Melville's "Typee," xviii.); abate or cease from (anger, displeasure, or other feeling: as, "She began to *remit* her curiosity," Johnson's "Rasselas," xxxv.); also, to relax the tension of†. **II.** *intr.* To transmit money, etc., as in payment; also, to relax, as from labor; also, to slacken or abate (as, "How often have I bless'd the coming day, When toil *remitting* lent its turn to play": Goldsmith's "Deserted Village," 16); abate for a time or at intervals, as a fever.—**re-mit'ment,** *n.* Remittance.—**re-mit'ta-ble,** *a.* That may be remitted.—**re-mit'tal,** *n.* Remission.—**re-mit'tance,** *n.* The remitting or transmitting of money, etc., to a recipient at a distance; also, that which is so remitted.—**re-mit'tance-man** (-man), *n.;* pl. *-men.* A man who lives abroad on remittances from home.—**re-mit'tent.** [L. *remittens* (*-ent-*), ppr.] **I.** *a.* Remitting; abating for a time or at intervals: used esp. of a fever in which the symptoms diminish considerably at intervals without disappearing entirely. **II.** *n.* A remittent fever.—**re-mit'ter¹,** *n.* One who or that which remits.—**re-mit'ter²,** *n.* [See *-er³*.] In *law*, the principle or operation by which a person who enters on an estate by a defective title, and who previously had an earlier and more valid title to it, is adjudged to hold it by the earlier and more valid one; also, the act of remitting a case to another court for decision; also, in general, restoration, as to a former right or condition.—**re-mit'tor,** *n.* In *law*, one who makes a remittance.

rem-nant (rem'nant). [OF. *remenant, remanant*, ppr. of *remanoir*: see *remain*.] **I.** *n.* That which remains or is left after a part has been taken away; the remainder or rest (as, "I had one morsel of bread yet, the *remnant* of a roll I had bought," C. Brontë's "Jane Eyre," xxviii.; "The sum exceeded the *remnant* of his savings," S. Butler's "Way of All Flesh," lxxv.); a part, quantity, or number, usually small, remaining or left (as, *remnants* of a once extensive forest; "Of the cattle only a *remnant* remains," W. H. Hudson's "Purple Land," xxv.); an end or odd piece of cloth, ribbon, lace, or the like, left over when the rest is sold or used; a fragment, bit, or scrap (as, "I saw Hosea's brindled cow feeding on fish *remnants*": H. Melville's "Moby-Dick," xv.); a person or a number of persons surviving from past time, events, etc. (as, " 'It is true, sir,' said the old *remnant* of the wars," Scott's "Castle Dangerous," viii.; "Still we watch . . . In this green place left all alone, A *remnant* of the days long gone," W. Morris's "Jason," xiv. 664); a small remaining amount, or a trace or vestige, of some quality, feeling, condition, or the like (as, to retain some *remnant* of dignity; without a *remnant* of shame; *remnants* of former greatness). **II.** *a.* Remaining. [Archaic.]

re-mod-el (rē-mod'el), *v. t.;* *-eled* or *-elled, -eling* or *-elling.* [See *re-*.] To model anew; reconstruct: as, "Philip *remodelled* and befriended the university of Louvain" (Motley's "Dutch Republic," Introd., vii.).—**re-mod'el-ment,** *n.*

re-mold, re-mould (rē-mōld'), *v. t.* [See *re-*.] To mold or shape anew.

re-mon-e-tize (rē-mon'e-tīz or rē-mun'-), *v. t.* [See *re-*.] To monetize again; restore to use as legal tender: as, to *remonetize* silver.—**re-mon″e-ti-za'tion** (-ti-zā'shon), *n.*

re-mon-strance (rē-mon'strans), *n.* [OF. *remonstrance* (F. *remontrance*).] Demonstration† or manifestation† (as, "*remonstrance* of my hidden power": Shakspere's "Measure for Measure," v. 1. 397); also, representation or statement of facts or circumstances† (as, "Mr. Clinker Lloyd has made humble *remonstrance* . . . setting forth the sincere love . . . mutually subsisting . . . and praying my consent": Smollett's "Humphry Clinker," Oct. 26); a formal statement of matters of public importance, esp. by way of protest, presented to a ruler, government, or the like (now hist.: as, "The *Remonstrance* [1641] was a bold manifesto to the public, setting out . . . the story of the Parliament, its past

gains, its future hopes, the standing perils with which it had to wrestle," Morley's "Oliver Cromwell," i. 7); [*cap*.] a document stating the points of divergence of the Dutch Arminians from strict Calvinism, presented to the States of Holland in 1610; also [*l. c*.], the act of remonstrating, or expostulation (as, to speak in *remonstrance*; "a tone of surprised *remonstrance*," Mallock's "New Republic," iv. 1); a remonstrating or expostulating utterance (as, to be deaf to *remonstrances*; "Almost every word . . . is . . . in the nature of a *remonstrance* for some breach of decorum," G. B. Shaw's "You Never Can Tell," i.); a protest.

re-mon-strant (rē-mon'strant). [ML. *remonstrans* (*-ant-*), ppr.] **I.** *a.* Remonstrating; expostulatory. **II.** *n.* One who remonstrates; specif., one of a party or body of persons presenting a remonstrance, as to a government (as, " ' 'Tis notorious,' said the *remonstrants*, 'that Antwerp was but yesterday the first . . . ornament of all Europe' ": Motley's "Dutch Republic," iv. 5); [*cap*.] one of the Dutch Arminians whose doctrines were set forth in the Remonstrance of 1610.—**re-mon'strant-ly,** *adv.*

re-mon-strate (rē-mon'strāt), *v.;* *-strated, -strating.* [ML. *remonstratus*, pp. of *remonstrare*, < L. *re-*, back, + *monstrare*, show.] **I.** *tr.* To demonstrate†, make manifest†, or show†; also, to point out or represent, as in a complaint or protest† (as, to *remonstrate* wrong done or sustained); also, to say in remonstrance or expostulation (as, "If I have wander'd . . . As something, loudly in my breast, *Remonstrates* I have done": Burns's "Prayer in the Prospect of Death," 8). **II.** *intr.* To make representations or present reasons in complaint or protest (as, "We must obey first, and *remonstrate* afterwards": Marryat's "King's Own," xxxiv.); protest (*against*: as, "The people of Connecticut . . . *remonstrated* against the bill," Bancroft's "Hist. of the U. S.," Amer. Revolution, i. 2); reason or plead in protest, or expostulate (*with*: as, "Christina did not *remonstrate* with Theobald concerning the severity of the tasks imposed upon their boy," S. Butler's "Way of All Flesh," xx.).—**re-mon-stra-tion** (rē-mon-strā'shon or rem-on-), *n.* [ML. *remonstratio*(*n-*).] Remonstrance.—**re-mon-stra-tive** (rē-mon'stra-tiv), *a.* Remonstrant; expostulatory.—**re-mon'-stra-tor** (-strā-tor), *n.*

re-mon-tant (rē-mon'tant). [F., ppr. of *remonter*, go up again, < *re-* (< L. *re-*), again, + *monter*, E. *mount²*.] In *hort.:* **I.** *a.* Blooming more than once in a season: said of certain roses. **II.** *n.* A remontant rose.

re-mon-toir (rē-môn-twor'), *n.* [F., < *remonter*, go up again, also wind up: see *remontant*.] In *horol.*, a device by which a uniform impulse is given to the pendulum or balance.

rem-o-ra (rem'ō-rä), *n.* [L., < *re-*, back, + *mora*, delay.] An obstacle, hindrance, or obstruction (obs. or archaic); also, any of various fishes (family *Echeneididæ*) having on the top of the head a suctorial disk by which they can attach themselves to

Remora.

ships, other fishes, etc. (formerly believed to have the power of delaying or stopping ships).

re-morse (rē-môrs'), *n.* [OF. *remors* (F. *remords*), < LL. *remorsus*, < L. *remordere*, torment, disturb, < *re-*, back, again, + *mordere*, bite.] Mental distress due to a tormenting or reproachful conscience (in the phrase 'remorse of conscience': archaic); deep and painful regret for wrongdoing (as, "They showed not the least *remorse* for the crime," Defoe's "Robinson Crusoe," ii. 4; "Dread *remorse* when you are tempted to err . . . *remorse* is the poison of life," C. Brontë's "Jane Eyre," xiv.); in a milder sense, compunction, regret, scruple, or relenting as to action (esp. in the phrase 'without remorse': as, "The critic else proceeds without *remorse*, Seizes your fame," Pope's "Essay on Criticism," 167); also, pity† or compassion† (as, "the tears of soft *remorse*": Shakspere's "King John," iv. 3. 50).—**re-morse'ful,** *a.* Full of remorse, as for wrong-doing, as a person, the heart, etc.; characterized by or due to remorse (as, a *remorseful* mood; "So groan'd Sir Lancelot in *remorseful* pain," Tennyson's "Lancelot and Elaine," 1417); also, compassionate†.—**re-morse'ful-ly,** *adv.*—**re-morse'ful-ness,** *n.*—**re-morse'-**

less, *a.* Without remorse; relentless; pitiless: as, a *re-morseless* foe; *remorseless* cruelty.—**re-morse'less-ly,** *adv.*—**re-morse'less-ness,** *n.*

re-mote (rẹ-mōt′), *a.*; compar. *remoter,* superl. *remotest.* [L. *remotus,* pp. of *removere,* E. *remove.*] Removed, far apart, or distant in space, as from a point or as one from another (as, "the side of the grate most *remote* from the entrance," Scott's "Guy Mannering," liv.; "Imperative exigencies . . . demanded the acquisition of Lorraine, as the only means of linking together provinces now dissevered and *remote,*" J. F. Kirk's "Charles the Bold," iv. 1); far off, or far distant, as with reference to one's own place or to some center of habitation or importance (as, "I was now alone in the *remotest* part of the world [Bengal]," Defoe's "Robinson Crusoe," ii. 10; *remote* heavenly bodies; a *remote* outpost of civilization); out-of-the-way, retired, or secluded (as, a *remote* village; "In *remote* And silent woods I wander," Cowper's "Task," iii. 117); also, distant in time (as, *remote* antiquity; the *remote* future; "an episode so *remote* and so completely of the past as his love affair," Mrs. Wharton's "Age of Innocence," xvi.); also, distant in relation, connection, or bearing (as, a *remote* fact, circumstance, or conclusion; a *remote* cause or effect); distant in kinship (as, a *remote* branch of the family; a *remote* kinsman); far removed, alien, or widely divergent (*from*: as, things *remote* from common experience or use; "These small waves raised by the evening wind are as *remote* from storm as the smooth reflecting surface," Thoreau's "Walden," v.); not close, as a relation, connection, resemblance, etc.; hence, slight or faint (as, not the *remotest* idea; a *remote* possibility of success; "Would a single one of those frescoes . . . have the *remotest* chance of being hung?" S. Butler's "Way of All Flesh," i.).—**re-mote'ly,** *adv.*—**re-mote'ness,** *n.*

re-mo-tion (rẹ-mō′shọn), *n.* [L. *remotio(n-),* < *removere,* E. *remove.*] The act of removing; removal; departure†; also, remoteness.

ré-mou-lade (rā-mö-läd′), *n.* [F.; from It.] A salad-dressing of oil, vinegar, mustard, etc., and sometimes chopped anchovies and herbs.

re-mould (rē-mōld′), *v. t.* See *remold.*

re-mount (rē-mount′), *v.* [See *re-.*] **I.** *intr.* To mount again; reascend; esp., to mount a horse or other animal again, as a rider; sometimes, to go back to a source, earlier point, or the like. **II.** *tr.* To mount, go up, or ascend again; esp., to mount (a horse, etc.) again, as a rider; also, to mount or set up again on a support, in position, etc. (as, to *remount* guns); restore (a rider) to his place on horseback, etc.; furnish with a fresh horse or with fresh horses (as, to *remount* a rider; to *remount* cavalry).—**re-mount′,** *n.* The act, work, or service of remounting, as with fresh horses for cavalry or artillery purposes; also, a fresh horse, or a supply of fresh horses, for use (as, "Some of the cavalry had received *remounts*": Conan Doyle's "Exploits of Brigadier Gerard," vii.).

re-mov-a-ble (rẹ-mö′vạ-bl), *a.* That may be removed.—**re-mov-a-bil'i-ty** (-bil′i-ti), **re-mov'a-ble-ness,** *n.*

re-mov-al (rẹ-mö′vạl), *n.* The act of removing, or the state or fact of being removed.

re-move (rẹ-möv′), *v.*; *-moved, -moving.* [OF. *removoir,* < L. *removere* (pp. *remotus*), < *re-,* back, + *movere,* E. *move.*] **I.** *tr.* To move from a place or position, take away, or take off (as, to *remove* furniture from a room; to *remove* an obstacle; to *remove* one's hat); move or shift to another place or position (as, to *remove* a camp to a better situation; to *remove* one's self to a distance); put out or send away, as from a place (as, to *remove* a tenant; "Adam . . . to *remove* thee I am come, And send thee from the garden forth," Milton's "Paradise Lost," xi. 260); displace from a position or office, depose, or dismiss (as, to *remove* an official for malfeasance); in general, to take, withdraw, or separate (*from*: as, to *remove* a person from temptation, or from any possibility of harm; "Being an inland county, I was *re-moved* from conversing among ships, sailors . . . ," Defoe's "Robinson Crusoe," ii. 1; "How . . . love the offender, yet detest th' offence? How the dear object from the crime *remove?*" Pope's "Eloisa to Abelard," 193); render more or less distant or remote (*from*) in relation, connection, kinship, resemblance, etc. (usually in the passive: as, "blood *re-*

moved but little from her own," Shakspere's "Romeo and Juliet," iii. 3. 96; a case far *removed* from the ordinary: see *removed*); also, to take away, do away with, or put an end to (as, to *remove* a stain; to *remove* causes of discontent; to *remove* doubt or fear); take from life, as by death (as, "Forgive my grief for one *removed*": Tennyson's "In Memoriam," Prologue); put out of the way by killing (as, to *remove* a person by poisoning or assassination); put away† or lay aside† (as, "Till I die I will not *remove* mine integrity from me": Job, xxvii. 5). **II.** *intr.* To move from one place to another, esp. to another locality or place of residence (as, "till Birnam wood *remove* to Dunsinane," Shakspere's "Macbeth," v. 3. 2; "Roland *removed* to France, and fixed his abode in the environs of Paris," Bulwer-Lytton's "Caxtons," xvi. 4; to *remove* to a hotel); also, to go away, depart, or disappear (now chiefly poetic: as, "when autumn-heats *remove,*" Pope's "Autumn," 29).—**re-move′,** *n.* The act or an act of removing; a removal from one place, as of residence, to another (as, "It is an English proverb that three *removes* are as bad as a fire": J. H. Newman's "Callista," xxx.); a promotion of a pupil to a higher class or division at school (Eng.: as, "He never missed a *remove* or failed to gain a prize," Mrs. H. Ward's "Robert Elsmere," ii.); also, a dish served and removed (instead of remaining) during the course of a meal; also, the distance by which one place or thing is removed or separated from another (as, "It's a far *remove* from Paradise Is Spanish port": Masefield's "Port of Holy Peter"; a step or degree, as in a graded scale of distance (as, an action but one *remove* from crime; "a man two *removes* from a baronetcy," G. Meredith's "Diana of the Crossways," iii.).—**re-moved′,** *p. a.* Moved or taken away; also, retired† or secluded† (as, "some still *removed* place": Milton's "Il Penseroso," 78); also, distant or remote (specif. used in expressing degrees of relationship: as, a first cousin once, or twice, *removed,* that is, a cousin's child, or grandchild; a cousin several times *removed*).—**re-mov′ed-ness** (-mö′ved-nes), *n.*—**re-mov′er,** *n.*

rem-pli (roṅ-plē), *a.* [F., pp. of *remplir,* fill up, < *re-* (< L. *re-*), again, + *emplir,* fill, < L. *implere:* see *impletion.*] In *her.,* filled or covered with a different tincture, except for a bordering space, as a chief.

re-mu-ner-ate (rẹ-mū′nẹ-rāt), *v. t.*; *-ated, -ating.* [L. *remuneratus,* pp. of *remunerari,* < *re-,* back, + *munerare,* give, < *munus,* gift.] To requite, recompense, or reward (a person) for services, work, trouble, etc. (as, "Is she not then beholding to the man . . . ? Yes, and will nobly him *remunerate*": Shakspere's "Titus Andronicus," i. 1. 398); yield or afford a recompense to (as, work, crops, or prices that will richly *remunerate* us); also, to give or afford a recompense for (services, work, etc.: as, "The better hour is near, That shall *remunerate* thy toils severe," Cowper's "Sonnet to Wilberforce"); also.—**re-mu-ner-a′tion** (-nẹ-rā′shọn), *n.* [L. *remuneratio(n-).*] The act of remunerating; also, that which is given to remunerate; recompense for services, work, etc.; reward; pay.—**re-mu′ner-a-tive** (-nẹ-rā-tiv), *a.* That remunerates; affording remuneration; profitable: as, *remunerative* work.—**re-mu′ner-a-tive-ly,** *adv.*—**re-mu′ner-a-tive-ness,** *n.*—**re-mu′ner-a-tor** (-nẹ-rā-tọr), *n.*—**re-mu′ner-a-to-ry** (-nẹ-rā-tō-ri), *a.* Serving to remunerate; affording recompense.

re-mur-mur (rē-mèr′mèr), *v.* [L. *remurmurare,* < *re-,* back, again, + *murmurare,* E. *murmur.*] **I.** *intr.* To murmur back or in response; respond or resound with murmurs. [Poetic.] **II.** *tr.* To repeat in murmurs: as, "The trembling trees . . . Her fate *remurmur* to the silver flood" (Pope's "Winter," 64). [Poetic.]

ren-ais-sance (ren-ạ-säns′ or rẹ-nā′sạns, F. rẹ-ne-säṅs). [F., < *renaître,* be born again, < *re-* (< L. *re-*), again, + *naître:* see *née.*] **I.** *n.* A new birth; a revival; specif. [*cap.*], the activity, spirit, or time of the great revival of art, letters, and learning in Europe during the 14th, 15th, and 16th centuries, marking the transition from the medieval to the modern world. **II.** *a.* [*cap.*] Of or pertaining to the Renaissance: as, *Renaissance* architecture (the style of building and decoration succeeding the medieval, based upon study and emulation of the outward forms and ornaments of

A Chief Rempli.

classical Roman art, and originating in Italy in the first half of the 15th century, afterward spreading over Europe, and attaining notable development in France, where it flourished in the 16th century); *Renaissance* sculpture (characterized primarily by seeking its models and inspiration in the works of Roman antiquity).—**Re-nais-sant** (rẹ-nā'sạnt), *a.* [F. *renaissant*, ppr. of *renaître*.] Of or pertaining to the Renaissance.

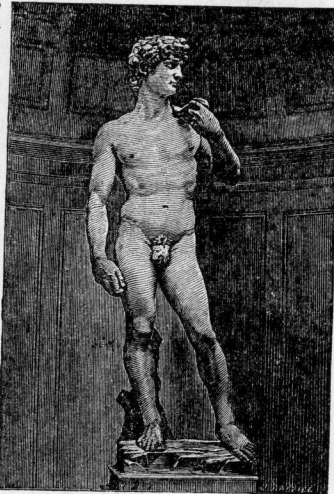
Renaissance Sculpture. — The "David" of Michelangelo, in the Accademia, Florence, Italy.

re-nal (rē'nạl), *a.* [LL. *renalis*, < L. *ren*, kidney: cf. *reins*.] Of or pertaining to the kidneys.
—**renal capsule** or **gland**, the suprarenal capsule. See *suprarenal, a.*

re-name (rē-nām'), *v. t.* [See *re-*.] To name anew.

Ren-ard (ren'ạrd), *n.* See *Reynard*.

re-nas-cence (rẹ-nas'ens), *n.* The state or fact of being renascent; rebirth, revival, or renewal (as, "a period of moral *renascence*": H. G. Wells's "Italy, France, and Britain at War," iv. 1); also, a new birth; a revival (as, "a *renascence* of religion": H. G. Wells's "Italy, France, and Britain at War," iv. 6); specif. [*cap.*], the Renaissance.

re-nas-cent (rẹ-nas'ent), *a.* [L. *renascens* (-*ent*-), ppr. of *renasci*, be born again, < *re-*, again, + *nasci*: see *native*.] Being born again; reviving; springing again into being or vigor.

ren-con-tre (ren-kon'tẹr, F. roṅ-kôṅtr), *n.* [F.] A rencounter; an encounter.

ren-coun-ter (ren-koun'tẹr), *v.* [F. *rencontrer*, < *re-* (< L. *re-*), again, + OF. *encontrer*, E. *encounter*.] **I.** *tr.* To meet or encounter in a hostile manner; meet in conflict; also, to meet with, fall in with, or come upon (as, "I had the good fortune to *rencounter* you at Durrisdeer": Stevenson's "Master of Ballantrae," iv.). **II.** *intr.* To encounter.—
ren-coun'ter, *n.* [OF. F. *rencontre*.] A hostile meeting or encounter; a battle; a conflict; a combat; a duel; hence, a contest of any kind; also, a meeting, as of two persons, or of a person with a thing, esp. a casual meeting (as, "All my acquaintance with him was confined to an occasional *rencounter* in the hall": C. Brontë's "Jane Eyre," xiv.); also, a coming in contact, or an impact or collision (obs. or rare).

rend (rend), *v.*; *rent, rending.* [AS. *rendan* = OFries. *renda.*] **I.** *tr.* To separate into parts with force or violence; tear (*asunder, in pieces*, etc.: as, "An evil beast hath devoured him; Joseph is without doubt *rent* in pieces," Gen. xxxvii. 33); tear (one's garments or hair) in rage, despair, grief, etc. (as, "Weep, weep, and *rend* your hair for those who never shall return": Macaulay's "Ivry"); fig., to tear apart, split, or divide (as, "The commons live, by no divisions *rent*": Dryden's tr. Virgil's "Georgics," iv. 309); disturb (the air) sharply with loud noise (as, "The air was *rent* by the shrieks and lamentations of the women": Irving's "Captain Bonneville," xviii.); harrow or distress (the heart, etc.) with painful feelings (as, "the sigh that *rends* thy constant heart": Goldsmith's "Hermit," xl.); also, to remove with force or violence (as, "I will surely *rend* the kingdom from thee": 1 Kings, xi. 11); pull or tear violently (*away, off, up*, etc.). **II.** *intr.* To rend or tear something; also, to become rent or torn (as, "He laid hold upon the skirt of his mantle, and it *rent*": 1 Sam. xv. 27); part asunder; split; break.—
rend'er¹, *n.*

ren-der² (ren'dẹr), *v. t.* [OF. F. *rendre*, < ML. *rendere*, for L. *reddere*, give back, yield, render, < *red-*, for *re-*, back, + *dare*, give.] To give back or restore (often with *back*: as, "Desirous to resign and *render* back All I received,"

Milton's "Paradise Lost," x. 749); give back as by reflection or echo (often with *back*: as, "hollow rocks that *render* back the sound," Dryden's tr. Virgil's "Georgics," iv. 69); also, to reproduce or represent in some way; depict, as in painting, etc.; bring out the meaning of by performance or execution, or interpret, as a part in a drama, a piece of music, etc.; reproduce in another language, or translate; also, to represent or describe as being what is stated† (as, "He did *render* him the most unnatural [brother] That lived amongst men": Shakspere's "As You Like It," iv. 3. 123); also, to give in return or requital (as, "receiving benefits, and *rend'ring* none": Cowper's "Task," vi. 959); often, to return (thanks); also, to give, deliver, or hand over (as, "Affirming that his father left him gold, And in my charge, which was not *render'd* to him": Tennyson's "Marriage of Geraint," 452); give up, resign, or relinquish (often with *up*); surrender, as in warfare; present for consideration, approval, action, etc., as an account; deliver officially, as judgment; furnish (assistance); do (a service); perform (a duty); exhibit or show (obedience, attention, etc.); pay as due (a tax, tribute, etc.); also, to present (one's self) at a particular place; also, to make, or cause to be or become, as specified (as, "O ye gods, *Render* me worthy of this noble wife!" Shakspere's "Julius Cæsar," ii. 1. 303; "Jasper's conjecture was *rendered* a certainty," Gissing's "New Grub Street," ii.); also, to melt (fat, etc.); clarify or extract by melting; also, in *building*, to cover (brickwork or stone) with a first coat of plaster.
—**ren'der²,** *n.* The act or an act of rendering (now rare); in *law*, a return; a payment in money, kind, or service, made by a tenant to his superior; also, in *building*, the first coat of plaster applied to brickwork or stone.—**ren'der-a-ble,** *a.* Capable of being rendered.—**ren'der-er,** *n.*—**ren'der-ing,** *n.* The act of one who or that which renders; restoring, giving, delivering, surrendering, etc., or something given or rendered; often, reproduction or representation; interpretation; translation; in *building*, the laying on of a first coat of plaster on brickwork or stone; also, the coat thus laid on.

ren-dez-vous (ron'dạ-vö or ren'dẹ-), *n.*; pl. *-vous* (-vöz). [F. *rendez-vous*, lit. 'render (or present) yourselves' (as at a place appointed).] An appointment or engagement made between two or more persons to meet at a fixed place and time (as, "I Have a *Rendezvous* with Death," the title of a poem by Alan Seeger; "Edwin would not have kept the *rendezvous* could he have found an excuse . . . for staying away," Arnold Bennett's "Clayhanger," iii. 11); also, a meeting arranged for by special appointment or engagement (as, "A general *rendezvous* is held, at some designated place in the mountains," Irving's "Captain Bonneville," i.; "He would not fail to give him the *rendezvous* at the hour he mentioned," Smollett's "Humphry Clinker," May 17); meeting or assembling (as, "Each tribe had usually some fixed place of *rendezvous*": Scott's "Guy Mannering," vii.); also, a place appointed for meeting or assembling, specif. for the assembling of troops or ships (as, "The Prince of Orange had raised six thousand infantry, whose *rendezvous* was the Isle of Bommel": Motley's "Dutch Republic," iv. 1); in general, a meeting-place, gathering-place, or place of common resort (as, "I . . . came into the drawing-room, which was the *rendezvous* of the little family": Bulwer-Lytton's "Caxtons," ix.); also, a retreat† or refuge†.—**ren'dez-vous,** *v. i.* or *t.*; *-voused* (-vöd), *-vousing* (-vö-ing). To assemble at a place previously appointed; in general, to come or bring together.

ren-di-tion (ren-dish'ọn), *n.* [Obs. F. *rendition*, for *reddition*, < L. *redditio*(*n*-), < *reddere*: see *render²*.] The act of rendering; interpretation, as of a rôle or a piece of music; translation, as of a work into another language; surrender (as, "the *rendition* of Douglas Castle to the owner," Scott's "Castle Dangerous," xix.; "the *rendition* of fugitive slaves," Charnwood's "Abraham Lincoln," v.).

rend-rock (rend'rok), *n.* An explosive mixture used chiefly in blasting, containing nitroglycerin, barium nitrate, kieselguhr, wood-pulp, etc.

ren-e-gade (ren'ẹ-gād). [Sp. *renegado*, < ML. *renegatus*, pp. of *renegare*: see *renege*.] **I.** *n.* An apostate from a religious faith; hence, one who deserts one party or cause and goes over to another; a turncoat; a traitor. **II.** *a.* Having the character of, or pertaining to, a renegade; apostate; traitorous.

ren-e-ga-do (ren-ē-gä'dō), n.; pl. -does (-dōz). [Sp.] A renegade. [Archaic.]

re-nege (rē-nēg'), v.; -neged, -neging. [ML. renegare, deny, renounce, < L. re-, back, again, + negare, deny.] **I.** tr. To deny; disown; renounce. [Archaic.] **II.** intr. To make denial†; in card-playing, to play a card that is not of the suit led; often, to revoke. Also **re-negue'** (-nēg'). —**re-nege'**, n. In card-playing, an act or instance of reneging.

re-nerve (rē-nėrv'), v. t. [See re-.] To nerve again; give new vigor to.

re-new (rē-nū'), v. [From re- + new.] **I.** tr. To make new, or as if new, again; restore to a former state, or to a good state after decay, impairment, deterioration, etc. (as, "Thou renewest the face of the earth": Ps. civ. 30); sometimes, to revive (as, "This renewed a contemplation which often had come to my thoughts in former times": Defoe's "Robinson Crusoe," i. 12); sometimes, to make spiritually new, or regenerate; also, to restore or reëstablish (as, "Mighty Cæsar . . . On the glad earth the Golden Age renews": Dryden's tr. Virgil's "Georgics," iv. 813); also, to assume anew, or recover (youth, strength, etc.: as, "Institutions may crumble and governments fall, but it is only that they may renew a better youth," Bancroft's "Hist. of the U. S.," Amer. Revolution, i. 1; "Thou wilt renew thy beauty morn by morn," Tennyson's "Tithonus," 74); also, to begin anew, take up again, or resume (as, "You must renew your acquaintance with the family": W. Churchill's "Modern Chronicle," i. 7); often, to resume (a speech, subject, etc.: as, "The subject was not renewed between them the next day or subsequently," Tarkington's "Magnificent Ambersons," xx.); also, to make or utter again, or repeat (as, "He once more renewed his often violated oaths," G. P. R. James's "Hist. of Charlemagne," iii.; "He did not hesitate . . . to renew his offers to her," Jane Porter's "Scottish Chiefs," x.); sometimes, to do again, or repeat (an action: as, "Awake remembrance of these valiant dead And with your puissant arm renew their feats," Shakspere's "Henry V.," i. 2. 116); also, to replace by something new of the same kind; restore, replenish, or maintain by replacement or additions (as, to renew a stock of goods); fill again (as, "Come, bumpers high, express your joy, The bowl we maun renew it": Burns's "Lines Written on a Tumbler"); also, to extend over a new or further period, as a lease, note, etc.; also, to obtain a renewal or extension of (a lease, note, etc.). **II.** intr. To become new, or as if new, again; grow afresh; also, to begin anew; recommence; also, to renew a lease, note, etc.—**re-new'a-ble**, a. Capable of being renewed.—**re-new'al**, n. The act of renewing, or the state of being renewed; an instance of this.—**re-new'ed-ly**, adv.—**re-new'er**, n.

ren-i-form (ren'i-fôrm or rē'ni-), a. [L. ren, kidney, + forma, form.] Kidney-shaped: as, a reniform leaf; hematite in reniform masses.

ren-i-tent (ren'i-tent or rē-nī'-), a. [F. rénitent, < L. renitens (-ent-), ppr. of reniti, resist, < re-, back, + niti, strive.] Resisting pressure; resistant; also, persistently opposing; recalcitrant.—**ren-i-ten-cy** (ren'i-ten-si or rē-nī'-), n.

Reniform Structure. — Hematite.

ren-net (ren'et), n. [ME. rennet, < rennen, E. run.] The lining membrane of the fourth stomach of a calf, or of the stomach of certain other young animals, or a preparation or extract of this membrane, used to curdle milk, as in making cheese, junket, etc.; also, anything used to curdle milk, as the plant Galium verum (our Lady's bedstraw).

ren-nin (ren'in), n. [From rennet.] In physiol. chem., a coagulating enzyme occurring in the gastric juice, forming the active principle of rennet, and having the power of curdling milk.

re-nom-i-nate (rē-nom'i-nāt), v. t. [See re-.] To nominate again or anew.—**re-nom-i-na'tion** (-nā'shon), n.

re-nounce (rē-nouns'), v.; -nounced, -nouncing. [OF. renoncier (F. renoncer), < L. renuntiare, disclaim, renounce, < re-, back, + nuntiare, announce, declare, < nuntius,

messenger.] **I.** tr. To give up, resign, abandon, or forsake by formal declaration (as, to renounce a right, claim, or title; at naturalization in the U. S. a person renounces allegiance to any foreign prince or state; "Question. Dost thou renounce the devil and all his works, the vain pomp and glory of the world . . . ? Answer. I renounce them all," Book of Common Prayer, Baptism of Those of Riper Years); abjure or forswear; repudiate (as, "He had . . . in express words, abrogated and renounced the treaty": J. F. Kirk's "Charles the Bold," iii. 1); disown (a relation, friend, etc.: as, "My brother has quarrelled with me . . . and renounced me," Dickens's "Our Mutual Friend," ii. 15); in general, to give up, abandon, relinquish, or put aside voluntarily (as, to renounce the pen for the sword; to renounce a practice or profession; to renounce an opinion, feeling, or intention); often, to give up, surrender, or resign by a greater or lesser sacrifice of one's own wishes or feelings (as, to renounce hopes or joys; "Oh teach me nature to subdue, Renounce my love, my life, myself—and you," Pope's "Eloisa to Abelard," 204). **II.** intr. To make formal resignation or surrender, as of a right; in card-playing, to play a card of a different suit from that led.—**re-nounce'**, n. In card-playing, an act or instance of renouncing.—**re-nounce'a-ble**, a. That may be renounced.—**re-nounce'ment**, n. The act of renouncing; renunciation: as, "if the taking of the cowl does not imply a complete renouncement of the world" (Kinglake's "Eothen," x.).—**re-noun'cer**, n.

ren-o-vate (ren'ō-vāt), v. t.; -vated, -vating. [L. renovatus, pp. of renovare, < re-, again, + novare, make new, < novus, new.] To make new, or as if new, again, after decay, impairment, deterioration, etc.; restore to the good condition or fresh appearance characteristic of what is new, as by repairs or freshening treatment (as, "He had cleaned and renovated the dark little hole of a cabin," J. Conrad's "Rover," vii.; to renovate a mattress; to renovate a garment); reinvigorate or refresh (as, "Every one awoke marvelously renovated": Irving's "Tales of a Traveler," i. 2); renew, restore, or revive (powers, qualities, etc.: as, "It [water] revived her, but could not renovate her courage," Hawthorne's "Twice-Told Tales," The Great Carbuncle; "Her beautiful eyes sparkled with renovated brilliancy," Cooper's "Spy," xii.); make over in a new and better form, or regenerate (as, "We want men and women who shall renovate life and our social state": Emerson's "Essays," Self-Reliance).—**ren'o-vate**, a. Renovated. [Archaic.]—**ren-o-va'tion** (-vā'shon), n. [L. renovatio(n-).] The act of renovating, or the state of being renovated; restoration to good condition, freshness, vigor, etc.; renewal.—**ren'o-va-tor**, n.

re-nown (rē-noun'), v. [OF. renomer (F. renommer), < L. re-, again, + nominare, name, E. nominate.] **I.** tr. To make famous: as, "The things of fame That do renown this city" (Shakspere's "Twelfth Night," iii. 3. 24): now chiefly in renowned, p. a. **II.** intr. To brag; swagger; play the swashbuckler: sometimes with impersonal it: as, "The student with the sword leaped to the floor . . . He was renowning it" (Longfellow's "Hyperion," ii. 4). [From German use.]—**re-nown'**, n. [OF. renon (F. renom), < renomer.] Widespread and high repute, or fame (as, "Short is my date, but deathless my renown": Pope's tr. Homer's "Iliad," ix.); also, reputation† (as, "a young gentlewoman . . . of a most chaste renown": Shakspere's "All's Well," iv. 3. 19); also, report† or rumor†.—**re-nowned'**, p. a. Famed; celebrated; famous: as, "a renowned patron of learning" (Swift's "Gulliver's Travels," i. 1); "a powerful family, renowned for their warlike exploits" (Parkman's "Oregon Trail," xi.).—**re-nown'er**, n. One who makes famous (obs. or rare); also, a swaggerer or swashbuckler (as, "He [a student] was a renowner, and a duellist," Longfellow's "Hyperion," ii. 4: see renown, v. ii.).

rens-se-laer-ite (ren'se-lėr-īt), n. [From Stephen Van Rensselaer (1765–1839), of New York.] A variety of talc with a fine, compact texture: worked in a lathe into inkstands and other articles.

rent[1] (rent). Preterit and past participle of rend.

rent[2] (rent), n. [From obs. or prov. rent, v., var. of rend.] An opening made by rending or tearing; a tear, as in a garment; a split, break, or fissure (as, "buildings . . . admitting the wind through wide rents and gaps": Scott's

"Castle Dangerous," xvii.); fig., a breach of relations or union; a rupture; a schism.

rent³ (rent), *n.* [OF. F. *rente*, < ML. *rendita*, return, revenue, for *reddita*, prop. pp. fem. of L. *reddere*: see *render²*.] Revenue† or income†, or an item or source of income† (as, "What are thy *rents*? what are thy comings in?" Shakspere's "Henry V.," iv. 1. 260); also, a return or payment made periodically by a tenant to an owner or landlord for the use of land or buildings; a similar return or payment for the use of property of any kind; also, a house or the like rented or for renting to a tenant (now colloq., U. S.: as, to find a good *rent*; few *rents* are to be had); in *polit. econ.*, the excess of the produce or return yielded by a given piece of cultivated land over that yielded by an equal area of the poorest land in cultivation under like conditions in respect to transportation, etc. ('economic rent'); also, profit or return derived from any differential advantage in production.—**rent³**, *v.* **I.** *tr.* To grant the possession and enjoyment of for rent; also, to take and hold by payment of rent; obtain or have the use or benefit of by paying rent. **II.** *intr.* To be leased or let for rent.—**rent′a-ble**, *a.* That may be rented; available for renting: as, "He sang eloquently the advantages of proximity of school-buildings to *rentable* homes" (Sinclair Lewis's "Babbitt," iv.).—**ren′tal**, *n.* [AF. *rental*.] A rent-roll; also, an income arising from rents received (as, "Mr. Brooke's estate, presumably worth about three thousand a year — a *rental* which seemed wealth to provincial families": George Eliot's "Middlemarch," i.); also, an amount received or paid as rent.

rente (roṅt), *n.* [F.: see *rent³*.] Revenue or income; esp., *pl.*, sums paid by a government as interest on public loans; also, the bonds, etc., on which such interest is paid.

ren-ten-mark (ren′ten-märk), *n.* [G., < *rente*, revenue (< F. *rente*: see *rente*), + *mark*, E. *mark¹*.] A temporary German mark for domestic use introduced in November, 1923, nominally representing a mortgage on all landed and industrial property, and having a value of 23.8 U. S. cents, and equivalent to 1,000,000,000,000 paper marks as previously issued: treated as of identical value with the reichsmark when succeeded by the latter in November, 1924.

rent-er (ren′tėr), *n.* One who rents; esp., one who holds, or has the use of, property by payment of rent.

ren-tier (roṅ-tyā), *n.* [F., < *rente*: see *rente*.] One who has a fixed income, as from lands, stocks, etc.

rent=roll (rent′rōl), *n.* A roll or list of rents received or due, as from tenants: as, "Godfrey Bertram . . . succeeded to a long pedigree, and a short *rent-roll*" (Scott's "Guy Mannering," ii.).

re-num-ber (rē-num′bėr), *v. t.* [See *re-*.] To number anew.

re-nun-ci-a-tion (rē-nun-si-ā′shon), *n.* [L. *renuntiatio(n-)*, < *renuntiare*, E. *renounce*.] The act of renouncing; the formal giving up or abandoning of a right, title, possession, or the like; the giving up of anything voluntarily, esp. with some sacrifice of one's own wishes or feelings (as, "The bonzes preach only patience, humility, and the *renunciation* of the world," Gibbon's "Decline and Fall of the Roman Empire," xliii.; "*Renunciation* remains sorrow, though a sorrow borne willingly," George Eliot's "Mill on the Floss," iv. 3).—**re-nun′ci-a-tive** (-ạ-tiv), **re-nun′ci-a-to-ry** (-ạ-tọ-ri), *a.* Pertaining to or characterized by renunciation.

re-oc-cu-py (rē-ok′ū-pī), *v. t.* [See *re-*.] To occupy again. —**re-oc-cu-pa′tion** (-pā′shon), *n.*

re-op-en (rē-ō′pn), *v. t. or i.* [See *re-*.] To open again.

re-or-der (rē-ôr′dėr), *v. t.* [See *re-*.] To order again or anew; in *com.*, to give a reorder for.—**re-or-der** (rē-ôr′dėr or rē′ôr″), *n.* In *com.*, an order for additional goods of the same kind as previously ordered, given to the same person or dealer.

re-or-gan-i-za-tion (rē-ôr″gan-i-zā′shon), *n.* The act or process of reorganizing, or the state of being reorganized; specif., the reconstruction or rehabilitation of a corporation that is in the hands of a receiver.

re-or-gan-ize (rē-ôr′gan-īz), *v. t. or i.* [See *re-*.] To organize anew.—**re-or′gan-iz-er** (-ī-zėr), *n.*

re-o-ri-ent (rē-ō′ri-ent), *a.* [See *re-* and *orient*.] Rising again: as, "the life *re-orient* out of dust" (Tennyson's "In Memoriam," cxvi.). [Poetic.]

rep¹ (rep), *n.* [F. *reps*; origin unknown.] A transversely

corded fabric of wool, silk, or cotton (woolen rep being used esp. for upholstery).

rep² (rep), *n.* Shortened form of *reputation*: as, upon *rep* (a phrase used in asseveration, in the 18th century); "We can't afford to have our *reps* ruined by being seen with you" (Sinclair Lewis's "Babbitt," v.). [Slang.]

re-pack (rē-pak′), *v. t.* [See *re-*.] To pack again or anew.—**re-pack′er**, *n.*

re-pa-gan-ize (rē-pā′gan-īz), *v. t. or i.* [See *re-*.] To render or become pagan again.—**re-pa″gan-i-za′tion** (-i-zā′shon), *n.*

re-paint (rē-pānt′), *v. t.* [See *re-*.] To paint again.—**re-paint′**, *n.* A part of a picture which has been repainted.

re-pair¹ (rē-pār′), *v. i.* [OF. *repairier*, return, < LL. *repatriare*, return to one's country: see *repatriate*.] To return†; also, to betake one's self or go, as to a place (as, "He soon *repaired* in person to St. Petersburg": De Quincey's "Revolt of the Tartars"); go frequently or customarily, or resort (as, "my little bower . . . whither daily I *repair*," Blackmore's "Lorna Doone," xvi.; "Young men *repaired* to the Druids for education," Froude's "Cæsar," xiv.).—**re-pair′¹**, *n.* [OF. *repaire*.] Repairing, going, or resort, as to a place (often in the phrase 'to make repair'); also, a place repaired to; a resort or haunt. [Archaic.]

re-pair² (rē-pār′), *v. t.* [OF. *reparer* (F. *réparer*), < L. *reparare* (pp. *reparatus*), < *re-*, again, + *parare*, make ready, prepare.] To restore to a good or sound condition after decay or damage, or mend (as, to *repair* a roof, a bridge, a road, or a machine; to *repair* broken jewelry or torn clothing); restore, renovate, or renew by any process of making good, strengthening, supplying, etc. (as, "the Cape (whither he had gone in an attempt to *repair* a broken constitution)," Hardy's "Two on a Tower," xviii.; "to *repair* his numbers thus impair'd," Milton's "Paradise Lost," ix. 144); also, to remedy (damage, harm, etc.); make good (loss, deficiency, etc.); make up for (as, "He . . . bade them not be cast down at a misadventure which they would soon *repair*": Froude's "Cæsar," xxii.); make amends for (as, "She seems desirous to *repair* the wrongs she has done": Miss Burney's "Evelina," i.).—**re-pair′²**, *n.* The act, process, or work of repairing (as, "artisans constantly employed in the erection or *repair* of buildings," Prescott's "Conquest of Mexico," iv. 1; "natives . . . whose ostensible business was the *repair* of broken necklaces," Kipling's "Kim," ix.); an instance, operation, or piece of repairing (esp. in *pl.*: as, while these *repairs* were going on; to make *repairs*; to work on *repairs*); also, the state of having been repaired, or good condition resulting from repairing (as, to keep roads in *repair*; "The Mile End cottages are out of *repair*," Mrs. H. Ward's "Robert Elsmere," xix.); condition (good or bad) with respect to repairing (as, "The property was always maintained in excellent *repair* by its landlords": Arnold Bennett's "These Twain," i.).—**re-pair′a-ble**, *a.* Capable of being repaired.—**re-pair′er**, *n.*—**re-pair′=link**, *n.* A link specially adapted for replacing a broken link in a chain.

re-pand (rē-pand′), *a.* [L. *repandus*, bent back, < *re-*, back, + *pandus*, bent, curved.] In *bot.*, having the margin slightly wavy, as a leaf; slightly wavy, as a margin.

re-pa-per (rē-pā′pėr), *v.t.* [See *re-*.] To paper anew.

rep-a-ra-ble (rep′ạ-rạ-bl), *a.* [L. *reparabilis*.] Capable of being repaired or remedied.

Repand Leaf.

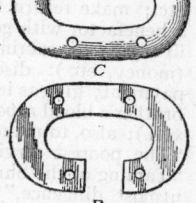

Repair-link for Round-link Chain.—*A*, section by a vertical plane; *B*, view showing the completed link with both halves in place; *C*, top view of one half-section; *D*, top view of other half-section. The interrupted side is open wide enough to pass the solid link adjacent to the repair-link on either side.

rep-a-ra-tion (rep-ạ-rā′shon), *n.* [OF. *reparation* (F. *réparation*), < L. *reparatio(n-)*.] The act of repairing, or the state of being repaired; repair, mending, or restoration, as of what is damaged or impaired (as, "The building stood from century to century . . . without need of *reparation*," Johnson's "Rasselas," i.: now rare); now, the making of amends for wrong or injury done (as, "There is a wrong which admits of no *reparation*": Kipling's "Light That Failed," xiv.); any amends, compensation, or indemnification for wrong or injury done (esp. in *pl.*: as, to demand *reparations* for the devastation of territory in war).—**re-par-a-tive, re-par-a-to-ry** (rḗ-par′a̯-tiv, -tō̞-ri), *a.* Tending to repair; pertaining to or involving reparation.

rep-ar-tee (rep-är-tē′), *n.* [F. *repartie*, prop. pp. fem. of *repartir*, retort, < *re-* (< L. *re-*), back, + *partir*, depart, start, E. *part*, *v.*] A ready and witty reply (as, "Droll allusions, good stories, and smart *repartees* . . . fell thick as hail": Lever's "Harry Lorrequer," xiii.); speech or talk characterized by smartness of reply (as, "framing comments . . . that would be sure to sting and yet leave no opening for *repartee*," H. G. Wells's "Soul of a Bishop," ix.; "Some droll *repartee* passed," Smollett's "Humphry Clinker," June 10); wit shown in smart rejoinder.

re-par-ti-mien-to (rä-pär-tē-myen′tō), *n.*; pl. *-tos* (Sp. -tōs). [Sp., < *repartir* = F. *répartir*: see *repartition*.] A partition or division; an allotment; an assessment; in Spanish America, etc., an allotment of territory, including the right to the labor of the native inhabitants, as granted by the early conquerors to their comrades and followers.

re-par-ti-tion (rē-pär-tish′on), *n.* [F. *répartition*, < *répartir*, divide, apportion, < L. *re-*, again, + *partire*, E. *part*, *v.*] Partition, distribution, or allotment; also, a fresh or additional partition; redistribution.

re-pass (rē-pås′), *v. i.* or *t.* [See *re-*.] To pass back or again.—**re-pas′sage** (-pas′ā̯j), *n.*

re-past (rē-påst′), *n.* [OF. *repast* (F. *repas*), < *repaistre*, < LL. *repascere*, feed again, < L. *re-*, again, + *pascere*, feed.] Food†; also, a quantity of food taken or provided for one occasion of eating (as, to eat a light *repast*; to serve a bountiful *repast*; "The *repast* . . . was made up of a parcel of kickshaws, contrived by a French cook," Smollett's "Humphry Clinker," Sept. 30); also, a taking of food such as serves or is provided for one occasion, or a meal (as, a brief *repast*; during or after the evening *repast*; "Their *repasts* were . . . unceremonious and irregular peckings, begun and finished in a few moments," Arnold Bennett's "Pretty Lady," xvii.); the taking of food, as at a meal (archaic: as, "if, before *repast*, it shall please you to gratify the table with a grace," Shakspere's "Love's Labour's Lost," iv. 2. 160).—**re-past′,** *v.* **I.**† *tr.* To supply or refresh with food; feed: as, "I'll . . . like the . . . pelican, *Repast* them with my blood" (Shakspere's "Hamlet," iv. 5. 147). **II.** *intr.* To feed; feast. [Archaic.]

re-pa-tri-ate (rē-pā′tri-āt), *v.*; *-ated, -ating.* [LL. *repatriatus*, pp. of *repatriare*, < L. *re-*, back, + *patria*, fatherland, native country: cf. *repair*[1].] **I.** *intr.* To return to one's own country. [Rare.] **II.** *tr.* To bring or send back (a person) to his own country; esp., to restore (prisoners of war, refugees, etc.) to the land of citizenship.—**re-pa-tri-a′tion** (-ā′shon), *n.*

re-pay (rē-pā′), *v.*; *-paid, -paying.* [OF. *repaier*, < *re-* (< L. *re-*), back, + *paier*, E. *pay*[2].] **I.** *tr.* To pay (a person, etc.) back for money lent or expended, goods, services, etc.; make return to, or requite, in any way (as, to *repay* a benefactor with gratitude or worthy performance; to feel ill *repaid* for sacrifices made); also, to pay back or refund (money, etc.): discharge or settle (a debt, loan, etc.) by payment; give as in payment or requital (as, "Come, for my brother's blood *repay* thy own": Pope's tr. Homer's "Iliad," xvii.); also, to make repayment or return for, or requite (as, "The poorest service is *repaid* with thanks," Shakspere's "Taming of the Shrew," iv. 3. 45; "I *repaid* his care by the utmost diligence," Howells's "Foregone Conclusion," x.); sometimes, to requite with the like, or return (as, to *repay* a visit or a salutation); also, of things, to yield a recompense or return to (a person) or for (efforts, pains, care, etc.). **II.** *intr.* To make repayment, return, or requital: as, "Vengeance is mine; I will *repay*, saith the Lord" (Rom. xii. 19).—**re-pay′a-ble,** *a.* That may or must be repaid.—**re-pay′er,** *n.*—**re-pay′ment,** *n.* The act of repaying; payment in return for something; requital; return; also, something given or serving to repay.

re-peal (rē-pēl′), *v. t.* [OF. *rapeler* (F. *rappeler*), recall, < *re-* (< L. *re-*), back, + *apeler*, E. *appeal*.] To call back, or recall, as from exile† (as, "I here . . . *repeal* thee home again": Shakspere's "Two Gentlemen of Verona," v. 4. 143); also, to revoke, withdraw, or remove formally or officially (as, to *repeal* a grant; to *repeal* a sentence given; "my banishment *repeal'd*," Shakspere's "Richard II.," iii. 3. 40); now, usually, to revoke or annul (a law, tax, duty, etc.) by express legislative enactment; abrogate; also, to retract (a statement)†; give up or abandon (a feeling, etc.)†.—**re-peal′,** *n.* The act of repealing; revocation; abrogation.—**re-peal′a-ble,** *a.* That may be repealed; revocable.—**re-peal′er,** *n.* One who or that which repeals; a legislative bill, or a clause of a bill, designed to repeal something (U. S.); also, one who advocates the repeal of something.

re-peat (rē-pēt′), *v. t.* [OF. *repeter* (F. *répéter*), < L. *repetere* (pp. *repetitus*), attack again, seek again, return to, repeat, < *re-*, again, + *petere*, fall on, seek.] To seek again†, or return to† (as, "Others in vain from sight of ruin run . . . With loathing eyes *repeat* what they would shun": Dryden's "Annus Mirabilis," cclvii.); also, to do, make, perform, or execute again (as, to *repeat* an action, attempt, or exploit; to *repeat* a ceremony; to *repeat* a passage of music); produce or present again, or reproduce (as, "portraits of the same man four times *repeated*," Amelia B. Edwards's "Thousand Miles up the Nile," xvi.; "Perhaps . . . that dream *repeats* for every one of us . . . the original temptation in Eden," De Quincey's "English Mail-Coach," ii.); go through or undergo again (as, I should not care to *repeat* the experience); also, to say or utter again, or iterate (something one has already said: as, to *repeat* a word for emphasis; "Oft he to her his charge of quick return *Repeated*," Milton's "Paradise Lost," ix. 400); also, to say or utter in reproducing the words, etc., of another (as, to *repeat* a sentence after a teacher; "'Have you heard of her, Philip?' . . . 'Heard of her?' he *repeated*," L. Merrick's "Worldlings," xviii.); reproduce (utterances, sounds, etc.) as an echo, a phonograph, or the like does; also, to tell (something heard) to another or others (as, "He that *repeateth* a matter separateth very friends," Prov. xvii. 9; please don't *repeat* this to anybody); also, to recite (a verse, passage, poem, etc.); relate (a story, etc.); tell one by one, or rehearse (as, to *repeat* the names of the months).—**to repeat itself,** to reproduce or duplicate itself in a later instance: as, history *repeats itself* (said when events of one period are like those of an earlier time); "The incidents of the previous evening were *repeating themselves*" (Mrs. Wharton's "Ethan Frome," iv.).—**to repeat one's self,** to do or say what one has done or said before.—**re-peat′,** *v. i.* To do or say something again; specif., to strike or sound again, when required, the hour (or division of an hour) last past, as a watch or clock; also, to appear again, or recur; also, to vote more than once at the same election (a form of fraud: U. S.).—**re-peat′,** *n.* The act or an act of repeating; repetition; also, something repeated, or due to repeating; a decorative figure, or portion of a pattern, repeated uniformly over the surface of cloth, paper, etc.; a duplicate or reproduction of something; in *com.*, a reorder for goods; in *music*, a passage to be repeated; also, a sign, as a vertical arrangement of dots, calling for the repetition of a passage.—**re-peat′a-ble,** *a.* That may be repeated.—**re-peat′ed,** *p. a.* Done, made, or uttered again, or again and again; renewed; persistent: as, *repeated* attempts; *repeated* assurances or solicitations.—**re-peat′ed-ly,** *adv.* With repetition; more than once; again and again.—**re-peat′er,** *n.* One who or that which repeats; a watch or clock, esp. a watch, which may be made to strike the hour (and sometimes the quarter-hour, etc.) last past; a device which automatically repeats or forwards telegraphic messages; a repeating firearm; a repeating decimal; one who fraudulently votes more than once at an election (U. S.).—**re-peat′ing,** *p. a.* That repeats: as, a *repeating* rifle or firearm (one capable of discharging a number of shots in succession without reloading); a *repeating* decimal (see under *decimal, n.*).

re-pel (rē-pel′), *v.*; *-pelled, -pelling.* [L. *repellere* (pp. *repulsus*), < *re-*, back, + *pellere*, drive.] **I.** *tr.* To drive or force back (an assailant, invader, etc.: as, "A hundred Indians . . . promised aid in *repelling* the French," Bancroft's "Hist. of the U. S.," Amer. Revolution, i. 4); thrust back or away (as, "Hester *repelled* the offered medicine": Hawthorne's "Scarlet Letter," iv.); cast or send back (as, the rocky shores *repel* the waves); resist effectually (an attack, onslaught, etc.: as, "The pond'rous wall and massy bar ... Have ... oft *repell'd* th' invader's shock," Burns's "Address to Edinburgh," 40); also, to force back or away by an inherent physical force, as one body acting upon another (opposed to *attract*); keep off or out, or fail to mix with (as, a surface that *repels* moisture; water and oil *repel* each other); also, fig., to put away from one, or refuse to have to do with (as, to *repel* temptation; "His look *repelled* such vanities," Bulwer-Lytton's "Caxtons," iii. 7); refuse to accept or admit, or reject, repudiate, or deny (as, to *repel* a suggestion; to *repel* a charge or insinuation; "Katy ... *repelled* this opinion with indignation," Cooper's "Spy," x.); repulse or rebuff, or discourage the advances of (a person: as, "But her with stern regard he thus *repell'd*: Out of my sight, thou serpent!" Milton's "Paradise Lost," x. 866); affect forbiddingly, or move to distaste or aversion (as, "Sir Wilfrid ... was half thrilled, half *repelled* by the flashing energy of the face beside him": Mrs. H. Ward's "Lady Rose's Daughter," iv.). **II.** *intr.* To repel something; act with a force that drives or keeps away something; fig., to cause distaste or aversion.—**re-pel′lent. I.** *a.* Repelling; driving back; fig., forbidding, repulsive; in *med.*, serving to prevent or reduce swellings, tumors, etc. **II.** *n.* Something that repels; a kind of waterproof cloth; in *med.*, a repellent medicine or agent. —**re-pel′lence, re-pel′len-cy,** *n.*—**re-pel′lent-ly,** *adv.*—**re-pel′ler,** *n.*

re-pent¹ (rē′pent), *a.* [L. *repens* (*repent-*), ppr. of *repere*, creep.] In *bot.*, creeping; growing along the ground, or horizontally beneath the surface, and rooting progressively; in *zoöl.*, reptant.

re-pent² (rē-pent′), *v.* [OF. F. *repentir*, refl., < L. *re-*, back, again, + *pænitere*, repent: cf. *penitent.*] **I.** *tr.* To remember or regard with self-reproach, compunction, or contrition (as, to *repent* one's injustice to another; to *repent* one's wrong-doing or sin); feel sorry for, or regret (as, "I had soon reason to *repent* those foolish words," Swift's "Gulliver's Travels," iii. 1; to *repent* one's choice); also, reflexively, to feel (one's self) to be repentant (archaic: as, "I *repent* me of all I did," Tennyson's "Edward Gray"); also, impersonally, to cause (one) to be repentant (archaic: as, " 'It *repents* me that I did not give a rupee to the shrine,' said the lama," Kipling's "Kim," iii.). **II.** *intr.* To feel self-reproach, compunction, or contrition for past conduct (often with *of*: as, "Sin not; but if you do, take heed to *repent* of it like Jonah," H. Melville's "Moby-Dick," ix.); feel regret, or change one's mind, with regard to past action in consequence of dissatisfaction with it or its results (often with *of*: as, "Those who had been most eager to trade, were readiest to *repent* of their bargains," Amelia B. Edwards's "Thousand Miles up the Nile," xiv.); specif., to feel such sorrow for sin or fault as disposes one to amendment of life (as, "Except ye *repent*, ye shall all likewise perish": Luke, xiii. 3); be penitent.—**re-pent′ance,** *n.* The act or fact of repenting; compunction or contrition for wrong-doing or sin, or the state of being penitent; regret for any past action.— **re-pent′ant,** *a.* Repenting, or experiencing repentance; penitent; regretful for past action; also, characterized by or showing repentance (as, a *repentant* mood; "my *repentant* tears," Shakspere's "Richard III.," i. 2. 216).—**re-pent′-ant-ly,** *adv.*—**re-pent′er,** *n.*

re-peo-ple (rē-pē′pl), *v. t.* [See *re-*.] To people anew; furnish again with people; also, to restock with animals.

re-per-cuss (rē-pėr-kus′), *v. t.* [L. *repercussus*, pp. of *repercutere*, < *re-*, back, + *percutere*, strike: see *percuss.*] To beat or drive back; hence, to reflect (light); reverberate (sound). [Obs. or rare.]—**re-per-cus′sion** (-kush′on), *n.* [L. *repercussio(n-).*] The act of driving back; the state of being driven back by a resisting body; rebounding or recoil; reflection of light, etc.; reverberation or echo; in *med.*, same as *ballottement*; in *music*, a reiteration or repetition, as of a tone or chord.—**re-per-cus′sive** (-kus′iv), *a.* Causing repercussion; reverberating; also, reflected; reverberated.

rep-er-toire, ré-per-toire (rep′ėr-twor, rā-per-twor), *n.* [F. *répertoire*: see *repertory.*] The list of dramas, operas,

parts, pieces, etc., which a company, or an actor, singer, or the like, is prepared to present or perform.

rep-er-to-ry (rep′ėr-tō-ri), *n.*; pl. *-ries* (-riz). [= F. *répertoire*, < LL. *repertorium*, inventory, catalogue, < L. *reperire*, find again, find: cf. *inventory.*] A catalogue or list of things; esp., a repertoire; also, a store or stock of things available; a storehouse.

rep-e-tend (rep′ē-tend or rep-ē-tend′), *n.* [L. *repetendus*, gerundive of *repetere*, E. *repeat.*] That part of a repeating or circulating decimal which is repeated indefinitely.

rep-e-ti-tion (rep-ē-tish′on), *n.* [OF. *repeticion* (F. *répétition*), < L. *repetitio(n-)*, < *repetere*, E. *repeat.*] The act of repeating; repeated action, performance, production, or presentation; recurrence; repeated utterance, or iteration; recital; a recitation, as of a lesson (Eng.: as, "The lower classes were called by the teachers; *repetitions* in history, grammar, &c., went on for an hour," C. Brontë's "Jane Eyre," v.); also, something made by or resulting from repeating (as, "Nature is an endless combination and *repetition* of a very few laws": Emerson's "Essays," History); a reproduction, copy, or replica of something.—**rep-e-ti′tion-a-ry** (-ā-ri), *a.* Of the nature of repetition; characterized by repetition.—**rep-e-ti′tious** (-tish′us), *a.* Abounding in repetition; tediously iterative.—**re-pet-i-tive** (rē-pet′i-tiv), *a.* Repetitionary.

re-pine (rē-pīn′), *v. i.*; *-pined, -pining.* [Appar. < *re-* + *pine²*.] To be fretfully discontented; fret; complain: as, to *repine* at one's lot.—**re-pin′er** (-pī′nėr), *n.*—**re-pin′ing-ly,** *adv.*

re-place (rē-plās′), *v. t.* [See *re-*.] To restore to a former or the proper place (as, "A hermit ... *replac'd* his book Within its customary nook": Cowper's "Moralizer Corrected," 7); also, to restore, return, or make good, as something borrowed; also, to provide a substitute or equivalent in the place of (as, a person or thing hard to *replace*); fill the place of with or by somebody or something else (as, "A conspiracy was carefully engineered to *replace* the Directory by three Consuls": H. G. Wells's "Outline of History," xxxviii. § 2); also, to take the place of, or become a substitute or equivalent for (a person or thing: as, "The successor ... cannot be ready to *replace* me for three months," C. Brontë's "Jane Eyre," xxxii.).—**re-place′a-ble,** *a.* Capable of being replaced.—**re-place′ment,** *n.* The act of replacing, or the state of being replaced; also, that which replaces, as a fresh supply of troops for replacing others; in *crystal.*, the replacing of an angle or edge by one face or more.—**re-pla′cer** (-plā′sėr), *n.*

re-plant (rē-plant′), *v. t.* [See *re-*.] To plant again.

re-plead (rē-plēd′), *v. i.* or *t.* [See *re-*.] To plead again.—**re-plead′er,** *n.* In *law*, a second pleading; also, the right or privilege of pleading again.

Replacement of the Solid Angles of a Cube.

re-plen-ish (rē-plen′ish), *v. t.* [OF. *re-plenir* (*repleniss-*), < *re-* (< L. *re-*), again, + *plenir*, fill: see *plenish.*] To fill, or supply abundantly, with something (obs. or archaic); stock, as with persons or animals (obs. or archaic); also, to occupy fully†; occupy as inhabitants do†, or people† (as, "Daily they grow, and daily forth are sent Into the world, it to *replenish* more": Spenser's "Faerie Queene," iii. 6. 36); also, to bring back to a state of fullness or completeness, as by supplying what is lacking (as, to *replenish* one's purse; to *replenish* a stock of goods); often, to supply (a fire, stove, etc.) with fresh fuel (as, "He turned to *replenish* the fire from a bucket": Arnold Bennett's "The Old Adam," ii.); also, to fill again or anew (as, "My glass has been empty for a considerable time; perhaps ... you will deign to *replenish* it?" Borrow's "Romany Rye," iii.); also, to render complete or perfect† (as, "the most *replenish'd* villain in the world": Shakspere's "Winter's Tale," ii. 1. 79).—**re-plen′-ish-er,** *n.*—**re-plen′ish-ment,** *n.*

re-plete (rē-plēt′), *a.* [OF. F. *replet*, < L. *repletus*, pp. of *replere*, refill, fill up, < *re-*, again, + *plere*, fill.] Filled, as with something (as, "A golden ewer ... *Replete* with water": Pope's tr. Homer's "Odyssey," xv.); abundantly supplied (*with*: as, "a little creek *replete* with frogs and young turtles," Parkman's "Oregon Trail," ii.); hence, in general, abounding, or abundantly provided, invested, or imbued (*with*: as, "London, in her idea, was . . . *replete* with temptations," H. Mackenzie's "Man of Feeling," xiv.; "a comedy . . . *replete* with wit and mirth," Sheridan's "Critic," i. 1); also, filled to satisfaction, sated, or gorged, with food or drink (as, "The old men would sit at their tables, *replete* and sleepy": H. G. Wells's "Mr. Britling," ii. 4. § 8); also, complete or perfect (obs. or rare).—**re-plete′ness**, *n.*

re-ple-tion (rḗ-plḗ′shǫn), *n.* [ŌF. *repletion* (F. *réplétion*), < LL. *repletio(n-)*, < L. *replere*: see *replete*.] The act of making replete (obs. or rare); also, the condition of being replete, or of being filled up, or filled to excess, with something; fullness, or superabundant fullness; often, overfullness resulting from eating or drinking to excess; in *pathol.*, plethora.

re-plev-i-a-ble (rḗ-plev′i-ạ-bl), *a.* Same as *replevisable*.

re-plev-in (rḗ-plev′in), *n.* [AF. *replevine*, < OF. *replevir*: see *replevy*.] In *law*, the recovery of goods or chattels taken or detained, on security given that the case shall be tried at law and the goods returned in case of an adverse decision; the writ by which goods are so recovered, or the action arising therefrom.—**re-plev′in**, *v. t.* To replevy.

re-plev-i-sa-ble (rḗ-plev′i-sạ-bl), *a.* [AF. *replevissable*, < OF. *replevir*: see *replevy*.] In *law*, capable of being replevied.

re-plev-y (rḗ-plev′i), *v. t.*; -*plevied*, -*plevying*. [OF. *replevir*, < re- (< L. re-), back, + *plevir*, < ML. *plevire*, to pledge: see *pledge*, *n.*] In *law*, to recover by replevin.

rep-li-ca (rep′li-kạ), *n.*; pl. -*cas* (-käz). [It., < *replicare*, repeat, < L. *replicare*: see *reply*.] A copy or reproduction of a work of art, esp. one by the maker of the original; hence, in general, a copy or reproduction (as, "looking alternately at a suit of stage armour and its *replica* in his picture": W. De Morgan's "Alice-for-Short," x.).

rep-li-cate (rep′li-kāt), *v. t.*; -*cated*, -*cating*. [L. *replicatus*, pp. of *replicare*: see *reply*.] To fold or bend back; also, to reproduce or copy; also, to say in reply.—**rep′li-cate**, *a.* Folded; folded back on itself, as a leaf.—**rep-li-ca′tion** (-kā′shǫn), *n.* [L. *replicatio(n-).*] A folding back; a fold; also, a reproducing or copying; a copy; also, replying; a reply; specif., a reply to an answer, esp. (in *law*) the reply of the plaintiff or complainant to the defendant's plea or answer; also, reverberation or echo.

re-pli-er (rḗ-plī′ėr), *n.* [See *reply*, *v.*] One who replies.

re-ply (rḗ-plī′), *v.*; -*plied*, -*plying*. [OF. F. *replier*, < L. *replicare* (pp. *replicatus*), fold back, turn back, repeat, reply, < re-, back, + *plicare*, fold: see *ply*.] **I.** *tr.* To fold back†; also, to return as an answer (as, "He . . . *replied* that no human consideration should tempt him to resume the gift which he had conferred": Gibbon's "Decline and Fall of the Roman Empire," xlix.). **II.** *intr.* To make answer in words or writing; answer; respond; also, to respond by some action, performance, etc. (as, "He sang his song, and I *replied* with mine": Tennyson's "Audley Court," 55); often, to return gun-fire (as, to *reply* to the enemy's fire); sometimes, to return a sound, or echo (as, "The nymph exulting fills with shouts the sky; The walls, the woods, and long canals *reply*": Pope's "Rape of the Lock," iii. 100); in *law*, to answer a defendant's plea.—**re-ply′**, *n.*; pl. -*plies* (-plīz′). The act of replying or responding; also, an answer or response in words or writing; also, a response made by some action, performance, etc.

re-pop-u-late (rē-pop′ū-lāt), *v. t.* [See *re-*.] To populate anew; repeople.—**re-pop-u-la′tion** (-lā′shǫn), *n.*

re-port (rḗ-pōrt′), *v.* [OF. F. *reporter*, carry back, carry, < L. *reportare*, carry or bring back, report, < re-, back, + *portare*, carry.] **I.** *tr.* To carry and repeat as an answer or message (as, "The voice of God To mortal ear is dreadful: they beseech That Moses might *report* to them his will": Milton's "Paradise Lost," xii. 237); repeat as what one has heard (as, "Who knows how he may *report* Thy words?" Milton's "Samson Agonistes," 1350); also, to relate as what has been learned by observation or investigation (as, "He would . . . return, and *report* what he had seen": Irving's "Captain Bonneville," xxvii.); also, to make report of, or announce (as, "Boat after boat *reported* full crews aboard," Kipling's "Captains Courageous," viii.; "The midshipman, who was looking round with his glass . . . *reported* three

gun-boats," Marryat's "Peter Simple," lviii.); also, to give or render a formal account or statement of (a matter or thing); state (something) in such an account (as, to *report* a deficit); make a formal report on (a bill, etc., officially referred); also, to lay a charge against (a person), as to a superior; also, to make known the presence or whereabouts of (one's self), or present (one's self), to a person in authority, as in accordance with requirements (as, "We . . . went on shore with the lieutenant to *report* ourselves to the admiral": Marryat's "Peter Simple," xxvi.); also, to take down (a speech, etc.) in writing; write an account of (a meeting, event, etc.), as for publication in a newspaper; also, to relate or tell (as, "Came The Lord of Astolat out, to whom the prince *Reported* who he was": Tennyson's "Lancelot and Elaine," 624); often, to tell or say in common or public talk (esp. in the passive: as, "It is *reported* thou didst eat strange flesh," Shakspere's "Antony and Cleopatra," i. 4. 67). **II.** *intr.* To make a report; draw up or submit a formal report; also, to act as a reporter, as for a newspaper; also, to report one's self, as to one in authority; present one's self duly, as at a place.—**re-port′**, *n.* An account brought back or presented (as, "This *report*, These tidings carry to the anointed King": Milton's "Paradise Lost," v. 869); a statement submitted as the result of investigation; a formal statement of facts concerning any matter on which information is required or due; statement or announcement made in reporting (as, to make *report* of changes observed); also, a statement of a judicial opinion or decision, or of a case argued and determined in a court of justice; also, an account of a speech, debate, meeting, etc., esp. as taken down for publication; also, in general, an account or statement (as, "We know, on Valentine's *report*, You are already Love's firm votary": Shakspere's "Two Gentlemen of Verona," iii. 2. 57); also, a statement generally made or circulated, or a rumor (as, "Even the common *reports* of the village would be some enlightenment to the darkness I was in about her": G. MacDonald's "Annals of a Quiet Neighbourhood," iv.); rumor, or common talk (as, "My brother Jaques he keeps at school, and *report* speaks goldenly of his profit": Shakspere's "As You Like It," i. 1. 6); also, repute or reputation (as, "a just man . . . and of good *report* among all the nation of the Jews": Acts, x. 22); also, a loud noise, esp. the sound of an explosion (as, "The still solitudes had echoed . . . with the *reports* of his gun": Irving's "Sketch-Book," Rip Van Winkle).—**re-port′a-ble**, *a.* Capable or worthy of being reported.—**re-port′er**, *n.* One who reports; one who prepares official reports, as of legal or legislative proceedings; one employed to seek and report news for a newspaper.—**re-por-to-ri-al** (rē-pǫr-tō′ri-ạl), *a.* Of or pertaining to a reporter.

re-po-sal (rḗ-pō′zạl), *n.* The act of reposing.

re-pose¹ (rḗ-pōz′), *v. t.*; -*posed*, -*posing*. [ME. *repose*: see *re-* and *pose¹*.] To put back† or replace†; also, to deposit, as in a place or repository (obs. or rare); fig., to put (confidence, trust, etc.) in a person or thing; place or vest (power, control, etc.) in a person or body.

re-pose² (rḗ-pōz′), *v.*; -*posed*, -*posing*. [OF. F. *reposer*, < ML. *repausare*, < L. re-, again, + *pausare*, halt, cease, LL. rest: cf. *pose¹*.] **I.** *tr.* To lay to rest; rest; refresh by rest: often used reflexively: as, "We stopped at a little public-house where we *reposed* ourselves" (R. Graves's "Spiritual Quixote," iii. 15). **II.** *intr.* To lie at rest (as, "Mr. Travers *reposed* at ease in a low bed-place": J. Conrad's "Rescue," vi. 9); take rest; also, to rest from exertion or toil (as, "They *reposed* during the winter season in the harbours of Greece": Gibbon's "Decline and Fall of the Roman Empire," xli.); be at peace or in tranquillity, as a land; lie in quiet (as, "The winds were hushed, and all nature *reposed* under the eye of the quiet moon": Mrs. Shelley's "Frankenstein," xx.); also, to lie or rest on something (as, "His right cheek *Reposing* on a cushion": Shakspere's "Cymbeline," iv. 2. 212); also, to depend or rely on a person or thing (as, "They had received him with a show of kindness . . . and, *reposing* on this, he had been decoyed into the snare": Prescott's "Conquest of Mexico," iii. 7).—**re-pose′²**, *n.* [OF. F. *repos*.] The state of reposing or resting; rest; sleep; also, restful ease after exertion or toil; peace or tranquillity (as, "to restore order and repose to an

Empire so great and so distracted as ours": Burke's "Conciliation with the Colonies"); dignified calmness, as of manner or demeanor (as, "Her manners had not that *repose* Which stamps the caste of Vere de Vere": Tennyson's "Lady Clara Vere de Vere"); absence of movement, animation, etc., or quiet (as, "Her face, which even in *repose* had a true nobility, now was alight with . . . inspiration": W. Churchill's "Coniston," ii. 5); quiescence or inactivity (as, a volcano in *repose*); in *painting*, etc., harmonious arrangement of colors, figures, etc., producing a restful effect upon the eye.—**re-pose′ful**, *a.* Full of repose; calm; quiet: as, "his deliberation suggesting a mighty force like the *reposeful* attitude of a lion" (J. Conrad's "Rover," x.).— **re-pose′ful-ly**, *adv.*—**re-pose′ful-ness**, *n.*—**re-pos′er** (-pō′zėr), *n.*

re-pos-it (rẹ-poz′it), *v. t.* [L. *repositus*, pp. of *reponere*, < *re-*, back, + *ponere*, place, put.] To put back; replace; also, to place or deposit (as, "They . . . examined the chest in which the body of the founder is supposed to have been *reposited*": Johnson's "Rasselas," xxxii.); lay up or store.— **re-po-si-tion** (rē-pọ-zish′ọn), *n.* [LL. *repositio(n-).*] Replacement, as of a bone; also, the act of depositing or storing.

re-pos-i-to-ry (rẹ-poz′i-tọ-ri), *n.; pl.* -ries (-riz). [L. *repositorium*, < *reponere* (pp. *repositus*): see *reposit*.] A receptacle or place where things are deposited or stored (as, "Somebody must attend on Miss Bertram's part, when the *repositories* of the deceased are opened": Scott's "Guy Mannering," xxxv.); a place in which a dead body is deposited; a place where things are kept or offered for sale, or a warehouse, store, or shop; also, a person to whom something is intrusted or confided (as, "Pepper alone had been the *repository* of my secret": Aldrich's "Story of a Bad Boy," xx.).

re-pos-sess (rē-pọ-zes′), *v. t.* [See *re-*.] To possess again; regain possession of; also, to put again in possession of something.—**re-pos-ses′sion** (-zesh′ọn), *n.*

re-post (rẹ-pōst′), *n.* and *v.* Same as *riposte.*

re-pous-sé (rẹ-pö-sā′). [F., pp. of *repousser*, push back, < *re-* (< L. *re-*), back, + *pousser*, E. *push.*] **I.** *a.* Raised in relief, as a design on thin metal, by hammering on the reverse side; ornamented or made in this manner, as work. **II.** *n.* Repoussé work.

repped (rept), *a.* Transversely corded, like rep.

rep-re-hend (rep-rẹ-hend′), *v. t.* [L. *reprehendere* (pp. *reprehensus*), hold back, seize, check, reprove, < *re-*, back, + *prehendere*, seize.] To reprove (a person), as for fault; reprimand; rebuke; also, to censure (a thing, action, etc.) as being blameworthy.

rep-re-hen-si-ble (rep-rẹ-hen′si-bl), *a.* [LL. *reprehensibilis.*] Deserving to be reprehended; blameworthy: as, "These proceedings, however *reprehensible*, had yet the semblance of legality" (Macaulay's "Hist. of Eng.," ii.).—**rep-re-hen-si-bil′i-ty** (-bil′i-ti), **rep-re-hen′si-ble-ness**, *n.*—**rep-re-hen′si-bly**, *adv.*

rep-re-hen-sion (rep-rẹ-hen′shọn), *n.* [L. *reprehensio(n-).*] The act of reprehending; reproof; censure.—**rep-re-hen′sive** (-siv), *a.* Of the nature of or containing reprehension.

re-pre-sent[1] (rē-prẹ-zent′), *v. t.* [See *re-*.] To present again or anew. Also written *re-present.*

rep-re-sent[2] (rep-rẹ-zent′), *v. t.* [OF. *representer* (F. *représenter*), < L. *repræsentare* (pp. *repræsentatus*), bring back, bring before one, show, < *re-*, back, + *præsentare*, E. *present*[2].] To present (one's self or another) before a person†; also, to present to the eye, esp. by a picture, image, or the like; portray, depict, or figure (as, "My wife desired to be *represented* as Venus": Goldsmith's "Vicar of Wakefield," xvi.); present the likeness or semblance of, as a picture, image, or the like does (as, "These statues . . . *represent* Rameses II. and . . . his queen": Amelia B. Edwards's

Gold Etui, decorated with Repoussé Work; time of Louis XV.

"Thousand Miles up the Nile," xvi.); also, to present to the mind; place clearly before or picture to the mind (as, his fears *represented* to him the perils of the journey; the imagination *represents* a scene); also, to present in words, set forth, describe, or state (as, to *represent* the facts in a case; "He found means . . . to send . . . a full account of my story to a merchant at London, who *represented* it effectually to her," Defoe's "Robinson Crusoe," i. 3); set forth or describe as having a particular character (with *as*, *to be*, etc.: as, "He *represented* his parsimony as disinterestedness because it only enriched his children," Bancroft's "Hist. of the U. S.," Amer. Revolution, ii. 3; we found him all that he was *represented* to be); often, to set forth clearly or earnestly with a view to influencing opinion or action or making protest (as, "The Jesuits strongly *represented* to the King the danger which he had so narrowly escaped": Macaulay's "Hist. of Eng.," vi.); also, to present, produce, or perform (a play, etc.), as on the stage; personate (a character, etc.), as in acting; also, to express or designate by some term, character, symbol, or the like (as, to *represent* ideas by words, or speech by writing; to *represent* musical sounds by notes; to *represent* an unknown quantity by x); serve to express or designate, or stand for or denote, as a word, symbol, or the like does; symbolize; also, to stand or act in the place of, as a substitute, proxy, or agent does; speak and act for by delegated authority (as, to *represent* a principal in negotiations; to *represent* one's government in a foreign country); specif., to act for (a constituency, etc.) by deputed right in exercising a voice in legislation or government (often in the passive with special reference to the participation in government thus enjoyed: as, "The Colonies . . . complain that they are taxed in a Parliament in which they are not *represented*," Burke's "Conciliation with the Colonies"); also, to serve as an example or specimen of, or exemplify (as, a genus *represented* by two species); be the equivalent of, correspond to, or replace (as, the llama *represents* the camel in the New World).—**rep-re-sent′a-ble**, *a.* Capable of being represented.

rep-re-sen-ta-tion (rep″rẹ-zen-tā′shọn), *n.* [OF. *representation* (F. *représentation*), < L. *repræsentatio(n-).*] The act of representing, or the state of being represented; portrayal, picturing, or other rendering in visible form, or a picture, figure, statue, or the like made to represent something; presentation to the mind, or a mental image or idea presented; presentation in words, or a description or statement, as of things true or alleged (often in *pl.*: as, "All *representations* of the smallness of his chance were fruitless," Kingsley's "Alton Locke," xxi.; glowing *representations* of advantages offered; to deceive by false *representations*); a statement of facts, reasons, etc., made in appealing or protesting, or a protest or remonstrance (as, "He had made *representations* to the local authority to get the footpath closed, but in vain": H. G. Wells's "Bealby," vii.); the production, or a performance, of a play or the like, as on the stage; expression or designation by some term, character, symbol, or the like; the representing of a person, body, business house, district, or the like by an agent, deputy, or representative; the state or fact of being so represented (as, to demand *representation* on a directing board; a house without *representation* in a certain territory); specif., the state, fact, or right of being represented by delegates having a voice in legislation or government (as, popular *representation*, representation of the people by their own chosen delegates having a voice in legislation, etc.); also, the body or number of representatives, as of a constituency.—**rep″re-sen-ta′tion-al**, *a.*—**rep″re-sen-ta′tion-al-ly**, *adv.*

rep-re-sen-ta-tive (rep-rẹ-zen′tạ-tiv). [OF. *representatif* (F. *représentatif*), < ML. *repræsentativus.*] **I.** *a.* Serving to represent; representing; esp., standing or acting for another or others; specif., representing a constituency or community or the people generally in legislation or government (as, a *representative* delegation; a *representative* assembly); characterized by, founded on, or pertaining to representation of the people in government (as, "The government was a *representative* one, in which all those who had the inclination possessed, in one mode or another, a voice," Motley's "Dutch Republic," iv. 4; the *representative* system or principle of government); also, exemplifying a

---

(variable) ḏ as d or j, ş as s or sh, ṯ as t or ch, ẓ as z or zh; *o*, F. cloche; ü, F. menu; ċh, Sc. loch; ṅ, F. bonbon; ′, primary accent; ″, secondary accent; †, obsolete; <, from; +, and; =, equals. See also lists at beginning of book.

class, or typical (as, the *representative* genus of a family; "the *representative* Pharaoh of a line of monarchs whose history covers a space of fifty centuries," Amelia B. Edwards's "Thousand Miles up the Nile," xv.); corresponding to or replacing some other species or the like, as in a different locality. **II.** *n.* One who or that which represents another or others; esp., an agent or deputy (as, a legal or a business *representative*); specif., one who represents a constituency or community in a legislative body; in the U. S., a member of the lower house in Congress ('House of Representatives') or in a State legislature; also, an example or specimen; a type; a typical embodiment, as of some quality.—**rep-re-sen'ta-tive-ly**, *adv.*—**rep-re-sen'ta-tive-ness**, *n.*

rep-re-sent-er (rep-rę-zen'tėr), *n.* One who represents.

re-press¹ (rē-pres'), *v. t.* [See *re-*.] To press again. Also written *re-press*.

re-press² (rę-pres'), *v. t.* [L. *repressus*, pp. of *reprimere*, < *re-*, back, + *premere*, press.] To press or drive back†; also, to reduce (persons) to subjection (as, "Charlemagne instantly prepared to *repress* his rebellious subjects": G. P. R. James's "Hist. of Charlemagne," ii.); put down or quell (sedition, disorder, etc.); keep down or suppress (anything objectionable: as, "Thus long succeeding critics justly reign'd, Licence *repress'd*, and useful laws ordain'd," Pope's "Essay on Criticism," 682); also, to restrain or check (a person, or his passions, tendencies, etc.: as, "The unseasonableness of the hour did not *repress* the impatience of the islanders," H. Melville's "Typee," xxvii.); often, to keep under control or suppress (one's own desires, feelings, etc.: as, "They rigorously *repress* the instinctive feeling as a temptation of the evil one," W. H. Hudson's "Far Away and Long Ago," xvii.); keep back or check (a smile, thought, action, tears, etc.: as, "To save his life he could not *repress* a chuckle," Tarkington's "Gentleman from Indiana," ix.; "The boy could not *repress* a start," Dickens's "Oliver Twist," xx.); also, in general, to keep back or down, or keep from coming into action or manifestation (as, "Chill penury *repress'd* their noble rage," Gray's "Elegy." xiii.; "a motive to *repress* speculative inquiry," Bancroft's "Hist. of the U.S.," Amer. Revolution, i. 6).—**re-press'er**, *n.*—**re-press'i-ble**, *a.* That may be repressed.—**re-pres'sion** (-presh'ọn), *n.* The act or an act of repressing; the state of being repressed.—**re-pres'sive** (-pres'iv), *a.* Tending or serving to repress.—**re-pres'sive-ly**, *adv.*—**re-pres'sive-ness**, *n.*—**re-pres'sor**, *n.*

re-priev-al (rę-prē'val), *n.* A reprieving; reprieve.

re-prieve (rę-prēv'), *v. t.*; *-prieved*, *-prieving*. [Earlier *reprie*, *repry*, perhaps < OF. *repris*, pp. of *reprendre*, take back, also reprehend, reprove (see *reprisal*), the modern E. form being appar. due to *reprieve*, obs. var. of *reprove*.] To take back or remand to prison†; also, to respite (a person) from impending punishment; esp., to grant a delay of the execution of (a condemned person: as, "You shall not die: She has *reprieved* you," Swinburne's "Chastelard," v. 2); hence, to relieve temporarily from any evil; also, to postpone (punishment, etc.)†.—**re-prieve'**, *n.* The act of reprieving, or the state of being reprieved; a respite from impending punishment, esp. from execution of a sentence of death; a warrant authorizing this; in general, respite, or a temporary relief, from some evil or trouble.

rep-ri-mand (rep'ri-mȧnd), *n.* [F. *réprimande*, < L. *reprimendus*, gerundive of *reprimere*, press back, check: see *repress²*.] A severe reproof, esp. one given formally as by a person in authority (as, "the sharp *reprimands* that were sure to follow every act of negligence": J. F. Kirk's "Charles the Bold," iii. 1); also, reprehension, private or public (as, words of *reprimand*).—**rep-ri-mand** (rep-ri-mȧnd' or rep'ri-mȧnd), *v. t.* To address a reprimand to; reprove severely, esp. in a formal way: as, "Captain Wilson sent for the master, and *reprimanded* him for his oppression" (Marryat's "Mr. Midshipman Easy," xiii.).—**rep-ri-mand'er**, *n.*

re-print (rē-print'), *v. t.* [See *re-*.] To print again; print a new impression of.—**re-print** (rē'print or rē-print'), *n.* A reproduction in print of matter already printed; a new impression, without alteration, of any printed work.—**re-print'er**, *n.*

re-pri-sal (rę-prī'zạl), *n.* [OF. *reprisaille* (F. *représaille*), ult. < L. *reprendere*, *reprehendere*, seize (see *reprehend*):

cf. OF. *repris*, pp. of *reprendre*, take back, < L. *reprendere*.] The act or practice of using force, short of war, against another nation, to secure redress of a grievance, orig. the forcible seizing of its property or subjects for this purpose; an instance of this; also, the infliction of similar or severer injury on the enemy in warfare, in retaliation for some injury, as by the punishment or execution of prisoners of war; in general, retaliation, or an act of retaliation; also, a return or compensation (now rare).—**letters of marque and reprisal.** See *marque*.

re-prise (rę-prīz'), *n.* [OF. F. *reprise*, < *reprendre*, take back: see *reprisal*.] In *law*, an annual deduction, duty, or payment out of a manor or estate, as an annuity or the like (usually in *pl.*); in *music*, a repetition; esp., a return to the first theme or subject.

re-pris-ti-nate (rę-pris'ti-nāt), *v.t.*; *-nated*, *-nating*. [See *re-* and *pristine*.] To restore to the pristine state.—**re-pris-ti-na'tion** (-nā'shọn), *n.*

re-proach (rę-prōch'), *v. t.* [OF. *reprochier* (F. *reprocher*), prob. < L. *re-*, back, again, + *propius*, compar. of *prope*, near: cf. *approach*.] To address words, looks, etc., to (a person, etc.) by way of imputing fault; upbraid; blame; censure; often, to upbraid (*with*: as, "It is common to *reproach* the Southern leaders with reckless folly," Charnwood's "Abraham Lincoln," vi.); sometimes, to reprove or censure (an act, etc.: as, "Mezentius . . . *reproach'd* their shameful flight," Dryden's tr. Virgil's "Æneid," x. 976); also, to impute (a thing) as a fault (now rare); also, to be a cause of blame or discredit to (as, "Imputation, For that he knew you, might *reproach* your life": Shakspere's "Measure for Measure," v. 1. 426).—**re-proach'**, *n.* The act of reproaching or upbraiding, or blame or censure conveyed by reproaching (as, a term of *reproach*; "Your conduct was . . . above *reproach*," J. Conrad's "Rescue," v. 1); an expression of upbraiding, censure, or reproof (as, "Mr. Travers . . . overwhelmed him with *reproaches*": J. Conrad's "Rescue," iii. 2); also, disgrace, discredit, or blame incurred or sustained (as, to bring *reproach* on one's family; "She . . . bare a son; and said, God hath taken away my *reproach*," Gen. xxx. 23); also, a cause or occasion of disgrace or discredit (as, "I think it is a *reproach* on me . . . to have lived so long without making an excursion to the other side of the Tweed": Smollett's "Humphry Clinker," May 8); also, an object of scorn or contempt†.—**re-proach'a-ble**, *a.* Deserving of or open to reproach.—**re-proach'er**, *n.*—**re-proach'ful**, *a.* Full of or expressing reproach or censure; upbraiding; also, deserving of reproach or censure†; shameful† or disgraceful†.—**re-proach'ful-ly**, *adv.*—**re-proach'ful-ness**, *n.*—**re-proach'ing-ly**, *adv.*—**re-proach'less**, *a.* Without reproach; irreproachable.

rep-ro-ba-cy (rep'rō-bạ-si), *n.* Reprobate state.

rep-ro-bate (rep'rō-bāt), *v. t.*; *-bated*, *-bating*. [LL. *reprobatus*, pp. of *reprobare*, disapprove, reject, < L. *re-*, back, + *probare*, try, approve: see *prove*, and cf. *reprove*.] To disapprove, condemn, or censure (as, "This is what my uncle *reprobates*, as a monstrous jumble of heterogeneous principles": Smollett's "Humphry Clinker," April 30); also, to reject or refuse; specif., of God, to reject (a person), as for sin; exclude from the number of the elect, or from salvation.—**rep'ro-bate. I.** *a.* Disapproved, condemned, or rejected (now rare); specif., rejected by God, or excluded from the number of the elect (as, "Had it not been decided from all eternity? We were elect, or we were *reprobate*": Kingsley's "Alton Locke," i.); hence, morally abandoned; unprincipled; bad. **II.** *n.* A reprobate person; one rejected by God or beyond hope of salvation; an abandoned, unprincipled, graceless, or reprehensible person (as, "a penniless drunken *reprobate*," Watts-Dunton's "Aylwin," ii. 3; "Within a few weeks the incorrigible *reprobate* was at his tricks again," Lytton Strachey's "Queen Victoria," v.).—**rep-ro-ba'tion** (-bā'shọn), *n.* [LL. *reprobatio(n-)*.] The act of reprobating, or the state of being reprobated; disapproval, condemnation, or censure (as, "a people who were coming to regard their fundamental institution [slavery] with growing *reprobation*," Charnwood's "Abraham Lincoln," vi.; "dispensing *reprobation* for misconduct," G. Meredith's "Diana of the Crossways," xxi.); rejection; in *theol.*; rejection by God, as of persons not admitted to the number of the elect or to salvation.—**rep′ro-ba-tive** (-bạ-tiv), *a.* Reprobating; expressing reprobation.—**rep′ro-ba-tive-ly**, *adv.*

re-pro-duce (rē-prọ-dūs′), *v.* [See *re-.*] **I.** *tr.* To produce again or anew by natural process (as, to *reproduce* a lost part or organ); also, to produce new individuals of (some animal or plant kind) by some process of generation or propagation, sexual or asexual (as, sexed animals *reproduce* their kind by fecundation; "the various modes in which plants *reproduce* their species," Encyc. Brit., 11th ed., XXIII. 120); produce another or more like (itself) by such a process, as an animal or plant does; cause or foster the reproduction of (animals or plants); also, to produce, form, make, or bring about again or anew in any manner (as, to *reproduce* a thing from its fragments or remains; to *reproduce* sound; to *reproduce* the conditions of an earlier period; to *reproduce* a former success); call up again before the mind or represent mentally (a past scene, etc.), as by the aid of memory or imagination; bring out or present again, or repeat (as, "He caught up the remark and *reproduced* it as his own": S. Butler's "Way of All Flesh," xlvi.); produce again (a play, etc., produced at an earlier time); often, to make a copy, duplicate, or close imitation of (as, to *reproduce* a medieval building, or a painting or statue; to *reproduce* 18th century costumes or styles; to *reproduce* a text without change; to *reproduce* the handwriting of another); esp., to make a copy or copies of (a picture, etc.) by photography, photo-engraving, or some similar process; also, to produce as a copy of something else (as, designs *reproduced* from old tapestry). **II.** *intr.* To reproduce its kind, as an animal or plant does; propagate; multiply; also, to turn out or appear (*well*, etc.) when reproduced or copied.—**re-pro-du′cer** (-dū′sėr), *n.*—**re-pro-du′ci-ble**, *a.* That may be reproduced.—**re-pro-duc′tion** (-duk′shọn), *n.* The act or process of reproducing, or the state of being reproduced; the natural process among animals and plants by which new individuals are generated and the species perpetuated; the process of producing, bringing about, or presenting anything again, or an instance of it (as, "And now in the perpetual *reproductions* of history, another German warrior occupied a spot of vantage in that same perilous region": Motley's "Dutch Republic," iii. 2); the making of a copy or copies of something; also, that which is made by reproducing; a copy or duplicate of something; esp., a copy of a picture or the like made by photo-engraving or some similar process.—**re-pro-duc′tive** (-tiv), *a.* Serving to reproduce; concerned with or pertaining to reproduction.—**re-pro-duc′tive-ly**, *adv.*—**re-pro-duc′tive-ness**, *n.*

re-proof (rē-prȫf′), *n.* [OF. *reprove*, *reprowe*, < *reprover*, E. *reprove*.] The act of reproving, censuring, or rebuking (as, "stern . . . in his public *reproof* of such transgressions," Hawthorne's "Scarlet Letter," viii.; to speak in *reproof*; a glance of *reproof*); an utterance or expression of censure or rebuke (as, frequent *reproofs*; "Prue raises her eyes . . . with a *reproof* so delicate that it could not be trusted to words," G. W. Curtis's "Prue and I," ii.); a censure or rebuke; also, reproach incurred†, or disgrace†; also, disproof† or refutation†.

re-prov-a-ble (rē-prȫv′ạ-bl), *a.* Deserving of reproof.

re-prov-al (rē-prȫv′ạl), *n.* The act of reproving; a reproof.

re-prove (rē-prȫv′), *v.*; -*proved*, -*proving.* [OF. *reprover* (F. *réprouver*), < LL. *reprobare*, disapprove, reject: see *reprobate*.] **I.** *tr.* To express disapproval of, or censure (actions, words, errors, etc.: as, "There's something in me that *reproves* my fault," Shakspere's "Twelfth Night," iii. 4. 223); also, to address words of disapproval or censure to (a person, etc.), as for some action or fault (as, "How good is it, when thou art *reproved*, to shew repentance!" Ecclus. xx. 3; "Dr. Sitgreaves . . . forgot to *reprove* his patient for imprudence," Cooper's "Spy," xxi.); reprehend, rebuke, or blame; convey censure or blame to by any means, as by a look; also, to disprove†; refute†. **II.** *intr.* To speak in reproof; administer a reproof: as, "Presents and gifts . . . stop up his mouth that he cannot *reprove*" (Ecclus. xx. 29).—**re-prov′er** (-prȫ′vėr), *n.*—**re-prov′ing-ly**, *adv.*

reps (reps), *n.* [F.] Same as *rep¹.*

rep-tant (rep′tạnt), *a.* [L. *reptans* (*reptant-*), ppr. of *reptare*, freq. of *repere*, creep.] Creeping or crawling, as animals; also, repent, as plants.

rep-tile (rep′til or -tīl). [LL. *reptilis*, adj., *reptile*, n., < L. *repere*, creep.] **I.** *a.* Creeping or crawling; of the nature of or pertaining to a reptile or reptiles; fig., groveling, or base, or insidious and malignant (as, a *reptile* press; a *reptile* fund, for despicable and evil purposes). **II.** *n.* Any of various creeping or crawling animals, as the lizards, snakes, etc.; specif., any of the *Reptilia*, a class of cold-blooded vertebrates, including the lizards, snakes, turtles, alligators, etc.; fig., a groveling or mean person; a base or despicable person.—**rep-til′i-an** (-til′i-ạn). [NL. *Reptilia*, prop. pl. of LL. *reptile*, a reptile.] **I.** *a.* Belonging or pertaining to the *Reptilia*, a class of cold-blooded vertebrates (see *reptile*); reptile-like; fig., mean; base; malignant. **II.** *n.* Any of the *Reptilia*; a reptile.—**rep′til-i-form**, *a.* [See -*form.*] Having the form of a reptile; reptile-like.—**rep-ti-liv′o-rous** (-ti-liv′ọ-rus), *a.* [See -*vorous.*] Feeding on reptiles.

re-pub-lic (rē-pub′lik), *n.* [F. *république*, < L. *respublica*, *res publica*, < *res*, thing, affair, + *publica*, fem. of *publicus*, E. *public*.] The commonwealth† or state†; also, a state in which the supreme power rests in the body of citizens entitled to vote and is exercised by representatives chosen directly or indirectly by them (cf. *democracy*); also, any body of persons, etc., viewed as a commonwealth (as, the *republic* of letters, the collective body of persons engaged in literary work, or the field of literature).—**re-pub′li-can. I.** *a.* Of, pertaining to, or of the nature of a republic; also, favoring a republic; [*cap.*] in U. S. *politics*, noting or pertaining to a party which advocates generally a broad construction of the Constitution, extension of the powers of the national government, and a high protective tariff; [*l. c.*] in *ornith.*, living in communities (as, the *republican* grosbeak, or sociable weaver-bird, *Philetærus socius*, of South Africa, many pairs of which build in common an enormous umbrella-like nest: see cut, also cut of nest at *hive-nest*). **II.** *n.* One who favors a republican form of government (as, a red *republican*: see phrase under *red¹*, *a.*); [*cap.*] in U. S. *politics*, a member of the Republican party; [*l. c.*] in *ornith.*, any of various birds that nest in communities, as *Petrocheli-don lunifrons*, an American swallow which inhabits cliffs.

Republican Grosbeak (*Philetærus socius*), with its hive-nest.

—**re-pub′li-can-ism**, *n.* Republican government; republican principles or adherence to them; [*cap.*] in U. S. *politics*, the principles or policy of the Republican party.—**re-pub′li-can-ize**, *v. t.*; -*ized*, -*izing.* To render republican.

re-pub-li-ca-tion (rē-pub-li-kā′shọn), *n.* [See *re-.*] Publication anew; a fresh publication; also, a book or the like published again.

re-pub-lish (rē-pub′lish), *v. t.* [See *re-.*] To publish anew.—**re-pub′lish-er**, *n.*

re-pu-di-ate (rē-pū′di-āt), *v.t.*; -*ated*, -*ating.* [L. *repudiatus*, pp. of *repudiare*, < *repudium*, the casting off of one's spouse or betrothed, appar. < *re-*, back, + *pudere*, feel shame.] To put away by divorce, as a wife; in general, to cast off or disown (as, "He felt it necessary . . . to *repudiate* and denounce his father": Dickens's "Martin Chuzzlewit," xvi.); also, to refuse to accept or entertain, or reject, as something offered; reject with disapproval or condemnation, as a doctrine, etc.; reject with denial, as a charge, etc. (as, "The old man shook his head, gently *repudiating* the imputation": Dickens's "Our Mutual Friend," iii. 1); reject as having no authority or binding force, as a claim, etc.; refuse to acknowledge and pay, as a debt (said specif. of a state, municipality, etc.).—**re-pu-di-a′tion** (-ā′shọn), *n.* [L. *repudiatio(n-).*] The act of repudiating, or the state of being repudiated; specif., refusal, as by a state or municipality, to pay a debt lawfully contracted.— **re-pu-di-a′tion-ist**, *n.* One who advocates repudiation, as of a public debt.—**re-pu′di-a-tive** (-ā-tiv), *a.* Characterized by repudiation.—**re-pu′di-a-tor** (-ā-tor), *n.*

re-pugn (rē-pūn′), *v.* [OF. *repugner* (F. *répugner*), < L. *repugnare*, < *re-*, back, + *pugnare*, fight.] **I.** *intr.* To make opposition; object; also, to be opposed; be contradictory or inconsistent. [Obs. or rare.] **II.** *tr.* To oppose; be opposed to; also, to affect with repugnance.

re-pug-nance (rē-pug′nạns), *n.* The state of being repugnant; objection, distaste, or aversion (as, "I have no absolute *repugnance* to being a clergyman": S. Butler's "Way of All Flesh," viii.); contradictoriness or inconsistency (as, *repugnance* between statements). Also **re-pug′nan-cy.**

re-pug-nant (rē-pug′nạnt), *a.* [OF. *repugnant* (F. *répugnant*), < L. *repugnans* (-ant-), ppr. of *repugnare*: see *repugn.*] Making opposition, objecting, or averse (as, "Circumstances of recent occurrence . . . have rendered her . . . utterly *repugnant* to a personal interview with Mr. Glossin": Scott's "Guy Mannering," xxxv.); also, opposed or contrary, as in nature or character (as, "any vessel constructed on principles so *repugnant* to science," Cooper's "Prairie," xxiv.; "Tax exemption in a democracy such as ours is *repugnant* to every Constitutional principle," A. W. Mellon's "Taxation," viii.); contradictory or inconsistent (as, statements *repugnant* to each other); also, distasteful or objectionable (as, "Great exertion was *repugnant* to him": Lytton Strachey's "Queen Victoria," iv.).—**re-pug′nant-ly,** *adv.*

re-pulse (rē-puls′), *v. t.*; -pulsed, -pulsing. [L. *repulsus*, pp. of *repellere*, E. *repel.*] To drive back, or repel, as an assailant, etc. (as, "Thy faithful dogs . . . who, for the fold's relief, Will . . . *Repulse* the prowling wolf": Dryden's tr. Virgil's "Georgics," iii. 620); repel by force of arms (as, "The Roman cavalry thrice passed the rivulet; they were thrice *repulsed*": Gibbon's "Decline and Fall of the Roman Empire," xli.); also, to repel with denial, discourtesy, or the like, or rebuff (as, "The little lady drew her head back and *repulsed* him with the dignity of a young princess": Mrs. Stowe's "Oldtown Folks," xxiv.); refuse or reject (as, "He . . . *repulsed* their invitations," Johnson's "Rasselas," ii.; "She *repulsed* the idea with violent disdain," Arnold Bennett's "Lion's Share," ii.).—**re-pulse′,** *n.* [L. *repulsus*, a driving back, *repulsa*, a refusal, < *repellere.*] The act of repelling, or the fact of being repelled, as in hostile encounter; also, a repelling with denial, discourtesy, or the like, or a rebuff; refusal or rejection.—**re-puls′er,** *n.*—**re-pul′sion**, *n.* [LL. *repulsio*(n-), < L. *repellere.*] The act of repelling or driving back, or the state of being repelled; specif., the action of bodies that repel each other physically, or an inherent physical force by which bodies, electric charges, or the like, are forced apart (opposed to *attraction*); also, the state or feeling of being repelled, or distaste, repugnance, or aversion (as, "Gloria . . . stops, looking at Crampton with a certain *repulsion*": G. B. Shaw's "You Never Can Tell," ii.).—**re-pul′sive** (-siv), *a.* Tending to repel, or drive back; specif., of the nature of or characterized by physical repulsion (as, "The stone is endued at one of its sides with an attractive power, and at the other with a *repulsive*": Swift's "Gulliver's Travels," iii. 3); also, tending to repel by denial, discourtesy, or the like; forbidding; also, causing repugnance or aversion.—**re-pul′sive-ly,** *adv.*—**re-pul′sive-ness,** *n.*

re-pur-chase (rē-pėr′chạs), *v. t.* [See *re-.*] To purchase again; regain by purchase.—**re-pur′chase,** *n.* The act of repurchasing.

rep-u-ta-ble (rep′ū-tạ-bl), *a.* Held in good repute; estimable; honorable; respectable: as, "They were *reputable*, public-spirited, and religious men" (Charnwood's "Abraham Lincoln," vi.); "The parents of Barbara had been in *reputable* circumstances" (Lamb's "Barbara S——").—**rep″u-ta-bil′i-ty** (-bil′i-ti), **rep′u-ta-ble-ness,** *n.*—**rep′u-ta-bly,** *adv.*

rep-u-ta-tion (rep-ū-tā′shọn), *n.* [L. *reputatio*(n-), < *reputare*: see *repute.*] The consideration or estimation in which a person or thing is held, esp. by the community or the public generally; repute, favorable or unfavorable (as, a man

of good *reputation*; "The hospital bore a blameless *reputation* among the citizens," Arnold Bennett's "Pretty Lady," xiv.); also, favorable repute; good name (as, to ruin one's *reputation* by misconduct); credit or note with the public (as, to seek *reputation*; "Love of *reputation* is a darling passion in great men," Steele, in "Tatler," 92); a favorable and publicly recognized name or standing for merit, achievement, etc. (as, to build up a *reputation*; "He won for himself a *reputation* which his later cruelties might stain but could not efface," Froude's "Cæsar," vii.); sometimes, a person of note (as, "That is Baron Gozelius, one of our great *reputations*": Disraeli's "Lothair," xxxi.); also, the estimation or name of being, having, having done, etc., something specified (as, "Alexander Duncan, who had the *reputation* of being the richest man in the state": W. Churchill's "Coniston," i. 8).

re-pute (rē-pūt′), *v. t.*; -puted, -puting. [L. *reputare*, count over, reckon, consider, < *re-*, again, + *putare*, reckon: see *putative.*] To consider or esteem (a person or thing) to be as specified; account or regard (*to be, to have*, etc.): now used commonly in the passive, and with reference to the estimate or opinion formed by the community or the public generally: as, "I was *reputed* as a mighty diligent servant to my master" (Defoe's "Captain Singleton," i.); "Adamson, the American newspaper correspondent, who . . . was *reputed* to have 'inside information'" (Mrs. Wharton's "Son at the Front," viii.).—**re-pute′,** *n.* Manner of being reputed, estimation in the view of others, or reputation (as, persons of good or ill *repute*; "a weekly paper of fair *repute*," Gissing's "New Grub Street," vii.); also, favorable reputation; good name; credit or note.—**re-put′ed** (-pū′ted), *p. a.* Accounted or supposed to be such: as, his *reputed* son; the *reputed* author of a book; "the *reputed* marvels of Mr. Blaine's memory" (Bok's "Americanization of Edward Bok," xviii.).—**re-put′ed-ly,** *adv.*

re-quest (rē-kwest′), *n.* [OF. *requeste* (F. *requête*), through ML. < L. *requirere* (pp. *requisitus*): see *require.*] The act of asking, or solicitation or petition made, for something to be given, granted, or done, esp. as a favor or courtesy (as, to make *request* for an interview; further information will be sent on *request*; a poem reprinted by *request*); an utterance or communication asking for or requesting something (as, a dying *request*; many *requests* for tickets have been received; "To what *request* for what strange boon . . . Are these your pretty tricks . . . the preamble?" Tennyson's "Merlin and Vivien," 262); also, that which is asked for or requested (as, to obtain one's *request*; "He gave them their *request*," Ps. cvi. 15; "Let the *request* be fifty talents," Shakspere's "Timon of Athens," ii. 2. 201); also, the state of being asked for or sought after much or generally, or demand (esp. in the phrase 'in request': as, a coin in *request* among collectors; to be in great *request* as an after-dinner speaker).—**re-quest′,** *v. t.* [OF. *requester.*] To make a request for, ask for, or solicit (something), esp. politely or formally (as, to *request* one's aid or indulgence; "The first lieutenant *requested* my presence in the cabin," Marryat's "Peter Simple," lx.; "The deputies . . . *requested* permission to adjourn," Motley's "Dutch Republic," i. 3); ask or beg (with a clause or an infinitive: as, to *request* that no flowers be sent; to *request* to be excused from answering; "Charles Hazlewood . . . *requested* to know upon what account he had thought it necessary," Scott's "Guy Mannering," xlvii.); also, to make request to, ask, or beg (a person, etc., to do something: as, "You're *requested* to ring at the rear door," Howells's "Rise of Silas Lapham," v.; "Did I *request* thee, Maker, from my clay To mould me man?" Milton's "Paradise Lost," x. 743).—**re-quest′er,** *n.*

re-qui-em (rē′kwi-em or rek′wi-), *n.* [L., acc. of *requies*, rest: the first word of the introit of the Latin mass for the dead.] The mass sung, in the Roman Catholic Church, for the repose of the souls of the dead, or a celebration or service of this mass (also called 'requiem mass'); a musical setting of this mass; hence, any musical service, hymn, or dirge for the repose of the dead (often fig.: as, the winds chanted a *requiem* over the slain; "Every bird thy *requiem* sings," Burns's "To Miss Cruikshank," 18).

re-qui-es-cat (rek-wi-es′kat), *n.* [From L. *requiescat in pace*, 'may he (or she) rest in peace.'] A wish or prayer for the repose of the dead.

---

fat, fāte, fär, fâll, ȧsk, fāre; net, mē, hėr; pin, pīne; not, nōte, mŏve, nôr; up, lūte, pull; oi, oil; ou, out; (lightened) aviȧry, ēlect, agŏny, intŏ, ūnite; (obscured) errȧnt, operȧ, ardȧnt, actȯr, natūre; ch, chip; g, go; th, thin; ᴛʜ, then; y, you;

re-quir-a-ble (rẹ-kwīr′ạ-bl), *a.* That may be required.

re-quire (rẹ-kwīr′), *v.*; *-quired, -quiring.* [L. *requirere* (pp. *requisitus*), seek again, seek for, ask, ask for, want, need, < *re-*, again, + *quærere*, seek.] **I.** *tr.* To seek†, or search for†; also, to seek to know, inquire, or ask (obs. or archaic: as, "She *required* his pleasure," Cooper's "Spy," i.); also, to ask for, solicit, or request (archaic: as, to *require* a favor; "I spoke . . . *Requiring* at her hand the greatest gift, A woman's heart," Tennyson's "Gardener's Daughter," 224); more commonly, now, to ask for authoritatively or imperatively, or demand (as, "We *required* of them the names in writing of their principal men," 1 Esdras, vi. 12; "The duke . . . *requires* your haste-post-haste appearance, Even on the instant," Shakspere's "Othello," i. 2. 37); call for or exact as obligatory (as, the law *requires* annual income-tax returns; "He could not, in conscience, take the oath *required*," Motley's "Dutch Republic," ii. 10); hence, to impose need or occasion for, or render necessary or indispensable (as, "Rapid movements with a large force *required* supplies," Froude's "Cæsar," xix.; "a heavy expenditure, *requiring* accounts of a complicated . . . nature," Prescott's "Conquest of Mexico," iv. 1); have need of, or need (as, he *requires* medical care; how much time do you *require?* "Ev'n in his pastimes he *requires* a friend, To warn," Cowper's "Tirocinium," 607); also, to ask (one) for something†, or ask or request (one) to do something†; now, to call on authoritatively, order, or enjoin (a person, etc.) to do something (as, to *require* an agent to account for money spent; to *require* aliens to register); hence, to place under an obligation or necessity (as, "the duties of your profession, which *require* you to keep your bodies strong," Ruskin's "Crown of Wild Olive," iii.; circumstances may *require* us to submit). **II.** *intr.* To make request†; also, to make demand, or impose obligation or need (as, to do as a superior, or as the law, *requires*; ready to act if circumstances *require*); also, to be needful or requisite (now rare).—**re-quire′ment**, *n.* The act or an instance of requiring; a demand (as, to make excessive *requirements*); a need (as, to meet the *requirements* of daily life); also, that which is required; a thing demanded or obligatory (as, money is their first *requirement*; a knowledge of Spanish is among the *requirements*); an essential condition; a requisite.—**re-quir′er** (-kwīr′ẻr), *n.*

re-qui-site (rek′wi-zit). [L. *requisitus*, pp. of *requirere*, E. *require*.] **I.** *a.* Required by the nature of things or by circumstances; needful; indispensable: as, he possesses the *requisite* qualifications; qualities *requisite* to a leader; the number of votes *requisite* for election. **II.** *n.* Something requisite; a thing needful or indispensable: as, "a place where the three grand *requisites* of water, fuel and fodder were to be obtained" (Cooper's "Prairie," i.); "Activity was the great *requisite* to success" (G. P. R. James's "Hist. of Charlemagne," iv.).—**re′qui-site-ness**, *n.*

re-qui-si-tion (rek-wi-zish′ọn), *n.* [L. *requisitio(n-)*, < *requirere*, E. *require.*] The act of requiring or demanding, or a demand made (as, "Let me see you no more. I have a right . . . to expect your compliance with this *requisition*": Godwin's "Caleb Williams," xxxix.); esp., the demanding authoritatively or formally of something to be done, given, furnished, etc. (as, the *requisition* of supplies for a military force); an authoritative or official demand (as, "to obtain a revenue by royal *requisitions*": Bancroft's "Hist. of the U. S.," Amer. Revolution, i. 2); also, the state of being required for use or called into service (as, "The young messenger was put in ceaseless *requisition*": Thackeray's "Newcomes," lxi.); also, a requirement, or essential condition.—**re-qui-si′tion**, *v. t.* To make requisition for (something); demand or take as by authority for military purposes, public needs, etc. (as, to *requisition* supplies, horses, or labor; "There was a report abroad that private motors were to be *requisitioned*," Mrs. Wharton's "Son at the Front," vii.); require or take for use, or press into service (as, "There were seniors who had *requisitioned* a chance-met Rajah's elephant": Kipling's "Kim," vii.); also, to make requisition upon (a community, etc.), as for something required.—**re-quis-i-to-ry** (rẹ-kwiz′i-tọ-ri), *a.* Conveying a requisition or demand: as, "The Duke addressed a *requisitory* letter to the . . . judges of Castile, empowering them to carry the sentence into execution" (Motley's "Dutch Republic," iii. 5).

re-quit-a-ble (rẹ-kwī′tạ-bl), *a.* That may be requited.

re-qui-tal (rẹ-kwī′tạl), *n.* The act or an act of requiting; return or reward for service, kindness, etc.; retaliation for a wrong, injury, etc.; repayment; also, something given or serving to requite (as, "as though the only *requital* he would ever dare to dream of were a word of decent politeness, a glance of tolerance or good-will": Du Maurier's "Trilby," ii.).

re-quite (rẹ-kwīt′), *v. t.*; *-quited, -quiting.* [From *re-* + *quite*, obs. var. of *quit*[1], *v.*] To make repayment or return for (service, benefits, etc.: as, "God . . . *requite* to you all the kindness of your instructions to your poor pupil," Scott's "Guy Mannering," xv.; "Never were courtesy and gentleness so ill *requited*," Motley's "Dutch Republic," iii. 9); recompense or reward; make retaliation for (a wrong, injury, etc.: as, "He would take such vengeance as should amply *requite* the injuries done," Prescott's "Conquest of Mexico," iii. 6); also, to make return to (a person) for service, etc. (as, "My father will be glad to *requite* you for this night's hospitality": Bret Harte's "Princess Bob and Her Friends"); (as, "When we gave up our share of the gold at Vera Cruz, it was on the assurance that we should be amply *requited* in Mexico": Prescott's "Conquest of Mexico," iv. 5); make retaliation on (a person) for a wrong, etc. (as, "Not so much for the injury he offered me . . . hath Faustus worthily *requited* this injurious knight": Marlowe's "Doctor Faustus," x.); also, to give or do in return (as, to *requite* like for like).—**re-quite′ment**, *n.* Requital.—**re-quit′er** (-kwī′tẻr), *n.*

re-ra-di-ate (rē-rā′di-āt), *v.* [See *re-*.] **I.** *intr.* To radiate again or anew; specif., in *wireless teleg.* and *teleph.*, of a radio receiving set, antenna, steel chimney, or the like, to send out again into the surrounding air signals or energy received from broadcasting stations, such unintentional or undesired signals often being the cause of distorted reception in neighboring receiving sets; also, loosely, to radiate. **II.** *tr.* To radiate again or anew; specif., in *wireless teleg.* and *teleph.*, to send out again unintentionally (signals or energy received from broadcasting stations); also, loosely, to radiate.—**re-ra-di-a′tion** (-ā′shọn), *n.*

re-read (rē-rēd′), *v. t.*; pret. and pp. *-read* (-red). [See *re-*.] To read again or anew.

rere-brace (rēr′brās), *n.* [Cf. F. *arrière-bras*, lit. 'rear arm,' the arm from shoulder to elbow, also a rerebrace: cf. *vambrace*.] A piece of armor for the upper arm, from the shoulder to the elbow.

a, Rerebrace; *b*, Elbow-piece; *c*, Vambrace.

rere-dos (rēr′dos), *n.* [OF. *rere* (< L. *retro*, at] the back, + *dos* (< L. *dor- sum*), back.] The back of a fireplace or open hearth (archaic); also, a screen or a decorated part of the wall be hind an altar in a church.

rere-mouse (rēr′mous), *n.*; pl. *-mice* (-mīs). [AS. *hrēremūs*: cf. AS. *hrēran*, move, stir, shake.] A bat (animal). [Archaic or prov. Eng.]

re-rise (rē-rīz′), *v. i.*; pret. *-rose*, pp. *-risen*, ppr. *-rising.* [See *re-*.] To rise again.

Reredos and Altar of Lichfield Cathedral, England.

re-roll (rē-rōl′), *v. t.* [See *re-*.] To roll again; roll up (something unrolled).

re-route (rē-röt′, also -rout′), *v. t.* [See *re-*.] To route anew; send or forward by a new or different route.

---

re-sail (rē-sāl′), v. [See re-.] **I.** intr. To sail back; also, to sail again. **II.** tr. To sail again, as a race.

re-sale (rē-sāl′), n. [See re-.] The act of reselling.—**re-sal′a-ble** (-sā′la̤-bl), a.

re-scind (rĕ-sind′), v. t. [L. rescindere (pp. rescissus), < re-, back, + scindere, cut.] To cut off, take away, or remove (obs. or rare); also, to abrogate; annul; revoke; repeal.—**re-scind′a-ble**, a. That may be rescinded.—**re-scind′er**, n.—**re-scind′ment**, n.

re-scis-sion (rĕ-sizh′ọn), n. [LL. rescissio(n-), < L. rescindere, E. rescind.] The act of rescinding.—**re-scis′so-ry** (-sis′ọ̄-ri), a. Serving to rescind.

re-script (rē′skript), n. [L. rescriptum, prop. pp. neut. of rescribere, < re-, back, + scribere, write.] A written answer, as of a Roman emperor or a pope, to a query or petition; also, any edict, decree, or official announcement; also, the act or an act, or the product, of rewriting (as, "I wrote it three times—chastening and subduing the phrases at every rescript": C. Brontë's "Villette," xxxii.).

res-cue (res′kū), v. t.; -cued, -cuing. [OF. rescourre (F. recourre), < L. re-, back, + excutere, shake out or off, < ex, out of, + quatere, shake.] To free or deliver from confinement, violence, danger, or evil (as, to rescue a man from the hands of his enemies; to rescue sailors from destruction by shipwreck; to rescue a manuscript from destruction by fire); sometimes, to take back by force (something taken away); in law, to liberate or take by forcible or illegal means from lawful custody (as, to rescue a prisoner from a constable).—**res′cue**, n. The act or an act of rescuing; in law, the forcible or illegal taking of a person or thing out of the custody of the law.—**res′cue-grass**, n. [Appar. < rescue, n.] A tall brome-grass, Bromus unioloides, cultivated for forage.—**res′cu-er**, n.

re-search¹ (rē-sėrch′), v. t. or i. [See re-.] To search again. Also written re-search.—**re-search′¹**, n.

re-search² (rĕ-sėrch′), v. [OF. recerchier, search through, search (F. rechercher, seek for), < re- (< L. re-), again, + cerchier, E. search.] **I.** tr. To search into; investigate carefully. [Now rare.] **II.** intr. To pursue a course of research; make researches.—**re-search′²**, n. A searching for something or somebody, esp. with care (as, "She had left Thornfield Hall in the night; every research after her course had been vain": C. Brontë's "Jane Eyre," xxxiii.); also, a continued careful inquiry or investigation into a subject, in order to discover facts or principles (often in pl.: as, scientific or historical researches); inquiry or investigation directed to such ends (as, "recent geographical and philological research," Amelia B. Edwards's "Thousand Miles up the Nile," xv.; "Modern research adds little in the way either of correction or of amplification to Cromwell's own story," Morley's "Oliver Cromwell," iv. 2).—**re-search′er**, n.—**re-search′-ful**, a. Full of, characterized by, or devoted to research.

re-seat (rē-sēt′), v. t. [See re-.] To seat again (as, "For the third time I reseated myself on the same spot": W. H. Hudson's "Green Mansions," iii.); also, to provide with a new seat or new seats.

ré-seau (rā-zō′, F. rä-zō), n.; pl. réseaux (-zōz′, F. -zō). [F., dim. < L. rete, net.] A network; specif., a netted or meshed ground in lace; in astron., a network of fine lines on a glass plate, used in a photographic telescope in order to produce a corresponding network (for measuring purposes) on photographs of the stars.

re-sect (rĕ-sekt′), v. t. [L. resectus, pp. of resecare, < re-, back, + secare, cut.] In surg., to cut away or pare off; excise a portion of.—**re-sec′tion** (-sek′shọn), n. [L. resectio(n-).] In surg., the act of resecting; excision of a portion of some structure, as a bone or nerve; esp., removal of the articular extremity of a bone.—**re-sec′tion-al**, a.

re-se-da (rĕ-sē′dä), n. [NL. Reseda, < L. reseda, kind of plant.] Any plant of the genus Reseda, esp. R. odorata, the garden mignonette; also, mignonette color; a grayish green. —**res-e-da-ceous** (res-ē-dā′shius), a. Belonging to the Resedaceæ, or mignonette family of plants.

re-sell (rē-sel′), v. t. or i.; pret. and pp. -sold. [See re-.] To sell again.

re-sem-blance (rĕ-zem′blans), n. The state or fact of resembling or being like (as, points of resemblance); likeness or similarity; a degree, kind, or point of likeness (as, "The child . . . bore a remarkable resemblance to her grandfather," Lytton Strachey's "Queen Victoria," ii.; a family resemblance; there are certain resemblances between the two cases); also, the likeness, appearance, or semblance of something (as, "He is then described as gliding through the Garden, under the resemblance of a mist," Addison, in "Spectator," 351: now rare); also, a person or thing made in or having the likeness or appearance of some other, or a copy, image, or reproduction (as, "Fairest resemblance of thy Maker fair, Thee all things living gaze on," Milton's "Paradise Lost," ix. 538: now rare); also, a simile†; also, a likelihood† or probability†.

re-sem-blant (rĕ-zem′blant), a. Resembling; similar; having resemblance. [Now rare.]

re-sem-ble (rĕ-zem′bl), v. t.; -bled, -bling. [OF. resembler (F. ressembler), < re- (< L. re-), again, + sembler, be like: see semblance.] To be like or similar to (as, "The sand-drift . . . curiously resembles the glacier . . . In size, in shape, in position, in all but colour and substance, it is the same": Amelia B. Edwards's "Thousand Miles up the Nile," xvi.); also, to make like or similar to something (obs. or archaic); also, to liken or compare (archaic: as, "Unto what is the kingdom of God like? and whereunto shall I resemble it?" Luke, xiii. 18); also, to make a likeness or image of†, or represent†.—**re-sem′bler**, n.

re-send (rē-send′), v. t.; pret. and pp. -sent. [See re-.] To send back; also, to send again or anew.

re-sent (rĕ-zent′), v. t. [F. ressentir, feel, resent, < L. re-, back, + sentire, feel.] To feel†, or be affected by†; feel keenly or painfully†; also, to feel aggrieved at, or feel displeasure or indignation at from a sense of injury or insult (as, "How bitterly must such a measure have been resented by the Senate, which . . . robbed them of their . . . profitable privileges," Froude's "Cæsar," iii.; "The Barbarians resented the indignity which had been offered to their king," Gibbon's "Decline and Fall of the Roman Empire," xli.); hence, to manifest such feeling at, as by action or speech (as, "His nobles had more than once importuned him to resent his injuries by taking arms against the Spaniards," Prescott's "Conquest of Mexico," iv. 3; "M. Du Bois . . . put his hand upon his sword, and threatened to resent this indignity," Miss Burney's "Evelina," xxv.).—**re-sent′er**, n.—**re-sent′ful**, a. Full of or marked by resentment.—**re-sent′ful-ly**, adv.—**re-sent′ful-ness**, n.—**re-sent′ment**, n. [F. ressentiment.] A feeling† or emotion†; also, the feeling of one who resents; displeasure or indignation at something regarded as an injury or insult, or against the author or source of it (as, resentment at the treatment given to one's self or one's friends; "He . . . felt no resentment against me for using such intemperate words," W. H. Hudson's "Purple Land," xv.); hence, the manifestation of such feeling, as by action.

res-er-va-tion (rez-ėr-vā′shọn), n. [OF. reservation (F. réservation), < ML. reservatio(n-).] The act of reserving; a keeping back, withholding, or setting apart; the allotting or the securing of accommodations of a kind, on a train or boat, etc., as for a traveler (often in pl.: as, to write for reservations; to make reservations in advance for an entire trip); the making of some exception or qualification, or an exception or qualification made, expressly or tacitly (as, "making this admission with all due reservation," W. De Morgan's "Joseph Vance," xv.; a mental reservation, a qualification or limitation made mentally or tacitly by one making a statement, taking an oath, etc.); also, something reserved; a tract of public land set apart for a special purpose, as for the use of an Indian tribe (U. S.).

re-serve (rĕ-zėrv′), v. t.; -served, -serving. [OF. reserver (F. réserver), < L. reservare (pp. reservatus), < re-, back, + servare, keep.] To keep back or save for future use, disposal, treatment, etc. (as, to reserve grain for sowing; to reserve a sum for incidentals; to reserve one's strength for a struggle; "The reply of Ursula I reserve for another chapter," Borrow's "Romany Rye," x.); keep, withhold, or postpone till a certain time (as, "These jests are out of season; Reserve them till a merrier hour," Shakspere's "Comedy of Errors," i. 2. 69; "a God . . . that oftentimes suffers wicked men to go on a long time, and even reserves damnation to the general day of retribution," Defoe's "Robinson Crusoe," ii. 6); keep back or withhold for the present (as, to *reserve* one's fire; to *reserve* criticism; "Take each man's censure, but reserve thy judgement," Shakspere's "Hamlet," i. 3. 69); keep back or withhold (a matter) from knowledge or disclosure†; also, to keep back, withhold, or set apart for possession or allotment (as, "I have *reserved* To myself nothing," Shakspere's "Antony and Cleopatra," v. 2. 143; to *reserve* seats for holders of tickets); retain or secure (a right, etc.) by express stipulation; also, to keep or set apart for disposition, judgment, etc. (as, "when Paul had appealed to be *reserved* unto the hearing of Augustus," Acts, xxv. 21; to *reserve* a case for a higher authority); also, to set apart for a particular use, purpose, service, etc. (as, ground *reserved* for gardening; time *reserved* for recreation); also, to keep for some fate, lot, experience, etc. (as, to be *reserved* for a noble end; "His doom *Reserved* him to more wrath," Milton's "Paradise Lost," i. 54); also, to keep or preserve from death, destruction, etc. (obs. except as in 'to reserve alive'); also, to make an exception of†, or except†.—**re-serve′**, *n.* [F. *réserve*.] The act of reserving, or keeping back, withholding, setting apart, or excepting (esp. in 'without reserve': see phrase following); a reservation, exception, or qualification (as, "Whenever we come to discuss what may be called Christian evidence, I do it with *reserves*," Mrs. H. Ward's "Robert Elsmere," xxii.; "She knew that he meant it, without any *reserves*," Arnold Bennett's "Hilda Lessways," iii. 4); also, the state of being reserved, as for future use or for some purpose or person (as, to keep or have money in *reserve*; "a happiness greater than I had ever imagined to be in *reserve* for me," George Eliot's "Middlemarch," v.); also, something reserved, as for future use or some purpose or object; a store or stock; an amount of capital retained, as by a banker, to meet probable demands; a body of troops held in readiness to sustain the main body of an army as occasion may require (often in *pl.*); the part of a country's fighting force not in active service; a member of this, or a reservist; a tract of public land set apart for a special purpose (as, a forest *reserve*); also, self-restraint in action or speech; avoidance of familiarity in intercourse, or distance (as, "His manner had something of shyness and *reserve*," J. H. Newman's "Callista," i.; "His demeanour varied between a shy cordiality and a dignified *reserve*," Gissing's "New Grub Street," iii.); reticence or silence (as, "The islanders always maintained a discreet *reserve* with regard to my own peculiar views on religion": H. Melville's "Typee," xxiii.).—**without reserve,** without keeping back, withholding, or excepting anything; unqualifiedly: as, "We would obey him *without reserve*, on pain of death" (Defoe's "Captain Singleton," ii.); "The boys had liked him *without reserve*" (H. G. Wells's "Mr. Britling," iii. 2. § 3).—**re-serve′,** *a.* Kept in reserve; forming a reserve: as, a *reserve* stock or force.—**re-served′,** *p. a.* Kept in reserve; set apart for a particular use or purpose; kept by special arrangement for some person or persons (as, a *reserved* seat; a *reserved* compartment in a railroad-car); also, self-restrained in action or speech, or disposed to keep one's feelings, thoughts, or affairs to one's self (as, "a *reserved* man, whose inner life was intense and sufficient to him": Arnold Bennett's "Book of Carlotta," i. 5); avoiding familiarity, or distant; reticent or uncommunicative; characterized by reserve, as the disposition, manner, etc.—**re-serv′ed-ly,** *adv.* —**re-serv′ed-ness,** *n.*—**re-serv′er,** *n.*—**re-serv′ist,** *n.* [F. *réserviste*.] One who belongs to a reserve force of a country: as, French *reservists*; "orders to Army and Naval *reservists*" (A. S. M. Hutchinson's "If Winter Comes," iii. 4). **res-er-voir** (rez′ĕr-vwor), *n.* [F. *réservoir*, < *réserver*: see *reserve*.] A place where water is collected and stored for use, esp. water for supplying a community, irrigating land, furnishing power, etc.; hence, a place or area in which water collects naturally in great quantity, or a lake or the like supplying a stream (as, Lake Victoria Nyanza, the chief *reservoir* of the Nile); any natural receptacle or source of fluid matter (as, volcanic *reservoirs* of molten rock); a receptacle or chamber for holding a liquid or fluid, as oil or gas; a cavity or part, in an animal or plant, which holds some fluid or secretion; also, fig., a place where anything is collected or accumulated in great amount (as, "this great *reservoir* of folly, knavery, and sophistication [London]": Smollett's "Humphry Clinker," June 2); a great supply,

store, or reserve of something.—**res′er-voir,** *v. t.* To store in or as in a reservoir.
re-set (rē-set′), *v. t.*; *-set, -setting.* [See *re-*.] To set again or anew; esp., to fix (gems) in or provide (jewelry) with a new setting; in *printing*, to set (type, matter, etc.) again or anew; in *surg.*, to set (a broken bone, etc.) again.—**re-set** (rē-set′ or rē′set), *n.* The act of resetting; also, that which is reset; in *printing*, matter set over again.—**re-set′ta-ble,** *a.* Capable of being reset.
re-set-tle (rē-set′l), *v. t.* or *i.* [See *re-*.] To settle again.— **re-set′tle-ment,** *n.*
re-sew (rē-sō′), *v. t.* [See *re-*.] To sew again.
re-shape (rē-shāp′), *v. t.* [See *re-*.] To shape anew.
re-ship (rē-ship′), *v. t.*; *-shipped, -shipping.* [See *re-*.] To ship again.—**re-ship′ment,** *n.*
re-side (rē-zīd′), *v. i.*; *-sided, -siding.* [OF. *resider* (F. *résider*), < L. *residere*, remain behind, stay, reside, < *re-*, back, + *sedere*, sit.] To dwell permanently or for a considerable time, as in a settled or recognized place of abode (as, "His ancestors had for centuries *resided* on their estates in Norfolk," Bulwer-Lytton's "Pelham," iii.; to visit friends *residing* in Boston); have one's abode, or live, for a time (as, "There's four places where a person can be summoned: at his dwelling-house; at a place where he has *resided* forty days . . . ": Stevenson's "David Balfour," ix.); live or stay, as in a place, for the discharge of official or other duties (as, to require a clergyman to *reside* in his benefice; to *reside* as diplomatic agent at a foreign court); fig., of things, qualities, etc., to abide, lie, or be present habitually (as, "A certain dignity *resided* on his eyebrows": H. Mackenzie's "Man of Feeling," xi.); exist or be inherent (*in*); rest or be vested (*in*), as powers, rights, etc.—**res-i-dence** (rez′i-dens), *n.* The act or fact of residing; dwelling or abode, as in a place; living or staying in a place of official or other duty (as, the *residence* of a rector in his benefice; "The boy was eager to come into *residence* at once, though he would matriculate too late to keep the term," Mrs. H. Ward's "Robert Elsmere," iv.); also, a period of residing, or the time during which one resides, in a place; also, the place, esp. the house, in which one resides; a dwelling-place or dwelling; esp., a house of a more or less pretentious kind, or a mansion (as, "The land fronting the main road was destined not for cottages, but for *residences*": Arnold Bennett's "Clayhanger," ii. 3); fig., the seat of some power, principle, activity, or the like.—**res′i-den-cy** (-den-si), *n.*; pl. *-cies* (-siz). Residence; in India, the official residence of a representative of the British governor-general at a native court; in the Dutch East Indies, an administrative division.—**res′i-dent** (-dent). [L. *residens* (-*ent*-), ppr.] **I.** *a.* Residing; dwelling in a place; living or staying at a place in discharge of duty (cf. *non-resident, a.*); of birds, etc., not migratory. **II.** *n.* One who resides in a place; specif., a diplomatic representative, esp. one inferior in rank to an ambassador, residing at a foreign court; in India, a representative of the British governor-general at a native court; in the Dutch East Indies, the governor of a residency.—**res′i-dent-er** (-den-tėr), *n.* A resident; an inhabitant: as, "speaking like an old *residenter*" (Barrie's "Sentimental Tommy," xii.). [Sc. and U. S.]— **res-i-den′tial** (-den′shạl), *a.* Of or pertaining to residence or residences; adapted or used for residence (as, "Bleakridge, *residential* suburb of Bursley": Arnold Bennett's "These Twain," i.).—**res-i-den′tia-ry** (-den′shạ-ri). [ML. *residentiarius*.] **I.** *a.* Residing; resident; specif., bound to or involving official residence (as, a *residentiary* canon or canonry in a cathedral church). **II.** *n.*; pl. *-ries* (-riz). A resident; specif., an ecclesiastic bound to official residence. —**res′i-dent-ship,** *n.*—**re-sid′er** (-zī′dėr), *n.*
re-sid-u-al (rē-zid′ū-ạl). **I.** *a.* Pertaining to or constituting a residuum; remaining, or left over; remaining unexplained; left uncorrected; in *math.*, formed by the subtraction of one quantity from another (as, a *residual* quantity, in *alg.*, a binomial having one of its terms negative, as a—b). **II.** *n.* A residuum; a remainder; a residual quantity.
re-sid-u-a-ry (rē-zid′ū-ạ-ri), *a.* Pertaining to or of the nature of a residue, remainder, or residuum; entitled to the residue of an estate (as, a *residuary* legatee).
res-i-due (rez′i-dū), *n.* [OF. *residu* (F. *résidu*), < L. *residuum*: see *residuum*.] That which remains after a part

is taken, disposed of, or gone, or the remainder or rest of something (as, "The *residue* of the conquered people fled," Defoe's "Robinson Crusoe," ii. 3; "to . . . keep to my trade . . . and so work out the *residue* of my days," H. G. Wells's "Tono-Bungay," ii. 4. § 10); a portion remaining or left; specif., a quantity of matter remaining after evaporation, combustion, or some other process, or a residuum; in *law*, the part of a testator's estate that remains after the payment of all debts, charges, and particular devises and bequests; in *chem.*, an atom or group of atoms considered as a radical or part of a molecule.

re-sid-u-um (rẹ-zid′ū-um), *n.*; pl. -*ua* (-ū̇-ạ̈) or -*uums*. [L., neut. of *residuus*, remaining, < *residere*: see *reside.*] The residue, remainder, or rest of something (as, "He spoke in the tone of one who selects a truth from a heap of falsehoods, but isn't concerned with the quality of the *residuum*": W. De Morgan's "Alice-for-Short," i.); a portion or thing remaining or left (as, "After elimination of all verbiage, this fact was the only *residuum*": Motley's "Dutch Republic," ii. 6); specif., a quantity or body of matter remaining after a process of evaporation, combustion, distillation, or the like, as a sediment or deposit, an ash, various by-products or waste products, etc.; a residual product; in *law*, the residue of an estate.

re-sign¹ (rē-sīn′), *v. t.* [See *re-.*] To sign again. Also written *re-sign.*

re-sign² (rẹ-zīn′), *v.* [OF. *resigner* (F. *résigner*), < L. *resignare* (pp. *resignatus*), < *re-*, back, + *signare*, E. *sign, v.*] **I.** *tr.* To give up formally, as an office or commission to the person or authority that conferred it; relinquish, as a right or claim; surrender, as a thing (as, "They would have killed their captives rather than have *resigned* them": Johnson's "Rasselas," xxxiii.); abandon or consign (as, "Some rude handicrafts were entirely *resigned* to these itinerants": Scott's "Guy Mannering," vii.); yield (one's self, one's will, etc.) in confidence or reliance; submit (one's self, one's mind, etc.) without resistance (as, to *resign* one's self to what is inevitable). **II.** *intr.* To give up an office or position; also, to yield or submit (as, "Amazed, confused, he found his power expired, *Resign'd* to fate, and with a sigh retired," Pope's "Rape of the Lock," iii. 146: now rare).—**res-ig-na-tion** (rez-ig-nā′shọn), *n.* [ML. *resignatio(n-).*] The act of resigning; relinquishment; surrender; esp., the act or an instance of giving up an office, etc. (as, "In consequence of the *resignations* . . . the way to greatness was left clear to a new set of aspirants": Macaulay's "Hist. of Eng.," ii.); also, the fact of resigning one's self, or the state of being resigned or submissive (as, "He . . . gave her a hearty kiss on each side of the face, to which Lucy submitted in blushing *resignation*": Scott's "Guy Mannering," xlix.); submission; unresisting acquiescence; often, quiet submission to the will of Providence.—**re-signed′**, *p. a.* Submissive or acquiescent (as, "a meek, *resigned* sufferer": Macaulay's "Hist. of Eng.," xviii.); characterized by or indicative of resignation (as, "He should insist on the most *resigned* obedience from his daughter," Fielding's "Tom Jones," vi. 3; "'Very well,' he agreed with a *resigned* smile," J. Conrad's "Rescue," iv. 5).—**re-sign′ed-ly**, *adv.*—**re-sign′ed-ness**, *n.*—**re-sign′er**, *n.*

re-sile (rẹ-zīl′), *v. i.*; -*siled*, -*siling*. [L. *resilire*, < *re-*, back, + *salire*, leap.] To spring back, recoil, or rebound; return to the original form or position, as an elastic body; also, to draw back or recede, as from an agreement, purpose, etc.; also, to shrink back or recoil, as with aversion.

re-sil-i-ence (rẹ-zil′i-ens), *n.* Resilient action; rebound; recoil; also, resilient power; elasticity. Also **re-sil′i-en-cy.**

re-sil-i-ent (rẹ-zil′i-ent), *a.* [L. *resiliens* (-ent-), ppr. of *resilire*: see *resile.*] Springing back or rebounding; returning to the original form or position after being bent, compressed, or stretched (as, "thin *resilient* steel": Arnold Bennett's "Lion's Share," xxx.); fig., readily recovering, as from depression; buoyant or cheerful.

re-sil-i-om-e-ter (rẹ-zil-i-om′e-tėr), *n.* [From *resilience* + *-meter.*] An instrument for testing resilience.

res-in (rez′in), *n.* [OF. *resine*, also *rasine, rosine*, < L. *resina*: cf. *rosin.*] Any of a class of non-volatile, solid or semisolid organic substances (as copal, mastic, etc.) obtained directly from certain plants as exudations or derived from

various vegetable products by special processes, and used in medicine, varnish-making, etc.; esp., a substance (rosin) of this type obtained from certain pines.—**res′in**, *v. t.* To treat or rub with resin.—**res′in=gnat**, *n.* A small dipterous insect, *Diplosis resinicola*, whose larvæ live in exuding masses of resin on pine-trees and feed on the abraded bark.

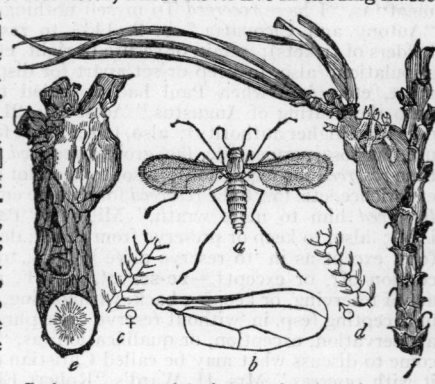

—**res-in-if′er-ous** (-i-nif′ẹ-rus), *a.* [See *-ferous.*] Yielding resin.—**res′-in-i-fy** (-i-fī), *v. t.* or *i.*; -*fied*,-*fying.* [See *-fy.*] To change into resin; make or become resinous.—**res′in-oid.** **I.** *a.* Resin-like. **II.** *n.* A resinoid substance.—**res′in-ous**, *a.* Full of or containing resin; of the nature of or resembling resin; pertaining to or characteristic of resin.—**res′in-ous-ly**, *adv.*—**res′in-y**, *a.* Resinous.

Resin-gnat.— *a*, adult female; *b*, wing of same; *c*, cross-section of antenna of female; *d*, same of male; *e*, section of pine twig showing work of larvæ; *f*, same showing extruded pupa-cases: *a*, *e*, *f*, enlarged; *b*, *c*, *d*, still more enlarged.

res-i-pis-cence (res-i-pis′ẹns), *n.* [LL. *resipiscentia*, < L. *resipiscens*: see *resipiscent.*] Restoration to one's right mind; change to a better frame of mind; repentance.

res-i-pis-cent (res-i-pis′ẹnt), *a.* [L. *resipiscens* (-ent-), ppr. of *resipiscere*, recover one's senses, < *re-*, again, + *sapere*, be wise.] Being restored to one's right mind.

re-sist (rẹ-zist′), *v.* [OF. *resister* (F. *résister*), < L. *resistere*, stand back, withstand, resist, < *re-*, back, + *sistere*, stand.] **I.** *intr.* To make a stand or make efforts in opposition; act in opposition; offer resistance. **II.** *tr.* To withstand, strive against, or oppose (as, "*Resist* the devil, and he will flee from you," Jas. iv. 7; "Pardon was freely extended to all who had *resisted* the invasion," Green's "Short Hist. of the Eng. People," iv. 3; "My servants . . . *resisted* the adoption of this plan," Kinglake's "Eothen," xxiii.); sometimes, to refrain or abstain from (as, to be unable to *resist* a smile; "Lady Flora could not *resist* a caustic observation," Lytton Strachey's "Queen Victoria," ii.); also, of things, to withstand the action or effect of (as, "as rocks *resist* the billows and the sky," Goldsmith's "Deserted Village," 430; "The feathers of these birds must be well preened to *resist* so much wet," G. White's "Nat. Hist. of Selborne," ii. 21).—**re-sist′**, *n.* A substance applied to a surface to enable it to resist corrosion or the like; in *calico-printing*, a preparation applied to parts of a fabric not to be colored, in order to prevent the color from fixing.—**re-sist′ance**, *n.* The act of resisting, opposing, or withstanding; opposition; also, power of resisting (as, "They, astonish'd, all *resistance* lost, All courage": Milton's "Paradise Lost," vi. 838); also, the opposition offered by one thing to another thing, a force, etc.; in *mech.*, etc., an opposing force, esp. one tending to prevent motion; in *elect.*, that property of a conductor in virtue of which the passage of a current is opposed, causing electric energy to be transformed into heat ('true resistance' or 'ohmic resistance'); also, a conductor or coil offering such opposition; also, impedance ('apparent resistance').—**re-sist′ance=box**, *n.* In *elect.*, a box containing one or more resistance-coils.—**re-sist′ance=coil**, *n.* In *elect.*, a coil of wire which offers a definite resistance to the passage of a current of electricity.—**re-sist′ant.** [F. *résistant*, ppr.] **I.** *a.*

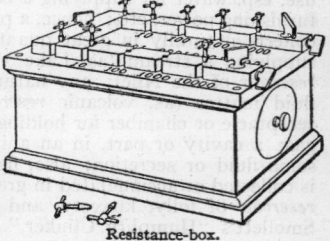

Resistance-box.

Resisting. **II.** *n.* One who or that which resists; in *calico-printing*, a resist.—**re-sist′ent**, *a.* [L. *resistens* (-*ent*-), ppr.] Resisting.—**re-sist′er**, *n.*—**re-sist′i-ble**, *a.* That may be resisted.—**re-sist′ing-ly**, *adv.*—**re-sis′tive** (-zis′-tiv), *a.* Resisting; capable of or inclined to resistance.— **re-sis-tiv-i-ty** (rē-zis-tiv′i-ti), *n.*—**re-sist′less**, *a.* That cannot be resisted, or irresistible (as, "A *resistless*, and almost frantic impulse, urged me forward": Mrs. Shelley's "Frankenstein," iv.); also, powerless to resist, or unresisting (as, "*Resistless*, tame, Am I to be burn'd up?" Keats's "Endymion," iii.).—**re-sist′less-ly**, *adv.*—**re-sist′less-ness**, *n.*—**re-sist′or**, *n.* In *elect.*, a conducting body or device used in a circuit, etc., because of its resistance.

re-sole (rē-sōl′), *v. t.* [See *re-*.] To put a new sole on (a shoe, etc.).

res-o-lu-ble (rez′ō-lū-bl), *a.* [LL. *resolubilis*, < L. *resolvere*, E. *resolve*.] Capable of being resolved.—**res″o-lu-bil′i-ty** (-bil′i-ti), **res′o-lu-ble-ness**, *n.*

res-o-lute (rez′ō-lūt). [L. *resolutus*, pp. of *resolvere*, E. *resolve*.] **I.** *a.* Firmly resolved or determined, or set in purpose or opinion (as, "*resolute* to stand out against such things, as are not lawful," 2 Mac. vi. 20; "Scipio, Cato, Labienus . . . were *resolute* to fight on to the last," Froude's "Cæsar," xxiv.; to be *resolute* against, or for, war); in general, of a firm, determined temper, or firm and bold in pursuing purposes (as, "all stout *resolute* fellows, and very well armed," Defoe's "Captain Singleton," xvi.; "a handful of *resolute* men and women who can dare," H. G. Wells's "Men Like Gods," ii. 2); characterized by firmness and determination, as the temper, spirit, actions, etc. (as, "a singularly smart boy . . . with a fine *resolute* temper that systematic spoiling had nearly turned to mulish obstinacy," Kipling's "Captains Courageous," iii.; *resolute* attempts or opposition); indicative or suggestive of firmness and determination (as, "a square, sharply outlined, *resolute* chin, of that type which gives character and determination to the whole physiognomy": Miss Mulock's "John Halifax," i.). **II.** *n.* A resolute or determined person: as, "a list of lawless *resolutes*" (Shakspere's "Hamlet," i. 1. 98).—**res′o-lute-ly**, *adv.*—**res′o-lute-ness**, *n.*

res-o-lu-tion (rez-ō-lū′shọn), *n.* [OF. *resolution* (F. *résolution*), < L. *resolutio*(n-), < *resolvere*, E. *resolve*.] The act or process of resolving or separating into constituent or elementary parts, or the resulting state; breaking up; reduction to a simpler form; conversion; also, solution or explanation, as of a problem, a doubtful point, etc.; also, assurance or certainty, as of the truth of something† (see Shakspere's "King Lear," i. 2. 108); also, the act or an act of resolving or determining as to action, etc.; a resolve or determination (as, "He now made a firm *resolution* to avoid and to forget her," Marryat's "King's Own," xli.; *resolutions* of reform; good *resolutions*); also, a formal determination, or expression of opinion, of a deliberative assembly or other body of persons (as, "Strong *resolutions* were adopted [in Parliament] against the Queen," Macaulay's "Hist. of Eng.," ii.; to propose *resolutions* of sympathy with a bereaved family); also, the mental state or quality of being resolved or resolute, or determination, or firmness of purpose (as, "the stern look of inflexible *resolution*," Cooper's "Prairie," xxx.; "That thought . . . gives me *resolution* to bid you fly from me for ever," Fielding's "Tom Jones," vi. 8); in *med.*, the reduction or disappearance of a swelling or inflammation without suppuration; in *music*, progression of a voice-part or of the harmony as a whole from a discord to a concord; also, the note or chord by which this is effected.— **res-o-lu′tion-er**, *n.* One accepting or approving particular resolutions (specif. in *Sc. hist.*); also, a resolutionist.—**res-o-lu′tion-ist**, *n.* One joining in or subscribing to a resolution.

re-solv-a-ble (rē-zol′vạ-bl), *a.* That may be resolved.—**re-solv-a-bil′i-ty** (-bil′i-ti), *n.*

re-solve (rē-zolv′), *v.*; -solved, -solving. [L. *resolvere* (pp. *resolutus*), loosen, relax, dissolve, lay open, disclose, < *re-*, again, + *solvere*, loosen.] **I.** *tr.* To loosen† or relax†; also, to dissolve† or melt†; also, to separate into constituent or elementary parts, break up, or disintegrate; separate or break up (*into*: as, "The cloud, as one drew near, *resolved* itself into innumerable garments, sheets and quilts . . . fluttering from long lines," W. H. Hudson's "Far Away and

Long Ago," vii.); reduce or convert by or as by breaking up or disintegration (*into* or *to*: as, "Earth, that nourished thee, shall claim Thy growth, to be *resolved* to earth again," Bryant's "Thanatopsis"); convert or transform by any process (often reflexive: as, the assembly *resolved* itself into a committee of the whole; "Little doubts grew into big ones —big doubts *resolved* themselves into downright negations," Du Maurier's "Trilby," v.); reduce by mental analysis (*into*: as, to *resolve* virtue into a form of selfishness; "*Resolving* all events . . . into the will And arbitration wise of the Supreme," Cowper's "Task," ii. 163); also, to deal with (a question, a matter of uncertainty, etc.) in a conclusive manner; solve (a problem); explain or decide (a doubtful point); clear away or dispel (doubts, etc.); also, to free from doubt†, make certain†, or convince† (a person: as, "You are amazed; but this shall absolutely *resolve* you," Shakspere's "Measure for Measure," iv. 2. 225); inform† or tell† (as, "*Resolve* me, Reason, which of these is worse?" Pope's "Moral Essays," iii. 319); also, to fix or settle on by deliberate choice and will, or determine on (a course of action, etc.: as, "ere a crime *resolved* is done," Lowell's "Legend of Brittany," ii. 18); determine (to do something: as, "I *resolved* to cease from sin in all its forms," Mark Twain's "Life on the Mississippi," liv.); also, to settle, determine, or declare by a formal resolution, as of a deliberative or other assembly or body; also, to bring to or fix in a determination or resolve (chiefly in the passive: as, "I run to meet th' alarms, *Resolv'd* on death, *resolv'd* to die in arms," Dryden's tr. Virgil's "Æneid," ii. 424; "His mind was *resolved*," Marryat's "King's Own," xli.); in *med.*, to cause (swellings, inflammation, etc.) to disappear without suppuration; in *music*, to cause (a voice-part or the harmony as a whole) to progress from a discord to a concord. **II.** *intr.* To dissolve† or melt†; also, to break up or disintegrate; be reduced or changed by breaking up or otherwise (*into* or *to*: as, "The roof [in a dream] *resolved* to clouds, high and dim," C. Brontë's "Jane Eyre," xxvii.); also, to feel certain, assured, or convinced†; also, to come to a determination, or make up one's mind (as, "I was not long *resolving*": Defoe's "Robinson Crusoe," ii. 1); determine (*on* or *upon*: as, "consultations . . . in which much was proposed, but nothing *resolved* on," Scott's "Quentin Durward," xxx.; to *resolve* upon an undertaking); in *music*, to progress from a discord to a concord.—**re-solve′**, *n.* A resolution or determination made, as to follow some course of action (as, "In pursuance of this *resolve*, he took up his residence in the Puritan town," Hawthorne's "Scarlet Letter," ix.; to forget one's noble *resolves*); also, a formal resolution of a deliberative or other body (as, "The general dissatisfaction had produced . . . several strong public *resolves* against the Stamp Act": Burke's "American Taxation"); also, determination, or firmness of purpose (as, "the very essence of high martial *resolve* and heroic self-confidence": Du Maurier's "Trilby," vi.).—**re-solved′**, *p. a.* Determined on, or deliberately purposed, as a course of action; also, determined or firm in purpose, as a person; resolute; characterized by or showing resolution, as the temper, bearing, etc.—**re-solv′-ed-ly**, *adv.*—**re-solv′ed-ness**, *n.*—**re-sol′vent** (-zol′vẹnt). [L. *resolvens* (-*ent*-), ppr.] **I.** *a.* Resolving; causing solution; solvent. **II.** *n.* Something resolvent; in *med.*, a remedy that causes resolution, as of swellings, etc.—**re-solv′er**, *n.*

res-o-nance (rez′ō-nạns), *n.* The state or quality of being resonant (as, "His voice lacked *resonance*": Galsworthy's "Saint's Progress," iii. 11); specif., the prolongation of sound by reflection; reverberation; also, the prolongation or increase of sound by the sympathetic vibration of other bodies; in *elect.*, that condition of a circuit with respect to a given frequency or the like in which the total reactance is zero and the current flow a maximum, as when an antenna circuit is so adjusted as to respond with maximum effect to a certain wave-length.

res-o-nant (rez′ō-nạnt), *a.* [L. *resonans* (-*ant*-), ppr. of *resonare*: see *resound²*.] Resounding, reëchoing, or continuing to sound or ring, as sounds; reëchoing with sound, as places; having the property of prolonging or increasing sound, as by sympathetic vibration, as bodies; pertaining to resonance.—**res′o-nant-ly**, *adv.*

---

res-o-nate (rez′ō-nāt), *v. i.*; -nated, -nating. [L. *resonatus*, pp. of *resonare*: see *resound*[2].] To resound; exhibit resonance; act as a resonator.—**res′o-na-tor** (-nā-tọr), *n.* [NL.] Something that produces resonance; an appliance for increasing sound by resonance; also, an instrument for detecting the presence of a particular tone by means of resonance; also, in *elect.*, a device for detecting Hertzian waves.—**res′o-na-to-ry** (-nạ-tō-ri), *a.* Producing resonance.

re-sorb (rē-sôrb′), *v. t.* [L. *resorbere* (pp. *resorptus*), < *re-*, back, + *sorbere*, suck in.] To absorb again, as an exudation.—**re-sorb′ent**, *a.* Absorbing again.—**re-sorb′ence**, *n.*

re-sor-cin (re-zôr′sin), *n.* [From *res(in)* + *orcin.*] In *chem.*, a colorless crystalline benzene derivative, orig. obtained from certain resins: used in medicine and in making dyes. Also **re-sor′ci-nol** (-si-nol or -nōl).—**re-sor′ci-nal** (-nạl), *a.*

re-sorp-tion (rē-sôrp′shọn), *n.* [= F. *résorption*, < L. *resorbere*, E. *resorb.*] The act of resorbing, or the fact of being resorbed; in *petrog.*, in the formation of igneous rocks, the process by which a crystal becomes partially or wholly remelted and hence reabsorbed by the molten magma from which it crystallized.—**re-sorp′tive** (-tiv), *a.*

re-sort (rē-zôrt′), *v. i.* [OF. *resortir* (F. *ressortir*), < *re-* (< L. *re-*), back, + *sortir*, go out: see *sortie.*] To return†; revert†; also, to betake one's self, repair, or go (as, "To Argos' realms the victor god *resorts*, And enters old Crotopus' humble courts": Pope's tr. Statius's "Thebais," i. 668); go frequently or customarily (as, "Head-waiter of the chop-house here, To which I most *resort*": Tennyson's "Will Waterproof's Lyrical Monologue," 210); also, to betake one's self for aid, as to a person; have recourse for use or service, as to a thing (as, "I have no opinion of flogging, and therefore I do not *resort* to it," Marryat's "Mr. Midshipman Easy," v.; "one of the devices to which he *resorted* for the purpose of obtaining an ascendency in the English counsels," Macaulay's "Hist. of Eng.," ii.); also, sometimes, to stay, as in a place.—**re-sort′**, *n.* [OF. *resort* (F. *ressort*).] Resorting, repairing, or going, as to a place (obs. or rare: as, "Nor from the heaven of heavens Hath he excluded my *resort* sometimes," Milton's "Paradise Regained," i. 367); habitual or general going or repairing, as to a place or person (as, "Oxford was a school of great *resort* in the reign of Henry II.," Hallam's "Literature of Europe," i. 1. § 20; "the Opera, or any other place of public *resort*," Marryat's "King's Own," xi.); also, concourse or assemblage of people†; an assemblage† or crowd†; also, a place frequented, as by a person or persons (as, "But chiefly the woods were her fav'rite *resort*": Burns's "Caledonia," 15); a place frequented by the public generally (as, a pleasure *resort*; a summer *resort*; a winter *resort*; a health *resort*); also, a resorting to some person or thing for aid, service, etc., or recourse (as, to have *resort* to force or to subterfuge; in the last *resort*, as a last expedient); a person or thing resorted to for aid, service, etc. (as, "a knowledge of the expedients and *resorts* in times of hazard," Dana's "Two Years before the Mast," xxiii.; one's last *resort*, or ultimate means of aid or relief).—**re-sort′er**, *n.*

re-sound[1] (rē-sound′), *v. i.* or *t.* [See *re-.*] To sound again. Also written *re-sound.*

re-sound[2] (rē-zound′), *v.* [OF. *resoner* (F. *résonner*), < L. *resonare*, < *re-*, back, again, + *sonare*, sound.] **I.** *intr.* To reëcho or ring with sound, as a place (as, "The dingle *resounded* with my strokes": Borrow's "Romany Rye," i.); also, to make an echoing sound, or sound loudly, as a thing (as, "Then through the dell his horn *resounds*," Scott's "Lady of the Lake," i. 10; "Cable cars *resounded* in Burton Street," W. Churchill's "Inside of the Cup," i.); also, to be echoed, or ring, as sounds (as, "The shouts of a furious mob *resounded* far and wide": Scott's "Guy Mannering," xlviii.); fig., to be much mentioned or repeated, or be famed or celebrated (as, "What *resounds* In fable or romance of Uther's son," Milton's "Paradise Lost," i. 579; "Milton, a name to *resound* for ages," Tennyson's "Milton"). **II.** *tr.* To give back or reëcho (a sound: as, "Albion's cliffs *resound* the rural lay," Pope's "Spring," 6); also, to give forth or utter loudly (as, "Tho' nations, which consult Their gain, at thy expense, *resound* applause," Young's "Night Thoughts," vii. 176: now rare); also, to proclaim loudly (praises, etc.); celebrate (a person or thing: as, "The man for wisdom's various arts

renown'd . . . O Muse! *resound*," Pope's tr. Homer's "Odyssey," i.).—**re-sound′er**, *n.*—**re-sound′ing**, *p. a.* That resounds; making an echoing sound, or sounding loudly (as, "He struck his breast a *resounding* blow": J. Conrad's "Rover," viii.); echoing, ringing, or sonorous (as, "a speech . . . in which . . . plain talk and *resounding* eloquence were mingled together": Lytton Strachey's "Queen Victoria," v.).—**re-sound′ing-ly**, *adv.*

re-source (rē-sōrs′), *n.* [F. *ressource*, < OF. *resourdre*, < L. *resurgere*, rise again: see *resurge*[2], and cf. *source.*] A source of supply, support, or aid (as, a class of persons forming the chief *resource* of a country for purposes of taxation; "the new *resources* of thought and language which literature felt to be at its disposal," Green's "Short Hist. of the Eng. People," vii. 5); *pl.*, the collective means of a country, an organization, etc., available for its purposes (as, "to prosecute that foreign commerce which brings all the *resources* of a country into profitable action": Irving's "Captain Bonneville," xxxviii.); often, pecuniary means, or funds; money, or any property which can be converted into money; also, available means afforded by the mind or the personal capabilities (as, "He always had the full command of all the *resources* of one of the most fertile minds that ever existed": Macaulay's "Essays," Warren Hastings); also, *sing.*, an action or measure to which one may have recourse in an emergency (as, "I had no *resource* but to request to be shown into a private room": C. Brontë's "Jane Eyre," xi.); an expedient or shift; also, capability in dealing with a situation or meeting difficulties (as, "*Resource* in difficulties is the distinction of great generals": Froude's "Cæsar," xxii.); also, a means of relaxation or diversion (as, "the amusements of letters and of devotion, which afford so many *resources* in solitude": Gibbon's "Decline and Fall of the Roman Empire," xiii.).—**re-source′ful**, *a.* Abounding in resources (as, a *resourceful* country); also, full of resource, or fertile in expedients (as, "His next thought was that women were very *resourceful*": J. Conrad's "Rescue," vi. 5); characterized by or showing resource (as, "mastery . . . of *resourceful* and evasive debate": Charnwood's "Abraham Lincoln," v.).—**re-source′ful-ness**, *n.*—**re-source′less**, *a.* Destitute of resources; without resource.—**re-source′less-ness**, *n.*

re-spect (rē-spekt′), *v. t.* [L. *respectus*, pp. of *respicere*, look back, look at, regard, respect, < *re-*, back, + *specere*, look at.] To look at or on†; front on†; also, to pay attention to†, or heed†; regard† or consider†; also, to relate to, or have reference to (as, "The first case . . . *respected* a bargain . . . between a butcher and a candle-maker": Scott's "Guy Mannering," xlii.); also, to hold in esteem or honor (as, "This good honest old gaucho we all *respected*": W. H. Hudson's "Far Away and Long Ago," xxiii.); show esteem or respect for (as, "It was pleasant to find how his [holy man's] cloth was *respected*": Kipling's "Kim," xi.); show regard or consideration for (as, "You . . . should have *respected* my wishes": Eden Phillpotts's "Grey Room," iii.); refrain from interfering with (as, to *respect* a person's privacy).—**re-spect′**, *n.* [L. *respectus* n., < *respicere*.] Attentive look, gaze, or regard† (as, "At that day shall a man look to his Maker, and his eyes shall have *respect* to the Holy One of Israel": Isa. xvii. 7); hence, attention† or heed†; also, regard or consideration (as, "Onely for honour and for high regard, Without *respect* of richesse or reward": Spenser's "Faerie Queene," iii. 2. 7); discrimination or partiality in the regarding of persons or things (as, "It is not good to have *respect* of persons in judgment": Prov. xxiv. 23); also, a consideration, motive, or end (as, "All the honours and worldly *respects* for which I formerly risked my life, were now my aversion": H. Brooke's "Fool of Quality," xviii.); also, relation or reference (as, "Their independence . . . had *respect* only to their own sovereign," De Quincey's "Revolt of the Tartars"; to make inquiries with *respect* to a matter); also, a particular, detail, or point (in phrases with *in*: as, "Suppose the analogy did . . . fail in this *respect*," J. Butler's "Analogy of Religion," ii. 3; "In some *respects* this was true," Mrs. Wharton's "Age of Innocence," xv.); also, esteem or deferential regard felt or shown (as, "I have a great *respect* for any man who makes his own way in life": W. Churchill's "Modern Chronicle," i. 10); deferential or respectful treatment (as, "Some voluntary *respect* was yielded to age and valour," Gibbon's "Decline and Fall of the Roman Empire," xlii.; "According to his virtue let us use him, With all *respect* and rites of burial," Shakspere's "Julius Cæsar," v. 5. 77); the condition of being esteemed or honored (as, "Let some part of government be kept in *respect!*" Burke's "American Taxation"); rank† or standing† (as, "many of the best *respect* in Rome": Shakspere's "Julius Cæsar," i. 2. 59); also, *pl.*, sentiments of esteem as conveyed in polite messages (as, "Give her my best *respects*": W. H. Hudson's "Purple Land," xiv.); deferential or respectful compliments, as paid by making a call on a person or otherwise (in 'to pay one's respects': as, "My wife and I are come to pay our *respects*," Borrow's "Romany Rye," vi.: the phrase being sometimes used ironically, esp. of making uncomplimentary references in a speech or the like).—**in respect of,** in consideration of†, or because of†; also, with respect or reference to; also, in comparison with† (as, "*In respect of* a fine workman, I am but . . . a cobbler": Shakspere's "Julius Cæsar," i. 1. 10).

re-spect-a-bil-i-ty (rẹ-spek-tạ-bil′i-ti), *n.*; pl. *-ties* (-tiz). The state or quality of being respectable; respectable social standing; respectable character or repute on moral grounds (as, "He . . . remarked . . . that he should want references of *respectability*": Besant's "All Sorts and Conditions of Men," iv.); also, those who are respectable (as, "Nearly the whole *respectability* of the town was either fussily marshalling processions or gazing down at them": Arnold Bennett's "Clayhanger," ii. 11); also, a respectable person (commonly in *pl.*); also, *pl.*, things accepted as respectable.

re-spect-a-ble (rẹ-spek′tạ-bl), *a.* Worthy of respect or esteem, estimable, or worthy (as, "I honoured and esteemed the *respectable* Laura like a mother," Godwin's "Caleb Williams," xxxix.; "His administrative talents, and his *respectable* and conciliatory character, made him well fitted to preside over the Government," Lecky's "Hist. of Eng. in the 18th Century," i.); of good or fair social standing, as persons; pertaining or appropriate to such standing, as things; honest and decent, irrespective of social standing, as persons or their character, etc. (as, "He was a *respectable* man . . . he had been chief-officer of home ships, with a spotless character," J. Conrad's "Rescue," iii. 9; "She's at least *respectable,* I hope!" Du Maurier's "Trilby," iv.); of good or fair repute (as, a *respectable* neighborhood); proper or decent (as, conduct or language which is not *respectable*); seemly or decent in appearance, or as the appearance (as, "It will be necessary to find a milliner . . . Something must be done with Maggy too, who at present is . . . barely *respectable*," Dickens's "Little Dorrit," i. 35; *respectable* clothes); of moderate excellence, fairly good, or fair (as, "He was a *respectable* military administrator": Lecky's "Hist. of Eng. in the 18th Century," viii.); considerable in size, number, or amount, or as size, etc. (as, "His father . . . had . . . left him a *respectable* fortune": Arnold Bennett's "Pretty Lady," vi.).—**re-spect′a-bly,** *adv.*

re-spect-er (rẹ-spek′tẹr), *n.* One who respects.—**respecter of persons,** one who considers individual persons in his dealings, so as to discriminate in favor of some or against others instead of being impartial or just: as, "I perceive that God is no *respecter of persons*" (Acts, x. 34).

re-spect-ful (rẹ-spekt′fụl), *a.* Full of, characterized by, or showing respect: as, to be *respectful* to age; "Had they brought money with them they might have had a *respectful* hearing" (Froude's "Cæsar," xv.).—**re-spect′ful-ly,** *adv.*—**re-spect′ful-ness,** *n.*

re-spect-ing (rẹ-spek′ting), *prep.* [Orig. ppr.] Considering†, or taking into account†; also, regarding or concerning, or relating to (as, "Every one is informed . . . respecting the supposed most skilful way of conducting his defence," Godwin's "Caleb Williams," xxiii.; "to ask a few questions *respecting* the seminary," Borrow's "Bible in Spain," i.).

re-spec-tive (rẹ-spek′tiv), *a.* Attentive†, heedful†, or regardful†; also, discriminating†; partial†; also, having relation or reference to something†; also, pertaining severally or individually to each of a number of persons, things, etc. (as, "He and I will talk together for our *respective* principals," J. H. Newman's "Callista," ix.; "In two hours all were at their *respective* destinations," Marryat's "King's Own," lvii.); pertaining to one particular person, thing, etc., of a number, or particular (as, each went his *respective* way; each house is marked with its *respective* number); also, respectful† or courteous†; also, worthy of respect†; respectable†.—**re-spec′tive-ly,** *adv.* In a respective manner; now, with respect to each of a number (as, these are distinguished *respectively* as A, B, and C; "if . . . the child's mother could see . . . the child's memories *respectively* of her husband and herself," W. De Morgan's "Alice-for-Short," xiii.); severally.

re-spell (rē-spel′), *v. t.* [See *re-.*] To spell anew.

re-spir-a-ble (rẹ-spīr′ạ-bl or res′pi-rạ-), *a.* Capable of being respired; also, capable of respiring.—**re-spir-a-bil′i-ty** (-bil′i-ti), *n.*

res-pi-ra-tion (res-pi-rā′shọn), *n.* [L. *respiratio(n-).*] The act of respiring; the inhalation and exhalation of air; breathing; specif., in animals, the process by which oxygen is absorbed into the system and the oxidation products (esp. carbon dioxide) are given off; also, in plants, the process by which oxygen is absorbed and carbon dioxide is released; also, a single act of breathing (as, "He [a lion] still breathed regularly, as his flanks heaved with each *respiration*": J. H. Patterson's "Man-Eaters of Tsavo," xxii.).—**res′pi-ra-tor,** *n.* [NL.] A device, usually of gauze, worn over the mouth, or nose and mouth, to prevent the inhalation of noxious substances, etc.—**re-spir-a-to-ry** (rẹ-spīr′ạ-tọ̄-ri or res′pi-rạ-), *a.* Pertaining to or serving for respiration.

re-spire (rẹ-spīr′), *v.*; *-spired, -spiring.* [L. *respirare* (pp. *respiratus*), < *re-,* back, + *spirare,* breathe.] **I.** *tr.* To breathe out or exhale; also, to breathe in and out; inhale and exhale; breathe. **II.** *intr.* To inhale and exhale air for the purpose of maintaining life; breathe; also, to breathe freely again, after anxiety, trouble, etc. (as, "The Imperial City stands released From bondage threatened by the embattled East, And Christendom *respires*": Wordsworth's "Siege of Vienna Raised by John Sobieski"); also, to take breath, or rest (as, "Pause, then; and, for a moment, here *respire*": Young's "Night Thoughts," ix. 1741).

res-pite (res′pit), *n.* [OF. *respit* (F. *répit*), < L. *respectus, n.*] Respect† or regard†; also, a delay, or extension of time, asked or allowed (as, "Give us seven days' *respite,* that we may send messengers unto all the coasts of Israel": 1 Sam. xi. 3); esp., temporary suspension of the execution of a person condemned to death; a reprieve; hence, delay or cessation for a time of anything distressing or trying (as, "No reversal or *respite* of their sufferings had followed," J. H. Newman's "Callista," xvi.; to toil without *respite*); an interval of relief from something (as, "I was just thanking Providence for the *respite* from hob-nobbing which I imagined was to follow," Lever's "Harry Lorrequer," xix.; a brief *respite* from care).—**res′pite,** *v. t.*; *-pited, -piting.* [OF. *respiter.*] To grant a respite to, esp. from execution or death, or reprieve (as, "Every one is informed whether he shall be acquitted, *respited,* or pardoned": Godwin's "Caleb Williams," xxiii.); relieve temporarily from anything distressing or trying, as from pain or toil; also, to grant delay in the carrying out of (an obligation, punishment, etc.: as, "Gregg . . . was sentenced to be hung, but his execution was *respited* for nearly three months," Lecky's "Hist. of Eng. in the 18th Century," i.); give an interval of relief from, or cause to cease for a time (as, "Care may be *respited,* but not repealed": Wordsworth's "Evening Voluntaries," iv. 24); also, to cease from† or suspend†.

re-splend (rẹ-splend′), *v. i.* [L. *resplendere,* < *re-,* back, again, + *splendere,* shine.] To shine brilliantly; be radiant or splendid.

re-splen-dence, re-splen-den-cy (rẹ-splen′dẹns, -dẹn-si), *n.* Resplendent state; splendor.

re-splen-dent (rẹ-splen′dẹnt), *a.* [L. *resplendens* (-*ent-*), ppr. of *resplendere*: see *resplend.*] Shining brilliantly, or gleaming (as, "In the dining-room, the sideboard flashed *resplendent* with plate," C. Brontë's "Jane Eyre," xvii.; "The moon shone with a pure and *resplendent* whiteness," Irving's "Knickerbocker's New York," iii. 4); hence, splendid, gorgeous, or showily fine in appearance (as, "A coach-and-four, *resplendent* in liveries, stopped at the door": Miss Mulock's "John Halifax," xv.); strikingly fine or admirable

---

(variable) ḏ as d or j, ṣ as s or sh, ṭ as t or ch, ẕ as z or zh; *o,* F. cloche; ü, F. menu; c̩h, Sc. loch; ṅ, F. bonbon; ′, primary accent; ″, secondary accent; †, obsolete; <, from; +, and; =, equals. See also lists at beginning of book.

in character (as, *resplendent* virtues or achievements).—**re-splen'dent-ly**, *adv.*

re-spond (rĕ-spond'), *v.* [OF. *respondre* (F. *répondre*), < L. *respondere* (pp. *responsus*), < *re-*, back, + *spondere*, promise.] **I.** *tr.* To say in answer or reply (as, he *responded* that no more could be done; "Miss Lucy Morgan . . . *responded* cheerfully: 'I'm willing to learn wisdom,'" Tarkington's "Magnificent Ambersons," v.); also, to answer or satisfy, as by payment (as, the prisoner was held to *respond* the judgment of the court: U. S.); also, to answer or correspond to† (as, "His great deeds *respond* his speeches great": Fairfax's tr. Tasso's "Jerusalem Delivered," x. 40). **II.** *intr.* To make answer, or give a reply in words (as, to *respond* briefly to a question); utter a response; hence, to make a return by some action as if in answer (as, to *respond* by a nod; to *respond* to a cry for help by going to the rescue; to *respond* generously to a call for contributions); exhibit some action or effect as if in answer, or react (as, nerves *respond* to a stimulus; the system *responds* to a drug, or to treatment; "My feelings . . . were dead indeed if they did not *respond* to such an inspiration," W. Churchill's "Modern Chronicle," i. 9); also, to answer, meet liability, or give satisfaction (as, the defendant is held to *respond* in damages: U. S.); also, to answer or correspond (*to*: as, "The service in no way *responded* to her expectations," Arnold Bennett's "Hilda Lessways," ii. 1).—**re-spond'**, *n.* An answer or reply (now rare); *eccles.*, a response; specif., a short anthem chanted at intervals during the reading of a lection; also, a responsory; in *arch.*, a half-pillar or the like engaged in a wall to support an arch.—**re-spond'ence**, *n.* The act of responding, or response (as, *respondence* to a stimulus); also, agreement or correspondence (obs. or rare).—**re-spond'ent.** [L. *respondens* (-*ent*-), ppr.] **I.** *a.* Answering; responsive; also, correspondent†. **II.** *n.* One who responds, or makes reply; in *law*, a defendant, esp. in a divorce case.—**res-pon-den-ti-a** (res-pon-den'shi-ä), *n.* [NL.] A loan on the cargo of a vessel, payment being contingent on the safe arrival of the cargo or some part of it at the port of destination.—**re-spond'er**, *n.* One who or that which responds; in *elect.*, a device for detecting Hertzian waves.

re-sponse (rĕ-spons'), *n.* [OF. *response* (F. *réponse*), earlier *respons*, < L. *responsum*, prop. neut. of *responsus*, pp. of *respondere*, E. *respond*.] An answer or reply, whether in words or in some other form (as, "A fierce cheer was their *response*," H. Melville's "Moby-Dick," liv.; "Her ladyship . . . smiled to him, but obtained no *response*," Barrie's "Sentimental Tommy," viii.; "The mother's *response* was a grieving silence," Tarkington's "Alice Adams," iii.); often, an answer or reply in the form of some action or proceeding (as, his *response* was a vigorous blow; the vote of confidence was a *response* to these charges); a responsive action, or reaction, as to some stimulus or affecting agency; also, the act of responding, answering, or replying (as, to listen without *response*; temporarily incapable of *response*; "In *response* to his knock the door was opened," W. Churchill's "Modern Chronicle," ii. 10); *eccles.*, a verse, sentence, phrase, or word said or sung by the choir or congregation in reply to the officiant (cf. *versicle*); also, a responsory.

re-spon-si-bil-i-ty (rĕ-spon-si-bil'i-ti), *n.*; pl. *-ties* (-tiz). The state or fact of being responsible; an instance of being responsible, or a particular burden of obligation resting upon one who is responsible (as, "He . . . felt the *responsibilities* of his position": H. G. Wells's "Mr. Polly," iv.); also, something for which one is responsible or which entails obligation (as, a child is a *responsibility* to its parents; the horse proved to be a *responsibility* rather than an advantage).—**on one's own responsibility**, with the responsibility resting solely upon one's self, as for something one does; on one's own authority: as, "He promulgates his system . . . entirely *on his own responsibility*" (Hawthorne's "Blithedale Romance," vii.).

re-spon-si-ble (rĕ-spon'si-bl), *a.* [Obs. F. *responsible*, < L. *respondere*, E. *respond*.] Answerable or accountable, as for something within one's power of choice or control or under one's management or care (as, to be *responsible* for one's own actions or for the actions of one's subordinates; "I am *responsible* for the ship's safety," Stevenson's "Treasure Island," ix.); under obligation to account (*to*: as, "The

people had given him his command, and to the people alone he was *responsible*," Froude's "Cæsar," xiv.); involving accountability or responsibility (as, a *responsible* position or office); also, chargeable with being the author, cause, or occasion of something (with *for*: as, who is *responsible* for all these changes? his methods are *responsible* for the general dissatisfaction; the weather is *responsible* for the delay); also, having a mental or moral capacity for knowing right from wrong, in virtue of which one may be held accountable for his acts (as, man is a *responsible* being); capable of rational thought or action (as, wrought upon by passion or fear until no longer *responsible*); also, able to discharge obligations or pay debts (as, "I let his houses; I told him who were *responsible* tenants": Besant's "All Sorts and Conditions of Men," iv.); reliable in business or other dealings; showing or suggesting reliability (as, to have a *responsible* appearance; "his studious and *responsible* face," W. De Morgan's "Somehow Good," iv.).—**re-spon'si-ble-ness**, *n.* —**re-spon'si-bly**, *adv.*

re-spon-sion (rĕ-spon'shon), *n.* [L. *responsio(n-)*, < *respondere*, E. *respond*.] The act of responding or answering, or a response (now rare); *pl.*, at Oxford University, England, the first examination which candidates for the degree of B. A. have to pass.

re-spon-sive (rĕ-spon'siv), *a.* [LL. *responsivus*.] Responding; making answer or reply (as, "Celestial voices . . . Sole, or *responsive* each to other's note": Milton's "Paradise Lost," iv. 683); acting in response, as to some stimulus; often, responding readily to influences, friendly advances, or the like (as, "This Mr. Arthur Russell was a much more *responsive* person than one had supposed": Tarkington's "Alice Adams," x.); also, characterized by the use of responses (as, *responsive* worship); also, correspondent (now rare).—**re-spon'sive-ly**, *adv.*—**re-spon'sive-ness**, *n.*

re-spon-so-ry (rĕ-spon'sō-ri), *n.*; pl. *-ries* (-riz). [ML. *responsorium*.] *Eccles.*, an anthem sung after a lection by a soloist and choir alternately.

rest[1] (rest), *n.* [AS. *rest*, *ræst*, rest, resting-place, = OHG. *rasta* (G. *rast*), rest, also stage of a journey, = Icel. *röst* and Goth. *rasta*, stage of a journey, mile.] The refreshing quiet or repose of sleep (as, to retire to *rest*; to have a good night's *rest*); also, refreshing ease or inactivity after exertion or labor (as, to allow an hour for *rest*; wayfarers at *rest* in the shade; *rest* for the weary body or mind); intermission of labor or activity (as, "Six days shall work be done: but the seventh day is the sabbath of *rest* . . . ye shall do no work therein": Lev. xxiii. 3); an interval or period of relief from exertion or labor (as, "Having but one horse, he had to go in a leisurely way with many *rests*," W. H. Hudson's "Far Away and Long Ago," xxiv.; "He [a doctor] would order you a *rest*. He would send you off to some holiday resort," H. G. Wells's "Soul of a Bishop," v.); also, in general, relief or freedom from anything that wearies, troubles, or disturbs (as, *rest* after pain; "Oh that I had wings like a dove! for then would I fly away, and be at *rest*," Ps. lv. 6); comfortable ease (as, "ignoble *rest*": Cowper's "To Miss Macartney," 7); mental or spiritual ease or tranquillity (as, to set one's mind at *rest*; care and remorse allow us no *rest*); undisturbed quiet, or peace (as, a period of *rest* between wars; a land or a people at *rest*); relief or freedom (from something specified: as, to have *rest* from one's labors; "The Lord shall give thee *rest* from thy sorrow, and from thy fear, and from the hard bondage wherein thou wast made to serve," Isa. xiv. 3); also, the repose of death or of the grave (as, "This pale faint swan, Who . . . sings His soul and body to their lasting *rest*," Shakspere's "King John," v. 7. 24; to lay the dead to *rest*); often, the ease and peace of the blessed after death (as, the heavenly *rest*; entered into *rest*, an expression used of one who has died; "Hang the sad verse on Carolina's urn, And hail her passage to the realms of *rest*," Pope's "Epilogue to the Satires," i. 81); also, cessation or absence of motion (as, a body at *rest*; to bring a machine to *rest*); stillness, as of water, the air, etc.; quiet, quiescence, or inactivity, as of some physical agency (as, a volcano at *rest*); subsidence, complete abatement, or final settlement (esp. in certain phrases: as, to lay or put fears to *rest*; to set a question at *rest*); also, stay or abode, as in a place† (as, "I entreat you . . . That you vouchsafe your *rest* here in our court Some little time":

Shakspere's "Hamlet," ii. 2. 13); a place of abode, or resting-place (as, "Till we end In dust, our final *rest* and native home": Milton's "Paradise Lost," x. 1085); specif., an establishment for providing shelter or lodging for some class of persons (as, a *rest* for sailors ashore); also, a piece or thing for something to rest on (as, a foot-*rest*; a *rest* for a firearm or a billiard-cue in use; a *rest* for the cutting tool in a lathe); a support, or supporting device; in *music*, an interval of silence between tones, or a mark or sign indicating it; in *pros.*, a short pause in reading; a cæsura.—**rest¹**, *v. i.* [AS. *restan*, *ræstan*.] To take rest, or refresh one's self with rest, as by sleeping, lying down, or relaxing the body or mind; recruit the powers or relieve weariness by cessation of exertion or labor; cease from exertion, labor, or activity (often with *from*: as, "On the seventh day God ended his work . . . and he *rested* on the seventh day from all his work," Gen. ii. 2); also, to be at ease, or have tranquillity or peace (as, "We would not let Mrs. Mirvan *rest* till she consented to go": Miss Burney's "Evelina," x.); also, to repose or lie in death or in the grave (as, "In the same cemetery *rest* the mortal remains of Doddridge": Borrow's "Bible in Spain," i.); also, to cease from motion, come to rest, or stop; be quiet or still (as, "like the troubled sea, when it cannot *rest*": Isa. lvii. 20); become or remain inactive; be discontinued, or go without further action or notice (as, to let a matter *rest*; "An if I wist he did,—but let it *rest*; Other affairs must now be managed," Shakspere's "1 Henry VI.," iv. 1. 180); also, to stay or abide, as in a place (archaic: as, "to *rest* awhile within her court," Tennyson's "Geraint and Enid," 854); also, to lie, recline, sit, or lean for rest or ease (*in*, *on*, *against*, etc.: as, "He was suffering from some internal malady, and spent most of the day . . . *resting* in an easy-chair," W. H. Hudson's "Far Away and Long Ago," xiii.); lie or be set for support (*on*, *against*, etc.: as, his arm *rested* on the table; the ladder *rested* against the wall); be imposed (*on* or *upon*), as a burden or responsibility; rely (*on* or *upon*: as, "Help us, O Lord our God; for we *rest* on thee," 2 Chron. xiv. 11); trust (*in*: as, "Nor did he doubt her more, But *rested* in her fealty," Tennyson's "Geraint and Enid," 966); be based or founded, or depend (*on* or *upon*: as, "The power of the house of commons in Great Britain *rested* on its exclusive right to grant annually the supplies necessary for carrying on the government," Bancroft's "Hist. of the U. S.," Amer. Revolution, i. 1); have its ground or seat (*in*: as, "I then inquired in what *rested* his hope of protection," Borrow's "Bible in Spain," iii.); lie, be found, or be (where specified: as, the blame *rests* with them; "No stain had ever *rested* on the name of Metellus," Froude's "Cæsar," v.); be present, dwell, or linger (*on* or *upon*: as, a light or shadow *rests* on a spot; a smile *rests* on the lips); be fixed or directed on something, as the gaze, eyes, etc.; in *law*, to terminate voluntarily the introduction of evidence in a case.—**to rest on one's oars.** See under *oar*, *n.*—**rest¹**, *v. t.* To give rest to, or refresh with rest (as, to *rest* one's self; a halt to *rest* the horses); also, to grant rest or peace to (the soul, a person, etc.), as after death (much used in pious wishes: as, "Is my boy, God *rest* his soul, alive or dead?" Shakspere's "Merchant of Venice," ii. 2. 75); also, to bring to rest, or to a halt or stop; let stand; allow to remain inactive or without further action; also, to lay or place for rest, ease, or comfortable support (as, to *rest* the head on a pillow, or on another's breast; to *rest* one's back against a tree); in general, to place or set for support or for a firm position (as, "Straight he took his bow of ash-tree, On the sand one end he *rested*": Longfellow's "Hiawatha," ix. 147); base, or let depend, as on some ground of reliance (as, to *rest* one's hopes on assurances received); fix (the eyes, etc.: as, "She *rested* her eyes on him, steadily," H. James's "Portrait of a Lady," xliii.); in *law*, to terminate voluntarily the introduction of evidence on (as, to *rest* one's case).

rest² (rest), *v. i.* [OF. F. *rester*, < L. *restare*, stop behind, stay, remain, < *re-*, back, + *stare*, stand.] To be left, or remain (archaic: as, "There *rests* no other shift but this," Shakspere's "1 Henry VI.," ii. 1. 75); also, to continue to be, or remain (as specified: as, *rest* assured that it is true; "He *rested* well content that all was well," Tennyson's "Geraint and Enid," 951).—**rest²**, *n.* [OF. F. *reste*.] That which is left or remains after separation of a part; the remainder (as,

the *rest* of the money, of the day, or of the sentence); the others (as, he is just like all the *rest*; one horse was in advance of the *rest*).

rest³ (rest), *v. t.* [For *arrest*.] To arrest. [Now chiefly prov.]—**rest³**, *n.* In medieval armor, a contrivance fixed to the side of the breastplate or cuirass for receiving and supporting the butt of a lance when couched for charging: as, to set or lay one's lance in *rest*; "Each ready lance is in the *rest*" (Scott's "Lord of the Isles," vi. 22).

re-state (rē-stāt'), *v. t.* [See *re-*.] To state again or anew.—**re-state'ment**, *n.*

res-tau-rant (res'tọ-rạnt), *n.* [F., prop. ppr. of *restaurer*, OF. *restorer*, E. *restore²*.] An establishment where refreshments of food and drink, or meals, are served, as to customers.—**res-tau-ra-teur** (res-tō-rȧ-tèr'), *n.* [F.] The keeper of a restaurant.

rest=cure (rest'kūr), *n.* A treatment for nervous disorders, consisting of a complete rest, usually combined with systematic feeding, massage, etc.

rest-er (res'tèr), *n.* One who rests.

rest-ful (rest'fúl), *a.* Full of, fraught with, or giving rest (as, "Tired with all these, for *restful* death I cry," Shakspere's "Sonnets," lxvi.; a *restful* hour); also, being at rest; quiet; tranquil; peaceful.—**rest'ful-ly**, *adv.*—**rest'ful-ness**, *n.*

rest=har-row (rest'har″ō), *n.* [See *rest³*.] A low, pink-flowered, leguminous European shrub, *Ononis arvensis*, with tough roots which hinder the plow or harrow.

res-tiff (res'tif), *a.* Earlier form of *restive*.

res-ti-form (res'ti-fôrm), *a.* [NL. *restiformis*, < L. *restis*, rope, cord, + *forma*, form.] Cord-like: as, the *restiform* bodies (in *anat.*, a pair of cord-like bundles of nerve-fibers lying one on each side of the medulla oblongata and connecting it with the cerebellum).

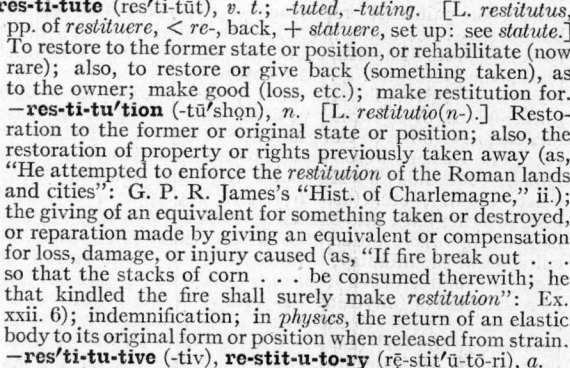

Flowering Branch of Rest-harrow.—*a*, a flower; *b*, the leaf.

rest-ing (res'ting), *p. a.* In *bot.*, dormant: applied esp. to spores which germinate after a period of dormancy.

rest-ing =place (res'ting-plās), *n.* A place for resting, as in sleep or in halting for rest on a journey; also, one's grave or tomb (often 'last, or final, resting-place'); also, a place of abode (archaic: as, "My people shall dwell . . . in sure dwellings, and in quiet *resting places*," Isa. xxxii. 18).

res-ti-tute (res'ti-tūt), *v. t.*; *-tuted*, *-tuting.* [L. *restitutus*, pp. of *restituere*, < *re-*, back, + *statuere*, set up: see *statute*.] To restore to the former state or position, or rehabilitate (now rare); also, to restore or give back (something taken), as to the owner; make good (loss, etc.); make restitution for.—**res-ti-tu'tion** (-tū'shọn), *n.* [L. *restitutio(n-).*] Restoration to the former or original state or position; also, the restoration of property or rights previously taken away (as, "He attempted to enforce the *restitution* of the Roman lands and cities": G. P. R. James's "Hist. of Charlemagne," ii.); the giving of an equivalent for something taken or destroyed, or reparation made by giving an equivalent or compensation for loss, damage, or injury caused (as, "If fire break out . . . so that the stacks of corn . . . be consumed therewith; he that kindled the fire shall surely make *restitution*": Ex. xxii. 6); indemnification; in *physics*, the return of an elastic body to its original form or position when released from strain.—**res'ti-tu-tive** (-tiv), **re-stit-u-to-ry** (rē-stit'ū-tọ-ri), *a.*

res-tive (res'tiv), *a.* [OF. *restif* (F. *rétif*), < L. *restare*, E. *rest²*.] Inactive or sluggish (obs. or rare); also, refusing to go forward, as a horse; hence, refractory (as, "The animal was *restive*, and . . . strenuously resisted being mounted": Motley's "Dutch Republic," vi. 6); impatient of control, restraint, or delay, as persons (as, "The army . . . had grown uncontrollably *restive* at the slow and tortuous course of the dealings": Morley's "Oliver Cromwell," iii. 6); sometimes, restless or uneasy.—**res′tive-ly,** *adv.*—**res′tive-ness,** *n.*

rest-less (rest′les), *a.* Without rest or sleep, or without unbroken, refreshing sleep (as, "I *restless* lie frae e'en to morn," Burns's "How Lang and Dreary"; a *restless* night); also, taking no rest, or averse to quiet or inaction, as persons; characterized by unceasing activity (as, "condemned by nature and fortune to an active and *restless* life": Swift's "Gulliver's Travels," ii. 1); also, unable to rest, unquiet, or uneasy, as a person or animal, the mind, heart, etc.; characterized by or showing inability to remain at rest (as, a *restless* mood; a *restless* twitch of the hand); also, never at rest, motionless, or still, or never ceasing (as, "watching . . . the shuttle's *restless* play": Whittier's "Mary Garvin"); also, affording no rest (as, "*Restless* was the chair": Cowper's "Task," i. 44); preventing rest (as, "Ease to the body some, none to the mind From *restless* thoughts": Milton's "Samson Agonistes," 19).—**rest′less-ly,** *adv.*—**rest′less-ness,** *n.*

re-stock (rē-stok′), *v. t.* [See *re-*.] To stock anew.

re-stor-a-ble (rē-stōr′a̤-bl), *a.* That may be restored.

res-to-ra-tion (res-tō̤-rā′shọn), *n.* [Earlier *restauration,* < OF. F. *restauration,* < LL. *restauratio(n-)*.] The act of restoring, or the state or fact of being restored; a bringing back to a former, original, normal, or unimpaired condition; a bringing back to or recovery of health or strength; a putting back into a former position, dignity, etc.; renewal, revival, or reëstablishment; restitution of something taken away or lost; also, something which is restored; specif., a representation of an ancient building, extinct animal, or the like, showing it in its original state; also [*cap.*], with *the,* in *Eng. hist.,* the reëstablishment of the monarchy in England with the return of Charles II. in 1660; hence, the period of the reigns of Charles II. (1660–85) and James II. (1685–88).—**res-to-ra′tion-ism,** *n.* The doctrine of the final restoration of all men to a state of happiness in the future life.—**res-to-ra′tion-ist,** *n.*

re-stor-a-tive (rē-stōr′a̤-tiv). [OF. F. *restauratif.*] **I.** *a.* Serving to restore; pertaining to restoration; esp., capable of renewing health or strength. **II.** *n.* A restorative agent; a food, cordial, or medicine which recruits the vital powers; esp., a means of restoring a person to consciousness.—**re-stor′a-tive-ly,** *adv.*

re-store[1] (rē-stōr′), *v. t.* [See *re-*.] To store anew. Also written *re-store.*

re-store[2] (rē-stōr′), *v. t.*; *-stored, -storing.* [OF. *restorer, restaurer* (F. *restaurer*), < L. *restaurare,* restore, repair, rebuild, < *re-,* back, + *-staurare,* occurring also in *instaurare,* renew, restore: see *instauration.*] To bring back to a former, original, or normal condition (as, to *restore* a country to order after a revolution; to *restore* a person to consciousness); bring back from a state of decay, injury, or harmful alteration, to the original condition or form, as a building, statue, or painting; reproduce or represent (an ancient building, extinct animal, etc.) in the original state; bring back to a state of health, soundness, or vigor (as, "The quiet place, the pure air . . . will *restore* you in a few days": Dickens's "Oliver Twist," xxxii.); also, to put back to a former place, or to former position, rank, etc. (as, "Release me, and *restore* me to the ground," Tennyson's "Tithonus," 72; "The Bishops were *restored* to their seats in the Upper House," Macaulay's "Hist. of Eng.," ii.); reinstate in an office, dignity, etc. (as, to *restore* an emperor or king); also, to bring back into existence, use, or the like, or reëstablish (as, to *restore* order; "to *restore* the helmets and the cuirasses of the infantry," Gibbon's "Decline and Fall of the Roman Empire," xxvii.); also, to give back, or make return or restitution of (anything taken away or lost: as, to *restore* stolen or lost goods to the owner); also, to make compensation or amends for† (as, "But if the while I think on thee, dear friend, All losses are *restored* and sorrows end": Shakspere's "Sonnets," xxx.).—**re-stor′er** (-stōr′ẽr), *n.*

re-strain (rē-strān′), *v. t.* [OF. F. *restreindre,* < L. *restringere* (pp. *restrictus*), bind back, confine, restrain, < *re-,* back, + *stringere,* draw tight: cf. *restrict.*] To draw tight†; also, to hold back from action, or keep in check or under control (as, to *restrain* a person from interference; to *restrain* a horse by a bridle; he *restrained* himself as long as he could); put a check upon, keep down, or repress (as, "His authority

had *restrained* the pride and oppression of the royal officers," Gibbon's "Decline and Fall of the Roman Empire," xxxix.; to *restrain* one's curiosity; "She *restrained* tears with difficulty," Eden Phillpotts's "Children of Men," i. 6); restrict or limit (obs. or archaic: as, "natural knowledge, in the more common *restrained* sense of the words," J. Butler's "Analogy of Religion," ii. 3); deprive of liberty, as a person; also, to withhold, as from a person†; also, to forbid† or prohibit†.—**re-strain′a-ble,** *a.* That may be restrained.—**re-strain′ed-ly,** *adv.*—**re-strain′er,** *n.* One who or that which restrains; specif., a chemical, as potassium bromide, added to a photographic developer to retard its action.—**re-straint′** (-strānt′), *n.* [OF. *restrainte.*] The act of restraining, or holding back, controlling, or checking; restraining action or influence (as, freedom from *restraint*); a means of restraining (as, "They threw off all *restraints,* conventions, pretences": Arnold Bennett's "Leonora," i.); also, the state or fact of being restrained; deprivation of liberty, or confinement; also, constraint or reserve (as, "a stout, merry little woman, whose informal welcome had banished his *restraint* almost at once": L. Merrick's "Position of Peggy Harper," ii.); also, restriction† or limitation†; also, a prohibition†.

re-strict (rē-strikt′), *v. t.* [L. *restrictus,* pp. of *restringere*: see *restrain.*] To confine or keep within limits, as of space, action, choice, quantity, etc. (as, to *restrict* a practice to a particular area; "a pardon, so *restricted* that none were likely to be forgiven save those who had done no wrong," Motley's "Dutch Republic," ii. 8; to *restrict* the number of officers to five; often, to attach limitations of application to (a meaning, etc.).—**re-strict′ed,** *p. a.* Confined within limits; limited.—**re-strict′ed-ly,** *adv.*—**re-stric′tion** (-strik′shọn), *n.* [LL. *restrictio(n-)*.] The act of restricting, or the state of being restricted; limitation; also, something that restricts; a restricting or limiting condition or regulation; a limitation.—**re-stric′tive** (-tiv), *a.* Tending or serving to restrict; of the nature of a restriction; also, expressing or implying restriction or limitation of application, as terms, expressions, etc.—**re-stric′tive-ly,** *adv.*

re-strike (rē-strīk′), *v. t.*; pret. and pp. *-struck.* [See *re-*.] To strike again; esp., to stamp (a coin) anew, with a different impression.

re-sult (rē-zult′), *v. i.* [ML. *resultare,* arise, result, L. spring back, freq. of *resilire*: see *resile.*] To spring back† or rebound†; also, to spring, arise, or proceed as a consequence from actions, circumstances, premises, etc. (as, from these measures much good may *result*; if they are molested, trouble will *result*); be the outcome; also, to terminate or end in a specified manner or thing (as, the affair *resulted* badly for him; the match *resulted* in a draw); also, in *law,* to revert (*to*).—**re-sult′,** *n.* That which results; the outcome, consequence, or effect of some action, circumstance, etc., or a particular consequence or effect (as, "If they had refused, the *result* would not have been greatly different," Froude's "Cæsar," xxvii.; "Judging from the *results* I have seen . . . I cannot say . . . that I agree with you," Mallock's "New Republic," iii. 2); also, a decision or determination, as of a council or a deliberative assembly (obs. or rare: as, "If our proposals once again were heard, We should compel them to a quick *result,*" Milton's "Paradise Lost," vi. 619); in *math.,* a quantity, value, etc., obtained by calculation.—**re-sult′ant. I.** *a.* That results; following as a result or consequence; specif., resulting from the combination of two or more agents (as, a *resultant* force). **II.** *n.* That which results; specif., a resultant force, velocity, or the like (see *composition of forces*).—**re-sult′ful,** *a.* Fraught with results; fruitful; effective.—**re-sult′less,** *a.* Without results; fruitless; ineffective.

re-sum-a-ble (rē-zū′ma̤-bl), *a.* That may be resumed.

re-sume (rē-zūm′), *v.*; *-sumed, -suming.* [OF. *resumer* (F. *résumer*), < L. *resumere* (pp. *resumptus*), < *re-,* again, + *sumere,* take.] **I.** *tr.* To take back (as, "He . . . replied that no human consideration should tempt him to *resume* the gift which he had conferred," Gibbon's "Decline and Fall of the Roman Empire," xlix.; "concessions which the sovereign had freely made and might at his pleasure *resume,*" Macaulay's "Hist. of Eng.," i.); also, to take, or take on, again (as, to *resume* one's maiden name; "ere russet fields their green *resume*," Bryant's "Yellow Violet"; "*resuming* . . . my own nationality," W. H. Hudson's "Purple Land," xvii.); take up or go on with again after interruption (as, to *resume* a journey; to *resume* official duties; "This official . . . *resumed* what was evidently an interrupted discourse," H. G. Wells's "Mr. Britling," i. 1. § 3); take again into use, or return to the use of (as, "She idly *resumed* the great Venetian fan which hung from her waist": Howells's "Foregone Conclusion," viii.); take or occupy again (as, "He *resumed* his old place at my side," W. H. Hudson's "Green Mansions," xix.; "Bob Pierson *resumed* his seat," Galsworthy's "Saint's Progress," ii. 10); also, to recapitulate or summarize. **II.** *intr.* To begin again; go on or continue after interruption.

ré-su-mé (rā-zü-mā), *n.* [F., prop. pp. of *résumer*, recapitulate, sum up: see *resume*.] A summing up; a summary: as, "to make a *résumé* of the rise and progress of the Greek drama" (S. Butler's "Way of All Flesh," xlvi.).

re-sum-er (rē-zū′mėr), *n.* One who resumes.

re-sum-mon (rē-sum′ǫn), *v. t.* [See *re-*.] To summon again.—**re-sum′mons**, *n.* A second or repeated summons.

re-sump-tion (rē-zump′shǫn), *n.* [LL. *resumptio(n-)*, < L. *resumere*: see *resume*.] The act of resuming; a taking back, as of something previously granted; a taking, or taking on, again, as of something given up or lost; a taking up or going on with again, as of something interrupted; specif., in *U. S. hist.* and *politics*, the return to specie payments by the government (as, the *Resumption* Act of 1875, providing for resumption on Jan. 1, 1879).—**re-sump′tive** (-tiv), *a.* Tending to resume; that recapitulates or summarizes.—**re-sump′tive-ly**, *adv.*

re-su-pi-nate (rē-sū′pi-nāt), *a.* [L. *resupinatus*, pp. of *resupinare*, bend back, < *re-*, back, + *supinare*: see *supinate*.] Bent backward; inverted; appearing as if upside down: chiefly in *bot.*—**re-su-pi-na′tion** (-nā′shǫn), *n.* Resupinate condition.

re-su-pine (rē-sū-pīn′), *a.* [L. *resupinus*, < *re-*, back, + *supinus*, E. *supine*.] Lying on the back; supine.

re-surge[1] (rē-sėrj′), *v. i.* [See *re-*.] To surge back. Also written *re-surge*.

re-surge[2] (rē-sėrj′), *v. i.*; *-surged*, *-surging*. [L. *resurgere* (pp. *resurrectus*), < *re-*, again, + *surgere*, rise.] To rise again, as from the dead.—**re-sur′gence** (-sėr′jens), *n.* The act of resurging.—**re-sur′gent. I.** *a.* Rising or tending to rise again. **II.** *n.* One who has risen again.

res-ur-rect (rez-u-rekt′), *v.* [Back-formation from *resurrection*.] **I.** *tr.* To raise from the dead; bring to life or view again. **II.** *intr.* To rise from the dead.

res-ur-rec-tion (rez-u-rek′shǫn), *n.* [LL. *resurrectio(n-)*, < L. *resurgere*: see *resurge*[2].] The act of rising again from the dead; specif., the rising again of Christ after his death and burial; also, the rising again of men on the judgment-day; also, the state of those risen from the dead; also, in general, a rising again, as from decay, disuse, etc.; revival.—**res-ur-rec′tion-al**, *a.* Of or pertaining to resurrection.—**res-ur-rec′tion-a-ry** (-ā-ri), *a.* Pertaining to or of the nature of resurrection; also, pertaining to resurrectionism.—**res-ur-rec′tion-ism**, *n.* The practice of exhuming and stealing dead bodies, esp. for dissection.—

res-ur-rec′tion-ist, *n.* One who exhumes and steals dead bodies, esp. for dissection; also, one who brings something to life or view again; also, a believer in resurrection.—**res-ur-rec′tion=plant**, *n.* A pteridophyte, *Selaginella lepidophylla*, forming when dry a nest-like ball, which unfolds when moistened; also, any of various other plants having the same property.

re-sur-vey (rē-sėr-vā′), *v. t.* [See *re-*.] To survey again or anew.—**re-sur-vey** (rē-sėr′vā or -sėr-vā′), *n.* A new survey.

re-sus-ci-tate (rē-sus′i-tāt), *v. t.* or *i.*; *-tated*, *-tating*. [L. *resuscitatus*, pp. of *resuscitare*, < *re-*, again, + *suscitare*, lift up, rouse, < *sub*,

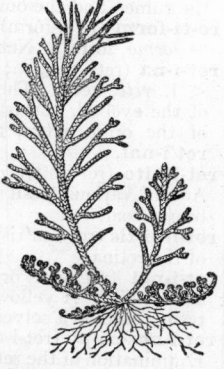

Resurrection-plant (*Selaginella lepidophylla*).

under, + *citare*, drive, urge.] To revive, esp. from apparent death or from unconsciousness.—**re-sus-ci-ta′tion** (-tā′shǫn), *n.* [LL. *resuscitatio(n-)*.] The act of resuscitating, or the state of being resuscitated; revival; restoration.—**re-sus′ci-ta-tive** (-tā-tiv), *a.* Serving to resuscitate.—**re-sus′ci-ta-tor** (-tā-tǫr), *n.*

ret (ret), *v. t.*; *retted*, *retting*. [ME. *retten*, *reten*, akin to D. *reten*, *roten*, ret: cf. *rot*.] To expose to moisture or soak in water, as flax, in order to soften by partial rotting.

re-ta-ble (rē-tā′bl), *n.* [F., prob. < OF. *rere*, at the back (cf. *reredos*), + *table*, E. *table*.] A decorative structure raised above an altar at the back, often forming a frame for a picture, bas-relief, or the like, and sometimes including a shelf or shelves, as for ornaments.

re-tail (rē′tāl), *n.* [AF. *retail*, retail, OF. a cutting, < OF. *retaillier*, cut, clip, pare, < *re-* (< L. *re-*), again, + *taillier*, cut: see *tail*[1].] The sale of commodities in small quantities: opposed to *wholesale*.—**at** (or **by**) **retail** (or, elliptically, simply **retail**), in small quantities, or a little at a time, as in the sale of commodities.—**re′tail**, *a.* Pertaining to, connected with, or engaged in sale at retail: as, the *retail* price; *retail* trade; a *retail* store; a *retail* dealer.—**re-tail** (rē-tāl′ or rē′tāl), *v.* **I.** *tr.* To sell at retail; sell directly to the consumer; also, to tell over again, relate in detail, or repeat to others (as, "a pious inclination to *retail* those doctrines which he had heard," R. Graves's "Spiritual Quixote," i. 5; "Methinks the truth should live from age to age, As 'twere *retail'd* to all posterity," Shakspere's "Richard III.," iii. 1. 77). **II.** *intr.* To be sold at retail: as, an article that *retails* at 50 cents.—**re-tail-er** (rē-tā′lėr or rē′tā-lėr), *n.*—**re-tail′ment**, *n.*

re-tain (rē-tān′), *v. t.* [OF. F. *retenir*, < L. *retinere* (pp. *retentus*), hold back, keep, < *re-*, back, + *tenere*, hold.] To hold back† or restrain†; also, to hold in place or position; also, to keep engaged in one's service; engage by the payment of a preliminary fee, as a lawyer; also, to keep possession of (as, "The executor . . . is allowed to pay himself first, by *retaining* in his hands so much as his debt amounts to": Blackstone's "Commentaries," II. 511); continue to hold or have (as, a thing *retains* its heat, moisture, or color; to *retain* an appearance of youth); continue to use, practise, etc. (as, to *retain* a system or method; to *retain* an old custom); also, to keep in mind, or remember (as, "The tune I still *retain*, but not the words": Dryden's tr. Virgil's "Pastorals," ix. 61).—**re-tain′a-ble**, *a.* That may be retained.—**re-tain′er**[1], *n.* One who or that which retains; also, one kept in service by a person of rank or position, or attached to a house and owing it service (hist. or archaic: as, "A vast number of the nobility, with their feudal *retainers*, had gathered around the royal standard at Beauvais," J. F. Kirk's "Charles the Bold," iii. 2; "the simple habiliments in which the *retainers* of the greatest houses were arrayed in that country," Motley's "Dutch Republic," ii. 4); in general, one kept in service, an attendant, or a dependent (as, "that old *retainer*, Bridget the cook": W. Churchill's "Modern Chronicle," i. 2).—**re-tain′er**[2], *n.* [See *-er*[3].] The act of retaining in one's service, or the fact of being so retained; an authorization given to an attorney to proceed in an action; also, a fee paid to secure services, as of a lawyer; also, the act of retaining or withholding (now rare).—**re-tain′ing**, *p. a.* That retains: as, a *retaining* wall (a wall built to hold back a mass of earth, etc.); a *retaining* fee (a retainer).—**re-tain′-ment**, *n.*

re-take (rē-tāk′), *v. t.*; pret. *-took*, pp. *-taken*, ppr. *-taking*. [See *re-*.] To take again; take back; recapture. —**re-take′**, *n.* A retaking, as of a picture.—**re-tak′er** (-tā′kėr), *n.*

a, b, c, Retaining Walls.

re-tal-i-ate (rē-tal′i-āt), *v.*; *-ated*, *-ating*. [L. *retaliatus*, pp. of *retaliare*, < *re-*, back, + *talis*, such.] **I.** *tr.* To make return for or requite (kindness, service, etc., or, now usually, wrong, injury, etc.) with the like; also, to inflict in return (as, "He *retaliated* on the Avars, or Huns of Pannonia, the same calamities which they had inflicted on the nations": Gibbon's "Decline and Fall of the Roman Empire," xlix.). **II.** *intr.* To return like for like, esp. (now usually) evil for evil: as, to *retaliate* for an injury.—**re-tal-i-a′tion** (-ā′shọn), *n.* The act of retaliating; the return of like for like, now esp. of evil for evil; reprisal; an act or instance of reprisal: as, "These cruelties naturally provoked *retaliation*" (Besant's "Coligny," viii.); "A severe *retaliation* [for a rebellion] was inflicted on the peasants" (Gibbon's "Decline and Fall of the Roman Empire," xiii.).—**re-tal′i-a-tive** (-ā-tiv), *a.* Disposed to retaliate; retaliatory.—**re-tal′i-a-tor** (-ā-tọr), *n.*—**re-tal′i-a-to-ry** (-ā-tọ-ri), *a.* Pertaining to or serving for retaliation; retaliative.

re-tard (rē-tärd′), *v.* [L. *retardare* (pp. *retardatus*), < *re-*, back, + *tardare*, make slow, < *tardus*, slow.] **I.** *tr.* To make slow, or delay the progress of (an action, process, etc.: as, "the increasing hatred, which *retarded* the execution of his great designs," Gibbon's "Decline and Fall of the Roman Empire," xlii.); hinder or impede in respect to movement, progress, etc., as a person or thing; also, to defer or postpone (as, "to advance or *retard* the hour of refection beyond the time," Scott's "Monastery," xvi.: now rare). **II.** *intr.* To be delayed.—**re-tard′**, *n.* Retardation; delay.—**in retard**, retarded; delayed.—**re-tar-da′tion** (rē-tär-dā′shọn), *n.* [L. *retardatio(n-).*] The act of retarding, or the state of being retarded; specif., decrease in velocity; negative acceleration (see *acceleration*); also, that which retards; a hindrance.—**re-tar-da-tive, re-tar-da-to-ry** (rē-tär′dạ-tiv, -tọ-ri), *a.* Tending to retard.—**re-tard′er**, *n.*—**re-tard′ment**, *n.* Retardation.

retch (rech), *v. i.* [AS. *hrǣcan*, clear the throat.] To make efforts to vomit.

re-te (rē′tē), *n.; pl. retia* (rē′shi-ạ or -ti-ạ). [L., net.] A network, as of fibers, nerves, or blood-vessels.

re-tell (rē-tel′), *v. t.;* pret. and pp. *-told.* [See *re-*.] To tell again.

ret-ene (ret′ēn or rē′tēn), *n.* [Gr. ῥητίνη, resin.] In *chem.*, a crystalline hydrocarbon, $C_{18}H_{18}$, obtained from the tar of resinous woods, certain fossil resins, etc.

re-tent (rē-tent′), *n.* [L. *retentus*, pp. of *retinere*, E. *retain*.] That which is retained.

re-ten-tion (rē-ten′shọn), *n.* [L. *retentio(n-)*, < *retinere*, E. *retain*.] The act of retaining, or the state of being retained; a holding in place or position; a keeping in possession; a continuing to hold, have, use, practise, etc.; also, power to retain; capacity for holding or keeping something; esp., the act of retaining things in mind; the power of doing this, or memory.

re-ten-tive (rē-ten′tiv), *a.* [OF. *retentif*, < L. *retinere*, E. *retain*.] Tending or serving to retain something; having power or capacity to retain; esp., of the mind, etc., having power or ability to remember, or good at remembering (as, "His memory is surprisingly *retentive*": Smollett's "Humphry Clinker," Sept. 6); of a person, having a good memory. —**re-ten′tive-ly**, *adv.*—**re-ten′tive-ness**, *n.*—**re-ten-tiv-i-ty** (rē-ten-tiv′i-ti), *n.* Power to retain; retentiveness; in *magnetism*, the power of resisting demagnetization; also, the power of resisting magnetization.

re-te-nue (rė-tė-nü′), *n.* [F.: see *retinue*.] Restraint; self-restraint; discreet reserve.

re-te-pore (rē′tẹ-pōr), *n.* [NL. *Retepora*, the typical genus, < L. *rete*, net, + *porus*, E. *pore²*.] Any of the *Reteporidæ*, a family of polyzoans which form colonies with a network-like or fenestrate structure.

re-ti-a-ri-us (rē-shi-ā′ri-us or

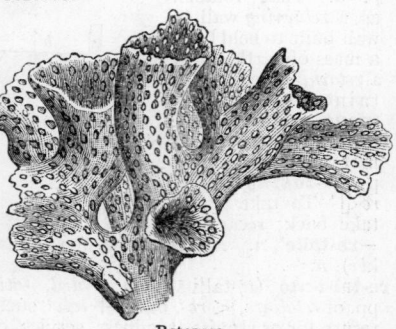
Retepore.

rē-ti-), *n.; pl. -rii* (-ri-i). [L.: see *retiary*.] In *Rom. antiq.*, a gladiator equipped with a net for casting over his opponent.

re-ti-a-ry (rē′shi-ạ-ri), *a.* [ML. *retiarius* (as n., L., a retiarius), < L. *rete*, net.] Using a net or any entangling device; also, making a net or web, as a spider; also, net-like.

ret-i-cent (ret′i-sẹnt), *a.* [L. *reticens* (*-ent-*), ppr. of *reticere*, remain silent, < *re-*, back, + *tacere*, be silent.] Disposed to be silent; not inclined to speak freely; reserved: as, "She had been shy and *reticent* with me, and now . . . she was telling aloud the secrets of her inmost heart" (W. H. Hudson's "Green Mansions," xii.).—**ret′i-cence, ret′i-cen-cy**, *n.*—**ret′i-cent-ly**, *adv.*

ret-i-cle (ret′i-kl), *n.* [= *reticule, reticulum.*] A network of fine lines, wires, or the like, placed in the focus of the objective of a telescope.

re-tic-u-lar (rē-tik′ụ-lạr), *a.* [See *reticulum.*] Having the form of a net; net-like; hence, intricate or entangled.—**re-tic′u-lar-ly**, *adv.*

re-tic-u-late (rē-tik′ụ-lāt), *a.* [L. *reticulatus*, < *reticulum*: see *reticulum.*] Netted; net-like; covered with a network; in *bot.*, of leaves, etc., having the veins or nerves disposed like the threads of a net.—**re-tic′u-late**, *v.; -lated, -lating.* **I.** *tr.* To form into a network; cover or mark with a network: used esp. in *reticulated*, *p. a.* **II.** *intr.* To form a network.—**re-tic′u-lat-ed** (-lā-ted), *p. a.* Formed into or like a network; having lines crossing like the threads of a network; reticulate: as, a *reticulated* decoration on porcelain; *reticulated* work in masonry (characterized by the use of square or diamond-shaped pieces set diagonally).—**re-tic′u-late-ly**, *adv.*—**re-tic-u-la′tion** (-lā′shọn), *n.* Reticulated formation, arrangement, or appearance; also, a reticulated system of parts; a network of lines; also, one of the meshes or open spaces of a network.

[illustration caption] Vase with Reticulated Decoration. — Pennsylvania Museum, Philadelphia.

[illustration caption] Ancient Roman Reticulated Work.

ret-i-cule (ret′i-kūl), *n.* [F. *réticule*, < L. *reticulum*: see *reticulum.*] A small bag, orig. of network but later of silk, etc., carried by women for use like a pocket (as, "women in cloaks, bearing *reticules* and bundles": H. James's "Europeans," i.); also, a reticle.

re-tic-u-lum (rē-tik′ụ-lum), *n.; pl. -la* (-lä). [L., dim. of *rete*, net.] A network; any reticulated system or structure; in *zoöl.*, the second stomach of ruminating animals, between the rumen and the omasum.

re-ti-form (rē′ti-fôrm), *a.* [NL. *retiformis*, < L. *rete*, net, + *forma*, form.] Net-like; reticulate.

ret-i-na (ret′i-nä), *n.; pl. -nas* (-nạz) or *-næ* (-nē). [ML., < L. *rete*, net.] The innermost coat of the posterior part of the eyeball, consisting of an expansion and modification of the optic nerve, and serving to receive the image.—**ret′i-nal**, *a.*

ret-i-nite (ret′i-nīt), *n.* [F. *rétinite*, < Gr. ῥητίνη, resin.] Any of various fossil resins, esp. one of those derived from brown coal.

ret-i-ni-tis (ret-i-nī′tis), *n.* [NL.] In *pathol.*, inflammation of the retina.

ret-i-nol (ret′i-nol or -nōl), *n.* [Gr. ῥητίνη, resin, + L. *oleum*, oil.] A yellowish oil obtained by the distillation of resin: used as a solvent, a mild antiseptic, etc.

ret-i-nos-co-py (ret-i-nos′kọ-pi), *n.* [See *retina* and *-scopy.*] Examination of the retina with the aid of an ophthalmoscope.—**ret″i-no-scop′ic** (-nọ-skop′ik), *a.*—**ret-i-nos′co-pist**, *n.*

ret-i-nue (ret′i-nū), n. [OF. *retenue*, a retaining, a retinue (F. restraint, reserve), < *retenir*, E. *retain*: cf. *retenue*.] A body of retainers in attendance upon an important personage; a train of followers; a suite: as, "Robert of Sicily . . . With *retinue* of many a knight and squire" (Longfellow's "King Robert of Sicily," 4).

re-tir-a-cy (rẹ-tīr′a-si), n. Retirement; seclusion.

re-tir-al (rẹ-tīr′al), n. The act of retiring; retirement.

re-tire (rẹ-tīr′), v.; -tired, -tiring. [F. *retirer*, < *re-* (< L. *re-*), back, + *tirer*, draw, E. *tire*[1].] **I.** *tr.* To draw back (now rare); withdraw or remove (now rare except as in the following senses); withdraw or lead back (troops, etc.), as from battle or danger; withdraw from operation or circulation by taking up and paying, as bonds, bills, etc.; remove from active service or the usual field of activity, as an officer in the army or the navy; in *baseball*, etc., to put out (a batsman). **II.** *intr.* To go back† or return† (as, "He'll say in Troy when he *retires*, The Grecian dames are sunburnt": Shakspere's "Troilus and Cressida," i. 3. 281); withdraw, go away, or remove one's self (as, "One of his two servants . . . *retired*, and came back bearing a priceless goblet and flask": F. M. Crawford's "Mr. Isaacs," i.); withdraw, or go away or apart, to a place of abode, shelter, or seclusion (as, "The Roman senators still *retired* in the winter season to the warm sun, and salubrious springs, of Baiæ," Gibbon's "Decline and Fall of the Roman Empire," xxxix.; "Miss Atkins now *retired* to her chamber," H. Mackenzie's "Man of Feeling," xxix.); betake one's self to rest or bed (as, "It is my usual hour for *retiring*": W. Churchill's "Modern Chronicle," ii. 10); withdraw from office, business, or active life (as, to *retire* at the age of sixty; to *retire* on a pension); fall back or retreat, as from battle or danger; recede, or appear to recede, as a shore.—**re-tire′**, n. Retirement; also, a place of retirement. [Obs. or rare.]—**re-tired′**, p. a. Withdrawn into seclusion or away from contact with others, as persons (as, "I kept myself . . . more *retired* than ever, and seldom went from my cell": Defoe's "Robinson Crusoe," i. 12); apart from public view or notice, as life, occupations, etc.; secluded or sequestered, as places (as, "a lover of nooks and *retired* corners": Borrow's "Lavengro," i.); withdrawn into one's self, or reserved (as, "You have censured me in your kindness for being too gentle, too *retired*": Scott's "Fair Maid of Perth," x.); withdrawn from or no longer occupied with one's business or profession (as, a *retired* sea-captain; a *retired* physician).—**retired list**, a list of persons, esp. of officers or men in the army or navy, who have been retired from active service, as because of disability or age, or upon voluntary application after a certain number of years of service.—**re-tire′ment**, n. The act of retiring, or the state of being retired; withdrawal or retreat, as of troops; retiring of bonds, etc.; removal or retiring from service, office, or business; withdrawal into privacy or seclusion; the state of being withdrawn from society or publicity; privacy or seclusion; also, a retired or secluded place; a place to which one withdraws for privacy; a retreat.—**re-tir′ing** (-tīr′ing), p. a. That retires; esp., withdrawing, or disposed to withdraw, from contact with others; shrinking from society or publicity; reserved; shy; also, characterized by or showing a shy reserve, as the disposition, manners, etc.—**re-tir′ing-ly**, adv.—**re-tir′ing-ness**, n.

re-told (rẹ-tōld′). Preterit and past participle of *retell*.

re-took (rẹ-tùk′). Preterit of *retake*.

re-tor-sion (rẹ-tôr′shon), n. [ML. *retorsio(n-)*, var. of *retortio(n-)*: see *retortion*.] Retaliation; in *international law*, retaliation in kind by one state upon the subjects of another, as for disabilities or restrictions imposed.

re-tort[1] (rẹ-tôrt′), v. [L. *retortus*, pp. of *retorquere*, twist back, cast back, < *re-*, back, + *torquere*, twist.] **I.** *tr.* To turn or cast back†; also, to reflect†; also, to make return of or retaliate (an injury, etc.) upon the originator; return (an accusation, epithet, etc.) upon the person uttering it; reply in kind to (a sarcasm, etc.); answer (an argument or the like) by another to the contrary; also, to say by way of retort (as, "'What does this mean?' said he. 'What do you think it means?' *retorted* Cynthia": W. Churchill's "Coniston," ii. 9). **II.** *intr.* To reply in retaliation; make a retort or retorts.—**re-tort′**[1], n. The act of retorting; also, a retaliatory act or remark; a severe, incisive, or witty reply,

esp. one that counters a first speaker's statement, argument, etc.

re-tort[2] (rẹ-tôrt′), n. [F. *retorte*, < L. *retorta*, fem. of *retortus*, pp.: see *retort*[1].] A vessel, commonly a glass bulb with a long neck bent downward, used for distilling or decomposing substances by heat.—**re-tort′**[2], v. t. To heat in a retort in order to distil, remove volatile ingredients, or the like.

Retort (*a*) and Receiver (*b*).

re-tor-tion (rẹ-tôr′shon), n. [ML. *retortio(n-)*, < L. *retorquere*: see *retort*[1], and cf. *retorsion*.] The act of turning or bending back; also, a retorting, as in argument†; also, retaliation; in *international law*, retorsion.

re-touch (rẹ-tuch′), v. t. [F. *retoucher*, < *re-* (< L. *re-*), again, + *toucher*, E. *touch*.] To improve by new touches or the like, as a painting; in *photog.*, to correct or improve (a photographic negative) by the use of a pencil, scraping-knife, etc.—**re-touch′**, n. An added touch to a painting, etc., by way of improvement.—**re-touch′er**, n.

re-trace[1] (rẹ-trās′), v. t.; -traced, -tracing. [See *re-*.] To trace again, as lines in writing or drawing. Also written *re-trace*.

re-trace[2] (rẹ-trās′), v. t.; -traced, -tracing. [F. *retracer*, < *re-* (< L. *re-*), back, + *tracer*, E. *trace*[2], v.] To trace backward, or go back over (as, to *retrace* one's steps; "He was about to turn, and *retrace* his path to his quarters," Cooper's "Spy," xix.); also, to trace back to an origin or source (as, "If the line of Turnus you *retrace*, He springs from Inachus of Argive race": Dryden's tr. Virgil's "Æneid," vii. 520); also, to go back over with the memory; also, to go over again with the sight or attention.—**re-trace′a-ble**, a. That may be retraced.

re-tract (rẹ-trakt′), v. [Partly < L. *retractus*, pp. of *retrahere*, draw back, < *re-*, back, + *trahere*, draw; partly < L. *retractare* (pp. *retractatus*), withdraw, freq. of *retrahere*: cf. *retreat*.] **I.** *tr.* To draw back or in (as, "The other . . . suddenly *retracted* his lips and exhibited his teeth": J. Conrad's "Victory," ii. 5); also, to withdraw or revoke (a decree, promise, etc.); withdraw (a statement, opinion, etc.) as unjustified. **II.** *intr.* To draw or shrink back; also, to withdraw a promise, etc.; make disavowal of a statement, opinion, etc., or recant.—**re-tract′a-ble**, a. That may be retracted.—**re-trac-ta-bil′i-ty** (-bil′i-ti), n.—**re-trac-ta-tion** (rẹ-trak-tā′shon), n. [L. *retractatio(n-)*, < *retractare*.] The act of retracting a promise, etc.; recantation of a statement, opinion, etc.—**re-trac-tile** (rẹ-trak′til), a. Capable of being drawn back or in, as the head of a tortoise; exhibiting the power of retraction.—**re-trac-til-i-ty** (rẹ-trak-til′i-ti), n.—**re-trac-tion** (rẹ-trak′shon), n. [L. *retractio(n-)*, < *retrahere*.] The act of retracting, or drawing back or in, or the state of being retracted; retractile power; also, the retractation or withdrawal of a promise, etc.; the recantation of a statement, opinion, etc.—**re-trac′tive** (-tiv), a. Tending or serving to retract.—**re-trac′tor**, n. One who or that which retracts or draws back something; in *anat.*, a muscle that retracts an organ, protruded part, etc.; in *surg.*, an instrument or appliance for drawing back an impeding part.

re-trans-form (rē-trans-fôrm′), v. t. [See *re-*.] To transform back to a previous state; also, to transform again or anew.—**re-trans-for-ma′tion** (-fôr-mā′shon), n.

re-trans-mit (rē-trans-mit′), v. t.; -mitted, -mitting. [See *re-*.] To transmit back; also, to transmit again or anew.—**re-trans-mis′sion** (-mish′on), n.

re-tread (rē-tred′), v. t. or i.; pret. -trod, pp. -trodden or -trod. [See *re-*.] To tread again; put a new tread on (a tire).

re-treat (rẹ-trēt′), n. [OF. *retret*, *retrete*, also (as in F.) *retrait*, *retraite*, < *retraire*, draw back, withdraw, retire, < L. *retrahere*: see *retract*.] The act of withdrawing or retiring, as into safety or privacy; retirement or seclusion; a retirement, or a period of retirement, for religious exercises and meditation; also, a place of refuge; a place of seclusion or privacy; an asylum, as for the insane; *milit.* and *naval*, the forced or strategic retirement of an armed force before an enemy, or the withdrawing of a ship or fleet from action; hence, the signal given for such a retirement or withdrawing; also, a signal given in the army or navy, by beat of drum or sound of bugle or trumpet, at sunset; in *aëronautics*, the backward slope of a plane or the like.—**re-treat′**, *v.* **I.** *intr.* To withdraw, retire, or draw back (as, "Zenobia and her companion had *retreated* from the window," Hawthorne's "Blithedale Romance," xviii.; "He took a step toward her, and she *retreated*," W. Churchill's "Coniston," i. 6); make a retreat, as an army; retire for shelter or seclusion; also, to slope backward, or recede (as, a *retreating* chin). **II.** *tr.* To draw or lead back; move backward, as a piece in chess.— **re-treat′ant**, *n.* One who takes part in a religious retreat. —**re-treat′er**, *n.*

re-tree (rę̄-trē′), *n.* [Cf. F. *retrait*, withdrawal, shrinkage: see *retreat*.] In *paper-making*, broken, wrinkled, or imperfect paper.

re-trench (rę̄-trench′), *v.* [F. (obs.) *retrencher* (now *retrancher*), < *re-* (< L. *re-*), back, + *trencher*, OF. *trenchier*, cut, E. *trench*, *v.*] **I.** *tr.* To cut down, reduce, or diminish; curtail (expenses); also, to cut off or remove; do away with; omit; *milit.*, to protect by a retrenchment. **II.** *intr.* To economize; reduce expenses: as, "I determined to *retrench* while I had yet a trifle left" (Irving's "Tales of a Traveler," ii. 7).—**re-trench′er**, *n.*—**re-trench′ment**, *n.* The act or an act of retrenching; a cutting down or off; a reduction of expenses; in *fort.*, an interior work which cuts off a part of a fortification from the rest, and to which a garrison may retreat; also, an intrenchment.

re-tri-al (rē-trī′al), *n.* [See *re-*.] A second or new trial.

re-trib-ute (rę̄-trib′ūt), *v. t.*; *-uted*, *-uting*. [L. *retributus*, pp. of *retribuere*, < *re-*, back, + *tribuere*, give, pay.] To give in return or requital (obs. or rare); also, to make return for†, or requite†.—**ret-ri-bu-tion** (ret-ri-bū′shǫn), *n.* [LL. *retributio(n-)*.] Repayment or recompense (now rare); also, requital according to merits or deserts, now esp. for evil; something given or inflicted in such requital (as, "His crime had been visited by a terrible *retribution* from Heaven": Cooper's "Prairie," xxxii.); in *theol.*, the distribution of rewards and punishments in a future life.—**re-trib′u-tive** (-ū-tiv), **re-trib′u-to-ry** (-tǫ-ri), *a.* Characterized by or involving retribution.—**re-trib′u-tive-ly**, *adv.*—**re-trib′u-tor**, *n.* One who makes retribution.

re-triev-a-ble (rę̄-trē′va-bl), *a.* That may be retrieved.— **re-triev′a-bly**, *adv.*

re-triev-al (rę̄-trē′val), *n.* The act of retrieving; retrieve.

re-trieve (rę̄-trēv′), *v.*; *-trieved*, *-trieving*. [OF. *retrover* (*retruev-*), < *re-* (< L. *re-*), again, + *trover*, find: see *trover*.] **I.** *tr.* To recover or regain (as, "He . . . began to breathe regularly, and soon *retrieved* his recollection": Smollett's "Humphry Clinker," after Oct. 4); also, to rescue or save (as, "to *retrieve* the nations sitting in darkness from eternal perdition": Prescott's "Conquest of Mexico," iii. 7); save (time), as from other occupations; also, to bring back to a former and better state, or restore (as, to *retrieve* one's fortunes); also, to make amends for (an error, etc.: as, "a false step that he was never able to *retrieve*," Morley's "Oliver Cromwell," iv. 6); make good, or repair (a loss, etc.: as, "By a brilliant coup he has *retrieved* . . . a rather serious loss," S. Butler's "Way of All Flesh," liv.); in *hunting*, of dogs, to find and fetch (killed or wounded game). **II.** *intr.* In *hunting*, to retrieve game.—**re-trieve′**, *n.* The act of retrieving; recovery; possibility of recovery (as, beyond *retrieve*).—**re-trieve′ment**, *n.*—**re-triev′er**, *n.* One who or that which retrieves; esp., a dog trained to retrieve game.

retro-. [L. *retro-*, repr. *retro*, adv., backward, back, behind, < *re-*, back.] A prefix meaning 'backward,' 'back,' 'behind,' occurring orig. in words from the Latin, but used also as a modern formative, as in *retrochoir*, *retrocognition*, *retroject*.

re-tro-act (rē-trǫ-akt′ or ret-rǫ-), *v. i.* [See *retro-*.] To act backward; act upon or affect what is past.—**re-tro-ac′tion** (-ak′shǫn), *n.*—**re-tro-ac′tive** (-tiv), *a.* Retroacting; esp., operative with respect to past occurrences, as a statute; retrospective.—**re-tro-ac′tive-ly**, *adv.*—**re‴tro-ac-tiv′i-ty** (-tiv′i-ti), *n.*

re-tro-cede[1] (rē-trǫ-sēd′ or ret-rǫ-), *v. t.*; *-ceded*, *-ceding*. [F. *rétrocéder*, < L. *retro*, back, + *cedere*, E. *cede*.] To cede back (territory, etc.).

re-tro-cede[2] (rē-trǫ-sēd′ or ret-rǫ-), *v. i.*; *-ceded*, *-ceding*. [L. *retrocedere* (pp. *retrocessus*), < *retro*, back, + *cedere*, go.]

To go back; recede; retire.—**re-tro-ced′ent** (-sē′dẹnt), *a.* Going back; retrograde; relapsing.

re-tro-ces-sion[1] (rē-trǫ-sesh′ǫn or ret-rǫ-), *n.* [F. *rétrocession*.] The act of retroceding or ceding back.

re-tro-ces-sion[2] (rē-trǫ-sesh′ǫn or ret-rǫ-), *n.* [LL. *retrocessio(n-)*.] The act of retroceding or going back; recession; retrogression.—**re-tro-ces′sion-al**, *a.*

re-tro-choir (rē′trǫ-kwīr or ret′rǫ-), *n.* [See *retro-*.] That part of the interior of a cathedral or similar church behind the choir or the main altar.

re-tro-cog-ni-tion (rē″trǫ-kog-nish′ǫn or ret″rǫ-), *n.* [See *retro-*.] Supernormal cognition of past events, actions, etc., without recourse to any of the ordinary means of information. —**re-tro-cog′ni-tive** (-ni-tiv), *a.*

re-tro-flex (rē′trǫ-fleks or ret′rǫ-), *a.* [L. *retroflexus*, pp. of *retroflectere*, < *retro*, back, + *flectere*, bend.] Bent backward; exhibiting retroflexion. Also **re′tro-flexed.**—**re-tro-flex′ion** (-flek′shǫn), *n.* A bending backward; in *pathol.*, a bending backward of the body of the uterus. Cf. *anteflexion*.

ret-ro-gra-da-tion (ret″rǫ-grā-dā′shǫn or rē″trǫ-), *n.* [LL. *retrogradatio(n-)*.] The act of retrograding; backward movement; retirement or retreat; decline or deterioration.

ret-ro-grade (ret′rǫ-grād or rē′trǫ-), *v.*; *-graded*, *-grading*. [L. *retrogradi* (LL. *retrogradare*), < *retro*, back, + *gradi*, walk, go.] **I.** *intr.* To move or go backward; retire or retreat; also, to fall back toward a worse condition, decline, or deteriorate (as, "He caused this branch of philosophy to *retrograde* rather than advance": Hallam's "Literature of Europe," iii. 3. § 2); in *astron.*, to have a retrograde motion. **II.** *tr.* To cause to go backward; turn back. [Now rare.] —**ret′ro-grade**, *a.* [L. *retrogradus*.] Moving backward; having a backward motion or direction; retiring or retreating; also, inverse or reversed, as order; also, tending to fall back toward a worse condition; deteriorating; also, opposed† or contrary† (as, "It is most *retrograde* to our desire": Shakspere's "Hamlet," i. 2. 114); in *astron.*, noting an apparent or actual motion in a direction contrary to the order of the signs, or from east to west; also, having such a motion, as a planet.—**ret′ro-grade-ly**, *adv.*

re-tro-gress (rē′trǫ-gres or ret′rǫ-), *v. i.* [L. *retrogressus*, pp. of *retrogradi*, E. *retrograde*, *v.*] To move backward; go back.—**re′tro-gress**, *n.* [LL. *retrogressus*, n.] Retrogression.—**re-tro-gres′sion** (-gresh′ǫn), *n.* The act of retrogressing or retrograding; backward movement; decline or deterioration.—**re-tro-gres′sive** (-gres′iv), *a.* Moving or going backward; retrograde.—**re-tro-gres′sive-ly**, *adv.*

re-tro-ject (rē′trǫ-jekt or ret′rǫ-), *v. t.* [From *retro-* + *-ject* as in *project*.] To cast or throw back.—**re-tro-jec′tion** (-jek′shǫn), *n.*

re-trorse (rę̄-trôrs′), *a.* [L. *retrorsus*, for *retroversus*, < *retro*, back, + *versus*, pp. of *vertere*, turn.] Turned backward; turned in a direction opposite to the usual one.— **re-trorse′ly**, *adv.*

ret-ro-spect (ret′rǫ-spekt or rē′trǫ-), *v.* [L. *retrospectus*, pp. of *retrospicere*, < *retro*, back, + *specere*, look at.] **I.** *tr.* To look back upon, contemplate, or think of (something past). **II.** *intr.* To look back in thought; reflect; also, to refer back (*to*).—**ret′ro-spect**, *n.* A look or view backward (rare); hence, contemplation of the past, as with reference to particular events or experiences (as, "to sit still and throw away the time in our possession, by *retrospect* on what is past": Steele, in "Spectator," 374); a survey of past time, events, etc. (as, "My *retrospect* of life recalls to my view many opportunities of good neglected": Johnson's "Rasselas," xlv.); also, a reference back (as, "He deprecated any invidious *retrospect* as to what had passed in former debates": Lecky's "Hist. of Eng. in the 18th Century," viii.).—**ret-ro-spec′tion** (-spek′shǫn), *n.* The action of looking back on things past; a survey of past events or experiences, or a retrospect; the faculty of looking back on the past; also, reference back to something.—**ret-ro-spec′tive** (-tiv), *a.* Looking or directed backward (as, "Frequent *retrospective* glances . . . served to assure me that our retreat was not cut off": H. Melville's "Omoo," lv.); seen or lying to the rear (as, a *retrospective* view); also, directed to the past; contemplative of past events, etc.; also, retroactive, as a statute.—**ret-ro-spec′tive-ly**, *adv.*

re-trous-sé (rē-trö-sā′), a. [F., pp. of retrousser, < re- (< L. re-), back, + trousser, E. truss.] Turned up: said esp. of the nose.

re-tro-vert (rē-trō-vėrt′ or ret-rō-), v. t. [L. retro, back, + vertere (pp. versus), turn.] To turn backward; in pathol., to displace (the uterus) as by tipping backward. Cf. antevert.—**re-tro-ver′sion** (-vėr′shon), n.

re-try (rē-trī′), v. t.; pret. and pp. -tried. [See re-.] To try again or anew, as before a court.

ret-ter-y (ret′ėr-i), n.; pl. -ies (-iz). [See ret.] A place where flax is retted.

re-turn¹ (rē-tėrn′), v. t. or i. [See re-.] To turn again. Also written re-turn.

re-turn² (rē-tėrn′), v. [OF. retorner (F. retourner), < re- (< L. re-), back, + torner, turn: see turn.] I. tr. To turn back or in the reverse direction; turn away from, or at an angle to, the previous line of direction (esp. in arch.); reflect (light, sound, etc.); also, to put, bring, take, or send back (as, to return a book to its shelf, or to a library; to return a lost child to its parents; to return prisoners to their country); restore; give back; also, to bring back and make known, or report (as, "Moses returned the words of the people unto the Lord": Ex. xix. 8); report or announce officially; render (a verdict, etc.); elect, as to a legislative body (as, "Only one Papist had been returned to the Irish Parliament since the Restoration": Macaulay's "Hist. of Eng.," vi.); also, to send or give back in reciprocation, recompense, or requital (as, to return shot for shot; to return good for evil; "Thanks, The slightest, easiest, readiest recompense From them who could return him nothing else," Milton's "Paradise Regained," iii. 129); yield (a profit, revenue, etc.), as in return for labor, expenditure, or investment; give back in response, or say in reply (as, to return an answer to a question; " 'Oh no, thank you,' returned Mr. Toots," Dickens's "Dombey and Son," xxviii.); also, to reciprocate, repay, or requite (something sent, given, done, etc.) with something similar (as, to return the enemy's fire; to return another's affection; to return a compliment, a salute, or a visit); sometimes, to repay or requite with anything specified (as, to return kindness with ingratitude); in card-playing, to respond to by a similar lead. II. intr. To turn back or away†; also, to go or come back, as to a former place, position, state, practice, etc.; go back or revert to a former owner; revert or recur in thought or discourse, as to a subject; also, to make reply, or retort.—

re-turn′². I. n. The act or fact of returning; a bringing, sending, or giving back; a going or coming back (as, "They . . . set out on their return to the camp": Irving's "Captain Bonneville," x.); a recurrence (as, to wish one many happy returns of the day); reciprocation, repayment, or requital (as, "As rich men deal gifts, Expecting in return twenty for one," Shakspere's "Timon of Athens," iv. 3. 517; profits in return for outlay; thanks in return for aid); response or reply (as, to speak or write in return); also, that which is returned; a report, esp. a formal or official report (as, "In other nations having income tax laws, privacy of returns is respected," A. W. Mellon's "Taxation," iii.; election returns); a recompense or requital (as, words are a poor return for such a service); a yield or profit, as from labor, land, business, investment, etc. (as, "Twenty-four and a half per cent. was the smallest possible return the shareholders could anticipate," Bulwer-Lytton's "Caxtons," ii. 2: often in pl.); a response (as, "To her compliments he makes very laconic and dry returns": Smollett's "Humphry Clinker," June 2); in arch., the continuation of a molding, projection, etc., in a different direction; also, a side or part which falls away from the front of any straight work; in mech., etc., a bend or turn, or a part between two bends; in law, the bringing or sending back of a writ or process, with a brief report usually indorsed

Return of a Molding. — From apse of a Romanesque church at Agen, France.

upon it, as by a sheriff, to the court from which it issued; also, the report or certificate indorsed on the document. II. a. Of or pertaining to return or returning (as, the return trip back to the point of starting; the return fare; the return stroke of a piston; a return passage for a fluid); also, sent, given, or done in return (as, a return shot or thrust; a return game or match).

re-turn-a-ble (rē-tėr′na-bl), a. That may be returned; also, required to be returned.

re-turn-er (rē-tėr′nėr), n. One who or that which returns.

re-turn-less (rē-tėrn′les), a. Without return, or not returning (as, "Gone to the mould now, whither all that be Vanish returnless": Lowell's "Under the Old Elm," i. 2); also, not admitting of return (as, "The boat had put a returnless distance between them": Mrs. Stowe's "Uncle Tom's Cabin," xxxvii.).

re-tuse (rē-tūs′), a. [L. retusus, blunted, pp. of retundere, < re-, back, + tundere, beat.] Of a leaf, etc., having an obtuse or rounded apex with a shallow notch.

Retuse Leaf.

re-u-nion (rē-ū′nyon), n. [See re-.] Union again; a renewed union; specif., a gathering of relatives, friends, or associates meeting after separation (as, "She had never come to the family reunion before": Eden Phillpotts's "Grey Room," i.).—**re-u′nion-ism**, n. Advocacy of reunion; the principles of reunionists.—**re-u′nion-ist**, n. An advocate of reunion; specif., one who advocates the reunion of the Anglican Church with the Roman Catholic Church.—**re-u-nion-is′tic**, a.

re-u-nite (rē-ū-nīt′), v. t. or i. [See re-.] To unite again, as after separation.—**re-u-nit′ed-ly** (-nī′ted-li), adv.—**re-u-nit′er**, n.

re-use (rē-ūz′), v. t. [See re-.] To use again.—**re-use′** (-ūs′), n. Use a second time; a using again.

re-val-ue (rē-val′ū), v. t. [See re-.] To value again.—**re-val-u-a′tion** (-ū-ā′shon), n.

re-vamp (rē-vamp′), v. t. [See re-.] To vamp or furbish afresh; renovate.—**re-vamp′**, n. Something revamped.

re-veal (rē-vēl′), v. t. [OF. reveler (F. révéler), < L. revelare (pp. revelatus), unveil, reveal, < re-, back, + velum, veil.] To lay open to view, display, or exhibit (as, "an open mouth revealing the upper teeth": Lytton Strachey's "Queen Victoria," ii.); also, to make known, disclose, or divulge (as, "He was glad it was to him she had revealed her secret," Mrs. Wharton's "Age of Innocence," xiii.; "Margery spoke with her mother and revealed a growing interest," Eden Phillpotts's "Children of Men," i. 9); specif., to make known by supernatural means (as, "The wrath of God is revealed from heaven against all ungodliness and unrighteousness of men": Rom. i. 18).—**re-veal′**, n. A revealing; revelation; disclosure; in arch., that part of a jamb or vertical face of an opening for a window or door, included between the face of the wall and that of the frame containing the window or door; also, the whole jamb or vertical face of an opening.—**re-veal′a-ble**, a. That may be revealed.—**re-veal′er**, n.—**re-veal′ment**, n. The act of revealing; revelation.

re-veg-e-tate (rē-vej′ē-tāt), v. i. [See re-.] To vegetate or grow again, as plants; put forth vegetation again, as land.—**re-veg-e-ta′tion** (-tā′shon), n.

re-veil-le (rē-vāl′yā, also U. S. rev-ē-lē′, Brit. rę-vel′i), n. [F. réveillez, impv. pl. of réveiller, awaken, < L. re-, again, + ex, out of, + vigilare, watch, wake: see vigilant.] A signal, as of a drum or bugle, given about sunrise, to waken soldiers or sailors for the day's duties.

rev-el (rev′el), v. i.; -eled or -elled, -eling or -elling. [OF. reveler, revel, orig. rebel, < L. rebellare, E. rebel, v.] To make merry; indulge in boisterous festivities; take part in a revel; also, to take great pleasure or delight (in: as, "I revelled in the vastness of the opened horizon," J. Conrad's "Lord Jim," xxxv.).—**rev′el**, n. [OF. revel.] Boisterous merrymaking or festivity; revelry; an occasion of merrymaking or boisterous festivity; specif., formerly, an occasion or course of noisy festivity with dancing, masking, and other forms of entertainment (often in pl.).

rev-e-la-tion (rev-ē-lā′shon), n. [OF. revelation (F. révélation), < LL. revelatio(n-).] The act or an act of revealing or disclosing; disclosure; something revealed or disclosed;

a striking disclosure, as of something not before realized; specif., the communication of religious truth by supernatural means; God's disclosure of himself and of his will to his creatures; an instance of such communication or disclosure, or something thus communicated or disclosed; that which contains such disclosure, as the Bible; also [*cap.*], the last book of the New Testament ("The Revelation of St. John the Divine": often in *pl.*); the Apocalypse.—**rev-e-la′-tion-ist**, *n.* One who makes a revelation, as the author of the Apocalypse; also, one who believes in revelation.

rev-e-la-tor (rev′ē-lā-tor), *n.* [LL.] One who makes a revelation.—**rev′e-la-to-ry** (-lā-tō-ri), *a.* Affording a revelation.

rev-el-er, rev-el-ler (rev′el-ėr), *n.* One who revels.

rev-el-ry (rev′el-ri), *n.* Reveling; boisterous festivity.

rev-e-nant (rev′ē-nant), *n.* [F., prop. ppr. of *revenir*, return: see *revenue.*] One who returns; esp., one who returns as a spirit after death; a ghost.

re-venge (rē-venj′), *v.*; -venged, -venging. [OF. *revengier* (F. *revancher*), < *re-* (< L. *re-*), back, + *vengier*, E. *venge.*] **I.** *tr.* To take vengeance or exact expiation on behalf of (a person, etc.) or for (a wrong, etc.), esp. in a resentful or vindictive spirit; avenge vindictively: as, to *revenge* a kinsman; to *revenge* one's self on another for an injury; "Every malecontent embraced the fair opportunity of *revenging* his private or imaginary wrongs" (Gibbon's "Decline and Fall of the Roman Empire," xli.). **II.** *intr.* To take revenge.—**re-venge′**, *n.* The act of revenging; retaliation for injuries or wrongs; vengeance; a particular act or way of revenging; something done in revenging; also, the desire to revenge; vindictiveness; also, an opportunity of retaliation or satisfaction, as a game or match in return played with a defeated opponent (as, to give one his *revenge*).—**re-venge′ful**, *a.* Full of revenge; vindictive: as, "I had a keen, *revengeful* sense of the insult" (Hawthorne's "Blithedale Romance," xix.).—**re-venge′ful-ly**, *adv.*—**re-venge′ful-ness**, *n.*—**re-venge′ment**, *n.* Revenging; revenge.—**re-ven′ger** (-ven′jėr), *n.*—**re-ven′ging-ly**, *adv.*

rev-e-nue (rev′ē-nū), *n.* [OF. F. *revenu*, OF. also *revenue*, orig. pp. of *revenir*, return, < L. *revenire*, < *re-*, back, + *venire*, come.] The return or yield from any kind of property (as, a source of *revenue*); income; also, an amount of money regularly coming in, or an income (as, "A thousand a year was thought a large *revenue* for a barrister": Macaulay's "Hist. of Eng.," iii.); also, a particular item of income; a source of income; *pl.*, the collective items or amounts of income of a person, a state, etc.; also, *sing.*, the income of a government from taxation, excise duties, customs, or other sources, appropriated to the payment of the public expenses (as, "the idea of taxing America for the purpose of *revenue*": Burke's "American Taxation"); the government department charged with the collection of such income.—**revenue cutter.** See *cutter.*

re-ver-a-ble (rē-vēr′ạ-bl), *a.* Worthy to be revered.

re-verb (rē-verb′), *v. t.* or *i.* Shortened form of *reverberate.* [Archaic.]

re-ver-ber-ant (rē-vėr′bẹ-rant), *a.* Reverberating; reëchoing.

re-ver-ber-ate (rē-vėr′bẹ-rāt), *v.*; -ated, -ating. [L. *reverberatus*, pp. of *reverberare*, < *re-*, back, + *verberare*, to lash, beat, < *verber*, a lash, whip.] **I.** *tr.* To beat or drive back (as, "smoke, forced down the chimneys by the gusts of wind *reverberated* from the hill behind," Smollett's "Humphry Clinker," April 23: obs. or rare); echo back or reëcho (sound); cast back or reflect (light, etc.); deflect (flame or heat) on something, as in a reverberatory furnace; also, to treat (a substance) in a reverberatory furnace or the like. **II.** *intr.* To rebound or recoil; echo back, reëcho, or resound, as sound (as, "A tremendous explosion of thunder followed, *reverberating* among the precipices": Parkman's "Oregon Trail," xx.); be reflected, as light, etc.; be deflected, as flame in a reverberatory furnace.—**re-ver′ber-ate**, *a.* Reverberated; also, reverberant.—**re-ver-ber-a′tion** (-bẹ-rā′shọn), *n.* The act or an instance of reverberating, or of driving or turning back; echoing back or return of sound; reflection of light or heat; the fact of being reverberated or reflected; also, that which is reverberated; a reëchoed sound (as, "Shoutings and pistol-shots sent their hollow reverbera-

tions to the ear": Mark Twain's "Tom Sawyer," xxx.); a reflection of light or color; also, the action or process of subjecting something to heat as in a reverberatory furnace.—**re-ver′ber-a-tive** (-bẹ-rā-tiv), *a.* Reverberating.—**re-ver′ber-a-tor** (-bẹ-rā-tọr), *n.* One who or that which reverberates; specif., a reflecting lamp.—**re-ver′ber-a-to-ry** (-bẹ-rā-tọ-ri), *a.* Characterized or produced by reverberation; deflected, as flame; esp., noting a furnace, kiln, or the like, in which the fuel is not in direct contact with the ore, metal, etc., to be heated, but furnishes a flame that plays over the material, esp. by being deflected downward from the roof.

Section of Reverberatory Furnace.

re-vere (rē-vēr′), *v. t.*; -vered, -vering. [L. *revereri*, < *re-*, back, again, + *vereri*, feel awe of, fear.] To regard with respect tinged with awe, as in recognition of exalted character or merit; venerate: as, "At least one-third of the population . . . *reverés* every sort of holy man" (Kipling's "Kim," xi.); "Whose word is truth, as sacred and *revered*, As Heaven's own oracles from altars heard" (Pope's "Satires and Epistles of Horace Imitated," Epistles, ii. 1. 27).

rev-er-ence (rev′ẹ-rens), *n.* [OF. *reverence* (F. *révérence*), < L. *reverentia*, < *reverens*, E. *reverent.*] The feeling or mental attitude of revering, deep respect tinged with awe, or veneration (as, *reverence* for the priesthood; "He had . . . a sincere *reverence* for the laws of his country," Macaulay's "Hist. of Eng.," ii.); also, the outward manifestation of this feeling (as, to pay *reverence*; "Now lies he [Cæsar] there, And none so poor to do him *reverence*," Shakspere's "Julius Cæsar," iii. 2. 125); also, a gesture indicative of deep respect; an obeisance, bow, or curtsy (as, "He made a profound *reverence* to the ladies": Miss Burney's "Evelina," xxiii.); also, the state of being revered; also, with *your* or *his*, a title used in addressing or mentioning a clergyman.—**rev′er-ence**, *v. t.*; -enced, -encing. To regard or treat with reverence; venerate: as, "Ye shall keep my sabbaths, and *reverence* my sanctuary" (Lev. xix. 30); "the man who *reverenced* all women, simply for their womanhood" (Miss Mulock's "John Halifax," xi.).—**rev′er-en-cer** (-ẹ-ren-sėr), *n.*

rev-er-end (rev′ẹ-rend), *a.* [L. *reverendus*, gerundive of *revereri*, E. *revere.*] Worthy to be revered, or entitled to reverence (as, "*reverend* Goddesses," W. Morris's "Jason," xv. 390; "The *reverend* walls In which of old I wore the gown," Tennyson's "In Memoriam," lxxxvii.); specif., an epithet of respect applied to, or prefixed to the name of, a clergyman (as, "The *reverend* abbot, With all his convent, honourably received him," Shakspere's "Henry VIII.," iv. 2. 18; *Reverend*, or the *Reverend*, John Smith, the epithet in such cases being often abbreviated *Rev.*); also, pertaining to or characteristic of the clergy; also, reverent (now rare).

rev-er-ent (rev′ẹ-rent), *a.* [L. *reverens* (-*ent-*), ppr. of *revereri*, E. *revere.*] Feeling, exhibiting, or characterized by reverence, or deeply respectful (as, "Hermes and Apollo *reverent* stood Before Jove's throne," Shelley's tr. Homer's "Hymn to Mercury," lv.; "the *reverent* attention which is usually rendered to the clergy in Scotland," Scott's "Guy Mannering," xlvii.); also, reverend (obs. or rare).

rev-er-en-tial (rev-ẹ-ren′shạl), *a.* Of the nature of or characterized by reverence; feeling or showing reverence; reverent: as, *reverential* awe; *reverential* affection; "He was at once *reverential* and affectionate" (Lytton Strachey's "Queen Victoria," iii.).—**rev-er-en′tial-ly**, *adv.*—**rev-er-en′tial-ness**, *n.*

rev-er-ent-ly (rev′ẹ-rent-li), *adv.* In a reverent manner.

re-ver-er (rē-vēr′ėr), *n.* One who reveres.

rev-er-ie (rev′ẹ-ri), *n.* [F. *rêverie*, < *rêver*, dream: see *rave*[1].] A state of dreamy meditation or fanciful musing (as, "to indulge in *reverie*," Hardy's "Return of the Native," i. 7; lost in *reverie*); a fit of such meditation or musing, or a day-dream (as, "plunged in a profound *reverie*": H. Melville's "Typee," iv.); also, a fantastic, visionary, or unpractical idea; also, in *music*, an instrumental composition of a vague and dreamy character.—**rev′er-ist**, *n.* One given to reverie; a dreamer.

re-vers (rẹ-vār′, commonly rẹ-vēr′, F. rė-vär), *n.*; pl. *revers* (rẹ-vārz′, commonly rẹ-vērz′, F. rė-vär). [F.: see *reverse*.] A part of a garment turned back to show the lining or facing, as a lapel; a trimming simulating such a part; the facing used.

re-ver-sal (rẹ-vėr′sạl), *n.* The act or an instance of reversing; the state of being reversed.

re-verse (rẹ-vėrs′), *a.* [OF. *revers*, adj. (as n., OF. F. *revers*), < L. *reversus*, pp. of *revertere*, turn back, turn about: see *revert*.] Opposite or contrary in position, direction, order, or character (as, "a little village on the *reverse* slope," J. Conrad's "Rover," v.; *reverse* motion; a *reverse* arrangement or disposition of things; an impression *reverse* to what was intended); also, acting in a manner opposite or contrary to that which is usual, as an appliance or apparatus.—**re-verse fire**, *milit.*, fire directed upon a fortification, body of troops, etc., from the rear; specif., a fire in which the shot strikes the interior slope of the parapet or the back of the line of troops exposed to its effects, at a horizontal angle of more than 30°.—**reverse shell**, a spiral shell in which the whorl rises from right to left, in the reverse of the usual direction; a sinistral (rather than dextral) shell.—**re-verse′**, *n.* The opposite or contrary of something (as, "My temper was the *reverse* of cruel and imperious": C. B. Brown's "Wieland," vii.); also, that side of a coin, medal, etc., which does not bear the principal design (opposed to *obverse*); the back or rear of anything; also, a backhanded stroke, as in fencing†; also, reversal (now rare); also, an adverse change of fortune, or a misfortune, check, or defeat (as, to meet with an unexpected *reverse*; "Cæsar was never more calm than under a *reverse*," Froude's "Cæsar," xix.); in *mech.*, a reversing mechanism, etc.—**re-verse′**, *v.*; *-versed*, *-versing*. [OF. *reverser*, < L. *reversare*, freq. of *revertere*.] **I.** *tr.* To turn in an opposite position; transpose; turn inside out; turn upside down, or invert (as, "*revers′d* that spear, redoubtable in war": Burns's "On the Death of Sir J. H. Blair," 21); turn in the opposite direction, or send on the opposite course (as, "As if in her the stream of mild Maternal nature had *revers′d* its course": Cowper's "Task," iii. 436); turn in the opposite order (as, "He had *reversed* the usual order, and had been in the fire — now he was going to the frying-pan": W. Churchill's "Coniston," ii. 14); alter to the opposite in character or tendency, or change completely (as, "The concluding portion of his reign had *reversed* all its previous glories": Motley's "Dutch Republic," i. 1); also, to revoke, repeal, or annul (a decree, judgment, etc.); in *mech.*, to cause to revolve or act in an opposite or contrary direction or manner. **II.** *intr.* To turn or move in the opposite or contrary direction, as in dancing.—**re-verse′ly**, *adv.*—**re-verse′ment**, *n.* Reversal.—**re-vers′er**, *n.*—**re-vers′i-ble**, *a.* Capable of being reversed or of reversing; of fabrics, finished on both sides so that either may be exposed.—**re-vers-i-bil′i-ty** (-bil′i-ti), *n.*—**re-vers′i-bly**, *adv.*

re-ver-sion (rẹ-vėr′shọn), *n.* [OF. *reversion* (F. *réversion*), < L. *reversio(n-)*, < *revertere*: see *revert*.] The act of turning something the reverse way, or the state of being so turned; reversal; also, the act of reverting or returning; return to a place†; return to a former practice, belief, etc.; return to a former state or condition; return to an earlier or primitive type, or atavism (in *biol.*); esp., the returning of an estate to the grantor or his heirs after the grant expires (in *law*); an estate which so returns, often such an estate as transferable to another party, as on the death of the original grantee (in *law*); hence, the right of succeeding to an estate, etc. (in *law*); the right of succeeding to the future possession of anything, as after another is done with it (as, "An old baronetage in actual possession is worth something more than the *reversion* of a new coronet": Maria Edgeworth's "Belinda," xv.); also, a payment, etc., which falls to a person upon the happening of some future event; also, the remains† or remainder†.—**in reversion**, conditional upon the expiring of a grant or upon the death of a person (as, an interest *in reversion*; an annuity *in reversion*); in general,

conditional upon something future.—**re-ver′sion-al**, *a.* Reversionary.—**re-ver′sion-a-ry** (-ạ-ri), *a.* Of, pertaining to, or involving a reversion.—**re-ver′sion-er**, *n.* One who possesses the reversion to an estate, etc.

re-vert (rẹ-vėrt′), *v.* [OF. *revertir*, < L. *revertere*, turn back, turn about, return, < *re-*, back, + *vertere*, turn.] **I.** *tr.* To turn back; direct backward; also, to turn the other way; reverse; invert. [Now rare.] **II.** *intr.* To go or come back, or return, as to a former place or position (now rare); return to a former habit, practice, belief, etc. (as, "Part of them . . . *reverted* to their former prejudices in regard to Lincoln": Charnwood's "Abraham Lincoln," v.); return to a former state or condition; return to an earlier or primitive type, or reproduce the characteristics of antecedent stages of development (in *biol.*); go back or return to the former proprietor or his heirs, or to any former possessor (esp. in *law*); go back in thought or discourse, as to a subject (as, "My thoughts *reverted* immediately to that scene," Bulwer-Lytton's "Pelham," xli.; to *revert* in a speech to a subject already treated); also, to look back (rare).—**re-vert′er**[1], *n.* One who or that which reverts.—**re-vert′er**[2], *n.* [See *-er*[3].] In *law*, reversion, as of an estate.—**re-vert′i-ble**, *a.* Capable of reverting; subject to reversion.

rev-er-y (rev′ẹ-ri), *n.* See *reverie*.

re-vest (rē-vest′), *v.* [See *re-*.] **I.** *tr.* To vest (a person, etc.) again, as with ownership or office; reinvest; reinstate; also, to vest (powers, etc.) again, as in a person. **II.** *intr.* To become vested again in a person; revert to a former owner.

re-vet (rẹ-vet′), *v. t.*; *-vetted*, *-vetting.* [F. *revêtir*, lit. 'clothe,' < LL. *revestire*, < L. *re-*, again, + *vestire*, clothe, E. *vest*, *v.*] To face, as an embankment, with masonry or other material.—**re-vet′ment**, *n.* [F. *revêtement*.] A facing of masonry or the like, as for protecting an embankment; a retaining wall.

re-vict-ual (rē-vit′l), *v. t.* or *i.*; *-ualed* or *-ualled*, *-ualing* or *-ualling.* [See *re-*.] To victual again.—**re-vict′ual-ment**, *n.*

re-view (rẹ-vū′), *n.* [F. *revue*, orig. pp. fem. of *revoir*, see again, examine anew, review, < L. *revidere* (pp. *revisus*), < *re-*, again, + *videre*, see.] A viewing again, or a second or repeated view of something; also, a looking over something again with a view to correction or improvement (formerly often used with reference to revision of literary matter); specif., a judicial reëxamination, as by a higher court, of the decision or proceedings in a case; also, the process of going over a subject again in study or recitation in order to fix it in the memory or summarize the facts, or an exercise of this kind (as, to allow a week for *review* of the term's work; monthly *reviews* in Latin); also, an inspection, or examination by viewing; esp., a formal inspection of military or naval forces by a commander or official in order to observe their condition, strength, skill in evolutions, etc.; hence, a formal inspection of any force or body, of a public parade, or the like; also, a viewing of the past, or a retrospective view or survey (as, "My intercourse with Brightwel was not, in the *review*, without its portion of comfort": Godwin's "Caleb Williams," xxv.); in general, contemplation or consideration of past events, of circumstances or facts in a case, or of any matter or subject (as, "Walked and talked . . . passing lightly in *review* What seemed hits and what seemed misses in a certain fence-play": Browning's "La Saisiaz"; a general survey of something (as, a mental *review* of a situation); often, a survey in words, or a report or account, of something (as, "The document was a nervous and rapid *review* of the course of late events in the provinces," Motley's "Dutch Republic," iii. 9; to publish regular *reviews* of the progress made in the sciences); also, critical examination or discussion, by a writer in some publication, of the character and merits and defects of a literary work (as, "Her book is clever . . . If it's put into capable hands for *review*! that's all it requires": G. Meredith's "Diana of the Crossways," xvii.); a critical article or report, as in a periodical, on some literary work, commonly some work of recent appearance; a critique; also, a periodical publication containing articles on current events or affairs, books, art, or other subjects of general or special interest (as, a literary, medical, or financial *review*: orig. used in the sense of 'survey,' as in the title of a paper started by Defoe in 1704, called in full "A Review of the

Affairs of France and of all Europe, as influenced by that Nation," but in modern use often implying, esp. as applied to literary periodicals, a mainly critical character).—**re-view′**, v. [Prob. partly < *review*, n., and partly < *re-* + *view*, v.] **I.** *tr.* To see again† (as, "I shall *review* Sicilia, for whose sight I have a woman's longing": Shakspere's "Winter's Tale," iv. 4. 680); also, to view, look at, or look over again (as, "Mrs. Reed . . . at far intervals, visited it [a room] to *review* the contents of a certain secret drawer in the wardrobe": C. Brontë's "Jane Eyre," ii.); look over (a book, etc.) in revision†; reëxamine judicially (as, a court of appeal *reviews* the judgment of an inferior court); also, to go over (lessons, studies, etc.) in review; also, to inspect, esp. formally or officially; hold a review of (troops, etc.); also, to look back upon, or view retrospectively (as, "Let me *review* the scene, And summon from the shadowy Past The forms that once have been": Longfellow's "Gleam of Sunshine"); survey mentally, or take a survey of (as, to *review* progress made; "Now let's *review* the situation," W. H. Hudson's "Purple Land," vi.); present a survey of in speech or writing (as, "The Emperor proceeded to address the states . . . He *reviewed* rapidly the progress of events . . . up to that day": Motley's "Dutch Republic," i. 1); also, to discuss (a book, etc.) in a critical review; write a critical report upon. **II.** *intr.* To write reviews; review books, etc., as for some periodical.—**re-view′a-ble**, a. That may be reviewed.—**re-view′al**, n. The act of reviewing; a review. —**re-view′er**, n. One who reviews; esp., one who writes reviews of new books, etc.

re-vile (rẹ-vīl′), v.; *-viled, -viling*. [OF. *reviler*, treat or regard as vile, < L. *re-*, back, again, + *vilis*, E. *vile*.] **I.** *tr.* To assail with contemptuous or opprobrious language; address, or speak of, abusively: as, "Blessed are ye, when men shall *revile* you, and persecute you . . . for my sake" (Mat. v. 11); "Lord Halifax used to *revile* him as 'a knave and a fool' " (Bancroft's "Hist. of the U. S.," Amer. Revolution, i. 1). **II.** *intr.* To speak abusively.—**re-vile′ment**, n. The act of reviling; a reviling utterance or speech.—**re-vil′er** (-vīl′ẹr), n.—**re-vil′ing-ly**, adv.

re-vin-di-cate (rẹ-vin′di-kāt), v. t. [See *re-*.] To vindicate again; reclaim, as a rightful possession.—**re-vin-di-ca′tion** (-kā′shọn), n.

re-vis-a-ble (rẹ-vī′zạ-bl), a. That may be revised.

re-vi-sal (rẹ-vī′zạl), n. The act of revising; revision.

re-vise (rẹ-vīz′), v. t.; *-vised, -vising*. [F. *reviser*, < L. *revisere*, go to see again, < *re-*, again, + *visere*, freq. of *videre*, see.] To see or view again†; also, to look carefully over with a view to correction or improvement, or correct or amend on a careful perusal (as, to *revise* a manuscript or a proof-sheet; to *revise* a translation; to *revise* a book for a new edition); go over and amend or alter in a systematic way (as, to *revise* a law or a treaty; to *revise* the tariff; to *revise* estimates or statistics); in general, to amend or alter (as, to find it necessary to *revise* one's opinion of a person; "if I had prolonged to this time of day the task of *revising* my life," Scott's "Castle Dangerous," xix.).—**Revised Version** (of the Bible). See under *version*.—**re-vise′**, n. A revising; also, a revised form of something; in *printing*, a proof-sheet taken after corrections or alterations have been made. —**re-vis′er** (-vī′zẹr), n. One who revises; esp., one who corrects or amends literary matter, etc.

re-vi-sion (rẹ-vizh′ọn), n. [F. *revision*, < LL. *revisio(n-)*, < L. *revidere*, see again (see *review*); in use now associated with L. *revisere*, E. *revise*.] The act or work of revising, or examination and correction or amendment (as, "Our political contrivances . . . need to undergo constant *revision* as knowledge and understanding grow": H. G. Wells's "Outline of History," xxxvii. § 6); a process of revising (as, "The fortunate condition of the Government's finances in 1924 justifies not only a *revision* but a reduction of taxes": A. W. Mellon's "Taxation," vii.); also, a revised form or version, as of a book.—**re-vi′sion-al, re-vi′sion-a-ry** (-ạ-ri), a. Of or pertaining to revision.—**re-vi′sion-ist**, n. An advocate of revision; also, a reviser; esp., one of those who made the Revised Version of the Bible.

re-vis-it (rẹ-viz′it), v. t. [See *re-*.] To visit again; come back for a visit to; return to: as, "like a ghost that *revisits* the familiar fireside" (Hawthorne's "Scarlet Letter," v.).

—re-vis′it-ant, a. Revisiting.—**re-vis-i-ta′tion** (-i-tā′-shọn), n.

re-vi-sor (rẹ-vī′zọr), n. Same as *reviser*.

re-vi-so-ry (rẹ-vī′zọ-ri), a. Pertaining to revision.

re-vi-tal-ize (rē-vī′tạl-īz), v. t. [See *re-*.] To restore vitality to; put new life into.—**re-vi″tal-i-za′tion** (-i-zā′-shọn), n.

re-viv-a-ble (rẹ-vī′vạ-bl), a. That may be revived.

re-viv-al (rẹ-vī′vạl), n. The act of reviving, or the state of being revived; restoration to life or consciousness, or to vigor, strength, a flourishing condition, etc.; esp., restoration to use, acceptance, or currency (as, the *revival* of old customs, sports, methods, or styles); the reproduction of an old play; specif., an awakening, in a church or a community, of interest in and care for matters relating to personal religion (in full, 'revival of religion'); a service or a series of services for the purpose of effecting a religious awakening (as, to hold a *revival*.—**Revival of Learning**, the Renaissance in its relation to learning.—**re-vi′val-ism**, n. The tendency to revive what belongs to the past; also, that form of religious activity which manifests itself in revivals.—**re-vi′val-ist**, n. One who revives former customs, methods, etc.; also, one who promotes or holds religious revivals.—**re-vi-val-is′-tic**, a.

re-vive (rẹ-vīv′), v.; *-vived, -viving*. [OF. F. *revivre*, < L. *revivere*, < *re-*, again, + *vivere*, live.] **I.** *intr.* To return to life, or live again (as, "Henry is dead and never shall *revive*": Shakspere's "1 Henry VI.," i. 1. 18); also, to return to consciousness, as after a swoon; also, to gain fresh life and vigor, regain strength, or return to a flourishing condition, as after drooping, languishing, or declining (as, plants *revive* with the rain; an age in which commerce and arts *revived*); recover from depression (as, "With this thought my spirits began to *revive*": Defoe's "Robinson Crusoe," i. 5); be quickened, restored, or renewed, as hope, confidence, suspicions, memories, etc.; also, to return to notice, use, or currency, as a subject, practice, doctrine, etc.; also, to become operative or valid again; in *chem.*, to recover its natural or uncombined state, as a metal. **II.** *tr.* To restore to life; also, to restore to consciousness, or resuscitate; also, to restore to vigor, strength, or a flourishing condition (as, "flow'r-*reviving* rains," Burns's "On Cessnock Banks," 23; to *revive* declining industries); reanimate or cheer (the spirit, heart, etc., or the person: as, "Your coming, friends, *revives* me," Milton's "Samson Agonistes," 187); quicken or renew in the mind (as, to *revive* feelings, thoughts, or memories); bring back before the mind (as, "a boy in heart, able after long years to *revive* the past mentally, and picture it in its true, fresh, original colours": W. H. Hudson's "Far Away and Long Ago," xvii.); also, to bring back into notice, use, or currency (as, to *revive* a subject of discussion; "If I could have had my way I would have *revived* prize-fighting," Gissing's "New Grub Street," ii.); produce (an old play) again; set going or in activity again (as, to *revive* old feuds); also, to make operative or valid again; in *chem.*, to restore or reduce to its natural or uncombined state, as a metal.—**re-viv′er** (-vī′vẹr), n.

re-viv-i-fy (rẹ-viv′i-fī), v. t.; *-fied, -fying*. [F. *revivifier*, < LL. *revivificare*, < L. *re-*, again, + LL. *vivificare*, E. *vivify*.] To restore to life; give new life to; quicken or animate anew.—**re-viv″i-fi-ca′tion** (-fi-kā′shọn), n.—**re-viv′i-fi-er** (-fī-ẹr), n.

rev-i-vis-cent (rev-i-vis′ẹnt), a. [L. *reviviscens* (-ent-), ppr. of *reviviscere*, become alive again, < *revivere*, E. *revive*.] Returning to life; reviving; gaining fresh vigor.—**rev-i-vis′-cence**, n.

re-vi-vor (rẹ-vī′vọr), n. In *law*, the reviving of a suit abated by the death of a party or by other cause.

rev-o-ca-ble (rev′ọ-kạ-bl), a. [L. *revocabilis*.] That may be revoked; revokable.—**rev″o-ca-bil′i-ty** (-bil′i-ti), n.

rev-o-ca-tion (rev-ọ-kā′shọn), n. [L. *revocatio(n-)*.] The act of revoking; recall; withdrawal; repeal or annulment (as, the *revocation* of the Edict of Nantes by Louis XIV. of France in 1685: see *Edict of Nantes*, under *edict*).—**rev′o-ca-to-ry** (-kạ-tọ-ri), a.

re-voice (rē-vois′), v. t. [See *re-*.] To voice again or in return; echo; also, to readjust the tone of (as, to *revoice* an organ-pipe).

re-vok-a-ble (rę-vō′ką-bl), *a.* That may be revoked; revocable.

re-voke (rę-vōk′), *v.*; *-voked, -voking.* [OF. *revoquer* (F. *révoquer*), < L. *revocare* (pp. *revocatus*), < *re-*, back, + *vocare*, call.] **I.** *tr.* To call or summon back (now rare); also, to bring back as by recalling (what is past: as, "if he could have *revoked* his life and prearranged his destiny," Hawthorne's "Twice-Told Tales," The Prophetic Pictures); also, to take back or withdraw (as, to *revoke* a privilege or a grant); rescind or repeal (as, to *revoke* a decree or edict); annul, cancel, or reverse (as, to *revoke* a will; "Let them . . . on a safer judgement all *revoke* Your ignorant election," Shakspere's "Coriolanus," ii. 3. 226); also, to retract† or recant†. **II.** *intr.* In card-playing, to fail to follow suit when one can and should do so.—**re-voke′**, *n.* In *card-playing*, an act or instance of revoking.—**re-vok′er** (-vō′kėr), *n.*

re-volt (rę-vōlt′, also -volt′), *v.* [F. *révolter*, < It. *rivoltare*, < L. *re-*, back, + *volutare*, freq. of *volvere*, roll, turn.] **I.** *intr.* To turn away from one party, leader, cause, or religion, or go over to another (as, "Home to your cottages, forsake this groom [Jack Cade]: The king is merciful, if you *revolt*," Shakspere's "2 Henry VI.," iv. 2. 133: obs. except as in the following sense); esp., to break away from or rise against constituted authority, as by open rebellion (as, "Edom *revolted* from under the hand of Judah, and made a king over themselves," 2 Kings, viii. 20; "The household troops openly *revolted*," Burke's "American Taxation"); cast off allegiance or subjection to a ruler or government, officers, or others in authority; rebel; mutiny; fig., to turn away in involuntary mental rebellion or utter disgust or abhorrence (*from*: as, "an extremity from which . . . his mind *revolted*," Stevenson's "Master of Ballantrae," xii.); feel disgust or horror (*at*); rebel in feeling (*against*: as, "Our whole hearts *revolt* against the way in which women have hitherto been treated," Mallock's "New Republic," iv. 1). **II.** *tr.* To affect with disgust or abhorrence: as, "There were several . . . whom this brutality *revolted*" (Stevenson's "Master of Ballantrae," xi.); "Its dogmas are . . . too odious to be believed. They *revolt* me" (J. H. Newman's "Callista," xix.).—**re-volt′**, *n.* [F. *révolte*.] The act of revolting, or the state of those revolting (as, "A portion of the fleet was already in *revolt*": Morley's "Oliver Cromwell," iii. 4); an insurrection or rebellion; any breaking out against authority or control; fig., a revolting in mind or feeling (as, "Fort had begun to feel something of the *revolt* which the man of action so soon experiences when he listens to an artist talking," Galsworthy's "Saint's Progress," ii. 8; "It was not possible to think of such things without a *revolt* of his whole being," Mrs. Wharton's "Ethan Frome," vii.).—**re-volt′er**, *n.*—**re-volt′ing**, *p. a.* That revolts; rebellious; also, causing disgust or abhorrence; disgusting; repulsive.—**re-volt′ing-ly**, *adv.*

rev-o-lute[1] (rev′ǫ-lūt), *a.* [L. *revolutus*, pp. of *revolvere*, E. *revolve*.] In *bot.*, *zoöl.*, etc., rolled backward or downward; rolled backward at the tip or margin, as a leaf.

rev-o-lute[2] (rev-ǫ-lūt′), *v. i.*; *-luted, -luting.* [Back-formation from *revolution*.] To engage in or effect a (political) revolution. [Colloq.]

rev-o-lu-tion (rev-ǫ-lū′shǫn), *n.* [OF. *revolution* (F. *révolution*), < LL. *revolutio(n-)*, < L. *revolvere*, E. *revolve*.] A turning round or rotating, as on an axis; a single turn of this kind; also, a moving in a circular or curving course, as about a central point; a single movement in such a course; specif., of a heavenly body, the action or fact of going round in an orbit, also an apparent movement round the earth; a single course of such movement; the time required to complete such a course; also, procedure or course as if in a circuit, as back to a starting-point in time (as, "the daily *revolution* of affairs": Hawthorne's "House of the Seven Gables," xxi.); a round or cycle of events in time, or a recurring period of time; also, the act of turning something over in the mind†; consideration†; reflection†; also, a complete or marked change in something (as, "a new and terrible *revolution* of my

fortune," Godwin's "Caleb Williams," xli.; "Religions . . . and usages of private life, and modes of thinking, all have undergone a succession of *revolutions*," Macaulay's "Essays," Moore's Byron); also, a complete overthrow of an established government or political system; esp. [*cap.*], with *the*, (*a*) in *Eng. hist.*, the convulsion of 1688–89 by which James II. was expelled and the sovereignty conferred on William and Mary ('English Revolution'); (*b*) in *Amer. hist.*, the series of movements during 1775–83 by which the thirteen colonies overthrew British rule and established their independence ('American Revolution'); (*c*) in *Fr. hist.*, the series of movements during 1789–95, by which the old monarchy was overthrown and a republican government established ('French Revolution').—**rev-o-lu′tion-a-ry** (-ą-ri), *a.* Pertaining to or marked by revolution or revolving; also, pertaining to, characterized by, or of the nature of a revolution, or complete or marked change (as, "the novel and *revolutionary* experience of playing for money — and winning": W. Churchill's "Modern Chronicle," ii. 7); tending to produce such a change, or subversive to established procedure, principles, etc.; esp., pertaining to a political revolution (often *cap.*, with reference to the American Revolution or the French Revolution: see *revolt*).—**Revolutionary calendar.** Same as *calendar of the first French republic*, under *calendar*, *n.*—**rev-o-lu′tion-a-ry**, *n.*; pl. *-ries* (-riz). A revolutionist: as, "the heated and headlong *revolutionary*" (Morley's "Oliver Cromwell," iii. 2).—**rev-o-lu′tion-ist**, *n.* An advocate of revolution; one who takes part in a revolution.—**rev-o-lu′tion-ize**, *v.*; *-ized, -izing.* **I.** *tr.* To bring about a revolution in; effect a radical change in (as, "Advertisement has *revolutionised* trade and industry": H. G. Wells's "Tono-Bungay," ii. 3. § 2); subject to a political revolution (as, to *revolutionize* a government). **II.** *intr.* To undergo a revolution.

re-volv-a-ble (rę-vol′vą-bl), *a.* Capable of being revolved.

re-volve (rę-volv′), *v.*; *-volved, -volving.* [L. *revolvere* (pp. *revolutus*), roll back, revolve, < *re-*, back, + *volvere*, roll, turn.] **I.** *tr.* To roll or turn back†; also, to cause to turn round, as on an axis; also, to cause to move in a circular or curving course, as about a central point; also, to turn over in the mind or thoughts, or consider (as, "Jones . . . having *revolved* this matter much in his thoughts, at last came to a resolution," Fielding's "Tom Jones," vii. 13; "Tommy sat on the fender *revolving* this problem," Barrie's "Sentimental Tommy," v.); also, to search through†, study†, or read† (as, "Straight I again *revolved* The law and prophets, searching what was writ Concerning the Messiah": Milton's "Paradise Regained," i. 259). **II.** *intr.* To turn round or rotate, as on an axis; also, to move in a circular or curving course, or orbit; also, to proceed in a round or cycle; come round in the process of time; also, to be revolved in the mind; also, to consider†; meditate on something†.—**re-volv′er**, *n.* One who or that which revolves; specif., a firearm, esp. a pistol, having a revolving chambered cylinder for holding a number of cartridges which may be discharged in succession without reloading.—**re-volv′ing**, *p. a.* That revolves; in *mach.*, noting or pertaining to an internal-combustion engine for an aëroplane, whose cylinders revolve about a stationary crank-shaft.

re-vue (rę-vū′, F. rė-vü), *n.* [F.: see *review*.] A form of theatrical entertainment of the nature of a medley, with singing, dancing, etc., in which are represented in review, and often parodied, recent plays, events, popular fads, etc.

re-vul-sion (rę-vul′shǫn), *n.* [L. *revulsio(n-)*, < *revellere*, pluck away, < *re-*, back, + *vellere*, pluck.] The act of drawing something back or away, or the fact of being so drawn (as, the *revulsion* of capital from an industry); also, a sudden and violent change of feeling or reaction in sentiment (as, "With a sudden *revulsion* his heart recoiled from its purpose": Longfellow's "Courtship of Miles Standish," v.); a sudden reverse tendency, as in business, etc. (as, "to sustain the credit of the merchants under the *revulsion* consequent on peace," Bancroft's "Hist. of the U. S.," Amer. Revolution, ii. 3; "where the penalties of progress and refinement are constantly exacted in financial *revulsions*," J. F. Kirk's "Charles the Bold," iv. 2); in *med.*, the diminution of morbid action in one part of the body by developing

1. Revolute-margined Leaf. 2. The leaf as shown in transverse section.

it artificially in another.—**re-vul'sive** (-siv). **I.** *a.* Tending to produce revulsion. **II.** *n.* A revulsive agent.

re-ward (rē-wârd'), *v. t.* [OF. *rewarder*, var. of *regarder*, E. *regard, v.*] To regard†; observe†; consider†; also, to recompense or requite (a person, etc.) for service, merit, achievement, etc.; make return for, or requite (service, merit, etc.: as, "She *rewarded* his past services with liberality," Lytton Strachey's "Queen Victoria," iii.); sometimes, to requite (a person, etc.) for wrong, evil, etc. (as, "The Lord shall *reward* the doer of evil according to his wickedness": 2 Sam. iii. 39); make return for (wrong, evil, etc.: rare); also, to serve as recompense to (as, excellent results *rewarded* him for his efforts); serve as recompense for (as, "Gold and silver . . . *rewarded* the struggle of the conquerors": G. P. R. James's "Hist. of Charlemagne," iii.); also, to give as a recompense† (as, "Thou hast *rewarded* me good, whereas I have *rewarded* thee evil": 1 Sam. xxiv. 17).—**re-ward'**, *n.* [OF. *reward, rewart*.] Regard†; consideration†; also, the act of rewarding, recompensing, or requiting (as, the *reward* of good and the punishment of evil; to confer a gift in *reward* of service); also, something given or received in return or recompense for service, merit, hardship, etc. (as, "the best of all earthly *rewards*, the love and admiration of his fellow-citizens": Burke's "American Taxation"); a recompense; specif., a sum of money offered for the detection or capture of a criminal, the recovery of lost or stolen property, etc.; also, sometimes, something given or received in recompense or retribution for wrong, evil, etc. (as, "Hanging was the *reward* of treason and desertion": Stubbs's "Constitutional Hist. of Eng.," ii. § 16).—**re-ward'a-ble**, *a.* That may be or is to be rewarded; worthy of reward.—**re-ward'er**, *n.*—**re-ward'ful**, *a.* Yielding a reward.—**re-ward'less**, *a.* Without reward.

re-weigh (rē-wā'), *v. t.* [See *re-*.] To weigh again.

re-wind (rē-wīnd'), *v. t.*; pret. and pp. *-wound*. [See *re-*.] To wind again.—**re-wind'er**, *n.*

re-word (rē-wėrd'), *v. t.* [See *re-*.] To word again; repeat; reëcho; put into other words.

re-work (rē-wėrk'), *v. t.* [See *re-*.] To work again.

re-write (rē-rīt'), *v. t.*; pret. *-wrote*, pp. *-written*, ppr. *-writing*. [See *re-*.] To write again or anew; write in a different form. —**re-write** (rē-rīt' or rē'rīt), *n.* A rewriting; also, a new or revised form of a writing or document.

rex (reks), *n.*; pl. *reges* (rē'jēz). [L., < *regere*, rule: see *regent*.] King: abbreviated *R.*, as, Carolus (Charles) *R.*

Rey-nard (rā'närd or ren'ärd), *n.* [OF. *renart* (F. *renard*); from Teut.] A name for the fox, orig. in the medieval beast epic "Reynard the Fox"; [*l. c.*] a fox.

rhab-do-man-cy (rab'dō-man-si), *n.* [Gr. ῥαβδομαντεία, < ῥάβδος, rod, + μαντεία, divination.] Divination by means of a rod or wand; esp., the art of discovering things in the earth, as ores, springs of water, etc., by means of a divining-rod.

rha'chis, rha-chi'tis, etc. See *rachis*, etc.

Rhad-a-man-thus (rad-a-man'thus), *n.* [From *Rhadamanthus*, in Greek mythology, one of the judges in the lower world.] An inflexibly just or severe judge: as, "the very *Rhadamanthus* of schoolmasters" (J. H. Newman's "Callista," viii.).—**Rhad-a-man'thine** (-thin), *a.*

Rhæ-tian (rē'shian), *a.* Of or pertaining to Rhætia, the ancient name for a district comprising southeastern Switzerland, part of Tyrol, and adjoining regions; also, Rhæto-Romanic.—**Rhæ'tic**, *a.* In *geol.*, noting or pertaining to certain strata, extensively developed in the Rhætian Alps, having features characteristic of both the Triassic and the Jurassic.—**Rhæ-to-Ro-man-ic** (rē''tō-rō-man'ik). **I.** *a.* Noting or pertaining to a group of Romance dialects spoken in the Rhætian Alps. **II.** *n.* The Rhæto-Romanic dialects.

rham-na-ceous (ram-nā'shius), *a.* [NL. *Rhamnus*, the typical genus, < Gr. ῥάμνος, kind of prickly shrub.] Belonging to the *Rhamnaceæ*, or buckthorn family of plants.

rha'phe, rha'phis. See *raphe*, *raphis*.

-rhaphy. A noun termination from Gr. ῥαφή, a sewing, suture, used in surgical terms, as *hysterorrhaphy*, *tenorrhaphy*.

rhap-sode (rap'sōd), *n.* [Gr. ῥαψῳδός, lit. 'one who sews songs together,' < ῥάπτειν, sew, + ᾠδή, song, E. *ode*.] An ancient Greek rhapsodist.

rhap-sod-ic, rhap-sod-i-cal (rap-sod'ik, -i-kal), *a.* [Gr. ῥαψῳδικός.] Pertaining to, characteristic of, or of the nature of rhapsody; extravagantly enthusiastic; ecstatic.—**rhap-sod'i-cal-ly**, *adv.*

rhap-so-dist (rap'sō-dist), *n.* A reciter of epic poetry among the ancient Greeks, esp. a professional reciter of the Homeric poems; hence, any professional reciter or singer of poems; also, one who speaks or writes in a rhapsodic manner. —**rhap-so-dis'tic**, *a.*

rhap-so-dize (rap'sō-dīz), *v.*; *-dized*, *-dizing*. **I.** *tr.* To recite as a rhapsody. **II.** *intr.* To utter rhapsodies; talk rhapsodically: as, "*rhapsodising* on this and that — poetry, politics, life and death" (M. Hewlett's "Open Country," xx.).

rhap-so-dy (rap'sō-di), *n.*; pl. *-dies* (-diz). [Gr. ῥαψῳδία, < ῥαψῳδός, E. *rhapsode*.] An epic poem, or a part of such a poem, as a book of the Iliad, suitable for recitation at one time; also, an exalted or exaggerated expression of feeling or enthusiasm; an utterance or writing marked by extravagant enthusiasm; sometimes, rhapsodic language (as, "Spend all the pow'rs Of rant and *rhapsody* in virtue's praise": Cowper's "Task," v. 677); also, a medley† or jumble† (as, "He . . . had uttered nothing but a *rhapsody* of nonsense": Fielding's "Joseph Andrews," i. 13); in *music*, an instrumental composition irregular in form and somewhat suggestive of improvisation (as, Liszt's Hungarian *rhapsodies*).

rhat-a-ny (rat'a-ni), *n.* [Pg. *ratanhia* or Sp. *ratania*; from Peruvian.] A procumbent South American shrub, *Krameria triandra*, the root of which is used as an astringent and tonic in medicine and also to color portwine; also, the root; also, some other plant of this genus, or its similarly used root.

rhe-a[1] (rē'ä), *n.* [NL. use of L. *Rhea*, < Gr. Ῥέα, the goddess Rhea, mother of Zeus and other deities.] A bird of the genus *Rhea*, which consists of South American ratite birds resembling the African ostrich but smaller and having three toes instead of two. Sometimes called *American ostrich*.

rhe-a[2] (rē'ä), *n.* [E. Ind.] Ramie (plant or fiber).

-rhea, -rhœa. [Gr. ῥοία or -ροια, < ῥεῖν, flow.] A noun termination meaning 'a flow,' 'a discharge,' used in pathological terms, as *diarrhea* or *diarrhœa*, *galactorrhea*, *pyorrhea*.

Rhatany (*Krameria triandra*).

Rhea (*R. americana*).

rhe-mat-ic (rē-mat'ik), *a.* [Gr. ῥηματικός, < ῥῆμα, word, verb, lit. 'something said,' akin to ῥήτωρ, speaker: see *rhetor*.] Pertaining to the formation of words; also, pertaining to or derived from a verb.

Rhen-ish (ren'ish), *a.* [MHG. *rīnisch* (G. *rheinisch*); with E. spelling affected by L. *Rhenus*, Rhine.] Of or pertaining to the river Rhine or the regions bordering on it.—**Rhenish architecture**, the local form assumed by Romanesque or round-arched architecture in the 11th and 12th centuries in the regions bordering on the Rhine. See cut on following page.—**Rhen'ish**, *n.* Rhine wine: as, "He drains his draughts of *Rhenish* down" (Shakspere's "Hamlet," i. 4. 10).

rheo-. Form of Gr. ῥέος, something flowing, a stream, used in combination.—**rhe-om-e-ter** (rē-om'e-tėr), *n.* [+

-*meter*.] An instrument for measuring the velocity of the blood-flow; also, an instrument for measuring electric currents.—**rhe-o-scope** (rē'ō-skōp), *n.* [+ *-scope*.] An instrument which indicates the presence of an electric current.—**rhe'-o-stat** (-stat), *n.* [+ *-stat*.] A device for regulating an electric current by introducing a resistance (esp. one that can be varied) into the circuit.—**rhe-o-stat'ic**, *a.*—**rhe-o-tax'is** (-tak'sis), *n.*

Rhenish Architecture.—Apse of the Church of the Apostles, Cologne.

[NL.: see *-taxis*.] In *biol.*, the property in a cell or organism of responding by movement to the stimulus of a current of water.—**rhe-ot-ro-pism** (rē-ot'rō-pizm), *n.* [+ *-tropism*.] The effect of a current of water upon the direction of plant-growth.

rhe-sus (rē'sus), *n.* [NL.] A macaque, *Macacus rhesus*, common in India.

rhe-tor (rē'tor), *n.* [L., rhetorician, < Gr. ῥήτωρ, speaker, orator, from the root of εἴρειν, say, speak: cf. *irony²*.] A master or teacher of rhetoric; also, an orator.

rhet-o-ric (ret'ō-rik), *n.* [OF. *rhetorique* (F. *rhétorique*), < L. *rhetorica*, < Gr. ῥητορική, prop. fem. of ῥητορικός, pertaining to an orator; < ῥήτωρ: see *rhetor*.] Orig., the art of oratory; now, more broadly,

Rhesus.

the art of the effective use of words in speaking and writing; also, effective, artistic, or oratorical use of language, or the language used (as, "Blifil suffered himself to be overpowered by the forcible *rhetoric* of the squire": Fielding's "Tom Jones," vii. 6); often, artificial oratory; mere display in language; also, a treatise or text-book on the art of rhetoric.—**rhe-tor-i-cal** (rē-tor'i-kạl), *a.* Of or pertaining to the art of rhetoric; also, belonging to or concerned with mere rhetoric; of language, etc., intended especially or merely for artistic effect.—**rhe-tor'i-cal-ly**, *adv.*—**rhet-o-ri'cian** (-rish'ạn), *n.* One versed in the art of rhetoric; also, one given to empty rhetoric or display in language.

rheum¹ (rōm), *n.* [OF. *reume* (F. *rhume*), < LL. *rheuma*, < Gr. ῥεῦμα, a flow, flux, rheum, < ῥεῖν, flow: see *stream*, and cf. *rhythm*.] A mucous or catarrhal discharge; hence, catarrh; a cold; also, any serous fluid or humid matter secreted by the mucous glands, etc.; also, tears (poetic: as, "A few drops of women's *rheum*, which are As cheap as lies," Shakspere's "Coriolanus," v. 6. 46).

rhe-um² (rē'um), *n.* [NL., < Gr. ῥῆον, rhubarb.] Any plant of the genus *Rheum*. See *rhubarb*.

rheu-mat-ic (rȯ-mat'ik), *a.* [OF. *reumatique* (F. *rhumatique*), < L. *rheumaticus*, < Gr. ῥευματικός, < ῥεῦμα, E. *rheum¹*.] **I.** *a.* Pertaining to or of the nature of rheum†; affected with rheum, catarrh, or a cold†; also, pertaining to or of the nature of rheumatism (as, *rheumatic* symptoms; "a slight *rheumatic* feel in one of his shoulders," Jane Austen's "Sense and Sensibility," viii.); affected with or subject to rheumatism (as, "Silk mittens . . . covered her *rheumatic* hands":

Mrs. Wharton's "Age of Innocence," xvii.); causing rheumatism. **II.** *n.* One affected with or subject to rheumatism; *pl.*, rheumatic pains, or rheumatism (colloq.: as, "a new cure for the *rheumatics*," Stevenson's "Treasure Island," i.).—**rheu-mat'i-cal-ly**, *adv.*

rheu-ma-tism (rö'mạ-tizm), *n.* [L. *rheumatismus*, < Gr. ῥευματισμός, < ῥευματίζεσθαι, have a flux, < ῥεῦμα, E. *rheum¹*.] In *pathol.*, a disease ('acute rheumatism' or 'inflammatory rheumatism') characterized by inflammation of the joints, accompanied by constitutional disturbances, and now usually thought to be due to a micro-organism; also, any of various other diseases of the joints or muscles, as certain chronic joint inflammations ('chronic rheumatism') and certain painful affections of the muscles ('muscular rheumatism').—**rheu'ma-toid**, *a.* [See *-oid*.] Resembling rheumatism; rheumatic. Also **rheu-ma-toi'dal.**—**rheu-ma-toi'dal-ly**, *adv.*

rheum-y (rö'mi), *a.* Of the nature of, full of, or causing rheum.

rhig-o-lene (rig'ō-lēn), *n.* [Gr. ῥῖγος, cold, + L. *oleum*, oil.] An extremely volatile liquid obtained from petroleum: used to produce local anæsthesia by freezing.

rhi-nal (rī'nạl), *a.* [Gr. ῥίς (ῥιν-), nose.] Of or pertaining to the nose; nasal.

rhi-nen-ceph-a-lon (rī-nen-sef'ạ-lon), *n.*; pl. *-la* (-lä). [NL.: see *rhino-* and *encephalon*.] In *anat.*, the olfactory portion of the brain when regarded as a distinct segment, and not as an anterior division of the prosencephalon.—**rhi'nen-ce-phal'ic** (-se-fal'ik), *a.*

rhine-stone (rīn'stōn), *n.* [Tr. F. *caillou du Rhin*, 'pebble of the Rhine.'] An artificial gem made of paste or strass, often cut to imitate the diamond.

Rhine (rīn) **wine.** Wine (of many varieties) produced in the valley of the Rhine, esp. any of a class of white wines, mostly light, still, dry, and acid.

rhi-ni-tis (ri-nī'tis or rī-), *n.* [NL., < Gr. ῥίς (ῥιν-), nose.] In *pathol.*, inflammation of the nose or its mucous membrane.

rhi-no¹ (rī'nō), *n.* [Origin obscure.] Money; cash. [Slang.]

rhi-no² (rī'nō), *n.*; pl. *-nos* (-nōz) or *-no.* Shortened form of *rhinoceros*: as, "We saw two *rhino* come down to the river to drink" (J. H. Patterson's "Man-Eaters of Tsavo," xii.). [Colloq.]

rhino-, rhin-. Forms of Gr. ῥίς (ῥιν-), nose, used in combination.

rhi-no-ce-ros (rī-nos'ẹ-ros), *n.*; pl. *-roses* or *-ros.* [L., < Gr. ῥινόκερως, < ῥίς (ῥιν-), nose, + κέρας, horn.] Any of various large, ungainly, thick-skinned mammals (family *Rhinocerotidæ*) with one or two upright horns on the snout.—**rhi-no-ce-rot-ic** (rī-nos-ẹ-rot'ik), *a.*

rhi-nol-o-gy (rī-nol'ọ-ji), *n.* [See *rhino-* and *-logy*.] The science dealing with the nose and its diseases.—**rhi-no-log-i-cal** (rī-nọ-loj'i-kạl), *a.*—**rhi-nol'o-gist**, *n.*

One-horned Rhinoceros (*Rhinoceros unicornis*).

rhi-no-plas-ty (rī'nọ-plas-ti), *n.* [See *rhino-* and *-plasty*.] Plastic surgery of the nose.—**rhi-no-plas'tic**, *a.*

rhi-no-scope (rī'nọ-skōp), *n.* [See *rhino-* and *-scope*.] An instrument for examining the nasal passages.—**rhi-no-scop'ic** (-skop'ik), *a.*—**rhi-nos'co-py** (-nos'kọ-pi), *n.*

rhizo-. Form of Gr. ῥίζα, root, used in combination.—**rhi-zo-car-pous** (rī-zō-kär'pus), *a.* [+ *-carpous*.] In *bot.*, having the root perennial but the stem annual, as the perennial herbs.—**rhi'zo-caul** (-kâl), *n.* [+ Gr. καυλός, stalk.] In *zoöl.*, that part of a polyp by which it is affixed to some support.

rhi-zo-ceph-a-lous (rī-zō-sef'ạ-lus), *a.* [NL. *Rhizocephala*, pl., < Gr. ῥίζα, root, + κεφαλή, head.] Belonging to the *Rhizocephala*, a group of degenerate hermaphrodite crustaceans which are parasitic chiefly on crabs, attaching themselves to the host by means of modified antennæ resembling root-like processes.

rhi-zo-gen-ic (rī-zō-jen′ik), a. [See rhizo- and -genic.] In bot., producing roots, as certain cells or tissues. Also **rhi-zog′e-nous** (-zoj′e-nus).

rhi-zoid (rī′zoid). [Gr. ῥιζοειδής, < ῥίζα, root, + εἶδος, form.] **I.** a. Root-like. **II.** n. In mosses, etc., one of the root-like filaments by which the plant is attached to the substratum.—**rhi-zoi′dal**, a.

rhi-zome (rī′zōm), n. [Gr. ῥίζωμα, mass of roots, < ῥιζοῦν, cause to take root, < ῥίζα, root.] In bot., a root-like stem, commonly horizontal or oblique in position, lying on the ground or being subterranean, which usually produces roots below and sends up shoots progressively from the upper surface.—**rhi-zo′ma-tous** (-zō′ma-tus), **rhi-zo′mic**, a.

rhi-zo-mor-phous (rī-zō-môr′fus), a. [See rhizo- and -morphous.] In bot., root-like in form.

rhi-zoph-a-gous (rī-zof′a-gus), a. [Gr. ῥιζοφάγος, < ῥίζα, root, + φαγεῖν, eat.] Feeding on roots.

rhi-zo-pho-ra-ceous (rī″zō-fō-rā′shius), a. [NL. Rhizophora, the typical genus, < Gr. ῥίζα, root, + φέρειν, bear.] Belonging to the Rhizophoraceæ, the mangrove family of trees and shrubs.

Forms of Rhizome. — 1, Solomon's-seal (Polygonatum commutatum); 2, jack-in-the-pulpit (Arisæma triphyllum); 3, trillium (Trillium sessile).

rhi-zo-pod (rī′zō-pod), n. [NL. Rhizopoda, pl., < Gr. ῥίζα, root, + πούς (ποδ-), foot.] Any of the Rhizopoda, a class of protozoans having pseudopods.—**rhi-zop′o-dous** (-zop′ō-dus), a.

rho (rō), n. [Gr. ῥῶ.] The seventeenth letter (Ρ, ρ, = English R, r) of the Greek alphabet.

rho-dam-ine (rō-dam′in), n. [Gr. ῥόδον, rose, + E. amine.] A red dye obtained by heating an amino derivative of phenol with phthalic anhydride and concentrated sulphuric acid; any of various related dyes.

Rho-di-an (rō′di-an). **I.** a. Of or pertaining to Rhodes, an island of the Mediterranean, southwest of Asia Minor. **II.** n. A native or inhabitant of Rhodes.

rho-di-um (rō′di-um), n. [NL., < Gr. ῥόδον, rose.] Chem. sym., Rh; at. wt., 102.9; sp. gr., 12.1. A grayish-white metallic element, forming salts which give rose-colored solutions.— **rho′dic**, a.

rho-do-chro-site (rō-dō-krō′sīt), n. [G. rhodochrosit, < Gr. ῥοδόχρως, rose-colored, < ῥόδον, rose, + χρόα, color.] A mineral consisting essentially of manganese carbonate, and usually rose-red in color.

rho-do-den-dron (rō-dō-den′dron), n.; pl. -drons. [NL., < Gr. ῥοδόδενδρον, oleander, < ῥόδον, rose, +

δένδρον, tree.] Any plant of the ericaceous genus Rhododendron, comprising evergreen shrubs and trees with handsome pink, purple, or white flowers and oval or oblong leaves, as R. maximum ('great rhododendron'), abounding from Nova Scotia to Georgia, and R. catawbiense, of the southern Alleghanies: much cultivated for ornament. See cut in preceding column.

rho-do-lite (rō′dō-līt), n. [Gr. ῥόδον, rose, + λίθος, stone.] A rose-red variety of garnet, sometimes used as a gem.

rhod″o-mon-tade′, n. and v. See rodomontade.

rho-do-nite (rō′dō-nīt), n. [G. rhodonit, < Gr. ῥόδον, rose.] A mineral, usually rose-red, consisting essentially of manganese silicate, and crystallizing in the triclinic system but commonly found massive: sometimes used as an ornamental stone.

rho-do-phy-ceous (rō-dō-fī′shius), a. [NL. Rhodophyceæ, pl., < Gr. ῥόδον, rose, + φῦκος, seaweed.] Belonging to the Rhodophyceæ, or red algæ, a class of algæ containing forms that are red or purplish in color, and practically all marine.

rho-do-ra (rō-dō′rä), n. [NL., with form < L. rhodora, kind of plant, but with sense < Gr. ῥόδον, rose.] A low ericaceous shrub, Rhodora canadensis, of North America, with rose-colored flowers which appear before the leaves.

-rhœa. See -rhea.

rhomb (romb or rom), n. [L. rhombus, < Gr. ῥόμβος, spinning top or wheel, rhomb, lozenge, < ῥέμβειν, turn round, roll.] An oblique-angled equilateral parallelogram; also, a rhombohedron; also, a circle† or wheel†.— **rhom-bic** (rom′bik), a. Having the form of a rhomb (plane figure); also, having a rhomb as base or cross-section; also, bounded by rhombs, as a solid; in crystal., orthorhombic.—**rhom-bo-he′dron** (-bō-hē′dron), n.; pl. -drons or -dra (-drä). [See -hedron.] A solid bounded by six rhombic planes.—**rhom-bo-he′dral**, a.—**rhom′boid**. [Gr. ῥομβοειδής: see -oid.] **I.** a. Having a form like or approaching that of a rhomb; also, shaped like a rhomboid. **II.** n. An oblique-angled parallelogram with only the opposite sides equal.—**rhom-boi′dal**, a.— **rhom′bus** (-bus), n.; pl. -buses or -bi (-bī). [L.] A rhomb (plane figure).

Rhomb.

Rhomboid.

rhon-chus (rong′kus), n.; pl. -chi (-kī). [L., a snoring, akin to Gr. ῥέγκειν, snore.] A râle, esp. when produced in the bronchial tubes.—**rhon′chal, rhon′chi-al** (-kal, -ki-al), a.

rho-ta-cism (rō′ta-sizm), n. [= F. rhotacisme, < Gr. ῥωτακίζειν, make overmuch or wrong use of rho, < ῥῶ, rho.] Peculiar pronunciation of the letter r, as by rolling or trilling; also, conversion of some other sound, as of s, into that of r.

rhu-barb (rö′bärb), n. [OF. reubarbe (F. rhubarbe), < ML. reubarbarum, also rhabarbarum, < Gr. ῥῆον, ῥᾶ, rhubarb, + βάρβαρον, neut. of βάρβαρος, foreign, E. barbarous.] Any of the herbs constituting the polygonaceous genus Rheum, as R. officinale, a plant with a medicinal rhizome, and R. rhaponticum, a garden-plant with edible leafstalks; also, the rhizome of any medicinal species of this plant, forming a combined cathartic and astringent; also, the edible fleshy leafstalks of any of the garden species, used in making pies, etc.

rhumb (rumb or rum), n. [F. rumb = Sp. rumbo = Pg. rumbo, rumo, < L. rhombus, E. rhomb.] A loxodromic curve or line ('rhumb-line'); also, a point of the compass.—**rhumb′=sail′ing**, n. Sailing on a rhumb-line.

rhyme (rīm), etc. See rime², etc.

Medicinal Rhubarb (Rheum officinale).

Rhododendron (R. grande, native in the Himalayas).

rhyn-cho-ce-pha-li-an (ring″kō-se-fā′li-an). [NL. Rhynchocephalia, n. pl., < Gr. ῥύγχος, snout, + κεφαλή, head.] **I.** a. Belonging to the Rhynchocephalia, an order of nearly extinct small, lizard-shaped reptiles. **II.** *n.* A rhyncho-cephalian reptile.

rhyn-choph-o-rous (ring-kof′ō-rus), *a.* [Gr. ῥύγχος, snout, + -φόρος, < φέρειν, bear.] Of beetles, having a snout or rostrum, as a snout-beetle or weevil.

rhy-o-lite (rī′ō-līt), *n.* [G. rhyolit, irreg. < Gr. ῥύαξ, stream (esp. of lava), + λίθος, stone.] A kind of volcanic rock with a texture showing the lines of flow.—**rhy-o-lit′ic** (-lit′ik), *a.*

rhyp-a-rog-ra-phy (rip-a-rog′ra-fi), *n.* [Gr. ῥυπαρογράφος, painting foul or mean objects, < ῥυπαρός, dirty, sordid, + γράφειν, mark, draw, write.] The painting or description of low or commonplace subjects.—**rhyp-a-rog′ra-pher**, *n.*—**rhyp-a-rog′ra-phist**, *n.*—**rhyp″a-ro-graph′ic** (-rō-graf′ik), *a.*

Rhynchophorous Beetle (the Potato-stalk Weevil *Trichobaris trinotata*). (Line shows natural size.)

rhythm (riᵀʜm or rithm), *n.* [F. rhythme, < L. rhythmus, < Gr. ῥυθμός, < ῥεῖν, flow: see stream, and cf. rheum[1].] Measured movement, as in dancing, music, verse, etc.; movement or procedure with uniform recurrence of a beat, accent, or the like; in general, procedure marked by the regular recurrence of particular elements, phases, etc.; specif., in *music*, the structure of a composition with reference to the distribution of its successive beats or accents, as distinguished from melody and harmony; also, a particular form of this (as, duple *rhythm*, triple *rhythm*, etc.: see *duple time, triple time*, etc., at *time, n.*); in *pros.*, metrical movement; also, metrical or rhythmical form; meter; also, a particular kind of metrical form; in *art*, a proper relation and interdependence of parts with reference to one another and to an artistic whole.—**rhythmed**, *a.* Having rhythm; rhythmic.—**rhyth-mic** (riᵀʜ′mik or rith′mik). [Gr. ῥυθμικός.] **I.** *a.* Of or pertaining to rhythm; also, characterized by rhythm; often, having a flowing rhythm; also, periodic, as motion, etc. **II.** *n.* Rhythmics.—**rhyth′mi-cal**, *a.* Rhythmic.—**rhyth′mi-cal-ly**, *adv.*—**rhyth-mi′ci-ty** (-mis′i-ti), *n.* Rhythmic character.—**rhyth′mics**, *n.* The science of rhythm and rhythmic forms.—**rhyth′mist**, *n.* One versed in, or having a fine sense of, rhythm.

rhy-ton (rī′ton), *n.*; pl. *-ta* (-tä). [Gr. ῥυτόν, < ῥεῖν, flow.] In *Gr. antiq.*, a kind of drinking-vessel commonly shaped somewhat like a horn, with one handle, and often having the lower end in the form of an animal's head.

ri-a (rē′ä), *n.* [Sp. ría, mouth of a river: cf. rio.] A long, narrow arm of the sea formed by a submerged valley with no indications of glacial action.

Rhyton.

Ri-al-to (rē-al′tō), *n.* [From the *Rialto* district in Venice, in which the exchange was formerly located, and from which the famous bridge of the same name crosses the Grand Canal to the island of San Marco.] [Also *l. c.*] An exchange or mart; [*cap.*] a part of or a region along Broadway, in New York City, frequented by theatrical people and the center of many theatrical enterprises (cf. Shakspere's "Merchant of Venice," i. 3. 39).

ri-ant (rī′ant, F. rē-äṅ), *a.* [F., ppr. of rire, < L. ridere, laugh.] Laughing; smiling; cheerful; gay.—**ri-an-cy** (rī′an-si), *n.*—**ri-ante** (rē-äṅt), *a.* [F.] Fem. of *riant.*—**ri′ant-ly**, *adv.*

ri-a-ta (rē-ä′tä), *n.* See *reata.*

rib (rib), *n.* [AS. ribb = D. rib = G. rippe = Icel. rif, rib.] One of a series of long, slender, curved bones, occurring in pairs, more or less inclosing the thoracic cavity, and articulated with the vertebræ (in man consisting of twelve pairs, the upper seven pairs, or 'true ribs,' being attached in front to the sternum, and the lower five, or 'false ribs,' not so attached, the first three of these being joined at their forward ends by cartilages to the ribs above, and the last two, or 'floating ribs,' being left free: see cut in next column); also, a cut of meat, as beef, containing a rib; also, some thing or part resembling a rib in form, position, or use, as a supporting or strengthening part in a framework or structure; one of the curved timbers or members in a ship's frame which spring upward and outward from the keel; an arch or arched member, plain or molded, forming a support of a vault, or a merely decorative feature of like appearance on the surface of a vault or ceiling; a primary vein of a leaf; a ridge or raised stripe in cloth, knitted work, etc.; also, a wife (in humorous allusion to the creation of Eve from one of Adam's ribs: see Gen. ii. 21–22: as, "A *rib*'s a thorn in a wed gallant's side," Byron's "Don Juan," xi. 46).—**rib**, *v. t.*; ribbed, ribbing. To furnish or strengthen with ribs; inclose as with ribs; mark with rib-like ridges or markings (as, "The print of its first rush-wrapping, Wound ere it dried, still *ribbed* the thing": Rossetti's "Burden of Nineveh").

Human Ribs, left side (rear view), the first, second, seventh, ninth, and twelfth shaded in detail, the others in outline — all without their costal cartilages.

rib-ald (rib′ald). [OF. ribalt, ribaut (F. ribaud), = ML. ribaldus; prob. from Teut.] **I.** *n.* Orig., one of a class of medieval retainers of a low grade in household and military service†; hence, a low, ruffianly fellow†; a person of lewd habits or abandoned character†; now, one who uses offensive or scurrilous language, or jeers irreverently or blasphemously. **II.** *a.* Ruffianly or profligate (as, "Offensive by their licentious and *ribald* habits of life . . . these troops had become an intolerable burthen to the people": Motley's "Dutch Republic," i. 3); more commonly, offensive or scurrilous in speech, or as speech, writing, etc.; coarsely mocking or abusive; wantonly irreverent or blasphemous.—**rib′ald-ry** (-ri), *n.* Profligacy† or vice†; also, ribald character, as of language; scurrility; ribald speech (as, "Those further off . . . assailed them with insulting *ribaldry*": Wiseman's "Fabiola," ii. 21).

rib-and, rib-band[1] (rib′and), *n.* and *v.* Archaic forms of *ribbon.*

rib-band[2] (rib′band or rib′and), *n.* [Appar. < rib + band[2].] In *ship-building*, a lengthwise timber or the like used to secure a ship's ribs in position while the outside planking or plating is being put on.

ribbed (ribd), *p. a.* Having ribs; having, or marked with, ridges or rib-like markings.

rib-bing (rib′ing), *n.* Ribs collectively; an assemblage or arrangement of ribs.

rib-bon (rib′on), *n.* [OF. riban, ruban (F. ruban); origin uncertain.] A woven strip or band of fine material, as silk, finished off at the edges, and varying in width from less than one fourth of an inch to nine inches or more, used for ornament, tying, etc. (as, "Get . . . new *ribbons* to your pumps," Shakspere's "Midsummer Night's Dream," iv. 2. 37; a child's hair-*ribbon*); material in such strips (as, a yard of *ribbon*; a bow of *ribbon*; grosgrain, satin, velvet, or tinsel *ribbon*); also, a strip or piece of such material used as a badge of an order of knighthood or of other distinction (as, the red *ribbon* of the French Legion of Honor: see *blue ribbon*, under *blue, a.*, also *cordon bleu*); in general, a narrow strip or band of woven or other material; a band of material charged with ink, for supplying ink for the impression in a typewriter; a long, thin, flexible band of metal, as for a spring, a band-saw, a tape-line, etc.; *pl.*, reins for driving; *sing.*, anything resembling or suggesting a ribbon or woven band; a long, narrow strip of something (as, "The houses stood well back, leaving a *ribbon* of waste land on either side of the road": Stevenson's "Inland Voyage," vi.); *pl.*, torn or ragged strips, or shreds (as, clothes torn or worn to *ribbons*; sails hanging in *ribbons*); *sing.*, in *her.*, a diminutive of the bend, one eighth of its width.—**rib′bon**, *v.* **I.** *tr.* To adorn with ribbon; also, to streak or mark with something suggesting ribbon (as, "I could see all the inland valleys *ribboned* with broad waters": Blackmore's "Lorna Doone," xlviii.); also, to separate into or reduce to ribbon-like strips. **II.** *intr.* To stretch out in ribbon-like form; form ribbon-like strips.

Ribbon (*a*).

(variable) ḍ as d or j, ṣ as s or sh, ṭ as t or ch, ẓ as z or zh; o, F. cloche; ü, F. menu; ch, Sc. loch; ṅ, F. bonbon; ′, primary accent; ″, secondary accent; †, obsolete; <, from; +, and; =, equals. See also lists at beginning of book.

rib-bon=fish (rib′on-fish), *n.* Any of certain deep-sea fishes with a long, compressed, ribbon-like body, as the deal-fish and the oar-fish.

rib-bon=grass (rib′on-gràs), *n.* A striped green and white garden variety of the reed canary-grass, *Phalaris arundinacea.*

Rib-bon-man (rib′on-man), *n.*; pl. *-men.* A member of a secret society (Ribbon Society) formed in the north of Ireland early in the 19th century in opposition to the Orangemen, and named from the green ribbon worn as a badge.

rib-bon=seal (rib′on-sēl), *n.* A seal, *Histriophoca fasciata,* of the north-ern Pacific, the male of which is curi-ously banded with yellow-ish white on a dark ground.

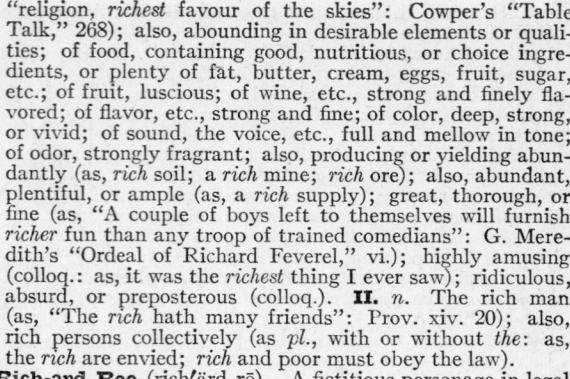

Ribbon-seal.

rib-bon=snake (rib′on-snāk), *n.* A small striped gar-ter-snake, *Eutaenia saurita,* common in the U. S.

ri-bo-fla-vin (rī-bō-flā′vin), *n.* [From *ribo(se)* + *flavin.*] Vitamin B₂, a growth-producing compound.

rib=roast (rib′rōst), *v. t.* To belabor with blows; beat; drub; thrash. [Colloq.]—**rib′=roast″ing,** *n.* A beating or thrashing: as, to get a sound *rib-roasting.* [Colloq.]

rib-wort (rib′wėrt), *n.* A plantain, *Plantago lanceolata,* having narrow leaves with prominent ribs; also, any of various similar plantains.

Ri-car-di-an (ri-kär′di-an). **I.** *a.* Of, pertaining to, or adhering to the English political economist David Ricardo (1772–1823) or his theories. **II.** *n.* A follower of Ricardo.

rice (rīs), *n.* [OF. *ris* (F. *riz*), < It. *riso,* < L. *oryza,* < Gr. ὄρυζα, rice; of Eastern origin.] The starchy seeds or grain of a species of grass, *Oryza sativa,* cultivated in warm climates and constituting an important food; also, the plant itself.—**rice,** *v. t.*; *riced, ricing.* To reduce to a form resembling that of rice: as, to *rice* potatoes (see *ricer*).—**rice′= bird,** *n.* The Java sparrow; also, the bob-olink (southern U. S.).—**rice=pa″per,** *n.* A thin paper made from the straw of rice, in China, etc.; also, a Chinese paper con-sisting of the pith of certain plants cut and pressed into thin sheets.—**ri-cer** (rī′sėr), *n.* An implement for ricing potatoes, etc., by pressing them through small holes.—**rice= stitch,** *n.* A stitch in embroidery or crocheting resembling a grain of rice.

rich (rich). [AS. *rīce,* powerful, rich, = D. *rijk,* G. *reich,* rich, = Icel. *rīkr,* powerful, rich, = Goth. *reiks,* powerful, = OF. F. *riche* (from Teut.), rich; prob. from Celtic, and ult. akin to L. *rex,* king.] **I.** *a.* Powerful† or mighty†; also, having wealth or great possessions, or wealthy, affluent, or opulent, as persons (as, "The *rich* man had exceeding many flocks and herds": 2 Sam. xii. 2); abundantly supplied with resources, means, or funds (as, a *rich* city or nation; a †*rich* institution or organization); abounding in natural resources (as, a *rich* territory); often, having wealth or valuable resources (*in:* as, "Abram was very *rich* in cattle, in silver, and in gold," Gen. xiii. 2; a tract *rich* in minerals); in general, abounding (*in* or *with:* as, "All this part of the river is *rich* in Indian history and traditions," Mark Twain's "Life on the Mississippi," lviii.; "the meadows *rich* with corn," Whittier's "Barbara Frietchie"); also, of great value or worth, or valuable (as, a *rich* harvest; *rich* cargo); costly, or expensively elegant or fine, as dress, jewels, silks, hangings, etc.; sumptuous, as a feast; of valuable materials or elaborate workmanship, as buildings, furniture, ornamentation, etc.; of great moral worth, or precious (as,

Panicle of Rice.— *a,* a spikelet; *b,* the empty glumes; *c,* the flowering glume; *d,* the palet; *e,* the lodicules, the stamens, and the pistil.

"religion, *richest* favour of the skies": Cowper's "Table Talk," 268); also, abounding in desirable elements or quali-ties; of food, containing good, nutritious, or choice ingre-dients, or plenty of fat, butter, cream, eggs, fruit, sugar, etc.; of fruit, luscious; of wine, etc., strong and finely fla-vored; of flavor, etc., strong and fine; of color, deep, strong, or vivid; of sound, the voice, etc., full and mellow in tone; of odor, strongly fragrant; also, producing or yielding abun-dantly (as, *rich* soil; a *rich* mine; *rich* ore); also, abundant, plentiful, or ample (as, a *rich* supply); great, thorough, or fine (as, "A couple of boys left to themselves will furnish *richer* fun than any troop of trained comedians": G. Mere-dith's "Ordeal of Richard Feverel," vi.); highly amusing (colloq.: as, it was the *richest* thing I ever saw); ridiculous, absurd, or preposterous (colloq.). **II.** *n.* The rich man (as, "The *rich* hath many friends": Prov. xiv. 20); also, rich persons collectively (as *pl.,* with or without *the:* as, the *rich* are envied; *rich* and poor must obey the law).

Rich-ard Roe (rich′ärd rō). A fictitious personage in legal proceedings.

rich-en (rich′n), *v. t.* or *i.* To make or become rich or richer.

rich-es (rich′ez), *n. pl.,* orig. *sing.* [OF. *richece* (F. *richesse*), < *riche,* rich: see *rich.*] The state of being rich or having wealth (orig. and properly *sing.,* but later construed as *pl.:* as, "He that is honoured in poverty, how much more in *riches?*" Ecclus. x. 31); also, abundant and valuable posses-sions, or wealth (formerly construed as *sing.,* now as *pl.:* as, "Alas, alas that great city . . . ! For in one hour so great *riches* is come to nought," Rev. xviii. 17; "*Riches,* rightly used, are instruments of happiness," Peacock's "Nightmare Abbey," i.); fig., rich or precious stores of something im-material (as, the *riches* of knowledge; "On her he spent the *riches* of his wit," Spenser's "Astrophel," 62); intellectual or spiritual treasure.

rich-ly (rich′li), *adv.* In a rich manner; wealthily; sumptu-ously; finely; abundantly or amply.—**rich′ness,** *n.*

rich-weed (rich′wēd), *n.* A common urticaceous plant, *Adicea* (or *Pilea*) *pumila,* of the U. S. and Japan; also, a labiate plant, *Collinsonia canadensis,* of eastern North Amer-ica, used medicinally as a diuretic, tonic, etc.; also, any of several ragweeds, esp. *Ambrosia trifida.*

ri-ci-no-le-ic (ris″i-nō-lē′ik or ris-i-nō′lē-ik), *a.* [NL. *Ricinus,* the castor-oil plant genus, + L. *oleum,* oil.] In *chem.,* noting or pertaining to an organic acid occurring in castor-oil in the form of a glyceride.—**ri-ci-no′le-in,** *n.* In *chem.,* a glyceride of ricinoleic acid: the chief constituent of castor-oil.

rick¹ (rik), *n.* [AS. *hrēac.*] A stack of hay, straw, or the like, esp. one regularly built and thatched or covered for protection from rain.—**rick¹,** *v. t.* To pile up in ricks.

rick² (rik), *v.* and *n.* See *wrick.*

rick-ets (rik′ets), *n.* [Origin uncertain.] In *pathol.,* a disease of childhood, characterized by softening of the bones through perverted nutrition, and often resulting in deformities. —**rick′et-y,** *a.* Affected with or suffering from rickets; pertaining to or of the nature of rickets; also, feeble in the joints, tottering, or infirm; hence, in general, liable to fall or collapse, or shaky (as, "a *rickety* chair," Lever's "Harry Lorrequer," xxvi.; "a large *rickety* wooden building," Irving's "Sketch-Book," Rip Van Winkle); weak, feeble, or unsound (as, "I wish those impertinent fellows, with their *rickety* understandings, would keep their advice for those that ask for it," Smollett's "Humphry Clinker," April 20; *rickety* notions); irregular, as motion or action (as, *rickety* movements).—**rick′et-i-ness,** *n.*

rick-ey (rik′i), *n.*; pl. *-eys* (-iz). [From a Colonel *Rickey.*] A drink in which spirituous liquor (esp. gin), lime-juice, and carbonated water are the principal ingredients.

rick-rack (rik′rak), *n.* [Cf. *rack¹.*] A kind of openwork trimming made, with needle and thread, out of a narrow zigzag braid.

rick-shaw (rik′shâ), *n.* Same as *jinrikisha.*

ric-o-chet (rik-ō-shā′ or -shet′), *n.* [F.; origin uncertain.] The motion of an object which rebounds one or more times from a flat surface over which it is passing; the method of firing by which a projectile is made to rebound in this manner. —**ric-o-chet′,** *v. i.*; *-cheted* (-shād′) or *-chetted* (-shet′ed), *-cheting* (-shā′ing) or *-chetting* (-shet′ing). To move with a glancing rebound or a series of such rebounds, as a projectile.

ric-tus (rik′tus), *n.* [L., < *ringi*, open the mouth wide: cf. *ringent*.] The cleft of the open mouth; the gape; also, an open position of the mouth (as, "the teeth disclosed in a perpetual *rictus*": Stevenson's "Master of Ballantrae," xii.).—**ric′tal**, *a.*

rid[1] (rid), *v. t.*; rid or ridded, ridding. [ME. *ridden, rydden, ruden*: cf. Icel. *rydhja*, clear, also AS. *hreddan*, rescue, save.] To clear (a way or space, land, etc.: now prov. Eng.); also, to clear, disencumber, or free of something objectionable (with *of*: as, to rid a house of vermin; "I cannot *rid* my hands of him," Shakspere's "2 Henry IV.," i. 2. 226); to *rid* a manuscript of errors; disembarrass or relieve (*of*: as, to rid one's self of a contract; to *rid* the mind of doubt); also, to deliver, rescue, or save (*out of, from*, etc.: as, "I will *rid* you out of their bondage," Ex. vi. 6: obs. or archaic); also, to clear away or out, expel, or remove (as, "I will rid evil beasts out of the land," Lev. xxvi. 6: now prov. Eng.); kill† or destroy†; also, to despatch or accomplish (work, etc.: now prov. Eng.).—**to be well rid of**, to be completely or safely rid of (as, "I would we *were well rid of* this knavery": Shakspere's "Twelfth Night," iv. 2. 73); also, to be fortunate in being rid of (as, you *are well rid of* the fellow).—**to get rid of**, to get free, quit, or relieved of (as, to *get rid of* a burden, an unwelcome guest, a cold, or one's worries; "Her voice is in my ears; I can't *get rid of* it," H. James's "Portrait of a Lady," xlvii.); get (a thing or person) off one's hands; dispose of effectually so as no longer to be encumbered or annoyed; do away with, or put an end to (as, "What I want is to *get rid of* all that nonsense": G. B. Shaw's "You Never Can Tell," ii.); sometimes, to dispose of by killing (as, to *get rid of* kittens).

rid[2] (rid). Archaic or prov. preterit and past participle of *ride*.

rid-a-ble (rī′da-bl), *a.* Capable of being ridden, as a horse; also, capable of being ridden over, through, etc., as a road or a stream.

rid-dance (rid′ans), *n.* The act of ridding; clearance, as of a space or place (obs. or archaic: as, "Thou shalt not make clean *riddance* of the corners of thy field when thou reapest . . . thou shalt leave them unto the poor," Lev. xxiii. 22); a clearing away or out, as of anything undesirable (as, "Those blossoms also, and those dropping gums . . . Ask *riddance*, if we mean to tread with ease," Milton's "Paradise Lost," iv. 632; "He shall make even a speedy *riddance* of all them that dwell in the land," Zeph. i. 18); a relieving or deliverance from something, or a mode or means of deliverance (as, "That's the late man . . . no bad *riddance* his death, if all's true that's said of him," J. H. Newman's "Callista," v.: see phrase *good riddance*, following).—**good riddance**, clearing away or removal that is to good purpose or gives satisfaction (as, " 'Good riddance to bad rubbish,' said my grandmother": Mrs. Stowe's "Oldtown Folks," xlvi.); also, a welcome relief or deliverance from something (much used as an expression of satisfaction or thankfulness: as, "*Ther.* I will see you hanged . . . ere I come any more to your tents . . . *Patr.* A *good riddance*," Shakspere's "Troilus and Cressida," ii. 1. 132); hence, something of which one is well or fortunately rid (as, "He may be a *good riddance* in the main": Scott's "Abbot," vi.).

rid-den (rid′n). Past participle of *ride*.

rid-dle[1] (rid′l), *n.* [AS. *hriddel*.] A coarse sieve; also, a board with a zigzag row of pins through which wire is passed to be straightened.—**rid′dle**, *v. t.*; -dled, -dling. To sift through a riddle, as gravel; also, to pierce with many holes suggesting those of a riddle (as, to *riddle* a door with shot; "The moat . . . was *riddled* at the sides with rat-holes," W. H. Hudson's "Far Away and Long Ago," xvi.); fig., to impair or refute completely by persistent verbal attacks (as, to *riddle* a person's reputation; to *riddle* testimony or statements).

rid-dle[2] (rid′l), *n.* [ME. *redels* (sing. misunderstood as pl.), < AS. *rǽdels*, riddle, < *rǽdan*, E. *read*.] A question or statement so framed as to exercise one's ingenuity in answering it or discovering its meaning (see Judges, xiv. 8–18); an enigma or conundrum; hence, any enigmatic or dark saying or speech (as, "You speak in *riddles*, learned Sir,"

Hawthorne's "Scarlet Letter," x.; "All that Silver said was a *riddle* to him," Stevenson's "Treasure Island," xx.); a puzzling question, problem, or matter (as, "How a brilliant and beautiful girl could have committed this rashness, was the perplexing *riddle*": G. Meredith's "Diana of the Crossways," vi.); a puzzling or inexplicable thing or person (as, "The world is one wide *riddle* to them," Ruskin's "Crown of Wild Olive," i.; "His eldest son was a *riddle* that he had long given up," Galsworthy's "Patrician," i. 1).—**rid′dle**[2], *v.*; -dled, -dling. **I.** *intr.* To propound riddles; also, to speak enigmatically. **II.** *tr.* To solve or interpret as a riddle (as, "*Riddle* me this, and guess him if you can, Who bears a nation in a single man?" Dryden's tr. Juvenal's "Satires," iii. 135); in general, to explain.—**rid′dler**, *n.*—**rid′dling-ly**, *adv.*

ride (rīd), *v.*; pret. *rode* (archaic or prov. rid), pp. *ridden* (archaic or prov. rid), ppr. *riding.* [AS. *rīdan* = D. *rijden* = G. *reiten* = Icel. *rīdha*, ride.] **I.** *intr.* To be carried on the back of an animal; sit on and manage a horse or other animal in motion; also, to be borne along on or in a vehicle or any kind of conveyance; also, to be carried on something as if on horseback (as, "I saw him beat the surges under him, And *ride* upon their backs": Shakspere's "Tempest," ii. 1. 115); also, to move or float on the water (as, "While proudly *riding* o'er the azure realm In gallant trim the gilded vessel goes": Gray's "Bard," ii. 2); lie at anchor, as a vessel (as, "a windy, tossing anchorage where yawls and ketches *ride*": Masefield's "Wanderer's Song"); also, in general, to move along in any way, or be carried or supported; appear to float in space, as a heavenly body (as, "The moon was *riding* high and clear": Stevenson's "Travels with a Donkey," v. 7); turn or rest on something (as, "Strong as the axletree On which heaven *rides*": Shakspere's "Troilus and Cressida," i. 3. 67); extend or project over something, as the edge of one thing over the edge of another thing; also, to work or move (*up*) from the proper position, as a part of the dress; also, to admit of being ridden, or carry a rider, as a horse. **II.** *tr.* To sit on and manage (a horse or other animal, or a bicycle or the like) so as to be carried along; also, to sit or be mounted on (something) as if on horseback; be carried or borne along on (as, "The eagle *rode* the rising blast": Byron's "Prisoner of Chillon," xiii.); rest on, esp. by overlapping; also, fig., to control, dominate, or tyrannize over (esp. in *ridden, pp.*), in composition: as, "What chance was there of reason being heard in a land that was king-*ridden*, priest-*ridden*, peer-*ridden?*" C. Brontë's "Shirley," iv.); harass or torment (slang); also, to separate (an animal) from a herd by riding (with *off* or *out*); to ride over, along, or through (a road, boundary, region, etc.); also, to execute by riding (as, to *ride* a race); also, to cause to ride; carry (a person) on something as if riding on a horse (as, to *ride* a person on a rail as a punishment); keep (a vessel) at anchor or moored.—**to ride a hobby.** See *hobby*[2], *n.*—**to ride down**, to knock down or overthrow by riding against; bear down or overcome as if by such action (as, to *ride down* all resistance or opposition); also, to overtake by riding in pursuit; also, to exhaust by excessive riding, as a horse. —**to ride out**, to sustain (a gale, etc.) without damage, as while riding at anchor, as a vessel; hence, fig., to sustain or endure successfully.—**ride**, *n.* A journey or excursion on the back of a horse, etc., or on or in a vehicle or conveyance; also, a way, road, etc., made esp. for riding.—**ride′a-ble**, *a.* See *ridable*.

ri-deau (rē-dō′), *n.* [F., curtain, screen.] In *fort.*, a small elevation or ridge of earth, as one thrown up to cover a camp from the approach of an enemy.

ri-dent (rī′dent), *a.* [L. *ridens* (*rident-*), ppr. of *ridere*, laugh.] Laughing; smiling; cheerful: as, "a smile so wide and steady, so exceedingly *rident*" (Thackeray's "Newcomes," xxiv.).

rid-er (rī′dėr), *n.* One who or that which rides; one who rides a horse or other animal, or a bicycle

Obverse.   Reverse.
Rider of Charles of Egmont, Duke of Gelderland. — British Museum.

or the like; a riding master†; a gold coin bearing the figure of a horseman, formerly current in the Netherlands, or any of certain other gold coins (see cut on preceding page); any of various objects or devices straddling, mounted on, or attached to something else; an addition or amendment to a document, etc., esp. an additional clause attached to a legislative bill in passing it; *naut.*, one of an additional set of timbers or iron plates used to strengthen the frame of a ship.—**rid′er-less**, *a.* Having no rider.

ridge (rij), *n.* [AS. *hrycg* = D. *rug* = G. *rücken* = Icel. *hryggr*, the back.] The back or spine in man or an animal†; also, the long and narrow upper part or crest of something, as of an animal's back, a hill, a wave, etc. (as, "The whole line of buffalo . . . gradually disappeared over the *ridge* of the hill," Parkman's "Oregon Trail," vii.; "a nose with a decided *ridge*," W. Churchill's "Modern Chronicle," i. 1); a long, narrow elevation of land, or a chain of hills or mountains (as, "a small *ridge* of mountains," Irving's "Captain Bonneville," xxx.; the Blue *Ridge* of the Appalachian Mountains, in Virginia, North Carolina, etc.); the horizontal line in which the tops of the rafters of a roof meet; any raised narrow strip, as in plowed ground or on cloth, etc.—**ridge**, *v.*; ridged, ridging. **I.** *tr.* To provide with or form into a ridge or ridges; mark with or as with ridges. **II.** *intr.* To form ridges.—**ridge′=piece, ridge′=plate**, *n.* Same as *ridge-pole.*—**ridge′=pole**, *n.* The horizontal timber or member at the top of a roof, to which the upper ends of the rafters are fastened; also, the horizontal pole at the top of a tent.—**ridg′y**, *a.* Rising in a ridge or ridges: as, "the *ridgy* summits of the eastern mountains of Clydesdale" (Jane Porter's "Scottish Chiefs," xlix.).

rid-i-cule (rid′i-kūl). [F. *ridicule*, a. and n., < L. *ridiculus*, laughable, ridiculous (as n., *ridiculum*, something laughable, a jest), < *ridere*, laugh.] **I.**† *a.* Laughable; absurd; ridiculous. **II.** *n.* Something ridiculous (now rare); also, ridiculous character (as, "to see the *ridicule* of this monstrous practice," Addison, in "Spectator," 18: now rare); also, words or actions intended to excite contemptuous laughter at a person or thing; derision.—**rid′i-cule**, *v. t.*; -culed, -culing. To treat with ridicule; deride; make fun of: as, "My father discouraged me by *ridiculing* my performances" (B. Franklin's "Autobiography," i.).—**rid′i-cul-er** (-kū-lèr), *n.*—**ri-dic-u-lous** (ri-dik′ū-lus). [L. *ridiculosus* or *ridiculus*.] **I.** *a.* Such as to excite ridicule or derision, or absurd, preposterous, or laughable (as, "a *ridiculous* piece of missionary quixotism," Godwin's "Caleb Williams," xxix.; "Clara's conceited assumption of a universal interest in her dull children was *ridiculous*," Arnold Bennett's "These Twain," v.); also, derisive†; mocking†. **II.**† *n.* With *the*, that which is ridiculous: as, "a man . . . keenly sensible of the *ridiculous*" (Macaulay's "Hist. of Eng.," ii.).—**ri-dic′u-lous-ly**, *adv.*—**ri-dic′u-lous-ness**, *n.*

ri-ding[1] (rī′ding), *n.* [For *thriding*, from Scand.: cf. Icel. *thridhjungr*, third part; an initial *th* being lost in Eng. after *north*, etc.] Each of the three administrative divisions into which Yorkshire, England, is divided (the North Riding, East Riding, and West Riding); also, each of a similar group of divisions elsewhere.

ri-ding[2] (rī′ding), *n.* The act of one who or that which rides; also, a way or road intended esp. for persons riding. —**rid′ing=hab″it**, *n.* A costume or dress worn while riding, esp. one for women.—**rid′ing=hood**, *n.* A kind of hood or hooded cloak, orig. one worn while riding or traveling, but afterward an outdoor garment for women or children. —**rid′ing=light**, *n.* *Naut.*, a light hung in the rigging of a vessel at night while it is riding at anchor.

ri-dot-to (ri-dot′ō), *n.*; pl. *ridottos* (-ōz). [It., a retreat, resort: see *redoubt*[1].] A public ball or social gathering, often in masquerade: common in the 18th century: as, "They now thrust themselves into all assemblies, from a *ridotto* at St. James's to a hop at Rotherhithe" (Smollett's "Humphry Clinker," June 5).

riet-bok (rēt′bok), *n.* [S. Afr. D., 'reed buck.'] Any of various medium-sized African antelopes of the genus *Cervicapra*, esp. *C. arundineum*, a reddish species inhabiting the marshy regions of central and southern Africa, of which the males alone have horns.

ri-fa-ci-men-to (rē-fä-chē-men′tō), *n.*; pl. -*ti* (-tē). [It.,

a remaking.] A recast or adaptation, as of a literary or musical work.

rife (rīf), *a.* [Late AS. *rȳfe* = MLG. *rīve* = Icel. *rīfr*, abundant.] Of common or frequent occurrence, or prevalent (as, "that blood-guiltiness which is so *rife* in this our day and generation," Scott's "Castle Dangerous," xix.; "all those noises so *rife* in a Portuguese inn," Borrow's "Bible in Spain," ii.); in widespread existence, activity, or use (as, "The speculation which for some time was *rife* concerning its [a book's] authorship made many turn to it," S. Butler's "Way of All Flesh," lxxxv.; "The drinking of tea . . . now . . . became very *rife*," Galt's "Annals of the Parish," ii.); commonly repeated, or current in speech or report (as, a rumor *rife* throughout the city; "Here I cannot avoid relating a story, *rife* among the natives," H. Melville's "Omoo," lvi.); also, abundant, plentiful, or numerous (as, "great store of deer and wild boars *rife* as flies at midsummer": Reade's "Cloister and the Hearth," xxxvi.); also, abounding (*with*, formerly *in*: as, "Whose life was work, whose language *rife* With rugged maxims hewn from life," Tennyson's "Ode on the Death of the Duke of Wellington," vii.).—**rife′ness**, *n.*

rif-fle[1] (rif′l), *n.* [Cf. *ripple*[2].] A ripple, as upon the surface of water; also, a rapid. [Local, U. S.]

rif-fle[2] (rif′l), *n.* [Cf. *riffle*[1].] In *mining*, the lining at the bottom of a sluice or the like, made of blocks or slats of wood, or stones, arranged in such a manner that grooves or openings are left between them for catching and collecting particles of gold; also, one of the slats of wood or the like so used, or one of the grooves or openings formed.

rif-fler (rif′lèr), *n.* [F. *rifloir*, < *rifler*, scrape, file: see *rifle*[1].] A file with a curved extremity, for working in depressions.

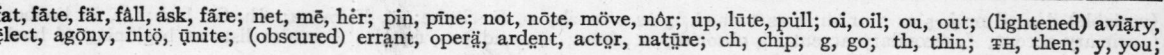
Riffler.

riff-raff (rif′raf). [ME. *rif* (*and*) *raf*, < OF. *rif* (*et*) *raf*, every bit.] **I.** *n.* Worthless material, trash, or rubbish (now chiefly prov.); also, worthless or low persons (as, a pack of *riffraff*); the refuse of a community, class, etc. (as, "the *riffraff* of the city, who lived by their wits, or by odd jobs": J. H. Newman's "Callista," xii.); the worthless or disreputable element of society, or the rabble. **II.** *a.* Worthless or trashy, as things; also, low or disreputable, as persons; belonging to the rabble.

ri-fle[1] (rī′fl), *v. t.*; -fled, -fling. [OF. *rifler*, scrape, graze, strip, plunder (F. scrape, file): cf. *rifle*[2].] To ransack and rob (a place, receptacle, etc.: as, "The city shall be taken, and the houses *rifled*," Zech. xiv. 2; "The drawers of a bureau . . . had been . . . *rifled*," Poe's "Murders in the Rue Morgue"); search and rob (a person: as, "We'll make you sit and *rifle* you," Shakspere's "Two Gentlemen of Verona," iv. 1. 4); often, to plunder or strip bare (a place, person, etc.) of something specified (as, "The roadside garden and the secret glen Were *rifled* of their sweetest flowers," Bryant's "Sella"; "The rascal insisted on *rifling* her of her ear-rings and necklace," Smollett's "Humphry Clinker," June 26); also, to carry off as booty (as, "the rich spoil *rifled* from the Cholulans": Prescott's "Conquest of Mexico," iii. 7); fig., to steal or take away (as, "till Time shall *rifle* every youthful grace": Pope's tr. Homer's "Iliad," i.).

ri-fle[2] (rī′fl), *v. t.*; -fled, -fling. [Cf. G. *reifeln, riefeln*, groove, rifle, also F. *rifler*, scrape, file (see *rifle*[1].)] To cut spiral grooves within (a gunbarrel, etc.).—**ri′fle**[2], *n.* One of the spiral grooves cut in the inner surface of a gun-barrel to give the bullet a rotatory motion and thus render its flight more accurate; also, a gun or firearm with such grooves, esp. one fired from the shoulder; also, a soldier armed with such a weapon.—**ri′fle=bird**, *n.* An Australian bird, *Ptilorhis paradisea* (family *Paradiseidæ*),

Rifle-bird (*Ptilorhis paradisea*).

the male of which has a velvety-black plumage splendidly iridescent with purple, blue, green, etc.; any bird of the genus *Ptilorhis*: said to have been so named by the early colonists because the coloration suggested the uniform of a British rifle brigade.—**ri′fle-man** (-man), *n.*; pl. *-men.* A soldier armed with a rifle; also, a man skilled in the use of a rifle (as, "The supply of fresh meat depends mainly on the skill of the *riflemen*": Roosevelt's "Hunting Trips of a Ranchman," i.).—**ri′fle=pit,** *n.* A pit or short trench affording shelter to riflemen in firing at an enemy.

ri-fler (rī′flėr), *n.* One who rifles or plunders.

ri-fling (rī′fling), *n.* The act or process of cutting rifles or spiral grooves in a gun-barrel; also, the system of spiral grooves in a rifle.

rift (rift), *n.* [ME. *rift*; from Scand., and akin to *rive.*] An opening made by riving or splitting; a fissure; a cleft; a chink.—**rift,** *v.* **I.** *intr.* To form fissures; burst open; split. **II.** *tr.* To rive; split; cleave.

rig¹ (rig), *n.* Sc. and prov. Eng. form of *ridge.*

rig² (rig), *v. t.*; *rigged, rigging.* [Cf. Norw. *rigga,* bind up, wrap round, rig, Sw. *rigga,* rig.] To fit (a vessel, or a mast, etc.) with the necessary shrouds, stays, etc.; fit (shrouds, stays, braces, etc.) to the proper mast, yard, or the like; also, in general, to furnish or provide with equipment, etc., or fit (usually with *out* or *up*: as, "The free trappers being newly *rigged* out and supplied, were in high spirits," Irving's "Captain Bonneville," xvii.); also, to put in proper order for working or use (chiefly *naut.*: as, "Forward there! *rig* the head-pump!" Dana's "Two Years before the Mast," ii.); also, to prepare, put together, or get up, esp. as a makeshift (often with *up*: as, "an intermediate dressing station, *rigged* up with wood and tarpaulings," H. G. Wells's "Italy, France, and Britain at War," iii. 1); also, to fit or deck with clothes or personal adornments (often with *out* or *up*: as, "You shall see how I *rigged* my 'squire out, with the remains of my shipwrecked wardrobe," Wycherley's "Plain Dealer," iv. 1: now colloq.).—**rig²,** *n.* The arrangement of the masts, spars, sails, etc., on a boat or ship; also, equipment; outfit; apparatus for some purpose; the derrick of an oil-well, with its engine-house, etc.; also, a vehicle with a horse or horses, for driving (colloq., U. S.); also, costume or dress, esp. when odd or conspicuous (colloq.).

rig³ (rig), *n.* [Origin obscure.] A prank; a trick; also, a fraudulent scheme; a swindle. [Prov. or colloq.]—**rig³,** *v. t.*; *rigged, rigging.* To play tricks on (prov.); hoax (prov.); also, to manipulate fraudulently (colloq.: as, to *rig* the market).

rig-a-doon (rig-a-dön′), *n.* [F. *rigaudon, rigodon*; said to be named from *Rigaud,* the originator.] A lively dance, formerly popular, for one couple, characterized by a peculiar jumping step, and usually in quick duple rhythm; also, a piece of music for this dance, or in its rhythm.

rigged (rigd), *a.* Having a (specified) rig: as, a fore-and-aft *rigged* ship.

rig-ger¹ (rig′ėr), *n.* [See *rig²,* *v.*] One who rigs; one whose occupation is the fitting of the rigging of ships; one who works with hoisting-tackle, etc.

rig-ger² (rig′ėr), *n.* [See *rig³,* *v.*] One who manipulates something fraudulently; one who rigs the market; a thimblerigger.

rig-ging (rig′ing), *n.* [See *rig²,* *v.*] The ropes, chains, etc., employed to support and work the masts, yards, sails, etc., on a ship; hence, tackle in general; also, equipment or outfit; also, clothing or dress (colloq.).

Riggs's (rigz′ez) **dis-ease′.** [From John M. *Riggs* (1810–85), American dentist.] In *pathol.,* pyorrhea alveolaris.

right (rīt). [AS. *riht* = D. and G. *recht* = Icel. *rēttr* = Goth. *raihts,* straight, right; akin to L. *rectus,* straight, right, *regere,* keep straight, direct, rule, Skt. *rju,* straight, right, Gr. ὀρέγειν, reach out.] **I.** *a.* Straight (as, a *right* line); also, formed by, or with reference to, a line or a plane extending to another line or a surface by the shortest course (as, a *right* angle, see *angle³,* *n.*; at *right* angles, of a line or lines, etc., so placed with reference to another or to each other that at the place of actual crossing, or of crossing if prolonged, four right angles are or would be produced; a *right* cone, one with the axis perpendicular to the base); not oblique; also, upright or righteous, as a person, the character, etc.

(now rare); in accordance with what is just or good, as conduct, etc.; in conformity with fact, reason, or some standard or principle, or correct or proper (as, the *right* answer to a problem; "a *right* description of our sport," Shakspere's "Love's Labour's Lost," v. 2. 522; the *right* method of procedure); fitting or appropriate (as, to say the *right* thing; the *right* man for the place); most advantageous or desirable (as, "a widow on the *right* side of thirty": Malkin's tr. Le Sage's "Gil Blas," x. 10); principal, front, or upper (as, the *right* side of cloth); correct in judgment, opinion, or action (as, "When the people complain, says Mirabeau, the people are always *right*," Froude's "Cæsar," viii.; "A fool must now and then be *right,* by chance," Cowper's "Conversation," 96); sound or normal, as the mind, etc. (as, to be in one's *right* senses); mentally sound, or sane, as persons (as, not *right* in one's head); in good health or spirits, as persons (as, he is all *right* again); in a satisfactory state, or in good order (as, to put things *right*; "God's in his heaven—All's *right* with the world!" Browning's "Pippa Passes," i.); also, legitimate or rightful (archaic: as, the *right* owner); true, real, or genuine (as, "The Houyhnhnms . . . could hardly believe me to be a *right* Yahoo," Swift's "Gulliver's Travels," iv. 3: chiefly archaic, except as in 'right whale,' etc.: see under *whale²,* *n.*); also, belonging or pertaining to the side of a person or thing which is turned toward the east when the face is toward the north, or to that part of anything faced which appears on this side of the spectator (opposed to *left*: as, one's *right* hand or *right* glove; the *right* side of a deliberative assembly, that to the presiding officer's right; the *right* bank of a river, that to the right as one faces down the stream). **II.** *n.* That which is right or in accordance with morality or equity (as, "Because *right* is *right,* to follow *right* Were wisdom": Tennyson's "Œnone," 147); just or equitable treatment, or justice (as, "King Charles, and who'll do him *right* now?" Browning's "Cavalier Tunes," ii. 1); that which accords with fact, reason, or propriety (as, "Thou hast spoke the *right*": Shakspere's "Henry V.," ii. 1. 129); the right or proper way of thinking (as, "a historical question about which they were in the *right*": Macaulay's "Hist. of Eng.," xviii.); also, justifiable claim, or a just claim or title, whether legal, prescriptive, or moral (as, "Who . . . hath full *right* to exempt Whom so it pleases him," Milton's "Samson Agonistes," 310; "The people have a *right* supreme To make their kings," Dryden's "Absalom and Achitophel," i. 409; "I'm a champion for the *Rights* of Woman," Maria Edgeworth's "Belinda," xvii.); specif., a privilege of subscribing for a stock or bond, esp. a privilege whereby a stockholder in a company may purchase stock of a new issue of that company in a fixed proportion to the amount of his holdings of the old stock, such privileges being bought and sold like stock, and dealt in on the markets (often in *pl.*); also, that which is due to any one by just claim (as, to give one his *right,* or his *rights*); also, the right side, or what is on the right side (as, to the *right,* toward the right side, also clockwise); specif., the starboard of a ship; also [usually *cap.*], in continental Europe, that part of a legislative assembly which sits on the right side of the chamber as viewed by the president, a position customarily assigned to representatives holding conservative views; hence, a party holding such views.—**by right,** or **by rights,** with justice or reason, or properly (as, "I should have been a woman *by right,*" Shakspere's "As You Like It," iv. 3. 177; "a villain who should have swung, *by rights,* at Tyburn, last autumn," Whyte-Melville's "Katerfelto," xxvi.); also, by just claim or title (as, "She belonged to Tobias *by right* of inheritance," Tobit, iii. 17; it is ours *by right,* or *by rights*).—**right of way,** a right of passage, as over another's land; also, a path that may lawfully be used; specif., the strip of land traversed by a railroad; also, the right to pass over a path or way, to the temporary exclusion of others.—**to have a right** or **no right** (to do something), to have a, or no, just claim or title (to do something); also (prov.), to be required, or not required, in justice or reason (to do something: equivalent to *ought,* or *ought not*: as, he *has a right* to mind his own business; "You'd *have a right* to be leaving him alone, Molly," Synge's "Well of the Saints," i.; I *have no right* to pay, that is, I should not be compelled to pay).—**to rights,** to or into the proper condition or order:

as, "Perhaps you'll let the gentleman know, how you would set this muddle . . . *to rights*" (Dickens's "Hard Times," ii. 5).—**right**, *adv.* [AS. *rihte*.] In a right or straight line, straight, or directly (as, "Let thine eyes look *right* on," Prov. iv. 25; "*Right* up Ben-Lomond could he press," Scott's "Lady of the Lake," ii. 25); directly and quite (*to*, *into*, *through*, etc.: as, "*Right* down to Paradise descend," Milton's "Paradise Lost," x. 398); quite or completely (as, his hat was knocked *right* off); immediately (as, *right* after dinner); exactly, precisely, or just (as, *right* here; "*Right* adjoining the chapel is an immense, rickety building," H. Melville's "Omoo," lxxix.; *right* now); very or extremely (archaic or colloq.: as, "I was *right* glad . . . to stop and take shelter," Roosevelt's "Hunting Trips of a Ranchman," vi.: also used specif. in certain titles, as '*right* honorable' and '*right* reverend'); also, uprightly or righteously (as, "Thou satest in the throne judging *right*": Ps. ix. 4); correctly or accurately (as, "She had guessed *right*," Arnold Bennett's "Lion's Share," xl.; if I remember *right*); properly or fittingly (as, to behave *right*; it serves you *right*); advantageously, favorably, or well (as, to turn out *right*).—**right**, *v.* [AS. *rihtan*.] **I.** *tr.* To bring or restore to an upright or the proper position (as, "The man . . . *righted* him on to the seat and said, 'Paddington' to the driver": A. S. M. Hutchinson's "If Winter Comes," iv. 3); also, to do justice to, or relieve from wrong (as, "I know the Captain'll see folks *righted* if he can": George Eliot's "Adam Bede," xxxiv.); redress (wrong, etc.: as, "The wrongs you are so pitiful over will be *righted*," Mallock's "New Republic," v. 1); also, to bring into conformity with fact, or correct (as, to *right* one's accounts; to *right* errors); inform (a person) correctly (as, he was in error but I *righted* him); also, to set in order or put right (as, "Things have got all wrong, and can't be *righted!*" Du Maurier's "Trilby," iv.). **II.** *intr.* To resume an upright or the proper position (as, "The Arethusa . . . whipped under the tree, *righted*, and went merrily away down stream": Stevenson's "Inland Voyage," xi.); also, to resume a satisfactory state (as, "For a few days he was really ill, but after this he *righted*": S. Butler's "Way of All Flesh," lxxx.).

right-a-ble (rī′tạ-bl), *a.* That may be righted.

right=a-bout (rīt′ạ-bout″), *n.* The opposite direction as faced after turning about to the right: as, to send to the *right-about* (fig., to dismiss summarily).

right=an-gled (rīt′ang″gld), *a.* Containing a right angle or right angles; rectangular.

right-en (rī′tn), *v. t.* To set right; right.

right-eous (rī′chus), *a.* [AS. *rihtwīs*, appar. < *riht*, a., right, + *wīs*, wise, way, E. *wise*[2], *n.*, or perhaps < *riht*, n., right, + *wīs*, E. *wise*[1], *a.*] Upright or virtuous, or obedient to the divine or the moral law (as, "A *righteous* man hateth lying": Prov. xiii. 5); also, in accordance with right, or characterized by uprightness or morality (as, "Lord God Almighty, true and *righteous* are thy judgments": Rev. xvi. 7); morally right or justifiable (as, "He was . . . stirred by *righteous* wrath," Galsworthy's "Dark Flower," i. 15; "to rise against his father in a rebellion which he recognised as *righteous*," S. Butler's "Way of All Flesh," xxxvii.).—**right′eous-ly**, *adv.*—**right′eous-ness**, *n.*

right-er (rī′tėr), *n.* One who rights, or redresses, sets right, etc.

right-ful (rīt′fụl), *a.* [AS. *rihtfull*.] Righteous, as a person†; also, equitable or just, as actions, etc. (as, a *rightful* cause); also, having a right, or just claim, as to some possession or position (as, the *rightful* owner; "the deposing of a *rightful* king," Shakspere's "Richard II.," v. 1. 50); belonging by right, or just claim (as, one's *rightful* property); also, correct or proper (as, "Such is the *rightfull* Courtier in his kinde," Spenser's "Mother Hubberds Tale," 793: now rare).—**right′-ful-ly**, *adv.*—**right′ful-ness**, *n.*

right=hand (rīt′hand), *a.* Of, for, or with the right hand; also, on or to the right; also, most efficient or useful as a helper (as, one's *right-hand* man).—**right′=hand′ed**, *a.* Having the right hand or arm more serviceable than the left; preferably using the right hand; also, adapted to or performed by the right hand; also, situated on the side of the right hand; moving or rotating from left to right, or in the same direction as the hands of a clock (as, a *right-handed* screw, a screw which is advanced by turning from left to

right, and whose thread runs upward from left to right when viewed from the side with the axis vertical; a *right-handed* helix or spiral, one that ascends or advances like the thread of a right-handed screw).—**right′=hand′ed-ness**, *n.*—**right′=hand′er**, *n.* A right-handed person; also, a blow with the right hand.

right-less (rīt′les), *a.* Without rights.

right-ly (rīt′li), *adv.* [AS. *rihtlīce*.] In accordance with morality or equity, or uprightly; in accordance with truth or fact, or correctly; properly, fitly, or suitably.

right=mind-ed (rīt′mīn″ded), *a.* Having right opinions or principles.—**right′=mind′ed-ness**, *n.*

right-ness (rīt′nes), *n.* [AS. *rihtnes*.] The state or quality of being right; straightness or directness; uprightness or rectitude; correctness or accuracy; propriety or fitness.

right-ward (rīt′wärd), *adv.* and *a.* Toward or on the right.

rig-id (rij′id). [L. *rigidus*, < *rigere*, be stiff: cf. *rigor*.] **I.** *a.* Stiff or unyielding; not pliant or flexible; hard; hence, firmly fixed, set, or not moving (as, "Her eyes grew *rigid*," M. Hewlett's "Open Country," xx.; "his hat . . . hiding all the face except the *rigid* mouth and chin," Miss Mulock's "John Halifax," viii.); stiff in outline or aspect (as, "The broken landscape, by degrees Ascending, roughens into *rigid* hills": Thomson's "Seasons," Spring, 960); also, inflexible, strict, or severe, as a person, the disposition, etc. (as, "The young man is under the dictates of a *rigid* schoolmaster or instructor," Steele, in "Tatler," 175; "a *rigid* disciplinarian," Aldrich's "Story of a Bad Boy," vi.); strictly or rigorously performed, maintained, etc. (as, "a *rigid* discipline," Gibbon's "Decline and Fall of the Roman Empire," xli.; "a *rigid* and elaborate drill," Buchan's "Hist. of the Great War," liii.; "*rigid* precautions," G. P. R. James's "Hist. of Charlemagne," iv.); often, strict in opinion or observance, as a person, etc. (as, a *rigid* Calvinist; a *rigid* sect); of a rigorously strict character, as principles, notions, conduct, etc. (as, "My morals will appear to you far from *rigid*," C. B. Brown's "Wieland," xxiii.; "*rigid* ideas of duty," W. De Morgan's "Joseph Vance," xix.); also, severely exact, or rigorous (as, a *rigid* examination); also, in *aëronautics*, noting or pertaining to an airship or dirigible whose form is maintained by a rigid structure contained within the envelop. **II.** *n.* In *aëronautics*, a rigid airship or dirigible (see *rigid*, *a.*).—**ri-gid-i-ty** (ri-jid′i-ti), **rig′id-ness**, *n.*—**rig′id-ly**, *adv.*

rig-ma-role (rig′mạ-rōl), *n.* [Corruption of obs. *ragman roll*, a roll, list, or catalogue (*ragman*, of unknown origin, being first applied, in 1276, to a particular statute of Edward I., and subsequently to legal documents).] A succession of confused or foolish statements; incoherent or rambling discourse.

rig-ol† (rig′ọl), *n.* [Cf. F. *rigole*, channel for water, furrow.] A ring, circle, or diadem.

rig-o-lette (rig-ọ-let′), *n.* [Perhaps < F. *Rigolette*, woman's name.] A kind of scarf, commonly knitted or crocheted of wool, worn as a head-covering by women.

rig-or (rig′ọr, also, as L., rī′gọr), *n.* [OF. *rigor*, *rigour* (F. *rigueur*), < L. *rigor*, < *rigere*, be stiff: cf. *rigid*.] Stiffness or rigidity (as, "The rest his look Bound with Gorgonian *rigour* not to move," Milton's "Paradise Lost," x. 297: now only technical); also, strictness, severity, or harshness, as in dealing with persons; the full or extreme severity of laws, rules, etc. (as, "Let him have all the *rigour* of the law": Shakspere's "2 Henry VI.," i. 3. 199); strict or severe character, as of discipline, etc.; severity of life, or austerity; extreme strictness, as of principles, etc.; severe exactness, or strict accuracy (as, to employ terms with the utmost *rigor*); also, an instance of strictness or severity; a severe or harsh act, proceeding, or circumstance (as, "The *rigours* of his prison-house in the Tower could not break that dauntless spirit": Morley's "Oliver Cromwell," i. 4); also, severity of weather or climate, or an instance of this (as, the *rigor*, or *rigors*, of winter; "the rage and *rigour* of a polar sky," Cowper's "Hope," 462); painful extremity (as, the *rigor* of famine); in *pathol.* (pron. rī′gọr or rig′ọr), a sudden coldness, as that preceding certain fevers; a chill.—**rigor mortis** (rī′gọr môr′tis). [L., 'stiffness of death.'] The stiffening of the body following upon death.—**rig′or-ism**, *n.* Extreme strictness; in *Rom. Cath. theol.*, the doctrine that in doubtful cases of conscience the strict course is always to be followed.—

rig′or-ist, *n.* A believer in or adherent of rigorism.—

rig′or-ous, *a.* [OF. *rigoreux* (F. *rigoureux*), < ML. *rigorosus*.] Characterized by rigor; rigidly severe or harsh, as persons, rules, discipline, etc. (as, "*rigorous* laws," Burke's "Conciliation with the Colonies"; "A *rigorous* censorship of the press was established," Morley's "Oliver Cromwell," iv. 1); extremely strict, as principles, observance, etc.; severely exact or rigidly accurate (as, *rigorous* accuracy); severe, sharp, or bitter, as weather or climate (as, "A *rigorous* winter was approaching," Irving's "Conquest of Granada," xcvi.; "in this *rigorous* climate, where the snows seldom melt," Gibbon's "Decline and Fall of the Roman Empire," xl.).—**rig′or-ous-ly**, *adv.*—**rig′or-ous-ness**, *n.*

rig′our, *n.* British preferred form of *rigor* (except as Latin).

Rigs-dag (rigz′däg), *n.* [Dan.: cf. *Reichstag*.] The parliament of Denmark.

rigs-da-ler (rigz′dä″lėr), *n.* [Dan.: see *rix-dollar*.] A Danish silver coin of the value of two kroner.

Rig=Ve-da (rig-vā′dä or -vē′dä), *n.* [Skt., < *ric*, a hymn of praise, + *vēda*: see *Veda*.] See *Veda*.

Obverse.   Reverse.
Rigsdaler of Frederick VII., 1854.— British Museum.

Riks-dag (riks′däg), *n.* [Sw.: cf. *Reichstag*.] The parliament of Sweden.

rile (rīl), *v. t.*; *riled, riling*. [Var. of *roil*.] To render (water, etc.) turbid by stirring up sediment; fig., to disturb the temper of, irritate, or vex (as, "To be shot at wouldn't *rile* me so much": J. Conrad's "Rescue," iii. 9). [Prov. or colloq.]

ri-lie-vo (rē-lyā′vō), *n.*; pl. *-vos* (-vōz), It. *-vi* (-vē). [It.] In *sculpture, painting*, etc., relief.

rill (ril), *n.* [Cf. LG. *rille*, channel, rill, G. *rille*, D. *ril*, furrow.] A small stream; a brook; a rivulet: as, "the blue *rill* glittering as it twined itself through its rude and solitary dell" (Scott's "Guy Mannering," xxv.).—**rill**, *v. i.* To flow in a rill.

rille (ril), *n.* [G.: see *rill*.] In *astron.*, any of certain long, narrow trenches or valleys observed on the surface of the moon.

rill-et (ril′et), *n.* A little rill; a streamlet: as, "Each *rillet* was swollen to a gushing stream" (Eden Phillpotts's "Children of Men," Prologue, iii.).

rim (rim), *n.* [AS. *rima*.] The outer edge, border, or margin, esp. of a circular object; the circular part of a wheel, furthest from the axle; any edge or margin, often a raised one.—**rim**, *v. t.*; *rimmed, rimming*. To furnish with a rim, border, or margin: as, "a broad lake *rimmed* with a desolation of mud and bleached refuse and dead trees" (H. G. Wells's "Tono-Bungay," iii. 4. § 4).

rime¹ (rīm), *n.* [AS. *hrīm* = D. *rijm* = Icel. *hrīm*, rime.] White frost (see *frost*, *n.*) or hoar-frost (as, "Evening cloud and whitening sunrise *rime* Told of the coming of the wintertime": Whittier's "Bridal of Pennacook," vi.); specif., in *meteor.*, a hoary, white icy covering deposited on trees, etc., somewhat resembling white frost but formed only from fog or vapor-bearing air.—**rime¹**, *v. t.*; *rimed, riming*. To cover with rime or hoar-frost.

rime², **rhyme** (rīm), *n.* [OF. F. *rime*, < L. *rhythmus*, < Gr. ῥυθμός, E. *rhythm*.] Agreement in the terminal sounds of lines of verse or words; also, an instance of this; a word agreeing with another in terminal sound; also, verse or poetry having correspondence in the terminal sounds of the lines; also, a poem or piece of verse having such correspondence.—**feminine rime.** See under *feminine*, *a.*—**masculine rime.** See under *masculine*, *a.*—**rime²**, **rhyme**, *v.*; *rimed, rhymed, riming, rhyming*. [OF. F. *rimer*.] **I.** *tr.* To treat in rime, or verse having rimes, as a subject; turn into

rime, as something in prose; compose (verse, etc.) in metrical form with rimes; also, to use (a word) as a rime to another word; use (words) as rimes; also, to bring by riming (as, "those fellows of infinite tongue, that can *rhyme* themselves into ladies' favours": Shakspere's "Henry V.," v. 2. 164). **II.** *intr.* To make rime or verse; versify; also, to use rime in writing verse, as a poet; also, to form a rime, as one word or line with another, or as two or more words or lines; also, to be composed in metrical form with rimes, as verse.—

rim-er, **rhym-er** (rī′mėr), *n.*—**rime′=roy′al**, *n.* In *pros.*, a form of verse introduced into English by Chaucer, consisting of seven-line stanzas in which there are three rimes, the first line riming with the third, the second with the fourth and fifth, and the sixth with the seventh.—**rime′ster**, **rhyme′ster** (-stėr), *n.* A maker of rime or verse, esp. of an inferior order; a poetaster.

rim-less (rim′les), *a.* Without a rim or rims: as, "*rimless* eye-glasses" (Mrs. Wharton's "Son at the Front," xii.).

rimmed (rimd), *a.* Having a rim or rims, esp. as specified: as, "ornamental gilt *rimmed* blue candlesticks" (G. B. Shaw's "You Never Can Tell," i.).

ri-mose (rī′mōs or rī-mōs′), *a.* [L. *rimosus*, < *rima*, chink.] Full of chinks or crevices.

rim-ple (rim′pl), *n.* [ME. *rymple* = MLG. and D. *rimpel*.] A wrinkle; a ripple. [Now prov.]—**rim′ple**, *v. t.* or *i.*; *-pled, -pling*. To wrinkle; ripple. [Now prov.]

rim-rock (rim′rok), *n.* In *mining*, rock rising like a rim from bed-rock hollowed out by the action of water, and serving to retain accumulations of auriferous detritus.

rim=saw, *n.* A saw with an annular toothed cutting part which is mounted on the rim of a central disk.

rim-y (rī′mi), *a.* Covered with or abounding in rime or hoar-frost: as, *rimy* trees; "a *rimy* morning in departing November" (George Eliot's "Adam Bede," lv.).

rind (rīnd), *n.* [AS. *rind* = G. *rinde*.] A thick and firm outer coat or covering, as of animals, plants, fruits, cheeses, etc.; a thick skin or integument; the cortex or bark of a plant.—**rind**, *v. t.* To strip of the rind.—**rind′ed**, *a.* Having a rind: as, smooth-rinded.

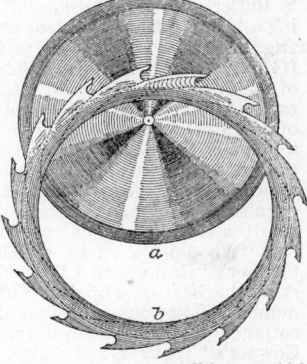

Rim-saw.— *a*, central disk upon which the cutting part *b* is mounted, attached to the disk by rivets.

rin-der-pest (rin′dėr-pest), *n.* [G., 'cattle pest.'] An acute, usually fatal, infectious disease of cattle, sheep, etc., characterized by high fever, diarrhea, lesions of the skin and mucous membranes, cough, etc.

rin-for-zan-do (rēn-fôr-tsän′dō), *a.* [It., gerund of *rinforzare*, strengthen, reinforce.] In *music*, with special or increased emphasis: usually applied to a single phrase or voice-part to be made specially prominent.

ring¹ (ring), *v.*; pret. *rang* (also *rung*), pp. *rung*, ppr. *ringing*. [AS. *hringan* = Icel. *hringja*, ring; prob. imit.] **I.** *intr.* To give forth a clear, resonant sound when set in sudden vibration by a blow or otherwise, as a bell or other metal object, or glass or some other substance; hence, to give forth a sound proper or not proper to genuine metal in striking on something; fig., to seem (true, false, etc.) in the effect produced on the mind, as his words *ring* true, or false); also, to cause a bell or bells to sound; convey a summons by means of a bell (as, to *ring* for a messenger); also, to sound loudly, or make a resonant sound, as things (as, "He heard the chieftain's horn *ringing* through the woods," Scott's "Fair Maid of Perth," xxix.; "The blow *rang* as if I had struck upon an anvil," W. H. Hudson's "Purple Land," xix.); also, to be loud or resonant, or resound, as a sound (as, "Lady Henry's voice *rang* imperiously through the room"; Mrs. H. Ward's "Lady Rose's Daughter," v.); also, to be filled with sound, reëcho with sound, or resound, as a place (as, "The woods round Fort Duquesne *rung* with the halloos of the red men":

Bancroft's "Hist. of the U. S.," Amer. Revolution, i. 8); hence, be filled with report or talk (as, "The whole world inside the ocean was *ringing* with the infamy of the Roman senatorial tribunals": Froude's "Cæsar," ix.); also, of the ears, to have a sensation as of the sound of bells. **II.** *tr.* To cause to ring, as a bell, etc.; test (coin, etc.) by the sound produced in striking on something (as, "He *rang* his silver money upon the counter": Wister's "Virginian," iv.); also, to produce (sound) by or as if by ringing (as, "Sea-nymphs hourly *ring* his knell": Shakspere's "Tempest," i. 2. 402); also, to announce or proclaim, usher in or out, summon, signal, etc., by or as by the sound of a bell (as, "The city bells were just *ringing* one," Dana's "Two Years before the Mast," xxxvi.; "*Ring* out the old, *ring* in the new," Tennyson's "In Memoriam," cvi.; "She had been *rung* down into the glass room," Dickens's "Dombey and Son," iii.; to *ring* up, or *ring* down, a theater-curtain); also, to utter sonorously or proclaim aloud (as, to *ring* a person's praises); also, to bring or put (*in*) artfully or fraudulently (slang: as, "Them fellows at Red Dog would swap it [an infant], and *ring* in somebody else on us," Bret Harte's "Luck of Roaring Camp"). **—to ring the changes.** See *change*, *n.*—**ring**[1], *n.* A ringing sound, as of a bell, etc. (as, "the *ring* of sleigh-bells": Mrs. Stowe's "Oldtown Folks," xxxvii.); a sound or tone resembling the ringing of a bell, as in the voice, etc. (as, "He spoke rather sadly than otherwise, yet there was a *ring* in his voice": Stevenson's "Master of Ballantrae," v.); a characteristic sound, as of a coin, or, fig., a characteristic quality, as of other things, indicating genuineness or the reverse (as, "This [a remark] had the true Theobald *ring*": S. Butler's "Way of All Flesh," lxxxii.); also, an act of ringing a bell, etc.; also, a set or peal of bells.

ring[2] (ring), *n.* [AS. *hring* = OFries. *hring* = OHG. *hring* (G. *ring*) = Icel. *hringr*, ring: cf. *rank*[2].] A circular band of metal or other material (as, a key-*ring*, a napkin-*ring*); esp., a small circular band, as of gold or other precious metal, often set with gems, for wearing on the finger as an ornament, a token of betrothal or marriage, etc.; also, anything having the form of a circular band; one of the concentric layers of wood produced yearly in the trunks of exogenous trees; a circular line or mark; a circular course (as, to dance in a *ring*); a single turn in a spiral or helix or in a spiral course (as, "Woodbine . . . In spiral *rings* ascends the trunk," Cowper's "Retirement," 231; "In airy *rings* they [lapwings] skim the heath," Pope's "Windsor Forest," 131); also, a number of persons or things disposed in a circle (as, "A cottage . . . close Environ'd with a *ring* of branching elms": Cowper's "Task," i. 223); also, a group of persons coöperating for selfish, sometimes illicit, purposes, as to control a business or market, politics, or the like (as, "I had always understood that the theatrical '*ring*' was impenetrable to an outsider": Arnold Bennett's "Truth about an Author," xiii.); also, an inclosed circular or other area, as one in which some sport or exhibition takes place (as, the *ring* of a circus); an inclosure in which prize-fights take place (now usually a square area marked off by stakes and ropes); a space devoted to betting at a race-course; also, specif., in *geom.*, the area or space between two concentric circles; also, a tore; in *chem.*, a number of atoms so united that they may be graphically represented in circular form.—**ring**[2], *v.* **I.** *intr.* To form a ring or rings; move in a ring or a constantly curving course. **II.** *tr.* To surround with a ring, or encircle (as, "He was *ringed* round with unseen celestial defences," S. R. Crockett's "Stickit Minister," ii.; "the circling sea that *rings* the world," W. Morris's "Jason," xii. 225); hem in (animals) by riding or circling about them; draw a ring around; also, to form into a ring (as, "They [a class at a clinic] *ring* themselves Round the first bed": Henley's "In Hospital," xi.); also, to provide with a ring or rings; put a ring in the nose of (an animal); mark or decorate with rings; cut away the bark in a ring about (a tree, branch, etc.), as to check too luxuriant growth and induce a state of fruitfulness, or to cause decay.

ring=ar-mor (ring'är″mọr), *n.* Armor composed of interlinked metal rings, or chain-mail; also, armor made by fastening metal rings on leather or cloth (see cut in next column).

ring=bark (ring'bärk), *v. t.* To ring or girdle (a tree, branch, etc.).

ring=bolt (ring'bōlt), *n.* A bolt with a ring fitted in an eye at its head.

ring=bone (ring'bōn), *n.* A morbid bony growth on the pastern-bones of a horse.

ring=dove (ring'duv), *n.* A European pigeon, *Columba palumbus*, with two whitish patches on the neck; also, a small old-world pigeon, *Turtur risorius*, with a black half-ring around the neck, allied to the turtle-dove.

Ring-armor (in 2d sense).

ringed (ringd), *a.* Having or wearing a ring or rings; marked or decorated with a ring or rings; surrounded by a ring or rings; formed of or with rings; ring-like or annular.

rin-gent (rin'jẹnt), *a.* [L. *ringens* (*ringent-*), ppr. of *ringi*, open the mouth wide: cf. *rictus*.] Gaping; having the lips widely spread, as certain corollas.

ring-er[1] (ring'ẹr), *n.* [See *ring*[1].] One who or that which rings; a device for ringing a bell; also, an athlete, horse, etc., entered in a competition under false representations as to identity or ability; a person or thing that closely resembles another (slang).

ring-er[2] (ring'ẹr), *n.* [See *ring*[2].] One who or that which rings, or surrounds with a ring, encircles, etc.; in *quoits*, a quoit so thrown as to encircle the peg aimed at, or the throw itself.

ring=fence (ring'fens), *n.* A fence completely inclosing an estate or piece of ground.

ring=fin-ger (ring'fing″gẹr), *n.* [AS. *hringfinger*.] The third finger of the hand (next to the little finger); esp., the third finger of the left hand, on which the wedding-ring is worn.

ring-ing (ring'ing), *p. a.* [See *ring*[1].] That rings; giving or having the sound of a bell or some similar resonant body; resounding; loud or resonant.—**ring'ing-ly**, *adv.*

ring-lead-er (ring'lē″dẹr), *n.* A leader†; now, one who leads others in some form of opposition to authority or law, or in anything deemed objectionable (as, "the principal *ringleader* of the mutiny": Defoe's "Robinson Crusoe," i. 18).

ring-less (ring'les), *a.* Without rings: as, "her *ringless* hands" (Arnold Bennett's "Helen with the High Hand," xxii.).

ring-let (ring'let), *n.* A small ring or circle; also, a curled lock of hair, esp. when long and spirally curled (as, "Her long hair, escaped from its band, fell in jetty *ringlets*": Jane Porter's "Scottish Chiefs," ii.).—**ring'let-ed**, *a.*

ring=mas-ter (ring'mȧs″tẹr), *n.* One in charge of the performances in the ring of a circus.

ring=necked (ring'nekt), *a.* Having the neck marked by a ring or rings of color, as a bird.

ring=ou-zel (ring'-ö″zl), *n.* See *ouzel*.

ring=ster (ring'stẹr), *n.* A member of a ring, esp. a political ring. [Colloq., U. S.]

ring=straked, ring=streaked (ring'strākt, -strēkt), *a.* Having streaks or bands of color round the body.

ring=tailed (ring'-tāld), *a.* Having

Ring-necked Bird (*Ægialitis meloda*, species of plover).

the tail or the tail-feathers ringed or barred transversely with alternating colors; also, having the tail curled into a ring at the end.

ring-worm (ring′wẽrm), *n.* In *pathol.*, any of certain contagious skin-diseases due to vegetable parasites and characterized by the formation of ring-shaped eruptive patches.

rink (ringk), *n.* [Orig. Sc.; appar. < OF. *renc*, row, rank; see *rank²*.] A ground or course for justing, racing, etc.†; also, an area of ice marked off for the game of curling; a set of players on one side in this game; also, a sheet of ice for skating, often one artificially prepared and under cover; a smooth floor for roller-skating; a building or inclosure containing a surface prepared for skating.—**rink,** *v. i.* To skate on or in a rink.

rinse (rins), *v. t.; rinsed, rinsing.* [OF. *rincier, raincier* (F. *rincer*); origin uncertain.] To wash lightly, as by pouring water into or over or by dipping in water; esp., to put through clean water, as a final stage in cleansing; also, to remove (impurities, etc.) thus.—**rinse,** *n.* A rinsing, esp. a final application of water to remove impurities.—**rins′er,** *n.* —**rins′ing,** *n.* The act of one who rinses; also, the liquid with which anything has been rinsed (chiefly in *pl.*).

ri-o (rē′ō), *n.* [Sp. *río*, < L. *rivus*, stream.] A river.

ri-ot (rī′ọt), *n.* [OF. *riote* (F. *riotte*), dispute, quarrel; origin unknown.] A disturbance of the peace by an assembly of persons (in *law*, at least three); a disorderly public outbreak; a tumult; also, violent or wild disorder or confusion; also, loose, wanton, or profligately luxurious living (as, "Governors held their provinces for one, two, or three years; they went out bankrupt from extravagance, they returned with millions for fresh *riot*": Froude's "Cæsar," ii.); unrestrained revelry; also, an instance or course of loose or profligate living; a noisy revel (as, "And hark! the *riots* of the Green begin, That spring at first from yonder noisy inn": Crabbe's "Village," ii.); an unbridled outbreak, as of emotions, passions, etc.; a brilliant display (as, a *riot* of color); in *hunting*, the action of a hound in following the scent of the wrong animal.—**Riot Act,** an English statute of 1715 providing that if twelve or more persons assemble unlawfully and riotously, to the disturbance of the public peace, and refuse to disperse upon proclamation being made (called 'reading the Riot Act'), they shall be considered guilty of felony.—**to run riot,** to run wild, as hounds forsaking the right scent; hence, to act without control or restraint, or disregard all limits (as, "Honora's imagination *ran riot* until the seeming possibilities of life became infinite": W. Churchill's "Modern Chronicle," i. 7); grow luxuriantly or wildly (as, "And overhead the wandering ivy and vine, This way and that, in many a wild festoon *Ran riot*": Tennyson's "Œnone," 99).—**ri′ot,** *v.* **I.** *intr.* To take part in a riot or disorderly public outbreak; also, to live in a loose, wanton, or profligately luxurious manner; indulge in unrestrained revelry; indulge unrestrainedly in anything; act unrestrainedly, or run riot (as, "no pulse that *riots*, and no blood that glows": Pope's "Eloisa to Abelard," 252); also, to revel, or take great pleasure or delight (*in*: as, "He straightway began to *riot* in the possession of vast meadows of salt marsh and interminable patches of cabbages," Irving's "Knickerbocker's New York," ii. 4). **II.** *tr.* To spend (money, etc.) or pass (time, etc.) in riotous living: with *away* or *out*: as, "He . . . Had *rioted* his life out, and made an end" (Tennyson's "Aylmer's Field," 391).—**ri′ot-er,** *n.*—**ri′ot-ous,** *a.* Characterized by or of the nature of rioting, or disturbance of the peace, as actions; inciting to or taking part in a riot, as persons; also, loose, wanton, or profligately luxurious, as conduct, living, etc. (as, "The younger son . . . wasted his substance with *riotous* living": Luke, xv. 13); marked by unrestrained revelry; boisterous or uproarious (as, *riotous* glee); unrestrained (as, "Colors were in *riotous* discord": Bok's "Americanization of Edward Bok," xxii.); also, given to wantonness or profligately luxurious living, as persons (as, "Lord Baltimore . . . dissolute and *riotous*, fond of wine to madness and of women to folly": Bancroft's "Hist. of the U. S.," Amer. Revolution, i. 6); indulging in unrestrained revelry; unrestrained in action (as, "a fierce and *riotous* gust of wind": Hawthorne's "Twice-Told Tales," The Gentle Boy).—**ri′ot-ous-ly,** *adv.*—**ri′ot-ous-ness,** *n.*

rip¹ (rip), *v.; ripped, ripping.* [Late ME.: cf. Fries. *rippe,* tear, rip, MLG. *reppen,* stir up.] **I.** *tr.* To cut or tear apart in a rough or vigorous manner; slash; slit; often, to undo (a seam) by breaking, cutting, or pulling out the thread; specif., to saw (wood) in the direction of the grain; fig., to lay open, as for discussion (now usually with *up*: as, "Don't stand there *ripping* up old stories, to make one ashamed before one's love," Sheridan's "Trip to Scarborough," iv. 1); also, to cut or tear away from something in a rough or vigorous manner (as, "Macduff was from his mother's womb Untimely *ripp'd*": Shakspere's "Macbeth," v. 8. 16); also, to utter with violence, as an oath (with *out*: colloq.). **II.** *intr.* To become torn apart or split open; also, to move along with violence or great speed (colloq.); also, to break (*out*) angrily, as with an oath (colloq.); use strong language, or swear (colloq.: as, "Captain Peleg *ripped* and swore astern in the most frightful manner," H. Melville's "Moby-Dick," xxii.).—**rip¹,** *n.* A rent made by ripping; a tear.

rip² (rip), *n.* [Earlier *rep*: cf. *reprobate*.] A dissolute or worthless person (as, "the old *rip*, bewigged and gouty, ornate and enormous, with his jewelled mistress by his side": Lytton Strachey's "Queen Victoria," ii.); also, a worthless or worn-out horse; also, anything of little or no value. [Colloq.]

rip³ (rip), *n.* [Cf. *rip¹, v.,* also *ripple²*.] A heavy wave or current in water, or a stretch of broken water at sea or in a river: as, "I dip and I surge and I swing In the *rip* of the racing tide" (Kipling's "Bell Buoy").

ri-pa-ri-al (rī-pā′ri-ạl or ri-), *a.* Riparian.

ri-pa-ri-an (rī-pā′ri-ạn or ri-). [L. *riparius,* belonging to a river-bank or shore: see *river²*.] **I.** *a.* Of, pertaining to, or situated on, the bank of a river or other body of water. **II.** *n.* One who dwells, or owns property, on the banks of a river, etc.; a riparian proprietor.

rip=cord (rip′kõrd), *n.* In *aëronautics,* a cord fastened in the bag of a balloon or dirigible in such a way that a sharp pull upon it will rip the bag or tear off the rip-panel, and let the gas escape, thus causing the balloon to descend rapidly.

ripe (rīp), *a.; compar. riper; superl. ripest.* [AS. *rīpe* = D. *rijp* = G. *reif*, ripe.] Ready for reaping or gathering, as grain, fruits, etc.; complete in natural growth or development, as when arrived at the stage most fit for eating or use; also, resembling ripe fruit, as in ruddiness and fullness (as, "O, how *ripe* in show Thy lips, those kissing cherries, tempting grow!" Shakspere's "Midsummer Night's Dream," iii. 2. 139); also, fully grown or developed, as animals when ready to be killed and used for food; fully developed in body or mind, as persons; advanced to the point of being in the best condition for use, as cheese, beer, etc.; ready for some operation or process (as, a *ripe* abscess, one ready for lancing; a *ripe* fish, one ready for spawning); in general, arrived at the highest or a high point of development or excellence, or mature (as, "I . . . saw, beneath his jaunty air, true mettle, and *ripe* bravery," Blackmore's "Lorna Doone," xxi.; "the *ripe* administrative experience which he gained," Charnwood's "Theodore Roosevelt," iii.; *ripe* scholarship); of mature judgment or knowledge (as, "He was a scholar, and a *ripe* and good one": Shakspere's "Henry VIII.," iv. 2. 51); completed or perfected by the mind (as, *ripe* deliberation); also, characterized by full development of body or mind (as, of *ripe* years); sometimes, advanced in years (as, a *ripe* old age); also, ready for action, execution, etc. (as, "Our legions are brim-full, our cause is *ripe*," Shakspere's "Julius Cæsar," iv. 3. 215; "When the deed is *ripe*, he'll do it," Eden Phillpotts's "Children of Men," i. 3); fully prepared or ready to do or undergo something, or for some action, purpose, or end (as, "I hope I am not *ripe* to pass sentence on the gravest public bodies," Burke's "Conciliation with the Colonies"; a deed *ripe* to be done; "The Roman province in Asia Minor . . . was *ripe* for revolt," Froude's "Cæsar," ix.; "a young fellow . . . *ripe* for the gallows," H. Kingsley's "Geoffry Hamlyn," xlii.); of time, fully or sufficiently advanced (as, "When time is *ripe* . . . I'll steal to Glendower": Shakspere's "1 Henry IV.," i. 3. 294).—**ripe,** *v. i. or t.; riped, riping.* [AS. *rīpian*.] To ripen. [Archaic.]—**ripe′ly,** *adv.*—**rip-en** (rī′pn), *v. i. or t.* To become or make ripe; come or bring to maturity, the proper condition, etc.; mature.—**ripe′ness,** *n.*

ri-pid-o-lite (rī-pid′ō-līt or ri-), *n.* [G. *ripidolith,* < Gr. ῥιπίς (ῥιπιδ-), fan, + λίθος, stone.] Same as *clinochlore.*

ri-pie-no (rē-pyā′nō). [It., < L. *re-,* again, + *plenus,* full.] In *music:* **I.** *a.* Supplementary or reinforcing. **II.** *n.;* pl. *-ni* (-nē). A supplementary instrument or performer.

ri-poste (ri-pōst′), *n.* [F., < It. *risposta,* response, < *rispondere,* < L. *respondere,* E. *respond.*] In *fencing,* a quick thrust given after parrying a lunge; fig., a quick, sharp reply or return.—**ri-poste′,** *v. i.;* -posted, -posting. To make a riposte; fig., to reply or retaliate.

rip-pan-el (rip′pan″el), *n.* In *aëronautics,* a panel in the envelop of a balloon or dirigible, which can be ripped or torn out to let out the gas, as when a quick descent is necessary or in order to deflate the bag.

rip-per (rip′ėr), *n.* [See *rip*[1].] One who or that which rips; a tool for ripping; a rip-saw; also, a double-ripper; also, something especially strong, fine, or good of its kind (slang: as, "a perfect *ripper* of a gust," Mark Twain's "Huckleberry Finn," ix.; "a reg'lar *ripper* of a robber," Mark Twain's "Tom Sawyer," xxxv.); also, in *U. S. politics,* a legislative bill or act for taking powers of appointment to and removal from office away from the usual holders of these powers and conferring them unrestrictedly on a chief executive, as a governor or a mayor, or on a board of officials (also called *ripper bill* or *ripper act*).—**rip′ping,** *p. a.* That rips; also, excellent, splendid, or fine (slang: as, "a *ripping* girl," G. B. Shaw's "Misalliance": also used adverbially, as, "*ripping* good business," H. G. Wells's "Tono-Bungay," ii. 3. § 2).— **rip′ping=cord,** *n.* Same as *rip-cord.*—**rip′ping-ly,** *adv.*— **rip′ping=pan″el,** *n.* Same as *rip-panel.*

rip-ple[1] (rip′l), *n.* [Cf. D. and LG. *repel,* G. *riffel.*] A toothed or comb-like device for removing seeds or capsules from flax, etc.—**rip′ple**[1], *v. t.;* -pled, -pling. To remove the seeds or capsules from (flax, etc.) with a ripple.

rip-ple[2] (rip′l), *v.;* -pled, -pling. [Origin uncertain: cf. *rip*[1] and *rimple.*] **I.** *intr.* To form small waves or undulations on the surface, as water when agitated by a gentle breeze or by running over a rocky bottom; flow with a light ruffling of the surface (as, "The rivulet at her feet *Ripples* on in light and shadow": Tennyson's "Maud," ii. 4. 6); also, in general, to form or have small undulations; also, of sound, to go on or proceed with an effect like that of water flowing in ripples (as, "A mocking-bird chuckle *rippled* in her throat": G. W. Cable's "Cavalier," xiv.). **II.** *tr.* To form small waves or undulations on (as, "A cool sea-breeze came *rippling* and darkening the surface of the water": Dana's "Two Years before the Mast," xvii.); agitate lightly; also, to mark as with ripples; cause to undulate slightly, or give a wavy form to (as, "She shook her head, And shower'd the *rippled* ringlets to her knee": Tennyson's "Godiva," 47).—

rip′ple[2], *n.* A small wave or undulation, as on water; hence, any similar movement or appearance; a small undulation, as in hair; a ripple-mark; also, a sound as of water flowing in ripples (as, a *ripple* of laughter); also, a stretch of rough water, as over a rocky bottom, or a small rapid (U. S.).—**rip′ple=mark,** *n.* One of the wavy lines or ridges produced on sand, etc., by the action of waves, wind, or the like.

rip-pler (rip′lėr), *n.* One who ripples flax, etc.; also, an implement for rippling; a ripple.

rip-plet (rip′let), *n.* A little ripple.

rip-pling (rip′ling), *p. a.* That ripples; flowing in ripples, as water; having small undulations, or wavy (as, "*rippling* brown hair": Kingsley's "Yeast," xv.); sounding like water flowing in ripples (as, *rippling* laughter).—**rip′pling-ly,** *adv.*

rip-ply (rip′li), *a.* Characterized by ripples; rippling.

rip-rap (rip′rap), *n.* [Origin uncertain: cf. *rap*[1].] Broken stones used for foundations, etc.; also, a foundation or wall of stones thrown together irregularly.—**rip′rap,** *v. t.;* -rapped, -rapping. To construct with or strengthen by loose stones or a riprap.

rip-saw (rip′så), *n.* A saw for cutting wood in the direction of the grain.

Rip-u-a-ri-an (rip-ū-ā′ri-an). [ML. *Ripuarius, Ribuarius;* origin uncertain: cf. *riparian,* also *Salian*[2].] **I.** *a.* Designating or pertaining to the group of Franks who dwelt along the Rhine in the neighborhood of Cologne, or the code of laws observed by them. **II.** *n.* A Ripuarian Frank.

rise (rīz), *v.;* pret. *rose,* pp. *risen,* ppr. *rising.* [AS. *rīsan* = D. *rijzen* = OHG. *rīsan* = Icel. *rīsa* = Goth. *-reisan:* cf. *raise.*] **I.** *intr.* To get up from a lying, sitting, or kneeling posture, as a person or an animal; assume a standing position; in general, to assume an upright position; become erect and stiff, as the hair; often, to get up after falling or being thrown down (as, "Truth, crushed to earth, shall *rise* again": Bryant's "Battle-Field"); get up from sleep or rest (as, "With early dawn Lord Marmion *rose*": Scott's "Marmion," i. 31); adjourn, or close a session, as a deliberative body or a court; arise or return from the grave or the dead, or be restored to life (as, "how that Christ died for our sins . . . that he was buried, and that he *rose* again the third day": 1 Cor. xv. 4); also, to become active in opposition or resistance; revolt or rebel (as, "At our heels all hell should *rise* With blackest insurrection": Milton's "Paradise Lost," ii. 135); also, to be built up, erected, or constructed (as, "Bastions and ravelins were everywhere *rising,*" Macaulay's "Hist. of Eng.," iii.; "a restaurant then *rising* in Piccadilly," Arnold Bennett's "Roll-Call," ii.); spring up or grow, as plants or trees; become prominent on a surface, as a blister on the skin; have its spring or source, as a river; also, to come into being or appear, as persons (as, "Of the royal stock Of David . . . shall *rise* A son": Milton's "Paradise Lost," xii. 326); come into action, as a wind, storm, etc.; come into existence (as, "He can . . . make scenes *rise* up before us and seem present to the eye": Addison, in "Spectator," 421); come to pass, come about, or occur (as, "Then *rose* a little feud betwixt the two": Tennyson's "Princess," Conclusion, 23); originate, issue, or be derived (as, "From Study will no comforts *rise?*" Crabbe's "Borough," xxiv.); also, to move from a lower to a higher position, move upward, mount up, or ascend (as, a fog *rises* from a river; a bird *rises* in the air); come up to the surface of the water to take bait, etc., as a fish; come above the horizon, as a heavenly body; also, to extend directly upward (as, the tower *rises* to the height of 60 feet); have an upward slant or curve (as, the walk *rises* as it approaches the house); also, to attain higher rank, importance, etc., or advance in position, consequence, wealth, or social standing (as, "to have *risen* all the way from an errand boy in the bank to a lawyer," W. Churchill's "Modern Chronicle," i. 4; "Mrs. Stanhope . . . accomplished in . . . the art of *rising* in the world, had, with but a small fortune, contrived to live in the highest company," Maria Edgeworth's "Belinda," i.); advance to a higher level of action, thought, feeling, expression, etc. (as, "Horace . . . always *rises* above himself, when he has Homer in his view": Addison, in "Spectator," 417); prove one's self equal to a demand, emergency, etc. (as, "They *rose* to the occasion and sometimes above the occasion": J. Conrad's "Rescue," v. 3); also, to become animated or cheerful, as the spirits (as, "his spirits *rising* as his toils increase": Cowper's "Table Talk," 279); become stirred or roused (as, one's indignation *rises;* "Arthur felt his temper *rising,*" George Eliot's "Adam Bede," xxvii.); also, to increase in height, as water (as, "The river sometimes *rose* 30 feet in eight hours": A. R. Wallace's "Darwinism," ii.); swell or puff up, as dough from the action of yeast; also, to increase in amount, as prices, etc.; increase in price or value, as commodities; increase in degree, intensity, or force, as color, fever, etc.; become louder or of higher pitch, as the voice. **II.** *tr.* To cause to rise; cause (birds) to start up into the air; cause (fish) to come to the surface of the water; also, to ascend or mount (a hill, etc.: as, "The Americans had to descend into a little hollow, and *rise* a hill on its opposite side," Cooper's "Spy," xxxiii.); also, *naut.,* to cause (something) to rise above the visible horizon by approaching nearer to it; raise.—**rise** (rīz), *n.* The act or an act of rising; upward movement, or ascent; the coming of a fish to the surface of the water to seize bait, etc. (as, to get a *rise:* often fig., of success in artful dealing with a victim or in making a butt of a person); appearance above the horizon, as of the sun or moon; elevation in rank, position, fortune, etc., or a means of such elevation (as, "The match was considered . . . a *rise* in life for the girl": W. De Morgan's "Alice-for-Short," iii.); advance toward a flourishing condition (as, the *rise* and fall of a party or a movement); an increase in height, as of water, or the amount of such increase (as, "We met a great *rise* coming down the river": Mark Twain's "Life on the Mississippi," x.); an increase in amount, as of prices; an increase in price or value, as of commodities; an increase in degree or intensity, as of temperature; an increase in loudness or in pitch, as of the voice; also, origin, source, or beginning (as, the *rise* of a stream in a mountain); occasion (as, to give *rise* to suspicion); a coming into existence or notice (as, the *rise* of a question); also, extension upward, or the amount of this; the vertical height of a step, arch, etc.; a flight of steps; the vertical face of a step, or a riser; upward slope, as of ground or a road; a piece of rising or high ground (as, "On getting to the top of the next *rise*, I saw the plain in front of me," J. H. Patterson's "Man-Eaters of Tsavo," xxiii.; "Slatter's Hill . . . was a *rise* of ground covering, perhaps, an acre and a quarter," Aldrich's "Story of a Bad Boy," xiii.); in *mining*, an excavation begun from below and directed upward.—**ris-er** (rī′zẽr), *n.* One who or that which rises; often, one who rises from bed (as, "The next morning we were early *risers*": H. Melville's "Typee," vi.); specif., the vertical face of a stair-step.

ris-i-bil-i-ty (riz-i-bil′i-ti), *n.*; pl. *-ties* (-tiz). Risible character; ability or disposition to laugh; faculty of laughing (often in *pl.*).

ris-i-ble (riz′i-bl). [F. *risible*, < LL. *risibilis*, < L. *ridere* (pp. *risus*), laugh.] **I.** *a.* Having the faculty or power of laughing, as man; inclined to laughter (as, "He is the most *risible* misanthrope I ever met with. A lucky joke, or any ludicrous incident, will set him a-laughing immoderately": Smollett's "Humphry Clinker," April 30); also, pertaining to or connected with laughing (as, "By and by something would be said to touch his *risible* faculties": W. H. Hudson's "Far Away and Long Ago," xi.); also, capable of exciting laughter, laughable, or ludicrous (as, "a few wild blunders, and *risible* absurdities, from which no work of such multiplicity was ever free": Johnson's "Dictionary," Preface). **II.** *n. Pl.*, the risible faculties: as, "These provincialisms might have excited the *risibles* of so keen a set of grammarians as we were" (Mrs. Stowe's "Oldtown Folks," xxxiii.).

ris-ing (rī′zing), *n.* The act of one who or that which rises; specif., an insurrection or revolt (as, "There was a *rising* now in Kent, my Lord of Norwich being at the head of them": Evelyn's "Diary," May 30, 1648); also, something that rises; a projection or prominence; a morbid swelling, as an abscess, boil, etc. (now prov.); a piece of rising or high ground; also, yeast or leaven (prov.); a quantity of dough set to rise at one time (U. S.); also, in *mining*, a rise.—**ris′ing**, *p. a.* That rises; ascending or mounting; appearing above the horizon, as a heavenly body; advancing in position, influence, fortune, etc. (as, "Dr. Henry Fraser, the *rising* physician of Cairn Edward": S. R. Crockett's "Stickit Minister," i.); increasing in amount, degree, intensity, pitch, etc.; coming into existence or notice; growing, or advancing to adult years (as, the *rising* generation); sloping upward, or being elevated above the surrounding level, as ground.—**ris′ing**, *prep.* [Orig. ppr.] Approaching in amount, age, etc. (as, *rising* a thousand men; a horse *rising* five years old); also, somewhat more than; above. [Colloq.]

risk (risk), *n.* [F. *risque*, < It. *risco, risico,* risk; origin uncertain.] Exposure to the chance of injury or loss (as, a trip made at great *risk*; where there is *risk* there may be loss); hazard or danger; a hazard or dangerous chance (as, to run *risks*; "I promise to take care of myself . . . I won't take any *risks*," J. Conrad's "Lord Jim," xxiii.); the hazard or chance (*of*: as, to persist at the *risk* of being fined or imprisoned; to run the *risk* of failure); in *com.*, the hazard or chance of loss, esp. of insured goods or property; the degree of probability of such loss; the amount which the insurance company may lose; a person or thing with reference to the risk involved in insuring him or it.—**risk,** *v. t.* [F. *risquer*.] To expose to the chance of injury or loss, or hazard (as, to *risk* one's life to save another; to *risk* money in speculation; "the foolhardiness which had *risked* so valuable an army on a single blow," Motley's "Dutch Republic," i. 2); also, to take or run the risk of (something adverse: as, to *risk* a fall in climbing; to *risk* defeat or loss); also, to venture upon (something involving risk: as, to *risk* an attempt; to *risk* a battle).—**risk′er,** *n.*—**risk′y,** *a.*; compar. *riskier*, superl. *riskiest*. Attended with or involving risk,

or hazardous (as, a *risky* undertaking; "It's a *risky* thing getting mixed in any matters with the like of you," Synge's "Tinker's Wedding," ii.); also, venturesome or daring, as persons; also, risqué.—**risk′i-ly,** *adv.*—**risk′i-ness,** *n.*

ri-sor-gi-men-to (rē-sôr-jē-men′tō), *n.* [It.] A resurrection; a revival; [*cap.*] the Renaissance as developed in Italy.

ris-ot-to (rē-sot′tō), *n.* [It., < *riso,* < L. *oryza,* E. *rice.*] A dish of rice with grated cheese and other seasoning.

ris-qué (rēs-kā), *a.* [F. (fem. *risquée*), lit. 'risked,' 'ventured,' pp. of *risquer*, E. *risk, v.*] Daringly close to indelicacy or impropriety; intentionally suggestive of indecency: as, a *risqué* remark or story; a *risqué* situation in a play.

ris-sole (ris′ōl, F. rē-sol), *n.* [F., perhaps < LL. *russeolus*, reddish, < L. *russus,* red.] A small fried ball, roll, or cake of minced meat or fish mixed with bread-crumbs, egg, etc., and usually inclosed in paste.

ri-tar-dan-do (rē-tär-dän′dō), *a.* [It., gerund of *ritardare*, retard.] In *music*, becoming gradually slower.

rite (rīt), *n.* [L. *ritus*.] A formal or ceremonial act or procedure prescribed or customary in religious or other solemn use (as, *rites* of baptism, marriage, or burial; sacrificial *rites*; *rites* of initiation into a society); a ceremony; any customary observance or practice (as, "No doubt they rose up early to observe The *rite* of May," Shakspere's "Midsummer Night's Dream," iv. 1. 138; "He omitted such empty *rites* as saying 'Yes' or 'Please,'" Arnold Bennett's "Old Wives' Tale," ii. 4); also, a particular form or system of religious or other ceremonial practice (as, "The Admiral rejoiced the hearts of the Huguenots by publicly christening his new-born son after the Genevan *rite*," Besant's "Coligny," viii.; the Roman or the Anglican *rite*; the Scottish *rite* in freemasonry).—**rite′less,** *a.* Without rites or ceremonies: as, *riteless* burial.

ri-tor-nel-lo (rē-tôr-nel′lō), *n.*; pl. *-li* (-lē). [It., dim. of *ritorno,* a return.] In *music*, an instrumental refrain, interlude, or prelude in a vocal work; also, one of the tutti passages in an instrumental concerto.

ri-tour-nelle (rē-tör-nel), *n.* [F.] Same as *ritornello*.

rit-ter (rit′ẽr), *n.*; pl. *ritters*, G. *ritter*. [G., var. of *reiter, rider*: see *reiter*.] A mounted warrior; a knight; also, a member of a lower order of nobility in Germany and Austria.

rit-u-al (rit′ū-al). [L. *ritualis*, < *ritus*, E. *rite*.] **I.** *a.* Of or pertaining to rites (as, *ritual* laws; "As through a zodiac, moves the *ritual* year Of England's Church," Wordsworth's "Ecclesiastical Sonnets," iii. 19); of the nature of, or practised as, a rite or rites (as, a *ritual* dance; *ritual* observances; *ritual* murder, the sacrifice of human beings as a religious rite). **II.** *n.* A form or system of religious or other rites (as, "the English service for the dead, one of the most beautiful and impressive parts of the *ritual* of the church": Scott's "Guy Mannering," xxxvii.); also, a book of rites or ceremonies; specif., in the Roman Catholic Church, a book containing the offices to be used by priests in administering the sacraments and for visitation of the sick, burial of the dead, etc.; also, a ritual proceeding or service (as, "Come . . . And hear the *ritual* of the dead": Tennyson's "In Memoriam," xviii.); also, ritual acts or features collectively, as in religious services; observance of set forms in public worship.—**rit′u-al-ism,** *n.* The study of ritual practices or religious rites; also, adherence to or insistence on ritual (specif. with reference to the Anglican ritualists: as, "*Ritualism* was still [in 1858] unknown by the general provincial public," S. Butler's "Way of All Flesh," xlvii.); fondness for ritual (as, "Perhaps her touch of *ritualism* came from mere love of any form she could make sure of": Howells's "Foregone Conclusion," v.).—**rit′u-al-ist,** *n.* A student of or authority on ritual practices or religious rites; also, one who practises or advocates observance of ritual, as in religious services; specif. [often *cap.*], a member of a branch of the High-church party in the Anglican Church that in the 19th century revived the ritual of the time of Edward VI., insisting particularly upon the eastward position of the celebrant at the eucharist, and the use of vestments, lights, waferbread, incense, etc.—**rit″u-al-is′tic,** *a.* Pertaining to or characteristic of ritualists or ritualism; devoted to ritual.—**rit′u-al-ly,** *adv.*

ri-vage (rī′vāj or riv′āj), *n.* [F., < *rive*, < L. *ripa*, bank, shore.] A bank, shore, or coast: as, "From the green *rivage* many a fall Of diamond rillets musical" (Tennyson's "Recollections of the Arabian Nights," 47). [Archaic.]

ri-val (rī′val). [F. *rival*, < L. *rivalis*, orig. one dwelling by or using the same stream as another, < *rivus*, stream.] **I.** *n.* One who is in pursuit of the same object as another, or strives to equal or outdo another (as, "There were no *rivals*: I had no competitor, none to dispute sovereignty or command with me," Defoe's "Robinson Crusoe," i. 9; "This brilliant youth might be a dangerous *rival* to his sons," Froude's "Cæsar," iv.); a competitor; often, a competitor in love, or a fellow-suitor (as, "Sullen . . . return'd Leolin's rejected *rivals* from their suit": Tennyson's "Aylmer's Field," 493); also, one who is in a position to dispute preëminence or superiority with another (as, a painter without a *rival* in his own field); an equal or peer; anything that will bear comparison with something else. **II.** *a.* Being a rival (as, "my *rival* cousin, who had . . . elbowed me out of my expectations": Irving's "Tales of a Traveler," ii. 9); competing or standing in rivalry (as, *rival* suitors; *rival* business houses or enterprises); made or shown in rivalry (as, "Fair scenes! whereto the Day and Night Make *rival* love," Whittier's "Summer by the Lakeside," ii.; "The steed With *rival* ardour beats the dusty plain," Akenside's "Pleasures of Imagination," i. 471).—

ri′val, *v.*; *-valed* or *-valled*, *-valing* or *-valling.* **I.** *tr.* To compete with in rivalry; strive to equal or outdo; also, to prove to be a worthy rival, or the equal or peer, of (as, he soon *rivaled* the others in skill); equal (something) as if in rivalry (as, "The fame of Archimedes was *rivalled* by Proclus and Anthemius": Gibbon's "Decline and Fall of the Roman Empire," xl.); of things, to bear comparison with, or be a match for (as, "The simple summer silk, of a deep and glowing pink, *rivalled* the colour in her cheeks": W. Churchill's "Modern Chronicle," i. 7). **II.** *intr.* To engage in rivalry; compete (*with*). [Archaic.]—**ri-val′i-ty** (-val′i-ti), *n.* Rivalry. [Now rare.]—**ri′val-less**, *a.* Without a rival. —**ri′val-ry** (-ri), *n.*; pl. *-ries* (-riz). The action, position, or relation of a rival or rivals; competition; emulation; a course of effort to rival another or each other (as, "fruitful strifes and *rivalries* of peace": Tennyson's "Idylls of the King," Dedication, 37).—**ri′val-ship**, *n.* The state or character of a rival; rivalry.

rive (rīv), *v.*; pret. *rived*, pp. *rived* or *riven* (riv′n), ppr. *riving.* [ME. *riven*, from Scand.: cf. Icel. *rīfa*, rive, rend, also E. *rift.*] **I.** *tr.* To tear or rend apart; split; cleave; strike asunder; also, to tear or wrench away; pull or remove with violence; split off; also, fig., to rend, harrow, or distress (the heart, etc.: as, "the anguish and despair that are . . . *riving* thousands of hearts," Mrs. Stowe's "Uncle Tom's Cabin," xlv.). **II.** *intr.* To become rent or split apart; part asunder.

riv-el (riv′l), *v. t.* or *i.*; *-eled* or *-elled*, *-eling* or *-elling.* [AS. *rifelede* (also *gerifod*), wrinkled.] To wrinkle; shrivel. [Archaic or prov.]

riv-en (riv′n), *p. a.* [See *rive.*] Rent or split asunder: as, "It [a tree] stood up, black and *riven*; the trunk, split down the centre, gaped ghastly" (C. Brontë's "Jane Eyre," xxv.).

riv-er[1] (rī′vėr), *n.* One who rives or splits.

riv-er[2] (riv′ėr), *n.* [OF. *rivere, riviere* (F. *rivière*), bank, shore, later river, < ML. *riparia*, prop. fem. of L. *riparius*, belonging to a river-bank or shore, < *ripa*, bank, shore.] A considerable natural stream of water flowing in a definite course or channel (as, the Amazon in South America, the largest *river* in the world; the Hudson *River*); hence, a similar stream of something other than water (as, Phlegethon, the fabled *river* of fire in Hades); any abundant stream or copious flow (lit. or fig.: as, *rivers* of lava; *rivers* of blood; "the full-flowing *river* of speech," Tennyson's "Œnone," 67); also, a stream figured to separate life from death, and

River-crab (*Thelphusa depressa*).

to be crossed in dying (often called 'the river of death,' or 'the dark river'); [*cap.*] in *astron.*, the southern constellation Eridanus.—**riv′er-ain** (-ān), *a.* [F.] Riverine; riparian.—**riv′er=crab**, *n.* Any of the fresh-water crabs of the family *Thelphusidæ*, inhabiting rivers and lakes, as *Thelphusa depressa*, of southern Europe, much esteemed for food. See cut in preceding column.—**riv′ered**, *a.* Having a river or rivers.—**riv′er=hog**, *n.* Any of the African wild hogs constituting the genus *Potamochœrus*; also, the capibara.—**riv′er=horse**, *n.* The hippopotamus. —**riv′er-ine** (-in or -īn), *a.* Of or pertaining to a river; situated or dwelling beside a river; riparian.—

Red River-hog (*Potamochœrus penicillatus*).

riv′er-less, *a.* Without rivers: as, a *riverless* region.— **riv′er-side.** **I.** *n.* The bank of a river: as, "She had . . . come up to a little flat on the *riverside* not far from Westminster" (Galsworthy's "Patrician," ii. 6). **II.** *a.* On the bank of a river: as, "a *riverside* hotel at Maidenhead" (H. G. Wells's "Men Like Gods," i. 1).—**riv′er=weed**, *n.* Any of the small submerged fresh-water plants constituting the genus *Podostemon*, as the North American species *P. ceratophyllum.*

riv-et (riv′et), *n.* [OF. F. *rivet*, a rivet, < *river*, fix, rivet; origin uncertain.] A metal pin or bolt for passing through holes in two or more plates or pieces to hold them together, usually made with a head at one end, the other end being hammered into a head after insertion.—**riv′et**, *v. t.*; *-eted, -eting.* To fasten with a rivet or rivets; also, to hammer or spread out the end of (a pin, etc.), in order to form a head and secure something; clinch; also, in fig. use, to fasten or fix firmly (as, "Equally unable to fly or to advance, he stood *riveted* to the spot," Cooper's "Prairie," xix.; "All the precepts of father Ignatius were *riveted* in her faithful memory," Cooper's "Prairie," xxvi.); fix (the eye, mind, etc.) intently on something (as, "Their eyes were *riveted* on each other," Mrs. H. Ward's "Robert Elsmere," xviii.; "The wizard . . . directed him to *rivet* his attention to these marks," Kinglake's "Eothen," xviii.); hold (the eye or attention) firmly (as, "His face *riveted* the eye," C. Brontë's "Jane Eyre," xxix.; "a . . . man, whose fate it was . . . to *rivet* and indeed fatigue the attention of civilized mankind," Charnwood's "Theodore Roosevelt," i.); hold the attention of (a person).—**riv′et-er**, *n.*—**riv′et-ing**, *n.* The act or work of one who rivets; also, a fastening made with rivets.

Rivets and Hand-riveting Tools. — *a*, round-headed rivets, one riveted and the other inserted ready for riveting; *b*, round-headed rivet, with washer *d* under the riveted end; *b*, riveting-hammer; *c*, chisel, for trimming off the ends of rivets before riveting.

ri-vière (rē-vyär′), *n.* [F., lit. 'river': see *river*[2].] A necklace of diamonds or other gems, esp. in more than one string.

riv-u-let (riv′ū-let), *n.* [It. *rivoletto*, dim. of *rivolo*, < L. *rivulus*, streamlet, dim. of *rivus*, stream.] A small stream; a streamlet; a brook: as, "A fine stream, fed by *rivulets* and mountain springs, pours through the valley" (Irving's "Captain Bonneville," vi.).

rix=dol-lar (riks′dol″är), *n.* [For D. *rijksdaalder*, Dan. *rigsdaler*, G. *reichsthaler*, etc., lit. 'dollar of the kingdom.'] Any of various silver coins of Holland, Denmark, Germany, etc., now mostly disused, varying in value but commonly worth about $1. See *rigsdaler.*

Ro (rō), *n.* An artificial language for international use, devised by Rev. Edward P. Foster, of Marietta, Ohio, and later of Waverly, West Virginia, first put forth in 1906.

roach[1] (rōch), *n.*; pl. *roaches* or (esp. collectively) *roach.* [OF. *roche, roque*; origin uncertain.] A European fresh-water fish, *Rutilus rutilus*, of the carp family; also, any of various similar American fishes, as certain fresh-water sunfishes.

roach² (rōch), *n.* Same as *cockroach*.

road (rōd), *n.* [AS. *rād*, a riding, raid, journey, course, < *rīdan*, E. *ride*.]

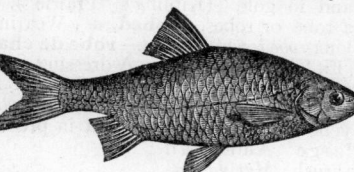

Roach (*Rutilus rutilus*).

The act of riding on horseback†; a ride or journey on horseback† (as, "At last, with easy *roads*, he came to Leicester": Shakspere's "Henry VIII.," iv. 2. 17); also, a hostile incursion of mounted men†, a raid†, or a foray†; also, a protected place near the shore where ships may ride at anchor, or a roadstead (often in *pl.*: as, Hampton *Roads*; "The ship continued a fortnight in the *roads*, repairing some damage which had been done her in the late storm," Defoe's "Captain Singleton," i.); also, an open way for passage or travel, usually one wide enough for vehicles, and esp. one between distant points; a highway; also, a railroad (U. S.); also, any path or way (as, "in climes beyond the solar *road*": Gray's "Progress of Poesy," ii. 2); fig., a way or course (as, "There is one *road* To peace and that is truth," Shelley's "Julian and Maddalo," 347; the *road* to ruin); also, a way or course taken or pursued (as, their *road* lay through an open country; a thing in one's *road*; get out of my *road*); also, the usual course or practice (as,"Nothing goes down with her, that is quaint, irregular, or out of the *road* of common sympathy": Lamb's "Mackery End").—**on the road,** traveling; esp., traveling on business, as to make sales (as, "He had been *on the road* for Birkinshaws for several years": Arnold Bennett's "Old Wives' Tale," i. 4); also on tour, as a theatrical company (as, "I was Blanche Wilmot, *on the road* for ten years,—never got a show in London": Arnold Bennett's "The Old Adam," vi.).—**to take to the road,** to become a highwayman: as, "Martin . . . could not supply his occasions any other way than by *taking to the road*" (Smollett's "Humphry Clinker," June 11).—**road-a-bil-i-ty** (rō-dạ-bil'i-ti), *n.* Ability to hold or keep to the road, and to travel over roads of all kinds easily and smoothly: said of automobiles.—**road′=a″gent,** *n.* A highwayman. [U. S.]—**road′=bed,** *n.* The bed or foundation of a railroad, on which the ties, rails, etc., rest; also, the whole material (foundation, etc.) of an ordinary road.—**road′=cart,** *n.* A light, two-wheeled, one-horse vehicle.—**road′=horse,** *n.* A horse used on the road; a roadster.—**road′=house,** *n.* An inn or hotel at the roadside, used as a place of refreshment by those traveling along the road by carriage, automobile, etc.—**road′less,** *a.* Without roads: as, "the *roadless* plain" (W. H. Hudson's "Far Away and Long Ago," x.).—**road′=met″al,** *n.* Broken stone, etc., used for making roads.—**road′=run″ner,** *n.* The chaparral-cock.—**road′side,** *n.* The side or border of the road; the wayside.—**road′stead** (-sted), *n.* A protected place near the shore where ships may conveniently ride at anchor: as, "the inner *roadstead* of the Port of Toulon" (J. Conrad's "Rover," i.).—**road′ster** (-stėr), *n.* A horse for riding or driving on the road; also, a person accustomed to traveling on the road; a coach-driver; also, a bicycle or the like for road use; also, an automobile of the open-car type for use on ordinary roads, and having a single seat for two or more persons.—**road′way,** *n.* A way used as a road; a road; also, the central part of a road, used by vehicles, etc.

roam (rōm), *v.* [ME. *romen*; origin uncertain: cf. *ramble*.] **I.** *intr.* To walk, go, or travel about without fixed purpose or direction; ramble; wander; rove: as, "Round the wide world in banishment we *roam*" (Dryden's tr. Virgil's "Pastorals," i. 3); "Herds of horses and cattle *roamed* at will over the plain" (G. W. Cable's "Bonaventure," i. 1); "Her eyes were *roaming* about the room" (Hawthorne's "Twice-Told Tales," The Gentle Boy). **II.** *tr.* To wander over or through: as, "to *roam* the moors" (C. Brontë's "Jane Eyre," xxx.).—**roam,** *n.* The act of roaming; a ramble: as, "The boundless space, thro' which these rovers take Their restless *roam*" (Young's "Night Thoughts," ix. 1173).—**roam′er,** *n.*

roan¹ (rōn). [F. *rouan*; origin unknown.] **I.** *a.* Of a sorrel, chestnut, or bay color sprinkled with gray or white: used chiefly of horses: as, "a *roan*-gelding" (Butler's "Hudibras," ii. 1). **II.** *n.* A roan horse or other animal (as, "Beaufort's . . . brougham, drawn by a big *roan*": Mrs. Wharton's "Age of Innocence," ix.); also, a roan coloring.

roan² (rōn), *n.* [Origin uncertain.] A soft, flexible leather made of sheepskin, much used in bookbinding, and often made in imitation of morocco.

roar (rōr), *v.* [AS. *rārian* = MLG. *rāren* = OHG. *rēren* (G. *röhren*), bellow, roar; prob. imit.] **I.** *intr.* To utter a loud, deep cry, esp. of excitement, distress, or anger (as, "You . . . *roared* for mercy": Shakspere's "1 Henry IV.," ii. 4. 286); behave in a noisy or riotous manner†; laugh loudly or boisterously; also, to cry with a loud, deep sound, as a lion, a bull, etc.; also, to make a loud noise or din, as a horse (see *roaring*, *n.*); also, to make a loud noise in breathing, as thunder, cannon, waves, wind, etc. (as, "Loud *roar'd* the blast," Coleridge's "Ancient Mariner," i.; "I know a ruin on a hill, Where once there *roared* a great wind-mill," Eden Phillpotts's "Cherry-Stones," The Old Mill); resound with noise, as a place (as, "Confounded Chaos *roar'd*": Milton's "Paradise Lost," vi. 871). **II.** *tr.* To utter loudly (as, "The song, *roared* out in grand chorus by the midshipmen, was caught up . . . by the marines": Marryat's "King's Own," xxxviii.); also, to express by roaring (as, "The audience . . . *roared* its amusement": Arnold Bennett's "Great Man," xvii.); also, to bring, put, make, etc., by roaring (as, to *roar* one's self hoarse).—**roar,** *n.* The sound of roaring; a loud, deep cry, as of a person or persons, or of a lion or other large animal; a loud outburst of laughter; a loud noise, as of thunder, waves, etc. (as, "the *roar* of the surf breaking upon the beach": H. Melville's "Typee," xxxiii.).—**roar′er,** *n.* One who or that which roars; esp., a horse affected with roaring.—**roar′ing,** *n.* The act of one who or that which roars; a loud, deep cry or sound; in *vet. science*, a disease of horses causing them to make a loud noise in breathing under exertion.—**roar′ing,** *p. a.* That roars, as a person or an animal, or as thunder, waves, etc.; extremely loud, as sound; characterized by loud noise or din, or by noisy revelry (as, "The pelt of hoofs Out in the *roaring* darkness told Of Herne the Hunter," Henley's "Arabian Nights' Entertainments"; "He kept . . . a *roaring* table at which were collected the loose livers of the country round," Irving's "Tales of a Traveler," ii. 9); behaving in a noisy or riotous manner (archaic: as, "the wild life of a *roaring* cavalier," Scott's "Woodstock," viii.); brisk or highly successful, as trade (colloq.).—**the roaring forties,** a notably rough part of the northern Atlantic Ocean, between 40° and 50° north latitude; also, the region between 40° and 50° south latitude in the southern Atlantic, the Indian Ocean, and the Pacific Ocean.—**roar′ing-ly,** *adv.*

roast (rōst), *v.* [OF. *rostir* (F. *rôtir*), roast; from Teut.] **I.** *tr.* To prepare (meat or other food) for eating by direct exposure to dry heat, as on a spit; bake (meat or other food), as in an oven; brown by exposure to heat, as coffee; hence, to heat (any material) more or less violently; heat (an ore, etc.) with access of air, as to cause oxidation; also, to torture by exposure to flame or heat (as, "The Lord make thee like Zedekiah and like Ahab, whom the king of Babylon *roasted* in the fire": Jer. xxix. 22); heat to excess, as a person; sometimes, to warm (one's self, etc.) at a hot fire (as, "Making a roaring fire, I *roasted* myself for half an hour, turning like a duck on a spit": Weir Mitchell's "Hugh Wynne," xviii.); also, to ridicule or criticize severely or mercilessly (colloq.). **II.** *intr.* To roast meat, etc.; also, to undergo the process of becoming roasted (as, "a pair of chickens *roasting* at the fire": C. Brontë's "Jane Eyre," xxxviii.).—**roast,** *a.* [Obs. pp. of *roast*, *v.*] Roasted, as meat.—**roast,** *n.* Something that is roasted, esp. a piece of roast meat; a piece of meat for roasting; also, roast meat (as, "On holidays an egg, or two at most; But her ambition never reach'd to *roast*": Dryden's "Cock and the Fox," 36); also, the act or an operation of roasting; also, a ridiculing or criticizing severely (colloq.).—**to rule the roast.** See under *rule*, *v. t.*—**roast′er,** *n.* One who or that which roasts; a contrivance for roasting something; also, a pig or other animal or article fit for roasting.—**roast′ing,** *p. a.* That roasts; also, exceedingly hot; scorching.

rob (rob), *v. t.*; *robbed, robbing*. [OF. *rober*, rob; from Teut. (cf. G. *rauben*), and akin to E. *reave*.]   To deprive of something by unlawful force or violence; commit robbery upon (see *robbery*); deprive of something legally belonging or due; in general, to deprive of something unjustly or injuriously (as, "The shock of the explosion had *robbed* him of speech and movement": J. Conrad's "Rescue," vi. 7); also, to plunder or rifle (a house, etc.: as, "one that is likely to be executed for *robbing* a church," Shakspere's "Henry V.," iii. 6. 106); also, to carry off unlawfully, or steal (as, "a sideboard *robbed* out of the carved work of a church in the Low Countries," Thackeray's "Pendennis," i. 37: now rare).— **to rob Peter to pay Paul**, to take something away from one in order to pay another; incur a new debt in order to discharge an old one; sacrifice one interest for the advancement of another.—**rob**, *v. i.*   To commit or practise robbery.

ro-ba-lo (rō′ba̤-lō or rob′a̤-), *n.*; pl. *-los* (-lōz). [Sp. *róbalo.*] Any of the acanthopterygian marine fishes constituting the family *Centropomidæ*, esp. *Centropomus undecimalis*, a valuable food-fish of West Indian and adjacent waters.

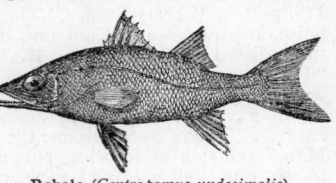

Robalo (*Centropomus undecimalis*).

rob-and (rob′and), *n.* [Cf. D. *raband* (< *ra*, yard, + *band*, band), Dan. *raabaand*.] *Naut.*, a short piece of spun yarn or other material, used to secure a sail to a yard, gaff, or the like.

rob-ber (rob′ėr), *n.*   One who robs, or commits robbery.— **rob′ber=fly**, *n.*   Any of the swift, often large, predatory flies constituting the family *Asilidæ*, given to preying upon other insects.—**rob′ber-y** (-i), *n.*; pl. *-ies* (-iz).   The action or practice, or an instance, of robbing; specif., in *law*, the felonious taking of the property of another from his person or from his immediate presence, against his will, by violence or intimidation.

Robber-fly (*Asilus sericeus*), natural size.

rob-bin (rob′in), *n.*   Same as *roband*.

robe (rōb), *n.* [OF. F. *robe*, orig. spoil, booty, < *rober*, E. *rob*.]   A long, loose or flowing gown or outer garment worn by men or women, esp. for formal or stately occasions; an official vestment, as of a judge; a woman's gown, esp. of the more elaborate kind; a portion of material suitably shaped and ornamented, for making a woman's gown; an infant's long dress; any long, loose garment (as, a bath-*robe*); fig., any vesture or covering (as, "Another [cottage] wore A close-set *robe* of jasmine sown with stars": Tennyson's "Aylmer's Field," 158); also, a piece of fur, cloth, knitted work, etc., used as a covering or wrap (as, a buffalo-*robe*; a lap-*robe*).—**the long robe**, fig., the legal or sometimes the clerical profession: as, "If the profits respectively gained by military and clerical speculators in that day should be compared, the disadvantage would hardly be found to lie with those of *the long robe*" (Motley's "Dutch Republic," ii. 1). —**the robe**, fig., the legal profession: as, "rich advocates and other gentlemen of *the robe*" (Motley's "Dutch Republic," ii. 1).—**the short robe**, fig., the military profession.—**robe**, *v.*; *robed, robing*. **I.** *tr.*   To clothe or invest in a robe or robes; dress or apparel; array: as, "He returned in a few minutes *robed* in loose garments from Kashmir" (F. M. Crawford's "Mr. Isaacs,"

European Robin (*Erythacus rubecula*).

viii.); "I behold My faithful seasons *robe* the year in silver and in gold" (Kipling's "Prairie"). **II.** *intr.*   To put on a robe or robes.—**robed**, *a.*   Wearing a robe or robes: as, long-*robed*; white-*robed*.—**robe de chambre** (rob dė shän̈br). [F., 'chamber robe.']   A dressing-gown.

rob-in (rob′in), *n.* [OF. *Robin*, for *Robert*, Robert, man's name.]   A small European bird, *Erythacus rubecula*, with a yellowish-red breast (see cut in preceding column); also, a large American thrush, *Merula migratoria*, with chestnut-red under parts; also, any of various related or similar birds.

Rob-in Good-fel-low (rob′in gŭd′fel″ō).   The sprite or fairy Puck, or Hobgoblin: as, "That shrewd and knavish sprite Call'd *Robin Goodfellow*" (Shakspere's "Midsummer Night's Dream," ii. 1. 34).   See *puck*.

American Robin (*Merula migratoria*).

rob-in=red-breast (rob′in-red′brest), *n.*   The European or the American robin.

ro-ble (rō′blä), *n.* [Sp., oak, < L. *robur*: see *roborant*.]   A Californian oak, *Quercus lobata*.

rob-o-rant (rob′ō-ṛant). [L. *roborans* (-ant-), ppr. of *roborare*, strengthen, < *robur* (*robor-*), strength, orig. a hard kind of oak.] **I.** *a.*   Strengthening. **II.** *n.*   A roborant medicine; a tonic.

Rob-ot (rub′ut), *n.*   [Name of a kind of manufactured man (worker) in the fantastic melodrama "R. U. R." ("Rossum's Universal Robots") (1920, Eng. tr. 1923), by Karel Čapek, Czechish dramatist.] [Also *l. c.*]   A manufactured or machine-made man; a merely mechanical being.

ro-bur-ite (rō′bėr-īt), *n.* [L. *robur*, strength.]   An explosive containing a nitro derivative of benzene and ammonium nitrate.

ro-bust (rō-bust′), *a.* [L. *robustus*, oaken, hard, strong, < *robur*: see *roborant*.]   Strong and healthy, hardy, or vigorous (as, "He is pretty well advanced in years, but hale, *robust*, and florid," Smollett's "Humphry Clinker," after Oct. 4; "his *robust* and vigorous frame," J. F. Kirk's "Charles the Bold," iv. 1); strongly or stoutly built; sturdy; sound, as health; also, suited to or requiring bodily strength or endurance (as, "*robust* and warlike exercises": G. P. R. James's "Hist. of Charlemagne," i.); also, rough, rude, or boisterous (as, "Romp-loving miss Is hauled about in gallantry *robust*": Thomson's "Seasons," Autumn, 529); also, fig., of a naturally strong or vigorous kind (as, a *robust* mind or thinker); not easily affected or overcome (as, a *robust* ignorance); rudely vigorous (as, "the *robuster* sorts of evangelism": Galsworthy's "Saint's Progress," iii. 5).

ro-bus-tious (rō-bus′chus), *a.* [From *robust*.]   Robust, strong, or stout, as persons, the body, etc.; also, big, thick, or heavy (as, "These redundant locks, *Robustious* to no purpose": Milton's "Samson Agonistes," 569); also, rough, rude, or boisterous (as, "The old hall . . . echoed to bursts of *robustious* fox-hunting merriment": Irving's "Tales of a Traveler," i. 2); violent or severe, as storms, etc. [Now chiefly archaic or humorous.]—**ro-bus′tious-ly**, *adv.*—**ro-bus′tious-ness**, *n.*

ro-bust-ly (rō-bust′li), *adv.*   In a robust manner; strongly; stoutly.—**ro-bust′ness**, *n.*

roc (rok), *n.* [Ar. and Pers. *rukh*.]   A fabulous bird of enormous size and strength, famous in Arabian mythology.

roc-am-bole (rok′am-bōl), *n.* [F., = G. *rockenbolle*; origin uncertain.]   A European liliaceous plant, *Allium scorodoprasum*, used like garlic.

Ro-chelle (rō-shel′) **pow′der.** [From La *Rochelle*, seaport in western France.]   Same as *Seidlitz powder.*—**Ro-chelle′ salt.**   A tartrate of sodium and potassium, used as a laxative.

roche mou-ton-née (rosh mö-to-nā); pl. *roches mouton-nées* (rosh mö-*to*-nā). [F., 'rock shaped like a sheep.'] A knob of rock rounded and smoothed by glacial action; a sheep-back.

roch-et (roch′et), *n.* [OF. F. *rochet*, dim. < OHG. *roc* (G. *rock*) = AS. *rocc*, outer garment.] A mantle or cloak (obs. or prov.); *eccles.*, a vestment of linen or lawn, resembling a surplice, worn esp. by bishops and abbots.

rock[1] (rok), *n.* [OF. *roke*, *roque*, also *roche* (F. *roche*), = ML. *rocca*; origin unknown.] A large mass of stone form-ing an eminence, cliff, or the like; a large detached mass of stone, as a boulder; a stone of any size (prov. or colloq.); also, stone in the mass (as, "As strong As shore of *rock*": Shakspere's "Henry VIII.," i. 1. 158); also, fig., something resembling or suggesting a rock; a source of peril or disaster, as with allusion to shipwreck (as, the *rock* on which they split; on the *rocks*, see phrase below); a firm foundation or support, or a means of safety (as, "The Lord is my *rock*": 2 Sam. xxii. 2); a piece of money (usually in *pl.*: as, "Old man's piling up the *rocks*," Kipling's "Captains Courageous," i.: slang, U. S.); also, a kind of hard sweetmeat, variously flavored; also, the striped-bass; also, the rock-pigeon, *Columba livia*; in *geol.*, mineral matter of various composi-tion, consolidated or unconsolidated, assembled in masses or considerable quantities in nature, as by the action of fire ('igneous rock') or of water ('aqueous rock'); a particular kind of such matter.—**on the rocks**, on rocks, as a ship-wrecked vessel; fig., into or in a state of disaster or ruin; destitute of funds, or 'broke' (colloq.: as, "You're *on the rocks* . . . Let me give you a hundred to set you right," L. Merrick's "Conrad in Quest of His Youth," xvii.).—**rock**[1], *v. t.* To throw stones at; stone. [Colloq.]

rock[2] (rok), *v.* [Late AS. *roccian*, rock: cf. Dan. *rokke*, move, shake, Icel. *rykkja*, G. *rücken*, pull.] **I.** *tr.* To move or sway to and fro or from side to side as on a support (as, to *rock* a cradle or a rocking-chair; to *rock* a boat in the water; "A slight breeze *rocked* the tops of the pine-trees," Bret Harte's "Outcasts of Poker Flat"); move to and fro in a cradle, chair, the arms, etc., esp. gently and soothingly (as, "Go, *rock* the little wood-bird in his nest": Bryant's "Eve-ning Wind"); put (to sleep, etc.) with swaying movements, as in a cradle (as, "a young French mother . . . darning socks by a cradle, and *rocking* her baby to sleep with her foot": Du Maurier's "Trilby," vi.); fig., to lull in security, hope, etc.; also, to move or sway powerfully with emotion, etc. (as, "She beheld the Theatre Royal . . . *rocked* by enthusiasm for Mr. Christopher Tatham's melodrama": L. Merrick's "Position of Peggy Harper," ii. 5); in *engraving*, to abrade the surface of (a copperplate, etc.) with a cradle or rocker. **II.** *intr.* To move or sway to and fro or from side to side (as, the trees *rock* in the wind; "The ruins of the ancient church seemed actually to *rock* and threaten to fall," Scott's "Castle Dangerous," xx.); fig., to be moved or swayed powerfully with emotion, etc. (as, "His soul *rocked* with passion": W. Churchill's "Coniston," i. 6).—**rock**[2], *n.* A rocking movement.

rock[3] (rok), *n.* [ME. *roc* = OHG. *rocco* (G. *rocken*) = Icel. *rokkr*.] A distaff. [Archaic or prov.]

rock-a-way (rok′a-wā″), *n.* [Appar. < *Rockaway*, place-name.] A light four-wheeled carriage with two (or three) seats, a standing top, and open sides which may be closed by curtains; later, a kind of four-wheeled carriage with a door on each side, com-bining features of the preceding vehicle and the coupé.

Rockaway (in 2d sense).

rock=bass (rok′bȧs′), *n.* An American food-fish, *Am-bloplites rupestris*, common in the northern lakes and rivers (see cut in next column); also, the striped-bass; also, a ser-ranoid fish, *Paralabrax clathratus*, found off the coast of California.

rock=bound (rok′bound), *a.* Hemmed in by rocks; rocky: as, "a stern and *rock-bound* coast" (Mrs. Hemans's "Landing of the Pilgrim Fathers").

rock=can-dy (rok′kan′di), *n.* Sugar in hard cohering crystals of con-siderable size.

rock=crys-tal (rok′kris′tal),*n.* Transparent quartz, esp. of the colorless kind.

rock=dove (rok′duv), *n.* A rock-pigeon.

rock-er (rok′ér). *n.* One who or that which rocks; one of the curved pieces on which a cradle or a rocking-chair rocks; a rocking-chair; any of various devices that operate with a rocking motion; in *engraving*, a cradle (engravers' tool).—**rock′er=arm**, *n.* In *mach.*, an arm-like piece attached to a rock-shaft.

rock-er-y (rok′ér-i), *n.*; pl. *-ies* (-iz). A mound built of fragments of rock with earth interspersed, for the growing of ferns or other plants.

rock-et[1] (rok′et), *n.* [It. *rocchetto*, lit. 'bobbin,' dim. < *rocca*, distaff; from Teut., and akin to E. *rock*[3].] A cylin-drical tube containing combustibles which on being ignited liberate gases whose action propels the tube through the air: used for pyrotechnic effect, signaling, carrying a life-line, etc.—**rock′et**[1], *v. i.* To move like a rocket (as, "with a sudden movement strikes the can from the Saint's hand and sends it *rocketing* across stage": Synge's "Well of the Saints," iii.); of game-birds, to fly straight up rapidly when flushed.

rock-et[2] (rok′et), *n.* [F. *roquette*, < It. *ruchetta*, dim. of *ruca*, < L. *eruca*, kind of colewort.] Orig., a European bras-sicaceous plant, *Eruca sativa*, eaten as a salad; now, any of various other (chiefly brassicaceous) plants, esp. *Hesperis matronalis*, a garden-plant with white, pinkish, or purple flowers which are fra-grant after dark.

rock-fish (rok′fish), *n.* Any of various fishes found about rocks; specif., the striped-bass, *Roccus lineatus*; any fish of the marine family *Scorpænidæ*, certain of which are common food-fishes of the Pacific coast of North America; any of several groupers, as a bonasi, *Myctero-perca venenosa*; a killifish, *Fundulus majalis*, of the Atlantic coast of the U. S.

rock=gar-den (rok′gär″dn), *n.* A garden on rocky ground or among rocks, for the growing of alpine or other plants: as, "It [a house] lay about two-thirds up be-tween the main road and cliffs, and had a *rock-garden*" (Galsworthy's "Saint's Progress," iv. 2).

rock-i-ness (rok′i-nes), *n.* The state of being rocky.

rock-ing=chair (rok′ing-chãr), *n.* A chair mounted on rock-ers, or on springs, so as to permit of rocking back and forth.

rock-ing=horse (rok′ing-hôrs), *n.* A toy horse, as of wood, mounted on rock-ers, on which chil-dren play at riding.

rock-ing=stone (rok′ing-stōn), *n.* Same as *logan-stone.*

rock=oil (rok′oil′), *n.* Petroleum.

rock=pi-geon (rok′pij″ọn), *n.* A wild pigeon, *Columba livia*, of the Old World, of which many domesticated pigeons are varie-ties; also, a sand-grouse.

rock=ribbed (rok′ribd), *a.* Having ribs or ridges of rock (as, "The hills *Rock-ribbed* and ancient as the sun": Bryant's

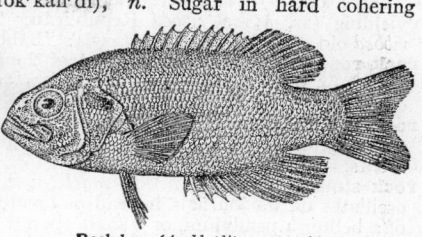

Rock-bass (*Ambloplites rupestris*).

Inflorescence of Rocket (*Hesperis ma-tronalis*).

Rock-pigeon (*Columba livia*).

"Thanatopsis"); fig., exceedingly strong or firm, or un-yielding (as, a *rock-ribbed* Republican; "Jake is a *rock-ribbed* old die-hard," Sinclair Lewis's "Babbitt," xxxii.).

rock=rose (rok′rōz), n. Any plant of the genus *Cistus* (see *cistus*) or some allied genus, as *Helianthemum*; any cistaceous plant.

rock=salt (rok′sâlt′), n. Common salt (sodium chloride) occurring native in solid form; salt in large crystals or fragments.

rock=shaft (rok′shȧft), n. In *mach.*, a shaft that rocks or oscillates on its journals instead of revolving, as the shaft of a bell or a pendulum, or a shaft operating the valves of a steam-engine.

rock=tem-ple (rok′tem′pl), n. A temple cut out of solid rock, as in India.

rock=weed (rok′-wēd), n. Any of various seaweeds (genera *Fucus*, *Ascophyllum*, etc.) common on rocks exposed at low tide: as, "a wagon-load of live lobsters, packed in *rock-weed*" (Hawthorne's "Twice-Told Tales," The Village Uncle).

Rock-temple. — An interior at Ellora, India.

rock-work (rok′-wêrk), n. A natural mass of rocks; also, stonework or masonry left or made rough to imitate natural rock; also, a rockery.

rock-y[1] (rok′i), a.; compar. *rockier*, superl. *rockiest*. Full of or abounding in rocks; consisting of rock; rock-like; fig., firm as a rock; of the heart, etc., hard or unfeeling.

rock-y[2] (rok′i), a. Inclined to rock, tottering, or shaky (as, "Don't upset the cruet, it's *rocky*": L. Merrick's "Position of Peggy Harper," i. 5); hence, unpleasantly uncertain (as, "Things look a bit *rocky*, but we must hope for the best": L. Merrick's "Conrad in Quest of His Youth," xiv.); also, out of sorts physically. [Colloq. or slang.]

ro-co-co (rō-kō′kō). [F., < *rocaille*, decorative work made of or representing pebbles, shells, etc., < *roc*, masc. of *roche*, rock: see *rock*[1].] **I.** n. A style of architectural and other decoration prevalent in France and elsewhere in the first half of the 18th century, combining shellwork, scrolls, foliage, etc., with florid and bizarre or tasteless effect. Also fig. **II.** a. In the style called rococo; tastelessly or clumsily florid; also, antiquated.

rod (rod), n. [Late AS. *rodd*, appar. the same word as *rōd*, E. *rood*.] A straight, slender shoot or stem of any woody plant, whether growing upon or cut from the plant (as, "So thick a swarm Of flow'rs, like flies clothing her slender *rods*, That scarce a leaf appears," Cowper's "Task," vi. 166; "Jacob took him *rods* of green poplar, and of the hazel and chestnut tree," Gen. xxx. 37);

Rococo. — An interior in Schloss Bruchsal, Baden, Germany.

hence, fig., in Biblical use, an offshoot or branch of a family; a scion; a tribe; in general, a stick, wand, staff, bar, shaft, or the like, of wood, metal, or other material; a piece, part, or structure of elongated slender form; specif., a stick, or a bundle of sticks or switches bound together, used as an instrument of punishment (as, "Theodoric . . . declaring, that the child who had trembled at a *rod*, would never dare to look upon a sword": Gibbon's "Decline and Fall of the Roman Empire," xxxix.); hence, a means of punishment, or punishment or chastisement; a stick, wand, or staff carried in the hand, as a shepherd's stick; an enchanter's wand; a divining-rod; a wand or staff carried as a symbol of office, authority, power, etc. (as, "hands, that the *rod* of empire might have sway'd": Gray's "Elegy," xii.); a long, light, tapering, elastic pole used in angling, or a fishing-rod; a stick used to measure with; also, a linear measure of 5½ yards or 16½ feet; a perch or pole; also, a square perch or pole (30¼ square yards).—**a rod in pickle**, fig., punishment in reserve: as, to have *a rod in pickle* for a person.

rode (rōd). Preterit of *ride*.

ro-dent (rō′dent). [L. *rodens* (rodent-), ppr. of *rodere*, gnaw.] **I.** a. Gnawing; belonging or pertaining to the *Rodentia*, an order of gnawing or nibbling mammals, including the hares, rats, mice, squirrels, etc. **II.** n. A rodent mammal.

ro-de-o (rō-dā′ō), n. [Sp., a going round, < *rodear*, go round, < L. *rota*, a wheel.] A round-up of cattle. [Western U. S.]

rod-man (rod′man), n.; pl. *-men*. The man whose duty it is to carry the leveling-rod in surveying.

rod-o-mon-tade (rod″ō-mon-tād′), n. [F., < It. *rodomontata*, < *Rodomonte*, name of a boastful Moorish king in Ariosto's "Orlando Furioso."] Vainglorious boasting (as, "A day it was, of boast, swagger, and *rodomontade*": Irving's "Captain Bonneville," vii.); inflated, bragging speech; a piece of vainglorious boasting or bragging, or of pretentious, blustering talk (as, "He . . . almost raised mobs by his insolent *rodomontades*": Macaulay's "Hist. of Eng.," vi.). —**rod″o-mon-tade′**, v. i.; *-taded*, *-tading*. To indulge in rodomontade; boast; brag; talk big.

rod-ster (rod′ster), n. One who fishes with a rod.

roe[1] (rō), n. [ME. *rowe*, also *rowne*, akin to MLG. *roge*, *rogen*, OHG. *rogo*, G. *rogen*, Icel. *hrogn*, roe.] The mass of eggs, or spawn, within the ovarian membrane of the female fish ('hard roe'); also, the milt or sperm of the male fish ('soft roe'); also, the spawn of various crustaceans, as the coral of the lobster.

roe[2] (rō), n.; pl. *roes* or (esp. collectively) *roe*. [AS. *rā*, *rāha*, = D. *ree* = G. *reh* = Icel. *rā*, roe.] The roe-deer.—**roe′buck**, n. A male roe-deer; less properly, any roe-deer.—**roe′=deer**, n. [AS. *rāhdēor*.] A small, agile old-world deer, *Capreolus capræa*.

Roent-gen (rent′gen), etc. See *Röntgen*, etc.

ro-ga-tion (rō-gā′shon), n. [L. *rogatio*(n-), < *rogare*, ask.] In *Rom. antiq.*, the proposing by the consuls or tribunes of a law to be passed by the people; also, a law so proposed; *eccles.*, solemn supplication, esp. as

Roebuck.

chanted during procession on the three days ('Rogation Days') before Ascension Day (usually in *pl.*).

rog-a-to-ry (rog′a-tō-ri), a. [= F. *rogatoire*, < ML. *rogatorius*, < L. *rogare*, ask.] Pertaining to asking or requesting: as, a *rogatory* commission (a commission with request to act,

---

fat, fāte, fär, fâll, ȧsk, fāre; net, mē, hėr; pin, pīne; not, nōte, mȯve, nȯr; up, lūte, pȧll; oi, oil; ou, out; (lightened) aviȧry, ēlect, agōny, intŏ, ūnite; (obscured) errȧnt, operä, ardȧnt, actȯr, natüre; ch, chip; g, go; th, thin; ᴛʜ, then; y, you;

issued by one judge or court to another, as in a foreign country, as for the examination of witnesses or the ascertaining of facts).

rogue (rōg), *n.* [Origin obscure; first in slang of 16th century vagabonds.] A vagabond or vagrant (archaic: as, "To hovel thee with swine, and *rogues* forlorn, In short and musty straw," Shakspere's "King Lear," iv. 7. 39); also, a dishonest person, or knave (as, "the *rogue* that cheats": Pope's "Moral Essays," iii. 238); a rascal or scamp (sometimes used with humorous tolerance: as, "The jovial *rogues* had the run of my lord's kitchen, stables, cellars, and cigar-boxes," Thackeray's "Newcomes," lix.); also, a playfully mischievous person (often applied to a child or young person); also, an elephant or other animal of savage disposition and solitary life (also 'rogue elephant,' 'rogue hippopotamus,' etc.).—**rogues' gallery,** a collection of portraits of criminals, as at police headquarters.—**rogues' march,** derisive music played to accompany the expulsion of a person from a regiment, community, etc.—**rogue,** *v.*; rogued, roguing. **I.** *intr.* To live or act like a rogue; play the rogue. **II.** *tr.* To practise roguery upon; cheat.—**ro-guer-y** (rō′gėr-i), *n.*; pl. *-ies* (-iz). Conduct characteristic of rogues; rascality; a rascally act; playful mischief.—**ro′guish** (-gish), *a.* Pertaining to, characteristic of, or acting like a rogue; knavish or rascally (as, "These are the ideas of a *roguish* merchant rather than a statesman": H. G. Wells's "Outline of History," xxxviii. § 3); playfully mischievous (as, a *roguish* smile or glance).—**ro′guish-ly,** *adv.*—**ro′guish-ness,** *n.*

roil (roil), *v. t.* [Origin uncertain.] To render (water, etc.) turbid by stirring up sediment (as, "I had . . . made a well of clear gray water, where I could dip up a pailful without it": Thoreau's "Walden," xii.); fig., to disturb or disquiet; disturb the temper of, irritate, or vex. Cf. *rile.*—**roil,** *n.* A roiling, stirring up, or agitation, as of water.—**roil′y,** *a.* Turbid; muddy.

rois-ter (rois′tėr), *n.* [OF. *ruistre, ruiste,* rude, violent (F. *rustre,* a boor), < L. *rusticus,* E. *rustic.*] A swaggering bully; a riotous fellow; a noisy reveler. [Archaic.]—**rois′-ter,** *v. i.* To act in a swaggering, boisterous, or uproarious manner; revel noisily or without restraint: used esp. in *roistering,* *p. a.*: as, "these genial, *roistering* dare-devils [soldiers], who . . . are supposed to carry their lives in their hands" (Du Maurier's "Trilby," iv.); "troops of *roistering* graduates trotting about arm in arm, and singing" (Tarkington's "Gentleman from Indiana," iii.).—**rois′-ter-er,** *n.*—**rois′ter-ing-ly,** *adv.*

roke (rōk), *n.* [ME. *roke;* akin to E. *reek.*] Smoke; mist; drizzling rain. [Now prov. Eng. and Sc.]—**rok-y** (rō′ki), *a.* Misty; foggy; damp: as, "In a *roky* hollow, belling, heard The hounds of Mark" (Tennyson's "Last Tournament," 501). [Now prov. Eng. and Sc.]

Ro-land (rō′land), *n.* [OF., = It. *Orlando.*] One of Charlemagne's legendary paladins, famous for his prowess and death in the battle of Roncesvalles (778), and also for his five days' combat with Oliver, another paladin, in which neither gained the advantage, whence the expression 'a Roland for an Oliver' (used of one thing deemed a full match or equivalent for another).

rôle (rōl), *n.* [F., roll (as of paper), transcription of an actor's part: see *roll, n.*] The part or character which an actor presents in a play; hence, in general, a part or function sustained by any one (as, "She was proud and happy in her *rôle* of benefactor": Arnold Bennett's "Hilda Lessways," iii. 2).

roll (rōl), *v.* [OF. *roller* (F. *rouler*), < ML. *rotulare,* roll, revolve, < L. *rotula, rotulus,* little wheel, dim. of *rota,* wheel.] **I.** *intr.* To move along a surface by turning over and over, as a ball or a wheel; move or be moved on wheels, as a vehicle or its occupants (as, "A carriage was *rolling* on the more westerly road down to Steignton," G. Meredith's "Lord Ormont and His Aminta," xvi.; "Oliver found himself . . . in a travelling-carriage *rolling* fast towards his native town," Dickens's "Oliver Twist," li.); also, to go along or proceed easily or smoothly, as if with a revolving movement; move onward or advance in a stream or with an undulating motion, as water, waves, or smoke; extend in undulations, as land (as, "Around me the prairie was *rolling* in steep swells and pitches": Parkman's "Oregon Trail," vii.); also, to move

(on, etc.) or pass (*away,* etc.), as time; move (*round*) as in a cycle, as seasons; also, to perform a periodical revolution in an orbit, as a heavenly body (as, "Philosophy . . . Sees planetary wonders smoothly *roll* Round other systems under her control": Cowper's "Charity," 317); also, to flow or run (often with *on*), as sound, language, etc.; continue with or have a deep, prolonged sound, as thunder, etc. (as, "All day long the noise of battle *roll'd*": Tennyson's "Passing of Arthur," 170); trill, as a bird; also, to turn over, or over and over, as a person or animal lying down (as, "Kittenlike he [a leopard] *roll'd* And paw'd about her sandal": Tennyson's "Princess," iii. 165); sometimes, to turn one's self over and over in something specified; fig., to luxuriate or abound (in wealth, money, etc.); also, to become piled (*up*) as if by turning over and over (as, "The deeper his inquiries went, the stronger the evidence *rolled* up": Bok's "Americanization of Edward Bok," xxix.); also, to turn round in different directions, as the eyes in their sockets; revolve upon an axis, as a heavenly body; also, to sway or rock from side to side, as a ship (opposed to *pitch*); sail with a rolling motion; walk with a rolling or swaying gait; also, to form into a roll, or curl up upon itself; admit of being rolled up, as a material; also, to spread out from being rolled up (with *out,* etc.); also, to spread out as under a roller. **II.** *tr.* To cause to move along a surface by turning over and over, as a cask, a ball, or a hoop; move along on wheels or rollers; convey in a wheeled vehicle; also, to drive, impel, or cause to flow onward with a sweeping motion (as, "The tide was coming in, *rolling* quite big waves on to the rocks": W. H. Hudson's "Far Away and Long Ago," vii.); also, to utter or give forth with a full, flowing, continuous sound (as, "Pen . . . *rolled* out these verses in his rich sweet voice," Thackeray's "Pendennis," i. 16; "The organ *rolled* out hymns and anthems," W. Churchill's "Inside of the Cup," v.); trill (as, to *roll* one's r's); beat (a drum) with rapid, continuous strokes; also, to turn over, or over and over (as, "In the house of Aphrah *roll* thyself in the dust": Micah, i. 10); pile (*up*) by or as if by turning over and over (as, to *roll* up a reserve for future use); turn round in different directions, as the eyes (as, "to go *rolling* your eyes about in the frivolous, irresponsible way affected by some people": Besant's "All Sorts and Conditions of Men," i.); cause to revolve upon an axis; also, to turn over or revolve in thought or consideration (as, "*Rolling* in his mind Old waifs of rhyme": Tennyson's "Brook," 198); also, to cause to sway or rock from side to side, as a ship; also, to wrap round an axis or round upon itself (as, "Mrs. Poyser . . . *rolling* and unrolling her knitting": George Eliot's "Adam Bede," xxxii.); form into a roll, ball, or the like; coil, wind, or fold (*up:* as, "He *rolled* up his dressing-gown for a pillow," Eden Phillpotts's "Grey Room," ii.); make by forming a roll (as, to *roll* a cigarette); also, to spread out from being rolled up (with *out,* etc.); also, wrap, infold, or envelop, as in some covering (as, "Gerard *rolled* himself in the bed-clothes": Reade's "Cloister and the Hearth," lxii.); also, to spread out, level, compact, or the like, with a rolling-pin, cylinder, etc.; operate upon with a roller or rollers.—**roll,** *n.* [Partly < OF. *rolle* (F. *rôle*), < ML. *rotulus,* roll (of parchment, etc.), record, list, L. little wheel (see *roll, v.*); partly < *roll, v.*] A piece of parchment, paper, or the like, as for writing, etc., which is or may be rolled up; a scroll; esp., such a piece inscribed with some formal or official record; hence, a list, register, or catalogue (as, "Happy king, whose name The brightest shines in all the *rolls* of fame!" Pope's tr. Homer's "Odyssey," viii.); a list containing the names of the persons belonging to any company, class, society, etc.; a muster-roll; such a list as read to ascertain if all named in it are present (as, to call the *roll*); also, anything rolled up in cylindrical form; a number of papers or the like rolled up together (as, "a large wrinkled *roll* of yellowish sea charts," H. Melville's "Moby-Dick," xliv.; "He pulled out a *roll* of bills as if to count them," Kipling's "Captains Courageous," i.); a quantity of cloth, wall-paper, or the like, rolled up in cylindrical form (often forming a definite measure); a cylindrical twist of tobacco, or tobacco in this form; a case consisting of a piece of leather or other material, sometimes with pockets, which when closed is rolled up about its contents; specif., some article of cookery which is rolled up; meat rolled up and cooked;

---

thin cake spread with jelly or the like and rolled up; a small cake of bread, orig. and still often rolled or doubled on itself before baking; also, a quantity of some other material, as butter, made into cylindrical or rounded form; a cylindrical or rounded mass of something (as, "her tiny hands, with . . . *rolls* of aged fat encircling the wrist like ivory bracelets": Mrs. Wharton's "Age of Innocence," iv.); in general, some article of cylindrical or rounded form, as a molding; also, a cylindrical piece upon which something is rolled along to facilitate moving; a cylinder upon which something is rolled up; a roller with which something is spread out, leveled, crushed, compacted, or the like; a revolving wheel-like tool used by bookbinders for impressing and gilding book-covers; also, the act or an act of rolling; undulation of surface (as, the *roll* of a prairie); sonorous or rhythmical flow of words; a deep, prolonged sound, as of thunder, etc. (as, "the deep *roll* of a breaking wave": Conan Doyle's "Micah Clarke," i.); the continuous sound of a drum rapidly beaten; the trill of certain birds; a rolling motion, as of a ship; a rolling or swaying gait.

Bookbinders' Roll.— *a*, roll, pivoted to furcate handle *b* at *c*.

roll-a-ble (rōl′la-bl), *a.* Capable of being rolled.

roll=call (rōl′kål), *n.* The calling over of a roll or list of names, as of soldiers or students, to find out who are present; also, a military signal for this, as one given by a drum.

roll-er (rōl′lėr), *n.* One who or that which rolls; a cylinder, wheel, or the like, upon which something is rolled along; a cylindrical body, revolving on a fixed axis, employed to facilitate the movement of something passed over or around it, as a cylindrical piece of wood over which a roller-towel is passed; a cylindrical body upon which cloth or other material is rolled up; a cylindrical body for rolling over something to be spread out, leveled, crushed, compacted, impressed, inked, etc.; a similar body revolving on a fixed axis, or one of a set of such bodies, forming part of some machine or apparatus, and operating on something to be similarly acted upon; any of various other revolving cylindrical bodies, as the barrel of a music-box; a bandage, as for surgical use, esp. one in the form of a roll, to be unrolled as used; a long, swelling wave advancing steadily (as, "the southern *rollers* tumbling in over the reefs like cascades": H. Kingsley's "Geoffry Hamlyn," xxxiii.); in *ornith.*, a variety of canary-bird, remarkable for rolling or trilling; a variety of tumbler pigeon; any of the old-world non-passerine birds constituting the family *Coraciidæ*, esp. the common species *Coracias garrula.* —

roll′er=bear′ing, *n.* In *mach.*, a bearing in which the shaft or journal turns upon a number of steel rollers running in an annular track. —**roll′ered,** *a.* Mounted on or having rollers. —**roll′er=skate′,** *n.* A

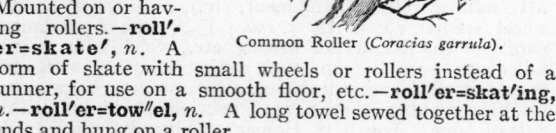

Common Roller (*Coracias garrula*).

form of skate with small wheels or rollers instead of a runner, for use on a smooth floor, etc. —**roll′er=skat′ing,** *n.* —**roll′er=tow″el,** *n.* A long towel sewed together at the ends and hung on a roller.

rol-lick (rol′ik), *v. i.* [Origin uncertain: cf. *roll* and *frolic*.] To move or act in a careless, frolicsome manner; behave or enjoy one's self in a free, hearty, gay or jovial way: used esp. in *rollicking*, *p. a.*: as, "He was a joyous, spirited, jolly, *rollicking* young fellow" (Mrs. Stowe's "Oldtown Folks," v.); "A giddy and *rollicking* company were gathered at Judge Thatcher's" (Mark Twain's "Tom Sawyer," xxix.). —**rol′lick-er,** *n.* —**rol′lick-ing-ly,** *adv.*

roll-ing (rō′ling), *n.* The action, motion, or sound of anything that rolls. —**roll′ing,** *p. a.* That rolls (in any sense); rising and falling in gentle slopes, as land; producing a deep, continuous sound; rocking or swaying from side to side; turning or folding over, as a collar. —**rolling circle,** a circle which, by rolling, generates a cycloid, epicycloid, or other

curve. —**rolling hitch,** a kind of hitch which is made round a spar or the like with the end of a rope, and which jams when the rope is pulled. —**rolling stone,** fig., a person who is ever roving from place to place: from the proverb "a rolling stone gathers no moss." —**roll′ing=mill,** *n.* A mill or establishment where (heated) iron or other metal is rolled into sheets, bars, or the like; also, a machine or set of rollers for rolling out or shaping metal, etc. —**roll′ing=pin,** *n.* A cylinder of wood or other material for rolling out dough, etc. —**roll′ing=stock,** *n.* The wheeled vehicles of a railroad, including locomotives, cars, etc.

roll-way (rōl′wā), *n.* A way or place on which things are rolled, or moved on rollers; esp., a place where logs are rolled into a stream for transportation; also, a pile of logs at the side of a stream awaiting transportation.

ro-ly=po-ly (rō′li-pō′li). [A riming formation based on *roll*.] **I.** *n.*; pl. *-lies* (-liz). A sheet of paste spread with jam, fruit, or the like, rolled up and cooked as a pudding; also, a roly-poly person or thing. **II.** *a.* Short and plumply round, as a person, a young animal, etc.: as, "His wife, Jinny, was a fat, *roly-poly* little body" (Mrs. Stowe's "Oldtown Folks," v.).

Ro-ma-ic (rō-mā′ik). [Gr. Ῥωμαϊκός, Roman, Latin, hence, later, pertaining to the Eastern Empire, Greek.] **I.** *a.* Being, or pertaining to, the vernacular language of modern Greece. **II.** *n.* The Romaic language.

ro-ma-i-ka (rō-mā′i-kä), *n.* [NGr. ρωμαϊκή: cf. *Romaic*.] A popular dance of modern Greece.

ro-maine (rō-mān′) **let′tuce.** [F. *romaine*, fem. of *romain*, E. *Roman*.] A variety of Cos lettuce with long, comparatively narrow, crisp leaves. —**ro-maine′ sal′ad.** Romaine lettuce served as a salad.

Ro-man (rō′man), *a.* [OF. F. *romain*, < L. *Romanus*, < *Roma*, Rome.] Of or pertaining to Rome, ancient or modern, or its inhabitants; specif., of language, etc., Latin; sometimes, of a kind or character regarded as typical of the ancient Romans (as, "the ancient *Roman* honour": Shakspere's "Merchant of Venice," iii. 2. 297); also, of or pertaining to the Roman Catholic Church; also [usually *l.c.*], designating or pertaining to the style of printing-types most commonly used in modern books, etc., of which the text of this dictionary is an example (cf. *Italic*, *a.*). —**Roman architecture,** the architecture of the ancient Romans, characterized by admirable development and application of

Roman Architecture. — Section of the Pantheon, illustrating the use of vaulting, arches, and columns.

the round arch and vault, and of stone and esp. brick masonry of all varieties, and by adoption of the Greek orders in general as mere exterior ornaments. —**Roman candle,** a kind of firework consisting of a tube which sends out a shower of sparks and a succession of balls of fire. —**Roman Catholic,** of or pertaining to the Roman Catholic Church; as a noun, a member of the Roman Catholic Church. —**Roman Catholic Church,** the Christian church of which the Pope, or Bishop of Rome, is the supreme head. —**Roman Empire,** the empire of ancient Rome, dating from 27 B.C., and divided into the Eastern Empire and the Western Empire in A.D. 395; also, a later empire, as that of Charlemagne, regarded as a restoration or continuation of this ancient empire or of one of its branches. See *Eastern Empire*, under *eastern*, *a.*; *Holy Roman Empire*, under *holy*, *a.*; *Western Empire*, under *western*, *a.* —**Roman law,** the system of jurisprudence elaborated by the ancient Romans, forming the basis of civil law in many countries. —**Roman nose,** a nose having a prominent upper part or bridge. —**Roman numeral,** a numeral in the Roman system of notation, of which the common symbols are I (for 1), V (5), X (10), L (50), C (100), D (500), M (1,000).—**Roman punch,** a lemon water-ice flavored with rum or other spirit.—**Roman snail,** a European edible snail, *Helix pomatia,* formerly supposed to have been introduced into Britain by the Romans.—**Ro′man,** *n.* A native, inhabitant, or citizen of ancient or modern Rome; also, a member of the Roman Catholic Church; also [usually *l.c.*], roman type or letters; a roman type, letter, or character; also, *pl.* [*cap.*], the book of the New Testament called in full "The Epistle of Paul the Apostle to the Romans."

ro-mance[1] (rō-mans′). [OF. *romans,* a romance or tale, orig. one in the vulgar tongue (French, as opposed to Latin),

Roman Snail (*Helix pomatia*), natural size.

also the vulgar tongue (F. *roman,* a novel), < ML. *Romanice,* adv., in the vulgar tongue of France (derived from the Romans), < L. *Romanicus,* E. *Romanic.*] **I.** *n.* A medieval tale, orig. one in verse (and in some Romance dialect), treating of heroic personages or events (as, the Arthurian *romances,* the *romances* of Alexander; the *romances* of Amadis of Gaul); hence, in general, a tale depicting heroic or marvelous achievements, colorful events or scenes, chivalrous devotion, unusual experiences, or other matters of a kind to appeal to the imagination; a tale or novel dealing less with real or familiar life than with extraordinary adventures, fortunes, or occurrences or with imaginary or ideal conditions; romantic literature (as, "I soon found . . . that the world in reality was very different from what it appeared in poetry and *romance*": R. Graves's "Spiritual Quixote," iii. 10); the world, life, or conditions depicted in such literature (as, "Lady of the Mere, Sole-sitting by the shores of old *romance,*" Wordsworth's "Poems on the Naming of Places," iv. 38; the atmosphere of *romance*); romantic character or quality (as, "This thing [lighting of river] has knocked the *romance* out of piloting": Mark Twain's "Life on the Mississippi," xxviii.); romantic spirit or sentiment (as, "You have no *romance* in you," G. B. Shaw's "Man and Superman," iii.; "of an ugliness to chill and kill *romance,* and scatter young love's dream," Du Maurier's "Trilby," i.); a romantic affair or experience, as a love-affair (as, "Miss Ailie had her *romance*": Barrie's "Sentimental Tommy," xiv.); also, a made-up story, or a statement proceeding wholly or chiefly from the imagination; fanciful or extravagant invention or exaggeration (as, "This knight was indeede a valiant gentleman, but not a little given to *romance* when he spake of himselfe": Evelyn's "Diary," Sept. 6, 1651); also [*cap.*], the group of dialects or languages of southern Europe, including the French, Provençal, Spanish, Portuguese, Italian, Rhæto-Romanic, etc., descended from the Latin. **II.** *a.* [*cap.*] Belonging or pertaining to the group of languages called Romance; composed in or using some language of this group.—**ro-mance′**[1], *v. i.;* -manced, -mancing. To invent or relate romances; indulge in fanciful or extravagant stories; also, to think or talk romantically (as, "That I am a '*romancing* chit of a girl' is a mere conjecture on your part: I never *romanced* to you": C. Brontë's "Shirley," xxiii.).

ro-mance[2] (rō-mans′), *n.* [F. *romance,* < Sp. *romance,* kind of poem, ballad, = OF. *romans,* E. *romance*[1].] In *Spanish lit.,* a short epic narrative poem, or historical ballad; later, a short lyric poem; in *music,* a short, simple melody, vocal or instrumental, of tender character.

ro-man-cer (rō-man′sėr), *n.* A writer of romance; also, one who invents false or extravagant stories.

Ro-man-esque (rō-man-esk′). [See -*esque*.] **I.** *a.* Of languages, etc., Romance; also, noting or pertaining to the early medieval style of art and ornament developed in western Europe from that of the later Roman Empire; noting or pertaining to the style of architecture which, developing from that of the later Roman Empire (cf. *Roman architecture*), prevailed in western Europe until the middle of the

12th century (cf. *Gothic, a.*), being characterized esp. by the round arch and vault. **II.** *n.* The Romance group of languages; also, the Romanesque style of art or architecture.

Romanesque Architecture. — Great doorway of the abbey church of Vézelay, France, 12th century.

Ro-man-ic (rō-man′ik), *a.* [L. *Romanicus,* < *Romanus,* E. *Roman.*] Derived from the Romans, or from Latin; of languages, etc., Romance.

Ro-man-ism (rō′man-izm), *n.* [See *Roman.*] The spirit or institutions of ancient Rome; also, the polity, doctrines, etc., of the Roman Catholic Church.—**Ro′man-ist,** *n.* One versed in Roman institutions, law, etc.; also, a member of the Roman Catholic Church.—**Ro-man-is′tic,** *a.*—**Ro′man-ize,** *v.;* -ized, -izing. **I.** *tr.* To make Roman in character; also, to render Roman Catholic. **II.** *intr.* To follow Roman practices; also, to conform to Roman Catholic doctrine, etc.; become Roman Catholic.—**Ro″man-i-za′tion** (-i-zā′shọn), *n.*

Ro-mansh (rō-mansh′), *a.* and *n.* [Native *romansch, rumansch.*] Same as *Rhæto-Romanic.*

ro-mant (rō-mänt′), *n.* See *romaunt.*

ro-man-tic (rō-man′tik). [F. *romantique,* < *roman,* OF. *romant, romans,* E. *romance*[1].] **I.** *a.* Of, pertaining to, or of the nature of romances or romance; also, characteristic or suggestive of the world of romance (as, a *romantic* quest; *romantic* devotion; "a *romantic* visage, wistful, full of sad subtleties," Arnold Bennett's "Hilda Lessways," ii. 3; "I have never heard a more *romantic* story," W. H. Hudson's "Purple Land," xvi.); of a kind to appeal to the imagination; looking like a place in romance (as, "deep and *romantic* glens," H. Melville's "Typee," iii.; "Scarborough . . . is *romantic,* from its situation along a cliff that overhangs the sea," Smollett's "Humphry Clinker," July 4); also, proper to romance rather than to real or practical life (as, *romantic* ideas; *romantic* motives or projects); fanciful, unpractical, or quixotic; also, imbued with or dominated by the ideas, spirit, or sentiment prevailing in romance (as, a *romantic* school-girl; "This kind of person is not nearly so sensitive as my *romantic* Henry supposes," Watts-Dunton's "Aylwin," ii. 11; "a . . . dark-eyed maiden, with a *romantic* imagination," Lever's "Harry Lorrequer," xxxiii.); also, imaginary, fictitious, or fabulous (obs. or rare); also, of or pertaining to a style of literature and art characterized by freedom of treatment, subordination of form to matter, imagination, picturesqueness, etc. (opposed to *classical*). **II.** *n.* *Pl.,* romantic ideas, ways, etc.; also, *sing.,* a romantic person; specif., a romanticist.—**ro-man′-ti-cal,** *a.* Romantic. [Archaic.]—**ro-man′ti-cal-ly,** *adv.* —**ro-man′ti-cism** (-ti-sizm), *n.* Romantic spirit or tendency; specif., the romantic style or movement in literature and art, or adherence to its principles (as contrasted with *classicism*).—**ro-man′ti-cist** (-sist), *n.* An adherent of romanticism in literature or art.—**ro-man′ti-cize** (-sīz), *v.;* -cized, -cizing. **I.** *tr.* To make romantic; invest with a romantic character. **II.** *intr.* To be romantic; act, talk, or write in a romantic manner.

Rom-a-ny (rom′a-ni). [Gipsy *Romani,* fem. and pl. of *Romano,* adj. < *Rom,* Gipsy, *rom,* man, husband.] **I.** *n.;* pl. -nies (-niz). A Gipsy (as, "Dulverton Revels . . . afforded to every true *Romany* many opportunities for gain":

Whyte-Melville's "Katerfelto," xxi.); also, the language of the Gipsies (as, "to . . . speak *Romany*": Borrow's "Romany Rye," x.). **II.** *a.* Belonging or pertaining to the Gipsies: as, "And the *Romany* lass to the *Romany* lad By the tie of a roving breed" (Kipling's "Gipsy Trail"); "the wildest *Romany* beliefs and superstitions" (Watts-Dunton's "Aylwin," i. 6).

ro-man-za (rō-man′zä), *n.* [It.] In *music*, same as *romance*[2].

ro-maunt (rō-mânt′), *n.* [For *romant*, < OF. *romant*, var. of *romans*, E. *romance*[1].] A romance, or romantic poem or tale: as, "The *Romaunt* of the Rose" (title of Chaucer's translation of a French allegorical poem of the 13th century). [Archaic.]

Rom-ish (rō′mish), *a.* Of or pertaining to Rome†; now, of or pertaining to Rome as the center of the Roman Catholic Church, or Roman Catholic (usually depreciatory).

romp (romp), *v. i.* [Var. of *ramp*[1].] To play or frolic in a lively or boisterous manner (as, "boys and girls *romping* together and running after one another," S. Butler's "Way of all Flesh," lxxxiv.; "*romping* under the mistletoe," Macaulay's "Hist. of Eng.," ii.); also, to run or go rapidly and without effort, as in racing.—**romp**, *n.* A romping frolic (as, "that Uncle Bill should start a full-fledged *romp* among the girls and children": Mrs. Stowe's "Oldtown Folks," xxvii.); also, a romping person, esp. a girl (as, "a brisk young creature of seventeen, who was of the order of *romps* or tomboys": Thackeray's "Newcomes," xxxii.).—**romp′ers**, *n. pl.* A loose outer garment combining a waist and knickerbockers, worn by young children, as at play.—**romp′ish**, *a.* Given to romping.—**romp′ish-ness**, *n.*

ron-ca-dor (rong-ka-dôr′), *n.* [Sp., < *roncar*, < LL. *rhonchare*, snore.] Any of several carnivorous fishes (family *Sciænidæ*) of the Pacific coast of North America, as *Roncador stearnsi*, a large food-fish.

ron-deau (ron′dō), *n.*; pl. -*deaux* (-dōz). [F.: see *rondel*.] A short poem of fixed form,

Roncador (*Roncador stearnsi*).

consisting of thirteen (or ten) lines on two rimes and having the opening words or word used in two places as an unrimed refrain.

ron-del (ron′del), *n.* [OF. *rondel* (F. *rondeau*), dim. < *rond*, round: see *roundel*.] A short poem of fixed form, consisting usually of fourteen lines on two rimes, of which four are made up of the initial couplet repeated in the middle and at the end (the second line of the couplet sometimes being omitted at the end).

ron-de-let (ron′dę-let), *n.* [OF., dim. of *rondel*: see *rondel*.] A short poem of fixed form, consisting of five lines on two rimes, and having the opening words or word used after the second and fifth lines as an unrimed refrain.

ron-do (ron′dō), *n.*; pl. -*dos* (-dōz). [It., < F. *rondeau*: see *rondeau, rondel*.] In *music*, a work or movement having one principal subject to which return is made after the introduction of each subordinate theme.

ron-dure (ron′dūr), *n.* [F. *rondeur*, < *rond*, E. *round*[2].] A round, circle, or round space (as, "All things rare That heaven's air in this huge *rondure* hems": Shakspere's "Sonnets," xxi.); also, roundness, or rounded form. [Archaic and poetic.]

ron-ion†, ron-yon† (run′yon), *n.* [Origin obscure: cf. F. *rogne*, scab, mange.] A term of abuse for a woman. See Shakspere's "Macbeth," i. 3. 6.

ron-quil (rong′kil), *n.* [Sp. *ronquillo*, slightly hoarse, dim. of *ronco*, hoarse.] An acanthopterygian fish, *Ronquilus jordani* (family *Bathymasteridæ*), of the northern Pacific Ocean; also, any fish of the same family.

Rönt-gen (rėnt′gen, commonly rent′-), *a.* Pertaining to the German physicist Wilhelm Konrad Röntgen (1845–1923), or [also *l.c.*] to the Röntgen rays, which were discovered by him. —**Röntgen rays**, the highly penetrative rays formed when cathode rays impinge upon a solid body (as the wall of a

vacuum-tube), supposedly consisting of pulses in the ether: used to photograph or examine objects (as bones) through substances (as flesh) opaque to ordinary light, and also to treat disease. Also called X-rays.—**rönt′gen-ize**, *v. t.*; -*ized*, -*izing*. To subject to the action of the Röntgen rays.—**rönt′gen-o-gram** (-ō-gram), *n.* [See -*gram*.] A picture or photograph taken by means of the Röntgen rays. Also **rönt′gen-o-graph** (-gräf).—**rönt-gen-og′ra-phy** (-og′ra-fi), *n.* [See -*graphy*.] The art of producing röntgenograms.—**rönt″gen-o-graph′ic** (-graf′ik), *a.*—**rönt″gen-o-graph′i-cal-ly**, *adv.*—**rönt-gen-ol′o-gy** (-ol′ō-ji), *n.* [See -*logy*.] The study of the Röntgen rays.—**rönt″gen-o-log′i-cal** (-loj′i-kal), *a.*—**rönt″gen-o-log′i-cal-ly**, *adv.*—**rönt-gen-ol′o-gist**, *n.*—**rönt′gen-o-scope** (-skōp), *n.* [See -*scope*.] An apparatus for examining parts of the body by means of the Röntgen rays.—**rönt-gen-os′co-py** (-os′kō-pi), *n.* [See -*scopy*.] The art of examining opaque bodies by means of the Röntgen rays.—**rönt″gen-o-scop′ic** (-skop′ik), *a.*—**rönt″gen-o-scop′i-cal-ly**, *adv.*—**rönt″gen-o-ther′a-py** (-ther′a-pi), *n.* Treatment of disease by means of the Röntgen rays.—**rönt″gen-o-ther′a-pist**, *n.*

Röntgen Ray Photograph (of a foot in a shoe).

ron-yon† (run′yon), *n.* See *ronion*.

rood (rōd), *n.* [AS. *rōd*, cross, rod or pole (cf. *seglrōd*, sailyard), measure of land, = OS. *ruoda* = D. *roede* = G. *rute*, rod: cf. *rod*.] A cross as used in crucifixion, specif. the cross on which Christ died (archaic: as, "Good hope I have Of help from Him that died upon the *rood*," W. Morris's "Earthly Paradise," April, The Proud King; "No, by the holy *rood*," Shakspere's "Richard III.," iv. 4. 165); also, a crucifix, esp. a large crucifix at the entrance to the choir or chancel of a medieval church, often supported on a roodbeam or rood-screen; also, a linear measure of 1 rod or 5½ yards, but varying locally from 6 to 8 yards; also, a square measure of 40 square rods, also one of 1 square rod, both varying locally.—**rood′-beam**, *n.* A beam extending across the entrance to the choir or chancel of a church to support the rood, and usually forming the head of a rood-screen.—**rood′-loft**, *n.* In a church, a loft or gallery over a rood-screen.—**rood′-screen**, *n.* A screen, often of elaborate design and properly surmounted by a rood, separating the nave from the choir or chancel of a church.—**rood′-stee″ple**, *n.* A steeple or spire built over the position of the rood at the entrance to the choir, or over the intersection of the nave and transepts, of a cruciform church.—**rood′-tow″er**, *n.* A tower in the position of a rood-steeple.

roof (rōf), *n.* [AS. *hrōf*, roof, top, = D. *roef*, cover, cabin, = Icel. *hrōf*, shed.] The external

Rood-steeple. — Cathedral of Notre Dame, Paris, from the southeast.

upper covering of a house or other building; hence, a house (as, "Lady Clara Pulleyn could bear his tyranny no longer, and had left his *roof*": Thackeray's "Newcomes," lviii.); fig., the highest part or summit of something; also, some thing or part which in form or position resembles the roof of a house, as the top of a carriage or car, or the upper part of the mouth or of a cavern or subterranean excavation.—**roof**, *v. t.* To provide or cover with or as with a roof (as, "rude log cabins, *roofed* with bark," Bancroft's "Hist. of the U. S." Amer. Revolution, i. 5; "a long narrow canal-boat, *roofed* with tarpaulins," Arnold Bennett's "Clayhanger," i. 1); also, to form a roof over (something: as, "Huge fir-trees *roofed* it [a gully] in, and made a night of noon," Kingsley's "Hereward," ii.).— **roofed,** *a.* Having a roof or roofs: as, flat-*roofed*; "green-*roofed* Mecca of the many gates" (Dunsany's "Tents of the Arabs," ii.).—**roof′er,** *n.* One who makes or repairs roofs.— **roof′=gar″den,** *n.* A garden on the flat roof of a house or other building; the top, or top story, of a building, ornamented with plants, etc., and fitted up for restaurant, theatrical, or other like purposes.—**roof′ing,** *n.* The act of covering with a roof; also, material used or suitable for roofs; also, a roof.—**roof′less,** *a.* Having no roof; also, without the shelter of a house.—**roof′=tree,** *n.* The ridge-pole of a roof; hence, a roof as affording a shelter and home to those beneath it (as, "Their vile cabal had driven him from his happy home, and sent him in his old age to seek shelter under a strange *roof-tree*": Trollope's "Warden," xx.).— **roof′=truss,** *n.* A truss in the framework of a roof, as the triangular one formed by two principal rafters and a tie-beam.

rook[1] (rŭk), *n.* [OF. F. *roc*; from Pers.] In *chess*, a piece having the power to move in a right line forward, backward, or sidewise, but not diagonally, over any number of un-occupied squares; a castle.

rook[2] (rŭk), *n.* [AS. *hróc* = D. *roek* = OHG. *hruoh* = Icel. *hrōkr*, rook; prob. imit.: cf. Goth. *hrūkjan*, to crow.] A black European bird, *Corvus frugilegus*, of the crow family, of a gregarious disposition and given to nesting in colonies in trees about buildings (as, "The *rooks* cawed peacefully in the old elms": Galsworthy's "Country House," i. 2);

Rook.

also, a sharper, as at cards or dice; a swindler; also, a simpleton† or gull†.—**rook**[2], *v. t.* To cheat; fleece; swindle. —**rook′er-y** (-ér-i), *n.*; pl. *-ies* (-iz). A place where rooks congregate to breed; a colony of rooks; hence, a breeding-place or colony of other birds or animals, as penguins, seals, etc.; also, a cluster of mean tenements inhabited by people of the lowest class; any mean, crowded tenement-house.— **rook′ie, rook′y,** *n.*; pl. *-ies* (-iz). A raw recruit, orig. in the army, and hence in any service: as, "The men that fought at Minden, they was *rookies* in their time" (Kipling's "Men That Fought at Minden"). [Slang.]—**rook′y,** *a.* Abounding in or frequented by rooks: as, "Light thickens; and the crow Makes wing to the *rooky* wood" (Shakspere's "Macbeth," iii. 2. 51).

room (rōm), *n.* [AS. *rūm* = D. *ruim* = G. *raum* = Icel. *rūm* = Goth. *rūms*, room.] Space, or extent of space, great or small, occupied by or available for something (as, the desk takes up too much *room*; much stowed in little *room*; there is plenty of *room* for all; "I am pent up in frouzy lodgings, where there is not *room* enough to swing a cat," Smollett's "Humphry Clinker," June 8); sufficient or convenient space (as, there is *room* for one more in the car; "Lady Ambrose . . . made *room* for him at her side," Mallock's "New Republic," iii. 4; "Stand back; *room*; bear back," Shakspere's "Julius Cæsar," iii. 2. 172); fig., opportunity or scope for or to do something (as, *room* for improvement, doubt, or originality; "During a week there is *room* for much reflection," Marryat's "Mr. Midshipman Easy," vii.; "My improvement was greater than my condition in life afforded *room* to expect," Godwin's "Caleb Williams," i.); also, a portion of space within a building or other structure or place, separated by walls or partitions from other parts (as, a dining-*room*; a school-*room*; an engine-*room* in a factory; a greenroom in a theater; a state-*room* on a

ship or a railroad-train; "I worked to make this *room* or cave spacious enough to accommodate me as a warehouse," Defoe's "Robinson Crusoe," i. 5); a chamber; a compartment; *pl.*, lodgings or quarters, as in a house or building (as, "He travelled . . . to Islington, the locality of Mrs. Harper's latest '*rooms*,'" L. Merrick's "Position of Peggy Harper," iii. 1; the *rooms* of a society); *sing.*, the persons present in a room of a building or the like (as, "The *room* applauded vociferously": Thackeray's "Newcomes," i.); also, a particular place or station, as for a person or thing†; a place or seat in a theater†; a position†, post†, or office†; also, place or stead (as, "I wish you would cast about for some creditable body to be with me in her *room*," Smollett's "Humphry Clinker," Nov. 20; "The inland counties had not been required to furnish ships, or money in the *room* of ships," Macaulay's "Essays," Nugent's Hampden: now chiefly British).—**room,** *v.* **I.** *intr.* To occupy a room or rooms; lodge; share a room or rooms with another. [U. S.] **II.** *tr.* To provide (lodgers or guests) with a room or rooms. [U. S.]—**room-age** (rö′māj), *n.* Room or space afforded.—**roomed,** *a.* Having a room or rooms: as, one-roomed.—**room′er,** *n.* A lodger. [U. S.]—**room′ful** (-fúl), *n.*; pl. *-fuls.* An amount or number sufficient to fill a room: as, "a *roomful* of books" (G. B. Shaw's "Arms and the Man," i.).—**room′i-ly,** *adv.* In a roomy manner. —**room′i-ness,** *n.*—**room′=mate,** *n.* One who shares a room with another or others.—**room′y,** *a.*; compar. *roomier,* superl. *roomiest.* Affording ample room; spacious; large: as, "He lived . . . in a great *roomy* log-house" (Roosevelt's "Winning of the West," i. 3); "a sort of family canoe—wide and *roomy*" (H. Melville's "Omoo," lxxi.).

roop, roop-y (röp, rö′pi). See *roup*[2], *roupy.*

roor-back (rör′bak), *n.* [Also *roorbach*; from an instance of the kind in 1844, when an alleged extract from an account of travel by a Baron Roorback was published as an attack upon James K. Polk, then a candidate for the Presidency.] A false and more or less damaging report circulated for political effect. [U. S.]

roose (röz), *v. t.*; *roosed, roosing.* [From Scand.] To praise; commend highly; flatter. [Now Sc. and north. Eng.]

roost (röst), *n.* [AS. *hróst.*] A perch upon which domestic fowls rest at night; a house or place for fowls to roost in (as, a hen-*roost*); any place used by a bird or an assemblage of birds for roosting or customary rest; hence, in general, a place used for sitting, resting, or staying (as, "Sam Lawson . . . continued to occupy his usual *roost* in the chimney-corner," Mrs. Stowe's "Oldtown Folks," xxvi.; a robbers' *roost*); also, an assemblage of birds roosting together.—**to rule the roost.** See *to rule the roast,* under *rule, v. t.*—**roost,** *v. i.* To take rest on a roost, perch, or other support or place, as birds; hence, to sit or rest as if on a perch (as, "A dozen young imps were *roosting*, like so many crows, on the verandah railings": Mrs. Stowe's "Uncle Tom's Cabin," vi.); settle or stay, esp. for the night (as, "Pedlars, gipsies, tinkers . . . *roosted* about his outhouses, or harboured in his kitchen": Scott's "Guy Mannering," ii.).—**roost′er,** *n.* The male of the domestic fowl; a cock.

root[1] (röt), *v.* [AS. *wrótan* (= D. *wroeten*), akin to *wrót,* snout.] **I.** *intr.* To turn up the soil with the snout, as swine; dig with the snout, as in search of food; hence, in general, to poke, pry, or search, as if to find something; also, to exert one's self, give encouragement, or applaud for a contestant, etc. (slang: as, "Who you *rootin'* for Republican candidate, Mr. Babbitt?" Sinclair Lewis's "Babbitt," iii.; to *root* for one of the teams at a game of baseball). **II.** *tr.* To turn over with the snout; dig up with the snout (often with *up*: as, "Her own [parsley] was all *rooted* up when the pigs broke into her garden," W. H. Hudson's "Purple Land," viii.); fig., to unearth, or bring to light (with *up*, etc.).

root[2] (röt), *n.* [Late AS. *rót* = Icel. *rót*, root; akin to E. *wort*[1].] A part of the body of a plant which, typically, develops from the radicle, and grows downward into the soil, fixing the plant and absorbing nutriment and moisture (see cut on following page); a similar organ ('adventitious root') developed from some other part of the plant, as one of those by which ivy clings to its support; loosely, any underground part of a plant, as a rhizome; often, an underground part of a plant as used for food or in medicine;

also, something resembling or suggesting the root of a plant in position or function; the embedded or basal portion of a hair, tooth, nail, etc.; the bottom or base of anything; the basis upon which something rests or is established (as, "a courage of unshaken *root*": Cowper's "TableTalk," 15); the fundamental or essential part (as, the *root* of a matter; to get at the *root* of things); the source or origin of a thing (as, "The love

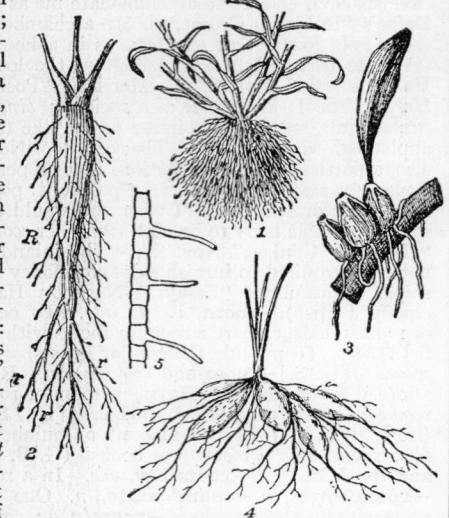

Various forms of Roots. — 1, fibrous roots of meadow-grass (*Poa annua*); 2, root of carrot (*Daucus carota*) — R, tap-root, *r, r, r*, rootlets; 3, aërial roots of orchid (*Oncidium*); 4, tuberous roots of rue-anemone (*Syndesmon thalictroides*); 5, root-hairs of yucca (*Yucca gloriosa*), highly magnified.

of money is the *root* of all evil": 1 Tim. vi. 10); a person or family as the source of offspring or descendants (as, "It was said . . . that myself should be the *root* and father Of many kings": Shakspere's "Macbeth," iii. 1. 5); sometimes, an offshoot or scion (as, "In that day there shall be a *root* of Jesse, which shall stand for an ensign of the people": Isa. xi. 10); specif., in *math.*, a quantity which, when multiplied by itself a certain number of times, produces a given quantity (as, 2 is the square *root* of 4, the cube *root* of 8, and the fourth *root* of 16: cf. *power*); also, a quantity which, when substituted for the unknown quantity in an algebraic equation, satisfies the equation; in *philol.*, an ultimate word-element of a language, accepted as the source or basis of derived words; in *music*, the fundamental tone of a compound tone or of a series of harmonics; also, the fundamental tone of a chord, or, simply, the lowest one of a chord in its normal position. — **to take** (or **strike**) **root**, to send out roots and begin to grow; fig., to become fixed or established. — **root²**, *v.* **I.** *intr.* To take or strike root, as a plant; fig., to settle or establish one's self or itself; obtain a permanent footing. **II.** *tr.* To fix by the roots; fig., to fix or attach firmly as if by roots (as, "I saw something which . . . *rooted* me to the spot with astonishment": S. J. Weyman's "Gentleman of France," xxi.); implant or establish deeply (as, "The principle . . . was firmly *rooted* in the public mind": Macaulay's "Hist. of Eng.," iv.); also, to pull, tear, or dig (*up, out*, etc.) by the roots; hence (with *up, out*, etc.), to remove as if by the roots, extirpate, or exterminate (as, "We'll *root* out the very nation of them from the earth": Defoe's "Robinson Crusoe," ii. 9).

root-age (rō′tāj), *n.* The act of taking root; firm fixture by means of roots.

root=beer (rōt′bēr′), *n.* A drink containing the extracted juices of various roots, as of sarsaparilla, sassafras, etc.

root-ed (rōt′ed), *a.* Having roots; also, having taken root; firmly implanted or infixed (as, "a *rooted* belief": Mrs. H. Ward's "Robert Elsmere," ii.). — **root′ed-ly**, *adv.* — **root′ed-ness**, *n.*

root-er¹ (rōt′ėr), *n.* A pig that roots; also, one who roots for a contestant, etc. (slang: as, "The amateur baseball-team . . . made a schedule of games . . . The citizens accompanied it as '*rooters*,'" Sinclair Lewis's "Main Street," xxxv.).

root-er² (rōt′ėr), *n.* A plant, etc., that takes root; also, one who or that which roots up or extirpates.

root-less (rōt′les), *a.* Without roots.

root-let (rōt′let), *n.* A little root; a small or fine branch of

a root; one of the adventitious roots by which ivy or the like clings to rocks, etc.

root-stock (rōt′stok), *n.* A rhizome.

root=tu-ber-cle (rōt′tū″bėr-kl), *n.* In *bot.*, one of the small tuber-like growths produced on the roots of leguminous plants by nitrogen-fixing bacteria.

root-y (rō′ti), *a.* Abounding in roots.

rope (rōp), *n.* [AS. *rāp* = D. *reep* = G. *reif-* = Icel. *reip* = Goth. *-raips*, rope.] A strong, thick line or cord, commonly one composed of twisted or braided strands of hemp, flax, or the like, or of wire or other material; specif., a hangman's cord or halter; a line stretched between two points, for a rope-dancer; a lasso; *pl.*, the cords used to inclose a prize-ring or other space; also, *sing.*, a quantity of material or a number of things twisted or strung together in the form of a thick cord (as, a *rope* of hair; a *rope* of tobacco; a *rope* of onions; a *rope* of pearls); something elongated and cord-like; a stringy viscid or glutinous formation in a liquid (as, "I count him no more than the *ropes* in beer": Blackmore's "Lorna Doone," vii.). — **rope of sand**, something that cannot hold together; something delusively appearing like a bond, tie, or means of union: as, "the only man who could have used aright such a *rope of sand* as was the Creek confederacy" (Roosevelt's "Winning of the West," i. 3). — **to know the ropes.** See under *know, v. t.* — **rope, v. t.**; *roped, roping.* To tie, bind, or fasten with a rope; also, to inclose or mark off with a rope; also, to catch with a lasso (as, "He dexterously *roped* a horse": Wister's "Virginian," xxxii.); also, to pull back or restrain (a horse) in order to prevent it from winning a race. — **to rope in**, fig., to draw, entice, or inveigle into something: as, "I knew the first house would keep mum and let the rest of the town get *roped in*" (Mark Twain's "Huckleberry Finn," xxiii.). [Colloq.] — **rope, v. i.** To be drawn out into a filament or thread; become ropy. — **rope′=dan″cer**, *n.* One who dances, walks, etc., on a rope stretched at some height above the floor or ground; a funambulist. — **rope′=dan″cing**, *n.* — **rop-er** (rō′pėr), *n.* One who makes ropes; also, one who ropes; one who uses a lasso (as, "A good *roper* will hurl out the coil with marvelous accuracy and force": Roosevelt's "Ranch Life and the Hunting-Trail," iv.). — **rop′er-y** (-i), *n.*; *pl. -ies* (-iz). A place where ropes are made; also, knavery or roguery (as, "What saucy merchant was this, that was so full of his *ropery?*" Shakspere's "Romeo and Juliet," ii. 4. 154: archaic). — **rope′walk**, *n.* A long, usually covered, course, or a long, low building, where ropes are made. — **rope′=walk″er**, *n.* A rope-dancer. — **rope′=yarn**, *n.* See *yarn, n.* — **rop′ing**, *n.* The action of one who ropes; also, ropes collectively (as, "We had on board pretty good store of *roping* made of mats and flags": Defoe's "Captain Singleton," v.); also, a rope-like or ropy formation. — **rop-y** (rō′pi), *a.* Resembling a rope or ropes; forming viscid or glutinous threads, as a liquid. — **rop′i-ly**, *adv.* — **rop′i-ness**, *n.*

roque (rōk), *n.* [Arbitrary reduction of *croquet.*] A form of croquet played on a specially prepared court and modified so as to demand greater skill.

Roque-fort (rōk′fort, F. rok-fôr) **cheese.** A strongly flavored variety of cheese, veined with mold, made wholly or in part of sheep's milk and ripened in caves at Roquefort, in the department of Aveyron, in southern France.

ro-que-laure (rok′e-lōr), *n.* [F.; from the Duc de *Roquelaure* (1656–1738).] A cloak reaching to the knees, much worn by men during the 18th century: as, "a closely buttoned . . . *roquelaure* which enveloped him" (Poe's "Man of the Crowd").

Roquelaure, time of George II.

ro-quet (rō-kā′), *v.*; -queted (-kād′), -queting (-kā′ing). [Prob. an arbitrary reduction of *croquet.*] In croquet: **I.** *tr.* To cause one's ball to strike (another player's ball); of a ball, to strike (another ball). **II.** *intr.* To roquet a ball. — **ro-quet′**, *n.* An act of roqueting.

ro-ric (rō′rik), *a.* [L. *ros* (*ror-*), dew.] Of or pertaining to dew; dew-like.

ror-qual (rôr′kwạl), *n.* [Norw.] Any of the whalebone whales constituting the genus *Balænoptera*, having a dorsal fin, certain of which are of great size; a finback.

Rorqual.

ro-sa-ceous (rọ-zā′shius), *a.* [L. *rosaceus*, < *rosa*, E. *rose²*.] Rose-like; rose-colored; having a corolla of five broad petals, like that of the rose; specif., belonging to the *Rosaceæ*, or rose family of plants, which includes also the blackberry, raspberry, strawberry, potentilla, agrimony, spiræa, etc.

ro-sa-lia (rō-zä′lyä), *n.* [It.] In *music*, a form of melody in which a phrase or figure is repeated two or three times, each time a step or a half-step higher.

ros-an-i-line (roz-an′i-lin), *n.* [From *rose²* + *aniline*.] In *chem.*, a crystalline base derived from aniline, forming salts which yield red and other dyes.

ro-sa-ri-an (rō-zā′ri-ạn), *n.* [See *rosary*.] A cultivator of roses.

ro-sa-ri-um (rō-zā′ri-um), *n.*; pl. *-riums* or *-ria* (-ri-ạ). [L.: see *rosary*.] A rose-garden.

ro-sa-ry (rō′zạ-ri), *n.*; pl. *-ries* (-riz). [L. *rosarium*, rose-garden, ML. rosary, prop. neut. of L. *rosarius*, of roses, < *rosa*, E. *rose²*.] A rose-garden; a bed of roses; also, in the *Rom. Cath. Ch.*, a series of prayers or devotions consisting (in the usual form) of fifteen decades of aves, each decade being preceded by a paternoster and followed by a gloria (Gloria Patri), one of the mysteries or events in the life of Christ and of the Virgin Mary being recalled at each decade; also, a string of beads used to assist the memory in reciting these prayers; also, among other religious bodies, a string of beads similarly used in praying (as, "The lama . . . fingered his *rosary* awhile": Kipling's "Kim," i.).

rose¹ (rōz). Preterit of *rise*.

rose² (rōz), *n.* [AS. *róse*, < L. *rosa*, akin to Gr. ῥόδον, rose.] Any of the wild or cultivated, usually prickly-stemmed, showy-flowered shrubs constituting the genus *Rosa*, having in the wild state a corolla of five roundish pétals (as, the dog-rose; the damask rose; the moss-rose; the musk-rose; the China or Indian rose, *Rosa indica*, an Asiatic species from which many important cultivated varieties have been derived); the flower of any such shrub, of a red, pink, white, or yellow color, and often fragrant (as, "Red as a *rose* is she," Coleridge's "Ancient Mariner," i.; "That which we call a *rose* By any other name would smell as sweet," Shakspere's "Romeo and Juliet," ii. 2. 43); also, any of various related or similar plants, or the flower (as, the rock-rose; the Christmas *rose*, black hellebore); also, rose-color, or a soft pink or pinkish red (as, a pale or a deep *rose*; old *rose*, see *old*, *a*.); rosy color in the cheek (usually with reference to young women, and often in *pl.*: as, "shows in her cheek the *roses* of eighteen," Pope's "Rape of the Lock," iv. 32); also, the fragrance of roses (as, "Fresh gales and gentle airs . . . from their wings Flung *rose*, flung odours from the spicy shrub": Milton's "Paradise Lost," viii. 517); a perfume obtained from roses, or imitating the fragrance of roses; also, a person, esp. a woman, of great beauty, loveliness, or excellence; also, a representation or figure of a rose (flower), as in painting, embroidery, heraldry, carving, metalwork, etc.; also, something shaped like or suggesting a rose; a rosette of ribbon or the like; a rose-window; the compass-card of the mariners' compass, or some similar card or diagram with markings, as for showing barometric pressure,

Tudor Rose. — From gate of St. John's College, Cambridge, England.

conditions as to winds, etc.; a perforated cap or plate closing the spout of a watering-pot, the end of a water-pipe, etc.; a form of cut gem formerly much used, with faceted top and flat under side (hence, the 'rose cut'; a 'rose diamond'); also, with *the*, erysipelas (so called from the redness of the skin in this disease); in *Eng. hist.*, the red or the white flower of the rose as used as the emblem respectively of the Lancaster branch or the rival York branch of the reigning family during the 15th century (as, the Wars of the *Roses*, the prolonged armed struggle between the houses of Lancaster and York, beginning in 1455 in the reign of the last Lancastrian king, Henry VI., and terminating in 1485 in the overthrow of the last Yorkist king, Richard III., by Henry Tudor, Earl of Richmond, of the house of Lancaster, and the union of the two houses in the accession to the throne of the latter as Henry VII., with a niece of Richard III. as his queen). — **bed of roses**, fig., a situation of luxurious ease; an easy and highly agreeable position. — **golden rose**. See under *golden*, *a*. — **rose of Jericho**, an Asiatic brassicaceous plant, *Anastatica hierochuntica*, which has the property, after drying and curling up, of expanding when moistened and appearing to revive: one of the so-called resurrection-plants. — **rose of Sharon**, a plant mentioned in the Bible (see Cant. ii. 1: the Hebrew word being explained in the Revised Version, marginal note, as "the autumn crocus"); also, the althæa, *Hibiscus syriacus*. — **under the rose** (tr. L. *sub rosa*, the rose being taken as an emblem of secrecy), in secret or private; in strict confidence: as, "There was even a story told, with great mystery, and *under the rose*, of his having shot the devil with a silver bullet" (Irving's "Knickerbocker's New York," vi. 6). — **rose²**, *a*. Of the color called rose; rose-pink or rose-red. — **rose²**, *v. t.*; rosed, rosing. To render rose-colored (as, "Till all the sails were darken'd in the west, And *rosed* in the east": Tennyson's "Sea Dreams," 40); make rosy, or flush (the cheeks, face, etc.); also, to scent or perfume with rose.

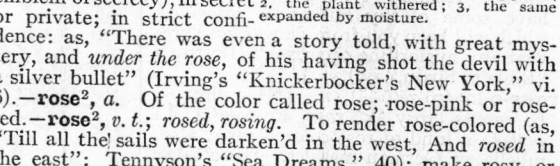

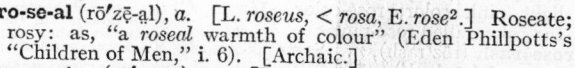

Rose of Jericho. — 1, the living plant; 2, the plant withered; 3, the same expanded by moisture.

ro-se-al (rō′zẹ-ạl), *a*. [L. *roseus*, < *rosa*, E. *rose²*.] Roseate; rosy: as, "a *roseal* warmth of colour" (Eden Phillpotts's "Children of Men," i. 6). [Archaic.]

ro-se-ate (rō′zẹ-āt), *a*. [L. *roseus*: see *roseal*.] Rose-colored or rosy (as, the *roseate* glow of dawn; the *roseate* spoonbill, *Ajaja rosea*, of warm or tropical parts of America, with plumage chiefly pink deepening in parts to red); fig., bright or promising (as, "The future might turn out to be not quite so simple and *roseate* as a delighted public dreamed," Lytton Strachey's "Queen Victoria," iii.; *roseate* prospects); optimistic (as, to take a *roseate* view of a case); also, made or consisting of roses, or fragrant as with roses (obs. or rare). — **ro′se-ate-ly**, *adv*.

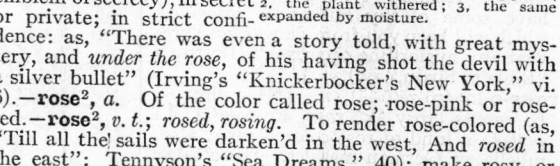

Roseate Spoonbill.

rose=bay (rōz′bā), *n*. The oleander; also, the rhododendron; also, the willow-herb, *Chamænerion angustifolium*.

rose-bud (rōz′bud), *n*. The bud of a rose; fig., a girl in the first bloom of womanhood.

rose=cam-pi-on (rōz′kam′pi-ọn), *n*. See *campion*.

rose=cold (rōz′kōld), *n*. A form of hay-fever appearing early in summer.

rose=col-or (rōz′kul″ọr), *n*. A soft pink with a slight tinge of purple. — **rose′=col″ored**, *a*. Of rose-color; pink, roseate, or rosy; fig., bright or promising (as, *rose-colored* prospects);

cheerful or optimistic (as, "The colonel was . . . full of his *rose-colored* plans for the future," F. H. Smith's "Colonel Carter of Cartersville," iv.; "You take . . . a rather more *rose-coloured* view of things than you did last night," Mallock's "New Republic," iv. 1).

rose=en-gine (rōz'en″jin), *n.* A form of lathe or machine for executing rose-like or other decorative combinations of curved lines, as on watchcases and on engraved plates for printing banknotes, bonds, etc. See *engine-turning.*

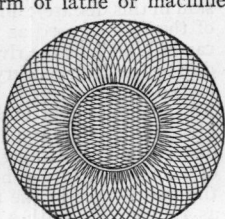

Work of Rose-engine.

rose=fish (rōz'fish), *n.* A marine food-fish, *Sebastes marinus*, mostly red in color, common on both coasts of the northern Atlantic.

rose=ge-ra-ni-um (rōz'jē-rā'ni-um), *n.* Any of a class of geraniums (*Pelargonium*) cultivated for their fragrant lobed or narrowly subdivided leaves rather than for their small pink or purplish flowers.

rose=leaf (rōz'lēf), *n.*; pl. *-leaves* (-lēvz). A petal of a rose.

rose=mal-low (rōz'mal″ō), *n.* Any of various plants of the malvaceous genus *Hibiscus*, bearing rose-colored flowers; also, the hollyhock, *Althæa rosea.*

rose-ma-ry (rōz'mā-ri), *n.* [For earlier *rosmarine,* < L. *ros marinus,* lit. 'marine dew,' 'dew of the sea.'] An evergreen menthaceous shrub, *Rosmarinus officinalis,* native in the Mediterranean region, and yielding a fragrant essential oil: traditionally taken as a symbol of remembrance, or invested with other significance or special virtue: as, "There's *rosemary,* that's for remembrance" (Shakspere's "Hamlet," iv. 5. 175); "You shall have some of my husband's *rosemary,* which will keep you from danger, and prevent any misfortune occurring" (Borrow's "Bible in Spain," iv.).

Rosemary.— 1, the upper part of the stem, with flowers; 2, the lower part of the stem; *a,* a flower; *b,* a leaf.

ro-se-o-la (rō-zē'ō-lä), *n.* [NL., dim. < L. *roseus,* rosy, < *rosa,* E. *rose*².] In *pathol.,* a kind of rose-colored rash; also, rubella, or German measles.—**ro-se'o-lar** (-lär), *a.*

rose=pink (rōz'pingk'). **I.** *n.* A soft, light pink color; rose-color. **II.** *a.* Of the color called rose-pink.

rose=rash (rōz'rash), *n.* Same as *roseola.*

rose=red (rōz'red'). **I.** *n.* The color of a red rose; red with a tinge of purple. **II.** *a.* Of the color called rose-red.

ro-sette (rō-zet'), *n.* [F., dim. of *rose,* < L. *rosa,* E. *rose*².] A rose-shaped arrangement of ribbon or other material, used as an ornament or badge (as, "The quaint little shoes . . . had large *rosettes* on them": W. H. Hudson's "Purple Land," xxiv.); also, an architectural ornament resembling a rose or having a generally circular combination of parts; sometimes, a rose-window; in general, any arrangement, part, object, or formation more or less resembling a rose; in *bot.,* a circular cluster of leaves or other organs.—**ro-set'ted,** *a.* Ornamented with or formed into a rosette or rosettes.

rose=wa-ter (rōz'wâ″tėr). **I.** *n.* Water tinctured with the essential oil of roses. **II.** *a.* Having the odor of rose-water; fig., affectedly delicate, nice, or fine; sentimental.

Architectural Rosette.— Early Italian medieval work.

rose=win-dow (rōz'win'dō), *n.* An ornamental circular window, esp. one with rose-like tracery or radiating mullions. See cut in next column.

rose=wood (rōz'wud), *n.* Any of various reddish cabinet-woods (sometimes with a rose-like odor) yielded by certain fabaceous tropical trees, esp. of the genus *Dalbergia*; also, a tree yielding such wood.

Ro-si-cru-cian (rō-zi-krō'shian). [L. *rosa,* rose, + *crux* (*cruc-*), cross; prob. referring to the 'rose cross' (G. *rosenkreuz*) used as a Rosicrucian emblem, but also alleged to represent the name of a mythical 15th century founder, Christian *Rosenkreuz.*] **I.** *n.* One of a number or body of persons (an alleged secret society) prominent in the 17th and 18th centuries, laying claim to various forms of occult knowledge and power and professing esoteric principles of religion; also, a member of any of several later or modern bodies or societies professing principles derived from or attributed to the earlier Rosicrucians, esp. of an organization known as the Rosicrucian Order or the Ancient Mystic Order Rosae Crucis (AMORC) which is active in America. **II.** *a.* Of, pertaining to, or characteristic of the Rosicrucians.—**Ro-si-cru'cian-ism,** *n.*

Rose-window in North Transept of Church of St. Denis, France.

ros-i-ly (rō'zi-li), *adv.* With a rosy color; in a rosy manner.

ros-in (roz'in), *n.* [OF. *rosine,* var. of *resine,* E. *resin.*] Resin; esp., the hard, brittle resin left after distilling off the oil of turpentine from the crude oleoresin of the pine, used in making varnish, for rubbing on violin-bows, etc. —**ros'in,** *v. t.* To cover or rub with rosin.

Ros-i-nan-te (roz-i-nan'tē), *n.* [Sp. *Rocinante,* name of Don Quixote's steed, < *rocín,* jade, hack.] A sorry or worn-out horse.

ros-in-dol (rōz-in'dol or -dōl), *n.* [From *rose*² + *indol.*] In *chem.,* any of various red dyestuffs produced by heating certain indols with benzoyl chloride and zinc chloride.

ros-i-ness (rō'zi-nes), *n.* Rosy state or hue.

ros-in=weed (roz'in-wēd), *n.* Any of the coarse North American composite plants with a resinous juice which constitute the genus *Silphium,* esp. the compass-plant, *S. laciniatum.*

ros-in-y (roz'i-ni), *a.* Abounding in rosin; resinous.

ros-ma-rine (roz'mā-rēn or -rīn), *n.* [Dan. *rosmar,* walrus.] An old name for the walrus, formerly imagined as a sea-monster which climbed cliffs to feed on dew: as, "greedy *Rosmarines* with visages deforme" (Spenser's "Faerie Queene," ii. 12. 24).

An early representation (1560) of the Rosmarine, or Walrus.

ro-so-lio (rō-zō'liō), *n.* [It., appar. < L. *ros solis,* 'dew of the sun,' the plant sundew (formerly used in cordials).] A cordial made from raisins, etc., popular in southern Europe.

ros-tel-lum (ros-tel'um), *n.*; pl. *rostella* (-ä). [L., dim. of *rostrum,* beak.] In *bot.,* any small, beak-like process, esp. a modification of the stigma in many orchids.—**ros'tel-late** (-te-lāt), *a.*

---

ros-ter (ros'tẽr), *n.* [D. *rooster*, list, table, orig. gridiron, < *roosten*, roast; prob. with allusion to parallel lines or columns.] A military or naval list or register showing the rotation in which officers and men are subject to duty; hence, any list or table giving the names of persons or groups with their turns, periods, or hours of duty; in general, a list, roll, or register (as, "Many 'servants' are mentioned in the *roster* of the Mayflower," H. G. Wells's "Outline of History," xxxvii. § 2; "a golden *roster* of cities," Sinclair Lewis's "Babbitt," xiv.).

ros-tra (ros'trä), *n.* Plural of *rostrum*.

ros-tral (ros'trạl), *a.* [LL. *rostralis*.] Of or pertaining to a rostrum; also, of columns, pillars, etc., adorned with rostrums or beaks of ships or representations of them (orig. in honor of a naval victory).

ros-trate (ros'trāt), *a.* [L. *rostratus*.] Furnished with a rostrum.

ros-trum (ros'trum), *n.*; *pl.* *-trums* or *-tra* (-trä). [L., beak, bill, snout, pointed end, pl. platform for speakers, < *rodere*, gnaw.] A beak, snout, or similar part in birds, quadrupeds, fishes, insects, etc.; a beak-like process or extension of some part (specif. in *anat.*, *zoöl.*, and *bot.*); also, a beak-like projection from the prow of a ship, esp. one on an ancient war-vessel for ramming an enemy's ship; also, *pl.* (*rostra*), the platform or elevated place (adorned with the beaks of captured war-vessels) in the ancient Roman forum, from which orations, pleadings, etc., were delivered (as, "Cato flew to the *Rostra* and railed at the consul": Froude's "Cæsar," xii.); hence, *sing.*, any platform, stage, or the like, for public speaking (as, the *rostrum* of a hall; "Mr. Tappertit mounted on an empty cask which stood by way of *rostrum* in the room," Dickens's "Barnaby Rudge," xxxix.); sometimes, a pulpit (as, "He had been encouraged to mount the *rostrum* by the example and success of a weaver, who was much followed as a powerful minister": Smollett's "Humphry Clinker," June 10).

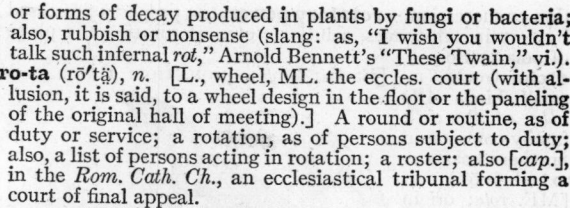
Rostral Column.

ros-u-late (roz'ụ-lāt), *a.* [LL. *rosula*, dim. of L. *rosa*, E. *rose²*.] In *bot.*, arranged in a rosette, as leaves.

ros-y (rō'zi), *a.*; compar. *rosier*, superl. *rosiest*. Pink or pinkish-red, like the color of many roses (as, a *rosy* cloud; the *rosy* tints of sunset; a bird with *rosy* plumage); often, of persons, the cheeks, lips, etc., having a fresh, healthy redness of complexion or color (as, "The Captain is still hale and *rosy*": Aldrich's "Story of a Bad Boy," xxii.); flushed with exercise (as, "My mother entered, *rosy* from a shopping expedition": Bulwer-Lytton's "Caxtons," vii. 2); blushing, as with emotion or confusion; fig., bright or promising (as, a *rosy* future); cheerful or optimistic (as, *rosy* anticipations); also, made or consisting of roses (as, a *rosy* wreath); abounding with roses (as, *rosy* ways); also, fragrant as with roses (obs. or rare).

rot (rot), *v.*; *rotted*, *rotting*. [AS. *rotian* = D. and LG. *rotten*, rot: cf. *rotten* and *ret*.] **I.** *intr.* To undergo natural decomposition; decay; often, to undergo foul decomposition or decay; putrefy; sometimes, to pass or fall (*away*, *off*, etc.) by decay; fig., to undergo decay or impairment; become morally corrupt or offensive; also, to become affected with a putrescent or wasting disease, as through confinement in jail; become affected with the rot, as sheep, etc.; also, to talk rubbish or nonsense (slang, Eng.). **II.** *tr.* To cause to rot; affect with decay or putrescence; specif., to ret (flax, etc.); fig., to cause to undergo decay or impairment; also, to affect with a rotting disease; affect with the rot, as sheep; also, a term used in imprecations, now without precise meaning (as, "*Rot* him, I forgot he was a preacher," Mark Twain's "Huckleberry Finn," xxvi.: cf. *drat*); also, to chaff or banter (slang, Eng.).—**rot**, *n.* The process of rotting, or the state of being rotten; decay; putrefaction; also, rotting or rotten matter; also, a putrescent or wasting disease in persons; any of certain parasitic tissue-destroying diseases affecting animals, esp. sheep; any of various diseases or forms of decay produced in plants by fungi or bacteria; also, rubbish or nonsense (slang: as, "I wish you wouldn't talk such infernal *rot*," Arnold Bennett's "These Twain," vi.).

ro-ta (rō'tä), *n.* [L., wheel, ML. the eccles. court (with allusion, it is said, to a wheel design in the floor or the paneling of the original hall of meeting).] A round or routine, as of duty or service; a rotation, as of persons subject to duty; also, a list of persons acting in rotation; a roster; also [*cap.*], in the *Rom. Cath. Ch.*, an ecclesiastical tribunal forming a court of final appeal.

ro-tam-e-ter (rō-tam'e-tẽr), *n.* [L. *rota*, wheel: see *-meter*.] An instrument containing a small wheel and an attachment for indicating the distance traversed by the wheel when it is rolled along a surface: used in measuring curved lines, etc.

Ro-ta-ri-an (rō-tā'ri-ạn). **I.** *a.* Belonging or pertaining to the Rotary organization or a Rotary Club. **II.** *n.* A member of a Rotary Club.

ro-ta-ry (rō'tạ-ri). [L. *rota*, wheel.] **I.** *a.* Taking place round an axis, as motion; turning round as on an axis, as an object; having a part or parts that rotate, as a machine; specif., noting or pertaining to a steam-engine in which the piston or analogous part rotates or moves in a circular path in the cylinder instead of moving in a straight line, or in which the cylinder rotates upon the piston (cf. *reciprocating*); also, noting or pertaining to an internal-combustion engine for an aëroplane, having radially arranged cylinders which move about a stationary crank-shaft (cf. *reciprocating*); also, passing or acting in rotation (rare); also [*cap.*], designating or pertaining to an organization (so named because the meetings of the first club were held in rotation at the places of business of the members) which originated at Chicago in 1905, and which comprises a great number of clubs (Rotary Clubs) located in different cities and towns of the United States and other countries and united through a central international association founded and incorporated in 1910 (the membership of each club consisting of representative business and professional men of its city or town, one member from each trade, business, or profession; and the purpose of the clubs being to develop the highest ideal of unselfish service and make practical application of this to their business and professional life and to their communities, and to advance international peace and good-will through a fellowship of business and professional men of all nations united in this ideal). **II.** *n.*; *pl.* *-ries* (-riz). [*cap.*] The Rotary organization; a Rotary Club.

ro-tat-a-ble (rō-tā'tạ-bl or rọ-tā'-), *a.* Capable of being rotated.—**ro'tat-a-bly**, *adv.*

ro-tate¹ (rō'tāt), *a.* [L. *rota*, wheel.] Wheel-shaped: applied esp. to a gamopetalous short-tubed corolla with a spreading limb.

ro-tate² (rō'tāt or rọ-tāt'), *v.*; *-tated*, *-tating*. [L. *rotatus*, pp. of *rotare*, < *rota*, wheel.] **I.** *tr.* To cause to turn round like a wheel on its axis; fig., to cause to go through a round of changes; cause to pass or follow in a fixed routine of succession (as, to *rotate* men in office; to *rotate* crops, see *rotation*). **II.** *intr.* To turn round as on an axis (as, "a wheel which was to *rotate* forever on its axis in a vacuum": W. De Morgan's "Joseph Vance," xix.); fig., to proceed in rotation, or in a fixed routine of succession.—**ro-ta-tion** (rō-tā'shọn), *n.* [L. *rotatio(n-)*.] The act of rotating; a turning round as on an axis; fig., a proceeding through a round of changes, or in a fixed routine of succession (as, "All being summoned in *rotation*, my own turn came at last": H. Melville's "Omoo," xxx.); regularly recurring succession, as of persons in office; in *agric.*, the process or the method of varying, in a definite order, the crops grown on the same ground, so as to avoid exhausting the soil.—**ro-ta'tion-al**, *a.* Pertaining to or characterized by rotation.—**ro-ta-tive** (rō'tạ-tiv), *a.* Rotating; pertaining to rotation.—**ro-ta-tor** (rō-tā'tọr), *n.*; *pl.* *rotators*, L. (in *anat.*) *rotatores* (rō-tạ-tō'rēz). [L.] One who or that which rotates; in *anat.*, a muscle serving to rotate a part of the body.—**ro-ta-to-ry** (rō'tạ-tō-ri), *a.* Pertaining to or of the nature of rotation on an axis (as, *rotatory* motion); rotating, as an object; causing rotation, as a muscle; also, passing or following in rota-

Rotate Corolla of Potato (*Solanum tuberosum*).

tion or succession.—**rotatory power**, the property possessed by certain substances, solutions, etc., of rotating the plane of polarization.

rotche (roch), *n*. [Earlier *rotge*; prob. from Dutch.] A small bird, *Alle alle*, of the auk family, common on northern coasts.

Rotche.

rote[1] (rōt), *n*. [ME. *rote*; origin uncertain.] Routine; fixed or mechanical course of procedure: now only in the phrase *by rote*, with reference to learning, knowing, repeating, etc., and commonly indicating an unthinking exercise of memory: as, "The hearers of such literature . . . had to get it *by rote*" (M. Hewlett's "Open Country," xiv.); "I used to say my own prayers then. Now I speak them but *by rote*" (Thackeray's "Newcomes," xlvii.).

rote[2] (rōt), *n*. [OF. F. *rote*; of Celtic origin, and akin to *crowd*[1].] A kind of medieval stringed musical instrument.

rote[3] (rōt), *n*. [Origin uncertain.] The sound of the sea or surf: as, "The *rote* of the sea from its sandy coast . . . Seemed the murmurous sound of the judgment host" (Whittier's "Preacher").

ro-ti-fer (rō'ti-fėr), *n*. [NL., < L. *rota*, wheel, + *ferre*, bear.] Any of the animalcules constituting the class *Rotifera*, found in fresh and salt water, and characterized by rings of cilia, which often appear like rotating wheels; a wheel-animalcule.—**ro-tif-er-al, ro-tif-er-ous** (rō-tif'ẹ-ral, -ẹ-rus), *a*.

rô-tisse-rie (rō-tēs-rē), *n*. [F.] A restaurant at which meats, poultry, etc., are roasted in the sight of customers.

ro-to-gra-vure (rō''tō-gra-vūr' or rō-tō-grā'vụr), *n*. [L. *rota*, wheel, + F. *gravure*, engraving.] A photomechanical process in which pictures, letters, etc., are printed from an engraved copper cylinder, the ink-bearing lines, etc., which print, being depressed (etched in) instead of raised as in ordinary metal type, etc.; a print made by this process.

A Rotifer (*Floscularia ornata*), magnified 500 times.

ro-tor (rō'tọr), *n*. [For *rotator*.] The rotating part of a machine or apparatus, esp. the rotating element (armature or field) of a motor or dynamo (opposed to *stator*); also, a kind of high, tower-like, cylindrical structure of sheet-metal, rising above the deck of a vessel and rotated by a small electric motor, which so operates in connection with the wind as to propel the vessel (invented by Anton Flettner, German engineer: see *rotor-ship*).—

ro'tor=ship, *n*. A wind-propelled vessel employing rotors instead of sails, and having auxiliary means of propulsion by propeller when wind is lacking: recommended as superior to the sailing-vessel because of cheaper construction and greater speed, and esp. because requiring only a small crew for operation.

Rotor-ship "Buckau" (1924).

rot-ten (rot'n), *a*. [From Scand.: cf. Icel. *rotinn*, Sw. *rutten*, Dan. *raadden*, rotten, akin to AS. *rotian*, E. *rot*.] In a state of decomposition or decay, or decomposed; in a state of foul decay, or putrid; of soil, rocks, etc., soft, yielding, or friable as the result of decomposition (as, "steep banks of *rotten* ice, which were breaking off and falling in all the time": Roosevelt's "Ranch Life and the Hunting-Trail," viii.); sometimes, tainted, foul, or ill-smelling, as water, air, etc.; also, affected with the rot, as sheep; also, fig., impaired or unsound (as, "It is a reasoning weak, *rotten*, and sophistical": Burke's "Conciliation with the Colonies"); corrupt or offensive morally, politically, or otherwise (as, "Something is *rotten* in the state of Denmark": Shakspere's "Hamlet," i. 4. 90); hence (slang), wretchedly bad, unsatisfactory, or unpleasant (as, to feel *rotten*; *rotten* work; "I'm absolutely *rotten* at meeting new people," A. S. M. Hutchinson's "If Winter Comes," ii. 5; to have a *rotten* time); mean or contemptible (as, "I am a *rotten* little snob": Arnold Bennett's "Lion's Share," xliii.).—**rotten borough**, formerly, in England, any of certain boroughs which had fallen into decay and had only a few voters, but which still retained the privilege of sending members to Parliament.—**rot'ten-ly**, *adv*.—**rot'ten-ness**, *n*.—**rot'ten-stone**, *n*. A friable stone resulting from the decomposition of a siliceous limestone: used as a powder for polishing metals.

rot-ter (rot'ėr), *n*. [From *rot*.] One who is thoroughly bad or base; a good-for-nothing or worthless person; an objectionable person. [Slang, orig. Eng.]

ro-tund (rọ-tund'), *a*. [L. *rotundus*, round: see *round*[2].] Round, circular, or globular; now, esp., rounded out or plump (as, "this pink-faced *rotund* specimen of prosperity," George Eliot's "Felix Holt," xxx.; "his *rotund* helpmate," Hawthorne's "Blithedale Romance," iv.); also, full-toned or sonorous, as utterance.

ro-tun-da (rọ-tun'dạ), *n*.; pl. *-das* (-dạz). [L., fem. of *rotundus*, round, E. *rotund*.] A round building, esp. one with a dome; also, a large and high circular hall or room in a building, esp. one surmounted by a dome (as, the *rotunda* of the Capitol at Washington); loosely, any large, high central space in a building, as a hotel or a store, esp. one rising through openings in the floors above.

ro-tun-di-ty (rọ-tun'di-ti), *n*.; pl. *-ties* (-tiz). The condition of being rotund; roundness; sphericity; plumpness of the body or its parts; rounded fullness, as of language; also, something round or spherical.

ro-tund-ly (rọ-tund'li), *adv*. In a rotund manner.

ro-ture (rō-tür), *n*. [F., < ML. *ruptura*, land plowed or cleared for cultivation, L. a breaking, < *rumpere*, break.] Plebeian rank; also, plebeian tenure; in *French-Canadian law*, tenure of real property subject to an annual rent or charge.—**ro-tu-rier** (rō-tü-ryā), *n*. [F.] A person of low rank; a plebeian; in *French-Canadian law*, one who holds land by roture.

rou-ble (rö'bl), *n*. See *ruble*.

rou-é (rö-ā), *n*. [F., orig. pp. of *rouer*, break on the wheel, < *roue*, < L. *rota*, wheel: first applied by the Duke of Orleans, regent of France 1715—23, to his companions in dissipation.] A debauchee or rake.

rouge (rözh), *n*. [F., prop. adj., red, < L. *rubeus*, red: cf. *ruby*.] Any of various red cosmetics for coloring the cheeks or lips; also, a reddish powder, chiefly ferric oxide, used for polishing metal, etc.—**rouge**, *v*.; *rouged, rouging*. **I.** *tr*. To color with rouge (as, "She was admirably *rouged* and powdered": Arnold Bennett's "Old Wives' Tale," iii. 2); fig., to cause to become red, as from blushing. **II.** *intr*. To use rouge on the face (as, "Fanny Minafer, who *rouged* a little": Tarkington's "Magnificent Ambersons," v.); fig., to blush.

rouge et noir (rözh ā nwor). [F., 'red and black.'] A certain gambling-game at cards: so called because played at a table marked with two red and two black diamond-shaped spots indicating the colors upon which the players place their stakes.

rough (ruf). [AS. *rūh* = D. *ruig* = G. *rauh*, rough.] **I.** *a*. Uneven from projections, irregularities, or breaks of surface, or not smooth (as, *rough* boards; *rough* bark; *rough* cloth; a *rough* skin); shaggy (as, a dog with a *rough* coat; *rough* eyebrows); having irregularities of surface, obstructions, etc., that render passage difficult (as, "Beneath her feet the way was *rough* enow," W. Morris's "Jason," vii. 149; "After crossing some *rough* and hilly ground, the army entered on the wide plain," Prescott's "Conquest of Mexico,"

iii. 6); violently disturbed or agitated, as the sea, water, etc.; performed over ground, water, etc., not admitting of smooth passage (as, *rough* driving or going; "The crossing [from Calais to Dover] was a very *rough* one," Lytton Strachey's "Queen Victoria," iv.); violently irregular, as motion; also, acting with or characterized by violence; stormy or tempestuous, as wind, weather, etc.; rudely violent or harsh (as, "a fiend, a fury, pitiless and *rough*," Shakspere's "Comedy of Errors," iv. 2. 35; "My temper is *rough*, and will not be controlled," Godwin's "Caleb Williams," iv.; to have a *rough* tongue); rudely or carelessly ungentle, as treatment, handling, usage, etc.; unmannerly or rude (as, "Cyril was 'getting *rough*' . . . He shouted, whistled, sang, stamped": Arnold Bennett's "Old Wives' Tale," ii. 4); disorderly or riotous; violent in action or effect, as remedies; severe, hard, or unpleasant (chiefly colloq.: as, to have a *rough* time of it; this was *rough* on the losing side); also, harsh to the ear, grating, or jarring, as sounds; also, harsh to the taste, sharp, or astringent, as wines; also, lacking culture or refinement (as, "A *rough* sailor's lad Made orphan by a winter shipwreck": Tennyson's "Enoch Arden," 14); without refinements, luxuries, or ordinary comforts or conveniences (as, "Our landlord's housekeeping is equally *rough* and hospitable," Smollett's "Humphry Clinker," Sept. 3; "He said the life was *rough*, but it made him feel extraordinarily well," H. G. Wells's "Mr. Britling," ii. 2. § 7); coarse, as fare, food, materials, etc.; requiring mere exertion or strength rather than intelligence or skill, as work; unpolished or rude, as language, verse, style, etc.; also, crude, unwrought, undressed, or unprepared (as, a *rough* diamond; *rough* rice, rice in the husk, or paddy); not elaborated, perfected, or corrected (as, a *rough* draft or sketch; "It [a proof] was the *rough* galley of a circular . . . that they were correcting together," Arnold Bennett's "Hilda Lessways," i. 7); made or done in an unprecise, general way or without any attempt at exactness, completeness, or thoroughness (as, "It is impossible to make any but the *roughest* guess at the numbers of these northwestern Indians," Roosevelt's "Winning of the West," i. 4; "We started to make a *rough* search through the thicket," J. H. Patterson's "Man-Eaters of Tsavo," xxvii.); in *gram.*, with aspiration, or having the sound of *h* (as, the *rough* breathing : see *breathing*). **II.** *n.* That which is rough; rough ground (lit. or fig.: as, "And love there was to lead her o'er the *rough* Of life," W. Morris's "Jason," ix. 348); the rough, hard, or unpleasant side or part of anything; also, a disorderly, lawless fellow, esp. one given or disposed to acts of violence in public places (as, "preaching and singing hymns among the Whitechapel *roughs*, taking as part of the day's work all the rotten eggs, brickbats, and kicks," Besant's "All Sorts and Conditions of Men," v.; "Without an army Pompey could do little against the *roughs* in the streets," Froude's "Cæsar," xv.); a rowdy; also, the rough, crude, unwrought, or unfinished state (esp. in the phrase 'in the rough').—**rough,** *adv.* In a rough manner; roughly.— **rough,** *v.* **I.** *tr.* To make rough, or roughen (as, "You are water *roughed* by every wind that stirs": Masefield's "Daffodil Fields," vii.); also, to treat roughly or harshly (as, "How tenderly the years touched him . . . all the more tenderly, it seemed, for having *roughed* him so cruelly in other days": Aldrich's "Story of a Bad Boy," xvi.); also, to subject to some rough preliminary process of working or preparation; cut, shape, or sketch (*out*), or sketch or fill (*in*), roughly (as, to *rough* out building-stones; to *rough* out a plan; to *rough* in the outlines of a face). **II.** *intr.* To become rough, as of surface; also, to behave roughly; also (with indefinite *it*), to live in a rough way, without luxuries or ordinary comforts or conveniences, or put up with hardships or discomforts in living (as, "He looked old . . . as if he had *roughed* it all his life, and had found living a desperate long, hard grind": Du Maurier's "Trilby," viii.).

rough-age (ruf′āj), *n.* Rough or coarse material; specif., the coarser kinds or parts of fodder or food, of less nutritive value, as distinguished from those affording more concentrated nutriment.

rough=and=read-y (ruf′and-red′i), *a.* Rough, rude, or crude, but ready and good enough for the purpose (as, a *rough-and-ready* contrivance); roughly effective (as, to do a thing in a *rough-and-ready* fashion; "Nor did he make himself an exact lawyer; a *rough and ready* familiarity with practice . . . contented him," Charnwood's "Abraham Lincoln," iv.); also, exhibiting or showing rough vigor rather than refinement or delicacy (as, a *rough-and-ready* person; "He had a bluff, *rough-and-ready* face," Stevenson's "Treasure Island," vi.).

rough=and=tum-ble (ruf′and-tum′bl). **I.** *a.* Characterized by rough tumbling, falling or throwing down, struggling, etc. (as, a *rough-and-tumble* fight; *rough-and-tumble* play); given to such action, as a fighter, etc.; in general, rough, violent, or rudely vigorous (as, "The squire in his most *rough-and-tumble* days at Berlin had always felt himself the grandee as well as the student," Mrs. H. Ward's "Robert Elsmere," xxii.; *rough-and-tumble* controversy; "a *rough-and-tumble* drama," L. Merrick's "Position of Peggy Harper," ii. 1); in disorderly or confused masses (as, "*rough-and-tumble* hills": Stevenson's "Travels with a Donkey," ii. 1). **II.** *n.* Rough-and-tumble fighting, struggling, or strife (lit. or fig.: as, "the *rough and tumble* of popular debate," Charnwood's "Abraham Lincoln," v.); a rough-and-tumble fight (as, "a *rough-and-tumble* between the officers": Arnold Bennett's "Pretty Lady," xvi.).

rough=cast (ruf′kȧst), *n.* A coarse plaster for outside surfaces, usually thrown against the wall.—**rough′=cast,** *v. t.;* -cast, -casting. To cover or coat with rough-cast; also, to make, shape, or prepare in a rough form (as, to *rough-cast* a plan or a story).

rough=dry (ruf′drī′), *v. t.;* -dried, -drying. To dry (clothes, etc.) after washing, without smoothing, ironing, etc.— **rough′=dry′,** *a.* Dry after being washed, but not smoothed or ironed, as clothes.

rough-en (ruf′n), *v.* **I.** *tr.* To make rough: as, "Thou hast been . . . Riding all day the wild blue waves . . . *Roughening* their crests" (Bryant's "Evening Wind"). **II.** *intr.* To become rough; change with increasing roughness (*into*: as, "The broken landscape, by degrees Ascending, *roughens* into rigid hills," Thomson's "Seasons," Spring, 960).

rough-er (ruf′ėr), *n.* One who roughs, or roughs out.

rough=hew (ruf′hū′), *v. t.;* pret. -hewed, pp. -hewed or -hewn, ppr. -hewing. To hew (timber, stone, etc.) roughly or without smoothing or finishing; shape roughly by or as by hewing (as, "There's a divinity that shapes our ends, Rough-hew them how we will": Shakspere's "Hamlet," v. 2. 11); give crude form to.—**rough′=hew′er,** *n.*—**rough′=hewn′** (-hūn′), *p. a.* Roughly hewn or shaped; fig., of a rough, rude, or crude kind; without refinement or polish, as persons.

rough=house (ruf′hous), *n.* Rough or disorderly behavior, as among the occupants of a house; rough play; rowdy conduct. [Slang.]—**rough′=house** (-hous), *v.;* -housed, -housing. **I.** *intr.* To engage or take part in rough-house. [Slang.] **II.** *tr.* To disturb or harass by rough-house: as, to *rough-house* a meeting or a speaker. [Slang.]

rough-ish (ruf′ish), *a.* Rather rough: as, "a *roughish* sea" (Lever's "Harry Lorrequer," xxxiii.).

rough-ly (ruf′li), *adv.* In a rough manner.

rough=neck (ruf′nek), *n.* A rough, coarse fellow. [Slang.]

rough-ness (ruf′nes), *n.* The state or quality of being rough; also, a rough part or place (as, "There were other breaks and *roughnesses* on that flat green expanse": W. H. Hudson's "Far Away and Long Ago," v.).

rough=rid-er (ruf′rī′dėr), *n.* One who breaks horses to the saddle; also, one accustomed to rough or hard riding (as, "the *rough-rider* of the plains, the hero of rope and revolver": Roosevelt's "Ranch Life and the Hunting-Trail," ii.); hence, pl. [caps.], commonly Rough *Riders*], the members of a volunteer regiment of cavalry, composed partly of Western cowboys, organized by Theodore Roosevelt and Leonard Wood for service in the Spanish-American War of 1898.

rough=shod (ruf′shod′), *a.* Shod with shoes having projecting nails or points, as horses to prevent slipping: often fig., in the phrase 'to ride roughshod over' (to override roughly, harshly, or unfeelingly; pursue one's own course domineeringly over).

rou-lade (rö-läd′), *n.* [F., < *rouler*, roll: see *roll, v.*] A musical embellishment consisting of a rapid succession of tones sung to a single syllable; also, a slice of meat rolled about a filling of minced meat and cooked.

(variable) d̦ as d or j, ș as s or sh, ț as t or ch, z̦ as z or zh; o, F. cloche; ü, F. menu; ċh, Sc. loch; ṅ, F. bonbon; ′, primary accent; ″, secondary accent; †, obsolete; <, from; +, and; =, equals. See also lists at beginning of book.

rou-leau (rö-lō′), *n.*; pl. *-leaux* (-lōz′) or *-leaus*. [F. *rouleau,* OF. *rolel,* dim. of *rolle:* see *roll, n.*] A roll of something; a cylindrical mass or arrangement; specif., a number of coins put up in cylindrical form in a paper wrapping (as, *rouleaux* of gold pieces).

rou-lette (rö-let′), *n.* [F. *roulette,* OF. *roelete,* dim. of *roele,* little wheel: see *rowel.*] A small wheel, esp. one with sharp teeth, mounted in a handle, for making lines of marks, dots, or perforations (as, engravers' *roulettes*; a *roulette* for perforating sheets of postage-stamps); also, a wheel or revolving disk used in playing a game of chance (as, "She had a *roulette* at her elbow, where the peasants risked a kreutzer for a cake": Longfellow's "Hyperion," iv. 5); hence, a game of chance played at a table in the center of which is a revolving disk with numbered compartments, into one of which a ball in motion finally comes to rest.—**rou-lette′,** *v. t.*; *-letted,* *-letting.* To mark, impress, or perforate with a roulette.

roul-roul (röl′röl), *n.* [Native name.] Any of the partridge-like birds of the genus *Rollulus,* of Java, Sumatra, Borneo, etc., as *R. cristatus,* the male of which is of a rich green color, with a long red crest.

Rou′man, Rou-ma′ni-an. See *Ruman, Rumanian.*

rounce (rouns), *n.* [D. *ronds, rons:* cf. D. *rond,* round.] In *printing,* a device on a hand printing-press by which the bed (supporting the form of type) is run in and out under the platen, and consisting essentially of a pulley fitted with bands or thongs and turned by a handle.

Roulroul (*Rollulus cristatus*).

round¹ (round), *v.* [For *roun,* < AS. *rūnian,* < *rūn,* mystery, secret: see *rune.*] **I.** *intr.* To whisper: as, to *round* in one's ear. [Archaic or prov.] **II.** *tr.* To whisper (something: as, "The 'Ghosts of Life' *rounded* strange secrets in his ear," Carlyle's "Sartor Resartus," iii. 6); also, to whisper to (a person). [Archaic or prov.]

round² (round), *a.* [OF. F. *rond,* < L. *rotundus,* round, lit. 'wheel-shaped,' < *rota,* wheel: cf. *rotund.*] Circular, as a disk, or approximately so; annular or ring-shaped, as a hoop; curved or curving like a part of a circle or the like, as an outline; having the form of a circle or the like in section, as a cylinder; spherical or globular, as a ball, or approximately so; rounded more or less like a part of a sphere; in general, free from angularity; plump, as parts of the body; sometimes, stout or corpulent (as, "In person he was not very tall, but exceedingly *round*": Irving's "Knickerbocker's New York," v. 9); also, executed with or involving circular or revolving motion (as, a *round* dance: see phrase below); also, completed by passing through a course which finally returns to the place of starting (as, a *round* trip); also, full, complete, or entire (as, "a *round* dozen of epics," Peacock's "Headlong Hall," xii.; "a *round* score of muskets," Stevenson's "Treasure Island," xxi.); forming, or expressed by, an integer or whole number (with no fraction), or expressed in tens, hundreds, thousands, or the like, as a number or sum (as, "He returned me immediately an order on the paymaster for the *round* sum of one thousand pounds, leaving the remainder to the next account," B. Franklin's "Autobiography," xi.: see also phrase *in round numbers,* below); roughly correct, as an estimate (as, "I may form a *round* guess . . . what I might have to fear": Scott's "Castle Dangerous," vii.); also, considerable in amount (as, "a good *round* sum of money," Defoe's "Captain Singleton," xiii.; "There was a *round* bounty offered," H. Melville's

"Omoo," xxxviii.); also, brought to completeness or perfection (as, "If sentiment were sacrific'd to sound, And truth cut short to make a period *round*": Cowper's "Table Talk," 517); full and sonorous, as sound (as, "the *round,* bold, bullying voice with which he usually spoke": Scott's "Guy Mannering," xli.); also, vigorous, brisk, or smart (as, "I passed at a *round* trot over the plains": Parkman's "Oregon Trail," x.); also, plain, honest, or straightforward (as, "I will a *round* unvarnish'd tale deliver," Shakspere's "Othello," i. 3. 90; *round* dealing); plain-spoken or candid, as a person (as, "'My dear lord, I will be *round* with you like a soldier,' said the Colonel": Stevenson's "Master of Ballantrae," ii.); outspoken or uncompromising, as speech (as, "Paul would almost certainly have condemned tobacco in good *round* terms": S. Butler's "Way of All Flesh," l.); downright or unmodified, as an oath; positive or unqualified, as an assertion; in *phonetics,* uttered with the lips drawn together with a circular opening between them, as a vowel. **—in round numbers,** employing a round number (see *round², a.,* above) by way of approximate statement, with disregard of the exact number of units, or of smaller elements of the actual number: as, a city having a population, *in round numbers,* of 100,000.—**round dance,** orig., a dance with the dancers arranged in or moving about in a circle or ring; now, commonly, a dance performed by couples and characterized by circular or revolving movement, as the waltz.—**Round Table,** the celebrated table of medieval legend, made round to avoid quarrels as to precedence, about which King Arthur and his knights sat; also, King Arthur and his knights as a body; also [*l. c.,* as *round table*], a number of persons seated, or conceived as seated, about a round (or other) table, esp. for the discussion of some subject (often used attributively in the form *round-table:* as, a *round-table* conference).—**round²,** *n.* Something round (circular, ring-shaped, curved, cylindrical, globular, etc.); a circle, or a circular object or structure; a ring, or a ring-like object; a curve, or something curved; something circular or round in section, as a rung of a ladder, or a rounded crosspiece, as between the legs of a chair, or a rounded molding; a spherical or globular body (as, "this great terrestrial and celestial *Round*": Carlyle's "Sartor Resartus," i. 4); specif., the portion of the thigh of beef below the rump and above the leg; also, rounded form; specif. (with *the*), the form of sculpture in which figures are executed apart from any background (contrasted with *relief*); also, a dance with the dancers arranged or moving in a circle or ring; also, movement in a circle or about an axis; a round or

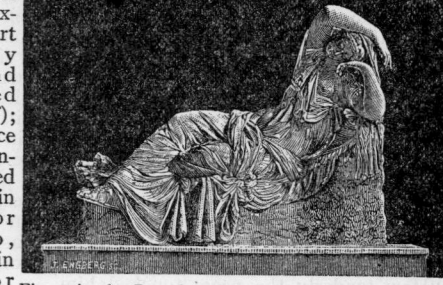

Figure in the Round. — The Sleeping Ariadne, in the Vatican Museum.

roundabout way or course (as, "You took them in a *round,* while they supposed themselves going forward": Goldsmith's "She Stoops to Conquer," v.); also, a completed course of time, ending at a point corresponding to that at which it began; a recurring period of time; also, a series of events, operations, etc., ending at a point corresponding to that at which it began; a recurring succession of events, duties, etc.; any complete course, series, or succession; hence, the complete extent or range of something (as, the whole *round* of human knowledge or endeavor); also, a fixed or customary circuit, as of a military officer and men inspecting the sentinels of a camp, or of a policeman, a postman, etc.; a military party making such a circuit; also, a circuit of any place, series of places, etc.; a going about from place to place in a more or less definite course; also, a completed course or spell of activity, commonly one of a series, in some play or sport; one of a series of bouts making up a prize-fight or boxing-match; also, a single outburst of applause, cheers, etc.; also, a single discharge of shot by each of a number of guns, rifles, etc., or by a single piece; a charge of ammunition for a single shot; also, a portion of drink, etc., served to all the members of a company (as, "Serve out a *round* of brandy to all hands": Stevenson's "Treasure Island," xxi.); in *music*, a short rhythmical canon at the unison, in which the several voices enter at equal intervals of time; also, *pl.*, in *change-ringing*, the order followed in ringing a peal of bells in diatonic sequence from the highest to the lowest.—**round²**, *adv.* In a circle, ring, or the like, or so as to surround something (as, "The ambient air wide interfused, Embracing *round* this florid earth": Milton's "Paradise Lost," vii. 90); on all sides, or about, whether circularly or otherwise (as, "So twice five miles of fertile ground With walls and towers were girdled *round*": Coleridge's "Kubla Khan"); also, in all directions from a center (as, "As Lord Marmion cross'd the court, He scatter'd angels [coins] *round*," Scott's "Marmion," i. 10; every house within a mile *round*); in the region about a place (as, the country *round*); also, in circumference (as, a tree 40 inches *round*); also, in a circular or rounded course (as, "It [albatross] ate the food . . . And *round* and *round* it flew": Coleridge's "Ancient Mariner," i.); through a round, circuit, or series, as of places or persons (as, to show a person *round*; "when a money-subscription is going *round*," Lamb's "Popular Fallacies," ix.; enough to go *round*); through a round, or recurring period, of time, esp. to the present or particular time (as, time rolls *round*; "when, year by year, these glorious days came *round*," W. Morris's "Jason," xvii. 73); throughout, or from beginning to end of, a recurring period of time (as, "It fetched us a dollar a day apiece all the year *round*": Mark Twain's "Huckleberry Finn," i.); also, by a circuitous or roundabout course (as, "The horse-way . . . was five miles *round*, though the footway was but two": Goldsmith's "Vicar of Wakefield," x.); to a place or point as by a circuit or circuitous course (as, "going at least two miles farther north, so as to get *round* into the navigable channel at the other side," Amelia B. Edwards's "Thousand Miles up the Nile," xvii.; "I'm off to Barbizon, to paint the forest; I was coming *round* to tell you," Du Maurier's "Trilby," iii.); also, about, or in circulation, action, etc. (chiefly U. S.: as, "those unwholesome, weak-eyed, half-fed creatures, that look not fit to be *round* among live folks," Holmes's "Elsie Venner," xvi.); also, with a rotating course or movement (as, "*Round* went the wheels": Cowper's "John Gilpin," 41); also, with change to another or the opposite direction, course, opinion, etc. (as, "She continued to sit very still, without looking *round*," Galsworthy's "Saint's Progress," iii. 6; "He brought me *round* to his opinion," S. Butler's "Way of All Flesh," lxx.).—**all round**, round something on all sides; in all directions from a center; over the whole place; also, in all respects, or for all purposes (as, "It would be a very desirable thing *all round!*" Du Maurier's "Trilby," iv.).—**round²**, *prep.* So as to encircle, surround, or envelop (as, "I . . . *round* thee . . . bind my belt," Tennyson's "Holy Grail," 159; to wrap paper *round* an article); on the circuit, border, or outer part of; around; about; also, in all or various directions from (as, to stand still and look *round* one); in the vicinity of (as, the country *round* Boston); also, so as to encircle, or make the circuit of, in moving (as, "He . . . saw ghosts dancing *round* him," Peacock's "Nightmare Abbey," i.; "Those have their course to finish, *round* the earth," Milton's "Paradise Lost," iv. 661); in a round, circuit, or course through, or to all or various parts of (as, to wander *round* the country; to take a visitor *round* the city); also, throughout (a period of time: as, "Verdant olives flourish *round* the year," Pope's tr. Homer's "Odyssey," vii.); also, here and there in (as, there are boxes for mail all *round* the city); also, so as to make a turn or partial circuit about or to the other side of (something: as, to sail *round* a cape; to go *round* a corner); reached by making a turn or partial circuit about (something: as, the church *round* the corner); also, so as to revolve or rotate about (a center or axis: as, the earth's motion *round* its axis).—**to get**, or **come, round a person**, to circumvent or outwit him; cajole or wheedle him.—**round²**, *v. t.* To make round (circular, ring-shaped, curved, cylindrical,

globular, convex, concave, etc.); in general, to free from angularity; fill out symmetrically; make plump; also, to bring to completeness or perfection; finish off; end (a sentence, etc.) with something specified; also, to drive or bring (cattle, etc.) together (commonly with *up*); also, to encircle or surround (as, "The hollow crown That *rounds* the mortal temples of a king": Shakspere's "Richard II.," iii. 2. 161); also, to make the complete circuit of, or pass completely round; also, to make a turn or partial circuit about, or to the other side of (as, "In 1486 a Portuguese, Diaz, reported that he had *rounded* the south of Africa," H. G. Wells's "Outline of History," xxxv. § 8; to *round* the corner of a street); also, to cause to move in a circle or turn round; also, in *phonetics*, to utter (a vowel) with a narrow circular opening between the lips.—**to round in**, *naut.*, to haul in.—**round²**, *v. i.* To become round (circular, curved, globular, etc.); assume or have a curved or rounded form; in general, to become free from angularity; become plump; also, to develop to completeness or perfection; also, to take a circular course; proceed through a round, or recurring period, of time (as, "I see . . . The *rounding* seasons come and go": Whittier's "Questions of Life"); make a circuit; go the rounds, as a guard; make a turn or partial circuit about something (as, "He . . . kept on till he could *round* into the backwater": Galsworthy's "Dark Flower," ii. 19); turn round as on an axis (as, "The men who met him *rounded* on their heels And wonder'd after him": Tennyson's "Pelleas and Ettarre," 135).—**to round to**, *naut.*, to come head up to the wind, as before heaving to or anchoring: as, "We *rounded-to* and let go our anchor" (Dana's "Two Years before the Mast," xxxvi.).

round-a-bout (round′a-bout″). **I.** *a.* Round; cut circularly at the bottom, without tails or the like, as a coat or jacket; encircling or surrounding; plump or stout, as a person; also, comprehensive, or taking a wide survey (rare); also, circuitous or indirect, as a road or journey, methods or procedure, utterances or language, or persons with respect to their methods or utterances (as, "I heard in a *roundabout* way that she's going to marry an old neighbour of theirs," A. S. M. Hutchinson's "If Winter Comes," iv. 8; "Runi . . . made some *roundabout* remarks, apparently with the object of eliciting an account of what I had seen," W. H. Hudson's "Green Mansions," iv.). **II.** *n.* A round or circular object or course; a merry-go-round (as, "a steam '*round-about*,' where wooden horses revolved to the blare of an organ": Eden Phillpotts's "Children of Men," i. 8); a short, closely fitting coat or jacket, without skirts, for men or boys (as, "His close-buttoned blue cloth *roundabout* was new and natty": Mark Twain's "Tom Sawyer," i.); also, a circuitous or indirect way or course; an indirect utterance, or a circumlocution.—**round′a-bout″ness**, *n.*

roun-del (roun′del), *n.* [OF. *rondel*, dim. < *rond*, round: see *round²*, and cf. *rondel*.] Something round or circular; a small disk or rounded piece; a small round shield; a small round pane or window; a decorative plate, panel, tablet, or the like, round in form; also, a dance in a circle or ring; also, a rondel or rondeau; specif., a modification of the rondeau consisting of nine lines with two refrains.

Roundel by Luca della Robbia.

roun-de-lay (roun′dẹ-lā), *n.* [OF. *rondelet*, dim. of *rondel*: see *roundel*.] A song in which a phrase, line, or the like, is continually repeated; the music for such a song; also, a dance in a circle.

round-er (roun'dėr), *n.* [See *round*[2].] One who or that which rounds something; also, one who goes round, or makes a round; esp., a habitual drunkard or criminal (colloq.); an idle frequenter of public resorts (colloq.); also, *pl.* (construed as *sing.*), a game, somewhat resembling baseball, played with a bat and a ball.

round-hand (round'hand), *n.* A style of handwriting in which the letters are round and full.

Round-head (round'hed), *n.* In *Eng. hist.*, a member or adherent of the Parliamentarians or Puritan party during the civil wars of the 17th century (so called in derision by the Cavaliers because they wore their hair cut short): as, "When, in October, 1641, the Parliament reassembled . . . two hostile parties . . . appeared confronting each other. During some years they were designated as Cavaliers and *Roundheads*. They were subsequently called Tories and Whigs" (Macaulay's "Hist. of Eng.," i.).

round-house (round'hous), *n.* A lockup (now rare); a building for locomotives, usually round or semicircular, and built about a turn-table; *naut.*, a cabin on the after part of a quarter-deck.

round-ish (roun'dish), *a.* Somewhat round.

round-let (round'let), *n.* [OF. *rondelet*: see *roundelay*.] A small circle or circular object.

round-ly (round'li), *adv.* In a round manner; in a circle, ring, curve, globe, or the like; in a roughly correct manner, or as a general estimate; in a finished or perfected style; vigorously, briskly, or smartly; honestly, openly, or without concealment; outspokenly, or without mincing matters; sharply, severely, or unsparingly; positively, unqualifiedly, or without qualification.—**round'ness**, *n.*

round=rob-in (round'rob'in), *n.* A petition, remonstrance, or the like, having the signatures arranged in circular form, so as to disguise the order of signing.

round=shoul-dered (round'shōl'dėrd), *a.* Having the shoulders bent forward, giving a rounded form to the upper part of the back.

rounds-man (roundz'man), *n.*; pl. *-men.* One who makes rounds, as of inspection; esp., a police officer who inspects the policemen on duty in a particular district.

round-up (round'up), *n.* The driving together of cattle, etc., for inspection, branding, or the like, as in the western U. S. (as, "The missing ones [cattle] are generally recovered in the annual *round-ups*, when the calves are branded": Roosevelt's "Hunting Trips of a Ranchman," i.); the men and horses who do this, or the herd so collected; also, any similar driving or bringing together.

round-worm (round'werm), *n.* A nemathelminth or a nematode, esp. *Ascaris lumbricoides*, a parasite infesting the human intestine.

roup[1] (roup), *v.* [From Scand.] **I.** *intr.* To cry or shout. [Sc.] **II.** *tr.* To sell or let by auction: as, "An auctioneer . . . *rouped* the kirk seats . . . beginning by asking for a bid" (Barrie's "Auld Licht Idylls," ii.). [Sc.]—**roup**[1], *n.* An auction. [Sc.]

roup[2] (rõp), *n.* [Prob. imit.] Hoarseness or huskiness (Sc. and north. Eng.); also, an infectious purulent catarrh of poultry.—**roup'y**, *a.* Hoarse or husky (chiefly prov.); also, affected with the disease roup.

rous-ant (rou'zant), *a.* [From *rouse*[2].] In *her.*, of a bird, starting up, as if about to take flight.

rouse[1] (rouz), *n.* [Prob. for *carouse*.] A full draft or measure of liquor, or a bumper (as, "*Cas.* 'Fore God, they have given me a *rouse* already. *Mon.* Good faith, a little one; not past a pint": Shakspere's "Othello," ii. 3. 66); also, a bout or revel of drinking, or a carouse (as, "Fill the cup and fill the can, Have a *rouse* before the morn": Tennyson's "Vision of Sin," iv.). [Archaic.]

Swan Rousant.

rouse[2] (rouz), *v.*; *roused, rousing.* [Late ME. *rowse*; origin uncertain.] **I.** *tr.* To cause (game) to start from a covert or lair; also, to cause (sleepers) to awaken and rise (as, to be *roused* from one's bed by a cry of fire); bring out of a state of sleep or unconsciousness (as, to *rouse* a person from sleep or a swoon; "Frae his harp sic strains did flow, Might

rous'd the slumbering dead to hear," Burns's "A Vision," 26); also, to bring out of a state of inactivity, fancied security, abstraction, apathy, depression, etc. (as, "His mother, the high-spirited sultana . . . endeavored to *rouse* him from this passive state," Irving's "Conquest of Granada," xxviii.; "The Franks forgot their first panic, *roused* themselves, rallied, resisted, overcame," G. P. R. James's "Hist. of Charlemagne," iv.); stir or excite to activity, vigor, animation, enthusiasm, etc. (as, "England was *roused* —on every side Courier and post and herald hied": Scott's "Lord of the Isles," vi. 4) stimulate or incite (*to*: as, "Ethan, with a touch of his whip, *roused* the sorrel to a languid trot," Mrs. Wharton's "Ethan Frome," ix.; "They were *roused* to action by the progress of Totila and the reproaches of Justinian," Gibbon's "Decline and Fall of the Roman Empire," xliii.); stir to strong indignation or anger (as, "When Thomas Newcome was once *roused* . . . woe to the offender!" Thackeray's "Newcomes," lvi.); excite (feelings, etc.: as, to *rouse* indignation or hatred; "The ocean-going steamers . . . *roused* in him wild and painful longings," Arnold Bennett's "Roll-Call," vii.); also, to stir up, or set in motion (as, "Blustering winds, which all night long Had *roused* the sea": Milton's "Paradise Lost," ii. 287); set in action, or set going (as, "He lifted the . . . knocker, and gave such a rat tat tat as must have *roused* all the echoes of the old house": Mrs. Stowe's "Oldtown Folks," xvii.); also, to raise or lift up†; also, *naut.*, to pull by main strength, or haul. **II.** *intr.* To start up from a covert or lair, as game; also, to awaken and rise, as from bed or sleep (as, "Morpheus *rouses* from his bed": Pope's "Ode on St. Cecilia's Day," ii.); come out of a state of sleep or unconsciousness; also, to rouse one's self from inaction, apathy, depression, etc.: become active; start up, or rise, as feelings, etc.; also, to rise or stand up, as the hair† (see Shakspere's "Macbeth," v. 5. 12).—**rouse**[2], *n.* A rousing; also, a signal for rousing or action; the reveille.—**rous-er** (rou'zėr), *n.*—**rous'ing**, *p. a.* That rouses; stirring (as, a *rousing* political speech; a *rousing* song); stirringly active or vigorous (as, a *rousing* campaign; *rousing* cheers); brisk, lively, smart, or "roaring" (as, a *rousing* trade; a *rousing* fire); great, extraordinary, or outrageous (colloq.: as, a *rousing* lie).—**rous'ing-ly**, *adv.*

roust (roust), *v. t.* [Appar. a combination of *rouse*[2] and *rout*[2].] To rout (*out*), as from a place: as, "I'm a-going up . . . to *roust* out my engineer" (Mark Twain's "Huckleberry Finn," xiii.). [Colloq.]—**roust'a-bout**″ (-a-bout″), *n.* A wharf-laborer or deck-hand, as on the Mississippi River (as, "no pitiful handful of deck-hands, firemen, and *roust-abouts*": Mark Twain's "Life on the Mississippi," vi.); also, a rough fellow who lives by odd jobs. [U. S.]

rout[1] (rout), *v. i.* [From Scand.] To roar; bellow; make a loud noise. [Now prov.]—**rout**[1], *n.* A roar; a loud noise; an uproar. [Now prov.]

rout[2] (rout), *v.* [Var. of *root*[1].] **I.** *intr.* To root, as swine; hence, to poke, search, or rummage (as, "He had been *routing* among the piled newspapers under the kitchen dresser": H. G. Wells's "Mr. Polly," i.). **II.** *tr.* To turn over or dig up with the snout, as swine; also, to hollow out or furrow (a surface) as with a scoop, gouge, or machine, or deepen or form (a hollow) by such action; also, to bring or get (*out*) in poking about, searching, etc. (as, "Foraging about . . . I *routed* out some biscuit . . . and a piece of cheese": Stevenson's "Treasure Island," xxv.); fetch or get (*out*), as from a place, by vigorous action (as, "I went down . . . *routed* him out with a little trouble from that centre, made things right with him": H. G. Wells's "Tono-Bungay," iii. 4. § 2); force or drive out (as, "From even this stronghold the unlucky Rip was at length *routed* by his termagant wife": Irving's "Sketch-Book," Rip Van Winkle); cause to get (*up* or *out*) from bed (as, "He'll have you *routed* up by four o'clock in the morning": Mrs. Stowe's "Oldtown Folks," ix.).

rout[3] (rout), *n.* [OF. *route*, troop, band, < ML. *rupta*, lit. 'a division,' prop. pp. fem. of L. *rumpere*, break: cf. *rout*[4] and *route*.] A troop, company, or band (archaic: as, "a *rout* of roisterers," Tennyson's "Geraint and Enid," 274; "a *rout* of armed men," W. Morris's "Jason," v. 65); a train or retinue (archaic); a pack, herd, or other assemblage of animals (archaic); also, a tumultuous or disorderly crowd of persons, or a rabble or mob (as, "like a band of freed prisoners who head the *rout* to fire a city": G. Meredith's "Lord Ormont and His Aminta," xv.); the common herd of persons, or the rabble; also, riot, disturbance, or uproar; also, a large evening party or social gathering (archaic); in *law*, an assemblage of three or more persons proceeding to commit an unlawful act.

rout⁴ (rout), *n.* [Obs. F. *route*, < It. *rotta*, break-up, rout, < L. *rupta*, pp. fem. of *rumpere*, break: cf. *rout³* and *route*.] Dispersal or flight of a defeated armed or opposing force in complete disorder (as, to put an army to *rout*; defeat ending in *rout*; the enemy was in full *rout*); a defeat attended with disorderly flight (as, "All the military skill of Frederick was required to prevent the defeat becoming an absolute *rout*": Lecky's "Hist. of Eng. in the 18th Century," viii.). Also *fig.* —**rout⁴**, *v. t.* To put to rout, or disperse in defeat and disorderly flight (as, to *rout* an army; "Twenty-two of the Prince's vessels being captured, and the rest totally *routed*, Bossu swept across the lake in triumph," Motley's "Dutch Republic," iii. 8); *fig.*, to put to confusion, or discomfit (as, to *rout* one's accusers); put to flight, or drive away (as, "to *rout* the brood of cares": Tennyson's "In Memoriam," lxxxix.).

rout=cake (rout′kāk), *n.* [See *rout³*.] A kind of rich sweet cake orig. made for routs or evening parties. [Eng.]

route (rōt, also rout), *n.* [OF. F. *route*, < ML. *rupta*, lit. 'a way broken,' another use of *rupta*, E. *rout³*.] A way or road for passage or travel (as, "Others . . . were for taking the more northerly *route*," Prescott's "Conquest of Mexico," iii. 6; "on the great *route* from Piccadilly Circus to Putney," Arnold Bennett's "Roll-Call," i.); also, a way or course taken, or to be taken (as, "They came up by a *route* of their own," J. H. Newman's "Callista," xxv.; to fix a *route* for a procession); a customary or regular line of passage or travel (as, "They [Indians] know the *routes* and resorts of the trappers; where to waylay them," Irving's "Captain Bonneville," i.; "They . . . arrived at the next inn upon the *route* of the stage-coach," H. Mackenzie's "Man of Feeling," xxxiii.); the line of direction of a road, railroad, canal, or the like, existing or proposed (as, "I had a contract to survey a *route* for a great mining ditch in California": Mark Twain's "Life on the Mississippi," xxxvi.); also, *milit.*, an order to move from one station or place to another.—**route**, *v. t.*; *routed*, *routing*. To fix the route of; send or forward by a particular route.

rout-er (rou′tẽr), *n.* [See *rout²*.] Any of various tools or machines for routing, hollowing out, or furrowing; a tool or machine for routing out parts of an etched plate, electrotype, etc.

routh (routh), *n.* [Origin obscure.] Plenty. [Sc.]

rou-tine (rö-tēn′), *n.* [F., < *route*, E. *route*.] **I.** *n.* A customary or regular course of procedure (as, "The common business of the nation . . . is carried on in a constant *routine* by the clerks of the different offices," Smollett's "Humphry Clinker," June 5; "All this sort of thing was fresh and exciting at first, and then it began to fall into a *routine* and became habitual," H. G. Wells's "Soul of a Bishop," iii.); the customary course or round of proceedings in a particular instance (as, to be familiar with the *routine* of an office or business; "The examinations were over, and the *routine* of the half year began," S. Butler's "Way of All Flesh," xxx.); also, regular, unvarying, or mechanical procedure (as, "Old forms remould, and substitute . . . For blind *routine*, wise-handed skill," Whittier's "Snow-Bound"; "the hypnotising effect of *routine*," Mrs. Wharton's "Ethan Frome," Introd.). **II.** *a.* Of the nature of, proceeding by, or adhering to routine: as, *routine* methods or duties; *routine* workers.—**rou-tin′ism** (-tē′nizm), *n.* Adherence to routine.—**rou-tin′ist**, *n.*

rout=seat (rout′sēt), *n.* [See *rout³*.] A light bench let out for use at evening parties: as, "The waltz was over. He could see her now, on a *rout seat* against the wall" (Galsworthy's "Dark Flower," iii. 12). [Eng.]

roux (rō), *n.* [F., red, reddish, russet: see *russet*.] Butter and flour cooked together, orig. until brown, used to thicken sauces, etc.

rove¹ (rōv). Preterit and past participle of *reeve²*.

rove² (rōv), *v. t.*; *roved, roving.* [Origin uncertain.] To form (slivers of wool, cotton, etc.) into slightly twisted strands in a preparatory process of spinning.—**rove²**, *n.* A strand of wool, cotton, or the like, formed by roving.

rove³ (rōv), *v.*; *roved, roving.* [Origin uncertain.] **I.** *intr.* To wander or travel about without definite destination; move hither and thither at random, esp. over a wide area; roam: as, "For ten years I *roved* about, living first in one capital, then another" (C. Brontë's "Jane Eyre," xxvii.); "The cattle *rove* free over the hills and prairies" (Roosevelt's "Hunting Trips of a Ranchman," i.); "My eyes *roved* over the level area we were standing on" (W. H. Hudson's "Green Mansions," xi.). **II.** *tr.* To wander over or through; traverse: as, "Their young men . . . *roved* the spurs of the Alleghanies, in quest of marketable skins" (Bancroft's "Hist. of the U. S.," Amer. Revolution, i. 6).—**rove³**, *n.* The act of roving; a ramble.

rove=bee-tle (rōv′bē″tl), *n.* [Cf. *rove³*.] Any beetle of the family *Staphylinidæ*, which comprises numerous insects having a long, slender body and very short elytra, and capable of running swiftly.

rov-er¹ (rō′vẽr), *n.* One who roves; a wanderer; in *archery*, a mark selected at random; in *croquet*, a ball that has gone through all the arches and needs only to strike the winning-peg to be out of the game.

rov-er² (rō′vẽr), *n.* [D. *roover*, < *rooven*, rob: see *reave*, and cf. *rob*.] A sea-robber or pirate (as, "the *rovers* whom Scandinavia had sent forth to ravage Western Europe": Macaulay's "Hist. of Eng.," i.); also, a ship employed in cruising for plunder (as, "Our ship . . . was surprised . . . by a Turkish *rover* of Sallee, who gave chase to us with all the sail she could make": Defoe's "Robinson Crusoe," i. 2).

Rove-beetle (*Ocypus olens*), natural size.

row¹ (rō), *v.* [AS. *rōwan* = D. *roeien* = LG. *rojen* = Icel. *rōa*, row; akin to L. *remus*, Gr. ἐρετμόν, oar: cf. *rudder*.] **I.** *intr.* To use oars or the like for propelling a boat, etc.; also, to be propelled by such means, as a boat. **II.** *tr.* To propel (a boat, etc.) by or as by the use of oars; also, to convey in a boat, etc., so propelled (as, "The General and I . . . got into the boat and were slowly *rowed* towards the shore": Kinglake's "Eothen," xxix.); convey or propel (something) in a manner suggestive of rowing; also, to perform (a race, etc.) by rowing; also, to use (oars or oarsmen) for rowing; also, to row against in a race.—**row¹**, *n.* A spell of rowing; an excursion in a rowboat.

row² (rō), *n.* [AS. *rāw, rǣw*, prob. akin to D. *rij*, G. *reihe*, row.] A number of persons or things arranged in a line, esp. a straight line; a rank; a file; often, a line of seats facing the same way and placed one alongside of another, in a theater, etc.; also, a line of plants in a field, etc.; also, a line of buildings facing the same way and standing contiguously or near together; esp., such a line of buildings more or less alike or forming an architectural whole; hence, a street formed by two continuous lines of buildings.

row³ (rou), *n.* [Origin obscure.] A violent disturbance or commotion (as, "What's the *row* there? Who's banging? What do you want?" Mark Twain's "Tom Sawyer," xxix.); a noisy dispute or quarrel (as, "It wasn't any ordinary difference of opinion; it was a '*row*'": H. G. Wells's "Tono-Bungay," ii. 4. § 2); also, noise or clamor. [Colloq.]—**row³**, *v.* **I.** *tr.* To assail roughly; upbraid severely: as, "If I had got up and gone out of the room . . . she would have *rowed* me in a nasty way" (J. Conrad's "Victory," iii. 4). [Colloq.] **II.** *intr.* To make a row or disturbance, engage in a noisy quarrel: as, "I don't want no row with you, and I don't want you to *row* with me" (H. G. Wells's "Mr. Polly," vii.). [Colloq.]

row-an (rō′an or rou′an), *n.* [From Scand.] The European mountain-ash, *Sorbus aucuparia*, a tree with red berries; either of two American mountain-ashes, *S. americana* and *S. sambucifolia*; also, the berry of any of these trees.—**row′an=tree**, *n.*

row-boat (rō′bōt), *n.* A boat propelled by rowing.

row-dy (rou′di). [Origin obscure.] **I.** *n.*; pl. -*dies* (-diz). A rough, disorderly person; one given to quarreling or fighting: as, "*Rowdies* imported from New York . . . filled the

---

(variable) ḍ as d or j, ş as s or sh, ṭ as t or ch, ẓ as z or zh; o, F. *cloche*; ü, F. *menu*; ċh, Sc. *loch*; ṅ, F. *bonbon*; ′, primary accent; ″, secondary accent; †, obsolete; <, from; +, and; =, equals. See also lists at beginning of book.

streets with noise" (Charnwood's "Abraham Lincoln," v.).
II. *a.* Of the nature of or characteristic of a rowdy; rough and disorderly.—**row′di-ness,** *n.*—**row′dy-ish,** *a.* Like, or characteristic of, a rowdy; disposed to or characterized by rowdyism.—**row′dy-ism,** *n.* Conduct characteristic of rowdies.

rowed (rōd), *a.* Having rows: as, six-*rowed* barley.

row-el (rou′el), *n.* [OF. *rouele, roele,* little wheel (F. *rouelle,* round slice), < ML. *rotella,* dim. of L. *rota,* wheel.] A small wheel with radiating points, forming the extremity of a horseman's spur (as, "Striking his *rowels* into his horse, he was out of sight in an instant": Jane Porter's "Scottish Chiefs," lxxviii.); in *vet. science,* a piece of leather or the like inserted beneath the skin of a horse or other animal to cause a discharge.—

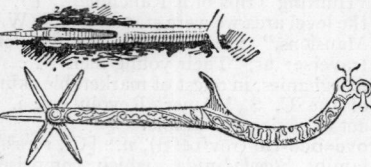

Spur with Rowel, 14th century.

row′el, *v. t.;* -*eled* or -*elled,* -*eling* or -*elling.* To prick, or urge on, with a rowel; in *vet. science,* to insert a rowel in.

row-en (rou′en), *n.* [ME. *roweyn, raweyne, rewayn,* akin to OF. F. *regain.*] The second crop of grass or hay in a season; the aftermath.

row-er (rō′ẽr), *n.* One who rows a boat.

row-lock (rō′lok, colloq. rul′ok), *n.* A contrivance on a boat's gunwale in or on which the oar rests and swings.

rox-burghe (roks′bur-ọ), *n.* [From the third Duke of *Roxburghe* (1740–1804), a famous bibliophile.] A style of bookbinding having a plain leather back with gilt lettering, cloth or paper sides, and the leaves gilt at the top and uncut at the front and bottom edges.

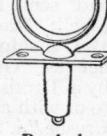

Rowlock.

roy-al (roi′al), *a.* [OF. *roial, reial* (F. *royal*), < L. *regalis,* E. *regal.*] Of or pertaining to a king, queen, or sovereign; pertaining to a sovereign with reference to his dignity or office (as, *royal* power or authority); pertaining to the sovereign as head of the state (as, a *royal* council; the *royal* army or navy); established or chartered by, or existing under the patronage of, a sovereign (as, a *royal* society, academy, or hospital); belonging to or used by a sovereign (as, a *royal* park; a *royal* palace); proceeding from or performed by a sovereign (as, a *royal* warrant; a *royal* progress); also, originating from or connected with a king or a line of kings (as, the *royal* family); belonging to the royal family (as, a *royal* prince); having the rank of a king or queen; also, befitting, or appropriate to, a sovereign, or princely, magnificent, or splendid (as, *royal* splendor; *royal* munificence); fine, first-rate, or excellent (colloq.: as, in *royal* spirits); also, having the character proper to a sovereign (as, "Cæsar was mighty, bold, *royal,* and loving": Shakspere's "Julius Cæsar," iii. 1. 127); majestic, noble, or generous; king-like, or having characteristics suggesting those of a king (as, that *royal* beast the lion); beyond the common or ordinary in size, quality, etc. (used as a specific qualification of many things of various kinds).—**royal antler,** the third branch (from the base) of a stag's horn.—**royal flush,** in *poker,* a straight flush in which the highest card is an ace.—**roy′al,** *n.* A royal person, or a member of the royal family (now colloq.); also, any of various obsolete coins†; also, a size of writing-paper, 19×24 inches, and of printing-paper, 20×25 inches; also, a royal antler; also, *naut.,* a small sail set on the royal-mast (as, "The order was given to loose the *royals*": Dana's "Two Years before the Mast," xxix.).—**roy′al-ism,** *n.* Adherence to a king, a royal government, or monarchical principles.—**roy′al-ist. I.** *n.* A supporter or adherent of a king or a royal government, esp. in times of rebellion or civil war. **II.** *a.* Of or pertaining to royalists.—**roy′al-ly,** *adv.*—**roy′al-mast,** *n.* *Naut.,* the mast next above the topgallantmast.—**roy′al-ty** (-ti), *n.;* pl. -*ties* (-tiz). [OF. *roialte* (F. *royauté*), < ML. *regalitas:* cf. *regality.*] Royal status, dignity, or power; sovereignty; also, character or quality proper to or befitting a sovereign; kingliness; nobility; generosity; also, a royal person, or royal persons collectively (as, "Crowds of the surrounding *royalties* [in

Germany] swooped down to welcome her," Lytton Strachey's "Queen Victoria," iv.; "a separate car, specially reserved for the accommodation of *royalty,*" H. Melville's "Moby-Dick," xc.); also, a royal domain; a kingdom; a realm; also, a prerogative or right belonging to a king or sovereign (as, "Wherefore do I assume These *royalties,* and not refuse to reign?" Milton's "Paradise Lost," ii. 451); also, a royal right, as over minerals, granted by a sovereign to a person or corporation; the payment made for such a right; also, a compensation or portion of proceeds paid to the owner of a right, as a patent, for the use of it; a fixed portion of the proceeds from his work, paid to an author, composer, etc.

roys-ter (rois′tẽr), etc. See *roister,* etc.

rub (rub), *v. t.;* *rubbed, rubbing.* [ME. *rubben* = LG. *rubben.*] To subject (an object) to the action of something moved over it with pressure; often, to subject to pressure and friction in order to clean, smooth, polish, etc.; treat by pressure and friction, as with something in a soft or liquid form (as, to *rub* the arm with liniment); also, to move (something) with pressure and friction over something else (as, "The cattle were free to *rub* their hides on the tree trunks": W. H. Hudson's "Far Away and Long Ago," xii.); also, to move (things) with pressure and friction over each other (with *together,* etc.: as, a cricket produces its characteristic sound by *rubbing* together certain parts of the body); sometimes, to move (the hands) over each other in showing satisfaction (as, "Solomon Gills *rubbed* his hands with an air of stealthy enjoyment," Dickens's "Dombey and Son," iv.; "I *rubbed* my hands, I sung aloud in my glee," Stevenson's "Master of Ballantrae," v.); also, to apply, spread, force, etc., by rubbing (with *over, in, into,* etc.: as, to *rub* a remedy over or into the skin); also, to remove by rubbing (with *off, out,* etc.: as, to *rub* off rust; to *rub* out marks).—**to rub it in,** *fig.,* to emphasize or reiterate something unpleasant: as, "'You said he wasn't a concert-player and never would be —' 'Don't *rub* it in, Madam,' said Mr. Shinner merrily" (Arnold Bennett's "Lion's Share," xlvi.). [Slang.]—**rub,** *v. i.* To exert pressure and friction on something; move with pressure against something (as, "Stray, homeless cats *rubbed* against his legs": W. Churchill's "Modern Chronicle," i. 2); fig., to proceed, continue in a course, or keep going, with effort or difficulty (with *on, along, through,* etc.: as, "We . . . now just *rubbed* on from hand to mouth," B. Franklin's "Autobiography," iii.; "We'll *rub* along," Mrs. H. Ward's "Robert Elsmere," xix.); also, to admit of being rubbed (*off,* etc.).—**rub,** *n.* An act or the act of rubbing (as, "The rest of the servants were giving a final *rub* to the weapons of the chase": F. M. Crawford's "Mr. Isaacs," ix.); also, something irritating to the feelings; a reproof, gibe, sarcasm, or the like (as, "I had the management of the paper; and I made bold to give our rulers some *rubs* in it": B. Franklin's "Autobiography," i.); an annoying experience or circumstance (as, "those little *rubs* which Providence sends to enhance the value of its favours": Goldsmith's "Vicar of Wakefield," i.); also, an obstacle, impediment, or difficulty (as, "She knew every hard *rub* . . . in the Latin grammar by heart," Mrs. Stowe's "Oldtown Folks," xxxiii.; "To sleep: perchance to dream: ay, there's the *rub,*" Shakspere's "Hamlet," iii. 1. 65); also, an unevenness† or inequality†; also, a rough or abraded spot due to rubbing.

rub-a-dub, rub=a=dub (rub′a-dub′), *n.* [Imit.] The sound of a drum when beaten.—**rub′a-dub′, rub′=a=dub′,** *v. i.;* -*dubbed,* -*dubbing.* To give forth the sound of a drum when beaten: as, "I heard a drum go rolling, *Rub-a-dubbing* in the distance" (Henley's "In Hospital," xxi.).

ru-bá-i (rö-bä′i), *n.;* pl. *rubáiyát* (rö-bäi′yät). [Ar. and Pers. *rubā′i,* pl. *rubā′iyát.*] A quatrain: as, the "*Rubáiyát*" of Omar Khayyam (rendered into English from the Persian by Edward FitzGerald in 1859).

ru-basse (rö-bas′), *n.* [F. *rubasse, rubace,* akin to *rubis,* ruby.] A beautiful variety of rock-crystal containing minute particles of specular iron ore which reflect a bright red color: used as a gem.

ru-ba-to (rö-bä′tō), *a.* [It., 'robbed.'] In *music,* having certain notes of a measure arbitrarily lengthened while others are correspondingly shortened.

---

rub-ber[1] (rub'ėr), *n.* One who rubs; one who practises rubbing, as in order to smooth or polish something; one who makes rubbings; one who practises massage, or who rubs persons down, as at a bath; one who rubs horses down, as those used for racing; also, an instrument, implement, etc., used for rubbing something; a coarse file; a towel or piece of cloth for rubbing the body after bathing or for rubbing horses down; a kind of brush consisting of wool, felt, or the like, fastened to a back, for erasing chalk from a blackboard or slate; a piece of caoutchouc, or india-rubber, for erasing pencil marks, etc.; also, caoutchouc or india-rubber; also, something made of india-rubber; an india-rubber band, or elastic, as for holding things together; an overshoe (usually in *pl.*); in *baseball*, the home base or plate, or the slab marking the pitcher's position, both made (properly) of whitened rubber.—**rub'-ber**[1], *v. i.* [Cf. **rubberneck**.] To stretch the neck or turn the head in order to look at something; hence, to pry into the affairs of others. [Slang, U. S.]

rub-ber[2] (rub'ėr), *n.* [Origin uncertain.] In certain games, as whist, a series of games of an odd number, usually three, the last of which is played to decide the contest when each side has won the same number of games; two games out of three (or three out of five, etc.) won by the same side; the decisive game in a series of this kind.

rub-ber-ize (rub'ėr-īz), *v. t.; -ized, -izing.* To coat or impregnate with india-rubber or some preparation of it.

rub-ber-neck (rub'ėr-nek), *n.* One given to stretching the neck in looking at things, esp. in idle or impertinent curiosity. [Slang, U. S.]

rub-ber=plant (rub'ėr-plant), *n.* Any plant yielding caoutchouc or india-rubber; esp., a moraceous plant, *Ficus elastica,* with oblong, shining, leathery leaves, growing native as a tall tree in India, the Malay Archipelago, etc., and much cultivated in Europe and America as an ornamental house-plant.

rub-ber-y (rub'ėr-i), *a.* Like india-rubber; elastic; tough.

rub-bing (rub'ing), *n.* The act of one who or that which rubs; also, a reproduction of an incised or sculptured surface made by laying paper or the like upon it and rubbing with some marking substance.

rub-bish (rub'ish), *n.* [ME. *robous, robys*; origin obscure: cf. *rubble.*] Waste or refuse material; debris; litter; fig., worthless stuff, or trash (as, "What trash is Rome, What *rubbish* and what offal!" Shakspere's "Julius Cæsar," i. 3. 109; "selling slightly injurious *rubbish* at one-and-three-halfpence . . . a bottle," H. G. Wells's "Tono-Bungay," ii. 3. § 1); often, worthless or nonsensical ideas, talk, writing, etc., or nonsense (as, "all this modern newspaper *rubbish* about a New York aristocracy," Mrs. Wharton's "Age of Innocence," vi.; "Do you suppose I am not aware that my books are *rubbish?*" Gissing's "New Grub Street," iv.).—**rub'bish-ing**, *a.* Rubbishy; trashy: as, "*rubbishing* novels" (W. De Morgan's "Joseph Vance," x.).—**rub'-bish-y**, *a.* Abounding in or covered with rubbish; also, of the nature of rubbish; trashy; paltry.

rub-ble (rub'l), *n.* [ME. *robyl, robel*: cf. *rubbish.*] Rough fragments of broken stone, formed by geological action, in quarrying, etc., and sometimes used in masonry; masonry built of such stone; also, any solid substance, as ice, in irregularly broken pieces.—**rub'ble=work**, *n.* Masonry built of rubble or roughly dressed stones.—**rub'bly**, *a.* Abounding in, consisting of, or of the nature of rubble.

rube (rōb), *n.* [Abbr. of *Reuben*, man's name.] An unsophisticated countryman. [Slang.]

ru-be-fa-cient (rō-bē-fā'shent), *a.* [L. *rubefaciens* (-ent-), ppr. of *rubefacere*, make red, < *rubere*, be red, + *facere*, make.] **I.** *a.* Producing redness, esp. of the skin, as a medicinal application. **II.** *n.* A rubefacient application, as a mustard-plaster.—**ru-be-fac'tion** (-fak'shon), *n.* A making red, esp. with a rubefacient; redness of the skin produced by a rubefacient.

ru-bel-la (rō-bel'ä), *n.* [NL., prop. fem. of L. *rubellus*, reddish, dim. of *ruber*, red.] In *pathol.*, a contagious disease characterized by a reddish eruption like that of measles, but usually with only slight catarrhal and febrile symptoms; German measles.

ru-bel-lite (rō'be-līt), *n.* [L. *rubellus*, reddish: see *rubella.*] A red variety of tourmalin, used as a gem.

ru-be-o-la (rō-bē'ọ-lä), *n.* [NL., dim. < L. *rubeus*, red.] In *pathol.*, measles; also, rubella.—**ru-be'o-lar** (-lär), *a.*

ru-bes-cent (rō-bes'ent), *a.* [L. *rubescens* (-ent-), ppr. of *rubescere*, become red, < *rubere*, be red.] Becoming red; blushing.—**ru-bes'cence**, *n.*

ru-bi-a-ceous (rō-bi-ā'shius), *a.* [L. *rubia*, madder.] Belonging to the *Rubiaceæ*, or madder family of plants, including also the coffee, cinchona, and ipecacuanha plants, the gardenia, partridge-berry, houstonia, bedstraw, etc.

Ru-bi-con (rō'bi-kon), *n.* [From the river *Rubicon*, a southern limit of Cæsar's province of Cisalpine Gaul, by crossing which, in 49 B.C., he began a civil war.] A limit the crossing of which is a decisive and irrevocable step.

ru-bi-cund (rō'bi-kund), *a.* [L. *rubicundus*, < *rubere*, be red.] Red or reddish (now chiefly with reference to the face or complexion); ruddy: as, "the cheery, *rubicund* faces of children" (Mrs. Stowe's "Oldtown Folks," xxxiv.); "He was sixty-five, pompous, large, and *rubicund*" (Eden Phillpotts's "Grey Room," i.).—**ru-bi-cun'di-ty** (-kun'di-ti), *n.*

ru-bid-i-um (rō-bid'i-um), *n.* [NL., < L. *rubidus*, red, < *rubere*, be red; named from red lines in its spectrum.] Chem. sym., Rb; at. wt., 85.45; sp. gr., 1.52. A silver-white metallic element resembling potassium.

ru-bied (rō'bid), *p. a.* Colored like the ruby.

ru-big-i-nous (rō-bij'i-nus), *a.* [L. *rubiginosus*, < *rubigo, robigo*, rust.] Rusty; rust-colored; of plants, affected with the disease rust.

ru-bi-ous (rō'bi-us), *a.* Ruby-colored; red.

ru-ble (rō'bl), *n.* [Russ. *rubl.*] The monetary unit and a

Ruble, 1862. — British Museum.

Obverse.   Reverse.

silver coin of Russia, equal to 100 kopecks, and normally equivalent to about 51¼ U. S. cents.

ru-bric (rō'brik). [OF. F. *rubrique*, < L. *rubrica*, red earth, < *ruber*, red.] **I.** *n.* Red earth or ocher (archaic); also, a title, heading, direction, or the like, in a manuscript, book, etc., written or printed in red or otherwise distinguished from the rest of the text; the title or a heading of a statute, etc. (orig. written in red); a direction for the conduct of divine service or the administration of the sacraments, inserted in liturgical books (orig. and properly in red). **II.** *a.* Red; reddish; rubrical.—**ru'bri-cal**, *a.* Red; marked with red; also, of, pertaining to, or enjoined by liturgical rubrics.—**ru'bri-cal-ly**, *adv.*

ru-bri-cate (rō'bri-kāt), *v. t.; -cated, -cating.* [L. *rubricatus*, pp. of *rubricare*, < *rubrica*: see *rubric.*] To mark or color with red; also, to furnish with or regulate by rubrics.—**ru-bri-ca'tion** (-kā'shon), *n.* The act of rubricating; also, that which is rubricated, or colored with red, as a title or heading in a manuscript.—**ru'bri-ca-tor**, *n.*

ru-bri-cose (rō'bri-kōs), *a.* [L. *rubricosus*, < *rubrica*: see *rubric.*] Marked with red; reddish.

ru-by (rō'bi). [OF. *rubi*, also *rubin* (F. *rubis*), < L. *rubeus* or *ruber*, red; akin to E. *red*[1].] **I.** *n.; pl. -bies* (-biz). A red variety of corundum, highly prized as a gem ('true ruby' or 'oriental ruby'); a piece of this stone; any of various other red gems, as a variety of spinel ('spinel ruby'); also, a deep, glowing red color (as, "the natural *ruby* of your cheeks": Shakspere's "Macbeth," iii. 4. 115); also, something resembling a ruby or having a color similar to that of the ruby; a pimple, as on the face; *pl.*, the lips (see Shakspere's "Cymbeline," ii. 2. 17); *sing.*, red wine (as, "Still the Vine her ancient *Ruby* yields": FitzGerald's tr. Omar Khayyam's "Rubáiyát," v.); in *horol.*, a jewel or bearing of a watch, made of ruby or other material; in *printing*, a type (about 5½ point) nearly corresponding in size to American agate (Eng.). **II.** *a.* Of the color called ruby: as, "*ruby* lips" (Shakspere's "Julius Cæsar," iii. 1. 260).—**ru′by,** *v. t.*; *rubied*, *rubying*. To make of ruby color.—**ru′by-tail,** *n.* Any of numerous small, solitary, brilliantly colored, parasitic, aculeate hymenopterous insects (family *Chrysididæ*) which lay their eggs in the nests of other insects, as *Chrysis ignita*, a European species having the abdomen of a ruby color.

ru-cer-vine (rŏ-sėr′vin), *a.* [NL. *Rucervus*, < Malay *rūsa*, deer, + L. *cervus*, deer.] Of or pertaining to the genus *Rucervus*, comprising East Indian deer with doubly dichotomous antlers.

ruche (rösh), *n.* [F., beehive, ruche; from Celtic.] A full pleating or frilling of lace, net, muslin, ribbon, etc., used as a trimming or finish for women's dress.—**ruch-ing** (rö′-shing), *n.* Material made into a ruche.

ruck[1] (ruk), *n.* [Cf. Icel. *hrukka*, a wrinkle.] A fold, crease, or wrinkle, as in a garment.—**ruck**[1], *v. i.* or *t.* To draw up into creases; wrinkle.

ruck[2] (ruk), *n.* [Prob. from Scand.: cf. Icel. *hraukr*, small stack, rick.] A heap or pile of material (now chiefly prov.); hence, a large number or quantity; a crowd or throng; also, the great mass of undistinguished or inferior persons or things (as, "Here in the *ruck*, anyhow, Surging along, Louts, duffers, exquisites, students, and prigs": Henley's "In Hospital," xi.); also, the horses left behind in a race (as, "a brillant young charioteer in the *ruck* of the race": G. Meredith's "Diana of the Crossways," xv.).

ruck-sack (rŭk′sak), *n.* [G., lit. 'back sack.'] A kind of knapsack carried by tourists, etc.

ruck-us (ruk′us), *n.* Same as *rucus*. [Slang, U. S.]

ruc-tion (ruk′shọn), *n.* [Perhaps a corruption of *eruption*.] A disturbance, quarrel, or row: as, "when the racial *ructions* rise" (Kipling's "Et Dona Ferentes"). [Colloq.]

ru-cus (rö′kus), *n.* [Also *rookus*, *ruckus*; origin obscure.] A disturbance; a rumpus; a row. [Slang, U. S.]

rud (rud), *n.* [AS. *rudu*, akin to *rēad*, E. *red*[1].] Red or ruddy color (archaic or prov.); also, complexion†; also, ruddle (now prov.).

ru-das (rö′das). [Origin obscure.] **I.** *n.* A coarse, ill-natured old woman; a hag; a beldam. [Sc.] **II.** *a.* Hag-like; coarse; unmannerly. [Sc.]

rud-beck-i-a (rud-bek′i-ạ), *n.* [NL.; from *Rudbeck*, name of Swedish botanical writers.] Any of the showy-flowered asteraceous herbs constituting the genus *Rudbeckia*, as *R. hirta*, the yellow daisy, whose flower-head has a dark disk and yellow rays; a coneflower.

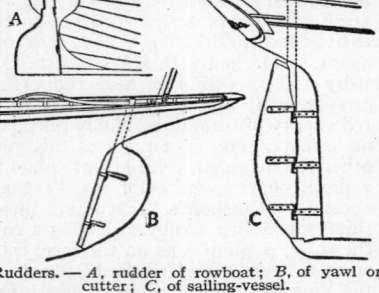
Rudbeckia (*R. hirta*).—1, upper part of the stem with the heads; 2, lower part of the stem; *a*, the achenium.

rudd (rud), *n.* [Prob. = *rud*.] A European fresh-water fish, *Scardinius erythrophthalmus*, of the carp family.

rud-der (rud′ėr), *n.* [AS. *rōther* (= D. *roer* = G. *ruder*), from the stem of *rōwan*, E. *row*[1].] A movable flat piece hinged vertically at the stern of a boat or ship as a means of steering; also, an analogous device for steering an aëroplane, etc., hinged vertically (for right-and-left steering) or horizontally (for up-and-down steering); fig., one who or that which guides or directs.—**rud′dered,** *a.* Having a rudder.—**rud′der-less,** *a.* Without a rudder.

Rudders.—*A*, rudder of rowboat; *B*, of yawl or cutter; *C*, of sailing-vessel.

rud-di-ly (rud′i-li), *adv.* In a ruddy manner; with a ruddy hue.—**rud′di-ness,** *n.*

rud-dle (rud′l), *n.* [From *rud*.] A red variety of ocher, used for marking sheep, coloring, etc.—**rud′dle,** *v. t.*; *-dled*, *-dling.* To mark or color with ruddle.

rud-dock (rud′ọk), *n.* [AS. *rudduc*: cf. *rud*.] The European robin: as, "The sweet And shrilly *ruddock*, with its bleeding breast" (Hood's "Midsummer Fairies," lv.).

rud-dy (rud′i), *a.*; compar. *ruddier*, superl. *ruddiest*. [AS. *rudig*, < *rudu*, E. *rud*.] Of a fresh, healthy red or reddish color, as the complexion, cheeks, face, etc.; having a fresh red color in the cheeks, etc., as a person (as, "a short, stout, *ruddy* young fellow": H. Melville's "Moby-Dick," xxvii.); red or reddish, as color (as, "Notwithstanding his age there was a *ruddy* tinge upon his features": Borrow's "Bible in Spain," v.); in general, of a red or reddish color (as, "As dear to me as are the *ruddy* drops That visit my sad heart," Shakspere's "Julius Cæsar," ii. 1. 289; the *ruddy* glow of a fire; "the *ruddier* orange, and the paler lime," Cowper's "Task," iii. 573).—**ruddy duck,** a North American fresh-water duck, *Erismatura rubida* (or *jamaicensis*), the adult male of which has the sides and upper parts of a brownish-red color.—**rud′dy,** *v. t.*; *-died*, *-dying.* To make ruddy; redden: as, "A wondrous blaze was seen to gleam . . . It *ruddied* all the copse-wood glen" (Scott's "Lay of the Last Minstrel," vi. 23).

Ruddy Duck.

rude (röd), *a.*; compar. *ruder*, superl. *rudest.* [OF. F. *rude*, < L. *rudis*, unwrought, unformed, raw, rough, uncultivated, unskilled, inexperienced.] Unwrought, raw, or crude (as, *rude* stone or metal; iron in the *rude* state); uncultivated or wild, esp. roughly wild, or rugged, as land, etc. (as, "this island, spot of unreclaim'd *rude* earth," Cowper's "Expostulation," 468; *rude* hills); also, roughly wrought, built, or formed, or of a rough or crude make or kind (as, *rude* tools; a *rude* cabin or boat; "a *rude* bed upon the floor," Dickens's "Oliver Twist," xix.; "limbs . . . very much swelled with the *rude* bandage he had been tied with," Defoe's "Robinson Crusoe," i. 16); imperfectly or unskilfully made or done, rough, or clumsy (as, a *rude* drawing or inscription; a *rude* handwriting); without literary or rhetorical elegance or merit, or unpolished (as, *rude* rimes or ballads; *rude* oratory); without artistic elegance, or of a primitive crudeness or simplicity (as, "The temple . . . is of *rude* design and indifferent execution," Amelia B. Edwards's "Thousand Miles up the Nile," xiv.; "The *rude* magnificence of the inner court amply corresponded with the grandeur of the exterior," Scott's "Guy Mannering," iv.); also, without culture, learning, or refinement (as, "the *rude* forefathers of the hamlet," Gray's "Elegy," iv.; "a *rude* and unlearned age," J. Butler's "Analogy of Religion," ii. 7); uncivilized or barbarous (as, *rude* tribes; the *rudest* savages); without refined elegance or delicacy, rough, or homely (as, the *rude* life of the frontier; *rude* comfort; *rude* sympathy); coarse, or not fine or choice (as, *rude* clothing; *rude* fare; "the *rude* and scanty produce of their own mountains," Scott's "Castle Dangerous," i.); also, rough in manners or behavior, or unmannerly (as, "In far less polished days, A time when rough *rude* man had naughty waỳs," Burns's "Rights of Woman," 18; "The *rude* mob reviled them in the street," Hawthorne's "Twice-Told Tales," Old Esther Dudley); grossly uncivil, discourteous, or impolite (as, to be *rude* to a person; a *rude* reply; "I knew it was very *rude* to stare at people," Watts-Dunton's "Aylwin," i. 2); also, rough, harsh, or ungentle (as, *rude* hands; a *rude* grasp, blow, or shock; "Futile proceedings in the House of Commons had been brought to a *rude* close," Morley's "Oliver Cromwell," iii. 6); violent or tempestuous, as the wind, waves, etc.; also, robust, sturdy, or vigorous (as, *rude* health; *rude* strength; "The morning air has given me a *rude* appetite," Longfellow's "Hyperion," iii. 4); also, harsh to the ear, as sounds.—**rude′ly**, *adv.*—**rude′ness**, *n.*—**rudes-by** (rödz′bi), *n.*; pl. *-bies* (-biz). A rude or unmannerly fellow: as, "*Rudesby*, be gone!" (Shakspere's "Twelfth Night," iv. 1. 55). [Archaic.]

Rü-des-heim-er (rü′des-hī′mèr), *n.* [G., < *Rüdesheim*, town on the Rhine.] A fine white Rhine wine.

ru-di-ment (rö′di-ment), *n.* [L. *rudimentum*, a first attempt, beginning (esp. of military training: *rudimentum ponere*, to 'lay down,' or complete, the elementary training), first principle, < *rudis*, unwrought, raw, inexperienced, E. *rude*.] A beginning or elementary part of learning or education (chiefly in *pl.*: as, "But first I mean To exercise him in the wilderness: There he shall first lay down the *rudiments* [see etym.] Of his great warfare, ere I send him forth To conquer Sin and Death," Milton's "Paradise Regained," i. 157; "Mr. Geoffry Wildgoose received the first *rudiments* of his education at a little free-school," R. Graves's "Spiritual Quixote," i. 1; to be taught one's *rudiments*); *pl.*, the elements or first principles of a subject (as, the *rudiments* of grammar, algebra, or painting; "This boy . . . hath been tutor'd in the *rudiments* Of many desperate studies," Shakspere's "As You Like It," v. 4. 31); also, *sing.*, a mere beginning, first slight appearance, or undeveloped or imperfect form of something (often in *pl.*: as, "a youth . . . who apparently had not in him even the *rudiments* of worldly successfulness," Arnold Bennett's "Helen with the High Hand," ii.); in *biol.*, an organ or part incompletely developed in size or structure, as one in an embryonic stage, one arrested in growth, or one with no functional activity, as a vestige.—**ru-di-men′tal** (-men′tal), *a.* Rudimentary.—**ru-di-men′ta-ry** (-ta-ri), *a.* Pertaining to rudiments or first principles; elementary; also, of the nature of a rudiment; undeveloped; imperfect.—**ru-di-men′ta-ri-ly**, *adv.*—**ru-di-men′ta-ri-ness**, *n.*

rue¹ (rö), *n.* [OF. F. *rue*, < L. *ruta*, < Gr. ῥυτή, rue.] Any of the strongly scented plants constituting the genus *Ruta*, esp. *R. graveolens*, a yellow-flowered herb with decompound leaves formerly much used in medicine; also, any of various other plants (as, meadow-*rue*; goat's-*rue*).

Rue (*Ruta graveolens*).

rue² (rö), *v.*; *rued*, *ruing*. [AS. *hrēowan* = D. *rouwen* = G. *reuen*, rue: cf. *ruth*.] **I.** *tr.* To make sorrowful†, or grieve†; make repentant or sorry†; affect with pity or compassion†; also, to feel sorrow over (as, "Was ever son so *rued* a father's death?" Shakspere's "3 Henry VI.," ii. 5. 109); repent of or feel remorse for (wrong-doing, etc.); be sorry for or regret bitterly (one's own action, conduct, etc.) as bringing unpleasant consequences (as, "Thou shalt *rue* this treason," Shakspere's "1 Henry VI.," iii. 2. 36; "If you attempt it, you shall never cease to *rue* your folly," Godwin's "Caleb Williams," xx.); repent of or regret (a bargain, promise, etc.); in general, to regret as unfortunate, or regard as something that one wishes might never have been done, taken place, etc. (without or with self-reproach: as, "In all her gates Abaddon *rues* Thy bold attempt," Milton's "Paradise Regained," iv. 624; to *rue* the day one was born; "to make us *rue* the hour we let ourselves forget this wasn't our private war," G. W. Cable's "Cavalier," xxxi.); also, to pity†. **II.** *intr.* To feel sorrow; be repentant; feel regret or dissatisfaction; also, to have pity or compassion (archaic: as, "*Rue* on thy despairing lover!" Burns's "Fair Eliza").—**rue²**, *n.* [AS. *hrēow*.] Sorrow; repentance; regret; also, pity or compassion. [Archaic or prov.]

rue-a-nem-o-ne (rö′a-nem′ō-nē), *n.* A small ranunculaceous plant, *Syndesmon thalictroides*, of North America, bearing white or pinkish flowers.

rue-ful (rö′fúl), *a.* Sorrowful, unhappy, or dejected, as persons (as, "A small *rueful* disillusioned . . . little Bealby crept back into the visible universe again": H. G. Wells's "Bealby," iv.); mournful or doleful, as the face, looks, utterances, etc. (as, the Knight of the *Rueful* Countenance,

Don Quixote, the hero of Cervantes's romance; "with *rueful* cry," Milton's "Samson Agonistes," 1553); often, feeling, showing, or expressing a regretful or self-reproachful dismay (as, "He looked so genuinely *rueful* and abashed that Sabre laughed," A. S. M. Hutchinson's "If Winter Comes," ii. 1; "Here is Cromwell's *rueful* admission. 'Truly I will now come and tell you a story of my own weakness and folly,'" Morley's "Oliver Cromwell," iv. 7); also, such as to excite sorrow or pity, deplorable, or pitiable (as, a *rueful* spectacle; in a *rueful* plight).—**rue′ful-ly**, *adv.*—**rue′ful-ness**, *n.*

ru-fes-cent (rö-fes′ent), *a.* [L. *rufescens* (-ent-), ppr. of *rufescere*, become reddish, < *rufus*, E. *rufous*.] Somewhat rufous or reddish.—**ru-fes′cence**, *n.*

ruff¹ (ruf), *n.* [Origin uncertain: cf. *ruffle¹*.] A neck-piece or collar of lace, lawn, etc., gathered or drawn into deep, full, regular folds, much worn in the 16th century

Ruff. — Close of 16th century.

by both men and women; also, something resembling such a piece in form or position; in *mach.*, an annular ridge on a shaft or the like, as at a journal, to prevent motion endwise; in *zoöl.*, a collar, or set of lengthened or specially marked hairs or feathers, on the neck of an animal; also, one of a breed of domestic pigeons having a ruff on the neck.

ruff² (ruf), *n.* [Cf. *ruff¹* and *reeve³*.] A sandpiper, *Pavoncella pugnax*, the male of which has an enormous frill of feathers on the neck during the breeding season: the female is called a *reeve*.

ruff³ (ruf), *n.* [ME. *ruf*, *roffe*; origin uncertain.] A small European freshwater fish, *Acerina cernua*, of the perch family.

Ruff (*Pavoncella pugnax*).

ruff⁴ (ruf), *n.* [Cf. obs. F. *roufle*, *ronfle*, It. *ronfa*, card-game, perhaps corruptions of F. *triomphe*, It. *trionfo*, E. *triumph*.] An old game at cards, resembling whist†; in *card-playing*, the act of trumping when one cannot follow suit.—**ruff⁴**, *v. t.* or *i.* In *card-playing*, to trump when unable to follow suit.

ruffed (ruft), *a.* Having a ruff.—**ruffed grouse**, a North American game-bird, *Bonasa umbellus*, having a tuft of feathers on each side of the neck: called *partridge* in the northeastern U. S., and *pheasant* in the southern U. S.

ruf-fian (ruf′ian), *n.* [F. *rufian*, *rufien*; origin uncertain.] **I.** *n.* A rough, lawless fellow; a brutal bully: as, "Have you a *ruffian* that will swear, drink . . . rob, murder?" (Shakspere's "2 Henry IV.," iv. 5. 125); "an abominable lot of lawless *ruffians*" (J. Conrad's "Rover," i.). **II.** *a.* Having the character of a ruffian or ruffians (as, "the most *ruffian* enemy": Borrow's "Lavengro," iv.); also, belonging or pertaining to, or characteristic of, a ruffian or ruffians (as, "some *ruffian* voice," J. H. Newman's "Callista," xvii.; "*ruffian* faces," Parkman's "Oregon Trail," xxvi.).—**ruf′fian**, *v. i.* To play the ruffian.—**ruf′fian-ism**, *n.* Conduct befitting a ruffian; ruffianly character.—**ruf′fian-ly**, *a.* Having the character of, also, characteristic of or befitting a ruffian.

ruf-fle¹ (ruf′l), *v.*; *-fled*, *-fling*. [ME. *ruffelen* = LG. *ruffelen* = D. *ruifelen*, wrinkle.] **I.** *tr.* To destroy the smoothness or evenness of, or wrinkle (as, "My mother's brow, before somewhat *ruffled*, grew smooth on the instant": Bulwer-Lytton's "Caxtons," v. 1); roughen or abrade (the skin, etc.); cause to rise in ripples or waves (as, "But what if the stormy cloud should come, And *ruffle* the silver sea?" Holmes's "Star and the Water-Lily"); throw or form into uneven masses (as, "the breeze, *ruffling* the desert sand": Galsworthy's "Saint's Progress," iv. 6); disarrange, as the hair, feathers, etc. (as, "He *ruffled* up his gray moustache with thumb and forefinger": Tarkington's "Alice Adams," xvi.); erect (the feathers), as in anger, as a bird; in general, to disorder; disturb; often, to disturb (the mind, one's composure, peaceful relations, etc.: as, "The usual serenity of his disposition was slightly *ruffled*," W. Churchill's "Modern Chronicle," i. 9); discompose, annoy, or irritate (a person: as, "By nature she was of an even temper, more willing to be pleased than *ruffled*," S. Butler's "Way of All Flesh," lxxxiii.; "He was not *ruffled* by the immense disappointment," Arnold Bennett's "Roll-Call," ii.); also, to draw up (cloth, lace, etc.) into a ruffle, as by gathering along one edge; trim with ruffles; also, to turn over (the pages of a book) rapidly; pass (cards) through the fingers rapidly. **II.** *intr.* To rise unevenly; form folds, ripples, etc.; flutter, as a flag in the breeze; also, to show annoyance or irritation (as, " 'Of course you consider it would have been so,' sighed the lady, *ruffling*": G. Meredith's "Ordeal of Richard Feverel," xiii.).—**ruf′fle**[1], *n.* A break in the smoothness or evenness of some surface, as of water; also, a strip of cloth, lace, etc., drawn up by gathering along one edge, and used as a trimming on dress, etc.; some object resembling this, as the ruff of a bird; also, a disturbed state of the mind; perturbation; also, a disturbing experience, or an annoyance or vexation (as, "the ordinary rubs and *ruffles* which disturb even the most uniform life": Scott's "Heart of Midlothian," xlvii.).

ruf-fle[2] (ruf′l), *v.*; *-fled, -fling.* [ME. *ruffelyn*; origin uncertain.] **I.** *intr.* To contend or struggle (as, "She had lords and lairds that would *ruffle* for her": Scott's "Abbot," xxvi.); act in a contentious, bullying, or arrogant way; fig., of winds, waves, etc., to be violent or rough; also, of persons, to act proudly or ostentatiously, swagger, or make a display (often with indefinite *it*: as, "If I go not brave myself, those whom I trust have ever the means to *ruffle it* with the best," Scott's "Quentin Durward," xi.; "Here he was, a provincial man of business, *ruffling it* with the best of them!" Arnold Bennett's "The Old Adam," vii.). [Archaic.] **II.†** *tr.* To handle roughly; bully.—**ruf′fle**[2], *n.* A struggle; a fight; a brawl: as, "the *ruffle* betwixt the Scottish Archers and the provost-marshal's guard" (Scott's "Quentin Durward," vii.). [Archaic.]

ruf-fle[3] (ruf′l), *n.* [Also earlier *ruff*: cf. Pg. *rufla, rufo*, roll of a drum, *rufar*, beat a roll.] A low, continuous beating of a drum, less loud than the roll.—**ruf′fle**[3], *v. t.*; *-fled, -fling.* To beat a ruffle on (a drum).

ruf-fler[1] (ruf′lėr), *n.* [See *ruffle*[1], *v.*] One who or that which ruffles (as, "that enemy of all repose and *ruffler* of even tempers — the mosquito": H. Melville's "Typee," xxviii.); esp., a sewing-machine attachment for gathering cloth into ruffles.

ruf-fler[2] (ruf′lėr), *n.* [See *ruffle*[2], *v.*] One of a class of bullying vagabonds common in the 16th century†; also, a swaggering fellow (archaic: as, "the meanest *ruffler* who, with broken feather and tarnished lace, swaggered at the heels of Turenne," S. J. Weyman's "Gentleman of France," i.).

ru-fous (rö′fus), *a.* [L. *rufus*, red, reddish; akin to E. *red*[1].] Of a reddish or reddish-brown color.

rug[1] (rug), *n.* [Prob. from Scand.] A piece of thick, warm cloth used as a coverlet, lap-robe, etc.; also, a square or oblong piece of carpeting, often elaborate in design and workmanship, used as a floor-covering or a hanging; also, a mat or the like made from the pelt of an animal.

rug[2] (rug), *v. t.* or *i.*; *rugged, rugging.* [ME. *ruggen, roggen*; prob. from Scand.] To pull roughly; tug. [Sc. and north. Eng.]—**rug**[2], *n.* A pull; a tug. [Sc.]

ru-ga (rö′gä), *n.*; pl. *-gæ* (-jē). [L.] A wrinkle, fold, or ridge.—**ru′gate** (-gāt), *a.* Wrinkled; rugose.

Rug-by (rug′bi) **foot′ball.** [From the *Rugby* public school, in Warwickshire, England.] An English form of the game of football (of which the common American game is a development) in which handling and carrying of the ball are permitted. Cf. *soccer.*

rug-ged (rug′ed), *a.* [ME. *rugged, roggyd*; prob. from Scand.: cf. *rug*[1].] Rough or shaggy, as with hair or as hair† (as, "the *rugged* Russian bear": Shakspere's "Macbeth," iii. 4. 100); also, rough with projections or irregularities of surface (as, *rugged* rocks; "the *rugged* bark of some broad elm," Milton's "Comus," 354); of ground, etc., roughly broken, rocky, hilly, or otherwise difficult of passage (as, "a quarter of a mile's slow and toilsome advance up a broken and *rugged* ascent," Scott's "Legend of Montrose," iii.; "So onward, o'er the *rugged* way That runs through rocks and sand," Holmes's "Agnes," ii.); of the brow, face, etc., wrinkled or furrowed; of the features, face, etc., roughly irregular, heavy, or hard in outline or form, rather than smoothly rounded or delicately shaped (as, "a tall rawboned man, of an extremely *rugged* countenance": Scott's "Castle Dangerous," vii.); also, rough or tempestuous, as weather; severe, hard, or trying, as times, life, etc.; rough, harsh, or stern, as persons, the nature, etc. (as, "By slow prudence to make mild A *rugged* people," Tennyson's "Ulysses," 37; "the *rugged*, dour, and unyielding persistency of the northern Covenanters," Morley's "Oliver Cromwell," iii. 3); ungentle, or roughly rude, as actions, etc. (as, "When offended, his customary behaviour was exceedingly *rugged*," Godwin's "Caleb Williams," xix.; "a creature incapable, by nature, of a *rugged* tone or a coarse gesture," Reade's "Christie Johnstone," i.); also, harsh to the ear, as sounds; also, rude, unpolished, or unrefined (as, *rugged* rimes; *rugged* manners); often, homely or plain, but with a rough force or effectiveness (as, "*rugged* maxims hewn from life," Tennyson's "Ode on the Death of the Duke of Wellington," vii.; "He spoke with the *rugged* earnestness of his place and character," Dickens's "Hard Times," ii. 5); sturdy or strong, rather than elegant (as, "a *rugged* figure in rawhide boots and coonskin cap": W. Churchill's "Coniston," ii. 1); robust or vigorous (U. S.).—**rug′ged-ly**, *adv.* —**rug′ged-ness**, *n.*

ru-gose (rö′gōs or rö-gōs′), *a.* [L. *rugosus*, < *ruga*, wrinkle.] Having rugæ or wrinkles; wrinkled; ridged.—**ru-gos-i-ty** (rö-gos′i-ti), *n.*; pl. *-ties* (-tiz). The state of being rugose; also, a wrinkle.—**ru-gous** (rö′gus), *a.* Rugose.—**ru′gu-lose** (-gū-lōs), *a.* Finely rugose; having small wrinkles.

Ruhm-korff (röm′kôrf) **coil.** [From H. D. *Ruhmkorff* (1803–77), the inventor.] An induction-coil.

ru-in (rö′in), *n.* [OF. F. *ruine*, < L. *ruina*, fall, downfall, ruin, < *ruere*, fall with violence, rush or dash down.] A falling or tumbling down, esp. of a building (now rare); also, fallen and wrecked or decayed state, or ruinous condition (as, a building falls to *ruin*); also, that which remains after destruction or decay (as, "one who, having alone escaped destruction in an earthquake . . . contemplates the silent, corpse-strewn *ruin* of a vast city": Arnold Bennett's "Hilda Lessways," v. 2); a ruined building, town, etc.; a person as the wreck of his former self (as, "A paralysis had ravaged his stately form, and left it a shaking *ruin*": Irving's "Tales of a Traveler," i. 9); *pl.*, the remains of a fallen building, town, etc., or of anything in a state of destruction or decay (as, the *ruins* of an ancient city; "the *ruins* of thy linen," Shakspere's "2 Henry IV.," ii. 2. 27); also, *pl.*, injuries or damage done or sustained (as, "Till thy father hath made good The *ruins* done to Malta and to us": Marlowe's "Jew of Malta," v.); also, *sing.*, the downfall, decay, or destruction of anything (as, "the wanton butchery, the *ruin* of property": Prescott's "Conquest of Mexico," iii. 7); the downfall of a person, or the complete loss of means, position, or the like; the dishonoring of a woman; also, the condition resulting from downfall or destruction; ruined or hopeless state; also, something that causes downfall or destruction (as, "Retreat would be *ruin*," Prescott's "Conquest of Mexico," iii. 6; "Her ladyship and Mrs. Stanhope between them were the *ruin* of this poor old man," Maria Edgeworth's "Belinda," viii.).—**ru′in**, *v.* [F. *ruiner*, < ML. *ruinare* (pp. *ruinatus*), < L. *ruina*.] **I.** *tr.* To reduce to ruins; lay waste; hence, to overthrow or destroy (as, "In them is plainest taught . . . What *ruins* kingdoms": Milton's "Paradise Regained," iv. 363); also, to bring irreparable disaster upon (a person, etc.); bring (a person, etc.) to financial ruin; dishonor (a woman); demoralize (a person); also, to injure (a thing) irretrievably (as, to *ruin* one's clothes; to *ruin* one's health); spoil; involve in disaster, or render abortive (as, "to *ruin* years of industry by one impulsive moment's folly," Arnold Bennett's "Roll-Call," vii.; "Do you wish to *ruin* everything with your imprudence?" W. H. Hudson's "Purple Land," xiii.). **II.** *intr.* To fall with violence, or go down with a crash (archaic: as, "Hell saw Heaven *ruining* from heaven," Milton's "Paradise Lost," vi. 868); also, to fall into ruins; also, to come to ruin.—**ru′i-nate** (-i-nāt), *v. t.* or *i.*; *-nated, -nating.* [ML. *ruinatus*, pp.] Same as *ruin, v.* [Archaic.]—**ru-i-na′tion** (-nā′shọn), *n.* The act of ruining, or the state of being ruined; also, something that ruins.—**ru′in-er**, *n.* —**ru′i-nous**, *a.* [L. *ruinosus*.] Fallen into ruin, or dilapidated (as, "The house was old and partly *ruinous*," S. J. Weyman's "Gentleman of France," xii.; "a *ruinous* wooden fence," Hawthorne's "House of the Seven Gables," i.); consisting of ruins (as, "Damascus . . . shall be a *ruinous* heap": Isa. xvii. 1); also, bringing or tending to bring ruin, or destructive or disastrous (as, "a *ruinous* war," Gibbon's "Decline and Fall of the Roman Empire," xlii.; *ruinous* expense; "Of all those expensive and uncertain projects . . . there is none perhaps more perfectly *ruinous* than the search after new silver and gold mines," Adam Smith's "Wealth of Nations," iv. 7. 1).—**ru′i-nous-ly**, *adv.* —**ru′i-nous-ness**, *n.*

rul-a-ble (rö′lạ-bl), *a.* That may be ruled; governable. **rule** (röl), *n.* [OF. *riule* (F. *règle*), < L. *regula*, rule, ruler, straight stick, bar, pattern, model, < *regere*, keep straight, direct, rule: see *right*.] A straight strip of wood, metal, or other material, used for measuring, as a guide in drawing, etc.; also, fig., a standard or criterion (as, "a knave, when tried on honesty's plain *rule*": Cowper's "Hope," 566); also, a principle or regulation governing conduct, action, procedure, arrangement, etc.; a principle regulating personal conduct (as, "If thou well observe The *rule* of — Not too much: by temperance taught": Milton's "Paradise Lost," xi. 531); a principle regulating practice or procedure (as, the *rules* of the road); one of the regulations of a game or the like; one of the regulations adopted by some body for governing its conduct and that of its members; also, *pl.*, formerly, a fixed area in the neighborhood of certain prisons, within which certain prisoners were allowed to live on giving security; the freedom of such an area; also, *sing.*, a principle regulating the procedure to be followed in order to obtain some desired result; a prescribed mathematical method for performing a calculation or solving a problem; also, the code of regulations observed by a religious order or congregation, or the order or congregation itself (as, the *rule* of St. Benedict); also, that which customarily or normally occurs or holds good (as, obedience is the *rule* rather than the exception; as a *rule*, that is, customarily or usually); also, order† or discipline†, esp. good discipline†; also, conduct† or behavior† (as, "If you prized my lady's favour . . . you would not give means for this uncivil *rule*": Shakspere's "Twelfth Night," ii. 3. 132); sometimes, misrule† or disorder†; also, control, government, or dominion (as, "A wife's *rule* should only be over her husband's house, not over his mind," Ruskin's "Crown of Wild Olive," iii.; "The *rule* of the democracy meant anarchy," Froude's "Cæsar," ix.); in *printing*, a thin, type-high strip of metal, usually brass, for printing a line or lines; in *law*, a formal order or direction made by a court and limited in application to the case for which it is given ('special rule'); also, an order or regulation governing the procedure of a court ('general rule').—**out of rule**, contrary to practice or custom: as, "Miss Portman . . . blushes for you . . . when you propose that she, who is not yet a married woman, should chaperon a young lady. It is quite *out of rule*" (Maria Edgeworth's "Belinda," xiv.). —**rule of three**, in *math.*, the method of finding the fourth term in a proportion when three terms are given.—**rule of thumb**, a rule based on experience or practice rather than on scientific knowledge; a rough, practical method of procedure: as, "People were not so introspective then . . . they lived more according to a *rule of thumb*" (S. Butler's "Way of All Flesh," vi.).—**rule**, *v. t.*; *ruled, ruling.* [OF.

riuler, rieuler, < LL. *regulare*, < L. *regula*: cf. *regulate*.] To mark with lines, esp. parallel straight lines, with the aid of a ruler or the like; also, to mark out or form (a line) by this method; also, to control or direct, or exercise dominating power or influence over (as, "My blood begins my safer guides to *rule*," Shakspere's "Othello," ii. 3. 205; "the evil influence that *rules* your fortunes," Hawthorne's "Twice-Told Tales," The Haunted Mind); prevail on, persuade, or advise (in the passive: as, "But listen to me, and by me be *ruled*," Tennyson's "Geraint and Enid," 623); restrain or curb by the exercise of self-control (as, "He that *ruleth* his spirit [is better] than he that taketh a city": Prov. xvi. 32); exercise authority or dominion over, or govern (as, "She *ruled* her husband and her children as a matter of course," Eden Phillpotts's "Children of Men," Prologue, i.; "Thou art not king, Nor fit to govern and *rule* multitudes," Shakspere's "2 Henry VI.," v. 1. 95); also, to decide or declare judicially or authoritatively; decree; put or shut (*out*) by formal decision (as, "I lock up my Grey Room and *rule* it *out* of our scheme of existence": Eden Phillpotts's "Grey Room," i.).—**to rule the roast**, to have the chief direction of affairs; have full sway; be master: as, "His wife '*ruled the roast*,' and, in governing the governor, governed the province" (Irving's "Knickerbocker's New York," iv. 4). [Now sometimes understood as *to rule the roost*, in allusion to the domineering manner of a cock.]—**rule**, *v. i.* To exercise dominating power or influence (as, "this love of life, which in our nature *rules*": Crabbe's "Borough," vii.); exercise authority, dominion, or sovereignty (as, "Let them obey that know not how to *rule*": Shakspere's "2 Henry VI.," v. 1. 6); also, to prevail or be current, as prices (as, prices *ruled* high yesterday); maintain a particular current price or value, as commodities; be, prevailingly, as specified; also, to make a formal decision or ruling, as on a point at law. **rule=joint** (röl′joint), *n.* A pivoted joint by which two thin flat strips are so joined end to end that each strip will turn or fold only edgewise in one direction: so called from its employment in folding rules. **rul-er** (rö′lėr), *n.* A strip of wood, metal, or other material with a straight edge, used in drawing lines, etc.; also, one who or that which rules paper, etc.; also, one who or that which rules or governs; a sovereign. **rul-ing** (rö′ling), *n.* Ruled lines; also, an authoritative decision, as by a judge on a point at law. —**rul′ing**, *p. a.* That rules; governing; predominating; prevalent or current.—**rul′-ing-ly**, *adv.*

Rule-joint. — *a* and *b*, strips joined; *c*, rule-joint.

ru-ly (rö′li), *a.* [Cf. *unruly*.] Conforming to rule; orderly; not unruly.

rum[1] (rum), *n.* [Origin uncertain.] An alcoholic liquor or spirit distilled from molasses or some other sugar-cane product; hence (colloq.), alcoholic drink in general; intoxicating liquor.

rum[2] (rum), *a.* [Origin obscure; first in slang of 16th century vagabonds.] Good or fine; also, odd, strange, or queer (as, "It's *rum*! At least I can't make it out," W. De Morgan's "Alice-for-Short," xxv.; "Deuced *rum* sensation!" Galsworthy's "Saint's Progress," i. 4). [Slang.]

Ru-man (rö′man or rọ̈-män′). [Rumanian *Român*, < L. *Romanus*, E. *Roman*.] **I.** *a.* Rumanian. **II.** *n.*; pl. *-mans*. A native or inhabitant of Rumania; also, the language of Rumania; Rumanian.

Ru-ma-ni-an (rọ̈-mā′ni-ạn). **I.** *a.* Of or pertaining to Rumania, its inhabitants, or their language. **II.** *n.* A native or inhabitant of Rumania; also, the language of Rumania, belonging to the Romance group (although containing many additions from the Slavic and other sources).

Ru-mansh (rọ̈-mansh′), *a.* and *n.* [See *Romansh*.] Same as *Rhæto-Romanic*.

rum-ble (rum′bl), *v.*; *-bled, -bling.* [ME. *romblen* = D. *rommelen* = G. *rummeln* = Dan. *rumle*, rumble; of imit. origin.] **I.** *intr.* To make a deep, heavy, continuous, jarring sound, as thunder, etc.; also, to move or travel with such a sound (as, "The train *rumbled* on through a landscape of fiery furnaces": Arnold Bennett's "Book of Carlotta," i. 4). **II.** *tr.* To cause to make, or move with, a rumbling sound; give forth or utter with a rumbling sound; also, to subject to the action of a rumble, as for the purpose of polishing.—**rum′ble,** *n.* A rumbling sound, as of thunder or a heavy vehicle; also, a rear part of a carriage containing seating accommodations as for servants or space for baggage; a smaller seat behind the principal seat in an automobile ('rumble seat'); also, a tumbling-box.—**rum′bler,** *n.*—**rum′bling-ly,** *adv.*—**rum′bly,** *a.* Rumbling; attended with, making, or causing a rumbling sound.

rum-bus-tious (rum-bus′chus), *a.* [Var. of *robustious*: cf. *rambunctious*.] Boisterous; unruly. [Colloq.]

ru-men (rö′men), *n.*; pl. *rumina* (rö′mi-nạ̈). [L. *rumen* (*rumin-*), throat, gullet.] The first stomach of ruminating animals, lying next to the reticulum; also, the cud of a ruminant.

ru-mi-nant (rö′mi-nạnt). [L. *ruminans* (-*ant-*), ppr.] **I.** *a.* Ruminating; chewing the cud; belonging or pertaining to the *Ruminantia*, a section of ungulate mammals, including the ox, sheep, camel, etc., which chew the cud, and have a complex stomach of several compartments (see *stomach, n.*); also, given to or characterized by meditation; meditative. **II.** *n.* A ruminant animal.—**ru′mi-nant-ly,** *adv.*

ru-mi-nate (rö′mi-nāt), *v.*; -*nated,* -*nating.* [L. *ruminatus,* pp. of *ruminari,* chew the cud, chew over again, think over, < *rumen,* throat, gullet: cf. *rumen.*] **I.** *intr.* To chew the cud, as a ruminant; also, to meditate or muse (as, "Mr. Wendover . . . stood gloomily *ruminating* in front of the fire," Mrs. H. Ward's "Robert Elsmere," xxvi.; "The old warrior king was . . . *ruminating* on his gloomy fortunes," Irving's "Conquest of Granada," lxxxi.); sometimes, to meditate with a view to action (as, "I *ruminated* incessantly upon plans of deliverance": Godwin's "Caleb Williams," xix.). **II.** *tr.* To chew again; also, to turn over in the mind, or meditate on (as, "Conduct me where, from company, I may revolve and *ruminate* my grief": Shakspere's "1 Henry VI.," v. 5. 101); meditate on (a plan, etc.) with a view to action (as, "to *ruminate* strange plots of dire revenge": Shakspere's "Titus Andronicus," v. 2. 6).—**ru′mi-nat-ing-ly** (-nā-ting-li), *adv.*—**ru-mi-na′tion** (-nā′shọn), *n.* [L. *ruminatio(n-).*] The act or process of ruminating, or chewing the cud; also, meditation.—**ru′mi-na-tive** (-nạ-tiv), *a.* Given to rumination; meditative.—**ru′mi-na-tor** (-nā-tọr), *n.*

rum-mage (rum′āj), *n.* [Obs. F. *arrumage* (now *arrimage*), < *arrumer* (now *arrimer*) = Sp. and Pg. *arrumar,* stow; origin obscure.] The stowage of cargo in a ship's hold†; a place of stowage or storage†; also, miscellaneous articles; odds and ends; also, a rummaging search; also, a commotion (obs. or Sc.).—**rummage sale,** a sale of unclaimed goods at a wharf or warehouse, or of odds and ends of merchandise at a shop ; hence, the sale of miscellaneous articles (old or new) contributed to raise money for charity.—**rum′mage,** *v.*; -*maged,* -*maging.* **I.** *tr.* To stow or arrange (cargo) in a ship†; stow or arrange cargo in (a ship or hold)†; also, to search thoroughly or ransack (a ship, etc.), as for goods or persons to be seized; in general, to search thoroughly or actively through (a place, receptacle, etc.), esp. by moving about, turning over, or looking through contents (as, to *rummage* a closet or a trunk; "He *rummaged* his pockets," Mark Twain's "Huckleberry Finn," xlii.); hunt through (sometimes fig.: as, to *rummage* one's memory for a name or date); also, to bring or fetch (*out* or *up*) by searching (lit. or fig.: as, "The hostess was engaged in *rummaging* out silver in change of half-a-guinea," Scott's "Guy Mannering," xxiii.; "Theobald had *rummaged* up a conclusion from some odd corner of his soul," S. Butler's "Way of All Flesh," xiii.). **II.** *intr.* To search actively, as in a place or receptacle, or among contents, etc.: as, "He *rummaged* in the drawer for a sheet of paper" (Mrs. Wharton's "Ethan Frome," viii.); "They then proceeded to *rummage* about the city . . . in quest of what they called evidence" (Irving's "Knickerbocker's New York," v. 6).—**rum′mag-er** (-ạ-jėr), *n.*

rum-mer (rum′ėr), *n.* [D. *roemer.*] A kind of large drinking-glass, or its contents: as, "Then Rhenish *rummers*

walk the round; In bumpers ev'ry king is crown'd" (Dryden's "Letter to Sir George Etherege," 45).

rum-my¹ (rum′i). [See *rum¹.*] **I.** *a.* Of or like rum: as, a *rummy* flavor. **II.** *n.*; pl. *rummies* (-iz). A drinker of rum or liquor, or a drunkard (as, "I'd ben a-runnin' a little temperance revival . . . I was makin' it mighty warm for the *rummies*": Mark Twain's "Huckleberry Finn," xix.); also, one who favors the liquor traffic, or opposes prohibition. [Slang.]

rum-my² (rum′i), *a.* [See *rum².*] Odd; strange; queer: as, "There seemed to be some *rummy* mystery about his absence" (A. S. M. Hutchinson's "If Winter Comes," iv. 2). [Slang.]

ru-mor (rö′mọr), *n.* [OF. *rumour* (F. *rumeur*), < L. *rumor,* common talk, rumor.] Unconfirmed public report (as, "*Rumour* doth double, like the voice and echo, The numbers of the fear'd": Shakspere's "2 Henry IV.," iii. 1. 97); the report of a particular thing (whether merely asserted or actual), without confirmation or certainty as to facts (as, "The faint *rumour* of something big being in preparation followed him into every harbour," J. Conrad's "Rescue," ii. 5; "The *rumour* of what had happened . . . had spread about the premises," Arnold Bennett's "Clayhanger," i. 13); a report or statement in general circulation without confirmation or certainty as to facts (as, "He had, if the persistent *rumors* were true, accomplished an almost incomprehensible feat," W. Churchill's "Coniston," ii. 18; *rumors* of an impending change); also, reputation or fame (archaic: as, "Great is the *rumour* of this dreadful knight," Shakspere's "1 Henry VI.," ii. 3. 7); also, a murmur, confused noise, or din (archaic).—**ru′mor,** *v.* **I.** *tr.* To circulate, report, or assert by a rumor: as, "*Rumour* it abroad That Anne, my wife, is sick and like to die" (Shakspere's "Richard III.," ii. 2. 51); "I was *rumoured* to be dreadfully 'clever'" (H. G. Wells's "Tono-Bungay," ii. 4. § 1). **II.** *intr.* To make a murmuring sound.—**ru′mor-er,** *n.*—**ru′mor=mong″er** (-mung″gėr), *n.* One given to spreading rumors.—**ru′mor-ous,** *a.* Of the nature of rumor or unconfirmed report (rare); also, murmurous, as sound or things sounding (archaic).

ru′mour, ru′mour-er. British preferred forms of *rumor,* etc.

rump (rump), *n.* [ME. *rumpe,* prob. from Scand.: cf. Icel. *rumpr,* Dan. *rumpe,* Sw. *rumpa,* rump, D. *romp,* G. *rumpf,* trunk.] The hinder part of the body of an animal; the buttocks; also, a cut of beef from this part of the animal, behind the sirloin and above the round; also, fig., the last and unimportant part, or fag-end, of something, esp. of a parliamentary or other assembly or body; specif. [*cap.*], with *the,* in Eng. *hist.,* the remnant of the 'Long Parliament,' 1640–53, restored 1659–60, after the expulsion of many of its members in 1648 or during its final period (as, "the few members who made up what was contemptuously called the *Rump* of the House of Commons," Macaulay's "Hist. of Eng.," i.; "The *Rump* alone was left to stand for the old tradition of Parliament," Morley's "Oliver Cromwell," iv. 6).—**rump=bone,** *n.* The bone of the rump; the aitchbone; the sacrum.

rum-ple (rum′pl), *n.* [Cf. MLG. *rumpele,* a wrinkle, D. *rompelig,* wrinkled, also E. *rimple.*] A wrinkle or irregular fold, esp. in cloth or the like that has been crushed or crumpled.—**rum′ple,** *v.*; -*pled,* -*pling.* **I.** *tr.* To draw or crush into wrinkles, or crumple (as, to *rumple* the clothes; a *rumpled* sheet of paper); in general, to bring into an uneven or disordered condition; ruffle (the hair, feathers, etc.: often with *up*); tousle. **II.** *intr.* To become wrinkled or crumpled.—**rum′ply,** *a.* Rumpled; crumply.

rum-pus (rum′pus), *n.* [Origin uncertain.] A noisy or violent disturbance or commotion, or a row (as, "He . . . knocked down so many students and easels and drawing-boards . . . and made such a terrific *rumpus*," Du Maurier's "Trilby," ii.; "I should think twice about it before making a *rumpus,* Heath," W. De Morgan's "Alice-for-Short," x.); also, disturbing noise, or uproar (as, children, don't make so much *rumpus*; the affair caused considerable *rumpus*). [Colloq.]

rum=run-ner (rum′run″ėr), *n.* A person or a vessel engaged in running or smuggling rum or liquors, as for illicit sale. [Colloq.]—**rum′=run″ning,** *n.* and *a.*

---

run (run), *v. i.*; pret. *ran* (also *run*), pp. *run*, ppr. *running*. [ME. *rinnen*, *rennen*, < AS. *rinnan* (pret. *ran*, pp. *ge-runnen*) = OHG. *rinnan* (G. *rinnen*) = Icel. *rinna*, later *renna*, = Goth. *rinnan*, run.] To move the legs quickly, so as to go more rapidly than in walking (in bipedal locomotion, so that for an instant in each step neither foot is on the ground); hasten, as to some end or object, or to do something (as, "What need a man . . . *run* to meet what he would most avoid?" Milton's "Comus," 363); have recourse for help, as to some person or thing; go about without restraint (often with *about*: as, to *run* about at will; children allowed to *run* about the streets); make off quickly, or take to flight; rush (*at*, etc.) with hostile intent; take part in a race; stand as a candidate for election; also, to move swiftly by other means of locomotion than legs, as an animal (as, "When the fish first *run* up the rivers, they are fat": Irving's "Captain Bonneville," viii.); in general, to move rapidly through space; move swiftly, as a vessel, vehicle, etc.; sail or be driven (*ashore*, *aground*, etc.), as a vessel or those on board; ply between places, as a vessel or conveyance; make a more or less rapid journey for a short stay at a place (as, "The Doctor would *run* up from Sacramento once in a while": Bret Harte's "Miggles"); also, to pass quickly (as, "There *ran* a rumour Of many worthy fellows that were out," Shakspere's "Macbeth," iv. 3. 182; a thought *runs* through one's mind; "The eyes of the Lord *run* to and fro throughout the whole earth," 2 Chron. xvi. 9); also, to creep, trail, or climb, as vines, etc.; also, to move easily, freely, or smoothly (as, a rope *runs* in a pulley); be in operation, or continue operating, as machinery; continue in or return to the mind persistently (as , "That bit of a tune's been *running* in my head": Arnold Bennett's "These Twain," vii.); also, to come undone or unravel, as stitches or a fabric; also, to flow, as a liquid (as, blood *runs* from a wound); flow along, esp. strongly, as a stream, a tide, the sea, etc. (as, "with a strong tide *running*": Cooper's "Two Admirals," xi.); melt and flow, as varnish, etc.; spread on being applied to a surface, as a liquid; spread over a material when exposed to moisture (as, the colors in a fabric *run*); pass from one bulb of an hour-glass to the other, as sand (often fig.: as, "while the sands o' life shall *run*," Burns's "My Love is Like a Red Red Rose"); also, to flow, stream, or be wet with a liquid (as, "Mine eye shall . . . *run* down with tears": Jer. xiii. 17); discharge, or give passage to, a liquid or fluid; overflow or leak, as a vessel; allow the sand to pass from one bulb to the other, as an hour-glass; also, to coagulate or curdle, as milk, etc. (now prov.); also, to pass or go by, as time; sometimes, to come to an end, as a period of time; also, to have currency or be current, as practices, etc.; have legal force or effect, as a writ; also, to continue or last, or remain in operation or existence (as, a lease to *run* ten years); keep the stage or be played continuously, as a play; also, to go or proceed (as, so the story *runs*; the series of numbers *running* 2, 4, 6, 8, etc.); also, to extend or stretch (as, "Narrow shelves . . . *ran* round the walls," J. Conrad's "Lord Jim," xx.; "Our front now *ran* behind what had once been Hooge village," Buchan's "Hist. of the Great War," liii.); also, to have a specified character, quality, form, etc.; be of a certain average size, number, etc. (as, potatoes *running* large, or *running* a certain number to the pound); also, to pass into a certain state or condition, get, or become (as, to *run* into debt; a well *runs* dry; one's funds *run* low). —**to run amuck.** See *amuck*.—**to run down**, to have the motive power exhausted; cease to go; stop working, as a mechanism; also, to decline in vigor or health; also, to fall off, diminish, or decrease; deteriorate; fall into decay.—**to run out**, to come to an end, as a period of time; expire; also, to become expended or exhausted, as a supply of something.—**to run out of,** to come to the end of, or exhaust (a supply).—**to run riot.** See under *riot*, *n.*—**to run through**, to consume or spend rapidly or recklessly.—**to run wild.** See under *wild*, *a.*—**run**, *v. t.* To run along (a way, path, etc.); traverse in running; run about in (as, to *run* the streets); perform by or as by running (as, to *run* a race); also, to sew (something) by passing the needle in and out repeatedly with even stitches in a line; also, to flee from (a place, etc.: now colloq. or prov.); also, to run or get past or through (as, to *run* a blockade); also, to expose one's self to, or be exposed to (a chance, risk, etc.); also, to pursue, chase, or hunt (game, etc.: as, "The chief difficulty in *running* buffalo . . . is that of loading the gun . . . at full gallop," Parkman's "Oregon Trail," xxiv.); also, to contend with in a race; also, to cause to run, as a horse ridden or led (as, "men *running* horses up and down the street for sale": Dickens's "Old Curiosity Shop," xlvi.); enter (a horse, etc.) in a race; put up (a person) as a candidate for election; also, to bring into a certain state by running (as, to *run* one's self out of breath); bring, lead, or force into some state, action, etc. (as, "to *run* myself into trouble," Scott's "Monastery," xxv.; "He *runs* his father in debt," Thoreau's "Walden," i.); also, to cause to move rapidly or otherwise (as, "The lugger had been *run* into a narrow creek": Conan Doyle's "Micah Clarke," xxiv.); cause to ply between places, as a vessel or conveyance; convey or transport, as in a vessel or vehicle; smuggle (contraband goods); also, to drive, force, or thrust (as, "I . . . chanced to *run* my nose directly against a post," Steele, in "Spectator," 268; to *run* a dagger into a man); pierce or stab (with *through*: as, "I *ran* one of the assassins through the body," H. Brooke's "Fool of Quality," xviii.); also, to cause to pass quickly (as, to *run* one's eyes over a letter); also, to cause to move easily, freely, or smoothly (as, to *run* up a sail); keep operating or going, as a machine; conduct or manage, as a business, an establishment, etc.; also, to cause (a liquid) to flow; melt, fuse, or smelt, as ore; cast in a mold, as cannon; also, to give forth or flow with (a liquid); pour forth or discharge; also, to extend (a thing), as in a particular direction (as, to *run* a partition across a room); draw or trace, as a line.—**to run down**, to pursue until caught or killed, as game; pursue and overtake, as a criminal; hunt down or trace out, as a clue; also, to knock down or overthrow by running against; collide with and sink (a vessel); also, to disparage; defame; vilify; also, to reduce in vigor or health (as, to be *run down* by overwork).—**to run into the ground**, to carry to an extreme; overdo. [Colloq.]—**to run the gantlet.** See *gantlet*[1].—**run**, *n.* The act of running, as in hastening to some point or in rapid flight (esp. in 'on the run': as, "You could see the people tearing down on the *run*," Mark Twain's "Huckleberry Finn," xxv.); a running pace (as, "I set out . . . at a *run*": W. H. Hudson's "Green Mansions," x.); power of running (as, "They have . . . little *run* left in themselves": Hughes's "Tom Brown's School Days," i. 7); also, in general, onward movement, progress, course, etc. (as, the *run* of the sea or the waves); the direction or lie of something (as, the *run* of the grain of wood); the particular course or tendency of something (as, the *run* of events; to get or keep the *run* of a thing, that is, to become or keep informed about it); also, freedom to range over, go through, or use something; free access to, or free use or enjoyment of, something (as, "The jovial rogues had the *run* of my lord's kitchen, stables, cellars, and cigar-boxes": Thackeray's "Newcomes," lix.); also, an act or spell of running, or the distance covered; an act or spell of moving rapidly, as in sailing, moving on wheels, etc., or the distance covered (as, "After a *run* of six weeks, the Aspasia entered the Channel," Marryat's "King's Own," xxxviii.; the train makes a *run* of 100 miles); a rapid journey for the purpose of a short stay at a place (as, to take a *run* to the seashore); any rapid or easy course or progress; also, a line or place in knitted work where a series of stitches have slipped out or come undone; also, a flow or rush of water, etc.; a small stream, or a brook or rivulet (as, Bull *Run*, in northeastern Virginia); also, a continuous spell or course of some condition of affairs, etc. (as, a *run* of good or bad luck; a *run* of power); a continuous extent or stretch of something, as a vein of rock or ore; a continuous series or succession of something (as, "a *run* of wet seasons": G. White's "Nat. Hist. of Selborne," ii. 19); a series of successful shots, strokes, or the like, in a game; a set of things in numerical or other regular order, as a sequence at cards; a series of sudden and urgent demands, as on a bank, for payment; any continued or extensive demand, call, or the like (as, "Never was such a *run* upon the haberdashers": Motley's "Dutch Republic," ii. 4); a spell of being in demand or favor with the public (as, "A history of the Bloody Assizes . . . was expected to have as great a *run* as the

Pilgrim's Progress": Macaulay's "Hist. of Eng.," xix.); a continuous course of performances, as of a play; also, a spell or period of causing something, as a machine, to run or continue operating; the amount of anything produced in such a period; also, a spell of causing something liquid to run or flow, or the amount which runs; also, a landing of smuggled goods; also, a kind or class, as of goods; the ordinary or average, or not superior, kind of goods or material; the ordinary or average kind or class of anything (often preceded by *common*, *ordinary*, *general*, etc.: as, the *run*, or the common *run*, of mankind; "As for the usual *run* of concerts, he hated them," S. Butler's "Way of All Flesh," lxxiii.); also, a number of animals moving together; a school of fish in motion, esp. inshore from deep water or up a river for spawning; also, that in or on which something runs or may run; a stretch or range of grazing-ground for cattle, etc.; an inclosure within which domestic animals or fowls may range about (as, a poultry *run*); a regular track made by certain animals, as, "a hippo '*run*' ": J. H. Patterson's "Man-Eaters of Tsavo," xii.); the bower of a bower-bird or gardener-bird; a way, track, or the like along which something runs or moves; a trough or pipe through which water, etc., runs; in *baseball*, the score unit, made by successfully running around all the bases and reaching the home plate; in *cricket*, the score unit, made by the successful running of both batsmen from one wicket to the other; in *music*, a rapid succession of tones; a roulade; *naut.*, the extreme after part of a ship's bottom.—**in the long run.** See under *long¹, a.*—**run,** *p. a.* Smuggled (as, "*run* goods": Scott's "Guy Mannering," ix.); also, melted or liquefied; poured in a melted state; run into and cast in a mold.

run-a-bout (run′a̯-bout″), *n.* One who runs about from place to place; also, a light open wagon; also, an automobile of the open-car type intended to accommodate two persons upon a single seat; also, a small motor-boat.

run-a-gate (run′a̯-gāt), *n.* [= *renegade*.] A renegade†; also, a fugitive or runaway (archaic); also, a vagabond or wanderer (archaic).

run-a-round (run′a̯-round″), *n.* A mild form of whitlow encircling a nail.

run-a-way (run′a̯-wā″). **I.** *n.* One who runs away; a fugitive; a deserter; also, a horse or team which has broken away from control and bolted; also, an act of running away; specif., an elopement. **II.** *a.* Having run away; escaped; fugitive; of a horse, etc., having escaped from the control of the rider or driver; also, pertaining to or accomplished by running away or eloping (as, a *runaway* match or marriage); also, easily won, as a race.

run-ci-nate (run′si-nāt), *a.* [NL. *runcinatus*, < L. *runcina*, plane (but taken as 'saw').] In *bot.*, of a leaf, etc., pinnately incised, with the lobes or teeth curved backward.

run-dle (run′dl), *n.* [Var. of *roundel*.] A circlet†; a circular arrangement†; something circular†; also, a rung of a ladder; one of the bars of a lantern-wheel; also, a wheel or similar rotating object.

rund-let, run-let¹ (rund′let, run′let), *n.* [ME. *rondelet*, dim. < OF. *rondelle*, small cask, < *rond*, E. *round²*.] A small cask or barrel (as, "twelve small *rundlets* of fine powder for our small-arms": Defoe's "Captain Singleton," x.); also, an old measure of capacity, usually reckoned at about 18 gallons. [Archaic.]

Runcinate Leaf of Dandelion (*Taraxacum taraxacum*).

rune (rön), *n.* [From Scand.: cf. Icel. *rūn* = AS. *rūn*, written character, writing, orig. mystery, secret, = Goth. *rūna*, mystery: cf. *round¹*.] Any of the letters or characters of an alphabet (in varying forms) used by the ancient Teutonic peoples, esp. the Scandinavians; hence, something written or inscribed in such characters; an old Scandinavian poem or song (as, "Of the Troll of the Church they sing the *rune* By the Northern Sea in the harvest moon": Whittier's "Kallundborg Church"); in general, a poem, song, or verse (chiefly poetic); also, a character or mark, inscription, verse, or the like, of mystic significance or

Part of Cross with Runes at Ruthwell, Dumfriesshire, Scotland.

magic power (as, "Wise he was, and many curious arts, Postures of *runes*, and healing herbs he knew": M. Arnold's "Balder Dead," i.).—**runed,** *a.* Inscribed with runes.

rung¹ (rung), *n.* [AS. *hrung* = D. *rong* = G. *runge*.] A stout stick, rod, or bar, esp. one of rounded section, forming a piece in something framed or constructed (as, a *rung* or rail on the side of a cart; the *rungs* or spokes of a wheel); one of the rounded crosspieces forming the steps of a ladder; a rounded or shaped piece fixed horizontally, for strengthening purposes, between the legs of a chair or the like, or one set, esp. vertically, as part of the back or arm of a chair; also, a cudgel or stout staff (Sc. and north. Eng.).

rung² (rung). Preterit and past participle of *ring¹*.

ru-nic (rö′nik), *a.* Of the nature of an alphabetic rune, or consisting of or set down in runes (as, a *runic* character; the *runic* alphabet; *runic* inscriptions or writing); inscribed with runes (as, *runic* stones or monuments); pertaining to or concerned with runes (as, *runic* knowledge or study); also, such as might have been written in runes (as, *runic* rimes); specif., of the ancient Scandinavian class or type, as literature, poetry, etc.; also [usually *cap.*], of or from ancient Scandinavia (as, "The Northmen came, Fix'd on each vale a *Runic* name": Scott's "Rokeby," iv. 1); also [*l. c.*], of ornamental knots, figures, etc., of an interlaced form seen on ancient monuments, metalwork, etc., of the northern European peoples.—**runic staff.** Same as *clog-almanac*.

run′let¹, *n.* See *rundlet*.

run-let² (run′let), *n.* A little run or stream; a runnel: as, "*runlets* babbling down the glen" (Tennyson's "Mariana in the South," 44).

run-nel (run′el), *n.* [For ME. *rynel*, < AS. *rynel*.] A small stream or brook, or a rivulet (as, "hearing no sound except . . . the various gurgling noises of innumerable *runnels*": W. H. Hudson's "Green Mansions," x.); also, a small channel, as for water.

run-ner (run′ėr), *n.* One who or that which runs; a racer; a fugitive† or deserter†; a messenger; one acting as collector, agent, or the like for a bank, broker, etc.; one whose business it is to solicit patronage or trade; a policeman or detective (now rare: Eng.); a smuggler, or a smuggling vessel; an operator or manager, as of a machine; a small stream (chiefly north. Eng.); a long, narrow rug, suitable for a hall or passageway; a long, narrow strip of linen, embroidery, lace, or the like, placed across a table; in a grinding-mill, the stone which is turned, in distinction from the fixed stone; also, something in or on which something else runs or moves; a channel along which metal runs in founding; a roller on which something moves along; either of the long pieces of wood or metal on which a sled or the like slides; the blade of a skate; also, specif., in *ichth.*, a jurel, *Carangus chrysos*, ranging from Cape Cod southward; in *bot.*, a slender, prostrate stem which throws out roots at its nodes or end, thus producing new plants; also, a plant that spreads by such stems.—**scarlet runner.** See under *scarlet, a.*—

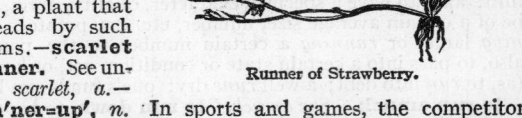

Runner of Strawberry.

run′ner-=up′, *n.* In sports and games, the competitor, player, or team finishing next to the winner or taking second place.

run-net (run′et), *n.* Obs. or prov. form of *rennet*.

run-ning (run′ing), *n.* The act of one who or that which runs; competition, as in a race (as, to be out of the *running*); also, that which runs, as a flow of liquid (as, "And from the dregs of life think to receive What the first sprightly *running* could not give": Dryden's "Aurengzebe," iv. 1).—**running,** *p. a.* That runs; moving or passing rapidly; creeping or climbing, as plants; moving or proceeding easily or smoothly; moving when pulled or hauled, as a rope; slipping or sliding easily, as a knot or a noose (see phrases below); operating, as a machine; cursive, as handwriting; flowing, as a stream; liquid or fluid; discharging matter, as a sore; also, that is going on, or current (as, the *running* month);

---

fat, fāte, fär, fåll, åsk, fāre; net, mē, hėr; pin, pīne; not, nōte, mŏve, nôr; up, lūte, pull; oi, oil; ou, out; (lightened) aviary, ėlect, agŏny, intŏ, ŭnite; (obscured) errant, operä, ardent, actŏr, natŭre; ch, chip; g, go; th, thin; ᴛʜ, then; y, you;

prevalent, as a condition, etc.; also, going or carried on continuously, or continuous or sustained (as, a *running* commentary); extending or repeated continuously (as, a *running* pattern); also, following in succession (placed after the noun: as, for three nights *running*); also, performed with or during a run (as, "He had taken a *running* leap . . . and with all his might had thrown himself clear over our palisades," Defoe's "Captain Singleton," vii.; a *running* fight, one carried on during a pursuit or flight).—**running board**, a narrow platform, as along the side of a locomotive, or along the ridge of a box-car, or along the side of an open street-car just above the ground.—**running bowline**, a bowline-knot made round a part of the same rope so as to form a noose.—**running knot**, a knot made round and so as to slide along a part of the same rope, thus forming a noose which tightens as the rope is pulled.—**running noose**, a noose with a running knot.—**running part**, of a rope, etc., a part which is not made fast to something, as a part of a tackle running between sheaves or pulleys. Cf. *standing part*, under *standing*, *p. a.*

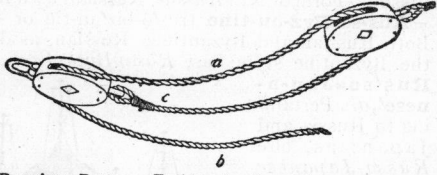
Running Part. — Tackle showing (*a*) running part, (*c*) standing part, (*b*) end hauled on.

running title, in *printing*, a descriptive head-line placed continuously at the top of pages of type, esp. a general title of a volume placed at the top of the left-hand pages or all the pages of the volume.—**running=gear**, *n.* The wheels and axles of a vehicle, and their attachments, as distinguished from the body; also, all the working parts of a locomotive or the like.—**run′ning-ly**, *adv.* In a running manner.

run-nion† (run′yọn), *n.* See *ronion*.

run-off (run′ôf), *n.* Something which runs off, as rain which flows off from the land in streams; also, a deciding final race held after a dead heat; a deciding final contest held after a principal one.

run-round (run′round), *n.* Same as *runaround*.

runt (runt), *n.* [Origin uncertain.] A stump, as of a tree (now prov. Eng.); the stalk of a cabbage (Sc. and north. Eng.); also, an ox or cow of a small breed; any stunted or dwarfish animal, person, or thing; also, a vague term of opprobrium for a person; also, one of a breed of large, stout domestic pigeons.—**runt′y**, *a.* Stunted; dwarfish.

run-way (run′wā), *n.* A way along which something runs; the beaten track of deer or other animals; a way, track, groove, trough, or the like, along which something moves, slides, etc.; the bed of a stream.

ru-pee (rö-pē′), *n.* [Hind. *rūpiya*, < Skt. *rūpya*, silver.] A silver coin and the monetary unit of British India, equal to 16 annas, and equivalent to about 32½ U. S. cents.

Obverse. Reverse.
Rupee, 1862. — British Museum.

ru-pes-tri-an (rö-pes′tri-ạn), *a.* [L. *rupes*, rock.] Pertaining to or found on rocks: as, *rupestrian* inscriptions.—**ru-pes′trine** (-trin), *a.* In *zoöl.* and *bot.*, living or growing among rocks.

rup-ture (rup′ṭūr), *n.* [OF. F. *rupture*, < L. *ruptura*, < *rumpere* (pp. *ruptus*), break.] The act of breaking or bursting, or the state of being broken or burst (as, the *rupture* of a blood-vessel); fig., breach of harmonious or friendly relations, or a breach or break, as between persons, parties, or nations (as, "The smothered dissensions among the emigrants suddenly broke into open *rupture*," Parkman's "Oregon Trail," vi.; "The soldiers . . . far from desiring a *rupture* with those of Cortés, would willingly coöp-

erate with them," Prescott's "Conquest of Mexico," iv. 6); in *pathol.*, hernia, esp. abdominal hernia.—**rup′ture**, *v.*; *-tured*, *-turing*. **I.** *tr.* To break or burst (a blood-vessel, etc.); fig., to cause a breach of (relations, etc.); in *pathol.*, to affect with hernia. **II.** *intr.* To suffer a break or rupture.

ru-ral (rö′rạl), *a.* [OF. F. *rural*, < LL. *ruralis*, < L. *rus* (*rur*-), the country: cf. *rustic*.] Of, pertaining to, or characteristic of the country as distinguished from towns or cities (as, *rural* life; *rural* free delivery of mail; "The smell of grain, or tedded grass, or kine, Or dairy, each *rural* sight, each *rural* sound," Milton's "Paradise Lost," ix. 451); having the character of the country (as, the *rural* districts; "I do love quiet, *rural* England," G. Meredith's "Diana of the Crossways," v.); living in the country (as, the *rural* portion of the population; "The *rural* clergy were even more vehement in Toryism than the *rural* gentry," Macaulay's "Hist. of Eng.," iii.); also, characteristic of country life or country people, or rustic (as, *rural* manners; "Adieu, ye shepherds' *rural* lays and loves," Pope's "Winter," 90); also, of or pertaining to agriculture (as, *rural* economy).—**rural dean.** See *dean²* and *archpriest*.—**ru-ra-les** (rö-rä′lās), *n. pl.* [Sp. (*guardias*) *rurales*, rural (guards).] A class of mounted police in Mexico.—**ru′ral-ism**, *n.* Rural character or life.—**ru′ral-ist**, *n.* One who leads or advocates a rural life; also, one versed in the conduct or management of rural affairs, the cultivation or development of country regions, etc.—**ru-ral-i-ty** (rö-ral′i-ti), *n.*; pl. *-ties* (-tiz). Rural character; also, a rural characteristic, matter, or scene.—**ru′ral-ize**, *v.*; *-ized*, *-izing*. **I.** *tr.* To render rural. **II.** *intr.* To spend time in the country; rusticate.—**ru′ral-ly**, *adv.*

ru-sa (rö′sä), *n.* [NL., < Malay *rūsa*, deer.] Any of the large, maned East Indian deer which constitute the genus *Rusa*.

ru-sal-ka (rö-sal′kạ), *n.* [Russ.] In Russian folklore, a water-nymph.

ruse (röz), *n.* [F., < *ruser*, use artifice.] A trick, stratagem, or artifice: as, "It was a *ruse* on the part of the governing authorities . . . to get the rioters out of the city" (J. H. Newman's "Callista," xx.).—**ru-sé** (rü-zā′), *a.* [F.] Artful; cunning; sly.

rush¹ (rush), *v.* [ME. *ruschen*, rush, dash: cf. D. *ruischen*, MLG. *rūschen*, G. *rauschen*, rush, move with noise, roar.] **I.** *intr.* To move or go with speed, impetuosity, or violence (as, "Our sail was now set, and, with the still rising wind, we *rushed* along," H. Melville's "Moby-Dick," xlviii.; an avalanche *rushes* down); dash; dash forward for an attack or onslaught (as, to *rush* at a person; to *rush* upon the enemy); go or plunge with headlong or rash haste (lit. or fig.: as, "Fools *rush* in where angels fear to tread," Pope's "Essay on Criticism," 625; "this sort of crazy impulse to *rush* into other people's rows," Mrs. Wharton's "Son at the Front," xvii.); in general, to go, come, pass, etc., rapidly (as, color *rushes* over the face; tears *rush* to the eyes; thoughts *rush* through the mind; "O'er the shaded landscape *rush′d* the night," Pope's tr. Homer's "Odyssey," iii.). **II.** *tr.* To send or drive with speed or violence (as, the wind *rushes* a sail-boat along); carry or convey with haste, or hurry (as, to *rush* an injured person to the hospital); send, push, force, etc., with unusual speed or undue haste (as, to *rush* a message; to *rush* a bill through the legislature; too much inclined to *rush* matters); sometimes, to urge or force (a person, etc.) to great or excessive haste; also, to attack with a rush; overcome (a person, force, etc.) or take or carry (a place, position, etc.) by a sudden rush and attack (as, "They *rushed* the German trenches and found the enemy with bayonets unfixed": Buchan's "Hist. of the Great War," liii.); enter or occupy (a place, etc.) or pass (a barrier, etc.) by a sudden dash; also, to heap attentions on (slang, U. S.: as, to *rush* a girl; to *rush* a student desirable for membership in a college fraternity).—**rush¹.** **I.** *n.* The act of rushing, or the sound made (as, "The roar and *rush* of the swollen river were heard below": Bret Harte's "Tennessee's Partner"); a rapid, impetuous, or headlong onward movement, or a dash (as, "There was a general *rush* of the men towards the beach": H. Melville's "Typee," xxvii.); a hostile dash, or an onset, charge, or onslaught (as, "The infantry *rush* which followed them captured them": Buchan's "Hist. of the

Great War," liii.); an eager rushing of numbers of persons to some region to be occupied or exploited (as, a *rush* to newly opened public lands; the *rush* to the Klondike gold-fields); a stampede, as of cattle (Australia); a sudden coming or access (as, a *rush* of blood to the face, or of tears to the eyes; a *rush* of emotion); specif., an attempt to carry the ball through the opposing line in football, or a player in the forward line who makes such attempts; also, a scrimmage held as a form of sport between classes or bodies of students in American colleges; also, hurried activity or busy haste (as, the *rush* of city life); a hurried state, or a hurry, as from pressure of affairs (as, "So sorry to have kept you waiting, but we're rather in a *rush* to-day": Chesterton's "Magic," i.); press of work, business, traffic, etc., requiring extraordinary effort or haste; also, an eager demand, as for something in request; a run, as on a commodity or stock. **II.** *a.* Requiring haste (as, a *rush* order for goods); also, characterized by rush or press of work, traffic, etc. (as, the *rush* hours on a street railway).

rush² (rush), *n.* [AS. *rysc*, *risc*, akin to D. and G. *rusch*, rush.] Any plant of the genus *Juncus* (family *Juncaceæ*), which comprises grass-like herbs with pithy or hollow stems, found in wet or marshy places; any plant of the same family, or any of various similar plants; also, a stem of such a plant, such stems being used for making chair-bottoms, mats, baskets, etc., and for other purposes, formerly esp. for strewing on bare floors (as, "a heap of dried leaves and *rushes* . . . for rest at night," J. H. Newman's "Callista," iii.; "Is supper ready, the house trimmed, *rushes* strewed?" Shakspere's "Taming of the Shrew," iv. 1. 48); often, such a stem taken as a type of something of little or no value (as, not worth a *rush*).—**rush′=can′dle,** *n.* A candle made by dipping a dried and peeled pithy-stemmed rush in tallow.

rush-er (rush′ẽr), *n.* One who or that which rushes; in *football*, a player in the forward line; a rush.

rush-ing (rush′ing), *p. a.* That rushes; moving or going with speed or impetuosity; dashing along; fig., proceeding with great activity (as, a *rushing* business).—**rush′ing-ly,** *adv.*

rush-light (rush′līt), *n.* A rush-candle.

rush=line (rush′līn), *n.* In *football*, the forward line or row of players of a team.

rush-y (rush′i), *a.* Abounding with rushes (as, "Artemis haunted streams and *rushy* pools": M. Hewlett's "Open Country," vi.); covered or strewed with rushes (as, "the *rushy* floor": Scott's "Lay of the Last Minstrel," i. 2); consisting or made of rushes (as, "my *rushy* couch": Goldsmith's "Hermit"); rush-like (as, *rushy* herbs).

ru-sine (rö′sin), *a.* [NL. *Rusa*: see *rusa*.] Of or pertaining to the genus *Rusa*, comprising East Indian maned deer, as the sambar, having rounded antlers with a simple brow-tine (brow-antler) and the beam simply forked at the summit.

rusk (rusk), *n.* [Sp. *rosca*, twist or roll (of bread), lit. 'screw.'] Bread dried for ships' use by a second baking†; also, a piece of bread or cake dried and browned in the oven; also, a kind of light, soft, sweetened biscuit.

Russ (rus). [= F. *Russe*; from Russ.] **I.** *n.*; pl. *Russ* or *Russes.* A Russian; also, the Russian language. **II.** *a.* Russian.

rus-set (rus′et). [OF. *rousset*, dim. of *rous* (F. *roux*), red, reddish, russet, < L. *russus*, red.] **I.** *n.* A coarse reddish-brown or brownish homespun cloth formerly in use (as, "They [the peasantry of Scotland] are clothed with a coarse kind of *russet* of their own making": Smollett's "Humphry Clinker," Sept. 15); also, a yellowish-brown or light-brown color; also, a kind of winter apple with a rough brownish skin; also, in *leather-manuf.*, leather finished but not polished or colored except as colored by the tanning liquor. **II.** *a.* Made of russet (cloth); hence, rustic, homely, or simple; also, yellowish-brown or light-brown in color (as, "ere *russet* fields their green resume": Bryant's "Yellow Violet"); of shoes, etc., made of leather which has not been blackened.—**rus′set-y,** *a.* Inclining to a russet color.

Rus-sia (rush′ä) **leath′er.** A fine, smooth leather produced by careful tanning and dyeing, esp. in dark red: orig. prepared in Russia, but imitated elsewhere. Also called *russia*.

Rus-sian (rush′an), *a.* Of or pertaining to Russia, its people, or their language.—**Russian Church,** the national church

of Russia, a branch of the Orthodox Eastern Church.—**Rus′sian,** *n.* A native or inhabitant of Russia; esp., a member of the dominant, Slavic race of Russia; also, the language of this race, belonging to the Slavic group.—**Great Russians,** the main stock of the Russian people, dwelling chiefly in the northern and central parts of European Russia. —**Little Russians,** a division of the Russian people dwelling in southern and southwestern European Russia and in adjoining regions. Cf. *Ruthenian.*—**White Russians,** a division of the Russian people dwelling in the western part of European Russia (east of Poland and Lithuania) and in adjoining regions.

Rus-sian-ize (rush′an-īz), *v. t.*; *-ized, -izing.* To make Russian; impart Russian characteristics to.—**Rus″sian-i-za′tion** (-i-zā′shon), *n.*

Russ-ni-ak (rus′ni-ak), *n.* and *a.* [Ruthenian *Rusnyak.*] Same as *Ruthenian.*

Russo-. Form of NL. *Russus*, Russian, used in combination. —**Rus-so-Byz-an-tine** (rus′ō-biz′an-tin or -bi-zan′tin), *a.* Both Russian and Byzantine; Russian, as developed from the Byzantine style: as, *Russo-Byzantine* architecture.—

Rus′so-Jap-a-nese′, *a.* Pertaining to Russia and Japan: as, the *Russo-Japanese* War of 1904-05 (in which the Russians were defeated).—**Rus-so-phil, Rus-so-phile** (rus′ō-fil), *n.* [+ *-phil*, *-phile*.] One who admires or favors Russia or anything Russian.—**Rus-soph-i-lism** (ru-sof′i-lizm), *n.*—**Rus′so-phobe** (-fōb), *n.* [+ *-phobe*.] One who fears or hates Russia or anything Russian.—**Rus-so-pho′bi-a** (-fō′-bi-ä), *n.*

Russo-Byzantine Architecture. — Cathedral of the Assumption, Kremlin, Moscow.

rust (rust), *n.* [AS. *rust* = D. *roest* = G. *rost*, rust.] The red or orange coating which forms on the surface of iron when exposed to air and moisture, consisting chiefly of ferric hydroxide and ferric oxide; any film or coating on metal due to oxidation, etc.; also, rust-color; also, any of various plant-diseases caused by fungi, in which the leaves and stems become spotted or discolored; a fungus producing such a disease; also, fig., any growth, habit, influence, or agency tending to injure the mind, character, abilities, usefulness, etc.—**rust,** *v.* **I.** *intr.* To contract rust, or grow rusty, as iron does; also, to become rust-colored; also, fig., to deteriorate or become impaired, as through inaction or disuse (as, "Neglected talents *rust* into decay": Cowper's "Table Talk," 546). **II.** *tr.* To affect with rust; also, to make rust-colored; also, to affect (plants) with the disease rust; also, fig., to impair as if with rust.—**rust′=col″or,** *n.* The reddish-yellow or reddish-brown color of iron-rust.—**rust′=col″ored,** *a.*

rus-tic (rus′tik). [L. *rusticus*, < *rus*, the country: cf. *rural.*] **I.** *a.* Of, pertaining to, or living in the country as distinguished from towns or cities, or rural (as, "Others took long rambles among the *rustic* lanes," Hawthorne's "Blithedale Romance," xiv.; "that *rustic* aristocracy which constituted the main strength of the armies of Charles the First," Macaulay's "Hist. of Eng.," iii.); characteristic of country life or country people (as, *rustic* sports; *rustic* ways; "some *rustic* phrases which I had learned at the farmer's house," Swift's "Gulliver's Travels," ii. 3); esp., simple, artless, or unsophisticated, after the manner of the country (as, *rustic* grace or innocence; a *rustic* beauty); countrified; uncouth, rude, or boorish; also, made or built in country fashion or of simple materials, after a plain or rude design, etc.; esp., made of roughly dressed limbs or roots of trees, as summer-houses, garden seats, etc.; of masonry, having the surface rough or the joints deeply sunk or chamfered. **II.** *n.* A country person; esp., an unsophisticated countryman or countrywoman.— **rus′ti-cal**, *a.* and *n.* Same as *rustic.* [Archaic.]— **rus′ti-cal-ly**, *adv.*

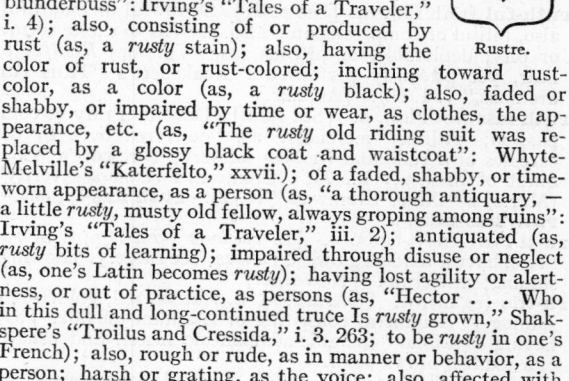

Rustic Masonry.—*A*, plain; *B*, beveled; *C*, vermiculated; *D*, frosted.

rus-ti-cate (rus′ti-kāt), *v.*; *-cated, -cating.* [L. *rusticatus*, pp. of *rusticari*, < *rusticus*, E. *rustic.*] **I.** *intr.* To go to the country; stay or sojourn in the country. **II.** *tr.* To send to or domicile in the country; hence, to send (a student) away from a university or college for a time by way of punishment (as, "his eldest son, who has just been *rusticated* from Christ Church for riding one of Simmons's hacks through a china-shop window": Kingsley's "Yeast," Epilogue); also, to render rustic or countrified, as persons, manners, etc.; also, to construct or finish (masonry, etc.) in the rustic manner.—**rus-ti-ca′tion** (-kā′shon), *n.* The act of rusticating, or the state of being rusticated; residence, or a period of residence, in the country (as, "the sudden transition from a town life to such a melancholy state of *rustication*": Smollett's "Humphry Clinker," Oct. 11); temporary dismissal of a student from a university or college by way of punishment; treatment of masonry in the rustic manner.

rus-ti-ci-ty (rus-tis′i-ti), *n.*; pl. *-ties* (-tiz). The state or quality of being rustic; rural character or life (as, "a pretty piece of *rusticity* — domestic arcadia on a small scale": Miss Mulock's "John Halifax," xii.); esp., rustic or countrified quality, or rustic unsophistication, awkwardness, or uncouthness (as, "There was not the slightest trace of *rusticity* in her manner": W. H. Hudson's "Purple Land," xxiv.); a rustic characteristic or peculiarity (as, "Any little *rusticity* of gait or pronunciation which he had brought from Paleham, was . . . completely lost": S. Butler's "Way of All Flesh," ii.).

rust-i-ly (rust′i-li), *adv.* In a rusty manner.—**rust′i-ness**, *n.*

rus-tle (rus′l), *v.*; *-tled, -tling.* [ME. *rustel*; prob. imit.] **I.** *intr.* To make a succession of slight, soft sounds as of parts rubbing gently one on another, as leaves or bushes, silks, papers, etc., or sometimes as lightly dropping rain; cause such sounds to be made by moving or stirring something (as, "Coveys of young partridges ran *rustling* over the leaves below": Parkman's "Oregon Trail," xxvii.); move, go, or pass with such sounds (as, the wind *rustles* through the woods; a boat *rustles* through the reeds; "Madame Piriac and Audrey *rustled* off," Arnold Bennett's "Lion's Share," xxx.); often, to go about or be dressed in materials that produce such sounds (as, "*rustling* in unpaid-for silk": Shakspere's "Cymbeline," iii. 3. 24); also, to move, proceed, or work energetically or vigorously (slang, U. S.). **II.** *tr.* To move or stir (something) so as to cause a rustling sound (as, the wind *rustles* the leaves; "I just *rustled* the newspaper," A. S. M. Hutchinson's "If Winter Comes," ii. 1); send, cast, turn, etc., with a rustling sound (as, "Air-swept lindens . . . *rustle* down their perfumed showers Of bloom," M. Arnold's "Scholar-Gipsy"; "Memory was turning over the leaves of her volume, *rustling* them to and fro," Hawthorne's "Twice-Told Tales," Fancy's Show-Box); also, to move, bring, get, etc., by energetic action (slang, U. S.; as, "I'll sure buy Pedro back . . . just as soon as ever I *rustle* some cash," Wister's "Virginian," xxv.); also, to steal (cattle, etc.: western U. S.).—**rus′tle**, *n.* The sound made by anything that rustles: as, the *rustle* of leaves; the *rustle* of garments; "Your ear . . . will hear . . . on the lichen-crusted leads above The *rustle* of the eternal rain of love" (M. Arnold's "Church of Brou," iii.).—**rus′tler**, *n.* One who or that which rustles; an active, energetic person (slang, U. S.); a cattle-thief (western U. S.: as, "The cattle thieves — the *rustlers* — were gaining in numbers and audacity," Wister's "Virginian," xxxv.).

rust-less (rust′les), *a.* Free from rust; rust-proof.

rus-tling (rus′ling), *p. a.* That rustles; making a succession of slight, soft sounds as of moving parts (as, *rustling* leaves or boughs); having the character of sound so produced (as, a *rustling* murmur or noise); active, energetic, or hustling (slang, U. S.).—**rus′tling-ly**, *adv.*

rust=proof (rust′prōf), *a.* Not subject to rusting.

rus-tre (rus′tėr), *n.* [F.] In *her.*, a bearing in the form of a lozenge with a relatively large circular hole in the middle.

rust-y¹ (rus′ti), *a.*; compar. *rustier*, superl. *rustiest.* [AS. *rustig.*] Covered or affected with rust, or rusted, as iron (as, "a *rusty* blunderbuss": Irving's "Tales of a Traveler," i. 4); also, consisting of or produced by rust (as, a *rusty* stain); also, having the color of rust, or rust-colored; inclining toward rust-color, as a color (as, a *rusty* black); also, faded or shabby, or impaired by time or wear, as clothes, the appearance, etc. (as, "The *rusty* old riding suit was replaced by a glossy black coat and waistcoat": Whyte-Melville's "Katerfelto," xxvii.); of a faded, shabby, or time-worn appearance, as a person (as, "a thorough antiquary, — a little *rusty*, musty old fellow, always groping among ruins": Irving's "Tales of a Traveler," iii. 2); antiquated (as, *rusty* bits of learning); impaired through disuse or neglect (as, one's Latin becomes *rusty*); having lost agility or alertness, or out of practice, as persons (as, "Hector . . . Who in this dull and long-continued truce Is *rusty* grown," Shakspere's "Troilus and Cressida," i. 3. 263; to be *rusty* in one's French); also, rough or rude, as in manner or behavior, as a person; harsh or grating, as the voice; also, affected with the disease rust, as a plant.

Rustre.

rus-ty² (rus′ti), *a.* [= *restive.*] Restive or refractory (as, a *rusty* horse; to ride or run *rusty*, fig., of persons, to act in a perversely stubborn, contrary, or disagreeable way); also, in an unpleasant temper, ill-tempered, or cross (as, "The people got *rusty* about it, and would not deal," Scott's "Guy Mannering," xxviii.: commonly in the phrase 'to turn rusty').

rus-ty³ (rus′ti), *a.* [Var. of obs. or prov. *resty, reasty*, prob. < OF. *resté*, left over, pp. of *rester*, E. *rest².*] Rancid: used esp. of bacon: as, "shreds of *rusty* meat" (C. Brontë's "Jane Eyre," v.). [Now chiefly prov.]

rut¹ (rut), *n.* [Appar. a var. of *route.*] A furrow or track made or worn in the ground by the passage of a vehicle or vehicles (as, "A sleepy land, where under the same wheel The same old *rut* would deepen year by year": Tennyson's "Aylmer's Field," 34); sometimes, any furrow or track hollowed out in the ground (as, "From hills rain-waters headlong fall, That all ways eat huge *ruts*": Chapman's tr. Homer's "Iliad," iv.); in general, a furrow, lengthened depression, groove, etc.; also, in fig. use, a fixed or established mode of procedure or course of life; a groove.—**rut¹**, *v. t.*; *rutted, rutting.* To make a rut or ruts in; furrow: as, "The road was beaten into paste and *rutted* two feet deep by the artillery" (Conan Doyle's "Exploits of Brigadier Gerard," vii.).

rut² (rut), *n.* [OF. F. *rut*, < L. *rugitus*, a roaring, < *rugire*, roar.] The periodically recurring sexual excitement of deer, goats, sheep, etc.—**rut²**, *v. i.*; *rutted, rutting.* To be in the condition of rut.

ru-ta-ba-ga (rö-ta̯-bā′ga̯), *n.* [Sw. dial. *rotabagge.*] The Swedish or yellow turnip.

ru-ta-ceous (rö-tā′shius), *a.* [L. *rutaceus*, < *ruta*, E. *rue¹.*] Of or like rue; belonging to the *Rutaceæ*, a family of plants including the rue, dittany, Angostura bark tree, orange, lemon, shaddock, cumquat, etc.

ruth (röth), *n.* [ME. *ruthe, rewthe*, < *rewen*, < AS. *hrēowan*, E. *rue².*] Sorrow or grief (as, "Reign thou above the storms of sorrow and *ruth* That roar beneath": Tennyson's "Sonnet," Though Night hath climbed); also, repentance or regret; also, pity or compassion (as, "I came back to her now with no other emotion than a sort of *ruth* for her great sufferings": C. Brontë's "Jane Eyre," xxi.). [Archaic.]

Ru-the-ni-an (rö-thē′ni-an), *n.* [ML. *Ruthenia*, Russia.] **I.** *a.* Of or pertaining to the Little Russians, specif. and commonly a division of them dwelling in Galicia and neighboring regions. **II.** *n.* One of the Ruthenian people; also, their (Slavic) language; specif., the dialect employed by the Ruthenians of Galicia and neighboring regions, being a variety of the form of Russian used by the Little Russians.

ru-the-ni-um (rö-thē′ni-um), *n.* [NL., < ML. *Ruthenia*, Russia; the metal being found first in ore from the Ural Mountains.] Chem. sym., Ru; at. wt., 101.7; sp. gr., 12.26. A difficultly fusible, steel-gray metallic element, belonging to the platinum group of metals, and very little acted on by aqua regia.—**ru-then′ic** (-then′ik), *a.*—**ru-the′ni-ous**, *a.*

ruth-ful (röth′fúl), *a.* [See *ruth.*] Sorrowful or mournful; also, pitiful or compassionate; also, such as to excite sorrow or pity, deplorable, or piteous (as, "Villanies *Ruthful* to hear, yet piteously perform'd": Shakspere's "Titus Andronicus," v. 1. 66). [Archaic.]

ruth-less (röth′les), *a.* [See *ruth.*] Devoid of pity or compassion; pitiless; merciless: as, "delivered over to the excesses of a rude and *ruthless* soldiery" (Prescott's "Conquest of Mexico," iii. 7); "Cromwell's *ruthless* severity" (Morley's "Oliver Cromwell," iv. 2).—**ruth′less-ly**, *adv.*—**ruth′less-ness**, *n.*

ru-ti-lant (rö′ti-lant), *a.* [L. *rutilans* (-*ant*-), ppr. of *rutilare*, have a reddish glow, < *rutilus*: see *rutile.*] Glowing; shining; glittering. [Now rare.]

ru-tile (rö′til), *n.* [G. *rutil*, < L. *rutilus*, red, golden-red, shining.] A mineral consisting of titanium dioxide, TiO_2, having a brilliant metallic-adamantine luster, and usually of a reddish-brown color.

rut-tish (rut′ish), *a.* [See *rut*[2].] Lustful; lascivious.

rut-ty (rut′i), *a.* [See *rut*[1].] Full of or abounding in ruts, as a road.

-ry. [Reduced form of *-ery.*] A suffix of nouns denoting occupation, calling, or art, state or condition, action or practice, things or persons collectively, etc., as in *blazonry, chivalry, dentistry, husbandry, jewelry, ribaldry, rivalry, tenantry, yeomanry.*

rye[1] (rī), *n.* [AS. *ryge*, akin to D. *rogge*, G. *roggen*, Icel. *rūgr*, rye.] A widely cultivated cereal grass, *Secale cereale*; also, the seeds or grain of this plant, used for making flour, etc.; also, whisky made from this grain.

rye[2] (rī), *n.* [Gipsy.] A gentleman: as, "The Romany *Rye*" (the title of a book by George Borrow, published in 1857).

rye=grass (rī′gras), *n.* [Earlier *ray-grass*; origin obscure.] A commonly cultivated forage-grass, *Lolium perenne.*

rynd (rīnd), *n.* [ME. *rynd* = D. *rijn*.] A piece of iron running across the hole of an upper millstone and serving to support the stone.

ry-ot (rī′ot), *n.* [Hind. *raiyat*, from Ar.] In India, a peasant; one who holds land as a cultivator of the soil.

Rye.—I, the plant; 2, the spike; *a*, a spikelet; *b*, the empty glumes; *c*, the flowering glume; *d*, the palet; *e*, one of the lodicules, highly magnified.

S

S[1], **s**[1] (es); pl. *S's, s's* (es′ez). A consonant, the 19th letter of the English alphabet.

S[2] (es), *n.*; pl. *S's, SS* (es′ez). Something having a shape like that of the letter S. Cf. *ess.*—**collar of S's**, or **SS**. See under *collar, n.*

-s[1]. [ME. -*es*, < AS. -*as*.] A suffix used to form the plural of most nouns, as in *bats, boys, dogs, halos, pleas, Tupis.* See -*es*[1].

-s[2]. [For earlier -*eth, -th*.] Ending of the third person singular present indicative of verbs, as in *asks, lies, sees, tells.* See -*es*[2] and -*eth.*

-s[3]. [AS. -*es*, orig. genitive ending: see -'*s*.] A suffix serving to form adverbs, as *always, betimes, needs, unawares.* Cf. -*wards* and -*ways.*

's. A form of *is* or of *has* due to reduction in colloquial speech: commonly written or printed (as also pronounced) continuously with the preceding word, as in 'he's here' or 'he's just gone.'

-'s. [AS. -*es*, genitive sing. ending: cf. -*s*[3].] A suffix used to form the possessive case of nouns in the singular, as *ass's, horse's, man's,* and of plural nouns not ending in -*s*, as *men's.* See *possessive case,* under *possessive, a.*

sab-a-dil-la (sab-a-dil′ä), *n.* [Sp. *cebadilla*, dim. of *cebada*, barley.] A liliaceous plant of Mexico, *Schœnocaulon officinale* (or *Asagræa officinalis*), with long grass-like leaves and bitter seeds; also, the seeds, which are used medicinally and as a source of veratrine and veratridine.

Sa-bæ′an[1], **Sa-bæ′an**[2], etc. See *Sabean*[1], *Sabean*[2], etc.

Sa-ba-ism (sā′bā-izm), *n.* Same as *Sabianism.*

Sab-a-oth (sab′ā-oth or sa-bā′oth), *n. pl.* [LL., < Gr. Σαβαώθ, < Heb. *tsebāōth*, pl. of *tsābā*, army, host.] Armies; hosts: as, "the Lord of *Sabaoth*" (Rom. ix. 29).

Sab-ba-ta-ri-an (sab-a-tā′ri-an), *n.* [L. *sabbatarius.*] **I.** *a.* Pertaining to the Sabbath, or to the tenets of the Sabbatarians. **II.** *n.* One who observes the seventh day of the week (Saturday) as the Sabbath, as the Jews do; also, a Christian who observes the first day of the week (Sunday) according to the regulations of the Jewish Sabbath, or one who adheres to or favors a strict observance of Sunday.—**Sab-ba-ta′ri-an-ism**, *n.*

Sab-bath (sab′ath). [= F. *sabbat*, < L. *sabbatum*, < Gr. σάββατον, < Heb. *shabbāth*, < *shābath*, to rest from labor.] **I.** *n.* The seventh day of the week (Saturday) as the day of rest and religious observance among the Jews and certain Christian sects (see Ex. xx. 8–11); also, the first day of the week (Sunday), similarly observed by most Christians in commemoration of the resurrection of Christ; also [*l. c.* or *cap.*], the sabbatical year of the ancient Jews (see Lev. xxv. 4); a time or period of rest, quiet, etc. (as, "This blessed Ann. Dom. [1770] was one of the *Sabbaths* of my ministry. When I look back upon it, all is quiet and good order": Galt's "Annals of the Parish," xi.); in medieval lore, a midnight meeting of demons, sorcerers, and witches, presided over by Satan, supposed to have been held annually as an orgy or festival (more fully, 'witches' sabbath'). **II.** *a.* Pertaining to or characteristic of the Sabbath: as, *Sabbath* duties; a *Sabbath* stillness.—**Sabbath=day's journey**, the distance that anciently a Jew might lawfully travel on the Sabbath: as, "Then returned they . . . from the mount called Olivet, which is from Jerusalem a *sabbath day's journey*" (Acts, i. 12).—**Sab′bath-less**, *a.* Having no Sabbath, or day of rest: as, "*Sabbathless* Satan! he who his unglad Task ever plies" (Lamb's "Work").

sab-bat-ic, sab-bat-i-cal (sa-bat′ik, -i-kal), *a.* [Gr. σαββατικός.] Of, pertaining to, or appropriate to the Sabbath; bringing an intermission of labor.—**sabbatical river**, in Jewish legend, a river which, according to one account, stopped flowing on the Sabbath, or, according to another, flowed only on the Sabbath.—**sabbatical year**, among the ancient Jews, every seventh year, during which fields were to be left untilled, debtors were to be released, etc.; also, in certain universities, etc., a year, usually every seventh, of freedom from teaching, granted to a professor, as for study or travel.—**sab-bat′i-cal-ly**, *adv.*

Sab-ba-tism (sab′a-tizm), *n.* [LL. *sabbatismus*, < Gr. σαββατισμός.] Observance of the Sabbath; also [*l. c.*], sabbatic rest.

Sa-be-an[1], **Sa-bæ-an**[1] (sạ-bē'ạn). [L. *Sabæus*, Sabean (*Sabæa*, the Sabean country), < Gr. Σαβαῖος, < Σάβα, Ar. *Saba'*, Heb. *Shebā*, the Sabean people (but erroneously taken as the name of their chief city).] **I.** *a.* Of or pertaining to Sabæa, an ancient kingdom of southern Arabia, noted for its extensive trade in spices, gems, etc.: as, "*Sabæan* odours from the spicy shore Of Araby the bless'd" (Milton's "Paradise Lost," iv. 162). **II.** *n.* An inhabitant of Sabæa.

Sa-be-an[2], **Sa-bæ-an**[2] (sạ-bē'ạn), etc. Same as *Sabian*, etc.

sa-ber, sa-bre (sā'bėr), *n.* [F. *sabre*, for *sable*, < G. *sabel* (now *säbel*); prob. of Oriental origin.] A heavy one-edged sword, usually slightly curved, used esp. by cavalry; also, a soldier armed with such a sword.—**sa'ber, sa'bre**, *v. t.*; -bered, -bred, -bering, -bring. To strike, wound, or kill with a saber.—**sa'bered, sa'bred**, *a.* Armed or equipped with a saber.—**sa'ber= toothed, sa'bre=toothed**, *a.* Having saber-like teeth, as the extinct feline mammals of the subfamily *Machærodontinæ*, whose upper canine teeth were greatly elongated and sometimes extended below the margin of the lower jaw.

Sa-bi-an (sā'bi-ạn), *n.* [Also (by confusion with *Sabean*[1]) *Sabean, Sabæan*; Ar. *Çābi'*, a Sabian.] A member of a religious sect in Babylonia classed in the Koran with the Moslems, Jews, and Christians, as believers in the true God; also, a member of a sect in Mesopotamia which in the 9th century, in order to profit by Mohammedan tolerance for the original Sabians, assumed the same name, while their own religion, though comprising Christian and Neoplatonic elements, was notably marked by star-worship.—**Sa'bi-an-ism**, *n.* The religious doctrines or practices of the Sabians, esp. the star-worshiping sect; star-worship.

United States Light-cavalry Saber, as used in 1864.

Sa-bine (sā'bīn). [L. *Sabinus*.] **I.** *a.* Belonging or pertaining to an ancient people of central Italy who lived chiefly in the Apennines to the northeast of Rome and who were subjugated by the Romans about 290 B.C. (as, the rape of the *Sabine* women, a seizure of Sabine women for wives traditionally ascribed to the early Romans of the time of Romulus); also, pertaining to the language of this people. **II.** *n.* One of the Sabine people; also, their language.

sa-ble (sā'bl). [OF. F. *sable*, sable, also black; from Slavic: cf. Russ. and Pol. *sobol*, also E. *zibeline*.] **I.** *n.* An old-world carnivorous mammal, *Mustela zibellina*, of cold regions, valued for its dark-brown or blackish fur; any of various similar species, esp. an American marten, *M. americana*; also, the fur of the sable, or some similar fur (as, Alaska *sable*, the fur of the common American skunk); also, black, as one of the heraldic colors; the color black; black clothing; *pl.*, mourning garments. **II.** *a.* Made of the fur or hair of the sable; also, black; very dark. —**sa'ble**, *v. t.*; -bled, -bling. To make black; darken. [Chiefly poetic.]—**sa'ble-ness**, *n.*

Sable (*Mustela zibellina*).

sa-bot (sạ-bō'), *n.* [F. *sabot*, OF. *çabot*: cf. F. *savate*, old shoe (see *savate*).] A wooden shoe, made of a single piece of wood hollowed out, worn by peasants in France, Belgium, etc.; also, a kind of shoe consisting

Breton Sabot, with straw inserted for warmth and to serve as a cushion.

of a thick wooden sole with sides and top of coarse leather.

sab-o-tage (sab-ō-täzh', F. sȧ-bo-täzh), *n.* [F., the making of sabots, the doing of work quickly and badly, the intentional garbling of work by a printer, sabotage, < *sabot*: see *sabot*.] Malicious injury to work, tools, machinery, etc., or any underhand interference with production or business, caused by employees of an industrial establishment or the like as a form of attack or intimidation directed against the employer; fig., malicious attacking of or secret working against any cause to which coöperation is due.—**sab-o-tage'**, *v. t.*; -taged, -taging. To injure or attack by sabotage. Often fig.—**sab-o-teur** (sab-ō-tėr', F. sȧ-bo-tėr), *n.* [F.] One who commits or practises sabotage.

sa'bre, etc. See *saber*, etc.

sab-re-tache, sab-re-tash (sab'ėr-tash or sā'bėr-), *n.* [F. *sabretache*, < G. *säbeltasche*, 'saber pocket.'] A case, as of leather, suspended by long straps from the sword-belt of a cavalryman, and hanging beside the saber.

sa-breur (sȧ-brėr'), *n.* [F.] One who uses a saber.

sab-u-lous (sab'ū-lus), *a.* [L. *sabulosus*, < *sabulum*, sand.] Sandy; gritty.

sac (sak), *n.* [F. *sac*, < L. *saccus*: see *sack*[1].] A bag-like structure in an animal or plant, as one containing a fluid; a pouch.

British Cavalryman wearing Sabretache. (After drawing by Lady Elizabeth Butler.)

sac-a-ton (sak-ạ-tōn'), *n.* Same as *zacaton*.

sac-cate (sak'āt), *a.* [ML. *saccatus*, < L. *saccus*, E. *sac*, *sack*[1].] Having the form of, or furnished with, a sac or pouch. Also **sac-cat-ed** (sak'ā-ted).

sac-cha-rate (sak'ạ-rāt), *n.* [From *saccharic*.] In *chem.*, a salt of any saccharic acid; also, a sucrate.

sac-cha-rat-ed (sak'ạ-rā-ted), *a.* [ML. *saccharum*, sugar: see *saccharine*.] Mixed or prepared with some variety of sugar: as, *saccharated* pepsin.

sac-char-ic (sạ-kar'ik), *a.* [ML. *saccharum*, sugar: see *saccharine*.] Pertaining to or derived from sugar: as, *saccharic* acid (any of certain acids derived from sugars).

sac-cha-ride (sak'ạ-rīd or -rid), *n.* [ML. *saccharum*, sugar: see *saccharine*.] In *chem.*, a sucrate.

sac-cha-rif-er-ous (sak-ạ-rif'e-rus), *a.* [ML. *saccharum*, sugar: see *-ferous*.] Yielding or containing sugar.

sac-char-i-fy (sạ-kar'i-fī), *v. t.*; -fied, -fying. [ML. *saccharum*, sugar: see *-fy*.] To convert (starch, etc.) into sugar.—**sac-char"i-fi-ca'tion** (-fi-kā'shọn), *n.*—**sac-char'i-fi-er** (-fī-ėr), *n.*

sac-cha-rim-e-ter (sak-ạ-rim'e-tėr), *n.* [ML. *saccharum*, sugar: see *-meter*.] An optical instrument for determining the strength of sugar solutions by measuring the amount they rotate the plane of polarization of light; also, any of certain other devices for determining the amount of sugar in a solution.

sac-cha-rin (sak'ạ-rin), *n.* [ML. *saccharum*, sugar: see *saccharine*.] In *chem.*, a crystalline compound derived from levulose; also, an intensely sweet, crystalline benzene derivative, used as a substitute for sugar, as in cases of diabetes.

sac-cha-rine (sak'ạ-rin or -rīn). [ML. *saccharum*, L. *saccharon*, or Gr. σάκχαρ, σάκχαρον, sugar, from the same ult. source as E. *sugar*: see *sugar*.] **I.** *a.* Pertaining to, of the nature of, containing, or resembling sugar; sugary; of a sugary sweetness (often fig.: as, "Nellie's *saccharine* assurances . . . that Edward Henry really needed a change," Arnold Bennett's "The Old Adam," iii.). **II.** *n.* Saccharine matter; sugar.—**sac'cha-rine-ly,** *adv.*—**sac-cha-rin'-i-ty** (-rin'i-ti), *n.*

sac-cha-rize (sak'ạ-rīz), *v. t.*; -rized, -rizing. [ML. *saccharum,* sugar: see *saccharine.*] To convert into sugar; saccharify.—**sac″cha-ri-za'tion** (-ri-zā'shọn), *n.*

sac-cha-roid, sac-cha-roi-dal (sak'ạ-roid, sak-ạ-roi'dạl), *a.* [Gr. σάκχαρον, sugar: see -*oid.*] In *geol.,* having a granular texture like that of loaf-sugar.

sac-cha-rom-e-ter (sak-ạ-rom'e-tèr), *n.* Same as *saccharimeter* (esp. in second sense).

sac-cha-rose (sak'ạ-rōs), *n.* [ML. *saccharum,* sugar: see *saccharine.*] In *chem.,* a crystalline compound, $C_{12}H_{22}O_{11}$, being the ordinary sugar obtained from the sugar-cane, the sugar-beet, and sorghum, and forming the greater part of maple sugar.

sac-ci-form (sak'si-fôrm), *a.* [NL. *sacciformis,* < L. *saccus,* bag, + *forma,* form.] Sac-shaped; sac-like.

sac-cu-lar (sak'ū-lär), *a.* Pertaining to or having the form of a saccule or sac.

sac-cu-late (sak'ū-lāt), *a.* [NL. *sacculatus.*] Formed into or with a saccule or sac or a number of sac-like dilatations. Also **sac'cu-lat-ed** (-lā-ted).—**sac-cu-la'tion** (-lā'shọn), *n.* The formation of a saccule or saccules; also, a sacculate part.

sac-cule (sak'ūl), *n.* [L. *sacculus,* dim. of *saccus,* bag, E. *sac, sack¹.*] A little sac; specif., in *anat.,* the smaller of two sacs in the membranous labyrinth of the internal ear (cf. *utricle*).

sac-cu-lus (sak'ū-lus), *n.*; pl. -li (-lī). [L.: see *saccule.*] Same as *saccule.*

sa-cer-do-cy (sas'èr-dọ-si), *n.* [= F. *sacerdoce,* < L. *sacerdotium,* < *sacerdos:* see *sacerdotal.*] Sacerdotal or priestly character or dignity; also, a priestly office or system.

sa-cer-do-tal (sas-èr-dō'tạl), *a.* [L. *sacerdotalis,* < *sacerdos* (*sacerdot-*), priest, < *sacer,* sacred, + -*dos,* connected with *dare,* give.] Of or pertaining to priests or the priesthood; priestly.—**sa-cer-do'tal-ism,** *n.* The sacerdotal system; the spirit or methods of the priesthood; in an unfavorable sense, priestcraft.—**sa-cer-do'tal-ly,** *adv.*

sa-chem (sā'chem), *n.* [Algonquian: cf. *sagamore.*] Among some tribes of American Indians, the chief; in *U. S. politics,* one of a body of high officials in the Tammany Society of New York City.—**sa'chem-ship,** *n.*

sa-chet (sa-shā'), *n.* [F., dim. of *sac,* bag, < L. *saccus,* E. *sack¹.*] A small bag, case, pad, or other device inclosing a perfuming powder or the like, placed among clothes, etc., to perfume them; also, sachet-powder.—**sa-chet'=pow″der,** *n.* Perfuming powder for sachets.

sack¹ (sak), *n.* [AS. *sacc* = OF. F. *sac* = It. *sacco,* < L. *saccus,* < Gr. σάκκος, bag, sack, sackcloth; of Semitic origin.] A large bag of some stout woven material, as for grain, flour, potatoes, coal, etc.; such a bag with its contents (as, "a heap of *sacks* of meal": W. H. Hudson's "Far Away and Long Ago," xxii.); sometimes, any bag, often with its contents (chiefly prov.: as, "the little *sack* of tobacco," Tarkington's "Alice Adams," x.; a *sack,* or small paper bag, of peanuts); also, the amount which a sack will hold, constituting a varying unit of measure; also (with *the*), the punishment of drowning in a sack, inflicted in ancient Rome on parricides; also, dismissal or discharge, as from employment (in 'to give one the sack' and 'to get the sack': slang); also, sackcloth†.—**sack¹,** *v. t.* To put into a sack or sacks; pocket, as money (colloq.); also, to dismiss or discharge, as from employment (slang); defeat in a contest (slang).

sack² (sak), *n.* [F. *sac,* < It. *sacco,* sack, pillage; origin uncertain: cf. It. *sacco,* bag, sack, = E. *sack¹.*] The plundering or pillaging of a captured place (as, "The city was sure to be delivered over to fire, *sack,* and outrage": Motley's "Dutch Republic," ii. 9); also, the spoil so obtained.—**sack²,** *v. t.* To pillage or loot after capture, as a city; strip of possessions or goods; plunder; despoil.

sack³ (sak), *n.* [F. *sec,* dry (*vin sec,* dry wine), < L. *siccus,* dry.] Any of various strong light-colored wines formerly brought from Spain, the Canary Islands, etc.

sack⁴ (sak), *n.* [Also *sacque;* appar. another use of *sack¹,* or from the equivalent F. *sac.*] A kind of loose gown formerly worn by women, or a long back piece attached to the gown at the shoulders and forming a train; also, a loose-fitting coat or jacket, esp. for women and children.

sack-but (sak'but), *n.* [F. *saquebute,* sackbut, OF. *saqueboute,* hooked lance for pulling riders from their horses, < *saquier,* pull, + (?) *bouter,* strike, thrust.] A medieval musical instrument of the trumpet class, resembling the trombone; also, in Biblical use (Dan. iii.), an ancient stringed musical instrument.

sack-cloth (sak'klôth), *n.* Coarse cloth for making sacks or bags; sacking: formerly worn as a sign of mourning or penitence.

Woman wearing a Sack (middle of the 18th century).

sack=coat (sak'kōt), *n.* A man's short, more or less loose-fitting coat for ordinary wear.

sack-er (sak'èr), *n.* One who sacks or plunders.

sack-ful (sak'fūl), *n.*; pl. -*fuls.* A quantity sufficient to fill a sack or bag.

sack-ing (sak'ing), *n.* Stout or coarse woven material of hemp, jute, or the like, such as is used for making sacks.

sack-less (sak'les), *a.* [AS. *sacleas,* < *sacu,* strife, dispute, guilt: see *sake¹.*] Secure† or unmolested†; also, guiltless or innocent (archaic or prov.); also, guileless, harmless, foolish, feeble-minded, lacking energy, or dispirited (Sc. and north. Eng.).

sacque (sak), *n.* [See *sack⁴.*] A woman's sack (gown or jacket).

sa-cral¹ (sā'krạl), *a.* [NL. *sacralis,* < *sacrum:* see *sacrum.*] Of or pertaining to the sacrum.

sa-cral² (sā'krạl), *a.* [L. *sacra,* sacred things or rites, pl. of *sacrum,* prop. neut. of *sacer,* sacred.] Pertaining to sacred rites or observances.

sac-ra-ment (sak'rạ-ment), *n.* [OF. F. *sacrement,* < L. *sacramentum,* oath, solemn engagement, LL. sacrament, mystery, < L. *sacrare,* make sacred: see *sacre.*] A sworn or solemn engagement (now rare); also, any of certain solemn religious ceremonies of the Christian church, as the eucharist, baptism, etc., enjoined by Christ or the church, and regarded as outward and visible signs of inward and spiritual grace; [often *cap.*] the eucharist, or Lord's Supper (with *the*); the consecrated elements of the eucharist, esp. the bread (often called 'the blessed sacrament'); also [*l. c.*], something regarded as possessing a sacred character or a mysterious significance; also, a sign, token, or symbol.—**sac-ra-men'tal** (-men'tạl). **I.** *a.* Of, pertaining to, or of the nature of a sacrament, specif. the sacrament of the eucharist; also, peculiarly sacred, as an obligation; also, pertaining to or of the nature of an outward sign or symbol. **II.** *n.* A rite, observance, or the like, similar to but not included among the recognized sacraments of the church.—**sac-ra-men'tal-ly,** *adv.*—**sac″ra-men-ta'ri-an** (-tā'ri-ạn). **I.** *a.* Pertaining to the sacraments or to the sacramentarians. **II.** *n.* One of the Protestant theologians, as Zwingli, maintaining that the bread and wine of the eucharist can be said to be the body and blood of Christ only in a sacramental, that is, symbolical or metaphorical, sense; also, one who holds that there is in the sacraments a direct spiritual efficacy to confer grace upon the recipient.—**sac-ra-men'ta-ry** (-tạ-ri). **I.** *a.* Sacramental; sacramentarian. **II.** *n.*; pl. -*ries* (-riz). A sacramentarian; also, an office-book formerly in use in the Western Church, containing the rites and prayers connected with the sacraments and other ceremonies.

sa-cra-ri-um (sạ-krā'ri-um), *n.*; pl. -*ria* (-ri-ạ). [L., < *sacer* (*sacr-*), sacred.] In *Rom. antiq.,* a shrine; a sanctuary; an adytum; *eccles.,* the sanctuary or chancel; in the *Rom. Cath. Ch.,* a piscina.

---

fat, fāte, fär, fåll, ȧsk, fāre; net, mē, hèr; pin, pīne; not, nōte, mŏve, nôr; up, lūte, pu̇ll; oi, oil; ou, out; (lightened) aviȧry, ēlect, agŏny, intọ, ūnite; (obscured) errạnt, operä, ardẹnt, actọr, natụre; ch, chip; g, go; th, thin; ᴛʜ, then; y, you;

sa-cre (sā′kèr), *v. t.*; *sacred, sacring*. [OF. F. *sacrer*, < L. *sacrare*, make or declare sacred, consecrate, also declare accursed, < *sacer* (*sacr-*), sacred, holy: see *sanction*, and cf. *sacré*.] To consecrate; hallow: now only as in *sacred* and *sacring*.

sa-cré (sȧ-krā′), *a.* [F., pp. of *sacrer*: see *sacre*.] Sacred; also, profanely or as a colloquial intensive, damned; cursed; confounded.

sa-cred (sā′kred), *a.* [Orig. pp. of *sacre*.] Appropriated or dedicated to a deity or to some religious purpose; consecrated; entitled to veneration or religious respect by association with divinity or divine things; hallowed; holy; pertaining to or connected with religion (opposed to *profane* and *secular*: as, *sacred* music; *sacred* history); also, reverently dedicated to some person or object (as, a monument *sacred* to the memory of a person); regarded with reverence similar to that due to holy things (as, the *sacred* memory of a dead hero); also, secured against violation, infringement, etc., by reverence, sense of right, or the like (as, *sacred* oaths; *sacred* rights); properly immune from violence, interference, etc., as a person or his office (as, "The persons of Saturninus and Glaucia were doubly *sacred*, for one was tribune and the other prætor": Froude's "Cæsar," v.); also, accursed (obs. or rare: as, "For *sacred* hunger of my gold I die," Dryden's "Cock and the Fox," 254).—**Sacred College.** See *college*.—**Sacred Heart,** in the *Rom. Cath. Ch.*, the physical heart of Jesus Christ, to which devotion is offered as being the symbol of his love and spiritual life.—**Sacred Writ,** the Scriptures.—**sa′cred-ly,** *adv.*—**sa′cred-ness,** *n.*

sac-ri-fice (sak′ri-fīs), *n.* [OF. F. *sacrifice*, < L. *sacrificium*, < *sacer* (*sacr-*), sacred, + *facere*, make.] The offering of an animal, a possession, etc., to a deity, as in propitiation or homage; that which is so offered; also, the surrender or destruction of something prized or desirable for the sake of something considered as having a higher or more pressing claim; the thing so surrendered or devoted; also, a loss of profit incurred in selling something below its value, as in order to get rid of it (as, "Going for seven ten — a cruel *sacrifice*": Lever's "Harry Lorrequer," xxxiv.).—**sacrifice hit,** in *baseball*, a bunt which allows a runner to gain a base while the batsman is (or could be) put out before reaching first base; also, a fly ball which results in a run being scored though the batsman is (or could be) put out by its being caught.—**the supreme sacrifice.** See under *supreme, a.* —**sac′ri-fice,** *v.*; *-ficed, -ficing*. **I.** *tr.* To make a sacrifice or offering of (as, "From the herd or flock Oft *sacrificing* bullock, lamb, or kid": Milton's "Paradise Lost," xii. 20); also, to surrender or give up, or permit injury or disadvantage to, for the sake of something else (as, "He would have *sacrificed* his life for the saving mine," Defoe's "Robinson Crusoe," i. 14; "Every feeling has been *sacrificed* to worldly considerations," Marryat's "Peter Simple," xl.); also, to dispose of (goods, etc.) regardless of profit. **II.** *intr.* To offer or make a sacrifice.—**sac′ri-fi-cer** (-fī-sèr), *n.*—**sac-ri-fi′cial** (-fish′al), *a.* Pertaining to or concerned with sacrifice.—**sac-ri-fi′cial-ly,** *adv.*

sac-ri-lege (sak′ri-lej), *n.* [OF. *sacrilege* (F. *sacrilège*), < L. *sacrilegium*, < *sacrilegus*, stealing sacred things, sacrilegious, < *sacer* (*sacr-*), sacred, + *legere*, gather.] The stealing of anything consecrated to the service of God; hence, the violation or profanation of anything sacred or held sacred; an instance of this.—**sac-ri-le′gious** (-lē′jus), *a.* Guilty of or involving sacrilege; impious: as, a *sacrilegious* person; *sacrilegious* practices.—**sac-ri-le′gious-ly,** *adv.*—**sac-ri-le′gious-ness,** *n.*—**sac′ri-le-gist** (-lē-jist), *n.* One guilty of sacrilege.

sa-cring (sā′kring), *n.* [See *sacre*.] The act or ceremony of consecrating; esp., the consecrating of the eucharistic elements in the mass. [Archaic.]—**sa′cring=bell,** *n.* A small bell rung at the elevation of the host in the mass.

sa-crist (sā′krist), *n.* [ML. *sacrista*, < L. *sacer* (*sacr-*), sacred (neut. pl. *sacra*, sacred things).] A sacristan.—**sac-ris-tan** (sak′ris-tan), *n.* [ML. *sacristanus*.] An official in charge of the sacred vessels, vestments, etc., of a church or a religious house; also, a sexton (obs. or archaic).—**sac′ris-ty** (-ti), *n.*; pl. *-ties* (-tiz). [ML. *sacristia*.] An apartment in or a building connected with a church or a religious house, in which the sacred vessels, vestments, etc., are kept.

sa-cro- (sā′krō-). Form of *sacrum* used in combination, as in *sacro-iliac* (pertaining to the sacrum and the ilium), *sacrosciatic, sacrospinal.*

sac-ro-sanct (sak′rō-sangkt or sā′krō-), *a.* [L. *sacrosanctus*, < *sacro*, abl. of *sacrum*, sacred rite (prop. neut. of *sacer*, sacred), + *sanctus*, pp. of *sancire*, make sacred: see *sanction*.] Made sacred or inviolable by special religious sanction; of established sacredness or inviolability.—**sac-ro-sanc′ti-ty** (-sangk′ti-ti), **sac′ro-sanct-ness,** *n.*

sa-cro-sci-at-ic (sā″krō-sī-at′ik), *a.* [See *sacro-* and *sciatic*.] In *anat.*, pertaining to the sacrum and the ischium: as, the *sacrosciatic* ligament (either of two stout ligaments connecting the sacrum with the ischium).

sa-crum (sā′krum), *n.*; pl. *-cra* (-krä) or *-crums*. [NL., for LL. *os sacrum*, 'sacred bone': *sacrum*, neut. of L. *sacer*, sacred; the name being said to refer to the offering of this part in sacrifice.] In *anat.*, a bone resulting from the ankylosis of two or more vertebræ between the lumbar and the coccygeal regions, in man forming the posterior wall of the pelvis.

sad (sad), *a.*; compar. *sadder*, superl. *saddest*. [AS. *sæd*, sated, = D. *zat* = G. *satt* = Icel. *saðr* = Goth. *saths*, all orig. pp. from a root *sa-*, 'satisfy,' whence also L. *sat, satis*, enough, *satur*, sated, Gr. ἄδην, enough: cf. *sate*[2], *satisfy*, and *saturate*.] Sated†; wearied or tired of something†; also, solid, compact, or heavy (obs. or prov.); soggy or doughy, as bread (now prov.); also, firm† or steadfast†; also, grave† or serious†; also, sorrowful or mournful, as persons; expressive of or characterized by sorrow (as, *sad* looks; a *sad* occasion); causing sorrow, distressing, or grievous (as, a *sad* accident; a *sad* disappointment); also, deplorably bad (as, a *sad* attempt; "They bore the character of being *sad* scoundrels," Kinglake's "Eothen," xxi.: often humorous); also, of color, somber, dark, or dull (as, "The general colouring was uniform and *sad*": Stevenson's "Treasure Island," xiii.).

sad-den (sad′n), *v.* **I.** *tr.* To make sad; specif., to make dark-colored; tone down or dull (a color or dye), as by mixing with another color or some chemical. **II.** *intr.* To become sad.

sad-dle (sad′l), *n.* [AS. *sadol* = D. *zadel* = G. *sattel* = Icel. *söðhull*, saddle; perhaps from the root of E. *sit*.] A contrivance secured on the back of a horse or other animal to serve as a seat for a rider; a similar seat, as on a bicycle; a pack-saddle; a part of a harness which is laid across the back of the animal and girded under the belly, and to which the terrets are attached and the check-rein is secured; also, something resembling a saddle in shape or position; a ridge connecting two higher elevations; the bearing resting on the journal of the axle of a railroad-car wheel; a block with a hollowed top to sustain a round object which is being worked upon; of mutton, venison, etc., a cut including part of the backbone and both loins; of poultry, the posterior part of the back.—**sad′dle,** *v.*; *-dled, -dling*. **I.** *tr.* To put a saddle upon (a horse, etc.); also, to load or charge as with a burden (as, "Mr. Simpson was *saddled* with a wife who was little but a drag on him": S. R. Crockett's "Stickit Minister," xv.); also, to impose as a burden (as, "If you like not my company, you can '*saddle*' yourself on some one else": Stevenson's "Master of Ballantrae," iii.). **II.** *intr.* To get into the saddle: as, "Every churl who owns a manor . . . must needs arm and *saddle*, and levy war on his own behalf" (Kingsley's "Hereward," i.).

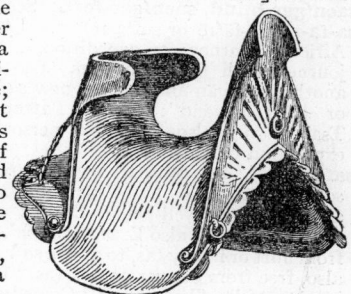
War-saddle of the 14th century.

sad-dle=backed (sad′l-bakt), *a.* Having the back or upper surface concavely curved like a saddle; also, having a saddle-like marking on the back, as certain birds; in *arch.*, noting a roof or a coping with a slope on both sides; also, noting a tower with a gable-roof.

sad-dle=bag (sad′l-bag), *n.* A bag carried at the saddle to hold various objects; esp., one of a pair of bags laid over the back of an animal behind the saddle.

sad-dle=bow (sad′l-bō), *n.* The arched front part of a saddle or saddletree.

sad-dle=cloth (sad′l-klôth), *n.* A cloth placed between a horse's back and the saddle.

sad-dler (sad′lėr), *n.* One who makes or deals in saddles or saddlery; also, a horse used for riding.—**sad′dler-y** (-i), *n.*; pl. *-ies* (-iz). The work or business of a saddler; also, the establishment of a saddler; also, saddles and other articles pertaining to the equipment of horses, etc.

sad-dle=shell (sad′l-shel), *n.* A shell suggesting a saddle in shape, as that of *Placuna sella*, a bivalve mollusk of East Indian seas; also, a mollusk with such a shell.

sad-dle-tree (sad′l-trē), *n.* The frame of a saddle.

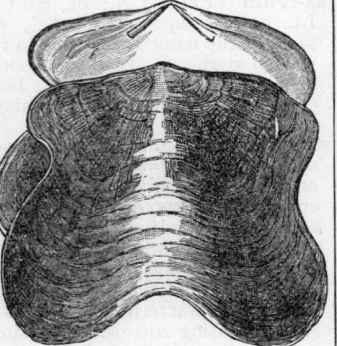

Saddle-shell (*Placuna sella*).

Sad-du-cee (sad′ū-sē), *n.* [LL. *Sadducæi*, pl., < Gr. Σαδδουκαῖοι, < Heb. *Tsedūqīm*, pl.] One of an ancient Jewish sect or party whose views and practices were opposed to those of the Pharisees, and who denied the resurrection of the dead, the existence of angels, the authority of oral tradition, etc.—**Sad-du-ce′an, Sad-du-cæ′an** (-sē′an), *a.*—**Sad′du-cee-ism**, *n.*

sad-i-ron (sad′i″ėrn), *n.* A solid flat-iron.

sad-ism (säd′izm), *n.* [From Comte D. A. F. de *Sade* (1740–1814), French writer, infamous for the licentiousness of his life and writings.] In *pathol.*, a form of sexual perversion marked by a love of cruelty. Cf. *masochism.*—**sad′ist**, *n.* One affected with sadism.—**sad-is′tic**, *a.*

sad-ly (sad′li), *adv.* In a sad manner.—**sad′ness**, *n.*

sae (sā), *adv.* Scotch form of *so.*

saen′ger-bund, saen′ger-fest. See *sängerbund*, etc.

sa-fa-ri (sạ-fä′rẹ or suf′ạ-rē), *n.* [Ar. *safarī*.] In eastern Africa, a journey; an expedition, as for hunting; a caravan journey with native porters (as, "The Swahili . . . join another caravan and begin a new *safari* to the Great Lakes, or even beyond": J. H. Patterson's "Man-Eaters of Tsavo," xi.); also, a body of persons employed on such an expedition or journey.

safe[1] (sāf), *a.*; compar. *safer*, superl. *safest*. [OF. *sauf*, *salf* (F. *sauf*), < L. *salvus*, safe, unharmed, sound, well, akin to *salus*, well-being, health: cf. Gr. ὅλος, whole, Skt. *sarva*, whole, all, also E. *sage[2], salve[3], salute*, and *save*.] Free from hurt or injury (as, to arrive *safe* and sound); unharmed; also, free from danger or risk (as, "I greatly fear my money is not *safe*": Shakspere's "Comedy of Errors," i. 2. 105); secure from liability to harm, injury, etc.; also, affording freedom from danger or risk (as, a *safe* place; a *safe* distance); involving no risk of mishap, error, etc. (as, a *safe* undertaking; a *safe* estimate); also, dependable or trustworthy (as, a *safe* guide or adviser); cautious in avoiding danger (as, a *safe* player); also, sure or certain (colloq.: as, "an extremely clear-headed . . . young man, who was *safe* to rise in the world," Dickens's "Hard Times," ii. 1); also, in secure custody (as, a criminal *safe* in jail); placed beyond the power of doing harm.

safe[2] (sāf), *n.* [Orig. *save*, < *save*, *v.*] A receptacle or structure for the safe-keeping of articles (as, a meat-*safe*; a match-*safe*: see these entries); esp., a steel or iron box or repository for the storage of money, jewels, papers, etc., in safety from theft or fire.—**safe′=blow″er**, *n.* A safe-breaker who blows open safes by means of explosives.—**safe′=break″er**, *n.* One who breaks into safes to commit theft.

safe=con-duct (sāf-kon′dukt), *n.* [OF. *sauf conduit* (F. *sauf-conduit*).] A conducting or convoying in safety; also,

the privilege of safe passage through a region, as in time of war; also, a document securing this privilege.—**safe=con-duct′** (-kǫn-dukt′ or -kon′dukt), *v. t.* To conduct or convoy safely, as through a hostile region.

safe-de-pos-it (sāf′dẹ-poz′it). **I.** *n.* A depositing in safety; also, a place where valuables may be stored in safety. **II.** *a.* Providing safe-keeping for valuables: as, *safe-deposit* vaults.

safe-guard (sāf′gärd), *n.* [OF. *salve garde* (F. *sauvegarde*).] Safe-keeping, protection, or defense; also, something serving as a protection or defense, or ensuring safety; sometimes, a permit for safe passage; also, a guard or convoy for protection.—**safe′guard**, *v. t.* To guard; protect.

safe=keep-ing (sāf′kē′ping), *n.* The action of keeping safe; secure preservation.

safe-ly (sāf′li), *adv.* In a safe manner; without harm; without risk; in secure custody.—**safe′ness**, *n.*

safe-ty (sāf′ti), *n.*; pl. *-ties* (-tiz). [OF. *sauvete* (F. *sauveté*), < ML. *salvitas*, < L. *salvus*, E. *safe[1]*.] The state of being safe; freedom from hurt or injury, or from danger or risk; the quality of insuring against hurt or injury, of affording freedom from danger or risk, or of being dependable or trustworthy; close confinement or custody†; also, a protection† or safeguard†; a contrivance or device to prevent injury or avert danger; a safety-bicycle; in *football*, an action of a player in touching the ball down behind his own goal-line when the impetus has been given to the ball by his own side, in order to prevent the making of a touchdown by the other side (also called *safety touchdown*).—**safe′ty=bi″cy-cle**, *n.* The type of bicycle in later use, with two low wheels, as distinguished from the old type with one high and one small wheel.—**safe′ty=fuse**, *n.* A fuse filled or saturated with a slow-burning composition; in *elect.*, a fuse (see *fuse[2]*).—**safe′ty=lamp**, *n.* A miner's lamp in which the flame is protected by wire gauze, thus preventing the ignition of explosive gases.—**safe′ty=match**, *n.* A match designed to ignite only when rubbed on a specially prepared surface.—**safe′ty=pin**, *n.* A pin bent back on itself to form a spring, and having a guard to cover the point and prevent accidental unfastening.—**safe′ty=ra″zor**, *n.* A razor provided with a guard or guards to prevent cutting the skin.—**safe′ty=valve**, *n.* A valve in a steam-boiler or the like, which, when the pressure becomes abnormal or dangerous, opens automatically and allows the steam or fluid to escape. Also fig.

saf-fi-an (saf′i-ạn), *n.* [Russ. *safyan*; from Pers.] A kind of leather made from goatskins or sheepskins tanned with sumac and dyed in various colors without a previous stuffing with fats.

saf-flow-er (saf′lou″ėr), *n.* [D. *saffloer*, < OF. *safleur*, *safour*, appar. ult. < Ar. *'uçfur*, safflower: cf. *saffron*.] A thistle-like composite herb, *Carthamus tinctorius*, a native of the Old World, bearing large orange-red flower-heads; also, its dried florets, used medicinally or as a red dyestuff.

saf-fron (saf′rọn). [OF. F. *safran*, ult. < Ar. *za'farān*, saffron.] **I.** *n.* An orange-colored product consisting of the dried stigmas of a species of crocus, used to color confectionery, for flavoring, etc.; also, a crocus, *Crocus sativus*, having handsome purple flowers, and yielding this product; also, the color of the stigmas, an orange-yellow. **II.** *a.* Orange-yellow: as, "a *saffron* sky" (Arnold Bennett's "Hilda Lessways,"

Upper part of Stem of Safflower, with the Heads.— *a*, a flower; *b, c*, the two different kinds of involucral leaves.

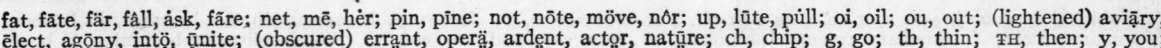

iii. 3).—**saf'froned**, *a.* Colored or flavored with saffron.

saf-ra-nine (saf'rạ-nin), *n.* [G. *safranine*, < *safran*, saffron.] In *chem.*, any of a class of (chiefly red) organic dyes, derivatives of azonium compounds, used for dyeing wool, silk, etc.

saf-rol (saf'rol or -rōl), *n.* [From (*sas*)*safr*(*as*) + -*ol*.] In *chem.*, a colorless or faintly yellow liquid, $C_{10}H_{10}O_2$, obtained from oil of sassafras, etc., and used for flavoring and in perfumery.

saft (saft), *a.* and *adv.* Scotch form of *soft*.

sag (sag), *v.*; *sagged*, *sagging.* [ME. *saggen*: cf. D. *zakken*, MLG. *sacken*, Sw. *sacka*, sink.] **I.** *intr.* To sink or bend downward by weight or pressure, esp. in the middle; hang down unevenly, as a door or a skirt; droop, or hang loosely, as a part of the body; also, to yield through weakness, lack of effort, or the like (as, "The mind I sway by . . . Shall never *sag* with doubt": Shakspere's "Macbeth," v. 3. 10); decline, as in price; also, to drag one's self along feebly; *naut.*, to drift out of the intended course (as, "We're *sagging* south on the Long Trail": Kipling's "Long Trail"). **II.** *tr.* To cause to sag; cause to sink downward in the middle.— **sag**, *n.* The act, state, or degree of sagging; also, a place where anything sags; a depression.

sa-ga (sä'gạ or sā'-), *n.*; pl. -*gas* (-gạz). [Icel. *saga*, story, tale, legend, history: see *saw²*.] A medieval Icelandic or Norse prose narrative of achievements and events in the history of a personage, family, etc.; hence, any narrative or legend of heroic exploits.

sa-ga-cious (sạ-gā'shus), *a.* [L. *sagax* (*sagac-*), < *sagire*, perceive acutely (cf. *presage*); akin to E. *seek*.] Having keen sense-perception, esp. keen-scented (obs. or rare: as, "With might and main they chas'd the murd'rous fox . . . Nor wanted horns t' inspire *sagacious* hounds," Dryden's "Cock and the Fox," 752); also, gifted with acute mental discernment, having keen practical sense, or shrewd, as a person; due to or exhibiting acute mental discernment (as, "He was observant and thoughtful, and given to asking *sagacious* questions": Galt's "Annals of the Parish," xlii.); of animals, intelligent.— **sa-ga'cious-ly**, *adv.*— **sa-ga'cious-ness**, *n.*— **sa-ga'ci-ty** (-gas'i-ti), *n.* The quality of being sagacious; acuteness of mental discernment; keenness and soundness of judgment; shrewdness; of animals, intelligence.

sag-a-more (sag'ạ-mōr), *n.* [Of Algonquian origin, and akin to *sachem*.] Among some tribes of American Indians, a chief or great man.

sage¹ (sāj). [OF. F. *sage*, from a Latin adj. (recorded in the negative *nesapius*, unwise; *ne*, not) < *sapere*, be wise: cf. *sapient*.] **I.** *a.*; compar. *sager*, superl. *sagest.* Wise, judicious, or prudent (as, "My *sage* counsellor was gone, I was like a ship without a pilot": Defoe's "Robinson Crusoe," ii. 1); often, having been made wise or prudent by experience (as, "Let time, that makes you homely, make you *sage*," T. Parnell's "Elegy to an Old Beauty"; "For most men (till by losing render'd *sager*) Will back their own opinions with a wager," Byron's "Beppo," xxvii.); of conduct, advice, etc., exhibiting wisdom or sound judgment (as, "The lawyers gave a *sage* reply": Morley's "Oliver Cromwell," ii. 4); also, grave† or solemn† (as, "And if aught else great bards beside In *sage* and solemn tunes have sung": Milton's "Il Penseroso," 117). **II.** *n.* A profoundly wise man; a man of high repute for wisdom; often, a man who is venerated for the store of wisdom that he has accumulated during a long life: as, the seven *sages* of ancient Greece (as commonly given, Thales, Solon, Bias, Chilon, Cleobulus, Periander, and Pittacus).

sage² (sāj), *n.* [OF. F. *sauge*, < L. *salvia*, sage, < *salvus*, safe, well: see *safe¹*, and cf. *salvia*.] A shrubby menthaceous perennial, *Salvia officinalis* (see cut in next column), whose grayish-green leaves are used in medicine and for seasoning in sausage-making, cookery, etc.; the leaves themselves; also, any species of salvia, as *S. splendens*, a garden-plant with racemes of scarlet flowers ('scarlet sage'); also, the sage-brush.— **sage'=brush**, *n.* Any of various sage-like bushy plants of the asteraceous genus *Artemisia*, common on the dry plains of the western U. S.— **sage'=green'**, *n.* A dull grayish green.— **sage'=grouse**, *n.* A large grouse, *Centrocercus urophasianus*, common in the sage-brush regions of western America.

sage-ly (sāj'li), *adv.* In a sage manner. — **sage'-ness**, *n.*

sag-gar (sag'är), *n.* [Prob. a reduced form of *safeguard*.] A box or case made of baked clay in which the finer ceramic wares are inclosed and protected while baking; also, the clay of which such boxes are made.— **sag'gar**, *v. t.* To place in or upon a saggar.

sag-it-tal (saj'-i-tạl or sạ-jit'ạl), *a.* [ML. *sagittalis*, < L. *sagitta*, arrow.] Pertaining to an arrow; resembling an arrow or arrow-head; in *anat.*, noting, or pertaining to, a suture between the parietal bones of the skull; noting, or situated in, the plane of this suture (the median longitudinal anteroposterior plane of the body) or a plane parallel to it.— **sag'it-tal-ly**, *adv.*

Sag-it-ta-ri-us (saj-i-tā'ri-us), *n.* [L.: see *sagittary*.] The Archer (a centaur drawing a bow), a zodiacal constellation; also, the ninth sign of the zodiac. See *zodiac*.

sag-it-ta-ry (saj'i-tạ-ri), *n.*; pl. -*ries* (-riz). [L. *sagittarius*, archer, orig. adj., pertaining to arrows, < *sagitta*, arrow.] An archer (also, formerly, with *cap.*, same as *Sagittarius*); also, a centaur; specif. [*cap.*], a centaur fabled in medieval romance to have fought in the Trojan army against the Greeks.

sag-it-tate (saj'i-tāt), *a.* [NL. *sagittatus*, < L. *sagitta*, arrow.] Shaped like an arrow-head. Also **sa-git-ti-form** (sạ-jit'i-fôrm).

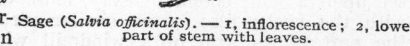

Sage (*Salvia officinalis*). — 1, inflorescence; 2, lower part of stem with leaves.

Sagittate Leaf of Calla Lily (*Aroides æthiopicum*).

sa-go (sā'gō), *n.*; pl. -*gos* (-gōz). [Malay *sāgū*.] A starchy foodstuff derived from the soft interior of the trunk of various palms and cycads (see *sago-palm*), used in making puddings, etc.; also, a sago-palm.— **sa'go=palm**, *n.* Any tree yielding sago, as certain large palms of the genus *Metroxylon*, the gomuti, various cycads, etc.

sa-gua-ro (sạ-gwä'rō), *n.*; pl. -*ros* (-rōz). [Amer. Sp.] An extremely tall cactus, *Cereus giganteus*, of Arizona and neighboring regions, yielding a useful wood and an edible fruit.

sa-gum (sā'gum), *n.*; pl. -*ga* (-gä). [L. *sagum*, *sagus*; said to be from Celtic.] In *Rom. antiq.*, a kind of cloak worn by Roman soldiers and inferior officers.

Sa-ha-ra (sạ-hä'rä, commonly sạ-hār'ä), *n.* [From the great desert in northern Africa.] A desert; an arid waste.

Sago-palm (*Metroxylon læve*).

sa-hib (sä'ib), *n.* [Hind. use of Ar. *çāhib*, master, lord, orig. companion, friend.] In India, a term of respect applied by natives to a European: as, "The servant announced a *sahib* who wanted to see me" (F. M. Crawford's "Mr. Isaacs," ii.). Cf. *mem-sahib*.

sa-hua-ro (sạ-hwä'rō), *n.* Same as *saguaro*.

sa-ic (sā′ik), *n.* [F. *saïque*, < Turk. *shāïqā*.] *Naut.*, a kind of ketch very common in the Levant.

said (sed). Preterit and past participle of *say*[3].—**said**, *p. a.* Named or mentioned before: used chiefly in legal style: as, the *said* witness; the *said* sum of money.

sai-ga (sī′gä), *n.* [Russ.] An antelope, *Saiga tartarica*, of western Asia and eastern Russia, having the nose parts peculiarly inflated or expanded.

Saiga.

sail (sāl), *n.* [AS. *segel, segl,* = D. *zeil* = OHG. *segal* (G. *segel*) = Icel. *segl,* sail.] A piece or extent of canvas or the like spread to the wind to cause a vessel to move through the water (called a *square sail* when quadrilateral and extended by a yard, normally at right angles to the keel, and a *fore-and-aft sail* when set upon a gaff, boom, or stay, more or less in a line with the keel); also, some similar piece or apparatus; the part of an arm of a windmill which catches the wind; a wing of a bird (poetic); the large dorsal fin of the sailfish; also, sails for a vessel or vessels, collectively; also, a sailing-vessel or ship (as, "I spied a *sail,* and gave her chase": Defoe's "Captain Singleton," xii.); sailing-vessels collectively (chiefly with a numeral: as, "the Spanish armada . . . numbering now thirty *sail,*" Motley's "Dutch Republic," iii. 9); also, a voyage or excursion in a sailing-vessel or other vessel.—**sail,** *v.* [AS. *seglan, siglan.*] **I.** *intr.* To move along or be conveyed on water by the action of wind on sails, or, by extension, by means of steam, etc.; also, to begin a journey by water (as, "I have taken my berth in an East Indiaman which *sails* on the twentieth of June": C. Brontë's "Jane Eyre," xxxiv.); also, to travel through the air, as an airship; also, to move along in a manner suggestive of a sailing-vessel, as a swan on the surface of water or clouds through the air; move along with dignity, as a person (as, "Madame Beck . . . *sailed* from the room": C. Brontë's "Villette," viii.); also, to go boldly into action (with *in*: colloq.). **II.** *tr.* To sail upon, over, or through; also, to perform by sailing, as a race; also, to navigate (a ship, etc.).

sail=boat (sāl′bōt), *n.* A boat propelled by a sail or sails.

sail=cloth (sāl′klôth), *n.* Canvas or other material such as is used for making sails.

sailed (sāld), *a.* Having sails: as, white-*sailed.*

sail-er (sā′lėr), *n.* One who sails (now rare: see *sailor*); a sailing-vessel; a ship or vessel with reference to powers or manner of sailing (as, "The ship . . . proved the best *sailer* in the fleet," B. Franklin's "Autobiography," xiv.; "a very fast *sailer* and a noble craft," H. Melville's "Moby-Dick," ci.).

sail-fish (sāl′fish), *n.* Any of the large marine fishes constituting the genus *Histiophorus* (or *Istiophorus*), characterized by a very large dorsal fin likened to a sail, and related to the swordfishes, as *H.* (or *I.*) *nigricans,* a species of the warmer parts of the Atlantic; also, any of various other fishes with a large dorsal fin, as the basking-shark.

Sailfish (*Histiophorus nigricans*).

sail-ing (sā′ling), *n.* The act of one who or that which sails; *naut.*, the art of navigation; also, the method of determining a ship's course and related problems.—**great=circle sailing,** a method of navigation by which the courses of a ship are so laid as to carry it over an arc of a great circle of the globe, such being the shortest path between two points.—**oblique sailing,** sailing on loxodromic lines; rhumb-sailing.—**plane sailing,** a method of navigation in which the surface of the ocean is assumed to be plane instead of spherical: used in calculations, etc., in which only short distances are concerned.—**spherical sailing,** a method of navigation in which the curvature of the earth is taken into consideration.—**sail′ing=ves″sel,** *n.* A vessel propelled by means of a sail or sails.

sail-less (sāl′les), *a.* Without sails.

sail=liz-ard (sāl′liz″ärd), *n.* A large lizard, *Histiurus amboinensis,* of the Molucca Islands, with a crested tail.

sail-mak-er (sāl′mā″kėr), *n.* One who makes or repairs sails; specif., in the U. S. navy, a warrant-officer whose duty it is to take charge of and keep in repair sails, awnings, etc.

Sail-lizard.

sail-or (sā′lọr), *n.* One whose occupation is sailing or navigation; a mariner; a seaman; specif., a common seaman, or one below the rank of officer; also, a person with reference to freedom from seasickness (as, a good *sailor*; a bad *sailor*; "Paquíta proving a very indifferent *sailor,*" W. H. Hudson's "Purple Land," i.); also (orig. *sailor hat*), a woman's flat-brimmed hat having a crown of moderate height with a flat or slightly rounded top; a similar hat worn by children, having a turned-up brim.—**sailor collar,** a large collar, broad and square across the back, with ends tapering to a point to meet on the breast.—**sail′or-ing,** *n.* The work or life of a sailor.—**sail′or-ly,** *a.* Like or befitting a sailor.—**sail′or=man** (-man), *n.*; pl. *-men.* A sailor: as, "an ancient *sailor-man*" (Stevenson's "Master of Ballantrae," viii.). [Colloq.]—**sail′or′s=choice′,** *n.* A pinfish; also, the pigfish, *Orthopristis chrysopterus*; also, a grunt, *Hæmulon parra,* ranging from Florida to Brazil.

sail-plane (sāl′plān), *n.* A gliding-machine or motorless aëroplane.—**sail′plane,** *v. i.*; *-planed, -planing.* To move through the air in a sailplane.

sain (sān), *v. t.* [AS. *segnian,* < L. *signare,* mark, E. *sign, v.*] To make the sign of the cross on, as to protect against evil influences; also, to protect by prayer, etc.; also, to bestow divine favor on, or bless (as, "God *sain* us": Scott's "Heart of Midlothian," xxix.). [Archaic or prov.]

sain-foin (sān′foin), *n.* [F. *sainfoin,* also formerly *saintfoin,* appar. < *saint,* holy (see *saint*), or perhaps *sain,* wholesome (< L. *sanus,* E. *sane*), + *foin,* < L. *fænum,* hay.] A European fabaceous herb, *Onobrychis sativa,* cultivated as a forage-plant.

saint (sānt), *a.* [OF. F. *saint* (fem. *sainte*) = Sp. and It. *santo, san* (fem. *santa*), = Pg. *santo, são* (fem. *santa*), < L. *sanctus* (fem. *sancta*), sacred, holy, prop. pp. of *sancire,* make sacred: see *sanction.*] Sacred; holy: prefixed to proper or quasi-proper names, as in *Saint* Paul, *Saint* Sophia ('Holy Wisdom'), and hence now commonly regarded as a noun. Abbreviated *St.*—**St. Agnes's Eve,** the night of Jan. 20 (before St. Agnes's Day): the traditional time for rites to reveal a woman's future husband. —**St. Andrew's cross,** an X-shaped cross.—**St. Anthony's cross,** a T-shaped cross.—**St. Anthony's fire,** erysipelas.—**St. Bartholomew's Day,**

Sainfoin. — 1, the inflorescence; 2, the lower part of the stem with the leaves; *a,* the pod with the persistent calyx.

Aug. 24; esp., this day of the year 1572, on which a great massacre of Huguenots was begun in Paris by order of King Charles IX. at the instigation of Catharine de' Medici.—**St. Bernard dog,** one of a breed of large dogs with a massive head, noted for their intelligence: named from the hospice of St. Bernard, on the pass of the Great St. Bernard in the Alps, where kept by the monks for rescuing travelers from the snow.—**St. Elmo's fire,** a corposant.—**St. George's cross,** a +-shaped red cross on a white field: used esp. in flags of Great Britain.—**St. George's Day,** April 23: observed by the English in honor of St. George, the patron saint of England.—**St. John's bread,** the fruit of the carob.—**St. John's Day,** June 24; Midsummer Day: named for St. John the Baptist.—**St. John's Eve,** the night before St. John's Day: long celebrated with bonfires and other festivities in various countries of Europe, apparently in continuation of an ancient heathen festival of the summer solstice.—**St. Luke's summer,** a period of mild weather occurring about St. Luke's Day, Oct. 18.—**St. Martin's summer,** a period of mild weather occurring about St. Martin's Day, Nov. 11.—**St. Nicholas's clerk†,** a highwayman; a thief.—**St. Patrick's Day,** March 17: observed by the Irish in honor of St. Patrick, the patron saint of Ireland.—**St. Swithin's Day,** July 15: rain on this day being popularly reputed to betoken rain for 40 days continuously.—**St. Valentine's Day,** Feb. 14. See *valentine*.—**St. Vitus's dance,** the disease chorea.—**to braid St. Catharine's tresses.** See under *braid*[1], *v.*—**saint,** *n.* One of the blessed dead in heaven; also, one of certain persons of exceptional holiness of life formally recognized by the Christian church as having attained an exalted position in heaven and as being entitled to veneration on earth; a canonized person; hence, one who is the object of similar veneration in a non-Christian religion; also, one of God's chosen people; in the Old Testament, an Israelite; in the New Testament, a member of the Christian church; in certain religious bodies, a designation applied by the members to themselves; sometimes, an angel; in general, a person of great holiness.—**saint,** *v.* **I.** *tr.* To give the name of saint to; reckon as a saint; specif., to enroll formally among the saints recognized by the church. **II.** *intr.* To live or act as a saint (often with indefinite *it*).—**saint′ed,** *p. a.* Enrolled among the saints; being a saint in heaven; also, of saintly life or character (as, "a most *sainted* king": Shakspere's "Macbeth," iv. 3. 109); also, sacred or hallowed (as, "the enthroned Gods on *sainted* seats": Milton's "Comus," 11).—**saint′hood** (-hŭd), *n.* The character or status of a saint.—**St.=John's=wort,** *n.* Any of various herbs or shrubs of the genus *Hypericum,* having yellow flowers. —**saint′like,** *a.* Saintly.— **saint′ly,** *a.;* compar. *saintlier,* superl. *saintliest.* Like, proper to, or befitting a saint. —**saint′li·ness,** *n.*—**saint′ship,** *n.*

Saint=Si·mon·ism (sänt-sī′mon-izm), *n.* The socialistic system founded by Claude Henri de Rouvroy, Comte de Saint-Simon (1760–1825), advocating state control of all property, distribution of the products of the common labor according to individual vocation and capacity, etc.

Branch of St.-John's-wort (*Hypericum aureum*), with flower and young fruit.—*a*, cluster of stamens; *b*, fruit.

sair (sãr), etc. Scotch form of *sore*[2], etc.
sais (sīs), *n.* [Hind. and Ar. *sāis.*] A groom. [India.]
saith (seth). Third person sing. pres. ind. of *say*[3]: now only in poetic or solemn use.
sai·yid (sī′yid), *n.* See *sayyid.*
sake[1] (sāk), *n.* [AS. *sacu,* strife, lawsuit, guilt, = D. *zaak,* G. *sache,* lawsuit, cause, affair, thing, = Icel. *sök,* charge, lawsuit, offense, cause; akin to AS. *sacan,* contend (see *forsake*), and perhaps to E. *seek*.] Cause, account, or interest; often, purpose or end: now chiefly in 'for the sake of,' 'for one's (its, etc.) sake,' or 'for our (their, etc.) sakes': as, to die for the *sake* of another, or for another's *sake*; to go for the sake

of appearances, or for appearances' *sake*; to do a thing for the *sake* of money, or for money's *sake*; put yourself to no trouble for our *sakes.*—**for old sake's sake,** for the sake of old times or old friendship; for auld lang syne: as, "Rail me then, on my decease, To the Hills *for old sake's sake!*" (Kipling's "Ballad of Burial").
sa·ke[2] (sä′kạ or sak′i), *n.* [Jap.] A Japanese fermented alcoholic beverage made from rice.
sa·ker (sā′kėr), *n.* [OF. F. *sacre,* prob. < Ar. *çaqr,* hawk.] An old-world falcon, *Falco sacer,* used in falconry; also, an old form of cannon.
sa·ki[1] (sä′ki), *n.* [F.; from S. Amer. name.] Any of various South American monkeys with a bushy tail, mostly of the genus *Pithecia.*
sa·ki[2] (sä′ki or sak′i), *n.* Same as *sake*[2].
sa·ki-a, sa·ki-eh (sä′ki-ạ), *n.* [Ar. *sāqiyah.*] A device used in Egypt and elsewhere for raising water, consisting essentially of a large vertical wheel to which a series of buckets or the like are attached, and to which motion is imparted by a horizontal wheel.

Black Saki (*Pithecia satanas*).

sal[1] (sal), *n.* [L.] Salt: used esp. in pharmaceutical terms. —**sal ammoniac.** See *ammoniac,* *a.*—**sal volatile** (vō-lat′i-lē). [NL., 'volatile salt.'] Ammonium carbonate, or an aromatic alcoholic solution of this salt.
sal[2] (säl), *n.* [Hind. *sāl.*] A large dipterocarpaceous tree, *Shorea robusta,* of India, yielding a valuable timber.
sa·laam (sạ-läm′), *n.* [Ar. *salām,* peace.] In the Orient, a salutation meaning 'peace'; also, a very low bow or obeisance, esp. with the palm of the right hand placed on the forehead. —**sa·laam,** *v. t.* or *i.* To salute with or perform a salaam.
sal·a·ble (sā′lạ-bl), *a.* Subject to or suitable for sale; readily sold.—**sal·a·bil′i·ty** (-bil′i-ti), **sal′a·ble·ness,** *n.*—**sal′a·bly,** *adv.*
sa·la·cious (sạ-lā′shus), *a.* [L. *salax* (*salac-*), < *salire,* leap.] Lustful or lecherous, as persons, the disposition, etc.; of writings, etc., wantonly lewd or obscene.—**sa·la′cious·ly,** *adv.*—**sa·la′cious·ness, sa·la′ci·ty** (-las′i-ti), *n.*
sal·ad (sal′ạd), *n.* [OF. F. *salade,* < Pr. *salada,* < ML. *salata,* pp. fem. of *salare,* season with salt, < L. *sal,* salt.] A dish of lettuce or other herbs, or vegetables, meat or fowl, fish, eggs, fruit, etc., prepared with various kinds of seasoning or dressing and served cold; also, any herb or plant used for such a dish, as lettuce or cress.—**salad days,** days of youthful inexperience: as, "My *salad days,* When I was green in judgement" (Shakspere's "Antony and Cleopatra," i. 5. 73).
sa·lade (sạ-läd′), *n.* [F.] Same as *sallet.*
sal·al (sal′ạl), *n.* [Chinook jargon.] An evergreen ericaceous shrub, *Gaultheria shallon,* of California, Oregon, etc., having an edible berry.
sal·a·man·der (sal′ạ-man-dėr), *n.* [OF. F. *salamandre,* < L. *salamandra,* < Gr. σαλαμάνδρα.] A lizard or other reptile formerly supposed to be able to live in fire; also, any of various lizard-

Spotted Salamander (*Salamandra maculosa*).

like amphibians with a long tail and short limbs, certain of which are aquatic, as the tritons, and others terrestrial; esp., a terrestrial amphibian of this kind, as *Salamandra maculosa* (see cut on preceding page), a spotted species of Europe; also, an imaginary being inhabiting fire; also, any of various articles that are used in connection with fire, or that withstand fire or great heat without damage. — **sal-a-man′drine** (-drin), *a.* Pertaining to, characteristic of, or resembling a salamander; capable of living in or enduring fire.

sa-la-me (sä-lä′mä), *n.*; pl. *-mi* (-mē). [It., ult. < L. *sal*, salt.] A kind of sausage common in Italy, often flavored with garlic.

sa-la-ri-at (sạ-lä′ri-at), *n.* [F.: cf. *proletariat*.] The salaried class; the class of workers receiving a salary.

sal-a-ry (sal′ạ-ri), *n.*; pl. *-ries* (-riz). [AF. *salarie*, OF. F. *salaire*, < L. *salarium*, stipend, salary, orig. money allowed soldiers to buy salt, prop. neut. of *salarius*, pertaining to salt, < *sal*, salt: cf. *salt-cellar*.] A fixed compensation periodically paid to a person for regular work or services, esp. work other than that of a manual, mechanical, or menial kind: as, "The fees annually paid to lawyers . . . amount, in every court, to a much greater sum than the *salaries* of the judges" (Adam Smith's "Wealth of Nations," v. 1. 2). Cf. *wage*. — **sal′a-ry**, *v. t.*; *-ried*, *-rying*. To pay or attach a salary to. — **sal′a-ry-less**, *a.* Without a salary.

sale (sāl), *n.* [AS. *sala* = OHG. and Icel. *sala*, sale: cf. *sell*[1].] The act or an act of selling; also, opportunity to sell; demand; market; also, an auction; also, a special disposal of goods, as at reduced prices. — **for sale**, or **on sale**, offered to be sold; offered to purchasers. — **sale′a-ble**, etc. See *salable*, etc.

sal-ep (sal′ep), *n.* [Turk. *sālep*, prob. < Ar. *tha′lab*, fox, in a name meaning 'fox's testicles,' for the orchis.] A starchy drug or foodstuff consisting of the dried tubers of certain orchids.

sal-e-ra-tus (sal-ẹ-rā′tus), *n.* [NL. *sal aëratus*, 'aërated salt.'] Orig., potassium bicarbonate; now, usually, sodium bicarbonate: used in cookery and in the manufacture of baking-powders.

sales-la-dy (sālz′lā″di), *n.*; pl. *-dies* (-diz). A saleswoman.

sales-man (sālz′man), *n.*; pl. *-men*. [See *sale*.] A man whose occupation it is to sell goods, as in a shop or on the road. — **sales′man-ship**, *n.* The function or art of a salesman; skill as a salesman. — **sales′peo″ple**, *n.* Salespersons. — **sales′per″son**, *n.* One engaged in selling goods, as in a shop. — **sales′room**, *n.* A room in which goods are sold; specif., an auction-room. — **sales′wom″an**, *n.*; pl. *-women* (-wim″en). A woman who sells goods, esp. in a shop.

sale-work (sāl′wėrk), *n.* Work or things made for sale, and hence made in a routine or perfunctory manner: as, "I see no more in you the ordinary Of nature's *sale-work*" (Shakspere's "As You Like It," iii. 5. 43).

Sa-li-an[1] (sā′li-ạn). [L. *Salius*, < *salire*, leap.] **I.** *a.* Of or pertaining to the Salii or priests of Mars in ancient Rome. **II.** *n.* One of these priests.

Sa-li-an[2] (sā′li-ạn). [LL. *Salii*, n. pl., perhaps < L. *sal*, salt, from their dwelling near the salt sea: cf. *Ripuarian*.] **I.** *a.* Of or pertaining to the Salii, a tribe of Franks who dwelt in the regions of the Rhine near the North Sea. **II.** *n.* A Salian Frank.

Sal-ic (sal′ik or sā′lik), *a.* [OF. F. *salique*, < ML. *Salicus*, < LL. *Salii*: see *Salian*[2].] Of or pertaining to the Salian Franks. — **Salic law**, a code of laws of the Salian Franks and other Germanic tribes; also, a provision in this code excluding females from the inheritance of land; hence, the alleged fundamental law of the French monarchy by which females were excluded from succession to the crown, or any law to the same effect.

sal-i-ca-ceous (sal-i-kā′shius), *a.* [L. *salix* (*salic-*), willow: see *sallow*[1].] Belonging to the *Salicaceæ*, a family of trees and shrubs containing the willows and poplars.

sal-i-cin (sal′i-sin), *n.* [F. *salicine*, < L. *salix* (*salic-*), willow.] In *chem.*, a bitter crystalline glucoside obtained from the bark of various species of willow and poplar, used medicinally in the treatment of rheumatism, as a tonic, etc.

sal-i-cyl (sal′i-sil), *n.* [From *salic(in)* + *-yl*.] In *chem.*, the radical, $C_6H_4.OH.CO$, of salicylic acid. — **sal-i-cyl-ate** (sal′i-sil-āt or sạ-lis′i-lāt), *n.* In *chem.*, a salt of salicylic acid. — **sal-i-cyl′ic**, *a.* In *chem.*, noting or pertaining to an acid, $C_6H_4.OH.CO_2H$, prepared from salicin or from phenol, and used esp. as a remedy for rheumatic and gouty affections, usually in the form of a salicylate.

sa-li-ence (sā′li-ẹns), *n.* The state or condition of being salient; also, a salient or projecting object, part, or feature. Also **sa′li-en-cy.**

sa-li-ent (sā′li-ẹnt). [L. *saliens* (*salient-*), ppr. of *salire*, leap: cf. *sally*.] **I.** *a.* Leaping or jumping; saltatorial; specif., in heraldic use, of an animal, represented on an escutcheon with the hind legs in the sinister base and the fore paws raised in the dexter chief, as if leaping; also, jetting up or out, as water; also, projecting or pointing outward, as an angle; standing out beyond the general surface (as, "Jerusalem . . . was built upon and surrounded by sharp, *salient* rocks, intersected by deep ravines": Kinglake's "Eothen," xvi.); prominent or conspicuous (as, "He had neither *salient* traits, nor general comprehensiveness": Bancroft's "Hist. of the U. S.," Amer. Revolution, ii. 3). **II.** *n.* A salient angle or part, as the central, outward projecting angle of a bastion, or an outward projection in a line of intrenchments: as, "The only serious fighting in the first half of the year [1916] took place in and around the Ypres *Salient*" (Buchan's "Hist. of the Great War," liii.). — **sa′li-ent-ly,** *adv.*

A Lion Salient.

sa-lif-er-ous (sạ-lif′ẹ-rus), *a.* [L. *sal*, salt: see *-ferous*.] Containing or producing salt, as strata.

sal-i-fy (sal′i-fī), *v. t.*; *-fied*, *-fying*. [L. *sal*, salt: see *-fy*.] To form into a salt, as by chemical combination. — **sal′i-fi-a-ble** (-fī-ạ-bl), *a.* — **sal″i-fi-ca′tion** (-fi-kā′shọn), *n.*

sa-lim-e-ter (sạ-lim′e-tėr), *n.* [L. *sal*, salt: see *-meter*.] Same as *salinometer.*

sa-li-na (sạ-lī′nạ), *n.*; pl. *-nas* (-nạz). [Sp., < L. *salinæ*: see *saline*.] A saline marsh, spring, or the like; also, a salt-works.

sa-line (sā′līn). [L. *sal*, salt; as n., in part < L. *salinæ*, salt-works, salt-pits, < *sal*, salt.] **I.** *a.* Of, like, or containing salt; also, of or pertaining to a chemical salt, esp. a salt of sodium, potassium, magnesium, etc., as used in medicine. **II.** *n.* A saline spring, well, or marsh; also, a saline medicine. — **sa-lin-i-ty** (sạ-lin′i-ti), *n.* — **sal-i-nom-e-ter** (sal-i-nom′e-tėr), *n.* [See *-meter*.] A form of hydrometer for measuring the percentage of salt in a solution.

Sa-lique (sa-lēk′), *a.* Same as *Salic.*

sa-li-va (sạ-lī′vạ), *n.* [L.: cf. Gr. σίαλον, saliva.] A fluid consisting of the secretions produced by various glands which discharge into the mouth, serving to keep the mouth moist, aid mastication, etc., and containing in man and certain other animals the diastatic enzyme ptyalin; spittle. — **sal-i-va-ry** (sal′i-vạ-ri), *a.* Of or pertaining to saliva; secreting or conveying saliva. — **sal′i-vate** (-vāt), *v. t.*; *-vated, -vating.* [L. *salivatus*, pp. of *salivare*, < *saliva*.] To produce an excessive secretion of saliva in, as by the use of mercury. — **sal-i-va′tion** (-vā′shọn), *n.* [LL. *salivatio(n-)*.] The act or process of salivating; also, the secretion of saliva, esp. an abnormally abundant flow of saliva.

salle (sål), *n.* [F.; from Teut.: cf. *salon*.] A hall; a room. — **salle à manger** (ä män-zhā). [F.] A dining-room.

sal-len-ders (sal′ẹn-dėrz), *n. pl.* [Origin obscure: cf. F. *solandre*.] In *vet. science*, an eczematous eruption occurring on the hock of a horse.

sal-let (sal′et), *n.* [OF. F. *salade*, < It. *celata*, < L. *cælata*, pp. fem. of *cælare*, engrave.] In medieval armor, a light, rounded helmet, either without or with a visor.

sal-low[1] (sal′ō), *n.* [ME. *salwe*, < AS. *sealh* = G. *sal-* (as in *salweide*) = Icel. *selja*, sallow; akin to L. *salix*, Gr. ἑλίκη, willow.] A willow, esp. *Salix caprea* ('great sallow'), an old-world shrub or bushy tree used in making charcoal for gunpowder; also, a willow twig; an osier.

Sallet, without Vizor, of form worn by horsemen in the first half of the 15th century.

sal-low² (sal′ō), *a.* [AS. *salo* = OHG. *salo* (G. dial. *sal*) = Icel. *sölr*: cf. F. *sale*, dirty (from Teut.).] Of a yellowish hue or complexion (rather than of the normal healthy or ruddy color): as, "*sallow* cheeks" (Shakspere's "Romeo and Juliet," ii. 3. 70); "a man . . . lean and *sallow*, with hollow eyes" (J. Conrad's "Rescue," iii. 2).—**sal′low²**, *v. t.* To make sallow.—**sal-low-ish** (sal′ō-ish), *a.* Somewhat sallow.—**sal′low-ness**, *n.*

sal-low-y (sal′ō-i), *a.* Abounding in sallows or willows.

sal-ly (sal′i), *n.*; pl. *sallies* (-iz). [F. *saillie*, < *saillir*, < L. *salire*, leap: cf. *assail*, *exult*, *insult*, *salient*.] A sudden rushing forth, esp. a sortie of troops from a besieged place upon an enemy; also, an excursion or expedition; also, a sudden start into activity (as, "Nature goes by rule, not by *sallies* and saltations": Emerson's "Conduct of Life," iii.); also, an outburst or flight, as of passion, fancy, etc. (as, "a little *sally* of anger": Burke's "Conciliation with the Colonies"); also, a sprightly or brilliant utterance or remark; also, an escapade (now rare); in *arch.*, a projecting part.—**sal′ly**, *v. i.*; *-lied*, *-lying*. To make a sally, as a body of troops from a besieged place; also, to set out on an excursion or expedition (as, "She saw him . . . *sally* forth towards the river, with his rod," Galsworthy's "Dark Flower," i. 16; "They *sally* off, armed with their rifles, into the wilderness," Irving's "Captain Bonneville," ii.); set out briskly or energetically; also, of things, to issue forth; issue suddenly.

sal-ly=lunn (sal′i-lun′), *n.* [From *Sally Lunn*, a woman who sold such cakes through the streets of Bath, England, about the end of the 18th century.] A kind of slightly sweetened tea-cake served hot with butter.

sal-ma-gun-di (sal-ma-gun′di), *n.* [F. *salmigondis*, earlier *salmiguondin*; origin uncertain: cf. *salame*.] A mixed dish consisting of chopped meat, anchovies, eggs, onions, oil, etc.; hence, any mixture, medley, or miscellany.

sal-mi (sal′mi), *n.* [F. *salmis*, appar. short for *salmigondis*, E. *salmagundi*.] A ragout of roasted or partly roasted game, fowl, or the like, cut up and stewed with wine and other ingredients. Also (F.) **sal-mis** (sál-mē′).

sal-mon (sam′on), *n.*; pl. *salmons* or (esp. collectively) *salmon*. [OF. F. *saumon*, < L. *salmo(n)-*, perhaps < *salire*, leap: cf. *sally*.] A marine and fresh-water food-fish, *Salmo salar* (family *Salmonidæ*), with yellowish-pink flesh, common in the northern Atlantic Ocean near the mouths of large rivers, which it ascends in order to spawn; a

Atlantic Salmon (*Salmo salar*).

variety of this species confined to lakes, etc. ('landlocked salmon'); also, any of various other fishes of the same family; esp., any of these fishes belonging to the genus *Oncorhynchus*, which are common in the northern Pacific Ocean and the rivers flowing into it; also, any of certain other fishes resembling those of this family; also, a yellowish-pink color.—**Mackenzie River salmon.** See *inconnu*.—**sal′mon**, *a.* Of the color salmon; yellowish-pink.—**sal′mon=ber″ry**, *n.* The salmon-colored edible fruit of *Rubus spectabilis*, a raspberry with large red or purple flowers, of the Pacific coast of North America; also, the plant.—**sal′mon=col″ored**, *a.* Salmon.—**sal-mo-noid** (sal′mō-noid). [L. *salmo(n)-*: see *-oid*.] **I.** *a.* Resembling a salmon; belonging or pertaining to the *Salmonidæ*, or salmon family of fishes. **II.** *n.* A salmonoid fish.—**sal″mon=trout′**, *n.* A European trout, *Salmo trutta*, an anadromous fish belonging to the salmon family and resembling the common salmon; also, any of various American trouts resembling the common salmon.

sal-ol (sal′ol or -ōl), *n.* [From *sal(icyl)* + *-ol*.] In *phar.*, a white crystalline substance, phenyl salicylate, prepared by the interaction of salicylic acid and phenol, and used as an antipyretic, antiseptic, etc.

sa-lon (sà-lôn′), *n.* [F., < It. *salone*, aug. of *sala* (= F. *salle*), hall; from Teut.: cf. *saloon* and *salle*.] A drawing-room or reception-room; a large and more or less elegant apartment for the reception of guests, as in the house of a Parisian lady of fashion; hence, an assembly of guests in such an apartment, or the company present; esp., a periodical social gathering of men and women representative of the fashion, wit, literature, art, politics, etc., of the time, at the house of a Parisian lady of fashion (as during the 17th and 18th centuries and later), or a similar gathering elsewhere (as, "Medora Manson . . . had inaugurated a 'literary *salon*'; but it had soon died out owing to the reluctance of the literary to frequent it": Mrs. Wharton's "Age of Innocence," xii.); also, a hall or place used for the exhibition of works of art; hence, an exhibition of works of art, esp. [*cap.*] either of two exhibitions of paintings, sculptures, etc., by living artists held annually in Paris.

sa-loon (sa-lön′), *n.* [F. *salon*: see *salon*.] A drawing-room or reception-room, as in a house (archaic); a salon, or social gathering, as at the house of a lady of fashion (archaic: as, "Her *saloons* were always attended, and by 'nice people,'" Disraeli's "Lothair," xii.); also, a large apartment for general or public use or resort, as in a hotel or other establishment (as, "A group of Italians took their seats at a table on the opposite side of the *saloon* [in a casino]": Irving's "Tales of a Traveler," i. 8); a hall or gallery for things on exhibition (as, "It [the British Museum collection] would appear more striking if it were arranged in one spacious *saloon*": Smollett's "Humphry Clinker," June 2); a large cabin for the common use of passengers on a passenger-vessel; an apartment, room, or place for common or public resort for a specific purpose (as, a dining-*saloon*; an ice-cream *saloon*); specif., a place for the sale of intoxicating liquors to be drunk on the premises (U. S.).

sa-loop (sa-löp′), *n.* [Altered form of *salep*.] Salep; also, a hot drink prepared from salep, or later sassafras, etc., formerly popular in London.

sal-pa (sal′pä), *n.* [NL.: cf. L. *salpa*, Gr. σάλπη, kind of sea-fish.] Any of the free-swimming oceanic tunicates constituting the genus *Salpa*, common in warm regions, and having a transparent, more or less fusiform body.

sal-pi-con (sal′pi-kon, F. sál-pē-kôn′), *n.* [F., < Sp. *salpicón*, < *salpicar*, sprinkle, < *sal*, salt, + *picar*, pick.] Cooked meat, mushrooms, truffles, etc., cut into small pieces and mixed with a rich sauce: used as a filling for pâtés, etc., or served separately.

sal-pin-got-o-my (sal-ping-got′ō-mi), *n.* [See *salpinx* and *-tomy*.] In *surg.*, the operation of cutting into a Fallopian tube; also, excision of a Fallopian tube.

sal-pinx (sal′pingks), *n.*; pl. *salpinges* (sal-pin′jēz). [NL., < Gr. σάλπιγξ (σαλπιγγ-), trumpet.] In *anat.*, a Eustachian tube; also, a Fallopian tube.

sal-si-fy (sal′si-fi), *n.* [Also *salsafy*; F. *salsafis*, earlier *sercifi*: cf. It. *sassefrica*, goat's-beard.] A purple-flowered cichoriaceous plant, *Tragopogon porrifolius*, whose root has an oyster-like flavor and is used as a culinary vegetable; oyster-plant.

sal-sil-la (sal-sil′ä), *n.* [Sp., dim. of *salsa*, sauce, < ML. *salsa*: see *sauce*.] Any of the plants of the amaryllidaceous genus *Bomarea*, of tropical America, which yield edible tubers.

sal=so-da (sal-sō′dä), *n.* [ML. *sal sodæ*, salt of soda.] Crystalline sodium carbonate, Na_2CO_3. $10 H_2O$: used as a cleansing agent.

sal-su-gi-nous (sal-sū′ji-nus), *a.* [L. *salsugo* (*salsugin-*), saltness, < *salsus*, pp. of *salire*, to salt, < *sal*, salt.] Of plants, growing in salty soil.

salt¹ (sált), *a.* [From obs. *assault*, *assaut*, adv., < F.

Salsify.—Upper part of the stem, with heads; *a*, a flower; *b*, the fruit.

à saut, 'to leaping.'] In heat, as female animals (obs. or prov. Eng.); also, salacious†; lecherous†.

salt² (sâlt), *n.* [AS. *sealt* = D. *zout* = G. *salz* = Icel. and Goth. *salt,* salt; akin to L. *sal,* Gr. ἅλς, salt.] A crystalline compound, sodium chloride, NaCl, occurring as a mineral, a constituent of sea-water, etc., and used for seasoning food, as a preservative, etc. ('common salt'); in fig. use, that which gives liveliness, piquancy, or pungency to anything (as, "We have some *salt* of our youth in us," Shakspere's "Merry Wives of Windsor," ii. 3. 50; Attic *salt,* see *Attic, a.*); the seasoning, excellent, or best element (as, "the *salt* of the earth": Mat. v. 13); reserve or allowance, as in accepting a statement (chiefly in 'with a grain of salt'); also, a salt-cellar; also, a salt-marsh; also, a sailor, esp. an experienced one (colloq.: as, "Nor, though I am something of a *salt,* do I ever go to sea as a Commodore, or a Captain, or a Cook," H. Melville's "Moby-Dick," i.); also, in chemical use, a compound derived from an acid by replacing the hydrogen wholly or partly by a metal or an electropositive radical (as, a normal *salt,* one in which all the hydrogen of an acid has been replaced; an acid *salt,* one in which only a part of the hydrogen of an acid has been replaced; a basic *salt,* one in which the hydroxyls of the base of which it is a derivative have not been wholly replaced by the acid radical, or one in which the metal or electropositive radical is united partly to an acid radical and partly to oxygen; a double *salt,* one containing two different metals or electropositive radicals, or one regarded as a combination of two other salts); *sing.* or (colloq.) *pl.,* any of various compounds of this nature used as purgatives (as, Epsom *salt;* Rochelle *salt*); *pl.,* smelling-salts.—**worth one's salt.** See under *worth², a.*—**salt², *a.** Impregnated with or containing salt; having the taste of salt; overflowed with or growing in salt water; cured or preserved with salt; fig., pungent or sharp, as speech.—**salt junk,** hard salt meat used for food on shipboard.— **Salt River.** See entry in alphabetical place.—**salt², *v. t.** To impregnate, season, cure, preserve, or treat with salt; furnish with salt (as, to *salt* cattle); in chemical processes, etc., to treat with common salt or with any chemical salt; add common salt to (a solution) in order to precipitate a dissolved substance; precipitate (a dissolved substance) by the addition of common salt (usually with *out*); in fig. use, to lay or store away in reserve (slang: as, "I know he's anything but miserly; still I can't help thinking he must be *salting* a lot of money away," Tarkington's "Magnificent Ambersons," xvii.); season or mingle (*with*) so as to affect or improve the general character; give piquancy or pungency to (language, etc.); specif., to introduce rich ore or other valuable matter secretly and fraudulently into (a mine, ground, etc.) in order to create a false impression of value or prospective yield.

sal-tant (sal'tant), *a.* [L. *saltans* (*saltant-*), ppr. of *saltare:* see *saltate.*] Dancing; leaping; jumping.

sal-ta-rel-lo (sal-ta-rel'ō), *n.;* pl. *-relli* (-rel'ē). [It., < L. *saltare:* see *saltate.*] A lively Italian dance for one person or a couple; also, the music for such a dance.

sal-tate (sal'tāt), *v. i.; -tated, -tating.* [L. *saltatus,* pp. of *saltare,* dance, freq. of *salire,* leap.] To dance; skip; leap; jump.—**sal-ta'tion** (-tā'shọn), *n.* [L. *saltatio(n-).*] Dancing; leaping; a leap; fig., an abrupt movement or transition. —**sal-ta-to'ri-al** (-ta-tō'ri-al), *a.* Pertaining to saltation; in *zoöl.,* characterized by or adapted for leaping.—**sal'ta-to-ry** (-tọ-ri), *a.* [L. *saltatorius.*] Pertaining to saltation; dancing; leaping; fig., proceeding by abrupt movements.

salt=cel-lar (sâlt'sel″är), *n.* [With *-cellar* for earlier *seler, saler,* < OF. *saliere* (F. *salière*), < ML. *salaria,* salt-cellar, prop. fem. of L. *salarius,* pertaining to salt, < *sal,* salt: cf. *salary.*] A vessel for holding salt, used on the table.

salt-ed (sâlt'ted), *p. a.* Impregnated, seasoned, cured, or otherwise treated with salt; fig., of horses, etc., seasoned, as from having survived attacks of disease (colloq.); of

Salt-cellar, of Henri Deux ware (16th century).

persons, experienced in some occupation, etc. (colloq.); also, of a mine or the like, fraudulently made to appear richer than it is.

salt-er (sâl'tèr), *n.* One who makes or deals in salt; also, a drysalter (Eng.); also, one who salts meat, fish, or the like.

salt-ern (sâl'tèrn), *n.* [AS. *sealtern.*] A salt-works; esp., a plot of land laid out in pools for the evaporation of sea-water to produce salt.

salt=grass (sâlt'grâs), *n.* Any of various grasses, as of the genus *Spartina,* growing in salt meadows or alkaline regions.

salt=horse (sâlt'hôrs'), *n.* Salt beef: as, "There is nothing left us but *salt-horse* and sea-biscuit" (H. Melville's "Typee," i.). [Sailors' slang.]

sal-tier, sal-tire (sal'tēr, -tér or -tīr), *n.* [ME. *sawtire,* < OF. F. *sautoir,* orig. a cord hanging in a loop from a saddle for aid in mounting (cf. *sautoir*), < *sauter,* leap, < L. *saltare:* see *saltate.*] In *her.,* an ordinary in the form of a St. Andrew's cross.

sal-ti-grade (sal'ti-grād). [L. *saltus,* a leap, + *gradi,* walk.] In *zoöl.:* **I.** *a.* Moving by leaping; belonging to the *Saltigradæ,* a group of saltatorial spiders. **II.** *n.* A saltigrade spider.

Saltier.

salt-ing (sâl'ting), *n.* The act of one who or that which salts; also, a tract of land overflowed at times by the sea (local, Eng.: as, "At the bridge of the lower *saltings* the cattle gather and blare," Kipling's "The Dykes").

sal'tire, *n.* See *saltier.*

salt-ish (sâl'tish), *a.* Somewhat salt; salty.

salt-less (sâlt'les), *a.* Without salt; fig., insipid.

salt=lick·(sâlt'lik), *n.* See *lick, n.*

salt-ly (sâlt'li), *adv.* With a salt taste or smell.

salt=marsh (sâlt'märsh'), *n.* A marsh, or marshy tract, wet with salt water, as from the sea.

salt-ness (sâlt'nes), *n.* The quality of being salt.

salt=pan (sâlt'pan), *n.* A large, shallow vessel in which salt water is evaporated to yield salt; also, a shallow depression in the ground in which salt water is evaporated in salt-making; *pl.,* salt-works; *sing.,* any dried-up salt lake or marsh.

salt-pe-ter, salt-pe-tre (sâlt-pē'tèr), *n.* [For ME. *salpetre,* < OF. *salpetre* (F. *salpêtre*), < ML. *salpetra,* for *sal petræ,* 'salt of rock' (because found as an incrustation on rocks).] Niter (nitrate of potassium); also, nitrate of sodium, $NaNO_3$, a crystalline compound used as a fertilizer ('Chile saltpeter').

salt=pit (sâlt'pit), *n.* A pit where salt is obtained.

salt=rheum (sâlt'röm'), *n.* [See *rheum¹.*] Any of various common cutaneous eruptions, as eczema. [Colloq.]

Salt Riv-er (sâlt riv'èr). An imaginary river up which defeated political candidates and parties are supposed to be sent to oblivion. [U. S.]

salt=spoon (sâlt'spön), *n.* A small spoon, usually having a round, deep bowl, used in taking salt at table.

sal-tus (sal'tus), *n.;* pl. *-tus.* [L., a leap, < *salire,* leap.] A breach of continuity, as in a process of reasoning; a leap from premises to conclusion.

salt=wa-ter (sâlt'wâ″tèr), *a.* Of or pertaining to water impregnated with salt, as that of the ocean and of certain lakes; living in or frequenting salt water, as animals.

salt=works (sâlt'wèrks), *n. pl.* or *sing.* A building or place where salt is made, as for the market.

salt=wort (sâlt'wèrt), *n.* Any of various plants of sea-beaches, salt-marshes, and alkaline regions, esp. of the chenopodiaceous genus *Salsola,* as *S. kali,* a bushy plant with prickly leaves, or of the chenopodiaceous genus *Salicornia.* See *glasswort.*

salt-y (sâl'ti), *a.;* compar. *saltier,* superl. *saltiest.* Impregnated with, containing, or tasting of salt.

sa-lu-bri-ous (sạ-lū'bri-us), *a.* [L. *salubris,* < *salus,* well-being, health: see *salute.*] Favorable to health; promoting health: now used esp. of air, climate, etc.

Saltwort (*Salsola kali*).

—sa-lu′bri-ous-ly, *adv.* **—sa-lu′bri-ous-ness, sa-lu′bri-ty** (-bri-ti), *n.*

sal-u-ta-ry (sal′ū-tạ-ri), *a.* [L. *salutaris*, < *salus* (*salut-*), well-being, health: see *salute*.] Conducive to health, healthful, health-giving, or healing (as, "The warm baths of Anchialus in Thrace were rendered as safe as they were *salutary*": Gibbon's "Decline and Fall of the Roman Empire," xl.); now, esp., conducive to moral or general well-being, morally wholesome, or beneficial (as, "afraid . . . that too great familiarity might diminish a *salutary* awe in the natives," Prescott's "Conquest of Mexico," iii. 8; "The conversion of the Saxon colonists to Christianity was the first of a long series of *salutary* revolutions," Macaulay's "Hist. of Eng.," i.). **—sal′u-ta-ri-ly,** *adv.* **—sal′u-ta-ri-ness,** *n.*

sal-u-ta-tion (sal-ū-tā′shọn), *n.* [L. *salutatio*(*n*-).] The act or an act of saluting; also, something uttered, written, or done by way of saluting (as, "Mr. Petulengro and his wife took their leave, with many *salutations*," Borrow's "Romany Rye," vi.; "The tall gentleman waved a gracious *salutation* to George," Tarkington's "Magnificent Ambersons," iv.).

sa-lu-ta-to-ri-an (sạ-lū-tạ-tō′ri-ạn), *n.* In American colleges and schools, the student who delivers the salutatory oration.

sa-lu-ta-to-ry (sạ-lū′tạ-tō-ri). [L. *salutatorius*.] **I.** *a.* Pertaining to or of the nature of a salutation: as, a *salutatory* oration (in American colleges and schools, an address of welcome, commonly by a member of the graduating class, with which the commencement exercises begin). **II.** *n.*; pl. *-ries* (-riz). An address of salutation; a salutatory oration.

sa-lute (sạ-lūt′), *v.*; *-luted, -luting.* [L. *salutare* (pp. *salutatus*), < *salus* (*salut-*), well-being, health, akin to *salvus*, safe, well: see *safe*[1].] **I.** *tr.* To address with expressions of good-will, respect, etc., or greet in words (as, "The glorious procession . . . was *saluted* by the acclamations of the senate and people," Gibbon's "Decline and Fall of the Roman Empire," xli.; "He knew the pretty girls upon the street and *saluted* them by name," Howells's "Chance Acquaintance," ii.); greet or hail by a particular title (as, to be *saluted* emperor); also, to make a bow, gesture, or the like to in greeting or farewell, respect, etc. (as, "I took off my hat to *salute* her": W. H. Hudson's "Purple Land," xxii.); kiss, as in greeting, farewell, etc. (as, "He . . . ventured to *salute* the withered cheek of the spinstress": Scott's "Pirate," xii.); fig., to greet, come to, or meet, as something that affects the senses (as, "if the noise of revelry . . . *saluted* their ears," Godwin's "Caleb Williams," xxviii.; "On all sides various scents *saluted* me," Mrs. Shelley's "Frankenstein," xi.); *milit.* and *naval*, to pay respect to or honor by some formal act, as by raising the right hand to the side of the head, presenting arms, firing cannon, dipping colors, or the like. **II.** *intr.* To perform a salutation; *milit.* and *naval*, to give a salute. **—sa-lute′,** *n.* An act of saluting; a salutation; a greeting; sometimes, a kiss; *milit.* and *naval*, a special act of respect paid to a person, flag, etc., as the raising of the right hand to the side of the head, the presenting of arms, the firing of cannon, the dipping of colors, or the like; the position of the hand, gun, or the like, or the attitude of the person, in saluting. **—sa-lut′er** (-lū′tėr), *n.*

sal-u-tif-er-ous (sal-ū-tif′ẹ-rus), *a.* [L. *salutifer*, < *salus* (*salut-*), well-being, health, + *ferre*, bear.] Salutary. [Now rare.]

salv-a-ble (sal′vạ-bl), *a.* [See *salve*[2].] That may be salved or salvaged.

sal-vage (sal′vāj), *n.* [F. *salvage*, < OF. *salver, sauver*, < LL. *salvare*, E. *save*.] The act of saving a ship or its cargo from wreck, capture by an enemy, etc.; the saving of anything, as from fire or other danger; also, property so saved; also, an allowance or compensation to which those are entitled who by voluntary effort have saved a ship or its cargo. **—sal′vage,** *v. t.*; *-vaged, -vaging.* To save or salve from shipwreck, fire, etc.; make salvage of. **—sal′vag-er** (-vā-jėr), *n.*

sal-var-san (sal′vạr-san), *n.* [G., < LL. *salvare*, save, + L. *arsenicum*, E. *arsenic*.] An organic arsenical compound used in the treatment of syphilis: orig. introduced under the name "606" (the number of the substance in a series of experiments). [Proprietary name.]

sal-va-tion (sal-vā′shọn), *n.* [OF. F. *salvation*, < LL. *salvatio*(*n*-), < *salvare*, E. *save*.] The act of saving or delivering, or the state of being saved or delivered; specif., in theological use, deliverance from the power and penalty of sin; redemption; also, a source, cause, or means of deliverance. **— Salvation Army,** a religious organization, on a quasi-military model, for the revival of religion among the masses: founded in England in 1865 by William Booth (1829–1912), the present system having been adopted in 1878 and the name in 1880. **—Sal-va′tion-ist,** *n.* A member of the Salvation Army.

salve[1] (säv), *n.* [AS. *sealf* = D. *zalf* = G. *salbe*, salve: cf. Skt. *sarpis*, clarified butter.] An adhesive composition or substance to be applied to wounds and sores for relief or healing; a healing ointment; fig., something that soothes or mollifies. **—salve**[1], *v. t.*; *salved, salving.* [AS. *sealfian*.] To apply salve to; fig., to soothe as if with salve; also, to heal† or cure†.

salve[2] (salv), *v. t.*; *salved, salving.* [Back-formation from *salvage*.] To save from loss or destruction by wreck, fire, etc., as a ship, its cargo, or any property; make salvage of.

sal-ve[3] (sal′vē). [L., impv. of *salvere*, be well, < *salvus*, well, E. *safe*[1].] **I.** *interj.* Hail! — used in salutation. **II.** *n.* An exclamation of the word 'salve'; a salutation or greeting; [often *cap.*] in the *Rom. Cath. Ch.*, an antiphon beginning in Latin "Salve, Regina" ('Hail, Queen'); a musical setting for this antiphon.

salv-er[1] (sal′vėr), *n.* Same as *salvor*.

sal-ver[2] (sal′vėr), *n.* [Sp. *salva*, salver, orig. the assay of food or drink before presenting it at table, < *salvar*, < LL. *salvare*, E. *save*: cf. *credence*, def.] A tray, as for serving dishes or presenting letters or cards: as, "The first footman brought in a letter on a silver *salver*" (Galsworthy's "Country House," ii. 4).

sal-vi-a (sal′vi-ạ), *n.* [L., sage: see *sage*[2].] Any of the menthaceous herbs or shrubs constituting the genus *Salvia*, as *S. splendens*, the scarlet sage, an ornamental garden-plant, and *S. officinalis*, the common sage.

sal-vo[1] (sal′vō), *n.*; pl. *-vos* (-vōz). [L. *salvo*, abl. of *salvus*, safe, as used in law phrases, as *salvo jure*, the right being safe (or unimpaired).] A saving clause; a reservation; also, an excuse or evasion; also, something to save a person's reputation, feelings, etc.

sal-vo[2] (sal′vō), *n.*; pl. *-vos* (-vōz). [It. *salva*, < L. *salve*, hail: see *salve*[3].] A simultaneous discharge of artillery or other firearms, intended as a salute; any simultaneous discharge of artillery or other firearms; also, a round of cheers, applause, etc.

sal vo-lat-i-le (sal vō-lat′i-lē). See under *sal*[1].

sal-vor (sal′vọr), *n.* One who salves or helps to salve a ship, cargo, etc.

sam-a-ra (sam′ạ-rä), *n.* [L. *samara, samera*, the seed of the elm.] In *bot.*, an indehiscent, usually one-seeded, winged fruit, as of the elm.

Sa-mar-i-tan (sạ-mar′i-tạn). [LL. *Samaritanus*.] **I.** *a.* Pertaining to Samaria (a district of ancient Palestine, also the chief city of this district), or to the Samaritans. **II.** *n.* A native or inhabitant of Samaria; also, one who is compassionate and helpful to a fellow-being in distress (often 'good Samaritan': in allusion to the Samaritan in the parable: see Luke, x. 30–37).

sa-ma-ri-um (sạ-mā′ri-um), *n.* [NL.; named from *samarskite*.] Chem. sym., Sm or Sa; at. wt., 150.4. A rare metallic element discovered in samarskite.

sa-mar-skite (sạ-mär′skīt), *n.* [G. *samarskit*; named from *Samarski*, a Russian.] A black mineral containing niobium, uranium, cerium, etc.

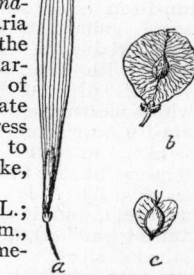

Samara. — (a) of white ash (*Fraxinus americana*); (b) of slippery-elm (*Ulmus fulva*); (c) of black birch (*Betula lenta*).

sam-bar, sam-bur (sam′bėr), *n.* [Hind. *sāmbar*.] A large, maned deer, *Rusa aristotelis*, of India. See cut on following page. See *rusine*.

sam-bo (sam′bō), *n.*; pl. *-bos* (-bōz). [Sp. *zambo*.] A half-breed; the offspring of negro and Indian parents; the offspring of a negro and a mulatto; also [*cap.*], a nickname for a negro.

Sam Browne (sam broun) **belt.** [Named from General Sir Samuel J. Browne (1824–1901), of the British army in India, the inventor.] A military belt having a supporting piece passing over the right shoulder, worn by officers.

Sambar.

sam-bu-ca (sam-bū′kä), n. [L., < Gr. σαμβύκη.] A kind of ancient stringed musical instrument.

sam′bur, n. See *sambar*.

same (sām). [ME. *same*, from Scand.: cf. Icel. *samr*, Sw. *samma*, Dan. *samme*, OHG. *sam*, Goth. *sama*, same, akin to Skt. *sama*, even, like, equal, L. *similis*, like, Gr. ὀμός, same, also E. *seem*, *simple*, and *some*.] **I.** *a.* Not being any other than that or those indicated or implied; identical with what is about to be or has just been mentioned; being the identical (person, thing, etc.), and no other; also, being one or identical, though referred to under different names, in different aspects, or as related to different things (as, these are one and the *same* thing; he and I rode in the *same* car); also, agreeing in kind, amount, etc.; corresponding; also, unchanged in character, condition, etc. **II.** *pron.* The same person, or the same thing; the forementioned person or thing (now chiefly in legal or commercial use). Often used in the adverbial phrase *the same*, meaning 'in the same manner': as, a cause which operates the *same* everywhere.—**all the same,** notwithstanding; nevertheless; for all that.—**just the same,** in the same manner; also, nevertheless.—**same′ly,** *a.* Unvaried; monotonous: as, "The earth is so *samely* that your eyes turn towards heaven" (Kinglake's "Eothen," xvii.).—**same′ness,** n. The state of being the same; identity; oneness of nature; uniformity; monotony.

Sa-mi-an (sā′mi-an). [L. *Samius.*] **I.** *a.* Of or pertaining to Samos, an island in the Ægean Sea, west of Asia Minor. **II.** *n.* A native or inhabitant of Samos.

sam-iel (sam′iel), n. [Turk.] Same as *simoom*.

sam-i-sen (sam′i-sen), n. [Jap.; from Chinese.] A Japanese guitar-like musical instrument with three strings, played with a plectrum.

Samisen.—*a*, plectrum.

sam-ite (sam′īt or sā′mīt), n. [OF. *samit*, < ML. *examitum*, < MGr. ἑξάμιτον, lit. 'six-threaded,' < Gr. ἕξ, six, + μίτος, thread: cf. *dimity.*] A heavy silk fabric, sometimes interwoven with gold, worn in the middle ages.

sam-let, n. [Dim. < *salmon*.] A young or small salmon; a parr.

Sam-nite (sam′nīt). [L. *Samnites*, pl.] **I.** *n.* A native of Samnium, an ancient country of central Italy whose people were allied to the Sabines. **II.** *a.* Pertaining to the Samnites or to Samnium.

Sa-mo-an (sa-mō′an). **I.** *a.* Pertaining to Samoa, a group of islands in the Pacific, or its (Polynesian) people. **II.** *n.* A native or inhabitant of Samoa; also, the Samoan language.

Sam-o-thra-cian (sam-ō-thrā′shan). **I.** *a.* Pertaining to the island of Samothrace, in the northern Ægean Sea: as, the *Samothracian* (or Winged) Victory (a famous statue, now in the Louvre, at Paris). **II.** *n.* A native or inhabitant of Samothrace.

sam-o-var (sam-ō-vär′ or sam′ō-vär), n. [Russ., lit. 'self-boiler.'] A metal urn, commonly of copper, used in Russia and elsewhere for heating the water for making tea.

Sam-o-yed, Sam-o-yede (sam-ō-yed′), n. [Russ.] A member of a Ural-Altaic people dwelling in northwestern Siberia and along the northeastern coast of Russia; also, the language of this people; also, one of a breed of Russian dogs.—**Sam-o-yed′ic. I.** *a.* Of or pertaining to the Samoyeds; also, noting or pertaining to a division of the Ural-Altaic family of languages consisting of the language or group of dialects spoken by the Samoyeds. **II.** *n.* The language of the Samoyeds.

Antique Russian Samovar.

samp (samp), n. [Algonquian.] Coarsely ground Indian corn, or a porridge made of it. [U. S.]

sam-pan (sam′pan), n. [Chinese, lit. 'three boards.'] Any of various small boats of China, etc., as one propelled by a single scull over the stern and provided with a roofing of mats.

Sampan.

sam-phire (sam′fīr), n. [Earlier *sampire, sampere*, < F. (*herbe de*) *saint Pierre*, '(herb of) St. Peter.'] A succulent apiaceous herb, *Crithmum maritimum*, of Europe, growing in clefts of rocks near the sea; also, the glasswort (*Salicornia*).

sam-ple (sam′pl). [OF. *essample*, var. of *example*, E. *example*.] **I.** *n.* A small portion of anything or a single object of a number, intended to show the quality, style, etc., of the whole; a specimen; also, an example† or instance†; also, a model for imitation†. **II.** *a.* Serving as a sample or specimen: as, a *sample* copy.—**sam′ple,** *v. t.*; -pled, -pling. To take a sample or samples of; test or judge by a sample: as, "Each of us . . . seems to have *sampled* all the different varieties of human experience" (Mark Twain's "Life on the Mississippi," xlv.).—**sam′pler[1],** n.

sam-pler[2] (sam′plėr), n. [OF. *essamplaire, exemplaire*, < LL. *exemplarium*, < L. *exemplum*, E. *example*.] An illustrative instance†; also, a pattern† or model†; also, a piece of cloth embroidered with various devices, serving to show a beginner's skill in needlework.

sam-ple=room (sam′pl-rōm), n. A room where samples are kept or shown; also, a room or place for the sale of alcoholic liquor by the glass (colloq., U. S.).

sam-shu (sam′shö), n. [Chinese.] A Chinese spirituous liquor distilled chiefly from rice.

Sam-son (sam′son), n. [From *Samson* in the Bible (see Judges, xiv.–xvi.).] A man, sometimes a blind man, of extraordinary strength.

sam-u-rai (sam′ö-rī), n.; pl. *rai*. [Jap.] In feudal Japan, a member of the military class, esp. a retainer of a daimio.

san-a-tive (san′a-tiv), a. [ML. *sanativus*, < L. *sanare*: see *sanatory*.] Having the power or tendency to heal; pertaining to healing; curative.

Sampler.

san-a-to-ri-um (san-a-tō′ri-um), *n.*; pl. *-riums* or *-ria* (-ri-ą). [NL., prop. neut. of LL. *sanatorius*, health-giving: see *sanatory*, and cf. *sanitarium* (a different word, from L. *sanitas*, health).] An establishment for the reception and treatment of invalids, convalescents, etc., esp. in a locality where climatic and other conditions are favorable (as, a tuberculosis *sanatorium*); also, a health resort.

san-a-to-ry (san′ą-tō-ri), *a.* [LL. *sanatorius*, health-giving, < L. *sanare* (pp. *sanatus*), cure, heal, < *sanus*, sound, healthy, E. *sane*: cf. *sanitary* (a different word).] Conducive to health; curative; healing; pertaining to healing.

san-be-ni-to (san-be-nē′tō), *n.*; pl. *-tos* (-tōz). [Sp. *sambenito*, < *San Benito*, St. Benedict; from its resemblance to the scapular introduced by St. Benedict.] Under the Spanish Inquisition, a penitential garment worn by a confessed heretic; also, a garment ornamented with flames, devils, etc., worn by a condemned heretic at an auto da fé.

sanc-ti-fi-ca-tion (sangk″ti-fi-kā′shon), *n.* [LL. *sanctificatio(n-)*.] The act of sanctifying, or the state of being sanctified.

sanc-ti-fied (sangk′ti-fīd), *p. a.* Made holy, or freed from sin; consecrated, or set apart as sacred; also, affecting holiness; sanctimonious.

sanc-ti-fy (sangk′ti-fī), *v. t.*; *-fied, -fying.* [OF. F. *sanctifier*, < LL. *sanctificare*, < L. *sanctus*, sacred, holy, + *facere*, make.] To make holy, as a person; purify or free from sin; also, to set apart as sacred; consecrate; observe as sacred, as a day; also, to honor, celebrate, or confess as holy; manifest as holy; also, to impart religious sanction to; render legitimate or binding; hence, to entitle to reverence or respect; justify (as, "Does the end *sanctify* the means?" W. H. Hudson's "Purple Land," xi.); also, to render productive of or conducive to spiritual blessing (as, to *sanctify* sufferings).—**sanc′ti-fi-er** (-fī-ėr), *n.*—**sanc′ti-fy-ing-ly,** *adv.*

sanc-ti-mo-ni-ous (sangk-ti-mō′ni-us), *a.* [See *sanctimony*.] Holy†; sacred†; also, characterized by sanctimony, making a show of sanctity, or affecting the appearance of sanctity (as, "No solemn *sanctimonious* face I pull, Nor think I'm pious when I'm only bilious": Hood's "Ode to Rae Wilson," 43).—**sanc-ti-mo′ni-ous-ly,** *adv.*—**sanc-ti-mo′ni-ous-ness,** *n.*

sanc-ti-mo-ny (sangk′ti-mō-ni), *n.* [OF. *sanctimonie*, < L. *sanctimonia*, < *sanctus*, sacred, holy: see *sanction*.] Sanctity†; sacredness†; also, pretended, affected, or hypocritical holiness or devoutness.

sanc-tion (sangk′shon), *n.* [L. *sanctio(n-)*, < *sancire*, make sacred, establish as inviolable, ordain, ratify (pp. *sanctus*, often as adj., sacred, holy: cf. *saint, sanctity,* and *sanctum*), akin to L. *sacer*, sacred, holy: cf. *sacre*.] An ordaining as authoritative or binding; solemn ratification; also, authoritative permission; countenance or support given to an action, etc.; also, something serving to support an action, etc.; also, a decree, ordinance, or law; also, a provision of a law or the like enacting a penalty for disobedience to it or a reward for obedience; the penalty or the reward (as, to impose *sanctions* on a country violating a covenant); also, a consideration or motive operating to enforce obedience to a rule of conduct; also, binding force given, or something which gives binding force, as to an oath.—**sanc′tion,** *v. t.* To ratify or confirm (as, to *sanction* a law or a covenant); also, to permit authoritatively; authorize; hence, to countenance or approve.—**sanc′tion-er,** *n.*

sanc-ti-tude (sangk′ti-tūd), *n.* [L. *sanctitudo*.] Sanctity; holiness. [Now rare.]

sanc-ti-ty (sangk′ti-ti), *n.*; pl. *-ties* (-tiz). [OF. *sainctete* (F. *sainteté*), < L. *sanctitas*, < *sanctus*, sacred, holy: see *sanction*.] Holiness, saintliness, or godliness (as, "The general fate of sects is to obtain a high reputation for *sanctity* while they are oppressed": Macaulay's "Hist. of Eng.," ii.); also, sacred or hallowed character (as, "the majesty and inviolable *sanctity* of the temple, honoured over all the world": 2 Mac. iii. 12); sacredness; inviolability (as, "The *sanctity* of private property is being menaced": W. Churchill's "Inside of the Cup," iii.); also, a sacred thing (as, "the *sanctities* of obedience and faith": Emerson's "Essays," Self-Reliance).—**odor of sanctity.** See under *odor*.

sanc-tu-a-rize (sangk′tū-ą-rīz), *v. t.*; *-rized, -rizing.* To shelter as in a sanctuary. [Obs. or rare.]

sanc-tu-a-ry (sangk′tū-ą-ri), *n.*; pl. *-ries* (-riz). [OF. *sanctuarie* (F. *sanctuaire*), < LL. *sanctuarium*, < L. *sanctus*, sacred, holy: see *sanction*.] A sacred or holy place, as a church, a temple, or a sacred grove; also, an especially holy place in a temple or church; specif., the part of a church about the altar; the chancel; also, a church or other sacred place as a place in which fugitives were formerly entitled to immunity from arrest; in general, an asylum; hence, immunity from the ordinary operations of the law afforded by refuge in such a place; refuge; protection.

sanc-tum (sangk′tum), *n.*; pl. *-tums,* L. *-ta* (-tą). [LL., prop. neut. of L. *sanctus*, sacred, holy: see *sanction*.] A sacred or holy place; also, a private retreat where a person is free from intrusion.—**sanctum sanctorum** (sangk-tō′rum); pl. *sancta sanctorum.* [LL.] The 'holy of holies' of the Jewish tabernacle and temple; also, any especially private place or retreat.

Sanc-tus (sangk′tus), *n.* [L. *sanctus*, sacred, holy, the first word of the hymn in Latin: see *sanction*.] In *liturgics*, the hymn beginning "Holy, holy, holy, Lord God of hosts," with which the eucharistic preface culminates; also, a musical setting for this hymn.

sand (sand), *n.* [AS. *sand* = D. *zand* = G. *sand* = Icel. *sandr*, sand: cf. Gr. ἄμαθος, sand.] The more or less fine debris of rocks, consisting of small, loose grains, often of quartz; also, a tract or region, as a desert, a beach, or a shoal, composed principally of such material (usually in *pl.*); also, the sand in an hour-glass or sand-glass, or a grain of this (often fig.: as, the *sands* of time, or of life; "Now our *sands* are almost run," Shakspere's "Pericles," v. 2. 1); also, pluck, or indomitable spirit (colloq., U. S.: as, "She had more *sand* in her than any girl I ever see," Mark Twain's "Huckleberry Finn," xxviii.).—**rope of sand.** See under *rope, n.*—**sand,** *v. t.* To sprinkle with or as with sand; overlay or bury under sand; fill up with sand, as a harbor; also, to add sand to (as, to *sand* sugar); also, to drive (a ship, etc.) upon a sand-bank.

san-dal[1] (san′dąl), *n.* [OF. F. *sandale*, < L. *sandalia*, pl. of *sandalium*, < Gr. σανδάλιον, dim. of σάνδαλον, sandal.] A kind of shoe, consisting of a sole of leather or other material fastened to the foot by thongs or straps; also, any of various kinds of low shoes or slippers; also, a

Sandals. — The pair in the middle are Roman, those on the sides are Greek.

kind of light, low rubber overshoe; also, a band for fastening a low shoe or slipper on, by passing over the instep or round the ankle.—**san′dal**[1], *v. t.*; *-daled* or *-dalled, -daling* or *-dalling.* To furnish with sandals.

san-dal[2] (san′dąl), *n.* [ML. *sandalum, santalum,* = LGr. σάνταλον, σάνδανον, ult. < Skt. *candana*.] Sandalwood.—**san′dal=tree,** *n.* The white sandalwood-tree, *Santalum album*; also, an evergreen meliaceous tree, *Sandoricum indicum*, of the East Indies, having a red close-grained heartwood which takes a fine polish.—**san′dal-wood,** *n.* The fragrant heart-wood of any of certain Asiatic trees of the genus *Santalum* (family *Santalaceæ*), used for ornamental carving and burned as incense; any of these trees, esp. *S. album* ('white sandalwood'), an evergreen of India; also, any of various related or similar trees or their woods, esp. an East Indian fabaceous tree, *Pierocarpus santalinus* ('red sandalwood'), or its heavy dark-red wood, which is used as a dyestuff.

san-da-rac (san′dą-rak), *n.* [L. *sandaraca*, < Gr. σανδαράκη.] Realgar; also, a brittle, usually

White Sandalwood (*Santalum album*).

pale-yellow, more or less transparent, faintly aromatic resin exuding from the bark of the tree *Callitris quadrivalvis* (see *sandarac-tree*), and used chiefly as incense and in making varnish; also, the sandarac-tree.—**san′da-rac=tree**, *n.* A pinaceous tree, *Callitris quadrivalvis*, native in northwestern Africa, yielding the resin sandarac, and having a fragrant, hard, dark-colored wood much used in building.

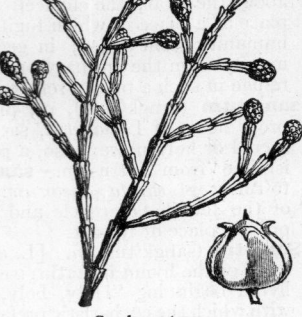

Sandarac-tree.

sand=bag (sand′bag), *n.* A bag filled with sand, used in fortification, as ballast, etc.; often, such a bag used as a weapon; esp., a weapon consisting of a cylindrical bag or the like filled with sand, by which a heavy blow may be struck which leaves little or no mark.—**sand′bag**, *v. t.*; *-bagged*, *-bagging.* To furnish with sand-bags (as, "two lines of *sand-bagged* breastworks": H. G. Wells's "Italy, France, and Britain at War," iii. 1); also, to hit or stun with a sand-bag.—**sand′bag″ger**, *n.*

sand=bank (sand′bangk), *n.* A bank of sand, esp. one formed by tides or currents, as in water.

sand=bar (sand′bär), *n.* A bar of sand formed in a river or sea by the action of tides or currents: as, "Those who navigate the Platte invariably spend half their time upon *sandbars*" (Parkman's "Oregon Trail," vii.).

sand=bath (sand′båth), *n.* A receptacle containing hot sand, in which a chemical retort or the like is heated; also, a therapeutic treatment in which the body is covered with warm sand; also, the rolling of fowls in sand.

sand=blast (sand′blåst), *n.* A blast of air or steam laden with sand, used to clean, grind, cut, or decorate hard surfaces, as of glass, stone, or metal; also, the apparatus used to apply such a blast.

sand=blind (sand′blīnd), *a.* [ME. *sand-blynde*: cf. AS. *sām-*, half, in *sām-cwic*, 'half-quick,' half-alive.] Partially blind; dim-sighted. See Shakspere's "Merchant of Venice," ii. 2. 37. Cf. *stone-blind*. [Archaic or prov.]

sand=box (sand′boks), *n.* A box or receptacle for holding sand intended for various purposes, as (formerly) for sprinkling on wet ink as a blotter, or for dropping from a locomotive or a street-car to the rails in front of the wheels to prevent slipping; also, the fruit of the sand-box tree, or the tree itself.—**sand=box tree**, a euphorbiaceous tree, *Hura crepitans*, of tropical America, bearing a furrowed roundish fruit about the size of an orange which when ripe and dry bursts with a sharp report and scatters the seeds.

Branch of Sand-box Tree, showing the fruit (at bottom).

sand=bur (sand′bėr), *n.* Any of several bur-bearing weeds growing in sandy places, as *Solanum rostratum*, a species of nightshade of the western U. S., or *Cenchrus tribuloides*, a species of grass of the U. S., Mexico, etc.

sand=crack (sand′krak), *n.* A crack or fissure in the hoof of a horse, extending from the coronet downward toward the sole, and occurring mostly on the inner quarters of the fore feet and on the toes of the hind feet: due to a diseased condition, and liable to cause lameness.

sand=dol-lar (sand′dol″år), *n.* Any of various flat, disk-like sea-urchins, esp. *Echinarachnius parma*, which lives on sandy bottoms off the eastern coast of the U. S.

Sand-dollar (*Echinarachnius parma*).

sand-ed (san′ded), *p. a.* Sprinkled with sand (as, "a *sanded* floor": C. Brontë's "Jane Eyre," xxxi.); covered with sand; also, adulterated with sand; also, of a sandy color† (see Shakspere's "Midsummer Night's Dream," iv. 1. 125).

sand=eel (sand′ēl), *n.* Any of various marine fishes (genus *Ammodytes*) with a cylindrical, eel-like body, found buried in the sand at low tide.

sand=er (san′dėr), *n.* One who or that which sprinkles with sand; also, one who sandpapers; an apparatus for sandpapering something.

sand=er-ling (san′dėr-ling), *n.* [Also *sandling*: see *-ling*[1].] A small sandpiper, *Calidris arenaria*, found on sandy beaches.

sand=flea (sand′flē), *n.* A flea found in sandy places; a chigo; a beach-flea or sand-hopper.

sand=glass (sand′glås), *n.* An instrument for measuring time, consisting of two glass receptacles joined by a narrow passage through which a quantity of sand will run from the receptacle placed uppermost into that placed below in a certain space of time.

Sanderling, in breeding-plumage.

sand=grop-er (sand′grō″pėr), *n.* A native of Western Australia. [Australia.]

sand=grouse (sand′grous), *n.* Any of certain birds, inhabiting sandy tracts of the Old World, which constitute the family *Pteroclidæ*, structurally allied to the pigeons, but having the legs more or less covered with feathers after the fashion of the grouse. Also called *rock-pigeon*.

sand=hog (sand′hog), *n.* A laborer who digs or works in sand; esp., one who works in a caisson in tunneling under water.

Sand-grouse (*Pterocles arenaria*).

sand=hop-per (sand′hop″ėr), *n.* A beach-flea.

sand-i-ness (san′di-nes), *n.* Sandy character.

san-di-ver (san′di-vėr), *n.* [ME. *saundyver*, < OF. F. *suint de verre*, 'suint of glass': cf. *suint*.] A scum which rises upon melted glass in the furnace.

sand=lance (sand′låns), *n.* Same as *sand-eel*.

sand=lark (sand′lärk), *n.* Any of various small limicoline birds or sandpipers, as the sanderling.

sand-ling (sand′ling), *n.* Same as *sanderling*.

sand-man (sand′man), *n.* A fabled personage said to make children sleepy, in allusion to their rubbing the eyes when sleepy, as if to rub out particles of sand.

sand=mole (sand′mōl), *n.* A large South African mole-rat, *Bathyergus maritimus*, which burrows in the sand; also, a smaller related species, *Georychus capensis*, of South Africa, very troublesome in gardens.

sand-pa-per (sand′pā″pėr), *n.* Stout paper upon which a layer of sand has been fixed with glue, used for smoothing or polishing.—**sand′pa″per**, *v. t.* To smooth or polish with or as with sandpaper.

Cape Sand-mole (*Georychus capensis*).

sand-pip-er (sand′pī″pėr), *n.* Any of various small limicoline birds of the snipe family (*Scolopacidæ*), typically having a piping note and a bill shorter than that of the true snipe, as *Tringoides hypoleucus* (the common European species), *T. macularius* ('spotted sandpiper,' the common American species), or *Actodromas* (or *Pisobia*) *maculata* ('pectoral sandpiper,' a species seen in the U.S. chiefly during its migration, the male of which is notable for inflating its breast and throat: sometimes to more than twice the natural size: also called *grass-snipe* and *jack-snipe*).

Spotted Sandpiper (*Tringoides macularius*).

sand=spit (sand'spit), *n.* [See *spit¹, n.*] A low sandy point projecting from a shore into the water.

sand-spout (sand'spout), *n.* A pillar of sand resembling a waterspout, produced by a whirlwind, as on a desert: as, "High in heaven upcurl'd The dreadful *sand-spouts* moved" (Southey's "Thalaba," iv. 31).

sand=star (sand'stär), *n.* A starfish; also, specif., an ophiuran.

sand-stone (sand'stōn), *n.* A rock formed by the consolidation of sand, the grains being held together by a cement of silica or the like.—**New Red Sandstone**, in *geol.*, a mass of strata in England and elsewhere, which consists largely of red shales and sandstones, and which lies above the Carboniferous.—**Old Red Sandstone**, in *geol.*, a group of predominantly red marls, sandstones, conglomerates, etc., esp. in England, lying above the Silurian and below the Carboniferous, and corresponding to the Devonian or a part of it.

sand=storm (sand'stôrm), *n.* A storm of wind that bears along clouds of sand.

sand=vi-per (sand'vī"pèr), *n.* A hognose (snake) (local, U. S.); also, the horned viper, *Cerastes cornutus*.

sand-wich (sand'wich), *n.* [From the 4th Earl of *Sandwich* (1718–92), who is said to have once spent 24 hours at the gaming-table without other refreshment than sandwiches of toast and beef.] Two slices of bread (or toast), plain or buttered, with a layer of meat, fish, cheese, or some other filling between them; also, something formed by a similar combination.—**club sandwich**, a sandwich of toast with a filling of cold chicken or turkey, pieces of bacon or ham, and lettuce with mayonnaise dressing.—**sand'wich**, *v. t.* To put into a sandwich; fig., to insert between two other things (as, "Toby slept away . . . as soundly as though he had been *sandwiched* between two Holland sheets": H. Melville's "Typee," vii.).—**sand'wich=board**, *n.* A board carried by a sandwich-man. [Colloq.] — **sand'wich=man** (-man), *n.*; pl. *-men.* A man carrying two advertising-boards suspended from his shoulders, one before him and one behind (colloq.).

sand-wort (sand'wèrt), *n.* Any of the plants constituting the silenaceous genus *Arenaria*, mostly low, tufted, white-flowered herbs, many of which grow in sandy soil.

San-dy¹ (san'di), *n.*; pl. *-dies* (-diz). A familiar form of *Alexander*, man's name, esp. in Scotch use; hence, a Scotchman (colloq.). Cf. *Sawney.*

sand-y² (san'di), *a.*; compar. *sandier*, superl. *sandiest.* [AS. *sandig.*] Of the nature of or consisting of sand; containing sand; covered with sand; also, fig., shifting or unstable, like sand (as, "But mark how *sandy* is your own pretence": Dryden's "Hind and the Panther," ii. 105); also,

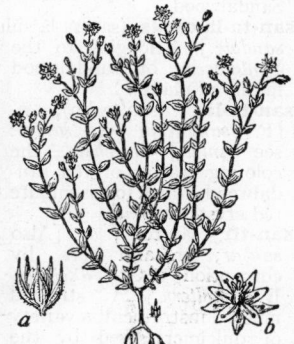

Thyme-leaved Sandwort (*Arenaria serpyllifolia*).—*a*, capsule surrounded by the scarious calyx; *b*, expanded flower.

of a yellowish-red color, as hair; having such hair (as, "The ladies Fitz-Warene were *sandy* girls": Disraeli's "Sybil," ii. 11).

sane (sān), *a.*; compar. *saner*, superl. *sanest.* [L. *sanus*, sound, healthy: cf. Gr. σάος, σῶς, sound, safe.] Sound or healthy (now rare); esp., of sound mind, or free from mental derangement, as a person; characterized by soundness of mind (as, a *sane* condition or period); also, having or exercising reason, sound judgment, or good sense (as, "There was a chance, if she had married Sir James, of her becoming a *sane*, sensible woman": George Eliot's "Middlemarch," vi.); proceeding from or showing reason or sound judgment (as, "*sane* and equitable historic verdicts": Morley's "Oliver Cromwell," v. 10); regulated by reason, or rational (as, "It is the American woman who is primarily responsible for the safe and *sane* Fourth": Bok's "Americanization of Edward Bok," xxxi.).—**sane'ly**, *adv.*—**sane'ness**, *n.*

sang¹ (sang). Preterit of *sing.*

sang² (sang), *n.* Scotch form of *song.*

san-gar (sung'gär), *n.* [Afghan.] A breastwork of stone on a hillside or elsewhere, as for defense: orig. used on the northwestern frontier of India.

san-ga-ree (sang-gạ-rē'), *n.* [Sp. *sangria*, lit. 'bleeding' (with reference to the color), < *sangre*, < L. *sanguis*, blood.] A cooling drink composed of wine, esp. red wine, diluted, sweetened, and spiced.

säng-er-bund (zeng'ér-bunt), *n.* [G.] A German male singing society.—**säng'er-fest** (-fest), *n.* [G.] A German song festival; esp., a gathering of German singing societies for competition.

sang=froid (sän-frwo'), *n.* [F., 'cold blood.'] Coolness of mind; calmness; composure: as, "He started violently . . . then at once assumed the *sangfroid* of a hero of romance" (Arnold Bennett's "Clayhanger," iv. 12).

San-graal, San-gre-al (sang-grāl', sang'grē-ạl), *n.* [OF. *saint graal*, also later *sangreal*, 'holy vessel': see *saint* and *Grail*.] The Holy Grail. See *Grail*.

san-guic-o-lous (sang-gwik'ō-lus), *a.* [L. *sanguis*, blood: see *-colous*.] Living in the blood, as a parasite.

san-guif-er-ous (sang-gwif'ẹ-rus), *a.* [L. *sanguis*, blood: see *-ferous*.] Conveying blood, as a blood-vessel.

san-gui-fi-ca-tion (sang"gwi-fi-kā'shọn), *n.* [F. *sanguification*, < L. *sanguis*, blood, + *facere*, make.] The production of blood.

san-gui-na-ri-a (sang-gwi-nā'ri-ạ), *n.* [NL., prop. fem. of L. *sanguinarius*, pertaining to blood, E. *sanguinary*.] The bloodroot, *Sanguinaria canadensis*, or its medicinal rhizome.

san-gui-na-ry (sang'gwi-nạ-ri), *a.* [L. *sanguinarius*, < *sanguis* (*sanguin-*), blood.] Of or pertaining to blood; also, attended with or characterized by bloodshed, or bloody (as, a *sanguinary* struggle; *sanguinary* events); also, bloodthirsty, as persons, the disposition, etc.; inciting to or sanctioning bloodshed (as, "*sanguinary* counsels," Irving's "Conquest of Granada," lxiv.; "misinterpretations of *sanguinary* texts from the Old Testament" [cf. Num. xxxv. 33], Morley's "Oliver Cromwell," iii. 7).—**san'gui-na-ri-ly**, *adv.*—**san'gui-na-ri-ness**, *n.*

san-guine (sang'gwin), *a.* [OF. F. *sanguin*, < L. *sanguineus*, < *sanguis* (*sanguin-*), blood.] Of or pertaining to blood, bloody, or bloodthirsty (now literary); also, blood-red, or red (now esp. literary, or in names of animals); ruddy (as, "a middle-aged little man, with a *sanguine* complexion": L. Merrick's "Conrad in Quest of His Youth," iv.); also, in the old physiology, having blood as the predominating humor (see *humor*, *n.*), and hence characterized by the bodily habit, ruddy face, and cheerful and ardent disposition attributed to the predominance of this humor (said of persons, the 'complexion' or constitution, etc.); hence, in modern use, naturally cheerful and hopeful, as persons, the disposition, etc. (as, "The invincible hopefulness of his *sanguine* temperament had now got Mr. Britling well out of the pessimistic pit again": H. G. Wells's "Mr. Britling," ii. 3. § 12); hopeful or confident with respect to something in particular (as, "I am not so *sanguine* as you in my expectation of the result," Godwin's "Caleb Williams," xl.; "He wishes he were as *sanguine* of his success . . . as of yours," Bulwer-Lytton's "Caxtons," xiv. 3); confidently ardent, as hopes, expectations, etc.—**san'guine-ly**, *adv.*—**san'guine-ness**, *n.*

san-guin-e-ous (sang-gwin'ē-us), *a.* [L. *sanguineus*: see *sanguine.*] Of, pertaining to, or containing blood; of the nature of or resembling blood; of the color of blood; also, bloody, bloodthirsty, or sanguinary (now rare); also, sanguine, as temperament.

san-guin-o-lent (sang-gwin'ō-lent), *a.* [L. *sanguinolentus*, < *sanguis* (*sanguin-*), blood.] Of or pertaining to blood; containing, or tinged with, blood; bloody.

san-guiv-o-rous (sang-gwiv'ō-rus), *a.* [L. *sanguis*, blood: see *-vorous.*] Feeding on blood, as a bat.

san-he-drim, san-he-drin (san'hē-drim, -drin), *n.* [Late Heb. *sanhedrīn*, < Gr. συνέδριον, council, < σύν, with, + ἕδρα, seat.] The supreme council and highest ecclesiastical and judicial tribunal of the ancient Jewish nation; also, a similar lower tribunal.

san-i-cle (san'i-kl), *n.* [OF. F. *sanicle*, < ML. *sanicula*, appar. a dim. < L. *sanus*, sound, healthy, E. *sane.*] Any of the umbelliferous herbs constituting the genus *Sanicula*, as *S. europæa*, an old-world species once credited with great remedial virtues, and *S. marilandica*, an American species with medicinal properties; also, any of various plants of other genera.

sa-ni-es (sā'ni-ēz), *n.* [L.] In *pathol.*, a thin serous fluid, often greenish, discharged from ulcers, etc.

san-i-fy (san'i-fī), *v. t.*; *-fied, -fying.* [L. *sanus*, sound, healthy: see *-fy.*] To make healthy; improve in sanitary conditions.

sa-ni-ous (sā'ni-us), *a.* [L. *saniosus*, < *sanies.*] Pertaining to, of the nature of, containing, or discharging sanies.

san-i-ta-ri-an (san-i-tā'ri-an). **I.** *n.* One versed or engaged in sanitary work. **II.** *a.* Sanitary.

san-i-ta-ri-ly (san'i-tā-ri-li), *adv.* In a sanitary manner or respect.—**san'i-ta-ri-ness**, *n.*

Flowering Plant of Sanicle (*Sanicula marilandica*).— *a*, a male flower; *b*, the fruit.

san-i-ta-ri-um (san-i-tā'ri-um), *n.*; pl. *-riums* or *-ria* (-ri-ä). [NL., < L. *sanitas*, health: see *sanity*, and cf. *sanatorium.*] A sanatorium.

san-i-ta-ry (san'i-tā-ri), *a.* [= F. *sanitaire*, < L. *sanitas*, health: see *sanity.*] Of or pertaining to health; concerned with conditions affecting health, esp. with reference to cleanliness, precautions against disease, etc.; pertaining to sanitation; also, designed to promote health or prevent disease; conducive or favorable to health.—**sanitary cordon**, a line of troops, guards, or the like on the borders of a region or district infected with disease, to cut off communication and thus prevent the disease from spreading: often fig., with reference to anything serving as a barrier to check some objectionable influence.—**san'i-ta-ry**, *n.*; pl. *-ries* (-riz). A public water-closet, urinal, and lavatory.

san-i-tate (san'i-tāt), *v.*; *-tated, -tating.* [Back-formation from *sanitation.*] **I.** *tr.* To subject to sanitation; make sanitary. **II.** *intr.* To introduce sanitation: as, "Rustum Beg . . . began to *sanitate.* Built a Gaol and Hospital—nearly built a City drain" (Kipling's "Legend of the Foreign Office").

san-i-ta-tion (san-i-tā'shon), *n.* [L. *sanitas*, health (see *sanity*), + E. *-ation.*] The working out and practical application of sanitary measures.

san-i-tize (san'i-tīz), *v. t.*; *-tized, -tizing.* [From *sanit(ary)* + *-ize.*] To render sanitary; disinfect.

san-i-ty (san'i-ti), *n.* [OF. *sanite* (F. *santé*), < L. *sanitas*, health, < *sanus*, sound, healthy, E. *sane.*] The state of being sane; soundness of mind; fig., soundness of judgment.

san-jak (san'jak), *n.* [Turk. *sanjāq*, lit. 'banner.'] In Turkey, one of the administrative districts into which a vilayet or eyalet is divided.

San Jo-sé (san hō-zā') **scale.** A scale-insect, *Aspidiotus perniciosus*, native in China, and very injurious to many deciduous fruit and other trees and shrubs: so called because first found in the United States at San José, California.

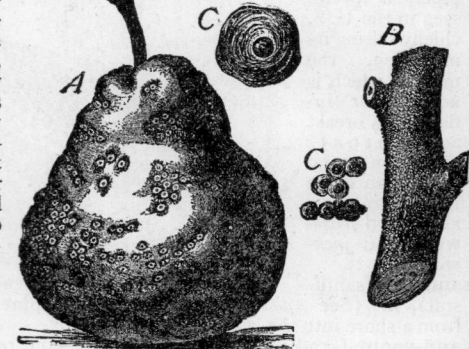

San José Scale. — *A*, infested fruit; *B*, branch; *C, C*, enlarged scales.

sank (sangk). Preterit of *sink.*

san-nup (san'up), *n.* [Algonquian.] Among North American Indians, a married man.

sans (sanz, F. säṅ), *prep.* [F., < L. *sine.*] Without: as, "*sans* teeth, *sans* eyes, *sans* taste, *sans* everything" (Shakspere's "As You Like It," ii. 7. 166). [Archaic, or as French.]

San-scrit (san'skrit), etc. See *Sanskrit*, etc.

sans-cu-lotte (sanz-kū-lot', F. säṅ-kü-lot), *n.* [F. *sans-culotte*, 'without breeches'; from the discarding by the republicans of (short) breeches in favor of (long) pantaloons.] In the French Revolution, a contemptuous designation for a republican of the poorer class (see etym.), adopted by the revolutionists as a designation of honor, as if synonymous with 'patriot'; hence, any extreme republican or revolutionary.—**sans-cu-lot-tic** (sanz-kū-lot'ik), *a.* Pertaining to the sansculottes or to sansculottism.—**sans-cu-lot-tide** (sanz-kū-lot'id, F. säṅ-kü-lo-tēd), *n.* [F. *sans-culottide.*] In the calendar of the first French republic, one of the 5 (in leap-year 6) complementary days added at the end of the month Fructidor, as the result of dividing the year into 12 months of 30 days each.—**sans-cu-lot-tism** (sanz-kū-lot'izm), *n.* The principles or practices of sansculottes.

San-skrit (san'skrit). [Skt. *samskrita*, prepared, cultivated; applied to the literary language as opposed to the common or vernacular dialects: see *Prakrit.*] **I.** *n.* The ancient literary language of India, belonging to the Aryan or Indo-European family, in which most of the literature of India from the Vedas downward is written. **II.** *a.* Of, pertaining to, or written in Sanskrit.—**San-skrit'ic**, *a.* Pertaining to or derived from Sanskrit.—**San'skrit-ist**, *n.* One versed in the Sanskrit language or literature.

san-tal (san'tal), *n.* [F., < ML. *santalum*: see *sandal²*.] Sandalwood.

san-ta-la-ceous (san-ta-lā'shius), *a.* [ML. *santalum*: see *sandal²*.] Belonging to the *Santalaceæ*, or sandalwood family of plants.

san-ta-lin (san'ta-lin), *n.* [F. *santaline*, < *santal*: see *santal*.] In *chem.*, the coloring matter of red sandalwood, which forms minute red crystals.

san-tir (sän-tēr'), *n.* [Also *santur*; Ar. and Pers., by corruption < Gr. ψαλτήριον, E. *psaltery.*] A stringed musical instrument, a variety of dulcimer, used by the Arabs and Persians.

san-ton (san'ton), *n.* [Sp. *santón*, < *santo*, saint: see *saint.*] One of a class of Mohammedan holy men ven-

Santir, after a Persian painting.

erated as saints; a marabout: as, "one of those holy men termed *santons*, who pass their lives in hermitages, in fasting, meditation, and prayer" (Irving's "Conquest of Granada," iv.).

san-ton-i-ca (san-ton'i-kä), *n.* [NL., prop. fem. of L. *Santonicus*, pertaining to the *Santoni*, a people of Aquitania, in southwestern Gaul.] A species of wormwood, *Artemisia pauciflora*; also, an anthelmintic drug consisting of the dried flower-heads of this plant.

san-to-nin (san'tō-nin), *n.* [From *santonica*.] In *chem.*, a crystalline compound, the active principle of the drug santonica.

sap¹ (sap), *n.* [AS. *sæp* = D. *sap* = G. *saft*, sap.] The juice or vital circulating fluid of a plant; hence, any vital fluid, as blood; also, sap-wood.

sap² (sap), *v.*; *sapped*, *sapping*. [F. *sapper*, now *saper* (= It. *zappare*), < OF. *sappe* (F. *sape*) = It. *zappa*, < ML. *sappa, sapa*, hoe, mattock.] **I.** *tr.* To undermine; render unstable by digging into or removing the foundations of; fig., to weaken or destroy insidiously (as, to *sap* one's strength; "The fidelity of the people was *sapped*," Motley's "Dutch Republic," Introd., iv.); *milit.*, to approach (a besieged place, etc.) with trenches protected by gabions or parapets; dig such trenches in (ground). **II.** *intr. Milit.*, to dig protected trenches, or approach a besieged place or an enemy's position by means of such trenches: as, "At Hooge the Germans had *sapped* out, and linked up their sap-heads into a connected line 150 yards from our front" (Buchan's "Hist. of the Great War," liii.).—**sap²**, *n.* [F. *sappe*, now *sape*, = It. *zappa*.] *Milit.*, the process of constructing trenches protected by gabions or parapets, in order to approach a besieged place or an enemy's position; also, a trench of this kind (as, "They were now pushing forward *saps* into No Man's Land, linking them across, and so continually creeping nearer to the enemy and a practicable jumping-off place for an attack": H. G. Wells's "Italy, France, and Britain at War," i.).

sap³ (sap), *v. i.*; *sapped*, *sapping*. [Prob. another use of *sap²*.] To study hard; 'dig.' [Slang, chiefly Eng.]—**sap³**, *n.* One who studies hard or is absorbed in books: as, "When I once attempted to read Pope's poems out of school hours, I was laughed at, and called 'a *sap*'" (Bulwer-Lytton's "Pelham," ii.). [Slang, chiefly Eng.]

sap⁴ (sap), *n.* [Cf. *saphead¹*.] A simpleton or fool. [Colloq.]

sap-a-jou (sap'a-jö), *n.* [F.; of S. Amer. origin.] A capuchin (monkey).

sa-pan=wood (sa-pan'wůd or sap'an-), *n.* [Malay *sapang*.] A dyewood yielding a red color, produced by a small East Indian cæsalpiniaceous tree, *Biancæa sappan*.

sap=green (sap'grēn), *n.* A green coloring matter derived from the juice of buckthorn berries; also, its color.

sap-head¹ (sap'hed), *n.* [From *sap¹* (cf. *sappy*) + *head*.] A simpleton; a fool: as, "You don't seem to know anything, somehow — perfect *saphead*" (Mark Twain's "Huckleberry Finn," iii.). [Colloq.]

sap-head² (sap'hed), *n.* [From *sap²* + *head*.] *Milit.*, the foremost end of a sap (trench), toward the enemy.

sap=head-ed (sap'hed"ed), *a.* [See *saphead¹*.] Silly; foolish. [Colloq.]

sa-phe-na (sa-fē'nä), *n.*; pl. *-næ* (-nē). [ML., < Ar. *çâfin*.] Either of two large superficial veins of the leg, one ('long' or 'internal saphena') on the inner side of the leg, and the other ('short,' 'external,' or 'posterior saphena') on the outer and posterior sides.—**sa-phe'nous**, *a.*

sap-id (sap'id), *a.* [L. *sapidus*, < *sapere*, have a taste: see *sapient*, and cf. *insipid*.] Having taste or flavor; esp., having a pleasant taste; savory; palatable; fig., agreeable to the mind; to one's taste or liking.—**sa-pid-i-ty** (sa-pid'i-ti), *n.*

sa-pi-ence (sā'pi-ens), *n.* [OF. F. *sapience*, < L. *sapientia*, < *sapiens*, E. *sapient*.] The quality of being sapient; wisdom: often used ironically.

sa-pi-ent (sā'pi-ent), *a.* [OF. *sapient*, < L. *sapiens* (*sapient-*), ppr. of *sapere*, have a taste or flavor, have discernment, be wise: cf. *sapid* and *sage¹*.] Wise or sage: often used ironically.

sa-pi-en-tial (sā-pi-en'shal), *a.* [LL. *sapientialis*, < L. *sapientia*, E. *sapience*.] Pertaining to or characterized by wisdom.

sa-pi-ent-ly (sā'pi-ent-li), *adv.* In a sapient or wise manner: often used ironically.

sap-in-da-ceous (sap-in-dā'shius), *a.* [NL. *Sapindus*, the typical genus, for *sapo Indicus*, 'Indian soap.'] Belonging to the *Sapindaceæ*, or soapberry family of plants.

sap-less (sap'les), *a.* Destitute of sap, as a plant; withered; hence, lacking vitality, energy, or the like; insipid; trivial.

sap-ling (sap'ling), *n.* A young tree; fig., a young person.

sap-o-dil-la (sap-ō-dil'ä), *n.* [Sp. *zapotillo*, dim. of *zapote*: see *sapota*.] A large evergreen tree, *Sapota zapotilla*, of tropical America, bearing an edible fruit ('sapodilla-plum') and yielding chicle; also, the fruit.

sap-o-na-ceous (sap-ō-nā'shius), *a.* [L. *sapo*(*n-*), soap; from Teut., and akin to E. *soap*.] Of the nature of soap; soap-like; soapy.—**sap-o-na'ceous-ness, sap-o-na'ci-ty** (-nas'i-ti), *n.*

sa-pon-i-fi-a-ble (sa-pon'i-fī-a-bl), *a.* Capable of being saponified.

sa-pon-i-fi-ca-tion (sa-pon"i-fi-kā'shon), *n.* [F. *saponification*.] The act of saponifying, or the state of being saponified.

Sapodilla. — *a*, the fruit; *b*, the same, transversely cut.

sa-pon-i-fy (sa-pon'i-fī), *v.*; *-fied*, *-fying*. [F. *saponifier*, < L. *sapo*(*n-*), soap, + *facere*, make.] **I.** *tr.* To convert (a fat) into soap by treating with an alkali; hence, to decompose (any ester) with the formation of a corresponding alcohol and acid or salt. **II.** *intr.* To become converted into soap.—**sa-pon'i-fi-er** (-fī-ėr), *n.*

sap-o-nin (sap'ō-nin), *n.* [F. *saponine*, < L. *sapo*(*n-*), soap.] In *chem.*, any of a class of glucosides occurring in soapwort and many other plants, and forming a soapy-looking froth when shaken with water.

sap-o-nite (sap'ō-nīt), *n.* [Sw. *saponit*, < L. *sapo*(*n-*), soap.] A mineral, a hydrous silicate of magnesium and aluminium, occurring in soft, amorphous masses with a soapy feel in serpentine, trap-rock, etc.

sa-por (sā'por), *n.* [L., < *sapere*: see *sapient*, and cf. *savor*.] That quality in a substance which affects the sense of taste; savor; flavor.—**sap-o-rous** (sap'ō-rus), *a.* [LL. *saporosus, saporus*.] Having flavor or taste; yielding some kind of taste.

sa-po-ta (sa-pō'tä), *n.* [NL., < Sp. *zapote*; from Mex.] Same as *sapodilla*.—**sap-o-ta-ceous** (sap-ō-tā'shius), *a.* Belonging to the *Sapotaceæ*, or sapodilla family of plants.

sap-per (sap'ėr), *n.* One who saps; *milit.*, a soldier employed in the construction of trenches, fortifications, field-works, etc.

Sap-phic (saf'ik). **I.** *a.* Pertaining to Sappho, a Greek lyric poetess of Lesbos (about 600 B.C.), or to certain meters or a form of strophe or stanza used by or named after her. **II.** *n.* A Sapphic verse; *pl.*, Sapphic verses or strophes.

sap-phire (saf'īr). [OF. *safir* (F. *saphir*), < L. *sapphirus*, < Gr. σάπφειρος; of Eastern origin.] **I.** *n.* A variety of corundum, esp. a transparent blue kind valued as a gem; a gem of this kind; also, the color of this gem, a deep blue (as, "His waves in milder tints unfold Their long array of *sapphire* and of gold": Byron's "Corsair," iii. 1). **II.** *a.* Of or pertaining to sapphire; resembling sapphire; esp., deep-blue (as, "a *sapphire* sky": Pope's tr. Homer's "Odyssey," xx.).—**sap-phi-rine** (saf'i-rin or -rīn). **I.** *a.* Consisting of sapphire; like sapphire, as in color (as, "She looked at the sky overhead, and saw that the *sapphirine* hue . . . had completely gone": Hardy's "Return of the Native," iv. 5). **II.** *n.* A pale-blue or greenish, usually granular mineral, consisting of a silicate of magnesium and aluminium; also, a blue variety of spinel.

sap-pho (saf'ō), *n.*; pl. *sapphos* (-ōz). [NL., < Gr. Σαπφώ, Sappho, the Greek poetess: see *Sapphic, a.*, def.] Any of the humming-birds of the South American genus *Sappho* (or *Cometes*), with long forked tail and brilliant red plumage. See cut on following page.

(variable) **d** as d or j, **ş** as s or sh, **ţ** as t or ch, **ẓ** as z or zh; *o*, F. *cloche*; **ü**, F. *menu*; **ch**, Sc. *loch*; **ṅ**, F. *bonbon*; **'**, primary accent; **"**, secondary accent; †, obsolete; <, from; +, and; =, equals. See also lists at beginning of book.

sap-py (sap'i), *a.* Abounding in sap, as a plant; fig., full of vitality, energy, or the like (as, "a *sappy* preacher of the word": Galt's "Ayrshire Legatees," viii.); also, juicy, as a fruit†; also, silly or foolish (colloq.: as, "a committee of *sappy* women," Mark Twain's "Tom Sawyer," xxxiii.). —**sap'pi-ness,** *n.*

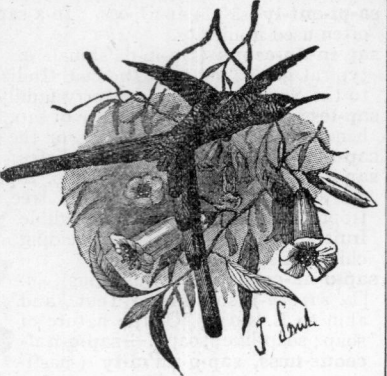

Sappho (*Sappho sparganura*).

sa-pre-mi-a, sa-præ-mi-a (sa-prē'mi-ạ), *n.* [NL., < Gr. σαπρός, rotten, + αἷμα, blood.] In *pathol.*, a form of blood-poisoning, esp. that due to the absorption of the toxins produced by certain micro-organisms. —**sa-pre'mic, sa-præ'mic,** *a.*

sap-ro-gen-ic (sap-rō-jen'ik), *a.* [Gr. σαπρός, rotten: see *-genic*.] Producing putrefaction or decay, as certain bacteria; also, formed by putrefaction. Also **sa-prog-e-nous** (sa-proj'e-nus).

sap-ro-lite (sap'rō-līt), *n.* [Gr. σαπρός, rotten, decayed, + λίθος, stone.] In *petrog.*, soft, disintegrated, usually more or less decomposed rock, remaining in its original place. — **sap-ro-lit'ic** (-lit'ik), *a.*

sa-proph-a-gous (sa-prof'ạ-gus), *a.* [NL. *saprophagus*, < Gr. σαπρός, rotten, decayed, + φαγεῖν, eat.] Feeding on decaying matter, as certain beetles.

sap-ro-phyte (sap'rō-fīt), *n.* [Gr. σαπρός, rotten, decayed, + φυτόν, plant.] Any vegetable organism that lives on decaying organic matter, as certain fungi, etc. —**sap-ro-phyt'ic** (-fit'ik), *a.*

sap-sa-go (sap-sā'gō), *n.* [Corruption of G. *schabzieger*, < *schaben*, shave, grate, + *zieger*, curd, cheese.] A kind of hard, greenish cheese flavored with melilot, made in Switzerland.

sap-suck-er (sap'suk″ėr), *n.* Any of various small American woodpeckers, esp. of the genus *Sphyrapicus*, which feed on the sap and sap-wood of trees.

sap=wood (sap'wud), *n.* Alburnum.

sar-a-band (sar'ạ-band), *n.* [F. *sarabande*, < Sp. *zarabanda*; origin uncertain.] A slow, stately Spanish dance in triple rhythm; also, a piece of music for, or in the rhythm of, this dance, usually forming one of the movements in the suite, following the courante.

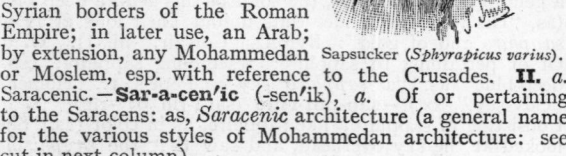

Sapsucker (*Sphyrapicus varius*).

Sar-a-cen (sar'ạ-sẹn). [LL. *Saraceni*, pl.] **I.** *n.* Among the later Romans and Greeks, a member of the nomadic tribes on the Syrian borders of the Roman Empire; in later use, an Arab; by extension, any Mohammedan or Moslem, esp. with reference to the Crusades. **II.** *a.* Saracenic. —**Sar-a-cen'ic** (-sen'ik), *a.* Of or pertaining to the Saracens: as, *Saracenic* architecture (a general name for the various styles of Mohammedan architecture: see cut in next column).

-sarc. Noun termination from Gr. σάρξ (σαρκ-), flesh.

sar-casm (sär'kazm), *n.* [LL. *sarcasmos*, < Gr. σαρκασμός, < σαρκάζειν, tear flesh, bite the lips in rage, sneer, < σάρξ (σαρκ-), flesh.] Harsh or bitter irony or derision; also, an ironical taunt or gibe; a sneering or cutting remark.

sar-cas-tic (sär-kas'tik), *a.* [= F. *sarcastique*, < Gr. σαρκάζειν: see *sarcasm*.] Characterized by, of the nature of, or pertaining to sarcasm; using, or given to the use of, sarcasm. —**sar-cas'ti-cal-ly,** *adv.*

sarce-net (särs'net), *n.* See *sarsenet*.

sar-co-carp (sär'kọ-kärp), *n.* [Gr. σάρξ (σαρκ-), flesh, + καρπός, fruit.] In *bot.*, the fleshy mesocarp of certain fruits, as the peach.

sar-code (sär'kōd), *n.* [F. *sarcode*, < Gr. σαρκώδης, fleshy, < σάρξ (σαρκ-), flesh, + εἶδος, form.] In *biol.*, animal protoplasm. —**sar-cod'ic** (-kod'ik), *a.*

Indian-Saracenic Architecture. — Tomb of Sultan Humayun, Delhi.

sar-col-o-gy (sär-kol'ọ-ji), *n.* [Gr. σάρξ (σαρκ-), flesh: see *-logy*.] The branch of anatomy that deals with the fleshy parts of the body.

sar-co-ma (sär-kō'mạ), *n.*; pl. *-mas* or *-mata* (-mạ-tạ). [NL., < Gr. σάρκωμα, < σαρκοῦν, make fleshy, < σάρξ (σαρκ-), flesh.] In *pathol.*, any of various malignant tumors originating in the connective tissue, attacking esp. the bones. —**sar-com'a-tous** (-kom'ạ-tus), *a.*

sar-coph-a-gous (sär-kof'ạ-gus), *a.* [L. *sarcophagus*, < Gr. σαρκοφάγος, < σάρξ (σαρκ-), flesh, + φαγεῖν, eat.] Flesh-eating; carnivorous.

sar-coph-a-gus (sär-kof'ạ-gus), *n.*; pl. *-gi* (-jī) or *-guses.* [L., < Gr. σαρκοφάγος, orig. adj., flesh-eating: see *sarcophagous*.] Among the ancient Greeks, a kind of stone supposed to consume the flesh of corpses laid in it, and consequently used for coffins; hence, in general, a stone coffin, esp. one ornamented with sculptures or bearing inscriptions, etc.

sar-cous (sär'kus), *a.* [Gr. σάρξ (σαρκ-), flesh.] Consisting of or pertaining to flesh or muscular tissue.

Sarcophagus (restored), from the Street of Tombs at Assos, in the Troad (in northwestern Asia Minor).

sard (särd), *n.* [L. *sarda*, LL. *sardius*, = Gr. σάρδιος, σάρδιον, lit. 'stone of Sardis' (L. *Sardis*, Gr. Σάρδεις, capital of Lydia, in Asia Minor).] A brownish-red chalcedony, or a piece of it: used in jewelry, etc.

Sar-da-na-pa-li-an (sär″dạ-nạ-pā'li-ạn), *a.* Of, pertaining to, or befitting Sardanapalus (Asurbanipal, died 626? B.C.), an Assyrian king who, from the stories of the ancient Greek writers, has become a proverbial example of inordinate luxury and effeminacy.

sar-dine[1] (sär-dēn'), *n.* [OF. F. *sardine*, < L. *sardina*, also *sarda*, kind of fish: cf. L. *Sardus*, Sardinian.] The common pilchard, much used preserved in oil as a table delicacy; any of various allied or similar fishes used for this purpose, as the young menhaden.

sar-dine[2] (sär'din or -dīn), *n.* [LL. (*lapis*) *sardinus*, < Gr. σάρδινος (λίθος), 'sardine (stone)': cf. *sard*.] A precious stone of the ancients, perhaps sard.

Sar-din-i-an (sär-din'i-ạn). **I.** *a.* Of or pertaining to Sardinia, a large island in the Mediterranean, west of Italy, or the former kingdom of Sardinia, which included the island of Sardinia, Savoy, Piedmont, etc. **II.** *n.* A native or inhabitant of the island or the former kingdom of Sardinia.

sar-di-us (sär'di-us), *n.* [LL.: see *sard*.] A sard.

sar-don-ic (sär-don′ik), *a.* [F. *sardonique*, < L. *Sardonius*, < Gr. Σαρδόνιος, Sardinian, substituted (from the notion of a Sardinian plant said to distort the face of one eating it) for σαρδάνιος, adj. applied to laughter: cf. σαίρειν, grin like a dog.] Bitter, scornful, or mocking, as a laugh or smile, and hence the expression, humor, utterances, etc., or a person: as, "a peculiar, *sardonic*, and somewhat primitive sense of humour" (W. H. Hudson's "Far Away and Long Ago," viii.); "He was proud, *sardonic*, harsh to inferiority of every description" (C. Brontë's "Jane Eyre," xv.).—**sar-don′i-cal-ly**, *adv.*

sar-do-nyx (sär′dō-niks), *n.* [L., < Gr. σαρδόνυξ, < σάρδιον, sard, + ὄνυξ, E. *onyx*.] A kind of onyx containing layers or bands of sard.

sa-ree (sä′rē), *n.* See *sari*.

sar-gas-so (sär-gas′ō), *n.* [Pg. *sargaço*, *sargasso*, < *sarga*, kind of grape.] The gulfweed.—**Sargasso Sea**, a large area in the northern Atlantic, in which there is an abundance of floating gulfweed.

sar-gas-sum (sär-gas′um), *n.* [NL., < Pg. *sargaço*: see *sargasso*.] Any seaweed of the genus *Sargassum*, the species of which are widely distributed in the warmer waters of the globe, as *S. bacciferum*, the common gulfweed.—**sar-gas′sum=fish,** *n.* Any of the frogfishes of the genus *Pterophryne*, often found among floating masses of sargassum, as *P. tumida*, common in warm parts of the Atlantic.

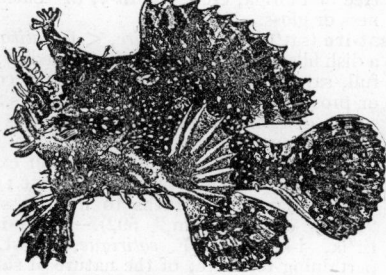
Sargassum-fish (*Pterophryne tumida*).

sa-ri (sä′rē), *n.* [Hind.] A long piece of cotton or silk, constituting the principal garment of Hindu women, worn wound round the body with one end thrown over the head.

sark (särk), *n.* [AS. *serc*, *syrce*, = Icel. *serkr* = Sw. *särk* = Dan. *særk*.] A body-garment for either sex; a shirt or chemise. [Chiefly Sc. and north. Eng.]

Sar-ma-tian (sär-mā′shian). [L. *Sarmatia* (see def.), < *Sarmatæ*, pl., the Sarmatians.] **I.** *a.* Of or pertaining to Sarmatia, an ancient region in Europe extending from the Vistula to the Volga, sometimes identified poetically with Poland; pertaining to the inhabitants of this region. **II.** *n.* A native or inhabitant of Sarmatia.

sar-ment (sär′ment), *n.* [L. *sarmentum*, < *sarpere*, trim, prune.] A scion† or cutting†; also, a sarmentum.—**sar-men′tose, sar-men′tous** (-men′tōs, -tus), *a.* [L. *sarmentosus*.] In *bot.*, having sarmenta or runners; of the nature of or resembling a runner.—**sar-men′tum** (-tum), *n.*; pl. *-ta* (-tä). [L.] In *bot.*, a runner (stem).

sa-rong (sa-rong′), *n.* [Malay *sārung*.] The principal garment for both sexes in the Malay Archipelago, etc., consisting of a piece of cloth enveloping the lower part of the body like a skirt (as, "an elderly grim Javanese servant in a sort of livery of white jacket and yellow *sarong*": J. Con-

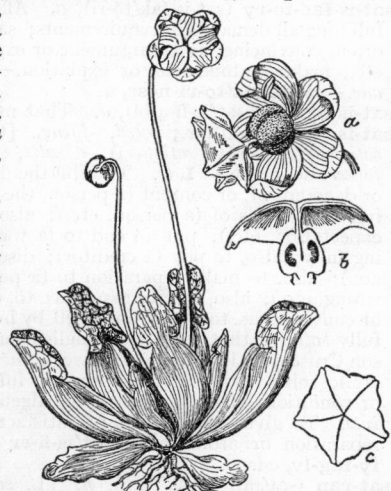
Sarracenia (*S. purpurea*). — *a*, a flower, the petals removed; *b*, longitudinal section of the whole pistil; *c*, the umbrella of the style, seen from above.

rad's "Lord Jim," xx.) also, a kind of cloth for such garments.

sar-ra-ce-ni-a (sar-a-sē′ni-ä), *n.* [NL.; named from Dr. *Sarrazin* of Quebec, who first sent specimens of the plant to Europe.] Any plant of the genus *Sarracenia*, comprising American marsh-plants with hollow leaves of a pitcher-like form in which insects are trapped and digested, as *S. purpurea*, a common pitcher-plant (see cut in preceding column).—**sar-ra-ce-ni-a′ceous** (-ā′shius), *a.* Belonging to the *Sarraceniaceæ*, the American pitcher-plant family.

sar-sa-pa-ril-la (sär″sa-pa-ril′ä), *n.* [Sp. *zarzaparrilla*, < *zarza*, bramble, + *-parrilla*, perhaps dim. of *parra*, vine.] Any of various climbing or trailing tropical American plants of the genus *Smilax*, having a root which has been much used in medicine as an alterative; also, the root, or an extract or other preparation made of it; also, any of various allied or similarly used plants.—**sar″sa-pa-ril′lin,** *n.* In *chem.*, same as *parillin*.

sarse-net, sarce-net (särs′net), *n.* [AF. *sarzinett*, perhaps < OF. *sarrazin*, Saracen: cf. OF. *drap sarrazinois*, Saracen (Oriental) cloth.] A soft, fine, thin silk fabric formerly much used, esp. for lining.

sar-tor (sär′tor), *n.* [L., < *sarcire*, patch, mend.] A tailor.—**sar-to′ri-al** (-tō′ri-al), *a.* Of or pertaining to a tailor or his art; in *anat.*, pertaining to the sartorius.—**sar-to′ri-us** (-ri-us), *n.*; pl. *-rii* (-ri-ī). [NL., < L. *sartor*.] In *anat.*, a flat, narrow muscle, the longest in the human body, running from the ilium to the top of the tibia, and crossing the thigh obliquely in front: so called because it is the chief muscle concerned in producing the cross-legged position in which a tailor sits when at work.

Branch of Sarsaparilla (*Smilax medica*), with fruits.

sash[1] (sash), *n.* [Earlier *shash*, < *shashes*, for *chassis*, pl.: see *chassis*.] A framework in which panes of glass are set in a window or the like; also, such frameworks collectively; also, a frame in which a saw is put to prevent bending.—**sash**[1], *v. t.* To furnish with sashes or with windows having sashes.

sash[2] (sash), *n.* [Ar. *shāsh*, muslin, head-cloth.] A band of muslin or other material worn wrapped about the head as a turban by Orientals; also, a long band or scarf of silk, etc., worn over one shoulder or round the waist, as by military officers as a part of the costume, or by women and children for ornament.—**sash**[2], *v. t.* To dress or ornament with a sash.

sa-shay (sa-shā′), *v. i.* [Corruption of *chassé*.] To chassé in dancing; hence, to glide, move, or go. [Colloq., U. S.]

sas-in (sas′in), *n.* [Native name in Nepal.] An agile antelope, *Antilope cervicapra*, of India.

sas-ka-toon (sas-ka-tön′), *n.* [N. Amer. Ind.] The service-berry, *Amelanchier canadensis*, or its fruit.

sas-sa-by (sa-sā′bi), *n.*; pl. *-bies* (-biz). [S. Afr.] A large South African antelope, *Bubalis* (or *Damaliscus*) *lunatus*.

sas-sa-fras (sas′a-fras), *n.* [Sp. *sasa-*

Sasin.

frás; origin uncertain: cf. *saxifrage*.] An American lauraceous tree, *Sassafras
sassafras*; also, the aromatic bark of its root,
used medicinally and
esp. for flavoring bever-
ages, confectionery, etc.
Sas-se-nach (sas'ę-
nȧċh), *n.* [Gael. *Sas-
unnach*, Saxon.] A
Saxon or Englishman:
a name applied by the
Gaelic inhabitants of
the British Isles.
sas-sy=bark (sas'i-
bärk), *n.* [Appar. from
W. Afr. name.] The
bark of a large African
cæsalpiniaceous tree,
*Erythrophleum guine-
ense*, used by the na-
tives as a poison in
ordeals; also, the tree
itself.
sas-tra, shas-tra (säs'-
trȧ, shäs'-), *n.*; pl. *-tras*
(-trȧz). [Skt. *çāstra*, <
çās-, instruct, direct.]
In Hindu use, any of certain sacred books constituting the
sources of Hindu law; any of various authoritative books
for instruction in some science or art.

Sassafras.— 1, branch with fruits;
2, branch with sterile flowers; *a, b, c*, different forms of leaves.

sas-tru-ga (sas-trö'gȧ), *n.*; pl. *-gi* (-gē). Same as *zastruga*.
sat (sat). Preterit and past participle of *sit*.
Sa-tan (sā'tan), *n.* [LL. *Satan, Satanas*, < Gr. Σατᾶν,
Σατανᾶς, < Heb. *sātān*, adversary, < *sātan*, oppose.] The
chief evil spirit; the great adversary of man; the devil. Cf.
Lucifer.—**sa-tan-ic** (sȧ-tan'ik), *a.* Of or pertaining to
Satan; also, characteristic of or befitting Satan; extremely
wicked; diabolical; infernal. Also **sa-tan'i-cal.—sa-tan'-
i-cal-ly,** *adv.*—**sa'tan-ism,** *n.* Satanic disposition or practice; also [*cap.*], the worship of Satan.—**sa'tan-ist,** *n.* An
adherent of Satan (now rare); also [*cap.*], a worshiper of
Satan.—**sa-tan-oph'a-ny** (-of'ȧ-ni), *n.* [See *-phany*.] The
visible manifestation of Satan.
satch-el (sach'ęl), *n.* [OF. *sachel*, < L. *saccellus*, dim. of
saccus, E. *sack*[1].] A small bag, as of leather, for carrying
necessaries, etc., as in traveling; a handbag; sometimes, a
bag for carrying school-books.
sate[1] (sāt). Archaic pret. and pp. of *sit*.
sate[2] (sāt), *v. t.*; *sated, sating.* [Appar. an altered form (by
association with *satiate, satiety*, etc.) of obs. or prov. *sade*,
satiate, < AS. *sadian*, satiate, connected with *sæd*, sated, E.
sad.] To gratify to the full by the satisfaction of hunger or
any appetite or desire; hence, to surfeit; glut.
sa-teen (sa-tēn'), *n.* [From *satin*.] A cotton or woolen
fabric resembling satin in weave and gloss.
sate-less (sāt'les), *a.* That cannot be sated: as, "his *sateless*
thirst of pleasure, gold, and fame" (Young's "Night
Thoughts," vii. 512).
sat-el-lite (sat'ę-līt), *n.* [F. *satellite*, < L. *satelles* (*satellit-*),
an attendant, follower.] A follower or attendant upon a
person of importance, often a subservient or obsequious
follower (as, "Three thousand armed *satellites* escorted his
steps," Motley's "Dutch Republic," Introd., xii.; "Legree
encouraged his two black *satellites* to a kind of coarse familiarity with him," Mrs. Stowe's "Uncle Tom's Cabin," xxxii.);
in *astron.*, a small planet which revolves round a larger or
primary planet; a secondary planet; a moon.—**sat-el-lit'ic**
(-lit'ik), *a.*
sa-ti-a-ble (sā'shi-ȧ-bl), *a.* That can be satiated.—**sa″ti-a-
bil'i-ty** (-bil'i-ti), **sa'ti-a-ble-ness,** *n.*
sa-ti-ate (sā'shi-āt), *v. t.*; *-ated, -ating.* [L. *satiatus*, pp. of
satiare, < *satis*, enough: see *satiety*.] To gratify to the
full, as with food or with anything that satisfies desire; hence,
to supply with anything to excess, so as to disgust or weary;
surfeit; cloy.—**sa'ti-ate,** *a.* Satiated. [Archaic.]—**sa-ti-
a'tion** (-ā'shọn), *n.*
sa-ti-e-ty (sȧ-tī'ę-ti), *n.* [F. *satiété*, < L. *satietas*, < *satis*,

enough; akin to E. *sad*.] The state of being satiated; now,
usually, the state of being surfeited with food or with anything that satisfies desire; disgust or weariness caused by
excess; surfeit.
sat-in (sat'in). [OF. F. *satin*, < It. *setino*, < *seta*, silk,
< L. *seta, sæta*, bristle: cf. *seta*.] **I.** *n.* A silk fabric so
woven and finished as to have a characteristic smoothness
and gloss on one surface, or sometimes on both ('double-faced
satin'). **II.** *a.* Of or like satin; smooth or glossy as satin;
satiny.—**sat'in,** *v. t.* To give a satin-like finish to.—**sat-i-
net'** (-i-net'), *n.* [Cf. F. *satinette*.] A thin, light satin†;
an inferior kind of satin containing cotton; also, a fabric
having a cotton warp and a woolen filling, woven with
a satiny surface.—**sat'in=pod,** *n.* Either of two European
brassicaceous plants constituting the genus *Lunaria*, *L.
annua* and *L. rediviva*, often cultivated for their showy
flowers and large, round, flat, satiny pods.—**sat'in=stitch,**
n. A mode of embroidery in which portions of surface are
covered with long stitches in close parallel lines somewhat
resembling satin.—**sat'in-wood,** *n.* The satiny wood of
an East Indian meliaceous tree, *Chloroxylon swietenia*, used
for cabinet-work, etc.; the tree itself; also, any of various
similar woods or trees, as *Fagara flava*, a small rutaceous
tree of Florida, etc.—**sat'in-y,** *a.* Satin-like, as in smoothness or gloss.
sat-ire (sat'īr), *n.* [F. *satire*, < L. *satira*, earlier *satura*, orig.
a dish filled with various fruits, a medley, prop. fem. of *satur*,
full, sated: see *saturate*.] A literary composition, in verse
or prose, in which vices, abuses, follies, etc., are held up to
scorn, derision, or ridicule; the species of literature constituted by such compositions; the use of irony, sarcasm, ridicule, etc., in writing or speaking, in exposing, denouncing,
or deriding vice, folly, indecorum, etc.; also, a satirist† (as,
"Leave dangerous truths to unsuccessful *satires*": Pope's
"Essay on Criticism," 592).—**sa-tir-ic, sa-tir-i-cal** (sȧ-
tir'ik, -i-kȧl), *a.* [F. *satirique*, < LL. *satiricus*.] Of or
pertaining to satire; of the nature of satire; marked by satire; indulging in or given to satire, as a person.—**sa-tir'i-
cal-ly,** *adv.*—**sa-tir'i-cal-ness,** *n.*—**sat-i-rist** (sat'i-rist), *n.*
A writer of satires; one who indulges in satire.—**sat'i-rize**
(-rīz), *v. t.*; *-rized, -rizing.* To assail with satire; make
the object of satire.—**sat'i-riz-er** (-rī-zėr), *n.*
sat-is-fac-tion (sat-is-fak'shọn), *n.* [OF. F. *satisfaction*, <
L. *satisfactio*(*n-*).] The act of satisfying, or the state of
being satisfied; fulfilment of desires, demands, needs, etc.;
gratification or pleasure occasioned by some fact, circumstance, etc., or the cause of such gratification; payment, as
for debt; discharge, as of obligations; reparation, as of a
wrong or injury; the opportunity of repairing a supposed
wrong, as by a duel; release from doubt, or conviction; *eccles.*,
the performance by a penitent of the penal acts enjoined by
ecclesiastical authority.
sat-is-fac-to-ry (sat-is-fak'tọ-ri), *a.* Affording satisfaction;
fulfilling all demands or requirements; satisfying; adequate;
often, convincing, as an argument or explanation; in *theol.*,
etc., making atonement or expiation.—**sat-is-fac'to-ri-ly,**
adv.—**sat-is-fac'to-ri-ness,** *n.*
sat-is-fi-a-ble (sat'is-fī-ȧ-bl), *a.* That may be satisfied.
sat-is-fy (sat'is-fī), *v.*; *-fied, -fying.* [OF. *satisfier*, < L.
satisfacere (passive *satisfieri*), < *satis*, enough (see *sad*), +
facere, do, make.] **I.** *tr.* To fulfil the desires, expectations,
or demands of, or content (a person, the mind etc.); supply
full. the needs of (a person, etc.); also, to fulfil (a desire,
expectation, etc.); put an end to (a want, etc.) by supplying fully; also, to pay (a creditor); discharge fully (a debt,
etc.); also, to make reparation to (a person, etc.) or for (a
wrong, etc.); also, to give assurance to, set free from doubt,
or convince (as, to *satisfy* one's self by investigation; "I was
fully *satisfied* that they were Englishmen," Defoe's "Robinson Crusoe," i. 17); also, to answer sufficiently (an objection,
etc.); solve (a doubt, etc.); also, to fulfil the requirements
or conditions of (as, to *satisfy* an algebraic equation). **II.**
intr. To give contentment or satisfaction; also, to make
reparation or atonement.—**sat'is-fi-er** (-fī-ėr), *n.*—**sat'is-
fy-ing-ly,** *adv.*
sat-rap (sat'rap or sā'trap), *n.* [L. *satrapes, satrapa*, <
Gr. σατράπης; from OPers.] A governor of a province
under the ancient Persian monarchy; hence, in general, a

fat, fāte, fär, fȧll, ȧsk, fāre; net, mē, hėr; pin, pīne; not, nōte, mȯve, nȯr; up, lūte, pl̇ull; oi, oil; ou, out; (lightened) aviȧry,
ęlect, agǫny, intǫ, ụnite; (obscured) errȧnt, operȧ, ardęnt, actǫr, natųre; ch, chip; g, go; th, thin; ƬH, then; y, you;

subordinate ruler, often a despotic one.—**sat-ra-py** (sat′-rạ-pi or sā′trạ-), *n.*; pl. *-pies* (-piz). [L. *satrapia*, < Gr. σατραπεία.] The province or jurisdiction of a satrap.

Sat-su-ma (sat′sǭ-mä) **ware.** A kind of glazed pottery (faience), often cream-colored or yellowish and decorated with gold and colored enamels, made in the province of Satsuma, in the island of Kiushiu, Japan.

sat-u-ra-ble (saṭ′ū-rạ-bl), *a.* That may be saturated.—**sat″u-ra-bil′i-ty** (-bil′i-ti), *n.*

sat-u-rate (saṭ′ū-rāt), *v. t.*; *-rated, -rating.* [L. *saturatus*, pp. of *saturare*, satisfy, sate, saturate, < *satur*, full (of food), sated, akin to *satis*, enough, also to E. *sad*.] To satisfy†, sate†, or satiate†; also, to soak, impregnate, or imbue thoroughly or completely (lit. or fig.: as, "Its [a house's] timbers were *saturated* with dew," Thoreau's "Walden," ii.; "The whole spiritual atmosphere was *saturated* with cant," Froude's "Cæsar," i.); specif., to cause (a substance) to unite with the greatest possible amount of another substance, through solution, chemical combination, or the like; also, to bring (a vapor) to a state where any increase of pressure or lowering of temperature will cause it to be more or less condensed to a liquid; also, to charge to the utmost, as with magnetism.—**sat′u-rate**, *a.* Saturated; also, of colors, deep or intense.—**sat′u-rat-ed** (-rā-ted), *p. a.* Soaked, impregnated, or imbued thoroughly; charged thoroughly or completely; brought to a state of saturation; of colors, free from admixture of white.—**sat-u-ra′tion** (-rā′shọn), *n.* [LL. *satura-tio(n-).*] The act or process of saturating, or the resulting state; specif., the degree of freedom of a color from white (as, the *saturation* of a color increases as the amount of white is diminished.—**sat′u-ra-tor**, *n.*

Sat-ur-day (sat′ėr-dā), *n.* [AS. *Sæterdæg, Sæternesdæg* (L. *Saturni dies*), 'Saturn's day.'] The seventh day of the week, following Friday.—**Holy Saturday.** See under *holy, a.*

Sat-urn (sat′ėrn), *n.* [L. *Saturnus*, prob. from the root of *serere* (pp. *satus*), sow: see *sow*1.] An ancient Italian deity, the god of agriculture and vegetation; in *astron.*, a major planet, the sixth in order from the sun, remarkable for the thin rings surrounding it; in *alchemy*, the metal lead.

The Planet Saturn, with its Rings.

Sat-ur-na-lia (sat-ėr-nā′liạ), *n. pl.* [L.] In ancient Rome, the festival of Saturn, celebrated in December, and observed as a time of general feasting and unrestrained merrymaking; [*l. c.*] any period of unrestrained revelry and license (sometimes construed as *sing.*: as, "the trapper's holiday, when he is all for fun and frolic, and ready for a *saturnalia* among the mountains," Irving's "Captain Bonneville," xx.).—**Sat-ur-na′lian**, *a.* Of or pertaining to the Roman Saturnalia; [*l. c.*] pertaining to or characterized by unrestrained revelry and license.

Sa-tur-ni-an (sạ-tėr′ni-ạn), *a.* [L. *Saturnius*.] Of or pertaining to the god Saturn, whose reign is referred to as 'the golden age'; hence, prosperous, happy, or peaceful; also, noting or pertaining to a form of verse used in early Roman poetry before the introduction of Greek meters; also, of or pertaining to the planet Saturn.

sat-ur-nine (sat′ėr-nīn), *a.* [OF. F. *saturnin*, through ML. < L. *Saturnus*, E. *Saturn*.] [*cap.*] Pertaining to the planet Saturn; [*l. c.*] born under, or affected by the influence of, the planet Saturn (supposed in astrology to cause sluggishness and gloominess of temperament); hence, having or showing a sluggish, gloomy temperament; gloomy; taciturn; also, of or pertaining to lead; due to absorption of lead, as bodily disorders; suffering from lead-poisoning, as a person.—**sat′ur-nine-ly**, *adv.*—**sat′ur-nine-ness, sat-ur-nin′i-ty** (-nin′i-ti), *n.*

sat-urn-ism (sat′ėr-nizm), *n.* [See *Saturn*.] Lead-poisoning.

sat-yr (sat′ėr or sā′tėr), *n.* [L. *satyrus*, < Gr. σάτυρος.] In *classical myth.*, one of a class of sylvan deities, attendant on Bacchus, represented as partly human and partly bestial in form, and noted for riot and lasciviousness; hence, a lascivious person.—**sat-y-ri-a-sis** (sat-i-rī′ạ-sis), *n.* [LL., < Gr. σατυρίασις.] In *pathol.*, morbid and uncontrollable

sexual desire in men. Cf. *nymphomania.*—**sa-tyr-ic** (sạ-tir′ik), *a.* [L. *satyricus*, < Gr. σατυρικός.] Of or pertaining to satyrs: as, the *satyric* drama (a particular type of ancient Greek drama of a somewhat burlesque character, the chorus representing satyrs). Also **sa-tyr′i-cal.**

sauce (sâs), *n.* [OF. *sausse*, *salse* (F. *sauce*), < ML. *salsa*, sauce, lit. 'something salted,' prop. fem. of L. *salsus*, pp. of *salire*, to salt, < *sal*, salt.] Any preparation, usually liquid or soft, of distinctive flavor, eaten as a relish or appetizing accompaniment to food; fig., something that adds piquancy to a thing; also, garden vegetables, etc., such as are eaten with meat (prov. Eng. and U. S.); also, stewed fruit (as, apple-*sauce*); also, sauciness or impertinence (colloq.: as, "It never pays to stand any *sauce*," Arnold Bennett's "Old Wives' Tale," iv. 3).—**sauce**, *v. t.*; *sauced, saucing.* To dress or prepare with sauce; season; flavor; fig., to give zest to; also, to rebuke smartly (obs. or prov.); speak impertinently to (colloq.).—**sauce′=boat**, *n.* A small boat-shaped vessel for serving sauce, commonly having a spout or lip at one end and a handle at the other.—**sauce′box**, *n.* A saucy or impertinent person, esp. a girl or a child. [Colloq.]—**sauce′pan**, *n.* A metallic vessel of moderate depth, usually having a long handle and sometimes a cover, for stewing, etc.

sau-cer (sâ′sėr), *n.* [OF. *saussier*, *saussiere* (F. *saucière*), vessel for sauce, < *sausse*, E. *sauce*.] A vessel or dish for holding sauce, etc.†; also, a small, round, shallow dish to hold a cup and catch any liquid which may be spilled from it; any similar dish, plate, or the like; also, something round and shallow like a saucer; a saucer-like rounded track, as for bicycle or motor-car races.—**sau′cer=eye**, *n.* A large, round eye.—**sau′cer=eyed**, *a.*—**sau′cer-ful** (-fúl), *n.*; pl. *-fuls.* A quantity sufficient to fill a saucer.

sau-cy (sâ′si), *a.*; compar. *saucier*, superl. *sauciest.* [From *sauce.*] Insolent, impertinent, or pert; also, archly or piquantly pert; smart; also, wanton†.—**sau′ci-ly**, *adv.*—**sau′ci-ness**, *n.*

sauer-kraut (sour′krout), *n.* [G., < *sauer*, sour, + *kraut*, plant, vegetable, cabbage.] A favorite German preparation of cabbage cut fine, salted, and allowed to ferment until sour.

sau-ger (sâ′gėr), *n.* [Origin uncertain.] A North American pike-perch, *Stizostedion canadense.*

sault (sō, commonly sö), *n.* [Canadian F. *sault* (F. *saut*), lit. 'a leap,' < L. *saltus*, < *salire*, leap: cf. *saltus*.] A rapid in a river: as, the *Sault* Ste. Marie. [North America.]

saun-ter (sân′tėr), *v. i.* [Origin obscure.] To walk with a leisurely or careless gait; stroll: as, "Crowds of Aztec nobles were *sauntering* up and down . . . loitering away their hours in attendance on the court" (Prescott's "Conquest of Mexico," iii. 9).—**saun′ter**, *n.* A leisurely or careless gait (as, "The other . . . walked slowly, with a sort of *saunter*, towards Adam": George Eliot's "Adam Bede," xxvii.); also, a leisurely walk or ramble, or a stroll (as, "a week-day *saunter* through the less busy parts of the metropolis": Lamb's "Superannuated Man").—**saun′ter-er**, *n.*—**saun′ter-ing-ly**, *adv.*

-saur, -saurus. [NL. *-saurus*, < Gr. σαῦρος, lizard.] Noun terminations occurring in names of reptiles, esp. extinct reptiles (many being of extraordinarily large size), as in *dinosaur, ichthyosaur, ichthyosaurus, tyrannosaurus.*

sau-rel (sâ′rẹl or sà-rel′), *n.* [F.] Any of the small carangoid marine fishes constituting the genus *Trachurus*, as *T. trachurus*, the scad, a common species of the northern Atlantic, esp. off the coasts of Europe.

Saurel (*Trachurus trachurus*).

sau-ri-an (sâ′ri-ạn). [NL. *Sauria*, pl., < Gr. σαῦρος, σαύρα, lizard.] **I.** *a.* Belonging or pertaining to the *Sauria*, a group of reptiles orig. including the lizards, crocodiles, etc., but commonly restricted to the lizards or lacertilians; lizard-like. **II.** *n.* A saurian animal, as a dinosaur.

---

sau-roid (sâ'roid), *a.* [Gr. σαυροειδής, < σαῦρος, lizard, + εἶδος, form.] Resembling a lizard or saurian; lizard-like.

sau-ro-pod (sâ'rō-pod). [NL. *Sauropoda*, pl., < Gr. σαῦρος, lizard, + πούς (ποδ-), foot.] **I.** *n.* Any of the *Sauropoda*, a group of herbivorous dinosaurs with small head, long neck and tail, and five-toed limbs, comprising the largest of all known land animals. **II.** *a.* Belonging or pertaining to the *Sauropoda.*—**sau-rop'o-dous** (-rop'ō-dus), *a.*

-saurus. See *-saur.*

sau-ry (sâ'ri), *n.*; pl. *-ries* (-riz). [Origin uncertain.] A long-snouted fish, *Scomberesox saurus*, of the Atlantic; also, any of various related fishes.

Saury (*Scomberesox saurus*).

sau-sage (sâ'sāj), *n.* [OF. *saussiche, saussice* (F. *saucisse*), < ML. *salsicia*, sausage, < L. *salsus*, pp., salted: see *sauce*.] Minced pork, beef, or other meats (often combined), with various added ingredients and seasonings, commonly stuffed into a container (typically cylindrical, and often tied at regular intervals to form 'links') consisting usually of a prepared intestine; also, a single stuffed container of this kind with its contents, or a single link of such a container; also, something of similar form or appearance; esp., a large sausage-shaped bag forming the sustaining part of a balloon; a balloon with such a bag, as an observation balloon used in warfare.

saus-su-rite (sâ-sū'rīt or sâs'ū-), *n.* [F.; named from H. B. de *Saussure* (1740—99), Swiss naturalist, who described it.] A compact, tough substance, greenish-white or grayish in color, consisting chiefly of epidote and zoisite.—**saus-su-rit-ic** (sâs-ū-rit'ik), *a.*

sau-té (sō-tā). [F., pp. of *sauter*, leap, cause to leap, toss, < L. *saltare*: see *saltate.*] **I.** *a.* Cooked or browned in a pan containing a little fat, as chicken or potatoes. **II.** *n.* A dish of food sauté.—**sau-té'**, *v. t.*; *-téd* (-tād'), *-téing* (-tā'ing). To cook as a sauté.

Sau-terne (sō-tärn), *n.* [F. *Sauternes*, district in southwestern France, near Bordeaux.] [Often *l. c.*] Any of a class of French white wines, sweet or dry.

sau-toir (sō-twor), *n.* [F. (*en sautoir*, said of a ribbon, chain, etc., worn with ends crossed, or drawn together, on the breast): see *saltier.*] A long ribbon, chain, beaded band, or the like, worn about the neck and drawn together on the breast some distance above the lower ends or part.

sauve=qui=peut (sōv-kē-pè), *n.* [F., 'save who can.'] A general rout, as of troops, in which each person seeks to save himself.

sav-a-ble (sā'va-bl), *a.* That may be saved.

sav-age (sav'āj). [OF. F. *sauvage*, < L. *silvaticus*, belonging to a wood, wild, < *silva, sylva*, wood, forest: cf. *sylva.*] **I.** *a.* Wild or rugged, as country or scenery (as, "a wild *savage* land of mountains, rivers, and forests": W. H. Hudson's "Green Mansions," xxi.); also, uncultivated, as a plant†; also, uncivilized, barbarous, wild, or rude, as races or tribes, life, manners, etc. (as, "the barriers, which had so long separated the *savage* and the civilized nations of the earth": Gibbon's "Decline and Fall of the Roman Empire," xxx.); also, undomesticated or untamed, as animals (now rare); also, fierce, ferocious, or cruel, as animals, persons, or their actions, etc. (as, "a roaring voice of most *savage* wild beasts," Wisdom of Solomon, xvii. 19; "a great hulking fellow, of a *savage* temper," S. Butler's "Way of All Flesh," lviii.); also, enraged, or furiously angry, as a person; rough or harsh, as in speech. **II.** *n.* A member of a race or tribe in the lowest stage of development or cultivation (as, "nations of *savages* . . . barbarous and brutish to the last degree": Defoe's "Captain Singleton," iv.); an uncivilized human being; also, a fierce, brutal, or cruel person (as, "Witness the patient ox . . . Driv'n to the slaughter . . . while the *savage* at his heels Laughs at the frantic suff'rer's fury": Cowper's "Task," vi. 422); also, a wild animal† (as, "When the grim *savage* [the lion], to his rifled den Too late returning, snuffs the track of men": Pope's tr. Homer's "Iliad," xviii.). —**sav'age-ly**, *adv.*—**sav'age-ness**, *n.*—**sav'age-ry** (-ri), *n.*; pl. *-ries* (-riz). The state, disposition, or conduct of a savage; wildness; barbarism; barbarity; a savage proceeding.— **sav'ag-ism** (-āj-izm), *n.* The condition of savages.

sa-van-na (sa-van'ä), *n.* [Also *savannah*; Sp. (obs.) *zavana*, now *sabana*; said to be from Carib.] A treeless plain, esp. one of those in the southern U. S.—**sa-van'na=spar"row**, *n.* Any of several North American sparrows of the genus *Passerculus*, as *P. savanna*, common in the eastern part of the continent.

sa-vant (sä-vän), *n.* [F., noun use of *savant*, ppr. of *savoir*, know, < L. *sapere*, be wise: see *sapient.*] A man of learning or science.—**sa-vante** (sä-vänt), *n.* [F.] Fem. of *savant.*

sa-vate (sä-vät), *n.* [F., lit. 'old shoe': cf. *sabot.*] A method of fighting, employed either alone or in conjunction with boxing, in which the feet are used.

Savanna-sparrow (*Passerculus savanna*).

save (sāv), *v. t.*; *saved, saving.* [OF. *sauver, salver* (F. *sauver*), < LL. *salvare*, save, < L. *salvus*, safe, unharmed: see *safe*[1].] To rescue from danger; preserve from harm, injury, loss, destruction, or the like; in theological use, to deliver from the power and consequences of sin; in general, to protect, guard, or keep safe; preserve from anything which would cause discomfort or annoyance; keep intact or unhurt, as honor or credit; safeguard, as a right or possession; keep from being lost, as a game or match; avoid missing, or be in time for, as the tide or the post; also, to set apart, reserve, or lay by, as for future use; store up or put by as the result of economy, as money; avoid the spending, consumption, or waste of, as money, goods, time, etc.; use sparingly, as food, etc.; treat carefully in order to reduce wear, fatigue, etc., as one's nerves or eyes or one's self; also, to prevent the occurrence of, as something undesirable (as, "We must *save* all scandal": Stevenson's "Master of Ballantrae," v.); obviate the necessity of (as, a stitch in time *saves* nine).— **(God) save the mark!** See under *mark*[2], *n.*—**to save appearances**, formerly, to explain in a satisfactory manner observed appearances or facts, as of astronomy, in accordance with a theory; now, to keep up an appearance of propriety, solvency, or the like, as by contrivance or shift; avoid giving an appearance of embarrassment, discomfiture, or the like.—**to save one's bacon**, to escape bodily harm, or any damage or loss.—**to save one's face.** See *face*, *n.*— **to save one's skin.** See under *skin*, *n.*—**save**, *v. i.* To lay up money, etc., as the result of economy; be economical in expenditure; also, to admit of being kept without spoiling, as food (colloq.).—**save.** [OF. F. *sauf*, prop. adj. (as used in absolute constructions), safe, expected, < L. *salvus.*] **I.** *prep.* With the exception of; except; but: as, "He heard no other sound *save* . . . his own breathing" (Barrie's "Sentimental Tommy," xv.). **II.** *conj.* Except; but; also, unless.—**save'=all**, *n.* A means, contrivance, or receptacle for preventing loss or waste.

sav-e-loy (sav'e-loi), *n.* [Corruption of *cervelat.*] A kind of sausage. See *cervelat.*

sav-er (sā'vėr), *n.* One who or that which saves.

sav-ey (sav'i), *v.* and *n.* See *savvy.*

sav-in, sav-ine (sav'in), *n.* [OF. *savine* (F. *sabine*), < L. *Sabina (herba)*, 'Sabine (herb).'] A juniper, *Juniperus sabina*, whose dried tops are used as a drug; the drug itself; also, the red cedar (see *cedar*).

sav-ing (sā'ving), *n.* The act of one who or that which saves; also, that which is saved, as a sum of money; *pl.*, sums of money saved by the exercise of economy and hoarded up; also, *sing.*, in *law*, a reservation or exception.—**sav'ing**, *p. a.* That saves; rescuing; preserving; redeeming; also, accustomed to save; economical; also, making a reservation (as, a *saving* clause).—**sav'ing.** [Orig. ppr.] **I.** *prep.* Excepting or save (as, none *saving* imperfect ones); also, with all due respect to or for (as, *saving* your reverence; *saving* your presence). **II.** *conj.* Save.—**sav'ing-ly**, *adv.* —**sav'ing-ness**, *n.*—**sav'ings=bank**, *n.* An institution for the encouragement of the practice of saving money and for the secure investment of savings.

sav-ior, sav-iour (sāv′yọr), *n.* [OF. *sauveour* (F. *sauveur*), < LL. *salvator*, < *salvare*, E. *save*.] One who saves, rescues, or delivers (as, "He was extolled as the *savior* of the country": Irving's "Conquest of Granada," l.); specif. [*cap*.], a title of God, and esp. of Christ (in this use commonly spelled *Saviour*).

sa-voir=faire (sȧ-vwor-fār′), *n.* [F., lit. 'to know how to do.'] The instinctive knowledge of just what to do in any emergency; tact: as, "He had great confidence in his own *savoir faire*" (Scott's "Guy Mannering," xxxv.).

sa-voir=vivre (sȧ-vwor-vēvr), *n.* [F., lit. 'to know how to live.'] Knowledge of the world and the usages of polite society: as, "Our society is to have the utmost polish, ease, and grace of manner, and the completest *savoir-vivre*" (Mallock's "New Republic," iii. 1).

sa-vor (sā′vọr), *n.* [OF. *savor*, *savour* (F. *saveur*), < L. *sapor*, taste, flavor: see *sapor*.] The quality in a substance which affects the sense of taste or of smell; a particular taste or smell; fig., distinctive quality or property; also, repute or estimation (archaic: as, "a name of evil *savour* in the land," Tennyson's "Gareth and Lynette," 377).—**sa′vor,** *v.* [OF. F. *savourer*, < ML. *saporare*, < L. *sapor*.] **I.** *intr.* To have savor, taste, or odor; fig., to exhibit the peculiar characteristics of something specified; show traces of the presence or influence (*of*); smack (*of*). **II.** *tr.* To give a savor to; season; flavor; also, to perceive by taste or smell; taste or smell with relish; fig., to give one's self to the enjoyment of (as, "He *savoured* anew . . . the beauty and stateliness of its architecture": Arnold Bennett's "Mr. Prohack," ii.); also, to care for or like (archaic); also, to perceive† or discern†; also, to show traces of the presence or influence of (as, "Wilful barrenness, That . . . *savours* only Rancour and pride": Milton's "Paradise Lost," x. 1043).—**sa′vor-i-ly,** *adv.* In a savory manner; with a pleasing savor.—**sa′vor-i-ness,** *n.*—**sa′vor-less,** *a.* Without savor; flavorless; insipid.—**sa′vor-y¹.** **I.** *a.* Having savor; agreeable in taste or smell (as, "A *savoury* smell is wafted from the kitchen": Amelia B. Edwards's "Thousand Miles up the Nile," xvii.); also, giving a relish; appetizingly seasoned (esp. of food-dishes that are not sweet); fig., pleasing or agreeable; often, morally pleasing. **II.** *n.*; pl. *-ies* (-iz). A savory or appetizing dish served at the beginning or end of a dinner. [Chiefly Eng.]

sa-vor-y² (sā′vọr-i), *n.* [ME. *saverey*, ult. < L. *satureia*, savory.] Any of the aromatic plants constituting the menthaceous genus *Satureia*, esp. *S. hortensis* ('summer savory'), an herb native in southern Europe and much cultivated for seasoning in cookery.

sa′vour, etc., **sa′vour-y.** British preferred forms of *savor*, etc., *savory¹*.

sa-voy (sạ-voi′), *n.* [For *Savoy cabbage*; named from *Savoy*, region in southeastern France.] A variety of the common cabbage with a compact head and leaves reticulately wrinkled.

Sa-voy-ard (sạ-voi′ärd). [F.] **I.** *n.* A native or inhabitant of Savoy, a region in southeastern France. **II.** *a.* Of or pertaining to Savoy.

sav-vy (sav′i), *v. t.* or *i.*; *-vied, -vying.* [Sp. *sabe* (*sabe usted,* 'do you know,' *no sabe,* 'he does not know,' etc.), < *saber,* know, < L. *sapere,* be wise: see *sapient*.] To know; understand: as, "You think you are wise, but there's a lot of things you don't *savvy*" (Wister's "Virginian," xxxi.). [Slang.]—**sav′vy,** *n.* Understanding; intelligence; sense: as, "I said he had *savvy* enough to find the index in 'Gray's

Anatomy' " (Sinclair Lewis's "Main Street," xiv.). [Slang.]

saw¹ (sâ). Preterit of *see²*.

saw² (sâ), *n.* [AS. *sagu* = OHG. *saga* (G. *sage*) = Icel. *saga* (see *saga*); from the root of E. *say³*.] A speech†; discourse†; also, a decree†; now, a sententious saying, a maxim, or a proverb (as, "The justice . . . Full of wise *saws* and modern instances": Shakspere's "As You Like It," ii. 7. 156).

saw³ (sâ), *n.* [AS. *sagu, saga,* = D. *zaag* = OHG. *saga* = Icel. *sög,* saw; akin to L. *secare,* cut: see *secant,* and cf. *sax*.] A tool or device for cutting, consisting typically of a thin blade or plate of metal, usually steel, armed on the edge with sharp teeth; such a device together with its handle or frame; a machine operating such a device.—**circular saw.** See under *circular, a.*—**saw³,** *v. t.*; pret. *sawed,* pp. *sawed* or *sawn,* ppr. *sawing.* To cut or divide with a saw; also, to form by cutting with a saw; also, to cleave as if in using a saw (as, "Do not *saw* the air too much with your hand": Shakspere's "Hamlet," iii. 2. 5); also, to work (something) from side to side like a saw.—**to saw wood,** fig., to work steadily at one's task, without attention to anything else. [Colloq.]—**saw³,** *v. i.* To use a saw; cut with or as with a saw; also, to cut as a saw does; also, to admit of being sawed. —**saw′bill,** *n.* Any of several birds with serrate bill; esp., a motmot.—**saw′bones,** *n.* A surgeon. [Slang.]—**saw′-buck,** *n.* [= D. *zaagbok*.] A sawhorse.

saw-der (sâ′dėr), *n.* [= *solder*.] Flattery; blarney: in the phrase *soft sawder*: as, "My Lord Jermyn seems to have his insolence as ready as his *soft sawder*" (George Eliot's "Felix Holt," xxi.). [Colloq.]

saw-dust (sâ′dust), *n.* Small fragments of wood produced in the process of sawing.

saw-er (sâ′ėr), *n.* One who saws; a sawyer.

saw-fish (sâ′fish), *n.* Any of various shark-like elasmobranchiate fishes (genus *Pristis*) having a snout prolonged into a flat, saw-like projection; also, any of various similar fishes.

Saw-fish (*Pristis pectinatus*). — 1, side view; 2, under view.

saw-fly (sâ′flī), *n.*; pl. *-flies* (-flīz). Any of the hymenopterous insects constituting the family *Tenthredinidæ*, the females of which are characterized by a saw-like organ for cutting slits in plants to hold their eggs.

saw-grass (sâ′gràs), *n.* Any of various cyperaceous plants, esp. of the genus *Cladium*, with the margins of the leaves toothed like a saw.

saw-horse (sâ′hôrs), *n.* A frame for holding wood that is being sawed.

saw-mill (sâ′mil), *n.* An establishment in which timber is sawed into planks, boards, etc., by machinery.

sawn (sân). Past participle of *saw³.*

Saw-ney, Saw-ny (sâ′ni), *n.*; pl. *-neys, -nies* (-niz). [Sc. var. of *Sandy¹,* for *Alexander.*] A nickname for a Scotchman; also [*l. c.*], a fool or simpleton (as, "He's a *sawney,* but you must not drive him to bay": J. H. Newman's "Callista," vii.). [Colloq.]

Sawhorse and Saw.

saw=pal-met-to (sâ′pal-met″ō), *n.* A shrub-like palmetto, *Serenoa serrulata,* of the southern U. S., having the leafstalks set with spiny teeth.

saw-set (sâ′set), *n.* An instrument used to set a saw.

saw-yer (sâ′yėr), *n.* [ME. *sawyer, sawier,* for *sawer*.] One who saws; one whose occupation it is to saw timber (see *pit-saw*); also, a tree with one end caught in the bed of a stream and the other swaying with the current (U. S.: as, "abundance of water from shore to shore, and no bars, snags, *sawyers,* or wrecks in his road," Mark Twain's "Life on the Mississippi," xl.).

sax (saks), *n.* [AS. *seax,* knife, dagger; akin to E. *saw³*: see *Saxon*.] A tool for trimming, and for making nail-holes in, slates for roofs.

sax-a-tile (sak′sạ-til), *a.* [L. *saxatilis,* < *saxum,* rock.] In *zoöl.* and *bot.,* saxicolous.

Summer Savory (*Satureia hortensis*). — *a*, corolla; *b*, calyx; *c*, pistil.

(variable) ḍ as d or j, ş as s or sh, ţ as t or ch, ẓ as z or zh; o, F. *cloche*; ü, F. *menu*; c̵h, Sc. *loch*; ṅ, F. *bonbon*; ′, primary accent; ″, secondary accent; †, obsolete; <, from; +, and; =, equals. See also lists at beginning of book.

ax-horn (saks′hôrn), *n.* Any of a group of brass musical instruments of the trumpet class, with valves, invented by Antoine Joseph (known as Adolphe) Sax (1814–94).

sax-ic-a-vous (sak-sik′ạ-vus), *a.* [NL. *saxicavus*, < L. *saxum*, rock, + *cavare*, hollow out, < *cavus*, hollow.] Hollowing out rocks, as certain mollusks.

sax-ic-o-lous, sax-ic-o-line (sak-sik′ō-lus, -lin), *a.* [L. *saxum*, rock, + *colere*, inhabit.] In *zoöl.* and *bot.*, living or growing on or among rocks.

sax-i-fra-ga-ceous (saks″si-frạ-gā′shius), *a.* Belonging to the *Saxifragaceæ*, or saxifrage family of plants, which includes the alumroot, miterwort, etc.

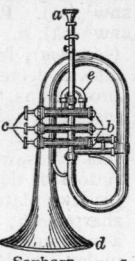

Saxhorn. — *a,* mouthpiece; *b,* valves; *c,* keys; *d,* bell; *e,* crook.

sax-i-frage (sak′si-frāj), *n.* [OF. F. *saxifrage*, < L. *saxifraga*, prop. fem. of *saxifragus*, rock-breaking, < *saxum*, rock, + *frangere*, break.] Any of the plants, mostly perennial herbs, constituting the genus *Saxifraga*, many of which grow wild in the clefts of rocks, others being cultivated for their flowers; also, any of various related or similar plants.

Sax-on (sak′sọn), *n.* [OF. F. *Saxon*, < LL. *Saxo(n-)*, pl. *Saxones*, Saxons, from Teut.: cf. AS. *Seaxan*, G. *Sachsen*, pl.; perhaps named from the weapon used (AS. *seax*, knife, dagger): see *sax*, and cf. *Frank*[1].] A member of a Teutonic people anciently dwelling in the regions near the mouth of the Elbe, a portion of which invaded and occupied parts of Britain in the 5th and 6th centuries; hence, an Anglo-Saxon; also, a person of the English race or of English descent; an Englishman as distinguished from an Irishman or a Welshman; a Lowland Scot as distinguished from a Highlander; also, a native or inhabitant of Saxony in modern Germany; also, the language of the early Continental Saxons ('Old Saxon'); also, Anglo-Saxon; also, modern English speech of Saxon or Anglo-Saxon origin. — **West Saxon.** See under *west*, *a.* — **Sax′on**, *a.* Of or pertaining to the early Continental Saxons or their language; also, Anglo-Saxon; also, English; also, of or pertaining to Saxony in modern Germany. — **Saxon architecture**, a rude variety of Romanesque architecture prevailing in England before the Norman period. — **Sax-on-ic** (sak-son′ik), *a.* Of or pertaining to the Saxons or Anglo-Saxons, or their language. — **Sax′on-ism**, *n.* Saxon or Anglo-Saxon character, or attachment to what is Anglo-Saxon; also, an Anglo-Saxon idiom. — **Sax′on-ize** (-īz), *v. t.*; *-ized, -izing.* To render Saxon, esp. Anglo Saxon. — **Sax″on-i-za′tion** (-i-zā′shọn), *n.*

sax-o-ny (sak′sō-ni), *n.* Fine wool produced in Saxony, Germany; cloth or flannel made of it or of similar wool; also, a fine woolen yarn for knitting, etc.

Saxifrage (*Saxifraga virginiensis*). — *a,* a flower; *b,* the fruit.

Saxon Architecture. — Earl's Barton Church, Northamptonshire, England: *a,* tower; *b,* window; *c,* angle of structure.

sax-o-phone (sak′sō-fōn), *n.* [From *Sax* (see def.) + Gr. φωνή, sound.] A keyed musical instrument of brass with a clarinet mouthpiece, invented by Antoine Joseph (known as Adolphe) Sax (1814–94). See cut in next column. — **sax-o-phon′ic** (-fon′ik), *a.* — **sax′o-phon-ist** (-fō-nist), *n.*

sax=tu-ba (saks′tū″bạ), *n.* [Cf. *saxhorn* and *tuba*[1].] A large (bass) form of saxhorn.

say[1] (sā), *n.* [For *assay*.] Assay; trial; a taste; a sample. [Obs. or prov.]

say[2] (sā), *n.* [OF. F. *saie*, < L. *saga*, pl. of *sagum*, military cloak: cf. *sagum*.] A light-weight woolen fabric resembling serge, formerly in use.

say[3] (sā), *v.*; pres. 1 *say*, 2 *sayest* or *sayst*, 3 *says* (sez) or *saith* (seth), pl. *say*; pret. and pp. *said* (sed); ppr. *saying*. [AS. *secgan* (pret. *sægde, sæde*) = D. *zeggen* = G. *sagen* = Icel. *segja*, say: cf. *saw*[2].] **I.** *tr.* To utter or pronounce, as a word or words; speak; also, to express in words; state; declare; sometimes, to state as an opinion, or with assurance (as, it is hard to *say* what is wrong); also, to recite or repeat (as, to *say* one's prayers); also, to assume as a hypothesis or an estimate (in imperative expressions: as, to learn in, *say*, ten lessons). **II.** *intr.* To speak; declare; express an opinion. — **say**[3], *n.* What a person says or has to say (as, "Do let me say my *say*": Mallock's "New Republic," iii. 2); also, the right or opportunity to say, speak, or decide (colloq.). — **say′a-ble**, *a.* That may be said. — **say′er**, *n.*

say-id (sī′id), *n.* See *sayyid*.

say-ing (sā′ing), *n.* Something said; a statement; an apothegm; a proverb.

say-nète (se-net′), *n.* [F., < Sp. *sainete*, lit. 'titbit,' < *saín*, fat, = E. *seam*[2].] In Spanish use, a short, amusing dramatic piece with few characters; also, in French use, a short dramatic piece of somewhat similar character.

say=so (sā′sō), *n.* One's personal statement or assertion. [Colloq.]

say-yid, sai-yid (sī′yid), *n.* [Ar., 'lord': cf. *Cid*.] In Mohammedan countries, a person supposed to be descended from Mohammed through his daughter Fatima.

sbir-ro (sbēr′rō), *n.*; pl. *-ri* (-rē). [It.] An Italian police officer.

'sblood (sblud), *interj.* A reduced form of *God's blood*, used as an oath. [Archaic.]

scab (skab), *n.* [ME. *scab*, from Scand.: cf. Sw. *skabb*, Dan. *skab*, scab, = AS. *sceabb*, E. *shab*.] Any of various cutaneous diseases in man, as the itch (obs. or rare); a mangy disease in animals, esp. sheep; any of various fungous diseases of plants, usually producing dark crust-like spots; also, the incrustation which forms over a sore during healing; also, a rascal or scoundrel (slang); in opprobrium, a workman who refuses to become a member of or to act with a labor-union, who takes a striker's place, or the like. — **scab**, *v. i.*; *scabbed, scabbing.* To become covered with a scab, as a sore; also, in opprobrium, to act or work as a scab.

scab-bard (skab′ärd), *n.* [AF. *escaubers, escauberz*, pl.; prob. from Teut.] A sheath or cover for the blade of a sword, dagger, or the like. — **scab′bard**, *v. t.* To put into a scabbard; sheathe. — **scab′bard=fish**, *n.* A fish, *Lepidopus caudatus*, with a long, compressed, silvery body and a long dorsal fin, of the coasts of Europe and of New Zealand.

Scabbard-fish.

scabbed (skabd or skab′ed), *a.* Diseased with the scab; also, covered with a scab or scabs; also, mean or contemptible (obs. or prov.).

scab-bi-ly (skab′i-li), *adv.* In a scabby manner. — **scab′bi-ness**, *n.* Scabby condition.

scab-ble (skab′l), *v. t.*; *-bled, -bling.* [Var. of *scapple*, < OF. *eskapeler, eschapler*, dress roughly: cf. F. *chapeler*, chip.] To shape or dress (stone) roughly.

scab-by (skab′i), *a.* Affected with the scab; also, covered with or consisting of scabs; blotchy; also, mean or contemptible (colloq.).

sca-bi-es (skā′bi-ēz), *n.* [L., < *scabere*, scratch, scrape; prob. akin to E. *shave*[1].] In *pathol.*, a skin-disease, the itch, due to the itch-mite. — **sca-bi-et′ic** (-et′ik), *a.*

sca-bi-ous[1] (skā′bi-us), *a.* [L. *scabiosus*, < *scabies*: see *scabies*.] Pertaining to or of the nature of scabies; also, scabby.

sca-bi-ous² (skā′bi-us), *n.* [OF. F. *scabieuse*, < ML. *scabiosa* (so called from its repute as a cure for skin-diseases), prop. fem. of L. *scabiosus*, E. *scabious¹*.] Any plant of the genus *Scabiosa*, which comprises a large number of more or less hairy herbs with flowers in dense heads.

sca-brous (skā′brus), *a.* [LL. *scabrosus*, for L. *scaber* (*scabr-*), rough, scurfy, < *scabere*: see *scabies*.] Rough with minute points or projections; hence, fig., harsh; full of difficulties; also, bordering upon the indelicate, or risqué, as books, etc.—**sca′brous-ness**, *n.*

scad¹ (skad), *n.* [Origin unknown.] The saurel (fish), *Trachurus trachurus*; also, any of various other fishes of the same genus or allied genera.

scad² (skad), *n.* [Cf. *squad*, in prov. Eng. sense 'a quantity of anything.'] A large quantity of anything: usually in *pl.* [Slang, U. S.]

scaf-fold (skaf′old), *n.* [From a var. of OF. *eschafaut* (F. *échafaud*), < *es-* (< L. *ex-*, out) + *chafaut*, platform, stage, ult. the same word as *catafalque* (see *catafalque*), appar. < Gr. κατά, down, + L. *fala*, *phala*, scaffold, high wooden structure.] A temporary structure for holding workmen and materials during the erection, repair, or decoration of a building; a raised platform, stage, or stand for exhibiting spectacles, seating spectators, or the like; an elevated platform on which a criminal is executed; any raised framework.—**scaf′fold**, *v. t.* To furnish with a scaffold or scaffolding (as, "The walls were *scaffolded* for the use of fire-arms": Scott's "Legend of Montrose," iv.); support by or place on a scaffold.—**scaf′fold-ing**, *n.* A scaffold or system of scaffolds, as for use in building; also, materials for scaffolds.

sca-glia (skal′yä), *n.* [It., scale, chip of marble, = E. *scale¹*.] An Italian limestone, usually reddish.

sca-glio-la (skal-yō′lä), *n.* [It. *scagliuola*, dim. of *scaglia*: see *scaglia*.] Plaster-work imitating marble, granite, or the like, used for interior walls, etc.

scal-a-ble (skā′la-bl), *a.* That may be scaled.

sca-lade (ska-lād′), *n.* Same as *escalade*. [Obs. or archaic.]

sca-lar (skā′lär), *n.* [L. *scalaris*, < *scala*, flight of steps, ladder, E. *scale³*.] **I.** *a.* Resembling a ladder; in *math.*, real (as, a *scalar* number). **II.** *n.* In *math.*, a scalar number.

sca-lar-i-form (ska-lar′i-fôrm), *a.* [L. *scalaria*, pl., flight of steps, + *forma*, form.] Of the form of a ladder; ladder-like.

scal-a-wag (skal′a-wag), *n.* [Origin obscure.] An undersized or ill-conditioned animal (U. S.); also, a scamp, rascal, or good-for-nothing fellow (colloq.); in *U. S. hist.*, a native white Southerner of the reconstruction period after the Civil War, who acted with the Republican party (a term used in contempt by Southern Democrats).

scald¹ (skåld), *v.* [OF. *escalder*, *eschalder* (F. *échauder*), scald, < LL. *excaldare*, wash in hot water, < L. *ex-*, out, + *caldus*, *calidus*, hot: cf. *caldron*.] **I.** *tr.* To burn or affect painfully with or as with hot liquid or steam; also, to subject to the action of boiling or hot liquid, as for cleansing purposes; also, to heat to a temperature just short of the boiling-point (as, to *scald* milk). **II.** *intr.* To be or become scalded. —**scald¹**, *n.* A burn caused by hot liquid or steam.

scald² (skåld), *a.* [Earlier *scalled*, < *scall*.] Affected with scall; scabby; fig., mean or contemptible (obs. or rare).

scald³, skald (skåld), *n.* [From Scand.: Icel. *skáld*, Norw. and Sw. *skald*, Dan. *skjald*: cf. *scold*.] An ancient Scandinavian poet: as, "Never was I so enthralled Either by Saga-man or *Scald*" (Longfellow's "Saga of King Olaf," vi.).

scald-ed† (skål′ded), *a.* Same as *scald²*.

scald=head (skåld′hed), *n.* A popular name for ringworm of the scalp and similar scalp affections.

scald-ic, skald-ic (skål′dik), *a.* Pertaining to the scalds, or ancient Scandinavian poets.

scal-di-no (skäl-dē′nō), *n.*; pl. *-ni* (-nē). [It., < *scaldare*, to heat, = E. *scald¹*, *v.*] A small earthenware brazier used in Italy: as, "He took my poor plaything, and thrust it down among the coals of his *scaldino*" (Howells's "Foregone Conclusion," x.). See cut in next column.

scale¹ (skāl), *n.* [OF. *escale*, *eschale*, scale, shell (F. *écale*, shell, *écaille*, scale); from Teut., and akin to E. *scale²*.] One of the thin, flat, horny or hard plates that form the covering of certain animals, as fishes; also, any thin plate-like piece, lamina, or flake such as peels off from a surface; also, a plate or thin piece of metal or other material; also, a thin scarious or membranous part of a plant, as a bract of a catkin; also, the shield covering the body of certain female insects (see *scale-insect*); a scale-insect (as, the San José *scale*: see entry in alphabetical place); also, a coating or incrustation, as on the inside of a boiler; also, *pl.*, something that causes blindness (see Acts, ix. 18).—**scale¹**, *v.*; *scaled*, *scaling*. **I.** *tr.* To remove the scales or scale from; also, to remove in scales or thin layers; also, to cover with an incrustation or scale, as the inside of a boiler. **II.** *intr.* To come off in scales; also, to become coated with scale, as the inside of a boiler.

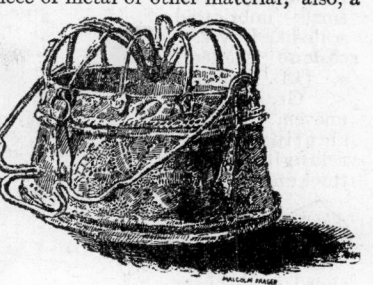

Old Venetian Scaldino.

scale² (skāl), *n.* [ME. *scale*, *scole*, from Scand.: cf. Icel. *skál*, bowl, scale for weighing, akin to OHG. *scâla*, bowl, *scala*, shell (G. *schale*), AS. *scealu*, dish, shell (see *shale¹*), also to E. *scale¹* and *shell*.] A bowl† or cup†; also, the pan, or either of the pans or dishes, of a balance; hence, *sing.* or, usually, *pl.*, a balance, or any of various other more or less complicated devices for weighing; *pl.* [*cap.*], in *astron.*, the zodiacal constellation or sign Libra; the Balance.—**scale²**, *v. t.*; *scaled*, *scaling*. To weigh in or as in scales; also, to have a weight of (as, the fish *scaled* seven pounds).

scale³ (skāl), *n.* [L. *scala*, usually pl. *scalæ*, flight of steps, ladder, < *scandere*, climb: see *scan*.] A ladder†; also, a flight of stairs†; also, a succession or progression of steps or degrees; a graduated series; a graduated table, as of prices; also, a series of marks laid down at determinate distances, as along a line, for purposes of measurement or computation; a graduated line, as on a map, representing proportionate size; also, an instrument with graduated spaces, for measuring, etc.; also, the proportion which the representation of an object bears to the object (as, a model on a *scale* of one inch to a foot); a system of proportion by which definite magnitudes represent definite magnitudes, as in drawing or sculpture (as, a drawing made to *scale*); hence, a certain relative or proportionate size or extent (as, "Not content with the spacious residence of his father, Montezuma erected another on a yet more magnificent *scale*": Prescott's "Conquest of Mexico," iv. 1); also, fig., a standard of measurement or estimation (as, "Even mean self-love becomes, by force divine, The *scale* to measure others' wants by thine": Pope's "Essay on Man," ii. 292); in *arith.*, a system of numerical notation (as, the decimal *scale*); in *music*, a definite series or succession of tones ascending or descending according to fixed intervals, esp. such a series beginning on a particular note (as, a diatonic *scale*; the major and minor *scales*; the major *scale* of C; the chromatic *scale*).—**scale³**, *v.*; *scaled*, *scaling*. **I.** *tr.* To climb by or as by a ladder; climb up or over; ascend; mount; also, to measure by or as if by a scale; esp. in lumbering, to measure (logs), or estimate the amount of (standing timber); hence, of trees, to furnish (so much timber); also, to make according to scale; also, to reduce in amount according to a fixed scale or proportion (often with *down*). **II.** *intr.* To climb; ascend; mount.

scale=board (skāl′bōrd, commonly skab′ord), *n.* [See *scale¹*.] A very thin board, as for the back of a picture; in *printing*, a thin strip of wood used in justifying.

scaled (skāld), *a.* Furnished with scales, as a fish.

scale=dove (skāl′duv), *n.* [Also *scaled dove*.] Any of the doves or pigeons of the genus *Scardafella*, of tropical or warm parts of America, of small size and having plumage so marked as to suggest scales. See cut on following page.

scale=in-sect (skāl′in″sekt), *n.* Any of various small plant-destroying insects of the homopterous family *Coccidæ*, the females of which mostly have the body and eggs covered by a large scale or shield formed by secretions.

scale-less (skāl′les), *a.* Without scales, as a fish.

scale=moss (skāl′môs), *n.* Any of certain liverworts (class *Hepaticæ*) with small, imbricated, scale-like leaves.

sca-lene (skā-lēn′), *a.* [LL. *scalenus*, < Gr. σκαληνός, uneven, unequal, slanting.] Of a triangle, having three unequal sides; of a cone, etc., hav-ing the axis in-clined to the base.

Scalene Tri-angle.

Scale-dove (*Scardafella squamosa*).

scal-er (skā′lėr), *n.* One who or that which scales.

scal-i-ness (skā′li-nes), *n.* Scaly condition.

scal-ing (skā′ling), *n.* Scales collectively; the arrangement of scales, as on a fish.

scall (skål), *n.* [ME. *scall*: cf. Icel. *skalli*, bald head.] A scaly or scabby cutaneous eruption, esp. on the scalp.—**scalled**, *a.* See *scald*[2].

scal-la-wag (skal′a-wag), *n.* See *scalawag*.

scal-lion (skal′yon), *n.* [OF. *escaloigne, eschaloigne*, < ML. *ascalonia*, n., for L. *cæpa Ascalonia*, onion of Ascalon (in Palestine): cf. *shallot*.] The shallot; also, the leek; also, any onion which does not form a large bulb.

scal-lop (skol′op or skal′-), *n.* [OF. *escalope*, shell, from Teut.: cf. D. *schelp*, shell, and E. *scalp*.] Any of various bivalve mollusks of the genus *Pecten* and allied genera; also, the adductor muscle of certain species of such mollusks, esteemed as an article of food; also, one of the valves of such a mollusk, usually having radial ribs and a wavy outer edge; a scallop-shell as the badge of a pilgrim; a scallop-shell or a dish in which flaked fish or the like is baked and served; also, one of a series of convex rounded projections along an edge, as for ornament.—**scal′lop**, *v. t.* To mark or cut the border of into scallops; ornament with scallops; also, to bake (fish, etc.) in scallop-shells; cook (oysters, vegetables, etc., suitably prepared) in a baking-dish.—**scal′lop=shell**, *n.* The shell or valve of a scallop, often 'as the badge of a pilgrim: as, "In thy hand retaining yet The pilgrim's staff and *scallop-shell!*" (Whittier's "Daniel Wheeler").

Scallop (genus *Hinniles*).

scal-ly-wag (skal′i-wag), *n.* See *scalawag*.

scalp (skalp), *n.* [ME. *scalp*, appar. from Scand.: cf. Icel. *skalpr*, sheath, also D. *schelp*, shell, and E. *scalp*.] The top of the head, or the skull (now only prov.); also, the integument of the upper part of the head, usually including the associated subcutaneous structures; also, a part of this integument with the accompanying hair, cut from a person's head by the North American Indians as a trophy of victory (as, "when the warriors . . . returned, carrying the *scalps* of their slain foes on branches of evergreen pine": Roosevelt's "Winning of the West," i. 3); also, a small profit made in quick buying and selling (colloq.).—**scalp**, *v.* **I.** *tr.* To cut or tear the scalp from (as, "A party of St. Francis Indians . . . *scalped* one of his companions": Bancroft's "Hist. of the U. S.," Amer. Revolution, i. 4); hence, to remove the top, covering, etc., of; also, to buy cheap and sell at less than official rates, as railroad-tickets (colloq.); buy and sell so as to make small, quick profits, as stocks (colloq.). **II.** *intr.* To scalp railroad-tickets, etc.; buy and sell stocks, etc., so as to make small, quick profits. [Colloq.]

scal-pel (skal′pel), *n.* [L. *scalpellum*, dim. of *scalprum*, knife, < *scalpere*, cut, carve, engrave, scrape: cf. *sculp*.] A small, light, usually straight knife used in sur-gical and anatomical opera-tions.

Scalpel.

scalp-er (skalp′ėr), *n.* One who or that which scalps; esp., one who scalps railroad-tickets, stocks, etc. (colloq.).

scalp=lock (skalp′lok), *n.* A long lock or tuft of hair left on the scalp by North American Indians as an implied challenge to their enemies: as, "The men were hunters and warriors, who painted their bodies and shaved from their crowns all the hair except the long *scalp-lock*" (Roose-velt's "Winning of the West," i. 4).

scal-y (skā′li), *a.* Covered with or abounding in scales or scale; characterized by scales; consisting of scales or scale; of the nature of scales; also, shabby or despicable (slang); mean or stingy (slang).—**scaly ant=eater**, or **scaly lizard**, a pangolin.

scam-ble (skam′bl), *v. i.* or *t.*; *-bled, -bling*. [Origin obscure: cf. *scramble* and *shamble*[2].] To scramble. [Obs. or prov.]

scam-mo-ny (skam′ō-ni), *n.* [OF. *escamonie* (F. *scam-monée*), < L. *scammonia*, < Gr. σκαμμωνία, scammony.] A twining Asiatic species of con-volvulus, *Convolvulus scammonia*, or the cathartic gum-resin obtained from its root.

Scammony.—*R*, the root.

scamp[1] (skamp), *n.* [Appar. akin to *scamper*[2].] A highway robber (archaic); also, a worthless per-son, or a rascal or rogue (as, "Old Dodd had a *scamp* of a son who had run away from school," Margaret Kennedy's "Constant Nymph," xii.: often used play-fully).

scamp[2] (skamp), *v. t.* [Prob. akin to *scant*.] To perform (work, etc.) in a hasty, careless, or slipshod manner: as, "I will undertake to say he never *scamped* a job in the whole course of his life" (S. Butler's "Way of All Flesh," i.).—**scamp′er**[1], *n.*

scam-per (skam′pėr), *v. i.* [Cf. F. *escamper*, It. *scampare*, decamp, run away.] To run away† or decamp† (as, "The wagoners took each a horse out of his team and *scampered*": B. Franklin's "Autobiography," xi.); also, to run or go hastily or quickly; run about nimbly (as, "Young lambs *scamper* through the fold": Eden Phillpotts's "Cherry-Stones," Triads).—**scam′per**[2], *n.* A scampering; a quick run or excursion.

scamp-ish (skam′pish), *a.* Like or befitting a scamp; rascally.

scan (skan), *v.*; *scanned, scanning.* [LL. *scandere*, scan, L. climb; akin to Skt. *skand-*, spring, Gr. σκάνδαλον, a trap: cf. *ascend, scale*[3], and *scandal*.] **I.** *tr.* To analyze (verse) as to its prosodic or metrical structure; read or recite so as to indicate or test the metrical form; hence, to examine minutely; scrutinize; look at searchingly; also, to interpret†; also, to perceive† or discern†. **II.** *intr.* Of verse, to con-form to the rules of meter.—**scan**, *n.* The act of scanning; close examination or scrutiny.

scan-dal (skan′dal), *n.* [F. *scandale*, < LL. *scandalum*, < Gr. σκάνδαλον, a trap, stumbling-block, offense: see *scan*, and cf. *slander*.] An obstacle to religious faith or to obedi-ence to divine law; also, discredit to religion caused by irreligious conduct or moral lapse; also, damage to reputa-tion; a disgraceful or discreditable action, circumstance, etc.; a person whose conduct brings disgrace, or offends public morals or sense of decency; also, general indignation at something that offends moral feelings or sense of decency (as, he persisted in his course to the *scandal* of the entire community); also, defamatory talk; malicious gossip.—**scan′dal**, *v. t.*; *-daled* or *-dalled, -daling* or *-dalling.* To disgrace†; also, to spread scandal concerning (archaic or prov.).

scan-dal-ize (skan′dal-īz), *v. t.*; *-ized, -izing.* [F. *scan-daliser*, < LL. *scandalizare*, < Gr. σκανδαλίζειν, cause to stumble, < σκάνδαλον: see *scandal*.] To disgrace (obs. or rare); also, to defame or slander (now rare); also, to shock or horrify by something considered immoral or improper. —**scan″dal-i-za′tion** (-i-zā′shon), *n.*—**scan′dal-iz-er** (-ī-zėr), *n.*

scan-dal-mong-er (skan′dal-mung″gėr), *n.* One who spreads or retails scandal.

scan-dal-ous (skan′dal-us), *a.* [F. *scandaleux*, < ML. *scan-dalosus*, < LL. *scandalum*, E. *scandal*.] Disgraceful to repu-tation; also, extremely offensive to moral feelings or sense of decency (as, "The contending of preachers in their pulpits, one against another . . . became most *scandalous*": Strype's "Memorials of Cranmer," i. 30); shocking; also, defamatory or libelous, as a speech or writing; addicted to scandal, as a person.—**scan′dal·ous·ly,** *adv.*—**scan′dal·ous·ness,** *n.*

scan·dent (skan′dent), *a.* [L. *scandens* (*scandent-*), ppr. of *scandere*, climb: see *scan*.] Climbing, as a plant.

scan·di·a (skan′di-ä), *n.* [NL., < *scandium*.] In *chem.*, oxide of scandium, Sc₂O₃, a white infusible powder.

Scan·di·an (skan′di-an), *a.* and *n.* [L. *Scandia*, also *Scandinavia*.] Same as *Scandinavian*.

scan·dic (skan′dik), *a.* In *chem.*, of or pertaining to scandium.

Scan·di·na·vi·an (skan-di-nā′vi-an). [L. *Scandinavia*: cf. Icel. *Skāni*, *Skāney*, southernmost district of the Scandinavian peninsula.] **I.** *a.* Of or pertaining to Scandinavia (Norway, Sweden, Denmark, and Iceland) or the inhabitants or languages of Scandinavia. **II.** *n.* A native or inhabitant of Scandinavia; also, the Scandinavian languages.—**Scan·di·na′vi·an·ism,** *n.*

scan·di·um (skan′di-um), *n.* [NL., < L. *Scandia*, Scandinavia: cf. *Scandian*.] Chem. sym., Sc; at. wt., 44.1. A rare trivalent metallic element present in the Scandinavian mineral euxenite, etc.

scan·ner (skan′ėr), *n.* One who scans.

scan·sion (skan′shon), *n.* [LL. *scansio(n-)*, scanning, L. climbing, < L. *scandere*: see *scan*.] The scanning of verse.—**scan′sion·ist,** *n.* One versed in scansion.

scan·so·ri·al (skan-sō′ri-al), *a.* [L. *scansorius*, < *scandere*, climb: see *scan*.] Pertaining to or adapted for climbing, as the feet of birds, etc.; habitually climbing, as a bird.

scant (skant). [ME. *scant*, from Scand.: cf. Icel. *skamr*, neut. *skamt*, short, brief, *skamta*, dole out, also E. *scamp*².] **I.** *a.* Inadequate or barely sufficient in amount or quantity; stinted in amount, or not abundant; less than enough, or very little (as, to do a thing *scant* justice); limited or not large, as an amount or quantity; barely amounting to as much as indicated (as, a *scant* two hours' notice); limited in extent (as, *scant* domains); also, having an inadequate or limited supply (*of*: as, "He's fat, and *scant* of breath," Shakspere's "Hamlet," v. 2. 298); also, deficient in quality, poor, or meager (as, "Although the verse be somewhat *scant*, God doth supply the want": Herbert's "Temple," A True Hymn); also, sparing† or parsimonious†; chary†. **II.** *adv.* Scarcely; barely; hardly: as, "His manner was *scant* civil" (Stevenson's "David Balfour," viii.); "*Scant* three miles the band had rode" (Scott's "Marmion," v. 33). [Now archaic or prov.]—**scant,** *v. t.* To make scant; cut down; diminish; also, to stint the supply of; be niggardly of; keep back or withhold; also, to treat slightingly or inadequately; also, to furnish with an inadequate supply; put on scant or short allowance.

scant·i·ly (skan′ti-li), *adv.* In a scanty manner; insufficiently; meagerly.—**scant′i·ness,** *n.*

scant·ling (skant′ling), *n.* [OF. *escantillon*, *eschantillon* (F. *échantillon*), gage, sample, scantling: cf. It. *scandaglio*, sounding-line.] Measured or fixed size or dimensions; also, limited measure, space, or amount†; also, an allotted quantity or amount (as, "The muleteer . . . thought not of tomorrow . . . provided he got but his *scantling* of Burgundy": Sterne's "Tristram Shandy," vii. 21); esp., a small quantity or amount; a modicum; also, a sample† or specimen†; also, a rough draft†; also, a timber of comparatively small cross-section, as a rafter or a purlin; such timbers collectively.

scant·ly (skant′li), *adv.* In a scant manner or measure; scantily; also, scarcely, barely, or hardly (archaic: as, "Marmion, whose soul could *scantly* brook, Even from his King, a haughty look," Scott's "Marmion," iii. 14).—**scant′ness,** *n.*

scant·y (skan′ti), *a.*; compar. *scantier*, superl. *scantiest*. Scant in amount, quantity, etc.; barely sufficient; not abundant; lacking amplitude in extent or compass; also, parsimonious†.

scape¹ (skāp), *n.* [L. *scapus*, shaft, stem, akin to Gr. σκῆπτρον, staff, E. *scepter*: cf. *shaft*².] In *bot.*, a leafless peduncle rising from the ground; in *zoöl.*, a stem-like part, as the shaft of a feather; in *arch.*, the shaft of a column.

scape² (skāp), *v.* and *n.* Same as *escape*. [Archaic.]

scape³ (skāp), *n.* [Detached from *landscape*.] A scene or view, whether pictured or in nature. Cf. *cloudscape*, *seascape*, *skyscape*, *treescape*, *waterscape*.

scape-goat (skāp′gōt), *n.* [See *scape*².] In the ancient Jewish ritual, a goat which was sent alive into the wilderness after the chief priest on the Day of Atonement had symbolically laid the sins of the people upon it (see Lev. xvi.); hence, one who is made to bear the blame for the misdeeds or errors of others, or to suffer in the place of others.

Scape. — 1, bluebell (*Scilla nonscripta*); 2, oxlip (*Primula elatior*); *s, s,* scapes.

scape-grace (skāp′grās), *n.* [See *scape*².] A graceless person; a reckless, good-for-nothing person; a ne'er-do-well; a scamp.

scape-ment (skāp′ment), *n.* Same as *escapement* (in a timepiece).—**scape′-wheel,** *n.* In the escapement of a timepiece, a toothed wheel which actuates the pendulum or balance.

scaph-oid (skaf′oid). [Gr. σκαφοειδής, < σκάφη, boat, + εἶδος, form.] **I.** *a.* Boat-shaped; esp., in *anat.*, noting a bone of the radial side of the carpus, or a bone on the inner side of the tarsus. **II.** *n.* In *anat.*, a scaphoid bone.

scap-o-lite (skap′ō-līt), *n.* [F. *scapolite*, < Gr. σκᾶπος, rod, + λίθος, stone.] Any of a group of minerals of variable composition, essentially silicates of aluminium, calcium, and sodium, occurring in tetragonal crystals and also massive, and usually of a white or grayish-white color.

sca-pose (skā′pōs), *a.* [See *scape*¹ and *-ose*¹.] In *bot.*, having scapes; consisting of or resembling a scape.

scap-ple (skap′l), *v. t.*; *-pled, -pling.* Same as *scabble*.

scap-u-la (skap′ū-lä), *n.*; pl. *-læ* (-lē). [NL.; in L. as pl. *scapulæ*, shoulder-blades, in LL. as sing., *scapula*, shoulder.] In *anat.* and *zoöl.*, a bone of the pectoral arch; in man, either of two flat triangular bones each forming the back part of a shoulder; a shoulder-blade.—**scap′u·lar**¹. [NL. *scapularis*.] **I.** *a.* Of or pertaining to the shoulders or the scapula or scapulæ; in *ornith.*, noting any of the feathers on the wing of a bird at or near its insertion into the body. **II.** *n.* In *ornith.*, a scapular feather.

scap-u-lar² (skap′ū-lär), *n.* [ML. *scapulare*, also *scapularium*, < LL. *scapula*, shoulder: see *scapula*.] *Eccles.*, a kind of loose, sleeveless monastic garment depending from the shoulders; also, two small quadrilateral pieces of woolen cloth, joined by strings passing over the shoulders, worn under the ordinary clothing as a badge of affiliation with a religious order, a token of devotion, etc. Also **scap′u·la·ry** (-lä-ri); pl. *-ries* (-riz).

scar¹ (skär), *n.* [OF. *escarre* (F. *eschare*), < LL. *eschara*, < Gr. ἐσχάρα, orig. 'hearth': see *eschar*.] The mark left by a healed wound, sore, or burn, or a cicatrix (as, "He jests at *scars* that never felt a wound": Shakspere's "Romeo and Juliet," ii. 2. 1); hence, any blemish remaining as a trace or result (as, "stairs by the side of which holes had been knocked through the faded wall-paper — *scars* of frequent movings": W. Churchill's "Inside of the Cup," xi.); also, a mark indicating a former point of attachment, as where a leaf has fallen from a stem or branch.—**scar**¹, *v.*; scarred, scarring. **I.** *tr.* To mark with a scar. **II.** *intr.* To heal with a scar.

scar² (skär), *n.* [ME. *skarre*, *skerre*: cf. Icel. *sker*, rock in the sea, E. *skerry*.] A precipitous rocky place on the side of a mountain; a precipice or cliff; also, a low or submerged rock in the sea.

scar-ab (skar′ab), *n.* [Earlier *scarabe*, *scarabee*, < F. *scarabée*, < L. *scarabæus*, scarab: cf. Gr. κάραβος, kind of beetle.] A beetle; esp., the scarabæus, *Scarabæus sacer*, which was regarded as sacred by the ancient Egyptians; also, a representation or image of a beetle, much used among the ancient Egyptians as a symbol, seal, amulet, or the like; esp., a gem (as of emerald, green feldspar, etc.) cut in the form of a beetle and engraved on the under face, common among the Egyptians and other ancient peoples.—**scar-a-bæ′id** (-ạ-bē′id). **I.** *a.* Of or pertaining to the *Scarabæidæ*, a family of lamellicorn beetles containing the scarabæi, cockchafer, June-bugs, etc. **II.** *n.* A scarabæid beetle.—**scar-a-bæ′oid.** [See *-oid.*] **I.** *a.* Of the nature of a scarabæid; pertaining to or resembling the scarabæids; also, resembling a scarab (image or gem). **II.** *n.* A scarab (image or gem) but remotely resembling the natural insect, or an imitation or counterfeit scarab (gem).—**scar-a-bæ′us** (-us), *n.*; pl. *-bæi* (-bē′ī). [L.] Any beetle of the genus *Scarabæus*, as *S. sacer*, a large beetle of Egypt and the Mediterranean countries; also, a scarab (image or gem).—**scar′ab-oid.** [See *-oid.*] **I.** *a.* Resembling a scarab (image or gem); of the nature of a scarabæoid. **II.** *n.* A scarabæoid.

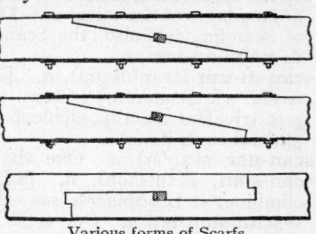

Ancient Egyptian Scarab (gem); about 1600 B.C.

Scar-a-mouch (skar′ạ-mouch), *n.* [F. *Scaramouche*, < It. *Scaramuccia*, lit. 'skirmish': see *skirmish.*] A stock character in Italian comedy and farce, a cowardly braggart who is constantly beaten by Harlequin; [*l. c.*] a masquerader or buffoon representing this character (as, "The habit of this greasy Don was very proper for a *scaramouch*, or merryandrew; being a dirty calico, with all the tawdry and trapping of a fool's coat": Defoe's "Robinson Crusoe," ii. 13); also [*l. c.*], a rascal or scamp (as, "He swore no *scaramouch* of an Italian robber would dare to meddle with an Englishman": Irving's "Tales of a Traveler," iii. 4).

scarce (skārs), *a.*; compar. *scarcer*, superl. *scarcest.* [OF. *escars*, *eschars*, scanty, stingy (F. *échars*, below the standard, light), = It. *scarso*, scanty, stingy, prob. through ML. < L. *ex*, out of, + *carpere*, pick: cf. *excerpt.*] Scanty or inadequate, as in amount, size, etc.†; existing or available in less than the usual amount, or not plentiful or abundant (as, many commodities become *scarce* in wartime); seldom met with, or rare (as, a *scarce* book or coin); also, scantily supplied, or short (with *of*: now rare); also, stingy† or niggardly†; chary (*of*)†.—**to make one's self scarce,** to go or keep away: as, "Please do *make yourself scarce.* You are in my way, and I'm very busy" (Arnold Bennett's "Helen with the High Hand," vii.). [Colloq.]—**scarce,** *adv.* Scarcely: as, "If old, they are *scarce* capable of enterprise" (G. Meredith's "Ordeal of Richard Feverel," xiii.); "I *scarce* kept myself from shedding tears" (Gissing's "Private Papers of Henry Ryecroft," ii. 23). [Now chiefly literary.]—**scarce′ly,** *adv.* Scantily†; also, barely, or only just; hardly, or not quite.

scarce-ment (skārs′ment), *n.* [Origin uncertain: cf. *scarce.*] In *building*, a set-off in the face of a wall, or in a bank of earth; a footing or ledge formed by a set-off in a wall.

scarce-ness (skārs′nes), *n.* The state or fact of being scarce; scarcity.

scar-ci-ty (skār′si-ti), *n.*; pl. *-ties* (-tiz). The state or fact of being scarce; insufficiency or smallness of supply; dearth, or a period of dearth, as of the necessaries of life; rarity or infrequency; stinginess† or niggardliness†.

scare[1] (skār), *n.* [Orig. Sc.: cf. Icel. *skör*, joint, *skara*, clinch (planks).] In *golf*, the part of a club where the head joins the shaft.

scare[2] (skār), *v. t.*; *scared*, *scaring.* [ME. *skerren*, from Scand.: cf. Icel. *skirrask*, refl., shrink from, *skjarr*, shy, timid.] To frighten; terrify; strike with sudden fear or terror; also, to drive by frightening (with *away*, etc.).—**to scare up,** fig., to raise; get; procure: as, to *scare up* money. —**scare**[2], *v. i.* To become frightened; be scared. [Now colloq.]—**scare**[2], *n.* A sudden fright or alarm, esp. with little or no ground: as, "Peyrol actually laughed at his momentary *scare*" (J. Conrad's "Rover," x.).—**scare′-crow,** *n.* An object, usually a crude figure of a man dressed in old and ragged clothes, set up in a field to frighten crows, etc., away from growing crops; fig., anything of terrifying aspect but not really dangerous; also, one who resembles a scarecrow, as in dress (as, "There ranged themselves in front

of the schoolmaster's desk, half-a-dozen *scarecrows*," out at knees and elbows": Dickens's "Nicholas Nickleby," viii.). —**scare′=head,** *n.* A newspaper heading in large type and of a sensational character. [Colloq.]—**scare′mong″er** (-mung″gėr), *n.* One given to creating or spreading scares; an alarmist.—**scar-er** (skār′ėr), *n.*

scarf[1] (skärf), *n.*; pl. *scarfs* or *scarves* (skärvz). [OF. *escarpe*, *escharpe*, bag worn hanging from the neck, scrip, later sash or scarf (F. *écharpe*); from Teut.: cf. *scrip*[1].] A military sash; a long, broad strip of silk, lace, gauze, or other material worn about the neck, shoulders, or head for ornament or protection; a necktie or cravat with hanging ends; a long cover of linen, etc., for a bureau, sideboard, etc. —**scarf**[1], *v. t.* To cover or wrap with or as with a scarf; also, to wrap round or about a person in the manner of a scarf.

scarf[2] (skärf), *n.*; pl. *scarfs.* [Appar. from Scand.: cf. Sw. *skarf*, joint, scarf.] A joint by which the ends of two timbers or the like are united so as to form a continuous piece; also, either of the chamfered or specially cut ends of the pieces forming such a joint.—**scarf**[2], *v. t.* To join by a scarf or overlapping joint; also, to form a scarf, chamfer, or the like, on.—**scarf′= joint,** *n.* A joint formed by scarfing; a scarf.

Various forms of Scarfs.

scarf=skin (skärf′skin), *n.* [From *scarf*[1] (as an outer covering).] The outermost layer of the skin; the epidermis.

scar-i-fi-ca-tion (skar″i-fi-kā′shọn), *n.* [LL. *scarificatio*(n-).] The act of scarifying; also, that which is produced by scarifying, as a scratch or a number of scratches.—**scar′i-fi-ca-tor,** *n.* One who scarifies; a surgical instrument for scarifying.

scar-i-fi-er (skar′i-fī-ėr), *n.* One who or that which scarifies; a scarificator; a form of cultivator with prongs, used for loosening the soil; a similar apparatus for tearing up roads, as in preparation for making new ones.

scar-i-fy (skar′i-fī), *v. t.*; *-fied*, *-fying.* [OF. F. *scarifier*, < LL. *scarificare*, for L. *scarifare*, scarify, < Gr. σκαριφᾶσθαι, scratch, < σκάριφος, stylus.] To make scratches or superficial incisions in (the skin, a wound, etc.), as in surgery; fig., to lacerate or harrow, as the feelings; criticize severely; also, in general, to make incisions in; loosen (the soil) with a scarifier; tear up (a road) with a scarifier.

sca-ri-ous (skā′ri-us), *a.* [NL. *scariosus*; origin uncertain.] In *bot.*, thin, dry, and membranous, as certain bracts; in *zoöl.*, scaly; scurfy; furfuraceous.

scar-la-ti-na (skär-lạ-tē′nä), *n.* [NL., < It. *scarlattina*, < *scarlatto*, scarlet: see *scarlet.*] In *pathol.*, scarlet fever; popularly, a mild form of scarlet fever.—**scar-la-ti′nal,** *a.* Pertaining to or of the nature of scarlatina.—**scar-la-ti′noid,** *a.* [See *-oid.*] Resembling scarlatina or its eruption.

scar-less (skär′les), *a.* Bearing no scar; unscarred; also, producing or leaving no scar.

scar-let (skär′let), *n.* [OF. *escarlate* (F. *écarlate*) = It. *scarlatto* = ML. *scarlatum*; perhaps from Pers.] **I.** *n.* A rich fabric, often of a red color, in use during the middle ages; hence, a brilliant red color inclining toward orange; cloth or garments of this color. **II.** *a.* Of the color scarlet; clothed in scarlet, as a person; red, as with shame; fig., glaring, flagrant, or notorious (as, *scarlet* sins, see Isa. i. 18; the *scarlet* woman, see phrase below).—**scarlet fever,** in *pathol.*, a contagious febrile disease characterized by a scarlet eruption; scarlatina.—**scarlet letter,** a scarlet letter A worn for punishment by one convicted of adultery, as by Hester Prynne in Hawthorne's story "The Scarlet Letter." —**scarlet runner,** a high-twining bean, *Phaseolus multiflorus*, of tropical America, commonly having scarlet flowers. —**scarlet sage.** See *sage*[2].—**scarlet woman,** the woman described in Rev. xvii.: variously explained as symbolizing pagan Rome, or (esp. formerly, in religious controversy) the Church of Rome, or some other place, power, or the like. Allusively, an epithet for anything regarded as a great source of or power for evil.

scarp (skärp), *n.* [It. *scarpa*, prob. from Teut. and akin to E. *sharp*: cf. *escarp*.] In *fort.*, an escarp; in general, a steep slope (as, "sheer *scarps* of grey rock": H. Kingsley's "Geoffry Hamlyn," xxvii.).—**scarp**, *v. t.* To escarp; slope steeply.

scar-y (skär'i), *a.* Such as to scare, or causing fright or alarm (as, "If any can pretend . . . to have seen *scary* sights, it is myself!" Cooper's "Prairie," xxii.); also, easily frightened; timorous. [Colloq.]

scat¹ (skat), *n.* [From Scand.: cf. Icel. *skattr*.] A tax or tribute; in the Orkney and Shetland Islands, a land-tax paid to the crown.

scat² (skat), *interj.* [Appar. < *cat*, preceded by a hissing sound.] An exclamation used to drive away cats, etc.—**scat**², *v. t.* or *i.*; *scatted*, *scatting*. To drive or be driven away by a cry of 'scat!'

scath (skāᴛʜ), etc. See *scathe*, etc.

scathe (skāᴛʜ), *n.* [From Scand.: cf. Icel. *skadhi*, Sw. *skada*, Dan. *skade*, G. *schade*, harm, damage, Goth. *skathis*, wrong, also AS. *sceatha*, doer of harm.] Hurt, harm, or injury (as, "Sirs, ye have heard News of your *scathe* and of shame done to God": Swinburne's "Bothwell," i. 2); also, matter for regret. [Archaic or prov.]—**scathe**, *v. t.*; *scathed*, *scathing*. To hurt, harm, or injure (archaic or prov.); also, to injure by fire, lightning, etc., or scorch or sear (as, "a place where the tree had been *scathed* by lightning": Irving's "Sketch-Book," Sleepy Hollow).—**scathe'ful**, *a.* Hurtful, harmful, or injurious. [Archaic.]—**scathe'less**, *a.* Without scathe or harm.—**scath-ing** (skā'ᴛʜing), *p. a.* That scathes, scorches, or sears; fig., bitterly severe, as a remark.—**scath'ing-ly**, *adv.*

scatt (skat), *n.* See *scat*¹.

scat-ter (skat'ėr), *v.* [ME. *scateren*; origin obscure: cf. *shatter*.] **I.** *tr.* To separate and drive off in various directions; disperse; also, to squander (archaic); also, to throw loosely about; strew; sprinkle; diffuse; distribute here and there at irregular intervals; also, to strew or sprinkle with something. **II.** *intr.* To separate and disperse; proceed in different directions.—**scat'ter**, *n.* The act or an act of scattering: as, "There was a general *scatter* of the party who had come to see the duel" (Lover's "Handy Andy," iv.).—**scat'ter=brain**, *n.* One incapable of serious, connected thought; a thoughtless, giddy person: as, "The little *scatterbrain* had, of course, forgotten her cloak" (Mrs. H. Ward's "Robert Elsmere," vii.).—**scat'ter=brained**, *a.*—**scat'ter-er**, *n.*—**scat'ter=good**, *n.* A spendthrift.—**scat'ter-ing**, *n.* The act of one who or that which scatters; also, that which is scattered; esp., a small amount or number scattered or interspersed (as, "The bulk of them were mainly Gloucester boats, with a *scattering* from Provincetown, Harwich, Chatham, and some of the Maine ports": Kipling's "Captains Courageous," v.).—**scat'ter-ing**, *p. a.* That scatters or is scattered; dispersing in different directions; distributed here and there at irregular intervals; occurring sparsely or irregularly; straggling, as an assemblage of parts; of votes, cast in small numbers for various candidates.—**scat'ter-ing-ly**, *adv.*—**scat'ter=rug**, *n.* A rug suitable in size for placing here or there on a floor rather than for carpeting a room.

sca-tu-ri-ent (skạ-tū'ri-ẹnt), *a.* [L. *scaturiens* (-ent-), ppr. of *scaturire*, stream forth, < *scatere*, gush.] Streaming; flowing; gushing. Also fig.

scaup (skåp), *n.* [Origin uncertain.] Any of certain ducks of the genus *Æthyia* (*Aythya*), esp. *Æ. marila*, the male of which has a black head and neck and a white belly. Also **scaup'=duck**.

scaur (skår), *n.* Same as *scar*².

scav-enge (skav'ẹnj), *v.*; *-enged*, *-enging.* [Back-formation from *scavenger*.] **I.** *tr.* To cleanse from dirt or filth, as a street; also, to expel or sweep out burnt gases from (the

Scaup (*Æthyia marila*).

cylinder of an internal-combustion engine), as by a stroke of the piston, an incoming charge, or an admission of air; expel (burnt gases) from the cylinder in such a manner. **II.** *intr.* To act as a scavenger; also, to become scavenged of burnt gases.

scav-en-ger (skav'ẹn-jẻr), *n.* [For earlier *scavager*, officer who took *scavage*, or toll on goods brought in by merchant strangers, and later had charge of street-cleaning, < AF. *scawage* = OF. *escauwage*, inspection, < *escauwer*, inspect, akin to AS. *scēawian*, look at: see *show*.] A person whose employment it is to clean streets, etc., by scraping or sweeping together and carrying off dirt or filth (as, "An army of *scavengers* . . . was cleansing the asphalt roadway": Du Maurier's "Trilby," viii.); also, any of various animals feeding on decaying matter.

sce-na-ri-o (sē-nä'ri-ō, It. shä-nä'rē-ō), *n.*; pl. *-rios* (-ri-ōz), It. *-ri* (-rē). [It., < LL. *scenarius*, pertaining to stage scenes, < L. *scena*, E. *scene*.] An outline of the plot of a dramatic work, giving particulars as to the scenes, characters, situations, etc.; specif., the outline or manuscript of a moving-picture play, giving the action in the order in which it takes place, the description of scenes and characters, the printed matter to be shown on the screen, etc.—**sce-na-rist** (sē-nä'rist), *n.* A writer of scenarios for moving pictures.

scend (send), *v.* and *n.* *Naut.*, see *send*.

scene (sēn), *n.* [F. *scène*, < L. *scena*, *scæna*, stage, scene, < Gr. σκηνή, tent, stage.] The stage of a theater (obs. or rare); hence, the stage as standing for the drama or the theatrical profession (archaic); also, the place in which the action of a play or part of a play is supposed to occur; also, a division of a play or of an act of a play, now commonly representing what passes between certain of the actors in one place; hence, some particular incident or situation represented in the course of a play; also, the painted hangings, slides, etc., used to represent a place in which action is occurring in a play; sometimes, any one of these hangings, slides, etc.; also, the place where any action is carried on or anything takes place (as, "Paris, the *scene* of her former happiness," Mrs. Radcliffe's "Romance of the Forest," i.; to appear upon the *scene*); often, the setting of a story or the like; also, any view or picture presented to the eye, or to the mind (as, "See what delights in sylvan *scenes* appear!" Pope's "Summer," 59); also, an action, incident, or situation in real life; an episode, situation, or the like, as described in writing; also, an exhibition or outbreak of excited or violent feeling before others (as, "She lost her temper and made a fearful *scene* with Sarah": Arnold Bennett's "Hilda Lessways," v. 2).

scen-er-y (sē'nėr-i), *n.*; pl. *-ies* (-iz). [For earlier *scenary* (< It. *scenario*: see *scenario*), taken as if < *scene* + *-ery*.] The painted hangings, slides, etc., of a stage intended to represent the scene of the action; also, the general appearance of a place, regarded from a picturesque or pictorial point of view; the aggregate of features that give character to a landscape.

scene=shift-er (sēn'shif″tėr), *n.* One who shifts and arranges the scenes in a theater in accordance with the requirements of the play.

sce-nic (sē'nik or sen'ik). [F. *scénique*, < L. *scenicus*, *scænicus*, < Gr. σκηνικός, < σκηνή, E. *scene*.] **I.** *a.* Of or pertaining to the stage; dramatic; theatrical; also, of or pertaining to stage scenery or effect; also, of or pertaining to natural scenery; abounding in, or affording views of, fine scenery (as, a *scenic* railway, in an amusement-park or the like, a railway passing over or through structures formed in imitation of natural scenery); also, representing a scene, action, incident, or the like, as painting or sculpture. **II.** *n.* A moving picture of natural scenes.—**sce'ni-cal**, *a.* Scenic. —**sce'ni-cal-ly**, *adv.*

sce-nog-ra-phy (sē-nog'rạ-fi), *n.* [F. *scénographie*, < L. *scenographia*, < Gr. σκηνογραφία, < σκηνή, E. *scene*, + γράφειν, mark, draw, write.] The representing of objects, as buildings, according to the rules of perspective; also, scene-painting (used esp. with reference to ancient Greece). —**sce-nog'ra-pher**, *n.*

scent (sent), *v.* [OF. F. *sentir*, < L. *sentire* (pp. *sensus*), perceive, feel: see *sense*.] **I.** *tr.* To perceive or recognize by the sense of smell; hence, to perceive in any way; detect;

often, to have a suspicion of (as, "The people, *scenting* a dramatic situation, lingered": W. Churchill's "Coniston," i. 11); also, to impregnate with an odor; perfume. **II.** *intr.* To hunt by the sense of smell, as a hound; also, to have odor; be scented.—**scent,** *n.* The sense or faculty of smell; also, an odor left in passing, by means of which an animal or person may be traced; hence, a track or trail as indicated by such an odor or otherwise (often fig.); the small pieces of paper scattered to mark the trail in the game of hare and hounds; also, distinctive odor, esp. when agreeable; smell; fragrance; also, a fragrant liquid for perfuming; a perfume.—**scent′ed,** *a.* Having scent, or the faculty of smell (as, keen-*scented*); also, having a scent or odor (as, sweet-*scented*); esp., fragrant; perfumed.—**scent′less,** *a.* Having no scent or odor.

scep-ter, scep-tre (sep′tėr), *n.* [OF. *ceptre* (F. *sceptre*), < L. *sceptrum*, < Gr. σκῆπτρον, staff, scepter, < σκήπτειν, to prop: cf. *scape*[1].] A rod or wand, as of gold with jewels, borne in the hand as an emblem of regal or imperial power; hence, royal or imperial power or authority; sovereignty; supremacy.—**scep′tered, scep′tred,** *a.* Furnished with or bearing a scepter; hence, invested with regal authority; regal.

scep-tic (skep′tik), etc. See *skeptic*, etc.

schanz (skäns), *n.* [D. *schans*: see *sconce*[2].] A redoubt or similar protective work made of stones, earth, etc. [South Africa.]

Scha-per (shä′pėr) **glass.** A drinking-glass of a low cylindrical form, named from its originator, Johann Schaper, a German glass-painter of the 17th century.

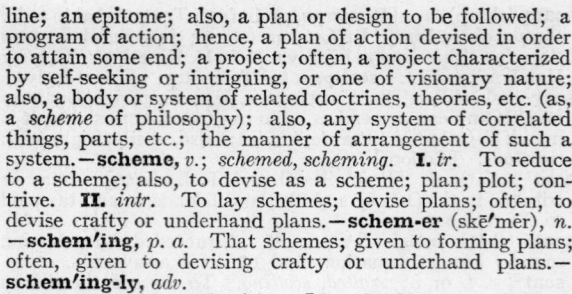

Schaper Glass. — Victoria and Albert Museum, London.

schat-chen (shät′shen), *n.* [Yiddish.] Among the Jews, one who arranges marriages for a fee; a marriage-broker.

sched-ule (sked′ūl, Brit. shed′ūl), *n.* [OF. *sedule* (F. *cédule*), < LL. *schedula*, ML. *scedula*, dim. of L. *scheda, scida*, leaf of paper, strip of papyrus, prob. < *scindere*, cut, split: see *shed*[2].] A slip or piece of parchment or paper containing writing†; also, a written or printed statement of details, often in classified or tabular form, forming an appendix or explanatory addition to another document; in general, a classified or tabular statement; a list, catalogue, or table; esp., a time-table.—**sched′ule,** *v. t.*; *-uled, -uling.* To make a schedule of; enter in a schedule; fix by a schedule.

scheel-ite (shēl′īt), *n.* [G. *scheelit*; named from K. W. *Scheele* (1742–86), Swedish chemist.] A mineral consisting of calcium tungstate, $CaWO_4$, occurring in tetragonal crystals and also massive, and usually of a yellowish, white, or brownish color.

schef-fer-ite (shef′ėr-īt), *n.* [Sw. *schefferit*; named from H. T. *Scheffer* (1710–59), Swedish chemist.] A variety of pyroxene, usually of a brownish color, containing manganese and often iron.

sche-ma (skē′mä), *n.*; pl. *-mata* (-mạ-tä). [L. *schema* or Gr. σχῆμα (σχηματ-): see *scheme*.] A diagram, plan, or scheme.—**sche-mat-ic** (skē-mat′ik), *a.* Pertaining to or of the nature of a schema, diagram, or scheme; diagrammatic.—**sche-mat′i-cal-ly,** *adv.*

sche-ma-tism (skē′mạ-tizm), *n.* [Gr. σχηματισμός, < σχηματίζειν, E. *schematize*.] The particular form or disposition of a thing; also, a schematic arrangement; also, schematic presentation.

sche-ma-tize (skē′mạ-tīz), *v. t.*; *-tized, -tizing.* [Gr. σχηματίζειν, form, arrange, < σχῆμα, E. *scheme*.] To reduce to or arrange according to a scheme.—**sche″ma-ti-za′tion** (-ti-zā′shọn), *n.*

scheme (skēm), *n.* [L. *schema*, < Gr. σχῆμα, form, figure, plan, outline, akin to ἔχειν, have, hold.] A diagram, map, or the like; esp., formerly, an astrological diagram of the heavens; also, an analytical or tabular statement; an out-line; an epitome; also, a plan or design to be followed; a program of action; hence, a plan of action devised in order to attain some end; a project; often, a project characterized by self-seeking or intriguing, or one of visionary nature; also, a body or system of related doctrines, theories, etc. (as, a *scheme* of philosophy); also, any system of correlated things, parts, etc.; the manner of arrangement of such a system.—**scheme,** *v.*; *schemed, scheming.* **I.** *tr.* To reduce to a scheme; also, to devise as a scheme; plan; plot; contrive. **II.** *intr.* To lay schemes; devise plans; often, to devise crafty or underhand plans.—**schem-er** (skē′mėr), *n.*—**schem′ing,** *p. a.* That schemes; given to forming plans; often, given to devising crafty or underhand plans.—**schem′ing-ly,** *adv.*

schenk=beer (shengk′bēr), *n.* [G. *schenkbier*, < *schenken*, pour out, retail, + *bier*, beer.] A mild German beer brewed for immediate use, and not stored like lager-beer.

scher-zan-do (sker-tsän′dō), *a.* [It., gerund of *scherzare*, to play, sport, < *scherzo*: see *scherzo*.] In *music*, playful; sportive.

scher-zo (sker′tsō), *n.*; pl. *-zos* (-tsōz), It. *-zi* (-tsē). [It., play, sport; from Teut. (cf. G. *scherz*).] In *music*, a movement or passage of light or playful character, esp. when forming the second or third division of a sonata or a symphony.

Schie-dam (skē-dam′), *n.* [From *Schiedam*, town in Holland.] Holland gin. See *gin*[3].

schil-ler (shil′ėr), *n.* [G., play of colors.] A peculiar, almost metallic luster, sometimes with iridescence, occurring on certain minerals.—**schil′ler-ize** (-īz), *v. t.*; *-ized, -izing.* To give a schiller to (a crystal) by developing microscopic inclusions along certain planes.—**schil″ler-i-za′tion** (-i-zā′shọn), *n.*

schip-per-ke (skip′ėr-kė), *n.* [D., 'little boatman.'] One of a breed of small black tailless dogs much used as watch-dogs on boats in Holland and Belgium.

schism (sizm), *n.* [OF. *scisme, cisme* (F. *schisme*), < LL. *schisma*, < Gr. σχίσμα, cleft, division, later schism, < σχίζειν, split, cleave: see *shed*[2].] Division, separation, or disunion; esp., a division into mutually opposed or hostile parties; sometimes, a breach or discord; specif., *eccles.*, a formal division within or separation from a church or religious body, on account of some difference of opinion with regard to matters of faith or discipline; also, the offense of causing or seeking to cause such a division; also, a sect or body formed by division within a church.—**schis-mat-ic** (siz-mat′ik), *n.* [OF. *scismatique* (F. *schismatique*), < LL. *schismaticus*, < Gr. σχισματικός.] **I.** *a.* Of or pertaining to schism; of the nature of schism; guilty of schism. **II.** *n.* One who promotes schism; one guilty of the sin of schism; an adherent of a schismatic body.—**schis-mat′i-cal,** *a.* Schismatic.—**schis-mat′i-cal-ly,** *adv.*—**schis-ma-tize** (siz′mạ-tīz), *v. i.*; *-tized, -tizing.* To act as a schismatic; advocate schismatic principles; belong to a schismatic body.

schist (shist), *n.* [F. *schiste*, < L. *schistos*, splitting readily, < Gr. σχιστός, adj. < σχίζειν, split: see *schism*.] Any of a class of crystalline rocks whose constituent minerals have a more or less parallel or foliated arrangement, due mostly to metamorphic action: as, mica-*schist* (a rock made up of quartz and mica).—**schis-tose, schis-tous** (shis′tōs, -tus), *a.*

schiz-o-carp (skiz′ō-kärp), *n.* [Gr. σχίζειν, split, + καρπός, fruit.] In *bot.*, a dry fruit which at maturity splits into two or more one-seeded indehiscent carpels.—**schiz-o-car′pous** (-kär′pus), *a.*

schiz-o-gen-e-sis (skiz-ō-jen′e-sis), *n.* [Gr. σχίζειν, split, + γένεσις, genesis.] In *biol.*, reproduction by fission.

schiz-o-my-cete (skiz″ō-mī-sēt′), *n.* [NL. *Schizomycetes*, pl., < Gr. σχίζειν, split, + μύκης (μυκητ-), fungus.] Any of the *Schizomycetes*, a class or group of vegetable organisms comprising the bacteria.—**schiz″o-my-ce′tous** (-sē′tus), *a.*—**schiz″o-my-co′sis** (-kō′sis), *n.* [NL.] In *pathol.*, any disease due to schizomycetes.

schiz-o-pel-mous (skiz-ō-pel′mus), *a.* [Gr. σχίζειν, split, + πέλμα, sole of the foot.] In *ornith.*, nomopelmous.

schiz-o-phre-ni-a (skiz-ō-frē′ni-ä), *n.* [Gr. σχίζειν, split, + Gr. φρήν, mind.] Cleavage of the personality.

schiz-o-phy-ceous (skiz-ō-fī′shius), *a.* [NL. *Schizophyceæ*, pl., < Gr. σχίζειν, split, + φῦκος, seaweed.] In *bot.*, belonging to the *Schizophyceæ*, a class or group of unicellular and multicellular green or bluish-green algæ, occurring in both salt and fresh water, and often causing pollution of drinking-water.

schiz-o-phyte (skiz'ō-fīt), *n.* [NL. *Schizophyta*, pl., < Gr. σχίζειν, split, + φυτόν, plant.] Any of the *Schizophyta*, a group of plants comprising the schizomycetes and the schizophyceous algæ, characterized by a simple structure and by reproduction by simple fission or by spores.—**schiz-o-phyt-ic** (-fīt'ik), *a.*

schiz-o-pod (skiz'ō-pod), *n.* [NL. *Schizopoda*, pl., < Gr. σχίζειν, split, + πούς (ποδ-), foot.] **I.** *n.* Any of the *Schizopoda*, an order or division of crustaceans with a soft carapace and with branched and apparently double thoracic appendages, which comprises the opossum-shrimps and their allies. **II.** *a.* Belonging or pertaining to the *Schizopoda.*—**schi-zop-o-dous** (ski-zop'ō-dus), *a.*

schlaf-rock (shläf'rok), *n.* [G., < *schlafen*, sleep, + *rock*, coat, gown.] A dressing-gown.

schlie-ren (shlē'ren), *n. pl.* [G., prop. pl. of (dial.) *schlier*, a boil.] In *petrog.*, streaks or irregularly shaped masses in an igneous rock, which differ in texture or composition from the main mass.—**schlie'ric**, *a.*

schloss (shlos), *n.* [G., lock, castle, akin to *schliessen*, shut, lock: cf. *slot*[1].] In German use, a castle.

schmier-kä-se (shmēr'kä"zè), *n.* [G., 'smear-cheese.'] Cottage cheese (see under *cottage*); smearcase.

schna-bel-kan-ne (shnä'bel-kän"è), *n.* [G., lit. 'beak can.'] A jug or vessel with a long, beak-like spout: specif. in *archæol.*

Schnabelkanne (Trojan).

schnap-per (shnap'ėr), *n.* [Altered form of the earlier name *snapper*, appar. under German influence.] A sparoid food-fish, *Pagrus unicolor*, abundant off the coasts of Australia and New Zealand.

schnapps, schnaps (shnaps), *n.* [G., dram or 'nip,' liquor, akin to *schnappen*, snap: cf. *snap*.] Holland gin (see *gin*[3]); hence, any spirituous liquor.

schnit-zel (shnit'sel), *n.* [G., akin to *schneiden*, cut.] A cutlet, esp. of veal.

schnor-rer (shnor'ėr), *n.* [Yiddish, < G. *schnurrer*, < *schnurren*, hum, go begging.] Among Jews, a beggar; also, one who sponges on others.

schol-ar (skol'är), *n.* [OF. *escoler* (F. *écolier*), < LL. *scholaris*, belonging to a school, < L. *schola*, E. *school*[2].] One who receives instruction in a school, or from a teacher; a pupil; a student; also, a person with reference to his ability at learning (as, an apt *scholar*; a poor *scholar*); also, in certain universities, colleges, and schools, a student who, because of merit, etc., is granted money or other aid to enable or assist him to pursue his studies; also, one who has acquired learning; a learned or erudite person.

schol-arch (skol'ärk), *n.* [Gr. σχολάρχης, < σχολή, school, + ἄρχειν, lead, rule.] The head of a school, esp. of an Athenian school of philosophy.

schol-ar-ly (skol'är-li), *a.* Pertaining to, characteristic of, or befitting a scholar (as, *scholarly* habits; *scholarly* attainments); having the qualities or attainments of a scholar, or learned or erudite (as, a *scholarly* person).—**schol'ar-li-ness**, *n.*—**schol'ar-ly**, *adv.* In the manner of a scholar: as, "Speak *scholarly* and wisely" (Shakspere's "Merry Wives of Windsor," i. 3. 2).

schol-ar-ship (skol'är-ship), *n.* The attainments of a scholar; learning; erudition; also, the position of a student in a university, college, or school who, because of merit or for some other reason, is granted money or other aid to support him or to assist him in the prosecution of his studies; the sum of money or other aid granted; a foundation to provide such money or aid.

scho-las-tic (skō-las'tik). [L. *scholasticus*, < Gr. σχολαστι-κός, < σχολάζειν, have leisure, devote one's time to learning, < σχολή: see *school*[2].] **I.** *a.* Of or pertaining to schools, scholars, or education (as, "She opened each *scholastic* day by reading fifteen verses from the Bible," Barrie's "Sentimental Tommy," xiv.; *scholastic* attainments); also, in accordance with the methods of schools; sometimes, pedantic; also, of, pertaining to, or characteristic of the teaching or methods of the schoolmen. **II.** *n.* A scholastic person; [sometimes *cap.*] a schoolman, a disciple of the schoolmen, or an adherent of scholasticism.—**scho-las'ti-cal-ly**, *adv.*—**scho-las'ti-cism** (-sizm), *n.* The doctrines of the schoolmen; the system of theological and philosophical teaching predominant in the middle ages, based chiefly upon the authority of the church fathers and of Aristotle and his commentators, and characterized by marked formality in methods; hence, narrow adherence to the teachings of the schools or to traditional doctrines and methods.

scho-li-a (skō'li-ä), *n.* Plural of *scholium.*

scho-li-ast (skō'li-ast), *n.* [MGr. σχολιαστής.] One who writes scholia upon an author; esp., an ancient commentator upon the classics.—**scho-li-as'tic**, *a.*

scho-li-um (skō'li-um), *n.*; pl. *-lia* (-li-ä). [ML., < Gr. σχόλιον, < σχολή, E. *school*[2].] An explanatory note or comment; esp., an ancient annotation upon a passage in a Greek or Latin author; also, a note added by an author or editor by way of illustration or amplification, as in a mathematical work.

school[1] (sköl), *n.* [ME. *scole, sculle*, prob. < MD. *schole* (D. *school*), school or shoal of fish, = AS. *scolu*, troop, multitude: cf. *shoal*[1].] A large number of fish, porpoises, whales, or the like, feeding or migrating together; hence, in general, a flock or company of animals.—**school**[1], *v. i.* To form into, or go in, a school, as fish.

school[2] (sköl), *n.* [AS. *scōl* = OF. *escole* (F. *école*), < L. *schola*, < Gr. σχολή, leisure, employment for leisure, learned discussion, lecture, school.] A place or establishment where instruction is given; a regular course of meetings of a teacher or teachers and students for exercises of instruction (as, a *school* held during the summer months); a session of an establishment for instruction (as, before *school*; after *school*; no *school* to-day); the body of students or pupils attending a school; fig., any place, situation, experience, etc., as a source of instruction or training (as, "the *school* of adversity": Scott's "Guy Mannering," xviii.); also, the body of pupils or followers of a particular master; a body or succession of persons who accept the same teachings or principles, as in philosophy, economics, etc., or who follow the same general method, as in painting, music, etc. (as, the Platonic *school* of philosophy; the Dutch *school* of painting); a set or body of persons who agree in certain principles, opinions, methods, etc., as those prevalent at a particular time (as, a politician of the new *school*; a gentleman of the old *school*); also, one of the various organized bodies of teachers and students which constituted a medieval university; a particular faculty or department of a modern university (as, the graduate *school*, medical *school*, or dental *school*); a building, room, etc., in a university, set apart for the use of one of the faculties or for some particular purpose; *pl.*, the faculties of a university; universities in general; the academic world; formerly, the schoolmen; also, *sing.*, *milit.* and *naval*, special drill regulations or drill applying to the individual ('school of the soldier'), the squad ('school of the squad'), or the like. —**common school, high school, primary school, public school, secondary school.** See under the first words. See also *grammar-school.*—**school**[2], *a.* Pertaining to or connected with a school or schools; also, pertaining to the schools or universities, or to the schoolmen.—**school**[2], *v. t.* To educate in or as in a school; teach; train; discipline; sometimes, to admonish; reprimand.—**school'a-ble**, *a.* Subject to the requirement of attendance at school.—**school'=board**, *n.* A local board or committee in charge of public education.—**school'=book**, *n.* A book for study in schools.—**school'=boy**, *n.* A boy attending a school.—**school'craft**, *n.* Knowledge taught in the schools. [Archaic.]—**school'=days**, *n. pl.* Days or time of attendance at school.—**school'=fel"low**, *n.* A schoolmate.—**school'=girl**, *n.* A girl attending school.—**school'=house**, *n.* A building in which a school is conducted.—**school'ing**, *n.*

The act of teaching, or the process of being taught, in or as in a school; education received in a school; also, cost of instruction; sometimes, reproof or reprimand.—**school'-ma'am, school'marm** (-mäm or -mam, -märm), *n.* A schoolmistress. [Colloq.]—**school'-maid,** *n.* A school-girl. See Shakspere's "Measure for Measure," i. 4. 47. [Obs. or archaic.]—**school'man** (-man), *n.*; pl. *-men.* [Sometimes *cap.*] A master in one of the schools or universities of the middle ages; one of the medieval writers who dealt with theology and philosophy after the methods of scholasticism; [*l. c.*] one versed in scholastic learning or engaged in scholastic pursuits.—**school'marm,** *n.* See *schoolma'am.*—**school'mas″ter,** *n.* A man who presides over or teaches in a school.—**school'mate,** *n.* A companion or associate at school.—**school'mis″tress,** *n.* A woman who presides over or teaches in a school.—**school'-room,** *n.* A room in which a school is conducted or pupils are taught. —**school'-ship,** *n.* A vessel used for the instruction and training of students of practical seamanship.—**school'-teach″er,** *n.* A teacher in a school.—**school'-teach″ing,** *n.*

schoon-er (skö'nėr), *n.* [Earlier *scooner, skooner*; said to be from a New England word (about 1713) *scoon,* skim along, as on water: cf. Sc. *scon,* skip over the surface of water, as stones.] A vessel with two or more masts and fore-and-aft sails, used for coasting, etc.; also, a prairie-schooner; also, a tall glass, as for beer, holding much more than an ordinary glass (colloq.).

s c h o r l (shôrl), *n.* [G. *schörl.*]

Four-masted Schooner.

Tourmalin, esp. a black variety.—**schor-la-ceous** (shôr-lā'shius), *a.* Of, resembling, or containing schorl.

schot-tische (shot'ish or sho-tēsh'), *n.* [G. *schottisch,* Scottish.] A round dance resembling the polka; its music.

schreck-lich-keit (shrek'lich-kīt), *n.* [G., < *schrecklich,* frightful, < *schreck,* fright, terror.] Frightfulness; frightful or terrifying methods or measures used as a means of coercion, as in war; terrorism.

schwa (shvä), *n.* [G.] In *phonetics,* a symbol (ə), an inverted e, denoting an obscured vowel sound.

sci-æ-nid (sī-ē'nid), *n.* [NL. *Sciænidæ,* pl., < *Sciæna,* the typical genus, < L. *sciæna,* < Gr. σκιαινα, kind of sea-fish.] **I.** *n.* Any of the *Sciænidæ,* a family of carnivorous acanthopterygian fishes including the drumfishes, certain kingfishes, etc. **II.** *a.* Belonging or pertaining to the sciænids. —**sci-æ'noid,** *a.* and *n.*

sci-a-gram (sī'a-gram), etc. Same as *skiagram,* etc.

sci-ag-ra-phy (sī-ag'ra-fi), *n.* [Gr. σκιαγραφια, < σκιαγράφος, drawing in light and shade, < σκιά, shadow, + γράφειν, mark, draw.] The art of delineating shadows in drawing, or of sketching objects with correct shading; also, skiagraphy (which see).—**sci-ag'ra-pher,** *n.*—**sci-a-graph'-i-cal** (-a-graf'i-kal), *a.*

sci-am-a-chy (sī-am'a-ki), *n.*; pl. *-chies* (-kiz). [Gr. σκιαμαχία, < σκιά, shadow, + μάχεσθαι, fight.] A fighting with a shadow; also, a sham combat, as for exercise.

sci-at-ic (sī-at'ik), *a.* [F. *sciatique,* < ML. *sciaticus, ischiaticus,* for L. *ischiadicus:* see *ischiadic.*] Of or pertaining to the hip; noting or pertaining to either of two nerves distributed along the back part of each thigh and leg; affecting the hip or the sciatic nerves.—**sci-at'i-ca** (-i-kä), *n.* [ML.] In *pathol.,* pain and tenderness in a sciatic nerve and its branches; sciatic neuritis; sciatic neuralgia.— **sci-at'i-cal,** *a.* Of, pertaining to, or affected with sciatica. —**sci-at'i-cal-ly,** *adv.*

sci-ence (sī'ens), *n.* [OF. F. *science,* < L. *scientia,* knowledge, < *sciens* (*scient-*), ppr. of *scire,* know.] Knowledge, as of facts or principles; knowledge gained by systematic study; skill resulting from training; also, a particular branch of knowledge; esp., a branch of knowledge or study dealing with a body of facts or truths systematically arranged and showing the operation of general laws (as, the *science* of botany; the mathematical *sciences*); also, systematized knowledge; esp., systematized knowledge of the facts and laws of the physical or material world.

sci-en-tial (sī-en'shal), *a.* [L. *scientia:* see *science.*] Of or pertaining to science or knowledge; also, having knowledge.

sci-en-tif-ic (sī-en-tif'ik), *a.* [LL. *scientificus,* < L. *sciens* (*scient-*), knowing, + *facere,* make.] Producing knowledge†; also, of or pertaining to science or the sciences (as, *scientific* studies; *scientific* nomenclature); occupied or concerned with science (as, *scientific* men; a *scientific* institution); also, regulated by or conforming to the principles of science (as, a *scientific* method; "Your Gaul is *scientific* about everything," H. Melville's "Omoo," xxix.); systematic; accurate.—**sci-en-tif'i-cal-ly,** *adv.*

sci-en-tism (sī'en-tizm), *n.* [See *scientist.*] The habit of thought or procedure of scientists; the mental attitude or the practice of scientists.

sci-en-tist (sī'en-tist), *n.* [L. *scientia,* E. *science.*] One versed in or devoted to science, esp. physical or natural science; also [*cap.*], a Christian Scientist (see under *Christian, a.*) (colloq.).—**sci-en-tis'tic,** *a.* Characteristic of, or having the character or methods of, a scientist.—**sci-en-tis'ti-cal-ly,** *adv.*

scil-i-cet (sil'i-set), *adv.* [L., for *scire licet,* 'it is permitted to know.'] To wit; namely: abbreviated *sc.* or *scil.*

scim-i-tar (sim'i-tär), *n.* See *simitar.*

scin-coid (sing'koid). [L. *scincus,* E. *skink:* see *-oid.*] **I.** *a.* Resembling the skinks, as certain lizards; also, belonging to the *Scincidæ,* the family of lizards comprising the skinks. **II.** *n.* A scincoid lizard.

scin-til-la (sin-til'ä), *n.* [L., a spark: cf. *tinsel* and *stencil.*] A spark; fig., a minute particle, or a trace (as, "There was approval in the lady's gaze. There was, however, not a *scintilla* of recognition in it": L. Merrick's "Conrad in Quest of His Youth," x.).

scin-til-lant (sin'ti-lant), *a.* [L. *scintillans* (*-ant-*), ppr.] Scintillating; sparkling: as, "But who can view the pointed rays, That from ·black eyes *scintillant* blaze?" (M. Green's "The Spleen").

scin-til-late (sin'ti-lāt), *v.*; *-lated, -lating.* [L. *scintillatus,* pp. of *scintillare,* < *scintilla,* a spark.] **I.** *intr.* To emit sparks; sparkle; flash. **II.** *tr.* To emit as or like sparks; flash forth.—**scin-til-la'tion** (-lā'shon), *n.* [L. *scintillatio*(*n-*).] The act of scintillating; a sparkling or flashing; a spark or flash; in *astron.,* the twinkling or tremulous motion of the light of the stars.—**scin'til-la-tor,** *n.*

sci-o-graph (sī'ō-gräf), etc. See *skiagraph,* etc.

sci-o-lism (sī'ō-lizm), *n.* [See *sciolous.*] Superficial knowledge: as, "the *sciolism* of literary or political adventurers" (George Eliot's "Middlemarch," xxxvii.).—**sci'o-list,** *n.* One who has only superficial knowledge; a pretender to deep knowledge.—**sci-o-lis'tic,** *a.*

sci-o-lous (sī'ō-lus), *a.* [LL. *sciolus,* a smatterer, dim. < L. *scius,* knowing, < *scire,* know.] Having only superficial knowledge; shallow.

sci-o-man-cy (sī'ō-man-si), *n.* [Gr. σκιά, shadow, shade, + μαντεία, divination.] Divination by means of the shades of the dead.

sci-on (sī'on), *n.* [OF. *cion* (F. *scion*); origin uncertain.] A shoot or twig, esp. one cut for grafting or planting; a cutting; hence, a descendant (as, "The present Mr. Chadwick was a worthy *scion* of a worthy stock": Trollope's "Warden," i.).

sci-re fa-ci-as (sī'rē fā'shi-as), *n.* [L., 'that you cause to know.'] In *law,* a writ requiring the party against whom it is brought to show cause why a judgment, letters patent, etc., should not be executed, vacated, or annulled.

scir-rhoid (sir'oid or skir'-), *a.* [See *-oid.*] Resembling a scirrhus.

scir-rhos-i-ty (si-ros'i-ti or ski-), *n.*; pl. *-ties* (-tiz). Scirrhous condition; a morbid induration, as of an organ.

scir-rhous (sir'us or skir'-), *a.* [NL. *scirrhosus.*] Proceeding from, of the nature of, or resembling a scirrhus; in general, indurated or hard (as, "Blow, flute, and stir the

---

fat, fāte, fär, fåll, åsk, fāre; net, mē, hėr; pin, pīne; not, nōte, mŏve, nôr; up, lūte, půll; oi, oil; ou, out; (lightened) aviȧry, ėlect, agȯny, intȯ, ụnite; (obscured) errȧnt, operȧ, ardȩnt, actȯr, natụre; ch, chip; g, go; th, thin; ᴛʜ, then; y, you;

stiff-set sprigs, And *scirrhous* roots and tendons!" Tennyson's "Amphion," 64).

scir-rhus (sir'us or skir'-), *n.*; pl. *scirrhuses* or *scirrhi* (-ī). [NL., for L. *scirros*, < Gr. σκίρρος, σκίρος, connected with σκιρός, hard.] In *pathol.*, a hard, indolent tumor; a hard cancer.

scis-sel (sis'el), *n.* [F. *cisaille*, connected with *ciseaux*, scissors, *cisoires*, large shears: see *scissors*.] The metal clippings or scrap left after certain operations; the plates from which circular blanks for coins have been cut.

scis-sile (sis'il), *a.* [L. *scissilis*, < *scindere*: see *scission*.] Capable of being cut or divided.

scis-sion (sish'on or sizh'-), *n.* [LL. *scissio(n-)*, < L. *scindere* (pp. *scissus*), cut, split: see *shed²*.] A cutting, dividing, or splitting; division; separation.

scis-sor (siz'or), *v. t.* [From *scissors*.] To cut with scissors. —**scis'sor-er**, *n.*

scis-sors (siz'orz), *n.* pl. or *sing.* [ME. *sisoures* (later spelling being due to confusion with L. *scissor*, one who cuts, < *scindere*: see *scission*), < OF. *cisoires* (in F. large shears), < LL. *cisoria*, pl. of *cisorium*, a cutting instrument, < L. *cædere*, cut.] A cutting instrument consisting of two blades (with handles) so pivoted together that their edges work against each other from opposite sides of material to be cut: often called a *pair of scissors*. Cf. *shears*.

scis-sor-tail (siz'or-tāl), *n.* A bird, *Milvulus forficatus*, a species of flycatcher of the southern U. S. and Mexico, with a deeply cleft tail which it opens and closes like a pair of scissors.

scis-sure (sish'ūr or sizh'-), *n.* [L. *scissura*, < *scindere*: see *scission*.] A longitudinal opening in a body, made by cutting; a fissure; fig., a division or schism; in *anat.*, etc., a natural cleft in an organ or part.

sci-u-rine (sī'ū-rin), *a.* [L. *sciurus*, squirrel: see *squirrel*.] Of or pertaining to the squirrels. —**sci-u-roid** (sī-ū'roid or sī'ū-), *a.* [See *-oid*.] Squirrel-like; belonging to the squirrel family (*Sciuridæ*); in *bot.*, resembling a squirrel's tail, as the spikes of certain grasses.

Scissortail.

sclaff (sklaf), *v. i.* or *t.* [Orig. Sc., and prob. imit.] In *golf*, to scrape (the ground) with the club before hitting the ball in striking; hit (the ball) after having scraped the ground with the club.—**sclaff**, *n.* In *golf*, a sclaffing stroke.

Sclav (skläv), etc. See *Slav*, etc.

scle-ren-chy-ma (sklē-reng'ki-mä), *n.* [NL., < Gr. σκληρός, hard, + *-enchyma* as in *parenchyma*.] In *bot.*, tissue composed of thickened and indurated cells from which the protoplasm has disappeared.

scle-ri-a-sis (sklē-rī'a-sis), *n.* [NL., < Gr. σκληρίασις, < σκληρός, hard.] In *pathol.*, hardening or induration of a tissue or part.

scle-rite (sklē'rīt), *n.* [Gr. σκληρός, hard.] In *zoöl.*, any chitinous, calcareous, or similar hard part, plate, spicule, or the like.—**scle-rit-ic** (sklē-rit'ik), *a.*

sclero-. Form of Gr. σκληρός, hard, used in combination, sometimes with special reference to the sclerotic coat of the eyeball.

scle-ro-der-ma, scle-ro-der-mi-a (sklē-rō-dėr'mä, -mi-ä), *n.* [NL., < Gr. σκληρός, hard, + δέρμα, skin.] In *pathol.*, a disease in which the skin becomes hard and rigid.

scle-roid (sklē'roid), *a.* [Gr. σκληροειδής, < σκληρός, hard, + εἶδος, form.] In *bot.* and *zoöl.*, hard or indurated.

scle-ro-ma (sklē-rō'mä), *n.*; pl. *-mata* (-ma-tä). [NL., < Gr. σκλήρωμα, < σκληρός, hard.] In *pathol.*, an induration of tissues; scleriasis.

scle-rom-e-ter (sklē-rom'e-tėr), *n.* [See *sclero-* and *-meter*.] An instrument for determining with precision the degree of hardness of a substance, esp. a mineral.

scle-ro-sal (sklē-rō'sal), *a.* Pertaining to sclerosis.

scle-ro-scope (sklē'rō-skōp), *n.* [See *sclero-* and *-scope*.] An instrument for testing the hardness of metal.

scle-rose (sklē-rōs'), *v. t.* or *i.*; *-rosed*, *-rosing*. To affect or become affected with sclerosis; harden.

scle-ro-sis (sklē-rō'sis), *n.*; pl. *-roses* (-rō'sēz). [NL., < Gr. σκλήρωσις, < σκληρός, hard.] In *pathol.*, a hardening or induration of a tissue or part; increase of connective tissue or the like at the expense of more active tissue; in *bot.*, a hardening of a tissue or cell-wall by thickening or lignification.

scle-rot-ic (sklē-rot'ik). [= OF. *sclirotique* (F. *sclérotique*), adj. and n., through ML. (cf. *sclerotica*) < Gr. σκληρός, hard.] **I.** *a.* In *anat.*, designating or pertaining to the hard, white outer coat (sclerotica) of the eyeball; in *pathol.* and *bot.*, pertaining to or affected with sclerosis; indurated. **II.** *n.* In *anat.*, the sclerotica.—**scle-rot'i-ca** (-i-kä), *n.* [ML.] In *anat.*, a dense, white, fibrous membrane forming with the cornea the external covering of the eyeball.—**scle-ro-ti-tis** (sklē-rō-tī'tis), *n.* [NL.] In *pathol.*, inflammation of the sclerotica.—**scle-ro-tit'ic** (-tit'ik), *a.*

scle-rot-o-my (sklē-rot'ō-mi), *n.* [See *sclero-* and *-tomy*.] In *surg.*, incision into the sclerotica, as for the extraction of foreign bodies.

scoff¹ (skôf or skof), *n.* [Orig. in South African use: cf. D. *schofttijd*, meal-time.] Food; a meal. [Slang.]

scoff² (skôf or skof), *n.* [ME. *scof*, *skof*: cf. Icel. *skop*, *skaup*, mockery, Dan. *skuffe*, deceive, delude.] Mockery or derision (now rare); also, an expression of mockery, derision, or derisive scorn, or a jeer or gibe (as, "with *scoffs* and scorns and contumelious taunts": Shakspere's "1 Henry VI.," i. 4. 39); also, an object of mockery or derision (as, "The principles of liberty were the *scoff* of every grinning courtier": Macaulay's "Essays," Milton).—**scoff²**, *v.* **I.** *intr.* To speak derisively; mock; jeer: often with *at*: as, "Fools, who came to *scoff*, remain'd to pray" (Goldsmith's "Deserted Village," 180); "The one preserved an open mind, the other *scoffed* at apparitions" (Eden Phillpotts's "Grey Room," ii.). **II.** *tr.* To jeer at; deride. [Now rare.] —**scoff'er**, *n.*—**scoff'ing-ly**, *adv.*—**scoff'law**, *n.* [A word coined in 1924.] One who scoffs at and disobeys the law prohibiting the manufacture and sale of intoxicating liquors for beverage purposes (18th Amendment to the Constitution of the U. S.); a lawless drinker. [Colloq., U. S.]

scold (skōld), *n.* [ME. *scold*; appar. from Scand., and the same word as *scald³*, *skald*: cf. Icel. *skáldskapr*, a libel in verse.] A person, esp. a woman, addicted to vituperative or abusive speech; also, a scolding or rebuke (obs. or Sc.). —**scold**, *v.* **I.** *intr.* To use abusive language; chide or find fault, esp. with vehemence or persistence. **II.** *tr.* To address with angry reproaches or reproofs; berate; chide: as, "She *scolds* the servants from morning till night" (Thackeray's "Vanity Fair," lxi.).—**scold'er**, *n.*

scol-e-cite (skol'ē-sīt), *n.* [G. *scolezit*, < Gr. σκώληξ (σκωληκ-), worm; from its curling up sometimes before the blowpipe.] A mineral, a hydrous silicate of calcium and aluminium, occurring in (usually) acicular crystals and also massive, and commonly white.

sco-lex (skō'leks), *n.*; pl. *scoleces* (skō-lē'sēz), erron. *scolices* (skol'i-sēz). [NL., < Gr. σκώληξ (pl. σκώληκες), worm.] In *zoöl.*, the larva of a tapeworm or similar parasitic worm; hence, the part (the head) into which such a larva develops in the adult form, situated at one extremity of the tapeworm or the like, and serving as an organ of attachment.

sco-li-on (skō'li-on), *n.*; pl. *-lia* (-li-ä). [Gr. σκόλιον, < σκολιός, curved, crooked.] In *Gr. antiq.*, a short song sung in turn by the guests at a banquet.

scol-i-o-sis (skol-i-ō'sis), *n.* [NL., < Gr. σκολίωσις, < σκολιός, curved, crooked.] In *pathol.*, lateral curvature of the spine.

scol-lop (skol′ọp), etc. See *scallop*, etc.

scol-o-pen-drid (skol-ọ-pen′drid), *n.* [NL. *Scolopendridæ*, pl., < L. *scolopendra*, < Gr. σκολόπενδρα, kind of multiped.] In *zoöl.*, any of the *Scolopendridæ*, a family of myriapods including many large and poisonous centipedes.

scom-broid (skom′broid), *a.* [Gr. σκόμβρος, mackerel: see *-oid*.] Resembling the mackerel; belonging or pertaining to the mackerel family (*Scombridæ*) or the superfamily (*Scombroidea*) containing the mackerel family.

sconce[1] (skons), *n.* [OF. *esconse*, < ML. *absconsa*, dark lantern, prop. fem. of L. *absconsus*, pp. of *abscondere*, hide: see *abscond*.] A form of lantern or candlestick formerly carried in the hand; now, a more or less ornamental bracket projecting from a wall, etc., for holding one or more candles or other lights (as, "There were *sconces* on the walls for candles," Besant's "All Sorts and Conditions of Men," ix.; "Their leader took off an electric bulb from a *sconce* on the wall," Eden Phillpotts's "Grey Room," ii.).

sconce[2] (skons), *n.* [D. *schans* = MLG. *schantze* = G. *schanze*, sconce; origin uncertain: cf. *schanz*.] In *fort.*, a small detached fort or earthwork, as for defense of a pass or ford; hence, in general, a shelter, screen, or protection (obs. or rare).—**sconce**[2], *v. t.*; *sconced*, *sconcing*. To fortify; shelter; ensconce. [Obs. or rare.]

sconce[3] (skons), *n.* [Origin uncertain: cf. *sconce*[1] and *sconce*[2].] The head or skull, esp. the top of the head (archaic: as, "Peter Stuyvesant dealt him a thwack over the *sconce* with his wooden leg," Irving's "Knickerbocker's New York," vi. 8); also, sense or wit (archaic); also, a mulct or fine, as among undergraduates at Oxford University, England.— **sconce**[3], *v. t.*; *sconced*, *sconcing*. To mulct or fine, as among Oxford University undergraduates for some breach of conventional usage.

scone (skōn or skon), *n.* [Cf. MD. *schoonbrot*, fine bread.] A flat, round cake of wheat-flour, barley-meal, or the like, cooked on a griddle; one of the four quadrant-shaped pieces into which it is often cut. [Sc.]

scoop (sköp), *n.* [ME. *scope*: cf. MLG. and MD. *schōpe*, scoop, also MD. *schoppe*, D. *schop*, shovel.] A ladle or ladle-like utensil; a kind of shovel with a deep, hollow receptacle, and commonly with a short handle, for taking up and carrying loose materials, as flour or sugar; a spoon-shaped or gouge-like instrument for removing or hollowing out something; also, the quantity taken up at one time by any such instrument; also, a place scooped or hollowed out; sometimes, a natural hollow; also, an act of scooping; a movement as of scooping; also, in fig. use, a big haul, as of money made in speculation or in some other way (colloq.); in journalistic slang, a beat (as, "The editor hears 'stories' that, if printed, would be a '*scoop*' which would cause his publication to be talked about": Bok's "Americanization of Edward Bok," xxvii.).—**scoop**, *v. t.* To take up or out with or as with a scoop; gather or collect with a scoop; gather or appropriate as if with a scoop (often with *in*: colloq.); also, to empty with a scoop; form a hollow or hollows in, with or as with a scoop (as, "The ground . . . was *scooped* into valleys and dales": C. B. Brown's "Wieland," v.); also, to form with or as with a scoop (as, "a hollow *scooped* out of the living rock": Kinglake's "Eothen," xvi.); also, in journalistic slang, to get the better of by a scoop or beat, as a rival newspaper.—**scoop′er**, *n.*

scoot (sköt), *v.* [Appar. orig. Sc.; perhaps from Scand. and akin to E. *shoot*.] **I.** *tr.* To squirt (liquid: Sc.); also, to send or impel at high speed (colloq.). **II.** *intr.* To spurt, as liquid (Sc.); also, to dart, go, or make off swiftly or hastily (colloq.).—**scoot**, *n.* The act or an act of scooting; a swift, darting movement or course. [Colloq.]—**scoot′er**, *n.* One that scoots, or goes swiftly (colloq.); esp., a kind of sailboat with runners, for use on either water or ice (local, U. S.: see cut in next column); also, a swift, powerful motor-boat which skims over the surface of the water like a hydroplane,

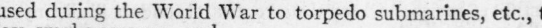
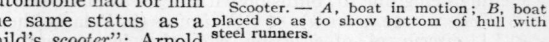

used during the World War to torpedo submarines, etc., to lay smoke-screens, and for other purposes; also, a kind of low vehicle with two wheels, one in front of the other, and a tread or footboard between them, and sometimes with a saddle or seat, which is steered by a handle-bar, and propelled by pushing against the ground with one foot or both feet, as in simple forms used by children, or by motor, as in more elaborate forms (as, "An automobile had for him the same status as a child's *scooter*": Arnold Bennett's "Mr. Prohack," v.).—**scoot′er**, *v. i.* To sail, go, or travel in or on a scooter.

Scooter.— *A*, boat in motion; *B*, boat placed so as to show bottom of hull with steel runners.

scope (skōp), *n.* [It. *scopo*, < L. *scopos*, < Gr. σκοπός, mark, aim, also watcher, < σκοπ-: see *-scope*.] A mark for shooting or aiming at†; also, an aim, purpose, or object (now rare: as, "Thy coming hither, though I know thy *scope*, I bid not, or forbid," Milton's "Paradise Regained," i. 494); also, extent or range of view, outlook, application, operation, effectiveness, etc. (as, a mind of limited *scope*; an investigation of wide *scope*; to act within the *scope* of one's powers; beyond the *scope* of speculation); also, space for movement or activity (as, "O, cut my lace in sunder, that my pent heart May have some *scope* to beat!" Shakspere's "Richard III.," iv. 1. 35); opportunity for operation (as, to give one's fancy full *scope*; "I could find you an occupation . . . in which your talents would have free *scope*," Borrow's "Romany Rye," iv.); also, extent in space; a tract or area; length, or a length (as, "The yacht's gig was towing easily at the end of the long *scope* of line": J. Conrad's "Rescue," i. 3); specif., the length of cable at which a vessel rides when at anchor.

-scope. [NL. *-scopium*, < Gr. -σκοπος, adj. formative (see *telescope*) < σκοπ-, σκεπ-, as in σκοπεῖν, view, σκέπτεσθαι, look (see *spy*); many E. words in *-scope* being referred to Gr. σκοπεῖν.] A noun termination occurring in many names of instruments or devices for use in viewing, observing, or showing something, as in *anemoscope*, *gyroscope*, *kaleidoscope*, *microscope*, *periscope*, *stethoscope*, *telescope*. Cf. *-scopy*.

sco-po-lam-ine (skō-pō-lam′in), *n.* [G. *scopolamin*, < NL. *Scopola* or *Scopolia*, genus of plants (named from G. A. *Scopoli*, of Pavia), + G. *amin*, amine.] In *chem.* and *phar.*, a crystalline alkaloid obtained from the rhizome of a low European plant, *Scopola* (or *Scopolia*) *carniolica*, and from certain other solanaceous plants: used as a depressant and mydriatic, and in producing the so-called 'twilight sleep,' and to some extent, because of its effect upon the mind, upon criminals and others from whom confessions are desired. Cf. *hyoscine*.

sco-po-line (skō′pō-lin), *n.* [See *scopolamine*.] In *chem.*, a crystalline alkaloid obtained by decomposing scopolamine.

scop-u-late (skop′ū-lāt), *a.* [L. *scopulæ*, little broom, dim. of *scopæ*, twigs, broom.] In *zoöl.*, broom-shaped; brush-like.

-scopy. [Gr. -σκοπία, < -σκοπος: see *-scope*.] A noun termination meaning 'viewing,' 'observation,' 'examination,' or the like, as in *aëroscopy*, *cranioscopy*, *microscopy*, *telescopy*, many such words being associated with nouns ending in *-scope*.

scor-bu-tic (skôr-bū′tik), *a.* [F. *scorbutique*, < *scorbut*, scurvy, prob. from LG. or D.: cf. MLG. *schorbūk*, D. *scheurbuik*, Icel. *skyrbjūgr*, scurvy.] Pertaining to, of the nature of, or affected with scurvy.

scorch (skôrch), *v.* [ME. *scorchen*; perhaps from Scand.] **I.** *tr.* To burn superficially or slightly; affect in color, taste, etc., by slightly burning; parch or shrivel with heat; hence, to affect injuriously as if by heat. **II.** *intr.* To be or become scorched; also, to ride at high speed, as on a bicycle or in a motor vehicle (colloq.).—**scorched earth**, a state in which all things useful to an invading army are destroyed, as by fire: also used adjectively.—**scorch**, n. A superficial burn; also, scorching effect; also, a fast ride, as on a bicycle or in a motor vehicle (colloq.).—**scorch'er**, n. One who or that which scorches; a very hot day (colloq.); one who rides at an excessive speed, as on a bicycle or in a motor vehicle (colloq.).—**scorch'ing**, p. a. That scorches; burning; withering; very hot; caustic or scathing, as a criticism; moving at a high rate of speed (colloq.).—**scorch'ing-ly**, adv.

scor-da-to (skôr-dä′tō), a. [It., pp. of scordare, put out of tune.] In music, put out of tune; tuned in an unusual manner, for the purpose of producing particular effects. —**scor-da-tu'ra** (-tö′rä), n. [It.] In music, an intentional deviation from the usual tuning of a stringed instrument for some special effect.

score (skōr), n.; pl. scores or (see def.) score. [From Scand.: cf. Icel. skor, notch, incision, tally (notched for each twenty), hence twenty, akin to E. shear.] A notch, groove, cut, or scratch; a stroke, mark, or line; a line drawn as a boundary, as a mark at which competitors stand in beginning a race, etc.; esp., a notch cut or a mark made in keeping an account or record; hence, a reckoning or account, as of charges, kept by means of notches, marks, etc.; any account showing indebtedness; an amount recorded as due; also, account, reason, or ground (as, to be excused on the score of illness); also, the record of points made by the competitors in a game or match; the aggregate of points made by a side or individual; the scoring of a point or points; also, a group or set of twenty (pl. scores or, as after a numeral, score); in music, a written or printed piece of music with all the vocal and instrumental parts arranged on staves, one under another; the written or printed piece of music for a particular voice or instrument in a concerted composition.—**score**, v.; scored, scoring. **I.** tr. To make notches, cuts, etc., in; mark with strokes or lines (as, "He . . . scored the ground with his stick": H. Mackenzie's "Man of Feeling," xl.); also, to draw a line through in order to cancel; also, fig., to censure severely (U. S.: as, "The first citizen should have been scored as he deserved, and held up to the contempt of his fellow-townsmen," W. Churchill's "Coniston," ii. 16); also, to produce by cutting, marking, etc., as marks or figures; also, to record by notches, marks, etc., or in any way, as something of which an account is to be kept; esp., to write down as a debt; record (a person) as a debtor; also, to gain for addition to one's score in a game; make a score of; hence, to gain or win (a success, etc.: as, "A farcical comedy had scored a great success," L. Merrick's "Conrad in Quest of His Youth," vii.); in music, to write out in score; also, to orchestrate. **II.** intr. To make notches, cuts, marks, or lines on something; also, to keep score, as of a game; also, to make a point or points in a game or contest; hence, to win an advantage; achieve a success.—**scor-er** (skōr′ėr), n.

sco-ri-a (skō′ri-ạ), n.; pl. scoriæ (-ē). [L., < Gr. σκωρία, dross, < σκῶρ, dung.] The refuse, dross, or slag left after smelting or melting metals; also, a clinker-like cellular lava. —**sco-ri-a'ceous** (-ā′shius), a. Of the nature of or resembling scoria.—**sco'ri-fi-ca'tion** (-fi-kā′shọn), n. The act of scorifying; in assaying, a process by which a gold or silver ore is fused with lead, borax, etc., in order to form scoria or slag and a lead button containing the silver and gold; the fusion of such a lead button (or a lead button obtained in other ways) in order to make it smaller or to remove more impurities and thus make it more adaptable for cupellation. —**sco'ri-fi-er** (-fī-ėr), n. That which scorifies; a flat bowl-like vessel used in scorification.—**sco'ri-form**, a. In the form of scoria; scoria-like.—**sco'ri-fy** (-fī), v. t.; -fied, -fying. [See -fy.] To reduce to scoria; subject to scorification.

scorn (skôrn), n. [ME. scorn, for scarn, < OF. escarn, escharn; from Teut.] Orig., mockery or derision; hence, in modern use, derisive, open, or unqualified contempt (as, "Mr. Rossiter had the most withering scorn for ordinary sentimental nonsense": Mrs. Stowe's "Oldtown Folks," xxxiii.); also, a derisive or contemptuous action or speech (archaic: as, "Unto him did fall Full many a scorn upon that day to get," W. Morris's "Jason," ii. 129); also, an object of derision or contempt (as, "Oh! aren't you the scorn of women?" Synge's "Tinker's Wedding," ii.).—**scorn**, v.

[OF. escarnir, escharnir.] **I.**† intr. To mock; scoff; jeer. **II.** tr. To deride†; also, to treat or regard with scorn (as, to scorn a hypocrite; to scorn all meanness); reject or refuse with scorn (as, "I scorn the counterfeit sentiment you offer," C. Brontë's "Jane Eyre," xxxiv.; "We scorn to take any unfair advantage," Marryat's "King's Own," vii.).—**scorn'er**, n.—**scorn'ful**, a. Full of scorn; derisive; contemptuous.—**scorn'ful-ly**, adv.—**scorn'ful-ness**, n.

scor-o-dite (skor′ọ-dīt), n. [G. skorodit, < Gr. σκόροδον, garlic; from its odor when heated.] A mineral, a hydrous ferric arsenate, occurring in orthorhombic crystals and also in earthy form, and usually of a leek-green or brown color.

scor-pæ-nid (skôr-pē′nid), n. [NL. Scorpænidæ, pl., < L. scorpæna: see scorpene.] Any of the Scorpænidæ, a family of marine acanthopterygian fishes.—**scor-pæ'noid**, a. and n.

scor-pene (skôr′pēn), n. [= F. scorpène = Sp. escorpina, < L. scorpæna, < Gr. σκόρπαινα, kind of spiny fish, < σκορπίος, scorpion: cf. sculpin.] A scorpænoid fish, Scorpæna guttata, abundant off the southern coast of California.

Scorpene.

Scor-pi-o (skôr′pi-ō), n. [L. scorpio, also scorpius: see scorpion.] The Scorpion, a zodiacal constellation; also, the eighth sign of the zodiac. See zodiac.

scor-pi-oid (skôr′pi-oid), a. [Gr. σκορπιοειδής, < σκορπίος, scorpion, + εἶδος, form.] Resembling a scorpion; belonging to the Scorpionida, the order of arachnids comprising the scorpions; also, curved (at the end) like the tail of a scorpion or in a flat spiral; circinate.

scor-pi-on (skôr′pi-ọn), n. [OF. F. scorpion, < L. scorpio(n-), scorpius, < Gr. σκορπίος, scorpion.] Any of the arachnids, of warm and tropical countries, constituting the order Scorpionida, somewhat resembling miniature lobsters in form, and having an abdomen ending in a slender tail-like part (often curled up over the back) which is tipped with a poisonous sting; also, any of various other arachnids (see whip-scorpion) or other animals (as certain lizards) likened to the arachnids of the order Scorpionida; also, an old military engine for throwing stones, etc.; also, a (supposed) whip or scourge armed with spikes or the like (cf. 1 Kings, xii. 11); also [cap.], in astron., the zodiacal constellation or sign Scorpio.—**Scorpion's Heart**, in astron., the bright (red) star Antares, in the constellation Scorpio.—**scor-pi-on'ic** (-on′ik), a.

Scorpion (Buthus carolinus), natural size.

scot[1] (skot), n. [ME. scot, prob. from Scand.: cf. Icel. skot, contribution, also the related OF. escot (F. écot), AS. gescot, and E. shot[3] and shot[2].] A payment or charge; one's share of a payment; an assessment or tax.—**scot and lot**, a municipal tax assessed proportionately upon the members of a community; fig., full payment.

Scot[2] (skot), n. [LL. Scotus, Scottus.] One of an ancient Gaelic people who came from northern Ireland about the 6th century and settled in the northwestern part of Great Britain, and from whom Scotland was named; hence, a native or inhabitant of Scotland; a Scotchman.

scotch[1] (skoch), v. t. [ME. scocchen; origin uncertain.] To cut, gash, or score; also, to inflict such hurt upon as to render harmless for the time (from the use in Shakspere's "Macbeth," iii. 2. 13); also, to crush, or stamp out, as something dangerous.—**scotch**[1], *n.* A cut, gash, or score; also, a line scored or marked on the ground in the game of hop-scotch.

scotch[2] (skoch), *n.* [Origin uncertain.] A block or wedge put under a wheel, barrel, or the like, to prevent moving or slipping.—**scotch**[2], *v. t.* To block or prop with a scotch, as a wheel.

Scotch[3] (skoch), *a.* [Contr. of *Scottish*.] Of or pertaining to the Scots, Scotland, or the dialect of English spoken in Scotland.—**Scotch cap,** any of several forms of brimless cap worn in Scotland, as the glengarry or the balmoral. —**Scotch mist,** a very dense, wet, penetrating mist like that common in the Highlands of Scotland; also (humorously), a steady, soaking rain.—**Scotch pebble,** any of various kinds of agate, jasper, etc., found in Scotland, used in jewelry.—**Scotch terrier,** one of a breed of terriers with short legs and shaggy hair, of Scotch origin.—**Scotch woodcock,** a dish composed of eggs, milk, butter, etc., cooked together, seasoned with anchovy paste, and served on toast. —**Scotch**[3], *n.* The people of Scotland collectively; also, the dialect of English spoken by the people of Scotland; also, Scotch whisky (colloq.).—**Scotch'=I'rish,** *a.* Belonging or pertaining to a part of the population of northern Ireland descended from Scotch settlers.—**Scotch'man** (-man), *n.*; pl. *-men.* A man of Scotch origin.— **Scotch'wom''an,** *n.*; pl. *-women* (-wim''en).

sco-ter (skō'tėr), *n.* [Origin uncertain.] Any of the large ducks constituting the genus *Œdemia,* common in northern regions and seas: in the U. S. commonly called *coot.*

Male Black Scoter (*Œdemia nigra*).

scot=free (skot'frē'), *a.* [See *scot*[1].] Free from payment of scot; hence, exempt from injury, punishment, etc., or unharmed (as, "Another always got off *scot-free* whatever mischief he did": W. De Morgan's "Joseph Vance," xi.).

sco-ti-a (skō'ti-ä or skō'shiạ), *n.* [L., < Gr. σκοτία, lit. 'darkness.'] In *arch.,* a concave molding, as in the base of a column.

Sco-tism (skō'tizm), *n.* [From *Scotus* (see def.).] The doctrines of Joannes Duns Scotus (about 1265– about 1308), the scholastic theologian.—**Sco'tist,** *n.*

Scot-o- (skot'ō- or skō'tō-). Form of LL. *Scotus,* a Scot, used in combination, in the sense of 'Scotch,' as in *Scoto-Celtic, Scoto-Irish.*

Base of Column (Ionic) of the Erechtheum, Athens. — *a,* scotia.

sco-to-ma (skō-tō'mä), *n.*; pl. *-mata* (-mạ-tä). [LL., < Gr. σκότωμα, < σκότος, darkness.] In *pathol.,* loss of vision in a part of the visual field.

Scots (skots). [Earlier *Scottis,* for *Scottish*.] **I.** *a.* Scottish or Scotch. **II.** *n.* The Scottish dialect of English.— **Scots'man** (-man), *n.*; pl. *-men.* A Scotchman: as, "I think my father was a *Scotsman*" (Barrie's "Sentimental Tommy," xv.).

Scot-ti-cism (skot'i-sizm), *n.* [LL. *Scotticus, Scoticus,* Scottish.] An idiom peculiar to the Scottish dialect of English; also, Scottish character or sympathies.

Scot-tish (skot'ish). **I.** *a.* Of or pertaining to the Scots, their country, the dialect of English spoken there, or its literature. **II.** *n.* The Scottish dialect of English.

scoun-drel (skoun'drel). [Origin obscure.] **I.** *n.* A thoroughly unprincipled or dishonorable man; an unscrupulous villain: as, "He saw these high-born *scoundrels* . . . when brought to trial, purchasing the consciences of their judges" (Froude's "Cæsar," xv.). **II.** *a.* Scoundrelly: as, "these *scoundrel* Doones" (Blackmore's "Lorna Doone," xv.); *scoundrel* behavior. [Now rare.]—**scoun'drel-dom** (-dom), *n.* Scoundrels collectively, or their ways or habits.— **scoun'drel-ism,** *n.* The character or conduct of a scoundrel; also, a scoundrelly action (as, "A dirty little boy! Capable no doubt of a thousand kindred *scoundrelisms*": H. G. Wells's "Soul of a Bishop," i.).—**scoun'drel-ly,** *a.* Having the character of a scoundrel; also, pertaining to or characteristic of a scoundrel.

scour[1] (skour), *v.* [ME. *scouren,* prob. through D. or LG. < OF. *escurer* (F. *écurer*), cleanse, scour, < L. *ex-,* out, + *curare,* care for.] **I.** *tr.* To cleanse or polish by hard rubbing, as with some suitable implement or substance (as, to *scour* pots and pans; "the . . . female who was *scouring* the steps," Thackeray's "Vanity Fair," liv.); remove dirt, grease, etc., from by rubbing or by any cleansing process (as, to *scour* soiled clothing; to *scour* woolens); clear out (a channel, drain, etc.) by removing dirt, etc., or by flushing with water; also, to purge thoroughly, as an animal; also, in general, to clear or rid of what is undesirable (as, "*Scour* me this famous realm of enemies," Beaumont and Fletcher's "Knight of the Burning Pestle," v.; "to *scour* the seas of these cruel marauders," Marryat's "King's Own," xlvi.); also, to sweep with gun-fire; also, to remove by or as by cleansing; cleanse away; get rid of; efface. **II.** *intr.* To rub a surface in order to cleanse or polish it; remove dirt, grease, etc., by rubbing or by any cleansing process; also, to act as a purge; also, to be purged; of cattle, to have diarrhea.—**scour**[1], *n.* A scouring; esp., the action of a current or flow of water in clearing away deposits; also, the current itself, or the place scoured; also, an apparatus or a material used in scouring; also, a kind of diarrhea in cattle.

scour[2] (skour), *v.* [ME. *scouren, scuren*; origin uncertain.] **I.** *intr.* To move rapidly or energetically (as, "The horsemen . . . gave reins to their steeds and *scoured* for the frontier," Irving's "Conquest of Granada," xvi.; "Aston, the general in command, *scoured* up a steep mound," Morley's "Oliver Cromwell," iv. 2); range about, as in search of something. **II.** *tr.* To run or pass quickly over or along; range over, as in quest of something (as, "They were soldiers or mounted policemen, *scouring* the country in search of recruits": W. H. Hudson's "Purple Land," x.).

scour-er[1] (skour'ėr), *n.* One who scours or cleanses; an implement or contrivance for scouring; a purgative agent.

scour-er[2] (skour'ėr), *n.* One who scours or ranges about; in the 17th and 18th centuries, one who made a practice of roistering through the streets at night committing various kinds of mischief.

scourge (skėrj), *n.* [AF. *escorge, escurge,* for OF. *escorgee* (F. *écourgée*), leather scourge, < L. *excoriare,* strip skin from: see *excoriate.*] A whip or lash, esp. for the infliction of punishment or torture upon human beings; hence, any means of punishment; also, a cause of affliction or calamity.— **scourge,** *v. t.*; *scourged, scourging.* To whip with a scourge; lash; drive or force by or as by blows of a whip (as, "Some slaves are *scourged* to their work by whips": Ruskin's "Crown of Wild Olive," iii.); hence, to punish or chastise severely; afflict; torment.—**scourg'er,** *n.*

scour-ing (skour'ing), *n.* Dirt, refuse material, etc., removed by scouring; refuse removed from grain before milling: now commonly in *pl.*—**scour'ing=rush,** *n.* Any of certain species of the plant horsetail, esp. *Equisetum hyemale,* used for scouring and polishing.

scouse (skous), *n.* Same as *lobscouse.*

scout[1] (skout), *n.* [OF. *escoute* (F. *écoute*), < *escouter, asculter* (F. *écouter*), listen to, < L. *auscultare*: cf. *auscultate.*] The action or an act of going about or watching, in order to obtain information (as, "I set myself upon the *scout* . . . to see for canoes, but none appeared," Defoe's "Robinson Crusoe," i. 14; "If an officer planned a *scout* or campaign, those who thought proper accompanied him, and the others stayed at home," Roosevelt's "Winning of the West," i. 5); also, one sent out to obtain information; esp., in military use, one sent out to obtain information about an enemy's position, movements, etc. (as, "*Scouts* brought the intelligence that the Scots and Langdale's force . . .

were marching southward": Morley's "Oliver Cromwell," iii. 5); also, a war-vessel, aëroplane, or the like, employed in reconnoitering; also, a scouting party†; also, one employed to keep watch upon the actions of others; formerly, a spy†; also, a male college servant, as at Oxford, England; also, a fellow (slang: as, "George, old *scout*, you were sore-headed about something," Sinclair Lewis's "Babbitt," xxxiii.; a good old *scout*); also, in *cricket*, a fielder.—**Boy Scout.** See under *boy*.—**Girl Scout.** See under *girl*.—**scout**[1], *v.* **I.** *intr.* To act as a scout; reconnoiter. **II.** *tr.* To examine, inspect, or observe for the purpose of obtaining information; reconnoiter.

scout[2] (skout), *v.* [Prob. from Scand.: cf. Icel. *skūta*, a taunt.] **I.** *tr.* To reject with scorn; dismiss as absurd; treat with disdain; flout: as, "Granvelle *scouted* the idea of her being ignorant of Anjou's scheme" (Motley's "Dutch Republic," v. 5). **II.** *intr.* To scoff: as, "They might *scout* at Moby Dick as a monstrous fable" (H. Melville's "Moby-Dick," xlv.).—**scout'ing-ly**, *adv.*

scout=mas-ter (skout′mȧs″tėr), *n.* The leader or officer in charge of a band of scouts; esp., the adult leader of a troop of Boy Scouts.

scow (skou), *n.* [D. *schouw*.] A large flat-bottomed boat used chiefly for transporting freight, mud, etc.; a flat-bottomed lighter or barge.

scowl (skoul), *v.* [ME. *skoulen*, prob. from Scand.: cf. Dan. *skule*, scowl.] **I.** *intr.* To draw down or contract the brows in a sullen or angry manner; look with a scowl (*at*, etc.: as, "They found . . . men lounging about the entrance, who *scowled* and swore at Offit for being late," John Hay's "Bread-Winners," v.); fig., to have a gloomy or threatening aspect. **II.** *tr.* To send forth or express with a scowl.—**scowl**, *n.* A scowling expression, look, or aspect.—**scowl′er**, *n.*—**scowl′ing-ly**, *adv.*

scrab-ble (skrab′l), *v.*; *-bled, -bling.* [D. *schrabbelen*, freq. of *schrabben*, scratch, scrape; akin to E. *scrape*.] **I.** *intr.* To scratch or scrape about, as with the claws or hands (as, "Gangs of the prying gull That shriek and *scrabble* on the riven hatches," Kipling's "The Derelict"; "She *scrabbled* among the papers," H. G. Wells's "Soul of a Bishop," ix.); also, to scramble; struggle; also, to scrawl or scribble. **II.** *tr.* To scratch or scrape (as, "But Tubal got him a pointed rod, And *scrabbled* the earth for corn": Kipling's "Jubal and Tubal Cain"); gather (*up, together*, etc.) hastily; also, to scrawl.—**scrab′ble**, *n.* A scrabbling or scramble; also, a scrawled character, writing, etc.

scrag[1] (skrag), *n.* [Origin obscure: cf. *crag*[1].] A lean or scrawny person or animal; also, the lean end of a neck of mutton, etc.; also, the neck of a human being (slang: as, "I have your little pearl necklace at this moment fastened round my bronze *scrag* under my cravat," C. Brontë's "Jane Eyre," xxxvii.).—**scrag**[1], *v. t.*; *scragged, scragging.* To put to death by hanging; wring the neck of; garrote. [Slang.]

scrag[2] (skrag), *n.* [Origin obscure: cf. ME. *schragge*, jagged end, rag.] A rough projecting part of a tree, rock, etc. [Chiefly prov.]

scrag-gi-ness (skrag′i-nes), *n.* Scraggy condition. See *scraggy*[1] and *scraggy*[2].

scrag-gling (skrag′ling), *a.* [Cf. *scrag*[2] and *straggle*.] Projecting or scattered irregularly; straggling; scraggy. Also **scrag-gly** (skrag′li).

scrag-gy[1] (skrag′i), *a.*; compar. *scraggier*, superl. *scraggiest.* [From *scrag*[1].] Lean or thin (as, "gaunt and *scraggy* limbs," Mrs. Shelley's "Frankenstein," xix.; "his sinewy, *scraggy* neck," Scott's "Guy Mannering," ii.); also, meager or scanty.

scrag-gy[2] (skrag′i), *a.*; compar. *scraggier*, superl. *scraggiest.* [From *scrag*[2].] Rough or broken in surface or outline; jagged, ragged, or rugged; irregular or straggling: as, "old *scraggy* bushes" (W. H. Hudson's "Far Away and Long Ago," iv.); *scraggy* rocks; "The note was written in Meshach's *scraggy* and irregular hand" (Arnold Bennett's "Leonora," i.).

scram-ble (skram′bl), *v.*; *-bled, -bling.* [Origin obscure: cf. *scamble* (recorded earlier), of like meaning.] **I.** *intr.* To get one's self into a place or position by a struggling use of the hands and feet; make one's way by clambering, crawling, jumping, etc., as over rough ground; also, to struggle with others for the possession of something; struggle or strive rudely with others, as for a share of something. **II.** *tr.* To collect in a hurried or disorderly manner (with *up*, etc.); also, to mix together confusedly; cook (eggs) in a pan, mixing whites and yolks with butter, milk, etc.; also, to struggle with others for (something); also, to scatter (money, etc.) for others to struggle for.—**scram′ble**, *n.* An act of scrambling; a progression or journey in which there is clambering, crawling, jumping, etc. (as, "My *scramble* through the wood had fatigued me": W. H. Hudson's "Green Mansions," ix.); a struggle for the possession of something; any disorderly struggle or proceeding.—**scram′bler**, *n.*—**scram′bling-ly**, *adv.*

scran (skran), *n.* [Origin obscure: cf. Icel. *skran*, rubbish.] Miscellaneous or broken victuals; scraps of food; provisions; fare; also, luck (in 'bad scran': Ir.). [Prov. or slang.]

scran-nel (skran′el), *a.* [Origin obscure: cf. Norw. *skran*, thin, lean, Sw. *skrangel*, 'bag of bones,' *skranglig*, gaunt, also E. *scrawny*.] Thin or slight (as, "Their lean and flashy songs Grate on their *scrannel* pipes of wretched straw": Milton's "Lycidas," 124); hence (from Milton's use), squeaky or unmelodious (as, "From the stone lungs sighed the *scrannel* voice": Browning's "Ring and the Book," vi.).

scrap[1] (skrap), *n.* [Cf. *scrape*.] A fight; a scrimmage; a contest. [Slang.]—**scrap**[1], *v. i.*; *scrapped, scrapping.* To fight: as, "Well, let's not *scrap* about it" (Sinclair Lewis's "Main Street," xxxix.). [Slang.]

scrap[2] (skrap), *n.* [ME. *scrappe*, from Scand.: cf. Icel. and Sw. *skrap*, Dan. *skrab*, akin to E. *scrape*.] A fragment of food; *pl.*, the remains of a meal; also, *sing.*, in general, a small detached piece or portion, or a fragment (as, "the floor strewn with *scraps* of mortar," S. J. Weyman's "Gentleman of France," xv.; "The girls haven't a *scrap* of imagination," Galsworthy's "Country House," i. 9); often, a detached piece of something written or printed; also, *pl.*, refuse of fish after the oil has been extracted; the remains of animal fat after the oil has been tried out; also, *pl.*, fragments or remnants of metal; esp., *sing.*, scrap-iron.—**scrap of paper**, a small bit of paper; a mere fragment of paper: sometimes applied to a written agreement or the like when regarded or treated as without binding force (esp., in recent use, with reference to a remark attributed to the German imperial chancellor Theobald von Bethmann-Hollweg, in August, 1914, in a conversation with Sir W. E. Goschen, the British ambassador at Berlin, to the effect that Great Britain, in coming to the assistance of Belgium, whose neutrality, violated by Germany, Great Britain was pledged by treaty to defend, was making war on a kindred nation "just for a scrap of paper").—**scrap**[2], *a.* Consisting of scraps or fragments; in the form of fragments or remnants of use only for reworking, as metal.—**scrap**[2], *v. t.*; *scrapped, scrapping.* To make into scraps or scrap; break up into scrap-iron, as worn-out machinery; consign to the scrap-heap; hence, to discard as useless or worthless.—**scrap′=book**, *n.* A book in which pictures, short extracts from newspapers, etc., are pasted for preservation.

scrape (skrāp), *v. t.*; *scraped, scraping.* [ME. *scrapen*, prob. from Scand.: cf. Icel. and Sw. *skrapa*, Dan. *skrabe*, D. *schrapen*, scrape; prob. akin to E. *sharp*.] To deprive of or free from an outer layer, adhering matter, etc., by drawing or rubbing something, esp. a sharp or rough instrument, over the surface; remove (an outer layer, adhering matter, etc.) in this way; also, to scratch; produce as by scratching; also, to collect by or as by scraping, or laboriously, or with difficulty (with *up* or *together*: as, "He had *scraped* up the last crumbs of cheese from his plate," Arnold Bennett's "Clayhanger," i. 8; "By fear and favour he had *scraped* together near upon a dozen men," Stevenson's "Master of Ballantrae," i.); also, to rub harshly on or across (something), as in passing; also, to draw or rub (a thing) roughly across something else.—**to scrape acquaintance,** to gain acquaintance, as with a person, by deliberate effort or by going beyond the conventional procedure of introduction, etc.—**scrape**, *v. i.* To scrape something; also, to practise laborious economy or saving (chiefly prov.); also, to rub against something in a grating manner; also, to draw back the foot in making an obeisance.—**to scrape through,** to get through by or as if by scraping against something; get through barely or by a very narrow margin: as, to *scrape through* a narrow opening; he only just *scraped through* the examination.—**scrape**, *n.* An act of scraping; sometimes, something scratched, as with a pen, or a small scrap of writing (chiefly Sc.: as, "It [a letter] said, 'I send you these few *scrapes* to say I am dying,'" Barrie's "Sentimental Tommy," xi.; "not a line . . . not the *scrape* of a pen," F. H. Smith's "Colonel Carter of Cartersville," vii.); often, a drawing back of the foot in making a bow; also, a scraping sound (as, "the *scrape* of an overworked gramophone": Mrs. Wharton's "Son at the Front," xxii.); also, a scraped place (as, "a *scrape* on a tree trunk": Roosevelt's "Winning of the West," i. 4); also, a scraper; also, an embarrassing predicament or situation, esp. one due to imprudence or thoughtlessness (as, "Cool thinkers were beginning to believe that Cæsar was in a *scrape* from which his good fortune would this time fail to save him": Froude's "Cæsar," xxii.).—**scrap-er** (skrā′pẽr), *n.* One who or that which scrapes; esp., any of various implements for scraping something; specif., an iron implement placed at or near the door of a house, on which to scrape the dirt from the soles of the shoes.

scrap=heap (skrap′hēp), *n.* A heap of scraps, esp. of disused or broken ironwork for re-melting or reworking.—**scrap′=heap**, *v. t.* To consign to the scrap-heap; hence, to discard as useless or worthless.

Scraper.

scrap-ing (skrā′ping), *n.* The act of one who or that which scrapes; the sound produced by this; also, that which is scraped off, up, or together (usually in *pl.*).

scrap=i-ron (skrap′ī′ẽrn), *n.* Old iron, as cuttings, broken fragments, etc., used for remelting or reworking.

scrap-per (skrap′ẽr), *n.* One who scraps or fights; a pugilist; one given to fighting. [Slang.]

scrap-pi-ly (skrap′i-li), *adv.* In a scrappy or fragmentary manner.—**scrap′pi-ness**, *n.*

scrap-ple (skrap′l), *n.* [Dim. of *scrap²*.] A sausage-like preparation of minced pork, herbs, rye or other meal, etc., fried in slices: of Pennsylvania-German origin: as, "the *scrapple* so dear to the heart of the Philadelphian as a breakfast dish" (Bok's "Americanization of Edward Bok," xix.).

scrap-py (skrap′i), *a.*; compar. *scrappier*, superl. *scrappiest*. Made up of scraps, or of odds and ends; fragmentary; disconnected: as, "Maisie's letters are *scrappy*" (Kipling's "Light That Failed," x.).

scratch¹ (skrach), *n.* [Cf. Icel. *skratti*, wizard, goblin, monster, mod. devil, G. *schrat*, goblin.] The devil: usually [*cap.*] in '(the) old Scratch': as, "He that would cozen a Scot, mun get oop betimes, and take *old Scratch* for his counsellor" (Smollett's "Humphry Clinker," July 4).

scratch² (skrach), *v.* [Appar. a mixture of earlier (ME.) *scrat* and *cratch*, both meaning 'scratch': cf. OHG. *krazzōn* (G. *kratzen*), scratch, also OF. *grater* (F. *gratter*), scratch, scrape, E. *grate²*.] **I.** *tr.* To wound superficially, or break or mark the surface of, by the rubbing, scraping, or tearing action of something sharp or rough; rub or scrape lightly with the finger-nails, etc., as to relieve itching (as, "He *scratched* his head": W. Churchill's "Coniston," ii. 17); make with the claws, the nails, etc., as a hole; tear (*out*, *off*, etc.) by the action of the claws, the nails, etc. (as, "If you say another word I'll *scratch* your eyes out!" Arnold Bennett's "Old Wives' Tale," i. 3); also, to produce by or as by scratches or irregular marks, as something written or drawn (as, "He *scratched* hieroglyphics with his stick on the gravel": L. Merrick's "Position of Peggy Harper," ii. 9); also, to erase or strike out (writing, a name, etc.); withdraw (a horse, etc.) from the list of entries in a race or competition; also, to rub gratingly, as a match, on something; also, in *U. S. politics*, of a voter, to strike out or reject a particular name or names on (a party ticket); reject (a candidate) on a ticket. **II.** *intr.* To use the nails, the claws, or the like, for tearing a surface, for digging, etc.; relieve itching by rubbing with the nails, etc.; also, to make scratches or marks; also, to make a slight grating noise, as a pen; also, to withdraw from a contest, as a competitor.—**scratch²**. **I.** *n.* An act of scratching; also, the sound produced by scratching; also, a slight tear or incision in the skin, as from a sharp instrument; *pl.* (construed as *sing.*),

a disease of horses, in which dry rifts or chaps appear on the skin near the fetlock; *sing.*, any furrow or mark produced by scratching; also, a rough or irregular mark of a pen, etc.; also, the line or mark from which competitors start, jump, etc., in a race or other contest; a line to which pugilists are brought for encounter; the starting-place, time of starting, or status, of a competitor in a handicap who has no allowance and no penalty, or the competitor himself; also, a scratch-wig (as, "Don't pull his hair, Because he wears a *scratch*": Holmes's "Treadmill Song"); also, in *billiards*, etc., a fluke. **II.** *a.* Starting from scratch, or without allowance or penalty, as a competitor; also, gathered together hastily and indiscriminately (colloq.: as, a *scratch* crew); done by or dependent on chance (colloq.: as, a *scratch* shot).—**scratch′er**, *n.*—**scratch′=wig**, *n.* A wig covering only part of the head.—**scratch′y**, *a.* Consisting of mere scratches, as a drawing; also, that scratches, scrapes, or grates.

scrawl (skrål), *v.* [Appar. a particular use of obs. or prov. *scrawl*, crawl, sprawl, for *crawl²*.] **I.** *tr.* To write or draw in a sprawling, awkward manner; also, to mark irregularly, as a surface. **II.** *intr.* To write awkwardly.—**scrawl**, *n.* Something scrawled, as a letter or a note (as, "the Anabasis, the little Oxford edition which I used at school, with . . . its blots and underlinings and marginal *scrawls*": Gissing's "Private Papers of Henry Ryecroft," ii. 9); also, awkward or careless handwriting.—**scrawl′er**, *n.*—**scrawl′y**, *a.* Awkwardly written or drawn.

scraw-ny (skrå′ni), *a.*; compar. *scrawnier*, superl. *scrawniest*. [Var. of prov. Eng. and Sc. *scranny*: cf. *scrannel*.] Lean; thin; scraggy: as, "He was tall . . . with a long, *scrawny* neck that rose out of a very low collar" (W. Churchill's "Coniston," i. 13).—**scraw′ni-ness**, *n.*

screak (skrēk), *v. i.* [= *screech*.] To emit a sharp, shrill cry; screech; scream; also, to creak. [Now chiefly prov.] —**screak**, *n.* A screaking; a sharp, shrill cry; a creak. [Now chiefly prov.]

scream (skrēm), *v.* [ME. *scræmen*, *screamen*; origin uncertain.] **I.** *intr.* To utter a loud, sharp, piercing cry, as of pain, fright, mirth, etc. (as, "He immediately began to *scream* with pain," F. M. Crawford's "Mr. Isaacs," x.; "the desperate *screaming* of a frightened woman," J. Conrad's "Lord Jim," xxv.); of a bird or beast, to give forth a characteristic shrill cry (as, "White owls . . . often *scream* horribly as they fly along," G. White's "Nat. Hist. of Selborne," ii. 15; "The mules *screamed*," Borrow's "Bible in Spain," ii.); also, in general, to emit a shrill, piercing sound, as a whistle, etc. **II.** *tr.* To utter with a scream or screams (as, "The witch, the witch,' the mob *screamed* out": J. H. Newman's "Callista," xxxiv.); also, to make or render by screaming (as, "I seemed to *scream* myself hoarse with warnings": Stevenson's "Master of Ballantrae," ix.).—**scream**, *n.* A loud, sharp, piercing cry, as of pain, fright, mirth, etc. (as, "loud *screams* of laughter": W. H. Hudson's "Purple Land," xix.); a shrill cry of a bird or beast (as, "A gull flew away with an angry *scream*": J. Conrad's "Rover," vii.); in general, a shrill, piercing sound (as, "The *screams* of the engines announced that the day was done": L. Merrick's "Worldlings," i.); also, something so funny as to evoke screams of mirth (slang: as, "Ted observed that her friends were 'a *scream* of a bunch,'" Sinclair Lewis's "Babbitt," ii.). —**scream′er**, *n.* One who or that which screams; also, something apt to evoke screams, as of astonishment, delight, or mirth (slang); something

Horned Screamer (*Palamedea cornuta*).

first-rate (slang); in *ornith.*, any of the long-toed South and Central American birds, sometimes larger than a turkey, which constitute the family *Palamedeidæ*, including *Palamedea cornuta* ('horned screamer': see cut on preceding page), and *Chauna chavaria* and *C. derbiana* (both known as 'crested screamer'); also, the seriema (also known as 'crested screamer').—**scream'ing**, *p. a.* That screams; fig., startling in effect; also, such as to evoke screams of mirth (as, a *screaming* farce); first-rate (slang).—**scream'ing-ly**, *adv.*

scree (skrē), *n.* [Cf. Icel. *skridha*, landslide.] A steep mass of detritus on the side of a mountain: as, "The path ascends and passes round the side of the mountain upon loose *screes*, which descend steeply to a lower wall of precipices" (H. G. Wells's "Italy, France, and Britain at War," ii. 2).

screech (skrēch), *v.* [For earlier *scritch*, ME. *scrichen*; ult. imit.: cf. *screak* and *shriek*.] **I.** *intr.* To utter a loud, harsh, shrill cry or sound; scream; shriek. **II.** *tr.* To utter with a screech: as, " 'Leave me alone!' he *screeched*" (Stevenson's "Master of Ballantrae," x.).—**screech**, *n.* A loud, harsh, shrill cry or sound.—**screech'er**, *n.*—**screech'=owl**, *n.* An owl that screeches, as distinguished from one that hoots; specif., any of various small owls of the genus *Megascops*, having horn-like tufts of feathers; the barn-owl, *Strix flammea* (Eng.).—**screech'y**, *a.* Loud, harsh, and shrill: as, "a shrill, *screechy* voice" (W. H. Hudson's "Green Mansions," x.).

screed (skrēd), *n.* [Var. of *shred*.] A shred or fragment (obs. or prov.); also, a long, narrow strip (now chiefly prov.); also, a long list or roll; a long piece of writing; a long letter; a lengthy discourse or harangue; also, in *plastering*, a strip of plaster (or wood) of the proper thickness, applied to a wall as a guide or gage for the rest of the work.

screen (skrēn), *n.* [ME. *screne*: cf. OF. *escren, escran* (F. *écran*), screen, prob. from Teut.] A covered framework or some other device, movable or fixed, and of various forms, for sheltering from heat, air, observation, etc., or serving as a partition or the like; an

Fire-screen, covered with tapestry. — Louis Seize style.

ornamental partition of wood, stone, etc., as in a church (see cut in next column); something affording a surface for displaying stereopticon views, moving pictures, or the like; also, anything that serves to shelter, protect, or conceal (lit. or fig.: as, "A semi-circular *screen* of great beeches masks the church and village," H. G. Wells's "Tono-Bungay," i. 1. § 3; "an impenetrable *screen* of secrecy," W. De Morgan's "Joseph Vance," viii.); also, a sieve or riddle, as for grain, sand, etc.; in *photo-engraving*, a transparent plate containing two sets of fine parallel lines, one crossing the other, used to produce the minute dots in the half-tone process; *milit.*, a body of men detached to cover the movements of an army.—**screen**, *v. t.* To shelter, protect, or conceal with or as with a screen (as, "Mrs. Bellew had taken up a palm-leaf fan to *screen* her face from the fire": Galsworthy's "Country House," i. 3); hence, fig., to shield or protect; save from punishment or exposure; also, to project (pictures, etc.) on a screen, as with a stereopticon or a moving-picture machine; sometimes, to photograph with a moving-picture camera, for presentation on a screen; film; also, to sift by passing through a screen.—**screen'er**, *n.*—**screen'ing**, *n.* The act or work of one who screens; also, *pl.*, matter separated out by sifting with a screen.

screw (skrö), *n.* [OF. *escroue, escro* (F. *écrou*), female screw: cf. MLG. *schrûve*, MHG. *schrûbe*, G. *schraube*, screw.] A

mechanical device consisting of a cylinder of wood or metal having a helical ridge (the thread) winding round it ('external screw' or 'male screw'); a corresponding part into which such a device advances and fits when turned, consisting of a cylindrical socket in whose wall is cut a helical groove ('internal screw' or 'female screw'); also, a metal device resembling and serving as a nail, having a slotted head and a tapering spiral thread, and driven into wood, etc., with the aid of a

Screen. — Lady Chapel of Gloucester Cathedral, England, looking toward the nave.

screw-driver ('wood-screw'); also, a screw-propeller (see *propeller*), or a vessel propelled by one; also, a former instrument of torture for compressing the thumbs to extort a confession (usually called 'the screws'); hence, a means of pressure or coercion (as, to put the *screw* on a debtor); also, something having a spiral form or course; also, an act of screwing, or a turn of a screw; a screwing or twisting movement or motion; a contortion, as of the body or face (as, "The Englishman . . . listened to them all with a certain *screw* of the mouth, expressive of incredulity": Irving's "Tales of a Traveler," iii. 1); also, a small portion, as of tobacco, wrapped up in a twisted paper; also, one who drives sharp bargains (as, "He's a terrible *screw* at a bargain": Mrs. Stowe's "Oldtown Folks," xxxvi.); a miserly person (as, "They both agreed in calling him an old *screw*," which means a very stingy, avaricious person": Thackeray's "Vanity Fair," viii.); also, an unsound or broken-down horse; also, salary or wages (British slang: as, "I shall have something left out of this week's *screw*," L. Merrick's "Worldlings," ii.).—**a screw loose**, fig., something amiss or wrong (as, "There's *a screw loose* in your affairs": Dickens's "Martin Chuzzlewit," xiii.); often, something wrong mentally, as with a person (as, a man with *a screw loose*).—**screw**, *v.* **I.** *tr.* To force, press, hold fast, stretch tight, etc., by or as by means of a screw (as, to *screw* a block in a vise; to *screw* up the strings of a musical instrument); operate or adjust by turning a screw, as a press; also, to attach with a screw or screws (as, to *screw* a bracket to a wall); also, to put compulsion on; oppress by exactions; force (a seller) to lower a price (often with *down*); also, to extract or extort by pressure or coercion (as, to *screw* information or money out of a person); also, to work (a screw, etc.) by turning; fix (*on, in*, etc.), or take (*off, out*, etc.), by a twisting movement which operates a screw; also, to twist; twist round; twist awry; contort; distort; also, to force or propel by a spiral movement; also, to provide with a helical ridge or groove. **II.** *intr.* To turn as or like a screw; be adapted for being connected or taken apart by means of a screw or screws (with *on, together, off*, etc.); also, to wind or move spirally; also, to turn with a twisting motion; also, to become contorted or distorted; also, to make exactions; practise extortion; also, to be parsimonious.

screw-a-ble (skrö'a-bl), *a.* That may be screwed.

screw=bean (skrö'bēn), *n.* A mimosaceous tree, *Prosopis pubescens*, of the southwestern U. S., bearing twisted pods which are used as fodder; also, the pod itself.

screw=driv-er (skrö'drī''vèr), *n.* A tool for driving in or withdrawing screws by turning them.

screwed (skröd), *p. a.* Fastened with a screw or screws; also, furnished with a screw or screws; also, twisted round or awry; also, somewhat intoxicated (slang).

screw-er (skrö′ėr), *n.* One who or that which screws.

screw=pine (skrö′pīn), *n.* A pandanus (plant): so called from its leaves, which have a spiral arrangement and resemble those of the pineapple.

screw=pro-pel-ler (skrö′prọ-pel′ėr), *n.* See *propeller*.

screw=thread (skrö′thred), *n.* The helical ridge which forms the essential part of an external or male screw, or a corresponding ridge formed by the groove of an internal or female screw.

screw=worm (skrö′wėrm), *n.* The larva of a fly, *Lucilia macellaria*, a dipterous insect which sometimes deposits its eggs in sores, etc., of living animals, the eggs developing rapidly into larvæ, which bore into the tissues of the animal attacked, often with fatal results.

screw-y (skrö′i), *a.* Winding or twisting about like the thread of a screw; also, mean or stingy; also, unsound, as a horse; also, somewhat intoxicated (slang).

scri-bal (skrī′bạl), *a.* Of or pertaining to a scribe; due to a scribe or copyist (as, a *scribal* error).

scrib-ble[1] (skrib′l), *v. t.*; *-bled, -bling.* [Prob. from LG. and akin to E. *scrub*[1].] To card or tease coarsely, as wool.

scrib-ble[2] (skrib′l), *v.*; *-bled, -bling.* [ME. *scribyl, scrible*, prob. freq. < L. *scribere*, write: cf. L. *conscribillare*, scribble over, freq. of *conscribere*, E. *conscribe*.] **I.** *tr.* To write hastily or carelessly (as, to *scribble* a message or a letter; to *scribble* verses); draw (marks, lines, etc.) hastily or carelessly; also, to cover with writing or marks of a careless or purposeless kind (often with *over*: as, walls *scribbled* over with names). **II.** *intr.* To scribble something; write literary matter in a hasty, careless way (as, "some poor devil in Grub Street, *scribbling* for his dinner": Stevenson's "Master of Ballantrae," x.); make purposeless or meaningless marks (as, a child *scribbles* on the pages of a book).— **scrib′ble**[2], *n.* Something scribbled; a hasty or careless piece of writing; a paltry composition.—**scrib′bler**, *n.* One who scribbles; hence, a petty writer or author.— **scrib′bling**, *n.* The act of one who scribbles; also, something scribbled; a scribble; a scrawl.

scribe (skrīb), *v.*; *scribed, scribing.* [Appar. < L. *scribere* (pp. *scriptus*), write, draw, prob. in part through *scribe, n.*, and perhaps *describe*: cf. *shrive*.] **I.** *tr.* To write down (now rare); also, to mark or score (wood, etc.) with a pointed instrument; draw (a line) by scoring or the like; fit (a piece of wood, metal, etc.) closely to another piece or part, as by marking and then cutting. **II.** *intr.* To write. [Now rare.]—**scribe**, *n.* [L. *scriba*, < *scribere*.] One who writes; a penman; a copyist; an amanuensis; specif., any of various officials of ancient or former times who performed clerical or secretarial duties; also, one of a class of doctors or teachers among the Jews, whose office it was to interpret the Jewish law to the people; also, sometimes, a writer or author.— **scrib-er** (skrī′bėr), *n.* A tool or instrument for scribing.

scrim (skrim), *n.* [Origin obscure.] A cotton or linen fabric of open, canvas-like weave, used for curtains, etc.

scrim-mage (skrim′āj), *n.* [Var. of *skirmish*.] A skirmish†; hence, a rough or vigorous fight or struggle, esp. between numbers of persons (as, "one of those chums that stand up for a fellow in a *scrimmage* and look after him should he be hurt": J. Conrad's "Rover," xv.); in *football*, orig., a confused struggle among players round the ball (in Rugby football); now, specif., the action between contesting lines of players in definite formation when the ball is put in play. Cf. *scrummage*.—**scrim′mage**, *v. i.*; *-maged, -maging.* To engage in a scrimmage.

scrimp (skrimp), *v.* [Cf. MLG. *schrimpen, schrempen*, wrinkle, contract, G. *schrumpfen*, shrink, also E. *shrimp* and *skimp*.] **I.** *tr.* To keep on short allowance, as of food; also, to stint or scant the amount of; be sparing of or in. **II.** *intr.* To use severe economy; be parsimonious or niggardly.—**scrimp. I.** *a.* Scanty; meager; deficient. **II.** *n.* A niggard; a pinching miser. [Colloq.]—**scrimp′y**, *a.*; compar. *scrimpier*, superl. *scrimpiest.* Scanty; meager. —**scrimp′i-ness**, *n.*

scrim-shank (skrim′shangk), *v. i.* [Origin obscure.] To shirk duty; soldier; malinger. [Military slang, Eng.]— **scrim′shank**[″]**er**, *n.*

scrim-shaw (skrim′shâ), *n.* [Origin obscure.] Carved or other work or articles of shell, ivory, wood, etc., executed by sailors in leisure time: often called *scrimshaw work.*— **scrim′shaw**, *v. t.* or *i.* To make into, or make, scrimshaw work.

scrip[1] (skrip), *n.* [ME. *scrippe*, prob. < OF. *escrepe*, var. of *escarpe, escharpe*, bag, scrip: see *scarf*[1].] A bag or wallet carried by pilgrims or other wayfarers, shepherds, etc.: as, "the primitive pilgrims, with *scrip*, and staff, and cockleshell" (Irving's "Tales of a Traveler," iii. 3). [Archaic.]

scrip[2] (skrip), *n.* [Appar. for *script*.] A writing, esp. a receipt or certificate; a provisional certificate, as for shares of stock, issued on payment of an instalment of the amount due; a certificate of a right to a fractional part of a share of stock (such certificates in sufficient amount usually being convertible into regular certificates of stock with full voting and dividend rights); certificates of any such kind collectively; also, paper currency in denominations of less than $1, formerly issued in the U. S.

script (skript), *n.* [L. *scriptum*, something written, prop. neut. of *scriptus*, pp. of *scribere*, write.] A writing (now rare); also, handwriting; the characters used in handwriting; a mode of writing; in *law*, an original or principal document; in *theatrical use*, the manuscript of a play or of a player's rôle; in *printing*, a style of type imitating handwriting (see *type*).

scrip-to-ri-um (skrip-tō′ri-um), *n.*; pl. *-riums* or *-ria* (-ri-ạ). [ML., a place for writing, prop. neut. of L. *scriptorius*, of or for writing, < *scribere*, write.] A writing-room; esp., a room in a monastery set apart for the writing or copying of manuscripts.

scrip-tur-al (skrip′țụr-ạl), *a.* Of or pertaining to writing; also [often *cap.*], of, pertaining to, or in accordance with the Scriptures.—**scrip′tur-al-ism**, *n.* Literal adherence to the Scriptures.—**scrip′tur-al-ist**, *n.*—**scrip′tur-al-ly**, *adv.* —**scrip′tur-al-ness**, *n.*

scrip-ture (skrip′țụr), *n.* [L. *scriptura*, writing, < *scribere*, write.] The act of writing, written characters, or a writing (now rare); an inscription, motto, or legend (archaic); specif. [usually *cap.*], the sacred writings of the Old and the New Testament or of either of them (often called 'Holy Scripture' and 'the Scriptures'); Holy Writ; the Bible; also, a passage from the Bible (now rare); also [*l. c.*], any sacred writing or book (as, "Most men do not know that any nation but the Hebrews have had a *scripture*": Thoreau's "Walden," iii.).—**scrip′tured**, *a.* Covered with writing; also, versed in or well acquainted with the Scriptures†; also, warranted by the Scriptures†.

scri-vel-lo (skri-vel′ō), *n.*; pl. *-velloes* or *-vellos* (-vel′ōz). [Pg. *escrevelho*: cf. F. *escarbeille*.] An elephant's tusk of comparatively small size and light weight, such as is used for making billiard-balls.

scriv-en (skriv′n), *v. t.* or *i.* [Back-formation from *scrivener*.] To write or work as a scrivener. [Archaic.]

scriv-en-er (skriv′nėr), *n.* [ME. *scriveyner*, for *scriveyn*, < OF. *escrivain* (F. *écrivain*), < ML. *scribanus*, < L. *scriba*, E. *scribe, n.*] A professional or public writer, as of letters or documents for others; a clerk or scribe; a notary; also, one making a business of receiving and placing money at interest and supplying money on security. [Archaic or hist.]

scro-bic-u-late (skrọ-bik′ụ-lāt), *a.* [L. *scrobiculus*, dim. of *scrobis*, ditch, trench.] In *bot.* and *zoöl.*, furrowed or pitted.

scrod (skrod), *n.*; pl. *scrods* or (esp. collectively) *scrod.* [Origin uncertain; perhaps from Dutch.] A young codfish, esp. one that is split for cooking. [U. S.]

scrof-u-la (skrof′ụ-lä), *n.* [ML., < LL. *scrofulæ*, pl., scrofulous swellings, scrofula, dim. < L. *scrofa*, a breeding sow.] In *pathol.*, a constitutional disorder of a tuberculous nature, characterized chiefly by swelling and degeneration of the lymphatic glands, esp. of the neck, and by inflammation of the joints, etc.; king's evil.—**scrof′u-lous**, *a.* Pertaining to or of the nature of scrofula; affected with scrofula.—**scrof′u-lous-ly**, *adv.*—**scrof′u-lous-ness**, *n.*

scroll (skrōl), *n.* [ME. *scrowle*, for *scrowe*, < AF. *escrowe*: see *escrow*.] A roll of parchment or paper, esp. one with writing on it; hence, a piece of writing; a list or schedule; a draft or rough copy (as, "a letter . . . of which . . . I have preserved the *scroll*": Stevenson's "Master of Ballantrae," vi.); also, something, esp. an ornament, resembling a partly unrolled sheet of paper or having a spiral or coiled form; a ribbon-like figure bearing a motto or other inscription; a flourish appended to a person's signature, sometimes serving the purpose of a seal.—**scroll**, *v.* **I.** *tr.* To write down on a scroll; inscribe; also, to form into a scroll; also, to ornament with scrolls. **II.** *intr.* To roll or curl up.— **scroll'=saw,** *n.* A narrow saw mounted vertically in a frame and operated with an up-and-down motion: used for cutting thin boards or the like in curved ornamental designs. —**scroll'work,** *n.* Decorative work in which scrolls form an important element; also, ornamental work cut out with a scroll-saw.

scrooge (skrööj), *v.* See *scrouge.*

scroop (skröp), *v. i.* [Imit.] To emit a harsh, scraping or grating sound, as a gate on its hinges; creak; grate.— **scroop,** *n.* A scrooping sound.

scroph-u-la-ri-a-ceous (skrof-ū-lā-ri-ā'shius), *a.* [NL. *Scrophularia,* the typical genus, reputed a remedy for scrofula, < LL. *scrofulæ:* see *scrofula.*] Belonging to the *Scrophulariaceæ,* or figwort family of plants, including the snapdragon, foxglove, toad-flax, mullein, eyebright, pentstemon, etc.

scro-tum (skrō'tum), *n.;* pl. *-ta* (-tä). [L.] In *anat.,* the pouch that contains the testicles.—**scro'tal,** *a.*

scrouge (skrouj or skröj), *v. t.* or *i.;* *scrouged, scrouging.* [Origin obscure.] To squeeze, press, or crowd. [Colloq. or prov.]

scroyle† (skroil), *n.* [Origin obscure.] A rascal; a wretch. See Shakspere's "King John," ii. 1. 373.

scrub¹ (skrub), *v.;* *scrubbed, scrubbing.* [Cf. MLG. *schrubben, schrobben,* scratch, rub, scrub, D. *schrobben,* scrub: cf. *scribble¹.*] **I.** *tr.* To scratch or rub, as a part of the body†; also, to rub hard with a brush, cloth, or the like, or against a rough surface, as in washing or cleansing (as, to *scrub* a floor; to *scrub* clothes on a washboard); in general, to wash or cleanse. **II.** *intr.* To cleanse things by hard rubbing, as with a brush and water or on a washboard.—**scrub¹,** *n.* A scrubbing: as, "She . . . inflicted a merciless, but, happily, brief *scrub* on my face and hands with soap, water, and a coarse towel" (C. Brontë's "Jane Eyre," iv.).

scrub² (skrub). [= *shrub².*] **I.** *n.* A low or stunted tree; low trees or shrubs collectively, or an extended growth of them (as, "I had ridden . . . into *scrub,* high enough to brush my horse's belly," H. Kingsley's "Geoffry Hamlyn," xxiv.; "a small glen, grown over with a low oak *scrub,*" Lever's "Harry Lorrequer," v.); hence, anything undersized, inferior, or small and mean (as, *scrubs* among domestic animals; "The ungrateful little *scrub* [a sparrow] bolted without a word of thanks," Barrie's "Auld Licht Idylls," i.); a mean, insignificant person; in *sports,* a scrub team, etc., or a member of it. **II.** *a.* Stunted or undersized; inferior, poor, or scrubby (as, "We got together a *scrub* wagon team of four . . . unkempt, dejected, and vicious-looking broncos": Roosevelt's "Ranch Life and the Hunting-Trail," x.); in *sports,* composed of inferior, substitute, or untrained players or members, as a team, etc.; belonging or pertaining to such a team, etc.; participated in by such teams, as a game or contest. —**scrub'bed,** *a.* Stunted; scrubby. [Archaic.]

scrub-ber (skrub'ėr), *n.* One who or that which scrubs; an instrument for scrubbing; an apparatus for washing a gas or gaseous mixture.

Scrub-bird (*Atrichornis rufescens*).

scrub=bird (skrub'bėrd), *n.* One of the passerine birds of the genus *Atrichornis* (or *Atrichia*), inhabiting the dense scrub of Australia, as *A. clamosa,* of Western Australia, or *A. rufescens,* of New South Wales. See cut in preceding column.

scrub-by (skrub'i), *a.;* compar. *scrubbier,* superl. *scrubbiest.* [See *scrub².*] Low or stunted, as trees and shrubs; consisting of or covered with stunted trees, etc., or scrub (as, "a little *scrubby* wood on the hillside," H. G. Wells's "Italy, France, and Britain at War," ii. 1; a *scrubby* region); undersized, inferior, or poor, as animals; in general, sorry, wretched, or shabby; mean, paltry, or insignificant.— **scrub'bi-ness,** *n.*

scruff (skruf), *n.* [Also *scuff;* origin uncertain.] The nape or back of the neck of a person or animal: as, "He took Buck [a dog] by the *scruff* of the neck, and . . . dragged him to one side" (Jack London's "Call of the Wild," iv.).

scrum (skrum), *n.* [Shortened form of *scrummage.*] A scrimmage in football. [Colloq., Eng.]

scrum-mage (skrum'āj), *n.* and *v.* Same as *scrimmage:* chiefly in British use, specif. in *football.*

scrump-tious (skrump'shus), *a.* [Origin obscure.] Superlatively fine or nice; elegant; splendid; first-rate: as, a *scrumptious* hat; "Probably the lumber-yard isn't as *scrumptious* as all these Greek temples" (Sinclair Lewis's "Main Street," ii.); to have a *scrumptious* time. [Slang.]

scrunch (skrunch), *v.* [Imit.: cf. *crunch.*] **I.** *tr.* To chew with a crushing sound, or crunch, as food; also, to tread with a crushing sound, as gravel; tread on with crushing force; also, to crush or crumple (as, "She *scrunched* the pieces of the letter in her powerful hand": Arnold Bennett's "Riceyman Steps," iv. 7); squeeze compactly (often with *up*). **II.** *intr.* To make a sound of crunching or crushing; also, to squeeze one's self (*up:* as, "Don't *scrunch* up like that, Huckleberry—set up straight," Mark Twain's "Huckleberry Finn," i.).—**scrunch,** *n.* An act or sound of scrunching.

scru-ple¹ (skrö'pl), *n.* [L. *scrupulus, scrupulum, scripulum,* unit of weight or measure, by some identified with *scrupulus,* small stone: see *scruple².*] An ancient Roman unit of weight equivalent to $\frac{1}{24}$ of an ounce or $\frac{1}{288}$ of an as or pound; also, a modern unit of weight equivalent to 20 grains or $\frac{1}{3}$ of a dram, apothecaries' weight; also, a small fraction, esp. a sixtieth part, as of a degree; hence, a very small portion or amount of anything (as, "the smallest *scruple* of her excellence": Shakspere's "Measure for Measure," i. 1. 38).

scru-ple² (skrö'pl), *n.* [L. *scrupulus,* cause or feeling of uneasiness, scruple, lit. 'small, sharp stone,' dim. of *scrupus,* sharp or rough stone, fig. uneasiness, anxiety.] A feeling of uneasiness affecting the conscience or the sense of propriety, fitness, or the like, tending to restrain one's action (as, *scruples* of conscience; "the *scruples* of an exaggerated delicacy," J. Conrad's "Lord Jim," xvii.; a mind little troubled by *scruples*); a feeling of hesitation or reluctance to do something regarded as not right or proper (as, "Mr. Parr had *scruples* . . . about using the carriage on the Sabbath," W. Churchill's "Inside of the Cup," ii.; "My father's old-fashioned notions boggled a little at first to this arrangement . . . but his *scruples* were in the end overruled," Galt's "Ayrshire Legatees," ii.); hesitation or reluctance from conscientious or other restraining reasons (as, "The gipsies, without *scruple,* entered upon measures of retaliation," Scott's "Guy Mannering," vii.; "Most English people have a kind of diffidence and *scruple* at calling in the evening," Bulwer-Lytton's "Pelham," xii.); also, a doubt† or doubting objection†; disbelief†.—**to make scruple,** to have hesitation or reluctance on conscientious or other like grounds: often with a negative: as, "The grooms *made no scruple* . . . to state all that had passed" (Marryat's "King's Own," xlviii.); "She *made no scruple* of oversetting all human institutions" (Hawthorne's "Blithedale Romance," vi.).—**scru'ple²,** *v.;* *-pled, -pling.* **I.** *intr.* To have scruples about something (as, "Perhaps you may *scruple* out of a regard to truth": Godwin's "Caleb Williams," xxxviii.); now, usually, to hesitate or be reluctant (to do something) on conscientious or other like grounds (as, "He . . . did not *scruple* to equivocate and to deceive": Bancroft's "Hist. of the U. S.," Amer. Revolution, i. 2). **II.** *tr.* To have scruples about; hesitate at, as on conscientious grounds: as, "or even *scruple* the refusal of quarter to prisoners" (Scott's "Castle Dangerous," iv.).—**scru′pler**, *n.*

scru-pu-los-i-ty (skrö-pū-los′i-ti), *n.*; pl. *-ties* (-tiz). The state or quality of being scrupulous; strict regard for what is right; scrupulous care; also, an instance of being scrupulous.

scru-pu-lous (skrö′pū-lus), *a.* [L. *scrupulosus.*] Having scruples, or troubled by scruples, as of conscience; restrained by scruples (as, "When was it ever seen that fear, armed with power, was *scrupulous* in the exercise of it?" Prescott's "Conquest of Mexico," iii. 7); carefully conforming or conformed to the dictates of conscience, as persons, actions, etc.; having or showing a strict regard for what is right; hence, in general, punctiliously or minutely careful, precise, or exact (as, "Cynthia was *scrupulous* in her efforts to give no trouble," W. Churchill's "Coniston," ii. 8; *scrupulous* courtesy, neatness, or nicety).—**scru′pu-lous-ly**, *adv.*—**scru′pu-lous-ness**, *n.*

scru-ta-ble (skrö′ta̤-bl), *a.* [L. *scrutari:* see *scrutiny*, and cf. *inscrutable.*] That may be penetrated or understood by investigation.

scru-ta-tor (skrö-tā′tọr), *n.* [L., < *scrutari:* see *scrutiny.*] One who examines or investigates; sometimes, a scrutineer at an election.

scru-ti-neer (skrö-ti-nēr′), *n.* [From *scrutiny.*] An official examiner, specif. of votes at an election.

scru-ti-nize (skrö′ti-nīz), *v. t.*; *-nized, -nizing.* To subject to scrutiny; examine closely or critically (as, "A collection of facts . . . is to be made out . . . These are to be selected, compared, and *scrutinized*": Hallam's "Literature of Europe," iii. 3. § 43); study with the eye, or look at searchingly or attentively (as, "He continued to *scrutinize* the drawing minutely," Poe's "Gold-Bug"; "I *scrutinized* my new acquaintances with unconcealed curiosity," Aldrich's "Story of a Bad Boy," vi.).—**scru′ti-niz-er** (-nī-zėr), *n.*—**scru′ti-niz-ing-ly**, *adv.*

scru-ti-nous (skrö′ti-nus), *a.* Scrutinizing; searching; critical. [Now rare.]—**scru′ti-nous-ly**, *adv.*

scru-ti-ny (skrö′ti-ni), *n.*; pl. *-nies* (-niz). [L. *scrutinium,* < *scrutari,* search, examine, perhaps orig. 'search even to the rags,' < *scruta,* pl., trash, frippery.] Searching examination or investigation (as, to subject a proposed measure to rigid *scrutiny*; conduct that will not bear *scrutiny*); a minute or critical examination or inquiry; specif., an official examination of the votes cast at an election; also, examination with the eye (as, "Montresor put up his glasses and bestowed on him a few moments of *scrutiny*": Mrs. H. Ward's "Lady Rose's Daughter," vi.); a searching or attentive gaze.

scry (scrī), *v.*; *scried, scrying.* [For *descry.*] **I.** *tr.* To descry, see, or perceive. [Now prov. Eng.] **II.** *intr.* To see images revealing the future, etc., by looking into crystal or the like; practise crystal-gazing.—**scry′er**, *n.*

scud (skud), *v.*; *scudded, scudding.* [Origin obscure.] **I.** *intr.* To run or move quickly or hurriedly along (as, "I heard . . . the lighter feet of chambermaids *scudding* along the passages": Hawthorne's "Blithedale Romance," xvii.); go, dart, or fly hastily off or away (as, "The intruder . . . *scudding* out at the eastern gate, was soon lost in the passes of the mountain," J. H. Newman's "Callista," xxvi.; "The prairie fowl rose . . . *scudding* with spread wings toward the thickest cover," Roosevelt's "Hunting Trips of a Ranchman," iv.); be driven by the wind, as clouds, spray, etc.; *naut.*, to run before a gale with little or no sail set (as, "We were *scudding* before a heavy gale, under bare poles": Marryat's "Peter Simple," xxxviii.). **II.** *tr.* To pass quickly over: as, "The startled red-deer *scuds* the plain" (Scott's "Cadyow Castle").—**scud**, *n.* The act of scudding; also, clouds, spray, or the like, driven by the wind (as, "When the smoking *scud* is blown — When the greasy wind-rack lowers": Kipling's "Bell Buoy"); a driving shower; a gust of wind.—**scud′der**, *n.*

scu-do (skö′dō), *n.*; pl. *-di* (-dē). [It., < L. *scutum,* shield: cf. *écu* and *escudo.*] A former silver coin and money of account of various Italian states, usually equivalent to about 97 U. S. cents; also, a former Italian gold coin, usually of the same value. See cut in next column.

scuff[1] (skuf), *v.* [Origin uncertain: cf. *scuffle*[2].] **I.** *intr.* To walk without raising the feet; shuffle. **II.** *tr.* To graze in passing; scrape with the feet; also, to mar the surface of by scraping or hard usage, as shoes, furniture, etc.—**scuff**[1], *n.* The act or sound of scuffing; also, a slight glancing blow (Sc.).

scuff[2] (skuf), *n.* Same as *scruff.*

scuf-fle[1] (skuf′l), *n.* [D. *schoffel,* hoe, = E. *shovel.*] A form of hoe which is pushed instead of pulled, and which commonly has the blade set in line, or nearly in line, with the handle.

Obverse.

Reverse.
Silver Scudo of Pope Gregory XVI.—British Museum.

scuf-fle[2] (skuf′l), *v. i.*; *-fled, -fling.* [Prob. from Scand., and akin to E. *shove* and *shuffle.*] To struggle or fight in a rough, confused manner; also, to go or move in hurried confusion; also, to move in a shuffling manner.—**scuf′fle**[2], *n.* A scuffling; a rough, confused struggle or fight (as, "The mob followed . . . a *scuffle* ensued, and a riot was in progress": J. H. Newman's "Callista," xvi.); a shuffling (as, "They could hear a *scuffle* of feet": Whyte-Melville's "Katerfelto," i.).—**scuf′fler**, *n.*

scul-dud′der-y, scul-dug′ger-y. See *skulduddery, skulduggery.*

sculk (skulk), etc. See *skulk*, etc.

scull (skul), *n.* [ME. *sculle, skulle;* origin uncertain.] An oar worked from side to side over the stern of a boat as a means of propulsion; also, one of a pair of oars operated, one on each side, by one person; also, a boat propelled by sculls; esp., a light racing-boat propelled by one rower with a pair of oars or by two or more rowers each with a pair of oars.—**scull,** *v.* **I.** *tr.* To propel or convey by means of a scull or sculls. **II.** *intr.* To propel a boat with a scull or sculls.—**scull′er,** *n.* One who sculls; also, a boat propelled by sculling.

Scull.

scul-ler-y (skul′ėr-i), *n.*; pl. *-ies* (-iz). [OF. *escuelerie,* < *escuele* (F. *écuelle*), dish, < L. *scutella,* salver: see *scuttle*[1].] Orig., the room or place in which the dishes and kitchen utensils of a household were kept and cleaned; in modern use, a small adjoining room, or back kitchen, where the rough or dirty work of a kitchen is done (as, "Through a doorway . . . you could see the kitchen, and beyond that the *scullery*," Arnold Bennett's "Helen with the High Hand," vi.; "A tiny *scullery* . . . sufficed for the coarser domestic operations," Gissing's "New Grub Street," iv.).

scul-lion (skul′yọn), *n.* [Perhaps (with form modified by association with *scullery*) < F. *souillon,* scullion, < *souiller,* E. *soil*[2].] A domestic servant who does menial work in a kitchen (as, "to hear the clinking of the plates in the far-off kitchen as the *scullion* rinsed them and put them by": S. Butler's "Way of All Flesh," lxxx.); hence, a low or contemptible person. [Archaic.]

sculp (skulp), *v. t.* or *i.* [L. *sculpere* (pp. *sculptus*), carve, engrave, sculpture: cf. *scalpel.*] To sculpture, or execute sculptural work. [Now humorous.]

scul-pin (skul′pin), n. [Cf. *scorpene*.] Any of various marine fishes of the family *Cottidæ*, esp. of the genus *Myoxocephalus*, with large spiny head, wide mouth, and repulsive appearance; also, a scorpænoid fish, *Scorpæna guttata*, of the coast of southern California; a scorpene; also, a worthless person or animal.

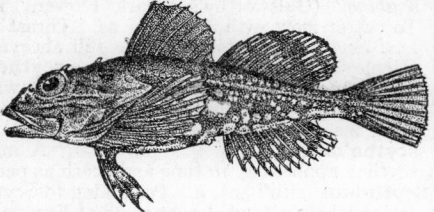

Sculpin (*Myoxocephalus grœnlandicus*).

sculp-sit (skulp′sit). [L.] ′(The person specified) carved or engraved (this)′: used in giving the artist's name on sculpture or engraving.

sculpt (skulpt), v. Same as *sculp*.

sculp-tor (skulp′tọr), n. [L., < *sculpere*: see *sculp*.] One who practises the art of sculpture.—**sculp′tress**, n. A female sculptor.

sculp-tur-al (skulp′tūr‿al), a. Of or pertaining to sculpture (as, *sculptural* works); suggestive of or suitable for sculpture (as, "one rolled-up sleeve baring a *sculptural* forearm": J. Conrad's "Rescue," iii. 1).—**sculp′tur-al-ly**, adv.

sculp-ture (skulp′tūr), n. [L. *sculptura*, < *sculpere*: see *sculp*.] Orig., the act or art of cutting or carving more or less hard substances so as to form figures or designs, whether in relief, in intaglio, or in the round; in later use, the fine art concerned with forming figures in the round or in relief by cutting marble or the like, by fashioning plastic materials, or by making molds for casting in bronze or other metal; also, sculptured work, or a piece of such work (as, temples adorned with *sculpture*; the Æginetan *sculptures*, see *Æginetan*, a.); in *zoöl.* and *bot.*, marking on a shell, skin, etc., resembling carving.—**sculp′ture**, v. t.; *-tured, -turing.* To carve, make, or execute by sculpture, as a figure, design, etc.; represent in sculpture, as a subject; also, to cover or adorn with sculpture, as rocks, architectural parts, monuments, ornamental objects, etc.; in *phys. geog.*, to change the form of by erosion.—**sculp′tur-er**, n.—**sculp-tu-resque′** (-tū-resk′), a. [See *-esque*.] In the manner of, or suggestive of, sculpture.

scum (skum), n. [ME. *scume* = MLG. *schūm* = D. *schuim* = G. *schaum*, foam: cf. *meerschaum* and *skim*.] Foam† or froth†; also, a film of extraneous matter formed upon the surface of a liquid, as in boiling or fermentation; a film of foul matter, as on stagnant water; hence, fig., refuse or offscourings (as, "rascals, the *scum* of the earth," Godwin's "Caleb Williams," xxvi.; "poachers and petty thieves — the *scum* of misery, ignorance, and rascality throughout the country," Kingsley's "Alton Locke," xxx.); low, worthless persons.—**scum**, v.; *scummed, scumming.* I. *tr.* To remove the scum from; also, to remove as scum. II. *intr.* To form scum; become covered with scum.

scum-ble (skum′bl), v. t.; *-bled, -bling.* [Appar. freq. of *scum*.] In *painting* and *drawing*, to soften the effect of (color or the harder lines), as by overlaying with a thin coat of opaque or semiopaque color or by spreading the lines.—**scum′ble**, n. A softened effect produced by scumbling.

scun-ner (skun′ẻr), v. i. or t. [Origin uncertain.] To feel, or cause to feel, disgust or loathing; sicken. [Sc. and north. Eng.]—**scun′ner**, n. A feeling of disgust or loathing; also, an object of disgust; an abomination. [Sc. and north. Eng.]

scup (skup), n. [N. Amer. Ind.] A sparoid marine food-fish, *Stenotomus chrysops*, of the eastern coast of the U. S., having a compressed body and a high back. Also **scup-paug** (sku-pâg′).

Scup.

scup-per[1] (skup′ẻr), n. [ME. *skopper, skopor*; origin uncertain.] *Naut.*, an opening in the side of a ship at or just below the level of the deck, to allow water to run off; also, a gutter bordering the deck and leading to such an opening.

scup-per[2] (skup′ẻr), v. t. [Origin uncertain: cf. *scupper*[1].] To overwhelm; surprise and massacre. [British military slang.]

scup-per-nong (skup′ẻr-nong), n. [From the *Scuppernong* River, in eastern North Carolina; N. Amer. Ind. name.] A cultivated variety of the fox-grape of the southern U. S.

scur (skẻr), v. See *skirr*.

scurf (skẻrf), n. [AS. *scurf, sceorf*, = D. *schurft* = G. *schorf*, scurf.] The scales or small shreds of epidermis that are continually exfoliated from the skin; esp., dandruff; hence, any scaly matter or incrustation on a surface; fig., scum, as of population.—**scurf′y**, a. Covered with scurf; also, of the nature of or resembling scurf.—**scurf′i-ness**, n.

scur-rile, scur-ril (skur′il), a. [L. *scurrilis*, < *scurra*, buffoon, jester.] Scurrilous: as, "Peace with thy *scurrile* jests" (Scott's "Talisman," xx.). [Archaic.]

scur-ril-i-ty (sku-ril′i-ti), n.; pl. *-ties* (-tiz). [L. *scurrilitas*, < *scurrilis*: see *scurrile*.] The quality of being scurrilous; buffoonish jocularity; indecent abusiveness; also, scurrilous language; a scurrilous remark, attack, or the like.

scur-ri-lous (skur′i-lus), a. [From *scurrile*.] Characterized by or using the license of a low buffoon, as language or persons; coarsely jocular or derisive (as, a *scurrilous* jest or jester); grossly or indecently abusive (as, "so indiscreet as to print *scurrilous* reflections on the government of neighboring states," B. Franklin's "Autobiography," vi.; a *scurrilous* speaker or writer).—**scur′ri-lous-ly**, adv.—**scur′ri-lous-ness**, n.

scur-ry (skur′i), v.; *-ried, -rying.* [Origin uncertain: cf. *scour*[2] and *skirr*.] I. *intr.* To go or run in haste (as, "We *scurried* away and gave the alarm," Mark Twain's "Life on the Mississippi," liv.; "There was a *scurrying* to and fro in the camp," F. M. Crawford's "Mr. Isaacs," xii.); rush hurriedly or precipitately; of things, to go or pass rapidly, as if in haste (as, "a flight of sparks *scurrying* up the chimney": F. H. Smith's "Colonel Carter of Cartersville," ii.). II. *tr.* To send scurrying or hurrying along; drive rapidly onward.—**scur′ry**, n.; pl. *scurries* (-iz). A scurrying rush or flight; a flurry; also, a scurrying throng or assemblage.

scur-vy[1] (skẻr′vi), a.; compar. *scurvier*, superl. *scurviest.* [= *scurfy*.] Scurfy†; hence, fig., low, mean, or contemptible (as, a *scurvy* fellow; a *scurvy* trick); sorry, wretched, or paltry (as, "a lot of *scurvy* institutions": M. Hewlett's "Open Country," xiv.).—**scur′vi-ly**, adv.—**scur′vi-ness**, n.

scur-vy[2] (skẻr′vi), n. [Appar. a noun use of *scurvy*[1]: cf. F. *scorbut*, scurvy, and E. *scorbutic*.] In *pathol.*, a disease characterized by swollen and bleeding gums, livid spots on the skin, prostration, etc., and due esp. to an unvaried diet, esp. one without vegetables.—**infantile scurvy.** See under *infantile*.—**scur′vy=grass**, n. A brassicaceous plant, *Cochlearia officinalis*, used as a remedy for scurvy.

scut (skut), n. [Origin obscure.] A short tail, esp. that of a hare, rabbit, or deer.

scu-ta (skū′tä), n. Plural of *scutum*.

scu-tage (skū′tāj), n. [ML. *scutagium*, < L. ′*scutum*, shield.] In the feudal system, a payment exacted in lieu of military service.

scu-tate (skū′tāt), a. [L. *scutatus*, armed with a shield, < *scutum*, shield.] In *zoöl.*, having scutes, shields, or large scales; in *bot.*, formed like an ancient round buckler.

scutch (skuch), v. t. [Cf. F. *écoucher*, scutch, *écouche*, OF. *escouche*, implement for scutching.] To dress (flax, cotton, etc.) by beating.—**scutch**, n. A scutcher.

scutch-eon (skuch′ọn), n. [For *escutcheon*.] An escutcheon.—**scutch′eoned**, a. Furnished or decorated with scutcheons.

scutch-er (skuch′ẻr), n. One who or that which scutches; a device for scutching fiber.

scute (skūt), n. [L. *scutum*, shield: cf. *scutum*.] An escutcheon†; in *zoöl.*, a dermal plate, as on an armadillo, tortoise, etc.; a large scale; a scutum.

scu-tel-la (skū-tel′ä), n. Plural of *scutellum*.

scu-tel-lar (skū′tẹ-lạr or skū-tel′är), a. Of or pertaining to a scutellum.

scu-tel-late (skū′tę-lāt), *a.* Having scutella; also, formed into a scutellum. Also **scu′tel-lat-ed** (-lā-ted).—**scu-tel-la′tion** (-lā′shǫn), *n.* Scutellate state or formation; arrangement of scutella or scales; a scaly covering, as of a bird's leg.

scu-tel-lum (skū-tel′um), *n.*; pl. *scutella* (-ä). [NL., dim. of L. *scutum*, shield: cf. *scutum*.] In *zoöl.* and *bot.*, a small plate, scutum, or other shield-like part.

scu-ti-form (skū′ti-fôrm), *a.* [NL. *scutiformis*, < L. *scutum*, shield, + *forma*, form.] Shield-shaped.

scut-tle¹ (skut′l), *n.* [AS. *scutel*, < L. *scutella*, salver, dim. of *scutra*, tray, platter: cf. *scullery.*] A shallow dish†; a platter†; also, a kind of broad, shallow basket (now chiefly prov. Eng.); also, a deep vessel of sheet-iron, copper, or the like, for holding coal in small amounts.

scut-tle² (skut′l), *n.* [OF. *escoutille* (F. *écoutille*) = Sp. *escotilla*; prob. from Teut.] A small rectangular opening in the deck of a ship, furnished with a movable lid or cover; a similar opening in a ship's side; also, a similar opening in a roof, wall, etc.; also, the lid or cover for any such opening. —**scut′tle²**, *v. t.*; *-tled, -tling.* To cut a hole or holes through the bottom, sides, or deck of (a ship or boat) for any purpose, esp. through the bottom or sides for the purpose of sinking it.

scut-tle³ (skut′l), *v. i.*; *-tled, -tling.* [Perhaps from *scuddle*, obs. or prov. freq. of *scud.*] To run with quick, hurried steps (as, "Divers negroes . . . were *scuttling* about, hither and thither": Mrs. Stowe's "Uncle Tom's Cabin," xi.); run or hurry (*away, off*, etc.) in an undignified manner (as, "The few scattered men . . . were *scuttling* away like hunted ostriches," W. H. Hudson's "Purple Land," xviii.: often fig.: see *scuttle³, n.*).—**scut′tle³**, *n.* The act or performance of scuttling; often, fig., the act or the policy, on the part of a government, of withdrawing with undignified haste from the occupation or control of a country.

scut-tler¹ (skut′lėr), *n.* One who scuttles a ship or boat.

scut-tler² (skut′lėr), *n.* One who scuttles, or goes at a hurried pace; one who makes off in an undignified manner; one who advocates a policy of scuttle on the part of a government.

scu-tum (skū′tum), *n.*; pl. *-ta* (-tä). [L.] A shield or shield-like part; in *Rom. antiq.*, a large, oblong shield, as of heavy-armed legionaries; in *zoöl.*, a shield-like plate; a scute.

scye (sī), *n.* [Orig. prov. (Sc. and north. Ir.); origin obscure.] The armhole of a garment, into which the sleeve is set.

Scyl-la (sil′ä), *n.* [L., < Gr. Σκύλλα.] A dangerous rock on the Italian side of the Strait of Messina, facing Charybdis, a whirlpool on the Sicilian side, both personified in classical mythology as female monsters: often used allusively in connection with Charybdis, as presenting an alternative of dangers: as, "When I shun *Scylla*, your father, I fall into *Charybdis*, your mother" (Shakspere's "Merchant of Venice," iii. 5. 19).

Various forms of the Roman Scutum.

scy-phi-form (sī′fi-fôrm), *a.* [L. *scyphus*, < Gr. σκύφος, cup: see *-form.*] In *bot.*, shaped like a cup or goblet.

scy-pho-zo-an (sī-fō-zō′ạn). [NL. *Scyphozoa*, pl., < Gr. σκύφος, cup, + ζῷον, animal.] **I.** *a.* Belonging or pertaining to the *Scyphozoa*, a group or class of cœlenterates comprising many of the large jellyfishes. **II.** *n.* A scyphozoan animal.

scythe (sīᴛʜ), *n.* [AS. *sīthe, sigthe*, = MLG. *segede* = Icel. *sigdhr*; akin to G. *sense*, scythe, also to E. *saw³*.] An agricultural implement consisting of a long, curving blade fastened at an angle to a handle, for mowing grass, etc., by hand; also, a curved sharp blade anciently attached to

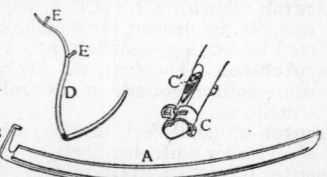

Scythe.—*A*, blade; *B*, tang; *C, C′*, fastening by which the scythe is attached rigidly to the snath; *D*, snath; *E, E*, handles grasped by the operator in mowing.

the wheels of some war-chariots.—**scythe,** *v.*; *scythed, scything.* **I.** *intr.* To use a scythe: as, "Far away . . . men were *scything*" (Galsworthy's "Dark Flower," ii. 18). **II.** *tr.* To cut or mow with a scythe: as, "Thrust in your sickles! . . . *Scything* and binding The full sheaves of sovranty" (Henley's "Song of the Sword").—**scythed,** *a.* Having scythes or sharp blades attached to the wheels: as, "Let Destiny drive forth her *scythed* car through the . . . trembling mass of humanity!" (Scott's "Black Dwarf," vi.).—**scythe′man** (-mạn), *n.*; pl. *-men.* A man who uses a scythe: applied fig. to time and death as personified.

Scyth-i-an (sith′i-ạn), *a.* Pertaining to Scythia, an ancient region which extended over parts of Europe and Asia north of the Black Sea and Caspian Sea and eastward, or to the nomadic, savage people who inhabited this region, or to their language.—**Scythian lamb,** a mythical creature, half animal, half plant, formerly supposed to inhabit Scythia; also, the shaggy rhizome of the Asiatic fern *Cibotium barometz*, which when inverted and suitably trimmed somewhat resembles a small lamb; also, the fern itself.—**Scyth′i-an,** *n.* A native or inhabitant of Scythia; also, the language of Scythia.

Scythian Lamb (*Cibotium barometz*).

'sdeath (sdeth), *interj.* A reduced form of *God's death*, used as an oath: as, "'*Sdeath!* sir, do you question my understanding?" (Peacock's "Headlong Hall," v.). [Archaic.]

sea (sē), *n.* [AS. *sǣ* = D. *zee* = G. *see* = Icel. *sær* = Sw. *sjö* = Dan. *sö* = Goth. *saiws*, sea.] The salt waters that cover the greater part of the earth's surface; a division of these waters, of considerable extent, more or less definitely marked off by land boundaries (as, the North *Sea*); a large lake or landlocked body of water (now only in 'inland sea' and certain proper names); also, the swell of the ocean or some other body of water (as, "The ship had fresh way, but a great *sea* rolling in upon us from the N.E.": Defoe's "Captain Singleton," xiv.); also, a large, heavy wave (as, "The wide river was running in *seas* that made the boat stagger in her course": Howells's "Chance Acquaintance," iv.); also, fig., a widely extended, copious, or overwhelming quantity or mass of something (as, a *sea* of upturned faces; "a *sea* of troubles," Shakspere's "Hamlet," iii. 1. 59); in *Jewish antiq.*, same as *brazen sea*, under *brazen, a.*—**at sea**, out on the ocean; fig., in a state of uncertainty or perplexity; also, wide of the truth; quite wrong.—**the four seas**, the waters bounding Great Britain on the north, south, east, and west.—**the seven seas**, the Arctic and Antarctic, north and south Atlantic, north and south Pacific, and Indian oceans: as, "Far and far our homes are set round *the Seven Seas*" (Kipling's "Flowers").

sea=an-chor (sē′angʺkǫr), *n.* A floating anchor used at sea to prevent a ship from drifting or to keep its head to the wind: commonly consisting of a framed cone of canvas dragged along with its large open base toward the ship.

sea=a-nem-o-ne (sē′-ạ-nem′ǫ-nē), *n.* Any of numerous flower-like polyps (order *Actiniaria*) with a fleshy, cylindrical body and a mouth surrounded by numerous tentacles.

sea=bass (sē′bȧs), *n.* A common serranoid marine food-fish, *Centropristes striatus*, with a peculiar caudal fin (see cut on following page); also, any of various allied fishes.

Sea-anemone (*Metridium marginatum*), open and closed.

---

fat, fāte, fär, fȧll, ȧsk, fâre; net, mē, hėr; pin, pīne; not, nōte, mŏve, nôr; up, lūte, pull; oi, oil; ou, out; (lightened) a-vi̇̄ary, ė̇lect, agǫny, intǫ, ūnite; (obscured) errạnt, operä, ardẹnt, actǫr, natūre; ch, chip; g, go; th, thin; ᴛʜ, then; y, you;

sea=bean (sē′bēn), *n.* The large, hard, bean-like seed of a tropical legumi-nous climbing plant, *Entada scandens*, often carried by ocean currents to dis-tant shores; the plant producing this seed; also, any of various small univale shells somewhat resembling coffee-beans.

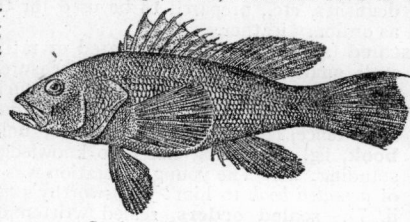

Sea-bass (*Centropristes striatus*).

sea=bear (sē′bār), *n.* The polar bear; also, any of various fur-seals, esp. the northern fur-seal.

sea=bird (sē′bėrd), *n.* A bird frequenting the sea or coast.

sea=board (sē′bōrd). [See *board, n.*] **I.** *n.* The line where land and sea meet; the seashore, or the land near the sea. **II.** *a.* Bordering on or adjoining the sea.

sea=born (sē′bôrn), *a.* Born in or of the sea; produced in or by the sea.

sea=borne (sē′bôrn), *a.* Conveyed by sea; carried on the sea.

sea=bread (sē′bred), *n.* Ship-biscuit; hardtack.

sea=bream (sē′brēm), *n.* Any of certain sparoid fishes, esp. *Pagellus centrodontus*, a European marine food-fish; some-times, any sparoid fish.

sea=breeze (sē′brēz), *n.* A breeze blowing from the sea; specif., a breeze of this kind felt near the coast, blowing from about 10 A.M. until sunset.

sea=calf (sē′käf or -kȧf), *n.*; pl. *-calves* (-kävz or -kȧvz). The harbor-seal.

sea=cap-tain (sē′kap″tạn), *n.* The captain or commanding officer of a ship.

sea=coal (sē′kōl), *n.* Coal dug from the earth, as distin-guished from charcoal: possibly so called because orig. brought to London by sea.

sea-coast (sē′kōst), *n.* The land immediately adjacent to the sea.

sea=cow (sē′kou), *n.* Any sirenian, as the manatee, dugong, etc.; also, the walrus; also, the hippopotamus.

sea=cu-cum-ber (sē′kū′kum-bėr), *n.* A holothurian: so called from the shape of certain species.

sea=dev-il (sē′dev″l), *n.* A devil-fish.

sea=dog (sē′dog), *n.* The harbor-seal; also, the dogfish, *Squalus acanthias*; also, a sailor, esp. one of long experience (as, "an old fighting *sea-dog*": J. Conrad's "Rover," ii.); also, a fog-dog.

sea=duck (sē′duk), *n.* Any duck of the subfamily *Fuligulinæ*, including the scoter, eider, etc., the members of which have a lobate hind toe and are mostly found on salt water.

Sea-cucumber (*Pentacta frondosa*).

sea=ea-gle (sē′ē″gl), *n.* Any of various eagles of the genus *Haliaëtus* which feed mostly on fish.

sea=ear (sē′ēr), *n.* An ear-shell.

sea=el-e-phant (sē′el″ē-fạnt), *n.* A large seal. *Macrorhinus elephantinus*, of the colder southern waters: so called from the prolonged trunk-like snout of the adult male.

sea=fan (sē′-fan), *n.* Any of certain actinozoans, esp. *Gorgonia flabellum* of the West Indies, in which the colony assumes a fan-like form.

Sea-elephant.

sea-far-er (sē′fār″ėr), *n.* A traveler on the sea; esp., a

sailor.—**sea′far″ing. I.** *n.* Traveling by sea; esp., the business or calling of a sailor. **II.** *a.* That travels by sea; esp., following the sea as a calling.

sea=feath-er (sē′feᴛʜ″ėr), *n.* A sea-pen.

sea=fight (sē′fīt), *n.* A fight between ships at sea; a naval battle.

sea=flow-er (sē′flou″ėr), *n.* A sea-anemone or some similar organism.

sea=foam (sē′fōm), *n.* The foam of the sea; also, meer-schaum.

sea=fowl (sē′foul), *n.* A sea-bird.

sea=gate (sē′gāt), *n.* A gate fronting, or giving access to, the sea; also, a place of entrance from the sea into a harbor or the like.

sea=girt (sē′gėrt), *a.* Girt or surrounded by the sea: as, "a green and *sea-girt* promontory" (Shelley's "Rosalind and Helen," 1050).

sea=god (sē′god), *n.* A god of the sea, as Neptune or Nereus. —**sea′=god″dess,** *n.* A goddess of the sea, as Amphitrite, wife of Poseidon.

sea=go-ing (sē′gō″ing). **I.** *n.* Going or traveling by sea; seafaring. **II.** *a.* That goes or travels on the sea; seafaring; designed or fit for going to sea, as a vessel; also, going to the sea; of fishes, catadromous.

sea=green (sē′grēn′). **I.** *a.* Of a clear, light bluish-green color. **II.** *n.* A sea-green color.

sea=gull (sē′gul), *n.* A gull, esp. any of the marine species.

sea=heath (sē′hēth), *n.* A heath-like shrub, *Frankenia lævis*, of European coasts; also, some other plant of the same genus.

sea=hedge-hog (sē′hej″hog), *n.* A sea-urchin.

sea=hog (sē′hog), *n.* A porpoise.

sea=hol-ly (sē′hol″i), *n.* The eryngo (plant), *Eryngium maritimum*.

sea=horse (sē′hôrs), *n.* A fabulous marine animal with the fore parts of a horse and the hinder parts of a fish; also, a walrus; also, any of various small marine fishes, mostly of the ge-nus *Hippocampus*, with a mailed body, a prehensile tail, and a head suggesting that of a horse.

sea=is-land (sē′ī″lạnd), *a.* Noting a long-staple variety of cotton grown on the islands off the coast of South Caro-lina and Georgia, and also elsewhere, or the plant producing it (see *cotton, n.*).

sea=kale (sē′kāl), *n.* A broad-leaved, maritime brassicaceous plant, *Crambe maritima*, of Europe, used as a pot-herb.

sea=king (sē′king), *n.* One of the pi-ratical Scandinavian chiefs who rav-aged the coasts of Europe during the early medieval period.

Sea-horse (genus *Hippo-campus*).

seal[1] (sēl), *n.* [OF. *seel* (F. *sceau*), < L. *sigillum* (usually pl., *sigilla*), small figure, seal: see *sigil*.] A device impressed on a piece of wax or the like, or an impression, wafer, mark, etc., representing this; affixed to a document as evidence of authenticity or attestation; hence, fig., some-thing that authenticates, confirms, or ratifies; some-times, a mark or the like serving as visible evidence of something; also, a piece of wax or similar substance, often impressed with a de-vice, affixed to a folded document, an envelop, a closed door, etc., which then cannot be opened without breaking this; some similar contrivance for effectually closing a thing; fig., some-thing for keeping a thing close or secret; a vow of secrecy; also, a stamp engraved with a special device for making impressions on wax, etc., as in attestation;

Seal of the United States.

(variable) ḏ as d or j, ş as s or sh, ṯ as t or ch, ẕ as z or zh; *o*, F. cloche; ü, F. menu; çh, Sc. loch; ṅ, F. bonbon; ′, primary accent; ″, secondary accent; †, obsolete; <, from; +, and; =, equals. See also lists at beginning of book.

a piece of stone, etc., so engraved, set in a finger-ring or worn as a pendant from a watch-chain or fob; also, in *plumbing*, a small amount of water left standing in a trap to prevent the escape of foul air from below.—**great seal.** See under *great.*—**privy seal.** See under *privy, a.*—**seal**[1], *v. t.* [OF. *seeler* (F. *sceller*).] To affix a seal to (a document) as evidence of authenticity, confirmation, or ratification; fig., to authenticate or attest solemnly as if by affixing a seal; also, to ratify or render binding (an agreement, etc.) by the affixing of seals, or by any ceremonial act; also, to decide irrevocably as if by the affixing of a seal (as, "The fate of the king was *sealed*": Morley's "Oliver Cromwell," iii. 6); also, to grant under or as under one's seal, as a charter or a pardon; also, to impose in a binding manner, as an obligation or a penalty; also, to mark as by a seal for a particular destination; designate or set apart (as, "the God . . . who had watched over the growth of a family into a nation, who had *sealed* that family for Himself": Seeley's "Ecce Homo," iv.); also, to impress a seal upon as an evidence of legal or standard exactness, measure, quality, etc.; also, to fasten (a letter, etc.) with a seal, or with sealing-wax, a wafer, mucilage, or the like; place a seal upon (a closed door, etc.) so that entrance cannot be effected without breaking the seal; fig., to fasten or close as if by a seal (as, "Through the town few eyes were *sealed* by sleep": W. Morris's "Jason," iv. 1); bind to silence or secrecy (as, to *seal* a person's lips); also, to close (a vessel, an aperture, etc.) with a coating of wax, cement, etc., or by any form of fastening that must be broken before access can be had; in general, to close effectually; also, to fix securely in a position, as with wax, cement, etc.; fig., to fix immovably (as, "She gave me never a look, For her eyes were *seal'd* to the holy book": M. Arnold's "Forsaken Merman"); also, to inclose in something secured by a seal; hence, to inclose effectually, confine, or imprison (as, "*seal'd* within the iron hills": Tennyson's "In Memoriam," lvi.).

seal[2] (sēl), *n.* [AS. *seolh* = Icel. *selr* = Sw. *säl* = Dan. *sæl* = OHG. *selah*, seal.] Any of the marine carnivorous mammals with flippers of the families *Phocidæ* ('true seals,' or 'earless seals') and *Otariidæ* ('eared seals,' or otaries) (see *harbor-seal, sea-lion, hair-seal, fur-seal*); esp., the common (earless) harborseal, *Phoca vitulina*; also, the skin of the seal, or leather made from it; often, the fur of the fur-seal; sealskin; also (with an epithet), some other fur used as a substitute for sealskin (as, Hudson *seal*, obtained from the muskrat).—**seal**[2], *v. i.* To hunt or take seals.

Gray Seal (*Halichœrus gryphus*, family *Phocidæ*).

Eared Seal, or Otary (*Otaria forsteri*).

sea=lav-en-der (sē'lav″en-dėr), *n.* An old-world plumbaginaceous plant, *Limonium limonium*, a seashore perennial bearing one-sided spikes of small lavender-colored flowers; also, some similar plant of the same genus, as *L. carolinianum* of the eastern coast of North America. See *statice.*

sea=law-yer (sē'lå″yėr), *n.* An argumentative, querulous, or captious sailor; a sailor given to criticizing orders and arguing about his work. [Colloq.]

seal=brown (sēl'broun′). **I.** *a.* Of a rich, dark brown color suggestive of dressed and dyed sealskin. **II.** *n.* A seal-brown color.

sea=leath-er (sē'leтн″ėr), *n.* The skin of sharks, porpoises, dogfishes, etc., prepared to be used for the same purposes as ordinary leather.

sealed (sēld), *p. a.* Authenticated or ratified by or as by a seal; guaranteed as to exactness, measure, quality, etc., by a seal; also, fastened with a seal, or in such a manner as not to be opened without breaking the fastening; closed by sealing; hence, fig., closed to knowledge; unknown.—**a sealed book,** fig., something closed to knowledge, or past understanding: as, "The young generation was always something of *a sealed book* to him" (Galsworthy's "Saint's Progress," ii. 7).—**sealed orders,** sealed written orders, not to be opened until after leaving port, given to the commander of a vessel to instruct him where to proceed on a voyage: as, "The captain came on board with *sealed orders*, with directions not to open them until off Ushant" (Marryat's "Peter Simple," xxix.).

sea=legs (sē'legz), *n. pl.* Legs habituated to walking steadily on a rolling or pitching ship: as, "Michel, who had good *sea-legs*, kept his balance to the movements of the craft" (J. Conrad's "Rover," xv.). [Colloq.]

sea=leop-ard (sē'lep″ärd), *n.* Any of certain spotted antarctic seals of the family *Phocidæ*, as of the genus *Leptonychotes*.

seal-er[1] (sē'lėr), *n.* One who seals; one who affixes a seal or stamps with a seal; in the U. S., an officer appointed to examine and test weights and measures, and to set a stamp upon such as are true to the standard.

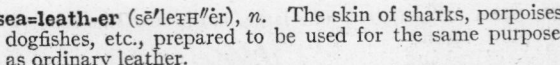

Sea-leopard (*Leptonychotes weddelli*).

seal-er[2] (sē'lėr), *n.* A person or a vessel engaged in hunting or taking seals.—**seal-er-y** (-i), *n.;* pl. *-ies* (-iz). The occupation of hunting or taking seals; also, a place where seals abound or are caught.

sea=let-ter (sē'let″ėr), *n.* A document formerly issued by the civil authorities of a port in which a vessel was fitted out, certifying her nationality, and specifying the kind, quantity, ownership, and destination of her cargo, and other particulars.

sea=let-tuce (sē'let″is), *n.* Any seaweed of the genus *Ulva*, whose green fronds are sometimes eaten like lettuce.

sea=lev-el (sē'lev″el), *n.* The surface of the sea; specif., the horizontal plane or level corresponding to the surface of the sea when half-way between mean high and low water.

sea=lil-y (sē'lil″i), *n.;* pl. *-ies* (-iz). A crinoid.

sea=line (sē'līn), *n.* The horizon at sea; also, a long line for fishing in deep water.

seal-ing (sē'ling), *n.* The process of hunting or taking seals.

seal-ing=wax (sē'ling-waks), *n.* A resinous preparation, soft when heated, used for sealing letters, etc.

sea=li-on (sē'lī″ọn), *n.* Any of various eared seals of large size, as *Eumetopias stelleri* of the northern Pacific, *Otaria jubata* of the Pacific coast of South America, or *Zalophus californianus* of the Pacific coast of North America.

seal=ring (sēl'ring′), *n.* A finger-ring bearing a seal.

seal-skin (sēl'skin), *n.* The skin of the seal; esp., the skin or fur of the fur-seal, dressed for use, constituting one of the choicest of furs; a garment or article made of this fur.

California Sea-lion (*Zalophus californianus*).

sea=lung-wort (sē'lung″wért), *n.* A boraginaceous herb, *Pneumaria maritima*, growing on northern seacoasts.

Seal-y-ham (sē'li-ham) **ter'ri-er.** [From *Sealyham*, name of an estate (now a sanatorium) between Haverfordwest and Fishguard, in Pembrokeshire, Wales, where the breed was originated about the middle of the 19th century by John Tucker-Edwardes, and used particularly for otter-hunting.] One of a breed of terriers of Welsh origin (see etym.), having short legs, long, powerful, level jaws, large black nose with wide nostrils, and rough or shaggy white coat with lemon, tan, or brindled markings on head and ears, and regularly having the tail docked.

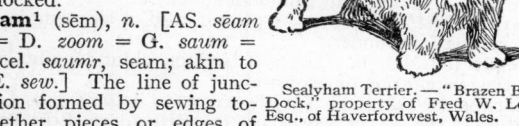

Sealyham Terrier. — "Brazen Barry Dock," property of Fred W. Lewis, Esq., of Haverfordwest, Wales.

seam¹ (sēm), *n.* [AS. *sēam* = D. *zoom* = G. *saum* = Icel. *saumr*, seam; akin to E. *sew*.] The line of junction formed by sewing together pieces or edges of cloth, leather, or the like; also, sewing or needlework (now prov.); also, any line of junction between abutting edges; a narrow crevice between edges or parts (as, to calk the *seams* of a ship, between planks or plates); a crack or fissure; a furrow or groove; any linear indentation or mark, as a wrinkle or a scar; in *knitting*, a line of stitches formed by purling; in *geol.*, a comparatively thin stratum; a bed, as of coal.—**seam¹,** *v.* **I.** *tr.* To sew the seam or seams of; join with a seam or seams; also, to cleave with seams, fissures, or the like (as, "volcanic hills . . . *seamed* with tremendous chasms," Irving's "Captain Bonneville," xliii.; "Marshes, *seamed* and crossed With narrow creeks," Whittier's "Tent on the Beach"); furrow; mark (the face, etc.) with wrinkles, scars, etc. (as, "a pale face *seamed* by a long scar got in a duel": G. W. Cable's "John March, Southerner," xiii.); in *knitting*, to knit with or in a seam. **II.** *intr.* To make seams; also, to become cracked, fissured, or furrowed; in *knitting*, to make a seam.

seam² (sēm), *n.* [OF. *saim* = Sp. *saín*, < ML. *sagimen*, fat, lard, connected with L. *sagina*, a fattening: cf. *saynète*.] Fat; grease; lard. See Shakspere's "Troilus and Cressida," ii. 3, 195. [Now prov.]

sea=maid (sē'mād), *n.* A mermaid; also, a goddess or nymph of the sea. Also **sea'=maid″en.**

sea=man (sē'man), *n.*; pl. *-men.* One whose occupation it is to assist in the navigation of a ship; a sailor, specif. one below the rank of officer.—**sea'man-like, sea'man-ly,** *a.* Like or befitting a seaman.—**sea'man-ship,** *n.* The art of navigating a ship at sea; skill in this art.

sea=mark (sē'märk), *n.* The boundary of the flow of the sea; also, a conspicuous object on land, visible from the sea, and serving to guide or warn mariners.

seamed (sēmd), *p. a.* Joined with a seam or seams, as by sewing; also, cleft, furrowed, or marked with seams (as, "a great ship, an East Indiaman, with rusty, *seamed*, blistered sides": G. W. Curtis's "Prue and I," iii.); often, of the face, etc., marked with lines or wrinkles.

seam-er (sē'mér), *n.* One who or that which seams; specif., a kind of sewing-machine for seaming fabrics together; also, a machine for bending two pieces of sheet-metal to unite them in a seam or joint.

sea=mew (sē'mū), *n.* [See *mew¹*.] A sea-gull, esp. a common European species, *Larus canus*.

sea=mile (sē'mīl), *n.* A geographical or nautical mile. See under *mile*.

sea=milk-wort (sē'milk″wért), *n.* See *milkwort*.

seam-i-ness (sē'mi-nes), *n.* The state or quality of being seamy.

seam-less (sēm'les), *a.* Without a seam.

sea=moss (sē'môs), *n.* Seaweed; also, carrageen; also, a polyzoön or bryozoön.

sea=mouse (sē'mous), *n.*; pl. *-mice* (-mīs). Any of various large marine annelids of the genus *Aphrodite* and allied genera: so called from their mouse-like appearance, due to a covering of long, fine, hair-like setæ.

seam-ster, semp-ster (sēm'stér, semp'-), *n.* [AS. *sēamestre*, fem. of *sēamere*, tailor, < *sēam*, E. *seam¹*: see *-ster*.] One whose occupation is sewing: orig. applied to a woman, but now only to a man.—**seam'stress, semp'stress,** *n.* A woman whose occupation is sewing; a needlewoman.

seam-y (sē'mi), *a.*; compar. *seamier*, superl. *seamiest.* Having or showing seams; of the nature of a seam.—**seamy side,** the under side of a garment or the like, showing the seams or the rough edges of the seams; hence, fig., the least pleasing or favorable, or the roughest or worst, side of anything (as, the *seamy side* of life: from the use in Shakspere's "Othello," iv. 2. 146, "Some such squire he was That turn'd your wit the *seamy side* without, And made you to suspect me").

Sean-ad (shan'aᴛʜ), *n.* Same as *Seanad Eireann*.

Sean-ad Eir-eann (shan'aᴛʜ ār'an). [Ir. *seanad*, senate, and *Éireann*, gen. of *Éire*, Erin.] The Senate of the State of Ireland. See *Oireachtas*.

sé-ance (sā'äns, F. sā-äns), *n.* [F., < *seoir*, sit, < L. *sedere*: see *see¹*.] A sitting or session, as of a learned society or other body of persons; specif., a meeting of spiritualists seeking to receive communications from spirits (as, "attending spiritualist lectures and *séances*, whenever a noted medium visited the place": John Hay's "Bread-Winners," ii.).

sea=net-tle (sē'net″l), *n.* A jellyfish: so called because of the stinging organs (nematocysts) in its tentacles.

sea=nymph (sē'nimf), *n.* A nymph of the sea; a Nereid.

sea=on-ion (sē'un″yon), *n.* A liliaceous plant, *Urginea maritima*, a native of the Mediterranean region, yielding the medicinal bulb squill.

sea=ot-ter (sē'ot″ér), *n.* A marine otter, *Enhydris marina* (or *lutris*), of the shores of the northern Pacific, with a very valuable fur.

Sea-otter.

sea=pen (sē'pen), *n.* Any of various polyps of the family *Pennatulidæ*, which form elongated, feather-like colonies.

sea=pie (sē'pī), *n.* A sailors' dish composed of meat, vegetables, etc., cooked between layers of paste.

sea=piece (sē'pēs), *n.* A picture representing a scene at sea: as, "a piece representing Sir F. Drake's action in the year 1580, an excellent *sea-piece*" (Evelyn's "Diary," July 10, 1656).

sea=plane (sē'plān), *n.* A hydro-aëroplane for use over the sea, esp. one provided with floats rather than a boat-like under part.

sea=por-cu-pine (sē'pôr″kū-pīn), *n.* Any of various globefishes having the skin covered with spiny processes, as *Diodon hystrix*, common in tropical seas.

sea=port (sē'pōrt), *n.* A port or harbor on the seacoast; a harbor or place conveniently accessible to and providing accommodation for sea-going vessels coming to discharge and take on cargoes, etc.; a town or city at such a place.

Sea-porcupine (*Diodon hystrix*).

sea=post (sē'pōst), *n.* The postal service conducted at sea, concerned with the sorting of mail on ocean steamers so as to be in readiness for prompt transmission to the various destinations on arrival in port.

sea=pow-er (sē'pou″ér), *n.* A nation or state having an important navy or great influence on the sea; also, the strength or ability of a nation for naval warfare, or naval strength (as, "The Influence of *Sea Power* upon History, 1660–1783," the title of a book by A. T. Mahan, published in 1890).

sea=purse (sē'pérs), *n.* The corneous egg-case of certain rays and sharks; also, a swirl of the undertow making a small whirlpool on the surface of the water, and dangerous to bathers.

sea=puss (sē′pùs), *n.* Corruption of *sea-purse* (undertow).

sea-quake (sē′kwāk), *n.* An agitation of the sea due to a submarine eruption or earthquake.

sear[1], **sere** (sēr), *a.* [AS. *sēar* = MLG. *sōr* = D. *zoor*, dry, withered.] Dry or withered: used esp. of vegetation: as, "My way of life Is fall'n into the *sear*, the yellow leaf" (Shakspere's "Macbeth," v. 3. 23); "The beautiful flower-garden . . . looked rather brown and *sere*, after the hot winds" (H. Kingsley's "Geoffry Hamlyn," i.). [Now chiefly poetic.] —**sear**[1], *v.* [Also (now only of drying or withering) *sere*; AS. *sēarian*, < *sēar*.] **I.** *intr.* To become dry, or wither, as vegetation; also, fig., to become hardened or callous (as, "Her conscience *sears*": W. Morris's "Defence of Guenevere," 147). [Now rare.] **II.** *tr.* To cause to dry up or wither; also, to burn or char the surface of, with heat, a hot iron, or the like; cauterize; burn or scorch injuriously or painfully (lit. or fig.: as, trees *seared* by the lightning; "The silly fuss of that man *seared* his very soul," J. Conrad's "Rescue," iii. 9); also, fig., to harden, or make callous or unfeeling (as, "manifesting . . . a more *seared* and callous conscience than even Nero himself": Fielding's "Tom Jones," viii. 1).

sear[2] (sēr), *n.* [Cf. OF. *serre*, lock, < L. *sera*, bar for fastening a door.] A pivoted piece in a gun-lock which holds the hammer at full cock or half-cock.

sea=ra-ven (sē′rā″vn), *n.* The cormorant; also, a marine fish, *Hemitripterus americanus*, common on the northern Atlantic coast of America, of large size and singular appearance, and having a long spinous dorsal fin.

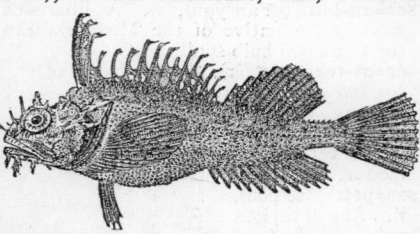

Sea-raven (*Hemitripterus americanus*).

search (sèrch), *v.* [OF. *cerchier* (F. *chercher*), < LL. *circare*, go about, traverse, < L. *circus*, circle: see *circus*.] **I.** *tr.* To go or look through carefully in seeking to find something; explore, as a place, in quest of something; examine, as a person, by going through his pockets, removing his garments, or the like, in order to ascertain whether he has some article concealed on his person; in general, to examine carefully or with earnest effort (as, to *search* one's own heart; "His eyes *searched* and *searched* her face," Galsworthy's "Dark Flower," ii. 14; "*Search* the scriptures," John, v. 39); probe (a wound, etc.); of wind, cold, gun-fire, etc., to pierce or penetrate; also, to seek or look for, or endeavor to find (archaic: as, "My fancy, ranging thro′ and thro′, To *search* a meaning for the song," Tennyson's "Day-Dream," 247); bring or find (*out*) by a search (as, "Edwin *searched* out the bicycle and brought it to the window," Arnold Bennett's "These Twain," v.; he *searched* out all the facts of the case). **II.** *intr.* To make search; seek; make examination or investigation.—**search**, *n.* [OF. *cerche* (F. *cherche*).] The act or an act of searching; a going or looking through a place or thing in seeking to find something; careful examination or investigation; specif., the searching of a neutral vessel, or the examining of its papers, cargo, etc., as at sea, by officers of a belligerent state, in order to verify its nationality and ascertain whether it carries contraband, etc. (as, the right of visit and *search*).—**search′a-ble**, *a.* That may be searched.—**search′er**, *n.*—**search′ing**, *p. a.* That searches; examining carefully or thoroughly; thorough or rigorous, as an examination; keenly observant, or penetrating, as the eyes, gaze, etc.; piercing or sharp, as the wind, etc.—**search′-ing-ly**, *adv.*—**search′ing-ness**, *n.*—**search′=light**, *n.* A device, usually consisting of an arc-light and a reflector, for throwing a powerful beam of light in any direction desired; also, a beam of light so thrown (as, "The *search-lights* had begun their nightly wanderings. It was a sky of ghosts and shadows": Galsworthy's "Saint's Progress," iii. 7).—**search′=war″rant**, *n.* In *law*, a warrant authorizing the searching of a house, etc., as for stolen goods.

sea=risk (sē′risk), *n.* Risk or hazard at sea; danger of injury or destruction by the sea.

sea=rob-in (sē′rob″in), *n.* Any of various gurnards (fishes), esp. certain reddish American species of the genus *Prionotus*.

Sea-robin (*Prionotus carolinus*).

sea=room (sē′rōm), *n.* Space at sea free from obstruction in which a ship can be easily maneuvered or navigated: as, "The sloop . . . at length . . . recovered *sea-room* enough to weather the Point of Warroch" (Scott's "Guy Mannering," ix.).

sea=rov-er (sē′rō″vèr), *n.* A pirate; also, a ship employed in cruising for plunder.

sea=salt (sē′sȧlt), *n.* The salt (sodium chloride) obtained by the evaporation of sea-water.

sea=scape (sē′skāp), *n.* [With *-scape* as in *landscape*.] A picture of the sea, or a sea-piece (as, "He adorned the Paris salon with a large *seascape* showing penguins in the foreground": Arnold Bennett's "Buried Alive," i.); also, a view or prospect of the sea.

sea=ser-pent (sē′sèr″pent), *n.* An enormous snake-like marine animal of popular tradition; also, any of the venomous marine snakes with a fin-like tail constituting the family *Hydrophidæ*; also [*cap.*], in *astron.*, the southern constellation Hydra.

sea=shell (sē′shel), *n.* The shell of any marine mollusk.

sea=shore (sē′shōr), *n.* The shore along, or the land lying adjacent to, the sea or ocean; also, the ground between the ordinary high-water and low-water marks.

Sea-serpent (genus *Hydrophis*).

sea=sick (sē′sik), *a.* Affected with nausea or other physical derangement from the motion of a vessel at sea or on rough water.—**sea′sick″ness**, *n.*

sea=side (sē′sīd), **I.** *n.* The margin of the sea; the sea-coast, esp. as resorted to for pleasure or health. **II.** *a.* Belonging to, situated at, or pertaining to the seaside: as, "a little *sea-side* place close to Caen" (G. Meredith's "Diana of the Crossways," xxii.).

sea sled (sē sled). A motor-boat of a more or less sled-like form, capable of great speed, having a square bow and stern, and characterized esp. by an inverted V-shaped longitudinal trough extending along the bottom of the hull. [Proprietary name.]

sea=slug (sē′slug), *n.* Any of various marine gastropods more or less resembling the terrestrial slugs, being without a shell in the adult state; also, a holothurian.

Sea-slug (gastropod : *Hermæa bifida*).

sea=snail (sē′snāl), *n.* Any of various spiral-shelled marine gastropods, as of the genera *Natica*, *Littorina*, etc.; a periwinkle.

sea=snake (sē′snāk), *n.* Same as *sea-serpent* (in first two senses).

sea=sol-dier (sē′sōl″jèr), *n.* A marine.

sea=son (sē′zn), *n.* [OF. *seson*, *saison* (F. *saison*), < L. *satio(n-)*, a sowing, < *serere* (pp. *satus*), sow: see *sow*[1].] A period of the year characterized by particular conditions of weather, temperature, etc.; esp., one of the four periods of the year, spring, summer, autumn, and winter, astronomically beginning each at an equinox or solstice, but popularly at different dates in different climates; also, a period or time of the year marked by a certain condition of affairs or

Sea-snail or Periwinkle (*Littorina littorea*).

by particular festivities, activities, etc. (as, the busy *season* or the dull *season* in trade; the Christmas holiday *season*; the *season* of harvest); the period of the year when something flourishes, is at its best, or is fit and available for use (as, the chrysanthemum *season*; the peach *season*; the oyster *season*); the period of the year when something is in vogue, going on, or particularly active (as, the hunting *season*; the baseball *season*; the theatrical *season*); the period of the year when a place is most frequented or active, often the period of greatest social activity (as, the *season* at Atlantic City; the London *season*); a period of time, experience, or activity, or one of a succession of such periods (as, "A bad king is like a bad *season*. The next may bring improvement," Froude's "Cæsar," ix.; "She had played in three Shakespearean *seasons*," L. Merrick's "Position of Peggy Harper," i. 5); in general, a period or time (as, "at a certain *season* of our life": Thoreau's "Walden," ii.); also, a space of time indefinitely, or a while (as, "Thou shalt be blind, not seeing the sun for a *season*": Acts, xiii. 11); also, a suitable or proper time (as, "But that was no *season* for internal dissensions": Macaulay's "Hist. of Eng.," i.); the fitting or right time; also, seasoning†.—**in good season,** in good time for something; sufficiently early.—**in season,** in the time or state for use, eating, etc.; in the best condition; in the period when lawfully to be killed or taken, as game; also, at the proper or right time; opportunely; sufficiently early.—**out of season,** not in season; not fit for use, eating, etc.; out of the period when lawfully to be killed or taken, as game; also, not at the proper or right time; unseasonably or unseasonable.—**sea′son,** v. [OF. *saisonner*.] **I.** *tr.* To bring to due or fine condition by a period of keeping, exposure to suitable conditions, or treatment (as, to *season* a cask by keeping liquor in it; to *season* a tobacco-pipe by smoking it); age, mature, or ripen; dry and harden (timber) by due process; harden or make fit physically (as, "an extremely vigorous person . . . tanned and *seasoned* by the life of his class, by the yachting, hunting, and shooting": Mrs. H. Ward's "Lady Rose's Daughter," x.); acclimatize; inure to service, a mode of life, etc. (as, troops *seasoned* by past campaigns); render experienced; also, to heighten or improve the flavor of (food) with some ingredient added, as condiments, spices, herbs, or the like; fig., to tincture or mix with something that gives relish or a certain character (as, conversation *seasoned* with wit or with profanity); temper, modify, or soften (as, "when mercy *seasons* justice": Shakspere's "Merchant of Venice," iv. 1. 197). **II.** *intr.* To become seasoned, or matured, hardened, inured, or the like.

sea-son-a-ble (sē′zn-a-bl), *a.* Suitable to the season of the year (as, *seasonable* weather); also, coming or occurring at the right season, timely, or opportune (as, "That was a very *seasonable* pamphlet of his on the Catholic Question": George Eliot's "Middlemarch," vii.); also, in good season, or early (as, "At a very *seasonable* hour a glow of crimson light came flooding through the window": Hawthorne's "House of the Seven Gables," v.).—**sea′son-a-ble-ness,** *n.* —**sea′son-a-bly,** *adv.*

sea-son-al (sē′zn-al), *a.* Pertaining to or dependent on the seasons of the year or some particular season; periodical. —**sea′son-al-ly,** *adv.*

sea-soned (sē′znd), *p. a.* Matured, hardened, or inured by some process of seasoning (as, *seasoned* timber; *seasoned* troops; "Even the *seasoned* old savage was affected [by liquor]," W. H. Hudson's "Green Mansions," i.); experienced; tested and approved by time, or of established merit or value, as securities; also, flavored with seasoning, as food.

sea-son-er (sē′zn-ėr), *n.* One who or that which seasons.

sea-son-ing (sē′zn-ing), *n.* The act of one who or that which seasons; also, something that seasons, or serves to season; esp., salt, spices, herbs, or the like added to food to give it flavor or relish; fig., a seasoning tincture or admixture (as, a *seasoning* of caution in one's plans).

sea=spi-der (sē′spī″dėr), *n.* Any of the spider-like marine arthropods of the group *Pycnogonida* (or *Pantopoda*), as *Nymphon hamatum* (see cut in next column); also, a spider-crab.

sea=squirt (sē′skwėrt), *n.* An ascidian: so called from its squirting water when contracting.

seat (sēt), *n.* [ME. *sete*, from Scand.: cf. Icel. *sæti*, Sw. *säte*, Dan. *sæde*, seat, also AS. *sæt*, ambush; akin to E. *sit*.] The place on or in which one sits; a place to seat one person; also, the right to use such a place, as in a theater; a right to sit as a member in a legislative or similar body; a right to the privileges of membership in a stock-exchange or the like; also, something made or used for sitting on, as a chair, bench, or throne; the particular part of a chair or the like on which one sits; also, that part of the body on which one sits; the buttocks or breech; also, that part

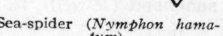

Sea-spider (*Nymphon hamatum*).

of a garment which covers the breech; also, manner of sitting, as on horseback (as "He . . . had the graceful *seat* of an experienced horseman": Dickens's "Barnaby Rudge," x.); also, that on which the base of anything rests; the base itself; also, site, location, or locality; abode or residence; a country-seat (as, "The family *seat* was in Gloucestershire": M. Hewlett's "Open Country," i.); established place or center, as of government; a place in which something prevails or is established (as, the *seat* of war; a *seat* of learning).—**seat,** *v. t.* To place on a seat or seats; cause to sit down; often, to settle in a seat or position of authority; put into a seat in a legislative body; also, to find seats for, or accommodate with seats; afford seats for (as, a hall that *seats* a thousand persons); also, to fix or settle in a particular place; locate; specif., to set or secure in the proper place; fix in proper position, as on a bed or support; also, to fit up (a room or the like) with seats; put a seat on (a chair, etc.); renew the seat of (a garment).

sea=tan-gle (sē′tang″gl), *n.* Any of various seaweeds, esp. of the genus *Laminaria*.

seat=cane (sēt′kān), *n.* A seat-stick.

seat-ed (sē′ted), *a.* Having a seat or seats: as, two-*seated*.

seat-ing (sē′ting), *n.* The act of furnishing with a seat or seats; the arrangement of the seats in a building, etc.; the seats themselves; material for seats, esp. haircloth for upholstering the seats of chairs, etc.; also, a support, as for the base of something; a part resting on such a support.

sea=trout (sē′trout), *n.* Any of various species of trout found in salt water, as the salmon-trout, *Salmo trutta*; also, any of various weakfishes.

seat=stick (sēt′stik), *n.* A stick or cane with an upper part which can be adjusted to form a seat, used by spectators at golf-matches, races, etc.

sea=turn (sē′tėrn), *n.* A gale or breeze coming from the sea, generally accompanied by mists.

sea=u-ni-corn (sē′ū″ni-kôrn), *n.* The narwhal: so called from its tusk.

sea=ur-chin (sē′ėr″chin), *n.* Any echinoderm of the class *Echinoidea*, comprising marine animals having a more or less globular or dis-coid form, and a spine-bearing shell composed of many calcareous plates.

Common New England Sea-urchin (*Strongylocentrotus drobachiensis*).

sea=view (sē′vū), *n.* A view or prospect of the sea, or at sea (as, "a room with a *sea-view*": L. Merrick's "Conrad in Quest of His Youth," ii.); also, a picture representing a scene at sea; a seascape.

sea=wall (sē′wâl), *n.* A strong wall or embankment to prevent the encroachments of the sea, act as a breakwater, etc.

sea-wan, sea-want (sē′won, -wont), *n.* [Algonquian, lit. 'scattered.'] Beads made from shells, used by North American Indians as money: properly denoting loose or unstrung beads as distinguished from strung beads. Cf. *peag* and *wampum*.

sea-ward (sē′wård). **I.** *adv.* Toward the sea: as, "The river . . . glided *seaward*" (Stevenson's "Inland Voyage," xx.). **II.** *a.* Lying, facing, or tending toward the sea (as,

---

(variable) d̦ as d or j, ș as s or sh, ț as t or ch, z̧ as z or zh; o, F. *cloche*; ü, F. *menu*; ċh, Sc. *loch*; ṅ, F. *bonbon*; ′, primary accent; ″, secondary accent; †, obsolete; <, from; +, and; =, equals. See also lists at beginning of book.

"the *seaward* wall," Tennyson's "Ode on the Death of the Duke of Wellington," vii.; "their *seaward* course," W. Morris's "Jason," xiv. 464); also, coming from the sea, as a wind. **III.** *n.* The direction or quarter toward the sea or away from the land: chiefly in 'to (the) seaward': as, "looking . . . out *to seaward*" (Whyte-Melville's "Katerfelto," xiv.); "I was scarce a quarter of a mile *to seaward*" (Stevenson's "Treasure Island," xxiv.).—**sea'wards,** *adv.* Seaward.

sea-ware (sē'wār), *n.* [See *ware*[1].] Seaweed.

sea-way (sē'wā), *n.* A way over the sea; the open sea; also, the progress of a ship through the waves; also, a rough sea (as, "a very safe boat . . . both buoyant and clever in a *seaway*": Stevenson's "Treasure Island," xxiii.).

sea-weed (sē'wēd), *n.* Any plant or plants growing in the sea; specif., a marine alga, as the gulfweed; sometimes, any alga.

sea-wolf (sē'wụlf), *n.* A pirate; also, a privateering vessel.

sea-wor-thy (sē'wèr″ᵮHi), *a.* Of a ship, in fit condition to go to sea and to encounter stormy weather. —**sea'wor″thi-ness,** *n.*

se-ba-ceous (sē-bā'shius), *a.* [NL. *sebaceus,* < L. *sebum:* see *sebum.*] Pertaining to, of the nature of, or resembling tallow or fat; fatty; greasy; specif., noting or pertaining to any of the cutaneous glands, follicles, or the like which secrete oily matter for lubricating the hair and the skin.

se-ba-cic (sē-bas'ik), *a.* [= F. *sébacique,* < NL. *sebaceus,* E. *sebaceous.*] In *chem.,* noting or pertaining to a white crystalline acid obtained from olein.

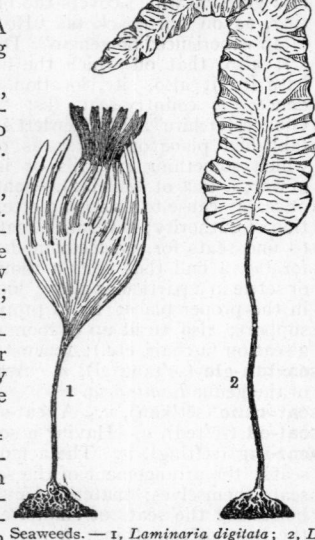

Seaweeds. — 1, *Laminaria digitata*; 2, *L. longicruris.*

se-bes-ten, se-bes-tan (sē-bes'ten, -tan), *n.* [Ar. *sebestān,* < Pers. *sapistān.*] A plum-like fruit borne by an East Indian tree, *Cordia myxa,* used in the East, and formerly in Europe, for medicinal purposes; also, the tree; also, the fruit of a related species, or the tree.

se-bif-er-ous (sē-bif'e-rus), *a.* [L. *sebum,* tallow: see *-ferous.*] Producing or secreting fat, as certain glands; in *bot.,* producing vegetable wax or tallow.

seb-or-rhe-a, seb-or-rhœ-a (seb-ọ-rē'ä), *n.* [NL., < L. *sebum,* tallow, + ῥοία, a flow, < ῥεῖν, flow.] In *pathol.,* an excessive and morbid discharge from the sebaceous glands, forming an oily coating or crust on the skin.—**seb-or-rhe'ic, seb-or-rhœ'ic** (-rē'ik), *a.*

se-bum (sē'bum), *n.* [L., tallow, suet, grease: cf. *suet.*] In *physiol.,* the fatty secretion of the sebaceous glands.

sec (sek), *a.* [F., < L. *siccus,* dry.] Of wines, dry; not sweet.

se-cant (sē'kant or -kạnt). [L. *secans* (*secant-*), ppr. of *secare* (pp. *sectus*), cut; akin to E. *saw*[3].] **I.** *a.* Cutting or intersecting, as one line or surface in relation to another. **II.** *n.* In *trigon.,* orig., a straight line drawn from the center of a circle through one extremity of an arc to the tangent from the other extremity of the same arc; now, the ratio of the length of this line to that of the radius of the circle; hence, of an acute angle of a right-angled triangle, a trigonometric function equal to the ratio of the length of the hypotenuse to that of the side adjacent to the angle; in *geom.,* an intersecting or secant line.

Secant. — The ratio of *AB* to *AD* is the secant of the angle *A*; and *AB* is the secant of the arc *CD.*

se-cede (sē-sēd'), *v. i.*; -ceded, -ceding. [L. *secedere* (pp. *secessus*), < *se-,* without, apart, + *cedere,* go.] To retire or withdraw (now rare); esp., to withdraw formally from an alli-

ance or association, as from a political or religious organization.—**se-ced'er** (-sē'dẻr), *n.*

se-cern (sē-sèrn'), *v. t.* [L. *secernere* (pp. *secretus*): see *secrete.*] To separate; distinguish or discriminate.—**se-cern'-ment,** *n.*

se-ces-sion (sē-sesh'ọn), *n.* [L. *secessio(n-),* < *secedere,* E. *secede.*] The act of seceding, or a body of seceders; [often *cap.*] in *U. S. hist.,* the attempted withdrawal from the Union of eleven Southern States in 1860–61, which brought on the Civil War; [*l. c.*] in the *fine arts,* any of various recent movements of protest against and divergence from the methods of older schools.—**se-ces'sion-ism,** *n.* The principles of secessionists.—**se-ces'sion-ist,** *n.* One who secedes or who favors secession: esp. in *U. S. hist.*

seck-el (sek'ẹl), *n.* [From *Seckel,* name of a grower of this fruit, near Philadelphia.] A small, sweet, reddish-brown kind of pear.

se-clude (sē-klöd'), *v. t.*; -cluded, -cluding. [L. *secludere* (pp. *seclusus*), < *se-,* without, apart, + *cludere, claudere,* shut.] To shut off or keep apart, as from company, society, etc.; place in or withdraw into solitude; also, to exclude†. —**se-clud'ed** (-klö'ded), *p. a.* Shut off or separated from others; withdrawn from public observation; retired or sequestered, as a place.—**se-clud'ed-ly,** *adv.*—**se-clud'ed-ness,** *n.*

se-clu-sion (sē-klö'zhọn), *n.* [ML. *seclusio(n-).*] The act of secluding, or the state of being secluded; retirement; solitude; also, a secluded place.—**se-clu'sive** (-siv), *a.* Serving or tending to seclude; affecting seclusion or retirement.

sec-ond[1] (sek'ọnd), *a.* [OF. F. *second,* < L. *secundus,* following, next, second, secondary, favorable, < *sequi,* follow: cf. *sequent.*] Next after the first in order, place, time, rank, value, quality, etc. (the ordinal of *two*); subordinate to the first (as, the *second* officer); inferior to the first (as, *second* quality); also, other or another (as, his *second* self; a *second* Solomon); also, helpful†; in *music,* next to the highest in pitch, as a part in concerted music; rendering such a part, as a voice or instrument.—**second advent,** the expected second coming of Christ to judge both the quick and the dead.—**Second Adventist.** Same as *Adventist.*—**second childhood.** See under *childhood.*—**second coming.** Same as *second advent.*—**second sight,** a supposed faculty enabling its possessor to perceive distant objects or occurrences and future events as if present before the eyes.—**sec'ond**[1], *n.* One who or that which is second; also, one who aids or supports another; an assistant; a backer; specif., one who acts as representative of and aid to a principal in a duel; one who acts as aid to a principal in a pugilistic encounter; also, *pl.,* in *com.,* products or goods of second grade, or below the first or perfect grade or quality; also, *sing.,* in *music,* a tone on the next degree from a given tone; the interval between such tones; the harmonic combination of such tones; in a scale, the supertonic; also, the next to the highest part in a piece of concerted music; a voice or instrument rendering such a part; often, the secondo (as, "She sang something . . . to which her brother sang a sort of *second* very nicely": F. M. Crawford's "Mr. Isaacs," vii.).—**sec'ond**[1], *v. t.* [F. *seconder,* < L. *secundare,* < *secundus.*] To support, back up, or assist, as a person or his efforts; further or advance, as aims (as, "He found his purpose *seconded* among his countrymen by the predatory habits of ages": G. P. R. James's "Hist. of Charlemagne," v.); reinforce, as a thing, activity, etc. (as, "Deeds must *second* words when needful": T. Arnold, To Rev. F. C. Blackstone, Sept. 28, 1828, in Stanley's "Life of Arnold," v.); act as second to, as a pugilist; also, to express approval of, as a proposal; specif., to express support of (a motion, etc.) as a necessary preliminary to further discussion of the motion or to a vote on it; also, to follow up with some second thing†; repeat, as an action† (as, "Mr. Great-heart *seconded* his blow, and smit the head of the giant from his shoulders": Bunyan's "Pilgrim's Progress," ii.).

sec-ond[2] (sek'ọnd), *n.* [F. *seconde,* < ML. *secunda* (for *secunda minuta,* 'second minute,' that is, a division of the second order), prop. fem. of L. *secundus,* E. *second*[1], *a.*] The sixtieth part of a minute of time; hence, a moment or instant; also, in *geom.,* etc., the sixtieth part of a minute of a degree (often represented by the sign ″: as, 12° 10′ 30″, that is, twelve degrees, ten minutes, and thirty seconds).

sec-on-da-ri-ly (sek′ọn-dā-ri-li), *adv.* In the second place in order or time, or secondly (obs. or rare); also, through an intermediate agency; indirectly; also, in a secondary or subordinate manner; subordinately; not primarily.— **sec′on-da-ri-ness,** *n.*

sec-on-da-ry (sek′ọn-dā-ri), *a.* [L. *secundarius,* < *secundus,* E. *second*[1], *a.*] Next after the first in order, place, or time; belonging or pertaining to a second order, division, stage, period, or the like; also, derived or derivative; not primary or original; also, next below the first in importance; belonging to the class that is second in importance; hence, of minor importance; subordinate; also, subsidiary or auxiliary; in *ornith.,* noting or pertaining to any of a set of flight-feathers situated on the second segment (that corresponding to the forearm in higher vertebrates) of a bird's wing; in *elect.,* noting or pertaining to the induced circuit, coil, or current in an induction-coil or the like; in *geol.,* noting or pertaining to a mineral produced from another mineral by decay, alteration, or the like.— **secondary planets.** See under *planet.*— **secondary school,** commonly, a high school or a school of corresponding grade, ranking between the lower schools and the college or university.— **sec′on-da-ry,** *n.*; pl. *-ries* (-riz). One who or that which is secondary; esp., a person or thing second or subordinate in importance; a delegate or deputy; in *ornith.,* a secondary feather; in *elect.,* a secondary circuit or coil; in *astron.,* a secondary planet.

sec-ond=class (sek′ọnd-klås′), *a.* Of or belonging to the class next after the first; specif., pertaining to the second grade of conveyances or accommodations for travel; in general, of second or inferior grade or quality; second-rate.

se-conde (se-kond′, F. sė-gônd), *n.* [F., fem. of *second,* E. *second*[1], *a.*] In *fencing,* the second in a series of eight parries.

sec-ond-er (sek′ọn-dėr), *n.* One who seconds: as, the *seconder* of a motion.

sec-ond=hand (sek′ọnd-hand′), *a.* Obtained from another (as, *second-hand* knowledge); not original; also, having been previously used or owned by another (as, *second-hand* clothes; *second-hand* books); also, dealing in previously used goods (as, a *second-hand* bookseller; a *second-hand* shop).

sec-ond-ly (sek′ọnd-li), *adv.* In the second place.

se-con-do (se-kōn′dō), *n.*; pl. *-di* (-dē). [It., < L. *secundus,* E. *second*[1], *a.*] In *music,* the second or subordinate part, as in a duet; also, its performer.

sec-ond=rate (sek′ọnd-rāt′), *a.* Of the second rate or class, as to size, quality, etc.; hence, not of the first grade of excellence or importance; inferior (as, "a very *second-rate* personage": Motley's "Dutch Republic," ii. 8).

sec-ond=sight-ed (sek′ọnd-sī′ted), *a.* Having the faculty of second sight. See *second sight,* under *second*[1], *a.*

se-cre-cy (sē′krẹ-si), *n.*; pl. *-cies* (-siz). The state or fact of being secret; concealment from the observation or knowledge of others (as, an affair conducted in strict *secrecy*); privacy; reticence or silence as to something (as, to give a promise of *secrecy;* to maintain *secrecy* as to one's plans); also, something kept secret, or a secret (archaic).

se-cret (sē′kret), *a.* [OF. F. *secret,* adj. and n., < L. *secretus,* pp. (as n., neut. *secretum*): see *secrete.*] Removed from general resort or knowledge, retired, or secluded, as a place (as, "Abide in a *secret* place, and hide thyself": 1 Sam. xix. 2); out of sight, hidden, or concealed (as, "A thousand rills . . . Winding a *secret* or an open course," Cowper's "Charity," 369); *secret* weapons; designed to escape observation or knowledge (as, a *secret* room, passage, or stairway; a *secret* drawer; a *secret* spring); unknown or unrevealed to any or to persons generally (as, "a page from the *secret* history of David Swan," Hawthorne's "Twice-Told Tales," David Swan; "That dream . . . publishes the *secret* frailty of human nature," De Quincey's "English Mail-Coach," ii.); withheld from the knowledge of others (as, to keep an affair *secret*); done, made, or conducted without the knowledge of others, or clandestine (as, a *secret* errand, visit, or marriage; *secret* negotiations; kept from the knowledge of any but the initiated or other particular persons (as, *secret* doctrines or rites; a *secret* sign or password); known only to the person or persons concerned, or private (as, a *secret*

thought or feeling; *secret* experiences); also, faithful or cautious in keeping secrets; close-mouthed, reticent, or secretive; keeping matters, one's movements, etc., from the knowledge of others (as, "I was *secret* in going forth next morning, waiting until the girl was out of the way": W. H. Hudson's "Green Mansions," x.).— **secret service,** official service of a secret nature, as secret investigation or observation, performed for a government; the branch of governmental service charged with secret investigation, etc.— **secret society,** a society whose members are sworn to secrecy.— **se′cret,** *n.* Something secret, hidden, or not generally known or revealed, or a mystery (as, the *secrets* of nature); something kept to one's self, or imparted only in confidence to others (as, "Each cherished a *secret,* which she did not confide to the other": Longfellow's "Kavanagh," xxiii.); a matter, affair, fact, or circumstance known or revealed to none or to few; the unrevealed truth, facts, or circumstances of something (as, "One great annal-book where after-years Will learn the *secret* of our Arthur's birth," Tennyson's "Coming of Arthur," 158; "The *secret* of the authorship was known to only one man," Bok's "Americanization of Edward Bok," xxiv.); the method or art of doing or attaining something as known only to the initiated, adepts, or the specially skilled or gifted few (as, the *secret* of transmuting base metals into gold; the *secret* of successful colonization; "He possessed beyond most men the *secret* of happiness, for he was always absorbed in the living moment," Galsworthy's "Saint's Progress," ii. 10); hence, the reason or explanation, not immediately or generally apparent, of something (as, "That is the *secret* of my fondness for the sea; I was born by it": G. W. Curtis's "Prue and I," iii.); also, a piece or suit of armor worn concealed (obs. or hist.: as, "a '*secret,*' or coat of linked mail, worn beneath the corslet," Scott's "Talisman," xxviii.); sometimes, a skullcap of steel worn under or over the camail (obs. or hist.); also, secrecy (now only in the phrase 'in secret': as, "I spake openly to the world . . . *in secret* have I said nothing," John, xviii. 20).

sec-re-ta-ri-al (sek-rẹ-tā′ri-ạl), *a.* Of, pertaining to, or proper to a secretary.

sec-re-ta-ri-at, sec-re-ta-ri-ate (sek-rẹ-tā′ri-at, -āt), *n.* [F. *secrétariat,* < ML. *secretariatus.*] The office or official position of secretary; also, the place where a secretary transacts business, preserves records, etc.; also, a body or department of secretaries.

sec-re-ta-ry (sek′rẹ-tā-ri), *n.*; pl. *-ries* (-riz). [ML. *secretarius,* confidential officer, < L. *secretum,* something secret or private: see *secret.*] One intrusted with secret or private matters†; also, a person who conducts correspondence, keeps records, etc., for an individual or an organization; also, an officer of state charged with the superintendence and management of a particular department of government (as, *Secretary* of State, see below; the *Secretary* of War of the U. S.); also, a piece of furniture for use as a writing-desk; also, the secretary-bird.— **Secretary of State,** an officer of state in charge of a particular department of government (as, the British *Secretary of State* for home affairs, for foreign affairs, for the colonies, for war, or for India); in the U. S. national government, the head of the Department of State, which has charge of all foreign relations; also, in certain States of the U. S., an officer whose chief duty is the making and filing of records.—

Secret.

sec′re-ta-ry=bird, *n.* A large, long-legged raptorial bird, *Serpentarius secretarius* (or *serpentarius*), of Africa, which feeds on reptiles: so called from its crest, which has been likened to pens stuck over the ear. — **sec′re-ta-ry-ship,** *n.* The office or position of secretary.

Secretary-bird.

se-crete (sē-krēt'), *v. t.*; *-creted, -creting*. [L. *secretus*, pp. of *secernere*, separate off, put apart, < *se-*, without, apart, + *cernere*, separate: see *certain*.] To separate off, prepare, or produce as in the physiological process of secretion; also, to hide; conceal; keep secret or hidden.—**se-cret'er** (-krē'tėr), *n.*

se-cre-tion (sē-krē'shon), *n.* [L. *secretio(n-)*, < *secernere*: see *secrete*.] The process or function of an animal body, executed in the glands, by which various substances, as bile, milk, etc., are separated and elaborated from the blood; a similar process in a plant; also, the product secreted.—**se-cre'tion-al, se-cre'tion-a-ry** (-ạ-ri), *a.*

se-cre-tive (sē-krē'tiv), *a.* [Partly < *secret*, *a.*, partly < *secrete*.] Having or showing a disposition to secrecy; reticent; also, causing or promoting secretion; secretory.—**se-cre'tive-ly**, *adv.*—**se-cre'tive-ness**, *n.* Secretive character; propensity to secrecy: in *phren.*, a special faculty.

se-cret-ly (sē'kret-li), *adv.* In a secret manner; without the observation or knowledge of others; not openly; sometimes, inaudibly (specif. in *liturgics*).—**se'cret-ness**, *n.*

se-cre-to-ry (sē-krē'tō-ri). **I.** *a.* Pertaining to secretion; performing the office of secretion. **II.** *n.* A secretory organ, vessel, or the like.

sect[1] (sekt), *n.* [Appar. < L. *sectum*, neut. of *sectus*, pp. of *secare*, cut.] A cutting or slip of a plant; a scion. See Shakspere's "Othello," i. 3. 336. [Obs. or archaic.]

sect[2] (sekt), *n.* [OF. F. *secte*, < L. *secta*, way, method, party, school, sect, < *sequi*, follow: cf. *sequent*.] A body of persons following certain principles or doctrines (as, a philosophical *sect*); esp., a body of persons adhering to a particular religious faith; a religious denomination; often, a party or school among the professors of a religion; sometimes, a party regarded as deviating from the general religious tradition, or as heretical; sometimes, a body separated from a particular church; a body of dissenters from an established church; also, a system or body of doctrines†; also, a party† or faction†; also, a class or kind, as of persons†; also, a religious order†; also, sex (now prov. or illiterate).

sec-ta-ri-al (sek-tā'ri-ạl), *a.* Sectarian.

sec-ta-ri-an (sek-tā'ri-ạn). [From *sectary*.] **I.** *a.* Of or pertaining to sectaries or sects; confined or devoted to a particular sect. **II.** *n.* A member of a sect; esp., a bigoted adherent of a sect.—**sec-ta'ri-an-ism**, *n.* The spirit or tendencies of sectarians; adherence or excessive devotion to a particular sect or party, esp. in religion.—**sec-ta'ri-an-ize**, *v. t.*; *-ized, -izing.* To render sectarian.

sec-ta-ry (sek'tạ-ri). [ML. *sectarius*, < L. *secta*, E. *sect*[2].] **I.** *n.*; pl. *-ries* (-riz). A member of a particular sect, esp. in religion; one zealously devoted to a particular sect; often, an adherent of a religious body regarded as heretical or schismatic; a member of a religious body separated from a particular church or dissenting from an established church. **II.** *a.* Of or pertaining to a sect; sectarian.

sec-tile (sek'til), *a.* [L. *sectilis*, < *secare*, cut.] Capable of being cut smoothly by a knife.

sec-tion (sek'shon), *n.* [F. *section*, < L. *sectio(n-)*, < *secare*, cut: see *secant*, and cf. *saw*[3].] The act or an act of cutting or dividing; separation by cutting; also, a part cut or separated from the rest; a division; a portion; esp., a thin slice of a tissue, mineral, or the like, as for microscopic examination; also, a distinct portion of a book, writing, or the like; a subdivision, as of a chapter; also, a mark (§) used in writing and printing to denote a section of a book, chapter, or the like, or as a mark of reference to a foot-note or the like (also called *section-mark*); also, a distinct part of a country, community, class, or the like; a region or district one mile square, forming a thirty-sixth part of a township, as used in U. S. surveys of public land; a division of a sleeping-car containing both an upper and a lower berth; also, the figure presented to the eye by the surface resulting from passing a plane through an object; a representation of an object as it would appear if cut by a plane, showing the internal structure (in mechanical drawing, a *longitudinal section* usually presenting the object as cut through its center lengthwise and vertically, a *cross-section* or *transverse section* as cut crosswise and vertically, and a *horizontal section* as cut through its center horizontally).—**sec'tion**, *v. t.* To

cut or divide into sections; also, to cut through so as to present a section.

sec-tion-al (sek'shon-ạl), *a.* Of or pertaining to a section or sections; esp., pertaining to a particular section of a country, community, etc; local; also, composed of several independent sections.—**sec'tion-al-ism**, *n.* Excessive regard for sectional or local interests; sectional spirit, prejudice, etc.—**sec'tion-al-ist**, *n.*—**sec'tion-al-ize** (-īz), *v. t.*; *-ized, -izing.* To render sectional; also, to divide into sections.—**sec''tion-al-i-za'tion** (-i-zā'shon), *n.*—**sec'tion-al-ly**, *adv.*

sec-tion=mark (sek'shon-märk), *n.* See *section, n.*

sec-tor (sek'tọr), *n.* [= F. *secteur*, < L. *sector*, cutter, LL. geometrical sector, < L. *secare*, cut: cf. *section*.] In *geom.*, a plane figure bounded by two radii and the included arc of a circle, ellipse, or the like; hence, a solid generated by the revolution of such a plane about one of its radii; in *mech.*, etc., a mathematical instrument consisting of two flat rulers hinged together at one end so as to move in their own plane, and bearing various scales; in *astron.*, an instrument for measuring differences of declination, etc.; *milit.*, one of the sections or districts of an area as divided for military operations, direction, etc.—**sec-to'ri-al** (-tō'ri-ạl), *a.* Pertaining to a sector; also, adapted for cutting, as certain teeth; carnassial.

DCB is a Sector of a Circle.

Sector.

sec-u-lar (sek'ū-lär). [OF. *seculer* (F. *séculier*, *séculaire*), < L. *sæcularis*, belonging to an age, LL. worldly, secular, < L. *sæculum*, race, generation, age, LL. the world.] **I.** *a.* Occurring or celebrated once in an age, century, or long period; also, going on from age to age; continuing through long ages; also, of or pertaining to the world or this world, or things not religious, sacred, or spiritual; lay; profane; temporal; worldly; not pertaining to or connected with religion, as literature, music, etc.; dealing with non-religious subjects, or, esp., excluding religious instruction, as education, etc.; also, of members of the clergy, living in the world; not belonging to a religious order (opposed to *regular*). **II.** *n.* A layman, or one not a clergyman; also, one of the secular clergy.—**sec'u-lar-ism**, *n.* Secular spirit or tendencies; esp., a system which rejects all forms of religious faith and worship, and accepts only the facts and influences derived from the present life; also, the view that public education and other matters of civil policy should be conducted without the introduction of a religious element.—**sec'u-lar-ist**, *n.*—**sec-u-lar'i-ty** (-lar'i-ti), *n.*; pl. *-ties* (-tiz). Secular spirit or quality; worldliness; also, a secular matter.—**sec'u-lar-ize** (-īz), *v. t.*; *-ized, -izing.* To make secular; separate from religious or spiritual connection or influences; make worldly or unspiritual; imbue with secularism; specif., to transfer (property) from ecclesiastical to civil possession or use; also, to change (clergy) from regular to secular.—**sec''u-lar-i-za'tion** (-i-zā'shon), *n.*—**sec'u-lar-ly**, *adv.*

se-cund (sē'kund or sē-kund'), *a.* [L. *secundus*, following, E. *second*[1], *a.*] In *bot.* and *zoöl.*, arranged on one side only; unilateral.

sec-un-dine (sek'un-din or -dīn), *n.* [LL. *secundinæ*, pl., afterbirth, in bot. NL. *secundina*, < L. *secundus*, following, E. *second*[1], *a.*] The afterbirth (usually in *pl.*); in *bot.*, the inner integument of an ovule (cf. *primine*).

se-cur-a-ble (sē-kūr'ạ-bl), *a.* That may be secured.

se-cure (sē-kūr'), *a.* [L. *securus*, free from care, untroubled, safe, < *se-*, without, + *cura*, care: cf. *sure*.] Free from care or apprehension; without anxiety; hence, careless; overconfident; also, free from doubt, or feeling certain or sure of something (obs. or rare); also, free from or not exposed to danger, as a person; safe; involving no danger, as an action; not liable to fail, yield, become displaced, etc., as a support or a fastening; affording safety, as a place; also, in safe custody or keeping (as, "In iron walls they deem'd me not *secure*": Shakspere's "1 Henry VI.," i. 4. 49); also, free from the risk of losing or not obtaining something (as, to be *secure* of victory); also, that can be counted on with certainty (as, victory is *secure*). — **se-cure'**, *v. t.*; *-cured, -curing.* To free from care or apprehension†; free from doubt†; also, to make secure from danger or harm; render safe; protect; also, to make firm or fast (as, "Having *secured* my boat, I took my gun and went on shore": Defoe's "Robinson Crusoe," i. 10); fix firmly in place; also, to seize and confine, as a prisoner (as, "They . . . formed a conspiracy to seize the ship and *secure* me": Swift's "Gulliver's Travels," iv. 1); place in safe custody or keeping; also, to get hold or possession of, as by effort or contrivance; obtain; gain; get; also, to make secure or certain, as of retaining or obtaining something; make (a creditor) sure of payment, as by a mortgage, bond, or the like; also, to make (something) secure, certain, or to be depended on; ensure; make the payment of (a debt, loan, etc.) certain, as by a mortgage or the like. — **to secure arms**, *milit.*, to hold a rifle or musket with the muzzle down and the lock well up under the arm, so as to protect the weapon from the wet. — **se-cure'ly**, *adv.* — **se-cure'ness**, *n.* — **se-cur'er** (-kūr'ĕr), *n.*

se-cu-ri-ty (sē-kū'ri-ti), *n.*; pl. *-ties* (-tiz). [L. *securitas:* cf. *surety.*] The state of being secure; freedom from care or apprehension; carelessness or overconfidence; freedom from doubt; well-founded confidence, or certainty; freedom from danger, risk, etc.; safety; stability or fixity; also, something that secures, or makes safe; a protection; a defense; an assurance or guarantee; something given or deposited as surety for the fulfilment of a promise or an obligation, the payment of a debt, etc.; one who becomes surety for another; an evidence of debt or of property, as a bond or a certificate of stock; a particular kind or issue of bonds, stock, or the like.

se-dan (sē-dan'), *n.* [Origin uncertain; commonly explained as from *Sedan,* town in northeastern France.] A portable covered chair for one person, borne on poles by two men, one before and one behind, much used during the 17th and 18th centuries (also called *sedan-chair*); also, a closed automobile seating four or more persons (including the driver) all in one compartment.

Sedan.

se-date (sē-dāt'), *a.* [L. *sedatus,* pp. of *sedare,* settle, allay, calm, causative of *sedere,* sit: see *see*[1].] Calm, quiet, or composed; sober; undisturbed by passion or excitement: as, a *sedate* matron; "one of those calm, quiet, *sedate* natures, to whom the temptations of turbulent nerves or vehement passions are things utterly incomprehensible" (Mrs. Stowe's "Oldtown Folks," i.); "I . . . lived a very *sedate,* retired life" (Defoe's "Robinson Crusoe," i. 10). — **se-date'ly**, *adv.* — **se-date'ness**, *n.*

sed-a-tive (sed'a-tiv). [OF. *sedatif* (F. *sédatif*), < ML. *sedativus,* < L. *sedare:* see *sedate.*] **I.** *a.* Tending to calm or soothe (as, "soothing the cares of Polynesian life in the *sedative* fumes of tobacco": H. Melville's "Typee," xxii.); in *med.,* allaying irritability or excitement; assuaging pain; lowering functional activity. **II.** *n.* A sedative agent or remedy.

sed-en-ta-ry (sed'en-ta-ri), *a.* [L. *sedentarius,* < *sedens* (*sedent-*), ppr. of *sedere,* sit: see *see*[1].] Characterized by or requiring continuance in a sitting posture (as, a *sedentary* life; a *sedentary* occupation); also, accustomed to sit much or take little exercise, as a person (as, "I am persuaded that all valetudinarians are too *sedentary*": Smollett's "Humphry

Clinker," Oct. 26); hence, inactive†; also, abiding in one place; not migratory; in *zoöl.,* remaining in one region, locality, or place; of spiders, spinning a web and lying in wait for prey (as, "I discovered that this was no web-spinning, *sedentary* spider, but a wandering hunter": W. H. Hudson's "Green Mansions," v.); of mollusks, etc., confined to one spot, or affixed or attached. — **sed'en-ta-ri-ly**, *adv.* — **sed'en-ta-ri-ness**, *n.*

se-de-runt (sē-dē'runt), *n.* [L., 'there sat' (as used in mentioning those present at a meeting).] A sitting or meeting of a judicial or deliberative body; also, any sitting, as for discussion, talk, enjoyment, etc. (as, "The bringing in of the toddy-bowl after supper . . . has a tendency to lengthen the *sederunt* to unseasonable hours": Galt's "Ayrshire Legatees," i.).

sedge (sej), *n.* [AS. *secg;* akin to E. *saw*[3].] Any of various rush-like or grass-like plants constituting the cyperaceous genus *Carex,* growing in wet places; hence, any cyperaceous plant; also, plants of this kind growing or taken together. — **sedged**, *a.* Made of sedge (as, "You nymphs, call'd Naiads . . . With your *sedged* crowns": Shakspere's "Tempest," iv. 1. 129); also, abounding or bordered with sedge (as, *sedged* brooks). — **sedg'y**, *a.* Abounding, covered, or bordered with sedge (as, a stream with *sedgy* banks; a *sedgy* brook); also, consisting of or resembling sedge (as, "The water . . . stirred a *sedgy* growth of reeds bordering its margin": H. Melville's "Omoo," lxvii.).

Sedges. — 1, the male plant of *Carex scirpoidea;* 2, the female plant of *Carex scirpoidea;* 3, the inflorescence of *Carex vulpinoidea;* 4, the inflorescence of *Carex crinita.*

se-di-le (sē-dī'lē), *n.*; pl. *-dilia* (-dil'i-ä). [L., < *sedere,* sit: see *see*[1].] *Eccles.,* one of the seats (usually three) on the south side of the chancel, often recessed in the wall, for the use of the officiating clergy: usually in *pl.*

sed-i-ment (sed'i-ment), *n.* [F. *sédiment,* < L. *sedimentum,* a settling, < *sedere,* sit: see *see*[1].] Matter, or a quantity of matter, which settles to the bottom of a liquid; lees; dregs; in *geol.,* matter deposited, as by water. — **sed'i-ment** (-ment), *v. t.* or *i.* To deposit as or form sediment. — **sed-i-men'tal** (-men'tal), *a.* Sedimentary. — **sed-i-men'ta-ry** (-ta-ri), *a.* Of, pertaining to, or of the nature of sediment; in *geol.,* formed by deposition of sediment, as rocks. — **sed"i-men-ta'tion** (-tā'shon), *n.* The deposition or accumulation of sediment.

Sedilia, Southwell Minster, England.

se-di-tion (sē-dish'on), *n.* [OF. *sedicion* (F. *sédition*), < L. *seditio(n-),* lit. 'a going apart,' < *sed-,* for *se-,* without, apart, + *ire,* go.] Violent party strife†, or a factious commotion in a state†; also, rebellious disorder, or a rebellion or revolt (archaic: as, "a rebellious city . . . they have moved *sedition* within the same of old time," Ezra, iv. 15; "He was suddenly oppressed by a *sedition* of the guards," Gibbon's "Decline and Fall of the Roman Empire," xliii.); now, usually, incitement of discontent or rebellion against the government; action or language promoting discontent with or opposition to the constituted authorities in a state.—**se-di′tion-a-ry** (-ā-ri). **I.** *a.* Pertaining to or involving sedition. **II.** *n.*; pl. *-ries* (-riz). One guilty of sedition.—**se-di′tious** (-dish′us), *a.* [OF. *sedicieus* (F. *séditieux*), < L. *seditiosus*.] Of, pertaining to, or of the nature of sedition; also, given to or guilty of sedition. —**se-di′tious-ly,** *adv.*—**se-di′tious-ness,** *n.*

Sed-litz (sed′lits) **pow′der.** See *Seidlitz powder.*

se-duce (sē̇-dūs′), *v. t.*; -duced, -ducing. [L. *seducere* (pp. *seductus*), < *se-*, without, apart, + *ducere*, lead.] To lead or draw away, as from one's chosen course, accepted principles, faith, allegiance, etc., by persuasions or inducements (as, "Cæcilius . . . *seduced* others from the religion he had left," J. H. Newman's "Callista," viii.; "The French King attempted by splendid offers to *seduce* him from the cause of the Republic," Macaulay's "Hist. of Eng.," ii.); win over or beguile (as, "Condé, won over and *seduced* by the sirens of the Court, signed it [a peace]": Besant's "Coligny," viii.); entice (*into, to,* etc.: as, "Or if not drive, *Seduce* them to our party," Milton's "Paradise Lost," ii. 368); lead astray, entice away from duty or rectitude, or corrupt (as, "Cælius . . . tried to *seduce* Cæsar's garrison, and was put to death for his treachery": Froude's "Cæsar," xxii.); specif., to entice (a woman) to a surrender of chastity.—**se-duce′ment,** *n.* The act of seducing, or the state of being seduced; also, a means of seducing.—**se-du′cer** (-dū′ser), *n.*—**se-du′ci-ble,** *a.* Capable of being seduced.—**se-du′cing-ly,** *adv.*

se-duc-tion (sē̇-duk′shon), *n.* [L. *seductio*(n-).] The act of seducing; specif., the act of inducing a woman to surrender her chastity; also, a means of seducing; an enticement or allurement.—**se-duc′tive** (-tiv), *a.* Tending to seduce; enticing; alluring; captivating: as, "a quick and extraordinarily *seductive* smile" (Arnold Bennett's "Hilda Lessways," iv. 3).—**se-duc′tive-ly,** *adv.*—**se-duc′tive-ness,** *n.*

sé-dui-sant (sā-dwē-zäṅ), *a.* [F., ppr. of *séduire*, < L. *seducere*, E. *seduce*.] Seductive; enticing; alluring; captivating.—**sé-dui-sante** (-zänt), *a.* [F.] Fem. of *séduisant.*

se-du-li-ty (sē̇-dū′li-ti), *n.* [L. *sedulitas.*] The quality of being sedulous; sedulous application or care.

sed-u-lous (sed′ū-lus), *a.* [L. *sedulus*, busy, diligent, assiduous, perhaps < *sedere*, sit: cf. *assiduous.*] Constant in application or attention, diligent, persevering, or assiduous (as, "While *sedulous* I seek t' improve . . . The mind he gave me," Cowper's "Task," iii. 367; "The most *sedulous* friend of union . . . was Benjamin Franklin," Bancroft's "Hist. of the U. S.," Amer. Revolution, i. 5); taking pains (to do something: as, "She wondered what sort of herbs they were, which the old man was so *sedulous* to gather," Hawthorne's "Scarlet Letter," xv.; "She neither felt respect for this lady, nor was she *sedulous* to evince it," Disraeli's "Coningsby," iv. 12); also, persistently or carefully maintained (as, *sedulous* application or attention; "I observed his conduct with *sedulous* particularity," Stevenson's "Master of Ballantrae," vi.).—**sed′u-lous-ly,** *adv.*—**sed′u-lous-ness,** *n.*

se-dum (sē′dum), *n.*; pl. *-dums.* [NL. use of L. *sedum*, houseleek.] Any plant of the crassulaceous genus *Sedum*, which comprises fleshy, chiefly perennial, herbs with cymes of usually yellow, white, or pink flowers. Cf. *stonecrop.*

see[1] (sē), *n.* [OF. *se, sie, sied,* < L. *sedes,* seat, < *sedere* (pp. *sessus*), sit; akin to E. *sit.*] A seat†; a seat of authority, as a throne†; *eccles.*, the seat, center of authority, office, or jurisdiction of a bishop (as, the Holy *See*, the see of Rome: see under *holy, a.*).

see[2] (sē), *v. t.*; pret. *saw*, pp. *seen*, ppr. *seeing.* [AS. *seon* = D. *zien* = G. *sehen* = Icel. *sjā* = Goth. *saihwan*, see.] To perceive with the eyes, or behold (as, "Whose house is that I *see?*" Tennyson's "Walking to the Mail," 7); also, to examine with the eyes; view; visit or attend as a spectator (as, "My father took me to *see* a show at Brookgreen Fair": Thackeray's "Vanity Fair," li.); also, fig., to per-

ceive mentally (as, to *see* the point of an argument); apprehend; discern; understand; sometimes, to judge or deem (as, you may go if you *see* fit to do so); also, to ascertain, learn, or find out (as, please *see* who it is; *see* what you can do about it); also, to bring about by supervision or vigilance (as, to *see* that work is done properly); make sure; also, to know by observation, or have knowledge or experience of (as, to *see* life; to *see* service; to have *seen* better days); also, to attend or escort (as, to *see* one to his door); also, to meet and converse with (as, to go to *see* a person); have an interview with (as, I must *see* you at once); sometimes, to interview or communicate with in order to influence, esp. improperly as by a bribe (colloq., U. S.); also, to receive as a visitor (as, if he comes, will you *see* him?); in *poker*, etc., to meet (a bet), or meet the bet of (a better), by staking an equal sum.—**to see out,** to go through with (a thing) to the end.—**to see the light.** See under *light*[1], *n.*—**to see through,** to continue to watch or take part in (a matter) until the end; also, to watch over or assist (a person) until he comes successfully through some difficulty.—**see**[2], *v. i.* To have the power of sight; also, to perceive objects by sight; also, fig., to have a mental perception; understand; also, to give attention, heed, or care (as, "He would *see* to it that his sons took a livelier interest in politics": H. G. Wells's "Men Like Gods," iii. 2); also, to look† (as, "I . . . went out . . . to the south-west corner of the island . . . to *see* for canoes": Defoe's "Robinson Crusoe," i. 14).—**to see through,** fig., to penetrate (a disguise, false appearance, etc.); detect (an imposture, etc.); perceive the real character or purpose of (a person): as, "She was quite indifferent whether Edwin *saw through* her dodge or not" (Arnold Bennett's "These Twain," iii.); "Any man old enough to have hair on his face ought to *see through* Trampas" (Wister's "Virginian," xxiii.).—**see′a-ble,** *a.* Capable of being seen.

see-catch (sē′kach), *n.*; pl. *seecatchie* (sē′kach″i). [Appar. native name.] The adult male of the fur-seal, *Callorhinus ursinus*, of Alaska.

seed (sēd), *n.*; pl. *seeds*, or (collectively) *seed* (see third def.). [AS. *sǣd* = D. *zaad* = G. *saat* = Icel. *sādh*, seed; from the root of E. *sow*[1].] The fertilized and matured ovule of a phanerogam, capable of development by germination into an individual similar to that from which it came; popularly, any small, seed-like part or fruit, as a grain of wheat; also, such ovules or parts collectively (as, "every herb bearing *seed*": Gen. i. 29); often, propagative parts of a plant or plants as preserved for growing a new crop, including ovules

Seeds cut vertically, showing their Embryos and Albumen.

and similar small bodies, and sometimes also tubers, bulbs, etc.; also, fig., the germ or beginning from which anything grows or develops (as, to sow the *seeds* of discord; "Every guilty deed Holds in itself the *seed* Of retribution and undying pain," Longfellow's "Masque of Pandora," viii.); also, semen or sperm; hence, offspring or progeny; race; also, the ovum or ova of certain animals, as the lobster and the silkworm-moth; the spat of oysters; very young oysters. —**to go to seed,** to pass to the stage of yielding seed, as a plant; fig., to approach the end of vigor, usefulness, prosperity, etc.—**seed,** *v.* **I.** *intr.* To produce seed; go to seed; shed seed; also, to sow seed. **II.** *tr.* To sow (land) with seed; also, to sow or scatter (seed); also, to remove the seeds from (fruit); also, fig., to modify (the ordinary drawing of lots for position in a tournament, as at tennis) by distributing a certain number of the ranking players so that they will not meet in the early rounds of play and thus leave the rest of the tournament lacking in interest;

distribute (ranking players) in this manner; fix (the positions of ranking players) by such distribution.—**seed'=bud,** *n.* In *bot.*, an ovule; also, a plumule.—**seed'=cake,** *n.* A sweet cake containing aromatic seeds; also, the cake left after the oil has been expressed from the seeds of cotton, etc.—**seed'=coat,** *n.* In *bot.*, the testa, or outer integument, of a seed.—**seed'ed,** *a.* Having a seed or seeds (as, one-seeded); also, modified, placed, or fixed by seeding, as at tennis (see *seed, v. t.*).—**seed'er,** *n.* One who or that which seeds; an apparatus for sowing or planting seeds; a device for removing seeds.—**seed'i-ness,** *n.* Seedy condition.—**seed'=lac,** *n.* The purer form of lac obtained from crude lac (see *lac¹*) by removing it from the twigs and triturating with water, this process removing the greater part of the coloring matter and rendering the product granular.—**seed'=leaf,** *n.* In *bot.*, a cotyledon.—**seed'less,** *a.* Having no seed.—**seed'ling. I.** *n.* A plant reared from a seed; in *forestry*, a tree which has grown from a seed; also, a tree of this kind which has not reached a height of three feet. **II.** *a.* Produced from the seed.—**seed'ness,** *n.* The sowing of seed; seed-time. See Shakspere's "Measure for Measure," i. 4. 42. [Obs. or prov. Eng.]—**seed'=pearl,** *n.* A very small pearl.—**seed'=plant,** *n.* Any plant bearing seeds; a spermatophyte.—**seeds'man** (-man), *n.*; pl. *-men.* A sower of seed; also, a dealer in seed.—**seed'=time,** *n.* The season for sowing seed.—**seed'=ves"sel,** *n.* In *bot.*, a pericarp.—**seed'y,** *a.*; compar. *seedier,* superl. *seediest.* Abounding in seed; gone to seed; hence, fig., no longer fresh or new, or shabby (as, "seedy habiliments," Mrs. Stowe's "Oldtown Folks," iv.; "a seedy old chest," Mark Twain's "Huckleberry Finn," ix.); wearing worn or shabby garments (as, "a seedy man who had evidently spent the night in a doorway": Aldrich's "Story of a Bad Boy," xx.); also, out of sorts physically (colloq.: as, "He had felt seedy all day and taken no food," Du Maurier's "Trilby," iii.).

see-ing (sē'ing), *conj.* [Orig. ppr.] In view of the fact (that); considering: as, "Seeing that the Democrats have split, this is more than an invitation to candidature" (Drinkwater's "Abraham Lincoln," i.); "Deep harm to disobey, Seeing obedience is the bond of rule" (Tennyson's "Passing of Arthur," 262).

seek (sēk), *v.*; sought, seeking. [AS. *sēcan* (pret. *sohte*) = D. *zoeken* = G. *suchen* = Icel. *sækja* = Goth. *sōkjan*, seek; akin to L. *sagire*, perceive acutely: cf. *ransack, sagacious*, and *sake¹*.] **I.** *tr.* To go in search or quest of (as, to seek a lost child; to seek a new home); endeavor to find; look for; endeavor to find out or learn (as, to seek the cause of a phenomenon); find (out) by searching or endeavor; also, to betake one's self or go to (as, to seek a place; to seek one's couch); also, to try to obtain (as, to seek fame; to seek relief); try to bring about (as, to seek a person's downfall); try or attempt (with an infinitive: as, to seek to convince a person); also, to ask for, request, or solicit (as, to seek one's advice); also, to search or explore (a place, etc.) in order to find something (now prov.). **II.** *intr.* To make search or inquiry (as, "Seek, and ye shall find," Mat. vii. 7; to seek for something lost or desired); also, to betake one's self, go, or resort (archaic: as, "Wisdom's self Oft seeks to sweet retired solitude," Milton's "Comus," 376).—**to seek,** to be sought (as, the reason is not far to seek, that is, one need not seek far to find it); hence, not yet found, or absent or lacking (as, men and money are still to seek; intelligence is sadly to seek among them); also, at a loss, puzzled, or without knowledge as to something (archaic); also, wanting or deficient (*in*: as, to be greatly to seek in practical wisdom).—**to seek after,** to go in search of; try to find or obtain; in the passive (to be sought after), to be desired or in demand.—**seek'er,** *n.*

seel (sēl), *v. t.* [OF. F. *siller, ciller,* < L. *cilium,* eyelid.] To close the eyes of (a hawk or other bird) by stitching the eyelids with a thread, as in the course of training in falconry; stitch up (a bird's eyes); hence, to close (a person's eyes, esp. fig.: as, "She that, so young, could give out such a seeming, To seel her father's eyes up close as oak," Shakspere's "Othello," iii. 3. 210); blind. [Archaic.]

seem (sēm), *v. i.* [From Scand.: cf. Icel. *sæma,* honor, conform to, *sama,* beseem, become, *sæmr,* becoming, fit; akin to E. *same.*] To be fitting, suitable, or becoming†; also, to have the appearance or semblance, or present the general effect, of being (with a complement: as, the work seems unfinished; he is not what he seems; this seems like old times); appear to be; appear (to be, feel, do, etc.: as, he seemed to realize his danger); appear to one's self, as in thought (to be, do, etc.: as, "As in a dream I seem'd to climb For ever," Tennyson's "Holy Grail," 833); appear to exist (as, there seems no need of further delay); appear to be true or the case (as, it would seem that he was right; only a copy, it seems, of the original painting).—**seem'er,** *n.*—**seem'ing,** *n.* Appearance; aspect; semblance; sometimes, outward appearance as distinguished from reality; deceptive appearance; also, opinion† or judgment† (as, in my seeming).—**seem'ing,** *p. a.* Fitting† or suitable†; also, apparent, or seeming to be such (whether truly or falsely: as, a seeming advantage; "'Do you see the mirage?' asked the Pacha . . . pointing to a seeming reach of water," G. W. Curtis's "Howadji in Syria," i. 9).—**seem'ing-ly,** *adv.*—**seem'ing-ness,** *n.*—**seem'ly,** *a.*; compar. *seemlier,* superl. *seemliest.* Fitting or suitable (as, "As rain in harvest, so honour is not seemly for a fool": Prov. xxvi. 1); esp., fitting or becoming with respect to propriety or good taste (as, "Lincoln in deference to the usual and seemly procedure took no part in the campaign," Charnwood's "Abraham Lincoln," v.; "In Germany . . . we do not dance like this. It could not be considered seemly," H. G. Wells's "Mr. Britling," i. 2. § 9); proper, decent, or decorous; also, of pleasing or fine appearance, or handsome (as, "a seemly Georgian residence," Arnold Bennett's "Lion's Share," ii.: archaic or prov.).—**seem'li-ness,** *n.*—**seem'ly,** *adv.* In a seemly manner; fittingly; becomingly; pleasingly or handsomely (archaic).

seen (sēn). Past participle of *see²*.—**seen,** *p. a.* Perceived, beheld, or discerned; also, experienced, versed, or skilled (archaic: as, "A schoolmaster Well seen in music," Shakspere's "Taming of the Shrew," i. 2. 134).

seep (sēp), *v. i.* [Var. of *sipe.*] To pass gradually, as liquid, through a porous substance; percolate; ooze: sometimes fig. (as, "The independence seeped out of him": Sinclair Lewis's "Babbitt," xxxii.).—**seep,** *n.* Moisture that seeps out; also, a small spring.—**seep-age** (sē'pāj), *n.* The act or process of seeping; leakage; also, that which seeps or leaks out.—**seep'y,** *a.* Full of moisture; poorly drained, as land.

se-er (sē'ėr or sēr), *n.* One who sees; also (usually pron. sēr), one who receives divine revelations; a prophet; one with deep spiritual insight; also, a person gifted with second sight; often, a crystal-gazer.—**seer'ess,** *n.* A female seer.—**seer'ship,** *n.*

seer-suck-er (sēr'suk"ėr), *n.* [Pers. *shīr o shakkar,* lit. 'milk and sugar,' with allusion to the stripes.] Orig., an East Indian striped fabric of linen or silk; now, a kind of (cotton) gingham, usually striped, alternate stripes being often crinkled in the weaving.

see-saw (sē'sâ). [Varied redupl. of *saw³.*] **I.** *n.* A children's sport in which they move alternately up and down when seated one or more at each end of a plank balanced on some support; a plank adjusted for this sport; hence, an up-and-down or a back-and-forth movement or procedure (often fig.); in *whist*, the playing of two partners so that each alternately trumps a non-trump card led by the other; a cross-ruff. **II.** *a.* Moving up and down or back and forth: sometimes fig. (as, "I don't remember ever being see-saw . . . when I'd made my mind up": George Eliot's "Adam Bede," xvi.).—**see'saw,** *v. i.* or *t.* To move or cause to move in a seesaw manner: as, "The ancient inn . . . Whose flapping sign these fifty years Has seesawed to and fro" (Holmes's "Agnes," ii.).

seethe (sēᵺ), *v.*; pret. *seethed,* pp. *seethed* (formerly sodden), ppr. *seething.* [AS. *sēothan* (pp. *soden*) = D. *zieden* = G. *sieden,* boil.] **I.** *tr.* To boil; prepare, cook, or extract the essence of, by boiling; also, to soak or steep. **II.** *intr.* To boil; hence, to surge or foam as if boiling (as, "The river . . . seethed in frothy streaks": J. Conrad's "Lord Jim," i.); fig., to be in a state of agitation or excitement.—**seethe,** *n.* The act or fact of seething; ebullition; a state of agitation or excitement.—**seeth'ing-ly,** *adv.*

se-gar (sē̦-gär'), *n.* See *cigar.*

seg-gar (seg'är), *n.* Same as *saggar.*

seg-ment (seg′ment), n. [L. segmentum, < secare, cut: see secant.] A piece or part cut, broken, or marked off; one of the parts into which anything naturally separates or is naturally divided; a division or section; in geom., a part cut off from a figure (esp. a circular or a spherical one) by a line or a plane, as a part of a circular area contained by an arc and its chord.—**seg′-ment** (-ment), v. t. or i. To separate or divide into segments.—**seg-men′tal** (-men′-tal), a. Pertaining to a segment or segments; composed of segments; of the nature of a segment; esp., having the form of a segment of a circle (as, a segmental arch).—**seg-men′tal-ly**, adv. — **seg′men-ta-ry** (-men-tā-ri), a. Segmental.—**seg-men-ta′-tion** (-men-tā′shon), n. Division into segments; in biol., cell-division; specif., the division of the egg or ovum into the many cells which form the body of the embryo.

Segment of a Circle, ACB.

se-gno (sā′nyō), n. [It., < L. signum, E. sign, n.] In music, a sign; esp., a sign or mark indicating the beginning or end of repetitions.

seg-re-gate (seg′rē-gāt), v.; -gated, -gating. [L. segregatus, pp. of segregare, lit. 'separate from the flock,' < se-, without, apart, + grex (greg-), flock.] **I.** tr. To separate or set apart from the others or from the rest; isolate. **II.** intr. To separate or go apart; separate from the main body and collect in one place.—**seg′re-gate**, a. Segregated; set apart; also, in zoöl., etc., separate; not aggregated.—**seg-re-ga′tion** (-gā′shon), n. [LL. segregatio(n-).] The act of segregating, or the state of being segregated; isolation; also, something segregated.—**seg′re-ga-tive** (-gā-tiv), a. Tending to segregate; characterized by segregation.—**seg′-re-ga-tor** (-gā-tor), n.

se-gui-dil-la (sā-gē-dēl′yä), n. [Sp.] A Spanish dance in triple rhythm for two persons, or the music (instrumental or vocal) for it.

sei-cen-to (sāi-chen′tō), n. [It., six hundred, short for mille seicento, one thousand six hundred.] The 17th century, with reference to Italy, and esp. to the Italian art or literature of that period.—**sei-cen′tist**, n.

seiche (sāsh), n. [F. (Swiss).] An occasional rhythmical movement from side to side of the water of a lake, with fluctuation of the water-level, thought to be due to sudden local variations in atmospheric pressure.

sei-del (zī′del), n. [G.] A mug, as for beer, holding about a pint.

Seid-litz (sed′lits) **pow′der.** [From Seidlitz, village in Bohemia, with mineral springs.] An aperient consisting of two powders, one tartaric acid and the other a mixture of sodium bicarbonate and Rochelle salt, which are dissolved separately and the solutions mixed and drunk while effervescing.

sei-gneur (se-nyėr), n. [F.: see seignior.] In old French use, a feudal lord; in Canada, formerly, one who held a landed estate by feudal tenure; one of the landed gentry.—**sei-gneu-ri-al** (sā-nyö′ri-al), a.

sei-gnior (sē′nyor or sā′-), n. [OF. seignor (F. seigneur) = Sp. señor = Pg. senhor = It. signore, < L. senior, elder: see senior.] A lord; a ruler; the lord of a manor; a gentleman: also formerly used as a title of respect.—**sei′gnior-age** (-aj), n. Lordship†; also, something claimed by a sovereign or superior as a prerogative; specif., a charge on bullion brought to the mint to be coined; the difference between the cost of bullion and the value as money of the pieces coined from it.—**sei′gnior-al**, a. Seigniorial.—**sei-gnio-ri-al** (sē-nyō′ri-al or sā-), a. Of or pertaining to a seignior.—**sei′-gnior-y** (-i), n.; pl. -ies (-iz). [OF. seignorie (F. seigneurie).] The power or authority of a seignior; feudal lordship; also, a lord's domain; also, a body of lords, as an Italian signory.

seine (sān or sēn), n. [AS. segne, < L. sagena < Gr. σαγήνη, large net, seine.] A fishing-net which hangs vertically in the water, having floats at the upper edge and sinkers at the lower, the fish being inclosed and taken by drawing the ends of the net together.—**seine**, v.; seined, seining. **I.** intr. To fish with a seine. **II.** tr. To catch with a seine; also, to use a seine in (water).—**seine′-boat,** n. A boat for carrying and paying out a seine. See cut in next column.

seise (sēz), v. Archaic form of seize, common in legal use.
sei-sin (sē′zin), n. See seizin.
seism (sīsm or sizm), n. [Gr. σεισμός, < σείειν, shake.] An earthquake.—**seis-mal** (sīs′mal or siz′-), a. Seismic.—**seis′mic**, a. Pertaining to, of the nature of, or caused by an earthquake or earthquakes. Also **seis′mi-cal.—seis′mi-cal-ly**, adv.—**seis-mi′ci-ty** (-mis′i-ti), n. Seismic character; liability to earthquakes; the relative frequency of earthquakes in a given area.—**seis′mism**, n. The phenomena of earthquakes, collectively.
seismo-. Form of Gr. σεισμός, earthquake, used in combination.—**seis-mo-gram** (sīs′mo-gram or siz′-), n. [+ -gram.] A record made by a seismograph.—**seis′mo-graph** (-graf), n. [+ -graph.] An instrument for recording the phenomena of earthquakes; a recording seismometer.—**seis-mog′ra-phy** (-mog′ra-fi), n. [+ -graphy.] The scientific description of earthquake phenomena; also, the use of the seismograph.—**seis-mog′ra-pher**, n.—**seis-mo-graph′ic** (-graf′ik), a.—**seis-mol′o-gy** (-mol′ō-ji), n. [+ -logy.] The science or study of earthquakes and their phenomena.—**seis-mo-log′i-cal** (-loj′i-kal), a.—**seis-mol′o-gist**, n.—**seis-mom′e-ter** (-mom′e-tėr), n. [+ -meter.] An instrument for measuring the direction, intensity, and duration of earthquakes.—**seis-mom′e-try**, n. [+ -metry.] The scientific recording and study of earthquake phenomena, esp. by means of the seismometer; the theory and use of the seismometer.—**seis-mo-met′ric, seis-mo-met′ri-cal** (-met′rik, -ri-kal), a.—**seis′mo-scope** (-skōp), n. [+ -scope.] An instrument for indicating the occurrence of earthquake shocks: a simple form of seismometer.—**seis-mo-scop′ic** (-skop′ik), a.
seiz-a-ble (sē′za-bl), a. That may be seized: as, "rich foreign lands, full of seizable wealth" (H. G. Wells's "Outline of History," xxxvii. § 13).
seize (sēz), v.; seized, seizing. [OF. seisir, saisir (F. saisir), < ML. sacire, take, seize; prob. from Teut.] **I.** tr. To put (one) in legal possession of something (usually spelled seise); also, to take possession of by legal authority, or confiscate (as, to seize smuggled goods); hence, to take possession of by force or at will (as, to seize enemy ships or towns; brigands seized the goods of traveling merchants); capture; take prisoner, or take into custody (as, "For a publication of simple ideas men were seized, tried at law, mulcted, imprisoned": G. Meredith's "Lord Ormont and His Aminta," xi.); also, to lay hold of suddenly or forcibly, clutch, or grasp (as, to seize a weapon or a life-preserver; to seize a person's hand; to seize a dog by the collar); catch or take (hold) suddenly or forcibly (as, "Lawless seized hold of the intruder to drag him out": Maria Edgeworth's "Belinda," iii.); fig., to take possession or control of as if by suddenly laying hold (as, a fever seized him; panic seized the crowd; "I was seized with sorrow for her," Stevenson's "Master of Ballantrae," v.); arrest (the attention), or impress (the mind, etc.) suddenly and forcibly; grasp with the mind (as, to seize an idea; to seize one's meaning); take advantage of promptly (as, to seize an opportunity or occasion); naut., to bind, lash, or make fast (as one thing to another), or fasten together (as two things), with several turns of small rope, cord, or the like (as, to seize one rope to another; to seize two fish-hooks back to back). **II.** intr. To take possession by force or at will (with on or upon: as, "Let us kill him, and let us seize on his inheritance," Mat. xxi. 38; to seize upon an abandoned farm); also, to lay hold suddenly or forcibly (lit. or fig.: as, to seize on a rope; to seize on a pretext, excuse, or opportunity; "The contagion of his confidence seized upon the prince," Johnson's "Rasselas," vi.).—**seiz′er**, n.
sei-zin, sei-sin (sē′zin), n. [OF. F. saisine, < saisir: see seize.] In law, orig., possession; in later use, possession of a freehold estate; possession of land, actual or constructive, under rightful title.
seiz-ing (sē′zing), n. The act of one who or that which seizes; naut., the act of binding, lashing, or making fast, or of fastening together, with several turns of small rope, cord, or

Seine-boat.

the like, or the fastening so made; also, cordage or a cord, or the like, used to seize with.

sei-zure (sē'zhụr), *n.* The act of seizing, or the fact of being seized; a taking possession, legally or by force; a sudden attack, as of disease (as, an epileptic *seizure*); also, something seized (as, "A part of them escorted the terrified revenue officers and their *seizure* to a neighbouring sea-port": Scott's "Guy Mannering," xxx.).

se-jant (sē'jạnt), *a.* [OF. *seant* (F. *séant*), ppr. of *seoir*, sit: cf. *séance*.] In *her.*, in a sitting posture; sitting with the forelegs upright, as a lion or other beast.

Lion Sejant.

se-la-chi-an (sē-lā'ki-ạn). [NL. *Selachii*, pl., < Gr. σέλαχος, cartilaginous fish, shark.] **I.** *a.* Belonging to the *Selachii*, a large group of elasmobranch fishes comprising the sharks and their allies. **II.** *n.* A shark or other selachian fish.

Nautical Seizings.

sel-a-choid (sel'ạ-koid), *a.* [Gr. σέλαχος, shark: see *-oid*.] Selachian.— Port Jackson Shark (*Heterodontus philippi*). Shark-like; of the shark kind.

se-lah (sē'lä). [Heb. *selāh*.] A word occurring frequently in the Psalms, supposed to be a liturgical or musical direction, perhaps indicating a pause.

se-lam-lik (sẹ-läm'lik), *n.* [Turk.] The part of a Turkish house reserved for the men; also, formerly, the ceremonial visit of the Sultan of Turkey to a place of worship every Friday.

sel-dom (sel'dọm). [AS. *seldum*, for *seldan* = D. *zelden* = G. *selten* = Icel. *sjaldan*, seldom, akin to Goth. *sildaleiks*, wonderful.] **I.** *adv.* Rarely; infrequently; not often: as, "She had *seldom* been there since her marriage" (Dickens's "Hard Times," ii. 9). **II.** *a.* Rare; infrequent: as, "blunting the fine point of *seldom* pleasure" (Shakspere's "Sonnets," lii.). [Now rare.]—**sel'dom-ness**, *n.*

se-lect (sẹ-lekt'), *v.* [L. *selectus*, pp. of *seligere*, < *se-*, without, apart, + *legere*, gather, choose: see *legion*.] **I.** *tr.* To choose in preference to another or others; pick out from a number. **II.** *intr.* To make choice or selection.—**se-lect'**, *a.* Selected; chosen in preference to others; hence, choice; of special value or excellence; superior; often, of persons, socially superior; also, careful or fastidious in selection, esp. of one's associates; exclusive.—**select council**, in certain cities of the U. S., the higher branch of the local legislative body: cf. *common council.*—**se-lect'**, *n.* One who or that which is selected, as a recruit obtained by selective draft; also, something select or choice.—**se-lec'-tee'**, *n.* One drafted for military service. [U. S.]

se-lec-tion (sẹ-lek'shọn), *n.* [L. *selectio(n-).*] The act of selecting, or the fact of being selected; choice; also, a thing or a number of things selected; often, a passage or piece, or a number of passages or pieces, selected from a book or a number of books, etc. (as, a volume of prose or poetical *selections*; a book containing a *selection* from an author's works); in *biol.*, the singling out of certain forms of animal and vegetable life for reproduction and perpetuation, by the operation of natural causes which, in the course of evolution, favor some organisms rather than others in consequence of differences in the organisms themselves ('natural selection'); the process resulting in the survival of the fittest (see under *survival*); also, man's agency in modifying the processes of natural selection and thereby changing its results, as in breeding animals and in cultivating fruits, vegetables, etc. ('artificial selection').—**se-lec'tion-ist**, *n.* One who adheres to a theory of selection.

se-lec-tive (sẹ-lek'tiv), *a.* Having the function or power of selecting; making selection; characterized by selection or choice; specif., in *mach.*, noting or pertaining to a system of transmission, as in automobiles, in which the speeds may be changed in any order, without the necessity of passing progressively through the different changes of gear; in *elect.*, having selectivity, as a radio receiving set.—**se-lec'tive-ly**, *adv.*—**se-lec'tive-ness**, *n.*—**se-lec-tiv-i-ty** (sē-lek-tiv'i-ti), *n.* The state or quality of being selective; in *elect.*, the property of a circuit, instrument, or the like, by virtue of which it responds to electric oscillations of a particular frequency; esp., of a radio receiving set, the ability to receive any one of a band of frequencies or waves to the exclusion of others.

se-lect-ly (sẹ-lekt'li), *adv.* In a select manner.

se-lect-man (sẹ-lekt'mạn), *n.*; pl. *-men*. One of a board of town officers, as in New England, chosen annually to manage certain public affairs.

se-lect-ness (sẹ-lekt'nes), *n.* The quality or character of being select.

se-lec-tor (sẹ-lek'tọr), *n.* [LL.] One who or that which selects; any of various mechanical, electrical, or other devices which have a more or less selective action.

sel-e-nate (sel'ẹ-nāt), *n.* In *chem.*, a salt of selenic acid.

Se-le-ne (se-lē'nē), *n.* [Gr. Σελήνη, personification of σελήνη, moon.] In *Gr. myth.*, the goddess of the moon. Cf. *Luna*.

se-len-ic (se-len'ik), *a.* [See *selenium*.] Of or containing selenium. See *selenious*.—**selenic acid**, a strong corrosive dibasic acid, H_2SeO_4, resembling sulphuric acid.—**sel-e-nide** (sel'ẹ-nīd or -nid), *n.* In *chem.*, a compound of selenium with a more electropositive element or radical.—**sel-e-nif'-er-ous** (-nif'ẹ-rus), *a.* [See *-ferous*.] Containing or yielding selenium, as ore.—**se-le'ni-ous** (-lē'ni-us), *a.* Containing selenium (in larger proportion than a corresponding selenic compound).—**selenious acid**, a dibasic acid, H_2SeO_3.—**sel'e-nite**[1] (-nīt), *n.* In *chem.*, a salt of selenious acid.

sel-e-nite[2] (sel'ẹ-nīt), *n.* [L. *selenites* < Gr. σεληνίτης (λίθος), '(stone) of the moon,' < σελήνη, moon.] A variety of gypsum, found in transparent crystals and foliated masses.—**sel-e-nit'ic** (-nit'ik), *a.*

se-le-ni-um (se-lē'ni-um), *n.* [NL. *selenium*, < Gr. σελήνη, moon; so named to correspond to *tellurium*, < L. *tellus*, the earth.] Chem. sym., Se; at. wt., 79.2. A non-metallic element resembling sulphur and tellurium in chemical properties, occurring in several allotropic forms (crystalline, amorphous, etc.), and having an electrical resistance which varies through the influence of light.

seleno-. Form of Gr. σελήνη, moon, used in combination.—**sel-e-nog-ra-phy** (sel-ẹ-nog'rạ-fi), *n.* [+ *-graphy*.] The science dealing with the moon, esp. with reference to its physical features.—**sel-e-nog'ra-pher**, *n.*—**sel-e-no-graph-ic** (se-lē-nọ-graf'ik), *a.*—**sel-e-nol'o-gy** (-nol'ọ-ji), *n.* [+ *-logy*.] The science of the moon; esp., that branch of astronomy which deals with the moon.—**se-le-no-log'i-cal** (-loj'i-kạl), *a.*—**sel-e-nol'o-gist**, *n.*—**se-le-no-trop'ic** (-trop'ik), *a.* [+ *-tropic*.] In *bot.*, turning toward the moon; taking a particular direction under the influence of the moon's light.—**sel-e-not'ro-pism** (-not'rọ-pizm), *n.* Selenotropic tendency.

self (self). [AS. *self* = D. *zelf* = G. *selb* = Icel. *sjálfr* = Sw. *sjelf* = Dan. *selv* = Goth. *silba*, self.] **I.** *a.* Same, identical, or very (archaic except when followed by *same*: cf. *selfsame*); also, being the same throughout, as a color (cf. *self-color*); uniform; unmixed; also, of a part, being of one piece or material with the rest; also, own† or personal†. **II.** *pron.*; pl. *selves* (selvz). The person or thing mentioned (formerly used as a separate word in connection with a noun or another pronoun, to express emphasis, as in "This is no Poetical fiction, but unfeynedly spoken of the Poete *selfe*," E. K., 1579, gloss on Spenser's "Shepheardes Calender," June, 18: cf. *himself, themselves*); often, elliptically, one's self (as, *self*-murder); sometimes (esp. colloq.), myself, yourself, himself, etc. (as, a check made out to *self*; tickets for *self* and wife). **III.** *n.*; pl. *selves* (selvz). A person or thing referred to, with respect to his, her, or its own person or individuality (following a possessive indicating the person or thing: as, one's *self*; his very *self*; our two *selves*; religion's *self*: cf. also *myself, ourselves*, etc.); also (esp. in philosophical use), the individual consciousness in its relations to itself; also, one's nature, character, etc., at a particular time or in a particular aspect, or as one of various conflicting personalities of which one is made up (as, one's former *self*; one's better *self*; "It seemed . . . as if he had

---

(variable) ḍ as d or j, ş as s or sh, ṭ as t or ch, ẕ as z or zh; *o*, F. *cloche*; ü, F. *menu*; ch, Sc. *loch*; ṅ, F. *bonbon*; ', primary accent: ", secondary accent; †, obsolete; <, from: +, and: =, equals. See also lists at beginning of book.

two distinct yet kindred *selves*, and that the former watched the latter," H. G. Wells's "Soul of a Bishop," vii.); also, personal interest or benefit; selfishness; also, a self-colored flower.

self-. Prefixal use of *self, a., pron.,* or *n.,* occurring in numerous compounds, as *self-color, self-control, self-evident, self-governed, self-governing, self-interest, self-will,* and others, including many that, being of obvious meaning, are not entered and defined in this book.

self=ab-ne-ga-tion (self″ab-nē-gā′shọn), *n.* Abnegation of self; self-denial; self-renunciation.

self=ab-sorbed (self-ab-sôrbd′), *a.* Absorbed in one's self or one's own thoughts, affairs, etc.—**self=ab-sorp′tion,** *n.*

self=a-buse (self-ạ-būs′), *n.* Abuse of one's self; specif., masturbation.

self=act-ing (self-ak′ting), *a.* Acting of or by itself; automatic: as, "Man is a *self-acting* machine" (G. Meredith's "Ordeal of Richard Feverel," xvi.).—**self=ac′tion,** *n.* Action that is independent of external impulse.—**self=ac′tive,** *a.* Acting of or by itself; acting independently of external impulse.—**self=ac-tiv′i-ty,** *n.*—**self=ac′tor,** *n.* A self-acting machine or part of a machine.

self=ad-dressed (self-ạ-drest′), *a.* Addressed to one's self: as, in writing for information inclose a *self-addressed* envelop.

self=ad-just-ing (self-ạ-jus′ting), *a.* Adjusting itself; requiring no external adjustment.

self=as-sert-ing (self-ạ-sėr′ting), *a.* Asserting one's self; putting one's self forward boldly and insistently; displaying self-assertion.—**self=as-ser′tion,** *n.* The asserting of one's self; insistence on one's own importance, claims, wishes, opinions, etc., esp. as conveyed indirectly in action or speech: as, "The hesitancy, the moral doubt of her conversation . . . seemed to have vanished wholly in a kind of acrid *self-assertion*" (Mrs. H. Ward's "Robert Elsmere," xv.).—**self=as-ser′tive,** *a.* Self-asserting.—**self=as-ser′tive-ly,** *adv.* —**self=as-ser′tive-ness,** *n.*

self=as-sur-ance (self-ạ-shör′ạns), *n.* A feeling of assurance as to one's self or one's own powers, etc.; self-confidence.—**self=as-sured′,** *a.* Self-confident.

self=cen-tered, self=cen-tred (self-sen′tėrd), *a.* Being itself fixed as a center; also, centered in one's self or itself; often, engrossed in self; selfish.

self=col-or (self-kul′ọr), *n.* [See *self, a.*] One uniform color, as of a dyed fabric; also, natural (undyed) color.—**self=col′ored,** *a.* Of one uniform color; also, of the natural color.

self=com-mand (self-kọ-månd′), *n.* Command or control of one's self or one's actions, feelings, etc.; self-control: as, "a combat between native ardour of temper and the habitual power of *self-command*" (Scott's "Guy Mannering," xviii.).

self=com-pla-cent (self-kọm-plā′sẹnt), *a.* Complacent as to one's self; pleased with one's self; self-satisfied.—**self=com-pla′cence, self=com-pla′cen-cy,** *n.*—**self=com-pla′cent-ly,** *adv.*

self=con-ceit (self-kọn-sēt′), *n.* Overweening opinion of one's self, one's abilities, etc.—**self=con-ceit′ed,** *a.* Having or showing self-conceit.—**self=con-ceit′ed-ness,** *n.*

self=con-fi-dent (self-kon′fi-dẹnt), *a.* Having or showing confidence in one's self or one's own powers, judgment, etc. —**self=con′fi-dence,** *n.*—**self=con′fi-dent-ly,** *adv.*

self=con-grat-u-la-tion (self″kọn-grat-ū-lā′shọn), *n.* Congratulation of one's self: as, "Her [his wife's] practical capacity was for him a matter for continual *self-congratulation*" (H. G. Wells's "Mr. Britling," i. 4. § 3).—**self=con-grat′u-la-to-ry** (-lā-tọ-ri), *a.*

self=con-scious (self-kon′shus), *a.* Conscious of one's self or one's own thoughts, actions, etc.; also, excessively or morbidly conscious of one's self; given to thinking of one's self as an object of observation to others.—**self=con′-scious-ly,** *adv.*—**self=con′scious-ness,** *n.*

self=con-se-quence (self-kon′sẹ-kwens), *n.* The sense of one's own consequence; self-importance.

self=con-sist-ent (self-kọn-sis′tẹnt), *a.* Consistent with one's self or itself; having its parts or elements in agreement. —**self=con-sist′en-cy,** *n.*

self=con-sti-tut-ed (self-kon′sti-tū-ted), *a.* Constituted by one's self or itself: as, a *self-constituted* board of inquiry.

self=con-tained (self-kọn-tānd′), *a.* Containing in one's self or itself all that is necessary; independent of what is external; of persons, not dependent on others; reserved or uncommunicative (as, "They are rather silent, *self-contained* men when with strangers": Roosevelt's "Hunting Trips of a Ranchman," i.); of a house, having approaches, entrances, and apartments restricted to the use of a single household (British); of a machine, etc., complete in itself (as, a *self-contained* engine, an engine and a boiler combined in one). —**self=con-tain′ment,** *n.*

self=con-tent (self-kọn-tent′), *n.* Contentment or satisfaction with one's self; self-complacency.—**self=con-tent′ed,** *a.* Self-satisfied.—**self=con-tent′ment,** *n.*

self=con-tra-dic-tion (self″kon-trạ-dik′shọn), *n.* The act or fact of contradicting one's self or itself; also, a statement or the like containing mutually contradictory elements.— **self″=con-tra-dic′to-ry,** *a.* Contradicting one's self or itself; involving self-contradiction.

self=con-trol (self-kọn-trōl′), *n.* Control of one's self or one's actions, feelings, etc.; self-command: as, "His handsome face had all the tranquillity of Indian *self-control*; a *self-control* which prevents the exhibition of emotion" (Parkman's "Oregon Trail," xviii.).—**self=con-trolled′,** *a.* Having or showing self-control.

self=de-ceit (self-dẹ-sēt′), *n.* Deceit practised on one's self; self-deception.—**self=de-ceit′ful,** *a.*—**self=de-ceived′,** *a.* Deceived by one's self; marked by self-deception.—

self=de-cep′tion, *n.* The act or fact of deceiving one's self; self-deceit; self-delusion.—**self=de-cep′tive,** *a.*

self=de-fense, self=de-fence (self-dẹ-fens′), *n.* The act of defending one's own person, property, reputation, etc.: as, "Homicide in *self-defence* . . . upon a sudden affray, is . . . excusable, rather than justifiable, by the English law" (Blackstone's "Commentaries," IV. 183); the manly art of *self-defense* (boxing or pugilism).—**self=de-fen′sive, self= de-fen′so-ry,** *a.*

self=de-lud-ed (self-dẹ-lū′ded), *a.* Deluded by one's self.— **self=de-lu′sion,** *n.* The act of deluding one's self; self-deception.

self=de-ni-al (self-dẹ-nī′ạl), *n.* The denial of one's self; the sacrifice of one's own desires.—**self=de-ny′ing,** *a.* Denying one's self; characterized by self-denial.—**self=de-ny′-ing-ly,** *adv.*

self=de-pend-ent (self-dẹ-pen′dẹnt), *a.* Depending on one's self, or on one's own efforts, etc.; self-reliant: as, "Left early to his own guidance, he had begun to be *self-dependent* while yet a boy" (Hawthorne's "House of the Seven Gables," xii.).—**self=de-pend′ence,** *n.*—**self=de-pend′ent-ly,** *adv.*

self=de-rived (self-dẹ-rīvd′), *a.* Derived from one's self or from itself.

self=de-spair (self-dẹ-spär′), *n.* Despair of one's self, one's prospects, etc.

self=de-struc-tion (self-dẹ-struk′shọn), *n.* The destruction of one's self or itself; esp., self-murder; suicide.—**self=de-struc′tive,** *a.* Tending to destroy one's self or itself, or each other.

self=de-ter-mi-na-tion (self″dẹ-tėr-mi-nā′shọn), *n.* Determination by one's self or itself, without constraint or influence from without; esp., the determining by a people or nationality of the form of government it shall have, without reference to the wishes of any other nation, even one to which it has been subject.—**self=de-ter′mined,** *a.* Determined by one's self or itself.—**self=de-ter′min-ing,** *a.* Determining one's own acts; having the power of self-determination.

self=de-vo-tion (self-dẹ-vō′shọn), *n.* Devotion of one's self; self-sacrifice: as, "the example of his life . . . one long act of *self-devotion*" (S. Butler's "Way of All Flesh," xvi.).— **self=de-vo′tion-al,** *a.*

self=di-ges-tion (self-di-jes′chọn), *n.* In *physiol.,* autodigestion; autolysis.

self=dis-trust (self-dis-trust′), *n.* Distrust of, or want of confidence in, one's self, one's abilities, etc.: as, "I . . . urge, in trembling *self-distrust,* A prayer without a claim" (Whittier's "Eternal Goodness").—**self=dis-trust′ful,** *a.*

self=ed-u-cat-ed (self-ẹd′ū-kā-ted), *a.* Educated by one's own efforts, without formal instruction, or without financial assistance.—**self″=ed-u-ca′tion,** *n.* Education by or through one's own efforts.

self=ef-face-ment (self-e-fās′ment), *n.* The act or fact of effacing one's self, or keeping one's self in the background, as in modesty or humility.—**self=ef-fa′cing** (-fā′sing), *a.* Effacing one's self, or keeping one's self in the background: as, "Susan was *self-effacing*, and she enjoyed listening to Honora's views on all topics" (W. Churchill's "Modern Chronicle," i. 6).

self=es-teem (self-es-tēm′), *n.* Esteem for one's self; favorable opinion of one's self: in *phren.*, a special faculty.

self=ev-i-dent (self-ev′i-dent), *a.* Evident in itself without proof; axiomatic.—**self=ev′i-dence,** *n.*—**self=ev′i-dent-ly,** *adv.*

self=ex-am-i-na-tion (self″eg-zam-i-nā′shon), *n.* Examination into one's own state, conduct, motives, etc., esp. as a religious duty.

self=ex-e-cut-ing (self-ek′sē-kū-ting), *a.* Providing for its own execution, and needing no legislation to enforce it: as, a *self-executing* treaty.

self=ex-ist-ent (self-eg-zis′tent), *a.* Existing by one's or its own virtue alone, independently of any other cause; also, having an independent existence.—**self=ex-ist′ence,** *n.*

self=ex-plan-a-to-ry (self-eks-plan′a-tō-ri), *a.* Explaining itself; needing no explanation; obvious. Also **self=ex-plain′ing.**

self=feed-er (self-fē′dėr), *n.* A machine or the like, as a printing-press, which feeds itself automatically.—**self=feed′ing,** *a.* That feeds itself automatically: as, a *self-feeding* printing-press.

self=fer-ti-li-za-tion (self″fėr-ti-li-zā′shon), *n.* In *bot.*, the fertilization of a flower by its own pollen: opposed to *cross-fertilization.*—**self=fer′ti-lized,** *a.* In *bot.*, of a flower, fertilized by its own pollen.

self=fig-ured (self-fig′ūrd), *a.* Woven with figures in its own color, as a self-colored fabric.

self=fill-er (self-fil′ėr), *n.* Any of various types of fountain-pen which can be filled by operating some mechanism while the lower part of the pen is dipped in ink.

self=for-get-ful (self-for-get′fùl), *a.* Forgetful of one's self; forgetful of, or showing no thought of, one's own advantage, interest, etc.—**self=for-get′ful-ly,** *adv.*—**self=for-get′ful-ness,** *n.*

self=gen-er-at-ed (self-jen′ė-rā-ted), *a.* Generated by one's self or itself, independently of any external agency.

self=gov-erned (self-guv′ėrnd), *a.* Governed by itself, or having self-government, as a state or community; also, governing one's own actions or affairs, or independent, as a person; also, exercising self-control.—**self=gov′ern-ing,** *a.* Governing itself; having self-government; autonomous.—**self=gov′ern-ment,** *n.* Government of a state, community, or other body of persons by its members jointly (as, *self-government* through elected representatives; local *self-government*): autonomy; also, government of one's actions, affairs, etc., by one's self or independently of others; also, self-control (as, "Virtuous *self-government* . . . improves the inward constitution or character": J. Butler's "Analogy of Religion," i. 5).

self=grat-i-fi-ca-tion (self″grat-i-fi-kā′shon), *n.* The gratification of one's self or one's desires, vanity, etc.

self=grat-u-la-tion (self″grat-ū-lā′shon), *n.* Self-congratulation.—**self=grat′u-la-to-ry** (-lā-tō-ri), *a.*

self=guid-ance (self-gī′dans), *n.* Guidance of one's self in one's own course, actions, etc.: as, "He may lose the powers of *self-guidance*, and in a wrong course his very vitalities hurry him to perdition" (G. Meredith's "Ordeal of Richard Feverel," xvi.).

self=hard-en-ing (self-här′dn-ing), *a.* Noting or pertaining to any of certain steels which, owing to their special composition, harden without the usual quenching, etc., necessary for ordinary steel.

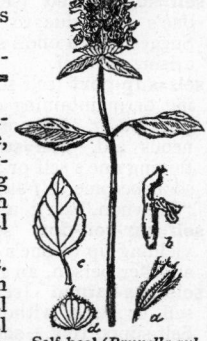

Self-heal (*Prunella vulgaris*), upper part of stem with flowers.— *a*, the calyx; *b*, the corolla; *c*, a leaf; *d*, a bract from the inflorescence.

self=heal (self′hēl), *n.* A menthaceous plant, *Prunella vulgaris*, a native of Europe, once credited with great remedial virtues; also, any of various other plants formerly supposed to possess healing properties, as the sanicle, *Sanicula europæa.*

self=help (self-help′), *n.* The act or the faculty of helping one's self, or getting along without assistance from others (as, "The first lesson the backwoodsmen learnt was the necessity of *self-help*": Roosevelt's "Winning of the West," i. 5); in *law*, the act or right of redressing or preventing wrongs by one's own action, without recourse to legal process.—**self=help′ful,** *a.*

self=hood (self′hùd), *n.* The character of being one's self; the mode of being of an individual person; personality.

self=i-den-ti-cal (self-ī-den′ti-kạl), *a.* Identical with itself.—**self=i-den′ti-ty,** *n.* The identity of a thing with itself.

self=im-mo-la-tion (self″im-ō-lā′shon), *n.* Immolation or sacrifice of one's self.

self=im-por-tant (self-im-pôr′tant), *a.* Having or showing an exaggerated opinion of one's own importance.—**self=im-por′tance,** *n.*—**self=im-por′tant-ly,** *adv.*

self=im-posed (self-im-pōzd′), *a.* Imposed on one by one's self: as, a *self-imposed* task.

self=im-prove-ment (self-im-pröv′ment), *n.* Improvement of one's self, one's mind, etc., by one's own efforts.—**self=im-prov′ing,** *a.*

self=in-duced (self-in-dūst′), *a.* Induced by one's self or itself; in *elect.*, produced by self-induction.—**self=in-duc′tion,** *n.* In *elect.*, the production of an induced current in a circuit by a varying current in that circuit.

self=in-dul-gent (self-in-dul′jent), *a.* Indulging one's own desires, passions, etc. (as, "a capricious and *self-indulgent* valetudinarian": Boswell's "Johnson," March 27, 1776); also, characterized by such indulgence, as conduct.—**self=in-dul′gence,** *n.*—**self=in-dul′gent-ly,** *adv.*

self=in-fec-tion (self-in-fek′shon), *n.* In *pathol.*, auto-infection.

self=in-flict-ed (self-in-flik′ted), *a.* Inflicted on one by one's self, as a wound.

self=in-oc-u-la-tion (self″in-ok-ū-lā′shon), *n.* In *pathol.*, auto-inoculation.

self=in-sur-ance (self-in-shör′ans), *n.* The insuring of one's self or one's property, etc., through one's self rather than through others, as by setting aside a fund for the purpose.—**self=in-sured′,** *a.*

self=in-ter-est (self-in′tėr-est), *n.* Personal interest or advantage; also, regard for one's own interest or advantage, esp. with disregard of the interest of others (as, "the *self-interest* of the calculating statesman": Morley's "Oliver Cromwell," iv. 2).—**self=in′ter-est-ed,** *a.* Actuated by regard for one's own interest or advantage; showing self-interest.—**self=in′ter-est-ed-ness,** *n.*

self=ish (sel′fish), *a.* Devoted to or caring only for self (as, "this *selfish*, well-fed and supremely indifferent old man": Mrs. Wharton's "Age of Innocence," xi.); influenced solely or chiefly by considerations of personal interest, well-being, desires, etc.; also, characterized by or showing care solely or chiefly for one's self, one's own interests, etc. (as, a *selfish* disposition; *selfish* motives; *selfish* conduct).—**self′ish-ly,** *adv.*—**self′ish-ness,** *n.*

self=knowl-edge (self-nol′ej), *n.* Knowledge of one's self, or one's character, abilities, etc.

self=less (self′les), *a.* Having no regard for or thought of self; unselfish.—**self′less-ly,** *adv.*—**self′less-ness,** *n.*

self=love (self-luv′), *n.* Love of one's self; the instinct by which man's actions are directed to the promotion of his own welfare.—**self=lov′ing,** *a.*

self=lu-mi-nous (self-lū′mi-nus), *a.* Luminous of itself; possessing in itself the property of emitting light.—**self″=lu-mi-nos′i-ty,** *n.*

self=made (self′mād′), *a.* Made by one's self; also, having attained success in life unaided (as, a *self-made* man).

self=mor-ti-fi-ca-tion (self″môr-ti-fi-kā′shon), *n.* Mortification of one's self, one's passions, etc.

self=moved (self-mövd′), *a.* Moved of itself, without external agency.—**self=mov′ing,** *a.* Moving of itself, without external agency.

self=mur-der (self-mėr′dėr), *n.* The murder of one's self; suicide.—**self=mur′der-er,** *n.*

self=o-pin-ion (self-ō-pin′yon), *n.* Opinion, esp. exaggerated opinion, of one's self; self-esteem; self-conceit; also,

obstinacy in one's own opinion.—**self=o·pin'ion-at-ed**, *a.*
Having an exaggerated opinion of one's self; self-conceited;
also, obstinate in one's own opinion. Also **self=o·pin'ioned.**

self=op-posed (self-o̯-pōzd'), *a.* Opposed to one's self or
itself; having parts or elements that are opposed one to
another.

self=per-cep-tion (self-pėr-sep'shon), *n.* Perception of the
soul by itself; immediate introspection.

self=pit-y (self-pit'i), *n.* Pity for one's self.—**self=pit'y-
ing**, *a.* Pitying one's self.—**self=pit'y-ing-ly**, *adv.*

self=poised (self-poizd'), *a.* Poised or balanced of itself or
without external aid (as, "Thy form *Self-poised* as if it
floated on the air": Longfellow's "Masque of Pandora," v.);
fig., having or showing mental poise, steadiness, or self-
possession, regardless of external circumstances (as, "Decorous and *self-poised*, he was only passionate before the
enemy": Motley's "Dutch Republic," vi. 1).

self=pol-lu-tion (self-po̯-lū'shon), *n.* Masturbation.

self=por-trait (self-pôr'trāt), *n.* A portrait of a person
executed by himself.—**self=por'trait-ist**, *n.*

self=pos-sessed (self-po̯-zest'), *a.* Having or showing control
of one's self or one's feelings, demeanor, behavior, etc.;
composed; characterized by self-possession: as, "as impenitent and *self-possessed* a young lady as one would desire
to see" (G. B. Shaw's "Man and Superman," i.); "In a
moment he recovered his usual *self-possessed* manner"
(W. H. Hudson's "Purple Land," xxviii.).—**self=pos-ses'-
sion**, *n.* Control of one's self or one's feelings, demeanor,
etc.; composure; coolness: as, "Their quiet *self-possession*
and dignified ease impressed me pleasurably" (S. Butler's
"Erewhon," vi.).

self=praise (self-prāz'), *n.* Praise of one's self.

self=pres-er-va-tion (self″prez-ėr-vā'shon), *n.* Preservation of one's self from harm or destruction: as, the instinct
of *self-preservation*; "He was not . . . acquainted with the
beautiful axiom that *self-preservation* is the first law of
nature" (Dickens's "Oliver Twist," x.).

self=pride (self-prīd'), *n.* Pride in one's self or one's own
importance, achievements, etc.

self=pro-duced (self-pro̯-dūst'), *a.* Produced by one's self
or itself.—**self=pro-duc'tion**, *n.*

self=prof-it (self-prof'it), *n.* One's own profit or advantage;
self-interest: as, "unbias'd by *self-profit*" (Tennyson's
"Œnone," 156).

self=pro-pelled (self-pro̯-peld'), *a.* Propelled by itself;
esp., of a vehicle, etc., containing an engine, motor, or the
like, within itself, by which it is propelled, as distinguished
from a vehicle, etc., which is drawn or pushed by a horse,
locomotive, or the like.

self=rais-ing (self-rā'zing), *a.* That raises itself: applied to
flour so prepared by mixing with suitable raising ingredients
that it may be used for making biscuits, etc., without adding
baking-powder or the like.

self=re-cord-ing (self-rē-kôr'ding), *a.* Recording automatically, as an instrument; self-registering; autographic.

self=reg-is-ter-ing (self-rej'is-tėr-ing), *a.* Registering automatically, as an instrument; self-recording.

self=reg-u-lat-ing (self-reg'ū-lā-ting), *a.* Regulating one's
self or itself.—**self″=reg-u-la'tion**, *n.* Regulation of one's
self or itself.—**self=reg'u-la-tive**, *a.*

self=re-li-ance (self-rē-lī'ans), *n.* Reliance on one's self or
one's own powers.—**self=re-li'ant**, *a.* Relying on one's
self; having or showing self-reliance.—**self=re-li'ant-ly**, *adv.*

self=re-nun-ci-a-tion (self″rē-nun-si-ā'shon), *n.* Renunciation of self, or of one's own will, interests, etc.; self-
sacrifice.

self=re-pres-sion (self-rē-presh'on), *n.* Repression of one's
self or one's own impulses, desires, etc.—**self=re-pressed'**, *a.*

self=re-proach (self-rē-prōch'), *n.* Reproach of one's self;
blame or censure by one's own conscience.—**self=re-proach'-
ful**, *a.*

self=re-spect (self-rē-spekt'), *n.* Respect for one's self;
proper esteem or regard for the dignity of one's character,
with recognition of its obligations of worthy conduct: as,
"With shame and repentance . . . had come a strange new
feeling — that of a dawning *self-respect*" (Du Maurier's
"Trilby," iii.); "a . . . little fellow whose clothes . . . were
always neatly mended, betokening a mother with *self-*

respect and character" (W. Churchill's "Inside of the Cup,"
xi.).—**self=re-spect'ing**, *a.* Having or showing self-
respect: as, "the shame of boasting that shuts the mouths
of *self-respecting* Scots" (Ian Maclaren's "Beside the Bonnie
Brier Bush," i. 2).

self=re-strained (self-rē-strānd'), *a.* Restrained by one's
self or itself; showing self-restraint.—**self=re-straint'**, *n.*
Restraint imposed on one by one's self; self-control.

self=right-eous (self-rī'chus), *a.* Righteous in one's own
esteem; affecting righteousness; pharisaic: as, "She's
narrow and *self-righteous*" (Eden Phillpotts's "Children of
Men," i. 5).—**self=right'eous-ly**, *adv.*—**self=right'eous-
ness**, *n.*

self=sac-ri-fice (self-sak'ri-fīs), *n.* Sacrifice of one's self or
one's own interests, desires, etc., as for the sake of duty or
the good of another.—**self=sac'ri-fi-cing**, *a.*

self=same (self'sām), *a.* (The) very same; identical: as,
"And his servant was healed in the *selfsame* hour" (Mat.
viii. 13); "I am made Of the *self-same* metal that my sister
is" (Shakspere's "King Lear," i. 1. 71).—**self'same-ness**, *n.*

self=sat-is-fied (self-sat'is-fīd), *a.* Satisfied with one's self,
one's achievements, etc.; feeling or showing satisfaction with
one's self; self-complacent.—**self″=sat-is-fac'tion**, *n.*

self=seek-er (self-sē'kėr), *n.* One who seeks his own interest
or selfish ends: as, "So the three *self-seekers* banded and
beset the one unselfish" (C. Brontë's "Villette," xxxix.).—
self=seek'ing. **I.** *n.* The seeking of one's own interest or
selfish ends: as, "the members of Parliament, who irritated
the army by their *self-seeking* and greediness" (Morley's
"Oliver Cromwell," iv. 5). **II.** *a.* Given to or characterized
by self-seeking; selfish in aims or purposes: as, *self-seeking*
politicians; "The *self-seeking* motives of many Protestant
princes had disgusted the nobles" (Motley's "Dutch Republic," iv. 4).—**self=seek'ing-ness**, *n.*

self=ser-vice (self-sėr'vis), *n.* Service by one's self; the
serving of one's self (to a greater or less extent) in a restaurant, shop, or the like, instead of being served by attendants.

self=sown (self-sōn'), *a.* Sown by itself, or without human
or animal agency; also, sown by any agency other than man,
as by birds, the wind, etc.

self=start-er (self-stär'tėr), *n.* A device which starts an
internal-combustion engine by some means that obviates the
necessity of cranking it by hand, as by the action of an electric
motor, a spring, gas-pressure, or the like; also, an automobile
whose engine is equipped with such a device.—**self=start'-
ing**, *a.*

self=striped (self-strīpt'), *a.* Woven with stripes in its own
color, as a self-colored fabric.

self=styled (self-stīld'), *a.* Styled or called by one's self
(as specified): as, a *self-styled* leader of advanced thought.

self=suf-fi-cient (self-su-fish'ent), *a.* Sufficient in or for one's
self or itself; able to supply one's own needs; also, having
undue confidence in one's own resources, powers, etc.;
overweeningly self-assured.—**self=suf-fi'cien-cy**, *n.*

self=suf-fi-cing (self-su-fī'sing), *a.* Sufficing in or for one's
self or itself; self-sufficient.—**self=suf-fi'cing-ness**, *n.*

self=sug-gest-ed (self-su-jes'ted), *a.* Suggested to or by
one's self; due to self-suggestion.—**self=sug-ges'tion**, *n.*
Suggestion to one's self; autosuggestion; also, a suggestion
arising of itself.

self=sup-port (self-su-pōrt'), *n.* The act or fact of supporting or maintaining one's self or itself unaided.—**self=sup-
port'ed**, *a.* Supported by one's self or itself without extraneous aid.—**self=sup-port'ing**, *a.* Supporting or maintaining one's self or itself unaided: as, "The children would
soon become *self-supporting* and independent" (S. Butler's
"Erewhon," xx.); a *self-supporting* charitable institution.

self=sur-ren-der (self-su-ren'dėr), *n.* The surrender or
yielding up of one's self, or one's will, affections, etc., as to
another person, an influence, etc.

self=sus-tained (self-sus-tānd'), *a.* Sustained by one's
self or itself without outside aid.—**self=sus-tain'ing**, *a.*
Self-supporting.—**self=sus-tain'ing-ly**, *adv.*

self=taught (self-tât'), *a.* Taught by one's self without aid
from others; self-educated; of knowledge, etc., acquired
by one's own unaided efforts.

self=tor-ture (self-tôr'tu̯r), *n.* Torture inflicted on one by
one's self.

self=will (self-wil′), n. [AS. selfwill.] One's own will; usually, obstinate or perverse insistence on one's own will or wishes; wilfulness; obstinacy.—**self=willed′**, a. Obstinately or perversely insistent on one's own will; characterized by self-will: as, "The children . . . were young and self-willed and rude, and would not learn to do as they were bid" (G. MacDonald's "Annals of a Quiet Neighbourhood," vii.); self-willed conduct.—**self=willed′ness**, n.

self=wind-ing (self-wīn′ding), a. Winding itself: applied to a kind of clock which is wound up automatically by a motor or the like.

self=wrong (self-rông′), n. Wrong done to one by one's self.

Sel-juk (sel-jōk′ or sel′jōk). [Prop. the name of an ancestor of these Turks.] **I.** a. Noting or pertaining to certain Turkish dynasties which ruled over large parts of Asia from the 11th to the 13th century. **II.** n. A member of a Seljuk dynasty or of the Seljuk tribe.—**Sel-juk′i-an**, a.

sell[1] (sel), v. t.; sold, selling. [AS. sellan (pret. sealde) = OS. sellian = MHG. sellen = Icel. selja, give, sell, = Goth. saljan, offer, sacrifice; from a noun represented by E. sale.] To give†; hand over†; also, to give up or make over to another for a consideration; dispose of for something else; esp., to dispose of for money; dispose of to a purchaser for a price; also, to deal in (a commodity); keep for sale; also, to accept a price or reward for, or make profit or gain of (something not a proper object for such action: as, "When perjury . . . Sells oaths by tale, and at the lowest price," Cowper's "Table Talk," 419); sometimes, to betray, esp. for a price or to gain some advantage (as, to sell a person, a party, or a cause); also, to give up or sacrifice (one's life, etc.) at some cost to an adversary (as, to sell one's life dearly); also (colloq., orig. in advertising use), to cause (something) to be accepted, approved, or adopted, as by representations and methods characteristic of salesmanship (often with to: as, to sell an idea to the public; to sell a candidate to the electorate); cause (a person, etc.) to accept, approve, or adopt something by representations and methods such as are used in selling goods (as, to sell the public on an idea; he is sold already on the proposition); also, to cheat, trick, or hoax (slang: as, "I'll bet you a sovereign you never see a poacher, and then how sold you will be in the morning!" Hughes's "Tom Brown at Oxford," xxxvii.).—**to sell off**, to dispose of by sale.—**to sell out**, to dispose of entirely by selling; also, in the passive, to have sold all of one's stock of something (as, a dealer is sold out); also, to sell the goods of (a debtor) for the benefit of his creditors (as, the sheriff sells out an insolvent merchant); also, to betray by a secret bargain (slang: as, the political leaders sold out their candidate for governor).—**to sell up**, to sell the goods of (a debtor) in order to pay his creditors (as, "He . . . would . . . drink his glass with a tenant and sell him up the next day": Thackeray's "Vanity Fair," ix.); sometimes, to sell (the goods of a debtor) to pay the creditors.—**sell**[1], v. i. To sell something; engage in selling commodities; also, to be on sale; be sold, as at a particular price (as, these goods sell at higher prices; this cloth sells at $3 a yard); find purchasers, or be in demand as an article of sale (as, this article sells well); also (colloq., orig. in advertising use), to win acceptance, approval, or adoption when presented as if by a salesman (as, an idea that will sell).—**to sell out**, to dispose of the whole of one's stock, property, etc., by sale; also, formerly, to dispose of one's commission in the army by sale under the purchase system (as, "James had sold out of the army": H. Kingsley's "Geoffry Hamlyn," iii.); also, to betray the interests of a party, cause, etc., for a price or to gain some advantage.—**sell**[1], n. A cheat; a hoax; a fraud. [Slang.]

sell[2] (sel), n. [OF. F. selle, < L. sella, seat, stool, later saddle, < sedere, sit: cf. see[1].] A seat; also, a saddle. [Obs. or archaic.]

sell-a-ble (sel′a-bl), a. That may be sold; salable.

sel-lan-ders (sel′an-dèrz), n. pl. See sallenders.

sell-er (sel′er), n. One who sells; a vender; also, an article of merchandise, as a book, considered with reference to its sale (as, a good seller; one of the best sellers; a poor seller); also, an article that sells well.

sell-ing (sel′ing), n. The act of one who sells.—**selling plate**, a selling race. Cf. plate, n.—**selling plater**, a horse that competes in selling plates. Cf. plater.—**selling price**, the price at which an article is offered for sale.—**selling race**, a race for horses which are to be offered for sale after the race at prices stated when they are entered.

Sel-ters (sel′tèrz, G. zel′tèrs) **wa′ter.** See Seltzer water.

Selt-zer (selt′sèr) **wa′ter.** [From (Nieder-)Selters, village in Hesse-Nassau, Prussia, with mineral springs.] A natural effervescent mineral water (see etym.) containing sodium chloride (common salt) and small quantities of sodium, calcium, and magnesium carbonates; also, an artificial water of similar composition. Also called Seltzer or seltzer, Selters, and Selters water.

sel-va (sel′vä), n.; pl. -vas (-väz). [Sp. and Pg., < L. silva, wood.] A wooded plain, esp. in the Amazon basin, in South America.

sel-vage, sel-vedge (sel′vej), n. [Appar. < self + edge, after D. or LG. equivalents.] The edge of a textile fabric finished off to prevent raveling; also, a narrow strip at each edge or side of a textile fabric, differing from the rest, and meant (usually) to be concealed in a finished seam; also, any similar strip or part, as a waste strip at the side of wallpaper; hence, in general, a margin or border (as, "Here's the Saint coming from the selvage of the wood," Synge's "Well of the Saints," i.; "Ducks gobble at the selvage of the brook," Masefield's "Daffodil Fields," i.).—**sel′vage, sel′vedge**, v. t.; -vaged, -vedged, -vaging, -vedging. To edge with or as with a selvage.

selves (selvz). Plural of self.

se-man-tic (sē-man′tik), a. [LL. semanticus, < Gr. σημαντικός, < σημαίνειν, indicate, signify, < σῆμα, sign.] Pertaining to signification or meaning.—**se-man′tics**, n. Semasiology.

sem-a-phore (sem′a-fōr), n. [Gr. σῆμα, sign: see -phore.] An apparatus for conveying information by means of signals; an upright post or structure for railroad signaling by means of lanterns, flags, movable arms, etc.—**sem′a-phore**, v. t. or i.; -phored, -phoring. To signal by semaphore or by some system of flags, etc.—**sem-a-phor′ic** (-for′ik), a.

se-ma-si-ol-o-gy (sē-mā-si-ol′ō-ji), n. [Gr. σημασία, signification (< σημαίνειν: see semantic): see -logy.] The branch of philology that deals with the meanings and sense-development of words.—**se-ma′′si-o-log′i-cal** (-ō-loj′i-kal), a.—**se-ma-si-ol′o-gist**, n.

se-mat-ic (sē-mat′ik), a. [Gr. σῆμα (σηματ-), sign.] In biol., serving as a sign or warning of danger, as the conspicuous colors or markings of certain poisonous animals.

sem-a-tol-o-gy (sem-a-tol′ō-ji), n. [Gr. σῆμα (σηματ-), sign: see -logy.] The science of signs or symbols, esp. of words as representing thought; also, semasiology.

sem-bla-ble (sem′bla-bl). [OF. F. semblable, < sembler: see semblance.] **I.** a. Like† or similar†; also, corresponding† or accordant†; also, seeming or apparent (obs. or rare). **II.**† n. Something that is like or similar; the like; (one's) like or fellow (as, "His semblable is his mirror": Shakspere's "Hamlet," v. 2. 124).—**sem′bla-bly**, adv.

sem-blance (sem′blans), n. [OF. F. semblance, < OF. sembler, be like, seem, F. seem, < L. similare, for simulare: see simulate.] The state or fact of being like or similar; likeness or resemblance; hence, a likeness, image, or copy of something (as, "Wax . . . Wherein is stamp'd the semblance of a devil": Shakspere's "Lucrece," 1246); also, outward aspect, appearance, or seeming (with or without truth or reality: as, to bear the semblance of an honest man; to have the semblance of modesty); hence, an assumed or unreal appearance of something, or a mere show (as, "Where vice has such allowance, that her shifts And specious semblances have lost their use": Cowper's "Task," iii. 107); sometimes, an apparition.

sem-blant (sem′blant), a. [OF. semblant, ppr. of sembler: see semblance.] Like† or similar†; also, seeming, apparent,

Railroad Semaphore. — a, lever, which operates both b, arm, and c, lantern.

or specious (rare: as, "a just real union . . . not a false and merely *semblant* one," Carlyle's "Past and Present," i. 2).

sem-ble (sem'bl), *v. i.* [F., 3d pers. sing. pres. ind. of *sembler*, seem: see *semblance*.] 'It seems': a legal term used impersonally in judicial utterances to precede an incidental statement of opinion on a point of law which it is not necessary to decide in the case.

sem-é, sem-ée (sem'ā, F. se-mā), *a.* [F. *semé*, masc., *semée*, fem., pp. of *semer*, sow, strew, < L. *seminare*: see *seminate*.] In *her.*, etc., strewn or covered with small figures of the same kind, as stars or flowers, arranged to form a sort of pattern: as, "heralds in blew velvet *semèe* with fleurs de lys" (Evelyn's "Diary," Sept. 7, 1651).

se-mei-ol-o-gy (sē-mī-ol'ō-ji), *n.* See *semiology*.

se-mei-ot-ic (sē-mī-ot'ik), etc. See *semiotic*, etc.

se-men (sē'men), *n.* [L., seed, from the root of *serere*, sow: see *sow*[1].] The impregnating fluid produced by the male reproductive organs; seed or sperm.

se-mes-ter (sē-mes'tėr), *n.* [G., < L. *semestris*, of six months, < *sex*, six, + *mensis*, month.] A period of six months; esp., a half of a university, college, or school year.—

A Shield Semé of Fleurs-de-lis.

se-mes'tri-al, se-mes'tral (-tri-al, -tral), *a.* [L. *semestris*.] Of or for a semester, or a period of six months; semiannual. —**se-mes'tri-al-ly**, *adv.*

semi-. [L. *semi-*, akin to Skt. *sāmi-*, Gr. ἡμι-, AS. *sām-*, half: cf. *hemi-* and *sand-blind*.] A prefix meaning 'half,' as in *semiannual*, *semicolumn*, and hence used to mean 'partly,' 'incompletely,' 'imperfectly,' as in *semicivilized*, *semidetached*, *semiofficial*, *semiprecious*, and many like formations: used at will to form new words, commonly at first with a hyphen, which tends to disappear from terms coming into general use. Cf. *hemi-*.

sem-i-an-nu-al (sem-i-an'ū-al), *a.* [See *semi-*.] Occurring or appearing every half-year; half-yearly; also, lasting for half a year.—**sem-i-an'nu-al-ly**, *adv.*

sem-i-a-quat-ic (sem″i-a-kwat'ik), *a.* [See *semi-*.] In *bot.* and *zoöl.*, partly aquatic; growing or living close to water, and sometimes found in or entering water.

sem-i-breve (sem'i-brēv), *n.* [See *semi-* and *breve*.] In *music*, a note having half the length of a breve, being the longest note in common use; a whole-note. See *note* under *note*, *n.*

sem-i-cen-ten-ni-al (sem″i-sen-ten'i-al). [See *semi-*.] **I.** *a.* Occurring at the end of, or celebrating the completion of, fifty years, or half a century. **II.** *n.* A semicentennial celebration.

sem-i-cho-rus (sem'i-kō-rus), *n.* [See *semi-*.] In *music*, a half-chorus; a number of voices chosen from a full chorus, whether from all or from some of the parts; also, a passage or piece to be sung by such a selection of voices.—**sem-i-cho'ric**, *a.*

sem-i-cir-cle (sem'i-sėr-kl), *n.* [L. *semicirculus*.] The half of a circle; the part of a circle comprehended between a diameter and the half of the circumference, or the half of the circumference itself; hence, anything having, or arranged in, the form of a half of a circle (as, "Around the waiting-room fire . . . sat a goodly *semicircle* of men": G. W. Cable's "Bonaventure," iii. 3).—**sem-i-cir'cu-lar** (-kū-lär), *a.* Having the form of a semicircle.—**semicircular canals**, in *anat.*, three curved tubular canals in the labyrinth of the ear. —**sem-i-cir'cu-lar-ly**, *adv.*

sem-i-cir-cum-fer-ence (sem″i-sėr-kum'fe-rens), *n.* [See *semi-*.] The half of a circumference.

sem-i-cirque (sem'i-sėrk), *n.* [See *semi-* and *cirque*.] A semicircle; a semicircular formation or arrangement: as, "a *semicirque* of turf-clad ground" (Wordsworth's "Excursion," iii. 50). [Poetic.]

sem-i-civ-il-ized (sem-i-siv'i-līzd), *a.* [See *semi-*.] Half-civilized.—**sem″i-civ″il-i-za'tion** (-i-li-zā'shon), *n.*

sem-i-co-lon (sem'i-kō-lon or sem-i-kō'lon), *n.* [See *semi-*.] A mark of punctuation (;) used to indicate a more distinct separation between parts of a sentence than that indicated by a comma.

sem-i-col-umn (sem'i-kol-um), *n.* [See *semi-*.] The half of a column (taken lengthwise); an engaged column of which one half projects from the wall.—**sem″i-co-lum'nar** (-kō-lum'när), *a.* Pertaining to or of the nature of a semicolumn; in *bot.*, of a stem, petiole, etc., shaped like the half of a cylinder cut lengthwise.

sem-i-con-scious (sem-i-kon'shus), *a.* [See *semi-*.] Half-conscious; not fully conscious.—**sem-i-con'scious-ness**, *n.*

sem-i-cyl-in-der (sem-i-sil'in-dėr), *n.* [See *semi-*.] The half of a cylinder (as divided longitudinally).—**sem″i-cy-lin'dric, sem″i-cy-lin'dri-cal** (-si-lin'drik, -dri-kal), *a.*

sem-i-de-tached (sem″i-dē-tacht'), *a.* [See *semi-*.] Partly detached: used esp. to designate either of a pair of houses joined together by a party-wall but detached from other buildings: as, "Whereas the Cedars was detached, No. 59 was not even *semi-detached*, but one of a gaunt, tall row of . . . dwellings" (Arnold Bennett's "Hilda Lessways," iii. 3).

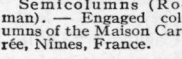

sem-i-di-am-e-ter (sem″i-dī-am'e-tėr), *n.* [See *semi-*.] The half of a diameter; a radius.

sem-i-di-ur-nal (sem″i-dī-ėr'nal), *a.* [See *semi-*.] Pertaining to, consisting of, or accomplished in half a day; also, occurring every twelve hours; in *astron.*, noting or pertaining to the arc described by a heavenly body in half the time between its rising and its setting; in *entom.*, partly diurnal; flying at twilight.

Semicolumns (Roman). — Engaged columns of the Maison Carrée, Nîmes, France.

sem-i-dome (sem'i-dōm), *n.* [See *semi-*.] Half a dome, esp. as formed by a vertical section, as over a semicircular apse.

sem-i-el-lip-ti-cal (sem″i-e-lip'ti-kal), *a.* [See *semi-*.] Shaped like the half of an ellipse, esp. one which is cut transversely.

sem-i-fi-nal (sem-i-fī'nal). [See *semi-*.] **I.** *a.* Designating a round, contest, or match which immediately precedes the final and decisive one (as in a tournament), or a last contest, match, or the like but one in a series; pertaining to such a round, contest, or the like. **II.** *n.* A semifinal round, contest, match, or the like.

Semidome, exterior (above) and interior (below). — Apse of Mosque of Sultan Suleiman, Constantinople (A.D. 1550).

sem-i-fit-ting (sem-i-fit'ing), *a.* [See *semi-*.] Half-fitting; partly or loosely fitting, as a garment.

sem-i-flu-id (sem-i-flö'id). [See *semi-*.] **I.** *a.* Imperfectly fluid; extremely viscous. **II.** *n.* A semifluid substance.—**sem″i-flu-id'i-ty** (-flö-id'i-ti), *n.*

sem-i-li-quid (sem-i-lik'wid). [See *semi-*.] **I.** *a.* Imperfectly liquid; semifluid. **II.** *n.* A semiliquid substance. —**sem″i-li-quid'i-ty** (-li-kwid'i-ti), *n.*

sem-i-lu-nar (sem-i-lū'när). [NL. *semilunaris*, < L. *semi-*, half, + *luna*, moon.] **I.** *a.* Shaped like a half-moon; crescentic: as, in *anat.*, the *semilunar* bone (the second bone of the proximal row of the carpus, counting from the thumb side); *semilunar* valves (a set of three crescentic valves at the orifice of the aorta which prevent the blood from flowing back into the ventricle, or a similar set of valves at the orifice of the pulmonary artery). **II.** *n.* Something of semilunar shape, as a semilunar bone or valve.—**sem'i-lu'nate** (-nāt), *a.* Semilunar.—**sem'i-lune** (-lūn), *n.* Something of semilunar shape; in *fort.*, a demilune.

sem-i-month-ly (sem-i-munth'li). [See *semi-.*] **I.** *a.* Occurring or appearing every half-month. **II.** *n.* A semimonthly publication. **III.** *adv.* Every half-month.

sem-i-nal (sem'i-nạl), *a.* [L. *seminalis*, < *semen* (*semin-*), seed: see *semen*.] Of, pertaining to, or of the nature of semen; also, pertaining to or of the nature of seed; also, pertaining to reproduction; in fig. use, having the possibility of future development.—**sem'i-nal-ly,** *adv.*

sem-i-nar (sem-i-när' or sem'i-när), *n.* [G., < L. *seminarium*, E. *seminary*.] A group of students, as in a university, engaged in advanced study and original research under an instructor.

sem-i-na-ri-an (sem-i-nā'ri-ạn), *n.* A seminarist.

sem-i-na-rist (sem'i-nạ-rist), *n.* A student in a seminary; specif., formerly, a Roman Catholic priest educated in a foreign seminary; also, an instructor in a seminary; also, a member of a seminar.

sem-i-na-ry (sem'i-nạ-ri), *n.*; pl. *-ries* (-riz). [L. *seminarium*, prop. neut. of *seminarius*, of or for seed, < *semen* (*semin-*), seed: see *semen*.] A plot of ground where plants are grown from seed, cuttings, etc., for transplanting†; hence, a place of origin and development; also, a place of education; a school, esp. one of higher grade; an academy or boarding-school, esp. one for young women; a school for the education of men for the priesthood or ministry; also, a seminar.

sem-i-nate (sem'i-nāt), *v. t.*; *-nated, -nating.* [L. *seminatus*, pp. of *seminare*, sow, < *semen* (*semin-*), seed: see *semen*, and cf. *semé*.] To sow (esp. fig.); propagate; disseminate.—**sem-i-na'tion** (-nā'shọn), *n.*

sem-i-nif-er-ous (sem-i-nif'ẹ-rus), *a.* [L. *semen* (*semin-*), seed: see *-ferous*.] Bearing or producing seed; in *anat.*, conveying or containing semen.

sem-i-oc-ca-sion-al (sem''i-ọ-kā'zhọn-ạl), *a.* [See *semi-.*] Occurring once in a while. [Colloq.]—**sem''i-oc-ca'sion-al-ly,** *adv.*

sem-i-of-fi-cial (sem''i-ọ-fish'ạl), *a.* [See *semi-.*] Half-official; having some degree of official authority.—**sem''i-of-fi'cial-ly,** *adv.*

se-mi-ol-o-gy, se-mei-ol-o-gy (sē-mi-ol'ọ-ji, sē-mī-), *n.* [Gr. σημεῖον, sign: see *-logy*.] The science of signs; also, sign-language; also, the branch of medical science dealing with symptoms.

sem-i-o-paque (sem''i-ọ-pāk'), *a.* [See *semi-.*] Half-opaque; imperfectly opaque.

se-mi-ot-ic, se-mei-ot-ic (sē-mi-ot'ik, sē-mī-), *a.* [Gr. σημειωτικός, < σημεῖον, sign, < σῆμα, sign: cf. *sematic*.] Pertaining to signs or symptoms; symptomatic.—**se-mi-ot'ics, se-mei-ot'ics,** *n.* The science of signs or symptoms; semiology.

sem-i-pal-mate (sem-i-pal'māt), *a.* [See *semi-.*] Partially or imperfectly palmate, as a bird's foot; half-webbed. Also **sem-i-pal'mat-ed** (-mā-ted).—**sem''i-pal-ma'tion** (-mā'shọn), *n.*

sem-i-ped (sem'i-ped), *n.* [L. *semipes* (*semiped-*), < *semi-*, half, + *pes* (*ped-*), foot.] In *pros.*, a half-foot.

sem-i-per-me-a-ble (sem-i-pèr'mē-ạ-bl), *a.* [See *semi-.*] Partly permeable; permeable to some substances more than to others: as, a *semipermeable* membrane, septum, or diaphragm (an animal or vegetable membrane, a sheet of unglazed fine-grained porcelain, or the like, which when placed between the solution of a substance and the pure solvent, allows the solvent, but not much of the dissolved substance, to pass through).

sem-i-plas-tic (sem-i-plas'tik), *a.* [See *semi-.*] Imperfectly plastic; in a state between plasticity and rigidity.

sem-i-porce-lain (sem-i-pôrs'lạn or -pôr'sẹ-lạn), *n.* [See *semi-.*] An inferior grade of porcelain; also, earthenware made to resemble porcelain.

Semipalmate Foot of Willet (*Symphemia semipalmata*).

sem-i-pre-cious (sem-i-presh'us), *a.* [See *semi-.*] Having value, but not strictly precious; specif., belonging to a class of stones (as the amethyst, garnet, etc.) ranked below the so-called precious stones (the diamond, ruby, etc.).

sem-i-pub-lic (sem-i-pub'lik), *a.* [See *semi-.*] Partly or to some degree public.

sem-i-qua-ver (sem'i-kwā''vèr), *n.* [See *semi-* and *quaver*, *n.*] In *music*, a sixteenth-note.

sem-i-rig-id (sem-i-rij'id), *a.* [See *semi-.*] Partly rigid; in *aëronautics*, designating or pertaining to a type of airship (dirigible balloon) whose shape is maintained by means of a rigid keel-like structure.

sem-i-sol-id (sem-i-sol'id). [See *semi-.*] **I.** *a.* Half-solid; of a somewhat firm consistence; extremely viscous. **II.** *n.* A semisolid substance.

sem-i-spher-i-cal (sem-i-sfer'i-kạl), *a.* [See *semi-.*] Hemispherical.

Sem-ite (sem'īt), *n.* [NL. *Semita*, < LL. *Sem*, < Gr. Σήμ, Shem.] A member of a race of mankind (corresponding inexactly to the peoples said in Gen. x. to be descended from Shem, son of Noah) comprising the Hebrews and kindred peoples, as the Arabians, Assyrians, etc.—**Se-mit-ic** (sẹ-mit'ik). **I.** *a.* Of or pertaining to the Semites or their languages. **II.** *n.* The Semitic family of languages, including the Hebrew, Phenician, Aramaic, Assyrian, Arabic, Amharic, etc.—**Se-mit'ics,** *n.* The study of the Semitic languages, literature, etc.—**Sem-it-ism** (sem'i-tizm), *n.* Semitic character or characteristics; esp., the ways, ideas, influence, etc., of the Jewish people; also, a Semitic word or idiom.—**Sem'it-ist,** *n.* One versed in the Semitic languages, literature, etc.—**Sem'it-ize,** *v. t.*; *-ized, -izing.* To render Semitic, as in character, language, or religion.

sem-i-tone (sem'i-tōn), *n.* [See *semi-.*] In *music*, one of the smaller intervals of the modern scale (see *tone*, *n.*); a half-tone; a half-step.—**sem-i-ton'ic** (-ton'ik), *a.*

sem-i-trans-lu-cent (sem''i-trans-lū'sẹnt), *a.* [See *semi-.*] Imperfectly translucent.

sem-i-trans-par-ent (sem''i-trans-pär'ẹnt or -par'ẹnt), *a.* [See *semi-.*] Imperfectly transparent.

sem-i-trop-i-cal (sem-i-trop'i-kạl), *a.* [See *semi-.*] Half-tropical; subtropical.

sem-i-vit-re-ous (sem-i-vit'rẹ-us), *a.* [See *semi-.*] Partially vitreous; having more or less of a vitreous structure, as mineral constituents of volcanic rocks.—**sem-i-vit'ri-fied** (-ri-fīd), *a.* Partially or imperfectly vitrified.—**sem''i-vit''ri-fi-ca'tion** (-fi-kā'shọn), *n.*

sem-i-vow-el (sem'i-vou-ẹl), *n.* [See *semi-.*] A sound partaking of the nature of both a vowel and a consonant, as that of the English *w* or *y*; also, a letter or character representing such a sound.

sem-i-week-ly (sem-i-wēk'li). [See *semi-.*] **I.** *a.* Occurring or appearing every half-week. **II.** *n.* A semiweekly publication. **III.** *adv.* Every half-week.

sem-o-li-na (sem-ọ-lē'nạ), *n.* [It. *semolino*, < *semola*, bran: cf. L. *simila*, fine wheat flour.] The large, hard grains of wheat retained in the bolting-machine after the fine flour has passed through it: used for making puddings, etc.

sem-per-vi-rent (sem-pèr-vi'rẹnt), *a.* [L. *semper*, always, + *virens* (*virent-*), ppr. of *virere*, be green.] Evergreen, as plants. Also **sem-per-vir'id** (-vir'id).

sem-pi-ter-nal (sem-pi-tèr'nạl), *a.* [OF. F. *sempiternel*, < L. *sempiternus*, < *semper*, always.] Everlasting; eternal: as, "All truth is from the *sempiternal* source Of light divine" (Cowper's "Task," ii. 499).—**sem-pi-ter'nal-ly,** *adv.*

semp'ster, semp'stress. See *seamster, seamstress.*

sen (sen), *n.*; pl. *sen.* [Jap.] A Japanese monetary unit and copper or bronze coin, equal to the hundredth part of a yen, or about half of a United States cent.

Obverse.   Sen.   Reverse.

sen-a-ry (sen′a̱-ri), *a*. [L. *senarius*, < *seni*, six each, < *sex*, six.] Of or pertaining to the number six.

sen-ate (sen′āt), *n*. [OF. *senat* (F. *sénat*), < L. *senatus*, council of elders, senate, < *senex*, old: see *senior*.] An assembly or council of citizens having the highest deliberative functions in the government of a state; esp., the supreme council of state in ancient Rome, whose membership and functions varied at different periods; [*cap*.] the upper and less numerous branch of various legislatures, as of France, Italy, the U. S., the separate States of the U. S., etc.; also [*l. c*.], in general, a legislative assembly of a state or nation; also, a governing, advisory, or disciplinary body, as in certain universities and colleges.

sen-a-tor (sen′a̱-tọr), *n*. [OF. *senateur* (F. *sénateur*), < L. *senator*, < *senex*, old: cf. *senate*.] A member of a senate.—**sen-a-to′ri-al** (-tō′ri-a̱l), *a*. [L. *senatorius*.] Of or pertaining to a senator or senators; characteristic of or befitting a senator; consisting of senators; also, administered by the senate, as an ancient Roman province; also, entitled to elect a senator (U. S.: as, a *senatorial* district).—**sen-a-to′ri-al-ly**, *adv*.—**sen-a-to′ri-an**, *a*. Senatorial: chiefly with reference to the senators of ancient Rome.—**sen′a-tor-ship**, *n*. The office or dignity of a senator.—**sen′a-to-ry** (-tọ-ri), *a*.; pl. *-ries* (-riz). [Cf. F. *sénatorerie*.] In *French hist.*, a landed estate granted to a senator under the consulate and the first empire.

se-na-tus con-sul-tum (sē-nā′tus kọn-sul′tum); pl. *-ta* (-tä). [L.: *senatus*, gen. of *senatus*, senate; *consultum*, decree, prop. pp. neut. of *consulere*, deliberate: see *consult*.] A decree of the senate of ancient Rome. Also **se-na′tus-con-sult′**.

send (send), *v*.; pret. and pp. *sent* (naut., pret. *sended*), ppr. *sending*. [AS. *sendan* = D. *zenden* = G. *senden* = Icel. *senda* = Goth. *sandjan*, send, causative from a root meaning 'go': cf. AS. *sīth*, a going, journey.] **I.** *tr*. To cause to go; order or direct to go, as to a place or person (as, to *send* a messenger); compel or force to go (as, a volley of musketry *sent* the enemy flying); cause to be conveyed or transmitted to a destination (as, to *send* letters or tidings); cause to come, befall, etc. (as, "He . . . *sendeth* rain on the just and on the unjust": Mat. v. 45); cause to be or become (archaic: as, "God *send* him well!" Shakspere's "All's Well," i. 1. 190); drive, impel, cast, throw, etc., as a ball or missile; deliver, as a blow; give (*forth, out*, etc.), as light, odor, or sound. **II.** *intr*. To send or despatch a messenger, agent, message, etc.; *naut.* (also spelled *scend*), of a vessel in a rough sea, to have a rocking motion by which the bow alternately falls and rises; also, to pass through the downward portion of such a motion; also, sometimes, to pass through the upward portion of such a motion.—**to send for**, to send a messenger or message for; request or require by message to come or to be brought: as, to *send for* a physician; to *send for* a newspaper.—**send**, *n*. A sending†; also, a message or a messenger (chiefly Sc.); also, an impetus; *naut.*, the driving impulse of a wave or waves upon a ship (as, "The Mayflower . . . stood for the open Atlantic, Borne on the *send* of the sea": Longfellow's "Courtship of Miles Standish," v.); also (also spelled *scend*), the act or an act of sending (see *send, v. i.*); a sudden plunge of a vessel.

sen-dal (sen′da̱l), *n*. [OF. *cendal*, prob. ult. < Gr. σινδών, fine linen.] A silk fabric in use during the middle ages, or a piece or garment of it (archaic or hist.); sometimes, fine linen†, or a piece of it†.

send-er (sen′dėr), *n*. One who or that which sends; specif., a transmitter, as in telegraphy.

send=off (send′ôf), *n*. A friendly demonstration in honor of a person, etc., setting out on a journey, course, career, or the like (as, "'Give him a last *send-off*,' cried Teddy. 'One, Two, Three! *Auf Wiedersehen!*'" H. G. Wells's "Mr. Britling," i. 5. § 10); in general, a start (favorable or otherwise) given to a person or thing (as, the new play had a good, or a poor, *send-off*). [Colloq.]

sen-e-ca (sen′ē-kä), *n*. Same as *senega*.

sen-e-ga (sen′ē-gä), *n*. [NL., for *seneca*, so called from the *Seneca* Indians.] The dried root of a milkwort, *Polygala senega* (the Seneca snakeroot), of the eastern U. S.: used as an expectorant and diuretic.

sen-e-gal (sen′ē-ga̱l), *n*. [From *Senegal*, in western Africa.]

A dealers' name for any of various small, finch-like African birds of the genus *Lagonosticta* (family *Ploceidæ*), with plumage of a rich crimson shading into brown, gray, etc. (the species being often called 'blood-finches'), as *L. minima* (the 'little senegal'), with small white spots on the sides of the breast.

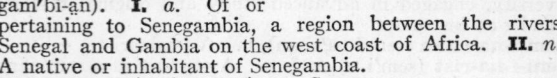

Sen-e-gal-ese (sen″ē-ga̱l-ēs′ or -ēz′). **I.** *a*. Of or pertaining to Senegal, a French colony in western Africa. **II.** *n*.; pl. *-ese*. A native or inhabitant of Senegal.

Sen-e-gam-bi-an (sen-ē-gam′bi-a̱n). **I.** *a*. Of or pertaining to Senegambia, a region between the rivers Senegal and Gambia on the west coast of Africa. **II.** *n*. A native or inhabitant of Senegambia.

Senegal (*Lagonosticta minima*).

sen-e-ga=root (sen′ē-gä-röt), *n*. Same as *senega*.

se-nes-cent (sē-nes′ent), *a*. [L. *senescens* (-*ent*-), ppr. of *senescere*, grow old, < *senex*, old: see *senior*.] Growing old; aging.—**se-nes′cence**, *n*.

sen-e-schal (sen′ē-sha̱l), *n*. [OF. *seneschal* (F. *sénéchal*) = ML. *seniscalcus*, from Teut., lit. 'old servant': cf. *marshal*.] An officer in the household of a prince or dignitary, who had full charge of domestic arrangements, ceremonies, etc.; a steward; also, a royal officer exercising certain administrative or judicial functions.—**sen′e-schal-ship**, *n*.

se-nhor (sā-nyōr′), *n*. [Pg., < L. *senior*: see *senior* and *seignior*.] In Portuguese use, a gentleman; as a term of address, sir; as a title, Mr.—**se-nho-ra** (sā-nyō′rä), *n*. [Pg.] In Portuguese use, a lady: also used as a term of address and as a title.—**se-nho-ri′ta** (-rē′tä), *n*. [Pg., dim. of *senhora*.] In Portuguese use, a young lady: also used as a term of address and as a title.

se-nile (sē′nil or -nīl), *a*. [L. *senilis*, < *senex*, old: see *senior*.] Of, pertaining to, or proceeding from old age; exhibiting the characteristics of old age; in *phys. geog.*, of topographical features, having advanced in reduction by erosion, etc., to a great extent.—**se′nile-ly**, *adv*.—**se-nil-i-ty** (sē-nil′i-ti), *n*. The state of being senile; old age; the weakness or mental infirmity of old age.

se-nior (sē′nyọr), *a*. [L., older, elder (as n., an elder, elderly person), compar. of *senex* (gen. *senis*), old, akin to Gr. ἕνος, Skt. *sana*, Goth. *sineigs*, old: cf. *seignior, senhor, señor, signor*, and *sire*.] Older or elder (often used, esp. as abbreviated *Sr.* or *Sen.*, after the name of a person who is the older of two persons bearing the name, as a father having the same name as his son: as, John Smith, *Sr.*); also, of earlier date; ranking before others by virtue of earlier entrance into office or service; of higher rank or standing; specif., in American universities, colleges, and schools, noting or pertaining to the highest class or the last year of the course.—**senior high school.** See *high school*, under *high, a.*—**se′nior**, *n*. A person who is older than another; also, an aged person; also, one ranking before others by virtue of earlier entrance into office or service; one of higher rank or standing; also, a member of the senior class in a university, college, or school.—**se-nior-i-ty** (sē-nyor′i-ti), *n*.; pl. *-ties* (-tiz). The state or fact of being senior; priority of birth; superior age; priority or precedence in office or service; also, a body of seniors.

sen-na (sen′a̱), *n*. [Ar. *sanā*.] A cathartic drug consisting of the dried leaflets of various

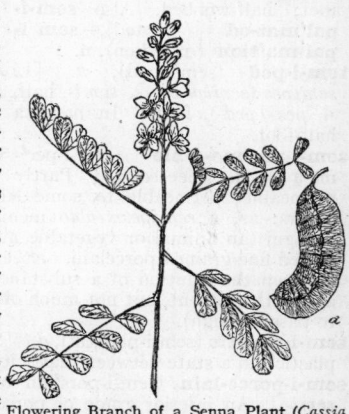

Flowering Branch of a Senna Plant (*Cassia obovata*). — *a*, a pod.

plants of the cæsalpiniaceous genus *Cassia* (see *cassia*) (as, Alexandrian *senna*, from *C. acutifolia*; Indian *senna*, from *C. angustifolia*; Aleppo, Italian, or Senegal *senna*, an inferior kind from *C. obovata*); also, any plant yielding this drug (see cut on preceding page); also, any of various similar plants.

sen-net† (sen′et), *n.* [Appar. a var. of *signet*, in old sense of 'signal.'] A particular set of tones on a trumpet or cornet: ordered in stage-directions of old plays, as upon a ceremonial entrance or exit.

sen-night (sen′īt), *n.* [ME. *sennygt, sevenygt,* < AS. *seofon niht,* seven nights: cf. *fortnight.*] The space of seven nights and days; a week: as, "She shall never have happy hour, unless she marry within this *sennight*" (Jonson's "Bartholomew Fair," i. 1). [Archaic.]

sen-nit (sen′it), *n.* [Earlier (naut.) *sinnet*; origin obscure.] A kind of flat braided cordage used on shipboard, formed by plaiting strands of rope-yarn or other fiber; also, a kind of plaited straw braid with a serrated edge, for making hats.

Plaiting of Sennit.

se-ñor (se-nyōr′), *n.* [Sp., < L. *senior*: see *senior* and *seignior*.] In Spanish use, a gentleman; as a term of address, sir; as a title, Mr.—**se-ño-ra** (se-nyō′rä), *n.* [Sp.] In Spanish use, a lady: also used as a term of address and as a title.—**se-ño-ri-ta** (sen-yō-rē′tä), *n.* [Sp., dim. of *señora.*] In Spanish use, a young lady: also used as a term of address and as a title.

sen-sate¹ (sen′sāt), *a.* [LL. *sensatus,* < L. *sensus,* E. *sense.*] Endowed with sense or sensation. Cf. *insensate.* [Obs. or rare.]

sen-sate² (sen′sāt), *v. t.*; *-sated, -sating.* [Back-formation from *sensation.*] To perceive by a sense or the senses; have a sensation of.—**sen′sate².** **I.** *a.* Perceived by a sense or the senses. **II.** *n.* That which is perceived by a sense or the senses.

sen-sa-tion (sen-sā′shon), *n.* [ML. *sensatio(n-),* < L. *sensus,* E. *sense.*] The operation or function of the senses; perception through the senses; physical feeling; also, mental apprehension or realization; also, a mental condition produced through an organ of sense or resulting from a particular condition of some part of the body; a physical feeling, as of cold, dizziness, etc. (as, "A strange *sensation* of numbing coldness seemed to pervade my whole arm": Borrow's "Lavengro," ii.); also, a mental feeling (as, "He got out with a blank *sensation,* as if those memories had played him false": Galsworthy's "Dark Flower," i. 11); an emotion; also, a state of excited feeling; often, a state of excited feeling or interest caused among a number of persons or throughout a community by some occurrence, etc. (as, this disclosure created a *sensation*); also, a cause of such feeling or interest (as, this event was the greatest *sensation* of its day; a play which was the *sensation* of the season).—**sen-sa′tion-al,** *a.* Of or pertaining to sensation or the senses; also, pertaining to philosophical sensationalism; also, such as to produce a sensation, or a startling or thrilling impression, or intended to do this (as, "Her nature . . . shrank from any act which might appear dramatic or *sensational,*" W. Churchill's "Coniston," ii. 15; a *sensational* novel); aiming at startling or thrilling impressions, as a writer, etc. (as, "Writing for the papers had made Miss Stackpole *sensational*": H. James's "Portrait of a Lady," xlviii.).—**sen-sa′tion-al-ism,** *n.* The philosophical theory or doctrine that all ideas are derived solely through sensation; also, sensational methods; sensational writing, language, etc.—**sen-sa′tion-al-ist,** *n.* A believer in philosophical sensationalism; also, a sensational writer, speaker, etc.; one aiming at making a sensation.—**sen-sa″tion-al-is′tic,** *a.*—**sen-sa′tion-al-ize,** *v. t.*; *-ized, -izing.* To render sensational; deal with or treat of in a sensational manner; make a sensation of.—**sen-sa′tion-al-ly,** *adv.*—**sen-sa′tion-ism, sen-sa′tion-ist.** Same as *sensationalism, sensationalist.*

sense (sens), *n.* [= F. *sens,* < L. *sensus,* < *sentire* (pp. *sensus*), perceive, feel: cf. *scent, sentient, sentence, sentiment, sensible, sensitive, assent, dissent, resent.*] Each of the special faculties connected with bodily organs by which man and other animals perceive external objects and their own bodily changes (commonly reckoned as five: sight, hearing, smell, taste, and touch); also, these faculties collectively; their operation or function, or sensation; also, the part of the nature which seeks or enjoys merely physical or carnal pleasures (as, the promptings of *sense*; "But small the bliss that *sense* alone bestows, And sensual bliss is all the nation knows," Goldsmith's "Traveller," 123); also, a faculty or function of the mind or soul analogous to sensation (as, the moral *sense*); any special capacity for perception, estimation, appreciation, etc. (as, "She had usually a keen *sense* of the ludicrous," Bret Harte's "Fool of Five Forks"; "One doesn't often find girls of her age with a *sense* for poetry," M. Hewlett's "Open Country," xxvi.; "Lynch . . . had been most carefully divested of an æsthetic *sense,*" Galsworthy's "Saint's Progress," i. 8); clear or sound mental faculties or mind (usually in *pl.*: as, "The astonished countenance of the valet restored the master to his *senses,*" Marryat's "King's Own," lviii.; "Had he been in his right *senses,* he could not have thought of such a thing," Jane Austen's "Sense and Sensibility," ii.); sound practical intelligence (as, a man of *sense*; "They had more *sense* than to secede from Christianity to become Utilitarians," Galt's "Annals of the Parish," xxxv.); also, a feeling or perception produced through the organs of touch, taste, etc., or resulting from a particular condition of some part of the body (as, to have a *sense* of cold); hence, any more or less vague perception or impression of something (as, a building that gives one a *sense* of solidity; to have a *sense* of security); a mental discernment, realization, or recognition of something (as, to have a just *sense* of the worth of a thing); the recognition of something as incumbent or fitting (as, to act from a *sense* of duty; to have no *sense* of gratitude; "I had no *sense* of virtue or religion upon me," Defoe's "Captain Singleton," i.); a keen appreciation of something (as, to have a *sense* of a person's kindness; "O brave Iago, honest and just, That hast such noble *sense* of thy friend's wrong!" Shakspere's "Othello," v. 1. 32); a consciousness of something as attaching to one's self (as, "Beware of too sublime a *sense* Of your own worth and consequence!" Cowper's "Retired Cat," 109); also, an opinion or judgment formed or held, now esp. by an assemblage or body of persons (as, "This notion . . . appears to be contrary to the general *sense* of mankind," J. Butler's "Analogy of Religion," ii. 5; the *sense* of a meeting); also, the meaning, or one of the meanings, of a word or phrase; the meaning, or one meaning, of some connected group of words, or passage (as, "He had barely enough Greek to make out the *sense* of the epigram": George Eliot's "Romola," vii.); in general, meaning or signification, as of a dream, etc.; also, gist or substance (as, "They proceeded to pass several votes, the *sense* of which was finally summed up in an address to the King": Macaulay's "Hist. of Eng.," xxi.); also, what is sensible or reasonable (as, "Against all *sense* you do importune her," Shakspere's "Measure for Measure," v. 1. 438; "There's a good deal o' *sense* in what you say," George Eliot's "Adam Bede," xxi.); intelligible or sensible discourse (as, now you are talking *sense*); also, in scientific use, a direction, course, or the like, as, in *geom.,* either of two directly opposite ways in which a line, surface, etc., may be generated, described, or conceived.—**in a** (**no,** etc.) **sense,** according to a (no, etc.) meaning or interpretation of the word or words used; in some (no, etc.) manner of speaking: as, "Detached *in a sense* from the life of men . . . he took yet a reasonable interest in the course of events" (J. Conrad's "Rescue," v. 3); "They . . . are *in no sense* the progenitors of a nobler race of men" (Thoreau's "Walden," i.).—**to make sense of,** to discover a meaning in: as, "Then I saw my rival's composition . . . I could not *make sense of* much of it" (Arnold Bennett's "Truth about an Author," ii.).—**sense,** *v. t.*; *sensed, sensing.* To perceive by or as by the senses; become aware of; also, to comprehend or understand (colloq.: as, "I cannot *sense* your meaning sometimes," Hardy's "Tess of the D'Urbervilles," xlviii.).—**sense′less,** *a.* Destitute or deprived of sensation; often, in a state of unconsciousness (as, "He pitched over upon the gravel, and lay *senseless,* stunned by the fall": Parkman's "Oregon Trail," ix.); also, destitute of mental perception or appreciation (as, "I am *senseless* of your wrath," Shakspere's "Cymbeline," i. 1. 135: now rare); stupid or foolish, as persons, or their actions, etc.; nonsensical or meaningless, as words.—**sense′less-ly,** *adv.*—**sense′less-ness,** *n.*—**sense′=or″gan,** *n.* An organ of sense;

---

specif., a collection of nerve-cells which receive impressions from without ('peripheral sense-organ'), such as one of the taste-buds or tactile corpuscles; also, a collection of nerve-cells in the cerebrospinal centers which translate such impressions into conscious sensation or reflex movement ('central sense-organ').—**sense'=per-cep'tion,** *n.* Perception by means of the senses; also, a perception of an object of sense.

sen-si-bil-i-ty (sen-si-bil'i-ti), *n.*; pl. *-ties* (-tiz). The state of being sensible, or capable of sensation; capacity for sensation or feeling; responsiveness, as of a bodily organ or part, to sensory stimuli; also, the property, as in plants or instruments, of being readily affected by external influences; also, mental susceptibility or responsiveness; quickness and acuteness of apprehension or feeling; sensitiveness (*to:* as, *sensibility* to the beauties of nature); *pl.*, emotional capacities (as, "Something intensely human, narrow, and definite pierces to the seat of our *sensibilities* more readily than huge occurrences and catastrophes": Holmes's "Autocrat of the Breakfast-Table," xii.); *sing.* or *pl.*, liability to feel hurt or offended, or sensitive feelings (as, to wound a person's *sensibility*, or *sensibilities*); also, *sing.*, capacity for the higher or more refined feelings; delicacy of feeling; delicate sensitiveness of taste (as, "those monuments . . . whose light, aërial forms still survive after the lapse of ages, the admiration of every traveller of *sensibility* and taste": Prescott's "Conquest of Mexico," iii. 5); sometimes, susceptibility to emotional appeal (as, "O, how I hate the cambric handkerchief *sensibility* that is brought out only to weep at a tragedy!" Maria Edgeworth's "Belinda," viii.); also, keen consciousness or appreciation (as, a person's *sensibility* of his own good fortune, or of another's loss).

sen-si-ble (sen'si-bl), *a.* [OF. F. *sensible*, < L. *sensibilis*, < *sentire*, perceive, feel: see *sense*.] Capable of being perceived by the senses (as, the *sensible* universe; "Art thou not, fatal vision, *sensible* To feeling as to sight? or art thou but A dagger of the mind?" Shakspere's "Macbeth," ii. 1. 36); also, perceptible to the mind; also, easy to perceive, or evident (as, evidence too *sensible* to be doubted); often, large enough to be perceived; appreciable or considerable (as, a *sensible* reduction in expenses); also, capable of feeling or perceiving; having sensation, as organs or parts of the body; hence, having acute power of sensation, or sensitive (now rare); capable of emotion, or sensitive to emotional influence (as, *sensible* of, or to, shame: now rare); readily affected by physical influences, as substances, instruments, etc. (now rare); also, actually having perception either by the senses or by the intellect; cognizant, conscious, or aware (as, "I was not in the least *sensible* of the progressive motion made in the air by the island," Swift's "Gulliver's Travels," iii. 2; "You ask a promise which you must be *sensible* I ought not to grant," Miss Burney's "Evelina," xxi.); often, keenly conscious or appreciative (usually with *of:* as, "an unenthusiastic youth, who ought to . . . be more *sensible* of his advantages," S. Butler's "Way of All Flesh," vii.; "He was . . . very *sensible* of his fault," Addison, in "Spectator," 166); responsive in feeling (*to:* as, to be *sensible* to kindness); also, in a state of consciousness, or not unconscious (as, "When Mrs. Newcome was found she was speechless, but still *sensible*": Thackeray's "Newcomes," iii.); also, having or using good sense or sound judgment (as, "She calmed down like a *sensible*, practical person," J. Conrad's "Rover," xiv.; now do be *sensible*); marked by or showing good sense, as actions, discourse, etc. (as, a *sensible* thing to do; a *sensible* proposal; "One hears very *sensible* things said on opposite sides," George Eliot's "Middlemarch," iii.).—**sen'si-ble-ness,** *n.*—**sen'si-bly,** *adv.*

sen-si-tive (sen'si-tiv), *a.* [OF. F. *sensitif*, < ML. *sensitivus*, < L. *sentire*, perceive, feel: see *sense*.] Pertaining to or connected with the senses or sensation (as, the *sensitive* perception of objects); also, endowed with sensation; esp., having quick or acute sensation or feeling, as a bodily organ or part; also, in general, readily affected by external agencies or influences; responding to stimulation, as leaves which curl up when touched; highly susceptible to certain agents, as photographic plates, films, or paper to light; so constructed as to indicate, measure, or be affected by small amounts or changes, as a balance, scientific instrument, etc.; also,

having acute mental or emotional sensibility (as, "The scenes of blood which followed shocked his *sensitive* nature," Irving's "Tales of a Traveler," i. 6; "He was keenly *sensitive* to personal slight or insult," Prescott's "Conquest of Mexico," iv. 4); easily affected, pained, annoyed, etc.—**sensitive fern,** a polypodiaceous fern, *Onoclea sensibilis*, common in eastern North America, whose fronds when detached and wilting tend to fold together.—
sen'si-tive, *n.* A sensitive person; esp., one sensitive to hypnotic or similar influences.—**sen'si-tive-ly,** *adv.*—**sen'si-tive-ness,** *n.*—**sen'si-tive=plant,** *n.* A tropical American plant, *Mimosa pudica*, cultivated in greenhouses, with bipinnate leaves whose leaflets fold together when touched; also, any of various other plants showing sensitiveness to touch.—**sen-si-tiv'i-ty** (-tiv'i-ti), *n.* The state or quality of being sensitive.

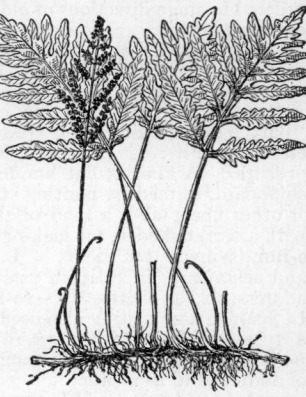

Sensitive Fern (*Onoclea sensibilis*).

sen-si-tize (sen'si-tīz), *v. t.*; *-tized, -tizing.* [From *sensit(ive)* + *-ize.*] To render sensitive; in *photog.*, to render (a plate, film, etc.) sensitive to the influence of light.—**sen''si-ti-za'tion** (-ti-zā'shon), *n.* —**sen'si-tiz-er** (-tī-zėr), *n.* One who or that which sensitizes; in *photog.*, a sensitizing agent.

sen-si-tom-e-ter (sen-si-tom'e-tėr), *n.* [From *sensit(ive)* + *-meter.*] In *photog.*, an apparatus or device for determining the degree of sensitiveness of plates, films, etc.—**sen-si-tom'e-try,** *n.*

sen-so-ri-um (sen-sō'ri-um), *n.*; pl. *-ria* (-ri-ạ) or *-riums.* [LL., < L. *sentire*, perceive, feel: see *sense*.] The supposed seat of sensation in the brain, usually taken as the cortex or gray matter; loosely, the brain or mind; also, the whole sensory apparatus of the body.—**sen-so'ri-al,** *a.*

sen-so-ry (sen'sọ-ri). [LL. *sensorium*: see *sensorium*.] **I.** *n.*; pl. *-ries* (-riz). The sensorium. **II.** *a.* Pertaining to the sensorium, or to sensation; conveying an impulse that results or tends to result in sensation, as a nerve.

sen-su-al (sen'shụ-ạl), *a.* [L. *sensualis*, < *sensus*, E. *sense*.] Of or pertaining to the senses or physical sensation (as, "The wide-stretcht realm of intellectual woe, Surpassing *sensual* far": Young's "Night Thoughts," vii. 747); also, pertaining to or given to the gratification of the senses or the indulgence of appetite (as, "Like all orthodox divines, he was tenacious of the only *sensual* enjoyment [eating] permitted to his cloth," Marryat's "Peter Simple," i.; the *sensual* man); esp., excessively inclined to the gratification of the senses; voluptuous; often, lewd or unchaste; of the face, features, etc., indicative of sensuality; also, pertaining to or concerned with the body, as distinguished from the spirit; fleshly; worldly; materialistic; also, pertaining to the doctrine of sensationalism.—**sen'su-al-ism,** *n.* Subjection to sensual appetites; sensuality; often, lewdness; also, the theory that the highest good consists in sensual gratification; also, the doctrine of sensationalism.—**sen'su-al-ist,** *n.* One given to the indulgence of the senses or appetites; one devoted to sensual pleasure; also, one who holds the doctrine of sensationalism.—**sen-su-al'i-ty** (-al'i-ti), *n.*; pl. *-ties* (-tiz). Sensual nature; also, excessive or unrestrained indulgence in sensual pleasures; often, lewdness; unchastity.—**sen'su-al-ize** (-īz), *v. t.*; *-ized, -izing.* To render sensual.—**sen''su-al-i-za'tion** (-i-zā'shon), *n.*—**sen'su-al-ly,** *adv.*

sen-su-ous (sen'shụ-us), *a.* [L. *sensus*, E. *sense*.] Of or pertaining to the senses (as, "Be near me when the *sensuous* frame Is rack'd with pangs that conquer trust": Tennyson's "In Memoriam," l.); perceived by or affecting the senses (as, the *sensuous* qualities of music); received through the senses (as, *sensuous* pleasure; "The *sensuous* joy from all things fair His strenuous bent of soul repressed," Whittier's "Sumner"); also, readily affected through the senses, as a person, the temperament, etc.; alive to the pleasure to be received through the senses; of the face, expression, etc., showing a tendency to be affected through the senses; also, of words, ideas, etc., connected with sensible or material objects.—**sen-su-os′i-ty** (-os′i-ti), **sen′su-ous-ness,** *n.*—**sen′su-ous-ly,** *adv.*

sent (sent). Preterit and past participle of *send.*

sen-tence (sen′tens), *n.* [OF. F. *sentence*, < L. *sententia*, opinion, judgment, sentence, saying, < *sentire*, perceive, feel: see *sense*.] Way of thinking†, or opinion† (as, "the selfsame portion and lot, which your manner hath been hitherto to lay on them that concur not in opinion and *sentence* with you": Hooker's "Ecclesiastical Polity," Preface, i. 1); also, an opinion pronounced on some particular question; also, an authoritative decision; a judicial judgment or decree; now, esp., the judicial determination of the punishment to be inflicted on a convicted criminal; hence, the punishment itself (as, "The remaining two months of his *sentence* slipped by . . . rapidly": S. Butler's "Way of All Flesh," lxviii.); also, a saying, apothegm, or maxim (as, "Who fears a *sentence* or an old man's saw Shall by a painted cloth be kept in awe," Shakspere's "Lucrece," 244: obs. or rare); also, a combination of words forming a grammatically complete expression of a single thought, in the form of a statement, inquiry, command, or the like; a connected series of words in speech or writing, consisting of a single expression of thought or of several connected clauses, which is grammatically independent of words preceding and following, and which in writing ends with a period or its equivalent; also, in *music*, a period.—**sen′tence**, *v. t.*; -tenced, -tencing. To pronounce sentence upon; condemn to punishment: as, "They were *sentenced* to death and immediately beheaded" (J. F. Kirk's "Charles the Bold," iii. 2).—**sen′ten-cer** (-ten-sèr), *n.*

sen-ten-tial (sen-ten′shal), *a.* [LL. *sententialis*, < L. *sententia*, E. *sentence*.] Pertaining to or of the nature of a judicial sentence; also, pertaining to a grammatical sentence.

sen-ten-tious (sen-ten′shus), *a.* [L. *sententiosus*, < *sententia*, E. *sentence*.] Abounding in or given to pithy sayings or apothegms; also, of the nature of an apothegm; pithy; also, sometimes, affectedly judicial in utterance; magisterial. —**sen-ten′tious-ly,** *adv.*—**sen-ten′tious-ness,** *n.*

sen-tience (sen′shiens), *n.* Sentient condition or character; capacity for sensation or feeling: as, "This opinion . . . was that of the *sentience* of all vegetable things" (Poe's "Fall of the House of Usher"). Also **sen′tien-cy.**

sen-tient (sen′shient). [L. *sentiens* (sentient-), ppr. of *sentire*, perceive, feel: see *sense*.] **I.** *a.* That feels; having the power of perception by the senses; also, characterized by sensation or feeling. **II.** *n.* One who or that which is sentient; also, the mind.—**sen′tient-ly,** *adv.*

sen-ti-ment (sen′ti-ment), *n.* [F. *sentiment*, < ML. *sentimentum*, < L. *sentire*, perceive, feel: see *sense*.] A personal opinion or view (as, to express one's *sentiments* on a subject); mental attitude with regard to something; also, a mental feeling, or an emotion (as, a *sentiment* of pity; "He leaned out of the window as the train rolled away, and waved and smiled to her, not concealing his *sentiments* now," Arnold Bennett's "The Old Adam," iii.); also, refined or tender emotion; manifestation of the higher or more refined feelings; display, often undue display, of emotional susceptibility; sometimes, exhibition or manifestation of feeling or sensibility, or appeal to the tender emotions, in literature, art, or music; also, a thought influenced by or proceeding from feeling or emotion; also, the thought or feeling intended to be conveyed by words as distinguished from the words themselves; also, the expression of some striking or agreeable thought or wish, esp. in epigrammatic or graceful language (as, "Come, Mr. Premium, I'll give you a *sentiment*; here's Success to usury!" Sheridan's "School for Scandal," iii. 3; "Now, here is a little girl who wants my autograph and a '*sentiment*,'" Longfellow, in Bok's "Americanization of Edward Bok," v.).—**sen-ti-men′tal** (-men′tal), *a.* Pertaining to or dependent on sentiment (as, to do a thing for *sentimental* reasons); also, expressive of or appealing to sentiment or the tender emotions (as, the *sentimental* comedy of the 18th century; a *sentimental* song); also, of persons, or their actions, etc., characterized by or exhibiting

sentiment or refined feeling (with a favorable implication: a use common in the 18th century: as, "Your squires are an agreeable race of people, refined, *sentimental*, formed for the *belle passion*," Mrs. Frances Brooke's "Hist. of Lady Julia Mandeville," 1763, Mrs. Barbauld ed., 34); now, usually, swayed by sentiment, or characterized by a weak yielding to sentiment (as, "a *sentimental* schoolgirl," Ruskin's "Crown of Wild Olive," iii.; "a *sentimental* mood," J. Conrad's "Lord Jim," xxxiv.); weakly emotional; mawkishly susceptible or tender.—**sen-ti-men′tal-ism,** *n.* Sentimental tendency or character; tendency to be governed by sentiment rather than reason; predominance of sentiment over reason; weak emotionalism; excessive indulgence in sentiment; also, a display of sentimentality.—**sen-ti-men′tal-ist,** *n.* One swayed by sentiment, or guided by sentiment rather than reason; one given to sentimentalism.—**sen″ti-men-tal′i-ty** (-tal′i-ti), *n.*; pl. -ties (-tiz). Sentimental quality, disposition, behavior, etc.; also, a sentimental notion or the like.—**sen-ti-men′tal-ize,** *v.*; -ized, -izing. **I.** *intr.* To indulge in sentiment; affect sentiment: as, "He had left his father tearfully *sentimentalising* about the Queen" (Arnold Bennett's "Clayhanger," iii. 9). **II.** *tr.* To render sentimental, as a person, etc.; also, to be sentimental over, or turn into an object of sentiment (as, "The leading novelists . . . seemed to enter into a conspiracy to *sentimentalize* the first-book episode in their brilliant careers": Arnold Bennett's "Truth about an Author," vii.). —**sen-ti-men′tal-ly,** *adv.*

sen-ti-nel (sen′ti-nel), *n.* [F. *sentinelle*, < It. *sentinella*; origin uncertain: cf. *sentry*.] A soldier stationed as a guard to challenge all comers and prevent a surprise attack (as, to stand *sentinel*; "The party now approached the *sentinels* on guard at the castle," Scott's "Castle Dangerous," v.); a sentry; hence, in general, one who or that which watches, or stands as if watching, like a sentinel (as, pines standing *sentinel* over a grave).—**sen′ti-nel**, *v. t.*; -neled or -nelled, -neling or -nelling. To watch over or guard as a sentinel does (as, "when the watches of the night were set, and the band on deck *sentinelled* the slumbers of the band below": H. Melville's "Moby-Dick," xxix.); also, to furnish with a sentinel or sentinels; also, to post as a sentinel.

sen-try (sen′tri), *n.*; pl. -tries (-triz). [Appar. related to *sentinel* (recorded earlier).] A soldier stationed at a place to keep guard and prevent the passage of unauthorized persons; a sentinel; also, the guard or watch kept.—**sentry go,** orig., the call made to announce the time of relieving the sentry on guard; now, the patrol or duties of a sentry.—**sen′try,** *v. t.*; -tried, -trying. To guard as a sentry does.—**sen′try=box,** *n.* A small structure for sheltering a sentry in bad weather.

sep-al (sep′al or sē′pal), *n.* [= F. *sépale*, < NL. *sepalum*, irreg. < Gr. σκέπη, a covering.] In *bot.*, each of the individual leaves or parts of the calyx of a flower.—**sep′aled,** **sep′alled,** *a.* Having sepals: as, four-*sepaled*.—**sep′al-ine** (-in), *a.* Pertaining to sepals. —**sep′a-lo-dy** (-a-lō-di), *n.* [With termination as in *petalody*.] In *bot.*, a condition in flowers in which certain organs, as petals, assume the appearance of or become metamorphosed into sepals.—**sep′a-loid,** *a.* [See -*oid*.] Resembling, or of the nature of, a sepal.—**sep′a-lous,** *a.* Having sepals.

sep-a-ra-ble (sep′a-ra-bl), *a.* [L. *separabilis*.] Capable of being separated. — **sep″a-ra-bil′i-ty** (-bil′i-ti), **sep′a-ra-ble-ness,** *n.*—**sep′a-ra-bly,** *adv.*

sep-a-rate (sep′a-rāt), *v.*; -rated, -rating. [L. *separatus*, pp. of *separare*, < *se*-, without, apart, + *parare*, make ready, prepare, E. *pare*.] **I.** *tr.* To put apart or asunder, or part,

Forms of Sepals. — *a*, flower of marsh-marigold (*Caltha palustris*), showing the petaloid sepals *s*, *b* being one of the sepals on a larger scale; *c*, flower of a chickweed (*Cerastium longipedunculatum*), seen from below, *s* being a sepal, and *d* the calyx showing the five free sepals.

---

as two or more persons or things or as one from another (as, to *separate* persons fighting; "In the darkness and confusion, the bands of these commanders became *separated* from each other," Irving's "Conquest of Granada," xii.); disconnect, disjoin, or disunite (what is connected, etc.: as, to *separate* church and state; to *separate* ideas in thought; "You have *separated* your religion from your life," Ruskin's "Crown of Wild Olive," ii.); put out of or remove from personal association or relations (as, "He that repeateth a matter *separateth* very friends," Prov. xvii. 9; "When Mr. Rainscourt was first *separated* from his wife, he felt himself released from a heavy burthen," Marryat's "King's Own," xxxvi.); also, to part, sunder, or keep apart as by an intervening barrier, space, or the like, or as something intervening does (as, nature has *separated* this land from others by mountains and deserts; the Atlantic *separates* Europe and America; the immense distances *separating* star from star; the long tract of time *separating* the ancient from the modern world); also, to part or divide (an assemblage, mass, compound, or whole) into individuals, components, or elements (as, to *separate* a mixture or tangle of things; to *separate* a substance into its chemical elements); take (*from* or *out*) by such parting or dividing (as, to *separate* metal from ore; to *separate* out the gold in a solution); also, to set apart, as for a special purpose (archaic: as, "Thou shalt *separate* three cities for thee in the midst of thy land," Deut. xix. 2; "Paul . . . called to be an apostle, *separated* unto the gospel of God," Rom. i. 1). **II.** *intr.* To draw or come apart or asunder; become disconnected or disunited; become parted or disengaged; often, to part company, as persons; withdraw from association or relations (as, the partners have *separated*; husband and wife have *separated*); withdraw (*from*), as by severing relations, seceding, etc. (as, to *separate* from a church or a political party).—**sep′a-rate** (-rāt). **I.** *a.* Separated, disconnected, or disjoined (as, fragments *separate* or partly detached); also, being or standing apart or by itself or one's self (as, a row of *separate* houses; "He sought them both, but wish'd his hap might find Eve *separate*," Milton's "Paradise Lost," ix. 422); shut off, one from another, as cells or prisoners, or characterized by such shutting off, as confinement; existing or maintained independently (as, a *separate* entity; *separate* organizations or establishments); unconnected or distinct (as, these are two *separate* questions; to keep private matters *separate* from official business); individual or particular (as, each *separate* item of an account; "a hundred trifles too insignificant for *separate* notice," Arnold Bennett's "Leonora," iv.). **II.** *n.* Something separate; an article or document issued separately; a copy of an article reprinted separately from a magazine, etc.—**sep′a-rate-ly**, *adv.*—**sep′a-rate-ness**, *n.*—**sep-a-ra′tion** (-rā′shon), *n.* [L. *separatio(n-)*.] The act of separating, or the state of being separated; specif., cessation of conjugal cohabitation by mutual consent or by judicial decree; also, a place, line, or point of parting or division; also, something that separates other things.—**sep′a-rat-ism** (-ra-tizm), *n.* The principle or policy of separation, esp. as opposed to ecclesiastical or political union.—**sep′a-rat-ist. I.** *n.* One who separates, withdraws, or secedes, as from an established church; also, an advocate of separation, esp. ecclesiastical or political separation. **II.** *a.* Of, pertaining to, or characteristic of separatists or separatism.—**sep″a-rat-is′tic**, *a.* —**sep′a-ra-tive**, *a.* [LL. *separativus*.] Tending to separate; causing separation.—**sep′a-ra-tor** (-rā-tor), *n.* [LL.] One who or that which separates; specif., an apparatus for separating one thing from another, as cream from milk, steam from water, or wheat from chaff, dirt, etc.—**sep′a-ra-to-ry** (-ra-tō-ri), *a.* Serving to separate; separative.—**sep-a-ra′tum** (-rā′tum), *n.*; pl. *-ta* (-tä). [NL.] A copy of an article reprinted from the transactions of a learned society or the like; a separate.

Se-phar-dim (sē-fär′dim), *n. pl.* [Heb.; named from *Sepharad*, a place mentioned in Obad. 20, and variously identified, being taken by the rabbis as the Spanish Peninsula.] Spanish-Portuguese Jews and their descendants, as distinguished from the Ashkenazim or German-Polish Jews and their descendants. See *Ashkenazim*.—**Se-phar′dic**, *a.*
se-pi-a (sē′pi-ä). [L., < Gr. σηπία.] **I.** *n.* A cuttlefish of the genus *Sepia* or some allied genus; also, a brown pigment

prepared from the inky secretion of various cuttlefishes; the color of this pigment, a dark brown; also, cuttlebone. **II.** *a.* Of the color of sepia; brown; also, executed in sepia, as a drawing.
se-pi-o-lite (sē′pi-ọ-līt), *n.* [G. *sepiolith*, < Gr. σήπιον, cuttlebone, + λίθος, stone.] Meerschaum (native hydrous silicate of magnesium).
se-poy (sē′poi), *n.* [Hind. *sipāhī*, < Pers. *sipāhī*, horseman, soldier, < *sipāh*, army: cf. *spahi*.] In India, a native soldier in the military service of Europeans, esp. of the British.—**Sepoy Mutiny**, a revolt of the sepoy troops in British India which broke out in 1857 and was suppressed in 1858, resulting in the transference of the administration of India from the East India Company to the crown.
sep-sine (sep′sin), *n.* [See *sepsis*.] In *physiol. chem.*, any of certain ptomaines causing septic poisoning.
sep-sis (sep′sis), *n.* [NL., < Gr. σῆψις, < σήπειν, make rotten: cf. *septic*.] Putrefaction; also, a poisoning of the system due to the entrance of putrefactive material or certain micro-organisms into the blood; septic poisoning.
sept (sept), *n.* [Perhaps a var. of *sect²*.] A clan: orig. with reference to tribes or families in Ireland.
sep-ta (sep′tä), *n.* Plural of *septum*.
sep-tal (sep′tal), *a.* Of or pertaining to a septum.
sep-tan-gu-lar (sep-tang′gū-lär), *a.* [L. *septem*, seven, + *angulus*, E. *angle³*.] Having seven angles.
sep-ta-ri-um (sep-tā′ri-um), *n.*; pl. *-ria* (-ri-ä). [NL., < L. *septum*: see *septum*.] In *geol.*, a concretionary nodule or mass, usually of calcium carbonate or of argillaceous carbonate of iron, traversed within by a network of cracks filled with calcite and other minerals.—**sep-ta′ri-an**, *a.*
sep-tate (sep′tāt), *a.* [NL. *septatus*.] Divided by a septum or septa. Also **sep′tat-ed** (-tā-ted).—**sep-ta′tion** (-tā′shon), *n.* Septate condition.
Sep-tem-ber (sep-tem′ber), *n.* [L. *September*, the seventh month of the Roman year, < *septem*, seven.] The ninth month of the year, containing 30 days.—**Sep-tem′brist**, *n.* In the French Revolution, one of those who instigated or took part in the massacre of royalist and other inmates of the prisons of Paris, Sept. 2–6, 1792.
sep-tem-vir (sep-tem′ver), *n.*; pl. *-viri* (-vi-rī) or *-virs*. [L., orig. pl., *septemviri*, < *septem*, seven, + *viri*, pl. of *vir*, man.] One of a body of seven men associated in some office or commission.—**sep-tem′vi-rate** (-vi-rāt), *n.* [L. *septemviratus.*] The office of a septemvir; government by septemviri; any association of seven in office or authority; any group or set of seven.
sep-te-na-ry (sep′te-na-ri). [L. *septenarius*, < *septeni*, seven each, < *septem*, seven.] **I.** *a.* Of or pertaining to the number seven; forming a group of seven; also, septennial. **II.** *n.*; pl. *-ries* (-riz). The number seven; also, a group or set of seven things; a period of seven years.
sep-ten-nate (sep-ten′āt), *n.* [F. *septennat*, < L. *septennis*: see *septennial*.] A period of seven years, as during which office is held.
sep-ten-ni-al (sep-ten′i-al), *a.* [L. *septennis*, *septuennis*, < *septem*, seven, + *annus*, year.] Of or for seven years; also, occurring every seven years.—**sep-ten′ni-al-ly**, *adv.*—**sep-ten′ni-um** (-ten′i-um), *n.*; pl. *-niums* or *-nia* (-ä). [L., < *septennis*.] A period of seven years.
sep-ten-tri-on (sep-ten′tri-ọn), *n.* [L. *septentrio(n-)*, sing. of *septentriones*, lit. 'seven plow-oxen' (seven stars of the Great Bear), < *septem*, seven, + *triones*, pl. of *trio(n-)*, plow-ox.] *Pl.* [*cap.*], the constellation of the Great Bear; *sing.* [*l. c.*], the north (as, "Thou art as opposite to every good . . . as the south to the *septentrion*": Shakspere's "3 Henry VI.," i. 4. 136); also, a northerner. [Archaic.]—**sep-ten′tri-o-nal** (-ọ-nal), *a.* Of the north; northern. [Archaic.]
sep-tet, sep-tette (sep-tet′), *n.* [G. *septett*, < L. *septem*, seven.] A musical composition for seven voices or instruments; also, a company of seven singers or players; also, any group of seven persons or things.
septi-. Form of L. *septem*, seven, used in combination, as in *septiform, septisyllable.*
sep-tic (sep′tik), *a.* [L. *septicus*, < Gr. σηπτικός, putrefactive, < σήπειν, make rotten: cf. *sepsis*.] **I.** *a.* Putrefactive; putrefying; also, pertaining to or of the nature of

sepsis. **II.** *n.* A substance which causes putrefaction or sepsis.—**sep'ti-cal-ly,** *adv.*

sep-ti-ce-mi-a, sep-ti-cæ-mi-a (sep-ti-sē'mi-ä), *n.* [NL., < Gr. σηπτικός, septic, + αἷμα, blood.] In *pathol.*, a form of blood-poisoning, esp. one in which micro-organisms as well as their toxins are absorbed by the blood.—**sep-ti-ce'mic, sep-ti-cæ'mic,** *a.*

sep-ti-ci-dal (sep'ti-sī-dal), *a.* [L. *septum* (see *septum*) + *cædere*, cut.] In *bot.*, characterized by splitting through the septa or dissepiments, as a mode of dehiscence.—**sep'ti-ci-dal-ly,** *adv.*

sep-ti-ci-ty (sep-tis'i-ti), *n.* Septic character or quality.

sep-ti-form (sep'ti-fôrm), *a.* [LL. *septiformis*, < L. *septem*, seven, + *forma*, form.] Sevenfold.

sep-tif-ra-gal (sep-tif'ra-gal), *a.* [L. *septum* (see *septum*) + *frangere*, break.] In *bot.*, characterized by the breaking away of the valves from the septa or dissepiments, as a mode of dehiscence.—**sep'tif-ra-gal-ly,** *adv.*

Septicidal Dehiscence.—*v*, valves; *d*, dissepiments; *c*, axis.

sep-til-lion (sep-til'yon), *n.* [F. *septillion*, < L. *septem*, seven, + F. (*m*)*illion*, million.] In Great Britain, the seventh power of a million, represented by 1 followed by 42 ciphers; in France and the U. S., a thousand sextillions, represented by 1 followed by 24 ciphers.—**sep-til'lionth,** *a.* and *n.*

sep-ti-mal (sep'ti-mal), *a.* [L. *septimus*: see *septime*.] Pertaining to or based on the number seven.

sep-time (sep'tēm), *n.* [L. *septimus*, seventh, < *septem*, seven: see *seven*.] In *fencing*, the seventh in a series of eight parries.

sep-tin-su-lar (sep-tin'sū-lär), *a.* [L. *septem*, seven, + *insula*, island.] Pertaining to or consisting of seven islands; [*cap.*] of or pertaining to the Ionian Islands (the 'Septinsular Republic' of 1800–07).

sep-ti-syl-la-ble (sep-ti-sil'a-bl), *n.* [See *septi-.*] A word of seven syllables.

sep-tu-a-ge-na-ri-an (sep″tū-a-je-nā'ri-an). [L. *septuagenarius*, < *septuageni*, seventy each, distributive of *septuaginta*, seventy: see *Septuagint*.] **I.** *a.* Of the age of 70 years, or between 70 and 80 years old. **II.** *n.* A septuagenarian person. Also **sep-tu-ag'e-na-ry** (-aj'e-na-ri), *a.* and *n.*

Sep-tu-a-ges-i-ma (sep″tū-a-jes'i-mä), *n.* [ML., prop. fem. of L. *septuagesimus*, seventieth, < *septuaginta*, seventy: see *Septuagint* and *Sexagesima*.] The third Sunday before Lent (more fully, 'Septuagesima Sunday').

Sep-tu-a-gint (sep'tū-a-jint), *n.* [L. *septuaginta*, seventy, related to *septem*, seven: see *seven*.] The Greek version of the Old Testament (often represented by the symbol LXX) traditionally said to have been made at the request of Ptolemy Philadelphus, king of Egypt (285–247? B.C.), by 72 Jewish scholars, and to have been completed by them in 72 days. Cf. *seventy*, *n.*—**Sep″tu-a-gin'tal,** *a.*

sep-tum (sep'tum), *n.*; pl. *-ta* (-tä). [L. *septum*, *sæptum*, inclosure, fence, wall, < *sæpire*, hedge in, inclose, < *sæpes*, a hedge, fence.] A partition; specif., a dividing wall, membrane, or the like in a plant or animal structure; a dissepiment.

sep-tu-or (sep'tū-ôr), *n.* [F. *septuor* (formed after F. *quatuor*, quartet), < L. *septem*, seven.] A septet.

sep-tu-ple (sep'tū-pl), *a.* [LL. *septuplus*, < *septem*, seven, + *-plus*: see *double*.] Sevenfold; seven times as great.—**sep'tu-ple,** *v. t.*; *-pled*, *-pling.* To make seven times as great.

sep-ul-cher, sep-ul-chre (sep'ul-kėr), *n.* [OF. *sepulcre* (F. *sépulcre*), < L. *sepulcrum*, *sepulchrum*, < *sepelire*, bury: cf. *sepulture*.] A building, vault, excavation, or other place for the reception and keeping of a dead body (as, "Joseph . . . laid him [the dead Jesus] in a *sepulchre* which was hewn out of a rock, and rolled a stone unto the door of the *sep-*

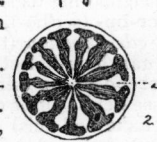

Septum.—1, fruit of poppy, cut transversely to show the 12 septa (S) with the seeds; 2, diagram of same, the seeds omitted.

ulchre": Mark, xv. 46); a tomb, grave, or burial-place (often *fig.*: as, "the maxim of antiquity, that the throne is a glorious *sepulchre*," Gibbon's "Decline and Fall of the Roman Empire," xl.; the *sepulcher* of one's hopes or ambitions); also, sepulture or burial (rare); *eccles.*, a structure or a recess in some old churches in which the sacred elements, the cross, etc., were deposited with due ceremonies on Good Friday to be taken out at Easter, in commemoration of Christ's entombment and resurrection (often called 'Easter sepulcher').—**Holy Sepulcher.** See under *holy*, *a.*—**whited sepulcher.** See under *white*, *v.*—**sep'ul-cher, sep'ul-chre,** *v. t.*; *-chered*, *-chred*, *-chering*, *-chring.* To place in a sepulcher; entomb; bury; also, to serve as a sepulcher or tomb for.

se-pul-chral (sē-pul'kral), *a.* [L. *sepulcralis*.] Of, pertaining to, or serving as a sepulcher or tomb (as, *sepulchral* inscriptions or monuments; "Our wasted oil unprofitably burns, Like hidden lamps in old *sepulchral* urns," Cowper's "Conversation," 358); also, of or pertaining to sepulture or burial (as, *sepulchral* rites); also, proper to or suggestive of a sepulcher or tomb (as, a *sepulchral* silence or gloom); hence, in general, funereal or dismal (as, "His demeanor in public was still, silent, almost *sepulchral*," Motley's "Dutch Republic," i. 1; "an old *sepulchral* man," H. Melville's "Moby-Dick," xxviii.); often, of sound, hollow and dismal (as, "He heard his own name spoken in the hollow, *sepulchral* tones of death," Cooper's "Spy," x.; "An owl answered with its *sepulchral* note," Mark Twain's "Tom Sawyer," xxv.).—**se-pul'chral-ly,** *adv.*

sep-ul-ture (sep'ul-tūr), *n.* [OF. *sepulture* (F. *sépulture*), < L. *sepultura*, < *sepelire* (pp. *sepultus*), bury.] The act of placing in a sepulcher or tomb; entombment; burial; also, a sepulcher, tomb, or burial-place (archaic).—**se-pul'tu-ral** (sē-pul'tū-ral), *a.*—**sep'ul-ture,** *v. t.*; *-tured*, *-turing.* To entomb; bury.

se-qua-cious (sē-kwā'shus), *a.* [L. *sequax* (sequac-), < *sequi*, follow.] Following, as after a person or thing (sometimes with *of*: as, "Orpheus could lead the savage race; And trees unrooted left their place, *Sequacious* of the lyre," Dryden's "Song for St. Cecilia's Day," vii.); also, disposed to follow a leader; given to following others in action, thought, etc., esp. in an unreasoning manner; also, following with smooth regularity one after another, as musical tones; proceeding smoothly and regularly, as movements.—**se-qua'cious-ly,** *adv.*—**se-qua'cious-ness, se-qua'ci-ty** (-kwas'i-ti), *n.*

se-quel (sē'kwel), *n.* [L. *sequela*, < *sequi*, follow.] A following†, or train of followers†; also, a train of events, proceedings, or circumstances, or an event or circumstance, following, or following from, something (as, the affair had an unexpected *sequel* in the surrender and confession of unsuspected persons; "She referred to the expected decease of her mother, and the gloomy *sequel* of funeral rites," C. Brontë's "Jane Eyre," xxi.; "Of love that never found his earthly close, What *sequel*? Streaming eyes and breaking hearts?" Tennyson's "Love and Duty," 2); the subsequence, consequence, result, or aftermath of something (as, "Our dreams are the *sequel* of our waking knowledge . . . Hideous dreams are exaggerations of the sins of the day": Emerson's "Essays," Spiritual Laws); the subsequent course of affairs, or the ensuing or later stages of the case (as, all these facts became clear in the *sequel*); also, the part of something yet to come (as, "I will not fail to make you acquainted, from time to time, with the *sequel* of our adventures": Smollett's "Humphry Clinker," May 8); esp., the following or remaining part of a narrative or the like (as, "I have experienced the excitement of a person to whom a tale has been half told, and who is impatient to hear the *sequel*": C. Brontë's "Jane Eyre," xxxiii.); specif., a literary work, complete in itself, but forming a continuation of a preceding work (as, Stevenson's "David Balfour," called in England "Catriona," a romance written as a *sequel* to his "Kidnapped"); in *pathol.*, a sequela.

se-que-la (sē-kwē'lä), *n.*; pl. *-læ* (-lē). [L.: see *sequel*.] A thing following or resulting; in *pathol.*, a disease or morbid affection following as the result of a previous disease.

se-quence (sē'kwens), *n.* [LL. *sequentia*, < L. *sequens* (sequent-), ppr.: see *sequent*.] The following or coming of one thing after another in order, or succession (as, three names in *sequence* on a list; events occurring in *sequence*); also, order of succession (as, a list of books in alphabetical *sequence*; "Tell Athens, in the *sequence* of degree From high to low throughout, that . . . ," Shakspere's "Timon of Athens," v. 1. 211); also, the following of one thing from another logically or as a natural consequence (as, "In this remarkable Volume . . . his adherence to the mere course of time produces . . . a certain show of outward method; but of true logical method and *sequence* there is too little": Carlyle's "Sartor Resartus," i. 4); connection or relation between successive events, facts, utterances, etc.; also, a number of things following one after another in order, or a continuous or connected series (as, a long *sequence* of unfavorable seasons; a *sequence* of sonnets); also, something that follows; a subsequent event; a result; a logical consequence; in *music*, a series of melodic or harmonic phrases or groups repeated three or more times at successive pitches upward or downward, usually without modulation or chromatic deviation from the key; in *card-playing*, a set of three or more cards following one after another in order of value; in *liturgics*, a hymn sung in the Western Church after the gradual and before the gospel.—**se'quen-cy**, *n.* The quality of being sequent; the fact of following as a logical or natural consequence.

se-quent (sē'kwęnt), *a.* [L. *sequens* (*sequent-*), ppr. of *sequi*, follow: cf. *second*[1], *sect*[2], *sue*, *suit*, also *execute*, *extrinsic*, *obsequious*, *persecute*, and *social*.] **I.** *a.* Following, succeeding, or subsequent (archaic: as, "a *sequent* king," Milton's "Paradise Lost," xii. 165); also, following one after another, or successive (as, "The galleys Have sent a dozen *sequent* messengers . . . at one another's heels": Shakspere's "Othello," i. 2. 41); characterized by continuous succession; occurring in or forming an uninterrupted series; consecutive; also, following as a logical or natural consequence; consequent. **II.** *n.* A follower†; also, that which follows in order; also, that which follows as a result.

se-quen-tial (sē-kwen'shął), *a.* [LL. *sequentia*: see *sequence*.] Following in sequence; succeeding; subsequent; resultant or consequent; also, forming a sequence or connected series; characterized by regular sequence of parts.— **se-quen'tial-ly**, *adv.*

se-ques-ter (sē-kwes'tèr), *v. t.* [LL. *sequestrare* (pp. *sequestratus*), < L. *sequester*, a depositary, trustee: cf. *sequestrate*.] In legal use, to remove (property) temporarily from the possession of the owner; seize and hold, as the property and income of a debtor, until legal claims are satisfied; also, to sequestrate the property of (a person); in general use, to confiscate, or take forcible possession of (as, "The soldiers . . . *sequestered* rents and assessed fines": Morley's "Oliver Cromwell," ii. 4); also, to remove or separate (as, "The virtue of art lies in detachment, in *sequestering* one object from the embarrassing variety": Emerson's "Essays," Art); esp., to remove or withdraw into solitude or retirement, or seclude (as, "A man might properly *sequester* himself, to review his life and purify his heart," Johnson's "Rasselas," xxii.; "So long he had been retired and *sequestered* from all his acquaintance," Smollett's "Humphry Clinker," Sept. 15).—**se-ques'tered**, *p. a.* Separated or withdrawn from others; living in retirement or seclusion, as persons; secluded or out-of-the-way, as places (as, "this dark *sequester'd* nook," Milton's "Comus," 500; "a *sequestered* village," R. Graves's "Spiritual Quixote," i. 1).

se-ques-trate (sē-kwes'trāt), *v. t.*; *-trated, -trating.* [LL. *sequestratus*, pp. of *sequestrare*: see *sequester*.] In legal use, to sequester (property); seize and hold until legal claims are satisfied; in general use, to confiscate; also, to separate, withdraw, or seclude (obs. or rare).—**se-ques-tra-tion** (sek-wes-trā'shǫn or sē-kwes-), *n.* [LL. *sequestratio(n-)*.] In legal use, the sequestrating or sequestering of property; a writ authorizing this; in general use, confiscation or seizure; also, removal or separation; banishment or exile; withdrawal, retirement, or seclusion.—**se-ques-tra-tor** (sek'wes-trā-tǫr or sē'kwes-), *n.*

se-ques-trum (sē-kwes'trum), *n.* [NL. use of ML. *sequestrum*, separation, L. deposit: cf. *sequester*.] In *pathol.*, a dead portion of bone separated from the living part, as in necrosis.

se-quin (sē'kwin), *n.* [F. *sequin*, < It. *zecchino*, < *zecca*, mint, < Ar. *sikkah*, die for coining.] A former Italian gold coin, worth about $2.25, first minted in Venice about 1280; also, a small disk or spangle used to ornament dress, etc.— **se'quined**, *a.* Ornamented with sequins (spangles).

se-quoi-a (sē-kwoi'ą), *n.* [NL.; named from *Sequoya*, an Indian (part white) of the Cherokee tribe, who invented an alphabet.] Either of two species of extremely tall pinaceous trees of California constituting the genus *Sequoia.* See *big tree* (under *big*[1], *a.*) and *redwood.*

se-rac (se-rak' or ser'ak), *n.* [F. (Swiss) *sérac.*] A large block or pinnacle-like mass of ice formed by the breaking of a glacier.

se-ra-glio (se-ral'yō or se-räl'-), *n.*; pl. *seraglios* (-yōz). [It. *seraglio*, inclosure, harem, palace, ult. < L. *sera*, bar for fastening a door (cf. *serry*), but with sense due in part to Turk. *serāï*: see *serai*.] The part of a Mohammedan house or palace in which the wives and concubines are secluded; a harem; also, a Turkish palace, esp. of the Sultan.

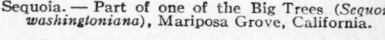

Sequoia. — Part of one of the Big Trees (*Sequoia washingtoniana*), Mariposa Grove, California.

se-rai (sē-rāï'), *n.* [Turk. and Hind. *serāī*, < Pers. *sarāī*.] In Eastern countries, a building for the accommodation of travelers; a caravansary; also, a Turkish palace, esp. of the Sultan.

se-rail (sē-rāl'), *n.* [F. *sérail.*] A seraglio. [Now rare.]

se-rang (sē-rang'), *n.* [Pers. *sarhang*, commander.] A native boatswain or head of a lascar crew. [E. Ind.]

se-ra-pe (se-rä'pā), *n.* [Mex. Sp. *sarape.*] A kind of shawl or wrap, often of gay colors, worn by Spanish-Americans.

ser-aph (ser'ąf), *n.*; pl. *-aphs* or *-aphim* (-ą-fim) (also erron. *-aphims*). [LL. *seraphim*, pl., < Heb. *serāphīm*, pl.] One of the celestial beings seen hovering above the throne of God in Isaiah's vision (see Isa. vi.); also, a member of the highest order of angels, distinguished by fervor of love, often represented as a child's head with two wings above, two below, and one on each side; also (pl. *seraphs*), a seraphic person. Cf. *cherub.*—**se-raph-ic** (sē-raf'ik), *a.* [LL. *seraphicus.*] Of, like, or befitting a seraph.—**se-raph'i-cal-ly**, *adv.*

ser'a-phim, *n. pl.* See *seraph.*

ser-as-kier (ser-ąs-kēr'), *n.* [Turk., < Pers. *ser*, head, + Ar. *'askar*, army.] A Turkish general, esp. the commander-in-chief.

Serb (sèrb). [Serbian *Srb*, *Serb*: cf. *Sorb*[2].] **I.** *n.* A native or inhabitant of Serbia (Servia); a Serbian; also, the (Slavic) language of Serbia. **II.** *a.* Serbian.—**Ser-bi-an** (sèr'bi-ąn). **I.** *a.* Of or pertaining to Serbia (or Servia), its inhabitants, or their language. **II.** *n.* A native or inhabitant of Serbia, esp. one belonging to the Slavic race inhabiting it; also, the Slavic language spoken in Serbia and neighboring regions.

Ser-bo- (sèr'bō-). Form of *Serb* used in combination, as in *Serbo-Croatian* (both Serbian and Croatian, as a particular branch or dialect of Slavic), *Serbo-Montenegrin.*

Ser-bo-ni-an (sèr-bō'ni-ąn), *a.* [Gr. Σερβωνίς (L. *Sirbonis*): see def.] Of or designating a large marshy (now dry) tract (Lake Serbonis) anciently existing in northern Egypt, surrounded and covered by shifting sands, in which entire armies are said to have been swallowed up: used in the phrase *Serbonian bog* (see Milton's "Paradise Lost," ii. 592: fig., anything causing inextricable difficulty and embarrassment).

ser-dab (sėr′dab or sėr-däb′), *n.* [Ar., < Pers. *serdāb*, cellar.] In western Asia, a cellar or underground chamber; also, in Egypt, a narrow chamber in a mastaba (tomb), in which a statue or other representation of the deceased person was kept.

sere (sēr), *a.* and *v.* See *sear*[1].

se-rein (sė-raṅ′), *n.* [F. *serein*, evening damp, OF. *serain*, evening, nightfall, ult. < L. *serum*, evening, prop. neut. of *serus*, late.] In *meteor.*, a very fine rain falling from a clear sky after sunset.

ser-e-nade (ser-ẹ-nād′), *n.* [F. *sérénade*, < It. *serenata*: see *serenata*.] A complimentary performance of vocal or instrumental music in the open air at night, as by a lover under the window of his lady; also, a piece of music suitable for such performance. Cf. *aubade*.—**ser-e-nade′**, *v. t.* or *i.*; *-naded*, *-nading.* To entertain with or perform a serenade.—**ser-e-nad′er** (-nā′dėr), *n.*

ser-e-na-ta (ser-e-nä′tạ), *n.* [It., serenade, appar. < *sereno*, open air (< L. *serenus*, E. *serene*), perhaps with sense affected by *sera*, evening, < L. *serus*, late: cf. *serein*.] In *music*, a form of secular cantata, often of a dramatic or imaginative character; also, an instrumental composition in several movements, forming an intermediate link between the suite and the symphony.

ser-en-dip-i-ty (ser-en-dip′i-ti), *n.* [Coined (1754) by Horace Walpole from *Serendip, Serendib*, old name for Ceylon, in a fairy-tale called "The Three Princes of Serendip," in which the princes are described as making such discoveries.] The faculty or habitual experience of making happy or interesting discoveries unexpectedly or by accident. —**ser-en-dip′per**, *n.* One who has or displays the faculty of serendipity.

se-rene (sẹ-rēn′), *a.* [L. *serenus*, clear, bright, serene.] Clear, fair, or without cloud or storm (as, a *serene* sky; *serene* air or weather; "one *serene* and moonlight night, when all the waves rolled by like scrolls of silver," H. Melville's "Moby-Dick," li.); clear and bright (as, "The moon, *serene* in glory, mounts the sky," Pope's "Winter," 6; "many a gem of purest ray *serene*," Gray's "Elegy," xiv.); also, calm or tranquil, as waters, the sea, etc.; peaceful, quiet, or without tumult or disturbance, as times, conditions, life, etc. (as, "The days were peaceful and *serene*," Dickens's "Oliver Twist," xxxii.; "She . . . wish'd . . . Some place of more *serene* repose," Cowper's "Retired Cat," 30); unaffected by disturbing emotions, or calm, placid, or unruffled, as a person or the mind, countenance, etc. (as, "He is kept *serene* and calm, by . . . knowing nothing of the dangers which surround him," Defoe's "Robinson Crusoe," i. 14; "His features were sunk in death, but they were yet *serene*," Mrs. Radcliffe's "Romance of the Forest," vii.); characteristic of or showing serenity of mind (as, "a certain *serene* self-possession," Longfellow's "Kavanagh," xxiv.; "She announced, in the *serenest*, simplest tone, that . . . ," H. James's "Portrait of a Lady," xlv.); also [often *cap.*], an epithet used in titles of honor of certain reigning princes, etc. (as, his *Serene* Highness).—**all serene**, all peaceful or quiet; hence, all satisfactory, or all right (as, "'I'm just going to walk about in the garden a minute.' . . . *'All serene!'* he agreed": Arnold Bennett's "Hilda Lessways," ii. 6). [Colloq.]—**se-rene′**, *n.* A time or condition of clear weather (obs. or rare); also, a clear or tranquil expanse, as of sky or sea (poetic: as, "No mist obscures, nor cloud . . . Breaks the *serene* of heaven," Southey's "Thalaba," i. 1); also, calm, tranquillity, or serenity (chiefly poetic).—**se-rene′**, *v. t.*; *-rened*, *-rening.* To make serene. [Archaic.]— **se-rene′ly**, *adv.*—**se-rene′ness**, *n.*—**se-ren′i-ty** (-ren′i-ti), *n.*; pl. *-ties* (-tiz). The state or quality of being serene; clearness, as of the sky, air, etc.; calmness, tranquillity, or peacefulness, as of a place, time, etc.; often, calmness of mind, placidity, or tranquil composure (as, "He was always a cool man; nothing could disturb his *serenity*": Mark Twain's "Life on the Mississippi," xlix.); also [usually *cap.*], with *his, your*, etc., a title of honor given to certain reigning princes, etc.

serf (sėrf), *n.* [OF. F. *serf*, < L. *servus*, slave: cf. *serve*.] A slave†; specif., a person in a condition of modified slavery, required to render certain services to his lord, and commonly attached to the lord's land and transferred with it from one owner to another.—**serf-age** (sėr′fạj), *n.* The condition of a serf; also, the serf system; also, the serf class.—**serf′- dom** (-dọm), *n.* The condition of a serf. Also **serf′hood** (-hụd), **serf′ship**, *n.*

serge (sėrj), *n.* [OF. *serge, sarge* (F. *serge*), orig. a silk fabric, < L. *sericus*: see *silk*.] Formerly, a woolen fabric used for hangings, clothing, etc.; now, a twilled fabric, commonly of worsted or wool, but also woven wholly or in part of silk or cotton.

ser-geant, ser-jeant (sär′jent), *n.* [OF. *serjant* (F. *sergent*), < L. *serviens* (*servient-*), ppr. of *servire*, E. *serve.*] A servant† or retainer†; a tenant by military service, below the rank of knight†; also, an officer who enforced the decrees or commands of a court, arrested offenders, etc.† (sometimes fig.: as, "This fell *sergeant*, death, Is strict in his arrest," Shakspere's "Hamlet," v. 2. 347); also, in England, a member of a superior order of barristers, now abolished (usually *serjeant*, often *serjeant at law*); also, any of various officers of the English royal household; also, in military use, a non-commissioned officer of the grade next above that of corporal (now *sergeant*); hence, a police officer of higher rank than a common policeman or constable (now *sergeant*). —**ser′gean-cy, ser′jean-cy** (-jen-si), *n.*—**ser′geant=at= arms′**, *n.*; pl. *sergeants-*. An executive officer of a legislative or other body, whose duty it is to enforce the commands of the body, preserve order, etc.—**ser′geant=fish**, *n.* A large, fusiform acanthopterygian fish, *Rachycentron canadus* (or *Elacate canada*), with a long black stripe along its side, found in warm seas, esp. on the southeastern coast of the

Sergeant-fish.

U. S. and in the East Indies.—**ser′geant=ma′jor**, *n.*; pl. *-jors.* A non-commissioned military officer of the highest grade.—**ser′geant-ship, ser′jeant-ship**, *n.*—**ser′gean-ty, ser′jean-ty** (-jen-ti), *n.* [OF. *serjantie.*] A form of feudal tenure in England, on condition of rendering some specified personal service to the king. [Now hist.]

se-ri-al (sē′ri-ạl), *a.* [NL. *serialis*, < L. *series*: see *series*.] **I.** *a.* Of or pertaining to a series (as, the *serial* number of a bond); arranged in or constituting a series; specif., occurring or appearing in instalments in successive issues of a periodical (as, *serial* publication; a *serial* story); pertaining to such publication (as, the *serial* rights of a novel). **II.** *n.* A literary work issued in successive parts; esp., a novel or the like published in instalments in successive numbers of a periodical.—**se′ri-al-ist**, *n.* A writer of serials.—**se-ri-al′i-ty** (-al′i-ti), *n.* Serial character; occurrence or arrangement in a series.—**se′ri-al-ize** (-īz), *v. t.*; *-ized, -izing.* To arrange in a series; also, to publish in serial form (as, "Gordon's Monthly was *serializing* the novel in America": Arnold Bennett's "Great Man," xxvi.).—**se″ri-al-i-za′tion** (-i-zā′-shọn), *n.*—**se′ri-al-ly**, *adv.* In a serial manner; in a series; as a serial.

se-ri-ate (sē′ri-āt), *a.* [ML. *seriatus*, pp. of *seriare*, arrange in a series, < L. *series*: see *series*.] Arranged or occurring in one or more series.—**se′ri-ate-ly**, *adv.*

se-ri-a-tim (sē-ri-ā′tim), *adv.* [ML., < L. *series*: see *series*.] In a series; one after another: as, "He announced his intention of thrashing the entire population of Medora *seriatim*" (Roosevelt's "Ranch Life and the Hunting-Trail," vi.).

se-ri-a-tion (sē-ri-ā′shọn), *n.* [Cf. F. *sériation.*] Succession or arrangement in a series.

se-ri-ceous (sẹ-rish′ius), *a.* [L. *sericeus*, < *sericus*, silken: see *silk*.] Silky; covered with silky down, as a leaf.

ser-i-ci-cul-ture (ser′i-si-kul″tụr), *n.* [F. *sériciculture*, < LL. *sericum*, silk (see *silk*), + L. *cultura*, culture.] The rearing and keeping of silkworms, for the production of raw silk; sericulture.—**ser″i-ci-cul′tur-al** (-tụr-ạl), *a.*—**ser″i-ci-cul′tur-ist**, *n.*

ser-i-cin (ser′i-sin), *n.* [LL. *sericum*, silk: see *silk*.] In *chem.*, a gelatinous organic compound obtained from silk.

ser-i-cul-ture (ser′i-kul-tụr), etc. Shorter form of *sericiculture*, etc.

ser-i-e-ma (ser-i-ē'mä̤), *n.* [S. Amer.] A large bird, *Cariama cristata*, with long legs and a crested head, native in southern Brazil, etc. Also called *crested screamer*.

se-ries (sē'rēz or sē'ri-ēz), *n.*; pl. *series*. [L., row or chain of things, series, < *serere* (pp. *sertus*), join: cf. *assert*, *desert*[2], *dissert*, *exert*, *insert*.] A number of things, events, etc., ranged or occurring in spatial, temporal, or other succession; a number of similar or related things in succession; a sequence; specif., a consecutively numbered issue of notes, bonds, or the like; a set, as of coins, stamps, etc.; a set of volumes, as of a periodical, or as issued in like form with similarity of subject or purpose; also, a continued

Seriema.

course, as of action, life, etc.† (as, "I looked forward without hope through the *series* of my existence": Godwin's "Caleb Williams," xxxiv.); also, the connected sequence of thought or discourse†; in *math.*, a succession of quantities or terms related in some definite way to one another or to another quantity or quantities.—**in series**, in *elect.*, with the positive pole, terminal, or the like, of one, joined to the negative of the next: said of batteries, etc.—**se'ries-dy″na-mo**, *n.* In *elect.*, a series-wound dynamo.—**se'ries-mo″tor**, *n.* In *elect.*, a series-wound motor.—**se'ries-wound**, *a.* In *elect.*, noting a dynamo or a motor of which the field-magnet coils are in series with the armature circuit, so that the whole or practically the whole armature current passes through the field-magnet coils. Cf. *shunt-wound*.

ser-if (ser'if), *n.* [Origin uncertain.] In *typog.*, a smaller line used to finish off a main stroke of a letter, as at the top and bottom of M.

ser-in[1] (ser'in), *n.* [F.; origin unknown.] A finch, *Serinus hortulanus*, of central and southern Europe, closely resembling the canary, but smaller.

ser-in[2], **ser-ine** (ser'in), *n.* [LL. *sericum*, silk: see *silk*.] In *chem.*, a white organic compound derived from sericin, etc., occurring in monoclinic crystals, and combining with both acids and bases.

se-rin-ga (sẹ-ring'gä), *n.* [F.] Same as *syringa*.

se-ri-o-com-ic (sē″ri-ọ-kom'ik). I. *a.* Partly

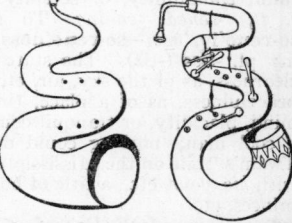

Serin (*Serinus hortulanus*).

serious and partly comic: as, "Irony . . . assumes that man is a *serio-comic* animal" (J. H. Robinson's "Mind in the Making," iv. 9). II. *n.* A serio-comic performer; an actor of serio-comic rôles; a singer of serio-comic songs.—**se″ri-o-com'i-cal**, *a.* Serio-comic.—**se″ri-o-com'i-cal-ly**, *adv.*

se-ri-ous (sē'ri-us), *a.* [OF. *serieux* (F. *sérieux*), < ML. *seriosus*, for L. *serius*, grave, earnest, serious.] Characterized by earnestness of purpose or thought, as persons, or their actions, etc.; of grave or solemn disposition or character; not light or superficial; often, being in earnest, or not trifling or jesting; not comic or humorous, as a play, a rôle, or an actor; also, earnestly or solemnly religious, as persons (sometimes taken as a mere cant expression: as, "And Peter Bell, when he had been With fresh-imported Hell-fire warmed, Grew *serious*," Shelley's "Peter Bell the Third," i. 1); also, of grave aspect (as, "a shallow brain behind a *serious* mask": Cowper's "Conversation," 297); also, demanding earnest

thought or application (as, *serious* reading; a *serious* occupation); also, weighty or important (as, a *serious* matter; *serious* reasons against a project); considerable in amount or extent (as, "He . . . *serious* sums in healing misery spent," Crabbe's "Borough," xiii.; *serious* damage); giving cause for apprehension, grave, or critical (as, a *serious* illness; "We live in *serious* times," Cooper's "Two Admirals," xi.). —**se'ri-ous-ly**, *adv.*—**se'ri-ous-ness**, *n.*

ser-jeant (sär'jẹnt), etc. See *sergeant*, etc.

ser-mon (sėr'mọn), *n.* [OF. F. *sermon*, < L. *sermo(n-)*, talk, discourse.] Talk† or discourse†; also, a discourse for the purpose of religious instruction or exhortation, esp. one based on a text of Scripture and delivered from a pulpit; hence, any similar serious discourse; a serious exhortation.— **Sermon on the Mount**, the discourse delivered by Christ and recorded in Mat. v.-vii. and Luke vi.—**ser-mon-esque'** (-esk'), *a.* [See -*esque*.] In the style or manner of a sermon. —**ser'mon-et, ser-mon-ette'** (-et'), *n.* [See -*et* and -*ette*.] A short sermon.—**ser-mon'ic, ser-mon'i-cal** (-mon'ik, -i-kạl), *a.* Pertaining to, of the nature of, or resembling a sermon.—**ser-mon'i-cal-ly**, *adv.*—**ser'mon-ize** (-īz), *v.*; -*ized*, -*izing*. I. *intr.* To deliver or compose a sermon; hence, to give serious exhortation, or discourse seriously (as, "In sailor fashion roughly *sermonizing* On providence and trust in Heaven": Tennyson's "Enoch Arden," 204). II. *tr.* To preach a sermon to; hence, to give serious exhortation to, or lecture (as, "I see no right you have to *sermonize* me": C. Brontë's "Villette," ix.); also, to bring into a particular condition by preaching.—**ser'mon-iz-er** (-ī-zėr), *n.*

se-ro- (sē'rọ-). Form of *serum* used in combination, as in *seromucous* (composed of both serum and mucus), *serovaccination*.

se-rol-o-gy (sẹ-rol'ọ-ji), *n.* [See *sero-* and -*logy*.] The scientific study of the serum of the blood.—**se-ro-log-i-cal** (sē-rọ-loj'i-kạl), *a.*—**se-rol'o-gist**, *n.*

se-ros-i-ty (sẹ-ros'i-ti), *n.*; pl. -*ties* (-tiz). The state of being serous or watery; also, a serous or watery fluid; serum.

se-ro-ther-a-py (sē-rọ-ther'ạ-pi), *n.* [See *sero-*.] Same as *serumtherapy*.

se-rot-i-nal, se-rot-i-nous (sẹ-rot'i-nạl, -nus), *a.* [See *serotine*.] In *bot.*, appearing or flowering late in the season.

ser-o-tine (ser'ọ-tin or -tīn), *a.* [L. *serotinus*, < *sero*, adv., late, < *serus*, adj., late.] Late, as in beginning or appearing; late in the day; in *bot.*, serotinal. [Now rare.]

se-rous (sē'rus), *a.* [F. *séreux*, < L. *serum*, E. *serum*.] Of the nature of or resembling serum; containing serum; secreting serum; pertaining to or characterized by serum.— **serous fluid**, any of various animal liquids resembling blood-serum, as the fluids of the serous membranes.— **serous membrane**, any of various thin membranes, as the peritoneum, which line certain cavities of the body and exude a serous fluid.

ser-ow (ser'ō), *n.* [Native name.] Any of the Asiatic goatlike antelopes constituting the genus *Nemorhædus*, as *N. bubalinus* (or *thar*), a native of the Himalayas.

ser-pent (sėr'pẹnt). [OF. F. *serpent*, < L. *serpens* (*serpent-*), creeping thing, serpent, orig. ppr. of *serpere*, creep, crawl, akin to Gr. ἕρπειν, Skt. *sarp-*, creep, *sarpa*, serpent: cf. *herpes* and *herpetology*.] I. *n.* A snake, esp. a large one; an ophidian reptile; also, Satan, or the devil (cf. Gen. iii. 1-5); fig., a wily, treacherous, or malicious person; also, a kind of firework which burns with serpentine motion or flame; also, an old wooden musical wind-instrument of serpentine form and deep tone (as, "The fiddles finished off with a screech, and the *serpent* emitted a last note that nearly lifted the roof": Hardy's "Return of the Native," ii. 5); also [*cap.*], in *astron.*, the constellation Serpens. II. *a.* Serpent-like; serpentine or winding.—**ser'pent**, *v. i.* To move like a serpent; wind.

Forms of Serpent. — The left-hand figure is an early form of the instrument.

ser-pen-ta-ri-a (sėr-pẹn-tā'ri-ä), *n.* [LL., < L. *serpens*, E. *serpent*.] The medicinal rhizome and rootlets of the Virginia snakeroot (see *snake-root*); also, the plant itself.

Ser-pent=bear-er (sėr'pent-bãr"ėr), *n.* In *astron.*, the constellation Ophiuchus, which is represented as a man holding in his hands a serpent (the representation of the constellation Serpens: see *serpent, n.*).

ser-pen-ti-form (sėr-pen'ti-fôrm), *a.* [L. *serpens* (*serpent-*), serpent: see *-form.*] Having the form of a serpent; serpent-like.

ser-pen-tine (sėr'pen-tīn or -tin). [OF. F. *serpentin*, adj. (as n., F. *serpentine*, the mineral), < LL. *serpentinus*, of a serpent, < L. *serpens*: see *serpent.*] **I.** *a.* Of, pertaining to, or resembling a serpent; also, having the qualities of a serpent; subtle, wily, or cunning; treacherous; also, moving in a wind-

A Serpentiform Mexican Lizard (*Chirotes canaliculatus*).

ing course or having a winding form; tortuous; winding. **II.** *n.* A mineral consisting chiefly of a hydrous silicate of magnesium, usually green and sometimes spotted like a serpent's skin, occurring in many varieties, from the more or less translucent ('noble' or 'precious serpentine') to the impure massive forms ('common serpentine') occurring as rock and extensively used (often under the name of 'serpentine marble') for architectural and decorative purposes (see *verd-antique*);

also, a kind of cannon formerly in use; also, something serpentine or winding; a winding path; a winding sheet of water (as [*cap.*, pron. sėr'pen-tīn] the artificial lake in Hyde Park and Kensington Gardens,

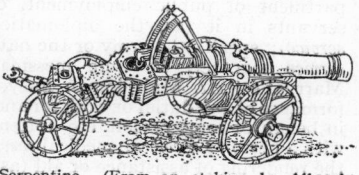

Serpentine. (From an etching by Albrecht Dürer.)

London).—**ser'pen-tine**, *v. i.* or *t.*; *-tined, -tining.* To wind like a serpent: as, "She saw a . . . figure *serpentining* upward by one of the little paths" (Hardy's "Return of the Native," ii. 7).—**ser'pen-ti-nous** (-tĭ-nus), *a.* Of the nature of, resembling, or pertaining to serpentine.

ser-pent-ry (sėr'pent-ri), *n.* Serpents collectively.

ser-pi-go (sėr-pī'gō), *n.* [ML. *serpigo* (*serpigin-*), < L. *serpere*, creep: see *serpent.*] In *pathol.*, a creeping or spreading skin-disease, as ringworm.—**ser-pig'i-nous** (-pij'i-nus), *a.*

ser-ra-dil-la, ser-ra-del-la (ser-a-dil'ä, -del'ä), *n.* [Sp. *serradilla* (Pg. *serradela*), dim. < *serrado*, < L. *serratus*, E. *serrate.*] A fabaceous plant, *Ornithopus sativus*, a species of bird's-foot, cultivated in Europe for forage, etc.

ser-ra-noid (ser'a-noid). [NL. *Serranus*, genus of fishes, < L. *serra*, saw, saw-fish: see *-oid.*] **I.** *a.* Belonging to the *Serranidæ*, a family of acanthopterygian fishes including the sea-bass, and groupers, jewfishes, etc. **II.** *n.* A serranoid fish.

ser-rate (ser'āt), *a.* [L. *serratus*, < *serra*, saw: cf. *sierra.*] Notched like the edge of a saw; toothed; specif., of a leaf, having small, sharp marginal teeth pointing toward the apex (cf. *dentate*). —**ser'rate**, *v. t.*; *-rated, -rating.* To render serrate; notch like a saw. —**ser-rat-ed** (ser'ā-ted), *p. a.* Serrate; notched like a saw.—**ser-ra-tion** (se-rā'shon), *n.* Serrated condition or form; also, a serrated edge or formation; also, one of the series of notches or teeth of such an edge or formation. Also **ser-ra-ture** (ser'a-tūr).

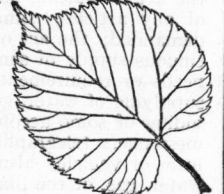

Serrate Leaf of American Linden (*Tilia americana*).

ser-re-file (ser'e-fīl), *n.* [F. *serre-file*, < *serrer*, close up (see *serry*), + *file*, E. *file*[3].] *Milit.*, any of the men forming a line behind the last regular rank at the rear of a body of troops.

ser-ri-corn (ser'i-kôrn). [NL. *serricornis*, < L. *serra*, saw, + *cornu*, horn.] **I.** *a.* Having serrate antennæ; belonging to the *Serricornia*, a group of beetles (including the ordinary fireflies) whose antennæ are usually serrate. **II.** *n.* A serricorn beetle.

ser-ried (ser'id), *p. a.* [See *serry.*] Crowded closely together, or in close order, as ranks or files of armed men, or objects likened to these: as, "On every side rose up the *serried* ranks of pine-trees" (Bret Harte's "Romance of Madroño Hollow").

1. A Serricorn Beetle (an elater). 2, 3. Enlarged Antennæ of other Serricorns.

ser-ri-form (ser'i-fôrm), *a.* [L. *serra*, saw: see *-form.*] Resembling a saw; serrate.

ser-ru-late (ser'ö-lāt), *a.* [NL. *serrulatus*, < L. *serrula*, dim. of *serra*, saw.] Finely or minutely serrate, as a leaf. Also **ser'ru-lat-ed** (-lā-ted).—**ser-ru-la'tion** (-lā'shon), *n.* Serrulate condition or form; also, a fine or minute serration.

ser-ry (ser'i), *v.*; *-ried, -rying.* [For earlier *serr*, < F. *serrer*, close up, press close, < LL. *serare*, to bar, bolt, < L. *sera*, bar for fastening a door: cf. *sear*[2], *seraglio*, and *serrefile*.] **I.** *tr.* To cause to stand closely together, or in close order, as ranks or files of armed men: as, "The little band of devoted cavaliers about the king *serried* their forces" (Irving's "Conquest of Granada," xvi.). **II.** *intr.* To crowd closely together, as ranks or files of men: as, the troops *serried* close together; "High shoulders, low shoulders . . . Round, square, and angular, *serry* and shove" (Henley's "In Hospital," xi.).

ser-tu-la-ri-an (sėr-tṳ-lā'ri-an). [NL. *Sertularia* (see def.), < L. *sertula*, dim. of *serta*, garland, prop. pp. fem. of *serere*, join: cf. *series.*] **I.** *a.* Belonging or pertaining to the genus *Sertularia*, or to the family *Sertulariidæ*, comprising hydromedusæ which form arborescent colonies. **II.** *n.* A sertularian hydromedusa.

se-rum (sē'rum), *n.*; pl. *-rums* or *-ra* (-rä). [L., whey, watery fluid, serum.] The whey of milk (also called, as L., *serum lactis*, 'serum of milk'); also, the clear, pale-yellow liquid which separates from the clot in the coagulation of blood ('blood-serum'); also, a fluid of this kind obtained from the blood of an animal which has been rendered immune to some disease by inoculation, used as an antitoxic or therapeutic agent; also, any watery animal fluid.—**se-rum-ther'a-py** (-ther'a-pi), *n.* [See *therapy.*] The treatment of disease by the injection of the serum of immunized animals.

A Sertularian.

serv-a-ble (sėr'va-bl), *a.* That may be served.

ser-val (sėr'val), *n.* [F. *serval*, for Pg. *lobo cerval*, lynx, < L. *lupus*, wolf, + *cervus*, deer.] An African quadruped, *Felis serval*, of the cat family, having a tawny coat spotted with black.

ser-vant (sėr'vant), *n.* [OF. *servant* (F. *servante*, fem.), servant, prop. ppr. of *servir*, < L. *servire*, E. *serve.*] A person of either sex who is under obligation to perform certain duties

Serval.

for, or to obey the orders of, another or others, usually in return for wages or salary; esp., such a person employed in the performance of certain domestic duties, etc.; a household or personal attendant; also, a bondman or bondwoman; a slave; also, a professed lover†; also, one devoted to any service, esp. that of God; also, fig., something affording useful aid (as, "In the conquest of the west the backwoods axe . . . was a *servant* hardly standing second even to the rifle": Roosevelt's "Winning of the West," i. 5).—**your (humble, obedient,** etc.) **servant,** a phrase of courtesy, now purely formal, used esp. in subscribing a letter.—**ser′vant-less,** *a.* Without a servant.—**ser′vant-ship,** *n.* The condition of being a servant.

serve (sėrv), *v.*; *served, serving.* [OF. F. *servir,* < L. *servire,* be a slave or servant, serve, < *servus,* slave, servant: cf. *serf, sergeant, servant, service*[2], *deserve,* and *subserve.*] **I.** *intr.* To perform domestic duties for another; act as a servant; also, to wait at table; hand food to guests; also, to attend to customers in a shop; also, to perform any duties for others; render assistance; go through a term of service; do duty as a soldier or sailor; perform official duty, as on a jury; also, to have a definite use or function; admit of being used for a particular purpose; be of use; also, to answer the purpose, or suffice (as, "Short greeting *serves* in time of strife": Scott's "Marmion," vi. 24); also, to be favorable, suitable, or convenient, as wind, weather, time, etc. (as, "We must take the current when it *serves,* Or lose our ventures": Shakspere's "Julius Cæsar," iv. 3. 223); also, in *tennis,* etc., to put the ball in play; also, *eccles.,* to act as server. **II.** *tr.* To attend or wait upon; be a servant to; be in the service of; work for; also, to go through (a term of service, or of imprisonment); also, to render assistance or service to (as, "Cranmer rose into favour by *serving* Henry in the disgraceful affair of his first divorce": Macaulay's "Essays," Hallam); render obedience or homage to (God, a sovereign, etc.); be a professed lover of†; gratify (desire, etc.); regulate one's conduct in accordance with the demands of (the time); render active service to (a king, commander, etc.) in the army or navy; perform the duties of (an office, etc.); assist at or take part in (a function, etc.); also, to be subservient or subordinate to (as, "In the soul Are many lesser faculties that *serve* Reason as chief": Milton's "Paradise Lost," v. 101); also, to be useful or of service to; answer the requirements of; also, to contribute or conduce to, or promote (as, "Christianity *served* these ends and purposes": J. Butler's "Analogy of Religion," ii. 1); also, to be favorable to (as, "If fortune *serve* me, I'll requite this kindness": Shakspere's "3 Henry VI.," iv. 7. 78); also, to satisfy or content (as, "He took such a fancy to me, that nothing would *serve* him but I must be his guest": Malkin's tr. Le Sage's "Gil Blas," iii. 1); suit or fit, as clothes do (now Sc.); also, to prompt or encourage to do something† (as, "Certainly my conscience will *serve* me to run from this Jew my master": Shakspere's "Merchant of Venice," ii. 2. 1); also, to wait upon at table; set food before; help to food; set food on (a table); also, to wait on or supply (a customer in a shop); supply with something necessary; provide with a regular or continuous supply of something; also, to set (food) on a table or before a person (as, "Soup is *served*": G. B. Shaw's "You Never Can Tell," ii.); deal out or distribute (often with *out*: as, "He . . . *served* it [water] out in a gourd," G. W. Cable's "John March, Southerner," xix.; to *serve* out ammunition); supply or furnish, or provide a regular or continuous supply of (as, "the pump . . . that *serves* water to his garden," Evelyn's "Diary," Oct. 25, 1695; to *serve* milk to a community); play or do (one a trick, turn, etc.: as, "He had before *served* me a scurvy trick," Swift's "Gulliver's Travels," ii. 3; he *served* me a good turn); also, to treat in a specified manner (as, "I could . . . deprive him of all his possessions and *serve* him as he *served* me," W. H. Hudson's "Green Mansions," xix.; it *serves* him right, that is, it gives him his deserts, esp. for folly or wrong-doing); also, to operate or work (a gun, etc.); also, of a male animal, to cover (the female); in *tennis,* etc., to put (the ball) in play; *naut.,* etc., to bind or wind (a rope, etc.) with small cord or the like, as to strengthen or protect it; in *law,* to make legal delivery of (a process or writ); present (a person) with a writ.—**serve,** *n.* The act, manner, or right of serving, as in tennis or handball: as, "He had beaten Inchcape Jones at tennis, with a nasty, unsporting *serve*" (Sinclair Lewis's "Arrowsmith," xxxi.).—**serv′er,** *n.* One who serves; the player who puts the ball in play in tennis, etc.; that which serves or is used in serving, as a salver; *eccles.,* an attendant on the priest at mass, who arranges the altar, makes the responses, etc.

Ser-vi-an (sėr′vi-an), *a.* and *n.* Same as *Serbian.*

ser-vice[1] (sėr′vis), *n.* [From *serves,* pl. of obs. *serve,* < AS. *syrfe,* < L. *sorbus,* service-tree: cf. *sorb*[1].] A service-tree, esp. the European tree *Sorbus domestica.*

ser-vice[2] (sėr′vis), *n.* [OF. *servise* (F. *service*), < L. *servitium,* < *servus,* slave, servant.] The condition of one who or that which serves; occupation or employment as a servant (as, to go into or be in *service*); employment in any duties or work for another or others, a government, etc. (as, to be in the *service* of a banking house); also, the work of one who serves; performance of duties as a servant; feudal allegiance†; a duty owed by a feudal tenant to his lord; the devotion or suit of a lover (as, "So well he wood her . . . With humble *service,* and with daily sute," Spenser's "Faerie Queene," vi. 10. 38: archaic); deferential regard or respect (in complimentary expressions: as, "Sir, my *service* to you," Goldsmith's "She Stoops to Conquer," ii.: archaic); also, in religious use, the serving of God by obedience, piety, etc. (as, "Our voluntary *service* he requires": Milton's "Paradise Lost," v. 529); public religious worship according to prescribed form and order (as, divine *service*); a celebration of public worship; a ritual or form prescribed for public worship or for some particular occasion (as, the marriage *service*); a musical setting of those portions of a liturgy which are sung; also, the serving of a sovereign, state, or government in some official capacity; the duty or work of public servants; specif., military or naval duty; the performance of such duty; participation in warfare; sometimes, a military or naval operation (obs. or rare: as, "Alexander the Great . . . received letters out of Greece, of some fights and *services* there," Bacon's "Advancement of Learning," i. 8. 1); also, a department of public employment, or the body of public servants in it (as, the diplomatic *service;* the customs *service*); specif., the army or the navy (as, "We entered the *service* together, we were messmates for many years": Marryat's "Mr. Midshipman Easy," viii.); also, the performance of any duties or work for another or others; activity in behalf of some person, etc. (often in *pl.*: as, to dispense with a person's *services;* medical *services*); hence, in general, the rendering of assistance or aid (as, to do good *service* in a cause); helpful activity for the advantage or welfare of others (as, "Myriads of souls were born again to ideas of *service* and sacrifice in those tremendous days": H. G. Wells's "Soul of a Bishop," iii.); an act of helpful activity or friendly assistance (as, "I prithee, Lucio, do me this kind *service*": Shakspere's "Measure for Measure," i. 2. 181); the affording of assistance or useful aid by something, or the work which it does (as, "I'll have the cudgel hallowed and hung o'er the altar; it hath done meritorious *service,*" Shakspere's "Merry Wives of Windsor," iv. 2. 218; these goods will give good *service*); assistance or use (in the phrase 'of service': as, "I hope you'll let me be of *service* to you in getting to a hotel," Howells's "Chance Acquaintance," iv.; "Analogy is . . . of great *service* in answering those objections," J. Butler's "Analogy of Religion," i. 7); also, often, the act or manner of waiting at table, or serving food to guests; that which is served for a meal, the food set before a person, or a portion of food (now rare); a course served at table†; a set of dishes, etc., required for a particular use (as, a tea *service;* "Deslauriers was arranging upon the ground our *service* of tin cups and plates," Parkman's "Oregon Trail," ii.); hence, a set of certain other articles, as of vessels for an altar; also, the act of waiting on customers, etc.; also, the supplying of any articles, commodities, activities, etc., required or demanded; the act or work of providing a regular or continuous supply of something, or of supplying regularly the needs or requirements of persons or the community; the supplying of water, gas, or the like to the public; the providing of some accommodation required by the public, as messengers, telegraphs, or telephones, or conveyance by some form of vehicle; also, the system of pipes, etc., by which water, gas, or the like is supplied; the organized system of apparatus, appliances, employees, etc., for supplying some accommodation required by the public; also, the covering of a female animal by the male; in *tennis,* etc., the act or manner of putting the ball in play; the ball as put in play; *naut.,* etc., small cord or the like wound about a rope, etc., as for strengthening or protection; in *law,* the serving of a process or writ upon a person.—**at one's service,** ready to serve one or obey one's commands (formerly much used elliptically as a phrase of civility: as, "My name is Matthew Bramble, *at your service,*" Smollett's "Humphry Clinker," July 13); also, at one's disposal, or ready for one's use, as things.—**ser′vice²,** *v. t.*; -viced, -vicing. To make fit for service, or restore to condition for service: as, to *service* the brakes or the generator of an automobile.

ser-vice-a-ble (sẻr′vis-ạ-bl), *a.* [OF. *servisable.*] Disposed to be of service, or diligent or attentive in serving (archaic: as, "The footmen might be aptly compared to the waiters of a tavern, if they were more *serviceable* and less rapacious," Smollett's "Humphry Clinker," June 26); also, being of service, or useful (as, "You are useful to Mrs. Gradgrind, and . . . you are *serviceable* in the family also": Dickens's "Hard Times," i. 14); also, capable of doing good service, or well suited for use (as, a *serviceable* horse; "his gold-headed cane . . . a *serviceable* staff of dark, polished wood," Hawthorne's "House of the Seven Gables," iv.; "It's a decent *serviceable* chair," W. De Morgan's "Alice-for-Short," xiv.); often, admitting of long or hard use, or durable, as materials, clothing, etc.—**ser″vice-a-bil′i-ty** (-bil′i-ti), **ser′vice-a-ble-ness,** *n.*—**ser′vice-a-bly,** *adv.*

ser-vice-ber-ry (sẻr′vis-ber″i), *n.*; pl. -berries (-iz). The fruit of any service-tree; also, a North American malaceous shrub or small tree, *Amelanchier canadensis,* with a berry-like fruit; the shad-bush or June-berry; any of various other species of *Amelanchier.*

ser-vice=book (sẻr′-vis-bùk), *n.* A book containing forms for divine service, as the Book of Common Prayer of the Anglican churches.

ser-vice=plate (sẻr′-vis-plāt), *n.* A kind of large, ornamental plate used, one at each place, on a formally arranged table: intended for decorative effect, and replaced by (or sometimes, in some

Service-berry (*Amelanchier canadensis*).— 1. branch with flowers; 2, branch with fruit; *a,* flower; *b,* fruit.

courses, remaining under) plates holding food during the course of the meal.

ser-vice=sta-tion (sẻr′vis-stā″shọn), *n.* A station or establishment for the accommodation of those requiring service of some kind, as the supplying of parts for or the making of repairs on automobiles, radio apparatus, etc.

ser-vice=tree (sẻr′vis-trē), *n.* [See *service¹.*] A European malaceous tree, *Sorbus domestica,* bearing a small, acid fruit that is edible when overripe, or the related European tree, *S. torminalis* (the 'wild service-tree'), with similar fruit; a checker-tree; also, the North American service-berry, *Amelanchier canadensis,* or some related species.

ser-vi-dor (sẻr′vi-dôr), *n.* [Coined word.] A specially devised cabinet, built usually in the entrance-door of a guest-room, as in modern hotels, clubs, etc., intended to afford a mechanically safeguarded passage through which the occupant of the room may be served in some way (as with respect to mail, telegrams, ice-water, laundry, the pressing of clothes, etc.) without needless intrusion by servants. [Proprietary name.]—**ser′vi-dor,** *v. t.* To serve through a servidor.

ser-vi-ent (sẻr′vi-ẹnt), *a.* [L. *serviens* (*servient-*), ppr. of *servire,* E. *serve.*] Subordinate. [Now chiefly legal.]— **servient tenement,** in *law,* a tenement which is subject to a servitude or easement in favor of a dominant tenement.

ser-vi-ette (sẻr-vi-et′, F. ser-vyet), *n.* [F., appar. < *servir,* E. *serve.*] A napkin, as for use at table: as, "His *serviette*

was tucked under his chin" (Arnold Bennett's "Old Wives' Tale," iv. 1).

ser-vile (sẻr′vil or, chiefly Brit., -vīl). [L. *servilis,* < *servus,* slave, servant.] **I.** *a.* Of, pertaining to, or connected with slaves (as, the *servile* condition; a *servile* insurrection; the *servile* wars of ancient Rome, against insurgent slaves); being in slavery (as, the *servile* class); politically enslaved, oppressed, or in subjection, as a people (archaic); also, proper to or customary for slaves (as, "*servile* food": Milton's "Samson Agonistes," 574); hence, of work, etc., laborious, mechanical, common, or menial (as, "On the first day shall be an holy convocation: ye shall do no *servile* work therein," Lev. xxiii. 35; "The squire's employment . . . was the *servile* task of cleaning Sir Aymer's arms," Scott's "Castle Dangerous," v.); also, characteristic of, befitting, or suggesting a slave, or slavish, abject, or ignoble (as, *servile* obedience or humility; *servile* fear); often, slavishly deferential or obsequious, as actions, speech, manner, etc., or persons (as, "I did not . . . aim at gaining his favor by paying any *servile* respect to him," B. Franklin's "Autobiography," vi.; *servile* complaisance; *servile* courtiers or flatterers); yielding slavishly, or truckling (*to:* as, judges *servile* to public opinion; "*servile* to a shrewish tongue," Tennyson's "Locksley Hall," 42); completely subject† (*to:* as, "A breath thou [life] art, *Servile* to all the skyey influences," Shakspere's "Measure for Measure," iii. 1. 9); also, slavishly faithful or exact, as imitation, reproduction, translation, etc., or an imitator, etc.; devoid of originality; in *philol.,* merely subsidiary or auxiliary, as a letter or a particle. **II.** *n.* A servile person; in *philol.,* a servile letter or particle.— **ser′vile-ly,** *adv.*—**ser′vile-ness,** *n.*—**ser-vil′i-ty** (-vil′i-ti), *n.* The state or character of being servile; servile attitude, spirit, or behavior; servile deference or submission.

serv-ing (sẻr′ving), *n.* The act of one who or that which serves; *naut.,* material used for serving a rope, etc.

Ser-vite (sẻr′vīt), *n.* [ML. *Servitæ,* pl., < L. *servus,* slave, servant.] A monk or nun of the mendicant order of "Servants of Mary," founded in Italy in 1233.

ser-vi-tor (sẻr′vi-tọr), *n.* [OF. *servitor* (F. *serviteur*), < LL. *servitor,* < L. *servire,* E. *serve.*] A man-servant (archaic: as, "There sat the lifelong creature of the house, Loyal, the dumb old *servitor,*" Tennyson's "Lancelot and Elaine," 1137); in general, one who serves, or is in or at the service of another, or a servant, attendant, or adherent (archaic: as, "My noble queen . . . henceforth I am thy true *servitor,*" Shakspere's "3 Henry VI.," iii. 3. 196); a lover (archaic); a soldier†; also, formerly, at Oxford University, an undergraduate supported in part by college funds and required to wait at table on the fellows and gentlemen commoners (as, "In moods of humility I can be a Sizar, or a *Servitor*": Lamb's "Oxford in the Vacation").—**ser-vi-to′ri-al** (-tō′ri-ạl), *a.*—**ser′vi-tor-ship,** *n.*—**ser′vi-tress,** *n.* A female servant or attendant.

ser-vi-tude (sẻr′vi-tūd), *n.* [OF. F. *servitude,* < L. *servitudo,* < *servus,* slave, servant.] The condition of being a slave; slavery, bondage, or serfdom; any condition of slavish, oppressive, or ignoble subjection (as, political *servitude*; intellectual *servitude*; moral *servitude,* as of those under the sway of the passions); complete subjection to the authority or influence of anything (as, the *servitude* of duty or of love); also, the condition or work of a servant or of one serving, or service (chiefly archaic: as, "Besides my daylight *servitude,* I served over again all night in my sleep," Lamb's "Superannuated Man"); specif., compulsory service or labor as a punishment for criminals (as, penal *servitude*); also, slaves or servants collectively† (as, "After him a cumbrous train Of herds and flocks, and numerous *servitude*": Milton's "Paradise Lost," xii. 132); in *law,* the condition of property subject to some right of enjoyment possessed by another than its owner or attaching to some other property; such a right of enjoyment.

Ser-vo- (sẻr′vọ-). Same as *Serbo-.*

ser-vo=mo-tor (sẻr″vọ-mō′tọr), *n.* [F. *servo-moteur,* < L. *servus,* slave, servant, + *motor,* E. *motor.*] In *mach.,* an auxiliary motor, as one for moving the reversing gear of a marine engine.

ses-a-me (ses′ạ-mē), *n.* [L. *sesamum, sesama,* < Gr. σησαμον, σησάμη.] A tropical herbaceous plant, *Sesamum* *indicum*, whose small oval seeds are edible and yield an oil (see *benne*); also, the seeds themselves; also, same as *open sesame.* **—open sesame.** See entry *open sesame.*—**ses′a-moid.** [Gr. σησαμοειδής: see *-oid*.] **I.** *a.* Shaped like a sesame-seed, as certain small, nodular bones and cartilages. **II.** *n.* A sesamoid bone or cartilage.—**ses′a-mum** (-mum), *n.* [L.] Sesame.

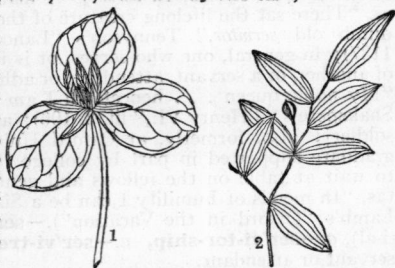

Sesame (*Sesamum indicum*).

sesqui-. [L. *sesqui-, sesque-,* contr. < *semis,* half, + *-que,* and: cf. *semi-*.] A prefix meaning 'and a half more,' or implying a ratio of 1½ to 1 (or 3 to 2), as in *sesquicentennial, sesquioxide.*

ses-qui-cen-ten-ni-al (ses″kwi-sen-ten′i-al). [See *sesqui-*.] **I.** *a.* Pertaining to, or marking the completion of, a period of a century and a half, or 150 years. **II.** *n.* A 150th anniversary, or its celebration.

ses-qui-ox-ide (ses-kwi-ok′sīd or -sid), *n.* [See *sesqui-*.] In *chem.,* an oxide containing three atoms or equivalents of oxygen to two of the other element or of some radical.

ses-qui-ped-al (ses′kwi-ped-al or ses-quip′ē-dal), *a.* Same as *sesquipedalian.*

ses-qui-pe-da-lian (ses″kwi-pē-dā′lian). [L. *sesquipedalis* (in neut. pl., *sesquipedalia verba,* words a foot and a half long: Horace's "Ars Poetica," 97), < *sesqui-* (see *sesqui-*) + *pes* (*ped-*), foot.] **I.** *a.* Measuring a foot and a half; hence, of words or expressions, very long; containing many syllables; of persons, given to using long words (as, "The words gathered size like snowballs, and towards the end of her letter Miss Jenkyns used to become quite *sesquipedalian*": Mrs. Gaskell's "Cranford," v.). **II.** *n.* A sesquipedalian word.—**ses″qui-pe-da′lian-ism,** *n.* The practice of using long words.

ses-sile (ses′il), *a.* [L. *sessilis,* sitting, low, < *sedere,* sit: see *see[1]*.] In *bot., zoöl.,* etc., attached by the base, or without any distinct projecting support, as a leaf issuing directly from the stem without a petiole or as a flower without a peduncle, or as certain crustaceans (see *acornshell* and *barnacle[1]*), or as parts or organs (*cf. stalk-eyed*).

1. Sessile Flower of Trillium (*Trillium sessile*). 2. Sessile Leaves of Bellwort (*Uvularia sessilifolia*).

ses-sion (sesh′on), *n.* [OF. F. *session,* < L. *sessio*(*n*-), a sitting, session, < *sedere,* sit: see *see[1]*.] The act of sitting, or the state or posture of being seated (now rare: as, "Vivien . . . Leapt from her *session* on his lap, and stood," Tennyson's "Merlin and Vivien," 842); also, the sitting together of a court, council, legislature, or the like, for conference or the transaction of business (as, Congress is now in *session*); a single continuous sitting, or period of sitting, of persons assembled for conference, business, or the like; a single continuous course or period of lessons, study, etc., in the work of a day at school (as, a school day consisting of one *session,* or of a morning and an afternoon *session*); a continuous series of sittings or meetings of a court, legislature, or the like, or the period or term during which such a series is held; a portion of the year during which instruction is given at a college or the like; specif., *pl.,* the sittings or a sitting of justices in court (as, *sessions* of the peace, in Great Britain, periodical sittings held by justices of the peace, as petty, special, or general *sessions,* or quarter-*sessions*; courts of special or of general *sessions,* in the U. S., local courts dealing esp. with lesser criminal offenses); the court so held; also, *sing.,* the lowest court in Presbyterian churches, composed of the pastor and the lay or ruling elders of the local

church.—**Court of Session,** the supreme civil tribunal of Scotland, established in 1532.—**ses′sion-al,** *a.*

ses-terce (ses′tèrs), *n.* [L. *sestertius,* prop. adj., 'two and a half,' < *semis,* half, + *tertius,* third.] An ancient Roman coin (orig. equivalent to 2½ asses, later to 4 asses) equal to a quarter of a denarius.—**ses-ter′ti-um** (-tèr′shi-um), *n.*; pl. *-tia* (-shi-ä). [L.] An ancient Roman money of account equal to a thousand sesterces.—**ses-ter′ti-us** (-shi-us), *n.*; pl. *-tii* (-shi-ī). A sesterce.

Obverse.   Reverse.
Sesterce (silver). — British Museum.

ses-tet (ses-tet′), *n.* [It. *sestetto,* dim. < *sesto,* < L. *sextus,* sixth, < *sex,* six: cf. *sextet.*] A musical sextet; also, the last six lines of a sonnet.

ses-ti-na (ses-tē′nä), *n.* [It., < *sesto,* sixth: see *sestet.*] A poem of six six-line stanzas and a three-line envoy, orig. without rime, in which each stanza repeats the end-words of the lines of the first stanza, but in different order, the envoy using the six words again, three in the middle of the lines and three at the end. Also **ses-tine′** (-tēn′).

set (set), *v. t.;* *set, setting.* [AS. *settan* = D. *zetten* = G. *setzen* = Icel. *setja* = Goth. *satjan,* set, lit. 'cause to sit'; causative of the verb (AS. *sittan,* etc.) represented by E. *sit.*] To cause to sit; seat; often, to put (a hen) to sit on eggs to hatch them; hence, to place (eggs) under a hen or in an incubator; also, to put in a particular or the proper place or position; place; often, to put into the ground to grow, as young plants; hence, to plant (ground), as with young trees; also, to stake or wager (archaic); also, to put on paper or the like, as in writing (usually with *down*); affix to a document, as one's signature; give an account, esp. an orderly or detailed account, of (with *forth*); also, to put into some condition or relation (as, to *set* a thing on fire; to *set* one free; to *set* one's heart on a thing; one thing *sets* another off to advantage by contrast); put (a price or value) upon something; also, to post, station, or appoint for the purpose of performing some duty (as, "I *set* my dog to guard it [land with a growing crop] in the night," Defoe's "Robinson Crusoe," i. 8; to *set* spies on a person); fix, appoint, or ordain (as, "Where bounds were *set* To darkness," Milton's "Paradise Lost," iii. 538; to *set* a time); present or fix for others to follow (as, to *set* an example; to *set* a fashion; to *set* the pace); prescribe or assign, as a task; lease or let (now prov. Eng. and Sc.: as, "He *set* his own house to Thomas Treddles the weaver," Galt's "Annals of the Parish," xxviii.); also, to put in the proper position, order, or condition for use (as, to *set* a trap, a table, or a stage); adjust or arrange; spread (sails) so as to catch the wind (hence, to *set* sail, to start on a voyage); also, to fix or mount (a gem, etc.) in gold or the like; place in a frame or setting; hence, to adorn with or as with precious stones; stud, strew, or cover with a number of objects (as, "The old knight . . . bid me observe how thick the city was *set* with churches": Addison, in "Spectator," 383); also, to give a fine edge to (a razor, etc.); incline the teeth of (a saw) alternately to the right and the left in order that the kerf may be wider than the blade; also, to adjust according to a standard (as, to *set* a clock, so that it will indicate the correct time); also, to place in thought or estimation (as, to *set* too early a date upon an occurrence; "Dante shall give Fame leave to *set* thee higher Than his Casella," Milton's "Sonnets," To H. Lawes); fix the value of at a certain amount or rate (as, "There shall no figure [statue] at such rate be *set* As that of true and faithful Juliet": Shakspere's "Romeo and Juliet," v. 3. 301); put (much, little, store, etc.) as the measure of esteem of a person or thing (used in certain phrases: as, to *set* little by a person; to *set* great store by a thing); also, to put into a fixed, rigid, or settled state, as the countenance, the muscles, or the mind; cause (something, as mortar) to become firm or hard; pose, perplex, or embarrass (now rare); also, to cause to take a particular direction; convey or transport (now rare: as, to *set* one across a ferry); propel by means of a pole, as a boat; also, to put to a duty, undertaking, etc. (as, "one *set* to watch the manners and behaviour of my countrymen," Addison in "Spectator," 435; "All my mind was *set* Serious to learn and know," Milton's "Paradise Regained," i. 202); encourage to an attack, pursuit, etc.

(esp. with *on* or *upon*: as, "It's good luck, if the house-dog be not *set* upon one," R. Graves's "Spiritual Quixote," ii. 3); cause to be hostile or antagonistic (with *against*: as, "He could . . . tell people his side of it, and *set* 'em against me," Tarkington's "Alice Adams," xviii.); also, of a hunting-dog, to indicate the position of (game) by standing stiffly and pointing with the muzzle; in *printing*, to arrange (type) in the order required for printing from; put together types corresponding to (words, etc.); in *music*, to fit, as words to music; arrange for musical performance; arrange (music) for certain voices or instruments; in *surg.*, to put (a broken or dislocated bone) in a position suitable for restoration to the normal condition; in *dyeing*, to make fast or permanent, as a color.—**to set aside**, to put to one side; put by, as for later use; also, to discard from use or service; dismiss from the mind, or leave out of consideration (as, *setting aside* this building, there is nothing in the town worth seeing); also, to reject as without value or pertinence (as, to *set aside* a law or a rule); annul or quash (as, to *set aside* a verdict). —**to set at naught.** See under *naught*, *n.*—**to set by the ears.** See *by the ears*, under *ear¹*.—**to set down**, to put down, as upon the ground, floor, etc.; deposit or let alight from a vehicle (as, "Mrs. Freke desired me to *set* her *down* at her sister's": Maria Edgeworth's "Belinda," iii.); also, to put down in writing or printing; put down in a schedule or the like; hence, to put down in estimation, or consider (as, "Clive *set* her *down* as a very haughty, spoiled, aristocratic young creature": Thackeray's "Newcomes," xx.); ascribe or attribute (as, "He could not *set* it *down* to caprice": Lamb's "Modern Gallantry").—**to set one's cap** at or for. See under *cap*, *n.*—**to set one's house in order.** See under *house²*, *n.*—**to set right**, to put or make right; restore (matters) to the right condition; put (a person, etc.) in the right light (as, "It would *set* him *right* in their eyes": H. G. Wells's "Men Like Gods," ii. 3); bring into conformity with fact, or correct (as, to *set* errors *right*); bring to right ideas (as, "I . . . found myself capable of *setting* him *right* as to many of his antiquated notions": Irving's "Tales of a Traveler," ii. 7).—**to set up**, to raise to an elevated position or situation; post up, or place in view (as, to *set up* a notice); also, to place in a superior or exalted position (as, "Whom he would he *set up*; and whom he would he put down": Dan. v. 19); raise to authority or power; also, to make (a person) elated or proud (as, " 'I'm not so *set up* with my pastry to-day,' observed Mrs. Baines": Arnold Bennett's "Old Wives' Tale," i. 3); also, to give forth or utter loudly a cry, etc.: as, "At this answer the good old man *set up* a roar of laughter," Malkin's tr. Le Sage's "Gil Blas," x. 10); also, to place in an erect position; erect for use; also, to arrange (types) for printing from, or put (words, etc.) into type; also, to make erect in bearing, or of strong, vigorous frame, as by drill or exercise (as, "a keen-looking young man, particularly well *set up*": A. S. M. Hutchinson's "If Winter Comes," ii. 7); also, to establish, or set in active existence or operation (as, to *set up* a government or a business; to *set up* housekeeping); establish or start (a person) in some business or profession; put in a position of prosperity; restore to health and strength (as, "little Alfred being perfectly *set up* by a month of Brighton air": Thackeray's "Newcomes," xiv.); also, to put into an attitude of opposition or hostility (as, "He was skilful enough to have lived still, if knowledge could be *set up* against mortality": Shakspere's "All's Well," i. 1. 35); also, to put forward (as, "this claim which the Pretender has *set up* to the throne": Cooper's "Two Admirals," xix.); propose for consideration or adoption (as, to *set up* a theory).—**set**, *v. i.* To sit, or be seated (now prov. or vulgar: as, "You must always go and be a-*settin* on our steps, must you!" Dickens's "Chimes," i.); sit on eggs, as a hen; hang or fit in a particular manner, as clothes; also, to decline toward or pass below the horizon, as the sun; fig., to sink, decline, or wane; also, to bet or gamble (archaic); also, to assume a fixed or rigid state, as the countenance, the muscles, etc.; become firm or solid, as mortar; become bent or twisted, as metal from strain; develop or grow as the result of fertilization, as a blossom or fruit; also, to begin to move, or start (*forth, off, out*, etc.: as, "He *set* off in hot pursuit," Irving's "Captain Bonneville," xlvii.; "He *set* out to cross the road," H. G. Wells's "Soul of a Bishop,"

v.); have a certain direction or course, as a wind, current, etc. (as, "It is the drifting icebergs *setting* with any current anywhere, that wreck the ships": Dickens's "Hard Times," ii. 8); have a certain tendency (as, opinion is *setting* against this practice); also, to begin to apply one's self to something (as, "Let me ask you how you have *set* to work," Mallock's "New Republic," iii. 1; to *set* to writing a letter); make an attack (as, robbers *set* upon them by the way); also, of a dog, to indicate the position of game; in *dancing*, to perform steps toward one's partner, another dancer, etc.—**to set about**, to start work upon; begin upon: as, "We had best *set about* our part of the contract" (Conan Doyle's "Micah Clarke," xxx.).—**to set in**, to blow or flow toward the shore, as a wind or a current; also, to begin (as, "Darkness had almost *set in*": Du Maurier's "Trilby," iv.).—**to set to**, to make a beginning; start work; specif., of pugilists, etc., to begin fighting.—**to set up**, to start in business; begin to practise some trade or profession; also, to lay claim or make pretensions (as, to *set up* to be superior to others).—**to set up for**, to put one's self forward as, or lay claim to being (as, to *set up for* a man of fashion); also, to lay claim to (as, "No doubt . . . you have known ladies *set up for* wit that had none": Goldsmith's "Vicar of Wakefield," xv.).—**set**, *p. a.* That has been set (placed, fixed in position, appointed or ordained, prescribed or assigned, adjusted or arranged, mounted, or put into a fixed or rigid state), or that has set (assumed a fixed or rigid form or condition); esp., fixed or appointed beforehand (as, a *set* time; a *set* sum); prescribed beforehand (as, *set* rules; a *set* form of words); deliberate (as, of *set* purpose); deliberately composed, or customary or usual, rather than spontaneous or original (as, *set* phrases; a *set* form of expression); composed in due form (as, a *set* discourse); formal, ceremonious, or regular (as, a *set* meal); also, fixed, rigid, unvarying, or settled (as, a *set* countenance; "He had a *set* smile on his face," Miss Burney's "Evelina," xi.; a *set* feeling or opinion); having one's mind or will fixed upon something (as, "Are you still *set* on this divorce?" Galsworthy's "Country House," i. 9); resolved or determined (to do something, or that something shall be done: now rare); habitually or stubbornly fixed (as, a man *set* in his opinions; "She's an old maid, and kind o' *set* in her ways," Mrs. Stowe's "Oldtown Folks," ix.; colloquially, an awfully *set* person); also, formed, built, or made (as specified), as a person (as, thick-*set*).—**set**, *n.* The act or an act of setting, or the state of being set; the setting of the sun or other heavenly body; the close, as of day or of life; the assumption of a fixed, rigid, or hard state, as by mortar, etc.; a determined attack, onslaught, or effort (as, to make a *set* at a person or thing; the woman is making a dead *set* at him, that is, a determined effort to gain his affections); also, the manner in which something sets or is set; the way in which an article of dress, etc., hangs or fits; the form which a body assumes in the process of solidification, etc.; the permanent change of form which a body undergoes as the result of tension, pressure, etc.; a bend, twist, or warp; the direction of a wind, current, etc. (as, "Ahab . . . knew the *sets* of all tides and currents": H. Melville's "Moby-Dick," xliv.); tendency, as of the mind, action, affairs, etc. (as, "This was the course things had taken in the Church of England . . . The *set* has been steadily in one direction": S. Butler's "Way of All Flesh," lxxxiii.); fixed direction or bent, as of the mind, etc.; build, as of the body; bearing or carriage, as of a part of the body (as, the *set* of one's shoulders); set expression, as of the features (as, "a grim *set* about his mouth": Conan Doyle's "Exploits of Brigadier Gerard," i.); the adjustment of the reeds of a loom for the making of a fabric of a particular weave, or the make of a fabric as so determined; the pattern of a tartan, or any of the squares in it (as, "The petticoat was formed of tartan silk, in the *set*, or pattern, of which the colour of blue largely predominated": Scott's "Legend of Montrose," ix.); the lateral deflection of a saw-tooth or saw-teeth that is produced by setting; also, something set; a young plant, or a slip, tuber, or the like, suitable for setting out, or putting in the ground to grow; a rudimentary fruit as it forms from the blossom; the stake at dice, etc.†; a game, as at cards†; a stage scene consisting of a number of pieces or parts set or arranged together; a construction representing a place in which action takes place in a moving picture; also, a place where something, as a net, is set; also, a device for setting something, as the teeth of a saw; also, a number or group of persons associating or classed together (as, "I do not know any *set* of men so likely to err as reviewers": Marryat's "King's Own," xxviii.); a social group or class (as, "the so-called fashionable *set* of the present day": W. Churchill's "Modern Chronicle," ii. 10); a number of things customarily used together or forming a complete assortment, outfit, or collection (as, a *set* of dishes, furs, teeth, books, etc.); a number of things connected together in some way, as by succession in space or time (as, a *set* of hills; a *set* of earthquake shocks); specif., a radio receiving apparatus; in *dancing*, etc., the number of couples required to execute a quadrille or the like; a series of movements or figures that make up a quadrille or the like, or the music adapted for this; in *tennis*, etc., a group of games counting as one of the units of a series.

se-ta (sē'tä), *n.*; pl. **setæ** (-tē). [L. *seta, sæta*, bristle: cf. *satin* and *seton*.] In *zoöl.* and *bot.*, a stiff hair; a bristle; a bristle-like part; also, in *bot.*, the stalk that supports the theca of mosses.—**se-ta-ceous** (sē-tā'shius), *a.* [NL. *setaceus.*] Bristle-like; bristle-shaped; also, furnished with bristles; bristly.—**se'tal** (-ṭạl), *a.* Of or pertaining to setæ.

set-back (set'bak), *n.* A check to progress, or a reverse (as, "some great *setback* to civilization": J. H. Robinson's "Mind in the Making," viii. 16); in *arch.*, a flat, plain set-off in a wall; also, a setting back of the outside wall of a building for some distance from the street-line; esp., in modern tall buildings, such a setting back at a particular height in the building, or one of a number of such settings back at different heights, for the purpose of allowing better light and ventilation in the street.

set=down (set'doun), *n.* A humiliating rebuke or rebuff: as, "I wish you had been there . . . to have given him one of your *set-downs*" (Jane Austen's "Pride and Prejudice," iii.).

se-tif-er-ous (sē-tif'ẹ-rus), *a.* [L. *seta*, bristle: see *-ferous*.] Having setæ or bristles; setigerous.

se-ti-form (sē'ti-fôrm), *a.* [L. *seta*, bristle: see *-form*.] Bristle-shaped; setaceous.

se-tig-er-ous (sē-tij'ẹ-rus), *a.* [L. *setiger*, < *seta*, bristle, + *gerere*, bear.] Having setæ or bristles.

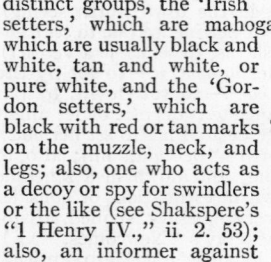

Building with Setbacks (seen on front and side), in New York City.

set-ness (set'nes), *n.* The state of being set.

set=off (set'ôf), *n.* Start or outset; also, an ornament or decoration; also, the setting off of one thing, as a debt or claim, as a counterbalance against another; something so set off; a counterbalancing debt or claim; anything that counterbalances or makes up for something else; a compensating circumstance; in *arch.*, a reduction in the thickness of a wall, etc.; a flat or sloping projection on a wall, buttress, or the like, below a part of less thickness; an offset; in *printing*, an offset.

se-ton (sē'ṭon), *n.* [= F. *séton*, appar. < L. *seta*, bristle.] In *surg.*, a thread or the like inserted beneath the skin in order to maintain an artificial passage or issue; also, the issue itself.

se-tose (sē'tōs), *a.* [L. *setosus*, < *seta*, bristle.] Covered with setæ or bristles; bristly.

sett (set), *n.* Archaic form of *set*, used in certain technical senses.

set-tee[1] (se-tē'), *n.* [= F. *sétie, scétie*, < It. *saettia*.] A decked vessel having a long, sharp prow and two or three masts with lateen sails, used on the Mediterranean. See cut in next column.

set-tee[2] (se-tē'), *n.* [Appar. an altered form of *settle*[1].] A

seat for two or more persons, with a back and usually arms.

set-ter (set'ẽr), *n.* One who sets (as, a *setter* of type, or of jewels); something that sets, or is used in setting; esp., one of a breed of long-haired hunting-dogs which originally had the habit of crouching when game was scented, but which are now trained to stand stiffly and point the muzzle toward the scented game, the breed being made up of three distinct groups, the 'Irish setters,' which are mahogany-red, the 'English setters,' which are usually black and white, tan and white, or pure white, and the 'Gordon setters,' which are black with red or tan marks on the muzzle, neck, and legs; also, one who acts as a decoy or spy for swindlers or the like (see Shakspere's "1 Henry IV.," ii. 2. 53); also, an informer against violators of law.

Settee.

English Setter.

set-ting (set'ing), *n.* The act of one who or that which sets; also, the manner or position in which anything is set; also, that in which something, as a jewel, is set or mounted; hence, the surroundings or environment of anything; the mounting (scenery, costumes, etc.) of a play; also, a piece of music composed for certain words.—**set'ting=up'**, *a.* Such as to make one erect in bearing or of strong, vigorous frame, as gymnastic exercises.

set-tle[1] (set'l), *n.* [AS. *setl*, seat; from the root of E. *sit*.] A seat (archaic); specif., a long seat, or bench, esp. one with arms and a high back (as, "A long hard-wood *settle* extended its uneasy length by the chimney": Mrs. Stowe's "Uncle Tom's Cabin," viii.); also, a ledge or platform (obs. or prov. Eng.: see Ezek. xliii. 14, 17).

set-tle[2] (set'l), *v.; -tled, -tling.* [AS. *setlan*, < *setl*, seat, E. *settle*[1].] **I.** *tr.* To seat†; also, to set, place, or fix firmly, as in a position to be retained (as, to *settle* one's feet in the stirrups); place in a position of repose, or dispose comfortably (as, to *settle* one's self in an easy-chair); place in a desired position or in order (as, "Mr. Featherstone, holding his stick between his knees and *settling* his wig," George Eliot's "Middlemarch," xii.; "They immediately began to *settle* their clothes, which were a little deranged," Scott's "Heart of Midlothian," i.); also, to install in a house or residence (as, "It was some time before I could *settle* myself in a house to my liking," Addison, in "Spectator," 12; "We were soon *settled* in barracks," Lever's "Harry Lorrequer," i.); cause to take up residence in a place, esp. to establish (a body of persons) as residents in a country, town, etc.; also, to fix (one's residence, abode, etc.) permanently in a place; also, to furnish (a place) with inhabitants or settlers; take up residence in (a new country or place) as settlers; also, to cause to sink down gradually or subside; render (soil) firm or compact; also, to cause (dregs, etc.) to sink to the bottom; cause (a liquid) to deposit dregs; also, to bring to rest after agitation; quiet (the nerves, stomach, etc.); also, to reduce to quiet, or cause to cease from opposition or annoyance, as by a blow or some other effective measure, or as the measure does (now chiefly colloq.: as, "There was an approving nod all around as this quiet snub dropped on the boaster and '*settled*' him," Mark Twain's "Life on the Mississippi," vii.); also, to render stable or permanent (as, " 'Tis hard to *settle* order once again": Tennyson's "Choric Song," vi.); set permanently in order, or place on a permanent basis (a government, an institution, etc.); put (a language) into permanent form; make (a person, the mind, etc.) steadfast or constant (as, "if ye continue in the faith grounded and *settled*": Col. i. 23); set (one's self) steadily, as to some employment (as, "Mr. Oakhurst *settled* himself coolly to the losing game before him": Bret Harte's "Outcasts of Poker Flat"); establish in a way of life, a business, an office, a charge, etc. (as, "He had made to himself a practice large enough to enable him to *settle* two sons well in his own profession," Kingsley's "Two Years Ago," i.; "I was placed and *settled* as the minister of Dalmailing," Galt's "Annals of the Parish," Introd.); establish (a person) in the matrimonial state (as, to *settle* one's daughter); secure (property, title, etc.) on or to a person by formal or legal process (as, to *settle* the crown on a person; to *settle* an annuity upon a relative); also, to appoint or fix definitely, or decide or agree upon (a time, a place, a price, conditions, etc.); decide, or come to a conclusion upon (a question, or a matter in doubt: as, "The lama waved a hand to show that the matter was finally *settled* in his mind," Kipling's "Kim," v.); be decisive of (a question), as a fact or argument is; bring (a dispute) to an end through agreement or intervention; close (an account) by payment; pay (a bill, etc.); close up, or dispose of finally (as, to *settle* an estate). **II.** *intr.* To come to rest from flight, or alight, as a bird on a bough; come down and remain (as, a heavy fog *settled*; "And silence *settled*, wide and still, On the lone wood," Scott's "Lady of the Lake," i. 3); come to rest in a particular place, as after wandering (as, a shifting wind finally *settles* in the west; a cold *settles* in one's head); take up a position to be retained, as one of repose; also, to take up a fixed habitation or abode, or become domiciled (sometimes with *down*); specif., to take up residence in a new country or place, as settlers; also, to sink down gradually to a lower level, or subside, as a structure, the ground, etc. (as, "There was the wagon up to the hub in mud, and visibly *settling* every instant": Parkman's "Oregon Trail," iv.); become firm or compact, as the ground; also, to sink to the bottom as sediment, as particles in a liquid; separate and collect, as a part or element of a liquid, by the effect of gravity; become clear, by the sinking or gathering together of particles, as a liquid; also, to come to rest after agitation; become calm or composed, as the mind, etc., or a person (sometimes with *down*); also, to assume a particular form, state, etc., at the end of a series of changes (as, the light took on one color after another and finally *settled* into red: sometimes with *down*); of the weather, to come gradually to a condition for something specified (as, it is *settling* for a storm); often, to become steadily clear (as, the weather is *settling*); also, to set one's self steadily to some object, employment, etc. (often with *down*: as, "the good Doctor . . . having just . . . *settled* to his microscope," Kingsley's "Two Years Ago," i.; "They *settled* down to their work in earnest," M. Hewlett's "Open Country," xxvi.); set one's self to a regular way of life (giving up an irregular one), esp. upon marrying (often with *down*: as, he has been wild, but he will *settle* down; to marry and *settle* down); also, to come to a decision, or decide (as, to *settle* on a plan of action); arrange matters in dispute, or come to an agreement (as, to *settle* with a person); make a financial arrangement or come to terms (as, "They had to *settle* with Tom Beatty for something like three hundred thousand": W. Churchill's "Inside of the Cup," x.); adjust accounts by payment, or make payment for something (as, "We shall be only too pleased to put the ticket down to you: and you can *settle* at your convenience": G. B. Shaw's "You Never Can Tell," iv.). —**set′tled,** *p. a.* Fixed in place or position; having a fixed abode, as a people; also, populated, as a region; also, fixed or established (as, "the *settled* course of things": J. Butler's "Analogy of Religion," ii. 5); placed on a permanent basis, as government; also, maintained or continuing without change, as weather of a particular kind, a wind, etc. (as, *settled* fair weather); sometimes, of weather, steadily clear or fine; also, fixed, firmly seated, or unchanging (as, "a *settled* melancholy," Bret Harte's "Romance of Madroño Hollow"; "his *settled* views," Arnold Bennett's "Clayhanger," i. 12); steadfast, staid, or sober, as the character, mind, etc.; indicating such a character, as the countenance; also, established in a regular way of life, or in fixed, humdrum ways, as after marriage or with increasing age (as, a *settled* married man; "The eye-glasses pinched her nose. She considered spectacles. They would make her seem older, and hopelessly *settled*," Sinclair Lewis's "Main Street,"

xxxix.); steady or orderly, as the life, etc.; established in an office, charge, etc.; also, secured to a person by a legal act or process, as an estate or property; also, appointed or fixed definitely, as a time, etc.; decided or determined definitely, as a question or a matter in doubt; adjusted or closed, as an account by payment. —**set′tled-ness,** *n.*

set-tle-ment (set′l-ment), *n.* The act of settling, or the state of being settled; a fixing firmly in position, or the position itself; a settling in a place or abode, or the state of being so settled; legal residence in a particular place, or the right to maintenance, if a pauper, acquired through this (British); the settling of persons in a new country or place as settlers; a gradual sinking down or subsidence, as of a structure or the ground; the sinking of dregs as sediment to the bottom of a liquid, or the sediment itself (now prov.); the settling or clearing of a liquid by the sinking or gathering together of particles; the act of rendering stable or permanent or putting on a permanent basis, or the resulting state, or an established order of things; the establishment of a person in an employment, office, or charge; the establishment of one in marriage; the settling of property, title, etc., upon a person, the terms of the arrangement, the deed or instrument incorporating the terms, or the property so settled (as, a marriage *settlement*, whereby certain property is secured to the wife; a *settlement* of succession to the crown; "She wished her husband to receive a *settlement* from the nation of £50,000 a year," Lytton Strachey's "Queen Victoria," iv.); the deciding or determining of a question or a matter in doubt; the arrangement or adjustment of a matter in dispute; the satisfying of a claim or demand, or a coming to terms; the settling of accounts by payment; the closing up or final disposition of an estate or the like; also, a body of persons settled together in a new country, or the tract of country settled by them; a colony, esp. in its early stages; also, a small village or collection of houses (as, "The houses of the colored people formed a little *settlement* by themselves in the north part of the village": Mrs. Stowe's "Oldtown Folks," v.); also, a house or establishment in a neglected or unfavored neighborhood, as in a large city, where men or women of education take up their abode to work, by means of various activities, for local social betterment (as, a university, college, or church *settlement*). —**set′tle-ment=work″er,** *n.* One who devotes his or her time to the work of a settlement established in an unfavored neighborhood for purposes of local social betterment.

set-tler (set′lėr), *n.* One who or that which settles; esp., one who settles in a new country; one of those who first settle in a place as residents; also, something, as a crushing blow or speech or some other effective measure, that 'settles,' reduces to quiet, or 'finishes' one (colloq.); also, a pan, vat, or the like, in which a liquid is run to settle and thus effect a separation of some part or element of it.

set-tling (set′ling), *n.* The act of one who or that which settles; also, sediment (chiefly in *pl.*).

set-tlor (set′lŏr), *n.* In *law*, one who makes a settlement of property.

set=to (set′tö′), *n.*; pl. -tos (-töz′). Orig., a pugilistic encounter; hence, in general, a fight (as, "The bulls and some of the steers . . . occasionally have most desperate and obstinate *set-tos* with one another": Roosevelt's "Ranch Life and the Hunting-Trail," iii.); a vigorous altercation or dispute; a smart contest or bout of any kind. [Colloq.]

sev-en (sev′n), *a.* [AS. *seofon* = D. *zeven* = G. *sieben* = Icel. *sjau* = Goth. *sibun*, seven; akin to L. *septem*, Gr. ἑπτά, Skt. *sapta*, seven.] One more than six. —**seven champions of Christendom,** in medieval tales, the national saints of England, Scotland, Wales, Ireland, France, Spain, and Italy (George, Andrew, David, Patrick, Denis, James, and Anthony). —**seven chief virtues,** the four cardinal virtues and the three theological virtues. See *virtue.* —**seven deadly sins.** See *deadly, a.* —**seven hills of Rome,** the seven hills (the Aventine, Cælian, Capitoline, Esquiline, Palatine, Quirinal, and Viminal) on and about which the ancient city of Rome was built. —**seven=league boots,** the magical boots in the fairy-tale of Hop o' my Thumb, which enabled the wearer to cover seven leagues at each stride. —**seven liberal arts,** the seven studies which constituted the quadrivium and trivium of the middle ages. See *quadrivium*

---

and *trivium*, and cf. *liberal arts* under *art*². — **seven sages of ancient Greece.** See *sage*¹, *n.* — **seven seas.** See under *sea*. — **seven sleepers (of Ephesus)**, seven Christian youths of Ephesus who, according to legend, fled during the persecution under the Roman emperor Decius (249–251), and hid in a cave, where they were discovered and walled in, and who then fell asleep, not to awaken until the cave was opened about two hundred years (or more) later, when the Christian religion had become generally accepted. — **seven stars**, the seven planets of the ancients (that is, the sun, the moon, Mercury, Venus, Mars, Jupiter, and Saturn)†; also, the Pleiades; also, the seven stars of the Dipper, or the whole constellation Ursa Major. — **seven wonders of the world.** See under *wonder*, *n.* — **Seven Years' War**, a war between Prussia under Frederick the Great (aided by British subsidies) and Austria, France, Russia, etc., which lasted from 1756 to 1763, and resulted in establishing Prussia in the front rank of European powers and in laying the foundations of England's colonial empire. — **sev′en**, *n.* A number composed of seven units (as, "The number *seven* was a magic number in Brussels, and was supposed . . . to denote the seven planets which governed all things terrestrial by their aspects and influences": Motley's "Dutch Republic," i. 1); a symbol, as 7 or vii, representing this number; a set of seven persons or things; a playing-card with seven pips. — **at sixes and sevens.** See under *six*, *n.* — **the Seven against Thebes**, in Greek legend, the seven heroes, Adrastus, Amphiaraus, Capaneus, Eteoclus (in some versions Hippomedon), Parthenopæus, Polynices, and Tydeus, who made an expedition against Thebes for the purpose of seating Polynices on the throne, during which all perished except Adrastus: the subject of a drama by Æschylus.

sev-en-fold (sev′n-fōld). [AS. *seofonfeald*.] **I.** *a.* Comprising seven parts or members; seven times as great or as much. **II.** *adv.* In sevenfold measure.

sev-en-night (sev′n-nīt), *n.* Same as *sennight*.

sev-en-teen (sev′n-tēn′). [AS. *seofontȳne*.] **I.** *a.* Seven more than ten. **II.** *n.* A number composed of seventeen units, or a symbol, as 17 or xvii, representing it. — **sev′enteenth′.** **I.** *a.* Next after the sixteenth; also, being one of seventeen equal parts. **II.** *n.* The seventeenth member of a series; also, a seventeenth part.

sev-enth (sev′nth), *a.* [ME. *seventhe*: cf. AS. *seofotha*.] Next after the sixth; also, being one of seven equal parts. — **seventh day**, the seventh day of the week (Saturday); the Jewish Sabbath: used esp. (attributively, with hyphen) in the designations of certain Christian religious bodies who make Saturday their chief day of rest and religious observance (as, *Seventh-day* Adventists; *Seventh-day* Baptists). — **seventh heaven.** See under *heaven*. — **sev′enth**, *n.* The seventh member of a series; also, a seventh part; in *music*, a tone on the seventh degree from a given tone (counted as the first); the interval between such tones; the harmonic combination of such tones; in a scale, the leading tone. — **sev′enth-ly**, *adv.*

sev-en-ti-eth (sev′n-ti-eth). [ME. *seventithe*.] **I.** *a.* Next after the sixty-ninth; also, being one of seventy equal parts. **II.** *n.* The seventieth member of a series; also, a seventieth part.

sev-en-ty (sev′n-ti). [AS. *(hund)seofontig*.] **I.** *a.* Seven times ten. **II.** *n.*; pl. *-ties* (-tiz). A number composed of seventy units, or a symbol, as 70 or lxx, representing it; also [*cap.*], with *the*, any of various groups of seventy persons, esp. the body of (seventy-two) scholars who, according to tradition, made the Septuagint.

sev-en=up (sev″n-up′), *n.* A card-game played by two or more persons, to each of whom six cards are dealt, in which there are four special chances of scoring a point (a player winning them all having 'all-fours'), seven points constituting a game. Also called *all-fours*, *high-low-jack*, and *old sledge*.

sev-er (sev′ėr), *v.* [OF. *sevrer*, separate (F. *wean*), < L. *separare*: see *separate*, *v.*] **I.** *tr.* To put apart or asunder, part, or separate, as two or more persons or things or as one from another (as, "Her lips are *sever′d* as to speak," Tennyson's "Day-Dream," 50; "a homeless hearthrug *severed* from its natural companion the fireside," Dickens's "Dombey and Son," ix.); disconnect or disjoin; disunite or dissociate; distinguish in thought; also, to keep apart as by

an intervening barrier or space, or as something intervening does (as, "Fens nearly one hundred miles long *severed* East Anglia from the midland counties": Green's "Short Hist. of the Eng. People," ii. 1); also, to divide into parts, esp. suddenly or forcibly, as by cutting; cut, cleave, split, or rend asunder (as, to *sever* a rope or fastening; "Cane . . . *sever'd* into stripes That interlac'd each other," Cowper's "Task," i. 40); cut, split, or tear (a part) from the rest (as, "His head was nearly *severed* from his body": H. G. Wells's "Mr. Britling," iii. 1. § 1); fig., to break off or dissolve (ties, connections, relations, etc.); break up or disperse (an assemblage, etc.: now rare). **II.** *intr.* To separate or part from each other or one from another; also, to act separately or independently, as defendants at law; also, to become divided into parts; also, to make a separation or division, as between things. — **sev′er-a-ble**, *a.* Capable of being severed.

sev-er-al (sev′ėr-al). [AF. *several*, < ML. *separalis*, < L. *separ*, separate, different: cf. L. *separare* and E. *separate*, *v.*] **I.** *a.* Separated†, separate†, or distinct† (as, "Uzziah . . . dwelt in a *several* house, being a leper": 2 Chron. xxvi. 21); also, considered separately, single, or particular (as, each *several* one of a group); also, individually separate, or different (as, on three *several* occasions); divers, various, or sundry (as, the *several* steps in a process); hence, being more than two or three, but not many (as, to gain *several* pounds in weight); also, pertaining to separate individuals or to a separate individual, or respective (as, they went their *several* ways; each went his *several* way); private, or privately owned (chiefly in *law*: as, a right of *several* fishery); in *law*, separate or separable, as opposed to *joint*; admitting of separate action; enforceable against each party separately, as an obligation to which a number of persons are parties. **II.** *pron.* or *n.* Several persons or things; a few; some: as, *several* have given their consent; *several* of us; *several* of the books. — **sev′er-al-ly**, *adv.* Separately, singly, or individually (as, consider these points, first *severally* and then collectively); also, apart from others, or independently (archaic); also, respectively. — **sev′er-al-ty** (-ti), *n.*; pl. *-ties* (-tiz). [AF. *severalte*.] The state of being separate or distinct; also, the condition, as of land, of being held or owned by separate or individual right; also, land so held.

sev-er-ance (sev′ėr-ạns), *n.* The act of severing, or the state of being severed; separation; division; cutting asunder or off; detachment; breaking off, as of relations.

se-vere (sẹ-vēr′), *a.*; compar. *severer*, superl. *severest*. [F. *sévère*, < L. *severus*, serious, grave, stern, harsh, severe.] Serious or grave in aspect, demeanor, manner, spirit, etc. (as, "And give good company a face *severe*, As if they met around a father's bier," Cowper's "Conversation," 873; "Happy, who in his verse can gently steer From grave to light, from pleasant to *severe*," Soame and Dryden's tr. Boileau's "Art of Poetry," i. 76); of a serious rather than a trifling or superficial kind (as, "Hitherto I have known few pleasures save of the *severer* kind," George Eliot's "Middlemarch," v.; *severe* studies or scholarship); also, austere, or austerely strict, as persons or the principles, life, etc. (as, "The habits of the household were simple and *severe*": Froude's "Cæsar," vi.); also, rigidly exact, accurate, or methodical (as, *severe* conformity to standards or principles; *severe* reasoning); also, rigidly restrained in style or taste, as persons, esp. writers or artists (as, "Lucilius, who was more *severe*, and more correct, and gave himself less liberty in the mixture of his verses in the same poem": Dryden's "Discourse concerning Satire"); austerely simple or plain, as style or taste, beauty, dress, etc.; chaste in conception or style, rather than florid, ornate, or highly elaborate, as architectural designs or any artistic work; also, harsh, stern, or unsparing, as persons, the temper or mood, treatment, language, etc. (as, "The magistrate . . . was very *severe* on cases of this description," S. Butler's "Way of All Flesh," lxi.; a *severe* critic or criticism; a *severe* reproof); showing a harsh temper or mood (as, a *severe* look or tone); harsh in effect, rigorous, or harshly extreme (as, *severe* laws, penalties, or punishment; *severe* discipline; *severe* measures); also, causing discomfort or distress by extreme character or conditions, as weather, cold, heat, etc.; unpleasantly violent, as rain or wind, a blow or shock, etc.; distressingly intense or acute, or sharp, as pain, grief, dis-

---

fat, fāte, fär, fȧll, ȧsk, fāre; net, mē, hėr; pin, pīne; not, nōte, mōve, nôr; up, lūte, pùll; oi, oil; ou, out; (lightened) aviȧry, ėlect, agȯny, intọ, ūnite; (obscured) errạnt, operä, ardẹnt, actọr, natụre; ch, chip; g, go; th, thin; ᴛʜ, then; y, you;

appointment, etc.; in an acute or extreme form, as an attack or case of disease; grievous, as loss; hard to endure, perform, fulfil, etc. (as, a *severe* test, experience, or strain; *severe* exercise; *severe* terms or conditions).—**se-vere′ly,** *adv.*—**se-vere′ness,** *n.*

sev-er-er (sev′ẻr-ẻr), *n.* One who or that which severs.

se-ver-i-ty (sẹ-ver′i-ti), *n.*; pl. *-ties* (-tiz). [F. *sévérité*, < L. *severitas*.] The character or state of being severe; gravity; austerity; rigid exactness or accuracy; austere simplicity, as of style or taste; harshness, sternness, or rigor; distressingly extreme character, or violence, sharpness, or acuteness, as of cold, storms, pain, disease, etc.; grievousness; hard or trying character or effect; also, something severe; esp., *pl.*, severe or harsh proceedings or measures, or severe criticisms or reproofs.

Sèvres (sāvr), *n.* [From *Sèvres*, town near Paris, France.] A choice and costly kind of porcelain made at Sèvres.

sew (sō), *v.*; *sewed* (pp. also *sewn*), *sewing*. [AS. *siwian* = OHG. *siuwan* = Icel. *sȳja* = Goth. *siujan*, sew; akin to L. *suere*, Gr. (κασ)σύειν, Skt. *sīv-*, sew: cf. *seam*[1], *suture*, and *sutra*.] **I.** *tr.* To join or attach by passing a thread or the like in and out through punctures in the material, as with a needle or an awl (as, to *sew* together the parts of a garment or a shoe, the sheets of a book, or the edges of a wound; to *sew* trimming, buttons, a patch, or a label on a garment); work on (a garment, etc.) with a needle and thread or the like, by hand or machine, as in making or repairing (as, "*Sewing* at once, with a double thread, A Shroud as well as a Shirt": Hood's "Song of the Shirt," 31); make (seams, stitches, etc.), as with a needle and thread; close (a hole, wound, etc.) by means of stitches (commonly with *up*); also, to make fast, or secure in place, with stitches, as something inclosed or inserted (with *in*, *into*, *between*, etc.: as, flour *sewed*, or *sewed* up, in bags; "The diamonds were *sewed* into her habit," Thackeray's "Vanity Fair," xxxii.; to *sew* money between the lining and the outer thickness of a garment). **II.** *intr.* To work with a needle and thread, or with a sewing-machine.

sew-age (sū′āj), *n.* [From *sewer*[3].] The waste matter which passes through sewers.—**sew′age,** *v. t.*; *-aged, -aging*. To irrigate or fertilize with sewage; also, to drain with sewers.

se-wel-lel (sẹ-wel′el), *n.* [N. Amer. Ind.] Any of the terrestrial burrowing rodents constituting the genus *Haplodon* (or *Aplodontia*), inhabiting the wooded regions west of the Rocky Mountains.

Sewellel (*Haplodon rufus,* or *Aplodontia rufa*).

sew-er[1] (sō′ẻr), *n.* One who or that which sews.

sew-er[2] (sū′ẻr), *n.* [AF. *asseour*, < OF. *asseoir*, seat, set, < L. *assidere*, sit at: see *assess*.] Formerly, a household officer or head servant in charge of the service of the table.

sew-er[3] (sū′ẻr), *n.* [OF. *sewiere*, channel for draining, < L. *ex-*, out, + *aqua*, water.] Orig., a ditch for draining a region; later, an artificial conduit, usually underground, for carrying off waste water and refuse, as from a town or city.—**sew′er**[3], *v.* **I.** *tr.* To drain by means of sewers; furnish with sewers. **II.** *intr.* To discharge sewage.—**sew′er-age** (-āj), *n.* The removal of waste water and refuse by means of sewers; also, a system of sewers; also, sewage.

sew-ing (sō′ing), *n.* The act or work of one who sews (by hand or machine); also, something done or made with a needle and thread; needlework; materials or articles to be sewed.—**sew′ing-cir″cle,** *n.* A society of women who meet regularly to sew for the benefit of charitable or religious objects; also, a meeting of such a society.—**sew′ing-machine,** *n.* A machine for sewing.

sewn (sōn). Past participle of *sew*.

sex (seks), *n.* [L. *sexus*, also *secus*, prob. lit. 'a division,' < *secare*, cut: see *secant*.] The character of being either male or female (as, the *sex* of a child; persons of different *sexes*); also, the physical distinction between male and female (as, organs of *sex*); the sum of the anatomical and physiological differences with reference to which the male and the female are distinguished, or the phenomena depending on these differences; sometimes, the instinct or attraction drawing one sex toward another, or its manifestation in life and conduct (as, novels dealing with *sex*; problems of *sex*); also, those of either the male or the female kind or gender collectively, esp. in the human race (as, the sterner *sex*, men; the fair, gentle, gentler, or weaker *sex*, women; a school for both *sexes*); sometimes, with *the*, the female sex; women.

sex-. Form of L. *sex*, six, used in combination, as in *sexangular*, *sexpartite*.

sex-a-ge-na-ri-an (sek″sạ-je-nā′ri-ạn). [L. *sexagenarius*: see *sexagenary*.] **I.** *a.* Of the age of 60 years, or between 60 and 70 years old. **II.** *n.* A sexagenarian person.

sex-ag-e-na-ry (sek-saj′e-nā-ri). [L. *sexagenarius*, < *sexageni*, sixty each, distributive of *sexaginta*, sixty, related to *sex*, six: see *six*.] **I.** *a.* Of or pertaining to the number 60; composed of or proceeding by sixties; also, sexagenarian (as, "a *sexagenary* bachelor": Longfellow's "Hyperion," iv. 2). **II.** *n.*; pl. *-ries* (-riz). A sexagenarian.

Sex-a-ges-i-ma (sek-sạ-jes′i-mä), *n.* [ML., prop. fem. of L. *sexagesimus*, sixtieth (see *sexagesimal*); the names *Sexagesima* and *Septuagesima* being appar. used, without appropriateness of sense, to form a series with *Quadragesima* and *Quinquagesima* (see these words).] The second Sunday before Lent (more fully, 'Sexagesima Sunday').

sex-a-ges-i-mal (sek-sạ-jes′i-mạl). [L. *sexagesimus*, sixtieth, < *sexaginta*, sixty: see *sexagenary*.] **I.** *a.* Pertaining to or based upon the number 60: as, a *sexagesimal* fraction (a fraction whose denominator is 60 or a power of 60). **II.** *n.* A sexagesimal fraction.—**sex-a-ges′i-mal-ly,** *adv.*

sex-an-gu-lar (sek-sang′gū-lär), *a.* [L. *sexangulus*, < *sex*, six, + *angulus*, E. *angle*[3].] Having six angles; hexagonal.

sex-cen-te-na-ry (seks-sen′te-nā-ri). [See *sex-* and *centenary*.] **I.** *a.* Pertaining to six hundred or a period of six hundred years; marking the completion of six hundred years. **II.** *n.*; pl. *-ries* (-riz). A six-hundredth anniversary, or its celebration.

sexed (sekst), *a.* Having sex; sometimes, belonging to a sex (used in compounds: as, her gentle-*sexed* humanity).

sex-en-ni-al (sek-sen′i-ạl), *a.* [L. *sexennis*, < *sex*, six, + *annus*, year.] Of or for six years; also, occurring every six years.—**sex-en′ni-al-ly,** *adv.*—**sex-en′ni-um** (-um), *n.*; pl. *-niums* or *-nia* (-ạ) [L., < *sexennis*.] A period of six years.

sex-less (seks′les), *a.* Without sex; having, or seeming as if having, no sex: as, "All beauty is *sexless* in the eyes of the artist at his work — the beauty of man, the beauty of woman" (Du Maurier's "Trilby," ii.).—**sex′less-ly,** *adv.*—**sex′less-ness,** *n.*

sex-par-tite (seks-pär′tīt), *a.* [See *sex-* and *partite*.] Divided into or consisting of six parts, as a vault, etc.

sext (sekst), *n.* [ML. *sexta*, prop. fem. of L. *sextus*, sixth, < *sex*, six: see *six*.] *Eccles.*, the fourth of the seven canonical hours, or the service for it, orig. fixed for the sixth hour of the day (or noon).

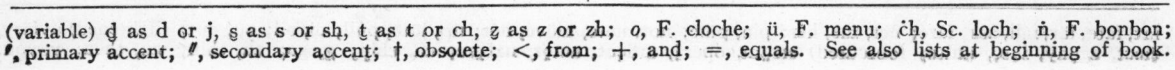
Sexpartite Vaulting. — Nave of Bourges Cathedral, France.

sex-tan (seks′-tạn). [L. *sextus*, sixth: see *sext*.] **I.** *a.* Of a fever, ague, etc., characterized by paroxysms which recur every sixth day, both days of consecutive occurrence being counted. **II.** *n.* A sextan fever or ague.

sex-tant (seks'tant), *n.* [L. *sextans* (*sextant-*), sixth part, < *sextus*, sixth: see *sext*.] The sixth part of a circle; also, an astronomical instrument containing a graduated arc (usually equal to a sixth part of a circle), used in measuring angular distances, esp. the sun's altitude at sea in determining latitude and longitude; also [*cap.*], in *astron.*, the constellation Sextans (south of Leo).

sex-tet, sex-tette (seks-tet'), *n.* [Altered form of *sestet*, after L. *sex*, six.] A musical composition for six voices or instruments; also, a company of six singers or players; also, any group of six persons or things.

sex-tile (seks'til), *a.* [= F. *sextil*, < L. *sextus*, sixth: see *sext*.] In *astrol.*: **I.** *a.* Noting or pertaining to the aspect or position of two heavenly bodies when 60° distant from each other. **II.** *n.* A sextile aspect.

sex-til-lion (seks-til'yon), *n.* [F. *sextillion*, < L. *sextus*, sixth, + F. (*m*)*illion*, million.] In Great Britain, the sixth power of a million, represented by 1 followed by 36 ciphers; in France and the U. S., a thousand quintillions, represented by 1 followed by 21 ciphers.—**sex-til'lionth**, *a.* and *n.*

sex-to-de-ci-mo (seks-tō-des'i-mō). [NL. *in sexto decimo*, 'in sixteenth.'] **I.** *n.*; pl. *-mos* (-mōz). The page size of a book in which each leaf is one sixteenth of a whole sheet of paper; a volume of this size. Abbreviated 16*mo* or 16°. **II.** *a.* In sextodecimo.

sex-ton (seks'ton), *n.* [OF. *secrestain*, *segrestein*, < ML. *sacristanus*, E. *sacristan*.] An official of a church charged with taking care of the edifice and its contents, ringing the bell, etc., and sometimes with digging graves; also, a sexton-beetle.—**sex'ton-bee"tle**, *n.* Any of the beetles of the genus *Necrophorus*, noted for their habit of burying the bodies of small dead animals in which they have deposited their eggs, the decaying flesh serving as food for the larvæ.—**sex'ton-ess**, *n.* A female sexton.—**sex'ton-ship**, *n.*

Sexton-beetles burying a dead bird.

sex-tu-ple (seks'tū-pl), *a.* [From L. *sex*, six, after *quintuple*, *septuple*, etc.] Sixfold; consisting of six parts; six times as great.—**sex'tu-ple**, *v. t.* or *i.*; *-pled*, *-pling*. To make or become six times as great.

sex-tu-plex (seks'tū-pleks), *a.* [From L. *sex*, six, after LL. *quintuplex*, fivefold, quintuple: cf. *duplex*.] Sixfold; specif., noting or pertaining to a system of telegraphy by which six messages may be transmitted simultaneously over one wire.

sex-u-al (sek'shū-al), *a.* [LL. *sexualis*.] Of, pertaining to, or distinctive of sex (as, *sexual* characteristics; the *sexual* organs, those peculiar to either sex which are concerned with generation or reproduction); pertaining to or existing between the two sexes or two individuals of opposite sex (as, "Her very frankness suggested a perfect *sexual* equality," Bret Harte's "Miggles"; *sexual* affinity); specif., occurring between or involving the two sexes in their distinctive physical (generative) functions and powers (as, *sexual* intercourse or union; *sexual* processes; *sexual* reproduction); pertaining to the physical intercourse between the sexes (as, *sexual* desire; *sexual* immorality); peculiar to or affecting the organs of sex (as, *sexual* diseases); also, having sex or sexual organs, or reproducing by processes involving both sexes, as animals or plants.—**sexual selection**, in *biol.*, the form or kind of natural selection in which sex is especially concerned, or in which certain characteristics (as beauty, strength, etc.) in one sex serve to attract the other and conduce to mating and reproduction, with perpetuation of the characteristics.—**sex-u-al'i-ty** (-al'i-ti), *n.* Sexual character; possession of sex; also, the recognition or emphasizing of sexual characteristics or matters.—**sex'u-al-ly**, *adv.*

sfor-zan-do (sfôr-tsän'dō), *a.* [It., gerund of *sforzare*, to force.] In *music*, forcing: used as a direction, to indicate that a tone or chord is to be rendered with special emphasis. Also **sfor-za'to** (-tsä'tō).

sh, 'sh (sh), *interj.* A shortened form of *hush*, used in enjoining silence: as, " '*Sh!*' she whispered. 'Never mind what you make' " (L. Merrick's "House of Lynch," iv.).

shab (shab), *n.* [AS. *sceabb*, scab; from the root of E. *shave*[1]: cf. *scab*.] A scab†; also, the scab, a disease of animals, esp. sheep (prov. Eng.).

shab-bi-ly (shab'i-li), *adv.* In a shabby manner.—**shab'bi-ness**, *n.*

shab-by (shab'i), *a.*; compar. *shabbier*, superl. *shabbiest*. [From *shab*.] Scabby, as sheep (prov. Eng.); also, having the appearance impaired by wear, use, decay, etc. (as, *shabby* clothes, carpets, furniture, or houses; "*shabby* fences," Hawthorne's "House of the Seven Gables," xix.; "a *shabby* horse in a *shabby* cab," W. De Morgan's "Somehow Good," iii.); wearing noticeably worn clothes, or seedy in appearance, as persons; in general, making a poor appearance or show (as, a *shabby* entertainment); of a poor or sorry kind (as, "I kept a poor, *shabby* pretence of a journal," Kinglake's "Eothen," xvii.; "Drowning's but a *shabby* way of going out of the world," H. Melville's "Omoo," xli.); meanly small or inadequate, as a gift, allowance, etc.; mean, meanly ungenerous or unfair, scurvy, or contemptible, as persons, actions, etc. (as, a *shabby* trickster; a *shabby* way to treat an old friend; "It would be *shabby* to let the avalanche fall without giving . . . warning," H. G. Wells's "Soul of a Bishop," vi.).—**shab"by=gen-teel'**, *a.* Shabby but genteel; making or showing an effort to keep up genteel appearances in spite of shabbiness: as, "a somewhat *shabby-genteel*, youngish man . . . wearing a silk hat and a too ample frock-coat" (Arnold Bennett's "Hilda Lessways," i. 6).—**shab"by=gen-til'i-ty**, *n.*

shab-le, shab-ble (shab'l), *n.* [It. *sciabla*, *sciabola*; akin to E. *saber*.] A saber; a curved sword. [Archaic or Sc.]

shab-rack (shab'rak), *n.* [= F. *schabraque*, < G. *schabracke*; prob. ult. from Turk.] A saddle-cloth used in European armies: as, "all . . . upon chestnut horses, with their leopard skin *shabracks* and their little red panaches" (Conan Doyle's "Exploits of Brigadier Gerard," v.).

shack (shak), *n.* [Origin uncertain.] A roughly built house or cabin (as, "The ranch-house may be only a mud dugout, or a '*shack*' made of logs stuck upright into the ground": Roosevelt's "Hunting Trips of a Ranchman," i.); a shanty; also, a railroad brakeman. [Colloq.]

shack-le[1] (shak'l), *n.* [AS. *sceacul*, shackle; = D. *schakel*, link of a chain.] A ring or fastening of iron or the like, usually one of a pair, for securing the wrist, ankle, or some other part of the body of a prisoner (often in *pl.*: as, "Haley, drawing out . . . a heavy pair of *shackles*, made them fast round each ankle," Mrs. Stowe's "Uncle Tom's Cabin," x.); a hobble or fetter for a horse or other animal (as, "a half-bred foal or two, straggling about with *shackles* on their hind legs": Scott's "Guy Mannering," xxiii.); any of various fastening or coupling devices, as the curved bar of a padlock which passes through the staple; in fig. use, anything that serves to prevent freedom of procedure, thought, etc., or a restraint (as, "The *shackles* of an old love straiten'd him," Tennyson's "Lancelot and Elaine," 870; "the bars and *shackles* of civilization," Mark Twain's "Tom Sawyer," xxxv.).—**shack'le**[1], *v. t.*; *-led*, *-ling.* To put a shackle or shackles on; confine or restrain with shackles, or fetter (as, "James More lies *shackled* in prison": Stevenson's "David Balfour," i.); fasten or couple with a shackle; in fig. use, to restrain, hamper, or trammel in action, thought, etc.

shack-le[2] (shak'l), *v. i.*; *-led*, *-ling.* [Cf. *shake* and *ramshackle*.] To shake; joggle; rattle as from looseness; also, to idle about; loaf; shirk work. [Prov.]—**shack'ling**, **shack'ly**, *a.* Shaky; loose-jointed; rickety; ramshackle: as, "his lanky jaws, protruding eyes, and *shackling* figure" (Mrs. Stowe's "Oldtown Folks," xlv.); "the country-people . . . in all kinds of old *shackly* wagons" (Mark Twain's "Huckleberry Finn," xxi.). [Prov. or colloq., esp. U. S.]

shad (shad), *n.*; pl. *shad*, occasionally (esp. with reference to different species) *shads*. [AS. *sceadd*.] Any of various fishes of the clupeid genus *Alosa*, as *A. sapidissima*, an American anadromous fish with a comparatively deep body, one of the most highly esteemed food-fishes of the

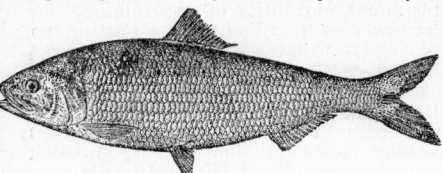

American Shad (*Alosa sapidissima*).

northern Atlantic coast.—**shad′=ber″ry,** *n.* The fruit of the shad-bush; also, the shad-bush itself.—**shad′=bush,** *n.* The North American service-berry, *Amelanchier canadensis,* a shrub or small tree with racemose white flowers and a berry-like fruit, which blossoms about the time when shad appear in the rivers; any of various other species of *Amelanchier.*

shad-dock (shad′ọk), *n.* [From a Captain *Shaddock* who brought the seed from the East Indies to the West Indies in the 17th century.] The large, roundish or pear-shaped, usually pale-yellow, orange-like edible fruit of the rutaceous tree *Citrus decumana;* strictly, the pear-shaped kind of this fruit, yielded by certain varieties of the tree (the roundish and more choice kind being usually known as *grape-fruit*); also, the tree itself, belonging to the same genus as the orange, lemon, etc., and cultivated in tropical and semitropical regions (see *citrus*).

shade (shād), *n.* [AS. *sceadu* (inflected *sceadw-,* whence E. *shadow*), akin to D. *schaduw,* G. *schatten,* Goth. *skadus,* shade, shadow: cf. Gr. σκότος, darkness.] The comparative darkness caused by the interception of rays of light (as, "Aloft, here, half a village shines, arrayed In golden light; half hides itself in *shade*": Wordsworth's "Descriptive Sketches," 98); an instance or area of comparative darkness, or a shadow (as, "Some delicious land Of lavish lights,

Leaf of Shad-dock (*Citrus decumana*).

and floating *shades*": Tennyson's "Eleänore," i.); *pl.*, the darkling shadows, or the darkness, gathering at the close of day (lit. or fig.: as, "The *shades* of night were falling fast," Longfellow's "Excelsior"; the *shades* of life's evening, or of death); *sing.,* fig., comparative obscurity (as, this last feat threw all others into the *shade*; the real leaders remained in the *shade*); a darkening look, expression, feeling, or the like, or a cloud (as, a *shade* crosses the face; "The first *shade* of doubt now fell across his mind," Trollope's "Warden," iii.); also, comparative darkness as represented pictorially; the dark part, or a dark part, of a picture; also, degree of depth of color; hence, any of the different varieties of a color (as, *shades* of blue, any of the many colors called blue differing from one another in hue, chroma, etc.), or, in a more restricted sense, any of the different varieties of a color produced by mixing it with black; fig., a very slightly differentiated variety of something (as, delicate *shades* of meaning; "quite intelligent enough to appreciate the exact *shade* of his attitude," J. Conrad's "Rescue," v. 3; "The North-country woman had found it very difficult to suit herself to a new *shade* of local character," Mrs. H. Ward's "Robert Elsmere," xx.); a minute amount, or a trace or tinge, of something (as, not a *shade* of remorse; "There was the slightest *shade* of asperity in the question," W. De Morgan's "Joseph Vance," i.); a slight degree, or a little bit (as, a *shade* too long; "He had begun to dread his visits to her a *shade*," L. Merrick's "Worldlings," v.); also, a shadow or dark figure cast on the ground or some surface by a body intercepting light (now chiefly poetic: as, "The low sun had lengthen'd every *shade*," Pope's "Autumn," 100; "Every one hath . . . one *shade*," Shakspere's "Sonnets," liii.); hence, a mere unsubstantial image or unreal appearance; a specter, phantom, or ghost (as, "There, where a sceptred Pictish *shade* Stalk'd round his ashes lowly laid": Burns's "Vision," 109); the spirit of one dead, esp., in the classical mythology, an inhabitant of Hades; *pl.,* with *the,* the spirits of the dead collectively, or the world or abode of the dead, or Hades (as, "This, my third victim, to the *shades* I send": Pope's tr. Homer's "Iliad," xiii.); also, *sing.,* the slight darkness and coolness, or the protection

from glare and heat, afforded by something that intercepts light, esp. sunlight (as, to sit in the *shade* of a tree, rock, or building; to seek the *shade* of an arbor); overshadowing foliage (in *sing.* or *pl.*: poetic: as, "In Vallombrosa, where the Etrurian *shades* High overarch'd imbower," Milton's "Paradise Lost," i. 303); a shady place (now chiefly in *pl.,* and poetic: as, "These *shades* Are still the abodes of gladness," Bryant's "Inscription for the Entrance to a Wood"); hence, a retired, sequestered, or obscure place (chiefly in *pl.,* and poetic or literary: as, "In the depth of college *shades* . . . the poor student shrunk from observation," Lamb's "Poor Relations"); also, something used for protection against excessive light, heat, etc.; a piece of cloth or other material, commonly mounted on a roller, fixed at a window to keep out light or prevent view; a globular, conical, or otherwise shaped screen of porcelain, silk, or other material, for surrounding the flame of a lamp or candle, a gas-jet, or the like, in order to soften and diffuse the light, to concentrate and reflect it, etc.—**shade,** *v.; shaded, shading.* **I.** *tr.* To produce shade in or on, or render shady (as, "The enclosure was . . . *shaded* by ancient trees": Prescott's "Conquest of Mexico," iv. 2); overspread with shade; fig., to obscure, dim, or darken; also, to screen or hide from view (as, "Leicester drew the curtain . . . so as completely to *shade* his face": Scott's "Kenilworth," xxxii.); also, to protect from light, heat, etc., with something serving as a screen, or as the screening object does (as, to *shade* the eyes with the hand; to *shade* the face with a broad-brimmed hat; his hat *shaded* his face); cover or screen (a light, candle, etc.) as with a shade; also, to represent pictorially the shade or shadow on (an object); paint or draw with indications of shade; also, to color in shades passing gradually one into another, as from light to dark or reversely; cause (color) to pass by slight gradations into another shade or color; fig., to change by imperceptible degrees into something else; soften by modification (with *away, down,* or *off*: as, "He had the characteristic national trait of *shading* off his most serious remarks," W. Churchill's "Modern Chronicle," iii. 1); lessen slightly, as a price (colloq.); also, to surpass, esp. by a shade or slight degree (colloq. or prov.: as, to *shade* an opponent in a contest). **II.** *intr.* To pass or change by slight gradations, as one color or one thing into another; pass gradually (*away* or *off*).—**shade′less,** *a.* Having or affording no shade.—**shad-er** (shā′dèr), *n.*—**shade′=tree,** *n.* A tree planted or valued for its shade.

shad=fly (shad′flī), *n.;* pl. *-flies* (-flīz). Any of various insects which appear about the time when shad enter the rivers, as a May-fly.

shad-i-ly (shā′di-li), *adv.* In a shady manner.—**shad′i-ness,** *n.*

shad-ing (shā′ding), *n.* The act of one who or that which shades; esp., the representation of shade, as in a picture; marking or color giving the effect of shade; a slight variation or difference of color, character, etc.

sha-doof, sha-duf (shä-döf′), *n.* [Ar. *shādūf*.] A contrivance used in the East for raising water, as from a river, esp. for irrigation, consisting of a long rod suspended on a frame, with a bucket hanging at one end and a weight at the other serving as a counterpoise.

shad-ow (shad′ō), *n.* [AS. *sceadw-:* see *shade*.] Shade or comparative darkness, or an instance or area of comparative darkness (as, "Some inscription ran along the front, But deep in *shadow*," Tennyson's "Princess," i. 210; "until the day break, and the *shadows* flee away," Cant. ii. 17); fig., obscurity (as, to dwell in *shadow*); a darkening look or expression, as on the face; a cloud, as on friendship or reputa-

Raising Water by Shadoofs.

tion; also, the dark part, or shade, or a dark part, of a picture; also, a dark figure or image cast on the ground or some surface by a body intercepting light (as, "Th' ascending villas . . . Project long *shadows* o'er the crystal tide": Pope's "Windsor Forest," 376); often, the figure so cast by a person (as, "He was careful not to step in Huneefa's blotched, squat *shadow* on the boards," Kipling's "Kim," x.; to be afraid of one's own *shadow*, to be excessively timid; may your *shadow* never be less! — a polite expression, of Oriental origin); hence, an inseparable follower or companion (as, "Sin and her *shadow* Death": Milton's "Paradise Lost," ix. 12); one who follows a person in order to keep watch upon him, as a spy or detective; also, a reflected image (as, "Let . . . The swan on still St. Mary's Lake Float double, swan and *shadow*!" Wordsworth's "Yarrow Unvisited," 44); a copy or counterpart; also, a shadowy or faint image, or adumbration (as, "These sights are the *shadows* of that fairer Paradise which is our home," J. H. Newman's "Callista," xiv.; *shadows* of things to come); one so emaciated or weakened as to suggest a mere shadowy form of a person (as, to be worn to a *shadow*; "When it [a fever] left me, a mere *shadow* of my former self, I was dumb," W. H. Hudson's "Far Away and Long Ago," xxii.); a slight appearance or suggestion, or a shade or trace, of something (as, a claim made without any *shadow* of reason or right; "There was . . . a grain of derision, a *shadow* of treachery, in his expression," Stevenson's "Treasure Island," xxv.); also, a mere unsubstantial image or semblance of something, or an unreality (as, to have but the *shadow* of power; "A dream itself is but a *shadow*," Shakspere's "Hamlet," ii. 2. 266); a specter, phantom, ghost, or shade; a shadowy or spectral being (as, "There sat the *Shadow* fear'd of man": Tennyson's "In Memoriam," xxii.); also, the cool shade, or the protection from glare and heat, afforded by something that intercepts light (as, "as rivers of water in a dry place, as the *shadow* of a great rock in a weary land": Isa. xxxii. 2); hence, shelter, cover, or protection (as, "Hide me under the *shadow* of thy wings": Ps. xvii. 8); range of influence or effect (as, to come within the *shadow* of one's power); in *physics*, a condition or an area of obstruction of sound-waves, electric waves, or the like, analogous to the shadow produced by the interception of light by some obstacle. — **shadow of death,** the darkness or gloom of death, esp. approaching or imminent death: a Biblical expression: as, "before I go . . . to the land of darkness and the *shadow of death*" (Job, x. 21); "Yea, though I walk through the valley of the *shadow of death*, I will fear no evil" (Ps. xxiii. 4). — **shad'ow,** *v.* **I.** *tr.* To overspread with shadow, or shade (as, "the great oak *shadowing* a bare place in mid-pasture": George Eliot's "Middlemarch," xii.); throw into shadow, or obscure with a shadow (as, "Her plumed hat *shadowed* a face which was no longer young in such a way as to hide all the lines possible": Mrs. H. Ward's "Robert Elsmere," xxvi.); fig., to cast a gloom over, cloud, or darken (as, events that have *shadowed* one's life); also, to hide from view or knowledge†; also, to screen or protect from light, heat, etc. (as, "Some . . . under arches of the marble bridge Hung, *shadow'd* from the heat": Tennyson's "Princess," ii. 435); hence, to shelter or protect as with something overshadowing (archaic: as, "You give his offspring life, *Shadowing* their right under your wings of war," Shakspere's "King John," ii. 1. 14); also, to shade in painting, drawing, etc.†; paint† or draw†; also, to represent by a shadowy or faint image, or in an imperfect, obscure, or prophetic way (often with *forth* or *out*); adumbrate, symbolize, or prefigure; also, to follow like a shadow; specif., to follow (a person) about secretly, in order to keep watch upon him (as, detectives *shadow* suspected persons). **II.** *intr.* To cast a shadow; also, to become dark or shadowy; also, to shade or pass by degrees, as into another color.

shad-ow=bird (shad'ō-bėrd), *n.* The umbrette.

shad-ow=box-ing (shad'ō-bok″sing), *n.* Boxing carried on with a shadow or an imaginary opponent, as for exercise.

shad-ow-er (shad'ō-ėr), *n.* One who or that which shadows.

shad-ow-graph (shad'ō-gráf), *n.* [+ -*graph*.] A picture produced by throwing a shadow, as of the hands, on a lighted screen; also, a radiograph.

shad-ow-i-ly (shad'ō-i-li), *adv.* In a shadowy manner. — **shad'ow-i-ness,** *n.*

shad-ow-land (shad'ō-land), *n.* A land or region of shadows, phantoms, unrealities, or uncertainties.

shad-ow-less (shad'ō-les), *a.* Casting no shadow; also, having no shadows or shade.

shad-ow-y (shad'ō-i), *a.* Abounding in shadow or shade, or shady, as places; dark with shadows, or having but dim light (as, "In a *shadowy* saloon, On silken cushions half reclined": Tennyson's "Eleänore," viii.); enveloped in shadow, as objects; dim, as light; also, casting a shadow, or affording shade (as, "The golden oriole . . . darted among the *shadowy* branches": Parkman's "Oregon Trail," xxvii.); also, resembling a shadow, as in being indistinct, faint, slight, or emaciated (as, a *shadowy* image; *shadowy* outlines; "Little Rima . . . now began to fade and look more *shadowy*," W. H. Hudson's "Green Mansions," xv.); unsubstantial, unreal, or illusory (as, "authority of a *shadowy* kind": Froude's "Cæsar," xiv.); spectral, phantom, or ghostly.

sha-duf', *n.* See *shadoof*.

shad=wait-er (shad'wā″tėr), *n.* A whitefish, *Coregonus quadrilateralis*, of lakes from New England to Alaska.

Shad-waiter.

shad-y (shā'di), *a.*; compar. *shadier*; superl. *shadiest.* Abounding in shade, or shaded (as, *shady* paths; a *shady* nook); also, affording shade (as, "The *shady* trees cover him with their shadow": Job, xl. 22); also, shadowy, indistinct, or spectral (as, "See, *shady* forms advance!" Pope's "Ode on St. Cecilia's Day," iv.: obs. or archaic); also, uncertain, questionable, or dubious as to excellence, promise, etc. (colloq.: as, a *shady* lot of candidates; *shady* prospects or chances); of dubious character or reputation, as persons (colloq.); of doubtful honesty, morally questionable, or such as will not bear investigation, as actions, character, etc. (colloq.: as, "He confessed that much to me in extenuation of the *shady* part he had played in Sherif Ali's plot," J. Conrad's "Lord Jim," xxxiii.). — **on the shady side of,** fig., on the less bright or youthful side of (as, "a tall, upright, florid man, a little *on the shady side of* life": Mrs. Stowe's "Oldtown Folks," v.); beyond in age (as, to be *on the shady side of* forty). [Colloq.] — **to keep shady,** to keep out of sight, or in hiding. [Slang.]

shaft[1] (shäft), *n.* [ME. *shaft*: cf. MLG. and G. *schacht*, shaft (of mine, etc.), also E. *shaft*[2].] A deep passage sunk through the earth, esp. vertically or nearly vertically, in mining, tunneling, etc.; any well-like passage or vertical inclosed space, as in a building (as, a *shaft* for air or light; an elevator *shaft*); also, the chamber of a blast-furnace above the hearth.

shaft[2] (shäft), *n.* [AS. *sceaft* = MLG. and D. *schaft*, *schacht*, = G. *schaft* = Icel. *skapt*, shaft (of spear, etc.): cf. L. *scapus*, shaft, stem, E. *scape*[1].] The long, slender rod forming the body of a spear or lance, or of an arrow; hence, a spear or lance; an arrow; loosely, any missile; fig., something directed as in sharp attack against a person or the mind, heart, etc. (as, *shafts* of wit or sarcasm; "a shield against the *shafts* of doubt," Whittier's "Questions of Life"; "The *shaft* of love . . . had struck me," Arnold Bennett's "Book of Carlotta," i. 4); also, something resembling an arrow or missile, as a ray of light; also, any long, slender body, piece, or part; the trunk of a tree (as, "the symmetrical *shaft* of the cocoa-nut tree, surmounted by its tuft of graceful branches": H. Melville's "Typee," xvii.); a pole; either of the bars of wood (thills) between which the animal drawing a vehicle is placed; the pole or tongue of a vehicle; the upright part of a cross; the handle of a hammer, ax, golf-club, or other long implement; the main stem or stock of a feather; the body of a column or pillar between the base and the capital; a column (as, "A glittering roof of gold Slim *shafts* of pale blue marble did uphold": W. Morris's "Jason," xvii. 236); a monument in the form of a column, obelisk, or the like; in *mach.*, a revolving bar (fitted with pulleys or the like) serving to transmit motion, as from an engine to various machines; also, a large axle (as, the *shaft* of a fly-wheel).

—shaft′ed, *a.* Having a shaft or shafts.—**shaft′ing,** *n.* In *mach.*, shafts for communicating motion, or material for such shafts; a system of such shafts.

shag[1] (shag). [AS. *sceacga,* shag of hair; akin to Icel. *skegg,* Sw. *skägg,* Dan. *skjæg,* beard: cf. *shaw*[1].] **I.** *n.* Rough, matted hair, wool, or the like, or a mass of this (as, "a mop of

Shafting.—*a,* shaft; *b, b′,* pulleys; *c, c′,* belts; *d, d′,* supports; *e,* cup to receive oil dropping from the bearing in *d′.*

hair not a little resembling the *shag* of a Newfoundland dog": Irving's "Knickerbocker's New York," v. 9); also, the nap of cloth, esp. when long or rough; a cloth with a nap, at times one of silk but commonly a heavy or rough woolen fabric, formerly in use; a rug†; also, a rough mass or growth of bushes or other vegetation; also, a coarse tobacco cut into fine shreds. **II.** *a.* Rough or shaggy, as hair; covered with shaggy hair (as, "old Trusty, my *shag* housedog": H. Mackenzie's "Man of Feeling," xxxiv.); also, made of shag, as garments.—**shag**[1], *v. t.; shagged, shagging.* To make rough or shaggy, esp. with vegetation (as, "the woods that . . . have *shagged* the hills with a stunted and meagre growth": Howells's "Chance Acquaintance," iii.); also, to render roughly or sharply broken in surface (as, "This vast mountain . . . was *shagged* by frightful precipices": Irving's "Captain Bonneville," xxv.).

shag[2] (shag), *n.* [Perhaps another use of *shag*[1], with reference to the crest.] A cormorant; esp., the crested cormorant, *Phalacrocorax graculus,* of Europe, which in the breeding season is crested with long, curly plumes.

shag-bark (shag′bärk), *n.* A species of hickory, *Hicoria ovata,* with rough bark, yielding the best hickory-nuts; also, the nut of this tree; also, the wood.

shag=eared (shag′ērd), *a.* Having shaggy or hairy ears: as, a *shag-eared* pony; "thou *shag-ear′d* [also *shag-hair′d*] villain" (Shakspere's "Macbeth," iv. 2. 83); "*shag-eared,* military, hirsute ruffians" (Motley's "Dutch Republic," vi. 7). [Now prov. Eng. or archaic.]

shag-ged (shag′ed), *a.* [AS. *sceacgede.*] Covered with or having shaggy hair, as animals, etc.; shaggy, as hair; also, covered with a rough growth of vegetation (as, "a deep mountain glen, wild, lonely, and *shagged*": Irving's "Sketch-Book," Rip Van Winkle); also, roughly or sharply broken in surface, or jagged.

shag-gy (shag′i), *a.;* compar. *shaggier,* superl. *shaggiest.* [See *shag*[1].] Rough and matted or tangled, or forming a thick, rough mass, as hair, etc. (as, "The hand of nature has . . . covered their [negroes'] heads with *shaggy* wool": Gibbon's "Decline and Fall of the Roman Empire," xlii.); often, long and rough, or forming a bushy, irregular mass, as the hair, beard, mane, eyebrows, etc.; consisting of a growth of long, rough hair, wool, or the like (as, a dog with a *shaggy* coat; a *shaggy* fleece); covered with or having long, rough hair (as, a *shaggy* dog; a *shaggy* pony; "our wild Seer, *shaggy,* unkempt, like a Baptist living on locusts and wild honey," Carlyle's "Sartor Resartus," i. 4); also, long or rough, as a nap on cloth (as, "velvet soft, or plush with *shaggy* pile": Cowper's "Task," i. 11); having a long or rough nap, as cloth, garments, etc. (as, "wrapping myself in my *shaggy* jacket of the cloth called bearskin": H. Melville's "Moby-Dick," vii.); also, forming a rough or ragged growth, as bushes, trees, etc.; covered with such a growth, as hills, etc.; also, having a rough or broken surface, as the bark of trees, etc.—**shag′gi-ly,** *adv.*—**shag′gi-ness,** *n.*—**shag′gy-mane,** *n.* A common edible fungus, *Coprinus comatus,* having an elongated pileus covered with shaggy appressed scales. See cut in next column.

sha-green (sha-grēn′), *n.* [F. *chagrin,* < Turk. *çāghrī,* back of a horse, hence leather made of the skin of this part.] A kind of untanned leather with a granular surface, prepared from the skin of the horse, ass, etc., and sometimes the shark, seal, etc.; an imitation of this; also, the rough skin of certain sharks and other selachians.

shah (shä), *n.* [Pers. *shāh.*] King: esp. used [usually *cap.*] as a title of the ruler of Persia. Cf. *padishah.*

Shai-tan (shī-tän′), *n.* [Ar., = E. *Satan.*] In Mohammedan use, Satan, or the devil; an evil spirit; hence [*l. c.*], a person of evil disposition; a vicious animal.

shak-a-ble (shā′ka-bl), *a.* That may be shaken.

shake (shāk), *v.;* pret. *shook,* pp. *shaken* (sometimes, esp. archaic or prov., *shook*), ppr. *shaking.* [AS. *sceacan, scacan* (pret. *scōc,* pp. *scacen*), shake, move, depart, = OS. *skakan,* depart, = Icel. and Sw. *skaka,* shake.] **I.** *intr.* To move or sway with short, quick, irregular vibratory movements, esp. under some force or from weakness (as, trees *shake* in the wind; "The whole hut *shook* when she walked," J.

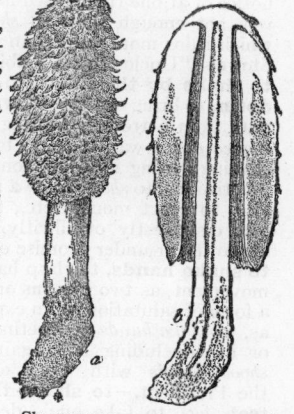

Shaggy-mane.—*a,* young specimen; *b,* section through a specimen older than *a.*

Conrad's "Lord Jim," xxxvii.; his hand *shakes* in writing; to *shake* with palsy): vibrate irregularly or tremulously; quiver; quake; tremble with emotion; shiver with cold; be stirred or convulsed with laughter (as, "She *shook* with laughter till her bracelets and anklets jingled": Kipling's "Kim," vii.); sound unsteadily (as, "Though he tried to speak firmly his voice *shook*": W. Churchill's "Coniston," i. 12); also, to totter, waver, or become unsteady, as if about to give way (as, the ranks *shook* under a heavy onslaught; his resolution begins to *shake*); also, to fall (*down, off,* etc.) as the result of some movement to and fro (as, fruit *shakes* down in a storm; sand *shakes* off readily; "Her brown hair had *shaken* low upon her temples," G. W. Cable's "Cavalier," xxxiii.); settle (*down*), as into place, a condition, relations, etc.; in *music,* to execute a shake or trill. **II.** *tr.* To move to and fro with short, quick, forcible movements (as, to *shake* a sieve or a tambourine; to *shake* a dusty rug; "Oliver . . . seized Noah by the throat; *shook* him . . . till his teeth chattered," Dickens's "Oliver Twist," vi.); brandish or flourish (a weapon, the fist, etc.); turn (the head) from side to side as an expression of dissent, refusal, disapproval, sorrow, or the like; bestir (one's self: as, "Get up and *shake* yourself," H. Melville's "Moby-Dick," xvii.); often, to set in vibratory or tremulous motion, or cause to quiver or tremble (as, the explosion *shook* the neighboring houses; the breeze *shakes* the aspen leaves; "A little clock-work steamer paddling . . . *shook* the lilies," Tennyson's "Princess," Prologue, 72); set quivering with nervous agitation, strong emotion, etc.; agitate or disturb profoundly in feeling (as, "One day a little swift brutality *shook* him to the very soul": Galsworthy's "Saint's Progress," iii. 4); also, to cause to totter or waver, as if about to give way (as, "An ever-fixed mark That looks on tempests and is never *shaken*," Shakspere's "Sonnets," cxvi.; a force that has *shaken* kingdoms; to *shake* the very foundations of society); unsettle, weaken, or make less firm (as, to *shake* one's reason; to *shake* a firm's credit; to *shake* one's faith, conviction, or resolution); render (a person) less set or determined (as, "Nor could either our prayers or our offers of money . . . avail to *shake* him": Stevenson's "Master of Ballantrae," iii.); also, to bring, throw, force, rouse, etc. (*down, off, out, up,* etc.) by or as by some vigorous movement to and fro (as, to *shake* snow off one's clothes; to *shake* off gloomy feelings; to *shake* out the contents of a bag; to *shake* a rose to pieces: see phrases *to shake down* and *to shake up,* following); also, to scatter or sprinkle by some shaking movement (as, to *shake* salt over food); also, to take (casks) to pieces for packing and transportation (cf. *shook*[2]); also, to cast off, or get rid of (slang: as, "His mother seized the property and '*shook*' him, as he phrased it," Mark Twain's "Life on the Mississippi," v.); in *music,* to trill (a note, etc.).—**to shake a leg,** to dance: as, "A lively customer at a dance! He can *shake a leg,* as they say" (M. Hewlett's "Open Country," xi.). [Prov. or colloq.]—**to shake a stick at**, to deal with or indicate as if by strokes of a stick; attend to or take notice of at one time: used in expressing quantity: as, there was not enough snow to *shake a stick at*; "laziness . . . which ruins more souls than you can *shake a stick at*" (Mrs. Stowe's "Uncle Tom's Cabin," xvi.). [Colloq., U. S.]—**to shake by the hand**, to shake hands with.—**to shake down**, to bring or throw down by shaking (as, to *shake down* nuts from a tree by beating the branches; an earthquake *shakes down* walls); also, to cause to settle down, as by shaking; bring into due condition or working order, as by practice (as, to *shake down* a naval cruiser by a first voyage); also, to exact money, etc., from (persons) by compulsion, esp. dishonestly or illicitly, as under pretense of official authority or under promise of political protection (slang).—**to shake hands**, to clasp hands, with or without a shaking movement, as two persons or as one person with another, as a form of salutation or an expression of friendly feeling, etc.: as, to *shake hands* at meeting or parting, in congratulation, or in concluding a bargain; the late combatants now *shook hands* with each other; to *shake hands* with the President.—**to shake the dust off** (or **from**) one's **feet**, fig., to take one's departure from a place, esp. in displeasure or with the determination not to return: from a New Testament use, as in Luke, ix. 5, "And whosoever will not receive you, when ye go out of that city, shake off the very dust from your feet for a testimony against them."—**to shake up**, to shake vigorously, as for the purpose of mixing ingredients, loosening material, etc. (as, to *shake up* a liquid medicine; to *shake up* hay); also, to rouse up by or as by shaking; fig., to stir up or upset by vigorous proceedings, unexpected changes, etc. (as, to *shake up* a business establishment or an official department); also, to jar in body or nerves by some physical shock (as, to be badly *shaken up* by a fall or in a collision); also, to scold roundly, or berate (as, "Thou shalt hear how he will *shake me up*," Shakspere's "As You Like It," i. 1. 30: now prov. Eng.).—**shake**, *n.* The act or an act of shaking something (as, a *shake* of a stick; a *shake* of the head; "a cordial *shake* of the hand," Smollett's "Humphry Clinker," May 17); also, vibratory or tremulous motion; a quiver or tremor; a fit of trembling or shivering; also, an unsettling or disturbing blow, or a shock (often fig.: as, to give a *shake* to one's confidence); also, the (brief) time required for a single shaking movement, or an instant or moment (slang: as, I'll be there in two *shakes* of a lamb's tail; wait a *shake*; "Fists and brickbats would have been going in a couple of *shakes*," S. R. Crockett's "Stickit Minister," xvii.); also, something resulting from shaking, a shock, or the like; a fissure in the earth; a crack or fissure in timber, produced during growth by wind, sudden change of temperature, or the like; a shook of staves, etc.; a drink made by shaking ingredients together (as, a milk-*shake*; an egg-*shake*); in *music*, a rapid alternation of a given tone with the tone above or below it; a trill.—**great shakes**, something extraordinary; something of great account or importance: usually with a negative: as, "My Mother said my Father was no such *great shakes* to boast on" (W. De Morgan's "Joseph Vance," xii.). [Slang.]—**the shakes**, ague, or some other disease characterized by shaking; also, the sensations of trembling or shivering caused by fear, dread, horror, etc. (as, "I've *the shakes* upon me for the gallows": Stevenson's "Treasure Island," xxx.). [Colloq.]

shake′a·ble, *a.* See *shakable*.

shake=down (shāk′doun), *n.* A bed made of straw, blankets, or other bedding spread on the floor; any makeshift bed, as for temporary use; also, a process of shaking down; esp., a bringing into due condition or working order by practice (as, to give a naval vessel a *shake-down*, as by a voyage which permits a trial of the engines, guns, etc., in use); also, an exaction of money, etc., by compulsion, esp. dishonestly or illicitly, as in various forms of official graft (slang).

shake=fork (shāk′fôrk), *n.* A large wooden fork, used esp. for lifting and shaking threshed straw to throw out the grain (now prov. Eng.); hence, in *her.*, a forked or Y-shaped bearing resembling the pall but with the three extremities, usually pointed bluntly, not reaching the edge of the escutcheon.

Shake-fork.

shak·er (shā′kėr), *n.* One who or that which shakes (as, "Neptune, *shaker* of the earth and sea": W. Morris's "Jason," v. 358); also, that with which something is shaken; also [*cap.*], one of an American communistic celibate religious sect ("United Society of Believers in Christ's Second Appearing"), so called, popularly, from the agitations or movements of the body which form part of their ceremonial.—**Shak′er·ess**, *n.* A female Shaker.—**Shak′er·ism**, *n.* The principles and practices of the Shakers.

Shake-spear′i·an, etc. See *Shaksperian*, etc.

shake=up (shāk′up), *n.* A shaking up; esp., a vigorous stirring up, or upsetting of existing conditions, in a business establishment, an official department, or the like, as by investigation, changes in system, transfer or dismissal of officials, etc.

shak·i·ly (shā′ki-li), *adv.* In a shaky manner.—**shak′i·ness**, *n.*

shak·ing (shā′king), *n.* The act of one who or that which shakes; also, that which is shaken down, off, etc.; *pl.*, *naut.*, small pieces of cordage, rope, canvas, etc., used for making oakum or paper (as, "a bale of *shakings*": J. Conrad's "Lord Jim," x.).—**shak′ing**, *p. a.* That shakes; characterized by shaking; quivering; quaking; trembling: as, "The '*shaking* prairie,' 'trembling prairie,' or *prairie tremblante*, is low, level, treeless delta land, having a top soil of vegetable mould overlying immense beds of quicksand" (G. W. Cable's "Bonaventure," iii. 1, note).—**shaking palsy.** See *palsy*, *n.*—**shak′ing·ly**, *adv.*

shak·o (shak′ō), *n.*; *pl.* *-os* (-ōz). [F. *shako*, *schako*, < Hung. *csákó*.] A kind of military cap or head-covering in the form of a cylinder or truncated cone, with a vizor and a plume or pompon: as, "I had taken the panache from my *shako* so that it might escape notice" (Conan Doyle's "Exploits of Brigadier Gerard," iv.).

Shak·sper·i·an (shak-spēr′i·an). [From *Shakspere*, the form of the name in one of Shakspere's own signatures, accepted by the New Shakspere Society of London, the Oxford English Dictionary, and other authorities, and used in this dictionary. The spelling *Shakespeare*, which occurs in the first folio edition (1623), is an alternative in common use, and numerous other spellings have appeared.] **I.** *a.* Of, pertaining to, or suggestive of William Shakspere, or Shakespeare (1564–1616), the great English dramatist and poet, or his works. **II.** *n.* A Shaksperian scholar; a specialist in the study of the works of Shakspere.—**Shak·sper·i·a′na** (-ā′nä), *n. pl.* [NL.: see *-ana*.] Items, details, publications, etc., relating to Shakspere.—**Shak·sper′i·an·ism**, *n.* Devotion to Shakspere; the influence of Shakspere; also, a form of expression peculiar to Shakspere.

shak·y (shā′ki), *a.*; compar. *shakier*, superl. *shakiest*. Given to shaking; shaking; trembling; tremulous, as the voice; also, liable to break down or give way, as a structure; weak or feeble, or not strong in health (as, "screaming unsuitable for the ears of an elderly, *shaky*, rich aunt": H. G. Wells's "Tono-Bungay," i. 1. § 7); insecure or unreliable, as one's position or credit; wavering or unsettled, as in allegiance or belief; uncertain, or not to be depended on, as one's knowledge of a subject; also, having shakes or cracks, as timber.

shale[1] (shāl), *n.* [AS. *scealu*, *scalu*, dish, shell: see *scale*[2].] A shell or husk; a scale, as of a fish; a scale-like piece, or flake. [Obs. or prov. Eng.]

shale[2] (shāl), *n.* [Appar. another use of *shale*[1], with reference to the fissile structure.] A rock of fissile or laminated structure formed by the consolidation of clay or argillaceous material: differing from slate in being less solid and in splitting along the planes of stratification.

shall (shal), *v.*; pres. 1 *shall*, 2 *shalt*, 3 *shall*, pl. *shall*; pret. 1 *should*, 2 *shouldest* or *shouldst*, 3 *should*, pl. *should*; imperative, infinitive, and participles lacking. [AS. *sceal*, *scal*, 1st and 3d pers. sing. pres. (orig. pret.) ind. (pret. *sceolde*, *scolde*), = OHG. *scal*, *sal* (G. *soll*, inf. *sollen*), = Icel. and Goth. *skal*; all from a root meaning 'owe,' whence also AS. *scyld*, G. *schuld*, debt, guilt.] **A.**† *tr.* To owe; be under obligation to pay or render. **B.** *auxiliary.* Ought (now only in the form *should*); also, must†; also, am (is, are, etc.) to (used to express command, as, 'thou *shalt* not steal,' inevitable certainty, as, 'what *shall* be, *shall* be,' determination, as, 'you *shall* not go,' etc., and in future constructions generally). As a future auxiliary, *shall* is used in connection with *will* as follows: In the first person (singular and plural) *shall* denotes futurity (as, we *shall* miss you); in the second and third persons, promise (as, you *shall* hear from us) or determination (as, he *shall* not do it). Conversely, in the first person *will* denotes promise or determination (as, I *will* not fail you; I *will* succeed); in the second and third persons, mere futurity (as, he *will* be here to-day). See *will*[1]. Interrogatively, *shall* is used in questions that admit of *shall* as an auxiliary in the answer: as, *shall* I go? yes, you *shall* (not *will*); *shall* he be told? yes, he *shall* (not *will*). In conditional, hypothetical, and other clauses denoting a future contingency, *shall* is used in all persons: as, if he *shall* come; whether I *shall* succeed; when you *shall* be forgotten. See *should*.

shal-loon (sha-lön′), *n.* [Appar. named from *Châlons*-sur-Marne, city in northeastern France.] A light, twilled woolen fabric used chiefly for linings.

shal-lop (shal′ǫp), *n.* [F. *chaloupe* = Sp. *chalupa*; origin uncertain: cf. *sloop*.] A heavy boat with one or more masts; a sloop; also, a small, light boat with or without a mast; a dinghy.

shal-lot (shạ-lot′), *n.* [= *eschalot*, < F. *eschalotte* (now *échalote*), altered form of OF. *eschaloigne*: see *scallion*.] A plant of the onion kind, *Allium ascalonicum*, whose bulb forms bulblets which are used for flavoring in cookery; also, the bulb or bulblet; also, a small onion.

shal-low (shal′ō). [ME. *schalowe*; prob. related to *shoal*[2].] **I.** *a.* Of little depth, or not deep (as, *shallow* water; a *shallow* dish; "The Ypres Salient now represented a *shallow* semicircle," Buchan's "Hist. of the Great War," liii.); fig., lacking depth, or superficial, as thought, observation, knowledge, feeling, etc. (as, "Ancient humour at its best was a *shallow* thing," Mallock's "New Republic," iii. 4; "The thought of treachery dried up the springs of his very *shallow* friendship," Stevenson's "Master of Ballantrae," vii.); wanting depth of thought, observation, knowledge, feeling, etc., as persons (as, "I do not take a great interest in many people . . . for I find most of them *shallow*": Tarkington's "Magnificent Ambersons," x.); indicative of shallowness of thought, feeling, etc. (as, a *shallow* boast). **II.** *n.* A shallow part of a body of water; a shoal. Also fig.: as, "Here was something beyond the *shallows* of ladies'-school literature" (George Eliot's "Middlemarch," iii.).—**shal′low**, *v. t.* or *i.* To make or become shallow.—**shal′low-ly**, *adv.*—**shal′low-ness,** *n.*

shal-lu (shal′ō or sha-lö′), *n.* [E. Ind.] A grain-sorghum (see *sorghum*), a variety of *Andropogon sorghum*, introduced into the U. S. from India about 1890. Also called *Egyptian wheat*.

shalm (shâm), *n.* See *shawm*.

shalt (shalt). Second person sing. pres. ind. of *shall*: now only in poetic or solemn use.

shal-y (shā′li), *a.* Of, like, or containing shale.

sham (sham). [Said to be a var. of *shame*.] **I.** *n.* A trick† or hoax†; also, something that is not what it purports to be; a spurious imitation; also, a cover or the like for giving a thing a different outward appearance; esp., a pillow-sham. **II.** *a.* Pretended; imitation; counterfeit: as, "a real lady, not a *sham* one" (W. Churchill's "Coniston," ii. 12); "to exercise the men in *sham* attacks upon *sham* forts" (B. Franklin's "Autobiography," xiv.); "*sham* pearls" (H. G. Wells's "Tono-Bungay," ii. 4. § 6).—**sham**, *v.*; *shammed*, *shamming*. **I.** *tr.* To trick† or hoax†; also, to impose by deceit†; also, to produce a deceptive imitation of, or pretend falsely to be (something); assume the appearance of (a condition, action, etc.: as, to *sham* illness; "They were just *shamming* attention," H. G. Wells's "Men Like Gods," i. 8). **II.** *intr.* To make a false pretense; pretend to be, do, etc., what one is not, does not, etc.: as, "You had better keep your pistol ready cocked, for they may be *shamming*" (Marryat's "Mr. Midshipman Easy," xviii.).

sha-man (shä′mạn or sham′ạn), *n.*; pl. *-mans* (-mạnz). [Tungusic.] A priest or sorcerer among various tribes of northern Asia, supposed to have the power to deal with and protect against spirits; also, a medicine-man.—**sha-man-ic** (shä-man′ik), *a.* Pertaining or proper to shamans or shamanism.—**sha′man-ism**, *n.* The primitive religion of northern Asia embracing a belief in controlling spirits who can be influenced only by shamans; hence, any similar religion.—**sha′man-ist**, *n.* A believer in shamanism.—**sha-man-is′tic**, *a.*

sham-ba (sham′bạ), *n.* [Swahili.] A piece of cultivated land. [East African.]

sham-ble[1] (sham′bl), *n.* [AS. *sceamel*, *scamel*, < L. *scamellum*, dim. of *scamnum*, bench, stool.] A stool†; also, a table or stall for the sale of meat; also, *pl.* (often construed as *sing.*), a meat-market; a slaughter-house; fig., a place of carnage (as, "the gloomy bigot . . . who . . . converted all these gay cities into *shambles*," Motley's "Dutch Republic," Introd., xiv.; "to make a *shambles* of the parliament-house," Shakspere's "3 Henry VI.," i. 1. 71).

sham-ble[2] (sham′bl), *v. i.*; *-bled*, *-bling*. [Origin obscure: cf. *scamble*.] To walk or go awkwardly or unsteadily; shuffle: as, "two policemen . . . between whom there *shambled* rather than walked our unhappy friend Ernest" (S. Butler's "Way of All Flesh," lx.).—**sham′ble**[2], *n.* A shambling gait.—**sham′bling-ly**, *adv.*

shame (shām), *n.* [AS. *sceamu*, *scamu*, = OHG. *scama* (G. *scham*) = Icel. *skömm* = Sw. Dan. *skam*, shame: cf. *shend* and *sham*.] The painful feeling arising from the consciousness of something dishonorable, improper, ridiculous, or the like done by one's self or another, or of being in a situation offensive to decency, self-respect, or pride (as, to feel *shame*; to blush with *shame*); also, susceptibility to this feeling (as, to be without *shame*; "There was no *shame* in the aristocracy to prevent them from committing crimes," Froude's "Cæsar," ix.); also, ignominy, disgrace, or dishonor (as, "Bear thine own *shame* for thy sins that thou hast committed": Ezek. xvi. 52); an instance of disgrace (as, "Let his *shames* quickly Drive him to Rome": Shakspere's "Antony and Cleopatra," i. 4. 72); specif., loss of chastity, or unchaste life, on the part of a woman (as, a child of *shame*, one born out of wedlock; to lead a life of *shame*); also, a fact or circumstance bringing disgrace or discredit, or much to be regretted or lamented (as, "It was now becoming a *shame* for a youth of gentle blood to be unlearned," Besant's "Coligny," ii.; it's a *shame* that you can't come; formerly, and still archaically, often used without an article, as, "It were *shame* to our profession were we to suffer it," Scott's "Ivanhoe," xl.); a person or thing that is a source or cause of disgrace (as, "Nature casts him off, who is her *shame*": Shelley's "Cenci," iii. 1. 287); also, the private parts of the body† (see Isa. xlvii. 3).—**to put to shame,** to cause to feel shame (as, "Never in his life had Isaac Worthington been so ignored, so *put to shame*": W. Churchill's "Coniston," ii. 19); also, to bring disgrace or discredit upon; fig., to cast into obscurity, eclipse, or outshine.—**shame**, *v.*; *shamed*, *shaming*. [AS. *sceamian*, *scamian*.] **I.** *intr.* To feel shame. [Now chiefly prov.] **II.** *tr.* To cause to feel shame; make ashamed; also, to cover with ignominy or reproach; disgrace; dishonor; also, to put to shame as by superior excellence, or eclipse or outshine (as, "She'll *shame* 'em with her good looks yet": Dickens's "Dombey and Son," lviii.); also, to drive, force, etc., through shame (as, "You would have *shamed* despotism from the earth": Burke's "Revolution in France," 53).

sha-me-a′nah, *n.* See *shamiana*.

shame-faced (shām′fāst), *a.* [For *shamefast*, by association with *face*.] Modest or bashful; also, characterized by or showing shame (as, "It was pitiful to see his confusion and hear his awkward and *shamefaced* apologies": Mark Twain's "Life on the Mississippi," xxxvi.).—**shame′faced-ly**, *adv.*—**shame′faced-ness,** *n.*

shame-fast (shām′fàst), *a.* [AS. *sceamfæst*, < *sceamu*, E. *shame*, *n.*, + *fæst*, E. *fast*[1], *a.*] Modest; bashful: as, "*Shamfast* she was in maydens shamfastnesse" (Chaucer's "Physician's Tale," 55). [Archaic.]—**shame′fast-ly**, *adv.*—**shame′fast-ness,** *n.*

shame-ful (shām′fúl), *a.* Full of shame†; ashamed†; also, modest†; also, that causes or ought to cause shame, or disgraceful or scandalous (as, "the *shameful* evacuation of Fort Cumberland," Bancroft's "Hist of the U. S.," Amer. Revolution, i. 8; *shameful* treatment).—**shame′ful-ly**, *adv.*—**shame′ful-ness,** *n.*

shame-less (shām′les), *a.* Destitute of shame, as a person; lacking in modesty, immodest, or audacious; insensible to disgrace; also, characterized by or indicating absence of shame (as, "this *shameless* falsehood," Burke's "American

Taxation"; *shameless* boldness).—**shame′less·ly**, *adv.*—**shame′less·ness**, *n.*

sham·er (shā′mėr), *n.* One who or that which shames.

sha·mi·a·na (shä-mē-ä′nä), *n.* [Hind. and Pers. *shāmiyāna*.] An awning set on poles, like a flat tent-roof, often with open sides. [India.]

sham·mer (sham′ėr), *n.* One who shams.

sham·my (sham′i), *n.*; pl. *shammies* (-iz). Same as *chamois*.

sham·poo (sham-pö′), *v. t.*; *-pooed*, *-pooing*. [Prob. < Hind. *chāmpo*, impv. of *chāmpnā*, press.] Orig., to massage (a person, the body, etc.); now, commonly, to treat (the scalp or hair), or to treat the scalp or hair of (a person), by rubbing with soap and water or some other cleansing agent, or by a dry process of massaging.—**sham·poo′**, *n.*; pl. *-poos* (-pöz′). The act or an act of shampooing; also, a preparation used for shampooing.—**sham·poo′er**, *n.*

sham·rock (sham′rok), *n.* [Ir. *seamrog*, dim. of *seamar*, trefoil.] A plant with trifoliate leaves (usually a yellow-flowered species of trefoil, *Trifolium dubium* or *minus*) taken as the national emblem of Ireland: supposedly used by St. Patrick to illustrate the doctrine of the Trinity.

shan·dry·dan (shan′dri-dan), *n.* [Origin obscure.] A light two-wheeled cart or gig; also, any old-fashioned rickety conveyance.

shan·dy·gaff (shan′di-gaf), *n.* [Origin obscure.] A mixed drink as of beer with ginger-beer.

shang·hai¹ (shang′hī), *n.* [From *Shanghai*, city and port of China.] One of a long-legged breed of domestic fowls supposedly introduced from Shanghai.

shang·hai² (shang′hī), *v. t.*; *-haied*, *-haiing*. [Appar. meaning 'to ship to Shanghai': cf. *shanghai¹*.] *Naut.*, to render insensible, as by drugs, and ship on a vessel wanting hands.

shank (shangk), *n.* [AS. *sceanca*, *scanca*, shank, akin to G. *schenkel*, thigh, *schinken*, ham.] That part of the leg in man between the knee and the ankle; also, a corresponding or analogous part in certain animals; that portion of the fore leg of a horse between the knee and the fetlock; that portion of the leg (anatomically, of the foot) of a bird between the point where the feathers usually end and the bases of the toes (also called *tarsus*); also, the whole leg (hence, *shanks' mare*, or *shanks's mare*, one's own legs as a means of conveyance); also, any leg-like, stem-like, or shaft-like part; the pedicel of a flower; that portion of an instrument, tool, etc., connecting the acting part with the handle or any like part; the body of a printing-type, between the shoulder and the foot; the narrow part of a shoe, connecting the broad part of the sole with the heel; a loop at the back of a button, serving for attachment; also, the latter end or part of anything (colloq.: as, the *shank* of the evening).—**shanked**, *a.* Having a shank or shanks: as, long-*shanked*.

shan't, sha'n't (shȧnt). Colloquial contraction of *shall not*.

shan·tung (shan-tung′), *n.* [For *Shantung pongee*; from *Shantung*, province of eastern China.] A silk fabric, a heavy grade of pongee.

shan·ty¹ (shan′ti), *n.*; pl. *-ties* (-tiz). [Canadian F. *chantier*, log hut, in F. supporting framework, open or roofed inclosure, shed, shop, < L. *cantherius*, gelding, framework.] A roughly built hut, cabin, or house, as in lumbering regions or frontier districts; in general, a building of flimsy or rough character; a rude dwelling.

shan·ty² (shan′ti), *n.* Same as *chantey*.

shan·ty=boat (shan′ti-bōt), *n.* A rude house-boat used on inland waters, esp. on the Mississippi River and its tributaries; in lumbering regions, a loggers' house-boat, or wanigan.

shap·a·ble (shā′pa̤-bl), *a.* That may be shaped.

shape (shāp), *v.*; *shaped* (pp. formerly also *shapen*), ppr. *shaping*. [ME. *shapen*, *schapen* (conformed to *shapen*, pp., from AS. pp.), for earlier *scheppen*, *schippen*, < AS. *scieppan*, *scyppan*, *sceppan* (pp. *sceapen*), create, form, ordain; akin to Goth. *gaskapjan*, Icel. *skapa*, D. *scheppen*, G. *schaffen*, create: cf. *-ship*.] **I.** *tr.* To create†; also, to fashion or form, as out of materials; esp., to give a definite form or shape to (as, to *shape* a vessel on the potters' wheel); adapt in form or shape (as, to *shape* a sleeve to a person's arm); hence, to give definite form or character to (as, "the great river-courses which have *shaped* the lives of men,"

George Eliot's "Romola," Proem; "Events began so to *shape* themselves as directly to point to the entrance of the United States into the Great War," Bok's "Americanization of Edward Bok," xxxiv.); couch or express in words (as, to *shape* a statement or a question); fashion or develop into something specified (as, "There I *shaped* The city's ancient legend into this," Tennyson's "Godiva," 3; "The idea of a general union was *shaping* itself into a reality," Bancroft's "Hist. of the U. S.," Amer. Revolution," i. 6); adjust or adapt (as, "So, as I grew, I rudely *shaped* my life To my immediate wants": Browning's "Pauline"); also, to direct (one's course: lit. or fig.: as, "Up this stream they now *shaped* their course," Irving's "Captain Bonneville," iv.; "It is so difficult to *shape* one's course in life," Mallock's "New Republic," i. 3); also, to contrive or devise (obs. or rare: as, "Can I *shape* no means for myself when I am deserted by these cravens?" Scott's "Ivanhoe," xxxiv.); also, to imagine (as, "Oft my jealousy *Shapes* faults that are not": Shakspere's "Othello," iii. 3. 148); picture (as, "The lone Seer . . . *Shaped* forth a disembodied world": Scott's "Lady of the Lake," iii. 7); also, to appoint†; decree†; destine†. **II.** *intr.* To take shape or form; assume a definite form or character (as, "He . . . was nearly fourteen years old, so that his character had begun to *shape*": S. Butler's "Way of All Flesh," xxxii.); develop (as specified, or into something specified); come out (as, "It's appalling, simply appalling! . . . Just when everything was *shaping* so well!" Arnold Bennett's "Hilda Lessways," iii. 4).—

shape, *n.* [ME. *shæpe*, *shap*, < AS. *gesceap*, creation, created thing, form, shape.] The quality of a thing depending on the relative positions of all the points in its outline or external surface; form; figure; a particular variety of this, or a particular form; the form of a particular thing, person, or being (as, "Thou comest in such a questionable *shape* That I will speak to thee": Shakspere's "Hamlet," i. 4. 43); also, something that has form or figure; a figure dimly seen (as, "Rowing [at night], he faced her, a hooded and cloaked *shape*": J. Conrad's "Rescue," iv. 1); an imaginary or ethereal form, or a phantom (as, "Awful *shape*, what art thou? Speak!" Shelley's "Prometheus Unbound," iii. 1. 51); also, an assumed appearance, guise, or disguise (as, "Oh, that deceit should steal such gentle *shapes*!" Shakspere's "Richard III.," ii. 2. 27); also, the particular form or character, or mode of being, which a thing has (as, a present in the *shape* of money; "The result of this conversation took a *shape* that amazed me," Watts-Dunton's "Aylwin," ii. 2); one of the various forms, or modes of being, in which a thing may exist (as, "Dangers of ev'ry *shape* and name Attend the followers of the Lamb": Cowper's "Olney Hymns," Temptation); also, definite form or character (as, things are beginning to take *shape*); proper form, or orderly arrangement (as, to put a thing into *shape*); condition, esp. good condition (as, his affairs are in bad *shape*; an athlete out of condition but training to get into *shape* again); also, something used to give form, as a mold or a pattern; also, a foundation form for a woman's hat; also, something shaped; a quantity of jelly, blancmange, or the like, shaped in a mold; a piece of rolled or hammered iron or steel of any of various special shapes or cross-sections, as an angle-iron, I-bar, or the like; a piece of metal roughly forged to approximately the shape it is to have when finished.

—**in any** (or **no**) **shape**, in any (or no) form; hence, in any (or no) way (as, "Are ye *in any shape* bound to this birkie Peppercull?" Scott's "Fortunes of Nigel," xxxv.).—**shaped**, *a.* Having a shape or shapes (as, many-*shaped*); also, fashioned by shaping; made into a particular shape; given a special ornamental form (as, a *shaped* mirror).—**shape′less**, *a.* Without shape; having no definite or regular shape or form; wanting

A Shaped Mirror, 18th century.

beauty or elegance of form.—**shape′less-ly,** *adv.*—**shape′-less-ness,** *n.*—**shape′ly,** *a.*; compar. *shapelier,* superl. *shapeliest.* Having a pleasing shape; well-formed: as, "an oak, which, though *shapely* and tall on the whole, bulged out into a large excrescence about the middle of the stem" (G. White's "Nat. Hist. of Selborne," i. 2); "a delicate, *shapely* little hand" (W. H. Hudson's "Green Mansions," viii.).—**shape′li-ness,** *n.*—**shap-er** (shā′pèr), *n.*

shaps (shaps), *n. pl.* Same as *chaps,* for *chaparejos.*

shard[1] (shärd), *n.* [AS. *sceard,* noun use of *sceard,* cut, notched, a pp. formation from the root of E. *shear.*] A gap, as in a hedge (now chiefly prov.); also, a fragment, esp. of broken earthenware; also, the wing-cover or elytrum of a beetle.

shard[2] (shärd), *n.* [Cf. obs. or prov. *sharn,* < AS. *scearn,* dung.] Excrement; a mass of cow-dung. [Now prov. Eng. and Sc.]—**shard′=bee″tle,** *n.* A dung-beetle, *Geotrypes stercorarius,* or some allied species.

shard=born (shärd′bôrn), *a.* [Also erron. *shard-borne:* see def.] Born or generated in shards or dung (as, "the *shard-born* beetle," Shakspere's "Macbeth," iii. 2. 42; commonly printed *shard-borne,* and hence interpreted as meaning 'borne on shards or wing-covers'). Cf. *shard-beetle.*

share[1] (shär), *n.* [AS. *scear;* from the root of E. *shear.*] The broad iron or blade of a plow, which cuts the ground at the bottom of the furrow, or a plowshare (as, "The sluggish clod, which the rude swain Turns with his *share*": Bryant's "Thanatopsis"); also, the analogous part of some other implement, as of a seed-drill.

share[2] (shär), *n.* [AS. *scearu,* cutting, division; from the root of E. *shear.*] The portion or part allotted or belonging to, or contributed or owed by, an individual among a number, all of whom receive or contribute (as, "They want father to let them have their *share* of the estate now," Tarkington's "Magnificent Ambersons," xiii.; "taking our turns to row, of which I reckon my *share* came to little less than 20 leagues," Evelyn's "Diary," July 5, 1646); also, a definite portion of some property owned by a number in common; specif., each of the equal parts into which the capital stock of a joint-stock company or a corporation is divided; also, a part taken in some action, etc. (as, to have a *share* in a good work); also, in general, a portion or part (as, "Half a dozen of noblemen . . . have engaged to spend a *share* of to-morrow in a party of pleasure upon the Thames": H. Brooke's "Fool of Quality," vii.).—**on shares,** in accordance with a plan by which two or more persons participate in the risks and the profits of some undertaking.—**to go shares,** to share in something, as two or more persons, or one person with another or others: as, two men *go shares* in a venture, participating in its risks and its profits.—**share**[2], *v.*; *shared,* *sharing.* **I.** *tr.* To divide and distribute in shares between two or more; apportion; also, to apportion to one as his share (archaic: as, "He part of his small feast to her would *share,*" Spenser's "Faerie Queene," iv. 8. 5); also, to divide into shares or parts (rare: as, "a thin oaten cake, *shared* into fragments," C. Brontë's "Jane Eyre," v.); also, to divide (what one has or receives) into shares, apportioning them to another or others as well as one's self (often with *with:* as, to *share* one's money; "There were few but would have *shared* their all with her," Barrie's "Sentimental Tommy," vii.); give or grant to another or others a share in (often with *with:* as, "Then *share* thy pain, allow that sad relief; Ah, more than *share* it, give me all thy grief," Pope's "Eloisa to Abelard," 49; to *share* one's room with another); also, of two or more persons, etc., to divide (something) into shares, each taking part (as, "You wrangling pirates, that fall out In *sharing* that which you have pill'd from me!" Shakspere's "Richard III.," i. 3. 159); use, occupy, etc., jointly (as, "They *shared* the same water-bottle," Kipling's "Light That Failed," ii.; several companies *share* the same building); participate in, enjoy, suffer, etc., jointly (as, "that love of admiration which all pretty women *share* less or more," Scott's "Guy Mannering," xvi.; a group of persons who *share* the same opinions; two persons who *shared* the same fate); also, of one or more persons, etc., to receive, use, occupy, etc., together with another or others (as, "So shall you *share* all that he doth possess," Shakspere's "Romeo and Juliet," i. 3. 93; "the sudden withdrawal from school of

. . . the Cincinnati girl who had *shared* her room," W. Churchill's "Modern Chronicle," i. 6); participate in along with another or others (as, "You English gentlefolk do not let us *share* your griefs; you keep them to yourselves," Galsworthy's "Saint's Progress," iii. 10; "Their wives and families *shared* their lot," Bancroft's "Hist. of the U. S.," Amer. Revolution, i. 8). **II.** *intr.* To have a share or part: participate; take part: often with *in:* as, "Every one shall *share* i' the gains" (Shakspere's "Macbeth," iv. 1. 40).—**share′crop″per,** *n.* A tenant farmer who pays as rent a share of the crop.—**share′crop″ping,** *n.*—**share′hold″er,** *n.* One who holds or owns a share or shares, as in a corporation.—**shar-er** (shär′èr), *n.*

shark[1] (shärk), *n.* [Origin uncertain: cf. *shark*[2].] Any of a group of elongate elasmobranchiate (mostly marine) fishes, certain species of which are large and ferocious, and destructive to other fishes and sometimes dangerous to man.

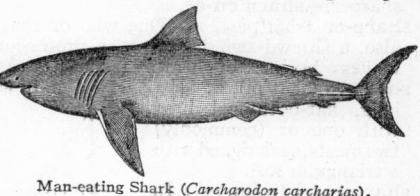

Man-eating Shark (*Carcharodon carcharias*).

shark[2] (shärk), *n.* [Origin uncertain; commonly associated with *shark*[1] (recorded earlier), but perhaps from a different source: cf. G. *schurke,* rascal, also E. *shirk.*] One who lives by sponging or petty swindling†; also, one who preys greedily on others; a rapacious sharper; an extortionate person, esp. a usurer; also, one who has unusual ability or proficiency in a particular field (slang: as, "You're a *shark* on this writing stuff," Sinclair Lewis's "Babbitt," xiii.).—**shark**[2], *v.* **I.** *intr.* To act or live as a shark; live by shifts and stratagems; play the sharper. **II.** *tr.* To obtain by trickery or fraud; steal; also, to collect hastily (with *up:* as, "Young Fortinbras . . . Hath in the skirts of Norway here and there *Shark'd* up a list of lawless resolutes," Shakspere's "Hamlet," i. 1. 98: now archaic).

sharp (shärp). [AS. *scearp* = D. *scherp* = G. *scharf* = Icel. *skarpr* = Sw. and Dan. *skarp,* sharp: cf. *scarp* and *scrape.*] **I.** *a.* Having a thin cutting edge or a fine point; well adapted for cutting or piercing; keen; acute; also, terminating in an edge or point; not blunt or rounded; characterized by sudden change of direction, as a turn; abrupt, as an ascent; angular, as the features (as, "Her features were decidedly handsome, though somewhat too *sharp* and aquiline": Bulwer-Lytton's "Pelham," xxv.); also, composed of hard, angular grains, as sand; also, clear or distinct in outline; strongly marked, as a contrast; also, keenly affecting the senses; pungent in taste; sour, biting, or acrid; piercing or shrill in sound; keenly cold, as weather, etc.; intensely painful or distressing (as, a *sharp* pain; "*Sharp* misery had worn him to the bones," Shakspere's "Romeo and Juliet," v. 1. 41); severe, harsh, or merciless (as, *sharp* words; a *sharp* rebuke; a *sharp* critic); also, fierce or violent (as, a *sharp* struggle); keen or eager (as, *sharp* desire); quick or brisk (as, a *sharp* walk or run); also, of keen perception (as, "I've *sharp* ears," H. Melville's "Moby-Dick," xliii.; "I never saw anybody with such *sharp* eyes!" Mrs. Wharton's "Ethan Frome," ix.); vigilant or attentive (as, a *sharp* watch); mentally acute or quick (as, a *sharp* lad; "a young man of *sharp* and active intellect," J. H. Newman's "Idea of a University," ii. 9); sagacious, subtle, or clever (as, "He pleaded still not guilty and alleged Many *sharp* reasons to defeat the law": Shakspere's "Henry VIII.," ii. 1. 14); shrewd or astute (as, *sharp* at making a bargain; a *sharp* bargain); sometimes, shrewd to the point of dishonesty (as, *sharp* practice); in *phonetics,* of a consonant, pronounced with breath and not with voice; surd; in *music* (opposed to *flat*), above an intended pitch, as a note; too high; also, raised a half-step in pitch (as, F *sharp*); also, either major or augmented, as an interval; also, having sharps in the signature, as keys or tonalities. **II.** *n.* Something sharp; a sharp weapon (archaic); a needle with a very sharp point; a sharper or swindler; an expert (colloq.); *pl.,* the hard parts of wheat, requiring a second grinding; middlings; *sing.,* in *music,* a tone one half-step above a given tone; in musical notation, the character (♯) which indicates this.—**sharp**, v. I. tr. To sharpen (now prov.); also, to cheat; obtain by cheating; in music, to raise in pitch, esp. one half-step. II. intr. To cheat; act as a sharper; in music, to sound above the true pitch.—**sharp**, adv. [AS. scearpe.] In a sharp manner; keenly or acutely; abruptly or suddenly (as, to pull a horse up sharp); punctually (as, at one o'clock sharp); quickly or briskly; vigilantly or attentively (as, look sharp!); in music, above the true pitch.

sharp=cut (shärp′kut′), a. Cut sharply or clearly; presenting a well-defined outline; hence, sharply defined; distinct; clear.

sharp=en (shär′pn), v. t. or i. To make or become sharp or sharper.—**sharp′en=er**, n.

sharp=er (shär′pèr), n. One who or that which sharpens; also, a shrewd swindler; esp., a professional gamester who makes a business of cheating (as, a card-sharper).

sharp=ie (shär′pi), n. [Appar. a dim. of sharp.] A kind of long, flat-bottomed boat with one or (commonly) two masts, each rigged with a triangular sail.

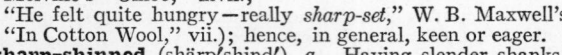
Sharpie.

sharp=ly (shärp′li), adv. In a sharp manner.—**sharp′-ness**, n.

sharp=set (shärp′set′), a. Keen or eager for food, or very hungry (as, "Being sharp-set, we told him to get breakfast," H. Melville's "Omoo," lxvii.; "He felt quite hungry—really sharp-set," W. B. Maxwell's "In Cotton Wool," vii.); hence, in general, keen or eager.

sharp=shinned (shärp′shind′), a. Having slender shanks: specif. applied to a small hawk, Accipiter velox (or fuscus), of North America, which often attacks poultry.

sharp-shoot-er (shärp′shö″tèr), n. [Cf. G. scharf-schütze.] One skilled in shooting, esp. with the rifle; a marksman of accurate aim, esp. one engaged in skirmishing and outpost duty.— **sharp′shoot″ing**, n. and a.

Sharp-shinned Hawk (Accipiter velox, or fuscus); adult female.

sharp=sight-ed (shärp′sī″ted), a. Having sharp, keen, or quick sight (as, "He is as sharp-sighted as a hawk": Scott's "Guy Mannering," xxix.); fig., having or proceeding from acute mental discernment (as, a sharp-sighted opponent; a sharp-sighted judgment).— **sharp′=sight′-ed-ness**, n.

sharp=tailed (shärp′tāld′), a. Having the tail or the tail-feathers sharp-pointed: as, the sharp-tailed grouse (a grouse, Pediœcetes phasianellus, of the northwestern U. S. and Canada; the

Sharp-tailed Grouse (Pediœcetes phasianellus).

pintail); the sharp-tailed finch (a small sparrow, Ammodromus caudacutus, of the eastern U. S. and Canada); the sharp-tailed sandpiper (a sandpiper, Actodromas acuminata, of Alaska and Asia).

sharp=wit-ted (shärp′wit′ed), a. Having or showing sharp or keen wits; mentally acute: as, "I found some of these heavy-looking, gaping rustics wake up into sharp-witted girls enough" (C. Brontë's "Jane Eyre," xxxii.).—**sharp′=wit′ted-ness**, n.

shas-tra, shas-ter (shäs′trä, -tèr), n. See sastra.

shat-ter (shat′ér), v. [ME. schateren; assibilated form of scatter.] I. tr. To scatter (as, "I come to pluck your berries . . . And . . . Shatter your leaves before the mellowing year," Milton's "Lycidas," 5: now prov. Eng.); also, to reduce to scattered or loose fragments, or break in pieces, as by a sudden blow or concussion, or as the blow or concussion does (as, "The bottles twain . . . Were shatter'd at a blow," Cowper's "John Gilpin," 124; "a concussion that should shatter the Pyramid," Johnson's "Rasselas," xxxi.); hence, to break up (an army, etc.) by violent onslaughts; damage or injure severely by some breaking or crushing action (as, ships shattered by shell-fire or by storms; "men . . . crawling out to save a comrade and being shattered to death on the return," Mrs. Wharton's "Son at the Front," xvi.); fig., to break down, demolish, or overthrow (as, "I rode, Shattering all evil customs everywhere," Tennyson's "Holy Grail," 477; to shatter an opponent's argument; "His conversation with the young man . . . shattered the idea," Eden Phillpotts's "Grey Room," v.); wreck or ruin (fortunes, happiness, lives, etc., or persons); impair (the constitution, health, nerves, etc.) seriously or completely; crush in spirit (as, "I'm afraid the grief cuts very deep . . . He looks terribly shattered": George Eliot's "Adam Bede," xl.). II. intr. To scatter, as grain when overripe; also, to break suddenly into fragments, or fly in pieces, as glass, etc.; break up, as a wave dashing against rocks; crumble, as soil, etc.—**shat′ter**, n. Pl., fragments due to shattering (as, to be dashed to shatters: now chiefly prov.); also, sing., a shattered state, as of the nerves.—**shat′ter-y**, a. Apt to be shattered; esp., crumbly or friable, as rock, soil, etc.

shave¹ (shāv), v.; pret. shaved, pp. shaved or shaven, ppr. shaving. [AS. sceafan, scafan, shave, scrape, = D. schaven = G. schaben = Icel. skafa = Goth. skaban, prob. akin to L. scabere, scratch, scrape: cf. scabies and shab.] I. tr. To cut or scrape away the surface of with a sharp-edged tool (as, "Men paint your long ship's prow, and shave the oars With sharpened planes," W. Morris's "Jason," iii. 281; to shave hides in preparing leather); cut down gradually by taking off thin slices; reduce to the form of shavings or thin slices (as, to shave wood, wax, or chocolate); take off (the surface layer or matter, a thin slice, etc.) by cutting or scraping (often with off: as, to shave off bark or rough projections from timber); often, to remove the hair from (the head, crown, chin, upper lip, etc., or the person) by cutting close to the skin; esp., to remove the beard, or a growth of beard, from with a razor (as, "We separated to dress and be shaved—my beard was a week old at least": F. M. Crawford's "Mr. Isaacs," xiii.); tonsure, as an ecclesiastic; cut off (the hair, esp. the beard) close to the skin with or as with a razor (often with off or away); in general, to cut or trim closely, or reduce to a smooth or bare surface (as, to shave a lawn; buildings shaved along the front to widen a street); cut off (vegetation, parts, etc.) closely or cleanly; also, to scrape or graze, or, now commonly, to pass so close as almost to graze (as, "The cab shaved a corner," L. Merrick's "Conrad in Quest of His Youth," xiii.; "The boat, shaving the low point close, seemed . . . to . . . hang over it like a mountain," J. Conrad's "Lord Jim," xliii.); also, to strip or defraud of money, etc., fleece, or cheat (now colloq. or prov.); also, to purchase (a note) at a rate of discount greater than is legal or customary (colloq., U. S.). II. intr. To shave something; esp., to shave one's self by removing a growth of beard with a razor; also, to scrape (through), or get (through) by a close shave.—**shave**¹, n. An act or process of shaving; esp., a shaving of a person by removing a growth of beard; also, a thin piece or slice shaved off, or a shaving; also, an approach so close as almost to graze (as, one vehicle passes another by a shave; the shot missed him, but it was a close *shave*); a (narrow) miss or escape (as, "A narrow *shave*; but a miss is as good as a mile": G. B. Shaw's "Arms and the Man," i.); also, a fleecing performance, or a cheat or swindle (colloq.); also, an unauthenticated report (colloq.); also, an exorbitant discount on a note (colloq., U. S.); in stock transactions, a premium or consideration paid for an extension of time for delivery or payment, or for the right to vary the terms of a contract.

shave² (shāv), *n.* [AS. *sceafa*, < *sceafan*, E. *shave¹*.] Any of various tools for shaving, scraping, removing thin slices, etc.; a drawing-knife; a spoke-shave.

shave-ling (shāv′ling), *n.* [See *-ling¹*.] A tonsured ecclesiastic (used opprobriously); also, a shaver, young fellow, or youngster.

shav-en (shā′vn), *p. a.* Shaved (as, a clean-*shaven* face); sometimes, tonsured (as, a *shaven* ecclesiastic).

shav-er (shā′vėr), *n.* One who shaves, esp. with a razor; also, an instrument for shaving something; also, a fellow or chap, now esp. a youngster or small boy (colloq.: as, "Young *shavers* like you don't have pipes," W. De Morgan's "Joseph Vance," xvi.).

shave-tail (shāv′tāl), *n.* A second lieutenant. [U. S. army slang.]

Sha-vi-an (shā′vi-ạn). [As if from a NL. *Shavius*, for E. *Shaw*; with *v* for *w*, there being no *w* in (classical) Latin.] **I.** *a.* Of, pertaining to, or characteristic of George Bernard Shaw, the Irish dramatist: as, *Shavian* humor. **II.** *n.* A devoted admirer of George Bernard Shaw or his works.

shav-ing (shā′ving), *n.* The act of one who or that which shaves; also, that which is shaved off, as a very thin piece or slice of something; esp., a very thin piece of wood cut off in planing (commonly in *pl.*).

shaw¹ (shâ), *n.* [AS. *sceaga*, akin to *sceacga*, E. *shag¹*.] A thicket, coppice, or small wood. [Archaic or Sc. and prov. Eng.]

shaw² (shâ), *n.* [Origin uncertain: cf. *shaw¹*.] The top, or stalk and leaves, of potatoes, turnips, etc. [Sc. and north. Eng.]

shawl (shâl), *n.* [Pers. *shāl*.] An article of dress, consisting usually of a square or oblong piece of material, worn about the shoulders, head, etc., chiefly by women, or otherwise used: as, a Cashmere *shawl* (see *cashmere*); a knitted *shawl*; a silk *shawl*; a lace *shawl*.—**shawl collar**, a plain (not notched) collar on a coat or the like, resembling a fold of a shawl turned back about the neck.—**shawl**, *v. t.* To wrap in a shawl: as, "George had meanwhile . . . *shawled* his wife, and brought her away" (Thackeray's "Vanity Fair," xxvii.).—**shawl′=pat″tern**, *n.* A pattern, as on fabrics, such as is characteristic of Oriental shawls. Cf. *cashmere*.—**shawl′=strap**, *n.* A device for carrying a rolled shawl, a parcel, etc., commonly consisting of a narrow, flat, stiff piece with a handle above and two leather straps, set some distance apart, for passing about the thing to be carried.

shawm (shâm), *n.* [ME. *schalme*, through OF. < L. *calamus*, reed.] A medieval musical wind-instrument of the oboe class, having a double reed inclosed in a globular mouthpiece. Cf. *chalumeau*. "Shawms" is inaccurately used in Ps. xcviii. 7 (6, in the Authorized Version) in the Psalter of the Book of Common Prayer, where the Authorized Version and the Revised Version have "sound of cornet."

shay, chay¹ (shā), *n.* [From *chaise*, taken as pl.] A chaise: as, "Here comes the wonderful one-hoss *shay*" (Holmes's "Deacon's Masterpiece"). [Colloq.]

she (shē), *pron.*; nom. *she*, poss. *her* or *hers*, obj. *her*, pl. nom. *they*, poss. *their* or *theirs*, obj. *them*. [ME. *she*, *sche*, *scheo*, *se*, < AS. *sēo*, fem. of *se*, demonstrative pronoun, later *the*: see *the¹*.] A personal pronoun of the third person, being the nominative singular feminine, and standing (1) for the female being in question or last mentioned, or (2) for 'the woman or female' (as, *she* who listens learns).—**she**, *n.*; pl. *shes* (shēz). A woman or any female person; a female, esp. of an animal (often used attributively or in composition: as, a *she*-goat).

shea (shē or shē′ą), *n.* [Mandingo.] An African sapotaceous tree, *Butyrospermum* (or *Bassia*) *parkii*, the kernels of which yield shea-butter.—**shea′=but′ter**, *n.* A butter-like fat obtained from the kernels of the shea: used as food and in making soap, etc.

sheaf (shēf), *n.*; pl. *sheaves* (shēvz). [AS. *scēaf* = D. *schoof* = G. *schaub*, sheaf, = Icel. *skauf*, fox's brush; prob. from the root of E. *shove*.] One of the bundles in which cereal plants, as wheat, rye, etc., are bound after reaping (as, "We were binding *sheaves* in the field": Gen. xxxvii. 7); hence, a bundle of stalks or sprays of some other plant or plants (as, a *sheaf* of lilies, ferns, or autumn leaves); also, a bundle or quiverful of 24 arrows (as, "At his belt, of arrows keen A furbish'd *sheaf* bore he": Scott's "Lay of the Last Minstrel," iii. 17); in general, a bundle or cluster, or a collection of things held or massed together (as, "a great palette, and a *sheaf* of painting-brushes," Thackeray's "Newcomes," xlviii.; a *sheaf* of papers).—**sheaf**, *v. t.* To bind into a sheaf or sheaves.—**sheaf′y**, *a.* Consisting of or resembling a sheaf or sheaves.

sheal¹ (shēl), *v. t.* To shell (peas, etc.). See Shakspere's "King Lear," i. 4. 219. [Now prov. Eng. and Sc.]

sheal², **sheal-ing** (shēl, shē′ling). See *shiel, shieling*.

shear (shēr), *v.*; pret. *sheared* (archaic *shore*), pp. *sheared* or *shorn*, ppr. *shearing*. [AS. *sceran* (pp. *scoren*) = D. *scheren* = G. *scheren* = Icel. *skera*, shear, cut; prob. akin to Gr. κείρειν, cut short, shear: cf. *corm*, also *score*, *shard¹*, *share¹*, *share²*, *shears*, *shore³*, and *short*.] **I.** *tr.* To cut with a sharp instrument, now chiefly with some form of shears (as, to *shear* metal); cut as a sharp instrument does (archaic: as, a sword that could *shear* a shield in two); pass through as by cutting, or cleave (archaic: as, a bird *shears* the air in flight; a ship *shears* the waves); also, to cut off or remove by or as by cutting with a sharp instrument (often with *off* or *away*: as, "The slender roots . . . Must smooth be *shorn* away," Cowper's "Task," iii. 613); esp., to cut off (hair, wool, nap, etc.); also, to cut (grain, grass, etc.) with a sickle or the like (now prov.); also, to deprive of some part or growth by cutting; esp., to cut or shave off the hair or beard from (the head, crown, a person, etc.); cut the wool or fleece from (sheep, etc.); remove superfluous nap from (cloth) in manufacturing; clip or trim (a plant, hedge, lawn, etc.), esp. closely or smoothly (as, "The rounded, *shorn* swells of the land hove upward to the eye, verdant and smooth": Cooper's "Two Admirals," x.); fig., to strip or deprive (*of*), as by cutting (as, "The assembly of the people had been *shorn* of its legislative powers": Froude's "Cæsar," viii.); strip of money by sharp practice, or fleece; in *mech.*, etc., to produce a shear in; break or distort by a shear. **II.** *intr.* To cut (*through*) with a sharp instrument (archaic: as, "Geraint . . . grasping at his sword . . . *Shore* thro' the swarthy neck," Tennyson's "Geraint and Enid," 727); also, to cleave a way (*through*: archaic); also, to cut grain, etc., with a sickle or the like (now prov.); also, in *mech.*, etc., to become fractured by a shear or shears.—**shear**, *n.* The act or process of shearing; esp., a shearing of sheep (used in stating the age of sheep: as, a sheep of one *shear*, or one year old; a two-*shear* sheep); also, that which is taken off by shearing; a quantity of wool, grass, or the like cut off at one shearing; also, in *mech.*, etc., a strain or deformation consisting of a compression in one direction with an elongation in the same ratio in a perpendicular direction; also, the stress involved in such a strain; a stress tending to cause one part of a body to slide by a contiguous part.—**shear′er**, *n.*—**shear′ing**, *n.* The action of one who or that which shears, or an instance of it; also, something cut off by such action (usually in *pl.*: as, the *shearings* of sheep; the *shearings* of cloth).—**shear′man** (-mạn), *n.*; pl. *-men*. One whose occupation it is to shear cloth.

shears (shērz), *n.* pl. or *sing*. [ME. *scheres*, pl., *schere*, sing., < AS. *scēar*, sing., *scēara*, *scērero*, pl.; from the root of E. *shear*.] Scissors of large size (often called a *pair of shears*); also, a similar cutting instrument, used in shearing sheep, etc., in which the blades are not

Shears for cutting Cloth.—*a*, screw-pivot on which as a fulcrum each blade with its handle works.

pivoted together but connected by an arched spring between their handles, pressure on the handles bringing the blades together and the spring causing them to open when the pressure has ceased; any of various other cutting implements or machines resembling or suggesting shears or scissors; also, sheers (apparatus for hoisting heavy weights); also, the two parallel parts forming the bed of a lathe.

shear-wa-ter (shēr'wä"tẽr), n. Any of various long-billed sea-birds (esp. of the genus *Puffinus*) allied to the petrels, as *P. major* ('greater shearwater,' or hagden), a species common on the Atlantic: so called from their appearing, when flying low, to shear or cleave the water with their long wings.

sheat=fish (shēt'fish), n. [Earlier *sheath-fish*: cf. G. *scheid*, *schaid*, the fish, *scheide*, sheath.] A large fresh-water fish, *Silurus glanis*, the great catfish of central and eastern Europe, sometimes having a weight of 400 pounds; also, any of various allied fishes.

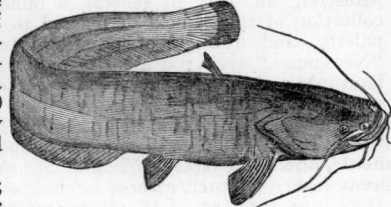

Sheat-fish (*Silurus glanis*).

sheath (shēth), n.; pl. *sheaths* (shēᴛнz). [AS. *scēath*, *scǣth*, = D. *scheede* = G. *scheide* = Icel. *skeidhir*, pl., sheath; from the root of E. *shed²*.] A case or covering for the blade of a sword, dagger, or the like, esp. one fitting closely and conforming to the shape of the blade; hence, any similar covering; a closely enveloping part or structure, as in an animal or plant organism.—**sheath** (shēth), v. t. To put into or provide with a sheath or sheathing; sheathe.—

sheath'bill, n. Either of two sea-birds with white plumage, *Chionis alba* and *C. minor*, inhabiting the colder parts of the southern hemisphere: so called from the horny case which partly sheathes the bill.

sheathe (shēᴛн), v. t.; *sheathed*, *sheathing*. [From *sheath*.] To put (a sword, etc.) into a sheath; hence, to plunge (a sword, etc.) in

Sheathbill (*Chionis alba*).

something as if in a sheath (as, "Not I, till I have *sheathed* My rapier in his bosom": Shakspere's "Titus Andronicus," ii. 1. 53); also, to inclose in or as in a case, casing, or covering (as, a mummy *sheathed* in wrappings); incase in or cover with a layer of some material (as, temple doors *sheathed* in silver); esp., to cover or provide with a protective layer or sheathing (as, to *sheathe* a ship's bottom with copper).—**sheath-er** (shē'ᴛнẽr), n.—**sheath'ing**, n. The act of one who sheathes; also, that which sheathes; a casing or covering; esp., a covering or layer of metal, wood, or other material, as a protective covering of metal plates on a ship's bottom, or the first covering of boards on a house or the like; material for forming any such covering.

sheath=knife (shēth'nīf), n.; pl. *-knives* (-nīvz). A knife carried in a sheath.

sheath-less (shēth'les), a. Having no sheath; not incased in a sheath.

sheath=winged (shēth'wingd), a. Having the wings sheathed or incased in elytra, as a beetle; coleopterous.

sheave¹ (shēv), v. t.; *sheaved*, *sheaving*. [From *shea..*.] To gather or collect into a sheaf or sheaves.

sheave² (shēv), n. [= *shive*.] A slice, as of bread (now prov.); also, a grooved wheel forming a pulley; any of various other wheels or disks with a grooved rim.

sheaves (shēvz), n. Plural of *sheaf*.

she-bang (shȩ-bang'), n. [Origin uncertain: cf. *shebeen*.] A shanty or hut; a dwelling; an establishment; indefinitely, a thing or affair. [Slang, U. S.]

She-bat (shȩ-bät'), n. [Heb.] In the Jewish calendar, the fifth month (30 days) of the civil year and the eleventh of the ecclesiastical year, beginning in January.

she-been (shȩ-bēn'), n. [Ir.] A shop or place where intoxicating liquors are sold without the license required by law. [Ireland and Scotland.]

She-chi-nah (shȩ-kī'nä), n. See *Shekinah*.

shed¹ (shed), n. [Prob. a var. of *shade*.] A slight or rude structure built for shelter, storage, etc., either attached to a house or building or separate (as, "under the pent roof of the cart *shed*," J. Conrad's "Rover," vii.; a wood*shed*); also, a large, strongly built structure, often open at the sides or end, for shelter, etc. (as, a train-*shed*; a *shed* for goods on a wharf); a hangar for aircraft; also, a hut or rude dwelling (archaic: as, "In lowly *sheds* With smoky rafters," Milton's "Comus," 323); also, a covering.

shed² (shed), v.; *shed*, *shedding*. [AS. *scēadan*, *scādan*, = D. *scheiden* = G. *scheiden* = Goth. *skaidan*, part, separate; prob. akin to L. *scindere*, Gr. σχίζειν, Skt. *chid-*, split: cf. *schedule*, *scission*, *schism*, and *sheath*.] **I.** *tr.* To separate or divide (now prov. Eng. and Sc.); make a parting in, as hair (now prov. Eng. and Sc.); also, to scatter or spill (as, "Break his glass, And *shed* the luscious liquour on the ground," Milton's "Comus," 652: now prov. Eng.); also, to throw off or let fall readily (something that does not penetrate or stick: as, thick foliage *sheds* rain; cloth that *sheds* water or dust); also, to pour forth (water, etc.), as a fountain or a vessel does; emit and let fall (tears: as, "If you have tears, prepare to *shed* them now," Shakspere's "Julius Cæsar," iii. 2. 173); let flow or cause to flow (blood: as, to *shed* one's blood for one's country, as by suffering wounds or being killed in war; "Whoso *sheddeth* man's blood, by man shall his blood be *shed*," Gen. ix. 6); hence, to pour out or expend in use (as, "We have *shed* much ink in vain, and wasted quires . . . if it be necessary now to tell the reader . . .": Cooper's "Prairie," xxix.); also, to send forth or cast (light, etc., lit. or fig.: as, the moon *sheds* a soft radiance; "Over all this the clouds *shed* a uniform and purplish shadow," Stevenson's "Travels with a Donkey," i. 3; this news *shed* light on the mystery); give or send forth (sound, fragrance, influence, etc.); shower (blessings, etc.); bestow (a gift, etc.: colloq.); also, to cast off or let fall by natural process (leaves, hair, feathers, skin, shell, etc.); discharge (seed, spawn, etc.); put off (garments, etc.: colloq.: as, "The duke *shed* his coat," Mark Twain's "Huckleberry Finn," xx.; "She had already *shed* a notable part of her own costume," Arnold Bennett's "Old Wives' Tale," i. 1); cast aside or discard (colloq.: as, to *shed* an old hat or umbrella). **II.** *intr.* To cast off hair, feathers, skin, or other covering or parts by natural process (as, the crab *sheds* in June); molt, as a bird; also, to fall off, as leaves, flowers, etc.; drop out, as seed, grain, etc.—**shed²**, n. A part or parting, as in the hair (now prov. Eng. and Sc.); also, a ridge of high ground between lower areas; a divide or watershed; in *weaving*, the opening between the sets of warp-threads (produced by the movement of the heddles) for the passage of the shuttle and the weft-thread.—**shed'der**, n.

sheen (shēn), a. [AS. *scēne*, *scīene*, *scȳne*, = D. *schoon* = G. *schön* = Goth. *skauns*, beautiful; from the root of AS. *scēawian*, look at, E. *show*, though in later English use associated with *shine*.] Beautiful; also, bright or shining (as, "by fountain clear, or spangled starlight *sheen*": Shakspere's "Midsummer Night's Dream," ii. 1. 29). [Archaic or poetic.]—**sheen**, v. i. To be bright; shine; gleam. [Archaic or Sc. and prov. Eng.]—**sheen**, n. Brightness, shining, radiance, or light (as, "throned in celestial *sheen*," Milton's "On the Morning of Christ's Nativity," 145; "The full moon . . . bathed every object in silver *sheen*," F. M. Crawford's "Mr. Isaacs," xii.); a gleam, or a gleaming light (as, "From quite a fair way off a *sheen* was visible, making points of brightness in the shrubbery": Stevenson's "Master of Ballantrae," v.); now, esp., the brightness or luster of something glossy or polished reflecting light (as, the *sheen* of satin or of pearls; "My grandmother's kitchen . . . was resplendent with the *sheen* of a set of scoured pewter plates and platters," Mrs. Stowe's "Oldtown Folks," vi.); also, gleaming or resplendent attire (chiefly poetic).—**sheen'y¹**, a. Bright; shining; lustrous: as, "his *sheeny* . . . sabre" (Scott's "Talisman," ii.).

shee-ny² (shē'ni), n.; pl. *-nies* (-niz). [Origin obscure.] A Jew. [Slang.]

sheep (shēp), *n.*; pl. *sheep*. [AS. *scēap, scēp,* = D. *schaap* = G. *schaf,* sheep.] Any of the ruminant mammals constituting the genus *Ovis* (family *Bovidæ*), closely allied to the goats, esp. *O. aries,* which has many domesticated varieties or breeds, valuable for their flesh, fleece, etc.; also, leather made from the skin of these animals; also, fig., a meek, timid, or stupid person.—**black sheep,** fig., a disreputable member of an otherwise respectable family or class.—**lost sheep,** fig. one who has strayed from the right way, as in conduct, religious belief, etc.: as, "I [Jesus] am not sent but unto the *lost sheep* of the house of Israel" (Mat. xv. 24). —**to cast** (or **make**) **sheep's eyes at,** to cast languishing, amorous glances at (a person of the other sex); sometimes, to cast longing glances at (a thing).

sheep=back (shēp′bak), *n.* Same as *roche moutonnée.*

sheep-ber-ry (shēp′ber″i), *n.*; pl. *-berries* (-iz). A caprifoliaceous shrub or small tree, *Viburnum lentago,* of North America, bearing cymes of small white flowers, and edible, berry-like black drupes; also, the fruit; also, the black-haw, *V. prunifolium.*

sheep=cote, sheep=cot (shēp′kōt, -kot), *n.* A slight covered structure for sheltering sheep: as, "scarce so much housing as a *sheep-cot*" (Bancroft's "Hist. of the U. S.," Amer. Revolution, ii. 1).

sheep=dog (shēp′dog), *n.* A dog trained to watch and tend sheep; esp., a dog of some variety commonly used for this purpose, as a collie, or as one of a large, shaggy, bobtailed breed ('old English sheep-dog') which usually has a blue-gray and white coat; fig., a chaperon.

sheep-fold (shēp′fōld), *n.* A fold or inclosure for sheep.

sheep-ish (shē′pish), *a.* Like sheep, as in meekness, timidity, etc. (as, "saying the downright things that the *sheepish* society around her is afraid to utter": Kinglake's "Eothen," viii.); characteristic or suggestive of sheep; now, esp., awkwardly bashful or embarrassed, as a person or the expression, manner, etc. (as, "He . . . was extremely bashful and *sheepish* in their presence," Parkman's "Oregon Trail," xviii.; to look *sheepish*; a *sheepish* smile).—**sheep′-ish-ly,** *adv.*—**sheep′ish-ness,** *n.*

sheep=lau-rel (shēp′lâ″rel), *n.* A North American laurel, *Kalmia angustifolia,* bearing flowers smaller than those of the mountain-laurel: reputed to be poisonous to sheep and other animals.

sheep=run (shēp′run), *n.* A large sheepwalk.

sheep=shank (shēp′shangk), *n. Naut.,* a kind of knot, hitch, or bend made on a rope to shorten it temporarily.

sheeps-head (shēps′hed), *n.* A deep-bodied sparoid marine food-fish, *Archosargus probatocephalus,* abundant on the Atlantic coast of the U. S.: so called from the fancied resemblance of its head to that of a sheep, due largely to its broad incisor teeth.

—Sheepshead.

sheep=shear-ing (shēp′-shēr″ing), *n.* The act of shearing sheep; also, the time or season of shearing sheep, or a feast held at that time.

sheep=skin (shēp′skin), *n.* The skin of a sheep, esp. such a skin dressed with the wool on, as for a garment; also, leather, parchment, or the like made from the skin of sheep; hence, a diploma (of parchment or the like) given to one taking a degree (colloq., U. S.).

sheep=walk (shēp′wâk), *n.* A tract of land on which sheep are pastured.

sheer¹ (shēr), *v.* [Perhaps another form of *shear.*] **I.** *intr.* To deviate from a course, as a ship or boat and hence any thing or person; swerve; draw (*off* or *away*: as, "They *sheered* off . . . and pulled back in the direction of the frigate," Marryat's "Mr. Midshipman Easy," xl.; "One or two *sheered* off from him with contemptuous smiles," Miss Mulock's "John Halifax," xvii.); turn off, go, or come obliquely (as, "They . . . *sheered,* with all speed, to the opposite side of the river," Irving's "Captain Bonneville," xli.; "Lingard made all sail and *sheered* alongside to say good-bye," J. Conrad's "Rescue," ii. 2). **II.** *tr.* To cause to sheer.—**sheer¹,** *n.* A deviation or divergence, as of a

ship from her course; a swerve; also, the position in which a ship at anchor is placed to keep her clear of the anchor; also, the upward longitudinal curve of a ship's deck or bulwarks.

sheer² (shēr). [ME. *schere*: cf. Icel. *skærr* and AS. *scīr,* bright, clear, pure, from the root of E. *shine.*] **I.** *a.* Bright, shining, or shiny (now prov. Eng.); also, clear or transparent, as water or ice (now prov. Eng.); transparently thin, or diaphanous, as fabrics, etc. (now U. S.); also, unmixed with anything else (as, *sheer* rock or sand); undiluted, as wine, ale, etc.; unqualified, pure, downright, or utter (as, *sheer* folly or waste; to interfere from *sheer* pity; "The old man slept from *sheer* weariness," H. Kingsley's "Geoffry Hamlyn," iii.); being that and nothing else, or mere (as, "At such a time the *sheer* adventurer has an excellent field before him": Charnwood's "Abraham Lincoln," iv.); also, extending straight down or up perpendicularly or very steeply (as, "a *sheer* descent of rock," J. H. Newman's "Callista," i.; "*Sheer* and high the great headland rose," H. G. Wells's "Men Like Gods," ii. 4). **II.** *adv.* Clear, completely, or quite (as, "Down the trunk, from top to bottom, *Sheer* he cleft the bark asunder": Longfellow's "Hiawatha," vii. 32); also, straight down or up perpendicularly or very steeply (as, "the gloomy walls that rose a thousand feet *sheer* above the circling pines": Bret Harte's "Outcasts of Poker Flat").

sheer=hulk (shēr′hulk), *n.* An old hulk or dismantled ship with sheers mounted on it, for hoisting purposes.

sheer=leg (shēr′leg), *n.* One of the spars forming sheers; *pl.,* sheers.

sheer-ly (shēr′li), *adv.* In a sheer manner; purely; utterly; completely; perpendicularly.—**sheer′ness,** *n.*

sheers (shērz), *n. pl.* or *sing.* [Another form of *shears.*] An apparatus for hoisting heavy weights, consisting of two or more spars fastened together near the top with their lower ends separated to form a base, the tackle being suspended from the top and the whole structure being steadied by guys.

Sheer-hulk.

sheet¹ (shēt), *n.* [AS. *scēte, scīete, scȳte,* sheet, cloth, related to *scēat,* projection, corner, fold or piece of cloth, *scēata,* lower corner of a sail (see *sheet²*), from the root of *scēotan,* E. *shoot.*] A large square or rectangular piece of linen, cotton, or other material, used as an article of bedding, commonly one of a pair spread immediately above and below the sleeper; any similar piece of cloth for covering, protection, etc.; a winding-sheet; a sail (chiefly poetic); also, an oblong or square piece of paper or parchment, esp. one on which to write or print; one of the separate pieces, of definite size, in which paper is made, and which in printing and bookbinding are folded to form pages of a required size; *pl.,* the pages or leaves of a book, etc.; *sing.,* a newspaper (as, "The other ladies would at times tackle that *sheet,* but only to read the births, marriages, and deaths on the front page": H. G. Wells's "Tono-Bungay," i. 1. § 4); also, an extent, stretch, or expanse, as of lightning, water, etc. (as, "Some of the deep gorges and defiles sent up *sheets* of flame": Irving's "Captain Bonneville," xliv.); a broad, thin mass, layer, or covering; a broad, relatively thin piece of iron, glass, etc.; in *geol.,* a more or less horizontal mass of rock (esp. eruptive rock intruded between strata or spread over a surface) which has great length and breadth as compared with its thickness.—**in sheets,** in the form of flat sheets, not folded; also, in the form of folded sheets, but not bound: used esp. of printed pages, as of books.—**sheet¹,** *v. t.* To furnish with sheets; also, to wrap in a sheet, often a winding-sheet (as, "a *sheeted* ghost": Longfellow's "Wreck of the Hesperus"); cover with a protective sheet of some material; cover with a sheet or layer of something (as, "The river was

---

(variable) ḍ as d or j, ṣ as s or sh, ṭ as t or ch, ẓ as z or zh; *o,* F. *cloche;* ü, F. *menu;* ċh, Sc. *loch;* ṅ, F. *bonbon;* ′, primary accent; ″, secondary accent; †, obsolete; <, from; +, and; =, equals. See also lists at beginning of book.

sheeted with ice": Irving's "Captain Bonneville," xxx.); also, to form into a sheet or sheets (as, "Then *sheeted* rain burst down": Scott's "Vision of Don Roderick," xxxvi.).

sheet² (shēt), *n.* [ME. *schete*, sheet (rope), < AS. *scēata*, lower corner of a sail (*scēatlīne*, sheet or rope): see *sheet¹*.] *Naut.*, a rope or chain fastened to a lower corner of a sail to extend the sail or change its direction; also, *pl.*, the spaces beyond the thwarts in the forward or the after end of an open boat (as, the fore-*sheets*; the stern-*sheets*).—**a sheet in the wind** (or **in the wind's eye**), somewhat tipsy: as, "Maybe you think we were all *a sheet in the wind's eye*. But . . . I was sober" (Stevenson's "Treasure Island," xx.). Hence, *three sheets in the wind*, very drunk.—**sheet²**, *v. t. Naut.*, to extend or secure by means of a sheet or sheets: as, to *sheet* sails home (to extend them to the utmost by hauling on the sheets).

sheet=an-chor (shēt′ang″kọr), *n.* [Earlier *shoote anker*, late ME. *shute anker*; appar. connected with *shoot*.] A large anchor used only in cases of emergency; fig., a final reliance or resource (as, "His [Archbishop Laud's] *sheet-anchor* was authority": Morley's "Oliver Cromwell," i. 2).

sheet-ing (shē′ting), *n.* The act of covering with or forming into sheets; also, linen or cotton cloth such as is used for bed-sheets; also, a lining or covering, as of timber or metal, serving as a protection; the sheathing on a house.

sheet=i-ron (shēt′ī′ẽrn), *n.* Iron in sheets or thin plates.

sheet=light-ning (shēt′līt″ning), *n.* Lightning appearing merely as a general illumination over a broad surface, due to the reflection of the lightning of a distant thunder-storm (commonly too far distant for the thunder to be heard), or sometimes possibly caused by a weak electrical discharge in the air at a considerable altitude.

sheet=met-al (shēt′met″ạl), *n.* Metal in sheets or thin plates.

sheet=mu-sic (shēt′mū″zik), *n.* Separate printed or written musical compositions on unbound sheets.

Shef-field (shef′ēld) **plate.** [From *Sheffield*, manufacturing city in Yorkshire, England.] Plate made by rolling out sheets of copper (or copper and brass) and silver fused together: a durable substitute for solid silver.

sheik, sheikh (shēk or shāk), *n.* [Ar. *shaikh*, old man, elder.] In Arab and other Mohammedan use, a chief or head; the head man of a village or tribe; the head of a religious body; a very learned or devout man; sometimes, a title of respect. Also (slang), a masterful man of irresistible romantic charm for the other sex; a lady-killer; a (male) lover or sweetheart: from the hero of "The Sheik," a popular novel by E. M. Hull, published in England in 1919 and in the U. S. in 1921.—**sheik ul Islam** (ul is-läm′). [Ar.] The chief authority in matters of Moslem religion and sacred law; in Turkey, the chief mufti.

shek-el (shek′el), *n.* [Heb. *sheqel*, < *shāqal*, weigh.] An ancient, orig. Babylonian, unit of weight, of varying value (taken as equal to the fiftieth or the sixtieth part of a mina, and to about half an ounce); also, a coin of this weight, esp. the chief silver coin of the Hebrews; hence, *pl.*, coins or money (slang).

Obverse.   Reverse.
Jewish Shekel. — British Museum.

She-ki-nah, She-chi-nah (shē-kī′nạ), *n.* [Late Heb. *shekīnāh*, lit. 'dwelling.'] In Jewish theology, the divine presence, or a radiance forming the visible manifestation of the divine presence.

shel-drake (shel′drāk), *n.* [ME. *sheldedrake, schelledrake*: cf. obs. or prov. *sheld*, party-colored, piebald.] Any of the old-world ducks constituting the genera *Tadorna* and *Casarca*, certain species of which are characterized by variegated coloring (see cut in next column); also, any of various other swimming birds, as a merganser.

shelf¹ (shelf), *n.*; pl. *shelves* (shelvz). [ME. *shelf, schelfe*: cf. MLG. *schelf*, shelf, AS. *scylfe*, ledge, floor, story.] A thin slab of wood or other material fixed horizontally to a wall, or in a frame, for supporting objects; also, a timber attached to the inner side of a ship, following the sheer, to

afford strength to the frame and support the deck-beams; also, a comparatively flat and approximately horizontal extent of something, raised above a general level; a shelf-like surface or projection, or a ledge (as, a continental *shelf*, a relatively shallow extent of sea-bottom bordering a continent, at whose outer edge there is a rapid descent to the deep ocean-floor); in *mining*, etc., bedrock, as under alluvial deposits.—**on the shelf,** put aside, as something discarded from use; out of active service, as a person.—**shelf¹**, *v. t.* Same as *shelve¹*.

Sheldrake (*Tadorna cornuta*).

shelf² (shelf), *n.*; pl. *shelves* (shelvz). [Origin uncertain: cf. *shelf¹*, also AS. *scylf*, crag, pinnacle.] A sand-bank or submerged extent of rock in the sea or a river, rendering the water shallow and dangerous to navigation.

shell (shel), *n.*; pl. *shells*, also (in sense of 'projectiles') *shell* (see def.). [AS. *scell, sciell, scyll*, = D. *schel, schil*, = Icel. *skel*, shell, = Goth. *skalja*, tile; akin to E. *scale²*.] A hard outer covering of an animal; the hard case or integument of a mollusk, or either half of the case of a bivalve mollusk, or, sometimes, a mollusk itself; the hard integument of a crustacean; the hard outside covering of a turtle or tortoise; the elytrum of a beetle; also, the hard exterior of an egg; also, a more or less hard outer covering of a seed, fruit, or the like; the hard outside portion of a nut; the pod of peas, etc.; also, the material constituting any of various kinds of shells; esp., the horny material (tortoise-shell) of which the hard covering of a turtle or tortoise is partly composed; also, any of various objects resembling a shell, as in shape, or in being more or less concave or hollow; the external ear, or conch; a light, long, narrow racing-boat rowed by means of outriggers; the thin film of copper which forms the face of an electrotype and is backed with type-metal; also, an inclosing case or cover suggesting a shell; a hollow projectile for a cannon, etc., filled with an explosive charge which is arranged to explode during flight or upon impact or after penetration (pl. *shells* or, collectively, *shell*: as, "storm'd at with shot and *shell*," Tennyson's "Charge of the Light Brigade," iii.); a metal or paper cartridge (empty or loaded), as for use in a shot-gun; a cartridge-like pyrotechnic device which explodes in the air; the casing containing the pulley or pulleys of a block; also, a mere exterior covering or framework; a slight hollow structure suggestive of a shell; also, something scale-like; a lamina; a thin metal plate, as in armor; also, a lyre (the first lyre having been made, according to legend, from a tortoise's shell: poetic: as, "Hast thou thy *shell* in order? Sing me a song of Sappho," Byron's "Sardanapalus," iii. 1). —**shell**, *v. t.* To remove the shell of; take out of the shell, pod, etc.; also, to separate (Indian corn) from the ear or cob; also, to inclose in or as in a shell; also, to cover or furnish with shells, as an oyster-bed; also, to throw shells or explosive projectiles into, upon, or among; bombard with shells.—**to shell out,** fig., to hand over; pay up. [Colloq.] —**shell**, *v. i.* To fall or come out of the shell, husk, etc.; also, to come away or fall off as a shell or outer coat.

shel-lac (she-lak′ or shel′ak), *n.* [For *shell lac*.] Lac which has been purified and formed into thin plates, used for making varnish, etc.; also, a varnish ('shellac-varnish') made by dissolving this material in alcohol or the like (in common use not called a varnish, the term *varnish* being used for the ordinary oil-varnishes).—**shel-lac′**, *v. t.*; *-lacked, -lacking.* To coat or treat with shellac.

shell-bark (shel′bärk), *n.* The shagbark.

shell=bean (shel′bēn), *n.* Any of various kinds of bean (plant) the seeds of which are removed from the pods before cooking; also, the seed itself: distinguished from *snap-bean* or *string-bean*.

shelled (sheld), *a.* Having a shell: as, hard-*shelled*.

shell·er (shel′ėr), *n.* One who shells something, or an implement or machine used in shelling.

shell·fire (shel′fīr), *n. Milit.*, the firing of explosive shells or projectiles, as shrapnel.

shell·fish (shel′fish), *n.*; pl. *-fishes* or (esp. collectively) *-fish*. An aquatic animal (not a fish in the ordinary sense) having a shell, as the oyster and other mollusks and the lobster and other crustaceans.

shell·game (shel′gām), *n.* A swindling game resembling thimblerig but employing walnut-shells or the like instead of thimble-like cups.

shell·heap (shel′hēp), *n.* Same as *kitchen-midden*.

shell·less (shel′les), *a.* Having no shell, as some mollusks.

shell·mound (shel′mound), *n.* Same as *kitchen-midden*.

shell·pink (shel′pingk′), *n.* A soft, delicate pink with a tinge of yellow.

shell·proof (shel′prōf), *a.* Proof against shells, bombs, etc.; bomb-proof.

shell·shock (shel′shok), *n.* Nervous or mental disorder in various forms, characterized by loss of self-command, memory, speech, sight, or other powers, at first supposed to be brought on by the explosion of shells in battle, but now explained as the result of the cumulative strain of modern warfare.—**shell′·shocked**, *a.* Suffering from shell-shock.

shell·work (shel′wėrk), *n.* Decorative work composed of or representing sea-shells.

shell·y (shel′i), *a.* Abounding in shells; consisting of a shell or shells; shell-like.

shel·ter (shel′tėr), *n.* [Connected with *shield*: cf. AS. *scyldtruma*, 'shield troop,' troop of men with shields.] Something which affords protection or refuge, as from rain, wind, etc., or from attack or danger; a place of refuge or safety; also, protection afforded, as from the weather or from attack: refuge.—**shel′ter**, *v.* **I.** *tr.* To be a shelter for; afford shelter to; also, to provide with a shelter; place under cover or shelter; hence, to protect as by a shelter; screen, as from punishment or censure; harbor, or take under one's protection. **II.** *intr.* To take shelter; find a refuge: as, "This is a night when polecats and rabbits would *shelter* together in peace" (H. Kingsley's "Geoffry Hamlyn," xiv.).—**shel′ter·er**, *n.*—**shel′ter·ing·ly**, *adv.*—**shel′ter·less**, *a.* Having no shelter; also, affording no shelter.—**shel′ter·y**, *a.* Affording shelter: as, "the warm and *sheltery* shores of Gibraltar and Barbary" (G. White's "Nat. Hist. of Selborne," i. 32).

shel·ty, shel·tie (shel′ti), *n.*; pl. *-ties* (-tiz). [Cf. Icel. *Hjalti*, Shetlander.] A Shetland pony: as, "a *shelty* waddling under a Highlander far bigger than itself" (Scott's "Legend of Montrose," xix.). [Chiefly Sc.]

shelve[1] (shelv), *v. t.*; *shelved, shelving*. [From *shelf*[1].] To furnish with shelves; also, to place on a shelf or shelves; also, to lay aside as on a shelf; put aside from consideration (as, "He . . . *shelves* the topic": W. De Morgan's "Alice-for-Short," vii.); remove from active service, as a person.

shelve[2] (shelv), *v. i.*; *shelved, shelving*. [Origin uncertain: cf. *shelf*[1] and *shelf*[2].] To slope gradually: as, "a *shelving* part of the shore" (Peacock's "Headlong Hall," viii.).

shelves (shelvz), *n.* Plural of *shelf*[1], *shelf*[2].

shelv·ing (shel′ving), *n.* Material for shelves; also, shelves collectively.

shelv·y (shel′vi), *a.* Shelving; sloping gradually.

Shem·ite (shem′īt), etc. Same as *Semite*, etc.

shend (shend), *v. t.*; *shent, shending*. [AS. *scendan* = D. *schenden* = G. *schänden*, bring to shame; akin to E. *shame*.] To put to shame or confusion; blame or reproach; defeat or overcome; ruin or destroy; damage or mar: now chiefly in

shent, *pp.*: as, "that they should be *shent* for suffering such preaching and contention" (Strype's "Memorials of Cranmer," i. 26). [Archaic.]

She·ol (shē′ōl or -ol), *n.* [Heb.] The abode of the dead or of departed spirits (common in the Revised Version of the Old Testament); hence [*l. c.*], hell, the abode of evil and condemned spirits (colloq.).

shep·herd (shep′ėrd), *n.* [AS. *scēaphyrde*: see *sheep* and *herd*[2].] A man who herds, tends, and guards sheep in pasture; also, fig., one exercising care or guidance over a body of persons, esp. a minister or clergyman with reference to his flock or congregation.—**Good Shepherd.** See under *good*, *a.*—**Shepherd Kings**, the Hyksos, a succession or dynasty of kings of Egypt, of foreign (probably Asiatic) origin, who ruled for an uncertain period (perhaps from about 2000 B.C.).—**shep′herd**, *v. t.* To tend or guard as a shepherd; hence, fig., to tend or guide as a shepherd does his sheep (as, "Jim took up an advantageous position and *shepherded* them [men] out in a bunch through the doorway": J. Conrad's "Lord Jim," xxxii.); watch over carefully.—**shep′herd·dog**, *n.* A sheep-dog.—**shep′herd·ess**, *n.* A woman or girl who tends sheep.—**shep′herd's·purse′**, *n.* A brassicaceous weed, *Bursa bursa-pastoris*, with white flowers and purse-like pods.

sher·ard·ize (sher′ạr-dīz), *v. t.*; *-ized, -izing*. [From *Sherard* Cowper-Coles, inventor of the process.] To coat (iron or steel) with zinc by heating with zinc-dust in a closed chamber.

Sher·a·ton (sher′ạ-tọn), *a.* Pertaining to Thomas Sheraton (1751–1806), an English designer of furniture; in the style of Sheraton.

sher·bet (shėr′bẹt), *n.* [Turk. *sherbet* = Pers. *sharbat*, < Ar. *sharbah* (*sharbat*), a drink, < *shariba*, to drink: cf. *shrub*[1] and *syrup*.] A favorite cooling drink in the East, made of fruit-juice diluted with water and sweetened, and often cooled with snow; also, a water-ice, variously flavored.

sherd (shėrd), *n.* Same as *shard*[1].

she·rif, she·reef (shẹ-rēf′), *n.* [Ar. *sharīf*, noble.] A descendant of Mohammed through his daughter Fatima; also, an Arab prince or ruler, esp. the sovereign of Morocco or the chief magistrate of Mecca.

sher·iff (sher′if), *n.* [AS. *scīrgerēfa*, 'shire reeve': see *shire* and *reeve*[1].] An important civil officer in a shire or county and in certain cities and boroughs, charged with the execution of the laws and the preservation of the peace, and now esp. with the keeping of prisoners in safe custody, the serving of processes, the preparation of jury panels, the execution of the judgments of the courts, etc.—**sher′iff·al·ty** (-ạl-ti), *n.*; pl. *-ties* (-tiz). Shrievalty.—**sher′iff·dom** (-dọm), *n.* The district or territory under a sheriff's jurisdiction; also, the office of sheriff.—**sher′iff·ship**, *n.*—**sher′iff·wick** (-wik), *n.* [See *wick*[2].] The district over which a sheriff has jurisdiction; also, the office of sheriff.

sher·ris (sher′is), *n.* Earlier form of *sherry*.

sher·ry (sher′i), *n.*; pl. *sherries* (-iz). [From earlier *sherris*, taken as pl., < *Xeres*, now *Jerez* de la Frontera, city in southern Spain.] Any of a class of strong white wines of southern Spain, or of various similar wines made elsewhere.—**sher′ry=cob′bler**, *n.* A cobbler (drink) made with sherry.

sheth (sheth), *n.* [ME. *schethe*; prob. from the root of E. *shed*[2].] The part of a plow which extends downward from the beam and to which the mold-board, share, etc., are attached.

Shet·land·er (shet′lạn-dėr), *n.* A native or inhabitant of the Shetland Islands, northeast of Scotland; also, a Shetland pony.—**Shet′land** (-lạnd) **po′ny.** One of a small, sturdy, rough-coated breed of horses, orig. from the Shetland Islands.—**Shet′land sheep.** One of a breed of sheep native in the Shetland Islands.—**Shet′land wool.** A thin, loosely twisted woolen yarn for knitting, etc., made from the wool of Shetland sheep.

Shell-work, Hôtel de Cluny, Paris.

Plant with Flowers and Fruits of Shepherd's-purse.— *a*, a flower; *b*, a pod.

shew (shū or shō), *v.* and *n.* Archaic or prov. form of *show.*—
shew-bread (shō'bred), *n.* Among the ancient Jews, the bread that was placed every Sabbath before Jehovah on the table beside the altar of incense, and that was eaten at the end of the week by the priests alone. See Ex. xxv. 30.

Shi-ah (shē'ä), *n.* [Ar. *shī'ah*, lit. 'followers.'] One of the two great religious divisions of Islam, centered in Persia, which regards Ali, the son-in-law of Mohammed, as the latter's legitimate successor, and rejects the first three califs and the Sunnite books of tradition handed down under their protection (cf. *Sunnite*); also, a Shiite.

shib-bo-leth (shib'ō-leth), *n.* [Heb. *shibbōleth*, ear of corn, stream.] A Hebrew word used by Jephthah, one of the judges of Israel, as a test-word by which to distinguish the fleeing Ephraimites (who could not pronounce the *sh*) from his own men, the Gileadites (see Judges, xii. 4–6); hence, any word or sound which one cannot pronounce properly, or which is used to detect persons by their pronunciation; a peculiarity of pronunciation, or a habit, mode of dress, etc., which distinguishes a particular class or set of persons; also, a watchword, catchword, or pet phrase of a party, sect, etc.

shied (shīd). Pret. and pp. of *shy*[1], *shy*[2].

shiel, sheal[2] (shēl), *n.* [ME. *schele*; prob. from Scand.] A temporary building; a shanty or hut; a small house or cottage. [Sc. and north. Eng.]

shield (shēld), *n.* [AS. *scild, scyld, sceld,* = D. *schild* = G. *schild* = Icel. *skjöldr* = Goth. *skildus,* shield: cf. *shelter.*] A piece of defensive armor (of various shapes, but often roughly triangular with sides curving to a point at the bottom) carried on the arm or in the hand to protect the body in battle; hence, anything used or serving as a defense or protection; a protective covering or shelter; a protective plate or the like on the body of an animal, as a scute, carapace, etc.; also, something shaped like a shield; in *her.,* a shield-shaped escutcheon on which armorial bearings are displayed; in *ordnance,* a steel screen attached to a heavy gun to protect its gunners, mechanism, etc.; in *mining,* a movable framework for protecting a miner at the place at which he is working.

Shield of Mounted Man-at-arms.—*A,* end of 14th century; *B,* end of 13th century; *C,* first half of 13th century.

—**Shield of Sobieski** (sō-byes'kē), in *astron.,* a constellation (Scutum Sobiescianum, or Scutum Sobieskii) over the bow of Sagittarius, represented as an escutcheon charged with a cross: named after John Sobieski (1624–96), king of Poland.—**shield,** *v.* [AS. *scildan, scyldan.*] **I.** *tr.* To protect with or as with a shield; protect or defend from danger, distress, annoyance, or the like; serve as a shield or protection for; also, to ward off†; also, to avert†, prevent†, or forbid† (as, "God *shield* I should disturb devotion!" Shakspere's "Romeo and Juliet," iv. 1. 41). **II.** *intr.* To offer protection or defense; act or serve as a shield.—**shield'er,** *n.*—**shield'less,** *a.* Without a shield; unprotected.

shiel-ing, sheal-ing (shē'ling), *n.* Same as *shiel.* [Sc. and north. Eng.]

shi-er[1], **shy-er**[1] (shī'ėr), *n.* [See *shy*[1], *v.*] A horse which shies.

shi-er[2], **shy-er**[2] (shī'ėr), *n.* [See *shy*[2], *v.*] One who shies or throws.

shi-er[3], **shi-est** (shī'ėr, shī'est). Occasional compar. and superl. of *shy*[1], *a.*

shift (shift), *v.* [AS. *sciftan,* arrange, appoint, divide, = D. *schiften,* divide, distinguish, = Icel. *skipta,* Sw. *skifta,* Dan. *skifte,* divide, share, change.] **I.** *tr.* To arrange†; appoint†; apportion, distribute, or divide (now prov. Eng.); also, to put by and replace by another or others; change (as, "I . . . insisted on his going home immediately to *shift* his clothes," Smollett's "Humphry Clinker," July 4; "'Tis time, high time, to *shift* this dismal scene," Young's "Night Thoughts," iii. 363); substitute one for another of (things indicated: as, "The peaky islet *shifted* shapes," Tennyson's "Voyage," v.); also, to change the clothes of, or put fresh clothing on (a person, esp. one's self: as, "I was wet, had no clothes to *shift* me," Defoe's "Robinson Crusoe," i. 3: now prov.); also, to transfer from one place, position, person, etc., to another (as, "Cæsar had *shifted* his camp continually," Froude's "Cæsar," xxii.; to *shift* a burden from one shoulder to the other; to *shift* blame or responsibility upon another); alter the direction of (as, to *shift* one's course); also, to get rid of, as by some expedient. **II.** *intr.* To manage to get along or succeed (as, "I had some inclination to give them their lives, if they thought they could *shift* on shore": Defoe's "Robinson Crusoe," i. 18); also, to get along as best one may (as, "As for bread, we were obliged to *shift* with some roots": Defoe's "Captain Singleton," v.); also, to get along by indirect methods; employ shifts or evasions; also, to change one's clothes, or put on fresh clothing; also, to change, or become different (as, the scene *shifts*); also, to move from one place, position, etc., to another (as, "On the 20th of March 1815, the family had to *shift* towards home," Carlyle's "Life of John Stirling," i. 3; "She *shifted* round suddenly on the chair," Arnold Bennett's "Roll-Call," i.); change direction, as the wind.—**to shift for one's self,** to get along by one's own efforts; provide for one's self: as, "Abraham, by this time, was of age, and in accordance with custom had been set free to *shift for himself*" (Charnwood's "Abraham Lincoln," i.).—**shift,** *n.* An expedient or resource (as, "the innumerable *shifts* that small wits put in practice to raise a laugh": Addison, in "Spectator," 44); an ingenious device for effecting some purpose; also, an evasion, artifice, or trick; also, a change or substitution, or something substituted (as, a *shift* of clothes); a woman's chemise (archaic or prov.); a set of workmen, etc., that relieves another set; the time during which such a set works; also, a change or alteration; also, a shifting from one place, position, person, etc., to another; a removal; a transfer; in *mining,* a slight fault or dislocation of a seam or stratum.—**to make shift** (or, esp. formerly, **a shift**), to manage to get along or succeed (as, "*Acres.* Your honour follows you to the grave. *David.* Now, that's just the place where I could *make a shift* to do without it": Sheridan's "Rivals," iv. 1); manage with effort or difficulty (as, "He *made a shift* at last to crawl home": Fielding's "Tom Jones," viii. 11); also, to do one's best, or be content, as with inferior means (as, "them flat-nosed chaps we have to *make shift* with, instead of a proper crew of decent Christians": J. Conrad's "Rescue," i. 2); make an effort, as to do something (as, "I'd *make a shift* . . . to give you more liberty": George Eliot's "Adam Bede," iii.).—**shift'er,** *n.*—**shift'i-ly,** *adv.* In a shifty manner.—**shift'i-ness,** *n.*—**shift'less,** *a.* Lacking in resource; incapable of shifting for one's self; hence, inefficient; improvident; lazy; also, indicating inefficiency, improvidence, or laziness, as actions.—**shift'less-ly,** *adv.*—**shift'less-ness,** *n.*—**shift'y,** *a.*; compar. *shiftier,* superl. *shiftiest.* Full of shifts; fertile in expedients; also, given to or characterized by evasions or artifices; not straightforward; tricky; also, shifting; changing; changeable.

Shi-ism (shē'izm), *n.* The principles or doctrines of the Shiites.

Shi-ite (shē'īt), *n.* A member of the Shiah sect of the Mohammedan religion.—**Shi-it-ic** (shē-it'ik), *a.*

shi-kar (shi-kär'), *n.* [Hind. and Pers. *shikār.*] In India, hunting, as of game.—**shi-ka/ri** (-kä'rē), *n.* [Hind. *shikārī.*] In India, a hunter or sportsman; esp., a native hunter, or a native who accompanies European sportsmen as aid or guide.

shil-la-lah, shil-le-lagh (shi-lā'lä), *n.* [From *Shillelagh,* town and barony in County Wicklow, Ireland.] In Ireland, a cudgel of blackthorn or oak.

shil-ling (shil'ing), *n.* [AS. *scilling* = D. *schelling* = G. *schilling* = Icel. *skillingr* = Goth. *skilliggs,* shilling.] A British money of account and silver coin of the value of 12 pence or one twentieth of a pound sterling, and equivalent to about 24⅓ U. S. cents; also, any of certain other denomi-

Obverse.　　　　　　　Reverse.
Shilling of Henry VIII. — British Museum.

nations of money, or coins, varying in value.—**to take the (King's** or **Queen's) shilling,** in Great Britain, to enlist as a soldier by accepting a shilling given by a recruiting-officer (a practice now discontinued).—**shil'ling=mark,** *n.* A mark (/) used in writing and printing. See *solidus.*

shil-ly-shal-ly (shil'i-shal″i). [Varied redupl. of *shall I,* as if said in indecision.] **I.** *adv.* In an irresolute or hesitating manner: as, "Don't stand *shilly-shally*" (Bulwer-Lytton's "Lucretia," ii. 2). **II.** *a.* Irresolute; undecided; vacillating. **III.** *n.* Irresolution; indecision; vacillation; also, an irresolute person.—**shil'ly=shal″ly,** *v. i.;* -shallied, -shallying. To be irresolute; vacillate: as, "He *shilly-shallied* and temporised an unconscionable time before he would fix the day and hour for the encounter" (S. Butler's "Way of All Flesh," xl.).

shil-pit (shil'pit), *a.* [Origin unknown.] Of a sickly paleness; feeble; puny; of drink, weak or insipid. [Sc.]

shim (shim), *n.* [Origin uncertain.] A thin strip of metal, wood, or the like, for filling in, as for bringing one part in line with another.—**shim,** *v. t.;* shimmed, shimming. To fill out or bring to a level by inserting a shim or shims.

shim-mer (shim'ėr), *v. i.* [AS. *scimrian* (= D. *schemeren,* G. *schimmern*), a freq. form related to *scīmian,* shine, from the root of E. *shine.*] To shine with a subdued, tremulous light; gleam faintly: as, "Everything about her *shimmered* and glimmered softly, as if her dress had been woven out of candle-beams" (Mrs. Wharton's "Age of Innocence," xviii.). —**shim'mer,** *n.* A shimmering light or gleam.—**shim'-mer-y,** *a.* Shimmering; shining with soft, faint gleams of light.

shim-my (shim'i), *n.;* pl. shimmies (-iz). [Corruption of *chemise,* prob. taken as pl.] A chemise. [Prov. or colloq.]

shi-mo-se (shi-mō'sä), *n.* [For *shimonose,* from the name of the Japanese inventor.] A Japanese explosive consisting largely of picric acid.

shin (shin), *n.* [AS. *scinu* = D. *scheen,* shin: cf. G. *schiene,* thin or narrow piece (of metal, wood, etc.), *schienbein,* shin-bone.] The front part of the leg from the knee to the ankle; also, the shin-bone or tibia, esp. its sharp edge or front portion; also, the lower leg, esp. the lower part of the fore leg in beef cattle.—**shin,** *v.;* shinned, shinning. **I.** *intr.* To climb by clasping or holding fast with the hands or arms and legs and drawing one's self up (as, to *shin* up a tree); also, to walk or go, esp. quickly (as, "I was up in the second and *shinning* down the hill": Mark Twain's "Huckleberry Finn," iv.). [Colloq.] **II.** *tr.* To climb by shinning (as, to *shin* a pole); also, to kick on the shins (as, "He had . . . been well *shinned* half a dozen times in scrimmages at football": S. Butler's "Way of All Flesh," xxx.). [Colloq.] —**shin'=bone,** *n.* [AS. *scinbān.*] The tibia.

shin-dig (shin'dig), *n.* [Cf. *shindy.*] A dance, party, or other festivity, esp. of a noisy kind. [Slang, U. S.]

shin-dy (shin'di), *n.;* pl. -dies (-diz). [Origin obscure.] A merrymaking or festivity; also, a row, rumpus, or disturbance (as, "a chair being the favourite projectile in the event of a *shindy*": Smedley's "Frank Fairlegh," i.).

shine (shīn), *v.;* shone (also *shined,* now chiefly archaic, prov., or as given in def.), shining. [AS. *scīnan* (pret. *scān*) = D. *schijnen* = G. *scheinen* = Icel. *skīna* = Goth. *skeinan,* shine; perhaps akin to Gr. σκιά, Skt. *chāyā,* shadow: cf. *sheer²* and *shimmer.*] **I.** *intr.* To give forth light, or glow with light, as the heavenly bodies, fire, fireflies, etc. (as, "With no lack of light, For moon and stars *shone* brightly overhead," W. Morris's "Jason," xii. 411; "Behind the

clouds is the sun still *shining,*" Longfellow's "Rainy Day"); shed or cast light (*down, in, into, through, on* or *upon, over,* etc.: as, the moon *shines* in at the window, or through the trees; "The August sun *shone* over Egdon, and fired its crimson heather to a scarlet glow," Hardy's "Return of the Native," iv. 1); be shed, appear, pass, or flash with brightness, as light, etc. (as, a light *shone* about the place; "the beams that thro' the oriel *shine,*" Tennyson's "Day-Dream," 54; "as the lightning cometh out of the east, and *shineth* even unto the west," Mat. xxiv. 27); also, to be bright with reflected light, as the sky, sea, fields, objects, etc.; gleam, glisten, sparkle, or glitter in the light, as polished metal or wood, glossy silks, gems, glass, etc.; also, to be unusually bright in appearance or expression, as the eyes, face, etc. (as, "His eyes *shone* like coals of fire," F. M. Crawford's "Mr. Isaacs," vii.; the face *shines* with happiness); appear with brightness or clearness, as feelings, qualities, etc. (as, "Pleasure *shone* on her face," Arnold Bennett's "Roll-Call," vii.; "Clive's happy friendly nature *shone* out of his face," Thackeray's "Newcomes," xxviii.); be radiant or resplendent with color, richness, etc. (as, "a beauty that *shone* with deep and vivid tints," Hawthorne's "Scarlet Letter," vii.; to *shine* in splendid array); also, to appear to great advantage, or be conspicuously admirable or fine (as, "There was a grace and dignity . . . in this farmer's wife, which would have *shined* in a palace," Lamb's "Mackery End"; good manners *shine* by contrast with bad); be brilliantly conspicuous or distinguished, or excel conspicuously (as, to *shine* in society; "Philip . . . was not considered, in that warlike age, as likely to *shine* as a warrior," Motley's "Dutch Republic," i. 2); also, to make (*up*) to a person by ingratiating advances, as to win favor, liking, or love (slang, U. S.: as, "tempted to *shine* up to some girl that has sense enough to take life as it is," Sinclair Lewis's "Main Street," xxv.). **II.** *tr.* To give forth or shed (light, etc.); also, to drive, put, or bring (*away, down,* etc.) by shining (lit. or fig.: as, "Like the sun, let bounty spread her ray, And *shine* that superfluity away," Pope's "Satires and Epistles of Horace Imitated," Satires, ii. 2. 116; to *shine* a person down, as by greater brilliance or splendor); also, to cause to shine, or direct the light of, as a lantern; also (pret. and pp. *shined*), to put a gloss or polish on (shoes, etc.); also (pret. and pp. *shined*), in hunting at night, to throw light on (an animal's eyes) with a lantern or the like, or locate (an animal) in this way.—**shine,** *n.* Shining, radiance, brightness, or light, as of something that gives light (as, "Cynthia for shame obscures her silver *shine,*" Shakspere's "Venus and Adonis," 728; "as we went forth in the *shine* of the candles," Stevenson's "Master of Ballantrae," v.); often, sunshine, or fair weather (lit. or fig.: as, I will come, rain or *shine;* "Shadow and *shine* is life, little Annie, flower and thorn," Tennyson's "Grandmother," xv.); also, luster or sheen, as of something that reflects light; a gloss or polish; esp., a polish given to shoes, or a giving of such a polish; also, brilliance, splendor, or fine show (as, "What signifies his barren *shine* Of moral pow'rs an' reason?" Burns's "Holy Fair," 127); a brilliant display or dash (colloq.: as, to cut or make a *shine*); a social gathering, or party (Sc.: as, a tea-*shine*); also, a disturbance, fuss, or row (slang: as, "There'd be a pretty *shine* made if I was to go a-visiting them," Dickens's "Bleak House," lvii.); an unpleasant outbreak or performance (slang, U. S.: as, "Old Crab a cuttin' up one of his *shines,* I s'pose?" Mrs. Stowe's "Oldtown Folks," xii.; "None o' your *shines,* gal! You've got to keep a pleasant face when I speak to ye," Mrs. Stowe's "Uncle Tom's Cabin," xxxi.); a caper, antic, prank, or trick (slang, U. S.: as, "It would make a cow laugh to see the *shines* that old idiot cut," Mark Twain's "Huckleberry Finn," xxiii.: cf. *monkey-shine*); also, a liking or fancy (slang, U. S.: as, "Brent seems to have taken quite a *shine* to you, Honora," W. Churchill's "Modern Chronicle," ii. 5). —**to take the shine out of** (or **off,** or **off of**), fig., to take the brightness or cheer from (as, "enough to *take* more of *the shine out of* things than church-going on Sundays could put in again": G. MacDonald's "Annals of a Quiet Neighbourhood," iv.); also, to deprive of luster, glory, or distinction as if by shining more brightly; outshine. [Colloq.]

shin-er (shī'nėr), *n.* One who or that which shines; a coin of gold or silver, esp. (in England) a guinea or sovereign (slang); specif., any of various small American fresh-water fishes, mostly cyprinoids, with glistening scales, as *Notemigonus* (or *Abramis*) *chrysoleucus*, a common species with a golden or silvery coloration; a minnow.

Shiner (*Notemigonus chrysoleucus*).

shin-gle[1] (shing′gl), *n.* [Cf. Norw. *singl*, MLG. *singele*, shingle.] Small, water-worn stones or pebbles such as lie in loose sheets or beds on the seashore (as, "Her feet sank at each step into descending ridges of loose *shingle*," Arnold Bennett's "Hilda Lessways," iii. 4: sometimes *pl.*, *shingles*, in same sense, as, "They go wandering on the *shingles*, picking up cockle-shells," Lamb's "Old Margate Hoy"); such stones or pebbles as a material for ballast, for laying walks, etc. (as, "A little garden . . . round it ran a walk Of *shingle*": Tennyson's "Enoch Arden," 733); also, an extent of small, loose stones or pebbles (as, "now through loose earth, then through a *shingle* of pebbles or sand, then over rough rocks": Roosevelt's "Ranch Life and the Hunting-Trail," xii.).

shin-gle[2] (shing′gl), *n.* [ME. *schingel*, *scingle*, *scincle*, perhaps < L. *scindula*, also *scandula*, a shingle.] A thin piece of wood, usually oblong and with one end thicker than the other, used in overlapping rows to cover the roofs and sides of houses; also, such pieces collectively; also, a small sign-board, esp. that of a professional man (colloq.).

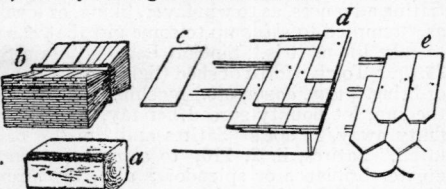

Shingles.— *a*, block prepared for splitting or sawing into shingles; *b*, shingles as bunched for market; *c*, a shingle; *d*, plain shingles laid on a roof; *e*, fancy shingles laid.

shin′gle[2], *v. t.*; -gled, -gling. To cover (a roof, etc.) with shingles; also, to cut (a person's hair) so that it gives the effect of overlapping shingles; also, to cut (hair) close to the head.

shin-gle[3] (shing′gl), *v. t.*; -gled, -gling. [Cf. F. *cingler*, G. *zängeln*, shingle (metal).] To hammer or squeeze (a mass of iron taken from a puddling-furnace) in order to press out the slag and impurities.

shin-gler[1] (shing′glẽr), *n.* One who shingles houses; also, one who or a machine which cuts and prepares shingles.

shin-gler[2] (shing′glẽr), *n.* One who or that which shingles iron.

shin-gles (shing′glz), *n. sing.* or *pl.* [ME. *schingles*, *cingules*, *sengles*, ult. < L. *cingulum*, girdle: cf. *zoster*, lit. 'girdle,' as a name for the disease.] In *pathol.*, a cutaneous disease characterized by vesicles which sometimes form a girdle about the body; herpes zoster.

shin-gly (shing′gli), *a.* Consisting of or covered with shingle, or small, loose stones or pebbles: as, "a *shingly* spit on the Hampshire shore" (Morley's "Oliver Cromwell," iii. 6); a *shingly* beach.

shin-i-ly (shī′ni-li), *adv.* In a shiny manner; glossily.—**shin′i-ness**, *n.*

shin-ing (shī′ning), *p. a.* That shines; luminous; radiant; gleaming or glistening; lustrous or glossy; bright; resplendent; brilliant (as, "a man of *shining* talents": Disraeli's "Lothair," ii.); conspicuously fine, or conspicuous (as, "a *shining* instance of youthful piety": George Eliot's "Silas Marner," i.).—**shin′ing-ly**, *adv.*—**shin′ing-ness**, *n.*

shin-leaf (shin′lēf), *n.* [Cf. *shinplaster*.] A North American herb, *Pyrola elliptica*, with elliptical or broadly oval leaves which are said to have been once used for plasters; sometimes, any plant of the same genus.

shin-ny[1] (shin′i), *n.*; pl. *shinnies* (-iz). [Origin obscure.]

A simple variety of hockey, played with a ball or the like and clubs curved at one end; also, the club used.—**shin′ny**[1], *v. i.*; -nied, -nying. To play shinny; drive the ball at shinny.

shin-ny[2] (shin′i), *v. i.*; -nied, -nying. [From *shin*.] To shin or climb. [Colloq.]

shin-plas-ter (shin′pläs″tẽr), *n.* A plaster for the shin or leg, as (in homely use) a piece of paper wet with vinegar, etc.; hence, humorously, a piece of paper money of low denomination or little value, as one issued on insufficient security or greatly depreciated in value (U. S.).

Shin-to (shin′tō). [Jap., < Chinese *shin tao*, 'way of the gods.'] **I.** *n.*; pl. *-tos* (-tōz). The native religion of Japan, primarily a system of nature-worship and ancestor-worship; also, an adherent of this religion. **II.** *a.* Of or pertaining to Shinto.—**Shin′to-ism** (-tō-izm), *n.* The Shinto religion.—**Shin′to-ist**, *n.*

shin-y (shī′ni), *a.*; compar. *shinier*, superl. *shiniest*. Characterized by shine or shining; bright (as, "Wouldn't you marry us for a half a sovereign, and it a nice *shiny* one with a view on it of the living king's mamma?" Synge's "Tinker's Wedding," i.); glistening; glossy; often, worn to a glossy smoothness, as clothes.

ship (ship), *n.* [AS. *scip* = D. *schip* = G. *schiff* = Icel. and Goth. *skip*, ship: cf. *skiff*.] A sea-going vessel of considerable size; any vessel intended or used for navigating the water, esp. one of some size and not propelled by oars, paddles, or the like; specif., in nautical use, a vessel with a bowsprit and three (or more) masts (foremast, mainmast, and mizzenmast), each consisting of a lower mast, a topmast, and a topgallantmast (the term *ship* in this sense having been formerly applied only to those vessels in which all the masts were square-rigged); also, a vessel for navigating the air; an airship; also, something suggestive of a ship (as, the *ship* of the desert, the camel); something shaped like the hull of a ship, as, formerly, a vessel in which incense was kept; also [*cap.*], in *astron.*, the southern constellation Argo (also called *Ship Argo*).—**ship of the line**, a ship large enough to be in the line of battle.—**ship's boat**, a rowboat, launch, or the like, carried on or towed by a ship for use in landing passengers and for other purposes.—**ship's husband**, a man who has the care of a ship while in port; one who oversees the general interests of a ship, as berthing, provisioning, repairing, entering and clearing, etc.—**ship's papers**. See *paper*, *n.*—**ship**, *v. t.*; *shipped*, *shipping*. To put or take on board a ship or the like, for transportation, as persons or goods; also, to send or transport by ship, or by rail or other means of conveyance (as, to *ship* goods by express); hence, to send away or get rid of (colloq.); also, to take in (water) over the side, as a vessel does when waves break over it (as, "We *shipped* a sea that drenched us all to the skin": Smollett's "Humphry Clinker," Aug. 8); also, to draw (an object) into a ship or boat (as, to *ship* the gang-plank; to *ship* oars, see phrase below; "He *shipped* his sculls and drifted," Galsworthy's "Dark Flower," ii. 11); also, to fix in a ship or boat in the proper place for use (as, "They had dropped the rudder overboard while attempting to *ship* it," J. Conrad's "Lord Jim," x.; to *ship* oars, see phrase below); also, to engage for service on a ship (as, "Captain Guy had gone on board his vessel for the purpose of *shipping* a new crew": H. Melville's "Omoo," xxxviii.).—**to ship oars**, to lift the oars out of the rowlocks and bring them into the boat (as, "The sailors *ship* their *oars*, and cease to row": Dryden's "Ceyx and Alcyone," 92); also, to fix the oars in the rowlocks in readiness to row (as, the boatmen *shipped* their *oars* and commenced pulling us ashore).—**ship**, *v. i.* To go on board a ship; embark; also, to engage to serve on a ship (as, "We never ask questions when a seaman *ships* for us": Marryat's "Frank Mildmay," xxi.).

-ship. [ME. *-schip*, *-schipe*, etc., < AS. *-scipe*, *-scype*, akin to D. *-schap*, G. *-schaft*; from the root of E. *shape*.] A suffix of nouns denoting state or condition, character, office, dignity, skill, etc., as in *clerkship*, *friendship*, *lordship*, *statesmanship*, *workmanship*, *worship*.

ship=bis-cuit (ship′bis″kit), *n.* A kind of hard biscuit used on shipboard; hardtack.

ship-board (ship′bōrd), *n.* The side of a ship†; also, a ship, or its deck or interior (in 'on shipboard').

ship=build-er (ship'bil″dèr), *n.* One whose occupation is the designing and constructing of ships.—**ship'=build″-ing,** *n.* The art of constructing ships.

ship=chan-dler (ship'chan″dlèr), *n.* One who deals in cordage, canvas, and other supplies for ships.—**ship'=chan″dler-y,** *n.*

ship-en-tine (ship'en-tēn), *n.* [From *ship*, after *barkentine*, *barkantine*.] A four-masted vessel having the first three masts square-rigged and the last one fore-and-aft rigged.

ship=fe-ver (ship'fē″vèr), *n.* Typhus fever as occurring on overcrowded ships.

ship-ful (ship'fúl), *n.*; pl. *-fuls.* A quantity or number sufficient to fill a ship.

ship-less (ship'les), *a.* Destitute of ships.

ship=load (ship'lōd), *n.* A full load or cargo for a ship.

ship-man (ship'man), *n.*; pl. *-men.* [AS. *scipmann.*] A seaman or sailor; also, the master of a ship. [Now chiefly poetic.]

ship-mas-ter (ship'màs″tèr), *n.* The master, commander, or captain of a ship.

ship-mate (ship'māt), *n.* One who serves with another in the same vessel.

ship-ment (ship'ment), *n.* The act of shipping goods, etc.; the delivery of goods, etc., to a carrier for transportation; also, that which is shipped; a consignment of goods for transportation.

ship=mon-ey (ship'mun″i), *n.* In *old Eng. law,* a tax levied in time of war on ports, maritime towns, etc., to provide ships for national defense.

ship=own-er (ship'ō″nèr), *n.* One who owns a ship or ships, or any share therein.

ship-per (ship'èr), *n.* [AS. *scipere,* seaman.] A seaman†; also, a skipper†; also, one who ships goods, or makes shipments; also, a commodity shipped, or suitable for export; also, a device for shifting a belt from one pulley to another.

ship-ping (ship'ing), *n.* The act of one who ships goods, etc.; the action or business of sending or transporting goods, etc., by ship, or by rail or other means of conveyance; also, ships collectively; a body of ships, as of a particular country; their aggregate tonnage; also, a ship or ships for the accommodation of one or more persons or things, or accommodation on board a ship or ships (obs. or archaic: as, "We had agreed to descend the Rhine in a boat from Strasburg to Rotterdam, whence we might take *shipping* for London," Mrs. Shelley's "Frankenstein," xviii.); also, a voyage† (as, "God send 'em good *shipping!*" Shakspere's "Taming of the Shrew," v. 1. 43).—**ship'ping=clerk,** *n.* A clerk who attends to shipments.

ship-rigged (ship'rigd), *a.* *Naut.,* rigged as a three-masted vessel, with square sails on all three masts; sometimes, square-rigged.

ship-shape (ship'shāp). **I.** *a.* In the state of order, neatness, etc., proper on shipboard; orderly; trim: as, "We'll try to make this barn a little more *shipshape*" (Kipling's "Light That Failed," iii.). **II.** *adv.* In a shipshape manner.

ship-worm (ship'wèrm), *n.* Any of various marine bivalve mollusks (genus *Teredo*) with small valves and a long worm-like body, which burrow into the timbers of ships, etc.

ship-wreck (ship'rek), *n.* The remains of a wrecked ship (now rare); also, the destruction or loss of a ship by foundering at sea, striking or stranding on a rock or shoal, or the like; fig., destruction or ruin (as, the *shipwreck* of one's hopes).—**ship'wreck,** *v.* **I.** *tr.* To cause to suffer shipwreck; subject to the perils of shipwreck; fig., to destroy or ruin. **II.** *intr.* To suffer shipwreck (lit. or fig.).

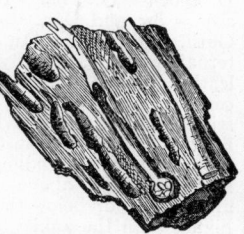

Ship-worm (*Teredo navalis*), about one fifth natural size.

Piece of Wood perforated by Ship-worms.

ship-wright (ship'rīt), *n.* One employed in the construction of ships: as, "She [a ship] has been built by French *shipwrights*" (J. Conrad's "Rover," vi.).

ship-yard (ship'yärd), *n.* A yard or inclosure near the water, in which ships are built or repaired.

shire (shīr or shēr), *n.* [AS. *scīr,* official charge, office, district, shire, = OHG. *scīra,* care, official charge: cf. *sheriff.*] A province†, district†, or region†; esp., an old English administrative district, made up of a number of smaller districts; in later use, one of the counties into which Great Britain is divided (now esp. one of those having names ending in *-shire*); also, one of the larger divisions elsewhere for purposes of local administration, as in Australian states. —**shire'=horse,** *n.* One of a breed of large, strong draft-horses with long hair on the back of the legs from the knees and hocks down, long cultivated in Lincolnshire and other midland counties of England.—**shire'=town,** *n.* The town where the business of a shire is transacted.

shirk (shèrk), *n.* [Origin uncertain: cf. G. *schurke,* rascal, also E. *shark².*] A parasite†, petty swindler†, or sharper†; also, one who seeks to avoid work, duty, etc. (as, "You think we're all a lot of *shirks*": Mrs. Wharton's "Son at the Front," xx.).—**shirk,** *v.* **I.** *intr.* To sponge or prey on others†; also, to evade work, duty, etc.; also, to slink or sneak (as, "He and his comrades had been obliged to *shirk* on board at night, to escape from their wives": Thackeray's "Pendennis," ii. 22). **II.** *tr.* To procure by sponging or trickery†; also, to evade (work, duty, obligations, etc.: as, "a man not being able to *shirk* work because it may happen to be dirty," G. MacDonald's "Annals of a Quiet Neighbourhood," i.; "Common men cannot *shirk* world politics and at the same time enjoy private freedom," H. G. Wells's "Outline of History," xxxvii. § 1); also, to avoid or elude (a person, etc.: obs. or rare).—**shirk'er,** *n.*

shirr (shèr), *v. t.* [Origin obscure.] To draw up or gather (cloth, etc.) on parallel threads; also, to bake (eggs removed from the shell) in a shallow dish or in individual dishes with butter, etc., sometimes serving with a sauce.—**shirr,** *n.* A shirred arrangement of cloth, etc. Also **shirr'ing.**

shirt (shèrt), *n.* [AS. *scyrte* = Icel. *skyrta,* shirt, = D *schort,* G. *schürze,* apron; prob. orig. meaning 'short garment,' from the Teut. adj. represented by E. *short*: cf. *skirt.*] An undergarment of cotton, linen, or other material, for the upper part of the body; a garment for the upper part of a man's body, without or with collar and special bosom, having long sleeves with wristbands or cuffs, and usually worn under a waistcoat, etc.; a woman's shirtwaist; a nightshirt; some similar garment.—**shirt,** *v. t.* To clothe with or as with a shirt.—**shirt'ing,** *n.* Material or a fabric for shirts.—**shirt'=sleeve,** *n.* A sleeve of a shirt: chiefly in *pl.,* often in the phrase 'in one's shirt-sleeves,' that is, with one's coat off so that the sleeves of one's shirt are visible: as, "Lincoln thought it friendly to open the door himself *in his shirt sleeves* when two most elegant ladies came to call" (Charnwood's "Abraham Lincoln," iii.).—**shirt'=waist,** *n.* A woman's loosely fitting waist of cotton, linen, silk, flannel, or other material, worn with a separate skirt: as, "She was dressed simply in a *shirtwaist* and a dark skirt" (W. Churchill's "Modern Chronicle," i. 7).—**shirt'y,** *a.* Ill-tempered; ill-natured. [Slang, Eng.]

shit-tah=tree (shit'a-trē), *n.* [Heb. *shittāh* (pl. *shittīm*).] A tree mentioned in the Bible (see Isa. xli. 19), probably a species of acacia with a hard, durable wood.

shit-tim=wood (shit'im-wùd), *n.* [Heb. *shittīm,* pl.: see *shittah-tree.*] The wood of the shittah-tree, of which the ark of the covenant and various parts of the Jewish tabernacle were made. See Ex. xxv.—xxvii.

Shi-va (shē'vä), *n.* Same as *Siva.*

shiv-a-ree (shiv-a-rē'), *n.* Corruption of *charivari.*

shive (shīv), *n.* [ME. *schive,* slice, = D. *schijf,* G. *scheibe,* slice, disk, sheave: cf. *sheave².*] A slice, esp. of bread (now chiefly prov.); also, a thin, flat cork or stopper.

shiv-er¹ (shiv'èr), *n.* [ME. *schivere, scifre,* = OHG. *scivero,* splinter, G. *schiefer,* splinter, flake, slate.] A fragment; a splinter: as, to shatter a spear to *shivers*; "thorns of the crown and *shivers* of the cross" (Tennyson's "Balin and Balan," 108).—**shiv'er¹,** *v.* **I.** *tr.* To break or split into fragments or splinters; shatter: as, "Their lances were *shivered,* and sent up splinters in the air" (Irving's "Conquest of Granada," xciii.); "Every statue was hurled from its niche . . . every painted window *shivered* to atoms"

(Motley's "Dutch Republic," ii. 7). Often used in imprecations attributed to sailors: as, *shiver* my timbers! "If fairer can be said by mortal seaman, *shiver* my sides!" (Stevenson's "Treasure Island," xxviii.). **II.** *intr.* To break into fragments; become shattered: as, "His statue fell, and *shivered* on the stones" (Froude's "Cæsar," xxvi.).

shiv-er[2] (shiv′ér), *v. i.* [ME. *chiveren*; origin uncertain.] To shake involuntarily or tremble with cold, fear, excitement, etc. (as, "He *shivered* as with an ague," Hawthorne's "Twice-Told Tales," Howe's Masquerade; "As a dog, withheld A moment . . . *shivers* ere he springs and kills," Tennyson's "Pelleas and Ettarre," 278); in general, to shake tremulously, tremble, or quiver, as leaves in the breeze; sound or resound tremulously or vibrantly (poetic: as, "a cry that *shiver′d* to the tingling stars," Tennyson's "Passing of Arthur," 367).—**shiv′er**[2], *n.* A shivering motion or state; an involuntary trembling, or a sensation of trembling, from cold, fear, etc. (as, "Cold *shivers* went down Trilby's back as she listened": Du Maurier's "Trilby," ii.); a tremulous motion, or a tremble or quiver, of anything (as, "the faintest *shiver* of leaf and limb": Whittier's "Mogg Megone," i.).—**the shivers,** ague or chills attended with shivering; a fit of shivering; also, the sensations of shivering caused by fear, etc.—**shiv′er-er,** *n.*—**shiv′er-ing-ly,** *adv.*

shiv-er-y[1] (shiv′ér-i), *a.* Readily breaking into shivers or fragments; brittle.

shiv-er-y[2] (shiv′ér-i), *a.* Inclined to shiver or shake with cold, etc. (as, "the frail, *shivery* . . . little being, enveloped in a tangle of black silk wraps": Mrs. Stowe's "Oldtown Folks," xxiv.); characterized by shivering; quivering; tremulous; also, causing shivering, as from chilliness.

shoal[1] (shōl), *n.* [= *school*[1].] A school of fish, porpoises, or the like; hence, a large number of persons or things gathered or considered together (as, "Here he met a *shoal* of Scots," Morley's "Oliver Cromwell," ii. 2; "The letters which followed her in *shoals* from Berlin flattered her to the skies," Mrs. H. Ward's "Robert Elsmere," xxiii.).—**shoal**[1], *v. i.* To collect or swim in a shoal; hence, to crowd together; throng.

shoal[2] (shōl). [Earlier *shoald*, ME. *schold, schald*, < AS. *sceald*, shallow: cf. *shallow*.] **I.** *a.* Of little depth, as water; shallow: as, "The entrance to this northern anchorage was . . . narrow and *shoal*" (Stevenson's "Treasure Island," xxvi.). **II.** *n.* A place where the water is of little depth; a shallow; also, a sand-bank or sand-bar in the bed of a body of water, esp. one which shows at low water.—**shoal**[2], *v.* **I.** *intr.* To become shallow or more shallow: as, "He anchored them fast where the Texel *shoaled*" (H. Newbolt's "Admirals All"). **II.** *tr.* To cause to become shallow; also, *naut.*, to proceed from a greater to a less depth of (water: as, "There was no apparent change in colour to indicate that they *shoaled* their water," Marryat's "King's Own," xlix.).—**shoal′i-ness,** *n.* Shoaly condition.—**shoal′ness,** *n.*—**shoal′y,** *a.* Full of shoals or shallows.

shoat (shōt), *n.* See *shote*.

shock[1] (shok), *n.* [ME. *schokke* = MLG. *schok*, shock, = G. *schock*, heap, sixty.] A group of sheaves of grain placed on end and supporting one another in order to permit the grain to dry and ripen before housing; a similar group of separate stalks of maize; hence, a heap or considerable collection.—**shock**[1], *v. t.* To make into shocks.

shock[2] (shok). [Origin uncertain: cf. *shough*.] **I.** *n.* A dog with long, shaggy hair, esp. a poodle; also, a thick, bushy mass, as of hair (as, "a huge man with . . . a great *shock* of orange-coloured hair": Conan Doyle's "Exploits of Brigadier Gerard," i.). **II.** *a.* Having rough, thick hair; also, shaggy, as hair.

shock[3] (shok), *v.* [Prob. < F. *choquer*, strike against, shock, appar. from Teut.: cf. *chuck*[3].] **I.** *tr.* To strike against suddenly and violently; shake or weaken as by violent impact; also, to attack violently, as in battle†; also, to affect mentally as by a blow; strike with intense and painful surprise (as, "Ernest was terribly *shocked* when he heard of the loss of his money": S. Butler's "Way of All Flesh," lxvi.); startle by outraging the sense of propriety or decency, or horrify or scandalize (as, "that period of disgrace when she had so *shocked* her family by her divorce": Galsworthy's "Saint's Progress," i. 8); also, to subject to bodily or nervous

shock; also, to give an electric shock to. **II.** *intr.* To come into violent contact; collide; encounter with a shock: as, "All at fiery speed the two *Shock′d* on the central bridge" (Tennyson's "Gareth and Lynette," 939).—**shock**[3], *n.* A violent collision or encounter, as of armed forces in battle (as, "In the English civil war the campaigns were few in which the *shock* of horse was not the deciding element": Morley's "Oliver Cromwell," ii. 1); a sudden, violent blow or impact; a sudden disturbance or commotion as from violent impact; fig., a sudden damaging effect, as to credit, belief, etc.; also, a sudden and startling effect on the mind; a feeling or state of painful, agitating surprise (as, "Here he sat sentenced to die. A *shock*, chill and painful, deprived me of speech": Wister's "Virginian," xxx.); a startled sense of outraged propriety or decency; something that shocks mentally (as, "He was, I must admit, a *shock* to me": H. G. Wells's "Tono-Bungay," i. 2. § 1); also, a sudden debilitating effect on the bodily functions due to some violent impression on the nervous system, as from a severe injury, a surgical operation, a violent emotional disturbance, or the like; the resulting condition of nervous depression or prostration; also, a sudden attack, or stroke, of paralysis (colloq.); also, the effect produced on the animal body by the sudden passage through it of a current of electricity.—**shock**[3]=**ab-sorb″er,** *n.* In *mech.*, a device for deadening shock or concussion, as when two bodies come together; esp., an appliance on an automobile for checking sudden or excessive movements of the springs, esp. in recoiling, or a device on an aëroplane for lessening the shock on landing.—**shock′er,** *n.* One who or that which shocks; esp., a highly sensational work of fiction (colloq.).

shock=head-ed (shok′hed″ed), *a.* Having the head covered with a shock or thick mass of hair: as, "a *shock-headed* urchin" (Mrs. H. Ward's "Robert Elsmere," xxii.).

shock-ing (shok′ing), *p. a.* That shocks; esp., causing intense and painful surprise; often, startlingly offensive to the sense of propriety or decency (as, "I do think, Augustine, you are so irreverent! . . . I think it's *shocking* to hear you talk": Mrs. Stowe's "Uncle Tom's Cabin," xvi.); exciting intense repugnance or horror, or revolting (as, "They say it was a *shocking* sight After the field was won; For many thousand bodies here Lay rotting in the sun": Southey's "Battle of Blenheim," ix.); sometimes, very bad (colloq.: as, *shocking* manners).—**shock′ing-ly,** *adv.*—**shock′ing-ness,** *n.*

shock-troops (shok′trōps), *n. pl.* [Cf. G. *stosstruppen*.] *Milit.*, troops especially selected and equipped for engaging in assault.

shod (shod). Preterit and past participle of *shoe*.

shod-dy (shod′i). [Origin uncertain; perhaps related to *shed*[2].] **I.** *n.*; pl. *shoddies* (-iz). A fibrous material obtained by shredding woolen rags or waste; also, a cloth made of or containing this material; hence, anything inferior made to resemble what is of superior quality; anything inferior but pretentious; pretense or sham. **II.** *a.*; compar. *shoddier*, superl. *shoddiest*. Made of or containing shoddy; hence, inferior but pretentious, or pretending to an excellence or superiority not possessed (as, "It [painting] was all false, insincere, *shoddy*": Maugham's "Moon and Sixpence," xix.); sham.—**shod′di-ly,** *adv.*—**shod′di-ness,** *n.*

shoe (shō), *n.*; pl. *shoes* (shōz), archaic or prov. *shoon* (shōn). [AS. *sceōh, scōh*, = D. *schoen* = G. *schuh* = Icel. *skōr* = Sw. and Dan. *sko* = Goth. *skōhs*, shoe.] An external covering, usually of leather, for the human foot, consisting of a more or less stiff or heavy sole and a lighter upper part; specif., such a covering ending a short distance above the

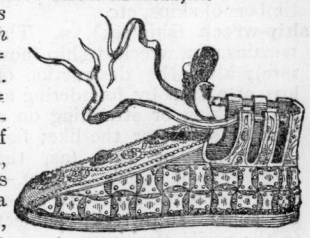
Shoe, 9th century.

ankle, or at or below the ankle (in British use, reaching no higher than the ankle), as distinguished from a *boot*; also, a horseshoe, or a similar plate for the hoof of some other animal; also, some thing or part resembling a shoe in form, position, or use; a drag or skid for a wheel of a vehicle;

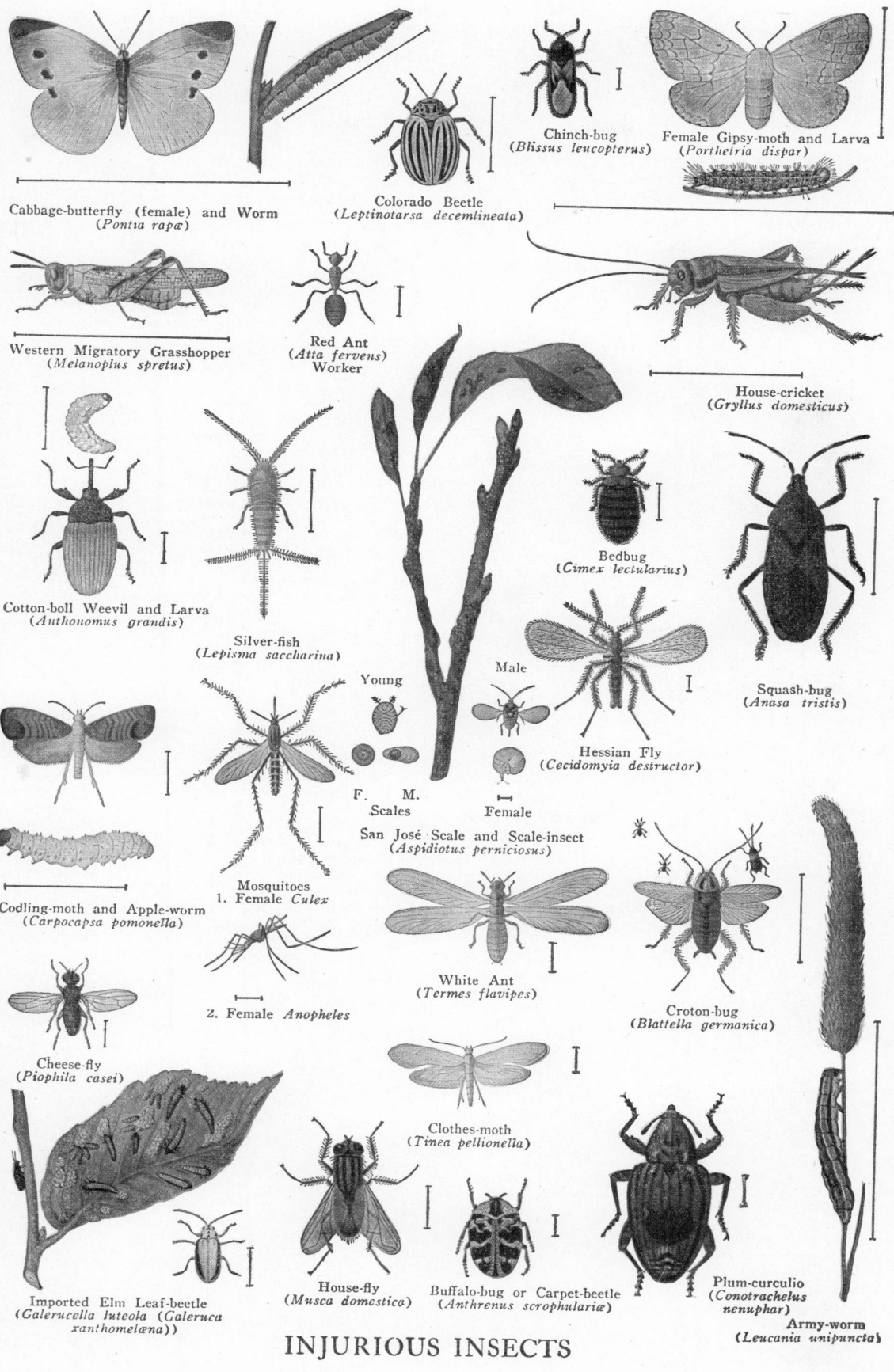

Cabbage-butterfly (female) and Worm
(*Pontia rapæ*)

Colorado Beetle
(*Leptinotarsa decemlineata*)

Chinch-bug
(*Blissus leucopterus*)

Female Gipsy-moth and Larva
(*Porthetria dispar*)

Western Migratory Grasshopper
(*Melanoplus spretus*)

Red Ant
(*Atta fervens*)
Worker

House-cricket
(*Gryllus domesticus*)

Cotton-boll Weevil and Larva
(*Anthonomus grandis*)

Silver-fish
(*Lepisma saccharina*)

Bedbug
(*Cimex lectularius*)

Squash-bug
(*Anasa tristis*)

Male

Young

Hessian Fly
(*Cecidomyia destructor*)

F.   M.
Scales   Female

San José Scale and Scale-insect
(*Aspidiotus perniciosus*)

Codling-moth and Apple-worm
(*Carpocapsa pomonella*)

Mosquitoes
1. Female *Culex*

2. Female *Anopheles*

White Ant
(*Termes flavipes*)

Croton-bug
(*Blattella germanica*)

Cheese-fly
(*Piophila casei*)

Clothes-moth
(*Tinea pellionella*)

Imported Elm Leaf-beetle
(*Galerucella luteola* (*Galeruca xanthomelæna*))

House-fly
(*Musca domestica*)

Buffalo-bug or Carpet-beetle
(*Anthrenus scrophulariæ*)

Plum-curculio
(*Conotrachelus nenuphar*)

Army-worm
(*Leucania unipuncta*)

INJURIOUS INSECTS

the part of a brake which acts upon the wheel; a ferrule or the like, as of iron, for protecting the end of a staff, pole, etc.; a band of iron fastened to the bottom of the runner of a sleigh; the outer casing of a pneumatic automobile-tire; the sliding plate or contact by which an electric car or locomotive takes its current from the third rail.—
shoe, v. t.; shod, shoeing. To provide or fit with a shoe or shoes (as, "He was shod in old, black leather slippers," Arnold Bennett's "Riceyman Steps," i. 1; "the shoeing of horses," Blackmore's "Lorna Doone," xii.); also, to protect or arm at the point, edge, or face with a ferrule, metal plate, or the like.

shoe-bill (shō′bil), n. A large African wading bird, Balæniceps rex, having a broad bill shaped somewhat like a shoe.

shoe-black (shō′blak), n. One who cleans and polishes shoes and boots for a livelihood.

shoe=horn (shō′hôrn), n. A shaped implement of horn, metal, or the like, for inserting in a shoe at the heel to facilitate the slipping on of the shoe.

shoe-ing=horn (shō′ing-hôrn), n. A shoe-horn; fig., something facilitating or bringing on something else; one used as a tool or a decoy by another; an appetizer.

shoe-lace (shō′lās), n. A shoe-string.

shoe-less (shō′les), a. Without shoes.

shoe-mak-er (shō′mā″kėr), n. One whose occupation it is to make shoes.

Shoebill.

shoe′mak″ing, n.

sho-er (shō′ėr), n. One who provides or fits with shoes; one who shoes horses, etc.

shoe=string (shō′string), n. A string or lace for fastening a shoe; fig., a very small amount of money or capital used to start or carry on an enterprise or business (colloq.).

sho-far (shō′fär), n. See shophar.

shog (shog), v. t. or i.; shogged, shogging. [ME. schoggen: cf. MLG. and MHG. schocken, to swing, shake, also E. jog².] To shake; jolt; jog. [Now chiefly prov.]—**shog,** n. A shake, jerk, or jog. [Now chiefly prov.]

sho-gun (shō′gōn), n. [Jap.] The hereditary commander-in-chief of the Japanese army, virtual ruler of Japan until the resignation of the last shogun in 1867. Also called tycoon.—**sho′gun-ate** (-āt), n. The office or rule of a shogun.

shone (shōn or shon). Preterit and past participle of shine.

shoo (shō), interj. [ME. schowe, ssou: cf. F. chou, G. schu, It. scio, Gr. σοῦ, interj.] An exclamation used to scare or drive away poultry, birds, etc.—**shoo,** v.; shooed, shooing. I. tr. To scare or drive away by calling out 'shoo': as, "If a cow came into this farmyard everybody in the place would be shooing it out again" (H. G. Wells's "Mr. Britling," i. 1. § 12). II. intr. To call out 'shoo,' as in driving away poultry; also, to hasten away in obedience to a call of 'shoo.'

shook¹ (shúk). Preterit and sometimes past participle of shake.

shook² (shúk), n. [From shook, archaic pp. of shake, as applied to casks taken to pieces.] A set of staves and headings sufficient for one hogshead, barrel, or the like; also, a set of the parts of a box, piece of furniture, or the like, ready to be put together.

shook³ (shúk), n. [= shock¹.] A shock of sheaves or the like.

shoon (shōn), n. Archaic or prov. plural of shoe.

shoot (shōt), v.; shot (pp. formerly also shotten), shooting. [AS. scéotan (pret. scéat) = D. schieten = G. schiessen = Icel. skjóta = Sw. skjuta = Dan. skyde, shoot: cf. shot², shut, shuttle, and sheet¹.] I. intr. To move swiftly through space; pass suddenly and swiftly; dart; also, to slide, as a

bolt into its fastenings; also, to pass suddenly or dart along the nerves, as pain (as, "She could not endure the shooting pains that she felt in her breast": Maria Edgeworth's "Belinda," x.); be affected with sharp, darting pains, as a part of the body; also, to come forth from the ground, a stem, etc., as a plant or a bud; grow; grow rapidly (often with up); also, to put forth buds or shoots, as a plant; germinate; also, to produce crystals, as a solution; form as crystals, as a salt; also, to project, extend, or jut (as, a cape which shoots out into the sea); also, to send forth missiles from a bow, firearm, or the like; take a shot, as with a firearm; also, to send forth missiles or be discharged, as a gun; also, to engage in or follow the sport of killing game with a gun; also, to propel a thing at something else or in a particular direction, as a marble or a ball in playing games; also, to take a snap-shot with a camera; take pictures with a moving-picture camera. II. tr. To send swiftly along or in a particular direction; dart; cast; push or thrust sharply; slide (a bolt, etc.) into or out of its fastenings (as, "He went to the door and shot back the great forged bolt": W. Churchill's "Coniston," i. 12); emit (rays, etc.) swiftly; put forth (buds, branches, etc.), as a plant does; dump or empty out, as from a receptacle; send (something) down a chute; let down (an anchor); lower and set (a net for fish); pull (one's cuffs) out so that they project beyond the sleeves of one's coat (colloq.); also, to cause to extend or project (as, "Two slim, tall poplars stood against the gable of the chapel, and shot their tops above its roof": Howells's "Chance Acquaintance," iv.); also, to send forth (arrows, bullets, etc.) from a bow, firearm, or the like; discharge (a bow, firearm, etc.: often with off); engage in (a shooting-match); decide (a tie) in such a match by additional shooting (with off); also, fig., to send forth like an arrow or a bullet (as, "Suddenly he shot a question at her," W. Churchill's "Coniston," i. 1; "She shot a grateful glance at him," Whyte-Melville's "Katerfelto," xv.); also, to hit, wound, or kill with a missile discharged from a weapon; also, to put to death as a penalty with such a missile; also, to carry, break, etc., by the discharge of such missiles (with away, off, etc.: as, "Her rudder, and a piece of her stern, were shot quite away," Defoe's "Robinson Crusoe," ii. 11); also, to make by the discharge of such missiles (as, to shoot a hole in a thing); also, to go over (country) in shooting game; also, to open, loosen, remove, etc., by setting off a charge of an explosive (as, to shoot an oil-well); also, to take a snap-shot of (something) with a camera; photograph with a moving-picture camera; also, in games, to propel (a marble) from the thumb and forefinger (as, "He . . . taught them to fly kites and shoot marbles": Irving's "Sketch-Book," Rip Van Winkle); kick or drive (the ball, etc.), as at the goal; hence, to accomplish by kicking or driving the ball, etc. (as, "He'd shot a goal": H. G. Wells's "Mr. Britling," i. 3. § 4); also, to pass rapidly through, over, down, etc. (as, to shoot a rapid); also, to give a changeable coloration to (fabrics) in weaving by using a warp and a weft of different colors; hence, to variegate by introducing threads, streaks, etc., of some different color (as, "The river . . . lay in pools of the most enchanting sea-green shot with watery browns," Stevenson's "Travels with a Donkey," v. 1: often fig.).—**to shoot off one's mouth,** or **shoot one's mouth off,** to talk, esp. freely and indiscreetly: as, "Don't you know better than to shoot your mouth off like that?" (G. W. Cable's "Cavalier," iv.). [Slang, U. S.]—**shoot,** n. [From shoot, v.; in some senses confused with chute.] A swift or sudden movement; a sharp twinge of pain; a cast or throw; one movement of the shuttle between the threads of the warp in weaving, or a thread so placed; also, a heavy rush, as of water down a steep channel; a rapid; also, an artificial channel, as for conveying water to a lower level by gravity; a sloping trough, upright shaft, or the like, for conveying coal, grain, etc., to a receptacle below; a chute; also, a growing or sprouting, as of a plant or a portion of a plant; the amount of such growth; also, a new or young growth which shoots off from some portion of a plant; a young branch, stem, twig, or the like; a new part growing out from a root, tuber, germinating seed, etc.; in forestry, a sprout which is not three feet high; in general, any growth from a main stock; an offshoot; also, an act of shooting with a bow, firearm, etc.; shooting distance† (as, "Nor could we any where see above a pistol *shoot* before us": Evelyn's "Diary," 1646); an expedition for shooting game; a shooting-party; the right to shoot game within a certain area, or the area itself; a match or contest at shooting.

shoot-a-ble (shö'tạ-bl), *a.* That may be shot; fit for shooting.

shoot-er (shö'tėr), *n.* One who shoots; in the petroleum industry, one who shoots oil-wells with nitroglycerin; also, something that shoots or is used in shooting; a gun, pistol, or the like (cf. *six-shooter*).

shoot-ing (shö'ting), *n.* The act of one who or that which shoots; also, a shoot or sprout; also, the exclusive right to kill game on a particular tract (as, "Gentlemen . . . combine and lease the *shooting* over wide areas": Jefferies's "Gamekeeper at Home," ii.); the tract itself.—**shoot'-ing=box,** *n.* A small house or lodge for the accommodation of a sportsman or sportsmen during the shooting-season.— **shoot'ing=i"ron,** *n.* A firearm, esp. a pistol or revolver: as, "What he called '*shooting-irons*' were his weapons" (J. Conrad's "Victory," iii. 7). [Slang.]—**shoot'ing=star,** *n.* A falling-star; a meteor.—**shoot'ing=stick,** *n.* An implement of hard wood or metal used by printers, by striking with a mallet, to tighten or loosen the quoins in a chase.

Shooting-stick.

shoot=off (shöt'ôf), *n.* A supplementary contest in shooting held to decide a tie in a shooting-match.

shop (shop), *n.* [ME. *shoppe*, shop, < AS. *sceoppa* (used of the 'treasury' in Luke, xxi. 1), akin to *scypen*, cattle-shed, OHG. *scopf*, porch, MLG. *schoppe*, G. *schoppen, schuppen*, shed, barn.] A building or room in which articles are made or prepared and sold; also, a building or room appropriated to the selling of goods; a store; also, a building or room set apart for the carrying on of some handiwork or mechanical industry (as, a carpenter's *shop*); a workshop; also, one's place of business or occupation (colloq.); also, an engagement or 'job' (theatrical slang, British: as, "I say . . . you'll be able to get me a *shop!* If Ross takes the piece, mind you tell him he's to give me an engagement in it," L. Merrick's "Position of Peggy Harper," ii. 2); also, matters pertaining to one's trade, occupation, or profession, as a subject of conversation (as, to talk *shop*, to converse about such matters, esp. unseasonably; "The girls had wanted to hear about the war, but the Major . . . put an absolute ban on *shop*," Arnold Bennett's "Pretty Lady," xxiii.).—**closed shop,** a shop or business establishment closed to the employment of all but a particular class of workers; esp., one in which only union workers and prospective union workers are employed. Cf. *open shop*.—**open shop,** a shop or business establishment open to the employment of both non-union and union workers, without discrimination; hence (as used by some), a non-union shop or business establishment (operated without regard to the rules of labor-unions), whether open to both non-union and union workers, or only to non-union workers. Cf. *closed shop*.—**shop,** *v.*; *shopped*, *shopping*. **I.** *tr.* To shut up as in a building, imprison, send to jail, or place under arrest (as, "He did not at all doubt but that they would find matter enough to *shop* the evidence himself before the next jail delivery," Smollett's "Humphry Clinker," June 11: now slang); also, to give a situation, engagement, or 'job' to (British, esp. in theatrical use: as, "I can't *shop* everybody; there aren't enough parts to go round," L. Merrick's "Position of Peggy Harper," i. 2). **II.** *intr.* To visit shops or stores for the purpose of purchasing or examining goods: as, "I thought Joan was going with you, and that you would be *shopping*" (Disraeli's "Sybil," vi. 4).—**shop'=girl,** *n.* A girl employed in a shop.

sho-phar (shō'fär), *n.* [Heb. *shōphar*.] An ancient Jewish musical instrument of the trumpet kind, usually made of the curved horn of a ram, still used in certain Jewish religious services, as on Yom Kippur.

shop-keep-er (shop'kē"pėr), *n.* One who carries on business in a shop or store; a tradesman.—**shop'keep"ing,** *n.*

shop-lift-er (shop'lif"tėr), *n.* One who steals goods from a shop, as while ostensibly making purchases.—**shop'lift"-ing,** *n.*

shop-man (shop'man), *n.;* pl. *-men.* A shopkeeper (now rare); also, a salesman in a shop.

shop-per (shop'ėr), *n.* One who shops; one who visits shops for the purpose of buying or examining goods.—

shop'ping, The act of one who shops; the act of practice of visiting shops for the purchase or examination of goods.

shop-py (shop'i), *a.* Pertaining to or characteristic of shops; also, abounding in shops; also, pertaining to or savoring of one's trade or profession; talking shop.

shop=walk-er (shop'wå"kėr), *n.* A floor-walker.

shop=worn (shop'wôrn), *a.* Worn or marred, as goods, from handling or exposure in a shop. Also fig.

shore¹ (shōr). Archaic preterit of *shear*.

shore² (shōr), *n.* [ME. *schore* = MLG. *schore* = D. *schoor*, shore, prop: cf. Icel. *scordha*, prop.] A supporting post or beam, esp. one placed obliquely against the side of a building, a ship in dock, or the like; a prop; a strut.—**shore²,** *v. t.;* *shored, shoring.* To support by a shore or shores; prop: commonly used with *up*: as, "We laid the ship aground upon a hard sand . . . and *shored* her up on each side" (Defoe's "Captain Singleton," xiv.).

Frame of a Vessel supported by Shores.

shore³ (shōr), *n.* [ME. *schore* = MLG. *schore*, shore, coast, = D. *schor*, land washed by the sea; prob. from the root of E. *shear*.] The land adjacent to a considerable body of water, as an ocean, sea, or large lake or river (as, a sandy or a rocky *shore*; a *shore* strewn with wreckage; "Far down the Beautiful River, Past the Ohio *shore* . . . Floated a cumbrous boat," Longfellow's "Evangeline," ii. 2: also fig.); the coast of some land, and hence the land itself (as *sing.* or *pl.*: as, "Adieu, adieu! my native *shore* Fades o'er the waters blue," Byron's "Childe Harold," i. 13. 1; "As one who long detain'd on foreign *shores* Pants to return," Cowper's "Task," v. 832); land, as opposed to sea (as, the marines serve both at sea and on *shore*); in *law*, the space between the ordinary high-water mark and low-water mark; the foreshore.—**shore³,** *v. t.;* *shored, shoring.* To put or set ashore.—**shore=bird,** *n.* A bird that frequents the seashore, estuaries, etc.; a limicoline wading bird.—**shore'=go"ing.** [Cf. *sea-going*.] **I.** *n.* Going, staying, or living on shore. **II.** *a.* Going or living on shore; pertaining to life on shore.—**shore'less,** *a.* Having no shore, and hence boundless, as a sea (lit. or fig.: as, "mad of doubt—a castaway on a *shoreless* sea," Mrs. H. Ward's "Robert Elsmere," xxv.); sometimes, without a shore that permits of landing, as a rocky island.—**shore'line,** *n.* The line followed in the course of a shore; the line where shore and water meet.

shor-er (shōr'ėr), *n.* One who shores or props; one whose work it is to prop up structures, etc., as during construction operations; also, something that shores; a shore or prop.

shore-ward (shōr'wärd), *adv.* and *a.* Toward the shore.— **shore'wards,** *adv.*

shor-ing (shōr'ing), *n.* Shores or props for supporting a building, a ship, etc.

shorn (shôrn). Past participle of *shear*.

short (shôrt), *a.* [AS. *sceort, scort,* = OHG. *scurz*, short, akin to Icel. *skorta*, be short of, *skortr*, shortness, want; referred by some to L. *curtus*, cut short (see *curt*), by others to the root of E. *shear*: cf. *shirt*.] Having little length, or of small extent from end to end (as, a *short* distance); not long; of relatively little extent (as, a *short* arm); low in stature, or not tall, as a person; having the greatest dimension unusually small in proportion; of the head or skull, of less than ordinary length from front to back (cf. *short-headed*); extending or reaching but a little way, as vision or memory; also, having little extent in duration or from beginning to end, or brief (as, a *short* time; a *short* life; a *short* interview; a *short* series of lectures); also, not far in the future (now chiefly legal and commercial: as, a *short* day); also, brief or concise, as writing or speaking or a writer or speaker; often, rudely or angrily brief or curt (as, a *short* answer; "Ingram was changed, and very *short* with his friend," M. Hewlett's "Open Country," xv.); hasty in temper or as the temper; also, below the standard in extent, quantity, duration, etc. (as, *short* measure or weight; a *short* ton, a ton of 2,000 pounds); low, reduced, or deficient in amount, or scanty (as, *short* allowance; "Provisions . . . by this time were very

fat, fāte, fär, fåll, åsk, fāre; net, mē, hėr; pin, pīne; not, nōte, mŏve, nôr; up, lūte, pull; oi, oil; ou, out; (lightened) aviạry, ẹlect, agọny, intọ, ụnite; (obscured) errạnt, opeṙä, ardẹnt, actọr, natụre; ch, chip; g, go; th, thin; ᴛʜ, then; y, you;

short with us," Defoe's "Captain Singleton," xv.); not reaching a mark or the like, as a throw or a missile; being within a specified distance (*of*: as, "He halted . . . at Malmesbury, twenty miles *short* of Bath," J. F. Kirk's "Charles the Bold," iii. 2); less than or inferior to (with *of*: as, a few *short* of a hundred; nothing *short* of perfection; little *short* of the best); also, having a scanty or insufficient amount or supply of something, as money, food, etc. (as, I'm rather *short* just now; to go *short* rather than ask for more); lacking the required amount (as, to be *short* in one's accounts; "He was . . . *short* with his rent for the approaching quarter day," H. G. Wells's "Mr. Polly," vii.); having an insufficient amount or a deficiency or shortage (*of*: as, to be *short* of ready money; "She was tired and *short* of sleep," Arnold Bennett's "Lion's Share," xxvii.; "Fine seasoned regiments were *short* of half their strength," Charnwood's "Abraham Lincoln," vii.); also, breaking or crumbling readily, as pastry that contains a large proportion of butter or lard; not tenacious in substance, as metal; friable; brittle; also, in *pros.* and *phonetics*, occupying a relatively short time in utterance, as vowels or syllables (used commonly in English orthoëpy to note the sounds of a, e, i, o, u exemplified in the words *fat, net, pin, not, up*); also, in *com.*, not possessing at the time of sale commodities or stocks that one sells; also, noting or pertaining to sales of commodities or stocks which the seller does not possess; depending for profit on a decline in prices.—**short and,** the character &. See *and, n.*—**short circuit.** See entry below.—**short commons,** short allowance of food; scanty fare: as, to be on *short commons.*—**short for,** being a shorter form for: as, the word 'phone' is *short for* 'telephone'; "Cousin Sallie was *short for* Confederate States" (G. W. Cable's "Cavalier," xv.). —**short shrift,** short shriving or time for shriving, or confession and absolution, given to a condemned person before execution (as, "Here they are like to meet *short shrift* and a tight cord": Scott's "Quentin Durward," viii.); hence, little mercy, respite, or delay given in dealing with or disposing of a person, a matter, etc.—**to make short work of,** to accomplish or finish (a task, etc.) quickly; also, to deal with or dispose of summarily (as, to *make short work of* false claims or statements; to *make short work of* an opponent).—**short,** *n.* Something that is short; *pl.*, knee-breeches or small-clothes, formerly worn by men (as, "a gentleman in black *shorts* and a laced waistcoat": Bulwer-Lytton's "Caxtons," xi. 5); breeches, knickerbockers, or short, loose trousers worn by men in sports, etc. (as, "He talked to me of aeronautics as I stood in jersey and *shorts* beside my machine, fresh from alighting": H. G. Wells's "Tono-Bungay," iii. 2. § 10); the shorter clothes in which a baby is dressed after the early months of infancy (as, "Six months passed . . . then he was put into *shorts*": Marryat's "Mr. Midshipman Easy," iii.); also, a mixture of the bran and coarse part of meal; also, what is deficient or lacking; *sing.*, in *pros.* and *phonetics*, a short sound or syllable; in *elect.*, a short circuit; in *com.*, one who has sold short; also, a short sale, or a commodity or stock sold short.—**for short,** by way of abbreviation: as, Robert, called Bob *for short.*—**in short,** in few words; in brief; briefly: as, "*In short* . . . I resolved to run quite away from him" (Defoe's "Robinson Crusoe," i. 1).—**short,** *adv.* So as to make or be short (as, to cut a thing *short*); also, abruptly or suddenly (as, "The little chap . . . after a few steps stopped *short*," J. Conrad's "Lord Jim," v.; "I turned *short* upon him, and said . . . ," Defoe's "Robinson Crusoe," ii. 11); also, briefly, concisely, or curtly (now rare); also, on the hither side of an intended or particular point (as, to come *short*; to fall *short*, see under *fall, v. i.*: often fig.); without going to the extent (*of*: as, to stop *short* of actual crime; "I don't see any other plan for you—*short* of leaving her alone," M. Hewlett's "Open Country," xxvi.); in *com.*, without possessing at the time the stocks, etc., sold (as, to sell *short*).—**short,** *v. t.* or *i.* To short-circuit.

short-age (shôr′tāj), *n.* Deficiency in quantity (as, a period of *shortage* in a commodity); a condition or period of deficiency in the quantity or supply of something (as, "There is still an acute *shortage* of housing facilities in the large cities of this country," A. W. Mellon's "Taxation," v.; "During a gold *shortage* he [Emperor Frederick II.] introduced and made a success of a coinage of stamped leather," H. G. Wells's

"Outline of History," xxxiii. § 12); also, an amount by which something is deficient (as, the total *shortage* was $500).

short-bread (shôrt′bred), *n.* A kind of bread, commonly in flat cakes, made short with butter or the like. Compare *shortcake.*

short-cake (shôrt′kāk), *n.* A cake made short with butter or lard; esp., a cake made of shortened and sometimes sweetened biscuit-dough baked or split in layers, with a filling of strawberries or other fruit; also, any layer-cake with such a filling.

short=change (shôrt′chānj′), *v. t.*; *-changed, -changing.* To give less change for money to (a person), esp. intentionally, than is properly due. [Colloq.]

short cir-cuit (shôrt sẽr′kit). In *elect.*, a side circuit or shunt of relatively low resistance connecting two points of an electric circuit so as to carry the greater part of the current.— **short′=cir′cuit,** *v.* I. *tr.* To establish a short circuit in; carry (a current) by acting as a short circuit, as a conducting body does; cut off by the establishment of a short circuit. II. *intr.* To form a short circuit.

short-com-ing (shôrt′kum′ing), *n.* A coming short of what should be attained; a failure to come up to a standard of excellence in achievement, conduct, character, condition, etc.; a fault or defect: as, "His distresses were intensified by a consciousness of his own *shortcomings*" (Lytton Strachey's "Queen Victoria," iii.); "profoundly unconscious of any *shortcoming* in his education" (G. W. Cable's "Cavalier," ii.); "It is cruel to enumerate the *shortcomings* of her attire" (Besant's "All Sorts and Conditions of Men," i.).

short-en (shôr′tn), *v.* I. *tr.* To make shorter, abridge, or curtail; also, to make to seem shorter (as, "Thus were the hours of labour *shortened* for Peyrol by shrewd remarks and bits of local gossip": J. Conrad's "Rover," vii.); also, to lessen the extent or amount of, take in, or reduce (as, to *shorten* sail; to *shorten* an allowance); reduce the reach or power of (the hand or arm: in fig. uses, orig. in the Bible: as, "Behold, the Lord's hand is not *shortened*, that it cannot save," Isa. lix. 1); also, to render short† or deprive† (*of*: as, "*shorten'd* of his ears," Dryden's tr. Virgil's "Æneid," vi. 669); also, to make (pastry, etc.) short, as with butter or lard; also, to treat or pronounce (a vowel or syllable) as short. II. *intr.* To become shorter; diminish in length (as, the days *shorten* in November); of odds or prices, to decrease. —**short′en-er,** *n.*—**short′en-ing,** *n.* Butter, lard, or the like, used to make pastry, etc., short.

short-hand (shôrt′hand), *n.* A method of rapid writing employing shortened forms or arbitrary symbols in place of letters, sounds, words, etc.; stenography; also, writing consisting of such forms or symbols. Cf. *phonography.*

short-hand-ed (shôrt′han′ded), *a.* Not having the full or necessary number of hands, workmen, or helpers.—**short′=hand′ed-ness,** *n.*

short-head-ed (shôrt′hed′ed), *a.* Having a short head; brachycephalic.—**short′=head′ed-ness,** *n.*

short-horn (shôrt′hôrn), *n.* One of a breed of cattle with short horns, valued more for their beef than for dairy purposes.—**short′=horned,** *a.*

shor-ti-a (shôr′ti-ä), *n.* [NL.; named from C. W. Short (1794–1863), American botanist.] Any plant of the genus *Shortia*, comprising two species, *S. uniflora* of Japan, and *S. galacifolia* of the mountains of North and South Carolina, long thought the rarest of North American plants, with evergreen radical leaves and white nodding flowers: esteemed in cultivation.

Flowering Plant of Shortia (*S. galacifolia*).
— *a*, the corolla, laid open.

short-ish (shôr′tish), *a.* Rather short.

short=legged (shôrt′legd or -leg″ed), *a.* Having short legs.

short=lived (shôrt′līvd), *a.* Having but a short life, or not living long (as, *short-lived* insects); also, lasting but a short time, or of brief duration (as, "So *short-lived* is human happiness in this frail world!" Kinglake's "Eothen," xxiii.; "Philip's *short-lived* military ardor had already exhausted itself," Motley's "Dutch Republic," i. 2).

short-ly (shôrt′li), *adv.* In a short manner; briefly; concisely; curtly; also, in a short time, or soon (as, I will be with you *shortly*); a short time (*after* or *before*: as, he went *shortly* before they came).—**short′ness**, *n.*

short=sight-ed (shôrt′sī′ted), *a.* Unable to see far; nearsighted; myopic; also, lacking in foresight, as persons; characterized by or showing lack of foresight (as, a *short-sighted* policy; "Heaven mocks the *short-sighted* views of man," Walpole's "Castle of Otranto," ii.).—**short′=sight′-ed-ly**, *adv.*—**short′=sight′ed-ness**, *n.*

short=spok-en (shôrt′spō′kn), *a.* Speaking in a short, brief, or curt manner; curt in speech.

short-stop (shôrt′stop), *n.* In *baseball*, a player stationed between second and third base.

short=tem-pered (shôrt′tem′pėrd), *a.* Having a short or hasty temper; quick-tempered.

short=waist-ed (shôrt′wās′ted), *a.* Comparatively short from neck to waist-line, as a person or a garment.

short=wind-ed (shôrt′win′ded), *a.* Short of breath; liable to difficulty in breathing; becoming soon out of breath under exertion.—**short′=wind′ed-ness**, *n.*

Sho-sho-ne-an (shō-shō′nē-an), *a.* Belonging to or constituting a linguistic stock of North American Indians of the western U. S., including the Shoshoni, Comanche, Ute, Hopi, and other tribes.

shot[1] (shot). Preterit and past participle of *shoot.*—**shot**[1], *p. a.* Woven so as to present a play of colors, as silk; changeable; of changing colors.

shot[2] (shot), *n.*; *pl. shots* or (see defs.) *shot.* [AS. *sceot, scot, shooting, gesceot, gescot,* missile (also contribution, payment: see *shot*[3]), akin to Icel. *skot,* shooting, missile (also contribution: see *scot*[1]), D. *schot,* G. *schoss, schuss, geschoss;* all from the root seen in AS. *scēotan,* shoot, also contribute, pay: see *shoot,* and cf. *shot*[3] and *scot*[1].] The act or an act of shooting; a rapid movement or motion; the sliding of a bolt; esp., the discharge or a discharge of a bow, firearm, etc.; the range of the discharge, or the distance passed over by the missile in its flight; hence, range in general (as, "And keep you in the rear of your affection, Out of the *shot* and danger of desire": Shakspere's "Hamlet," i. 3. 35); also, an attempt to hit with a projectile discharged from a gun or the like; fig., a remark aimed at some person or thing (as, "The speaker . . . presently delivered a *shot* which went home, and silence and attention resulted": Mark Twain's "Life on the Mississippi," lvii.); also, a guess at something; also, an attempt or try at something; also, an aimed stroke, throw, or the like, as in games, etc.; also, the taking of a snap-shot with a camera; the taking of a photograph with a moving-picture camera; the picture so obtained; also, a blast with an explosive, as in mining; also, that which is discharged in shooting; a projectile for discharge from a firearm or cannon, esp. a solid ball or bullet as distinguished from a *shell* (*pl.*, as with numerals, commonly *shot*); such projectiles collectively (as, "storm'd at with *shot* and shell": Tennyson's "Charge of the Light Brigade," iii.); a heavy metal ball which competitors cast as far as possible in the sport of 'putting the shot'; a small ball or pellet of lead, of which a number are used for one charge of a sportsman's gun (*pl.*, as with numerals, commonly *shot*); such pellets collectively (as, a charge of *shot*); also, an injection or dose of a drug, as cocaine (slang); also, one who shoots, with reference to his skill as a marksman (as, a poor *shot*; "The old hunters . . . were skilful *shots,*" Roosevelt's "Hunting Trips of a Ranchman," i.; "a notorious duellist and a dead *shot,*" Bret Harte's "Fool of Five Forks''); an expert in shooting; also, a soldier armed with a firearm†; such soldiers collectively†.—**a long shot,** fig., an attempt at something apparently beyond the reach of easy attainment; something apparently offering no great assurance of success (as, to bet on *a long shot*).—**by a long shot,** fig., by a great deal: esp. with *not*: as, this one is not so good as the other *by a long shot.*—**like a shot,** with great rapidity; with the utmost promptness; at once: as, "If anybody can suggest to me anything else that I can do—I'll do it *like a shot*" (Arnold Bennett's "Hilda Lessways," iii. 4).—**Parthian shot.** See *Parthian, a.*—**shot**[2], *v. t.; shotted, shotting.* To load or supply with shot (as, "Her [a vessel's] *shotted* guns were discharging": Scott's "Guy Mannering," x.); also, to weight with shot or a shot, as in order to cause to sink in water (as, "to have his body stitched up in a *shotted* hammock and dropped into the harbor": Aldrich's "Story of a Bad Boy," xxii.).

shot[3] (shot), *n.* [ME. *schott,* appar. < AS. *gesceot, gescot,* contribution, payment: see *shot*[2], and cf. *scot*[1].] An amount due or to be paid, esp. at a tavern.—**to stand shot,** to meet the expense; pay the bill: as, "Are you to *stand shot* to all this good liquor?" (Scott's "Kenilworth," xix.).

shote, shoat (shot), *n.* [ME. *shote;* origin uncertain.] A young weaned pig; also, a thriftless, worthless person (prov.).

shot=gun (shot′gun), *n.* A smooth-bore gun for firing small shot: used for killing birds and small quadrupeds.—**shot=gun prescription,** a medical prescription which combines a great number of drugs of different properties. [Humorous.]

shot=proof (shot′pröf), *a.* Proof against shot: as, "an enormous vessel, with *shot-proof* bulwarks" (Motley's "Dutch Republic," iv. 2).

shot-ten (shot′n), *p. a.* [Old pp. of *shoot.*] That has recently spawned: as, a *shotten* herring (fig., a person who is spent, exhausted, or worthless: see Shakspere's "1 Henry IV.," ii. 4. 143).

shot=tow-er (shot′tou′ėr), *n.* A high tower for making small shot by dropping molten lead from the top into water at the bottom.

shot-ty (shot′i), *a.* Like shot, or small balls of lead.

shough† (shok), *n.* [Origin uncertain: cf. *shock*[2].] A kind of dog with shaggy hair, said to have come from Iceland. See Shakspere's "Macbeth," iii. 1. 94.

should (shud). [AS. *sceolde, scolde:* see *shall.*] Preterit of *shall:* specially used to denote duty, propriety, or expediency (as, you *should* not do that; you *should* hear him talk), to make a statement less direct or blunt (as, I *should* think so; I *should* hardly say that), and to bring out the element of uncertainty in conditional and hypothetical clauses (as, if it *should* be true; suppose he *should* come).

shoul-der (shōl′dėr), *n.* [AS. *sculdor* = D. *schouder* = G. *schulter,* shoulder.] Either of two corresponding parts of the human body, situated at the top of the trunk and extending respectively from the right side and left side of the neck to the upper joint of the corresponding arm; *pl.,* these two parts together with the portion of the back joining them, forming a place where burdens are sometimes carried (hence used fig., as, to take the blame on one's *shoulders*); also, *sing.,* a corresponding part in animals; the upper fore leg and adjoining parts of a sheep, etc., prepared for market; also, the joint connecting the arm or the fore leg with the trunk; also, a shoulder-like part or projection; a part of an object where it widens out more or less abruptly, as from a neck or narrower part; in *printing,* the flat surface on a type extending beyond the base of the letter or other character; in *fort.,* the angle of a bastion included between the face and the flank.—**shoul′der,** *v.* **I.** *tr.* To push against with the shoulder, esp. unceremoniously or roughly; force or thrust with or as with the shoulder (as, "The Zelanders dashed into

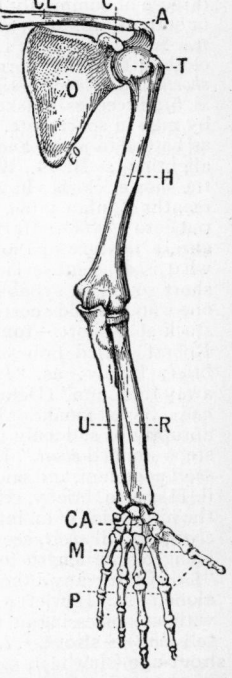

Bones of the Left Shoulder and Upper Extremity, from the front.—*A,* acromion; *C,* coracoid; *CA,* carpus; *CL,* clavicle; *H,* humerus; *M,* metacarpals; *O,* ventral surface of the scapula; *P,* phalanges, proximal row; *R,* radius; *T,* head of humerus; *U,* ulna.

the sea, and with sheer strength *shouldered* every vessel through," Motley's "Dutch Republic," iv. 2; "Custom and prejudice . . . *should'ring* aside The meek and modest truth," Cowper's "Task," vi. 839); make (one's way) by pushing with the shoulders; also, to take upon or support with the shoulder or shoulders (as, "Caleb . . . *shouldered* the round box, and took a hurried leave": Dickens's "Cricket on the Hearth," i.); place (a weapon) upon or against the shoulder (as, to *shoulder* arms, to hold a rifle or other weapon in a nearly vertical position, with the barrel resting in the hollow of the shoulder and the butt in the hand); also, fig., to assume as a burden (as, to *shoulder* responsibility or expense); also, to furnish with one or more shoulder-like parts or projections. **II.** *intr.* To push with the shoulder; make one's way by pushing with the shoulders (as, "A policeman and the coroner's officer came *shouldering* through the press": A. S. M. Hutchinson's "If Winter Comes," iv. 4); also, to project as a shoulder; form a shoulder-like projection.— **shoul'der=belt,** *n. Milit.*, a belt worn over the shoulder and across the breast.— **shoul'der=blade,** *n.* The scapula. — **shoul'der=brace,** *n.* An appliance for correcting or preventing round shoulders.— **shoul'dered,** *a.* Having shoulders: as, round-*shouldered.*— **shoul'der=knot,** *n.* A knot of ribbon or lace worn on the shoulder, as by men of fashion in the 17th and 18th centuries, by servants in livery, or by women or children.— **shoul'der=strap,** *n.* A strap worn over the shoulder, as to support a garment; also, an ornamental strip fastened on the shoulder of a uniform to distinguish the rank, etc., of an officer.

shout (shout), *v.* [ME. *schoute, schowte*; origin uncertain.] **I.** *intr.* To call or cry out loudly and vigorously, as in joy, applause, anger, etc., or in order to make one's self heard (as, "All the people *shouted,* and said, God save the king," 1 Sam. x. 24; "They all *shouted* and screamed at me," F. M. Crawford's "Mr. Isaacs," i.; to *shout* for help); speak loudly and vehemently; also, to give forth unrestrainedly loud sounds in laughing (as, to *shout* with laughter; at this slip of the tongue the audience fairly *shouted*). **II.** *tr.* To utter with a loud and vigorous voice (as, "The one who is head of the gang *shouts* his directions at the top of his voice": W. H. Hudson's "Far Away and Long Ago," xiv.); express by a shout or shouts (as, to *shout* one's joy); also, to salute with shouts†, or acclaim† (as, "The statesman . . . comes. Some *shout* him, and some hang upon his car": Cowper's "Task," vi. 698).— **shout,** *n.* A loud, vigorously uttered call or cry (as, "Westminster Hall . . . resounded with their hoarse *shouts* for justice": Morley's "Oliver Cromwell," iii. 7); a shouted utterance; also, a loud, unrestrained burst (of laughter: as, "There was a *shout* of laughter from the full tent," Kipling's "Kim," v.).— **shout'er,** *n.*— **shout'ing-ly,** *adv.*

shove (shuv), *v.*; *shoved, shoving.* [AS. *scūfan* = D. *schuiven* = G. *schieben* = Icel. *skūfa, skȳfa,* = Goth. *-skiuban,* shove, push: cf. *scuffle², sheaf, shovel,* and *shuffle.*] **I.** *tr.* To move (something) forward or along by the application of force from behind; push with effort; often, to propel (a boat) by pushing it from outside the stern, or by pushing from the inside on something outside it; also, to push or thrust roughly, unceremoniously, or carelessly (as, "He . . . just *shoved* me out of the room," Arnold Bennett's "The Old Adam," v.; to *shove* away a dish at table); push roughly or rudely against, or jostle (a person, etc.). **II.** *intr.* To exert force against a thing in order to move it; push; often, to cause a boat to move along by pushing, as from the inside on something outside it (as, to *shove* off: see phrase below); also, to push or jostle in a crowd; make one's way by pushing or jostling (as, "So saying, he *shoved* to another corner of the room": Smollett's "Humphry Clinker," June 2).— **to shove off,** to push a boat off, as from the bank; fig. (in slang use), to leave a place; start on one's way.— **shove,** *n.* An act of shoving; a forcible push (as, "He gave a vigorous *shove* which sent the little boat into the water": J. Conrad's "Rescue," vi. 9); a rough or careless push or thrust.

shov-el (shuv'l), *n.* [AS. *scofl* = MLG. *schuffele,* shovel, = D. *schoffel,* hoe (see *scuffle¹*), akin to G. *schaufel,* shovel; from the root of E. *shove.*] An implement consisting of a broad blade or scoop attached to a handle, used for taking up and removing loose matter, as earth, snow, coal, etc.; a

contrivance or machine for shoveling, removing matter, etc. (as, a steam-*shovel*); also, a part or formation suggesting the blade of a shovel (in first sense: cf. *shovelbill* and *shovelnose*); a shovel-hat (colloq.); also, a shovelful.— **shov'el,** *v.*; *-eled* or *-elled, -eling* or *-elling.* **I.** *tr.* To take up and cast or remove with a shovel (as, to *shovel* earth into a hole; to *shovel* coal on the fire; to *shovel* snow from the sidewalk); also, to gather, throw, or put, in quantities, or quickly and carelessly, as with a shovel (as, to *shovel* up food, or *shovel* food into the mouth, with a knife); also, to dig up or clear (ground, etc.) with a shovel; make (a hole, path, etc.) with a shovel. **II.** *intr.* To work with a shovel.

shov-el-bill (shuv'l-bil), *n.* A duck, the shoveler.

shov-el-board, shuf-fle=board (shuv'l-bōrd, shuf'l-), *n.* [Also earlier *shove-board:* see *shove.*] A game in which coins or disks are driven along a smooth board, table, or other surface, toward certain lines, etc., on it; also, the board, table, or the like; also, a similar game played with large disks pushed with a kind of cue on the deck of a ship.

shov-el-er, shov-el-ler (shuv'l-ėr), *n.* One who or that which shovels; also, a widely distributed fresh-water duck, *Spatula clypeata,* with a broad shovel-like bill.

shov-el-ful (shuv'l-fûl), *n.*; pl. *-fuls.* A quantity sufficient to fill a shovel; as much as a shovel can hold.

shov-el-hat (shuv'l-hat'), *n.* A hat with a broad brim turned up at the sides and projecting with a shovel-like curve in front and behind: worn by some ecclesiastics: as, "Suddenly he [a bishop] was back in his gaiters and his apron and his *shovel hat*" (H. G. Wells's "Soul of a Bishop," v.).

Shoveler (*Spatula clypeata*).

shov-el-head (shuv'l-hed), *n.* A shark, *Reniceps* (or *Sphyrna*) *tiburo,* of the hammerhead family, with a kidney-shaped head; also, the shovelnose (sturgeon).— **shov'el-head"ed,** *a.*

Shovelhead (*Reniceps tiburo*).

shov-el-nose (shuv'l-nōz), *n.* Any of various animals with a shovel-like snout or head, as a shark, *Hexanchus corinus,* of the Pacific, and an American sturgeon, *Scaphirhynchus platyrhynchus.*— **shov'el-nosed,** *a.*

Shovelnose (*Scaphirhynchus platyrhynchus*).

shov-er (shuv'ėr), *n.* One who or that which shoves.

show (shō), *v. t.*; pret. *showed,* pp. *shown* or *showed,* ppr. *showing.* [ME. *showen, sheawen, shewen,* look at, also let see, show, < AS. *scēawian,* look at, = D. *schouwen* = G. *schauen,* look at, view; akin to Gr. κοεῖν, perceive, L. *cavere,* take heed, Skt. *kavi,* wise: cf. *scavenger, sheen,* and *caution.*] To look at†; also, to cause or allow to be seen; manifest to the sight; present or expose to view; exhibit, as for inspection, amusement, or sale; display; also, to point out or indicate, as to a person (as, "Conscience . . . *Shows,* with a pointing finger . . . A pale procession of past sinful joys," Cowper's "Hope," 221; "I pray you, *show* my youth old Shylock's house," Shakspere's "Merchant of Venice," iv. 2. 11; a guide *showed* us the way); hence, to guide or conduct (one) as specified (as, "*Show* Mr. Milvain into the study," Gissing's "New Grub Street," viii.; "He . . . *showed* him up a steep and narrow stone staircase," Scott's "Guy Mannering," xliv.; to *show* one in, or out); also, to make evident by appearance, behavior, etc. (as, "He *showed* all the outward signs of a mind at ease," George Eliot's "Romola," x.; "She hated to *show* her feelings," Galsworthy's "Saint's Progress," ii. 1; to *show* determination, or good judgment); manifest (kindness, malice, etc.) by action; accord or grant (favor, etc.); offer or attempt (resistance); also, to make clear by statement, evidence, reasoning, etc.; make known; explain; prove or demonstrate; sometimes, to declare, narrate, or tell (archaic); allege, as in a legal document; plead, as a reason or cause; also, of things, to serve to make evident (as, "You must needs learn, lord, to amend this fault: Though sometimes it *show* greatness, courage, blood": Shakspere's "1 Henry IV.," iii. 1. 181).— **to show off,** to display ostentatiously: as, "to *show off* before them his new wealth and splendour" (Thackeray's "Vanity Fair," l.).—**to show one the door,** to bid one leave the room or house: as, "I shall make bold to *show you the door*" (Miss Burney's "Evelina," xxi.).—**to show up,** to expose to view or knowledge; esp., to lay bare the faults, delinquencies, etc., of.—**show,** *v. i.* To be seen; be or become visible; appear; also, to make one's or its appearance (now chiefly colloq.: cf. *to show up,* below); give an exhibition or performance (colloq.); also, to look or appear (as indicated: as, to *show* well or to advantage).—**to show off,** to make an ostentatious display of one's accomplishments, cleverness, etc. [Colloq.]—**to show up,** to appear conspicuously; stand out; also, to put in an appearance, or turn up (colloq.: as, "Major Harper wants you as quick as you can *show up,*" G. W. Cable's "Cavalier," iv.; he promised to come, but did not *show up*).—**show,** *n.* The act or an act of showing, exhibiting, or displaying (as, a *show* of hands, a raising of hands to show the sentiments of a gathering of persons upon some proposition); also, the appearance or aspect of something (as, "The outward *shows* of sky and earth, Of hill and valley, he has viewed": Wordsworth's "Poet's Epitaph," 45); also, a particular kind of appearance (as, a thing makes a fine *show,* or a sorry *show*); sometimes, a fine or striking appearance; an imposing display; also, ostentatious display, or parade (as, "He disliked *show,* with a calm and deep aversion": Arnold Bennett's "Helen with the High Hand," ii.); also, an appearance or display of something which has at least some basis of reality (as, "A certain *show* of freedom was allowed him": S. Butler's "Way of All Flesh," vii.); also, an indication, trace, or sign of something, as a sign of the presence of gold, oil, or the like in a region; also, an unreal or empty appearance, as of something that does not exist; often, a misleading or deceptive display of something, or a pretense (as, to do little while making a *show* of zeal; "We kept up such an outward *show* that . . . Smithie thought our household the most amiable in the world," H. G. Wells's "Tono-Bungay," ii. 4. § 5); a half-hearted appearance or beginning of something (as, he made a *show* of going, but did not go); also, something shown or exhibited; something exhibited as an object of admiration, curiosity, etc., or of mockery or derision (as, "that marble arch, our sexton's favourite *show,*" Crabbe's "Borough," ii.; "Then yield thee, coward, And live to be the *show* and gaze o' the time," Shakspere's "Macbeth," v. 8. 24; to make a *show* of, to exhibit to public view or public contempt); a person or thing which attracts attention by odd appearance, etc.; a sight or spectacle (as, "She . . . took them to see her collection of bric-à-brac across the yard, a gorgeous *show*": Du Maurier's "Trilby," vi.); a display of objects for public inspection, as a temporary exhibition of flowers, dogs, or automobiles; a public spectacle on a large scale, as a procession, pageant, or the like; an exhibition of strange objects, wild animals, equestrian and acrobatic feats, or the like, often one held in a booth or a tent; in general, any kind of public exhibition or display (chiefly colloq.); a theatrical performance, or a theatrical company (colloq.); also, a chance or opportunity (colloq.: as, to give one a fair *show*;

to have no *show* of succeeding).—**for show,** for mere appearance or display rather than use: as, "a lamp that was kept *for show,* and had never been used" (Ian Maclaren's "Beside the Bonnie Brier Bush," iv. 2).

show-a-ble (shō′a̱-bl), *a.* That may be shown.

show=bill (shō′bil), *n.* A poster, placard, or the like advertising a show or other matter for public attention.

show=box (shō′boks), *n.* A box in which objects of interest or curiosity are exhibited; a box containing a peep-show (as, "Fancy's *Show-Box,*" the title of one of Hawthorne's "Twice-Told Tales").

show-bread (shō′bred), *n.* See shewbread.

show=case (shō′kās), *n.* A glass case for the display and protection of articles in shops, museums, etc.

show=down (shō′doun), *n.* The laying down of one's cards, face upward, in a card-game; hence, a disclosure of actual resources, power, etc., as required by an opponent or as enforced by some decisive test.

show-er[1] (shō′ėr), *n.* One who or that which shows.

show-er[2] (shou′ėr), *n.* [AS. *scūr* = D. *schoer* = G. *schauer* = Icel. *skūr,* shower, = Goth. *skūra,* storm (of wind).] A brief fall of rain, or of hail, sleet, or, sometimes, snow; hence, a similar fall, as of tears, sparks, or bullets; fig., a copious supply or quantity bestowed (as, "He discharged a *shower* of blows upon his mules," Parkman's "Oregon Trail," iv.; "The two greeted Noel with a *shower* of cordial questions," Galsworthy's "Saint's Progress," iii. 3); specif., a bestowal of presents, usually of a particular kind, on a prospective bride (as, a linen *shower*); also, a shower-bath; in *pyrotechny,* a device for producing a shower-like mass of small stars of a slow-burning composition, which fall from a rocket or the like.—**show′er**[2], *v.* **I.** *intr.* To rain in a shower or showers; fall or come in a shower or a copious supply or quantity (as, "The withered leaves came *showering* down," Dickens's "Dombey and Son," v.; congratulations *showered* upon him); also, to shed tears, or weep (as, "What, still in tears? Evermore *showering?*" Shakspere's "Romeo and Juliet," iii. 5. 131; "Her dark eyes *showered,*" G. Meredith's "Diana of the Crossways," xlii.). **II.** *tr.* To pour down in a shower; send down abundantly and rapidly (as, "The women, from the roofs and windows, *showered* stones on the heads of the soldiers": Gibbon's "Decline and Fall of the Roman Empire," xl.); bestow liberally or lavishly (as, "She . . . *showered* upon him . . . the greetings due to her father's oldest friend," Mrs. H. Ward's "Lady Rose's Daughter," i.; "his recklessness of money *showered* upon him by . . . doting grandfathers," Tarkington's "Magnificent Ambersons," x.); also, to wet or sprinkle with or as with a shower.—**show′er=bath,** *n.* A bath in which water is showered upon the body from above; also, an apparatus for such a bath.—**show′er-er,** *n.*—**show′er-i-ness,** *n.* The state of being showery.—**show′er=proof,** *a.* Proof against showers, as a garment or fabric; waterproof in showers.—**show′er-y,** *a.* Raining or falling in showers; characterized by frequent falls of rain (as, "a *showery* summer afternoon": Morley's "Oliver Cromwell," ii. 2); also, pertaining to or resembling a shower or showers.

show-i-ly (shō′i-li), *adv.* In a showy manner; with display.—**show′i-ness,** *n.*

show-ing (shō′ing), *n.* The act of one who or that which shows; exhibition; display; show; a setting forth or presentation, as of facts or conditions (as, he is wrong by his own *showing*).

show-man (shō′man), *n.*; pl. *-men.* One who exhibits a show; esp., the proprietor of a traveling exhibition.

shown (shōn). Past participle of show.

show=room (shō′rōm), *n.* A room used for the display of goods or merchandise.

show-y (shō′i), *a.*; compar. *showier,* superl. *showiest.* Making a show, striking appearance, or imposing display (as, *showy* flowers; "She's *showier* and better-looking than they are," Tarkington's "Alice Adams," xiii.); hence, of excessively striking appearance, or gaudy; given to show or ostentatious display, as persons; of qualities, manners, actions, etc., striking or conspicuous, often ostentatiously so (as, *showy* talents; "His manners, without being *showy,* were gentleman-like and pleasing," Scott's "St. Ronan's Well," v.; "He was disposed to settle the Netherland difficulty in some *showy*, off-hand fashion," Motley's "Dutch Republic," v. 1; "They want to do vulgar, *showy* things," H. G. Wells's "Men Like Gods," i. 7).

shrank (shrangk). Preterit of *shrink*.

shrap-nel (shrap′nel), *n.* [From the inventor, H. *Shrapnel* (1761–1842), officer in the British army.] A hollow projectile containing a collection of bullets or the like and a bursting-charge, arranged to explode before reaching the object, in order to set free a shower of missiles; also, more commonly, such projectiles collectively.—**shrap′nel**, *v. t.*; *-neled* or *-nelled*, *-neling* or *-nelling.* To shell with shrapnel.

shred (shred), *n.* [AS. *screáde*, akin to G. *schrot*, piece, block; from a root meaning 'cut,' whence also E. *shroud*[1]: cf. *screed* and *escrow*.] A small piece cut or torn off, esp. in a narrow strip as from cloth or any fibrous substance; fig., a bit or scrap (as, there is not a *shred* of evidence; "He had gained some *shred* of comfort from this thought," W. Churchill's "Inside of the Cup," xix.).—**shred**, *v.*; *shredded* or *shred*, *shredding.* [AS. *screádian*.] **I.** *tr.* To prune (a tree, etc.)†; also, to cut or lop off, as branches†; also, to cut or tear into small pieces, esp. into small, narrow strips; reduce to shreds; also, to sever or cleave (rare). **II.** *intr.* To become reduced to shreds.—**shred′der**, *n.*—**shred′dy**, *a.* Consisting of or resembling shreds; torn into shreds; ragged.

shrew[1] (shrō), *n.* [AS. *screáwa*: cf. *shrew*[2].] Any of various small insectivorous mammals of the genus *Sorex* and allied genera, having a long, sharp snout and a mouse-like form, as *Sorex vulgaris* of Europe (see *shrew-mouse*) or *Neosorex palustris* of North America.

shrew[2] (shrō), *n.* [ME. *shrewe*, *schrewe*, *screwe*; commonly supposed to be another use of *shrew*[1], from an old belief that the animal was venomous or exercised a malignant influence.] A wicked or malignant person†;

American Shrew (*Neosorex palustris*).

also, a woman of violent temper and speech, a termagant, or an ill-tempered scold (as, "Tricks . . . To tame a *shrew* and charm her chattering tongue," Shakspere's "Taming of the Shrew," iv. 2. 58; "She shrieked like a common *shrew*," Arnold Bennett's "Old Wives' Tale," ii. 5).—**shrew**[2], *v. t.* To curse†; also, to treat or scold as a shrew does.

shrewd (shrōd), *a.* [ME. *shrewed*, *schrewed*, appar. < *shrewe*, *schrewe*, E. *shrew*[2], *n.*] Malignant, malicious, or mischievous (archaic or prov.: as, "That *shrewd* and knavish sprite Call'd Robin Goodfellow," Shakspere's "Midsummer Night's Dream," ii. 1. 33; to do one a *shrewd* turn); evil or bad (obs. or archaic); troublesome or vexatious (obs. or archaic); grievous, severe, or hard (archaic: as, to get some *shrewd* knocks); sharp, keen, or piercing, as wind, weather, pangs, etc. (archaic: as, "The night was *shrewd* and windy," Irving's "Tales of a Traveler," i. 3; "a sting of *shrewdest* pain," Tennyson's "St. Simeon Stylites," 195); also, shrewish† (as, "Thou wilt never get thee a husband, if thou be so *shrewd* of thy tongue": Shakspere's "Much Ado about Nothing," ii. 1. 20); also, cunning† or artful†; esp., in modern use, astute or sagacious, or sharp in discernment or grasp of practical considerations, as a person, the mind, etc. (as, "He was too *shrewd* to go along with them upon a road which could lead only to their overthrow," Froude's "Cæsar," x.; a *shrewd* politician; *shrewd* wits); characterized by or showing such discernment, as an action, move, speech, guess, etc.—**shrewd′ly**, *adv.*—**shrewd′-ness**, *n.*

shrew-ish (shrō′ish), *a.* Having the disposition or ways of a shrew (as, a *shrewish* woman); behaving or scold-

Shrew-mole (*Scalops aquaticus*).

ing like a shrew (as, "My wife is *shrewish* when I keep not hours": Shakspere's "Comedy of Errors," iii. 1. 2); characteristic of or befitting a shrew (as, a *shrewish* disposition; a *shrewish* tongue; *shrewish* complaints); in general, bad-tempered; ill-tempered.—**shrew′ish-ly**, *adv.*—**shrew′ish-ness**, *n.*

shrew=mole (shrō′mōl), *n.* Any of the American mole constituting the genera *Scalops* and *Scapanus.* See cut in preceding column.

shrew=mouse (shrō′mous), *n.*; pl. *-mice* (-mīs). A shrew, esp. *Sorex vulgaris*, the common shrew of Europe.

Shrew-mouse (*Sorex vulgaris*).

shriek (shrēk), *v.* [= *screak* and *screech*.] **I.** *intr.* To utter a loud, sharp, shrill cry (as, "Night-owls *shriek* where mounting larks should sing," Shakspere's "Richard II.," iii. 3. 183; "Hark the Phantom of the house That ever *shrieks* before a death," Tennyson's "Lancelot and Elaine," 1016); of persons, to cry out sharply at a high pitch of voice, often wildly or frantically, as with terror, rage, pain, delight, etc.; utter loud, high-pitched sounds in laughing violently; of a musical instrument, a whistle, the wind, etc., to give forth a loud, shrill sound. **II.** *tr.* To utter or cry in a shriek (as, to *shriek* defiance; "In the midst of the confusion and uproar . . . Cicero could only *shriek* that he had saved his country," Froude's "Cæsar," xii.); also, to make or render by shrieking (as, to *shriek* one's self hoarse).—**shriek**, *n.* An act or sound of shrieking; a loud, sharp, shrill cry; a loud, high-pitched sound of violent laughter; any loud, shrill sound, as of a whistle.—**shriek′er**, *n.*—**shriek′ing-ly**, *adv.*

shriev-al (shrē′val), *a.* [From *shrieve*.] Of or pertaining to a sheriff.—**shriev′al-ty** (-ti), *n.*; pl. *-ties* (-tiz). The office, jurisdiction, or term of office of a sheriff.

shrieve† (shrēv), *n.* Old form of *sheriff*.

shrift (shrift), *n.* [AS. *scrift*, < *scrīfan*, E. *shrive*.] The act of shriving; the imposition of penance by a priest on a penitent after confession; absolution or remission of sins granted after confession and penance; confession to a priest; hence, in general, confession.—**short shrift.** See under *short*, *a.*

shrike (shrīk), *n.* [AS. *scrīc*, kind of bird.] Any of numerous predaceous birds (family *Laniidæ*), as the butcher-birds, with a strong hooked and toothed bill, which feed on insects and sometimes small birds and other animals (as, the *shrikes* of the genus *Lanius*, see *butcher-bird*; the thick-headed *shrikes* of the genus *Pachycephala*, of the Australian region); also, any of various more or less similar birds, as the drongos (or drongo-shrikes).

Thick-headed Shrike (*Pachycephala mentalis*).

shrill (shril). [ME. *shrille* = G. *schrill*, shrill.] **I.** *a.* High-pitched and piercing, as the voice, utterances, or any sound (as, a *shrill* cry; a *shrill* laugh; the *shrill* piping of birds; "the *shrill* whistle of the fifes," Conan Doyle's "Exploits of Brigadier Gerard," vi.); uttering or producing such sound (as, she became *shrill* with passion; "Farewell . . . the *shrill* trump, The spirit-stirring drum," Shakspere's "Othello," iii. 3. 351); characterized by or resounding with such sound (as, "the voice of an invisible hag . . . scolding with *shrill* fury," J. Conrad's "Rescue," ii. 6; "ringing for waiters, in a *shrill* and busy hotel," Kinglake's "Eothen," i.); also, in general, sharp, keen, or piercing (chiefly poetic: as, "The northern summer air is *shrill* and cold," Henley's "In Hospital," i.; "The Lady's-head upon the prow Caught the *shrill* salt," Tennyson's "Voyage," ii.). **II.** *adv.* With a shrill sound: as, "The hounds and horn . . . Through the high wood echoing *shrill*" (Milton's "L'Allegro," 56).—**shrill**, *v.* **I.** *intr.* To sound shrilly, as the voice, bird-notes, etc.; utter or produce shrill sounds, as a person or animal, an instrument, the wind, etc. (as, "clouds of venomous insects perpetually *shrilling* in my ears": W. H. Hudson's "Green Mansions,"ᵏ xxii.). **II.** *tr.* To utter, cry, or give forth shrilly: as, " 'Go,' *shrill'd* the cotton-spinning chorus" (Tennyson's "Edwin Morris," 122); "The locust *shrills* his song of heat" (Whittier's "Summons").—**shrill**, *n.* A shrill sound.—**shrill'ish**, *a.* Somewhat shrill.—**shrill'ness**, *n.*—**shrill-y** (shril'i), *a.* Shrill: as, "*Shrilly* notes and clear Of waking cocks" (W. Morris's "Jason," vii. 288). [Chiefly poetic.]—**shril-ly** (shril'li), *adv.*

shrimp (shrimp), *n.* [ME. *schrimpe*: cf. MLG. *schrimpen*, wrinkle, contract, and E. *scrimp*.] Any of various small, long-tailed, chiefly marine decapod crustaceans of the genus *Crangon* and allied genera (suborder *Macrura*), as *C. vulgaris*, a European species esteemed as a table delicacy; any of various similar crustaceans; fig., a diminutive or insignificant person (contemptuous: as, "Could she possibly care for a *shrimp* like himself?" Du Maurier's "Trilby," v.).—**shrimp'=pink'**, *n.* A bright yellowish pink.

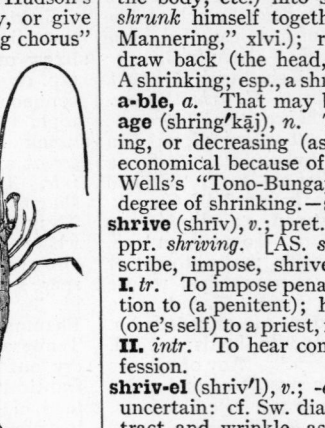

Shrimp (*Crangon vulgaris*), natural size.

shrine (shrīn), *n.* [AS. *scrīn*, < L. *scrinium*, case or box for books, papers, etc.] A box† or chest†; also, a receptacle for sacred relics; a reliquary; esp., an erection, often of a stately or sumptuous character, inclosing the remains or relics of a saint and forming an object of religious veneration and pilgrimage (as, the *shrine* of Edward the Confessor in Westminster Abbey; "an humble petition for aid at the *shrine* of St. Martin of Tours, which had been rendered famous as a place of marvellous cure," G. P. R. James's "Hist. of Charlemagne," i.); any receptacle or

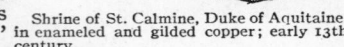

Shrine of St. Calmine, Duke of Aquitaine, in enameled and gilded copper; early 13th century.

place for an object of religious veneration, as a niche for a sacred image; any structure or place consecrated or devoted to some saint or deity, as an altar, chapel, church, or temple (as, "My knees are bow'd in crypt and *shrine*," Tennyson's "Sir Galahad," 18; "The goddess that in rural *shrine* Dwell'st here," Milton's "Comus," 267); also, in general use, a tomb or cenotaph erected in special commemoration or honor; a place in which anything is enshrined, preserved, or cherished (often fig., as of the heart); any place or object hallowed by its history or associations.—**shrine**, *v. t.*; *shrined*, *shrining.* To inclose in or as in a shrine; enshrine.

shrink (shringk), *v.*; pret. *shrank* or *shrunk*, pp. *shrunk* (now chiefly as p. a.) *shrunken*, ppr. *shrinking.* [AS. *scrincan* (pret. *scranc*, pp. *scruncen*) = MD. *schrinken*, shrink, = Sw. *skrynka*, wrinkle.] **I.** *intr.* To draw up by the wrinkling or contracting of parts or substance; shrivel; contract with heat, cold, moisture, etc.; esp., to contract from wetting, as a fabric or garment; in general, to become reduced in extent or compass (as, the pond has *shrunk* to a mere pool; capital *shrinks* with a continuous drain upon it); also, to draw back, as in retreat or avoidance (as, "He

shrinks out of my way whenever he sees me coming near him": S. Butler's "Way of All Flesh," xxix.); esp., to start back by an instinctive movement, as from something alarming or unpleasant; draw back in fear, horror, dislike, etc. (often fig.: as, to *shrink* from a painful duty); recoil. **II.** *tr.* To cause to shrink, shrivel, or contract; draw (one's self, the body, etc.) into smaller compass (as, "The poor man *shrunk* himself together . . . from terror": Scott's "Guy Mannering," xlvi.); reduce in extent or compass; also, to draw back (the head, hand, etc.: now rare).—**shrink**, *n.* A shrinking; esp., a shrinking movement; a recoil.—**shrink'-a-ble**, *a.* That may be shrunk; liable to shrink.—**shrink-age** (shring'kāj), *n.* The act or fact of shrinking, contracting, or decreasing (as, "This divine . . . was vindictively economical because of some *shrinkage* of his tithes": H. G. Wells's "Tono-Bungay," i. 1. § 3); also, the amount or degree of shrinking.—**shrink'er**, *n.*—**shrink'ing-ly**, *adv.*

shrive (shrīv), *v.*; pret. *shrove* or *shrived*, pp. *shriven* or *shrived*, ppr. *shriving.* [AS. *scrīfan* (pret. *scrāf*, pp. *scrifen*), prescribe, impose, shrive, < L. *scribere*, write: see *scribe*.] **I.** *tr.* To impose penance for sin; hence, to grant absolution to (a penitent); hear the confession of; also, to confess (one's self) to a priest, for the purpose of obtaining absolution. **II.** *intr.* To hear confessions; also, to go to or make confession.

shriv-el (shriv'l), *v.*; *-eled* or *-elled*, *-eling* or *-elling.* [Origin uncertain: cf. Sw. dial. *skryvla*, wrinkle.] **I.** *intr.* To contract and wrinkle, as from great heat or cold; hence, to become withered or atrophied (often fig.). **II.** *tr.* To cause to contract and wrinkle; hence, to wither; make impotent.

shriv-en (shriv'n). Past participle of *shrive.*

shriv-er (shrī'vėr), *n.* One who shrives.

shroff (shrof), *n.* [Ar. *çarrāf*.] In India, a banker or money-changer; in China, etc., a native expert employed to test coins and separate the base from the genuine.—**shroff**, *v. t.* To test (coins) in order to separate the base from the genuine.

shroud[1] (shroud), *n.* [AS. *scrūd*, garment, clothing, = Icel. *skrūdh*, fittings, gear, furniture, ornament, = Sw. *skrud*, attire: see *shred*, and cf. *shroud*[2].] A garment†; esp., a white cloth or sheet in which a corpse is wrapped for burial; a winding-sheet; hence, a long robe or gown for the dead; also, something which covers, envelops, or conceals like a garment (as, "a grey *shroud* of rain sweeping up from the westward": Kingsley's "Alton Locke," xxvi.); also, a place of shelter†; shadow† or shade†; protection†; a branch or branches as affording shade (chiefly in *pl.*: now prov.); a crypt or vault (chiefly in *pl.*).—**shroud**[1], *v.* **I.** *tr.* To clothe†; esp., to wrap or clothe (a corpse) in a shroud for burial; also, to cover or envelop as with a garment; often, to cover so as to conceal; hide from view; screen from observation; veil, as in obscurity or mystery; also, to provide with shelter (archaic); give protection to†. **II.** *intr.* To take shelter: as, "One who, forced from storms to *shroud*, Felt the loose walls of this decayed Retreat Rock" (Wordsworth's "Guilt and Sorrow," xx.). [Archaic.]

shroud[2] (shroud), *n.* [ME. *srowde*, pl. *srowdes*; prob. another use of *shroud*[1].] *Naut.*, one of a set of strong ropes extended from the mastheads to the sides of a ship to help support the masts: usually in *pl.*: as, "Jonah . . . stumbling to the deck, grasps a *shroud*, to look out upon the sea" (H. Melville's "Moby-Dick," ix.); "In an instant, every one sprung into the rigging, up the *shrouds*, and out on the yards" (Dana's "Two Years before the Mast," xxiii.).—**shroud'-knot**, *n. Naut.*, a knot joining the two parts of a broken or severed shroud.—**shroud'=laid**, *a.* Of a rope, made with four strands and (usually) a central core or heart.

shroud-less (shroud'les), *a.* Without a shroud or winding-sheet; also, unveiled; unobscured.

shrove[1] (shrōv). Preterit of *shrive.*

shrove[2] (shrōv), *n.* [Connected with *shrive.*] Shrift; shriving: used only in certain compounds or combinations, as *Shrove Sunday, Shrove Monday, Shrove Tuesday* (the three days of Shrovetide).—**Shrove'tide** (-tīd), *n.* The three days

Shroud-knots.

preceding Ash Wednesday, as a time for confession and absolution; esp., Shrove Tuesday: long observed as a season of merrymaking before the fast of Lent.

shrub¹ (shrub), *n.* [Ar. *sharāb*, drink, beverage, < *shariba*, to drink: cf. *sherbet* and *syrup*.] Any of various beverages made from the juice of fruit, sugar, and other ingredients.

shrub² (shrub), *n.* [ME. *shrubbe, shrobbe*: cf. AS. *scrybb, shrubbery,* also E. *scrub²*.] A woody perennial plant smaller than a tree, usually having permanent stems branching from or near the ground; also, the strawberry-shrub (commonly 'sweet shrub,' or 'sweet-scented shrub').—**shrub-ber-y** (shrub'ĕr-i), *n.*; pl. *-ies* (-iz). A plantation of shrubs, as in a garden or pleasure-ground (as, "She would give her advice as to the trees which were to be lopped in the *shrubberies*": Thackeray's "Vanity Fair," x.); also, shrubs collectively (as, "Planted amid *shrubbery* on a fine knoll, stands a very tasteful cottage": H. Melville's "Omoo," lviii.).—**shrub'by**, *a.* Abounding in shrubs; consisting of shrubs; of the nature of a shrub; shrub-like.—**shrub'bi-ness**, *n.*

shrug (shrug), *v.*; *shrugged, shrugging.* [ME. *schruggen*; origin uncertain.] **I.** *intr.* To shiver, as with cold or fear†; also, to shrug the shoulders (as, "Ewan ... *shrugged*, as one who would express by that sign that what he was doing was none of his own choice": Scott's "Rob Roy," xxxiii.). **II.** *tr.* To raise and contract (the shoulders) in a brief movement, esp. as an expression of indifference, disdain, impatience, etc., or instead of an explicit comment or reply (as, "My uncle sometimes *shrugs* up his shoulders, and sometimes bursts out a laughing," Smollett's "Humphry Clinker," May 6; "The official fiercely *shrugged* his shoulders and threw up his arms," Arnold Bennett's "Lion's Share," viii.); also, to draw or pull (*up*).—**shrug,** *n.* An act of shrugging; a brief raising and contracting of the shoulders, as to express indifference, etc.

shrunk (shrungk). Preterit and past participle of *shrink.*—**shrunk'en**, *p. a.* [Pp. of *shrink.*] Shriveled; contracted; reduced in extent or compass.

shu-ba (shö'bä), *n.* [Russ.] A long fur coat or outer garment. [Russian.]

shuck (shuk), *n.* [Origin obscure.] A husk or pod, as the outer covering of maize, hickory-nuts, chestnuts, etc. (as, "a half load of corn in the *shuck*": G. W. Cable's "John March, Southerner," iv.); also, the shell of an oyster or clam; also, the case of certain larvæ: often used colloquially, esp. in *pl.*, to represent something worthless (as, not worth *shucks*), or interjectionally, in *pl.*, to express contempt or disgust (as, oh, *shucks!*).—**shuck,** *v. t.* To remove the shucks from (as, "Sometimes they divided into parties, each bending all its energies to be first in *shucking* a given heap of corn": Roosevelt's "Winning of the West," i. 5); also, to remove as or like shucks.—**shuck'er,** *n.*

shud-der (shud'ĕr), *v. i.* [ME. *shoddren* = MLG. *schoderen* = G. *schaudern*, shudder; freq. from a verb-stem (cf. MLG. *schoden, schudden*) meaning 'shake.'] To tremble with a sudden convulsive movement, as from horror, fear, or cold (as, "She starts, like one that spies an adder ... The fear whereof doth make him shake and *shudder*": Shakspere's "Venus and Adonis," 880); also, to move tremulously, quiver, vibrate, or shake (as, "When the strong neighings of the wild White Horse Set every gilded parapet *shuddering*": Tennyson's "Lancelot and Elaine," 298).—**shud'der,** *n.* An act of shuddering; a convulsive movement of the body, as from horror, fear, or cold; a quiver or vibration.—**shud'der-ing-ly,** *adv.*—**shud'der-y,** *a.* Characterized by or causing shudders.

shuf-fle (shuf'l), *v. t.*; *-fled, -fling.* [A freq. form related to *shove*: cf. *scuffle²*.] To move this way and that (as, "Yon cottager, who weaves at her own door ... *Shuffling* her threads about the live-long day": Cowper's "Truth," 320); shift from one place to another; also, to push along, about, or together in a disorderly mass or heap (as, "There is a slight sound as of fallen leaves *shuffled* by approaching feet": Chesterton's "Magic," i.); also, to jumble together; mingle indiscriminately; esp., to mix (cards in a pack) so as to change their relative position; put, bring, etc., in doing this (as, to *shuffle* one card in with others; to *shuffle* a person a good hand); also, to put, thrust, or bring (*in, out, away,* etc.) trickily or surreptitiously, or in a shirking manner, or by

haphazard, or carelessly or clumsily (as, "Glossin had *shuffled* among the papers some writings which really did belong to Bertram," Scott's "Guy Mannering," xliii.; "She *shuffled* away the subject ... and bounded onward into loftier spheres of thought," Kinglake's "Eothen," viii.; a thing which has been *shuffled* out of its place by accident; to *shuffle* one's clothes on); also, to move (the feet, etc.) along the ground or floor without lifting them (as, "An audience of the lower middle class would *shuffle* their feet and want a crime to happen," L. Merrick's "Position of Peggy Harper," ii. 2; "Men, women ... *Shuffled* their sandals o'er the pavement white," Keats's "Lamia," i.); perform (a dance, etc.) with such movements.—**to shuffle off,** to thrust aside or get rid of (as, "when we have *shuffled off* this mortal coil": Shakspere's "Hamlet," iii. 1. 67); also, to put off, as upon another person (as, "to *shuffle off* upon him their responsibilities": Froude's "Cæsar," xiii.).—**shuf'fle,** *v. i.* To shift about, as the wind; also, to act in a shifting or evasive manner; employ deceitful pretenses; equivocate; also, to get (*in, out of,* etc.) in an underhand or evasive manner (as, to *shuffle* out of responsibilities); get (*through*) by some means or other, or in a haphazard manner (as, to *shuffle* through a task); get (*into,* etc.) in a clumsy manner (as, to *shuffle* into one's clothes); also, to make scrambling efforts†, or get along as best one may† (as, "Your life, good master, Must *shuffle* for itself": Shakspere's "Cymbeline," v. 5. 105); also, to move the feet without lifting them, so as to make a scraping noise; move unlifted with a scraping noise, as the feet do; walk with such movements of the feet, or with slovenly or clumsy steps or a shambling gait (as, "There *shuffled* round the corner ... such a man as Kim ... had never seen," Kipling's "Kim," i.; "The bear ... comes ... *shuffling* along at a strange rate," Defoe's "Robinson Crusoe," i. 20; "One of his [a dog's] hind legs had been ... injured, so that he limped and *shuffled* along in a peculiar lopsided fashion," W. H. Hudson's "Far Away and Long Ago," i.); scrape the feet over the floor in dancing; also, to mix cards in a pack so as to change their relative positions.—**shuf'fle,** *n.* The act or an act of shuffling; a shuffling of cards in a pack, or the right or turn to shuffle in card-playing; a tricky shifting of arguments, expedients, etc.; an evasive trick; a scraping movement of the feet; a dragging gait, characterized by such movements; a dance in which the feet are shuffled along the floor (as, "We all turned-to and had a regular sailor's *shuffle,*" Dana's "Two Years before the Mast," xxiii.; a double *shuffle,* one in which each movement is executed twice in succession with the same foot).

shuf'fle=board, *n.* See *shovel-board.*

shuf-fler (shuf'lĕr), *n.* One who shuffles.—**shuf'fling,** *p. a.* That shuffles; shifty or evasive, as persons or their actions, etc. (as, "a mean-spirited *shuffling* rascal in the very agonies of detection," Scott's "Guy Mannering," xli.; "her *shuffling* excuses," Jane Austen's "Sense and Sensibility," l.); that moves the feet over the ground or floor without lifting them, or characterized by such movement (as, "the forced gait of a *shuffling* nag," Shakspere's "1 Henry IV.," iii. 1. 135; "Sounds like the *shuffling* steps of those that bear Some heavy thing," W. Morris's "Jason," xv. 1092).—**shuf'fling-ly,** *adv.*

Shu-lam-ite, Shu-lam-mite (shö'lam-īt), *n.* [Commonly explained as meaning 'native of *Shulem,*' for *Shunem* (cf. Josh. xix. 18), and by some taken as containing an allusion to "Abishag a Shunammite," mentioned in 1 Kings, i. 3.] In the Bible, epithet of the bride in the Song of Solomon (vi. 13). See etym.

shun (shun), *v. t.*; *shunned, shunning.* [AS. *scunian*: cf. *shunt.*] To shrink from in horror or loathing†, or abhor†; hence, to keep away from (a place, person, etc.), from dislike, caution, or some other feeling or consideration (as, "He *shunned* the Clubs as nests of scandal," G. Meredith's "Ordeal of Richard Feverel," xviii.; "Family friends ... she *shunned* like the plague," Galsworthy's "Saint's Progress," ii. 7); take pains or seek to avoid (anything undesirable or unwelcome: as, to *shun* danger or temptation; to *shun* publicity; "He *shunned* the congratulations of Gordon Atterbury," W. Churchill's "Inside of the Cup," vi.); abstain from or eschew (an action, practice, etc.: as, "He *shunned* uttering a direct falsehood, but did not scruple to equivocate," Bancroft's "Hist. of the U. S.," Amer. Revolution, i. 2); forbear, neglect, or refuse (to do something: as, "I have not *shunned* to declare unto you all the counsel of God," Acts, xx. 27; "Do not *shun* To speak the wish most near to your true heart," Tennyson's "Lancelot and Elaine," 908); also, to elude, evade, or escape (as, "Weak we are and cannot *shun* pursuit," Shakspere's "3 Henry VI.," ii. 3. 13: now rare).—**shun′less**, *a.* That cannot be shunned; inevitable: as, "*shunless* destiny" (Shakspere's "Coriolanus," ii. 2. 116).—**shun′ner**, *n.*

shunt (shunt), *v.* [ME. *schunten*; perhaps related to *shun.*] **I.** *intr.* To start aside† or shrink back†; also, to move or turn aside or out of the way (as, "Trucks clanged and *shunted*, great lorries rumbled smoothly by": Galsworthy's "Saint's Progress," iii. 9); of a train, to move from one line of rails to another (chiefly Eng.). **II.** *tr.* To elude† or avoid†; also, to shove or turn aside or out of the way; shift (a train, or part of it) from one line of rails to another or from the main track to a siding (chiefly Eng.); fig., to side-track; put aside; get rid of; in *elect.,* to divert (a part of a current) by means of a shunt; place on or furnish with a shunt.—**shunt**, *n.* An act of shunting; a turning aside; a shift; also, a railroad-switch (chiefly Eng.); in *elect.,* a conductor joining two points in a circuit and forming a path through which a part of the current will pass.—**shunt′=dy″na-mo**, *n.* In *elect.,* a shunt-wound dynamo.—**shunt′er**, *n.*—**shunt′=mo″tor**, *n.* In *elect.,* a shunt-wound motor.—**shunt′=wound**, *a.* In *elect.,* noting a dynamo or a motor so wound that a portion of the armature current is shunted into the field-magnet coils. Cf. *series-wound.*

shut (shut), *v. t.;* shut, shutting. [AS. *scyttan* = D. *schutten,* shut; from the root of E. *shoot.*] To shoot or slide (a bolt or bar) into position in fastening a door, etc.†; fasten (a door, etc.) with a bolt or bar†; also, to put (a door, gate, cover, etc.) in position to obstruct an entrance, passage, or aperture; also, to close by bringing together the outward covering parts of, as the eyes or the mouth; close by bringing or folding together the parts of, as a book or a knife; weld, as two pieces of metal; also, to obstruct or block (an entrance, passage, or aperture) by means of a door, gate, or other barrier; also, to close the doors or apertures of (as, "When the bell . . . jangled six, he *shut* and darkened the shop," Arnold Bennett's "Riceyman Steps," i. 4: often with *up*); prevent ingress to or egress from; also, to confine or inclose in a place, receptacle, etc. (with *in, up,* etc.); bar, exclude, or cut off (with *out, off,* etc.: as, "From such contentment poor Dorothea was *shut* out," George Eliot's "Middlemarch," iii.); in games, to keep from scoring (with *out*): also, to free from or relieve of something troublesome (now only as in *shut, p. a.*).—**to shut down**, to shut or close by lowering, as a window or cover; also, to close (a factory or the like) for a time, as during a dull season.—**shut**, *v. i.* To become shut or closed; close.—**to shut down**, to come or be put down so as to close an aperture, as a cover; hence, to settle down so as to cover or envelop (as, "Night *shut down* on the settlement," Bret Harte's "How Santa Claus Came to Simpson's Bar"; "when winter *shut down* on Starkfield," Mrs. Wharton's "Ethan Frome," Introd.); also, to stop work; close for a time, as a factory during a dull season (as, "There's an overstock in everything, and . . . we've got to *shut down* till the home demand begins again": Howells's "Rise of Silas Lapham," vii.); also, to put a stop or check to something (followed by *on* or *upon*: colloq.).—**to shut up**, to shut doors, etc., or close a place, as for the night; also, to shut one's mouth, or stop talking (colloq.).—**shut**, *p. a.* Closed; fastened up; inclosed; free, clear, or rid (with *of:* now prov. or colloq.: as, "I'd seen all I wanted to of them, and wanted to get entirely *shut* of them," Mark Twain's "Huckleberry Finn," xxxi.); in *phonetics,* same as *stopped;* also, having the sound suddenly stopped by a consonant at the end of the syllable, as the *i* in *pit* or the *o* in *got.*—**shut**, *n.* The act or time of shutting or closing; also, the place of shutting; the line where two pieces of welded metal are united; also, something which shuts, as a sliding door for an aperture.—**shut′=down**, *n.* A shutting down; a closing of a factory or the like for a time, as during a dull season.

shute (shōt), *n.* See *chute* and *shoot, n.*

shut=in (shut′in), *n.* A person who is shut in or confined, as by infirmity or disease, to the house, a hospital, etc.

shut=out (shut′out), *n.* The act or an act of shutting out, or the state of being shut out; esp., a preventing of the opposite side from scoring, as in the game of baseball.

shut-ter (shut′ėr), *n.* One who or that which shuts; a hinged or other movable wooden or iron screen or cover for a window; a movable cover, slide, or the like, for closing an aperture; in *photog.,* a mechanical device on a camera, for opening and closing the aperture of a lens in order to expose a plate or film.—**shut′ter**, *v. t.* To close with or as with a shutter; provide with shutters.

shut-tle (shut′l), *n.* [ME. *schutylle, schetylle,* weaver's shuttle, < AS. *scytel,* dart, missile; from the root of E. *shoot.*] A device in a loom, for passing or shooting the weft-thread through the shed from one side of the web to the other, usually consisting of a boat-shaped piece of wood containing a bobbin on which the weft-thread is wound; also, an implement on

Shuttle.—*a, a,* body of shuttle; *b,* yarn wound on the bobbin *d; c,* eye through which the yarn is led, and then passed out through hole *f; e, e,* metal points.

which the thread is wound, used in tatting; also, the sliding container that carries the lower thread in a sewing-machine; also, a shuttle-train.—**shut′tle**, *v. t.* or *i.; -tled, -tling.* To move quickly to and fro like a shuttle.—**shut′tle-cock**, *n.* A piece of cork, or of similar light material, with feathers stuck in one end, intended to be struck into the air with a battledore in play; also, the play or game ('battledore and shuttlecock').—**shut′tle-cock**, *v. t.* To send, or bandy to and fro, like a shuttlecock.—**shut′tle=shell**, *n.* The elongated fusiform shell of a marine gastropod of the genus *Radius* (family *Ovulidæ*), or the gastropod itself: so called from the resemblance to a weaver's shuttle. —**shut′tle=train**, *n.* A train running for a short distance to and fro, as on a branch line.

Shuttle-shell (*Radius volva*), one third natural size.

shy[1] (shī), *a.;* compar. *shyer,* also *shier,* superl. *shyest,* also *shiest.* [AS. *scēoh,* akin to D. *schuw,* G. *scheu,* Sw. *skygg,* Dan. *sky,* timid, shy: cf. *eschew.*] Easily frightened away; timid; sometimes, skittish, as a horse (prov. Eng.); also, keeping away from or avoiding some person or thing, through timidity or caution (with *of*); suspicious; distrustful; also, wary, chary, or reluctant (with *of, about, at,* etc.: as, "As for Jarvis, he was very *shy* of taking charge of my letter," Smollett's "Humphry Clinker," April 6); also, shrinking from familiarity or self-assertion, retiring, or bashful (as, "The poor man was *shy* and hated society": G. B. Shaw's "Man and Superman," ii.); also, not bearing or breeding freely, as plants or animals; also, short of something (colloq.: as, to be *shy* of funds); failing to pay something due, as one's ante in poker (colloq.); short in amount, degree, etc., to a certain extent (colloq.: as, the supply is rather *shy*); also, of dubious character, or 'shady' (colloq.: as, "two men, very *shy* characters," Dickens's "Our Mutual Friend," i. 12).—**shy**[1], *v.;* shied, shying. **I.** *intr.* To start back or aside, as in sudden fear (now esp. of a horse: as, "Katerfelto [a horse] *shied* at an object moving in the brushwood," Whyte-Melville's "Katerfelto," ix.); hence, to shrink; draw back; recoil. **II.** *tr.* To frighten; also, to shun or avoid (as, "I . . . had a straitened, money-borrowing air, upon which the world began to *shy* me": Irving's "Tales of a Traveler," ii. 7).—**shy**[1], *n.;* pl. *shies* (shīz). A sudden start aside, as in fear, esp. as made by a horse.

shy[2] (shī), *v. i.* or *t.; shied, shying.* [Origin uncertain.] To throw (a missile) with a swift, sudden movement; fling.—**shy**[2], *n.;* pl. *shies* (shīz). A quick, sudden throw; a fling; fig., a gibe or sneer (colloq.); also, a try at something (colloq.).

shy-er[1], **shy-er**[2] (shī′ėr), *n.* See *shier*[1], *shier*[2].

Shy-lock (shī′lok), *n.* A relentless and revengeful Jewish money-lender in Shakspere's "Merchant of Venice"; hence, an extortionate usurer.

shy-ly (shī′li), *adv.* In a shy manner.—**shy′ness**, *n.*

shy-ster (shī′stėr), *n.* [Origin obscure.] One who gets along by petty, sharp practices in a business or profession; esp., a lawyer who uses unprofessional or questionable methods in seeking and handling cases. [Slang, U. S.]

si (sē), *n.* In *music*, the syllable used for the seventh tone of the scale (B, in the major scale of C), and sometimes for the tone B. See *sol-fa*.

si-al-a-gogue (sī-al′ạ-gog). [Gr. σίαλον, saliva, + ἀγωγός, leading, < ἄγειν, lead.] **I.** *a.* Promoting the flow or secretion of saliva. **II.** *n.* A sialagogue agent or medicine.—**si″a-la-gog′ic** (-ạ-lạ-goj′ik), *a.* and *n.*

si-a-lid (sī′ạ-lid). [NL. *Sialidæ*, pl., < *Sialis*, the typical genus, < Gr. σίαλις, kind of bird.] **I.** *n.* Any of the *Sialidæ*, a family of neuropterous insects with aquatic larvæ, as *Sialis infumata*, common in the eastern U. S., and *Corydalus cornutus* (see *hellgrammite*). **II.** *a.* Belonging to the *Sialidæ*.—**si-al′i-dan** (-al′i-dạn), *a.* and *n.*

si-a-loid (sī′ạ-loid), *a.* [Gr. σίαλον, saliva: see *-oid*.] Resembling saliva.

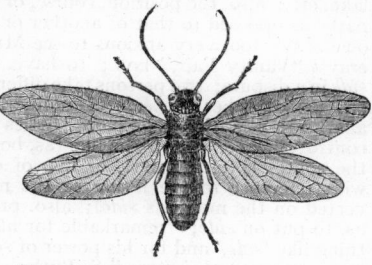
Sialid (*Sialis infumata*), twice natural size.

si-a-mang (sē′ạ-mang or sī′-), *n.* [Malay.] A black anthropoid ape, *Hylobates syndactylus* (or *Siamanga syndactyla*), of Sumatra and the Malay Peninsula, the largest of the gibbons, with very long arms and having the second and third digits united to some extent.

Si-a-mese (sī-ạ-mēs′ or -mēz′), *a.* Of or pertaining to Siam, a kingdom in southeastern Asia, or its people or their language; sometimes (in allusion to the Siamese twins), twin; closely connected; similar.—

Siamang.

Siamese twins, two Siamese men, Chang and Eng (1811–74), who were joined to each other by a short tubular cartilaginous band.—**Si-a-mese′,** *n.*; pl. *-mese.* A native of Siam; also, the language of Siam.—**Si-a-mese′,** *v. t.*; *-mesed, -mesing.* [Also *l. c.*] To join or unite in the manner of, or in a manner suggesting that of, the Siamese twins.

sib (sib). [AS. *sibb* = OFries. *sib* = OHG. *sippi* = Goth. *-sibjis*, related, akin: cf. G. *sipp, sippe*, relative, kinsman, and E. *gossip*.] **I.** *a.* Related by blood; akin; hence, closely related in any way. [Now chiefly archaic or prov.] **II.** *n.* A kinsman or relative; also, one's kin or kindred. [Now chiefly archaic or prov.]

Si-be-ri-an (sī-bē′ri-ạn). **I.** *a.* Of or pertaining to Siberia, a large Russian possession extending across northern Asia. **II.** *n.* A native or inhabitant of Siberia.

sib-i-lant (sib′i-lạnt). [L. *sibilans* (-ant-), ppr. of *sibilare*: see *sibilate*.] **I.** *a.* Hissing; making, having, or representing a hissing sound. **II.** *n.* A sibilant sound, letter, or symbol, as *s* or *sh*.—**sib′i-lance, sib′i-lan-cy,** *n.*—**sib′i-lant-ly,** *adv.*

sib-i-late (sib′i-lāt), *v.*; *-lated, -lating.* [L. *sibilatus*, pp. of *sibilare*, < *sibilus*, a hissing; prob. of imit. origin: cf. *siffle*.] **I.** *intr.* To hiss. **II.** *tr.* To utter or pronounce with a hissing sound.—**sib′i-la′tion** (-lā′shọn), *n.* [LL. *sibilatio(n-)*.] The act of sibilating; also, a hissing sound.—**sib′i-la-to-ry** (-lạ-tọ-ri), *a.*

sib-yl (sib′il), *n.* [L. *sibylla*, < Gr. σίβυλλα.] Any of certain women of antiquity reputed to possess powers of prophecy or divination; hence, a prophetess; a female fortune-teller; a witch.—**si-byl-lic** (si-bil′ik), *a.* Sibylline.—**sib-yl-line** (sib′i-lin or -līn), *a.* [L. *sibyllinus*.] Pertaining to, or uttered or written by, a sibyl; hence, oracular; occult; mysterious; also, resembling a sibyl.—**Sibylline Books,** in *Rom. hist.*, a collection of oracular utterances, written in Greek hexameters, containing directions as to the worship of the gods and the policy of the Romans, which were kept with great care at Rome. According to legend, these books were bought by Tarquinius Superbus from the Cumæan sibyl, who at first offered him nine books; when he refused them, she burned three, and offered him the remaining six at the original price; when he again refused, she burned three more, and offered him the remaining three, still at the original price, and these he bought.—**Sibylline Oracles,** a collection of apocalyptic writings, consisting partly of Jewish and partly of Christian material, composed in imitation of the Sibylline Books.

sic[1] (sik), *adv.* [L.] So; thus: often inserted within brackets in a text to vouch for the reproduction of a word, spelling, date, etc., exactly as in the original.

sic[2] (sik), *a.* and *pron.* Sc. form of *such.* Also **sic-can** (sik′ạn).

sic[3] (sik), *v. t.* See *sick*[1].

sic-ca-tive (sik′ạ-tiv). [LL. *siccativus*, < L. *siccare*, make dry, < *siccus*, dry.] **I.** *a.* Causing or promoting absorption of moisture; drying. **II.** *n.* A siccative substance; esp., a drier used in painting.

sice[1] (sīs), *n.* [OF. *sis* (F. *six*), < L. *sex*, six: see *six*.] The number six at dice.

sice[2] (sīs), *n.* See *sais*.

Si-cel-i-ot (si-sel′i-ot), *n.* [Gr. Σικελιώτης.] An ancient Greek settler in Sicily; a Sicilian Greek.

Si-cil-ian (si-sil′ian). [L. *Sicilia* = Gr. Σικελία, Sicily.] **I.** *a.* Of or pertaining to Sicily: as, *Sicilian* architecture (a special development of medieval architecture peculiar to Sicily, characterized by a fusion of the Norman and the later French pointed styles of the foreign race dominant from the 11th to the 13th century, with local Byzantine and Saracenic elements); the *Sicilian* Vespers (a general massacre of the French in Sicily by the natives, begun at the sound of the vesper-bell on Easter Monday, 1282, and resulting in the superseding of French by Spanish rule). **II.** *n.* A native or inhabitant of Sicily; also, sicilienne.

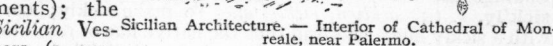
Sicilian Architecture. — Interior of Cathedral of Monreale, near Palermo.

si-cil-i-enne (si-sil-i-en′), *n.* [F., fem. of *sicilien*, Sicilian.] A heavy variety of mohair (fabric).

sick[1] (sik), *v. t.* [Var. of *seek*.] To seek, set upon, or attack (chiefly in the imperative, as a command to a dog: as, *sick* him, Towser!); also, to incite to set upon or attack (chiefly with *on*: as, "The boys . . . *sicked* the dogs on him," Tarkington's "Gentleman from Indiana," viii.).

sick[2] (sik), *a.* [AS. *sēoc* = D. *ziek* = G. *siech* = Icel. *sjúkr* = Goth. *siuks*, sick.] Affected with any disorder of health; ill, unwell, or ailing; esp., affected with nausea, or sickness at the stomach; inclined to vomit, or vomiting; hence, deeply affected with some feeling comparable to physical disorder, as sorrow, longing, repugnance, weariness, etc. (as, *sick* at heart; *sick* for old scenes; "I get very *sick* sometimes of our conventional society manners," Mallock's "New Republic," iii. 1); sometimes, mortified or chagrined (slang); also, not in proper condition; impaired; spoiled;

in the spawning stage, as fish, etc.; out of repair, as ships, boats, etc.; also, of a sickly hue; pale; wan; also, pertaining to or attended with sickness (as, "Now comes the *sick* hour that his surfeit made": Shakspere's "Richard II.," ii. 2. 84); pertaining or appropriated to sick persons (as, on *sick* leave; a *sick*-room).—**the Sick Man, or the Sick Man of the East** (or **of Europe**), the Turkish or Ottoman Empire, or the Sultan of Turkey: used from the middle of the 19th century in allusion to the moribund condition of the Turkish Empire (which ceased to exist in 1923).—**sick′=bay,** *n.* A compartment of a ship used as a hospital.—**sick′=bed,** *n.* A bed upon which a person lies sick.

sick-en (sik′n), *v.* [From *sick*².] **I.** *intr.* To become sick; feel faint with nausea, horror, disgust, etc.; experience a feeling of revulsion; grow weary or tired of something; grow pale. **II.** *tr.* To make sick; render faint with nausea, horror, disgust, etc. (as, "The horrible news of Escovedo's assassination had *sickened* him to the soul": Motley's "Dutch Republic," v. 5); make weary or tired of something. —**sick′en-er,** *n.*—**sick′en-ing,** *p. a.* Becoming sick; also, making sick; causing nausea, faintness, disgust, or loathing. —**sick′en-ing-ly,** *adv.*

sick-er (sik′ėr), *a.* [AS. *sicor* = G. *sicher*, < L. *securus*: see *secure*.] Secure; safe; certain; sure; firm; settled; also, prudent; also, hard or severe. [Now Sc. and north. Eng.]

sick=head-ache (sik′hed′āk), *n.* Headache accompanied by nausea; megrim.

sick-ish (sik′ish), *a.* Somewhat sick or ill; also, somewhat sickening or nauseating.—**sick′ish-ly,** *adv.*—**sick′ish-ness,** *n.*

sick-le (sik′l), *n.* [AS. *sicol*: cf. L. *secula*, sickle, < *secare*, cut.] An implement for cutting grain, grass, etc., consisting of a curved, hook-like blade mounted in a short handle; also [*cap.*], in *astron.*, a group of stars in the constellation Leo, likened to this implement.—**sick′le-bill,** *n.* Any of various birds with a curved bill suggestive of the blade of a sickle, as a curlew.—**sick′le-pod,** *n.* An American cress, *Arabis canadensis*, with long, curved pods.—**sick′le=shaped,** *a.* Shaped like a sickle; of a curved, hook-like form; falcate.

Sickle with Serrated Edge.

sick-ly (sik′li), *a.*; compar. *sicklier*, superl. *sickliest*. Habitually ailing or indisposed; not robust or strong; unhealthy; also, pertaining to, connected with, or arising from ill health (as, a *sickly* complexion); marked by the prevalence of ill health, as a region or a period; also, causing sickness; nauseating; also, fig., morbid or unwholesome; weak or mawkish (as, *sickly* sentimentality); also, faint or feeble, as light, color, etc. (as, "the sky clearing in patches, with a flicker of *sickly* sun from time to time": Kipling's "Captains Courageous," iv.).—**sick′li-ly,** *adv.*—**sick′li-ness,** *n.*—**sick′ly,** *v. t.*; *sicklied*, *sicklying*. To make sickly; cover with a sickly hue: as, "And thus the native hue of resolution Is *sicklied* o'er with the pale cast of thought" (Shakspere's "Hamlet," iii. 1. 85).—**sick′ly,** *adv.*

sick-ness (sik′nes), *n.* The state of being sick; illness; esp., nausea; fig., disgust or weariness; also, a particular disease or malady.

sick=nurse (sik′nėrs), *n.* A nurse for sick persons.

sick=room (sik′röm), *n.* A room occupied by a sick person.

Sic-u-lo- (sik′ū-lō-). Form of L. *Siculus*, Sicilian, used in combination, as in *Siculo-Arabian* (Sicilian and Arabian, Arabian as found in Sicily), *Siculo-Moresque*, *Siculo-Punic*.

si-da (sī′dä), *n.* [NL., < Gr. *σίδη*, kind of water-plant.] A plant of the malvaceous genus *Sida*, which comprises annual and perennial herbs and shrubs, mostly of warm climates, with (usually) small yellow or white flowers, many species affording demulcents, and some, as *S. rhombifolia* (Queensland hemp), yielding useful fibers.

side (sīd), *n.* [AS. *sīde* = D. *zijde* = G. *seite* = Icel. *sīdha* = Sw. *sida* = Dan. *side*, side: cf. AS. *sīd*, long, large, spacious.] One of the surfaces or lines bounding a thing, esp. of the longer ones as distinguished from the ends; one of the two surfaces of an object other than the front, back, top, and bottom; either of the two surfaces of paper, cloth, or the like; a particular surface, or part of the total surface,

of anything (as, the outer and inner *sides* of a hollow ball; the *side* of the moon turned toward us); fig., an aspect or phase (as, to study all *sides* of a question); also, either of the two lateral (right and left) parts of a thing; either lateral half of the body of a person or an animal, esp. of the trunk; also, an area or region in one direction from a central line, space, or point (as, the east *side* of the city; "in our *side* of the country," Galt's "Annals of the Parish," xxx.); hence, direction or position with reference to a central line, space, or point (as, to turn to one *side*; from or on every *side*); in special uses, either of the two lateral parts of the framework of a ship; a slope, as of a bank or hill; a bounding or inclosing part, as of a cave; the bank or shore of a river, lake, etc.; also, the position, course, or part of one person or party as opposed to that of another or others (as, "He was, on his *side* too, very anxious to see Mrs. Osborne," Thackeray's "Vanity Fair," lxvi.; to have, or be on, the losing *side* in a dispute; two persons take different *sides* in a quarrel; one person takes the *side* of another, or takes *sides* with another); one of two or more parties concerned in a case, controversy, contest, or the like (as, both *sides* are ready for the contest); either part, or line of descent, of a family, with reference to the father or the mother (as, well connected on the mother's *side*); also, pretentious airs (slang: as, to put on *side*; "remarkable for his entire want of anything like '*side*,' and for his power of setting those whom he came across at their ease," S. Butler's "Way of All Flesh," xlviii.); in *billiards*, a spinning motion imparted to a ball by a quick stroke on one side of its center (in American billiards called *English*).—**side by side**, in the position of being one beside another; esp., with sides adjoining, and abreast.—**side**, *a.* Being at or on one side (as, the side aisles of a theater); coming from or directed toward one side (as, a *side* blow; a *side* glance); seen or taken from the side (as, a *side* view); fig., subsidiary or subordinate (as, a *side* issue).—**side**, *v.*; *sided*, *siding*. **I.** *tr.* To be, stand, or move by the side of; also, to dress the sides of (timber); also, to put aside or away (prov.: as, "Mrs. Wilson was '*siding*' the dinner things," Mrs. Gaskell's "Mary Barton," x.); also, to place or range with a side or party. **II.** *intr.* To turn or move sideways; also, to place one's self with a side or party, or take sides (as, "She . . . *sided* with the doctor against him," Arnold Bennett's "Riceyman Steps," iv. 9; "a . . . Scotchman, who *sided* alternately with the French and English interests," Roosevelt's "Winning of the West," i. 3).

side-arms (sīd′ärmz), *n. pl. Milit.*, weapons (as sword, bayonet, etc.) carried at the side or in the belt, in contradistinction to musket, lance, etc.

side-board (sīd′bōrd), *n.* A side-table, esp. in a dining-room; also, a piece of furniture, as in a dining-room, often with shelves, drawers, etc., for holding articles of table-service.

side-car (sīd′kär), *n.* A car-like device for attachment to a motor-cycle, being supported on one side by the motor-cycle and on the other by a wheel or wheels of its own: used for carrying a passenger, baggage, or the like.

sid-ed (sī′ded), *a.* Having a side or sides: as, three-*sided*.

side-dish (sīd′dish), *n.* A dish served in addition to the principal dish of a course.

side=hill (sīd′hil), *n.* The side or slope of a hill; a hillside. [U. S.]

side-less (sīd′les), *a.* Without sides; open at the sides, as a garment.

side-light (sīd′līt), *n.* Light coming from the side; fig., incidental light or information on a subject (as, "such information may throw *side-light* upon my story": H. Melville's "Moby-Dick," liv.); also, either of two lights carried by a vessel under way at night, a red one on the port side and a green one on the starboard side; also, a window or other aperture for light, in the side of a building, ship, etc.; a window at the side of a door or another window.

side-line (sīd′lin), *n.* A line at the side of something; a line or rope used for hobbling a horse or other animal by tying together the fore and hind leg on one side; a line or mark which defines the limit of play on the side of the field in football, etc.; also, an additional or auxiliary line of goods or of business.

---

side-ling (sīd′ling), *adv.* and *a.* [See *-ling*[2].] Toward one side; sidewise; sidelong; at a slope. [Archaic or prov.]

side-long (sīd′lông). [Altered form of *sideling*, after *long*[1].] **I.** *adv.* Toward the side; obliquely; also, at the side of, or with the side to, something; also, on the or its side (as, "*Sidelong* the plough beside the field-gate lay": W. Morris's "Earthly Paradise," November, The Story of Rhodope). **II.** *a.* Directed to one side (as, "Mrs. Bellew gave him a *sidelong* glance": Galsworthy's "Country House," i. 1); oblique; hence, indirect; also, slanting or sloping; also, lying on the side.

side=oats (sīd′ōts), *n.* A grama-grass, *Atheropogon curtipendulus*, bearing many short spikes along the sides of the stem, ranging from New Jersey to the Rocky Mountains and southward: used for forage.

side=piece (sīd′pēs), *n.* A piece forming a side or a part of a side, or fixed by the side, of something.

sid-er (sī′dėr), *n.* One who sides with a person, party, or cause; a partizan; an adherent.

sid-er-al (sid′ę-ṛạl), *a.* [L. *sideralis*, < *sidus*: see *sidereal*.] Sidereal; also, due to the stars.

si-de-re-al (sī-dē′rę̄-ạl), *a.* [L. *sidereus*, < *sidus* (*sider-*), constellation, star.] Of or pertaining to the constellations or fixed stars; also, determined by the stars (as, *sidereal* time, time as measured by the apparent diurnal motion of the stars; *sidereal* day, the fundamental unit of sidereal time, the interval between two successive passages of the vernal equinoctial point over the meridian, being about 4 minutes shorter than a mean solar day; *sidereal* hour, one twenty-fourth of a sidereal day; *sidereal* year, see *year*).—**si-de′re-al-ly**, *adv.*

sid-er-ite (sid′ę-rīt), *n.* [L. *siderites*, lodestone, < Gr. σιδηρίτης, of iron, < σίδηρος, iron.] Lodestone†; also, a native carbonate of iron, usually of a brownish color, valued as an ore of iron; also, a meteorite consisting mainly of metallic iron.—**sid-er-it′ic** (-ę-rit′ik), *a.*

sidero-. Form of Gr. σίδηρος, iron (hence used also for 'steel'), in combination.—**sid-er-og-ra-phy** (sid-ę-rog′ṛa-fi), *n.* [+ *-graphy*.] The art of engraving on steel, esp. a process in which the design is subsequently transferred by pressure to other steel surfaces.—**sid′er-o-lite** (-ę-rọ̄-līt), *n.* [+ *-lite*.] A meteorite consisting mainly of metallic iron and stony matter.

sid-er-o-stat (sid′ę-rọ̄-stat), *n.* [L. *sidus* (*sider-*), constellation, star: see *-stat*.] A device on a telescope, etc., for reflecting the rays of a heavenly body in a constant direction, consisting mainly of a mirror operated by clockwork.—**sid″er-o-stat′ic**, *a.*

sid-er-ur-gy (sid′ę-rėr-ji), *n.* [Gr. σιδηρουργία, < σιδηρουργός, worker in iron, < σίδηρος, iron, + -εργός, working, worker.] The art of working in iron and steel.—**sid-er-ur′gi-cal**, *a.*

side-sad-dle (sīd′sad″l), *n.* A saddle on which the rider sits with both feet on the same (usually the left) side of the horse: used chiefly by women.—**side′sad″dle=flow″er**, *n.* Any of various marsh-plants of the American genus *Sarracenia*, esp. the common pitcher-plant, *S. purpurea*.

side=show (sīd′shō), *n.* A small or minor show or exhibition in connection with a principal one; fig. (in colloq. use), any minor proceeding or affair connected with a more important one; a subordinate matter.

side-slip (sīd′slip), *n.* A slip or slipping to one side; specif., in aëronautics, the act or an act of sideslipping.—**side′-slip**, *v. i.* ; *-slipped*, *-slipping*. To slip to one side; specif., in aëronautics, of an aëroplane when banked excessively, to slide sideways in a downward direction, toward the center of the curve executed in turning.

sides-man (sīdz′man), *n.*; pl. *-men.* An assistant to a churchwarden (as, "Daniel Povey . . . a *sidesman* at St. Luke's": Arnold Bennett's "Old Wives' Tale," ii. 2); also, a partizan†.

side-step (sīd′step), *n.* A step or stepping to one side, as to avoid or evade something; also, a step at the side of a ship, vehicle, etc.—**side′step**, *v. i.* or *t.*; *-stepped*, *-stepping*. To step, or avoid by stepping, to one side. Often fig.

side-swipe (sīd′swīp), *n.* [Cf. *swipe*.] A sweeping stroke or blow with or along the side of something; a collision in which the side of one train, car, or the like strikes or grazes against the side of another.—**side′swipe**, *v. t.*; *-swiped*, *-swiping*. To give a sideswipe to; collide with in a sideswipe.

side=ta-ble (sīd′tā″bl), *n.* A table placed near the wall of an apartment, esp. a dining-room; a table smaller than a principal table, esp. a dining-table, and placed to one side of it.

side=track (sīd′trak), *n.* A railroad-siding.—**side′=track**, *v.* **I.** *tr.* To shift (a train, etc.) to a side-track; fig., to divert to one side or set aside; divert from a subject (as, "He could not *sidetrack* her": Sinclair Lewis's "Arrowsmith," vi.). **II.** *intr.* To pass to a side-track; fig., to diverge from the main course.

side-walk (sīd′wâk), *n.* A walk, esp. one paved or otherwise prepared, at the side of a street or road.

side-ward (sīd′wạrd), *adv.* and *a.* Toward one side.—**side′wards**, *adv.*

side-way (sīd′wā), *n.* A byway; also, a sidewalk.—**side′-way.** **I.** *adv.* Sideways. **II.** *a.* Directed toward or from one side; oblique; hence, indirect.—**side′ways.** **I.** *adv.* Toward or from one side; obliquely; hence, indirectly; also, with the side foremost; facing to the side. **II.** *a.* Sideway: as, "Michel . . . executed an instantaneous *sideways* leap" (J. Conrad's "Rover," xii.).

side-wheel (sīd′hwēl), *a.* Having a paddle-wheel on each side, as a steamboat.—**side′=wheel″er**, *n.* A side-wheel steamer.

side-whisk-er (sīd′hwis′kėr), *n.* The hair growing on the side of a man's face when worn long and with the chin cleanshaven: usually in *pl.*—**side′=whisk′ered**, *a.* Having side-whiskers: as, "the sainted but *side-whiskered* Nathaniel Mugford" (Sinclair Lewis's "Arrowsmith," xxii.).

side-wipe (sīd′wīp), *n.* and *v.* Same as *sideswipe*.

side-wise (sīd′wīz). **I.** *adv.* Toward one side; obliquely; hence, indirectly; also, from the side; also, on the side; also, with the side foremost. **II.** *a.* Directed toward one side; sidelong: as, "I made a long *sidewise* reach, secured the paper, and read it" (G. W. Cable's "Cavalier," xx.).

sid-ing (sī′ding), *n.* The boarding forming the sides of a timber building; also, a short additional railroad-track to which a train may be shifted from a main line.

si-dle (sī′dl), *v.*; *-dled*, *-dling*. [Appar. < *sideling*, taken as ppr.] **I.** *intr.* To move sidewise or obliquely; edge along furtively, as while looking in another direction. **II.** *tr.* To move or direct sidewise.—**si′dle**, *n.* A sidling movement.

Si-do-ni-an (sī-dō′ni-ạn). **I.** *a.* Of or pertaining to Sidon, a famous seaport of ancient Phenicia. **II.** *n.* A native or inhabitant of Sidon.

siege (sēj), *n.* [OF. *siege*, *sege* (F. *siège*), through LL. < L. *sedes*, seat: see *see*[1].] A seat†; also, the encampment of an investing army about a fortified place to reduce and capture it by cutting off supplies, undermining, bringing guns to bear, and other offensive operations; beleaguerment; fig., any prolonged or persistent endeavor to overcome resistance.—**siege**, *v. t.*; *sieged*, *sieging*. To lay siege to; besiege.—**siege′=piece**, *n.* A coin, commonly of unusual shape and rude workmanship, struck and issued in a place during a siege, when the operations of the ordinary mints are suspended or their issues are not available. See cut on following page.—**siege′=train**, *n.* The equipment of guns, carriages, ammunition, etc., carried with an army for the purpose of besieging.

Si-e-nese, Si-en-nese (sē-e-nēs′ or -nēz′). **I.** *a.* Of or pertaining to the city or the province of Siena (Sienna), in central Italy. **II.** *n.*; pl. *-nese.* A native or inhabitant of Siena.

Side-oats.— *a*, spike; *b*, spikelet; *c*, spikelet with glumes removed.

si-e-nite (sī′ẹ-nīt), etc. See *syenite*, etc.

si-en-na (si-en′ä), *n.* [For It. *terra di Siena*, 'earth of Siena': cf. *Sienese*.] A ferruginous earth used as a yellowish-brown pigment ('raw sienna') or, after roasting in a furnace, as a reddish-brown pigment ('burnt sienna'); also, the color of such a pigment.

Obverse.   Reverse.
Newark Siege-piece (one shilling). — British Museum.

si-er-ra (si-er′ä), *n.* [Sp., lit. 'saw,' < L. *serra*, saw: cf. *serrate*.] A chain of hills or mountains the peaks of which suggest the teeth of a saw (as, "The road wound up the bold *sierra* which separates the great plateaus of Mexico and Puebla": Prescott's "Conquest of Mexico," iii. 8); also, the pintado (fish).—**si-er′ran**, *a.*

si-es-ta (si-es′tä), *n.* [Sp., < L. *sexta* (*hora*), sixth (hour) (that is, the sixth hour after sunrise, midday).] A midday or afternoon rest or nap, esp. as taken in Spain and other hot countries: as, "The king having dined, was taking his *siesta*, or afternoon's sleep" (Irving's "Conquest of Granada," lix.).

sieur (syẻr), *n.* [OF. F. *sieur*, orig. acc. of OF. *sire*, lord: see *sire*.] An old French title of rank or of respect for a man, now occurring chiefly in French legal use.

sieve (siv), *n.* [AS. *sife* = D. *zeef* = G. *sieb*, sieve: cf. *sift*.] An instrument with a meshed or perforated bottom, used for separating the coarser from the finer parts of loose matter, for straining liquids, etc., esp. one with a circular frame and fine meshes or perforations; also, something resembling this, as a form of basket with small meshes or openings; fig., a person who tells all that he knows, or who cannot keep a secret.—**sieve**, *v. t.*; *sieved*, *sieving*. To sift. —**sieve′=cell**, *n.* In *bot.*, an elongated cell whose walls contain perforations (called *sieve-pores*) which are arranged in circumscribed areas (called *sieve-plates*) and which afford communication with abutting or adjacent cells of a similar nature. See *sieve-tube*.—**sieve′=plate**, **sieve′= pore**, *n.* See *sieve-cell*.—**sieve′=tis″sue**, *n.* In *bot.*, tissue composed of sieve-cells or sieve-tubes.—**sieve′=tube**, *n.* In *bot.*, a tube-like structure composed of sieve-cells placed end to end.

sif-fle (sif′l), *v. i.*; *-fled*, *-fling*. [F. *siffler*, < L. *sifilare*, *sibilare*, hiss: see *sibilate*, and cf. *persiflage*.] To blow with or make a sibilant sound; whistle.—**sif′fle**, *n.* In *pathol.*, a sibilant râle.

sift (sift), *v.* [AS. *siftan* = D. *ziften*, sift; related to E. *sieve*.] **I.** *tr.* To separate the coarser from the finer parts of (meal, ashes, etc.) by shaking in a sieve; free from coarser particles, impurities, etc., by passing through a sieve; let fall through or scatter by means of a sieve (as, to *sift* sugar upon cake); separate by or as by a sieve (as, "to *sift* the wheat from the chaff": Du Maurier's "Trilby," v.); hence, in fig. use, to examine with close scrutiny, as evidence; subject to minute analysis, as a proposition; also, to make trial of (a person); question (a person) closely (as, "He multiplied his questions, and *sifted* me thoroughly upon every part of this head," Swift's "Gulliver's Travels," ii. 6; "It . . . occurred to him to *sift* her on the subject," Wal-

Sieve-cells of Pumpkin (*Cucurbita pepo*), highly magnified.

pole's "Castle of Otranto," v.). **II.** *intr.* To use a sieve; fig., to make close investigation; also, to pass or fall through or as through a sieve.—**sift′er**, *n.*—**sift′ing**, *n.* The act of one who or that which sifts; *pl.*, parts of matter sifted out.

sigh (sī), *v.* [ME. *sighen*, *sihen*, for *sichen* (pret. *sihte*), < AS. *sican*, sigh; prob. ult. imit.] **I.** *intr.* To emit a prolonged and more or less audible respiration after a deeply drawn inspiration, as from sorrow, weariness, relief, yearning, etc.; hence, to yearn or long (as, "She *sighed* for the air, the liberty, the quiet of the country": Jane Austen's "Sense and Sensibility," xxxix.); also, of the wind, etc., to make a sound resembling or suggesting a sigh (as, "The sails did *sigh* like sedge": Coleridge's "Ancient Mariner," v.). **II.** *tr.* To utter or express with a sigh; give forth by sighing; also, to spend (time) in sighing; also, to bring, make, etc., by sighing; also, to lament with sighing (poetic: as, "I *sigh* the lack of many a thing I sought," Shakspere's "Sonnets," xxx.).—**sigh**, *n.* An act or sound of sighing; hence, any similar sound, as of the wind, etc. (as, "the *sigh* of the near pines": Bret Harte's "How Santa Claus Came to Simpson's Bar").—**sigh′er**, *n.*—**sigh′ing-ly**, *adv.*

sight (sīt), *n.* [AS. *sihth* (also *gesihth*) = D. *zicht* = G. *sicht*, sight; from the Teut. verb represented by E. *see²*.] The power or faculty of seeing; the sense whereby objects are perceived with the eye; vision; also, range or field of vision (as, land was in *sight*; to pass out of one's *sight*); also, position affording a view (chiefly with *in* or *within*: as, to come in *sight* of land); also, the act or fact of seeing, or perceiving with the eye (as, "Who ever loved that loved not at first *sight?*" Shakspere's "As You Like It," iii. 5. 82); view; a view or glimpse of something; sometimes (now less frequently), mental view, regard, or estimation (as, "Let my life . . . be precious in thy *sight*": 2 Kings, i. 13); also, look, glance, or gaze (now rare); an observation taken with a surveying or other instrument; an aim with a gun, etc.; also, something seen or to be seen, esp. something striking or remarkable (as, to see the *sights* of the town; "I am fond of *sights* and shows," Galt's "Ayrshire Legatees," v.); a spectacle; something presenting an extraordinary appearance (as, the children, or their clothes, were a *sight*; "You're a perfect *sight* and a fright," Arnold Bennett's "Riceyman Steps," iv. 7); also, appearance† or aspect†; also, a great display, number, or quantity, or a great deal (now colloq.: as, a *sight* of people; "an awful *sight* of money," Mark Twain's "Huckleberry Finn," i.; a *sight* better than before); also, the pupil of the eye (now prov.); *pl.*, spectacles (now prov.); *sing.*, a vizor of a helmet†; also, a device on or used with a surveying instrument, a firearm, etc., serving to guide the eye; also, the open space in a picture-frame, or the part of a picture exposed within this.—**at sight**, as soon as one sees a thing; immediately upon seeing (as, to shoot *at sight*; to read music *at sight*); in *com.*, on presentment (as, a draft payable *at sight*).—**on** or **upon sight**. Same as *at sight*. —**sight unseen**. Same as *unsight*, *unseen* (see *unsight*). —**to know by sight**, to know or recognize (a person or thing) when seen; esp., to know only sufficiently to recognize when seen.—**sight**, *v.* **I.** *tr.* To get sight of (as, "We were overjoyed to *sight* a small ship on the horizon": Stevenson's "Master of Ballantrae," iii.); come in sight of; also, to take a sight or observation of, esp. with an instrument (as, to *sight* a star); also, to direct by means of a sight or sights, as a firearm; also, to provide with sights, or adjust the sights of, as a gun. **II.** *intr.* To take a sight, as in shooting.

sight-ed (sī′ted), *a.* Having sight or vision (as, dim-*sighted*); also, having a sight or sights, as a firearm.

sight=hole (sīt′hōl), *n.* A hole to see through, as in a surveying instrument or the like.

sight-less (sīt′les), *a.* Lacking sight; blind; also, out of sight; invisible; also, unsightly† (as, "full of unpleasing blots and *sightless* stains": Shakspere's "King John," iii. 1. 45).

sight-ly (sīt′li), *a.* Pleasing to the sight; also, affording a fine sight or view (U. S.: as, "There ain't a *sightlier* place in the world for a house," Howells's "Rise of Silas Lapham," ii.).—**sight′li-ness**, *n.*

sight=se-er (sīt′sē″ẻr), *n.* One who goes about to see sights, or objects or places of interest.—**sight″=see″ing**, *n.* and *a.*

sight=wor-thy (sīt′wẻr″ᵺi), *a.* Worthy of being seen, or of being visited as a sight.

sig-il (sij′il), *n.* [L. *sigillum* (usually pl., *sigilla*), small figure, seal, dim. of *signum*, E. *sign*, *n.*: cf. *seal*[1].] A seal or signet; also, an occult sign or mark, as in astrology or magic (as, "Sign and *sigil*, word of power, From the earth raised keep and tower": Scott's "Bridal of Triermain," iii. 16).—**sig-il-la-ry** (sij′i-lạ-ri), *a.* Pertaining to seals.

sig-il-late (sij′i-lāt), *v. t.*; -*lated*, -*lating.* [L. *sigillatus*, pp. of *sigillare*, < *sigillum*: see *sigil*.] To mark with or as with impressions of a seal; also, to close by or as by sealing.—**sigillated earth,** Lemnian earth, because made into cakes stamped with a seal. Cf. *terra sigillata*, under *terra.*—**sig′il-late,** *a.* In *ceram.*, decorated with impressed patterns; in *bot.*, marked as with impressions of a seal.—**sig-il-la′tion** (-lā′shọn), *n.* The act of marking or the state of being marked with or as with a seal; also, a mark or marking so made.

sig-il-log-ra-phy (sij-i-log′rạ-fi), *n.* [L. *sigillum*, seal, sigil: see -*graphy.*] The study or science of seals.—**sig-il-log′ra-pher,** *n.*

sig-ma (sig′mạ), *n.* [L., < Gr. σίγμα.] The eighteenth letter (Σ, σ, s, = English S, s) of the Greek alphabet, in its uncial form resembling the letter C; also, something shaped like C or like S. In Greek the form s is used at the end of a word, the form σ in any other position, as in στάσις, a standing.—**sig′mate** (-māt), *a.* Having the form of the Greek sigma or of the letter S.—**sig′ma-tism** (-mạ-tizm), *n.* Marked recurrence of the letter *s* or the *s*-sound.—**sig′moid,** *a.* [Gr. σιγμοειδής: see -*oid.*] Shaped like the uncial sigma or the letter C; also, shaped like the letter S (as, the *sigmoid* flexure of the colon, its last curve before terminating in the rectum); hence, pertaining to the sigmoid flexure of the colon (as, the *sigmoid* artery, which supplies this flexure). Also **sig-moi′dal.**—**sig-moi′dal-ly,** *adv.*

sign (sīn), *n.* [OF. F. *signe*, < L. *signum*, mark, token, indication, ensign, signal, image, figure, seal, constellation: cf. *sigil.*] Any mark, impress, or the like used or serving to convey a particular meaning; a symbol; esp., a conventional mark, figure, or symbol used technically instead of the word or words which it represents, as in mathematics, music, etc.; also, a badge†, ensign†, or banner†; a characteristic figure or representation attached to or placed before an inn or shop as a means of distinguishing it or attracting attention to it (as, "a little tavern with a large brass telescope for *sign*," Stevenson's "Treasure Island," viii.; "a note addressed to John Silver, at the *sign* of the 'Spy-glass,'" Stevenson's "Treasure Island," viii.); now, usually, an inscribed board,

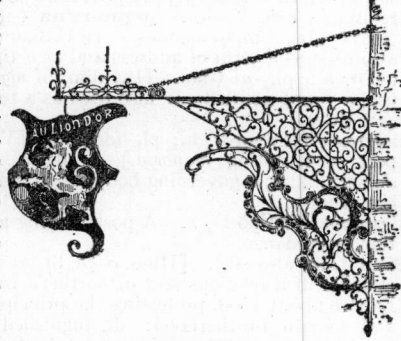

Swinging Sign, style of 18th century.

plate, space, or the like serving for information, guidance, advertisement, etc., as on or before a building or a place of business, or along a street or road; also, a motion or gesture intended to express or convey an idea (as, "I . . . talked with them by *signs*," Defoe's "Robinson Crusoe," i. 3; "Then Hudibras, with face and hand, Made *signs* for silence," Butler's "Hudibras," ii. 2); a signal (as, "Mark Antony, shall we give *sign* of battle?" Shakspere's "Julius Cæsar," v. 1. 23); also, a token or indication (as, "The exile of Gaveston was the *sign* of the barons' triumph": Green's "Short Hist. of the Eng. People," iv. 5); sometimes, a trace or vestige; specif., the trace or trail of wild animals, etc. (as, "These game paths . . . showed very little fresh goat *sign*": Roosevelt's "Ranch Life and the Hunting-Trail," xii.); also, an indication of a coming event (as, "Seamen much believe in *signs*": Cowper's "Tale," 61); an omen or portent; also, a miraculous act or occurrence indicative of divine power or authority (as, "Many wonders and *signs*

were done by the apostles": Acts, ii. 43); also, in *astron.*, any of the twelve divisions of the zodiac, each denoted by the name of a constellation or its symbol, and each (because of the precession of the equinoxes) now containing the constellation west of the one from which it took its name (see *zodiac*).—**sign manual,** an autograph signature, esp. that of a sovereign or magistrate on an official document; fig., a distinctively individual sign, stamp, or quality.—**sign,** *v.* [OF. F. *signer*, < L. *signare*, < *signum*.] **I.** *tr.* To mark with a sign, esp. the sign of the cross (as, "There sprung A light that *sign'd* the heav'ns," Dryden's tr. Virgil's "Æneid," ix. 130; "We receive this Child into the congregation of Christ's flock; and do *sign* him with the sign of the Cross," Book of Common Prayer, Public Baptism of Infants); cross (one's self); also, to mark or impress (something) as a sign; make the sign of (the cross: as, "He pray'd, and *sign'd* the cross between," Scott's "Lady of the Lake," iii. 4); also, to affix a signature to (a document, etc.); write as a signature (as, to *sign* one's name); designate (one's self) in a signature; dispose of by affixing one's signature to a document (with *away*, etc.); engage by written agreement (as, a baseball club *signs* a new player); also, to communicate by a sign (as, "He . . . *signed* a mournful greeting to Tressilian": Scott's "Kenilworth," xii.); direct by a sign (as, "She was on the threshold *signing* me to enter": Stevenson's "Master of Ballantrae," v.); also, to indicate or betoken. **II.** *intr.* To write one's signature, as in token of agreement or obligation or of the receipt of something (as, "If you'll hand me up a jacket and pair of shoes I'll *sign* for them": G. W. Cable's "Cavalier," v.); also, to make a sign or signal (as, "Louis . . . *signed* to Dunois . . . to come up," Scott's "Quentin Durward," ix.; "She . . . *signed* to the driver to stop," L. Merrick's "Worldlings," xvii.).—**to sign off,** to announce the end of a radiobroadcasting program, or a cessation of radiobroadcasting until some future time: as, Station XYZ is now *signing off* until eight o'clock this evening.

sig-nal (sig′nạl), *n.* [OF. F. *signal*, < ML. *signale*, < L. *signum*, E. *sign*, *n.*] A sign† or symbol†; also, a token or indication (as, "in *signal* of my love to thee": Shakspere's "1 Henry VI.," ii. 4. 121); also, something, as a gesture, action, light, sound, or object, used or serving to give warning, information, direction, etc.; specif., *pl.*, the impulses, waves, sounds, etc., transmitted or received in telegraphy, radiotelephony, etc.; also, *sing.*, anything agreed upon or understood as the occasion for concerted action (as, "They were to rise at a *signal* and massacre all their Protestant neighbours": Macaulay's "Hist. of Eng.," ii.); hence, an exciting cause (as, this tyrannous act was the *signal* for revolt).—**Signal Corps,** a branch of the military service of the U. S., concerned with all methods of signaling, and having charge of communication by means of telegraphs, telephones, wireless apparatus, etc.—**signal service,** an organized system of service concerned with communicating by means of signals, esp. in the military service; the organization or body having charge of such a system.—**sig′nal,** *v.*; -*naled* or -*nalled*, -*naling* or -*nalling.* **I.** *tr.* To make a signal or signals to; direct by a signal or signals (as, "The girl came out . . . *signalling* me to enter": Watts-Dunton's "Aylwin," xii. 3); also, to make known or announce by a signal or signals (as, "The Foas . . . had been *signalling* to her and Audrey an intention to meet them in the foyer," Arnold Bennett's "Lion's Share," xliii.; "The whistle blew, *signalling* that this episode was concluded," Tarkington's "Magnificent Ambersons," ix.); hence, to mark out clearly; signalize; also, to provide with signals, as a railroad. **II.** *intr.* To make communication by a signal or signals.—**sig′nal,** *a.* [Cf. F. *signalé*, signalized, signal, pp. of *signaler*, signalize.] Conspicuous or notable (as, "I had an opportunity of doing his Majesty . . . a most *signal* service," Swift's "Gulliver's Travels," i. 5; "a *signal* exploit," Parkman's "Oregon Trail," vi.); also, serving as a sign.—**sig′nal-er, sig′nal-ler,** *n.*—**sig′nal-ize,** *v.*; -*ized*, -*izing.* **I.** *tr.* To make signal; render conspicuous or notable (as, to *signalize* one's reign by beneficent reforms); distinguish (one's self: as, "He *signalised* himself . . . by holding a fort with thirty men against a whole corps," Besant's "Coligny," vii.); be a conspicuous feature or circumstance of (as, many reforms *signalized* his reign); also, to point out or indicate particu-larly; also, to make signals to (obs. or rare). **II.** *intr.* To make signals. [Obs. or rare.]—**sig′nal-ly**, *adv.*—**sig′nal-man** (-man), *n.*; pl. *-men.* A man employed in signaling, as in the army or navy or on a railroad.—**sig′nal-ment**, *n.* [F. *signalement.*] A description of a person, as for police purposes. [A French use.]

sig-na-ta-ry (sig′na̤-tā̤-ri), *n.*; pl. *-ries* (-riz). [F. *signataire.*] A signatory.

sig-nate (sig′nāt), *a.* [L. *signatus*, pp. of *signare*, E. *sign, v.*] Distinguished in some way; in *zoöl.*, having spots or marks resembling letters.

sig-na-to-ry (sig′na̤-tō̤-ri). [L. *signatorius*, < *signare*, E. *sign, v.*] **I.** *a.* That has signed, or has joined in signing, a document: as, the *signatory* powers to a treaty. **II.** *n.*; pl. *-ries* (-riz). A signer, or one of the signers, of a document, as a treaty.

sig-na-ture (sig′na̤-tṳr), *n.* [F. *signature*, < ML. *signatura*, < L. *signare*, E. *sign, v.*] A person's name, or a mark repre-senting it, as signed or written by himself or by deputy, as in subscribing a letter or other document; also, the act of signing a document; also, a distinctive marking or other characteristic of a plant, mineral, or other natural object, formerly supposed to indicate its qualities, esp. for medicinal purposes; in general, a distinguishing mark; a stamp or impression (also *fig.*: as, "Goodness celestial, whose broad *signature* Is on the universe," Cary's tr. Dante's "Paradise," vii. 103); also, an image or figure (now rare); in *printing*, one of a series of letters or numbers placed by a printer at the foot of the first page (and sometimes of certain of the succeeding pages) of every sheet (as folded) of a book, etc., to aid the binder in arranging the sheets; a sheet as thus marked, esp. when folded; in *music*, a sign or set of signs at the beginning of a staff to indicate the key or the time of a piece; in *phar.*, that part of a prescription which gives the directions to be marked on the container of the medicine.—**sig′na-ture**, *v. t.*; *-tured*, *-turing.* To sign one's name to; put a signature on.

sign=board (sīn′bōrd), *n.* A board or the like bearing a device, inscription, notice, or the like, serving for informa-tion, guidance, advertisement, etc.

sign-er (sī′nėr), *n.* One who signs; esp., one who writes his name as a signature, as in token of agreement, obligation, etc. (as, to obtain *signers* to a petition; the 56 *signers* of the Declaration of Independence).

sig-net (sig′net), *n.* [OF. *signet*, signet (F. book-mark), < ML. *signetum*, dim. of L. *signum*, seal, E. *sign, n.*] A small seal, as in a finger-ring; esp., a small official seal; specif., a smaller official seal formerly used by the sovereigns of England and Scotland for private purposes and for certain official documents; also, the impression made by a signet or seal; any impressed stamp; in general, a mark or sign (as, "I fancied that this smile . . . was the devil's *signet* on the Professor": Hawthorne's "Blithedale Romance," xviii.); also, a signal† (cf. *sennet*).—**writer to the signet.** See under *writer.*—**sig′net=ring**, *n.* A finger-ring containing a signet.

sig-ni-fi-a-ble (sig′ni-fī-a̤-bl), *a.* That may be signified.

sig-nif-i-cance (sig-nif′i-kans), *n.* The quality of being significant or having a meaning; hence, meaning or import; also, importance or consequence. Also **sig-nif′i-can-cy.**

sig-nif-i-cant (sig-nif′i-kant). [L. *significans* (-ant-), ppr. of *significare*, E. *signify.*] **I.** *a.* Signifying something; having or expressing a meaning; expressive or indicative (*of*); esp., having a special or covert meaning (as, a *sig-nificant* gesture or smile); meaning, expressive, or suggestive; also, important, or of consequence (as, "I thought I was presently to go out into a larger and quite important world and do *significant* things there": H. G. Wells's "Tono-Bungay," i. 3. § 2). **II.** *n.* Something significant; a sign; an indication: as, "Since you are tongue-tied and so loath to speak, In dumb *significants* proclaim your thoughts" (Shakspere's "1 Henry VI.," ii. 4. 26). [Archaic.]—**sig-nif′i-cant-ly,** *adv.*

sig-ni-fi-ca-tion (sig″ni-fi-kā′shon), *n.* [OF. F. *significa-tion*, < L. *significatio(n-)*, < *significare*, E. *signify.*] The act or fact of signifying; indication or intimation of some-thing; possession or conveyance of a meaning; hence,

meaning, as of a sign, symbol, word, etc.; import; sense; also, importance, consequence, or significance (now prov. Eng.); also, a thing that signifies something†; a sign† or token†.—**sig-nif′i-ca-tive** (-nif′i-ka̤-tiv), *a.* [OF. F. *signi-ficatif*, < LL. *significativus.*] Serving to signify; having a signification; also, significant or suggestive (as, "Egmont received another most *significative* and mysterious warn-ing": Motley's "Dutch Republic," iii. 1).

sig-nif-i-ca-tor (sig-nif′i-kā-tor), *n.* [ML.] One who or that which signifies or indicates something; in *astrol.*, the planet that rules a house.—**sig-nif′i-ca-to-ry** (-ka̤-tō̤-ri), *a.* [LL. *significatorius.*] Serving to signify; significative.

sig-nif-ics (sig-nif′iks), *n.* [From *significance.*] The science or the systematic study of the exact significance of terms in any department of education or learning.

sig-ni-fi-er (sig′ni-fī-ėr), *n.* One who or that which signifies.

sig-ni-fy (sig′ni-fī), *v.*; *-fied, -fying.* [OF. F. *signifier*, < L. *significare*, < *signum*, sign, indication, + *facere*, make.] **I.** *tr.* To make known by signs, speech, or action (as, "With courteous brevity, I *signify* my indifference to contraband trade," Carlyle's "Sartor Resartus," ii. 8; to *signify* one's assent by a nod); indicate; intimate; also, to be a sign or indication of; represent, as a symbol does; denote or mean, as a word does; betoken or portend, as an omen does. **II.** *intr.* To have import; be of importance or consequence; matter: often with adverbial adjunct: as, the precise hour does not *signify*, or *signifies* little; "Pray now — not that it *signifies* — what might the gentleman say?" (Sheridan's "Critic," i. 1); "Pooh, what *signifies* what I am?" (God-win's "Caleb Williams," xxviii.).

si′gnior, *n.* See *signor.*

si-gnor (sē′nyor, It. sē-nyôr′), *n.* [It., reduced form of *signore*, < L. *senior*: see *senior* and *seignior.*] In Italian use, a title of respect used before a man's name, equivalent to the English 'Mr.'; also, in loose rendering of Italian use, same as *signore.*—**si-gno-ra** (sē-nyō′rä), *n.*; pl. *-re* (-rä). [It.] In Italian use, a lady: also used as a term of address and as a title.—**si-gno′re** (-rä), *n.*; pl. *-ri* (-rē). [It.: see *signor.*] In Italian use, a lord; a nobleman; a gentleman; as a term of address (without a proper name following), sir. See also *signor.*—**si-gno-ri-a** (sē-nyō-rē′ä), *n.* [It., = OF. *seignorie*, E. *seigniory.*] A governing body in old Italian republics, esp. Venice.—**si-gno-ri′na** (-rē′nä), *n.*; pl. *-ne* (-nä). [It., dim. of *signora.*] In Italian use, a young lady: also used as a term of address and as a title.—**si-gno-ri′no** (-nō), *n.*; pl. *-ni* (-nē). [It., dim. of *signore.*] In Italian use, a young gentleman: also used as a term of address and as a title.

si-gnor-y (sē′nyor-i), *n.*; pl. *-ies* (-iz). [Var. of *seigniory*, in part representing *signoria.*] Lordship or rule; also, a domain; also, a governing body, as in old Italian republics, esp. Venice.

sign=post (sīn′pōst), *n.* A post bearing a sign for informa-tion or guidance.

Sikh (sēk, also sik). [Hind. *Sikh*, lit. 'disciple.'] **I.** *n.* A member of a religious sect of northern India, founded near Lahore about 1500, professing the principles of monotheism and human brotherhood: distinguished as fighters, and furnishing a notable contingent to the British Indian army. **II.** *a.* Of or pertaining to the Sikhs.—**Sikh′ism,** *n.* The religious system and practices of the Sikhs.

si-lage (sī′lāj), *n.* [See *silo.*] Fodder preserved in a silo; ensilage.—**si′lage,** *v. t.*; *-laged, -laging.* To make silage of; ensile.

si-le-na-ceous (sī-lē̤-nā′shius), *a.* [NL. *Silene*, a genus of catchflies; origin uncertain.] Belonging to the *Silenaceæ* (or *Caryophyllaceæ*), a family of plants including the catch-flies, campions, pinks, chickweeds, sandworts, soapwort, ragged-robin, etc.

si-lence (sī′lens), *n.* [OF. F. *silence*, < L. *silentium*, < *silens*: see *silent.*] The state or fact of being silent; for-bearance of speech or utterance (as, "*Silence* gives consent": Goldsmith's "Good-Natured Man," ii.); muteness; reti-cence; omission of mention (as, to pass over a matter in *silence*); absence of any sound or noise, or stillness (as, "The music all is ground, And *silence*, like a poultice, comes To heal the blows of sound": Holmes's "Music-Grinders"); a state or period of being silent or still (as, "All talk died . . .

---

fat, fāte, fär, fȧll, ȧsk, fāre; net, mē, hėr; pin, pīne; not, nōte, mȯve, nôr; up, lūte, pu̇ll; oi, oil; ou, out; (lightened) aviȧry, ēlect, agȯny, intȯ, ūnite; (obscured) erraṇt, operȧ, ardeṇt, actoṛ, natūre; ch, chip; g, go; th, thin; ᴛʜ, then; y, you:

Then a long *silence* came upon the hall," Tennyson's "Pelleas and Ettarre," 596; "a cry between the *silences*," Whittier's "Questions of Life"); also, a silent or still place (as, "glad to escape from the noisy dusty city into the sweet green *silences*": W. H. Hudson's "Far Away and Long Ago," viii.); also, fig., the state or sphere of existence beyond the clamor or turmoil of this life (as, "the eternal *Silence*," Wordsworth's "Intimations of Immortality," ix.: often in *pl.*); in *music*, a rest.—**tower of silence.** See under *tower*[2], *n.*—Be silent! cease from all noise!—**si'lence,** *v. t.*; *-lenced, -lencing.* To put or bring to silence; restrain from speech or utterance, or from the expression of opinion, etc.; reduce to silence in a controversy, as by an unanswerable argument; restrain from making noise of any kind; stop the noise of; still; also, to stop or repress (utterances, sound, noise, etc.); also, to put to rest (doubts, scruples, etc.); quiet (the conscience, etc.); quell (opposition, etc.); *milit.*, to still (enemy guns, batteries, gun-fire, etc.), as by a more effective fire.—**si'lence=cloth,** *n.* A sheet of thick cotton cloth or the like placed under the linen cloth on a dining-table.—**si'len-cer** (-len-sèr), *n.* One who or that which silences; specif., the muffler on an internal-combustion engine; also, a device for deadening the report of a firearm.

si-lent (sī'lent), *a.* [L. *silens* (*silent-*), ppr. of *silere*, be silent.] Refraining from speech or utterance (as, "Be *silent*, boy; I profit not by thy talk": Shakspere's "Troilus and Cressida," v. 1. 16); speechless, mute, or dumb; taciturn or reticent; omitting mention of something, as in a narrative; also, making no sound of any kind (as, "The grasshopper is *silent* in the grass," Tennyson's "Œnone," 25; the bells have become *silent*; "the *silent* wheels of time," Burns's "To Miss Logan, with Beattie's Poems"); noiseless, quiet, or still; also, characterized by absence of speech or sound (as, a *silent* prayer; *silent* tears; a *silent* house); tacit (as, a *silent* assent); not sounded or pronounced (as, a *silent* letter, such as the *b* in *doubt*); fig., taking no open or active part in something (as, a *silent* partner, see *partner, n.*; the *silent* vote, see phrase below); inactive or quiescent, as a volcano.—**silent drama,** the drama as presented in moving pictures.—**silent system,** a system of prison discipline that imposes complete silence on the prisoners.—**silent treatment,** the maintaining of complete silence toward a person by those about him as a form of ostracism or a mode of expressing disapproval.—**silent vote,** the collective vote of those who take no avowed part in a campaign; sometimes, the vote represented by the number of persons qualified to vote who do not vote.

si-len-ti-a-ry (sī-len'shi-ā-ri), *n.*; pl. *-ries* (-riz). [LL. *silentiarius*, < L. *silentium*, E. *silence*.] One who practises or advocates silence, esp. from religious motives; also, an official appointed to enforce silence, as in a public assembly; specif., an officer of the Byzantine court charged with maintaining silence within the imperial palace, and often acting as confidential adviser or agent.

si-lent-ly (sī'lent-li), *adv.* In a silent manner; without speech or sound; mutely; noiselessly.—**si'lent-ness,** *n.*

Si-le-nus (sī-lē'nus), *n.*; pl. *-ni* (-nī). [L., < Gr. Σειληνός.] In *Gr. myth.*, the foster-father of Bacchus, and leader of the satyrs; also [*l. c.*], a satyr.

si-le-sia (si-lē'shä or -shiä), *n.* [From *Silesia*: see *Silesian*.] A lightweight, smooth-finished, twilled cotton fabric, used esp. for linings.

Si-le-sian (si-lē'shạn or -shiạn). **I.** *a.* Of or pertaining to Silesia, a region of central Europe, in eastern Germany, Czechoslovakia, and Poland. **II.** *n.* A native or inhabitant of Silesia.

si-lex (sī'leks), *n.* [L., stone, flint.] Silica.

sil-hou-ette (sil-ö-et'), *n.* [From Étienne de *Silhouette*, French controller of finances in 1759.] An out-

Silenus. — Marble in the Glyptothek, Munich.

line portrait or representation filled in with black or some other single color; an outline portrait cut out of black paper; hence, a dark image outlined against a lighter background (as, "the cat's dark *silhouette* on the wall": Whittier's "Snow-Bound").—**sil-hou-ette'**, *v. t.*; *-etted, -etting.* To represent or show in or as in a silhouette: as, "a view of the distant western hills *silhouetted* in black against a flaming western sky" (W. Churchill's "Modern Chronicle," i. 7).—**sil-hou-et'tist,** *n.* A maker of silhouettes.

Silhouette of George Washington.

sil-i-ca (sil'i-kạ), *n.* [NL., < L. *silex* (*silic-*), stone, flint.] Silicon dioxide, SiO_2, a hard, white or colorless substance occurring in nature as quartz, etc.—**sil'i-cate** (-kāt), *n.* In *chem.*, a salt of silicic acid.—**si-li-ceous** (si-lish'us), *a.* [L. *siliceus*, < *silex*.] Containing, consisting of, or resembling silica.—**si-li'cic** (-lis'ik), *a.* In *chem.*, of or pertaining to silica; noting any of certain acids regarded as derivatives of silica.—**sil'i-cide** (-sīd or -sid), *n.* In *chem.*, a compound of silicon with another element or a radical.—**si-li-cif'er-ous** (-sif'e-rus), *a.* [See *-ferous*.] Yielding or containing silica; united with silica.—**si-li'ci-fy** (-lis'i-fī), *v. t. or i.*; *-fied, -fying.* [See *-fy*.] To convert or be converted into silica; make or become siliceous.—**si-li″ci-fi-ca'tion** (-fi-kā'shọn), *n.*—**si-li'cious** (-lish'us), *a.* Same as *siliceous*.

si-li-ci-um (si-lish'i-um), *n.* [NL.] Earlier name for *silicon*.

sil-i-cle (sil'i-kl), *n.* [L. *silicula*, dim. of *siliqua*, pod.] In *bot.*, a short siliqua.

sil-i-con (sil'i-kọn), *n.* [NL., < *silica*.] Chem. sym., Si; at. wt., 28.3. A non-metallic element, having amorphous and crystalline forms, occurring in the combined state in minerals and rocks and constituting more than one fourth of the earth's crust: used in steel-making, etc.

sil-i-co-sis (sil-i-kō'sis), *n.* [NL., < *silica*.] In *pathol.*, a disease of the lungs due to the inhaling of siliceous particles, as by stone-cutters.—**sil-i-cot'ic** (-kot'ik). **I.** *a.* Pertaining to or affected with silicosis. **II.** *n.* A person affected with silicosis.

si-lic-u-lose (si-lik'ū-lōs), *a.* [NL. *siliculosus*, < L. *silicula*, E. *silicle*.] In *bot.*, bearing silicles; also, having the form or appearance of a silicle.

sil-i-qua (sil'i-kwạ), *n.*; pl. *-quæ* (-kwē). [L., pod; hence F. *silique*.] In *bot.*, the long two-valved seed-vessel or pod of brassicaceous plants. Also **si-lique** (si-lēk').—**sil'i-quose** (-kwōs), *a.* Bearing siliquæ; also, resembling a siliqua or silicle.

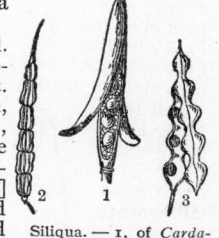

Siliqua. — 1, of *Cardamine bulbosa* (a cress); 2, of *Raphanus raphanistrum* (jointed charlock); 3, of *Heliophila crithmifolia* (of South Africa).

silk (silk), *n.* [AS. *sioloc, seoloc*, = Icel. *silki* = Sw. and Dan. *silke*, silk; appar. < LL. *sericum*, silk, prop. neut. of L. *sericus* (Gr. σηρικός), silken, special use of *Sericus* (Gr. Σηρικός, of or pertaining to an Asiatic people (L. *Seres*, Gr. Σῆρες), prob. the Chinese, from whom silk was obtained.] The fine, soft, lustrous fiber obtained from the cocoon of the silkworm, used for making thread, textile fabrics, etc.; thread, or a particular kind of thread, made of this fiber (as, to stitch seams with *silk*; sewing-*silk*; embroidery *silks*); cloth or any fabric or material made of this fiber (as, a square of *silk*; "The *silks* which had been closely woven in China were sometimes unravelled by the Phœnician women, and the precious materials were multiplied by . . . the intermixture of linen threads," Gibbon's "Decline and Fall of the Roman Empire," xl.); a garment of such material (as, "The little lady . . . had on, ma'am, rather an old black *silk*": Mrs. Gaskell's "Cranford," viii.); specif., such material, or the gown of such material, worn distinctively by a king's or queen's counsel at the English bar (as, to take *silk*: see phrase following); hence, a king's or queen's counsel (Eng.); also, some similar fiber or filamentous matter; a silk-like fiber produced by some other animal, as certain spiders; an artificial material resembling and used like silk, manufactured for commercial purposes, as a prod-uct ('fiber silk') made from cellulose; the hair-like styles on an ear of maize. — **to take silk,** to assume the silk gown, and hence to take the rank, of a king's or queen's counsel at the English bar: as, "He has made a big practice, and has *taken silk*" (L. Merrick's "Worldlings," iii.). — **silk,** *a.* Consisting or made of silk; silken; also, resembling silk; silky; also, of or pertaining to silk. — **silk,** *v. i.* Of maize, to be in the course of forming silk.

silk-a-line, silk-a-lene (sil′ka-lēn), *n.* [Arbitrary forma-tion based on *silk.*] A soft, thin cotton fabric with a smooth finish, and often with a printed floral or other design, used for curtains, quilt-coverings, etc.

silk=cot-ton (silk′kot′n), *n.* The silky covering of the seeds of certain tropical trees ('silk-cotton trees') of the family *Bombacaceæ:* used for stuffing cushions, etc. Cf. *kapok.*

silk-en (sil′kn), *a.* [AS. *seolocen.*] Consisting or made of silk; also, clad in silk; also, abounding in silk (poetic: as, "*silken* Samar-cand," Keats's "Eve of St. Agnes," xxx.); also, resem-bling or suggesting silk, as in luster, smoothness, soft-ness, richness, etc.; silky; smooth; soft; ingratiating; elegant; luxurious. — **silk′-en-ly,** *adv.*

silk-i-ly (sil′ki-li), *adv.* In a silky manner. — **silk′i-ness,** *n.*

silk′o-line, silk′o-lene, *n.* See *silkaline.*

silk=stock-ing (silk′stok′-ing). **I.** *n.* One who wears silk stockings; a person of the elegant or luxurious class; an aristocrat. **II.** *a.* Wearing silk stockings; ele-gant; luxurious; aristocratic: as, the *silk-stocking* gentry; *silk-stocking* reformers or politicians. Cf. *kid-glove.*

silk-weed (silk′wēd), *n.* Any milkweed of the family *Asclepiadaceæ:* so called from the silky down in the pod.

silk-worm (silk′wẽrm), *n.* [AS. *seolcwyrm.*] The larva or caterpillar of any of various moths (esp. *Bombyx mori*) which spin a fine, soft filament (silk) to form a cocoon, in which they are inclosed while in the chrysalis state. — **silk′worm=moth,** *n.* Any moth whose larva is a silk-worm.

silk-y (sil′-ki), *a.;* compar. *silkier,* superl. *silkiest.* Of, like, or suggesting silk; lustrous or glossy; smooth; soft; suave or ingratiating; also, covered with fine, soft, closely set hairs, as a leaf.

sill (sil), *n.* [AS. *syll* = Icel. and Sw. *syll* = G. *schwelle,* sill.] A horizontal timber, block, or the like, serving as a foundation of a wall, house, etc.; also, the horizontal piece or member beneath an opening, esp. a window or door opening.

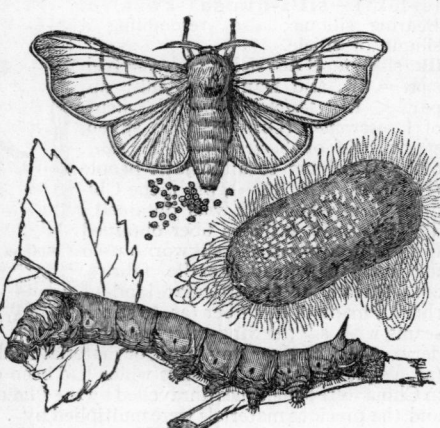

silk-stocking (silk′stok′- Pod of a Silk-cotton Tree (*Ceiba pentan-dra*).

Silkworm (*Bombyx mori*), about natural size.

sil-la-bub, syl-la-bub (sil′a-bub), *n.* [Origin obscure.] A dish made of milk or cream mixed with wine, cider, or the like so as to form a curd, and often sweetened and flavored.

sil-li-man-ite (sil′i-man-īt), *n.* [From Benjamin *Silliman* (1779–1864), American scientist.] A mineral consisting of a silicate of aluminium, of the same chemical composition as andalusite and cyanite, and occurring in long, slender crystal-line needles or compact, fibrous masses: valuable commer-cially as a refractory or fire-resisting material.

sil-ly (sil′i). [Var. of earlier *seely,* ME. *seli,* happy, blessed, good, innocent, helpless, < AS. *(ge)sælig* (= D. *zalig* = G. *selig*), happy, blessed, < *sæl,* happiness.] **I.** *a.;* compar. *sillier,* superl. *silliest.* Good, innocent, guileless, or harmless, as persons or animals (esp. sheep: as, "Gives not the haw-thorn-bush a sweeter shade To shepherds looking on their *silly* sheep?" Shakspere's "3 Henry VI.," ii. 5. 43: now archaic or prov.); also, helpless, weak, or frail, as persons, animals, or things (as, "After long stormes . . . With which my *silly* barke was tossed sore," Spenser's "Amoretti," lxiii.: now Sc. and north. Eng.); feeble or sickly (as, "She was but of a *silly* constitution," Galt's "Annals of the Parish," i.: Sc. and north. Eng.); deserving of pity or sympathy, or poor (as, "The *silly* owner of the goods Weeps over them," Shakspere's "2 Henry VI.," i. 1. 225: now Sc. and north. Eng.); also, plain, simple, or homely (as, "a fourth man, in a *silly* habit," Shakspere's "Cymbeline," v. 3. 86: obs. or archaic); simple-minded, unsophisticated, or ignorant (obs. or archaic); now, esp., deficient in strength of intellect or in good, strong common sense, or showing such deficiency, as persons, the mind, actions, speech, etc. (as, a pretty woman, but undeniably *silly*; *Silly* Billy, a nickname given to William IV. of England; a *silly* simper or expression; "Edwin's own suggestions never seemed very brilliant . . . but they were never *silly,*" Arnold Bennett's "Clayhanger," ii. 3); weakly foolish or stupid; opposed to or remote from sound or sober sense (as, a *silly* book; *silly* games; the *silly* season, in newspaper use, a season when there is little real news and its place is supplied by any available matter, however trivial); often, absurdly foolish, or senseless (as, "Nonsense, Effie. You must . . . Don't be *silly,*" A. S. M. Hutchinson's "If Winter Comes," iv. 2; "They would think she was lost, or run over, or something *silly!*" Galsworthy's "Saint's Progress," i. 6); hence, absurd or ridiculous (as, "when I saw colliers unloading, watched the workers in the hold filling up *silly* little sacks": H. G. Wells's "Tono-Bungay," i. 2. § 1); also, feeble-minded or imbecile; also, stunned or dazed (colloq.: as, to knock one *silly*). **II.** *n.;* pl. *sillies* (-iz). A silly person: as, "You're such a *silly*" (George Eliot's "Mill on the Floss," i. 5). [Colloq.] — **sil′li-ly,** *adv.* — **sil′li-ness,** *n.*

si-lo (sī′lō), *n.;* pl. *-los* (-lōz). [Sp., < L. *sirus,* < Gr. σιρός, pit to keep grain in.] A pit or underground chamber for storing grain, etc.; specif., a pit or chamber, now commonly an air-proof tower-like structure, in which green fodder, usually tightly packed and undergoing slight (or greater) fermen-tation, is preserved for fu-ture use as silage or ensilage. — **si′lo,** *v. t.;* -*loed,* -*loing.* To put into or preserve in a silo; ensile.

sil-phid (sil′fid). [NL. *Silphidæ,* pl., < Gr. σίλφη, beetle, bookworm.] **I.** *n.* Any of the *Silphidæ,* a fam-ily of clavicorn beetles which live mainly on carrion. **II.** *a.* Belonging or pertaining to the *Silphidæ.*

Silo.

silt (silt), *n.* [ME. *cylte;* origin uncertain.] Earthy matter, sand, or the like carried by moving or running water and deposited as a sediment: as, a harbor choked up with *silt.* — **silt,** *v.* **I.** *intr.* To be-come filled or choked up with silt; also, to drift or pass as or like silt. **II.** *tr.* To fill or choke up with or as with silt. — **silt′y,** *a.* Consisting of, containing, or resembling silt.

Si-lu-ri-an (si-lū'ri-ạn). [L. *Silures*, pl.: see def.] **I.** *a.* Of or pertaining to the Silures, an ancient British people, or their country, in southeastern Wales; in *geol.*, noting or pertaining to the geological period or the system of rocks which precedes the Devonian. **II.** *n.* In *geol.*, the Silurian period or system.

si-lu-rid (si-lū'rid). [NL. *Siluridæ*, pl., < L. *silurus*, < Gr. σίλουρος, kind of river-fish.] **I.** *n.* Any of the *Siluridæ*, or catfish family, comprising chiefly fresh-water fishes with long barbels and without true scales, and including many species used for food. **II.** *a.* Belonging or pertaining to the *Siluridæ*.—**si-lu'ri-dan** (-ri-dạn), *a.* and *n.*—**si-lu'roid.** [See *-oid*.] **I.** *a.* Catfish-like; of the catfish family (*Siluridæ*). **II.** *n.* A siluroid fish.

sil'va, sil'van, etc. See *sylva, sylvan,* etc.

sil-ver (sil'vėr), *n.* [AS. *siolfor, seolfor,* = D. *zilver* = G. *silber* = Icel. *silfr* = Goth. *silubr,* silver.] Chem. sym., Ag (see *argentum*); at. wt., 107.88; sp. gr., 10.42 to 10.57. A white ductile metallic element, used for making coins, ornaments, table utensils, etc.; also, coin made of this metal; money; also, silverware; also, something resembling this metal in color, luster, etc. (as, "O'er the friths that branch and spread Their sleeping *silver* thro' the hills": Tennyson's "In Memoriam," Conclusion); also, the color of silver, a lustrous grayish white or whitish gray (as, "noting the touch of *silver* in his dark hair": Galsworthy's "Dark Flower," ii. 8).—**German silver.** See under *German*², *a.*—**oxidized silver.** See under *oxidized.*—**sil'ver,** *a.* Consisting or made of silver; also, producing or yielding silver; also, of or pertaining to silver; also, resembling silver; having the whiteness or luster of silver (as, "the *silver* waves": Shakspere's "Comedy of Errors," iii. 2. 48); white or gray with age (as, "O, blessings . . . on his *silver* hair!" Tennyson's "May Queen," Conclusion, 13); having a clear, ringing, or melodious sound suggesting that of silver (as, "And let your *silver* chime Move in melodious time": Milton's "On the Morning of Christ's Nativity," 128); fig., eloquent or persuasive (as, a *silver* tongue).—**silver age,** the second of the mythological ages of mankind, inferior to the first or golden age, and a period of luxury and impiety (see *ages in mythology,* under *age, n.*); hence, in general, a period following, and inferior to, a so-called 'golden age.'—**silver certificate.** See under *certificate, n.*—**silver hake.** See *hake.*—**silver lining,** of a cloud, a silvery or bright side existing even though turned away from those who see only the dark side (chiefly in fig. use): as, "Was I deceived, or did a sable cloud Turn forth her *silver lining* on the night?" (Milton's "Comus," 222); "The clouds of ennui themselves for you have *silver linings*" (Mallock's "New Republic," i. 4).—**silver nitrate,** in *chem.,* a salt obtained by treating silver with nitric acid, and appearing in commerce as colorless crystals or white fused or molded masses (lunar caustic): used in photography, medicine, etc. —**silver screen,** the screen upon which moving pictures are shown. [Colloq.]—**silver standard.** See *standard, n.* —**sil'ver,** *v.* **I.** *tr.* To coat with silver, or with some substance resembling silver; also, to give a silvery color or luster to (as, "There is the sea . . . with the full moon *silvering* the waves": Marryat's "Mr. Midshipman Easy," xxiv.); often, to turn (the hair, etc.) gray or white. **II.** *intr.* To take on the color or luster of silver; become silvery: as, "Over Enoch's early-*silvering* head The . . . seasons came and went" (Tennyson's "Enoch Arden," 618).

sil-ver-bell (sil'vėr-bel), *n.* Any of the handsome North American shrubs or small trees, with white bell-shaped flowers, constituting the styracaceous genus *Mohrodendron* (or *Halesia*). Often called *silverbell-tree.*

sil-ver-ber-ry (sil'vėr-ber″i), *n.;* pl. *-berries* (-iz). A

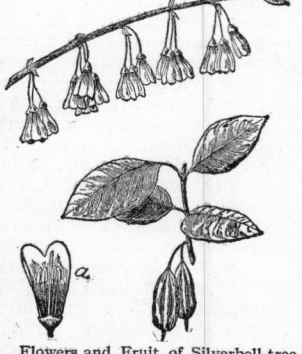

Flowers and Fruit of Silverbell-tree (*Mohrodendron carolinum*). — *a,* flower cut longitudinally.

shrub, *Elæagnus argentea*, of the northern central part of North America, having silvery leaves and flowers and silvery edible berries.

sil-ver-fish (sil'vėr-fish), *n.* A variety of the goldfish, *Carassius auratus*, of a white or silvery color; any of various other silvery fishes, as the tarpon, *Tarpon atlanticus*, or the silversides, *Menidia notata*, or the shiner, *Notemigonus chrysoleucus*; also, any of certain small wingless insects (genus *Lepisma*) occurring in houses and damaging books, wall-paper, etc.

sil-ver-gilt (sil'vėr-gilt″), *n.* Silver or silverware gilded; also, an imitation gilding consisting of silver-leaf coated with a yellow lacquer.

sil-ver-gray (sil'vėr-grā′). **I.** *a.* Of a clear, lustrous, silvery gray. **II.** *n.* A silver-gray color.

sil-ver-i-ness (sil'vėr-i-nes), *n.* Silvery quality or appearance.

sil-ver-ing (sil'vėr-ing), *n.* The act or process of coating with silver, or with some substance resembling silver; also, the coating thus applied.

Silver-fish (*Lepisma saccharina*).

sil-ver-leaf (sil'vėr-lēf), *n.* Silver beaten into a very thin sheet.

sil-ver-ly (sil'vėr-li), *adv.* With a silvery appearance or sound: as, "the dinn'd air vibrating *silverly*" (Keats's "Hyperion," ii.). [Chiefly poetic.]

sil-vern (sil'vėrn), *a.* [AS. *seolfren.*] Of or like silver: as, speech is *silvern,* silence is golden. [Archaic or poetic.]

sil-ver-print (sil'vėr-print), *n.* A photographic print or positive made on paper sensitized with a silver salt.

sil-ver-sides (sil'vėr-sīdz), *n.* Any of the small fishes, with a silvery stripe along the sides, which constitute the family *Atherinidæ*, as *Menidia notata*, a species abundant along the Atlantic coast of the U. S.; also, any of certain minnows.

Silversides (*Menidia notata*).

sil-ver-smith (sil'vėr-smith), *n.* [AS. *seolforsmith.*] One who makes articles of silver.—**sil'ver-smith″ing,** *n.*

sil-ver-tongued (sil'vėr-tungd), *a.* Having a silver tongue or a melodious, pleasing, or effective utterance; eloquent: as, "the *silver-tongued* Murray — the most graceful, luminous, and subtle of all legal speakers" (Lecky's "Hist. of Eng. in the 18th Century," viii.).

sil-ver-ware (sil'vėr-wār), *n.* Articles, esp. for table use, made of silver.

sil-ver-weed (sil'vėr-wēd), *n.* A rosaceous plant, *Potentilla anserina*, with pinnate leaves having on the under side a silvery pubescence.

sil-ver-y (sil'vėr-i), *a.* Resembling silver in appearance; of a lustrous grayish-white color (as, a *silvery* fish; *silvery* foliage; *silvery* moonbeams); hoary, as the hair, beard, etc.; also, having a clear, ringing sound suggesting that of silver (as, *silvery* bells; a *silvery* tinkle; a *silvery* voice or laugh); also, containing silver; covered with silver.

sil-vi-cul-ture, etc. See *sylviculture,* etc.

si-mar (si-mär′), *n.* [F. *simarre,* < It. *cimarra, zimarra,* robe, cassock; = Sp. *chamarra, zamarra,* sheepskin coat: cf. the related OF. *chamarre* (from Sp.) and AL. *chimera,* E. *chimere.*] A loose, light garment or robe worn by women. [Archaic or poetic.]

sim-a-ru-ba (sim-ạ-rö′bä), *n.* [NL.; from native name in Guiana.] Any of the trees of the simarubaceous genus *Simaruba,* of tropical America, with pinnate leaves and a drupaceous fruit, and with a root whose bark contains a tonic principle; also, the bark. See *mountain-damson* and *paradise-tree.*—

Branch of Simaruba (*S. amara*), with female flowers. — *a,* a male flower; *b,* a female flower.

sim″a-ru-ba′ceous (-rö-bā′shius), *a.*

Belonging to the *Simarubaceæ*, a family of trees and shrubs, mostly tropical, which includes the mountain-damson, paradise-tree, ailantus, quassia, etc.

sim-bil (sim'bil), *n.* [Afr.] An African stork, *Sphenorhynchus abdimii* (or *Abdimia sphenorhyncha*), having a greenish and brownish-purple plumage with white under parts.

Simbil.

sim-i-an (sim'i-an). [L. *simia*, ape.] **I.** *a.* Pertaining to an ape or monkey; characteristic of apes; ape-like; specif., belonging or pertaining to the family *Simiidæ*, comprising the anthropoid apes (see *ape*). **II.** *n.* An ape or monkey; specif., an ape of the family *Simiidæ* (see *ape*).

sim-i-lar (sim'i-lär). [F. *similaire*, < L. *similis*, like: see *same*.] **I.** *a.* Having likeness or resemblance, esp. in a general way or in some respects (as, dogs, foxes, and *similar* animals of the family *Canidæ*; on a *similar* occasion; this plan is very *similar* to the others; the cases are somewhat *similar*); like or alike to a greater or less degree; also, of the same nature or structure throughout†, or homogeneous†; in *geom.*, of figures, alike in shape, irrespective of size. **II.** *n.* A similar thing or person.—**sim-i-lar'i-ty** (-lar'i-ti), *n.*; pl. -*ties* (-tiz). The state of being similar; likeness; resemblance; also, a point of resemblance.—**sim'i-lar-ly**, *adv.*

sim-i-le (sim'i-lē), *n.*; pl. -*les* (-lēz). [L., prop. neut. of *similis*: see *similar*.] In *rhet.*, a figure of speech directly expressing a resemblance, in one or more points, of one thing to another, as in "The wicked are like the troubled sea" (Isa. lvii. 20); also, an instance of this figure, or a use of words exemplifying it (as, "The sea hissed 'like twenty thousand kettles.' That's his *simile*, not mine": J. Conrad's "Lord Jim," x.).

si-mil-i-tude (si-mil'i-tūd), *n.* [OF. F. *similitude*, < L. *similitudo*, < *similis*: see *similar*.] Likeness, resemblance, or similarity (as, "A striking *similitude* between the brother and sister now first arrested my attention": Poe's "Fall of the House of Usher"); also, a likening or comparison; a parable or allegory; also, a person or thing that is the like, match, or counterpart of another (as, "Begotten Son, Divine *Similitude*, In whose conspicuous countenance . . . the Almighty Father shines": Milton's "Paradise Lost," iii. 384); also, the likeness, semblance, or image of a person or thing (as, to make one thing in the *similitude* of another; "Take ye therefore good heed . . . Lest ye . . . make you a graven image, the *similitude* of any figure," Deut. iv. 16).

sim-i-ous (sim'i-us), *a.* [L. *simia*, ape.] Ape-like; apish; simian.

sim-i-tar, scim-i-tar (sim'i-tär), *n.* [Cf. F. *cimeterre*, It. *scimitarra*, Sp. and Pg. *cimitarra*, simitar; origin uncertain; supposed to be from Persian.] A short, curved, single-edged sword used by the Turks, Persians, etc.

sim-lin (sim'lin), *n.* [Var. of *simnel*.] A variety of summer squash shaped somewhat like a round cake with a scalloped edge. [U. S.]

sim-mer (sim'ér), *v.* [Var. of earlier *simper*; perhaps imit.] **I.** *intr.* To make a gentle murmuring sound under the action of continued heat, as liquids just below the boiling-point; continue in a state approaching boiling, as liquids subjected to a gentle heat; fig., to continue in a state of subdued activity, suppressed

Simitar. Persian, 17th century.

excitement, or the like; develop slowly toward the point of breaking forth (as, a *simmering* spirit of revolt). **II.** *tr.* To cause to simmer; keep in a state approaching boiling, as liquids subjected to a gentle heat.—**sim'mer**, *n.* A process or condition of simmering.

sim-nel (sim'nel), *n.* [OF. *simenel*, < L. *simila*, fine wheat flour.] A kind of bread or biscuit made of fine wheat flour (now chiefly hist.); also, a kind of cake containing currants, etc., eaten esp. on Mid-Lent Sunday (local, Eng.).

si-mo-le-on (si-mō'lē-on), *n.* [Origin obscure.] A dollar. [Slang, U. S.]

si-mo-ni-ac (si-mō'ni-ak), *n.* [ML. *simoniacus*, < *simonia*, E. *simony*.] One who practises simony.—**sim-o-ni-a-cal** (sim-ō-nī'a-kal), *a.* Of, pertaining to, or involving simony; guilty of or tainted by simony.—**sim-o-ni'a-cal-ly**, *adv.*

Si-mo-ni-an (si-mō'ni-an), *n.* A member of an early Christian (Gnostic) sect named after Simon Magus (see etym. of *simony*) and regarded as heretical.

si-mon=pure (sī'mon-pūr'), *a.* [From *Simon Pure*, a Quaker in Mrs. Centlivre's comedy, "A Bold Stroke for a Wife" (1718), who is impersonated by an impostor.] Real; genuine; authentic; true: as, the *simon-pure* Mr. Smith (not an impostor or another person); the *simon-pure* heir; the *simon-pure* imported article.

sim-o-ny (sim'ō-ni), *n.* [OF. F. *simonie*, < ML. *simonia*, simony; so called from *Simon Magus* (the sorcerer), who sought to buy from the apostles the power of imparting the Holy Ghost: see Acts, viii. 9–24.] The act or practice of trafficking in sacred things; esp., the buying or selling of ecclesiastical preferments, benefices, etc.

si-moom (si-möm'), *n.* [Ar. *samūm*, < *samm-*, poison.] A hot, suffocating, sand-laden wind of the deserts of Arabia, Syria, northern Africa, etc. Also **si-moon'** (-mön').

simp (simp), *n.* [Appar. short for *simpleton*.] A simpleton; a fool: as, "I guess it's a joke on me, I was such a *simp*" (Sinclair Lewis's "Main Street," xxxii.). [Slang.]

sim-per (sim'pér), *v.* [Origin uncertain: cf. G. *zimper*, finical, dainty, coy.] **I.** *intr.* To smile in an affected, self-conscious manner: as, "She stood before the mirror courtesying and *simpering* to her own image" (Hawthorne's "Twice-Told Tales," Dr. Heidegger's Experiment); "the nurse, a *simpering* piece of faded gentility" (Dickens's "Dombey and Son," i.). **II.** *tr.* To utter or say with a simper: as, to *simper* one's thanks; "We have friends of yours here, Miss Nickall,' *simpered* Mrs. Spatt" (Arnold Bennett's "Lion's Share," xxiv.).—**sim'per**, *n.* The smile or the facial expression of one who simpers: as, "the unmeaning *simper* of a dangling coxcomb" (H. Mackenzie's "Man of Feeling," xxxiii.).—**sim'per-er**, *n.*—**sim'per-ing-ly**, *adv.*

sim-ple (sim'pl), *a.*; compar. *simpler*, superl. *simplest*. [OF. F. *simple*, < L. *simplus* or *simplex*, simple, < *sim-*, akin to *singulus*, single, *semel*, once, *simul*, at once, together, and E. *same*; for L. -*plus* and -*plex*, see *double* and *duplex*.] Not divided into parts (as, a *simple* leaf, one having only a single blade; a *simple* stem, one that does not branch); not compound (as, a *simple* ascidian); composed of but one substance or element (as, a *simple* substance); also, occurring or considered alone or with nothing added (as, a *simple* negative; the *simple* truth or fact); bare or mere; also, having few parts; rudimentary, as forms of animal or plant life; not complex, complicated, or intricate (as, a *simple* design); easy to understand, deal with, use, etc. (as, "the faculty . . . of reducing his thought on any subject to the *simplest* and plainest terms possible," Charnwood's "Abraham Lincoln," iv.; a *simple* matter; *simple* tools); not elaborate or artificial (as, *simple* verse or meters; a *simple* style); not ornate, elegant, or luxurious, as dress, furniture, food, tastes, mode of life, etc.; plain, homely, or unpretentious; unostentatious, unaffected, or unassuming, as persons, the manner, etc. (as, "Those of highest worth and breeding are most *simple* in manner and attire": Parkman's "Oregon Trail," xi.); also, of modest pretensions or station (as, "A fair large diamond . . . Such be for queens, and not for *simple* maids": Tennyson's "Lancelot and Elaine," 230); humble or lowly (often opposed to *gentle*); common or ordinary (as, a *simple* citizen; a *simple* soldier); unimportant or insignificant; also, not complex, subtle, or overrefined mentally, as in ideas, tastes, etc. (as, "It was worth a guinea to see the *simple*

Colonel and his delight at the music," Thackeray's "New-comes," i.; "He was one of those *simple* men that love and sympathize with children," W. H. Hudson's "Far Away and Long Ago," i.); artless or unsophisticated (as, "A *simple* Child . . . What should it know of death?" Wordsworth's "We Are Seven," 1); innocent, guileless, or sincere, as persons, the heart, etc.; unlearned or ignorant (as, "Among *simple* people she had the reputation of being a prodigy of information": Mrs. Stowe's "Oldtown Folks," xxx.); often, lacking in mental acuteness or shrewd sense; weakly credulous or easily imposed on; proceeding from or showing a lack of acuteness or sense, as an action or speech; sometimes, feeble-minded; imbecile.—**simple contract,** in *law*, a contract or agreement not under seal.—**simple fraction.** See *fraction, n.*—**simple interest.** See *compound interest, under interest, n.*—**simple machine.** See *machine, n.*—**simple sentence,** a sentence having but one subject and one predicate.—**sim'ple,** *n.* Something simple; an uncompounded or unmixed thing, substance, or constituent; a medicine consisting of a single constituent, esp. one made from a single herb or plant†; hence, an herb or plant used for medicinal purposes (archaic: as, "Upon the margin of celestial streams alone those *simples* grow which cure the heartache," Longfellow's "Hyperion," ii. 5); also, a person of humble condition (now usually opposed to *gentle*: archaic).—**sim'ple,** *v. i.*; *-pled, -pling.* To seek for or gather simples or medicinal herbs. [Archaic.]

sim-ple=heart-ed (sim'pl-här'ted), *a.* Having or showing a simple heart; guileless; sincere; ingenuous.—**sim'ple=heart'ed-ness,** *n.*

sim-ple=mind-ed (sim'pl-mīn'ded), *a.* Having or showing a simple mind; artless or unsophisticated (as, "He was . . . *simple-minded* like a child": Stevenson's "Travels with a Donkey," iii. 2); lacking in mental acuteness or shrewd sense; sometimes, feeble-minded; mentally deficient.—**sim'ple=mind'ed-ness,** *n.*

sim-ple-ness (sim'pl-nes), *n.* The state or quality of being simple.

sim-pler (sim'plėr), *n.* One who gathers simples or medicinal herbs, or is versed in their properties; a herbalist. [Archaic.]

sim-ple-ton (sim'pl-tọn), *n.* [From *simple.*] A simple-minded person, or one lacking in intelligence or sense; a silly person; a fool: as, "My niece . . . is a poor, good-natured *simpleton,* as soft as butter" (Smollett's "Humphry Clinker," April 17).

sim-plex (sim'pleks). [L.: see *simple.*] **I.** *a.* Simple; consisting of or characterized by a single element, action, or the like: as, *simplex* telegraphy (in which but one message at a time is sent over a single wire). **II.** *n.* An uncompounded word.

sim-pli-ci-den-tate (sim"pli-si-den'tāt). [L. *simplex* (*simplic-*), simple, + *dens* (*dent-*), tooth.] **I.** *a.* Belonging or pertaining to the *Simplicidentata,* a suborder or division of rodents (including all except the hares, rabbits, and pikas) in which there is only one pair of upper incisor teeth. **II.** *n.* A simplicidentate rodent.

sim-pli-ci-ty (sim-plis'i-ti), *n.*; pl. *-ties* (-tiz). [L. *simplicitas,* < *simplex*: see *simple.*] The state or quality of being simple; condition free from division into parts, or from compounding or compositeness; freedom from complexity, intricacy, or elaborateness; absence of ornament, luxury, or pretentiousness; plainness; unaffectedness; artlessness; sincerity; ignorance; lack of mental acuteness or shrewdness; also, *pl.,* instances of what is simple; simple forms of expression; plain or homely ways (as, "the *simplicities* of cottage life" Wordsworth's "Prelude," vi. 2).

sim-pli-fi-ca-tion (sim"pli-fi-kā'shọn), *n.* The act of simplifying, or the state of being simplified; reduction to a simple or more simple state or form.—**sim'pli-fi-ca-tive** (-kā-tiv), *a.* Tending to simplify.

sim-pli-fy (sim'pli-fī), *v. t.*; *-fied, -fying.* [F. *simplifier,* < ML. *simplificare,* < L. *simplus,* simple, + *facere,* make.] To make simple or more simple; render less complex or complicated; make plainer, more intelligible, or easier.—**sim'pli-fi-er** (-fī-ėr), *n.*

sim-ply (sim'pli), *adv.* In a simple manner; without complexity, elaboration, or ornament; plainly; unaffectedly;

artlessly; without intelligence or sense; also, without addition or qualification; merely or only (as, "The creature did not *simply* live in the house; she pervaded it": Arnold Bennett's "These Twain," i.); absolutely (as, "She must be *simply* irresistible!" Du Maurier's "Trilby," vii.).

sim-u-la-cre (sim'ū-lā-kėr), *n.* [OF. F.] A simulacrum or image, as of a deity or of a person or thing.

sim-u-la-crum (sim-ū-lā'krum), *n.*; pl. *-cra* (-krä) or *-crums.* [L., < *simulare,* make like: see *simulate.*] An image or material representation of a deity or of some person or thing; hence, a mere, faint, or unreal semblance (as, "He was a mere *simulacrum* of his former self": Lytton Strachey's "Queen Victoria," iv.).

sim-u-lar (sim'ū-lạr). [Irreg. < L. *simulare*: see *simulate.*] **I.**† *n.* One who or that which simulates. **II.** *a.* Simulated; counterfeit; false: as, "*simular* proof" (Shakspere's "Cymbeline," v. 5. 200). [Obs. or archaic.]

sim-u-late (sim'ū-lāt), *v.*; *-lated, -lating.* [L. *simulatus,* pp. of *simulare,* make like, imitate, assume the appearance of, < *similis,* like: see *similar* and *same.*] **I.** *tr.* To assume falsely the appearance or character of (a person or thing); make a pretense of (a quality, condition, feeling, action, etc.: as, "I . . . lay there *simulating* death," W. H. Hudson's "Purple Land," xii.); counterfeit; feign; also, to take on or have the semblance of (something else) without conscious imitation (as, "A fallacious and verdant scum upon the surface of deep pools *simulated* the turf that had been removed," Motley's "Dutch Republic," iii. 2; certain insects *simulate* flowers or leaves; the spelling 'frontispiece' *simulates* 'piece'). **II.** *intr.* To make pretense; feign: as, "He could neither *simulate* nor dissimulate" (H. James's "Europeans," x.).—**sim'u-late,** *a.* Simulated; feigned. [Archaic.]—**sim-u-la'tion** (-lā'shọn), *n.* [L. *simulatio(n-).*] The act of simulating; false assumption of a particular appearance or character; pretending or feigning; sometimes, assumption of a particular appearance or form as if by unconscious imitation.—**sim'u-la-tive** (-lạ-tiv), *a.* Characterized by simulation.—**sim'u-la-tor** (-lā-tor), *n.*

sim-ul-ta-ne-ous (sim-ul-tā'nē-us or sī-mul-), *a.* [From L. *simul,* at once, at the same time, together (see *simple*), + *-taneus* as in *momentaneus, subitaneus*: cf. *momentaneous, subitaneous.*] Existing, occurring, or operating at the same time; coincident in time: as, *simultaneous* outbreaks in several districts; *simultaneous* shots sounding as one.—**sim"ul-ta-ne'i-ty** (-tạ-nē'i-ti), **sim-ul-ta'ne-ous-ness,** *n.* —**sim-ul-ta'ne-ous-ly,** *adv.*

si-murgh (si-mörg'), *n.* [Pers.] A monstrous bird of Persian mythology, corresponding to the Arabian roc.

sin¹ (sin), *n.* [AS. *synn, syn,* akin to D. *zonde,* G. *sünde,* Icel., Sw., and Dan. *synd,* sin: cf. L. *sons* (*sont-*), guilty.] Transgression of divine law (as, "*Sin* is a reproach to any people": Prov. xiv. 34); an act regarded as such transgression, or any violation, esp. a wilful or deliberate one, of some religious or moral principle (as, a venial *sin,* or a mortal or deadly *sin*: see the adjectives); hence, any serious transgression or offense; anything deemed utterly wrong; also, depravity, or tendency to evil (as, original *sin*: see under *original, a.*).—**sin¹,** *v.*; *sinned, sinning.* [AS. *syngian.*] **I.** *intr.* To commit sin; do a sinful act; hence, to offend against a principle, standard, or the like (as, "Faces *sinning* Against proportion": Byron's "Don Juan," vi. 52). **II.** *tr.* To do or perform sinfully; commit (a sin: as, "a man . . . who had *sinned* all the sins," H. G. Wells's "Tono-Bungay," iii. 3. § 2); also, to be ungrateful for (mercies); also, to bring, drive, etc., by sinning.

sin² (sin), *adv., prep.,* and *conj.* [Contr. of *sithen.*] Since. [Now prov.]

Si-næ-an (si-nē'ạn or sī-), *a.* [See *Sinic.*] Chinese.

Si-na-ic (sī-nā'ik), *a.* Same as *Sinaitic.*

Si-na-it-ic (sī-nạ-it'ik), *a.* Pertaining to Mount Sinai.

si-nal-bin (si-nal'bin), *n.* [L. *sin(api),* mustard, + *alb(us),* white.] In *chem.,* a colorless crystalline glucoside contained in the seeds of white mustard.

sin-a-pine (sin'ạ-pin), *n.* [L. *sinapi,* mustard: see *sinapism.*] In *chem.,* an unstable alkaloid contained in the seeds of white and black mustard.—**si-nap-ic** (si-nap'ik), *a.*

sin-a-pism (sin'ạ-pizm), *n.* [LL. *sinapismus,* < Gr. σιναπισμός, < σιναπίζειν, treat with a mustard-plaster, <

σίναπι (L. *sinapi, sinapis*), mustard.] In *med.*, a mustard-plaster.

since (sins). [Contr. of *sithence, sithens*.] **I.** *adv.* From then till now (often preceded by *ever*); also, at some or any time between a particular past time and the present (as, he at first refused, but has *since* consented); subsequently; also, ago, or before now (as, long *since*). **II.** *prep.* Continuously from or counting from (a past time or event) to the present (as, the package has been ready *since* noon; the period *since* the birth of Christ); also, at some or any time between (a past time or event) and the present (as, we have not seen him *since* Monday; many changes have taken place *since* the war). **III.** *conj.* Continuously from or counting from the time when (as, he has been busy ever *since* he came; it is a year to-day *since* he came); also, in the course of the period following the time when (as, he has written but once *since* he left us); also, when† (after *remember*, etc.: see Shakspere's "2 Henry IV.," iii. 2. 206); also, as a consequence of the fact that, or seeing that (as, *since* you ask, I will tell you; they rose, *since* such was the custom); inasmuch as; because.

sin-cere (sin-sēr'), *a.*; compar. *sincerer*, superl. *sincerest*. [L. *sincerus*, pure, sound, genuine, honest, sincere, perhaps related to *sim-* in *simplex*: see *simple*.] Pure, unmixed, or unadulterated (archaic: as, "As newborn babes, desire the *sincere* milk of the word," 1 Peter, ii. 2); without admixture (*of*: rare); sound† or unimpaired†; true, veracious, or correct (obs. or archaic); now, usually, free from any element of deceit, dissimulation, or duplicity, as persons, feelings, intentions, statements, work, etc.; honest.—**sin-cere'ly**, *adv.*—**sin-cere'ness**, *n.*—**sin-cer'i-ty** (-ser'i-ti), *n.*; pl. *-ties* (-tiz). The state or character of being sincere; freedom from deceit, dissimulation, or duplicity; honesty; *pl.*, sincere feelings, actions, etc.

sin-ci-put (sin'si-put), *n.* [L., < *semi-*, half, + *caput*, head.] In *anat.*, the fore part of the head or skull (cf. *occiput*); also, the upper part of the skull.—**sin-cip'i-tal** (-sip'i-tal), *a.*

sine[1] (sīn), *n.* [NL. *sinus*, sine, special use (rendering an Ar. term) of L. *sinus*, a bend, fold, hanging fold of a toga: see *sinus*.] In *trigon.*, orig., a perpendicular line drawn from one extremity of an arc of a circle to the diameter which passes through its other extremity; now, the ratio of the length of this line to that of the radius of the circle; hence, of an acute angle of a right-angled triangle, a trigonometric function equal to the ratio of the length of the side opposite the angle to that of the hypotenuse.

Sine.

BE is the sine of the arc *AB*; and the ratio of *BE* to *CB* is the sine of the angle *ACB*.

si-ne[2] (sī'nē), *prep.* [L.: cf. *sans*.] Without.—**sine die** (dī'ē). [L.] 'Without day'; without a day fixed for future action: used with *adjourn, postpone*, etc.—**sine qua non** (kwā non). [L.] 'Without which not': a phrase often used as an adjective (meaning 'indispensable,' 'absolutely necessary') or as a noun (meaning 'an indispensable condition': as, "He always insisted, as the absolute *sine qua non*, that verbal complaints should be presented to him with the fullest pomp," Chesterton's "Napoleon of Notting Hill," ii. 2).

si-ne-cure (sī'nē-kūr, also sin'ē-). [L. *sine*, without, + *cura*, E. *cure*, *n.*] **I.** *n.* An ecclesiastical benefice without cure of souls; hence, any office requiring little or no work, esp. one yielding profitable returns. **II.** *a.* Of the nature of a sinecure (as, "a half-pay officer who held the *sinecure* position of under-butler": Lytton Strachey's "Queen Victoria," iv.); also, holding a sinecure.—**si'ne-cur-ism** (-kūr-izm), *n.* The practice of holding or permitting sinecures.—**si'ne-cur-ist**, *n.*

sin-ew (sin'ū), *n.* [AS. *sionw-, seonw-*, in inflectional forms of *sionu, seonu*, akin to D. *zenuw*, G. *sehne*, Icel. *sin*, Sw. *sena*, Dan. *sene*, sinew.] A tendon; also, a nerve†; fig., that which supplies the strength or sustains the activities of anything (often in *pl.*: as, the *sinews* of war, that is, money as necessary for the carrying on of war, after the Latin *nervos belli, pecuniam infinitam*, "the sinews of war, unlimited money," Cicero's "Philippics," v. 2. 5); hence, strength,

vigor, or energy (often in *pl.*).—**sin'ew**, *v. t.* To furnish with sinews; strengthen as by sinews; also, to bind as with sinews (rare: as, "So shalt thou *sinew* both these lands together," Shakspere's "3 Henry VI.," ii. 6. 91).—**sin'ew-less**, *a.* Destitute of sinews; hence, lacking vigor; feeble.—**sin'ew-y**, *a.* Furnished with or full of sinews; also, having strong sinews, or strong or vigorous (as, "his *sinewy* frame, which showed him formed for hardy deeds of arms": Irving's "Conquest of Granada," ii.); derived from or characteristic of strong sinews (as, "*sinewy* strength": Scott's "Lady of the Lake," i. 28); hence, vigorous or forcible, or nervous, as language, writings, literary style, etc.; also, like a sinew; tough; stringy.

sin-fo-ni-a (sēn-fō-nē'ä), *n.*; pl. *-nie* (-nē'ā). [It.] In *music*, a symphony.

sin-ful (sin'fúl), *a.* [AS. *synfull*.] Full of sin, as a person; wicked; also, involving sin, as an action.—**sin'ful-ly**, *adv.*—**sin'ful-ness**, *n.*

sing (sing), *v. i.*; pret. *sang* or *sung*, pp. *sung*, ppr. *singing*. [AS. *singan* (pret. *sang*, pp. *sungen*) = D. *zingen* = G. *singen* = Icel. *syngja* = Goth. *siggwan*, sing.] To utter words or sounds in succession with musical modulations of the voice; tell of something in song; chant or intone, as in divine service†; call (*out*: colloq.); also, to admit of being sung, as verses; also, to compose verse; tell of something in verse; also, to produce tuneful sounds, as certain birds, insects, etc. (as, "Redbreasts *sing* all through the spring, summer, and autumn": G. White's "Nat. Hist. of Selborne," i. 40); give out a continuous ringing, whistling, murmuring, or other sound of musical quality, as a tea-kettle, a brook, etc.; move with such a sound, as a bullet, etc. (as, "A stone *sang* past my head": Conan Doyle's "Exploits of Brigadier Gerard," vi.); also, to have the sensation of a ringing or humming sound, as the ears (as, "I had forgotten the buffet, though mine ear *sung* after it for a whole day": Scott's "Ivanhoe," xl.).—**to sing small.** See under *small, adv.*—**sing**, *v. t.* To utter with musical modulations of the voice, as a song; give forth in sounds of musical quality, as a bird its song; chant or intone (as, "On Christmas Eve the mass was *sung*": Scott's "Marmion," vi., Introd.); call (*out*: colloq.); also, to frame or utter in poetic form; also, to relate or celebrate in song or in verse (as, "Arms and the man I *sing*": Dryden's tr. Virgil's "Æneid," i. 1); also, to proclaim enthusiastically (as, to *sing* a person's praises); also, to bring, send, put, etc., with or by singing (as, to *sing* a child to sleep).—**to sing another** (or **a different**) **song** or **tune**, fig., to speak or act in a very different manner, esp. with greater modesty or humility.—**sing**, *n.* The act, or an act or performance, of singing; a meeting of persons for singing; also, a singing, ringing, or whistling sound, as of a bullet in its flight. [Chiefly colloq.]—**sing'a-ble**, *a.* That may be sung.

singe (sinj), *v. t.*; *singed, singeing*. [AS. *sengan* = D. *zengen* = G. *sengen*, singe; perhaps orig. a causative form, meaning 'cause to sing' (with reference to the sound of burning), from the Teut. verb represented by E. *sing*.] To burn superficially; burn the ends or projections of (hair, etc.); subject (a carcass, as of a plucked fowl) to flame in order to remove the hair; also, to remove by superficial burning (as, "The doctor, Whose beard they have *singed* off with brands of fire": Shakspere's "Comedy of Errors," v. 1. 171).—**singe**, *n.* The act or an act of singeing; also, a superficial burn.

sing-er[1] (sing'ėr), *n.* One who or that which sings; a trained or professional vocalist; a poet; a singing bird.

sin-ger[2] (sin'jėr), *n.* One who or that which singes.

Sin-gha-lese (sing-gạ-lēs' or -lēz'). [Skt. *Sinhala*, Ceylon.] **I.** *a.* Pertaining to the island of Ceylon, or to its principal native race or their language. **II.** *n.*; pl. *-lese*. A member of the Singhalese race; also, the Singhalese language, an Aryan dialect closely related to Pali.

sing-ing (sing'ing), *n.* The act or sound of one who or that which sings; a sensation of ringing in the ears or head.—**sing'ing**, *p. a.* That sings; also, of the nature of singing; having the musical quality of song.—**singing bird**, a bird that sings; a song-bird; specif., any oscine bird whether it sings or not.

sin-gle (sing'gl), *a.* [OF. *single, sengle*, < L. *singulus*, single, separate, individual: see *simple*.] Alone, solitary,

---

or without others (as, "Each man apart, all *single* and alone, Yet an arch-villain keeps him company": Shakspere's "Timon of Athens," v. 1. 110); separate or distinct (as, *single* pieces; to bind *single* sheets into a volume); considered separately, individual, or particular (as, each *single* citizen; to recall *single* instances of heroism); pertaining to an individual, personal, or private (as, one's *single* will must yield to the will of the majority); unmarried, or pertaining to the unmarried state (as, a *single* man or woman; *single* life; *single* blessedness, see phrase below); also, one only (as, a *single* hope remained; not a *single* word was said); sole; only; sometimes, singular or unique (obs. or archaic); also, consisting of one part, element, or member, or being of unit size or extent, as distinguished from *double*, *triple*, etc.; having but one set of petals, as a flower; of a size suitable for one person, as a room or bed; requiring the use of but one hand, as a weapon (see *single-stick*); of one against one, as combat or fight; of only moderate strength or body, as ale, etc.; slight† or poor† (as, "Is not . . . your wit *single?*" Shakspere's "2 Henry IV.," i. 2. 207); simple†, plain†, or mere†; also, sincere, honest, or single-minded (as, a *single* heart; *single* devotion); of the eye, seeing rightly or justly (from Biblical use: as, "If therefore thine eye be *single*, thy whole body shall be full of light," Mat. vi. 22).— **single blessedness,** orig., in Shakspere's use, the state of one who forgoes marriage, or becomes a celibate, for religious reasons, and is hence regarded as blessed (see "Midsummer Night's Dream," i. 1. 67–78); hence, in general, with more or less allusion to the blessings attached, the unmarried state (humorous: as, "She was left unplucked on the stalk of *single blessedness*," Galt's "Ayrshire Legatees," vii.). — **single entry.** See under *entry*.—**single file,** a file or line of persons or things arranged one by one behind another; Indian file.—**single tax,** in *econ.*, a tax on a single object of taxation, as land, capital, or income; specif., taxation solely on land-value, to the exclusion of other taxation by the same state.—**single track,** a single line of railroad-track between points, for travel in either direction. Hence **sin'gle=track',** *a.* Having only a single track, as a railroad; fig., able to go or act but one way at a time, as the mind; hence, sometimes, limited in capacity for changing opinion or purpose. —**sin'gle,** *n.* Something single, or alone, separate, sole, consisting of one part or element, being of unit size or extent, etc.; a single one; in *falconry*, a claw or talon; in *hunting*, the tail of an animal, esp. of a deer; in *baseball*, a hit which allows the batter to reach first base only; in *cricket*, a hit for which one run is scored; in *lawn-tennis*, etc., a game or match played with only one person on each side; in *theatrical use*, a player or performer who appears alone in a vaudeville act. —**sin'gle,** *v.*; -gled, -gling. **I.** *tr.* To separate (now chiefly in *hunting*: as, a hound *singles* a deer from the herd); pick or choose out from others (commonly with *out*: as, "Romance had *singled* Jim for its own," J. Conrad's "Lord Jim," xxix.; "Looking for the complement and counterpart of Lady Casterley, one would perhaps have *singled* out her brother," Galsworthy's "Patrician," i. 8; to *single* out a fact for special mention, or a person for a particular duty); thin (young growing plants) so as to leave each one separate; also, to make single or reduce to one; unite into one. **II.** *intr.* To separate from others; become single, as a railroad-track; also, of a horse, to go at the gait called single-foot.

sin-gle-breast-ed (sing'gl-bres'ted), *a.* Of a garment, overlapping across the breast only sufficiently to allow of fastening. Cf. *double-breasted*.

sin-gle-eyed (sing'gl-īd'), *a.* Having but one eye; also, seeing rightly; just, honest, or straightforward in views, aims, etc.

sin-gle-foot (sing'gl-fūt), *n.* A certain gait of a horse, also called *rack*. See *rack*[5].—**sin'gle=foot,** *v. i.* Of a horse, to go at the gait called single-foot.—**sin'gle=foot″er,** *n.*

sin-gle-hand-ed (sing'gl-han'ded), *a.* Having, using, or requiring the use of, but one hand; also, acting or working alone or unaided (as, "*Single-handed*, and without a servant, she performed all the labors of Mr. Jonathan Rossiter's little establishment": Mrs. Stowe's "Oldtown Folks," xxxiii.); carried on or performed by one alone or unaided (as, *single-handed* efforts); sometimes, of a combat, carried on by one on each side.—**sin'gle=hand'ed-ly,** *adv.*

sin-gle=heart-ed (sing'gl-här'ted), *a.* Having or showing a single or sincere heart; sincere in feeling or spirit; also, single-minded or undivided in feeling or purpose (as, "He was *single-hearted* in his aim": Maugham's "Moon and Sixpence," xliii.).—**sin'gle=heart'ed-ly,** *adv.*—**sin'gle=heart'ed-ness,** *n.*

sin-gle=leaf (sing'gl-lēf), *n.* A piñon or pine, *Pinus monophylla*, of western North America, with leaves growing singly.

sin-gle=mind-ed (sing'gl-mīn'ded), *a.* Having or showing a single or sincere mind; single-hearted; also, having or showing a mind undivided in feeling or purpose. —**sin'gle=mind'ed-ly,** *adv.*—**sin'gle=mind'ed-ness,** *n.*

sin-gle-ness (sing'gl-nes), *n.* The state or quality of being single; solitariness; unmarried state; oneness; sincerity, honesty, or integrity; freedom from duplicity or deceit.

Single-leaf.

sin-gle=phase (sing'gl-fāz), *a.* In *elect.*, noting or pertaining to an alternating current of one phase.

sin-gle=stick (sing'gl-stik), *n.* A stick requiring the use of but one hand, employed in fencing, etc.; also, fencing, etc., with such a stick (as, "an exciseman, whom he challenged to a bout at *singlestick*": Smollett's "Humphry Clinker," June 26).

sin-glet (sing'glet), *n.* [From *single*, after *doublet*.] A kind of undershirt or jersey worn by men.

sin-gle-ton (sing'gl-ton), *n.* [From *single*: for the termination, cf. *simpleton*.] Something occurring singly, or apart from others; in *card-playing*, a card which is the only one of a suit in a hand.

sin-gle-tree (sing'gl-trē), *n.* Same as *swingletree*.

sin-gly (sing'gli), *adv.* As a single person or thing; apart from others, separately, or individually (as, consider each point *singly*); by one's own efforts solely, or single-handed (as, to strive *singly* against a general evil); also, as single units; one by one, or one at a time (as, misfortunes never come *singly*); also, solely† or only†.

sing=sing (sing'sing), *n.* [Afr.] An African antelope, *Kobus sing-sing*.

sing-song (sing'sông). **I.** *n.* Verse, or a piece of verse, of a jingling or monotonous character; also, monotonous rhythmical cadence, tone, or sound (as, "the rapt *singsong* of the wayside fortune-teller": Kipling's

Sing-sing.

"Kim," iii.); also, a social gathering with singing (colloq.).
II. *a.* Making mere jingling verse or singsong, as a poet; also, of the nature of jingling verse or singsong; also, monotonous in rhythm, as utterance (as, "repeating in true *sing-song* vernacular the legend of St. George and his fight": Hughes's "Tom Brown's School Days," i. 1).—**sing'-song,** *v.* **I.** *intr.* To make verses, speak, etc., in singsong. **II.** *tr.* To express or utter in singsong.

sing-spiel (zing'shpēl), *n.* [G., < *singen*, sing, + *spiel*, play.] A kind of semi-dramatic work or performance, formerly common in Germany, in which singing and spoken dialogue alternate.

sin-gu-lar (sing'gū-lạr). [OF. *singuler* (F. *singulier*), < L. *singularis*, < *singulus*, E. *single*.] **I.** *a.* Alone† or solitary†; separate, individual, or particular (now chiefly in the legal phrase 'all and singular,' all collectively and individually); pertaining to an individual†, or private†; also, one only, or single (obs. or archaic); being the only one of the kind, unparalleled, or unique (as, an event *singular* in the history of the world); extraordinary or remarkable, as in character, extent, etc. (as, "a scene of *singular* beauty," Mrs. Shelley's "Frankenstein," ix.; *singular* favor or success); unusual or strange (as, a *singular* occurrence; "the *singular* history of the former heir," Marryat's "King's Own," l.); peculiar, odd, eccentric, or bizarre (as, a *singular* person; *singular* behavior, taste, or dress); also, pertaining or relating to but one person or thing, or not general (specif. in *logic*: as, "A *Singular* term is one which can denote only a single object . . . William Shakspeare, the most precious of the metals, are *singular* terms," Jevons's "Elementary Lessons in Logic," iii.); in *gram.*, signifying or implying but one person or thing (as, the *singular* number; a *singular* verb-form: cf. *plural, a.*, and *dual, a.*). **II.** *n.* That which is singular; a single person or thing; in *gram.*, the singular number; a noun, verb, or other word in this number. —**sin-gu-lar'i-ty** (-lar'i-ti), *n.*; pl. *-ties* (-tiz). The state, fact, or quality of being singular; solitariness†; oneness; uniqueness; extraordinary or remarkable character; unusualness or strangeness; oddness or eccentricity (as, "He affected *singularity*, in order to establish his claims to genius": Maria Edgeworth's "Belinda," i.); also, something singular; an individual or unusual feature or characteristic, or a peculiarity (as, "One of the larger *singularities* of the great war is its failure to produce great and imposing personalities": H. G. Wells's "Italy, France, and Britain at War," i.).—**sin'gu-lar-ize** (-īz), *v. t.*; *-ized, -izing.* To make singular or single; individualize; also, to distinguish or signalize.—**sin″gu-lar-i-za'tion** (-i-zā'shọn), *n.*—**sin'gu-lar-ly,** *adv.* In a singular manner; to a singular extent or degree; extraordinarily; unusually; strangely; peculiarly.—**sin'gu-lar-ness,** *n.*

Sin-ha-lese (sin-hạ-lēs' or -lēz'), *a.* and *n.* Same as *Singhalese.*

Sin-ic (sin'ik), *a.* [ML. *Sinicus*, < L. *Sinæ*, < Gr. Σῖναι, pl., the Chinese.] Chinese.—**Sin'i-cism** (-i-sizm), *n.* Chinese methods or customs; a Chinese usage.—**Sin'i-cize** (-sīz), *v. t.*; *-cized, -cizing.* To invest with a Chinese character.—**Sin″i-ci-za'tion** (-si-zā'shọn), *n.*

sin-is-ter (sin'is-tèr), *a.* [OF. F. *sinistre*, < L. *sinister*, left, on the left, adverse, unfavorable.] Pertaining to or situated on the left side; left; left-hand; also, on or toward the left as the side or direction of ill omen; hence, portending misfortune, as an omen; of ominous import or character, as occurrences, rumors, meaning, etc.; suggestive of threatened or intended evil, as looks, utterances, actions, etc.; also, of an unfortunate or disastrous kind, as an accident, chance, or fate; unfavorable (*to*); also, malign in purpose, as suggestions; evil, bad, or base, as influences, practices, motives, etc.; also, in *her.*, situated to the left of the bearer, and hence to the right of the spectator (opposed to *dexter*).—**sin'is-ter-ly,** *adv.*—**sin'is-ter-ness,** *n.*—**sin'is-trad** (-trad), *adv.* [See *-ad.*] To the left: opposed to *dextrad.*—**sin'is-tral** (-trạl), *a.* Of or pertaining to the left side; left; left-handed; of a spiral shell, having the whorl rising from right to left, as viewed from the outside.—**sin'is-tral-ly,** *adv.*—**sin'is-trorse** (-trôrs), *a.* [L. *sinistrorsus*, toward the left, < *sinister*, left, + *versus*, toward.] Rising spirally from right to left (from a point of view at the center of the spiral), as a

stem: by some authorities taken in the opposite sense (from a point of view on the outside of the spiral). Cf. *dextrorse.* —**sin'is-trous,** *a.* Sinistral; also, ill-omened; unlucky; disastrous; also, malign†; evil†; base†.

sink (singk), *v.*; pret. *sank* or *sunk*, pp. *sunk* or (now chiefly as p. a.) *sunken*, ppr. *sinking.* [AS. *sincan* (pret. *sanc*, pp. *suncen*) = D. *zinken* = G. *sinken* = Icel. *sökkva* = Goth. *siggan*, sink.] **I.** *intr.* To go under or to the bottom, as in water (often opposed to *float* or *swim*); go down until wholly or partly covered over, as in a quicksand, a bog, snow, etc.; become submerged; also, to settle or fall gradually or gently downward, as from insufficiently supported weight, as a heavy structure, a portion of the earth's crust, a partially deflated balloon, etc.; fall slowly from weakness, fatigue, etc., as a person or an animal; settle down into a reclining, sitting, or kneeling posture (as, "She pushed a chair up to the tea-table and Mrs. Struthers *sank* into it": Mrs. Wharton's "Age of Innocence," ix.); also, to descend gradually to a lower level, as water, flames, a heavy gas, etc.; go down (apparently) toward or below the horizon, as a heavenly body or as land seen from a departing ship; settle down, as darkness upon the earth; have a downward slope, as ground; also, to fall in, or assume a hollow form or appearance, as the cheeks, etc. (often with *in*: cf. *sunken*); also, to enter (*in, into,* etc.), as a permeating liquid, a weapon, or, fig., ideas or truth penetrating into the mind; also, to pass gradually into some state, as of slumber, reverie, silence, oblivion, etc. (as, "I finished a happy day by *sinking* to sleep in a soft, clean bed": W. H. Hudson's "Purple Land," xxi.); pass or fall into some lower or worse state, as of fortune, estimation, moral being, etc.; decline or degenerate; fail markedly or seriously in physical strength or vital power, esp. in approaching death; fall in depression, as the heart or spirits (as, "My spirits began to *sink* under the burthen of a strong distemper": Defoe's "Robinson Crusoe," i. 6); give way under misfortune or affliction, as a person; also, to decrease in amount, extent, degree, etc., as value, prices, rates, etc.; become lower in tone or pitch, as sound, the voice, etc.; also, to sink a shaft, well, etc., by excavating or boring. **II.** *tr.* To cause to sink or become submerged, as in water (as, to *sink* the enemy's ships; to *sink* a caisson for engineering work); also, to cause to fall, descend, or go to a lower level (as, rivers *sunk* by drought; to *sink* a weapon to the ground); see (land, a ship, etc.) sink beneath the horizon with increasing distance (as, "In a few hours we *sank* them [islands] in the north-east": Dana's "Two Years before the Mast," iv.); put down (a pipe, post, etc.), as into the ground; insert (a screw, part, etc.) into something; depress (a part, area, etc.) below the general level, as by excavating or hollowing; hence, to make (a hole, shaft, well, etc.) by excavating or boring downward; hollow out (any cavity); cut the design into (a die, etc.: cf. *die-sinker*); also, to cause to fall into some state (as, "The gloom of the hour . . . *sunk* him in silent reverie": Mrs. Radcliffe's "Romance of the Forest," i.); bring to some lower or worse state; reduce, lower, or degrade; bring to ruin or perdition (formerly much used in imprecation: as, "*Sink* the public, madam, when the fair are to be attended," Goldsmith's "Good-Natured Man," ii.); depress or deject, as in spirit; also, to reduce in amount, extent, etc., as value or prices (as, "whatever regulations tend to *sink* the price . . . below what it naturally would be": Adam Smith's "Wealth of Nations," iv. 8); decrease or extinguish (a debt) by payment (as, "the funds given for *sinking* the debt," Burke's "Conciliation with the Colonies": cf. *sinking-fund*); lower (the voice, etc.: as, "*sinking* her voice almost to a whisper," W. H. Hudson's "Purple Land," xxii.); also, to merge, as one thing in another (as, to *sink* the official in the friend, that is, to subordinate one's own official character to one's relation as friend); give up or abandon, as a name or title; suppress, as facts; omit, ignore, or avoid mentioning; leave out of consideration; also, to invest (money), now esp. unprofitably (as, "The money *sunk* here unproductively would have quite restored the family": Stevenson's "Master of Ballantrae," ii.); lose (money) in an unfortunate investment, etc. —**sink,** *n.* A pit or cesspool, or a drain or sewer, as for dirty water, liquid filth, etc. (now rare); a basin or receptacle, esp. in a kitchen, connected with a drain, for receiving and carrying off dirty water; hence, fig., a place of vice or corruption; a resort or abode of depraved persons; also, a low-lying area or basin in land where waters collect, or where they disappear by sinking downward or by evaporation; sometimes, (as, a sink-hole; also, the act or an act of sinking (as, "The patient *sink* and swell Of winds among the leaves": Lowell's "Legend of Brittany," ii. 19).

sink-a-ble (sing′ką-bl), *a.* That may be sunk.

sink-er (sing′kèr), *n.* One who or that which sinks; a die-sinker; a weight of lead, etc., for sinking a fishing-line, fishing-net, or the like in the water; also, a doughnut or a cruller (slang, U. S.).

sink=hole (singk′hōl), *n.* A hole or funnel-like cavity formed in rock, etc., by the action of water, and serving to conduct surface water to an underground passage; a swallow or swallow-hole.

sink-ing=fund (sing′king-fund), *n.* A fund formed by a government, a corporation, or the like, as by periodically setting aside certain amounts of money to accumulate at interest, for the sinking or extinguishing of a debt: as, "The *Sinking Fund*, which is part of the Budget of regular governmental expenditures, reduces the debt by about three hundred million dollars a year" (A. W. Mellon's "Taxation," iii.).

sink-less (singk′les), *a.* Unsinkable, as a ship.

sin-less (sin′les), *a.* [AS. *synlēas.*] Free from or without sin.—**sin′less-ly**, *adv.*—**sin′less-ness**, *n.*

sin-ner (sin′èr), *n.* One who sins; a transgressor; an offender.

sin-net (sin′et), *n.* Same as *sennit* (cordage).

Sinn Fein (shin fān). [Ir. *sinn féin,* 'we ourselves.'] A political organization in Ireland, founded about 1905, advocating the advancement of Ireland along national lines and its complete political separation from Great Britain.—**Sinn Fein′er,** *n.* A member or supporter of the Sinn Fein.

Sino-. Form of L. *Sinæ,* Gr. Σῖναι, the Chinese, used in combination, as in *Sino-Japanese, Sinology.*

sin=of-fer-ing (sin′of′èr-ing), *n.* A sacrifice or other offering made as an atonement for sin. See Ex. xxix. 14.

Sin-o=Jap-a-nese (sin′ọ̄-jap-ạ-nēs′ or -nēz′, or sī′nọ̄-), *a.* [See *Sino-.*] Chinese and Japanese; of both China and Japan: as, *Sino-Japanese* art.

Sin-o-log-i-cal (sin-ọ̄-loj′i-kạl), *a.* Of or pertaining to Sinology.—**Si-nol-o-gist** (si-nol′ọ̄-jist), *n.* One versed in Sinology.—**Sin′o-logue** (-log), *n.* A Sinologist.

Si-nol-o-gy (si-nol′ọ̄-ji), *n.* [See *Sino-* and *-logy.*] The branch of knowledge or study that deals with the language, literature, history, institutions, customs, etc., of China.

Si-non (sī′non), *n.* [From that *Sinon* who, during the siege of Troy, induced the Trojans to take into their city the wooden horse, filled with armed Greeks.] A treacherous or perfidious betrayer: as, "Mr. Osbaldistone inveighed . . . against the arts of these modern *Sinons*" (Scott's "Rob Roy," iv.).

Sin-o-phil, Sin-o-phile (sin′ọ̄-fil). [See *Sino-* and *-phil.*] **I.** *a.* Friendly to the Chinese; fond of Chinese ways, customs, etc. **II.** *n.* A friend or admirer of the Chinese.

sin-ter (sin′tèr), *n.* [G., = E. *cinder.*] Siliceous or calcareous matter deposited by springs, as that formed around the vent of a geyser.

sin-u-ate, sin-u-at-ed (sin′ū-āt, -ā-ted), *a.* [L. *sinuatus,* pp. of *sinuare,* bend, wind, < *sinus:* see *sinus.*] Bent in and out; winding; sinuous; in *bot.,* having the margin strongly or distinctly wavy, as a leaf.—**sin′u-ate-ly,** *adv.*—**sin-u-a′tion** (-ā′shọn), *n.* A winding; a sinuosity.

sin-u-os-i-ty (sin-ū-os′i-ti), *n.;* pl. *-ties* (-tiz). Sinuous form or character; winding; also, a curve, bend, or turn, as of a winding road or river or of any sinuous formation or cavity (commonly in *pl.*): as, "The long stretch of the Alpine coast continued beyond sight its endless sinuosities," J. Conrad's "Rover," xvi.); fig., *pl.,* intricacies.

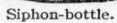
Sinuate Leaf.

sin-u-ous (sin′ū-us), *a.* [L. *sinuosus,* < *sinus:* see *sinus.*] Abounding in curves, bends, or turns, or winding (as, "gardens bright with *sinuous* rills": Coleridge's "Kubla Khan"); fig., intricate; indirect; devious; morally crooked.—**sin′u-ous-ly,** *adv.*—**sin′u-ous-ness,** *n.*

si-nus (sī′nus), *n.;* pl. *sinuses,* L. *sinus.* [L., a bend, fold, inner place, hollow, bay or gulf: cf. *sine*[1].] A curve, bend, or fold; a curving part or recess; a bay† or gulf†; in *anat.,* any of various cavities, recesses, or passages, as a hollow in a bone, or a reservoir or channel for venous blood; in *pathol.,* a narrow, elongated abscess with a small orifice; a narrow passage leading to an abscess or the like; in *bot.,* a small, rounded depression between two projecting lobes, as of a leaf.

-sion. See *-ion.*

Siou-an (sö′ạn), *a.* Belonging to or constituting a linguistic stock of North American Indians formerly widespread through the central U. S. and northward into British America, and including the Sioux (Dakota), Crow, Iowa, Mandan, Omaha, Osage, Winnebago, and other tribes.

sip (sip), *v.;* *sipped, sipping.* [ME. *sippen*; prob. a modified form of *sup*[1].] **I.** *intr.* To take up liquid with the lips in small quantities for swallowing; drink by sips: as, "Peyrol . . . *sipped* from his mug" (J. Conrad's "Rover," ix.). Also fig. **II.** *tr.* To drink by sips, or little by little (as, "The water's boiling! Now *sip* a good glass slowly": Galsworthy's "Dark Flower," ii. 3); fig., to take in, absorb, or enjoy as if by sips (as, "every herb that *sips* the dew," Milton's "Il Penseroso," 172; "He was a man of taste, and *sipped* the arts and other knowledge, as he sauntered Europe round," Reade's "Christie Johnstone," i.); also, to take honey from as by sips (poetic: as, "They [bees] . . . *sip* the purple flow'rs," Dryden's tr. Virgil's "Georgics," iv. 76).—**sip,** *n.* An act of sipping; also, a small quantity taken by or as by sipping; a small draft or drink (as, "I . . . dismounted to give my horse a *sip* of clear water": W. H. Hudson's "Purple Land," vii.).

sipe (sīp), *v. i.;* *siped, siping.* [AS. *sīpian,* soak: cf. *seep.*] To percolate or ooze through something; seep. [Chiefly Sc. and north. Eng.]

si-phon (sī′fọn), *n.* [L. *sipho(n-),* < Gr. σίφων, tube, pipe.] A bent tube of glass, metal, rubber, or the like, by which a liquid is conducted over something higher, as the side of a receptacle, by means of atmospheric pressure, one leg of the tube being in the liquid and the other outside and reaching lower than the surface of the liquid, and the tube being filled with the liquid by suction or otherwise in order to start the flow; also, a fluid-conducting tubular organ, as that by which water is conveyed to the gills, etc., of a bivalve mollusk or that by which the waste water passes out; also, a siphon-bottle.—**si′phon,** *v. t.* or *i.* To convey or pass through a siphon.—**si′phon-age** (-āj), *n.* The action of a siphon.—**si′phon-ate** (-āt), *a.* Of a mollusk, etc., having a siphon or siphons.—**si′phon=bot″tle,** *n.* A bottle for aërated water, fitted with a tube extending from near the interior bottom of the bottle out through the neck and terminating in a short, bent nozzle, the water being forced out, when a valve is opened, by the pressure on its surface of the gas accumulating within the bottle.

Siphons.—At left, ordinary siphon; at right, siphon with exhausting-tube (*a*) to start flow by sucking liquid to cock (*b*), which is closed, the cock then being opened and the flow beginning, the exhausting-tube being closed while the liquid is running.

si-pho-no-phore (sī′fọ-nọ̄-fōr), *n.* [NL. *Siphonophora,* pl., < Gr. σίφων, tube, + -φόρος, bearing: see *-phorous.*] Any of the *Siphonophora,* an order of pelagic hydrozoans occurring in many diverse forms but consisting typically of a hollow stem or stock budding into a number of appendages.

si-phun-cle (sī′fung-kl), *n.* [L. *siphunculus,* dim. of *sipho(n-),* E. *siphon.*] In *zoöl.,* a small tube passing through the partitions in the shell of certain cephalopods; in *entom.,* either of two small tubular organs on the abdomen

Siphon-bottle.

of an aphid, through which a waxy secretion is exuded.—**si-phun'cu-lar** (-kū-lạr), *a*. Of, pertaining to, or of the nature of a siphuncle.—**si-phun'cu-late, si-phun'cu-lat-ed** (-lāt, -lā-ted), *a*. Having a siphuncle.

sip-id (sip'id), *a*. [Back-formation from *insipid*: cf. *sapid*.] Having a pleasing taste or flavor; fig., of agreeably distinctive character.

sip-per (sip'ėr), *n*. One who sips, or drinks by sips; also, a straw or a small tube through which to sip or suck up a beverage.

sip-pet (sip'et), *n*. [Appar. dim. < *sop*: cf. *sip*.] A small piece of toasted or fried bread, esp. as served in soup or with meat; hence, a small piece or bit of anything; a fragment.

sip-pi-o (sip'i-ō), *n*. [Cf. *Mississippi*, name of an old game similar to bagatelle.] A game of the bagatelle kind, played with eight balls, which are to be driven into numbered holes or pockets by means of a cue-ball struck with an ordinary cue.

sir (sėr), *n*. [Shortened form of *sire*.] A master, lord, or gentleman (obs. or archaic: as, "some *sir* of note," Shakspere's "Twelfth Night," iii. 4. 81); also, a title of respect or honor used before a man's name, esp. formerly [*l. c.* or *cap.*] in designating a priest, a bachelor of arts, or some notable personage of ancient times (as, *Sir* Pandarus of Troy), and [*cap.*] in regular modern use (before the Christian name) as the distinctive title of a knight or a baronet (as, *Sir* Henry Irving, Knight; *Sir* Walter Scott, Baronet); [*l. c.*] a title of respect prefixed to a noun designating a man's profession, rank, etc. (archaic: as, *sir* priest; *sir* knight); also, a respectful or formal term of address used to a man, as to a superior or elder or at the beginning of a letter.—**sir**, *v. t.*; **sirred** (also sir'd), **sirring**. To address as 'sir': as, "The regiment of natty servants respectfully *'sir'd'* me" (Mark Twain's "Life on the Mississippi," vi.).

sir'car, *n*. See *sirkar*.

sir-dar (sėr'där or sėr-där'), *n*. [Hind. *sardār*, < Pers. *sardār*, < *sar*, head, + *-dār*, holder.] In India, etc., a military chief or leader; specif., the British commander of the Egyptian army.—**sir'dar-ship**, *n*.

sire (sīr), *n*. [OF. F. *sire*, lord, < L. *senior*, elder: see *senior*, and cf. *messire*, *sieur*, and *sir*.] A master†, lord†, or sovereign†; a person of importance†; also, an aged or elderly man (as, "that bearded, staff-supported *Sire*," Wordsworth's "White Doe of Rylstone," i.: now chiefly poetic); a father or forefather (as, "Few sons attain the praise Of their great *sires*," Pope's tr. Homer's "Odyssey," ii.: now chiefly poetic); specif., the male parent of a quadruped (often with *dam* for the female parent); esp., a stallion; also, a respectful term of address used to a man, formerly (like *sir*) to any superior or elder, but now only (esp. archaically) to a king or other sovereign (as, " 'We shall then proceed into the wood together,' said the Emperor . . . 'I understand, *sire*' ": Conan Doyle's "Exploits of Brigadier Gerard," ii.); also, in old French use (F. pron. sēr), the title of certain seigneurs or feudal lords (as, the *Sire* de Joinville).—**sire**, *v. t.*; **sired**, **siring**. To become the sire of; beget: now used esp. of stallions.

si-re-don (sī-rē'don), *n*. [NL., < Gr. σειρηδών, siren.] An axolotl, or larval salamander of the genus *Amblystoma*.

sire-less (sīr'les), *a*. Without a sire; fatherless. [Poetic.]

si-ren (sī'ren). [Also *syren*; L. *siren*, < Gr. σειρήν, siren.]
I. *n*. One of several fabulous sea-nymphs of classical mythology, part woman and part bird, who were supposed to lure mariners to destruction by their seductive singing; hence, a woman or other female being that sings sweetly (as, "In deep of

Ulysses and the Sirens, from a Greek red-figured hydria.

night . . . then listen I To the celestial *sirens'* harmony": Milton's "Arcades," 63); more commonly, a woman who exercises an alluring or dangerous charm (as, "If Mr. Haim stayed away from home of an evening Mrs. Lobley was the *siren* who deflected him from the straight domestic path": Arnold Bennett's "Roll-Call," ii.); also, an acoustical instrument for producing musical tones, consisting essentially of a disk pierced with holes arranged equidistantly in a circle, which is rotated over a jet or stream of compressed air, steam, or the like, so that the stream is alternately allowed to pass and interrupted; a device of this kind used as a whistle, fog-signal, etc.; also, any of certain eel-like amphibians (family *Sirenidæ*) with small fore limbs and no hind ones, and with external gills persistent throughout life. **II.** *a*. Pertaining to or characteristic of a siren (as, a *siren* voice or song); dangerously alluring (as, *siren* beauty or fascinations).

si-re-ni-an (sī-rē'ni-ạn), *n*. [NL. *Sirenia*, pl., < L. *siren*, E. *siren*.] Any of the *Sirenia*, an order of aquatic herbivorous mammals, including the manatee, dugong, etc., with a fish-like body, flipper-like fore limbs, rudimentary or no hind limbs, and a flat, horizontally expanded tail.

si-ren-ic (sī-ren'ik), *a*. Siren-like; seductive; alluring.

sir-gang (sėr'gang), *n*. A corvine bird, *Cissa sinensis*, of southern Asia, with plumage of a light green (when newly molted) later changing to blue.

Sir-i-us (sir'i-us), *n*. [L., < Gr. Σείριος, Sirius.] The dog-star, in the constellation Canis Major: the brightest (fixed) star in the heavens.—**Sir'i-an**, *a*.

Sirgang.

sir-kar (sėr'kär or sėr-kär'), *n*. [Hind. *sarkār*, < Pers. *sarkār*, < *sar*, head, + *kār*, action, business.] In India, the government; the state.

sir-loin (sėr'loin), *n*. [For *surloin*, from a var. of OF. *surlonge*, sirloin, < *sur*, over, + *longe*, loin; not so called, as often alleged, from a humorous knighting of the piece as 'Sir Loin' by James I. or some other king of England.] The portion of the loin of beef in front of the rump.

si-roc (si-rok' or sī'rok), *n*. Same as *sirocco*. [Archaic or poetic.]

si-roc-co (si-rok'ō), *n*.; pl. *siroccos* (-ōz). [It. *sirocco*, *scirocco*, < Ar. *sharq*, east.] A hot, dry, dust-laden wind blowing from northern Africa across the Mediterranean, and affecting certain parts of southern Europe; also, a warm, sultry south or southeast wind accompanied by rain, occurring in the same regions; hence, any hot, oppressive wind elsewhere.

sir-rah (sir'ä), *n*. [Extended form of *sir*.] A term of address used to men and boys (sometimes formerly to women) in impatience, contempt, anger, etc.: as, " 'Silence, *sirrah!*' said Jos" (Thackeray's "Vanity Fair," xxxi.); " 'Answer, *sirrah!*' he continued, working himself rapidly into a passion" (S. J. Weyman's "Gentleman of France," xxiv.). [Archaic.]

sir=rev-er-ence†, *n*. [For *save reverence*, that is, saving (one's) reverence, with all respect (as for a hearer).] An expression used apologetically, as before unseemly or indelicate words. See Shakspere's "Comedy of Errors," iii. 2. 93.

sir-up (sir'up), etc. See *syrup*, etc.

sir-vente (sėr-vont'), *n*. [F., < Pr. *sirventes*, *sirventesc*, appar. orig. a poem by a *sirvent*, lit. 'one serving' (fighting or contending in the service of another), < L. *serviens*, ppr., E. *servient*.] A kind of poem of the medieval troubadours, often satirical, and usually devoted to political or moral subjects.

sis (sis), *n*. A colloquial abbreviation of *sister*, also used in familiar address to any girl. Cf. *bub*.

Sis-al (sis'ạl or sē-säl') **hemp**. [From *Sisal*, port of Yucatan.] Any of certain fibers yielded by species of agave, esp.

Agave rigida sisalana of Yucatan, used for making ropes, etc.; also, a plant yielding such fiber. Also called *sisal*. Cf. *henequen*.

sis-co-wet (sis′kō-wet), *n.* [N. Amer. Ind.] A very fat, thick-skinned variety of the namaycush (trout), found in Lake Superior.

sis-kin (sis′kin), *n.* [Cf. G. *zeischen, zeisig*, MLG. *ziseke*, Dan. *sisgen*, siskin, prob. from Slav.] A small old-world fringilline bird, *Chrysomitris* (or *Spinus*) *spinus*; also, any of certain related or similar birds, as the pine-siskin.

Siskin (*Chrysomitris spinus*).

sis-mo-gram (sis′mō-gram), etc. Same as *seismogram*, etc.

siss (sis), *v. i.* [Imit.] To hiss.—**siss,** *n.* A hiss.

sis-sy (sis′i), *n.*; pl. *sissies* (-iz). [Dim. of *sis*.] A familiar term of address to a little girl; also, an effeminate boy or man. [Colloq.]

sis-ter (sis′tėr). [Prob. from Scand.: cf. Icel. *systir*, Sw. *syster*, Dan. *söster*, also AS. *sweostor, swuster*, D. *zuster*, G. *schwester*, Goth. *swistar*, sister, akin to L. *soror* and Skt. *svasar-*, sister.] **I.** *n.* A female relative, a daughter of the same parents or parent; also, a female member of a religious order, society, etc. (as, a *Sister* of Charity, a member of any of various religious organizations of women devoted to works of mercy, esp. of a Roman Catholic congregation established in 1633 by St. Vincent de Paul and bound only by yearly vows); a female fellow-member, as of a church; one of a number or group (female, or regarded as feminine) considered as linked by some relation resembling that of children of one family; a thing associated as if by kinship with something else (as, "Happiness and Intelligence are seldom *sisters*": Peacock's "Headlong Hall," v.). **II.** *a.* Being a sister; related by or as by sisterhood (as, *sister* churches; *sister* ships, ships built at the same time and of the same type).— **sis′ter,** *v. t.* To stand in the relation of a sister to; also, to treat or address as a sister.—**sis′ter-hood** (-húd), *n.* The state of being a sister; sisterly relation; also, a group or body of sisters; an association of women bound by monastic vows or otherwise devoted to religious life or work; a number of women with some common aim, characteristic, etc.— **sis′ter=in=law″,** *n.*; pl. *sisters-in-law.* One's husband's or wife's sister; one's brother's wife.—**sis′ter-ly,** *a.* Of, like, or befitting a sister.—**sis′ter-li-ness,** *n.*—**sis′ter-ly,** *adv.* In the manner of a sister or of sisters.

Sis-tine (sis′tēn or -tin), *a.* [It. *Sistino*, < *Sisto*, Sixtus.] Of or pertaining to any of various popes named Sixtus: as, the *Sistine* Chapel (the chapel of the Pope in the Vatican at Rome, built for Pope Sixtus IV., and decorated with frescoes by Michelangelo and others); the *Sistine* Madonna (a famous Madonna painted by Raphael for the Church of St. Sixtus at Piacenza, Italy, now in the museum at Dresden).

sis-trum (sis′trum), *n.*; pl. *-trums* or *-tra* (-trä). [L., < Gr. σεῖστρον, < σείειν, shake.] An ancient musical instrument, a form of metal rattle, used esp. in Egypt in the worship of Isis.

Sis-y-phe-an (sis-i-fē′an), *a.* Of or pertaining to Sisyphus, a mythical king of Corinth, condemned in Hades to roll a heavy stone up a steep hill, only to have it always roll down again when he approached the top; hence, endless and unavailing, as labor or a task.

sit (sit), *v. i.*; *sat* (archaic *sate*), *sitting*. [AS. *sittan* (pret. *sæt*) = D. *zitten* = G. *sitzen* = Icel. *sitja* = Goth. *sitan*, sit; akin to L. *sedere*, Gr. ἕζεσθαι, Skt. *sad-*, sit, Gr. ἕδρα, seat, base: cf. *seat, set, settle¹, see¹, session, cathedra*, and *-hedron*.] To take or have the posture in which the weight of the body rests upon the haunches or buttocks; be seated; also, of a bird, to perch or roost; assume or continue in the position necessary for hatching eggs; also, to occupy a seat in an official capacity, as a judge or bishop; have a seat in a legislative assembly, etc. (as, "Its [Council of State's]

Sistrum.

members were named in the Act and *sat* for life": Morley's "Oliver Cromwell," v. 1); be convened or in session, as an assembly; also, to place one's self in position for having one's portrait painted, one's photograph taken, or the like (as, "If she was well enough to *sit* he must certainly have her portrait painted": S. Butler's "Way of All Flesh," lxxxiii.); also, to have one's seat or place; dwell or abide; be situated (as, "a cluster of black roofs . . . *sitting* among vineyards and meadows and orchards": Stevenson's "Travels with a Donkey," v. 3); rest or lie on something; blow from a particular direction, as the wind (as, "*Sits* the wind in that corner?" Shakspere's "Much Ado about Nothing," ii. 3. 102); fit or be adjusted in a specified manner, as a garment.— **to sit on** or **upon,** to sit in judgment or council on, or consider officially (as, "Three magistrates arrived and *sat on* my case," Arnold Bennett's "Lion's Share," xxi.; the coroner's jury *sat on* the case); also, to have a seat on (a jury, commission, etc.: as, "a law . . . disabling the senators from *sitting on* juries of any kind," Froude's "Cæsar," iii.); also, to check, rebuke, or snub (slang: as, to *sit upon* a forward or presumptuous person).—**to sit pretty,** fig., to occupy a position that suits or pleases one; be in a favorable or eminently satisfactory position of affairs. [Slang.]—**to sit tight,** to sit firmly; hence (colloq.), to maintain a position or attitude taken; refuse to abandon one's position; hold on or wait quietly, without acting.—**to sit under,** to attend the preaching, etc., of; listen to, as a customary hearer: as, "Members of Parliament, even Cabinet Ministers, *sit under* him [a clergyman]" (Thackeray's "Newcomes," xi.).—**to sit up,** to raise the body from a recumbent to a sitting posture; maintain a sitting posture, instead of lying down; stay up, instead of going to bed; watch, as with a sick person during the night; also, to sit upright or start up in astonishment (often fig., as in the colloq. phrase 'to make one sit up': as, "I thought I'd retire for five years . . . and then come back and make 'em *sit up*," Arnold Bennett's "Hilda Less-ways," iii. 2).—**sit,** *v. t.* To cause (now usually one's self) to sit (often with *down*); seat; also, to sit upon (a horse, etc.: as, "He . . . *sat* his horse easily," F. M. Crawford's "Mr. Isaacs," viii.).—**to sit out,** to remain seated through (a dance, etc.), instead of taking part; remain seated or present throughout (a performance, etc.), instead of withdrawing; also, to sit longer than or outstay (another), as in making a call.—**sit,** *n.* The manner in which an article of dress sits or fits; also, a sinking or settling, as of a wall.

site (sīt), *n.* [L. *situs*, position, situation, < *sinere* (pp. *situs*), let, put, lay: cf. *situate*.] The position or place of anything (now only as in the following); the position of a town, building, etc., esp. with reference to environment (as, "A structure fair, Its *site* uncertain, if in earth or air": Pope's "Temple of Fame," 421); the ground or area upon which anything, as a building, is, has been, or is to be located (as, "The chapel . . . stands on the *site* of the ancient church burnt not long ago": Howells's "Chance Acquaintance," xiii.).—**site,** *v. t.*; *sited, siting.* To place or locate.

sit-fast (sit′fàst), *n.* In *vet. science*, a callosity, often tending to ulceration, on the back of a horse or similar animal, due to pressure or friction of the saddle.

sith (sith), *adv., prep.,* and *conj.* [ME. *sith* (by reduction), also *sithens* (by extension: see -s³), for *sithen*, < AS. *sith-than*, for *sīth than*, after that: cf. Icel. *sīdhan*, Dan. *siden*, G. *seitdem*, after that, G. *seit*, since, also E. *sin²* and *since*.] Since. Also **sith′en, sith′ens, sith′ence.** [Obs., archaic, or prov.]

sito-. Form of Gr. σῖτος, food, used in combination.— **si-tol-o-gy** (sī-tol′ō-ji), *n.* [+ *-logy*.] The science of food or diet; dietetics.—**si-to-ma-ni-a** (sī-tō-mā′ni-a), *n.* In *pathol.*, insane craving for food.—**si-to-pho′bi-a** (-fō′bi-ä), *n.* [+ *-phobia*.] In *pathol.*, insane aversion to food.—**si-to-tox′in** (-tok′sin), *n.* A toxin or poison generated by a micro-organism in vegetable food.

sit-ter (sit′ėr), *n.* One who sits, or occupies a seat; a person who sits or poses for a portrait, photograph, or the like; also, a brooding bird.

sit-ting (sit′ing), *n.* The act of one who or that which sits; a brooding, as of a hen upon eggs, or the number of eggs on which a bird sits during one hatching; a session, as of a court or legislature; a period of remaining seated, as for continuous action or work (as, "You should question me for half-a-dozen hours at a *sitting*, and welcome": Dickens's "Old Curiosity Shop," xlvi.); a period of sitting for a portrait, photograph, or the like (as, "The girl was giving *sittings* to Lavendie [a painter] in the drawing-room": Galsworthy's "Saint's Progress," iii. 4); also, that on or in which one sits; a seat for one person in a church, or the right to use such a seat (as, "The church is enlarged by at least five hundred *sittings*": George Eliot's "Janet's Repentance," ii.).—**sit'ting=room**, *n.* A room to sit in, as distinguished from a bedroom, kitchen, etc.; a parlor: as, "The house . . . contained room for about eight boarders, who had one *sitting-room* in common" (Besant's "All Sorts and Conditions of Men," i.).

sit-u-ate (sit'ū-āt), *v. t.*; *-ated*, *-ating*. [LL. *situatus*, pp. of *situare*, < L. *situs*, position, E. *site*.] To give a site to, locate, or place (as, "this renowned island on which is *situated* the city of New York": Irving's "Knickerbocker's New York," i. 2); fig., to place in a particular position with reference to circumstances, or subject to circumstances (as, "something which society would . . . deem unpardonable in a girl *situated* as I was": Arnold Bennett's "Book of Carlotta," i. 3): now usually in the passive.—**sit'u-ate,** *a.* Situated: as, "Athens, though *situate* in a barren soil, possessed a pure air" (Gibbon's "Decline and Fall of the Roman Empire," xl.); "We are so falsely *situate*, we dare not show the man the door" (Stevenson's "Master of Ballantrae," vi.). [Archaic.]

sit-u-a-tion (sit-ū-ā'shọn), *n.* [ML. *situatio(n-).*] The state or manner of being situated; the location or position of a town or the like with reference to environment (as, "Beautiful for *situation* . . . is mount Zion . . . the city of the great King": Ps. xlviii. 2); a position or place with reference to environment or character (as, a camp in a sheltered *situation*); in general, a place or locality, esp. a place of abode or sojourn (obs. or archaic); fig., position with reference to circumstances (as, to be in the *situation* of a rudderless boat, or of a bankrupt); condition, case, or plight; a position in life, experience, or the like, in which one is or might be (as, to be in or to avoid an embarrassing *situation*; "New *situations* give a diff'rent cast Of habit, inclination, temper, taste," Cowper's "Tirocinium," 440); often, a position or post of employment (as, to apply for a *situation*; to be out of a *situation*; "James Gloag's father, who . . . flung up his *situation*," Barrie's "Sentimental Tommy," vi.); also, the position or state of affairs, or the combination of circumstances (as, to meet the demands of the *situation*; to be master of the *situation*; "The European *situation* was now at a pitch to get upon Mr. Britling's nerves," H. G. Wells's "Mr. Britling," i. 5. § 9); a particular state of affairs, or combination of circumstances (as, the investigation revealed a strange *situation*); specif., a state of affairs of special significance or effective value in the course of a play, novel, or the like (as, "The play turned upon a typical French *situation*," Mrs. H. Ward's "Robert Elsmere," xii.; the book abounds in *situations*).

sit-u-la (sit'ū-lạ), *n.*; pl. *-læ* (-lē). [L., bucket, urn.] In *class. antiq.*, a deep, bucket-like vessel, vase, or urn.

si-tus (sī'tus), *n.* [L.: see *site*.] Position, situation, or location; esp., the proper or original position, as of a part or organ.

sitz=bath (sits'bȧth), *n.* [For G. *sitzbad*, < *sitzen*, sit, + *bad*, bath.] A tub or vessel to bathe in, in which the user sits so that only the hips and the lower part of the trunk are submerged; also, the bath so taken.

Si-va (sē'vạ), *n.* [Euphemistic use of Skt. *çiva*, kind, gracious.] In *Hindu religion*, one of the three chief divinities, the third member of the Hindu trinity: known also as 'the Destroyer.' See cut in next column. See also *Trimurti*, and cf. *Brahma*[2] and *Vishnu*.—**Si'va-ism**, *n.* The worship of Siva.—**Si'va-ist**, *n.* A worshiper of Siva.—**Si-va-is'tic**, *a.*

Situla (Greco-Egyptian).

Si-van (sē-vän'), *n.* [Heb.] In the Jewish calendar, the ninth month (30 days) of the civil year and the third of the ecclesiastical year, beginning in the latter part of May or the first part of June.

siv-a-there (siv'ạ-thēr), *n.* [NL. *sivatherium*: see *Siva* and *-there*.] A large, four-horned mammal of the extinct genus *Sivatherium*, having a skull of the size of an elephant's and probably allied to the giraffe, found in the Tertiary strata of India. Also **siv-a-the'ri-um** (-thē'ri-um).

si-wash (sī'wosh). [Chinook jargon, < F. *sauvage*, E. *savage*.] [Often *cap.*] **I.** *a.* Indian: with reference to the northern Pacific coast of North America. **II.** *n.* An Indian of the northern Pacific coast of North America: often used [*cap.*] as if referring to a particular tribe.

six (siks). [AS. *six, siex, seox*, = D. *zes* = G. *sechs* = Icel. *sex* = Goth. *saihs*, six; akin to L. *sex*, Gr. ἕξ, Skt. *shash*, six.] **I.** *a.* One more than five. **II.** *n.* A number composed of six units, or a symbol, as 6 or vi, representing it; a set of six persons or things; a playing-card, die-face, etc., with six pips.—**at sixes and sevens** [orig. from an expression used in dicing], in disorder or confusion: as, "While doing one thing with heart and soul, he was too apt to leave every thing else *at sixes and sevens*" (Irving's "Knickerbocker's New York," vii. 6).—**six'fold** (-fōld). **I.** *a.* Comprising six parts or members; six times as great or as much. **II.** *adv.* In sixfold measure.—**six'pence** (-pẹns), *n.* A sum of money of the value of six English pennies, or about 12 U. S. cents; also, a British silver coin of this value.—**six'pen-ny** (-pẹ-ni), *a.* Of the amount or value of sixpence; costing sixpence; hence, of trifling value; cheap; paltry.—**six'=shoot'er**, *n.* A revolver with which six shots can be fired without reloading.

sixte (sikst), *n.* [F., < L. *sextus*, sixth, < *sex*, six: see *six*.] In *fencing*, the sixth in a series of eight parries.

six-teen (siks'tēn'). [AS. *sixtȳne*.] **I.** *a.* Six more than ten. **II.** *n.* A number composed of sixteen units, or a symbol, as 16 or xvi, representing it.—**six'teen'mo** (-mō), *n.* and *a.* [See *-mo*.] Same as *sextodecimo*.—**six'teenth'**. **I.** *a.* Next after the fifteenth; also, being one of sixteen equal parts. **II.** *n.* The sixteenth member of a series; also, a sixteenth part.—**six'teenth=note**, *n.* In *music*, a note having one sixteenth of the time-value of a whole-note; a semiquaver.

sixth (siksth). [AS. *sixta*.] **I.** *a.* Next after the fifth; also, being one of six equal parts. **II.** *n.* The sixth member of a series; also, a sixth part; in *music*, a tone on the sixth degree from a given tone (counted as the first); the interval between such tones; the harmonic combination of such tones; in a scale, the submediant.—**sixth'ly**, *adv.*

six-ti-eth (siks'ti-eth). [AS. *sixteogotha*.] **I.** *a.* Next after the fifty-ninth; also, being one of sixty equal parts. **II.** *n.* The sixtieth member of a series; also, a sixtieth part.

six-ty (siks'ti). [AS. *sixtig, siextig*.] **I.** *a.* Six times ten. **II.** *n.*; pl. *-ties* (-tiz). A number composed of sixty units, or a symbol, as 60 or lx, representing it.

siz-a-ble (sī'zạ-bl), *a.* Of suitable or convenient size†; also, of fair size; fairly large.—**siz'a-ble-ness**, *n.*—**siz'a-bly**, *adv.*

siz-ar (sī'zạr), *n.* [From an allowance of food, etc., granted: see *size*[1], *n.*] In the colleges of the University of Cambridge, England, and at Trinity College, Dublin, one of a class of undergraduates who receive from the college assistance toward maintenance.—**siz'ar-ship**, *n.*

size[1] (sīz), *n.* [For *assize*.] An assize for administering justice (now prov. Eng. and Sc.); also, a fixed standard, as for food or drink†; a quantity or portion of food or drink† (as, "'Tis not in thee To grudge my pleasures . . . to scant my *sizes*," Shakspere's "King Lear," ii. 4. 178: cf. *sizar*); also, the dimensions, proportions, or magnitude (linear, square, solid, numerical, etc.) of anything (as, the *size* of a

Siva.

pencil, map, book, tree, house, city, or army; men of the same *size*); sometimes, considerable or great magnitude (as, to seek *size* rather than quality); often, the magnitude of a thing, as a manufactured article, in terms of some conventional system of measurement (as, the *size* of a hat, glove, or shoe); hence, one of a series of graduated measures for articles of manufacture or trade (as, children's, women's, or men's *sizes* of shoes; *sizes* of paper or of coal); in general, extent, amount, rate, range, or scope (as, the *size* of an undertaking or an industry; the *size* of one's efforts, ambitions, powers, or understanding); pitch or volume, as of sound (as, "clamours of all *size*, both high and low": Shakspere's "Lover's Complaint," 21); grade or class (as, the common *size* of men).—**size**[1], *v.*; *sized*, *sizing*. **I.** *tr.* To regulate according to a standard†; also, to make of a certain size; regulate with respect to size; also, to separate or sort according to size; also, to take the size or measure of, or form an estimate of (usually with *up*: colloq.: as, "A fellow ought to . . . look 'em [candidates] all over and *size* 'em up, and then decide carefully," Sinclair Lewis's "Babbitt," iii.). **II.** *intr.* To have or assume size; also, to come (up) to some size, grade, etc., as in comparison with a standard (colloq.: as, the corn *sizes* up well this season; "Maybe you can give me your opinion how it [a letter] *sizes* up with the letters they write back East?" Wister's "Virginian," v.).

size[2] (sīz), *n.* [ME. *syse*, *cyse*; perhaps related to *size*[1].] Any of various gelatinous or glutinous preparations made from glue, starch, or other material, used for glazing or coating paper, cloth, etc.—**size**[2], *v. t.*; *sized*, *sizing*. To coat or treat with size.

size′a-ble. See *sizable*, etc.

sized (sīzd), *a.* [See *size*[1].] Having size, esp. as specified: as, fair-*sized*; middle-*sized*; variously *sized*.—**siz-er** (sī′zèr), *n.* A device for sizing articles, esp. for sorting them according to size.

siz-ing (sī′zing), *n.* [See *size*[2].] Size, as for glazing paper. —**siz′y**, *a.* Of or like size; thick and viscous.

sizz (siz), *v. i.* [Imit.] To hiss; sizzle.

siz-zle (siz′l), *v.*; *-zled*, *-zling.* [Imit.: cf. *sizz*.] **I.** *tr.* To burn or scorch so as to produce a hissing sound. **II.** *intr.* To make a hissing sound, as in frying or burning; also, to be very hot (colloq.).—**siz′zle**, *n.* A sizzling sound; also, extreme heat (colloq.).—**siz′zler**, *n.* An excessively hot day. [Colloq.]

sjam-bok (shäm′bok), *n.* [S. Afr. D., through Malay < Hind. *chābuk*, whip: cf. *chabouk*.] A strong, heavy whip made from the hide of a rhinoceros, hippopotamus, or the like, used in South Africa for driving cattle, etc.

skald (skåld), etc. See *scald*[3], etc.

skat (skät), *n.* [G., the game, also cards put aside in playing, < It. *scarto*, a discard, < *scartare*, to discard: cf. *écarté*.] A card-game, originating in Germany and much played there, in which there are three active players (without or with other players), 32 cards being used, two of which are dealt to the table; also, these two cards.

skate[1] (skāt), *n.* [ME. *scate*, *schate*, from Scand.: cf. Icel. and Norw. *skata*, skate.] Any of certain rays, or fishes of the genus *Raia*, usually having a pointed snout; also, a term of contempt for a person, a horse, etc. (slang: as, "Dave's a cheap *skate*, all right," Sinclair Lewis's "Main Street," xxv.).

skate[2] (skāt), *n.* [D. *schaats* (pl. *schaatsen*), skate: cf. OF. *escache*, *escace*, F. *échasse*, stilt.] A device consisting of a steel blade or runner supporting a frame for attaching to the sole of a shoe, used to enable a person to glide on ice; also, a similar device, mounted on small rollers instead of a runner, for use on a floor,

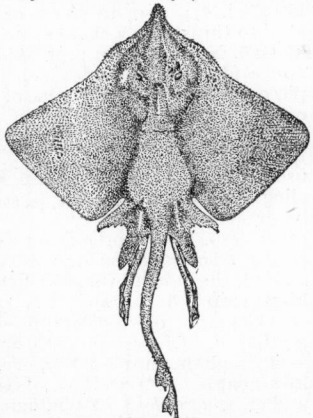

Barn-door Skate (*Raia lævis*).

the ground, etc.; a roller-skate; sometimes, a ski; also, a spell of skating; fig., a fit of intoxication (slang, U. S.). —**skate**[2], *v. i.*; *skated*, *skating.* To glide over ice or a floor, the ground, etc., on skates; hence, to glide or slide smoothly along (as, "Insects *skated* on ⸤the water": Longfellow's "Hiawatha," xviii. 58).—**skat-er** (skā′tèr), *n.* One who skates; also, any of various long-legged aquatic insects that glide over the surface of water as if skating; a water-strider.

skat-ol (skat′ol or -ōl), *n.* [Gr. σκατός, gen. of σκῶρ, dung: see *-ol*.] In *chem.*, a crystalline compound produced in the decomposition of albuminous matter, found in the intestine and in feces.

skean, skene (skēn), *n.* [Ir. and Gael. *sgian*.] A kind of knife or dagger formerly used in Ireland and among the Scottish Highlanders.

ske-dad-dle (skĕ-dad′l), *v.*; *-dled*, *-dling.* [Origin obscure.] **I.** *tr.* To spill or scatter. [Sc. and north. Eng.] **II.** *intr.* To disperse or make off precipitately in flight; run away. [Colloq.]— **ske-dad′dle**, *n.* A precipitate dispersion or flight. [Colloq.]

skee (skē), *n.* and *v.* See *ski*.

skeet (skēt), *n.* [Said to be named from an old Scand. word meaning 'shoot.'] A form of trap-shooting in which clay targets are thrown from different traps and the shooter moves to different stations, thus firing from various angles as in real game-shooting.

Skeans.— From specimens in the Museum of the Royal Irish Academy, Dublin.

skee-zicks, skee-sicks (skē′ziks), *n.* [Origin obscure.] Fellow; 'chap': used contemptuously or playfully: as, little *skeezicks* (said to a child). [Slang, U. S.]

skeg (skeg), *n.* [Prob. from Dutch.] The after part of a ship's keel; specif., a projection abaft a ship's keel for the support of a rudder.

skein (skān), *n.* [OF. *escaigne* (F. *écagne*), skein; perhaps from Celtic.] A quantity of thread or yarn disposed in loops or rounds of uniform size, formed by winding upon a reel, removing, and fastening together; also, a flight or company of wild-fowl.

skel-e-tal (skel′ẹ-tạl), *a.* Of or pertaining to a skeleton.

skel-e-ton (skel′ẹ-tọn), *n.* [NL., < Gr. σκελετόν, dried body, mummy, skeleton, prop. neut. of σκελετός, dried, < σκέλλειν, dry up.] The bones of a human or other animal body considered together, or assembled or fitted together as a framework; the bony or cartilaginous framework of a vertebrate animal; the framework or hard protective portion of an invertebrate animal, as the shell of a mollusk, crustacean, etc.; fig., a very lean or much emaciated person or animal (as, "still but a *skeleton*, a shadow of my former self," W. H. Hudson's "Far Away and Long Ago," xxii.; "an unhappy *skeleton* of a horse," Arnold Bennett's "Clayhanger," i. 1); the mere lifeless, dry, meager, or poor remains of anything; a supporting framework, as of a leaf, a building, or a ship; an outline, as of a literary work (as, "In a few days' time I sketched out the *skeleton* of my poem": Irving's "Tales of a Traveler," ii. 4); *milit.*, etc., the small number of men representing a regiment or other body when reduced far below its full strength.—**family skeleton.** See *skeleton in the closet*, below.—**skeleton at the feast**, a reminder of gloomy or depressing things in the midst of pleasure: in allusion to the Egyptian custom of having a skeleton (or rather a mummy) at feasts as a reminder of death.—**skeleton in the closet, cupboard,** or **house,** a secret source of grief or shame, esp. to a family; a hidden domestic trouble.— **skel′e-ton,** *a.* Of or pertaining to a skeleton; of the nature of a skeleton or mere framework or outline; *milit.*, etc., being the skeleton or greatly reduced form of a regiment, crew, or the like.—**skeleton key,** a key with nearly the whole substance of the bit filed away, so that it may open various locks.—**skel′e·ton·ize** (-īz), *v. t.*; *-ized, -izing.* To reduce to a skeleton; also, to construct in outline.—**skel′e·ton·iz·er** (-ī-zėr), *n.* Any of certain moths whose larvæ eat the parenchyma of leaves, leaving only the skeleton.—**skel′e·ton·less**, *a.* Having no skeleton.

skel·lum (skel′um), *n.* [D. *schelm*, < G. *schelm*, rascal.] A rascal, scamp, or scoundrel: as, "worthless *skellums*" (Burns's "To the Rev. John M′Math," 34). [Archaic or prov.]

skelp (skelp), *v.* [ME.; perhaps imit.] **I.** *tr.* To strike, beat, slap, or spank: as, "In the year you refer to, Mr. Macgregor, I was getting *skelped* in the parish school" (Stevenson's "David Balfour," v.). [Chiefly Sc. and north. Eng.] **II.** *intr.* To go quickly; run; dash: as, "*skelping* about here, destroying the few deer that are left in the country" (Scott's "Black Dwarf," vi.). [Chiefly Sc. and north. Eng.]—**skelp,** *n.* A blow, esp. with the flat of the hand; a slap; a smack. [Chiefly Sc. and north. Eng.]

skel·ter (skel′tėr), *v. i.* [From *helter-skelter*.] To dash along; rush; hurry.

skene (skēn), *n.* See *skean.*

skep (skep), *n.* [Cf. Icel. *skeppa*, measure, bushel.] A specific quantity of coal, grain, etc., being that contained in a basket or vessel of a certain size; also, a basket, hamper, or the like; also, a beehive, esp. one of straw. [Chiefly prov. Eng. and Sc.]

skep·tic, scep·tic (skep′tik). [L. *Sceptici*, pl., < Gr. Σκεπτικοί, the Skeptics, prop. pl. of σκεπτικός, adj., considering, reflective, < σκέπτεσθαι, look, view, consider: see *spy.*] **I.** *n.* [*cap.*] A member of a philosophical school of ancient Greece, the earliest group of which consisted of Pyrrho and his immediate followers (see *Pyrrhonism*), who maintained that real knowledge of things is impossible; [*l. c.*] any later philosopher or thinker who doubts or questions the possibility of real knowledge of any kind; also, one who questions the validity or authenticity of something purporting to be knowledge; one who maintains a doubting attitude in regard to a particular matter; a person of doubting temper; often, one who doubts the truth of the Christian religion or of important elements of it. **II.** *a.* [*cap.*] Pertaining to the Skeptics; also [*l. c.*], pertaining to skeptics or skepticism; skeptical.—**skep′ti·cal, scep′ti·cal,** *a.* Of or pertaining to skeptics or skepticism; imbued with or inclined to skepticism; having doubt or incredulity as to something (as, "The Major was *skeptical.* 'Dream on, fair son!' he said": Tarkington's "Magnificent Ambersons," xix.); characterized by or showing doubt or incredulity (as, a *skeptical* attitude or remark; "By his faint *sceptical* smile he seemed to insinuate that he knew better," De Quincey's "English Mail-Coach," i.).—**skep′ti·cal·ly, scep′ti·cal·ly,** *adv.*—**skep′ti·cism, scep′ti·cism** (-sizm), *n.* The doctrines or opinions of philosophical skeptics; universal doubt; also, skeptical attitude in regard to a particular matter (as, "Much of the farmer's *scepticism* on the subject was affected, as evincing a liberality of thinking": Scott's "Black Dwarf," i.); doubt; skeptical temper; often, doubt or unbelief with regard to the Christian religion.—**skep′ti·cize, scep′ti·cize** (-sīz), *v. i.*; *-cized, -cizing.* To act the sceptic; profess doubt.

sker·ry (sker′i), *n.*; pl. *skerries* (-iz). [Icel. *sker* = Sw. *skär:* cf. *scar²*.] An isolated rock, rocky island, or reef in the sea: as, "watching . . . the seals . . . that slipped off the *skerries* at our approach" (Buchan's "Three Hostages," xi.). [Chiefly Sc.]

sketch (skech), *n.* [D. *schets*, < It. *schizzo*, sketch: cf. L. *schedius*, Gr. σχέδιος, sudden, offhand, impromptu.] A rough drawing or delineation of something, giving the essential features without the details, as for the artist's use in a more elaborate or finished work; also, a simply or hastily executed drawing or painting; in general, a rough design or plan; a rough draft, as of a literary work; a brief or hasty outline of facts, occurrences, etc.; a short or slight description, account, or narrative, often in the form of a literary work (as, Dickens's "*Sketches* by Boz"); also, a short play or slight dramatic performance, as one forming part of a vaudeville program; in *music,* a preliminary memorandum or study for a finished work; also, a short composition of

descriptive character.—**sketch**, *v.* **I.** *tr.* To make a sketch of; draw or delineate roughly, as for an aid to more finished work; make a slight or simple drawing or picture of (as, "A figure . . . was seated on a bench, *sketching* the old tree": George Eliot's "Middlemarch," ix.); set forth in a brief or general description or account (as, "Montesquieu *sketched* a government which should make liberty its end": Bancroft's "Hist. of the U. S.," Amer. Revolution, ii. 1); outline. **II.** *intr.* To make a sketch or sketches.—**sketch′a·ble,** *a.* Suitable for being sketched.—**sketch′=block,** *n.* A pad of paper for sketching on.—**sketch′=book,** *n.* A book for making sketches in; also, a book of literary sketches (as, Washington Irving's "*Sketch-Book* of Geoffrey Crayon"). —**sketch′er,** *n.*—**sketch′y,** *a.* Resembling, suggesting, or giving only a sketch; having or giving only outlines, main features, etc., with little detail; hence, in general, slight, incomplete, imperfect, or superficial (as, a *sketchy* meal; *sketchy* accommodations; "He stood with a towel . . . concluding some *sketchy* ablutions," Tarkington's "Magnificent Ambersons," xvi.).—**sketch′i·ly,** *adv.*—**sketch′i·ness,** *n.*

skete (skēt), *n.* [NGr. σκῆτος, < Gr. ἀσκητής, monk, ascetic: see *ascetic.*] A settlement of monks or ascetics of the Greek Church.

skew (skū), *v.* [ME. *skewen*, < OF. *eskiuver, escuer,* var. of *eschuer*, escape, avoid, E. *eschew.*] **I.** *intr.* To escape†; also, to start aside, or shy (now prov.); also, to turn aside or swerve, as from a course; take an oblique course or direction; twist, as out of position; also, to look obliquely, esp. in suspicion or disdain. **II.** *tr.* To give an oblique direction or position to; shape or form obliquely; hurl, throw, or fling, esp. obliquely (prov. Eng.).—**skew,** *a.* Having an oblique direction or position; slanting; turned to one side; also, having a part which deviates from a straight line, right angle, or the like, as a tool, etc. (as, *skew* gearing); also, twisted askew or awry; distorted. —**skew arch,** an arch whose axis is not perpendicular to the faces of its abutments.—**skew curve,** a curve in three dimensions.—**skew,** *adv.* Askew.—**skew,** *n.* An oblique movement, direction, or position; a slant; a twist, as out of position; also, something askew or awry; in *arch.*, a stone or member presenting a sloping surface, as for another part to abut against.—**skew′back,** *n.* In *arch.*, a sloping surface against which the end of an arch rests; a stone, course of masonry, or the like, presenting such a surface.

Skew Gearing.

skew-bald (skū′bâld), *a.* [Cf. obs. or prov. *skewed*, skewbald (of uncertain origin), and *piebald.*] Of horses, etc., having patches of different colors, esp. of white and brown or red. Cf. *piebald.*

skew-er (skū′ėr), *n.* [Also (prov.) *skiver;* perhaps connected with *shiver¹*.] A long pin of wood or metal for putting through meat to hold it together or in place while being cooked; a brochette; hence, any similar pin for some other purpose.—**skew′er,** *v. t.* To fasten with or as with skewers (as, "I . . . jammed the hat on my head and *skewered* it savagely with the pins": Arnold Bennett's "Book of Carlotta," i. 4); also, to pierce or transfix as with a skewer; also, to thrust like a skewer into or through something.

ski (skē, Norw. shē), *n.*; pl. *ski* or *skis* (skēz). [Norw. *ski,* also *skid, skida,* = Sw. *skida,* Icel. *skīdh,* snow-shoe, orig. piece of wood: cf. *skid.*] One of a pair of long, slender pieces of hard wood, one fastened to each shoe, used for traveling or gliding over snow,

Ski.— *a*, profile view; *b*, view from above.

often (esp. as a sport) down declivities.—**ski,** *v. i.*; *skied, skiing.* To travel on or use ski: as, "They tramped, they skated, they *skied*" (Sinclair Lewis's "Arrowsmith," v.).

ski-a-gram (skī′a̤-gram), *n.* [See *skiagraph* and *-gram.*] A skiagraph or radiograph.—**ski″a·gram·mat′ic** (-gra-mat′ik), *a.* Of, pertaining to, or of the nature of a skiagram. —**ski″a·gram·mat′i·cal·ly,** *adv.*

ski-a-graph (skī′a̤-gräf), *n.* [Gr. σκιά, shadow: see *-graph,* and cf. *sciagraphy.*] A photograph taken with the Röntgen rays; a radiograph.—**ski′a·graph,** *v. t.* To take a skiagraph of.—**ski-ag'ra-pher** (-ag'ra̤-fẽr), *n.*—**ski-a-graph'ic** (-graf'ik), *a.* Of or pertaining to skiagraphy.—**ski-ag'ra-phy,** *n.* [See *-graphy.*] The process or art of making skiagraphs.

ski-am-a-chy (skī-am'a̤-ki), *n.* Same as *sciamachy.*

skid (skid), *n.* [Origin uncertain: cf. AS. *scīd,* Icel. *skīdh,* piece of wood.] A piece of timber, a plank, or the like, esp. one of a number, on which something rests or is supported, or by which something is held in position; also, a plank, bar, log, or the like, esp. one of a pair, on which something heavy may be slid or rolled along; one of a number of such logs or timbers forming a skidway; also, one of a pair of runners on the under part of some aëroplanes, enabling the machine to slide along the ground when alighting; also, a shoe or some other device for preventing the wheel of a vehicle from rotating, as when descending a hill; fig., a retarding agency or influence; also, an act of skidding; also, *pl., naut.,* a wooden framework fitted to the outside of a ship to prevent injury while loading, etc.—**skid,** *v.;* skidded, skidding. **I.** *tr.* To place on or slide along a skid or skids; also, to check with a skid, as a wheel. **II.** *intr.* To slide along without rotating, as a wheel to which a skid or brake has been applied; also, to slip or slide sideways while in motion, as an automobile in turning a corner rapidly; in *aëronautics,* of an aëroplane when not banked sufficiently, to slide sideways, away from the center of the curve executed in turning.—**skid'der,** *n.*—**skid'way,** *n.* Two or more logs laid parallel at right angles to a road, on which logs are piled for loading; also, a way prepared with skids, as for use in transporting logs.

skied[1] (skēd). Preterit and past participle of *ski.*

skied[2] (skīd). Preterit and past participle of *sky.*

ski-er (skē'ẽr), *n.* [See *ski, v.*] One who skis.

skiff (skif), *n.* [F. *esquif,* < It. *schifo;* from Teut., and akin to E. *ship.*] Orig., a small boat adapted for both sailing and rowing; hence, any small, light boat; a light rowboat; specif., a kind of long, narrow racing-boat for one oarsman.

skil-ful, *a.* [ME. *skilful:* see *skill*[2] and *-ful.*] Having or exercising skill, as a person; able through knowledge, practice, etc., to do something well; expert; clever; dexterous; adroit; also, characterized by, showing, or involving skill, as performance, execution, work, etc.—**skil'ful-ly,** *adv.*—**skil'ful-ness,** *n.*

skill[1] (skil), *v.* [ME. *skilen, skelien,* from Scand.: cf. Icel. and Sw. *skilja,* Dan. *skille,* separate, distinguish, and E. *skill*[2].] **I.** *tr.* To separate†; also, to understand or comprehend (now prov. Eng.); know how (with an infinitive: archaic). **II.** *intr.* To make a difference, or matter (archaic: as, "I am to get a man, — whate'er he be, It *skills* not much, we'll fit him to our turn," Shakspere's "Taming of the Shrew," iii. 2. 134); avail or help (archaic); also, to have knowledge of or be versed in something†.

skill[2] (skil), *n.* [ME. *skil, skele,* from Scand.: cf. Icel. *skil,* distinction, discernment, Sw. *skäl,* reason, Dan. *skjel,* boundary, limit, reason, justice; akin to E. *skill*[1].] The discriminating or reasoning faculty†; discernment† or understanding†; also, knowledge, conversance, or experience in a specified instance (usually with *of:* archaic or prov.); now, usually, the ability that comes from knowledge, practice, aptitude, etc., to do something well (as, "In a lottery it is not *skill* and intelligence which take the lead, but blind chance": Ruskin's "Crown of Wild Olive," ii.); competent excellence in performance, execution, workmanship, the practice of an art, etc.; expertness; cleverness; dexterity, adroitness, or address, as in handling matters, dealing with others, etc. (as, "He had conducted an important negotiation with *skill* and tact": Lytton Strachey's "Queen Victoria," iv.); also, an art† or science†; also, reason, right, or justice, as in conduct†; also, a reason†, ground†, or cause† (as, "I think you have As little *skill* to fear as I have purpose To put you to 't": Shakspere's "Winter's Tale," iv. 4. 152). —**skilled,** *a.* Having skill; trained or experienced; also, showing, involving, or requiring skill, as work.—**skil'less,** *a.* Ignorant (archaic); unskilled or inexpert, as a person; rude or crude, as work.

skil-let (skil'et), *n.* [ME. *skelet;* origin uncertain.] A long-handled saucepan or stewpan; also, a frying-pan.

skill'ful, etc. See *skilful,* etc.

skim (skim), *v.;* skimmed, skimming. [ME. *skym, skeme,*

prob. < OF. *escumer* (F. *écumer),* skim, from Teut., and akin to E. *scum.*] **I.** *tr.* To clear (liquid) of floating matter, as with a spoon, ladle, or the like (as, to *skim* milk, by taking off the cream); take up, remove, or collect (floating matter) thus (as, to *skim* cream); also, to cover (liquid, etc.) with a thin layer, as of scum or ice (as, "At night the frost *skimmed* with thin ice the edges of the ponds and small lakes": Roosevelt's "Ranch Life and the Hunting-Trail," xii.); also, to move or glide lightly over or along the surface of (the ground, water, etc.: as, "a crippled privateer, which but three short days ago had left Dieppe to *skim* the sea," Borrow's "Lavengro," ii.); pass lightly along over or near (a surface); cause (a thing, esp. something flat) to fly or move lightly along over or near a surface or in a smooth, even course through the air (as, to *skim* stones over the water; to *skim* a disk or plate horizontally across the room); also, fig., to go over in reading, study, treatment, etc., in a superficial or cursory manner (as, "Like others, I had *skimmed,* and sometimes read With care, the master-pamphlets of the day": Wordsworth's "Prelude," ix. 96). **II.** *intr.* To become covered with a thin layer, as of scum or ice, as a liquid (often with *over);* also, to pass or glide lightly along over or near a surface or through the air (as, "I saw several cuckoos *skimming* over a large pond": G. White's "Nat. Hist. of Selborne," ii. 7); also, fig., to go, pass, glance, etc., over something in a superficial or cursory way (as, to *skim* over a book or a list of names).—**skim,** *n.* The act of skimming a liquid, or that which is skimmed off, as cream; skim-milk; scum†; also, the movement of skimming lightly or smoothly along; also, a superficial or hasty survey, as of facts.

skim-ble=scam-ble, skim-ble=skam-ble (skim'bl-skam'bl). [Varied redupl. of *scamble.*] **I.** *a.* Rambling; confused; incoherent; nonsensical: as, "A couching lion and a ramping cat, And such a deal of *skimble-skamble* stuff As puts me from my faith" (Shakspere's "1 Henry IV.," iii. 1. 154). **II.** *n.* Rambling or nonsensical discourse: as, "a good deal of *skimble-skamble* of this nature" (Motley's "Dutch Republic," ii. 2).

skim-mer (skim'ẽr), *n.* One who or that which skims; a shallow utensil, usually perforated, used in skimming liquids; a superficial reader or student; any of various tern-like marine birds (genus *Rhynchops*) which skim the surface of the water with the lower mandible to obtain food, as *R. nigra,* a species common on the southern Atlantic and Gulf coasts of the U. S. ('black skimmer').

skim=milk (skim'-milk'), *n.* Milk from which the cream has been skimmed.

skim-ming (skim'-ing), *n.* The act of one who or that which skims; also, that which is removed by skimming

Black Skimmer (*Rhynchops nigra*).

(usually in *pl.*).—**skim'ming,** *p. a.* That skims; esp., passing lightly along over or near a surface; gliding or flying smoothly along; fig., dealing with a thing in a superficial way; superficial; cursory.—**skim'ming-ly,** *adv.*

skim-ming-ton (skim'ing-tŏn), *n.* [Origin obscure.] A burlesque procession or serenade in ridicule of a henpecked husband or a shrewish wife, an unfaithful husband or wife, or some other offender, formerly common in villages and country districts of England; also, a charivari or mock serenade for newly married persons (local, U. S.).

skimp (skimp), *v.* [Cf. *scrimp* and *scamp*[2].] **I.** *tr.* To scrimp; keep (a person, etc.) on short allowance of something; stint the amount of (something); also, to scamp (work, etc.); do carelessly. **II.** *intr.* To use severe or niggardly economy; also, to scamp work.—**skimp,** *a.* Skimpy.—**skimp'i-ly,** *adv.* In a skimpy manner.—**skimp'i-ness,** *n.*—**skimp'ing-ly,** *adv.*—**skimp'y,** *a.* Skimped in amount, as of material; lacking due size, length, breadth, fullness, etc.; scanty; meager.

skin (skin), *n.* [ME. *skin*, from Scand.: cf. Icel. and Sw. *skinn*, Dan. *skind*, skin, akin to OHG. *scindan*, G. *schinden*, to skin, flay.] The external covering or integument of an animal body, esp. when soft and flexible; also, such an integument stripped from the body of an animal (sometimes that obtained from a small animal as distinguished from the *hide* of a large animal); a hide or pelt; also, the skin or hide of a sheep, calf, or other animal, prepared for writing on (cf. *parchment* and *vellum*); also, a vessel made of the skin of a goat or other animal, used for holding liquids (cf. *wineskin*); in general, any integumentary covering, outer coating, or surface layer, as an investing membrane, the rind or peel of fruit, or a film on liquid; the planking or iron plating which covers the ribs of a ship; also, a skinflint (slang); also, a swindler or cheat (slang); a fleecing or swindling proceeding (slang).—**by** (orig. **with**) **the skin of one's teeth**, by a very narrow margin; barely: as, "I am escaped *with the skin of my teeth*" (Job, xix. 20).—**in** or **with a whole skin**, in or with complete safety of body; safe and sound: as, to sleep *in a whole skin*; to get off *with a whole skin*.—**skin game**, a game in which some one is fleeced or cheated; hence, any proceeding in which a person is fleeced, cheated, or swindled. [Slang.]—**to save one's skin**, to escape bodily or personal harm: as, "He was taken prisoner . . . and had to turn Dervish to *save his skin*" (Conan Doyle's "Tragedy of the Koroskó," v.).—**skin,** *v.*; skinned, skinning. **I.** *tr.* To furnish or cover with or as with skin; also, to strip or deprive of skin; flay; peel; also, to strip (*off*), as or like skin; pull (*off*), as gloves or stockings by turning back and drawing off inside out; also, to strip of money or belongings, or fleece, as in gambling, swindling, or any sharp practice (slang). **II.** *intr.* To become covered with skin, as a wound (often with *over*); also, to shed the skin; also, to slip away or make off hastily (slang: often with *out*: as, "I used to *skin* out of the ole Sunday School . . . every chance I got," Sinclair Lewis's "Babbitt," xvi.).—**skin′=bound**, *a.* Having the skin drawn tightly over the flesh, as in scleroderma.—**skin′=deep′. I.** *a.* Penetrating no deeper than the skin; superficial; shallow; slight. **II.** *adv.* In a superficial manner; slightly.—**skin′=dis-ease″**, *n.* A disease affecting the skin.—**skin′flint**, *n.* One who resorts to mean, petty ways of getting or saving money; a mean, niggardly person. —**skin′ful** (-fúl), *n.*; pl. *-fuls.* As much as a skin (vessel) for liquids can hold; also, as much as a person's skin can hold; one's fill of anything, esp. of drink.—**skin′=graft″ing**, *n.* In *surg.*, the transplanting of pieces of healthy skin from the patient's or another's body to a wound or burn, to form new skin.

skink (skingk), *n.* [L. *scincus*, < Gr. σκίγκος, kind of lizard.] Any of the harmless, generally smooth-scaled lizards constituting the family *Scincidæ*, as *Scincus officinalis*, a species common in northern Africa and formerly much used (dried) for medicinal purposes.

Skink (*Scincus officinalis*).

skin-less (skin′les), *a.* Having no skin, or but a very thin skin.

skinned (skind), *a.* Having a skin, esp. as specified: as, dark-*skinned.*

skin-ner (skin′ér), *n.* One who prepares skins, as for the market; a worker or dealer in skins; also, one who skins.—**skin′ner-y** (-i), *n.*; pl. *-ies* (-iz). Skins or furs collectively†; also, a place where skins are prepared, as for the market.

skin-ny (skin′i), *a.*; compar. *skinnier,* superl. *skinniest.* Of or like skin; cutaneous; membranous; also, lean or emaciated; also, niggardly or stingy.—**skin′ni-ness**, *n.*

skin=tight (skin′tīt′), *a.* Fitting as tightly as the skin.

skip[1] (skip), *n.* [Var. of *skep.*] A bucket, box, cage, or the like, for raising ore, etc., in a mine.

skip[2] (skip), *v.*; skipped, skipping. [ME. *skippen;* prob. from Scand.] **I.** *intr.* To spring, jump, or leap lightly from the ground as in joy or sport; caper, gambol, or frisk (often with *about*); go or pass along with light, springing movements; sometimes, to ricochet, as a missile passing with rebounds along a surface; fig., to pass from one point, thing, subject, etc., to another, with disregard or omission of what intervenes, as in reading, discourse, etc. (often with *about*); pass (*over*) without notice, mention, action, etc.; also, to go hastily away, make off, or abscond (colloq.); go or depart (colloq.: as, "Well, I must *skip!*" L. Merrick's "Position of Peggy Harper," iii. 5). **II.** *tr.* To spring or jump lightly over (as, to *skip* the rope: see *skipping-rope*); fig., to pass over without reading, notice, mention, action, etc.; disregard, ignore, or omit; also, to cause to skip; send (a missile) ricocheting along a surface; also, to leave hastily, or flee from, as a place (colloq.).—**skip**[2], *n.* A skipping movement; a light spring, jump, or leap; a gait marked by such springs; also, a passing from one point or thing to another, with disregard of what intervenes, as in reading, narrating, reckoning, etc.; also, that which is or may be skipped, as in reading (as, "In his books there are scarcely any of those passages which, in our school days, we used to call *skip*": Macaulay's "Essays," Horace Walpole).

skip[3] (skip), *n.* [Cf. *skipper*[2].] The captain of a team or side at curling or bowling.

skip-jack (skip′jak), *n.* [From *skip*[2] + *jack*[3].] A lively, pert, pretentious fellow, conceited fop, or whipper-snapper (archaic or prov.); also, any of various fishes which sometimes leap out of the water, as the scad, bluefish, bonito, etc.; also, an elaterid (beetle).

skip-per[1] (skip′ér), *n.* One who or that which skips; specif., any of the quick-flying lepidopterous insects constituting the family *Hesperiidæ;* also, a maggot found in cheese, etc., the larva of a small dipterous insect, *Piophila casei;* also, the saury (fish).

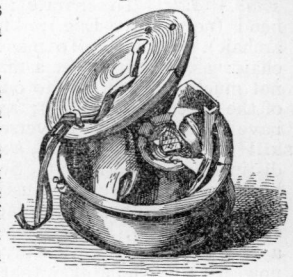

Skipper (family *Hesperiidæ*). (Line shows natural size.)

skip-per[2] (skip′ér), *n.* [ME. *skypper,* < MD. D. *schipper,* < *schip,* ship: see *ship.*] The master or captain of a ship, esp. of a small trading or fishing vessel; in general, a captain or leader, as of a sporting team.—**skip′per**[2], *v. t.* To act as skipper of.

skip-pet (skip′et), *n.* [Origin uncertain.] A small round box for protecting a seal as formerly attached by a ribbon or cord to a document.

skip-ping=rope (skip′ing-rōp), *n.* A piece of rope, often with a wooden handle at each end, held slackly (either by the skipper or by two persons some distance apart) and kept in rapid revolution over the head and under the feet of one who skips over it as it passes the ground in each revolution: used for sport, esp. by young girls.

Skippet.

skip=stop (skip′stop). **I.** *a.* Designating or pertaining to a method by which street-cars and omnibuses stop only at every second ordinary stopping-place along a route, skipping or ignoring the intermediate one, as in order to reduce delays or to save power: as, the *skip-stop* system; *skip-stop* regulations. **II.** *n.* The skip-stop system.

skirl (skérl), *v. i.* or *t.* [Prob. from Scand., and related to *shrill.*] To shriek; scream; also, to sound loudly and shrilly (used esp. of the bagpipe). [Sc. and north. Eng.] —**skirl,** *n.* A shrill cry or sound; esp., the sound of the bagpipe. [Sc. and north. Eng.]

skir-mish (skér′mish), *n.* [ME. *skyrmysh, skarmich, skarmuch,* < OF. *escarmuche* (F. *escarmouche,* < It. *scaramuccia,* skirmish; appar. from Teut., from the same source as OF. *eskermir* (eskermiss-), *escremir,* to fight, fence, which has influenced the E. spelling *skirmish:* cf. G. *schirmen,* defend, *schirm,* a shield, screen, defense,] An irregular engagement between small bodies of troops, esp. advanced or outlying detachments of opposing armies; a petty or preliminary hostile encounter; hence, any brisk encounter or contest (as, "They never meet but there's a *skirmish* of wit between them": Shakspere's "Much Ado about Nothing," i. 1. 64).—**skir′mish,** *v. i.* [OF. *escarmucher* (F. *escarmoucher*), < *escarmuche*; also, in part, OF. *eskermir* (*eskermiss-*): see *skirmish*, *n.*] To engage in a skirmish or skirmishes; also, to fence†, or make strokes with a weapon†. —**skir′mish-er,** *n.*

skirr (skėr), *v.* [Cf. *scour*².] **I.** *intr.* To go rapidly; rush; fly; scurry: as, "And make them *skir* away, as swift as stones Enforced from the old Assyrian slings" (Shakspere's "Henry V.," iv. 7. 64). **II.** *tr.* To go rapidly over; scour: as, "Mount ye, spur ye, *skirr* the plain, That the fugitive may flee in vain" (Byron's "Siege of Corinth," xxii.).

skir-ret (skir′et), *n.* [ME. *skirwhit*: cf. F. *chervis*, skirret, akin to *carvi*, caraway.] An apiaceous plant, *Sium sisarum,* formerly much cultivated in Europe for its edible tuberous root, which in flavor somewhat resembles the parsnip.

skirt (skėrt), *n.* [ME. *skirt,* from Scand.: cf. Icel. *skyrta,* Sw. *skjorta,* Dan. *skjorte,* shirt, = AS. *scyrte,* E. *shirt.*] The lower part of a gown, coat, or the like, hanging from the waist; also, a separate garment (outer or under) worn by women and girls, extending from the waist downward; hence, a woman or girl (slang: as, "She's as nice a looking *skirt* as there is in town," Sinclair Lewis's "Main Street," xxxix.); also, some part resembling or suggesting the skirt of a garment; one of the flaps hanging from the sides of a saddle; the bordering, marginal, or outlying part of a place, area, assemblage of persons, etc. (as, "as I came out of the *skirts* of the wood," Stevenson's "Travels with a Donkey," ii. 1; "a few heavy drops from the *skirt* of the passing cloud," Parkman's "Oregon Trail," xix.; "The *skirts* of the Cimbri had encountered a small Roman force near Trieste," Froude's "Cæsar," v.: now usually in *pl.*: cf. *outskirt*, *n.*); a skirting or bordering finish in building; also, the diaphragm or midriff of an animal, esp. of one butchered for food.—**skirt,** *v.* **I.** *tr.* To lie on or along the border of (as, "An extensive belt of woodland *skirted* the seacoast": Motley's "Dutch Republic," Introd.); also, to border or edge with something (as, the sun *skirted* the clouds with gold); also, to pass along or around the border or edge of (as, to *skirt* a town, a mountain, or a marsh in one's course; "They *skirted* the woodland on their homeward way," Longfellow's "Kavanagh," xxv.). **II.** *intr.* To be, lie, live, etc., on or along the border or edge of something; also, to pass or go along or around the border of something (as, "We *skirted* round the edge of the grove": F. M. Crawford's "Mr. Isaacs," xi.).— **skirt′=dance,** *n.* A form of spectacular dance in which the effect is heightened by graceful movements of the skirt or draperies.—**skirt′=dan″cing,** *n.*—**skirt′ed,** *a.* Having a skirt: as, short-*skirted.*—**skirt′er,** *n.*—**skirt′ing,** *n.* Cloth for making skirts; also, a bordering finish of wood or other material placed along the base of an interior wall of a building; a baseboard.

skit¹ (skit), *v. i.*; *skitted, skitting.* [Perhaps from Scand. and akin to *shoot*: cf. *skittish.*] To dart, leap, or spring; skip or caper. [Sc. and prov. Eng.]

skit² (skit), *n.* [Cf. *skit*¹.] A derisive or satirical hit or fling, as at a person or thing; a piece of light satire or caricature; often, a literary trifle of humorous or satirical character (as, "He had written . . . some . . . political *skits* relating to some question about taxes": Charnwood's "Abraham Lincoln," iii.).—**skit**², *v.:* *skitted, skitting.* **I.** *tr.* To make a derisive or satirical fling at; assail in a skit. **II.** *intr.* To make a derisive or satirical fling, as at a person or thing.

skit-ter (skit′ėr), *v.* [Freq. of *skit*¹.] **I.** *intr.* To go, run, or glide lightly or rapidly; skim or skip along a surface; in *angling,* to draw a spoon or a baited hook over the surface of the water with a skipping motion. **II.** *tr.* To cause to

skitter; in *angling,* to draw (a spoon or a baited hook) over the water with a skipping motion.

skit-tish (skit′ish), *a.* [ME. *skittish:* cf. *skit*¹.] Restlessly or excessively lively or frolicsome, as a person or the mood, disposition, behavior, etc.; giddy or frivolous; also, apt to start or shy, as a horse; disposed to draw back from advances, or coy, as a young girl; also, fickle or changeable (as, "How some men creep in *skittish* fortune's hall!" Shakspere's "Troilus and Cressida," iii. 3. 134); uncertain, ticklish, or tricky (as, *skittish* diseases).—**skit′tish-ly,** *adv.*—**skit′-tish-ness,** *n.*

skit-tle (skit′l), *n.* [Origin uncertain.] *Pl.* (construed as *sing.*), a game played with a number of wooden pins which the player endeavors to knock down by throwing or rolling a kind of disk or a ball at them; ninepins; also, *sing.,* one of the pins used (as, "This [beverage] is brought in a pewter stoop, shaped like a *skittle*": Smollett's "Humphry Clinker," Sept. 3).—**beer** (or **ale**, or the like) **and skittles,** fig., enjoyment or pleasure: as, "Life isn't all *beer and skittles* for a rank outsider, I'm told!" (Du Maurier's "Trilby," v.).

skive¹ (skīv), *n.* [D. *schijf,* disk, skive, = E. *shive.*] A rotating iron wheel or disk used with diamond-powder in grinding diamonds and other gems.

skive² (skīv), *v. t.;* *skived, skiving.* [From Scand., and akin to E. *shive.*] To split or cut (leather, etc.) into layers or slices; shave (hides, etc.); also, to pare off.—**skiv-er** (skī′vėr), *n.* One who or that which skives; also, a thin leather split from the grain side of sheepskin, used for bookbinding, etc.

skoal (skōl), *n.* [Dan. and Norw. *skaal,* Icel. *skāl,* bowl.] A health in drinking: as, "There from the flowing bowl Deep drinks the warrior's soul, *Skoal!* to the Northland! skoal!" (Longfellow's "Skeleton in Armor," 159).

Sko-da-ic (skọ-dā′ik), *a.* Of or pertaining to Joseph Skoda (1805–81), a Bohemian-Austrian physician.—**Skodaic resonance,** in *pathol.,* a sound of tympanitic quality heard above a pleuritic effusion.

skoo-kum (skö′kum), *a.* [Chinook jargon.] Strong; fine; excellent; good. [Northwestern U. S., British Columbia, etc.]

skrim′shank, etc. See *scrimshank,* etc.

sku-a (skū′ä), *n.* [From Scand.] A jäger, esp. *Megalestris skua,* a blackish-brown gull-like bird of northern Atlantic, esp. European, waters ('great skua').

Skirret.

skul-dud-der-y (skul-dud′ėr-i), *n.* [Origin obscure.] Immorality or unchastity; also, obscenity. [Sc.]

skul-dug-ger-y (skul-dug′ėr-i), *n.* [Var. of *skuldud-dery.*] Dishonorable proceedings; mean dishonesty or trickery: as, political *skulduggery.* [U. S.]

Great Skua (*Megalestris skua*).

skulk (skulk), *v. i.* [ME. *sculken,* prob. from Scand.: cf. Dan. *skulke,* Sw. *skolka,* play truant, shirk.] To move or go in a mean, stealthy manner, as from fear, cowardice, or shame, or with some evil purpose (as, to *skulk* through dark streets); sneak; slink; also, to lie or keep in hiding, as for some discreditable reason or evil purpose; lurk; also, to shelter one's self or take refuge in a cowardly manner (as, "I withdrew from the road, and *skulked* behind a hedge till it [carriage] should have completely gone by," Godwin's "Caleb Williams," xxxi.; to *skulk* behind others in time of danger); hence, to shirk duty; esp., to malinger.—**skulk,** *n.* One who skulks; a shirk (as, "You are certainly no *skulk* when duty is to be done": Cooper's "Two Admirals," xix.); also, an act of skulking.—**skulk′er,** *n.*—**skulk′ing-ly,** *adv.*

skull¹, etc. See *scull,* etc.

skull² (skul), *n.* [ME. *scolle;* origin uncertain.] The bony framework of the head, inclosing the brain and supporting the face; the skeleton of the head; in a restricted sense, the part of this that incloses the brain; the cranium; also, the head as the seat of intelligence or knowledge (usually in disparagement: as, "With various readings stor'd his empty *skull*, Learn'd without sense, and venerably dull," Churchill's "Rosciad," 591).—**skull′cap,** *n.* A brimless cap of silk, velvet, or the like, fitting closely to the head (as, "a Presbyterian clergyman . . . wearing a black silk *skull-cap*, covering his short hair so closely that it could scarce be seen at all": Scott's "Legend of Montrose," xi.); also, a cap-like metal head-piece formerly worn for defense; also, the upper, domed part of the skull, covering the brain; also, in *bot.*, any of various menthaceous herbs (genus *Scutellaria*) in which the calyx of the flower suggests a helmet. —**skulled,** *a.* Having a skull: as, the *skulled* vertebrates; thick-*skulled.*—**skull′=less,** *a.* Having no skull; acranial.

Upper part of the Flowering Stem of Skullcap (*Scutellaria serrata*). — *a*, the calyx.

skunk (skungk), *n.* [Algonquian.] A small, fur-bearing, bushy-tailed North American quadruped, *Mephitis mephitica*, which ejects a fetid fluid when attacked; the fur of this animal; also, any of various allied or similar animals; fig., a thoroughly contemptible person (colloq.: as, "He must think me the most awful *skunk*," Galsworthy's "Saint's Progress," iii. 14). —**skunk,** *v. t.* In games, to beat so completely as to keep from scoring; shut out. [Slang, U. S.]—**skunk′=cab″bage,** *n.* A low, fetid, broad-leaved araceous plant, *Spathyema*

Common Skunk (*Mephitis mephitica*).

fœtida, of North America, growing in moist ground; also, a similar araceous plant, *Lysichitum camtschatcense*, found on the western coast of North America and in Siberia, Japan, etc.—**skunk′er-y** (-ėr-i), *n.*; pl. *-ies* (-iz). A place where skunks are kept and bred, as for their fur.—**skunk′weed,** *n.* Skunk-cabbage.

Skup-shti-na (skŭp′shti-nä), *n.* [Serbian (*Narodna*) *Skupshtina*, (National) Assembly.] The former national assembly of Serbia or of Montenegro, consisting in each case of a single chamber; also, the national assembly of Jugoslavia, likewise consisting of a single chamber.

sky (skī), *n.*; pl. *skies* (skīz). [ME. *sky*, from Scand.: cf. Icel. *skȳ*, Sw. and Dan. *sky*, cloud.] A cloud†; hence, the region of the clouds or the upper air (often in *pl.*: as, "Heavily the low *sky* raining Over tower'd Camelot," Tennyson's "Lady of Shalott," iv.; "The *skies* look grimly And threaten present blusters," Shakspere's "Winter's Tale," iii. 3. 3); the heavens or firmament, appearing as a great arch or vault, blue when unclouded, above the earth (often in *pl.*: as, a cloudless *sky*; the starry *sky* or *skies*; under alien *skies*; "the blue rim where *skies* and mountains meet," Cowper's "Hope," 49); hence, the supernal or celestial heaven (often in *pl.*, and chiefly poetic: as, mansions in the *sky* or *skies*; to be translated to the *skies*); also, the space occupied by the upper row or rows of pictures in a gallery (colloq.).—**sky,** *v. t.*; skied, skying. To raise aloft or toward the sky; strike (a ball) high into the air; also, to hang (a picture, etc.) high up on the wall or near the ceiling of a gallery, as at an exhibition (colloq.).—**sky′=blue′. I.** *a.* Of a clear, soft blue color like that of the unclouded sky by day; azure. **II.** *n.* A sky-blue color.

Skye (skī) **ter′ri-er.** [From the Isle of *Skye*, off the west coast of Scotland.] One of a breed of small, short-legged, very shaggy terriers.

sky-ey (skī′i), *a.* Of or from the sky (as, "the *skyey* vault with its everlasting Luminaries above," Carlyle's "Sartor Resartus," ii. 9; "A breath thou art, Servile to all the *skyey* influences," Shakspere's "Measure for Measure," iii. 1. 9); also, in, reaching, or approaching the sky; lofty; also, sky-like, as in color; sky-blue; azure. [Chiefly poetic.]

sky=high (skī′hī′), *adv.* and *a.* As high as the sky; very high.

sky hook, a flattish device that spirals slowly to earth when dropped from a plane: used to supply medicines, etc.

sky-ish (skī′ish), *a.* Skyey; lofty. [Chiefly poetic.]

sky-lark (skī′lärk), *n.* The common European lark, *Alauda arvensis*, which sings as it mounts in flight toward the sky; also, any of certain allied or similar birds.—**sky′-lark,** *v. i.* [Appar. orig. a sailors' word for frolicking in the rigging or elsewhere aboard ship: cf. *lark²*.] To frolic; play pranks; indulge in boisterous or rough sport: as, "No *skylarking* in my rooms. You two smashed half my furniture last time you threw the cushions about" (Kipling's "Light That Failed," viii.). [Colloq.]—**sky′-lark-er,** *n.*

Skylark (*Alauda arvensis*).

sky-less (skī′les), *a.* Without visible sky; dark.

sky-light (skī′līt), *n.* Light from the sky, as for illuminating a room; also, an opening in a roof or ceiling, fitted with glass, for admitting daylight; the frame set with glass fitted to such an opening.—**sky′light,** *v. t.* To furnish with or light by a skylight or skylights.

sky-line (skī′līn), *n.* The boundary-line between earth and sky; the horizon; also, the outline of mountains, trees, buildings, etc., as seen against the sky (as, "Often I had to crawl on all-fours to avoid appearing against the *sky-line* on the ridge," Roosevelt's "Ranch Life and the Hunting-Trail," xi.; "the whole crowded *sky-line* from Notre Dame to the Panthéon [in Paris]," Mrs. Wharton's "Son at the Front," xix.).

sky-man (skī′man), *n.*; pl. *-men.* An aviator or aëronaut. [Colloq.]

sky-par-lor (skī′pär′lọr), *n.* A garret or attic. [Colloq.]

sky-pi-lot (skī′pī′lọt), *n.* A chaplain or other clergyman (orig. in sailors' use); also, a pilot of an aëroplane or the like; an aviator. [Colloq.]

sky=rock-et (skī′rok″et), *n.* A rocket (firework) that ascends into the air and explodes at a height.—**sky′=rock″et,** *v. i.* To move like a sky-rocket; rise suddenly, make a brilliant show, and disappear. [Colloq.]

sky-sail (skī′sāl), *n. Naut.*, in a square-rigged vessel, a light sail next above the royal.

sky-scape (skī′skāp), *n.* [With *-scape* as in *landscape*.] A picture or a view of the sky.

sky-scrap-er (skī′skrā″pėr), *n.* Something that (apparently) scrapes the sky, as by reason of great height; esp., a very tall building, such as many seen in the larger American cities; *naut.*, a triangular skysail.—**sky′=scrap″ing,** *a.* So high as (apparently) to scrape the sky; very high; lofty.

sky=sign (skī′sīn), *n.* Any sign, as for advertisement, announcement, or direction, set up so as to be visible against the sky, as on the top of a building. [Chiefly Eng.]

sky-ward (skī′wạrd), *adv.* and *a.* Toward the sky.—**sky′wards,** *adv.*

sky=writ-ing (skī′rī″ting), *n.* The act or practice of tracing words, etc., against the sky, so that they may be read from the ground, in characters of great size (often a mile high), by means of smoke of a white or other color, produced chemically and ejected from an aëroplane as it moves in a course corresponding to the form of the characters traced (used esp. for advertising purposes); also, the words, etc., traced.—**sky′=writ″er,** *n.*

slab[1] (slab). [Prob. from Scand.] **I.** *n.* A wet place or puddle (now prov. Eng.); also, wet or slimy matter. **II.** *a.* Thick in consistence: as, "make the gruel thick and *slab*" (Shakspere's "Macbeth," iv. 1. 32).

slab[2] (slab), *n.* [ME. *slabbe, sclabbe*; origin uncertain.] A broad, flat, somewhat thick piece of stone, wood, or other solid material (as, "for the sake of him who sleeps beneath the marble *slab* in yonder quiet chancel": Borrow's "Lavengro," iii.); also, a rough outside piece cut from a log, as in sawing it into boards; also, a thick slice of anything (as, a *slab* of bread, meat, or cheese; "Harmon drew a *slab* of tobacco from his pocket," Mrs. Wharton's "Ethan Frome," Introd.).—**slab**[2], *v. t.*; *slabbed, slabbing.* To make into a slab or slabs; also, to cover or lay with slabs; also, to cut the slabs or outside pieces from (a log, etc.).

slab-ber (slab'ėr), etc. Same as *slobber*, etc.

slab-sid-ed (slab'sī'ded), *a.* Having the sides long and flat, like slabs; tall and lank: as, "long-legged, *slab-sided*, lean, sunburnt . . . lads" (H. Kingsley's "Geoffry Hamlyn," xxxiii.). [Colloq.]

slack[1] (slak), *n.* [Cf. G. *schlacke*, dross, slag, slack, also E. *slag*.] The finer screenings of coal; small or refuse coal.

slack[2] (slak). [AS. *slæc, sleac*, = OHG. *slach* (G. dial. *schlack*) = Icel. *slakr* = Sw. *slak*, slack: see *lax*.] **I.** *a.* Lacking in energy or diligence, as persons, actions, etc. (as, "I think our friend of Morton had grown *slack* But for my spurring," Swinburne's "Bothwell," i. 4; *slack* service; *slack* ways); indolent; negligent; remiss (often in a specified particular: as, *slack* in fulfilling a promise; not *slack* to resent an affront); also, lacking in activity, vigor, or strength; slow, as the pace; sluggish, as the water, tide, or wind; gentle or moderate, as heat, an oven, etc.; weak in action or operation, as the pulse; dull, or not brisk, as business, work, etc., or the season or times with respect to work (as, "After harvest there comes *slack* times for the likes of me": G. MacDonald's "Annals of a Quiet Neighbourhood," iii.); having little work, as an establishment; also, not drawn tightly, as a rein, rope, or sail; loose; not tense or taut; relaxed, as the hand or grasp (as, "Her *slack* hands fell lifeless by her side": Mrs. Stowe's "Uncle Tom's Cabin," xii.); also, not firm or compact, as a substance; loose, crumbly, or soft. **II.** *n.* A slack condition, interval, or part; a cessation in a strong flow, as of a current or of the tide at its turn, or a stretch of water with little or no current; a decrease in activity, as in business, work, etc., or a period of decreased activity (as, "It was a still summer evening in the *slack* between hay and harvest on the farm of Drumquhat": S. R. Crockett's "Stickit Minister," x.); looseness, as in something not drawn tight, or a loose part; esp., a part of a rope, sail, or the like, that hangs loose, without strain upon it; a loose, baggy part of clothing, esp. the seat of trousers or the like (colloq.); hence, *pl.*, trousers, esp. of sailors (colloq.); also, *sing.*, loose, overfree, or impertinent talk (slang).—**slack**[2], *adv.* In a slack manner; slackly.—**slack**[2], *v.* **I.** *tr.* To be slack or remiss in respect to (some matter, duty, etc.); neglect, shirk, or leave undone; also, to make slack, or allow to become slack, or less active, vigorous, intense, etc.; relax or abate (efforts, labor, speed, etc.: as, "He . . . without *slacking* his pace for an instant, stalked on," Stevenson's "Travels with a Donkey," i. 2); moderate; slacken; also, to make slack or loose, or less tense or taut, as a rope; loosen; also, to slake (lime). **II.** *intr.* To be slack or remiss; shirk one's duty or part (cf. *slacker*); also, to become slack, or less active, vigorous, rapid, etc. (as, "Still she went . . . *slacking* not, pausing not": Mrs. Stowe's "Uncle Tom's Cabin," vii.); moderate; slacken; also, to become less tense or taut, as a rope; also, to become slaked, as lime.

slack[3] (slak), *n.* [ME. *slak*; from Scand.] A depression between hills, in a hillside, or in the surface of ground; also, a boggy or wet hollow, or a morass (as, "Between the farmhouse and the hill-pasture was a deep morass, termed in that country a *slack*": Scott's "Guy Mannering," xxv.). [Sc. and prov. Eng.]

slack-baked (slak'bākt), *a.* Insufficiently baked, as bread.

slack-en (slak'n), *v.* **I.** *tr.* To make slack; make less active, vigorous, rapid, intense, etc., as efforts, action, pace, speed, etc.; abate; moderate; make looser or less taut, as a rein,

rope, sail, etc. (as, "*Slackening* the reins, I let my horse take his own course": Parkman's "Oregon Trail," x.); relax (as, "Her fingers white *Slackened* their hold upon the coverlet": W. Morris's "Jason," vii. 449). **II.** *intr.* To become slack; become less active, vigorous, brisk, etc.; moderate, as in activity, force, or speed; become less tense or taut, as a rope. —**slack'en-er**, *n.*

slack-er (slak'ėr), *n.* One who shirks or evades his duty; esp., one who in time of war seeks to evade military service (as, "Every shirker, every coward and *slacker* in the country decided at once to be a conscientious objector": H. G. Wells's "Italy, France, and Britain at War," iv. 2). [Colloq., orig. Eng.]—**slack'er-ism**, *n.* The conduct of a slacker.

slack-ly (slak'li), *adv.* In a slack manner; without energy, diligence, activity, or vigor; not tightly, tensely, or tautly; loosely.—**slack'ness**, *n.*

slade (slād), *n.* [AS. *slæd*, valley.] A valley or dell; also, a piece or strip of greensward, as in a wood or in plowed land. [Now chiefly prov. Eng.]

slag (slag), *n.* [MLG. *slagge* = G. *schlacke*, dross, slag, slack: cf. *slack*[1].] The more or less completely fused and vitrified refuse matter separated during the reduction of a metal from its ore; also, the scoria from a volcano.—**slag**, *v.*; *slagged, slagging.* **I.** *tr.* To free from slag; also, to convert into slag. **II.** *intr.* To form slag; become a slag-like mass. —**slag'gy**, *a.* Consisting of, resembling, or pertaining to slag.

slain (slān). Past participle of *slay*[2].

slake (slāk), *v.*; *slaked, slaking.* [AS. *sleacian, slacian*, < *slæc*, E. *slack*[2].] **I.** *intr.* To become slack, or less active, vigorous, intense, etc. (now rare); of lime, to become slaked. **II.** *tr.* To make slack, or less active, vigorous, intense, etc.; now, esp., to allay (thirst, desire, wrath, etc.) by satisfying; cool or refresh with or as with water (as, "The clouds . . . *slake* Our thirsty souls with rain": Whittier's "All's Well"); also, to make loose or less tense†; also, to disintegrate or treat (lime, CaO) with water or moist air, causing it to change chemically into calcium hydroxide, $Ca(OH)_2$ ('slaked lime'). —**slake'less**, *a.* Incapable of being slaked; not to be allayed or satisfied, as thirst; insatiable.

slam[1] (slam), *v.*; *slammed, slamming.* [Prob. from Scand.] **I.** *tr.* To shut (a door, gate, etc.) with force and noise; thrust or cast (a window, lid, etc.) violently and noisily (*down, up, to*, etc.); dash or throw (anything) with a bang (*on, against, through*, etc.: as, "Why, he'd have *slammed* you through the window," Mark Twain's "Life on the Mississippi," viii.); also, to strike or hit violently (prov. or slang); fig., to criticize severely or captiously (slang, U. S.). **II.** *intr.* To close with a bang, as a door (as, "Tommy . . . heard the door *slam*": Barrie's "Sentimental Tommy," i.); dash, strike, etc., with violent and noisy impact (as, shutters *slamming* against a house in a high wind).—**slam**[1], *n.* A slamming, as of a door; a violent and noisy closing, dashing, or impact, or the noise made (as, "The window . . . was thrown open with a *slam*": Stevenson's "Treasure Island," v.); a bang; a violent blow (prov. or slang); fig., a severe or captious criticism (slang, U. S.).

slam[2] (slam), *n.* [Origin obscure.] In *card-playing*, the winning of all the tricks in one deal, as at whist (in bridge, called 'grand slam'), or of all the tricks but one (in bridge, and called 'little slam'); in *euchre*, the winning of five points before the other side has scored, sometimes counting as two games.—**slam**[2], *v.*; *slammed, slamming.* **I.** *tr.* To beat by winning a slam, as at whist. **II.** *intr.* To win a slam.

slam-bang (slam'bang'). **I.** *adv.* With a slam and a bang; with noisy or headlong violence. [Colloq.] **II.** *a.* Violent and noisy. [Colloq.]—**slam'-bang'**, *v. i.* To go with a slam and a bang; be violent and noisy. [Colloq.]

slan-der (slan'dėr), *n.* [OF. F. *esclandre*, scandal, < LL. *scandalum*: see *scandal*, and cf. *esclandre*.] The malicious putting forth or circulating of false statements tending to defame; calumny; defamation; specif., in legal use, defamation by oral utterance rather than by writing, etc. (cf. *libel, n.*); also, false and defamatory matter, as about a person, maliciously uttered or circulated; a malicious, false, and defamatory statement or report (as, to trace a *slander* to its author; base or spiteful *slanders*); also, ill report or repute† (as, "You shall not find me, daughter, After the *slander* of most stepmothers, Evil-eyed unto you": Shakspere's "Cymbeline," i. 1. 71); also, discredit†, dishonor†, or shame†, or a source of discredit or shame† (see Shakspere's "Richard III.," i. 3. 231).—**slan′der**, *v.* **I.** *tr.* To utter slander concerning; calumniate; defame; also, to charge or reproach with something discreditable†; also, to bring into discredit or disgrace†. **II.** *intr.* To utter or circulate slander.—**slan′der-er**, *n.*—**slan′der-ous**, *a.* Of the nature of or involving slander, as utterances, reports, language, attacks, etc.; calumnious; defamatory; given to or uttering slander, as persons, tongues, etc.; also, discreditable† or disgraceful†.—**slan′der-ous-ly**, *adv.*—**slan′der-ous-ness**, *n.*

slang (slang), *n.* [Origin obscure.] Orig., the special vocabulary of thieves, vagabonds, etc.; argot; later, the jargon of a particular class, profession, etc. (as, lawyers' *slang*); also, esp., language of a markedly colloquial character, regarded as below the standard of cultivated speech, and made up of new words, and of ordinary words or phrases employed in special or arbitrary senses; also, insincere or conventional cant, or stock phraseology (obs. or archaic); also, abusive language (prov. or colloq.).—**slang**, *v.* **I.** *intr.* To use slang or abusive language; rail violently: as, "We rowed, swore, *slanged*, with a Christian meekness and forbearance" (Bulwer-Lytton's "Pelham," xlix.). [Colloq.] **II.** *tr.* To assail with abusive language; rail at violently: as, "It is not consistent with my paternal duty to sit here and listen to you *slanging* your mother" (Arnold Bennett's "Mr. Prohack," vi.). [Colloq.]—**slang′y**, *a.* Pertaining to or of the nature of slang (as, "Trilby's French was . . . droll, *slangy*, piquant, quaint, picturesque": Du Maurier's "Trilby," ii.); of persons, addicted to the use of slang (as, "She's *slangy*, and she'd shock your sort of woman out of her wits": L. Merrick's "Conrad in Quest of His Youth," xvi.).—**slang′i-ly**, *adv.*—**slang′i-ness**, *n.*

slank (slangk). Occasional preterit of *slink²*.

slant (slänt), *v.* [Var. of earlier *slent*, ME. *slenten*, *sclenten*, from Scand.: cf. Sw. *slinta*, to slip, glance, *slänt*, *n.*, slope, slant.] **I.** *intr.* To have or take an oblique direction or position with reference to some line or plane, as lines, stitches, handwriting, sides, facets, etc.; slope, esp. from the horizontal, as ground, roofs, etc.; fall or strike obliquely, as light, shadows, rain, missiles, etc. (as, "The sun *slanted* through the south window on the girl's moving figure": Mrs. Wharton's "Ethan Frome," iv.); turn off or go obliquely, as from a straight or direct course, as a path or road, persons moving, etc. (often with *off*); fig., to have a mental leaning or bias. **II.** *tr.* To give an oblique direction or position to (as, "the dim peak of a hill, with grass . . . *slanted* as if by a breeze": C. Brontë's "Jane Eyre," xiii.); incline or direct obliquely; form or cut with a slant.—**slant**, *n.* Slanting or oblique direction or position (as, the *slant* of handwriting, or ground, or of a roof); inclination; slope; also, a slanting line, side, surface, stretch of ground, or the like; a slanting ray (of light); a slanting course or movement; fig., a mental leaning or tendency; a bias; also, an indirect reflection, or sly hit or gibe (chiefly colloq.); also, in slang use, a glance or look; a trial or attempt, as at something; a chance or opportunity; a way of looking at or regarding something.—**slant**. **I.** *adv.* In a slanting direction; aslant. **II.** *a.* Slanting; oblique.

slan-tin-dic-u-lar, slan-ten-dic-u-lar (slăn-tin-dik′ū-lär, slän-tĕn-), *a.* [Earlier *slantingdicular*, from *slanting*, after *perpendicular*.] Slanting; oblique. Often fig. [Humorous.]—**slan-tin-dic′u-lar-ly, slan-ten-dic′u-lar-ly**, *adv.*

slant-ing (slän′ting), *p. a.* That slants; oblique: as, "*slanting* roofs" (Borrow's "Lavengro," iv.); "*slanting* sunlight" (W. Churchill's "Coniston," ii. 11).—**slant′ing-ly**, *adv.*

slant-ly (slänt′li), *adv.* In a slant or slanting direction.

slant-wise (slänt′wiz). **I.** *adv.* Aslant; obliquely. **II.** *a.* Slanting; oblique: as, "The *slantwise* rain Of light through the leaves" (Whittier's "Telling the Bees").

slap¹ (slap), *v.*; *slapped*, *slapping*. [Imit.: cf. LG. *slapp*, G. *schlapp*, used interjectionally to express the sound of a blow.] **I.** *tr.* To strike smartly, esp. with the open hand or with something flat; also, to bring (the hand, etc.) upon or against something with a smart blow (as, "*slapping* his hand familiarly on Shelby's shoulder": Mrs. Stowe's "Uncle Tom's Cabin," i.); dash or cast forcibly (as, "Mrs. Beeton

slapped the muffins into the dish": Kipling's "Light That Failed," xiv.); slam. **II.** *intr.* To strike or beat with a sharp, resounding impact, as waves; aim a smart blow, as at something.—**slap¹**, *n.* A smart blow, esp. with the open hand or with something flat: a smack; fig., a sarcastic or censuring hit; a direct rebuke, rebuff, or affront.—**slap¹**, *adv.* With or as with a slap; smartly; suddenly; also, directly or straight (as, "He'll run *slap* into the sentries": Kipling's "Kim," v.). [Colloq.]

slap² (slap), *n.* [ME. *slop* = MLG. and D. *slop*.] A breach, gap, or opening in a wall, hedge, or the like (as, "They forced a passage through a *slap* in a dyke": Ian Maclaren's "Beside the Bonnie Brier Bush," vii. 2); a narrow pass between hills. [Sc., Ir., and prov. Eng.]

slap=dash (slap′dash). **I.** *adv.* In a dashing, haphazard manner; hastily and carelessly: as, "I talked, and rattled, and said a thousand silly things, *slapdash*" (Irving's "Tales of a Traveler," ii. 7). **II.** *a.* Acting, proceeding, or done in a dashing, haphazard manner; carelessly hasty or offhand. **III.** *n.* Slap-dash action, methods, or work; also, roughcast (plaster).

slap-jack (slap′jak), *n.* A flapjack or griddle-cake (U. S.); also, a simple card-game in which the object of each player is to be the first to slap a jack when played.

slap-per (slap′er), *n.* One who or that which slaps; an instrument used to slap with.

slap-stick (slap′stik). **I.** *n.* A stick or lath used by harlequins, clowns, etc., as in pantomime, for striking other performers, often a combination of laths so arranged as to make a loud, clapping noise without hurting a person struck (cf. *lath*, *n.*); any stick or the like to strike with, used by performers in broad comedy; hence, the type of broad comedy in which rough play and knockabout methods prevail. **II.** *a.* Using, or marked by the use of, the slapstick, or rough or knockabout methods: as, a *slapstick* artist; a *slapstick* moving-picture comedy.

slash¹ (slash), *n.* [Cf. *slosh* and *slush*.] A tract of wet or swampy ground overgrown with bushes or trees: often in *pl.* [Local, U. S.]

slash² (slash), *v.* [ME. *slaschen*, cut, hew: cf. OF. *esclachier*, break.] **I.** *tr.* To cut or wound with a sweeping stroke of an edged instrument or the like; gash; also, to make slits in (a garment) in order to show an underlying fabric of different color or kind; line or fill the slits of with a specified fabric or color (as, "His doublet, shaped of buff, With satin *slash'd* and lined": Scott's "Lay of the Last Minstrel," v. 16); also, to lash, as with a whip (as, "He *slashed* his horse across the flank with his whip": Conan Doyle's "Exploits of Brigadier Gerard," viii.); crack or snap, as a whip; fig., to assail sharply, as with criticism; also, to cut, abridge, or alter (a manuscript, text, etc.) unsparingly, as in editing, or in preparing a play for the stage. **II.** *intr.* To deliver a sweeping, cutting stroke, as at something (as, "Sir Wilfrid walked along, *slashing* at the railings with his stick": Mrs. H. Ward's "Lady Rose's Daughter," iv.); lay about one with sharp strokes, as of a sword in battle; also, to make one's way by or as by cutting, as through the waves; dash furiously along.—**slash²**, *n.* A sweeping stroke with an edged instrument, a whip, or the like (as, "The crowd jostled and fought to get a *slash* or thrust at a victim": H. G. Wells's "Outline of History," xxxvii. § 10); also, a cut or wound made with such a stroke; a long, roughly inflicted cut; a gash; also, an ornamental slit in a garment serving to show an underlying fabric, often of different color; also, in forest land, an open area strewn with debris of trees from felling or from wind or fire; the debris itself.—**slash′er**, *n.*—**slash′ing**, *n.* The act of one who or that which slashes, cuts, lashes, etc.; the slitting of a garment to show an underlying fabric, or one of the slits made, or the part or color revealed by a slit; also, a slash or open area in forest land strewn with the debris of trees, or the debris itself.—**slash′ing**, *p. a.* That slashes; dealing sweeping, cutting strokes (often fig.); sharp and violent, as a stroke or blow; unsparingly severe, as criticism, epithets, etc. (as, "It is pretty safe to be sure that these *slashing* superlatives are never true": Morley's "Oliver Cromwell," i. 2); dashing, impetuous, or recklessly rapid (as, a *slashing* rider or run; "a *slashing* pace," Kinglake's "Eothen," xxviii.); very large, great, or fine (colloq.: as, "some fair creature with a *slashing* fortune," Dickens's "Hard Times," ii. 7).—**slash'ing-ly,** *adv.*

slash=pine (slash′pīn), *n.* [See *slash*[1].] A pine, *Pinus heterophylla* with a hard, durable wood, common in slashes and swamps in the southeastern U. S.

slat[1] (slat), *v.:* *slatted, slatting.* [Origin uncertain: cf. Icel. *sletta,* to slap.] **I.** *tr.* To throw, dash, knock, etc., with force or violence. [Now prov. or colloq.] **II.** *intr.* To flap violently, as sails: as, "The main-sail was blowing and *slatting* with a noise like thunder" (Dana's "Two Years before the Mast," xxxii.).—**slat**[1], *n.* A slap; a sharp blow or stroke. [Chiefly prov. or colloq.]

slat[2] (slat), *n.* [ME. *slat, sclat,* < OF. *esclat* (F. *éclat*), fragment, piece, also bursting, burst, < *esclater,* to shiver, burst; origin uncertain: cf. *éclat* and *slate*[2].] A roofing-slate or thin slab of stone (now chiefly prov.); also, a long, thin, narrow strip of wood, metal, or the like; a lath; specif., one of a number of wooden bars laid across a bedstead to form a support for the bed; also, one of the horizontal laths of a Venetian blind or the like.—**slat**[2], *v. t.; slatted, slatting.* To furnish or make with slats.

slate[1] (slāt), *v. t.; slated, slating.* [Origin uncertain.] To thrash severely; also, to take to task harshly; berate; often, to criticize severely, as a book. [Colloq., chiefly Eng.]

slate[2] (slāt), *n.* [OF. *esclate,* fem. corresponding to *esclat,* masc.: see *slat*[2].] A fine-grained rock formed by the compression of clay, shale, etc., that tends to split along parallel cleavage-planes which are usually at an angle to the planes of stratification (cf. *shale*[2]); also, a thin piece or plate of this rock or a similar material, used esp. for roofing, or (when framed) for writing on with a slate-pencil or the like; hence, a tentative list of candidates, officers, etc., prepared, as by party managers, for acceptance by a nominating convention or the like (political slang, U. S.); also, slate-color.—**slate**[2], *v. t.; slated, slating.* To cover or roof with slates; also, to write or set down on or as on a writing-slate; set down for nomination or appointment, as on a political slate.—**slate′=col″or,** *n.* A dark bluish-gray color.—**slate′=col″ored,** *a.* —**slate′=pen″cil,** *n.* A pencil of soft slate or similar material, used for writing on a slate.—**slat-er** (slā′tėr), *n.* One who makes or lays slates; also, any of various small isopods, esp. a wood-louse or sow-bug (chiefly Sc. and north. Eng.).

slath-er (slaTH′ėr), *n.* [Origin obscure.] A large quantity of anything: usually in *pl.:* as, "They get *slathers* of money—most a dollar a day, Ben Rogers says" (Mark Twain's "Tom Sawyer," vii.). [Slang, U. S.]

slat-ing (slā′ting), *n.* The slates of a roof or the like; slates collectively; also, a liquid preparation for coating black-boards.

slat-ter (slat′ėr), *v. t.* [Origin uncertain: cf. *slattern.*] To spill; slop; scatter carelessly; waste. [Prov. Eng.]

slat-tern (slat′ėrn). [Cf. *slatter.*] **I.** *n.* A woman or girl (or, rarely, a man) who is slovenly or untidy in dress, habits, etc. **II.** *a.* Slatternly: as, "his *slattern* spouse, the once trim and dimpling Columbine" (Irving's "Tales of a Traveler," ii. 7).—**slat′tern-ly,** *a.* Having the appearance or ways of a slattern; characteristic or suggestive of a slattern; slovenly: as, "a *slatternly* girl, in shoes down at heel" (Dickens's "Oliver Twist," iv.); "A *slatternly* calico wrapper hung from her shoulders" (Mrs. Wharton's "Ethan Frome," Conclusion).—**slat′tern-li-ness,** *n.*

slat-y (slā′ti), *a.* Consisting of, resembling, or pertaining to slate; slate-colored (as, "*slaty* skies": Lowell's "Pictures from Appledore," v.).

slaugh-ter (slâ′tėr), *n.* [ME. *slaghter;* from Scand., from the root seen in E. *slay*[2].] The killing or butchering of oxen, sheep, pigs, etc., for food or for the market; also, the killing or slaying of a person, as in a brutal or violent manner (as, "How will my wife for *slaughter* of my son Shed seas of tears!" Shakspere's "3 Henry VI.," ii. 5. 105); more commonly, the killing, or a killing, by violence, of great numbers of persons, as in a battle or a massacre (as, the *slaughter* of the Innocents: see *innocent, n.*); carnage; a massacre; sometimes, the killing of animals in great numbers (as, the wanton *slaughter* of game-birds); also, a sweeping reduction of prices, as in a bargain-sale (colloq.).—**slaugh′ter,** *v. t.* To kill or butcher (animals) for food or for the market; also, to slay (a person), as in a brutal or violent manner (as, "Condé was in prison; he could be *slaughtered* at any moment": Besant's "Coligny," vi.); more commonly, to slay (persons or animals) in great numbers, as in war or in any campaign of destruction; massacre; also (colloq.), to reduce (prices) greatly; reduce the price of (goods, etc.) greatly.—**slaugh′ter-er,** *n.*—**slaugh′-ter=house,** *n.* A house or place where animals are slaughtered or butchered for food; an abattoir. Also fig.—**slaugh′ter-man** (-man), *n.; pl. -men.* A man whose work it is to slaughter animals for food; also, one who slays human beings; an executioner.—**slaugh′ter-ous,** *a.* Murderous; destructive: as, "Direness, familiar to my *slaughterous* thoughts, Cannot once start me" (Shakspere's "Macbeth," v. 5. 14).

Slav (släv or slav). [G. *Slave, Slawe,* F. *Slave* = ML. *Slavus, Sclavus;* from Slavic: cf. *Slovene.*] **I.** *n.* One of a race of peoples widely spread over eastern, southeastern, and central Europe, including the Russians and Ruthenians (eastern Slavs), the Bulgars, Serbs, Croats, Slavonians, Slovenes, etc. (southern Slavs), and the Poles, Czechs, Moravians, Slovaks, etc. (western Slavs). **II.** *a.* Of, pertaining to, or characteristic of the Slavs; Slavic.

slave (slāv), *n.* [OF. F. *esclave,* < ML. *sclavus,* a slave, orig. (ML. *Sclavus*) a Slav; many Slavs having been reduced to slavery by Germanic conquerors.] One who is the property of, and wholly subject to, another; a bond-servant; hence, a submissive or devoted follower; one entirely under the domination of some influence (as, a *slave* to the use of a drug; "Give me that man That is not passion's *slave,*" Shakspere's "Hamlet," iii. 2. 77); also, one who labors like a slave; a drudge; also, in contempt, a base wretch (archaic: as, "Though the deist rave, And think, if earth bear so base a *slave,*" Cowper's "Progress of Error," 615).—**white slave.** See under *white, a.*—**slave,** *v.; slaved, slaving.* **I.** *tr.* To reduce to the condition of a slave; enslave; also, to treat like a slave; force to perform hard or servile labor. **II.** *intr.* To work like a slave, or toil or drudge (as, "If the property isn't managed right, I may find myself *slaving* when I'm your age, mother": Arnold Bennett's "Hilda Lessways," i. 2); also, to traffic in or hold slaves (as, "He'd give his life to persuade the state against *slaving*": Drinkwater's "Abraham Lincoln," i.).—**slave′=driv″er,** *n.* An overseer of slaves at their work; hence, a harsh or exacting taskmaster.—**slave′=fork,** *n.* A long, heavy piece of wood with a forked end used in Africa for securing a slave, as when on the march, the forked end being made fast about the neck of the slave.—**slave′-hold″er,** *n.* One who owns slaves.—**slave′hold″-ing,** *n.* and *a.* —**slave′less,** *a.* Without slaves: as, "a *slaveless* land" (Whittier's "Panorama").—**slav-er**[1]

Slave-fork.

(slā′vėr), *n.* A dealer in or an owner of slaves; also, a vessel engaged in the traffic in slaves.—**white slaver.** See under *white, a.*

slav-er[2] (slav′ėr), *v.* [ME. *slaveren,* prob. from Scand.: cf. Icel. *slafra,* slaver, also E. *slabber* and *slobber.*] **I.** *intr.* To let saliva run from the mouth; slobber; drivel; fig., to fawn; also, to issue like slaver. **II.** *tr.* To wet or smear with saliva; fig., to fondle or flatter in a disgusting manner.—**slav′er**[2], *n.* Saliva running or fallen from the mouth (as, "He [a dog] staggered limply about . . . his beautiful coat . . . flecked with bloody *slaver*": Jack London's "Call of the Wild," i.); fig., drivel; twaddle; also, gross flattery.—**slav′er-er,** *n.*

---

slav-er-y (slā'vẽr-i), *n.* The condition of a slave; servitude; bondage; hence, a state of subjection resembling or suggesting that of a slave; also, severe toil like that of a slave; drudgery; also, the keeping of slaves as a practice or institution.—**white slavery.** See under *white, a.*

slav-ey (slā'vi), *n.*; pl. *slaveys* (-viz). A female domestic servant; a maid of all work: as, "You touch that bell . . . and we'll make the artful *Slavey* get us a cup o' tea" (W. De Morgan's "Joseph Vance," xvi.). [Colloq., chiefly Eng.]

Slav-ic (slăv'ik or slav'-). **I.** *a.* Of or pertaining to the Slavs, or their languages, etc. **II.** *n.* The language or group of languages spoken by the Slavs.

slav-ish (slā'vish), *a.* Pertaining to, characteristic of, or befitting a slave (as, *slavish* submission); hence, base, mean, or ignoble (as, *slavish* fears); also, consisting of or characterized by laborious toil or drudgery (as, *slavish* service; a *slavish* life); also, being or resembling a slave or slaves (as, "a *slavish* race": Pope's tr. Homer's "Iliad," i.); abjectly or basely submissive; also, servilely imitative, or lacking originality or due independence (as, a *slavish* copyist; a *slavish* reproduction).—**slav'ish-ly,** *adv.*—**slav'ish-ness,** *n.*

Slav-ism (slăv'izm or slav'-), *n.* The racial character, spirit, or tendencies of the Slavs.

Slav-o- (slăv'ọ or slav'ọ-). Form of *Slav* used in combination, as in *Slavo-Germanic* (Slav and Germanic), *Slavo-Hungarian.*

slav-oc-ra-cy (slăv-ok'rạ-si), *n.* [See *slave* and *-cracy.*] The rule or domination of slaveholders; also, a dominating body of slaveholders.—**slav-o-crat** (slăv'ọ-krat), *n.* [See *-crat.*] A member of a slavocracy.—**slav-o-crat'ic,** *a.*

Sla-vo-ni-an (slạ-vō'ni-ạn). **I.** *a.* Of or pertaining to Slavonia, a region east of Croatia and south of Hungary, or its inhabitants; also, Slavic. **II.** *n.* A native or inhabitant of Slavonia; also, a Slav; also, the Slavic language or languages.—**Sla-von'ic** (-von'ik). **I.** *a.* Slavonian; also, Slavic. **II.** *n.* The language or languages of the Slavs; Slavic.—**Slav-o-nize** (slav'ọ-nīz), *v. t.*; *-nized, -nizing.* To render Slavonian or Slavic in character, sentiment, language, etc.—**Slav″o-ni-za'tion** (-ni-zā'shọn), *n.*

Slav-o-phil, Slav-o-phile (slăv'ọ-fil or slav'-). [See *Slavo-* and *-phil.*] **I.** *a.* Friendly to or admiring the Slavs; favoring the Slavic interests, aims, etc. **II.** *n.* A friend or admirer of the Slavs.—**Slav-o-phil'ic,** *a.*—**Sla-voph-i-lism** (slạ-vof'i-lizm), *n.*

Slav-o-phobe (slăv'ọ-fōb or slav'-), *n.* [See *Slavo-* and *-phobe.*] One who fears the Slavs, or their influence or ascendancy. Also **Sla-voph-o-bist** (slạ-vof'ọ-bist).

slaw, *n.* [D. *sla,* for *salade,* salad.] Sliced or chopped cabbage served uncooked or cooked (cold or hot) with seasoning or dressing.

slay¹, sley (slā), *n.* [AS. *slege,* akin to *slēan,* strike, E. *slay².*] The reed of a weaver's loom.

slay² (slā), *v. t.*; pret. *slew,* pp. *slain,* ppr. *slaying.* [AS. *slēan* (pret. *slōg, slōh,* pp. *slægen, slegen*), strike, smite, slay, = D. *slaan* = G. *schlagen* = Icel. *slā* = Goth. *slahan,* strike: cf. *overslaugh, slaughter, slay¹, sledge²,* and *sly.*] To strike† or smite†; hence, to strike so as to kill; kill by means of a weapon or by some form of violence (as, to *slay* a foe in battle; to *slay* a helpless victim; to *slay* wild beasts); sometimes, to slaughter (an animal) for food; in general, to kill, deprive of life, or occasion the death of (as, "*slain* with hunger": Lam. iv. 9); fig., to destroy, put an end to, or extinguish (as, "having *slain* the enmity thereby": Eph. ii. 16).—**slay'er,** *n.*

sla-zy (slā'zi), etc. Same as *sleazy,* etc.

sleave (slēv), *v. t.*; *sleaved, sleaving.* [Related to *sliver.*] To divide or separate into filaments, as silk.—**sleave,** *n.* A filament of silk obtained by separating a thicker thread; silk in the form of such filaments. Also fig.: as, "sleep that knits up the ravell'd *sleave* of care" (Shakspere's "Macbeth," ii. 2. 37). [Archaic.]

slea-zy (slē'zi or slā'-), *a.* [Origin obscure.] Thin and poor in texture, as a fabric; flimsy: as, "Wise pulled down the *sleazy* window-shades" (Sinclair Lewis's "Arrowsmith," xiv.). Sometimes fig.—**slea'zi-ly,** *adv.*—**slea'zi-ness,** *n.*

sled (sled), *n.* [ME. *sledde* = MLG. *slẹdde,* sled; akin to E. *slide:* cf. *sledge¹* and *sleigh.*] A vehicle mounted on runners (instead of wheels), or sometimes without runners (cf.

toboggan), for conveying loads over snow, ice, rough ground, etc.; a sledge; also, a small vehicle of this kind used in coasting, etc.; also, a sleigh.—**sled,** *v.*; *sledded, sledding.* **I.** *tr.* To convey on a sled. **II.** *intr.* To ride or be carried on a sled.—**sled'der,** *n.* One who conveys loads on or rides on a sled; also, a horse or other animal that draws a sled.—**sled'ding,** *n.* The act of conveying or riding on a sled; also, the going, or kind of travel, for sleds, as determined by the condition of the ground, etc. (as, good, rough, or hard *sledding:* often fig.).

sledge¹ (slej), *n.* [From Dutch, and akin to E. *sled.*] A sled for conveying loads over snow, ice, rough ground, etc.; also, a vehicle mounted on runners, and of various forms, used for traveling over snow and ice, as in northern countries (as, a reindeer *sledge;* a Russian *sledge*); sometimes, a light form of such a vehicle used in more temperate climates for pleasure-driving, etc. (Eng.:

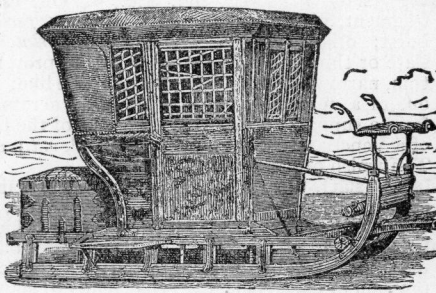

Traveling-sledge of Peter the Great.

in the U. S. called *sleigh*).—**sledge¹,** *v. t.* or *i.*; *sledged, sledging.* To convey or travel by sledge.

sledge² (slej), *n.* [AS. *slecg,* akin to *slēan,* strike, E. *slay².*] A large, heavy hammer, commonly wielded with both hands, used chiefly by blacksmiths.—**sledge²,** *v. i.* or *t.*; *sledged, sledging.* To strike or beat with or as with a sledge.

sledge=ham-mer (slej'ham″ẽr), *n.* A sledge, or large, heavy hammer.—**sledge'=ham″mer,** *v. t.* To beat with or as with a sledge-hammer.

sleek (slēk). [Var. of *slick¹.*] **I.** *a.* Smooth to the touch or in appearance, as hair, fur, skin, or the head, an animal, etc.; glossy; without roughness; hence, having a well-fed or well-groomed appearance, as a person (as, "A *sleek,* comfortably dressed man arose smilingly": W. Churchill's "Coniston," i. 14); also, smooth of manners, speech, etc. (as, "I saw That equal baseness lived in *sleeker* times With smoother men": Tennyson's "Princess," v. 375); suave; plausible; insinuating; artful or sly. **II.** *n.* A slick, or smooth place, as an oil-covered area on the ocean: as, "The sea presented that smooth satin-like surface, called a *sleek,* produced by the subtle moisture thrown off by the whale" (H. Melville's "Moby-Dick," lxxxvii.).—**sleek,** *v. t.* To make sleek; smooth (as, "She brought the . . . carter, *sleeking* down his hair, into the drawing-room": Mrs. Gaskell's "Cranford," ii.); fig., to calm or soothe.—**sleek'er,** *n.* One who or that which sleeks; an implement for smoothing something, as leather during preparation.—**sleek'ly,** *adv.*—**sleek'ness,** *n.*—**sleek'y,** *a.* Sleek; smooth; fig., plausible; artful; sly.

sleep (slēp), *v.*; *slept, sleeping.* [AS. *slǣpan* = D. *slapen* = G. *schlafen* = Goth. *slēpan,* sleep.] **I.** *intr.* To take the repose or rest afforded by a suspension of the voluntary exercise of the bodily functions and the natural suspension, complete or partial, of consciousness; be in a state of sleep; slumber; also, to lie in death, or rest in the grave (as, "So David *slept* with his fathers, and was buried in the city of David": 1 Kings, ii. 10); also, to be 'asleep' or numb, as the foot, hand, etc.; also, to rest or lie quietly (as, the sword *sleeps* in its scabbard; "How sweet the moonlight *sleeps* upon this bank!" Shakspere's "Merchant of Venice," v. 1. 54; "Pools both clear and deep, Wherein the images of trees did *sleep,*" W. Morris's "Jason," xv. 112); be quiet or still, as the sea; spin with a smooth, scarcely perceptible motion, as a top; be dormant, quiescent, or inactive, as faculties, passions, powers, matters at issue, etc.; be slothful, negligent, or remiss (as, "Authority herself not seldom *sleeps,* Though . . . witness of the wrong": Cowper's "Task," iv. 593); in *bot.,* of plants, to assume, esp. at night, a state similar to the sleep of animals, marked by closing of petals, etc. (cf. *nyc-*

titropic). **II.** *tr.* To take rest in (sleep); spend or pass (time, etc.) in sleep (with *away* or *out*); get rid of (a headache, etc.) by sleeping (with *off* or *away*).—**sleep,** *n.* [AS. *slǣp.*] The state of a person or an animal that sleeps (as, sound or dreamless *sleep*; "Tired nature's sweet restorer, balmy *sleep!*" Young's "Night Thoughts," i. 1); slumber; a period of sleeping or slumber (as, a brief *sleep*; between *sleeps*; to measure a journey by nightly *sleeps*, as the Indians do); also, the repose of death, or rest in the grave (as, "The morningless and unawakening *sleep* Under the flowery oleanders pale": M. Arnold's "Thyrsis"); also, the numb state of a foot, hand, etc., when 'asleep'; also, reposeful quiet or stillness; dormancy or inactivity; in *bot.*, the condition of a plant when sleeping.

sleep-er (slē′pẽr), *n.* One who or that which sleeps; a slumberer; a dead person; an inactive or indolent person; something in a dormant or inactive state; also, a railroad sleeping-car; also, a horizontal beam or stone serving as a foundation or support, as a tie of a railroad-track.—**seven sleepers.** See under *seven, a.*

sleep-i-ly (slē′pi-li), *adv.* In a sleepy manner.—**sleep′i-ness,** *n.*

sleep-ing (slē′ping), *n.* The condition of being asleep.—**sleep′ing,** *p. a.* That sleeps; slumbering; dormant; inactive (as, a *sleeping* partner: see *partner, n.*).—**sleep′ing-bag,** *n.* A large bag made of fur or the like, for sleeping in out of doors.—**sleep′ing-car,** *n.* A railroad-car fitted with berths, etc., for sleeping in.—**sleep′ing-porch,** *n.* A sleeping apartment arranged from or on a porch, veranda, or other like part of a house, often on an upper story, open on one or more sides to the outdoor air: as, "Had to have a couple blankets, on the *sleeping-porch* last night" (Sinclair Lewis's "Babbitt," iii.).—**sleep′ing-sick″ness,** *n.* In *pathol.*, a disease, generally fatal, common in certain parts of Africa, characterized usually by fever, wasting, and progressive lethargy, and caused by a parasitic protozoan, *Trypanosoma gambiense*, the infection being transferred from one person to another through the bites of a tsetse-fly, *Glossina palpalis*; also, encephalitis lethargica (see under *encephalitis*).

sleep-less (slēp′les), *a.* Going without sleep, or not sleeping, as a person; characterized by absence of sleep, as nights, watching, diligence, etc.; wakeful; ever alert; also, continually active or in motion (as, "the *sleepless* ocean": Wordsworth's "Excursion," ix. 212).—**sleep′less-ly,** *adv.*—**sleep′less-ness,** *n.*

sleep-walk-er (slēp′wâ″kẽr), *n.* One who walks about while asleep; a somnambulist.—**sleep′walk″ing,** *n.* and *a.*

sleep-y (slē′pi), *a.*; compar. *sleepier*, superl. *sleepiest*. Inclined to sleep, drowsy, or somnolent (as, to feel *sleepy*; a *sleepy* child); characterized by or showing drowsiness (as, a *sleepy* fit; a *sleepy* tone; "The Vicar acquiesced with a *sleepy* laugh," H. Kingsley's "Geoffry Hamlyn," xi.); languid or languorous, as if from drowsiness (as, "dark, rather *sleepy* eyes," H. G. Wells's "Italy, France, and Britain at War," i.; "*sleepy,* languishing manners," Emerson's "Essays," Manners); lethargic or sluggish; quiet, as if from drowsiness (as, "They drove through the village, with its old houses and its *sleepy* streets": W. Churchill's "Modern Chronicle," i. 7); also, inducing sleep (as, "a *sleepy* potion," Swift's "Gulliver's Travels," i. 1: now rare).—**sleep′y-head** (-hed), *n.* A sleepy or drowsy person.

sleet (slēt), *n.* [ME. *slete*, akin to MLG. *slote*, G. *schlosse*, hail.] Snow or rain in a half-frozen state, falling through the air or driven by the wind: as, "A wet snow, melting to *sleet,* had fallen in the night" (Mrs. Wharton's "Ethan Frome," vi.).—**sleet,** *v.* **I.** *intr.* To send down sleet; fall as sleet. **II.** *tr.* To send down like sleet; also, to beat or cover with sleet.—**sleet′y,** *a.* Of or like sleet (as, "*sleety* showers": Whittier's "Legend of St. Mark"); characterized by sleet (as, "The weather was wet and *sleety*": Galt's "Annals of the Parish," v.).

sleeve (slēv), *n.* [AS. *slíefe, sléfe.*] The part of a garment that covers the arm, varying in form and length but commonly tubular; sometimes, a detachable or separate article of dress for the arm (as, a pair of embroidered *sleeves*; the knight wore his lady's *sleeve* as a favor in the tournament) (see cut in next column); also [*cap.*], with *the* (tr. F. *la Manche*), the English Channel, between England and France; also [*l. c.*], in *mech.*, a tubular piece, as of metal, fitting over a rod or the like.—**to laugh in one's sleeve.** See under *laugh, v. i.*—**to wear one's heart upon one's sleeve.** See under *wear²*, *v. t.*—**up one's sleeve.** See under *up, prep.*—**sleeve,** *v. t.*; *sleeved, sleeving.* To furnish with sleeves; in *mech.*, to fit with a sleeve; join or fasten by means of a sleeve.—**sleeved,** *a.* Having sleeves: as, long-*sleeved*.—**sleeve′=dog,** *n.* A toy dog small enough to be carried in the sleeve, as among the Chinese, Japanese, etc.—**sleeve′less,** *a.* Having no sleeves; also, futile, fruitless, or useless (archaic or prov.: as, "a *sleeveless* errand," Shakspere's "Troilus and Cressida," v. 4. 9).

Sleeve worn as a favor at knight's left shoulder.

sleigh (slā), *n.* [D. *slee*; akin to E. *sled*.] A vehicle on runners for carrying travelers or passengers over snow and ice (cf. *sledge¹, n.*); esp., a light, usually open vehicle on runners, generally drawn by a horse or horses, used for pleasure-driving, etc., in snowy weather (in England commonly called *sledge*); also, a sled or sledge for conveying loads.—**sleigh,** *v. i.* To travel or ride in a sleigh.—**sleigh′=bell,** *n.* A small bell, commonly a hollow ball of metal pierced by a slit and containing a loose pellet of metal: a number of such bells commonly being attached to the harness of a horse drawing a sleigh, and jingling when in motion.—**sleigh′er,** *n.*—**sleigh′ing,** *n.* The act or the pastime of riding in a sleigh; also, the going, or kind of travel, for sleighs, as determined by the state of the snow, etc. (as, good *sleighing*).

sleight (slīt), *n.* [ME. *sleyght, sleyth*, from Scand.: cf. Icel. *slægdh*, slyness, cunning (< *slægr*: see *sly*), also Sw. *slöjd*, craft, industrial art, woodworking (see *sloyd*).] Cunning, craft, or artful contrivance (obs. or rare); an artifice, stratagem, or ruse (obs. or rare); also, skill, dexterity, or cleverness, as in doing something; adroitness or nimbleness, as of mind or body; esp., skill in jugglery or legerdemain (as, "As lookers-on feel most delight, That least perceive a juggler's *sleight*," Butler's "Hudibras," ii. 3: see *sleight of hand*, below); a feat of jugglery or legerdemain; a clever performance or trick achieved by great dexterity, as in manipulation.—**sleight of hand,** skill or dexterity in using the hands (as, "The throwing the hides upon the pole . . . required a *sleight of hand* which was only to be got by long practice": Dana's "Two Years before the Mast," xxix.); now, specif., skill in feats of jugglery or legerdemain; hence, the performance of such feats; jugglery or legerdemain; a feat of legerdemain (as, to perform new *sleights of hand*).

slen-der (slen′dẽr), *a.* [ME. *slendre, sclendre*; origin uncertain.] Small in girth or circumference in proportion to height or length, usually with graceful effect, as persons or animals, the body, or parts of the body; slim or slight of form; not stout or fleshy; hence, of things generally, small in diameter, thickness, or width in proportion to length (as, *slender* columns, spires, stalks, chains, or bands; a *slender* strip of land); thin, as a book; small in size, amount, extent, etc. (as, a *slender* income; *slender* means or possessions; "the *slender* but still sufficient contents of his wine-cellar," Trollope's "Warden," xx.; *slender* abilities); inconsiderable, meager, or scanty; thin or weak, as sound; also, having little value, force, or justification (as, *slender* arguments or claims; "at best but very *slender* probabilities," Adam Smith's "Wealth of Nations," v. 1. 3. 2; "The Prince . . . had *slender* hopes of a peaceful result," Motley's "Dutch Republic," ii. 8); slight or poor.—**slen′der-ize** (-īz), *v. t.*; *-ized, -izing.* To make slender, or more slender; cause to appear slender: as, modes of dress that *slenderize* the figure. **—slen″der-i-za′tion** (-i-zā′shǫn), *n.*—**slen′der-ly**, *adv.*—**slen′der-ness,** *n.*

slept (slept). Preterit and past participle of *sleep.*

sleugh (slö), *n.* See *slough*[1].

sleuth (slöth), *n.* [ME. *sleuth, sloth,* from Scand.: cf. Icel. *slōdh,* track, trail, also E. *slot*[3].] The track or trail of a person or animal†; also, a sleuth-hound or bloodhound; fig., a detective (colloq.: as, "I read story-books of crime in which the detectives are '*sleuths,*'" Eden Phillpotts's "Red Redmaynes," v.).—**sleuth,** *v. t.* or *i.* To track or trail (a person, etc.) as a detective does. [Colloq.] **—sleuth′-hound,** *n.* A bloodhound; fig., a detective (colloq.).

slew[1] (slö). Preterit of *slay*[2].

slew[2], **slew**[3], **slew**[4] (slö). See *slough*[1], *slue*[2], *slue*[3].

sley (slā), *n.* See *slay*[1].

slice (slīs), *n.* [OF. *esclice* (F. *éclisse*), < *esclicier,* split, reduce to pieces; from Teut., and akin to E. *slit.*] A splinter† or fragment†; also, a relatively thin, broad, flat piece cut from something (as, a *slice* of bread or meat); hence, a part, portion, or share of something (as, to get a *slice* of the profits; "He's seen his *slice* of luck, has Dick," Stevenson's "Treasure Island," xxix.); also, any of various implements with a thin, broad blade or part, as for turning food in a frying-pan, for serving fish at table, for taking up printing-ink, etc.; also, a cut or movement as in slicing; in *golf,* a slicing stroke.—**slice,** *v.; sliced, slicing.* **I.** *tr.* To cut into slices; divide into parts, portions, or shares (as, "The ground will be curiously *sliced* into acres, and roods, and perches": Kinglake's "Eothen," xii.); also, to cut through or cleave like a knife (as, our ship *sliced* the sea); cut (a way) as with a knife; also, to cut (*off, away, from,* etc.) as or like a slice; also, to remove by means of a slice (implement), slice-bar, or the like; in *golf,* to hit (the ball)

Printer's Slice.

with a glancing stroke that causes it to curve off to the right (or, in the case of a left-handed player, the left). **II.** *intr.* To cut a slice or slices; also, to cut through something, like or as with a knife; in *golf,* to slice the ball.—**slice′-bar,** *n.* A long-handled instrument with a blade at the end, for clearing away or breaking up clinkers, etc., in a furnace.—**sli-cer** (slī′sẽr), *n.* One who slices; also, an implement or apparatus for slicing.

slick[1] (slik). [ME. *slike, slyk:* cf. Icel. *slīkr,* sleek, smooth, also E. *sleek.*] **I.** *a.* Sleek, smooth, or glossy; fig., smooth of manners, speech, etc.; plausible or insinuating; artful or sly; shrewdly adroit, clever, or smart; also, ingenious, cleverly devised, or neat (as, "That's a pretty *slick* arrangement on the radiator, so you can adjust it at any temperature you want": Sinclair Lewis's "Main Street," xvii.); excellent or first-rate. [Now prov. or colloq.] **II.** *n.* A smooth place or spot, as an oil-covered area on the ocean; in *carp.,* a wide chisel.—**slick**[1], *adv.* In a slick manner; smoothly; cleverly; quickly; also, completely, just, or right. [Prov. or colloq.]—**slick**[1], *v. t.* To make sleek or smooth; smooth; also, to make smart or fine (often with *up:* as, "Come down when you are *slicked* up enough," Mark Twain's "Tom Sawyer," xxxiii.). [Now chiefly prov. or colloq.]

slick[2] (slik), *n.* [G. *schlich.*] In *metal.,* ore in fine particles. **slick-en** (slik′n), *a.* [From *slick*[1].] Smooth; polished. [Prov. Eng.]

slick-ens (slik′nz), *n. pl.* [Cf. *slick*[2].] Fine or powdered ore, debris, or the like, as from a stamp-mill.

slick-en-side (slik′n-sīd), *n.* [See *slicken.*] In *geol.,* a rock surface which has become more or less polished and striated from the sliding or grinding motion of an adjacent mass of rock.—**slick′en-sid″ed** (-sī″ded), *a.*

slick-er (slik′ẽr), *n.* A sleeker, or smoothing implement; also, a long, loose oilskin or waterproof outer coat (U. S.: as, "I wore a great flapping yellow *slicker,* or oilskin overcoat," Roosevelt's "Ranch Life and the Hunting-Trail," ix.).

slick-ly (slik′li), *adv.* In a slick manner.—**slick′ness,** *n.*

slide (slīd), *v.; pret. slid, pp. slidden* or *slid, ppr. sliding.* [AS. *slīdan* = MHG. *slīten,* slide: cf. G. *schlitten,* a sledge, sled, and E. *sled.*] **I.** *intr.* To move along in continuous

contact with a smooth or slippery surface, under the impetus of a thrust or initial effort, the force of weight, etc. (as, to *slide* on ice; to *slide* down a snow-covered hill, as on a sled); move smoothly along on a surface or thing, or in a groove, etc.; slip (*down, off,* etc.); sometimes, to slip as one losing foothold, or as a vehicle skidding; fig., to slip morally, as into fault (as, "I find myself a learner yet, Unskilful, weak, and apt to *slide,*" Cowper's "Olney Hymns," Peace after a Storm: cf. *backslide*); in general, to glide or pass smoothly onward, as over ground or water or through the air, or as a stream in its course (chiefly archaic: as, "Swiftly through the water Argo *slid,*" W. Morris's "Jason," xii. 438); slip easily, quietly, or unobtrusively (*in, out, away,* etc.), as a person (as, "Mr. Fred . . . had *slid* in unobserved through the half-open door": George Eliot's "Middlemarch," xi.); make off or decamp (slang); go unregarded, or take its or their own course (as, "He [Lord Melbourne] was lazy and easy-going . . . he let things *slide,*" Lytton Strachey's "Queen Victoria," iii.; "Let the world *slide,*" Shakspere's "Taming of the Shrew," Induction, i. 6); pass quietly or imperceptibly (*away, by,* etc.), as time; pass or fall gradually into a specified state, character, practice, etc.; in *music,* to pass from one tone to another without perceptible step or break, as by a portamento. **II.** *tr.* To cause to slide, as over a surface or with a smooth, gliding motion; slip (something) easily or quietly (*in, into,* etc.); also, to slide or glide over, along, or down (obs. or rare).—**slide,** *n.* The act or an act of sliding; a landslide or the like, or the mass of matter sliding down; also, a sliding piece or part, as in a mechanism; a plate of glass or other material on which objects are placed for microscopic examination; a plate of glass on which is a prepared picture for projection by a stereopticon, etc.; a photographic plate-holder; a sledge or sled; also, a smooth surface, esp. of ice, for sliding on; an inclined plane for goods, etc., to slide on; a chute; a rail, groove, or the like, on or in which something slides; in *music,* an embellishment or grace consisting of an upward or downward series of three or more tones, the last of which is the principal tone; also, a portamento; also, in instruments of the trumpet class, a U-shaped section of the tube, which can be pushed in or out so as to alter the length of the air-column and thus the pitch of the tones.—**slide′-bar,** *n.* In *mech.,* etc., a sliding bar in a machine, etc., as for opening or closing an aperture; also, a bar which serves as a guide, track, or the like, for a sliding or reciprocating part.—**slid-er** (slī′dẽr), *n.* One who slides; also, a sliding thing or part; also, a turtle, *Pseudemys rubriventris,* an inferior kind of terrapin found chiefly about the Susquehanna River and other streams flowing into Chesapeake Bay (also called *red-bellied terrapin*).—**slide′-rule,** *n.* A device used in engineering, etc., for rapid calculation, consisting essentially of a rule having a sliding piece moving along it, both parts being marked with graduated logarithmic scales. —**slide′-valve,** *n.*

Slider (*Pseudemys rubriventris*).

In *mech.,* a valve that slides (without lifting) to open or close an aperture, as the valves that control the ports in the cylinders of certain steam-engines.—**slid′ing,** *p. a.* That slides (as, a *sliding* rule, a slide-rule); varying (as, a *sliding* scale, a scale of wages, prices, etc., varying according to circumstances).

sli-er, sli-est (slī′ẽr, slī′est). Compar. and superl. of *sly, a.*

slight (slīt), *a.* [ME. *slight, sleght,* from Scand.: cf. Icel. *slēttr,* Sw. *slät,* also Goth. *slaihts,* smooth, flat, G. *schlicht,* smooth, plain, *schlecht,* plain, low, base, bad.] Smooth or glossy (now Sc. and north. Eng.); also, slender or slim, as in form (as, "a short, *slight* woman": Gissing's "New Grub Street," vii.); hence, light in structure, texture, substance, etc., so as to be unequal to a severe strain, as an erection, a fabric, etc. (as, "The bridge, which . . . was a very *slight* one, was broke down": Sterne's "Tristram Shandy," iii. 24); frail; flimsy; fig., lacking in solid or substantial qualities, as a literary production, intellectual parts, a person, etc.; of little weight, importance, or consequence, as a matter, cause, excuse, etc.; trifling, petty, or paltry (as, "His offence in itself seemed *slight* in so loose an age": Froude's "Cæsar," xiii.); small in amount, degree, etc. (as, a *slight* increase, extent, or effect; a *slight* glance; a *slight* odor); low, as esteem or consideration; also, indifferent, slighting, or contemptuous (obs. or archaic: as, "*Slight* was his answer, 'Well — I care not for it,'" Tennyson's "Aylmer's Field," 238).—**slight**, *v. t.* To make smooth, as linen or ground†; level, raze, or demolish, as buildings†; also, to treat (persons or things) as of slight importance; treat with indifference or disrespect; disregard or ignore, as in contempt; do negligently, or scamp, as work; slur (*over*), as a point or matter†; put (*off*) with contempt† (as, "My letters . . . were *slighted* off": Shakspere's "Julius Cæsar," iv. 3. 5); throw contemptuously† (as, "The rogues *slighted* me into the river with as little remorse as they would have drowned a blind bitch's puppies": Shakspere's "Merry Wives of Windsor," iii. 5. 9).—**slight**, *n.* A slight or trifling matter†; also, slighting indifference or treatment (as, "Mr. Bounderby, swelling with a sense of *slight*": Dickens's "Hard Times," ii. 9); an instance of slighting treatment (as, "thwarted or stung by a fancied *slight*": Bret Harte's "Mliss," i.); a pointed and contemptuous ignoring; an affront of neglect or omitted courtesy.—**slight′er,** *n.*—**slight′ing-ly,** *adv.*—**slight′ly,** *adv.* In a slight manner; also, to a slight extent or degree; in some small measure; somewhat.—**slight′ness,** *n.*

sli-ly (slī′li), *adv.* See *slyly*.

slim (slim), *a.*; compar. *slimmer,* superl. *slimmest.* [Cf. MLG. *slim,* oblique, crooked, not in due condition, sorry, bad, D. *slim,* crooked, sly, bad, G. *schlimm,* sly, bad, ill.] Slender, as in girth or form (as, a *slim* young girl; a *slim* waist); slight in build or structure; thin, as a book (as, "two *slim* volumes of poems": Buchan's "Three Hostages," iv.); frail or flimsy (chiefly prov.); poor (as, a *slim* chance; a *slim* excuse); small, inconsiderable, or scanty (as, a *slim* audience; a *slim* income); also, sly or crafty (prov.).

slime (slīm), *n.* [AS. *slīm* = D. *slijm* = G. *schleim* = Icel. *slīm,* slime: cf. L. *limus,* slime, mud.] Thin, glutinous mud; any ropy or viscous liquid matter, esp. of a foul or offensive kind; sticky liquid filth (often fig.: as, "An honest man he is, and hates the *slime* That sticks on filthy deeds," Shakspere's "Othello," v. 2. 148); a viscous secretion of animal or vegetable origin (as, the trail of *slime* left by a snail; a *slime*-mold or *slime*-fungus); liquid bitumen (archaic: see Ex. ii. 3); in *mining* and *metal.,* ore reduced to a very fine powder and held in suspension in water (usually in *pl.*).—**slime,** *v. t.; slimed, sliming.* To cover or smear with or as with slime; also, to remove slime from, as fish for canning.—**slime′=fun″gus,** *n.;* pl. *-gi* (-jī). Same as *slime-mold.*—**slime′=mold,** *n.* Any of the fungus-like vegetable organisms of the myxomycetous group, occurring in slimy masses on decaying logs, etc. See *myxomycetous.*—**slime′=pit,** *n.* A pit yielding liquid bitumen (archaic: see Gen. xiv. 10); also, in *mining* and *metal.,* a tank or reservoir in which slimes are settled or stored.

slim-i-ly (slī′mi-li), *adv.* In a slimy manner.—**slim′i-ness,** *n.*

slim-ly (slim′li), *adv.* In a slim manner; slenderly; slightly; poorly; scantily.—**slim′ness,** *n.*

slimp-sy, slim-sy (slimp′si, slim′zi), *a.* [Appar. a mixture of *slim* and *flimsy.*] Flimsy; frail. [U. S.]

slim-y (slī′mi), *a.*; compar. *slimier,* superl. *slimiest.* Of or like slime; abounding in or covered with slime (as, "Yea,

Slime-mold (*Cribraria piriformis*).

slimy things did crawl with legs Upon the *slimy* sea": Coleridge's "Ancient Mariner," ii.); fig., foul; vile.

sling (sling), *v. t.; slung, slinging.* [Prob. orig. from Scand.: cf. Icel. *slyngva* (pret. *slöng, slungu*), Sw. *slunga,* Dan. *slynge,* throw, sling, also MHG. *slingen,* throw, wind, G. *schlingen,* wind, twist; the E. verb being early affected in meaning by *sling, n.*] To throw, cast, or hurl; fling, as from the hand; throw or cast (stones or other missiles) with a sling (as, "like David, who was accustomed to *sling* smooth stones taken from the brook": Scott's "Legend of Montrose," xvi.); also, to place in or secure with a sling in order to raise or lower; raise, lower, etc., by such means; also, to hang in a sling or so as to swing loosely (as, to *sling* a rifle over one's shoulder); suspend (as, "Order one of the quarter-masters to get a hammock *slung*": Marryat's "Mr. Midshipman Easy," ix.); *naut.,* to secure by a sling.—**to sling ink,** to write; esp., to write for publication. [Slang.]—**sling,** *v. i.* To cast missiles with a sling; also, to move with long, swinging strides (prov. or colloq.).—**sling,** *n.* [Cf. Icel. *slanga,* Dan. *slynge,* OF. *eslingue* (from Teut.), OHG. *slinga* (G. *schlinge*), a sling.] An instrument for hurling stones, etc., by hand, consisting of a strap or piece for holding the missile, with two strings attached, the ends of which are held in the hand (or attached to a staff), the impulse being given by whirling the whole rapidly before discharging the missile (in general use as a weapon among the ancients: see 1 Sam. xvii. 50, 2 Chron. xxvi. 14); hence, a similar instrument used in sport by boys; a catapult; sometimes, formerly, a ballista, or military engine for throwing stones, etc.; also, the act of slinging; the stroke of something coming as if cast from a sling (in first sense: as, "The deadly *sling* of the hailstones Beats down the farmer's corn," Longfellow's "Evangeline," i. 4); a throw, cast, or fling; a draft, as of liquor (colloq.); a drink consisting of spirits and water sweetened and flavored (as, "You won't take a glass of *sling* . . . with a countryman?" Marryat's "Mr. Midshipman Easy," xxxix.); also, a device consisting commonly of a rope, band, chain, or the like in the form of a loop, for holding heavy articles, as casks, bales, etc., while being raised or lowered; a strap, band, or the like forming a loop by which something is suspended or carried, as a strap attached to a rifle and passed over the shoulder; a hanging loop, as of cloth, in which an injured limb is supported (as, "One of his arms was supported by a *sling,* and lay motionless across his breast": H. Mackenzie's "Man of Feeling," xxxiv.); *naut.,* a rope or chain supporting a yard (usually in *pl.*); hence, *pl.,* that part of a yard (its middle portion) at which it is thus supported (as, "They observed that the mainyard was shot in the *slings,* and that the vessel was disabled": Scott's "Guy Mannering," x.).—**sling′er,** *n.* One who slings; esp., a soldier armed with a sling (as, "Cæsar . . . sent back his cavalry and his archers and *slingers*": Froude's "Cæsar," xiv.).—**sling′=shot,** *n.* A boy's sling or catapult.

slink¹ (slingk), *v. t.* or *i.; slinked* or *slunk, slinking.* [Cf. *sling, v.,* 'cast.'] Of cows, etc., to bring forth (young) prematurely.—**slink¹,** *n.* A prematurely born calf or other animal.

slink² (slingk), *v. i.;* pret. *slunk* (occasionally *slank*), pp. *slunk,* ppr. *slinking.* [AS. *slincan,* creep, crawl, = Sw. *slinka,* slink, = MLG. and D. *slinken,* shrink.] To creep or go quietly or stealthily (as, "When the Master looked away again . . . Mountain *slunk* stealthily back": Stevenson's "Master of Ballantrae," xi.); now, usually, to go in a furtive, abject manner, as from fear, cowardice, or shame (as, "As boys that *slink* From ferule and the trespass-chiding eye, Away we stole": Tennyson's "Princess," v. 35); sneak; sometimes, to skulk, or lie in hiding (as, "I'd crawl somewhere to a cave, and *slink* there": H. Melville's "Moby-Dick," cxxxv.).—**slink²,** *n.* A slinking person; a sneak; also, a slinking movement or gait.—**slink′ing-ly,** *adv.*

slip¹ (slip), *n.* [AS. *slyppe,* paste, slime: cf. *cowslip* and *oxlip.*] Slime† or mud†; also, curdled milk; also, in *ceram.,*

Staff-sling, about the 10th century.

potters' clay reduced to a semifluid state with water, used for coating or decorating pottery, cementing handles, etc.

slip² (slip), *v.*; *slipped*, *slipping*. [ME. *slippen* = MLG. and D. *slippen*, slip; akin to AS. *slipor*, slippery, E. *slipper¹*: cf. AS. *slūpan*, slip, glide, move smoothly, and E. *slope*.] **I.** *intr.* To pass or go smoothly or easily, glide, or slide (*along, away, down, off, over, through*, etc.: as, water *slips* off a smooth surface; a ship *slips* through the waves); often, to go quietly, or steal (as, "He . . . *slipped* in by a side entrance," W. Churchill's "Coniston," i. 16; "the jackals . . . *slipping* back to the hills," Dunsany's "Tents of the Arabs," ii.); fig., to pass insensibly, as from the mind or memory; pass quickly or imperceptibly (*away, by*, etc.), as time; pass superficially, carelessly, or without attention, as over a matter; also, to slide suddenly and involuntarily, as on a smooth surface, or lose one's foothold (as, "He had *slipped* one day on some rocks and twisted . . . his ankle": H. G. Wells's "Men Like Gods," iii. 2); fig., to make a slip, mistake, or error; also, to move, slide, or start from place, position, fastenings, the hold, etc. (as, an ax-head *slips* from the handle; a knife, or the hand, *slips* in cutting; a pen *slips* from the fingers); fig., to get away, escape, or be lost (as, wealth or power *slips* from one; to let an opportunity *slip*); become known (as, "If he let *slip* his secret, he knew well it was the warrant for his death": Stevenson's "Master of Ballantrae," xi.); also, to go, come, get, etc., easily or quickly (as, the ring *slips* on and off; to *slip* into or out of a garment). **II.** *tr.* To cause to slip; pass, put, draw, etc., with a smooth, easy, or sliding motion (as, to *slip* one's hand into a drawer; to *slip* back a bolt); put or draw quietly or stealthily (as, to *slip* a letter into a person's hand; to *slip* a thing out of sight); put (*on*) or take (*off*) easily or quickly, as a garment; cast (the skin, etc.); also, to let or have (the foot) slip (as, "Bertram, in his haste, *slipped* his foot upon the uneven rock": Scott's "Guy Mannering," liv.); let slip from fastenings, the hold, etc.; release from a leash or the like, as a hound or a hawk; untie or undo (a knot); fig., to let pass unheeded, neglect, or miss (as, "Let us not *slip* the occasion": Milton's "Paradise Lost," i. 178); also, to pass over or omit, as in speaking or writing; also, to slip away from; escape from or elude, as a pursuer; get loose or free from (a halter, collar, etc.); fig., to escape (one's memory, notice, knowledge, etc.); also, to bring forth (offspring) prematurely (said of animals); also, to take slips or cuttings from (a plant); take (a part) as a slip from a plant; *naut.*, to let go entirely, as an anchor-cable or an anchor.—**slip²**, *n.* The act of slipping; a landslide; a slipping of the feet, as on slippery ground; fig., a mishap; a mistake, often a slight mistake inadvertently made, as in speaking or writing (as, a *slip* of the tongue, or of the pen; *slips* in one's grammar or spelling); an error in conduct, often an indiscretion or a venial transgression; also, the slipping away from a pursuer, guard, or other person (chiefly in 'to give one the slip,' to slip quietly or stealthily away from him); also, something easily slipped on or off; a kind of leash for a dog (as, "The dogs . . . strained at the *slips*, which prevented them from joining their companions": Scott's "Guy Mannering," xxv.); a child's dress or frock; a woman's garment, now an underdress worn under a dress of lace or the like; a pillow-case; also, an artificial slope beside navigable water, serving as a landing-place; an inclined plane sloping to the water, on which vessels are built or repaired; a space between two wharves or in a dock, for vessels to lie in (U. S.); a narrow passage or roadway (chiefly prov.); also, a piece suitable for propagation cut from a plant; a scion or cutting; hence, a descendant; a young person of either sex, esp. one of slender form (as, "To him she was a *slip* of a girl": Arnold Bennett's "Old Wives' Tale," ii. 7); also, any long, narrow piece or strip, as of wood, paper, land, etc.; a long seat or narrow pew, as in a church (U. S.: as, "He entered quietly, and sat in the rear *slip*," W. Churchill's "Coniston," i. 2); in *geol.*, a small fault due to the sinking of one section of strata; in *mech.*, the moving on each other of two surfaces or parts which are intended to be immovable with respect to each other (as, the *slip* of the plates in a riveted joint); in *marine engin.*, the difference between the speed at which a screw-propeller or paddle-wheel would move forward if it were working against a solid and the actual speed at which it advances

through the water; in *cricket*, the position of a fielder who stands behind and to the off side of the wicket-keeper, or the fielder himself; in *printing*, a galley-proof.

slip=knot (slip′not), *n.* A knot which may easily be slipped or undone; also, a knot which slips easily along the cord or line round which it is made.

slip=noose (slip′nös), *n.* A running noose (see under *running, p. a.*).

slip=on (slip′on). **I.** *a.* Designed to be slipped on easily, as a kind of loose overcoat or cloak or a kind of glove loose at the wrist; also, designed for slipping on over the head, as a blouse or a sweater; slip-over. **II.** *n.* A slip-on garment or article of dress.

slip=o•ver (slip′ō″vėr). **I.** *a.* Designed for slipping over the head, as a blouse or a sweater that does not open from top to bottom (as the ordinary buttoned garment does). **II.** *n.* A slip-over garment.

slip-page (slip′āj), *n.* The act of slipping; also, the amount or extent of slipping.

slip-per¹ (slip′ėr), *a.* [AS. *slipor*: see *slip²*.] Slippery (lit. or fig.): as, "a *slipper* and subtle knave" (Shakspere's "Othello," ii. 1. 246). [Obs. or prov.]

slip-per² (slip′ėr), *n.* [From *slip²*.] One who or that which slips; also, a kind of light shoe into which the foot may be easily slipped, worn chiefly indoors; also, a kind of skid or shoe for a wheel.—**slip′per²**, *v. t.* To provide with slippers; also, to strike or beat with a slipper.—**slip′pered**, *a.* Shod with or wearing slippers: as, "the lean and *slipper'd* pantaloon" (Shakspere's "As You Like It," ii. 7. 158).

slip-per-i-ly (slip′ėr-i-li), *adv.* In a slippery manner.—**slip′per-i-ness**, *n.*

slip-per-ing (slip′ėr-ing), *n.* A beating with a slipper: as, "to give me a good *slippering* for my misbehavior" (H. Melville's "Moby-Dick," iv.).

slip-per-less (slip′ėr-les), *a.* Without slippers: as, "His feet were *slipperless*, Eastern fashion" (F. M. Crawford's "Mr. Isaacs," iii.).

slip-per-y (slip′ėr-i), *a.* [Extended form of *slipper¹*.] Tending to cause slipping or sliding, as ground, places, surfaces, things, etc. (as, "The hills were *slippery* with ice and snow," Irving's "Captain Bonneville," xxxi.; "Green slime Made the way *slippery*," W. B. Yeats's "Wanderings of Oisin," ii.; *slippery* pavements or rails); also, tending to slip from the hold or grasp or from position, by reason of smooth or greasy surface, oily character, etc. (as, a *slippery* rope; wet soap becomes *slippery*); fig., likely to slip away or escape (as, a *slippery* captive); also, not to be depended on; fickle; shifty, tricky, or deceitful, as persons or their actions, etc. (as, "the *slippery* politicians in the capital," Froude's "Cæsar," xxii.; a *slippery* trick); unstable or insecure, as conditions, etc.; also, wanton or licentious (see Shakspere's "Winter's Tale," i. 2. 273); also, liable to slip, or lose foothold† (as, "*slippery* standers": Shakspere's "Troilus and Cressida," iii. 3. 84).—**slip′per-y=elm′**, *n.* A species of elm, *Ulmus fulva*, of eastern North America, with a mucilaginous inner bark; also, the bark, used as a demulcent.

slip-py (slip′i), *a.* Slippery (now colloq. or prov.: as, "steep, *slippy*-feeling rocks," Synge's "Well of the Saints," i.); also, nimble, quick, or sharp (colloq. or prov., British: chiefly in 'to be, or look, slippy,' as, "Bring us two liqueur brandies, miss . . . And look *slippy*, if ye please," Arnold Bennett's "Lion's Share," xxiii.).—**slip′pi-ness**, *n.*

slip-shod (slip′shod), *a.* Wearing slippers or loose shoes, esp. such as are down at the heel, as a person; down at the heel, or worn, loose, and untidy, as shoes; shuffling, as from the wearing of such shoes (as, "The *slipshod* tread of the old porter . . . alone broke the silence": S. J. Weyman's "Gentleman of France," xxiii.); hence, in general, untidy or slovenly (as, *slipshod* dress or habits; "the new owners' camp . . . a *slipshod* and slovenly affair, tent half stretched, dishes unwashed," Jack London's "Call of the Wild," v.); often, slovenly or careless in statement, mode of expression, etc. (as, *slipshod* writers or writing; "*slipshod* talk," George Eliot's "Mr. Gilfil's Love-Story," Epilogue).—**slip′shod″-ness**, *n.*

slip-slop (slip′slop). [Varied redupl. of *slop¹*.] **I.** *n.* A sloppy food or drink; also, a blunder in the use of words, or the making of such blunders; also, loose or trifling talk or writing (as, "The second-rate actors have their . . . admirers, with whom they . . . spout tragedy and talk *slipslop*": Irving's "Tales of a Traveler," ii. 10). **II.** *a.* Sloppy; slovenly; feeble or trifling (as, "Furlong talked *slip-slop* common-places with them": Lover's "Handy Andy," xv.).

slip=up (slip′up), *n.* A slip, mishap, or failure, as in a course of proceedings; a mistake or error. [Colloq.]

slit (slit), *v. t.; slit* or *slitted, slitting.* [ME. *slitten* = OHG. *slizzan* (G. *schlitzen*), slit; akin to AS. *slitan*, OHG. *slizan* (G. *schleissen*), slit, split: cf. *slice.*] To cut apart or open along a line (as, to *slit* one's throat from ear to ear; to *slit* the uncut leaves of a book); make a long (or relatively long) cut, fissure, or opening in (as, to *slit* a garment for ornament, as in slashing, or in order to permit of freer movement); cut or rend into strips (as, the gale has *slit* the sails into ribbons); split; also, to cut or sever, as a thread† (as, "Comes the blind Fury with the abhorred shears, And *slits* the thinspun life": Milton's "Lycidas," 76).—**slit,** *n.* A straight, narrow cut, opening, or aperture: as, "The postman . . . had . . . pushed the letters, as usual, through the *slit* in the door" (Arnold Bennett's "Helen with the High Hand," xiii.); "pretending to doze . . . and out of the narrow *slits* of my half-closed eyes seeing the others" (W. H. Hudson's "Green Mansions," i.).

slith-er (sliTH′er), *v.* [ME. *slitheren*, var. of *slideren*, < AS. *slidrian*, freq. of *slidan*, E. *slide.*] **I.** *intr.* To slide down or along a surface, esp. unsteadily or with more or less friction or noise (as, "The detached crystals *slithered* down the rock face for a moment and then made no further sound": H. G. Wells's "Men Like Gods," ii. 3); go or walk with a sliding motion; slip along. **II.** *tr.* To cause to slither or slide. —**slith′er,** *n.* A slithering movement or passage; a slide.

slit-ter (slit′er), *n.* One who or that which slits.

sliv-er (sliv′er), *n.* [ME. *slivere*, < *sliven*, < AS. *slifan*, split: cf. *sleave.*] A piece, as of wood, split, broken, or cut off, usually lengthwise or with the grain; a slender fragment or piece; a splinter; also, a continuous strand or band of wool, cotton, or other fiber in a loose, untwisted condition, ready for roving or slubbing.—**sliv′er,** *v.* **I.** *tr.* To split or cut off, as a sliver; split or cut into slivers; also, to form (wool, cotton, etc.) into slivers. **II.** *intr.* To split.— **sliv′er-er,** *n.*

slob (slob), *n.* [Ir. *slab*, mud: cf. *slab*[1].] Mud or ooze, or a stretch of mud, esp. along a shore (Ir. and Eng.); also, a stupid, clumsy, or slovenly person (slang: as, "careless, ignorant, foreign *slobs*," Sinclair Lewis's "Arrowsmith," xix.).

slob-ber (slob′er), *v.* [Also *slabber*: cf. D. *slobberen, slabberen*, LG. *slabbern*, G. *schlabbern*, also the related E. *slaver*[2] and *slubber*[2].] **I.** *intr.* To let saliva, etc., run from the mouth; slaver; drivel. **II.** *tr.* To wet or make foul by slobbering; sometimes, to wet with kissing; also, to utter with slobbering (as, "The king . . . *slobbers* out a speech, all full of tears and flapdoodle": Mark Twain's "Huckleberry Finn," xxv.).—**slob′ber,** *n.* Saliva or liquid dribbling from the mouth; slaver.—**slob′ber-er,** *n.*— **slob′ber-ing-ly,** *adv.*— **slob′ber-y,** *a.* Characterized by slobbering; also, disagreeably wet; sloppy.

sloe (slō), *n.* [AS. *slāh* = D. *slee* = G. *schlehe*, sloe.] The small, sour, blackish fruit (drupe) of the black-thorn, *Prunus spinosa*, or the shrub itself; also, any of various other species or plants, as *P. alleghaniensis*, a shrub or small tree with a dark-purple drupe.— **sloe′=eyed,** *a.* Having eyes like sloes; black-eyed.

slog (slog), *v.; slogged, slogging.* [Cf. *slug*[1].] **I.** *tr.* To hit hard, as in boxing, cricket, etc.; also, to drive with blows. [Colloq.]

Sloe (*Prunus spinosa*). — 1, flowering branch; 2, branch with fruit; *a*, a flower, longitudinal section.

II. *intr.* To deal heavy blows; also, to walk or plod heavily; also, to work hard; toil. [Colloq.]

slo-gan (slō′gan), *n.* [Gael. *sluagh-ghairm*, 'army-cry.'] A war-cry or gathering-cry, as formerly used among the Scottish clans (as, "The Border *slogan* rent the sky! A Home! a Gordon! was the cry": Scott's "Marmion," vi. 27); hence, in general, a war-cry, battle-cry, or rallying-cry; a distinctive cry of any party, class, body, or person; a watchword.

slog-ger (slog′er), *n.* One who slogs, as in boxing or cricket. [Colloq.]

sloid, slojd (sloid), *n.* See *sloyd.*

sloop (slöp), *n.* [D. *sloep*, related to (and perhaps derived from) F. *chaloupe*, E. *shallop.*] A small, fore-and-aft rigged, one-masted vessel, usually carrying a jib, mainsail, and gaff-topsail; also, a small ship-rigged war-vessel with guns on the upper deck only ('sloop of war').

Sloop.

slop[1] (slop), *n.* [Cf. ME. *sloppe*, a muddy place, AS. *slyppe*, slime, E. *slip*[1].] Liquid mud; also, a quantity of liquid carelessly spilled or splashed about (as, "The wall-paper was defaced, in spots, by *slops* of beer and wine": Mrs. Stowe's "Uncle Tom's Cabin," xxxv.); also, weak or unappetizing liquid or semiliquid food, as gruel for invalids (often in *pl.*); also, the dirty water, liquid refuse, etc., of a household or the like (often in *pl.*); swill, or the refuse of the kitchen, etc., often used as food for pigs or the like; the watery or other vegetable remains from certain industrial processes, much used as food for animals.—**slop**[1], *v.; slopped, slopping.* **I.** *tr.* To spill or splash (liquid); spill liquid upon; also, to drink or eat (*up*) greedily (now prov. Eng.). **II.** *intr.* To walk or go through mud, slush, or water (as, "Then he *slopped* right along": Mark Twain's "Huckleberry Finn," xviii.); also, to spill or splash liquid (sometimes with *about*); of liquid, to run (*over*) in spilling; hence (colloq.), of persons, etc., with *over*, to overrun due limits, esp. in the expression of feeling or enthusiasm; be unduly effusive; indulge in maudlin gush.

slop[2] (slop), *n.* [ME. *sloppe*: cf. AS. *oferslop*, overgarment, Icel. *sloppr*, gown.] A loose outer garment, as a jacket, tunic, or smock-frock (as, "Tawno had on a clean white *slop*": Borrow's "Romany Rye," viii.); *pl.*, loose breeches or trousers, worn by seamen and others (as, "a soldier in his blue *slops* and red tie": Galsworthy's "Saint's Progress," iii. 3); clothing, bedding, etc., supplied to seamen from the ship's stores; also, cheap ready-made clothing in general.— **slop′=chest,** *n.* A store of seamen's clothing, etc., kept on board a ship for sale to the crew during a voyage.

slope (slōp). [Appar. < AS. *slopen*, pp. of *slūpan*, slip, glide, = Goth. *sliupan* = OHG. *sliofan* (G. *schliefen*), slip: cf. *slip*[2].] **I.** *a.* Proceeding or extending obliquely; slanting; esp., inclining downward or upward from the horizontal, as surfaces, ground, etc. (as, "Murmuring waters fall Down the *slope* hills": Milton's "Paradise Lost," iv. 261); sloping. [Archaic.] **II.** *adv.* At an inclination; aslant; aslope. [Obs. or archaic.]—**slope,** *n.* Inclination or slant, esp. downward or upward (as, "As our pony's back had a forward *slope* we slipped further and further forward": W. H. Hudson's "Far Away and Long Ago," xxi.); deviation from the horizontal; also, an inclined surface; an extent of ground marked by gradual descent or ascent (as, "He began to mount the gentle *slope* leading to its pleasant uplands,"

(variable) d̦ as d or j, ș as s or sh, ț as t or ch, z̦ as z or zh; o, F. *cloche*; ü, F. *menu*; ċh, Sc. *loch*; ṅ, F. *bonbon*; ′, primary accent; ″, secondary accent; †, obsolete; <, from; +, and; =, equals. See also lists at beginning of book.

George Eliot's "Adam Bede," ii.; "He limped down the *slope* of Montmartre," Mrs. Wharton's "Son at the Front," v.).—**slope,** *v.*; *sloped, sloping.* **I.** *intr.* To take or have an inclined or slanting direction, esp. downward or upward from the horizontal (as, "To their minds it had never occurred that the land *sloped* the same way the water ran!" G. W. Cable's "Cavalier," ix.); descend or ascend at a slant (as, "great Orion *sloping* slowly to the west": Tennyson's "Locksley Hall," 8); also, to depart or decamp (colloq.). **II.** *tr.* To direct at a slope or inclination; incline from the horizontal; also, to form with a slope or slant.—**slop-ing-ly** (slō′ping-li), *adv.*

slop-py (slop′i), *a.*; compar. *sloppier,* superl. *sloppiest.* [See *slop*[1].] Muddy, slushy, or very wet, as ground, walking, weather, etc.; also, wet from slopping (as, "*sloppy,* beery tables": Thackeray's "Vanity Fair," lxvi.); splashed or soiled with liquid; also, of the nature of slops, as food; watery and unappetizing; fig., weak, silly, or maudlin (as, *sloppy* sentiment); loose, careless, or slovenly (as, to use *sloppy* English; "*Sloppy* phrases are characteristic of an age of newspapers," M. Hewlett's "Open Country," xiv.; "I do not see how the *sloppiest* reasoner can evade that," H. G. Wells's "In the Fourth Year," v.); untidy, as dress.—**slop′pi-ly,** *adv.*—**slop′pi-ness,** *n.*

slop=shop (slop′shop), *n.* [See *slop*[2].] A shop where cheap clothing is sold.

slop=work (slop′wėrk), *n.* [See *slop*[2].] The manufacture of cheap clothing; clothing of this kind; also, any work done cheaply or poorly.—**slop′=work″er,** *n.*—**slop′=work″ing,** *n.*

slosh (slosh), *n.* [Cf. *slush.*] Slush, or watery snow or mud; also, watery or weak drink, or slops (colloq. or prov.); fig., poor or rubbishy work or writing (colloq.).—**slosh,** *v. i.* To splash in slush, mud, or water (as, "Then on we went, dripping and *sloshing*": Kinglake's "Eothen," ii.); also, to go idly about (colloq., U. S.: as, "Devils don't *slosh* around much of a Sunday, I don't reckon," Mark Twain's "Tom Sawyer," vi.).—**slosh′y,** *a.* Slushy.

slot[1] (slot), *n.* [ME. *slot;* from Dutch or Low German, and akin to G. *schloss,* lock, castle: see *schloss.*] A bolt or bar for securing a door or the like; also, a bar of wood, esp. one set as a crosspiece in a framework or structure; also, a metal rod or pin. [Now chiefly north. Eng. and Sc.]

slot[2] (slot), *n.* [ME. *slot;* origin uncertain.] A narrow, elongated depression or aperture, esp. one to receive or admit something: as, "The patrons [on a street-car] . . . put their fares into a *slot*" (Tarkington's "Magnificent Ambersons," i.).—**slot**[2], *v. t.; slotted, slotting.* To provide with a slot or slots; make a slot in.

slot[3] (slot), *n.* [OF. *esclot;* prob. akin to E. *sleuth.*] The track or trail of a deer or other animal, as shown by the marks of the feet (as, "The Deer Hath left his *slot* beside the way": Southey's "Thalaba," xi. 23); hence, the track, trace, or trail of anything; also, the foot of a deer (as, "the '*slot,*' or forefoot, carefully severed for preservation, in memorial of so fine a run": Whyte-Melville's "Katerfelto," xxv.).—**slot**[3], *v. t.; slotted, slotting.* To track by the slot: as, "May be you never heard of '*slotting*' a stag . . . into a lone quiet coombe" (Whyte-Melville's "Katerfelto," xvi.).

sloth (slōth, also slôth), *n.* [ME. *slowth, slawth,* < *slow, slaw,* E. *slow.*] Sluggishness of disposition, or habitual disinclination to exertion, as a moral fault; indolence; laziness; also, self-indulgent inactivity or idleness (as, "Solicitous how best He may compensate for a day of *sloth*": Cowper's "Task," iv. 434); also, slowness or tardiness (obs. or archaic: as, "These cardinals trifle with me: I abhor This dilatory *sloth,*" Shakspere's "Henry VIII.," ii. 4. 237); also, any of various sluggish arboreal edentate mammals (family *Bradypodidæ*) of tropical America, some having three toes on each fore foot ('three-toed sloths,' genus *Bradypus*), and some only two ('two-toed sloths,' genus *Cholopus*), but all having three on each hind foot; any of various allied extinct edentates, as the megathere or the mylodon.—**sloth′=bear,** *n.* A long-haired bear, *Melursus labiatus,* of India. See cut in next column.—**sloth′ful,** *a.* Full of or characterized by sloth; sluggardly; indolent; lazy.—**sloth′ful-ly,** *adv.*—**sloth′ful-ness,** *n.*

slot=hound (slot′hound), *n.* [See *slot*[3].] A sleuth-hound.

slot=ma-chine (slot′ma-shēn″), *n.* A machine for vending small articles, weighing, or the like, operated by dropping a coin in a slot.

slot-ter (slot′ėr), *n.* A person or a machine that makes slots.

slouch (slouch), *n.* [Origin obscure.] An awkward, ungainly, or slovenly person (as, "Samuel . . . looked transformed from the *slouch* of every day. He wore his

Sloth-bear.

best clothes": Eden Phillpotts's "Children of Men," i. 8); also, an inefficient or inferior person or thing (esp. with a negative: as, he's no *slouch* at this game: slang, U. S.); also, a slouch-hat (colloq.); also, a drooping or bending forward of the head and shoulders; an awkward, drooping carriage of the person, or a slouchy gait (as, "He was clumsily put together, and he walked with a slight *slouch*": Lytton Strachey's "Queen Victoria," iv.); also, a drooping or hanging down of the brim of a hat, etc. (as, "the jaunty *slouch* of this Spanish sombrero": H. Melville's "Omoo," lxi.).—**slouch,** *v.* **I.** *intr.* To sit or stand in an awkward, drooping posture (as, "Most of the men *slouched* in their chairs and wriggled": Sinclair Lewis's "Babbitt," xxx.); carry one's self with a slouch, as in walking; move or walk with loosely drooping body and careless gait (as, "every burly rough who *slouched* through Fishbourne High Street," H. G. Wells's "Mr. Polly," vii.; "A Punjabi constable . . . *slouched* across the road," Kipling's "Kim," iv.); also, to have a droop or downward bend, as a hat. **II.** *tr.* To cause to droop or bend down, as the shoulders or a hat: as, "*slouching* his hat over his face" (Bulwer-Lytton's "Pelham," iv.).—**slouch′=hat′,** *n.* [Earlier *slouched hat.*] A soft hat, esp. one with a broad, flexible brim.—**slouch′i-ly,** *adv.* In a slouchy manner.—**slouch′i-ness,** *n.*—**slouch′ing,** *p. a.* That slouches; carrying one's self with a slouch (as, "a tall *slouching* fellow": Parkman's "Oregon Trail," vi.); characterized by a slouch (as, "I adopted, along with my beggar's attire, a peculiar *slouching* and clownish gait": Godwin's "Caleb Williams," xxxi.); slouchy.—**slouch′ing-ly,** *adv.*—**slouch′y,** *a.* Like or befitting a slouch; slouching; slovenly.

slough[1] (slou), *n.* [AS. *slōh.*] A piece of soft, muddy ground; a hole full of mud or mire, as in a road; a marsh or swamp (as, "bogged up to the middle in the *slough* of Lochend, in attempting to gather a water-lily," Scott's "Guy Mannering," viii.; "He . . . not having followed properly in our tracks, stumbled into a deep part of the *slough* where it was mostly water," Stevenson's "Master of Ballantrae," iii.); in the U. S. and Canada (pron. slö, and also spelled *sleugh, slew,* and *slue*), a marshy or reedy pool, pond, inlet, or the like (as, "trying our rifles on the mallards in the reedy *sloughs,*" Roosevelt's "Ranch Life and the Hunting-Trail," ix.; "They ate their sandwiches by a prairie *slew*: long grass reaching up out of clear water, mossy bogs . . . the scum a splash of gold-green," Sinclair Lewis's "Main Street," v.); also, fig., a condition of degradation, embarrassment, or helplessness (as, "Education lifts the citizens more and more out of the original *slough,*" Motley's "Dutch Republic," Introd., vi.; "floundering desperately in a very *slough* of multifarious knowledge," Mrs. Shelley's "Frankenstein," ii.).—**Slough of Despond,** in Bunyan's "Pilgrim's Progress," i., a "miry slough . . . whither the scum and filth that attends conviction for sin doth continually run . . . many fears, and doubts, and discouraging apprehensions, which all of them get together, and settle in this place," in which Christian, falling in, struggles in vain until drawn out by Help; hence, fig. [often *l. c.*], a state of profound despondency or dejection.

slough[2] (sluf), *n.* [ME. *slughe, sloghe, slouh*: cf. MHG. *slūch,* G. *schlauch,* skin, bag.] The skin of a snake, esp. the outer skin which is shed periodically; any part of an animal that is naturally shed or molted; hence, anything that is shed or cast off; in *pathol.,* a mass or layer of dead tissue which separates from the surrounding or underlying living tissue.—

slough², v. I. *intr.* To be shed or cast off, as the slough or skin of a snake; fall off or away like a slough; also, to cast off a slough; in *pathol.*, to separate from the sound flesh as a slough; also, to develop a slough. **II.** *tr.* To shed as or like a slough (as, "a great modern liberal nation seeking to *slough* an exceedingly tough and tight skin": H. G. Wells's "Italy, France, and Britain at War," iv. 4); cast or throw (*off*).

slough-y¹ (slou'i), *a.* Of or like a slough, as of mud; abounding in sloughs; miry.

slough-y² (sluf'i), *a.* Of the nature of or characterized by a slough, as of skin or of dead tissue.

Slo-vak (slō-vak' or slō'vak). [Slovak and Bohem. *Slovak*: cf. *Slovene.*] **I.** *n.* One of a Slavic people dwelling in a region (Slovakia) to the southeast of Moravia, and closely related to the Czechs proper, or Bohemians, and the Moravians; also, the (Slavic) language of this people, closely connected with Czech, or Bohemian. **II.** *a.* Of or pertaining to the Slovaks, or their language, etc.—**Slo-vak'i-an,** *a.* and *n.*

slov-en (sluv'n). [ME. *sloveyn*: cf. D. *slof*, careless, negligent.] **I.** *n.* A knave† or rascal†; also, a lazy, idle fellow†; now, one who is habitually negligent of neatness or cleanliness in dress, personal appearance, habits, etc. (as, "Since he had never taken any care of his personal appearance he became every known variety of *sloven*": Kipling's "Light That Failed," xiv.); also, one who works, or does anything, in a negligent, slipshod manner or without care, thoroughness, system, etc. **II.** *a.* Slovenly.

Slo-vene (slō-vēn'). [From the old native name of the Slavs: cf. LL. *Sclaveni*, pl., Slavs, also E. *Slav* and *Slovak.*] **I.** *n.* One of a Slavic people dwelling in a region (Slovenia) to the north of Croatia (and comprising Carniola, and parts of Styria, etc.), and closely related to the Croats, Serbians, and other southern Slavs; also, the (Slavic) language of this people, closely allied to Croatian and Serbian. **II.** *a.* Of or pertaining to the Slovenes, or their language, etc.—**Slo-ve'ni-an** (-vē'ni-an), *a.* and *n.*

slov-en-ly (sluv'n-li), *a.* Having the habits of a sloven; characteristic or suggestive of a sloven; untidy, as persons or the dress, appearance, etc.; careless or slipshod, as a person in doing anything, or as the performance, work, etc.; negligent or devoid of care, thoroughness, system, etc.—**slov'en-li-ness,** *n.*—**slov'en-ly,** *adv.* In a slovenly manner.

slov-en-ry (sluv'n-ri), *n.* Slovenly character, condition, or procedure. See Shakspere's "Henry V.," iv. 3. 114. [Now rare.]

slow (slō), *a.* [ME. *slow, slaw,* < AS. *slāw*, sluggish, dull, = D. *sleeuw* = OHG. *slēo* = Icel. *sljōr* = Sw. *slö* = Dan. *slöv*, blunt: cf. *sloth.*] Sluggish in nature or disposition; naturally inactive, or lacking in energy; sluggish in function, as a bodily organ; slothful (obs. or archaic: cf. *slow-belly*); also, dull of perception or understanding, as a person, the mind, etc.; also, tardy or dilatory (as, *slow* in arriving; "He hath . . . wrung from me my *slow* leave By laboursome petition," Shakspere's "Hamlet," i. 2. 58); not prompt, readily disposed, or in haste (with *to* or an infinitive: as, "*slow* to wrath," Prov. xiv. 29; *slow* to take offense; *slow* to accept a statement); also, taking or requiring a comparatively long time for moving, going, acting, occurring, etc. (as, a *slow* walker, worker, speaker, or thinker; a *slow* boat or train; *slow* motion; a *slow* process; a *slow* rate of progress); not fast, rapid, or swift; leisurely; gradual, as change, growth, etc.; burning or heating with little speed or intensity, as a fire or an oven; slack, as trade; causing a low or lower rate of speed (as, *slow* ground; a *slow* track); sometimes, running at less than the proper rate of speed; indicating a time earlier than the correct time, as a clock or watch; passing heavily, or dragging, as time; fig., unprogressive, or behind the times (as, a *slow* old town); dull, humdrum, uninteresting, or tedious (as, *slow* company; a *slow* book; to have a *slow* evening).—**slow,** *adv.* In a slow manner; slowly.—**slow,** *v.* **I.** *tr.* To make slow or slower; retard; reduce the speed of. **II.** *intr.* To become slow or slower; move or go more slowly; slacken in speed.

slow=bel-ly (slō'bel"i), *n.;* pl. *-bellies* (-iz). A slothful or lazy glutton; in general, a sluggard: from the Biblical use, "One of themselves, even a prophet of their own, said, The Cretians are alway liars, evil beasts, slow bellies"

(Titus, i. 12, with quotation supposedly from Epimenides).

slow=coach (slō'kōch), *n.* One who is slow in moving, acting, working, thinking, etc.; one deficient in quickness, energy, briskness, etc.; sometimes, an unprogressive person; a fogy.

slow=go-ing (slō'gō"ing), *a.* Slow in moving, proceeding, or acting; leisurely.

slow=hound (slō'hound), *n.* Same as *sleuth-hound.*

slow-ly (slō'li), *adv.* [AS. *slāwlīce.*] In a slow manner; tardily; without promptness or haste; at a low rate of speed.

slow=match (slō'mach), *n.* A match or fuse that burns very slowly, often consisting of a rope or cord which has been soaked in a solution of saltpeter.

slow-ness (slō'nes), *n.* The state or quality of being slow.

slow=paced (slō'pāst), *a.* Slow of pace, gait, or motion; also, passing slowly, as time.

slow=wit-ted (slō'wit"ed), *a.* Slow of wit or intelligence; dull of understanding.

slow=worm (slō'wėrm), *n.* [AS. *slāwyrm*, with *slā-* perhaps related to *slēan*, strike, E. *slay².*] The blindworm.

sloyd (sloid), *n.* [Sw. *slöjd*, craft, industrial art, woodworking, = E. *sleight.*] A system of manual training in woodworking, etc., orig. developed and taught in Sweden.

slub (slub), *v. t.;* *slubbed, slubbing.* [Origin obscure.] To draw out and twist slightly after carding or slivering, as wool or cotton.—**slub,** *n.* The partially twisted wool or the like produced by slubbing; also, a lump of cotton which becomes attached to or twisted into the yarn during the process of spinning.—**slub'ber¹,** *n.*

slub-ber² (slub'ėr), *v. t.* [Akin to *slobber.*] To daub; stain or soil; also, to perform or deal with in a hasty or careless manner (as, "*Slubber* not business for my sake, Bassanio": Shakspere's "Merchant of Venice," ii. 8. 39). [Now chiefly prov.]

sludge (sluj), *n.* [Also (prov.) *slutch*; origin uncertain: cf. *slush.*] Mud, mire, or ooze; slush; specif., imperfectly formed or broken ice, as on the surface of the sea; also, any of various more or less mud-like deposits or mixtures; a mixture of some finely powdered substance and water.—**sludg'y,** *a.*

slue¹ (slö), *n.* See *slough¹.*

slue², slew³ (slö), *n.* [Origin obscure.] A considerable quantity or number; a lot: as, "a *slew* of bright young fellows" (Sinclair Lewis's "Babbitt," vi.). [Slang.]

slue³, slew⁴ (slö), *v.;* *slued* or *slewed, sluing* or *slewing.* [Origin uncertain: first recorded in nautical use.] **I.** *tr.* To turn (a mast, etc.) round upon its own axis, or without removing it from its place; in general, to swing round (as, "Mr. Vane, seeing the direction of all their eyes, *slewed* himself round in his chair": Reade's "Peg Woffington," x.); fig., to intoxicate (colloq.). **II.** *intr.* To turn about; swing round: as, "As he called again the boat *slewed* around" (Weir Mitchell's "Hugh Wynne," xviii.).—

slue³, slew⁴, *n.* The act or an act of sluing, or turning or swinging round (as, "The pack . . . would take an ugly *slew* to one side or the other": Stevenson's "Travels with a Donkey," i. 2); a position slued to.—**slued, slewed,** *p. a.* Intoxicated: as, "He came into our place . . . rather *slued,* but not much" (Dickens's "Martin Chuzzlewit," xxviii.). [Colloq.]

slug¹ (slug), *v. t.;* *slugged, slugging.* [Origin uncertain: cf. *slog.*] To strike heavily; hit hard, esp. with the fist: as, "Who's afraid of half a dozen cops? . . . We'll *slug* 'em this time!" (John Hay's "Bread-Winners," xiv.). [Colloq.] —**slug¹,** *n.* A heavy blow, esp. with the fist. [Colloq.]

slug² (slug), *v.;* *slugged, slugging.* [ME. *sluggen*; prob. from Scand.] **I.** *intr.* To be inactive or slothful; pass the time in slothful inactivity (as, to *slug* in one's bed); also, to move slowly. [Archaic or prov.] **II.** *tr.* To spend (time) in sloth (archaic); also, to make sluggish†; also, to retard or hinder (obs. or prov.); also, to load with slugs, as a gun.—

slug², *n.* An inactive, lazy person, or sluggard (obs. or prov.); also, a slow-moving animal, vehicle, or the like; specif., any of various slimy, elongated terrestrial gas-

Slug (genus *Limax*), crawling and at rest.

tropods related to the terrestrial snails, but having no shell or only a rudimentary one; also, a sea-slug; also, a slug-worm; also, a piece of lead or other metal for firing from a gun (as, "most of our pieces being loaded with two or three *slugs* or bullets apiece": Defoe's "Captain Singleton," vii.); any heavy piece of crude metal; in *printing*, a thick strip of type-metal less than type-high; such a strip containing a type-high number, etc., for temporary use; a line of type in one piece, as produced by a linotype machine.

slug-a-bed (slug'ạ-bed), *n.* [See *slug*[2].] One given to lying long in bed, as from laziness. See Shakspere's "Romeo and Juliet," iv. 5. 2.

slug-gard (slug'ärd). [See *slug*[2].] **I.** *n.* One who is habitually inactive or slothful: as, "For *sluggard's* brow the laurel never grows; Renown is not the child of indolent repose" (Thomson's "Castle of Indolence," ii. 50). **II.** *a.* Sluggardly: as, "*sluggard* negligence" (Shakspere's "Lucrece," 1278).—**slug'gard-ly,** *a.* Like or befitting a sluggard; slothful; lazy.

slug-ger (slug'ėr), *n.* [See *slug*[1].] One who slugs, or strikes hard, esp. with the fists; hence, a pugilist. [Colloq.]—**slug'ging,** *n.* The act of one who slugs, or strikes hard; hard hitting; a beating. [Colloq.]

slug-gish (slug'ish), *a.* [See *slug*[2].] Indisposed to action or exertion, esp. by nature, as persons or animals; inactive, slow, or of little energy or vigor (as, a *sluggish* nature or temperament; a *sluggish* mind); not acting or working with full vigor, as bodily organs; also, moving slowly, or having little motion, as a stream (as, "The boat was rowed up the *sluggish* waters of the Maes": Scott's "Quentin Durward," xix.); slow or tardy, as motion (as, "the *sluggish* pace of the continental posts": Macaulay's "Hist. of Eng.," iii.).—**slug'gish-ly,** *adv.*—**slug'gish-ness,** *n.*

slug-horn (slug'hôrn), *n.* Old form of *slogan,* erroneously used to mean a kind of horn (wind-instrument): as, "Dauntless the *slug-horn* to my lips I set And blew" (Browning's "Childe Roland," xxxiv.).

slug-worm (slug'wėrm), *n.* The slimy slug-like larva of any of various saw-flies.

sluice (slös), *n.* [OF. *escluse* (F. *écluse*), < ML. *exclusa,* prop. fem. of L. *exclusus,* pp. of *excludere,* shut out, shut off, E. *exclude.*] A structure forming a barrier for holding back the water of a river, canal, etc., and provided with a gate or the like by which the water may be allowed to pass; the gate, or the body of water held back or controlled; hence, any contrivance for regulating a flow from or into a receptacle; also, a channel, esp. one carrying off surplus water; a drain; a stream of surplus water; in *mining*, a long, sloping trough or the like, with riffles or grooves in its bottom, into which a current of water is directed to separate gold from gravel or sand.— **sluice,** *v.*; *sluiced, sluicing.* **I.** *tr.* To let out (water, etc.), or draw off the contents of (a pond,

Sluice in Mining.

etc.), by or as by the opening of a sluice; send (logs, etc.) down a sluiceway; also, to open a sluice upon; flush or cleanse with a rush of water; throw or pour water over; in *mining,* to wash in a sluice. **II.** *intr.* To flow or pour through or as through a sluice.—**sluice'=gate,** *n.* The gate of a sluice, by which the water may be let out or retained.—**sluice'way,** *n.* A channel controlled or fed by a sluice; any small artificial channel for running water.—**slui-cy** (slö'si), *a.* Pouring abundantly, as if from a sluice (as, "And oft whole sheets descend of *sluicy* rain": Dryden's tr. Virgil's "Georgics," i. 437); also, wet, as if sluiced (as, "the cool and *sluicy* sands": Keats's "Endymion," i.). [Chiefly poetic.]

slum[1] (slum), *n.* [Cf. *slumgullion.*] A stew of meat, etc. [Soldiers' and sailors' slang.]

slum[2] (slum), *n.* [Origin obscure.] A thickly populated, squalid part of a city, inhabited by the poorest or lowest class of the people: as, "a small and shabby room in a Folkestone *slum*" (H. G. Wells's "Kipps," i. 4): often in *pl.*—**slum**[2], *v. i.*; *slummed, slumming.* To go into or visit slums, as for philanthropic purposes or from curiosity.

slum-ber (slum'bėr), *v.* [ME. *slumeren,* freq. of *slumen,* to slumber, doze, < AS. *slūma,* n., slumber: cf. D. *sluimeren,* G. *schlummern,* to slumber.] **I.** *intr.* To sleep; esp., to sleep lightly; doze; drowse; fig., to live in a state of inactivity or negligence (as, "The successors of Alaric had *slumbered* in a long peace": Gibbon's "Decline and Fall of the Roman Empire," li.); be in a state of quiescence (as, "Now conscience wakes despair That *slumber'd*": Milton's "Paradise Lost," iv. 24); be calm or still (as, "lakes that *slumber* in the storm": Goldsmith's "Traveller," 312); move calmly or peacefully (*along*), as a stream. **II.** *tr.* To cause to slumber†; also, to spend (time) in slumbering (with *away,* etc.); drive (*away*) by slumbering.—**slum'ber,** *n.* Sleep; esp., light sleep; also, a period of sleep, esp. of light sleep; fig., a state of inactivity or quiescence.—**slum'ber-er,** *n.*—**slum'ber-less,** *a.* Without slumber; sleepless.— **slum'ber-ous, slum'brous,** *a.* Inclined to slumber; lethargic; heavy with drowsiness, as the eyelids; also, causing or inducing sleep (as, "The timely dew of sleep, Now falling with soft *slumbrous* weight, inclines Our eyelids": Milton's "Paradise Lost," iv. 615); also, pertaining to, characterized by, or suggestive of slumber; fig., inactive or sluggish; calm or quiet.—**slum'ber-y,** *a.* Pertaining to or characterized by slumber; of the nature of slumber.

slum-gul-lion (slum-gul'yọn), *n.* [Appar. a made word: cf. *slum*[1].] Offal or refuse of fish; the watery refuse, mixed with blood and oil, which drains from blubber; also, a kind of stew (slang); an insipid, watery beverage (slang); also, a muddy deposit in a mining sluice.

slum-gum (slum'gum), *n.* [Origin uncertain.] The propolis and other impurities which remain as a residue after the wax is extracted from honeycombs.

slum-mer (slum'ėr), *n.* One who slums.—**slum'ming,** *n.* The visiting of slums, as for philanthropic purposes or from curiosity.

slump[1] (slump), *v. i.* [Appar. imit.] To sink into a bog, muddy place, etc., or through ice or snow; drop heavily (as, "The wagon, under a load . . . had *slumped* into a hole," G. W. Cable's "John March, Southerner," vi.; "She *slumped* into a chair and gasped with the heat," Sinclair Lewis's "Main Street," xxv.); hence, to go down, as the wind; fall suddenly and markedly, as prices, the market, etc.; have a decided falling off in progress, as an enterprise, a competitor, etc.; sink heavily, as the spirits, etc.; also, to move or walk heavily or with difficulty. [Colloq.]—**slump**[1], *n.* The act or an act of slumping; a heavy drop or fall; a sudden, marked decline in prices, etc.; a decided falling off in progress, as in an undertaking. [Colloq.]

slump[2] (slump), *n.* [Cf. LG. *slump,* D. *slomp,* heap, mass.] A large quantity; the whole mass; the lump. [Chiefly Sc.]—**slump**[2], *v. t.* To bring into or treat as a mass or whole; lump. [Chiefly Sc.]

slung (slung). Preterit and past participle of *sling.*— **slung'=shot,** *n.* A shot, a piece of metal, a stone, etc., fastened to a short strap, chain, or the like, used as a weapon, as by roughs or criminals: as, "a burly ruffian, who carried a *slung-shot*" (John Hay's "Bread-Winners," xiv.).

slunk (slungk). Preterit and past participle of *slink*[1], *slink*[2].

slur (slėr), *v.*; *slurred, slurring.* [Appar. from obs. or prov. *slur,* ME. *sloor, slore,* mud; origin uncertain: cf. *slurry.*] **I.** *tr.* To smear; smudge; blur; fig., to smirch or sully (as, "to *slur* the honour of a spotless family": Arnold Bennett's "Old Wives' Tale," ii. 4); asperse or calumniate; disparage or depreciate; also, to pass over lightly, or without due mention or consideration (often with *over*: as, "*slurring* with an evasive answer the question concerning the endurance of his own possession," Scott's "Guy Mannering," xli.; "He felt inclined to *slur* things over, but I wanted to get at the facts," S. Butler's "Way of All Flesh," lxxii.); treat lightly, or make little of (as, "Studious to please the genius of the times, With periods, points, and tropes, he *slurs* his crimes": Dryden's tr. Persius's "Satires," i. 167); also, to go through hurriedly or carelessly; often, to pronounce (a syllable, word, etc.) indistinctly, as in hurried or careless utterance; in *music*, to sing to a single syllable or play without a break (two or more tones of different pitch); also, to mark with a slur. **II.** *intr.* To go through anything hurriedly and carelessly.—**slur**, *n.* A smear; a smudge; a blur; fig., a blot or stain, as upon reputation; a discredit incurred or cast; also, a disparaging or slighting remark; a slight; also, the act of slurring, or passing over hurriedly or carelessly; a slurred utterance or sound; in *music*, the combination of two or more tones of different pitch sung to a single syllable or played without a break; also, a curved mark indicating this.—**slur′ring-ly**, *adv.*

slur-ry (slur′i), *n.*; pl. *slurries* (-iz). [ME. *slory*, < *slore*, mud: see *slur*, *v.*] Thin mud, slush, or the like (prov. Eng.); also, any of various semifluid mixtures or substances, esp. as employed or formed in the arts; the levigated matter which forms under a grindstone; in *ceram.*, inequalities in the interior of a vessel, smoothed away by the potter as his wheel rotates.

slush (slush), *n.* [Appar. a var. of *sludge*, in part imit.: cf. *slosh* and *slash[1]*.] Snow in a partly melted, watery state, or snow and water mixed (as, "There was no traffic to turn the snow to *slush*": Barrie's "Auld Licht Idylls," ii.); also, liquid mud, or watery mire; also, refuse fat, grease, etc., from the cook's galley on board ship; also, a mixture of grease and other materials for lubricating; also, a mixture of white lead and lime for covering bright parts of machinery to prevent rusting; in fig. use, rubbishy, silly, or weakly emotional talk, writing, etc. (colloq.: as, "calling him about a thousand old mans and that sort of *slush*," A. S. M. Hutchinson's "If Winter Comes," iv. 2).—**slush**, *v.* **I.** *tr.* To splash with slush or mud; also, to grease, polish, or cover with slush (as, "The officer . . . ordered me to *slush* the main-mast . . . So I took my bucket of grease and climbed up": Dana's "Two Years before the Mast," ii.); also, to fill or cover with mortar or cement; also, to wash with much water, as by dashing it on. **II.** *intr.* To go through slush or mud with a splashing sound; rush or dash with splashes.—**slush′-fund**, *n.* A fund derived from the sale of slush, refuse fat, or the like, aboard ship or in a camp or garrison, as formerly on U. S. war-vessels, where it was commonly expended at the discretion of the officers; hence, a fund available for use, as in a campaign, propaganda, or the like, esp. secretly or illicitly, as in bribery.—**slush′y**, *a.* Abounding in or covered with slush (as, "Quin and his friends . . . went swinging on through the *slushy* grass": Chesterton's "Napoleon of Notting Hill," i. 3); consisting of or resembling slush.—**slush′i-ness**, *n.*

slut (slut), *n.* [ME. *slutte*, *slotte*; origin uncertain.] A dirty, slovenly woman; a slattern; also, a woman of loose character; a bold or impudent girl; sometimes, a playful term for any woman or girl (now rare); also, a female dog, or bitch; also, a greased rag burned for light.—**slut′ter-y**, *n.* The practice of a slut; gross neglect of cleanliness and neatness.—**slut′tish**, *a.* Having the habits of a slut; characteristic of or befitting a slut; dirty and slovenly.—**slut′-tish-ly**, *adv.*—**slut′tish-ness**, *n.*

sly (slī), *a.*; compar. *slyer* or *slier*, superl. *slyest* or *sliest*. [ME. *sly*, *sley*, from Scand.: cf. Icel. *slœgr*, sly, cunning, Sw. *slög*, dexterous, also E. *sleight* and *sloyd*; prob. related to Icel. *slā*, strike, and E. *slay[2]*.] Skilful or clever (obs. or north. Eng.); also, cunning, artful, crafty, or wily, as persons or animals, actions, ways, etc. (as, "You think he's open and blunt — he's as *sly* as a mink," G. W. Cable's "Cavalier," lvi.; "Finney, the attorney, had been among them, asking *sly* questions," Trollope's "Warden," iv.); often, playfully artful, mischievous, or roguish (as, a *sly* jest or wink; *sly* humor); also, stealthy, insidious, underhand, or secret (as, to advance by *sly* approaches; "Skilful alike to seem devout and just, And stab religion with a *sly* side-thrust," Cowper's "Retirement," 690); carried on, sold, etc., secretly and illicitly, as trade, liquor, or the like (slang).—**on the sly**, in a sly, stealthy, or secret manner; secretly: as, "I'm doubting Gavinia's reading ill books *on the sly*" (Barrie's "Sentimental Tommy," xx.).—**sly′boots**, *n.* A sly, cunning, or

artful person or animal: as, "Harry is an old *sly-boots*" (Mrs. Stowe's "Oldtown Folks," xxxii.). [Colloq.]—**sly′ish**, *a.* Rather sly.—**sly′ly**, **sli′ly**, *adv.*—**sly′ness**, *n.*

slype (slīp), *n.* [Prob. related to *slip[2]*.] In *arch.*, a covered passage, esp. one from the transept of a cathedral to the chapter-house.

smack[1] (smak), *n.* [AS. *smæc* = MLG. *smak* = G. dial. *schmack* (G. *geschmack*), taste.] A taste or flavor (as, "This . . . wine . . . has a little *smack* which is most agreeable": Thackeray's "Newcomes," xxviii.); esp., a slight flavor distinctive or suggestive of something; fig., a trace, touch, or suggestion of something (as, "He was not sailorly, and yet he had a *smack* of the sea about him," Stevenson's "Treasure Island," ii.; "These words had the true *smack* of an Irish accent," Lever's "Harry Lorrequer," xxvi.); a smattering (as, "He hath a *smack* of all neighbouring languages": Shakspere's "All's Well," iv. 1. 18); also, a taste, mouthful, or small quantity of liquor or the like.—**smack[1]**, *v. i.* To have a taste or flavor as specified (often with *of*: as, wine *smacking* of the cask); fig., to savor or be suggestive (*of*: as, "Strange was the sight and *smacking* of the time," Tennyson's "Princess," Prologue, 89); have a trace or touch (*of*: as, "All sects, all ages *smack* of this vice," Shakspere's "Measure for Measure," ii. 2. 5).

smack[2] (smak), *v.* [Cf. D. *smakken*, MLG. *smacken*, G. *schmatzen*, smack; prob. imit.] **I.** *tr.* To separate (the lips) smartly so as to produce a sharp sound, often as a sign of relish, as in eating (as, "I have heard him *smack* his lips over dinners": Hawthorne's "Scarlet Letter," The Custom House); taste (wine, etc.) with relish; also, to kiss loudly; also, to crack (a whip, etc.); also, to bring, put, throw, send, etc., with a sharp, resounding blow or a smart stroke (as, "She brought down her lifted right arm and *smacked* the ball into the net [at tennis]": Arnold Bennett's "Clayhanger," iii. 11); also, to strike smartly, esp. with the open hand or anything flat (as, "'You sneak!' I said, and *smacked* his face hard": H. G. Wells's "Tono-Bungay," i. 2. § 1); slap smartly. **II.** *intr.* To smack the lips; part in a smack, as the lips (as, "Hot mutton pasty . . . to hear them talk of it made my lips *smack*": Blackmore's "Lorna Doone," iii.); also, to kiss loudly; also, to come or strike smartly or forcibly, as against something (as, "The motor cyclist *smacked* against something . . . The wall seemed to rush up at them": H. G. Wells's "Mr. Britling," i. 3. §7); make a sharp sound as of striking against something.—**smack[2]**, *n.* A smacking of the lips, as in relish (as, "Lord Bellinger . . . emptied his glass with a *smack*": Whyte-Melville's "Katerfelto," viii.); also, a resounding or loud kiss (as, "He . . . kiss'd her lips with such a clamorous *smack* That at the parting all the church did echo": Shakspere's "Taming of the Shrew," iii. 2. 180); also, the crack of a whip, lash, etc.; also, a smart, resounding blow, esp. with something flat; a smart slap.—**smack[2]**, *adv.* With or as with a smack; suddenly and sharply; plump; fig., directly; straight. [Colloq.]

smack[3] (smak), *n.* [D. *smak*.] A sailing-vessel, usually one rigged like a sloop or a cutter, used chiefly in coasting and fishing; also, a fishing-vessel with a well in which to keep fish alive.

smack-er (smak′ėr), *n.* [See *smack[2]*, *v.*] One who or that which smacks; a loud kiss, or smack; a resounding blow; also, a dollar (slang, U. S.).

smack-ing (smak′ing), *p. a.* [See *smack[2]*, *v.*] That smacks; resounding sharply, as a kiss or a smart blow; also, smart, brisk, or strong, as a breeze; also, unusually big or large (prov. Eng.).

smacks-man (smaks′man), *n.*; pl. *-men*. [See *smack[3]*.] One who owns, or is employed on, a smack.

small (smâl), *a.* [AS. *smæl* = D. *smal* = G. *schmal* = Icel. *smal-* = Goth. *smals*, small.] Slender, thin, or narrow (as, a *small* waist; a *small* line or cord; the *small* intestine); hence, in general, of limited size; of comparatively restricted dimensions; not big; little; not large as compared with other things of the same kind (as, *small* arms; *small* letters; *small* capitals: see phrases below); also, composed of fine particles, drops, etc., as rain; also, not great in amount, degree, extent, duration, value, etc. (as, a *small* dose; a *small* fortune; of *small* power; to have *small* hope of success;

a *small* distance; a *small* vacation; *small* bills or change); not great numerically (as, a *small* army; a *small* group); of low numerical value, or denoted by a low number (as, a *small* trump; the *small* hours, see phrase below); also, low in rank or station (as, "The king made a feast unto all the people . . . both unto great and *small*": Esther, i. 5); having but little land, capital, etc., or carrying on business on a limited scale (as, a *small* farmer; a *small* tradesman); of minor note or importance (as, "the *small* poets of the time": Jonson's "Alchemist," i. 2.); also, of little moment, weight, or consequence (as, a *small* matter; *small* talk, see phrase below); trifling; trivial; also, humble, modest, or unpretentious (as, "Though thy beginning was *small*, yet thy latter end should greatly increase," Job, viii. 7; to be an author in a *small* way); also, characterized by or indicative of littleness of mind or character, or mean-spirited or un-generous (as, "For there was nothing base or *small* Or craven in his soul's broad plan": Whittier's "Sumner"); also, ashamed or mortified (as, "He had a damnable trick of making you feel *small*": J. Conrad's "Lord Jim," vi.); also, of little strength or force (as, a *small* pulse); of low alcoholic strength, weak, or diluted, as liquors or beverages (as, *small* beer: see phrase below); of sound or the voice, gentle, soft, or low (as, "a still *small* voice," 1 Kings, xix. 12); "the *small* crumbling sound of the dying embers," Lover's "Handy Andy," xxxviii.); sometimes, thin and clear.—**small arms**, firearms carried in the hand or on the person, as distinguished from those requiring carriages.—**small beer**, weak beer; fig., matters of little or no consequence (with allusion to Shakspere's "Othello," ii. 1. 161); persons of little or no importance.—**small capitals**, in *printing*, letters of the form of the ordinary capitals of a font of roman text-type, but smaller, used along with the other letters of the font for special purposes, as in 'Virgil was born in 70 B.C.' and 'Jupiter rises at 10 P.M.'—**small circle**. See *great circle*, under *circle*, *n*.—**small fry**. See *fry*[1].—**small hours**, the early hours of the morning, denoted by the small numbers one, two, etc.—**small letters**, the ordinary letters which commonly constitute the bulk of a written or printed text, as opposed to capitals.—**small pica**. See under *pica*[2].—**small potatoes**, insignificant things or persons; some-thing insignificant or of little consequence (as, "That cor-vette, the big factor of everyday life on that stretch of coast, would become very *small potatoes* indeed": J. Conrad's "Rover," x.); something meanly petty. [Colloq.]—**small stuff**, *naut.*, yarn, marline, and small ropes.—**small talk**, light, unimportant, or trifling talk or conversation; chit-chat.—**small**, *n*. That which is small; the small or narrow part, as of the back (as, "Sixteen hours in bed! the *small* of my back ached to think of it": H. Melville's "Moby-Dick," iv.); something small; *pl.*, small-clothes (as, "her footman, in large plush *smalls* and waistcoat": Thackeray's "Vanity Fair," lvi.); also, at Oxford University, responsions. —**small**, *adv.* To a small degree or extent† (as, "If thou dost weep . . . it *small* avails my mood": Shakspere's "Lucrece," 1273); also, in low tones; softly; sometimes, in a thin, clear voice; in a high key.—**to sing small**, fig., to adopt a humble tone or manner; play a less assertive part.

small-age (smâl′āj), *n.* [ME. *smalege, smalache*, < *smal, small*, + *ache*, < OF. *ache*, < L. *apium*, parsley.] Celery, *Apium graveolens*, esp. in its wild state.

small=clothes (smâl′klōꝥHz), *n. pl.* Knee-breeches, esp. the close-fitting knee-breeches formerly worn: as, "He wore a waistcoat and *small-clothes*, meeting the stockings at the knee with a . . . buckle" (Howells's "Foregone Conclusion," v.).

small-ish (smâl′ish), *a.* Rather small: as, "a *smallish* sort of small boy" (H. G. Wells's "Bealby," vi.).

small-ness (smâl′nes), *n.* The state or quality of being small; also, a small part, etc.

small-pox (smâl′poks), *n.* [Orig. *small pocks*: see *pock*.] An acute, highly contagious febrile disease characterized by a pustular eruption which often leaves permanent pits or scars.

small=sword (smâl′sōrd), *n.* A light sword for thrusting, tapering from the hilt to the point, and used esp. in fencing.

smalt (smâlt), *n.* [It. *smalto*, kind of glass, enamel; from Teut., and akin to E. *smelt*[2]: cf. *enamel*.] A deep-blue pigment prepared by powdering a glass colored with cobalt.— **smal-tine** (smâl′tin), *n.* [F.] Same as *smaltite*.—**smal′-**

tite (-tīt), *n.* A tin-white to steel-gray mineral consisting essentially of cobalt arsenide but usually containing also iron and nickel, and occurring in crystals or in compact or granular masses.

smar-agd (smar′agd), *n.* [L. *smaragdus*: see *emerald*.] A green stone or gem; an emerald. [Now rare.]—**sma-rag-dine** (smạ-rag′din), *a.* [L. *smaragdinus*.] Of the color of a smaragd; emerald-green.—**sma-rag′dite** (-dīt), *n.* An emerald-green variety of amphibole.

smart (smärt), *v.* [AS. *smeortan* = D. *smarten* = G. *schmerzen*, smart; prob. akin to L. *mordere*, bite: cf. *mor-dant*.] **I.** *intr.* To be a source of sharp local and usually superficial pain, as a wound; cause a sharp pain, as an irritating application, a blow, etc.; fig., to wound the feelings, as words; also, to feel a sharp pain, as in a wounded surface; fig., to suffer keenly from wounded feelings (as, "I was still *smarting* at his too candid criticism": W. H. Hudson's "Green Mansions," Prologue); also, to suffer in punishment or in return for something (as, he shall *smart* for this). **II.** *tr.* To cause a sharp pain to or in.—**smart**, *a.* [AS. *smeart*.] Causing sharp pain, stinging, or smarting (obs. or archaic: as, "Poison be their drink! . . . Their softest touch as *smart* as lizards' stings!" Shakspere's "2 Henry VI.," iii. 2. 325); sharp or keen, as pain; pungent or cutting, as speech (obs. or archaic); sharply severe, as blows, strokes, etc.; hence, sharply brisk, vigorous, or active (as, a *smart* wind or storm; a *smart* skirmish; a *smart* pace); quick or prompt in action, as persons (as, "Be *smart*, my lads, you work for your lives": Marryat's "King's Own," liii.); physi-cally vigorous or well (prov. or colloq.); also, having or showing quick intelligence or ready capability (as, a *smart* boy; a *smart* performance); clever; sometimes, shrewd or sharp, as a person in dealing with others, or as dealings, bargains, etc.; also, cleverly ready or effective, as a speaker or a speech, rejoinder, etc.; witty, esp. in a superficial way; also, dashingly or effectively neat or trim in appearance, as persons, uniform or dress, etc. (as, "a . . . girl . . . with . . . a disposition to be . . . *smart* in her dress;" H. G. Wells's "Tono-Bungay," ii. 4. § 1; "a *smart* white merino dress trimmed with blue," Lytton Strachey's "Queen Victoria," iv.); spruce; also, fine, elegant, or stylish (as, a *smart* equipage; *smart* hotels or shops; a *smart* profession); socially elegant, or fashionable (as, *smart* society; the *smart* set); also, considerable, or fairly large, as in amount, extent, etc. (prov. or colloq.: as, a *smart* sum; a *smart* distance).— **smart Aleck** (al′ek, popularly el′ek). [Also *l. c., aleck*; for *Alexander*, man's name.] A would-be smart, clever, or shrewd fellow. [Colloq.]—**smart**, *adv.* In a smart manner; smartly.—**smart**, *n.* Sharp local pain, usually superficial, as from a wound or sting (as, "a sort of ointment . . . which . . . removed all the *smart* of their arrows": Swift's "Gulli-ver's Travels," i. 1); fig., keen mental suffering, as from wounded feelings, affliction, grievous loss, etc. (as, "Fellow-ship in pain divides not *smart*, Nor lightens aught each man's peculiar load": Milton's "Paradise Regained," i. 401); also, smart-money; also (esp. in the 18th century), one who is smart or affects smartness in speech or talk, or a person of elegance or fashion.

smart-en (smär′tn), *v.* **I.** *tr.* To make smart or more smart; make more brisk, as the pace; make more trim or spruce, as one's self, the dress, etc.; improve in appearance. **II.** *intr.* To become smart or more smart.

smart-ly (smärt′li), *adv.* In a smart manner; sharply; briskly; promptly; cleverly; sprucely; elegantly.

smart=mon-ey (smärt′mun″i), *n.* Money allowed to soldiers and sailors for injuries received while on service; hence, any compensation for injury; legal damages in excess of the injury done, as for gross misconduct on the part of the defendant; also, money paid to escape some unpleasant engagement or painful situation; money paid to obtain the discharge of a recruit.

smart-ness (smärt′nes), *n.* The quality of being smart.

smart=weed (smärt′wēd), *n.* The plant *Polygonum hydro-piper*, a weed growing in wet places, which causes smarting or inflammation of the skin; water-pepper; also, some allied species.

smart-y (smär′ti), *n.*; pl. *smarties* (-tiz). A would-be smart, clever, or witty person. [Colloq.]

---

fat, fāte, fär, fâll, ȧsk, fāre; net, mē, hėr; pin, pīne; not, nōte, môve, nôr; up, lūte, pull; oi, oil; ou, out; (lightened) aviȧry, ēlect, agōny, intọ, ụnite; (obscured) errạnt, operạ, ardẹnt, actọr, natụre; ch, chip; g, go; th, thin; ꝥH, then; y, you;

smash (smash), *v.* [Prob. imit.] **I.** *tr.* To break to pieces with violence and often with a crashing sound, as by striking, letting fall, or dashing against something (as, to *smash* a window, a plate, or a child's toy; the boat was *smashed* on the rocks; both cars were *smashed* in the collision); shatter; crush; also, to flatten by a crushing force (sometimes with *flat* or *down*: as, to *smash* a hat flat); also, to break, beat, or dash (*in, off, down*, etc.) with great violence (as, to *smash* a door in; to *smash* a lock off; to *smash* a hat down over one's eyes); break up or break through (hostile forces, the enemy's front, etc.) by crushing onslaughts, as in battle; break (a way) through opposing forces, or obstructions, etc., by a crushing action; fig., to defeat utterly, as a person; overthrow or destroy, as a thing; sometimes, to ruin financially (colloq.); in *lawn-tennis*, to strike (the ball) hard and fast with an overhand stroke. **II.** *intr.* To break to pieces from a violent blow or collision; also, to dash with a shattering or crushing force or with great violence (*against, into, through*, etc.); crash; also, to become ruined financially, or bankrupt (often with *up*: colloq.).—**smash**, *n.* A smashing or shattering, or the sound of it (as, "There was the sound of a fall — a *smash* of broken glass": S. Butler's "Way of All Flesh," xvii.); a destructive collision (as, a *smash* on a railroad); smashed or shattered condition (as, to break a thing to *smash*; "You cannot imagine a house in such a state of *smash*; the very clock had been thrown down," Stevenson's "Treasure Island," v.); also, a crushing or violent blow (colloq.); also, a breaking violently through opposing forces, obstructions, etc.; fig., a crushing defeat, as of an enemy or opponent; a process or a state of collapse, ruin, or destruction (as, affairs went completely to *smash*); often, financial failure or ruin (colloq.); also, a drink made of brandy, or the like, with sugar, water, mint, and ice.—**smash'er**, *n.*—**smash'=up**, *n.* A smashing to pieces; a complete smash; a collapse. [Colloq.]

smatch (smach), *n.* [Var. of *smack*[1].] A smack, taste, or flavor; fig., a trace or touch (as, "Thy life hath had some *smatch* of honour in it": Shakspere's "Julius Cæsar," v. 5. 46); a smattering (as, "some Latin, and a *smatch* of Greek": Cowper's "Progress of Error," 365). [Archaic or prov. Eng.]

smat-ter (smat'ér), *v.* [ME. *smateren*; perhaps imit.] **I.** *intr.* To chatter† or babble† (as, "*Smatter* with your gossips, go": Shakspere's "Romeo and Juliet," iii. 5. 172); talk ignorantly or superficially of something†; also, to have a slight or superficial knowledge, as of a subject; dabble, as in a pursuit or at something. **II.** *tr.* To speak (a language) or utter (words, etc.) with but superficial knowledge or understanding (as, "She could read, and write, and dance, and sing . . . and *smatter* French": Smollett's "Humphry Clinker," Sept. 30); also, to have or get a superficial knowledge of (a subject); dabble in.—**smat'ter**, *n.* Slight or superficial knowledge; a smattering.—**smat'ter-er**, *n.* One who smatters; one who has only superficial knowledge; a dabbler: as, "All the people in his government are lawyers, or *smatterers* in law" (Burke's "Conciliation with the Colonies").—**smat'ter-ing**, *n.* A slight or superficial knowledge of something: as, "a mere man of science, who was without even a *smattering* of Greek" (Mallock's "New Republic," iii. 3).—**smat'ter-ing-ly**, *adv.*

smear (smēr), *n.* [AS. *smeoru* = D. *smeer* = G. *schmer* = Icel. *smjör*, fat, grease.] Fat† or grease†; also, an ointment (obs. or Sc.); also, something smeared, or to be smeared, on a thing, as a glaze for pottery; a small quantity of something smeared on a slide for microscopic examination; also, a mark or stain made by or as by smearing.—**smear**, *v. t.* [AS. *smerian, smirian, smierwan*, < *smeoru*.] To anoint ceremonially (obs. or rare); also, to rub or spread with oil, grease, paint, etc.; overspread thickly or irregularly with something unctuous, sticky, or dirty; daub with anything; also, to spread or daub (oil, grease, etc.) on or over something; also, to rub or draw (something) over a thing so as to produce a smear (as, "*smearing* his sleeve across his mouth": Dickens's "Our Mutual Friend," iv. 15); also, to rub or wipe (*away, out*, etc.) so as to leave a smear (as, "Her penitence started his tears . . . He wanted to *smear* them away": L. Merrick's "Conrad in Quest of His Youth," ix.).

smear-case (smēr'kās), *n.* [See *schmierkäse*.] Cottage cheese (see under *cottage*).

smear-y (smēr'i), *a.* Showing smears; smeared; bedaubed; also, tending to smear or soil.—**smear'i-ness**, *n.*

smell (smel), *v. t.*; *smelled* or *smelt, smelling*. [ME. *smellen, smullen*; origin and connections uncertain.] To perceive through the nose, by means of the olfactory nerves; perceive the scent of; inhale the odor of; test by the sense of smell; hence. to perceive as if by smell; detect or discover by shrewdness or sagacity (as, "He *smelt* mischief in this sudden conversion": S. Butler's "Way of All Flesh," l.); search or find (*out*) as if by smell (as, "What a man cannot *smell* out, he may spy into": Shakspere's "King Lear," i. 5. 23).—**to smell a rat**, fig., to suspect something; have an inkling of some mischief, plot, underhand proceeding, etc.: as, "Quoth Hudibras, — 'I *smell a rat*; Ralpho, thou dost prevaricate'" (Butler's "Hudibras," i. 1).—**smell**, *v. i.* To exercise the sense of smell; inhale or try the odor of a thing (with *at, of*, or formerly *to*); sniff; search or investigate as if by smell (usually with *about*); also, to give out an odor, esp. as specified (as, to *smell* sweet; to *smell* like violets); sometimes, to give out an offensive odor (as, "The lamp *smelt*, and gave off a stuffy warmth": Arnold Bennett's "Clayhanger," i. 11); also, to have the odor (*of*: as, "the days when the old house was new and clean and *smelt* of recent plaster," W. De Morgan's "Alice-for-Short," xiv.); fig., to have a trace or suggestion (*of*: as, "It was expedient that this errand should not *smell* of haste," W. Churchill's "Coniston," ii. 2).—**to smell of the lamp**, to be suggestive of nocturnal or protracted labor, as a literary work; be labored or pedantic: as, "Hardly any poet *smells of the lamp* less disagreeably than Spenser" (Saintsbury's "Hist. of Elizabethan Literature," iv.).—**smell**, *n.* [ME. *smel, smul*.] The faculty or sense of smelling (as, "The sagacity and *smell* of this bird enable him to discover his quarry at a great distance": Swift's "Gulliver's Travels," ii. 8); also, that quality of a thing which is or may be smelled; odor, or a particular kind of odor (as, "There was a strong *smell* of gas in the passage": W. De Morgan's "Joseph Vance," xxxv.); scent, perfume, or stench; fig., a trace or suggestion of something; also, an act of smelling; a sniff.—**smell'a-ble**, *a.* Capable of being smelled.—**smell'er**, *n.* One who or that which smells; one who tests by smelling; the nose or, *pl.*, the nostrils (slang); also, a tactile hair or process, as one of the whiskers of a cat; a feeler.—**smell'=feast**, *n.* One who smells out feasting in order to join in it; a sponger for good food. [Archaic.]—**smell'ing=salts**, *n. pl.* A preparation for smelling, consisting essentially of ammonium carbonate with some agreeable scent, used as a restorative in cases of faintness, headache, etc.—**smell'=less**, *a.* Having no sense of smell; also, emitting no smell or odor; odorless.—**smell'y**, *a.* Emitting a strong or offensive smell: as, "I wonder what makes the sea so *smelly*. I don't like it" (Kipling's "Light That Failed," i.).

smelt[1] (smelt), *n.* [AS. *smelt*.] Any of various food-fishes (family *Argentinidæ*) having a salmon-like structure but small in size, esp. those of the genus *Osmerus*, as *O. eperlanus* (the sparling, or European smelt) and *O. mordax* (the frostfish, or common American smelt); also, any of various similar fishes.

Common American Smelt (*Osmerus mordax*).

smelt[2] (smelt), *v. t.* [MD. D. *smelten* = MLG. *smelten* = G. *schmelzen*, melt, smelt: see *melt*, and cf. *enamel* and *smalt*.] To fuse or melt (ore), or treat (ore) by a process involving fusion, in order to separate the metal contained; also, to obtain or refine (metal) in this way.—**smelt'er**, *n.* One who or that which smelts; the owner of, or a workman in, a smeltery; a smeltery.—**smelt'er-y** (-i), *n.*; pl. *-ies* (-iz). A place or establishment where ores are smelted.

smew (smū), *n.* [Origin uncertain.] A small merganser, *Mergus* (or *Mergellus*) *albellus*, inhabiting the northerly parts of the eastern hemisphere, the adult male of which has a pure white plumage varied with black and gray, and tinged with green on the crested head. See cut on next page.

smi-la-ca-ceous (smī-lạ-kā′shius), *a.* [See *smilax*.] Belonging to the *Smilacaceæ*, the smilax or greenbrier family of plants.

smi-lax (smī′-laks), *n.* [L. *smilax*, < Gr. σμῖλαξ, bindweed.] Any plant of the genus *Smilax*, consisting mostly of woody vines,

Smew, adult male.

often with prickly stems, and widely distributed through most temperate and tropical regions, as *S. rotundifolia*, a common species of the eastern U.S. (see *greenbrier*), or *S. medica* (see *sarsaparilla*); a greenbrier; also, a fine, delicate, twining convallariaceous plant, *Asparagus asparagoides*, with glossy, bright-green leaves (cladodes), native in South Africa, and much cultivated by florists for use in decoration.

Flowering Branch of Smilax (*S. rotundifolia*). — *a*, the fruit.

smile (smīl), *v.*; *smiled, smiling.* [ME. *smilen* = MHG. *smielen* = Sw. *smila* = Dan. *smile*, smile.] **I.** *intr.* To assume a facial expression, characterized esp. by a widening of the mouth, indicative of pleasure, favor, kindliness, amusement, derision, scorn, etc. (as, "One may *smile*, and *smile*, and be a villain": Shakspere's "Hamlet," i. 5. 108); look with such an expression, esp. (with *at, on,* or *upon*) in a pleasant or kindly way, or (with *at*) in amusement; hence, to look (*on* or *upon*) with favor (as, society *smiled* on the enterprise; "Heaven *smiled* upon the efforts of this righteous cavalier," Irving's "Conquest of Granada," xxvi.); also, fig., to have a pleasant or agreeable aspect, as natural scenes, objects, etc. (as, "This same flower that *smiles* to-day To-morrow will be dying": Herrick's "Gather Ye Rosebuds"); also, to take a drink, as of whisky (slang, U. S.). **II.** *tr.* To assume or give (a smile: as, "She *smiled* the sunniest smile that she had given to him yet," L. Merrick's "Position of Peggy Harper," ii. 7); also, to bring, put, drive, etc., by smiling (as, to *smile* a person out of countenance; to *smile* one's tears away); also, to express by a smile (as, to *smile* approval); sometimes, to say with a smile (as, "'I shall give you a rap over the knuckles in a minute,' *smiled* Mrs. Hamps": Arnold Bennett's "Clayhanger," iv. 1); also, to smile at† (as, "*Smile* you my speeches, as I were a fool?" Shakspere's "King Lear," ii. 2. 88).—**smile**, *n.* An act of smiling; a smiling expression of the face (as, "She met his eye with her sweet hospitable *smile*," H. James's "Portrait of a Lady," xlviii.); "Tom saw a *smile* of contempt pass over the young curate's features," H. Kingsley's "Geoffry Hamlyn," xii.); favoring look or regard (as, fortune's *smile*); pleasant or agreeable look or aspect (as, the *smiles* of spring; nature's *smile*); also, a drink, as of whisky (slang, U. S.).—**smile′less**, *a.* Without a smile; unsmiling; grave; gloomy; cheerless.—**smil-er** (smī′lėr), *n.*—**smil-et** (smī′let), *n.* A little or faint smile: as, "Those happy *smilets*, That play'd on her ripe lip" (Shakspere's "King Lear," iv. 3. 21).—**smil′ing**, *p. a.* That smiles; wearing, or accompanied with, a smile; bright; cheerful; pleasant.—**smil′ing-ly**, *adv.*—**smil′ing-ness**, *n.*

smirch (smėrch), *v. t.* [Earlier *smorch*; origin uncertain.] To discolor or soil with some substance, as soot, dust, dirt, etc., or as the substance does (as, "I'll . . . with a kind of umber *smirch* my face": Shakspere's "As You Like It,"

i. 3. 114); make dirty; smudge; fig., to sully or tarnish, as with disgrace (as, to *smirch* one's honor or reputation).—**smirch**, *n.* A dirty mark or smear; fig., a stain or blot, as on reputation.—**smirch′er**, *n.*

smirk (smėrk), *v.* [AS. *smearcian*.] **I.** *intr.* To smile in an affected, would-be agreeable, or offensively familiar way: as, "Nodding and *smirking* at Morsfield's approach, she entreated Aminta to step up" (G. Meredith's "Lord Ormont and His Aminta," xviii.). **II.** *tr.* To utter or say with a smirk: as, "Charles Honeyman . . . *smirked* a blessing over the plenteous meal" (Thackeray's "Newcomes," lxii.). —**smirk**, *n.* The smile or the facial expression of one who smirks.—**smirk′er**, *n.*—**smirk′ing-ly**, *adv.*

smit (smit). Past participle and obs. or archaic preterit of *smite*.

smitch (smich), *n.* [Cf. AS. *smīc, smēc*, smoke, akin to *smoca*, E. *smoke, n.*] A particle of soot, grime, or the like (prov. Eng. and Sc.); hence, a speck, particle, or least bit of anything (colloq.).

smite (smīt), *v.*; pret. *smote* (obs. or archaic *smit*), pp. *smitten* or *smit*, ppr. *smiting*. [AS. *smītan* (pret. *smāt*, pp. *smiten*), smear, smite, = D. *smijten*, G. *schmeissen*, smite, throw, = Goth. *-smeitan*, smear.] **I.** *tr.* To strike or hit hard, as with the hand, a stick or weapon, etc., or as the hand or a weapon does; deal (a blow, etc.) by striking hard; strike, knock, break, or cut (*away, off, down, asunder,* etc.) by a forcible blow (as, "He imagined . . . how he would himself run out with a spade and *smite* the Germans down," H. G. Wells's "Mr. Britling," ii. 3. § 11: also fig.); render by or as by a blow (as, to *smite* a person dead; "Here were the emissaries of the dread power . . . suddenly *smitten* helpless," Kipling's "Kim," xiii.); in general, to strike (as, to *smite* a drum or a harp in playing; "Push off, and sitting well in order *smite* The sounding furrows," Tennyson's "Ulysses," 58); strike against or upon, as wind, waves, light, etc., do; also, to strike down or slay (as, "The men of Ai *smote* of them about thirty and six men": Josh. vii. 5); afflict, chasten, or punish in a grievous manner (as, "I *smote* you with blasting and with mildew and with hail . . . yet ye turned not to me, saith the Lord": Haggai, ii. 17); fall upon or attack with deadly or disastrous effect, as lightning, blight, pestilence, etc., do; affect mentally with a sudden pang (as, "I was *smitten* to the heart to see the empty seats that were in my kirk," Galt's "Annals of the Parish," l.; his conscience *smote* him; the recollection *smote* his heart); hence, to affect suddenly and strongly with a specified feeling or sentiment (as, to be *smitten* with terror, jealousy, hatred, or admiration); esp., to impress favorably, charm, or enamour (now chiefly in the passive: as, to be *smitten* with a person's charms; "Miss Thornton seems to have made a conquest already. Young Hawker seems desperately *smitten*," H. Kingsley's "Geoffry Hamlyn," vii.). **II.** *intr.* To strike; deal a blow or blows; also, to come, dash, fall, etc., with or as with the force of a blow (as, "His heart turned within him, and his knees *smote* together," Irving's "Sketch-Book," "Rip Van Winkle," "Iron clang and hammer's ringing *Smote* upon his ear," Whittier's "Fountain"). [*Smite, tr.* and *intr.*, is now chiefly a literary, rhetorical, or non-colloquial word.]—**smite**, *n.* A hard blow. [Now rare.]—**smit-er** (smī′tėr), *n.*

smith (smith), *n.* [AS. *smith* = D. *smid* = G. *schmied* = Icel. *smidhr* = Sw. and Dan. *smed*, smith: cf. Goth. *aiza-smitha*, coppersmith.] A worker in metal (as, a goldsmith; a tinsmith; a locksmith); esp., a blacksmith.—**smith**, *v.* **I.** *tr.* To fashion out of metal, as by forging or hammering; treat by forging or hammering. **II.** *intr.* To work as a smith.

smith-ers, smith-er-eens (smiᴛʜ′ėrz, smiᴛʜ-ėr-ēnz′), *n. pl.* [Origin obscure.] Small fragments: as, to knock a thing to *smithers*, or *smithereens*; "It [an aëroplane] went right over and flew to pieces, all to *smithereens*" (H. G. Wells's "Mr. Britling," ii. 4. § 13). Also fig. [Colloq.]

smith-er-y (smith′ėr-i), *n.*; pl. *-ies* (-iz). The work or craft of a smith; also, a smithy.

Smith-so-ni-an (smith-sō′ni-ạn), *a.* Of or pertaining to James Smithson (1765–1829), an English scientific man and philanthropist, who left a legacy to the United States government to found at Washington an institution ('Smithsonian Institution') "for the increase and diffusion of knowledge among men"; also, of or pertaining to this institution (as, *Smithsonian* reports).

smith-son-ite (smith′son-īt), *n.* [From James *Smithson*: see *Smithsonian*.] A mineral, a native carbonate of zinc, occurring in crystals but more commonly massive or earthy, and forming an important ore of zinc; also, native hydrous silicate of zinc. Cf. *calamin* and *hemimorphite*.

smith-y (smiTH′i or smith′i), *n.*; pl. -*ies* (-iz). [ME. *smithi*: cf. Icel. *smidhja*, also AS. *smiththe* (ME. *smithe*), smithy.] The workshop of a smith, esp. a blacksmith; a forge; a stithy: as, "Off came one of the mare's shoes, and I had to lead her to the village *smithy*" (Conan Doyle's "Exploits of Brigadier Gerard," vi.).—**smith′y,** *v.*; -*ied*, -*ying.* **I.** *tr.* To make or forge in or as in a smithy: as, "The forge Where hate was *smithying* tools" (Masefield's "Daffodil Fields," iv.). **II.** *intr.* To work as a smith.

smit-ten (smit′n). Past participle of *smite*.—**smit′ten,** *p. a.* Struck, as with a hard blow; also, stricken with affliction, disease, etc.; also, enamoured.

smock (smok), *n.* [AS. *smoc.*] A woman's chemise (archaic or prov.); also, a laborer's smock-frock; hence, any similar overgarment, esp. one worn to protect the clothing while at work (as, an artist's *smock*; a woman's gardening *smock*).—**smock,** *v. t.* To clothe in a smock; also, to draw (silk, etc.) by needlework into a honeycomb pattern with diamond-shaped recessed compartments (from the needlework sometimes seen on smock-frocks).—**smock′=frock,** *n.* A loose overgarment of linen or cotton worn by European field-laborers, etc.—**smock′=frocked,** *a.* Wearing a smock-frock: as, "the *smock-frock'd* boors" (M. Arnold's "Scholar-Gipsy").—**smock′ing,** *n.* Smocked needlework.

smog (smog), *n.* [From *sm(oke)* + *(f)og*².] A combination of smoke and fog in the atmosphere. [Colloq.]

smok-a-ble (smō′ka-bl), *a.* That may be smoked.

smoke (smōk), *n.* [AS. *smoca*, smoke, akin to *smēocan*, to smoke, also to D. *smook*, G. *schmauch*, smoke.] The visible exhalation given off by a burning or smoldering substance, esp. the gray, brown, or blackish mixture of gases and suspended carbon particles resulting from the combustion of wood, peat, coal, or other organic matter; hence, something resembling this, as vapor or mist, flying particles, etc. (as, the *smoke* of a waterfall; "I heard the rumbling thunder of the falling avalanche, and marked the *smoke* of its passage," Mrs. Shelley's "Frankenstein," ix.); fig., something unsubstantial, evanescent, or without result (as, "This helpless *smoke* of words doth me no right," Shakspere's "Lucrece," 1027; "I take it for granted this whole affair will end in *smoke*," Smollett's "Humphry Clinker," June 10); sometimes, obscuring conditions (as, perceptions dimmed by the *smoke* of controversy); also, a colored person (slang); also, an act or spell of smoking tobacco or the like (as, "I . . . had a *smoke* out of a pipe that one of them left in reach": Mark Twain's "Life on the Mississippi," iii.); that which is smoked, as a cigar or cigarette (as, "A woman is only a woman, but a good Cigar is a *Smoke*": Kipling's "Betrothed").—**London smoke.** See entry in alphabetical place.—**smoke,** *v.*; smoked, smoking. [AS. *smocian*.] **I.** *intr.* To give off or emit smoke, as burning matter; sometimes, to give out smoke offensively or improperly, as a lamp, a stove, or a chimney that allows smoke to pass into a house (as, "For a wonder, the chimney did not *smoke*": Roosevelt's "Ranch Life and the Hunting-Trail," xi.); send forth steam or vapor, dust, or the like (as, "On two long tables *smoked* basins of something hot": C. Brontë's "Jane Eyre," v.); move or pass like smoke, as clouds across the sky; ride or travel (*along*) with great speed; also, fig., to burn, or be hot or intense (obs. or archaic: as, "The anger of the Lord and his jealousy shall *smoke* against that man," Deut. xxix. 20); fume with anger†; also, to suffer for something, orig. by burning† (as, "This . . . will I keep safe, Or some of you shall *smoke* for it in Rome": Shakspere's "Titus Andronicus," iv. 2. 111); also, to get an inkling or suspicion (archaic); also, to draw into the mouth and puff out again the smoke of tobacco or the like, as from a pipe, cigar, or cigarette (as, "As it [a tobacco-pipe] . . . would draw the smoke, I was exceedingly comforted with it; for I had been always used to *smoke*": Defoe's "Robinson Crusoe," i. 10). **II.** *tr.* To expose to the action of smoke;

fumigate (rooms, etc.), as for the purpose of purifying or disinfecting; cure (meat, fish, etc.) by exposure to smoke; color or darken by the action of smoke; scent (a place, etc.) with smoke (often with *up*); subject (persons, animals, etc.) to an annoying or stifling smoke; drive (*out*, etc.) by means of smoke, as an animal from its hole; fig., to force or bring (*out*), as into public view or knowledge (colloq.: as, "a set of traitors, who shall and will be *smoked* out like a nest of wasps," J. H. Newman's "Callista," xxii.; to *smoke* out a person's real purposes); also, to ridicule or banter (a person: archaic); smell, get an inkling of, or suspect (archaic: as, to *smoke* a plot); observe or notice (archaic); also, to draw into the mouth and puff out again the smoke of (tobacco, opium, etc.), as from a pipe or (in case of tobacco) a cigar or cigarette; use (a pipe, etc.) in this process; bring, pass, etc., by smoking (as, to *smoke* one's self drowsy; to *smoke* time away).

smoke=col-ored (smōk′kul″ọrd), *a.* Of a dull-gray or brownish-gray color.

smoked (smōkt), *p. a.* Treated or cured with smoke, as meat or fish; also, darkened by smoke, as glass; also, gray, as pearl.

smoke=dry (smōk′drī), *v. t.*; -dried, -drying. To dry or cure by exposure to smoke: as, "He cut up and *smoke-dried* the flesh" (W. H. Hudson's "Green Mansions," xviii.).

smoke=eat-er (smōk′ē″tėr), *n.* A fireman (belonging to a public fire department). [Colloq.]

smoke=house (smōk′hous), *n.* A building or place in which things are treated with smoke, esp. one in which meat or fish is cured with smoke.

smoke=jack (smōk′jak), *n.* [See *jack*³.] An apparatus for turning a roasting-spit, set in motion by the current of ascending gases in a chimney.

smoke-less (smōk′les), *a.* Emitting, producing, or having no (or but little) smoke: as, a *smokeless* flame; *smokeless* coal; *smokeless* air.—**smokeless powder,** any of various substitutes for ordinary gunpowder which give off little or no smoke on exploding, esp. one composed wholly or mostly of guncotton.

smok-er (smō′kėr), *n.* One who or that which smokes; also, a railroad-car, or a compartment in one, for travelers who wish to smoke (colloq.); also, an informal gathering for smoking and entertainment (colloq.).

smoke=room (smōk′rŏm), *n.* A smoking-room.

smoke=screen (smōk′skrēn), *n.* A mass of dense smoke specially produced over the surface of the sea in time of war as a means of screening a vessel from the enemy's aim or attack; a mass of smoke similarly used as a screen elsewhere, as in the air (to screen an aëroplane) or on land; hence, fig., anything used, done, or said as a means of concealing the truth or facts of a case.

Smoke-jack. — *a, a,* the chimney, contracted in a circular form; *b,* strong bar placed over the fireplace, to support the jack; *c,* wheel with vanes radiating from its center, set in motion by the ascent of the heated air, and communicating, by the pinion *d* and the crown-wheel *e,* with the pulley *f,* from which motion is transmitted to the spit by the chain passing over it.

Smoke-tree (*Cotinus cotinus*). — 1, branch with fruit and sterile pedicels; 2, the inflorescence; *a,* a flower; *b,* a fruit.

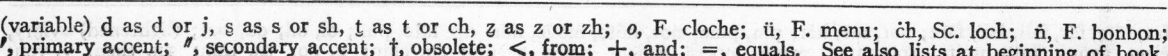

smoke=stack (smōk′stak), *n.* A pipe serving for the escape of the smoke or gases of combustion, as on a steamboat, a locomotive, or a building; a tall chimney, as of a factory.

smoke=tree (smōk′trē), *n.* An anacardiaceous tree-like shrub, *Cotinus cotinus*, native in southern Europe and Asia Minor, bearing small flowers in large panicles that develop a light, feathery appearance suggestive of smoke (see cut on preceding page); also, a related American species, *Cotinus cotinoides*.

smok-i-ly (smō′ki-li), *adv.* In a smoky manner; with much smoke; like smoke.—**smok′i-ness**, *n.*

smok-ing (smō′king), *n.* The act of one who or that which smokes; specif., the act or practice of smoking tobacco (as, "Captain Nutter gradually gave up *smoking*, which is an untidy, injurious, disgraceful, and highly pleasant habit": Aldrich's "Story of a Bad Boy," xii.).—**smok′ing=car**, *n.* A railroad-car for travelers who wish to smoke.—**smok′ing=room**, *n.* A room set apart for smoking, as in a hotel, club-house, or the like.

smok-y (smō′ki), *a.*; compar. *smokier*, superl. *smokiest.* Emitting smoke, or much smoke, as a fire, a torch, etc.; apt to emit smoke offensively or in the wrong way, as a stove or a chimney; sending forth smoke-like vapor, or steaming; also, abounding in smoke (as, the *Smoky* City, Pittsburgh, Pa., so called from the smoke arising from its extensive industrial establishments); hazy; darkened or begrimed with smoke; also, having the character or appearance of smoke (as, a *smoky* cloud or fog; "The *smoky* mist had begun to rise from the water," W. Churchill's "Coniston," ii. 19); pertaining to or suggestive of smoke (as, a *smoky* appearance or flavor); smoke-like in color; of a dull or brownish gray; cloudy; also, given or pertaining to the smoking of tobacco.

smol-der, smoul-der (smōl′dėr), *n.* [ME. *smolder*: cf. D. *smeulen*, to smolder.] Dense smoke resulting from slow or suppressed combustion; also, smoldering matter; a smoldering fire; fig., an inward burning or continued heat of feeling (as, "The man . . . felt a *smoulder* of indignation": Eden Phillpotts's "Children of Men," Prologue, ii.).—**smol′der, smoul′der**, *v.* **I.**† *tr.* To stifle, orig. as smoke does; suffocate; smother. **II.** *intr.* To burn and smoke without flame; fig., to exist or continue in a suppressed state or without outward demonstration (as, "Betwixt these two Division *smoulders* hidden": Tennyson's "Princess," iii. 63).—**smol′der-ing-ly, smoul′der-ing-ly**, *adv.*

smolt (smōlt), *n.* [Cf. *smelt*¹.] A young salmon, with silvery scales, which has ceased to be a parr and is ready to descend, or has descended, to the sea for the first time, next becoming a grilse.

smooch (smōch), *v. t.* and *n.* Same as *smutch*.

smoor, smore (smōr, smōr), *v. t.* or *i.* [AS. *smorian*: see *smother*.] To smother. [Sc. and prov. Eng.]

smooth (smōᵺ), *a.* [AS. *smōth*, also *smoethe, smēthe*; connections uncertain.] Free from projections or irregularities of surface such as would be perceived in touching or stroking (as, *smooth* stones, planks, or bark; coins worn *smooth* by use; a *smooth* forehead; *smooth* hair: often opposed to *rough*); free from hairs or a hairy growth (as, a *smooth* face; *smooth* leaves); in general, free from inequalities of surface, ridges or hollows, obstructions, etc. (as, *smooth* ground; a *smooth* slope; a *smooth* road); even; flat; generally flat or unruffled, as water or a calm sea; performed over ground, water, etc., free from unevenness or roughness (as, *smooth* driving or sailing; a *smooth* voyage); also, of uniform consistence, or free from lumps, as a batter, a sauce, etc.; also, free from or proceeding without breaks, abrupt bends, etc. (as, *smooth* curves or contours; a *smooth* sweep of the pen); easy and uniform, as motion, the working of a machine, etc.; free from hindrances or difficulties (as, "Unforeseen Contingence might . . . disturb The *smooth* and equal course of his affairs": Cowper's "Task," ii. 173); easy, flowing, elegant, or polished, as speech, verse, style, or a speaker or writer; undisturbed, tranquil, or equable, as the feelings, temper, etc.; also, pleasant, agreeable, or ingratiatingly polite, as speech, manner, persons, etc. (as, "*Smooth* words he had to wheedle simple souls": Wordsworth's "Excursion," ii. 254); bland or suave; plausible; free from harshness or sharpness of taste, as wine; not harsh to the ear, as sound; in *gram.*, without aspiration, or the sound of *h* (as, the *smooth*

breathing: see *breathing*).—**smooth**, *adv.* In a smooth manner; smoothly: as, "The course of true love never did run *smooth*" (Shakspere's "Midsummer Night's Dream," i. 1. 134).—**smooth**, *v.* **I.** *tr.* To make smooth of surface, as by scraping, planing, pressing, stroking, etc.; make even, flat, or easy for travel, as a way (often fig.: as, to *smooth* one's path in life); remove (projections, wrinkles, obstructions, etc.) in making something smooth (often with *away* or *out*, and also fig.: as, to *smooth* away difficulties); also, to make more smooth or elegant, as wording, verse, etc.; polish; refine (manners, or the person); also, to tranquilize, calm, or soothe, as the feelings or temper; also, to make smooth, agreeable, or plausible, as the speech, tongue, etc.; soothe, compliment, or flatter with smooth words, as a person†; gloss over or palliate, as something unpleasant or wrong (as, "To *smooth* his fault I should have been more mild," Shakspere's "Richard II.," i. 3. 240: now usually with *over*). **II.** *intr.* To become smooth; also, to use smooth words†, or flatter†.—**smooth**, *n.* An act of smoothing (as, "She . . . gave one *smooth* to her hair, and finally let in her visitor": Thackeray's "Vanity Fair," lxv.); also, an implement for smoothing; also, that which is smooth; a smooth part of anything; a smooth place.

smooth=bore (smōᵺ′bōr), *a.* Of firearms, having a smooth bore; not rifled.

smooth-en (smō′ᵺn), *v. t.* or *i.* To make or become smooth.

smooth-er (smō′ᵺėr), *n.* One who or that which smooths.

smooth=faced (smōᵺ′fāst), *a.* Having a smooth face; beardless or clean-shaven, as persons; having a smooth surface, as cloth; fig., smooth, agreeable, or ingratiating in aspect or manner (as, a *smooth-faced* hypocrite).

smooth-ly (smōᵺ′li), *adv.* In a smooth manner.—**smooth′ness**, *n.*

smooth=spok-en (smōᵺ′spō′kn), *a.* Smooth, agreeable, or plausible in speech, or as speech; smooth-tongued.

smooth=tongued (smōᵺ′tungd), *a.* Smooth of tongue or speech, as a person; agreeable, suave, or plausible, as a speaker or his utterances, etc.: as, "The *smooth-tongued* rascal found no difficulty to insinuate himself into . . . her heart" (Smollett's "Humphry Clinker," July 18).

smore (smōr), *v.* See *smoor*.

smote (smōt). Preterit of *smite*.

smoth-er (smuᵺ′ėr), *n.* [ME. *smorther*, < AS. *smorian*, to smother, = D. and MLG. *smoren*, G. *schmoren*, to smother, stifle, also cook in a close vessel: cf. *smoor*.] Dense, stifling smoke (as, "Thus must I from the smoke into the *smother*; From tyrant duke unto a tyrant brother": Shakspere's "As You Like It," i. 2. 299); a smoking or smoldering state, as of burning matter; a smoldering fire; also, dust, fog, spray, or the like in a dense or enveloping cloud; hence, an overspreading profusion of anything.—**smoth′er**, *v.* **I.** *tr.* To stifle, as smoke does; stifle or suffocate with smoke, or by any means of impeding respiration; kill by depriving of the air necessary for life, often by closely covering the mouth and nose; hence, to extinguish or deaden (fire, etc.) by covering so as to exclude air; cover closely or thickly (often with *up*); envelop (*in*: as, a house *smothered* in vines); fig., to suppress as by covering up (as, to *smother* a scandal); repress, as feelings, impulses, etc. (as, "He . . . *smothered* his resentment": Cooper's "Two Admirals," iii.); check or quell, as attempts, outbreaks, etc.; deaden or muffle, as sound; in *cookery*, to cook in a close vessel (as, a dish of *smothered* chicken); also, to cover thickly with something (as, beefsteak *smothered* with onions). **II.** *intr.* To become stifled or suffocated; be prevented from breathing freely by smoke or otherwise; also, to smolder, as a fire (now prov. Eng.).—**smoth′er-er**, *n.*—**smoth′er-y**, *a.* Tending to smother; stifling.

smoul-der (smōl′dėr), etc. See *smolder*, etc.

smudge¹ (smuj), *v. t.*; *smudged, smudging.* [Late ME. *smoge*; origin uncertain: cf. *smutch*.] To mark with dirty streaks or smears; smirch; smear.—**smudge**¹, *n.* A dirty mark or smear; also, a smeary state.

smudge² (smuj), *n.* [Origin obscure.] A stifling smoke; also, a smoky fire, esp. one made for the purpose of driving away mosquitoes, etc.—**smudge**², *v.*; *smudged, smudging.* **I.** *intr.* To smolder. [Prov. Eng.] **II.** *tr.* To fill with smoke from a smudge, as to drive away insects.

smudg-y[1] (smuj′i), *a.* Marked with smudges; smeared; smeary.

smudg-y[2] (smuj′i), *a.* Emitting a stifling smoke; smoky; also, close or sultry, as the air (prov. Eng.).

smug (smug), *a.*; compar. *smugger*, superl. *smuggest*. [Origin uncertain: cf. MLG. *smuk*, G. *schmuck*, trim, spruce, smart.] Smooth or sleek (now only with reference to personal appearance, esp. the face, and usually implying complacency); trim, spruce, or smart (as, "a beggar, that was used to come so *smug* upon the mart": Shakspere's "Merchant of Venice," iii. 1. 49); now, usually, consciously and complacently nice or proper; complacent from a sense of respectability or righteousness; affecting or wearing an air of conventional or commonplace respectability.

smug-gle (smug′l), *v.*; -gled, -gling. [LG. *smuggeln*, *smukkeln*, smuggle.] **I.** *tr.* To import or export (goods) secretly, without payment of legal duty or in violation of law; hence, to bring, take, put, etc., surreptitiously (as, "He had been *smuggled* to the Hall inside a tea-chest," Arnold Bennett's "Lion's Share," xxiii.; "Somehow a bag must be packed and *smuggled* out of the house," H. G. Wells's "Men Like Gods," i. 1; to *smuggle* a letter into a person's hand). **II.** *intr.* To smuggle goods.—**smug′gler,** *n.* One who smuggles; also, a vessel employed in smuggling.

smug-ly (smug′li), *adv.* In a smug manner.—**smug′ness,** *n.*

smut (smut), *v.*; *smutted, smutting*. [Cf. earlier (ME.) *smot*, besmirch, also G. *schmutzen*, soil.] **I.** *tr.* To soil with some black or dirty substance; smirch; smudge; fig., to make obscene; also, to affect (a plant) with the disease called smut. **II.** *intr.* To become affected with smut, as a plant.—**smut,** *n.* A black or dirty mark; a smudge; also, a particle of soot; sooty matter; earthy, worthless coal; fig., indecent or obscene talk or writing; obscenity; also, a fungous disease of plants, esp. cereals, in which the affected parts are converted into a black powdery matter; a fungus causing such disease.

smutch (smuch), *v. t.* [Cf. *smudge*[1] and *smooch*.] To mark with dirt or the like; smudge; soil.—**smutch,** *n.* A dirty mark; a smudge; a stain; also, dirt, grime, or smut.—**smutch′y,** *a.* Marked with smutches; smudgy; smeary; dirty.

smut-ty (smut′i), *a.*; compar. *smuttier*, superl. *smuttiest.* Soiled with smut, soot, or the like; grimy; dirty; also, dusky or dark; fig., indecent or obscene, as talk or writing, stories, etc.; given to such talk, etc., as a person; also, affected with the disease smut, as a plant.—**smut′ti-ly,** *adv.* —**smut′ti-ness,** *n.*

Smyr-ni-ot, Smyr-ni-ote (smẽr′ni-ot, -ōt). [See *-ot* and *-ote*.] **I.** *n.* A native or inhabitant of Smyrna, the chief city and seaport of Asia Minor. **II.** *a.* Of or pertaining to Smyrna.

snack (snak), *n.* [Related to *snatch.*] A snap or bite, as by a dog (now Sc. and prov. Eng.); also, a small portion of food or drink, or a light repast (now colloq.: as, "When you want to go . . . he'll put up a *snack* for you to take along," Stevenson's "Treasure Island," xii.); also, a share or portion (now colloq.: as, to go *snacks*, to share).

snaf-fle (snaf′l), *n.* [Cf. D. *snavel*, beak, muzzle, snout, and E. *snap*, *v.*] A slender, jointed bit used on a bridle. Also called *snaffle-bit.*—**snaf′fle,** *v. t.*; *-fled, -fling.* To put a snaffle on (a horse, etc.); control by or as by a snaffle.

Snaffle.

snag (snag), *n.* [Prob. from Scand.: cf. Norw. *snag*, *snage*, sharp point, projection, Icel. *snagi*, peg.] A short, projecting stump, as of a branch broken or cut off; any sharp or rough projection; often, a stump of a tooth; a projecting tooth, or snaggletooth; also, a branch or tine of a deer's antler; also, a tree or part of a tree held fast in the bottom of a river or other water and forming an impediment or danger to navigation (as, "It required all his attention and skill . . . to pilot her [a boat] clear of sand-bars and *snags*, or sunken trees": Irving's "Captain Bonneville," xli.); any obstacle or impediment (as, to strike a *snag* in carrying out plans).—

snag, *v. t.*; *snagged, snagging.* To run or catch upon, or damage by, a snag (as, "one of these [steamboats], the Radnor, since *snagged* and lost": Parkman's "Oregon Trail," i.); also, to obstruct or impede, as a snag does; also, to clear of snags.—**snag′=boat,** *n.* A vessel equipped with apparatus for removing snags or other obstacles to navigation, as from rivers.—**snagged** (snagd or snag′ed), *a.* Having snags, or sharp or rough projections; jagged.

snag-gle=tooth (snag′l-töth), *n.*; pl. *-teeth* (-tēth). [With *snaggle* appar. as a dim. of *snag.*] A tooth growing out beyond or apart from others.—**snag′gle=toothed,** *a.*

snag-gy (snag′i), *a.* Having snags or sharp projections, as a tree; abounding in snags or obstructions, as a river; also, snag-like; projecting sharply or roughly.

snag=tooth (snag′töth), *n.*; pl. *-teeth* (-tēth). A snag-like tooth; a snaggle-tooth.

snail (snāl), *n.* [AS. *snægl*, *snegl*, = G. dial. *schnegel* (cf. G. *schnecke*) = Icel. *snigill* = Dan. *snegl*, snail.] Any of various terrestrial air-breathing gastropods of the family *Helicidæ*, with a spiral or helicoid shell, as *Helix pomatia*, an edible European species (see *Roman snail*, under *Roman, a.*) or *H. desertorum*; also, any of various related or similar mollusks, as the spiral-shelled fresh-water gastropods of the genus *Limnæa*, or the sea-snails; also, a shell-less gastropod, or slug; fig., a slow or

Snail (*Helix desertorum*) crawling on the extended foot or podium.

lazy person; a sluggard.—**snail's pace,** a very slow pace or rate of progress: as, "We started in single file and at a *snail's pace* up the valley" (S. J. Weyman's "Gentleman of France," xxviii.).—**snail,** *v.* **I.** *intr.* To go or travel slowly, like a snail. **II.** *tr.* To give the spiral form of a snail-shell to.—**snail′er-y** (-ẽr-i), *n.*; pl. *-ies* (-iz). A place where edible snails are kept and bred for food purposes.—**snail′=paced** (-pāst), *a.* Slow of pace or motion, like a snail; slow-paced; sluggish: as, "Delay leads impotent and *snail-paced* beggary" (Shakspere's "Richard III.," iv 3. 53).

snake (snāk), *n.* [AS. *snaca* = MLG. *snake* = G. dial. *schnake*, snake.] Any of the scaly, limbless, long-bodied reptiles, with a slender forked tongue, constituting the order *Ophidia*; an ophidian; a serpent; also, any of various ophidian-like lizards and amphibians, as *Amphiuma means* (see *Congo snake*); hence, any object, part, strip, line, or the like, suggesting a snake or serpent, as in form or movement; fig., a treacherous person; an insidious enemy; a lurking danger; also, a groveling or sorry creature (as, "I see love hath made thee a tame *snake*": Shakspere's "As You Like It," iv. 3. 71).

snake, *v.*; *snaked, snaking.* **I.** *intr.* To move in a creeping or stealthy manner, like a snake; also, to wind or curve like a snake (as, "the well-trodden track . . . that *snaked* among the mountains": Kipling's "Kim," xiii.). **II.** *tr.* To move, twist, or wind in the manner of a snake; make (one's way) in a creeping or sinuous manner; also, to drag or haul, as a log by means of a chain or rope fastened around one end (U. S.); pull forcibly or jerk (with *out*, *off*, etc.: U. S.); *naut.*, to wind or bind with small stuff; worm (a rope).

Common Ringed Snake of Europe (*Tropidonotus natrix*), with head showing forked tongue below.

snake=bird (snāk′bẽrd), *n.* Any of various swimming birds of the genus *Plotus* (or *Anhinga*) with a long, snaky neck. See cut on following page.

snake=fence (snāk′fens′), n. A fence of zigzag outline made of rails laid horizontally with the ends resting one across another at an angle, and often held in place by slanting posts at the point of meeting; a worm-fence, or Virginia fence.

snake=fish (snāk′fish), n. Any of various fishes more or less resembling a snake, as the lizard-fish and the oar-fish.

snake=head (snāk′hed), n. A turtlehead (plant).

snake=neck (snāk′nek), n. A snake-bird.

American Snake-bird (*Plotus anhinga*).

snake=root (snāk′rōt), n. Any of various plants whose roots have been regarded as a remedy for snake-bites, as *Aristolochia serpentaria* ('Virginia snakeroot'), an herb with medicinal rhizome and rootlets, and *Polygala senega* ('Seneca snakeroot'), a white-flowered plant with a medicinal root; also, the root or rhizome of such a plant (see *serpentaria* and *senega*).

snake=stone (snāk′stōn), n. An ammonite; also, a porous substance supposed to extract the venom from snake-bites.

snake=weed (snāk′wēd), n. The herb bistort, *Polygonum bistorta*; also, the Virginia snakeroot (see *snakeroot*).

snake=wood (snāk′wud), n. Any of certain East Indian shrubs or trees (genus *Strychnos*) whose wood is supposed to cure snakebites; the wood itself; also, a South American tree, *Brosimum* (or *Piratinera*) *guianensis*, with a beautiful mottled wood used for veneering, etc.; the wood itself.

Seneca Snakeroot.—1, the upper part of the stem with the flowers; 2, the root and the base of the stem; *a*, the fruit.

snak=y (snā′ki), a. Consisting of, entwined with, or bearing snakes or serpents (as, the *snaky* locks of the Furies; the *snaky* caduceus of Mercury); abounding in snakes, as a place; of or pertaining to snakes; also, snake-like; twisting, winding, or sinuous; venomous; treacherous or insidious.— **snak′i-ly**, adv.—**snak′i-ness**, n.

snap (snap), v.; snapped, snapping. [MD. D. *snappen* = MLG. and MHG. *snappen* (G. *schnappen*), snap; prob. related to D. *snavel*, G. *schnabel*, beak, snout, but in part of imit. origin.] **I.** intr. To make a quick or sudden bite or snatch (often with *at*); also, to utter a quick, sharp speech, reproof, retort, or the like (often with *at*); also, to make a sudden, sharp sound; crack, as a whip; crackle (as "a clear and cheerful fire crackling and *snapping* on a rude hearth": Cooper's "Spy," xxx.); click, as a mechanism; move, strike, shut, catch, etc., with a sharp sound, as a door, lid, or lock; also, to break suddenly, esp. with a sharp, cracking sound, as something slender and brittle; part asunder suddenly from tension (as, "Screw not the chord too sharply lest it *snap*": Tennyson's "Aylmer's Field," 469); also, to flash, as the eyes; in *photog.*, to take instantaneous photographs. **II.** tr. To seize with or as with a quick bite or snatch (now commonly with *up*, and often fig.: as, a dog *snaps* up a morsel; a bargain is promptly *snapped* up; "She was *snapped* up, of course, the moment she entered the room," G. Meredith's "Diana of the Crossways," ii.); take (*off*) at or as at one bite or snatch (as, "We had like to have had our two noses *snapped* off with two old men without teeth": Shakspere's "Much

Ado about Nothing," v. 1. 116); secure hastily, as a decision, legislation, etc., not subjected to due deliberation (cf. *snap*, a.); also, to address or interrupt (a person) quickly and sharply (usually with *up*); utter or say in a quick, sharp manner (as, "'Who said I was going to the show?' he *snapped*," W. Churchill's "Coniston," i. 15: sometimes with *out*); also, to cause to make a sudden, sharp sound (as, to *snap* the fingers: see phrase below); crack (a whip); bring, strike, shut, open, operate, etc., with a sharp sound or movement (as, to *snap* the jaws together; to *snap* a lid down; to *snap* a catch or lock; to *snap* an unloaded pistol); also, to break suddenly, esp. with a cracking sound (as, to *snap* a pipe-stem; branches *snapped* off by the wind); cause (a rope, etc.) to part suddenly; in *photog.*, to take an instantaneous photograph of.—**to snap the fingers**, to rub the fingers smartly against the inner surface of the thumb so as to strike against the ball with a sharp sound, often as a sign of contempt: as, "Fanny disdained a reply in words. She made a hissing sound of utter contempt and *snapped* her *fingers*" (Tarkington's "Magnificent Ambersons," xiii.); to *snap* one's *fingers* in a person's face, or at a person. Often fig.—**snap.** **I.** n. A quick or sudden bite or snatch, as at something; something obtained by or as by biting or snatching; a snack, or light repast (now prov.); a bit, morsel, portion, or share (now chiefly prov.); a short spell, as of cold weather (as, "The spirit in the thermometer during winter often sinks to fifty degrees below zero . . . the cattle become thin during such a *snap* of weather": Roosevelt's "Ranch Life and the Hunting-Trail," ii.); an easy and profitable or agreeable position, piece of work, or the like (slang); also, a quick, sharp speech, or manner of speaking; also, a sharp, cracking or clicking sound, or a movement or action causing such a sound (as, a *snap* of a whip; the *snap* of a catch or lock; a *snap* of the fingers); a catch or the like operating with such a sound; a riveters' tool for rounding or finishing the heads of rivets; also, a sudden breaking, as of something brittle or tense, or a sharp, cracking sound caused by it; a small, thin, brittle or crisp cake (as, a ginger*snap*; a brandy-*snap*); crispness, smartness, or liveliness, as of language, writings, or style; briskness, vigor, or energy, as of persons or actions; a sharper† or swindler†; in *photog.*, a snap-shot. **II.** a. Made, done, taken, etc., suddenly, off-hand, or without preparation or deliberation (as, a *snap* judgment; *snap* legislation); also, that is a 'snap,' or easy and agreeable (slang: as, a *snap* course at college).

snap=back (snap′bak), n. In *football*, the snapping or passing back of the ball by the center, which puts it in play; also, the snapper-back.

snap=bean (snap′bēn), n. Any of various kinds of bean (plant) whose unripe pods (which break with a snap) are used as food; the pod itself; a string-bean.

snap=drag-on (snap′drag″on), n. A plant of the scrophulariaceous genus *Antirrhinum*, esp. *A. majus*, an herb long cultivated for its spikes of showy flowers, of various colors, with a corolla that has been supposed to look like the mouth of a dragon; also, the game of flapdragon.

snap=hance (snap′hans), n. [D. *snaphaan*, < *snappen*, snap, + *haan*, cock.] An early form of flintlock worked by a spring, or a gun or pistol having such a lock: as, "The *snaphance* or flintlock was little used, at least in the early stages of the war" (Morley's "Oliver Cromwell," ii. 1).

snap=per (snap′er), n. One who or that which snaps (as, "a *snapper*-up of unconsidered trifles": Shakspere's "Winter's Tale," iv. 3. 26); a snappish person; specif., any of various large marine fishes of the family *Lutianidæ*, of warm seas, as *Lutianus aya* ('red snapper'), a highly esteemed food-fish, of a rose-red color, abundant off the coast of Florida; any of various other fishes; also, a snapping-turtle; also, a snapping-beetle.—**snap′per=back′**, n. In *football*, the center, or middle player in the forward line, who snaps or passes back the ball, thus putting it in play.

Florida Red Snapper (*Lutianus aya*).

---

fat, fāte, fär, fâll, ȧsk, fāre; net, mē, hèr; pin, pīne; not, nōte, mȯve, nôr; up, lūte, pull; oi, oil; ou, out; (lightened) avīạry, ēlect, agōny, intọ, ūnite; (obscured) errạnt, operä, ardẹnt, actọr, natūre; ch, chip; g, go; th, thin; ʈʜ, then; y, you;

snap-pi-ly (snap′i-li), *adv.* In a snappy manner.—**snap′pi-ness**, *n.*

snap-ping (snap′ing), *p. a.* That snaps; making quick attempts to bite, as an animal; snappish, as persons or language; making a sharp, cracking or clicking sound, as a beetle; flashing, as eyes.—**snap′ping=bee″tle**, *n.* A click-beetle or elaterid.—**snap′ping-ly**, *adv.*—**snap′ping=tur″tle**, *n.* A large and savage turtle, *Chelydra serpentina*, of American rivers, having powerful jaws with which it is given to snapping at prey, etc.; also, any of certain other turtles.

Snapping-turtle (*Chelydra serpentina*).

snap-pish (snap′ish), *a.* Apt to snap or bite, as a dog; also, disposed to speak or reply quickly and sharply, as a person (as, "I found him morose and *snappish*": Borrow's "Bible in Spain," xlii.); proceeding from or showing such a disposition, as the speech, manner, or tone; impatiently or irritably sharp or curt; also, smart or 'snappy' (as, "The smart And *snappish* dialogue, that flippant wits Call comedy": Cowper's "Task," iv. 198).—**snap′pish-ly**, *adv.*—**snap′pish-ness**, *n.*

snap-py (snap′i), *a.*; compar. *snappier*, superl. *snappiest.* Snappish, as a dog, or as a person, the speech, etc. (as, "She's been very kind to us, though lately she's been a little *snappy*": Margaret Kennedy's "Constant Nymph," xviii.); also, snapping or crackling in sound, as a fire; also, quick or sudden in action or performance; also, having snap, or crispness, smartness, liveliness, briskness, etc. (colloq.: as, "It was a 'tent show, presenting *snappy* new dramas under canvas,' " Sinclair Lewis's "Main Street," xviii.; "*snappy* young men," Tarkington's "Alice Adams," xii.).

snap=shot (snap′shot), *n.* A quick shot taken without deliberate aim (as, "The Major caught a carbine . . . and took a *snap-shot*, quick as lightning, at a man whom they saw running": H. Kingsley's "Geoffrey Hamlyn," xlii.); in *photog.*, the taking of an instantaneous photograph, or such a photograph.—**snap′shot**, *v. t.*; -*shotted*, -*shotting.* In *photog.*, to take a snap-shot of.—**snap′shot″ter**, *n.*

snare (snār), *n.* [AS. *sneare* = Icel. and Sw. *snara*, noose, snare; also, in part, the related D. *snaar* = MLG. *snare*, string of a musical instrument: cf. *snarl*².] A device, usually consisting of a noose or a set of nooses of cord or the like, for capturing birds or small animals; hence, in general, anything serving to entrap, entangle, or catch unawares, or a trap (lit. or fig.: as, "Something was to be resolved on . . . to draw the men on board into some *snare* for their surprise," Defoe's "Robinson Crusoe," i. 17; "the *snares* youth is exposed to," B. Franklin's "Autobiography," ii.); also, one of the strings of gut or rawhide on a snare-drum.—**snare**, *v. t.*; *snared*, *snaring.* To catch with a snare; insnare; entrap; entangle.—**snare′=drum**, *n.* A small, double-headed drum carried at the side, having snares or strings stretched across the lower head which produce a rattling or reverberating effect.—**snar-er** (snār′ėr), *n.*

snark (snärk), *n.* [Coined by C. L. Dodgson ("Lewis Carroll"), in "The Hunting of the Snark" (1876).] An imaginary animal.

snarl¹ (snärl), *v.* [From earlier *snar*, snarl = MLG. *snarren*, G. *schnarren*; prob. imit.: cf. *gnar* and *gnarl*¹.] **I.** *intr.* To growl angrily or viciously, as a dog (as, "The cur *snarled*, showed his teeth": Irving's "Sketch-Book," Rip Van Winkle); also, to speak in a savagely sharp, angry tone; speak or complain in a viciously ill-natured or quarrelsome manner. **II.** *tr.* To utter or say with a snarl: as, " 'Look here!' he *snarled*" (Arnold Bennett's "Helen with the High Hand," xxvii.).—**snarl**¹, *n.* An act of snarling; a snarling sound or utterance.

snarl² (snärl), *n.* [From *snare.*] A snare or noose (now prov. Eng.); also, a tangle, as of thread or hair; fig., a complicated or confused condition or matter; also, a knot in wood.—**snarl**², *v.* **I.** *tr.* To catch in a snare or noose (now prov. Eng.); also, to bring into a tangled condition, as thread, hair, etc.; tangle; fig., to render complicated or confused. **II.** *intr.* To become tangled; get into a tangle.

snarl³ (snärl), *v. t.* [Perhaps another use of *snarl*².] To raise or emboss, as parts of a thin metal vessel, by hammering on a tool (*snarling-iron*) held against the inner surface of the vessel.

snarl-er¹ (snär′lėr), *n.* An animal or a person that snarls; an ill-natured faultfinder.

snarl-er² (snär′lėr), *n.* One who snarls metal; also, a tool used in snarling (also called *snarling-iron*).

snarl-ing (snär′ling), *p. a.* That snarls; growling angrily; speaking or complaining in a sharp, ill-natured way.—**snarl′ing-ly**, *adv.*

snarl-y¹ (snär′li), *a.* Disposed to snarl or growl.

snarl-y² (snär′li), *a.* Snarled; tangled; knotted.

snatch (snach), *v.* [ME. *snacchen, snecchen*; origin uncertain: cf. *snack.*] **I.** *intr.* To make a snap with the jaws, as in order to bite (as, "And like a dog that is compell'd to fight, *Snatch* at his master": Shakspere's "King John," iv. 1. 117); also, to make a sudden motion or effort to seize something, as with the hand (usually with *at*, and often fig.: as, to *snatch* at a support when falling; to *snatch* at an excuse or opportunity); catch or grasp (*at*). **II.** *tr.* To seize or take by a sudden or hasty grasp (often with *up*, *from*, *out of*, *away*, etc.: as, to *snatch* up a weapon; to *snatch* a purse from a person); fig., to take, get, secure, etc., suddenly or hastily (as, to *snatch* a kiss; "At half-past four he had *snatched* a cup of tea," Galsworthy's "Saint's Progress," ii. 1; "I . . . resolved to *snatch* this opportunity of seeing the manners of other nations," Johnson's "Rasselas," viii.; "He *snatched* a few hours' repose," J. F. Kirk's "Charles the Bold," iii. 2); remove suddenly (with *away*, *from*, etc.: as, "And, unregretted, are soon *snatch'd* away From scenes of sorrow into glorious day," Cowper's "Retirement," 167); rescue or save by prompt action (as, to be *snatched* from danger or death).—**snatch**, *n.* An act of snatching; a snap with the jaws, as of an animal (see Spenser's "Faerie Queene," iii. 1. 22); a sudden motion to seize something (as, to make a *snatch* at a flying ball: also fig.); a hasty catch, grasp, or grab; also, something snatched, or taken hastily; a snack, or light repast (now prov.); a bit, scrap, or fragment of something (as, a *snatch* of verse or of a song; to overhear *snatches* of conversation; "if he caught now and then some *snatches* of these wild legends," Lamb's "Old Margate Hoy"); a glimpse, as of scenery; a brief spell of effort, activity, or any experience (as, to work or read by, or in, *snatches*; "A *snatch* of sleep were like the peace of God," Tennyson's "Harold," v. 1. 103); a brief period or space of time (as, "so that the sailors might not be idle in the *snatches* between the frequent squalls": Dana's "Two Years before the Mast," iii.); also, a quibble† (as, "Come, sir, leave me your *snatches*, and yield me a direct answer": Shakspere's "Measure for Measure," iv. 2. 6).

snatch=block (snach′blok), *n. Naut.*, a block with an opening in one side to receive the bight of a rope.

snatch-er (snach′ėr), *n.* One who or that which snatches.

snatch-y (snach′i), *a.* Consisting of, occurring in, or characterized by snatches; spasmodic; irregular: as, *snatchy* reading.—**snatch′i-ly**, *adv.*

Snatch-block.

snath, snathe (snath, snāᴛʜ), *n.* [Var. of *snead.*] The shaft or handle of a scythe: as, "O mower, lean on thy bended *snath*" (Whittier's "Wreck of Rivermouth").

snead (snēd), *n.* [AS. *snǣd.*] A snath. [Prov.]

sneak (snēk), *v.* [Origin uncertain: cf. AS. *snīcan*, creep, crawl, as a reptile.] **I.** *intr.* To go (*about, along, in, off, out*, etc.) in a stealthy or furtive manner, as if afraid or ashamed to be seen; slink; skulk; also, to go away quickly and quietly (colloq.); also, to act in a furtive, underhand, or mean way (as, "See how he cowers and *sneaks*": Thoreau's "Walden," i.); cringe or truckle (*to*: obs. or archaic). **II.** *tr.* To move, put, pass, etc., in a stealthy or furtive manner (as, to *sneak* a thing out of the house; to *sneak* a bill through the legislature); also, to take surreptitiously, or steal (colloq.).—**sneak**, *n.* One who sneaks; a sneaking, underhand, or contemptible person (as, "I had recognised him as a poltroon and a *sneak*": Conan Doyle's "Exploits of Brigadier Gerard," iv.); a sneak-thief; also, an act of sneaking; a going quietly away, or a departure (colloq.:

as, "How about taking a *sneak*?" Sinclair Lewis's "Main Street," xvii.); in *cricket*, a ball bowled so as to roll along the ground.—**sneak'=boat, sneak'=box**, *n.* A small, shallow, decked boat used in hunting wild-fowl: commonly masked with brush, etc., when in use. [U. S.]—**sneak'er**, *n.* One who sneaks; a sneak; also, a shoe with a rubber or other sole that makes little noise in walking (colloq.).—**sneak'ing**, *p. a.* That sneaks; acting in a furtive or underhand way; meanly or deceitfully underhand, as actions, etc.; contemptible; sometimes, with a deprecating force, secret, or not generally avowed, as a feeling, notion, suspicion, etc.—**sneak'ing-ly**, *adv.*—**sneak'=thief**, *n.* One who goes about in search of opportunities for thieving, as by sneaking into houses through open doors.—**sneak'y**, *a.* Like or suggestive of a sneak; sneaking: as, "They dropped their eyes and looked *sneaky*" (Mark Twain's "Huckleberry Finn," xxii.).

sneap (snēp), *v. t.* [From Scand.] To nip or pinch (as, "An envious *sneaping* frost That bites the first-born infants of the spring": Shakspere's "Love's Labour's Lost," i. 1. 100); also, to check, reprove, or snub (as, "She had a tongue for the *sneaping* of too casual boys": Arnold Bennett's "Hilda Lessways," i. 10). [Archaic or prov. Eng.]—**sneap**, *n.* A check; a reproof; a snub: as, "My lord, I will not undergo this *sneap* without reply" (Shakspere's "2 Henry IV.," ii. 1. 133). [Archaic or prov. Eng.]

sneck (snek), *n.* [ME. *snekke*; perhaps related to *snatch*.] The latch or catch of a door, etc. [Chiefly Sc. and prov. Eng.]—**sneck**, *v. t.* or *i.* To fasten by means of a latch or catch. [Chiefly Sc. and prov. Eng.]—**sneck'=draw″er, sneck'=draw**, *n.* One who draws or lifts a sneck or latch, as to enter stealthily; hence, a crafty, thievish, or grasping person (as, "a skinflint and a *sneckdraw*, sitting, with his nose in an account book, to persecute poor tenants": Stevenson's "Master of Ballantrae," i.). [Sc. and north. Eng.]

sneer (snēr), *v.* [Origin uncertain: cf. *snore* and *snort*.] **I.** *intr.* To snort, as a horse (now Sc. and prov. Eng.); also, to draw the face into a grin or grimace (now prov. Eng.); esp., to smile, or curl the lip, in a scornful or contemptuous manner; manifest scorn, contempt, etc., by the expression of the face; speak or write in a manner expressive of derision, scorn, or contempt (as, "Cato had *sneered* at his exploits as victories over women": Froude's "Cæsar," xii.). **II.** *tr.* To utter or say in a sneering manner (as, " 'A ship of fools,' he *sneer'd*": Tennyson's "Voyage," x.); also, to sneer at (now prov. Eng.); also, to bring, put, force, etc., by sneering (as, to *sneer* a person out of countenance).—**sneer**, *n.* An act of sneering; a look or expression suggestive of derision, scorn, or contempt (as, "The Highlander . . . had regarded the ceremony of his antagonist's knighthood with a *sneer* of sullen scorn": Scott's "Legend of Montrose," xix.); a derisive or scornful utterance or remark, esp. one more or less covert or insinuative.—**sneer'er**, *n.*—**sneer'ing-ly**, *adv.*

sneesh-ing (snē'shing), *n.* [= *sneezing*.] Snuff; also, a pinch of snuff. [Sc., Ir., and north. Eng.]

sneeze (snēz), *v.; sneezed, sneezing.* [ME. *snesen*, for *fnesen*, < AS. *fnēosan* = D. *fniezen*, sneeze, = Icel. *fnȳsa*, Sw. *fnysa*, Dan. *fnyse*, snort.] **I.** *intr.* To emit air or breath suddenly, forcibly, and audibly through the nose and mouth by involuntary, spasmodic action (as, "He had caught cold, and was beginning to *sneeze*": Arnold Bennett's "Clayhanger," ii. 18); also (with *at*), to show contempt for, or treat with contempt (colloq., and usually in negative expressions: as, the offer was not to be *sneezed* at). **II.** *tr.* To utter with or as with a sneeze.—**sneeze**, *n.* An act or sound of sneezing; also, snuff (north. Eng.).—**sneeze'=gas**, *n.* Sneezing-gas.—**sneez'er**, *n.*—**sneeze'weed**, *n.* The false sunflower, *Helenium autumnale*, a North American asteraceous plant the powdered leaves and flowers of which when snuffed up produce violent sneezing (see cut in next column); also, any of various other plants of the genus *Helenium*.—**sneeze'wort** (-wėrt), *n.* An asteraceous plant, *Achillea ptarmica*, a native of Europe, the powdered leaves of which are said to be used to cause sneezing (also called 'sneezewort yarrow'); also, sneezeweed.—**sneez'ing**, *n.* The act of one who sneezes; also, something used to cause sneezing, esp. snuff (obs. or prov.).—**sneez'ing=gas**, *n.* A substance, an organic derivative of arsine, liberated in clouds of fine particles by the bursting of specially prepared shells in which it is contained: used in modern warfare to produce sneezing among enemy soldiers, sometimes forcing them to remove their gas-masks and become exposed to more dangerous gases. Also called *sneeze-gas*.

Sneezeweed (*Helenium autumnale*).

snell[1] (snel). [AS. *snel, snell*, = D. *snel* = G. *schnell*, quick, swift, = Icel. *snjallr*, Sw. *snäll*, clever, good.] **I.** *a.* Quick, brisk, or active, as persons; also, keen, clever, or smart; also, sharp, as weather, etc. (as, "Bleak December's winds . . . Baith *snell* an' keen": Burns's "To a Mouse," 24); also, harsh, biting, or caustic, as speakers, speech, etc.; also, severe or hard, as blows, afflictions, etc. [Now Sc. and north. Eng.] **II.** *adv.* Quickly; sharply; strongly. [Now Sc.]

snell[2] (snel), *n.* [Origin obscure.] A short piece of gut or the like by which a fish-hook is attached to a longer line.

snib (snib), *v. t.; snibbed, snibbing.* [ME. *snibben*; from Scand., and akin to E. *snub*.] To check; reprove; rebuke; reprimand. [Now Sc. and prov. Eng.]

snick[1] (snik), *v. t.* [Origin uncertain: cf. *nick*[1], also *snicker-snee*.] To cut, snip, or nick; also, to strike sharply.—**snick**[1], *n.* A small cut; a nick; in *cricket*, a light, glancing blow given to the ball by the batsman, or the ball so hit.

snick[2] (snik), *v.* [Imit.] **I.** *tr.* To cause to make a clicking sound; snap (a gun, etc.). **II.** *intr.* To make a slight, sharp sound; click: as, "And ye may hear a breech-bolt *snick* where never a man is seen" (Kipling's "Ballad of East and West").—**snick**[2], *n.* A snicking sound; a click: as, "Hurree was no game shot, — the *snick* of a trigger made him change colour" (Kipling's "Kim," xiii.).

snick=a=snee (snik'ạ-snē″), *n.* See *snickersnee*.

snick-er (snik'ėr), *v.* [Imit.: cf. *nicker*[2].] **I.** *intr.* To laugh in a half-suppressed and often indecorous or disrespectful manner. Cf. *snigger*. **II.** *tr.* To utter with a snicker. —**snick'er**, *n.* A snickering laugh: as, "not able to repress a self-conscious *snicker*" (W. Churchill's "Coniston," i. 10). —**snick'er-er**, *n.*—**snick'er-ing-ly**, *adv.*

snick-er-snee (snik'ėr-snē″), *n.* [From an old phrase, *snick or snee* (also *snick and snee*), by corruption from D. *steken*, stick, stab, and *snijden*, cut.] A combat with cut-and-thrust knives (obs. or archaic); also, a cut-and-thrust knife, or a large knife for use as a weapon (now archaic or humorous).

snide (snīd). [Origin obscure.] **I.** *a.* Spurious, sham, counterfeit, or false, as jewelry, coin, etc.; not honestly done, as work; characterized by mean fraud or trickery; of persons, dishonest in a mean, tricky way. [Slang.] **II.** *n.* Something spurious or counterfeit, as an imitation gem; anything made or done dishonestly or fraudulently; also, a mean, tricky, or dishonest person; a cheat. [Slang.]

sniff (snif), *v.* [ME. *snyffen*: cf. *snuff*[2].] **I.** *intr.* To draw air through the nose in short, audible inspirations; clear the nose by so doing; sniffle, as with emotion; also, to smell by short inspirations (as, "My camel . . . lifted his head toward the desert and *sniffed*, as if he tasted home . . . in the unpolluted air": G. W. Curtis's "Howadji in Syria," i. 5); also, to show disdain, contempt, etc., by a sniff (often with *at*, and also fig.). **II.** *tr.* To draw in or up through the nose by sniffing, as air, odor, liquid, powder, etc.; inhale; also, to inhale or perceive the odor of, or smell (as, "They strolled out after dinner to *sniff* the sea": Galsworthy's "Patrician," ii. 10); fig., to perceive or detect as if by smelling (as, to *sniff* treachery); also, to express (disdain, etc.) by or as by a sniff; say with a sniff; also, to put (*aside*) with a sniff, as of contempt (as, "Thy wishes have all been *sniffed* aside": Carlyle's "Sartor Resartus," ii. 8).—

sniff, *n.* An act of sniffing; a single short, audible inspiration, as in clearing the nose, or the sound made; a single inhalation of something (as, a *sniff* of fresh air, or of the fragrance of flowers); a smell taken of something (as, a *sniff* of smelling-salts or of a vinaigrette); hence, a scent or odor perceived; also, a portion or quantity of anything to be sniffed (as, a *sniff* of cocaine); also, a short, audible inspiration serving to express disdain, contempt, or the like.— **sniff′er**, *n.* — **sniff′ing-ly**, *adv.*

snif-fle (snif′l), *v. i.*; *-fled*, *-fling*. [Freq. of *sniff*: cf. *snivel*.] To sniff repeatedly, as from a cold in the head or in repressing tearful emotion: as, "*Sniffling* a little to swallow his grief, he turned from the heartrending spectacle" (Scott's "Legend of Montrose," xiv.).— **snif′fle**, *n.* An act or sound of sniffling; *pl.*, with *the*, a condition marked by sniffling.— **snif′fler**, *n.*

sniff-y (snif′i), *a.* Inclined to sniff, as in disdain; disdainful; supercilious: as, "Some [hostesses] will sweep 'em [guests] in like a dustman, and some are very *sniffy*" (M. Hewlett's "Open Country," xi.). [Colloq.]

snift (snift), *v. and n.* Same as *sniff*. [Now chiefly prov. Eng.]

snig (snig), *n.* [ME. *snygge*; origin obscure.] An eel, esp. a young or small eel. [Prov. Eng.]

snig-ger (snig′ėr), etc. Same as *snicker*, etc. [The form *snigger* is more common in England, *snicker* in the U. S.]

snig-gle[1] (snig′l), *v. i. and n.* Same as *snigger* and *snicker*.

snig-gle[2] (snig′l), *v.*; *-gled*, *-gling*. [From *snig*.] **I.** *intr.* To fish for eels by thrusting a baited hook or the like into their holes or lurking-places. **II.** *tr.* To take, as an eel, by sniggling; catch; hook.— **snig′gler**, *n.*

snip (snip), *v.*; *snipped*, *snipping*. [D. *snippen*, snip, clip, = G. *schnippen*, snip, snap.] **I.** *tr.* To cut with a small, quick stroke, or a succession of such strokes, with scissors or the like (as, to *snip* cloth, paper, thread, etc.); also, to take off by or as by cutting thus (as, to *snip* off ragged ends; "His mother was *snipping* dead leaves from the window plants," Hardy's "Return of the Native," iii. 2); also, to cut out, shape, or make by cutting thus. **II.** *intr.* To cut with small, quick strokes, with scissors or the like.— **snip**, *n.* An act of snipping, as with scissors; also, a small cut made by snipping; also, a small piece snipped off; in general, a small piece, bit, or amount of anything; a young, small, or insignificant person (used in disparagement: colloq.); a share or snack (as, "a younger brother that is afraid to be mumped of his *snip*," Wycherley's "Love in a Wood," i. 2: now prov.); also, a white or light-colored spot or mark on a horse, esp. on the face; also, a tailor (colloq.). See also *snips*.

snipe (snīp), *n.*; *pl.* *snipes* or (esp. collectively) *snipe*. [ME. *snype*: cf. Icel. *snīpa*, MD. and MLG. *snippe*, G. *schnepfe*, snipe.] Any of the long-billed limicoline birds that constitute the genus *Gallinago*, frequenting marshy places and much sought by game-shooters, as *G. delicata* (the common American species, also called *jack-snipe* and *Wilson's snipe*), *G. cælestis* (the common European species, also called *whole-snipe*), or *S. gallinula* (a smaller European species, also called *jack-snipe* and *half-snipe*); sometimes, any bird of the same family (*Scolopacidæ*); also, a term of contempt for a person (see Shakspere's "Othello," i. 3. 391).— **snipe**, *v.*; *sniped*, *sniping*. **I.** *intr.* To shoot or hunt snipe; also, to shoot at soldiers, etc., at will, as opportunity offers, like a sportsman picking off game (said of scattered troops, civilians, etc., firing from under cover or at long range, otherwise than in regular battle). **II.** *tr.* To shoot at or shoot by sniping.— **snip-er** (snī′pėr), *n.*

Common American or Wilson's Snipe (*Gallinago delicata*).

snip-per (snip′ėr), *n.* One who snips; a tailor; *pl.*, scissors, shears, or the like.

snip-pet (snip′et), *n.* [Dim. of *snip*, *n.*] A small piece snipped off; a small bit, scrap, or fragment; also, a little or young snip (person) (colloq.: as, "Do you suppose these *snippets* would treat Alice the way they do if she could afford to entertain?" Tarkington's "Alice Adams," xiii.).— **snip′pet-y**, *a.* Of the nature of a snippet; consisting of snippets; scrappy.

snip-py (snip′i), *a.* [From *snip*, *v.* and *n.*] Sharp or curt in speech or manner, esp. in a supercilious way (colloq.); also, scrappy or fragmentary.

snips (snips), *n. pl.* or *sing.* [Pl. of *snip*, *n.*] Small, stout hand-shears for the use of workers in sheet-metal.

Snips.

snitch[1] (snich), *v. t.* [Cf. *snatch*.] To snatch, pilfer, or steal. [Prov. or slang.]

snitch[2] (snich), *n.* [Origin obscure.] An informer; one who turns state's evidence. [Slang.]— **snitch**[2], *v. i.* To turn informer; inform or tell on one. [Prov. or slang.]— **snitch′er**, *n.*

sniv-el (sniv′l), *v.*; *-eled* or *-elled*, *-eling* or *-elling*. [ME. *snyvelen*, *snevelen*: cf. AS. *snyflung*, sniveling, < *snofl*, mucus of the nose.] **I.** *intr.* To run at the nose; also, to draw up mucus audibly through the nose; also, to weep or cry with sniffing (as, "to take a lad from grammar . . . and . . . send him crying and *snivelling* into foreign countries": Steele, in "Spectator," 364); affect a tearful state; whine. **II.** *tr.* To utter with sniveling or sniffing.— **sniv′el**, *n.* Mucus running from the nose; also, a sniveling; a light sniff as in weeping; weak, forced, or pretended weeping; hypocritical show of feeling.— **sniv′el-er**, **sniv′el-ler**, *n.*

snob (snob), *n.* [Origin obscure.] A shoemaker, cobbler, or shoemaker's apprentice (prov. Eng., Sc., or colloq.); also, a person belonging to the lower classes of society, or lacking breeding or refinement; now, esp., one who is unduly influenced in his judgments or conduct by rank, wealth, etc., or their absence, servilely admiring, imitating, or cultivating those who possess these advantages, and looking down upon, ignoring, or acting in an overbearing manner toward those who do not; also, one who affects social importance and exclusiveness.— **snob-ber-y** (snob′ėr-i), *n.*; *pl.* *-ies* (-iz). The character or conduct of a snob; a snobbish trait or act.— **snob′bess**, *n.* A female snob.— **snob′bish**, *a.* Of, pertaining to, or characteristic of a snob (as, "Some writers, even American writers . . . display a *snobbish* shame of something homespun about these makers of America": H. G. Wells's "Outline of History," xxxvii. § 6); also, having the character of, or resembling, a snob (as, "That which we call a Snob, by any other name would still be *Snobbish*": Thackeray's "Book of Snobs," xviii.).— **snob′bish-ly**, *adv.* — **snob′bish-ness**, *n.*

snood (snöd), *n.* [AS. *snöd*.] A band or fillet for confining the hair; esp., the distinctive hair-band formerly worn by young unmarried women in Scotland and northern England; also, a snell or the like for a fish-hook.— **snood**, *v. t.* To bind or confine (the hair) with a snood; also, to attach (a fish-hook) to a snood or snell.

Snood.

snoop (snöp), *v. i.* [D. *snoepen*.] To prowl or pry in order to help one's self stealthily to dainties or other things; in general, to go about in a sneaking, prying way (as, "He did not remain . . . where he belonged, but *snooped* all over the island": Sinclair Lewis's "Arrowsmith," xxxi.); pry in a mean, sly manner. [Colloq.]— **snoop**, *n.* An act or instance of snooping; also, one who snoops. [Colloq.]— **snoop′er**, *n.*

snoot (snöt), *n.* Prov. or colloq. form of *snout*.

snooze (snöz), *v. i.*; *snoozed*, *snoozing*. [Origin obscure.] To sleep; slumber; doze; nap: as, "He tarried till the next morning, smoking and *snoozing*" (H. Melville's "Omoo," lii.). [Colloq.]— **snooze**, *n.* A sleep; a doze; a nap: as, "I . . . fell into the sweetest *snooze* that ever I was in in all my life" (Borrow's "Lavengro," iv.). [Colloq.]—**snooz′er,** *n.*

snoo-zle (snö′zl), *v.*; *-zled, -zling*. [Cf. *nuzzle* and *snooze*.] **I.** *intr.* To nuzzle, nestle, or snuggle; also, to snooze. [Colloq. or prov.] **II.** *tr.* To thrust (the nose, etc.) into something, as an animal does. [Colloq. or prov.]

snore (snōr), *v.*; *snored, snoring.* [ME. *snoren*, snort, snore; prob. imit.: cf. *snort.*] **I.** *intr.* To snort, as a horse or other animal (obs. or prov.); also, to roar, or move with a roaring sound, as the wind, a ship, etc. (chiefly Sc.); now, esp., to breathe during sleep through the open mouth, or the mouth and nose, with hoarse or harsh sounds. **II.** *tr.* To spend or pass (time) in snoring (with *away* or *out*); also, to bring, drive, etc., by snoring (as, "lazy nurse, who *snores* the sick man dead": Cowper's "Task," i. 97); also, to utter or express with or as with snores.—**snore,** *n.* An act of snoring, or the sound made; a loud, harsh respiration during sleep.—**snor-er** (snōr′ėr), *n.*

snort (snórt), *v.* [ME. *snorten*, snort, snore; prob. imit.: cf. *snore.*] **I.** *intr.* To force the breath violently through the nostrils with a loud, harsh sound, as a horse, etc.; hence, to make some sound resembling this (as, "The engine *snorted* . . . and the train Moved": Masefield's "Daffodil Fields," ii.); often, to express contempt, indignation, or the like by such a sound; also, to laugh outright or boisterously (colloq.); also, to snore†. **II.** *tr.* To utter with a snort (as, " 'Indeed!' *snorted* the great-aunt": Wister's "Virginian," xxix.); also, to expel or force out by or as by snorting (as, "The island . . . *snorting* a cataract Of rage-froth from every cranny and ledge": Lowell's "Pictures from Appledore," v.).—**snort,** *n.* An act or sound of snorting: as, "Mr. Beard . . . swung around with a *snort* of pain" (W. Churchill's "Coniston," ii. 4); "She heard a loud *snort* of shattering contempt from Louisa" (Arnold Bennett's "Hilda Lessways," v. 1).—**snort′er,** *n.*

snot (snot), *n.* [ME. *snotte* = D. *snot.*] Nasal mucus; also, a term of contempt for a person. [Prov. or vulgar.]

snot-ter (snot′ėr), *n.* [Origin uncertain.] *Naut.*, a small rope attached at one end to a light yard-arm, passing under the eye of the yard's lift and brace, and attached at the other end to the tripping-line (see *tripping-line*); also, a becket fitted on a mast to hold the lower end of a sprit.

snot-ty¹ (snot′i), *a.* [From *snot.*] Foul with snot (prov. or vulgar); hence, dirty, mean, or contemptible (prov. or vulgar); also, pert, saucy, or impudent (prov. Eng. and Sc.).

snot-ty² (snot′i), *n.*; pl. *snotties* (-iz). [Cf. *snotty¹.*] In the British navy, a midshipman. [Colloq.]

snout (snout), *n.* [ME. *snoute, snute,* = D. *snuit* = MLG. *snūte* = G. *schnauze*, snout.] A part of an animal's head projecting forward and containing the nose, or the nose and jaws (as, the *snout* of a hog, fox, dog, or crocodile); the muzzle; sometimes, the trunk of an elephant; the proboscis of any animal; a beak or beak-like part, as of a turtle; a rostrum, as of an insect; also, a person's nose, esp. when large or prominent (humorous or contemptuous); also, anything that resembles or suggests an animal's snout in shape, function, etc.; a nozzle or spout; the beak of a ship; a projecting part of land, rock, etc.; the front or lower end of a glacier.—**snout,** *v. t.* or *i.* To push, dig, root, etc., with or as with the snout: as, "They *snout* the bushes and stones aside" (Kipling's "Hyænas").—**snout′=bee″tle,** *n.* Any of a group of beetles (*Rhynchophora*) having the head more or less prolonged into a snout or rostrum, as *Epicærus imbricatus*, a species common in the eastern U. S. and often highly injurious to plants; a weevil or

Snout-beetle (*Epicærus imbricatus*). (Line shows natural size.)

Crystals of Snow.

Snotter (becket). — *a*, sprit with the lower end in the snotter *b*.

curculio.—**snout′ed,** *a.* Having a snout: as, "the *snouted* mole" (Whittier's "Barefoot Boy").

snow¹ (snō), *n.* [D. *snauw* = LG. *snau*.] An old type of sailing-vessel with a foremast, mainmast, and trysail-mast.

snow² (snō), *n.* [AS. *snāw* = D. *sneeuw* = G. *schnee* = Icel. *snær* = Goth. *snaiws*, snow; akin to L. *niv*- (nom. *nix*), Gr. νίφα (acc.), snow.] The aqueous vapor of the atmosphere precipitated in partially frozen crystalline form and falling to the earth in white flakes; these flakes as forming a layer on the ground, etc.; the fall of these flakes; also, a fall of snow; a snow-fall; a snow-storm; also, a winter or year (as, "Thirty *snows* had not yet shed Their glory on the warrior's head": Longfellow's "Burial of the Minnisink"); also, an expanse of snow (as, "Yonder, where the far *snows* blanch Mute Mont Blanc": Browning's "La Saisiaz"); also, something resembling snow; any of various congealed or other chemical substances of snow-like appearance (as, carbon-dioxide *snow*); cocaine or heroin (slang); the white hair of age (as, "attiring herself like summer though her head was covered with *snow*": Thackeray's "Henry Esmond," i. 2); white blossoms; the white color of snow (chiefly poetic).—**snow²,** *v.* **I.** *intr.* To send down snow; fall as snow; hence, to descend like snow. **II.** *tr.* To let fall as or like snow; also, to cover, bury, obstruct, etc., with or as with snow (with *over, under, up,* etc.); also, to cause (the hair, etc.) to turn white like snow.

snow-ball (snō′bâl). **I.** *n.* A ball made of snow; a round mass of snow pressed or rolled together; also, any of various dishes, confections, etc., having the appearance of a ball of snow; also, a shrub, a cultivated variety of the cranberry-tree, *Viburnum opulus*, with white flowers in large globular clusters. **II.** *a.* Snowball-like; growing or increasing like a snowball rolled along in the snow: applied to a system of obtaining contributions whereby each contributor asks a certain number of other persons to contribute and also requests each of them to ask as many more to contribute, and so on.—**snow′ball,** *v. t.* or *i.* To pelt with or throw snowballs.—**snow′ball″ing,** *n.* The act or sport of throwing snowballs; also, any process of growing or increasing in amount or extent analogous to the increase of a snowball rolled along in the snow.

Snowball (*Viburnum opulus*).

snow-ber-ry (snō′ber″i), *n.*; pl. *-berries* (-iz). A caprifoliaceous shrub, *Symphoricarpos racemosus*, native in North America, cultivated for its ornamental (but not edible) white berries; the berry itself; also, a rubiaceous shrub, *Chiococca racemosa*, native in tropical and subtropical America, bearing similar berries.

snow-bird (snō′bėrd), *n.* A junco, esp. *Junco hiemalis*, a small slate-gray bird commonly seen in flocks in certain localities during winter; also, the snow-bunting; also, a small

Snowbird (*Junco hiemalis*).

coal-mine, worked by only a few men (colloq.); also, a habitual user of cocaine or heroin (slang).

snow=blind (snō′blīnd), *a.* Having the sight dimmed or affected by exposure of the eyes to the glare of snow.—**snow′=blind″ness**, *n.*

snow=blink (snō′blingk), *n.* The peculiar reflection that arises from fields of snow or ice; ice-blink.

snow=bound (snō′bound), *a.* Shut in or blocked by snow.

snow=broth (snō′brôth), *n.* Melting or melted snow; water produced by the melting of snow.

snow=bun-ting (snō′bun″ting), *n.* A fringilline bird, *Plectrophanes nivalis*, inhabiting cold regions, commonly of a white color varied with black or brown.

snow-bush (snō′bush), *n.* Any of several ornamental shrubs bearing a profusion of white flowers, as *Ceanothus velutinus*, a tall rhamnaceous shrub of western North America.

snow=drift (snō′drift), *n.* A mass or bank of snow driven together by the wind (as, "As against the warmth of Titan's fire, *Snowdrifts* consume": Fairfax's tr. Tasso's "Jerusalem Delivered," xx. 136); also, snow driven before the wind (as, "The moon was full, and its beams struggled through scudding clouds and *snow-drift*": Roosevelt's "Ranch Life and the Hunting-Trail," xi.).

Snow-bunting, male, in breeding-plumage.

snow-drop (snō′drop), *n.* A European amaryllidaceous plant, *Galanthus nivalis*, bearing pendulous white flowers which appear very early in spring: as, "Fair-handed Spring unbosoms every grace — Throws out the *snow-drop* and the crocus first" (Thomson's "Seasons," Spring, 530).

snow-fall (snō′fâl), *n.* A fall of snow; the snow falling at one time; also, the amount of snow falling at a particular place, as in a given time.

snow=fence (snō′fens′), *n.* A fence built, as along the side of a railroad, to check the drifting of snow.

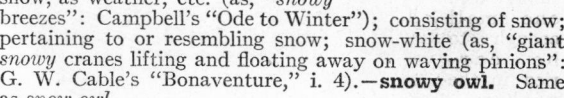

Snow-fence.

snow-flake (snō′flāk), *n.* One of the small feathery masses or flakes in which snow falls; also, the snow-bunting; also, any of certain European amaryllidaceous plants (genus *Leucoium*) resembling the snowdrop; also, a pattern in weaving by which small knots or tufts are produced, distributed over a fabric, somewhat resembling a sprinkling of snow.

snow-i-ly (snō′i-li), *adv.* In a snowy manner.—**snow′i-ness**, *n.*

snow=leop-ard (snō′lep″ärd), *n.* The ounce, *Felis uncia.*

snow=lim-it (snō′lim″it), *n.* See *snow-line.*

snow=line (snō′līn), *n.* The line, as on mountains, above which there is perpetual snow, varying locally in the same latitudes, but, in general, descending as one proceeds from the equator toward either pole, and being at an altitude of from 15,000 to 18,000 feet

Snow-owl.

in the tropics and touching sea-level in the polar regions; sometimes, the line on the earth north of the equator or that south of the equator marking the limit of the fall of snow at sea-level.

snow=owl (snō′oul), *n.* A large owl, *Nyctea nyctea*, inhabiting arctic and northerly regions of both hemispheres, and having the plumage more or less white. See cut in preceding column.

snow=plow (snō′plou), *n.* An implement or machine for clearing away snow from highways, railroads, etc.

snow=scape (snō′skāp), *n.* [With *-scape* as in *landscape.*] A picture or a view of a snowy scene.

snow=shed (snō′shed), *n.* A structure, as over an extent of railroad on a mountain-side, for protection against snow.

snow=shoe (snō′shö), *n.* A contrivance attached to the foot to enable the wearer to walk on deep snow without sinking in, as a ski, or, esp., a light racket-shaped frame across which is stretched a network of rawhide.—**snow′=shoe**, *v. i.*; -shoed, -shoeing. To walk or travel on snowshoes.—**snow″=sho″er**, *n.*

snow-slide (snō′slīd), *n.* The sliding down of a mass of snow on a steep slope; also, the mass of snow. Also **snow′slip.**

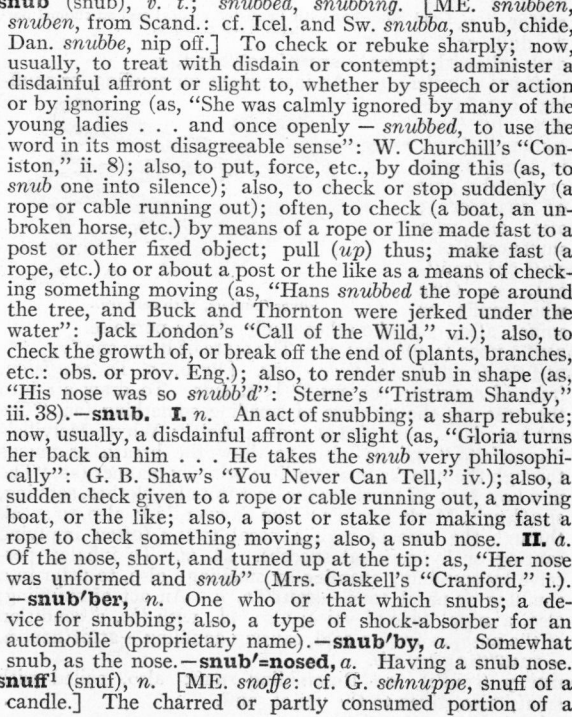

Canadian Snow-shoe.

snow=storm (snō′stôrm), *n.* A storm accompanied by a heavy fall of snow.

snow=white (snō′hwīt′), *a.* [AS. snāwhwīt.] White as snow.

snow-y (snō′i), *a.*; compar. *snowier*, superl. *snowiest*. [AS. snāwig.] Abounding in or covered with snow (as, "The *snowy* top Of cold Olympus": Milton's "Paradise Lost," i. 515); characterized by snow, as weather, etc. (as, "*snowy* breezes": Campbell's "Ode to Winter"); consisting of snow; pertaining to or resembling snow; snow-white (as, "giant *snowy* cranes lifting and floating away on waving pinions": G. W. Cable's "Bonaventure," i. 4).—**snowy owl.** Same as *snow-owl.*

snub (snub), *v. t.*; snubbed, snubbing. [ME. *snubben*, *snuben*, from Scand.: cf. Icel. and Sw. *snubba*, snub, chide, Dan. *snubbe*, nip off.] To check or rebuke sharply; now, usually, to treat with disdain or contempt; administer a disdainful affront or slight to, whether by speech or action or by ignoring (as, "She was calmly ignored by many of the young ladies . . . and once openly — *snubbed*, to use the word in its most disagreeable sense": W. Churchill's "Coniston," ii. 8); also, to put, force, etc., by doing this (as, to *snub* one into silence); also, to check or stop suddenly (a rope or cable running out); often, to check (a boat, an unbroken horse, etc.) by means of a rope or line made fast to a post or other fixed object; pull (*up*) thus; make fast (a rope, etc.) to or about a post or the like as a means of checking something moving (as, "Hans *snubbed* the rope around the tree, and Buck and Thornton were jerked under the water": Jack London's "Call of the Wild," vi.); also, to check the growth of, or break off the end of (plants, branches, etc.: obs. or prov. Eng.); also, to render snub in shape (as, "His nose was so *snubb'd*": Sterne's "Tristram Shandy," iii. 38).—**snub. I.** *n.* An act of snubbing; a sharp rebuke; now, usually, a disdainful affront or slight (as, "Gloria turns her back on him . . . He takes the *snub* very philosophically": G. B. Shaw's "You Never Can Tell," iv.); also, a sudden check given to a rope or cable running out, a moving boat, or the like; also, a post or stake for making fast a rope to check something moving; also, a snub nose. **II.** *a.* Of the nose, short, and turned up at the tip: as, "Her nose was unformed and *snub*" (Mrs. Gaskell's "Cranford," i.).—**snub′ber**, *n.* One who or that which snubs; a device for snubbing; also, a type of shock-absorber for an automobile (proprietary name).—**snub′by**, *a.* Somewhat snub, as the nose.—**snub′=nosed**, *a.* Having a snub nose.

snuff[1] (snuf), *n.* [ME. *snoffe*: cf. G. *schnuppe*, snuff of a candle.] The charred or partly consumed portion of a candle-wick or the like; also, a candle almost burned out†. —**snuff**[1], *v. t.* To cut off or remove the snuff of (a candle, etc.); also (with *out*), to extinguish (as, "The lamps . . . were visible — slight yellow specks, that seemed to be rapidly *snuffed* out . . . as intervening obstacles hid them from the sight": Dickens's "Barnaby Rudge," iii.); cause to disappear from view: put an end to suddenly and completely.

snuff[2] (snuf), *v.* [Prob. < MD. D. *snuffen*, snuff, sniff: cf. *sniff*.] **I.** *tr.* To draw in through the nose by inhaling (as, "The pack impatient *snuff* the tainted gale," Pope's tr. Homer's "Odyssey," xix.; to *snuff* up liquid for medicinal purposes); also, to perceive by or as by smelling (as, "The cow . . . from afar can find The change of heav'n, and *snuffs* it in the wind": Dryden's tr. Virgil's "Georgics," i. 519); also, to examine by smelling, as an animal does. **II.** *intr.* To draw air, etc., into the nostrils by inhaling, as in order to smell something (as, "'Smell that . . . Isn't it good?' Dick *snuffed* luxuriously": Kipling's "Light That Failed," xi.); also, to express disdain, contempt, displeasure, etc., by snuffing or sniffing (often with *at*: now rare); also, to inhale powdered tobacco; take snuff.—**snuff**[2], *n.* An act of snuffing; an inhalation; a sniff; sometimes, a sniff of disdain, displeasure, etc.; hence, offense or umbrage, or a fit of displeasure (archaic or Sc.); also, smell, scent, or odor (as, "All whiffs, and sniffs, and puffs, and *snuffs*, From metals, minerals, and dyewood stuffs": Hood's "Turtles," 34); also, a preparation of powdered tobacco taken into the nostrils by inhalation; a pinch of such tobacco (as, "Hendry once offered Mr. Dishart a *snuff* from his mull": Barrie's "Auld Licht Idylls," iii.); also, a quantity of anything snuffed up (as, a *snuff* of cocaine); hence, a small quantity of anything.—**up to snuff**, not easily deceived; wideawake. [Colloq.]—

snuff'=box, *n.* A box for holding snuff, esp. one small enough to be carried in the pocket.—**snuff'=color**, *n.* A dull or dark yellowish brown.—**snuff'=colored**, *a.*

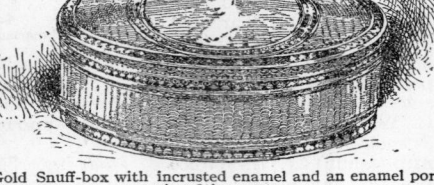
Gold Snuff-box with incrusted enamel and an enamel portrait, 18th century.

snuff-er[1] (snuf'er), *n.* An instrument for snuffing, or snuffing out, candles, etc. (now commonly in *pl.* in same sense, or called a *pair of snuffers*); also, one who snuffs candles.

snuff-er[2] (snuf'er), *n.* One who snuffs or

Silver Snuffers, 18th century.

sniffs; also, one who takes snuff; also, a porpoise.

snuff-i-ness (snuf'i-nes), *n.* The state of being snuffy.

snuf-fle (snuf'l), *v.*; *-fled, -fling.* [Prob. < D. *snuffelen*, freq. of *snuffen*: see *snuff*[2].] **I.** *intr.* To draw air into the nose for the purpose of smelling something (as, "The old hound . . . *snuffled* at every pebble": Whyte-Melville's "Katerfelto," xxiv.); also, to draw the breath or mucus through the nostrils in an audible or noisy manner (as, "The new boy went off brushing the dust from his clothes, sobbing, *snuffling*": Mark Twain's "Tom Sawyer," i.); also, to speak through the nose or with a nasal twang (often implying canting or hypocritical speech). **II.** *tr.* To inhale; perceive by snuffling; examine by smelling; also, to utter in a snuffling or nasal tone.—**snuf'fle**, *n.* An act of snuffling; also, a nasal tone of voice; also, *pl.*, with *the*, a condition of the nose, as from a cold, causing snuffling.—**snuf'fler**, *n.* —**snuf'fling-ly**, *adv.*

snuff-y (snuf'i), *a.* Resembling snuff; also, soiled with snuff; also, given to the use of snuff.

snug (snug). [Origin uncertain.] **I.** *a.*; compar. *snugger*, superl. *snuggest.* Trim, neat, or compactly arranged, as a ship or its parts (as, "We had all hands at work to strike our topmasts, and make everything *snug* and close, that the ship might ride as easy as possible": Defoe's "Robinson Crusoe," i. 1); adequately protected from the weather; also, fitting closely, but not too closely, as a garment; also, comfortable or cozy, as a place, accommodations, etc., more or less compact or limited in size and sheltered or warm (as, "She had a *snug*, well-furnished house": Irving's "Sketch-Book," Rip Van Winkle); comfortably placed or circumstanced, as persons, etc. (as, "It was a kind of afternoon on which nice people . . . like to be *snug* at home": S. Butler's "Way of All Flesh," xxix.); pleasant or agreeable, esp. in a small, exclusive way (as, "They did occasionally give *snug* dinners to three or four literary men at a time": Irving's "Tales of a Traveler," ii. 2); also, enabling one to live in comfort (as, a *snug* fortune); sometimes, moderately well-to-do, as persons (chiefly Ir.: as, "You're a *snug* man, Mat," Lover's "Handy Andy," viii.); also, in concealment or hiding (as, to lie *snug*); secret (as, "*Snug*'s the word, I shrug and am silent": Congreve's "Way of the World," i.). **II.** *adv.* In a snug manner; snugly.—**snug**, *v.*; *snugged, snugging.* **I.** *intr.* To lie closely or comfortably; snuggle; nestle. **II.** *tr.* To make snug; put in a snug position.—**snug-ger-y** (snug'ėr-i), *n.*; *pl. -ies* (-iz). A snug place or position (as, "In the kitchen each member of the family had established unto him or her self some little pet private *snuggery*, some chair or stool, some individual nook": Mrs. Stowe's "Oldtown Folks," vi.); a comfortable or cozy room, esp. a small one into which a person retires for seclusion (as, "I . . . fled . . . to the sanctuary of my uncle's study, his *snuggery*": H. G. Wells's "Tono-Bungay," iii. 2. § 2); a comfortable or cozy house or dwelling; sometimes, a comfortable position or post (as, "ecclesiastical *snuggeries*": Trollope's "Warden," iii.).

snug-gle (snug'l), *v.*; *-gled, -gling.* [Freq. of *snug*.] **I.** *intr.* To lie or press closely, as for warmth or comfort or from affection; assume a snug position; nestle; cuddle. **II.** *tr.* To draw or press closely, as for comfort or from affection; also, to wrap closely.

snug-ly (snug'li), *adv.* In a snug manner.—**snug'ness**, *n.*

so (sō), *adv.* [ME. *so, so, sow, swa*, < AS. *swā* = D. *zoo* = G. *so* = Icel. *svā* = Goth. *swa*, so: cf. *also, as*[1], and *such*.] In the way or manner indicated, described, or implied (as, do it *so*); in that or this manner or fashion; thus; also, as stated or reported (as, is that *so*? "That is not *so*, sire," S. J. Weyman's "Gentleman of France," xx.); sometimes, equivalent to 'is that so?' (as, 'He says he will not come.' '*So*?'); also, in the aforesaid state or condition (as, it is broken, and has long been *so*); also, used in expressing assent, approval, or the like, as equivalent to 'so be it' or 'it is well' (as, "For my sake read it over, And if it please you, *so*; if not, why, *so*": Shakspere's "Two Gentlemen of Verona," ii. 1. 137); also, to that extent, or in that degree (as, do not walk *so* fast; has it been *so* long? she was *so* ill that she could not come, or *so* ill as to be unable to come); hence, very or extremely (as, you are *so* kind); very greatly (as, my head aches *so!*); also, used as the antecedent in the correlation *so . . . as* expressing comparison, in the sense 'to such a degree or extent' (as, *so* [or *as*] far *as* I know; "Arrows were shot by the English *so* late as at the Isle of Ré in 1627," Morley's "Oliver Cromwell," ii. 1: now often in negative and interrogative constructions, as, it is not *so* bad *as* it was [this form of expression now being considered preferable by some authorities to 'it is not *as* bad *as* it was']; is there anything *so* [or *as*] bad *as* that?).—**and so,** a continuative used to confirm or emphasize a previous statement (as, I said I would come, *and so* I will); also, likewise or correspondingly (as, he is going, *and so* am I); consequently or accordingly (as, she is ill, *and so* cannot come); thereupon or thereafter (as, *and so* they were married).—**or so,** about thus, or about that amount or number: as, a day *or so* ago; "a mile *or so* from home" (W. H. Hudson's "Far Away and Long Ago," xx.).—**so as,** with the result or purpose (followed by an infinitive, or, now only in provincial use, by a clause); also, provided that (as, "He could play 'em a tune on any sort of pot you please, *so as* it was iron or block tin": Dickens's "Bleak House," xxvi.).—**so called,** called or designated thus, or by this name or term (as, the Smithsonian Institution, *so called* after James Smithson, an English scientist who left the money to found it); sometimes, called or styled thus, but not properly or correctly (as, their liberty, *so called,* is only license): when used attributively, written with a hyphen (see *so-called*).—**so that,** with the effect or result that (as, "The turf roof . . . had fallen entirely in; *so that* the hut was of no use to me": Stevenson's "Kidnapped," xiv.); also, in order that (as, he wrote *so that* they might expect him); also, provided that (as, "*So that* ye do not serve me sparrow-hawks For supper, I will enter": Tennyson's "Marriage of Geraint," 304).—**so to speak** (or **say**), to use such a manner of speaking; to use that expression: a phrase used parenthetically as if in apology for the use of some current, figurative, or unprecise expression.— **so,** *conj.* As†; also, used elliptically for *and so* (see phrase above); also, used elliptically for *so that* (see phrase above).— **so,** *interj.* A word of checking or command, equivalent to 'that will do!' or, as to a restless animal, 'stand still!'

soak (sōk), *v.* [AS. *socian,* soak, related to *sūcan,* E. *suck.*] **I.** *intr.* To lie in and become saturated or permeated with water or some other liquid; hence, to be thoroughly wet (used in *soaking, ppr.*: as, "The place was *soaking* with the dew," Stevenson's "Master of Ballantrae," vii.); also, to pass, as a liquid, through pores or interstices (usually with *in, through, out,* etc.); esp., to enter by so doing; penetrate by saturation; also, to drink immoderately (colloq.: as, "You do nothing but *soak* with the guests all day long," Goldsmith's "Vicar of Wakefield," xxi.). **II.** *tr.* To place and keep in liquid in order to saturate thoroughly; steep; also, to wet thoroughly, or drench (as, "It rained very hard all the day; I was thoroughly *soaked*": B. Franklin's "Autobiography," ii.); permeate thoroughly, as liquid or moisture does; also, to intoxicate with liquor (slang); also, to bake thoroughly, as bread (now prov.); subject (an ingot, etc.) to prolonged heating, as to make the temperature uniform throughout; also, to put in pawn (slang); also, to beat hard, punish severely, charge exorbitantly, etc. (slang, U. S.); also, to draw (*out*) by or as by soaking; hence, to drain† or exhaust†; also, to take in or up by absorption (lit. or fig., and often with *up*: as, blotting-paper *soaks* up ink; "The day was still glowing, and . . . his refreshed senses *soaked* up its beauty," Galsworthy's "Saint's Progress," iii. 7); absorb; also, to drink, esp. to excess (colloq.). —**soak,** *n.* The act of soaking, or the state of being soaked; also, the liquid in which anything is soaked; also, a heavy drinker (slang).—**soak-age** (sō′kåj), *n.* The act of soaking, or of soaking through or up; also, liquid which has oozed out; also, liquid absorbed by soaking.—**soak′a-way″,** *n.* A place through which water soaks or drains away: as, "On an offensive front they [trenches] have vertical sides of unsupported earth and occasional *soakaways* for rain covered by wooden gratings" (H. G. Wells's "Italy, France, and Britain at War," iii. 3).—**soak′er,** *n.* One who or that which soaks; often, an immoderate drinker (colloq.).— **soak′ing-ly,** *adv.*

so=and=so (sō′ănd-sō″), *n.* Some one or something not definitely named: as, Mrs. *So-and-so;* "She would say that she had intended to do *so-and-so* and to buy *so-and-so*" (Arnold Bennett's "Mr. Prohack," ix.).

soap (sōp), *n.* [AS. *sāpe* = D. *zeep* = G. *seife,* soap: cf. L. *sapo(n-),* soap, from the same Teut. source, and E. *saponaceous, saponify,* etc.] A substance used for washing and cleansing purposes, usually made by treating a fat with an alkali (as sodium or potassium hydroxide), and consisting chiefly of the sodium or potassium salts of the acids contained in the fat; hence, any metallic salt of an acid derived from a fat; also, fig., smooth words, or flattery (colloq.: more commonly 'soft soap,' see phrase following); also, money, esp. as used for bribery in politics (slang, U. S.).—**Castile soap.** See entry in alphabetical place.—**green soap,** a soap made chiefly from potassium hydroxide and linseed-oil, used in treating skin-diseases.—**soft soap,** the semifluid soap produced when potassium hydroxide is used; also, smooth words, or flattery (colloq.: as, "He and I are great chums, and a little *soft soap* will go a long way with him," Hughes's "Tom Brown at Oxford," xxxiii.).—**soap,** *v. t.*

To rub, cover, or treat with soap; also, to ply with smooth words, or flatter (colloq.: cf. *soft-soap, v. t.*).

soap=bark (sōp′bärk), *n.* The inner bark of a tree, *Quillaia saponaria,* of Chile, used as a substitute for soap; any of various other saponaceous barks, as of several tropical American shrubs of the mimosaceous genus *Pithecolobium;* also, a plant yielding such bark.

soap-ber-ry (sōp′ber″i), *n.;* pl. *-berries* (-iz). The fruit of any of certain tropical and subtropical trees of the genus *Sapindus,* used as a substitute for soap; also, any of the trees bearing such fruit, as *S. drummondi,* of the southwestern U. S., which yields a useful wood.

soap=box (sōp′boks), *n.* A box, esp. a wooden box, in which soap is packed; often, an empty wooden box of this kind used as a convenient temporary platform, as by agitators addressing gatherings of persons on the public streets (also attrib.: as, a *soap-box* orator).—**soap′=box,** *v. i.* To address or harangue an audience from a soap-box or the like serving as a platform, as on the street.—**soap′= box″er,** *n.*

Branch with Fruits of Soapberry (*Sapindus drummondi*).— *a*, a flower.

soap-er-y (sō′pėr-i), *n.;* pl. *-ies* (-iz). An establishment for manufacturing soap.

soap-i-ly (sō′pi-li), *adv.* In a soapy manner.—**soap′i-ness,** *n.*

soap=plant (sōp′plant), *n.* Any of various plants of which some portion may be used as a substitute for soap; esp., a liliaceous plant, *Chlorogalum pomeridianum,* of California, whose bulbs are so used.

soap-root (sōp′röt), *n.* Any of certain old-world silenaceous herbs (genus *Gypsophila*) whose roots are used as a substitute for soap.

soap-stone (sōp′stōn), *n.* A massive variety of talc with a soapy or greasy feel, used for hearths, foot-warmers, griddles, etc.

soap=suds (sōp′sudz), *n. pl.* Suds made with water and soap.

soap-wort (sōp′wèrt), *n.* A silenaceous herb, *Saponaria officinalis,* whose leaves are used as a cleansing agent.

soap-y (sō′pi), *a.;* compar. *soapier,* superl. *soapiest.* Containing, or impregnated with, soap (as, *soapy* water); covered with soap or lather; of the nature of soap; resembling soap; pertaining to or characteristic of soap (as, a *soapy* feel); also, fig., unctuous, ingratiating, or smooth-tongued (slang).

soar (sōr), *v.* [OF. F. *essorer,* < L. *ex-,* out, + *aura,* air.] **I.** *intr.* To fly upward, as a bird (as, "the thrilling strains of the skylark . . . as she *soared* towards the heavens": R. Graves's "Spiritual Quixote," ii. 5); mount upward in the air to a great height with little advance in any other direction; also, to fly at a great height, without visible movements of the pinions, as a bird; glide along at a height, as an aëroplane; in general, to rise or ascend to a height; rise imposingly to a great altitude, as a mountain (as, "Far away to the east was seen the conical head of Orizaba *soaring* high into the clouds": Prescott's "Conquest of Mexico," iii. 6); fig., to rise to a higher or more exalted level; aspire

Upper part of Stem with Flowers of Soapwort.

beyond the commonplace or ordinary level. **II.** *tr.* To perform (a flight) by soaring; reach in soaring (as, "stupendous heights to *soar*": Young's "Night Thoughts," iv. 611); fly upward through (the air: as, "*soaring* th' air sublime," Milton's "Paradise Lost," vii. 421).—**soar,** *n.* The act or an act of soaring; the height attained in soaring.—**soar′er,** *n.*—**soar′ing-ly,** *adv.*

sob[1] (sob), *v. t.*; *sobbed, sobbing.* [Cf. *sop, v.*] To soak or saturate, as with water. [Prov.]

sob[2] (sob), *v.*; *sobbed, sobbing.* [ME. *sobben*; perhaps imit.] **I.** *intr.* To utter a sound caused by a convulsive catching of the breath, under the influence of violent emotion, esp. grief; weep with such sounds (as, "*sobbing* and crying, and wringing her hands as if her heart would break": Sterne's "Tristram Shandy," iv. 16); hence, to make a sound resembling this (as, "The wild Winds flew round, *sobbing* in their dismay": Shelley's "Adonais," xiv.). **II.** *tr.* To utter with sobs; also, to put, send, etc., by sobbing or with sobs (as, to *sob* one's self to sleep).—**sob**[2]. **I.** *n.* An act of sobbing; a convulsive catching of the breath as under the influence of grief (as, "Her body was shaken with *sobs*, though the tears came not": W. Churchill's "Coniston," ii. 11); any sound suggesting this (as, "The anchor came up with a *sob*": Kipling's "Captains Courageous," iii.). **II.** *a.* Seeking, designed, or fitted to call forth sobs or to appeal strongly to the emotions, as of readers or hearers (orig. in journalistic use); pathetic; emotional: as, a *sob* sister (orig., a woman writer of pathetic or emotional newspaper articles); a *sob* story; *sob* stuff. [Slang.]—**sob′bing,** *n.* The act of one who sobs; the sound produced by this.—**sob′bing-ly,** *adv.*

sob-by (sob′i), *a.* [From *sob*[1]: cf. *soppy.*] Soaked, as with water; wet, as ground. [Prov.]

so-be-it (sō-bē′it), *conj.* [Orig. three words, *so be it.*] If it be so that; provided. [Archaic.]

so-ber (sō′bėr), *a.* [OF. F. *sobre,* < L. *sobrius,* sober, not drunk, temperate, moderate, prudent, appar. < *so-,* for *se-,* without, apart, + *ebrius,* drunk: cf. *solve* and *ebriety.*] Free from the influence of intoxicating liquor; not intoxicated or drunk; also, not given to the use of strong drink; habitually temperate in the use of liquor; hence, temperate in general; not given to the indulgence of the appetite; characterized by absence of excess or indulgence, as diet; also, quiet or sedate in demeanor, as persons (as, "a *sober* thoughtful man": Trollope's "Barchester Towers," xxiv.); serious; grave; solemn; not mirthful or jocular; marked by seriousness, gravity, solemnity, etc., as demeanor, speech, etc. (as, "I do not assert that in *sober* earnest he expects to be shown all these wonders at once": Lamb's "Old Margate Hoy"); also, free from haste, excitement, violence, etc. (as, "Legions . . . move to meet their foes with *sober* pace": Dryden's tr. Virgil's "Georgics," ii. 380); showing self-control; also, free from excess, extravagance, or exaggeration (as, *sober* facts; a *sober* estimate; "cruelties which even in the most accurate and *sober* narrative excite just detestation," Macaulay's "Hist. of Eng.," ii.); subdued in tone, as color; not gay or showy, as clothes (as, "Aunt Mary's *sober* bonnet and brooch and gown": W. Churchill's "Modern Chronicle," i. 1); also, sane or rational (as, "people in their *sober* senses": Lover's "Handy Andy," xliv.); also, small, slight, or poor (chiefly Sc.).—**so′ber,** *v. t.* or *i.* To make or become sober.—**so′ber-ly,** *adv.*—**so′ber=mind′ed,** *a.* Having or showing a sober mind; self-controlled; sensible. —**so′ber=mind′ed-ness,** *n.*—**so′ber-ness,** *n.*—**so′ber-sid″ed** (-sī″ded), *a.* Being a sobersides; of a serious disposition: as, "She's not a *sober-sided* woman for all her calm" (Eden Phillpotts's "Red Redmaynes," vi.).—**so′ber-sides,** *n.* A sedate or serious person: as, "a melancholy *sober-sides*" (C. Brontë's "Villette," xxviii.).

So-bran-je (sō-brän′ye), *n.* [Bulg., 'assembly.'] The national assembly of Bulgaria, consisting of a single chamber of elected deputies.

so-bri-e-ty (sō-brī′ẹ-ti), *n.* [L. *sobrietas.*] The state or quality of being sober; temperance or moderation in the use of strong drink; moderation in the indulgence of the appetite generally; seriousness, gravity, or solemnity; avoidance of excess or extravagance in any respect; saneness or soundness, as of judgment.

so-bri-quet (sō′bri-kā, F. so-brē-kä), *n.* [F.; origin uncertain.] A nickname.

soc (sok), *n.* Same as *soke.*

soc-age (sok′ạj), *n.* [AF. *socage,* < ML. *soca,* E. *soke.*] A former tenure of lands in England by the performance of certain determinate services.—**soc′ag-er** (-ạ-jėr), *n.* One who held land by socage.

so=called (sō′kâld′), *a.* Called or designated thus; usually, called or styled thus (by the name or term used), but not properly or with admitted truth: chiefly in attributive use (as, their *so-called* liberty is only license). See also phrase *so called,* under *so, adv.*

soc′cage, etc. See *socage,* etc.

soc-cer (sok′ėr), *n.* [From *assoc.,* abbr. of *association.*] A form of the game of football in which the use of the hands and arms either for playing the ball or for interfering with an opponent is prohibited. Also called *Association football.* Cf. *Rugby football.*

so-cia-ble (sō′shạ-bl), *a.* [F. *sociable,* < L. *sociabilis,* < *sociare,* associate, join, < *socius,* companion: see *social.*] Inclined to associate with or be in the company of others (as, "Man is said to be a *sociable* animal": Addison, in "Spectator," 9); also, disposed to be friendly or agreeable in company; companionable; also, characterized by or pertaining to intercourse or companionship with others, esp. friendly intercourse (as, *sociable* habits).—**sociable weaver=bird.** See *weaver-bird.*—**so′cia-ble,** *n.* An informal gathering of people for social purposes, esp. a meeting of the members of a church: as, "You'll see her settled down one of these days, and teaching Sunday School and helping at *sociables*" (Sinclair Lewis's "Main Street," xxxix.). [U. S.]—**so″cia-bil′i-ty** (-bil′i-ti), **so′cia-ble-ness,** *n.*—**so′cia-bly,** *adv.*

so-cial (sō′shạl), *a.* [F. *social,* < L. *socialis,* < *socius,* companion, associate, partner, ally, as adj. sharing, associated, allied: akin to L. *sequi,* follow, Skt. *sakhi,* companion, *sac-,* accompany, follow: cf. *sequent.*] Pertaining to, devoted to, or characterized by friendly companionship, intercourse, or relations (as, *social* pleasures; a *social* evening or gathering; a *social* club); inclined toward friendly intercourse or relations, or sociable, as persons or the disposition, tastes, spirit, etc.; sometimes, pertaining to, connected with, or suited to the intercourse of polite or fashionable society (as, a *social* function; *social* prominence; *social* graces); also, living, or disposed to live, in companionship with others, or in a community, rather than in isolation (as, man is naturally a *social* being); of animals, living together in communities, as bees, wasps, ants, etc. (opposed to *solitary*); compound, as ascidians; of plants, growing in patches or clumps; characterized by or pertaining to life in communities (as, many wasps approach the bees in their *social* manner of life); specif., of or pertaining to the life and relations of human beings in a community, or of human beings generally viewed as members of a community (as, the *social* state; *social* conditions or institutions; *social* problems; *social* science, see phrase below; *social* work, see phrase below); of or pertaining to human society; also, of or pertaining to society as a body divided into classes graded according to worldly status (as, *social* rank; one's *social* equals); also, pertaining to or advocating socialism (as, a *Social* Democrat: see phrase below); socialistic; also, of or pertaining to allies or confederates, as a war (as, in *Gr. hist.,* the *Social* War between Athens and its confederates in 357–355 B.C.; in *Rom. hist.,* the *Social* War between Rome and its Italian allies in 90–88 B.C.).—**social contract,** a supposed expressed or implied agreement regulating the relations of ⸤citizens with one another and with the government, and forming the foundation of political society. The phrase (in the French form *contrat social*) was used by J. J. Rousseau as the title of a political treatise (1762) which exercised great influence in France and elsewhere previous to the Revolution.—**Social Democrat,** a member of any of certain political parties with socialistic principles, in Germany and elsewhere.—**Social Democratic party** (in Russian politics). See *Bolshevik,* *n.*—**Social Revolutionary party** (in Russian politics). See *Bolshevik,* *n.*—**social science** or **sciences,** the science or group of sciences concerned with all that relates to the social condition of man, or to his existence and well-being as a member of an organized community.—**social settlement,** a settlement or establishment conducted in a neglected or unfavored neighborhood for local social betterment. See *settlement.*—**social unit,** an individual, a family, or a larger group of persons, taken as a unit in social organization; specif., in recent use, the residents collectively of any of a number of districts into which a community is divided in organizing for the betterment of social conditions, the residents of each district conducting their own welfare-work through elected representatives, and all having a voice or a part in the work. —**social work,** work directed toward the betterment of social conditions in the community, as by organizations or individuals seeking to improve the condition of the poor, to promote the welfare of children, or to carry on other philanthropic activities.—**social worker,** a person engaged in social work.—**the social evil,** prostitution.—**so′cial,** *n.* A social gathering or party; also, a club or association for social purposes (U. S.).

so-cial-ism (sō′shạl-izm), *n.* [= F. *socialisme.*] A theory or system of social organization which aims at securing better distribution and more effective production of wealth by the vesting of the ownership and control of the means of production, capital, land, etc., in the community as a whole; also, procedure or practice in accordance with this theory; also, the socialistic movement.—**Christian socialism,** any of various socialistic theories or systems designed to secure practical adjustments for the benefit of all by the application of the principles of Christianity to the ordinary business of life; esp., such a system promulgated in England about 1850 by F. D. Maurice, Charles Kingsley, and others, opposed to the existing system of competition and favoring instead coöperation in production and distribution.—**gild** (or **guild**) **socialism,** a socialistic theory or system put forth and developed in England in the early part of the 20th century, which advocates the reorganization of society, on the basis of function, in 'national gilds,' or associations of persons connected with the various trades, industries, and professions (suggested by the gilds of the middle ages), these associations to be self-governing and the basis of representation in the government to be gild, trade, or profession rather than political area or division, and which aims at decentralization in industry and politics, and the placing of as large a part as possible of governmental activity in the hands of local communities.—**state socialism,** socialism, or any system of measures of socialistic character, esp. for the benefit of the working class, established and directed by the existing state or government.—**so′cial-ist. I.** *n.* An advocate or supporter of socialism. **II.** *a.* Of or pertaining to socialists; socialistic.—**so-cial-is′tic,** *a.* Of or pertaining to socialists or socialism; in accordance with socialism; advocating or supporting socialism.—**so-cial-is′ti-cal-ly,** *adv.*

so-ci-al-i-ty (sō-shi-al′i-ti), *n.*; pl. *-ties* (-tiz). [F. *socialité,* < L. *socialitas.*] The state or quality of being social; social companionship or intercourse; a social affair, gathering, or the like (esp. in *pl.*); also, social nature or tendencies as shown in the assembling of individuals in communities; the action on the part of individuals of associating together in communities.

so-cial-ize (sō′shạl-īz), *v. t.*; *-ized, -izing.* To render social; make fit for life in companionship with others; also, to render socialistic; establish or regulate according to the theories of socialism.—**so′cial-i-za′tion** (-i-zā′shon), *n.*

so-cial-ly (sō′shạl-i), *adv.* In a social manner or respect.—**so′cial-ness,** *n.*

so-ci-e-ta-ri-an (sō-sī-ẹ-tā′ri-ạn), *a.* Of or pertaining to society; social. Also **so-ci′e-ta-ry** (-tạ-ri).

so-ci-e-ty (sō-sī′ẹ-ti), *n.*; pl. *-ties* (-tiz). [F. *société,* < L. *societas,* < *socius:* see *social.*] Companionship or company (as, to seek or enjoy one's *society;* to be on a desert island without other *society* than that of animals); friendly association, intercourse, or relations (as, "Among unequals what *society* Can sort, what harmony, or true delight?" Milton's "Paradise Lost," viii. 383); those with whom one has companionship or intercourse; a body of persons associated in intercourse by their calling, interests, etc. (as, diplomatic *society;* official *society*); often, the social intercourse, activities, or life of the polite or fashionable world (as, accomplish-

ments fitting one for *society;* to shine in *society;* **to make** one's début in *society*); the body of those associated in the intercourse of the polite or fashionable world; the upper, richer, or more fashionable class in a community in their social intercourse and relations; also, the condition of those living in companionship with others, or in a community, rather than in isolation; the social mode of living; a body of individuals living as members of a community (as, a *society* of human beings; a *society* of wasps); a community; the body of human beings generally, associated or viewed as members of a community (as, the evolution of human *society;* to work for the welfare of *society;* *society* demands the punishment of crime); sometimes, human beings collectively regarded as a body divided into classes graded according to worldly status (as, the higher or lower ranks or classes of *society*); also, association†, alliance†, or confederation†; hence, an organization of persons associated together for the promotion of common purposes or objects, whether religious, benevolent, literary, scientific, political, patriotic, or other (as, "a *society* . . . for helping the deserving poor": Barrie's "Sentimental Tommy," xvii.); an association for usefulness, profit, or pleasure.—**Society of Friends.** See *friend, n.*—**Society of Jesus.** See *Jesuit.*—**so-ci′e-ty,** *a.* Of or pertaining to society or societies; esp., belonging or pertaining to those associated in the intercourse of the polite or fashionable world, or the upper, richer, or more fashionable class in a community (as, "I went over to paint a portrait of a *Society* woman," L. Merrick's "House of Lynch," vi.; "We are told so in the *society* papers," Du Maurier's "Trilby," iii.).—**society verse** [tr. F. *vers de société*], light, graceful, entertaining poetry, such as to appeal to polite society.

So-cin-i-an (sō-sin′i-ạn). **I.** *n.* A follower of Lælius Socinus (1525–62) and his nephew Faustus Socinus (1539–1604), Italian Protestant theologians, who denied the divinity of Christ, although holding that he was miraculously begotten and thus entitled to adoration. **II.** *a.* Of or pertaining to the Socinians or their doctrines.—**So-cin′i-an-ism,** *n.*

so-ci-o- (sō′shi-ọ-). Form of L. *socius,* companion, associate (see *social*), used in combination, often as if representing *social,* or having reference to society, as in *socio-economic* (both social and economic), *socio-political.*

so-ci-o-log-ic, so-ci-o-log-i-cal (sō″shi-ọ-loj′ik, -i-kạl), *a.* [See *sociology.*] Of or pertaining to sociology; pertaining to human society, or to subjects or questions relating to it. —**so″ci-o-log′i-cal-ly,** *adv.*—**so-ci-ol′o-gist** (-ol′ọ-jist), *n.* One versed in sociology; a student of sociology.—**so-ci-ol′o-gize** (-jīz), *v. i.*; *-gized, -gizing.* To study or investigate matters of sociology.

so-ci-ol-o-gy (sō-shi-ol′ọ-ji), *n.* [See *socio-* and *-logy.*] The science or study of the origin, development, and constitution of human society; the science of the fundamental laws of social relations, institutions, etc.; sometimes, the whole group of social sciences.

sock[1] (sok), *n.* [AS. *socc,* < L. *soccus,* kind of light, low-heeled shoe, slipper.] A light shoe, a slipper, or the like (now rare); esp., a light shoe worn by ancient Greek and Roman comic actors, sometimes taken as a symbol of comedy (cf. *buskin*); also, a short stocking reaching about half-way to the knee.

sock[2] (sok), *v. t.* [Origin obscure.] To strike or hit hard. [Slang.]—**sock**[2], *n.* A hard blow. [Slang.]

sock-dol-o-ger (sok-dol′ọ-jèr), *n.* [Also *sockdolager;* origin obscure.] A heavy, knock-down, or finishing blow; fig., a reply, argument, or the like that decisively settles a matter; also, something unusually large, heavy, etc. [Slang, U. S.]

sock-er (sok′èr), *n.* See *soccer.*

sock-et (sok′et), *n.* [ME. *soket, sokette;* origin uncertain.] A hollow part or piece for receiving and holding some part or thing; esp., the hollow part of a candlestick, in which the candle is set (as, "The candles had burned down to their *sockets*": H. James's "Portrait of a Lady," xlii.); in *anat.,* a hollow in one part, which receives another part (as, the *socket* of the eye); the concavity of a joint (as, the *socket* of the hip).—**sock′et,** *v. t.* To place in or fit with a socket.

Socket.—Right scapula, seen from in front, with G, glenoid fossa or socket.

so-cle (sō'kl or sok'l), *n.* [F., < It. *zoccolo*, socle, orig. wooden shoe, patten, < L. *socculus*, dim. of *soccus*, E. *sock*[1].] In *arch.*, a low, plain member supporting a wall, pedestal, or the like.

soc-man (sok'man), *n.*; pl. *-men*. One who held land in socage.

So-crat-ic (sō-krat'ik), *a.* Of or pertaining to the Athenian philosopher Socrates (469?–399 B.C.), or his philosophy, followers, etc.—**Socratic irony.** See *irony*[2].—**Socratic method,** the use of a series of questions as employed by Socrates to develop a latent idea, as in the mind of a pupil, or to elicit admissions, as from an opponent, tending to establish or to confute some proposition.—**So-crat'ic,** *n.* A disciple or follower of Socrates.—**So-crat'i-cal-ly,** *adv.*

sod (sod), *n.* [ME. *sod*, *sodde*, = D. *zode* = MLG. and G. *sode*, sod.] A piece (usually square or oblong) cut or torn from the surface of grassland, containing the roots of grass, etc.; also, the surface of the ground, esp. when covered with grass; turf; sward.—**the old sod,** one's native country or district: used esp. with reference to Ireland. [Colloq.] —**sod,** *v. t.*; *sodded*, *sodding.* To cover with sods: as, "a newly *sodded* grave" (C. Brontë's "Villette," xxvi.).

so-da (sō'dä), *n.* [ML. and It. *soda* = F. *soude*, earlier *soulde*, orig. plant (as saltwort or glasswort) yielding soda-ash, hence soda; origin uncertain.] Sodium carbonate, soda-ash, or sal-soda ('washing-soda'); also, sodium bicarbonate ('baking-soda'); also, sodium hydroxide ('caustic soda'); also, the oxide of sodium; also, sodium (in phrases, as 'carbonate of soda'); also, soda-water.—**so'da=ash,** *n.* Partially purified sodium carbonate, as that formerly obtained from the ashes of various plants growing by the seashore.—**so'da=foun''tain,** *n.* A vessel or apparatus for holding soda-water and provided with means of drawing it off as required; esp., an apparatus from which it is drawn off by faucets and which contains also receptacles for ice and flavoring syrups.—**so'da=lime,** *n.* A mixture of sodium hydroxide (caustic soda) and calcium hydroxide (slaked lime).

so-da-list (sō'dä-list), *n.* A member of a sodality.

so-da-lite (sō'dä-līt), *n.* [From *soda* + *-lite*.] A mineral, a silicate of sodium and aluminium with sodium chloride, occurring in crystals and massive, and having usually a blue color: found in certain igneous rocks.

so-dal-i-ty (sō-dal'i-ti), *n.*; pl. *-ties* (-tiz). [L. *sodalitas*, < *sodalis*, mate, fellow, comrade.] Fellowship or association; also, an association, society, or fraternity (as, "There were . . . military *sodalities* of musketeers, cross-bowmen, archers, swordsmen in every town": Motley's "Dutch Republic," Introd., xiv.); in the *Rom. Cath. Ch.*, a society with religious or charitable objects.

so-da-wa-ter (sō'dä-wâ''tėr), *n.* Orig., a beverage made with soda (sodium bicarbonate); now, an effervescent beverage consisting of water charged with carbon dioxide; also, this beverage variously served with the addition of fruit or other syrups, ice-cream, etc.

sod-den (sod'n), *p. a.* [Old pp. of *seethe*.] Boiled (now rare); also, soaked with liquid or moisture; hence, heavy, doughy, or soggy, as food; also, having the appearance of having been soaked; bloated, as the face; also, expressionless, dull, or stupid.—**sod'den,** *v. t.* or *i.* To make or become sodden: as, "The feet sink into *soddened* masses of decaying leaves" (Jefferies's "Gamekeeper at Home," ii.).—**sod'den-ness,** *n.*

sod-dy (sod'i). **I.** *a.* Of or like sod; made of sods. **II.** *n.*; pl. *soddies* (-iz). A house made of sods. [Western U. S.]

sod-er (sod'ėr), *n.* and *v.* Old spelling of *solder.* See *Isa.* xli. 7.

so-dic (sō'dik), *a.* Of or containing sodium.

so-di-um (sō'di-um), *n.* [NL., < ML. *soda*: see *soda*.] Chem. sym., Na (see *natrium*); at. wt., 23; sp. gr., 0.97. A soft, silver-white metallic element which oxidizes rapidly in moist air, occurring in nature only in the combined state.—**sodium bicarbonate,** a white crystalline compound, $NaHCO_3$, used in cooking, medicine, etc.—**sodium carbonate,** a compound of sodium, Na_2CO_3, occurring in an anhydrous form as a white powder or in a crystalline state as sal-soda, etc.—**sodium chloride,** common salt, $NaCl$.—**sodium hydroxide,** a white caustic solid, $NaOH$, used in making soap, etc.—**sodium hyposulphite.** See *hyposulphite.*

Sod-om (sod'om), *n.* An ancient city which, according to the account in the Bible, was destroyed by fire from heaven because of the wickedness of its inhabitants (see Gen. xviii.–xix.); hence, any extremely wicked place. See *Gomorrah.*—**Sod'om-ite** (-īt), *n.* An inhabitant of Sodom; also [*l. c.*], one who practises sodomy (see Deut. xxiii. 17).—**sod'om-y,** *n.* [F. *sodomie*.] Unnatural sexual intercourse, esp. of one man with another or of a human being with an animal.

so-ev-er (sō-ev'ėr), *adv.* [From *so* + *ever*.] At all; in any case; of any kind: in any way: used with generalizing force after *who, what, when, where, how, any, all,* etc. (sometimes separated by intervening words), often in composition: as, choose what person, time, or place *soever* you please; choose what*soever* person, etc., you please; "how little *soever* it may satisfy our curiosity" (J. Butler's "Analogy of Religion," i. 1); in any way *soever*.

so-fa (sō'fä), *n.* [Ar. *çuffah*.] A long, upholstered seat or couch with a back and raised ends (or end).

sof-fit (sof'it), *n.* [F. *soffite*, < It. *soffitto*, masc., *soffitta*, fem., < *sof-* (< L. *sub*), under, + *fitto*, pp. of *figgere* (< L. *figere*), fix: cf. *suffix*.] In *arch.*, the under surface or face of an architrave, arch, or the like.

So-fi (sō'fi), etc. Same as *Sufi*, etc.

soft (sôft), *a.* [AS. *sōfte*, var. of *sēfte*, akin to OHG. *semfti*, G. *sanft*, D. *zacht*, soft.] Producing agreeable sensations (as, *soft* slumber); pleasant, easeful, or comfortable (as, "a *soft* retreat from sudden vernal showers": Pope's "Spring," 98); also, low or subdued in sound; sometimes, gentle and melodious; also, not harsh or unpleasant to the eye; not glaring, as light or color; not hard or sharp, as outlines; also, gentle or mild, as wind, rain, etc.; genial or balmy, as climate, air, etc. (as, "It was a lovely *soft* spring morning at the end of March": S. Butler's "Way of All Flesh," lxxvi.); not rough or turbulent, as a stream; also, leisurely or easy, as pace or movement; gradual, as a slope or ascent; also, not hard, trying, or severe; involving little effort or work (colloq.: as, a *soft* job): also, gentle, mild, lenient, or compassionate, as persons (as, "The *soft* Napæan race will soon repent Their anger": Dryden's tr. Virgil's "Georgics," iv. 776); characterized by gentleness or tenderness, as the disposition, look, feelings, actions, etc.; also, smooth, soothing, or ingratiating, as words; not harsh or severe, as terms; also, yielding readily to the tender emotions, as persons; impressionable; sentimental, as language; also, easily influenced or swayed, as a person, the mind, etc.; easily imposed upon (colloq.); effeminate or unmanly; also, of delicate constitution, not strong or robust, or incapable of great endurance or exertion (as, the *soft*, or *softer*, sex, the female sex; "a certain kind of pulpit eloquence . . . powerful with the *softer* sex," Trollope's "Barchester Towers," iv.); also, foolish or silly; sometimes, weak-minded (colloq.); also, yielding readily to touch or pressure; easily penetrated, divided, or altered in shape; not hard; not stiff; relatively deficient in hardness, as metal; specif., of money, in paper currency rather than coin; also, smooth and agreeable to the touch, as the skin or hair; not rough or coarse; also, of water, relatively free from mineral salts that interfere with the action of soap; of beverages, not alcoholic or intoxicating; of the weather, etc., rainy, wet, or damp (prov.); thawing (U. S.); in *phonetics*, having a more or less sibilant sound, as the *c* and *g* in *cite* and *gin* (as distinguished from the 'hard' *c* and *g* in *corn* and *get*); also, sonant or voiced, as *g, b,* and *d,* in distinction from *k, p,* and *t,* which are hard, surd, or breathed.—**soft coal,** bituminous coal.—**soft pedal,** a pedal, as in a pianoforte, for softening musical tones. Also *fig.* Cf. *soft-pedal, v.*—**soft rays.** See under *ray*[3], *n.*—**soft sawder.** See *sawder.*—**soft soap.** See under *soap, n.*—**soft tube.** See under *tube, n.*—**soft,** *n.* That which is soft or yielding; the soft part of anything; softness; also, a foolish or silly person (prov. or colloq.:

s, s, Soffits.

as, "I know what the men like — a poor *soft*, as 'ud simper at 'em," George Eliot's "Adam Bede," liii.).—**soft**, *adv.* [AS. *sōfte*.] In a soft manner; softly.—**soft**, *interj.* Be quiet! hush! also, not so fast! stop! [Archaic.]

sof-ta (sof'tä), *n.* [Turk.; from Pers.] In Turkey, a Mohammedan student of theology and sacred law.

soft=bod-ied (sôft'bod''id), *a.* Having a soft body, as the mollusks.

soft-en (sôf'n), *v. t.* or *i.* To make or become soft or softer. —**soft'en-er**, *n.*—**soft'en-ing**, *n.* A making or becoming soft: as, *softening* of the brain (in *pathol.*, a degenerative process in the brain substance; in popular use, general paralysis, or paresis).

soft=head-ed (sôft'hed'ed), *a.* Foolish or silly; weak in intellect.—**soft'=head'ed-ness**, *n.*

soft=heart-ed (sôft'här'ted), *a.* Having a soft or tender heart: as, "I . . . had my own way, for my grandmother was . . . *soft-hearted* to children" (Mrs. Stowe's "Oldtown Folks," iii.).—**soft'=heart'ed-ness**, *n.*

soft-ish (sôf'tish), *a.* Somewhat soft.

soft-ly (sôft'li), *adv.* In a soft manner; in ease or comfort; in a subdued tone; quietly or silently; without force or violence; gently or tenderly.—**soft'ness**, *n.*

soft=ped-al (sôft'ped'al), *v.*; *-aled* or *-alled*, *-aling* or *-alling*. **I.** *intr.* To use the soft pedal, as in playing the pianoforte; fig., in colloq. use, to tone down language or statements; be particularly cautious or reticent on a subject. **II.** *tr.* To soften the sound of by means of the soft pedal; fig., to tone down, or make less strong, uncompromising, noticeable, or the like (colloq.: as, to *soft-pedal* a statement; to *soft-pedal* an issue in a political campaign).

soft=shell, soft=shelled (sôft'shel, -sheld), *a.* Having a soft shell: as, the *soft-shelled* crab (the common edible crab, *Callinectes hastatus*, when it has shed its hard shell and not yet grown another).

soft=soap (sôft'sōp'), *v. t.* [See *soft soap*, under *soap*, *n.*] To ply with smooth words; cajole; flatter. [Colloq.]

soft=spok-en (sôft'spō'kn), *a.* Of persons, speaking with a soft or gentle voice; mild; of words, softly or mildly spoken; persuasive.

soft-wood (sôft'wůd), *n.* Any wood which is relatively soft or easily cut; a tree yielding such wood; in *forestry*, the wood of a coniferous tree; such a tree itself.

soft-y (sôf'ti), *n.*; pl. *softies* (-tiz). A soft, silly, or weak-minded person; also, one who is easily imposed upon; also, an effeminate or unmanly person. [Colloq.]

sog (sog), *v. i.* or *t.*; *sogged, sogging.* [Origin uncertain: cf. *soak*.] To soak; become or make soggy. [Now chiefly prov.]—**sog**, *n.* A piece of wet or marshy ground; a bog. [Prov. Eng.]—**sog'gy**, *a.*; compar. *soggier*, superl. *soggiest*. Soaked; soppy; thoroughly wet; also, humid or sultry, as weather; also, damp and heavy, as ill-baked bread; sodden; also, spiritless, dull, or stupid.—**sog'gi-ness**, *n.*

soh (sō), *interj.* See *so*, *interj.*

so-ho (sō-hō'), *interj.* Ho there! hello! a shout of hailing, encouragement, discovery, etc., orig. used by huntsmen. See Shakspere's "Romeo and Juliet," ii. 4. 136.

soi=di-sant (swo-dē-zäṅ'), *a.* [F., < *soi* (< L. *se*), one's self, + *disant*, ppr. of *dire* (< L. *dicere*), say.] Calling one's self thus, or self-styled (as, a *soi-disant* marquis); also, so-called or pretended (as, a *soi-disant* science).

soil[1] (soil), *n.* [ME. *soyle*, < AF. *soile*, appar. with sense < L. *solum*, ground, earth (see *sole*[1]), but with form due to OF. *soil*, mire (see *soil*[3]), or other words.] The ground or earth (as, "Three years I lived upon a pillar, high Six cubits . . . last . . . this, That numbers forty cubits from the *soil*": Tennyson's "St. Simeon Stylites," 90); also, the ground of a particular country or region, or a country, land, or region (as, to set foot on foreign *soil*; "Must I thus leave thee, Paradise? thus leave Thee, native *soil*?" Milton's "Paradise Lost," xi. 270); a piece of ground or tract of territory (obs. or archaic); also, the ground as producing vegetation or cultivated for its crops (as, fruitful, fertile, or barren *soil*; to till the *soil*); that portion of the earth's surface in which plants grow, usually consisting of a mixture of disintegrated rock and decayed organic matter; earth; a particular kind of earth (as, a light, loose, or sandy *soil*).

soil[2] (soil), *v.* [OF. *soillier* (F. *souiller*), soil, OF. also roll in mire, as swine, perhaps < L. *suculus*, dim. of *sus*, swine: cf. *soil*[3].] **I.** *tr.* To make dirty or foul, esp. on the surface (as, to *soil* the hands, clothes, table-cloth, or carpet; to *soil* a book by handling); smirch, smudge, or stain; fig., to sully or tarnish, as with disgrace (as, to *soil* one's name or reputation); defile morally, as with sin; also, to manure†. **II.** *intr.* To become soiled, or smirched, stained, tarnished, etc.—

soil[2], *n.* A soiling or being soiled (as, to protect clothes from *soil*); also, a spot, mark, or stain due to soiling (lit. or fig.: as, "The only *soil* of his fair virtue's gloss . . . Is a sharp wit match'd with too blunt a will," Shakspere's "Love's Labour's Lost," ii. 1. 47); also, dirty or foul matter; filth; sewage; ordure; manure or compost.

soil[3] (soil), *n.* [OF. *soil*, *souil*, < *soillier*: see *soil*[2].] A marshy or muddy place used by a wild boar for wallowing in†; also, a pool, stream, or the like in which a hunted deer or other animal takes refuge (as, "John Garnet could not but hope that now the deer had taken *soil*": Whyte-Melville's "Katerfelto," xxiii.).—**soil**[3], *v. i.* To take to water or marshy ground, as a hunted deer: as, "He's a heavy deer . . . He'll hang in Badgeworthy woods, or *soil* in Badgeworthy water" (Whyte-Melville's "Katerfelto," xxiii.).

soil[4] (soil), *v. t.* [Origin uncertain.] To feed (horses, cattle, etc.) on green food, for purging; also, to feed on freshly cut green fodder, for fattening.

soiled (soild), *a.* Having soil or earth (as specified): as, a black-*soiled* plain.

soil'less, *a.* Without soil.—**soilless growth**, the growing of plants without soil, the nutrition being supplied by a water solution containing fertilizing chemicals.

soil-ure (soil'ūr), *n.* The act of soiling, smirching, or staining, or the state of being soiled; also, a stain. [Archaic.]

soi-rée (swo-rā), *n.* [F., < *soir*, evening, < L. *serum*, evening, prop. neut. of *serus*, late.] An evening party or social gathering, often for a particular purpose: as, a musical or a dancing *soirée*.

so-ja (sō'jä), *n.* [NL.] The soy-bean plant.

so-journ (sō'jėrn or sō-jėrn', Brit. soj'ėrn or suj'-), *v. i.* [OF. *sojorner* (F. *séjourner*), < L. *sub*, under, + *diurnus*, of the day, daily: see *diurnal*.] To dwell for a time in a place; make a temporary stay: as, "One law . . . shall be for you, and for the stranger that *sojourneth* with you" (Num. xv. 16).—**so'journ**, *n.* A temporary stay at a place (as, "During his *sojourn* at Trèves . . . Charles was constantly attended by the ambassadors of Lorraine": J. F. Kirk's "Charles the Bold," iv. 2); also, a place of temporary stay (as, "Escaped the Stygian pool, though long detain'd In that obscure *sojourn*": Milton's "Paradise Lost," iii. 15). —**so'journ-er**, *n.*—**so'journ-ment**, *n.*

soke (sōk), *n.* [ML. *soca*, < AS. *sōcn*, seeking, inquiry, jurisdiction, related to *sēcan*, E. *seek*.] A former right of local jurisdiction of causes in England; also, a district over which such a right was exercised; a minor local division.

soke-man (sōk'man), *n.*; pl. *-men*. A socman.

Sol[1] (sol), *n.* [L. *sol*, sun; akin to Gr. ἥλιος, Skt. *svar*, Goth. *sauil*, Icel. *sōl*, sun, and also E. *sun*[2].] The sun, personified by the Romans as a god; in *alchemy*, gold; in *her.*, same as *or*[3].

sol[2] (sol), *n.* [OF. *sol* (F. *sou*), < ML. *solidus*, a coin, LL. a gold coin: see *solidus*, and cf. *sou* and *soldier*.] An old French coin and money of account, equal to the twentieth part of a livre.

sol[3] (sōl), *n.* In *music*, the syllable used for the fifth tone of the scale (G, in the major scale of C), and sometimes for the tone G. See *sol-fa*.

so-la[1]† (sō-lä'), *interj.* [Cf. *soho*.] A call to attract attention. See Shakspere's "Merchant of Venice," v. 1. 39–44.

so-la[2] (sō'lä), *n.* [Bengali *solā*.] An East Indian leguminous plant, *Æschynomene aspera*, whose stems yield a pithy material much used for making light hats and helmets. See *topi*.

so-la[3] (sō'lä), *a.* [L.] Fem. of *solus*.

sol-ace (sol'ās), *n.* [OF. *solas* (F. *soulas*), < L. *solacium*, *solatium*, < *solari*, comfort, soothe: cf. *solatium* and *console*[2].] Comfort in sorrow or trouble; alleviation of distress or discomfort; consolation; relief; hence, something that gives comfort, consolation, or relief (as, "The evening pipe was the conclusion and *solace* of the day": Besant's "All

Sorts and Conditions of Men," i.); also, pleasure† or enjoy-ment†, or something that gives pleasure† (as, "Though sight be lost, Life yet hath many *solaces*, enjoy'd Where other senses want not their delights": Milton's "Samson Agonistes," 915).—**sol′ace**, *v.; -aced, -acing.* **I.** *tr.* To comfort, console, or cheer (a person, one's self, the heart, etc.: as, "Mrs. Corney was about to *solace* herself with a cup of tea," Dickens's "Oliver Twist," xxiii.); alleviate or relieve (sorrow, distress, etc.: as, "fevered with ivy poison, and *solacing* his woes with tobacco and Shakspere," Parkman's "Oregon Trail," xiv.); also, to entertain† or amuse† (as, "We will with some strange pastime *solace* them": Shakspere's "Love's Labour's Lost," iv. 3. 377). **II.** *intr.* To give comfort or consolation; also, to take comfort or pleasure† (as, "But one thing to rejoice and *solace* in, And cruel death hath catch'd it from my sight!" Shakspere's "Romeo and Juliet," iv. 5. 47).—**sol′ace-ment**, *n.*—**sol′a-cer** (-ā-sėr), *n.*

so-lan (sō′lạn), *n.* [From Scand.] The gannet, *Sula bassana*.

sol-a-na-ceous (sol-ạ-nā′shius), *a.* [See *solanum*.] Belonging to the *Solanaceæ*, or nightshade family of plants, which includes, besides the many species of *Solanum* (see *solanum*), the belladonna, henbane, mandrake, stramonium, tobacco, capsicum pepper, tomato, petunia, etc.

so-lan=goose (sō′lạn-gös), *n.* The solan.

sol-a-nine (sol′ạ-nin), *n.* [F., < L. *solanum*, nightshade.] In *chem.*, an alkaloidal substance obtained from the black nightshade and other species of solanum.

so-la-no (sō-lä′nō), *n.* [Sp., < L. *solanus*, < *sol*, sun.] A hot easterly wind of the Mediterranean, esp. on the eastern coast of Spain, or a moist easterly wind of the same regions.

so-la-num (sō-lä′num), *n.* [L., nightshade.] Any plant of the genus *Solanum*, which comprises gamopetalous herbs, shrubs, and small trees, including the nightshades, egg-plant, common potato, etc.

so-lar (sō′lär), *a.* [L. *solaris*, < *sol*, sun.] Of or pertaining to the sun (as, *solar* phenomena; the *solar* system, see phrase below); determined by the sun (as, *solar* hour, the twenty-fourth part of a solar day; *solar* day, see *day*; *solar* month, see *month*; *solar* year, see *year*; *solar* time, see *apparent solar time* and *mean solar time*, under *time*, *n.*); indicating time by means of or with reference to the sun (as, a *solar* chronometer); proceeding from the sun, as light or heat; operating by the light or heat of the sun, as a mechanism; resembling or suggesting the sun; also, sacred to the sun, or connected with the worship of the sun (as, a *solar* temple); representing or symbolizing the sun (as, a *solar* deity); in *astrol.*, subject to the influence of the sun; having the character determined by the sun.—**solar disk**, in *Egyptian art*, a disk used as a symbol of the sun, and often borne upon the head in representations of solar deities. Cf. *sun-disk* and *Ra*.—**solar plexus**, in *anat.*, a network of nerves situated at the upper part of the abdomen, behind the stomach and in front of the aorta.—**solar system**, the sun together with all the planets, etc., directly or indirectly revolving round it.—**so′lar-ism**, *n.* The interpretation of myths by reference to the sun, esp. such interpretation carried to an extreme.—**so′lar-ist**, *n.*

so-la-ri-um (sō-lä′ri-um), *n.; pl. -ria* (-ri-ą). [L., < *sol*, sun: cf. *sollar*.] A sun-dial; also, a room, gallery, or the like exposed to the sun's rays, as at a seaside hotel or for convalescents in a hospital.

so-lar-ize (sō′lär-īz), *v.; -ized, -izing.* [From *solar*.] **I.** *tr.* To affect by sunlight; in *photog.*, to injure or alter by excessive exposure to light. **II.** *intr.* In *photog.*, to become injured by overexposure.—**so″lar-i-za′-tion** (-i-zā′shọn), *n.*

so-la-ti-um (sō-lä′shi-um), *n.; pl. -tia* (-shi-ą). [L.: see *solace*.] A solace or compensation, as for suffering or loss; specif., in *law*, an additional sum, beyond actual damages, paid as a solace for injured feelings.

Egyptian Solar Deity, with Solar Disk on head.— Metropolitan Museum of Art, New York.

sold (sōld). Preterit and past participle of *sell*[1].

sol-dan (sol′dạn), *n.* [OF.: see *sultan*.] [Also *cap.*] The sovereign of a Mohammedan country; a sultan: as, "the *soldan* of Egypt" (Hume's "Essays," Of the First Principles of Government). [Archaic or hist.]

sol-der (sod′ėr or sol′dėr), *n.* [OF. *soldure, soudure* (F. *soudure*), < *solder, souder* (F. *souder*), to solder, < L. *solidare*, make solid, < *solidus*, E. *solid*.] Any of various fusible alloys, some ('soft solders') fusing readily, and others ('hard solders') fusing only at red heat, applied in a melted state to metal surfaces, joints, etc., to unite them; fig., anything that joins or unites.—**sol′der**, *v.* **I.** *tr.* To unite with solder; hence, to unite closely and firmly by means of some other substance or device; fig., to join closely and intimately; also, to mend; repair; patch up. **II.** *intr.* To unite things with solder; also, to become soldered; become united as if by soldering; grow together (as, "Their [children's] little brittle bones quickly *solder*": W. H. Hudson's "Far Away and Long Ago," i.).—**sol′der-er**, *n.*

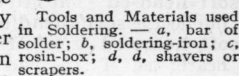

Tools and Materials used in Soldering.— *a*, bar of solder; *b*, soldering-iron; *c*, rosin-box; *d, d*, shavers or scrapers.

sol-dier (sōl′jėr), *n.* [OF. *soldier, soldeier*, < *solde, soldee*, pay (as of soldiers), < ML. *solidus*, a coin, piece of money: see *sol*[2].] One who serves in an army for pay; one engaged in military service; specif., one of the rank and file in such service, sometimes including non-commissioned officers (as, "That in the captain's but a choleric word, Which in the *soldier* is flat blasphemy": Shakspere's "Measure for Measure," ii. 2. 131); also, a man of military skill or experience; fig., one who contends or serves in any cause; in *zoöl.*, in colonies of certain ants, one of a type of workers with large head and powerful jaws; in colonies of termites, one of a kind of large-headed individuals.—**soldier of fortune**, a military adventurer; one ready to serve as a soldier wherever there is promise of profit, adventure, or other advantage. Also fig.—**sol′dier**, *v. i.* To act or serve as a soldier (as, "I suppose I've got to go *soldiering* for a bit": H. G. Wells's "Mr. Britling," ii. 2. § 6); also, to make a mere show of working (colloq.); feign illness, or malinger (colloq.).—**sol′dier=bee″tle**, *n.* Any of various serricorns, as *Chauliognathus pennsylvanicus*, a beetle whose larva destroys other insects.—**sol′dier=bug**, *n.* Any of various predaceous hemipterous insects, esp. of the genus *Podisus*, as *P. spinosus*, a common North American species which preys upon cutworms and other destructive larvæ.—**sol′dier=crab**, *n.* A hermit-crab.—**sol′dier-ly**, *a.* Of, like, or befitting a soldier.—**sol′-dier-li-ness**, *n.*—**sol′dier-ship**, *n.* The condition or profession of a soldier; soldierly qualities or skill (as, "Wallace . . . was now going to pitch his *soldiership* against that of the greatest general in Christendom": Jane Porter's "Scottish Chiefs," xlix.).—**sol′dier-y**, *n.* Soldiers collectively; a body of soldiers (as, "These mercenaries were . . . a fierce and rapacious *soldiery*": Scott's "Quentin Durward," xvii.); also, military training; knowledge of military matters.

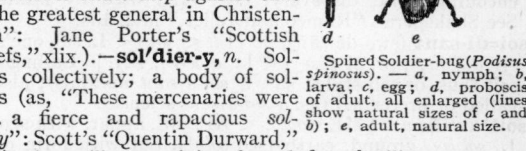

Spined Soldier-bug (*Podisus spinosus*).— *a*, nymph; *b*, larva; *c*, egg; *d*, proboscis of adult, all enlarged (lines show natural sizes of *a* and *b*); *e*, adult, natural size.

sol-do (sol′dō), *n.; pl. -di* (-dē). [It., < ML. *solidus*: see *sol*[2].] An Italian copper coin and money of account, the twentieth part of a lira (or 5 centesimi), equal to about 1 U. S. cent.

sole[1] (sōl), *n.* [OF. F. *sole*, < ML. *sola*, for L. *solea*, sole, sandal, < *solum*, ground, earth, foundation, sole of foot or shoe: cf. *soil*[1] and *sole*[2].] The bottom or under surface of the foot; also, the corresponding under part of a shoe, boot, or the like; or this part exclusive of the heel; also, a separate shaped piece, as of felt, for placing in the bottom of a shoe, etc.; also, the bottom, under surface, or lower part of anything; in *golf*, the under surface or part of a golf-club, which rests on the ground.—**sole**[1], *v. t.; soled, soling.* To furnish with a sole, as a shoe, a stocking, etc.; also, in *golf*, to place the sole of (a club) on the ground, as in preparation for a stroke.

sole² (sōl), *n.*; pl. *soles* or (esp. collectively) *sole*. [OF. F. *sole*, < ML. *sola*, for L. *solea*, sole (fish), another use (from the flat shape) of *solea*, sandal, whence E. *sole¹*.] Any of various flatfishes (family *Soleidæ*) with a more or less oval or elliptical body, as *Solea solea*, a food-fish common along European coasts; also, any of various other flat-fishes, as *Eopsetta jordani* and *Psettichthys melanostictus* of the Pacific coast of North America.

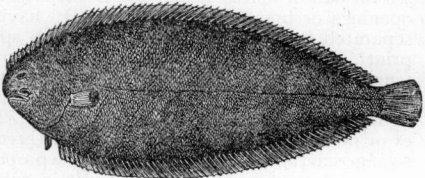

European Sole (*Solea solea*).

sole³ (sōl), *a.* [OF. *sol*, fem. *sole* (F. *seul*, fem. *seule*), < L. *solus*, fem. *sola*, alone, single: cf. *solus*, *solo*, and *sullen*.] Unaccompanied by others, alone, or solitary (archaic: as, "I should be *sole* in this sweet solitude," Byron's "Manfred," ii. 2); also, single or unmarried (now only in law: as, a feme *sole*, see under *feme*); also, consisting of one person only (as, a corporation *sole*: see *corporation*); also, being the only one or ones, or only (as, "The *sole* wall decoration of his studio was a Japanese print," Arnold Bennett's "Old Wives' Tale," ii. 8; "the *sole* grounds of the repeal of the five duties," Burke's "American Taxation"); sometimes, being the only one of the kind, or unique (as, "To all the fowls he seems A phœnix . . . that *sole* bird": Milton's "Paradise Lost," v. 272); also, belonging or pertaining to one individual or group to the exclusion of all others (as, to have the *sole* right to a thing; a fund for one's *sole* use; the *sole* work of two men); exclusive; also, uniform, as color.

sol-e-cism (sol′ē-sizm), *n.* [F. *solécisme*, < L. *solœcismus*, < Gr. σολοικισμός, < σολοικίζειν, violate the rules of grammar; said to have referred orig. to the bad Greek spoken at Soli, Gr. Σόλοι, town in Cilicia.] A violation of the grammatical or other settled usages of a language; a construction or expression at variance with grammatical or approved usage (as, 'it was him,' for 'it was he'); also, a breach of good manners or etiquette (as, "unused to society, and . . . afraid of making herself . . . conspicuous by some *solecism* or blunder": C. Brontë's "Jane Eyre," xxvii.); any error, impropriety, or inconsistency.—**sol′e-cist** (-sist), *n.* One who is guilty of solecisms.—**sol-e-cis′tic**, *a.* Of the nature of a solecism; characterized by solecisms.—**sol-e-cis′ti-cal-ly**, *adv.*

soled (sōld), *a.* Having soles: as, thin-*soled*.

sole=leath-er (sōl′leᴛн″er), *n.* A strong, thick leather used esp. for the soles of shoes.

sole-ly (sōl′li), *adv.* [See *sole³*.] Without companionship†, or in solitude†; also, as the only one or ones (as, "left *solely* heir to all his lands," Shakspere's "Taming of the Shrew," ii. 1. 118; the employers are *solely* responsible); also, exclusively or only (as, plants found *solely* in the tropics; questions relating *solely* to personal experience); wholly; merely.

sol-emn (sol′em), *a.* [OF. *solemne*, *solempne*, < L. *solemnis*, *sollemnis*, also *sollennis*, established, appointed, solemn.] Marked by or observed with religious rites, as feasts, feast-days, etc.; having a religious character, as rites, ceremonies, etc.; hence, of a formal or ceremonious character (as, "Proclaim A *solemn* council forthwith to be held": Milton's "Paradise Lost," i. 755); sometimes, grand, stately, or sumptuous, as entertainments, dress, etc.†; of great dignity or importance, as persons, places, etc.†; also, made according to religious forms, as a vow or oath (applied specif. in the Roman Catholic Church to certain vows, as in religious orders, of a more serious nature than others known as 'simple vows'); also, made in due legal or other express form, as a declaration, agreement, etc.; characterized by dignified or serious formality, as proceedings; serious or earnest, as assurances, feelings, purposes, etc.; grave, sober, or mirthless, as a person, the face, speech, tone, mood, etc. (as, "No *solemn* sanctimonious face I pull":

Hood's "Ode to Rae Wilson," 43); such as to cause serious thoughts or a grave mood (as, a *solemn* sight; a *solemn* silence; *solemn* music); gravely or somberly impressive; also, somber, as in color† (as, "suits of *solemn* black": Shakspere's "Hamlet," i. 2. 78).—**Solemn League and Covenant.** See *covenant*, *n.*—**so-lem-ni-ty** (sō-lem′ni-ti), *n.*; pl. *-ties* (-tiz). Observance of rites or ceremonies (religious or other), as on an important occasion (as, "They ordained . . . in no case to let that day pass without *solemnity*": 2 Mac. xv. 36); solemn celebration; a solemn observance, ceremonial proceeding, or special formality (often in *pl.*: as, to commemorate an event with all due *solemnities*); a course or occasion of ceremonial proceeding (as, "Ye shall have a song, as in the night when a holy *solemnity* is kept": Isa. xxx. 29); a formal celebration or festivity (as, "A fortnight hold we this *solemnity*, In nightly revels and new jollity": Shakspere's "Midsummer Night's Dream," v. 1. 376); also, the state or character of being solemn; seriousness or earnestness; gravity; impressiveness; in *law*, a formality requisite to render an act or document valid.—**sol′em-nize** (-em-nīz), *v. t.*; *-nized*, *-nizing.* To observe (a day, occasion, etc.) or commemorate (an event, etc.) with rites or ceremonies; also, to hold or perform (ceremonies, services, etc.) in due manner; esp., to celebrate (a marriage); perform the ceremony of (marriage); in general, to go through with ceremony or formality; also, to render solemn, serious, or grave (as, "The sight of the awful and majestic in nature had . . . the effect of *solemnising* my mind": Mrs. Shelley's "Frankenstein," x.).—**sol′em-ni-za′tion** (-ni-zā′shon), *n.*—**sol′emn-ly**, *adv.*—**sol′emn-ness**, **sol′em-ness**, *n.*

sole-ness (sōl′nes), *n.* The state or condition of being sole, alone, or without others.

so-le-no-don (sō-lē′nō-don), *n.* [NL., < Gr. σωλήν, channel, + ὀδούς (ὀδοντ-), tooth.] Either of the two species of the genus *Solenodon*, the agouta of Haiti and the almiqui of Cuba, opossum-like insectivorous animals with a long snout, coarse fur, and a long, scaly tail; an opossum-shrew.—**so-le′no-dont** (-dont), *a.* and *n.*

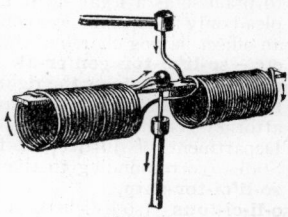

Solenodon (the Agouta, *Solenodon paradoxus*).

so-le-noid (sō-lē′noid or sō′lē-noid), *n.* [Gr. σωλήν, channel, pipe: see *-oid*.] In *elect.*, a conducting coil which acts like a magnet when an electric current is passed through it, and which consists of a cylindrical helix of copper or other wire, typically with one end brought back through the hollow center, or with both ends returned in like manner to a middle point.—**sol-e-noi-dal** (sol-ē-noi′dal or sō-lē-), *a.* Of or pertaining to a solenoid; of the nature of, or resembling, a solenoid.—**sol-e-noi′dal-ly**, *adv.*

Solenoid.

sol-fa (sol′fä′), *n.* [See *sol³* and *fa*.] In *music*, the set of syllables, do or ut, re, mi, fa sol, la, and si (most of which are attributed to Guido d'Arezzo), sung to the respective tones of the scale; the system of singing tones to these syllables; a scale or exercise sung in this way. See also *tonic sol-fa system*, under *tonic*, *a.*—**sol=fa**, *v.*; *-faed*, *-faing.* **I.** *intr.* To use the sol-fa syllables in singing. **II.** *tr.* To sing to the sol-fa syllables, as a tune.—**sol=fa-ist**, *n.* One who uses, or advocates the use of, the sol-fa syllables in singing.

sol-fa-ta-ra (sol-fä-tä′rä), *n.* [It., < *solfo*, < L. *sulfur*, E. *sulphur*.] A volcanic vent or area which gives off only sulphurous gases, steam, and the like.—**sol-fa-ta′ric**, *a.*

sol-feg-gio (sol-fed′jō), *n.*; pl. *solfeggios* (-jōz), It. *solfeggi* (-jē). [It.] In *music*, an exercise for the voice in which the sol-fa syllables are used; also, the use of these syllables.

sol-fe-ri-no (sol-fẹ-rē′nō), *n.* [From *Solferino*, in northern Italy, where a battle was won by French and Sardinians over Austrians in 1859, the year when the color was introduced: cf. *magenta*.] A dye-color obtained from rosaniline; a vivid purplish pink.

so-li (sō′lē), *n.* Italian plural of *solo.*

so-li-cit (sọ-lis′it), *v.* [OF. *soliciter* (F. *solliciter*), < L. *sollicitare*, disturb, rouse, incite, urge, < *sollicitus*, thoroughly moved, disturbed: see *solicitous*.] **I.** *tr.* To disturb† or disquiet† (as, "Anxious fears *solicit* my weak breast": Dryden's "Spanish Friar," iii. 3); also, to excite the interest, desire, etc., of (as, "*Solicit* Henry with her wondrous praise": Shakspere's "1 Henry VI.," v. 3. 190); tempt or entice; invite, attract, or allure, as things do (as, "That fruit, which . . . *Solicited* her longing eye": Milton's "Paradise Lost," ix. 743); also, to seek to influence or incite to action, esp. unlawful or wrong action (as, to *solicit* a subject people to rebellion; to *solicit* a person to commit a crime); endeavor to influence by bribery; also, to entreat or petition (a person, etc.), as for something, or to do something; urge or importune; specif., to importune with immoral intention; also, to seek after, or try to obtain (as, "To *solicit* by labour what might be ravished by arms, was esteemed unworthy of the German spirit": Gibbon's "Decline and Fall of the Roman Empire," ix.); seek for by entreaty, earnest or respectful request, formal application, etc. (as, to *solicit* a favor, an interview, contributions, or business orders; "I have the honour to *solicit* your votes," Bulwer-Lytton's "Pelham," xxxv.); call for or require (action, attention, etc.), as things do; also, to urge or plead (a cause, etc.: obs. or rare: as, "By way of *soliciting* his cause more effectually, he soon repaired in person to St. Petersburg," De Quincey's "Revolt of the Tartars"); conduct (a lawsuit, etc.) as a solicitor (obs. or rare); prosecute or manage (business, etc.)†. **II.** *intr.* To make petition or request, as for something desired; solicit orders or trade, as for a business house; specif., to importune a person with immoral intention; also, to act as a legal solicitor.—**so-li′cit-ant. I.** *a.* Soliciting. **II.** *n.* One who solicits.—**so-li-ci-ta-tion** (sọ-lis-i-tā′shọn), *n.* [OF. *solicitation* (F. *sollicitation*), < L. *sollicitatio(n-)*.] The act of soliciting; enticement or allurement; entreaty, urging, or importunity; a petition or request; specif., an importuning with immoral intention.

so-li-ci-tor (sọ-lis′i-tọr), *n.* [OF. *soliciteur* (F. *solliciteur*), < *soliciter*, E. *solicit*.] One who solicits; one who entreats or requests; one whose business it is to solicit custom, trade, etc.; in *law*, in England, formerly, one practising law in a court of equity; later, one properly qualified and admitted to practise as a legal agent in any court, but permitted to plead only in certain lower courts (cf. *barrister*); in the U. S., an officer having charge of the legal business of a city, town, etc.—**so-li′ci-tor=gen′er-al,** *n.*; pl. *solicitors-*. A law-officer who maintains the rights of the state in suits affecting the public interest, in England being next in rank to the attorney-general; in the U. S., the second officer of the Department of Justice, or the chief law-officer in some States (corresponding to the attorney-general in others).—**so-li′ci-tor-ship,** *n.*

so-li-ci-tous (sọ-lis′i-tus), *a.* [L. *sollicitus*, thoroughly moved, disturbed, anxious, careful, < *sollus*, whole, + *citus*, pp. of *ciere*, move: cf. *excite*.] Disturbed, troubled, or uneasy in mind† (as, "There, without sign of boast, or sign of joy, *Solicitous* and blank, he thus began": Milton's "Paradise Regained," ii. 120); hence, anxious or concerned over something (with *about*, *for*, etc., or a clause: as, to be *solicitous* about a person's health; *solicitous* for one's children; *solicitous* how best to meet a difficulty); also, anxiously desirous (*of*: as, to be *solicitous* of the esteem of others); eager (with infinitive: as, to be *solicitous* to please, or to avoid giving offense); also, careful or particular.—**so-li′ci-tous-ly,** *adv.*—**so-li′ci-tous-ness,** *n.*

so-li-ci-tress (sọ-lis′i-tres), *n.* A woman who solicits. Also fig.

so-li-ci-tude (sọ-lis′i-tūd), *n.* [OF. *solicitude* (F. *sollicitude*), < L. *sollicitudo* (*sollicitudin-*), < *sollicitus*: see *solicitous*.] The state of being solicitous; anxiety or concern; anxious

desire or care; *pl.*, feelings or causes of anxiety or care (as, "a simple and affectionate character, full of homely *solicitudes*": Morley's "Oliver Cromwell," i. 1).—**so-li-ci-tu′di-nous** (-tū′di-nus), *a.* Characterized by or showing solicitude.

sol-id (sol′id), *a.* [OF. F. *solide*, < L. *solidus*, solid: cf. L. *sollus*, whole, entire, unbroken.] Having the interior completely filled up, free from cavities, or not hollow (as, a *solid* ball of matter; the *solid* horns of the deer); without openings or breaks (as, a *solid* wall); having the lines not separated by leads, or having few open spaces, as type or printing; written without a hyphen, as a compound word (such as *catcall*, *earthworm*); also, having three dimensions (length, breadth, and thickness), as a geometrical body or figure; cubic (as, a *solid* foot contains 1,728 *solid* inches); of or pertaining to bodies or figures of three dimensions (as, *solid* geometry); sometimes, having the property of occupying space; also, firm, hard, or compact in substance (as, *solid* ground; *solid* snow); specif., having relative firmness, coherence of particles, or persistence of form, as matter that is not liquid or gaseous (as, *solid* particles floating in a liquid); pertaining to such matter (as, ice is water in a *solid* state); also, dense, thick, or heavy in nature or appearance (as, *solid* masses of cloud or smoke; "A ray of reason stole Half through the *solid* darkness of his soul," Pope's "Dunciad," iii. 226); substantial, or not flimsy, slight, or light, as buildings, furniture, fabrics, food, etc. (as, "This course of *solid* dishes was succeeded by another of sweetmeats and pastry": Prescott's "Conquest of Mexico," iv. 1); fig., of a substantial character, or not superficial, trifling, or frivolous (as, *solid* learning; "The books were of a *solid* kind — chiefly theology and classics," Gissing's "Private Papers of Henry Ryecroft," i. 13; "You know enough of him to do justice to his *solid* worth," Jane Austen's "Sense and Sensibility," iv.); real or genuine (as, *solid* comfort); of dance music, rhythm, etc., perfect (swing slang); sound or good, as reasons, arguments, etc. (as, "a poor pretence instead of a *solid* reason": Burke's "American Taxation"); of substantial intellectual powers, as a writer or thinker (as, "the ripest and *solidest* sort of scholars": Strype's "Memorials of Cranmer," i. 1); sober-minded or sensible; financially sound or strong, or well-to-do (as, "a *solid* householder": Carlyle's "Sartor Resartus," iii. 5); also, undivided or continuous (as, the *solid* hoofs of the horse; a *solid* row of buildings; a *solid* stretch of level ground); whole or entire (as, for one *solid* hour); forming the whole, or being the only substance or material (as, vessels of *solid* silver; *solid* gold, ivory, mahogany, or marble); uniform in tone or shade, as a color; thorough, vigorous, great, big, etc. (colloq., with emphatic force, often after *good*: as, a good *solid* blow, scolding, oath, or dose); also, firmly united or consolidated (as, a *solid* combination); united in opinion, policy, etc., or unanimous (as, the *solid* South; a *solid* party vote; the party is *solid* for, or against, the measure); hence, of individuals, firm in opinion, approval, support, etc. (colloq., U. S.: as, he is *solid* for the whole party ticket); also, on a friendly, favorable, or advantageous footing (colloq., U. S.: as, to get *solid* with a person; to make one's self *solid* with the authorities).—**solid angle.** See *angle*[3], *n.*—**sol′id,** *n.* A body or magnitude having three dimensions (length, breadth, and thickness); also, a solid (or not liquid or gaseous) substance or body.

sol-i-da-go (sol-i-dā′gō), *n.*; pl. *-gos* (-gōz). [NL. use of ML. *solidago*, plant of reputed healing virtue, < L. *solidus*, E. *solid*.] Any plant of the asteraceous genus *Solidago*, mostly native in North America; a goldenrod.

sol-i-dar-i-ty (sol-i-dar′i-ti), *n.* [F. *solidarité*, < *solidaire*, E. *solidary*.] Solidary character or relation; union or fellowship arising from common responsibilities and interests, as between members of a class or body of persons, or between classes, peoples, etc.; community of interests, feelings, purposes, action, etc.: as, "A downtrodden class . . . will never be able to make an effective protest until it achieves *solidarity* by the development of some common general idea" (H. G. Wells's "Outline of History," xxxvi. § 12).

sol-i-da-ry (sol′i-dạ-ri), *a.* [F. *solidaire*, both joint and several (as an obligation), solidary, < L. *solidus*, E. *solid*.] Characterized by or involving community of responsibilities and interests. Cf. *solidarity*.

sol-id=hoofed (sol′id-höft), *a.* Having solid (not cloven) hoofs, as the horse.

sol-id=horned (sol′id-hôrnd), *a.* Having solid (not hollow) horns, as deer.

so-lid-i-fy (sō-lid′i-fī), *v.*; *-fied, -fying.* [F. *solidifier*: see *-fy*.] **I.** *tr.* To make solid; make into a hard or compact mass; change from a liquid or gaseous to a solid form; unite firmly or consolidate. **II.** *intr.* To become solid: as, "The young wood will *solidify* and harden about the wire" (Jefferies's "Gamekeeper at Home," iii.).—**so-lid′i-fi-a-ble** (-fī-a̯-bl), *a.* —**so-lid″i-fi-ca′tion** (-fi-kā′shon), *n.*

so-lid-i-ty (sō-lid′i-ti), *n.*; pl. *-ties* (-tiz). The state, property, or quality of being solid; freedom from cavities, openings, etc.; extension in three dimensions; occupancy of space; firmness or hardness of substance; solid (as opposed to liquid or gaseous) state or form; density; substantialness (lit. or fig.: as, "The house had an air of *solidity*, and well-to-do-ness about it," Bulwer-Lytton's "Caxtons," ii. 3); also, something solid (see Shakspere's "Hamlet," iii. 4. 49); in *geom.*, the amount of space occupied by a solid body; volume.

sol-id-ly (sol′id-li), *adv.* In a solid manner; firmly; compactly; substantially; soundly; thoroughly; in a body.— **sol′id-ness,** *n.*

sol-i-dun-gu-late (sol-i-dung′gū-lāt). [L. *solidus*, solid, + *ungula*, hoof.] **I.** *a.* Solid-hoofed; belonging to the *Solidungula*, a group of mammals with solid (not cloven) hoofs, including the horse, ass, etc. **II.** *n.* A solidungulate animal.

sol-i-dus (sol′i-dus), *n.*; pl. *-di* (-dī). [LL., noun use of L. *solidus*, E. *solid*: cf. *sol*[2].] A Roman gold coin introduced by Constantine, which continued to be coined under the Byzantine Empire, and received in western Europe the name *bezant* (see *bezant*); also, a shilling†; also, the 'shilling-mark,' a sloping line (/) representing the old long form of the

Obverse.   Reverse.
Solidus of Constantine the Great. — British Museum.

letter *s* (abbreviation of *solidus*), as used to separate shillings from pence (as in 2/6, for 2 shillings, 6 pence), and generally as a dividing line, as in dates, fractions, etc.

sol-i-fid-i-an (sol-i-fid′i-a̯n or sō-li-), *n.* [L. *solus*, alone, + *fides*, faith.] In *theol.*, one who maintains that faith alone, without works, is all that is necessary for justification.— **sol-i-fid′i-an-ism,** *n.*

so-lil-o-quize (sō-lil′ō-kwīz), *v.*; *-quized, -quizing.* [From *soliloquy*.] **I.** *intr.* To utter a soliloquy; talk to one's self. **II.** *tr.* To utter in a soliloquy; say to one's self: as, "'There is something in that,' I *soliloquized*, (mentally, be it understood)" (C. Brontë's "Jane Eyre," x.).—**so-lil′o-quiz-er** (-kwī-zèr), *n.*—**so-lil′o-quiz-ing-ly,** *adv.*

so-lil-o-quy (sō-lil′ō-kwi), *n.*; pl. *-quies* (-kwiz). [LL. *soliloquium*, < L. *solus*, alone, + *loqui*, speak.] The act or an act of talking when alone or as if alone; an utterance or discourse by one who is talking to himself or is regardless of any hearers present (as, "He wandered like a ghost about the town, bursting into *soliloquies* in public places": Lytton Strachey's "Queen Victoria," iv.); also, a literary composition representing a discourse to one's self.

sol-i-ped (sol′i-ped), *a.* and *n.* [= F. *solipède*, contr. < L. *solidipes* (-ped-), < *solidus*, solid, + *pes* (ped-), foot.] Same as *solidungulate.*

sol-ip-sism (sol′ip-sizm), *n.* [L. *solus*, alone, + *ipse*, self.] In *metaph.*, the theory that self is the only object of real knowledge, or that nothing but self exists.—**sol′ip-sist,** *n.*

sol-i-taire (sol-i-tār′), *n.* [F., < L. *solitarius*, E. *solitary*.] One who lives in solitude or seclusion; a recluse; also, a precious stone, esp. a diamond, set by itself, or without other stones, as in a ring; also, a ring with a stone so set; also, a game which can be played by one person alone, as a game played with marbles or pegs on a board having hollows or holes, or any of various card-games (cf. *patience*); also, any of various shy song-birds (genus *Myiadestes*) of the thrush family.

sol-i-ta-ry (sol′i-ta̯-ri), [L. *solitarius*, < *solus*, alone, E.

sole[3].] **I.** *a.* Quite alone, without companions, or unattended (as, "The Indian holds his course, silent, *solitary*, but undaunted, through the boundless bosom of the wilderness": Irving's "Sketch-Book," Traits of Indian Character); living alone, or avoiding the society of others (as, "The *solitary* saint Walks forth to meditate at even tide": Cowper's "Task," vi. 948); also, alone by itself (as, "The Omnipotent . . . Who . . . with *solitary* hand . . . at one blow, Unaided, could have finish'd thee": Milton's "Paradise Lost," vi. 139); also, being the only one or ones (as, a *solitary* instance; with a few *solitary* exceptions); also, characterized by the absence of companions (as, a *solitary* walk or ride; *solitary* confinement; "the reading of poetry and romance in the long, silent, *solitary* winter evenings," Longfellow's "Kavanagh," xvi.); also, characterized by solitude, as a place; unfrequented, secluded, or lonely; giving no indications of human life (as, "Let that night be *solitary*, let no joyful voice come therein": Job, iii. 7); specif., in *zoöl.*, not social, as certain wasps; also, simple, or not compound, as certain ascidians; in *bot.*, occurring or growing singly, as a flower. **II.** *n.*; pl. *-ries* (-riz). One who lives alone or in solitude, or avoids the society of others (as, "The last glimmer of the twilight placed her before the hut of the *Solitary*": Scott's "Black Dwarf," xvi.); esp., one who lives in solitude from religious motives; sometimes, one who is left alone (as, "an orphan and a *solitary* whose mother's death . . . had amounted to a tragedy": Arnold Bennett's "Hilda Lessways," ii. 4).—**sol′i-ta-ri-ly,** *adv.*—**sol′i-ta-ri-ness,** *n.*

sol-i-tude (sol′i-tūd), *n.* [OF. F. *solitude*, < L. *solitudo*, < *solus*, alone, E. *sole*[3].] The state of being or living alone (as, "O, might I here In *solitude* live savage, in some glade Obscured": Milton's "Paradise Lost," ix. 1085); seclusion; also, remoteness from habitations, as of a place; absence of human life or activity (as, "Daylight followed swiftly, disclosing . . . the *solitude* of the shore": J. Conrad's "Rescue," iv. 5); also, a lonely, unfrequented, or uninhabited place (as, "The river was an awful *solitude*," Mark Twain's "Life on the Mississippi," ii.; "here and there in the *solitudes* . . . a log fort with a picketed enclosure," Bancroft's "Hist. of the U. S.," Amer. Revolution, ii. 4).

sol-lar, sol-ler (sol′är, -èr), *n.* [ME. *solar, soler*, upper room, orig. one exposed to the sun, < OF. *solier*, < L. *solarium*: see *solarium*.] An upper room or part of a house, or a loft, garret, or attic (archaic or prov. Eng.); also, an elevated chamber or loft in a church, esp. in a steeple or belfry.

sol-ler-et (sol′èr-et), *n.* [OF., dim. of *soller, souler* (F. *soulier*), shoe.] A steel shoe, as of overlapping plates, which formed a part of medieval armor.

sol-mi-za-tion (sol-mi-zā′shon), *n.* [F. *solmisation*, < *solmiser*, use the syllables *sol, mi*, etc., in singing.] In *music*, the act, process, or system of using certain syllables, esp. the sol-fa syllables, to represent the tones of the scale in singing.

so-lo (sō′lō). [It., < L. *solus*, alone, E. *sole*[3].] **I.** *n.*; pl. *solos* (-lōz), It. *soli* (-lē). A musical composition performed by or intended for one singer or player, with or without accompaniment; also, any performance, as a dance, by one person; in *aëronautics*, a flight in an aëroplane during which the aviator is unaccompanied by an instructor or other person; also, in *card-playing*, any of certain games in which one person plays alone against others; also, a bid to play without a partner or without discarding. **II.** *a.* Alone (as, to dance *solo*); without a companion or partner (as, a *solo* flight in an aëroplane: see *solo*, *n.*); in *music*, performing alone, as an instrument or its player; also, performed alone; not combined with other parts of equal importance; not concerted.—**so′lo,** *v. t.*; *-loed, -loing.* To perform or treat as a solo.—**so′lo-ist,** *n.* One who performs a solo or solos.

Sol-o-mon (sol′ō-mo̯n), *n.* [From *Solomon*, king of Israel (10th century B.C.): see 1 Kings, iii. 5–28.] An extraordinarily wise man; a sage.—**Sol-o-mo′ni-an, Sol-o-mon′ic** (-mō′ni-a̯n, -mon′ik), *a.* Of or pertaining to Solomon, king of Israel; suggestive of Solomon, or of his wisdom.

Solleret (*a*) and Jambe (*b*), 14th century.

—Sol'o-mon's=seal', *n.* Any of various plants of the convallariaceous genus *Polygonatum*, with a thick rootstock bearing seal-like scars, as *P. multiflorum*, a commonly cultivated English species with drooping flowers, or *P. commutatum*, an American species with similar flowers; also [commonly as two words], a figure resembling a six-pointed star, formed of two triangles interlaced, or placed one upon the other (used esp. as a Jewish emblem: see *magen-David*).

So-lon (sō'lon), *n.* [From *Solon*, the Athenian lawgiver (about 638 – about 558 B.C.).] A wise lawgiver; a sage.

so=long, so long (sō'lông'), *interj.* Good-by! as, "*So-long*, my dear!" (Masefield's "Valediction"); "I won't keep you now. *So long!*" (L. Merrick's "Worldlings," xvii.). [Colloq.]

Solomon's-seal
(*Polygonatum commutatum*).— I, the upper part of the flowering stem; 2, the lower part of the stem; *a*, a flower; *b*, a fruit.

So-lo-ni-an, So-lon-ic (sō-lō'ni-an, -lon'ik), *a.* Of, pertaining to, or associated with Solon, the Athenian lawgiver.

sol-stice (sol'stis), *n.* [OF. F. *solstice*, < with the rootstock; L. *solstitium*, < *sol*, sun, + *sistere*, stand.] In *astron.*, either of the two times in the year when the sun is at its greatest distance from the equator and apparently stands still with respect to its declination, about June 21, when it enters Cancer, and about Dec. 22, when it enters Capricorn (called respectively, in the northern hemisphere, *summer solstice* and *winter solstice*); also, either of the two points in the ecliptic reached by the sun at these times; also, in fig. use, a furthest or culminating point; a turning-point.—**sol-sti'tial** (-stish'al), *a.* Of or pertaining to a solstice or the solstices (as, the *solstitial* points: see *solstice*); also, occurring at or about the time of a solstice; specif., characteristic of the summer solstice (as, "the *solstitial* heats being over now": W. H. Hudson's "Purple Land," xvii.); appearing about the time of the summer solstice, as plants, etc.—**sol-sti'tial-ly**, *adv.*

sol-u-bil-i-ty (sol-ū-bil'i-ti), *n.*; pl. *-ties* (-tiz). The quality of being soluble, solvable, or explainable (rare); also, the quality or property of being soluble, or capable of being dissolved; relative capability of being dissolved; in *bot.*, capability of easy separation into parts.

sol-u-ble (sol'ū-bl), *a.* [OF. F. *soluble*, < L. *solubilis*, < *solvere*: see *solve*.] That may be loosed or untied (now rare: as, "More *soluble* is this knot By gentleness than war," Tennyson's "Princess," v. 129); also, relaxed or open, as the bowels (obs. or rare); also, capable of being solved or explained, as a problem; also, capable of being dissolved or liquefied.—**soluble glass.** See *water-glass.*—**sol'u-ble-ness**, *n.*—**sol'u-bly**, *adv.*

so-lus (sō'lus), *a.* [L. (fem. *sola*): see *sole*[3].] Alone; by one's self: used of a male person, esp. in stage directions. The feminine form is *sola.*

so-lute (sō-lūt'). [L. *solutus*, pp. of *solvere*: see *solve*.] **I.** *a.* Dissolved; in a state of solution; in *bot.*, not adhering; free. **II.** *n.* The substance dissolved in a given solution.

so-lu-tion (sō-lū'shon), *n.* [OF. *solucion* (F. *solution*), < L. *solutio(n)-*, < *solvere*: see *solve*.] The act of solving a problem, etc., or the state of being solved (as, "a mystery beyond *solution*": Dickens's "Hard Times," ii. 9); a particular instance or method of solving; an explanation or answer; also, payment or discharge, as of an obligation; also, a dissolving or liquefying; the conversion of a substance from the solid or gaseous to the liquid state by treatment with a liquid or solvent; the act or process by which two or more substances unite to form a physically homogeneous mixture, usually a liquid mixture; sometimes, the dissolving of a substance attended with a chemical reaction ('chemical solution'); also, the fact of being dissolved; dissolved state (as, salt in *solution*); also, the liquid or mixture formed by dissolving; a liquid preparation made by dissolving something in water or some other solvent (as, a *solution* of salt or of ammonia); also, a separation of parts usually joined or continuous (as, a *solution* of continuity, a breach or break in anything, esp. one in parts of the body normally continuous, as from fracture or laceration); also, a breaking up or dis-solution; also, in *med.*, the termination of a disease; the crisis of a disease.—**so-lu'tion-al**, *a.*

solv-a-ble (sol'va-bl), *a.* Capable of being solved, as a problem; also, capable of being dissolved; also, solvent†, or able to pay†.—**solv-a-bil'i-ty** (-bil'i-ti), **solv'a-ble-ness**, *n.*

solve (solv), *v. t.*; *solved, solving.* [L. *solvere* (pp. *solutus*), loosen, release, dissolve, break up, remove, solve, appar. < *so-*, for *se-*, without, apart, + *luere*, loose: cf. *sober* and *loss*.] To loosen†; untie†; also, to clear up or explain (something perplexing); find the answer to (a question, riddle, etc.); work out the answer or solution to (a mathematical problem); resolve or dispel (difficulties, doubts, etc.: as, "That doubt . . . was soon *solved*," Besant's "Coligny," v.); also, to settle (controversy, strife, etc.: as, "He . . . would . . . *solve* high dispute With conjugal caresses," Milton's "Paradise Lost," viii. 55); also, to pay or discharge, as a debt; also, to dissolve; liquefy; melt.

sol-ven-cy (sol'ven-si), *n.* Solvent condition; ability to pay all just debts.

sol-vent (sol'vent). [L. *solvens* (*solvent-*), ppr. of *solvere*: see *solve*.] **I.** *a.* Able to pay all just debts; also, having the power of dissolving; causing solution. **II.** *n.* Something that solves or explains; also, a substance, usually a liquid, having the power of dissolving other substances (as, water is the most common of all *solvents*; alcohol is the appropriate *solvent* of resins; aqua regia is a *solvent* of gold; the alkahest, or universal *solvent* sought by the alchemists).—**sol'vent-ly**, *adv.*

solv-er (sol'ver), *n.* One who solves.

so-ma[1] (sō'mä), *n.*; pl. *somata* (-ma-tä). [NL., < Gr. σῶμα, body.] In *zoöl.*, the axial part of an animal's body, comprising the head, neck, trunk, and tail; in *biol.*, the body of an organism as contrasted with its germ-cells.

so-ma[2] (sō'mä), *n.* [Skt., < *su-*, press out, extract.] An intoxicating drink prepared from the juice of a plant, used in religious ceremonies in ancient India, and supposed to be drunk by gods as well as men and to possess life-giving power (see Whittier's "Brewing of Soma"); also, the plant yielding this drink, commonly identified with *Sarcostemma acidum* (or *Asclepias acida*), a shrubby asclepiadaceous climber with an acidulous milky juice; also [*cap.*], the drink or the plant personified and worshiped as a god.

So-ma-li (sō-mä'lē), *n.*; pl. *-li* or *-lis* (-lēz). A member of a Hamitic race showing an admixture of Arab, negro, and other blood, and dwelling in eastern Africa (Somaliland and adjacent regions); also, their language.

so-mat-ic (sō-mat'ik), *a.* [Gr. σωματικός, < σῶμα, body.] Of or pertaining to the body; bodily, corporeal, or physical; in *anat.* and *zoöl.*, pertaining to the cavity of the body of an animal, or, more especially, to its walls; in *biol.*, pertaining to the soma.—**somatic cell**, in *biol.*, one of the cells which take part in the formation of the body, becoming differentiated into the various tissues, organs, etc.—**so-mat'i-cal-ly**, *adv.*

somato-. Form of Gr. σῶμα (σωματ-), body, used in combination.—**so-ma-tol-o-gy** (sō-ma-tol'ō-ji), *n.* [+ *-logy*.] The science of the human body, esp. as a branch of anthropology; also, the science of material bodies or substances; physics.—**so"ma-to-log'i-cal** (-tō-loj'i-kal), *a.*—**so-ma-tol'-o-gist**, *n.*—**so"ma-to-pleure** (-plör), *n.* [+ Gr. πλευρά, side.] In *embryol.*, the outer of the two layers into which the mesoderm of craniate vertebrates splits, and which forms the body-wall. Cf. *splanchnopleure.*—**so"ma-to-pleu'ral** (-plö'ral), *a.*

som-ber, som-bre (som'ber), *a.* [F. *sombre*, appar. < L. *umbra*, shade, with some prefix.] Dark, shadowy, or dimly lighted (as, "She . . . past afar, Thridding the *sombre* boskage of the wood": Tennyson's "Dream of Fair Women," 243); hence, gloomy from deficiency of light or brightness, as places, scenes, the sky, etc.; dark and dull, as color, or as things in respect to color; characterized by a settled or sullen gloom, as persons, the face, etc. (as, "Her face had grown as *sombre* as a tragic mask": Mrs. Wharton's "Age of Innocence," xii.); in general, gloomy, depressing, or dismal (as, "No more *sombre* thoughts; chase dull care away, Janet," C. Brontë's "Jane Eyre," xxv.; a *somber* existence; a *somber* tale).—**som'ber, som'bre**, *v. t.* or *i.*; *-bered, -bred, -bering, -bring.* To make or become somber: as, "Rain clouds had *sombred* the sky" (L. Merrick's "House of Lynch," vii.).— **som′ber-ly, som′bre-ly,** *adv.*—**som′ber-ness, som′bre-ness,** *n.*

som-bre-ro (som-brā′rō), *n.*; pl. *-ros* (-rōz). [Sp., < *sombra*, shade: cf. *somber*.] A broad-brimmed hat, usually of felt, worn in Spain, Mexico, the southwestern U. S., etc.

som-brous (som′brus), *a.* Somber. [Archaic.]

some (sum), *a.* [AS. *sum* = OS. and OHG. *sum* = Icel. *sumr* = Goth. *sums*, some: see *same*.] Being an undetermined or unspecified one (as, *some* poor fellow; *some* time or other); certain (with plural nouns: as, *some* friends of mine); also, of a certain unspecified number, amount, degree, etc. (as, *some* nuts; *some* water; *some* variation); often, unspecified but considerable in number, amount, degree, etc. (as, he was here *some* weeks; a town of *some* size); hence, of considerable account or consequence, or notable of the kind (colloq., U. S.: as, *some* pumpkins, see phrase below; that was *some* storm; he is *some* swimmer); also, used with numerals and with words expressing extent, etc., to indicate an approximate amount (as, *some* four or five of us; "*some* forty thousand francs a year," H. James's "Portrait of a Lady," xliii.; *some* mile and a half away; *some* fortnight ago).—**some one.** See entry in alphabetical place.—**some pumpkins,** fig., persons or a person, or things or a thing, of considerable consequence: as, "She is *some punkins*, thet I wun't deny, (For ain't she some related to you 'n' I?)" (Lowell's "Biglow Papers," ii. 2. 155). [Colloq., U. S.]—**some,** *pron.* Somebody† or some one†; also, certain persons, instances, etc., not specified (as, *some* think he is dead; *some* of the charges are false); also, an unspecified number, amount, etc., as distinguished from the rest (as, "A sower went out to sow his seed: and as he sowed, *some* fell by the way side," Luke, viii. 5; we ate *some* of our provisions and gave the rest).—**some,** *adv.* To some degree or extent, or somewhat (colloq.: as, he is *some* better to-day; to be troubled *some* with rheumatism; to work *some* and play *some*); also, to a great degree or extent, or considerably (colloq., U. S.: as, that's going *some!*).

-some[1]. [AS. *-sum*, akin to D. *-zaam*, G. *-sam*, Icel. *-samr*, Sw. *-sam*, Dan. *-som*, Goth. *-sams*; akin to E. *same* and *some*.] A suffix used to form adjectives, orig. from nouns and adjectives, often indicating the possession of a considerable degree of some quality or a disposition or tendency toward something, as in *blithesome, burdensome, lonesome, quarrelsome, venturesome*.

-some[2]. [AS. *sum*, E. *some*.] A suffix used with a collective force in combination with numerals, as in *twosome, threesome, foursome*.

-some[3]. Noun termination from Gr. σῶμα, body, as in *chromosome, karyosome*.

some-bod-y (sum′bod-i or sum′bod-i), *n.*; pl. *-ies* (-iz). Some person (as, "*Somebody*, surely, some kind heart will come To bury me": Tennyson's "Maud," ii. 5. 11); also, a person of some note, consequence, or importance (as, "I'm always trying to make people think I'm *somebody*. I'm not": Sinclair Lewis's "Arrowsmith," v.).

some-deal (sum′dēl), *n.* and *adv.* [See *deal*[2], *n.*] Somewhat. [Archaic or prov.]

some-gate (sum′gāt), *adv.* [See *gate*[2].] Somewhere; also, somehow. [Sc. and north. Eng.]

some-how (sum′hou), *adv.* In some way not specified, apparent, or known (as, "He managed *somehow*": W. H. Hudson's "Green Mansions," Prologue): often in the phrase *somehow or other* (in one way or another: as, "Let any one be known to be a man of virtue, *somehow or other* he will be favoured," J. Butler's "Analogy of Religion," i. 3).

some one (sum wun). Some person; somebody: sometimes as one word, *someone*.

som-er-sault (sum′er-sált), *n.* [OF. *sombresaut, soubresaut* (F. *soubresaut*), < Pr. *sobresaut*, < L. *supra*, above, + *saltus*, a leap.] A movement of the body, as of an acrobat or of a boy at play, in which it describes a complete revolution, heels over head, in the air or along a surface; fig., a complete overturn or reversal, as of opinion.—**som′er-sault,** *v. i.* To turn a somersault.

som-er-set (sum′er-set), *n.* and *v.* Same as *somersault*.

some-thing (sum′thing). **I.** *n.* Some thing; a certain undetermined or unspecified thing; also, a certain part, amount, etc., esp. a small part or amount (as, "*Something* yet of doubt remains": Milton's "Paradise Lost," viii. 13); a person or thing that is to a certain extent an example of what is specified (as, "Sir Roger . . . is *something* of an humourist": Addison, in "Spectator," 106); also, a thing or person of some value or consequence (as, if we can get back half what we paid, that will be *something*; "If a man think himself to be *something*, when he is nothing, he deceiveth himself," Gal. vi. 3). **II.** *adv.* In some degree; to some extent; somewhat: as, "I was *something* impatient . . . to have the use of my boat" (Defoe's "Robinson Crusoe," i. 11); "They told us below, we should find settlers *something* thinnish, hereaway" (Cooper's "Prairie," ii.).

some-time (sum′tīm). **I.** *adv.* On a certain occasion in the past†; also, for a certain period in the past, at one time, or formerly (archaic: as, "Herne the hunter, *Sometime* a keeper here in Windsor forest," Shakspere's "Merry Wives of Windsor," iv. 4. 29); also, at some indefinite or indeterminate point of time (as, this happened *sometime* last March; he will arrive *sometime* next week); also, at an indefinite future time (as, come over *sometime*); also, sometimes, or on some occasions (now rare). **II.** *a.* Having been formerly; former: as, "our *sometime* sister, now our queen" (Shakspere's "Hamlet," i. 2. 8).—**some′times,** On some occasions; at times; now and then; also, once†; formerly†.

some-way (sum′wā), *adv.* In some way; somehow.

some-what (sum′hwot). **I.** *n.* Something not specified (archaic or prov.: as, "There's *somewhat* in this world amiss Shall be unriddled by and by," Tennyson's "Miller's Daughter," 19); also, some part, portion, amount, etc. (as, "The pair . . . fell into a conversation of which he could not help hearing *somewhat*": Thackeray's "Vanity Fair," lxvi.); a person or thing that is to some extent an example of what is specified (as, "I am *somewhat* of a fighting man": Watts-Dunton's "Aylwin," iv. 2); also, a thing or person of importance, note, etc. (as, "They think that I am *somewhat* . . . The silly people take me for a saint": Tennyson's "St. Simeon Stylites," 124). **II.** *adv.* In some measure or degree; to some extent: as, "a situation *somewhat* like to this" (J. Butler's "Analogy of Religion," ii. 6); " 'Yes,' said Allen . . . raising his voice *somewhat*" (Mallock's "New Republic," i. 3).

some-when (sum′hwen), *adv.* At some indefinite time: as, "a single tongue, spoken somewhere and *somewhen* in the past" (W. D. Whitney's "Life and Growth of Language," ix.).

some-where (sum′hwār), *adv.* In or at some place not specified, determined, or known (as, he lives *somewhere* in this neighborhood); to some place not specified or known (as, "He said that he had to go *somewhere* to see some one about something": W. H. Hudson's "Far Away and Long Ago," xviii.); also, at or to some point in amount, degree, etc. (followed by *about*, etc.: as, he is *somewhere* about 60; he stayed *somewhere* about an hour); also, at some point of time (followed by *about* or *in*: as, this happened *somewhere* about 1580, or *somewhere* in Elizabeth's reign).

some-while (sum′hwīl), *adv.* At some former time; formerly; also, at some indefinite or indeterminate point of time; at one time or another; sometime; also, at times; sometimes; also, for some time. [Now rare.]—**some′whiles,** *adv.* Sometimes: as, "*Somewhiles* I think to myself I'd like to be even with that Sweep, *somewhiles* that I ought to make him a handsome consideration" (W. De Morgan's "Joseph Vance," xvi.). [Archaic or prov.]

some-whith-er (sum′hwɪᴛ**ᴛ**′ėr), *adv.* To some place (as, "*Somewhither* would she have thee go with her": Shakspere's "Titus Andronicus," iv. 1. 11); in some direction.

so-mite (sō′mīt), *n.* [Gr. σῶμα, body.] In *zoöl.*, any of the longitudinal series of segments or parts into which the body of certain animals is divided; a metamere.—**so-mit-ic** (sō-mit′ik), *a.*

som-nam-bu-lant (som-nam′bū-lant). [L. *somnus*, sleep, + *ambulans* (*-ant-*), ppr. of *ambulare*, walk.] **I.** *a.* Walking in sleep; characterized by somnambulism. **II.** *n.* A somnambulist.—**som-nam′bu-lance,** *n.*

som-nam-bu-lar (som-nam′bū-lär), *a.* Pertaining to a somnambule or somnambulist, or to somnambulism.

som-nam-bu-late (som-nam′bū-lāt), *v.*; *-lated, -lating*. [L. *somnus*, sleep, + *ambulatus*, pp. of *ambulare*, walk.]

I. *intr.* To walk during sleep, as a somnambulist does. **II.** *tr.* To traverse during sleep: as, "His Eminence again *somnambulates* the Promenade de la Rose" (Carlyle's "Essays," The Diamond Necklace, xiv.).—**som-nam-bu-la′tion** (-lā′shọn), *n.*—**som-nam′bu-la-tor,** *n.*

som-nam-bule (som-nam′būl), *n.* [F. *somnambule,* < L. *somnus,* sleep, + *ambulare,* walk.] One who walks about, and often performs other acts, during sleep; a somnambulist.—**som-nam′bu-lic** (-bū-lik), *a.* Somnambular.

som-nam-bu-lism (som-nam′bū-lizm), *n.* [F. *somnambulisme,* < *somnambule:* see *somnambule.*] The fact or habit of walking about, and often of performing various other acts, while asleep; sleep-walking; noctambulism.—**som-nam′bu-list,** *n.* One who has the habit of somnambulism; a sleep-walker; a somnambule.—**som-nam-bu-lis′tic,** *a.* Pertaining to a somnambulist or to somnambulism.—**som-nam-bu-lis′ti-cal-ly,** *adv.*

som-nif-er-ous (som-nif′ẹ-rus), *a.* [L. *somnifer,* < *somnus,* sleep, + *ferre,* bear.] Bringing or inducing sleep, as drugs, influences, etc.; also, sleepy or somnolent (as, "fat, *somniferous,* respectable burghers": Irving's "Knickerbocker's New York," v. 2).—**som-nif′er-ous-ly,** *adv.*

som-nif-ic (som-nif′ik), *a.* [L. *somnificus,* < *somnus,* sleep, + *facere,* make.] Causing sleep; soporific; somniferous.

som-nil-o-quism, som-nil-o-quy (som-nil′ọ-kwizm, -kwi), *n.* [L. *somnus,* sleep, + *loqui,* speak.] The act or habit of talking while asleep.—**som-nil′o-quist,** *n.* One who talks while asleep.

som-no-lent (som′nọ-lẹnt), *a.* [L. *somnolentus, somnulentus,* < *somnus,* sleep: see *sopor.*] Inclined to sleep, sleepy, or drowsy (as, "a lazy, rather *somnolent* youth": Mrs. H. Ward's "Lady Rose's Daughter," iii.); also, tending to cause sleep.—**som′no-lence, som′no-len-cy,** *n.*—**som′no-lent-ly,** *adv.*

son (sun), *n.* [AS. *sunu* = D. *zoon* = G. *sohn* = Icel. *sunr* = Goth. *sunus,* son; akin to Skt. *sūnu* and Gr. *viós,* son.] A male child or person in relation to his parents; also, a son-in-law; also, a familiar term of address to a man or boy from an older person, an ecclesiastic, etc.; also, any male descendant (as, "Adam's *sons* are my brethren": Shakspere's "Much Ado about Nothing," ii. 1. 66); one related as if by ties of sonship (as, *sons* of Æsculapius, physicians; "England's greatest *son,*" Tennyson's "Ode on the Death of the Duke of Wellington," vi.); a male person looked upon as the product or result of particular agencies, forces, influences, etc. (as, *sons* of liberty; *sons* of darkness; "a true *son* of chivalry," Scott's "Castle Dangerous," xiii.); also [*cap.*], with *the,* the second person of the Trinity; Jesus Christ (also called 'the Son of God' and 'the Son of man').

so-nant (sō′nạnt), *a.* [L. *sonans (sonant-),* ppr. of *sonare,* sound: see *sound⁵, v.*] **I.** *a.* Sounding; having sound; in *phonetics,* uttered with voice or vocal sound, as the sounds *a, l, n, b, z, v,* etc. (opposed to *surd*). **II.** *n.* In *phonetics,* a sonant speech-sound.—**so′nance, so′nan-cy,** *n.*

so-na-ta (sō-nä′tạ), *n.* [It., < *sonare,* < L. *sonare,* sound: see *sound⁵, v.*] In *music,* an instrumental composition, usually for the pianoforte, in several (commonly three or four) movements in contrasted rhythms but related keys.—**so-na-ti-na** (sō-nạ-tē′nạ), *n.* [It., dim. of *sonata.*] In *music,* a short or simplified sonata.

son-de-li (son-dā′lẹ), *n.* [Canarese.] An East Indian shrew, *Crocidura myosura,* with a strong musky odor.

son-der (zon′dẽr), *a.* [Detached from *sonderclass.*] Belonging or pertaining to the sonderclass.

son-der-class (zon′dẽr-klás), *n.* [G. *sonderklasse,* 'special class.'] A special class of small racing-yachts originating in Germany,

Sondeli.

and restricted as to size, sail area, cost of construction, etc., and also as to the crew, which must consist of three amateurs, citizens of the country in which the yacht was built.

song (sông), *n.* [AS. *sang, song,* = D. *zang* = G. *sang* = Icel. *söngr* = Goth. *saggws,* song; from the verb represented by E. *sing.*] The act or art of singing; vocal music; that which is sung; sometimes, poetical composition, or poetry (as, "This subject for heroic *song* Pleased me": Milton's "Paradise Lost," ix. 25); also, a short metrical composition intended or adapted for singing, esp. one in rimed stanzas; a lyric; a ballad; sometimes, any poem (as, "I thence Invoke thy aid to my adventurous *song*": Milton's "Paradise Lost," i. 13); also, a piece of music adapted for singing or simulating a piece to be sung (as, a part-*song*; Mendelssohn's *songs* without words); also, the musical or tuneful sounds produced by certain birds, insects, etc. (as, "From the stove there shrills The Cricket's *song*": Keats's "On the Grasshopper and Cricket"); some continuous ringing, whistling, murmuring, or other sound suggesting singing, as of a tea-kettle, a brook, etc. (as, "that falling stream's Lethean *song*": Shelley's "Triumph of Life," 463); also, a mere trifle (in certain expressions with reference to worth: as, "Two men . . . bought them [dogs], harness and all, for a *song,*" Jack London's "Call of the Wild," v.).—**Song of Solomon,** or **Song of Songs,** a certain book of the Old Testament. Also called *Canticles.*—**song′=bird,** *n.* A bird that sings; hence, a person, esp. a woman, who sings.—**song′fest,** *n.* [See *fest.*] A festival or entertainment of singing. [Colloq.] —**song′ful,** *a.* Abounding in song; melodious.—**song′less,** *a.* Devoid of song; lacking the power of song, as a bird.—**song′=spar′row,** *n.* A small fringilline song-bird, *Melospiza fasciata* (or *melodia*), of North America.—**song′ster** (-stẽr), *n.* One who sings; a singer; also, a writer of songs or poems; a poet; also, a song-bird (as, "Swifts are no *songsters,* and have only one harsh screaming note": G. White's "Nat. Hist. of Selborne," ii. 21); also, a book or other printed collection of songs.—**song′stress** (-stres), *n.* A female singer; also, a poetess; also, a female song-bird.—**song′=thrush,** *n.* A song-bird, the common thrush, *Turdus musicus,* of Europe.

Song-sparrow.

son-hood (sun′hud), *n.* The state or relation of being a son.

son-ic (son′ik), *a.* [L. *sonus,* sound: see *sound⁵, n.*] Of or pertaining to sound or sound-waves; noting or pertaining to certain methods of determining ocean depths, etc., as by measuring the time required for sound-waves to travel to the ocean bottom and be returned after the manner of an echo (as, *sonic* sounding; a *sonic* depth-finder); noting or pertaining to a method of transmitting power through a tube of confined liquid, in which strokes or blows of a plunger or the like at the transmitting end of the tube set up pulsations in the liquid ('sonic waves') which travel at the same rate as ordinary sound-waves and which, upon reaching the receiving end of the tube, can be made to operate a rock-drill or other device.

so-nif-er-ous (sō-nif′ẹ-rus), *a.* [L. *sonus,* sound, + *ferre,* bear.] Conveying or producing sound.

son=in=law (sun′in-lâ″), *n.*; pl. *sons-in-law.* The husband of one's daughter.

son-less (sun′les), *a.* Having no son.

son-net (son′et), *n.* [F. *sonnet,* < It. *sonetto,* dim. of *sono, suono,* sound, song, < L. *sonus,* E. *sound⁵, n.*] A short poem (obs. or rare); now, a poem, properly expressive of a single, complete thought, idea, or sentiment, of 14 lines (usually in 5-foot iambic meter) with rimes arranged according to one of certain definite schemes, being in the strict or Italian form divided into a major group of 8 lines (the *octave*) followed by a minor group of 6 lines (the *sestet*), and in a common English form into 3 quatrains followed by a couplet.—**son′net,** *v.*; -neted, -neting. **I.** *intr.* To compose sonnets. **II.** *tr.* To celebrate in a sonnet or sonnets.—

son-net-eer (son-e-tēr′), *n.* A composer of sonnets: often with a disparaging force (as, "I have heard many a little *sonneteer* called a fine genius": Addison, in "Spectator," 160).—**son-net-eer′**, *v. i.* To compose sonnets.—**son′net-ing**, *n.* The composing of, or a celebrating in, sonnets.

son-ny (sun′i), *n.*; pl. *sonnies* (-iz). [Dim. of *son*.] Little son: often used as a familiar term of address to a boy (as, "'Come here, *sonny*,' says he": Stevenson's "Treasure Island," ii.).

so-nom-e-ter (sō-nom′e-tèr), *n.* [L. *sonus*, sound: see *-meter*.] An acoustical device for experimenting with vibrating strings; also, an audiometer.

Sonometer.

so-no-rif-ic (sō-nǭ-rif′ik), *a.* [L. *sonor*, sound, noise, + *facere*, make.] Producing sound or noise, as the stridulating organs of a cricket.

so-no-rous (sǭ-nō′rus), *a.* [L. *sonorus*, < *sonor*, sound, < *sonare*: see *sound*⁵, *v.*] Giving out, or capable of giving out, a sound, esp. a deep or resonant sound, as a thing or a place (as, "*sonorous* metal blowing martial sounds": Milton's "Paradise Lost," i. 540); also, loud, deep, or resonant, as a sound (as, "With a summons *sonorous* Sounded the bell from its tower," Longfellow's "Evangeline," i. 4; "a round, deep, *sonorous* voice," Dickens's "Dombey and Son," i.); also, rich and full in sound, as language, verse, etc. (as, "Spanish, the most *sonorous* tongue in existence": Borrow's "Bible in Spain," i.); also, having a resounding voice, as a person.—**so-nor′i-ty** (-nor′i-ti), **so-no′rous-ness**, *n.*—**so-no′rous-ly**, *adv.*

son-ship (sun′ship), *n.* The state, fact, or relation of being a son; sonhood.

son-sy (son′si), *a.* [Gael. *sonas*, good fortune, prosperity.] Bringing luck or good fortune; also, thriving or plump; buxom or comely; comfortable-looking; cheerful; jolly. [Sc., Ir., and north. Eng.]

son-tag (son′tag), *n.* [From Henriette *Sontag* (1806–54), German singer.] A woman's knitted cape with long ends crossed over the breast and tied or fastened together at the back.

soo (sö), *n.* See *sault*.

soon (sön), *adv.* [AS. *sōna* = OS. *sāna*, immediately: cf. Goth. *suns*, immediately, soon.] Immediately†, or at once†; hence, within a short period after this (or that) time, event, etc. (as, we shall *soon* know; they were *soon* to learn the truth; this happened *soon* after dinner); before long; in the near future; at an early date; also, early in a period of time (now prov.: as, *soon* in the morning); also, promptly or quickly (as, no *sooner* said than done; least said *soonest* mended; as *soon* as I hear I will let you know); readily or willingly (as, I would as *soon* walk as ride; he would *sooner* die than yield).—**soon,** *a.* Coming or occurring soon; early; prompt; quick; speedy. [Now chiefly prov.]—**soon′er,** *n.* One who settles on government land before it is legally opened to settlers in order to gain the choice of location; hence, one who gains an unfair advantage by getting ahead of others. [Slang, U. S.]—**soon′ness,** *n.*

soot (sùt or söt), *n.* [AS. *sōt* = Icel. *sōt* = Sw. *sot* = Dan. *sod*, soot.] A black carbonaceous substance produced during the combustion of coal, wood, oil, etc., rising in fine particles and adhering to the sides of the chimney or pipe conveying the smoke.—**soot,** *v. t.* To mark, cover, or treat with soot.

sooth (söth), *a.* [AS. *sōth*, akin to Icel. *sannr*, Goth. *sunjis*, true, also Skt. *satya*, real, true, and *sant*, real, true, prop. ppr., 'being': see *suttee*.] True† or real†; also, in accordance with truth (archaic: as, "if thy speech be *sooth*," Shakspere's "Macbeth," v. 5. 40); also, truthful or veracious (archaic: as, "A destined errant-knight I come, Announced by prophet *sooth* and old," Scott's "Lady of the Lake," i. 24); also, soothing, soft, or delicious (poetic: as, "*soothest* Sleep," Keats's "To Sleep").—**sooth,** *n.* [AS. *sōth*.] Truth, reality, or fact (archaic: as, in *sooth*; to say the *sooth*; *sooth* to tell); also, a true thing or statement†; also, soothsaying†

or prognostication†; also, soothing or smooth speech† (as, "words of *sooth*": Shakspere's "Richard II.," iii. 3. 136).—

sooth, *adv.* [AS. *sōthe*.] Truly; in truth: as, "And, *sooth*, men say that he was not the sonne Of mortall Syre" (Spenser's "Faerie Queene," iii. 3. 13). [Archaic.]

soothe (söTH), *v.*; *soothed*, *soothing*. [AS. *sōthian*, < *sōth*, E. *sooth*, *a.*] **I.** *tr.* To prove to be true†; also, to declare (a statement, etc.) to be true†; support (a person) in a statement†; hence, to humor (a person) by assenting or agreeing† (as, "Good my lord, *soothe* him; let him take the fellow": Shakspere's "King Lear," iii. 4. 182); cajole† or flatter†; now, to put in or restore to good humor, or soften, mollify, or appease (as, "Music has charms to *soothe* a savage breast": Congreve's "Mourning Bride," i. 1); also, to tranquilize or calm, as a person, the feelings, nerves, etc. (as, "You have often *soothed* me when I was frightened": Dunsany's "Laughter of the Gods," iii.); relieve, ease, comfort, or refresh (as, "A cloud may *soothe* the eye made blind by blaze": Browning's "Ring and the Book," x.); mitigate, assuage, or allay, as pain, sorrow, doubt, etc.; affect in an agreeably quieting or restful way (as, "Scenes that *sooth'd* Or charm'd me young . . . I find Still soothing": Cowper's "Task," i. 141); bring, drive, etc., by soothing influence (as, "The murmuring wind, the moving leaves, *Soothed* him at length to sleep," Southey's "Thalaba," iv. 10; to *soothe* a person into tranquillity; to *soothe* away pain); also, to smooth or gloss over, as an offense† (see Shakspere's "3 Henry VI.," iii. 3. 175). **II.** *intr.* To exert a soothing influence; bring tranquillity, calm, ease, or comfort.—**sooth-er** (sö′THèr), *n.*

sooth-fast (söth′fast), *a.* [AS. *sōthfæst*, < *sōth*, E. *sooth*, *n.*, + *fæst*, E. *fast*¹, *a.*] True, as statements; also, truthful or veracious, as persons; also, faithful or loyal. [Archaic or Sc.]—**sooth′fast-ly,** *adv.*—**sooth′fast-ness,** *n.*

sooth-ful (söth′fùl), *a.* True; also, truthful; trustworthy. [Archaic or Sc.]

sooth-ing (sö′THing), *p. a.* That soothes; mollifying; tranquilizing; affording relief or ease.—**sooth′ing-ly,** *adv.*—**sooth′ing-ness,** *n.*

sooth-ly (söth′li), *adv.* [AS. *sōthlīce*: cf. *sooth*, *a.*] With truth; in truth; truly; verily: as, "*Soothly*, other shores I fain would see" (W. Morris's "Jason," iii. 282). [Archaic.]

sooth-say (söth′sā), *v. i.* [Back-formation from *soothsayer* or *soothsaying*.] To foretell future events; make predictions; prophesy.—**sooth′say,** *n.* A prediction or prophecy; also, omen or presage (as, "but God turne the same [signs] to good *sooth-say*": Spenser's "Faerie Queene," iii. 8. 50). [Now rare.]

sooth-say-er (söth′sā″èr), *n.* [ME. *sothseyere*, *sothseggere*: cf. AS. *sōthsecgan*, to 'say sooth,' speak truly.] One who tells the truth†; also, one who professes to foretell future events (as, "A *soothsayer* bids you beware the ides of March": Shakspere's "Julius Cæsar," i. 2. 19); also, a mantis (insect). —**sooth′say″ing,** *n.* The practice or art of a soothsayer; the foretelling of future events; also, a prediction or prophecy (as, "Divinations, and *soothsayings*, and dreams, are vain": Ecclus. xxxiv. 5).

soot-y (sùt′i or sö′ti), *a.* Covered, blackened, or smirched with soot; consisting of or resembling soot; of a black, blackish, or dusky color (as, the *sooty* tern: see *tern*¹).—**soot′i-ly,** *adv.*—**soot′i-ness,** *n.*

sop (sop), *n.* [AS. *sopp*, sop (of bread), akin to *sūpan*, sup, drink, and F. *soupe*, sop, soup: cf. *sup*¹ and *soup*.] A piece of bread or the like dipped, or for dipping, in liquid food (as, "The prudent Sibyl had before prepar'd A *sop*, in honey steep'd, to charm the guard": Dryden's tr. Virgil's "Æneid," vi. 567); hence, anything thoroughly soaked; a soppy mass or spot; a soppy condition; also, a milk-sop; also (from the sop thrown to quiet Cerberus during Æneas's visit to the lower world: see first def., with quotation), something given to pacify or quiet, or as a bribe (as, "He . . . takes the sacrament duly once a year as a *sop* to Nemesis": S. Butler's "Way of All Flesh," lxxxvi.).—**sop,** *v.*; *sopped*, *sopping.* [AS. *soppian*.] **I.** *tr.* To dip or soak (bread, etc.) in some liquid (as, "I gave him some milk . . . and let him see me drink it before him, and *sop* my bread in it": Defoe's "Robinson Crusoe," i. 14); also, to drench; also, to take up (water, etc.) by absorption (usually with *up*: as, "He returned with a little sponge and a basin, and had begun *sopping* up the waters," S. Butler's "Way of All Flesh," xvii.). **II.** *intr.* To become or be soaking wet; also, of a liquid, to soak (*in*, etc.: as, "*Sopping* and soaking in among the leaves . . . oozing down into the boggy ground . . . went a dark, dark stain," Dickens's "Martin Chuzzlewit," xlvii.).

soph[1] (sof), *n.* Shortened form of *sophister* (in university use): as, "soon after he had been created senior *soph* [at Oxford]" (R. Graves's "Spiritual Quixote," i. 1). [Colloq.]

soph[2] (sof), *n.* Shortened form of *sophomore* (in college use, etc.). [Colloq., U. S.]

so-phi (sō′fi), *n.* See *sophy*.

soph-ism (sof′izm), *n.* [OF. *sophisme, sophime* (F. *sophisme*), < L. *sophisma*, < Gr. σόφισμα, clever device, trick, sophism, < σοφίζεσθαι, deal subtly, < σοφός, skilled, clever, wise.] A specious but fallacious argument, used either to display ingenuity in reasoning or for the purpose of deception (cf. *paralogism*); sometimes, any false argument; a fallacy; also, sophistry.

soph-ist (sof′ist), *n.* [= F. *sophiste*, < L. *sophista, sophistes*, < Gr. σοφιστής, adept, wise man, sophist, < σοφίζεσθαι: see *sophism*.] [Often *cap.*] Any of a class of professional teachers in ancient Greece who, for pay, gave instruction in various fields, as in general culture, rhetoric, politics, or disputation; often, any member of a portion of this class at a later period who, while professing to teach skill in reasoning, concerned themselves with ingenuity and specious effectiveness rather than soundness of argument; hence [*l. c.*], one who reasons adroitly and speciously rather than soundly; also, a man of learning.—**soph′is-ter,** *n.* [OF. *sofistre*, < L. *sophista.*] An ancient Greek sophist†; also, a specious but unsound reasoner; also, in certain universities and colleges, as at Cambridge, England, a student after the completion of his first year, esp. one in his second or third year ('junior sophister' or 'senior sophister': now chiefly hist., or in the shortened form *soph*: see *soph*[1]).—**so-phis-tic, so-phis-ti-cal** (sō-fis′tik, -ti-ḳal), *a.* [L. *sophisticus*, < Gr. σοφιστικός.] Of or pertaining to sophists or sophistry; given to the use of sophistry; characteristic or suggestive of sophistry (as, "From the point of a modern's carnal reasoning all this has a thoroughly *sophistic* flavour": Morley's "Oliver Cromwell," iii. 6); of the nature of sophistry, or fallacious (as, "It is a reasoning weak, rotten, and *sophistical*": Burke's "Conciliation with the Colonies").—**so-phis′ti-cal-ly,** *adv.*

so-phis-ti-cate (sō-fis′ti-kāt), *v.*; -*cated, -cating.* [ML. *sophisticatus*, pp. of *sophisticare*, < L. *sophisticus*, E. *sophistic.*] **I.** *tr.* To delude by sophistry or untruth, as a person, the mind, etc.; mislead or pervert; also, to falsify, as truth, statements, etc. (as, "I have . . . *Sophisticated* no truth, Nursed no delusion": M. Arnold's "Empedocles on Etna," ii.); alter unwarrantably, as a text, spelling, etc.; also, to render (commodities) impure by admixture; adulterate; hence, fig., to impair or debase by addition or change; make less pure or genuine; also, to change from the natural character or simplicity, as a person, the mind, etc.; make less natural, simple, or ingenuous. **II.** *intr.* To use sophistry; quibble; act disingenuously.—**so-phis′ti-cat-ed** (-kā-ted), *p. a.* Falsified; also, adulterated; also, changed from the natural character or simplicity; artificial; esp., of a person, the ideas, tastes, manners, etc., altered by education, worldly experience, etc.—**so-phis-ti-ca′tion** (-kā′shọn), *n.* [ML. *sophisticatio*(*n-*).] The use of sophistry; delusion or falsification by sophistry; a sophism, quibble, or fallacious argument; also, unwarrantable alteration, as of a text; also, adulteration, as of a commodity; an adulterated form or preparation of a commodity; a substance used for adulterating something; also, fig., impairment or debasement, as by some change affecting purity or genuineness (as, the *sophistication* of religion); also, change from the natural character or simplicity, or the resulting condition; sophisticated character, ideas, tastes, or ways as the result of education, worldly experience, etc. (as, "Every thing I see . . . in this great reservoir of folly, knavery, and *sophistication* [London], contributes to enhance the value of a country life": Smollett's "Humphry Clinker," June 2).—**so-phis′-ti-ca-tor,** *n.*

soph-is-try (sof′is-tri), *n.*; pl. -*tries* (-triz). [OF. F. *sophis-*

terie.] The art, practice, or learning of the ancient Greek sophists (as, "Four principal varieties are distinguishable . . . the *sophistries* of culture, of rhetoric, of politics, and of 'eristic,' i.e. disputation": Encyc. Brit., 11th ed., XXV. 418); also, the art or practice of disputation; dialectic exercise; also, specious but fallacious reasoning (as, "Gross *sophistry* has scarce ever had any influence upon the opinions of mankind, except in matters of philosophy and speculation": Adam Smith's "Wealth of Nations," v. 1. 3. 2); a false argument, or sophism (as, "Can your intellect be deluded by such barefaced *sophistries?*" Kingsley's "Yeast," x.).

Soph-o-cle-an (sof-ō-klē′ạn), *a.* Of, pertaining to, or characteristic of Sophocles (495?–406? B.C.), the Greek tragic poet.

soph-o-more (sof′ō-mōr), *n.* [Prob. orig. < *sophom*, *sophim*, obs. var. of *sophism*, + *-or*[2], but with form perhaps affected by a supposed derivation from Gr. σοφός, wise, + μωρός, foolish.] A student in the second year of the course at a university, college, or school; also, a sophomoric person. [Chiefly U. S.]—**soph-o-mor′ic, soph-o-mor′-i-cal** (-mor′ik, -i-ḳal), *a.* Of or pertaining to a sophomore or sophomores; suggestive of or resembling the traditional sophomore, as in bombastic language, complacent pretensions, or complete assurance, coupled with crudeness and ignorance. [Chiefly U. S.]—**soph-o-mor′i-cal-ly,** *adv.*

so-pho-ra (sō-fō′rä), *n.* [NL.; from Ar.] Any plant of the fabaceous genus *Sophora*, native in warm regions of both hemispheres, consisting mostly of trees and shrubs with odd-pinnate leaves and racemes or panicles of white, yellow, or violet flowers, and including species much cultivated for ornament.

so-phy (sō′fi), *n.*; pl. *-phies* (-fiz). [Pers. çafī, < Ar. çafī-ud-dīn, 'purity of religion,' used as a personal epithet.] [Often *cap.*] A former title of the ruler (shah) of Persia. See Shakspere's "Merchant of Venice," ii. 1. 25.

so-pite (sō-pīt′), *v. t.*; -*pited, -piting.* [L. *sopitus*, pp. of *sopire*, put to sleep, related to *sopor*: see *sopor.*] To put to sleep; make drowsy or dull; fig., to set at rest, put an end to, or settle, as a dispute. [Now rare.]—**so-pite′,** *a.* Put to sleep; fig., set at rest; settled. [Now rare.]

so-por (sō′pọr), *n.* [L., deep sleep, akin to *somnus*, also Gr. ὕπνος, Skt. *svapna*, AS. *swefn*, sleep.] In *pathol.*, a deep, unnatural sleep; lethargy.—**so-po-rif-er-ous** (sō-pō-rif′e̱-rus or sop-ọ-), *a.* [L. *soporifer*: see *-ferous.*] Bringing sleep; soporific.—**so-po-rif′er-ous-ness,** *n.*—**so-po-rif′ic.** [See *-fic.*] **I.** *a.* Causing or tending to cause sleep; also, pertaining to or characterized by sleep or sleepiness; sleepy or drowsy. **II.** *n.* Something causing sleep, esp. a medicine. —**so′po-rose** (-rōs), *a.* In *pathol.*, characterized by morbid sleep or stupor, as certain diseases.

sopped (sopt), *p. a.* [See *sop.*] Soaked or steeped in a liquid; also, drenched with water or rain.—**sop′ping,** *p. a.* Soaking; soaked or drenched, as with rain.—**sop′py,** *a.* Soaked, drenched, or very wet, as ground; rainy, as weather, a day, etc.

so-pra-no (sō-prä′nō). [It., < *sopra*, above, < L. *supra*: see *supra.*] In *music*: **I.** *n.*; pl. -*nos* (-nōz), It. -*ni* (-nē). The highest singing voice in women and boys; a part for or sung by such a voice; also, a singer with such a voice. **II.** *a.* Of or pertaining to the soprano; having the compass of a soprano.—**so-pra′nist,** *n.*

so-ra (sō′rä), *n.* [Origin uncertain.] A small, short-billed North American rail, *Porzana carolina*, the Carolina rail; also, a related bird, *Gallinula galeata*, the Florida gallinule ('king sora').

sorb[1] (sôrb), *n.* [L. *sorbus*, service-tree, *sorbum*, its fruit: cf. *service*[1].] A European service-tree, *Sorbus domestica*; also, the European rowan, *S. aucuparia*; also, the fruit of either.

Sora (*Porzana carolina*).

Sorb[2] (sôrb), *n.* [G. *Sorbe*, var. of *Serbe*, representing the native Slav. name: cf. *Serb* (Serbian).] A member of a Slavic people dwelling in Saxony and adjoining parts of Prussia; a Wend; also, the language spoken by this people (see *Sorbian, n.*).

sor-be-fa-cient (sôr-bẹ-fā′shẹnt). [L. *sorbere*, suck in, + *faciens* (*facient-*), ppr. of *facere*, do, make.] **I.** *a.* Promoting absorption. **II.** *n.* A sorbefacient agent.

sor-bet (sôr′bẹt), *n.* [F., = E. *sherbet*.] The sherbet of the East; also, water-ice (of various flavors).

Sor-bi-an (sôr′bi-ạn). **I.** *a.* Of or pertaining to the Sorbs or their language. **II.** *n.* A Sorb; also, the Sorbian language, having two varieties (Upper, or High, Sorbian, and Lower, or Low, Sorbian), and belonging to the western branch of the Slavic family.

sor-bite (sôr′bīt), *n.* [From H. C. *Sorby* (1826–1908), English geologist.] In *metal.*, a constituent of steel related to pearlite.—**sor-bit′ic** (-bit′ik), *a.* Pertaining to or containing sorbite: as, *sorbitic* steel rails.

Sor-bon-ist (sôr′bọn-ist), *n.* [F. *sorboniste*.] A student or a doctor of the Sorbonne, a celebrated theological college founded in Paris in 1257 by Robert de Sorbon (the name *Sorbonne* now being given to the seat of the faculties of letters and science of the University of Paris).

sor-cer-er (sôr′sėr-ėr), *n.* [For earlier *sorcer*, < OF. F. *sorcier*, < ML. *sortiarius*, fortune-teller, sorcerer, < L. *sors* (*sort-*), lot, E. *sort*[1], *n.*] One who (professedly) practises magic arts; a magician or enchanter; esp., one supposed to exercise supernatural powers through the aid of evil spirits: as, "dark-working *sorcerers*" (Shakspere's "Comedy of Errors," i. 2. 99).—**sor′cer-ess**, *n.* A female sorcerer: as, "Again she [Medea] grew to be the *sorceress*, Worker of fearful things" (W. Morris's "Jason," xvii. 440).—**sor′-cer-ous**, *a.* Of the nature of or involving sorcery (as, "*sorcerous* spells": Kinglake's "Eothen," viii.); also, using sorcery.—**sor′cer-ous-ly**, *adv.*—**sor′cer-y** (-i), *n.*; pl. -*ies* (-iz). [OF. *sorcerie*, < *sorcier*.] The art, practices, or spells of a sorcerer; magic or enchantment; esp., the black art, or black magic, in which supernatural powers are supposed to be exercised through the aid of evil spirits; a piece of magic or a spell wrought by a sorcerer (as, "Of long time he had bewitched them with *sorceries*": Acts, viii. 11); fig., magical action or influence; witchery.

sor-da-men-te (sôr-dä-men′tā), *adv.* [It., < *sordo*, deaf, dull: see *sordino*.] In *music*, in a muted or muffled manner; softly.

sor-des (sôr′dēz), *n.* [L., < *sordere*, be dirty: cf. *sordid*.] Dirt; filth; esp., foul matter gathering on or in the body, as on the teeth, in the stomach, in an ulcer, etc.; specif., in *pathol.*, foul crusts forming on the lips and teeth in typhoid and other fevers.

sor-did (sôr′did), *a.* [F. *sordide*, < L. *sordidus*, < *sordere*, be dirty: cf. *sordes*.] Dirty or filthy (as, "His dress . . . was torn and *sordid*": Borrow's "Romany Rye," x.); foul (as, a *sordid* ulcer; a *sordid* discharge from an ulcer); squalid, as places; also, menial, abject, or low, as offices, uses, etc.†; also, morally mean, ignoble, or base (as, *sordid* actions, vices, or gains); esp., meanly selfish, self-seeking, or mercenary (as, "His ambitions are a little *sordid* . . . he is too intent upon growing rich," W. Churchill's "Modern Chronicle," i. 9; *sordid* motives or considerations; *sordid* persons; a *sordid* age); in *bot.* and *zoöl.*, of a dull or dirty hue.—**sor′did-ly**, *adv.*—**sor′did-ness**, *n.*

sor-dine (sôr′dēn), *n.* Same as *sordino*.

sor-di-no (sôr-dē′nō), *n.*; pl. -*ni* (-nē). [It., < *sordo*, deaf, dull, < L. *surdus*, E. *surd*.] In *music*, a device for deadening the sound of a stringed instrument; a mute.

sor-dor (sôr′dọr), *n.* [From L. *sordere*, be dirty, with -*or* as in *squalor*.] Sordid character or characteristics: as, "the *sordor* of civilisation" (Byron's "Island," ii. 4).

sore[1] (sōr). [OF. *sor* (F. *saur*) = ML. *saurus*; origin uncertain: cf. *sorrel*[1].] **I.** *a.* Reddish-brown, as a hawk in the plumage of the first year, or as some other bird or animal. [Obs. or archaic.] **II.**† *n.* A buck (male deer) of the fourth year. See Shakspere's "Love's Labour's Lost," iv. 2. 59.

sore[2] (sōr), *a.*; compar. *sorer*, superl. *sorest*. [AS. *sār* = D. *zeer* = Icel. *sárr* = Norw. *saar*, sore.] Physically painful, as a wound, hurt, diseased part, etc.; aching, smarting, or painfully sensitive; also, suffering bodily pain from wounds, bruises, diseased parts, etc., as a person; hence, suffering mental pain, grieved, distressed, or sorrowful (as, to be *sore* at heart; to have a *sore* heart or conscience); irritated, offended, or feeling aggrieved (as, to be *sore* over supposed injustice; "What are you *sore* about?" Sinclair Lewis's "Babbitt," xx.); irritable, touchy, or in a mood to take offense; being an occasion of irritation (as, a *sore* subject); also, causing great bodily suffering, or grievous (as, *sore* blows; "A pain . . . came upon him, and *sore* torments of the inner parts," 2 Mac. ix. 5); hence, causing great mental pain, distress, or sorrow (as, a *sore* bereavement; "*sore* news," Galt's "Ayrshire Legatees," vi.); in general, causing suffering, misery, hardship, etc. (as, a *sore* famine; a *sore* tax; "From having had all her own way . . . and money to spend, it was a *sore* change to her," G. MacDonald's "Annals of a Quiet Neighbourhood," vii.); severe, as pain, distress, trouble, displeasure, etc.; fierce or violent, as battle, storms, etc.; extreme, or very great (as, a *sore* offense; *sore* need).— **sore throat**, inflammation of the lining membrane of the gullet, pharynx, fauces, or upper air-passages, attended with pain, as in swallowing.—**sore**[2], *n.* [AS. *sār*: cf. *sorry*.] Bodily pain†; also, disease†; also, a sore spot or place on the body, as from wounding, ulceration, etc.; fig., a source or cause of grief, distress, ill feeling, trouble, etc. (as, "Having no desire to rip up old *sores*, I shall say no more anent it": Galt's "Annals of the Parish," xxviii.).—**sore**[2], *adv.* [AS. *sāre*.] Sorely; painfully; grievously; severely; extremely. [Now chiefly archaic or prov.]

so-re-di-um (sō-rē′di-um), *n.*; pl. -*dia* (-di-ạ). [NL., < Gr. σωρός, a heap.] In *bot.*, a single gonidium or group of gonidia enveloped in hyphal tissue, breaking through the surface of the thallus of a lichen and capable, after detachment, of developing into a new thallus.—**so-re′di-al**, *a.*

sore=fal-con (sōr′fâ″kn), *n.* [See *sore*[1].] A falcon in the reddish-brown plumage of the first year, before molting. Also **sore′=hawk**. [Obs. or archaic.]

sore-head (sōr′hed), *n.* A person who is sore or offended over some grievance; often, a disgruntled member of a political party. [Slang, U. S.]—**sòre′head′ed**, *a.* Feeling sore or aggrieved: as, "You were *soreheaded* about something" (Sinclair Lewis's "Babbitt," xxxiii.). [Slang.]

sore-hon (sōr′hon), *n.* See *sorren*.

sore-ly (sōr′li), *adv.* In a sore manner; painfully; grievously; severely; extremely.—**sore′ness**, *n.*

sor-ghum (sôr′gum), *n.* [NL., < It. *sorgo*; origin uncertain.] A cereal grass, *Andropogon sorghum*, of many varieties, which may be divided into four groups, the sweet or saccharine sorghums (which have a sweet, sugar-bearing juice and a rather poor grain, and are used especially for making a kind of molasses or syrup and for forage), the grain-sorghums or non-saccharine sorghums (which have a grain of high feeding value and a usually scanty or poor juice, and are used for forage, the grain sometimes being used also as a food for man), the grass-sorghums (which are leafy and fine-stemmed, and are used principally for producing hay), and the broom-corns (which have dry, pithy stalks and long, stiff panicles, and are used for making brooms and brushes); also, the syrup made from the sweet or saccharine sorghums.

Sorghum. — 1, wild form; 2, panicle of same.

sor-go (sôr′gō), *n.*; pl. -*gos* (-gōz). [It.: see *sorghum*.] Any of the sweet or saccharine sorghums. See *sorghum*.

so-ri (sō′rī), *n.* Plural of *sorus*.

sor-i-cine (sor′i-sin), *a.* [L. *soricinus*, < *sorex*, shrew.] Of, pertaining to, or resembling the shrews. See *shrew*[1].

so-ri-tes (sō-rī′tēz), *n.*; pl. *sorites*. [L., < Gr. σωρείτης, < σωρός, a heap.] In *logic*, a form of argument having several premises and one conclusion, and resolvable into a number of syllogisms, the conclusion of each of which is a premise of the next.—**so-rit′ic** (-rit′ik), *a.*

sorn (sôrn), *v. i.* [From *sorren.*] To obtrude one's self on another for food or lodging; sponge: as, "gillies that . . . maun gang thigging and *sorning* about on their acquaintance" (Scott's "Rob Roy," xxvi.). [Sc.]—**sorn′er,** *n.*

so-ro-ral (sọ-rō′ral). *a.* [L. *soror,* sister: see *sorority.*] Pertaining to or characteristic of a sister; sisterly.

so-ror-i-cide (sọ-ror′i-sīd), *n.* [L. *sororicida,* LL. *sororicidium,* < L. *soror.* sister: see *-cide.*] One who kills his or her sister; also, the act of killing one's own sister.

so-ror-i-ty (sọ-ror′i-ti), *n.;* pl. *-ties* (-tiz). [ML. *sororitas,* < L. *soror,* sister, akin to E. *sister:* see *sister.*] A sisterhood; esp., a society or club of women or girls, as in a college. Cf. *fraternity.*

so-ro-sis (sọ-rō′sis), *n.;* pl. *soroses* (-sēz). [NL., < Gr. σωρός, a heap; in last sense now perhaps associated with L. *soror,* sister.] In *bot.,* a fleshy multiple fruit composed of many flowers, seed-vessels, and receptacles consolidated, as in the pineapple and mulberry. Also, a woman's club.

sor-rel[1] (sor′el). [OF. *sorel,* < *sor,* E. *sore*[1].] **I.** *a.* Reddish-brown. **II.** *n.* A reddish-brown color; also, a horse of this color (as, "The horse was . . . a *sorrel* with long mane and tail": Borrow's "Bible in Spain," lvi.); also, a buck (male deer) of the third year (obs. or archaic: see Shakspere's "Love's Labour's Lost," iv. 2. 60).

sor-rel[2] (sor′el), *n.* [OF. *surele* (F. *surelle*), < *sur,* sour; from Teut., and akin to E. *sour.*] Any of various plants of the genus *Rumex,* having succulent acid leaves used in salads, sauces, etc.; also, any of various sour-juiced plants of the genus *Oxalis* (also called *wood-sorrel*); also, any of various similar plants.—**sor′rel=tree,** *n.* A North American ericaceous tree, *Oxydendrum arboreum,* having leaves with an acid flavor and racemes of white flowers.

sor-ren (sor′en), *n.* [ME. *sorryn;* from Ir.: cf. *sorn.*] Formerly, in Ireland and Scotland, an exaction of hospitality or maintenance due from a vassal to the lord or his men; also, a tax imposed in lieu of this.

sor-ri-ly (sor′i-li), *adv.* In a sorry manner.—**sor′ri-ness,** *n.*

sor-row (sor′ō), *n.* [AS. *sorg, sorh,* = D. *zorg* = G. *sorge* = Icel., Sw., and Dan. *sorg* = Goth. *saurga,* care, sorrow.] Distress of mind caused by loss, affliction, disappointment, etc.; grief, sadness, or regret; a feeling or experience of grief (as, "a man of *sorrows,* and acquainted with grief": Isa. liii. 3); also, a cause or occasion of grief or regret (as, "Call ignorance my *sorrow,* not my sin!" Browning's "Ring and the Book," x.); an affliction, misfortune, or trouble; hence, in imprecations, etc., mischief or ill fortune (as, "*Sorrow* on thee and all the pack of you!" Shakspere's "Taming of the Shrew," iv. 3. 33); the devil (esp. Sc. and Ir.: as, *sorrow,* or the *sorrow,* take him!); also, the manifestation of grief; lamentation or mourning; tears (poetic: as, "Down his white beard a stream of *sorrow* flows," Pope's tr. Homer's "Iliad," ix.).—**sor′row,** *v.* [AS. *sorgian.*] **I.** *intr.* To feel sorrow, or grieve; also, to manifest grief, lament, or mourn. **II.** *tr.* To feel or manifest sorrow over (now usually followed by a clause); also, to cause to sorrow or grieve, or make sorrowful (now rare).—**sor′row-er,** *n.*—**sor′row-ful,** *a.* Full of or feeling sorrow, as a person, the heart, etc.; grieved; sad; also, indicative or expressive of sorrow, as the looks, voice, words, etc.; mournful; plaintive (as, "a pretty dove-coloured bird with pretty *sorrowful* song": W. H. Hudson's "Far Away and Long Ago," vi.); also, fraught with, involving, or causing sorrow, as a place, sight, occurrence, occasion, etc.; distressing.—**sor′row-ful-ly,** *adv.*—**sor′row-ful-ness,** *n.*—**sor′row-ing-ly,** *adv.*

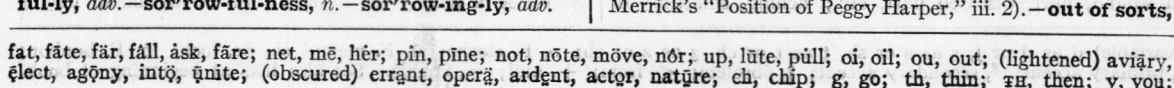

Female Flowering Plant of Field-sorrel (*Rumex acetosella*).—*a,* a male flower; *b,* a female flower.

sor-ry (sor′i), *a.;* compar. *sorrier,* superl. *sorriest.* [AS. *sārig,* < *sār,* E. *sore*[2], *n.*] Sorrowful, grieved, or sad (as, "Neither be ye *sorry;* for the joy of the Lord is your strength": Neh. viii. 10); now, more commonly, feeling regret, compunction, sympathy, pity, etc., for some reason expressed or understood (as, to be *sorry* for a loss, a fault, another's ill fortune, or the person himself; to be *sorry* to hear a thing: much used in courteous expressions of regret, etc.); also, fraught or associated with, or causing, sorrow (as, "The melancholy vale, The place of death and *sorry* execution": Shakspere's "Comedy of Errors," v. 1. 121); hence, of a deplorable, pitiable, or miserable kind (as, to be in a *sorry* plight; to come to a *sorry* end; "A *sorry* thing life seemed to him to be," W. Morris's "Jason," xvii. 537); wretched, poor, mean, or pitiful (as, a *sorry* horse; a *sorry* meal; a *sorry* jest; "I showed him a lot of this sort of literature . . . he confessed that it was poor stuff, exceedingly *sorry* rubbish," Mark Twain's "Life on the Mississippi," lix.).

sort[1]† (sôrt), *n.* [OF. F. *sort,* < L. *sors* (*sort-*), lot, share, destiny, condition: cf. *sort*[2].] A lot, or something awarded by lot (see Shakspere's "Troilus and Cressida," i. 3. 376); also, one's lot, as in life or experience; fate; destiny.—**sort**[1]†, *v.* [OF. *sortir,* < L. *sortire, sortiri,* < *sors.*] **I.** *tr.* To allot; assign; also, to ordain (as, "If God *sort* it so, 'Tis more than we deserve": Shakspere's "Richard III.," ii. 3. 36). **II.** *intr.* To come to pass; turn out: as, "*Sort* how it will, I shall have gold for all" (Shakspere's "2 Henry VI.," i. 2. 107).

sort[2] (sôrt), *n.* [OF. F. *sorte,* fem. (beside *sort,* masc., E. *sort*[1]), < L. *sors* (*sort-*), lot, condition, rank, LL. class, order: see *sort*[1].] Condition†, station†, or rank†, esp. high rank† (as, "a gentleman of great *sort*": Shakspere's "Henry V.," iv. 7. 142); also, character, quality, or nature (as, "The fire shall try every man's work of what *sort* it is": 1 Cor. iii. 13); hence, a particular kind, species, variety, or description, as distinguished by the character or nature (and comprising either a single individual or more: as, to discover a new *sort* of mineral; several *sorts* of fruit; we have no more of that *sort* in stock; "Thou shalt not wear a garment of divers *sorts,* as of woollen and linen together," Deut. xxii. 11); a class or number of persons or things ranked together as being of the same general character or as having attributes in common (as, the cases fall naturally into two *sorts*; this *sort* of fish is, or sometimes are, abundant along our coast; colloquially and irregularly, these, or those, *sort* of fish, people, books, etc.: cf. *kind*[1] in similar uses); sometimes, specif., a particular class or order of persons (as, the younger *sort*; the poorer or meaner *sort*); also, a person or thing as being of a particular character, kind, or class (as, he is a good *sort* of man, or, colloquially, a good *sort*; his face wore an odd *sort* of smile; he is a poor *sort* of teacher); a more or less adequate or inadequate example of something (as, to travel in a *sort* of litter; the unicorn is represented as a *sort* of horse with a single horn); also, a company, band, troop, or flock, as of persons or animals (obs. or archaic: as, "a *sort* of shepheards," Spenser's "Astrophel," 139); a number or quantity of persons or things (now prov. Eng. and Sc.: as, a good *sort,* a good many); also, manner, fashion, or way (as, "apparell'd in exactest *sort,*" Cowper's "Retired Cat," 19: archaic except in certain phrases, as *in a sort,* etc., see below); in *printing,* one of the kinds of characters of a font of type (usually in *pl.*).—**after a sort.** Same as *in a sort.*—**in a sort,** in a manner; after a fashion: as, "She . . . kept up the dignity of the great house *in a sort* while she lived" (Lamb's "Dream-Children").—**in some sort,** in some way or other, or after a fashion (as, "We began already to converse together *in some sort*": Swift's "Gulliver's Travels," i. 2); also, to some extent, or in some measure (as, "You have, as you say, become less prosperous, *in some sort* through me": Mrs. H. Ward's "Robert Elsmere," xxx.).—**of sorts,** of various kinds (now rare); also, of one sort or another, or of an indefinite kind (as, "The Alcalde . . . was . . . police officer, petty magistrate *of sorts*": W. H. Hudson's "Far Away and Long Ago," viii.); hence, of a mediocre or poor kind (as, a writer or a novel *of sorts*; "We've a fountain, *of sorts*; we're very vain of our shabby fountain!" L. Merrick's "Position of Peggy Harper," iii. 2).—**out of sorts,**

not in the normal condition of good health, spirits, or temper (as, "We've had a hot day, and are all tired and *out of sorts*": Stevenson's "Treasure Island," xiii.); in *printing*, short of certain characters of a font of type.—**sort of** (used adverbially). Same as *kind of* (see under *kind*[1]). [Colloq.] —**sort**[2], *v.* I. *tr.* To arrange according to sort, kind, or class; separate into sorts; classify; also, to assign to a particular sort or class; class, group, or place (*with, together,* etc.); also, to separate or take (*out*) from other sorts, or from others; hence, to select† or choose† (as, "I'll *sort* some other time to visit you": Shakspere's "1 Henry VI.," ii. 3, 27); also, to suit or adapt (*to*) or cause to accord (*with*) (obs. or archaic); also, to associate (one's self) in company or intercourse, as with others (now Sc. and prov. Eng.); also, to furnish or supply, as with something suitable or desired (now Sc.); feed and litter (an animal: Sc. and north. Eng.); put to rights (Sc., Ir., and north. Eng.); fig., to punish (Sc. and north. Eng.). II. *intr.* To agree, accord, or comport (archaic: as, "Different styles with different subjects *sort*," Pope's "Essay on Criticism," 322); occur or exist fittingly† (as, "Among unequals what society Can *sort*, what harmony, or true delight?" Milton's "Paradise Lost," viii. 384); also, to associate or consort (now Sc. and prov. Eng.).—**sort′a·ble,** *a.* That may be sorted; also, assorted†, or of various sorts†; also, suitable† or appropriate†.—**sort′-ance†,** *n.* Agreement; accord. See Shakspere's "2 Henry IV.," iv. 1. 11.—**sor·ta′tion** (sôr-tā′shọn), *n.* The process of sorting.—**sort′er,** *n.*

sor·tie (sôr′tē), *n.* [F., < F. and OF. *sortir,* go out; origin uncertain: cf. *resort.*] A sally of troops from a besieged place to attack the besiegers (as, "The troops . . . were not less annoyed by the frequent and vigorous *sorties* of the besieged": J. F. Kirk's "Charles the Bold," iii. 2); also, a body of troops making such a sally (as, "They were a *sortie* of the besieged": Chesterton's "Napoleon of Notting Hill," iv. 3); also, one aircraft on one flight against the enemy. Also fig.—**sor′tie,** *v. i.; -tied, -tieing.* To make a sortie.

sor·ti·lege (sôr′ti·lej), *n.* [OF. *sortilege* (F. *sortilège*), < ML. *sortilegium,* < L. *sortilegus,* divining (by lot or otherwise), < *sors* (*sort-*), lot, + *legere,* gather, see, read.] The casting or drawing of lots for divination or in order to decide something; divination by this or other means; hence, sorcery†; magic†.—**sor·ti·le′gic** (-lē′jik), *a.*

sor·ti·tion (sôr-tish′ọn), *n.* [L. *sortitio*(*n-*), < *sortiri,* E. *sort*[1], *v.*] The casting or drawing of lots; determination or selection by lot; an instance of determining by lot.

so·rus (sō′rus), *n.; pl. sori* (-rī). [NL., < Gr. σωρός, a heap.] In *bot.,* one of the clusters of sporangia on the back of the fronds of ferns.

S O S (es ō es). The letters represented by the radiotelegraphic code-signal used, as by ships in distress, to call for help; hence, in general, a signal of distress, or an urgent call for help (colloq.).

so·so (sō′sō). I. *adv.* In an indifferent, mediocre, or passable manner; indifferently; tolerably: as, "Touch. Art rich? Will. Faith, sir, *so so*" (Shakspere's "As You Like It," v. 1. 28). II. *a.* Indifferent or mediocre; neither very good nor very bad, but generally inclining toward bad: as, "The sermon was only *so-so,* but they enjoyed the singing" (G. W. Cable's "John March, Southerner," lx.).

Pinnules of various Ferns, showing the Sori.— *a,* pinnule of frond of genus *Asplenium; b,* genus *Woodwardia; c,* genus *Polypodium; d,* genus *Adiantum; e,* genus *Trichomanes.*

sos·te·nu·to (sos-tā-nö′tō), *a.* [It., pp. of *sostenere,* < L. *sustinere,* E. *sustain.*] In *music,* sustained; prolonged.

sot (sot), *n.* [OF. F. *sot* (fem. *sotte*), as adj. foolish, as n. fool; origin unknown.] A foolish or stupid person†; also, one whose mind is dulled by excessive drinking; a confirmed drunkard (as, "Boswell was a wine-bibber, and indeed little

better than a habitual *sot*": Macaulay's "Essays," Samuel Johnson).—**sot,** *v.; sotted, sotting.* I. *tr.* To make foolish or stupid; also, to stupefy, as with drink. II. *intr.* To play the sot; drink to excess: as, "He had acquired a habit of *sotting* with brandy" (B. Franklin's "Autobiography," ii.).

so·te·ri·ol·o·gy (sō-tē-ri-ol′ọ-ji), *n.* [Gr. σωτηρία, saving, preservation, salvation: see -*logy.*] In *theol.,* the doctrine of salvation through Jesus Christ.—**so·te″ri·o·log′i·cal** (-ō-loj′i-kạl), *a.*

So·thi·ac (sō′thi-ak), *a.* Same as *Sothic.*

So·thic (sō′thik or soth′ik), *a.* [Gr. Σῶθις, Sothis, representing an Egyptian name of the dog-star.] Of or pertaining to Sothis or Sirius, the dog-star: as, the *Sothic* year (the fixed year of the ancient Egyptians, determined by the heliacal rising of Sirius, and equivalent to 365¼ days, as distinguished from the ordinary Egyptian year of 365 days); the *Sothic* cycle or period (a period of 1,460 Sothic years, being equal to 1,461 ordinary years of 365 days).

sot·ni·a (sot′ni-ä), *n.* [Russ. *sotnya,* hundred.] A squadron of Cossack cavalry.

so·tol (sō-tōl′), *n.* [Mex.] Any plant of the liliaceous genus *Dasylirion,* of the southwestern U. S. and northern Mexico, resembling the yucca.

sot·tish (sot′ish), *a.* [From *sot.*] Foolish or stupid; also, stupefied, as with drink; given to excessive drinking, or being a sot (as, "He grew up *sottish,* coarse, and brutal": Wiseman's "Fabiola," i. 9); pertaining to or befitting a sot (as, a *sottish* appearance; *sottish* habits).—**sot′tish·ly,** *adv.*—**sot′tish·ness,** *n.*

sot·to vo·ce (sōt′tō vō′chā). [It., 'under voice.'] In an undertone, or aside (as, "'She makes herself too cheap,' Mrs. Van Buren said *sotto voce*": L. Merrick's "Conrad in Quest of His Youth," ix.): a phrase also used adjectively, *sotto-voce* (as, "'God forbid!' said the Justice, in a tone of *sotto-voce* deprecation": Scott's "Rob Roy," viii.).

sou (sö), *n.; pl. sous* (söz, F. sö). [F. *sou,* OF. *sol:* see *sol*[2].] A former French coin, orig. of gold, then of silver, and finally of copper; also, popularly, in France, the present bronze 5-centime piece, worth about 1 U. S. cent, or the bronze 10-centime piece ('big sou'); also, in Canada, a bronze 1-cent piece or a halfpenny.—**sou marqué** (F. mär-kā). [F., 'marked sou.'] An old French copper coin worth about 1½ sous; also, a coin or anything of little value (U. S.: as, not worth a *sou marqué*: in this sense commonly written *sou marquee* or *sou markee,* and pronounced sö mär-kē′).

Obverse. Reverse.
Sou, 1793.— British Museum.

sou·a·ri·nut (sou-ä′rē-nut or sö-), *n.* [Also *saouari-nut;* from native name in Guiana.] The large, edible, oily nut of a tall tree, *Caryocar nuciferum,* of tropical South America.

sou·bise (sö-bēz), *n.* [From Prince Charles de *Soubise* (1715–87), marshal of France.] A strained onion sauce for meats, etc.

sou·brette (sö-bret′), *n.* [F., < Pr. *soubreto,* fem. of *soubret,* coy.] Orig., a maid-servant or lady's maid as a character in a play or opera, esp. one displaying coquetry, pertness, and a spirit of intrigue, as in the older comedies (as, "Congreve has here [in Mincing and Foible, female attendants in 'The Way of the World'] made more use than . . . had been common in England, of the all-important *soubrette,* on whom so much depends in French comedy": Hallam's "Literature of Europe," iv. 6. § 52); hence, any lively or pert young woman character; also, an actress playing such a rôle; sometimes, any maid-servant or lady's maid.

sou·bri·quet (sö′bri-kā), *n.* Same as *sobriquet.*

sou·chong (sö′shong), *n.* [From Chinese, lit. 'small (or fine) sort.'] A kind of black tea.

souf-fle (sö′fl), *n.* [F., < *souffler*: see *soufflé*.] In *pathol.*, a murmuring or blowing sound.

souf-flé (sö-flā′). [F. *soufflé* (fem. *soufflée*), pp. of *souffler*, blow, puff, < L. *sufflare*: see *sufflate*.] In *cookery*: **I.** *a.* Puffed up; made light, as by beating and cooking. **II.** *n.* Any of various dishes made of ingredients beaten to a froth with whites of eggs and baked in an oven until puffed up light.

sou-fri-ère (sö-frē-yär′), *n.* [F., < *soufre*, < L. *sulfur*, E. *sulphur*.] A solfatara.

sou-gan (sö′gạn), *n.* See *sugan*.

sough (suf or sou), *v.* [AS. *swōgan*.] **I.** *intr.* To make a rushing, rustling, or murmuring sound (as, "The wind rose and *soughed* drearily through the rhododendrons and the pines," F. M. Crawford's "Mr. Isaacs," i.; "The water *soughed* amongst the stones," J. Conrad's "Rescue," iv. 4); also, to breathe heavily, as in sleep; sigh deeply; with *away*, to breathe one's last breath, or die (Sc.: as, "He . . . *soughed* awa' in the spring," Ian Maclaren's "Beside the Bonnie Brier Bush," i. 3). **II.** *tr.* To express or convey by a soughing sound (as, "The bow-wash murmurs and sighs and *soughs* A message from the angels' song": Masefield's "Christmas Eve at Sea"); also, to hum (a tune: Sc.); also, to utter in a whining tone (Sc.).—**sough**, *n.* A rushing, rustling, or murmuring sound (as, "the *sough* of the wind among the bracken": Scott's "Old Mortality," xxxiii.); also, a deep breath or sigh; also, a report or rumor (chiefly Sc.: as, "A *sough* reached us that the Americas were seized with the rebellious spirit of the ten tribes," Galt's "Annals of the Parish," x.); also, a whining or canting mode of speaking, esp. in preaching or praying (Sc.: as, "He's a speeritually minded man, Maister Cosh, and has the richt *sough*," Ian Maclaren's "Beside the Bonnie Brier Bush," ii. 1).

sought (sôt). Preterit and past participle of *seek*.

soul (sōl), *n.* [AS. *sāwl*, *sāwol* = D. *ziel* = G. *seele* = Icel. *sāla* = Goth. *saiwala*, soul.] The principle of life, feeling, thought, and action in man, regarded as a distinct entity separate from the body, and commonly held to be separable in existence from the body; the spiritual part of man as distinct from the physical; sometimes, the corresponding or analogous principle in animals or plants (as, "To hold opinion with Pythagoras, That *souls* of animals infuse themselves Into the trunks of men": Shakspere's "Merchant of Venice," iv. 1. 132); also, the emotional part of man's nature, or the seat of the feelings or sentiments (as, "Breathes there the man, with *soul* so dead, Who never to himself hath said, This is my own, my native land!" Scott's "Lay of the Last Minstrel," vi. 1); esp., capacity for exalted or noble emotions or feelings (as, "The mouse that always trusts to one poor hole, Can never be a mouse of any *soul*": Pope's "Wife of Bath," 299); high-mindedness, noble warmth of feeling, spirit or courage, etc.; in fig. use, the animating principle or essential element or part of something (as, "the hidden *soul* of harmony," Milton's "L'Allegro," 144; "Brevity is the *soul* of wit," Shakspere's "Hamlet," ii. 2. 90); the inspirer or moving spirit of some action, movement, etc. (as, "Dr. Mandeville, author of the 'Fable of the Bees,' who had a club there, of which he was the *soul*": B. Franklin's "Autobiography," iii.); the embodiment of some quality (as, "My brother, indeed, was the *soul* of honour": Goldsmith's "Vicar of Wakefield," xxxi.); also, the spiritual part of man regarded in its moral aspect, or as believed to survive death and be subject to happiness or misery in a life to come (as, "For what shall it profit a man, if he shall gain the whole world, and lose his own *soul*?" Mark, viii. 36; "My *soul*, which is a scourge, will I resign Into the hands of him who wielded it," Shelley's "Cenci," iv. 1. 63); also, a disembodied spirit of a deceased person (as, "Then of his wretched friend The *Soul* appear'd; at ev'ry part the form did comprehend His likeness": Chapman's tr. Homer's "Iliad," xxiii.); also, a human being, or person (as, "All the *souls* of the house of Jacob, which came into Egypt, were threescore and ten," Gen. xlvi. 27; "*Humph.* Where had you this intelligence? *Tom.* From a foolish fond *soul* that can keep nothing from me," Steele's "Conscious Lovers," i. 1).

souled (sōld), *a.* Having a soul: as, great-*souled*; mean-*souled*.

soul-ful (sōl′fül), *a.* Full of soul; of a deeply emotional nature or character; expressive of deep feeling or emotion (as, *soulful* eyes).—**soul′ful-ly**, *adv.*—**soul′ful-ness**, *n.*

soul=house (sōl′hous), *n.* A small clay model of a house placed in a tomb by the ancient Egyptians for the accommodation of the soul of the departed.

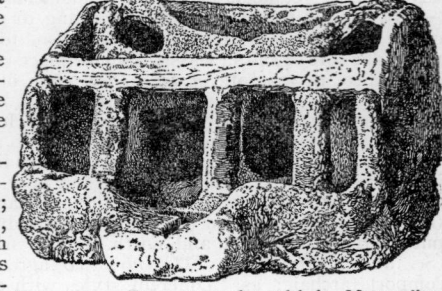

Soul-house. — From restored model in Metropolitan Museum of Art, New York.

soul-less (sōl′les), *a.* Without a soul; sometimes, from which the soul has departed; lifeless; dead; also, wanting in elevation of soul, as persons; destitute of nobility of feeling; without spirit or courage; also, lacking animation or expression, as the eyes; without life, vivacity, liveliness, etc., as action, writings, etc.; dull; uninteresting.—**soul′less-ly**, *adv.*—**soul′less-ness**, *n.*

sound[1] (sound), *a.* [ME. *sund*, < AS. *gesund* = D. *gezond* = G. *gesund*, sound: cf. L. *sanus*, sound, healthy, E. *sane*.] Free from disease, bodily injury, etc. (as, a *sound* body or mind; *sound* health; a horse warranted *sound*); healthy or robust; hence, more generally, free from injury, damage, decay, or defect (as, *sound* walls, timbers, or ships; *sound* fruit; *sound* goods); in good condition; undamaged or unimpaired; hence, stout, solid, or massive (now rare: as, "one *sound* cudgel of four foot," Shakspere's "Henry VIII.," v. 4. 19; *sound* rock); substantial or strong, as food or liquor; financially strong, secure, or reliable (as, a *sound* business house; *sound* credit; "Your father's always . . . taken such pride in his *sound* investments," Tarkington's "Magnificent Ambersons," xi.); unbroken and deep, as sleep; vigorous, hearty, or thorough, as a beating; also, fig., of substantial or enduring character (as, *sound* value or worth; "School-friendships are not always found, Though fair in promise, permanent and *sound*," Cowper's "Tirocinium," 437); solidly good or reliable (as, *sound* judgment or sense); also, without defect as to truth, justice, or reason (as, *sound* advice; *sound* rules or principles); just, right, well-founded, or valid; in special uses, without logical defect, as reasoning; without legal defect, as a title; theologically correct or orthodox, as doctrines or a theologian; hence, orthodox with reference to any doctrines or principles (as, "Albert was a calm and utterly *sound* Conservative": Arnold Bennett's "Clayhanger," iii. 4); also, free from moral defect or weakness; upright, honest, or good; honorable; loyal.—**sound**[1], *adv.* Soundly: esp. with reference to sleeping: as, to be *sound* asleep; "Roland Græme slept long and *sound*" (Scott's "Abbot," xiii.).

sound[2] (sound), *n.* [Prob. from Scand.: cf. Icel., Sw., and Dan. *sund*, sound, also AS. *sund*, swimming, water, sea, and E. *sound*[3].] A relatively narrow passage of water, not a stream, between larger bodies or between the mainland and an island (as, the *Sound*, between the Baltic Sea and the Cattegat; Long Island *Sound*); also, an inlet, arm, or recessed portion of the sea (as, Puget *Sound*; Norton *Sound*, Alaska).

sound[3] (sound), *n.* [Cf. AS. *sund*, swimming (see *sound*[2]), also Icel. *sundmagi*, 'swimming-maw,' fish's sound.] The swimming-bladder of a fish.

sound[4] (sound), *v.* [OF. F. *sonder*, < *sonde*, sounding-lead; prob. from Scand.: cf. *sound*[2] and *sound*[3].] **I.** *tr.* To measure or try the depth of (water, a deep hole, etc.) by letting down a lead or plummet at the end of a line (see *sounding-line*), or by some equivalent means; measure (depth) in such a manner, as at sea; examine or test (the bottom of water, etc.) with a lead that brings up adhering bits of matter; fig., to examine or investigate as if with a lead and line (as, to *sound* the depths of a person's character); make trial of (as, "And casts between Ambiguous words and

jealousies, to *sound* Or taint integrity": Milton's "Paradise Lost," v. 703); seek to fathom or ascertain (as, to *sound* a person's views or inclinations; "hesitating, half story-tellers . . . who go on *sounding* your belief, and only giving you as much as they see you can swallow at a time," Lamb's "Old Margate Hoy"); seek to elicit the views or sentiments of (a person) by indirect inquiries, suggestive allusions, etc. (as, "He has even *sounded* me on the subject; but I have given him no encouragement": Smollett's "Humphry Clinker," Oct. 14); in *surg.*, to examine, as the bladder, with a sound (see *sound*[4], *n.*). **II. intr.** To use the lead and line (or some other device) for measuring depth, etc., as at sea; go down or touch bottom, as a lead; hence, to plunge downward or dive, as a whale (as, "*Sounding* with his head in one direction, he [a whale] nevertheless, while concealed beneath the surface . . . swims off in the opposite quarter": H. Melville's "Moby-Dick," xlvii.); in fig. use, to make investigation; seek information, esp. by indirect inquiries, etc.—
sound[4], *n.* In *surg.*, a long, slender instrument for sounding or exploring cavities of the body; a probe.

sound[5] (sound), *n.* [OF. F. *son*, < L. *sonus*, sound: cf. Skt. *svan-*, to sound, and E. *swan*.] The sensation produced in the organs of hearing when certain vibrations ('sound-waves') are caused in the surrounding air or other elastic medium, as by a vibrating body; also, the vibrations or vibrational energy producing this sensation; also, the particular auditory effect produced by a given cause (as, the *sound* of music, of fighting, of thunder, or of the human voice); any auditory effect, or vibrational disturbance such as to be heard (as, to hear strange *sounds*; to make a sweet *sound*; deaf to the *sounds* of nature); a noise, vocal utterance, musical tone, or the like; esp., one of the simple elements ('speech-sounds') composing vocal utterance; the element or elements of this nature corresponding to a letter, word, etc.; also, mere noise, without meaning (as, "A tale Told by an idiot, full of *sound* and fury, Signifying nothing": Shakspere's "Macbeth," v. 5. 27); also, a report, or news or tidings (obs. or archaic: as, "A *sound* was bruited about that the king's forces would have a hot and a sore struggle," Galt's "Annals of the Parish," xviii.; "God gives the word— the preachers throng around, Live from his lips, and spread the glorious *sound*," Cowper's "Hope," 454); also, the distance within which the noise of something may be heard (as, "in *sound* of the swallowing sea": M. Arnold's "The Future").—**sound**[5], *v.* [OF. *soner* (F. *sonner*), < L. *sonare*, to sound, < *sonus*.] **I. intr.** To make or emit a sound, as a bell or trumpet does; sometimes, to give forth a sound as a call or summons (as, "The gongs were *sounding* for luncheon": W. Churchill's "Modern Chronicle," i. 9); also, to be filled with sound, or resound (as, "the great hall of the castle . . . *sounding* to strains of soft and delicious music": Scott's "Kenilworth," xxxi.); also, to make a sound on an instrument, etc. (as, "The singers sang, and the trumpeters *sounded*": 2 Chron. xxix. 28); also, to be heard, as a sound (as, "listening . . . to that statesman, as if the words of an oracle *sounded* in his ears": Scott's "Quentin Durward," xxx.); issue or pass as sound (as, "From you *sounded* out the word of the Lord": 1 Thes. i. 8); be mentioned (as, "The name of Flinter had long *sounded* amongst the Carlist ranks": Borrow's "Bible in Spain," xxxiv.); also, to convey a certain impression when heard or read (as, "How oddly will it *sound* that I Must ask my child forgiveness!" Shakspere's "Tempest," v. 1. 197); also, to tend† or incline†. **II. tr.** To cause (an instrument, etc.) to make or emit a sound (as, "A baggepype wel coude he blowe and *sowne*": Chaucer's "Prologue to the Canterbury Tales," 565); also, to give forth (a sound: as, "When winter's roar *Sounded* o'er earth and sea its blast of war," Shelley's "Prince Athanase," 186); announce, order, or direct by a sound, as of a trumpet (as, to *sound* a retreat); also, to utter audibly, pronounce, or express (as, "I, as one that am the tongue of these To *sound* the purposes of all their hearts": Shakspere's "King John," iv. 2. 48); pronounce in a particular manner (as, e *sounded* as in *me*); also, to announce or proclaim (as, "Thou sun . . . Acknowledge him thy greater; *sound* his praise": Milton's "Paradise Lost," v. 172); celebrate or honor by speech, etc. (as, "She loves aloft to *sound* The man for more than mortal deeds renown'd": Congreve's "Pindaric

Ode to the Earl of Godolphin"); also, to signify† or import†; also, to examine by percussion or auscultation.
sound-er[1] (soun'dĕr), *n.* One who or that which sounds the depth of water, etc.; also, a surgical sound or probe.
sound-er[2] (soun'dĕr), *n.* One who or that which makes a sound or noise, or sounds something; in *teleg.*, a receiving instrument by the sounds of which the message is read.
sound-ing[1] (soun'ding), *n.* The act or process of measuring depth, examining the bottom of water, etc., with or as with a lead and line; a single operation of this kind (often in *pl.*: as, to take *soundings*); *pl.*, depths of water ascertained by means of a lead and line, as at sea; also, parts of the water in which the ordinary deep-sea lead will reach bottom (as, "Up to the very brink of the coral rampart, there are no *soundings*": H. Melville's "Omoo," xxiii.); *sing.*, in *surg.*, the process of examining with a sound.
sound-ing[2] (soun'ding), *p. a.* Emitting or producing a sound or sounds, esp. of a loud kind; resounding; sonorous; also, having an imposing sound (as, "She used to repeat *sounding* phrases from books": C. Brontë's "Jane Eyre," xviii.); high-sounding; pompous.
sound-ing=bal-loon (soun'ding-ba̤-lön″), *n.* A small balloon equipped with self-registering instruments, sent up without an aëronaut to ascertain atmospheric and meteorologic conditions aloft.
sound-ing=board (soun'ding-bōrd), *n.* A thin, resonant plate of wood forming part of a musical instrument, and so placed as to enhance the power and quality of the tones; also, a board or reflecting structure placed over, or behind and above, a speaker, orchestra, etc., to direct the sound toward the audience; also, a board used in the deafening of floors, partitions, etc.
sound-ing=box (soun'ding-boks), *n.* A chamber in a musical instrument, as the body of a violin, for increasing the sonority of its tone.
sound-ing=lead (soun'ding-led), *n.* The lead or plummet at the end of a sounding-line.
sound-ing=line (soun'ding-līn), *n.* A line weighted at one end with a lead or plummet and bearing at fixed intervals marks to show the length paid out, used for sounding, as at sea.
sound-ing-ly (soun'ding-li), *adv.* In a sounding or resounding manner; sonorously; with imposing sound.
sound-ing=ma-chine (soun'ding-ma̤-shēn″), *n.* Any of various machines for taking deep-sea or other soundings.

Sounding-board over Pulpit.

sound-less[1] (sound'les), *a.* That cannot be sounded or fathomed; unfathomable: as, "Your shallowest help will hold me up afloat, Whilst he upon your *soundless* deep doth ride" (Shakspere's "Sonnets," lxxx.).
sound-less[2] (sound'les), *a.* Making or having no sound; noiseless; still.—**sound'less-ly**, *adv.*—**sound'less-ness**, *n.*
sound-ly (sound'li), *adv.* In a sound manner; esp., without weakness or defect; with unbroken, deep sleep; vigorously, heartily, or thoroughly; with sound judgment or reasoning. —**sound'ness**, *n.*
sound=proof (sound'pröf), *a.* Impervious to sound.
sound=ran-ging (sound'rän″jing), *n.* The process or art of locating causes or sources of sound, as an enemy's gun or the place where a shell bursts, by exactly recording the facts concerning the sounds, as at a number of stations supplied with delicate instruments, and by subsequent calculations.
sound'=track, *n.* A sound record on a moving-picture film.
soup (söp), *n.* [F. *soupe*, sop (of bread, as in broth), soup, related to *souper*, take supper; from Teut.: cf. *sop*, *sup*[1], *sup*[2], and *supper*.] A liquid food made from meat, fish, or vegetables, with various added ingredients, by boiling; broth; also, nitroglycerin (slang).
soup-çon (söp-sȯṅ), *n.* [F., < LL. *suspectio(n-)*, < L. *suspicere*: see *suspect*.] A suspicion; a slight trace or flavor; a very small amount.

(variable) ḍ as d or j, ṣ as s or sh, ṭ as t or ch, ẓ as z or zh; o, F. *cloche*; ü, F. *menu*; ċh, Sc. *loch*; ṅ, F. *bonbon*; ′, primary accent; ″, secondary accent; †, obsolete; <, from; +, and; =, equals. See also lists at beginning of book.

soup-y (sö′pi), *a.* Like soup; having the consistence or appearance of soup.

sour (sour), *a.* [AS. *sūr* = D. *zuur* = G. *sauer* = Icel. *sūrr* = Sw. and Dan. *sur*, sour: cf. *sorrel²*.] Having an acid taste, such as that of vinegar, lemon-juice, etc.; tart; also, rendered acid by fermentation; fermented; affected or spoiled by fermentation; characteristic of what is so affected (as, a *sour* smell); also, fig., distasteful or disagreeable; unpleasant; of persons, harsh in spirit or temper (as, "*Sour* to them that loved him not; But to those men that sought him sweet as summer": Shakspere's "Henry VIII.," iv. 2. 53); austere; morose; peevish; of the temper, looks, words, etc., marked by or showing austerity, moroseness, or peevishness (as, "*sour* visages," Gray's "Long Story," 106; "He said a *sour* thing to Laura at dinner the other day; upon which she burst into tears," Steele, in "Tatler," 54); also, cold and wet, or retaining stagnant moisture, as soil; wet or inclement, as weather, etc. (prov.: as, "A sleety rain was coming down . . . It was what Jotham called a *sour* morning for work," Mrs. Wharton's "Ethan Frome," vi.).— **sour grapes,** something that a person pretends to despise, only because he cannot have it: from Æsop's fable of "The Fox and the Grapes," in which a fox, after vain efforts to reach some grapes on a high vine, finally gives up the attempt with the declaration, "The grapes are sour!"—**sour,** *n.* That which is sour; something sour (lit. or fig.); esp., an acid drink, as whisky or the like with lemon-juice, sugar, etc., added (U. S.); in *bleaching, dyeing,* etc., a bath of an acid nature.—**sour,** *adv.* Sourly; disagreeably; morosely.— **sour,** *v.* **I.** *intr.* To become sour or acid; turn sour; fig., to become harsh, morose, or peevish. **II.** *tr.* To make sour or acid; esp., to render acid by fermentation; spoil by fermentation; also, fig., to make disagreeable or unpleasant; render harsh, morose, or peevish, or embitter (as, "Fourteen years of exile, with all its privations, contumelies, and heartsickness . . . had *soured* him," Morley's "Oliver Cromwell," v. 10; "Such suffering would probably have *soured* the kindest temper," Godwin's "Caleb Williams," iii.).

sour=ball (sour′bâl), *n.* A hard, round sweetmeat strongly flavored with lemon or the like.

source (sōrs), *n.* [OF. *sourse* (F. *source*), orig. pp. fem. of *sourdre,* < L. *surgere,* rise: see *surge,* and cf. *resource.*] A rising, as of a bird in the air†; also, a spring or issue of water from the earth, etc., or the place of issue; a fountain or fountainhead; now, esp., the beginning or the place of origin of a stream or river (as, "the Alpine *sources* of the Rhine": J. F. Kirk's "Charles the Bold," iv. 1); hence, the place from which anything comes or is obtained (as, the South African mines are the chief *source* of diamonds); anything from which something proceeds or arises (as, "one great original *source* of revenue . . . the wages of labour," Adam Smith's "Wealth of Nations," iv. 7. 3; to be a *source* of anxiety to one's family); an originating cause or ground, or an origin; a substance from which something is derived (as, pitchblende is a *source* of radium); specif., that from which information or evidence, esp. of an original character, in regard to some fact, event, subject, etc., is obtained; a book, passage, statement, or the like, supplying such information. —**source′=book,** *n.* A book or compilation of matter, as extracts, documents, or other special information, setting forth sources of knowledge in a particular field or on a particular subject.

sour=crout (sour′krout), *n.* See *sauerkraut.*

sour-dine (sör-dēn′), *n.* [F.] Same as *sordino.*

sour=dough (sour′dō), *n.* Leaven (obs. or prov. Eng.); also, a prospector or pioneer experienced in life in the Alaska region (in allusion to the use there of sour dough for raising bread: colloq.: cf. *chechaco*).

sour=gourd (sour′gōrd), *n.* The acid fruit of a bombacaceous tree, *Adansonia gregorii,* of northern Australia, or the tree itself; also, the fruit of the baobab, *A. digitata,* of Africa, or the tree itself.

sour=gum (sour′gum), *n.* The tupelo (tree), *Nyssa sylvatica.*

sour-ly (sour′li), *adv.* In a sour manner; with acidity; disagreeably or unpleasantly; morosely or peevishly.— **sour′ness,** *n.*

sour=sop (sour′sop), *n.* [Cf. *sweet-sop*.] The large, prickly,

slightly acid, pulpy fruit, of a greenish color, borne by a small anonaceous tree, *Anona muricata,* native in the West Indies; also, the tree.

Sour-sop.

sour-wood (sour′wùd), *n.* The sorrel-tree.

souse¹ (sous), *n.* [OF. *sous;* from Teut., and akin to E. *salt²*.] Something kept or steeped in pickle, esp. the head, ears, and feet of a pig; also, a liquid used as a pickle; also, an act of sousing; a plunging into or drenching with water, etc. (as, "Keeping her hand on his collar, she gave him two or three good *souses* in the watery fluid": Scott's "Monastery," v.); also, a fit of intoxication (slang); a drunkard (slang). —**souse¹,** *v.*; soused, sousing. **I.** *tr.* To steep in pickle; also, to plunge into water or other liquid (as, "He *soused* me head and ears into a pail of water": Steele, in "Tatler," 15); drench with water, etc.; also, to dash or pour, as water; also, to intoxicate (chiefly in *soused, pp.*: slang). **II.** *intr.* To be steeping or soaking in something; be soaked or drenched; plunge into water, etc.; fall with a splash; also, to drink to intoxication (slang).—**souse¹,** *adv.* With a sudden plunge, as into water.

souse² (sous), *v.*; soused, sousing. [Origin obscure; prob. from confusion of several words.] **I.** *tr.* To strike, beat, or dash violently (now colloq. or prov.); also, to swoop or pounce on (archaic). **II.** *intr.* To fall heavily (now colloq. or prov.); also, to swoop (archaic: as, "the sacred eagle . . . *sousing* on the quivering hare," Pope's tr. Homer's "Iliad," xvii.).—**souse²,** *n.* A heavy blow or fall. [Now colloq. or prov.]—**souse²,** *adv.* With a violent fall or impact (colloq. or prov.: as, "I hoped it would have fallen *souse* on your heads": Scott's "Bride of Lammermoor," xix.); also, with a swoop (archaic).

sou-tache (sö′tash), *n.* [F., < Hung. *szuszak,* curl of hair, etc.] A narrow braid, commonly of mohair or silk, used for trimming, often in fanciful designs.

sou-tane (sö-tän), *n.* [F., < It. *sottana,* < *sotto,* < L. *subtus,* underneath, < *sub,* under.] *Eccles.,* a cassock.

sou-ter (sö′tėr), *n.* [AS. *sūtere,* < L. *sutor,* < *suere,* sew: see *sew.*] A maker or mender of shoes; a shoemaker; a cobbler: as, "At his elbow, *Souter* Johnny, His ancient, trusty, drouthy crony" (Burns's "Tam o' Shanter," 41). [Now Sc. and north. Eng.]

south (south), *adv.* [AS. *sūth* = Icel. *sudhr,* earlier *sunnr,* = OHG. *sund* (cf. G. *süd,* n.); perhaps akin to Goth. *sunnō,* AS. *sunne,* E. *sun²*.] In the direction which is to the left of a person facing the setting sun or west; toward or in the south; also, from the south (as with reference to wind). —**south,** *n.* A cardinal point of the compass directly opposite to the north; the direction in which this point lies; also [*l. c.* or *cap.*], a quarter or territory situated in this direction; [*cap.*] that part of the U. S. which in general lies south of Pennsylvania and the Ohio River; also [*l. c.*], the south wind (chiefly poetic: as, "Breathing all gently . . . As o'er a bed of roses the sweet *south,*" Byron's "Don Juan," ii. 168).—**south,** *a.* Lying toward or situated in the south; directed or proceeding toward the south; also, coming from the south, as a wind; *eccles.,* designating, situated in, or lying toward that side of a church to the right of one facing the altar or high altar.—**South Sea,** the southern Pacific Ocean; formerly, the Pacific Ocean as a whole (so called as first seen toward the south from the Isthmus of Darien, where it was discovered by Balboa in 1513).—**south** (souᴛʜ or south), *v. i.* To move or veer toward the south; in *astron.,* of a heavenly body, to cross the meridian of a place.

South Af-ri-can (south af′ri-kạn). **I.** *a.* Of or pertaining to South Africa, that is, southern Africa (southward from the neighborhood of the Zambezi River), or, esp., the British possessions of this region, more particularly the colonies of this region settled by the English and the Dutch, which in 1910, as the provinces of the Cape of Good Hope, Natal, the Transvaal, and the Orange Free State, were united in the Union of South Africa, a part of the British Empire. **II.** *n.* A native or inhabitant of South Africa, esp. one of European descent.

South-down (south′doun), *n.* One of a noted English breed of sheep, orig. reared on the South Downs of Sussex and Hampshire.

south-east (south′ēst′). [AS. *sūthēast.*] **I.** *adv.* In the direction which is midway between south and east; also, from this direction. **II.** *n.* The point or direction midway between south and east; also, a region in this direction. **III.** *a.* Lying toward or situated in the southeast; directed or proceeding toward the southeast; also, coming from the southeast, as a wind.—**south′east′er,** *n.* A wind, gale, or storm from the southeast.—**south′east′er-ly,** *a.* and *adv.* Toward or from the southeast.—**south′east′ern,** *a.* Situated or going toward the southeast; also, coming from the southeast, as a wind; also, of or pertaining to the southeast.—**south′east′ward** (-wärd). **I.** *adv.* and *a.* Toward the southeast. **II.** *n.* The southeast.—**south′east′-ward-ly,** *adv.* and *a.*

south-er (sou′ᴛʜėr), *n.* A wind, gale, or storm from the south.

south-er-ly (suᴛʜ′ėr-li). **I.** *a.* Moving, directed, or situated toward the south; also, coming from the south, as a wind. **II.** *adv.* Toward the south; also, from the south.

south-ern (suᴛʜ′ėrn), *a.* [AS. *sūtherne.*] Lying toward or situated in the south; directed or proceeding toward the south; also, coming from the south, as a wind; also, of or pertaining to the south, esp. [*cap.*] the South of the U. S.; in *astron.*, south of the celestial equator or of the zodiac (as, the *southern* signs of the zodiac; a *southern* constellation).—**Southern Cross,** in *astron.*, the southern constellation Crux, which has its four chief stars arranged in the form of a cross.—**Southern Crown,** in *astron.*, the southern constellation Corona Australis.—**Southern Fish,** in *astron.*, the southern constellation Piscis Australis, containing the bright star Fomalhaut.—**southern lights,** the aurora australis. See *aurora.*—**Southern Triangle,** in *astron.*, the southern constellation Triangulum Australe.—**south′ern,** *n.* One living in a southern region or country.—**south′ern-er,** *n.* A native or inhabitant of the south, esp. [*cap.*] of the southern U. S.—**south′ern-most,** *a. superl.* Furthest south: as, "the more open part of the wood, on its *southern-most* border" (W. H. Hudson's "Green Mansions," xiv.).

south-ern-wood (suᴛʜ′ėrn-wủd), *n.* [AS. *sūtherne wudu.*] A woody-stemmed species of wormwood, *Artemisia abrotanum,* native in southern Europe, and cultivated for its aromatic, finely dissected leaves.

south-ing (sou′ᴛʜing), *n.* Movement or deviation toward the south; also, distance due south; the distance due south made by a ship on any course tending southward; also, in *astron.*, the transit of the moon or a star across the meridian of a place; also, south declination.

south-land (south′lạnd), *n.* [AS. *sūthland.*] The land or region in the south; the southern part of a country.—**south′land-er,** *n.*

south-most (south′mōst), *a. superl.* Southernmost.

south-paw (south′pâ), *n.* In *baseball,* a left-handed pitcher. [Slang.]

south-ron (suᴛʜ′rọn). [Var. of *southern.*] **I.** *a.* Southern; esp. [*cap.* or *l. c.*], English as distinguished from Scottish. [Orig. and chiefly Sc.] **II.** *n.* A native or inhabitant of a southern region or country; a southerner; esp. [usually *cap.*], an Englishman as distinguished from a Scotchman (as, "It has made the *Southrons* feel, there is yet one man in Scotland, who does not fear to resist oppression": Jane Porter's "Scottish Chiefs," ii.). [Orig. Sc.]

south-ward (south′wạrd). [AS. *sūthweard.*] **I.** *adv.* Toward the south; south. **II.** *a.* Moving, bearing, facing, or situated toward the south. **III.** *n.* The southward part, direction, or point.—**south′ward-ly. I.** *a.* Having a southward direction or situation; also, coming from the south, as a wind. **II.** *adv.* Toward the south; also, from the south.—**south′wards,** *adv.* Southward.

south-west (south′west′). [AS. *sūthwest.*] **I.** *adv.* In the direction which is midway between south and west; also, from this direction. **II.** *n.* The point or direction midway between south and west; also, a region in this direction;

also, a wind from this direction (poetic). **III.** *a.* Lying toward or situated in the southwest; directed or proceeding toward the southwest; also, coming from the southwest, as a wind.—**south′west′er,** *n.* A wind, gale, or storm from the southwest; also, a waterproof hat having the brim very broad behind, so as to protect the neck, worn esp. by seamen (as, "shaking the wet off an oilskin hat known by the name of a '*south-wester*'": Disraeli's "Sybil," ii. 14).—**south′west′er-ly,** *a.* and *adv.* Toward or from the southwest.—**south′west′ern,** *a.* Situated or going toward the southwest; also, coming from the southwest, as a wind; also, of or pertaining to the southwest.—**south′west′ward** (-wärd). **I.** *adv.* and *a.* Toward the southwest. **II.** *n.* The southwest.—**south′west′ward-ly,** *adv.* and *a.*

sou-ve-nir (sö′ve-nēr, F. söv-nēr), *n.* [F., remembrance, memento, noun use of *souvenir,* refl., remember, < L. *subvenire,* come to mind, also come to one's aid: see *subvention.*] A remembrance or memory (as, "Suspicions, sinister trifling *souvenirs,* crowded into her mind," Arnold Bennett's "Hilda Lessways," v. 2: chiefly as French); also, something given or kept for remembrance, as of a person, place, or occasion; a memento.

sov-er-eign (sov′ẹ-rẹn or suv′-). [OF. F. *souverain,* < ML. *superanus,* < L. *super,* over: see *super-.*] **I.** *a.* Being above all others, or supreme, in character, importance, excellence, etc. (as, the *sovereign* good; "*sovereign* artists," Tennyson's "Princess," v. 187); also, greatest in degree, utmost, or extreme (as, "a *sovereign* contempt for every one": H. James's "Portrait of a Lady," xlii.); also, efficacious or potent above all others, as a remedy (as, "a *sovereign* cure for all colds and catarrhs": H. Melville's "Moby-Dick," iii.); also, having supreme rank or power, or exercising supreme authority (as, a *sovereign* prince, a ruling prince; a *sovereign* lord or lady; a *sovereign* state or people, one whose government is independent of any superior or external control; a *sovereign* tribunal: also *fig.*); supreme, as power, authority, etc.; belonging to or characteristic of a sovereign or sovereignty. **II.** *n.* One who has sovereign power or authority (lit. or *fig.*); a supreme ruler (sometimes used of God: as, "When the great *Sov′reign* would his will express, He gives a perfect rule," Cowper's "Truth," 551); specif., a monarch; a king or queen; sometimes, a group or body of persons or a state possessing sovereign authority; formerly, in general, a person in authority†; one's lord or master†; also, a current British gold coin, worth 20 shillings or 1 pound, equivalent to about $4.86⅔.—**sov′er-eign-ly,** *adv.*—**sov′er-eign-ty** (-ti), *n.*; pl. *-ties* (-tiz). The quality or state of being sovereign; supreme excellence or efficacy (obs. or archaic); supremacy in rank or power (lit.

Obverse. Reverse.
Sovereign, 1817. — British Museum.

or *fig.*); the status, power, or authority of a sovereign; esp., royal authority or dominion; often, supreme and independent power or authority in government as possessed or claimed by a state or community (specif. with reference to the individual States of the U. S.: as, "It was the Federal system and the doctrine of State *sovereignty* grounded thereon . . . which led to the secession of 1861," Bryce's "American Commonwealth," xxix.; "This doctrine of State *sovereignty* had come to be held as universally in the South as the strict Unionist doctrine in the North," Charnwood's "Abraham Lincoln," vi.); also, a state, community, or political unit possessing independent power.

so-vi-et (sō-vi-et′). [Russ. *sovyet,* council.] **I.** *n.* In Russian use, a council or committee; an assembly of delegates; specif., any of the councils representing industrial workers and other classes of the community, or any of the local, provincial, or national assemblies, forming elements of the socialistic governmental system instituted in Russia by ultraradical communists in 1917 (cf. *Bolshevik*); hence, any similar council or assembly connected with a socialistic governmental system elsewhere. **II.** *a.* Of or pertaining to a soviet or soviets; specif., pertaining to the soviets of the

---

socialistic governmental system instituted in Russia in 1917, or to this system or government itself; governed through such soviets (as, *soviet* Russia); hence, pertaining to similar councils or assemblies, or a similar socialistic system, elsewhere.—**so″vi-et-eer′** (-e-tēr′), *n.* An adherent of the Russian or any similar soviet system.—**so-vi-et′ism,** *n.* The soviet system of government; government by soviets.—**so-vi-et′ist. I.** *n.* An adherent of a soviet system, as in Russia. **II.** *a.* Pertaining to or characteristic of sovietists or sovietism; governed by soviets.—**so-vi-et′ize** (-īz), *v. t.*; *-ized, -izing.* To bring under the influence or domination of soviets.—**so-vi-et′iz-er** (-ī-zėr), *n.*

sov-ran (sov′ran or suv′-), etc. Variant form of *sovereign,* etc. [Chiefly poetic.]

sow[1] (sō), *v. t.*; pret. *sowed,* pp. *sown* or *sowed,* ppr. *sowing.* [AS. *sāwan* = D. *zaaien* = G. *säen* = Icel. *sā* = Goth. *saian,* sow; akin to L. *serere* (perf. *sevi*), sow: see *Saturn, season, semen,* and cf. *seed.*] To scatter seed over (land, earth, etc.), for the purpose of growth; hence, to strew or sprinkle with anything (as, "And Abimelech . . . beat down the city, and *sowed* it with salt": Judges, ix. 45); stud or dot (as, a sky *sown* with stars); also, to scatter (seed) over land, earth, etc., for growth; plant (seed, and hence a crop); hence, to distribute or introduce for development, as germs (lit. or fig.), or anything capable of producing consequences (as, to *sow* distrust or dissension); seek to propagate or extend (as, to *sow* the gospel among all nations); disseminate; also, to scatter about (as, "Oh, Israel . . . o'er ev'ry country *sown,* With none on earth that thou canst call thine own": Cowper's "Expostulation," 265).—**to sow one's wild oats.** See under *oat.*—**to sow the wind and reap the whirlwind,** to act wrongly or recklessly, with severe or disastrous consequences to one's self. See Hos. viii. 7.—**sow**[1], *v. i.* To sow seed, as for the production of a crop: as, "I resolved . . . to *sow* but once a year" (Defoe's "Robinson Crusoe," i. 9).

sow[2] (sou), *n.* [AS. *sugu,* akin to D. *zeug,* G. *sau,* sow, also to L. *sus,* Gr. *σῦς, ὗς,* swine, hog: see *suilline, hyena, hyoscyamine,* and cf. *swine.*] The female of swine; an adult female hog; also, a sow-bug; also, in *metal.,* a large, oblong mass of iron which has solidified in the common channel through which the molten metal flows from a blast-furnace to the series of smaller channels or grooves in which the pigs solidify; a similar mass of other metal; also, *milit.,* a movable structure formerly used to protect men engaged in sapping, mining, etc.—**to get (have, or take) the wrong** (or **right) sow by the ear,** fig., to get hold of or hit upon the wrong (or right) person or thing; have the wrong (or right) idea: as, "I can tell you that you've *got the wrong sow by the ear* this time" (Conan Doyle's "Exploits of Brigadier Gerard," iv.). [Colloq.]—**sow**[2], *a.* Female: applied to animals.

so-war (sọ-wär′), *n.* [Hind. use of Pers. *sawār,* horseman.] A mounted native soldier (trooper or orderly) in the British Indian service: as, "The verandah . . . was crowded with servants and *sowars* in gorgeous but rather tawdry liveries" (F. M. Crawford's "Mr. Isaacs," v.).

sow=bug (sou′bug), *n.* Any of various small terrestrial isopods, esp. of the genus *Oniscus.* See *wood-louse.*

sow-ens (sō′ẹnz), *n. pl.* [Prob. from Gaelic.] An article of food prepared by boiling the farinaceous matter extracted from the husks or siftings of oats steeped in water until sour. [Chiefly Sc.]

sow-er (sō′ėr), *n.* One who or that which sows.

sowl (soul), *v. t.* [Origin obscure.] To pull by the ears (as, "He'll go, he says, and *sowl* the porter of Rome gates by the ears": Shakspere's "Coriolanus," iv. 5. 213); pull (the ears); hence, to handle roughly. [Now prov. Eng.]

sown (sōn). Past participle of *sow*[1].

sow-this-tle (sou′this′l), *n.* Any plant of the cichoriaceous genus *Sonchus,* esp. *S. oleraceus,* a common weed having thistle-like leaves, yellow flowers, and a milky juice. See cut in next column.

soy (soi), *n.* [Jap., from Chinese.] A sauce for fish, etc.,

---

made in the East from the bean or seed of a fabaceous herb, *Soia soja* (or *Glycine hispida*); also, this herb or its edible seed ('soy-bean'). See cut below.

so-ya (sō′yạ or soi′ạ), *n.* Same as *soy.*

so-zal (sō′zal), *n.* [Gr. σώζειν, save.] A crystalline salt of aluminium with a strongly astringent taste: used as an antiseptic.

so-zin (sō′zin), *n.* [Gr. σώζειν, save.] Any proteid normally present in the animal body and serving as a defense against disease.

spa (spä, also, esp. formerly, spà), *n.* [From *Spa,* town in eastern Belgium, with mineral springs.] A mineral spring, or a locality in which such springs exist: as, "There are fifty *spas* in England as efficacious and salutary as that of Scarborough" (Smollett's "Humphry Clinker," July 4).

Sow-thistle (*Sonchus oleraceus*). — 1, upper part of the stem with the heads; 2, one of the basal leaves; *a,* a flower; *b,* the achene with the pappus.

space (spās), *n.* [OF. F. *espace,* < L. *spatium,* space.] The unlimited or indefinitely great general receptacle of things, commonly conceived as an expanse extending in all directions (or having three dimensions), in which, or occupying portions of which, all material objects are located (as, "Stars countless . . . Fast-anchor'd in the deep abyss of *space*": Cowper's "Retirement," 84); the portion or extent of this in a given instance (as, the *space* occupied by a body; the *space* within a hollow sphere; to allow a *space* of ten cubic feet); extent or room in three dimensions; also, superficial extent, or area, or a particular extent of surface (as, forests covering acres of *space;* to reach a level *space* on a hillside; to fill out blank *spaces* in a document); also, linear distance, or a particular distance (as, a road continuing for the *space* of ten miles; trees set at equal *spaces* apart); also, extent, or a particular extent, of time (as, "Rameses II. reigned . . . for the *space* of sixty-seven years," Amelia B. Edwards's "Thousand Miles up the Nile," xv.; a *space* of two hours; during a long *space* of time); an interval of time, or a while (as, after a *space* he continued his story; wait a *space*); also, time allowed or available for some purpose† (as, "I gave her *space* to repent": Rev. ii. 21); respite† (as, "Come on; thou art granted *space*": Shakspere's "All's Well," iv. 1. 98); in *printing,* one of the blank types used to separate words, etc.; in *music,* one of the degrees or intervals between the lines of the staff.—**space,** *v. t.*; *spaced, spacing.* To fix the space or spaces of; divide into spaces; also, to set some distance apart (as, "They reached a part of the wood where the pines were more widely *spaced*": Mrs. Wharton's "Ethan Frome," ix.); specif., in *printing,* etc., to separate (words, letters, or lines) by space or spaces; also, to extend by inserting more space or spaces (usually with *out*).—**space′less,** *a.* Independent of space; infinite; also, occupying no space.—**spa-cer** (spā′sėr), *n.* One who or that which spaces; a device for spacing words, etc., as in a type-setting machine.—**spa′cing** (-sing), *n.* The act of one who or that which spaces; the fixing or arranging of spaces, as in the separating of words in type-setting; also, the manner in which spaces are arranged (as, even, close, or open *spacing* in printed matter); also, a space or the spaces collectively in printed matter or other work.

Soy-bean. — *a,* leaf, and spray with pods; *b,* beans.

---

fat, fāte, fär, fåll, åsk, fāre; net, mē, hėr; pin, pīne; not, nōte, mōve, nôr; up, lūte, pùll; oi, oil; ou, out; (lightened) aviạry, ẹlect, agọny, intọ, ụnite; (obscured) errạnt, operạ, ardẹnt, actọr, natụre; ch, chip; g, go; th, thin; ᴛʜ, then; y, you;

spa-cious (spā′shus), *a.* [L. *spatiosus*, < *spatium*, E. *space*.] Containing much space, as a house, room, court, street, etc.; amply large; roomy; commodious; also, occupying much space, or vast (as, "chief lord of all this *spacious* world," Shakspere's "Pericles," iv. 3. 5; "the *spacious* firmament on high," Addison, in "Spectator," 465); of great extent or area, or extensive, as land, grounds, etc.; broad; large; great; fig., broad in scope, range, inclusiveness, etc., or not narrow or limited (as, a *spacious* mind; "leading what even you would call full and *spacious* lives," H. G. Wells's "Men Like Gods," i. 5; "the *spacious* times of great Elizabeth," Tennyson's "Dream of Fair Women," 7).—**spa′cious-ly,** *adv.*—**spa′cious-ness,** *n.*

spade¹ (spād), *n.* [It. *spada*, spade at cards, orig. sword, < L. *spatha*, < Gr. σπάθη, broad blade: see *spathe*, and cf. *spade²*.] A black figure shaped like a heart placed with the point upward and supported beneath by a short stem at the cusp opposite the point, used on playing-cards; hence, a card of the suit bearing such figures.

spade² (spād), *n.* [AS. *spadu* = D. *spade* = G. *spaten*, spade; akin to L. *spatha*, Gr. σπάθη, E. *spade¹* and *spathe*.] A tool for digging, having an iron blade adapted for pressing into the ground with the foot, and a long handle commonly with a grip or crosspiece at the top; hence, some implement, piece, or part resembling this.—**to call a spade a spade,** to call a thing by its real name, without any attempt at delicacy of expression; speak plainly or bluntly, without mincing matters.—**spade²,** *v. t.*; *spaded, spading.* To dig, cut, or remove with a spade.—**spade′=fish,** *n.* An acanthopterygian food-fish, *Chætodipterus faber,* abundant on the Atlantic coast of the U. S.; also, the paddle-fish.—

spade′ful (-fůl), *n.*; pl. *-fuls.* As much as a spade can hold.—

spad-er (spā′-dẽr), *n.*

spa-di-ceous (spā-dish′ius), *a.* [NL. *spadiceus,* < L. *spadix,* < Gr. σπάδιξ, palm-colored, brown, as n. palm-branch: cf. *spadix.*] Of a bright-brown color; chestnut; in *bot.,* of the nature of a spadix; bearing a spadix.

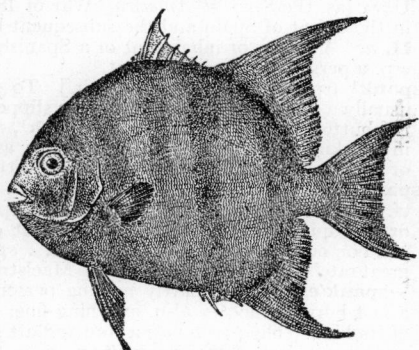

Spade-fish (*Chætodipterus faber*).

spa-dix (spā′diks), *n.*; pl. *spadixes,* L. *spadices* (spā-dī′sēz). [NL. use of L. *spadix,* < Gr. σπάδιξ, palm-branch: cf. *spadiceous.*] In *bot.,* an inflorescence consisting of a spike with a fleshy or thickened axis, usually inclosed in a spathe.

spae (spā), *v. t.* or *i.*; *spaed, spaeing.* [From Scand.: cf. Icel. *spá,* Norw. and Dan. *spaa,* prophesy.] To foretell or prophesy. [Chiefly Sc.]—**spae′man** (-man), *n.*; pl. *-men.* A prophet, soothsayer, or fortune-teller. [Sc.] —**spae′wife** (-wīf), *n.*; pl. *-wives* (-wīvz). A female fortune-teller. [Sc.]

spa-ghet-ti (spa-get′i), *n.* [It., pl. of *spaghetto,* dim. of *spago,* packthread, cord.] A kind of paste of Italian origin in long, slender, solid, cord-like pieces, to be cooked for food (intermediate in size between ordinary macaroni and vermicelli); in *elect.,* an insulating tubing of small diameter into which bare wire can be slipped, consisting typically of cotton impregnated or coated with varnish, etc., and used in the wiring of radio sets, etc.

spa-gir-ic, spa-gyr-ic (spa-jir′ik). [NL. *spagiricus;* prob. coined by Paracelsus.] **I.** *a.* Pertaining to alchemy. [Now rare.] **II.** *n.* An alchemist. [Now rare.]

spa-hi (spä′hē), *n.*; pl. *-his* (-hēz). [= F. *spahi,* < Turk. *sipāhī,* from Pers.: see *sepoy.*] One of a body of Turkish cavalry of former times; also, one of a body of native Algerian cavalry in the French service.

spake (spāk). Archaic preterit of *speak.*

spall (spâl), *n.* [ME. *spalle,* a chip: cf. ME. *spalden,* MLG.

spalden, to splinter, split, G. *spalten,* split.] A chip or splinter, as of stone or ore.—**spall,** *v.* **I.** *tr.* To break into smaller pieces, as ore; split or chip. **II.** *intr.* To break or split off in chips or fragments.

spal-peen (spal-pēn′), *n.* [Ir. *spailpín.*] A common laborer or workman; also, a mean fellow; a rascal; also, a boy. [Ir.]

span¹ (span), *n.* [AS. *spann* = D. *span* = G. *spanne* = Icel. *spönn,* span.] The distance between the tip of the thumb and the tip of the little finger when the hand is fully extended; hence, a measure of length corresponding to this distance, commonly taken as 9 inches (as, "a very little young leopard, about two *spans* high": Defoe's "Captain Single-ton," vi.); also, a distance, amount, piece, etc., of this length, or of some small extent (as, a *span* of earth; "every *span* of shade," Tennyson's "In Memoriam," cxvii.); also, a short space of time (esp. with reference to the duration of life: as, "A life's but a *span*," Shakspere's "Othello," ii. 3. 74); hence, the term or period of living (as, "Improve the remnant of his wasted *span,* And, having liv'd a trifler, die a man": Cowper's "Retirement," 13); also, the distance or space between two supports, as the abutments or springers of an arch, the piers of a bridge, etc.; a part between two supports, as an arch of a bridge; in general, the full extent, stretch, or reach of anything (as, the *span* of a beach between head-lands; the *span* of memory: "This argument, Which strove to grasp in its mighty *span* The purpose of God and the fate of man!" Whittier's "Preacher").—**span¹,** *v. t.*; *spanned, spanning.* To measure by or as by the hand with the thumb and little finger extended as far as possible; encompass or encircle with the hand or hands, as the waist; also, to extend over or across (a space, a river, etc.), as an arch, a bridge, or the like does (as, "a little bridge that *spanned* a horrible rushing white stream": Barrie's "Tommy and Grizel," xxvii.); provide with something that extends over (as, to *span* a doorway with an arch; to *span* a river with a bridge); in general, to extend, reach, or pass over (space or time: as, his thoughts *spanned* the miles before him; memory *spans* the past).

span² (span), *v.*; *spanned, spanning.* [D. *spannen;* akin to E. *span¹.*] **I.** *tr.* To harness or attach (horses, etc.) to a vehicle, or furnish (a vehicle) with animals to draw it (now chiefly South Africa); also, to stretch, or make taut (archaic); *naut.,* to draw tight or make fast in some way. **II.** *intr.* Of horses, etc., to form a span. [U. S.]—**span²,** *n.* [D. *span.*] A pair of horses or other animals harnessed and driven together (as, "comfortable carry-alls drawn by steady *spans,*" Tarkington's "Gentleman from Indiana," vii.: U. S. and Canada); also, a team of horses, oxen, etc., harnessed in pairs to a wagon, plow, or the like (South Africa); *naut.,* a rope fastened at both ends to afford a bight for securing a purchase; also, a rope fastened in the middle so that the ends may be used.

span³ (span). Archaic preterit of *spin.*

spa-næ′mi-a, etc. See *spanemia,* etc.

span-cel (span′-sel), *n.* [D. *spansel,* < *span-nen,* E. *span².*] A fetter or hobble; esp., a rope for tying together the hind legs of a cow during milking. [Chiefly prov.]—**span′cel,** *v. t.*; *-celed* or *-celled, -celing* Sculptured Spandrel. — Cloisters of Mont St. Michel, Normandy; 13th century.

or -*celling.* To fetter or hobble with a spancel (chiefly prov.); hence, to tie the flippers of (a turtle) or peg the claws of (a lobster, etc.) in order to restrain movement.

span=dogs (span'dogz), *n. pl.* A pair of iron bars linked together at one end and having sharp hooks at the other, used for grappling timber.

span-drel (span'drel), *n.* [ME. *spaundrell*; origin uncertain.] In *arch.*, the triangular space between either half of the extrados of an arch and a rectangular molding or part inclosing the arch; also, the space included between the extradoses of two adjacent arches and a horizontal molding or part above (see cut on preceding page).

spa-ne-mi-a, spa-næ-mi-a (spa-nē'mi-ä), *n.* [NL., < Gr. σπανός, scarce, scanty, + αἷμα, blood.] In *pathol.*, an abnormal condition of the blood characterized by deficiency of red corpuscles.—**spa-ne'mic, spa-næ'mic** (-nē'mik or -nem'ik), *a.*

spang (spang), *v.* [Origin obscure.] **I.** *intr.* To spring; bound; go rapidly. [Sc. and prov. Eng.] **II.** *tr.* To jerk; fling; throw violently; slam. [Sc. and prov. Eng.]— **spang,** *n.* A spring or bound; also, a jerk; also, a smart blow; a bang. [Sc. and prov. Eng.]

span-gle (spang'gl), *n.* [ME. *spangele*, dim. of *spang*, spangle, = D. *spang* = G. *spange*, brooch, clasp, stud.] A small, thin, often circular piece of glittering material, as metal, used for decorating garments, etc.; hence, any small, bright bit, drop, object, spot, or the like (as, *spangles* of mica in rock; *spangles* of dew on leaves, or of light on waves); often, a star as seen shining in the sky (poetic: as, "See, round the poles where keener *spangles* shine," Pope's "Dunciad," iii. 69); also, a spot or marking of color, as on a bird.—**span'gle,** *v.*; -*gled, -gling.* **I.** *tr.* To decorate (a garment, etc.) with spangles; hence, to sprinkle or stud with small, bright pieces, objects, spots, etc.; spot or dot (*with*); also, to sprinkle like spangles (as, "A good deal of gold lay *spangled* among the sand of the river": Defoe's "Captain Singleton," ix.); also, to be sprinkled like spangles over (as, "Stars, that then appear'd *Spangling* the hemisphere": Milton's "Paradise Lost," vii. 384). **II.** *intr.* To glitter with spangles, or like spangles.—**span'gler,** *n.*— **span'glet,** *n.* A little spangle.—**span'gly,** *a.* Like spangles; glittering.

Span-iard (span'yärd), *n.* [OF. *Espaniard, Espaignart*.] A native of Spain; a member of the Spanish race.

span-iel (span'yel), *n.* [OF. *espaignol* (F. *épagneul*), spaniel, orig. lit. 'Spanish (dog),' = F. *espagnol*, Sp. *español*, Spanish, < L. *Hispania*, Spain.] A dog of any of various breeds of small or medium size, usually with a long, silky coat and drooping ears, certain of which are used in hunting and others as pets (sometimes divided into three classes: the 'field-spaniels,' more or less adapted for hunting, see *clumber* and *cocker*; the 'water-spaniels,' having aquatic propensities, see *water-spaniel*; and the 'toy spaniels,' kept as pets, see *Blenheim*); fig., a submissive, fawning, or cringing person (as, "Perish shall all which makes A *spaniel* of the man!" Whittier's "Astræa").

Span-ish (span'ish), *a.* Of or pertaining to Spain, its people, or their language. —**Spanish Armada.** See *armada.*—**Spanish bayonet,** any of certain plants of the liliaceous genus *Yucca,* with narrow, rigid, spine-tipped leaves.— **Spanish broom,** a species of broom, *Spartium junceum,* a European fabaceous shrub native in the Mediterra-

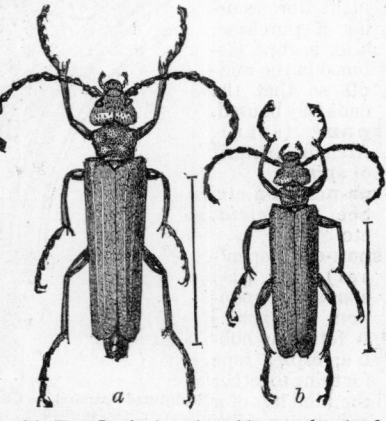

Spanish Fly (*Cantharis vesicatoria*).— *a*, female; *b*, male. (Vertical lines show natural sizes.)

nean region, whose flexible twigs are used in basketry and whose yellow flowers afford a yellow dye.—**Spanish cedar.** See *cedar.*—**Spanish dagger.** Same as *Spanish bayonet.* —**Spanish flag,** a rockfish, *Sebastichthys rubrivinctus* (family *Scorpænidæ*), of the coast of California, having crimson cross-bars.—**Spanish fly,** a blister-beetle, esp. *Cantharis vesicatoria,* used in medicine, after drying and powdering, for raising blisters and for other purposes. See cuts in preceding column.—**Spanish grass,** esparto. —**Spanish Inquisition.** See *inquisition.*—**Spanish mackerel.** See *mackerel.*—**Spanish Main,** formerly, the mainland of America adjacent to the Caribbean Sea, esp. between the mouth of the Orinoco River and the Isthmus of Panama; also, in later use, loosely, the Caribbean Sea.—**Spanish moss.** Same as *Florida moss.*—**Spanish n,** in *printing,* the letter *n* with a curved line, or tilde, over it, as in the word *cañon.* See *tilde.*—**Spanish needles,** an asteraceous plant, *Bidens bipinnata,* having achenes with downwardly barbed awns.—**Spanish omelet,** an omelet made with a filling or sauce of tomato, green pepper, onion, etc.—**Spanish Peninsula,** the peninsula in southwestern Europe consisting of Spain and Portugal.—**Span'ish,** *n.* The Spanish people collectively; also, the language of Spain, which belongs to the Romance group, and which is the prevailing language in Mexico, Central America, and the countries of South America settled by Spaniards, and is largely used in the Philippines. Cf. *Castilian.*—**Span'ish= A-mer'i-can. I.** *a.* Noting or pertaining to the parts of America where Spanish is the prevailing language; also, pertaining to Spain and America, sometimes to Spain and the U. S. (as, the *Spanish-American* War of 1898, which ended in the defeat of Spain and the subsequent freeing of Cuba). **II.** *n.* A native or inhabitant of a Spanish-American state, esp. a person of Spanish descent.

spank[1] (spangk), *v. t.* [Prob. imit.] To strike (a person, usually a child) with the open hand, a slipper, etc., esp. upon the buttocks, as in punishment.—**spank**[1], *n.* A blow given in spanking; a smart or resounding slap: as, "slaps, *spanks*, or boxes on the ear" (W. De Morgan's "Alice-for-Short," iv.).

spank[2] (spangk), *v. i.* [First recorded in *spanking, p. a.*; cf. *spang.*] To move quickly and with spirit; ride, drive, or go rapidly and smartly: as, "We set out with a fresh wind on our starboard quarter, and . . . *spanked* along at a great rate" (Poe's "Descent into the Maelström"). [Colloq.] —**spank'er,** *n.* A smartly moving person or animal, esp. a fast horse (colloq.); also, anything fine, large, or striking of its kind (colloq.); *naut.*, a fore-and-aft sail on the aftermost mast of a ship.—**spank'ing,** *p. a.* Moving rapidly and smartly (as, "a *spanking* horse": A. S. M. Hutchinson's "If Winter Comes," i. 2); quick and vigorous, as the pace; blowing briskly, as a breeze; in general, dashing, smart, or showy; unusually fine, great, large, etc. (as, "We'll have some *spanking* sport": Lover's "Handy Andy," iv.). [Colloq.]—**spank'ing-ly,** *adv.*

span-less (span'les), *a.* That cannot be spanned: as, "*spanless* girth" (Tennyson's "Princess," vi. 20).

span-ner (span'er), *n.* One who or that which spans; also, a tool for clasping and turning a nut or the like; a wrench, esp. one with fixed jaws.

span-new (span'nū'), *a.* [From Scand.: cf. Icel. *spānnȳr*, span-new, fresh (< *spānn*, chip, + *nȳr*, new), also E. *brand-new.*] Quite new; brand-new. [Now chiefly prov.]

span-roof (span'röf), *n.* A roof that has two equal inclined planes or sides.—**span'=roofed,** *a.*

span-worm (span'werm), *n.* A measuring-worm.

spar[1] (spär), *n.* [MLG. *spar, sper,* akin to AS. *spær-* in *spærstān,* gypsum.] Any of various more or less lustrous crystalline minerals: in many instances distinguished by a specific epithet, as in *dog-tooth spar, fluor-spar, heavy-spar, Iceland spar,* etc.

spar[2] (spär), *v. i.*; *sparred, sparring.* [Origin uncertain.] To strike or fight with the feet or spurs, as cocks do (as, "A young cuckoo . . . *sparring* and buffeting with its wings like a game-cock": G. White's "Nat. Hist. of Selborne," ii. 7); also, to make the motions of attack and defense with the arms and fists; use the hands as in boxing, without or with gloves; box; sometimes, to box defensively, without attacking, as to recover one's wind (also fig.); also, to bandy words, or dispute.—**spar²**, *n.* A boxing-match; also, a motion of sparring; also, a wordy contest; a dispute.

spar³ (spär), *n.* [ME. *sparre* = D. *spar* = G. *sparren* = Icel. *sparri* = Sw. and Dan. *sparre*, spar.] A piece of timber of considerable length in proportion to its thickness; a stout pole; a bar for fastening a gate, etc. (now prov. Eng.); one of the common rafters of a roof (now chiefly prov. Eng.); specif., *naut.*, a stout pole or round stick of timber such as those used for masts, etc.; a mast, yard, boom, gaff, or the like; in *aëronautics*, a principal lateral member of the framework of a plane of an aëroplane.—**spar³**, *v. t.*; *sparred*, *sparring.* To fasten (a gate, etc.) with a bar (archaic or prov.); also, in general, to fasten securely†; inclose†, confine†, or imprison†; also, to furnish or make with spars; *naut.*, to provide or fit with spars.

spar-a-ble (spär′ạ-bl), *n.* [For *sparrow-bill*.] A kind of small, headless nail used in the soles and heels of boots and shoes.

spa-ra-da (spạ-rä′dạ or -rā′dạ), *n.* [Appar. from Sp.] A small surf-fish, *Cymatogaster aggregatus*, common on the Pacific coast of North America.

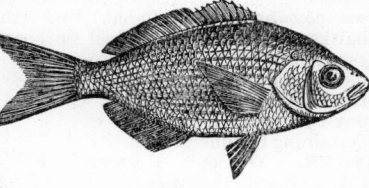

Sparada.

spar-deck (spär′dek), *n. Naut.* the upper deck of a vessel, extending from stem to stern: so called because the spars are disposed on or above it.

spare (spär), *v.*; *spared*, *sparing.* [AS. *sparian* = D. and G. *sparen* = Icel. and Sw. *spara* = Dan. *spare*, spare.] **I.** *tr.* To refrain from using, using up, or wasting (as, to *spare* one's stock of provisions; to *spare* coal or gas); use economically or frugally; also, to refrain from employing, as some instrument, means, aid, etc. (as, "He that *spareth* his rod hateth his son," Prov. xiii. 24; to *spare* no pains, time, or expense to make a thing a success); refrain from, forbear, omit, or withhold, as action or speech (as, "We might have *spared* our coming hither," Milton's "Paradise Lost," ix. 647; to *spare* useless remonstrances); sometimes, to forbear (to do something: archaic: as, "But *spare* to speak, and *spare* to speed," Burns's "Blue-Eyed Lassie"); also, to dispense with or do without (as, "On no other hand . . . could he so ill have *spared* her patient face," Dickens's "Hard Times," i. 12; "A certain degree of taste is not to be *spared* in those we sit with," Emerson's "Essays," Manners); part with or let go, as from a supply, esp. without inconvenience or loss (as, "I could have better *spared* a better man": Shakspere's "1 Henry IV.," v. 4. 104); set aside or allow for a particular use or purpose (as, to *spare* land for a garden; to *spare* time or money for an undertaking); give or grant, as to another (as, to *spare* a sum to a friend; to *spare* [to] one a small sum; *spare* us a thought now and then); also, to refrain from harming or destroying, or leave uninjured (as, to *spare* a fallen adversary, or his life; the storm *spared* few of the plants; time has *spared* the beauty of the place); forbear to punish (as, to *spare* a guilty person); deal gently or leniently with, or show consideration for (as, a tongue that *spares* nobody; to seek to *spare* a person's feelings); save from strain, discomfort, annoyance, or the like, or from a particular cause of it (as, "They were obliged to travel slowly, to *spare* their horses," Irving's "Captain Bonneville," xxix.; to *spare* the eyes from a glare of light; to *spare* one from listening to a tedious story); release or exempt, as from duty, attendance, etc.; save or relieve (a person, etc.) from (something) (as, to *spare* one's self trouble; to *spare* the world the miseries of war). **II.** *intr.* To use economy, or be frugal or saving; also, to refrain from action, or forbear (as, "Throw down the screen — *spare* not for cup or goblet": Scott's "Quentin Durward," x.); also, to refrain from inflicting injury or punishment; exercise lenience or mercy.—**spare,** *a.*; compar. *sparer,* superl. *sparest.* [Cf. AS. *spær,* sparing, frugal.] Kept in reserve, as for possible future need or extra use (as, a *spare* umbrella; a *spare* tire for an automobile; a *spare* bedroom, for guests); additional or extra; also, being in excess of present need, or free for

other use (as, *spare* cash; *spare* time); also, sparing, economical, or temperate, as persons†; also, frugally restricted, or meager, as living, diet, fare, etc. (as, "*spare* feast! — a radish and an egg!" Cowper's "Task," iv. 173); also, scanty or scant, as in amount, fullness, etc. (as, "Sir Launfal's raiment thin and *spare* Was idle mail 'gainst the barbèd air," Lowell's "Vision of Sir Launfal," ii. 3; "She hated her *spare* black frock," Arnold Bennett's "Hilda Lessways," ii. 5); often, scant of flesh, or without superfluous flesh, or lean or thin, as a person, the bodily frame, etc. (as, "an old man, very tall and *spare*, with an ascetic aspect": Mallock's "New Republic," iii. 4).—**spare,** *n.* Sparing or economical use, as of something; stint; also, forbearance†, lenience†, or mercy†; also, a spare thing, part, etc., as an extra tire carried for emergency use on an automobile; in *American bowling*, the knocking down of all the pins with two bowls (instead of three allowed, the third being thus a spare or extra one).

spare-ly (spär′li), *adv.* In a spare manner.—**spare′ness,** *n.*

spar-er (spär′ėr), *n.* One who spares.

spare-rib (spär′rib), *n.* A cut of pork containing ribs from the upper or fore end of the row, where there is little meat adhering.

sparge (spärj), *v. t.*; *sparged, sparging.* [L. *spargere* (pp. *sparsus*), scatter, sprinkle: cf. *sparse.*] To scatter or sprinkle; specif., in *brewing*, to sprinkle (malt) with hot water in order to wash out the wort remaining in the grains.—**spar-ger** (spär′jėr), *n.* A sprinkler; esp., an automatic sprinkler for sparging the malt in brewing.

spar-hawk (spär′hȧk), *n.* A sparrow-hawk. [Archaic.]

spar-ing (spär′ing), *p. a.* That spares; exercising economy in using, spending, etc.; economical (*in*) or chary (*of*: as, "Fortune alone has . . . been sparing of her gifts," Miss Burney's "Evelina," xxvii.); forbearing; lenient or merciful; also, economically or frugally restricted (as, "a very *sparing* diet," Parkman's "Oregon Trail," xi.; a *sparing* use of sugar); scanty; limited or moderate (as, "My uncle at the most *sparing* estimate must have possessed . . . two million pounds'-worth of property": H. G. Wells's "Tono-Bungay," iii. 1. § 3).—**spar′ing-ly,** *adv.*—**spar′ing-ness,** *n.*

spark¹ (spärk), *n.* [AS. *spærca, spearca,* = MLG. *sparke* = D. *spark,* spark.] An ignited or fiery particle such as is thrown off by burning wood, etc., or produced by one hard body striking against another (as, "His sister sat . . . by the fireside . . . looking at the bright *sparks* as they dropped upon the hearth": Dickens's "Hard Times," i. 8); a small mass of fiery matter in a body or mass otherwise inert; hence, in fig. use, a small amount or trace of something, esp. as comparable to a spark in its possible extension of activity (as, "to try if it was possible to get a *spark* of human spirit out of you," Scott's "Woodstock," v.; "They still keep alive the *sparks* of future friendship," Irving's "Sketch-Book," English Writers on America); often, a trace of life or vitality, as in a person (as, "O speak, if any *spark* of life remain": Kyd's "Spanish Tragedy," ii. 5. 17); the vital principle in man (as, "Will my tiny *spark* of being wholly vanish in your deeps and heights?" Tennyson's "God and the Universe"); also, a small diamond; a glittering bit of ore, etc.; also, a scintillation, gleam, or flash, as of light (as, "Beneath their oars the ocean's might Was dash'd to *sparks* of glimmering light": Scott's "Lord of the Isles," v. 12); in *elect.*, the luminous effect produced by a sudden discontinuous discharge of electricity through air or other dielectric; also, a small arc at a point where the continuity of a circuit is interrupted.—**spark¹,** *v.* **I.** *intr.* To emit sparks of fire; also, to send forth gleams or flashes; also, to issue as or like sparks; in *elect.*, to produce sparks. **II.** *tr.* To emit as sparks; in *elect.*, to affect by sparks.

spark² (spärk), *n.* [Appar. a fig. use of *spark¹*.] A gay, elegant, or showy young man (or, formerly, woman) (as, "A fop came . . . a fine *spark*, and gave them fine words": S. J. Weyman's "Gentleman of France," viii.); also, a beau, lover, or suitor.—**spark²,** *v.* **I.** *intr.* To engage in courtship; play the beau or suitor: as, "His master was courting, or, as it is termed, 'sparking,' within" (Irving's "Sketch-Book," Sleepy Hollow). [Prov., U. S.] **II.** *tr.* To pay attentions to (a woman); court. [Prov., U. S.]

(variable) ḏ as d or j, ş as s or sh, ṭ as t or ch, ẕ as z or zh; o, F. cloche; ü, F. menu; ċh, Sc. loch; ṅ, F. bonbon; ′, primary accent; ″, secondary accent; †, obsolete; <, from; +, and; =, equals. See also lists at beginning of book.

spark=ar-res-ter (spärk'a-res″tẻr), *n.* A device consisting of wire netting or other material used to stop or deflect sparks thrown from an open fireplace, a smoke-stack, or the like; in *elect.*, a sparker.

spark=coil (spärk'koil), *n.* In *elect.*, a coil of many turns of insulated wire on an iron core, used for producing sparks; also, an induction-coil for producing sparks.

sparked (spärkt), *a.* [Appar. < *spark*[1].] Spotted; speckled; mottled; variegated. [Prov.]

spark-er (spär'kẻr), *n.* Something that produces sparks; also, in *elect.*, a device for preventing injurious sparking in electrical apparatuses at points where frequent interruptions of the circuit occur.

spark=gap (spärk'gap), *n.* In *elect.*, an open space in any electric circuit, across which a discharge in the form of a spark takes place.

spar-kle (spär'kl), *v.*; -kled, -kling. [Freq. < *spark*[1].] **I.** *intr.* To issue in or as in little sparks, as fire, light, etc.; also, to emit little sparks, as burning matter; hence, to send forth or shine with little gleams or flashes of light, as a brilliant gem or star, dew or waves in the sunlight, etc.; glisten brightly; glitter; move or flow with gleams or flashes of light, as a stream; be bright as with flashes, as the eyes (as, "the pleasure that made Ruth's eyes *sparkle*": Archibald Marshall's "Anthony Dare," ii.); appear as if with flashing brightness (as, "Joy *sparkled* in all their eyes": Milton's "Paradise Lost," ii. 388); effervesce with small, glistening bubbles, as wine; also, fig., to be brilliant, showily clever, or smart, as wit, conversation, etc., or a speaker or writer; be lively or vivacious, as a person. **II.** *tr.* To cause to sparkle or glisten (as, "the jovial sun . . . *sparkling* the landscape with a thousand dewy gems": Irving's "Knickerbocker's New York," vi. 4); also, to emit in or as in sparks (as, "Women's eyes . . . They *sparkle* still the right Promethean fire": Shakspere's "Love's Labour's Lost," iv. 3. 351); show by sparkling or brightness (as, eyes *sparkling* joy).—**spar'kle,** *n.* A little spark or fiery particle (as, "And drove his heel into the smoulder'd log, That sent a blast of *sparkles* up the flue": Tennyson's "Morte d'Arthur," 287); hence, a small bit, amount, or trace of something (obs. or archaic); also, a little gleam, flash, or point of light (as, "Swift as the *sparkle* of a glancing star I shoot from heaven": Milton's "Comus," 80); sparkling appearance, luster, or flashing play of light (as, the *sparkle* of a diamond; fig., brilliance, cleverness, or smartness, as of wit; liveliness, animation, or vivacity, as of manner or disposition.—**spar'kler,** *n.* One who or that which sparkles; a firework that emits little sparks; a sparkling gem, esp. a diamond; a sparkling or bright eye (colloq.).

spark-less (spärk'les), *a.* Free from sparks; emitting no sparks: as, "*sparkless* ashes" (Shelley's "Adonais," xl.).

spark-let (spärk'let), *n.* A little spark or sparkle.

spar-kling (spär'kling), *p. a.* That sparkles; shining with little gleams or flashes; glistening brightly; effervescent, as wine; fig., brilliant; vivacious.—**spar'kling-ly,** *adv.*—**spar'kling-ness,** *n.*

spark=plug (spärk'plug), *n.* A device inserted in the cylinder of an internal-combustion engine, containing the two terminals between which passes the electric spark for igniting the explosive gases.

Sparks (spärks), *n.* [Prop. pl. of *spark*[1], *n.*] A colloquial name for a wireless operator, as on a ship.

spar-ling (spär'ling), *n.*; pl. *sparlings* or (esp. collectively) *sparling.* [OF. *esperlenc* (F. *éperlan*); from Teut.: cf. G. *spierling*, smelt.] The European smelt, *Osmerus eperlanus* (now chiefly north. Eng. and Sc.); also, a young herring (U. S.).

spa-roid (spä'roid). [L. *sparus*, < Gr. σπάρος, kind of sparoid fish: see -*oid*.] **I.** *a.* Resembling a sea-bream; belonging or pertaining to the *Sparidæ*, a family of acanthopterygian fishes including the sea-breams, the scup, etc. **II.** *n.* A sparoid fish.

spar-rer (spär'ẻr), *n.* One who spars or boxes.—**spar'ring,** *n.* The act or art of one who spars or boxes; boxing; also, the bandying of words, or disputing (as, "There was some amiable *sparring* between the worthy man and Mr. Britling about bringing Mr. Direck to church": H. G. Wells's "Mr. Britling," i. 2. § 2).

spar-row (spar'ō), *n.* [AS. *spearwa* = Goth. *sparwa* = OHG. *sparo* = Icel. *spörr*, sparrow: cf. G. *sperling*, sparrow.] A small, hardy, pugnacious fringilline bird, *Passer domesticus*, of Europe, introduced into America, Australia, etc., as a destroyer of insects, but now commonly regarded as a pest ('English sparrow'); also, any of various allied or similar birds (see *chipping sparrow, Java sparrow,* and *Texas sparrow,* also *Peabody bird*); also, the game of mah-jongg.

English Sparrow (*Passer domesticus*).

spar-row=grass (spar'ō-gràs), *n.* Corruption of *asparagus.* [Prov. or vulgar.]

spar-row=hawk (spar'ō-hâk), *n.* Any of certain small hawks or falcons which feed on sparrows and other prey, esp. *Accipiter nisus,* a European hawk, and *Falco sparverius,* an American falcon.

spar-ry (spär'i), *a.* Of or pertaining to mineral spar.

SPARS. Women's Reserve, Coast Guard Reserve.

sparse (spärs), *a.*; compar. *sparser,* superl. *sparsest.* [L. *sparsus,* pp. of *spargere,* scatter: cf. *sparge.*] Thinly scattered or distributed, or occurring here and there at considerable intervals (as, a *sparse* population; "a party which as yet was . . . an unorganised mob — thick in one place, *sparse* in another," Besant's "Coligny," v.); thin, or not thick or dense (as, *sparse* hair; "a poor, *sparse* hedge," Arnold Bennett's "Hilda Lessways," ii. 6); hence, scanty; meager.—**sparse'ly,** *adv.* —**sparse'ness,** *n.*—**spar-sim** (spär'sim), *adv.* [L., < *sparsus.*] At scattered points; here and there.—**spar'si-ty** (-si-ti), *n.* Sparse or scattered condition; thinness of distribution; relative fewness.

Spar-ta-can (spär'ta-kan). [From *Spartacus,* the name signed to certain political writings put forth in Germany, during the World War, under the direction of Karl Liebknecht (1871–1919), leader of the Spartacans: being orig. the name of a Thracian who became a slave and gladiator in Italy, and in 73–71 B.C. led an insurrection of slaves against Rome.] **I.** *n.* A member of a party of extreme socialists, ultraradical communists, or revolutionists in Germany (corresponding in general to the Bolsheviki of Russia), which arose about 1916, and was especially prominent in 1918–19. **II.** *a.* Belonging or pertaining to, or characteristic of, the Spartacans.—**Spar'ta-can-ism,** *n.* The doctrines, methods, or procedure of the Spartacans.—**Spar'ta-cide** (-sīd), *n.* and *a.* Same as *Spartacan.*—**Spar'ta-cism** (-sizm), *n.* Same as *Spartacanism.*—**Spar'ta-cist** (-sist), *n.* and *a.* Same as *Spartacan.*—**Spar'ta-cus** (-kus), *a.* Spartacan: as, the *Spartacus* group; *Spartacus* forces.

Spar-tan (spär'tan), *a.* Of or pertaining to Sparta (or Lacedæmon), an ancient city of southern Greece, and the capital of ancient Laconia; pertaining to its people, who were noted for their simplicity, austerity, fortitude, courage, and brevity of speech; hence, suggestive of or befitting the ancient Spartans (as, "a rigid economy, a stern and more than *Spartan* simplicity of life": Thoreau's "Walden," ii.); rigorously simple, frugal, or austere; sternly disciplined; characterized by fortitude; brave; brief, concise, or laconic. —**Spartan dog,** a bloodhound; fig., a cruel or bloodthirsty person (see Shakspere's "Othello," v. 2. 361).—**Spar'tan,** *n.* A native or inhabitant of Sparta; also, a person of Spartan characteristics.

---

fat, fāte, fär, fåll, ȧsk, fāre; net, mē, hẻr; pin, pīne; not, nōte, mȯve, nór; up, lūte, púll; oi, oil; ou, out; (lightened) aviȧry, ẹlect, agȯny, intọ, ūnite; (obscured) errạnt, operạ, ardẹnt, actọr, natūre; ch, chip; g, go; th, thin; ᴛʜ, then; y, you;

spar-te-ine (spär′tē-in), n. [NL. *Spartium*, genus of broom (now only Spanish broom), < Gr. σπάρτος, broom.] A bitter, poisonous liquid alkaloid obtained from the common broom, *Cytisus scoparius*: used in medicine, esp. in the form of its sulphate, as a heart-stimulant, etc.

spasm (spazm), n. [OF. F. *spasme*, < L. *spasmus*, < Gr. σπασμός, < σπᾶν, draw, convulse.] A sudden, abnormal, involuntary muscular contraction; an affection consisting of a continued muscular contraction ('tonic spasm'), or of a series of alternating muscular contractions and relaxations ('clonic spasm'); a convulsion; hence, any sudden movement or occurrence of a convulsive character (as, "an earthquake's *spasm*": Shelley's "Revolt of Islam," ix. 5); any sudden, brief fit or spell of unusual energy or activity (as, "Between the *spasms* of violence there were long quiet intervals when the ordinary occupations of men went on as usual": Froude's "Cæsar," viii.); a sudden, brief access of strong feeling or emotion (as, "I felt a *spasm* of petulant annoyance at this unexpected catastrophe": H. G. Wells's "Tono-Bungay," ii. 4. § 7).—**spas-mod-ic** (spaz-mod′ik), a. [Gr. σπασμώδης.] Pertaining to or of the nature of a spasm; characterized by spasms; hence, resembling a spasm or spasms; convulsive; sudden and violent, but brief; occurring or proceeding by fits and starts (as, "*spasmodic* toil": H. Melville's "Moby-Dick," liv.); given to or characterized by bursts of excitement.—**spas-mod-i-cal-ly**, adv.

spas-tic (spas′tik), a. [L. *spasticus*, < Gr. σπαστικός, < σπᾶν: see *spasm*.] In *pathol.*, pertaining to, of the nature of, or characterized by spasm, esp. tonic spasm.—**spas′ti-cal-ly**, adv.—**spas-ti′ci-ty** (-tis′i-ti), n.

spat¹ (spat), n. [Origin uncertain; perhaps related to *spit²*.] The spawn of an oyster or similar shell-fish; young oysters collectively; a young oyster.—**spat¹**, v. i. or t.; *spatted*, *spatting*. To spawn.

spat² (spat), n. [Prob. imit.] A light blow; a slap; a smack; also, a petty quarrel, or tiff (as, "They got into kind of a *spat* about which one'd make the best actress": Tarkington's "Alice Adams," ix.). [Chiefly colloq.]—**spat²**, v.; *spatted*, *spatting*. **I.** tr. To strike lightly; slap. [Chiefly colloq.] **II.** intr. To administer slaps; strike sharply; also, to engage in a petty quarrel or dispute. [Chiefly colloq.]

spat³ (spat), n. [Abbr. of *spatterdash*.] A short gaiter worn over the instep, usually fastened under the foot with a strap: usually in pl.

spat⁴ (spat). Preterit and past participle of *spit²*.

spa-tan-gus (spa-tang′gus), n.; pl. *-tangi* (-tan′jī). [NL., < Gr. σπατάγγης, kind of sea-urchin.] Any of the sea-urchins constituting the genus *Spatangus*, some of which are heart-shaped.—**spa-tan′goid** (-goid), a.

spatch-cock (spach′kok), n. [Origin uncertain; said to be for *despatch-cock*: cf. *spitchcock*.] A freshly killed fowl split and broiled.—**spatch′cock**, v. t. To cook in the manner of a spatchcock; also, to insert or interpolate, or to modify by interpolation (colloq., Eng.).

spate (spāt), n. [ME. *spate*; origin uncertain.] A flood or inundation; a freshet; a state of flood (as, "Is the torrent in *spate?* He must ford it or swim": Kipling's "Overland Mail"); also, a sudden, heavy downpour of rain; also, fig., any sudden, flood-like outburst, flow, etc. [Orig. Sc. and north. Eng.]

Violet Spatangus (*S. purpureus*), one half being shown with its spines removed.

spath (spath), n. [G.] Same as *spar¹*.

spa-tha-ceous (spā-thā′shius), a. In *bot.*, of the nature of or resembling a spathe; having a spathe.

spathe (spāᵺ), n. [L. *spatha*, < Gr. σπάθη, broad blade, spatula, spathe: cf. *spade¹*, *spade²*, and *spatula*.] In *bot.*, a bract or pair of bracts, often large and colored, subtending or inclosing a spadix or flower-cluster.—**spathed**, a. In *bot.*, having a spathe.

spath-ic (spath′ik), a. In *mineral.*, like spath or spar. Also **spath′ose** (-ōs).

spath-u-late (spath′ū-lāt), a. Same as *spatulate*.

spa-tial (spā′shạl), a. [L. *spatium*, E. *space*.] Of or pertaining to space; also, existing or occurring in space; having extension in space.—**spa-ti-al′i-ty** (-shi-al′i-ti), n. Spatial character.—**spa′tial-ly**, adv.

spat-ter (spat′ėr), v. [Cf. D. *spatten*, spatter, sprinkle.] **I.** tr. To scatter or dash in small particles or drops (as, to *spatter* mud, water, or ink); also, to splash with something in small particles (as, to *spatter* the ground with water); esp., to sprinkle or spot with something that soils or stains (as, to *spatter* a person with mud, or, fig., with slander or disgrace); also, to fall upon in scattered particles or drops (as, "One wave breaking far aft *spattered* the quarterdeck": Kipling's "Light That Failed," xv.). **II.** intr. To send out small particles or drops, as boiling matter; sometimes, to sputter, or eject particles of saliva, food, etc., from the mouth; also, to fly out or fall in small particles or drops (as, "a large umbrella upon which the rain *spattered*": Arnold Bennett's "Clayhanger," iv. 5); strike as in a shower, as bullets.—**spat′ter**, n. The act or the sound of spattering (as, the *spatter* of rain on a roof; the *spatter* of bullets); also, that which is spattered; a splash or spot of something spattered.—**spat′ter-dash**, n. A kind of long gaiter worn to protect the trousers or stockings from mud, etc., as in riding: usually in pl. Cf. *spat³*.—**spat′ter=dock**, n. A yellow pond-lily, esp. *Nymphæa advena*, a coarse yellow-flowered plant common in stagnant waters.—**spat′ter-work**, n. Decorative work in which a (blank) design is produced on a surface by spattering ink or the like over exposed parts.

spat-u-la (spat′ū-lä), n. [L. *spatula*, for *spathula*, dim. of *spatha*, broad blade: see *spathe*.] An implement with a broad, flat, more or less flexible blade, used for mixing drugs, spreading plasters and paints, etc.—**spat′u-lar** (-lär), a. Pertaining to or resembling a spatula.—**spat′u-late** (-lāt), a. Shaped like a spatula; often, rounded more or less like the outlines of a spoon; in *bot.*, having a broad, rounded end and a narrow, attenuate base, as a leaf.—**spat-u-la′tion** (-lä′shọn), n. Spatulate condition or form; a spatulate formation.

Spatter-dock (*Nymphæa advena*).—*a*, a stamen; *b*, the fruit.

spav-in (spav′in), n. [OF. *espavain*, *esparvain* (F. *éparvin*); origin uncertain.] Any of certain diseases of horses affecting the hock, esp. one in which a bony excrescence forms at the joint; also, an excrescence or enlargement so formed.—**spav′ined**, a. Affected with spavin; fig., lame; crippled; halting.

Spatulate Leaves.

spawl¹ (spâl), v. i. [Origin obscure.] To spit; expectorate. [Obs. or archaic.]

spawl² (spâl), n. and v. See *spall*.

spawn (spân), v. [Appar. < OF. *espandre* (F. *épandre*). spread, pour out, shed, < L. *expandere*, E. *expand*.] **I.** intr. Of fishes, amphibians, etc., to produce eggs or spawn; hence, in general, to be reproductive; also, to issue like spawn. **II.** tr. To produce (spawn); hence, in general, and usually in contempt, to give birth to; bring forth; produce; give rise to.—**spawn**, n. The eggs of fishes, amphibians, mollusks, crustaceans, etc., when small and numerous, or extruded in masses; also, the young from such eggs, while in an early stage of development; sometimes, a single egg, or a single young animal, of this kind; hence, in general, and usually in disparagement or contempt, a swarming brood or numerous progeny; persons, or a person, regarded as the offspring of some stock, or as imbued with some quality or principle (as, "Tyrants are but the *spawn* of Ignorance, Begotten by the slaves they trample on": Lowell's "Prometheus," 109); any product or result; sometimes, the source or origin of something; in *bot.*, the mycelium of fungi.

—spawn'=eat"er, *n.* A fish that feeds on spawn; esp., a large minnow, *Notropis hudsonius,* common in streams in New York, Pennsylvania, etc.**—spawn'-er,** *n.*

Spawn-eater (*Notropis hudsonius*).

spay (spā), *v. t.;* spayed, spaying. [Appar. < OF. *espeer,* cut with a sword, < *espee* (F. *épée*), sword, < L. *spatha:* see *spade*[1] and *spathe.*] To remove the ovaries of (a female animal).

speak (spēk), *v. i.;* pret. *spoke* (archaic *spake*), pp. *spoken* (archaic or prov. *spoke*), ppr. *speaking.* [AS. *specan,* earlier *sprecan* = OS. *sprekan* = D. *spreken* = G. *sprechen,* speak: cf. *speech.*] To utter words or articulate sounds with the ordinary (talking) voice; exercise the faculty of speech; hence, to make oral communication or mention (as, to *speak* to a person of various matters); hold talk or discourse; converse; sometimes, to be on speaking terms, as persons who are not estranged; also, to deliver an address, discourse, etc.; make a plea or recommendation in behalf of somebody or something (with *for:* as, "Why don't you *speak* for yourself, John?" Longfellow's "Courtship of Miles Standish," iii.); also, to make a statement in written or printed words; make communication or disclosure by any means; convey significance, or appeal (as, "The intruder's glance kept straying to the Canaletto prints . . . it was a rare thing for Mr. Irquetson to have a visitor to whom they *spoke*": L. Merrick's "Conrad in Quest of His Youth," v.); also, to emit a sound, as a musical instrument; make a noise or report (as, "their pursuers, whose guns were beginning to *speak*": Tarkington's "Gentleman from Indiana," xi.); of dogs, to bark when ordered.**—so to speak.** See under *so, adv.*—**to speak of,** worth mentioning: as, "Supper was to follow with scarcely any interval *to speak of*" (Du Maurier's "Trilby," iii.).**—speak,** *v. t.* To utter orally and articulately (as, to *speak* words of praise; to *speak* a person's name); hence, to express with the voice, or make known in uttered words (as, to *speak* the truth; "when he might *speak* his mind," Strype's "Memorials of Cranmer," i. 25); also, to declare in writing or printing, or by any means of communication; announce by sound, as a trumpet does; make known, indicate, or reveal (as, "the loud laugh that *spoke* the vacant mind": Goldsmith's "Deserted Village," 122); show to be (archaic: as, "His whole person is finely turned, and *speaks* him a man of quality," Addison and Steele, in "Tatler," 75); describe or characterize (archaic: as, "To *speak* him true . . . No keener hunter after glory breathes," Tennyson's "Lancelot and Elaine," 153); also, to speak of† or make mention of†; also, to use, or be able to use, in oral utterance, as a language (as, to *speak* French; to *speak* good English); also, to speak to or with (as, to *speak* a person fair, to speak to him in a courteous or kindly manner); address; converse with; communicate with (a passing vessel, etc.) at sea, as by voice or signal (as, "I've got to *speak* a homeward-bound ship or a man-of-war": J. Conrad's "Rescue," i. 2); also, to send, put, bring, render, etc., by speaking (as, to *speak* a world into being; "Impartially severe; Too just to wink, or *speak* the guilty clear," Cowper's "Expostulation," 256).

speak-a-ble (spē'kạ-bl), *a.* That may be spoken; also, able to speak†.

speak=eas-y (spēk'ē"zi), *n.;* pl. *-easies* (-ē"ziz). A place where intoxicating liquors are sold without a license or otherwise contrary to law. [Slang, U. S.]

speak-er (spē'kėr), *n.* One who speaks; esp., one who speaks formally before an audience; one who practises public speaking; an orator; [usually *cap.*] the presiding officer of the House of Commons of Great Britain, the House of Representatives of the U. S., or some other similar assembly; also [*l. c.*], a book of selections for practice in declamation.**—speak'er-ship,** *n.*

speak-ing (spē'king), *n.* The act, utterance, or discourse of one who speaks.**—speak'ing,** *p. a.* That speaks; giving information as if by speech (as, a *speaking* proof or example of a thing); highly expressive (as, a *speaking* face; "What *speaking* eyes!" Mallock's "New Republic," i. 2); lifelike (as, a *speaking* likeness); also, used in, suited to, or involving speaking or talking (as, the *speaking* voice; to be within *speaking* distance of a person; to have a *speaking* part in a play); permitting of speaking as in greeting or conversation (as, to have a *speaking* acquaintance with a person; they are no longer on *speaking* terms).**—speak'ing-ly,** *adv.*

—speak'ing=trum"pet, *n.* A trumpet-shaped instrument by which the sound of the human voice is reinforced so that it may be heard at a great distance or above other sounds, as in hailing ships at sea or giving orders at a fire.**—speak'ing=tube,** *n.* A tube or pipe for conveying the voice to a distance, as from one part of a building to another.

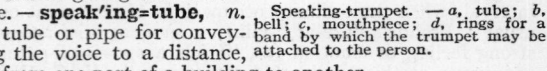

Speaking-trumpet. — *a,* tube; *b,* bell; *c,* mouthpiece; *d,* rings for a band by which the trumpet may be attached to the person.

spear[1] (spēr), *n.* [Var. of *spire*[1].] A sprout or shoot of a plant; an acrospire of grain; a blade of grass, etc.; also, an individual hair growing on the head (as, to have few remaining *spears* of hair); also, a spire of a church or other building†.**—spear**[1], *v. i.* To sprout; shoot; send up or rise in a spear or spears.

spear[2] (spēr), *n.* [AS. *spere* = D. and G. *speer,* spear (Icel. *spjör,* pl.): cf. L. *sparus,* hunting-spear.] A weapon for thrusting or throwing, consisting of a long wooden staff to which a sharp head, as of iron or steel, is fixed; a soldier or other person armed with such a weapon; also, some similar weapon or instrument, as one for spearing fish; also, the act of spearing.**—spear side,** the male side, or line of descent, of a family: opposed to *distaff side* or *spindle side.*—**spear**[2], *v.* **I.** *tr.* To pierce with or as with a spear: as, "I . . . think it a gain to be *speared* by a foe, rather than to be stabbed by a friend" (J. H. Newman's "Idea of a University," ii. 5). **II.** *intr.* To go or penetrate like a spear: as, "the long shafts of light which the rising sun sent . . . *spearing* right down into the hidden mysterious night below" (Margaret Kennedy's "Constant Nymph," ix.).**—spear'er,** *n.*—**spear'=fish,** *n.* A large marine fish, *Tetrapturus albidus,* with a long, spear-like beak.**—spear'=grass,** *n.* Any of various grasses with a spear-like leaf, inflorescence, or other part, as the couch-grass, *Agropyron repens.*—**spear'=head,** *n.* The sharp-pointed head which forms the piercing end of a spear.**—spear'man** (-mạn), *n.;* pl. *-men.* One who is armed with or uses a spear; a soldier whose spear is his principal weapon.**—spear'mint,** *n.* The common mint, *Mentha spicata,* an aromatic herb much used for flavoring.**—spear'wort** (-wėrt), *n.* Any of certain species of crowfoot with long, narrow leaves, as *Ranunculus flammula* ('lesser spearwort') and *R. lingua* ('great spearwort').**—spear'y,** *a.* Spearlike; sharp-pointed.

Hunting-spears, 15th or 16th century.

Spear-fish.

Spearmint, upper part of the stem with the inflorescence. — *a,* a flower.

spec (spek), *n.* Short for *speculation* (in financial matters): as, "If tradesmen will run up houses on *spec* in a water-meadow, who can stop them?" (Kingsley's "Two Years Ago," xxv.). [Colloq.]

spe-cial (spesh′ạl), *a.* [OF. *special, especial* (F. *spécial*), < L. *specialis,* special, particular, not general, < *species:* see *species,* and cf. *especial.*] Constituting a species or distinct sort (as, a *special* kind or form of key; a *special* type or pattern); of a distinct or particular kind or character; hence, being a particular one (as, a *special* day; of no *special* color; have you any *special* case in mind?); particular, individual, or certain; also, pertaining or peculiar to a particular person, thing, instance, etc. (as, "The Lord thy God hath chosen thee to be a *special* people unto himself," Deut. vii. 6; one's *special* province; the *special* features or merits of a plan); having a particular function, purpose, application, etc. (as, a *special* messenger or agent; a *special* train; *special* legislation; *special* knowledge or study); dealing with particulars, or specific, as a statement; also, distinguished or different from what is ordinary or usual (as, a *special* occasion; a *special* honor; a *special* edition of a book; *special* cause or reason); extraordinary; exceptional; sometimes, exceptional in amount or degree, or especial (as, *special* care or zeal; *special* importance; *special* interest); great; being such in an exceptional degree (as, a *special* friend or favorite). —**special pleading,** in legal use, pleading that alleges special or new matter in avoidance of the allegations made by the opposite side; hence, fig., pleading or arguing that ignores unfavorable features of a case; one-sided or unfair presentation of one's case.—**spe′cial,** *n.* A special person or thing; esp., a special constable (appointed for a particular duty or occasion); a special train; a special edition of a newspaper.—**in special,** specially; particularly; in particular: as, "He loved all maidens, but no maid *In special*" (Tennyson's "Pelleas and Ettarre," 40). [Obs. or archaic.]

spe-cial-ism (spesh′ạl-izm), *n.* Devotion to a special branch of study, etc.; restriction to one division of a general subject or pursuit.—**spe′cial-ist,** *n.* One who devotes himself to one subject, or to one particular branch of a subject or pursuit; esp., a medical practitioner who devotes his attention to a particular class of diseases, etc.—**spe-cial-is′tic,** *a.*

spe-ci-al-i-ty (spesh-i-al′i-ti), *n.;* pl. *-ties* (-tiz). [OF. *especialite* (F. *spécialité*), < LL. *specialitas,* < L. *specialis:* see *special,* and cf. *specialty.*] Special or particular character; also, a special quality or characteristic; a peculiarity; the distinctive characteristic or feature of a thing; also, a special point or item; a particular or detail; also, a specialty, in study, work, trade, etc., or in law (as, "Dean Alford . . . who had made the New Testament his *speciality*": S. Butler's "Way of All Flesh," lxv.).

spe-cial-ize (spesh′ạl-īz), *v.; -ized, -izing.* [F. *spécialiser.*] **I.** *tr.* To mention specially; specify; particularize; also, to render special or specific; invest with a special character, function, etc. (as, "All the Allied infantrymen tend to become *specialised,* as bombers, as machine gun men, and so on": H. G. Wells's "Italy, France, and Britain at War," iii. 4); adapt to special conditions; restrict to specific limits. **II.** *intr.* To go into particulars; particularize; also, to assume a special character; also, to pursue some special line of study, work, etc.; make a specialty of (as, "The Daily Film *specialised* in theatrical photographs": Arnold Bennett's "The Old Adam," v.).—**spe″cial-i-za′tion** (-i-zā′shọn), *n.*—**spe′cial-iz-er** (-ī-zèr), *n.*

spe-cial-ly (spesh′ạl-i), *adv.* In a special manner or degree; particularly; specifically; exceptionally; especially.—**spe′cial-ness,** *n.*

spe-cial-ty (spesh′ạl-ti), *n.;* pl. *-ties* (-tiz). [OF. *especialte:* cf. *speciality.*] Special or particular character, or speciality; also, a special characteristic, or peculiarity; also, a special or particular point, item, matter, or thing; esp., a special subject of study, line of work, or the like; an article particularly dealt in, manufactured, etc., or one to which the dealer or manufacturer professes to devote special care; also, an article of trade of special character; a novelty; in *law,* a special agreement, contract, etc., expressed in an instrument under seal.

spe-cie (spē′shē), *n.* [L., abl. of *species* (see *species*), in the phrase *in specie,* in kind, hence (of money) in actual coin.] Coin; coined money.

spe-cies (spē′shēz), *n.;* pl. *species.* [L., sight, appearance, form, particular sort or kind, species, < *specere,* look at: see *spy, v.*] Appearance†; the visible form or image of something†; a spectacle†; also, a class of individuals having some common characteristics or qualities; a distinct sort or kind (as, "that *species* of writing which is called the marvellous": Fielding's "Tom Jones," viii. 1); also, specie† or coin†; *eccles.,* the visible form or appearance of the bread or the wine used in the eucharist; hence, either of the eucharistic elements; in *logic,* a number of individuals having common characteristics or attributes peculiar to them, and forming a group which with other similar groups is included in a higher group called a *genus;* in *zoöl.* and *bot.,* a classificatory group ranking next below a genus or subgenus, consisting of animals or plants which have certain distinctive and permanent characteristics in common.

spe-ci-fi-a-ble (spes′i-fī-ạ-bl), *a.* That may be specified.

spe-cif-ic (spē-sif′ik), *a.* [ML. *specificus,* < L. *species,* kind, + *facere,* make.] Having a special application, bearing, or reference (as, *specific* mention; *specific* directions or measures; to be *specific* in one's statements); specifying, explicit, or definite; also, specified, precise, or particular (as, a *specific* instance; a *specific* purpose; a *specific* sum of money); also, peculiar or proper to something, as qualities, characteristics, effects, etc.; specially belonging to and characteristic of a thing or a group of things; also, of a special or particular kind; in *med.,* of a disease, produced by a special cause or infection; of a remedy, having special effect in the cure of a certain disease; in *zoöl.* and *bot.,* of or pertaining to a species (as, *specific* characters; a *specific* name).—**specific duty,** a duty of a specified amount assessed on an article of a particular kind, or on a given quantity of an article, without reference to its value or market price. Cf. *ad valorem.*—**specific gravity,** the ratio of the weight of a given volume of any substance to that of the same volume of some other substance taken as a standard, water being the standard for solids and liquids, and hydrogen or air for gases; relative density.—**specific heat,** the quantity of heat required to raise 1 gram of a given substance through 1° C. of temperature.—**spe-cif′ic,** *n.* Something specific, as a statement, quality, etc.; in *med.,* a specific remedy (as, "an admirable *specific* against all diseases produced by repletion": Swift's "Gulliver's Travels," iv. 7).—**spe-cif′i-cal-ly,** *adv.* In a specific manner; with specific mention or reference; explicitly; definitely; particularly; in a particular sense; also, with reference to specific or peculiar qualities or characteristics, or to species, esp. zoölogical or botanical species.

spe-ci-fi-ca-tion (spes″i-fi-kā′shọn), *n.* [F. *spécification,* < ML. *specificatio(n-).*] The act of specifying; specific or definite mention; explicit or detailed statement or enumeration; also, a statement of particulars; a document submitted by the applicant for a patent, giving detailed information about the construction, use, etc., of his invention; a detailed description setting forth the dimensions, materials, etc., for a proposed building, engineering work, or the like; also, something specified, as in a bill of particulars; a specified particular, item, or article; also, the act of making specific, or the state of having a specific character.

spe-ci-fic-i-ty (spes-i-fis′i-ti), *n.* The state or fact of being specific. Also **spe-cif′ic-ness.**

spe-ci-fy (spes′i-fī), *v.; -fied, -fying.* [OF. *specifier* (F. *spécifier*), < ML. *specificare,* < *specificus,* E. *specific.*] **I.** *tr.* To mention or name specifically or definitely; state in detail; also, to name or state as a condition or requisite; also, to give a specific character to. **II.** *intr.* To make a specific mention or statement.—**spe′ci-fi-er** (-fī-èr), *n.*

spe-ci-men (spes′i-men). [L., an indication, evidence, example, < *specere,* look at: cf. *species.*] **I.** *n.* A part or an individual taken as exemplifying a whole mass or number; something that represents or typifies all of its kind; an illustrative example; specif., an animal, plant, mineral, part of an organism, or the like, preserved as an example of its kind, as for scientific study; sometimes, a person as an example of the human race or as exemplifying some trait, tendency, proceeding, etc. (as, a fine *specimen* of manhood; he is a fair *specimen* of the manners and morals of the time); hence, a person as a specified kind, or in some respect a peculiar kind, of human being (colloq.: as, "a small, wrinkled, dark *specimen,* with jet-black, bead-like eyes," W. H. Hudson's "Purple Land," vii.; he is a pretty poor *specimen;* he's a *specimen!*). **II.** *a.* Serving as a specimen: as, "a strong desire to see something more of Christendom than a *specimen* whaler or two" (H. Melville's "Moby-Dick," xii.).

spe-cious (spē'shus), *a.* [L. *speciosus*, good-looking, fair-seeming, plausible, specious, < *species*: see *species*.] Pleasing to the eye, handsome, or fair (archaic); also, pleasing to the eye, but deceptive (as, "The next I took to wife . . . Dalila, That *specious* monster," Milton's "Samson Agonistes," 230; a *specious* appearance or exterior); in general, fair-seeming, superficially pleasing, or apparently good or right, without real merit (as, a *specious* hypocrite; *specious* promises; "These arguments, though *specious* . . . are really . . . shallow and unphilosophical," Mallock's "New Republic," ii. 1); plausible.—**spe-ci-os-i-ty** (spē-shi-os'i-ti), **spe'cious-ness**, *n.*—**spe'cious-ly**, *adv.*

speck[1] (spek), *n.* [AS. *specca*: cf. *speckle*.] A small spot differing in color or substance from that of the surface or material upon which it appears; a minute discoloration; a very small mass of something adhering to a surface; hence, any small or minute particle of matter (as, "the wind which all day had blown strong and full from the south, without, however, bringing a *speck* of rain": C. Brontë's "Jane Eyre," xxv.); fig., a very little bit, or the smallest quantity (as, he has not a *speck* of humor, or of sense); also, a small piece or portion (as, to own a *speck* of land); often, something appearing small by comparison or by distance (as, "forests . . . so vast that all this space your eyes look on is a mere *speck* of earth in comparison," W. H. Hudson's "Green Mansions," xi.; "Robert Fraser saw a couple of black *specks* which moved smoothly and evenly along the top of the distant dyke," S. R. Crockett's "Stickit Minister," i.); a small cloud; also, a small spot indicative of defective condition, as one on a fruit denoting decay; fig., any blemish or defect (as, "Can all the pearls of the East atone for a *speck* upon England's honour?" Scott's "Talisman," xvii.).—**speck**[1], *v. t.* To mark with or as with a speck or specks: as, "A few fishing vessels alone *specked* the water" (Mrs. Shelley's "Frankenstein," xx.).

speck[2] (spek), *n.* [D. *spek* or G. *speck*: cf. AS. *spic*, bacon, lard, Icel. *spik*, fat, blubber.] Fat meat, esp. pork (now local, U. S.); also, the blubber of a whale; also, the fat of a hippopotamus (South Africa).

speck-le (spek'l), *n.* [Dim. of *speck*[1].] A small speck, spot, or mark; a small natural marking, as on the skin; also, speckled coloring or marking (as, "the peculiar *speckle* of its [a chicken's] plumage": Hawthorne's "House of the Seven Gables," x.).—**speck'le**, *v. t.*; *-led*, *-ling.* To mark or dot with or as with speckles: as, "the blue bay of Cajeta . . . *speckled* by the white sails of its craft" (Wiseman's "Fabiola," i. 18).

speck-less (spek'les), *a.* Free from specks; without blemishes.

specs, specks (speks), *n. pl.* Spectacles (to aid vision): as, "If they think they're going to cure my eyesight for me with their beastly *specs* they just aren't" (Arnold Bennett's "These Twain," xvii.). [Colloq.]

spec-ta-cle (spek'tạ-kl), *n.* [OF. F. *spectacle*, < L. *spectaculum*, sight, spectacle, < *spectare*, look at or to, freq. of *specere*, look at: cf. *species*.] A public show or display, esp. on a large scale (as, "The magnificence of Justinian was displayed in the superior pomp of his public *spectacles*," Gibbon's "Decline and Fall of the Roman Empire," xl.; a military *spectacle*; a dramatic *spectacle*); also, a person or thing exhibited to public view as an object of wonder or of contempt (as, "We are made a *spectacle* unto the world": 1 Cor. iv. 9); also, anything presented to the sight or view, esp. something of a striking kind (as, "To see a head-master walking about the town during school-hours is a startling *spectacle*": Arnold Bennett's "Old Wives' Tale," ii. 4); hence, the sight or view of something specified (as, "The *spectacle* of their hurried and harassed retreat was far from restoring . . confidence": Scott's "Old Mortality," xxxii.); also, a window†; a mirror†; also, *pl.* (sometimes formerly *sing.*), a device to aid defective vision or to protect the eyes from light, dust, etc., consisting usually of two glass lenses set in a frame which rests on the nose and is held in place by pieces passing over or around the ears (often called a *pair of spectacles*); fig., something through which things are

viewed or regarded, or by which one's views or opinions are colored or affected; also, a marking on an animal's head resembling a pair of spectacles (as, "He [a dog] was a good-sized animal, with . . . a smooth black coat, tan feet, muzzle, and '*spectacles*,' and a face of extraordinary length": W. H. Hudson's "Far Away and Long Ago," i.); also, *pl.* or *sing.*, any of various devices suggesting a pair of spectacles, as one attached to a semaphore to display lights of different colors by means of colored glass.—**spec'ta-cled**, *a.* Provided with or wearing spectacles (as, "a scholar *spectacled* and slippered": Bulwer-Lytton's "Caxtons," vii. 7); in *zoöl.*, having a marking resembling a pair of spectacles (see phrases below).—**spectacled bear**, a bear, *Ursus* (or *Tremarctos*) *ornatus*, of the Andes, having a light-colored marking suggesting spectacles on the face.—**spectacled snake**, the cobra-de-capello, which typically has a black and white marking like spectacles on the back of the hood.

Spectacled Bear.

spec-tac-u-lar (spek-tak'ū-lär), *a.* [L. *spectaculum*: see *spectacle*.] Pertaining to or of the nature of a spectacle or show; marked by or given to great display or show (as, "a *spectacular* display of wrath," Arnold Bennet's "Clayhanger," ii. 9; a *spectacular* hero).—**spec-tac-u-lar'i-ty** (-lär'i-ti), *n.* Spectacular quality or character.—**spec-tac'u-lar-ly**, *adv.*

spec-ta-tor (spek-tā'tor), *n.* [L., < *spectare*: see *spectacle*.] One who looks on; an onlooker; a beholder; specif., one who is present at and views a spectacle or the like (as, "The Puritan hated bearbaiting, not because it gave pain to the bear, but because it gave pleasure to the *spectators*": Macaulay's "Hist. of Eng.," ii.).—**spec-ta-to'ri-al** (-tä-tō'ri-ạl), *a.*—**spec-ta'tress, spec-ta'trix**, *n.* A female spectator.

spec-ter, spec-tre (spek'ter), *n.* [F. *spectre*, < L. *spectrum*, appearance, image, apparition, specter, < *specere*, look at: cf. *species* and *spectrum*.] A visible incorporeal spirit, esp. one of a terrifying nature; a ghost; a phantom; an apparition; fig., some object or source of terror or dread; in *zoöl.*, a stick-insect.—**specter of the Brocken**, an optical phenomenon sometimes seen on a mountain-top, consisting of the shadow of an observer, etc., standing between the sun and a mass of mist or fog, as projected in gigantic size on the mist or fog: named from the Brocken, a mountain of the Harz range, in central Germany, where it has been frequently observed.

spec-tra (spek'trä), *n.* Plural of *spectrum*.

spec-tral (spek'trạl), *a.* Pertaining to or characteristic of a specter; of the nature of a specter (as, "a *spectral* apparition": Scott's "Guy Mannering," l.); resembling or suggesting a specter (as, "the *spectral* limbs of an old dead sycamore": Parkman's "Oregon Trail," ii.); also, of, pertaining to, or produced by a spectrum or spectra.—**spec-tral'i-ty** (-tral'i-ti), **spec'tral-ness**, *n.*—**spec'tral-ly**, *adv.*

spectro-. Form of *spectrum* used in combination.—**spec-tro-bo-lom-e-ter** (spek″trō-bọ-lom'e-tėr), *n.* An instrument consisting of a combined spectroscope and bolometer, for determining the distribution of radiant heat or energy in a spectrum.—**spec'tro-gram** (-gram), *n.* [+ *-gram*.] A representation or photograph of a spectrum.—**spec'tro-graph** (-gráf), *n.* [+ *-graph*.] An apparatus for making a representation or photograph of a spectrum; also, a spectrogram.—**spec-tro-graph'ic** (-graf'ik), *a.*—**spec-tro-he'li-o-gram** (-hē'li-ọ-gram), *n.* [See *-gram*.] A photograph of the sun made with a spectroheliograph.—**spec-tro-he'li-o-graph** (-gráf), *n.* [Cf. *heliograph*.] An apparatus for making photographs (spectroheliograms) of the sun with monochromatic light, in order to show the details of the sun's surface and surroundings as they would appear if only one kind of light were emitted.—**spec-trol'o-gy** (-trol'ọ-ji), *n.* [+ *-logy*.] The science of spectra or of spectrum analysis; also, the study of specters (as, "the frightful chimeras of witchcraft and *spectrology*": Irving's "Sketch-Book," Philip of Pokanoket).—**spec-trom'e-ter** (-trom'e-tėr), *n.* [+ *-meter*.] Any of certain optical instruments for observing a spectrum and measuring the deviation of the refracted rays: used for determining wave-lengths, angles between two faces of a prism, etc.—**spec-tro-met'ric** (-met'rik), *a.*—**spec″tro-pho-tom'e-ter** (-fọ-tom'e-tėr), *n.* An instrument for making photometric comparisons between corresponding parts of different spectra, or between parts of the same spectrum.

spec-tro-scope (spek'trọ-skōp), *n.* [= G. *spektroskop*, F. *spectroscope*: see *spectro-* and *-scope*.] An optical instrument for producing and examining the spectrum of the light or radiation from any source.—**spec-tro-scop'ic, spec-tro-scop'i-cal** (-skop'ik, -i-ḳạl), *a.* Of or pertaining to the spectroscope or spectroscopy.—**spec-tro-scop'i-cal-ly,** *adv.* —**spec-tros'co-py** (-tros'kọ-pi), *n.* [See *-scopy*.] The science dealing with the use of the spectroscope and with spectrum analysis.—**spec-tros'co-pist,** *n.*

spec-trum (spek'trum), *n.*; pl. *-tra* (-trä) or *-trums*. [L. *spectrum*, appearance, apparition, specter, NL. spectrum: see *specter*.] A specter (obs. or archaic); also, an image of something seen, continuing after the eyes are closed, covered, or turned away; also, in *physics*, the band of colors, or the colored lines or bands, formed when a beam of light from a luminous body or incandescent gas undergoes dispersion by being passed through a prism or reflected from a diffraction grating, as the series of colors, passing by insensible degrees from red to violet (ordinarily described as red, orange, yellow, green, blue, indigo, and violet), produced when white light (as sunlight) is passed through a prism, the white light being dispersed into rays of different color and wave-length, the rays of longest wave-length undergoing the least refraction and producing the color red, and the rays of shortest wave-length undergoing the greatest refraction and producing the color violet; more broadly, this band or series of colors together with extensions at the ends which are not visible to the eye, but which are studied by means of photography, heat effects, etc., and which are produced by the dispersion of radiant energy other than ordinary light-rays (see *infra-red* and *ultra-violet*).—**spectrum analysis,** the determination of the constitution or condition of bodies and substances by means of the spectra they produce.

spec-u-la (spek'ū-lä), *n.* Plural of *speculum*.

spec-u-lar (spek'ū-lär), *a.* [L. *specularis*, of or like a mirror, < *speculum*: see *speculum*. In the last two senses, < L. *speculari*, watch, observe, and *specula*, watch-tower: see *speculate*.] Pertaining to, or having the reflecting property of, a mirror; having a smooth, reflecting surface or a lustrous metallic appearance (see phrases below); also, pertaining to a speculum (in any sense); also, pertaining to sight or vision; of towers, heights, etc., affording a wide view (as, "Look once more, ere we leave this *specular* mount": Milton's "Paradise Regained," iv. 236).—**specular iron ore,** a variety of hematite with a brilliant metallic luster; iron-glance.—**specular schist,** a rock made up chiefly of quartz, specular iron ore, and mica.—**spec'u-lar-ly,** *adv.*

spec-u-late (spek'ū-lāt), *v.*; *-lated, -lating*. [L. *speculatus*, pp. of *speculari*, watch, observe, examine, < *specula*, watch-tower, < *specere*, look at: cf. *species*.] **I.** *tr.* To gaze at, observe, or inspect (obs. or archaic); also, to view or observe mentally, reflect upon, or consider (now chiefly with a clause as object: as, to *speculate* what course to pursue). **II.** *intr.* To engage in thought or reflection, or meditate (often with *on* or *upon*: as, "I certainly take my full share . . . in *speculating* on what has been done, or is doing, on the public stage," Burke's "Revolution in France," 5); indulge in conjectural thought (as, "How often they had *speculated* on what lay hidden behind that lofty old brick wall!" Du Maurier's "Trilby," vi.); pursue a course of abstract reasoning; also, to engage in the buying and selling of commodities, stocks, etc., in the expectation of profit through a change in their market value; engage in any business transaction or enterprise involving considerable risk, on the chance of large

gains.—**spec-u-la'tion** (-lā'shọn), *n.* [LL. *speculatio(n-)*.] Sight or vision (archaic: as, "His horny eye had lost the power of *speculation*," Scott's "Anne of Geierstein," xxxiv.); the act or an act of looking at, viewing, or observing something (obs. or archaic); also, the contemplation or consideration of some subject; a single instance or process of consideration, or a conclusion or opinion reached thereby; often, conjectural consideration of a matter, or a conjecture or surmise (as, "The hidden ways of the Sperm Whale . . . have originated the most curious and contradictory *speculations* regarding them": H. Melville's "Moby-Dick," xli.); often, abstract, hypothetical, or abstruse reasoning (as, metaphysical *speculation*; "In the middle ages, abstract *speculation*, another instrument of truth, was often frittered away in sophistical exercises," J. H. Newman's "Idea of a University," ii. 5); also, the act or practice of speculating in commodities, stocks, etc.; engagement in business transactions or enterprises involving considerable risk but offering the chance of large gains; a speculative commercial venture or undertaking (as, "He launched out into *speculations* in shipping and in a trade . . . in frozen meat brought from great distances": H. G. Wells's "Men Like Gods," i. 7).—**spec-u-la-tist** (-lạ-tist), *n.* One given to speculation or abstract reasoning: as, "a refining *speculatist*" (Burke's "American Taxation").—**spec'u-la-tive** (-tiv), *a.* [LL. *speculativus*.] Pertaining to sight or vision†; suitable for observing, or affording a good view (chiefly poetic: as, "High on her *speculative* tower Stood Science," Wordsworth's "Eclipse of the Sun," 1); also, pertaining to, of the nature of, or characterized by speculation, contemplation, conjecture, or abstract reasoning; often, theoretical, rather than practical (as, "a practical sense of things very different from a mere *speculative* knowledge": J. Butler's "Analogy of Religion," i. 5); given to speculation, as persons, the mind, etc.; devoted to speculation, as life, etc.; adapted for or employed in speculation, as mental faculties; also, of the nature of or involving commercial or financial speculation (as, "By telephoning twice to his stockbrokers . . . he had just made . . . three hundred and forty-one pounds in a purely *speculative* transaction concerning Rubber shares": Arnold Bennett's "The Old Adam," i.); engaging in or given to such speculation (as, a *speculative* trader).—**spec'u-la-tive-ly,** *adv.*—**spec'u-la-tive-ness,** *n.*—**spec'u-la-tor** (-lā-tọr), *n.* [L.] An observer† or watcher†; also, one devoted to mental speculation; also, one engaged in commercial or financial speculation; often, a person who purchases in advance tickets for theatrical performances, games, etc., likely to be in demand, in order to sell them later at an advance on the regular price ('ticket speculator').

spec-u-lum (spek'ū-lum), *n.*; pl. *-la* (-lä) or *-lums*. [L., mirror, < *specere*, look at: cf. *species*.] A mirror or reflector, esp. one of polished metal, as on a reflecting telescope; also, a lustrous or specially colored area on the wing of certain birds; also, a surgical instrument for rendering a part accessible to observation, as by enlarging an orifice.

sped (sped). Preterit and past participle of *speed*.

speech (spēch), *n.* [AS. *spǣc* (earlier *sprǣc*), < *specan* (earlier *sprecan*), E. *speak*.] The act of speaking; talk, discourse, or conversation (as, "She did not want to meet George Cannon, with whom she had not had *speech* since the interview at the Cedars": Arnold Bennett's "Hilda Lessways," ii. 7); sometimes, common talk, or rumor (archaic); also, manner of speaking, as of a person; often, the form of utterance characteristic of a particular people or region; a language or dialect; also, the faculty or power of speaking (as, "God's great gift of *speech*": Tennyson's "Dirge"); also, that which is spoken; words uttered; an utterance, remark, or declaration (as, a thoughtless, foolish, or cutting *speech*; polite *speeches*); specif., a more or less formal address, discourse, or the like; an oration (as, "Cicero in one of his *speeches* had painted him [Vatinius] as another Clodius or Catiline": Froude's "Cæsar," xviii.).—**speech,** *v.* **I.** *intr.* To make a speech or speeches. [Now rare.] **II.** *tr.* To make or deliver a speech to. [Rare.]

speech-ful (spēch'fùl), *a.* Full of speech; loquacious; talkative; also, speaking or expressive, as the eyes.—**speech'-ful-ness,** *n.*

speech-i-fy (spē'chi-fī), *v. i.*; *-fied, -fying*. [See *-fy*.] To make a speech or speeches; harangue: as, "Now, do not let them lure you to the hustings . . . A man always makes a fool of himself, *speechifying*" (George Eliot's "Middlemarch," vi.). [Humorous or depreciatory.]—**speech'i-fi-er** (-fī-ėr), *n.*

speech-less (spēch'les), *a.* Lacking the faculty of speech, or dumb (as, the *speechless* brutes); also, unable to speak, as from physical weakness, exhaustion, etc.; temporarily deprived of speech by strong emotion, something startling, etc. (as, to be *speechless* with horror or rage; "James, struck moveless and *speechless* by the extraordinary sight of her, offered no invitation to enter," Arnold Bennett's "Helen with the High Hand," xi.); also, refraining from speech, silent, or mute; sometimes, taciturn or reticent; also, not expressed in speech or words (as, "From her eyes I did receive fair *speechless* messages": Shakspere's "Merchant of Venice," i. 1. 164); unaccompanied by speech (as, "Valentine . . . takes refuge in a feeble, *speechless* smile": G. B. Shaw's "You Never Can Tell," iv.); characterized by absence or loss of speech (as, a *speechless* condition; *speechless* astonishment or rage).—**speech'less-ly**, *adv.*—**speech'less-ness**, *n.*

speed (spēd), *n.* [AS. *spēd*, success, speed (= D. *spoed*, speed, haste), < *spōwan*, succeed, prosper.] Success or prosperity (archaic); fortune (good or ill), as in an undertaking (as, to wish one *good speed*; "evill *speed*," Spenser's "Faerie Queene," iv. 5. 22); also, a promoter of success† (as, "Saint Denis be my *speed*!" Shakspere's "Henry V.," v. 2. 194); also, rapidity in moving, going, traveling, or any proceeding or performance (as, to run, fly, or revolve with *speed*; to act or work with *speed*); swiftness, celerity, or despatch; also, relative rapidity in moving, going, etc., or rate of motion or progress (as, at high or low *speed*; to signal full *speed* ahead).—**at speed**, in *her.*, in rapid movement: said of an animal represented as running.—

speed, *v.*; *sped* or *speeded, speeding*. [AS. *spēdan*.] **I.** *intr.* To succeed, prosper, or prove successful (archaic: as, "His errand *speeds*," Cowper's "Task," iv. 612); get on or fare in a specified or particular manner (as, to *speed* well or ill; "Well, my girls, how have you *sped?*" Goldsmith's "Vicar of Wakefield," x.); also, to move, go, pass, or proceed with speed or rapidity (as, "He *sped* through the passages with so swift a step that I could scarce keep up with him," Stevenson's "Master of Ballantrae," viii.; to *speed* through a task); hasten; with *up*, to increase the rate of speed or progress (as, to *speed* up in a race, or in work or production). **II.** *tr.* To cause (a person, etc.) to succeed or prosper (archaic: as, God *speed* you! cf. *God-speed*); promote the success of (an affair, undertaking, etc.); further, forward, or expedite; hence, to finish or despatch, as a duty (archaic); kill, as a person (archaic); less definitely, to do for, or settle the fate of (archaic: used in the passive: as, "We three are married, but you two are *sped*," Shakspere's "Taming of the Shrew," v. 2. 185); also, to cause to move, go, or proceed with speed (as, " 'No chance to *speed* a horse here, of course,' said Lapham," Howells's "Rise of Silas Lapham," i.; to *speed* an arrow; to *speed* workers or work); cause (time) to pass rapidly (as, "We *sped* the time with stories old": Whittier's "Snow-Bound"); expedite the going of (as, "True friendship's laws are by this rule express'd, Welcome the coming, *speed* the parting guest": Pope's tr. Homer's "Odyssey," xv.); direct (the steps, course, way, etc.) with speed; increase the rate of speed of (now commonly with *up*: as, to *speed* up industrial production); bring to a particular speed, as a machine.

speed=count-er (spēd'koun″tėr), *n.* A device for indicating the count of revolutions or other movements made by a moving part, as a revolving shaft: used in conjunction with a watch in order to determine speed.

speed-er (spē'dėr), *n.* One who or that which speeds.

speed-i-ly (spē'di-li), *adv.* In a speedy manner; with speed; rapidly; quickly; soon.—**speed'i-ness**, *n.*

speed-om-e-ter (spē-dom'e-tėr), *n.* [See *-meter*.] A device attached to an automobile or the like to indicate its speed.

speed-ster (spēd'stėr), *n.* An automobile of the roadster type, built especially for speed.

Hart at speed.

speed=up (spēd'up), *n.* A speeding up; an increasing of the rate of speed, as in some process or work.

speed-way (spēd'wā), *n.* A road or course for fast driving, motoring, or the like, or on which more than ordinary speed is allowed.

speed-well (spēd'wel), *n.* Any of various herbs of the scrophulariaceous genus *Veronica*, as *V. officinalis* (the common speedwell), a species with racemes of pale-blue flowers, formerly used in medicine, or *V. chamædrys* ('germander speedwell'), with bright-blue flowers.

Flowering Plant of Speedwell (*Veronica officinalis*). *a*, a flower; *b*, the fruit.

speed-y (spē'di), *a.*; *compar. speedier*, *superl. speediest*. Moving, going, or acting with speed (as, "Most of them [ponies] are small, wiry beasts, not very *speedy*," Roosevelt's "Hunting Trips of a Ranchman," i.; *speedy* workers); done with or characterized by speed (as, a *speedy* gallop or flight; *speedy* progress); rapid; swift; fast; also, rapidly coming or brought to pass (as, a *speedy* change; "The fact that a definite job was before a man gave him something better to think about than expectations of a *speedy* decease," Buchan's "Hist. of the Great War," liii.); coming, given, or arrived at, quickly or soon (as, *speedy* aid; a *speedy* reply; a *speedy* decision); prompt; not delayed.

speel (spēl), *v. i.* or *t.* [Origin uncertain.] To climb: as, "Sma' heart hae I to *speel* The steep Parnassus" (Burns's "Epistle to Colonel De Peyster"). [Sc. and north. Eng.]

speer (spēr), *v.* [AS. *spyrian*, inquire, seek, orig. follow a track: cf. *spoor*.] **I.** *intr.* To make inquiry; inquire; ask. [Now Sc. and north. Eng.] **II.** *tr.* To inquire or ask (something); also, to make inquiry of, or question (a person); also, to seek by inquiry (usually with *out*); also, to ask for, or make request for, as something desired. [Now Sc. and north. Eng.]

speiss (spīs), *n.* [G. *speise*, speiss, lit. 'food.'] A product consisting chiefly of one or more metallic arsenides (as of iron, nickel, etc.), obtained in smelting certain ores.

spe-læ-an, spe-le-an (spē-lē'an), *a.* [L. *spelæum*, < Gr. σπήλαιον, cave.] Inhabiting or frequenting caves; also, pertaining to or of the nature of a cave.

spe-le-ol-o-gy (spē-lē-ol'ọ-ji), *n.* [Also *spelæology*; F. *spéléologie*, < Gr. σπήλαιον, cave, + -λογία, < λέγειν, speak.] The scientific study of caves.—**spe″le-o-log'i-cal** (-ọ-loj'i-kal), *a.*—**spe-le-ol'o-gist**, *n.*

spell¹ (spel), *v.* [AS. *spelian*, act in the place of.] **I.** *tr.* To take the place of or relieve (a person, etc.) for a time by taking a turn at doing something (now chiefly U. S.); also, to give an interval of rest to (as, to *spell* a horse: Australia). **II.** *intr.* To take an interval of rest. [Australia.]—**spell¹**, *n.* A person or one set of persons taking a turn of work to relieve another (now rare); also, a turn of work so taken; hence, a continuous course or period of work or other activity (as, "His first *spell* of office had lasted uninterruptedly for twenty-one years": Lytton Strachey's "Queen Victoria," v.); in general, a turn, bout, fit, or period of anything experienced or occurring (as, a *spell* of uneasiness, crying, or coughing; a lazy *spell*; "We are in for a *spell* of Socialism," M. Hewlett's "Open Country," xiv.); an interval or period of rest (Australia); a period of weather of a specified kind (as, a hot, cold, or dry *spell*; "We had now a long '*spell*' of fine weather," Dana's "Two Years before the Mast," iii.); a fit of some personal ailment, disturbance of temper, or the like (colloq., U. S.: as, "When Hepsy does get beat out she has *spells*, and she goes on awful," Mrs. Stowe's "Oldtown Folks," xvi.); also, an interval or space of time, usually indefinite or of no great length (now colloq. or prov.: as, "You hold on

. . . for a *spell*, and I'll be back," Bret Harte's "How Santa Claus Came to Simpson's Bar").

spell[2] (spel), *n.* [AS. *spel, spell*, saying, discourse, narrative, message, = OHG. *spel* = Icel. *spjall* = Goth. *spill*: cf. *gospel*.] A discourse†, tale†, or narrative†; also, a form of words supposed to possess magic power (as, "One short *spell* therein he read, It had much of glamour might, Could make a ladye seem a knight": Scott's "Lay of the Last Minstrel," iii. 9); a charm, incantation, or any means of enchantment; hence, a magic or occult influence completely dominating or controlling (as, to be under a *spell*; "I'll put such a *spell* on ye that your bones shall shake apart," H. Kingsley's "Geoffry Hamlyn," viii.); fig., any enthralling, compelling, or irresistible influence (as, to be under the *spell* of music, eloquence, love, or fear; "The *spell* of the evening's beauty seemed to have fallen on them both," W. Churchill's "Coniston," i. 9); witchery; fascination; charm.—**spell**[2], *v. t.* To bind by or as by a spell; affect as a spell does; charm; also, to invest with magic properties (as, "This, gather'd in the planetary hour, With noxious weeds, and *spell'd* with words of pow'r, Dire stepdames in the magic bowl infuse": Dryden's tr. Virgil's "Georgics," iii. 445).

spell[3] (spel), *v.*; *spelled* or *spelt, spelling*. [OF. *espeller, espeler*, explain, spell (F. *épeler*, spell); from Teut., and akin to E. *spell*[2].] **I.** *tr.* To read letter by letter or with difficulty (often with *out*: as, "You *spell* out the words when you read the newspaper still," Thackeray's "Newcomes," xi.; to *spell* out a half obliterated inscription on a tombstone); hence, to make out, interpret, or understand, as if by reading (as, "The looks and gestures . . . He *spells* them true by intuition's light": Cowper's "Needless Alarm," 69); discern, discover, or find, as if by reading or study (often with *out*: as, to *spell* out the truth of a matter); study or scrutinize carefully (obs. or archaic); also, to name, write, or otherwise give (as by signals), in order, the letters of (a word, syllable, etc.); often, to write, print, or give the letters of (*well, ill*, etc.: as, an ill-*spelled* note); of letters, to form (a word, syllable, etc.); fig., to signify, have the force of, or amount to (as, the delay *spells* a refusal; "a position which I think *spells* ruin for me," Stevenson's "David Balfour," xvii.). **II.** *intr.* To make out words in laborious reading; hence, to gain knowledge, or learn (obs. or archaic: as, "Where I may sit and rightly *spell* Of every star that heaven doth shew, And every herb that sips the dew," Milton's "Il Penseroso," 170); also, to name, write, or give the letters of words, etc.; express words by letters, esp. correctly; also, to intimate a desire (*for*: now chiefly prov. Eng.).—**spell'a-ble**, *a.* Capable of being spelled.

spell-bind (spel'bīnd), *v. t.*; *-bound, -binding*. [Backformation from *spellbound, a.*] To render spellbound; bind or hold as by a spell; entrance.—**spell'bind**″**er**, *n.* An eloquent political orator; hence, any campaign orator. [Colloq., U. S.]

spell-bound (spel'bound), *a.* Bound by or as by a spell; enchanted, entranced, or fascinated: as, "this *spellbound* region" (Irving's "Sketch-Book," Sleepy Hollow); a *spellbound* audience.

spell-er (spel'ėr), *n.* One who spells words, etc.; also, a spelling-book.

spell-ing (spel'ing), *n.* The act of one who spells words, etc.; the manner of expressing words by letters; orthography; also, a combination of letters representing a word; a particular way in which a word is spelled.—**spelling reform**, regulation of the spelling of the words of a language according to systematic principles, as for the purpose of securing greater uniformity or simplicity or a more satisfactory representation of the sound of the spoken words.—**spell'ing=bee**, *n.* A spelling-match.—**spell'ing=book**, *n.* A book of exercises for teaching spelling.—**spell'ing=match**, *n.* A contest in spelling between two or more persons or sides.

spelt[1] (spelt). Preterit and past participle of *spell*[3].

spelt[2] (spelt), *n.* [AS. *spelt*, < LL. *spelta*.] A kind of wheat, *Triticum spelta* (or a race of *T. sativum*), anciently much cultivated, and still grown in parts of Europe.

spel-ter (spel'tėr), *n.* [Cf. OF. *espiautre, espeautre*, LG. *spialter*, D. *spiauter*, spelter; akin to E. *pewter*.] Zinc, esp. in the form of ingots.

spence (spens), *n.* [OF. *despense* (F. *dépense*), < ML. *dispensa*, < L. *dispendere*, weigh out, E. *dispend*.] A room or place where provisions are kept; a buttery or larder; a pantry; a cupboard. [Archaic or prov. Eng. and Sc.]

spen-cer[1] (spen'sėr), *n.* [From the 2d Earl *Spencer* (1758–1834).] A kind of short overcoat formerly worn by men; also, a man's short coat or jacket (as, "my travelling wear of country velveteen, pilot-coat, and knitted *spencer*": Stevenson's "Travels with a Donkey," i. 1); also, a kind of short jacket or outer bodice-like garment for women.

spen-cer[2] (spen'sėr), *n.* [Origin uncertain.] *Naut.*, a trysail.

Spen-ce-ri-an (spen-sē'ri-an), **I.** *a.* Of or pertaining to the English philosopher Herbert Spencer (1820–1903) or his philosophy (see *synthetic philosophy*, under *synthetic*); also, of or pertaining to P. R. Spencer (1800–64), an American educator, or his system of penmanship, characterized by clearly formed, rounded letters slanting to the right. **II.** *n.* A follower of Herbert Spencer, or an adherent of his philosophy.—**Spen-ce'ri-an-ism**, *n.* The philosophy of Herbert Spencer.

spend (spend), *v.*; *spent, spending*. [Late AS. *spendan*, < L. *expendere*, E. *expend*; or perhaps L. *dispendere*, E. *dispend*.] **I.** *tr.* To pay out, disburse, or expend, as money or some equivalent; dispose of (money, wealth, resources, etc.) by paying out, giving away, etc.; hence, in general, to give or devote in order to secure some result (as, "What! did my brother Henry *spend* his youth, His valour, coin and people, in the wars?" Shakspere's "2 Henry VI.," i. 1. 78); † give (one's blood, life, etc.) for some cause; employ (labor, thought, words, time, etc.) on some object, in some proceeding, etc.; also, to pass (time) in a particular manner, place, etc. (as, "My uncle . . . *spent* his evenings at home": H. G. Wells's "Tono-Bungay," i. 3. § 2); often, to pass (the day, evening, etc.) in a social visit or the like; also, to use (materials, food, crops, etc.) for the needs or purposes (now chiefly prov. Eng.); also, to use up, consume, or exhaust (as, "Thus they *spend* The little wick of life's poor shallow lamp," Cowper's "Task," iii. 163; the storm had *spent* its fury); exhaust of strength, force, etc. (as, to *spend* one's self in a cause: cf. *spent, p. a.*); also, to waste or squander (as, "While I play the good husband at home, my son and my servant *spend* all at the university": Shakspere's "Taming of the Shrew," v. 1. 72). **II.** *intr.* To spend money, etc.; make expenditure; also, to be consumed or exhausted†; waste away†; also, to hold out or last in expenditure or use (as, "I have no skill to make money *spend* well, no genius in my economy," Emerson's "Essays," Prudence: now chiefly prov. Eng.).—**spend'a-ble**, *a.* That may be spent.—**spend'er**, *n.*—**spend'ing=mon**″**ey**, *n.* Money available or used for spending, esp. for small personal expenses; pocket-money.

spend-thrift (spend'thrift). **I.** *n.* One who spends his substance or money extravagantly or wastefully (as, "He was a shiftless young *spendthrift* . . . full of careless generosities": Mark Twain's "Life on the Mississippi," xlix.); a prodigal; hence, a squanderer or waster (*of*: as, "A *spendthrift* of time, he was an economist of blood," Motley's "Dutch Republic," iii. 1). **II.** *a.* Wastefully extravagant; prodigal: as, "The wealth which the miser has amassed . . . a *spendthrift* heir may squander away" (Irving's "Knickerbocker's New York," vi. 9); *spendthrift* ways.

Spen-se-ri-an (spen-sē'ri-an), *a.* Of, pertaining to, or characteristic of the English poet Edmund Spenser (about 1552–99) or his work.—**Spenserian stanza**, the stanza used by Spenser in his "Faerie Queene," consisting of eight deca-syllabic lines and a final Alexandrine, with three rimes, the first and third lines forming one, the second, fourth, fifth, and seventh another, and the sixth, eighth, and ninth the third: also used in Thomson's "Castle of Indolence," Byron's "Childe Harold's Pilgrimage," Shelley's "Adonais," Keats's "Eve of St. Agnes," Tennyson's "Lotus-Eaters," etc.—**Spen-se'ri-an**, *n.* A Spenserian stanza; verse in Spenserian stanzas; also, a follower or imitator of Spenser.

spent (spent). Preterit and past participle of *spend*.—**spent**, *p. a.* Expended; passed or gone, as time; used up, consumed, or exhausted (as, "The water was *spent* in the bottle": Gen. xxi. 15); exhausted of strength, as by exertion, hardship, etc. (as, a *spent* swimmer; "a *spent* horse,"

Conan Doyle's "Exploits of Brigadier Gerard," vii.); exhausted of force, effective qualities, usefulness, etc. (as, a *spent* bullet; a *spent* match; the *spent* grains from brewing); of fishes, having recently spawned.

sper-ling (spėr'ling), *n.* Same as *sparling*.

sperm[1] (spėrm), *n.* [OF. *esperme* (F. *sperme*), < LL. *sperma*, < Gr. σπέρμα, seed, < σπείρειν, sow.] The generative fluid or substance of male animals; semen; milt; also, a male reproductive cell; a spermatozoön.

sperm[2] (spėrm), *n.* [Short for *spermaceti*, *sperm-whale*, or *sperm-oil*.] Spermaceti; also, a sperm-whale; also, sperm-oil.

-sperm. Noun termination from Gr. σπέρμα, seed, E. *sperm*[1], as in *angiosperm*, *oösperm*, *zoösperm*.

sper-ma-cet-i (spėr-ma-set'i or -sē'ti), *n.* [ML. *sperma ceti*, 'seed of the whale' (according to a former belief), < LL. *sperma*, seed, + L. *ceti*, gen. of *cetus*, whale.] A whitish waxy substance obtained from the oil in the head of the sperm-whale: used in making ointments, cosmetics, etc.

sper-ma-ry (spėr'ma-ri), *n.*; pl. *-ries* (-riz). [NL. *spermarium*.] A sperm-gland: an organ in which spermatozoa are generated.

sper-mat-ic (spėr-mat'ik), *a.* [LL. *spermaticus*, < Gr. σπερματικός.] Of pertaining to, or of the nature of sperm; seminal; generative; also, pertaining to a spermary.— **spermatic cord**, in *anat.*, the cord by which the testicle is suspended within the scrotum, containing the vas deferens, the blood-vessels and nerves of the testicle, etc.

sper-ma-ti-um (spėr-mā'shi-um), *n.*; pl. *-tia* (-shi-ä). [NL., < Gr. σπερμάτιον, dim. of σπέρμα, seed, E. *sperm*[1].] In *bot.*, the non-motile male gamete of the red algæ; also, a minute, colorless cell (conjectured to be a male reproductive body) developed within the spermogonia of certain thallophytic plants.

spermato-. Form of Gr. σπέρμα (σπερματ-), seed, E. *sperm*[1], used in combination.—**sper-ma-to-cyte** (spėr'ma-tō-sīt), *n.* [+ *-cyte*.] In *biol.*, a cell giving rise to spermatozoids or spermatozoa.—**sper″ma-to-gen′e-sis** (-jen'e-sis), *n.* In *biol.*, the genesis or origin and development of spermatozoa.—**sper″ma-to-ge-net′ic** (-jē-net'ik), *a.*—**sper″ma-to-go′ni-um** (-gō'ni-um), *n.*; pl. *-nia* (-ni-ä). [NL.: see *spermogonium*.] In *bot.*, a spermogonium; in *biol.*, one of the primitive germ-cells which give rise to the spermatocytes.—**sper″ma-to-go′ni-al**, *a.*—**sper″ma-toid**, *a.* [See *-oid*.] Resembling sperm.—**sper′ma-to-phore** (-fōr), *n.* [+ *-phore*.] In *zoöl.*, a special case or capsule containing a number of spermatozoa, produced by the male of certain insects, mollusks, annelids, etc., and some vertebrates.

sper-ma-to-phyte (spėr'ma-tō-fīt), *n.* [NL. *Spermatophyta*, pl., < Gr. σπέρμα (σπερματ-), seed, + φυτόν, plant.] Any of the *Spermatophyta*, a primary division or group of plants embracing those that bear seeds.—**sper″ma-to-phyt′ic** (-fit'ik), *a.*

sper-ma-tor-rhe-a, sper-ma-tor-rhœ-a (spėr″ma-tō-rē'ä), *n.* [NL., < Gr. σπέρμα (σπερματ-), seed, + ῥοία, a flow, < ῥεῖν, flow.] In *pathol.*, abnormally frequent involuntary emission of semen.

sper-ma-to-zo-al (spėr″ma-tō-zō'al), *a.* Pertaining to spermatozoa; of the nature of a spermatozoön. Also **sper″ma-to-zo′an**, **sper″ma-to-zo′ic**.

sper-ma-to-zo-id (spėr″ma-tō-zō'id), *n.* [= F. *spermatozoïde*: see *spermatozoön*.] In *bot.*, a motile male gamete produced in an antheridium. Also **sper″ma-to-zo′oid**.

sper-ma-to-zo-ön (spėr″ma-tō-zō'on), *n.*; pl. *-zoa* (-zō'ä). [NL., < Gr. σπέρμα (σπερματ-), seed, + ζῷον, animal.] In *biol.*, one of the numerous minute, usually actively motile bodies contained in semen or sperm, which serve to fertilize the ovum of the female; a male reproductive cell.

sper-mic (spėr'mik), *a.* [Gr. σπέρμα, seed, E. *sperm*[1].] Of or pertaining to sperm; spermatic.

sper-mine (spėr'min), *n.* [F., < *sperme*, E. *sperm*[1].] In *chem.*, a colorless, crystalline, basic compound found, in combination, in semen, etc.: used in medicine as a tonic.

sperm-ism (spėr'mizm), *n.* [From *sperm*[1].] In *biol.*, the theory or doctrine that the sperm or spermatozoön contains the whole germ of the future animal.

spermo-. Same as *spermato-*.

sper-mo-go-ni-um (spėr-mō-gō'ni-um), *n.*; pl. *-nia* (-ni-ä). [NL., < Gr. σπέρμα, seed, + *-gonium* as in *archegonium*.]

In *bot.*, one of the cup-shaped or flask-shaped receptacles in which the spermatia of certain thallophytic plants are produced.

sperm=oil (spėrm'oil), *n.* An oil from the sperm-whale.

sper-mo-phile (spėr'mō-fil), *n.* [NL. *Spermophilus*, < Gr. σπέρμα, seed, + φίλος, loving.] Any of various burrowing rodents of the squirrel family, esp. of the genus *Citellus* (or *Spermophilus*), sometimes sufficiently numerous to do much damage to crops. See *ground-squirrel*, *gopher*, and *suslik*.

Thirteen-lined Spermophile, or Gopher (*Citellus tridecemlineatus*).

sper-mo-phyte (spėr'mō-fīt), *n.* Same as *spermatophyte*.

-spermous. Adjective termination from Gr. σπέρμα, seed, as in *monospermous*, *dispermous*, *trispermous*.

sperm=whale (spėrm'hwāl), *n.* A large, square-headed whale, *Physeter macrocephalus*, valuable for its oil and spermaceti.

Sperm-whale.

sper-ry-lite (sper'i-līt), *n.* [From F. L. *Sperry*, of Sudbury, Ontario, Canada, where it was found.] A mineral, an arsenide of platinum, occurring in minute isometric crystals of a tin-white color: the only compound of platinum known to occur in nature.

spetch (spech), *n.* [Assibilated form of obs. or prov. *speck*, ME. *spekke*, patch, spetch; of uncertain origin.] One of the waste pieces or parings of hide, leather, or the like, used as a material for making glue, etc.

spew (spū), *v.* [AS. *spīwan*, also *spīowan*, = OHG. *spīwan* (G. *speien*) = Icel. *spȳja* = Goth. *speiwan*, spew, spit; akin to L. *spuere*, Gr. πτύειν, spit.] **I.** *intr.* To discharge the contents of the stomach through the mouth; vomit; also, to flow or run in or like a stream (now chiefly prov.). **II.** *tr.* To eject from the stomach through the mouth; vomit; hence, to throw out or cast up, as if by vomiting (as, "The encampment began to *spew* out men; here, there and everywhere they appeared": H. G. Wells's "Italy, France, and Britain at War," ii. 1).—**spew**, *n.* That which is spewed; vomit.—**spew′er**, *n.*—**spew′y**, *a.* Exuding moisture, wet, or moist, as ground.

spha-ce-late (sfas'e-lāt), *v. t.* or *i.*; *-lated*, *-lating*. In *pathol.*, to affect or be affected with sphacelus; mortify.—**spha-ce-la′tion** (-lā'shon), *n.*

spha-ce-lus (sfas'e-lus), *n.* [NL., < Gr. σφάκελος, gangrene, mortification, caries.] In *pathol.*, gangrene or mortification; also, a gangrenous or mortified mass of tissue.—**spha′ce-lous**, *a.*

sphag-nous (sfag'nus), *a.* Pertaining to, abounding in, or consisting of sphagnum.

sphag-num (sfag'num), *n.* [NL., < Gr. σφάγνος, kind of moss.] Any of the soft mosses constituting the genus *Sphagnum*, found chiefly on the surface of bogs: used in the mass by gardeners in potting and packing plants, and esp. in surgery, for dressing wounds, etc.

sphal-er-ite (sfal'e-rīt), *n.* [Gr. σφαλερός, slippery, uncertain.] A native zinc sulphide; blende.

sphene (sfēn), *n.* [F. *sphène*, < Gr. σφήν, wedge; from the shape of the crystals.] The mineral titanite, esp. a yellowish or greenish variety.

Sphagnum (various species): *a*, fertile plant; *b*, capsule; *c*, antheridium; *d*, cells of leaf.

sphe-nic (sfē'nik), *a.* [Gr. σφήν, wedge.] Wedge-shaped.—

---

fat, fāte, fär, fåll, åsk, fāre; net, mē, hėr; pin, pīne; not, nōte, mōve, nôr; up, lūte, pull; oi, oil; ou, out; (lightened) aviȧry, ēlect, agȯny, intȯ, ūnite; (obscured) errạnt, operä, ardẹnt, actọr, natūre; ch, chip; g, go; th, thin; ᴛʜ, then; y, you;

sphenic number, a number having three unequal factors.

sphe-noid (sfē′noid). [Gr. σφηνοειδής, wedge-shaped, < σφήν, wedge, + εἶδος, form.] **I.** *a.* Wedge-shaped; in *anat.*, noting or pertaining to a compound bone of the base of the skull. **II.** *n.* In *anat.*, the sphenoid bone.—**sphe-noi-dal** (sfē-noi′dạl), *a.*

spher-al (sfēr′ạl), *a.* [LL. *sphæralis.*] Of or pertaining to a sphere; having the form of a sphere, or spherical; fig., symmetrical, or perfect in form (as, "the poet, whose verses are to be *spheral* and complete": Emerson's "Essays," Intellect); also, pertaining to the heavenly bodies, or to their supposed revolving spheres or shells, sometimes as the supposed source of music (see *music of the spheres,* under *music*).—**sphe-ral-i-ty** (sfē-ral′i-ti), *n.*

sphere (sfēr), *n.* [OF. *espere* (F. *sphère*), < L. *sphæra,* later *sphera,* < Gr. σφαῖρα, ball, globe, sphere.] A solid geometrical figure generated by the revolution of a semicircle about its diameter; a round body whose surface is at all points equidistant from the center; hence, any rounded body approximately of this form; a globe; a ball; a globular or spherical mass, shell, etc.; esp., a heavenly body; a planet or star; also, the apparent surface of the heavens, conceived as a hollow globe inclosing the earth, in which the heavenly bodies appear to have their place ('celestial sphere'); also, a spherical representation of the apparent form of the heavens; a globe or the like representing the heavens, heavenly bodies, etc. (cf. *armillary sphere,* at *armillary*); also, any of the transparent spherical shells or 'heavens,' one within another, in which the planets, fixed stars, etc., were supposed to be set, and which the old astronomers conceived to revolve round the earth, thus producing the apparent motions of the heavenly bodies (see *primum mobile,* also *Ptolemaic system,* at *Ptolemaic,* and cf. *music of the spheres,* under *music*); also, the particular sphere or heaven in which a planet or the like was supposed to be set (as, "Certain stars shot madly from their *spheres*": Shakspere's "Midsummer Night's Dream," ii. 1. 153); an orbit, as of a planet†; also, sometimes, a place of abode above or beyond the earth or this world; in general, the place, region, or environment within which a person or thing exists or has being (as, "But thou wilt never move from hence, The *sphere* thy fate allots," Tennyson's "Will Waterproof's Lyrical Monologue," 218; "Admiration! In that blest *sphere* alone we live and move; There taste that life of life—immortal love," Burns's "Rights of Woman," 29); one's proper place, environment, or element (as, to be out of one's *sphere*); a particular social world, stratum of society, or walk of life (as, an exalted or a humble *sphere*); a field of activity or operation (as, "That school offered her for her powers too limited a *sphere*": C. Brontë's "Villette," viii.); a field of something specified (as, a *sphere* of usefulness; a *sphere* of influence, specif., a region, as in Africa or Asia, within which a nation claims to have, or is admitted to have, a special interest politically or economically); the whole field, province, domain, or realm of something (as, the *sphere* of vision; the *sphere* of science or of law).—**sphere,** *v. t.*; sphered, sphering. To inclose in or as in a sphere; also, to form into a sphere; also, to place among the heavenly spheres; hence, to set aloft.—**sphere′less,** *a.* Without spheres; starless; also, having no proper sphere.

spher-ic (sfer′ik), *a.* [LL. *sphæricus,* < Gr. σφαιρικός.] Pertaining to a sphere or spheres; also, having the form of a sphere; sphere-like; spherical; also, pertaining to the heavenly bodies, or to their supposed spheres.—**spher′i-cal,** *a.* Of or pertaining to a sphere or spheres (as, *spherical* trigonometry); formed in or on a sphere, as a figure; also, having the form of a sphere; globular; resembling a sphere; also, pertaining to the heavenly bodies, or to their supposed revolving spheres or shells; pertaining to the heavenly bodies regarded astrologically as exerting influence on mankind and events.—**spherical aberration.** See *aberration.* —**spherical angle.** See *angle*[3], *n.*—**spherical sailing.** See under *sailing.*—**spher-i-cal′i-ty** (-kal′i-ti), *n.* Spherical state or form.—**spher′i-cal-ly,** *adv.*—**spher′i-cal-ness,** *n.* —**sphe-ri-ci-ty** (sfē-ris′i-ti), *n.* Sphericity.—**spher′ics**[1], *n.* The geometry and trigonometry of figures formed on the surface of a sphere.

spher-ics[2] (sfer′iks), *n.* [(*atmo*)*spherics.*] The science of electronic detection of distant atmospheric disturbances.

sphe-roid (sfē′roid), *n.* [L. *sphæroides,* < Gr. σφαιροειδής, sphere-like, < σφαῖρα, sphere, + εἶδος, form.] A body resembling a sphere, but not perfectly spherical; esp., a solid generated by the revolution of an ellipse about one of its axes.—**sphe-roi-dal** (sfē-roi′dạl), *a.* Pertaining to a spheroid or spheroids; also, shaped like a spheroid; approximately spherical.—**sphe-roi′dal-ly,** *adv.*—**sphe-roi′dic,** *a.* Spheroidal.—**sphe-roi-di-ci-ty** (sfē-roi-dis′i-ti), *n.* Spheroidic or spheroidal state or form.

sphe-rom-e-ter (sfē-rom′e-tėr), *n.* [F. *sphéromètre,* < Gr. σφαῖρα, sphere, + μέτρον, measure.] An instrument for measuring the curvature of spheres and curved surfaces.

spher-u-lar (sfer′ö-lär), *a.* Having the form of a spherule.—**spher′u-lar-ly,** *adv.*

spher-ule (sfer′öl), *n.* [LL. *sphærula,* dim. of L. *sphæra,* E. *sphere.*] A small sphere or spherical body.—**spher′u-lite** (-ö-līt), *n.* One of the spherular bodies or concretions formed in certain igneous rocks.—**spher-u-lit′ic** (-lit′ik), *a.*

spher-y (sfēr′i), *a.* Having the form of a sphere; sphere-like; also, pertaining to the heavenly bodies, or to their supposed revolving spheres or shells; resembling a heavenly body, or star-like.

sphex (sfeks), *n.* [NL., < Gr. σφήξ, wasp.] Any of the large fossorial wasps constituting the genus *Sphex* (family *Sphegidæ*). Cf. *digger-wasp.*

sphinc-ter (sfingk′tėr), *n.* [LL., < Gr. σφιγκτήρ, < σφίγγειν, bind tight.] In *anat.* and *zoöl.*, a contractile ring-like muscle surrounding and capable of closing a natural orifice or passage.—**sphinc-te′ri-al** (-tē′ri-ạl), **sphinc-ter′ic** (-ter′ik), *a.*

sphin-gid (sfin′jid). [NL. *Sphingidæ,* pl., < *Sphinx,* the typical genus, < L. *sphinx:* see *sphinx.*] **I.** *n.* Any moth of the family *Sphingidæ,* comprising the sphinxes, sphinx-moths, or hawk-moths. **II.** *a.* Belonging to the family *Sphingidæ.* See *sphinx.*

sphinx (sfingks), *n.*; pl. *sphinxes,* L. *sphinges* (sfin′jēz). [L., < Gr. σφίγξ, sphinx, commonly explained as meaning 'strangler,' 'throttler,' < σφίγγειν, bind tight: cf. *sphincter.*] [*cap.* or *l. c.*] A fabulous monster of Greek mythology, variously repre-sented, commonly with the head of a woman, the body of a lion or a dog, and wings, which, near Thebes, proposed a riddle to passers-by, killing those unable to guess it; hence [*l. c.*], some similar monster; also, a sphinx-like person or thing, as one presenting diffi-cult questions or being of an in-scrutable nature; also, in *Egyptian antiq.*, a figure of an imaginary crea-ture having the head of a man or an animal and the body of a lion

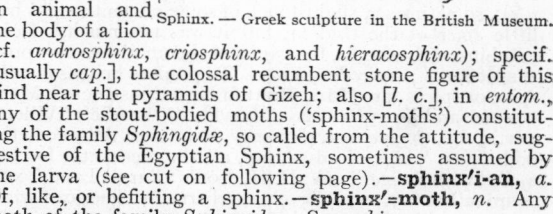

Sphinx. — Greek sculpture in the British Museum.

(cf. *androsphinx, criosphinx,* and *hieracosphinx*); specif. [usually *cap.*], the colossal recumbent stone figure of this kind near the pyramids of Gizeh; also [*l. c.*], in *entom.,* any of the stout-bodied moths ('sphinx-moths') constitut-ing the family *Sphingidæ,* so called from the attitude, sug-gestive of the Egyptian Sphinx, sometimes assumed by the larva (see cut on following page).—**sphinx′i-an,** *a.* Of, like, or befitting a sphinx.—**sphinx′=moth,** *n.* Any moth of the family *Sphingidæ.* See *sphinx.*

sphrag-ide (sfraj′id), *n.* [F., < L. *sphragis* (sphragid-), < Gr. σφραγίς (σφραγιδ-), lit. 'seal': cf. *sphragistic.*] Lem-nian earth, or terra sigillata. See under *Lemnian* and *terra.*

sphra-gis-tic (sfrạ-jis′tik), *a.* [Gr. σφραγιστικός, of or for sealing, < σφραγίζειν, to seal, < σφραγίς, seal, signet.] Of or pertaining to seals or signet-rings. — **sphra-gis′-tics**, *n.* The scientific study of seals or signet-rings.

Plum-tree Sphinx (*Sphinx drupiferarum*).

sphyg-mic (sfig′mik), *a.* [Gr. σφυγμικός, < σφυγμός, pulse, < σφύζειν, beat, throb.] In *physiol.*, etc., of or pertaining to the pulse.

sphygmo-. Form of Gr. σφυγμός, pulse, used in combination. — **sphyg-mo-gram** (sfig′mọ-gram), *n.* [+ -*gram.*] A tracing or diagram produced by a sphygmograph. — **sphyg′mo-graph** (-gråf), *n.* [+ -*graph.*] An instrument for recording the rapidity, strength, and uniformity of the arterial pulse. — **sphyg-mo-graph′ic** (-graf′ik), *a.* — **sphyg′moid**, *a.* [Gr. σφυγμοειδής: see -*oid.*] In *physiol.*, etc., resembling the pulse; pulse-like. — **sphyg″mo-ma-nom′e-ter** (-mạ-nom′e-tėr), *n.* [See *manometer.*] An instrument for measuring the pressure of the blood in an artery. — **sphyg′mom′e-ter** (-mom′e-tėr), *n.* [+ -*meter.*] An instrument for measuring the strength of the pulse. — **sphyg′mo-phone** (-fōn), *n.* [+ -*phone.*] An instrument by which pulse-beats are rendered audible. — **sphyg′mo-scope** (-skōp), *n.* [+ -*scope.*] An instrument by which pulse-beats are rendered visible.

Sphygmogram.

spi-cate (spī′kāt), *a.* [L. *spicatus*, pp. of *spicare*, furnish with spikes, < *spica*, E. *spike*[2].] In *bot.*, having or bearing spikes, as a plant; arranged in spikes, as flowers; having the form of a spike, as an inflorescence.

spic-ca-to (spēk-kä′tō), *a.* [It., pp. of *spiccare*, detach, separate.] In *music*, detached; in violin-playing, noting distinct tones produced by short, abrupt motions of the bow, without lifting it from the string.

spice (spīs), *n.* [OF. *espice*, *espece* (F. *épice*), spice, < LL. *species*, spice, L. sort, kind: see *species.*] Any of a class of pungent or aromatic substances of vegetable origin, as pepper, cinnamon, cloves, and the like, used as seasoning, preservatives, etc.; also, such substances as a material or collectively (as, "The dead . . . with precious gums and *spice* Fragrant, and incorruptibly preserved," Southey's "Madoc," i. 15. 242; a dealer in *spice*); also, a spicy or aromatic odor or fragrance (chiefly poetic: as, "The woodbine *spices* are wafted abroad," Tennyson's "Maud," i. 22. 1; "From the land now blew a gentle gale, *Spice*-laden, warm," W. Morris's "Jason," xiii. 11); also, in fig. use, something that gives zest (as, "Variety's the very *spice* of life, That gives it all its flavour": Cowper's "Task," ii. 606); a piquant element or quality; zest, piquancy, or interest; also, a slight touch or trace of something (as, "as I heard good Senecio, with a *spice* of the wit of the last age, say," Steele, in "Tatler," 45; "The world loves a *spice* of wickedness," Longfellow's "Hyperion," i. 7); sometimes, a slight touch of some ailment (as, "I had a little *spice* of the cold fit, but it was not much," Defoe's "Robinson Crusoe," i. 6; a *spice* of rheumatism: now prov.). — **spice**, *v. t.*; *spiced*, *spicing*. To prepare or season with a spice or spices (as, "Mrs. Bretton herself instructed Martha to *spice* and heat the wassail-bowl": C. Brontë's "Villette," xxv.); fig., to give zest, piquancy, or interest to by something added (as, "days of adventure, all the pleasanter for being *spiced* with danger": W. H. Hudson's "Purple Land," xvii.). — **spice′ber′ry**, *n.* The checkerberry or American wintergreen, *Gaultheria procumbens.* — **spice′=bush**, *n.* A yellow-flowered lauraceous shrub, *Benzoin benzoin*, of North America, whose bark and leaves have a spicy odor. — **spiced**, *p. a.* Seasoned or flavored with spice; also, fragrant as

with spice, or spicy (as, "*spiced* groves of ceaseless verdure": H. Melville's "Moby-Dick," cxix.). — **spi-cer** (spī′sėr), *n.* One who deals in spices†; an apothecary†; also, one who seasons with spice. — **spi′cer-y** (-i), *n.*; pl. -*ies* (-iz). Spices (in *sing.* or *pl.*: as, "the *spiceries* of the Moluccas," Adam Smith's "Wealth of Nations," iv. 5); also, spicy flavor or fragrance (as, "The pine forests exhaled the fresher *spicery*": Bret Harte's "Mliss," iv.); also, a room or place where spices are kept (obs. or hist.). — **spice′=tree**, *n.* A lauraceous timber-tree, *Umbellularia californica*, of California, etc., with aromatic leaves. — **spice′wood**, *n.* Same as *spice-bush.*

spi-ci-form (spī′si-fôrm), *a.* [L. *spica*, spike, ear: see -*form.*] In *bot.*, having the form of a spike.

spi-ci-ly (spī′si-li), *adv.* In a spicy manner; piquantly. — **spi′ci-ness**, *n.*

spick=and=span (spik′ạnd-span′), *a.* [From *spick-and-span-new.*] Perfectly new; fresh; hence, spruce or smart (as, "Never had she seen the judge so *spick and span*," W. Churchill's "Coniston," ii. 16; "young men in *spick-and-span* uniforms," Mrs. Wharton's "Son at the Front," vii.); neat and clean (as, "The studio is very *spick and span*": Du Maurier's "Trilby," viii.).

spick=and=span=new (spik′ạnd-span′nū′), *a.* [Extended form of *span-new*, with *spick-* perhaps equivalent to *spike*[1].] Perfectly new; brand-new; span-new. Also **spick′=span-new′.**

spick-e-ty (spik′ẹ-ti), *n.* and *a.* Same as *spiggoty.* [Slang.]

spic-u-la (spik′ū-lạ), *n.*; pl. -*læ* (-lē). [NL., dim. of L. *spica*, E. *spike*[2]: cf. *spiculum.*] A small, needle-like body or part; a spicule; an acicular crystal, as of ice: as, "Not a *spicula* of the frost is dissolved" (Tyndall's "Forms of Water," § 5). — **spic′u-lar** (-lạr), *a.* Pertaining to or of the nature of a spicula or spicule; slender and sharp-pointed; also, characterized by or having spicules. — **spic′u-late** (-lāt), *a.* Covered with or having spicules; consisting of spicules; also, having the form of a spicule. — **spic′ule** (-ūl), *n.* [NL. *spicula* or L. *spiculum.*] A small or minute, slender, sharp-pointed body or part; a small, needle-like crystal, process, or the like; specif., in *zoöl.*, one of the small, hard, calcareous or siliceous bodies which serve as the skeletal elements of sponges, etc.; in *bot.*, a floral spikelet. — **spic′u-lum** (-lum), *n.*; pl. -*la* (-lạ). [L., dim. of *spica*, E. *spike*[2].] A small, needle-like body, part, process, or the like; a spicule.

spi-cy (spī′si), *a.*; compar. *spicier*, superl. *spiciest.* Abounding in or yielding spices (as, "As when . . . north-east winds blow Sabæan odours from the *spicy* shore Of Araby the bless'd": Milton's "Paradise Lost," iv. 162); seasoned with or containing spice (as, "*spicy* nut-brown ale": Milton's "L'Allegro," 100); of the nature of or resembling spice (as, "The isles . . . whence merchants bring Their *spicy* drugs": Milton's "Paradise Lost," ii. 640); characteristic or suggestive of spice (as, a *spicy* flavor or odor); aromatic or fragrant (as, "Every *spicy* flower Of the laurel-shrubs": Tennyson's "Poet's Mind"); in fig. use, piquant or pungent (as, a *spicy* speech; *spicy* criticism); sometimes, of a somewhat improper or scandalous nature (as, a *spicy* story); also, full of spirit (slang: as, a *spicy* horse); smart or stylish (slang: as, to look *spicy*).

spi-der (spī′dėr), *n.* [ME. *spithre*, appar. < AS. *spinnan*, E. *spin.*] Any of the eight-legged, wingless, predaceous, insect-like arachnids which constitute the order *Araneida*, notable for the spinning of webs which serve as nests and as traps for prey; hence, any of various other arachnids resembling or suggesting these; also, a spider-crab; also, any of various things resembling or suggesting a spider; a frying-pan, orig. one with legs or feet; a trivet or tripod, as for supporting a pot or pan on a hearth; any of various mechanical structures or frames with radiating parts; a lightly built cart, phaëton, or wagon with a high body and disproportionately large

Spider. — Female of *Latrodectus mactans*, enlarged one quarter; *a*, under side of abdomen.

and slender wheels.—**spi′der=bug,** *n.* A heteropterous insect, *Emesa longipes,* of the U. S., having a very slender body with thread-like middle and hind legs, and spinous fore legs adapted for seizing. Also called *stick-bug.*—**spi′der=crab,** *n.* Any of various crabs with long, slender legs and comparatively small body, esp. of the class *Maioidea* (see *maioid*).—**spi′der=line,** *n.* One of the threads of a spider's web used in forming the reticle of a telescope or the like; a cross-hair.—**spi′der=mon″key,** *n.* Any of various tropical American monkeys of the genera *Ateles* and *Eriodes,* with a slender body, long, slender limbs, and a long, prehensile tail, and with the thumb either rudimentary or lacking.—**spi′der=wort,**

A Brazilian Spider-monkey (*Eriodes arachnoides*).

(-wẻrt), *n.* Any plant of the commelinaceous genus *Tradescantia,* comprising perennial herbs with blue, purple, or rose-colored flowers; also, any commelinaceous plant.—**spi′der=y,** *a.* Like or suggesting a spider; long and thin, as legs or arms; sometimes, suggesting a spider's web; also, full of or infested with spiders.

spied (spīd). Preterit and past participle of *spy.*

spie-gel (spē′gl), *n.* Same as *spiegeleisen.*

spie-gel-ei-sen (spē′gl-ī″zęn, G. shpē′gęl-), *n.* [G., 'mirror iron.'] A lustrous, crystalline pig-iron containing a large amount of manganese, sometimes fifteen per cent or more: used in making steel. Also **spie′gel=i″ron.**

spiel (spēl, G. shpēl), *n.* [G., < *spielen,* to play.] Play or playing; a game; a dance; also, a talk or speech (as, "You always hand out some *spiel* about the root.

Spiderwort (*Tradescantia virginiana*):—1, the inflorescence; 2, the lower part of the stem with the root.

my being so 'useful' ": Sinclair Lewis's "Main Street," xiv.); a story. [Slang.]—**spiel,** *v. i.* To play; dance; also, to talk or speak (as, "He's always *spieling* about the 'value of languages'": Sinclair Lewis's "Babbitt," vi.); 'orate.' [Slang.] —**spiel′er,** *n.* One who spiels; a gambler or sharper; a dancer; a talker or speaker; an announcer, crier, or barker. [Slang.]

spi-er (spī′ẻr), *n.* [See *spy, v.*] One who spies, watches, or discovers.

spif′fli-cate, etc. See *spifflicate,* etc.

spif-fy (spif′i), *a.* [Origin obscure.] Spruce; smart; fine: as, "I just simply can't get myself to fuss over my clothes, and here you're going to go and look so *spiffy*" (Sinclair Lewis's "Arrowsmith," vii.). [Slang.]

spif-li-cate (spif′li-kāt), *v. t.*; *-cated, -cating.* [Appar. a made word.] To confound or dismay; also, to overcome; do for; destroy; kill. [Colloq.]—**spif-li-ca′tion** (-kā′shǫn), *n.*

Spi-ge-li-an (spī-jē′li-ạn), *a.* Pertaining to Spigelius (Adrian van den Spieghel), a Belgian anatomist and botanist at Padua (died 1625): as, the *Spigelian* lobe (a small lobe of the liver).

spig-go-ty, spig-o-ty (spig′ǫ-ti), *n.* [Also *spickety*; said to be from a use of *speak*, in broken English.] **I.** *n.*; pl. *-ties* (-tiz). In the Panama Canal Zone and elsewhere, a term applied to a native. [Slang.] **II.** *a.* Of or pertaining to the natives in the Panama Canal Zone and elsewhere. [Slang.]

spig-ot (spig′ǫt), *n.* [ME. *spigot*; perhaps related to *spike¹* or *spike².*] A small peg or plug for stopping the vent of a cask, etc.; in devices for drawing off liquids from casks, etc., the small peg which stops the passage in the hollow plug or tube called the faucet; also, a faucet or cock for controlling the flow of liquid from a pipe or the like; also, the end of a pipe which enters the enlarged end or faucet of another pipe to form a joint.

spike¹ (spīk), *n.* [ME. *spike* = Sw. and Norw. *spik,* nail, spike, related to MLG. *spīker,* G. *spieker,* D. *spijker,* nail; all perhaps < L. *spica,* E. *spike².*] A large, strong nail or pin, as for fastening rails to ties; also, a sharp-pointed piece of metal, etc., fastened in something, with the point outward, as for defense; a sharp metal projection on the sole of a shoe, as of a baseball play-

Spikes.—*a,* dock-spike, used in building docks and piers; *b,* large nail; *c, d,* railroad-spikes, for fastening rails to sleepers; *e,* barbed spike; *f,* barbed and forked spike; *g, h,* types of forked spikes, the points of which spread and become hooked in the timber when driven.

er, to prevent slipping; also, the antler of a young deer, when straight and without branches; also, in general, a stiff, sharp-pointed piece or part; also, a workhouse, as for able-bodied paupers (slang, Eng.: as, "He [a tramp] discoursed of *spikes,* that is to say of workhouses," H. G. Wells's "Bealby," vi.).—**spike¹,** *v. t.*; *spiked, spiking.* To fasten or secure with a spike or spikes; also, to provide or set with a spike or spikes, as for protection or to prevent slipping; set or stud with something suggesting spikes (as, "A wild and broken landscape, *spiked* with firs, Roughening the bleak horizon's northern edge": Whittier's "Bridal of Pennacook," v.); also, to render (a gun) useless by driving a spike into the touch-hole (as, "He . . . wrenched the hammer from the armourer's hand, and seizing a nail . . . in a few moments he had *spiked* the gun": Marryat's "Peter Simple," xviii.); fig., to make ineffective, or frustrate the action or purpose of (as, to *spike* an attempt; to *spike* a rumor); also, to pierce with or impale on a spike; specif., to injure (another player or a competitor) with the spikes of one's shoe, as in baseball.

spike² (spīk), *n.* [L. *spica,* spike of grain, ear, top or tuft of a plant, orig. something sharp or pointed: cf. *spike¹.*] An ear, as of wheat or other grain (as, "The gleaners spread around, and here and there, *Spike* after *spike,* their sparing harvest pick": Thomson's "Seasons," Autumn, 166); also, in *bot.,* an inflorescence in which the flowers are sessile (or apparently so) along an elongated, unbranched common axis; also, spike-lavender (as, oil of *spike*: see *spike-lavender*).—**spike′=lav″en-der,** *n.* A species of lavender, *Lavandula spica,* having spikes of pale-purple flowers, and yielding an oil ('oil of spike') used in painting, etc.—**spike′let,** *n.* In *bot.,* a small or secondary spike; in true grasses, one of the flower-clusters (each consisting of two or more flowers and subtended by one or more glumes) variously disposed around a common axis.

a. Spike of Plantain (*Plantago major*); *b,* section of it, showing the sessile flowers.

Spike of Barley.

spike-nard (spīk′närd), *n.* [ML. *spica nardi,* 'spike of nard.'] An aromatic East Indian valerianaceous plant, *Nardostachys jatamansi* (see cut on following page), supposedly the same as the ancient nard; also, an aromatic substance used by the ancients, obtained from a plant supposed to be *Nardostachys jatamansi,* or the ointment nard prepared from this (as, "There came a woman having an alabaster box of ointment of *spikenard* very precious": Mark, xiv. 3); also, any of various other plants, esp. an American araliaceous herb, *Aralia racemosa,* with an aromatic root.

---

spik-er (spī'kėr), *n.* One who or that which spikes; esp., a workman who drives the spikes in the ties in laying railroad-tracks.

spike=rush (spīk'rush), *n.* Any plant of the cyperaceous genus *Eleocharis*, comprising sedges characterized by simple stems having a solitary terminal spike with closely imbricated scales.

spike=team (spīk'tēm), *n.* A team of three draft-animals of which two are harnessed abreast while the third leads. [U. S.]

spik-y (spī'ki), *a.* Having a spike or spikes; set with sharp, projecting points; also, having the form of a spike; spikelike.

spile (spīl), *n.* [Cf. MLG. *spile*, pointed stick, skewer, D. *spijl*, pin, bar, skewer, also E. *spill*[1].] A splinter of wood (now north. Eng.); also, a peg or plug of wood, esp. one used as a spigot; also, a

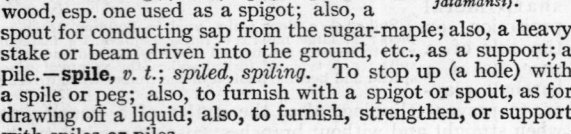

Spikenard (*Nardostachys jatamansi*).

spout for conducting sap from the sugar-maple; also, a heavy stake or beam driven into the ground, etc., as a support; a pile.—**spile**, *v. t.*; spiled, spiling. To stop up (a hole) with a spile or peg; also, to furnish with a spigot or spout, as for drawing off a liquid; also, to furnish, strengthen, or support with spiles or piles.

spil'i-kin, *n.* See *spillikin*.

spill[1] (spil), *n.* [ME. *spille*, splinter: cf. *spile*.] A sharp-pointed fragment of wood, etc.; a splinter; also, a slender piece of wood or of folded or twisted paper, for lighting candles, lamps, etc. (as, "candle-lighters, or '*spills*' . . . of coloured paper": Mrs. Gaskell's "Cranford," xiv.).

spill[2] (spil), *v.*; spilled or spilt, spilling. [AS. *spillan* = Icel. *spilla*, destroy, = MLG. and D. *spillen*, waste.] **I.** *tr.* To kill or slay (archaic); destroy (life: archaic); hence, to ruin†, wreck†, or undo† (as, "So full of artless jealousy is guilt, It *spills* itself in fearing to be *spilt*": Shakspere's "Hamlet," iv. 5. 20); spoil by damaging or injuring (now prov. Eng. and Sc.); waste† or squander†; also, to shed (blood), as in killing or wounding (as, "Not a single drop of blood had been *spilled* in the progress of a revolution which seemed already to be complete": J. F. Kirk's "Charles the Bold," iii. 2); in general, to cause or allow (liquid, or any matter in grains or loose pieces) to run or fall from a vessel or container, esp. accidentally or wastefully (as, to *spill* milk or salt); scatter (as, "Like the fair pearl-necklace of the Queen, That burst in dancing and the pearls were *spilt*": Tennyson's "Merlin and Vivien," 450); fig., to divulge, disclose, or tell (now slang); also, to cause to fall from a horse, vehicle, or the like (colloq.); also, *naut.*, to let the wind out of (a sail). **II.** *intr.* To perish† or be destroyed†; be ruined or spoiled†; also, of liquid, loose particles, etc., to run or escape from a vessel or container, esp. by accident or in careless handling; also, *naut.*, to become empty of wind, as a sail (as, "The ship turned slowly to the wind, pitching and chopping as the sails were *spilling*": Marryat's "Peter Simple," xv.).—**spill**[2], *n.* A spilling, as of liquid, or a quantity spilled or the mark made (as, "the *spill* of gravy on the cloth": Galsworthy's "Country House," i. 10); also, a throw or fall from a horse, vehicle, or the like (colloq.).—**spill'er**[1], *n.*

spil-ler[2] (spil'ėr), *n.* [Origin obscure.] In mackerel-fishing, a seine inserted into a larger seine to take out the fish, as over a rocky bottom where the larger seine cannot be hauled ashore.

spil-li-kin (spil'i-kin), *n.* [Also *spilikin*, *spilliken*: cf. *spill*[1].] A jackstraw, or strip of wood, bone, or the like used in the game of jackstraws; *pl.* (construed as *sing.*), the game itself (as, "Lewis . . . began to play *spillikens* with the wooden toothpicks on the table": Margaret Kennedy's "Constant Nymph," i.).

spill-way (spil'wā), *n.* A way or passage for the escape of surplus water, as from a dam.

spil-o-site (spil'ō-sīt), *n.* [Gr. σπῖλος, spot, speck.] A spotted rock resulting from local metamorphism of slate in contact with diabase or granite.

spilt (spilt). Preterit and past participle of *spill*[2].

spilth (spilth), *n.* [See -*th*[1].] The act of spilling, or that

which is spilled: as, "When our vaults have wept With drunken *spilth* of wine" (Shakspere's "Timon of Athens," ii. 2. 169). [Archaic.]

spin (spin), *v.*; pret. *spun* (also archaic *span*), pp. *spun*, ppr. *spinning*. [AS. *spinnan* = D. and G. *spinnen* = Icel. and Sw. *spinna* = Goth. *spinnan*, spin.] **I.** *tr.* To draw out and twist (wool, flax, cotton, or other fiber), either by hand or by machinery, into thread or yarn, for weaving or other purposes; form (any material) into thread (as, to *spin* gold or glass); hence, to make (thread or yarn) by drawing out, twisting, etc.; make or weave thread for (a fabric garment, etc.: as, "my sky-robes *spun* out of Iris' woof," Milton's "Comus," 83); of spiders, silkworms, etc., to produce (a thread, cobweb, gossamer, silk, etc.) by extruding from the body a long, slender filament of a natural viscous matter that hardens in the air; in fig. use, to produce, fabricate, or evolve in a manner suggestive of spinning thread (as, "I set me down, to pass the time, And *spin* a verse or twa o' rhyme": Burns's "Epistle to Davie," 5); tell (a yarn or story: see *yarn*, *n.*); draw out, protract, or prolong (often with *out*: as, to *spin* out proceedings; to *spin* out a story tediously); also, to cause to turn round rapidly, as on an axis (as, to *spin* a top; to *spin* a coin on a table); twirl; whirl; also, to fish (a pool, etc.) with a spinning or revolving bait, as a spoon-bait; in sheet-metal work, to shape into hollow, rounded form, during rotation on a lathe or wheel, by pressure with a suitable tool. **II.** *intr.* To draw out and twist wool, flax, or the like into thread or yarn, esp. with the distaff and spindle, with the spinning-wheel, or with spinning-machinery; also, to produce a thread from the body, as spiders, silkworms, etc.; also, to admit of being made into thread or yarn, as fiber; also, to issue in a rapid stream, or spurt, as liquid (now rare: as, "One razed Achilles' hand; the spouting blood *Spun* forth," Pope's tr. Homer's "Iliad," xxi.); also, to move, go, run, ride, or travel rapidly (as, "The horse . . . made the little wagon *spin* and bounce over the rough, stony road": Mrs. Stowe's "Oldtown Folks," viii.); roll rapidly along in a vehicle; pass quickly, as time; also, to turn round rapidly, as on an axis, as the earth, a top, etc. (as, "He . . . *spun* round, flung up his arms, and fell on his back, shot through": Galsworthy's "Saint's Progress," ii. 1); hence, to be affected with a sensation of whirling, as the head (as, "My head was *spinning* with unwonted Benedictine and Burgundy": H. G. Wells's "Tono-Bungay," ii. 2. § 1); be giddy; also, to fish with a spinning or revolving bait.—**spin**, *n.* The act of spinning fiber into thread, or the capacity of fiber for being spun; the thread made by spinning; also, the act of causing a spinning or whirling motion; a spinning motion given to a ball or the like when thrown; a spinning or whirling motion of anything; also, a moving or going rapidly along; a rapid run, ride, drive, or the like, as for exercise or enjoyment (as, "In the morning he had a *spin* in the ice-boat with his hostess": Mrs. Wharton's "Age of Innocence," xv.).

spi-na-ceous (spi-nā'shius), *a.* [ML. *spinacia*, spinach.] Pertaining to or of the nature of the spinach; belonging to the *Chenopodiaceæ*, or spinach or goosefoot family of plants.

spin-ach (spin'ạj or -ạch), *n.* [OF. *spinache*, *espinache*, *espinoche* (cf. F. *épinard*), = Sp. *espinaca* = ML. *spinachia*, *spinacia*, spinach; origin uncertain.] A chenopodiaceous herb, *Spinacia oleracea*, cultivated for its succulent leaves, which are eaten boiled; the leaves themselves; also, any of various allied or similar plants. Also **spin'age** (-ạj).

spi-nal (spī'nạl), *a.* [LL. *spinalis*.] Of or pertaining to the spine or backbone; also, resembling the spine or backbone; pertaining to a spine-like part; also, pertaining to a spine or spinous process.—**spinal column**, in a vertebrate animal, the series of small bones or vertebræ forming the axis of the skeleton and protecting the spinal cord; the spine; the backbone. See cut on following page.—**spinal cord**, the cord of nervous tissue extending through the spinal column.—**spi'nal-ly**, *adv.*

spi-nate (spī'nāt), *a.* [NL. *spinatus*.] Bearing spines or pointed processes.—**spi-na'tion** (-nā'shọn), *n.*

spin-dle (spin'dl), *n.* [AS. *spinel*, < *spinnan*, E. *spin*.] A rounded rod, usually of wood, tapering toward each end, used in spinning by hand to twist into thread the fibers drawn from the mass on the distaff, and to wind the thread on as it is spun; also, the rod or pin on a spinning-wheel by which the thread is twisted and on which it is wound; also, one of the rods of a spinning-machine which bear the bobbins on which the thread is wound as it is spun; also, as much thread or yarn as can be prepared on a spindle at one time; specif., a measure of yarn, containing for cotton 15,120 yards, and for linen 14,400 yards; also, any of various spindle-shaped (see below) or fusiform objects; a spindle-shaped figure, as one used as a charge in heraldry; also, any rod or pin suggestive of a spindle used in spinning, as one which turns round or on which something turns; an axle, axis, or shaft, esp. a small axis, arbor, or mandrel; either of the two shaft-like parts in a lathe which support the work to be turned, one ('live spindle') rotating and imparting motion to the work, and the other ('dead spindle') not rotating; either end of an axletree or the like; an iron rod or the like fixed

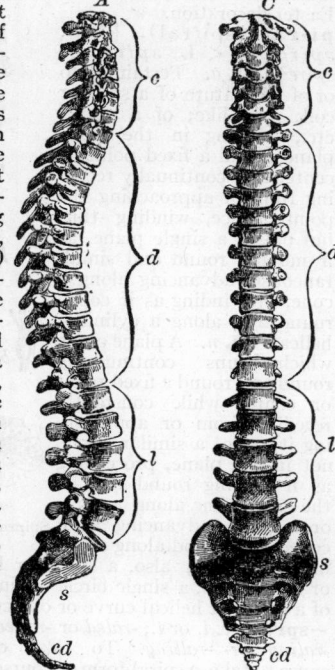

Human Spinal Column. — *A*, side view; *C*, front view; *c*, seven cervical vertebræ; *d*, twelve dorsal; *l*, five lumbar; *s*, five sacral, fused in a sacrum; *cd*, four caudal or coccygeal, forming a coccyx.

to a rock, sunken reef, etc., to serve as a guide in navigation; also, a stalk, stem, or shoot of a plant, esp. of a cereal (obs. or prov.).—**spindle side**, the female side, or line of descent, of a family; the distaff side: opposed to *spear side*. —**spin′dle,** *v. i.*; *-dled, -dling.* To shoot up, or grow, into a long, slender stalk or stem, as a plant; grow tall and slender, often disproportionately so; rise in slender form, as a tower. —**spin′dle-ful** (-fúl), *n.*; pl. *-fuls.* As much thread or yarn as a spindle can hold.—**spin′dle=legged,** *a.* Having long, slender legs: as, "a pale, sickly, *spindle-legged* generation of valetudinarians" (Addison, in "Tatler," 148).— **spin′dle=legs,** *n. pl.* Long, slender legs.—**spin′dle= shanked,** *a.* Spindle-legged: as, "a little, rivelled, *spindle-shanked* gentleman" (Addison, in "Guardian," 97).—**spin′- dle=shanks,** *n. pl.* Long, slender legs; also (construed as *sing.*), a tall, thin person with such legs.—**spin′dle=shaped,** *a.* Shaped like the spindle used in spinning by hand; rounded, and tapering from the middle toward each end; fusiform.—**spin′dle= tree,** *n.* A European celastraceous shrub, *Euonymus europæus*, whose wood was formerly much used for making spindles; also, any of various allied plants.—**spin′dling,** *p. a.* Growing into a long, slender stalk or stem, often a too slender or weakly one, as a plant; in general, long or tall and slender, often disproportionately so.—**spin′dly,** *a.* Spindling.

spin-drift (spin′drift), *n.* Same as *spoondrift*.

spine (spīn), *n.* [OF. *espine* (F. *épine*), < L. *spina*, thorn, prickle, spine, backbone.] A sharp-pointed, hard or woody outgrowth on a plant; a thorn; also, a stiff, pointed process or appendage on an animal, as a quill of a porcupine, or a sharp, unbranched and unjointed, bony rod or ray (see *ray*[3], *n.*, with cut) in a fish's fin; in

Spindle-shaped Root of Radish.

general, a pointed process or projection, as of a bone; also, the vertebral or spinal column (see under *spinal*); the backbone; hence, any backbone-like part (as, "The shock Of cataract seas that snap The three-decker's oaken *spine*": Tennyson's "Maud," ii. 2. 4); a ridge, as of ground, rock, etc., resembling the backbone in some way.—**spined,** *a.* Having a spine or spines.

spin-el (spin′el or spi-nel′), *n.* [F. *spinelle*, < It. *spinella*, dim. < L. *spina*, thorn; prob. with reference to the sharp angles of the crystals.] A mineral consisting chiefly of the oxides of magnesium and aluminium, and having varieties used as ornamental stones in jewelry. See *ruby*, *n.*, also *balas*, also *sapphirine*, *n.*

spine-less (spīn′les), *a.* Without spines or sharp-pointed processes; also, having no spine or backbone; also, having a weak spine; destitute of the natural strength of spine; limp; fig., without moral force, resolution, or courage; irresolute; feeble.

spi-nes-cent (spī-nes′ent), *a.* [LL. *spinescens* (-ent-), ppr. of *spinescere*, grow thorny, < L. *spina*, thorn, E. *spine*.] In *bot.*, becoming spine-like; ending in a spine; also, bearing spines; in *zoöl.*, somewhat spine-like; coarse, as hair.— **spi-nes′cence,** *n.*

spin-et (spin′et or spi-net′), *n.* [F. *espinette* (now *épinette*), < It. *spinetta*, spinet; prob. from the name of an early Venetian maker, Giovanni *Spinetti*, although commonly explained as dim. < L. *spina*, thorn, with reference to quills serving to pluck the strings.] An old keyed musical instrument resembling the harpsichord (the precursor of the piano) but smaller.

spine-tail (spīn′tāl), *n.* Any of various swifts (birds) with mucronate tail-feathers.—**spine′=tailed,** *a.*

spi-nif-er-ous (spī-nif′ẹ-rus), *a.* [L. *spinifer*, < *spina*, thorn, spine, + *ferre*, bear.] Bearing or having spines; spiny.

spin-i-fex (spin′i-feks), *n.* [NL., < L. *spina*, thorn, spine, + *facere*, make.] Any of the spiny grasses of the genus *Spinifex*, chiefly of Australia, often useful as binding sand on the seashore.

spi-ni-form (spī′ni-fôrm), *a.* [L. *spina*, thorn, spine: see *-form*.] Having the form of a spine; spine-like.

spi-nig-er-ous (spī-nij′ẹ-rus), *a.* [LL. *spiniger*, < L. *spina*, thorn, spine, + *gerere*, bear.] Bearing spines; spiniferous.

spi-ni-grade (spī′ni-grād), *a.* [NL. *spinigradus*, < L. *spina*, thorn, spine, + *gradi*, walk.] Moving by means of spines or spinous processes, as an echinoderm.

spin-i-ness (spī′ni-nes), *n.* Spiny character or state.

spink (spingk), *n.* [Imit.] The chaffinch. [Now chiefly prov.]

spin-na-ker (spin′ạ-kẻr), *n.* [Origin uncertain.] *Naut.,* a large triangular sail with a light boom ('spinnaker boom'), carried by yachts on the side opposite the mainsail when running before the wind.

spin-ner (spin′ẻr), *n.* One who or that which spins; a spider (now chiefly prov.); a revolving bait used in trolling for fish.

spin-ner-et (spin′ẻr-et), *n.* [Dim. of *spinner*.] An organ or part by means of which a spider, larva, or the like spins a silky thread for its web or cocoon.

spin-ner-y (spin′ẻr-i), *n.*; pl. *-ies* (-iz). A mill or establishment for spinning thread or yarn.

spin′net, *n.* See *spinet*.

spin-ney (spin′i), *n.*; pl. *spinneys* (-iz). [OF. *espinei*, *espinaye* (F. *épinaie*), thorny place, < *espine*, E. *spine*.] A thicket; a small wood with undergrowth, esp. one preserved for sheltering game-birds (as, "the first shooting-party of the season, devoted to *spinneys* and the outlying coverts": Galsworthy's "Country House," i. 1); a small plantation or group of trees. [Eng.]

spin-ning=jen-ny (spin′ing-jen″i), *n.*; pl. *-jennies* (-iz). An early type of spinning-machine having more than one spindle, whereby one person could spin a number of threads simultaneously.

spin-ning=wheel (spin′ing-hwēl), *n.* An old-fashioned device for spinning wool, flax, etc., into thread or yarn, consisting essentially of a single spindle driven by a large wheel operated by hand or foot. See cut on following page.

spin′ny, *n.* See *spinney*.

(variable) ḍ as d or j, ș as s or sh, ṭ as t or ch, ẓ as z or zh; *o*, F. *cloche*; ü, F. *menu*; ċh, Sc. *loch*; ṅ, F. *bonbon*; ′, primary accent; ″, secondary accent; †, obsolete; <, from; +, and; =, equals. See also lists at beginning of book.

spi-node (spī′nōd), n. [L. *spina*, thorn, spine, + *nodus*, E. *node*.] In *geom.*, that point on a curve where a point generating the curve has its motion precisely reversed; a cusp.

spi-nose (spī′nōs or spī-nōs′), a. [L. *spinosus*: see *spinous*.] Full of spines; spiniferous; spinous: chiefly in *bot.* and *zoöl.*—**spi′nose-ly,** *adv.*

spi-nous (spī′nus), a. [L. *spinosus*, < *spina*, thorn, E. *spine*.] Covered with or having spines; thorny, as a plant; armed with or bearing sharp-pointed processes, as an animal; spiniferous; also, spine-like or spiniform; slender and sharp-pointed, as a process of bone; fig., sharp or rough (as, "Coventry had a rough *spinous* humour": Lamb's "Old Benchers of the Inner Temple"); troublesome to deal with.—**spi-nos′i-ty** (-nos′i-ti), **spi′nous-ness,** *n.*

Spi-no-zism (spi-nō′zizm), n. The pantheistic philosophical doctrines or system of Baruch (or Benedict de) Spinoza (1632–77), the Dutch (Jewish) philosopher.—**Spi-no′zist,** *n.*

spin-ster (spin′stèr), n. [See *-ster*.] A woman (sometimes, any person) who spins, esp. as a regular occupation; also, a woman still unmarried (in England, a legal designation: as, "I, Anthony Lumpkin, Esquire, of blank place, refuse you, Constantia Neville, *spinster*, of no place at all," Goldsmith's "She Stoops to Conquer," v. 3); popularly, a woman still unmarried and beyond the usual age of marrying (as, "He was a beau of all the elder ladies and superannuated *spinsters*": Irving's "Sketch-Book," Christmas Eve); an old maid.—**spin′ster-hood** (-hud), n. The state of being a spinster, unmarried woman, or old maid.—**spin′ster-ish,** *a.* Like or befitting a spinster: as, "'Carrie' was . . . at once matronly and *spinsterish*" (Sinclair Lewis's "Babbitt," xxix.); "a *spinsterish* high-necked dress" (Sinclair Lewis's "Main Street," iv.).—**spin′ster-ish-ly,** *adv.*—**spin′ster-ship,** *n.* Spinsterhood.—**spin′stress,** *n.* A female spinner; also, a spinster, or unmarried woman (as, "He . . . ventured to salute the withered cheek of the *spinstress*": Scott's "Pirate," xii.).

spin-thar-i-scope (spin-thar′i-skōp), n. [Gr. σπινθαρίς, spark: see *-scope*.] An apparatus for observing the scintillations produced in a prepared screen, as of zinc sulphide, by the action of a radium compound, a tiny flash occurring as each of the particles of which the alpha rays are composed strikes the screen.—**spin-thar-i-scop′ic** (-skop′ik), *a.*

spin-ule (spin′ūl or spī′nūl), n. [L. *spinula*, dim. of *spina*, thorn, spine.] A small spine.—**spin-u-les′cent** (-ū-les′ent), *a.* [See *-escent*.] In *bot.*, producing small spines; somewhat spiny.—**spin′u-lose** (-lōs), *a.* Furnished with spinules; also, spinule-like.

spin-y (spī′ni), a. Abounding in or furnished with spines; thorny, as a plant; covered with or having sharp-pointed processes, as an animal; also, having the form of a spine; resembling a spine; spine-like.—**spin′y=finned,** *a.* Having fins with sharp, bony rays, or spines, as an acanthopterygian.

spir-a-cle (spir′a-kl or spīr′-), n. [L. *spiraculum*, < *spirare*, breathe.] A breathing-hole; an aperture or orifice through which air or water passes in the act of respiration, as the blow-hole of a cetacean (as, "Jet after jet of white smoke was agonizingly shot from the *spiracle* of the whale": H. Melville's "Moby-Dick," lxi.); also, an opening by which a confined space has communication with the outer air; an air-hole; an opening in the ground affording an outlet for subterranean vapors, etc.—**spi-rac-u-lar** (spī-rak′ū-lär), *a.*

spi-ræ-a (spī-rē′ä), n. [L., < Gr. σπειραία, meadow-sweet, < σπεῖρα, a coil, E. *spire*[2].] Any of the herbs or shrubs constituting the rosaceous genus *Spiræa* (see cut in next column), with racemes, cymes, panicles, or corymbs of small white or pink flowers, certain species of which are much cultivated for ornament; also, a saxifragaceous shrub, *Astilbe*

japonica, with large clusters of small white flowers, which is much cultivated, esp. for Easter decoration.

spi-ral (spī′ral). [ML. *spiralis*, < L. *spira*, E. *spire*[2].] **I.** *a.* Pertaining to or of the nature of a spire or coil; spire-like; of a curve, etc., winding in the same plane round a fixed point or center and continually receding from or approaching the point; hence, winding thus but out of a single plane, as if moving round and simultaneously advancing along a cone, or winding as if coiled round and along a cylinder; helical. **II.** *n.* A plane curve which runs continuously round and round a fixed point or center while constantly receding from or approaching it; also, a similar curve, not in one plane, proceeding as if moving round and at the same time along a cone, or a curve advancing as if coiled round and along a cylinder; a helix; also, a spiral or helical object, formation, or form; also, a single circle or ring of a spiral or helical curve or object.—**spi′ral,** *v. i.* or *t.*; *-raled* or *-ralled*, *-raling* or *-ralling*. To take, or cause to take, a spiral form or course.—**spi-ral′i-ty** (-ral′i-ti), *n.* Spiral character.—**spi′ral-ly,** *adv.*

spi-rant (spī′rant), n. [L. *spirans* (*spirant-*), ppr. of *spirare*, breathe.] In *phonetics*, a consonant uttered with perceptible expulsion of breath, as *f* or *v*.

Spiræa (*S. salicifolia*).—*a*, a flower; *b*, pistil.

Flat Spiral of an Ammonite.

spire[1] (spīr), n. [AS. *spīr* = D. and G. *spier* = Sw. *spira* = Dan. *spire*, spire, shoot: cf. *spear*[1].] A stalk or stem of a plant (now rare); the portion of the trunk of a tree which rises above the point where branching begins; a stalk of flowers (as, "The giant *spires* of yellow bloom Of the sun-loving gentian": M. Arnold's "Empedocles on Etna," i. 2); also, a sprout or shoot of a plant; an acrospire of grain; a blade or spear of grass, etc.; also, an elongated mass or body which tapers to a point; a tapering, pointed part of something; a tall, sharp-pointed summit, peak, or the like (as, "The hills ran up clear above the vegetation in *spires* of naked rock": Stevenson's "Treasure Island," xiii.); esp., a tall, tapering structure, practically an elongated, upright cone or pyramid, erected on a tower, roof, etc. (as, "The castle stands upon its crags . . . in a long line of *spires* and gable ends": Stevenson's "David Balfour," vii.); specif., such a structure erected on a tower of a church or the like, and forming the upper part of the steeple (as, "The steeple, which has a *spire* to it, is placed in the middle of the church": Sterne's "Tristram Shandy," vii. 5); sometimes, the whole steeple; fig., the highest point or summit of something (as, "To silence that, Which, to the *spire* and top of praises vouch'd, Would seem but modest": Shakspere's "Coriolanus," i. 9. 24).—**spire**[1], *v.*; *spired*, *spiring*. **I.** *intr.* To grow up into a tall stalk or stem, as a plant (now prov.); also, to sprout (obs. or prov.); also, to shoot or rise into spire-like form; rise or extend to a height in the manner of a spire. **II.** *tr.* To form like a spire; also, to furnish with a spire or spires.

Spire of Senlis Cathedral, France; early 13th century.

spire² (spīr), *n.* [L. *spira*, < Gr. σπεῖρα, a coil, twist, curl.] A coil; a connected series of concentric, spiral convolutions or curves; a spiral; also, one of the series of convolutions or rings of a coil or spiral; hence, a curl, twist, wreath, or the like; in *conch.*, the upper, convoluted part of a spiral shell, above the aperture.—**spire²**, *v. i.*; spired, spiring. To wind spirally; take a spiral form or course.

spi-re-a (spī-rē′ä), *n.* See *spiræa.*

spired¹ (spīrd), *a.* Having a spire, as a tower, steeple, etc.: as, "the large, high-*spired* church" (Arnold Bennett's "Hilda Lessways," ii. 1).

spired² (spīrd), *a.* In *conch.*, having a spire, as a univalve shell; turreted.

spi-reme (spī′rēm), *n.* [Gr. σπείρημα, σπείραμα, a coil, < σπειρᾶσθαι, be coiled, < σπεῖρα, E. *spire²*.] In *biol.*, the chromatin of a cell-nucleus, when it assumes a continuous or segmented thread-like form, during the process of mitosis.

a. Spire of a Univalve Shell.

spi-rif-er-ous (spī-rif′e-rus), *a.* [L. *spira*, a coil: see *-ferous*.] Having a spire, or spiral upper part, as a univalve shell; also, having spiral appendages, as a brachiopod.

spi-ril-lum (spī-ril′um), *n.*; pl. *spirilla* (-ä). [NL., dim. of L. *spira*, E. *spire²*.] Any of the bacteria constituting the genus *Spirillum*, characterized by spirally twisted forms; also, any of various similar micro-organisms.—**spi-ril′lar** (-ril′är), *a.*

spir-it (spir′it), *n.* [OF. *espirit* (F. *esprit*), < L. *spiritus*, breathing, breath, air, life, soul, spirit, NL. distilled or alcoholic spirit, < L. *spirare*, breathe, blow: cf. *sprite* and *esprit*.] Breath†; also, a wind or breeze (obs. or archaic: as, "while the balmy western *spirit* blows," Dryden's tr. Virgil's "Georgics," ii. 447); also, the principle of conscious life, orig. identified with the breath (as, "One doubt Pursues me . . . Lest that pure breath of life, the *spirit* of man Which God inspired, cannot together perish With this corporeal clod": Milton's "Paradise Lost," x. 784); the vital principle in man, animating the body or mediating between body and soul; hence, the incorporeal part of man (as, to be present in *spirit* though absent in body); the soul as separable from the body at death (as, "And the *spirit* shall return unto God who gave it": Eccles. xii. 7); also, conscious, incorporeal being, as opposed to matter (as, the world of *spirit*); also, an incorporeal or immaterial being (as, "God is a *Spirit*": John, iv. 24); often a supernatural, incorporeal being or presence inhabiting a place or thing or having a particular character (as, *spirits* of the air or water; a household *spirit*; good or evil *spirits*); a fairy, sprite, or elf; an angel or demon; specif., a disembodied soul, as of a person after death (as, "I am thy father's *spirit*, Doom'd for a certain term to walk the night": Shakspere's "Hamlet," i. 5. 9); a ghost; also, the soul, heart, or mind as the principle of psychical being, or as the seat of thought and feeling, and esp. of the moral or religious nature (as, "What delights can equal those That stir the *spirit's* inner deeps?" Tennyson's "In Memoriam," xlii.; "The Lord Jesus Christ be with thy *spirit*," 2 Tim. iv. 22); often, the soul or heart as the seat of feelings or sentiments, or as prompting to action (as, his *spirit* rebelled at the prospect; to break a person's *spirit*); hence, mettle or courage (as, a man of *spirit*; to show *spirit*); fine or brave vigor or liveliness, as in action, words, music, etc.; *pl.*, feelings with respect to exaltation or depression (as, "His army was in high *spirits* from its victory," Froude's "Cæsar," xiv.; to be in low *spirits*); hence, cheerfulness or liveliness (as, to be out of *spirits*; "The crew were thus kept lively till they recovered their *spirits*," Kipling's "Captains Courageous," vii.); *sing.*, temper or disposition (as, meek in *spirit*); a particular attitude or bent of mind (as, a friendly, impartial, or skeptical *spirit*); a person characterized according to character, disposition, action, etc. (as, "He was a brave *spirit*," W. H. Hudson's "Far Away and Long Ago," xiv.; "There was a little knot of choice *spirits* of us," Irving's "Tales of a Traveler," ii. 4; accompanied by several kindred *spirits*; the leading *spirit* in an undertaking); also, in Biblical use, a divine inspiring or animating influence (as, "When the *spirit* rested upon them, they prophesied," Num. xi. 25; "until the *spirit* be poured upon us from on high," Isa. xxxii. 15); [*cap.*] the divine influence as an agency working in the heart of man (as, "He

that raised up Christ from the dead shall also quicken your mortal bodies by his *Spirit* that dwelleth in you": Rom. viii. 11); the third person of the Trinity (the 'Holy Spirit,' or 'Holy Ghost'); also [*l. c.*], in general use, an inspiring or animating principle, such as pervades and tempers thought, feeling, or action (as, the *spirit* of love; a *spirit* of fanaticism or of reform); the dominant tendency of anything (as, the *spirit* of the age); the prevailing tone or character of anything (as, "A change came o'er the *spirit* of my dream": Byron's "Dream," iii.); the general meaning or intent of a statement, etc. (opposed to *letter*: see *letter²*, *n.*); also, any of certain subtle fluids formerly supposed to permeate the body (as, natural, animal, and vital *spirits*); a subtle principle formerly supposed to permeate a substance and impart to it its peculiar properties; also, the essence or active principle of a substance as extracted in liquid form, esp. by distillation; a liquor obtained by distillation, esp. a strong distilled alcoholic liquor (often in *pl.*: as, "'pegs'—those vile concoctions of *spirits*, ice, and soda-water," F. M. Crawford's "Mr. Isaacs," i.); alcohol (often in *pl.*); in *phar.*, a solution in alcohol of an essential or volatile principle; in *dyeing*, any of various mordant solutions, as of tin in an acid; in *gram.*, same as *spiritus*.—**spirit of hartshorn**, an aqueous solution of ammonia. See *hartshorn*.—**spirit, or spirits, of wine**, alcohol.—**sweet spirit of niter**. See under *niter*.—**tin spirit**. See under *tin*, *a.*—**spir′it**, *v. t.* To quicken with fresh vigor (as, "Shall our quick blood, *spirited* with wine, Seem frosty?" Shakspere's "Henry V.," iii. 5. 21); also, to animate with fresh ardor or courage; inspirit; encourage; urge (*on*) or stir (*up*), as to action; also, to conjure or bring (*up*) before the mental view, as something spirit-like or unreal (as, "The Marquesas! What strange visions of outlandish things does the very name *spirit* up!" H. Melville's "Typee," i.); also, to carry (*away*, *off*, etc.) mysteriously or secretly, as in kidnapping or abducting, or in removing from sight or reach (as, "There was a considerable trade in kidnapped children, who were '*spirited* away' to America to become apprentices or bond slaves," H. G. Wells's "Outline of History," xxxvii. § 2; to *spirit* away a prisoner, or witnesses or evidence in a case).

spir-it-ed (spir′i-ted), *a.* Having or showing spirit, or mettle, courage, vigor, liveliness, etc.; mettlesome; dashing; lively; also, having a spirit, or having spirits, as specified (as, mean-*spirited*; low-*spirited*).—**spir′it-ed-ly**, *adv.*—**spir′it-ed-ness**, *n.*

spir-it-ing (spir′i-ting), *n.* The action or service of a spirit: as, "Pardon, master; I [Ariel, "an airy spirit"] will be correspondent to command And do my *spiriting* gently" (Shakspere's "Tempest," i. 2. 298). Also fig. [Archaic.]

spir-it-ism (spir′i-tizm), *n.* Belief in the power of the spirits of the dead to communicate with the living; the doctrine or practices of spiritualism.—**spir′it-ist**, *n.* A believer in spiritism; a spiritualist.—**spir-it-is′tic**, *a.*

spir-it=lamp (spir′it-lamp), *n.* A lamp in which alcohol is burned.

spir-it-less (spir′it-les), *a.* Without spirit; without vital force, or lifeless (obs. or archaic); without spirit, ardor, vigor, animation, etc.; tame; dejected or depressed.—**spir′it-less-ly**, *adv.*—**spir′it-less-ness**, *n.*

spir-it=lev-el (spir′it-lev″el), *n.* See *level*, *n.*

spi-ri-to-so (spē-rē-tō′sō), *a.* [It.] In *music*, spirited; lively.

spir-i-tous (spir′i-tus), *a.* Of the nature of spirit; immaterial, ethereal, or refined (as, "One first matter all, Endued with various forms . . . But more refined, more *spiritous*, and pure, As nearer to him placed": Milton's "Paradise Lost," v. 475); of liquors, spirituous or alcoholic. [Obs. or archaic.]

spir-it=rap-ping (spir′it-rap″ing), *n.* Rapping or knocking purporting to be a form of communication from disembodied spirits.—**spir′it=rap″per**, *n.*

spir-i-tu-al (spir′i-tū-al). [OF. F. *spirituel*, < LL. *spiritualis*, < L. *spiritus*, E. *spirit*.] **I.** *a.* Of, pertaining to, or consisting of spirit or incorporeal being (as, "Millions of *spiritual* creatures walk the earth Unseen": Milton's "Paradise Lost," iv. 677); pertaining to incorporeal or disembodied spirits, esp. the spirits of the dead (as, communications from the *spiritual* world; "those aimless ghostly perambulations and performances which, according to

village legends, diversify the leisure of the *spiritual* state," Mrs. Stowe's "Oldtown Folks," xv.); also, of or pertaining to the spirit or soul as distinguished from the physical nature (as, *spiritual* activities; *spiritual* communion or love); characterized by or suggesting predominance of the spirit (as, "*spiritual* Adeline," Tennyson's "Adeline," ii.; a *spiritual* face); ethereal or delicately refined; sometimes, clever or witty (cf. *spirituel*); esp., of or pertaining to the spirit as the seat of the moral or religious nature (as, *spiritual* comfort; "*spiritual* understanding," Col. i. 9); symbolic or mystic, with reference to the spirit or to religious things (as, a *spiritual* meaning; "Our fathers . . . drank of that *spiritual* Rock . . . and that Rock was Christ," 1 Cor. x. 4 ; "Beyond the star I saw the *spiritual* city . . . the goal of all the saints," Tennyson's "Holy Grail," 526); religious; devotional; sacred; also, of or pertaining to sacred things; pertaining or belonging to the church, or ecclesiastical (as, lords *spiritual*, in the British House of Lords, the ecclesiastical or clerical members, as distinguished from the lay members, or lords temporal); also, spirituous† or alcoholic†.
II. *n.* A spiritual thing or matter (as, "John Cocks, the archbishop's . . . vicar-general in *spirituals*": Strype's "Memorials of Cranmer," i. 4); also, a spiritual or religious song (as, negro *spirituals*).

spir-i-tu-al-ism (spir′i-tū-al-izm), *n.* Spiritual quality or tendency; insistence on the spiritual side of things, as in philosophy or religion (as, "He often checked Seth's argumentative *spiritualism* by saying, 'Eh, it's a big mystery' ": George Eliot's "Adam Bede," iv.); also, the belief or doctrine that the spirits of the dead, surviving after the mortal life, can and do communicate with the living, esp. through a person (a medium) particularly susceptible to their influence; the practices or the phenomena associated with this belief; spiritism.—**spir″i-tu-al-ist,** *a.* One who concerns himself with or insists on the spiritual side of things; also, a believer in spiritualism, or in the power of the spirits of the dead to communicate with the living; a spiritist.—**spir″i-tu-al-is′tic,** *a.*

spir-i-tu-al-i-ty (spir″i-tū-al′i-ti), *n.*; pl. *-ties* (-tiz). [OF. *spiritualite*, F. *spiritualité*, < LL. *spiritualitas*: cf. *spiritualty*.] The quality or fact of being spiritual; incorporeal or immaterial nature; predominantly spiritual character, as shown in thought, teachings, life, or appearance; devotion to the things of the spirit; spiritual tendency or tone; also, something spiritual; property or revenue of the church or of an ecclesiastic in his official capacity (often in *pl.*); also, the clergy or spirituality (archaic: as, "to bring the matter before the justices, and certain of the *spirituality*," Strype's "Memorials of Cranmer," i. 26).

spir-i-tu-al-ize (spir″i-tū-al-īz), *v. t.*; *-ized*, *-izing*. To make spiritual, as in nature, character, or appearance; also, to invest with a spiritual meaning; understand or explain in a spiritual sense.—**spir″i-tu-al-i-za′tion** (-i-zā′shon), *n.*

spir-i-tu-al-ly (spir″i-tū-al-i), *adv.* In a spiritual manner or respect.—**spir″i-tu-al-ness,** *n.*

spir-i-tu-al-ty (spir′i-tū-al-ti), *n.*; pl. *-ties* (-tiz). [OF. *spiritualte*: cf. *spirituality*.] Spirituality† or spiritual character†; also, ecclesiastical property or revenue (often in *pl.*); also, the body of ecclesiastics; the clergy.

spir-i-tu-el (spir″i-tū-el′, F. spē-rē-tü-el), *a.* [F.: see *spiritual*.] Showing fineness of mind or wit; characterized by a refined and graceful intellectuality; witty.—**spir-i-tu-elle** (spir″i-tū-el′, F. spē-rē-tü-el), *a.* [F.] Fem. of *spirituel*: sometimes used as if meaning 'spiritual' or 'ethereal,' as in appearance.

spir-i-tu-ous (spir′i-tū-us), *a.* [= F. *spiritueux*, < L. *spiritus*, E. *spirit*.] Spiritual†, incorporeal†, or immaterial†; also, spirited, lively, or vivacious (obs. or archaic); also, containing, of the nature of, or pertaining to spirit or alcohol; alcoholic; specif., of liquors, distilled, as opposed to *fermented*.—**spir″i-tu-os′i-ty** (-os′i-ti), **spir′i-tu-ous-ness,** *n.*

spir-i-tus (spir′i-tus), *n.*; pl. *-tus*. [L. and NL.: see *spirit*.] In *gram.*, a breathing, or pronunciation with or without an *h*-sound; a sign indicating such a pronunciation. See *breathing*.—**spiritus asper** (as′pėr). [LL. (L. *asper*, rough).] In *gram.*, the rough breathing.—**spiritus lenis** (lē′nis). [LL. (L. *lenis*, soft, smooth).] In *gram.*, the smooth breathing.

spir-ket (spėr′ket), *n.* [Origin obscure.] In *ship-building*, a space forward or aft between the floor-timbers.—**spir′-ket-ing, spir′ket-ting,** *n.* In *ship-building*, the inside planking between the waterways and the ports of a vessel.

spi-ro-chæte, spi-ro-chete (spī′rō-kēt), *n.* [NL. *Spirochæta*, < Gr. σπεῖρα, a coil, + χαίτη, hair.] Any of the slender, thread-like micro-organisms, characterized by narrow, spiral or screw-like windings, which constitute the genus *Spirochæta* (formerly and still sometimes regarded as protozoans, but now usually as bacteria), various species of which cause certain diseases, as syphilis (due to *S. pallida*, also known as *Treponema pallidum*).—**spi-ro-chæ′tal, spi-ro-che′tal** (-kē′tal), *a.*—**spi-ro-chæ′ti-cide, spi-ro-che′ti-cide** (-ti-sīd), *n.* [See *-cide*.] An agent for destroying spirochætes.—**spi″ro-chæ-to′sis, spi″ro-che-to′sis** (-kē-tō′sis), *n.* [NL.] Any morbid condition due to spirochætes.

spi-ro-graph (spī′rō-gràf), *n.* [L. *spirare*, breathe: see *-graph*.] An instrument for recording the frequency and extent of respiratory movements.

spi-roid (spī′roid), *a.* [See *spire*[2] and *-oid*.] More or less spiral; resembling a spiral.

spi-rom-e-ter (spī-rom′e-tėr), *n.* [L. *spirare*, breathe: see *-meter*.] An instrument for determining the capacity of the lungs, or the total amount of air expired after the fullest possible inspiration.—**spi-ro-met′ric** (-rō-met′rik), *a.*—**spi-rom′e-try,** *n.*

spirt[1], **spirt**[2] (spėrt). See *spurt*[1], *spurt*[2].

spir-u-la (spir′ö-lä), *n.*; pl. *spirulæ* (-lē). [NL., dim. < L. *spira*, E. *spire*[2].] Any of the small decapod dibranchiate cephalopods of the genus *Spirula*, having in the hinder part of the body, but not completely internal, a shell in the form of a flat spiral with separated whorls, which is divided by partitions into a series of chambers.

spir-y[1] (spīr′i), *a.* Having the form of a spire, slender shoot, or tapering, pointed body; tapering up to a point like a spire; also, abounding in spires or steeples (as, "*spiry* towns": Thomson's "Seasons," Spring, 955).

spir-y[2] (spīr′i), *a.* Spiral; coiled; curling.

spis-sat-ed (spis′ā-ted), *a.* [L. *spissatus*, pp. of *spissare*, thicken, < *spissus*, thick, dense.] Made thick, dense, or compact; inspissated.

spis-si-tude (spis′i-tūd), *n.* [L. *spissitudo*, < *spissus*, thick, dense.] Thickness; density; compactness.

spit[1] (spit), *n.* [AS. *spitu* = D. *spit* = G. *spiess*, spit.] A sharply pointed, slender rod or bar for thrusting into or through and holding meat to be roasted at a fire; hence, any of various rods, pins, or the like used for particular purposes; also, a sword; also, a narrow point of land projecting into the water (as, "Hurst Castle, a desolate and narrow blockhouse standing at the edge of a shingly *spit* on the Hampshire shore": Morley's "Oliver Cromwell," iii. 6); a long, narrow shoal extending from the shore.—**spit**[1], *v. t.*; *spitted*, *spitting*. To thrust a spit into or through; hence, to pierce, stab, or transfix as with a spit; impale on something sharp (as, "my falcon . . . who *spitted* himself on a heron's bill": Scott's "Rob Roy," x.).

spit[2] (spit), *v.*; *spit or spat, spitting*. [AS. *spittan*, *gespittan*, spit: cf. AS. *spætan* and Icel. *spýta*, spit, also E. *spittle*.] **I.** *intr.* To eject saliva from the mouth; expectorate; often, to do this at or on a person, etc., to express hatred, contempt, etc. (as, " 'The more fool you !' said Legree, *spitting* scornfully at him": Mrs. Stowe's "Uncle Tom's Cabin," xxxviii.); also, to sputter (as, "She . . . took . . . a sausage, and . . . placed it in a frying-pan on the fire . . . The sausage began to '*spit*' ": Reade's "Peg Woffington," i.); also, to fall in scattered drops or flakes, as rain or snow (as, "He heard rain flatly *spitting* in big drops on the steps": Arnold Bennett's "Roll-Call," i.). **II.** *tr.* To eject (saliva, etc.) from the mouth; hence, to throw out or emit like saliva (as, "A gun *spat* fire from the higher ground": Tarkington's "Gentleman from Indiana," xi.); utter angrily or spitefully (as, "This was not . . . the same man as had a moment ago been *spitting* angry menaces at her," Arnold Bennett's "Old

Spirula (*S. lævis*).

Wives' Tale," iii. 4: often with *out*); say or speak (*out*) without hesitation or reserve (as, "What did he say then? *Spit* it out": W. De Morgan's "Joseph Vance," iv.).—**spit²**, *n.* Saliva, esp. when ejected; also, the act or an act of spitting; also, a frothy or spit-like secretion exuded by various insects, or any of these insects (cf. *cuckoo-spit*); also, a light fall of rain or snow; also, the image, likeness, or counterpart of a person, etc. (prov. or colloq.: as, he is the very *spit* of his father).

spit-al (spit′al), *n.* [= *hospital*.] A hospital, esp. one for lazars. [Obs. or archaic.]

spit-ball (spit′bâl), *n.* A small ball or lump of chewed paper used as a missile (colloq.); in *baseball*, a variety of curve pitched by moistening one side of the ball with saliva.

spitch-cock (spich′kok), *n.* [Origin uncertain: cf. *spatch-cock*.] An eel split, cut into pieces, and broiled or fried.— **spitch′cock**, *v. t.* To split, cut up, and broil or fry (an eel); fig., to treat severely.

spite (spīt), *n.* [For *despite*.] Contempt† or scorn†; also, keen, ill-natured desire to humiliate, annoy, or injure another (as, "She hath me bounden but in *spite*, And all to flout me": Tennyson's "Pelleas and Ettarre," 321); malice; venomous ill-will; a particular instance of such ill-will, or a grudge; also, ill-natured or malicious action†; an insult† or injury†; a misfortune† (as, "The time is out of joint: O cursed *spite*, That ever I was born to set it right!" Shakspere's "Hamlet," i. 5. 189); also, vexation or chagrin (archaic or Sc.: as, "For grief and *spite* Cast herself headlong from the Ismenian steep," Milton's "Paradise Regained," iv. 574); also, contemptuous disregard, or defiance (see phrase following).— **in spite of**, or **spite of**, in contemptuous or open disregard of; in defiance of; with complete indifference to: notwithstanding: as, I'll do it *in spite of* him; he persisted *in spite of* instructions, advice, promises, hopeless conditions, etc.; "Its [the United States's] civilization, *spite of* superficial resemblances, is not English" (Gissing's "Private Papers of Henry Ryecroft," ii. 22).—**spite**, *v. t.*; *spited, spiting.* To regard with contempt or spite†; also, to wreak one's spite or malice on (as, "I am reckless what I do to *spite* the world," Shakspere's "Macbeth," iii. 1. 111; to cut off one's nose to *spite* one's face, to indulge one's spite in such a way as to injure one's self); annoy or thwart, out of spite; also, to fill with spite, or vex or offend (archaic or Sc.: as, "one so *spited* against humanity, as to place his chief pleasure in defacing . . . her fairest works," Scott's "Black Dwarf," xvi.).—**spite′ful**, *a.* Contemptuous†; also, full of spite or malice; harboring or showing spite; malicious; malevolent; venomous.—**spite′ful-ly**, *adv.*—**spite′ful-ness**, *n.*

spit-fire (spit′fir), *n.* Something that emits fire, as a cannon; also, a person of fiery temper, easily provoked to outbursts, esp. a girl or woman; sometimes, an angry cat.

Spitfire. A British fighter plane.

spit=rack (spit′rak), *n.* An iron rack formerly in use for supporting a spit or spits before a fire.

spit-ter (spit′ėr), *n.* One who spits. See *spit¹*, *spit²*.

spit-tle (spit′l), *n.* [Altered form (conformed to *spit²*) of obs. or prov. *spattle*, < AS. *spātl*, saliva, < *spǣtan*, spit: cf. *spit²*.] Saliva; spit; also, the frothy or spit-like secretion exuded by various insects.—**spit′tle-in″sect**, *n.* Any of various small, leaping homopterous insects (family *Cercopidæ*) whose young exude a frothy secretion called cuckoo-spit; a froghopper.

Spit-rack.

spit-toon (spi-tön′), *n.* [From *spit²*.] A receptacle for convenience in spitting; a cuspidor.

spitz (spits), *n.* [G. *spitz* (also *spitzhund*, spitz-dog), < *spitz*, pointed.] A kind of small dog with long hair and pointed muzzle and ears; a small variety of Pomeranian dog. Also **spitz′=dog**.

spitz-en-burg (spit′sẹn-bẻrg), *n.* [Also *spitzenburgh*, *spitzenberg*; appar. from proper name.] Any of several varieties of apple, in color red more or less diversified with yellow, of

fine flavor and suitable for winter use: as, "His full-fed cheeks . . . were curiously mottled and streaked with dusky red, like a *spitzenberg* apple" (Irving's "Knickerbocker's New York," iii. 1).

splanch-nic (splangk′nik), *a.* [NL. *splanchnicus*, < Gr. σπλαγχνικός, < σπλάγχνον, pl. σπλάγχνα, inward parts, viscera.] Of or pertaining to the viscera or entrails; visceral.

splanch-no-pleure (splangk′nō-plör), *n.* [Gr. σπλάγχνον (see *splanchnic*) + πλευρά, side.] In *embryol.*, the inner or visceral one of the two layers into which the mesoderm of craniate vertebrates splits, and which gives rise to the musculature and connective tissue of most of the intestinal tract, etc. Cf. *somatopleure*.

splash (splash), *v.* [Altered form of *plash³*.] **I.** *tr.* To wet or soil by dashing masses or particles of water, mud, or other liquid or semiliquid substance; spatter; bespatter; fall upon (something) in scattered masses or particles, as a liquid does; hence, to cause to appear as if spattered; mark as if with splashes (as, "eggs . . . creamy white *splashed* with blood-red": W. H. Hudson's "Far Away and Long Ago," vi.); also, to cause (water, etc.) to fly about (as, "The carriage, *splashing* mud, drove away": Thackeray's "Vanity Fair," xxii.); dash (water, etc.) about in scattered masses or particles; also, to cause to dash or scatter a liquid about (as, "orders to go up the river with boats . . . *splashing* their oars, and making as much noise as possible": Froude's "Cæsar," xix.); also, to make (the way) with splashing (as, "The . . . vessel ploughed and *splashed* its way up the Hudson": Irving's "Knickerbocker's New York," iii. 5). **II.** *intr.* To dash a liquid or semiliquid substance about; fall, move, or go with a splash or splashes (as, "The heavy burden *splashed* in the dark-blue waters," Scott's "Rob Roy," xxxi.; "You may see the fish-hunters . . . *splashing* through the water," H. Melville's "Omoo," lxx.); also, of liquid, to dash with force in scattered masses or particles (as, "At the end of the pier, the water is *splashing* and beating against the piles": Arnold Bennett's "Hilda Lessways," iii. 4); also, fig., to make a show or display (colloq.).—**splash**, *n.* The act or an act of splashing (as, "You see that *splash*, and immediately afterwards hear the sound of the plunging ice": Tyndall's "Forms of Water," § 50); the sound of splashing (as, "the musical *splash* of the fountain in its quiet restlessness": Mallock's "New Republic," iii. 1); also, a quantity of some liquid or semiliquid substance splashed upon a thing; a spot caused by something splashed; hence, a patch, as of color or light (as, "Here and there great *splashes* of light lay on the ground": J. Conrad's "Victory," iii. 3); also, fig., a striking show, or an ostentatious display (colloq.: as, "a band . . . for making a *splash* in the first procession," Lover's "Handy Andy," xvii.).—**splash′board**, *n.* A board, guard, or screen to protect from splashing; a dash-board of a vehicle; a guard placed over a wheel to intercept water, dirt, etc.; a screen to prevent water or spray from coming on the deck of a boat.—**splash′er**, *n.* One who or that which splashes; also, something that protects from splashes, as a splashboard, or a screen behind a wash-stand. —**splash′y**, *a.* Making a splash or splashes (as, *splashy* rain); making the sound of splashing; also, full of or marked by splashes, or irregular spots; spotty; also, fig., making a show or display (colloq.: as, "It's the yellow carriage of that old lady with her diamonds, and her two *splashy* footmen!" Marryat's "Mr. Midshipman Easy," xxiv.).

splat (splat), *n.* [Prob. related to *split*.] A broad, flat piece of wood; esp., such a piece forming the central upright part of the back of a chair.

splatch (splach), *n.* and *v.* Same as *splotch*.

splat-ter (splat′ẻr), *v. i.* or *t.* [Appar. a mixture of *splash* and *spatter*.] To splash; spatter; sputter.

splay (splā), *v.* [For *display*.] **I.** *tr.* To unfold or unfurl, as a banner†; also, to spread out, expand, or extend (as, "The fore-hoofs [of a female moose] were upright and shapely, the hind flat and *splayed*": G. White's "Nat. Hist. of Selborne," i. 28); also, to form with an oblique angle; make slanting; bevel; make with a splay or splays. **II.** *intr.* To have an oblique or slanting direction.—**splay**, *n.* Spread or flare; in *arch.*, a surface which makes an oblique angle with another, as one where the opening through a wall for a window or door widens from the position of the window or door proper toward the face of the wall; a beveled surface at the side of a window or other opening; the bevel or slant.

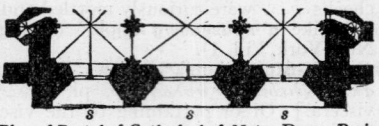

Plan of Portal of Cathedral of Notre Dame. Paris. *s, s, s,* splays.

—**splay,** *a.* Spread out; wide and flat; turned outward; fig., clumsy or awkward; oblique or awry.—**splay′=foot,** *n.* A broad, flat foot, esp. one turned more or less outward.—**splay′=foot″ed,** *a.*

spleen (splēn), *n.* [L. *splen,* < Gr. σπλήν, spleen.] A highly vascular organ or ductless gland in which the blood undergoes certain corpuscular changes, situated in man near the cardiac end of the stomach; formerly, this organ as supposed (variously) to be the seat of mirth, spirit or courage, ill humor, melancholy, etc.; hence, mirth† or gaiety† (as, "Haply my presence May well abate the over-merry *spleen*": Shakspere's "Taming of the Shrew," Induction, i. 137); also, spirit† or courage†; proud temper†; impetuosity† or eagerness†; also, ill humor, peevish temper, or spite (as, "retreating into some solitary corner, to vent their *spleen* on the first idle coxcomb they can find": Peacock's "Headlong Hall," xiii.); a grudge†; a fit of temper or passion (obs. or archaic); also, extreme depression of spirits, or melancholy (archaic: as, "When . . . *Spleen* With frightful figures spreads life's scene," M. Green's "The Spleen"); also, changeable temper† or caprice† (as, "Out, you mad-headed ape! A weasel hath not such a deal of *spleen* As you are toss'd with": Shakspere's "1 Henry IV.," ii. 3. 81); a whim† or caprice† (as, "A thousand *spleens* bear her a thousand ways": Shakspere's "Venus and Adonis," 907).—**spleen′ful,** *a.* Full of or displaying spleen; impetuous† or passionate†; ill-humored; irritable or peevish; spiteful. Also **spleen′ish.** —**spleen′wort** (-wėrt), *n.* Any of various ferns of the polypodiaceous genus *Asplenium,* having linear or oblong sori fixed obliquely on the upper side of a veinlet.—**spleen′y,** *a.* Spleenful; splenetic.

splen-dent (splen′dent), *a.* [L. *splendens* (*splendent-*), ppr. of *splendere,* shine, be bright: cf. *splendid, splendor,* and *resplend.*] Shining or radiant, as the sun; gleaming or lustrous, as metal, marble, etc.; hence, brilliant in appearance, color, etc.; gorgeous; magnificent; splendid.

splen-did (splen′did), *a.* [L. *splendidus,* < *splendere:* see *splendent.*] Shining, or very bright (now rare); hence, brilliant in appearance, color, etc. (as, *splendid* plumage; "It is a *splendid* sight to see . . . Their rival scarfs of mix'd embroidery, Their various arms that glitter in the air!" Byron's "Childe Harold," i. 40); gorgeous; magnificent; richly handsome, or sumptuous, as dress, jewels, a coach, a palace, etc.; luxuriously elegant, as entertainments, style, tastes, etc., or persons; grand; superb, as beauty; also, glorious, as a name, reputation, victory, etc.; in general, strikingly admirable or fine (as, *splendid* talents; a *splendid* conception); loosely, in enthusiastic commendation, excellent, fine, or very good (colloq.: as, a *splendid* chance; "He's a *splendid* old man," Archibald Marshall's "Anthony Dare," iii.; to have a *splendid* time, or a *splendid* sleep).—**splen′-did-ly,** *adv.*—**splen′did-ness,** *n.*

splen-dif-er-ous (splen-dif′e-rus), *a.* [Cf. OF. *splendifere,* also LL. *splendorifer,* splendor-bringing.] Splendid; magnificent; fine. [Now colloq.]

splen-dor (splen′dor), *n.* [OF. *splendur* (F. *splendeur),* < L. *splendor,* < *splendere:* see *splendent.*] Great brightness; brilliant light or luster (as, "The full moon . . . was filling the night with its mystic *splendour*": W. H. Hudson's

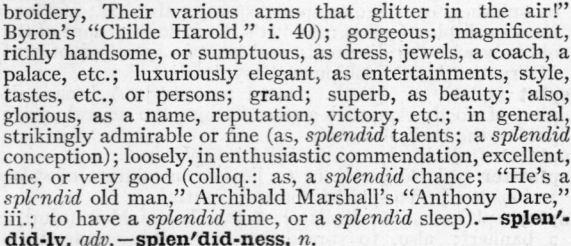

Spleenwort. — 1, 2, 3, fronds of various species.

"Purple Land," xxiii.); hence, brilliant or gorgeous appearance, coloring, etc.; magnificence, grandeur, or pomp, or an instance or display of it (as, "spectators, curious to behold the far-famed *splendors* of the Burgundian court": J. F. Kirk's "Charles the Bold," iv. 1); also, brilliant distinction; glory.—**splen′dor-ous,** *a.* Full of splendor.

splen′dour, *n.* British preferred form of *splendor.*

sple-net-ic (splē-net′ik), *a.* [LL. *spleneticus,* < L. *splen,* E. *spleen.*] Of or pertaining to the spleen; splenic; also, ill-humored, irritable or peevish, or spiteful, as persons, temper, etc.; arising from or showing spleen or ill humor (as, "*splenetic* opinions": Fielding's "Tom Jones," xi. 1); also, affected or marked by spleen or melancholy† (as, "The friend . . . Whose wit can brighten up a wintry day, And chase the *splenetic* dull hours away": Cowper's "Conversation," 582).—**sple-net′i-cal-ly,** *adv.*

sple-ni-al (splē′ni-al), *a.* In *anat.,* of or pertaining to the splenius.

splen-ic (splen′ik), *a.* [L. *splenicus,* < Gr. σπληνικός, < σπλήν, E. *spleen.*] Of or pertaining to, connected with, or affecting the spleen: as, *splenic* nerves; *splenic* fever (malignant anthrax, which is marked by enlargement of the spleen).

sple-ni-tis (splē-nī′tis), *n.* [NL., < Gr. σπληνῖτις, adj., of the spleen, < σπλήν, E. *spleen.*] In *pathol.,* inflammation of the spleen.

splen-i-tive (splen′i-tiv), *a.* [L. *splen,* E. *spleen.*] Spleenful†, impetuous†, or passionate† (as, "I am not *splenitive* and rash": Shakspere's "Hamlet," v. 1. 284); also, splenetic, ill-humored, or irritable (obs. or archaic).

sple-ni-us (splē′ni-us), *n.;* pl. *-nii* (-ni-ī). [NL., < Gr. σπληνίον, bandage.] In *anat.,* a broad, flat muscle of the upper dorsal region and the back and side of the neck, which divides into two sections in ascending the neck.

sple-noid (splē′noid), *a.* [Gr. σπλήν, spleen: see *-oid.*] Spleen-like.

sple-not-o-my (splē-not′ō-mi), *n.* [Gr. σπλήν, spleen: see *-tomy.*] In *surg.,* incision into or excision of the spleen.

spleu-chan (splū′chan), *n.* [Gael. *spliuchan.*] A pouch for holding tobacco, sometimes used as a purse: as, "There's some siller in the *spleuchan* that's like the Captain's ain" (Scott's "Guy Mannering," l.). [Sc. and Ir.]

splice (splīs), *v. t.;* spliced, splicing. [MD. *splissen* (D. *splitsen*); prob. akin to E. *split.*] To join together or unite, as two ropes or parts of a rope, by the interweaving of untwisted strands; also, to unite, as two pieces of timber, etc., by overlapping; hence, in general, to join or unite; sometimes, to join in marriage (slang: as, "Alfred and I intended to be married in this way . . . we never meant to be *spliced* in the humdrum way of other people," C. Brontë's "Villette," xl.).

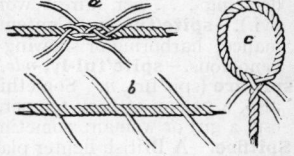

Splicing of Ropes. — *a,* short splice; *b,* long splice; *c,* eye-splice.

—**splice,** *n.* A joining together of two ropes or parts of a rope by splicing, or the union so effected; also, a joining or junction of two pieces of timber, etc., by overlapping and fastening the ends.—**spli-cer** (splī′sėr), *n.* One who or that which splices; specif., a tool used in splicing ropes.

spline (splīn), *n.* [Origin obscure.] A long, narrow, relatively thin strip of wood, metal, etc.; a slat; specif., a long, flexible strip of wood or the like used in drawing curves; in *mach.,* a flat, rectangular piece or key fitting into a groove or slot between parts; also, the groove for such a key.—**spline,** *v. t.;* splined, splining. In *mach.,* to fit with a spline or key; also, to provide with a groove for a spline or key.

Spline. — *a,* shaft; *b,* pulley; *c,* spline fitted into a groove in both *a* and *b.*

splint (splint), *n.* [ME. *splynte, splente,* = MD. and MLG. *splinte:* cf. *splinter.*] A splinter (now chiefly prov.); also, a thin strip or piece of wood, often flexible, serving a special purpose; a lath (prov. Eng.); one of a number of thin strips of wood woven together to make a chair-seat, basket, etc.; specif., a thin piece of wood or other material used to hold a fractured or dislocated bone in position when set, or to maintain any part of the body in a fixed position; any appliance

---

fat, fāte, fär, fȧll, ȧsk, fāre; net, mē, hėr; pin, pīne; not, nōte, mōve, nôr; up, lūte, pull; oi, oil; ou, out; (lightened) aviăry, ĕlect, agŏny, intŏ, ūnite; (obscured) errȧnt, operä, ardĕnt, actŏr, natūre; ch, chip; g, go; th, thin; ᴛʜ, then; y, you;

serving this purpose; also, one of a number of overlapping plates or strips of metal in armor, for protecting certain parts of the body, esp. one of the pieces of this kind for protecting the arm at the elbow (as, "The knees and feet were defended by *splints,* or thin plates of steel, ingeniously jointed upon each other": Scott's "Ivanhoe," ii.); also, an exostosis or bony enlargement of a splint-bone of a horse or an allied animal; sometimes, a splint-bone; also, splint-coal.—**splint,** *v. t.* To secure, hold in position, or support by means of a splint or splints, as a fractured bone; hence, to support as if with splints.—**splint'=ar″mor,** *n.* Armor made of splints, or overlapping plates or strips of metal.—**splint'=bone,** *n.* One of the rudimentary, splint-like metacarpal or metatarsal bones of the horse or some allied animal, closely applied one on each side of the back of each cannon-bone.—**splint'=coal,** *n.* A splintery variety of cannel-coal; also, a hard bituminous coal with a slaty structure, producing a hot fire.

a, a, Splints.

Splint-armor, 15th century.

splin-ter (splin′tėr), *n.* [ME. *splynter* = MD. D. *splinter;* related to E. *splint.*] A rough piece of wood, bone, etc., usually comparatively long, thin, and sharp, split or broken off from a main body, esp. by a violent blow (as, to get a *splinter* of wood into one's hand; "Into fiery *splinters* leapt the lance," Tennyson's "Princess," v. 483; "looking-glasses . . . shivered into ten thousand *splinters,*" Steele, in "Spectator," 32); sometimes, a thin strip or piece of wood prepared or used for a special purpose; a splint.—**splin′ter,** *v.* **I.** *tr.* To split or break into splinters (as, "The postern gate shakes . . . it crashes — it is *splintered* by his blows": Scott's "Ivanhoe," xxix.); break off in splinters; also, to secure or support by a splint or splints, as a broken limb† (as, "I bound and *splintered* up its [a goat's] leg, which was broke": Defoe's "Robinson Crusoe," i. 5). **II.** *intr.* To be split or broken into splinters (as, "a lance that *splinter'd* like an icicle": Tennyson's "Geraint and Enid," 89); break off in splinters.—**splin′ter=proof,** *a.* Proof against the splinters of bursting shells.—**splin′ter-y,** *a.* Apt to splinter (as, *splintery* wood); characterized by the production of small splinters, as a kind of fracture in minerals; rough and jagged as from splintering (as, "The ridgy precipices . . . showed their *splintery* and rugged edges": Scott's "Anne of Geierstein," i.); also, full of splinters; also, of the nature of or resembling a splinter.

split (split), *v. t.;* split (also splitted), splitting. [D. *splitten,* akin to *splijten,* MLG. *splēten,* G. *spleissen,* split: cf. *splice.*] To rend or cleave lengthwise; separate or part from end to end or between layers, often forcibly or by cutting; also, to separate off by rending or cleaving lengthwise (as, to *split* a piece from a block); also, less definitely, to tear or break asunder, rend, or burst (as, "Our helpful ship was *splitted* in the midst": Shakspere's "Comedy of Errors," i. 1. 104); hence, to divide into distinct parts or portions (as, "the practice of *splitting* freeholds for the purpose of multiplying votes": Macaulay's "Hist. of Eng.," ii.); separate (a part) by such division; divide (persons) into different groups, factions, parties, etc., as by discord; separate off (a group, etc.) by such division; divide between two or more persons, etc. (as, to *split* a bottle of wine with a friend; to *split* one's votes or vote, see phrase below); separate into parts by interposing something (as, to *split* an infinitive: see *split infinitive,* under *split, p. a.*); also, to disclose or reveal (something secret: slang).—**to split hairs,** to make excessively fine distinctions, as in reasoning.—**to split one's votes, vote,** or **ticket,** to vote for different candidates for an office or for candidates of different parties, as when one has more than one vote or is voting for candidates for a number of offices; in the U. S., commonly, to vote otherwise than for a straight party ticket.—**to split the difference,** to divide equally the difference between the claims of two parties, each party yielding half, in order to effect an agreement; compromise on the basis of a concession by each side of half of something claimed.—**split,** *v. i.* To break or part lengthwise, or suffer longitudinal division; also, to become

separated off by such division, as a piece or part from a whole; also, less definitely, to break asunder; part by striking on a rock, by the violence of a storm, etc., as a ship; hence, to part, divide, or separate in any way (as, "Presently they *split* into couples, drifting a little apart": Galsworthy's "Patrician," ii. 10); break up or separate through disagreement, etc. (as, a body *splits* into factions; "Seeing that the Democrats have *split,* this is more than an invitation to candidature," Drinkwater's "Abraham Lincoln," i.; a group *splits* from a party); also, to divide something with another or others (colloq.); also, to split one's votes, vote, or ticket (as, "I'll plump or I'll *split* for them as treat me the handsomest": George Eliot's "Felix Holt," xi.); also, to betray confidence, or turn informer (slang: as, "Lord strike you dead on the spot, if ever you *split,*" Dickens's "Great Expectations," xl.); also, to go with great speed (colloq.).—**split,** *n.* The act or an act of splitting; also, a crack, rent, or fissure caused by splitting; also, a piece or part separated by or as by splitting; a strip split from an osier, used in basket-making; one of the parallel strips forming the reed of a loom; one of the thicknesses of leather into which a skin is sometimes split or cut; often, a breach or rupture in a party, etc., or between persons (as, "The *split* among the Hussites was largely due to the drift of the extremer section towards a primitive communism": H. G. Wells's "Outline of History," xxxv. § 3); a schism; a faction, party, etc., formed by a rupture or schism; also, something split, as a fish; a split vote (colloq.); something combining different elements, as a drink composed of two liquors (colloq.); also, a drink containing only half the usual quantity (colloq.); a bottle, as of aërated water, half the usual size (colloq.); also, *sing.* or *pl.,* the feat of separating the legs while sinking to the floor, until they extend at right angles to the body, as in stage performances.—**at full split,** or **full split,** or **like split,** at full speed. [Colloq.]—**split,** *p. a.* That has undergone splitting; parted lengthwise; cleft; divided (as, a *split* vote or ticket: see phrase under *split, v. t.*); in *bot.,* deeply divided into segments; cleft.—**split infinitive,** in *gram.,* a simple infinitive with a modifier between the *to* and the verb, as 'to readily understand': a usage not grammatically incorrect, but commonly avoided by careful writers.

split=saw (split′sâ), *n.* A kind of rip-saw.

split-tail (split′tāl), *n.* A cyprinoid fish, *Pogonichthys macrolepidotus,* of California rivers: named from the form of the caudal fin.

split-ter (split′ėr), *n.* One who or that which splits.

split-ting (split′ing), *p. a.* That splits; overpoweringly noisy, as if to split the ears; violent or severe, as a headache; very fast or rapid (colloq.: as, "a *splitting* pace," Dickens's "Our Mutual Friend," iii. 15).

Splittail.

splodge (sploj), *n.* [Var. of *splotch.*] A splotch, or irregular spot; a splash; a blot: as, "that great *splodge* of ink" (W. De Morgan's "Joseph Vance," x.).—**splodg′y,** *a.*

splore (splōr), *n.* [Origin obscure.] A frolic; an escapade; also, a disturbance; a quarrel or fight. [Sc. and north. Eng.]

splotch (sploch), *n.* [Origin uncertain.] A large, irregular spot; a splash; a blot: a stain.—**splotch,** *v. t.* To mark with splotches.—**splotch′y,** *a.* Marked with splotches.

splurge (splėrj), *n.* [Appar. a made word, vaguely imit.] An ostentatious display; any pretentious proceeding or affair: as, to make a *splurge* in politics or in society; there was a big *splurge* at Mrs. Blank's last night. [Colloq.] —**splurge,** *v. i.;* splurged, splurging. To make a splurge. [Colloq.]—**splur-gy** (splėr′ji), *a.* Splurging; ostentatious. [Colloq.]

splut-ter (splut′ėr), *v.* [Appar. a var. of *sputter.*] **I.** *intr.* To talk hastily and confusedly or incoherently, as in excitement or embarrassment (as, "I wish . . . I could talk to her without *spluttering!*" Arnold Bennett's "Clayhanger," ii. 1); sputter; also, to make a sputtering sound, or emit particles of something explosively, as an apple in roasting or

---

a pen scattering ink; fly or fall in particles or drops, or spatter, as a liquid. **II.** *tr.* To utter hastily and confusedly or incoherently; sputter; also, to spatter (a liquid, etc.); bespatter (a person, etc.).—**splut′ter,** *n.* Spluttering utterance or talk; a dispute; a noise or fuss; also, a sputtering or spattering of liquid, etc.—**splut′ter-er,** *n.*

Spode (spōd), *a.* Pertaining to or made by Josiah Spode (1754–1827), a celebrated English potter.

spod-o-man-cy (spod′ō-man-si), *n.* [Gr. σποδός, ashes: see -*mancy*.] Divination by means of ashes.—**spod-o-man′tic,** *a.*

Spode Tea-pot, in colors and gold.

spod-u-mene (spod′ū-mēn), *n.* [F. *spodumène*, < Gr. σποδούμενος, ppr. of σποδοῦσθαι, be burned to ashes, < σποδός, ashes; from its action before the blowpipe.] A mineral, a silicate of aluminium and lithium, occurring usually in flattened prismatic crystals, some varieties, as hiddenite and kunzite, being used as gems.

spof-fish (spof′ish), *a.* [Origin obscure.] Bustling; fussy; officious. [Slang, Eng.]

spoil (spoil), *v. t.*; *spoiled* or *spoilt, spoiling.* [OF. *espoillier* (F. *spolier*), < L. *spoliare* (pp. *spoliatus*), strip, plunder, < *spolium,* booty, spoil. Some senses are prob. due to *spill*[2].] To strip (a defeated or fallen enemy, etc.) of arms, armor, or the like (as, "The Greeks with shouts press on, and *spoil* the dead": Pope's tr. Homer's "Iliad," iv.); strip (persons, places, etc.) of goods, valuables, etc., by force, as in war or robbery; plunder, pillage, or rob; despoil of possessions or property by extortion, fraud, or other means (as, "He desired . . . to conceal his riches, lest he should be *spoiled* by the governors of the province": Johnson's "Rasselas," viii.); rob or deprive (*of*: as, "He . . . of their fragrant physic *spoils* the fields," Pope's "Windsor Forest," 242); also, to take by force, or carry off as booty (obs. or archaic: as, "How can one enter into a strong man's house, and *spoil* his goods, except he first bind the strong man?" Mat. xii. 29); also (cf. *spill*[2], *v. t.*), to kill† or destroy†; ruin† or undo† (as, "O, I am *spoil'd*, undone by villains!" Shakspere's "Othello," v. 1. 54); hence, to damage or impair (a thing) irreparably as to excellence, value, usefulness, etc. (as, to *spoil* a cake in the making; tea *spoiled* by standing; to *spoil* one's clothes; to *spoil* a sheet of paper); in general, to mar completely (as, to *spoil* one's beauty, pleasure, or life; to *spoil* a kind act by an ungracious manner; to *spoil* style by mannerisms; "And so inconsiderate! *Spoiling* our pleasant walk!" Margaret Kennedy's "Constant Nymph," xx.); often, to impair in character or disposition by unwise treatment, benefits, etc., esp. by excessive indulgence (as, "He seems to be in no danger of being *spoilt* by good fortune," Gissing's "Private Papers of Henry Ryecroft," ii. 23; to spare the rod and *spoil* the child); treat with excessive kindness.—**to spoil the Egyptians,** fig. (with reference to Ex. iii. 22, xii. 36), to despoil the spoilers or oppressors, or those who are rich and powerful: as, "Easing a world of such misproud priests . . . of their jewels and their gimcracks, is a lawful *spoiling of the Egyptians*" (Scott's "Ivanhoe," xxxiii.).—**spoil,** *v. i.* To commit spoliation; plunder, pillage, or rob; also, to become spoiled, bad, or unfit for use, as food or other perishable substances (as, "Into this tent I brought everything that I knew would *spoil* either with rain or sun": Defoe's "Robinson Crusoe," i. 4); become tainted or putrid; decay; deteriorate.—**to be spoiling for,** to be suffering from want of or desire for; be pining for: as, he *was* evidently *spoiling for* a fight. [Colloq.]—**spoil,** *n.* [Partly < OF. *espoille,* < *espoillier,* partly < L. *spolium:* see *spoil, v.*] That which is taken in spoiling or despoiling; arms and armor stripped from a defeated enemy (usually in *pl.*); booty, loot, or plunder taken in war or robbery (as, "After contending for some time successfully with the enemy, they returned . . .

loaded with *spoil*," G. P. R. James's "Hist. of Charlemagne," iv.: often in *pl.*); fig., treasures won or accumulated (as, "But Knowledge to their eyes her ample page Rich with the *spoils* of time did ne'er unroll": Gray's "Elegy," xiii.); often, public offices with their emoluments and advantages viewed as won by a victorious political party (now usually in pl.: as, the *spoils* of office; the doctrine that to the victors belong the *spoils*); also, an object of spoliation, or a prey (as, "Chaldea shall be a *spoil*: all that spoil her shall be satisfied": Jer. l. 10); also, the act of spoiling or despoiling, or spoliation (obs. or archaic: as, "Soldiers, defer the *spoil* of the city until night," Shakspere's "2 Henry VI.," iv. 7. 142); also, destruction† or ruination†, or the cause of it† (as, "Company, villanous company, hath been the *spoil* of me": Shakspere's "1 Henry IV.," iii. 3. 11); irreparable or serious damage or harm, as to a thing or place (now rare); also, something spoiled, as in the process of manufacture; also, waste material, as that cast up in mining, excavating, quarrying, etc.; also, the cast skin, or slough, of a serpent or other animal (obs. or archaic).—**spoils system,** in *politics,* the system of practice in which public offices with their emoluments and advantages are treated as spoils of war, at the disposal of the victorious party for its own purposes and in its own (rather than the public) interest.

spoil-a-ble (spoi′la-bl), *a.* That can be spoiled.

spoil-age (spoi′lāj), *n.* The act of spoiling; also, that which is spoiled, esp. paper spoiled in printing.

spoil-er (spoi′lėr), *n.* One who or that which spoils; a plunderer or despoiler; a person or thing that spoils or seriously impairs excellence, value, etc.

spoil=five (spoil′fīv), *n.* A game of cards played by from three to ten persons having five cards each: the game being said to be 'spoiled' if no player can take three out of a possible five tricks.

spoils-man (spoilz′man), *n.*; pl. -*men.* One who seeks or receives a share in political spoils; an advocate of the spoils system in politics.

spoil=sport (spoil′spōrt), *n.* One who spoils the sport or enjoyment of others: as, "What harm will it do, just for once . . .? Don't let us be *spoil-sports*" (G. B. Shaw's "You Never Can Tell," iv.).

spoilt (spoilt). Preterit and past participle of *spoil.*

spoke[1] (spōk), *n.* [AS. *spāca* = D. *speek* = G. *speiche,* spoke.] One of the bars, rods, or rungs radiating from the hub or nave of a wheel and supporting the rim or felly; also, one of a number of pins or handles projecting from a cylinder or wheel, esp. from a steering-wheel; also, a rung of a ladder; also, a bar, rod, or pole for any of various purposes.—**to put a spoke in one's wheel,** to interpose an impediment to one's progress or action; do something to thwart one's purpose.—**spoke**[1], *v. t.*; *spoked, spoking.* To fit or furnish with or as with spokes.

spoke[2] (spōk). Preterit and archaic or prov. past participle of *speak.*

spok-en (spō′kn). Past participle of *speak.*—**spok′en,** *p. a.* Uttered or expressed by speaking; oral (opposed to *written*); also (in compounds), speaking, or using speech (as specified: as, fair-*spoken;* plain-*spoken*).

spoke=shave (spōk′shāv), *n.* A cutting tool having a blade set between two handles, orig. for shaping spokes, but now in general use for dressing wood.

spokes-man (spōks′man), *n.*; pl. -*men.* One who speaks for another or others; also, a public speaker.—**spokes′-wom″an,** *n.*; pl. -*women* (-wim″en).

spo-li-ate (spō′li-āt), *v. t.*; -*ated, -ating.* [L. *spoliatus,* pp. of *spoliare:* see *spoil, v.*] To spoil, plunder, or despoil.—**spo-li-a′tion** (-ā′shǫn), *n.* [L. *spoliatio(n-).*] The act of spoiling, plundering, or despoiling; specif., authorized plundering of neutrals at sea in time of war; also, in *law,* the act of destroying a document, or of tampering with it in such a way as to destroy its value as evidence.—**spo′li-a-tive** (-ā-tiv), *a.* Spoliatory; in *med.,* lessening the amount of the blood.—**spo′li-a-tor** (-ā-tǫr), *n.* One who commits spoliation; a spoiler or despoiler.—**spo′li-a-to-ry** (-a-tō-ri), *a.* Of the nature of or characterized by spoliation.

spon-da-ic (spon-dā′ik), *a.* [L. *spondaicus.*] Of or pertaining to a spondee; constituting a spondee; consisting of spondees; characterized by a spondee or spondees;

specif., noting a dactylic hexameter whose fifth foot is a spondee.

spon-dee (spon′dē), n. [L. *spondeus*, < Gr. σπονδεῖος, spondee, prop. adj., 'used at libations' (with reference to the meter of hymns), < σπονδή, libation, drink-offering, < σπένδειν, pour out.] In *pros.*, a foot consisting of two long syllables.

spon-du-lix, spon-du-licks (spon-dö′liks), n. [Prob. a made word.] Money; cash; funds. [Slang.]

sponge (spunj), n. [AS. *sponge*, < L. *spongia, spongea*, < Gr. σπογγιά, also σπόγγος, sponge.] Any of a group of aquatic (mostly marine) animals (phylum *Porifera*) which are characterized by a porous structure and (usually) a horny, siliceous, or calcareous skeleton or framework, and which, except in the larval state, are fixed, occurring in large, complex, often plant-like colonies; a colony of such animals; also, the light, yielding, porous, fibrous skeleton or framework of certain animals or colonies of this group, from which the living matter has been removed, characterized by readily absorbing water, and by swelling when wet and becoming soft while retaining toughness, and used when wet in bathing, in wiping or cleansing surfaces, in removing marks (as from a slate), and for other purposes; any piece of this material, as for wiping surfaces, etc.; the material itself; also, the fibrous interior of the fruit of the loofah, used in bathing, etc. ('vegetable sponge'); also, a mass of some absorbent material, as cotton gauze, employed to take up the blood and other fluids in surgical operations, etc.; also, dough raised with yeast, esp. before kneading, as for bread; a kind of light sweet pudding of spongy texture, made with gelatin, eggs, fruit-juice or other flavoring material, etc.; a metal, as platinum, when obtained as a porous or spongy mass consisting of fine, loosely cohering particles; any of various other sponge-like substances; also, a long-handled swab or brush for cleaning the bore of a cannon after its discharge; also, fig., one who or that which absorbs something freely, as a sponge does water; an immoderate drinker (as, "I will do any thing, Nerissa, ere I'll be married to a *sponge*": Shakspere's "Merchant of Venice," i. 2. 108); a person or thing as a source from which something may be readily extracted, as water from a sponge (as, "Thy monarchs . . . in distress Found thee a goodly *sponge* for pow'r to press": Cowper's "Expostulation," 531); esp., one who persistently lives at the expense of others; a parasite.—**to throw up the sponge.** See under *throw, v. t.*—**sponge,** *v.; sponged, sponging.* **I.** *tr.* To wipe or rub with a wet sponge, as in order to clean or moisten; hence, to dampen (cloth) before ironing, in manufacturing and tailoring processes, as to effect shrinkage or to dress the surface; also, to remove with a wet sponge (with *off, away*, etc.: as, "He *sponged* away blood, trickling fast down," C. Brontë's "Jane Eyre," xx.); wipe out or efface with or as with a sponge (as, "The disaster . . . was *sponged* clean from his mind like writing off a slate," Arnold Bennett's "Clayhanger," ii. 20: often with *out*); take up or absorb with a sponge or the like (often with *up*: as, to *sponge* up water); fig., to get from another or at another's expense by indirect exactions, trading on generosity or good nature, etc. (as, to *sponge* a dinner); also, to prey on or fleece (a person) in such a manner (as, "After *sponging* me well, he one morning played the part of a retrograde lover": H. Melville's "Omoo," xl.); also, to swab the bore of (a cannon). **II.** *intr.* To live meanly at the expense of others; make indirect exactions or depend or prey meanly (*on*) for what is needed or desired (as, "She only thought me a mean parasite, *sponging* on a duchess for presents above my station": Mrs. H. Ward's "Lady Rose's Daughter," iv.); also, to become spongy, as dough; also, to gather sponges.

sponge=cake (spunj′kāk), n. A very light kind of sweet cake, made with a comparatively large proportion of eggs but no shortening.—**white sponge=cake.** See *angel-cake.*

sponge=gourd (spunj′gōrd), n. The fruit of the loofah, or the plant itself.

spon-geous (spun′jus), a. [L. *spongeosus.*] Of the nature of a sponge; sponge-like; spongy.

spon-ger (spun′jėr), n. One who or that which sponges; a machine for sponging cloth in manufacture; a person who sponges on others; a person or a vessel engaged in gathering sponges.

spon-gi-ness (spun′ji-nes), n. Spongy character.

spon-ging=house (spun′jing-hous), n. Formerly, a house kept by a bailiff or sheriff's officer for the preliminary confinement of debtors, where they might have an opportunity of settling the debt before being lodged in prison: so called from the extortionate charges made on prisoners for their accommodation in such houses: as, "One of them he bailed out of a *sponging-house*, and afterward paid the debt" (Smollett's "Humphry Clinker," June 10).

spon-gi-ose (spun′ji-ōs), a. [L. *spongiosus.*] Spongy; porous. Also **spon′gi-ous.**

spon-gy (spun′ji), a.; compar. *spongier,* superl. *spongiest.* Of the nature of or resembling a sponge; light, yielding, and porous; without firmness, and readily compressible, as pith, flesh, etc.; porous but hard, as bone; absorbing or holding water or the like, **as a** sponge does, or yielding it as when pressed; deficient in solidity or substance, like a sponge; pertaining to a sponge.

spon-sion (spon′shon), n. [L. *sponsio(n-)*, < *spondere*: see *sponsor.*] An engagement or promise, esp. one made on behalf of another.

spon-son (spon′son), n. [Origin obscure.] Either of the triangular spaces or platforms before and abaft each of the paddle-boxes of a steamer; also, a gun-platform projecting from the side of a vessel.

a, a, Sponsons.

spon-sor (spon′sor), n. [L., < *spondere* (pp. *sponsus*), promise, engage, betroth: cf. *sponsion, espouse, spouse, despond,* and *respond.*] One who makes an engagement or promise on behalf of another; a surety; specif., one who answers for an infant at baptism, making the required professions and promises; a godfather or godmother; in general, one who vouches for or is responsible for a person or thing (as, to be a person's social *sponsor,* or the *sponsor* of a legislative measure).—**spon′sor,** *v. t.* To act as sponsor for; promise, vouch, or answer for.—**spon-so′ri-al** (-sō′ri-al), a. Of or pertaining to a sponsor.—**spon′sor-ship,** n. The position or office of a sponsor.

spon-ta-ne-i-ty (spon-ta-nē′i-ti), n.; pl. *-ties* (-tiz). The state, quality, or fact of being spontaneous (as, "that quality of *spontaneity* which so broadly distinguishes the best modern speaking from the prepared harangues of antiquity": Lecky's "Hist. of Eng. in the 18th Century," viii.); spontaneous activity; *pl.,* spontaneous impulses, movements, or actions.

spon-ta-ne-ous (spon-tā′nē-us), a. [LL. *spontaneus,* < L. *sponte,* of one's own accord.] Proceeding from a natural personal impulse, without external incitement or without effort or premeditation (as, *spontaneous* actions or utterances; a *spontaneous* tribute of esteem); acting freely in response to natural impulses, as a person (as, "Never before . . . had she so desired to be *spontaneous* and unrestrained": H. G. Wells's "Mr. Britling," ii. 4. § 24); natural and unconstrained, as literary style; of impulses, motion, activity, natural processes, etc., arising from internal forces or causes or independently of external agencies (as, "He thought that ideas came into clever people's heads by a kind of *spontaneous* germination": S. Butler's "Way of All Flesh," xlvi.); also, growing naturally or without cultivation, as plants, fruits, etc. (as, "The wild olive, the pomegranate, the citron . . . formed a sort of *spontaneous* orchard," J. H. Newman's "Callista," xxiv.; "But we, as if good qualities would grow *Spontaneous,* take but little pains to sow," Cowper's "Progress of Error," 364); produced by natural process; natural, as productions.—**spontaneous combustion,** the ignition of a substance or body from the rapid oxidation of its own constituents, without the application of heat from an external source.—**spontaneous generation,** in *biol.,* abiogenesis. —**spon-ta′ne-ous-ly,** *adv.*—**spon-ta′ne-ous-ness,** n.

spon-toon (spon-tön′), n. [F. *sponton, esponton,* < It. *spontone, spuntone,* spontoon, < *punto,* point.] *Milit.,* a kind of halberd, or short form of pike, formerly carried by British infantry officers and others.

spoof (spöf), *n.* [A made word.] A kind of game (Eng.); also, humbug, a piece of humbug, or a hoax (slang, orig. Eng.).—**spoof**, *v.* **I.** *tr.* To humbug; hoax; 'josh.' [Slang, orig. Eng.] **II.** *intr.* To humbug; play a hoax. [Slang, orig. Eng.]

spook (spök), *n.* [D. *spook* = MLG. *spōk, spūk*, = G. *spuk*, spook.] A ghost; a specter. [Colloq.]—**spook'ish, spook'y,** *a.* Like or befitting a spook or ghost; suited to or associated with spooks; suggestive of spooks; eerie. [Colloq.]

spool (spöl), *n.* [MD. *spoele* (D. *spoel*) = MLG. *spōle* = G. *spule*, spool.] A small cylindrical piece of wood or other material on which thread or yarn is wound in spinning, as for use in weaving; a bobbin; hence, a small cylinder of wood or other material, now typically expanded at each end and having a hole lengthwise through the center, on which thread is wound for sewing or other use; any cylindrical piece or appliance on which something is wound.—**spool,** *v. t.* To wind on a spool.—**spool'er,** *n.*

spoom (spöm), *v. i.* [Earlier *spoon*: origin obscure.] To run or scud, as a ship before the wind: as, "When virtue *spooms* before a prosp'rous gale, My heaving wishes help to fill the sail" (Dryden's "Hind and the Panther," iii. 96). [Obs. or archaic.]

spoon (spön), *n.* [AS. *spōn* = MLG. *spōn*, chip, shaving, = Icel. *spōnn*, spoon; akin to Icel. *spānn*, D. *spaan*, G. *span*, chip: cf. *span-new*.] A utensil consisting of a bowl or concave part and a handle, for taking up or stirring liquid or other food, or other matter; also, any of various implements, objects, or parts resembling or suggesting this; a spoon-like surgical instrument; a spoon-oar; a lure used in casting or trolling for fish, consisting of a bright spoon-shaped piece of metal or the like, swiveled above one or more fish-hooks, and revolving as it is drawn through the water; in *golf*, formerly, any of three clubs of different lengths, having a wooden head with a somewhat concave face; now, a club with a wooden head whose face is more lofted than that of the brassy, and with a shorter shaft; also, in colloq. use, a simple or foolish person; a sentimental lover or sweetheart; a fit of spooning.—**to be spoons on,** to have a sentimental fondness for (one of the other sex). [Colloq.]—**spoon,** *v.* **I.** *tr.* To take up or transfer in or as in a spoon; also, to fish for or catch with a spoon-bait; also, in games, to push or shove (the ball) along with a lifting motion instead of striking it smartly, as in croquet or golf; hit (the ball) up in the air, as in cricket; also, to hollow out or shape like a spoon; also, to make love to, esp. in an openly sentimental manner (colloq.: as, "He's *spooning* our schoolmarm!" Wister's "Virginian," x.). **II.** *intr.* To use a spoon; also, to fish with a spoon-bait; also, in games, to spoon the ball; also, to make love, esp. in an openly sentimental manner (colloq.).

spoon=bait (spön'bāt), *n.* A kind of artificial bait or lure used in fishing. See *spoon, n.*

spoon-bill (spön'bil), *n.* Any of the wading birds of the genera *Platalea* and *Ajaja*, closely related to the ibises, and having a long, flat bill dilated at the end like a spoon; any of various birds having a similar bill; also, the paddle-fish.—**roseate spoonbill.** See *roseate.*—**spoon'=billed,** *a.*

spoon-drift (spön'drift), *n.* [See *spoom.*] Spray swept by a violent wind along the surface of the sea; spindrift.

Spoonbill (*Platalea leucorodia*).

Spoon-er-ism (spö'nėr-izm), *n.* [From Rev. W. A. *Spooner* (1844–1930), of New College, Oxford, noted for such slips.] [Also *l. c.*] A slip of the tongue whereby initial or other sounds of words in a phrase are accidentally transposed, as in 'our queer old dean' for 'our dear old queen.'—**Spoon-er-is'tic,** *a.*

spoon'ey, *a.* and *n.* See *spoony.*

spoon-ful (spön'fúl), *n.*; pl. *-fuls.* As much as a spoon can hold; hence, a small quantity.

spoon=hook (spön'húk), *n.* A fish-hook with a spoon (lure) attached. See *spoon, n.*

spoon=meat (spön'mēt), *n.* Food taken with a spoon; soft or liquid food, esp. for infants or invalids.

spoon=oar (spön'ōr), *n.* An oar which is slightly curved lengthwise at the end of its broad blade.

spoon-y (spö'ni). **I.** *a.* Foolish; silly; also, foolishly or sentimentally amorous (as, "I never was in love myself, but I've seen many others *spoony*": Marryat's "Mr. Midshipman Easy," xxi.). [Colloq.] **II.** *n.*; pl. *spoonies* (-niz). A simple or foolish person (as, "I began the process of ruining myself in the received style — like any other *spoony*": C. Brontë's "Jane Eyre," xv.); also, one who is foolishly or sentimentally amorous. [Colloq.]

spoor (spör), *n.* [D. *spoor* = AS. and Icel. *spor*, track: cf. *speer.*] A track or trail, esp. that of a wild animal pursued as game: as, "We found the track of the wounded rhino clearly marked by great splashes of blood, and . . . the *spoor* could thus be easily followed" (J. H. Patterson's "Man-Eaters of Tsavo," xv.).—**spoor,** *v. t.* or *i.* To track by or follow a spoor.—**spoor'er,** *n.*

spo-rad-ic (spō-rad'ik), *a.* [ML. *sporadicus*, < Gr. σποραδικός, < σποράς (σποραδ-), scattered, < σπείρειν: see *spore.*] Appearing in scattered or isolated instances, as a disease; also, occurring singly, or widely apart, in locality (as, *sporadic* genera of plants); also, appearing or happening at intervals in time (as, *sporadic* recurrences or outbreaks); occasional; also, isolated, as a single instance of something; being or occurring apart from others.—**spo-rad'i-cal-ly,** *adv.*—**spor-a-dic'i-ty** (spor-ạ-dis'i-ti), *n.*

spor-a-do-sid-er-ite (spor″ạ-dō-sid'e-rīt), *n.* [Gr. σποράς (σποραδ-), scattered, + E. *siderite.*] A stony meteorite with disseminated grains of iron.

spo-ral (spō'rạl), *a.* Of or pertaining to spores.

spo-ran-gi-um (spō-ran'ji-um), *n.*; pl. *-gia* (-ji-ä). [NL., < Gr. σπορά, seed, + ἀγγεῖον, vessel.] In *bot.,* a receptacle containing spores; a spore-case.—**spo-ran'gi-al,** *a.*

spore (spör), *n.* [NL. *spora*, < Gr. σπορά (beside σπόρος), seed, orig. a sowing, < σπείρειν, sow, scatter: cf. *sperm*[1] and *sporadic.*] In *biol.,* any of various reproductive bodies or cells produced by plants and animals; esp., a reproductive body ('asexual spore') which is produced asexually and is capable of growth into a new individual, such individual often, as in ferns, etc., being one (a gametophyte) unlike that which produced the spore; less commonly, a reproductive body ('sexual spore') which is produced sexually (by the union of two gametes); hence, vaguely or figuratively, a germ, germ-cell, seed, or the like.—**spore'=case,** *n.* In *bot.,* a sporangium.—**spo-rif-er-ous** (spō-rif'e-rus), *a.* [See *-ferous.*] Bearing or producing spores.

sporo-. Form of Gr. σπορά, seed, E. *spore*, used in combination.—**spo-ro-carp** (spō'rō-kärp), *n.* [+ *-carp.*] In *bot.,* in ascomycetous fungi and red algæ, a pluricellular body developed as the product of a sexual act, serving essentially for the formation of spores; in mosses, a sporogonium.—**spo'ro-cyst** (-sist), *n.* [+ *cyst.*] In *zoöl.,* a sac or capsule which is developed when certain protozoans become encysted before sporulation; such an encysted protozoan; also, a cyst or sac containing spores, developed in the larval stage of certain trematodes; such a stage of a trematode; in *bot.,* a unicellular alga which produces spores.—**spo'ro-cyte** (-sīt), *n.* [+ *-cyte.*] In *bot.,* a cell from which a spore is derived.—**spo-ro-gen'e-sis** (-jen'e-sis), *n.* In *biol.,* the production of spores; also, reproduction by means of spores.—**spo-rog-e-nous** (spō-roj'e-nus), *a.* [+ *-genous.*] In *biol.,* producing spores, as tissue; also, reproducing or reproduced by means of spores.—**spo-ro-go'ni-um** (-gō'ni-um), *n.*; pl. *-nia* (-ni-ä). [NL. (with *-gonium* as in *archegonium*).] In *bot.,* the asexual generation in mosses, consisting of a capsule or theca within which spores are developed and which is usually borne on a stalk or seta.—**spo'ro-phore** (-fōr), *n.* [+ *-phore.*] In *bot.,* a spore-bearing process or stalk; that part of the thallus of certain fungi which develops spores; also, in ferns and mosses, the sporophyte.—**spo′ro-phyl, spo′ro-phyll** (-fil), *n.* [+ -*phyl*.] In *bot.*, a more or less modified leaf which bears spores or sporangia, as a sorus-bearing frond of a fern.—**spo′ro-phyte** (-fīt), *n.* [+ -*phyte*.] In *bot.*, the asexual form of a plant in the alternation of generations: opposed to *gametophyte*.

-sporous. Adjective termination from Gr. σπορά, seed, E. *spore*, as in *heterosporous, homosporous*.

spo-ro-zo-an (spō-rō̆-zō′an), **I.** *a.* Belonging or pertaining to the *Sporozoa*. See *sporozoön*. **II.** *n.* A sporozoön.

spo-ro-zo-ite (spō-rō̆-zō′īt), *n.* [See *sporozoön*.] In *zoöl.*, one of the minute active bodies or germs into which the spore of certain sporozoa divides, each finally developing into an adult individual.

spo-ro-zo-ön (spō-rō̆-zō′on), *n.*; pl. -*zoa* (-zō′ä). [NL., < Gr. σπορά, seed, E. *spore*, + ζῷον, animal.] In *zoöl.*, any member of the *Sporozoa*, a class or group of minute parasitic protozoans which reproduce by sporulation, and which are mouthless, absorbing fluid food osmotically.

spor-ran (spor′an), *n.* [Gael. *sporan*.] In Scottish Highland costume, a large purse, commonly of fur, worn hanging from the belt in front. See Scott's "Rob Roy," xxxiv.

sport (spōrt), *v.* [For *disport*.] **I.** *tr.* To divert† or amuse† (esp. one's self: as, "We will hence forthwith, To feast and *sport* us at thy father's house," Shakspere's "Taming of the Shrew," iv. 3. 185); pass (time) in amusement or sport (as, to *sport* the hours away); spend or squander lightly or recklessly (money or anything valuable: often with *away*); spend or stake (money) in betting, gambling, or the like†; also, to display freely in public (colloq.: as, to *sport* a roll of money, a fine horse, or a new hat; to *sport* radical opinions); have, bear, use, etc., with more or less ostentation (colloq.: as, to *sport* a title; to *sport* honorable scars; to *sport* a footman); also, to shut (one's door or 'oak'), as against visitors (Eng., chiefly university slang: as, "My rooms are . . . separated from all mankind by a great, iron-clamped, outer door, my oak, which I *sport* when I go out or want to be quiet," Hughes's "Tom Brown at Oxford," i.). **II.** *intr.* To amuse one's self with some pleasant pastime or recreation (as, "If all the year were playing holidays, To *sport* would be as tedious as to work": Shakspere's "1 Henry IV.," i. 2. 229); play, frolic, or gambol, as a child or an animal (as, "a shoal of fish *sporting* on the surface": H. Melville's "Typee," ii.); engage in some open-air or athletic pastime or sport; practise betting, gambling, or the like, or associate or interest one's self in sports or pursuits involving such practice (now chiefly as in *sporting*, *p. a.*); also, to dally, toy, or trifle playfully (as, "To *sport* with Amaryllis in the shade, Or with the tangles of Neæra's hair": Milton's "Lycidas," 68); also, to deal lightly, or too lightly, or trifle, as with something serious (as, "In irritating a madman you do but *sport* with your own life," Scott's "Castle Dangerous," xiii.; "It was selfishness which first made him *sport* with your affections," Jane Austen's "Sense and Sensibility," xlvii.); jest, as in fun or ridicule; in *biol.*, to develop as a sport, as an animal or a plant; produce sports. —**sport**, *n.* Diversion, amusement, or recreation; pleasant pastime; a particular form of pastime: esp., a pastime pursued in the open air or having an athletic character, as hunting, fishing, racing, baseball, tennis, golf, bowling, wrestling, boxing, etc.; a play† or theatrical entertainment† (see Shakspere's "Midsummer Night's Dream," iii. 2. 14); amorous dalliance† (see Shakspere's "Othello," ii. 1. 230); also, playful trifling, jesting, or mirth; mere jest or pleasantry (as, to do or say a thing in *sport*); derisive jesting, or ridicule; also, something sported with or tossed about like a plaything (as, to be the *sport* of the winds, or of circumstances; "He seemed to have been only the helpless *sport* of a sinister chance," Howells's "Chance Acquaintance," xiii.); an object of jesting, mirth, or derision (as, "Contending wits become the *sport* of fools": Pope's "Essay on Criticism," 517); a laughing-stock; also, one who is interested in sports

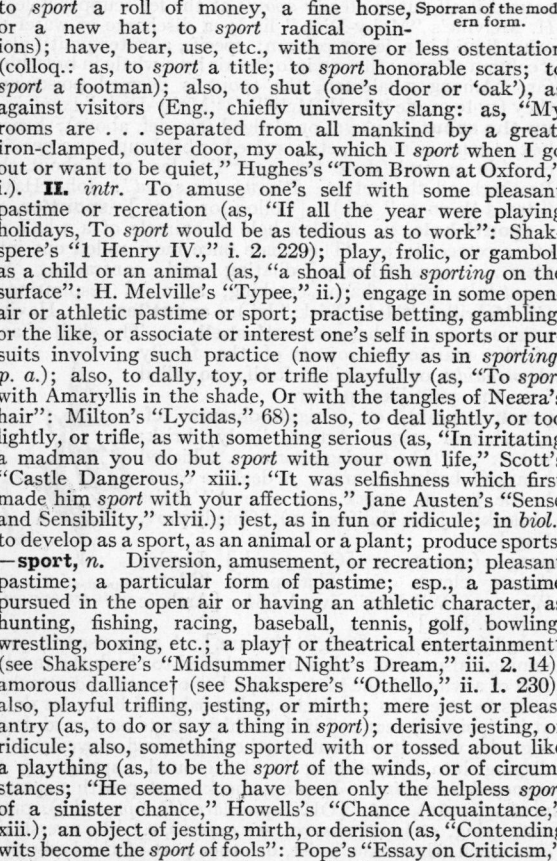

Sporran of the modern form.

or open-air pastimes; a sportsman; hence, a person of sportsmanlike or admirable qualities, or considered with reference to such qualities (slang: as, oh, be a *sport*, or a good *sport*; a cheap *sport*); hence, a fellow or man (slang); also, a sporting man, or one who is interested in pursuits involving betting or gambling (colloq.); hence, a flashy or vulgarly showy person (colloq.); any person who affects fine clothes, smart manners or pastimes, etc. (colloq.); in *biol.*, an animal or a plant, or a part of a plant, that shows an unusual or singular deviation from the normal or parent type.—**to make sport of**, to jest at; make fun of; ridicule; deride.—**to turn to sport**, to turn into or take as a matter for jesting or mirth: as, "Thrice I deluded her, and *turn'd to sport* Her importunity" (Milton's "Samson Agonistes," 396).—**sport, sports,** *a.* Of or pertaining to sport or sports, esp. of the open-air or athletic kind (as, "The Governors had recently made the discovery that a *sports* department was necessary to a good school, and had rented a field for cricket, football, and rounders": Arnold Bennett's "Old Wives' Tale," ii. 4); of garments, etc., suitable for use in open-air sports, or for outdoor or informal use generally.—**sport′er,** *n.*

sport-ful (spōrt′fúl), *a.* Full of or affording sport or diversion; amusing; also, inclined toward sport; playful; sportive; also, being or done merely in sport, rather than in earnest.—**sport′ful-ly,** *adv.*—**sport′ful-ness,** *n.*

sport-ing (spōr′ting), *p. a.* That sports; playing or frolicking; esp., engaging in, given to, or interested in open-air or athletic sports (as, a *sporting* team; a *sporting* family or community); pertaining to, concerned with, or suitable for such sports (as, *sporting* news, papers, or writers; *sporting* goods; "a few muskets and two *sporting* guns," J. Conrad's "Rescue," i. 2); sportsmanlike, as qualities, conduct, etc. (as, "By Jove, that's *sporting* of you": A. S. M. Hutchinson's "If Winter Comes," iii. 6); also, interested in or connected with sports or pursuits involving betting or gambling (as, *sporting* men; the *sporting* fraternity; *sporting* interests); also, involving or inducing the taking of risk as in sport (colloq.: as, a *sporting* proposition; to give one a *sporting* chance; to have no *sporting* blood or spirit).—**sport′ing-ly,** *adv.*

spor-tive (spōr′tiv), *a.* Inclined toward or characterized by sport; playful or frolicsome; jesting, jocose, or merry (as, "He is sometimes apt to indulge in *sportive* remarks concerning his first love": Aldrich's "Story of a Bad Boy," xix.); amorous or wanton (obs. or archaic); also, pertaining to or of the nature of sport or sports; also, done in sport, rather than in earnest; in *biol.*, tending to vary from the normal or parent type.—**spor′tive-ly,** *adv.*—**spor′tive-ness,** *n.*

sports (spōrts), *a.* See *sport, a.*

sports-man (spōrts′man), *n.*; pl. -*men.* A man who engages in sport, esp. in some open-air sport such as hunting, fishing, racing, yachting, etc.; hence, one who exhibits qualities especially esteemed in those who engage in sports, such as fairness, self-control, freedom from mercenary motives, etc.; a sportsmanlike person.—**sports′man-like, sports′man-ly,** *a.* Like or befitting a sportsman; showing the qualities proper to or esteemed in a sportsman; in keeping with the character of a sportsman, as qualities, conduct, etc.; fair or honorable.—**sports′man-ship,** *n.* The character, practice, or skill of a sportsman; sportsmanlike conduct.—**sports′wom″an,** *n.*; pl. -*women* (-wim″en).

sport-y (spōr′ti), *a.* Like or befitting a sport or sportsman; sportsmanlike; sporting; sometimes, flashy, or vulgarly showy; gay or fast (as, "He was certain that she knew he was associating with what Floral Heights called 'a *sporty* crowd' ": Sinclair Lewis's "Babbitt," xxx.); in a milder sense, smart in dress, appearance, manners, etc.; stylish. [Colloq.]

spor-u-late (spor′ọ-lāt), *v. t. or i.;* -*lated, -lating.* In *biol.*, to convert into or form sporules or spores.—**spor-u-la′tion** (-lā′shọn), *n.*

spor-ule (spor′ọl), *n.* [NL. *sporula,* dim. of *spora,* E. *spore*.] In *biol.*, a small spore; a spore; esp., a spore of certain fungi.

sposh (sposh), *n.* [Appar. imit.] Slush; watery matter; mud. [Local, U. S.]—**sposh′y,** *a.*

spot (spot), *n.* [ME. *spot* = MD. *spotte,* spot: cf. Icel. *spotti,* small piece, bit.] A mark made by foreign matter, as mud, blood, paint, ink, etc.; a stain, blot, or speck, as on a surface; hence, a moral stain, as on character or reputation; also, a blemish or flaw (as, "a lamb without blemish and without *spot*": 1 Peter, i. 19); a small scar, eruptive mark, or the like, upon the skin; in general, a relatively small, usually roundish, part of a surface differing from the rest in appearance or character (as, a *spot* of color or of light; the *spots*, or pips, on dice or playing-cards; a sun-*spot*); a patch, blotch, fleck, or dot; sometimes, a patch or beauty-spot worn on the face or elsewhere†; also, a limited portion or area of surface; a tract (as, "lab'ring well his little *spot* of ground": Dryden's tr. Virgil's "Georgics," iv. 191); a place or locality (as, the *spot* where a house stood, or where a ship sank; a monument marks the *spot*; "a lonely *spot* by a woodside," Gissing's "Private Papers of Henry Ryecroft," i. 3); a part, stage, or point in the course of something (as, a *spot* in a narrative or a book); also, a small piece or quantity of something; a particle, speck, or atom (as, "This earth, a *spot*, a grain, An atom, with the firmament compared": Milton's "Paradise Lost," viii. 17); also, one of a variety of domestic pigeons having white plumage with a spot of color on the forehead; also, a small sciænoid food-fish, *Leiostomus xanthurus*, of the eastern coast of the U. S., having dark bars on the upper part of the side and a dark spot on the shoulder (also called *lafayette*).—**blind spot.** See under *blind, a.*—**in spots,** in one spot, part, place, point, etc., and another (as, an argument weak *in spots*); also, at times, or by snatches (as, to sleep *in spots*). [Colloq.]—**on the spot,** on that very spot without waiting to change place (as, those who offered resistance were shot *on the spot*); there and then; at once; also, on that very spot, or in that place or locality, rather than elsewhere (as, to be *on the spot* when needed; "You know in business there's nothing like being *on the spot*," Dunsany's "If," i. 4).—**yellow spot.** See under *yellow, a.*—**spot,** *a.* Made, paid, delivered, etc., on the spot or at once: as, *spot* cash; *spot* freight (freight which is to be shipped at once).—**spot,** *v.*; *spotted, spotting.* **I.** *tr.* To make a spot or spots on; stain with spots; sully; blemish; also, to mark or diversify with spots, as of color; dot; stud; also, to note as of suspicious character (slang); detect or recognize (colloq.: as, "It was astonishing that a personage so notorious should not have been instantly '*spotted*' in such a resort," Arnold Bennett's "The Old Adam," ii.); single out beforehand, as the winner in a race (colloq.); also, to place on a particular spot, as a ball in billiards; scatter in various spots (as, "Stations either for sheep or cattle were *spotted* about ... over the whole country": S. Butler's "Erewhon," i.). **II.** *intr.* To make a spot; cause a stain; also, to become spotted, as some fabrics when spattered with water.

spot-less (spot'les), *a.* Free from spot, stain, blemish, marks, etc.; immaculate; unsullied.—**spot'less-ly,** *adv.*—**spot'less-ness,** *n.*

spot-light (spot'līt), *n.* In theatrical use, a strong light thrown upon a particular spot on the stage in order to render some object, person, or group especially conspicuous. Also fig.

spot-ted (spot'ed), *p. a.* Stained with a spot or spots; sullied; blemished; also, marked with or characterized by a spot or spots.—**spotted crake.** See *water-crake.*—**spotted deer.** Same as *axis².*—**spotted fever,** in *pathol.*, any of various fevers characterized by spots on the skin, esp. cerebrospinal fever or typhus fever.—**spotted moray.** See *moray.*—**spotted sandpiper.** See *sandpiper.*—**spot'ted-ness,** *n.*

spot-ter (spot'er), *n.* One who or that which spots; specif., one employed to keep watch on others, esp. on employees as for evidence of dishonesty (colloq.).

spot-ty (spot'i), *a.*; compar. *spottier,* superl. *spottiest.* Full of or having spots; spotted; characterized by or occurring in spots (as, *spotty* coloring; *spotty* vegetation); patchy; hence, lacking in uniformity or harmony of parts; irregular or uneven in quality or character (as, a *spotty* market).—**spot'ti-ly,** *adv.*—**spot'ti-ness,** *n.*

spou-sal (spou'zạl). [OF. *espousaille:* see *espousal.*] **I.** *n.* The ceremony of marriage, or nuptials (often in *pl.*); also, the married state†. **II.** *a.* Of or pertaining to marriage; nuptial; matrimonial.

spouse (spouz), *n.* [OF. *spus, spous, espous,* fem. *spuse,*

espouse (F. *époux,* fem. *épouse*), < L. *sponsus,* fem. *sponsa,* pp. of *spondere,* promise, betroth: cf. *espouse* and *sponsor.*] Either member of a married pair in relation to the other; one's husband or wife.—**spouse,** *v. t.*; *spoused, spousing.* To join, give, or take in marriage; marry: as, "He her *spous'd,* and made his joyous bride" (Spenser's "Faerie Queene," v. 3. 2). [Obs. or archaic.]—**spouse'less,** *a.* Having no spouse; unmarried or widowed: as, "The *spouseless* Adriatic mourns her lord" (Byron's "Childe Harold," iv. 11).

spout (spout), *v.* [ME. *spouten* = MD. *spouten* (D. *spuiten*), spout: cf. Icel. *spȳta,* spit, and E. *spit².*] **I.** *intr.* To discharge a liquid, etc., in a jet or continuous stream; specif., to throw up spray in breathing, as a whale; fig., to talk or speak at some length or in an oratorical manner (colloq.: as, "the dreary *spouting* of the Reverend Bartholomew Irons," Thackeray's "Vanity Fair," xxxiv.); also, to issue with force, as liquid through a narrow orifice. **II.** *tr.* To discharge or emit in a stream with some force; throw out as through a spout or pipe; fig., to utter or declaim in an oratorical manner (colloq.: as, "We *spouted* blank verse at each other": Mrs. Stowe's "Oldtown Folks," xxxix.); also, to put 'up the spout,' or pawn (slang: as, "He wouldn't *spout* the fenders and fire-irons — he ain't so bad as that," Thackeray's "Pendennis," ii. 22); also, to provide with a spout or spouts.—**spout,** *n.* A pipe or tube, or a tubular or lip-like projection, by which a liquid is discharged or poured, as from a roof or a pump, or a tea-pot or a pitcher; also, a trough or shoot for discharging or conveying grain, flour, etc.; also, a shoot or shaft formerly common in pawnbrokers' shops, up which articles pawned were sent for storage (see *up the spout,* below); hence, a pawnbroker's shop (slang); also, a blow-hole of a whale, etc.; also, a continuous stream of liquid, etc., discharged from, or as if from, a spout (as, "The rippling clear water ... ran across the deck, and poured itself out in steady *spouts* at the lee scupper-holes": H. Melville's "Moby-Dick," liv.); a discharge of water or other liquid in a jet or column; specif., a waterspout; also, a column of spray thrown into the air by a whale in breathing (as, "Among whalemen, the *spout* is deemed poisonous; they try to evade it": H. Melville's "Moby-Dick," lxxxv.).—**up the spout,** in pawn, or pledged (see def. above); hence, lost or gone, as money, etc.; ruined or bankrupt, as a person, etc.; in general, done for (as, "The less said about the Brotherhood the better. It's *up the spout*": John Hay's "Bread-Winners," xvi.). [Colloq. or slang.]—**spout'er,** *n.*—**spout'=hole,** *n.* A blow-hole or spiracle of a whale or other cetacean: as, "The whale once more rolled out into view ... spasmodically dilating and contracting his *spout-hole,* with sharp, cracking, agonized respirations" (H. Melville's "Moby-Dick," lxi.).—**spout'less,** *a.* Having no spout, as a pitcher.—**spout'=shell,** *n.* The shell of any of the marine gastropods of the family *Aporrhaidæ,* or the animal itself: so called from the spout-like aperture.

sprack (sprak), *a.* [Origin obscure: cf. *sprag¹* and *spry.*] Active; lively; brisk; smart: as, "The carriage-horse ... kicked him and broke his arm. A deal he cares: he be just as *sprack* ... as ever" (Miss Mulock's "John Halifax," x.). [Chiefly prov. Eng.]

sprag¹ (sprag), *a.* [Cf. *sprack.*] Lively; smart; clever. See Shakspere's "Merry Wives of Windsor," iv. 1. 84. [Archaic or prov. Eng.]

Spout-shell (*Aporrhais pes-pelecani*).

sprag² (sprag), *n.* [Origin obscure.] A prop used in coal-mining; also, a stout piece of wood used to check the revolution of a wheel or the like; also, a bar or metal rod attached at its front end to a vehicle, and capable of being let down at its (pointed) rear end if the vehicle starts backward down a grade, when it prevents further backward movement by digging into or catching in the ground.—**sprag²,** *v. t.*; *spragged, spragging.* To prop, check, or stop with a sprag.

sprain (sprān), *v. t.* [OF. *espreindre* (F. *épreindre*), press out, wring, < L. *exprimere:* see *express, v.*] To overstrain or wrench (the ankle, wrist, or other part of the body at a joint) so as to injure without producing dislocation.—

sprain, *n.* An act of spraining; a violent straining or wrenching of the parts surrounding a joint, without dislocation; the condition of being sprained.

sprang (sprang). Preterit of *spring.*

sprat (sprat), *n.*; pl. *sprats* or (esp. collectively) *sprat.* [Var. of earlier *sprot,* < AS. *sprot.*] A small, herring-like marine fish, *Clupea sprattus,* of European waters; also, any of various other small fishes, mostly resembling this.

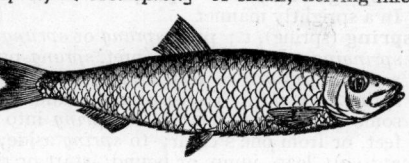

Sprat (*Clupea sprattus*).

sprat-tle (sprat′l), *v. i.*; *-tled, -tling.* [Cf. Sw. *sprattla,* sprawl, scramble.] To scramble; struggle: as, "Cattle, Or silly sheep, wha . . . thro' the drift . . . *sprattle*" (Burns's "Winter Night," 17). [Sc.]—**sprat′tle,** *n.* A scramble; a struggle: as, "in the deepest hole of the Nith, and making a *sprattle* for your life" (Scott's "Redgauntlet," ch. xii.). [Sc.]

sprawl (språl), *v.* [AS. *sprēawlian.*] **I.** *intr.* To toss or jerk the limbs about, as an infant or an animal lying on its back, or a person thrown down and struggling helplessly (as, "Jones . . . fell instantly upon the villain, and . . . laid him *sprawling* on the ground": Fielding's "Tom Jones," ix. 2); often, to struggle convulsively, as in agony (as, "First hang the child, that he may see it *sprawl*": Shakspere's "Titus Andronicus," v. 1. 51); be stretched out in irregular or ungraceful movements, as the limbs; also, to work one's way awkwardly along with the aid of all the limbs; scramble; also, to lie or sit with the limbs stretched out in a careless or ungraceful posture (as, "On painted ceilings you devoutly stare, Where *sprawl* the saints of Verrio or Laguerre," Pope's "Moral Essays," iv. 146; "*Sprawling* in the chair . . . he remained at ease," J. Conrad's "Rover," iii.); hence, to spread out in a straggling or irregular manner, as vines, buildings, handwriting, etc. (as, "Overgrown cities *sprawl* over the neighboring green fields," J. H. Robinson's "Mind in the Making," vi. 13; "The funeral sermon was written in the minister's large *sprawling* characters," S. R. Crockett's "Stickit Minister," xv.). **II.** *tr.* To stretch out (the limbs) as in sprawling (as, "The Dominie . . . had made bows . . . *sprawling* out his leg, and bending his back like an automaton": Scott's "Guy Mannering," xx.); also, to spread out or distribute in a straggling manner.—**sprawl,** *n.* The act of sprawling; a sprawling posture; also, a straggling array of something; also, activity, energy, or 'go' (prov. or colloq.).—**sprawl′er,** *n.* One who or that which sprawls; the larva of any of various moths, or the moth; esp., in the U.S., the hellgrammite, the larva of *Corydalus cornutus.*—**sprawl′y,** *a.* Tending to sprawl; straggly.

spray¹ (sprā), *n.* [ME. *spray, sprai*; origin uncertain.] Slender shoots or twigs of trees or shrubs, growing or cut, collectively (as, "He felled wood And from the trees did lop the needlesse *spray*": Spenser's "Faerie Queene," vii. 7. 42); more commonly now, a single slender shoot, twig, or branch (as, "Not a leaf nor vine Nor birch-*spray* trembling in the still moonshine": Whittier's "To C. S."); a small branch or piece of some plant with its leaves, flowers, or berries, growing or detached (as, a *spray* of oak, holly, or ivy; a *spray* of roses or of lily-of-the-valley; "I could be wishing I had brought you a *spray* of that heather," Stevenson's "David Balfour," i.); an artificial imitation of such a branch or piece, as in millinery, jewelry, etc., or a decorative figure representing one, as on a fabric.

Sprawler (Hellgrammite), two thirds natural size.

spray² (sprā), *n.* [Origin uncertain: cf. MD. *sprayen,* to sprinkle.] Water or other liquid broken up into small particles and blown or falling through the air (as, the *spray*

of a cataract; "The flying sea-*spray* drenches Fore and aft the rowers' benches," Longfellow's "Saga of King Olaf," xi.); also, a jet of fine particles of liquid discharged from an atomizer or other appliance, as for medicinal treatment, disinfecting, killing insects, etc.; a liquid to be discharged in such a jet, or an appliance for discharging it; also, a quantity of particles of matter, or of small objects, flying or discharged through the air (as, a *spray* of sand; a *spray* of bullets).—**spray²,** *v.* **I.** *tr.* To scatter in the form of spray or fine particles (as, "Where the niched snow-bed *sprays* down Its powdery fall": M. Arnold's "Switzerland," ii.); apply as a spray (as, to *spray* an insecticide upon plants); also, to sprinkle or treat with a spray (as, to *spray* plants with water or an insecticide; to *spray* the throat); direct a spray of particles, missiles, etc., upon (as, to *spray* the enemy's lines with artillery fire). **II.** *intr.* To scatter spray; discharge a spray; also, to take the form of spray; issue as spray.—**spray′er,** *n.* One who or that which sprays; an apparatus for spraying.

spray-ey¹ (sprā′i), *a.* Consisting of or resembling sprays, as of a plant.

spray-ey² (sprā′i), *a.* Forming or scattering spray; in the form of spray.

spread (spred), *v. t.*; *spread, spreading.* [AS. *sprǣdan* = D. *spreiden* = G. *spreiten,* spread.] To draw or stretch out to the full width, as a cloth, a rolled or folded map, folded wings, etc. (as, "They *spread* their blankets and lay down side by side," H. Kingsley's "Geoffry Hamlyn," xxx.: often with *out*); expand, unfold, or open; unfurl (as, "I bid ye *spread* the sail ye furled, And make on towards the straits": W. Morris's "Jason," iv. 700); extend (the arms, branches, oars, etc.); extend over a greater or a relatively great area, space, or period (often with *out*: as, to *spread* out handwriting; to *spread* out a group of persons; to *spread* payments over a term of years); force apart, as walls, rails, etc., under pressure; flatten out (as, "silver *spread* into plates," Jer. x. 9; to *spread* the end of a rivet by hammering); also, to lay out flat, as on the ground (as, "*Spread* beneath a rock, he sigh'd alone": Dryden's tr. Virgil's "Pastorals," x. 22); display in the full extent (as, "He look'd, and saw wide territory *spread* Before him, towns, and rural works between": Milton's "Paradise Lost," xi. 638); set forth in full, esp. on a record; also, to dispose or distribute in a sheet or layer (as, to *spread* hay to dry; to *spread* straw for a bed); apply in a thin layer or coating (as, "He carved . . . carvings of cherubims . . . and *spread* gold upon the cherubims": 1 Kings, vi. 32); smear (butter, jam, paint, plaster, etc.) on something; extend or distribute over a region, place, etc. (as, "O'er sandy wilds were yellow harvests *spread,*" Pope's "Windsor Forest," 88; this race is now *spread* all over the island); also, to overlay, cover, or coat with something (as, "The workman melteth a graven image, and the goldsmith *spreadeth* it over with gold": Isa. xl. 19); smear (bread, etc.) with butter or the like; set or prepare (a table, etc.), as for a meal; also, to extend over, or overspread (archaic: as, "Rich tap'stry *spread* the streets," Dryden's "Palamon and Arcite," iii. 104); also, to send out in various directions, as light, sound, mist, etc.; shed or scatter abroad; diffuse or disseminate, as knowledge, fame, news, terror, disease, etc.—**to spread one's self,** to display one's self in all one's greatness (as, "I have seen the wicked in great power, and *spreading himself* like a green bay tree": Ps. xxxvii. 35); also, to exert one's self to an unusual extent to produce a good effect or fine impression (colloq.: as, to *spread one's self* in giving a dinner; he *spread himself* on that contribution).—**spread,** *v. i.* To become stretched out or extended, as a flag in the wind; expand, as in growth (as, "And drooping chestnut-buds began To *spread* into the perfect fan": Tennyson's "Sir Launcelot and Queen Guinevere"); extend over a greater or a considerable area or period; be forced apart, as the rails of a car-track; also, to be or lie outspread or fully extended or displayed, as a landscape or scene; also, to admit of being spread or applied in a thin layer, as a soft substance; also, to become extended or distributed over a region, as population, animals, plants, etc.; become shed abroad, diffused, or disseminated, as light, influences, rumors, ideas, infection, etc.—**spread,** *n.* The act of spreading, or the state of being spread; expansion;

extension; diffusion; also, the extent of spreading (as, to measure the *spread* of the branches of a tree, or the *spread* of rails under heavy traffic); capacity for spreading (as, the *spread* of an elastic material); also, a stretch, expanse, or extent of something (as, "a vast *spread* of gorse and fern," Disraeli's "Coningsby," iii. 4; "a *spread* of level land, broad and beautiful," Wister's "Virginian," xxxiii.); also, something to be spread; a cloth covering for a bed, table, or the like; esp., a bedspread; also, any food-preparation used for spreading on bread, etc., as fruit jam or peanut butter; also, a repast set out, esp. a choice repast, or feast (colloq.); also, a pretentious display made (colloq.: as, to make a *spread*); also, in the stock-exchange, etc., a privilege consisting of a put and a call combined, giving the holder the right, at his option, either of delivering a certain amount of stock, etc., at a specified price, or of buying a certain amount of stock, etc., at another specified price, within a fixed time. —**spread**, *p. a.* Stretched out, expanded, or extended (as, *spread* sails; *spread* wings); of a precious stone, comparatively broad but shallow, or flat and thin.

spread ea-gle (spred ē'gl). A representation of an eagle with outspread wings (used as an emblem of the U. S.); also, a boastful person; also, a person tied with arms and legs outstretched, esp. to be flogged.—**spread'=ea'gle**, *a.* Having or suggesting the form of a spread eagle; also, boastful or bombastic, esp. in the display of patriotism or national vanity (as, *spread-eagle* oratory; "*spread-eagle* politicians," Sinclair Lewis's "Main Street," xxxiii.).—**spread'=ea'gle**, *v. t.*; *-gled, -gling.* To stretch out in the manner of a spread eagle (as, "I remember looking at my hand *spread-eagled* against the rock": Buchan's "Three Hostages," xxi.); tie in such a position, as a person to be punished.—**spread'=ea'gle-ism**, *n.* Boastfulness or bombast, esp. in the display of patriotism or national vanity.

spread-er (spred'ėr), *n.* One who or that which spreads; any of various devices or apparatuses for spreading something.

spree (sprē), *n.* [Origin uncertain.] A lively frolic (as, "young clerks on a mild *spree*, ready for fun": John Hay's "Bread-Winners," vii.); also, a bout or spell of drinking to intoxication; a fit of drunkenness.—**spree**, *v. i.*; *spreed, spreeing.* To go on a spree: as, "You travel together, you *spree* together" (Wister's "Virginian," xxxi.).

sprent (sprent), *pp.* [Pp. of *spreng* (otherwise obs.), < AS. *sprengan*, sprinkle, causative of *springan*, E. *spring, v.*] Sprinkled: as, "All the ground with purple bloud was *sprent*" (Spenser's "Faerie Queene," iv. 2. 18); "the brown hair *sprent* with grey" (M. Arnold's "Thyrsis"). [Archaic.]

sprew (sprö), *n.* See *sprue*[1].

sprig (sprig), *n.* [ME. *sprigge*: cf. MLG. *sprik*, dry twig.] A shoot, twig, or small branch (as, "It became a vine, and brought forth branches, and shot forth *sprigs*": Ezek. xvii. 6); a small spray of some plant with its leaves, flowers, etc. (as, a *sprig* of mint, lavender, or heather; "*sprigs* of rosemary," Shakspere's "King Lear," ii. 3. 16); an ornament or a decorative figure having the form of such a spray (as, "glasses covered with little gold *sprigs*": H. James's "Europeans," ii.); also, a person as a scion or offshoot of a family or class (as, a *sprig* of the nobility); hence, a youth or young fellow; also, a brad or headless nail with a projection on one side at the top; also, a brad or small wedge-shaped piece of tin-plate or the like, for holding glass in a sash.—**sprig**, *v. t.*; *sprigged, sprigging.* To decorate (fabrics, pottery, etc.) with a design of sprigs or small floral sprays (as, "a blue satin tie *sprigged* with gold": Kingsley's "Alton Locke," ii.); also, to fasten with sprigs or brads.—**sprig'ger**, *n.*—**sprig'gy**, *a.* Abounding in, consisting of, or resembling sprigs.

spright (sprīt), *n.* A former spelling of *sprite* (spirit).

spright-ful (sprīt'fůl), *a.* Full of spirit; spirited: as, "Spoke like a *sprightful* noble gentleman" (Shakspere's "King John," iv. 2. 177). [Obs. or archaic.]

spright-ly (sprīt'li), *a.*; compar. *sprightlier*, superl. *sprightliest.* Full of or characterized by spirit; spirited, mettlesome, or dashing (as, "that *sprightly* Scot of Scots, Douglas, that runs o' horseback up a hill perpendicular": Shakspere's "1 Henry IV.," ii. 4. 377); animated, vivacious, or cheerfully gay, as persons, the mood, looks, or air, talk, wit, etc. (as, "The young lady is very handsome, *sprightly*, and agreeable":

Smollett's "Humphry Clinker," Oct. 26); lively, as music, dances, etc.; bright, as colors; also, full of life, brisk, or fresh and sharp, as liquors, etc. (as, "And from the dregs of life think to receive What the first *sprightly* running could not give": Dryden's "Aurengzebe," iv. 1); piquant, as flavor. —**spright'li-ly**, *adv.*—**spright'li-ness**, *n.*—**spright'ly**, *adv.* In a sprightly manner.

spring (spring), *v.*; pret. *sprang* or *sprung*, pp. *sprung*, ppr. *springing.* [AS. *springan* (pret. *sprang*, pp. *sprungen*) = D. and G. *springen* = Icel. and Sw. *springa* = Dan. *springe*, spring.] **I.** *intr.* To rise or move suddenly and lightly as by some inherent power (as, to *spring* into the air, to one's feet, or from one's chair; to *spring* aside; a tiger about to *spring*); leap, jump, or bound; start or rise from cover, as partridges; go or come suddenly as if with a leap (as, the sword *springs* from its scabbard; blood *springs* to the face; "The tempest crackles on the leads, And, ringing, *springs* from brand and mail," Tennyson's "Sir Galahad," 54); shoot, dart, or fly; specif., to fly back or away in escaping from a forced position, as by resilient or elastic force or from the action of a spring (as, boughs drawn down *spring* back when released; a trap *springs*; a door *springs* to); start or work out of place, as parts of a mechanism, structure. etc.; split or crack, as a bat; become bent or warped, as boards; explode, as a mine; also, to issue suddenly, as water, blood, sparks, fire, etc. (often with *forth, out,* or *up*); spout, gush, or burst forth; well up or rise, as a stream from the earth; begin to appear, or dawn, as day, light, etc. (archaic); come into being, rise, or arise (often with *up*: as, towns, sects, or industries *spring* up; "Presently a breeze *sprang* up," H. Melville's "Moby-Dick," xci.; "Hope *springs* eternal in the human breast," Pope's "Essay on Man," i. 95); often, to arise by growth, as from a seed or germ, bulb, root, etc.; grow, as plants; proceed or originate, as from a source or cause (as, "Whence *springs* this deep despair?" Shakspere's "3 Henry VI.," iii. 3. 12); have one's birth, or be descended, as from a family, person, stock, etc. (as, "Piers Gaveston, a foreigner *sprung* from a family of Guienne": Green's "Short Hist. of the Eng. People," iv. 5); also, to rise or extend upward, as a spire; take an upward course or curve from a point of support, as an arch. **II.** *tr.* To cause to spring; rouse (partridges, etc.) from cover; cause to fly back, move, or act by elastic force, a spring, etc. (as, to *spring* a trap or a lock); cause to start out of place or work loose; split or crack (as, "The Druid has *sprung* her foremast": Cooper's "Two Admirals," xxiv.); come to have by cracking, etc. (as, to *spring* a leak, as a ship does); bend by force, or force (*in*) by bending, as a slat or bar; explode (a mine); fig., to bring out, disclose, produce, make, etc., suddenly (as, to *spring* a surprise or a piece of news on a person; to *spring* a joke); also, to cause to spring up or arise†; produce in growth†; also, to commence the upward course or curve of (an arch, etc.); also, to spring or leap over (as, "to *spring* the fence": Thomson's "Seasons," Autumn, 575); also, to fit with elastic springs, as a vehicle; also, to move by means of springs or ropes, as a ship.—**spring.** [AS. *spring, spryng.*] **I.** *n.* The act of springing; a leap, jump, or bound (as, "The dog made a *spring* at the horses' heads": Marryat's "King's Own," xlvii.); a flying back from a forced position (as, "the bow well bent, and smart the *spring*": Cowper's "Human Frailty"); an elastic or springy movement; elasticity or springiness; an elastic contrivance or body, as a strip or wire of steel coiled spirally, a strip of steel otherwise suitably shaped or adjusted, or any of various other devices, which, when compressed, bent, or otherwise forced from its normal shape, has the power of recovering this by virtue of its elasticity, and which is used for communicating motion, controlling movement, diminishing concussion, etc.; an elastic organ by which various insects are enabled to spring into the air; any moving or actuating agency (as, "Self-love, the *spring* of motion, acts the soul": Pope's "Essay on Man," ii. 59); also, a springing or starting from place; a split or crack, as in a mast; a bend or warp, as in a board; also, an issue of water from the earth, flowing away as a small stream or standing as a pool or small lake, or the place of such an issue (as, surface *springs*; mineral *springs*; hot *springs*); fig., a source of something (as, "On me, me only, as the source and *spring* Of all corruption, all the blame lights due": Milton's "Paradise Lost," x. 832); also, the act or time of springing or appearing; the dawn, as of day, light, etc. (archaic: as, "It came to pass about the *spring* of the day," 1 Sam. ix. 26; "at morning *spring* and even-fall," Whittier's "Mogg Megone," ii.); the first season of the year, in North America taken as comprising March, April, and May, in Great Britain February, March, and April; fig., the first and freshest period (as, the *spring* of life or of love); also, a springing up, arising, or originating (obs. or rare); a young growth of something, as trees (now prov. Eng.); a plantation or wood of young trees (now prov. Eng.); a shoot†, sprout†, small branch†, or young tree†; fig., a youth† or young fellow† (cf. *sprig*); also, a high tide, or spring-tide; also, the rise of an arch, or the point or line at which an arch springs from its support; also, a rope or hawser run out from some part of a ship to another vessel, a fixed object, etc., as to turn the ship into a desired position when hauled upon; also, a lively tune, esp. a dance-tune (obs. or Sc.). **II.** *a.* Of, pertaining to, characteristic of, or suitable for the season of spring (as, *spring* winds; *spring* flowers; *spring* millinery); of grain, etc., suitable for sowing in the spring.—**spring wheat.** See under *wheat.*

spring-al[1], **spring-ald**[1] (spring′al, -ald), *n.* [OF. *espringale*, prob. from Teut. and akin to E. *spring*.] A medieval military engine for throwing stones or other missiles.

spring-ald[2], **spring-al**[2] (spring′ald, -al), *n.* [Appar. < *spring*.] A youth; a young fellow: as, "A *springald* Can't, like ripe age, in gorman-dise excel" (Byron's "Don Juan," xv. 70). [Archaic.]

spring=beau-ty (spring′bū′ti), *n.*; pl. *-ties* (-tiz). An American spring flower of the portula-caceous genus *Claytonia,* esp. *C. virginica,* a low, succulent herb with a raceme of white or pink flowers.

spring=board (spring′bōrd), *n.* An elastic board used in vaulting, etc.; also, a projecting board from the end of which persons dive.

Flowers and Root of Spring-beauty (*Claytonia virginica*).

spring-bok (spring′bok), *n.* [S. Afr. D., 'spring-buck.'] A South African gazelle, *Gazella* (or *Antidorcas*) *euchore,* which has a habit of springing up-ward in play or when alarmed. Also called *springer.*

spring e (sprinj), *n.* [ME. *springe, sprenge*; prob. related to E. *spring*.] A snare for catch-ing small game: as, "*springes* to catch wood-cocks" (Shak-spere's "Ham-let," i. 3. 115). Often fig.—**springe,** *v.*; *springed, springeing.* **I.** *tr.* To catch in a springe. **II.** *intr.* To set springes; catch game with springes.

Springbok.

spring-er (spring′ėr), *n.* One who or that which springs; the springbok; a grampus; a spaniel of any of the larger breeds of field-spaniels, including the clumber, used to spring or flush game; in *arch.*, the impost of an arch, or the bottom stone of an arch resting upon the impost.

spring=gar-den (spring′gär′dn), *n.* A public pleasure-garden, as formerly in Hyde Park and at Vauxhall, London. [Now hist. or in place-names, etc.]

spring=gun (spring′gun), *n.* A gun set for trespassers, poachers, etc., or for large animals, to be discharged by accidental contact, as with a wire attached to the trigger.

spring=halt (spring′hålt), *n.* A nervous disorder in horses, causing an involuntary convulsive movement of the hind legs in walking; string-halt.

spring=head (spring′hed), *n.* The spring or fountainhead from which a stream flows; fig., the source of something.

spring=house (spring′hous), *n.* A small outbuilding con-structed over a spring or brook, used as a dairy or a place to keep meat, etc., cool. [U. S.]

spring-i-ly (spring′i-li), *adv.* In a springy manner; with a springy movement or step.—**spring′i-ness,** *n.*

spring-ing (spring′ing), *n.* The act of one who or that which springs; in *arch.*, the point or line from which an arch springs or rises; the spring.

spring-less (spring′les), *a.* Without spring or elasticity; also, without elastic springs, as a vehicle (as, "big *springless* carts": W. H. Hudson's "Far Away and Long Ago," vii.); also, without springs of water, as a region; also, having no spring season.

spring-let (spring′let), *n.* A little spring (of water): as, "Out from the little hill Oozes the slender *springlet* still" (Scott's "Marmion," vi. 37).

spring-like (spring′līk), *a.* Resembling or befitting the spring season: as, *springlike* weather; "A drowsy *springlike* sultriness pervaded the air" (Parkman's "Oregon Trail," ii.).

spring=lock (spring′lok), *n.* A lock which fastens automati-cally by a spring.

spring-tail (spring′tāl), *n.* Any of various wingless insects of the order *Thysanura,* having a pair of elastic tail-like appendages which are ordinarily folded under the abdomen, but when suddenly ex-tended enable the insect to spring into the air.—**spring′=tailed,** *a.*

spring=tide (spring′tīd), *n.* The excep-tionally high tide at or soon after the new or the full moon; fig., any great flood or swelling high rush (as, "Woe, wonder, and sen-sation high, In one *spring-tide* of ecstasy!" Scott's "Marmion," i., Introd.).

spring-tide (spring′tīd), *n.* Springtime: as, "Sounds as of the *springtide* they . . . While the chill months long for May" (Rossetti's "Love's Nocturn").

spring-time (spring′tīm), *n.* The season of spring; fig., the first or earliest period (as, the *springtime* of life; the *springtime* of the world).

Springtail, greatly enlarged.

spring-y (spring′i), *a.*; compar. *springier,* superl. *springiest.* Characterized by spring or elasticity (as, a *springy* step; "A laughing school-boy . . . Riding the *springy* branches of an elm," Keats's "Sleep and Poetry"); elastic; resilient; also, abounding in or having springs of water, as land.

sprin-kle (spring′kl), *v.*; *-kled, -kling.* [ME. *sprenklen* = D. *sprenkelen* = G. *sprenkeln,* sprinkle.] **I.** *tr.* To scatter, as a liquid or a powder, in drops or particles; let fall in minute quantities here and there; strew thinly or lightly; fig., to disperse or distribute here and there (as, "These, and such other reflections, are *sprinkled* up and down the writings of all ages": Steele, in "Spectator," 11); also, to overspread with drops or particles of water, powder, or the like; besprinkle; hence, to diversify or intersperse with objects scattered here and there (as, "A level plain Of spa-cious meads with cattle *sprinkled* o'er": Cowper's "Task," i. 164); also, to cleanse or purify, as with drops of water†. **II.** *intr.* To be sprinkled; issue in drops or particles; also, to rain slightly.—**sprin′kle,** *n.* The act or an act of sprin-kling; also, that which is sprinkled; a light rain; fig., a small quantity or number; also, a device for sprinkling something, esp. holy water†.—**sprin′kler,** *n.* One who or that which sprinkles; a device or apparatus for sprinkling.—**sprin′kling,** *n.* The act of one who or that which sprinkles; also, that which is sprinkled; a small quantity sprinkled or to be sprinkled; *fig.*, a small quantity or number scattered here and there (as, "The assembly room . . . already held a fair *sprinkling* of men": Arnold Bennett's "Clayhanger," i. 10).

sprint (sprint), *v. i.* [Cf. ME. *sprenten*, spring, leap, also E. *spurt*[1].] To spring† or leapt†; also, to go at full speed, esp. for a short distance, as in running, rowing, etc.; race in this manner. — **sprint,** *n.* A sprinting; a short spell of running, rowing, etc., at full speed; a short race at full speed. — **sprint′er,** *n.*

sprit (sprit), *n.* [AS. *sprēot* = D. *spriet*, pole; akin to E. *sprout*: cf. *bowsprit*.] A pole, esp. one for propelling a boat; *naut.*, a small pole or spar crossing a fore-and-aft sail diagonally from the mast to the upper aftmost corner, thus serving to extend the sail.

sprite (sprīt), *n.* [ME. *sprite, sprete*, < OF. F. *esprit*, < L. *spiritus*, E. *spirit*.] Spirit, or a spirit (obs. or archaic except as in the following); an elf, fairy, or goblin (as, "Of these am I, who thy protection claim, A watchful *sprite*, and Ariel is my name": Pope's "Rape of the Lock," i. 106).

Boat with Spritsail.

sprit-sail (sprit′sāl, *naut.* -sl), *n. Naut.*, a sail extended by a sprit.

sprock-et (sprok′et), *n.* [Origin obscure.] In *mach.*, one of a set of projections on the rim of a wheel, arranged so as to engage the links of a chain; hence, a sprocket-wheel. — **sprock′et=wheel,** *n.* In *mach.*, a wheel having sprockets for engaging the links of a chain passing over it.

Sprocket-wheel.

sprout (sprout), *v.* [ME. *spruten* = D. *spruiten* = MLG. *spruten* = G. *spriessen*, sprout: cf. *sprit*.] **I.** *intr.* To shoot forth, as a bud from a seed or stock; spring out or up by natural growth; also, of a seed, plant, etc., to put forth buds or shoots; specif., to germinate, or begin to grow, prematurely. **II.** *tr.* To cause to sprout forth or to put forth sprouts; also, to remove sprouts from. — **sprout,** *n.* A shoot of a plant; esp., a shoot or new growth developing from a germinating seed, or from a rootstock, tuber, bud, or the like; *pl.*, Brussels sprouts; *sing.*, in *forestry*, a tree which has grown from a stump or root; in general, something resembling or suggesting a sprout, as in growth; as applied to a person, a scion (as, "The noble Athelstane of Coningsburgh is no more—the last *sprout* of the sainted Confessor!" Scott's "Ivanhoe," xxxii.). — **a course of sprouts,** a disciplinary thrashing; a course of severe discipline. [Colloq., U. S.]

spruce[1] (sprös), *n.* [ME. *Spruce*, for *Pruce*, Prussia, used attributively to designate boards, coffers, leather, etc., from that country.] Any member of the pinaceous genus *Picea*, consisting of coniferous evergreen trees with needle-shaped leaves, as *P. abies* ('Norway spruce'), *P. canadensis* ('white spruce'), and *P. mariana* ('black spruce'); any of various allied trees, as the Douglas spruce (see *Douglas spruce*) and the hemlock-spruce (see *hemlock-spruce*); the wood of any such tree.

spruce[2] (sprös), *a.*; compar. *sprucer*, superl. *sprucest.* [Origin uncertain; perhaps the same word as *spruce*[1], through (obs.) *Spruce leather*,

Branchlet, with Cone, of Norway Spruce (*Picea abies*).

a leather from Prussia formerly used for jerkins, etc.] Smart in dress or appearance (as, "a good-looking man; *spruce* and dapper, and very tidy": Trollope's "Barchester Towers," iii.); trim; neat; dapper; fine; also, finical† or nice†. — **spruce**[2], *v.*; spruced, sprucing. **I.** *tr.* To make spruce or smart: often with *up*. **II.** *intr.* To make one's self spruce; become spruce: usually with *up*.

spruce=beer (sprös′bēr), *n.* [See *spruce*[1].] Beer from Prussia†; also, a fermented beverage made with the leaves and small branches of the spruce-tree, or with an extract prepared from them.

spruce=fir (sprös′fér′), *n.* A spruce (genus *Picea*), esp. the Norway spruce.

spruce=gum (sprös′gum′), *n.* A resinous exudation from various spruces and firs, used as a masticatory or chewing-gum, or an ingredient of chewing-gum.

spruce-ly (sprös′li), *adv.* In a spruce manner; smartly; trimly. — **spruce′ness,** *n.*

sprue[1] (sprö), *n.* [D. *spruw*.] In *pathol.*, the disease thrush; also, a tropical disease characterized by an inflamed condition of the mucous membranes of the mouth and tongue; psilosis.

sprue[2] (sprö), *n.* [Origin obscure.] In *founding*, an opening or passage through which molten metal is poured or run into a mold; also, the waste piece of metal cast in this opening.

spruit (sproit), *n.* [D., sprout, offshoot.] A small watercourse, often dry or nearly so; a small stream. [South Africa.]

sprung (sprung). Preterit and past participle of *spring*. — **sprung,** *p. a.* That has worked loose from a fastening, as a part of a tool; split or cracked, as a mast; bent or warped, as a board; tipsy or drunk (prov. or colloq.).

spry (sprī), *a.*; compar. *spryer*, superl. *spryest.* [Origin obscure: cf. *sprack*.] Active; nimble; brisk: as, "A *spry* fellow, your friend. He slipped through my hands like a shadow" (Chesterton's "Magic," i.). [Chiefly prov. or colloq.] — **spry′ly,** *adv.* — **spry′ness,** *n.*

spud (spud), *n.* [ME. *spudde*, knife; origin uncertain.] A knife† or dagger†; a spade-like instrument, esp. one with a narrow blade, as for digging up or cutting the roots of weeds; a kind of pronged instrument for digging; a small spade-like instrument used for various purposes in surgery; a chisel-like tool for removing bark; also, anything short and thick (prov. or colloq.); a potato (prov. or colloq.). — **spud,** *v. t.*; spudded, spudding. To remove with a spud. — **spud′der,** *n.* One who spuds; one who removes bark with a spud; also, a spud, or tool for removing bark.

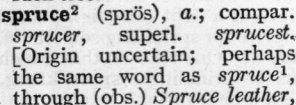

Spud for removing Bark.

spue (spū), *v.* See *spew*.

spume (spūm), *n.* [OF. F. *spume*, < L. *spuma*, foam.] Foam; froth; scum. — **spume,** *v.*; spumed, spuming. **I.** *intr.* To foam or froth. **II.** *tr.* To send forth as or like foam or froth.

spu-mes-cence (spū-mes′ens), *n.* Spumescent or foamy state; frothiness.

spu-mes-cent (spū-mes′ent), *a.* [L. *spumescens* (-ent-), ppr. of *spumescere*, grow foamy, < *spuma*, E. *spume*.] Foamy; foam-like; frothy.

spu-mo-ne (spö-mō′nä), *n.*; pl. *spumoni* (-nē). [It., < *spuma*, froth, foam, < L. *spuma*, E. *spume*.] A table delicacy of Italian origin, consisting of a cup-like or molded receptacle formed of layers of ice-cream or water-ice inclosing an inner mass of whipped cream containing bits of candied fruit, chopped nut-kernels, etc.: often made in the form of a truncated cone, which is cut vertically in wedge-shaped pieces for serving.

spu-mous (spū′mus), *a.* [L. *spumosus*, < *spuma*, E. *spume*.] Foamy; frothy; spumy: as, "a crazy boat, which made a *spumous* track upon the water as it jogged along" (Dickens's "Hard Times," ii. 1).

spum-y (spū′mi), *a.* Covered with, consisting of, or resembling spume; foamy; frothy.

spun (spun). Preterit and past participle of *spin.*—**spun,** *p. a.* That has undergone spinning; formed by or as by spinning.—**spun silk,** silk waste spun into yarn (in the manner of wool), and used for making fabrics, hosiery, etc.—**spun yarn,** *naut.,* cord formed of rope-yarns loosely twisted together: used for serving ropes, bending sails, etc.

spunk (spungk), *n.* [Orig. Sc.; origin obscure.] A spark or gleam, or a small fire (chiefly Sc.); touchwood, tinder, or punk; a friction match (Sc. and prov. Eng.); also (colloq.), courage or pluck; spirit or mettle.—**spunk,** *v. i.* With *out,* to come to light, or become known (Sc.); with *up,* to show spunk, pluck, or spirit (colloq., U. S.).—**spunk′y,** *a.;* compar. *spunkier,* superl. *spunkiest.* Full of spunk, pluck, or spirit; plucky; spirited: as, "He is a *spunky* fellow, and I'll be his second" (Marryat's "Peter Simple," iii.). [Colloq.] —**spunk′i·ly,** *adv.*—**spunk′i·ness,** *n.*

spur (spèr), *n.* [AS. *spora, spura,* = D. *spoor* = OHG. *sporo* (G. *sporn*) = Icel. *spori,* spur: cf. *spurn.*] A pricking instrument worn on a horseman's heel, for goading a horse onward; hence, anything which goads, impels, or urges to action or speed, or a stimulus, incitement, or incentive (as, "How Andy runs ! Fear's a fine *spur,*" Lover's "Handy Andy," iii.; "Necessity was the *spur* to invention," Defoe's "Captain Singleton," iii.); also, something projecting, and resembling or suggesting a spur; a sharp-pointed

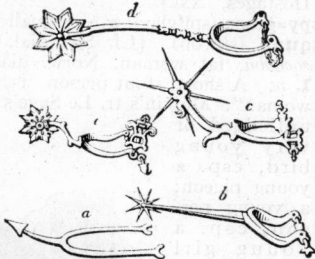

Forms of Spurs. — *a,* knight's spur (12th or 13th century); *b,* brass spur (Henry IV.); *c,* long-spiked rowel-spur (Edward IV.); *d,* long-necked brass spur (Henry VII.); *e,* steel spur (Henry VIII.).

process, formation, or growth; a stiff, usually sharp, horny process on the leg of various birds, as the domestic cock; a sharp piercing or cutting instrument fastened on the leg of a game-cock, for use in fighting; a slender, usually hollow, projection from some part of a flower, as from the calyx of the larkspur or the corolla of the violet; the disease ergot in rye and certain other cereals, characterized by horn-like growths often an inch in length; a short or stunted branch or shoot, as of a tree; any short or other branch, as of a railroad-line or railroad-track; in *carp.,* a brace, esp. one connecting or strengthening a post and some other part; in *arch.,* any offset from a wall, etc., as a buttress; specif., a griffe; in *phys. geog.,* a ridge or line of elevation projecting from or subordinate to the main body of a mountain or mountain-range (as, "The west side of the Judæan uplands consists of steep, bare *spurs* divided by narrow valleys": Buchan's "Hist. of the Great War," lxxxvii.).—**on** (or **upon**) **the spur of the moment,** on a momentary impulse; offhand; suddenly: as, "He had attempted *upon the spur of the moment* an explanation of just how much they differed" (H. G. Wells's "Soul of a Bishop," ix.).—**to set** (or **put**) **spurs to,** to start or impel by or as by applying spurs: as, "Hawker . . . *set spurs to* his noble chestnut mare" (H. Kingsley's "Geoffry Hamlyn," xliii.).—**to win one's spurs,** to win knighthood, as by prowess; hence, to win honorable recognition and reward, as by meritorious achievement; achieve one's first distinction or success.—**spur,** *v.;* spurred, spurring. **I.** *tr.* To prick with spurs or a spur, as in order to urge on; hence, in general, to urge on, impel, or incite (as, "He had *spurred* his party till he could no longer curb it": Macaulay's "Hist. of Eng.," ii.); also, to strike or wound with the spur, as one game-cock does another; also, to furnish with spurs or a spur. **II.** *intr.* To prick one's horse with the spur; ride quickly; hence, to proceed hurriedly; press forward; also, to fight or strike with the spur, as a cock.

spur=gall (spèr′gâl), *n.* A gall or sore on the side of a horse or other animal, due to the use of the spur.—**spur′=gall,** *v. t.* To gall or injure (a horse, etc.) by the use of the spur. Also fig.

spurge (spèrj), *n.* [OF. *espurge* (F. *épurge),* < *espurgier,* purge, < L. *expurgare:* see *expurgate.*] Any plant of the genus *Euphorbia,* some species of which have purgative properties; a euphorbia, esp. one of more or less inconspicuous habit; also, any of various related or similar plants.

spur=gear (spèr′gēr), *n.* In *mach.,* a gear in which spur-wheels are employed (also called *spur-gearing*); also, a spur-wheel.

spur=heeled (spèr′hēld), *a.* In *ornith.,* having a long, straight hind claw, as certain birds.

spu·ri·ous (spū′ri-us), *a.* [L. *spurius,* of illegitimate birth, false.] Of illegitimate birth; bastard; illegitimate; hence, not proceeding from the right source; irregular; unauthorized; also, not proceeding from the reputed or pretended source (as, a *spurious* document); not authentic; in general, not genuine or true; false, sham, or counterfeit (as, *spurious* gems; "He urged himself to a *spurious* curiosity about that trade," H. G. Wells's "Mr. Polly," i.).—**spurious fruit,** in *bot.,* a pseudocarp.—**spu′ri-ous-ly,** *adv.*—**spu′ri-ous-ness,** *n.*

spur-less (spèr′les), *a.* Without a spur.

Flowering Spurge (*Euphorbia corollata*) — *a,* a leaf; *b,* a flower-cluster of five male flowers and one female flower; *c,* flower-cluster, but younger, showing the cup-like base; *d,* part of the involucre; *e,* a male flower; *f,* the fruit, consisting of three carpels.

spurn (spèrn), *v.* [AS. *spornan, spurnan,* kick, reject, akin to OS. and OHG. *spurnan,* Icel. *sporna, spyrna, sperna,* kick, also to L. *spernere,* reject, and Skt. *sphur-,* jerk, dart, kick: cf. *spur.*] **I.** *tr.* To strike or tread with the foot; kick; trample; also, to reject with disdain (as, "The more she *spurns* my love, The more it grows": Shakspere's "Two Gentlemen of Verona," iv. 2. 14); treat with contempt; scorn; despise. **II.** *intr.* To kick†; also, to strike against something with the foot†; also, to manifest disdain or contempt, as in rejecting something (often with *at:* as, "I *spurn* at the slavish and bestial doctrine," Scott's "Black Dwarf," iv.); make contemptuous opposition or resistance (as, "They *spurned* at restraint and fretted under it": Roosevelt's "Winning of the West," i. 4).—**spurn,** *n.* A stroke or blow with the foot; a kick; also, disdainful rejection or contemptuous treatment, or an instance of this (as, "The insolence of office and the *spurns* That patient merit of the unworthy takes": Shakspere's "Hamlet," iii. 1. 73).—**spurn′er,** *n.*

spurred (spèrd), *a.* Having spurs or a spur.

spur-rer (spèr′ér), *n.* One who or that which spurs.

spur-rey (spur′i), *n.* See *spurry.*

spur-ri-er (spèr′i-ér), *n.* A maker of spurs.

spur=roy-al (spèr′roi′ạl), *n.* An English gold coin of the

Obverse.   Reverse.
Spur-royal of James I. — British Museum.

time of James I., worth 15 shillings: named from a figure on the reverse suggesting the rowel of a spur.

spur-ry (spur′i), *n.;* pl. *spurries* (-iz). [D. *spurrie:* cf. ML. *spergula,* spurry.] Any of various herbs of the silenaceous genus *Spergula;* esp., a white-flowered species, *S. arvensis,* with numerous whorled linear leaves, common as a weed in grain-fields, and sometimes cultivated for forage ('corn-spurry'); also, any of various allied or similar plants.

spurt[1] (spèrt), *v.* [Also *spirt*: cf. ME. *sprit* (rare), spring, dart, Icel. *spretta*, spring, dart, spurt (as water), Sw. *spritta*, spring, start, *sprätta*, spurt, G. *spritzen*, spurt.] **I.** *intr.* To gush or issue suddenly in a stream or jet, as a liquid: as, "I once more drove my weapon . . . in his prostrate form . . . the blood *spurted* afresh" (W. H. Hudson's "Green Mansions," xix.). **II.** *tr.* To throw or force out suddenly in a stream or jet, as a liquid; squirt.—**spurt**[1], *n.* [Also *spirt*: from *spurt*[1], *v.*] A forcible gush of water, etc., as from a confined place; a jet; any sudden burst, as of flame; a sudden outburst, as of feeling.

spurt[2] (spèrt), *n.* [Also *spirt*: cf. Icel. *sprettr*, a spring, run, spurt, also forms under *spurt*[1], *v.*] A sudden and brief spell of great activity or exertion (as, "He had ceased to be aggressive except in momentary *spurts*": H. G. Wells's "Tono-Bungay," i. 1. § 8); a marked increase of effort for a short period or distance, as in running, rowing, etc. (as, "She [a boat] dipped a little when they put on anything like a severe *spurt*": Hughes's "Tom Brown at Oxford," xiv.); a sudden advance or rise of prices, etc.; also, a short period of time (now prov.).—**spurt**[2], *v. i.* [Also *spirt*: from *spurt*[2], *n.*] To make a spurt (as, "The crowd . . . cheered as the St. Ambrose boat *spurted* from the Cherwell, and took the place of honour": Hughes's "Tom Brown at Oxford," xxvii.); show marked activity, or put forth one's utmost energy, for a short period.

spur=track (spèr′trak), *n.* In *railroading*, a short branch track leading from the main track, and connected with it at one end only.

spur=wheel (spèr′hwēl), *n.* In *mach.*, a wheel with projecting teeth on the periphery, which are placed radially about and parallel to the axis of the wheel: the ordinary and simplest form of gear-wheel or cog-wheel.

Spur-wheel.

spur=winged (spèr′wingd), *a.* In *ornith.*, having one or more horny spurs projecting from the bend of the wing, as certain birds.

sput-ter (sput′ėr), *v.* [Appar. a freq. form connected with *spout*.] **I.** *tr.* To eject (saliva, food, etc.) in small particles from the mouth explosively and involuntarily, as in excitement; emit (anything) in small particles as if by spitting; also, to utter hastily with emission of particles of saliva, food, or the like; utter explosively and incoherently (as, "He would *sputter* uneasy protest": Sinclair Lewis's "Main Street," xxxii.). **II.** *intr.* To eject particles of saliva, food, or the like from the mouth in an explosive manner; emit particles of anything in a similar manner, as a candle or a green stick in burning, often with explosive sounds (as, "I lighted all the fireworks at once, and tossed them whizzing and *sputtering* into the air": Parkman's "Oregon Trail," xv.); also, to utter words or sounds in an explosive, incoherent manner.—**sput′ter**, *n.* The act or the sound of sputtering; explosive, incoherent utterance; angry argument; clamor; also, matter ejected in sputtering.—**sput′ter-er**, *n.* —**sput′ter-ing-ly**, *adv.*

spu-tum (spū′tum), *n.*; pl. *-ta* (-tä). [L., spittle, prop. pp. neut. of *spuere*, spit: see *spew*.] That which is expectorated; spittle; esp., spittle mixed with mucus, purulent matter, or the like, as expectorated in certain diseased states of the lungs, etc.; a mass of such spittle.

spy (spī), *v.*; *spied*, *spying*. [OF. *espier* (F. *épier*), < OHG. *spehōn* (G. *spähen*), watch, spy; akin to L. *specere*, look at, Gr. σκέπτεσθαι, look, Skt. *spaç-*, *paç-*, *paç-*, see, look.] **I.** *tr.* To watch (a person, etc.) secretly or stealthily (now rare); make secret observations in (a place) with hostile intent (now usually with *out*); discover, or seek to discover, by secret observation; also, to view, inspect, or examine closely or carefully; view with a spy-glass or telescope; also, to find (*out*) by observation or scrutiny (as, "She had been *spying* out the riches and the poverty of the establishment": Arnold Bennett's "Helen with the High Hand," vii.); catch sight of, descry, or see (as, "At last we *spied* a sail to windward," Defoe's "Captain Singleton," xi.; "When the folk there *spy* me, They will all come up to me," W. B. Yeats's "Fiddler of Dooney"). **II.** *intr.* To make secret observations, or play the spy (as, "Do you think it right to ask a doorkeeper to *spy* on my movements?" W. Churchill's "Coniston," ii. 6);

also, to examine or search closely or carefully; make observations with a spy-glass or telescope; be on the lookout, or keep watch (as, "Several days I went about . . . *spying* for some juncture of talk to serve as introduction": Stevenson's "Master of Ballantrae," vi.).—**spy**, *n.*; pl. *spies* (spīz). [OF. *espie* (F. *épie*), < *espier*.] One who spies on others, or keeps secret watch on their actions, etc. (as, "the old man, cautious in all his movements, always acting as if surrounded by invisible *spies*": W. H. Hudson's "Green Mansions," xv.); one whose business it is to keep a person, place, etc., under close secret surveillance; one employed by a government to obtain secret information or intelligence, esp. with reference to military or naval affairs of other countries; specif., one who in time of war, acting clandestinely or on false pretenses, obtains, or seeks to obtain, information in the zone of operations of a belligerent, with the intention of communicating it to the hostile party; also, the act of spying; a careful view (as, "We had another *spy*, and made out two small lots of stags": Buchan's "Three Hostages," xxi.).

spy=glass (spī′glàs), *n.* A small telescope.

squab (skwob). [Cf. Sw. dial. *sqvabb*, loose or fat flesh, *sqvabba*, fat woman, Norw. dial. *skvabb*, soft wet mass.] **I.** *n.* A short, stout person (as, "a fat, laughing *squab* of a woman": Malkin's tr. Le Sage's "Gil Blas," v. 1); also, an unfledged or very young bird, esp. a young pigeon; a young person, esp. a young girl (slang); also, a sofa or couch; an ottoman; a thickly stuffed, soft cushion.

Squabs of Domestic Pigeon.

II. *a.* Short and stout (as, "a stout-made under-sized fellow, whose thick *squab* form had been rendered grotesque by a supplemental paunch": Scott's "Abbot," xiv.); short and thick or broad, or squat (as, "turning his *squab* nose up in the air": Scott's "Heart of Midlothian," xliv.); also, young and undeveloped; of birds, unfledged or lately hatched (as, "The *squab* young we brought down and placed on the grass-plot": G. White's "Nat. Hist. of Selborne," ii. 21).

squab-ble (skwob′l), *v.*; *-bled*, *-bling*. [Cf. Sw. dial. *sqvabbel*, a dispute.] **I.** *intr.* To engage in a petty quarrel or altercation; wrangle; brawl. **II.** *tr.* In *printing*, to disarrange and mix (composed type).—**squab′ble**, *n.* A petty quarrel or altercation; a wrangle; a brawl: as, "All the good wives of the village . . . took his part in all family *squabbles*" (Irving's "Sketch-Book," Rip Van Winkle).—**squab′bler**, *n.*

s q u a b - b y (skwob′i), *a.* Short and stout; squat; thick-set.

squac-co (skwak′ō), *n.* [It. *sguacco*.] A small, crested heron, *Ardeola* (or *Ardea*) *comata* (or *ralloides*), of southern Europe, parts of Asia, and esp. Africa.

Squacco.

squad (skwod), *n.* [F. *escouade*, earlier *esquade*, for *esquadre* (now *escadre*), < It. *squadra*: see *squadron*.] A small number of soldiers (commonly seven men and a corporal) grouped, as for drill, inspection, or duty; hence, any small group or party of persons engaged in a common enterprise, etc.; a set of persons in general; also, a quantity of anything (prov. Eng.: cf. *scad*[2]).—**squad**, *v. t.*; *squadded*, *squadding*. To form into squads; draw up in a squad; assign to a squad.

squad-ron (skwod'ron), *n.* [= F. *escadron*, < It. *squadrone*, aug. of *squadra*, a square, troop, squadron, = E. *square*, *n.*] A square†; a square of soldiers†; a relatively small body of soldiers, esp. when drawn up in regular formation; specif., in modern armies, a body of cavalry consisting usually of from 120 to 200 men; also, a portion of a naval fleet, or a detachment of war-ships employed on a particular service (as, "the flagship of the French Pacific *squadron*": J. Conrad's "Lord Jim," xiii.); also, a number of aëroplanes or other aircraft which operate together, or a military unit composed of a certain number of aëroplanes together with the necessary personnel, transportation equipment, etc. (as, "The little *squadron* of aeroplanes flew up a broad valley towards a pass": H. G. Wells's "Men Like Gods," i. 3); also, in non-military use, a number of persons grouped or united together for some purpose; a group or body in general (as, "A stately *squadron* of snowy geese were riding in an adjoining pond": Irving's "Sketch-Book," Sleepy Hollow). —**squad'ron**, *v. t.* To form into a squadron or squadrons; marshal or array in or as in squadrons: usually in *squadroned*, *pp.*—**squad'ron-al**, *a.*

squail (skwāl), *n.* [Origin uncertain.] One of a number of disks or counters in a certain table-game, driven by snapping toward a mark in the center of the table; *pl.* (construed as *sing.*), the game itself.

squal-id (skwol'id), *a.* [L. *squalidus*, < *squalere*, be stiff, rough, or dry, be filthy: cf. *squalor*.] Foul and repulsive, as from the want of care or cleanliness (as, "In the *squalid*, naked wretch who addressed him, he recognized Don Silvio!" Marryat's "Mr. Midshipman Easy," xxx.; "He would . . . prowl about the city by night, especially in the *squalid* quarters, where he would make the acquaintance of the very poor in their hovels," W. H. Hudson's "Far Away and Long Ago," viii.); dirty; filthy; hence, wretched, miserable, or degraded (as, "the *squalid* belief in witchcraft": J. H. Robinson's "Mind in the Making," vi. 12).—**squa-lid-i-ty** (skwo-lid'i-ti), **squal'id-ness**, *n.*—**squal'id-ly**, *adv.*

squall[1] (skwâl), *n.* [Cf. Sw. *sqval*, rush of water, *sqvalregn*, downpour.] A sudden, violent gust of wind, or a succession of such gusts, often accompanied by rain, snow, or sleet (as, "In crossing the bay, we met with a *squall* that tore our rotten sails to pieces," B. Franklin's "Autobiography," ii.; "Then a sharp *squall* of rain broke," Arnold Bennett's "Lion's Share," vii.); fig., a disturbance or commotion; a quarrel.— **squall**[1], *v. i.* To blow in a squall.

squall[2] (skwâl), *v.* [Imit.: cf. *squeal*.] **I.** *intr.* To cry out loudly and discordantly; scream violently: as, "Jenkins . . . was kicking her heels and *squalling* with great vociferation" (Smollett's "Humphry Clinker," May 24); "The parrot scream'd, the peacock *squall'd*" (Tennyson's "Day-Dream," 144). **II.** *tr.* To utter in a discordant, screaming tone.—**squall**[2], *n.* The act or sound of squalling; a loud, discordant cry (as, "The baby . . . set up . . . a terrific *squall*": Miss Mulock's "John Halifax," x.).—**squall'er**, *n.*

squall-y (skwâ'li), *a.* Characterized by squalls; disturbed with sudden and violent gusts of wind (as, "*squally*, misty weather": J. Conrad's "Lord Jim," xxxviii.); of the wind, blowing in squalls (as, "It was raining again, with a *squally* wind": Arnold Bennett's "Riceyman Steps," i. 7); fig., threatening or troublous (colloq.).

squa-loid (skwā'loid), *a.* [NL. *Squalus*, genus of sharks, < L. *squalus*, kind of sea-fish: see -*oid*.] Shark-like; pertaining to the sharks.

squal-or (skwol'or or skwā'lor), *n.* [L., < *squalere*: see *squalid*.] The state of being squalid; foulness; filthiness; degraded condition.

squa-ma (skwā'mä), *n.*; pl. -*mæ* (-mē). [L., scale.] A scale or scale-like part, as of epidermis or bone.—**squa-ma-ceous** (skwä-mā'shius), *a.* Scaly.—**squa-mate** (skwā'māt), *a.* [LL. *squamatus.*] Provided or covered with squamæ or scales; scaly; also, scale-like.—**squa-ma-tion** (skwä-mā'shon), *n.* The state of being squamate, or covered with

scales; also, the squamæ or scales of an animal, or their character or arrangement.

squa-mel-late (skwä-mel'āt), *a.* Same as *squamulate*.

squa-moid (skwā'moid), *a.* [L. *squama*, scale: see -*oid*.] Scale-like; scaly.

squa-mo-sal (skwä-mō'sal). [See *squamous.*] In *anat.*: **I.** *a.* Noting or pertaining to a thin scale-like bone (an element of the temporal bone) in the skull of man, or a corresponding bone in other vertebrates. **II.** *n.* A squamosal bone.

squa-mose (skwā'mōs), *a.* Same as *squamous*.

squa-mous (skwā'mus), *a.* [L. *squamosus*, < *squama*, scale.] Furnished or covered with, or formed of, squamæ or scales, or parts resembling scales; characterized by the development of scales; scale-like; specif., in *anat.*, squamosal.—**squa'mous-ly**, *adv.*—**squa'mous-ness**, *n.*

squam-u-late, squam-u-lose (skwam'ū-lāt, -lōs), *a.* [L. *squamula*, dim. of *squama*, scale.] Furnished or covered with small scales.

squan-der (skwon'dėr), *v.* [Origin obscure.] **I.** *tr.* To scatter or disperse (as, "Other ventures he hath, *squandered* abroad," Shakspere's "Merchant of Venice," i. 3. 22: now chiefly prov.); also, to spend (money, time, etc.) extravagantly or wastefully (often with *away*: as, "He had *squandered* her money in a speculation," Arnold Bennett's "Hilda Lessways," vi. 6; "They considered the time occupied in learning as so much *squandered* away," Borrow's "Bible in Spain," i.); waste; dissipate. **II.** *intr.* To scatter or disperse (now chiefly prov.); also, to wander aimlessly, or go at random (obs. or rare: as, "The wise man's folly is anatomized Even by the *squandering* glances of the fool," Shakspere's "As You Like It," ii. 7. 57).—**squan'der**, *n.* The act of squandering; extravagant or wasteful expenditure. —**squan'der-er**, *n.*—**squan'der-ing-ly**, *adv.*

square (skwār), *n.* [OF. *esquarre*, *esquerre* (F. *équerre*) = It. *squadra*, ult. < L. *ex-*, out, + *quadra*, a square: cf. *quadrate*, *v.*] A four-sided plane figure having all its sides equal and all its angles right angles; any space or area, or any flat object or piece, having this form or a form approximating it; a rectangular area, object, or piece; a cubical or rectangular block; also, a square, rectangular, or quadrilateral area in a city or town, marked off by neighboring and intersecting streets, and containing buildings, or sites for buildings, along each side; the distance along one side of such an area (as, a house two *squares* from here); an open area of this or other form, in a city or town, usually planted with grass, trees, etc. (as, Madison *Square*, in New York; Independence *Square*, in Philadelphia); any similar open space, as at the intersection of streets; the houses or buildings surrounding such an open area or space; also, an L-shaped or T-shaped instrument for determining or testing right angles, and for other purposes (cf. *T-square*); a similar instrument for measuring angles other than right angles or (with the arms movable) for measuring any angle; fig., a true measure, standard, or pattern (now rare); also, squared form or condition (see phrases below); *milit.*, a body of troops drawn up in quadrilateral form; in *agric.*, the leaf-like heart-shaped bracts (often four) surrounding the flower of the cotton plant, taken collectively; a bud of the cotton plant; in *arith.* and *alg.*, the second power of a number or quantity, that is, the product of the number or quantity multiplied by itself (as, the *square* of 4 is 4 × 4, or 16).—**on** (or **upon**) **the square**, at right angles; not obliquely; also, in an honest or upright manner (as, "I shall act *upon the square* with you": Malkin's tr. Le Sage's "Gil Blas," viii. 12); honest or straightforward (now slang: as, to be *on the square*); also, on equal terms, or on an equality (obs. or rare).—**out of square**, not at right angles; oblique; also, out of order; out of the proper condition; incorrect or incorrectly.— **square**, *a.* [Cf. OF. *esquarré*, pp. of *esquarrer*, E. *square*, *v.*] Having four equal sides and four right angles, as a figure or area; of a specified length on each side of a square (as, an area 2 feet *square*, which contains 4 square feet); designating a unit representing an area in the form of a square of the length of a specified linear unit along each edge, used in expressing surface measurement (as, a *square* inch, foot, or mile; an area of 4 *square* feet, which is equivalent to an area 2 feet square: cf. sense preceding); pertaining

---

to such units, or to surface measurement (as, *square* measure: see phrase below); having four sides and four right angles, but not equilateral; cubical or approximately so, or rectangular and of three dimensions (as, a *square* box); having a square section, or one that is merely rectangular (as, a *square* rod; a *square* file); having a solid, sturdy form with rectilinear and angular outlines (as, a man of *square* build); of the form of a right angle, or having some part or parts rectangular (as, a *square* corner; a *square* apse); at right angles, or perpendicular (as, one line *square* to another); straight, level, or even, as a surface, or as one surface with another; leaving no balance of debt on either side, or having all accounts settled (as, to make accounts *square*; to get *square* with a person); just, fair, or equitable (as, *square* dealing); honest, honorable, or upright, as a person (as, "I always found him true and *square* in everything": Mrs. Stowe's "Uncle Tom's Cabin," i.); straightforward, direct, or unequivocal (as, a *square* refusal); substantial or satisfying (colloq.: as, "Food was so abundant that farmers often gave their men a *square* meal which was not in the contract," W. R. Inge's "Outspoken Essays," i. 4); *naut.*, at right angles to the mast and the keel, as a yard; in *golf*, having an even or equal score; in *arith.* and *alg.*, being a square (see *square number*, below); pertaining to a square (see *square root*, below).—**square dance,** a dance, as a quadrille, performed by a set of couples arranged about a square space or in some set form. Cf. *round dance*, under *round*[2], *a.*—**square knot,** a common form of knot in which the ends of the cord or rope come out alongside of the standing parts. Also called *reef-knot*.—**square measure,** the measurement of area in square units; a system of such units, esp. the one in which 144 square inches = 1 square foot, 9 square feet = 1 square yard, etc. See *land-measure*.—**square number,** a number which is the square of some integer number, as 1, 4, 9, 16, 25, etc., with respect to 1, 2, 3, 4, 5, etc.—**square piano.** See under *piano*[2], *n.*—**square root,** the quantity of which a given quantity is the square: as, 4 is the *square root* of 16.—**square sail.** See *sail*, *n.*, and cf. entry *squaresail*.—**square wheel.** Same as *flat wheel*, under *flat*[2], *a.*—**square,** *adv.* So as to be square; in square or rectangular form; at right angles; fairly, honestly, or uprightly (now slang or colloq.: as, "I mean to act *square*," J. Conrad's "Lord Jim," xiv.).—**square,** *v.*; squared, squaring. [OF. *esquarrer* = It. *squadrare*, < L. *ex-*, out, + *quadrare*, make square, < *quadra*, a square.] **I.** *tr.* To reduce to square or rectangular form; make cubical, or approximately so; make square or rectangular in cross-section; mark out in one or more squares or rectangles (as, "the soil, *squared* off as usual like a gigantic chess-board": Amelia B. Edwards's "Thousand Miles up the Nile," vii.); bring to the form of a right angle or right angles; set at right angles to something else (as, to *square* the yards of a vessel, that is, to lay them at right angles to the mast and the keel); set (the shoulders, arms, etc.) so as to present a square or rectangular outline (as, "He held himself erect with head thrown back and shoulders *squared*": Tarkington's "Gentleman from Indiana," xvi.); make straight, level, or even; test the squareness of, as with a try-square; fig., to regulate, as by a standard (as, "The path of royal policy cannot be always *squared* . . . by the abstract maxims of religion and of morality": Scott's "Quentin Durward," xiii.); conform to or harmonize with something (as, "I cannot *square* my conduct to time, place, Or circumstance": Keats's "Otho the Great," ii. 1); adjust harmoniously or satisfactorily (as, to *square* matters with an aggrieved person); balance (accounts); settle (a debt, etc.: often with *up*); settle satisfactorily with (a person), esp. by a compensation or bribe, as in order to induce a favorable attitude or action (slang: as, "He would try not to offend them; perhaps an occasional penny or two might *square* them," S. Butler's "Way of All Flesh," lviii.); in *math.*, to find the equivalent of in square measure; also, to describe or find a square which is equivalent to (as, to *square* a circle, an operation which cannot be performed); also, to multiply (a number or quantity) by itself. **II.** *intr.* To accord or agree (often with *with*: as, his theory does not *square* with the facts; "His works are made to *square* with his faith," Thackeray's "Newcomes," xxxv.); also, to assume a posture

of defense, as in boxing (often with *off*); strut or swagger (obs. or prov. Eng.); also, to deviate† or diverge†; disagree† or quarrel†.

square-head (skwär'hed), *n.* A Scandinavian, or sometimes a German or a Dutchman. [Slang.]

square-ly (skwär'li), *adv.* In a square manner.—**square'-ness,** *n.*

squar-er (skwär'ėr), *n.* One who or that which squares.

square=rigged (skwär'rigd), *a.* *Naut.*, having the principal sails square sails.

square-sail (skwär'sāl), *n.* *Naut.*, a square sail (see *sail*, *n.*); specif., a square sail occasionally carried on the mast of a fore-and-aft rigged ship.

square=toed (skwär'tōd), *a.* Having a broad, square toe, as a shoe; fig., old-fashioned and homely in habits, ideas, etc.—**square'=toes,** *n.* An old-fashioned person; one who adheres to homely, old-fashioned ways, ideas, etc.: as, "You would have made a mock of me; you would never have spent ten civil words on such a *Square-toes*" (Stevenson's "Master of Ballantrae," ix.).

squar-ish (skwär'ish), *a.* Approximately square.

squar-rose (skwar'ōs or skwo-rōs'), *a.* [L. *squarrosus*, appar. erron. for *squamosus*, scaly, E. *squamous*.] In *bot.*, rough with spreading processes, or thickly set with divergent or recurved bracts or leaves, as a surface, stem, etc.; so disposed as to form a rough surface, as bracts or leaves; in *entom.*, noting a margin with an elevated fringe-like edge. Also **squar'rous.—squar-ru-lose** (skwar'ö-lōs), *a.* In *bot.*, somewhat squarrose.

squash[1] (skwosh), *n.* [Algonquian *askutasquash*, 'vegetables eaten green.'] The fruit or pepo (see *pepo*) of any of various vine-like, tendril-bearing plants of the genus *Cucurbita*, used as a culinary vegetable; also, any of the plants bearing this fruit. Cf. *pumpkin.*

squash[2] (skwosh), *v.* [Cf. OF. *esquachier*, *escachier* (F. *écacher*), crush, squash.] **I.** *tr.* To press into a flat mass or to pulp, or crush (as, "With the next step I should be *squashed* to death under his foot": Swift's "Gulliver's Travels," ii. 1); also, to suppress or put down (as, "the rapid *squashing* of the Senussi in western Egypt": H. G. Wells's "Italy, France, and Britain at War," iii. 4); quash; sometimes, to silence, as with a crushing retort (colloq.). **II.** *intr.* To be pressed into a flat mass or pulp; of a soft, heavy body, to fall heavily; also, to make a splashing sound; splash.—**squash**[2], *n.* The act of squashing, or the fact or sound of being squashed; the impact of a soft, heavy body falling on a surface, or the sound produced by this; something squashed or crushed, or a squashed or crushed mass; a crush or crowd, as of persons; something soft and easily crushed, esp. (obs. or archaic) the unripe pod of a pea (as, "as a *squash* is before 'tis a peascod": Shakspere's "Twelfth Night," i. 5. 166); also, a game resembling tennis and rackets, played in a walled court with rackets and a hollow rubber ball.

squash=bug (skwosh'bug), *n.* An ill-smelling, dark-colored heteropterous insect, *Anasa tristis*, of North America, injurious to the squash and other cucurbitaceous plants.

squash-er (skwosh'ėr), *n.* One who or that which squashes.

squash-y (skwosh'i), *a.* Easily squashed; lacking in firmness; pulpy; soft and wet, as ground, etc.; also, having a squashed or crushed appearance.—**squash'i-ness,** *n.*

Squash-bug, natural size.

squat (skwot), *v.*; squatted or squat, squatting. [OF. *esquatir*, < *es-* (< L. *ex-*, out) + *quatir*, press down, < L. *coactus*, pp. of *cogere*, drive together: see *cogent*.] **I.** *tr.* To flatten, crush, or bruise (now prov. Eng.); knock, dash, or throw (now prov. Eng.); also, to seat (one's self) in a low or crouching position, with the legs drawn up closely beneath or in front of the body (as, "I thought she intended to *squat* herself down on the floor": Smollett's "Humphry Clinker," June 12); also, to cause (a person, etc.) to squat; put in a squatting attitude or posture. **II.** *intr.* To sit down in a low or crouching position, with the legs drawn up closely beneath or in front of the body (as, "Wang . . . *squatting* on his heels, began to potter mysteriously about some plants":

J. Conrad's "Victory," iii. 3); also, to crouch or cower down, as an animal; also, to settle on land, esp. public or new land, without any title or right; also, to settle on public land under government regulation, as for the purpose of acquiring title.—**squat,** *a.* [Orig. pp. of *squat, v.*] Seated or being in a squatting position; squatting; crouching; also, short and thick-set or thick, as persons or animals, the body or figure, etc. (as, "a short *squat* Sicilian," Mrs. Wharton's "Son at the Front," xx.; "the *squat* . . . figure of Father Malachi," Lever's "Harry Lorrequer," vii.); hence, in general, low and thick or broad (as, "the *squat* spire of the village church": Galsworthy's "Country House," i. 7).—**squat,** *n.* A bump, jar, or jolt (now north. Eng.); a bruise (now prov. Eng.); also, the act or fact of squatting or crouching; a squatting attitude or posture; also, a short, stout person (colloq.).—**squat-tage** (skwot′āj), *n.* The occupation of land by squatting; also, a piece of land occupied or held by a squatter.—**squat′ter,** *n.* One who or that which squats; esp., one who settles on land, esp. public or new land, without any title or right; also, one who settles on land under government regulation, as for the purpose of acquiring title.—**squat′ty,** *a.* Squat; short and thick; low and broad (as, a *squatty* house; "He came at last to the *squatty* shelters," Sinclair Lewis's "Arrowsmith," ix.).

squaw (skwâ), *n.* [Algonquian.] A North American Indian woman or wife.—**squaw′=fish,** *n.* A large cyprinoid food-fish, *Ptychocheilus oregonensis,* common in rivers of the Pacific coast of the U. S. and Canada.

squawk (skwâk), *v.* [Imit.] **I.** *intr.* To utter a loud, harsh cry, as a duck or other fowl when frightened; of things, to emit a discordant sound. **II.** *tr.* To give forth with a squawk.—**squawk,** *n.* A loud, harsh cry or sound; also, the night-heron, *Nycticorax nycticorax nævius.*—**squawk′er,** *n.*

squaw=man (skwâ′man), *n.*; pl. *-men.* A white or other non-Indian man who has taken (or lives with) an Indian squaw as his wife.

squaw-root (skwâ′rŏt), *n.* A fleshy, leafless orobanchaceous plant, *Conopholis americana,* of eastern North America, having yellowish flowers, and found growing in clusters, esp. under oaks.

squeak (skwēk), *v.* [ME. *squeken;* imit.] **I.** *intr.* To utter a short, sharp, shrill cry, as a bird, rat, or pig (as, "the bats *squeaking* in the trees": Synge's "Tinker's Wedding," i.); emit a sharp, high-pitched sound, as a fiddle, or as a hinge that needs oiling (as, "The *squeaking* fiddle, and the soughing in the sail": Masefield's "Trade Winds"); also, to confess, or turn informer (slang). **II.** *tr.* To utter or produce with a squeak or squeaks (as, "His father *squeaked,* 'Now don't be too hard on the boy,'" Sinclair Lewis's "Arrowsmith," ix.; "Fiddles . . . were *squeaking* out the tune," Dickens's "Old Curiosity Shop," xix.); also, to make (one's or its way) with squeaking; also, to cause to squeak.—**squeak,** *n.* A short, sharp, shrill cry; a sharp, high-pitched sound; also, a bare chance (colloq.); a narrow escape (usually with *narrow, near,* etc.: colloq.).—**bubble and squeak.** See under *bubble, n.*—**squeak′er,** *n.*—**squeak′ing-ly,** *adv.*—**squeak′y,** *a.* Squeaking; tending to squeak: as, "a *squeaky* voice" (W. De Morgan's "Joseph Vance," ii.); "an ancient and *squeaky* bicycle" (Sinclair Lewis's "Arrowsmith," xii.).

Squawroot, parasitic on the root of oak.

squeal (skwēl), *v.* [ME. *squelen;* imit.] **I.** *intr.* To utter a more or less prolonged, sharp, shrill cry, as in pain, fear, etc., as persons or animals (as, "a litter of pigs . . . *squealing* in their carts": Synge's "Well of the Saints," i.); emit a shrill sound, as things; also, to turn informer (slang). **II.** *tr.* To utter or produce with a squeal; also, to tell, disclose, or reveal, as something secret (slang: as, "If I catch you knocking me to any other firm, I'll *squeal* all I know about you," Sinclair Lewis's "Babbitt," xix.).—**squeal,** *n.* A more or less prolonged, sharp, shrill cry or sound (as, "Miss Ingate gave

a little *squeal* of surprise": Arnold Bennett's "Lion's Share," xlvi.); also, a squealing, or turning informer (slang).—**squeal′er,** *n.*

squeam-ish (skwē′mish), *a.* [ME. *squaymysch,* var. of *squaymus, squoymous;* origin uncertain.] Easily nauseated; readily turned sick; also, slightly nauseated; qualmish; sickish; fig., easily shocked by anything approaching immodesty, or prudish (as, "our *squeamish* and shamefaced reluctance to recognize and deal frankly with the facts and problems of sex": J. H. Robinson's "Mind in the Making," v. 11); nice to excess in questions of propriety; excessively particular or scrupulous as to the moral aspect of things (as, "trifles magnified into importance by a *squeamish* conscience": Macaulay's "Hist. of Eng.," xiii.); fastidious or dainty in taste or requirements.—**squeam′ish-ly,** *adv.*—**squeam′ish-ness,** *n.*

squee-gee (skwē′jē or skwē-jē′), *n.* [Var. of *squilgee.*] An implement edged with rubber or the like, for sweeping water from wet decks, scraping water off windows after washing, etc.; any of various similar devices, as one for expressing water from photographic prints, etc.; a device with a rubber roller used in photography, etc., for like purposes ('squeegee-roller').—**squee′gee,** *v. t.;* *-geed, -geeing.* To sweep, scrape, or press with a squeegee.

squeez-a-ble (skwē′zȧ-bl), *a.* That may be squeezed.

squeeze (skwēz), *v.;* squeezed, squeezing. [Cf. AS. *cwēsan, cwȳsan,* squeeze, crush.] **I.** *tr.* To press forcibly together, or so as to force into smaller compass; compress; sometimes, to press (another's hand) tightly in one's own, as in friendliness or affection (as, "She *squeezed* his hand when she said good night": Galsworthy's "Saint's Progress," ii. 7); also, to apply pressure to in order to extract something (as, to *squeeze* a lemon); fig., to harass or oppress (a person, etc.) by exactions; also, to thrust forcibly, or force by pressure (as, to *squeeze* one's hand into a tight glove); also, to force out, extract, or procure by pressure (usually with *out* or *from*); extort as by pressure; also, to obtain a squeeze, or facsimile impression, of (see *squeeze, n.*). **II.** *intr.* To exert a compressing force; also, to force a way through some narrow or crowded place (with *through, in, out,* etc.: as, "He walked uneasily to and fro, *squeezing* between the table and the sideboard," Arnold Bennett's "Buried Alive," vii.); also, to admit of being compressed; yield to pressure. —**squeeze,** *n.* The act or an act of squeezing, or the fact of being squeezed; a tight pressure of another's hand within one's own, as in friendliness or affection (as, "My father assented with a silent *squeeze* of the hand": Bulwer-Lytton's "Caxtons," iv. 4); a hug or close embrace; the pressure of a crowd of persons; a crowded social gathering (colloq.); a situation from which extrication is difficult, or a narrow escape (often with *tight:* colloq.); also, a small quantity or amount of anything obtained by squeezing; also, a facsimile impression of an inscription, coin, or the like, obtained by pressing some plastic substance over or around it.—**squeeze′=play,** *n.* In *baseball,* a play executed when there is a runner on third base and usually not more than one man out, in which the runner starts for home as soon as the pitcher makes a motion to pitch, the batter bunting the ball when pitched.—**squeez′er,** *n.*

squelch (skwelch), *v.* [Prob. imit.] **I.** *tr.* To strike or press with crushing force; crush down; squash; fig., to put down or suppress completely; silence, as with a crushing retort (colloq.). **II.** *intr.* To become squelched or squashed; also, to fall heavily; also, to make a splashing sound, as of something wet under a heavy impact; tread heavily in water, mud, wet shoes, etc., with such a sound (as, "It will rain before eight o'clock, and I shall be *squelching* through miry Norfolk on my way to Ely": M. Hewlett's "Open Country," viii.).—**squelch,** *n.* A squelching; a crushing blow; a heavy fall; a crushing argument or retort (colloq.); a squelched or crushed mass of anything; also, a squelching sound.—**squelch′er,** *n.*

sque-teague (skwē-tēg′), *n.* [Algonquian.] The common weakfish, *Cynoscion regalis.*

squib (skwib), *n.* [Origin uncertain.] A firework consisting of a tube or ball filled with powder, which burns with a hissing noise terminated usually by a slight explosion; a fire-cracker broken in the middle so that when lighted it burns with a hissing noise; a kind of slow-match used in blasting; also, a short witty or sarcastic saying or writing (as, "Three-line editorial *squibs* dug at his tyranny, his ignorance": Sinclair Lewis's "Arrowsmith," xxiv.); a sharp sarcasm; a lampoon; also, one who writes squibs or lampoons†; also, a mean or paltry fellow†.—**squib**, *v. t.* or *i.*; *squibbed, squibbing.* To assail in or put forth squibs or lampoons.

squid (skwid), *n.*; pl. *squids* or (esp. collectively) *squid.* [Origin uncertain.] Any of various decapod dibranchiate cephalopods, esp. any of certain small species (as of the genera *Loligo* and *Ommastrephes*) having slender bodies and caudal fins and much used for bait; also, a kind of artificial bait made to imitate a squid, used in angling or trolling for fish.—**squid**, *v. i.*; *squidded, squidding.* To fish with a squid (bait).

squif-fy (skwif′i), *a.* [Origin obscure: cf. Sc. *squeefy*, mean-looking, disreputable.] Intoxicated; drunk. [Slang.]

squil-gee (skwil′jē or skwil-jē′), *n.* [Origin obscure: cf. *squeegee.*] A squeegee; also, *naut.*, a line bearing toggles, used in setting a studdingsail.—**squil′gee**, *v. t.*; *-geed, -geeing.* To squeegee.

squill (skwil), *n.* [L. *squilla, scilla*, sea-onion, also squilla, < Gr. σκίλλα, sea-onion: cf. *squilla.*] The bulb of the sea-onion, *Urginea maritima*, cut into thin slices and dried, and used in medicine chiefly as an expectorant and diuretic; the plant itself (see cut below); also, any of the plants of the liliaceous genus *Scilla*, as *S. nonscripta* (see *bluebell* and *harebell*), which bear blue, pink, or white racemose flowers on a leafless scape; also, any of the stomatopod crustaceans of the family *Squillidæ*, esp. of the genus *Squilla*, which burrow along the seashore.

Squid (*Loligo pealei*).

squil-la (skwil′ä), *n.*; pl. *squillas* (-äz), *squillæ* (-ē). [L.: see *squill.*] Any of the squills, or stomatopod crustaceans of the genus *Squilla* or family *Squillidæ.*

Squill (*Urginea maritima*).

squinch (skwinch), *n.* [Var. of obs. or prov. *scunch*, for *scuncheon*, < OF. *escoinson* (F. *écoinçon*), < *es-* (< L. *ex-*, out) + *coin*, corner, E. *coin.*] In *arch.*, a small arch, corbeling, or the like, built across the interior angle between two walls, as in a square tower for supporting the side of a superimposed octagonal spire.

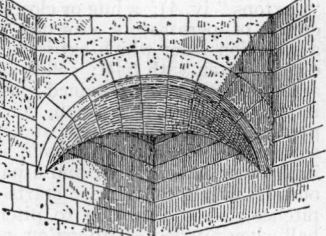

Squinch.

squin-ny (skwin′i), *v. i.* Same as *squint.* [Now prov. Eng.]

squint (skwint), *a.* [From *asquint.*] Directed obliquely, or having a cast, as the eye; affected with strabismus, as the eyes; also, looking obliquely; looking with a side glance; looking askance; hence, oblique; indirect.—**squint**, *v.* **I.** *intr.* To be directed obliquely, or have a cast, as the eye; be affected with strabismus, or be cross-eyed, as a person (as, "My Lady's own waiting-woman *squinted*, and was marked with the small-pox": Thackeray's "Henry Esmond," i. 7); also, to look or glance obliquely or sidewise; look askance; also, to glance hastily; also, to look with the eyes partly closed; also, *fig.*, to make or have an indirect reference; tend or incline (*toward*, etc.); also, to run or go obliquely. **II.** *tr.* To cause to squint; affect with strabismus; cause to look obliquely; also, to direct or divert obliquely; also, to close (the eyes) partly in looking.—**squint**, *n.* A permanent cast, or tendency to look obliquely, in the eye; an affection of the eyes consisting in non-coincidence of the optic axes; strabismus; also, a looking obliquely or askance;

a sidelong look or glance; a hasty glance, or a look (as, "Any one would have taken a second *squint* at old Sabre's face as I saw it then": A. S. M. Hutchinson's "If Winter Comes," iv. 3); *fig.*, an indirect reference; a leaning or inclination; also, an oblique or perverse tendency; in *arch.*, a hagioscope.—**squint′er**, *n.*—**squint′=eyed**, *a.* Having a squint eye or squint eyes; affected with or characterized by strabismus; also, looking obliquely or with a side glance; looking askance.—**squint′ing-ly**, *adv.*

squin′y†, *v. i.* See *squinny.*

squir′arch, etc. See *squirearch*, etc.

squire (skwīr), *n.* [OF. *esquier*: see *esquire.*] A young man of gentle birth who, as an aspirant to knighthood, attended upon a knight; an esquire; also, one who is neither a noble nor a knight but has received a grant of arms; in England, a country gentleman, esp. the chief landed proprietor in a district; in the U. S., esp. in country districts and small towns, a justice of the peace, local judge, or other local dignitary (chiefly used as a title); also, a personal attendant, as of a person of rank; also, a man who attends or escorts a lady in public.—**squire of dames**, a man very attentive to women and much in their company.—**squire**, *v. t.*; *squired, squiring.* To attend as or in the manner of a squire: as, "He . . . *squired* my aunt and me to every part of Bath" (Smollett's "Humphry Clinker," April 26).—**squire′arch, squir′arch** (-ärk), *n.* A member of the squirearchy: as, "Even the proudest of the neighbouring *squirearchs* always spoke of us as a very ancient family" (Bulwer-Lytton's "Caxtons," ii. 3).—**squire′ar-chy, squir′ar-chy** (-är-ki), *n.*; pl. *-chies* (-kiz). [See *-archy.*] The class of squires collectively; the country gentry; also, rule or government by a squire or squires.—**squir-een** (skwīr-ēn′), *n.* [See *-een.*] A petty squire; a small landed proprietor: as, "*Squireens* are persons who, with good long leases, or valuable farms, possess incomes from three to eight hundred a year" (Maria Edgeworth's "Absentee," vii.). [Orig. Ir.]—**squire′ling**, *n.* A petty squire; also, a young squire.—**squire′ly**, *a.* Of, pertaining to, or befitting a squire.

squirm (skwėrm), *v. i.* [Origin uncertain; perhaps imit.] To wriggle or writhe (as, "The chained dog . . . crouched and *squirmed* and gave low whines and his tail wagged with extreme rapidity": Arnold Bennett's "Lion's Share," xxvii.); *fig.*, to be sharply or painfully affected, as by reproof or sarcasm; also, to move or proceed by wriggling.—**squirm**, *n.* A squirming or wriggling movement.—**squirm′y**, *a.* Squirming or wriggling.

squir-rel (skwur′el or skwir′el), *n.* [OF. *esquireul* (F. *écureuil*), dim. < L. *sciurus*, < Gr. σκίουρος, squirrel, appar. < σκιά, shadow, + οὐρά, tail.] Any of the arboreal bushy-tailed rodents constituting the genus *Sciurus* (family *Sciuridæ*), as *S. vulgaris* (the common European squirrel), *S. hudsonius* ('red squirrel'), and *S. carolinensis* ('gray squirrel'); any of various other members of the family *Sciuridæ* ('squirrel family'), as the chipmunks, flying-squirrels, prairie-squirrels, etc.; any of certain African rodents (family *Anomaluridæ*) resembling flying-squirrels; any of various Australian flying-phalangers.—**squir′rel=corn**, *n.* An American papaveraceous herb, *Dicentra* (or *Bikukulla*) *canadensis*, with finely dissected leaves, cream-colored heart-shaped flowers, and a rootstock bearing numerous small tubers which resemble grains of Indian corn.—**squir′rel=fish**, *n.* Any of various spiny tropical fishes of the genus *Holocentrus* and allied genera.—**squir′rel=grass**, *n.* Squirreltail.—**squir′rel=mon″key**, *n.* Any of certain small South American monkeys (genus *Chrysothrix*) with a bushy, non-prehensile tail (see cut on following page); also, a marmoset.—

Common European Squirrel (*Sciurus vulgaris*).

squir'rel-tail, n. Any of various wild grasses of the genus *Hordeum*, related to the common barley.

squirt (skwėrt), v. [Late ME. *squyrt*: cf. earlier ME. *swirting*, n., squirting, also LG. *swirtjen*, squirt.] **I.** *intr.* To eject liquid in a jet or stream from a narrow orifice; also, to issue in a jet-like stream (as, "I see the white smoke *squirt* out of the ferryboat's side": Mark Twain's "Huckleberry Finn," viii.). **II.** *tr.* To cause (liquid) to issue in a jet from a narrow orifice; eject in a jet-like stream (as, "An aeroplane . . . is quite hard enough to hit, even if it is not *squirting* bullets from a machine gun": H. G. Wells's "Italy, France, and Britain at War," iii. 2); also, to wet or bespatter with a liquid so ejected; also, to cause to give out liquid in a jet-like stream.—**squirt,** n. An act of squirting; also, a jet, as of water; a small quantity of liquid squirted; also, an instrument for squirting, as a syringe; also, an insignificant, self-assertive fellow (colloq.: as, "a little *squirt* of a man," Sinclair Lewis's "Babbitt," v.).—**squirt'er,** n.—**squirt'ing,** p. a. That squirts; that ejects a jet-like stream, as of liquid.—**squirting cucumber,** a cucurbitaceous plant, *Ecballium elaterium*, native in the Mediterranean region, whose ripened fruit forcibly ejects the seeds and juice. Cf. *elaterium*.

Squirrel-monkey (*Chrysothrix sciureus*).

-st. See -*est*[2].

stab (stab), v.; *stabbed, stabbing*. [ME. (in *stabing*, n.); origin uncertain.] **I.** *tr.* To pierce or wound with or as with a pointed weapon, esp. with a knife or dagger; fig., to wound sharply or deeply in the feelings

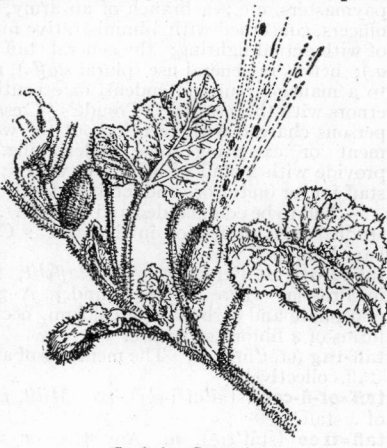

Squirting Cucumber.

(as, "She . . . was *stabbed* to the heart to see a haggard white face and eyes of deep despair regarding her": H. G. Wells's "Mr. Britling," ii. 4. § 23); penetrate sharply, like a knife (as, rays of light *stabbed* the gloom); also, to thrust or plunge (a knife, etc.), as into something (as, "*stab* poniards in our flesh": Shakspere's "3 Henry VI.," ii. 1. 98). **II.** *intr.* To thrust with or as with a knife or other pointed weapon (as, to *stab* at an adversary); deliver a wound as with a pointed weapon (lit. or fig.: as, "She speaks poniards, and every word *stabs*," Shakspere's "Much Ado about Nothing," ii. 1. 255).—**stab,** n. The act or an act of stabbing; a thrust or blow with or as with a pointed weapon; a wound made by stabbing (as, "his gash'd *stabs*": Shakspere's "Macbeth," ii. 3. 119); fig., a severe wound given to a person's feelings (as, "the *stab* of false Friendship and of false Love": Carlyle's "Sartor Resartus," ii. 7); sometimes, a flash of bright color.

Sta-bat Ma-ter (stā'bat mā'tėr). [ML. *stabat mater*, 'stood the mother': the opening words of the Latin text.] A celebrated 13th century Latin hymn on the Virgin Mary at the Cross (called more fully the 'Stabat Mater dolorosa'); a musical setting of this; also, any of certain other Latin hymns beginning with the same words, esp. one of the 15th(?) century (called more fully the 'Stabat Mater speciosa') on the Virgin Mary in contemplation of the infant Jesus; a musical setting of one of these hymns.

stab-ber (stab'ėr), n. One who or that which stabs; an instrument used in stabbing.

sta-bile (stā'bil or stab'il), a. [L. *stabilis*: see *stable*[2].] Fixed in position; firmly established, or stable; in *med.*, noting or pertaining to a mode of application of electricity in which the active electrode is kept stationary over the part to be acted upon (opposed to *labile*).

sta-bil-i-tate (stā-bil'i-tāt), v. t.; -*tated, -tating*. To give stability to; render stable. [Now rare.]

sta-bil-i-ty (stā-bil'i-ti), n.; pl. -*ties* (-tiz). [L. *stabilitas*, < *stabilis*: see *stable*[2].] The state or quality of being stable; fixedness or firmness in position; continuance in the same state or without change; endurance or permanence (as, "The name of Cæsar had become identified with the *stability* of the Empire": Froude's "Cæsar," xxv.); steadfastness, as of character or purpose; stable character of equilibrium; also, something stable.

stab-i-lize (stab'i-līz), v. t.; -*lized, -lizing*. [F. *stabiliser*, < L. *stabilis*: see *stable*[2].] To make stable; in *aëronautics*, to put or keep (an aircraft) in stable equilibrium, as by some special device or stabilizer.—**stab"i-li-za'tion** (-li-zā'shon), n.—**stab'i-liz-er** (-lī-zėr), n. One who or that which stabilizes; in *aëronautics*, a device for stabilizing an aircraft, as an air-inflated bag on a dirigible balloon, a plane on an aëroplane, etc. Cf. *gyro-stabilizer*.

sta-ble[1] (stā'bl), n. [OF. *estable* (F. *étable*), < L. *stabulum*, standing-place, habitation, inclosure for animals, < *stare*, stand.] A building fitted for the lodging and feeding of horses, cattle, etc., esp. of horses only; a collection of animals belonging in such a building; in racing use, an establishment where race-horses are kept and trained; the horses belonging to, or the persons connected with, such an establishment.—**sta'ble**[1], v.; -*bled, -bling*. **I.** *tr.* To put or lodge in or as in a stable: as, "I . . . *stabled* my horse at a little public-house" (H. Kingsley's "Geoffry Hamlyn," xlviii.). **II.** *intr.* To live in or as in a stable.

sta-ble[2] (stā'bl), a. [OF. *estable* (F. *stable*), < L. *stabilis*, standing firm, firm, steady, stable, < *stare*, stand: cf. *stabile*.] Able to stand firm, or not likely to fall or give way, as a structure, support, foundation, etc.; firmly fixed in position; firm; steady; stationary; also, able or likely to continue or last, or firmly established (as, a *stable* government; a *stable* peace; a *stable* condition of affairs); not liable to change, fail, or cease; enduring or permanent; also, firm, steadfast, or not wavering or changeable, as persons, the mind, etc.; in *physics*, having or showing an ability or tendency to maintain, or resist change in, position, form, etc.; specif., tending to keep the position, or to return to it after displacement, as a body; characterized by or showing such a tendency in a body, as position or equilibrium; in *chem.*, not readily decomposing, as a compound; resisting molecular or chemical change.—**sta'ble-ness,** n.

sta-bler (stā'blėr), n. One who provides stabling for horses, etc.; a stable-keeper.

sta-bling (stā'bling), n. The act of one who stables horses, etc.; also, accommodation for horses, etc., in a stable or stables (as, "There's *stabling* in this place for a dozen horses": Dickens's "Hard Times," ii. 7); stables collectively.

stab-lish (stab'lish), v. t. Same as establish. [Archaic.]

sta-bly (stā'bli), adv. In a stable manner; with stability.

stac-ca-to (stā-kä'tō, It. stäk-kä'tō), a. [It., pp. of *staccare*, for *distaccare*, detach.] In *music*, detached, disconnected, or abrupt; with breaks between the successive tones: opposed to *legato*. Also fig.: as, "Her manner to her husband was . . . a little *staccato*; she was nervous" (Margaret Kennedy's "Constant Nymph," xvii.).

stack (stak), n. [ME. *stac, stak*, from Scand.: cf. Icel. *stakkr*, Sw. *stack*, Dan. *stak*, stack.] A large, usually circular or rectangular, pile of hay, straw, or the like, often with a sloping thatched top; also, any more or less orderly pile or heap; a pile of sticks, poles, or the like; a number of muskets or rifles standing together in a conical group; a set of bookshelves ranged one above another, as in a library; a number of chimneys or flues grouped together; also, a single chimney or funnel for smoke (as, "Only the walls . . . and the *stack* of the furnace still stood": Eden Phillpotts's "Children of Men," i. 5); also, a high, detached rock rising out of the sea (Sc., etc.); also, an English measure for coal and wood, equal to 108 cubic feet; also, a great quantity or number (colloq.: as, "Sometimes a *stack* of people would come there," Mark Twain's "Huckleberry Finn," xviii.).—**stack**, *v. t.* To pile or arrange in the form of a stack (as, to *stack* hay; to *stack* firewood; to *stack* arms); also, to cover or load with something in stacks or piles (as, "The left-hand half of every step of the stairs was *stacked* with books": Arnold Bennett's "Riceyman Steps," i. 14); also, to arrange (playing-cards in the pack) in a particular manner, so as to secure an unfair advantage (also fig.: as, "The way the cards are *stacked* against a young fellow to-day, I can't say I approve of early marriages," Sinclair Lewis's "Babbitt," xxxiv.).—**stack'er**, *n.* One who or that which stacks; a device for stacking hay, straw, or the like.—**stack'=stand**, *n.* A stand or framework for supporting a stack of hay, grain, or the like.

stac-te (stak'tē), *n.* [L., < Gr. στακτή, < στάζειν, drop, drip.] A kind of fragrant spice known to the ancients, esp. fresh liquid myrrh, in the Bible, one of the sweet spices which composed the holy incense of the ancient Jews (see Ex. xxx. 34).

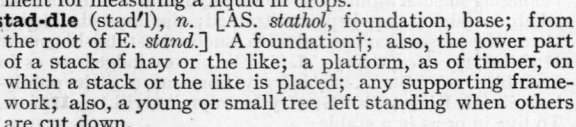
Stack-stand.

stac-tom-e-ter (stak-tom'e-tėr), *n.* [Gr. στακτός, oozing out in drops (< στάζειν, drop, drip), + μέτρον, measure.] An instrument for measuring a liquid in drops.

stad-dle (stad'l), *n.* [AS. *stathol*, foundation, base; from the root of E. *stand*.] A foundation†; also, the lower part of a stack of hay or the like; a platform, as of timber, on which a stack or the like is placed; any supporting framework; also, a young or small tree left standing when others are cut down.

stad-hold-er (stad'hōl″dėr), *n.* [For D. *stadhouder*, < *stad*, place (now city), + *houder*, holder.] Formerly, in the Netherlands, the viceroy or governor of a province (as, "All these *stadholders* were commanders-in-chief of the military forces in their respective provinces": Motley's "Dutch Republic," i. 3); also, the chief magistrate of the United Provinces of the Netherlands.—**stad'hold″er-ate** (-ạt), *n.* The office of stadholder; also, the rule or government of a stadholder (as, "The commonwealth which William had liberated . . . continued to exist . . . under the successive *stadholderates* of his sons and descendants": Motley's "Dutch Republic," vi. 7); also, a province or state governed by a stadholder.—**stad'hold″er-ship**, *n.* The office of stadholder.

sta-di-a (stā'di-ạ), *n.* [NL., < L. *stadium*: see *stadium*.] In *civil engin.*, an instrument, as a form of theodolite fitted with two horizontal parallel cross-hairs ('stadia hairs' or 'stadia wires'), used in connection with a vertical graduated rod ('stadia rod') to measure distances, the graduated rod being placed at one end of the distance to be measured and the theodolite or the like at the other; the stadia rod itself (chiefly Eng.); the method by which such measurements are made, the distance between the graduated rod and the theodolite or the like being figured from the number of divisions on the graduated rod subtended by the parallel cross-hairs; *milit.*, a device for roughly measuring distances, as a glass plate with figures of horsemen and foot-soldiers drawn at the size they appear to have at definite distances from the observer.

sta-dim-e-ter (stạ-dim'e-tėr), *n.* [See *stadium* and *-meter*.] An optical instrument for measuring distances of objects, esp. ships, of which the heights are known: invented and patented by Rear-Admiral Bradley A. Fiske in 1893.

sta-di-om-e-ter (stā-di-om'e-tėr), *n.* [See *stadium* and *-meter*.] In *surv.*, a modified theodolite in which the directions or bearings are not read off, but marked upon a small sheet, which is changed at each station.

sta-di-um (stā'di-um), *n.*; pl. *-diums* or *-dia* (-di-ạ). [L., < Gr. στάδιον, measure of length, race-course, < ἱστάναι, cause to stand: see *stand*.] An ancient Greek linear measure, equal at Athens to about 607 English feet; also, an ancient Greek course for foot-races, orig. a stadium in length, with banks or tiers of seats for spectators rising along its two sides and at one end, which was typically semicircular; a similar modern structure for athletic games, etc. (as, the Harvard *Stadium*); also, a stage or period, as of a disease.

stadt-hold-er (stat'hōl″dėr), etc. Same as *stadholder*, etc.

staff[1] (stâf), *n.* [Origin uncertain.] A kind of plaster combined with fibrous material, used for temporary ornamental buildings, etc.

staff[2] (stâf), *n.*; pl. *staves* (stāvz) or *staffs*. [AS. *stæf*, staff, stick, letter of the alphabet, = D. *staf* = G. *stab* = Icel. *stafr* = Sw. *staf* = Dan. *stav*, staff: cf. *stave*.] A stick, pole, rod, or wand, as one carried for aid in walking or climbing, or one used as a weapon, or for some other purpose; a rod or wand serving as an ensign of office or authority, as a crozier, baton, truncheon, or mace (as, "The Earl of Worcester Hath broke his *staff*, resign'd his stewardship": Shakspere's "Richard II.," ii. 2. 59); a pole on which a flag is hung or displayed; a graduated rod used in leveling or measuring; a stick or pole forming part of something, as the shaft of a spear, a rung of a ladder or a chair, etc. (now chiefly archaic or prov.); also, a steel surgical instrument, grooved and curved, used for guiding the knife in lithotomy; also, fig., something which serves to support or sustain (as, bread is the *staff* of life); also, a verse or stanza of a poem or song† (now *stave*); in *music*, a set of horizontal lines, now five in number, with the spaces between them, on which music is written; *milit.* and *naval* (plural *staffs*), a body of army or naval officers appointed to assist a commanding officer; a body of naval officers not in military command, as surgeons, paymasters, etc.; a branch of an army, or a body of army officers, concerned with administrative matters, etc., instead of with actual fighting; the general staff (see under *general*, *a.*); hence, in general use (plural *staffs*), a body of assistants to a manager, superintendent, or executive head (as, "governors with their *staffs*": Froude's "Cæsar," ii.); a body of persons charged with carrying out the work of an establishment or executing some undertaking.—**staff**[2], *v. t.* To provide with a staff of officers or others; also, to serve as a staff for, or officer or conduct as a staff does (as, "The armies . . . had to be commanded and *staffed* . . . by men who first studied their profession in that war": Charnwood's "Abraham Lincoln," vii.).

staf-fel-ite (staf'el-īt), *n.* [G. *staffelit*; named from *Staffel*, in Prussia, where it was found.] A greenish mineral, a phosphate and carbonate of calcium, occurring in botryoidal forms of a fibrous structure.

staff-ing (stâf'ing), *n.* The members of an official or working staff collectively.

staff=of-fi-cer (stâf'of″i-sėr), *n.* *Milit.* and *naval*, an officer of a staff.

staff=tree (stâf'trē), *n.* Any tree or shrub of the genus *Celastrus*, esp. the bittersweet, *C. scandens*.

stag (stag), *n.* [Late AS. *stagga*, stag: cf. Icel. *steggr*, male bird or animal.] The male of the deer, chiefly the red deer (*Cervus elaphus*), esp. after the fifth year; also, the male of various other animals; also, a man, esp. a man unaccompanied by a woman at a social gathering (colloq.: often used attributively or in composition, as of affairs in which only men take part, as a *stag* dinner, or a *stag*-party, which see).—**stag'=bee″tle**, *n.* Any of the lamellicorn beetles constituting the genus *Lucanus* (or family *Lucanidæ*), the males of which have mandibles resembling the antlers of a stag.—**stag'=bush**, *n.* The black-haw, *Viburnum prunifolium*.

stage (stāj), *n.* [OF. *estage* (F. *étage*), ult. < L. *stare*, stand: see *stand*.] A floor or story of a building (now rare); any of a series of levels rising one above another; also, a raised platform or floor for any of various purposes; esp., an elevated platform for speakers, performers, etc.; specif., the platform in a theater on which the actors perform, or this platform with all the parts of the theater and all the apparatus back of the proscenium; hence, the theater, the drama, or the dramatic profession; also, the scene of any action or career; also, a place of

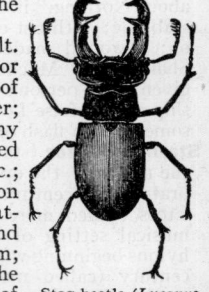
Stag-beetle (*Lucanus cervus*), one half natural size.

rest on a journey; a regular stopping-place of a stage-coach or the like, for the change of horses, etc.; also, the distance between two places of rest on a journey; each of the portions or periods of a journey (as, "and so on . . . by slow or swift *stages* . . . to the Atlantic at last": W. H. Hudson's "Green Mansions," xxi.); hence, a portion or period of a course of action, of life, etc. (as, "this early and necessarily blundering *stage* of the war": Charnwood's "Abraham Lincoln," ix.); a single step or degree in a process; a particular period in a process of development (as, "Lapham had not yet reached the picture-buying *stage* of the rich man's development": Howells's "Rise of Silas Lapham," ii.); also, a stage-coach; also, an omnibus (U. S.); in *microscopy*, the small platform of a microscope on which the object to be examined (or the glass slide or the like bearing it) is placed; in *biol.*, any of the several successive periods in the development of many animals and plants (as, the pupal *stage* of an insect).—**to be** (or **go**) **on the stage,** to follow (or take up) the profession of an actor or actress.—**up stage.** See *up-stage, a.*—**stage,** *v.*; *staged, staging.* **I.** *tr.* To furnish with a stage or staging; also, to put, represent, or exhibit on or as on a stage; mount (a play) for production on the stage. **II.** *intr.* To go by stages; travel by stage or stage-coach.—**stage=box,** *n.* A box in a theater, in or close to the proscenium-arch.—**stage=coach,** *n.* A coach that runs regularly by stages, or over a fixed route between two places, for the conveyance of passengers, parcels, etc.—**stage=craft,** *n.* Skill in or the art of writing, adapting, or mounting plays for effective representation on the stage.—**stage=fright,** *n.* Nervousness experienced on facing an audience, esp. for the first time.—**stage=land** (-land), *n.* The land or realm of the stage; the theatrical world.—**stage=man''age,** *v. t.*; *-aged, -aging.* To manage or regulate as a stage-manager does.—**stage=man''ag-er,** *n.* One who superintends the performance of a play and regulates the stage arrangements.—**stage=play,** *n.* A dramatic performance; also, a play adapted for representation on the stage; also, dramatic acting.—**stage=play''er,** *n.*—**sta-ger** (stā'jėr), *n.* An actor (obs. or archaic); also, a person of experience in some office, profession, way of life, etc. (usually in 'old stager,' a person of long experience); also, a horse used for drawing a stage-coach.—**stage=struck,** *a.* Smitten with a love for the stage; seized by a passionate desire to become an actor.—**stage=whis'per,** *n.* A loud whisper as used on the stage, intended to be heard by the audience; hence, in general, a whisper meant to be heard by others than the person addressed.—**sta'gey,** *a.* See *stagy.*

stag-ger (stag'ėr), *v.* [Var. of obs. or prov. *stacker,* ME. *stakeren,* stagger: cf. Icel. *stakra,* stagger, freq. of *staka,* push, stagger.] **I.** *intr.* To walk or stand unsteadily, as from weakness, intoxication, or a heavy burden (as, "I saw him *staggering* up the street in a state of intoxication," Borrow's "Bible in Spain," iv.; "She *staggered* on with her large jug," W. De Morgan's "Alice-for-Short," i.); reel; totter; move unsteadily, as a ship (as, "The little schooner *staggered* and shook": Kipling's "Captains Courageous," vii.); sway, rock, or shake (as, "Beneath me I can feel The great earth *stagger* and reel": Longfellow's "Golden Legend," i. 254); also, to become unsteady, or begin to give way, as a body of troops; fig., to begin to doubt or waver, as in opinion or purpose; falter; hesitate. **II.** *tr.* To cause to reel or totter; also, to cause to become unsteady; throw into confusion, as troops (as, "a fire from the militia, which . . . for a moment *staggered* the regulars": Cooper's "Spy," xxxiii.); fig., to shock, or render helpless with amazement or the like (as, "I was *staggered* . . . at her sudden vehemence of word and manner": Stevenson's "Master of Ballantrae," ii.); shake the stability or settled character of (as, "These news, fair cousin, have *staggered* your reason": Scott's "Quentin Durward," xxvii.); cause to waver or falter (as, to *stagger* a person's faith; to *stagger* a person in his purpose); also, to arrange in a zigzag order or manner, as spokes in the hub of a wheel; arrange in some other order or manner than the regular, uniform, or usual one, as in order to break up or distribute a combined or massed effect (as, to *stagger* the hours of opening and closing business houses, so that employees shall not all arrive, and all leave, at the same time — a method of preventing congestion in traffic; to

stagger traffic); in *aëronautics,* to arrange (the planes of a biplane, etc.) so that the entering edge of an upper plane is either in advance of or behind that of a corresponding lower plane.—**stag'ger,** *n.* The act or an act of staggering; a reeling or tottering movement or motion; *pl.* (construed as *sing.*), any of various forms of cerebral and spinal disease in horses, cattle, and other animals, characterized by a staggering gait, sudden falling, etc. (often called 'blind staggers'); also, *sing.,* a staggered order or arrangement (see *stagger, v. t.*); in *aëronautics,* the arrangement of the planes of a biplane, etc., produced by staggering; the amount by which the entering edge of an upper plane is in advance of or behind that of a corresponding lower one.—**stag'ger=bush,** *n.* An American ericaceous shrub, *Pieris mariana,* with a foliage poisonous to animals and fascicles of nodding white or pinkish flowers.—**stag'ger-er,** *n.*—**stag'ger-ing-ly,** *adv.* **stag=head-ed** (stag'hed''ed), *a.* Of a tree, having the upper branches bare and dead. **stag-hound** (stag'hound), *n.* One of a breed of hounds used for hunting stags, etc., resembling the foxhound, but larger. **sta-gi-ly** (stā'ji-li), *adv.* In a stagy manner; theatrically.—**sta'gi-ness,** *n.* **sta-ging** (stā'jing), *n.* A temporary platform or structure of posts and boards for support, as in building; scaffolding; also, the act or process of putting a play on the stage; also, the business of running stage-coaches; also, the act of traveling by stages or by stage-coach. **Stag-i-rite** (staj'i-rīt), *n.* A native or inhabitant of Stagira, a city of ancient Macedonia; specif., with *the,* the philosopher Aristotle (384—322 B.C.), who was born there. **stag-nant** (stag'nạnt), *a.* [L. *stagnans* (*stagnant-*), ppr. of *stagnare:* see *stagnate.*] Not running or flowing, as water, air, etc. (as, "As breezes break To sun-bright ripples a *stagnant* lake": Whittier's "Preacher"); without current or motion; often, foul from standing, as a pool of water (as, "The *stagnant* edge of the pool effaces itself into a slope of black slime": Ruskin's "Crown of Wild Olive," Preface); fig., inactive, sluggish, or dull (as, business is *stagnant;* "a dull, *stagnant* condition of mind," J. H. Newman's "Callista," iii.).—**stag'nan-cy,** *n.*—**stag'nant-ly,** *adv.* **stag-nate** (stag'nāt), *v.*; *-nated, -nating.* [L. *stagnatus,* pp. of *stagnare,* form a pool of standing water, stagnate, < *stagnum,* pool, pond: cf. *tank.*] **I.** *intr.* To cease to run or flow, as water, air, etc.; stand without motion or current; often, to become foul from standing, as a pool of water; fig., to become inactive, sluggish, or dull (as, "I felt my wits *stagnating* in the unwonted idleness of the autumn afternoon": F. M. Crawford's "Mr. Isaacs," ii.). **II.** *tr.* To cause to become stagnant.—**stag-na'tion** (-nā'shọn), *n.* A becoming or making stagnant (lit. or fig.); stagnant condition: as, "comparing the progressiveness of the North-Western European with the *stagnation* or decadence of the Latin races" (W. R. Inge's "Outspoken Essays," i. 4). **stag=par-ty** (stag'pär''ti), *n.* A party or entertainment in which only men participate; also, a party or company consisting of men only. [Colloq.] **sta-gy** (stā'ji), *a.* [Also *stagey.*] Of or pertaining to the stage; savoring or suggestive of the stage, theatrical, or theatrically artificial or pompous (as, "His laugh was *stagey,*"

Stagger-bush. — 1, flowering branch; 2, the fruits.

Sinclair Lewis's "Main Street," xxxvi.; *stagy* declamation); of persons, affecting theatrical mannerisms.

staid[1] (stād), *a.* [Earlier *stayed*; orig. pp. of *stay*[2].] Fixed, settled, or permanent (now rare); also, of settled or sedate character (as, "a grave and *staid* God-fearing man," Tennyson's "Enoch Arden," 112; "calm and *staid* deportment," Hawthorne's "Twice-Told Tales," The Gentle Boy); sober; serious; steady; not flighty or capricious.

staid[2] (stād). Preterit and past participle of *stay*[3].

staid-ly (stād'li), *adv.* In a staid manner.—**staid'ness**, *n.*

stain (stān), *v.* [For *distain*.] **I.** *tr.* To discolor with spots or streaks of dirt, blood, or other foreign matter; fig., to bring reproach upon, or blemish (as, "Among those politicians . . . very few can be named whose reputation is not *stained* by . . . gross perfidy and corruption": Macaulay's "Hist. of Eng.," ii.); sully with guilt or infamy, or corrupt (as, men *stained* with every vice); also, to color in a particular way; esp., to color with something which penetrates the substance; specif., to treat (a microscopic specimen) with some reagent or dye in order to color the whole or certain parts and so give distinctness, contrast of tissues, etc. **II.** *intr.* To produce a stain (as, "as the berry breaks before it *staineth*": Shakspere's "Venus and Adonis," 460); also, to become stained; take a stain.—**stain**, *n.* A discoloration produced by foreign matter; a spot; esp., one penetrating beneath the surface and not easily removable; also, a natural spot or patch of color different from the ground, as on the body of an animal; fig., a cause of reproach, or a blemish (as, a *stain* on one's reputation); a mark or taint of guilt or infamy (as, the *stain* of sin); also, a slight trace† (as, "You have some *stain* of soldier in you": Shakspere's "All's Well," i. 1. 122); also, coloration produced by staining anything; also, a dye, pigment, etc., used in staining; a reagent or dye used in staining microscopic specimens.—**stain'a-ble**, *a.* That may be stained.—**stained**, *p. a.* Discolored; colored by staining.—**stained glass**, colored glass as used in decorative windows, in mosaic or composite designs; sometimes, enameled or painted glass.—**stained window**, a window of stained glass.—**stain'er**, *n.*—**stain'less**, *a.* Free from stain; without blemish or taint (as, "the *stainless* honour of your cousin": Scott's "Black Dwarf," xiv.).—**stain'less-ly**, *adv.*—**stain'less-ness**, *n.*

stair (stār), *n.* [AS. *stæger*, < *stīgan*, ascend: see *stile*.] A series or flight of steps forming a means of passage from one story or level to another, as in a building (as, a winding *stair*; "There were two *stairs* in the house," Smollett's "Humphry Clinker," July 1); also, a single step of such a series; *pl.*, such steps collectively, esp. as forming a flight or a series of flights (as, "All is quiet . . . at least above *stairs*": Sterne's "Tristram Shandy," iii. 23).—**pair of stairs**, a flight of stairs: see *puir*, *n.* [Archaic or prov.]—**stair'-case**, *n.* Orig., the case or inclosing framework of a series of steps or stairs; hence, a flight of stairs with its framework, balusters, etc., or a series of such flights.—**stair'case-shell**, *n.* The shell of any of the gastropods of the genus *Solarium*, of tropical seas, or the animal itself: so called as suggesting in its appearance a spiral staircase.—**stair'=foot**, *n.* The foot or bottom of a stair or staircase.—**stair'=head**, *n.* The head or top of a stair or staircase.—**stair'way**, *n.* A way up and down by a series of stairs; a staircase.

Staircase-shell (*Solarium perspectivum*).

stake[1] (stāk), *n.* [AS. *staca* = D. *staak* = LG. *stake*, stake; from the root of E. *stick*[2].] A stick or post pointed at one end for driving into the ground as a boundary-mark, a part of a fence, a support for a plant, an upright for securing an animal to, etc.; in general, a post or upright; esp., a post to which a person is bound for execution, usually by burning; hence (with *the*), the punishment of death by burning; also, a post to which an animal is fastened to be baited; also, one of a number of vertical posts or bars fitting into sockets or staples on the edge of

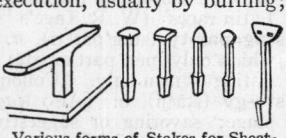

Various forms of Stakes for Sheet-metal Working.

the platform of a vehicle, as to retain the load; also, a small anvil used for working in thin metal, esp. one to be set upright by fitting into a socket on a bench (see cut in preceding column).—**to drive stakes**, to pitch one's tent or camp; stake off a claim; establish one's self; settle. [Colloq.]—**to pull up stakes**, to prepare to move one's camp or habitation; make ready to move on. [Colloq.]—**stake**[1], *v. t.*; *staked*, *staking*. To mark, or indicate the boundaries or divisions of, with stakes (often with *off* or *out*); also, to protect with a barrier of stakes; separate (*off*), shut (*in* or *out*), close (*up*), etc., by a barrier of stakes; also, to support with a stake or stakes, as a plant; also, to tether or secure to a stake, as an animal; fasten (*down*, etc.) with a stake or stakes; also, to impale on or transfix with a stake; also, to drive as or like a stake, as into the ground (as, "the whole being fenced in by a stout palisade of trunks and boughs of trees *staked* firmly in the ground": H. Melville's "Omoo," lii.).

stake[2] (stāk), *v. t.*; *staked*, *staking*. [Cf. MD. *staken*, fix, place, *staeck*, a stake played for.] To put at hazard upon the result of a game, the event of a contingency, etc.; wager; venture or hazard; also, to grub-stake (slang); furnish with necessaries or resources, orig. by way of a business venture with a view to a possible return (slang).—**stake**[2], *n.* That which is staked, wagered, or hazarded, as in a game; a sum of money or the like deposited, to be taken by the winner of a game, race, or other contest; also, *pl.* or *sing.*, the prize in a race or contest, esp. the sum staked or subscribed as the prize in a race between horses, etc.; hence, with a defining term, a particular race between horses, etc., for such a sum; also, *sing.*, an interest held in something (as, "a class of residents, men with a *stake* in the welfare of the country": Roosevelt's "Hunting Trips of a Ranchman," i.); something to gain or lose by the turn of events; also, a grub-stake, or any advance or supply of necessaries or resources (slang); also, the state of being staked or at hazard (now only in 'at stake': as, "Their lives and properties were at *stake*," Froude's "Cæsar," xiv.).

staked (stākt), *p. a.* Marked, separated, supported, secured, etc., with a stake or stakes.—**Staked Plain** (Sp. *Llano Estacado*), a vast arid plateau in northwestern Texas and southeastern New Mexico, bounded by palisades or steep escarpments.

stake=hold-er (stāk'hōl''dėr), *n.* The holder of the stakes of a wager, contest, etc.

stak-er (stā'kėr), *n.* One who stakes.

sta-lac-ti-form (stạ-lak'ti-fôrm), *a.* Having the form of a stalactite.

sta-lac-tite (stạ-lak'tīt or stal'ak-), *n.* [NL. *stalactites*, < Gr. σταλακτός, dropping, dripping, < σταλάσσειν, drop, drip.] A deposit of calcium carbonate, usually shaped like an icicle, hanging from the roof of a cave or the like, and formed by the dripping of percolating calcareous water (as, "a cavern whose walls were supported by many fantastic pillars which had been formed by the joining of great *stalactites* and stalagmites together, the result of the ceaseless water-drip of centuries": Mark Twain's "Tom Sawyer," xxxi.); also, a similar formation of other material, as lava. Cf. *stalagmite*.—**stal-ac-tit-ic** (stal-ak-tit'ik), *a.* Of the nature of or resembling a stalactite or stalactites; characteristic or suggestive of stalactites (as, the *stalactitic* structure of some minerals); having stalactites (as, a *stalactitic* cave).—**stal-ac-tit'i-cal-ly**, *adv.*

sta-lag-mite (stạ-lag'mīt or stal'ag-), *n.* [NL. *stalagmites*, < Gr. σταλαγμός, a dropping or dripping, < σταλάσσειν, drop, drip.] A deposit of calcium carbonate more or less resembling an inverted stalactite, formed on the floor of a cave or the like by the dripping of percolating calcareous water; also, a similar formation of other material, as lava.—**stal-ag-mit-ic** (stal-ag-mit'ik), *a.* Of the nature of, resembling, or characteristic of a stalagmite or stalagmites.—**stal-ag-mit'i-cal-ly**, *adv.*

Stalactitic Structure of Limonite.

stale[1] (stāl), *n.* [Cf. AF. *estale*, obs. F. *estalon*, a bird used as a decoy, AS. *stælhran*, a decoy reindeer, also E. *stall*[1].] A bird, or a figure of a bird, used as a decoy (now prov. Eng.):

hence, any thing or person serving to decoy or lure, esp. a prostitute or other person acting as a decoy for thieves or swindlers†; any thing or person craftily used as a means of carrying out or concealing designs†; also, a ridiculous dupe†.

stale² (stāl), *n.* [ME. *stale*, var. of *stele*, < AS. *stela*, stalk, stem.] A stalk or stem of a plant (now prov. Eng.); a long, straight handle, as of a broom, rake, or ax (now chiefly prov.); one of the long side-pieces (obs.), or a crosspiece or rung (now prov. Eng.), of a ladder.

stale³ (stāl), *a.*; compar. *staler*, superl. *stalest*. [ME. *stale*: cf. MD. *stel*, stale; prob. orig. 'having stood long,' and akin to E. *stall²*.] Old and strong, as ale, beer, or wine (obs. or prov. Eng.); also, affected, esp. unfavorably, by standing or keeping; not fresh; musty; vapid or flat, as beverages; dry or hardened (more or less), as bread that is no longer new; fig., having lost freshness, novelty, or interest (as, *stale* news; a *stale* jest; "I'm not here to do *stale* tricks," Chesterton's "Magic," ii.); hackneyed; trite; also, having passed the prime of life, as a person†; also, out of condition from overtraining or too long continued exertion, as an athlete or a racing animal; hence, having lost fresh vigor, quick intelligence, initiative, or the like, as from overstrain; in *law*, having lost force or effectiveness through absence of action, as a claim.—**stale³**, *v.*; *staled*, *staling*. **I.** *tr.* To make stale: as, "These are things which cannot be *staled* by repetition" (Gissing's "Private Papers of Henry Ryecroft," ii. 27). **II.** *intr.* To become stale: as, "To see her was a delight that never *staled*" (Maugham's "Moon and Sixpence," xxxix.).

stale⁴ (stāl), *v. i.*; *staled*, *staling*. [ME.: cf. D. and G. *stallen*, Sw. *stalla*, Dan. *stalle*, stale.] To urinate: used esp. of horses and cattle.—**stale⁴**, *n.* Urine, now only of horses and cattle.

stale⁵ (stāl), *n.* [Cf. OF. *estaler*, refl. and intr., come to a stand, stop, from Teut., and akin to E. *stall²*.] Same as *stalemate, n.*—**stale⁵**, *v. t.*; *staled*, *staling*. Same as *stalemate, v.*

stale-ly (stāl′li), *adv.* In a stale manner.

stale-mate (stāl′māt), *n.* [See *stale⁵* and *mate²*, and cf. *checkmate*.] A position of the pieces at chess when no move can be made without putting the king in check; hence, any position in which no action can be taken (as, "when the European powers had reached a hopeless *stalemate* after four years of war": J. H. Robinson's "Mind in the Making," vii. 15).—**stale′mate**, *v. t.*; *-mated*, *-mating*. To subject to a stalemate; bring to a standstill.

stale-ness (stāl′nes), *n.* The condition of being stale.

stalk¹ (stäk), *v.* [AS. *stealcian*, walk stealthily, akin to *stelan*, E. *steal*.] **I.** *intr.* To walk or go stealthily along†; also, to pursue or approach game, etc., stealthily, as behind a cover; also, to walk with slow, stiff, or haughty strides (said of persons or animals, or, fig., of ghosts, pestilence, famine, etc.: as, "Two immeasurable Phantoms, Hypocrisy and Atheism . . . *stalk* abroad over the Earth," Carlyle's "Sartor Resartus," iii. 12). **II.** *tr.* To pursue (game, a person, etc.) stealthily, as behind a cover: as, "He had *stalked* and shot a monster [crocodile]" (Amelia B. Edwards's "Thousand Miles up the Nile," xvii.); "Day by day, night by night, we *stalked* the enemy" (G. W. Cable's "Cavalier," lxi.).—**stalk¹**, *n.* An act or course of stalking game or the like (as, "By a careful *stalk* over rough ground I got within fifty yards [of deer feeding]": Roosevelt's "Ranch Life and the Hunting-Trail," ix.); also, a slow, stiff stride or striding gait.

stalk² (stäk), *n.* [ME. *stalke*, akin to *stale*, E. *stale²*.] The stem or main axis of a plant; any slender supporting or connecting part of a plant, as the petiole of a leaf, the peduncle of a flower, or the funicle of an ovule; a similar structural part of an animal (as, an eye-*stalk*; the *stalk*, or means of attachment, of the stalked barnacles, see *barnacle¹*); in general, a stem, shaft, or slender supporting part of anything (as, the *stalk* of a wineglass; "the *stalk* of a tobacco pipe," Stevenson's "Master of Ballantrae," vii.).—**stalked**, *a.* Having a stalk or stalks: as, the *stalked* barnacles (see *barnacle¹*).

stalk-er (stä′kėr), *n.* One who or that which stalks; esp., one who stalks game.

stalk=eyed (stäk′īd), *a.* Having the eyes set upon stalks, as certain crustaceans.

stalk-ing=horse (stä′king-hôrs), *n.* A horse, or a figure of a horse, behind which a hunter conceals himself in stalking game; fig., anything put forward to mask designs or endeavors; a pretext.

stalk-less (stäk′les), *a.* Having no stalk; sessile, as a leaf.

stalk-y (stä′ki), *a.* Abounding in stalks; also, stalk-like; long and slender.

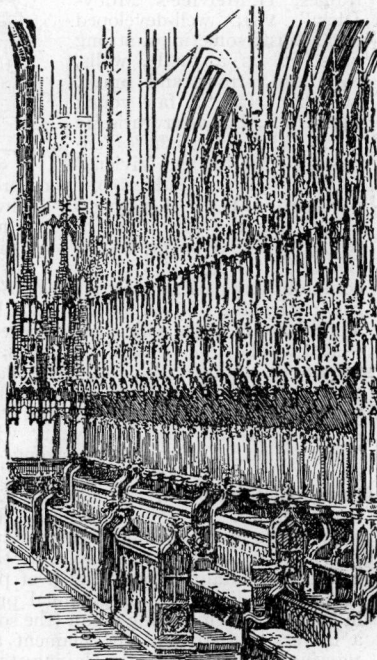

A Stalk-eyed Crustacean (genus *Ocypoda*). *a, a*, the long eye-stalks.

stall¹ (stäl), *n.* [Var. of *stale¹*.] A bird or a person serving as a decoy†; also, a confederate of a pickpocket or other thief, who distracts attention from the thief (slang); also, anything used as a pretext, pretense, or trick (slang: as, "She told her sister she wanted to go to Perry's to get some wool, instead o' which it was only a *stall* to get me a pint o' ale, bless her heart," S. Butler's "Way of All Flesh," lv.).—**stall¹**, *v.* **I.** *tr.* To divert attention from (a thief at work); also, to put off, evade, or deceive (often with *off*). [Slang.] **II.** *intr.* To act evasively or deceptively. [Slang.]

stall² (stäl), *n.* [AS. *steall*, stand, position, place, stall, = D. *stal* = OHG. *stal* (G. *stall*) = Icel. *stallr*, stall; from the same root as E. *stand*: cf. *forestall, install, stale³, stale⁵*, and *stallion*.] A standing-place†, station†, position†, or place†; also, a stable or shed for horses or cattle; a compartment in a stable or shed, for the accommodation of one animal (as, "a savage and vicious mare, whose *stall* it was dangerous to approach": Borrow's "Lavengro," ii.); also, a booth in which merchandise is exposed for sale, or in which some business is carried on (as, "It was Saturday, and all over the square little *stalls*, with yellow linen roofs, were being erected for the principal market of the week," Arnold Bennett's "Old Wives' Tale," i. 3; a butcher's *stall* in a market-house); a stand, table, or the like, on which goods are exposed for sale (as, a book-*stall*); also, one of a number of fixed inclosed seats, as in the choir or chancel of a cathedral or church, esp. for the use of the clergy; the position or dignity of one, as a canon, entitled to occupy such a seat (as, "He held a prebendal *stall* in the diocese": Trollope's "Barchester Towers," ix.); also, a chair-like seat in a theater, separated from others by arms or rails, esp. one in the front division of the parquet (as, "He thought vaguely of a little dinner . . . and a *stall* at the Alhambra": L. Merrick's "Conrad in Quest of His Youth," iv.); also, a compartment, chamber, sheath, or the like, for any of various purposes (as, a finger-*stall*); a working-place in a coal-mine; in aëronautics, a stalling (see *stall²*, *v. t.*); the condition of

Stalls.—Choir of Chester Cathedral, England.

being stalled.—**stall**[2], *v.* **I.** *tr.* To place† or set†; install in an official seat or in office†; also, to put or keep in a stall or stalls, as animals (as, "stables where hundreds of horses were *stalled* at night": Besant's "All Sorts and Conditions of Men," iv.); confine in a stall for fattening, as cattle; also, to furnish with stalls; also, to bring to a standstill; check the progress or motion of, esp. unintentionally; cause to stick fast, as in mire or snow; in *aëronautics*, to reduce the speed of (an aëroplane) so greatly that it is about to fall, out of control, as in climbing at so steep an angle that forward progress tends to become zero. **II.** *intr.* To dwell or live (obs. or prov. Eng.); occupy a stall, as an animal; also, to come to a standstill; be brought to a stop, esp. unintentionally; stick fast, as in mire; in *aëronautics*, of an aëroplane, to become stalled; of an aviator, to stall an aëroplane.—**stalled**, *p. a.* Kept in a stall, as an animal; confined in a stall for fattening before killing, as an ox; also, furnished with stalls; also, brought to a standstill or stop; stuck fast, as in mire.—**stall'=end**, *n.* The end of a stall or seat, as in the choir of a church, often richly carved.—**stall'=feed**, *v. t.; -fed, -feeding.* To keep and feed (an animal) in a stall; fatten by this process, as an animal for killing.

stal-lion (stal'yon), *n.* [OF. *estalon* (F. *étalon*); from Teut.: cf. OHG. *stal*, stall, stable, and E. *stall*[2].] A male horse not castrated; an entire horse, esp. one kept for breeding purposes.

stal-wart (stâl'wart). [Orig. Sc. form of *stalworth*.] **I.** *a.* Strongly and stoutly built, as persons or animals, the bodily form, etc. (as, "She was proud of her *stalwart*, good-looking son," Tarkington's "Magnificent Ambersons," xv.; "They are mostly young, of *stalwart* frames," H. Melville's "Moby-Dick," vi.); well-developed and robust; sometimes, strong or stout, as a castle, walls, etc.; also, strong and brave, or valiant (as, "A fair young squire . . . but afterwards He made a *stalwart* knight": Tennyson's "Merlin and Vivien,"

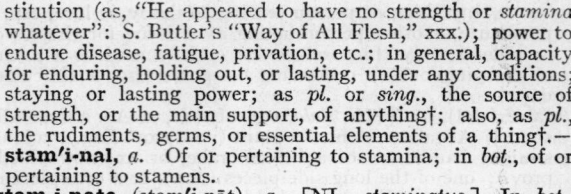

Stall-end (English).

480); also, firm, steadfast, or uncompromising (as, a *stalwart* partizan). **II.** *n.* A physically stalwart person (as, "One of the minor *stalwarts* entered and arranged a table . . . while the butler hovered . . . over the operation": Arnold Bennett's "Pretty Lady," xxvi.); also, a steadfast or uncompromising partizan; [*cap.*] in *U. S. politics*, a member of the controlling faction of the Republican party in New York State in 1881, which was opposed by the Half-breeds. —**stal'wart-ly**, *adv.*—**stal'wart-ness**, *n.*

stal-worth (stâl'werth), *a.* [AS. *stælwyrthe*, serviceable, appar. < *stæl*, place, + *wyrthe*, worth: cf. *stalwart*.] Stalwart, strongly built, or robust (as, "*Stalworth* and stately in form was the man of seventy winters": Longfellow's "Evangeline," i. 1); sturdy; strong; also, valiant (as, "a *stalworth* knight": Scott's "Marmion," i. 5). [Archaic.]

sta-men (stā'men), *n.; pl.* stamens, L. stamina (stam'i-nä) (see stamina). [L. *stamen* (stamin-), thread, fiber, orig. the warp in the upright loom, < *stare*, stand.] The thread of a person's life as fabled to be spun by the Fates†; hence, the measure of vitality†, or strength of physical constitution†; also, the rudimentary or germinal principle of anything†; in *bot.*, the pollen-bearing organ (the so-called male organ) of a flower, consisting of the filament and the anther. See stamina.—**sta'mened**, *a.* Having stamens.

stam-i-na (stam'i-nä), *n.* [L., pl. of *stamen*: see stamen.] As *pl.*, the vital powers as dependent on the physical constitution†; as *sing.* (orig. as *pl.*), strength of physical con-

stitution (as, "He appeared to have no strength or *stamina* whatever": S. Butler's "Way of All Flesh," xxx.); power to endure disease, fatigue, privation, etc.; in general, capacity for enduring, holding out, or lasting, under any conditions; staying or lasting power; as *pl.* or *sing.*, the source of strength, or the main support, of anything†; also, as *pl.*, the rudiments, germs, or essential elements of a thing†.—

stam'i-nal, *a.* Of or pertaining to stamina; in *bot.*, of or pertaining to stamens.

stam-i-nate (stam'i-nāt), *a.* [NL. *staminatus*.] In *bot.*, having a stamen or stamens; having stamens but no pistils.

stam-i-nif-er-ous (stam-i-nif'e-rus), *a.* [See *stamen* and *-ferous*.] In *bot.*, bearing or having a stamen or stamens.

stam-i-no-di-um (stam-i-nō'di-um), *n.; pl. -dia* (-di-ä). [NL., < L. *stamen* (stamin-), thread, + Gr. εἶδος, form.] In *bot.*, a sterile or abortive stamen, or a part resembling such a stamen. Also **stam'i-node** (-nōd).

stam-i-no-dy (stam'i-nō-di), *n.* [L. *stamen* (stamin-), thread, with termination as in E. *petalody*.] In *bot.*, the metamorphosis of any of various flower-organs (as a sepal or a petal) into a stamen.

stam-mel (stam'el). [Obs. F. *estamel*: cf. *etamine*.] **I.** *n.* A kind of coarse woolen fabric formerly in use, commonly dyed red; hence, a red color. [Archaic.] **II.** *a.* Made of stammel; of the color of stammel; red. [Archaic.]

stam-mer (stam'ėr), *v.* [AS. *stamerian*, < *stamer, stamor*, adj., stammering, akin to OHG. *stam*, Icel. *stamr*, Goth. *stamms*, stammering; from the root, meaning 'stop,' represented by E. *stem*[3]: cf. *stumble*.] **I.** *intr.* To falter in speaking, or speak with involuntary breaks and pauses, as from nervousness, confusion, or fear; often, to utter spasmodic repetitions of syllables or sounds in the effort to speak, as from a defect in the powers of speech; stutter. **II.** *tr.* To utter or say with a stammer: often with *out*: as, "He commanded himself sufficiently to *stammer* out his regrets" (Marryat's "King's Own," xlvii.).—**stam'mer**, *n.* A stammering mode of utterance; a habit of stammering; also, a stammered utterance.—**stam'mer-er**, *n.*—**stam'mer-ing-ly**, *adv.*

stam-nos (stam'nos), *n.* [Gr. στάμνος.] In *Gr. antiq.*, a kind of large jar or vessel typically wide-mouthed, short-necked, and having two small handles on opposite sides of the body, used for holding wine, oil, etc.

stamp (stamp), *v.* [ME. *stampen* = D. *stampen* = OHG. *stamfōn* (G. *stampfen*) = Icel. *stappa*, stamp: cf. the related AS. *stempan*, also OF. F. *estamper* (from Teut.), which has prob. affected the E. word.] **I.** *tr.* To crush or pound with or as with a pestle (as, "a stone mortar to *stamp* or beat some corn in": Defoe's "Robinson Crusoe," i. 9); crush (ore), as by means of a stamp-mill; bring (an implement, etc.) down heavily in crushing something; also, to strike or beat with a forcible downward thrust of the foot (as, "Under my feet I *stamp* thy cardinal's hat": Shakspere's "1 Henry VI.," i. 3. 49); trample; force, drive, etc., by or as by beating down with the foot (as, "filling the grave with sand, which they . . . *stamped* down with their naked feet," Amelia B. Edwards's "Thousand Miles up the Nile," xiv.; to *stamp* out, or extinguish, a fire, or, fig., disease, rebellion, etc.); bring (the foot) down forcibly or smartly on the ground, floor, etc. (as, "She . . . *stamped* her feet on the lobby tiles, partly to warm them . . . partly to announce clearly her arrival": Arnold Bennett's "Hilda Lessways," i. 10); shake off by bringing the feet down thus (as, "while he was still *stamping* the snow from his boots": W. Churchill's "Coniston," ii. 11); also, to impress a design on by striking; produce designs, numbers, etc., on with a die or the like; make (a coin, medal, etc.) by such means; cut out or shape (articles or pieces) with a die or the like; mark (paper or any surface) with characters, words, etc., impressed or printed; impress with a particular mark or device, as to indicate genuineness, quality, approval, official character, ownership, or the like (as, "The heaps of gold were cast into ingots and *stamped* with the royal arms": Prescott's "Conquest of Mexico," iv. 5); show or declare to be of a certain quality or character as if by a mark impressed (as, this act *stamped* him as a great statesman); impress with an official mark or device showing that

Typical form of Stamnos.

some duty or charge has been paid; affix an adhesive paper stamp to (a letter, etc.); impress with some conspicuous characteristic (as, a face *stamped* with sadness); be a conspicuous characteristic of (as, candor *stamps* his every utterance); also, to impress (a design, figure, words, etc.) on something; fix on the mind or memory; imprint deeply or permanently on anything (as, "There was a gravity beyond the usual expression of his years *stamped* upon his countenance": Wiseman's "Fabiola," ii. 22); also, to bring down upon something with a stroke or with pressure, in making an impression. **II.** *intr.* To come down forcibly in stamping something; also, to bring the foot down forcibly or smartly on the ground, floor, etc., as in crushing something, emphasizing a command, expressing rage, etc. (as, "Kim *stamped* with vexation": Kipling's "Kim," ix.); bring the foot down hard (*on*: as, "If your neighbour's foot obstructs you, *stamp* on it," Thackeray's "Newcomes," viii.); walk with forcible or heavy, resounding steps (as, "He . . . *stamped* violently out of the office": Bok's "Americanization of Edward Bok," xiv.).—**stamp**, *n.* The act or an act of stamping, as in crushing or in impressing something; a forcible downward thrust or stroke of the foot on the ground or floor (as " 'She shall go,' said Jos, with another *stamp* of his foot": Thackeray's "Vanity Fair," xxxii.); also, an instrument for stamping, crushing, or pounding; a heavy piece of iron or the like, as in a stamp-mill, for dropping on and crushing ore or other material; also, an instrument for making impressions on other bodies; a die, engraved block, or the like, for impressing a design, characters, words, or marks; a plate upon which is cut the design to be impressed on the sides or back of a book; an instrument or apparatus used for stamping coins, medals, etc.; a tool or machine for cutting out, shaping, or perforating articles by a blow or by pressure; also, an impression, a design, characters, words, etc., made with or as with a stamp; an official mark or the like impressed on a thing as an evidence of its genuineness, validity, etc.; a mark of authorization or approval (often fig.: as, a method upon which custom has set its *stamp*; "The South wants the *stamp* of national approval upon slavery," Drinkwater's "Abraham Lincoln," ii.); peculiar or distinctive impress or mark (as, a story which bears the *stamp* of truth); character, kind, or type (as, men of different *stamps*; "Clergymen of Robert's *stamp* are rare among us," Mrs. H. Ward's "Robert Elsmere," xiii.); an official mark or device impressed on a thing subject to a duty or charge, showing that this has been paid; the impression of a public seal required, for revenue purposes, to be obtained from a government office, for a fee, on the paper or parchment on which deeds, bills, receipts, etc., are written; in more recent use, a small adhesive piece of paper printed with a distinctive design, issued by a government for a fixed sum, for attaching to documents or goods subject to a duty, or to letters, etc., to show that a charge, as for postage, has been paid (as, a revenue-*stamp*; a postage-*stamp*); a similar piece of paper issued privately for various purposes (as, a trading-*stamp*, which see); *pl.*, government stamp duties; also, money, orig. paper money (slang, U. S.); also, *sing.*, a picture produced by impression, as from an engraved plate†; also, something stamped with a device, as a coin or a medal†.—**Stamp Act**, in *Amer. hist.*, an act passed by the British Parliament in 1765, providing for the raising of revenue in the American colonies by requiring the use of stamped paper and stamps for legal and official documents, commercial writings, and various articles. It was to go into effect on Nov. 1, 1765, but met with intense opposition, and was repealed in March, 1766. It is regarded as one of the causes leading to the Revolution.

stamp-age (stam′pāj), *n.* The act of stamping; also, an impression made by stamping; also, the amount charged or paid for stamps; postage.

stamped (stampt), *p. a.* Crushed by stamping; also, beaten down with the feet; also, impressed with a design, characters, etc.; ornamented with an embossed device or design; cut out or shaped by stamping; impressed with an official mark or device showing that a duty or charge has been paid; bearing an adhesive paper stamp, as a revenue-stamp or a postage-stamp; also, impressed on something by means of a stamp, as a device.

stam-pede (stam-pēd′), *n.* [Amer. Sp. *estampida*, stampede, Sp. crack, crash, connected with Sp. *estampar*, stamp, from Teut. and akin to E. *stamp*.] A sudden scattering or headlong flight of a body of cattle or horses in fright; any headlong general flight, as of troops in panic; an unconcerted general rush or movement, as of persons actuated by a common impulse (as, a *stampede* to newly discovered gold-fields; a *stampede* in favor of a particular candidate at a political convention).—**stam-pede′**, *v.*; -peded, -peding. **I.** *intr.* To scatter or flee in a stampede, as cattle or persons; make an unconcerted general rush, as persons actuated by a common impulse. **II.** *tr.* To produce a stampede among; cause to stampede: as, "those most trying times when . . . the cattle are *stampeded* by a thunderstorm at night"(Roosevelt's "Hunting Trips of a Ranchman," i.).—**stam-ped′er** (-pē′dėr), *n.*

stamp-er (stam′pėr), *n.* One who or that which stamps; one who applies the postmark and cancels the postage-stamps on letters, etc., in a post-office; an instrument for stamping; a pestle, esp. one in a stamp-mill.

stamp=mill (stamp′mil), *n.* In *metal.*, a mill or machine in which ore is crushed to a powder by means of heavy stamps or pestles which are automatically raised and dropped.

stance (stans), *n.* [Obs. F. *stance*, OF. *estance*, stand, stay, station, position, = It. *stanza*, < L. *stare*, stand: cf. *stanza*.] A standing-place, station, or position (Sc.); a site, as for a building (Sc.); in *golf*, etc., the position of the feet of a player when making a stroke.

stanch[1], **staunch**[1] (stänch, stȧnch or stänch), *v.* [OF. *estanchier* (F. *étancher*), ult. < L. *stagnum*, pool, pond: cf. L. *stagnare*, form a pool of standing water, also make stagnant, and E. *stagnate*.] **I.** *tr.* To stop the flow of (a liquid, esp. blood); stop the flow of blood from (a wound: as, "It was difficult . . . to fasten a bandage tightly enough to *staunch* the wound," Motley's "Dutch Republic," vi. 5); also, to check, appease, allay, or assuage (pain, appetite, desire, strife, etc.: archaic or prov.). **II.** *intr.* To stop flowing, as blood; be stanched.—**stanch**[1], **staunch**[1], *n.* A flood-gate in a river.

stanch[2], **staunch**[2] (stänch, stȧnch or stänch), *a.* [OF. *estanche*, fem. of *estanc* (F. *étanche*, masc. and fem.), < *estanchier*, E. *stanch*[1].] Impervious to water or liquids, or water-tight (as, "Build me . . . *Stanch* and strong, a goodly vessel": Longfellow's "Building of the Ship," 2); hence, sound or firm in structure, substance, etc. (as, *stanch* walls or defenses; "The *stanch* oaken logs were long ago burnt out," Hawthorne's "Blithedale Romance," ii.); strong; substantial; also, firm or steadfast in principle, adherence, loyalty, etc., as a person, the heart, etc. (as, "He lived and died a *stanch* loyalist," Mrs. Stowe's "Oldtown Folks," xxiv.; "I would think much less of you if you were not *staunch* to your employer," Stevenson's "Master of Ballantrae," viii.); characterized by firmness or steadfastness (as, "*stanch* fidelity," Prescott's "Conquest of Mexico," iii. 7; "*staunch* principles," Trollope's "Barchester Towers," xxii.); of a hunting-dog, that may be depended on to find or follow the scent.—**stanch**[2], **staunch**[2], *v. t.* To make stanch; render water-tight or close, as walls.

stanch-er, staunch-er (stän′chėr, stȧn′chėr or stän′-), *n.* One who or that which stanches.

stan-chion (stan′shọn), *n.* [OF. *estanchon* (F. *étançon*), < *estance*, a prop, also stand, station: see *stance*.] An upright bar, beam, post, or support, as in a window, in a stall for cattle, in a building, structure, or framework, in or on a ship, etc.—**stan′chion**, *v. t.* To furnish with stanchions; also, to secure by or to a stanchion or stanchions.

stanch-less, staunch-less (stänch′les, stȧnch′les or stänch′-), *a.* That cannot be stanched.

stanch-ly, staunch-ly (stänch′li, stȧnch′li or stänch′-), *adv.* In a stanch manner.—**stanch′ness, staunch′ness,** *n.*

stand (stand), *v. i.; stood, standing.* [AS. *standan* (pret. *stōd*) = OS. *standan* = OHG. *stantan* = Icel. *standa* = Goth. *standan*, stand; akin to L. *stare*, stand, *sistere*, cause to stand, stand, Gr. ἱστάναι, cause to stand, stand, Skt. *sthā*-, stand: cf. *assist, cost, rest*[2], *stadium, stage, stall*[2], *state, static, stead*.] Of persons or animals, to take or keep an upright position on the feet (opposed to *sit, lie*, etc.); have a specified height when in this position (as, he *stands* six feet in his socks); also, to remain motionless on the feet; cease walking or moving; halt; stop; of a hunting-dog, to point; also, to take a position or stand as indicated (as, to *stand* aside or back); also, to remain steady in an upright position on the feet; remain firm or steadfast, as in a cause; take up or maintain a position or attitude with respect to others or to some question or the like (as, to *stand* sponsor for a person or a movement); adopt a certain course, as of adherence, support, opposition, or resistance; be drawn up in battle array, as soldiers; become or be a candidate, as for office; also, of things, to be in an upright position (opposed to *lie*); be set on end; become erect or upright; rest on or as on a support; be set, placed, or fixed; be located or situated (as, "The Priory . . . *stood* on an island in the river": Kingsley's "Yeast," iii.); be placed or entered in a list, record, account, text, or the like, as names, figures, words, etc. (as, "As the passage really *stands* in the gospel, it is much stronger": J. Butler's "Analogy of Religion," ii. 1); be at a certain degree, as in a scale of measurement or valuation (as, the mercury, or the temperature, *stands* at 80°); of an account, score, etc., to show a specified position of the parties concerned (as, the account *stands* in my favor); also, to remain in an upright position, as an edifice; remain erect and entire; resist change, decay, or destruction; endure or last; continue in force or remain valid; also, to remain motionless, still, or stationary; stop moving; cease action of any kind; be or become stagnant, as water; also, of persons or things, to be or remain in a specified state, condition, relation, situation, etc. (as, he *stood* alone in that opinion; as matters *stand*; the relation in which abstract ideas *stand* to one another; he *stands* to win $100); also, to cost (with an indirect personal object and an adjunct of price: as, "My table alone *stands* me in a cool thousand a quarter," Smollett's "Humphry Clinker," June 26; how much will this *stand* me?); also, to move or tend steadily in a particular direction; esp., *naut.*, to take or hold a particular course at sea (as, "We weighed anchor . . . and *stood* out to sea," Defoe's "Captain Singleton," x.; "They beheld a little squadron of vessels far at sea, but *standing* towards the shore," Irving's "Conquest of Granada," lxxxviii.); sail; steer; also, in *card-playing*, to play with one's hand as dealt.—**to stand by.** (*a*) (With *by*, *prep.*) To stand beside (a person); side with; aid, uphold, or sustain (as, "His men promised to *stand by* him": Prescott's "Conquest of Mexico," iv. 6); also, to adhere to (an agreement, promise, etc.); abide by; maintain; also, *naut.*, to be or make ready to operate (as, to *stand by* an anchor, to prepare to let go of it; to *stand by* a rope, to take hold of it and be ready to ease it off or the like). (*b*) (With *by*, *adv.*) To stand near at hand; be present; also, to stand aside; also, *naut.*, to be or make ready, or stand or wait in a position of readiness, as in order to perform some act when a command or signal is given.—**to stand for,** to take the part of (a person); advocate or uphold (a cause, etc.: as, "This administration . . . must be regarded for its remaining months as *standing for* the Union," Charnwood's "Abraham Lincoln," vi.); also, to stand in place of; serve, or do duty, for; be a symbol of; represent; also, to answer, or be responsible, for (now chiefly slang); also, to put up with or tolerate (slang); also, *naut.*, to sail or steer toward.—**to stand in,** to be associated, leagued, or in partnership (as, a policeman who *stood in* with thieves); also, to be on good terms (as, to *stand in* with those in authority). [Slang or colloq.]—**to stand in one's own light.** See under *light*[1], *n.* —**to stand on.** (*a*) (With *on*, *prep.*) To base one's position on; rest or depend on; be based on; also, to be punctilious about (ceremony, etc.); assert, or claim respect for (one's rights, dignity, etc.). (*b*) (With *on*, *adv.*) *Naut.*, to continue on the same course or tack.—**to stand out,** to stand apart, in open view; project or protrude; be prominent or conspicuous (as, "Lingard struck a match . . . and his powerful face with narrowed eyes *stood out* for a moment in the night": J. Conrad's "Rescue," i. 2); also, to hold aloof; also, to persist in opposition or resistance; refuse to yield.—**to stand over,** to remain or be left for consideration, treatment, or settlement later: as, "That might *stand over* for the present" (S. Butler's "Way of All Flesh," lix.).— **to stand pat.** See under *pat*, *adv.*—**to stand to reason,** to be in accordance with reason.—**to stand up for,** to take

the part of; defend the cause of; support.—**to stand upon.** Same as *to stand on* (*a*).—**stand,** *v. t.* To cause to stand (as, "another plump and apple-faced boy, whom he *stood* down on the floor": Dickens's "Dombey and Son," ii.); set upright; set; also, to face or encounter (as, to *stand* an assault); endure, undergo, or submit to (as, to *stand* trial); endure or undergo without hurt or damage, or without giving way (as, material that will *stand* wear; "In Queensland the Italian colonists are said to *stand* the heat better than the English," W. R. Inge's "Outspoken Essays," i. 4); put up with or tolerate (as, "She was not prepared to *stand* patronage from such a man," Margaret Kennedy's "Constant Nymph," xv.; "Horace can't *stand* him!" Galsworthy's "Country House," i. 5); bear the expense of (colloq.: as, "Asked whether he would '*stand*' a bottle of champagne for the company, he consented," Thackeray's "Vanity Fair," liii.); also, *naut.*, to take or hold (a course) at sea (as, "The frigate was *standing* her course before a light breeze": Marryat's "King's Own," xlix.).—**to stand a chance** (or **a show**), to have a chance or possibility (as, to *stand a chance* of winning a race, of being expelled, or of defeat); esp., to have a chance of winning, surviving, or the like (as, he *stands* no chance).— **to stand off,** to keep off or at a distance; put off or evade. [Colloq.]—**to stand one's ground,** to stand firm; maintain one's position against attack or opposition.—**to stand shot.** See under *shot*[3].—**stand,** *n.* The act of standing; an assuming of, or a remaining in, an upright position; a coming to a position of rest, or a halt or stop; a halt of a theatrical company on tour, in order to give a performance or performances (as, a one-night *stand*); a halt, as of retreating troops, for defense or resistance (as, "The defeated Sherif Ali fled the country without making another *stand*": J. Conrad's "Lord Jim," xxviii.); a determined effort against or for something (as, "The most notable *stand* against actual secession was that which was made in Georgia by Stephens": Charnwood's "Abraham Lincoln," vi.); a state of rest or inaction, or a standstill; a state of hesitation, embarrassment, or perplexity (often in the phrase 'to be at a stand': as, "He is very ill at ease. The leeches are at a *stand*," Scott's "Kenilworth," xii.); also, the place where a person or thing stands, or a position or station (as, "I took my *stand* under the piazza of the post-office to wait for O'Flaherty": Lever's "Harry Lorrequer," xxii.); the post or station of a sentinel, watchman, or the like; a stall, booth, table, or the like, where articles are exposed for sale or some business is carried on (as, a fruit-*stand*; a news-*stand*); a site or location for business (as, "The shopkeeping nation, to use a shop word, has a good *stand*": Emerson's "English Traits," iii.); a place or station occupied by vehicles which ply for hire, or the vehicles occupying such a place; a raised platform or other structure, as for spectators at a race-course or an athletic field, or along the route of a parade, or for a band or the like; a raised platform for a speaker; the place where a witness stands to testify in court; fig., a position taken or maintained with respect to others or to some question (as, "He was preparing . . . to take a new political *stand* as the patron of Catholicism": Green's "Short Hist. of the Eng. People," vii. 4); also, something to stand things on; a framework on or in which articles are placed for support, exhibition, etc.; a piece of furniture of various forms, on or in which to put articles (as, a wash-*stand*; an umbrella-*stand*); a small, light table (as, "an ebony *stand* on which stood a cinerary urn": W. H. Hudson's "Green Mansions," Prologue); also, something that stands; a young tree left standing for timber; a tree growing from its own root, as distinguished from one produced from a scion set in the stock of another tree; the growing trees, or those of a particular species or grade, on a given area; a standing growth, as of grass, wheat, etc.; also, a complete set of articles of various kinds; a set of vestments, garments, or clothes (Sc.); the arms and accoutrements for one soldier ('stand of arms': pl. *stands* or *stand*); the colors or flag carried by a body of troops ('stand of colors': pl. *stands* or *stand*); a group of pikemen ('stand of pikes': obs. or hist.).

stan-dard (stan'därd). [Orig. < OF. *estandard*, *estandart*, *estendart*, ensign, flag, rallying-point (F. *étendard*, ensign), prob. < L. *extendere*, stretch out (see *extend*); some of the later E. senses being due to association with E. *stand*.] **I.** *n.*

A flag, emblematic figure (as the Roman eagle), or other object raised on a pole to indicate the rallying-point of an army, fleet, etc.; a distinctive flag or ensign, as of a king or a nation; any of various military or naval flags, sometimes, by restriction, a long, tapering one; also, an officer or soldier who carries a standard; a standard-bearer; also, the authorized exemplar of a unit of weight or measure; anything taken by general consent as a basis of comparison, or established as a criterion (as, "The Academy . . . rendered this dictionary the most received *standard* of the French language," Hallam's "Literature of Europe," iv. 7. § 11; "It wouldn't be quite fair to test him by our *standards*," Howells's "Rise of Silas Lapham," v.); the legal rate of intrinsic value for coins; the prescribed degree of fineness for gold or silver; a certain commodity treated as of invariable value and serving as a measure of value for all other commodities, as, in modern monetary systems, either gold or silver ('gold standard' or 'silver standard,' or 'single standard'), or both gold and silver in a fixed proportion to each other ('double standard': cf. *bimetallism*); a grade or level of excellence or advancement generally regarded as right or fitting (as, the *standard* of living in a community; *standards* of comfort; *standards* of education or of morals in the last century); any of the grades or degrees of attainment according to which school-children are classified (Great Britain); also, something which stands or is placed upright; a tall candlestick, candelabrum, or the like; an upright timber, bar, or rod; an upright support or supporting part (as, "Across the fields a line of gaunt iron *standards* . . . carried an electric cable": H. G. Wells's "Soul of a Bishop," ii.); in *hort.*, a tree, shrub, or other plant having a tall, erect stem, and not grown in bush form or trained upon a trellis or other support; in *forestry*, a tree or shoot left standing after a coppice is cut down; also, a tree from one to two feet in diameter, breast-high; in *bot.*, a vexillum; in *ornith.*, a lengthened wing-feather characteristic of certain birds. **II.** *a.* Serving as a standard of weight, measure, or value, or of comparison or judgment (as, "A yard or a foot has no meaning unless there be a definite *standard* yard or foot which fixes its meaning": Jevons's "Elementary Lessons in Logic," xxxiii.); also, conformed or conforming to any such standard; hence, of recognized excellence or established authority (as, a *standard* author; a *standard* book on chemistry); also, standing or set upright; in *hort.*, grown as a standard.—**standard time,** the time officially adopted for a country or a portion of a country, usually (but not always) based on one of the twenty-four standard meridians that start with the meridian of Greenwich, England, and extend 15° apart around the globe, the local time on each of these meridians differing from Greenwich time by a whole number of hours. In the U. S., this system divides the country into four sections, each section embracing 15° of longitude (15° of longitude making a difference in time of exactly one hour), although railroad use has caused irregularities in the boundaries, and each section having its time governed by its central meridian, the time prevailing in the first section being that of the 75th meridian west from Greenwich (called *eastern time*), in the second section that of the 90th meridian (called *central time*), in the third section that of the 105th meridian (called *mountain time*), and in the fourth and most westerly section that of the 120th meridian (called *Pacific time*).

stan-dard=bear-er (stan′dȧrd-bār″ėr), *n.* An officer or soldier of an army, company, or troop who bears a

Standard-bearer (*Macrodipteryx longipennis*).

standard; one who carries a banner in a procession; fig., a conspicuous leader of a movement, political party, or the like; also, an African bird, *Macrodipteryx longipennis*, of the goatsucker family, having one flight-feather of each wing extraordinarily prolonged as a bare shaft with barbs on the terminal portion (see cut in preceding column).

stan-dard-ize (stan′dȧr-dīz), *v. t.*; *-ized*, *-izing*. To conform to or regulate by a standard; bring to or make of an established standard size, shape, weight, quality, strength, or the like (as, to *standardize* manufactured articles or parts); also, to compare with or test by a standard.—**stan″dard-i-za′tion** (-dȧr-di-zā′shŏn), *n.*—**stan′dard-iz-er** (-dȧr-dī-zėr), *n.*

stand=by (stand′bī), *n.*; pl. *-bys* (-bīz). One who stands by another, as to render assistance; a stanch supporter or adherent; one who can be relied upon; also, something upon which one can rely (as, "The corn . . . was the *stand-by* and invariable resource of the western settler": Roosevelt's "Winning of the West," i. 5); a chief support; a ready, timely resource; *naut.*, a vessel kept in readiness for emergencies; also, an order or signal for a boat to stand by.

stand-ee (stand-ē′), *n.* One who stands, or has standing-room only, as at a theatrical performance. [Colloq.]

stand-er (stan′dėr), *n.* One who or that which stands.

stand-ing (stan′ding), *n.* The act of one who or that which stands; a remaining motionless or at a standstill; also, the period during which a person or thing stands; length of existence, continuance, residence, membership, experience, etc., or duration (as, "Between him and the licensers there was a feud of long *standing*," Macaulay's "Hist. of Eng.," xix.; "I know less geography than a schoolboy of six weeks' *standing*," Lamb's "Old and the New Schoolmaster"); also, a place where a person or thing stands; standing-room; also, position or status, as to rank, credit, reputation, etc. (as, men of good *standing*); esp., good position or credit (as, "Many of the emigrants . . . were persons of wealth and *standing*": Parkman's "Oregon Trail," i.).—**stand′ing**, *p. a.* That stands erect or upright; performed in or from an erect position (as, a *standing* jump); also, remaining motionless or at a standstill; still, not flowing, or stagnant, as water; stationary; also, continuing without cessation or change; lasting or permanent; continuing in operation, force, use, etc. (as, a *standing* rule); permanently established (as, a *standing* army, a permanently organized military force kept up by a country).—**standing part**, of a rope, etc., a part which is made fast to something. Cf. *running part*, under *running*, *p. a.*—**stand′ing=ground**, *n.* Ground to stand on; esp., fig., a basis for operations or argument.—**stand′-ing=room**, *n.* Room or space in which to stand; accommodation only for standing, as in a theater where all the seats have been taken.

stan-dish (stan′dish), *n.* [Appar. < *stand* + *dish*.] A stand for ink, pens, and other writing-materials; an ink-stand; also, an ink-well. [Now rare.]

stand=off (stand′-ôf). **I.** *n.* A standing off or apart; aloofness; also, a holding or keeping off; also,

Standish of Decorated Pottery, 18th century.

a situation involving a balance between opposing elements; a tie or draw, as in a game; also, something that counterbalances; a set-off. [Colloq.] **II.** *a.* Standing off or apart; holding aloof; reserved or distant: as, "Young Oliver . . . under Sylvia's spell, soon lost his *stand-off* air" (Galsworthy's "Dark Flower," iii. 6). [Colloq.]—**stand′=off′-ish,** *a.* Same as *stand-off*, *a.*: as, "A finicking sort of man — that was what she called him, *stand-offish*, stony" (Arnold Bennett's "Riceyman Steps," v. 3). [Colloq.]—**stand′=off′-ish-ness,** *n.*

stand=pat (stand′pat′). **I.** *n.* One who stands pat (see under *pat*, *adv.*); one who holds to an existing order of things, or to a policy, etc., in force, as in politics, refusing to consider proposals of change or reform. [Colloq.] **II.** *a.* Characterized by the principle of standing pat. [Colloq.]—

stand'=pat'ter, *n.* One who stands pat; a stand-pat. [Colloq.]—**stand'=pat'tism,** *n.* The principle of standing pat. [Colloq.]

stand=pipe (stand'pīp), *n.* A vertical pipe or tower into which water is pumped in order to obtain a required head.

stand-point (stand'point), *n.* [Tr. G. *standpunkt.*] A fixed point of standing; the point at which one stands to view something (as, "From my present *standpoint* I could see the upper part of the back of this house": S. J. Weyman's "Gentleman of France," ix.); esp., fig., the mental position from which one views and judges things, or a mental point of view (as, "Viewed from the *standpoint* of literary criticism their productions were not very commendable": Motley's "Dutch Republic," Introd., xiv.).

stand-still (stand'stil), *n.* A standing still; a state of cessation of movement or action; a halt; a pause; a stop: as, "The countess . . . stopped dead, bringing her escort to a *standstill* behind her" (Arnold Bennett's "The Old Adam," iii.); "Operations were at a *standstill*" (W. Churchill's "Coniston," ii. 14).

stand=up (stand'up), *a.* Standing erect; upright (not turn-down), as a collar; also, performed, taken, etc., while one stands (as, a *stand-up* meal); also, being one in which the combatants stand up fairly to each other without evasion of any kind (as, a *stand-up* fight in pugilism: "They wouldn't let us make a fair *stand-up* fight of it," G. B. Shaw's "Arms and the Man," ii.).

stane (stān), *n.*, *a.*, and *v.* Sc. and north. Eng. form of *stone.*

stang (stang), *n.* [ME. *stang, stong:* cf. Icel. *stöng* (gen. *stangar*), also AS. *steng,* pole, from the root of E. *sting.*] A pole, bar, or rail: as, to ride the *stang* (to be carried about in public mounted astride on a pole, in an old popular mode of punishment, as for wife-beating: the culprit being sometimes represented by an effigy or a proxy). [Prov. Eng. and Sc.]

stan-hope (stan'hōp or -ǫp), *n.* [From *Stanhope,* proper name.] A kind of light, open, one-seated carriage, formerly with two wheels, now usually with four.

stan-iel, stan-nel (stan'yel, stan'el), *n.* [AS. *stāngella,* < *stān,* stone, + *gellan,* yell.] The kestrel, *Tinnunculus alaudarius.*

stank (stangk). Preterit of *stink.*

stan-na-ry (stan'a-ri), *n.*; pl. *-ries* (-riz). [ML. *stannaria,* < LL. *stannum,* tin.] A tin-mining region or district; *pl.* [*cap.*], with *the,* the tin-mining districts of Cornwall and Devon, England, formerly under the jurisdiction of special courts; also, the customs and privileges attached to the mines.

stan-nate (stan'āt), *n.* In *chem.,* a salt of stannic acid.

stan'nel, *n.* See *staniel.*

stan-nic (stan'ik), *a.* [See *stannum.*] Of or containing tin. See *stannous.*—**stan-nif-er-ous** (sta-nif'e-rus), *a.* [See *-ferous.*] Yielding tin.—**stan-nite** (stan'īt), *n.* A mineral of an iron-black, steel-gray, or bronze-yellow color, with a metallic luster, consisting chiefly of the sulphides of tin, copper, and iron; tin pyrites.—**stan-no-type** (stan'ǫ-tīp), *n.* [See *-type.*] A tintype; also, a photomechanical process of printing in ink from a gelatin plate coated with tin-foil; also, the plate, or a print made from it.—**stan'nous,** *a.* Containing tin (in a larger proportion than a corresponding stannic compound).

stan-num (stan'um), *n.* [LL., tin, L. an alloy of silver and lead.] Tin: in *chem.,* abbreviated *Sn* (without period).

stan-za (stan'zä), *n.*; pl. *-zas* (-zäz). [It., < L. *stare,* stand: cf. *stance.*] In *pros.,* a group of lines of verse, commonly four or more in number, arranged according to a fixed plan as regards the number of lines, the meter, and the rime, and forming a poem or, esp., a division of a poem.—**stan'-zaed** (-zäd), *a.* Having stanzas: as, two-*stanzaed.*—**stan-za'ic** (-zā'ik), *a.* Of or pertaining to a stanza; forming a stanza; composed of stanzas. Also **stan'zic.**—**stan-za'i-cal-ly,** *adv.*

sta-pe-di-al (stạ-pē'di-ạl), *a.* Of or pertaining to the stapes.

sta-pe-li-a (stạ-pē'li-ạ), *n.* [NL.; named from J. B. van *Stapel* (died 1636), Dutch botanist.] Any of the plants constituting the asclepiadaceous genus *Stapelia,* native in South Africa and sometimes seen in cultivation, with short, fleshy, leafless stems, and flowers which are often oddly colored or mottled and in most species emit a fetid, carrion-like odor.

sta-pes (stā'pēz), *n.* [ML. *stapes* (*staped-*), stirrup.] In *anat.,* the innermost of three small bones in the middle ear of man and other mammals, having a stirrup-like shape; also, a corresponding bone in other animals. See *incus* and *malleus.*

Stapelia (*S. variegata*).

staph-y-lo-coc-cus (staf"i-lō-kok'us), *n.*; pl. *-cocci* (-kok'sī). [NL., < Gr. σταφυλή, bunch of grapes, + NL. *coccus:* see *coccus.*] Any of certain species of micrococcus in which the individual organisms form irregular clusters, as *Micrococcus* (or *Staphylococcus*) *pyogenes,* a species that causes the formation of pus.

staph-y-lo-ma (staf-i-lō'mä), *n.*; pl. *-mata* (-mạ-tä). [LL., < Gr. σταφύλωμα, < σταφυλή, bunch of grapes.] In *pathol.,* any of various local bulgings of the eyeball.

staph-y-lo-plas-ty (staf'i-lō-plas"ti), *n.* [Gr. σταφυλή, bunch of grapes, uvula: see *-plasty.*] The remedying of defects of the soft palate by plastic surgery.—**staph"y-lo-plas'tic,** *a.*

staph-y-lor-rha-phy (staf-i-lor'ạ-fi), *n.* [Gr. σταφυλή, bunch of grapes, uvula: see *-rhaphy.*] The uniting of a cleft palate by plastic surgery.

sta-ple[1] (stā'pl), *n.* [ME. *stapul, stapel,* appar. < AS. *stapol,* post, prop, = MLG. *stapel,* post, platform, pile (see *staple*[2]); prob. akin to E. *step.*] A loop of metal with pointed ends for driving into a surface to hold a hasp, hook, pin, bolt, or the like; also, some other device of similar shape or function; a bent piece of wire used to bind papers, sections of a book, etc., together.—**sta'ple**[1], *v. t.*; *-pled, -pling.* To secure or fasten by a staple or staples: as, "an iron ring that was *stapled* into a post" (H. Brooke's "Fool of Quality," xvii.).

sta-ple[2] (stā'pl). [OF. *estaple,* < MLG. *stapel,* post, platform, pile (of goods, etc.), mart, emporium: see *staple*[1].] **I.** *n.* A town or place appointed by royal authority as the seat of a body of merchants having the exclusive right of purchase of certain classes of goods for export (obs. or hist.); the body of merchants having this right (obs. or hist.); also, a town or place which is a principal market for some commodity (archaic, and often fig.: as, "Whitehall naturally became the chief *staple* of news," Macaulay's "Hist. of Eng.," iii.); a chief place of business in a country or district (archaic); an authorized place of trade for merchants of a foreign country (obs. or hist.); also, a principal commodity grown or manufactured in a locality, either for exportation or for home consumption (as, "Its [Ireland's] great *staple* was wool": Bancroft's "Hist. of the U. S.," Amer. Revolution, ii. 2); a commodity principally or largely dealt in; fig., a principal item, thing, feature, element, or part (as, "Haley . . . had been imbibing very freely of the *staple* of the evening," Mrs. Stowe's "Uncle Tom's Cabin," viii.; "Mummers, bacchanals, satyrs . . . formed the *staple* of the procession," J. H. Newman's "Callista," xx.); also, the fiber of wool, cotton, flax, etc., considered with reference to length and fineness; a particular length and degree of fineness of the fiber of wool, cotton, etc.; a lock of wool; unmanufactured wool; the fiber of which a thread or a textile fabric is composed (also fig.); also, a layer of mold (see *mold*[1]); a particular depth or quality of this. **II.** *a.* Pertaining to or of the nature of a staple (town or place); also, chief or prominent among the products exported or produced by a country or district; chiefly or largely dealt in or consumed; regularly produced in large quantities for the market; chief or principal, as industries; principally used (as, *staple* subjects of conversation).—**sta'ple**[2], *v. t.*; *-pled, -pling.* To receive (goods for export) at a staple (obs. or hist.); cause to be weighed, inspected, etc., in accordance with the regulations of the staple (obs. or hist.); also, to sort or classify according to the staple or fiber, as wool.—**sta'pled,** *a.* Having a staple (as specified): as, long-*stapled* wool.

sta-pler[1] (stā′plẻr), *n.* A wire-stitching machine used in bookbinding.

sta-pler[2] (stā′plẻr), *n.* A merchant of the staple (obs. or hist.); later, a wool-merchant; also, one who staples, or sorts according to the staple or fiber (as, a *stapler* of wool).

star (stär), *n.* [AS. *steorra* = D. *ster* = OHG. *sterro*, star; akin to L. *stella*, Gr. ἀστήρ, Skt. *tārā*, star.] Any of the heavenly bodies appearing as luminous points in the sky at night (as, the fixed *stars*, see following def.; the morning *star*, or the evening *star*, which are planets, see under *morning* and *evening*; a falling-*star* or shooting-*star*, a meteor); esp., as now usually restricted, any of the self-luminous bodies outside the solar system which apparently always retain about the same relative position with respect to one another (hence called 'fixed stars'), as distinguished from planets, comets, and meteors (the sun being sometimes classed with these fixed stars, as distinguished from the planets); sometimes, any heavenly body, as the sun or the moon (chiefly poetic: as, the *star* of day, the sun); a heavenly body, esp. a planet, considered as influencing mankind and events (as, "England was not yet at war, but all the *stars* were marching to that end," H. G. Wells's "Mr. Britling," ii. 1. § 3; to be born under a lucky *star*; "We thanked our *stars* that we had thus narrowly escaped," H. Melville's "Omoo," lxv.); hence, destiny or fortune (now rare); also, a person of brilliant qualities or achievements; one who is preëminent or distinguished in some art, profession, or other field (as, "the new *star* of society, Fulvius": Wiseman's "Fabiola," i. 6); often, a prominent or celebrated actor, singer, or the like, esp. a chief member of a company whose name is specially advertised and whom the rest of the company are considered as supporting; also, a conventional figure having rays (commonly five or six) proceeding from, or angular points disposed in a regular outline about, a central point, and considered as representing a star of the sky; some object or arrangement resembling or suggesting this; a star-shaped figure or ornament, worn as part of the insignia of an order of knighthood, as a military decoration, etc. (as, "The General was resplendent with *stars* and medals": Mrs. H. Ward's "Lady Rose's Daughter," ix.); the wearer of such a figure or ornament; a spot of white or light color on the forehead of an animal; a group of cracks or flaws radiating from a center, as in glass or ice; in *printing*, etc., an asterisk; in *zoöl.*, any of various more or less star-shaped echinoderms, as a starfish, a feather-star, etc.; in *elect.*, the star-shaped arrangement of connections in a polyphase apparatus which has one end of each of its windings joined at a common point (hence, *star-connected, star-current,* etc.); in *pyrotechny,* a small piece of inflammable composition used in rockets, etc., which, when burning high in the air, resembles a star.— **Stars and Bars,** the flag adopted by the Confederate States of America, consisting of two broad horizontal bars of red separated by one of white, with a blue union marked with as many white stars, arranged in a circle, as the number of Confederate States.—**Stars and Stripes,** the national flag of the United States, consisting of thirteen horizontal stripes, alternately red and white, equal to the number of the original States, with a blue union marked with white stars equal in number to the whole number of States.—**star,** *a.* Marked with or distinguished by a star or asterisk; also, having the character or position of a star, as in some art, profession, or other field; brilliant, prominent, or distinguished; conspicuous for standing or importance.—**Star Chamber.** See entry in vocabulary place.—**star route,** in the U. S. postal service, a route, other than the ordinary routes, over which mail is carried by special contract with private individuals, from default of the usual carriers: so called from asterisks used to mark such routes in official papers.—**star,** *v.;* **starred, starring. I.** *tr.* To set with or as with stars; stud or spangle, as with something starlike (as, "Blooms Which *star* the winds with points of coloured light": Shelley's "Prometheus Unbound," iii. 3. 138); be set or scattered like stars over (as, "When the first drift of white *Stars* the black branches of the spiky thorn": Masefield's "Daffodil Fields," i.); also, to mark with a star or asterisk, as for special notice; also, to fracture with cracks radiating from a center; also, to arrange in the form of a star; also, to make into a star or stars, or place among the stars; present (an actor, etc.) as a

star. **II.** *intr.* To shine as a star; be brilliant or prominent; of an actor, etc., to appear as a star (as, "the great actors who came down '*starring,*' as it is called, from London": Irving's "Tales of a Traveler," ii. 10).

star=ap-ple (stär′ap″l), *n.* The edible fruit of a West Indian sapotaceous tree, *Chrysophyllum cainito,* of the size of an apple, and when cut across presenting a star-shaped figure within; also, the tree.

star-board (stär′bõrd or -bẻrd). [AS. *stēorbord,* the side from which a vessel was steered: cf. *steer*[2] and *board.*] *Naut.:* **I.** *n.* The side of a ship to the right of a person looking from the stern toward the bow: opposed to *larboard* and *port,* and to some extent supplanted by *right.* **II.** *a.* Pertaining to the starboard; being on the right side of a vessel.—**star′board,** *v. t.* or *i. Naut.,* to turn (the helm) to the starboard or right side of a vessel.

Star-apple. — *a,* the fruit, transverse section.

starch (stärch), *n.* [ME. *starche,* akin to AS. *stearc,* stiff, rigid, E. *stark.*] A white, tasteless solid, chemically a carbohydrate, $(C_6H_{10}O_5)_n$, occurring in the form of minute granules in the seeds, tubers, and other parts of plants, and forming an important constituent of rice, corn, wheat, beans, potatoes, and many other vegetable foods; a commercial preparation of this substance, used (dissolved in water, boiling or cold) to stiffen linen, etc., in laundering, and employed also for many industrial purposes; fig., stiffness or formality, as of manner.—**starch,** *v. t.* To stiffen or treat with starch; fig., to make stiff or rigidly formal (sometimes with *up:* as, "She *starched* up her behaviour with a double proportion of reserve," Smollett's "Humphry Clinker," Sept. 12).

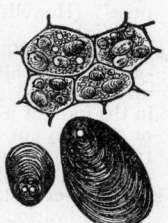

Cells of Potato (*Solanum tuberosum*) filled with Starch-granules; below, granules. (All greatly magnified.)

Star Cham-ber (stär chăm′bẻr). [Said to have been so called from a decoration of stars on its roof (ceiling).] In *Eng. hist.,* an apartment in the royal palace at Westminster, in which the king's council formerly sat to exercise jurisdiction; also, a court of civil and criminal jurisdiction developed from the judicial sittings of the king's council in this chamber, and abolished in 1641, concerned chiefly with controversies and offenses affecting the interests of the crown, and noted for its summary and arbitrary procedure; hence, in general [without *caps.,* and often with hyphen, *star-chamber*], any tribunal, committee, or the like which proceeds by arbitrary or unfair methods (also used attributively: as, *star-chamber* methods).

starched (stärcht), *p. a.* Stiffened with starch (as, a *starched* collar); fig., stiff, or rigidly formal (as, "throwing aside all the *starched* reserve of her ordinary manner," Hawthorne's "House of the Seven Gables," vii.; "transported from the conventionalities of a stiff and *starched* Anglo-Indian hotel," F. M. Crawford's "Mr. Isaacs," i.).

starch-er (stär′chẻr), *n.* One who starches; also, a machine for starching.

starch-y (stär′chi), *a.* Pertaining to, of the nature of, or resembling starch; abounding in or containing starch; stiffened with starch; fig., stiff or formal, as in manner. —**starch′i-ness,** *n.*

star=cor-al (stär′kor″ạl), *n.* Any of various stony corals with radiating septa that give the calicles a more or less starlike appearance.

star-craft (stär′kráft), *n.* Knowledge of the stars; astrology.

star-dom (stär′dọm), *n.* The

Star-coral, left branch shown in section.

world or class of professional stars, as of the stage; the status of a star.

star=drift (stär′drift), *n.* In *astron.*, a very slow actual motion common to a number of fixed stars in the same part of the heavens, entirely distinct from any apparent motion.

star=dust (stär′dust), *n.* Masses of stars so minute in appearance as to suggest particles of dust; also, particles of matter falling from space to the earth; cosmic dust.

stare (stār), *v.*; *stared, staring.* [AS. *starian* = D. *staren* = OHG. *starēn* = Icel. *stara,* stare.] **I.** *intr.* To gaze directly and fixedly with the eyes wide open, as in wonder, amazement, stupidity, or rudeness (as, "He continued to *stare* about him with dilated eyes": W. H. Hudson's "Green Mansions," iii.); be directed or fixed in such a gaze, as the eyes; also, to stand out boldly or obtrusively to view (used esp. in *staring, p. a.*); also, of hair, feathers, etc., to stand on end; bristle. **II.** *tr.* To stare at (as, "My lord *stared* him steadily in the eyes," Stevenson's "Master of Ballantrae," x.; to *stare* one up and down, that is, from head to foot); put, bring, etc., by staring (as, to *stare* one out of countenance; to *stare* one down, to abash one by staring).—**to stare one in the face,** to stare at one's face; also, to be directly before one's eyes; be glaringly evident to one.— **stare,** *n.* A staring gaze; a fixed look with the eyes wide open: as, "Kitty opened her eyes in a *stare* of dumb surprise" (Howells's "Chance Acquaintance," iii.).—**star=er** (stär′ėr), *n.*

star=fish (stär′fish), *n.*; pl. *-fishes* or (esp. collectively) *-fish.* Any echinoderm of the class *Asteroidea*, comprising marine animals having the body radially arranged, usually in the form of a star, with five or more rays or arms radiating from a central disk; an asteroid; also, an ophiuroid.

star=flow-er (stär′flou″ėr), *n.* Any of various plants with starlike flowers, as the star-of-Bethlehem or a plant of the primulaceous genus *Trientalis.*

star=gaze (stär′gāz), *v. i.* To gaze at or observe the stars; also, to gaze abstractedly; be absent-minded. — **star′=gaz″er** (-gā″zėr), *n.* One who gazes at the stars; also, any of various acanthopterygian marine fishes constituting the family *Uranoscopidæ,* having eyes set on the top of the head and directed vertically upward. —**star′=gaz″ing,** *n.* and *a.*

Starfish (genus *Asterias*).

Star-gazer (*Astroscopus guttatus*).

star=grass (stär′gräs), *n.* Any of various grass-like plants with star-shaped flowers or a stellate arrangement of leaves, as *Hypoxis hirsuta,* an American amaryllidaceous plant with small, yellow star-shaped flowers.

star=ing (stär′ing), *p. a.* That stares; of persons, etc., gazing with a stare; of things seen, standing out boldly to view (as, "printed in great black letters on a *staring* broadsheet": Dickens's "Hard Times," iii. 4); unduly conspicuous; glaring; of hair, feathers, etc., standing on end; bristling.— **star′ing-ly,** *adv.*

stark (stärk), *a.* [AS. *stearc,* stiff, hard, severe, strong, = D. *sterk* = G. *stark* = Icel. *sterkr,* strong, akin to Goth. *ga-staurknan,* dry up: cf. *starch.*] Stiff or rigid in substance, muscles, etc. (now chiefly archaic or prov., except as in the following sense); rigid in death (as, "lying, perhaps, *stark* and stained with blood on yon darkening moor," W. H. Hudson's "Purple Land," xviii.: often in the phrase 'stiff and stark'); also, hard, stern, or severe (archaic: as, "He is . . . *stark* as death To those that cross him," Tennyson's "Harold," ii. 2. 176); harsh or bleak, as weather, etc. (archaic or prov.: as, "Most pitiless and *stark* the winter grew," W. Morris's "Jason," xii. 1); also, strong, stout, or sturdy

(archaic or prov.: as, "some *stark* and sufficient man, who is not salt or sugar," Emerson's "Representative Men," iv.); also, harsh, grim, or desolate to the view, as places, as ("In the starlight their [peaks'] black shapes rose *stark* against the sky": Wister's "Virginian," xxxii.); also, sheer, utter, downright, or arrant (as, *stark* madness); also, stark (or absolutely) naked (as, "They . . . unbound me . . . And one did strip me *stark*": Shelley's "Revolt of Islam," iii. 13). —**stark,** *adv.* In a stark manner; stoutly or vigorously (prov.); utterly, absolutely, or quite (as, *stark* mad; *stark* naked; "The captain . . . was *stark* ignorant of his trade," Stevenson's "Master of Ballantrae," iii.).—**stark′ly,** *adv.*

star-less (stär′les), *a.* Without stars or starlight.

star-light (stär′līt). **I.** *n.* The light proceeding from the stars (as, "the faint glimmering *starlight*": W. Morris's "Jason," vii. 154); sometimes, the time when the stars shine. **II.** *a.* Of or pertaining to starlight; lighted by the stars, or by the stars only; also, bright as the stars.

star-like (stär′līk), *a.* Like a star; star-shaped; shining like a star.

star-ling[1] (stär′ling), *n.* [AS. *stærlinc,* < *stær* = OHG. G. *star* = Icel. *stari,* starling; akin to L. *sturnus.*] Any of the passerine birds constituting the genus *Sturnus,* esp. *S. vulgaris,* a common European species which often nests about buildings and is readily tamed; any of various related birds, esp. of the same family (*Sturnidæ*); also, any bird of the American blackbird family, *Icteridæ.*

star-ling[2] (stär′ling), *n.* [Origin uncertain.] A protecting work of piles, as for resisting waves.

star-lit (stär′lit), *a.* Lighted by stars.

star-lite (stär′lit), *n.* [See *-lite.*] A variety of zircon which on special treatment with heat affords a brilliant blue gem.

Common European Starling (*Sturnus vulgaris*).

star-nosed (stär′nōzd), *a.* Having a starlike ring of small, fleshy radiating processes about the end of the snout, as an American mole, *Condylura cristata.*

star=of=Beth-le-hem (stär′ọv-beth′lẹ-ẹm), *n.* [See Mat. ii. 1–10.] A liliaceous plant, *Ornithogalum umbellatum,* native

Star-nosed Mole (*Condylura cristata*).

in the Old World and common in gardens, with star-shaped flowers that are white within and greenish on the under side; also, some other plant of the same genus, or some other related or similar plant.

starred (stärd), *p. a.* Set or studded with or as with stars; decorated with a star, as of an order; marked with a starlike figure or spot; marked with an asterisk; fractured with cracks radiating from a center; also, star-shaped; also, made into a star or stars, or placed among the stars; presented as a star, as an actor; also, influenced by the stars (as, ill-*starred*).

star-ry (stär′i), *a.* Abounding with or lighted by stars (as, a *starry* sky; a *starry* night); of, pertaining to, or proceeding from the stars (as, "spirits of *starry* birth," H. Newbolt's "Nile"; *starry* light; *starry* influences); of the nature of or consisting of stars (as, *starry* worlds; the *starry* system); also, resembling a star; star-shaped or stellate; shining like stars (as, *starry* eyes); also, studded with starlike figures or markings.—**star′ri-ly,** *adv.*—**star′ri-ness,** *n.*

star=shaped (stär′shāpt), *a.* Shaped like a star (conventional figure); having rays (commonly five or six) proceeding from, or angular points disposed in a regular outline about, a central point.

star=shell (stär′shel), *n.* A shell loaded with stars, for firing into the air, where it is designed to burst: used in warfare to illuminate the enemy's position: as, "searchlights going like white windmill arms and an occasional flare or *star shell*" (H. G. Wells's "Mr. Britling," ii. 4. § 13).

star=shine (stär′shīn), *n.* Starlight: as, "The garden trees looked densely black in the *starshine*" (Galsworthy's "Saint's Progress," i. 10).

star=show-er (stär′shou″ėr), *n.* A shower of meteors.

star=span-gled (stär′spang″gld), *a.* Spangled with stars: as, the *star-spangled* banner (the national flag of the United States: a phrase made familiar by the national song, "The Star-Spangled Banner," written in 1814 by Francis Scott Key).

start¹ (stärt), *n.* [AS. *steort* = D. *staart* = G. *sterz* = Icel. *stertr*, tail.] The tail of an animal (obs. except in composition: as, a red*start*); also, the handle of an implement, vessel, or the like (now prov. Eng.).

start² (stärt), *v.* [ME. *sterten*: cf. AS. *steartlian*, stumble, also *sturtan*, leap, D. *storten*, G. *stürzen*, dash, plunge, fall: cf. *startle*.] **I.** *intr.* To leap† or jump†; also, to spring or move suddenly from a position or place (as, to *start* from one's seat; to *start* up, back, or aside); move with a sudden, involuntary jerk or twitch, as from a shock of surprise, alarm, or pain; flinch or recoil; rouse suddenly, as from sleep or reverie (as, to *start* out of a troubled dream; "I *started* wide awake on hearing a vague murmur," C. Brontë's "Jane Eyre," xv.); come suddenly into activity, life, view, etc.; come, rise, or issue suddenly (as, tears *started* to, or from, her eyes; "Perspiration *started* on her brow," Wiseman's "Fabiola," i. 7); burst out (as, eyes seeming to *start* from their sockets); spring, slip, or work loose from place or fastenings, as timbers or other structural parts (as, "An enormous sea broke over the vessel . . . causing every timber and knee in her to *start* from its place": Marryat's "King's Own," liv.); also, to begin to move, go, or act (often with *out*); set out, as on a journey; begin any course of action or procedure, or one's career, life, etc.; of a process or performance, to begin; also, to rush†, hasten†, or go†; depart†; escape†. **II.** *tr.* To cause to start involuntarily, or startle (archaic or prov.: as, "You boggle shrewdly, every feather *starts* you," Shakspere's "All's Well," v. 3. 232); rouse (game) from its lair or resting-place (also fig.); cause (timbers, structural parts, etc.) to start from place or fastenings; suffer the starting of (parts), as a ship or other structure; also, to set moving, going, or acting (as, to *start* a horse, an automobile, or a machine; to *start* a fire, a rumor, or a controversy; "They . . . gave a cheer that *started* the echo in a far-away hill," Stevenson's "Treasure Island," xiii.); set in operation, or establish (an enterprise, institution, etc.: as, to *start* a newspaper; "I've joined this league for *starting* a model public-house in the parish," Chesterton's "Magic," i.); cause or enable (a person, etc.) to set out on a journey, a course of action, a career, or the like (as, to *start* a person on his way; to *start* one's son in business); enter upon or begin (as, to *start* work; to *start* a speech or a letter); also, to draw or discharge (liquid or other contents) from a vessel or container, or empty (a container) thus.—**start**², *n.* A leap†; also, a sudden, springing movement from a position (as, a *start* aside; "He sprang up with a *start*," Mrs. H. Ward's "Robert Elsmere," xxix.); a sudden, involuntary jerking movement of the body (as, "The boy could not repress a *start*," Dickens's "Oliver Twist," xx.; to awake with a *start*); a spurt of activity (as, to work by *starts*, or by fits and *starts*: see under *fit*¹); a burst, outburst, or sally, as of emotion, wit, or fancy (archaic: as, "She had sometimes seen Lady Delacour in *starts* of passion that seemed to border on insanity," Maria Edgeworth's "Belinda," xv.); a starting of parts from their place or fastenings in a structure, or the resulting condition; also, a beginning to move, go, or act; a first movement or act in any course or process; the beginning or outset of anything; also, a setting in motion; an impulse to move or proceed; a signal to start, as on a course or in a race; a chance or opportunity given to one of starting on a course or career; also, the position or advantage of one who starts first, as in a race, competition, or other proceeding

(as, "She has got the *start* of the rest of us, and is already a resident of Blithedale": Hawthorne's "Blithedale Romance," i.); the lead; a lead or advance of specified amount, as over competitors or pursuers; also, a hasty journey†, or flight†.

start-er (stär′tėr), *n.* One who or that which starts; a person who gives the signal for starting, as in a race or in the running of a train, elevator, or the like.

star=this-tle (stär′this″l), *n.* A low, spreading asteraceous plant, *Centaurea calcitrapa*, a native of Europe, with purple flower-heads and spiny involucres and leaves; also, the related but more erect *C. solstitialis*, with yellow flowers; also, any plant of the genus *Centaurea*.

star-tle (stär′tl), *v.*; *-tled, -tling.* [ME. *stertlen*, freq. of *sterten*, E. *start*².] **I.** *intr.* To leap, spring, or rush about (now Sc. and prov. Eng.); also, to start involuntarily, or feel suddenly disturbed, as from a shock of surprise or alarm (archaic: as, "Some gentlemen *startle*—but it is true," Burke's "Conciliation with the Colonies"); start, spring, or rouse suddenly (with *back, from, up,* etc.: archaic). **II.** *tr.* To cause to start involuntarily, as under a sudden shock (as, "The applause *startled* him to his feet": Arnold Bennett's "Book of Carlotta," i. 2); disturb or agitate suddenly by a shock of surprise, alarm, or the like (as, "Neither self-possess'd Nor *startled*, but . . . in a graceful quiet": Tennyson's "Gardener's Daughter," 152); rouse suddenly, as from sleep or quiet; also, to cause to waver in firmness or steadfastness†.—**star′tle**, *n.* A startling or being startled; a sudden shock of surprise, alarm, or the like; also, something that startles.—**star′tler**, *n.*—**star′tling**, *p. a.* That startles; causing a shock, as of surprise or alarm; suddenly and forcibly arresting the gaze or attention.—**star′tling-ly**, *adv.*

star-va-tion (stär-vā′shon), *n.* The process of starving, or the condition of being starved.

starve (stärv), *v.*; *starved, starving.* [AS. *steorfan* = D. *sterven* = G. *sterben*, die.] **I.** *intr.* To die† or perish†; later, to die or perish from hunger; be in process of perishing, or suffer severely, from lack of food (as, "He eat it [bread] like a ravenous wolf that had been *starving* a fortnight in the snow": Defoe's "Robinson Crusoe," i. 13); pine or fail for want of proper nourishment, as animals or plants (also fig., as of the mind or heart, etc.); suffer from extreme poverty and want; pine or suffer for want of something specified (with *for*: as, to *starve* for sympathy or affection; "I . . . *starve* for a merry look," Shakspere's "Comedy of Errors," ii. 1. 88); also, to perish, be in process of perishing, or suffer extremely, from cold (now prov.). **II.** *tr.* To cause to starve; kill with hunger; weaken or reduce by lack of food or nourishment; treat (disease, a patient, etc.) by light diet; subdue, or force to some condition or action, by hunger or famine (as, to *starve* a besieged garrison into a surrender); cause to suffer for want of something needed or craved (as, "He was . . . mentally *starved*, *starved* of the good old milk of human kindness": A. S. M. Hutchinson's "If Winter Comes," iv. 1); also, to cause to perish, or to suffer extremely, from cold (now prov.).—**starve′ling.** **I.** *n.* A person, animal, or plant that is starving, or suffering from lack of nourishment. Also fig. **II.** *a.* Starving; suffering from lack of nourishment; pining with want; poverty-stricken (as, "dooming the *starveling* laborer as well as the opulent burgher": Motley's "Dutch Republic," iii. 2); fig., poor in condition or quality; also, such as to entail or suggest starvation (as, "abundance to me, though *starveling* pit-

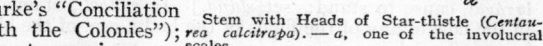

Stem with Heads of Star-thistle (*Centaurea calcitrapa*).— *a*, one of the involucral scales.

tance in the view of everyday prosperity," Gissing's "Private Papers of Henry Ryecroft," iv. 3; "*starveling* economy," Irving's "Tales of a Traveler," ii. 7); meager or scanty.—**starv′er,** *n.*

star-ward (stär′wạrd), *adv.* and *a.* Toward the stars.

star-wort (stär′wẽrt), *n.* Any of various chickweeds (genus *Alsine*) with white star-shaped flowers; also, any plant of the genus *Aster* (see *aster*); also, water-starwort.

stash (stash), *v. t.* [Origin obscure; appar. first as thieves' slang.] To stop, or leave off (sometimes with *up*: as, "She brought her playing [on the piano] to an end by—as school-boys say—'*stashing* it up,'"

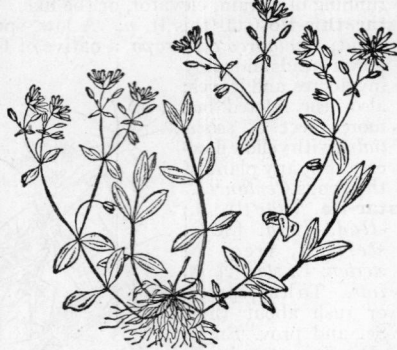

Starwort, or Great Chickweed (*Alsine pubera*).

H. G. Wells's "Tono-Bungay," iii. 4. § 2); also, to put out, or extinguish (as, "Tell him to *stash* his tomahawk there, or pipe, or whatever you call it; tell him to stop smoking, in short": H. Melville's "Moby-Dick," iii.); also, to quit (a place). [Slang, chiefly Eng.]

sta-sis (stā′sis), *n.* [NL., < Gr. στάσις, a standing, < ἱστάναι, cause to stand: see *stand.*] In *pathol.*, stagnation in the flow of any of the fluids of the body, esp. of the blood in an inflamed area.

-stat. [Gr. -στάτης, noun termination (as in ὑδροστάτης, hydrostatic balance), or στατός, adj., standing, < ἱστάναι, cause to stand: see *stand.*] A noun termination used to form names of scientific instruments, mechanical devices, etc., as in *aërostat, gyrostat, heliostat, rheostat, thermostat.*

stat-a-ble (stā′tạ-bl), *a.* That may be stated.

state (stāt), *n.* [OF. *estat* (F. *état*), < L. *status*, way of standing, posture, position, condition, rank, public affairs, the state, < *stare* (pp. *status*), stand: see *stand*, and cf. *estate.*] A mode or form of existence (as, the future *state*); the condition of a person or thing, as with respect to circumstances or attributes (as, "I have learned, in whatsoever *state* I am, therewith to be content," Phil. iv. 11; a prosperous *state*; a healthy *state*; a *state* of disrepair); a bad or unfavorable condition (colloq.: as, his affairs were in a *state!*); a particular condition of mind or feeling (as, to be in an excited or an irritable *state*); an excited condition of mind or feeling (colloq.: as, to be in quite a *state* over a matter); condition with respect to constitution, structure, or the like (as, a solid or a liquid *state*); any of the various forms in which a thing is found to exist (as, a crystalline or an amorphous *state* of a substance); any of the successive stages or phases of a thing (as, the larval, pupal, or imaginal *state* of an insect); also, a person's condition or position in life, or estate, station, or rank (as, "to do my duty in that *state* of life unto which it shall please God to call me," Book of Common Prayer, Catechism; "O wha wad leave this humble *state*, For a' the pride of a' the great?" Burns's "Bessy and Her Spinnin' Wheel," 27); high rank or standing†; high office†; the style of living befitting a person of high rank and great wealth; sumptuous, imposing, or ceremonious display of dignity, or pomp (as, "Ancient homes of lord and lady, Built for pleasure and for *state*," Tennyson's "Lord of Burleigh," 32; a chair, canopy, or coach of *state*; a dead person lying in *state*; a hall used on occasions of *state*); a seat of dignity†; a canopy†; also, the body of persons of a particular condition, class, etc.†; an estate of the realm†; *pl.*, the legislative assembly of a country, etc. (cf. *states-general*); *sing.*, the government or ruling body of a country, etc.†; a person of high rank, as a noble†; also, the condition of a country, the church, etc., with respect to its welfare, polity, etc.†; a particular form of polity or government†; the body politic as organized for supreme civil rule and government (often contrasted with the church, or ecclesiastical organiza-

tion and authority); the operations or activities of supreme civil government, or the sphere of supreme civil authority and administration (as, affairs of *state*; the British Secretary of *State* for home affairs, for foreign affairs, for the colonies, for war, or for India; the Department of *State* of the U. S., which has charge of all foreign relations); a body of people occupying a definite territory and organized under one government, esp. a sovereign government; the territory, or one of the territories, of a government; [often *cap.*] any of the commonwealths or bodies politic, each more or less independent as regards internal affairs, which together make up a federal union, as in the United States of America or the Commonwealth of Australia; also [*l.c.*], interest in property†; estate†; possessions†; also, a statement†; an account†; a report†; *milit.*, in the British service, a report of the number of officers and men in a body of troops, with details of casualties, etc.; in *engraving*, an impression taken from a plate at a particular stage of its progress and recognized by certain distinctive marks.—**state's evidence.** See *evidence, n.*—**state's prison.** Same as *state prison*, under *state, a.*—**States' rights,** the rights belonging to the separate States of the U. S., under the Constitution: used esp. with reference to the doctrine of strict construction of the Constitution, holding that all rights not specially delegated by the Constitution to the general government belong to the separate States.—**the States,** the United States of America. [Chiefly in British use.]—**state,** *a.* Characterized by, attended with, or involving state or ceremony (as, a *state* dinner; a *state* funeral; *state* occasions); used on or reserved for occasions of state or ceremony (as, *state* apartments; a *state* coach); also, of or pertaining to the state, or supreme civil government or authority; [often *cap.*] of or pertaining to one of the commonwealths which make up a federal union, as any of the States of the U. S.—**state bank,** a bank associated with the finances of a state; [often *State bank*] in the U. S., a bank chartered by the State in which it is located.—**state prison,** a prison maintained by a state, esp. for political offenders; [often *State prison*] a prison maintained by one of the States of a federal union, as in the U. S., for the regular confinement of felons under sentence of imprisonment.—**State rights.** Same as *States' rights*, under *state, n.*—**state socialism.** See under *socialism.*—**State sovereignty.** See *sovereignty.*—**state,** *v. t.*; *stated, stating.* To place† or station†; put in a specified condition†; also, to fix or settle, as by authority (now chiefly as in *stated, p.a.*); also, to set forth in proper or definite form (as, to *state* a question or a problem; "Every argument was *stated* with logical precision," Bulwer-Lytton's "Pelham," xxxvii.); set forth formally in speech or writing (as, to *state* a case; to *state* an account); declare in express terms, definitely, or specifically (as, to *state* one's views or intentions; "terrified . . . though she could not exactly *state* a reason why," Scott's "Castle Dangerous," xiv.); loosely, to say.

state-craft (stāt′kráft), *n.* The art of conducting affairs of state (as, "a man of ministerial tact . . . if no genius in *statecraft*": G. Meredith's "Diana of the Crossways," i.); state management; statesmanship; sometimes, crafty statesmanship.

stat-ed (stā′ted), *p. a.* Fixed or settled, as by authority, agreement, or custom (as, at *stated* times; for a *stated* fee; a *stated* meeting of a society); set; appointed; regular; recognized or official (as, a *stated* ministry); explicitly set forth, as a law or rule; declared as fact.—**stated clerk,** the principal clerk of Presbyterian church courts in the U. S.—**stat′ed-ly,** *adv.*

state-hood (stāt′hūd), *n.* The condition or status of a state, esp. a State of the U. S.

state=house (stāt′hous), *n.* A house or building of state†; [often *cap.*] in the U. S., the building in which the legislature of a State sits; the capitol of a State.

state-ly (stāt′li), *a.*; compar. *statelier*, superl. *stateliest.* Characterized by, proper to, or suggestive of high estate or lofty dignity; dignified or majestic, as persons, the bearing, manners, movements, etc.; imposing in magnificence, elegance, etc. (as, a *stately* palace, shrine, tomb, equipage, or banquet; "a *stately* refectory hung with paintings and rich with fantastic carving," Macaulay's "Hist. of Eng.," viii.); in general, of an imposing or majestic appearance or

---

character (as, a *stately* ship; a *stately* swan; a *stately* tree or river; *stately* music); elevated in thought or expression, as speech or a speaker.—**state′li-ly,** *adv.*—**state′li-ness,** *n.* —**state′ly,** *adv.* In a stately manner.

state-ment (stāt′ment), *n.* The act or the manner of stating something; also, something stated; a communication in speech or writing setting forth facts, particulars, etc.; a declaration, esp. of a formal, explicit, or specific character; a recital; an allegation; in *com.*, an abstract of an account, as one rendered periodically to show the balance due.

stat-er[1] (stā′tėr), *n.* One who states.

sta-ter[2] (stā′tėr), *n.* [L., < Gr. στατήρ, < ἱστάναι, cause to stand, weigh.] Any of various gold or silver coins of the ancient Greek states or cities; also, the gold daric of ancient Persia; also, an ancient unit of weight.

state=room (stāt′rōm), *n.* A room or apartment of state in a palace or the like; also, a private room or sleeping-apartment on a vessel; a private compartment on a railroad-train.

states=gen-er-al (stāts′jen′e̯-ral), *n. pl.* [Also *caps.*] An assembly of representatives of the estates of a whole realm or country (as distinguished from provincial assemblies), as in France before the Revolution; also, the parliament of the present kingdom of the Netherlands.

states-man (stāts′man), *n.*; pl. *-men.* A man who is versed in the management of affairs of state; one who exhibits political ability and sagacity of the highest kind in directing the affairs of a government or in dealing with important public issues.—**states′man-like, states′man-ly,** *a.* Having the qualifications of a statesman; worthy of or befitting a statesman.—**states′man-ship,** *n.* The character or procedure of a statesman; skill in the management of public affairs.

states-wom-an (stāts′wùm″an), *n.*; pl. *-women* (-wim″en). A woman with the skill or ability of a statesman.

stat-ic (stat′ik). [Gr. στατικός, causing to stand, pertaining to weighing, < ἱστάναι, cause to stand, weigh: see *stand.*] **I.** *a.* Pertaining to weighing or to weight†; acting by mere weight without producing motion (as, *static* pressure); pertaining to bodies at rest or forces in equilibrium, or to statics; fig., pertaining to or characterized by a fixed or stationary condition, as distinguished from a condition of motion or progress (as, "This mediæval idea of a *static* society yields only grudgingly, and the notion of inevitable vital change is as yet far from assimilated," J. H. Robinson's "Mind in the Making," v. 11; "Whatever she might become she would never be *static*," Sinclair Lewis's "Main Street," i.); in *elect.*, noting or pertaining to electricity at rest, as that produced by friction; noting or pertaining to atmospheric electricity, often present in such amount as to interfere with the sending and receiving of wireless messages, etc.; in *med.*, organic or structural, not merely functional, as a disease; also, characterized by stasis; also, pertaining to a standing posture; also, tending to maintain equilibrium. **II.** *n.* Statics (now rare); also, in *elect.*, static or atmospheric electricity, esp. when present in such amount as to cause interference with the sending and receiving of wireless messages, speeches, etc.; interference due to such electricity.—**stat′i-cal,** *a.* Static.—**stat′i-cal-ly,** *adv.*

stat-i-ce (stat′i-sē), *n.* [NL., in L. a kind of astringent herb, < Gr. στατική, prop. fem. of στατικός, causing to stand: see *static.*] Any of the small herbaceous plants constituting the plumbaginaceous genus *Statice*, with rosettes of narrow evergreen leaves on the ground and globular heads of pink, purplish, or white flowers, as *S. armeria*, the common thrift; also, any of the herbaceous or shrubby plants constituting the plumbaginaceous genus *Limonium* (also called *Statice*), native on the seashore and in desert sands, mostly of the Old World, and generally known as *sea-lavender* (which see).

North American Statice or Sea-lavender (*Limonium carolinianum*).—*a*, flower with its bracts.

stat-ics (stat′iks), *n.* [See *static.*] That branch of mechanics which deals with bodies at rest or forces in equilibrium.

sta-tion (stā′shon), *n.* [OF. F. *station*, < L. *statio(n-)*, a standing, position, post, station, < *stare*, stand: see *stand.*] The act or manner of standing; also, the fact or condition of standing still (obs. or archaic: as, "Her motion and her *station* are as one; She shows a body rather than a life," Shakspere's "Antony and Cleopatra," iii. 3. 22); a halt or stand (obs. or archaic); also, the place in which anything stands; position; a position assigned for standing or remaining in; specif., the correct relative position of a vessel in a squadron; a port, harbor, or roadstead for ships; a place at which ships of a navy are regularly stationed; a place or region to which a government ship or fleet is assigned for duty; also, a place where soldiers are garrisoned; a military post; also, a place in India where the British officials of a district or the officers of a garrison reside; the aggregate of society in such a place; also, the locality to which an official is appointed for the exercise of his functions; also, the headquarters of the police force in a municipality or a district thereof, usually containing a lockup for the temporary detention of accused or suspected persons; a place or building where men are stationed which is equipped for some particular kind of work, research, or the like (as, a postal *station*; a seismological *station*); an establishment with its buildings, lands, etc., for raising sheep or cattle, or a stock-farm, sheep-run, or cattle-run (Australia, New Zealand, etc.: as, "There is no place . . . where you can live so cheaply and so well as on a New Zealand sheep *station*," Lady Barker's "Station Life in New Zealand," xv.; "*Stations* either for sheep or cattle were spotted about . . . over the whole country," S. Butler's "Erewhon," i.); also, fig., standing, as of persons or things, in a scale of estimation or dignity (as, "He . . . wins mankind, as his attempts prevail, A prouder *station* on the gen'ral scale": Cowper's "Charity," 336); esp., relative position in the social scale (as, a man of high or low *station*; "How absurd it is of that class to educate their women above their *station!*" G. Meredith's "Ordeal of Richard Feverel," xx.); specif., high social position (as, "men . . . rais'd to *station* and command": Cowper's "Table Talk," 354); sometimes, a particular position, office, calling, or the like (archaic: as, "Canterbury being now without an archbishop, the dean, Dr. Wotton, acted in that *station*," Strype's "Memorials of Cranmer," iii. 5); also, the place at which something stops; a stopping-place; a regular stopping-place, as on a railroad; the building or collection of buildings erected at such a place on a railroad, for railroad business; *eccles.*, the fast observed in the early church on Wednesdays and Fridays; a service, esp. in the city of Rome, for which clergy and people assembled at one of a certain number of churches, each of which had its appointed day for the service; one of a number of holy places visited in succession by pilgrims; one of a number of churches or other holy places visited for the performance of an act of devotion; a procession or a visit to, or the service at, such a place; a special service held at a holy place; a church, or a visit to a church, where indulgences are to be gained on appointed days; a visit of a Roman Catholic priest to the house of a parishioner to say mass and to confess and communicate those living in the neighborhood (Ireland); one of the stations of the cross (see phrase below); in *surv.*, a point where an observation is taken, that is, the place where the transit or the like is planted; in *zoöl.* and *bot.*, the kind of place where a given animal or plant naturally lives or grows, as warm seas, mountain-tops, fresh waters, etc.; also, a particular spot or place where a given animal or plant is found.—**stations of the cross,** *eccles.*, a series of (usually) fourteen representations of successive incidents from the passion of Christ, each with a wooden cross, or a series of wooden crosses alone, set up in a church or, sometimes, in the open air, and visited in order, for prayer and meditation; also, the series of devotional exercises used for this purpose.—**sta′tion,** *v. t.* To assign a station to; place or post in a station or position: as, "A Gothic prince . . . was *stationed* with an army to guard the entrance of Italy" (Gibbon's "Decline and Fall of the Roman Empire," xli.); "They . . . *stationed* . . . musicians under the stairway in the 'front hall'" (Tarkington's "Magnificent Ambersons," i.);

"She *stationed* herself as near to the door as she well could" (Trollope's "Barchester Towers," xviii.).

sta-tion-a-ry (stā′shọn-ā-ri). [L. *stationarius*.] **I.** *a.* Having a fixed station or place; established in one place, or not itinerant or migratory (as, "I deemed it advisable to . . . change my late wandering life for a *stationary* one": Godwin's "Caleb Williams," xxxiv.); also, standing still, or not moving; also, having a fixed position, or not movable; noting or pertaining to an engine (steam-engine) which is permanently placed or which does not move from its position while in operation, as distinguished from a locomotive engine; also, remaining in the same condition or state, not changing, or neither progressing nor retrogressing (as, "Bacon has remarked that in ages when philosophy was *stationary*, the mechanical arts went on improving": Macaulay's "Essays," Lord Bacon); in *astron.*, of a planet, being at one of the points in its path through the heavens (as seen from the earth) at which it appears to have no motion; also, noting such a point. **II.** *n.*; pl. *-ries* (-riz). One who or that which is stationary; one of a force of stationary troops; one who opposes or resists progress.—**sta′tion-a-ri-ness**, *n.*

sta-tion-er (stā′shọn-ėr), *n.* [ML. *stationarius*, < *statio*(*n-*), shop, L. station: see *station*.] A bookseller†; also, a publisher†; also, one who sells the materials used in writing, as paper, pens, pencils, ink, etc.—**Company of Stationers**, or **Stationers' Company**, a company or gild of the City of London, incorporated in 1556, comprising booksellers, printers, bookbinders, and dealers in writing-materials, etc.—**Stationers' Hall**, the hall or building of the Stationers' Company in London, where formerly copyrights were required to be entered in a register kept for that purpose.—**sta′tion-er-y**, *n.* The articles usually sold by stationers; writing-materials.

sta-tion=house (stā′shọn-hous), *n.* A house or building at or serving as a station; esp., a police station.

sta-tion=mas-ter (stā′shọn-más″tėr), *n.* An official in charge of a station; esp., the person in charge of a railroad-station.

stat-ism (stā′tizm), *n.* Statecraft; politics. [Obs. or rare.] —**stat′ist**, *n.* A politician (obs. or rare); also, a statistician.

sta-tis-tic (stạ-tis′tik). [= F. *statistique*, < G. *statistik*, < L. *status*, E. *state*.] **I.** *n.* Statistics (rare); also, a statistical statement; also, a statistician. **II.** *a.* Statistical. —**sta-tis′ti-cal**, *a.* Of or pertaining to statistics; consisting of or based on statistics.—**sta-tis′ti-cal-ly**, *adv.*—**stat-is-ti-cian** (stat-is-tish′ạn), *n.* One versed in statistics; one engaged in compiling statistics.—**sta-tis′tics**, *n.* As *sing.*, the science which deals with the collection, classification, and use of facts or data, esp. such as can be stated numerically, bearing on a subject or matter, orig. on the condition of a state or community; as *pl.*, the numerical facts or data collected and classified (as, "Wherever *statistics* are kept, the numbers of births and of deaths rise and fall in nearly parallel lines": W. R. Inge's "Outspoken Essays," i. 4).

stat-o-blast (stat′ọ-blast), *n.* [Gr. στατός, standing, + βλαστός, sprout, germ.] In *biol.*, a germ or bud, inclosed in a chitinous envelop, developed within the body-cavity of many fresh-water polyzoans, and eventually, by the death of the parent colony, set free in the water, where it usually remains in a quiescent state through the winter, germinating and giving rise to a new individual in the spring.—**stat-o-blas′tic**, *a.*

sta-tor (stā′tọr), *n.* [NL., < L. *stare*, stand.] The stationary part of a machine or apparatus, esp. the stationary element (field or armature) of a motor or dynamo: opposed to *rotor*.

stat-o-scope (stat′ọ-skōp), *n.* [Gr. στατός, standing, + σκοπεῖν, view.] A form of aneroid barometer for registering minute variations of atmospheric pressure; in *aëronautics*, an instrument for detecting a small rate of rise or fall of an aircraft.

stat-u-a† (stat′ū-ä), *n.* [L.] A statue.

stat-u-a-ry (stat′ū-ā-ri). [L. *statuarius*.] **I.** *a.* Of or pertaining to statues; consisting of a statue or statues; of materials suitable for statues (as, "a tomb . . . composed of the most beautiful *statuary* marble": Scott's "Black Dwarf," xvii.). **II.** *n.*; pl. *-ries* (-riz). A maker of statues (in marble, bronze, etc.: as, "the companies of *statuaries*, lapidaries, and goldsmiths," J. H. Newman's "Callista," xxix.); also, the art of making statues; also, statues collectively.

stat-ue (stat′ū), *n.* [OF. F. *statue*, < L. *statua*, related to *statuere*, set up: see *statute*.] A representation of a person or an animal carved in stone or wood, molded in some plastic material, or cast in bronze or the like, properly one of some size and in the round: as, "on a noble pedestal, a brazen *Statue* of Lewis XIII." (Evelyn's "Diary," Feb. 4, 1644); "He sat rigid, immovable, like a *statue*" (F. M. Crawford's "Mr. Isaacs," iii.).—**stat′ued**, *a.* Adorned with statues; also, in the form of a statue or of statuary.—**stat-u-esque** (stat-ū-esk′), *a.* [See *-esque*.] Like or suggesting a statue, as in formal dignity, studied grace, or classic beauty: as, "the white *statuesque* immobility of her person" (J. Conrad's "Lord Jim," xxxiii.).—**stat-u-esque′ly**, *adv.*—**stat-u-esque′ness**, *n.*—**stat-u-ette′** (-et′), *n.* [F., dim. of *statue*.] A small statue; esp., one much smaller than life size.

stat-ure (stat′ūr), *n.* [OF. F. *stature*, < L. *statura*, < *stare*, stand.] The height of an animal body, esp. the human body, in its normal standing position (as, "He . . . was of middle *stature* . . . and very strong": B. Franklin's "Autobiography," i.); the height of some other object, as a tree, in its standing position; fig., elevation or development attained (as, "The men are of meaner moral *stature*. The very patriots work for lower objects": Stubbs's "Constitutional Hist. of Eng.," xvi. § 247).—**stat′ured**, *a.* Being of stature or height: as, low-*statured*.

sta-tus (stā′tus), *n.* [L.: see *state*.] State or condition; condition or position of affairs; esp., condition, position, standing socially, professionally, or otherwise (as, "making way for no one under the *status* of a priest," Kipling's "Kim," iv.; "Mr. Polly's *status* was that of a guest pure and simple," H. G. Wells's "Mr. Polly," iii.); in *law*, the standing of a person before the law in the class of persons indicated by his or her legal qualities; the relation fixed by law in which a person stands toward others or the state.—**status quo** (kwō). [L., 'state in which.'] The state in which anything was or is; the existing state of affairs.

stat-ut-a-ble (stat′ū-tạ-bl), *a.* Prescribed, authorized, or permitted by statute; also, conformed or conforming to statutes; also, of an offense, recognized by statute; legally punishable.—**stat′ut-a-bly**, *adv.*

stat-ute (stat′ūt), *n.* [OF. F. *statut*, < LL. *statutum*, prop. neut. of L. *statutus*, pp. of *statuere*, set up, establish, decree, < *stare*, stand: see *stand*.] An ordinance or law (as, "men that will not have Christ Jesus to rule over them, but have wilfully cast his *statutes* behind their backs": Hooker's "Ecclesiastical Polity," i. 1. 3); esp., a law made by a corporation for the conduct of its members; also, an enactment made by a legislature and expressed in a formal document; the document in which such an enactment is expressed; also, any of certain legal instruments and procedures based on the authority of a statute† (see phrases *statute merchant* and *statute staple*, below); also, *sing.* or *pl.*, an annual fair or gathering for the hiring of farm-laborers and house-servants (prov. Eng.).—**statute law**, law established by statutes or legislative enactments.—**statute merchant**, in *law*, a bond of record, now obsolete, acknowledged before the chief magistrate of a trading town, on which, if not paid at the appointed time, an execution might be awarded against the body, lands, and goods of the obligor or debtor.—**statute mile.** See under *mile*.—**statute staple**, in *law*, a bond of record, now obsolete, acknowledged before the mayor of the staple, operating against a debtor in like manner to the statute merchant.—**stat-u-to-ry** (stat′ū-tọ-ri), *a.* Of, pertaining to, or of the nature of a statute or statutes; prescribed or authorized by statute; conforming to statute; of an offense, recognized by statute; legally punishable.—**stat′u-to-ri-ly**, *adv.*

staunch[1], **staunch**[2] (stânch or stänch), etc. See *stanch*[1], *stanch*[2], etc.

stau-ro-lite (stâ′rọ-līt), *n.* [F. *staurolite*, < Gr. σταυρός, cross, + λίθος, stone.] A mineral consisting of a basic silicate of aluminium and iron, and occurring in brown to black prismatic crystals, which are often twinned in the form of a cross.—**stau-ro-lit′ic** (-lit′ik), *a.*

---

fat, fāte, fär, fâll, ȧsk, fāre; net, mē, hėr; pin, pīne; not, nōte, mȯve, nȯr; up, lūte, pu̇ll; oi, oil; ou, out; (lightened) aviȧry, ēlect, agȯny, intọ, ụnite; (obscured) errạnt, operä, ardẹnt, actọr, natūre; ch, chip; g, go; th, thin; ᴛʜ, then; y, you;

stau-ro-scope (stä′rō-skōp), *n.* [Gr. σταυρός, cross, + σκοπεῖν, view.] An optical instrument for determining the position of the planes of light-vibration in sections of crystals.

stave (stāv), *n.* [From *staves*, pl. of *staff*[2].] A stick, rod, pole, or the like; a rung of a ladder, chair, etc. (now prov. Eng.); one of the thin, narrow, shaped pieces of wood which form the sides of a cask, tub, or similar vessel; one of a number of boards joined laterally to form a hollow cylinder, a curb for a well or shaft, etc.; also, a verse or stanza of a poem or song (as, "The old squire . . . vociferating the first *stave*, they sang, or rather roared, the . . . chorus": Peacock's "Headlong Hall," xiii.); also, a staff for musical notation; also, a letter of the alphabet.—**stave**, *v.*; *staved* or *stove*, *staving*. **I.** *tr.* To break up (a cask, etc.) into staves; break in a stave or staves of, esp. with a letting out of contents (as, "an action at law, laid against a carman for having *staved* a cask of port": Smollett's "Humphry Clinker," June 8); cause (wine, etc.) to be lost by breaking the cask; also, to break a hole in, or crush inward (as, "If the boat was *staved* upon shore, he would make it good to their master," Defoe's "Robinson Crusoe," i. 1: often with *in*); break (to pieces, splinters, etc.: as, "He [a whale] had several times been known to turn round suddenly, and, bearing down upon them . . . *stave* their boats to splinters," H. Melville's "Moby-Dick," xli.); break (a hole) in a boat, etc.; also, to put together the staves of (a cask, etc.); renew the staves of; furnish with a stave or staves; also, to beat with a stave or staff; drive or force with or as with a stave (usually with *off*); put, ward, or keep (*off*), as by force or evasion (as, "He was still there, *staving* off the evil hour," Margaret Kennedy's "Constant Nymph," viii.; "in search of shellfish to *stave* off starvation," J. Conrad's "Lord Jim," i.); also, to shorten and thicken by hammering on the end, as a heated piece of iron; make firm by compression, as lead which has been run in to secure a joint. **II.** *intr.* To become staved in, as a boat; break in or up; also, to go with a rush (prov. or colloq.: as, "I lost no time, but down through the valley and by Stockbrig and Silvermills as hard as I could *stave*," Stevenson's "David Balfour," xi.).

staves (stāvz), *n.* Plural of *staff*[2] and *stave*.

staves-a-cre (stāvz′ā″kèr), *n.* [OF. *stafisagre* (F. *staphisaigre*), < ML. *staphisagria*, < Gr. σταφίς, raisin, + ἄγριος, wild.] A larkspur, *Delphinium staphisagria*, a native of Europe and Asia Minor, with bluish or purple flowers in terminal racemes and with violently emetic and cathartic poisonous seeds; also, the seeds. Cf. *delphinine*.

stave-wood (stāv′wud), *n.* Any of various trees whose wood has been used for making staves, as *Flindersia schottiana* of Australia and *Sterculia fœtida* of the East Indies, Australia, etc.

stay[1] (stā), *n.* [AS. *stæg* = D. and G. *stag* = Icel., Sw., and Dan. *stag*, stay (rope): cf. *s t a y*[2], *n.*] *Naut.*, a strong rope, now commonly of wire, used to support a mast of a vessel; hence, in general, any rope similarly used; a guy.— **in stays**, *naut.*, in the act of going about from one tack

Stavewood (*Sterculia fœtida*). — *a*, flower; *b*, ovary; *c*, stamens; *d*, fruit.

to the other.—**stay**[1], *v.*; *stayed*, *staying.* *Naut.*: **I.** *tr.* To support or secure with a stay or stays (as, to *stay* a mast; to *stay* a mast forward, aft, or otherwise, to secure it by stays so that it slants forward, aft, or otherwise); also, to put (a ship) on the other tack. **II.** *intr.* Of a ship, to change to the other tack.

stay[2] (stā), *n.* [OF. *estaie*, *estai* (F. *étai*), stay, prop; prob. from Teut.: cf. *stay*[1].] Something used or serving to support or steady a thing; a prop; a brace; fig., a thing or a person that sustains (as, "Obedience of creatures unto the law of nature is the *stay* of the whole world," Hooker's "Ecclesiastical Polity," i. 3. 2; "his son, the *stay* of his house," Roosevelt's "Winning of the West," i. 4); also, *pl.*, corsets.—**stay**[2], *v.*; *stayed*, *staying.* [Cf. OF. *estaier* (F. *étayer*), < *estaie*.] **I.** *tr.* To support or secure in position with stays, as parts of a structure; in general, to support, prop, or hold up (sometimes with *up*: as, "But Moses' hands were heavy . . . and Aaron and Hur *stayed* up his hands," Ex. xvii. 12); rest for support (as, "He *stay'd* his arms upon his knee": Tennyson's "Victim," v.); fig., to sustain or strengthen mentally or spiritually (as, "Once I could pray every morning, and go forth to my day's labour *stayed* and comforted": Mallock's "New Republic," v. 1); fix or rest in dependence or reliance (as, "Thou wilt keep him in perfect peace, whose mind is *stayed* on thee": Isa. xxvi. 3); also, to fix securely†, establish†, or settle† (cf. *staid*[1]). **II.**† *intr.* To rest or lean, as on a support; fig., to depend or rely: with *on* or *upon*.

stay[3] (stā), *v. i.*; *stayed* or *staid*, *staying.* [Prob. < OF. *ester*, stand, stop, remain (cf. *estant*, *estaiant*, *esteaunt*, *steant*, ppr.), < L. *stare*, stand: see *stand*.] To stop or halt (as, "He *staid* not for brake, and he stopp'd not for stone": Scott's "Marmion," v. 12); cease or desist (*from*: archaic); pause or wait, as for a moment, before proceeding or continuing (often used parenthetically in the imperative: as, "*Stay* though, I am speaking too fast," H. Kingsley's "Geoffry Hamlyn," xxvii.); linger or tarry (as, "Such sweetness . . . that . . . the merry rout That called on Bacchus, hearkening, *stayed* awhile": W. Morris's "Jason," i. 263); also, to remain in a place, situation, company, etc., instead of departing (as, uncertain whether to go or *stay*; we cannot *stay* long); remain (where or as specified: as, to *stay* at home; to *stay* out or up late; "She guessed that he had . . . *stayed* away through jealousy of his sister," Barrie's "Sentimental Tommy," ii.; "My stomach loathed the sugar, and brought it all up again; then I took a draught of water without sugar, and that *stayed* with me," Defoe's "Robinson Crusoe," ii. 8); continue to be (as specified), as to condition, etc. (as, to *stay* fastened; to *stay* clean, well, or young; to *stay* a bachelor); often, to remain in or at a place, with a person, etc., for a sojourn or visit (as, to *stay* in Paris for a week; to *stay* at a hotel; "Ernest shall go and *stay* with Figgins and meet the future Lord Lonsford," S. Butler's "Way of All Flesh," xxix.); dwell or reside for a time; also, to hold one's ground, or stand firm (archaic); hold out or endure, as in a race or other contest (colloq.); keep up, as with a competitor in a race or the like (colloq.).—**to stay put**, to remain where or as placed; remain fixed. [Colloq.] —**stay**[3], *v. t.* To bring to a stop or halt (as, "The master's silent signal *stays* The wearied cavalcade": Holmes's "Agnes," ii.); hold back, detain, or restrain, as from going or proceeding further (as, "No temptation that they could invent could *stay* him from following Claude," G. W. Cable's "Bonaventure," iii. 8; "News came which *stayed* his hand," Besant's "Coligny," viii.); check, arrest, or stop (movement, action, processes, etc.: as, to *stay* one's steps at a friend's door; "the gentle progression and growth of herbs, flowers, trees . . . which no force can *stay*," Longfellow's "Kavanagh," xiv.); suspend or delay (proceedings, etc.); suppress, quell, or allay (violence, strife, etc.: as, "Applications were in vain made to them that the havoc might be *stayed*," Motley's "Dutch Republic," iii. 7); appease or satisfy the cravings of (the stomach, appetite, etc., or the person) temporarily or in some measure (as, "He *stayed* his stomach on slabs of cold rice till the full dawn," Kipling's "Kim," xi.; "Father Michael . . . gave me a glass of liqueur to *stay* me until dinner," Stevenson's "Travels with a Donkey," iii. 2); also, to wait for, or await (archaic: as "My father *stays* my coming," Shakspere's "Two Gentlemen of Verona," ii. 2. 13); also, to remain for (a meal, performance, etc.: as, "The young gentleman and his mother insisted on our *staying* dinner," Smollett's "Humphry

Clinker," June 26; "We intended to *stay* the farce," Miss Burney's "Evelina," xx.); remain through or during (a period of time: as, "He *stayed* the night in the spare room," W. De Morgan's "Somehow Good," vi.); with *out*, to remain to the end of, or remain beyond, or outstay.—**stay**³, *n.* The act of staying or stopping; a coming or a bringing to a stop or halt; a stop, halt, or pause; a standstill (as, "if the plague . . . be at a *stay*, and the plague spread not in the skin": Lev. xiii. 5); a stoppage or arrest of action; a suspension of a judicial proceeding; a delay† or postponement†; also, a cause of stoppage or restraint†; a check†; also, continuance in a place; a sojourn or temporary residence (as, "Our *stay* with our hospitable friends at Rosebury was perforce coming to a close": Thackeray's "Newcomes," lxi.); also, continuance in a state†; duration†; a continuing or permanent state or condition†; also, staying power, or endurance (colloq.).

stay=at=home (stā′at-hōm″). **I.** *a.* Staying at home; not given to or characterized by roaming, gadding, or traveling. **II.** *n.* One who stays at home, esp. habitually: as, "If I wished to write a book for the *stay-at-homes* to read, I could easily invent a thousand lies far more entertaining" (W. H. Hudson's "Green Mansions," i.).

stay-er¹ (stā′ėr), *n.* One who stays or supports.

stay-er² (stā′ėr), *n.* One who or that which stays, stops, or checks; also, one who stays or remains; also, one who holds out or endures, or does not readily give in (colloq.).

stay-ing (stā′ing), *n.* The act of one who or that which stays, stops, remains, etc.; often, holding out or enduring, as in a race or other contest or under great exertion or strain (often used attributively: as, good *staying* qualities; "The old fellow's *staying* powers were really extraordinary," W. H. Hudson's "Purple Land," ii.).

stay-lace (stā′lās), *n.* A lace for drawing together the parts of stays or corsets.

stay-less¹ (stā′les), *a.* Without stay or support; unsupported; also, without stays or corsets.

stay-less² (stā′les), *a.* Without stay or stop; unceasing; ceaseless.

stay-sail (stā′sāl, naut. -sl), *n.* *Naut.*, any sail hoisted on a stay, as a triangular sail between two masts.

stead (sted), *n.* [AS. *stede* = OFries. *stede* = OHG. *stat* (G. *statt*) = Icel. *stadhr* = Goth. *staths*, place; from the root of E. *stand*.] A place, spot, or locality (archaic: as, "Fly therefore, fly this fearefull *stead* anon," Spenser's "Faerie Queene," ii. 4. 42; "And how to find within the marshy *steads* The stoutest reeds," W. Morris's "Jason," i. 230); a tract or area of ground, or a site, as for a particular use (archaic or prov.: cf. *homestead*); a piece of landed property, as a farm (archaic or prov.); the proper or appointed place of a person or thing (archaic: as, "The souldier may not move from watchfull *sted*, Nor leave his stand," Spenser's "Faerie Queene," i. 9. 41); hence, the place or room of a person or thing as occupied by a successor or substitute (as, "He [David] died . . . and Solomon his son reigned in his *stead*," 1 Chron. xxix. 28; "Why could not I have died in your *stead?*" Godwin's "Caleb Williams," v.; "a complete book of Christian principles, in the *stead* of the Scripture," Strype's "Memorials of Cranmer," i. 24: cf. *instead*); also, fig., a situation†, condition†, or plight†; also, a framework for supporting a bed† (cf. *bedstead*); also, a spot or mark on a surface, or an imprint or track (Sc.); also, service, advantage, or avail (now chiefly in the phrase 'to stand one in stead,' or 'in good stead,' that is, to be serviceable or advantageous to one: as, "An adroit diplomacy might stand him in *stead*," Motley's "Dutch Republic," i. 3; "They have brains which stand them in good *stead*," J. H. Robinson's "Mind in the Making," iii. 6).—**stead**, *v. t.* To place† or set†; fig., to put in a particular situation or plight†; also, to be of service or advantage to, profit, or avail (archaic: as, "In my dealing with my child . . . my accomplishments and my money *stead* me nothing," Emerson's "Essays," The Over-Soul).

stead-fast (sted′fast), *a.* [Also *stedfast*; AS. *stedefæst*, < *stede*, place, E. *stead*, + *fæst*, E. *fast*¹, *a.*] Firmly fixed in place or position, or not moving from or changing place (as, "a pillar *steadfast* in the storm," Tennyson's "In Memoriam," cxiii.; "I clung with my eyes to the dim, *steadfast*

line of the sea," Kinglake's "Eothen," xxviii.); fixed in direction, or steadily directed (as, a *steadfast* gaze; "searching his face with a *steadfast* eye," S. J. Weyman's "Gentleman of France," xx.); fig., firmly established, as an institution or a state of affairs; firm in purpose, resolution, faith, attachment, etc., as a person (as, "He that standeth *stedfast* in his heart . . . doeth well": 1 Cor. vii. 37); unwavering, as resolution, faith, adherence, etc.—**stead′fast-ly**, *adv.*—**stead′fast-ness**, *n.*

stead-i-er (sted′i-ėr), *n.* One who or that which steadies.

stead-i-ly (sted′i-li), *adv.* In a steady manner; firmly; evenly; uniformly; unwaveringly; steadfastly; with regularity in habits.—**stead′i-ness**, *n.*

stead-ing (sted′ing), *n.* [From *stead, n.*] A farm-house and outbuildings; sometimes, the outbuildings as distinguished from the farm-house; also, a site for a building. [Sc. and north. Eng.]

stead-y (sted′i). [Appar. < *stead, n.*] **I.** *a.*; compar. *steadier*, superl. *steadiest.* Firmly placed or fixed; stable in position or equilibrium; even or regular in movement; not tottering, swaying, shaking, faltering, etc. (as, "He . . . through the vast ethereal sky Sails . . . with *steady* wing," Milton's "Paradise Lost," v. 268; "His voice, and eye, and hand grew *steadier* and firmer as he repeated these words," Dickens's "Cricket on the Hearth," iii.); also, free from change, variation, or interruption, uniform, or continuous (as, a *steady* wind; *steady* progress; a *steady* rise in prices); constant, regular, or habitual (as, *steady* coöperation; to be a person's *steady* company, in slang use, to 'keep company' as a sweetheart with a person of the opposite sex); also, free from excitement or agitation (as, *steady* nerves; "Give them time to get *steady* a bit if you want them to fight," J. Conrad's "Rescue," iii. 9); also, firm, unwavering, or steadfast, as persons or their principles, policy, etc. (as, "This man seemed to be none of the *steadiest* in his religion," Strype's "Memorials of Cranmer," iii. 23; *steady* adherence or friendship); also, settled, staid, or sober, as a person or the character, habits, etc. (as, "a *steady* young business man, and a good church-goer": Tarkington's "Magnificent Ambersons," ii.); *naut.*, of a vessel, keeping nearly upright, as in a heavy sea. **II.** *n.*; pl. *-ies* (-iz). A person's 'steady company,' or regular companion and sweetheart: as, "I heard this Russell was supposed to be your . . . friend Mildred's *steady*" (Tarkington's "Alice Adams," xi.). [Slang.]—**stead′y**, *adv.* In a steady manner; steadily.—**stead′y**, *v.*; *steadied*, *steadying.* **I.** *tr.* To make steady, as in position, movement, action, character, etc.: as, "*steadying* his uncertain descent with a stick" (F. M. Crawford's "Mr. Isaacs," xi.); "The sense of responsibility had more than *steadied* him" (W. H. Hudson's "Purple Land," xvii.). **II.** *intr.* To become steady: as, "The breeze *steadied*" (J. Conrad's "Rescue," iv. 4).—**stead′y=go″ing**, *a.* Steady in action, habits, etc.: as, "a *steady-going* young man" (W. Churchill's "Coniston," i. 1).

steak (stāk), *n.* [ME. *steke, steike*, from Scand.: cf. Icel. *steik*, steak, *steikja*, roast on a spit.] A slice of meat or fish for broiling, frying, etc.—

steak′=maul, *n.* An implement for pounding steaks in order to soften the fiber.

Steak-maul.

steal (stēl), *v. t.*; pret. *stole*, pp. *stolen*, ppr. *stealing.* [AS. *stelan* = D. *stelen* = G. *stehlen* = Icel. *stela* = Goth. *stilan*, steal: cf. *stalk*¹.] To take, or take away, dishonestly or wrongfully, esp. secretly (as, to *steal* money or food; to *steal* a horse; to *steal* a document or a painting); kidnap or abduct (a child, etc.); appropriate (ideas, credit, words, etc.) without right or acknowledgment; also, to take as if by theft (something prized or not willingly lost: as, "When Time who *steals* our years away Shall *steal* our pleasures too," T. Moore's "Song," When Time); take by surprise or without permission (as, to *steal* a kiss); take (time) from duty or the usual occupation (as, "He *stole* occasional evenings for original research": Sinclair Lewis's "Arrowsmith," viii.); take, get, or win by insidious arts or subtle means (as, "Some enchantment old, Whose spells have *stolen* my spirit as I slept," Shelley's "Prometheus Unbound," ii. 1. 101); "She *steals* our affections awa, man," Burns's "Tarbolton

Lasses," 28); take, get, or effect surreptitiously (as, to *steal* a look at a person; to *steal* a nap during a sermon; "Much wondering how the subtle fiend had *stolen* Entrance unseen," Milton's "Paradise Lost," x. 20); make (one's way) stealthily; also, to move, bring, convey, or put secretly or quietly (*away, from, in, into*, etc.: as, "He tried once or twice to *steal* his hand away," G. Meredith's "Ordeal of Richard Feverel," x.; "He *stole* his arm about her," Mrs. Wharton's "Ethan Frome," ii.); also, in various games, to gain (a point, etc.) by strategy, or by chance or luck.—**to steal a march,** to accomplish a march, as of troops, without the knowledge of the enemy; in general, to gain an advantage secretly or slyly, as over a rival: often with *on* or *upon*.—**to steal one's thunder,** fig., to appropriate or use another's ideas, methods, etc., without asking leave or giving credit: from words attributed to John Dennis, the English dramatist, who devised a new kind of stage thunder for his play of "Appius and Virginia" in 1709, only to find that, while his play was unfavorably received, the thunder was appropriated by others for use in presenting "Macbeth."—**steal,** *v. i.* To commit or practise theft; also, to move, go, or come secretly, quietly, or unobserved (as, "A mink *steals* out of the marsh . . . and seizes a frog," Thoreau's "Walden," iv.; "I *stole* near, hushing my breath," Bulwer-Lytton's "Caxtons," viii. 1); pass, come, spread, etc., imperceptibly, gently, or gradually (as, the years *steal* by; sounds or odors *steal* upon the sense; a smile *steals* over the face; "A gentle light *stole* over the heavens," Mrs. Shelley's "Frankenstein," xi.). —**steal,** *n.* An act of stealing; a theft; also, the thing stolen. [Chiefly colloq.]—**steal′er,** *n.*—**steal′ing,** *n.* The act of one who steals; also, something stolen (chiefly in *pl.*). —**steal′ing-ly,** *adv.*

stealth (stelth), *n.* [ME. *stelthe, stalthe,* connected with AS. *stelan,* E. *steal.*] The act or practice of stealing†; a theft†; something stolen†; also, a stealing or going secretly† (as, "I told him of your *stealth* unto this wood": Shakspere's "Midsummer Night's Dream," iii. 2. 310); also, secret, clandestine, or surreptitious procedure (as, to resort to *stealth* to carry out one's purposes; "Let humble Allen, with an awkward shame, Do good by *stealth,* and blush to find it fame," Pope's "Epilogue to the Satires," i. 136).—**stealth′-ful,** *a.* Stealthy.—**stealth′y,** *a.*; compar. *stealthier,* superl. *stealthiest.* Done, characterized, or acting by stealth; furtive: as, to hear *stealthy* footsteps; a *stealthy* gesture or whisper; a *stealthy* foe.—**stealth′i-ly,** *adv.*—**stealth′i-ness,** *n.*

steam (stēm), *n.* [AS. *stēam* = D. *stoom,* steam, vapor.] Water in the form of an invisible gas or vapor; esp., water changed to this form by boiling, extensively used for the generation of mechanical power, for heating purposes, etc.; fig., power or energy (colloq.); also, the mist formed when the gas or vapor from boiling water condenses in the air, as the hot, white, smoke-like exhalation that issues from a tea-kettle ('condensed steam'); in general, an exhalation.— **steam,** *v.* **I.** *intr.* To emit or give off steam or vapor (as, "Their porridge was already *steaming* on the fire": George Eliot's "Adam Bede," iv.); generate or produce steam for mechanical purposes, as a boiler; also, to rise or pass off in the form of steam, as vapor; also, to become covered with condensed steam, as a surface; also, to move or travel by the agency of steam (as, "A ship with a cargo of wheat *steamed* off to Marseilles": Sinclair Lewis's "Arrowsmith," xxxi.). **II.** *tr.* To emit or exhale (steam or vapor); send out in the form of steam; also, to expose to the action of steam; treat with steam, as in order to heat, cook, soften, renovate, or the like; expose (a gummed letter, etc.) to the action of steam in order to soften the gum and facilitate opening (as, "If she [the postmistress] did not '*steam*' the letters . . . it is difficult to see how all the gossip got out": Barrie's "Auld Licht Idylls," ii.); also, to fill or cover with steam; also, to convey by the agency of steam, as in a steamship.—**steam′boat,** *n.* A boat propelled by steam-power.—**steam′boat″ing,** *n.* The process of traveling by or operating a steamboat.—**steam′=boil′er,** *n.* A receptacle in which water is boiled to generate steam.—**steam′=car,** *n.* A car driven or drawn by steam-power.—**steam′=chest,** *n.* In a steam-engine, the chamber from which the steam enters the cylinder.—**steam′=cyl′in-der,** *n.* The cylinder of a steam-engine. See *cylinder, n.*—**steam′=en′gine,** *n.* An

engine worked by steam, typically one in which a sliding piston in a cylinder is moved by the expansive action of the steam generated in a boiler.—**steam′er,** *n.* One who or that which steams; a device or vessel in which something is steamed; something propelled or operated by steam, as a steamboat or steamship, a steam-propelled road-locomotive, traction-engine, or automobile, or a fire-engine with pumps operated by steam.—**steam′er=chair,** *n.* A kind of reclining-chair used by passengers on the deck of a steamer.— **steam′=fit″ter,** *n.* One who installs and repairs steam-pipes and their accessories.—**steam′=fit″ting,** *n.*—**steam′=gage,** *n.* An attachment to a boiler to indicate the pressure of steam.—**steam′=ham′mer,** *n.* A powerful mechanical hammer for forging steel, etc., operated directly by steam.— **steam′=heat′,** *n.* Heat obtained by the condensation of steam in pipes, radiators, etc.—**steam′=jack″et,** *n.* An inclosure or jacket into which steam passes, built round a tank, kettle, or the like, in order to heat it.—**steam′=pipe,** *n.* A pipe through which steam is conveyed.—**steam′=pow″er,** *n.* The power of steam applied to move machinery or produce any other result.—**steam′=roll′er,** *n.* A heavy locomotive engine having a wide roller or a combination of rollers and operated by steam, for crushing, compacting, or leveling materials in road-making; fig., an agency for crushing opposition, esp. with ruthless disregard of rights (much used with reference to political measures or tactics). —**steam′=roll′er,** *v. t.* To go over or crush as with a steam-roller: chiefly fig., as in politics.—**steam′ship,** *n.* A ship propelled by steam-power.—**steam′=shov′el,** *n.* A machine for digging or excavating, operated by its own engine and boiler.—**steam′=tight,** *a.* Impervious to the passage of steam under pressure.—**steam′=whis′tle,** *n.* A whistle operated by the steam from a boiler.—**steam′y,** *a.* Consisting of or resembling steam (as, "The bubbling and loud-hissing urn Throws up a *steamy* column," Cowper's "Task," iv. 39; "I made my voyage to Africa, and came at last into a world of *steamy* fogs," H. G. Wells's "Tono-Bungay," iii. 4. § 3); full of or abounding in steam; emitting steam (as, "Their boots and mud-splashed uniforms . . . are wet and *steamy*": G. W. Cable's "Cavalier," xlvi.); covered with or as if with condensed steam.

stean (stēn), *n.* [AS. *stǣna, < stān,* E. *stone.*] A jar, pot, or vessel of earthenware. [Archaic or prov. Eng.]

ste-ap-sin (stē-ap′sin), *n.* [Formed, after *pepsin, <* Gr. στέαρ, fat, tallow.] In *chem.,* the lipase of the pancreatic juice.

ste-a-rate (stē′a-rāt), *n.* In *chem.,* a salt of stearic acid.

ste-ar-ic (stē-ar′ik), *a.* [F. *stéarique, <* Gr. στέαρ, fat, tallow.] Of or pertaining to suet or fat: as, *stearic* acid (a monobasic organic acid, $C_{18}H_{36}O_2$, the acid of which stearin is an ester, which forms white scaly crystals and is used for making candles, etc.: see *stearin*).

ste-a-rin (stē′a-rin), *n.* [F. *stéarine, <* Gr. στέαρ, fat, tallow.] Any of the three glyceryl esters of stearic acid, esp. the one with the formula $C_3H_5(C_{18}H_{35}O_2)_3$, which is a soft, white, odorless solid found in many natural fats; also, the crude stearic acid of commerce, used in making candles, etc.

ste-ar-rhe-a, ste-ar-rhœ-a (stē-a-rē′ä), *n.* [NL., < Gr. στέαρ, fat, tallow, + ῥοία, a flow, < ῥεῖν, flow.] Same as *seborrhea.*

ste-a-tite (stē′a-tīt), *n.* [L. *steatitis, <* Gr. στέαρ (στεατ-), fat, tallow.] Soapstone.—**ste-a-tit′ic** (-tit′ik), *a.*

ste-a-to-pyg-i-a, ste-a-to-py-ga (stē″a-tō-pij′i-ä, -pī′gä), *n.* [NL., < Gr. στέαρ (στεατ-), fat, tallow, + πυγή, rump.] Abnormal accumulation of fat on and about the buttocks, as among the Hottentots, Bushmen, and other African peoples, esp. the women.—**ste″a-to-pyg′ic** (-pij′ik), **ste″a-to-py′gous** (-pī′gus), *a.* Pertaining to, characterized by, or exhibiting steatopygia.

sted-fast (sted′fast), etc. See *steadfast,* etc.

steed (stēd), *n.* [AS. *stēda, < stōd,* E. *stud*[1].] A stud-horse† or stallion†; a high-spirited horse; in general, a horse, esp. one for riding. [Now chiefly literary or rhetorical.]— **steed′less,** *a.* Without a steed.

steel (stēl), *n.* [AS. *style,* earlier *stēli,* akin to D. *staal,* G. *stahl,* Icel. *stāl,* steel.] Iron in a modified form, artificially produced, containing a certain amount of carbon (more than in wrought-iron and less than in cast-iron) and other constituents, and possessing a hardness, elasticity, strength, etc., which vary with the composition and the heat treatment, commonly made by removing a certain amount of the carbon from pig-iron, as in the Bessemer process, and used in making tools, girders, etc.; also, something made of this material; a sword; a rod-shaped steel implement for sharpening knives; a piece of steel for striking fire with a flint; a flat strip of steel for stiffening corsets, etc.; also, steel-gray.—**high steel,** or **hard steel,** steel with a comparatively high percentage of carbon.—**low steel, mild steel,** or **soft steel,** steel with a comparatively low percentage of carbon.—**steel,** *v. t.* To fit with steel, as by pointing, edging, or overlaying (as, "In his hand two spears of cornel-wood, Well *steeled* and bound with brazen bands he shook": W. Morris's "Jason," ii. 9); also, to convert (iron) into steel; also, to cause to resemble steel in some way; make like steel in appearance: esp., fig., to make hard or strong like steel, or render insensible, inflexible, unyielding, determined, etc. (as, "Any good jury would . . . have been *steeled* against the appeal," Charnwood's "Abraham Lincoln," iv.; "The hearts of the Hollanders were rather *steeled* to resistance than awed into submission," Motley's "Dutch Republic," iii. 8).—**steel′=blue′. I.** *a.* Of a lustrous dark-bluish color, resembling steel tempered blue: as, "The *steel-blue* rim of the ocean" (Longfellow's "Courtship of Miles Standish," i.). **II.** *n.* A steel-blue color.—**steel′=gray′. I.** *a.* Of a dark metallic gray color. **II.** *n.* A dark metallic gray.—**steel′head,** *n.* A trout, *Salmo gairdneri*, of the Pacific coast from California northward.—**steel′i-ness,** *n.* Steely nature or quality.—**steel′ing,** *n.* The process of tipping, edging, or overlaying with steel; in *engraving,* the process of electroplating an engraved copperplate or the like with a film of iron to render it more durable.—**steel′work,** *n.* Work in steel; parts or articles made of steel.—**steel′=works,** *n. pl.* or *sing.* An establishment where steel is made, and often manufactured into girders, rails, parts of machinery, etc.—**steel′y,** *a.* Consisting or made of steel (as, "the *steely* helmet of the monarch": Jane Porter's "Scottish Chiefs," liii.); also, resembling or suggesting steel; like steel in appearance or color (as, "the beating of the *steely* sea": W. Morris's "Earthly Paradise," Apology); hard or strong like steel; unimpressionable, inflexible, or unyielding (as, "his *steely* calm . . . his imperturbable detachment from weak humanity": Arnold Bennett's "Old Wives' Tale," ii. 5).

Steel-yard[1] (stēl′yärd), *n.* [An erroneous translation of MLG. *stālhof,* < *stāl,* sample, specimen (confused with *stāl,* steel), + *hof,* yard, court.] [Also *l. c.*] A place in London where the Hanseatic merchants formerly had an establishment; also, the merchants themselves; also, a similar establishment elsewhere. [Now only hist.]

steel-yard[2] (stēl′yärd, commonly stil′yärd), *n.* [Appar. < *steel* + *yard*[2] (in sense of 'rod,' 'beam'), but explained by some as for *Steelyard beam,* that is, the balance used at the Steelyard: see *Steelyard*[1].] A portable balance with two unequal arms, the longer one having graduations and a movable counterpoise, and the shorter one bearing a hook or the like for holding the object to be weighed. Sometimes called *steelyards,* or a *pair of steelyards.*

steen (stēn), *n.* See *stean.*

steen-bok (stān′bok or stēn′-), *n.* [S. Afr. D., 'stone buck.'] Any of various small African antelopes of the genus *Nanotragus,* frequenting rocky places, as *N. tragulus,* common in South Africa.

steep[1] (stēp), *v.* [ME. *stepen*: cf. Sw. *stöpa,*

Steenbok (*Nanotragus tragulus*).

Dan. *stöbe,* cast, found, steep, Icel. *steypa,* pour out, cast, found, akin to E. *stoop*[3], also *steep*[2].] **I.** *tr.* To soak in water or other liquid, as for the purpose of softening, cleansing, or the like, or of extracting some constituent (as, to *steep* barley; to *steep* herbs in vinegar; to *steep* tea in boiling water); wet thoroughly in or with any liquid, or as a liquid does (as, swords *steeped* in blood; dew *steeps* the grass); drench, saturate, or imbrue; fig., to bathe, suffuse, or envelop, as in mist, smoke, or light, or as mist or the like does (as, "dark, rugged columns festooned with writhing creepers and *steeped* in gloom": J. Conrad's "Rescue," v. 2); immerse in some pervading, absorbing, or stupefying influence or agency (as, a mind *steeped* in romance; "Fancy . . . shall *steep* me in Elysian reverie," Cowper's "My Mother's Picture," 19); imbue or permeate (with *in*). **II.** *intr.* To lie soaking in a liquid. Also fig.—**steep**[1], *n.* The act or process of steeping, or the state of being steeped; also, a liquid in which something is steeped; also, rennet (prov. Eng.).

steep[2] (stēp). [AS. *stēap* = OFries. *stāp,* high, akin to Icel. *steypdhr,* high, also to E. *stoop*[3]: cf. *steep*[1].] **I.** *a.* High† or lofty†; also, having an almost perpendicular slope or pitch, or a relatively high gradient, as a hill, an ascent, stairs, etc.; fig., arduous, as an undertaking; also (chiefly in colloq. use), unduly high, or exorbitant, as a price or amount; extreme or extravagant, as a statement. **II.** *n.* A steep place; a declivity or slope, as of a hill: as, "the villages of the hill-folk . . . clinging like swallows' nests against the *steeps*" (Kipling's "Kim," xiii.).

steep-en (stē′pn), *v. i.* or *t.* To become or make steep or more steep.

steep-er (stē′pėr), *n.* One who or that which steeps or soaks; also, a vessel used in steeping.

steep-ish (stē′pish), *a.* Rather steep: as, "a bare valley . . . with *steepish* sides" (Roosevelt's "Ranch Life and the Hunting-Trail," v.).

stee-ple (stē′pl), *n.* [AS. *stēpel, stȳpel,* < *stēap,* high, E. *steep*[2].] A lofty tower or tower-like building†; also, a lofty tower attached to a church, temple, or the like, and often containing bells; such a tower with a spire or other superstructure surmounting it; also, a spire on the top of the tower or roof of a church or the like.—**stee′ple-bush,** *n.* The hardback.—**stee′ple-chase** (-chās), *n.* A horse-race across country, orig. one having as goal a church-steeple at some distance but in view; hence, now usually, a horse-race over a made course furnished with artificial ditches, hedges, and other obstacles; also, a race run on foot by persons across country or over a course furnished with ditches, hurdles, etc.—**stee′ple-chase,** *v. i.; -chased, -chasing.* To ride or run in a steeplechase.—**stee′ple-chas″er** (-chā″sėr), *n.*—**stee′ple-crowned,** *a.* Having a tall, pointed crown, as a hat: as, "a man . . . wearing a *steeple-crowned* hat and a skullcap beneath it" (Hawthorne's "Twice-Told Tales," Howe's Masquerade).—**stee′ple=cup,** *n.* A tall, ornamental cup, as of silver, having the cover surmounted by a steeple-like part.—**stee′pled,** *a.* Having a steeple or steeples, or abounding in steeples (as, "many a *steepled* town": Whittier's "Cobbler Keezar's Vision"); also, having the form of a steeple†.—**stee′ple=jack,** *n.* A man who climbs steeples, tall chimneys, or the like, to make repairs, etc.

steep-ly (stēp′li), *adv.* In a steep manner.—**steep′ness,** *n.*

steep-y (stē′pi), *a.* Steep: as, "the *steepy* hill" (Scott's "Lady of the Lake," iii. 13). [Archaic.]

steer[1] (stēr), *n.* [AS. *stēor* = D. and G. *stier* = Goth. *stiur,* steer.] A young male of the ox kind, esp. when castrated and raised for beef; also, a male animal of the beef-cattle class of any age.

steer[2] (stēr), *v.* [AS. *stēoran, stīeran,* = D. *sturen* = G. *steuern* = Icel. *stȳra,* steer: cf. AS. *stēor,* guidance, prob. also rudder, also E. *starboard* and *stern*[2].] **I.** *tr.* To guide the course of (a vessel) by means of a rudder, helm, or the like; guide the course of (anything in motion) by any means (as,

Steeple-cup.

to *steer* a sled, a motor-car, or an aëroplane; "I *steered* my dromedary close up alongside of the mounted Bedouin," Kinglake's "Eothen," xxi.); guide, pilot, or lead (a person: now colloq.); direct the course of (proceedings, affairs, etc.: now colloq.); govern† or rule†; restrain† or control†; also, to direct (the course, way, movements, etc.) by means of a rudder or helm or otherwise (as, to *steer* a ship's course to the nearest land; "With expanded wings he *steers* his flight Aloft," Milton's "Paradise Lost," i. 225; "She . . . oft her steps had hither *steered*," Wordsworth's "White Doe of Rylstone," v.); follow or pursue (a particular course) by means of a rudder or otherwise (as, "Heaving anchor . . . I *steered* the same course that I had done the day before, wherein I was directed by my pocket-compass": Swift's "Gulliver's Travels," i. 8). **II.** *intr.* To direct the course of a vessel, vehicle, aëroplane, or the like by the use of a rudder or other means (as, "The sail collapsed; the pilot *steered* for the bank," Amelia B. Edwards's "Thousand Miles up the Nile," xiv.; "automobiles . . . driven by chauffeurs . . . who reclined as they *steered*," Arnold Bennett's "The Old Adam," iii.); direct the course, or pursue a course (as specified: as, "I hear The tread of many feet *steering* this way," Milton's "Samson Agonistes," 111; "He . . . *steered* along the street by her side," Mrs. Gaskell's "Cranford," ii.); fig., to direct one's course of action (as, to *steer* between extremes); also, of a vessel, etc., to admit of being steered, or answer the helm (as, "Our ship would not *steer* at all, at least not so as to be depended upon": Defoe's "Captain Singleton," xiv.); be steered or guided in a particular direction.—**to steer clear of,** to keep away from; avoid.—**steer'a-ble,** *a.* That may be steered.—**steer'age** (-ạj), *n.* The act, practice, or method of steering a vessel, etc.; the manner in which a vessel or the like answers to the helm or steering apparatus; guidance in general; also, a course steered or held; also, the apparatus for steering a vessel, etc.; also, a part or division of a ship, orig. that containing the steering apparatus, later a certain part, division, or cabin not necessarily concerned with the steering, and varying in situation and use; in a passenger-ship, the part allotted to the passengers who travel at the cheapest rate.—**steer'age-way,** *n.* *Naut.,* the degree of forward movement of a ship which renders it subject to the helm: as, "In a few minutes it fell dead calm, the vessel lost her *steerage-way*" (Dana's "Two Years before the Mast," x.).—**steer'er,** *n.*—**steer'ing=gear,** *n.* The apparatus or mechanism for steering, as in a vessel, a motor-car, a bicycle, an aëroplane, etc.—**steer'ing=wheel,** *n.* A wheel by the turning of which a rudder or other device for steering is operated, as in a vessel, a motor-car, etc.—**steers'man** (-mạn), *n.*; pl. -*men*. One who steers a vessel (as, "By and by . . . nearly every pilot on the river had a *steersman*": Mark Twain's "Life on the Mississippi," xv.); sometimes, one who drives a motor-car or other machine.—**steers'man-ship,** *n.* The art or skill of a steersman.

steeve[1] (stēv), *v.*; steeved, steeving. [Origin uncertain.] *Naut.*: **I.** *intr.* Of a bowsprit, etc., to incline upward at an angle instead of extending horizontally. **II.** *tr.* To set (a bowsprit, etc.) at an upward inclination.—**steeve**[1], *n.* *Naut.,* the angle that a bowsprit or the like makes with the horizontal.

steeve[2] (stēv), *v. t.*; steeved, steeving. [F. *estiver* = Sp. *estivar* = It. *stivare,* < L. *stipare,* crowd, pack: cf. *stevedore* and *stive.*] To pack tightly; esp., to stow (cotton or other cargo) compactly in a ship's hold (as, "Each morning we . . . brought off as many hides as we could *steeve* in the course of the day": Dana's "Two Years before the Mast," xxix.).—**steeve**[2], *n.* A long derrick or spar, with a block at one end, used in stowing cargo.

steg-a-no-pod (steg'ạ-nō̱-pod). [NL. *Steganopodes,* pl., < Gr. στεγανόπους (-οπόδ-), web-footed, < στεγανός, covered, + πούς (ποδ-), foot.] **I.** *n.* Any of the *Steganopodes,* an order of natatorial birds comprising those with all four toes webbed, as the pelicans, gannets, cormorants, frigate-birds, snake-birds, and tropic-birds. **II.** *a.* Belonging to the *Steganopodes;* having all four toes webbed.—**steg-a-nop'o-dous** (-nop'ọ̄-dus), *a.*

steg-o-sau-rus (steg-ọ̄-sâ'rus), *n.*; pl. -*ri* (-rī). [NL., < Gr. στέγος, roof, + σαῦρος, lizard.] Any of the herbivorous dinosaurs constituting the genus *Stegosaurus,* reptiles of great size (sometimes nearly 40 feet long) with a heavy bony armor, as *S. ungulatus,* having on the back a double row of large, erect bony plates extending from the head almost to the tip of the tail.

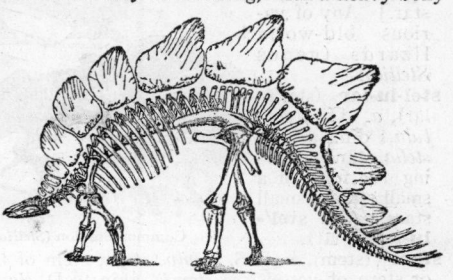

Stegosaurus (*S. ungulatus*). (Restoration.)

stein (stīn), *n.* [G., lit. 'stone': see *stone.*] An earthenware mug, esp. for beer.

stein-bock (stīn'bok), *n.* [G., 'stone buck': cf. *steenbok.*] The ibex; also, the steenbok.

stein-bok (stīn'bok), *n.* See *steenbok.*

ste-la (stē'lạ), *n.*; pl. *stelæ* (-lē) or *stelas* (-lạz). [L.: see *stele.*] In *archæol.,* a stele: as, "The *stela* of Dakkeh . . . speaks of him [Rameses II.] as already terrible in battle" (Amelia B. Edwards's "Thousand Miles up the Nile," xv.).

ste-le (stē'lē), *n.*; pl. *stelæ* (-lē) or *steles* (-lēz). [NL. *stele* (L. *stela*), < Gr. στήλη, upright block, post, akin to ἱστάναι, cause to stand.] In *archæol.,* an upright slab or pillar of stone bearing an inscription, sculptural design, or the like; sometimes, a prepared surface on the face of a building, a rock, etc., bearing an inscription or the like; in *bot.,* the central cylinder of vascular tissue, etc., in the stem or root of a plant, developed from the plerome.—**ste'lar** (-lär), *a.*

Sculptured Stele. — Monument of the Knight Dexileos (who fell before Corinth 394 B.C.), on the Sacred Way, Athens.

stell (stel), *v. t.* [AS. *stellan* = D. and G. *stellen,* place, set; akin to E. *stall*[2].] To place, set, or fix (now Sc.: as, "yonder round hillock . . . whereon an enemy might *stell* . . . a battery of cannon," Scott's "Legend of Montrose," x.); also, to prop or support (Sc.); also, to portray (archaic: as, "Mine eye hath play'd the painter and hath *stell'd* Thy beauty's form in table of my heart," Shakspere's "Sonnets," xxiv.).

stel-lar (stel'är), *a.* [LL. *stellaris,* < L. *stella,* star: see *star.*] Of or pertaining to the stars, astral, or sidereal; of the nature of, resembling, or suggesting a star; starlike; star-shaped; sometimes, pertaining to a professional star, as of the stage.

stel-late (stel'āt), *a.* [L. *stellatus,* < *stella,* star.] Being or arranged in the form of a conventional star; star-shaped. Also **stel-lat-ed** (stel'ā-ted).—**stel'late-ly,** *adv.*

stel-li-form (stel'i-fôrm), *a.* [L. *stella,* star, + *forma,* form.] Star-shaped.

stel-lion (stel′yon), n. [L. *stellio(n-)*, lizard with starlike spots, < *stella*, star.] Any of various old-world lizards (genus *Stellio*).

stel-lu-lar (stel′ū-lär), a. [LL. *stellula*, dim. of L. *stella*, star.] Having the form of a small star or small stars. Also **stel′-lu-late** (-lāt).

Common Stellion (*Stellio vulgaris*).

stem[1] (stem), n. [AS. *stemn, stefn*, stem of tree, also prow or stern of vessel (see *stem*[2]), akin to D. *stam*, OHG. *stam*, G. *stamm*, stem of tree, also D. *steven*, Icel. *stamn, stafn*, prow or stern; prob. from the root of E. *stand*.] The main body of that portion of a tree, shrub, or other plant which is above ground; the firm part which supports the branches; a trunk; a stock; a stalk; in scientific usage, the ascending axis of a plant, whether above or below ground, which ordinarily grows in an opposite direction to the root or descending axis; also, a branch† or shoot†; also, the stalk which supports a leaf, flower, or fruit; a petiole; a peduncle; a pedicel; also, the stock, or line of descent, of a family; ancestry or pedigree (as, "Where ye may all, that are of noble *stem*, Approach": Milton's "Arcades," 82); a race, or ethnic stock; a branch or offshoot of a family† (as, "And now declare, sweet *stem* from York's great stock . . .": Shakspere's "1 Henry VI.," ii. 5. 41); also, something resembling or suggesting the stem of a plant, flower, etc.; the main or relatively thick stroke of a letter in printing, etc.; a long, slender part of an object in distinction from the head or from branches or projections, as the tube of a tobacco-pipe, the shaft of a feather, etc.; the slender, upright part of a goblet, wineglass, or other vessel, which unites the body to the foot or base; the cylindrical projection on a watchcase, bearing a ring for attaching the watch to a chain, etc., and usually having a knob at the end for winding the watch; in *music*, the vertical line forming part of a note; in *philol.*, a part of a word (usually a derivative of a root rather than a root) which serves as the base of inflectional forms.—**stem**[1], v. t.; *stemmed, stemming*. To remove the stem from (a leaf, fruit, etc.); remove the stem and midrib from (tobacco-leaves).

stem[2] (stem), n. [AS. *stemn, stefn*: see *stem*[1].] *Naut.*, the (curved) piece of timber or metal to which the two sides of a ship are united at the foremost end; also, the bow or forward part of a vessel.—**stem**[2], v.; *stemmed, stemming*. **I.** *tr.* To dash against with the stem of a vessel, or ram (obs. or archaic: as, "As when two warlike Brigandines at sea . . . Do meete together . . . They *stemme* ech other," Spenser's "Faerie Queene," iv. 2. 16); also, to make headway against (a tide, current, gale, etc.) by sailing or the like (as, "To watch the well-built Argo *stem* The rushing tide": W. Morris's "Jason," xii. 176); in general, to make progress against (opposition of any kind). **II.** *intr.* To make headway, as a vessel or a navigator: as, "They on the trading flood . . . Ply, *stemming* nightly toward the pole" (Milton's "Paradise Lost," ii. 642).

stem[3] (stem), v. t.; *stemmed, stemming*. [ME. *stemmen* = Icel. *stemma* = OHG. G. *stemmen*, stop, stem: cf. *stammer*.] To stop or check (as, to *stem* proceedings; "his milk-porridge, which it was his old frugal habit to *stem* his morning hunger with," George Eliot's "Mill on the Floss," i. 12); dam up (a stream, etc.: as, "he who *stems* a stream with sand," Scott's "Lady of the Lake," iii. 28; "to *stem* the torrent of his eloquence," F. M. Crawford's "Mr. Isaacs," vii.); stanch (bleeding, etc.: Sc.); also, to tamp, plug, or make tight, as a hole or a joint.

stem-less[1] (stem′les), a. Having no stem; in *bot.*, having no visible stem; acaulescent.

stem-less[2] (stem′les), a. That cannot be stemmed or checked.

stem-let (stem′let), n. A little stem.

stemmed (stemd), a. Having a stem: as, long-*stemmed*.

stem-mer[1] (stem′ėr), n. One who stems (tobacco, etc.); a device for stemming (grapes, etc.).

stem-mer[2] (stem′ėr), n. An implement for stemming or tamping.

-stemonous. An adjective termination from Gr. στήμων, warp, thread, used in botanical terms having reference to stamens, as in *diplostemonous, isostemonous*.

stem-son (stem′son), n. [From *stem*[2], with -son as in *keelson*.] *Naut.*, a curved timber in a ship's bow, having its lower end scarfed into the keelson.

stem-ware (stem′wār), n. Vessels, as of glass, having a stem uniting the body to the foot or base, as goblets, wine-glasses, etc.

stem-wind-er (stem′wīn″dėr), n. A watch wound by turning a knob at the stem.—**stem′=wind″ing**, a.

stench (stench), n. [AS. *stenc*, < *stincan*, E. *stink*.] An ill smell or offensive odor (as, "A horrible *stench* of decayed fish filled the air": Kipling's "Captains Courageous," ii.); ill-smelling quality, or stink (as, "a narrow winding street, full of . . . *stench*": Dickens's "Tale of Two Cities," i. 5); also, something having an offensive odor.—**stench′ful, stench′y**, a.

sten-cil (sten′sil), n. [Prob. from obs. *stencel*, adorn with bright colors, < OF. *estenceler*, < *estencele* (F. *étincelle*), a spark, < L. *scintilla*: see *scintilla*.] A thin sheet, as of metal, having letters, designs, etc., cut through it, so that when it is laid on a surface and ink or color is applied, these letters, etc., are reproduced on the surface; also, the letters, designs, etc., produced.—**sten′cil**, v. t.; *-ciled* or *-cilled*, *-ciling* or *-cilling*. To mark or paint (a surface) or produce (letters, etc.) by means of a stencil.—**sten′cil-er, sten′-cil-ler**, n.

steno-. Form of Gr. στενός, narrow, confined, scanty, little, used in combination.—**sten-o-ce-phal-ic** (sten″ō-se-fal′ik), a. [+ Gr. κεφαλή, head.] Narrow-headed.—**sten′o-chro-my** (-krō-mi), n. [+ Gr. χρῶμα, color.] The art or process of printing in several colors at one impression.—**sten″o-chro-mat′ic** (-krō-mat′ik), a.

sten-o-graph (sten′ō-gráf), n. [See *steno-* and *-graph*.] A writing, as a report or memorandum, in shorthand; also, any of various keyboard instruments, somewhat resembling a typewriter, used for writing in shorthand, as by means of phonetic or arbitrary symbols.—**sten′o-graph**, v. t. or i. To write in shorthand.—**ste-nog-ra-pher** (ste-nog′ra-fėr), n. One who writes in shorthand; a person skilled in stenography.—**sten-o-graph′ic** (-graf′ik), a. Of or pertaining to stenography; written or produced by stenography; fig., of style, etc., concise.—**stenographic machine**, a machine for writing in shorthand; a stenograph.—**sten-o-graph′i-cal-ly**, adv.—**ste-nog′ra-phist**, n. A stenographer.—**ste-nog′ra-phy**, n. [See *-graphy*.] The art of writing in shorthand.

sten-o-pa-ic, sten-o-pæ-ic (sten-ō-pā′ik, -pē′ik), a. [Gr. στενός, narrow, + ὀπή, an opening.] In *optics*, pertaining to, characterized by, or of the nature of a small or narrow opening: as, *stenopaic* spectacles (spectacles in which each lens is covered by an opaque plate with a small central aperture); a *stenopaic* slit (a narrow slit in an opaque plate, placed before an eye in testing its astigmatism.

sten-o-pet-a-lous (sten-ō-pet′a-lus), a. [See *steno-*.] Having narrow petals.

sten-o-rhyn-chous (sten-ō-ring′kus), a. [Gr. στενός, narrow, + ῥύγχος, snout.] Having a narrow beak or bill.

ste-no-sis (ste-nō′sis), n.; pl. *stenoses* (-sēz). [NL., < Gr. στένωσις, < στενοῦν, make narrow, < στενός, narrow.] In *pathol.*, contraction of a passage or vessel.—**ste-not′ic** (-not′ik), a.

sten-o-type (sten′ō-tīp), n. [See *steno-* and *type*.] A simple keyboard instrument resembling a typewriter but smaller and with fewer keys, with which the letters of the alphabet are printed, in accordance with a system of phonetic shorthand, to form contracted representations of words. [Proprietary name.]—**sten′o-typ-ist** (-tī-pist), n. One who operates the stenotype; one skilled in stenotypy.—**sten′o-ty-py** (-tī-pi), n. Shorthand in which ordinary alphabetic letters or types are employed to produce shortened forms of words or groups of words; esp., the system of phonetic shorthand used on the stenotype; the use of the stenotype.

sten-tor (sten′tor), n. [From *Stentor*, a Greek herald in the Trojan War.] A person having a very loud or powerful voice.—**sten-to′ri-an** (-tō′ri-an), a. Of or befitting a stentor; very loud or powerful in sound (as, "The *stentorian* voice of Lawton rang through the valley," Cooper's "Spy," ix.; *stentorian* tones; a *stentorian* shout); uttering loud sounds (as, *stentorian* lungs; "After they had played a stave, a small *stentorian* choir . . . broke forth," Arnold Bennett's "Clayhanger," ii. 12).—**sten-to′ri-an-ly**, *adv.*

step (step), *v.*; stepped, stepping. [AS. *steppan, stæppan,* = OFries. *sleppa,* akin to D. *stappen,* G. *stapfen,* step.] **I.** *intr.* To move by lifting the foot and setting it down again in a new position, or by using the feet alternately in this manner (as, to *step* forward, aside, or back; to *step* from stone to stone across a brook; to *step* over obstacles); go or get (*in, into, out, off, up, down,* etc.) by bringing the foot or feet to a new position (as, to *step* into a boat; to *step* out of a garment; to *step* up on or down from a platform); move or use the feet or legs in a specified manner in going (as, a high-*stepping* horse; "He *stepped* out from the hip, swinging his arms with the free motion of a man starting out for a fifteen-mile walk," J. Conrad's "Rescue," i. 1); go briskly or fast, as a horse; move with measured steps, as in a dance; dance (slang); in general, to walk, or go on foot, esp. for a few steps or a short distance (as, please *step* this way; "waiting for the delinquent colonel, who had just *stepped* round to the Hotel St. Louis and was to be back presently," Howells's "Chance Acquaintance," x.); go or depart (colloq. or prov.: as, "If you have nothing more to say to me I will be *stepping*," Stevenson's "Master of Ballantrae," xi.); fig., to come as if by a step of the foot (as, to *step* into a fortune); also, to put the foot down, as on the ground, a support, etc.; tread (*on* or *upon*), by intention or accident (as, to *step* on a worm; to *step* on trailing draperies); press with the foot, as on a lever, spring, or the like, in order to operate some mechanism; *naut.,* etc., to be fixed in a step or support. **II.** *tr.* To take (a step, pace, stride, etc.); go through or perform the steps of (a dance); move or set (the foot) in taking a step; measure (a distance, ground, etc.) by steps (sometimes with *off* or *out:* as, "A speculative builder, too hurried to use a measure, 'stepped out' the foundations of fifteen cottages with his own bandy legs," Arnold Bennett's "These Twain," i.); also, to make or arrange in the manner of a series or flight of steps; *naut.,* to fix the foot of (a mast) in its step; in *mech.,* etc., to fix or place (something) in or on a step or support.—**to step down,** in *elect.,* to lower (the voltage of an alternating-current circuit) by means of a transformer.—**to step up,** in *elect.,* to raise (the voltage of an alternating-current circuit) by means of a transformer.—**step,** *n.* [AS. *stæpe.*] An act of stepping; a movement made by lifting the foot and setting it down again in a new position, as in walking, running, or dancing; a pace; the sound made by the foot in stepping (as, "He . . . heard but his own *steps*": Tennyson's "Pelleas and Ettarre," 407); a mark or impression made by the foot on the ground, or a footprint; manner of stepping, as in walking, marching, dancing, etc., or gait (as, "a true Dian in stature, *step,* and attributes," G. Meredith's "Diana of the Crossways," vii.; "Soames with his mousing, mincing *step,*" Galsworthy's "Man of Property," xiv.); pace in marching (as, double-quick *step*); pace uniform with that of another or others or in time with music (as, to be in *step,* or out of *step;* to keep *step;* "Jörgenson waited for him . . . and . . . fell into *step* at his elbow," J. Conrad's "Rescue," ii. 5); *pl.,* movements or course in stepping or walking (as, to direct or turn one's *steps* to a place; to retrace one's *steps;* to dog a person's *steps*); *sing.,* fig., a move or proceeding, as toward some end or in the general course of action (as, the first *step* toward failure; "He never took *steps* to make himself liked," C. Brontë's "Jane Eyre," viii.; "suspecting that he was taking a very imprudent *step,*" John Hay's "Bread-Winners," iv.); a measure; a stage in a process; also, the space passed over or measured by one movement of the foot in stepping (as, "He moved a *step* nearer," Barrie's "Sentimental Tommy," ii.; a *step* of 30 inches); hence, a very short distance; a distance easily walked; also, a degree in a scale; a grade in rank or promotion; also, a support, or a supporting piece, part, or place, for the foot in ascending or descending (as, a carriage-*step;* a *step* of a ladder or of a step-ladder; a *step* of a stair, consisting of a tread and a riser; to cut *steps* in rock; a door-*step;* "sitting out on the front *steps,*" Tarkington's "Alice Adams," xvi.); *pl.,* a

step-ladder (also called *pair of steps* and *set of steps*); *sing.,* in *music,* a degree of the staff or of the scale; also, the interval between two successive degrees of the scale (called *whole step* if one of the larger intervals, or *half-step* if one of the smaller); in *mech.,* etc., a part or offset resembling a step of a stair; also, any of various supports, frames, or bearings for receiving the lower end of something, as a vertical shaft; *naut.,* a socket, frame, or platform for supporting the lower end of a mast.

step-. [AS. *steop-* = D. and G. *stief-* = Icel. *stjūp-* = Sw. *styf-,* lit. 'bereaved,' 'orphaned': cf. OHG. *stiufan,* AS. *āstīepan,* bereave.] A prefix indicating connection between members of a family by the remarriage of a parent, and not by blood.—**step-broth-er** (step′bruTH″ėr), *n.* One's stepfather's or stepmother's son by a former marriage. Cf. *half-brother.*—**step′child,** *n.* [AS. *stēopcild.*] A child of one's husband or wife by a former marriage. Also fig. (cf. *stepmother*).—**step′dame,** *n.* A stepmother. [Archaic.]—**step′daugh″ter,** *n.* [AS. *stēopdohtor.*] A daughter of one's husband or wife by a former marriage.

step=down (step′doun), *a.* In *elect.,* serving to convert a current of higher voltage into one of lower voltage: as, a *step-down* transformer (see *transformer*).

step-fa-ther (step′fä″THėr), *n.* [AS. *stēopfæder:* see *step-.*] A man who occupies one's father's place by marriage to one's mother.

steph-a-ne (stef′a̤-nē), *n.* [Gr. στεφάνη, < στέφειν, put round.] In *Gr. antiq.,* a band-like head-dress or coronal widest at the front and narrowing toward the sides: often seen on representations of the goddess Hera.

steph-a-nos (stef′a̤-nos), *n.* [Gr. στέφανος: cf. *stephane.*] In *Gr. antiq.,* a wreath or crown serving as a prize, a mark of honor, a festal ornament, etc.; also, a coronal like the stephane but of the same width all around (see cut below).

steph-a-no-tis (stef-a̤-nō′tis), *n.* [NL., < Gr. στεφανωτίς, fit for a crown, < στέφανος, crown.] Any plant of the tropical asclepiadaceous genus *Stephanotis,* esp. *S. floribunda,* a favorite greenhouse climber with thick, glossy leaves and fragrant, waxy, white or cream-colored flowers; also, a kind of perfume.

Hera wearing Stephane.

step=lad-der (step′lad″ėr), *n.* A ladder having flat steps or treads in place of rungs, and often provided with a hinged supporting frame.

step-moth-er (step′muTH″ėr), *n.* [AS. *stēopmōdor:* see *step-.*] A woman who occupies one's mother's place by marriage to one's father. Often fig., with allusion to the unkindness traditionally attributed to stepmothers toward stepchildren: as, "Nature, barbarous nature! to me thou hast proved indeed the worst of *stepmothers*" (Godwin's "Caleb Williams," xxxiv.); "The world was her *stepmother,* vigilant to become her judge" (G. Meredith's "Diana of the Crossways," xxiii.).—**step′moth″er-ly,** *a.*

Head wearing Stephanos (in 2d sense).

step=par-ent (step′pãr′ent), *n.* [See *step-.*] A stepfather or stepmother.

steppe (step), *n.* [= F. and G. *steppe,* < Russ. *step.*] One of the vast, more or less level plains, devoid of trees, of southeastern Europe and Siberia; in general, an extensive plain, esp. one without trees.

stepped (stept), *a.* Having or forming a step or steps: as, a *stepped* pyramid (a form of pyramid, as in Egypt, having the faces formed into a more or less regular series of enormous steps).

Stepped Pyramid, Sakkara, Egypt.

step-per (step'ėr), *n.* A person or animal that steps, or has a particular step (as, a high-*stepper*, said esp. of a horse); a horse with a brisk, spirited gait (as, "Down the cobble-stones . . . came the ring of a *stepper's* hoofs": Mrs. Wharton's "Age of Innocence," ix.); also, a dancer (slang).

step-ping=stone (step'ing-stōn), *n.* A stone, or one of a line of stones, in shallow water, a marshy place, or the like, used for stepping on in crossing (as, "the *stepping-stones* in the shallow brook": Whittier's "Telling the Bees"); also, a stone for use in mounting or ascending; also, fig., anything serving as a means of advancing or rising (as, "You would make me a *stepping-stone* to your greatness," S. J. Weyman's "Gentleman of France," xix.; "That men may rise on *stepping-stones* Of their dead selves to higher things," Tennyson's "In Memoriam," i.).

step-sis-ter (step'sis″tėr), *n.* [See *step-*.] One's stepfather's or stepmother's daughter by a former marriage. Cf. *half-sister*.

step-son (step'sun), *n.* [AS. *stēopsunu*: see *step-*.] A son of one's husband or wife by a former marriage.

step-toe (step'tō), *n.* [Origin obscure.] A hill or mountain surrounded and isolated by a large flow or plain of lava. [Northwestern U. S.]

step=up (step'up), *a.* In *elect.*, serving to convert a current of lower voltage into one of higher voltage: as, a *step-up* transformer (see *transformer*).

Steptoe, Big Butte, Idaho.

step-way (step'wā), *n.* A way or passage formed by steps: as, "the little bridge that spanned the narrower canyon to a railed *stepway* from the crest on the further side" (H. G. Wells's "Men Like Gods," ii. 2).

-ster. [AS. *-estre*, *-istre*, fem. suffix of agent-nouns, corresponding to *-ere*, masc.: cf. *-er*1.] A suffix of nouns denoting a person, orig. a woman (now occasionally an animal, a vehicle, etc.), that does something by way of regular occupation or customary practice or is of a particular class or character, as in *brewster, gamester, rimester, roadster, songster, spinster, tonguester, trickster, youngster*. Many such formations, esp. words of modern origin, have a disparaging force.

ster-co-ra-ceous (stėr-kọ-rā'shius), *a.* [L. *stercus* (*stercor-*), dung.] Consisting of, resembling, or pertaining to dung or feces; also, frequenting or feeding on dung, as certain insects.

ster-co-ra-ry (stėr'kọ-rạ-ri). [L. *stercorarius*, < *stercus* (*stercor-*), dung.] **I.** *a.* Stercoraceous. **II.** *n.* A place for putting or storing dung or manure.

ster-cu-li-a-ceous (stėr-kū-li-ā'shius), *a.* [NL. *Sterculia*, the typical genus (with species having a fetid odor), < L. *stercus*, dung.] Belonging to the *Sterculiaceæ*, a family of trees and shrubs, mostly tropical, including the cacao and kola-nut trees, also species yielding gums and fibers.

stere (stēr), *n.* [F. *stère*, < Gr. στερεός, solid.] In the metric system, a cubic meter.

ster-e-o (ster'ē-ō), *n.*; pl. *-os* (-ōz). Shortened form of *stereotype*, also of *stereoscope*.

stereo-. Form of Gr. στερεός, hard, firm, solid, used in combination.

ster-e-o-bate (ster'ē-ọ-bāt, also stē'rē-), *n.* [L. *stereobata*, < Gr. στερεός, firm, solid, + *-βάτης* as in στυλοβάτης, E. *stylobate*.] In *arch.*, the foundation or base upon which a building or the like is erected; the solid platform or structure (including the stylobate) upon which the columns of a classical building rest.

ster-e-o-chem-is-try (ster″ē-ọ-kem'is-tri or stē″rē-), *n.* [See *stereo-*.] That branch of chemistry which deals with the relative arrangement in space of the atoms or groups of atoms constituting a molecule.—**ster″e-o-chem'i-cal**, *a.*

ster-e-o-chrome (ster'ē-ọ-krōm or stē'rē-), *n.* [G. *stereochrom*, < Gr. στερεός, solid, + χρῶμα, color.] A process of mural painting in which water-glass is used as a vehicle or as a preservative coating; also, a picture produced by this process.—**ster″e-o-chro'mic** (-krō'mik), *a.*—**ster'e-o-chro-my** (-mi), *n.* The stereochrome process.

ster-e-og-no-sis (ster″ē-og-nō'sis or stē″rē-), *n.* [NL., < Gr. στερεός, solid, + γνῶσις, a knowing.] In *psychol.*, apprehension of the form or corporeality of objects by touch.—**ster″e-og-nos'tic** (-nos'tik), *a.*

ster-e-o-gram (ster'ē-ọ-gram or stē'rē-), *n.* [See *stereo-* and *-gram*.] A diagram or picture representing objects in a way to give the impression of solidity; also, a stereograph.

ster-e-o-graph (ster'ē-ọ-gráf or stē'rē-), *n.* [See *stereo-* and *-graph*.] A single or double picture for a stereoscope.

ster-e-og-ra-phy (ster-ē-og'rạ-fi or stē-rē-), *n.* [See *stereo-* and *-graphy*.] The art of delineating the forms of solid bodies on a plane; a branch of solid geometry dealing with the construction of regularly defined solids.—**ster″e-o-graph'ic** (-ọ-graf'ik), *a.*—**ster″e-o-graph'i-cal-ly**, *adv.*

ster-e-o-i-som-er-ism (ster″ē-ọ-ī-som'ẹ-rizm or stē″rē-), *n.* [See *stereo-*.] In *chem.*, a kind of isomerism assumed to be due to the different relative positions in space of the atoms or groups of atoms in a molecule.

ster-e-om-e-try (ster-ē-om'ẹ-tri or stē-rē-), *n.* [Gr. στερεομετρία, < στερεός, solid, + *-μετρία*, < μέτρον, measure.] The mensuration of solid figures; solid geometry.—**ster″e-o-met'ric** (-ọ-met'rik), *a.*—**ster″e-o-met'ri-cal-ly**, *adv.*

ster-e-o-phon-ic (ster″ē-ọ-fon'ik), *a.* [< Gr. στερεός, solid, + Gr. φωνή, sound.] Noting or pertaining to a reproduction of sound which preserves the spatial relationships of the original sources: accomplished by a distribution of sound pick-up devices (microphones) connected one each to a geometrically similar array of sound-reproducing devices (loud-speakers). In recording, separate records are made synchronously for each channel. See *enhanced music*.

ster-e-o-op-ti-con (ster-ē-op'ti-kọn or stē-rē-), *n.* [NL., < Gr. στερεός, solid, + ὀπτικόν, neut. of ὀπτικός, of or for sight, E. *optic*.] An improved form of magic lantern.

ster-e-o-scope (ster'ē-ọ-skōp or stē'rē-), *n.* [See *stereo-* and *-scope*.] An optical instrument through which two pictures of the same object, taken from slightly different points of view, are viewed, one by each eye, and which produces the effect of a single picture of the object, with the appearance of solidity or relief.—**ster″e-o-scop'ic** (-skop'ik), *a.*—**ster″e-o-scop'i-cal-ly**, *adv.*—**ster-e-os'co-pist** (-os'kọ-pist), *n.*—**ster-e-os'co-py**, *n.*

Stereoscope.—The light-rays from corresponding points of the two pictures *P* and *P'* are refracted in passing through the lenses *L*, *L'*, and their directions changed so that they now seem to the eyes *E*, *E'*, to diverge from a common point *A* beyond the plane of the pictures.

ster-e-o-trope (ster'ē-ọ-trōp or stē'rē-), *n.* [See *stereo-* and *-trope*.] A device based on the same principle as a zoëtrope but fitted with a stereoscope, giving solidity and motion.

ster-e-o-type (ster'ē-ọ-tīp or stē'rē-), *n.* [F. *stéréotype*, < Gr. στερεός, solid, + τύπος, E. *type*.] A process of making metal plates for printing from by taking a mold of composed type or the like in plaster, paper-pulp, or other material, and then taking from this mold a cast (plate) in type-metal; also, a plate of type-metal made by this process.—**ster′e-o-type**, v. t.; -typed, -typing. To make a stereotype of (composed type); make stereotypes of (literary matter); fig., to give a fixed or settled form to.—**ster′e-o-typed**, p. a. Reproduced in stereotype plates; fig., fixed or settled in form; of an established conventional form or kind (as, "stereotyped phrases of encouragement," L. Merrick's "House of Lynch," xv.; a stereotyped smile).—**ster′e-o-typ″er** (-tī″pėr), n.—**ster′e-o-ty″py** (-tī″pi), n. The stereotype process.

ster-ile (ster′il), a. [L. sterilis, akin to Goth. stairō, Gr. στεῖρος, barren, Skt. starī, barren cow.] Incapable of producing, or not producing, offspring (used chiefly of females); barren; unproductive of vegetation, as soil (as, "the more sterile wastes of the rolling prairies": Cooper's "Prairie," xxv.); infertile; unfruitful; fig., unproductive of results, or fruitless (as, "verbal logic drawing sterile conclusions from untested authority": Morley's "Oliver Cromwell," ii. 3); lacking (in) or devoid (of); also, free from living germs or micro-organisms; in bot., etc., lacking reproductive elements that are normally present; incapable of reproduction.—**ster′ile-ly**, adv.—**ste-ril-i-ty** (ste-ril′i-ti), n. Sterile condition or character.—**ster′il-ize** (-īz), v. t.; -ized, -izing. To render sterile; esp., to free from living germs, as by heating.—**ster″il-i-za′tion** (-i-zā′shon), n.—**ster′il-iz-er** (-ī-zėr), n.

ster-let (stėr′let), n. [= F. and G. sterlet, < Russ. sterlyad.] A small sturgeon, Acipenser ruthenus, of the Black Sea, Caspian Sea, etc., highly esteemed for its flavor, and yielding roe from which a superior caviar is prepared.

Sterlet.

ster-ling (stėr′ling). [ME. sterling, the silver coin; of disputed origin; possibly < AS. steorra, star, + -ling (see -ling¹), with reference to some device on the coin.] **I.** n. A former English silver coin of the value of a penny (often in 'a pound of sterlings,' orig. a pound weight of such coins, later the English pound, equivalent to 240 pence, as a money of account); hence, money of the quality of this coin; genuine English money; also, English money as distinguished from foreign money; also, a former Scottish silver coin of the value of a penny. **II.** a. Orig., consisting of or reckoned in sterlings (English silver coins); hence, consisting of or pertaining to sterling, or English money (as, "two millions six hundred thousand pounds sterling money," Burke's "Conciliation with the Colonies"; one hundred pounds sterling); also, of silver, orig., being of the same quality as the silver in the sterling (English coin), and hence, now, being of standard quality; also, in general, conforming to the highest standard, or thoroughly excellent (as, a man of sterling worth; "people . . . of sterling morality," Howells's "Rise of Silas Lapham," i.; "Then the world seemed none so bad, And I myself a sterling lad," A. E. Housman's "Shropshire Lad," lxii.).

stern¹ (stėrn), a. [AS. styrne, stern, rigorous: cf. G. starr, stiff, rigid, Gr. στερεός, hard, solid.] Hard, harsh, or severe, as persons or their disposition, mood, action, speech, etc. (as, "Lady Feverel thought her husband a man fatally stern and implacable," G. Meredith's "Ordeal of Richard Feverel," xii.; "Gods and men Fear'd her stern frown," Milton's "Comus," 446); harshly firm, strict, or uncompromising (as, the sterner sex, the male sex, or men; "Stern Daughter of the Voice of God!" Wordsworth's "Ode to Duty," 1; "His discipline was of the sternest," Froude's "Cæsar," iv.); rigorous or austere; of an unpleasantly serious character (as, stern necessity; stern facts; stern times); also, grim or forbidding in aspect (as, a stern countenance; stern mountains; "the rude and stern scenes of the prairie and the mountains," Parkman's "Oregon Trail," ii.); also, cruel† or merciless†; bold or fierce in battle†; stubbornly or fiercely maintained, as battle or strife (archaic).

stern² (stėrn), n. [ME. sterne = OFries. stiarne, stiorne, rudder, = Icel. stjōrn, steering; akin to E. steer².] The rudder or steering apparatus of a vessel†; also, the hinder part of a ship or boat (often opposed to stem); hence, the hinder part of anything; the buttocks or rump; the tail of

an animal, esp. a hunting-dog.—**stern foremost,** with the stern or hinder part first or foremost; with the wrong end first.

ster-nal (stėr′nal), a. Of or pertaining to the sternum.

stern=board (stėrn′bōrd), n. Naut., a backward motion of a vessel.

stern=chase (stėrn′chās), n. Naut., a chase in which the pursuing vessel follows in the wake of the other (as, "The position became that of a stern chase, which proverbially is known as a long chase": J. Conrad's "Rover," xvi.); also, the stern-chasers of a vessel collectively (rare).—**stern=chas″er** (-chā″sėr), n. Naut., a cannon in a ship's stern, pointing backward, for use against pursuers.

sterned (stėrnd), a. Having a stern (as specified): as, a high-sterned vessel.

ster-nine (stėr′nin), a. [NL. sterninus, < Sterna, genus of terns: cf. AS. stearn, sea-bird, tern.] Of or like a tern; belonging to the Sterninæ, a subfamily of birds including the terns.

stern-ly (stėrn′li), adv. In a stern manner; severely.

stern-most (stėrn′mōst), a. superl. Furthest astern or in the rear; also, nearest the stern.

stern-ness (stėrn′nes), n. The quality of being stern.

stern=post (stėrn′pōst), n. Naut., the principal piece of timber or iron in the stern of a vessel, having its lower end fastened to the keel, and usually serving as a support for the rudder.

stern=sheets (stėrn′shēts), n. pl. [See sheet², n.] Naut., the rear part of an open boat, abaft the thwarts.

stern=son (stėrn′son), n. [From stern², with -son as in keelson.] Naut., the continuation of a vessel's keelson, to which the stern-post is bolted.

ster-num (stėr′num), n.; pl. -na (-nä) or -nums. [NL., < Gr. στέρνον, breast, chest.] In anat. and zoöl., a bone or series of bones extending along the middle line of the ventral portion of the body of most vertebrates, consisting in man of a flat, narrow bone connected with the clavicles and the true ribs; the breast-bone; also, in arthropods, the ventral part of a somite.

ster-nu-ta-tion (stėr-nū-tā′shon), n. [L. sternutatio(n-), < sternutare, freq. of sternuere, sneeze.] The act or an act of sneezing: as, "If she had not sneezed, she would have heard all . . . but that unlucky sternutation routed Dr. John" (C. Brontë's "Villette," xiii.).—**ster-nu′ta-to-ry** (-nū′ta-tō-ri). **I.** a. Causing or tending to cause sneezing; pertaining to sneezing. **II.** n.; pl. -ries (-riz). A sternutatory substance or drug, as snuff.

stern-ward, stern-wards (stėrn′wärd, -wärdz), adv. Toward the stern; astern.

stern-way (stėrn′wā), n. Naut., the movement of a ship backward, or with the stern foremost.

stern=wheel (stėrn′hwēl), a. Propelled by a paddle-wheel at the stern, as a steamboat. Cf. side-wheel.—**stern′=wheel″er**, n. A stern-wheel steamboat.

ster-tor (stėr′tor), n. [NL., < L. stertere, snore.] Snoring; in pathol., a heavy snoring sound accompanying respiration in certain diseases.—**ster′to-rous** (-tō-rus), a. Characterized by stertor or a heavy snoring sound: as, stertorous breathing.—**ster′to-rous-ly**, adv.—**ster′to-rous-ness**, n.

stet (stet). [L.] 'Let it stand': a direction on a printer's proof, a manuscript, or the like, to retain canceled matter (usually accompanied by a row of dots under or beside the matter).—**stet**, v. t.; stetted, stetting. To mark with the word 'stet,' or with dots, as for retention.

stetho-. Form of Gr. στῆθος, breast, chest, used in combination.—**steth-o-graph** (steth′ō-gráf), n. [+ -graph.] An instrument for recording the respiratory movements of the chest.—**steth-o-graph′ic** (-graf′ik), a.—**ste-thom-e-ter** (ste-thom′e-tėr or stē-), n. [+ -meter.] An instrument for measuring the respiratory movements of the walls of the chest.—**steth-o-met′ric** (-met′rik), a.

steth-o-scope (steth′ō-skōp), n. [F. stéthoscope, < Gr.

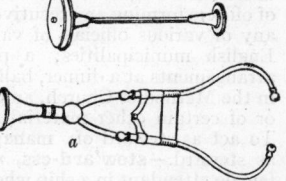

Stethoscopes. — a, binaural stethoscope.

στῆθος, breast, chest, + σκοπεῖν, view.] An instrument used in auscultation, to convey sounds in the chest, etc., to the ear of the examiner. See cut on preceding page.—**steth′o-scope**, v. t.; -scoped, -scoping. To examine with a stethoscope.—**steth-o-scop′ic** (-skop′ik), a. Pertaining to the stethoscope or to stethoscopy; made or obtained by the stethoscope. Also **steth-o-scop′i-cal.—steth-o-scop′-i-cal-ly**, adv.—**ste-thos-co-pist** (ste-thos′kǒ-pist or stę̄-), n. One skilled in the use of the stethoscope.—**ste-thos′-co-py**, n. The art or process of using the stethoscope.

ste-ve-dore (stē′vẹ-dōr), n. [Sp. estivador, < estivar, pack, stow: see steeve².] One whose occupation it is to stow goods in a ship's hold; one employed in loading and unloading vessels.—**ste′ve-dore**, v. t.; -dored, -doring. To stow or unload (cargo); load or unload the cargo of (a ship).

stew¹ (stū), n. [OF. estuve, hot-room or hothouse for bathing (F. étuve); akin to E. stove².] A hot-room or hothouse for sweating or bathing (often in pl., of a public establishment: archaic or hist.); a hot bath†; a heated room†; also (from the use often made of public stews or baths), a brothel or bagnio (often in pl., sometimes formerly construed as sing.: archaic); a prostitute†; also, a vessel for boiling or stewing†; a preparation of meat, fish, or other food cooked by stewing (as, a beef stew; an oyster stew; a vegetable stew; Irish stew, see under Irish, a.); also, an overheated or perspiring condition (colloq.); a state of uneasiness, agitation, or perturbation (colloq.: as, "They are all in a fine stew downstairs, I can tell you," W. De Morgan's "Alice-for-Short," x.). —**stew**¹, v. I. tr. To bathe in a vapor-bath or hot bath†; also, to cook (food) by simmering or slow boiling (as, "I would fain have stewed it [goat-flesh], and made some broth, but had no pot": Defoe's "Robinson Crusoe," i. 6); also, to bathe in perspiration†; steep†; also, to shut (up) in a close or stifling place. II. intr. To undergo cooking by simmering or slow boiling; also, to remain in a close or stifling place (as, "rushing into the open air from the justice's parlour, where I had been stewing in the crowd": Smollett's "Humphry Clinker," June 12); also, to fret, worry, or fuss (colloq.).—**to stew in one's own juice** or **grease**, fig., to remain in discomfort or trouble occasioned by one's self.

stew² (stū), n. [OF. estui, place of confinement, stew (F. étui, case, sheath), < estuier, shut up; origin uncertain: cf. etui.] A pond or tank in which fish are kept living until needed for the table (as, "like the stew in which the luxurious Lucullus kept his lampreys ready fattened for a banquet": Wiseman's "Fabiola," ii. 20); also, an artificial oyster-bed.

stew-ard (stū′ärd), n. [AS. stíweard, stigweard, < stig- (perhaps meaning 'house' and prob. akin to stigu, E. sty¹) + weard, keeper, E. ward, n.] One who has charge of the household of another, providing for the table, directing the servants, etc.; a member of a British college appointed to take charge of the table, or a college servant charged with the catering; an employee who has charge of the table, the servants, etc., in a club or other establishment; also, a ship's officer who keeps the stores and arranges for the table (as, "The steward is the captain's servant, and has charge of the pantry": Dana's "Two Years before the Mast," iii.); any attendant in a ship who waits on passengers (as, "A pair of stewards in white jackets . . . appeared on deck and began . . . laying the table for dinner": J. Conrad's "Rescue," iii. 5); also, any of various high officers of a royal household or of state (now chiefly hist.: as, "The lord steward and lord chamberlain looked after the expence of his [the sovereign's] family," Adam Smith's "Wealth of Nations," v. 2. 1); also, one who manages another's property or financial affairs; one who administers anything as the agent of another or others (often fig.); also, an officer in a gild, usually ranking next below the alderman; any of a number of officers forming an executive committee in certain societies; any of various officials of varying rank and function, as in English municipalities; a person appointed to supervise arrangements at a dinner, ball, etc.; an overseer of workmen; in the Methodist Church, an officer having charge of finances or of certain other material interests.—**stew′ard**, v. I. tr. To act as steward of; manage. II. intr. To act or serve as steward.—**stew′ard-ess**, n. A female steward; esp., a female attendant in a ship who waits on women passengers.—**stew′ard-ship**, n.

stewed (stūd), p. a. Cooked by stewing or slow boiling, as food; also, intoxicated or drunk (slang).

stew-pan (stū′pan), n. A pan for stewing; a saucepan.

stew=pond (stū′pond), n. Same as stew².

sthe-ni-a (sthē′ni-ą̈ or sthe-nī′ä), n. [NL., < Gr. σθένος, strength.] In pathol., strength; excessive vital force.—**sthen-ic** (sthen′ik), a. In pathol., attended with a morbid increase of vital or cardiac action.

stiac-cia-to (styät-chä′tō), a. [It., pp. of stiacciare, crush, flatten.] In art, in very low relief (like a bas-relief pressed flatter).

stib-i-um (stib′i-um), n. [L., the trisulphide (NL., the element), < Gr. στίβι, στίμμι, the trisulphide.] Antimony trisulphide; hence, antimony (in chem., abbreviated Sb, without period).—**stib′ic**, a.

stib-nite (stib′nīt), n. [F. stibine, stibnite, < NL. stibium: see stibium.] Native trisulphide of antimony, a mineral of lead-gray color with a metallic luster, occurring in orthorhombic, often acicular, crystals or massive, and forming an important ore of antimony.

Stibnite, in acicular crystals.

stich (stik), n. [Gr. στίχος, row, line, verse: see stile.] A verse or line of poetry; also, one of the lines of nearly equal length, corresponding to divisions in the sense, into which a manuscript prose text is divided; a line of average length assumed in measuring such a text.—**stich′ic**, a. Pertaining to or consisting of stichs; in pros., composed of lines of the same metrical form throughout.

sti-chom-e-try (sti-kom′e-tri), n. [Gr. στίχος, row, line, + -μετρία, < μέτρον, measure.] The measurement of a manuscript text by lines of fixed or average length into which the text is divided; also, a list or appendix stating such measurement; sometimes, the practice of writing a prose text in lines of nearly equal length corresponding to divisions in the sense.—**stich-o-met-ric** (stik-ǫ-met′rik), a.

stich-o-myth-i-a (stik-ǫ-mith′i-ą̈), n. [NL., < Gr. στιχο-μυθία, < στίχος, row, line, + μῦθος, word, speech.] In Gr. lit., dialogue in alternate lines, or pairs or groups of lines, of antithetical character.—**stich-o-myth′ic**, a.

stick¹ (stik), n. [AS. sticca = OHG. stecko (G. stecken), stick; from the root of E. stick².] A relatively long and slender piece of wood; a branch or shoot of a tree or shrub cut or broken off; an elongated piece of wood for burning, for carpentry, or for any special purpose; a rod or wand; a baton; a walking-stick or cane (as, "He came . . . hat on head and ebony stick in hand": Arnold Bennett's "Hilda Lessways," iv. 1); a club or cudgel; also, a log or tree-trunk, or a timber-tree (prov.: as, "a spot on the edge of a fir plantation where lies a fallen 'stick' of timber," Jefferies's "Gamekeeper at Home," ii.); pl., the backwoods, or any region distant from cities or towns (colloq., U. S.); also, sing., any of various elongated articles formed from sticks or resembling sticks; a drumstick; a fiddlestick; a joy-stick (colloq.); a candlestick; a piece (of furniture: often in pl.: colloq.); a pistol (slang); an elongated, stick-like piece of some material (as, a stick of candy; a stick of sealing-wax); also, a stiff, awkward, or stupid person (colloq.: as, "a prig, a stick, a petrified poser," G. Meredith's "Diana of the Crossways," xiii.); also, a portion of liquor, as brandy, added to a beverage, etc. (colloq.); naut., a mast, or a part of a mast; also, a yard; in printing, a composing-stick; also, a stickful.—**stick**¹, v. t. To furnish with a stick or sticks in order to support or prop, as a plant; in printing, to set (type) in a composing-stick.

stick² (stik), v. t.; stuck (earlier sticked), sticking. [AS. stician, pierce, stab, also remain fixed, stick fast, akin to G. stecken, stick, fix, stechen, D. steken, pierce, also to L. -stigare, -stinguere, Gr. στίζειν, prick, Skt. tij-, orig. stig-, be sharp: cf. instigate, distinguish, stigma, stimulus, etiquette, stake¹, stick¹, stitch, and style.] To pierce or puncture with a pointed instrument, as a dagger, spear, or pin; stab; kill by this means (as, to stick a pig); also, to thrust (something pointed) in, into, through, etc. (as, to stick a needle into one's flesh); fasten in position by thrusting the point or end into something (as, to *stick* a nail in a wall); fasten in position by or as by means of something thrust through (as, to *stick* a badge on one's coat); fix or impale upon something pointed (as, to *stick* a potato on a fork); in general, to thrust or put into a place or position indicated (as, "Mr. Sutton *stuck* his thumb into his vest pocket," W. Churchill's "Coniston," ii. 5; to *stick* one's head out of the window; to *stick* one's hat on the side of one's head); also, to fasten or attach by causing to adhere (as, to *stick* a label on with paste; to *stick* a stamp on a letter); bring to a stand, or render unable to proceed or go back (chiefly in the passive: as, to be *stuck* in the mud); nonplus or pose (colloq.); put into a position involving expense, loss, an unpleasant task, or the like (slang); impose upon or cheat (slang); charge (a person) as to amount, esp. exorbitantly (slang: as, " 'How much did they *stick* you for this lot?' asked Charlie," Arnold Bennett's "Clayhanger," ii. 7); also, to set with things piercing the surface (as, to *stick* a cushion full of pins; "Miss Jenkyns *stuck* an apple full of cloves, to be heated and smell pleasantly," Mrs. Gaskell's "Cranford," ii.); furnish or adorn with things attached or set here and there (as, a garden *stuck* full of statues); also, to stand or endure (slang, Eng.: as, "I can't *stick* shouting and smashing," A. S. M. Hutchinson's "If Winter Comes," iii. 2).—**to be stuck on**, to have one's fancy fixed on; be captivated with or enamoured of: as, "It's the younger one [sister] that he's so everlastingly *stuck on*" (G. W. Cable's "Cavalier," lvi.). [Slang.]—**to stick a thing out**, to stand or endure it to the end: as, "We could *stick it out*, and I would, except that life is short" (Sinclair Lewis's "Arrowsmith," xviii.). [Colloq.]—**to stick it**, to hold out or endure without giving way: as, "Your boy would have told you to *stick it* . . . you're not going to be downed, are you?" (Galsworthy's "Saint's Progress," ii. 5). [Slang, orig. Eng.]—**to stick up**, to hold up, or halt in order to rob; also, to rob (a bank, etc.: as, "My house has been *stuck up*," H. Kingsley's "Geoffry Hamlyn," xli.). [Slang, orig. Australia.]—**stick²**, *v. i.* To have the point piercing, or embedded in, something; be fixed in position by piercing, being inserted, being fastened on, etc.; remain attached by adhesion (as, the mud *sticks* to one's shoes; two papers *sticking* together); hold, cleave, or cling (as, to *stick* to, or on, a horse's back); remain persistently or permanently (lit. or fig.: as, "He *sticks* here instead of getting out into the world and enjoying the fight," Sinclair Lewis's "Arrowsmith," iv.; a fact that *sticks* in the mind); remain firm in resolution, opinion, statement, attachment, etc. (as, " 'Any way,' he said, 'I *stick* to Pompey' ": Froude's "Cæsar," xx.); hold faithfully, as to a promise or bargain; keep steadily or unremittingly at a task, undertaking, or the like (with *at* or *to*: as, to *stick* at a piece of work; "*sticking* close to my business," B. Franklin's "Autobiography," vi.); become held fast in mud, grounded on a sand-bar, or similarly hindered from moving; become fixed or stationary on account of some obstruction; become checked or arrested (as, the words *stuck* in his throat); be at a standstill, as from difficulties; be unable to proceed in a speech or the like, as from lapse of memory; be embarrassed or puzzled; hesitate or scruple (usually with *at*: as, "She's not a woman to *stick* at trifles," G. Meredith's "Diana of the Crossways," xix.); also, to be thrust, or extend, project, or protrude (*through, from, out, up,* etc.: as, "As for the horse, his legs *stuck* through the bridge," Lover's "Handy Andy," i.).—**to stick up for**, to stand up for; speak or act in defense of: as, "I'll *stick up for* the pretty women preachin' " (George Eliot's "Adam Bede," ii.). [Colloq.]—**stick²**, *n.* A thrust with a pointed instrument; a stab; also, a stoppage or standstill (as, "It is a strange thing that I should be at a *stick* for a date": Stevenson's "Master of Ballantrae," viii.); a demur; something causing delay or difficulty; also, the quality of adhering or of causing things to adhere; adhesiveness; something causing adhesion; something sticky.

stick=bug (stik′bug), *n.* A stick-insect; also, a spider-bug.

stick-er (stik′ėr), *n.* One who or that which sticks; one who kills swine by sticking or stabbing; a weapon for sticking or stabbing; a bur, thorn, or the like; one who causes something to adhere, as by pasting; an adhesive label, as one for pasting over a name on a ballot; one who remains constant or

attached; one who keeps steadily at a task, undertaking, etc.; something that nonplusses or puzzles one (colloq.).

stick-ful (stik′ful), *n.*; pl. *-fuls.* In *printing*, as much set type as a composing-stick will hold.

stick-i-ness (stik′i-nes), *n.* The state of being sticky.

stick-ing=plas-ter (stik′ing-plas″tėr), *n.* A material for covering and closing superficial wounds, etc., consisting of linen, silk, or the like coated with an adhesive substance.

stick=in-sect (stik′in″sekt), *n.* Any of certain orthopterous insects (family *Phasmidæ*) with a long, slender, twig-like body, esp. *Diapheromera femorata*, a wingless species of the U. S.

stick=in=the=mud (stik′in-thė-mud″), *n.* A slow, dull, or unprogressive person: as, "an old *stick-in-the-mud*" (Sinclair Lewis's "Babbitt," xxxii.). [Colloq.]

stick-it (stik′it), *p. a.* [Sc. form of *sticked*, old pp. of *stick²*.] Stuck; having failed, as in a calling or profession (as, "The *Stickit* Minister," the title of a story by S. R. Crockett); also, unfinished, imperfect, or bungled, as a task. [Sc.]

stick-le (stik′l), *v. i.*; *-led, -ling.* [Appar. < ME. *stiglten*, freq. of *stigten*, < AS. *stihtan*, arrange, regulate, = D. *stichten*, G. *stiften*, found, establish.] To act as umpire in a contest or the like†; interpose between contending parties†; also, to take an active part in a contest or for a contestant†; also, to contend insistently, as for a principle, opinion, or other matter at issue; insist pertinaciously, esp. on matters of mere form or little importance; also, to make difficulties or objections; scruple; demur.

stick-le-back (stik′l-bak), *n.* [ME. *stykylbak*, < AS. *sticel*, prickle, sting, + ME. *bak*, E. *back²*.] Any member of the family *Gasterosteidæ*, comprising small, pugnacious, spiny-backed fishes of the fresh waters and sea-inlets of northern Europe, Asia, and North America, remarkable for the elaborate nest which the male builds for the eggs.

Stick-insect (*Diapheromera femorata*).

Nest of Stickleback.

stick-ler (stik′lėr), *n.* One who stickles; an umpire (obs. or prov. Eng.); an insistent or pertinacious contender (as, a *stickler* for ceremony; "a gentleman of the old school— a *stickler* for the customs of a past . . . age," H. Melville's "Omoo," lxx.).

stick-seed (stik′sēd), *n.* Any of the boraginaceous herbs constituting the genus *Lappula*, characterized by prickly seeds which adhere to clothing.

stick-tight (stik′tīt), *n.* An asteraceous herb, *Bidens frondosa*, having flat, barbed achenes which adhere to clothing, etc.

stick=up (stik′up), *n.* A sticking or holding up, or one who sticks persons up, in order to rob (slang); also, something that sticks or stands up, as a stand-up collar or an ornament on a woman's hat (colloq.).

stick-y (stik′i), *a.*; compar. *stickier*, superl. *stickiest.* Having the property of sticking or adhering, as glue; adhesive; glutinous; covered or smeared with adhesive matter (as, *sticky* hands); also, of the weather, etc., humid.

stiff (stif), *a.* [AS. *stīf* = D. *stijf* = G. *steif*, stiff: cf. L. *stipare*, crowd, pack, *stipes*, stock, trunk.] Rigid or firm in substance, or not flexible, pliant, or easily bent (as, a *stiff* collar; *stiff* bristles; not moving or working easily (as, a *stiff* joint; a *stiff* hinge); often, of a person, etc., unable to move, or moving only with difficulty or pain, as from cold, age, exhaustion, etc. (as, "I was bruised and *stiff* . . . for I had been going on rough ground": S. Butler's "Erewhon," v.); rigid in death (as, *stiff* and stark); rigid or fixed in position or attitude (as, "He became aware of a policeman standing quite *stiff* and still at the corner": H. G. Wells's "Mr. Britling," i. 5. § 14); firm from tension, or taut (as, to keep a *stiff* rein); also, relatively firm in consistence, as semisolid matter (as, a *stiff* paste or batter; a *stiff* jelly); dense, compact, or tenacious (as, *stiff* soil; *stiff* clay); densely occupied or crowded with something specified (as, a harbor *stiff* with vessels); also, sturdy, stout, or strongly built (now prov. Eng. and Sc.); blowing violently, strongly, or with steady force, as the wind, etc. (as, "The weather would be *stiff* in the chops of the Channel and more than half a gale in the Bay": Kipling's "Light That Failed," xv.); strong, as liquors or beverages (as, "He mixed a glass of brandy-and-water, *stiff*": Besant's "All Sorts and Conditions of Men," viii.); also, fig., firm in purpose or resolution, or unyielding, stubborn, or pertinacious (as, "He . . . was as *stiff* about urging his point as ever you could be": C. Brontë's "Jane Eyre," xxxvii.); stubbornly maintained, as a struggle, contest, etc. (as, "The Royalist commander won a *stiff* fight at Tadcaster": Morley's "Oliver Cromwell," ii. 2); firm against any lowering action, as prices, rates, etc.; also, rigidly formal, as persons or manners, actions, proceedings, etc. (as, "The young gentlemen don't like a girl to be too *stiff*," John Hay's "Bread-Winners," iii.; "The etiquette was *stiff*," Lytton Strachey's "Queen Victoria," iii.); haughtily unbending or aloof; constrained; lacking ease and grace, as literary work or style; excessively regular, as a design; not graceful in form or arrangement; also (especially common in colloquial use), hard to deal with, accomplish, endure, pay, believe, etc.; steep, as an ascent or slope; laborious or difficult, as a task; heavy or tedious, as reading-matter; trying or unpleasant, as an experience; severe, as a penalty; unusually or excessively high or great, as a price, rate, demand, etc.; *naut.*, bearing the press of canvas or of wind without careening much (as, a *stiff* vessel).—**to keep a stiff upper lip**, fig., to keep up one's firmness or courage, as under trying circumstances: as, "Well, good-bye, Uncle Tom, *keep a stiff upper lip*" (Mrs. Stowe's "Uncle Tom's Cabin," x.). [Colloq.]—**stiff**, *n.* A dead body, or corpse (as, "They piled the *stiffs* outside the door": John Hay's "Mystery of Gilgal"); also, a stiff, formal, or priggish person (used as an opprobrious epithet, often with but vague meaning: as, "These old *stiffs* of teachers just give you a lot of junk about literature and economics," Sinclair Lewis's "Babbitt," xxvi.). [Slang.]

stiff=backed (stif′bakt), *a.* Having a stiff back; fig., rigid or set in ideas, ways, etc. (as, "delighting in his boyish way over the opposition some of his novelties excited among the older and more *stiff-backed* inhabitants": Mrs. H. Ward's "Robert Elsmere," xx.).

stiff-en (stif′n), *v.* **I.** *tr.* To make stiff (lit. or fig.): as, to *stiffen* linen with starch; to *stiffen* a coat-collar with a stiff interlining; "Bruce stood gazing on him, *stiffened* with astonishment" (Jane Porter's "Scottish Chiefs," lvii.). **II.** *intr.* To become stiff: as, "His bruised hand had *stiffened*" (Wister's "Virginian," xxvi.); the breeze *stiffens*; one's resolution *stiffens*.—**stiff′en-er**, *n.*—**stiff′en-ing**, *n.* A making or becoming stiff; also, something used to stiffen a thing.

stiff=heart-ed (stif′här′ted), *a.* Stubborn; contumacious. See Ezek. ii. 4. [Obs. or archaic.]

stiff-ly (stif′li), *adv.* In a stiff manner.

stiff=necked (stif′nekt), *a.* Having a stiff neck; fig., stubborn, perversely obstinate, refractory, or contumacious (as, "Now be ye not *stiffnecked* . . . but yield yourselves unto the Lord": 2 Chron. xxx. 8).

stiff-ness (stif′nes), *n.* The state or quality of being stiff.

sti-fle[1] (stī′fl), *v.*; *-fled, -fling.* [Late ME. *stifil*, also earlier *stufle, stuffle*: cf. OF. *estofer, estufer* (F. *étouffer*), stifle, suffocate, of uncertain origin.] **I.** *tr.* To kill by impeding respiration; stop the breath of; suffocate; smother; also, to prevent the emission of (as, to *stifle* a cry, laugh, or sob; "As he concluded, his voice was nearly *stifled* by his emotion," Prescott's "Conquest of Mexico," iv. 5); deaden or muffle (sound); keep back or repress (an action, impulse, feeling, etc.: as, to *stifle* a yawn; "This was a sinful curiosity, and I *stifled* it to the best of my ability," Galt's "Annals of the Parish," xxxvi.); keep from becoming known (as, to *stifle* a report); in general, to suppress, crush, or stop (as,

to *stifle* inquiry, enterprise, activities, or measures); also, to smother or extinguish (flame). **II.** *intr.* To become stifled or suffocated; also, to suffer from difficulty in breathing, as in a close atmosphere.

sti-fle[2] (stī′fl), *n.* [Origin uncertain.] The stifle-joint, as of a horse or dog.—**sti′fled**, *a.* Injured or diseased in the stifle.—**sti′fle=joint**, *n.* The joint of the hind leg of a horse, dog, etc., between the femur and the tibia, close to the belly.

sti-fling (stī′fling), *p. a.* That stifles; suffocating; oppressively close: as, a *stifling* atmosphere.—**sti′fling-ly**, *adv.*

stig-ma (stig′mä), *n.*; pl. *-mas* (-mäz) (chiefly in the earlier or literary senses and in bot.) or *-mata* (-mạ-tä). [L., < Gr. στίγμα (στιγματ-), a prick, mark, spot, brand, < στίζειν, prick: see *stick*[2].] A mark made upon the skin, as of a criminal, by burning with a hot iron; a brand; fig., a mark of disgrace or infamy; a stain or reproach, as on one's reputation (as, "They were suffering from the *stigma* of a crushing defeat": Motley's "Dutch Republic," iii. 4); also, a characteristic mark or sign of defect, degeneration, disease, etc.; also, a small mark, spot, pore, or the like, on an animal or organ; in *pathol.*, a spot or mark on the skin; esp., a place or point on the skin which bleeds during certain mental states, as in hysteria; *pl.*, in the *Rom. Cath. Ch.*, marks said to have been supernaturally impressed upon the bodies of certain persons in the semblance of the wounds on the crucified body of Christ; *sing.*, in *bot.*, that part of the pistil of a plant which receives the pollen.

stig-mat-ic (stig-mat′ik), **I.** *a.* Pertaining to or of the nature of a stigma or brand; ignominious; also, defective†, deformed†, or ugly†; also, pertaining to a stigma, mark, spot, or the like; pertaining to stigmata resembling the wounds of Christ; in *bot.*, pertaining to or having the character of a stigma (part of the pistil); also, in *optics*, designating a photographic lens or combination of lenses in which astigmatic defects have been overcome; anastigmatic. **II.** *n.* One who is branded†; a profligate†; also, one having some physical deformity†; also, one marked with stigmata resembling the wounds of Christ.

stig-ma-tif-er-ous (stig-mạ-tif′ẹ-rus), *a.* [See *stigma* and *-ferous*.] In *bot.*, stigma-bearing.

stig-ma-tism (stig′mạ-tizm), *n.* In *pathol.*, the condition in which stigmata are present (see *stigma*); in *optics*, a condition in which there is no astigmatism.—**stig′ma-tist**, *n.* A person marked with stigmata resembling the wounds of Christ.

stig-ma-tize (stig′mạ-tīz), *v. t.*; *-tized, -tizing.* [ML. *stigmatizare*, < Gr. στιγματίζειν, < στίγμα: see *stigma*.] To mark with a stigma or brand; fig., to set some mark of disgrace or infamy upon; censure or condemn in express terms (as, "The Prince of Orange . . . deplored the riots, and *stigmatized* the perpetrators": Motley's "Dutch Republic," ii. 7); characterize or describe in censure or condemnation (*as*: as, "The French . . . *stigmatised* the proceedings of the English as simple piracy," Lecky's "Hist. of Eng. in the 18th Century," viii.; "The Emperors of Austria and Russia were *stigmatised* as 'odious and detestable assassins,'" Lytton Strachey's "Queen Victoria," v.); also, to produce stigmata, marks, spots, or the like on; mark with stigmata resembling the wounds of Christ.—**stig″ma-ti-za′tion** (-ti-zā′shọn), *n.*

stil-bene (stil′bēn), *n.* [Gr. στίλβειν, glitter.] In *chem.*, a crystalline hydrocarbon, a toluene derivative, occurring in large, glistening monoclinic plates, used in the preparation of dyes.

stil-bite (stil′bīt), *n.* [F. *stilbite*, < Gr. στίλβειν, glitter.] A white to brown or red mineral with a pearly luster, consisting essentially of a hydrous silicate of aluminium and calcium, and occurring in sheaf-like aggregates of crystals and in radiated masses.

stile (stīl), *n.* [AS. *stigel*, < *stīgan* = OHG. *stīgan* (G. *steigen*) = Icel. *stīga* = Goth. *steigan*, ascend, go; akin to Gr. στείχειν, go, στίχος, row, line, Skt. *stigh-*, go, stride, L. *vestigium*, footstep: cf. *stair, stirrup, sty*[2], *stich*, and *vestige*.] A series of steps or the like for ascending and descending in getting over a fence or wall (as, "Pierson too stepped on, past the village, and down over the *stile*, into a field path": Galsworthy's "Saint's Progress," iii. 7); also, a turnstile; also, in *carp.*, a vertical member in a wainscot, paneled door, or other piece of framing; any principal member in framing or paneling.

sti-let-to (sti-let′ō), *n.*; pl. *stilettos* (-ōz). [It., dim. of *stilo*, dagger, < L. *stilus*: see *style*.] A dagger having a narrow blade thick in proportion to its width (as, "Don Silvio . . . had been whetting a sharp double-edged *stiletto*": Marryat's "Mr. Midshipman Easy," xxviii.); also, a small sharp-pointed instrument for making eyelet-holes, etc., as in needlework.—**sti-let′to**, *v. t.*; -toed, -toing. To stab or kill with a stiletto: as, "They [robbers] *stiletto* all the men" (Irving's "Tales of a Traveler," iii. 1).

still[1] (stil), *a.* [AS. *stille* = D. *stil* = G. *still*, still; akin to E. *stall*[2].] Remaining in place or at rest (as, to lie, sit, or stand *still*: in which expressions *still* may be regarded as either adjective or adverb); motionless; stationary; without waves or perceptible current, as water; not effervescent or sparkling, as wine; free from commotion of any kind, or quiet, tranquil, or calm (as, *still* air; "But after tempest . . . There came a day as *still* as heaven," Tennyson's "Guinevere," 290); gentle, as rain; also, free from sound or noise, as a place, time, etc.; making or uttering no sound (as, "Rust, rapier! be *still*, drum!" Shakspere's "Love's Labour's Lost," i. 2. 188; to keep a *still* tongue in one's head; to keep *still* about a matter); silent; hushed; sometimes, subdued or low in sound (as, "a *still* small voice": 1 Kings, xix. 12).— **still life,** inanimate objects, such as fruit, flowers, dead game, vases, and the like, as forming the subject of representation in art.—**still**[1], *n.* A condition of quiet or calm; also, stillness or silence (now chiefly poetic); also, a photographic picture of a person or other subject at rest or motionless, as distinguished from, or used in connection with, moving pictures.—**still**[1]. **I.** *adv.* At rest, or without movement (see *still*[1], *a.*, first sense); also, without commotion or noise†; quietly†; also, steadily, constantly, or always (now chiefly poetic or prov.); also, at this or that time, as previously (as, they are *still* here; "The things I loved once I love *still*," Mrs. H. Ward's "Robert Elsmere," xxvii.); up to this or that time (as, points *still* unsettled); in the future as in the past (as, objections will *still* be made); even or yet (with comparatives or the like: as, *still* more; *still* less; *still* rarer; "edifices of a *still* different character," Prescott's "Conquest of Mexico," iv. 2); also, with adversative force, even then, yet, or nevertheless (as, to be rich and *still* crave more). **II.** *conj.* And yet; but yet; but nevertheless: as, it was useless, *still* they came.—**still**[1], *v.* [AS. *stillan*.] **I.** *tr.* To make still; quiet (waves, winds, commotion, tumult, passion, pain, etc.); calm, appease, or allay; silence or hush (sounds, murmurs, cries, a crying child, etc.). **II.** *intr.* To become still or quiet; also, to keep silence†.

still[2] (stil), *v.* [Shortened form of *distil*.] **I.**† *intr.* To fall in drops; distil. **II.** *tr.* To give forth in drops†; also, to subject to distillation; extract or obtain by distillation.— **still**[2], *n.* A distilling apparatus consisting essentially of a vessel or retort in which the substance is heated and vaporized and a cooling device or coil for condensing the vapor; also, the vessel or retort alone; also, a distillery.

still=born (stil′-bôrn), *a.* Dead when born. Also fig.

Still. — *a*, alembic; *b*, hot-water jacket; *c*, head; *d*, rostrum or beak; *e e*, worm; *f*, refrigerator; *g*, funnel-tube for supplying cold water to the refrigerator; *h, h′*, tubes for conveying away the warm upper stratum of water, which is heated by the condensation of vapor in the worm.

still=burn (stil′-bẽrn), *v. t.* To burn in the process of distillation: as, to *still-burn* brandy.

still-er[1] (stil′ẽr), *n.* One who or that which stills or makes still.

still-er[2] (stil′ẽr), *n.* One who stills or distils; a distiller.

still=hunt (stil′hunt), *n.* A hunt for game carried on stealthily, as by stalking or under cover; hence, a quiet or secret pursuit of any object (colloq.).—**still′=hunt,** *v.* **I.** *tr.* To pursue by a still-hunt: as, "*Still-hunting* the big-horn is

always a toilsome and laborious task" (Roosevelt's "Hunting Trips of a Ranchman," vii.). **II.** *intr.* To carry on a still-hunt.—**still′=hunt″er,** *n.*

stil-li-cid-i-um (stil-i-sid′i-um), *n.* [L., < *stilla*, a drop, + *cadere*, fall.] In *pathol.*, a morbid dropping or trickling of a liquid, as of the urine in strangury.

stil-li-form (stil′i-fôrm), *a.* [L. *stilla*, a drop, + *forma*, form.] Drop-shaped.

still-ness (stil′nes), *n.* [AS. *stilnes*.] The state of being still; absence of motion, commotion, or sound; quiet; silence; hush.

still=room (stil′rōm), *n.* Orig., a room in a house in which cordials, etc., were distilled; later, a room where cordials, preserves, etc., are kept, and tea, coffee, etc., are prepared (Eng.).

stil-ly (stil′li), *adv.* [AS. *stillīce*.] In a still manner; quietly; silently.—**still-y** (stil′i), *a.* Characterized by stillness; still; quiet: as, "Oft, in the *Stilly* Night" (the title and first line of a poem by Thomas Moore). [Chiefly poetic.]

stilt (stilt), *n.* [ME. *stilte*, akin to D. *stelt*, G. *stelze*, Sw. *stylta*, Dan. *stylte*, stilt.] A crutch (now prov. Eng. and Sc.); also, one of two poles or props, each with a support for the foot at some distance above the ground, used in walking through shallow water, marshy places, etc., or (as by children) for amusement; in *ornith.*, any of various limicoline birds of the genus *Himantopus*, of both hemispheres, with very long legs and slender bill, and living esp. in marshes, as *H. mexicanus*, a North American species; also, a related and similar bird of the genus *Cladorhynchus*, of Australia, with webbed toes.—**stilt,** *v.* **I.** *tr.* To raise on or as on stilts (as, "a sort of raw curate . . . *stilted* up on his thick-soled high-lows": C. Brontë's "Jane Eyre," xxxvii.); fig., to render (speech, style, etc.) stiffly dignified or formal (chiefly as in *stilted*, p. a.); also, to cross (water, etc.) on stilts (Sc.). **II.** *intr.* To walk or go on or as on stilts.—**stilt′ed,** *p. a.* Raised on or as on stilts (as, a *stilted* arch: see below); fig., stiffly dignified or formal, as speech, literary style, etc. (as, "There were letters of *stilted* penitence to his father, for some wrong-doing": Mrs. Gaskell's "Cranford," v.); unnaturally elevated; pompous.—**stilted arch,** in *arch.*, an arch which does not spring immediately from the apparent imposts, but is raised above them by intervening courses or members.—**stilt′ed-ly,** *adv.*—**stilt′ed-ness,** *n.*

Stilt (*Himantopus mexicanus*).

Stil-ton (stil′ton) **cheese.** [From *Stilton*, in Huntingdonshire, England.] A rich, waxy, white cheese, veined with mold when well ripened.

stim-u-la-ble (stim′ū-la-bl), *a.* Capable of being stimulated.—**stim″u-la-bil′i-ty** (-bil′i-ti), *n.*

stim-u-lant (stim′ū-lant). **I.** *a.* Stimulating; esp., in *physiol.* and *med.*, temporarily

Stilted Arch.—Mosque of Sultan Hasan, Cairo.

quickening some vital process or functional activity. **II.** *n.* Something that stimulates; a stimulus or incentive (now rare); esp., in *physiol.* and *med.*, something that temporarily quickens some vital process or the functional activity of some organ or part; specif., an alcoholic liquor or beverage.

stim-u-late (stim′ū-lāt), *v.*; -lated, -lating. [L. *stimulatus*, pp. of *stimulare*, < *stimulus*: see *stimulus*.] **I.** *tr.* To rouse to action or effort as if by pricking or goading, or spur on, or incite (as, "Far different had been the motives which would have *stimulated* her unhappy mother to such a proceeding": Miss Burney's "Evelina," xxviii.); quicken (action, feeling, etc.) in vigor (as, "Our vigilance was *stimulated* by our finding traces of a large Comanche encampment," Parkman's "Oregon Trail," xxvi.; to *stimulate* production; to *stimulate* inquiry or curiosity); often, to incite to mental activity; quicken the mental powers of; in *physiol.*, *med.*, etc., to excite (an organ, etc.) to its functional activity; also, to quicken temporarily the vital activity or functional action of; sometimes, to affect thus by means of an alcoholic stimulant. **II.** *intr.* To act as a stimulus; rouse the mental powers; also, to act as a stimulant; sometimes, to indulge in alcoholic stimulants (colloq.).—**stim-u-la′tion** (-lā′shon), *n.* [L. *stimulatio(n-).*] The act of stimulating, or the state of being stimulated.—**stim′u-la-tive** (-lạ-tiv). **I.** *a.* Serving to stimulate. **II.** *n.* A stimulating agency.—**stim′u-la-tor** (-lā-tọr), *n.* One who or that which stimulates.

stim-u-lose (stim′ū-lōs), *a.* [NL. *stimulosus*, < L. *stimulus*: see *stimulus*.] In *bot.*, covered with stimuli or stings.

stim-u-lus (stim′ū-lus), *n.*; pl. *-li* (-lī). [L., goad, sting, incentive, stimulus; prob. from the same root as E. *stick*[2].] Something that incites to action or exertion as if by pricking or goading, or quickens action, feeling, thought, etc.; an incentive; a quickening impulse; stimulation; in *physiol.*, etc., something that excites an organ or part to functional activity; also, something that stimulates or temporarily quickens some vital process or organic activity; stimulating or quickening action or effect; in *bot.*, a sting, as a stinging hair on the nettle.

sti-my (stī′mi), *n.* and *v.* See *stymie*.

sting (sting), *v.*; stung, stinging. [AS. *stingan* = Icel. and Sw. *stinga* = Dan. *stinge*, sting: cf. *stang*.] **I.** *tr.* To pierce with a sharp-pointed instrument†; also, to prick or wound with some sharp-pointed, often venom-bearing organ, as a sting or fang, with which certain insects and other animals are furnished (as, to be *stung* by a bee, hornet, scorpion, or jellyfish; "What, wouldst thou have a serpent *sting* thee twice?" Shakspere's "Merchant of Venice," iv. 1. 69); affect painfully or irritatingly as the result of contact, as certain plants do (as, to be *stung* by nettles); in general, to pain sharply, hurt, or wound; cause to smart; affect with acute mental pain (as, to be *stung* with remorse; "This false evidence . . . *stung* me to the quick," Fielding's "Tom Jones," viii. 14); goad or drive as by sharp irritation (as, "The letter . . . *stung* him into a fit of frenzy": Kipling's "Light That Failed," xiv.); also, to 'stick,' or impose upon, charge exorbitantly, or the like (slang: as, to *sting* a person in a bargain; "Guess I'll have to get down to the office now and *sting* a few clients," Sinclair Lewis's "Babbitt," iii.). **II.** *intr.* To use or have a sting, as bees; cause a sharp, smarting pain, as some plants, an acrid liquid or gas, etc.; cause acute mental pain or irritation, as annoying thoughts or words, etc.; also, to feel a smarting pain, as from the sting of an insect or from a blow; feel acute mental pain or irritation (as, "the groans of a person *stinging* under defeat": Thackeray's "Vanity Fair," xxxi.).—**sting,** *n.* The act of stinging; a wound inflicted by stinging; the pain or smart caused by stinging; any sharp or smarting wound, hurt, or pain (physical or mental); also, any of various sharp-pointed, often venom-bearing organs of insects and other animals, capable of inflicting painful or dangerous wounds; a glandular hair on certain plants, as nettles, which emits an irritating fluid; anything, or an element in anything, that wounds, pains, or irritates (as, to feel the *sting* of defeat; "The speaker's smile took all the *sting* out of the words," Mrs. H. Ward's "Robert Elsmere," v.); capacity to wound or pain; sometimes, something that goads to action by

causing sharp irritation; a sharp stimulus or incitement (as, to be driven by the *sting* of hunger or of jealousy).

sting-a-ree (sting-ạ-rē′ or sting′ạ-rē), *n.* A corruption of *sting-ray*.

stinged (stingd), *a.* Having a sting, as an insect.

sting-er (sting′ėr), *n.* One who or that which stings; an animal or plant that stings; the sting of an insect or other animal; a stinging blow, remark, or the like (now colloq.).

stin-gi-ly (stin′ji-li), *adv.* In a stingy manner.—**stin′gi-ness,** *n.*

sting-ing (sting′ing), *p. a.* That stings; using or having a sting or stings; producing a smarting or pain; poignant, as remorse; keen or biting, as speech; painfully sharp or severe.—**sting′ing-ly,** *adv.*—**sting′ing-ness,** *n.*

sting-less (sting′les), *a.* Having no sting.

stin-go (sting′gō), *n.* [From *sting*.] Strong ale or beer. [Archaic, Eng.]

sting=ray (sting′rā), *n.* Any of the rays of the family *Dasyatidæ*, fishes with a long, flexible, lash-like tail armed near the base with a strong, serrated bony spine, or two or more such spines, with which they can inflict severe wounds.

sting-y[1] (sting′i), *a.* Having a sting; stinging.

stin-gy[2] (stin′ji), *a.*; compar. *stingier*, superl. *stingiest.* [Appar. connected with *sting*: cf. *stingy*[1].] Ill-tempered, snappish, or cross (prov. Eng. and Sc.); also, piercing, sharp, or cold, as wind or weather (prov. Eng.); also, more commonly, churlishly or meanly reluctant to give or spend, niggardly, or close-fisted (as, "At school, I quickly learned that to 'save money' was to be '*stingy*' ": Bok's "Americanization of Edward Bok," xxxviii.); meanly or excessively sparing or chary (*of*); also, meanly or unduly limited in amount (as, "The grant in Cicero's opinion was a *stingy* one": Froude's "Cæsar," xv.); in general, scanty or meager (as, "When your teams Drag home the *stingy* harvest": Longfellow's "Birds of Killingworth," 135).

Sting-ray (*Dasyatis sabina*).

stink (stingk), *v.*; pret. *stank* or *stunk*, pp. *stunk*, ppr. *stinking.* [AS. *stincan* = D. and G. *stinken*, stink: cf. *stench*.] **I.** *intr.* To emit a strong offensive smell; fig., to be in extremely ill odor or unsavory repute; be highly offensive. **II.** *tr.* To cause to stink; impart an offensive smell to; also, to put, drive, force, etc., by an offensive smell.—**stink,** *n.* A strong offensive smell; a disgusting odor; foul smell, or stench (as, "Instead of sweet smell there shall be *stink*": Isa. iii. 24).—**stink-ard** (sting′kärd), *n.* A stinking, disgusting, or objectionable person (obs. or prov.); also, any of various ill-smelling animals, as the polecat (prov. Eng.) or the stinking badger (see *stinking, p. a.*).—**stink′=ball,** *n.* A ball or missile containing explosives, etc., for generating offensive and suffocating vapors: used in warfare for throwing among the enemy.—**stink′=bug,** *n.* Any of various malodorous bugs; esp., any of the broad, flat insects of the family *Pentatomidæ*, including many species which feed on plant-juices.—**stink′er,** *n.* One who or that which stinks; an ill-smelling, disgusting, or objectionable person (slang); any of several large petrels.—**stink′=grass,** *n.* An ill-smelling grass, *Eragrostis major*, native in Europe and Asia and widely naturalized in the U.S.—**stink′horn,** *n.* Any of various ill-smelling fungi of the basidiomycetous genus *Phallus*, esp. *P. impudicus*.—**stink′ing,**

Stink-grass. — *a*, floret; *b*, glumes; *c*, leaf and culm; *d*, spikelet.

p. a. That stinks; having an offensive smell: specif. used in various names of plants and animals: as, the *stinking* hellebore (*Helleborus fœtidus*); the *stinking* badger (*Mydaus meliceps*, of Java and Sumatra).—**stink'ing-ly**, *adv.* —**stink'pot**, *n.* A vessel containing combustibles, etc., which generate offensive and suffocating vapors: used in warfare for throwing among the enemy: as, "One of our gunners made a *stink-pot*, as we called it, being a composition which only smokes, but does not flame or burn . . . This he threw into the tree" (Defoe's "Captain Singleton," xv.).—**stink'stone**, *n.* Any of various stones which emit a fetid odor on being struck or rubbed, as from embedded organic matter which has become decomposed.—**stink'-weed**, *n.* Any of various ill-smelling plants, as the jimson-weed.

stint¹ (stint), *n.* [ME. *stynte*; origin obscure.] Any of various small sand-pipers, as the dunlin and *Actodromas minutilla* (the 'least stint,' abounding in North America).

American Least Stint (*Actodromas minutilla*).

stint² (stint), *v.* [ME. *stinten*: cf. AS. *styntan*, to blunt, dull, Icel. *stytia*, Sw. dial. *stynta*, shorten, and E. *stunt¹*, *a.*] **I.** *tr.* To cut short, discontinue, or cease (one's own action, etc.: archaic: as, "The thin jackals . . . *Stinted* their hungry howls as he passed by," W. Morris's "Earthly Paradise," April, Doom of King Acrisius); bring to an end (another's action, a proceeding, etc.)†; also, to check, stop, or restrain from further action or movement (obs. or prov.); check (growth), check (plants, animals, etc.) in growth, or stunt (now chiefly prov.); also, to set limits to, or restrict (as, "His wisdom hath *stinted* the effects of his power in such sort, that it doth not work infinitely": Hooker's "Ecclesiastical Polity," i. 2. 3); limit (a person, etc.) to a certain amount, number, share, or allowance; often, to limit unduly, or keep on short allowance (as, "John never *stinted* her," Arnold Bennett's "Leonora," i.; "You have *stinted* yourself in a thousand ways to provide for their comfort and well-being," S. Butler's "Erewhon," xix.); scant (an allowance, supply, or thing: as, "The supply of provisions was *stinted*, on the ground that they were short of maize," Prescott's "Conquest of Mexico," iii. 6; "He *stints* neither time nor money," Kingsley's "Yeast," iii.); also, to assign (a person) to a definite amount or piece of work. **II.** *intr.* To cease action, leave off, or desist (archaic or prov.: as, "Hassan, finding his audience inattentive . . . *stinted* in his song," Scott's "Talisman," xxii.); halt or stop, as in a course (archaic or prov.); come to an end†; also, to stint one's self, or get along on a scanty allowance (as, "Why should we be pinching and *stinting* to keep him in idleness?" Gissing's "New Grub Street," i.).—**stint²**, *n.* Cessation†, pause†, or stop†; also, limitation or restriction, esp. as to amount (as, to give without *stint*); sometimes, undue limitation, as of amount or allowance (as, there is no need for *stint*); also, a limited or fixed amount; a prescribed quantity, share, allowance, rate, etc. (as, to exceed one's *stint*); an allotted amount or piece of work (as, to do one's daily *stint*). —**stint'er**, *n.*—**stint'ing-ly**, *adv.*—**stint'less**, *a.* Without stint or limit.

stipe (stīp), *n.* [F. *stipe*, < L. *stipes*: see *stipes*.] In *bot.*, a stalk or slender support, as the petiole of a fern-frond, the stem supporting the pileus of a mushroom, or a stalk-like elongation of the receptacle of a flower supporting a gynœcium or carpel. See cut in next column.

sti-pel (stī'pel), *n.* [NL. *stipella*, dim. of L. *stipula*: see *stipule*.] In *bot.*, a secondary stipule situated at the base of a leaflet of a compound leaf.—**sti'pel-late** (-pe-lāt), *a.* Having stipels.

sti-pend (stī'pend), *n.* [L. *stipendium*, < *stips* (*stip-*), gift, donation, + *pendere*, weigh, pay.] Fixed or regular pay, orig. that of a soldier; a salary, esp. that of a clergyman, a teacher, or a public or other official (as, "The *stipend* of the precentor of Barchester was eighty pounds a year": Trollope's "Warden," i.); any periodical payment, as a pension.—**sti-pen'di-a-ry** (-pen'di-ā-ri). [L. *stipendiarius*.] **I.** *a.* Receiving a stipend; per-

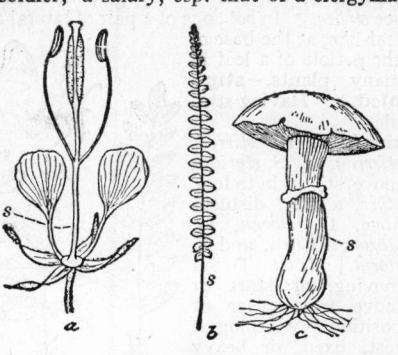

Stipe (*s*), in *a*, longitudinal section of flower, showing the calyx, two of the petals, two of the stamens, and the stipitate ovary; *b*, frond of fern; *c*, mushroom.

forming services for regular pay (as, "the insidious spy, the *stipendiary* informer": Hallam's "Europe during the Middle Ages," iii. 2); paid for by a stipend, as services; pertaining to or of the nature of a stipend. **II.** *n.*; pl. *-ries* (-riz). One who receives a stipend; a salaried clergyman, official, or the like: as, "the maintaining of a corps of *stipendiaries* in the courts of neighboring princes" (Prescott's "Conquest of Mexico," iv. 4).

sti-pes (stī'pēz), *n.*; pl. *stipites* (stip'i-tēz). [L. *stipes* (*stipit-*), stock, trunk, post; perhaps akin to E. *stiff*.] In *bot.*, a stipe; in *zoöl.*, a stem-like part, as a footstalk; a stalk.

stip-i-tate (stip'i-tāt), *a.* [NL. *stipitatus*, < L. *stipes*: see *stipes*.] Having, or supported by, a stipes or stipe: as, a *stipitate* ovary.

stip-i-ti-form (stip'i-ti-fôrm), *a.* [NL. *stipitiformis*, < L. *stipes* (see *stipes*) + *forma*, form.] Having the form of a stipes or stipe.

stip-ple (stip'l), *v. t.*; *-pled*, *-pling*. [D. *stippelen*, freq. of *stippen*, to dot, speckle, < *stip*, a point, dot.] To paint, engrave, or otherwise produce (a picture, etc.) by means of dots or small spots; produce gradation of color or shade in by means of dots; treat (a surface, etc.) or apply (paint, etc.) by this method.—**stip'ple**, *n.* The method of painting, engraving, etc., by stippling; also, stippled work; a painting, engraving, or the like executed by means of dots or small spots.—**stip'pler**, *n.*—**stip'pling**, *n.* The act, method, or work of one who stipples.

stip-u-la-ceous (stip-ū-lā'shius), *a.* Of the nature of stipules; stipular.

stip-u-lar (stip'ū-lär), *a.* Of or pertaining to stipules; stipule-like; having stipules.

stip-u-late¹ (stip'ū-lāt), *a.* Having stipules.

stip-u-late² (stip'ū-lāt), *v.*; *-lated*, *-lating.* [L. *stipulatus*, pp. of *stipulari*, stipulate.] **I.** *intr.* In ancient Roman use, to demand (or sometimes to make) a formal promise by way of giving legal validity to a contract; hence, in modern use, to make an express demand or arrangement (*for*), as a condition of agreement (as, to *stipulate* for an indemnity, or for full pardon; "I had *stipulated* for being allowed to take abundance of rugs and wrappings," S. Butler's "Erewhon," xxviii.). **II.** *tr.* To require as an essential condition in making an agreement (often with a clause or an infinitive as object: as, he *stipulated* that the charge should not be pressed; he *stipulated* to be released at once); arrange expressly or specify in terms of agreement (as, it is *stipulated* that each shall pay half the costs; to receive a *stipulated* price); sometimes, to promise, in making an agreement (chiefly with a clause or an infinitive as object: as, the Athenians *stipulated* to withdraw their troops).—**stip-u-la'tion** (-lā'shon), *n.* [L. *stipulatio(n-).*] The act of stipulating; also, something stipulated; a condition in an agreement or contract (as, "The *stipulations* of the treaty of Dover were accurately known to very few": Macaulay's "Hist. of Eng.," ii.).—**stip'u-la-tor**, *n.*—**stip'u-la-to-ry** (-lä-tọ-ri), *a.* Pertaining to or characterized by stipulation.

stip-ule (stip′ūl), n. [L. *stipula*, stalk, stem, dim. of *stipes*: see *stipes*.] In *bot.*, one of a pair of lateral appendages, often leaf-like, at the base of the petiole of a leaf in many plants.—**stip′-uled,** a. Having stipules.

stir (stėr), v.; stirred, stirring. [AS. *styrian,* move, stir, akin to Icel. *styrr,* a stir, disturbance, D. *storen,* G. *stören,* disturb, and E. *storm.*] **I.** *tr.* To set moving, or start or move from place or position (something at rest, fixed, or heavy and inert: as, "a great block of hard wood . . . one as big as I had strength to *stir,*" Defoe's "Robinson Crusoe," i. 9); move

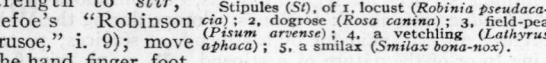

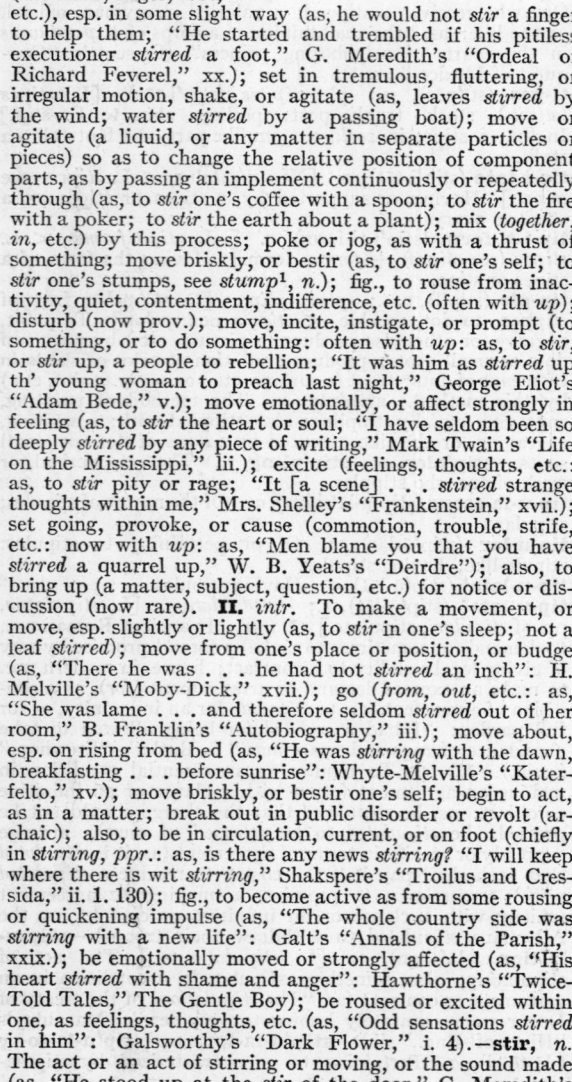

Stipules (*St*) of 1, locust (*Robinia pseudacacia*); 2, dogrose (*Rosa canina*); 3, field-pea (*Pisum arvense*); 4, a vetchling (*Lathyrus aphaca*); 5, a smilax (*Smilax bona-nox*).

(the hand, finger, foot, etc.), esp. in some slight way (as, he would not *stir* a finger to help them; "He started and trembled if his pitiless executioner *stirred* a foot," G. Meredith's "Ordeal of Richard Feverel," xx.); set in tremulous, fluttering, or irregular motion, shake, or agitate (as, leaves *stirred* by the wind; water *stirred* by a passing boat); move or agitate (a liquid, or any matter in separate particles or pieces) so as to change the relative position of component parts, as by passing an implement continuously or repeatedly through (as, to *stir* one's coffee with a spoon; to *stir* the fire with a poker; to *stir* the earth about a plant); mix (*together, in,* etc.) by this process; poke or jog, as with a thrust of something; move briskly, or bestir (as, to *stir* one's self; to *stir* one's stumps, see *stump¹, n.*); fig., to rouse from inactivity, quiet, contentment, indifference, etc. (often with *up*); disturb (now prov.); move, incite, instigate, or prompt (to something, or to do something: often with *up*: as, to *stir,* or *stir* up, a people to rebellion; "It was him as *stirred* up th' young woman to preach last night," George Eliot's "Adam Bede," v.); move emotionally, or affect strongly in feeling (as, to *stir* the heart or soul; "I have seldom been so deeply *stirred* by any piece of writing," Mark Twain's "Life on the Mississippi," lii.); excite (feelings, thoughts, etc.: as, to *stir* pity or rage; "It [a scene] . . . *stirred* strange thoughts within me," Mrs. Shelley's "Frankenstein," xvii.); set going, provoke, or cause (commotion, trouble, strife, etc.: now with *up*: as, "Men blame you that you have *stirred* a quarrel up," W. B. Yeats's "Deirdre"); also, to bring up (a matter, subject, question, etc.) for notice or discussion (now rare). **II.** *intr.* To make a movement, or move, esp. slightly or lightly (as, to *stir* in one's sleep; not a leaf *stirred*); move from one's place or position, or budge (as, "There he was . . . he had not *stirred* an inch": H. Melville's "Moby-Dick," xvii.); go (*from, out,* etc.: as, "She was lame . . . and therefore seldom *stirred* out of her room," B. Franklin's "Autobiography," iii.); move about, esp. on rising from bed (as, "He was *stirring* with the dawn, breakfasting . . . before sunrise": Whyte-Melville's "Katerfelto," xv.); move briskly, or bestir one's self; begin to act, as in a matter; break out in public disorder or revolt (archaic); also, to be in circulation, current, or on foot (chiefly in *stirring, ppr.*: as, is there any news *stirring?* "I will keep where there is wit *stirring,*" Shakspere's "Troilus and Cressida," ii. 1. 130); fig., to become active as from some rousing or quickening impulse (as, "The whole country side was *stirring* with a new life": Galt's "Annals of the Parish," xxix.); be emotionally moved or strongly affected (as, "His heart *stirred* with shame and anger": Hawthorne's "Twice-Told Tales," The Gentle Boy); be roused or excited within one, as feelings, thoughts, etc. (as, "Odd sensations *stirred* in him": Galsworthy's "Dark Flower," i. 4).—**stir,** n. The act or an act of stirring or moving, or the sound made (as, "He stood up at the *stir* of the door," G. Meredith's

"Lord Ormont and His Aminta," iv.; "a sudden *stir* of leaves, the crack of a dry branch," J. Conrad's "Victory," iv. 8); movement; brisk or busy movement, or bustle (as, "Although the day was Saturday there was no *stir* on Chelsea Pier": Arnold Bennett's "Roll-Call," vii.); a state or occasion of general excitement; a commotion; a sensation (as, "Roosevelt . . . had a great facility, when he chose, for doing things in a way that made a *stir*": Charnwood's "Theodore Roosevelt," iii.); a public disturbance, tumult, or revolt (archaic); fig., rousing or awakening activity of the mind; a mental impulse, sensation, or feeling (as, "He could never recall the boy's obstinate rosy face without a *stir* of irritation": Mrs. Wharton's "Son at the Front," xi.); also, an act of stirring something, as with an implement; a jog or thrust; also, a prison (thieves' slang).

stir-a-bout (stėr′a-bout″), n. A kind of porridge. [Prov. Eng., Ir., and Sc.]

stirk (stėrk), n. [AS. *stirc, stiorc, styrc, styric*: cf. AS. *stēor,* E. *steer¹.*] A young animal of the ox or cow kind, usually between one and two years old; fig., a stupid, ignorant person. [Now prov. Eng. and Sc.]

stir-less (stėr′les), a. Without stir or movement; not stirring; motionless: as, a *stirless* night; *stirless* air; "The mournful Princess . . . *stirless* stood" (Wiffen's tr. Tasso's "Jerusalem Delivered," iv. 70).

stirp (stėrp), n. [L. *stirps:* see *stirps.*] A stock or family; also, lineage (as, "Some maid Of royal *stirp*": Lowell's "Under the Willows," 141). [Now chiefly literary.]

stir-pi-cul-ture (stėr′pi-kul-tụr), n. [L. *stirps* (*stirp-*), stock, race, + *cultura,* culture.] The production of special stocks or strains by careful breeding.—**stir-pi-cul′tur-al,** a. —**stir-pi-cul′tur-ist,** n.

stirps (stėrps), n.; pl. *stirpes* (stėr′pēz). [L., stock, stem, root, race, family: cf. *extirpate.*] A stock; a family, or a branch of a family; a line of descent; in *law,* the person from whom a family is descended; in *bot.,* a race or permanent variety.

stir-rer (stėr′ėr), n. One who or that which stirs; an implement or device for stirring something.

stir-ring (stėr′ing), p. a. That stirs; moving; active, bustling, or lively (as, a *stirring* life); rousing, exciting, or thrilling (as, a *stirring* speech; *stirring* events).—**stir′-ring-ly,** adv.

stir-rup (stir′up or stur′up), n. [AS. *stīrāp, stigrāp,* < *stīgan,* ascend (see *stile*), + *rāp,* E. *rope.*] A loop, ring, or other contrivance of metal, wood, leather, etc., suspended from the saddle of a horse to support the rider's foot; hence, any of various similar supports, or any of various clamps, etc., used for special purposes; *naut.,* a short rope with an eye at the end, hung from a yard to support a foot-rope, the foot-rope being rove through the eye.—**stir′rup=bone,** n. In *anat.,* the stapes: so called from its shape.—**stir′rup=cup,** n. A cup of wine or other liquor presented to a rider already mounted for departure; a cup or drink at parting.

Stirrup.— 1, stirrup for pou-laine; 2, modern stirrup; 3, 4, Mexican stirrups.

stitch (stich), n. [AS. *stice* = OHG. *stih* (G. *stich*), stitch, stab, stitch, = Goth. *stiks,* a point of time; from the root of E. *stick².*] A sudden, sharp pain, esp. in the intercostal muscles (as, "I've a *stitch* in my side like a red-hot iron": Stevenson's "Kidnapped," xxiv.); also, one complete movement of a threaded needle through a fabric or material in hand-sewing (as in garment-making, embroidery, etc., or in surgical closing of wounds), such as to leave behind it a single, distinctly disposed portion of thread; a corresponding movement of a sewing-machine; a portion of thread disposed in place by one movement in sewing (as, to rip out *stitches;* coarse or uneven *stitches*); a particular mode of disposing the thread in sewing, or the style of work produced (as, basket-*stitch*, chain-*stitch*, cross-*stitch*, lock-*stitch*, or satin-*stitch*); also, one complete movement of the needle or other implement used in knitting, crocheting, netting, tatting, etc., or the portion of work produced; a particular mode of making such work, or the style of work made; also, a thread or bit of any fabric or of clothing, etc. (as, "She [a brig] expanded every *stitch* of canvas," Marryat's "Peter Simple," lv.; every *stitch* of clothes; he hadn't a dry *stitch* on him); also, a distance, as in walking (prov. Eng.).—**stitch**, *v.* **I.** *tr.* To work upon, join, or fasten with stitches; sew; ornament with stitches (now often by machine-sewing). **II.** *intr.* To make stitches; sew (by hand or machine).—**stitch′er**, *n.*—**stitch′er-y**, *n.* The process or the product of stitching or sewing; needlework: as, "Come, lay aside your *stitchery*" (Shakspere's "Coriolanus," i. 3. 75); "yards of fine *stitchery*" (Arnold Bennett's "Old Wives' Tale," iii. 2).—**stitch′-ing**, *n.* The act or the work of one who stitches; stitches collectively.

stitch-wort (stich′wėrt), *n.* Any of certain herbs of the genus *Alsine*, as *A. holostea*, an old-world white-flowered species: said to be so called from its use as a cure for stitch in the side.

stith-y (stiŧH′i), *n.*; pl. *-ies* (-iz). [ME. *stithi*, also *stith*, from Scand.: cf. Icel. *stedhi*, Sw. *städ*, anvil, akin to E. *stead*.] An anvil (as, "Sparks flew . . . as from the smith's *stithy*": Scott's "Castle Dangerous," v.); also, a forge or smithy.—**stith′y**, *v. t.*; *stithied*, *stithying*. To forge: as, "by the forge that *stithied* Mars his helm" (Shakspere's "Troilus and Cressida," iv. 5. 255). [Obs. or archaic.]

stive (stīv), *v.*; *stived*, *stiving*. [Orig. a var. of *steeve²* (F. *estiver*), appar. with sense later affected by *stifle¹*.] **I.** *tr.* To pack or stow (cargo, goods, etc.); also, to stuff or cram full (Sc. and north. Eng.); crowd with things or persons (often with *up*: now prov.); also, to shut up in a close or stifling place (often with *up*: now prov. or colloq.). **II.** *intr.* To remain shut up in a close or stifling place. [Colloq. or prov.]

sti-ver (stī′vėr), *n.* [D. *stuiver*.] A Dutch coin of small value, in present use a nickel coin worth about 2 U. S. cents; hence, any coin of small value (as, "paying the price of so many quarts of ale and not getting a *stiver* back for it": W. De Morgan's "Joseph Vance," iii.); a small sum of money; a small quantity of anything.

sto-a (stō′ä), *n.* [Gr. στοά: cf. *stoic*.] In *Gr. arch.*, a portico, usually a detached portico of considerable length used as a promenade or meeting-place; [*cap.*] with *the*, the Porch in ancient Athens (see *porch*).

stoat (stōt), *n.* [ME. *stote*; origin obscure.] The ermine, *Putorius ermineus*, esp. when in brown summer pelage; also, any of various allied species.

Stoat or Ermine (*Putorius ermineus*), in summer pelage.

stoc-ca-do (sto-kä′dō), *n.*; pl. *-dos* or *-does* (-dōz). [It. *stoccato*, < *stocco*, rapier; from Teut., and akin to E. *stock*.] In *fencing*, a thrust with a sword or the like. [Obs. or archaic.]

stock (stok), *n.* [AS. *stocc* = OFries. and D. *stok* = OHG. *stoc* (G. *stock*) = Icel. *stokkr*, stock: cf. *stoccado*.] The trunk or the stump of a tree left standing; a log or block of wood (now chiefly prov.); hence, something lifeless or senseless, or a dull or stupid person (as, "Such a *stock* of a child, such a statue! Why, he has no kind of feeling either of body or mind": H. Brooke's "Fool of Quality," iii.); also, the trunk or main stem of a tree or other plant, as distinguished from roots and branches (also fig.: as, "Thence doth doubt Spring, like a shoot, around the *stock* of truth," Cary's tr. Dante's "Paradise," iv. 126); sometimes, a rhizome or root-stock; a stem in which a graft is inserted, and which is its support; a stem, tree, or plant that furnishes slips or cuttings; also, the person from whom a given line of descent is derived;

the original progenitor of a family, tribe, or race; the person with whose ownership a given succession of inheritance is considered as commencing ('stock of descent'); hence, lineal descent, or lineage; a line of descent; a family, or body of descendants of a common ancestor; a tribe, race, or ethnic group; also, the original type from which a race or other group of animals or plants has been derived; a race or other related group of animals or plants; also, a related group of languages; also, a post, stake, or upright (now chiefly prov.: as, a whipping-*stock*, a whipping-post); *pl.*, an old instrument of punishment consisting of a framework (usually between two posts) with holes for confining the ankles and sometimes also the wrists of an offender placed in a sitting position and exposed to public derision (cf. *pillory*); *sing.*, a butt, or object of more or less unfavorable action or notice (usually in compounds: see *laughing-stock* and *gazing-stock*); also, the part

Stocks.

of a tally formerly given to a person making a payment to the English Exchequer; also, the main upright part of anything, as the vertical beam of a cross; a supporting structure of various kinds; a gun-carriage, or a certain portion of one; the support of the block on which an anvil is fitted, or of the anvil itself; the frame of a spinning-wheel; *pl.*, the timbers or frame on which a ship or boat rests while in course of construction (hence, fig., 'on the stocks,' in course of construction or preparation); a frame in which a horse or other animal is secured for shoeing or for a veterinary operation; *sing.*, a part of an object or instrument in which other parts are inserted or to which they are attached, as a body or handle supporting working parts (cf. *head-stock* and *tail-stock*); the wooden piece to which the barrel and lock of a rifle or like firearm are attached; the support upon which the bow of a crossbow is mounted; the part (beam) of a plow to which the irons, handles, etc., are attached; the hub of a wheel; the block of wood from which a bell is hung; the block of wood or piece of metal which constitutes the body of a carpenter's plane; the shorter and thicker piece of a T-square; the handle (brace) by which a boring-bit is held and rotated ('bit-stock'); an adjustable handle for holding and turning the dies used in cutting screw-threads; the handle of a whip, etc.; the heavy cross-bar of an anchor; also, a sum of money, or fund, set aside for a particular purpose†; the total property belonging to a person, etc., or held for public purposes by a municipality, nation, etc.†; money or property serving as capital, as that of a trader or a trading company; the subscribed capital of a company or corporation, divided into transferable shares of uniform amount; the shares of a particular company or corporation, esp. as a form of investment or as subject to fluctuations in market value; *sing.* and *pl.*, shares representing the capital of companies and corporations, as a form of property or investment or an article of purchase and sale (as, bank *stock*; railroad *stock*; *stocks* and bonds); *sing.*, a fund (or the securities representing it) constituting a debt due by a nation, a municipality, etc., to individuals who receive a fixed rate of interest, esp. a portion of the British national debt the principal of which is not repayable except at the pleasure of the government (chiefly in British use); also, the implements, etc. ('dead stock'), or the animals ('live stock'), used or kept on a farm, or employed in operating an establishment, etc. (cf. *rolling-stock*); esp., live stock; the horses, cattle, sheep, and other useful animals kept or raised on a farm or ranch; also, a quantity of something accumulated, as for future use, or a store which may be drawn upon as occasion demands (as, a *stock* of provisions, a *stock* of fuel; "a great *stock* of scientific knowledge," J. H. Robinson's "Mind in the Making," i. 1); an aggregate of goods kept on hand by a merchant or a commercial house for the supply of customers; that portion of a pack of cards which in certain games is not dealt out to the players, but left on the table, to be drawn from as occasion requires; the raw material from which anything is made (as, paper-*stock*, rags, fiber, wood-pulp, etc.); the liquor or broth prepared by boiling meat, with or without vegetables, etc., and used as a foundation for soups, sauces, etc.; also, a stocking (as, "a linen *stock* on one leg and a kersey boot-hose on the other," Shakspere's "Taming of the Shrew," iii. 2. 67: now prov. Eng.); also, a collar or a neck-cloth fitting like a band about the neck (as, "Around his throat he had negligently fastened a *stock* of black silk": Cooper's "Prairie," x.); also, a hollow receptacle used for various purposes, as a box for alms†, a basin for holy water†, or a box or trough in which cloth is beaten in fulling or one in which hides are beaten in tanning; in *bot.*, the stock-gilly-flower, or any of various other brassicaceous plants; in *zoöl.*, a compound animal organism; in *theatrical use*, the

Military Stock, 18th century.

repertoire of pieces produced by a stock company (see phrase under *stock, a.*) (as, a theater devoted to *stock*; an actor playing in *stock*).—**in stock,** in store or on hand, as for use or sale; esp., actually present in the stock of goods of a dealer.—**out of stock,** lacking, esp. temporarily, from a stock, esp. the stock of goods of a dealer.—**stock in trade,** the goods kept on hand for sale by a trader or a trading company; also, the tools, etc., of a workman; hence, one's resources for any work, undertaking, or purpose; one's mental equipment.—**to take stock,** in *com.*, to make an inventory of stock or goods on hand; hence, fig., to make an appraisal or estimate of resources, prospects, etc.; make an examination or inspection (*of*), as for the purpose of forming an opinion (as, "Mrs. Skinner . . . was *taking* pretty accurate *stock* of Christina": S. Butler's "Way of All Flesh," xxviii.).—**to take stock in,** to take a share or shares of stock in (a company, etc.); hence, to take an interest in, attach importance to, or put confidence in (colloq.: as, do you *take* any *stock in* spiritualism? to *take* no *stock in* a person's statements).—**stock,** *a.* Of or pertaining to stock (as the capital stock of a company, a government stock or debt, the stock of a farm or ranch, or the stock of goods of a trader); also, kept regularly in stock or on hand, as for use or sale (as, *stock* articles; *stock* sizes); staple; standard; of the common or ordinary type; in common use (as, the *stock* argument for prohibition); commonplace (as, a *stock* remark); in *theatrical use*, forming part of a repertoire, as a play or piece; appearing together in a repertoire, as a company (see phrase *stock company*, below); pertaining to stock plays or pieces, or to a stock company.—**stock company,** a company or corporation whose capital is divided into shares; in *theatrical use*, a company employed more or less permanently under the same management and appearing together in a repertoire, usually at a single theater or largely at a home theater.—**stock,** *v.* **I.** *tr.* To root up (stumps, weeds, etc.: often with *up*, and now chiefly prov. Eng.); also, to put in the stocks as a punishment†; also, to fasten to or provide with a stock, as a rifle, crossbow, plow, bell, anchor, etc.; also, to furnish with stock, as a farm with horses, cattle, etc., and sometimes with implements, etc. (as, "He had bought and *stocked* two cattle ranches": Charnwood's "Theodore Roosevelt," ii.); furnish with a stock or store of something (as, to *stock* one's cellar with wine); furnish (a shop) with a stock of goods; in general, to furnish or supply with something (as, "He had a library pretty well *stocked* with the elderly English authors": Howells's "Chance Acquaintance," ii.); sow (land) with seed of grass, etc.; also, to lay up in store, as for future use (as, "The wine was *stocked* in the deep vaults of Bracquemont": Scott's "Quentin Durward," xviii.); lay in a stock of. **II.** *intr.* To send out shoots, as a plant, esp. to tiller (Sc. and prov. Eng.); also, to lay in a stock or supply of something (often with *up*).

stock-ade (sto-kād′), *n.* [= F. *estacade*, < Sp. *estacada*, < *estaca*, a stake; from Teut., and akin to E. *stake*[1].] A defensive barrier consisting of strong posts or timbers fixed upright in the ground; a barricade, esp. of timber, with loopholes to fire from, employed in fortification; also, an inclosure or pen made with posts and stakes.—**stock-ade′,** *v. t.*; -aded, -ading. To protect, fortify, or encompass with a stockade.
stock-bro-ker (stok′brō″kėr), *n.* A broker who, for a commission, buys and sells stocks or shares (and commonly other securities) for clients.—**stock′=bro″king,** *n.*
stock-dove (stok′duv), *n.* [Appar. so called from its breeding in hollow stocks of trees.] A wild pigeon of Europe, *Columba œnas.*
stock-er (stok′ėr), *n.* One who or that which stocks; esp., a maker or fitter of stocks of rifles, etc.; also, an animal, as a young steer, to be kept until matured or fattened before killing.
stock=ex-change (stok′eks-chānj″), *n.* A building or place where stocks or shares, etc., are bought and sold; also, an association of brokers and dealers in stocks, bonds, etc., who meet together and transact business according to fixed rules. Cf. *stock-broker* and *stock-jobber.*
stock-farm (stok′färm), *n.* A farm devoted to the breeding of live stock.—**stock′=farm″er,** *n.*—**stock′=farm″ing,** *n.*
stock-fish (stok′fish), *n.* [Cf. D. and MLG. *stokvisch*, G. *stockfisch*, Sw. *stockfisk*, Dan. *stokfisk*, stockfish.] Any of various fishes, as cod or haddock, cured by splitting and drying in the air without salt.
stock=gil-ly-flow-er (stok′jil′i-flou″ėr), *n.* Any of various plants of the brassicaceous genus *Matthiola*, esp. *M. incana*: so called because of the woody stem.
stock-hold-er (stok′hōl″dėr), *n.* A holder or proprietor of stocks or shares; a proprietor of stock in the public funds, as in Great Britain; also, an owner of live stock (Australia). —**stock′hold″ing,** *n.* and *a.*
stock-i-ly (stok′i-li), *adv.* In a stocky manner.—**stock′i-ness,** *n.*
stock-i-net (stok-i-net′), *n.* [Prob. for earlier *stocking-net*.] An elastic machine-knitted fabric used for making undergarments, etc.
stock-ing (stok′ing), *n.* A close-fitting garment, usually knitted (by hand or machine) and of wool, cotton, or silk, for the foot and leg, esp. one reaching to or above the knee (as distinguished from a sock: see *sock*[1]); something resembling such a garment, as an elastic surgical covering or wrapping for the leg, or a noticeably different coloring (esp. white) of the lower part of a horse's leg; also, a repository or a hoard or store of money (colloq.: from the use of a stocking, in first sense, to hold savings).—**stock′inged,** *a.* Clad in or furnished with a stocking or stockings (as, "a hulking, obese Babu whose *stockinged* legs shook with fat": Kipling's "Kim," ix.); also, of the feet, having stockings as the only covering, without shoes (as, "She seized the candle, and in *stockinged* feet . . . descended the stairs": Arnold Bennett's "Riceyman Steps," iv. 7).—**stock′ing=feet′,** *n. pl.* Stockings as the only foot-covering (without shoes): used in the phrase 'in one's stocking-feet': as, "he . . . being at least six feet three inches in his *stocking-feet*" (Weir Mitchell's "Hugh Wynne," ii.).—**stock′ing-less,** *a.* Without stockings.
stock-ish (stok′ish), *a.* Like a stock or block of wood; dull; stupid: as, "I could never deny, in looking back upon what followed, that I was eminently *stockish*" (Stevenson's "David Balfour," v.).—**stock′ish-ly,** *adv.*—**stock′ish-ness,** *n.*
stock=job-ber (stok′job″ėr), *n.* A stock-exchange operator who acts as an intermediary between brokers but does not do business with the public (Eng.: also called simply *jobber*); also, a stock-broker (chiefly U. S.: often in contempt or with an implication of unscrupulousness).—**stock′=job″ber-y,** *n.* The business or practice of a stock-jobber.—**stock′=job″bing,** *n.* and *a.*
stock-less (stok′les), *a.* Having no stock.
stock=list (stok′list), *n.* A list published daily or periodically in connection with a stock-exchange, enumerating stocks dealt in, current prices, actual transactions, etc.
stock-man (stok′man), *n.*; pl. -men. A man who raises live stock; a stock-farmer; also, a man employed on a stock-farm; also, a man in charge of a stock of materials or goods.

fat, fāte, fär, fåll, åsk, fāre; net, mē, hėr; pin, pīne; not, nōte, mōve, nôr; up, lūte, púll; oi, oil; ou, out; (lightened) aviąry, ęlect, agǫny, intǫ, ŭnite; (obscured) errąnt, operä, ardęnt, actǫr, natūre; ch, chip; g, go; th, thin; ᴛʜ, then; y, you;

stock=mar-ket (stok′mär″ket), *n.* A market where stocks or shares, etc., are bought and sold; a stock-exchange; also, the purchase and sale of stocks or shares (as, the *stock-market* was dull to-day); sometimes, a cattle-market.

stock=pot (stok′pot), *n.* A pot in which stock for soup, etc., is made and kept.

stock=rid-er (stok′rī″dẻr), *n.* A mounted herdsman, esp. on an unfenced station. [Australia.]—**stock′=rid″ing,** *n.*

stock=room (stok′rŏm), *n.* A room in which is kept a reserved stock of materials or goods for use or sale; also, a room, as in a hotel, where travelers for commercial houses show their samples and take orders.

stock=still (stok′stil′), *a.* Still as a stock, or block of wood; motionless: as, "He stood *stock-still*, as if struck motionless by a discovery" (J. Conrad's "Lord Jim," xvii.).

stock-y (stok′i), *a.*; compar. *stockier*, superl. *stockiest.* Of solid and sturdy form or build; having a strong, stout stem, as a plant; thick-set (and often short), as a person (as, "a short, *stocky* young man": H. G. Wells's "Italy, France, and Britain at War," i.); also, intractable or stubborn (prov. Eng.).

stock=yard (stok′yärd), *n.* A yard for live stock; esp., an inclosure with pens, sheds, etc., connected with a slaughter-house, railroad, market, or the like, for the temporary keeping of cattle, sheep, swine, or horses.

stodge (stoj), *v. t.*; *stodged, stodging.* [Origin obscure.] To fill to distention; cram or stuff, esp. with food; fig., to satiate or weary with something heavy, dull, or stodgy (as, "He grabs the Leader and leaves me to *stodge* myself with his Times": G. B. Shaw's "Man and Superman," ii.). [Prov. or colloq., Eng.]—**stodge,** *n.* Any thick, semisolid matter, as mud or food; any heavy, substantial food. [Prov. or colloq., Eng.] —**stodg′y,** *a.*; compar. *stodgier*, superl. *stodgiest.* Of a thick, semisolid consistence; heavy, as food; fig., heavy, dull, or uninteresting; stupidly or tediously commonplace; also, heavy or bulky in appearance or figure. [Prov. or colloq.]—**stodg′i-ly,** *adv.*—**stodg′i-ness,** *n.*

stœ-chi-om-e-try (stē-ki-om′e-tri), etc. See *stoichiometry,* etc.

stoep (stŏp), *n.* [D.: see *stoop²*.] A raised outer platform at the front, and sometimes the sides, of a house. [South Africa.]

sto-gy (stō′gi). [Earlier *stoga*, < *Conestoga*, town in southeastern Pennsylvania: cf. *Conestoga wagon.*] **I.** *a.* Designating a kind of boot or shoe, also a kind of cigar: see the noun following. **II.** *n.*; pl. *-gies* (-giz). A rough, heavy boot or shoe; also, a long, slender, roughly made, inexpensive cigar (as, "He was lighting that terrible article, a Wheeling '*stogie*' ": Kipling's "Captains Courageous," i.).

sto-ic (stō′ik). [L. *stoicus*, < Gr. στωικός, < στοά, portico, porch: here with reference to the Porch, at Athens, in which Zeno taught.] **I.** *a.* [*cap.*] Pertaining to or named from the Stoa, or Porch, in ancient Athens, as the school of philosophy founded by Zeno of Citium (about 336 − about 264 B.C.), who taught that men should be free from passion, unmoved by joy or grief, and submit without complaint to unavoidable necessity; of or pertaining to this school, which has become proverbially known for the sternness and austerity of its ethical doctrines; [*l. c.*] stoical. **II.** *n.* [*cap.*] A member or adherent of the Stoic school of philosophy; hence [*l. c.*], one who maintains or affects the mental attitude required by the Stoics, of repression of emotion, indifference to pleasure or pain, and calm fortitude under all experiences (as, "The sternest-seeming *stoic* is human after all": C. Brontë's "Jane Eyre," xxxii.).—**sto′i-cal,** *a.* [*cap.*] Of or pertaining to the Stoics; [*l. c.*] resembling, suggesting, or befitting the Stoics, as in repression of emotion, or indifference to pleasure or pain (as, a *stoical* sufferer; "a *stoical* contempt of riches and power," Steele, in "Tatler," 170); impassive; characterized by calm or austere fortitude.—**sto′i-cal-ly,** *adv.*—**sto′i-cal-ness,** *n.*

stoi-chi-om-e-try (stoi-ki-om′e-tri), *n.* [Also *stoicheiometry*, and more properly *stœchiometry*, < G. *stöchiometrie*, < Gr. στοιχεῖον, element, +-μετρία, <μέτρον, measure.] The science of calculating the quantities of chemical elements or compounds involved in chemical reactions.—**stoi″chi-o-met′ric, stoi″chi-o-met′ri-cal** (-ō-met′rik, -ri-kạl), *a.*—**stoi″chi-o-met′ri-cal-ly,** *adv.*

sto-i-cism (stō′i-sizm), *n.* [*cap.*] The philosophy of the Stoics; [*l.c.*] conduct conforming to the precepts of the Stoics; repression of emotion; indifference to pleasure or pain; patient endurance; calm fortitude.

stoke (stōk), *v.*; *stoked, stoking.* [D. *stoken*, make or tend a fire, = MLG. *stoken*, poke and feed a fire.] **I.** *tr.* To poke, stir up, and feed (a fire); tend the fire of (a furnace, esp. one used with a boiler to generate steam for an engine); supply with fuel. Also fig. **II.** *intr.* To tend a fire or furnace; act as a stoker.—**stoke′=hold,** *n. Naut.*, the space or compartment containing the furnaces, boilers, etc., of a steamship.—**stoke′=hole,** *n.* A hole or aperture through which a furnace is stoked; also, a compartment where furnace-fires are worked, as in a steamship.—**stok-er** (stō′kẻr), *n.* [D. *stoker.*] One who or that which stokes; one employed to tend a furnace used in generating steam, as on a locomotive or a steamship; a mechanical device for stoking.

sto-la (stō′lä), *n.*; pl. *-læ* (-lē). [L.: see *stole²*.] In *Rom. antiq.*, a long, ample robe worn by Roman matrons.

stole¹ (stōl). Preterit of *steal.*

stole² (stōl), *n.* [AS. *stole*, < L. *stola*, < Gr. στολή, equipment, dress, garment, < στέλλειν, set, place, equip, array.] A long robe, worn by men or women (archaic or poetic); also, an ecclesiastical vestment, a narrow strip of silk or other material worn over the shoulders (by deacons, over the left shoulder only) and hanging down in front to the knee or below; also, a kind of collar of fur, marabou, or the like, extending downward in front in long bands, worn by women.

stole³ (stōl), *n.* A var. of *stool* (orig. with reference to a close-stool) in old titles of officers of a royal or princely household: as, groom of the *stole.*

stoled (stōld), *a.* Wearing a stole.

Roman Woman clad in the Stola (over which is draped the palla).

stol-en (stō′ln). Past participle of *steal.*

stol-id (stol′id), *a.* [L. *stolidus*, slow, dull, stolid.] Not easily moved or stirred mentally (as, "*stolid*, dull, vacant plough-boys": S. Butler's "Way of All Flesh," xiv.); lacking in sensibility; impassive as from dullness or stupidity; characterized by or indicating such impassiveness (as, "the *stolid* calm of the Indian," Whittier's "Mogg Megone," i.; "his joy overcoming the habitual *stolid* look," W. H. Hudson's "Green Mansions," iv.).—**sto-lid-i-ty** (stō-lid′i-ti), **stol′id-ness,** *n.*—**stol′id-ly,** *adv.*

sto-lon (stō′lon), *n.*; pl. *-lons* (-lonz). [L. *stolo(n)-*, shoot, sucker.] In *bot.*, a slender branch or shoot which takes root at the tip and eventually develops into a new plant; in *zoöl.*, a root-like extension in a compound organism, usually giving rise to new zoöids by budding.—**sto-lo-nif-er-ous** (stō-lọ-nif′ẹ-rus), *a.* [See *-ferous.*] Producing or bearing stolons.

sto-ma (stō′mä), *n.*; pl. *stomata* (stō′-mạ-tä or stom′ạ-). [NL., < Gr. στόμα, mouth, opening.] In *zoöl.*, a mouth or ingestive opening, esp. when in the form of a small or simple aperture; hence, a small opening of any kind; a pore; in *bot.*, any of various small apertures; esp., one of the minute orifices or slits in the epidermis of leaves, etc.

Sedge (*Carex goodenovii*), showing the Stolons.

stom-ach (stum'ak), n. [OF. F. *estomac*, < L. *stomachus*, < Gr. στόμαχος, throat, gullet, stomach, < στόμα, mouth, opening.] In man and other vertebrates, a more or less sac-like enlargement of the alimentary canal, forming the principal organ of digestion; such an organ, or an analogous portion of the alimentary canal, when divided into two or more sections or parts, or any one of these sections (the compound stomach of a ruminant — see cut below — consisting of four sections, which, taken in order from the esophagus to the intestines, are the rumen or first stomach, the reticulum or second stomach, the omasum or third stomach, and the abomasum or fourth or true stomach; the sections of a bird's two-part stomach being the glandular or

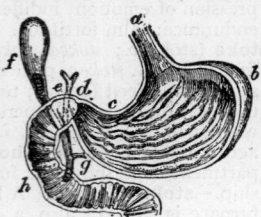

Human Stomach and Beginning of Intestine, laid open to show rugæ. — *a*, esophagus or gullet; *b*, cardiac (left) dilatation of stomach; *c*, lesser curvature of stomach, opposite which is the greater curvature; *d*, pylorus, at right extremity of stomach; *e*, biliary or hepatic duct; *f*, gall-bladder; *g*, pancreatic duct; *h, i*, duodenum, or beginning of small intestine.

true stomach, which is next to the esophagus or crop, and the grinding or muscular stomach, or gizzard, which is next to the intestines; any analogous digestive cavity or tract in invertebrates; also, the part of the body containing the stomach; the belly or abdomen; also, appetite or relish

Typical Ruminant Stomach (Sheep). — *Ru*, rumen; *Ret*, reticulum; *Ps*, omasum, psalterium, or manyplies; *A*, abomasum; *œ*, esophagus; *Du*, duodenum. (*Ru* unopened; other parts in section.)

for food (as, "I found Friday had still a hankering *stomach* after some of the flesh," Defoe's "Robinson Crusoe," i. 14; to have no *stomach* for one's meals); fig., desire, inclination, or liking (as, "It went against my *stomach* to work," H. Mackenzie's "Man of Feeling," xiv.; "The mercenaries . . . had little *stomach* for fight without wages," Motley's "Dutch Republic," vi. 1); also, temper† or disposition†; spirit† or courage† (as, "Let him take *stomach* to repel Troy's fiery threatenings": Chapman's tr. Homer's "Iliad," ix.); pride† (as, "He was a man Of an unbounded *stomach*, ever ranking Himself with princes": Shakspere's "Henry VIII.," iv. 2. 34); obstinacy†; resentment† or anger†; malice† or spite†.—**stom'ach**, v. **I.** *tr.* To take into or retain in the stomach; fig., to put up with, endure, or tolerate (as, "people in the North, who could hardly *stomach* the doctrine that slavery was good": Charnwood's "Abraham Lincoln," v.); also, to turn the stomach of; nauseate; also, to offend† or vex†; also, to be offended at† or resent†; also, to encourage†. **II.**† *intr.* To take offense; feel resentment: as, "What one . . . doth not *stomach* at such contradiction?" (Hooker's "Ecclesiastical Polity," i. 10. 7).

stom-ach=ache (stum'ak-āk), n. Pain in the stomach or abdomen; gastralgia; colic.

stom-ach-al (stum'a-kal), a. Pertaining to the stomach; gastric; good for the stomach, as a remedy; of the nature of a stomach.

stom-ached (stum'akt), a. Having a stomach (as specified): as, "There was my uncle . . . short, thin-legged, large-stomached" (H. G. Wells's "Tono-Bungay," iii. 2. § 10).

stom-ach-er[1] (stum'a-kér), n. One who stomachs.

stom-ach-er[2] (stum'a-kér or -chér), n. A piece of dress for covering the stomach and chest, formerly worn by both men and women; esp., an ornamental piece worn by women under the open (and often laced) front of a bodice.

sto-mach-ic (stō-mak'ik). [L. *stomachicus*, < Gr. στομαχικός.] **I.** *a.* Of or pertaining to the stomach; gastric; also, beneficial to the stomach; stimulating gastric digestion; sharpening the appetite. **II.** *n.* A stomachic agent or drug.

stom-ach=tooth (stum'ak-töth), n.; pl. *-teeth* (-tēth). A lower canine milk-tooth of infants: so called because there is often gastric disturbance at the time of its appearance.

sto-ma-ta (stō'ma-tä or stom'a-), n. Plural of *stoma*.

sto-ma-tal (stō'ma-tal or stom'a-), a. Of, pertaining to, or

of the nature of a stoma or stomata; also, having stomata.

sto-mat-ic (stō-mat'ik), a. [Gr. στοματικός, < στόμα (στοματ-), mouth.] Pertaining to the mouth; acting as a remedy for diseases of the mouth, as a drug; also, stomatal.

sto-ma-ti-tis (stō-ma-tī'tis or stom-a-), n. [NL., < Gr. στόμα (στοματ-), mouth.] In *pathol.*, inflammation of the interior of the mouth.—**sto-ma-tit'ic** (-tit'ik), a.

stomato-. Form of Gr. στόμα (στοματ-), mouth, opening, used in combination.—**sto-ma-tol-o-gy** (stō-ma-tol'ō-ji or stom-a-), n. [+ *-logy*.] The science dealing with the mouth and its diseases.—**sto″ma-to-log′i-cal** (-tō-loj'i-kal), a.—**sto′ma-to-plas″ty** (-plas″ti), n. [+ *-plasty*.] Plastic surgery of the mouth.—**sto″ma-to-plas′tic**, a.

sto-ma-to-pod (stō'ma-tō-pod or stom'a-). [NL. *Stomatopoda*, pl., < Gr. στόμα (στοματ-), mouth, + πούς (ποδ-), foot.] **I.** *n.* Any of the *Stomatopoda*, an order of crustaceans, including the squills, having some of the legs close to the mouth, and the gills borne on the abdominal segments. **II.** *a.* Belonging or pertaining to the *Stomatopoda*.

sto-mo-dæ-um (stō-mō-dē'um or stom-ō-), n.; pl. *-dæa* (-dē'ä). [NL., < Gr. στόμα, mouth, + ὁδαῖος, on the way, < ὁδός, way.] In *embryol.*, the oral or anterior part of the alimentary canal or digestive tract, beginning as an invagination of the ectoderm.—**sto-mo-dæ'al**, a.

-stomy. Noun termination from Gr. στόμα, mouth, opening, esp. in names of surgical operations for making an artificial opening, as in *ileostomy*.

stone (stōn), n. [AS. *stān* = D. *steen* = G. *stein* = Icel. *steinn* = Goth. *stains*, stone: cf. Gr. στία, στίον, pebble.] A piece of rock of small or moderate size; also, the hard substance of which rocks consist, as distinguished from wood, metal, etc.; a particular kind of rock; also, a piece of rock of definite size, shape, etc., used for a particular purpose; a gravestone or tombstone (as, "No *stone* was ever erected to the memory of Jean Myles": Barrie's "Sentimental Tommy," xii.); a grindstone; a millstone; an imposing-stone; also, a gem, or stone distinguished for its beauty and rarity and prized for use in jewelry, etc. ('precious stone'); also, something resembling a small stone or pebble; a hailstone; a calculous concretion in the body, esp. in the kidney, bladder, or gall-bladder, or the disease arising from such a concretion; a testicle (now vulgar); the hard endocarp of a drupe; any hard, stone-like seed; also, a measure of weight having various values, now commonly equal to 14 pounds (chiefly British: pl. commonly, as after a numeral, *stone*: as, "Mr. Frederick weighs fourteen *stone*," Thackeray's "Newcomes," xi.).—**a stone's throw,** the distance to which a stone may be thrown by the hand, and hence a short distance: as, "a labourer in the village who lived *a stone's throw* from the Rectory" (S. Butler's "Way of All Flesh," xxiii.).—**to leave no stone unturned,** fig., to use all practicable means to effect an object: as, "New crimes invented; *left unturn'd no stone*, To make my guilt appear, and hide his own" (Dryden's tr. Virgil's "Æneid," ii. 133).—**stone**, a. Made of or pertaining to stone; also, made of stoneware (as, a *stone* mug or bottle).—**stone age,** the age in the history of mankind (preceding the bronze and iron ages) marked by the use of stone implements. See *ages in archæology*, under *age*, n.—**stone**, v.t.; *stoned*, *stoning*. To throw stones at; drive by pelting with stones (as, "They *stoned* her out of Thrums": Barrie's "Sentimental Tommy," vi.); esp., to put to death by pelting with stones (as, "Some say he shall be *stoned*; but that death is too soft for him, say I": Shakspere's "Winter's Tale," iv. 4.

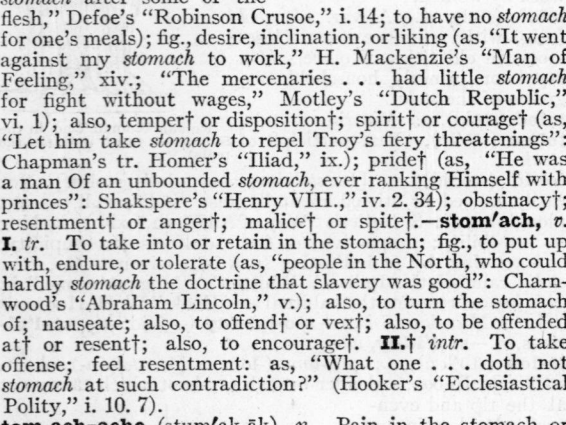

Implements of the Stone Age. — 1, saw-edged flint knife; 2, crescent-shaped flint knife; 3, stone ax; 4, flint knife; 5, harpoon-head of flint; 6, flint knife.

807); also, to turn into stone†; petrify†; also, to provide or fit with stones, as by paving, lining, facing, etc.; also, to rub with or on a stone, as to sharpen, polish, smooth, etc.; also, to free from stones, as fruit.

stone=blind (stōn'blīnd'), *a.* Blind as a stone; wholly blind. Cf. *sand-blind* and *gravel-blind.*

stone=bruise (stōn'brōz), *n.* A bruise, esp. on the sole of the foot, caused by a stone or the like.

stone-chat (stōn'chat), *n.* Any of various old-world chats, esp. of the genus *Pratincola*, as *P. rubicola*, whose alarm note resembles the sound of pebbles striking together.

Stonechat (*Pratincola rubicola*).

stone=coal (stōn'kōl), *n.* Mineral coal, or coal dug up from the earth, as distinguished from charcoal; esp., a hard variety of such coal; anthracite.

stone=cold (stōn'kōld'), *a.* Cold as a stone; quite cold.

stone=col-or (stōn'kul"ọr), *n.* A dark, dull bluish gray; also, a brownish gray.—**stone'=col"ored,** *a.*

stone-crop (stōn'krop), *n.* [AS. *stāncrop.*] A moss-like crassulaceous herb, a species of sedum, *Sedum acre*, with small, fleshy leaves and yellow flowers, frequently growing upon rocks and walls; any plant of the genus *Sedum* (see *sedum*); any of various plants of related genera.

stone=cut-ter (stōn'kut"ẽr), *n.* One who cuts or carves stone; also, a machine for cutting or dressing stone.—**stone'=cut"ting,** *n.*

stoned (stōnd), *a.* Having a stone or stones; also, deprived of stones, as fruit.

stone=dead (stōn'ded'), *a.* Dead as a stone; lifeless: as, "With a deep roar he [a lion] fell back . . . on the grass, *stone-dead*" (J. H. Patterson's "Man-Eaters of Tsavo," xxii.).

stone=deaf (stōn'def'), *a.* Deaf as a stone; totally deaf: as, "an acting Secretary of a leading Institute in London who is *stone deaf* but in receipt of £500 a year" (W. De Morgan's "Joseph Vance," xvi.).

stone=fly (stōn'flī), *n.*; pl. *-flies* (-flīz). Any of the numerous insects constituting the family *Perlidæ* or the order *Plecoptera*, whose larvæ abound under stones in streams.

stone=fruit (stōn'frōt), *n.* A fruit with a stone or hard endocarp, as a peach or a plum; a drupe.

stone=less (stōn'les), *a.* Having no stone or stones.

Stone-fly (genus *Perla*). — *a*, aquatic wingless larva; *b*, transitional stage to *c*, perfect insect, or imago.

stone=lil-y (stōn'lil"i), *n.*; pl. *-ies* (-iz). A fossil crinoid.

stone=mar-ten (stōn'mär"ten), *n.* A marten, *Mustela foina*, of Europe and Asia, having a white mark on the throat and breast.

stone=ma-son (stōn'mā"sn), *n.* A dresser of or builder in stone.

stone=pars-ley (stōn'pärs"li), *n.* An old-world apiaceous plant, *Sison amomum*, yielding aromatic seeds.

ston-er (stōn'ẽr), *n.* One who or that which stones.

stone=roll-er (stōn'rō"lẽr), *n.* The hammerhead (fish), *Hypentelium nigricans*; also, a small cyprinoid fish, *Campostoma anomalum*, of the United States.

Stone-roller (*Campostoma anomalum*).

stone=still (stōn'stil'), *a.* Still as a stone; absolutely motionless: as, "She lay *stone-still* in a trance of terror" (G. Meredith's "Ordeal of Richard Feverel," i.).

stone-ware (stōn'wãr), *n.* A coarse, hard, vitrified potters' ware; the material or substance of this ware.

stone-work (stōn'wẽrk), *n.* Work in stone; masonry of stone; in *printing*, work done on the imposing-stone.

stone=works (stōn'wẽrks), *n. pl.* or *sing.* An establishment where stone is prepared for building, etc.

stone-yard (stōn'yärd), *n.* A yard in which stone-cutting or stone-breaking is carried on.

Stoneware Mug, German, 18th century. — Pennsylvania Museum, Philadelphia.

ston-y (stō'ni), *a.* Full of or abounding in stones (as, "I chatter over *stony* ways": Tennyson's "Brook," 39); having a stone or stones, as a fruit; abounding in stone or rock (as, "*stony* ground": Mark, iv. 5); pertaining to or characteristic of stone; of the nature of stone; resembling or suggesting stone, esp. hard like stone; *fig.*, unfeeling; merciless; obdurate; also, motionless or rigid; without expression, as the eyes or look; also, seeming to turn one to stone (as, *stony* fear or grief).—**ston'i-ly,** *adv.*—**ston'i-ness,** *n.*—**ston'y=heart'ed,** *a.* Hard-hearted.

stood (stud). Preterit and past participle of *stand.*

stooge (stōj), *n.* [Origin uncertain.] One who acts as a foil, as for a comedian; a confederate, as of a magician.—**stooge,** *v. i.* To act as a stooge.

stook (stōk or stuk), *n.* [ME. *stouk*, *stowk*, akin to MLG. *stūke*, G. dial. *stauche*, bundle, truss.] A shock of grain. [Now chiefly prov.]—**stook,** *v. t.* To set up in stooks. [Now chiefly prov.]—**stook'er,** *n.*

stool (stōl), *n.* [AS. *stōl* = D. *stoel* = OHG. *stuol* (G. *stuhl*) = Icel. *stōll* = Goth. *stōls*, seat; prob. from the root of E. *stand.*] A seat for one person (obs. in general sense); a chair of authority, as a royal or episcopal throne†; a wooden seat, either low or high, without arms or a back, and for a single person; commonly, a simple seat of this kind consisting of a piece of wood mounted on three or four legs; sometimes, a high seat of this kind for use in writing at a high desk (as, "Oh! who would cast and balance at a desk, Perch'd like a crow upon a three-legg'd *stool?*" Tennyson's "Audley Court," 44); also, a short, low support of more or less similar construction, for resting the feet on, kneeling on, etc. also, a seat containing a chamber vessel; a commode; a close-stool; also, a privy; also, the act or an act of evacuating the bowels; the matter evacuated (chiefly in *pl.*); also, a base or support on which anything is placed to raise it above a surface; also, the stump of a tree which has been felled; the stump, base, or root of a tree or other plant which has been cut down, from which shoots are produced, as for coppice-wood, for saplings, or for layers; the base or root in plants which annually produce new stems, etc.; a cluster of shoots or stems springing up from a stool or from any root, or a single shoot or layer; also, a bird fastened as a decoy (cf. *stool-pigeon*); a decoy-duck or similar decoy.—**to fall between two stools**, to make a complete failure by hesitating between two opportunities or trying to use both. —**stool,** *v. i.* To evacuate the bowels; also, to throw up shoots from the base or root, as a plant; form a stool; tiller.

stool=pi-geon (stōl'pij"ọn), *n.* A pigeon used as a decoy; hence, a person employed as a decoy or secret confederate, as by gamblers; also, one who acts as a spy for the police.

stoop[1] (stōp), *n.* See *stoup.*

stoop[2] (stōp), *n.* [D. *stoep*, stoop (cf. *stoep*); akin to E. *step.*] A raised platform with seats, at the entrance of a house (see cut on following page); any raised entrance-platform with steps leading up to it; a porch; sometimes, a veranda. [U. S.]

stoop[3] (stōp), *v.* [AS. *stūpian* = MD. *stuypen* = Icel. *stūpa* = Sw. *stupa*, stoop, incline: cf. *steep*[1] and *steep*[2].] **I.** *intr.* To bend the head and shoulders, or the body generally, forward and downward from an erect position (as, to *stoop* over a desk; to *stoop* down to pick a flower); carry the head and shoulders habitually bowed forward (as, to *stoop* from age; "He was a tall man of about sixty, but *stooped* much," Borrow's "Bible in Spain," iv.); in general, to bend, bow, or lean (said of trees,

Stoop.

precipices, etc.); fig., to bow in submission, submit, or yield (archaic); esp., to descend from one's level of dignity, as to some position or action (as, "Louis *stooped* to any humiliation to reach his aim," Hallam's "Europe during the Middle Ages," i. 2; to *stoop* to flatter or to retaliate); condescend; deign; lower one's self morally; also, to come down from a height (obs. or archaic); swoop down, as a hawk at prey. **II.** *tr.* To bend (one's self, one's head, etc.) forward and downward (as, "A superb-looking warrior *stooped* the towering plumes of his head-dress beneath the low portal, and entered the house": H. Melville's "Typee," x.); bow; fig., to abase, humble, or subdue (archaic); bring down from the accustomed or proper level of dignity; also, to let down or lower (a sail, ensign, etc.)†.—**stoop**[3], *n.* An act of stooping; a stooping movement; a stooping attitude or carriage of body (as, "a hale, thin old man, six feet three inches tall, and without a *stoop*": Tarkington's "Magnificent Ambersons," xiii.); fig., a descent from dignity or superiority; a condescension; also, a downward swoop, as of a hawk at prey (as, "Once a kite hovering over the garden made a *stoop* at me": Swift's "Gulliver's Travels," ii. 5).—**stoop'er**, *n.*—**stoop'ing-ly**, *adv.*—**stoop'-shoul'dered**, *a.* Having a habitual stoop in the shoulders.

stop (stop), *v.*; *stopped*, *stopping*. [AS. *stoppian* (recorded in composition) = D. *stoppen* = G. *stopfen*, < ML. *stuppare*, *stupare*, stop, orig. with tow, < L. *stuppa*, tow: cf. *stupe* and *estop*.] **I.** *tr.* To close (a hole, opening, crevice, etc.) by filling, stuffing, plugging, or otherwise obstructing (often with *up*); fill the hole or holes in (a wall, a decayed tooth, etc.); stuff, press, or thrust (something) into a hole, place, or thing (now Sc. and north. Eng.); also, to close (a vessel, tube, etc.) with a cork, plug, bung, or the like; shut up (something) in a close vessel or place; also, to close the external orifice of (the ears, nose, mouth, etc.), as to prevent hearing, smelling, talking, etc. (often fig.: as, "There are many unruly and vain talkers . . . Whose mouths must be *stopped*," Titus, i. 11); also, to block or obstruct (a passage, way, channel, duct, etc.: often with *up*); close against passage, ingress, or egress; also, to hinder from passing; arrest the movement or progress of (a person, procession, stream, vehicle, etc.); bring to a stand; halt; in general, to prevent from proceeding, acting, operating, continuing, etc. (as, to *stop* a speaker or a worker; to *stop* a clock); check; restrain, hinder, or prevent (*from*: as, to *stop* a person from maltreating a horse); cut off, intercept, or withhold (as, to *stop* supplies; to *stop* letters on their way; "Sir, do you mean to *stop* any of William's wages, about the sack he lost . . . at Hinckley fair?" Shakspere's "2 Henry IV.," v. 1. 24); interrupt, arrest, or check (a course, proceeding, process, etc.: as, "He pressed on till the foot of the mountain *stopped* his course," Johnson's "Rasselas," iv.; to *stop* a run on a bank); cause to cease, or put an end to (anything going on, prevailing, etc.: as, to *stop* noise in the streets; to *stop* scandal, drunkenness, or vice); also, to cease from, leave off, or discontinue (as, to *stop* running; to *stop* crying; to *stop* useless efforts); also, to furnish with stops or punctuation-marks; punctuate; in *fencing*, *boxing*, etc., to check (a stroke, blow, etc.); parry; ward off; also, to defeat by a knock-out or the like (as, one pugilist *stopped* the other in the fifth round); hence, in *games*, etc., to defeat (an opponent); in *music*, to close (a finger-hole, etc.) in order to pro-

duce a particular note from a wind-instrument; also, to press down (a string of a violin, etc.) in order to alter the pitch of the tone produced from it; produce (a particular note) by so doing; *naut.*, to make fast with a piece of small line. **II.** *intr.* To come to a stand, as in a course or journey; halt; in general, to cease moving, proceeding, speaking, acting, operating, etc. (as, "*Stop!* Don't say anything more," G. B. Shaw's "You Never Can Tell," ii.; the machinery *stops* at noon); pause; desist; cease, or come to an end, as proceedings, activities, etc.; also, to make a stay at a place, as during a journey; sojourn as a guest; stay or remain (as, "Do you think a young lady of my pretensions can *stop* at home . . . and cut bread-and-butter?" Thackeray's "Newcomes," l.; "No wonder she looks pale, *stopping* up till this time of night!" Arnold Bennett's "Hilda Lessways," ii. 4).—**to stop off**, to halt for a brief stay at some point in the course of a journey.—**to stop over**, to make a brief stay at some point in the course of a journey, esp. with the privilege of proceeding by a later conveyance on the ticket originally issued for the journey.—**stop**, *n.* The act of stopping; a closing or filling up, as of a hole; a blocking or obstructing, as of a passage or way; a bringing to a stand, or an arrest of movement, action, operation, etc.; a check; an end put to anything; a coming to a stand, or to an end of movement, action, etc.; a halt, pause, or standstill; a cessation; a stay or sojourn made at a place, as in the course of a journey; also, something that stops; a plug or other stopper for an opening; an obstacle, impediment, or hindrance; any piece or device that serves to check or control movement or action in a mechanism; also, a punctuation-mark (as, a full *stop*, a period); in *music*, the act of closing a finger-hole, etc., or of pressing down a string, of an instrument, in order to produce a particular note; a device or contrivance, as on an instrument, for accomplishing this; also, in an organ, a graduated set of pipes of the same kind and giving tones of the same quality; a knob or handle which is drawn out or pushed back to permit or prevent the sounding of such a set of pipes or to control some other part of the organ; in *phonetics*, a sudden complete closure of the voice-organs in uttering certain sounds; also, a consonant, as *p*, *b*, *t*, or *d*, which involves a complete closure of the oral and nasal passages; also, sometimes, a consonant, as *m*, *n*, or *ng*, formed by complete closure of the oral but not the nasal passage; *naut.*, a piece of small line used to lash or fasten something, as a furled sail.

stop=cock (stop'kok), *n.* A short pipe with a valve of some sort operated by a handle, used to permit or arrest the flow of a liquid or gas from a receptacle or through a pipe; a cock; a faucet; a tap.

stope (stōp), *n.* [Prob. connected with *step*.] In *mining*, one of a group of horizontal workings which are made one higher than another in step-like arrangement; hence, any excavation made in a mine to remove the ore which has been rendered accessible by the shafts and drifts.—**stope**, *v. t.* or *i.*; *stoped*, *stoping*. To mine or work by stopes.

stop=gap (stop'gap). **I.** *n.* Something that stops a gap, or fills the place of something lacking; a temporary substitute; a makeshift: as, "She evidently considered Lady Ella a mere conversational *stop-gap*, to be dropped now that the real business could be commenced" (H. G. Wells's "Soul of a Bishop," vi.). **II.** *a.* Serving as a stop-gap; used merely to fill up; makeshift.

stop=o=ver (stop'ō″vér), *n.* A stopping over in the course of a journey, esp. with the privilege of proceeding later on the ticket originally issued for the journey.

stop=page (stop'āj), *n.* The act of stopping, or the state of being stopped; obstruction; halting or checking; discontinuance; cessation of movement, activity, etc.

stopped (stopt), *p. a.* Closed, filled up, or obstructed, as a hole, opening, or passage; closed with a cork, plug, or the like, as a vessel or tube; halted or checked; in *music*, having the upper end plugged or closed, as an organ-pipe (cf. *stopped diapason*, at *diapason*); also, acted upon by stopping, as a string (see *stop*, *v. t.*); produced by the stopping of a string, etc., as a note; in *phonetics*, formed by or uttered with a complete closure of the voice-organs (as, a *stopped* consonant: cf. *stop*, *n.*).

stop=per (stop'ér), *n.* One who or that which stops; specif., a plug or piece for closing a bottle, tube, or the like; a stopple;

fig., a check or quietus (colloq.: as, "The girl is beside herself with fear of something happening that would put a *stopper* on the Wajo expedition," J. Conrad's "Rescue," iii. 9).—

stop′per, *v. t.* To close, secure, or fit with a stopper.

stop-ple (stop′l), *n.* [Appar. < *stop*: cf. OF. *estoupail*, stopple.] A stopper for a bottle or the like.—**stop′ple**, *v. t.*; *-pled*, *-pling*. To close or fit with a stopple.

stop=watch (stop′woch), *n.* A watch which has a hand or hands that can be stopped or started at any instant, and which is adapted for indicating fractions of a second: used for timing races, etc.

stor-a-ble (stōr′a-bl), *a.* That may be stored.

stor-age (stōr′āj), *n.* The act of storing, or the state or fact of being stored (as, cold *storage*: see under *cold, a.*); capacity or space for storing; also, a place where something is stored; also, the price charged for storing goods.—**stor′-age=bat″ter-y**, *n.* A battery or device which, after having been subjected to an electric current for a certain time, will yield a limited current in the opposite direction and so serve as a source of electricity, the operation being dependent upon the reversal of the chemical changes produced by the charging current in the materials in the device.

sto-rax (stō′raks), *n.* [L. *storax, styrax*, < Gr. στύραξ, storax (resin and tree).] A solid resin with a vanilla-like odor obtained from a small styracaceous tree, *Styrax officinalis*, and formerly much used in medicine and perfumery; the tree itself; some related species, as *S. californica*, a handsome shrub of California; also, a liquid balsam ('liquid storax') obtained from species of liquidambar, esp. from the wood and inner bark of *Liquidambar orientalis*, a tree of Asia Minor, etc., and used in medicine (as an expectorant), perfumery, etc.

Branch with Flowers of Storax (*Styrax californica*). — *a*, a leaf, showing nervation.

store (stōr), *v. t.*; *stored, storing*. [OF. *estorer*, build, establish, supply, stock, < L. *instaurare*, renew, restore, erect, make: cf. *instauration* and *restore²*.] To supply or stock with something, as for future use (as, "He had *stored* himself with abundance of liquors . . . sugar, spices," Defoe's "Captain Singleton," i.; "He imagined . . . that he was *storing* himself with the knowledge that would best fit him for the work," S. Butler's "Way of All Flesh," l.); supply with anything in abundance (as, "a volume . . . *stored* with pictures": C. Brontë's "Jane Eyre," i.); also, to lay up or put away, as a supply for future use (often with *up* or *away*); deposit in a storehouse, warehouse, or other place, for keeping (as, "Mistress lets her have that room to *store* some boatgear in": Arnold Bennett's "Lion's Share," xxxiv.); also, of a repository, to hold or contain; afford room for.—**store**, *n.* [OF. *estor*, supplies, stock, < *estorer*.] The supply or stock of necessaries stored up, as for future use (archaic: as, the *store* of a household); *pl.*, supplies of food, clothing, or other requisites, as for a household or other establishment, a ship, naval or military forces, or the like (as, "long trains of government wagons, laden with *stores* for the troops": Parkman's "Oregon Trail," xxvii.); *sing.*, a supply or stock (of something), as for future use (as, "grapes . . . which I principally depended on for my winter *store* of raisins," Defoe's "Robinson Crusoe," i. 11; "Jim was the only one in Patusan who possessed a *store* of gunpowder," J. Conrad's "Lord Jim," xxxix.); in general, a stock of anything accumulated or possessed (as, a *store* of information, health, or strength; "I draw upon . . . my *stores* of observation [in writing]," Gissing's "New Grub Street," viii.); an accumulation of

wealth or money, or a hoard (archaic: as, "Here is gold in abundance, the saving of years: Give me oatcake and milk in return for my *store*," Peacock's "Headlong Hall," xiii.); also, quantity, esp. great quantity, abundance, or plenty (archaic: as, "They failed not to bring ashore Rich robes of price and of fair arms good *store*," W. Morris's "Jason," xiv. 684; "We wish them *store* of happy days," Tennyson's "In Memoriam," Conclusion); also, measure of esteem or regard (used in certain phrases: as, to set much, great, or little *store* by a thing); also, the state of being stored up, on hand, or in reserve (as, to keep a thing in *store*; he has a surprise in *store* for you, that is, kept for or awaiting you); also, a place where supplies are stored for future use or distribution, or a storehouse or warehouse; a place where goods are kept for sale, or a shop (esp. U. S. and British colonies); *pl.*, the departments collectively, each dealing in a particular class of goods, of a general (coöperative or other) trading establishment (esp. Eng.).

store-house (stōr′hous), *n.* A house or building in which things are stored; any repository or source of abundant supplies; a treasury, as of facts or knowledge.

store-keep-er (stōr′kē″pėr), *n.* One who has charge of a store or stores; specif., an officer or official in charge of naval or military stores; also, a shopkeeper (esp. U. S.).

stor-er (stōr′ėr), *n.* One who or that which stores.

store-room (stōr′röm), *n.* A room in which stores or supplies are kept, as for household use or on a ship; also, room or space for storage.

store-ship (stōr′ship), *n.* A government ship detailed to carry naval or military stores.

sto′rey, sto′reyed. See *story¹, storied¹*.

sto-ri-at-ed (stō′ri-ā-ted), *a.* Same as *historiated*.

sto-ried¹ (stō′rid), *a.* [Also *storeyed*.] Having stories or floors: as, "two-*storied* houses" (Barrie's "Auld Licht Idylls," ii.).

sto-ried² (stō′rid), *p. a.* Recorded or celebrated in history or story (as, "the *storied* Rhine": M. Arnold's "Calais Sands"); also, ornamented with designs representing historical, legendary, or similar subjects, by means of painting, sculpture, needlework, or other art (as, a *storied* urn; *storied* tapestries).

sto-ri-ette (stō-ri-et′), *n.* [Dim. of *story²*: see *-ette*.] A very short story.

sto-ri-ol-o-gy (stō-ri-ol′ọ-ji), *n.* [See *story²* and *-logy*.] The study of popular tales and legends, their origin, distribution, etc.—**sto″ri-o-log′i-cal** (-ọ-loj′i-kạl), *a.*—**sto-ri-ol′o-gist**, *n.*

stork (stôrk), *n.* [AS. *storc* = D. *stork* = G. *storch* = Icel. *storkr* = Sw. and Dan. *stork*, stork.] Any of the long-legged, long-necked, long-billed wading birds, allied to the ibis and heron, which constitute the genus *Ciconia* (family *Ciconiidæ*), esp. *C. alba* ('white stork') of Europe; also, any bird of the family *Ciconiidæ*, as the adjutant-bird or the marabou; also, the stork as popularly reputed (in Germany and elsewhere) to bring babies to the parents.

White Stork (*Ciconia alba*).

stork′s=bill (stôrks′bil), *n.* Any plant of the geraniaceous genus *Pelargonium*, or of the related genus *Erodium*, as *E. cicutarium* (the alfileria, or 'hemlock stork's-bill'): so called from the long-beaked fruit.

storm (stôrm), *n.* [AS. *storm* = D. *storm* = G. *sturm* = Icel. *stormr* = Sw. and Dan. *storm*, storm; from the root of E. *stir*.] A disturbance of the normal condition of the atmosphere, manifesting itself by winds of unusual force or direction, often accompanied by rain, snow, hail, thunder, lightning, or flying sand or dust; a tempest; also, a heavy fall of rain, snow, or hail, or a violent outbreak of thunder and lightning, unaccompanied by strong wind; also, a dis-

turbance resembling a storm of wind, rain, etc. (as, a magnetic *storm*: see under *magnetic*); also, fig., a heavy descent or discharge of missiles, blows, or the like; a violent disturbance of affairs, as a civil, political, social, or domestic commotion; a violent outburst or outbreak, as of sounds, speech, emotional expression, etc. (as, a *storm* of hisses or applause; "another *storm* of vile language," Wiseman's "Fabiola," ii. 24; a *storm* of weeping or laughter); a fit of violent emotion or other disturbance within the mind (as, "Ethan was ashamed of the *storm* of jealousy in his breast," Mrs. Wharton's "Ethan Frome," iv.; a brain-*storm*, which see); *milit.*, a violent assault on a fortified place, strong position, or the like (as, "He was first on the walls of the city in the final *storm*": Froude's "Cæsar," iii.).—**storm and stress.** [Tr. G. *sturm und drang*: with allusion to a drama of this title (1776), by F. M. von Klinger (1752–1831), taken as expressing the spirit of the movement.] A name applied to a movement and a period in German literature (about 1770–90) influenced by a group of younger writers whose works were characterized by vehement passion and by reaction from the old formal methods: hence used of any period of passionate or rebellious unrest, or (loosely) of turmoil or trouble, as in the life of a person.—**to take by storm,** to take (a fortified place, etc.) by assault, as in war; fig., to win or captivate (a person, the heart, an audience, etc.) as if by a successful assault.—**storm,** *v.* **I.** *intr.* To blow with unusual force, or to rain, snow, hail, etc., esp. with violence (used impersonally: as, it *stormed* all day); fig., to rage with violence or angry fury; complain or scold violently (as, "Christina cried bitterly — Theobald *stormed*": S. Butler's "Way of All Flesh," lxx.); also, to rush with violence (as, to *storm* out of a room); go or travel with furious speed (as, "The brig . . . was *storming* along . . . on her way": J. Conrad's "Rescue," ii. 4); also, to deliver a violent attack or fire, as with artillery (as, "*Storm'd* at with shot and shell, Boldly they rode and well": Tennyson's "Charge of the Light Brigade," iii.); *milit.*, to rush to an assault or attack. **II.** *tr.* To subject to or as to a storm (as, "A fickle maid . . . *Storming* her world with sorrow's wind and rain": Shakspere's "Lover's Complaint," 7); also, to utter or say with angry vehemence (as, "'Why can't you look where you are going?' *stormed* Florence": Margaret Kennedy's "Constant Nymph," xx.); *milit.*, to make a violent assault on (a fortified place, etc.) for the purpose of taking it, or take (a place, etc.) by assault or storm (often fig.).

storm=bound (stôrm′bound), *a.* Confined or detained by storms.

storm=cel-lar (stôrm′sel″är), *n.* A cellar or underground chamber for refuge during violent storms; a cyclone-cellar.

storm=cen-ter (stôrm′sen″tėr), *n.* The center of a cyclonic storm, being the area of lowest pressure and a place of comparative calm; fig., anything constituting a center of disturbance, tumult, trouble, or the like.

storm=door (stôrm′dōr), *n.* An outer or additional door for protection against inclement weather, as during the winter.

storm-er (stôr′mėr), *n.* One who storms.

storm-i-ly (stôr′mi-li), *adv.* In a stormy manner.—**storm′i-ness,** *n.*

storm-less (stôrm′les), *a.* Without storms.

storm=proof (stôrm′prōf), *a.* Proof against storms.

storm=troops (stôrm′trōps), *n. pl.* [Cf. G. *sturmtruppen*.] *Milit.*, troops specially chosen and equipped for carrying out storming operations.

storm-ward (stôrm′wärd), *adv.* and *a.* Toward the storm.

storm-y (stôr′mi), *a.*; compar. *stormier,* superl. *stormiest.* Affected or characterized by, or subject to, storms or tempests (as, a *stormy* sea; *stormy* weather; a *stormy* night; a *stormy* region); tempestuous; fig., characterized by violent commotion, actions, speech, passions, etc. (as, "His lot was thrown upon *stormy* times," De Quincey's "Revolt of the Tartars"; a *stormy* career, administration, or debate; "She looks made to be the heroine of some *stormy* romance," Howells's "Foregone Conclusion," vi.); disposed to violence or disorder, or turbulent (as, "the *stormy* chiefs of a desert, but extensive domain": Scott's "Guy Mannering," ii.); moved to or showing passionate emotion, as a person, the face or expression, etc. (as, "She straightened herself, still *stormy* with revolt":

Wister's "Virginian," xxvii.); also, associated with or supposed to portend storms (as, the *stormy* petrel: see under *petrel*).

Stor-thing, Stor-ting (stôr′ting), *n.* [Norw. *storting,* earlier *storthing,* < *stor,* great, + *thing, ting,* assembly: see *thing*[2].] The parliament of Norway.

sto-ry[1] (stō′ri), *n.*; pl. *-ries* (-riz). [Also *storey*; ME. *story,* < AL. *historia,* story or stage of a building, appar. the same word as L. *historia,* history, story: see *history,* and cf. *story*[2].] A complete horizontal section of a building, having one continuous or approximately continuous floor; the set of rooms on the same floor or level of a building; each of the stages, one above another, of which a building consists (as, "a large plain house . . . of three *storeys*": Arnold Bennett's "Pretty Lady," xxvi.); one of the structural architectural divisions in the height of a building; hence, each of a series of divisions or stages of anything, placed horizontally one above another; each of a number of rows or tiers of windows, columns, or the like, disposed horizontally one above another, and constituting an architectural detail.—**upper story.** See under *upper, a.*

sto-ry[2] (stō′ri), *n.*; pl. *-ries* (-riz). [AF. *storie, estorie,* OF. *estoire* (F. *histoire*), < L. *historia,* history, story: see *history.*] A history†, or connected account of events of the past†; history as a branch of knowledge†, or the events recorded in history† (as, "Who is so unread . . . in *story,* that hath not heard of many sects refusing books as a hindrance?" Milton's "Areopagitica"); also, a narration of a series of events, or a series of events that are or may be narrated (as, "Intent he hears Penelope disclose A mournful *story* of domestic woes": Pope's tr. Homer's "Odyssey," xxiii.); often, a narration of the events in the life of a person or the existence of a thing, or such events as a subject for narration (as, the *story* of a foundling; his is a sad *story*); also, a narrative, either true or fictitious, in prose or verse, designed to interest or amuse the hearer or reader; a tale; often, a fictitious tale, shorter and less elaborate than a novel; such narratives or tales as a branch of literature (as, a character famous in *story* and song); the plot, or succession of incidents, of a novel, poem, drama, etc. (as, "If you were to read [Samuel] Richardson for the *story,* your impatience would be so much fretted that you would hang yourself": Johnson, in Boswell's "Johnson," April 6, 1772); a real or fictitious incident related to interest or amuse or for the illustration of some point, or an anecdote (as, a speech full of good *stories*); also, a report or account of a matter (as, the *story* goes that he rejected the offer); a statement or allegation; a particular person's representation of the facts in a case; also, an account of something, as of some subject of news, in a newspaper (journalistic, U. S.); also, euphemistically, a falsehood or lie (as, "'I didn't recognize you,' he said. 'That's a *story.* Who did you think I was?'" J. Conrad's "Rover," xii.); also, a scene from history, legend, romance, etc., depicted by means of painting, sculpture, needlework, or other art†.—**sto′ry**[2], *v. t.*; *-ried, -rying.* To tell the history or story of, or tell as a story (now rare); also, to ornament with pictured scenes, as from history or legend, or with any decorative designs.

sto-ry-ol′o-gy, etc. See *storiology,* etc.

sto-ry=tell-er (stō′ri-tel″ėr), *n.* One who tells stories; a professional reciter of tales in public (as, the *story-tellers* of Arabia); a writer of stories; one given to relating anecdotes; euphemistically, one who tells falsehoods or lies (as, "He was . . . the greatest liar I had met with . . . none of your hesitating, half *story-tellers*": Lamb's "Old Margate Hoy"). —**sto′ry=tell″ing,** *n.* and *a.*

stot (stot), *n.* [Late AS. *stot,* horse: cf. Icel. *stūtr,* bull.] A horse†; also, a steer, or young castrated ox (north. Eng. and Sc.).

stoup (stöp), *n.* [ME. *stowpe, stope*: cf. Icel. *staup,* MD. *stoop,* MLG. *stōp,* cup.] A pail or bucket (now only Sc.); a drinking-vessel of various sizes, as a cup, flagon, or tankard, or the amount that it holds (now archaic or Sc. and north. Eng.: as, "He called to his attendants to fetch a *stoup* of wine and some refreshments," Scott's "Legend of Montrose," xvi.); also, a basin for holy water, as at the entrance of a church (see cut on following page).

stout (stout). [OF. *estout, estult,* proud, bold, stout; from Teut., and akin to G. *stolz,* proud, and perhaps also to E.

stilt.] **I.** *a.* Proud†, haughty†, or arrogant†; also, bold, hardy, or dauntless (as, a *stout* soldier; a *stout* heart); also, firm, determined, stubborn, or uncompromising (as, a *stout* opponent or advocate; *stout* resistance); also, strong of body, stalwart, or sturdy (as, *stout* fellows); in robust health (now prov. Eng. and Sc.); also, possessed of endurance or staying power, as a horse; also, strong in substance or construction (as, *stout* walls; a *stout* ship; "a *stout* loghouse," Stevenson's "Treasure Island," xvi.); strong and thick or heavy (as, a *stout* club; a *stout* branch; *stout* cloth); also, of persons, bulky in figure, solidly built, or thick-set; often, corpulent or fat; also, of liquor, strong (now Sc.). **II.** *n.* Strong ale or beer†; now, porter of extra strength; also, a stout or corpulent person, or a garment for

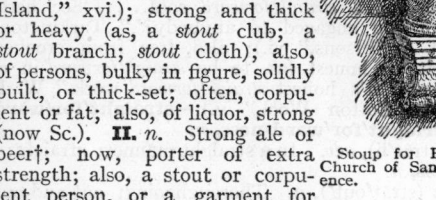
Stoup for Holy Water. — Church of San Miniato, Florence.

such a person (often in *pl.*: in trade use).—**stout'en,** *v. t.* or *i.* To make or become stout.—**stout'=heart'ed,** *a.* Having or showing a stout heart; brave and resolute; dauntless; also, stubborn†.—**stout'=heart'ed-ness,** *n.*—**stout'ish,** *a.* Somewhat stout (in various senses): as, "a coil of *stoutish* rope" (Stevenson's "Treasure Island."); "a short, *stoutish*, almost fat little man" (W. H. Hudson's "Far Away and Long Ago," ii.).—**stout'ly,** *adv.*—**stout'ness,** *n.*

sto-va-ine (stō'vȧ-in), *n.* [From stove (see *stove²*), used to translate F. *Fourneau* (lit. 'stove,' 'furnace'), name of the discoverer.] A crystalline organic compound used as a local anesthetic, resembling cocaine in action but said to be less toxic.

stove¹ (stōv). Preterit and past participle of *stave.*—**stove¹,** *v. t.*; *stoved, stoving.* [From *stove¹, pp.*] To stave or crush: often with *in*: as, "I'll *stove* in your old block-house like a rum puncheon" (Stevenson's "Treasure Island," xx.).

stove² (stōv), *n.* [ME. *stove*, prob. < MLG. or MD. *stove*, hot-room for sweating or bathing (D. *stoof*, stove or furnace), = OHG. *stuba*, hot-room (G. *stube*, room): cf. *stew¹*.] A hot-room or hothouse for sweating or bathing†; also, a heated sitting-room or bedroom†; also, a hothouse for plants; a heated chamber or box for some special purpose, as a drying-room, or a kiln for firing pottery; also, an apparatus, portable or fixed, and in many forms, for furnishing heat, as for comfort, cooking, or mechanical purposes, commonly by means of coal or other fuel burned in a closed chamber, but also by means of oil, gas, or electricity.—**stove²,** *v. t.*; *stoved, stoving.* To subject to the heat of a stove, hothouse, or heated chamber; also, to stew, as meat or vegetables (now Sc. and prov. Eng.); also, to fumigate with sulphur or the like; also, to heat with a stove or stoves, as a house.

stove-pipe (stōv'pīp), *n.* A pipe, as of sheet-metal, serving as the chimney of a stove or to connect a stove with a chimney-flue; also, a stovepipe hat (colloq.).—**stovepipe hat,** a tall silk hat. [Colloq.]

sto-ver (stō'vėr), *n.* [OF. *estover*: see *estovers*.] Winter fodder or litter for cattle.

stow (stō), *v. t.* [ME. *stowen*, < *stowe*, < AS. *stōw* = OFries. *stō*, a place; from the root of E. *stand*.] To place† or put†; lodge or quarter (obs. or rare); also, to put in a place or receptacle as for storage or reserve; place or arrange compactly, or pack; also, to fill (a place or receptacle) by packing (as, "the magazine of a pawnbroker, *stowed* with goods of every description": Scott's "Guy Mannering," xxxix.); also, of a place or receptacle, to afford room for; hold; also, to desist from (slang: as, "'*Stow* that,' cried Bendigo," Eden Phillpotts's "Red Redmaynes," vii.); also, specif., *naut.*, to place (cargo, etc.) in proper order in the hold or some other part of a ship; place (guns, oars, etc.) in the proper receptacles; furl (sails).—**to stow away,** to put away, as in a safe or convenient place or so as to be out of the way; sometimes, to put (a person) in a place of concealment. Also,

intransitively, to conceal one's self aboard a ship (or other conveyance), so as to obtain a free passage or to escape by stealth from a place.—**to stow down,** *naut.*, to put into the hold of a ship.—**stow'a-ble,** *a.* That may be stowed.—**stow'age** (-āj), *n.* The act or operation of stowing (as, "The *stowage* was clumsily done, and the vessel consequently crank": Poe's "MS. Found in a Bottle"); the state or manner of being stowed; also, room or accommodation for stowing something; a place in which something is or may be stowed; also, that which is stowed or to be stowed; also, a charge for stowing something.—**stow'a-way"**, *n.* One who conceals himself aboard a ship (or other conveyance), so as to obtain a free passage or to escape by stealth from a place.—**stow'er,** *n.*

strab-is-mom-e-ter (strab-iz-mom'e-tėr), *n.* [See *-meter.*] An instrument for measuring strabismus.

stra-bis-mus (strȧ-biz'mus), *n.* [NL., < Gr. στραβισμός, < στραβίζειν, to squint, < στραβός, oblique, squinting.] In *pathol.*, a disorder of vision due to the turning of one eye or both eyes from the normal position so that both cannot be directed at the same point or object at the same time; squint; cross-eye.—**stra-bis'mic,** *a.*

stra-bot-o-my (strȧ-bot'ọ-mi), *n.* [Gr. στραβός, oblique, squinting, + -τομία, < τέμνειν, cut.] In *surg.*, the operation of dividing one or more of the muscles of the eye for the cure of strabismus.

Strad (strad), *n.* Short for *Stradivarius.* [Colloq.]

strad-dle (strad'l), *v.*; *-dled, -dling.* [A freq. form connected with *stride.*] **I.** *intr.* To walk, stand, or sit with the legs wide apart (as, "The little courier *straddled* into the apartment": Irving's "Knickerbocker's New York," iii. 9); stand or sit astride; stand wide apart, as the legs; also, to take up or occupy an equivocal position in regard to something, or appear to favor both sides (colloq.: as, to *straddle* on the tariff question; "If Mr. Hill was going to speak at all, he was going to *straddle*," W. Churchill's "Coniston," ii. 15); in *poker*, to double the blind. **II.** *tr.* To spread (the legs) wide apart (as, "sitting on the floor, with the candlestick standing before him between his widely *straddled* legs": J. Conrad's "Rover," ii.); also, to walk, stand, or sit with one leg on each side of; stand or sit astride of (as, "Ingpen *straddled* the bicycle, with his left foot on one raised pedal and the other on the pavement": Arnold Bennett's "These Twain," v.); in general, to stand or lie across or on both sides of; also, to take up or occupy an equivocal position in regard to, or appear to favor both sides of (colloq.: as, to *straddle* a political question); in *poker*, to double (the blind).—**strad'dle,** *n.* The action or an act of straddling; the distance straddled over; also, a taking or holding of an equivocal or non-committal position (colloq.); in the stock-exchange, etc., a privilege consisting of a put and a call combined, giving the holder the right, at his option, either of delivering or of buying a certain amount of stock, etc., at a specified price, within a fixed time; in *poker*, a doubling of the blind.—**strad'dler,** *n.*

Strad-i-va-ri-us (strad-i-vā'ri-us), *n.* A violin or other stringed instrument made by Antonio Stradivari (Antonius Stradivarius) (about 1644–1737), of Cremona, Italy.

strafe (sträf or strāf), *v. t.*; *strafed, strafing.* [G. *strafen*, punish, chastise, much used in 1914 and following years in German maledictions directed against England.] To punish or chastise; bombard heavily (enemy lines, areas, etc.: as, "The Germans '*strafed*' this trench overnight," H. G. Wells's "Italy, France, and Britain at War," iii. 3); assail with gun-fire, shells, bombs, torpedoes, or the like; also, to utter maledictions upon. [Colloq.]—**strafe,** *n.* A strafing; a heavy bombardment, or other destructive assailing of the enemy, as in war. [Colloq.]—**straf'er,** *n.*

strag-gle (strag'l), *v. i.*; *-gled, -gling.* [Appar. a freq. form connected with ME. *straken*, move, go, perhaps related to E. *stretch.*] To wander about in a scattered fashion, as a number of persons or animals without a fixed common course; scatter from a road or a line of march; also, to wander away, as individuals, from a body (as of troops) pursuing a fixed common course; stray from the road, course, or line of march; also, to go, come, or travel in a scattered or rambling fashion (as, "Presently, down the hill, the servants appeared, *straggling* by twos and threes," H. G. Wells's "Tono-Bungay," i. 2. § 3; "The survivors

... *straggled* on to Langres, where they surrendered," Froude's "Cæsar," xiv.); in general, to wander, stray, or ramble; move, pass, come, etc., in an irregular, erratic, or random way (as, the pen or the writing *straggles* over the paper; "trusting to the faint gleams [of light] that *straggled* in from without," Amelia B. Edwards's "Thousand Miles up the Nile," xvi.); of plants, branches, etc., to spread in an irregular, rambling, or spindling manner; of a town, its houses, or any assemblage of parts, to extend irregularly in various directions, or without orderly and compact arrangement; of a road, river, etc., to wind irregularly.—**strag'gler**, *n.*—**strag'gling**, *p. a.* That straggles; wandering or straying (as, "any such casual accidental landing of *straggling* people from the main": Defoe's "Robinson Crusoe," i. 11); wandering apart from a line of march or a main body, as soldiers; spreading irregularly in growth, rambling, or spindling, as plants, etc.; extending or scattered irregularly over an area, as a village, houses, etc.; winding irregularly, as a road.—**strag'gling-ly**, *adv.*—**strag'gly**, *a.* Straggling; rambling; spreading or extending irregularly.

straight (strāt), *a.* [ME. *streigt*, *streiht*, orig. pp. of *strecchen*, E. *stretch*.] Stretched† or extended†; hence, having the linear form or uniform direction of a stretched string; of a line, lying evenly between its points, or, in other words, generated by a point moving constantly in the same direction; in general, without crooks, bends, or curvature (as, a *straight* path; a *straight* stick; *straight* hair; a *straight* nose; evenly formed or set (as, a *straight* floor; a *straight* back; *straight* shoulders; to hold the shoulders *straight*); direct, or leading or going directly to some point (as, a *straight* course; a *straight* aim, throw, hit, or ball); fig., without circumlocution, candid, or plain, as speaking or talk (colloq.: as, "I'm a bit doubtful of the piece — that's *straight!*" L. Merrick's "Conrad in Quest of His Youth," xiv.); straightforward, honest, honorable, or upright, as conduct, dealings, methods, persons, etc.; virtuous or chaste, as a woman; reliable, as reports, information, etc. (colloq.); right or correct, as reasoning, thinking, a thinker, etc.; in the proper order or condition (as, to set a room *straight*; our accounts are *straight*; to keep a *straight* face, to refrain from smiling); also, continuous or unbroken (as, in *straight* succession; a *straight* flush, in *poker*, a sequence of five cards of the same suit); thoroughgoing or unreserved (as, a *straight* Republican; to vote a *straight* party ticket, to vote for all of the party candidates); unmodified or unaltered (as, to play *straight* whist; a *straight* comedy); undiluted, as whisky (colloq.).—**straight angle**, a right angle†; also, an angle of 180°.—**straight**, *n.* The condition of being straight (as, to be out of the *straight*); a straight form or position; a straight line; also, a straight part, as of a race-course; in *poker*, a sequence of five cards of various suits.—**straight**, *adv.* In a straight line, or without crookedness, bending, or curving (as, to walk *straight*); in a straight or even form or position (as, to cut pieces *straight*; to sit *straight*; pictures hung *straight*); in a straight or direct course to some point, or directly (as, to go *straight* to a place or person; to look *straight* at one); fig., without circumlocution (often with *out*); straightforwardly, honestly, honorably, or virtuously (as, to go *straight*; "She intended to live *straight* for the future," Du Maurier's "Trilby," iii.); also, in a continuous course (as, to keep *straight* on); without delay, immediately, or straightway (archaic, except as followed by *off* or *away*: as, "Then *straight* she called her maidens," W. Morris's "Jason," viii. 5; "Your ma went *straight* off to see what was needed," Louisa M. Alcott's "Little Women," i. 2); also, without qualification of any kind (as, cigars selling at ten cents *straight*, that is, at ten cents each regardless of the number purchased).—**straight**, *v. t.* To straighten. [Now chiefly prov.]

straight-a-way (strāt'a̠-wā″). **I.** *a.* Straight onward, without turn or curve, as a course in horse-racing or yacht-racing. **II.** *n.* A straightaway course for racing, or a race over such a course.

straight=edge (strāt'ej), *n.* A bar or strip of wood or metal, of various sizes, having at least one edge of sufficiently reliable straightness, for use in obtaining or testing straight lines, plane surfaces, etc.

straight-en (strā'tn), *v.* **I.** *tr.* To make straight in direction, form, or position (as, to *straighten* crooked lines); to *straighten* a bent pin; to *straighten* the shoulders); fig., to make straight in character or conduct (as, "If a person could not be kept straight by these things, there was nothing that could *straighten* him": S. Butler's "Erewhon," xvii.); also, to set straight or in due order or condition (as, to *straighten* one's hair or dress; to *straighten* up a room); bring (*out*) of a confused or troublesome state (as, to *straighten* out accounts; to *straighten* out the difficulties in a case). **II.** *intr.* To become straight.—**straight'en-er**, *n.*

straight-for-ward (strāt'fôr′wạrd). **I.** *adv.* Straight forward; directly or continuously forward: usually as two words. **II.** *a.* Going or directed straight forward (as, a *straightforward* path or glance); fig., proceeding without circumlocution, roundaboutness, or indirection, or direct (as, "George was a *straightforward* soul . . . 'See here!' he said. 'Are you engaged to anybody?'" Tarkington's "Magnificent Ambersons," vi.); also, free from crookedness or deceit, or honest (as, to be *straightforward* in all one's dealings; "It's honest *straightforward* work," W. B. Maxwell's "In Cotton Wool," v.).—**straight'for'ward-ly**, *adv.*—**straight'for'ward-ness**, *n.*

straight-ly (strāt'li), *adv.* In a straight manner; straight.—**straight'ness**, *n.*

straight=out (strāt'out′), *a.* Thoroughgoing; out-and-out; straight: as, a *straight-out* Republican. [Chiefly U. S.]

straight-way (strāt'wā), *adv.* By a straight or direct way†; also, immediately, or at once (as, "They astound me . . . but *straightway* I forget my astonishment": Gissing's "Private Papers of Henry Ryecroft," iii. 9).

strain[1] (strān), *n.* [AS. *strēon*, *gestrēon*, gain, acquisition, begetting, progeny.] Begetting† or procreation†; also, offspring or progeny (obs. or archaic); also, ancestry or descent (as, a man of noble *strain*); the body of descendants of a common ancestor, as a family, stock, or race; any of the different lines of ancestry united in a family or an individual (as, "a youth . . . built as if he had come of two very different *strains*, one sturdy, the other wiry and light": Galsworthy's "Dark Flower," i. 1); an admixture of some family or racial element (as, "His son had through his mother a strong *strain* of the dark Irish in his composition": H. G. Wells's "Mr. Britling," i. 4. § 6); also, a group of animals or plants equivalent to, or forming a part of, a race, breed, or variety; an artificial variety, or a slight variation from a given breed or stock, of a domestic animal (as, "Bullstone bred a famous *strain* of red Irish terriers": Eden Phillpotts's "Children of Men," Prologue, i.); a group of cultivated plants distinguished from other plants of the race to which it belongs by some intrinsic quality, such as a tendency to yield heavily; also, hereditary or natural character or disposition; a hereditary tendency or trait (as, a *strain* of insanity in a family; "In Mr. Brooke the hereditary *strain* of Puritan energy was clearly in abeyance," George Eliot's "Middlemarch," i.); an element in one's make-up (as, to have a *strain* of melancholy); a streak or trace; also, a kind or sort (as, "His ambition was of a noble and generous *strain*": Burke's "American Taxation").

strain[2] (strān), *v. t.* [OF. *estreindre* (F. *étreindre*), < L. *stringere* (pp. *strictus*), draw tight: see *string*, and cf. *strait*, *strict*, and *stringent*.] To draw tight or taut, as a line; stretch; bring to a state of tension; stretch to the utmost tension (often fig.: as, to *strain* every nerve to accomplish something); exert to the utmost (as, "The remark had set us all on the alert, *straining* ears and eyes": Stevenson's "Treasure Island," xxi.); hence, to impair, injure, or weaken by stretching or overexertion, as a muscle or tendon; imperil the strength of by subjecting to too great stress; cause mechanical deformation in (a body or structure) as the result of stress; fig., to stretch or force beyond the proper point or limit (as, to *strain* one's authority; to *strain* the meaning of a word; "In one point I *strained* the case against your husband," S. J. Weyman's "Gentleman of France," xxi.); make excessive demands upon, or tax severely (resources, credit, etc.: as, "This poor man . . . has *strained* all his slender means to defend my person," Scott's "Legend of Montrose," xvi.); also, to bind tightly, as with bands or bonds†; attach firmly (obs. or archaic); clasp tightly in the arms, the hand, etc. (now chiefly as in 'to strain a person to one' or 'to one's heart,' or the like); constrict or compress painfully (obs. or archaic); afflict† or distress†; restrain†; constrain, as to a course of action†; urge (a thing)†; also, to squeeze out by or as by pressure†; extort, as by compulsion† (as, "The quality of mercy is not *strain'd*": Shakspere's "Merchant of Venice," iv. 1. 184); also, to press or pass (liquid matter) through a filter, colander, cloth, or the like, in order to separate the clear liquid from the denser or solid constituents (as, "The waters, impregnated with particles of gold, are carefully *strained* through sheep-skins": Gibbon's "Decline and Fall of the Roman Empire," xlii.); draw off (clear liquid) or take out (solid particles, etc.) from liquid matter by passing through a filter, colander, cloth, or the like; also, to play upon (an instrument)†; use (the voice) in singing†; utter in song†.—**to strain a point**, to exceed the proper or usual limit, as of procedure; go beyond the limit of one's obligation, duty, authority, or the like.—**to strain courtesy**, to insist too much on the observance of courtesy; stand too much upon form or ceremony; also, to act with less than due courtesy. [Archaic.]—**strain²**, *v. i.* To exert a stretching force; pull forcibly (as, a dog *straining* at a leash); stretch one's muscles, etc., to the utmost; make violent physical efforts; use one's utmost endeavors, or strive hard (as, "He had been *straining* for a glimpse of the dark head": Mrs. Wharton's "Ethan Frome," i.); also, to be subjected to tension or stress; suffer strain; also, to filter, percolate, or ooze (as, "The bottom of the basin . . . would not hold the water, which *strained* through the earth": Smollett's "Humphry Clinker," Sept. 30); trickle or flow; also, to sing†.—**to strain at a gnat and swallow a camel.** See under *gnat*.—**strain²**, *n.* A forcible straining or stretching of something; a force tending to pull a thing asunder; more broadly, any force or pressure tending to alter shape, cause fracture, etc.; stress; also, the condition of being strained or stretched; an injury to a muscle, tendon, etc., due to excessive tension or use; a sprain; an injury to or a distortion of any body or structure resulting from stress (in *mech.*, the deformation, or change of shape or dimensions, of a body, resulting from mechanical stress); also, strong muscular or physical effort, or great or excessive effort of any kind (as, "Every ear at *strain* Some sign of things that were to be to gain": W. Morris's "Earthly Paradise," November, The Lovers of Gudrun); extreme or excessive effort at or striving after some object or effect (as, "false taste and perpetual *strain* at something unexpected and paradoxical": Hallam's "Literature of Europe," iv. 7. § 5); also, in general, severe, trying, or wearing pressure or effect (as, to relieve *strain* on horses by lightening a load; to stand the *strain* of sleepless nights; to break down under the *strain* of heavy duties; relations that will not bear much further *strain*); trying or exhausting mental pressure or experience (as, "She must have taken alarm from the look of *strain* on his face": Galsworthy's "Dark Flower," iii. 10); a severe demand or tax, or something that makes such a demand, on powers, resources, feelings, a person, etc. (as, a *strain* on one's pocket-book; a *strain* on one's credulity or good nature; "They say a first speech is a great *strain*," Galsworthy's "Patrician," ii. 4); also, a particular degree, height, or pitch attained (now rare: as, a high *strain* of generosity); also, a passage of music or song as rendered or heard (in *sing.* or *pl.*, often collective *pl.*: as, "Canst thou . . . touch thy instrument a *strain* or two?" Shakspere's "Julius Cæsar," iv. 3. 257; "Thyrsis? whose artful *strains* have oft delay'd The huddling brook to hear his madrigal," Milton's "Comus," 494; to listen to the *strains* of the nightingale); a melody, tune, or song (as, "There is a hymn before the service, a wild *strain*, a remnant . . . of some pre-Reformation litany": S. Butler's "Way of All Flesh," xiv.); fig., a passage or piece of poetry (as, the *strains* of Homer; "Matthew [Prior] . . . Smooth'd and refin'd the meanest *strains*," Cowper's "Epistle to Robert Lloyd," 74); a flow or burst of language, eloquence, etc.; also, tone, style, or spirit in expression (as, to speak or write in a friendly, humorous, or moralizing *strain*; "Through many pages . . . Count Rumford continues in this *strain* to expound the ways and intentions of the Almighty," Tyndall's "Forms of Water," § 46); in *music*, a section of a piece of music which is more or less complete in itself.

strained (strānd), *p. a.* Subjected to strain or tension; ex-

erted to the utmost or an abnormal degree, as the nerves; injured by stretching or overexertion, as muscles, etc.; fig., affected or produced by effort, forced, or not natural or spontaneous (as, *strained* mirth); forced beyond the proper point or limit (as, to put a *strained* construction upon a person's words); subjected to a strain or severe pressure, demand, or tax (as, *strained* relations); suffering from or showing mental strain (as, a *strained* look); also, subjected to straining by means of a filter, colander, or the like.

strain-er (strā′ner), *n.* One who or that which strains; esp., a filter, colander, cloth, or the like for straining liquids.

strain-ing (strā′ning) *n.* The act of one who or that which strains.—**strain′ing=arch**, *n.* In *arch.*, an arch-like structure, as a flying buttress, designed to resist pressure like a strut.—**strain′ing=beam**, *n.* In *arch.*, a short piece of timber in a truss, for holding in place the ends of struts, etc.; esp., a horizontal beam between the heads of two queen-posts. Also **strain′ing=piece**.

strait (strāt). [OF. *estreit* (F. *étroit*), < L. *strictus*, pp. of *stringere*, draw tight: see *strain²*, and cf. *strict*.] **I.** *a.* Tight, as a knot, a garment, etc. (now chiefly prov.: cf. *strait-jacket*); also, narrow, or of little width (archaic or literary: as, "*Strait* is the gate, and narrow is the way, which leadeth unto life," Mat. vii. 14; "*strait* passes . . . overhung by high walls of rock," Carlyle's "Sartor Resartus," ii. 6); limited in space, or affording little room, as a place, bounds, etc. (archaic or literary: as, "The hunting and pasture grounds were too *strait* for the numbers crowded into them," Froude's "Cæsar," v.); straitened, as means or circumstances†; stingy†; also, close or intimate, as friendship or alliance (archaic); also, strict in requirements, obligations, principles, etc. (archaic: as, *strait* vows; "the most *straitest* sect of our religion," Acts, xxvi. 5); strictly or closely maintained, as imprisonment, guard, etc. (archaic); rigorous†, severe†, or harsh†. **II.** *n.* A narrow passage, space, or area (as, "It was in a narrow *strait*, between two . . . woods, that we pitched our little camp," Defoe's "Robinson Crusoe," ii. 15: obs. or archaic in general sense); a narrow passage of water connecting two large bodies of water (often in *pl.* with sense of *sing.*: as, the *Strait* or *Straits* of Malacca, whence the name of the adjacent 'Straits Settlements'); an isthmus (archaic); a narrow passage in the body (as, the *straits* of the pelvis, the two openings, superior and inferior, forming respectively the inlet and the outlet of the cavity); fig., *pl.*, narrow limits† (as, "to give them some larger scope and not to close them up in these *straits*": Hooker's "Ecclesiastical Polity," iii. 2. 2); also, *sing.*, a position of difficulty, distress, or need (as, "In this *strait* of life how he shrinks from them both!" Mrs. H. Ward's "Robert Elsmere," xxvii.: now infrequent in *sing.*); *pl.*, embarrassing or distressing circumstances (as, to be reduced to desperate *straits*; "In life's great *straits* and mighty griefs, ye feel but one sorrow," Mrs. Stowe's "Uncle Tom's Cabin," v.); often, pecuniary or financial difficulties (as, a house reported to be in *straits*).—**strait**, *adv.* Tightly (now chiefly prov.: cf. *strait-laced*); strictly†; rigorously†.

strait-en (strā′tn), *v.* **I.** *tr.* To draw tight†; also, to make strait or narrow (archaic or literary); confine within narrow limits (archaic); restrict in range, extent, amount, pecuniary means, etc.; hamper by insufficiency of something specified, now esp. money (with *for*: as, "They had all plantations . . . and were *straitened* for nothing so much as servants," Defoe's "Robinson Crusoe," i. 3; "Requesens was more than ever *straitened* for funds," Motley's "Dutch Republic," iv. 3); reduce to straits, esp. pecuniary or financial straits. **II.** *intr.* To become strait or narrow. [Archaic or literary.] —**strait′ened**, *p. a.* Drawn tight†; also, narrowed or contracted (archaic); narrowly confined (archaic); limited or reduced, esp. to insufficiency (as, *straitened* means, income, or circumstances); hampered by insufficiency of means; in straits.

strait=jack-et (strāt′jak″et), *n.* A kind of jacket or coat of strong material for confining violent lunatics or other persons, the arms being made fast within the jacket or within very long sleeves whose ends are secured.

strait=laced (strāt′lāst), *a.* Tightly laced, or wearing tightly laced garments (obs. or archaic); fig., excessively strict or rigid as to matters of conduct or morality (as, "I'm

---

(variable) ḍ as d or j, ş as s or sh, ṭ as t or ch, ẓ as z or zh; o, F. cloche; ü, F. menu; ch, Sc. loch; ṅ, F. bonbon; ′, primary accent; ″, secondary accent; †, obsolete; <, from; +, and; =, equals. See also lists at beginning of book.

not *strait-laced*, but I tell you we got to have decent women in our schools": Sinclair Lewis's "Main Street," xxxii.); narrowly scrupulous; puritanic; prudish.—**strait'=laced''=ness,** *n.*

strait-ly (strāt'li), *adv.* In a strait manner.—**strait'ness,** *n.*

strait=waist-coat (strāt'wāst''kōt), *n.* Same as *strait-jacket.*

strake (strāk), *n.* [ME. *strake,* strip of iron for a wheel, also streak: cf. *streak.*] A strip of iron used as a section of the rim of a cart-wheel; also, a streak or stripe (now prov. Eng. and Sc.); *naut.,* one of the continuous longitudinal lines or breadths of planking or plates on the side or bottom of a vessel.

stram (stram), *v. i.*; *strammed, stramming.* [Origin obscure.] To walk with ungraceful strides; tramp: as, "Don't go *stramming* off another afternoon" (Mrs. Stowe's "Oldtown Folks," xliii.). [Local, U. S.]—**stram,** *n.* A long, hard walk; a tramp. [Local, U. S.]

stra-mash (strạ-mash' or stram'ạsh), *n.* [Origin obscure.] A smash or crash; a noise, uproar, or disturbance. [Sc. and north. Eng.]

stra-min-e-ous (strạ-min'ē-us), *a.* [L. *stramineus,* < *stramen,* straw.] Consisting of or pertaining to straw; straw-like; straw-colored.

stra-mo-ni-um (strạ-mō'ni-um), *n.* [NL.; origin uncertain.] The jimson-weed, *Datura stramonium,* which yields a narcotic principle; the dried leaves of this plant, used in medicine as an analgesic, antispasmodic, etc.; also, some other species of *Datura,* as *D. tatula.*

strand[1] (strand), *n.* [AS. *strand* = D. and G. *strand* = Icel. *strönd* (*strand-*), strand, shore.] The land bordering the sea or ocean, or, formerly, a river (whence the name of the Strand in London, a street near the north bank of the Thames River); the shore: as, "Far in the Northern Land, By the wild Baltic's *strand*" (Longfellow's "Skeleton in Armor," 26). [Now chiefly poetic or prov.]—**strand**[1], *v.* I. *tr.* To drive aground on a shore, esp. of the sea, as a ship, a fish, etc.; fig. (usually in the passive), to bring into a position of helplessness, isolation, or the like; leave without resources. II. *intr.* To be driven or run ashore, as a ship, etc. (as, "You *stranding* just on that spot of the whole coast was my bad luck": J. Conrad's "Rescue," i. 2); run aground; fig., to become halted in difficulties.

strand[2] (strand), *n.* [ME. *strond;* origin uncertain.] A number of yarns or threads which together constitute one of the parts which are twisted together to form a rope, cord, or the like (as, a rope of three *strands*); a similar part of a wire rope; hence, a thread or the texture of anything, as cloth; a tress of hair; a fiber or filament, as in animal or plant tissue; a string of pearls, beads, etc.—**strand**[2], *v. t.* To break one or more of the strands of (a rope); also, to form (a rope, etc.) by the union or twisting of strands.—**strand'ed,** *a.* Composed of strands, esp. of a specified number of strands: as, a three-*stranded* rope.

strange (strānj), *a.*; compar. *stranger,* superl. *strangest.* [OF. *estrange* (F. *étrange*), < L. *extraneus,* that is without, foreign: see *extraneous.*] Foreign, as a country or the people or things belonging to it (archaic); situated, belonging, or coming from, outside of one's own or a particular locality or neighborhood (as, to move to a *strange* place; *strange* visitors); hence, outside of one's previous experience, hitherto unknown, or unfamiliar (as, "I do hate to be chucked in the dark aboard a *strange* ship. I wonder where they keep their fresh water," J. Conrad's "Rescue," iv. 2; *strange* faces; the writing is *strange* to me); unusual, singular, extraordinary, or curious (as, a *strange* accident, story, or notion; a *strange* practice); odd; queer; surprising; unaccountable; unusually great (now prov. Eng.); also, out of one's natural environment (as, to be or feel *strange* in a place); unacquainted; unaccustomed (*to*) or inexperienced (*at*); also, distant or reserved (now prov. Eng.); coy†, reluctant†, or unwilling†.—**strange to say** (or **relate** or **tell**), strange as the thing is for one to say (or relate or tell): used parenthetically, as, 'and then, *strange to say,* the claims were withdrawn.'—**strange woman,** a harlot: see Prov. xxiii. 27. [Archaic.]—**strange,** *adv.* In a strange manner: as, to act *strange.* [Colloq. or prov.]—**strange'ly,** *adv.*—**strange'ness,** *n.*

stran-ger (strān'jèr), *n.* [OF. *estrangier* (F. *étranger*),

< *estrange,* E. *strange.*] A foreigner or alien (archaic: as, "The *strangers* . . . were suffered to depart the kingdom," Strype's "Memorials of Cranmer," iii. 4); a newcomer in a place or locality, esp. one that is not yet known, or well known (used of a person, or sometimes a ship, an animal, etc.: as, "He and his crew . . . were soon alongside of the *stranger,*" H. Melville's "Moby-Dick," c.); hence, a person whose face is unfamiliar to one, or whose name, character, antecedents, etc., are unknown; a person with whom one has, or has hitherto had, no personal acquaintance (as, "It was highly improper for young women to dance with *strangers* at any public assembly": Miss Burney's "Evelina," xiii.); sometimes, a person with whom one has no longer any personal acquaintance (as, "Those who knew me best have suddenly become *strangers*": W. H. Hudson's "Purple Land," viii.); also, an outsider, as with reference to a family, society, or other associated body; a visitor or guest, as not belonging to the household; something alien, as to a thing†; also, a person or thing that is new or unaccustomed (*to*: as, to be no *stranger* to a place or to its people, ways, etc.; a *stranger* to hard work; a floor long a *stranger* to the broom); also, something popularly supposed to betoken the coming of a stranger or visitor, as a bit of tea-leaf floating in tea; a flake of soot hanging on the bar of a grate, or a knot in a candle-wick that causes guttering; also, in *law,* one not privy or party to an act, proceeding, etc.—**little stranger,** a baby recently arrived or born, as in a family: as, "A man generally hates the unwelcome *little stranger* for the first twelve months" (S. Butler's "Erewhon," xx.).

stran-gle (strang'gl), *v.*; *-gled, -gling.* [OF. *estrangler* (F. *étrangler*), < L. *strangulare,* < Gr. στραγγαλᾶν, strangle, < στραγγάλη, halter: see *string.*] I. *tr.* To kill by compression of the windpipe, as by means of a cord passed round the neck; also, to kill by stopping the breath in any manner; choke; stifle; suffocate; hence, to prevent the continuance, growth, rise, or action of, or suppress (as, "*Strangle* such thoughts as these," Shakspere's "Winter's Tale," iv. 4. 47; "He *strangled* an oath," L. Merrick's "House of Lynch," x.). II. *intr.* To be strangled; be choked, stifled, or suffocated.—**stran'gle,** *n.* The act of strangling†; also, a stranglehold.—**stran'gle=hold,** *n.* In *wrestling,* a hold by which the adversary's breathing is stopped or hampered. Also fig.—**stran'gler,** *n.*—**stran'gles,** *n.* [Orig. pl. of *strangle, n.*] An infectious febrile disease of equine animals, characterized by catarrh of the upper air-passages and suppuration of the submaxillary and other lymphatic glands; distemper.

stran-gu-late (strang'gū-lāt), *v. t.*; *-lated, -lating.* [L. *strangulatus,* pp. of *strangulare,* E. *strangle.*] To strangle (a person or animal); in *pathol.* and *surg.,* to compress or constrict (a duct, vessel, etc.) so as to prevent circulation or suppress function; also, to remove (a growth) by constricting with a ligature.—**stran'gu-lat-ed** (-lā-ted), *p. a.* In *pathol.* and *surg.,* compressed or constricted so as to prevent circulation or suppress function (as, a *strangulated* hernia, one in which the circulation in the protruded part is arrested); in *bot.,* irregularly contracted and expanded, as a stem.—**stran-gu-la'tion** (-lā'shọn), *n.* [L. *strangulatio(n-).*] The act of strangling, or the state of being strangled; a sudden and violent compression of the windpipe in such a manner as to prevent the passage of air and thereby suspend respiration, and, if continued, destroy life; in *pathol.* and *surg.,* the act of strangulating; a compression or constriction of a part so as to prevent circulation or suppress function; the removal of a growth by constricting with a ligature.

stran-gu-ry (strang'gū-ri), *n.* [L. *stranguria,* < Gr. στραγγουρία, < στράγξ (στραγγ-), a drop squeezed out, + οὖρον, urine.] In *pathol.,* a condition of the urinary organs in which the urine is emitted with great difficulty and pain, drop by drop.—**stran-gu-ri-ous** (strang-gū'ri-us), *a.*

strap (strap), *n.* [Var. of *strop.*] A narrow strip of leather, or of some other flexible material, used for any of various purposes; such a strip used to surround a thing and hold it together or fasten something to it, or for some other form of fastening, and often fitted with a buckle or the like, allowing of more or less close adjustment; a short band formerly attached to the bottom of each leg of a pair of trousers, passing from side to side under the boot; a looped band, as one attached to the top of a boot or shoe to draw it on by, or one to be grasped in order to steady one's self in a moving vehicle; a belt used to communicate motion in machinery; a strop for a razor; a strip of leather or other material used for flogging (as, "If I did ill he used the *strap* with little mercy": Weir Mitchell's "Hugh Wynne," ii.); in general, a strip, band, or long, narrow piece or object; a band of material applied in dressmaking, tailoring, etc., along a seam or edge or otherwise; a strap-like ornament, as a shoulder-strap; a narrow band of iron or other metal, in the form of a plate, loop, or ring, for fastening a thing in position, holding parts together, etc.; also, credit or trust (slang); *naut.*, a piece of rope with the ends spliced together, or a band of some other material, used as a fastening, etc.; a band of rope, iron, etc., fastened round a block, deadeye, or the like; in *bot.*, a ligula.—**strap**, *v. t.*; strapped, strapping. To fasten or secure with a strap or straps (as, "This servant had a good-sized portmanteau *strapped* on his horse": Stevenson's "Kidnapped," xvii.); furnish with a strap or straps; also, to fasten (a thing) around something in the manner of a strap; also, to sharpen on a strap or strop; also, to beat or flog with a strap (as, "Many and many a time had his own father . . . *strapped* and beaten him": Thackeray's "Newcomes," ii.).—**strap′hang′er**, *n.* A passenger who, for want of a seat in an overfull street-car or the like, has to cling for support to a strap suspended from above. [Colloq.]—**strap′-hinge**, *n.* A hinge with a long band of metal on each side, by which it is secured to a door and a post or the like.

strap-pa-do (stra-pā′dō), *n.*; pl. *-does* (-dōz). [= F. *estrapade*, < It. *strappata*, < *strappare*, pull; from Teut.] A form of punishment or torture in which the victim, attached to a rope (sometimes by his wrists, tied behind his back), was raised to a height and suddenly let fall almost to the ground; also, the instrument used for this purpose.—**strap-pa′do**, *v. t.*; *-doed, -doing.* To punish or torture with the strappado.

strapped (strapt), *p. a.* [See *strap.*] Fastened or provided with straps; finished with bands of cloth, etc., as seams or garments; also, pecuniarily embarrassed, or out of money (slang: as, "His dad said you could be a millionaire, and then you keep us *strapped* like this," Sinclair Lewis's "Arrowsmith," xiii.).—**strap′per**, *n.* One who or that which straps; also, a tall, robust person (colloq.).—**strap′ping**, *p. a.* Tall and robust (as, "Nicholas Snowe . . . with his three tall comely daughters, *strapping* girls": Blackmore's "Lorna Doone," xiii.); large and strongly built; in general, very large of its kind; whopping. [Colloq.]

strass (stras), *n.* [G. *strass*, from the name of the (German) inventor, Josef *Strasser*.] A brilliant, heavy glass used for making artificial gems; paste.

stra-ta (strā′tä), *n.* Plural of *stratum.*

strat-a-gem (strat′ä-jem), *n.* [F. *stratagème*, < L. *strategema*, < Gr. στρατήγημα, piece of generalship, stratagem, < στρατηγεῖν, act as general, < στρατηγός, general: see *strategy.*] A piece of generalship; an artifice in war; a plan, scheme, or trick for deceiving the enemy (as, "The Moors suspected some *stratagem* on the part of the Christians, and kept quietly within their walls": Irving's "Conquest of Granada," xcv.); in general, an artifice, ruse, or trick; also, the use of artifice to deceive or outwit an adversary or obtain any advantage (as, "Edward I . . . seized Berwick by *stratagem*": Jane Porter's "Scottish Chiefs," i.).

stra-tal (strā′tạl), *a.* Pertaining to a stratum or to strata.

strat-e-get-ic (strat-ē-jet′ik), *a.* Same as *strategic.*

stra-teg-ic (strạ-tej′ik or -tē′jik), *a.* [F. *stratégique*, < Gr. στρατηγικός, pertaining to a general, < στρατηγός, general: see *strategy.*] Pertaining to, characterized by, or of the nature of strategy (as, *strategic* movements); important in strategy (as, a *strategic* point, a point or position the occupation of which is of great military importance). Also **stra-teg′i-cal.—stra-teg′i-cal-ly**, *adv.*—**stra-teg′ics**, *n.* Strategy.

strat-e-gist (strat′ē-jist), *n.* One versed in strategy.

strat-e-gy (strat′ē-ji), *n.* [F. *stratégie*, < Gr. στρατηγία, office of general, generalship, < στρατηγός, general, < στρατός, army, + ἄγειν, lead.] Generalship; the science or art of combining and employing the means which the different branches of the art of war afford, for the purpose of planning and directing great military movements and operations (*strategy* and *tactics* being usually fairly distinct, the former dealing rather with the planning and carrying out of projects which involve the movements of forces, etc., the latter rather with the actual processes of moving, or the mere handling, of forces); the use, or a particular use, of this science or art; fig., the method of conducting operations, esp. by the aid of maneuvering or stratagem (as, "Mr. Direck was beginning to master the simple *strategy* of the sport [hockey]": H. G. Wells's "Mr. Britling," i. 3. § 4); skilful management in getting the better of an adversary or attaining an end.

strath (strath), *n.* [Gael. *srath.*] A wide valley: as, *Strath Spey* (the valley of the Spey River, in Scotland). [Sc.]

strath-spey (strath-spā′), *n.* [From *Strath Spey:* see *strath,* def.] A Scotch dance resembling the reel but slower and marked by sudden jerks (as, "Nor would my footstep spring more gay In courtly dance than blithe *strathspey*": Scott's "Lady of the Lake," ii. 11); also, the music for it.

stra-tic-u-late (strạ-tik′ū-lāt), *a.* [Dim. < *stratum.*] Arranged in thin strata or layers, as an agate.—**stra-tic-u-la′tion** (-lā′shon), *n.*

strat-i-fi-ca-tion (strat″i-fi-kā′shon), *n.* The act of stratifying; stratified state or appearance; in *geol.*, the formation of strata; deposition or occurrence in strata; also, a stratum.

strat-i-form (strat′i-fôrm), *a.* [See *stratum* and *-form.*] Forming a stratum or layer; arranged in strata; in *anat.*, not-

Stratification.

ing a cartilage occurring in thin layers in bones.

strat-i-fy (strat′i-fī), *v.*; *-fied, -fying.* [F. *stratifier,* < NL. *stratum* (see *stratum*) + L. *facere,* make.] **I.** *tr.* To form in strata or layers; in *geol.*, to deposit (sediment, etc.) in layers; form strata. **II.** *intr.* To form strata.

stra-tig-ra-phy (strạ-tig′rạ-fi), *n.* [See *stratum* and *-graphy.*] That branch of geology dealing with the order, etc., of strata; also, arrangement of strata.—**stra-tig′ra-pher**, *n.*—**strat-i-graph-ic, strat-i-graph-i-cal** (strat-i-graf′ik, -i-kạl), *a.*—**strat-i-graph′i-cal-ly**, *adv.*

stra-toc-ra-cy (strạ-tok′rạ-si), *n.* [= F. *stratocratie,* < Gr. στρατός, army, + -κρατία, < κρατεῖν, rule.] A form of government in which the army exercises the ruling power.

stra-to=cu-mu-lus (strā-tō-kū′mū-lus), *n.* [See *stratus* and *cumulus.*] A cloud consisting of large, dark, rounded masses, often covering the sky, esp. in winter.

stra-tog-ra-phy (strạ-tog′rạ-fi), *n.* [F. *stratographie,* < Gr. στρατός, army, + -γραφία, < γράφειν, write.] The description of armies or of whatever pertains to them.

stra-to-lin-er (strā′tō-lī-nėr), *n.* [(sub)*strato*(sphere) + *liner.*] A trademark name for any of certain multimotored commercial aircraft operated at high altitudes; commonly, a plane of this type fitted with air-pressure adjusting apparatus.—**stra′to-lin-er**, *a.* [Proprietary.]

stra-tose (strā′tōs), *a.* In *bot.*, arranged in strata or layers.

stra-to-sphere (strā′tō-sfēr), *n.* [See *stratum* and *sphere.*] A layer of the atmosphere, some distance above the surface of the earth (about 7 miles in middle latitudes), within which the temperature ceases to fall with increasing altitude (as in the troposphere below), but at first rises and then remains approximately constant.

stra-tum (strā′tum), *n.*; pl. *-ta* (-tä) or *-tums.* [NL. use of L. *stratum,* bed-covering, prop. neut. of *stratus,* pp. of *sternere,* spread out: see *strew,* and cf. *consternation, prostrate, stratus,* and *street.*] A layer of material, formed either naturally or artificially, often one of a number of parallel layers placed one upon another; also, one of any group of superposed layers, levels, or the like; fig., one of a number of portions of some body, mass, or the like, likened to layers or levels; a level or grade of a people or population with reference to social position or education (as, "They [children] proclaimed instantaneously the social *stratum* of their parents," L. Merrick's "Conrad in Quest of His Youth," vi.; the lowest *stratum* of society); in *geol.*, a bed of one kind of sedimentary rock or earth, usually consisting of a series of layers representing continuous periods of deposition; in *biol.*, a layer of tissue; a lamella.

stra-tus (strā'tus), *n.* [NL. use of L. *stratus*, a spreading out, a cover or spread, < *sternere*: see *stratum*.] A continuous horizontal sheet of cloud, usually of uniform thickness and comparatively low altitude.

Stratus.

stra-vaig (strạ-vāg'), *v. i.* [F. *extravaguer*, stray, wander, < ML. *extravagari*: see *extravagate*.] To wander about idly or aimlessly. [Sc. and north. Eng.]—**stra-vaig'er**, *n.*

straw[1] (strā), *n.* [AS. *strēaw* = D. *stroo* = G. *stroh* = Icel. *strā*, straw; from the root of E. *strew*.] The stalks or stems of certain species of grain, chiefly wheat, rye, oats, and barley, esp. after drying and threshing, used as litter or fodder, as filling for beds, as material for making hats, etc., and for various other purposes; also, the stalks or stems of certain other plants, as the pea and the buckwheat; also, the stalks or stems of wheat or the like, or the stalks, leaves, or other parts of various plants, plaited or woven to form a material for hats and bonnets; a hat or bonnet made of such material; also, a single stalk or stem of grain or the like, esp. when dry; a piece of such a stem; a piece of hollow plant-stem (esp. of wheat), or some substitute for it, used in sucking up beverages, etc.; a musical pipe of straw† (as, "when shepherds pipe on oaten *straws*": Shakspere's "Love's Labour's Lost," v. 2. 913); any bit or particle of straw or chaff, often mentioned as being of trifling value or consequence (as, "He . . . did not care two *straws* whether I was shocked or not": S. Butler's "Way of All Flesh," li.); also, something resembling a straw; a long, slender needle; a slender kind of clay pipe.—**last straw**, fig., the last of a number of burdens, annoyances, etc., and the one that finally brings about a collapse, outbreak, or the like (with allusion to the proverbial last straw which breaks the camel's back): as, "This letter of the squire's, with its imperious demands upon the tired irritable brain, was the *last straw*" (Mrs. H. Ward's "Robert Elsmere," xxv.).—**man of straw.** See under *man*, *n.*—**straw**[1], *a.* Of or pertaining to straw or straws; made or composed of straw; also, of little value or consequence; worthless; sham; fictitious.—**straw bail**, bail furnished by an irresponsible person, that is, a person not possessing the property he pretends to have.—**straw vote**, an unofficial vote taken, as at a casual gathering or in a particular district, to obtain some indication of the general drift of opinion (as if by straws showing which way the wind blows).

straw[2] (strā), *v. t.* Same as *strew*. [Archaic or prov.]

straw-ber-ry (strā'ber"i), *n.*; pl. *-berries* (-iz). [AS. *strēaw-berige*, < *strēaw*, straw, + *berige*, berry.] The fruit of any of the stemless herbs constituting the rosaceous genus *Fragaria*, consisting of an enlarged fleshy receptacle bearing achenes on its exterior; also, the plant bearing the fruit.—**crushed strawberry.** See under *crush*, *v. t.*—**wild strawberry.** See *potentilla*.—**straw'ber-ry=bass'**, *n.* Same as *calico-bass.*—**straw'ber-ry=bush**, *n.* An American celastraceous shrub, *Euonymus americanus*, with crimson pods, and

Strawberry (*Fragaria vesca*).

seeds with a scarlet aril; also, the wahoo, *E. atropurpureus.*—**straw'ber-ry=finch**, *n.* The amadavat.—**straw'ber-ry=leaves**, *n. pl.* The trifoliate leaf-like ornaments on the coronet of a duke, marquis, or earl: commonly taken as the symbol of the rank involved.—**straw'ber-ry=mark**, *n.* A reddish, vascular birth-mark.—**straw'ber-ry=shrub**, *n.* Any of various species of the genus *Calycanthus* (or *Butneria*), shrubs with dark brownish or purplish red flowers of distinctive fragrance, common in cultivation; Carolina allspice.—**straw'ber-ry=to-ma'to**, *n.* The small, edible, tomato-like fruit of any of various herbs of the solanaceous genus *Physalis*, as of *P. pubescens* or *P. alkekengi* (see *alkekengi*); also, the plant bearing it.—**straw'ber-ry=tree**, *n.* An evergreen ericaceous shrub or tree, *Arbutus unedo*, a native of southern Europe, bearing a scarlet, strawberry-like fruit.

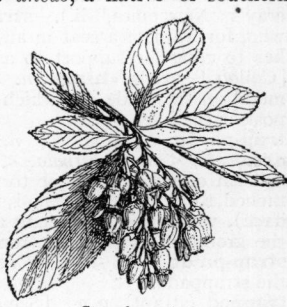
Flowering Branch of Strawberry-shrub (*Calycanthus floridus*).

straw-board (strā'bōrd), *n.* Coarse yellow paper board made of straw pulp, used in packing, and for making boxes, etc.

straw=col-or (strā'kul"ọr), *n.* A pale yellow.—**straw'=col"ored**, *a.*

straw=wine (strā'wīn), *n.* Wine (usually sweet and rich) made from grapes that have been dried or partly dried in the sun on a bed of straw.

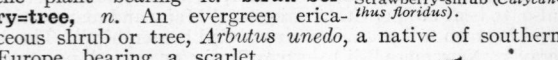
Strawberry-tree.

straw=worm (strā'wėrm), *n.* A caddis-worm; also, any of several joint-worms, as *Isosoma grande* and *I. hordei*, which infest the stalks of grain.

straw-y (strā'i), *a.* Of, containing, or resembling straw; strewed or thatched with straw.

stray (strā), *v. i.* [OF. *estraier*, stray, wander, < ML. *extravagari*: see *extravagate*, and cf. *astray* and *estray*.] To go from the proper course or place or beyond the proper limits, esp. without settled course or purpose, as travelers, soldiers on the march, domestic animals, etc. (as, "He gave Cicero strict directions to keep the legion within the lines, and not to allow any of the men to *stray*": Froude's "Cæsar," xvii.); wander (*away*, *off*, *from*, *into*, *to*, etc.); also, to wander about at will or without settled direction, or ramble or roam (as, "He's *straying* around saying prayers at the churches and high crosses": Synge's "Well of the Saints," i.); meander, as a stream; turn in one direction and another, as the eyes, gaze, etc. (as, "His eyes *strayed* about irresolutely": J. Conrad's "Victory," ii. 5); fig., to deviate, as from the set or right course; depart from the path of duty or rectitude; go astray; digress, as from a subject (as, "I ask pardon, I am *straying* from the question": Goldsmith's "Vicar of Wakefield," xiv.); proceed in an erratic fashion as if without settled purpose.—**stray. I.** *n.* A domestic animal found wandering at large or without an owner; an estray; also, a strayed or lost animal (as, to hunt for *strays* from a flock); hence, any homeless or friendless creature or person (as, waifs and *strays* of society); a person or thing that has strayed; anything found or occurring apart from other things or as an isolated or casual instance; also, an X in wireless telegraphy; a static disturbance or interference; also, a straying or wandering (obs. or rare); also, the right of letting cattle, etc., stray and feed on common land, or a piece of land open to such use (prov. Eng.). **II.** *a.* Straying, or having strayed, as a domestic animal (as, "I was abroad all day . . . riding after some *stray* beast": Blackmore's "Lorna Doone," ix.); hence, found or occurring apart from others, or as an isolated or casual instance (as, "a *stray* copy of Mr. Pope's ingenious translation of the Iliad": Bret Harte's "Outcasts of Poker Flat").—**stray'er**, *n.*

streak (strēk), *n.* [ME. *streke, strike,* < AS. *strica,* stroke, mark, line; from the root of E. *strike.*] A stroke, mark, or line, as in writing or drawing†; also, a relatively long, narrow, more or less irregular mark, smear, band of color, or the like, less distinctly or evenly formed than a stripe (as, *a streak* of grime, mud, ink, or paint; *streaks* of red and white); a long, more or less irregularly shaped portion or layer of substance, distinguished by color or nature from the rest (as, *streaks* of fat and lean in meat; a *streak* of ore in rock); hence, a vein, strain, or admixture of anything (as, to have a *streak* of humor in one; "He thinks she has a *streak* of genius," G. Meredith's "Diana of the Crossways," xl.); a run (of luck: colloq.: as, "We've had a *streak* of bad luck," Bret Harte's "Outcasts of Poker Flat"); also, anything seen as having the general shape of a line or band (as, a *streak* of light or of lightning; *streaks* of forest or of desert); in *mineral.,* the line of powder, of characteristic color, obtained by scratching a mineral or rubbing it upon a hard, rough white surface, often differing in color from the mineral in the mass, and forming an important distinguishing character; *naut.,* a strake.—**streak,** *v.* **I.** *tr.* To mark with a streak or streaks (as, "As when Apollo *streaks* With fire the op'ning eyelids of the morn": Wiffen's tr. Tasso's "Jerusalem Delivered," iv. 91); diversify with streaks; also, to dispose in the form of a streak or streaks. **II.** *intr.* To become streaked or streaky; also, to flash or move as a streak, as lightning; go rapidly, like a streak of lightning (colloq.: as, "You fairly *streaked* away, old chap," W. B. Maxwell's "In Cotton Wool," vii.).

streaked (strēkt or strē′ked), *p. a.* Marked or diversified with streaks; streaky; also, perturbed, uneasy, or alarmed (prov., U. S.).

streak-y (strē′ki), *a.* Occurring in streaks or a streak; also, marked with or characterized by streaks (as, "an old man with a *streaky* gray chin-beard": Tarkington's "Gentleman from Indiana," xix.); fig., varying or uneven in character, quality, etc. (colloq.).—**streak′i-ly,** *adv.*—**streak′i-ness,** *n.*

stream (strēm), *n.* [AS. *stréam* = D. *stroom* = G. *strom* = Icel. *straumr* = Sw. and Dan. *ström,* stream; akin to Gr. ῥεῖν and Skt. *sru-,* flow: cf. *rheum*[1] and *rhythm.*] A body of water flowing in a channel or bed; a watercourse, as a river, rivulet, or brook; also, a steady current in water, as in a river or the ocean (as, "The *stream* of the river was too gentle to aid us," Mrs. Shelley's "Frankenstein," xviii.; the Gulf *Stream,* see under *gulf, a.*); the course or direction of flow, as of a river (as, to row against the *stream*); also, any flow of water or other liquid or fluid (as, *streams* of tears or of blood; *streams* of lava); a current of air, gas, or the like; a beam or trail of light (as, "The day now began to send forth its first *streams* of light": Fielding's "Tom Jones," viii. 15); also, a continuous flow or succession of anything (as, "*Streams* of people pushed past him," Margaret Kennedy's "Constant Nymph," xxiv.; a *stream* of words, wealth, or influence); prevailing direction, or drift (as, the *stream* of tendency or opinion).—**stream,** *v.* **I.** *intr.* To flow, pass, or issue in or as in a stream, as water, tears, blood, etc.; move or proceed continuously like a flowing stream, as a procession or a succession of things (as, "Jacob strode away, the puppies *streaming* behind him," Eden Phillpotts's "Children of Men," Prologue, iii.; "Then suddenly the bombs had come *streaming* down," H. G. Wells's "Mr. Britling," ii. 3. § 11); extend in a beam or trail, as light (as, "Through each pass and hollow *streamed* The purpling lights of heaven": Whittier's "Among the Hills"); wave or float outward, as a flag in the wind (as, "The great banner of England . . . *streamed* from the highest part of the building": Scott's "Castle Dangerous," viii.); hang in a loose, flowing manner, as long hair; also, to send forth or throw off a stream, as of water, tears, blood, light, etc.; run or flow (*with*: as, "his eyes *streaming* with tears," G. Meredith's "Ordeal of Richard Feverel," xii.); in *mining,* to stream detrital matter (see *stream, v. t.*). **II.** *tr.* To send forth or discharge in or as in a stream; cause to stream or float outward, as a flag in the wind; overspread or suffuse with a stream or streams; in *mining,* to subject (detrital matter) to the action of a stream of water in order to separate ore, as of tin; work (a district) by this process.

stream-er (strē′mėr), *n.* Something that streams; a long, narrow flag or pennant; a long, flowing ribbon, feather, or the like, used for ornament, as in dress; any long, narrow piece or thing, as a spray of a plant or a strip of cloud; a stream of light, esp. one appearing in some forms of the aurora borealis; also, in *mining,* one who streams detrital matter to obtain ore.

stream-let (strēm′let), *n.* A small stream; a rivulet.

stream=line (strēm′līn). **I.** *n.* A line of motion in a fluid; the actual path of a particle in a flowing fluid mass whose motion is steady; also, a line of contour, as of an automobile, belonging to a stream-line shape (as, "a startling roadster, all *streamlines* and cream paint": Sinclair Lewis's "Arrowsmith," ix.). **II.** *a.* Pertaining to or of the nature of a stream-line; also, noting, pertaining to, or having a shape designed to offer the least possible resistance, or to reduce resistance, in passing through the air, etc., allowing an uninterrupted flow of the fluid about it (as, a projectile with a *stream-line* shape; an automobile with a *stream-line* body).

stream-y (strē′mi), *a.* Abounding in streams or watercourses; also, flowing in a stream; streaming; stream-like.

street (strēt), *n.* [AS. *strǣt* = D. *straat* = G. *strasse,* < LL. *strata,* paved way, street, prop. fem. of L. *stratus,* pp. of *sternere,* spread out: see *stratum.*] A paved way or road (now only in the proper names of certain ancient, chiefly Roman, roads in England: as, Watling *Street,* which extended from Dover to Chester); also, a public way or road, paved or unpaved, in a village, town, or city, usually including a sidewalk or sidewalks as well as a roadway, and having buildings or lots on one side or both sides; such a way or road together with the adjacent buildings or lots; the roadway, or way for vehicles, as distinguished from the sidewalk (as, to walk in the *street*); a main way or thoroughfare, in distinction from a lane, alley, or the like; also, a path or passageway between continuous lines of persons or things; also, the inhabitants of or the people in a street.—**man in the street.** See under *man, n.*—**street Arab.** See *Arab, n.*—**the street,** a street or locality where merchants or financiers of a city resort for business dealings, esp. [often *cap.,* 'the Street'] Wall Street in New York City; also, those engaged in business there, or the money-market.

street=car (strēt′kär), *n.* A car, esp. for passengers, running regularly through the streets, usually on rails. [U. S.]

street-ed (strē′ted), *a.* Provided with streets.

street=pi-an-o (strēt′pi-an″ō), *n.* An upright piano-like musical instrument set on wheels and operated mechanically, as by a crank, which is played in the streets for gratuities.

street=rail-way (strēt′rāl″wā), *n.* A railway constructed and operating on the surface of the street in a city or town; a street-car line.

street=walk-er (strēt′wȧ″kėr), *n.* One who walks the streets; esp., a soliciting prostitute.

strength (strength), *n.* [AS. *strengthu,* < *strang,* E. *strong.*] The quality or state of being strong; bodily or muscular power, whether for exertion or for endurance; bodily vigor, as in robust health; mental power, force, or vigor (as, "great *strength* of memory": Johnson's "Rasselas," viii.); moral power, firmness, fortitude, or courage (as, "If . . . Thou hast the *strength* of will to slay thyself": Shakspere's "Romeo and Juliet," iv. 1. 72); power by reason of influence, authority, resources, numbers, etc.; number, as of men or ships in a force or body (as, to recruit a regiment to its full *strength,* or to a *strength* of three thousand); effective force, potency, or cogency, as of inducements or arguments; power of resisting force, strain, wear, etc., upon material substance or structure (also fig.: as, *strength* of affection); vigor of action, procedure, language, feeling, etc.; large proportion of the effective or essential properties of a beverage, chemical, drug, or the like, or a particular proportion of these properties; intensity, as of light, color, sound, flavor, or odor; also, something that makes strong; a support or stay (as, "God is our refuge and *strength*": Ps. xlvi. 1); a stronghold or fastness (archaic: as, "This inaccessible high *strength,* the seat Of Deity supreme," Milton's "Paradise Lost," vii. 141). **—on** (or **upon**) **the strength of,** relying on, or by the support or aid of: as, "My father set out *upon the strength of* these two following axioms" (Sterne's "Tristram Shandy," ii. 19); "He did pretty well, *upon the strength of* being a tolerable antiquarian" (Lamb's "Old Benchers of the Inner Temple").

strength-en (streng'thn), *v.* **I.** *tr.* To give strength to; increase the strength, power, force, vigor, or intensity of; make stronger. **II.** *intr.* To gain strength; grow stronger. — **strength'en-er**, *n.*

strength-less (strength'les), *a.* Lacking strength.

stren-u-ous (stren'ū-us), *a.* [L. *strenuus*, brisk, active, vigorous; akin to Gr. στρηνής, strong, hard, rough.] Vigorous, energetic, or zealously active, as a person, the habit of mind, etc. (as, "a procession of *strenuous* master spirits, with Milton and Cromwell at their head," Morley's "Oliver Cromwell," v. 10); characterized by vigorous exertion, as action, efforts, life, periods, etc. (as, "a *strenuous* opposition to the Stamp Act," Burke's "American Taxation"; "I wish to preach, not the doctrine of ignoble ease, but the doctrine of the *strenuous* life, the life of toil and effort, of labor and strife," Roosevelt's "Strenuous Life," i.); of voice, etc., loud (archaic). — **stren-u-os'i-ty** (-os'i-ti), **stren'u-ous-ness**, *n.* — **stren'u-ous-ly**, *adv.*

Streph-on (stref'on), *n.* [From *Strephon*, a shepherd in Sidney's "Arcadia."] In pastoral and other literature, a name for a swain or lover (often of a Chloe).

strep-sir-rhine, strep-si-rhine (strep'si-rin). [Gr. στρεψι- (< στρέφειν, turn, twist) + ρίς (ρίν-), nose.] **I.** *a.* Having twisted or curved nostrils, as a lemur. **II.** *n.* A strep-sirrhine animal; a lemur.

strep-to-coc-cus (strep-tō-kok'us), *n.*; pl. *-cocci* (-kok'sī). [NL., < Gr. στρεπτός, twisted, + NL. *coccus*: see *coccus*.] Any member of the genus *Streptococcus*, comprising spherical bacterial organisms which divide in one direction only, frequently remaining attached and forming chains, and of which certain species cause disease. — **strep-to-coc'cal** (-kok'-al), **strep-to-coc'cic** (-kok'sik), *a.*

strep-to-my-cin (strep-tō-mī'sin), *n.* [Gr. στρεπτός, twisted, + μύκης, fungus, + *-in.*] A drug with powerful germicidal properties.

stress (stres), *n.* [Shortened form of *distress.*] Distress† or affliction†; also, distressing, painful, or adverse force or influence (as, to feel the *stress* of hunger or poverty); severe strain upon endurance, feelings, etc.; constraining or impelling force (as, "When the *stress* of national peril should be relaxed, arbitrary power would no longer go unquestioned," Morley's "Oliver Cromwell," i. 2; to do a thing under *stress*; driven by *stress* of circumstances); also, strong or straining exertion (now rare: as, won by *stress* of arms); also, the physical pressure, pull, or other force exerted on one thing by another (as, "aged firs — all grown aslant under the *stress* of mountain winds," C. Brontë's "Jane Eyre," xxx.; the *stress* of a load or weight; the *stress* of a ship pulling on her cables: see also mech. and elect. defs. below); strain; also, reliance placed upon a thing† (as, "I always put a great deal of *stress* upon his judgment": Defoe's "Captain Singleton," xiii.); also, importance or significance attached to a thing, marked insistence, or emphasis (as, "I never heard that the Methodists laid any *stress* upon those legal observances of fasting," R. Graves's "Spiritual Quixote," iv. 5; "One [way of telling a story] was to lay *stress* upon successive incidents," Archibald Marshall's "Anthony Dare," v.); also, emphasis in utterance, or increase of loudness or vocal force in pronouncing a particular syllable or word (as, "Whiskers! cried the queen, laying a greater *stress* upon the word": Sterne's "Tristram Shandy," v. 1); the relative loudness or force of utterance in the pronunciation of syllables or parts of syllables, words in a sentence, etc.; accent; hence, emphasis in verse, music, rhythm, etc.; in *mech.*, the action on a body of any system of balanced forces whereby strain or deformation results; a load, force, or system of forces producing a strain; the internal resistance or reaction of an elastic body to the external forces applied to it; in *elect.*, electromotive force. — **storm and stress.** See under *storm*, *n.* — **stress**, *v. t.* To distress† or afflict†; constrain†; also, to subject to stress or strain (in *mech.*, to mechanical stress); also, to lay stress or emphasis on; dwell upon insistently, or emphasize (as, "an exaggeration . . . of small foibles, that . . . should not have been *stressed*": G. Meredith's "Diana of the Crossways," xxiv.); emphasize in utterance; accent.

-stress. [From *-ster* + *-ess.*] A distinctively feminine suffix formed to correspond to *-ster* (itself orig. feminine), as in *seamstress*, *songstress.*

stress-less (stres'les), *a.* Having no stress; unstressed: as, a *stressless* syllable.

stretch (strech), *v. t.* [ME. *strecchen*, < AS. *streccan* = D. *strekken* = G. *strecken*, stretch: cf. *straight.*] To draw out or extend (one's self, the body, limbs, wings, etc.) to the full length or extent; lay at full length, as in a prostrate position (as, to *stretch* one's self on the bed for a nap; to *stretch* a person on the ground by a blow: often with *out*); hold out, reach forth, or extend (the hand or something held, the head, etc.: as, "Here and there I have *stretched* an arm and helped you to a ledge," Tyndall's "Forms of Water," § 67: often with *out* or *forth*); extend, spread, or place so as to reach from one point or place to another (as, to *stretch* a rope across a road; to *stretch* a curtain over an opening); also, to draw tight or taut (as, to *stretch* the strings of a violin or the membrane forming a drumhead); strain (nerves, etc.) to the utmost, as by exertion; exercise (one's self) by extending the body or limbs, straining the muscles, etc., in order to relieve stiffness, fatigue, etc. (as, "Kim yawned and *stretched* himself": Kipling's "Kim," x.); extend or use (the limbs) in movements or exercise for relief (as, "We . . . descended from our howdahs, glad to *stretch* our stiffened limbs in a brisk walk": F. M. Crawford's "Mr. Isaacs," ix.); also, to draw out to greater length or size by the application of force (as, to *stretch* a rubber band or a kid glove; to *stretch* a person's limbs, or the person, on the rack); lengthen, widen, distend, or enlarge by tension; open wide (the eyes, mouth, etc.); draw out, extend, or enlarge unduly (as, garments *stretched* at the elbows or knees); fig., to extend or force beyond the natural or proper limits (as, to *stretch* one's powers, or the law, to suit one's purposes; to *stretch* the truth or the facts in making a statement); strain. — to **stretch a halter** or **rope**, to be hanged. — to **stretch a point.** Same as *to strain a point*, under *strain*[2], *v. t.* — to **stretch one's legs**, to straighten the legs, as from a sitting position; relieve, by standing or walking, the stiffness or fatigue caused by sitting; take a walk for exercise. — **stretch**, *v. i.* To stretch one's self or recline at full length (usually with *out*: as, to *stretch* out on a couch); extend the hand, or reach, as for something; extend or continue over a distance or area or in a particular direction (as, the forest *stretches* for miles to the westward); sometimes, to continue over a tract of time; also, to make one's or its way, esp. rapidly or with effort (as, "Having a fresh gale, I *stretched* across this eddy, slanting north-west," Defoe's "Robinson Crusoe," i. 10; "It [an antelope] . . . *stretched* away at full speed," Parkman's "Oregon Trail," x.); also, to exert one's self to the utmost, as in running, rowing, etc. (as, to *stretch* to the oar: often with *out*); strain; stretch one's self by extending the limbs, straining the muscles, etc.; also, to become stretched, or admit of being stretched, to greater length, width, etc., as any elastic material; go beyond the strict truth, as in a statement (colloq.). — **stretch**, *n.* The act or an act of stretching, or the state of being stretched; a stretching to the full length, as of the body or limbs; a reclining at full length; a stretching out of the hand, or the length of reach; a drawing tight, or the resulting state of tension; strain (physical or mental: as, to keep the nerves or the mind on the *stretch*); forcible extension, as to greater length, or capacity for such extension (as, to take the *stretch* out of leather); fig., a stretching or straining beyond the natural or proper limits (as, a *stretch* of the imagination; a *stretch* of language); also, extent of ability as shown by straining, effort, or any test (as, "On we all came, each horse at his utmost *stretch*," Lever's "Harry Lorrequer," ii.; "shouted . . . at the utmost *stretch* of his voice," George Eliot's "Adam Bede," xxii.; "a mind of such a *stretch* of depravity, as . . . would appear utterly incredible," Godwin's "Caleb Williams," xxviii.); also, an extent of distance or area; a continuous length, distance, tract, or expanse (as, a *stretch* of road, meadow, forest, water, or ice; "*stretches* of sand and weedy pools," Gissing's "Private Papers of Henry Ryecroft," ii. 1); one of the two straight sides of a race-course, as distinguished from the bend or curve at each end, esp. that part of the course ('home stretch') between the last turn and the winning-post; also, an extent in time or duration; a tract of time (as, a *stretch* of ten years); a period, term, or spell (as, a long *stretch* of bad weather;

to write for hours at a *stretch*); a term of imprisonment (slang); also, a course or journey (as, a *stretch* of five miles; "I found Violette [a mare] ready for another twenty-league *stretch*," Conan Doyle's "Exploits of Brigadier Gerard," vii.); also, the direction in which a thing stretches or extends (as, the *stretch* of seams of coal).

stretch-er (strech'ėr), *n.* One who or that which stretches; any of various instruments or appliances for stretching, or extending, widening, distending, etc. (as, a glove-*stretcher*; a shoe-*stretcher*); a bar or rod serving to expand a part (as, the *stretchers* of an umbrella, which connect the ribs with the tube sliding upon the stick); a bar, beam, or the like, esp. a horizontal one, serving as a tie or brace; a brick or stone laid horizontally with its length in the direction of the face of a wall; fig., a statement that stretches or strains the truth, or a lie (colloq.: as, "mostly a true book, with some *stretchers*," Mark Twain's "Huckleberry Finn," i.); also, a kind of litter, usually of canvas stretched on a frame, esp. for carrying the sick, wounded, or dead.—**stretch'er-man** (-man), *n.*; pl. *-men*. A man whose work it is to take part in carrying a stretcher, as in removing the wounded from a battle-field. Also **stretch'er=bear"er.**

stretch-y (strech'i), *a.* Capable of being stretched; elastic; also, liable to stretch unduly.

strew (strö), *v. t.*; pret. *strewed*, pp. *strewed* or *strewn*, ppr. *strewing.* [AS. *strewian, strēowian,* = D. *strooien* = G. *streuen* = Icel. *strā* = Goth. *straujan,* strew; prob. akin to L. *sternere* (pp. *stratus*), Gr. στορνύναι, Skt. *star-,* spread out, strew: cf. *stratum* and *straw*[1].] To let fall in separate pieces or particles over a surface (as, to *strew* rushes or sand on a floor; to *strew* seed in a garden bed; "My master has . . . left all his finery *strewed* about his room," Scott's "Abbot," vi.); scatter or sprinkle; also, to cover or overspread (a surface, place, etc.) with something scattered or sprinkled (as, to *strew* a floor with rushes); be scattered or sprinkled over (a surface, etc.: as, rushes *strewed* the floor; "Photographs *strewed* the low tables," Mrs. Wharton's "Son at the Front," xix.); also, to throw down, prostrate, or lay low (archaic); make level, smooth, or calm, as water (archaic: as, "The harbour-bay was clear as glass, So smoothly it was *strewn!*" Coleridge's "Ancient Mariner," vi.).—**strew'er,** *n.* —**strew'ment,** *n.* Something strewed, as flowers: as, "She is allow'd . . . Her maiden *strewments*" (Shakspere's "Hamlet," v. 1. 256). [Archaic.]

stri-a (strī'ä), *n.*; pl. *striæ* (-ē). [L., a furrow, channel, flute.] A slight furrow or ridge; a linear marking; a narrow stripe or streak, as of color or texture, esp. one of a number in parallel arrangement; in *arch.,* a fillet between the flutes of columns, etc.—**stri'ate** (-āt), *v. t.*; *-ated, -ating.* [L. *striatus,* pp. of *striare,* to furrow, channel, < *stria.*] To mark with striæ; furrow; stripe; streak: used chiefly in *striated, pp.* —**stri'ate,** *a.* Marked with striæ; furrowed; striped; streaked.—**stri-a'tion** (-ā'shon), *n.* Striated condition or appearance; also, a stria; one of a number of parallel striæ. —**stri'a-ture** (-a-ṭūr), *n.* [L. *striatura.*] Disposition of striæ; striation; also, a stria.

strick (strik), *n.* [ME. *stric, strik;* connected with E. *strike.*] A strickle for leveling grain in a measure (now prov. Eng.); a measure of capacity, or a measuring vessel, for grain, etc. (see *strike, n.*: now prov. Eng.); also, a handful or bunch of flax or other fiber in the process of dressing.

strick-en (strik'n). Past participle of *strike.*—**strick'en,** *p. a.* Advanced or far gone (in age, etc.: archaic: as, "Abraham was old, and well *stricken* in age," Gen. xxiv. 1; "a man well *stricken* in years," Trollope's "Warden," xv.); also, struck; hit or wounded by a weapon, missile, or the like (as, "the *stricken* deer," Shakspere's "Hamlet," iii. 2. 282; "The harpoon was darted; the *stricken* whale flew forward," H. Melville's "Moby-Dick," cxxxv.); smitten or afflicted, as with disease, trouble, or sorrow (as, to flee from a *stricken* city; "They could not be of any service to the *stricken* household," Eden Phillpotts's "Grey Room," iii.); deeply affected, as with horror, fear, or other emotion; characterized by or showing the effects of affliction, trouble, misfortune, a mental blow, etc. (as, a *stricken* state; "The forlornness of the bookcase gave a *stricken* air to the whole room," Arnold Bennett's "Hilda Lessways," iii. 1; "They drew apart with *stricken* faces," Mrs. Wharton's "Ethan

Frome," ix.).—**stricken field,** a battle fought: as, "This was the issue of the first *stricken field* in the Netherlands, for the cause of religious liberty" (Motley's "Dutch Republic," ii. 9). [Archaic.]—**stricken hour,** a whole hour, as indicated by the striking of the clock. [Archaic.]—**strick'-en-ly,** *adv.*

strick-le (strik'l), *n.* [AS. *stricel,* connected with *strīcan,* E. *strike.*] A straight-edge used to sweep off heaped-up grain or the like to a level with the rim of a measure; also, a straight-edge used in founding to remove superfluous sand to a level with the top of a flask; a templet or piece of wood with a special profile, drawn over the sand in a flask to impart to it a required contour; also, a piece of wood covered with grease and sand, emery, or the like, used to sharpen scythes. —**strick'le,** *v. t.*; *-led, -ling.* To sweep or remove, or shape or form, with a strickle.

strict (strikt), *a.* [L. *strictus,* pp. of *stringere,* draw tight: see *strain*[2], and cf. *strait* and *stringent.*] Drawn tight, tight, or close (obs. or archaic: as, a *strict* ligature; "to strain her in a *strict* embrace," Dryden's tr. Ovid's "Metamorphoses," i. 975); taut or tense (obs. or archaic); also, narrow, contracted, or limited in space (obs. or archaic: as, "*Strict* passage, through which sighs are brought, And whispers," Wordsworth's "On the Power of Sound," i.); fig., narrowly or carefully limited or restricted (as, a *strict* construction of the Constitution); exact or precise (as, *strict* truth; the *strict* meaning of a word; a *strict* statement of facts); close, careful, or minute (as, "We closely scan the ice, and after an hour's *strict* search we discover the cause of the reports": Tyndall's "Forms of Water," § 36); absolute, perfect, or complete (as, *strict* neutrality; told in *strict* confidence); also, close or intimate, as connections, relations, etc. (obs. or archaic); also, characterized by or acting in close conformity to requirements or principles (as, *strict* reasoning; *strict* observance; a *strict* party-man; "the *strictest* of Mohammedans," F. M. Crawford's "Mr. Isaacs," vi.); stringent or exacting in requirements, obligations, etc. (as, *strict* laws, rules, or commands; *strict* vows; "The etiquette was very *strict*," H. G. Wells's "Tono-Bungay," i. 1. § 3); rigorous in rule, discipline, management, etc. (as, a *strict* judge or parent; to be *strict* with a child; "He [a schoolmaster] could not be severe nor even passably *strict*," W. H. Hudson's "Far Away and Long Ago," xviii.); rigorously scrupulous, strait-laced, or austere, as persons or their views, life, etc.; closely or rigorously enforced or maintained, as discipline, guard, imprisonment, etc.

stric-tion (strik'shon), *n.* [LL. *strictio(n-),* < L. *stringere,* draw tight: see *strain*[2].] The act of drawing tight, constricting, or straining.

strict-ly (strikt'li), *adv.* In a strict manner or sense; narrowly; exactly or precisely; closely or carefully; absolutely or completely; stringently; rigorously.—**strict'ness,** *n.*

stric-ture (strik'ṭūr), *n.* [L. *strictura,* < *stringere,* draw tight, also (perhaps a different word) touch, graze, touch upon: see *strain*[2], and cf. *strigil.*] A drawing or binding tightly, or something that binds tightly (obs. or rare: as, "A windless *stricture* of frost had bound the air," Stevenson's "Master of Ballantrae," v.); a morbid contraction of any passage or duct of the body; also, a touch or slight trace of something†; also, a remark or comment, now always of an unfavorable nature; an adverse criticism; also, strictness†.

stride (strīd), *v.*; pret. *strode,* pp. *stridden* (pret. and pp. also sometimes *strided*), ppr. *striding.* [AS. *strīdan* = MLG. *strīden,* stride: cf. *straddle.*] **I.** *intr.* To straddle (now fig.: as, an arch *striding* over the street); also, to walk with long steps, as with vigor, haste, impatience, or arrogance (as, "He moved freely . . . like a man accustomed to *stride* over plains and hills," J. Conrad's "Rescue," i. 1; "I turned about and *strode* to overtake him," H. G. Wells's "Tono-Bungay," iii. 3. § 2; "*Striding* in I demanded . . . to see the Prince instantly," Conan Doyle's "Exploits of Brigadier Gerard," vi.); take a long step; pass (*over* or *across*) by a long step (as, "He walked in resolutely, *striding* over the dead body": J. Conrad's "Lord Jim," xxxi.). **II.** *tr.* To straddle or bestride; also, to walk with long steps along, on, through, over, etc. (as, to *stride* the streets; to *stride* the deck of a ship; "Hannah . . . could not *stride* the drifts so well as I; her legs are not quite so long,"

(variable) ḏ as d or j; ş as s or sh, ṭ as t or ch, ẓ as z or zh; o, F. *cloche;* ü, F. *menu;* ċh, Sc. *loch;* ṅ, F. *bonbon;* ′, primary accent; ″, secondary accent; †, obsolete; <, from; +, and; =, equals. See also lists at beginning of book.

C. Brontë's "Jane Eyre," xxxiii.); take (a stride: as, "The Prince . . . fain To follow, *strode* a stride," Tennyson's "Marriage of Geraint," 376); pass over or across by one stride (as, to *stride* a ditch; "A prison for a debtor, that not dares To *stride* a limit," Shakspere's "Cymbeline," iii. 3. 35). —**stride,** *n.* A straddle, or a distance straddled over (obs. or rare); also, a striding, or progressing by long steps, or a striding gait (as, "The closeness of her skirt . . . permitted no natural *stride*": Tarkington's "Alice Adams," iii.); a long step in walking (also fig.: as, to walk, or, fig., to advance or progress, with rapid *strides*; "We boast that we . . . are making the most rapid *strides* of any nation," Thoreau's "Walden," iii.; "The stars rush out: At one *stride* comes the dark," Coleridge's "Ancient Mariner," iii.); the distance covered by such a step, sometimes used as a measure of distance; a single movement or step in running; the regular movement of a man or a horse in walking or running, of an oarsman in rowing, etc. (as, to get into one's *stride*, fig., to get into one's regular or steady course of procedure); in animal locomotion, an act of progressive movement completed when all the feet are returned to the same relative position as at the beginning; the distance covered by such a movement.

stri-dent (strī′dent), *a.* [L. *stridens* (*strident-*), ppr. of *stridere*, make a harsh sound.] Making or having a harsh sound; grating; creaking: as, "The *strident* voice sounded harsher than ever" (Mrs. H. Ward's "Robert Elsmere," xvii.).—**stri′dence, stri′den-cy,** *n.*—**stri′dent-ly,** *adv.*

strid-er (strī′dėr), *n.* One who or that which strides.

stri-dor (strī′dọr), *n.* [L., < *stridere*: see *strident*.] A harsh, grating, or creaking sound; in *pathol.*, a harsh respiratory sound due to any of various forms of obstruction.

strid-u-lant (strid′ū-lant), *a.* Stridulating.

strid-u-late (strid′ū-lāt), *v. i.*; *-lated, -lating*. [NL. *stridulatus*, pp. of *stridulare*, < L. *stridulus*: see *stridulous*.] To produce a shrill, grating sound, as a cricket or a katydid does, by rubbing together certain parts of the body; shrill; chirr. —**strid-u-la′tion** (-lā′shon), *n.* The action or the sound of stridulating.—**strid′u-la-tor,** *n.*—**strid′u-la-to-ry** (-la̩-tō̩-ri), *a.* Pertaining to stridulation; capable of stridulating.

strid-u-lous (strid′ū-lus), *a.* [L. *stridulus*, < *stridere*: see *strident*.] Making or having a harsh or grating sound; in *pathol.*, pertaining to or characterized by stridor.—**strid′u-lous-ly,** *adv.*—**strid′u-lous-ness,** *n.*

strife (strīf), *n.* [OF. *estrif*, connected with *estriver*, E. *strive*.] The striving or contending of opposing parties; contention, quarreling, fighting, or conflict; discord, dissension, or variance (as, to be at *strife*); a quarrel, struggle, clash, or dispute (as, "These *strifes* . . . And discords," Fairfax's tr. Tasso's "Jerusalem Delivered," i. 30; "*strifes* touching matters of Christian belief," Hooker's "Ecclesiastical Polity," i. 10. 14); also, strenuous effort or endeavor (obs. or rare: as, "Be your *strife* To lead on earth an Angel's life," Keble's "Christian Year," iv.); also, competition, emulation, or rivalry (obs. or rare: as, "Great was the *strife* betwixt the singing swains," Dryden's tr. Virgil's "Pastorals," vii. 23).

strig-il (strij′il), *n.* [L. *strigilis*, < *stringere*, touch, graze: see *stricture*.] An instrument with a curved blade, used by the ancient Greeks and Romans for scraping the skin at the bath and in the gymnasium; also, a brush or other article used later for a similar purpose; in *arch.*, one of a series of vertical flutings or channels curving in the form of an elongated S, used as a decoration, esp. in Roman architecture.—**strig-i-la′tion** (-i-lā′shon), *n.* Vigorous scraping or friction with a strigil or the like.

strig-il-ose (strij′i-lōs), *a.* In *bot.*, minutely strigose.

stri-gose (strī′gōs), *a.* [NL. *strigosus*, < *striga*, row of bristles, bristle, L.

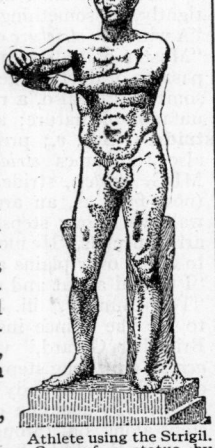
Athlete using the Strigil. — Copy of a statue by Lysippus; Vatican Museum, Rome.

swath, furrow.] In *bot.*, set with stiff bristles or hairs; hispid; in *zoöl.*, marked with fine, closely set ridges, grooves, or points.

strike (strīk), *v. i.*; pret. *struck*, pp. *struck* or *stricken*, ppr. *striking*. [AS. *strīcan*, intr. move, go, tr. rub, wipe, = OFries. *strīka* = OHG. *strīhhan* (G. *streichen*): cf. *streak*, *stroke*[1], and *stroke*[2].] To go, proceed, or advance, esp. in a new direction (as, "The islanders were now to be seen . . . *striking* across the valley," H. Melville's "Typee," xvi.; "Leaving the trail, we *struck* directly across the country," Parkman's "Oregon Trail," viii.); extend in a specified direction, as a boundary, path, or the like; also, to deal or aim a blow or stroke, as with the fist, a weapon, or a hammer (often fig.: as, to *strike* at one's reputation); deal blows; make an attack; knock, rap, or tap (as, he *struck* three times on the door); sound by percussion (as, the clock *strikes*); be indicated by such sounding (as, the hour has *struck*); be ignited by friction, as a match; pulsate or throb, as the heart; also, to make a vigorous movement as if dealing a blow; make a stroke, as with the arms or legs in swimming, or with an oar in rowing; pass suddenly and quickly (*in*, *through*, etc.: as, "till a dart *strike* through his liver," Prov. vii. 23; "The cry of some wild bird *struck* through the silence," Howells's "Chance Acquaintance," i.); thrust one's self suddenly, as into a conversation or discussion (as, "I *struck* in and boldly changed the subject": F. M. Crawford's "Mr. Isaacs," iv.); take root, as a slip of a plant; fasten to stones, shells, etc., as young oysters do; of dye or color, to sink in, also to run; also, to hit or dash on or against something, as a moving body does; impinge; come into forcible contact; run upon a bank, rock, or other obstacle, as a ship does (as, "The ship floated from the place where she first *struck*": Defoe's "Robinson Crusoe," i. 4); fall (*on* or *upon*), as light or sound does; make an impression on the mind, senses, etc., as something seen or heard (as, "All spread their charms, but charm not all alike; On different senses, different objects *strike*": Pope's "Essay on Man," ii. 128); come suddenly or unexpectedly (*on* or *upon*: as, to *strike* on a new way of doing a thing); also, to lower a sail, or the flag or colors, esp. as a salute or as a sign of surrender; also, of an employee or employees, to quit work along with others or as a body in order to compel the employer or employers to accede to some demand, as for increase of pay, or in protest against something, as a reduction of wages; sometimes, to leave off work, as at the close of the day or at meal-time; also, in army use, to act as an officer's servant.—**to strike out,** in *baseball*, of a batter, to make three strikes and be declared 'out.'—**to strike up,** to begin playing or singing (as, "*Strike up,* pipers": Shakspere's "Much Ado about Nothing," v. 4. 130); of music, to begin to sound (as, "The music *struck up* and away I waltzed": G. Meredith's "Diana of the Crossways," xxvi.).—**strike,** *v. t.* To go or proceed along (a path, course, etc., as specified: as, to *strike* a path across the fields); also, to stroke or rub lightly, as with the hand (now prov.); pass (the hand) lightly over something as in stroking† (as, "He will surely . . . *strike* his hand over the place, and recover the leper": 2 Kings, v. 11); smear (a substance) on a surface†, or spread or coat (a surface) with a substance†; make level or even, as a measure of grain, salt, etc., by drawing a straight-edge or strickle across the top, or, as in the case of potatoes, by making the projections equal to the depressions; make level or smooth, in various technical uses; also, to mark with or as with a line or lines†; draw (a line), esp. by mechanical means; draw (an arc, etc.) with or as with compasses; efface or cancel with or as with the stroke of a pen (with *off*, *out*, etc.: as, "His name was *struck* out of the Council Book," Macaulay's "Hist. of Eng.," vi.); form (a jury, committee, etc.) by canceling a certain number from a list of names considered; cut (a tally); also, to deal a blow or stroke to (a person or thing), as with the fist, a weapon, or a hammer; smite; hit; deal blows upon; make an attack upon; fight (a battle: archaic: as, "when Cressy battle fatally was *struck*," Shakspere's "Henry V.," ii. 4. 54); deal or inflict (a blow, stroke, etc.); force, drive, make, etc., with or as with a blow or blows; stamp (a coin, medal, etc.), or impress (a device), by a stroke; print from type, an engraving, or the like (chiefly with *off*); pierce or stab with or as with a sharp

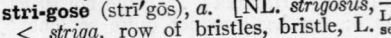

weapon (as, "The Templar *struck* him to the heart with a Turkish dagger": Scott's "Talisman," xxviii.); remove or separate with a cut (chiefly with *off*); harpoon (a whale: as, "The sperm whale, once *struck* . . . acts . . . with wilful, deliberate designs of destruction to his pursuers": H. Melville's "Moby-Dick," xlv.); hook (a fish) by a jerk or sudden movement of the tackle; broach (a cask)†; knock, rap, or tap (as, to *strike* a drum); touch (a string, etc.) so as to produce a tone; play upon (a harp, lyre, etc.); produce (a sound, music, etc.) by touching a string or playing upon an instrument; indicate (the hour of day) by a stroke or strokes, as a clock (as, "It was just *striking* midnight as we raced into Corbail," Conan Doyle's "Exploits of Brigadier Gerard," viii.; to *strike* twelve, see phrase below); cause (a repeater watch, etc.) to sound the time; produce (fire, sparks, light, etc.) by percussion, friction, etc.; cause (a match) to ignite by friction; also, to smite or blast with some natural or supernatural agency, or as such an agency does (as, *struck* with or by lightning); afflict suddenly, as with disease, suffering, or death; affect deeply or overwhelm, as with terror, fear, etc.; render (blind, dumb, etc.) suddenly, as if by a blow; cause (a feeling) to enter suddenly (as, to *strike* terror into a person); also, to deliver a blow, stroke, or thrust with (the hand, a weapon, etc.); stamp (the foot); drive or thrust forcibly (as, to *strike* the foot against a stone; to *strike* the hands together); also, to start suddenly into (vigorous movement: as, the horse *struck* a gallop); assume (an attitude or posture); cause (chill, warmth, etc.) to pass or penetrate quickly; send down or put forth (a root, etc.), as a plant, cutting, etc.; cause (a cutting, etc.) to take root; also, to hit, dash against, or impinge upon; come into forcible contact or collision with (as, the ship *struck* a rock); reach (ground or bottom) with a sounding-line; take (soundings); fall upon (something), as light or sound does; enter the mind of, or occur to (as, a happy thought *struck* him); catch or arrest (the eye, etc.: as, the first object that *strikes* one's sight); impress strongly (as, to be *struck* with the beauty of a thing; a picture which *struck* his fancy; impress in a particular manner (as, how does it *strike* you? "The thing *struck* her as somewhat strange," Arnold Bennett's "Grand Babylon Hotel," viii.); come upon or reach in traveling or in a course of procedure (as, "He *struck* it [Powder River] about three miles above its entrance into Snake River": Irving's "Captain Bonneville," xxix.); come across, meet with, or encounter suddenly or unexpectedly (as, to *strike* the name of a friend in a newspaper); come upon or find (ore, oil, etc.) in prospecting, boring, or the like; also, to make, conclude, or ratify (an agreement, treaty, etc.) by or as if by striking hands (as, "They shook hands and *struck* a bargain": Irving's "Tales of a Traveler," iv. 3); enter upon or form (an acquaintance, etc.: usually with *up*); fix (a price) by agreement; balance (a ledger, etc.: cf. phrase *to strike a balance*, below); estimate or determine (a mean or average); also, to make a sudden and pressing demand upon (a person), as for a loan (slang); also, to lower or take down (a sail, mast, etc.); lower (a sail, flag, etc.) as a salute or as a sign of surrender; lower (something) into the hold of a vessel by means of a rope and tackle (usually with *down*); hoist from the hold of a vessel and lower to a dock or the like (with *out*); take down or remove, as tents, scaffolding, scenery, etc.; break (camp); leave off (work), as a coercive measure, or as at the close of the day.—**to strike a balance,** to find the difference between the two sides of an account.—**to strike hands,** to clasp hands, as one party with another, in concluding an agreement; hence, to conclude an agreement; make a compact.—**to strike it rich,** to come upon a rich deposit, as in prospecting (as, "If Johnny would wait until he *struck it rich* in the tunnel, he'd have lots of money": Bret Harte's "How Santa Claus Came to Simpson's Bar"); hence, to meet with any unexpected rich return or good fortune.—**to strike out,** in *baseball*, of the pitcher, to cause (a batter) to strike out. See *to strike out*, under *strike, v. i.*—**to strike twelve,** to strike twelve times, as a clock does; fig., to display one's full powers, esp. in a first or early performance (as, "Mr. Avery ain't the kind of man that *strikes twelve* the fust time. He's a man that'll wear": Mrs. Stowe's "Oldtown Folks," xxxvii.); achieve a complete and surprising success.—**to strike up,** to begin to

play or sing (a tune, etc.: as, "The band *struck up* the opening bars of 'Ben Bolt,'" Du Maurier's "Trilby," vii.); also, to enter upon (an acquaintance, friendship, conversation, etc.). —**strike,** *n.* An act of striking; the discovery of a rich vein of ore in mining, of petroleum in boring, etc. (also fig., as of any sudden success); an attempt to obtain money or other personal advantage by initiating an attack with a view to being bought off, as by introducing into a legislature a bill hostile to some moneyed interest with the hope of being paid to let the matter drop (slang, U. S.); a concerted or general quitting of work by a body of employees in order to coerce their employer or employers in some way, as when higher wages or shorter hours are demanded, or a reduction of wages is resisted (often in the phrase 'on strike'); any general refusal to work or to continue some procedure, as a coercive measure; also, a strickle for leveling grain or the like in a measure; a piece of wood or other material used in various trades, etc., for leveling a surface by sweeping off superfluous material; an English dry measure usually identical with the bushel, but varying locally from half a bushel to four bushels; the measuring vessel containing such a measure; the unit proportion of malt in ale, etc.† (as, "a hogshead of ale . . . of the double *strike*": Scott's "Monastery," xviii.); a strick, or bunch of flax or other fiber in process of dressing; in *geol.* and *mining*, the direction of the line of intersection between the plane of an inclined stratum and a horizontal plane (see cut at *dip, n.*); in *baseball*, an unsuccessful attempt on the part of the batter to hit a pitched ball, or anything that is ruled to be equivalent to this; in *American bowling*, the knocking down of all the pins with the first bowl; in *coining*, a quantity or number struck at one time.

strike=break-er (strīk′brā″kẻr), *n.* One who takes part in breaking up a strike of workers, either by working or by furnishing workers for the employer.—**strike′=break″ing,** *n.* and *a.*

strik-er (strī′kẻr), *n.* One who or that which strikes (in any sense); esp., a strickle or strike for grain, etc.; one who strikes fish, etc., with a spear or harpoon; a worker who is on strike; in army use, a soldier who acts as an officer's servant.

strik-ing (strī′king), *p. a.* That strikes; esp., arresting the eye, attention, etc.; producing a marked or vivid impression on the mind; also, being on strike, as workmen.—**strik′-ing-ly,** *adv.*—**strik′ing-ness,** *n.*

string (string), *n.* [AS. *streng* = D. *streng* = Icel. *strengr*, akin to G. *strang*, string, and prob. also to Gr. στραγγάλη, halter, and L. *stringere*, draw tight: cf. *strangle* and *strain²*.] A line, cord, or thread, esp. a line of smaller thickness than a rope; a slender cord or thick thread; such cord or thread as a material, used for tying parcels, etc.; also, a cord for leading or dragging an animal, etc., along (as, to lead in or on a *string*, fig., to have under control, or be able to do what one pleases with); a cord for working a puppet (as, to pull the *strings*, fig., to control the course of any action ostensibly performed or directed by another); the line or cord of a bow (as, to have two *strings* to one's bow, fig., to have two alternative resources; second *string*, fig., a second resource available in case the first should fail); a piece of cord, tape, ribbon, or the like, or a narrow strip of cloth, leather, or other flexible material, used for binding, tying, lacing, drawing together, etc., often one of a pair of such pieces, as on a bonnet or an apron, for tying together in order to secure the article in place; in musical instruments, a tightly stretched cord or wire which produces a tone when caused to vibrate, as by plucking or striking or by the friction of a bow; *pl.*, stringed musical instruments, esp. such as are played with a bow, or the players on such instruments in an orchestra or band (often attrib., in *sing.*: as, a *string* quartet, a quartet of performers on stringed instruments); also, *sing.*, something resembling a string or thread; a ligament, tendon, nerve, or the like, in an animal body; a cord or fiber in a plant; a vein of a leaf; the tough piece uniting the two parts of a pod (as, the *strings* of beans); a tendril, runner, or the like; also, a number of objects, as beads or pearls, threaded or strung on a cord; a number of objects connected together in a line (as, "a *string* of apartments along one handsome thick-carpeted corridor": H. G. Wells's "Tono-Bungay," iii. 1. § 3); any series of things arranged in a line or following closely one

---

(variable) d̦ as d or j, ș as s or sh, ț as t or ch, z̦ as z or zh; *o*, F. cloche; ü, F. menu; ċh, Sc. loch; ṅ, F. bonbon; ′, primary accent; ″, secondary accent; †, obsolete; <, from; +, and; =, equals. See also lists at beginning of book.

after another (as, a *string* of islands or of vehicles; "The pyramids . . . were visited by *strings* of tourists," H. G. Wells's "Outline of History," xx. § 3; to ask a *string* of questions; to utter a *string* of oaths); a set or number, as of animals (as, to own a *string* of race-horses); in *arch.*, a string-course; also, one of the sloping sides of a stair, supporting the treads and risers; in *mining*, a thin vein or seam; a narrow branch of a lode; in *billiards*, etc., a number of wooden buttons strung on a wire to keep the score of the game; the score of either player or side at any stage of a game; a line from behind which the cue-ball is played after being out of play ('string-line'); a stroke made by each player from the head of the table to the opposite cushion and back, to determine, by means of the resultant positions of the balls, who shall open the game. — **to have a string to it,** to be subject to recall, as an offer, promise, or gift; hence, of anything ostensibly advantageous, to have some qualifying condition attached that may nullify the good effect. — **string,** *v.*; **strung** (occasionally **stringed**), **stringing. I.** *tr.* To furnish with or as with a string or strings; adjust the string of (a bow); tighten the strings of (a musical instrument) to the required pitch; also, to make tense, as the sinews, nerves, mind, etc. (as, "I suppose it was despair that *strung* my nerves": Poe's "Descent into the Maelström"); impart vigor or tone to; brace; also, to bring to a particular condition of tension or sensitiveness (as, nerves too highly *strung*); also, to bind, secure, suspend, etc., with a string or strings; tether (an animal); kill by hanging (usually with *up*); also, to thread on or as on a string (as, to *string* beads); connect in or as in a line; arrange in a series or succession (as, "I thought it necessary . . . to *string* together these few scattered recollections": Kingsley's "Alton Locke," i.); also, to extend or stretch (a cord, etc.) from one point to another; also, to provide or adorn with something suspended or slung (as, a room *strung* with festoons); also, to deprive of a string or strings; strip the strings from (as, to *string* beans); also, to fool or hoax (slang: as, "I watched you last night when you were *stringing* the Vicomte," W. Churchill's "Modern Chronicle," i. 9). **II.** *intr.* To form into a string or strings, as a glutinous substance does when pulled; extend or hang like a string; form into or move in a string or series (as, "Two or three . . . came *stringing* along, one after another, in unbroken procession": Mrs. Stowe's "Oldtown Folks," xxxvii.); be hanged, or die by hanging (Sc.: as, "You have confessed yourself a spy, and should *string* up to the next tree," Scott's "Rob Roy," xxx.); in *billiards*, etc., to hit one's ball so that it will go the length of the table and back, as in determining who shall open the game (see *string*, *n.*).

string-bean (string'bēn'), *n.* Any of various kinds of bean (plant) the unripe pods of which are used as food, usually after first stripping off the fibrous thread or string along the side; also, the pod itself.

string-board (string'bōrd), *n.* In *arch.*, a board or the like used to cover the ends of the steps in a staircase.

string-col-ored (string'kul″ọrd), *a.* Of a light grayish-brown color, as lace; ficelle.

string-course (string'kōrs), *n.* In *arch.*, a horizontal band or course of stone, etc., projecting beyond or flush with the face of a building, and often molded and sometimes richly carved. **stringed** (stringd), *a.* Having a string or strings, as a musical instrument; pertaining to such instruments (as, *stringed* music).

String-course (sculptured), 13th century. — From triforium of Amiens Cathedral, France.

strin-gent (strin'jẹnt), *a.* [L. *stringens* (*stringent-*), ppr. of *stringere* (pp. *strictus*), draw tight: see *strain*[2], and cf. *strict*.]

Drawing or binding tightly (now rare); also, astringent (obs. or rare); also, compelling, constraining, or urgent (as, *stringent* necessity); also, convincing or forcible, as arguments, etc.; also, narrowly binding, rigorously exacting, or strict, as regulations, requirements, obligations, etc. (as, "*Stringent* laws were passed, forbidding the use of meat in any form or shape," S. Butler's "Erewhon," xxvi.; "to support a demand for a revenue by *stringent* coercive measures," Bancroft's "Hist. of the U. S.," Amer. Revolution, ii. 5); rigorous; severe; also, of the money-market, tight. — **strin'gen-cy, strin'gent-ness,** *n.* — **strin'gent-ly,** *adv.*

string-er (string'ẻr), *n.* One who or that which strings; in *building*, etc., a long horizontal timber for connecting upright posts, supporting a floor, or the like; a tie in a truss or the like; the string of a stair; in *railroading*, a longitudinal timber on which a rail is fastened, and which rests on transverse sleepers.

string-halt (string'hâlt), *n.* Same as *spring-halt*.

string-i-ness (string'i-nes), *n.* Stringy character.

string-less (string'les), *a.* Without strings.

string-piece (string'pēs), *n.* In *building*, etc., a long piece of timber or the like (esp. a horizontal one) in a framework or structure, as for strengthening the structure or connecting or supporting parts.

string-y (string'i), *a.* Resembling a string; consisting of strings or string-like pieces; coarsely or toughly fibrous, as meat; ropy, as a glutinous liquid; sinewy or wiry, as a person (as, "a man of about sixty, tall, hard and *stringy*": G. B. Shaw's "You Never Can Tell," i.).

strip[1] (strip), *v.*; **stripped, stripping.** [AS. *strȳpan* (recorded in *bestrȳpan*, strip clean) = D. *stroopen* = G. *streifen*, strip.] **I.** *tr.* To rob, plunder, or dispossess (as, to *strip* a man of his possessions); deprive or divest (as, to *strip* a tree of its fruit); clear out or empty (as, to *strip* a house of its contents); deprive of equipment (as, to *strip* a ship of rigging); dismantle; deprive of covering (as, to *strip* a tree of its bark or a fruit of its rind); deprive of clothing (as, to *strip* a person naked or to the skin); make bare or naked; undress; divest of outer garments (as, to *strip* one's self of wrappings; "a party of fifteen or twenty . . . *stripped* to their shirts," Marryat's "King's Own," xl.); deprive of armor, insignia, etc. (as, to *strip* a soldier of his uniform); also, to take away or remove (possessions, equipment, a covering, a garment or garments, etc.: as, to *strip* pictures from a wall; "He *stripped* the skin from the banana," Galsworthy's "Dark Flower," ii. 5; "*Strip* the cloak from him," Synge's "Well of the Saints," i.); in specif. use, to draw the last milk from (a cow), esp. by a stroking and compressing movement of the hand; draw out (milk) thus; in *fish-culture*, to press or squeeze the ripe roe or milt from (a fish); in *tobacco-manuf.*, to separate the leaves from the stalks of (tobacco); remove the midrib, etc., from (tobacco-leaves); in *mach.*, to tear off the thread of (a screw, bolt, etc.) or the teeth of (a gear, etc.), as by applying too much force; in *steel-making*, to remove the mold from (a steel ingot). **II.** *intr.* To strip something; esp., to strip one's self of clothes (as, "Other lads than I *Strip* to bathe on Severn shore": A. E. Housman's "Shropshire Lad," lv.); also, to become stripped.

strip[2] (strip), *n.* [Appar. a var. of *stripe*[2].] A narrow piece, comparatively long and usually of uniform width (as, a *strip* of cloth, paper, board, metal, etc.); a long, narrow tract of land, forest, etc. (as, "a *strip* of dry land between the sea and the fens": Peacock's "Nightmare Abbey," i.); in recent use, a continuous series of pictures, as in a newspaper, illustrating incidents, conversation, etc., and usually of a comic character (as, "Babbitt looked up irritably from the comic *strips* in the Evening Advocate": Sinclair Lewis's "Babbitt," vi.). — **strip**[2], *v. t.*; **stripped, stripping.** To cut into strips.

strip[3] (strip), *v.*; **stripped, stripping.** [Origin uncertain: cf. *outstrip*.] **I.** *intr.* To go or pass swiftly; stride along. [Obs. or prov.] **II.**† *tr.* To outstrip.

stripe[1] (strip), *n.* [ME. *strype*: cf. D. *strips*, a whipping. *strippen*, to whip, MLG. *strippe*, strap, whip-lash, also E. *stripe*[2].] A stroke with a whip, scourge, rod, or the like, as in punishment (archaic); any stroke or blow, as with a weapon, a missile, a hoof or claw of an animal, etc.†; also, a mark or wale made by a stroke (obs. or archaic).—**stripe¹**, *v. t.*; *striped, striping*. To whip. [Now prov. Eng.]

stripe² (strīp), *n.* [Cf. MD. *strijpe*, stripe, MLG. *strîpe*, G. *streif*, stripe, strip, also E. *strip²* and *stripe¹*.] A relatively long, narrow band of a different color, appearance, weave, material, or nature from the rest of a surface or thing (as, the *stripes* of a zebra or a tiger; the stars and *stripes* of the U. S. flag; cloth woven with satin *stripes* or lace *stripes*; bayadere *stripes*: cf. *streak*); a particular style or pattern of such bands, as in a fabric or a wall-paper, or a striped fabric or material; also, a strip of braid or the like, or, *pl.*, a number or combination of such strips (cf. *chevron*), worn on a military, naval, or other uniform as a badge of rank, service, good conduct, wounds, etc.; also, a strip, or long, narrow piece of anything (as, "Cane . . . sever'd into *stripes* That interlac'd each other": Cowper's "Task," i. 40); also, a streak or layer of a different nature within a substance; also, fig., style, variety, sort, or kind (as, a man of quite a different *stripe*. See also *Stripes*.—**stripe²**, *v. t.*; *striped, striping*. To mark or furnish with a stripe or stripes; diversify with stripes.

striped (strīpt or strī′ped), *a.* Having stripes or bands, as of another color: as, "*striped* awnings in front of the windows" (Archibald Marshall's "Anthony Dare," xvi.).—**striped′= bass′**, *n.* An American game-fish, *Roccus lineatus*, with blackish stripes along the sides, common on the coasts of the U. S., and ascending rivers in spring to spawn.

Striped-bass.

Stripes (strīps), *n.* [Prop. pl. of *stripe²*, *n.*] A name for the tiger (as, "Spooner and I had . . . arguments in regard to the comparative courage of the lion and the tiger, he holding the view that '*Stripes*' was the more formidable foe": J. H. Patterson's "Man-Eaters of Tsavo," xxiii.); [*l. c.*] a tiger.

strip-ling (strip′ling), *n.* [Prob. < *strip²* + *-ling¹*.] A youth in the state of adolescence, or just passing from boyhood to manhood.

strip-per (strip′ėr), *n.* One who strips; that which strips, as an appliance or machine for stripping.

strip-ping (strip′ing), *n.* The act of one who or that which strips; also, something removed by this act; esp., *pl.*, the last milk drawn from a cow (see *strip¹, v. t.*).

strip-y (strī′pi), *a.* Having stripes; striped; occurring in or suggestive of stripes.

strive (strīv), *v. i.*; pret. *strove*, pp. *striven*, ppr. *striving*. [OF. *estriver*, contend, quarrel, struggle, strive; appar. from Teut.: cf. G. *streben*, strive, endeavor.] To contend in opposition or antagonism, or maintain strife (as, factions were constantly *striving* within the state); quarrel, wrangle, or dispute (archaic or prov.); contend in fight, battle, or any violent conflict (now chiefly fig.: as, to *strive* with Satan; love *strove* with hate); struggle vigorously, as in opposition or resistance (as, to *strive* against the stream; to *strive* against fate); hence, to make strenuous efforts toward any end (as, to *strive* to reach one's goal; to *strive* for self-control; to *strive* after effect); exert one's self or endeavor vigorously; try hard; endeavor to make one's way (as, to *strive* upward; to *strive* through the waves); also, to contend in rivalry, or vie, as with a competitor (obs. or archaic: as, "The rival chariots in the race shall *strive*," Dryden's tr. Virgil's "Georgics," iii. 28).—**striv-er** (strī′vėr), *n.*—**striv′ing-ly**, *adv.*

strob (strob), *n.* [Gr. στρόβος, a twisting or whirling round, akin to στρέφειν, turn, twist.] In *physics*, a unit of velocity for bodies moving in a circular path, equal to one radian per second.

strob-ic (strob′ik), *a.* [Gr. στρόβος: see *strob*.] Spinning or whirling, or appearing to spin or whirl: as, *strobic* circles (a group of concentric circles which appear to spin round or revolve when the paper or object they are drawn on is moved about); *strobic* disk (a disk containing strobic circles or the like).

strob-i-la-ceous (strob-i-lā′shius), *a.* In *bot.*, pertaining to, of the nature of, or resembling a strobile; also, bearing strobiles.

strob-ile (strob′il), *n.* [LL. *strobilus*, < Gr. στρόβιλος, pine-cone, akin to στρέφειν, turn, twist.] In *bot.*, a cone; the more or less conical multiple fruit of the pine, fir, etc.; the cone-like female inflorescence of the hop, consisting of imbricated scales.

strob-o-graph (strob′ō-gráf), *n.* [Gr. στρόβος, a whirling round: see *-graph*.] A device which makes a record of the phenomena observed with a stroboscope (instrument for studying the motion of a body) or similar instrument.—**strob-o-graph′ic** (-gráf′ik), *a.*

strob-o-scope (strob′ō-skōp), *n.* [Gr. στρόβος, a whirling round: see *-scope*.] A zoëtrope or similar device; also, an instrument used in studying the motion of a body (as one in rapid revolution or vibration) by rendering it visible at frequent intervals, as by illuminating it intermittently with an electric spark or the like, or by viewing it through openings in a revolving disk.—**strob-o-scop′ic** (-skop′ik), *a.*

strode (strōd). Preterit of *stride*.

stroke¹ (strōk), *n.* [ME. *strok, strak*, < AS. *strīcan*, E. *strike*.] An act of striking, as with the fist, a weapon, a hammer, etc.; a blow dealt or aimed; a hitting of or aiming at a ball or the like, as in a game; a hitting of or upon anything; a striking of a clapper or hammer, as on a bell, a gong, or the sounding part of a clock, or the sound produced by this; a throb or pulsation, as of the heart; a beat or accent, as in music or rhythm; also, something likened to a blow in its effect, as in causing pain, injury, or death; an act of divine chastisement; an attack of apoplexy or of paralysis (as, "John Baines had had a *stroke* . . . his left arm and left leg and his right eyelid were paralyzed": Arnold Bennett's "Old Wives' Tale," i. 3); a destructive discharge of electricity; a piece of luck, fortune, etc., befalling one (as, a *stroke* of bad or good luck); also, a vigorous movement as if in dealing a blow; a single complete movement, esp. one continuously repeated in some process; each of the succession of movements of the arms and legs in swimming; a vigorous attempt to attain some object (as, a bold *stroke* for liberty); a measure adopted for a particular purpose (as, "a *stroke* of policy": Prescott's "Conquest of Mexico," iii. 7); a feat or achievement (as, a *stroke* of genius); an act, piece, or amount of work, etc. (in phrases: as, "Father has never done a *stroke* of work since he has been here," Hugh Walpole's "Wooden Horse," ix.; that was a good or a poor *stroke* of work, or of business); also, a movement of a pen, pencil, brush, graver, or the like, as in writing, drawing, painting, engraving, etc.; a mark traced by or as if by a pen, pencil, brush, or the like; a distinctive or effective touch in a literary composition; a trait, as of character†; in *rowing*, a single pull of the oar; manner or style of moving the oars, as with reference to the length, speed, or frequency of the successive pulls; the oarsman nearest to the stern of the boat, to whose strokes those of the other oarsmen must conform; the position in the boat occupied by this oarsman; in *mech.*, one of a series of alternating continuous movements of something back and forth over or through the same line; the complete movement of a moving part (esp. a reciprocating part) in one direction, or the distance traversed (cf. *throw, n.*); travel.—**stroke¹**, *v. t.*; *stroked, stroking*. To row as stroke or strokesman of (a boat or crew); row as stroke in (a boat-race); also, to mark with a stroke or strokes, as of a pen; cancel, as by a stroke of a pen.

stroke² (strōk), *v. t.*; *stroked, stroking*. [AS. *strācian*, < *strīcan*, E. *strike*.] To pass the hand or an instrument over (something) lightly or with little pressure; rub with a gentle movement in a single direction, as in soothing or caressing, or for healing (as, "He was *stroking* her cat," Galsworthy's "Dark Flower," i. 3: also fig.); bring into a particular position, condition, etc., by stroking (as, "The old gentleman softly *stroked* the hair off her forehead": Louisa M. Alcott's "Little Women," i. 6); also, to pass (the hand or an instrument) lightly over something (as, "Molly *stroked* her hand down her chin to give it length": G. Meredith's "Ordeal of Richard Feverel," xx.); draw (a knife-blade, etc.) over a surface in order to sharpen it; in *masonry*, to work the face of (a stone) in such a manner as to produce a sort of fluted surface.—**to stroke the wrong way**, to stroke (an animal) in a direction contrary to that in which the fur naturally lies; fig., to ruffle or irritate (a person) as by going counter to his wishes.—**stroke²**, *n.* An act of stroking; a stroking movement, as of the hand.

stroke=oar (strōk'ōr), *n.* The oar nearest to the stern of a boat; also, the oarsman who pulls this oar; the stroke or strokesman.—**stroke'=oars'man**, *n.*; pl. *-men.* The oarsman who pulls the stroke-oar; the stroke or strokesman.

strok-er (strō'kėr), *n.* One who or that which strokes.

strokes-man (strōks'man), *n.*; pl. *-men.* The oarsman nearest to the stern of a boat, who sets the stroke for the other oarsmen.

stroll (strōl), *v.* [Origin uncertain: cf. G. dial. *strollen*, stroll, ramble, G. *strolch*, a vagabond.] **I.** *intr.* To wander or rove from place to place, as a vagrant or an itinerant (now chiefly in *strolling, p. a.:* as, *strolling* gipsies; a *strolling* player, an itinerant actor of a low class); roam; also, to walk leisurely as inclination directs (as, "A few infantry soldiers were *strolling* about under the trees": Howells's "Foregone Conclusion," xiv.); ramble; saunter; take a walk. **II.** *tr.* To stroll along or through: as, "He noticed three people *strolling* the muddy street" (Sinclair Lewis's "Arrowsmith," x.).—**stroll**, *n.* A leisurely walk; a ramble; a saunter: as, "Here . . . would the young men and maidens of the town take their evening *stroll*" (Irving's "Knickerbocker's New York," v. 7).—**stroll'er**, *n.* A wanderer; a vagrant; a strolling or itinerant player or performer; also, a saunterer.

stro-ma (strō'mą), *n.*; pl. *-mata* (-mạ-tä). [NL. use of LL. *stroma*, < Gr. στρῶμα, bed-covering, bed, < στρωννύναι, spread out.] In *anat.*, the sustentacular framework of an organ or part, usually consisting of connective tissue; also, the colorless, sponge-like framework of a red blood-corpuscle or other cell.—**stro-mat-ic** (strō-mat'ik), *a.*

stromb (stromb or strom), *n.* [L. *strombus*, < Gr. στρόμβος, spiral shell, akin to στρέφειν, turn, twist.] Any of the marine gastropods constituting the family *Strombidæ*, esp. those of the genus *Strombus*, as *S. gigas*, a large species of the West Indies whose delicate pink shell is used for ornament, cameo-cutting, etc.; also, the shell of such a gastropod.

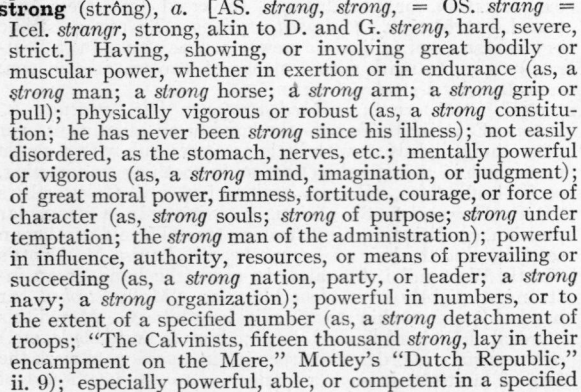

Stromb (*Strombus gigas*), one seventh natural size.

strom-bu-li-form (strom'bū-li-fôrm), *a.* [NL. *strombuliformis*, dim. adj. < L. *strombus*, spiral shell, + *forma*, form.] In *bot.*, twisted or coiled into the form of a screw, helix, or spiral.

stro-mey-er-ite (strō'mī"ėr-īt), *n.* [From F. *Stromeyer* (died 1835), German chemist and mineralogist.] A steel-gray mineral, a sulphide of silver and copper, with a metallic luster, occurring usually in compact masses, but also in crystals.

Strombuliform Pods (*a, b, c*) of different species of Medic (genus *Medicago*).

strong (strông), *a.* [AS. *strang*, *strong*, = OS. *strang* = Icel. *strangr*, strong, akin to D. and G. *streng*, hard, severe, strict.] Having, showing, or involving great bodily or muscular power, whether in exertion or in endurance (as, a *strong* man; a *strong* horse; a *strong* arm; a *strong* grip or pull); physically vigorous or robust (as, a *strong* constitution; he has never been *strong* since his illness); not easily disordered, as the stomach, nerves, etc.; mentally powerful or vigorous (as, a *strong* mind, imagination, or judgment); of great moral power, firmness, fortitude, courage, or force of character (as, *strong* souls; *strong* of purpose; *strong* under temptation; the *strong* man of the administration); powerful in influence, authority, resources, or means of prevailing or succeeding (as, a *strong* nation, party, or leader; a *strong* navy; a *strong* organization); powerful in numbers, or to the extent of a specified number (as, a *strong* detachment of troops; "The Calvinists, fifteen thousand *strong*, lay in their encampment on the Mere," Motley's "Dutch Republic," ii. 9); especially powerful, able, or competent in a specified

field or respect (as, a race *strong* on the sea; *strong* in mathematics; *strong* as a comedian; *strong* to save); well supplied or rich in something specified (as, a hand *strong* in trumps); of great force, effectiveness, potency, or cogency (as, *strong* influences, inducements, or arguments); also, of material things, able to resist force or stand strain, wear, etc. (as, *strong* walls; a *strong* castle; a *strong* box, for the safekeeping of valuables; a *strong* rope or cloth); not easily broken, demolished, injured, torn, worn through, or the like; fig., firm or unfaltering under trial (as, *strong* faith or friendship); also, moving or acting with force or vigor (as, a *strong* wind or tide; a *strong* pulse); strenuous or energetic (as, *strong* efforts; *strong* measures); forceful or vigorous (as, a *strong* speech; "The papal envoy urged, in *strong* language, the propriety . . . of succouring Rome," G. P. R. James's "Hist. of Charlemagne," iii.; a *strong* literary style; a *strong* picture of actual conditions); hearty, fervent, or thoroughgoing (as, *strong* liking, interest, or prejudice; a *strong* partizan; a *strong* Republican); also, having a large proportion of the effective or essential properties or ingredients (as, *strong* tea; *strong* acid; a *strong* solution); containing alcohol, or much alcohol (as, *strong* drink, alcoholic liquor of any kind; *strong* beer or wine); solid or substantial, as food; intense, as light or color; distinct, as marks or impressions; marked, as a resemblance or contrast; clear and firm, or loud, as the voice; having a high degree of flavor or odor (as, *strong* seasoning; *strong* onions; *strong* perfume); sometimes, of an unpleasant or offensive flavor or odor (as, *strong* butter; a *strong* breath); in *gram.*, designating or pertaining to verbs which are inflected by a change of the radical vowel, as, in English, *find* (*found*), *speak* (*spoke* or *spake*, *spoken*), *give* (*gave*, *given*), *swim* (*swam*, *swum*) (cf. *weak*); also, designating or pertaining to nouns and adjectives, as in German, etc., inflected with fuller retention of older case-distinctions (cf. *weak*); in *phonetics*, stressed; in *photog.*, dense; in *com.*, characterized by steady or advancing prices; tending upward in price.—**strong water.** See *water*, *n.*—**strong**, *adv.* [AS. *strange*, *stronge*.] In a strong manner; powerfully; forcibly; vigorously: as, a tide running *strong*; going *strong* (proceeding with vigor, or getting on fast or well: colloq.).

strong=arm (strông'ärm'), *a.* Having, using, or involving the use of, muscular or physical force: as, a *strong-arm* squad of police; *strong-arm* methods.

strong-bark (strông'bärk), *n.* Any of the trees or shrubs of the boraginaceous genus *Bourreria*, of tropical and subtropical America, as *B. havanensis*, a tree of the West Indies and southern Florida with a strong, hard wood of a brown color streaked with orange.

strong=head-ed (strông'hed'ed), *a.* Headstrong; also, having a strong intellect.—**strong'=head'ed-ness**, *n.*

strong-hold (strông'hōld), *n.* A strong or well-fortified place; a fortress; a fastness; a secure retreat or abode.

strong-ish (strông'ish), *a.* Somewhat or rather strong: as, "a simple-minded man, with a *strongish* will" (Kinglake's "Eothen," xxii.).

strong-ly (strông'li), *adv.* In a strong manner.

strong=mind-ed (strông'mīn'ded), *a.* Having or showing a strong mind or vigorous mental powers; of women, having or (seemingly) affecting to have the strong mentality supposed to belong more properly to the male sex, or holding views or claiming rights supposed to be exclusively masculine.—**strong'=mind'ed-ly**, *adv.*—**strong'=mind'ed-ness**, *n.*

strong-ness (strông'nes), *n.* The state or quality of being strong.

stron-gyle (stron'jil), *n.* [NL. *Strongylus*, the typical genus, < Gr. στρογγύλος, round.] Any of certain nematode worms constituting the family *Strongylidæ*, parasitic in the organs and tissues of man and many animals, and often giving rise to serious pathological conditions.—**stron-gy-lo'sis** (-ji-lō'sis), *n.* [NL.] In *pathol.*, a disease in man and animals, due to the presence of strongyles (genus *Strongylus*) in the organs and tissues.

stron-ti-a (stron'shi-ą), *n.* [NL.: see *strontian*.] In *chem.*, strontium oxide, SrO, a white amorphous powder resembling lime in its general character; also, strontium hydroxide; also, strontium (in phrases, as 'sulphate of strontia').

stron-ti-an (stron′shi-an), *n.* [Orig. in *Strontian mineral* or *spar*, strontium carbonate, first found in lead-mines at *Strontian*, in Argyllshire, Scotland.] Native strontium carbonate; strontianite; also, strontia; also, strontium.—
stron′ti-an-ite (-īt), *n.* A mineral consisting of strontium carbonate, occurring commonly in radiating, fibrous, or granular aggregates, and sometimes in orthorhombic crystals, and varying in color from white to yellow and pale green.
stron-ti-um (stron′shi-um), *n.* [NL., < *strontia*.] Chem. sym., Sr; at. wt., 87.63; sp. gr., 2.54. A bivalent metallic element whose compounds resemble those of calcium: found in nature only in the combined state, as in strontianite.—
stron′tic, *a.*
strop (strop), *n.* [AS. *strop* = MLG. and D. *strop*, < L. *stroppus*, *struppus*, band, thong, strap: cf. Gr. στρόφος, twisted band, also E. *strap*.] A strap, or narrow strip or band of leather or some other material (now only as in following defs.); esp., a strip of leather or other flexible material, or a long, narrow piece of wood having its faces covered with leather or an abrasive, or some similar device, used for sharpening razors; *naut.*, same as *strap*, *n.*—**strop**, *v. t.*; *stropped*, *stropping*. To sharpen on or as on a strop.
stro-phan-thin (strō-fan′thin), *n.* A bitter, poisonous glucoside obtained from the ripe seeds of various species of strophanthus, esp. *Strophanthus kombe*: used in medicine as a cardiac stimulant.
stro-phan-thus (strō-fan′thus), *n.* [NL. *Strophanthus*, < Gr. στρόφος, twisted band, + ἄνθος, flower; from the long, twisted segments of the corolla.] Any of the shrubs or small trees constituting the apocynaceous genus *Strophanthus*, mostly natives of tropical Africa, the ripe seeds of certain species of which, esp. of *S. kombe*, are used in the preparation of an arrow-poison and of the drug strophan-thin; also, the ripe seeds.
stro-phe (strō′fē), *n.*; pl. *-phes* (-fēz). [NL., < Gr. στροφή, a turning, strophe, < στρέφειν, turn.] The part of an ancient Greek choral ode sung by the chorus when moving from right to left (cf. *antistrophe*); also, the first of two metrically corresponding series of lines forming divisions of a lyric poem (the second being the *antistrophe*), or one of any number of such series; in modern poetry, a stanza.—**stroph-ic, stroph-i-cal** (strof′ik, -i-kal), *a.*

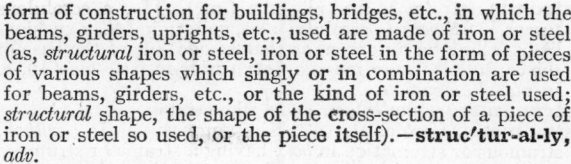

Strophanthus (*S. kombe*). — *a*, branch with leaves and flowers; *b*, corolla, laid open, the attenuate lobes removed; *c*, stamen, front and side view; *d*, pistil; *e*, portion of follicle.

stroph-i-ole (strof′i-ōl), *n.* [L. *strophiolum*, dim. of *strophium*, band, chaplet, < Gr. στρόφιον, dim. of στρόφος, twisted band, < στρέφειν, turn, twist.] In *bot.*, a cellular outgrowth in the region of the hilum in certain seeds; a caruncle.—**stroph′i-o-late** (-ō-lāt), *a.*
stroph-u-lus (strof′ū-lus), *n.* [NL., prob. for ML. *scrophulus*, red-gum, < LL. *scrofulæ*: see *scrofula*.] In *pathol.*, a papular eruption of the skin in infants, occurring in several forms (as red-gum and white-gum), and usually harmless.
strop-per (strop′ėr), *n.* One who strops; a device for stropping.
strove (strōv). Preterit of *strive*.
strow (strō), *v. t.*; pret. *strowed*, pp. *strowed* or *strown*, ppr. *strowing*. Same as *strew*: as, "when morn's roses o'er the skies are *strown*" (Wiffen's tr. Tasso's "Jerusalem Delivered," ii. 94). [Archaic.]
struck (struk). Preterit and past participle of *strike*.
struc-tur-al (struk′tūr-al), *a.* Of or pertaining to structure; pertaining or essential to a structure; in *biol.*, pertaining to organic structure; morphological; in *geol.*, pertaining to the structure of rock, etc.; in *chem.*, pertaining to or showing the arrangement or mode of attachment of the atoms which constitute the molecule of a substance (as, a *structural* formula); in *arch.* and *engin.*, pertaining to the art of building; used in construction; specif., pertaining to or used in a form of construction for buildings, bridges, etc., in which the beams, girders, uprights, etc., used are made of iron or steel (as, *structural* iron or steel, iron or steel in the form of pieces of various shapes which singly or in combination are used for beams, girders, etc., or the kind of iron or steel used; *structural* shape, the shape of the cross-section of a piece of iron or steel so used, or the piece itself).—**struc′tur-al-ly**, *adv.*
struc-ture (struk′tūr), *n.* [L. *structura*, < *struere* (pp. *structus*), pile up, build, make: cf. *construct*, *construe*, *destroy*, *instruct*, and *obstruct*.] The act or process of building or constructing (obs. or rare: as, "the scarcity of brick and stone at the period of its [a building's] *structure*," Disraeli's "Coningsby," vii. 3); also, mode of building, construction, or organization; arrangement of parts, elements, or constituents; make; constitution; a particular arrangement of parts or elements; also, something built or constructed; a building, esp. one of large size or imposing appearance (as, "Our house was a long low *structure*, built of brick," W. H. Hudson's "Far Away and Long Ago," i.; "There stands a *structure* of majestic frame," Pope's "Rape of the Lock," iii. 3); an edifice; a bridge, dam, framework, or the like; any construction; anything composed of parts arranged together in some way; an organization; in *biol.*, mode of organization; construction and arrangement of tissues, parts, or organs; also, a part, or the whole, of an organism; in *geol.*, the arrangement of the parts of which a mineral or rock is composed; various characteristic features of rocks, as stratification, cleavage, etc., considered collectively; the character of a mass of rock with regard to one or more of such features.—**struc′tured**, *a.* Having a definite structure.—**struc′ture-less**, *a.* Having no definite structure; amorphous.
strug-gle (strug′l), *v.*; *-gled*, *-gling*. [ME. *strugle*, *strogel*; origin uncertain.] **I.** *intr.* To contend with an adversary, as in wrestling; put forth violent bodily effort against any opposing force (as, "He was *struggling* gallantly with the waves": Borrow's "Bible in Spain," i.); offer obstinate opposition or resistance (as, "the kind of man who cannot *struggle* against adverse conditions": Gissing's "New Grub Street," v.); contend resolutely with a task, problem, etc.; make strenuous efforts toward an end, or strive (as, to *struggle* to do something difficult; to *struggle* for existence); also, to advance or progress with violent effort (as, to *struggle* through the snow; "From one or two offices *struggled* the dim gleam of an early candle," G. W. Curtis's "Prue and I," iv.). **II.** *tr.* To bring, put, etc., by struggling (as, to *struggle* one's self out of a tight place; "He there *struggled* down the last of his emotion," Stevenson's "Master of Ballantrae," iv.); make (one's way) with violent effort.—**strug′gle**, *n.* The act or process of struggling; a course of violently exerted bodily efforts, as between wrestlers or against an opposing force; a strong effort, or series of efforts, against any adverse agencies or conditions, as in order to maintain one's existence or to attain some end (as, "It is magnificent, the *struggles* she makes with her infirmities": Mrs. H. Ward's "Lady Rose's Daughter," iv.).—**strug′gler**, *n.*—**strug′gling**, *p. a.* That struggles; esp., having a struggle to make a living (as, "a *struggling* professional man," Charnwood's "Abraham Lincoln," i.; "a *struggling* periodical," L. Merrick's "Position of Peggy Harper," ii. 9).—**strug′gling-ly**, *adv.*
Struld-brug (struld′brug), *n.* [A made word.] One of a class of immortals described in Swift's "Gulliver's Travels," iii. 10, who after reaching the age of eighty, although regarded as legally dead, live on at the public expense in the imbecility of extreme age; hence [often *l. c.*], any person or thing that continues to exist although in a state of extreme decay.—**Struld-brug′gi-an**, *a.*
strum (strum), *v.*; *strummed*, *strumming*. [Imit.] **I.** *tr.* To play on (a stringed musical instrument) unskilfully or carelessly; produce (notes, etc.) by such playing (as, "He ... *strummed* a song she used to sing": L. Merrick's "Conrad in Quest of His Youth," viii.). **II.** *intr.* To play on a stringed instrument unskilfully or carelessly: as, "Lewis, on the piano-stool ... went on *strumming* softly" (Margaret Kennedy's "Constant Nymph," xx.).—**strum**, *n.* The act of strumming.

(variable) ḍ as d or j, ș as s or sh, ṭ as t or ch, ẓ as z or zh; *o*, F. cloche; ü, F. menu; čh, Sc. loch; ṅ, F. bonbon; ′, primary accent; ″, secondary accent; †, obsolete; <, from; +, and; =, equals. See also lists at beginning of book.

stru-ma (strö′mä), n.; pl. -mæ (-mē). [L., a scrofulous tumor.] In *pathol.*, scrofula; also, goiter; in *bot.*, a cushion-like swelling on an organ, as that at one side of the base of the capsule in many mosses.—**stru-mat-ic** (strö-mat′ik), a. In *pathol.*, strumous.

strum-mer (strum′ėr), n. One who strums.

stru-mose, a. [L. *strumosus*.] In *pathol.*, strumous or strumatic; in *bot.*, having a struma or strumæ.

stru-mous (strö′mus), a. [L. *strumosus*.] In *pathol.*, affected with struma; characteristic of struma; of the nature of struma.

strum-pet (strum′pet), n. [ME. *strumpet*; origin uncertain.] A prostitute; a harlot.

strung (strung). Preterit and past participle of *string*.

strut[1] (strut), v.; strutted, strutting. [ME. *strut*, also *stroute*: cf. Sw. *strutta*, Dan. *strutte*, strut, G. *strotzen*, swell out, strut.] **I.** *intr.* To swell† or bulge†; protrude† or jut forth† (as, "the foot of a promontory, which *strutted* forth boldly into the waves": Irving's "Knickerbocker's New York," ii. 4); also, to walk with a vain, pompous bearing, as with head erect and chest thrown out (as, "Brindley, inflated with the importance of controlling two establishments, *strutted* in and out": Arnold Bennett's "Old Wives' Tale," ii. 5); step or go along in a swaggering, vainglorious manner, as if expecting to impress observers. **II.** *tr.* To walk upon or over with a strut: as, "those strange monsters in lace and embroidery . . . which . . . strut the stage" (Fielding's "Tom Jones," xiv. 1).—**strut**[1], n. The act or state of strutting (as, "after our little hour of *strut* and rave": Lowell's "Commemoration Ode," iv.); a strutting walk or gait (as, "He had been a Janissary . . . and kept up the odd *strut* of his old corps": Kinglake's "Eothen," ii.).

strut[2] (strut), n. [From the root of *strut*[1]: cf. LG. *strutt*, stiff, rigid.] A piece of wood or iron, or some other member of a structure, designed for the reception of pressure or weight in the direction of its length, as a timber extending obliquely from a rafter to a king-post (see cut at *king-post*).—**strut**[2], v. t.; strutted, strutting. To brace or support by a strut or struts.

stru-thi-oid (strö′thi-oid), a. [LL. *struthio*, ostrich: see *struthious* and -oid.] Ostrich-like; struthious.

stru-thi-o-la-ri-a (strö′thi-ō-lā′ri-ä), n. [NL., < LL. *struthio*, ostrich: see *struthious*.] A gastropod mollusk of the genus *Struthiolaria*, of the southern Pacific waters, having a conical shell with an oval aperture and a lip said to have been compared to the foot of an ostrich.

stru-thi-ous (strö′thi-us), a. [LL. *struthio*, < Gr. στρουθίων, ostrich, < στρουθός, sparrow, bird: cf. *ostrich*.] Related to or resembling the ostrich; belonging or pertaining to the *Struthiones*, an order or group of birds including, in the restricted sense, the African ostriches only, or, in a wider sense, all the ratite birds (ostriches, cassowaries, emus, etc.).

Struthiolaria.

strut-ter (strut′ėr), n. One who or that which struts.

strut-ting (strut′ing), p. a. That struts; walking pompously; pompous.—**strut′ting-ly**, adv.

strych-ni-a (strik′ni-ä), n. [NL.] Same as strychnine.

strych-nic (strik′nik), a. Of, pertaining to, or obtained from strychnine.

strych-nine, strych-nin (strik′nin), n. [F. *strychnine*, < L. *strychnos*, < Gr. στρύχνος, nightshade.] A poisonous crystalline alkaloid obtained from nux vomica, etc.: used in medicine, usually in the form of a sulphate, as a tonic, etc.—**strych′nin-ism**, n. In *pathol.*, a morbid condition induced by an overdose, or by excessive use, of strychnine.

Stu-art (stū′ärt), a. Designating or pertaining to a royal house (family name Steward, Stewart, Steuart, or, in later times, Stuart) descended from Walter, steward of Scotland (died 1326), father of King Robert II., to which belonged the sovereigns of Scotland from Robert II. to James VI. (1371–1603), and the sovereigns of Great Britain and Ireland from James I. (previously James VI. of Scotland) to Anne (1603–1714).

stub (stub), n. [AS. *stubb* = MLG. *stubbe* = Icel. *stubbr* = Sw. *stubbe* = Dan. *stub*, stub, stump.] The end of a fallen tree, shrub, or plant left fixed in the ground; a stump; any remaining part resembling this (as, the *stub* of a docked tail or of a broken tooth); a short projecting part; a short remaining piece, as of a pencil, a candle, a cigar, etc. (as, "They were smoking large cigars and dropping ashes and *stubs* on the carpet": Sinclair Lewis's "Babbitt," xiii.); something unusually short, as a short, thick nail or a short-pointed, blunt pen; also, an old or worn horseshoe-nail, esp., in *pl.*, such nails and other similar bits of iron as material for making a tenacious kind of iron used for gun-barrels, etc.; also, *sing.*, in a check-book, etc., the inner end of each leaf, on which may be kept a record of the contents of the part torn away; a counterfoil.—**stub**, v. t.; stubbed, stubbing. To dig up by the roots; grub up (roots); also, to clear of stubs, as land; also, to reduce to a stub or stump, as a tree or a post; also, to cause (a horse) to be injured as by treading on or striking against a stub or stump; strike, as one's toe, against something projecting from a surface (chiefly U. S.).—**stub-bed** (stub′ed or stubd), a. Reduced to or resembling a stub; short and thick; stumpy; blunted; also, abounding in or rough with stubs (as, "a bit of *stubbed* ground, once a wood": Browning's "Childe Roland," xxv.).—**stub′ber**, n.

stub-bi-ness (stub′i-nes), n. Stubby state or form.

stub-ble (stub′l), n. [OF. *stuble, estuble* (F. *étouble, éteule*), < ML. *stupla*, for L. *stipula*, stalk, stem, stubble, E. *stipule*.] The stump or lower end of a grain-stalk or the like, left in the ground when the crop is cut (chiefly in *pl.*: as, "Gray mists were drifting silently across the woods and the wide *stubbles* of the now shaven cornfield," Mrs. H. Ward's "Robert Elsmere," xiv.); such stumps collectively (as, "The ground was covered with *stubble*": Borrow's "Lavengro," iv.); hence, any short, rough growth, as of beard (as, "the grey *stubble* on his unshaved chin": H. G. Wells's "Tono-Bungay," iv. 1. § 6); also, the straw of grain-stalks, etc., gathered after the crop has been harvested; also, a field covered with stubble, or stumps of grain-stalks, etc. (chiefly in *pl.*: as, "We trudged on, over wide *stubbles*, with innumerable weeds," Kingsley's "Alton Locke," xxviii.).—**stub′bled**, a. Covered with stubble.—**stub′bly**, a. Covered with stubble (as, "*stubbly* waste land": Sinclair Lewis's "Arrowsmith," x.); also, resembling stubble; bristly, as hair (as, "a *stubbly* gray moustache": Maugham's "Moon and Sixpence," xlvi.).

stub-born (stub′orn), a. [ME. *stuborn, stoburne, stibourne*; origin uncertain.] Fixed or set in purpose or opinion; inflexibly resolute; unyielding; esp., unreasonably obstinate, or obstinately perverse (as, "She was very *stubborn* when her mind was made up": S. Butler's "Way of All Flesh," xxxv.); also, obstinately maintained, as a course of action (as, a *stubborn* resistance); also, hard to deal with or manage (as, "Not a plough had ever disturbed a grain of that *stubborn* soil," Hardy's "Return of the Native," i. 3; facts are *stubborn* things); hard, tough, or stiff, as stone or wood. —**stub′born**, v. t. To make stubborn; render unyielding, firm, or the like. [Poetic.]—**stub′born-ly**, adv.—**stub′-born-ness**, n.

stub-by (stub′i), a. Of the nature of or resembling a stub; short and thick or broad; thick-set; also, consisting of or abounding in stubs; bristly, as the hair or beard.

stub=nail (stub′nāl), n. A short, thick nail; also, an old or worn horseshoe-nail; a stub (see *stub*, n.).

stub=pen (stub′pen′), n. A pen with a short, blunt nib.

stuc-co (stuk′ō), n.; pl. stuccoes or stuccos (-ōz). [It.; prob. from Teut.: cf. OHG. *stukki*, piece, crust, G. *stück*, piece.] Any of various plasters, cements, etc.; specif., a plaster (as of slaked lime, chalk, and pulverized white marble, or of plaster of Paris and glue) used for cornices and moldings of rooms and for other decorations; the last coat of plastering on a wall; a cement or concrete imitating stone, for coating exterior walls of houses, etc. (as, "The temples and principal buildings of the cities were covered with a hard white stucco, which glistened like enamel": Prescott's "Conquest of Mexico," iii. 9); hence, work made of such materials.— **stuc′co**, v. t.; -coed, -coing. To cover or ornament with stucco: as, "gabled houses, frescoed and stuccoed in imita-

tion of Italy" (Vernon Lee's "Genius Loci," Augsburg).—
stuc′co-er, *n.*—**stuc′co=work**, *n.*

stuck (stuk). Preterit and past participle of *stick*[2].—**stuck**, *p. a.* Pierced with a sharp instrument, or killed by this means: as, a *stuck* pig.—**stuck′=up′**, *a.* Superciliously proud; haughty: as, "two *stuck-up*, superior, impracticable young persons" (Mrs. H. Ward's "Robert Elsmere," ix.); "She . . . tells me not to talk in a *stuck-up* way" (Gissing's "New Grub Street," vii.). [Colloq.]

stud[1] (stud), *n.* [AS. *stōd* = OHG. *stuot* = Icel. *stōdh* = Dan. *stod*, stud of horses (Sw. *sto*, G. *stute*, brood-mare); from the root of E. *stand*.] An establishment in which horses are kept for breeding; the collection of horses kept there; also, a number of horses, as for racing or hunting, belonging to one owner; a collection of animals of some other kind, esp. a collection of dogs, belonging to one person; sometimes, a number of motor-cars or the like belonging to one owner; also, a stud-horse or stallion.

stud[2] (stud), *n.* [AS. *studu, stuthu,* = Icel. *stodh* = Sw. *stōd*, post, prop, akin to G. *stütze*, prop, support.] A post or upright prop, as in the wall of a building; esp., one of the smaller vertical timbers, of the height of a single story, to which laths or boards are nailed in forming partitions or walls in houses; also, a boss, knob, nail-head, or other protuberance projecting from a surface or part, esp. as an ornament; also, a kind of small button or fastener, commonly of metal, bone, or the like and in the form of a small knob and a disk connected by a stem, used (when passed through small buttonholes or the like) for holding together parts of dress (as shirts) or for ornament (as, "He possessed no jewellery save a set of gold *studs*": Arnold Bennett's "Old Wives' Tale," ii. 6); one of a number of knob-like projections around which a string, etc., is laced; also, any of various projecting pins, lugs, or the like on machines, etc.; *naut.*, a transverse piece of iron inserted in each link of a chain to prop the sides apart and thus increase the strength.—**stud**[2], *v. t.*; *studded*, *studding*. To furnish with or support by studs or upright props; also, to set with or as with studs, bosses, or the like (as, "a low door, *studded* with knobs of iron": Jane Porter's "Scottish Chiefs," xxxiv.); set with protuberant objects of any kind; scatter over with things set at intervals (as, "a blue mitre *studded* with gold stars": Amelia B. Edwards's "Thousand Miles up the Nile," xiv.); of things, to be set in, in the manner of studs; be scattered over the surface of (as, "Where are the islands of the blest? They *stud* the Ægean sea": J. H. Newman's "Callista," x.); also, to set or scatter (objects) at intervals over a surface.

stud=book (stud′buk), *n.* A genealogical register of a stud; a book giving the pedigree of thoroughbred or noted horses or other animals.

stud-ded (stud′ed), *a.* Of a room, story, etc., having studs or wall-uprights (as specified, as to height): as, "Have the parlours high-*studded* . . . Have the entrance-story low-*studded*" (Howells's "Rise of Silas Lapham," iii.). [U. S.]

stud-ding (stud′ing), *n.* Studs of a wall, partition, or the like, collectively; material for such studs; also, objects with which a surface is studded.

stud-ding-sail (stud′ing-sāl, naut. stun′sl), *n.* [Origin uncertain.] *Naut.*, a light sail sometimes set beyond either of the leeches of a square sail.

stu-dent (stū′dent), *n.* [L. *studens* (student-), ppr. of *studere*, be eager, apply one's self: cf. *study, n.*] One who is engaged in or given to study, or the acquisition of knowledge, as by reading or investigation (as, "The *students* of natural phenomena early realized the arduous path they had to travel": J. H. Robinson's "Mind in the Making," viii. 16); also, one who is engaged in a course of study and instruction, as at a college, university, or professional or technical school.—**student lamp**, an oil-lamp having an Argand burner and an elevated oil-reservoir connected with the burner by a downward curving tube, both mounted on an upright standard on which they may be raised and lowered. — **stu′dent-ship**, *n.* The state of being a student; also, a

Studfish (*Fundulus catenatus*).

position as a student having an allowance for maintenance.

stud-fish (stud′fish), *n.* Any of several American killifishes of the genus *Fundulus*, as *F. catenatus*, a species abundant in the Tennessee and Cumberland rivers. See cut in preceding column.

stud=horse (stud′hôrs), *n.* A stallion kept for breeding.

stud-ied (stud′id), *p. a.* Done by or resulting from deliberate effort (as, a *studied* insult; *studied* simplicity); marked by or suggestive of effort, rather than spontaneous or natural (as, "a *studied* laugh": Mrs. Wharton's "Son at the Front," viii.); carefully considered (as, "Your Majesty's statements are always clear and *studied*": Chesterton's "Napoleon of Notting Hill," iii. 3); also, learned (as, a *studied* man).—**stud′ied-ly**, *adv.*—**stud′ied-ness**, *n.*

stud-i-er (stud′i-ėr), *n.* One who studies; a student.

stu-di-o (stū′di-ō), *n.*; pl. *-os* (-ōz). [It., < L. *studium*, E. *study, n.*] The workroom or atelier of an artist, as a painter or sculptor; a room or place in which some form of art is pursued (as, a photographer's *studio*; a music *studio*; a moving-picture *studio*).

stu-di-ous (stū′di-us), *a.* [OF. *estudious* (F. *studieux*), < L. *studiosus*, eager, zealous, studious, < *studium*, E. *study, n.*] Zealous, assiduous, or painstaking (as, *studious* effort or care; *studious* application to business); solicitous (as, *studious* to please; *studious* of one's comfort); studied, deliberate, or carefully maintained (as, *studious* reserve; "The study was furnished with *studious* simplicity," Galsworthy's "Country House," ii. 2); also, disposed or given to study or the pursuit of learning (as, a *studious* boy; *studious* pupils); concerned with, characterized by, or pertaining to study (as, *studious* tastes, habits, or pursuits; *studious* hours); of places, used or frequented for purposes of study (chiefly poetic).—**stu′di-ous-ly**, *adv.*—**stu′di-ous-ness**, *n.*

stud-work (stud′wėrk), *n.* Construction with studs or upright scantlings; work containing or supported by studs; also, textile fabrics or leather set with studs or knobs.

stud-y (stud′i), *n.*; pl. *-ies* (-iz). [OF. *estudie, estude* (F. *étude*), < L. *studium*, eagerness, fondness, inclination, zeal, devotion, application, study, LL. a place for study, connected with L. *studere*, be eager, apply one's self, study: cf. *student* and *studio*.] Fondness, liking, or inclination for something†; zealous endeavor or assiduous effort, or the object of the endeavor or effort (as, his constant *study* is to avoid error; accuracy is his chief *study*); deep thought, reverie, or a state of abstraction (now usually in 'brown study': see under *brown, a.*); a state of perplexed or anxious thought†; often, application of the mind to the acquisition of knowledge, as by reading, investigation, or reflection (as, "I fixed on a page . . . and followed the lines . . . lazily at first . . . and finally in that absorbed effort of continued comprehension which constitutes real *study*": F. M. Crawford's "Mr. Isaacs," xi.); the pursuit of learning; the cultivation of a particular branch of learning, science, or art (as, the *study* of languages, chemistry, law, music, or painting); a particular course of effort to acquire knowledge or to become versed in some subject (as, to pursue medical or musical *studies*; to make a *study* of ferns); the process of memorizing something (as a part in a play), or a person with reference to facility in memorizing (as, an actor who is a quick *study*); also, something studied or to be studied (as, "These volumes were my *study* day and night," Mrs. Shelley's "Frankenstein," letter i.; "The proper *study* of mankind is man," Pope's "Essay on Man," ii. 2); a subject of acquired or desired knowledge; a matter for investigation or reflection; something deserving of attentive consideration (as, when he heard this his face was a *study*); also, a room, in a house or other building, set apart for private study, reading, writing, or the like (as, "He himself had been sitting . . . in a small apartment in which he had arranged his books, and which he called his *study*": H. James's "Portrait of a Lady," xli.); also, a university†; also, in *art*, something produced as an educational exercise, or as a memorandum or record of observations or effects, or as a guide for a finished production; sometimes, an artistic production intended to bring out in careful detail the characteristics of an object represented; in *literature*, a composition executed for exercise or as an experiment in a particular method of treatment, or one dealing in detail with a particular subject; in *music*, a composition, usually instrumental,

---

combining the instructive purpose of an exercise with a certain amount of artistic value; an étude.—**stud′y**, *v.*; *studied, studying.* [OF. *estudier* (F. *étudier*), < ML. *studiare*, < L. *studium*.] **I.** *intr.* To apply one's self or endeavor (to do something: as, "I *studied* to appear calm," W. H. Hudson's "Green Mansions," xix.); think deeply, reflect, or consider (as, "Friday stood musing . . . I asked him what it was he *studied* upon": Defoe's "Robinson Crusoe," i. 15); esp., to apply one's self to the acquisition of knowledge, as by reading, investigation, practice, etc.; pursue a course of study, as at a college or a professional or technical school or under some teacher. **II.** *tr.* To apply one's self to (any object of endeavor, thought, attention, etc.: as, "Nothing lovelier can be found In woman, than to *study* household good," Milton's "Paradise Lost," ix. 233); strive assiduously for (as, to *study* simplicity of style: cf. *studied*); devote care and thought to (an action, production, etc.); consider, as something to be achieved or devised (as, to *study* a way out of one's difficulties); think (*out*), as the result of careful consideration or devising; have thoughtful or solicitous consideration for (a person's wishes, interests, etc., or the person); also, to apply one's self to acquiring a knowledge of (a branch of learning, science, or art, or a subject), esp. systematically, as in general education or professional training; seek to learn or memorize, as a part in a play; read (a book, document, etc.) with careful effort to understand the full meaning or bearing; examine or investigate carefully and in detail (as, to *study* the political situation; to *study* a man's character); observe attentively, or scrutinize (as, to *study* a person's face; "Brendon *studied* the rugged cliff line," Eden Phillpotts's "Red Redmaynes," iv.); also, to instruct† or educate†.

stu-fa (stö′fä), *n.*; pl. *-fas*, It. *-fe* (-fä). [It., = E. *stove²*.] A jet of steam issuing from a fissure in the earth in a volcanic region.

stuff (stuf), *n.* [OF. *estoffe* (F. *étoffe*), stuff, materials; origin uncertain.] Equipments, belongings, baggage, goods, or stock (as, "Having settled my household *stuff* and habitation . . . I began to keep my journal," Defoe's "Robinson Crusoe," i. 4: now chiefly colloq.); also, the material of which anything is made (often fig.); material to be worked upon, or to be used in making something (as, bread*stuffs*); woven material, or a textile fabric; specif., woolen cloth (as, "I had brushed my black *stuff* travelling-dress": C. Brontë's "Jane Eyre," x.); fig., inward character, qualities, or capabilities (as, to have good *stuff* in one; "places where a man has got to show the *stuff* that's in him," J. Conrad's "Rescue," iii. 7); also, matter or material indefinitely (used as if to avoid specific characterization, and often disparaging: as, cushions filled with some soft *stuff*; "On my breakfast table there is a pot of honey. Not the manufactured *stuff* sold under that name," Gissing's "Private Papers of Henry Ryecroft," ii. 19); any of various substances, preparations, or compositions used in technical processes or operations, as a composition of tallow and other ingredients used to fill the pores of leather, or the working fluid for operating an engine; something to be swallowed, as food, drink, or medicine; matter produced as in agriculture or industries; literary or artistic matter or productions (as, "If I send in my *stuff* . . . to-morrow morning, it may be in time for next week's issue," Arnold Bennett's "Great Man," xii.: now chiefly colloq. or disparaging); loosely, actions, performances, talk, etc. (colloq. or slang: as, cut out the rough *stuff*); money (slang: often with *the*: as, "I'm out after the *stuff*," Arnold Bennett's "The Old Adam," v.); also, worthless matter or things; rubbish or trash; often, worthless or foolish ideas, talk, or writing (as, "With what *stuff* and nonsense hast thou filled thy head!" Fielding's "Tom Jones," viii. 9; "Nonsense, Netta, what *stuff* you talk," Trollope's "Barchester Towers," x.).—**small stuff.** See under *small*, *a.*—**stuff**, *v.* [OF. *estoffer* (F. *étoffer*).] **I.** *tr.* To equip, furnish, or stock with something†; also, to fill or line with some kind of material as a padding or packing; distend or expand with padding or packing; fill (a chicken, turkey, piece of meat, etc.) with seasoned bread-crumbs or other savory matter; fill out the skin of (a dead animal) with material so as to preserve the natural form and appearance; fill (a receptacle), esp. by packing the contents closely together; cram full; crowd (a

vehicle, room, etc.) with persons; put fraudulent votes into (a ballot-box: U. S.); fill or cram (one's self, one's stomach, etc.) with food; fill (an aperture, cavity, etc.) by forcing something into it; stop up or plug; block or choke (*up*); fill with something of an immaterial nature (as, to *stuff* a person's head with useless knowledge); impose upon the credulity of, or deceive, by false statements (slang: as, "I guess he has read a leader in The Flag and been *stuffed*," L. Merrick's "House of Lynch," ii.); also, to serve to pad, pack, fill, stop up, or the like, as a material or thing does; also, to thrust or cram (something) tightly into a receptacle, cavity, or the like (as, "I *stuffed* a shirt or two into my old carpet-bag": H. Melville's "Moby-Dick," ii.); pack tightly in a confined place; crowd together; gorge (food); also, in *leather-manuf.*, to treat (a skin, etc.) with a composition of tallow and other ingredients. **II.** *intr.* To cram one's self with food; eat gluttonously.

stuff-er (stuf′ėr), *n.* One who or that which stuffs.

stuff-i-ly (stuf′i-li), *adv.* In a stuffy manner.—**stuff′i-ness**, *n.*

stuff-ing (stuf′ing), *n.* The act of one who or that which stuffs; also, that with which anything is or may be stuffed; esp., seasoned bread-crumbs or other filling used to stuff a chicken, turkey, etc., before cooking.—**stuff′ing=box**, *n.* In *mach.*, a contrivance for securing a steam-tight, air-tight, or water-tight joint at the place or hole where a movable rod (as a piston-rod) enters a vessel, consisting typically of a cylindrical box or chamber through the middle of which the rod passes, the space between the rod and the walls of the box being filled with packing which is held in by a cover or adjustable member at one end of the box.

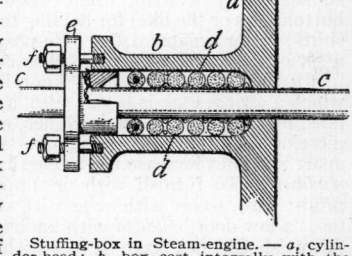

Stuffing-box in Steam-engine. — *a*, cylinder-head; *b*, box cast integrally with the head *a*; *c*, piston-rod; *d, d*, packing wound about the rod; *e*, cover for compressing the packing; *f, f*, bolts and nuts for forcing the cover against the packing.

stuff-y (stuf′i), *a.*; compar. *stuffier*, superl. *stuffiest.* Full of stuff or material†; also, close or ill-ventilated, as a room; oppressive from lack of freshness, as the air, etc.; fig., lacking in interest, as writing or discourse; also, affected with a sensation of obstruction in the respiratory passages, as a person; angry or sulky (colloq.).

Stu-ka (stö′kä), *n.* [G., *stu(rz)*, dive, + *ka(mpf)*, battle.] A powerful German plane of the dive-bomber type.

stull (stul), *n.* [Cf. G. *stollen*, prop. post.] In *mining*, a framework of timber covered with horizontal boards, built in an excavation or stope for a support or protection.

stul-ti-fy (stul′ti-fī), *v. t.*; *-fied, -fying.* [LL. *stultificare*, < L. *stultus*, foolish, + *facere*, make.] To make, or cause to appear, foolish or ridiculous (as, "The Prince could not . . . permit himself to be thus perpetually *stultified* by a weak, false, and imperious woman," Motley's "Dutch Republic," ii. 9; to *stultify* one's self or one's former acts or statements by gross inconsistency; reduce to foolishness or absurdity; render absurdly or wholly futile or ineffectual, as efforts; also, to regard as foolish (rare); in *law*, to allege or prove to be of unsound mind; allege (one's self) to be insane.—**stul″ti-fi-ca′tion** (-fi-kā′shon), *n.*—**stul′ti-fi-er** (-fī-ėr), *n.*

stul-til-o-quence (stul-til′ō-kwens), *n.* [L. *stultiloquentia*, < *stultus*, foolish, + *loqui*, speak.] Foolish or silly talk; senseless babble.—**stul-til′o-quent**, *a.*

stum (stum), *n.* [D. *stom*, noun use of *stom*, dumb.] Unfermented or partly fermented grape-juice; must, esp. that in which fermentation has been prevented or arrested by some ingredient mixed with it; must as used for renewing vapid wines; also, wine that has been renewed by an admixture of must.—**stum**, *v. t.*; *stummed, stumming.* To renew (wine) by an admixture of must which raises a new fermentation; also, to fumigate (a cask) with burning sulphur in order to prevent fermentation of the wine placed in it; stop the fermentation of (new wine) by such fumigation.

---

fat, fāte, fär, fåll, åsk, fāre; net, mē, hèr; pin, pīne; not, nōte, möve, nôr; up, lūte, pùll; oi, oil; ou, out; (lightened) aviạry, ẹlect, agọny, intọ, ụnite; (obscured) errạnt, operạ, ardẹnt, actọr, natụre; ch, chip; g, go; th, thin; ᴛʜ, then; y, you;

stum-ble (stum'bl), v.: -bled, -bling. [ME. stumblen, stomblen, prob. from Scand.: cf. Sw. dial. stomla, Dan. dial. stumle, Icel. stumra, stumble, akin to E. stammer.] **I.** intr. To strike the foot against something in walking, running, etc., so as to stagger or fall (as, "She ran faster . . . stumbling and nearly falling," H. G. Wells's "Mr. Britling," iii. 1. § 11; his horse stumbled over a stone and threw him); trip; walk or go unsteadily with frequent trips or stumbles (as, "Then blindly had he stumbled through the place": W. Morris's "Jason," xi. 295): fig., to trip morally, or fall into sin; make a slip, mistake, or blunder; proceed in a hesitating or blundering manner, as in action or speech; also, to come accidentally or unexpectedly (on, upon, across, etc.: as, "I could not have stumbled on more fascinating reading," W. H. Hudson's "Far Away and Long Ago," xxii.): also, to falter, hesitate, or stick, as at an obstacle to progress or belief. **II.** tr. To cause to stumble: trip: also, to give pause to; embarrass or nonplus; puzzle or perplex.—**stum'ble**, n. The act or an act of stumbling, a trip in walking, running, etc.; a moral lapse or error (as, "In the way of worldly honour I have no great stumble to reproach myself with": Stevenson's "David Balfour," iii.); a slip or blunder.—**stum'bler**, n.—**stum'bling-block**, n. A block, stump, or other object which causes one to stumble; a cause or occasion of moral stumbling; an obstacle or hindrance to progress, belief, etc. (as, "The question of miracles had been . . . my greatest stumbling-block": Kingsley's "Alton Locke," xxxviii.).—**stum'bling-ly**, adv.—**stum'bly**, a. Apt to stumble; also, apt to cause stumbling.

stu-mer (stū'mer), n. [Origin obscure.] A forged or worthless check; a counterfeit bank-note, coin, or the like; a sham. [Slang, Eng.]

stump¹ (stump), n. [ME. stumpe, stompe, = D. stomp = MLG. stump = G. stumpf, stump: cf. stub.] The lower end of a tree or plant left after the main part falls or is cut off; a standing tree-trunk from which the upper part and the branches have been removed; the base of a growing tree (as, to buy timber on the stump, that is, before it is felled); also, any basal part remaining after the main or more important part has been removed; the part of a limb of the body remaining after the rest has been cut off; a part resembling this, as a rudimentary or undeveloped limb or member; the remnant of a docked tail (as, "a shaggy, disreputable dog with a humorous stump of a tail": Hugh Walpole's "Wooden Horse," v.); a part of a broken or decayed tooth left in the gum (as, "It wasn't that tooth that was hurting me. It's an old stump at the back": Arnold Bennett's "Old Wives' Tale," i. 2); a stunted remnant of a pencil, candle, cigar, etc.; also, a leg (colloq.: chiefly in 'to stir one's stumps,' to move one's legs briskly, as in walking or dancing); a wooden leg (as, "He . . . set his wooden stump on my gouty toe": Smollett's "Humphry Clinker," May 5); also, a short, stumpy person (as, "a little, old, shabby stump of a man": Synge's "Well of the Saints," ii.); also, a post or small pillar (chiefly prov. Eng.); also, each of the three (formerly two) upright sticks which, with the two bails laid on the top of them, form a wicket in the game of cricket (as, to draw stumps, to pull the stumps out of the ground as indication of the discontinuance of play or of the termination of a match); also, the platform or place of political speech-making (as, to go on or take the stump; "the outpourings of an agitator upon the stump," Charnwood's "Abraham Lincoln," v.; attrib., a stump speech or speaker: orig. U. S., and at first with reference to a tree-stump as a rostrum in open-air political meetings); also, a challenge to do something (colloq., U. S.); also, a heavy step or gait, as of a wooden-legged or lame person.—**stump¹**, v. **I.** tr. To reduce to a stump; truncate; lop; also, to dig up by the roots, as trees, etc. (sometimes with up); also, to clear of stumps, as land; also, to stub, as one's toe (colloq., U. S.); also, to hand over (money), as in payment (usually with up: slang); also, to render penniless (slang); wear out or exhaust, as a horse, by excessive strain (sometimes with up); nonplus, embarrass, or render completely at a loss (colloq.: as, "Nobody could think of anything to do—everybody was stumped," Mark Twain's "Huckleberry Finn," ii.); challenge or dare to do something (colloq., U. S.); also, to make stump speeches in or to (colloq.: as, to stump a county or a constituency; "a man who had gone out of his way to . . . stump the country against her own son," Galsworthy's "Patrician," i. 7); in cricket, of the wicket-keeper, to put (a batsman) out by knocking down a stump or by dislodging a bail with the ball held in the hand, at a moment when the batsman is off his ground. **II.** intr. To walk heavily or clumsily, as if with a wooden leg (as, "Bendigo . . . stumped down his long flight of steps": Eden Phillpotts's "Red Redmaynes," vii.); also, to hand over or pay money (usually with up: slang: as, "You can't quarrel with a man for letting you off cheap when you thought you were bound to stump up," W. B. Maxwell's "In Cotton Wool," v.); also, to make stump speeches (colloq.).

stump² (stump), n. [Prob. < F. estompe, a stump: cf. D. stomp, blunt, obtuse, as n. stump of a tree, etc., = E. stump¹.] A rubbing instrument consisting of a short, thick roll of paper or soft leather, or a bar of india-rubber or other soft material, usually cut to a blunt point at each end, used for toning the lights and shades in crayon-drawing or charcoal-drawing and for other similar purposes.—**stump²**, v. t. To tone or modify (crayon-drawings, etc.) by means of a stump.

stump-age (stum'pāj), n. Standing timber considered with reference to its value; the right to cut such timber on the owner's land; the price paid for such timber; a tax levied on timber cut. [Local, U. S.]

stump-er (stum'per), n. One who or that which stumps; esp., something, as a task or problem, that stumps or nonplusses one (colloq.).

stump-y (stum'pi), a. Of the nature of or resembling a stump; short and thick: stubby; stocky; also, abounding in stumps.—**stump'i-ly**, adv.—**stump'i-ness**, n.

stun (stun), v. t.; stunned, stunning. [OF. estoner (F. étonner): see astonish.] To deprive of consciousness or strength by or as by a blow, fall, or the like, or as a blow does (as, "He was still dizzy from the heavy blow that had stunned him," F. M. Crawford's "Mr. Isaacs," viii.; "Their enemies had been stunned, not killed, by the western storm," Hallam's "Europe during the Middle Ages," i. 1); also, to strike with astonishment (as, "The dramatic swiftness of the revelation stunned her": Arnold Bennett's "Leonora," v.); astound; amaze; also, to daze or bewilder by distracting noise; also, to bruise (a stone, etc.) so that it splinters or exfoliates.—**stun**, n. The act of stunning, or the condition of being stunned; also, a flaw on the surface of stone, etc.

Stun-dist (shtun'dist), n. [Russ. shtundist, < G. stunde, hour; with reference to stated hours for Scripture-reading.] A member of a large Russian religious sect which originated among the peasants of southern Russia about 1860 and which takes the New Testament for its rule of faith and rejects the authority and practices of the Orthodox Church.—**Stun'dism**, n.

stung (stung). Preterit and past participle of sting.

stunk (stungk). Preterit and past participle of stink.

stun-ner (stun'er), n. One who or that which stuns; often, a person or thing of striking excellence, beauty, attractiveness, etc. (colloq.: as, "He considered her 'a stunner,'" Thackeray's "Pendennis," i. 38).

stun-ning (stun'ing), p. a. That stuns; often, of striking excellence, beauty, attractiveness, etc. (colloq.: as, "I was to have painted stunning pictures," Du Maurier's "Trilby," iv.).—**stun'ning-ly**, adv.

stun-sail (stun'sl), n. Contraction of studdingsail.

stunt¹ (stunt), a. [AS. stunt, dull, obtuse, stupid, = MHG. stunz, stumpy, = Icel. stuttr, short, scant: cf. AS. styntan, to blunt, dull, and E. stint², v.] Dull or stupid; blunt, curt, or rude; stubborn or obstinate; sullen; also, short and thick; stumpy; stunted or dwarfed. [Now prov. Eng.]—**stunt¹**, v. t. To check the growth or development of; dwarf; hinder the increase or progress of; also, to check (growth, development, etc.: as, "Open-air life . . . has the apparent effect of stunting growth in early youth," Jefferies's "Gamekeeper at Home," ii.).—**stunt¹**, n. A check in growth or development; a state of arrested development; also, a creature which has been hindered from attaining its proper growth.

stunt² (stunt), n. [Cf. stint², n., in sense of 'allotted piece of work.'] A performance serving as a display of strength, activity, skill, or the like, as in athletics, etc.; a feat; hence, any notable performance (as, "the chap that did the big *stunt . . .* with locomotion in dogs": Sinclair Lewis's "Arrowsmith," xxvii.). [Colloq.]—**stunt**[2], *v. i.* To do a stunt or stunts. [Colloq.]

stunt-ed (stun′ted), *p. a.* Checked in growth or development (as, "a knot of *stunted* hollies": Hardy's "Return of the Native," iv. 4); dwarfed; undeveloped; hence, disproportionately or abnormally short or small; also, of growth, etc., checked or arrested.—**stunt′ed-ly**, *adv.*—**stunt′ed-ness**, *n.*

stunt-y (stun′ti), *a.* Stunted.—**stunt′i-ness**, *n.*

stu-pa (stö′pä), *n.* [Skt. *stūpa.*] In Buddhist countries, a dome-shaped monumental structure erected to commemorate some event or to mark a sacred spot.

stupe (stūp), *n.* [L. *stupa, stuppa,* tow: cf. *stop.*] In *med.,* a pledget of tow or other soft material used in dressing a wound; also, a piece of flannel or other cloth wrung out of hot water and applied as a fomentation.

stu-pe-fa-cient (stū-pē-fā′shent). [L. *stupefaciens (-ent-),* ppr.] **I.** *a.* Stupefying; producing stupor. **II.** *n.* A drug or agent that produces stupor.

stu-pe-fac-tion (stū-pē-fak′shon), *n.* [F. *stupéfaction.*] The act of stupefying, or the state of being stupefied; stupor; numbness of the faculties; overwhelming amazement.—**stu-pe-fac′tive** (-tiv), *a.* Serving to stupefy.

stu-pe-fy (stū′pē-fī), *v. t.*; *-fied, -fying.* [F. *stupéfier,* < L. *stupefacere* (passive *stupefieri*), < *stupere,* be struck senseless (see *stupid*), + *facere,* make.] To put into a state of stupor; deprive of sensibility; benumb or dull the faculties of; make stupid, as with a narcotic, a shock, strong emotion, etc.; stun; often, to overwhelm with amazement; astound.—**stu′pe-fi-er** (-fī-ėr), *n.*—**stu′pe-fy-ing-ly**, *adv.*

stu-pend (stū-pend′), *a.* Stupendous. [Obs. or archaic.]

stu-pen-dous (stū-pen′dus), *a.* [L. *stupendus,* gerundive of *stupere,* be amazed at: see *stupid.*] Such as to cause amazement, astounding, or marvelous (as, "The British Museum . . . is a noble collection, and even *stupendous,* if we consider it was made by a private man," Smollett's "Humphry Clinker," June 2; "The whole thing was a *stupendous,* incomprehensible farce," Maugham's "Moon and Sixpence," xlii.); esp., amazingly large or great, or immense (as, "*Stupendous* as they are, nothing is more difficult than to see the colossi properly," Amelia B. Edwards's "Thousand Miles up the Nile," xvi.; a *stupendous* mass of information; "a task of *stupendous* difficulty," Charnwood's "Theodore Roosevelt," iii.).—**stu-pen′dous-ly**, *adv.*—**stu-pen′dous-ness**, *n.*

stu-pe-ous (stū′pē-us), *a.* [L. *stupeus, stuppeus,* of tow, < *stupa, stuppa,* tow.] In *entom.,* covered with long, loose scales, like tow; in *bot.,* woolly.

stu-pid (stū′pid). [L. *stupidus,* < *stupere,* be struck senseless, be stunned, also to be amazed at: cf. *stupefy, stupendous,* and *stupor.*] **I.** *a.* In a state of stupor; having the faculties benumbed or dulled; stupefied; also, lacking ordinary activity and keenness of mind, dull-witted, or obtuse (as, "a *stupid* silent dunce," Pope's "Moral Essays," i. 163; to be too *stupid* to learn or understand); characterized by, indicative of, or proceeding from mental dullness (as, *stupid* bewilderment; a *stupid* stare; a *stupid* act or speech; "It was very *stupid* of me to say yes," Du Maurier's "Trilby," viii.); also, tediously dull or uninteresting (as, a *stupid* book; to spend a *stupid* evening; a *stupid* place). **II.** *n.* A stupid person: as, "Hold your noise . . . Do you want to be grabbed, *stupid?*" (Dickens's "Oliver Twist," xii.). [Colloq.]—**stu-pid-i-ty** (stū-pid′i-ti), *n.*; pl. *-ties* (-tiz). The state, quality, or fact of being stupid; stupid action or behavior; a stupid act, notion, speech, etc.—**stu′pid-ly**, *adv.*—**stu′pid-ness**, *n.*

stu-por (stū′por), *n.* [L., < *stupere:* see *stupid.*] Suspension or great diminution of sensibility, as in disease or as caused by narcotics, intoxicants, etc.; a state of suspended or deadened sensibility; in a more general sense, a state in which the faculties are benumbed or dazed (as, "I was, in some degree, roused from the *stupor* which had seized my faculties," C. B. Brown's "Wieland," xxvii.; "The huge height of the buildings . . . the hubbub and endless stir . . . struck me into a kind of *stupor* of surprise," Stevenson's

"Kidnapped," xxx.); mental torpor, or apathy; stupefaction; amazement.—**stu′por-ous**, *a.* Characterized by or affected with stupor.

stu-pose (stū′pōs), *a.* [L. *stupa, stuppa,* tow.] In *bot.* and *zoöl.,* bearing tufts or mats of long hairs; composed of matted filaments like tow.

stur-died (stėr′did), *a.* Affected with the disease called sturdy.

stur-di-ly (stėr′di-li), *adv.* In a sturdy manner.—**stur′di-ness**, *n.*

stur-dy[1] (stėr′di), *a.*; compar. *sturdier,* superl. *sturdiest.* [OF. *estordi, estourdi,* stunned, dizzy, giddy, reckless, violent, pp. of *estordir, estourdir* (F. *étourdir*), stun, daze, make dizzy; origin uncertain.] Violent†, furious†, or fierce†; intractable†, refractory†, or rebellious†; perversely stubborn or obstinate (now prov. Eng.); also, firm, stout, or indomitable (as, *sturdy* defenders; *sturdy* resistance, courage, honesty, or common sense); also, possessed of or showing rugged bodily strength or endurance (as, a *sturdy* fellow; the *sturdy* ox; *sturdy* legs, blows, or vigor); strongly built, stalwart, robust, or lusty; in general, strong, as in substance, construction, texture, etc. (as, *sturdy* weapons, armor, walls, or fabrics; "*sturdy* russet boots," G. W. Cable's "Bonaventure," i. 3); of strong or hardy growth, as a plant.

stur-dy[2] (stėr′di), *n.* [OF. *estordie,* giddiness, < *estordir:* see *sturdy*[1].] In *vet. science,* same as *gid.*

stur-geon (stėr′jon), *n.*; pl. *sturgeons* or (esp. collectively) *sturgeon.* [OF. *sturgun* (F. *esturgeon*), < ML. *sturio(n-);* from Teut.] Any of various large ganoid fishes of the genera *Acipenser* and *Scaphirhynchus* (family *Acipenseridæ*), having a prolonged snout, barbels,

Common Sturgeon (*Acipenser sturio*).

and an elongate body set with five rows of bony plates: found in fresh and salt waters of the north temperate zone, and valued for their flesh and as a source of caviar and isinglass. See *beluga, sterlet,* and *shovelnose.*

stuss (stus, G. shtŭs), *n.* [G. colloq. and Yiddish *stuss,* nonsense.] A kind of gambling-game played with cards, resembling faro.

stut (stut), *v. i.* or *t.*; *stutted, stutting.* [ME. *stutten;* akin to D. *stooten,* G. *stossen,* push, strike.] To stutter. [Now prov. Eng. and Sc.]

stut-ter (stut′ėr), *v.* [Freq. of *stut:* cf. D. *stotteren,* MLG. *stoteren,* G. *stottern,* stutter.] **I.** *intr.* To utter involuntary or spasmodic repetitions of syllables or sounds in the effort to speak, esp. habitually, from a defect in the powers of speech; stammer. **II.** *tr.* To utter or say with a stutter: sometimes with *out.*—**stut′ter,** *n.* A stuttering mode of utterance; a habit of stuttering; also, a stuttered utterance. —**stut′ter-er,** *n.*—**stut′ter-ing-ly,** *adv.*

sty[1] (stī), *n.*; pl. *sties* (stīz). [AS. *stigu,* akin to Icel. *stīa,* Sw. *stia,* Dan. *sti,* sty: cf. *steward.*] A pen or inclosure for swine; hence, any filthy abode (as, "I see . . . human beings living in *sties*": Thoreau's "Walden," i.); also, a place of bestial debauchery.—**sty**[1], *v.*; *stied* or *styed, stying.* **I.** *tr.* To keep or lodge in or as in a sty: as, "the most beggarly, vile place that ever pigs were *styed* in" (Stevenson's "Kidnapped," xvi.). **II.** *intr.* To live in or as in a sty.

sty[2] (stī), *n.*; pl. *sties* (stīz). [For obs. or prov. *styan,* sty, or *styany,* ME. *styanye,* appar. 'styan eye,' later understood as 'sty on eye': *styan,* < AS. *stīgend,* sty, lit. 'riser,' < *stīgan,* rise, ascend: see *stile.*] In *pathol.,* a circumscribed inflammatory swelling, like a small boil, on the edge of the eyelid. Also **stye.**

Styg-i-an (stij′i-an), *a.* [L. *Stygius.*] Of or pertaining to the river Styx (see *Styx*) or the lower world; hence, dark or gloomy; also, infernal; hellish.

style (stīl), *n.* [OF. *style, stile* (F. *style*), < L. *stilus* (improperly *stylus*), stake, pale, pointed instrument, stylus, writing, mode of expression, style, prob. from the same root as E. *stick*[2]. The spelling *style* (in modern use) is due to a supposed connection with Gr. στῦλος, pillar, column.] An instrument of metal, bone, or the like, used by the ancients for writing on a waxed tablet, having one end pointed for incising the letters, and the other end blunt for rubbing out writing and smoothing the tablet; also, something resembling or suggesting such an instrument; a pen; a graver; an etching-needle; a pointed marking-instrument such as a phonographic stylus; a fixed pointer or indicator; the gnomon of a sun-dial; also, writing†; a literary composition†; an inscription†; also, mode of expression in writing or speaking; characteristic diction; a particular method of expressing thought by selection or collocation of words, distinct in some respect from other methods, as determined by nationality, period, literary form, individuality, etc. (as, the *style* of Johnson or of Dickens; a pedantic *style*; a nervous *style*); often, appropriate or suitable diction; conformity to an approved literary standard; also, a particular form of words used in expressing an idea†; also, a descriptive or distinguishing appellation; esp., a distinguishing appellation belonging to a person by right of rank, office, etc., or assigned as a mark of courtesy (as, "He always bare the title of primate of all England, as being the common *style* of the archbishop": Strype's "Memorials of Cranmer," i. 8); a legal, official, or recognized title (as, a firm trading under the *style* of Smith, Jones, & Co.); also, a particular, distinctive, or characteristic mode or form of construction or execution in any art or work; a particular type of architecture, having special characteristics of structure or ornamentation (as, the Doric order or *style*; the Norman *style*; the Gothic *style*); an assemblage of methods or rules with reference to spelling, capitalization, punctuation, etc., as observed by a particular publishing-house or the like; a particular kind, sort, or type, as with reference to form, appearance, or character (as, a *style* of countenance; *styles* of beauty); a particular, distinctive, or characteristic mode of action (as, *styles* of speaking, singing, running, riding, or rowing); a mode of deportment or behavior; one's bearing or demeanor; a mode of living, as with respect to expense or display; a mode or fashion, as in dress; often, good or approved mode, manner, or fashion; elegance; smartness; smartly effective manner; fine, elegant, or fashionable mode of living; also (with *the*), the prevailing mode; the fashion; also, a mode of reckoning time (as, Old *Style* or New *Style*, the reckoning of time according to the Julian calendar (see *Julian*) or the Gregorian calendar (see *Gregorian*) respectively, the dates in the former calendar being replaced in the latter calendar by dates 10 days later from 1582 to 1700, 11 days later from 1700 to 1800, 12 days later from 1800 to 1900, and 13 days later since 1900, so that now Sept. 3, Old Style, is the same as Sept. 16, New Style); in *zoöl.*, a small, slender, pointed process or part; a sponge-spicule sharp at one end; esp., in *entom.*, a bristle-like anal process; the bristle or seta of the antenna of a dipter; in *bot.*, a narrow, usually cylindrical and more or less filiform extension of the ovary, which, when present, bears the stigma at its apex.—**style**, *v. t.*; styled, styling. To call by a particular style or appellation (as specified); denominate: as, "one Hall, who styl'd himselfe his Majesty's printer" (Evelyn's "Diary," March 12, 1686); "A Frank of large estate was *styled* a noble" (Hallam's "Europe during the Middle Ages," ii. 1).

Style (*a*), with Stigma (*b*).

-style. A termination from Gr. στῦλος, pillar, column, serving to form adjectives and nouns, as *monostyle*, *dodecastyle*.

style-less (stīl′les), *a.* Without style; of no particular style.

sty-let (stī′let), *n.* [F. *stylet*, < It. *stiletto*: see *stiletto*.] A stiletto or dagger; some similar sharp-pointed instrument; in *surg.*, the stiffening wire or rod in a flexible catheter; also, a probe; in *zoöl.* and *entom.*, same as *style*.

styl-ish (stī′lish), *a.* Characterized by style, or conforming to the fashionable standard; fashionably elegant; smart.—**styl′ish-ly**, *adv.*—**styl′ish-ness**, *n.*

styl-ist (stī′list), *n.* A writer or speaker who is skilled in or who cultivates literary style; one who devotes much attention to his literary style; a writer or speaker with reference to his style.—**styl-is′tic**, *a.* Of or pertaining to style.—**styl-is′ti-cal-ly**, *adv.*

sty-lite (stī′līt), *n.* [LGr. στυλίτης, < Gr. στῦλος, pillar, column.] In *eccles. hist.*, one of a class of solitary ascetics who lived on the top of high pillars or columns.

styl-ize (stī′līz), *v. t.*; -ized, -izing. To conform to a particular style, as of representation or treatment in art; conventionalize.—**styl-i-za-tion** (stī-li-zā′shọn), *n.*

sty-lo (stī′lō), *n.*; pl. -los (-lōz). Shortened form of *stylograph*: as, "writing down the details of the order with his ivory-handled *stylo*" (Arnold Bennett's "Old Wives' Tale," i. 6).

sty-lo-bate (stī′lọ-bāt), *n.* [L. *stylobates*, *stylobata*, < Gr. στυλοβάτης, < στῦλος, pillar, column, + -βάτης, < βαίνειν, go, stand.] In *arch.*, a continuous base supporting a row of columns; that part of a stereobate immediately beneath the columns.

sty-lo-graph (stī′lọ-gràf), *n.* [L. *stylus*, prop. *stilus*, a style to write with: see *-graph*.] A stylographic pen.—**sty-lo-graph′ic** (-gràf′ik), *a.* Of or pertaining to stylography; also, designating or pertaining to a variety of fountain-pen in which the writing-point consists of a fine, hollow tube instead of a nib.—**sty-lo-graph′i-cal-ly**, *adv.*—**sty-log′ra-phy** (-log′rạ-fi), *n.* [See *-graphy*.] The art of writing, tracing, drawing, etc., with a style.

Doric Temple, showing Stylobate (*c*).

sty-loid (stī′loid), *a.* [See *style* and *-oid*.] Resembling a style; slender and pointed: applied esp. to several bony processes on the temporal bone, radius, ulna, etc.

sty-lo-lite (stī′lọ-līt), *n.* [Gr. στῦλος, pillar, column, + λίθος, stone.] In *geol.*, a longitudinally streaked, columnar structure occurring in various rocks, esp. limestone, and of the same material as the rock in which it occurs.—**sty-lo-lit′ic** (-lit′ik), *a.*

sty-lo-po-di-um (stī-lọ-pō′di-um), *n.*; pl. -dia (-di-ạ). [NL., < L. *stylus* (used to mean a style in bot.) + Gr. πούς (ποδ-), foot.] In *bot.*, a glandular disk or expansion surmounting the ovary in umbelliferous plants, and supporting the styles.

sty-lus (stī′lus), *n.*; pl. -luses, L. -li (-lī). [L., prop. *stilus*: see *style*.] A style or pointed instrument for writing on wax; also, the pointed piece which produces the indentations or incisions in making a phonograph record; a similar device in a phonograph, for reproducing sounds from such a record; in *zoöl.* and *bot.*, a style.

sty-mie, sti-my (stī′mi), *n.*; pl. -mies (-miz). [Cf. Sc. *stymie*, a dim-sighted person, *stime*, *styme*, a glimpse, glimmer.] In *golf*, an opponent's ball on a putting-green when it is directly between the player's ball and the hole for which he is playing, and when the distance between the balls is more than six inches; also, the occurrence of a ball in such a position, or the position of the ball.—**sty′mie, sti′my**, *v. t.*; -mied, -mieing, -mying. To hinder with a stymie or as a stymie does.

styp-sis (stip′sis), *n.* [LL., < Gr. στύψις, contraction, treatment with an astringent, < στύφειν, contract.] The employment or application of styptics.

styp-tic (stip′tik), *a.* [L. *stypticus*, < Gr. στυπτικός, astringent, < στύφειν, contract.] **I.** *a.* Contracting organic tissue; astringent; binding; esp., checking hemorrhage or bleeding, as a drug; hemostatic. **II.** *n.* A styptic agent or substance: as, "The physician . . . stopped with *styptics* and bandages the effusion of blood which followed" (Scott's "Talisman," xiv.).—**styp-ti′ci-ty** (-tis′i-ti), *n.*

sty-ra-ca-ceous (stī-rạ-kā′shius), *a.* [See *storax*.] Belonging to the *Styracaceæ*, or storax family of shrubs and trees.

sty-rene (stī′rēn), *n.* [L. *styrax*, storax: see *-ene*.] In *chem.*, a colorless liquid hydrocarbon with a fragrant, aromatic odor, obtained by the distillation of storax: used, when derived from benzol, in making synthetic rubber. Also called **sty′rol** (-rol or -rōl) and **sty′ro-lene** (-rọ-lēn).

stythe (stīth or stīᴛн), *n.* [Cf. *stive*.] Same as *choke-damp*. [Prov. Eng.]

Styx (stiks), *n.* [L., < Gr. Στύξ (Στυγ-), connected with στυγεῖν, hate.] In *Gr. myth.*, a river of the lower world, over which the souls of the dead were ferried by Charon, and by which the gods swore their most solemn oaths.

su-a-ble (sū′ạ-bl), *a.* Capable of being sued; liable to be sued.—**su-a-bil′i-ty** (-bil′i-ti), *n.*

---

sua-sion (swā'zhọn), *n.* [L. *suasio(n-)*, < *suadere*, advise, urge, akin to *suavis*, sweet, pleasant, and E. *sweet*: see *suave* and *sweet*.] The act of advising or urging, or attempting to persuade (as, "men governed by reasons, and *suasion* of speech," Kinglake's "Eothen," xxviii.; moral *suasion*, persuasive effort exerted through or acting upon the moral sense); also, an instance of this; a persuasive effort.—**sua'sive** (-siv). **I.** *a.* Advising or urging; tending to persuade; persuasive. **II.** *n.* A suasive speech, influence, or the like. —**sua'sive-ly,** *adv.*—**sua'sive-ness,** *n.*—**sua'so-ry** (-sō-ri), *a.* Suasive.

suave (swäv or swāv), *a.* [L. *suavis*, sweet, pleasant: see *sweet*, and cf. *suasion*.] Sweet to the senses (obs. or rare); pleasant or agreeable; now, usually, of persons or their manner, speech, etc., smoothly agreeable or polite (as, "Prince Aribert became *suave*, even deferential to Nella," Arnold Bennett's "Grand Babylon Hotel," v.; "a *suave* and deprecating gesture," J. H. Robinson's "Mind in the Making," viii. 17); agreeably or blandly urbane.—**suave'ly,** *adv.* —**suav-i-ty** (swav'i-ti or swä'vi-), *n.*; *pl.* -*ties* (-tiz). Sweetness, as to the senses†; pleasantness† or agreeableness†; *pl.*, delights†; now, *sing.*, suave or smoothly agreeable quality, as of persons, manner, etc. (as, "his *suavity* of manner and anxious desire to give one just the topic that pleased": W. Churchill's "Modern Chronicle," ii. 5); bland urbanity; *pl.*, suave or courteous actions or ways; amenities.

sub-. [L. *sub-* (also, by assimilation to a following consonant, *suc-*, *suf-*, *sug-*, *sup-*, *sur-*, etc.), repr. *sub*, prep., under, below, beneath, near, about; akin to Gr. ὑπό, under, and Skt. *upa-*, to, toward, near, under: see *hypo-*.] A prefix meaning 'under,' 'below,' 'near,' 'in a lower or inferior position,' 'in a lesser degree,' 'slightly,' 'somewhat,' 'moderately,' occurring in many words from the Latin, and also used freely as an English formative, as in *subacute*, *subarctic*, *subcellar*, *subclass*, *subhuman*, *subirrigate*, *sublet*, *subsoil*, *substation*, *substratosphere*, *subway*. In chemical terms *sub-* indicates a relatively small proportion of an ingredient, as in *subchloride*, or a basic salt, as in *subacetate*.

sub (sub), *n.* A shortened form of *subaltern*, *subeditor*, *sublieutenant*, *submarine*, *subordinate*, *substitute*, and various other words beginning with the same prefix. [Colloq.]— **sub,** *v.;* **subbed, subbing. I.** *intr.* To substitute, or act as substitute, for another. [Colloq.] **II.** *tr.* To submarine; attack with a submarine, or as a submarine does. [Colloq.]

sub-a-ce-tate (sub-as'ē-tāt), *n.* [See *sub-*.] In *chem.*, a basic acetate: as, *subacetate* of copper (verdigris).

sub-a-cid (sub-as'id), *a.* [L. *subacidus*: see *sub-* and *acid*.] Slightly or moderately acid or sour (as, a *subacid* fruit); fig., of speech, temper, etc., or a person, somewhat tart or sharp (as, "She was as . . . outspoken and pleasantly *sub-acid* as ever": Mrs. Stowe's "Oldtown Folks," xl.).—**sub-a-cid'i-ty** (-a-sid'i-ti), *n.*

sub-a-cute (sub-ạ-kūt'), *a.* [See *sub-*.] Somewhat or moderately acute.—**sub-a-cute'ly,** *adv.*

sub-a-ë-ri-al (sub-ạ-ē'ri-ạl), *a.* [L. *sub*, under, + *aër*, air.] In *geol.*, existing, operating, or produced in the open air or on the earth's surface.—**sub-a-ë'ri-al-ly,** *adv.*

su-bah-dar (sö-bạ-där'), *n.* [Hind.] The chief native officer of a company of native troops in the British Indian service.

sub-al-ka-line (sub-al'kạ-lin or -līn), *a.* [See *sub-*.] Slightly alkaline.

sub-al-pine (sub-al'pin or -pīn), *a.* [L. *subalpinus*: see *sub-* and *alpine*.] Pertaining to the regions at the foot of the Alps; also, in *bot.* and *zoöl.*, pertaining to, or growing or living in, mountain regions next in elevation below those known as alpine.

sub-al-tern (sub'ạl-tèrn or, esp. U. S., su-bâl'tèrn). [LL. *subalternus*, < L. *sub*, under, + *alternus*, one after the other, alternate.] **I.** *a.* Having an inferior or subordinate position or rank; subordinate; *milit.*, commissioned, but of a rank below that of captain (as, a *subaltern* officer). **II.** *n.* One who has a subordinate position; *milit.*, a subaltern officer.

sub-ant-arc-tic (sub-ant-ärk'tik), *a.* [See *sub-*.] Near, or just above, the antarctic region; pertaining to or occurring in a region just north of the antarctic circle.

sub-a-quat-ic (sub-ạ-kwat'ik), *a.* Subaqueous; also, partly aquatic, as plants or animals.

sub-a-que-ous (sub-ā'kwē-us), *a.* [L. *sub*, under, + *aqua*, water.] Existing or situated under water; occurring or performed under water; used under water.

sub-arc-tic (sub-ärk'tik), *a.* [See *sub-*.] Near, or just below, the arctic region; pertaining to or occurring in a region just south of the arctic circle.

sub-ar-id (sub-ar'id), *a.* [See *sub-*.] Moderately arid.

sub-as-trin-gent (sub-as-trin'jẹnt), *a.* [See *sub-*.] Slightly astringent.

sub-at-om (sub-at'ọm), *n.* [See *sub-*.] In *chem.* and *physics*, a constituent part of an atom: a term used when the atom is regarded as divisible.—**sub-a-tom'ic** (-ạ-tom'ik), *a.*

sub-au-di-tion (sub-â-dish'ọn), *n.* [LL. *subauditio(n-)*, < *subaudire*, understand (something omitted), < L. *sub*, under, + *audire*, hear.] The act of understanding or mentally supplying something not expressed; also, something mentally supplied; understood or implied meaning.

sub-ax-il-la-ry (sub-ak'si-lạ-ri), *a.* [See *sub-*.] In *anat.*, situated beneath the axilla; in *bot.*, situated or placed beneath an axil.

sub-base (sub'bās), *n.* [See *sub-*.] The lowest part of an architectural base (as of a column) which consists of two or more horizontal members; also, a base placed under the bottom of a machine, etc., to raise it higher from the ground; also, a secondary base of supplies.

sub-base-ment (sub'bās″mẹnt), *n.* [See *sub-*.] A basement, or one of a series of basements, below the main basement of a building.

sub-bass (sub'bās), *n.* [See *sub-*.] In *music*, a pedal stop producing the lowest tones of an organ.

sub-cal-i-ber, sub-cal-i-bre (sub-kal'i-bėr), *a.* [See *sub-*.] *Milit.*, of a projectile, having a diameter less than the caliber of the gun from which it is fired, the projectile being fitted with a disk large enough to fill the bore, or being fired from a small tube attached to the inside or the outside of the gun; hence, pertaining to such a projectile (as, a *subcaliber* gun; *subcaliber* practice).

Sub-car-bo-nif-er-ous (sub-kär-bọ-nif'ẹ-rus). [See *sub-*.] In *geol.*: **I.** *a.* Noting or pertaining to a geological period or a system of rocks which comprises the earlier or lower portion of the Carboniferous period or system; Mississippian. **II.** *n.* The Subcarboniferous period or system.

sub-car-ti-lag-i-nous (sub-kär-ti-laj'i-nus), *a.* [See *sub-*.] In *anat.* and *zoöl.*, situated below or beneath cartilage; also, partially or incompletely cartilaginous.

sub-ce-les-tial (sub-sē-les'tial), *a.* [See *sub-*.] Being beneath the heavens; terrestrial; mundane.

sub-cel-lar (sub'sel″ạr), *n.* [See *sub-*.] A cellar beneath another cellar.

sub-chlo-ride (sub-klō'rīd or -rid), *n.* [See *sub-*.] In *chem.*, a chloride that contains a relatively small proportion of chlorine.

sub-class (sub'klås), *n.* [See *sub-*.] A primary division of a class; specif., a zoölogical or botanical group or category ranking below a class.—**sub'class,** *v. t.* To place in a subclass.

sub-cla-vi-an (sub-klā'vi-ạn). [NL. *subclavius*, < L. *sub*, under, + *clavis*, key: cf. *clavicle*.] In *anat.*: **I.** *a.* Situated or extending beneath the clavicle, as certain arteries, veins, etc.; pertaining to such an artery, vein, or the like (as, the *subclavian* groove, either of two shallow depressions on the first rib, one for the subclavian artery and the other for the subclavian vein). **II.** *n.* A subclavian artery, vein, or the like.

sub-com-mit-tee (sub'kọ-mit″ē), *n.* [See *sub-*.] A secondary committee appointed out of a main committee, as for special duty.

sub-con-scious (sub-kon'shus), *a.* [See *sub-*.] Imperfectly or not wholly conscious; also, existing or operating beneath or beyond consciousness (as, the *subconscious* self; "Despite my determination to put the question off, my mind, or *subconscious* mind . . . went on revolving it," W. H. Hudson's "Far Away and Long Ago," xxiv.); present or occurring in the mind but not in consciousness (as, "Some train of *subconscious* suggestion brought a long-forgotten speech back into Mr. Britling's mind": H. G. Wells's "Mr. Britling," ii. 3. § 12).—**sub-con'scious-ly,** *adv.*—**sub-con'scious-ness,** *n.*

---

fat, fāte, fär, fâll, åsk, fāre; net, mē, hèr; pin, pīne; not, nōte, mŏve, nôr; up, lūte, půll; oi, oil; ou, out; (lightened) aviạry, ẹlect, agọny, intọ, ụnite; (obscured) errạnt, operä, ardẹnt, actọr, natụre; ch, chip; g, go; th, thin; ℞н, then; y, you;

sub-con-tract (sub′kon″trakt), *n.* [See *sub-*.] A contract under a previous contract; a contract for carrying out a previous contract or a part of it.—**sub-con-tract′** (-kon-trakt′), *v.* **I.** *tr.* To make a subcontract for. **II.** *intr.* To make a subcontract.—**sub′con-trac″tor**, *n.* One who contracts to carry out a previous contract or a part of it.

sub-cu-ta-ne-ous (sub-kū-tā′nē-us), *a.* [ML. *subcutaneus,* < L. *sub,* under, + *cutis,* skin.] Situated or lying under the skin, as tissue; living under the skin, as certain parasites; performed or introduced under the skin, as an injection or a syringe.—**sub-cu-ta′ne-ous-ly**, *adv.*

sub-dea-con (sub′dē″kon), *n.* [LL. *subdiaconus:* see *sub-*.] A member of the clerical order next below that of deacon. See *order, n.*

sub-del-e-gate (sub′del″ē-gāt), *n.* [See *sub-*.] A subordinate delegate; one to whom powers or functions are delegated by another to whom these have previously been delegated.— **sub-del′e-gate**, *v. t.*; *-gated, -gating.* To delegate (powers, etc.) to a subdelegate.—**sub-del-e-ga′tion** (-gā′shon), *n.*

sub-di-a-lect (sub′dī″a-lekt), *n.* [See *sub-*.] A subordinate dialect; a division or variety of a dialect: as, "The variety of *sub-dialects* . . . is very great" (W. D. Whitney's "Life and Growth of Language," xii.).

sub-dis-trict (sub′dis″trikt), *n.* [See *sub-*.] A division of a district.

sub-di-vide (sub-di-vīd′), *v.*; *-vided, -viding.* [LL. *subdividere* (pp. *subdivisus*), < L. *sub,* under, + *dividere,* E. *divide.*] **I.** *tr.* To divide (a part, or an already divided whole) into smaller parts; divide anew after a first division; sometimes, loosely, to divide into parts. **II.** *intr.* To separate into subdivisions.—**sub-di-vis′i-ble** (-viz′i-bl), *a.* Capable of being subdivided.—**sub-di-vi′sion** (-vizh′on), *n.* [LL. *subdivisio(n-).*] The act of subdividing, or the state or fact of being subdivided; also, a part resulting from subdividing; a division of a division; sometimes, loosely, a division.—**sub-di-vi′sion-al**, *a.*

sub-do-lous (sub′dō-lus), *a.* [LL. *subdolosus,* L. *subdolus,* < L. *sub,* under, + *dolus,* artifice, craft.] Crafty; artful; cunning; sly. [Now rare.]—**sub′do-lous-ly**, *adv.*

sub-dom-i-nant (sub-dom′i-nant), *n.* [See *sub-*.] In *music,* the fourth tone of a scale, being the next below the dominant.

sub-du-a-ble (sub-dū′a-bl), *a.* That may be subdued.

sub-du-al (sub-dū′al), *n.* The act of subduing, or the state of being subdued.

sub-duct (sub-dukt′), *v. t.* [L. *subductus,* pp. of *subducere,* draw from under, take away, < *sub,* under, + *ducere,* lead.] To take away or withdraw; subtract or deduct; also, to remove surreptitiously or fraudulently. [Now rare.]— **sub-duc′tion** (-duk′shon), *n.*

sub-due (sub-dū′), *v. t.*; *-dued, -duing.* [ME. *subdewe, sudewe, sodewe,* appar. with form < OF. *soduire, seduce* (< L. *subducere:* see *subduct*), but with meaning < L. *subdere,* subdue (pp. *subditus,* ME. *subdit,* subject), < *sub,* under, + *-dere,* put: see *do*[1].] To conquer and bring into subjection (as, "It cost them [Romans] two great wars, and three great battles, to *subdue* that little kingdom [Macedon]": Adam Smith's "Wealth of Nations," v. 1. 1); overpower by superior force; overcome; bring into moral subjection, as by persuasion or by inspiring awe or fear; render submissive (*to:* as, "the ability men have to *subdue* themselves to the conditions of life," Gissing's "Private Papers of Henry Ryecroft," iii. 7); repress (feelings, impulses, etc.); also, to bring (land) under cultivation; also, to allay (inflammation, etc.); reduce the intensity, force, or vividness of (sound, light, color, etc.); tone down; soften; also, to bring down or reduce, as to a low state†.—**sub-dued′**, *p. a.* Reduced to subjection; rendered submissive; also, reduced in intensity or force, or toned down (as, "a sort of boudoir, pervaded by a *subdued,* rose-coloured light": H. James's "Portrait of a Lady," xliii.).—**sub-dued′ly**, *adv.*—**sub-dued′ness**, *n.*—**sub-due′ment**, *n.* Subdual.—**sub-du′er**, *n.*

sub-ed-it (sub-ed′it), *v. t.* [See *sub-*.] To edit under the direction of a chief editor.—**sub′ed″i-tor**, *n.* A subordinate editor; one who subedits.—**sub″ed-i-to′ri-al** (-i-tō′ri-al), *a.* —**sub′ed″i-tor-ship**, *n.*

sub-e-qua-to-ri-al (sub-ē-kwa-tō′ri-al), *a.* [See *sub-*.] Near or adjoining the equatorial region.

su-ber (sū′bėr), *n.* [L., the cork-tree, cork.] Cork.— **su′ber-ate** (-āt), *n.* In *chem.,* a salt of suberic acid.— **su-be-re-ous** (sū-bē′rē-us), *a.* [L. *subereus.*] Of the nature of or resembling cork.—**su-bėr-ic** (sū-ber′ik), *a.* Of or pertaining to cork; in *chem.,* noting a crystalline acid derived from cork.—**su-bėr-in** (sū′bėr-in), *n.* A substance contained in and characteristic of cork tissue.—**su′ber-ize** (-īz), *v. t.*; *-ized, -izing.* In *bot.,* to convert into cork tissue. —**su″ber-i-za′tion** (-i-zā′shon), *n.*—**su′ber-ose, su′ber-ous** (-ōs, -us), *a.* Of the nature of cork; cork-like; corky.

sub-fam-i-ly (sub′fam″i-li), *n.*; pl. *-lies* (-liz). [See *sub-*.] In *zoöl.* and *bot.,* a group or category ranking below a family.

sub-fusc, sub-fusk (sub-fusk′), *a.* [L. *subfuscus, suffuscus:* see *sub-,* and cf. *fuscous.*] Somewhat dark or dusky in color; brownish: as, "a *subfusc* hue like that of old furniture" (Galsworthy's "Country House," i. 4). Also **sub-fus′cous** (-fus′kus).

sub-ge-ner-ic (sub-jē-ner′ik), *a.* Of, pertaining to, or constituting a subgenus.—**sub-ge-ner′i-cal-ly**, *adv.*

sub-ge-nus (sub′jē″nus), *n.*; pl. *-genera* (-jen″ē-rä) or *-genuses.* [See *sub-*.] A subordinate genus; specif., a zoölogical or botanical group or category ranking below a genus and above a species.

sub-gla-cial (sub-glā′shial), *a.* [See *sub-*.] Beneath a glacier: as, a *subglacial* stream.—**sub-gla′cial-ly**, *adv.*

sub-group (sub′gröp), *n.* [See *sub-*.] A subordinate group; a division of a group.

sub-head (sub′hed), *n.* [See *sub-*.] A subordinate head or title, under which is treated one of the divisions of a subject treated under a head; also, a subordinate division of a heading or title. Also **sub′head″ing.**

sub-hu-man (sub-hū′man), *a.* [See *sub-*.] Below the human race or type; less than or not quite human; also, almost human.

sub-in-dex (sub′in″deks), *n.*; pl. *-dices* (-di-sēz). [See *sub-*.] In *math.,* etc., a specifying or distinguishing figure or letter following and slightly below a figure, letter, or symbol: as, 2 is the *subindex* in b_2.

sub-in-feu-da-tion (sub-in-fū-dā′shon), *n.* [See *sub-*.] In *feudal law,* secondary infeudation; the granting of a portion of an estate by a feudal tenant to a subtenant, to be held of the tenant on terms similar to those of the grant to him; the tenure established by this; the estate or fief so created.— **sub-in-feu′da-to-ry** (-fū′da-tō-ri), *n.*; pl. *-ries* (-riz). One who holds by subinfeudation.

sub-ir-ri-gate (sub-ir′i-gāt), *v. t.*; *-gated, -gating.* [See *sub-*.] To irrigate beneath the surface of the ground, as with water passing through a system of underground pipes or transmitted through the subsoil from ditches, etc.— **sub-ir-ri-ga′tion** (-gā′shon), *n.*

sub-i-ta-ne-ous (sub-i-tā′nē-us), *a.* [L. *subitaneus:* see *sudden.*] Sudden; unexpected; hastily done, made, etc. [Now rare.]

su-bi-to (sö′bē-tö), *adv.* [It., < L. *subito,* abl. of *subitus,* sudden: see *sudden.*] In *music,* suddenly; quickly.

sub-ja-cent (sub-jā′sent), *a.* [L. *subjacens* (-ent-), ppr. of *subjacere,* lie under, < *sub,* under, + *jacere,* lie.] Situated or occurring underneath or below; underlying; hence, forming a basis; also, being in a lower situation, though not directly beneath.—**sub-ja′cen-cy**, *n.*—**sub-ja′cent-ly**, *adv.*

sub-ject (sub′jekt), *a.* [OF. *subject, subjet, suget* (F. *sujet*), < L. *subjectus,* pp. of *subjicere, subicere,* throw or place under, subject, < *sub,* under, + *jacere,* throw.] Placed or situated under or beneath (obs. or archaic); forming the substance of a thing†; also, being under dominion, rule, or authority, as of a sovereign or lord, a conqueror, a state, or some governing power; owing allegiance or obedience (*to*); hence, being under domination, control, or influence (often with *to:* as, "All that lives is *subject* to that law," Spenser's "Faerie Queene," iii. 6. 40); submissive† or obedient†; being under an obligation (to do something); being under the necessity of undergoing something (with *to:* as, all men are *subject* to death; accounts *subject* to periodical examination); liable, as to something (esp. something undesirable) that may or often does befall (as, "Human affairs are all *subject* to changes and disasters," Defoe's "Robinson Crusoe," i. 3; *subject* to headache; *subject* to earthquakes); open or exposed (*to*: as, *subject* to attack or ridicule); also, being dependent or conditional upon something (with *to*: as, his consent is *subject* to your approval).—**sub′ject**, *n*. [OF. *subjet*, *suget* (F. *sujet*), < L. *subjicius*, pp. (see *subject*, *a*.); some senses being derived through L. *subjectum*, underlying matter, the foundation or subject of a proposition, prop. neut. of *subjectus*, pp.] One who is under the dominion or rule of a sovereign; one who owes allegiance to a government and lives under its protection (as, "a French *subject* of military age": Mrs. Wharton's "Son at the Front," i.); the subjects of a realm collectively†; hence, one who or that which is under the domination, control, or influence of another (as, "Beauties are tyrants, and if they can reign They have no feeling for their *subjects*' pain": Crabbe's "Tales," v.); also, one who or that which undergoes, or may undergo, some action, or is regarded as the recipient of a certain treatment (as, "the most bold and fierce *subjects* of chase in the island of Britain": Scott's "Castle Dangerous," vi.); an object upon which one operates in some special manner; a person as an object of medical or surgical treatment, or of psychological experiment; a dead body as used for dissection; something that forms a matter of thought, discourse, investigation, etc. (as, a *subject* of conversation or negotiation; the *subjects* taught in a college course); the theme of a sermon, book, story, etc.; an object, scene, incident, or the like, chosen by an artist for representation, or as represented in art; a theme or melodic phrase on which a musical work or movement is based; a ground, motive, or cause (as, to give one a *subject* for complaint); also, the substance or material of which a thing consists†; in *gram.*, the word or words, in a sentence, denoting that of which something is predicated; in *logic*, that term of a proposition of which the other is affirmed or denied; in *philos.*, the substance in which attributes inhere; also, the self or ego to which all mental representations or operations are attributed.—**sub-ject** (sub-jekt′), *v. t.* [OF. *subjecter*, *subgetter*, < L. *subjectare*, place under, freq. of *subjicere*: see *subject*, *a*.] To place beneath something† or make subjacent†; also, to bring under dominion, rule, or authority, as of a conqueror or a governing power (usually with *to*); bring under domination, control, or influence (usually with *to*); cause to undergo or experience something (with *to*: as, to *subject* metal to a white heat; to *subject* a matter to critical analysis); make liable, lay open, or expose (*to*: as, to *subject* one's self to unpleasant comment).

sub-jec-ti-fy (sub-jek′ti-fī), *v. t.*; *-fied*, *-fying*. [L. *subjectum*, a subject: see *-fy*. Cf. *objectify*.] To make subjective; identify with the subject.—**sub-jec′ti-fi-ca′tion** (-fi-kā′shon), *n*.

sub-jec-tion (sub-jek′shon), *n*. [L. *subjectio(n-)*, < *subjicere*: see *subject*, *a*.] The act of subjecting, or the state or fact of being subjected.—**sub-jec′tion-al**, *a*.

sub-jec-tive (sub-jek′tiv), *a*. [L. *subjectivus*.] Pertaining to or befitting one who is subject to dominion, rule, or control†; also, pertaining to the subject or substance in which attributes inhere; essential; also, existing in the mind; belonging to the thinking subject rather than to the object of thought (opposed to *objective*: as, "Literature expresses, not objective truth, as it is called, but *subjective*; not things, but thoughts," J. H. Newman's "Idea of a University," ii. 2); sometimes, imaginary; also, pertaining to or characteristic of an individual thinking subject (as, "Sismondi never fully learned to judge men according to a *subjective* standard, that is, their own notions of right and wrong": Hallam's "Europe during the Middle Ages," i. 1, note); personal; individual; sometimes, habitually concerned with one's own mental states or processes; introspective; in *literature* and *art*, expressing or displaying the individuality of the author or artist (as, *subjective* poetry; a *subjective* painter); also, in *gram.*, pertaining to or constituting the subject of a sentence.—**sub-jec′tive-ly**, *adv*.—**sub-jec′tive-ness**, *n*.—**sub-jec′tiv-ism**, *n*. The philosophical theory that all knowledge is subjective, and that objective knowledge is impossible; hence, any theory that lays great stress on the subjective elements in experience; also, the ethical theory which conceives the aim of morality to be the attainment of states of feeling; also, subjectivity.—**sub-jec′tiv-ist**, *n*. One who believes in or advocates a theory of subjectivism.—**sub-jec-ti-vis′tic**, *a*.—**sub-jec-tiv′i-ty** (-tiv′i-ti), *n*. The state or quality of being subjective; existence in the mind only; absorption in one's own mental states or processes; the tendency to view things through the medium of one's own individuality; subjective quality in literary or artistic work; also, subjectivism.

sub-ject=mat-ter (sub′jekt-mat″ėr), *n*. The matter which is subjected to some operation, or out of which a thing is formed; esp., matter or material with which thought, discourse, investigation, study, or the like, is occupied; the substance of a discourse, book, writing, or the like, as distinguished from its form or style; the subject or theme.

sub-join (sub-join′), *v. t.* [OF. *subjoindre*, < L. *subjungere* (pp. *subjunctus*), < *sub*, under, + *jungere*, E. *join*.] To add at the end, as of something said or written; append; also, to place in immediate sequence or juxtaposition to something else.

sub-ju-gate (sub′jö-gāt), *v. t.*; *-gated*, *-gating*. [L. *subjugatus*, pp. of *subjugare*, < *sub*, under, + *jugum*, yoke.] To bring under the yoke or into subjection; subdue; conquer; hence, to bring under complete control (as, "Mrs. Morpher . . . had at last *subjugated* her naturally careless disposition to principles of 'order' ": Bret Harte's "Mliss," ii.); make submissive or subservient.—**sub-ju-ga′tion** (-gā′shon), *n*. [ML. *subjugatio(n-)*.] The act of subjugating, or the state of being subjugated.—**sub′ju-ga-tor**, *n*.

sub-junc-tion (sub-jungk′shon), *n*. [L. *subjungere* (pp. *subjunctus*): see *subjoin*.] The act of subjoining, or the state of being subjoined; also, something subjoined.

sub-junc-tive (sub-jungk′tiv). [LL. *subjunctivus*, < L. *subjungere* (pp. *subjunctus*): see *subjoin*.] In *gram.*: **I.** *a.* Serving to subjoin, as a mode of the verb used in subordinate clauses (expressing condition, contingency, etc.) and also in principal clauses; of or pertaining to this mode. **II.** *n.* The subjunctive mode, or a verb-form belonging to it.—**sub-junc′tive-ly**, *adv*.

sub-king-dom (sub′king″dom), *n*. [See *sub-*.] A primary division of the animal or vegetable kingdom: usually equivalent to *phylum*.

sub-lease (sub′lēs), *n*. [See *sub-*.] A lease granted by one who is himself a lessee of the property; an underlease.—**sub-lease′**, *v. t.*; *-leased*, *-leasing*. To grant a sublease of; sublet; also, to take or hold a sublease of.—**sub-les-see′** (-le-sē′), *n*. The receiver or holder of a sublease.—**sub-les′sor** (-les′or), *n*. The grantor of a sublease.

sub-let (sub-let′), *v. t.*; *-let*, *-letting*. [See *sub-*.] To let to another person, the party letting being himself lessee; grant a sublease of; underlet; of a contractor, to let (work, etc.) under a subcontract.

sub-lieu-ten-ant (sub-lū-ten′ant), *n*. [See *sub-*.] A subordinate lieutenant; now, specif., in the British navy, an officer ranking next below a lieutenant.—**sub-lieu-ten′-an-cy**, *n*.

sub-li-mate (sub′li-māt), *v*.; *-mated*, *-mating*. [L. and ML. *sublimatus*, pp. of *sublimare*: see *sublime*, *v*.] **I.** *tr.* To raise to high station or dignity†; also, to elevate or exalt in character; transmute into something higher, nobler, or purer; also, to refine away into something unreal or nonexistent; make unreal; in *chem.*, etc., to sublime (a solid substance); extract by or as by this process; also, to refine or purify (a substance). **II.** *intr.* To become sublimated; undergo sublimation.—**sub′li-mate** (-māt), *n*. [ML. *sublimatum*, prop. neut. of *sublimatus*, pp.] In *chem.*, the crystals, deposit, or material obtained when a substance is sublimed; esp., corrosive sublimate (see under *corrosive*, *a*.).—**sub-li-ma′tion** (-mā′shon), *n*. [LL. and ML. *sublimatio(n-)*.] The act or process of sublimating or subliming; the resulting state or product; esp., mental elevation or exaltation (as, "that enthusiastic *sublimation* which is the source of greatness and energy": Peacock's "Headlong Hall," v.); the highest stage or purest form of a thing; a chemical sublimate.

sub-lime (sub-līm′), *a*.; compar. *sublimer*, superl. *sublimest*. [L. *sublimis*, uplifted, lofty.] Raised aloft, or being high up (archaic: as, "He on the wings of cherub rode *sublime* On the crystalline sky," Milton's "Paradise Lost," vi. 771); rising to a great height, as towers, etc. (archaic); fig., exalted in rank or dignity (archaic); of lofty bearing or aspect, or, sometimes, haughty or proud (chiefly poetic); exalted in feeling†, or elated†; also, of an especially exalted moral character or excellence, or of the highest and noblest kind (as, a *sublime* Christian; *sublime* devotion; "Know how *sublime* a thing it is To suffer and be strong," Longfellow's "Light of Stars"); elevated or lofty in thought, sentiment, language, style, etc. (as, *sublime* poetry; the *sublime* Milton); belonging to the highest level of thought or knowledge, as ideas, subjects, etc.; striking the mind with a sense of grandeur or power, or awakening awe, veneration, or exalted feeling by reason of grandeur, beauty, or the like, as scenes in nature or works of art; in general, supreme or perfect (as, a *sublime* moment: sometimes used colloq. with ironical force, as, *sublime* indifference to the opinions of others; "I don't pretend to your *sublime* detachment," Mrs. Wharton's "Son at the Front," xviii.); also, sublimated, refined, or purified.—**Sublime Porte.** See *Porte* (etym. and def.).—**sub-lime′,** *n.* That which is sublime (usually with *the*: as, the *sublime* in literature or art; "No, never need an American look beyond his own country for the *sublime* and beautiful of natural scenery," Irving's "Sketch-Book," The Author's Account of Himself); also, the highest degree or example, or the supreme (*of*: as, "Your upward gaze at me now is the very *sublime* of faith, truth, and devotion," C. Brontë's "Jane Eyre," xxv.).—**sub-lime′,** *v.*; *-limed, -liming.* [L. *sublimare*, lift up on high, elevate, ML. sublime chemically, < L. *sublimis.*] **I.** *tr.* To raise or send aloft (archaic); fig., to raise to high rank†; also, to elevate or exalt in character (as, "If by worth *sublimed*, the dignity Of rule I need not envy": Wiffen's tr. Tasso's "Jerusalem Delivered," v. 14); make lofty or sublime; transmute into something higher, nobler, or purer; in *chem.*, etc., to convert (a solid substance) by heat into a vapor, which on cooling condenses again to solid form, without apparent liquefaction; also, to cause to be given off by this or some analogous process; extract by or as by sublimation. **II.** *intr.* To become sublimed; in *chem.*, etc., to undergo the process of subliming; also, to be given off or extracted by sublimation.—**sub-lime′ly,** *adv.*—**sub-lime′ness,** *n.*—**sub-lim′er** (-lī′mẻr), *n.*

sub-lim-i-nal (sub-lim′i-nạl), *a.* [L. *sub*, under, + *limen* (*limin-*), threshold.] In *psychol.*, below the limen or threshold of consciousness (see *threshold*); subconscious (which see): as, *subliminal* psychical processes; the *subliminal* memory; the *subliminal* self.

sub-lim-i-ty (sub-lim′i-ti), *n.*; pl. *-ties* (-tiz). The state or quality of being sublime; exalted moral character; lofty excellence; loftiness of conception, language, or style; grandeur or majesty (as, "There was an awful *sublimity* in the hoarse murmuring of the thunder": Parkman's "Oregon Trail," xiii.); also, something sublime; a sublime person or thing; a sublime feature; also, the or a supreme height of something (as, to attain the *sublimity* of wisdom).

sub-lin-e-ate (sub-lin′ē-āt), *v. t.*; *-ated, -ating.* [See *sub-* and *lineate.*] To underline; underscore.—**sub-lin-e-a′tion** (-ā′shọn), *n.*

sub-lin-gual (sub-ling′gwạl). [L. *sub*, under, + *lingua*, tongue.] In *anat.*: **I.** *a.* Situated under the tongue, or on the under side of the tongue (as, the *sublingual* gland, either of two saliva-producing glands situated on the floor of the mouth beneath the tongue, one on each side); pertaining to either sublingual gland. **II.** *n.* A sublingual gland, artery, or the like.

sub-lu-na-ry (sub′lū-nā-ri), *a.* [NL. *sublunaris*, < L. *sub*, under, + *luna*, moon.] Situated beneath the moon; hence, of, on, or being the earth, or terrestrial (as, this *sublunary* globe); esp., of this earth or world, earthly, mundane, or worldly (as, "the vanity of all *sublunary* things," Disraeli's "Coningsby," v. 3; "He began gradually to delight in *sublunary* pleasures," Johnson's "Rasselas," xlvi.). Also **sub-lu′nar** (-lū′när).

sub-ma-rine (sub′mạ-rēn, also sub-mạ-rēn′), *a.* [L. *sub*, under, + *mare*, sea.] Situated, occurring, or living under the surface of the sea, either at the bottom or elsewhere below the surface (as, a *submarine* volcano; a *submarine* plant); constructed, carried on, operating, or intended for use below the surface of the sea (as, a *submarine* telegraph; *submarine* navigation; a *submarine* boat; a *submarine* mine; *submarine* armor, the water-tight covering or dress worn by a

diver); also, of, pertaining to, or carried on by submarine boats (as, *submarine* warfare).—**sub′ma-rine,** *n.* A boat or vessel so designed that it can be submerged and navigated under water; esp., such a vessel used in warfare for the dis-

Submarine (for discharging torpedoes), at surface of water.

charge of torpedoes, etc.—**sub′ma-rine,** *v. t.*; *-rined, -rining.* To attack, torpedo, or sink through the agency of a submarine, or as a submarine does.—**sub′ma-rine-ly,** *adv.* —**sub′ma-rin-er** (-rē-nẻr), *n.*—**sub′ma-rin-ism,** *n.* The policy or practice of using submarines, esp. on a large scale or without restriction, as in warfare.—**sub′ma-rin-ist,** *n.*

sub-max-il-la (sub-mak-sil′ạ), *n.*; pl. *-maxillæ* (-ē). [NL.: see *sub-* and *maxilla.*] In *anat.* and *zoöl.*, the lower jaw or lower jaw-bone.—**sub-max′il-la-ry** (-mak′si-lā-ri). In *anat.*: **I.** *a.* Of or pertaining to the lower jaw or lower jaw-bone (as, the *submaxillary* gland, either of two saliva-producing glands situated beneath the lower jaw, one on each side); pertaining to or situated near the submaxillary gland. **II.** *n.*; pl. *-ries* (-riz). The lower jaw-bone; also, the submaxillary gland.

sub-me-di-ant (sub-mē′di-ạnt), *n.* [See *sub-.*] In *music*, the sixth tone of a scale, being midway between the subdominant and the upper tonic.

sub-merge (sub-mèrj′), *v.*; *-merged, -merging.* [L. *submergere* (pp. *submersus*), *summergere*, < *sub*, under, + *mergere*, dip, plunge, sink, E. *merge.*] **I.** *tr.* To put under water; sink below the surface of water or any enveloping medium (also fig.); also, to cover, as water or the like does something beneath it. **II.** *intr.* To sink or plunge under water, or beneath the surface of any enveloping medium. Also fig.—**sub-merged′,** *p. a.* Sunk under water or beneath the surface of something; fig., living in profound poverty and misery (as, the *submerged* classes of society, or the *submerged* tenth); in *bot.*, growing under water.—**sub-mer′-gence** (-mèr′jens), *n.* The act of submerging, or the state of being submerged.—**sub-mer′gi-ble** (-ji-bl), *a.* and *n.* Same as *submersible.*

sub-merse (sub-mèrs′), *v. t.*; *-mersed, -mersing.* [L. *submersus*, pp. of *submergere:* see *submerge.*] To submerge. —**sub-mersed′,** *p. a.* Submerged; esp., in *bot.*, growing under water.—**sub-mers′i-ble. I.** *a.* That may be submersed. **II.** *n.* A submersible boat: a term applied to submarines in general, particular types of submarines, or vessels used like but distinguished in some way from submarines, as submarines adapted for traveling great distances on the surface of the water or vessels capable of being only partly submerged.

sub-mer-sion (sub-mèr′shọn), *n.* [LL. *submersio(n-)*, < L. *submergere:* see *submerge.*] The act of submerging, or the state of being submerged; submergence.

sub-me-tal-lic (sub-me-tal′ik), *a.* [See *sub-.*] Imperfectly or partially metallic.

sub-miss (sub-mis′), *a.* [L. *submissus*, pp. of *submittere:* see *submit.*] Submissive or humble (archaic: as, "With *submiss* approach and reverence meek, As to a superior nature bowing low," Milton's "Paradise Lost," v. 359); also, of the voice, etc., subdued or low†.

sub-mis-sion (sub-mish′ọn), *n.* [OF. *submission* (F. *soumission*), < L. *submissio(n-)*, < *submittere:* see *submit.*] The act of submitting, or the condition of having submitted, as to power, authority, or requirements (as, "a Government to which *submission* is equivalent to slavery": Burke's "Conciliation with the Colonies"); submissive conduct or attitude; also, a submitting or being submitted for consideration, criticism, or approval; in *law*, an agreement to abide by a decision or obey an authority in some matter referred to arbitration.

sub-mis-sive (sub-mis′iv), *a.* Inclined or ready to submit; yielding to power or authority; unresistingly or humbly obedient; also, marked by or indicating submission (as, a *submissive* reply or tone; "The Czarina's yoke these wild nations bore with *submissive* patience," De Quincey's "Revolt of the Tartars").—**sub-mis′sive-ly**, *adv.*—**sub-mis′sive-ness**, *n.*

sub-mit (sub-mit′), *v.*; *-mitted*, *-mitting*. [L. *submittere* (pp. *submissus*), *summittere*, put under, lower, submit, < *sub*, under, + *mittere*, send.] **I.** *tr.* To yield in surrender, compliance, or obedience, as to another or to power, authority, laws, etc. (often used reflexively: as, "till . . . the parents had by repentance *submitted* themselves unto the Church," Hooker's "Ecclesiastical Polity," iii. 1. 12); subject (now esp. one's self) to conditions imposed; treatment, etc.; also, to refer to the decision or judgment of another or others (as, to *submit* a controversy to arbitrators); present for consideration, approval, or acceptance (as, to *submit* a plan; "I *submitted* it [a book] . . . to one of the big publishing houses," Bok's "Americanization of Edward Bok," xiii.); also, to represent or urge with deference (with a clause: as, I *submit* that full proof should be required); also, to lay or put down (obs. or rare). **II.** *intr.* To yield in surrender, compliance, or obedience (as, to *submit* to a conqueror; to *submit* to the authority or will of another); allow one's self to be subjected, or resign one's self, to something imposed or to be undergone (as, to *submit* to punishment or reproof; "He *submitted* to the decision of fate with . . . humility," Chesterton's "Napoleon of Notting Hill," iii. 1; "He must *submit* to this indignity," Du Maurier's "Trilby," ii.).—**sub-mit′tal**, *n.* The act of submitting.—**sub-mit′ter**, *n.*

sub-mon-tane (sub-mon′tān), *a.* [L. *sub*, under, + *mons* (*mont-*), mountain.] Under or beneath a mountain or mountains; also, at or near the foot of mountains; pertaining to the lower slopes of mountains.

sub-mul-ti-ple (sub-mul′ti-pl). [See *sub-*.] **I.** *a.* Being, or pertaining to, a number or quantity which divides another exactly, that is, without a remainder. **II.** *n.* A submultiple number or quantity.

sub-nor-mal (sub-nôr′mal), *a.* [See *sub-*.] Below the normal; less than or inferior to the normal.—**sub-normal′i-ty** (-mal′i-ti), *n.*

sub-o-ce-an-ic (sub″ō-shē-an′ik), *a.* [See *sub-*.] Beneath the ocean.

sub-of-fi-cer (sub′of″i-sėr), *n.* [See *sub-*.] A subordinate officer.

sub-or-bi-tal (sub-ôr′bi-tal), *a.* [See *sub-*.] In *anat.*: **I.** *a.* Situated below the orbit of the eye, or on the floor of the orbit, as a cartilage, nerve, etc. **II.** *n.* A suborbital cartilage, nerve, or the like.

sub-or-der (sub′ôr″dėr), *n.* [See *sub-*.] In *zoöl.* and *bot.*, a group or category ranking below an order.

sub-or-di-na-cy (sub-ôr′di-na-si), *n.* Subordinate position or state; subordination.

sub-or-di-nal (sub-ôr′di-nal), *a.* [NL. *subordo* (*subordin-*), a suborder: see *sub-* and *ordinal*.] Of, pertaining to, or ranked as a suborder.

sub-or-di-na-ry (sub-ôr′di-na-ri), *n.*; pl. *-ries* (-riz). [See *sub-*.] In *her.*, any of various simple charges or bearings regarded as less important than the ordinaries.

sub-or-di-nate (sub-ôr′di-nāt), *v. t.*; *-nated*, *-nating*. [ML. *subordinatus*, pp. of *subordinare*, < L. *sub*, under, + *ordinare*, order, arrange, E. *ordain*.] To place in a lower order or rank; make secondary (*to*), as in importance; hence, to make subject, subservient, or dependent (with *to*: as, "he to whose will our wills are to be *subordinated*," Carlyle's "On Heroes," vi.).—**sub-or′di-nate** (-nat). [ML. *subordinatus*, pp.] **I.** *a.* Placed in or belonging to a lower order or rank; occupying a lower position in a scale; of inferior importance; secondary; hence, subject to or under the authority of a superior; also, submissive† (cf. *insubordinate*); also, subservient, as to something of greater importance; dependent. **II.** *n.* A subordinate person or thing; esp., one who, being of lower rank, is under the authority of a superior.—**sub-or′di-nate-ly**, *adv.*—**sub-or′di-nate-ness**, *n.*—**sub-or-di-na′tion** (-nā′shọn), *n.* [ML. *subordinatio(n-)*.] The act of subordinating, or the state of being subordinate; secondary position or importance; subjection; submission to authority; subservience; de-

pendence.—**sub-or′di-na-tive** (-nā-tiv), *a.* Tending to subordinate; involving or expressing subordination or dependence.

sub-orn (sub-ôrn′), *v. t.* [L. *subornare* (pp. *subornatus*), < *sub*, under, + *ornare*, equip.] To furnish†, equip†, or adorn†; also, to prepare, provide, or procure, esp. in a secret or underhand manner†; also, to bribe or unlawfully procure (a person) to commit some act of wickedness; specif., to bribe or unlawfully procure (a person) to make accusations or give evidence; induce (a witness) to give false evidence or commit perjury (as, "He had no case without *suborning* witnesses": G. Meredith's "Diana of the Crossways," vii.); also, to procure (evidence) by bribery or other unlawful means; procure the performance or execution of (a thing) by bribery or the like.—**sub-or-na′tion** (-ôr-nā′shọn), *n.* [ML. *subornatio(n-)*.] The act of suborning; specif., the act of inducing a witness to commit perjury.—**sub-orn′er**, *n.*

sub-phy-lum (sub′fī″lum), *n.*; pl. *-la* (-lä). [See *sub-*.] In *zoöl.* and *bot.*, a group or category ranking below a phylum.—**sub′phy″lar** (-lär), *a.*

sub-pœ-na (sub-pē′nä or su-pē′-), *n.*; pl. *-nas* (-näz). [L. *sub pœna*, under penalty: see *sub-* and *pain*.] In *law*, a writ or process commanding the person on whom it is served to appear in court under a penalty for failure.—**sub-pœ′na**, **sub-pe′na**, *v. t.*; *-naed*, *-naing*. To serve with a subpœna.

sub-pre-fect (sub′prē″fekt), *n.* [See *sub-*.] An assistant or deputy prefect.—**sub′pre″fec-ture** (-fek-tụr), *n.*

sub-prin-ci-pal (sub′prin″si-pal), *n.* [See *sub-*.] An under, assistant, or deputy principal; in *carp.*, an auxiliary rafter or the like; in *music*, in an organ, a subbass of the open diapason class.

sub-re-gion (sub′rē″jọn), *n.* [See *sub-*.] A division or subdivision of a region, esp. a division of a zoögeographical region.—**sub-re′gion-al**, *a.*

sub-rep-tion (sub-rep′shọn), *n.* [L. *subreptio(n-)*, *surreptio(n-)*, < *subripere*, *surripere*, take secretly: see *surreptitious*.] The act of obtaining something, as an ecclesiastical dispensation, by suppression or fraudulent concealment of facts; also, a fallacious representation, or an inference derived from it.—**sub-rep-ti′tious** (-tish′us), *a.* [L. *subrepticius*, *surrepticius*: cf. *surreptitious*.] Obtained by subreption; also, clandestine or surreptitious.—**sub-rep-ti′tious-ly**, *adv.*

sub-ro-gate (sub′rō-gāt), *v. t.*; *-gated*, *-gating*. [L. *subrogatus*, pp. of *subrogare*, *surrogare*, put in another's place: see *surrogate*.] To put into the place of another; substitute for another; esp., to put (a person) into the place of another in respect to a legal right or claim.—**sub-ro-ga′tion** (-gā′shọn), *n.* [ML. *subrogatio(n-)*.] The act of subrogating; esp., the substitution of one person for another as a creditor.

sub-salt (sub′sâlt), *n.* [See *sub-*.] In *chem.*, a basic salt.

sub-scap-u-lar (sub-skap′ū-lär). [NL. *subscapularis*: see *sub-* and *scapula*.] In *anat.*: **I.** *a.* Situated beneath, or on the under (or anterior) surface of, the scapula, as a muscle, artery, etc. **II.** *n.* A subscapular muscle, artery, or the like.

sub-scribe (sub-skrīb′), *v.*; *-scribed*, *-scribing*. [L. *subscribere* (pp. *subscriptus*), < *sub*, under, + *scribere*, write.] **I.** *tr.* To write or inscribe (something) beneath or at the end of a thing; sign (one's name) to a document, etc. (as, "They must all *subscribe* their names as witnesses": Blackstone's "Commentaries," II. 377); write down or characterize (one's self) as specified, as at the end of a letter (as, I beg leave to *subscribe* myself Your obedient servant, John Smith: now rare); also, to sign one's name to (a document, etc.: as, "The prior and convent . . . solemnly *subscribed* an instrument for abolishing the pope's supremacy," Strype's "Memorials of Cranmer," i. 6); express assent or adhesion to (a contract, etc.) by signing one's name; attest by signing, as a statement; concur in† or sanction† (as, "Orestes . . . chose rather to encounter the rage of an armed multitude, than to *subscribe* the ruin of an innocent people": Gibbon's "Decline and Fall of the Roman Empire," xxxvi.); also, to sign away to another†; also, to promise, as by signing an agreement, to give or pay (a sum of money), whether as a contribution toward some object, or as in payment for something, as shares in some undertaking; give or pay in fulfilment of such a promise. **II.** *intr.* To sign one's name to something; assent by or as by signing one's name; give consent or sanction; also, to submit† or yield†; also, to make acknowledgment or admission (with *to*: obs. or rare); also, to undertake, as by signing an agreement, to give or pay money for some special purpose, whether as a contribution toward some object, or in payment for shares, a book, etc.; give or pay money as a contribution toward some object or in payment for shares, a periodical, etc. (as, "He *subscribes* liberally to the Associated Charities," Howells's "Rise of Silas Lapham," i.; to *subscribe* for a magazine).—**sub-scrib′er** (-skrī′bẽr), *n.*

sub-script (sub′skript). [L. *subscriptus*, pp. of *subscribere*: see *subscribe*.] **I.** *a.* Written below: distinguished from *adscript* (as, in *Gr. gram.*, an iota *subscript*, as in φ for ωι). **II.** *n.* Something written below.

sub-scrip-tion (sub-skrip′shǫn), *n.* [L. *subscriptio(n-).*] The act of subscribing; the signing of one's name, as to a document; something subscribed, or written beneath or at the end of a thing; a signature attached to a paper; a signed declaration (now rare); assent, agreement, or approval expressed by or as by signing one's name; submission† or obedience†; the subscribing of money as a contribution toward some object or in payment for shares, a book, a periodical, etc.; joint contribution as a means of carrying out some purpose (as, a public ball held by *subscription*; attrib., a *subscription* ball); a sum subscribed (as, "We read novels, plays, pamphlets, and newspapers, for so small a *subscription* as a crown a quarter": Smollett's "Humphry Clinker," April 26); a right obtained for a sum subscribed (as, one's *subscription* as a member of a society, or one's *subscription* to a magazine, has expired); a fund raised through sums of money subscribed by a number of persons (as, "I set on foot a *subscription* for opening and supporting an academy": B. Franklin's "Autobiography," ix.); specif., a method of ensuring the publication of a book by the promise of a sufficient number of persons in advance to purchase copies; also, the sale of books by canvassers (U. S.).

sub-sea (sub′sē), *a.* [See *sub-*.] Undersea; submarine.

sub-sec-tion (sub′sek″shǫn), *n.* [See *sub-*.] A part or division of a section.

sub-se-quence (sub′sē-kwẹns), *n.* The state or fact of being subsequent; also, that which is subsequent; the sequel of anything; a subsequent event or circumstance.

sub-se-quent (sub′sē-kwẹnt). [L. *subsequens* (-ent-), ppr. of *subsequi*, follow after, succeed, < *sub*, under, + *sequi*, follow.] **I.** *a.* Following in order or succession (as, a *subsequent* clause in a treaty; "But more of this in a *subsequent* chapter," Scott's "Waverley," ii.); coming or placed after; also, following in time (as, *subsequent* events; "a *subsequent* occasion," Pinero's "Wife without a Smile," ii.); coming or occurring after or later (often with *to*: as, "on the day *subsequent* to the despatch of the message," Trollope's "Barchester Towers," i.). **II.** *adv.* At a time subsequent (*to*).—**sub-se-quen′tial** (-kwen′shǎl), *a.* Subsequent.—**sub′se-quent-ly,** *adv.* At a subsequent or later time: sometimes followed by *to*.

sub-serve (sub-sẽrv′), *v.*; *-served, -serving.* [L. *subservire*, < *sub*, under, + *servire*, serve.] **I.** *intr.* To be of service or use as an instrument or means; also, to serve in a subordinate capacity† (as, "Not made to rule, But to *subserve* where wisdom bears command!" Milton's "Samson Agonistes," 57). **II.** *tr.* To be useful or instrumental in promoting (a purpose, action, function, etc.: as, "the temple of Mercury, which at that time *subserved* the purpose of a boy's school," J. H. Newman's "Callista," viii.); assist as an instrument or means; also, to serve under, or in subordination to†.

sub-ser-vi-ence (sub-sẽr′vi-ẹns), *n.* The condition of being subservient or serviceable; also, a serving or acting in subordination; subjection; hence, servility; obsequiousness. Also **sub-ser′vi-en-cy.**

sub-ser-vi-ent (sub-sẽr′vi-ẹnt), *a.* [L. *subserviens* (-ent-), ppr. of *subservire*: see *subserve*.] Of service or use as an instrument or means to promote a purpose or end, or serviceable (as, "a street of small shops *subservient* to the needs of poor people": Maugham's "Moon and Sixpence," xi.); also, serving or acting in a subordinate capacity; subordinate; subject; hence, of persons and their conduct, etc., servile;

meanly submissive; truckling; obsequious.—**sub-ser′vi-ent-ly,** *adv.*

sub-shrub (sub′shrub), *n.* [See *sub-*.] A plant with a somewhat woody base; a small shrub.—**sub′shrub″by,** *a.*

sub-side (sub-sīd′), *v. i.*; *-sided, -siding.* [L. *subsidere*, < *sub-*, down, + *sidere*, sit down, sink, settle.] To sink or fall to the bottom; settle, as lees; precipitate; also, to sink to a low or lower level, as a stream to its normal level; contract or become reduced after dilatation, swelling, or the like; also, to sink down, as into a chair (as, "Lord Bellinger . . . *subsided* into his seat": Whyte-Melville's "Katerfelto," viii.); also, to cease from action or agitation, as the sea, the wind, or a storm (as, "The wind, after several feeble gusts . . . *subsided* to a calm": Marryat's "King's Own," i.); fall into a state of quiet or of less violence or activity, as feeling, excitement, etc. (as, "The spirit which Joan of Arc had roused did not *subside*," Hallam's "Europe during the Middle Ages," i. 2; "The terrors of La Motte began to *subside*," Mrs. Radcliffe's "Romance of the Forest," i.); of an action, to be discontinued (as, "when the little titter had *subsided*," Kipling's "Kim," ii.); of a condition, to pass away (as, "as soon as the public danger had *subsided*": Gibbon's "Decline and Fall of the Roman Empire," xli.); of persons, to fall into an inactive or less active state (as, "After a few vicious efforts, they *subsided* into sullenness": Froude's "Cæsar," xiv.); cease from activity; often, to lapse into silence; stop talking.—**sub-sid-ence** (sub-sī′dẹns or sub′si-dẹns), *n.*

sub-sid-i-a-ry (sub-sid′i-ạ-ri). [L. *subsidiarius*, < *subsidium*: see *subsidy*.] **I.** *a.* Serving to assist or supplement; auxiliary; supplementary; tributary, as a stream; sometimes, subordinate or secondary (as, "a . . . body of highly cultivated languages, each with its legion of *subsidiary* dialectic forms": W. D. Whitney's "Life and Growth of Language," ix.); also, consisting of, pertaining to, or maintained by a subsidy or subsidies. **II.** *n.*; pl. *-ries* (-riz). A subsidiary thing or person; a commercial company which is subsidiary or auxiliary to another company; in *music*, a subordinate theme or subject.—**sub-sid′i-a-ri-ly,** *adv.*

sub-si-dize (sub′si-dīz), *v. t.*; *-dized, -dizing.* To furnish or aid with a subsidy; esp., to purchase the assistance of by the payment of a subsidy (as, "He collects His subject troops and *subsidized* allies": Wiffen's tr. Tasso's "Jerusalem Delivered," i. 90); hence, to secure the coöperation of by bribery; buy over.

sub-si-dy (sub′si-di), *n.*; pl. *-dies* (-diz). [L. *subsidium*, reserve troops, aid, assistance, < *subsidere*, sit down, remain, stay: cf. *subside*.] Aid or assistance, or a help or aid (obs. or archaic); a grant or contribution of money (as, "a *subsidy* for a prince in misfortune": Steele, in "Spectator," 53); esp., a pecuniary aid formerly granted by the English Parliament to the crown to meet special needs; a direct pecuniary aid furnished by a government to a private industrial undertaking, an eleemosynary institution, or the like; a sum paid, often in accordance with a treaty, by one government to another, sometimes to secure its neutrality, but more frequently to meet the expenses of carrying on a war.

sub-sist (sub-sist′), *v.* [L. *subsistere*, stand still, remain, continue, hold out, < *sub*, under, + *sistere*, stand.] **I.** *intr.* To stand firm†; also, to continue in existence (as, "a revolutionary group, installed by military force and by that force *subsisting*": Morley's "Oliver Cromwell," iv. 1); also, to have existence, or exist (as, "The diversity and contrast that *subsisted* in our characters drew us nearer together": Mrs. Shelley's "Frankenstein," ii.); exist as a substance or entity (as, "The young deities discussed . . . What *subsisteth*, and what seems": Emerson's "Uriel"); have existence in, or by reason of, something (as, "By ceaseless action all that is *subsists*": Cowper's "Task," i. 367); reside, lie, or consist (*in*: as, "The Universal Cause . . . makes what happiness we justly call *Subsist* not in the good of one, but all," Pope's "Essay on Man," iv. 38); also, to continue alive; live, as on food, resources, etc.; support or maintain one's self (as, "He borrowed occasionally of me to *subsist* while he was looking out for business": B. Franklin's "Autobiography," iii.). **II.** *tr.* To provide sustenance or support for; support; maintain: as, "They were . . . unacquainted with . . . modes of . . . *subsisting* themselves during long marches" (Irving's "Captain Bonneville," vi.).—**sub-sist′ence**, n. [LL. *subsistentia*.] The state or fact of subsisting; continuance; existence; existence as a substance or entity; also, something having existence; also, the providing of sustenance or support; the provision of food, etc., for persons or animals, esp. for an army; also, means of supporting life (as, "The principal part of our *subsistence* was to be had by our guns": Defoe's "Captain Singleton," ii.); a living or livelihood.—**sub-sist′ent**, a. [L. *subsistens* (-ent-), ppr.] Subsisting; existing; having existence.

sub-soil (sub′soil), n. [See *sub-*.] The bed or stratum of earth or earthy material which lies immediately under the surface soil.—**sub′soil**, v. t. To plow so as to cut into the subsoil.—**sub′soil″er**, n.

sub-spe-cies (sub′spē″shēz), n.; pl. *-species*. [See *sub-*.] A division of a species; specif., a zoölogical or botanical group or category ranking below a species.—**sub-spe-cif′ic** (-spē-sif′ik), a. Of, pertaining to, or of the nature of a subspecies.—**sub-spe-cif′i-cal-ly**, adv.

sub-stance (sub′stans), n. [OF. F. *substance*, < L. *substantia*, < *substans* (*substant-*), ppr. of *substare*, stand under, be present, < *sub*, under, + *stare*, stand.] In philosophical use, that which exists by itself, and in which accidents or attributes inhere; that which receives modifications, and is not itself a mode; also, something that has separate or independent existence; in general use, that of which a thing consists; matter or material; a particular kind of corporeal matter; a species of matter of definite chemical composition; also, the matter with which thought, discourse, study, or the like, is occupied; the material of a discourse, book, or the like, as distinguished from its form or style; subject-matter; also, the actual matter of a thing, as opposed to the appearance or shadow (often fig.: as, "The show of this intimacy had lasted longer than its *substance*," Motley's "Dutch Republic," ii. 2); the reality; also, substantial or solid character or quality (as, claims lacking in *substance*); body (as, soup without much *substance*); also, the mass, quantity, or amount of anything†; the greater number or main part†; also, possessions, means, or wealth (archaic: as, to squander one's *substance*; a man of *substance*; "my father being of good *substance*, at least as we reckon in Exmoor," Blackmore's "Lorna Doone," i.); also, the essential part, or essence, of a thing; the meaning, gist, or purport, as of speech or writing; in *theol.*, the divine nature or essence, common to the three persons of the Trinity.—**in substance**, in essence or essentials, or substantially (as, "They were good boys *in substance* he felt": H. G. Wells's "Men Like Gods," iii. 2); also, in purport or effect.—**sub′stance-less**, a. Without substance; unsubstantial.

sub-stan-tial (sub-stan′shal). [LL. *substantialis*, < L. *substantia*, E. *substance*.] **I.** a. In philosophical use, pertaining to or of the nature of substance rather than accidents; also, being a substance, or having independent existence; in general use, pertaining to the substance, matter, or material of a thing; also, of solid character or quality; firm, stout, or strong (as, a *substantial* cloth); of real worth or value (as, *substantial* criticism or reasons); of ample or considerable amount, quantity, size, etc. (as, "a *substantial* sum of money," Lytton Strachey's "Queen Victoria," iv.; *substantial* reinforcements; a work in three *substantial* volumes); wealthy or well-to-do, or influential (as, "a *substantial* farmer," R. Graves's "Spiritual Quixote," i. 2; one of the *substantial* men of the town); also, of a corporeal or material nature; real or actual, and not merely apparent or imaginary (as, "All this is but a dream, Too flattering-sweet to be *substantial*": Shakspere's "Romeo and Juliet," ii. 2. 141); also, of or pertaining to the essence of a thing; involving or being an essential part or feature; essential, material, or important; also, being such with respect to essentials, or in the main (as, "the *substantial* truth of the story," John Hay's "Bread-Winners," ix.; two stories in *substantial* agreement). **II.** n. Something substantial; a substantial article or kind of food; something real or actual; an essential part or feature: chiefly in pl.—**sub-stan′tial-ism**, n. The doctrine that there are substantial realities, or real substances, underlying phenomena.—**sub-stan′tial-ist**, n.—**sub-stan-ti-al′i-ty** (-shi-al′i-ti), n.; pl. *-ties* (-tiz). The quality of being substantial; solidity; firmness or stoutness; real

worth or value; materiality; real existence; also, something substantial; a substantial article of food.—**sub-stan′tial-ly**, adv. In the substance, or as a substantial thing or being; in a substantial, solid, or sound manner; really or actually; essentially or intrinsically; with respect to essentials, in the main, or for the most part (as, "It has maintained its own institutions . . . *substantially* unchanged": W. D. Whitney's "Life and Growth of Language," xii.).—**sub-stan′-tial-ness**, n.

sub-stan-ti-ate (sub-stan′shi-āt), v. t.; *-ated, -ating*. [ML. *substantiatus*, pp. of *substantiare*, < L. *substantia*, E. *substance*.] To make substantial, or give substantial existence to; also, to give solidity, firmness, or strength to; also, to present as having substance, or body forth (as, impressions too delicate to be *substantiated* in language); also, to establish by proof or competent evidence (as, to *substantiate* a charge or an allegation; "one of the most fully *substantiated* of historical facts," J. H. Robinson's "Mind in the Making," iii. 6).—**sub-stan-ti-a′tion** (-ā′shon), n. The act of substantiating, or the state of being substantiated; embodiment; proof.—**sub-stan′ti-a-tive** (-ā-tiv), a. Serving to substantiate.—**sub-stan′ti-a-tor** (-ā-tor), n.

sub-stan-ti-val (sub-stan-tī′val), a. In *gram.*, of, pertaining to, or consisting of a substantive or substantives.—**sub-stan-ti′val-ly**, adv.

sub-stan-tive (sub′stan-tiv). [OF. F. *substantif*, < LL. *substantivus*, < L. *substantia*, E. *substance*.] **I.** a. Standing of or by itself; having independent existence; independent; also, pertaining to the substance or material of a thing, as the tissue of an organ; also, having a solid basis; firm; enduring; permanent; also, of considerable amount or quantity; also, real or actual; also, belonging to the real nature or essential part of a thing; essential; in *dyeing*, of colors, attaching directly to the material without the aid of a mordant or the like (opposed to *adjective*); *milit.*, of an officer, actually or definitely appointed to a particular rank; of a rank, etc., to which one is definitely appointed; in *law*, pertaining to the rules of right which courts are called on to administer, as distinguished from rules of procedure (as, *substantive* law); in *gram.*, expressing existence (as, the *substantive* verb, the verb 'to be'); also, denoting a substance (as, a noun *substantive*); of the nature of, equivalent to, or employed as a substantive (as, a *substantive* adjective; a *substantive* clause). **II.** n. In *gram.*, the part of speech which is used as the name of a person or thing; a noun.—**sub′stan-tive-ly**, adv. Independently; actually; in substance or effect; in *gram.*, as a substantive.—**sub′stan-tive-ness**, n.—**sub′stan-tiv-ize** (-tiv-īz), v. t.; *-ized, -izing*. In *gram.*, to make a substantive of; use as a substantive.

sub-sta-tion (sub′stā″shon), n. [See *sub-*.] A subordinate station; a station subsidiary to a main station.

sub-stit-u-ent (sub-stit′ū-ent), n. [L. *substituens* (-ent-), ppr. of *substituere*: see *substitute*.] In *chem.*, an atom or atomic group which takes the place of another atom or group present in the molecule of the original compound.

sub-sti-tute (sub′sti-tūt), v.; *-tuted, -tuting*. [L. *substitutus*, pp. of *substituere*, set under, put instead, < *sub*, under, + *statuere*, set up, set.] **I.** tr. To invest with delegated authority†; depute† or delegate†; also, to put (one person or thing) in the place of another (as, "if they *substitute* human errors in the room of divine truth": J. Butler's "Analogy of Religion," ii. 6); put instead, as one thing for another (as, to *substitute* honey for sugar; to *substitute* one word for another; to *substitute* vivacity for wit); also, sometimes, to take the place of, or replace; act or serve as a substitute for. **II.** intr. To act as substitute.—**sub′sti-tute**. [L. *substitutus*, pp.] **I.** a. Substituted; put in or taking the place of another. **II.** n. One who or that which is substituted; a person or thing acting or serving in place of another; one who for a consideration serves in an army or navy in the place of a conscript; a substance, material, or article used or intended to replace something (as, an artificial *substitute* for butter or for silk; a simple *substitute* for a more complicated device).—**sub′sti-tut-er** (-tū-tėr), n.—**sub-sti-tu′tion** (-tū″shon), n. [L. *substitutio(n-)*.] The act of substituting, or the state of being substituted; in *chem.*, the replacing of one or more elements or radicals in a compound by other elements or radicals.—**sub-sti-tu′tion-al, sub-sti-tu′tion-a-ry** (-ā-ri), *a.* Pertaining to or characterized by substitution; acting or serving as a substitute.—**sub-sti-tu'tion-al-ly**, *adv.*—**sub'sti-tu-tive** (-tiv), *a.* Serving as, or capable of serving as, a substitute; pertaining to or involving substitution.—**sub'sti-tu-tor**, *n.*

sub-stra-tum (sub-strā'tum), *n.*; pl. *-ta* (-tä) or *-tums.* [NL., prop. neut. of L. *substratus*, pp. of *substernere*, spread under, < *sub*, under, + *sternere*, spread out: cf. *stratum.*] That which is spread or laid under something else; a stratum or layer lying under another; something which underlies, or serves as a basis or foundation (often fig.: as, "It is easy enough to say . . . that all ideas have a physical *substratum*," H. G. Wells's "Soul of a Bishop," v.; the story has a *substratum* of truth); in *agric.*, the subsoil; in *metaph.*, that which is regarded as supporting accidents or attributes; substance, as that in which qualities inhere.—**sub-stra'tal**, *a.*

sub-struc-tion (sub-struk'shon), *n.* [L. *substructio(n-)*, < *substruere*, build under, < *sub*, under, + *struere*, build.] An under structure, as of a building; a foundation; a substructure.

sub-struc-ture (sub'struk″tūr), *n.* [From *sub-* + *structure.*] A structure forming the foundation of a building or the like; the part of any structure supporting the superstructure.—**sub-struc'tur-al**, *a.*

sub-sul-tive, sub-sul-to-ry (sub-sul'tiv, -tō-ri), *a.* [L. *subsultus*, pp. of *subsilire*, leap up, < *sub*, under, + *salire*, leap.] Characterized by sudden leaps or starts, as motion or something moving; jerky; convulsive: sometimes used with reference to earthquake shocks.

sub-sume (sub-sūm'), *v. t.*; *-sumed, -suming.* [L. *sub*, under, + *sumere* (pp. *sumptus*), take.] To bring (one thing, as an idea, term, proposition, etc.) under another; bring (a case, instance, etc.) under a rule; take up into or include in a larger or higher class or the like.—**sub-sump'tion** (-sump'shon), *n.* The act of subsuming, or the state of being subsumed; also, that which is subsumed; a proposition subsumed under another.—**sub-sump'tive** (-tiv), *a.* Pertaining to or involving subsumption.

sub-sur-face (sub'sėr″fäs), [See *sub-.*] **I.** *n.* The part lying under, esp. immediately under, the surface. **II.** *a.* Lying, occurring, or operating under the surface, as of the earth or the water.

sub-tan-gent (sub'tan″jent), *n.* [See *sub-.*] In *geom.*, the part of the axis of a curve cut off between the tangent and the ordinate of a given point in the curve.

sub-tem-per-ate (sub-tem'pėr-āt), *a.* [See *sub-.*] Pertaining to or occurring in the colder parts of the temperate zone.

sub-ten-ant (sub'ten″ant), *n.* [See *sub-.*] A tenant under a tenant; one who rents land, a house, or the like from a tenant; an undertenant.—**sub-ten'an-cy**, *n.*

sub-tend (sub-tend'), *v. t.* [L. *subtendere*, < *sub*, under, + *tendere*, stretch.] In *geom.*, etc., to extend under, or be opposite to (as, the hypotenuse of a right-angled triangle *subtends* the right angle; a chord *subtending* an arc); in *bot.*, of a leaf, bract, etc., to inclose or embrace in its axil.

sub-tense (sub-tens'), *n.* [NL. *subtensa*, prop. pp. fem. of L. *subtendere*, E. *subtend.*] In *geom.*, etc., a subtending line, as the chord of an arc.

subter-. [L. *subter-*, repr. *subter*, adv. and prep., underneath, below, a compar. form < *sub*, under: see *sub-.*] A prefix meaning 'underneath,' 'beneath,' 'below,' 'less than,' occurring in words from the Latin, and used also as an English formative, as in *subternatural, subterposition*: opposed to *super-.*

sub-ter-fuge (sub'tėr-fūj), *n.* [F. *subterfuge*, < LL. *subterfugium*, < L. *subterfugere*, flee secretly, evade, < *subter*, underneath, + *fugere*, flee.] An artifice or expedient employed to escape the force of an argument or to evade any unfavorable consequences; an evasive or artful shift or expedient: as, "I . . . was compelled to as many arts and *subterfuges* as could have been entailed on the worst of villains" (Godwin's "Caleb Williams," Postscript).

sub-ter-nat-u-ral (sub-tėr-nat'ū-ral), *a.* [See *subter-.*] Below what is natural; less than natural.

sub-ter-po-si-tion (sub″tėr-pō-zish'on), *n.* [See *subter-.*] Position underneath; the state of being placed or of lying underneath something else.

sub-ter-rane (sub'tẹ-rān). **I.** *a.* Subterranean. [Now rare.] **II.** *n.* A subterranean chamber or place (now rare); in *geol.*, the underlying rock or rocks of a particular formation.

sub-ter-ra-ne-an (sub-tẹ-rā'nẹ-an). [L. *subterraneus*, < *sub*, under, + *terra*, earth, ground.] **I.** *a.* Existing, situated, or operating below the surface of the earth, or underground (as, "The daylight found its way to the *subterranean* dungeon only at noon," Scott's "Castle Dangerous," xiii.; *subterranean* forces); also, belonging to the lower world or the infernal regions; infernal; also, existing or operating out of sight or secretly, hidden, or secret (as, "It brought up almost to her tongue thoughts which would have remained *subterranean*": G. Meredith's "Lord Ormont and His Aminta," iii.). **II.** *n.* One who lives underground; also, an underground chamber or place (as, "The passage . . . was only one of several natural *subterraneans* . . . opening into each other": J. H. Newman's "Callista," xxx.).—**sub-ter-ra'ne-an-ly**, *adv.*

sub-ter-ra-ne-ous (sub-tẹ-rā'nẹ-us), *a.* Same as *subterranean*: as, "a *subterraneous* passage, which led from the vaults of the castle" (Walpole's "Castle of Otranto," i.).—**sub-ter-ra'ne-ous-ly**, *adv.*—**sub-ter-ra'ne-ous-ness**, *n.*

sub-ter-rene (sub-tẹ-rēn'). [L. *subterrenus*, < *sub*, under, + *terra*, earth, ground.] **I.** *a.* Underground; subterranean. **II.** *n.* A subterranean chamber or place.

sub-ter-res-tri-al (sub-tẹ-res'tri-al), *a.* [See *sub-.*] Underground; subterranean. [Now rare.]

sub-tile (sub'til or sut'l), *a.* [OF. F. *subtil*, earlier *soutil*: see *subtile.*] Same as *subtle*, now chiefly in the physical senses: as, a *subtile* fluid; a *subtile* fabric or fiber; a *subtile* powder.—**sub'tile-ly**, *adv.*—**sub'tile-ness**, *n.*—**sub-til-i-ty** (sub-til'i-ti), **sub-til-ty** (sub'til-ti or sut'l-), *n.* Subtile quality or character; subtlety.—**sub-til-ize** (sub'til-īz or sut'l-), *v.*; *-ized, -izing.* **I.** *tr.* To make thin or rare, or more fluid or volatile; rarefy; refine; fig., to elevate or exalt in character; sublimate; change as by a sublimating process (as, "By long brooding over our recollections, we *subtilize* them into something akin to imaginary stuff": Hawthorne's "Blithedale Romance," xii.); also, to introduce subtleties or nice distinctions into; argue subtly upon; also, to render (the mind, senses, etc.) acute or keen. **II.** *intr.* To make subtle distinctions; argue or reason in a subtle manner.—**sub'til-i-za'tion** (-i-zā'shon), *n.*

sub-ti-tle (sub'tī″tl), *n.* [See *sub-.*] A secondary or subordinate title of a literary work, usually of explanatory character; also, a repetition of the leading words in the full title of a book at the head of the first page of text; also, a bastard title, or a full-page half-title preceding a division of a book.

sub-tle (sut'l), *a.*; compar. *subtler*, superl. *subtlest.* [OF. *soutil* (later *subtil*: see *subtile*), < L. *subtilis*, fine, thin, delicate, nice, appar. orig. finely woven, < *sub*, under, + *-tilis*, akin to *tela*, web, *texere*, weave.] Thin, tenuous, or rarefied, as a fluid (as, "To swim is to fly in a grosser fluid, and to fly is to swim in a *subtler*": Johnson's "Rasselas," vi.); also, penetrating, pervasive, or elusive by reason of tenuity, as an effluvium or odor (as, "the softest, *subtlest* aroma": Gissing's "Private Papers of Henry Ryecroft," iv. 10); also, fine or delicate, as a fabric, texture, etc.; very thin or slender, as a thread; also, composed of fine or minute particles, as powder; fig., fine or delicate in character (as, "Thinking over a pleasure to come often gave him a *subtler* satisfaction than its realisation": Mrs. Wharton's "Age of Innocence," i.); so fine or delicate as to be likely to elude perception or understanding (as, "The irony was so *subtle*, that half the readers of the paper mistook his grave scorn for respect": Thackeray's "Newcomes," lxvi.); delicate or faint and mysterious (as, a *subtle* charm; a *subtle* smile); requiring mental acuteness, penetration, or discernment (as, a *subtle* point or distinction); also, characterized by mental acuteness or penetration (as, the *Subtle* Doctor, the scholastic theologian Joannes Duns Scotus; a *subtle* understanding or insight); discerning; discriminating; sometimes, characterized by excessive refinement of thought or argument (as, "His style of argument was neither trite and vulgar, nor *subtle* and abstruse": Burke's "American Taxation"); also, skilful, clever, or ingenious, as craftsmen, workmanship, or work (archaic: as, "Jacinth-work Of *subtlest* jewellery,"

Tennyson's "Passing of Arthur," 226); also, cunning, wily, or crafty (as, "This little knot of *subtle* schemers will control the convention": Hawthorne's "House of the Seven Gables," xviii.); insidious in operation, as poison, etc.—**sub′tle-ness,** *n.*—**sub′tle-ty** (-ti), *n.*; pl. *-ties* (-tiz). The state or quality of being subtle; tenuity; penetrating or elusive quality due to tenuity; fineness, as of texture; delicacy or nicety of character or meaning; acuteness or penetration of mind; delicacy of discrimination; skill† or cleverness†; cunning, craft, or guile; also, something subtle; a subtle or delicate point; a nicety of thought or argument; a fine-drawn distinction; an ingenious contrivance†; an artifice† or stratagem†; a carefully contrived dainty or dish for the table†.—**sub′tly,** *adv.*

sub-ton-ic (sub-ton′ik), *n.* [See *sub-.*] In *music*, the seventh tone of a scale, being the next below the upper tonic.

sub-tract (sub-trakt′), *v.* [L. *subtractus*, pp. of *subtrahere*, draw from under, withdraw, < *sub*, under, + *trahere*, draw.] **I.** *tr.* To withdraw or take away, as a part from a whole; in *math.*, to take (one number or quantity) from another; deduct. **II.** *intr.* To take away something or a part, as from a whole: as, "Marriage had . . . *subtracted* from the courage of this worthy officer" (Marryat's "King's Own," xli.); "By the payment of a heavy ransom, he had wofully *subtracted* from his hoard of pine-tree shillings" (Hawthorne's "Twice-Told Tales," The Great Carbuncle).—**sub-tract′er,** *n.*—**sub-trac′tion** (-trak′shon), *n.* [LL. *subtractio(n-).*] The act or operation of subtracting; in *math.*, the taking of one number or quantity from another; the operation of finding the difference between two numbers or quantities.—**sub-trac′tive** (-tiv), *a.* Tending to subtract; having power to subtract; in *math.*, of a quantity, that is to be subtracted; having the minus sign (−).

sub-tra-hend (sub′tra-hend), *n.* [L. *subtrahendus*, gerundive of *subtrahere:* see *subtract.*] In *math.*, the number or quantity to be taken from another (the *minuend*) in the operation of subtraction.

sub-treas-ur-y (sub-trezh′ūr-i), *n.*; pl. *-ies* (-iz). [See *sub-.*] A subordinate or branch treasury; specif., any of the branches of the U. S. treasury.—**sub-treas′ur-er,** *n.*

sub-tribe (sub′trīb), *n.* [See *sub-.*] A subordinate tribe; a division of a tribe; specif., a zoölogical or botanical group or category ranking below a tribe.

sub-trop-ic (sub-trop′ik), *a.* [See *sub-.*] Subtropical.—**sub-trop′i-cal,** *a.* Bordering on the tropics; nearly tropical; pertaining to or occurring in a region intermediate between tropical and temperate.—**sub-trop′ics,** *n. pl.* Subtropical regions.

sub-type (sub′tīp), *n.* [See *sub-.*] A subordinate type; in *zoöl.* and *bot.*, a more special type included in a more general type.

su-bu-late (sū′bū-lāt), *a.* [NL. *subulatus*, < L. *subula*, awl.] Awl-shaped; in *bot.*, *zoöl.*, etc., slender, more or less cylindrical, and tapering to a point. Also **su′bu-li-form** (-li-fôrm).

sub-urb (sub′èrb), *n.* [OF. *suburbe*, < L. *suburbium*, < *sub*, under, near, + *urbs*, city.] A district lying immediately outside a city or town, esp. a residential section outside of the city boundaries but adjoining them (often in *pl.*); such a residential section having a definite designation, boundary, or organization; in general, an outlying part (usually in *pl.*).—**sub-ur′ban** (-èr′ban). [L. *suburbanus.*] **I.** *a.* Pertaining to, inhabiting, or being in a suburb or the suburbs of a city or town; characteristic of a suburb or suburbs. **II.** *n.* One who lives in the suburbs of a city or town; also, a suburban residence (as, "Can truth give me a handsome *suburban* with some five hundred slaves?" J. H. Newman's "Callista," xxii.).—**sub-ur′ban-ism,** *n.* Suburban character (as, "a county, which is throughout a strange mixture of *suburbanism* and the desert": Mrs. H. Ward's "Robert Elsmere," xi.); also, a suburban characteristic.—**sub-ur′ban-ite** (-īt), *n.* A resident in the suburbs.

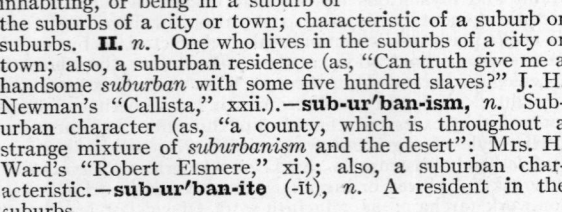
Subulate Leaves of Juniper (*Juniperus communis*).

sub-ur-bi-ca-ri-an (sub-èr-bi-kā′ri-an), *a.* [LL. *suburbicarius*, < L. *sub*, under, near, + *urbs*, city.] Being near the city (of Rome: as, *suburbicarian* regions); specif., noting or pertaining to the dioceses (now six in number) about Rome which are under the Pope as metropolitan and whose bishops are cardinals. Also **sub-ur′bi-ca-ry** (-kā-ri).

sub-va-ri-e-ty (sub′va-rī″ę-ti), *n.*; pl. *-ties* (-tiz). [See *sub-.*] A subordinate variety; in *zoöl.* and *bot.*, a further and minor modification of a variety.

sub-ven-tion (sub-ven′shon), *n.* [LL. *subventio(n-),* < L. *subvenire*, come to one's aid, < *sub*, under, + *venire*, come.] The furnishing of aid or relief; specif., the granting of pecuniary aid, esp. by a government or some other authority, in aid or support of some object, institution, or undertaking; a grant of this kind, or the sum granted; a subsidy.—**sub-ven′tion,** *v. t.* To aid by a subvention.—**sub-ven′tion-a-ry** (-ā-ri), *a.* Of the nature of a subvention.—**sub-ven′tion-ize,** *v. t.*; *-ized, -izing.* To subvention.

sub-ver-sal (sub-vèr′sal), *n.* Subversion.

sub-ver-sion (sub-vèr′shon), *n.* [LL. *subversio(n-),* < L. *subvertere:* see *subvert.*] The act of subverting, or the state of being subverted; overthrow; destruction; also, that which subverts or overthrows.—**sub-ver′sion-a-ry** (-ā-ri), *a.* Tending to cause subversion; subversive: as, "crude and *subversionary* books" (S. Butler's "Erewhon," xi.).

sub-ver-sive (sub-vèr′siv), *a.* Tending to subvert; such as to cause subversion or overthrow: often with *of:* as, doctrines *subversive* of all government.

sub-vert (sub-vèrt′), *v. t.* [L. *subvertere* (pp. *subversus*), < *sub*, under, + *vertere*, turn.] To overturn (as, "Here everything [rock strata] appeared to have been *subverted*, and thrown out of place," Irving's "Captain Bonneville," iv.: now rare in the literal sense); also, to throw down, demolish, or destroy (as, "Villages and hamlets were, with fire and pickaxe, utterly *subverted*," Stevenson's "Travels with a Donkey," v. 6: now rare); fig., to overthrow (something established or existing: as, to *subvert* a government, civil order, or religion; "What did they ever do but *subvert* received principles without substituting any others?" J. H. Newman's "Callista," viii.); cause the downfall, ruin, or destruction of; also, to undermine the principles of, or corrupt (now rare).—**sub-vert′er,** *n.*—**sub-vert′i-ble,** *a.* Capable of being subverted.

sub-way (sub′wā), *n.* [See *sub-.*] An artificial underground way or passage, as for pedestrians or traffic or for water-mains, electric wires, etc.; esp., an electric railway beneath the surface of the streets in a city.

suc-ce-da-ne-um (suk-sę-dā′nę-um), *n.*; pl. *-nea* (-nę-ą). [NL., prop. neut. of L. *succedaneus*, taking the place of something, < *succedere*, E. *succeed.*] A thing, or sometimes a person, that takes the place of another; a substitute: as, "being rid of these somewhat heavy boots, providing I can obtain any other *succedaneum*" (Scott's "Legend of Montrose," xiv.).

suc-ceed (suk-sēd′), *v.* [L. *succedere* (pp. *successus*), go under, go up, come next, follow, be successful, < *sub*, under, + *cedere*, go.] **I.** *intr.* To come next after and take the place of another, by descent, election, appointment, or the like, as in an office or estate (often with *to:* as, when Victoria died, Edward VII. *succeeded*; an heir *succeeds* to his father; "He had *succeeded* to a great estate early in his minority," Disraeli's "Coningsby," iii. 3); also, to come next after something else in an order or series; follow in the sequence of things or the course of events (as, "Enjoy, till I return, Short pleasures; for long woes are to *succeed*": Milton's "Paradise Lost," iv. 535); also, to come down by inheritance, as an estate†; also, to come to pass†, or happen†; also, to turn out or issue (well or ill), as an enterprise (as, "Yours be the thanks, for yours the danger is, If aught *succeed*, as much I fear, amiss": Fairfax's tr. Tasso's "Jerusalem Delivered," iv. 82); esp., to turn out or terminate according to desire; turn out successfully; have the desired result; do well or thrive, as a plant; of a person, etc., to have (good or ill) success (as, "I have *succeeded* very badly": G. MacDonald's "Annals of a Quiet Neighbourhood," vii.); esp., to accomplish what is attempted or intended; be successful in an endeavor or undertaking (as, "the man who had all but *succeeded* as a novelist": Gissing's "New Grub Street," vi.). **II.** *tr.* To come after and take the place of, as in an office or estate (as, "The son of a mandarin has no prescriptive right to *succeed* his father": H. G. Wells's "Outline of History," xx. § 7); also, to inherit†, or fall heir to†; also, to come next after in an order or series, or in the course of events, or follow (as, "Every occurrence in Nature is preceded by other occurrences which are its causes, and *succeeded* by others which are its effects," Tyndall's "Forms of Water," § 1; "When the quiet light *Succeeds* the keen and frosty night," Bryant's "To the Fringed Gentian"); also, to give success to†, or prosper†.—**suc-ceed′er**, *n.*

suc-cen-tor (suk-sen′tọr), *n.* [LL., < L. *succinere*, sing to, accompany, < *sub*, under, + *canere*, sing.] A precentor's deputy.

suc-cess (suk-ses′), *n.* [L. *successus*, < *succedere*, E. *succeed*.] Succession by descent or the like, as to office or estate†; also, succession† or sequence†; also, termination or issue, as of affairs†; the kind of outcome (good or ill) in a particular case (as, the ill *success* of the attempt deterred him from further efforts); the fortune (good or ill) befalling one in a particular affair (as, "perplex'd and troubled at his bad *success*": Milton's "Paradise Regained," iv. 1); esp., the favorable or prosperous termination of attempts or endeavors; the satisfactory accomplishment of something attempted; the attainment of an object desired; often, the gaining of wealth, position, or the like; also, a successful performance or achievement (as, political or military *successes*); a thing or a person that is successful (as, "The dinner was a *success*": S. Butler's "Way of All Flesh," xiii.).—**suc-cess′ful**, *a.* Resulting in or attended with success; achieving or having achieved success; that is a success; often, having succeeded in obtaining wealth, position, or the like.—**suc-cess′ful-ly**, *adv.*—**suc-cess′ful-ness**, *n.*

suc-ces-sion (suk-sesh′ọn), *n.* [L. *successio(n-)*, < *succedere*, E. *succeed*.] The act of succeeding to the place of another; the process by which one person succeeds to the office, rank, estate, or the like, of another, in accordance with custom or law; the act or fact of succeeding under established custom or law to the dignity and rights of a sovereign (as, a war of *succession*, a war to settle a disputed succession to a throne, as the War of the Spanish Succession, 1701–14, and the War of the Austrian Succession, 1740–48); the order or line of those entitled to succeed (as, "Mary . . . had been placed next in the *succession* to Edward by her father's will": Green's "Short Hist. of the Eng. People," vii. 2); the right of succeeding, as to an office, rank, or estate (as, "endangering both his *succession* and his life": Scott's "Fair Maid of Perth," xiv.); the descent or transmission, or the principle or mode of transmission, of a throne, dignity, estate, or the like; also, the coming of one after another in order, sequence, or the course of events (as, "The *succession* of his ideas was now rapid," Sterne's "Tristram Shandy," ii. 5; "A man diverts himself with the annual *succession* of pinks and tulips in his garden," Swift's "Gulliver's Travels," iii. 10); sequence; also, a passing from one act, state, or the like, to another; also, a series of persons succeeding one another, as in an office, dignity, or estate (as, "a brilliant *succession* of sovereigns": Amelia B. Edwards's "Thousand Miles up the Nile," xv.); a number of persons or things following one another in order or sequence; a series or line of things coming one after another; one's heirs, issue, or descendants†; a generation of men (chiefly in *pl.*)†; that which succeeds in the place of something else; *eccles.*, the act of succeeding to clerical office or receiving transmitted authority through ordination (see *apostolic succession*, under *apostolic*); in *agric.* and *hort.*, the rotation of crops; also, a continuous yield of crops of the same kind, as from successive sowings or plantings, or from the simultaneous sowing or planting of different varieties maturing at different times.—**suc-ces′sion-al**, *a.* Of or pertaining to succession; following or occurring in succession; passing by succession or descent.—**suc-ces′sion-al-ly**, *adv.*

suc-ces-sive (suk-ses′iv), *a.* [ML. *successivus*, < L. *succedere*, E. *succeed*.] Following in order or in uninterrupted course (as, "having renewed his defiance on three *successive* days": J. F. Kirk's "Charles the Bold," iii. 2); following another in a regular sequence (as, each *successive* occasion; on the second *successive* day); also, characterized by or

involving succession (as, "Our existence is not only *successive* . . . but one state of our life and being is appointed by God to be a preparation for another": J. Butler's "Analogy of Religion," ii. 4); also, hereditary†.—**suc-ces′sive-ly**, *adv.* In a successive manner; in succession or sequence.—**suc-ces′sive-ness**, *n.*

suc-cess-less (suk-ses′les), *a.* Without success; unsuccessful.—**suc-cess′less-ly**, *adv.*—**suc-cess′less-ness**, *n.*

suc-ces-sor (suk-ses′ọr), *n.* [OF. *successour* (F. *successeur*), < L. *successor*, < *succedere*, E. *succeed*.] One who or that which succeeds or follows; one who succeeds another in an office, position, or the like.—**suc-ces′sor-ship**, *n.*

suc-ci-nate (suk′si-nāt), *n.* In *chem.*, a salt of succinic acid.

suc-cinct (suk-singkt′), *a.* [L. *succinctus*, pp. of *succingere*, gird from below, < *sub*, under, + *cingere*, gird.] Girded up, or encircled as by a girdle (now chiefly poetic); also, compressed into a small compass; now, usually, of a statement, narrative, etc., expressed in few words, or concise or terse (as, "A tale should be judicious, clear, *succinct*": Cowper's "Conversation," 235); of persons, style, etc., characterized by conciseness or verbal brevity; also, short or scant, as garments (archaic: as, "Sister Ursula . . . exchanged her stole, or loose upper garment, for the more *succinct* cloak and hood of a horseman," Scott's "Castle Dangerous," xi.); brief or curt, as a bow or nod.—**suc-cinct′ly**, *adv.*—**suc-cinct′ness**, *n.*

suc-cinc-to-ri-um (suk-singk-tō′ri-um), *n.*; pl. -*ria* (-ri-ä). [LL., < L. *sub*, under, + *cinctorium*, girdle, < *cingere*, gird.] A vestment in the form of a band or strip resembling a maniple, which is worn by the Pope on certain occasions, hanging on his left side from the girdle or cincture. Also **suc-cinc′to-ry** (-tō-ri); pl. -*ries* (-riz).

suc-cin-ic (suk-sin′ik), *a.* [F. *succinique*, < L. *succinum*, *sucinum*, amber.] Pertaining to or obtained from amber; in *chem.*, noting or pertaining to a white crystalline acid, $C_4H_6O_4$, obtained by the distillation of amber and otherwise, and also an isomeric form of it.

suc-cise (suk-sīs′), *a.* [L. *succisus*, pp. of *succidere*, cut below, < *sub*, under, + *cædere*, cut.] In *bot.*, appearing as if cut or broken off at the lower end.

suc-cor (suk′ọr), *v. t.* [OF. *sucurre*, *secourre* (F. *secourir*), < L. *succurrere*, run under, run to aid, help, relieve, < *sub*, under, + *currere*, run.] To help or relieve in difficulty, want, or distress (as, "Mr. Harding thought . . . of the worn-out, aged men whom he had *succoured*": Trollope's "Barchester Towers," xii.); aid or assist; sometimes, specif., to furnish with military assistance, as a besieged place.—**suc′cor**, *n.* [ME. *sucurs*, *socurs* (sing., but later understood as pl.), < OF. *sucurs* (F. *secours*), < ML. *succursus*, aid, < L. *succurrere*.] Help; relief; aid; assistance; also, one who or that which succors; a means of assistance; an aid; often, *sing.* or *pl.*, military assistance in men or supplies; auxiliary forces; reinforcements.—**suc′cor-a-ble**, *a.* Affording succor or relief (archaic); also, capable of being succored or relieved.—**suc′cor-er**, *n.*—**suc′cor-less**, *a.* Without succor, help, or relief.

suc-co-ry (suk′ō-ri), *n.* Same as *chicory*.

suc-cose (suk′ōs), *a.* [L. *succosus*, *sucosus*, < *succus*, *sucus*, juice.] Juicy; succulent.

suc-co-tash (suk′ọ-tash), *n.* [Algonquian.] A dish of North American Indian origin, consisting of Indian corn (removed from the cob) and beans, variously prepared: now commonly made of green corn and (shelled) Lima beans.

suc-cour (suk′ọr), etc. British preferred form of *succor*, etc.

suc-cu-ba (suk′ū-bä), *n.*; pl. -*bæ* (-bē). [L., strumpet, < *succubare*, lie under, < *sub*, under, + *cubare*, lie.] A female demon fabled to have sexual connection with men in their sleep. Cf. *incubus*.—**suc′cu-bus** (-bus), *n.*; pl. -*bi* (-bī). [ML. *succubus*.] A succuba; sometimes, any demon or evil spirit; also, a low woman.

suc-cu-lent (suk′ū-lent), *a.* [L. *succulentus*, *suculentus*, < *succus*, *sucus*, juice.] Full of juice; juicy; of plants, etc., having fleshy and juicy tissues; fig., rich in desirable qualities; often, affording mental nourishment; not dry.—**suc′cu-lence**, **suc′cu-len-cy**, *n.*—**suc′cu-lent-ly**, *adv.*

suc-cumb (su-kum′), *v. i.* [L. *succumbere*, < *sub*, under, + -*cumbere*, lie.] To sink under pressure; give way to superior force; yield, as to something that overcomes (as,

"I didn't *succumb* without a struggle to my uncle's allurements": H. G. Wells's "Tono-Bungay," ii. 2. § 3); often, to yield to disease, wounds, old age, etc.; die.

suc-cur-sal (su-kėr′sạl). [F. *succursale*, fem. (as in *église succursale*, succursal church), < ML. *succursus*, aid, E. *succor*, *n.*] **I.** *a.* Subsidiary; esp., noting a religious establishment which is dependent upon a principal one. **II.** *n.* Something succursal; a subsidiary establishment, institution, or the like; a branch.

suc-cuss (su-kus′), *v. t.* [L. *successus*, pp. of *succutere*, < *sub*, under, + *quatere*, shake, strike.] To shake up; shake; in *med.*, to shake (a patient) in order to determine, as from a splashing sound elicited, if a fluid is present in the thorax or elsewhere.—**suc-cus-sion** (su-kush′ọn), *n.* [L. *succussio(n-).*] The act of succussing or shaking; in *med.*, a shaking for diagnostic purposes.—**suc-cus′sive** (-siv), *a.* Characterized by a shaking motion, esp. an up-and-down movement.

such (such). [AS. *swelc, swilc, swylc*, = OHG. *sulih* (G. *solch*) = Icel. *slíkr* = Goth. *swaleiks*, such; from the Teut. adv. (AS. *swā*, etc.) represented by E. *so*, with termination related to E. *-ly*[1] and *like*[1]: cf. *which*.] **I.** *a.* Of the kind, character, degree, extent, etc., of that or those indicated or implied (as, we cannot approve *such* a proceeding as that; *such* a man is dangerous; *such* men as he; men *such* as he); of that particular kind or character (as, the food, *such* as it was, was plentiful; they were forced to accept *such* terms as they could obtain); like or similar (as, tea, coffee, and *such* commodities); also, with a quasi-adverbial force (preceding an adjective used attributively), so, or in such a manner or degree (as, *such* terrible deeds; *such* a terrible deed); also, emphatically (with omission of an indication of comparison), of so extreme a kind, or so great, good, bad, etc. (as, he did not expect to come to *such* honor; never have I seen *such* crowds; *such* a time! he is *such* a liar!); also, being as stated or indicated (as, *such* is the case; a blade once sharp but no longer *such*); also, being the person or thing, or the persons or things, indicated (as, if any member be behind in his payments, *such* member shall be suspended); also, being definite or particular, but not named or specified (often in the form *such and such*, with either singular or plural: as, it happened at *such* a time in *such and such* a town; *such and such* persons). **II.** *pron.* Such a person or thing, or such persons or things; the person or thing, or the persons or things, indicated: as, he claims to be a friend but is not *such*; established for Christians and appealing only to *such*; a city once the capital but no longer *such*; *such* as have claims will please present them at once.—**as such**, as being what is indicated, or in that capacity (as, the leader, *as such*, is entitled to respect); hence, in itself or themselves (as, vice, *as such*, does not appeal to him).

such=like, such-like (such′līk). **I.** *a.* Of any such kind; of a like or similar kind: as, "They should ring no bells, nor adorn their churches . . . nor do other *such-like* things as belonged to the celebration of festivals" (Strype's "Memorials of Cranmer," i. 16); "a marvellous array of crockery, clocks, metal ornaments, and *suchlike* rewards" (H. G. Wells's "Mr. Britling," i. 5. § 11). **II.** *pron.* A person or thing, or, esp., persons or things, of such a kind: as, "A bard, sir, famed of yore, Went where *suchlike* used to go, Singing for a prize" (Browning's "Two Poets of Croisic," ii. 2); "deceptions, disguises, and *suchlike*" (J. Conrad's "Rover," viii.).

suck (suk), *v.* [AS. *sūcan*, akin to D. *zuigen*, G. *saugen*, also L. *sugere*, suck: see *suction* and *soak*.] **I.** *tr.* To draw into the mouth by action of the lips and tongue which produces a partial vacuum (as, an infant *sucks* milk from the breast or a bottle; to *suck* lemonade through a straw); draw (water, moisture, air, etc.) by any process resembling this (as, a sponge *sucks* in water; plants *suck* up moisture from the earth; a ventilator which *sucks* in fresh air); fig., to draw, extract, or take as if by sucking (as, to *suck* knowledge or profit from a thing; "All poor-laws . . . *suck* the independent spirit out of a man," Kingsley's "Yeast," xiii.); also, to apply the lips or mouth to, and draw upon by producing a partial vacuum, for the purpose of extracting fluid contents (as, an infant *sucks* the mother's breast; to *suck* an orange); apply the mouth to, or take into the mouth, and draw upon similarly, for some other purpose (as, to *suck*

one's thumb); take into the mouth and absorb by action of the tongue, etc. (as, to *suck* a piece of candy); draw upon by any similar process, as in extracting fluid or moisture (as, plants *suck* the earth; the sun *sucks* the streams); draw upon or drain as if by sucking, as in obtaining money, information, etc.; also, to render or bring (as specified) by or as by sucking (as, to *suck* a thing dry; the infant *sucks* himself to sleep); also, to suckle, as an infant†. **II.** *intr.* To draw something in by producing a partial vacuum in the mouth, esp. to draw milk from the breast; draw by or as by suction (as, "He *sucked* at his pipe for a space": H. G. Wells's "Tono-Bungay," ii. 1. § 3); of a pump, to draw air instead of water, as when the water is low or a valve is defective; also, to be drawn by or as by suction (as, "The crimson cheeks of the trumpeters *sucked* in and out," Arnold Bennett's "Clayhanger," ii. 10; "The water . . . Sank and *sucked* away in eddies," Longfellow's "Hiawatha," xvii. 140).—**suck**, *n.* The act or an act of sucking with the mouth or otherwise; a sucking force; the sound produced by sucking; also, that which is sucked; nourishment drawn from the breast; a small draft of liquid.

suck-er (suk′ėr), *n.* One who or that which sucks; an infant or a young animal that is suckled, esp. a sucking pig; a part or organ of an animal adapted for sucking nourishment, or for adhering to an object as by suction; the piston of a pump which works by suction (see *suction-pump*), or the valve of such a piston; a kind of toy consisting of a small piece of leather with a string attached to the center, which, when rendered flexible by wetting and pressed against a smooth object, adheres by reason of the vacuum created, and so firmly that an object of considerable weight may be lifted by means of it; a pipe or tube through which anything is drawn; also, a lump of hard candy for sucking; also, fig., a person easily imposed upon (slang); also, a sponger or parasite (slang); in *ichth.*, any of various fishes which suck in some way or are supposed to do so, or which have a suctorial organ for adhering to objects (see *remora*); esp., any member of the cyprinoid family *Catostomidæ*, comprising fresh-water fishes which are mostly of North America and little esteemed as food, and which are characterized by the habit

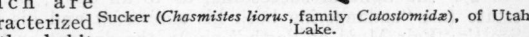

Sucker (*Chasmistes liorus*, family *Catostomidæ*), of Utah Lake.

of taking in their food by suction; in *bot.*, a shoot rising from a subterranean stem or a root; also, an adventitious shoot from the body or a branch of a tree; also, a haustorium.
—**suck′er**, *v.* **I.** *tr.* To strip off suckers or shoots from (a plant); remove superfluous shoots from (tobacco, etc.). **II.** *intr.* To send out suckers or shoots, as a plant.

suck-fish (suk′fish), *n.* A remora; also, an acanthopterygian fish, *Caularchus mæandricus*, of the Pacific coast of the U. S., having a suctorial disk on the under side of the body, by which it adheres to rocks, etc.

Suckfish (*Caularchus mæandricus*).

suck-ing (suk′ing), *p. a.* That sucks; not yet weaned; hence, very young; immature; unfledged.

suck-le (suk′l), *v.*; -led, -ling. [Appar. a back-formation from *suckling*.] **I.** *tr.* To give suck to; nurse at the breast; fig., to nourish, or bring up (as, "*suckled* on the literature of Spain": W. H. Hudson's "Green Mansions," Prologue); also, to put to suck. **II.** *intr.* To suck at the breast.—**suck′ler**, *n.*

suck-ling (suk′ling). [From *suck* + *-ling*[1].] **I.** *n.* An infant or a young animal that is given suck to, or is not yet weaned: as, "babes and *sucklings*" (Ps. viii. 2). **II.** *a.* Being a suckling; sucking; very young.

su-crate (sū′krāt), *n.* [F. *sucre*, sugar: see *sugar*.] In *chem.*, a compound of a metallic oxide with a sugar: as, calcium *sucrate* (a compound of calcium oxide with cane-sugar).

su-crose (sū'krōs), *n.* [F. *sucre*, sugar: see *sugar*.] In *chem.*, cane-sugar; saccharose.

suc-tion (suk'shọn), *n.* [= F. *succion*, < L. *sugere* (pp. *suctus*), suck: see *suck*.] The act, process, or condition of sucking; specif., the tendency to suck or draw a gas or liquid into an interior space, or to cause the parts surrounding an interior space to adhere more firmly together, when a more or less complete vacuum is produced in such a space; the production of a vacuum in order to cause such a sucking or adhering tendency; the act or process of sucking or drawing in a gas or liquid by such means.—**suc'tion=pump,** *n.* A pump for raising water or the like by suction, consisting essentially of a vertical cylinder in which a piston works up and down, the water or the like being drawn up into the cylinder during the upward stroke of the piston, and retained there during the downward stroke by means of valves in the piston and the bottom of the cylinder.

suc-to-ri-al (suk-tō'ri-ạl), *a.* [NL. *suctorius*, < L. *sugere* (pp. *suctus*), suck: see *suck*.] Adapted for sucking or suction, as an organ; functioning as a sucker, whether for imbibing or for adhering; also, having sucking-organs; imbibing or adhering by suckers; also, pertaining to or characterized by suction. Also **suc-to'ri-ous.**

Su-dan (sö-dan') **dur'ra.** Same as *feterita*.

Su-da-nese (sö-dạ-nēs' or -nēz'). **I.** *a.* Of or pertaining to the Sudan (in Africa, south of the Sahara) or its inhabitants. **II.** *n.*; pl. *-nese.* A native or inhabitant of the Sudan.

Su-dan (sö-dan') **grass.** A grass-sorghum (see *sorghum*), a variety of *Andropogon sorghum*, introduced into the U. S. from the Sudan in 1909, and grown for hay.

Suction-pump. *a*, piston; *b, b,* barrel or cylinder; *c, c,* suction-pipe; *d,* pump-box; *e,* valve in piston; *f,* valve which admits water into the barrel; *g,* spout.

su-da-ri-um (sū-dā'ri-um), *n.*; pl. *-ria* (-ri-ä). [L., < *sudor*, sweat, perspiration: see *sudor*.] A cloth for wiping the face; a handkerchief; specif., the cloth of St. Veronica, on which, according to a legend, was miraculously impressed a representation of the face of Christ (see *veronica*); hence, any similar cloth venerated as a relic; a portrait of Christ on a cloth; also, a sudatorium. Also **su-da-ry** (sū'dạ-ri).

su-da-to-ri-um (sū-dạ-tō'ri-um), *n.*; pl. *-ria* (-ri-ä). [L., prop. neut. of *sudatorius*, E. *sudatory*.] A hot-air bath for inducing sweating.

su-da-to-ry (sū'dạ-tō-ri). [L. *sudatorius*, < *sudare*, to sweat, perspire.] **I.** *a.* Pertaining to or causing sweating. **II.** *n.*; pl. *-ries* (-riz). A sudatorium.

sudd (sud), *n.* [Ar., 'barrier.'] Floating vegetable matter which often obstructs navigation in the White Nile; also, a temporary dam constructed in a river (Egypt.).

sud-den (sud'n). [OF. F. *soudain*, < L. *subitaneus*, < *subitus*, sudden, prop. pp. of *subire*, go under, approach stealthily, < *sub*, under, + *ire*, go.] **I.** *a.* Happening, coming, made, or done quickly, without warning or unexpectedly (as, *sudden* death; a *sudden* attack; a *sudden* flash of light; a *sudden* impulse, thought, cry, or action); quick and unexpected; abrupt (as, a *sudden* turn in a road); appearing or encountered unexpectedly (archaic: as, "A *sudden* little river crossed my path," Browning's "Childe Roland," xix.); arriving or acting without notice or unexpectedly (archaic: as, "the *sudden* guest," Tennyson's "Geraint and Enid," 284; "the *sudden* hand of death," Shakspere's "Love's Labour's Lost," v. 2. 825); also, unpremeditated, as actions (archaic); acting without premeditation or forethought, hasty, or rash (archaic: as, "How . . . the loud lie? For what, my *sudden* boy?" B. Jonson's "Alchemist," iv. 2); also, swift or prompt in action or effect (archaic); quickly made, prepared, provided, etc. (archaic: as, "Never was such a *sudden* scholar made," Shakspere's "Henry V.," i. 1. 32); impromptu† or extempore†; also, coming soon or at an early date† (as, a *sudden* opportunity). **II.** *n.* A sudden or unexpected occasion or occurrence:

now only in 'all of a sudden,' 'on a sudden,' etc. (all at once and without notice; unexpectedly; suddenly).—**sud'den,** *adv.* In a sudden manner; suddenly. [Chiefly poetic.]—**sud'den-ly,** *adv.*—**sud'den-ness,** *n.*

su-dor (sū'dọr), *n.* [L., < *sudare*, to sweat, perspire: see *sweat*.] Sweat; perspiration.—**su'dor-al,** *a.*—**su-do-rif-er-ous** (sū-dọ-rif'ẹ-rus), *a.* [LL. *sudorifer*: see *-ferous*.] Bearing or secreting sweat; also, causing sweat.—**su-do-rif'ic.** [See *-fic*.] **I.** *a.* Causing sweat; diaphoretic; also, sudoriparous. **II.** *n.* A sudorific or diaphoretic agent.—**su-do-rip'a-rous** (-rip'ạ-rus), *a.* [See *-parous*.] Producing or secreting sweat.

Su-dra (sö'drä), *n.* [Skt. *çūdra*.] A member of the lowest, or artisan and laboring, caste among the Hindus.

suds (sudz), *n. pl.* [Origin uncertain.] Water impregnated with soap; the frothy mass which forms on the top of soapy water; any froth or foam; the foam churned up by a wounded whale; also, beer (slang).—**suds'y,** *a.* Consisting of or containing suds; resembling or suggesting suds.

sue (sū), *v.*; sued, suing. [AF. *suir*, OF. *sievre, sivre* (F. *suivre*), < LL. *sequere*, for L. *sequi* (pp. *secutus*), follow: cf. *sequent, suit,* and *suitor*.] **I.** *tr.* To follow†; come after†; go in pursuit of†; follow as an attendant, or as a disciple or imitator†; follow (a manner of life, an occupation, etc.)†; carry out or continue (an action, etc.)†; institute (legal action)†; also, to institute a suit for, or make legal claim to (now rare); petition or appeal for (now rare: as, to *sue* peace); make application for (a writ, etc.), or apply for and obtain (a writ, etc.), from a court of law (often with *out*); execute or enforce (a legal process); also, to institute process in law against, or bring a civil action against (as, to *sue* one for debt or for damages); also, to make petition or appeal to; woo or court (archaic: as, "They would *sue* me, and woo me, and flatter me," Tennyson's "Mermaid," iii.). **II.** *intr.* To follow†; come after†; also, to institute legal proceedings, or bring suit (as, to *sue* for damages); also, to make petition or appeal (as, to *sue* for peace, or for pardon; "Do not *sue* to me for leniency," Dickens's "Oliver Twist," xlix.); pay one's court as suitor to a woman (archaic).

suède (swād, F. swed), *n.* [F. *Suède*, Sweden.] Kid or leather finished on the wrong or flesh side with a soft, not glossy surface, or on the outer side after removal of a thin outer layer; undressed kid; also, a woolen fabric with a similar finish or appearance.

su-er (sū'ẹr), *n.* One who sues.

su-et (sū'et), *n.* [ME. *sewet*, < OF. *siu* (F. *suif*), < L. *sebum*, tallow, suet, grease.] The comparatively hard fatty tissue about the loins and kidneys of the ox, sheep, etc.: used in cookery, etc., and prepared as tallow.—**su'et-y,** *a.*

suff (suf), *n.* A colloquial abbreviation of *suffragist*.

suf-fer (suf'ẹr), *v.* [OF. *soufrir* (F. *souffrir*), < L. *sufferre*, carry under, support, undergo, suffer, < *sub*, under, + *ferre*, bear.] **I.** *tr.* To undergo, experience, or be subjected to (pain, distress, injury, loss, or anything unpleasant: as, "not far from where we *suffered* shipwreck," Stevenson's "Kidnapped," xviii.); in general, to undergo (any action, process, etc., not necessarily unpleasant: as, to *suffer* change); also, to bear or endure with patience, fortitude, or composure (now prov.); bear with (a person, etc.) patiently (archaic: as, "For ye *suffer* fools gladly, seeing ye yourselves are wise," 2 Cor. xi. 19); put up with; also, to tolerate or allow (as, "No noise was *suffered* in their camp": Irving's "Conquest of Granada," v.); allow or permit (to do or be as stated: as, "*Suffer* the little children to come unto me," Mark, x. 14). **II.** *intr.* To undergo or feel pain or distress; undergo a penalty, esp. of death; sustain injury, detriment, disadvantage, or loss (as, the health *suffers* from overwork; to *suffer* in public esteem; one book *suffers* by comparison with another; "The revenue of the customs, instead of *suffering*, profits from such drawbacks," Adam Smith's "Wealth of Nations," iv. 4); be subject to unfortunate effects (from a disease, weakness, undesirable quality, etc.: as, to *suffer* from headaches, astigmatism, or insomnia; to *suffer* from excessive credulity); also, to be the object of some action; also, to endure patiently or bravely (as, "Charity *suffereth* long, and is kind": 1 Cor. xiii. 4).—**suf'fer-a-ble,** *a.* That may be suffered or endured; bearable; also, allowable†; also, capable of suffering or enduring patiently†.

—suf'fer-a-bly, *adv.* **—suf'fer-ance**, *n.* [OF. *soufrance* (F. *souffrance*).] The suffering of pain, distress, injury, etc. (archaic); patient endurance, or long-suffering (archaic); capacity to endure pain, hardship, etc.†; also, tolerance, as of a person or thing; tacit allowance, as through failure to object or hinder (as, "To stay where he was not wanted, on a sort of *sufferance*—never!" Galsworthy's "Saint's Progress," iii. 10; "I've been refused—scorned. I'm only here on *sufferance*," G. B. Shaw's "You Never Can Tell," iii.); permission or license. **—suf'fer-er**, *n.* **—suf'fer-ing**, *n.* The act of one who suffers; the undergoing or enduring of pain or distress, or a particular instance of this.

suf-fice (su-fīs'), *v.*; *-ficed, -ficing.* [OF. *soufire* (*soufis-*) (F. *suffire*), < L. *sufficere*, suffice, < *sub*, under, + *facere*, do, make.] **I.** *intr.* To be enough or adequate, as for wants or for the purpose or end: as, "I sent the money to *suffice* for one year" (Kipling's "Kim," vii.); a slight push would *suffice* to throw down the wall; *suffice* it (that is, let it suffice, or be sufficient) to say that the affair ended happily. **II.** *tr.* To be enough or adequate for, satisfy, or content (as, a small amount *sufficed* him; "Lord, shew us the Father, and it *sufficeth* us," John, xiv. 8); also, to provide with enough for needs or satisfaction†; also, to supply in adequate amount†. **—suf-fi'cien-cy** (-fish'ẹn-si), *n.* The state or fact of being sufficient; adequacy for wants or for the purpose; competency, qualification, or ability (archaic); self-sufficiency (archaic); also, a sufficient number or amount; enough; adequate provision, as of material comforts; an adequate supply of means or wealth (as, "An elegant *sufficiency*, content, Retirement, rural quiet, friendship, books": Thomson's "Seasons," Spring, 1161). **—suf-fi'cient** (-fish'ẹnt). [L. *sufficiens* (*-ent-*), ppr. of *sufficere*.] **I.** *a.* That suffices; enough or adequate for wants or for the purpose or end (as, a *sufficient* amount; *sufficient* proof or protection; "A hint was *sufficient* for Lord Orville," Miss Burney's "Evelina," xiii.); as much as is necessary; also, competent or capable, as a person (archaic); also, of adequate means†, or well-to-do†; also, self-sufficient†. **II.** *n.* A sufficient quantity or amount; enough. **—suf-fi'cient-ly**, *adv.* **—suf-fi'cing-ly** (-fī'sing-li), *adv.* **—suf-fi'cing-ness**, *n.*

suf-fix (su-fiks'), *v. t.* [L. *suffixus*, pp. of *suffigere*, fix below, fasten on, < *sub*, under, + *figere*, fix.] To fix or put under; also, to affix at the end of something (as, to *suffix* a syllable to a word). **—suf-fix** (suf'iks), *n.* [NL. *suffixum*, prop. neut. of L. *suffixus*, pp.] Something suffixed; esp., in *gram.*, a letter or syllable or a number of letters or syllables affixed to the end of a word or to a verbal stem or root to qualify the meaning or form a derivative word; a terminal formative element of a word, as *-th* in *warmth*, *-ly* in *godly*, or *-ation* in *flirtation*. **—suf-fix-al** (su-fik'sạl), *a.* Pertaining to or of the nature of a suffix. **—suf-fix'ion** (-fik'shọn), *n.* The act of suffixing, or the state of being suffixed; esp., the affixing of a suffix at the end of a word.

suf-flate (su-flāt'), *v. t.*; *-flated, -flating.* [L. *sufflatus*, pp. of *sufflare*, < *sub*, under, + *flare*, blow.] To blow up; inflate. [Obs. or rare.] **—suf-fla'tion** (-flā'shọn), *n.*

suf-fo-cate (suf'ọ-kāt), *v.*; *-cated, -cating.* [L. *suffocatus*, pp. of *suffocare*, < *sub*, under, + *fauces*, throat.] **I.** *tr.* To kill by preventing the access of air to the blood through the lungs or analogous organs, as gills (as, "The prison may catch fire, and he may be *suffocated* not with a rope, but with common ordinary smoke": S. Butler's "Erewhon," xiii.); stifle; also, to impede the respiration of, or oppress in breathing (as, to be *suffocated* with sobs or emotion; "The theatre, too small, shall *suffocate* Its squeez'd contents," Cowper's "Task," vi. 670); also, fig., to overcome or extinguish as if by excluding air; smother (fire, sound, etc.); suppress (an impulse, enterprise, etc.). **II.** *intr.* To become suffocated; stifle; smother. **—suf'fo-cat-ing-ly** (-kā-ting-li), *adv.* **—suf-fo-ca'tion** (-kā'shọn), *n.* [L. *suffocatio(n-)*.] The act of suffocating, or the condition of being suffocated. **—suf'fo-ca-tive** (-kā-tiv), *a.* Tending to suffocate; stifling.

Suf-folk (suf'ọk), *n.* One of a breed of heavy work-horses with rather short legs and a characteristic chestnut color, originating in the county of Suffolk, England; also, one of a breed of small, black English pigs, named from the same county.

suf-fra-gan (suf'rạ-gạn). [OF. *suffragan* (F. *suffragant*), <

ML. *suffraganeus*, < L. *suffragium*, vote, favorable decision, ML. assistance, aid: cf. *suffrage*.] *Eccles.*: **I.** *a.* Assisting or assistant: applied (*a*) to any bishop in relation to the archbishop or metropolitan who is his superior; (*b*) to an assistant or subsidiary bishop who performs episcopal functions in a diocese, but has no ordinary jurisdiction, as, in the Church of England, a bishop consecrated to assist the ordinary bishop of a see in a particular part of his diocese. Also, of a see or diocese, subordinate to an archiepiscopal or metropolitan see. **II.** *n.* A suffragan bishop (in either sense). **—suf'fra-gan-ship**, *n.*

suf-frage (suf'rạj), *n.* [OF. F. *suffrage*, < L. *suffragium*, vote, right of voting, favorable decision, ML. assistance, aid; origin uncertain.] A vote given in favor of a proposed measure, a candidate, or the like, or, more broadly, a vote whether favorable or unfavorable; an object, as a marked paper, used to indicate a vote given (now rare); also, an opinion in favor of, or, sometimes, with reference to, a person or thing; approval or sanction, or an expression or token of approval (archaic: as, "My Lord of Canterbury wrote to me for *suffrage* for Mr. Clarke's continuance . . . in the Boyle Lecture," Evelyn's "Diary," Dec., 1704); evidence or testimony in favor of something†; also, the collective vote of a body of persons (as, "The election of a new emperor was referred to the *suffrage* of the military order": Gibbon's "Decline and Fall of the Roman Empire," xii.); the collective opinion of a number of persons; also, the act of voting; also, the right of voting, as in political affairs (as, manhood *suffrage*; woman *suffrage*, or female *suffrage*); also, *eccles.*, a prayer, esp. a short intercessory prayer or petition (as, "occasional prayers and *suffrages*, to be used throughout all churches": Strype's "Memorials of Cranmer," i. 29). **—suf-fra-gette** (suf-rạ-jet'), *n.* [See *-ette*.] A woman who advocates female suffrage. [Colloq.] **—suf'fra-gism** (-jizm), *n.* The advocacy of the grant or extension of political suffrage, esp. to women. **—suf'fra-gist** (-jist), *n.* An advocate of the grant or extension of political suffrage, esp. to women.

suf-fu-mi-gate (su-fū'mi-gāt), *v. t.*; *-gated, -gating.* [L. *suffumigatus*, pp. of *suffumigare*, < *sub*, under, + *fumigare*: see *fumigate*.] To fumigate from below; apply fumes or smoke to. **—suf-fu-mi-ga'tion** (-gā'shọn), *n.*

suf-fuse (su-fūz'), *v. t.*; *-fused, -fusing.* [L. *suffusus*, pp. of *suffundere*, pour below, overspread, < *sub*, under, + *fundere*, pour.] To overspread with a liquid, color, etc., or as a liquid or the like does (as, "his eyes . . . with tears *suffused*," Fairfax's tr. Tasso's "Jerusalem Delivered," xii. 74; "A flush *suffused* his pallid visage," Howells's "Foregone Conclusion," xii.); also, to pour, as a liquid, over a surface. **—suf-fu'sion** (-fū'zhọn), *n.* [L. *suffusio(n-)*.] The act of suffusing, or the state of being suffused; also, that with which anything is suffused; a coloring spread over a surface; a flush of color in the face (as, "There was a healthful *suffusion* on their cheeks": Hawthorne's "Twice-Told Tales," Dr. Heidegger's Experiment). **—suf-fu'sive** (-siv), *a.* Tending to suffuse.

Su-fi (sö'fē), *n.*; pl. *-fis* (-fēz). [Ar. *çūfī*, prob. < *çūf*, wool, with reference to the woolen garments worn.] One of a sect of Mohammedan mystics which originated in the 8th century. **—Su'fic** (-fik), *a.* Of or pertaining to the Sufis or their mystical system. **—Su'fism**, *n.* The mystical system of the Sufis. **—Su-fis'tic**, *a.*

su-gan, sou-gan (sö'gạn), *n.* [Ir.] A straw rope (chiefly Ir.); also, a saddle of straw or rushes (chiefly Ir.); also, a heavy coverlet, as for a bed (Ir., western U. S., etc.).

sug-ar (shug'ạr), *n.* [OF. *çucre, zuchre* (F. *sucre*), < Ar. *sukkar*, akin to Gr. σάκχαρ, σάκχαρον, L. *saccharon*, ML. *saccharum*, Pers. *shakkar*, all < Prakrit *sakkara*, < Skt. *çarkara*, sugar, orig. grit, gravel: cf. *jaggery* and *saccharine*.] A sweet crystalline substance (saccharose, or 'cane-sugar'), $C_{12}H_{22}O_{11}$, obtained chiefly from the juice of the sugar-cane and sugar-beet, but present in sorghum, the maple, etc., and extensively used for food purposes; any of the class of carbohydrates to which this substance belongs, as glucose ('grape-sugar'), levulose ('fruit-sugar'), lactose ('milk-sugar,' or 'sugar of milk'), etc.; the brownish product derived from the sap of the maple ('maple sugar'), consisting of a mixture of saccharose and other substances; also, a sugar-like substance (as, *sugar* of lead, lead acetate, a poisonous crystalline compound); fig., agreeable or flattering language or treatment; also, money (slang).—**sug'ar**, v. **I.** tr. To cover, sprinkle, mix, or sweeten with sugar; fig., to sweeten as if with sugar; make agreeable. **II.** intr. To form sugar; also, to make maple sugar; in making maple sugar, to complete the boiling down of the syrup in preparation for granulation (with off).

sug-ar=beet (shŭg'är-bēt), n. A variety of beet with a white root, cultivated for the sugar it yields.

sug-ar-ber-ry (shŭg'är-ber″i), n. A hackberry, *Celtis occidentalis*.

sug-ar=cane (shŭg'är-kān), n. A tall grass, *Saccharum officinarum*, of tropical and warm regions, having a stout, jointed stalk, and constituting the chief source of sugar.

sug-ar=corn (shŭg'är-kôrn), n. Sweet corn (see under *sweet*, a.).

sug-ared (shŭg'ärd), p. a. Covered, mixed, or sweetened with sugar; fig., sweetened as if with sugar; made agreeable; honeyed, as words, speech, etc. (as, "the rain of *sugared* remonstrances and cajoleries that the two women directed upon him": Arnold Bennett's "Clayhanger," iii. 2).

sug-ar=house (shŭg'är-hous), n. An establishment in which crude or raw sugar is made from the sugar-cane, etc.

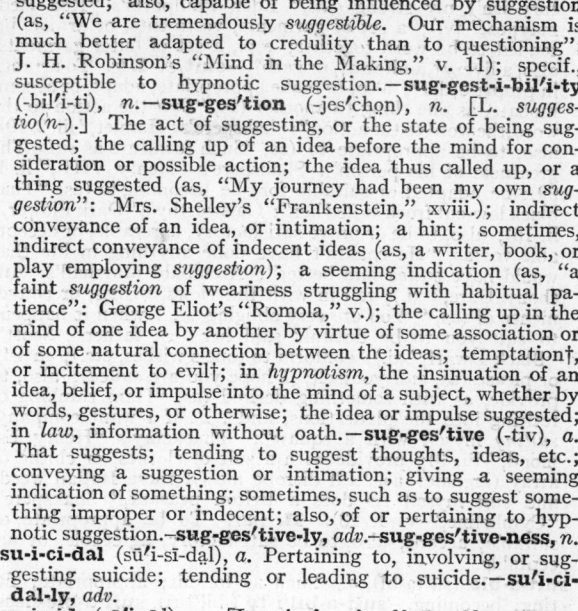

Sugar-cane.— *a*, part of the inflorescence; *b*, a spikelet.

sug-ar-i-ness (shŭg'är-i-nes), n. Sugary quality.

sug-ar-less (shŭg'är-les), a. Without sugar.

sug-ar=loaf (shŭg'är-lōf). **I.** n.; pl. *-loaves* (-lōvz). A large, approximately conical loaf or mass of hard refined sugar (now seldom made); also, something resembling this in shape; a kind of tall conical hat; a high conical hill (as, "here and there the outline of a wooded *sugar-loaf* in black": Stevenson's "Travels with a Donkey," i. 2). **II.** a. Resembling a sugar-loaf in shape.

sug-ar=ma-ple (shŭg'är-mā″pl), n. Any of several species of maple with a sweet sap, esp. *Acer saccharum*, of eastern North America, which yields an important timber and is the chief source of maple sugar. See cut at *maple*.

sug-ar=pine (shŭg'är-pīn), n. A tall pine, *Pinus lambertiana*, of California, Oregon, etc., from wounds in the heartwood of which a sweet, sugar-like, resinous substance exudes.

sug-ar=plum (shŭg'är-plum), n. A small sweetmeat made of sugar with various flavoring and coloring ingredients; a bonbon; fig., something especially agreeable or pleasing, as a bit of flattery.

sug-ar-y (shŭg'är-i), a. Consisting of or containing sugar; pertaining to or resembling sugar; sweet; sometimes, excessively sweet; fig., dulcet; honeyed; cloying; deceitfully agreeable.

sug-gan (sug'an), n. Same as *sugan*.

sug-gest (su-jest', also sug-), v. [L. *suggestus*, pp. of *suggerere*, put under, supply, suggest, < *sub*, under, + *gerere*, bear.] **I.** tr. To place or bring (an idea, proposition, plan, etc.) before a person's mind for consideration or possible action (as, "The doctor *suggested* a walk to the beach": H. Melville's "Omoo," lvi.); propose (a person or thing) as suitable or possible; of things, to prompt the consideration, making, doing, etc., of (as, the success of his first book *suggested* a second one); also, to bring before a person's mind indirectly or without plain expression; hint; intimate; also, of a thing, to call up in the mind (another thing) through association or natural connection of ideas; give the impression of (as, his actions *suggest* cowardice; "his erect and careless attitude *suggesting* assurance and power," J. Conrad's "Rescue," v. 2); also, to tempt† or seduce† (as, "I give thee not this to *suggest* thee from thy master": Shakspere's "All's Well," iv. 5. 47). **II.** intr. To make or offer a suggestion or suggestions: as, "statesmen . . . who act from day to day as immediate interests *suggest*" (Froude's "Cæsar," i.).—**sug-gest'er**, n.—**sug-gest'i-ble**, a. That may be

suggested; also, capable of being influenced by suggestion (as, "We are tremendously *suggestible*. Our mechanism is much better adapted to credulity than to questioning": J. H. Robinson's "Mind in the Making," v. 11); specif., susceptible to hypnotic suggestion.—**sug-gest-i-bil'i-ty** (-bil'i-ti), n.—**sug-ges'tion** (-jes'chon), n. [L. *suggestio(n-).*] The act of suggesting, or the state of being suggested; the calling up of an idea before the mind for consideration or possible action; the idea thus called up, or a thing suggested (as, "My journey had been my own *suggestion*": Mrs. Shelley's "Frankenstein," xviii.); indirect conveyance of an idea, or intimation; a hint; sometimes, indirect conveyance of indecent ideas (as, a writer, book, or play employing *suggestion*); a seeming indication (as, "a faint *suggestion* of weariness struggling with habitual patience": George Eliot's "Romola," v.); the calling up in the mind of one idea by another by virtue of some association or of some natural connection between the ideas; temptation†, or incitement to evil†; in *hypnotism*, the insinuation of an idea, belief, or impulse into the mind of a subject, whether by words, gestures, or otherwise; the idea or impulse suggested; in *law*, information without oath.—**sug-ges'tive** (-tiv), a. That suggests; tending to suggest thoughts, ideas, etc.; conveying a suggestion or intimation; giving a seeming indication of something; sometimes, such as to suggest something improper or indecent; also, of or pertaining to hypnotic suggestion.—**sug-ges'tive-ly**, adv.—**sug-ges'tive-ness**, n.

su-i-ci-dal (sū'i-sī-dal), a. Pertaining to, involving, or suggesting suicide; tending or leading to suicide.—**su'i-ci-dal-ly**, adv.

su-i-cide (sū'i-sīd), n. [L. *sui*, of one's self, + *-cida*, *-cidium*: see *-cide*.] One who intentionally takes his own life; also, the intentional taking of one's own life; fig., destruction of one's own interests or prospects.—**su'i-cide**, v.; *-cided*, *-ciding*. **I.** intr. To commit suicide. **II.** tr. To kill (one's self) by suicide; cause (any person) to die by or as by suicide.

su-i gen-e-ris (sū'ī jen'ę-ris). [L.] Of his, her, its, or their own or peculiar kind; unique.

su-il-line (sū'i-lin), a. [L. *suillus*, < *sus*, swine.] Of or pertaining to the swine family.

su-ine (sū'in), n. [L. *sus*, swine.] A mixture of oleomargarin with lard or other fatty substances, used as a substitute for butter.

suint (swint), n. [F., < *suer*, < L. *sudare*, to sweat.] The natural grease of the wool of sheep, consisting of a mixture of fatty matter and potassium salts: used as a source of potash and in the preparation of ointments.

Suisse (swis, F. swēs), n. [F.] A Swiss; also [sometimes l. c.], the porter of a large house (as, "The two great gates rolled back, a liveried *Suisse* appeared, and an open carriage and pair came out": Du Maurier's "Trilby," iii.); a beadle or similar officer of a church.

suit (sūt), n. [AF. *sute*, OF. *sieute* (F. *suite*), through LL. < L. *sequi* (pp. *secutus*), follow: cf. *sue*.] A following†, pursuing†, or pursuit†; also, a following or attendance, as of feudal tenants on their lord at his court; a company of followers, a train, or a retinue (as, "a gentleman of his *suit*, Count Rochepot," Motley's "Dutch Republic," vi. 6: now commonly *suite*); also, the act or process of suing in a court of law; legal prosecution; a process instituted in a court of justice for the enforcement or protection of a right or claim, or for the redress of a wrong, or a lawsuit (as, "The Plaintiff in the *suit* . . . was adjudged to have not proved his charge": G. Meredith's "Diana of the Crossways," xiv.); also, the act of making petition or appeal; a petition, as to a person of exalted station (as, "He gave audience . . . to such caciques as had *suits* to prefer to him": Prescott's "Conquest of Mexico," iv. 1); the wooing or courting of a woman; a solicitation in marriage; also, succession†, sequence†, or order†; also, a number of things of like kind forming a series or set, or a number of objects corresponding in general character or purpose and intended to be used together; one of the four sets or classes, spades, clubs, hearts, and diamonds, into which playing-cards are divided (as, to follow suit: see under *follow*, v. t.); the aggregate of cards belonging to one of these sets held in a player's hand at one time (as, to have a strong *suit* of trumps: often fig., as, "History isn't my strong *suit*," Eden Phillpotts's "Red Red-maynes," iv.); a set of garments, vestments, or armor, intended to be worn together; esp., a set of outer garments; also, a livery†, uniform†, or garb†.—**suit**, *v.* **I.** *tr.* To arrange in proper order†; also, to make appropriate, adapt, or accommodate, as one thing to another (as, "*Suit* the action to the word, the word to the action": Shakspere's "Hamlet," iii. 2. 19); also, to be appropriate to (as, "Such furniture as *suits* The greatness of his person": Shakspere's "Henry VIII.," ii. 1. 99); be adapted or suitable for; be becoming to (as, "That black low-cut frock *suited* her": Galsworthy's "Dark Flower," ii. 16); also, to be or prove satisfactory, agreeable, or acceptable to (as, "He couldn't have done anything in life that would have *suited* him better": Archibald Marshall's "Anthony Dare," xi.); fall in with the views, wishes, or convenience of (as, "'You are very obliging . . . when it happens to *suit* you to be dutiful,' said her . . . father": Scott's "Black Dwarf," xi.); conform to (one's wishes, etc.); satisfy or please (as, *suit* yourself; I hope you are *suited*); also, to provide, as with something desired (as, "I am thinking of retiring into the plantations, and . . . if I want company, *suiting* myself with a squaw": Thackeray's "Henry Esmond," iii. 3); provide with a suit of clothes, or clothe or array (archaic: as, "I'll disrobe me Of these Italian weeds and *suit* myself As does a Briton peasant," Shakspere's "Cymbeline," v. 1. 23). **II.** *intr.* To be appropriate or suitable; accord; also, to be satisfactory, agreeable, or acceptable.

suit-a-ble (sū'tạ-bl), *a.* Such as to suit; appropriate; fitting; becoming.—**suit-a-bil'i-ty** (-bil'i-ti), **suit'a-ble-ness**, *n.*—**suit'a-bly**, *adv.*

suit-case (sūt'kās), *n.* A kind of flat, oblong valise, orig. intended to contain a man's dress-suit (and hence called *dress-suit case*).

suite (swēt), *n.* [F.: see *suit.*] A company of followers or attendants (as, "He [a king] was accompanied by a numerous *suite* of nobles and inferior attendants": Prescott's "Conquest of Mexico," iii. 8); a train or retinue; also, a number of things forming a series or set; a connected series of rooms to be used together by one person or a number of persons; a set of furniture; in *music*, a definitely ordered series of instrumental dances, in the same key or related keys, commonly preceded by a prelude; hence, an ordered series of instrumental movements of any character.

suit-ed (sū'ted), *a.* Wearing a suit (of a kind specified): as, gray-*suited*.

suit-ing (sū'ting), *n.* Cloth for making suits of clothes.

suit-or (sū'tọr), *n.* [AF. *seutor, suitour,* < L. *secutor,* follower, < *sequi,* follow: cf. *sue.*] One who owed suit or attendance at a feudal court; one of a company of followers or attendants†; a petitioner or plaintiff in a suit at law; one who sues or petitions for anything (as, "The archbishop . . . was a *suitor* at court for some further preferment for him": Strype's "Memorials of Cranmer," iii. 23); one who courts a woman, or sues for her hand in marriage (as, "There were many *suitors* where women were not over-plenty": Roosevelt's "Winning of the West," i. 5).—**suit'or-ship**, *n.*—**suit'ress**, *n.* A female suitor.

sul-cate, sul-cat-ed (sul'kāt, -kā-ted), *a.* [L. *sulcatus,* pp. of *sulcare,* to furrow, < *sulcus,* a furrow.] Having long, narrow grooves or channels, as a stem; furrowed; cleft, as a hoof.—**sul-ca'tion** (-kā'shọn), *n.*

sul-cus (sul'kus), *n.*; pl. *-ci* (-sī). [L., a furrow.] A furrow or groove; specif., in *anat.*, a fissure between two convolutions of the surface of the brain.

sul-fate (sul'fāt), etc. See *sulphate*, etc.

sulk (sulk), *v. i.* [Origin uncertain.] To hold aloof in a sullenly ill-humored or offended mood; maintain an attitude of ill-humored reserve; be sulky: as, "The bride sat crying in one corner of the carriage; and the bridegroom *sulked* in the other" (S. Butler's "Way of All Flesh," xiii.).—**sulk**, *n.* A state or fit of sulking; *pl.*, often with *the*, ill humor shown by sulking (as, a fit of the *sulks*; to be in

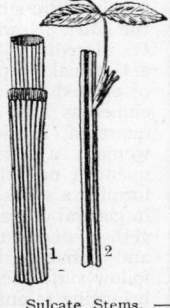

Sulcate Stems.—
1, of horsetail; 2, of blackberry.

the *sulks*); also, *sing.*, one who sulks.—**sulk'er**, *n.*—**sulk'i-ly**, *adv.* In a sulky manner.—**sulk'i-ness**, *n.*—**sulk'y**, *a.*; compar. *sulkier,* superl. *sulkiest.* Sulking; sullenly ill-humored or resentful; marked by ill-humored aloofness or reserve (as, "I resolved . . . upon a *sulky* silence": H. G. Wells's "Tono-Bungay," i. 1. § 8); fig., of weather, etc., gloomy; of soil, stone, timber, etc., hard to work (prov. Eng.).—**sulk'y**, *n.*; pl. *-ies* (-iz). [So called because the rider is alone.] A light two-wheeled one-horse carriage for one person: commonly used for trials of speed between trotting-horses. Also used in composition, as in *sulky-cultivator, sulky-harrow, sulky-plow, sulky-rake,* wheeled agricultural machines having a seat for the driver.

sul-len (sul'ẹn), *a.* [ME. *soleyn,* solitary, unsociable, through OF. < L. *solus,* alone, E. *sole*³.] Solitary†; also, unsociable†; also, showing ill humor by a gloomy silence or reserve (as, "The men returned, disappointed and *sullen,* for they had failed in their search": W. H. Hudson's "Green Mansions," xv.); silently and persistently ill-humored; morose; indicative of gloomy ill humor (as, "*sullen* silence," John Hay's "Bread-Winners," ii.; "a tone of *sullen* bitterness," Hawthorne's "Twice-Told Tales," The Gentle Boy); refractory, as an animal; fig., gloomy or dismal, as weather, places, sounds, etc. (as, "The night continued *sullen* and stormy": Scott's "Black Dwarf," vii.); somber, as in aspect or hue (as, "*sullen* skies": Cowper's "Task," ii. 212); sluggish, as a stream; malignant, as planets, influences, etc.†.—**sul'len-ly**, *adv.*—**sul'len-ness**, *n.*—**sul'lens**, *n. pl.* Sullen humor; ill humor shown by gloomy silence or reserve: as, a fit of *sullens,* or of the *sullens.*

sul-ly (sul'i), *v.*; *-lied, -lying.* [Appar. < F. *souiller:* see *soil*².] **I.** *tr.* To soil, stain, or tarnish (as, "when he had washed his face, which was a little *sullied* by his fall": R. Graves's "Spiritual Quixote," ii. 10); mar the purity or luster of; defile. Often fig.: as, to *sully* a victory by bloody executions. **II.** *intr.* To become sullied, soiled, or tarnished.—**sul'ly**, *n.*; pl. *sullies* (-iz). The act of sullying; a stain. [Obs. or rare.]

sulph-. See *sulpho-.*

sulph-a-nil'a-mide (sul-fạ-nil'ạ-mīd), *n.* [From *sulph-* (*ur*) + *anil*(*ine*) + *amide*.] A drug used in combating certain infections, as erysipelas, sore throat, etc.

sul-phate (sul'fāt), *n.* In *chem.,* a salt of sulphuric acid.—**sul'phate**, *v.*; *-phated, -phating.* **I.** *tr.* To combine, treat, or impregnate with sulphuric acid or with a sulphate or sulphates; convert into a sulphate; specif., to form a deposit of a lead sulphate compound on (the lead plates of a storage-battery). **II.** *intr.* To become sulphated.—**sul'phat-ize** (-fāt-īz), *v. t.*; *-ized, -izing.* To convert into a sulphate.—**sul'phat-i-za'tion** (-i-zā'shọn), *n.*

sul-phide, sul-phid (sul'fīd or -fid, -fid), *n.* In *chem.,* a compound of sulphur with a more electropositive element or radical.

sul-phite (sul'fīt), *n.* A salt of sulphurous acid; also, a person who is original in thought or speech, rather than conventional and commonplace (colloq.: cf. *bromide*).—**sul-phit'ic** (-fit'ik), *a.* Pertaining to a sulphite. [Colloq.]

sulpho-, sulph-. Combining-forms of *sulphur.* Cf. *thio-.*

sul-pho-nal (sul'fō-nạl), *n.* [G. *sulfonal,* < *sulfon,* E. *sulphone.*] In *phar.,* a crystalline organic compound containing sulphur, used as a hypnotic.

sul-phon-a-mide (sul-phon'ạ-mīd), *n.* In *chem.,* any of a class of organic compounds containing sulphanilamide, etc.

sul-phone (sul'fōn), *n.* [G. *sulfon,* < *sulfur,* sulphur.] In *chem.,* any of a class of organic compounds containing the bivalent SO_2 group united with two hydrocarbon radicals.—**sul-phon'ic** (-fon'ik), *a.* In *chem.,* noting or pertaining to the group SO_2OH; noting or pertaining to any of the acids, mostly organic, containing this group (as, ethyl *sulphonic* acid, $C_2H_5SO_2OH$).

sul-pho-ni-um (sul-fō'ni-um), *n.* [From *sulph*(*ur*) + (*amm*)*onium.*] In *chem.,* a hypothetical univalent radical, SH_3, present in certain organic compounds.

sul-phur (sul'fẹr), *n.* [L. *sulfur, sulphur, sulpur,* sulphur.] Chem. sym., S; at. wt., 32.06. A non-metallic element which exists in several forms, the ordinary one being a yellow crystalline solid, and which burns with a blue flame and a suffocating odor, and is used in making gunpowder and matches, in vulcanizing rubber, in medicine, etc.; also, a slightly greenish yellow color; also, any of various yellow or orange butterflies of the family *Pieridæ.*—**sulphur dioxide,** in *chem.,* a colorless suffocating gas, SO_2, formed when sulphur burns.—**sul'phur,** *v. t.* To treat with sulphur; sulphurize.—**sul'phu=rate** (-fū-rāt), *v. t.; -rated, -rating.* To combine, treat, or impregnate with sulphur, the fumes of burning sulphur, or the like.—**sul'phu=ra'tion** (-rā'shọn),

Orange Sulphur (*Phœbis agarithe*), one half natural size.

n.—**sul'phu=ra=tor,** *n.* An apparatus for treating, impregnating, or sprinkling something with sulphur; also, an apparatus for fumigating or bleaching with the fumes of burning sulphur.—**sul'phur=bot"tom,** *n.* A large rorqual, *Balænoptera* (or *Sibbaldius*) *sulfureus,* of the Pacific, with yellowish under parts; also, an allied species, *B. musculus,* of the northern Atlantic, which is whitish beneath.—**sul=phu're=ous** (-fū'rē-us), *a.* [L. *sulfureus.*] Consisting of, containing, pertaining to, or resembling sulphur; sulphur-colored.—**sul=phu're=ous=ly,** *adv.*—**sul=phu're=ous=ness,** *n.*—**sul'phu=ret** (-fū-ret), *n.* In *chem.,* a sulphide.—**sul'phu=ret=ed, sul'phu=ret=ted,** *a.* Combined or impregnated with sulphur.—**sul=phu'ric** (-fū'rik), *a.* Of or pertaining to sulphur; in *chem.,* containing sulphur (see *sulphurous*); noting or pertaining to a heavy, corrosive, colorless, oily acid, H_2SO_4, produced from sulphur trioxide.—**sul'phu=rize** (-fū-rīz), *v. t.; -rized, -rizing.* To combine, treat, or impregnate with sulphur; fumigate with the fumes of burning sulphur.—**sul"phu=ri=za'tion** (-rī-zā'shọn), *n.*—**sul=phu=rous** (sul'fū-rus, in chem. sul-fū'rus), *a.* [L. *sulfurosus.*] Full of sulphur; pertaining to or resembling sulphur; like the suffocating fumes or the heat of burning sulphur; hence, pertaining to the fires of hell; hellish or satanic; fiery or heated; blasphemous or profane, as language; in *chem.,* containing sulphur (in larger proportion than a corresponding sulphuric compound); noting or pertaining to an acid, H_2SO_3, produced from sulphur dioxide.—**sul'phur=whale,** *n.* The sulphur-bottom.—**sul'phur=y** (-fẽr-i), *a.* Sulphurous.—**sul'phu=ryl** (-fū-ril), *n.* [See *-yl.*] In *chem.,* the bivalent radical SO_2.

sul=phy=drate (sul-fī'drāt), *n.* [See *sulpho-, sulph-.*] In *chem.,* a hydrosulphide, which is commonly regarded as a salt of sulphydric acid: as, sulphydric acid forms two kinds of salts, the *sulphydrates* or hydrosulphides, in which only one of the hydrogen atoms has been replaced, and the sulphides, in which both hydrogen atoms have been replaced.—**sul=phy'dric,** *a.* In *chem.,* noting or pertaining to an acid, H_2S, which is more commonly called *hydrogen sulphide.*

Sul=pi=cian (sul-pish'ạn). **I.** *a.* Noting or pertaining to a Roman Catholic congregation of secular priests founded at Paris, in 1642, by Abbé (Jean Jacques) Olier, of the parish of St. Sulpice, for the purpose of training young men for the clerical office. **II.** *n.* A member of the Sulpician congregation.

sul=tan (sul'tạn), *n.* [F. *sultan* (OF. *soldan*) = It. *sultano,* < Ar. *sultān,* sovereign, ruler, orig. power, dominion.] [Usually *cap.*] The sovereign of a Mohammedan country, esp., formerly, the sovereign of Turkey; also, formerly, any Mohammedan prince; also [*cap.* or *l. c.*], any absolute ruler; a despot; a tyrant; also [*l. c.*], one of a breed of domestic fowls of small size, having white plumage and the legs profusely feathered; also, a sultana (gallinule).—**sul=ta'na** (-tä'nä), *n.* [It.] The wife, or a concubine, of a sultan; sometimes, the mother, sister, or daughter of

Black-backed Sultana (*Porphyrio melanotus*), of Australasia.

a sultan; also, a concubine or mistress; also, any of certain gallinules of the genera *Porphyrio* and *Ionornis,* notable for their brilliant plumage (see cut in preceding column); also, a kind of small seedless raisin.—**sul'tan=ate** (-āt), *n.* The office or rule of a sultan; the territory ruled over by a sultan; a state subject to a sultan (as, "Egypt was now a Turkish *sultanate*": H. G. Wells's "Outline of History," xxxiv. § 5D).—**sul'tan=ess,** *n.* A sultana (in first two senses).—**sul'tan=ic** (-tan'ik), *a.* Of, pertaining to, or suggestive of a sultan.—**sul'tan=ship,** *n.* The office or dignity of a sultan.

sul=try (sul'tri), *a.;* compar. *sultrier,* superl. *sultriest.* [Var. of *sweltry.*] Oppressively hot, as the weather, air, sun, etc.; esp., oppressively hot and close or moist (as, "There was no motion in the heavy *sultry* atmosphere," W. H. Hudson's "Green Mansions," vi.; "It was a cloudy, *sultry* afternoon," H. Melville's "Moby-Dick," xlvii.); sweltering; characterized by or associated with sweltering heat (as, "the reapers at their *sultry* toil": Tennyson's "Palace of Art," 77); fig., characterized by heat of temper or passion (as, "in a *sultry* chafe": Milton's "Samson Agonistes," 1246); also, uncomfortable or unpleasant (colloq.).—**sul'tri=ly,** *adv.*—**sul'tri=ness,** *n.*

Su=lu (sö-lö'), *n.* A member of the most numerous and most highly cultivated tribe of Moros, or Mohammedan Malays of the southern Philippine Islands, which is found chiefly in the islands of the Sulu Archipelago; also, the language or dialect of this tribe.

sum (sum), *n.* [OF. *summe, somme* (F. *somme*), < L. *summa,* highest point, culmination, completion, issue, total amount, an amount, principal matter, substance, ML. summary, prop. fem. of L. *summus,* highest, superl. of *superus,* being above: see *superior.*] The highest point, or culmination (archaic: as, the *sum* of earthly bliss); the issue or conclusion, as of an affair†; also, the total amount, or the whole (now only of things: as, "Sympathy . . . was extinct. Nor was this the *sum* of my misery," Godwin's "Caleb Williams," xl.); the aggregate (often in 'sum total': as, the *sum* total of all the items in an account); specif., the aggregate of two or more numbers, magnitudes, quantities, or particulars as determined by mathematical process (as, the *sum* of 5 and 7 is 12; the *sum* of a and b is $a + b$); a series of numbers or quantities to be added up; an arithmetical problem to be solved, or such a problem worked out and having the various steps shown; also, a particular aggregate or total, esp. with reference to money (as, the expenses came to an enormous *sum*); a quantity or amount, esp. of money (as, a *sum* of $500; to lend small *sums*); also, the substance or gist of a matter, comprehensively viewed or expressed (as, "The *sum* of his discourse was to this effect," Swift's "Gulliver's Travels," iii. 4: often in the phrase 'sum and substance,' as, the letter contains the *sum* and substance of his opinions); concise or brief form (as, in *sum,* in few words, in brief); a summary†.—**sum,** *v.; summed, summing.* [OF. F. *sommer,* < ML. *summare,* < L. *summa.*] **I.** *tr.* To combine into an aggregate or total (often with *up*); ascertain the aggregate or sum of, as by addition; reckon (*up*: as, to *sum* up advantages and disadvantages); also, to bring into or contain in a small compass (often with *up*: as, a man who *sums* up in himself the main characteristics of his time); esp., to bring into or contain in a brief and comprehensive statement (usually with *up*: as, the writer, or the article, *sums* up the work of the year; "In two masterly sentences he *summed* up Captain Guy's character," H. Melville's "Omoo," xxxvi.); express in a concise form; summarize; form a summary estimate of, as by observation (with *up*: as, "They were not obviously staring, but he knew that they were rapidly *summing* him up," Hugh Walpole's "Wooden Horse," ii.); also, to bring to completion or perfection†. **II.** *intr.* To amount, as to a total; also, to do sums, as in arithmetic (as, "He could read, write and *sum* better than any other boy of his age in the village," S. Butler's "Way of All Flesh," ii.: chiefly prov. Eng.); also, with *up,* to summarize facts or statements; recapitulate.

su=mac, su=mach (sū'mak), *n.* [OF. F. *sumac,* < Ar. *summāq,* sumac.] Any of the plants of the anacardiaceous genus *Rhus,* as, in North America, *R. hirta,* a shrub or small tree with long pinnate leaves and pyramidal panicles of crimson drupes, *R. glabra*, a shrub with panicles of small crimson drupes ('smooth sumac'), or *R. vernix* (see *poison-sumac*); also, a preparation of the dried and powdered leaves, etc., of certain species of *Rhus*, esp. *R. coriaria*, of southern Europe, used in tanning, etc.

sum-bul (sum′bul or sum′-bul), *n.* [Ar.] Any of several aromatic or medicinal plants, as the East Indian spikenard, or an Asiatic apiaceous plant, *Ferula sumbul* (see cut below); also, the root of such a plant; esp., the root of *Ferula sumbul*, used as a nerve-tonic and antispasmodic.

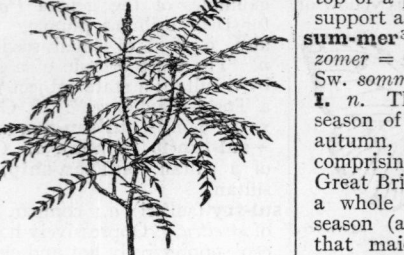

Smooth Sumac (*Rhus glabra*).

Su-me-ri-an (sū-mē′ri-ạn). [From *Sumer*, ancient name of Babylonia, or part of Babylonia.] **I.** *a.* Noting or pertaining to the primitive inhabitants of Babylonia, believed by most authorities to have been of non-Semitic origin; also, noting or pertaining to a certain language preserved in cuneiform inscriptions, and by most authorities held to be non-Semitic and ascribed to the primitive inhabitants of Babylonia. Cf. *Akkadian*, *a.* **II.** *n.* One of the Sumerian people; also, the Sumerian language.

sum-less (sum′les), *a.* That cannot be summed or reckoned up; incalculable: as, "Rich . . . As is the ooze and bottom of the sea With sunken wreck and *sumless* treasuries" (Shakspere's "Henry V.," i. 2. 165). [Chiefly poetic.]

sum-ma-ri-ly (sum′ạ-ri-li), *adv.* In a summary manner; concisely; briefly; without formalities; directly and promptly; without delay. **—sum′ma-ri-ness,** *n.*

sum-ma-rist (sum′ạ-rist), *n.* The maker of a summary.

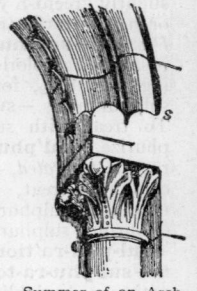

Sumbul (*Ferula sumbul*). —*a*, flower.

sum-ma-rize (sum′ạ-rīz), *v. t.*; *-rized, -rizing.* To make a summary of; state or express in a concise form; sometimes, to constitute a summary of.— **sum″ma-ri-za′tion** (-ri-zā′shọn), *n.*—**sum′ma-riz-er** (-rī-zėr), *n.*

sum-ma-ry (sum′ạ-ri). [ML. *summarius* (as n., L. *summarium*), < L. *summa*, E. *sum*, *n.*] **I.** *a.* Containing the sum or substance only, as a statement or account; brief and comprehensive; concise; also, of legal proceedings, jurisdiction, etc., conducted without or exempt from the various steps and delays of a formal trial (as when a magistrate deals directly with cases not requiring trial by jury); hence, in general, direct and prompt (as, a *summary* settlement of difficulties; "The inhabitants trembled at the danger of provoking a *summary* vengeance," Hallam's "Europe during the Middle Ages," iii. 1); characterized by unceremonious despatch (as, "He cleared the table by the *summary* process of tilting everything upon it into the fire-place": Dickens's "Martin Chuzzlewit," xiii.). **II.** *n.*; pl. *-ries* (-riz). A summary statement or account; a brief and comprehensive presentation of facts or statements; an abstract, compendium, or epitome: as, "He [Bacon] has hinted the Novum Organum to be a digested *summary* of his method" (Hallam's "Literature of Europe," iii. 3. § 58).

sum-ma-tion (su-mā′shọn), *n.* [NL. *summatio(n-)*, < ML. *summare*, E. *sum*, *v.*] The process of summing; combination into or ascertainment of an aggregate or total; also, the result of this; an aggregate or total (as, "He wanted to state England to Mr. Direck as the amiable *summation* of a grotesque assembly of faults": H. G. Wells's "Mr. Britling," i. 2. § 2).—**sum-ma′tion-al,** *a.*

sum-mer¹ (sum′ėr), *n.* One who sums.

sum-mer² (sum′ėr), *n.* [OF. *somier* (F. *sommier*), < ML. *sagmarius*, packhorse, orig. adj. < LL. *sagma*, < Gr. σάγμα, pack-saddle: cf. *sumpter*.] A packhorse†; also, a principal

timber or beam, as in a floor; a girder; a lintel; a stone at the top of a pier, column, or the like, as to support an arch.

sum-mer³ (sum′ėr). [AS. *sumor* = D. *zomer* = G. *sommer* = Icel. *sumar* = Sw. *sommar* = Dan. *sommer*, summer.] **I.** *n.* The second and the warmest season of the year, between spring and autumn, in North America taken as comprising June, July, and August, in Great Britain May, June, and July; also, a whole year as represented by this season (as, "Fair was she to behold, that maiden of seventeen *summers*": Longfellow's "Evangeline," i. 1); also, fig., the period of finest development, perfection, or beauty, previous to any decline (as, the *summer* of life; in the *summer* of her age); also, summer weather or warmth (as, "the lands of lasting *summer*, many-blossoming Paradises": Tennyson's "Boädicéa"); a summer-like season or period; specif., a period of mild, fine weather in late autumn or early winter (as, Indian *summer*; St. Luke's *summer*; St. Martin's *summer*: see under *Indian*, *a.*, and *saint*, *a.*). **II.** *a.* Of, pertaining to, or characteristic of summer (as, *summer* warmth; *summer* clothing; *summer* resorts; a *summer* sky or sea); having the weather or warmth of summer (as, "Some happy *summer* isle, Whereon the kind unburning sun doth smile For ever, and that knows no frost or drought": W. Morris's "Jason," ii. 665); of fruit, etc., of a kind that ripens during the summer.—**summer complaint,** diarrhea or cholera morbus occurring in summer. [U. S.]—**summer flounder,** a large flounder, *Paralichthys dentatus*, with more or less conspicuous dark spots, common along the Atlantic coast of the U. S. from Cape Cod southward.

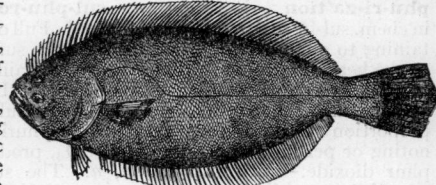

Summer of an Arch. 12th century.—*s*, summer.

Summer Flounder.

—summer savory. See *savory²*.—**summer school,** a school held during the summer, either in connection with a university or the like or independently, often one meeting amid agreeable outdoor surroundings.—**summer squash,** any of various squashes used as a summer vegetable, or not kept for use during the winter.—**summer time,** a method of reckoning time during the summer, as in connection with the practice known as 'daylight saving' (which see, under *daylight*). Cf. *summertime*, below.—**summer wheat.** See under *wheat*.—**sum′mer³,** *v.* **I.** *intr.* To spend or pass the summer. **II.** *tr.* To keep, feed, or manage during the summer; also, to make summer-like.

sum-mer=house (sum′ėr-hous), *n.* A house for summer residence, as in the country (now rare); also, a structure in a park or garden, usually of simple and often rustic character, intended to provide a shady and cool place in the heat of summer.

sum-mer-i-ness (sum′ėr-i-nes), *n.* Summery character.

sum-mer-less (sum′ėr-les), *a.* Having no summer; without summer weather.

sum-mer-ly (sum′ėr-li), *a.* Summer-like; summery.

sum′mer-sault, sum′mer-set. See *somersault, somerset.*

sum-mer-tide (sum′ėr-tīd), *n.* Summertime. [Now chiefly poetic.]

sum-mer-time (sum′ėr-tīm), *n.* The season of summer. Cf. *summer time*, under *summer³*, *a.*

sum-mer-y (sum′ėr-i), *a.* Of, like, or befitting summer.

sum-mit (sum′it), *n.* [OF. *somete*, also *somet* (F. *sommet*), dim. of *som*, < L. *summum*, highest point, top, prop. neut. of *summus*: see *sum*, *n.*] The highest point or part, as of a hill, a line of travel, or any object; the top; the apex; fig., the highest point of attainment or aspiration (as, "This [appointment] had been the *summit* of Mr. Bertram's ambition": Scott's "Guy Mannering," vi.); the highest stage or degree (as, "The *summits* of emotion can only be reached at rare intervals": Maugham's "Moon and Sixpence," xliii.); the culmination; the acme.—**sum′mit-al**, *a.*

sum-mon (sum′ọn), *v. t.* [OF. *somondre* (F. *semondre*), < ML. *summonere*, summon, L. remind privily, < L. *sub*, under, + *monere*, remind.] To call or notify by authority to appear at a place specified, esp. before a court (as, to *summon* a defendant or a witness); call together (an assembly, council, or other body) by authority, as for deliberation or action (as, to *summon* a parliament); call (a person) to a peerage (from the practice of summoning peers by a special writ to attendance at Parliament: Great Britain); in general, to call for the presence or attendance of, as by command, message, or signal; bid come; call (*to, away, from*, etc.: as, "His letters at Lugano *summoned* him to England instantly," G. Meredith's "Diana of the Crossways," xvi.); also, to call as with authority to some duty, task, or performance (as, to *summon* men to the defense of their country; the muezzin *summons* the people to prayer); call upon (to do something: as, "Orders were sent . . . to the commandant . . . to *summon* the intruder to depart," Bancroft's "Hist. of the U. S.," Amer. Revolution, i. 2; to *summon* a fortress to surrender); specif., to call upon to surrender (as, "The fortress . . . was immediately invested, and *summoned* by Oubacha": De Quincey's "Revolt of the Tartars"); also, to call into action (often with *up*: as, to *summon*, or *summon* up, all one's courage); rouse; call forth.—**sum′mon-er**, *n.* [OF. *somoneor* (F. *semonneur*).] One who summons; formerly, a petty officer charged with warning persons to appear in court.—**sum-mons** (sum′ọnz), *n.*; pl. *summonses* (-ọn-zez). [OF. *somonse* (F. *semonce*).] An authoritative call or notice to appear at a specified place, as for a particular purpose or duty; a call or citation by authority to appear before a court or a judicial officer, or the writ by which the call is made; a call issued for the meeting of an assembly or parliament; in general, an authoritative or peremptory call (as, "A very sudden and urgent *summons* of duty calls him to a great distance": C. Brontë's "Villette," xxxviii.); a command, message, or signal by which one is summoned (as, "Mrs. Thornburgh motioned to him to come . . . a *summons* which he obeyed with . . . alacrity": Mrs. H. Ward's "Robert Elsmere," iii.); also, a call to do something (as, a *summons* to surrender).—**sum′mons**, *v. t.* To serve with a summons; summon: as, "Say another word, and I'll *summons* you" (Dickens's "Nicholas Nickleby," xxxviii.). [Now prov. or colloq.]

sum-mum bo-num (sum′um bō′num). [L.] The highest or chief good.

sump (sump), *n.* [ME. *sompe* = D. *somp* = MLG. *sump* = G. *sumpf*, swamp: cf. *swamp*.] A swamp, bog, or muddy pool (now prov. Eng.); also, a pit, well, or the like in which water or other liquid is collected; in *mining*, a space at the bottom of a shaft where water is allowed to collect; in *mech.*, a reservoir for oil situated at the lowest point in a circulating system for lubricating-oil in an internal-combustion engine.

sumph (sumf), *n.* [Origin obscure.] A stupid person; a blockhead; a simpleton; also, a surly person. [Sc. and north. Eng.]

sum-pi-tan (sum′pi-tạn), *n.* [Malay.] A kind of blow-gun used by the Dyaks and Malays of Borneo for shooting darts, which are often poisoned.

sump-si-mus (sump′si-mus), *n.* [L., 'we have taken': see *mumpsimus*.] A correct expression for replacing an erroneous one in familiar use; a correct but undesired substitute for a habitual error. Cf. *mumpsimus.*

sump-ter (sump′tėr), *n.* [OF. *sommetier*, packhorse driver, packhorse, through ML. < LL. *sagma*, pack-saddle: see *summer²*.] A packhorse driver†; also, a packhorse or any animal for carrying baggage, etc. (archaic: often attrib., as in 'sumpter animals,' 'sumpter camels'); also, a pack or bag carried by a pack-animal†.—**sump′ter=horse**, *n.* A packhorse; a horse for carrying baggage, etc.: as, "Our aunt . . . advised her brother to provide a *sumpter-horse*, with store of hams, tongues, bread" (Smollett's "Humphry Clinker," July 18). [Archaic.]

sump-tu-a-ry (sump′tụ-ā-ri), *a.* [L. *sumptuarius*, < *sumptus*, expense: see *sumptuous*.] Pertaining to, dealing with, or regulating expense or expenditure: as, *sumptuary* laws (designed to curb luxury in dress, living, etc.); "When Sunday came, it was indeed a day of finery, which all my *sumptuary* edicts could not restrain" (Goldsmith's "Vicar of Wakefield," iv.).

sump-tu-ous (sump′tụ-us), *a.* [L. *sumptuosus*, < *sumptus*, expense, < *sumere*, take, use, spend, < *sub*, under, + *emere*, take, buy.] Entailing great expense, as from fine workmanship, choice or rich materials, or elegant appointments (as, a *sumptuous* residence, banquet, or funeral; *sumptuous* apparel or living; a *sumptuous* edition); costly; luxuriously fine or elegant; magnificent; rich; also, lavish or superb in appearance (as, *sumptuous* beauty; "She . . . turn'd her *sumptuous* head with eyes Of shining expectation," Tennyson's "Princess," iv. 134); also, lavish in expenditure†; luxurious in manner of living†.—**sump-tu-os′i-ty** (-os′i-ti), **sump′tu-ous-ness**, *n.*—**sump′tu-ous-ly**, *adv.*

sun¹ (sun), *n.* See *sunn.*

sun² (sun), *n.* [AS. *sunne* = D. *zon* = G. *sonne* = Icel. *sunna* = Goth. *sunnō*, sun; from the same root as L. *sol*, sun: see *Sol¹*, and cf. *south*.] The central body of the solar system (often classed with the fixed stars), around which the earth and the other planets revolve, and from which they receive light and heat (having a mean distance from the earth of about 93,000,000 miles, a diameter of about 866,500 miles, a volume about 1,300,000 times as great as the earth's, a mass about 330,000 times as great as the earth's, a mean density of about one fourth the earth's, and a period of surface rotation of about 25 days at its equator but of different values in other parts); also, some similar heavenly body; a fixed star; a star as the center of a system of worlds (as, "Other *suns* perhaps, With their attendant moons, thou wilt descry": Milton's "Paradise Lost," viii. 148); also, the sun considered with reference to its position in the sky, its visibility, the season of the year, the time at which or the place where it is seen, etc. (as, the rising or the setting *sun*; there was no *sun* to-day; the summer *sun*; the midnight *sun*, see under *midnight, a.*; under Eastern *suns*); the direct light of the sun, or sunshine (as, to be exposed to the *sun*; a place in the *sun*, see under *place, n.*); sunrise, also sunset (archaic: as, from *sun* to *sun*, from sunrise to sunset); a day (poetic: as, "by the fifth hour of the *sun*," Shakspere's "Troilus and Cressida," ii. 1. 134); a year as the period of the sun's apparent revolution in the zodiac (poetic: as, "Vile it were For some three *suns* to store and hoard myself," Tennyson's "Ulysses," 29); a parhelion, or sun-like spot or appearance in the sky; a figure or representation of the sun, as a heraldic bearing usually surrounded with rays and charged with the features of a human face; fig., something likened to the sun in brightness, splendor, etc.; that which is the chief source of light, honor, glory, or prosperity (as, "when the *sun* of my prosperity began to arise": Scott's "Bride of Lammermoor," xxi.).—**mean sun**, an imaginary or fictitious sun moving uniformly in the celestial equator and taking the same time to make its annual circuit as the true sun does in the ecliptic.—**mock sun**. Same as *parhelion.*—**under the sun**, on earth; in the world: as, "There is no new thing *under the sun*" (Eccl. i. 9).—**sun²**, *v.; sunned, sunning.* **I.** *tr.* To expose to the sun's rays (as, "Edwin and Mrs. Hamps were *sunning* themselves in the garden": Arnold Bennett's "Clayhanger," iii. 10); warm, dry, etc., in the sunshine; put, bring, make, etc. (as specified), by exposure to the sun's rays; also, to shine upon, as the sun does. **II.** *intr.* To expose one's self to the sun's rays (as, "We were *sunning* on the pier": A. S. M. Hutchinson's "If Winter Comes," iv. 3); bask in the sunshine; also, to shine as or like the sun.

Heraldic Sun.

sun=baked (sun′bākt), *a.* Baked by exposure to the sun, as bricks; also, excessively heated by the sun; parched, dried, or hardened by the heat of the sun.

sun-bath (sun′bath), *n.* An exposure of the body to the direct rays of the sun, esp. as a therapeutic measure.

sun-beam (sun′bēm), *n.* [AS. *sunbēam*.] A beam or ray of sunlight. Also fig., esp. as an epithet for a cheery person, esp. a child: as, little *sunbeam.*

sun=bear (sun'bār), *n.* A small bear, *Helarctos malayanus*, of southern Asia.

sun-bird (sun'bėrd), *n.* Any of various small, brilliantly colored, old-world birds of the family *Nectariniidæ*; also, the sun-bittern.

sun=bit-tern (sun'bit''ėrn), *n.* A South American bird, *Eurypyga helias*, with variegated plumage. See cut below.

Sun-bear.

sun-bon-net (sun'bon''et), *n.* A large bonnet of cotton or other light material shading the face and projecting down over the neck: worn by women and girls.

sun-bow (sun'bō), *n.* A bow or arc of prismatic colors like a rainbow, appearing in the spray of cataracts, etc.

sun-burn (sun'bėrn), *n.* Superficial inflammation of the skin, caused by exposure to the sun's rays; the discoloration or tan so produced.—**sun'burn,** *v. t.* or *i.* To affect or be affected with sunburn.—**sun'burned, sun'burnt,** *a.* Burned, scorched, or browned by the sun; tanned.

sun-burst (sun'bėrst), *n.* A burst of sunlight; a sudden shining of the sun through rifted clouds; also, a firework, a piece of jewelry, a decorative ornament, or the like, resembling the sun with its rays issuing in all directions.

sun-dae (sun'dā), *n.* [Origin unknown.] An individual portion of ice-cream with fruit or other syrup poured over it, and often whipped cream, minced nuts, or other additions.

sun=dance (sun'dàns), *n.* A religious ceremony associated with the sun, practised by North American Indians of the Plains, consisting of dancing attended with various symbolic rites, commonly including self-torture.

Sun-day (sun'dā), *n.* [AS. *sunnandæg,* 'sun's day,' used to render LL. *dies solis.*] The first day of the week; the Christian Sabbath.—**Sun'day=school,** *n.* A school, now usually in connection with a church, for religious (and formerly also secular) instruction on Sunday; also, the members of such a school.

sun-der (sun'dėr), *n.* [From the adv. phrase, ME. *in sunder,* for AS. *on sundran, onsundran,* asunder, < *on,* on, in, + *sundor,* adv., apart, = Icel. *sundr,* Goth. *sundrō,* OHG. *suntar,* apart (cf. G. *sonder,* adj., separate, as prep., without): cf. *asunder.*] The state of being put asunder, separated, parted, or severed: used in the phrase 'in sunder': as, "Gnawing with my teeth my bonds *in sunder,* I gain'd my freedom" (Shakspere's "Comedy of Errors," v. 1. 249).—**sun'der,** *v.* [AS. *sundrian, syndrian,* < *sundor.*] **I.** *tr.* To separate; part; divide; sever. **II.** *intr.* To become separated; part.—**sun'der-ance,** *n.* The act of sundering, or the resulting state; separation; severance. Also **sun'der-ment.**

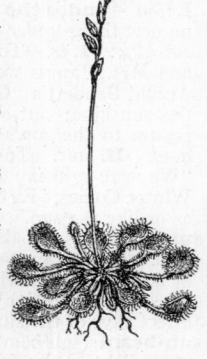
Sundew (*Drosera rotundifolia*).

Sun-bittern.

sun-dew (sun'dū), *n.* [= D. *zonnedauw,* G. *sonnentau,* tr. L. *ros solis,* 'dew of the sun': cf. *rosolio.*] Any of the small bog-inhabiting herbs constituting the genus *Drosera,* the species of which have leaves covered with glandular hairs which secrete viscid dew-like drops and give to the plant the means of capturing and retaining insects from which it eventually absorbs nutriment (see cut in preceding column); more broadly, any droseraceous plant.

sun=di-al (sun'dī''al), *n.* An instrument for indicating the time of day by the position of a shadow (as of a gnomon) cast by the sun on a graduated plate or surface; a dial.

sun=disk (sun'disk), *n.* The disk of the sun; also, a figure or representation of this, esp. in religious symbolism.

Sun-dial.—Face of horizontal dial, shadow pointing to one o'clock.

sun=dog (sun'dog), *n.* A parhelion; also, a small or incomplete rainbow.

sun-down (sun'doun), *n.* The going down of the sun, or sunset; the time of sunset (as, "By the time I reached home, it was *sundown*": C. Brontë's "Villette," xxxiv.); the region or quarter of sunset, or the west (as, "Have you been far towards the *sun-down?*" Cooper's "Prairie," ii.); also, a kind of broad-brimmed hat formerly worn by women (U. S.). —**sun'down''er,** *n.* A tramp who makes a practice of arriving at some station at sundown under the pretense of seeking work, so as to obtain food and a night's lodging. [Australia.]—**sun'down''ing,** *n.*

sun=dried (sun'drīd), *a.* Dried in the sun, as bricks, raisins, etc.; also, dried up, withered, or parched by the sun.

sun-dries (sun'driz), *n. pl.* Sundry things or items (not individually specified): as, "Mr. Giles, Brittles, and the tinker were recruiting themselves . . . with tea and *sundries*" (Dickens's "Oliver Twist," xxviii.).

sun-drops (sun'drops), *n.* Any of various plants of the onagraceous genus *Kneiffia,* related to the evening primrose but having yellow flowers that open by day, esp. *K. fruticosa,* a hardy species of eastern North America.

sun-dry (sun'dri), *a.* [AS. *syndrig,* < *sundor,* apart: see *sunder.*] Separate, distinct, or individual (now chiefly as in 'all and sundry': see phrase below); also, different†; hence, various or divers (as, *sundry* kinds or sorts); a number of, or several (without specification of individuals: as, *sundry* persons).—**all and sundry,** all, both collectively and individually (now usually without a noun following): as, to give notice to *all and sundry.*

sun=dry (sun'dri), *v. t.* or *i.,* *-dried, -drying.* [Back-formation from *sun-dried.*] To dry in the sun.

sun-fish (sun'fish), *n.* A large marine fish, *Mola mola,* with a deep body abbreviated behind; also, any of various small fresh-water acanthopterygian fishes of the genera *Eupomotis* and *Lepomis,* and allied genera, of North America, with a deep, compressed body; also, the basking-shark; also, a jellyfish.

sun=flow-er (sun'flou''ėr), *n.* Any plant of the asteraceous genus *Helianthus,* characterized by yellow-rayed flowers, as *H. annuus,* the common species of North America, a tall plant grown for its showy flowers, and for its seeds which are valued as food for poultry and as the source of an oil (see cut on following page); also, any of various other plants, as a yellow-

Sunfish (*Mola mola*).

Sundrops (*Kneiffia fruticosa*).—1, the upper part of the plant with the flowers; 2, the lower part of the plant; *a,* a flower; *b,* the fruit.

flowered asteraceous herb, *Heliopsis helianthoides*, of North America ('false sunflower,' or 'oxeye'), or a yellow-flowered asteraceous herb, *Helenium autumnale*, of North America (also called 'false sunflower,' 'swamp sunflower,' and 'sneezeweed').

sung (sung). Preterit and past participle of *sing*.

sun=glass (sun′glås), *n.* A burning-glass.

sun=glow (sun′glō), *n.* A diffused hazy light seen around the sun, due to particles of foreign matter in the atmosphere; also, the glow or warm light of the sun.

sun=god (sun′god), *n.* The sun considered or personified as a deity; a god identified or associated with the sun.

sunk (sungk). Preterit and past participle of *sink*.—**sunk,** *p. a.* Sunken; esp., depressed or lying below the general level (as, a *sunk* panel; a *sunk* fence, a ha-ha, or trench serving as a fence).—**sunk′en,** *p. a.* Having sunk or having been sunk beneath the surface, as of water; submerged, as a wreck or a rock; having settled down to a lower level, as walls; depressed or lying below the general level, as a garden or a military battery; having fallen in or become hollow, as cheeks or eyes (as, "the mourner's *sunken* eye": Scott's "Lady of the Lake," iii. 18).

sun=less (sun′les), *a.* Without sun or sunlight: as, "a region of *sunless*, tangled forests" (Roosevelt's "Winning of the West," i. 4).—**sun′less-ness,** *n.*

sun=let (sun′let), *n.* A little sun.

sun=light (sun′līt), *n.* The light of the sun.—**sun′lit,** *a.* Lighted or illuminated by the sun: as, "a far-seen, *sunlit* mountain-side" (Whittier's "Prophecy of Samuel Sewall").

sunn (sun), *n.* [Hind. *san*; from Skt.] A tall East Indian fabaceous shrub, *Crotalaria juncea*, with slender branches and yellow flowers, and an inner bark which yields a hemp-like fiber used for making ropes, sacking, etc.; also, the fiber.

Sun-na, Sun-nah (sun′ą), *n.* [Ar., lit. 'path.'] The traditionary portion of Moslem law, based on Mohammed's words and acts, but not written by him, which is accepted as authoritative by the so-called orthodox Mohammedans, or Sunnites.—**Sun-ni** (sun′ē), *n.*; pl. *Sunnis* (-ēz). [Ar.] A Sunnite.

sun-ni-ly (sun′i-li), *adv.* In a sunny manner.—**sun′ni-ness,** *n.*

Sun-nite (sun′īt), *n.* [See *Sunna.*] One of the so-called orthodox Mohammedans, who accept the Sunna as of equal importance with the Koran. Cf. *Shiite* and *Shiah.*

sun-ny (sun′i), *a.*; compar. *sunnier*, superl. *sunniest*. Abounding in sunshine (as, a *sunny* day); exposed to or lighted or warmed by the direct rays of the sun (as, "the *sunniest*, cosiest room in the city": W. Churchill's "Coniston," ii. 8); also, pertaining to or proceeding from the sun; solar; also, resembling the sun, as in brightness or color; shining; radiant; bright-yellow or golden (as, "Her *sunny* locks Hang on her temples like a golden fleece": Shakspere's "Merchant of Venice," i. 1. 169); fig., cheery, cheerful, or joyous (as, "the *sunniest* disposition": Hawthorne's "Scarlet Letter," The Custom House).

sun=par-lor (sun′pär′′lọr), *n.* A parlor or apartment exposed to the sun's rays; a solarium: as, "a sleeping-porch with a *sun-parlor* below" (Sinclair Lewis's "Babbitt," vii.).

sun=proof (sun′pröf), *a.* Proof against the sun; impervious to or unaffected by the rays of the sun.

sun-rise (sun′rīz), *n.* The rise or ascent of the sun above the horizon in the morning; the atmospheric phenomena accompanying this; also, the time when the sun rises; also, the region or quarter where the sun rises; the east.—**sun′ris′′ing** (-rī′′zing), *n.* Sunrise: as, "Jerry . . . was frequently whistling and singing . . . before *sun-rising*" (R. Graves's "Spiritual Quixote," ii. 8); "Toward the *sun-rising* it was bright and clear" (Bancroft's "Hist. of the U. S.," Amer. Revolution, i. 4). [Archaic.]

sun-set (sun′set), *n.* The setting or descent of the sun below the horizon in the evening; the atmospheric phenomena accompanying this; also, the time when the sun sets (as, "It was agreed that Alan should fend for himself till *sunset*": Stevenson's "Kidnapped," xxvii.); the close of day; fig., the close or final stage of any period (as, "the *sunset* of life": Campbell's "Lochiel's Warning"); also, the region or quarter where the sun sets; the west.—**sun′set′′ting,** *n.* Sunset.

sun-shade (sun′shād), *n.* Something used as a protection from the rays of the sun; esp., a parasol (as, "a new season's *sunshade* with a crooked handle": H. G. Wells's "Kipps," i. 6); also, a device of dark or colored glass used upon a sextant or telescope to diminish the intensity of the light in observing the sun.

sun-shine (sun′shīn), *n.* The shining of the sun; the direct light of the sun, uninterrupted by clouds or other obstacles (cf. *shade*); fig., brightness, radiance, or sunny appearance; cheerfulness or happiness; prosperity; genial or cheering influence; a source of cheer or happiness (as, the child is the *sunshine* of the house: cf. *sunbeam*).—**sun′shin′′y** (-shī′′ni), *a.* Abounding in sunshine; sunny.

sun-spot (sun′spot), *n.* One of the relatively dark patches which appear periodically on the surface of the sun, and which are supposed to have a certain effect on terrestrial magnetism and meteorological phenomena.

sun-star (sun′stär), *n.* Any of various starfishes having many rays, as *Brisinga coronata*, a deep-sea species.

sun-stroke (sun′strōk), *n.* In *pathol.*, a frequently fatal affection due to exposure to the sun's rays or to excessive heat, marked by sudden prostration, with or without fever, and symptoms resembling those of apoplexy; insolation.—**sun′struck,** *a.* Overcome by the heat of the sun; affected with sunstroke.

sun-up (sun′up), *n.* Sunrise: as, "It was after *sun-up*" (Mark Twain's "Huckleberry Finn," vii.). [Prov.]

sun-ward (sun′wạrd), *adv.* and *a.* Toward the sun.—**sun′-wards,** *adv.*

sun-wise (sun′wīz), *adv.* and *a.* In the direction of the sun's apparent daily motion; commonly, in a circuit from left to right about a point or object; clockwise.

sup[1] (sup), *v.*; *supped, supping.* [AS. *sūpan* = Icel. *sūpa*, sup, drink, = D. *zuipen*, G. *saufen*, drink: cf. *sip, sop, soup*, and *sup*[2].] **I.** *tr.* To take (liquid food, or any liquid) into the mouth in small quantities, as from a spoon or a cup (as, "At the head of his dinner-table . . . Horace Pendyce *supped* his soup," Galsworthy's "Country House," i. 1: now chiefly prov.); fig., to swallow up† or engulf†; also, to taste, or have experience of (used esp. in 'to sup sorrow': archaic or prov.). **II.** *intr.* To take liquid into the mouth in small quantities, as by spoonfuls or sips. [Now chiefly prov.]—

sup[1], *n.* A mouthful or small portion of liquid food or of drink: as, "As I was very thirsty too, I took a little *sup* of it [water]" (Defoe's "Robinson Crusoe," i. 16); "Drink a *sup* now" (Synge's "Tinker's Wedding," i.). [Now chiefly prov.]

sup[2] (sup), *v.*; *supped, supping.* [OF. *soper, super* (F. *souper*): cf. *supper, sup*[1], and *soup*.] **I.** *intr.* To eat the evening meal, or the last meal of the day; take supper: as, "When my uncle Toby dined or *supped* alone, he would never suffer the corporal to stand" (Sterne's "Tristram Shandy," vi. 6); "They were all to *sup* at Mr. Merrill's house" (W. Churchill's "Coniston," ii. 7). **II.** *tr.* To eat

Sunflower (*Helianthus annuus*).

Sunn (*Crotalaria juncea*).

Sun-star (*Brisinga coronata*).

(variable) d̦ as d or j, ş as s or sh, ț as t or ch, z̦ as z or zh; o, F. cloche; ü, F. menu; ċh, Sc. loch; ṅ, F. bonbon; ′, primary accent; ″, secondary accent; †, obsolete; <, from; +, and; =, equals. See also lists at beginning of book.

for supper (obs. or rare); also, to serve as a supper for†; also, to provide with supper; entertain at supper.

supe (sūp), *n.* A shortened form of *superintendent* and of *supernumerary.* Cf. *super, n.* [Slang.]

super-. [L. *super-,* repr. *super,* adv. and prep., over, above, beyond; akin to Gr. ὑπέρ, over, and E. *over:* see *hyper-* and *over.*] A prefix meaning 'over,' 'above,' 'beyond,' and hence 'more than usually,' 'exceedingly,' or 'to excess,' occurring in many words from the Latin, and also used freely as an English formative, as in *superclass, superdreadnought, super-heat, superman, supernormal, superphysical, supersensitive, superstate, supertax,* and many like combinations, mostly self-explanatory. In chemical terms *super-* (like *hyper-*), as indicating the maximum or a high proportion of an ingredient, is now commonly replaced by *per-*; in a few words it indicates an acid (rather than a basic) character. Cf. *supra-, sur-,* and *sub-.*

su-per (sū′pėr), *n.* A shortened form of *superintendent, supernumerary* (esp. in theatrical use), and various other words beginning with the same prefix. [Colloq. or slang.]—**su′per,** *a.* A shortened form of *superficial* and of *superfine* (esp. in trade use). [Colloq.]

su-per-a-ble (sū′pėr-ạ-bl), *a.* [L. *superabilis,* < *superare,* surmount, overcome, < *super,* over: see *super-.*] Capable of being overcome; surmountable.—**su″per-a-bil′i-ty** (-bil′-i-ti), *n.*

su-per-a-bound (sū″pėr-ạ-bound′), *v. i.* [LL. *superabundare,* < L. *super,* over, + *abundare,* E. *abound.*] To abound beyond something else; be even more abundant; also, to abound beyond the usual or proper measure; be very abundant or too abundant; abound greatly or excessively (*in* or *with*).—**su″per-a-bun′dance** (-bun′dạns), *n.* The state of being superabundant; great or excessive abundance; a superabundant quantity or amount (as, "a *superabundance* of evidence": W. D. Whitney's "Life and Growth of Language," ix.); an excess or surplus.—**su″per-a-bun′dant,** *a.* [LL. *superabundans* (-*ant-*), ppr.] Superabounding, or exceedingly or excessively abundant; being more than sufficient; excessive: as, "You must calm your *superabundant* energies, and be quiet" (Miss Mulock's "John Halifax," ix.).—**su″per-a-bun′dant-ly,** *adv.*

su-per-a-cid (sū-pėr-as′id), *a.* [See *super-.*] Excessively acid.

su-per-a-cute (sū″pėr-ạ-kūt′), *a.* [See *super-.*] Excessively acute.

su-per-add (sū-pėr-ad′), *v. t.* [L. *superaddere,* < *super,* over, + *addere,* E. *add.*] To add over and above; join as a further addition; add besides: as, "Jealousy was now *superadded* to a deeply-rooted enmity" (J. F. Kirk's "Charles the Bold," iii. 2).—**su″per-ad-di′tion** (-a-dish′ọn), *n.*

su-per-al-tar (sū′pėr-ȧl″tär), *n.* [ML. *superaltare,* < L. *super,* over, + *altare,* E. *altar.*] *Eccles.,* a portable stone slab consecrated for use upon an unconsecrated altar or upon a table or the like; also, a structure above and at the back of an altar, as a reredos or a gradin.

su-per-an-nu-ate (sū-pėr-an′ū-āt), *v.; -ated, -ating.* [First in *superannuated, pp.,* for earlier *superannated,* < ML. *superannatus,* more than a year old, < L. *super,* over, + *annus,* year: cf. F. *suranné,* orig. more than a year old, hence out of date, antiquated.] **I.** *tr.* To render out of date, antiquated, or obsolete, as time does; render too old, as for use, service, or a position; also, to set aside as out of date; remove or dismiss as too old; allow to retire from service or office on a pension, on account of age or infirmity: used esp. in *superannuated, p. a.* **II.** *intr.* To become too old, as for a position or office; reach the age of superannuation.—**su-per-an′nu-ate. I.** *a.* Superannuated. **II.** *n.* A superannuated person.—**su-per-an′nu-at-ed** (-ā-ted), *p. a.* Antiquated or obsolete (as, "*superannuated* worn-out Symbols": Carlyle's "Sartor Resartus," iii. 3); also, incapacitated or enfeebled by age, as a person or animal; too old for use, work, service, or a position held (as, "He left the house . . . for the support of twelve *superannuated* wool-carders": Trollope's "Warden," i.); also, retired from service or office on a pension, on account of age or infirmity.—**su-per-an-nu-a′tion** (-ā′shọn), *n.* The act of superannuating, or the state of being superannuated; also, a pension or allowance granted to a superannuated person.

su-perb (sū-pėrb′), *a.* [L. *superbus,* proud, haughty, arrogant, magnificent, splendid, < *super,* over: see *super-.*] Proud or haughty (obs. or archaic: as, "She ordered away grandees . . . informing them, with a *superb* manner, that she wished to speak to her cousin," Thackeray's "Newcomes," xli.; "that majestic dame who had conceded a *superb* recognition to him," Disraeli's "Coningsby," iv. 9); also, of a proudly imposing appearance or kind (as, "the *superb* mausoleums of sovereigns," Wiseman's "Fabiola," ii. 1; *superb* beauty; a *superb* air); stately, majestic, or grand; magnificent or splendid (as, *superb* jewels; a *superb* edition); admirably fine or excellent (as, a *superb* portrait; a *superb* performance; "a *superb* horsewoman," A. S. M. Hutchinson's "If Winter Comes," ii. 1; "Accident had given Doria *superb* opportunities," Eden Phillpotts's "Red Redmaynes," viii.).—**superb bird of paradise,** a bird of paradise, *Lophorhina superba,* of New Guinea, remarkable (in the male) for its breast-shield and neck-piece of feathers and for the beauty of its coloring, velvety-black with rich iridescence, metallic green,etc.—**superb′ly,** *adv.* —**su-perb′-ness,** *n.*

Superb Bird of Paradise (*Lophorhina superba*), male.

su-per-cal-en-der (sū-pėr-kal′ẹn-dėr), *v. t.* [See *super-.*] To give a high gloss or extra smoothness to (paper or the like) by passing it through an additional and special calender. —**su-per-cal′en-der,** *n.* The special calender used in supercalendering.

su-per-car-go (sū-pėr-kär′gō), *n.; pl. -goes* or *-gos* (-gōz). [Earlier *supracargo,* < Sp. *sobrecargo,* < *sobre* (< L. *super*), over, + *cargo,* E. *cargo.*] An officer on a merchant ship who is in charge of the cargo and the commercial concerns of the voyage: as, "The question was, whether I would go their *supercargo* in the ship, to manage the trading part upon the coast of Guinea" (Defoe's "Robinson Crusoe," i. 3).—**su-per-car′go-ship,** *n.*

su-per-cil-i-a-ry (sū-pėr-sil′i-ạ-ri), *a.* [NL. *superciliaris,* < L. *supercilium,* eyebrow: see *supercilious.*] In *anat.* and *zoöl.,* of or pertaining to the eyebrow; situated over the eye; also, having a conspicuous marking over the eye, as certain birds.

su-per-cil-i-ous (sū-pėr-sil′i-us), *a.* [L. *superciliosus,* < *supercilium,* eyebrow, pride, haughtiness, < *super,* over, + *cilium,* eyelid: cf. *cilia.*] Haughtily disdainful or contemptuous, as persons or their glance, expression, air, or bearing toward others (as, "The *supercilious*-looking man . . . is Mr. Luke, the great critic and apostle of culture," Mallock's "New Republic," i. 2; "He listened . . . with a *supercilious* smile," Cooper's "Spy," vii.); affecting or showing a haughty or scornful contempt, as for persons deemed greatly inferior or of little importance; also, overbearing† or dictatorial†.—**su-per-cil′i-ous-ly,** *adv.*—**su-per-cil′i-ous-ness,** *n.*

su-per-class (sū′pėr-klȧs), *n.* [See *super-.*] In *zoöl.* and *bot.,* a group or category ranking above a class.

su-per-cool (sū-pėr-köl′), *v.* [See *super-.*] In *physical chem.:* **I.** *tr.* To cool (a liquid) below its freezing-point without producing solidification. **II.** *intr.* To become supercooled.

su-per-dread-nought (sū′pėr-dred″nȧt), *n.* [See *super-.*] A battle-ship of the general type of the dreadnought, but much larger and with superior armament.

su-per-em-i-nent (sū-pėr-em′i-nẹnt), *a.* [L. *supereminens* (-*ent-*), ppr. of *supereminere,* < *super,* over, + *eminere,* stand out: see *eminent.*] Standing out or rising above others (now rare); fig., of superior eminence, rank, or dignity;

distinguished, conspicuous, or noteworthy above others; surpassingly eminent.—**su-per-em'i-nence**, *n.*—**su-per-em'i-nent-ly**, *adv.*

su-per-er-o-gate (sū-pėr-er'ọ-gāt), *v. i.*; *-gated, -gating.* [LL. *supererogatus*, pp. of *supererogare*, pay out over and above, < L. *super*, over, + *erogare*, pay out (from the public treasury, after asking consent of the people), < *e*, out of, + *rogare*, ask.] To do more than duty requires.—**su-per-er-o-ga'tion** (-gā'shọn), *n.* [LL. *supererogatio(n-)*.] The act of supererogating; performance of more than duty requires: as, works of supererogation (specif., in *Rom. Cath. theol.*, good works beyond what God requires, performed by some, but held to be of avail, by dispensation of the church, toward the salvation of others).—**su″per-e-rog'a-to-ry** (-e-rog'ạ-tọ-ri), *a.* Characterized by, or of the nature of, supererogation; going beyond the requirements of duty; superfluous: as, "He continued silent, as if he deemed discussion altogether *supererogatory*" (Cooper's "Two Admirals," vii.).

su-per-ex-cel-lent (sū-pėr-ek'sẹ-lẹnt), *a.* [LL. *superexcellens* (-ent-): see *super-* and *excellent*.] Of superior or surpassing excellence.—**su-per-ex'cel-lence**, *n.*—**su-per-ex'cel-lent-ly**, *adv.*

su-per-fam-i-ly (sū'pėr-fam″i-li), *n.*; pl. *-lies* (-liz). [See *super-*.] In *zoöl.* and *bot.*, a group or category ranking above a family.

su-per-fec-un-da-tion (sū″pėr-fek-un-dā'shọn), *n.* [See *super-*.] In *physiol.*, the fertilization of two ova at the same menstruation by two different acts of coition.

su-per-fe-ta-tion (sū″pėr-fẹ-tā'shọn), *n.* [= F. *superfétation*, < L. *superfetare*, < *super*, over, + *fetare*, breed.] In *physiol.*, a second conception occurring after a prior conception, but before the first one has run its course. Also fig.

su-per-fi-cial (sū-pėr-fish'ạl). [LL. *superficialis*, < L. *superficies*: see *superficies*.] **I.** *a.* Of or pertaining to the superficies or surface (as, *superficial* measurement or extent); being at, on, or near the surface (as, a *superficial* layer; a *superficial* wound); external or outward (as, a *superficial* resemblance); also, concerned with or comprehending only what is on the surface or obvious (as, a *superficial* view, examination, or judgment; a *superficial* observer); shallow, or not profound or thorough (as, a *superficial* education; a *superficial* scholar or writer; "Only the most *superficial* mind would assert nowadays that man is a reasonable creature," H. G. Wells's "Mr. Britling," i. 4. § 4); also, without profound effects or significance (as, *superficial* changes); also, apparent, rather than real (as, *superficial* piety). **II.** *n. Pl.*, superficial features or characteristics: as, "Excepting in the merest *superficials*, there is a far greater variety in women than in men" (Watts-Dunton's "Aylwin," ii. 4).—**su-per-fi-ci-al'i-ty** (-fish-i-al'i-ti), *n.*; pl. *-ties* (-tiz). The state or quality of being superficial; also, something superficial.—**su-per-fi'cial-ly**, *adv.*—**su-per-fi'cial-ness**, *n.*

su-per-fi-cies (sū-pėr-fish'iēz), *n.*; pl. *superficies*. [L., upper side, surface, < *super*, over, + *facies*, E. *face*.] The surface, outer face, or outside of a thing; specif., a geometrical surface; also, the extent or area of surface; fig., the outward appearance, esp. as distinguished from the inner nature.

su-per-fine (sū'pėr-fīn), *a.* [See *super-*.] Extra fine; of unusually fine quality, as goods; in general, more than ordinarily fine; also, excessively fine, refined, or nice (as, "How could any one expect such a *superfine* dreamer to turn bread-winner for a wife and household?" Mrs. H. Ward's "Robert Elsmere," xxxi.).—**su'per-fine-ly**, *adv.*—**su'per-fine-ness**, *n.*

su-per-flu-i-ty (sū-pėr-flö'i-ti), *n.*; pl. *-ties* (-tiz). The state of being superfluous; superabundant or excessive amount; also, something superfluous or not needed, as a luxury (as, "The Scots . . . seem to vie with each other in purchasing *superfluities* from England, such as broadcloth, velvets . . . jewels": Smollett's "Humphry Clinker," Sept. 20).

su-per-flu-ous (sū-pėr'flö-us), *a.* [L. *superfluus*, < *superfluere*, overflow, < *super*, over, + *fluere*, flow.] Superabundant†, excessive†, or inordinate† (as, "A proper title of a peace; and purchased At a *superfluous* rate!" Shakspere's "Henry VIII.," i. 1. 99); also, being over and above what is sufficient or required (as, to lop off *superfluous* branches; omit all *superfluous* words); hence, in general, unnecessary or needless (as, "He blew out the now quite *superfluous* light," Wister's "Virginian," xxi.; "She had grown feeble and *superfluous*," Arnold Bennett's "Hilda Lessways," iv. 1; "It is *superfluous* to argue a point so clear," Macaulay's "Essays," Utilitarian Theory of Government); also, going further or doing more than is necessary (rare); lavish† or extravagant†.—**su-per'flu-ous-ly**, *adv.*—**su-per'flu-ous-ness**, *n.*

su-per-flux (sū'pėr-fluks), *n.* [ML. *superfluxus*, < L. *superfluere*: see *superfluous*.] An overflowing, or an excessive flow, as of water; fig., a superabundant amount; also, a superfluous amount, or surplus.

su-per-fœ-ta-tion (sū″pėr-fẹ-tā'shọn), *n.* See *superfetation*.

su-per-fuse[1] (sū-pėr-fūz'), *v.*; *-fused, -fusing.* [L. *superfusus*, pp. of *superfundere*, < *super*, over, + *fundere*, pour.] **I.** *tr.* To pour (a liquid, etc.) over or on something; also, to sprinkle or cover (something) with a liquid or the like poured on. **II.** *intr.* To be poured over or on something.—**su-per-fu'sion**[1] (-fū'zhọn), *n.*

su-per-fuse[2] (sū-pėr-fūz'), *v. t.*; *-fused, -fusing.* [See *super-* and *fuse*[1].] To heat (a substance, such as a basaltic rock) far above its fusing-point, so that it may remain molten for a long time; also, in *physical chem.*, to cool (a liquid) below its melting-point without producing solidification; supercool.—**su-per-fu'sion**[2] (-fū'zhọn), *n.*

su-per-gla-cial (sū-pėr-glā'shiạl), *a.* [See *super-*.] On the surface of a glacier.—**su-per-gla'cial-ly**, *adv.*

su-per-heat (sū-pėr-hēt'), *v. t.* [See *super-*.] To heat to an extreme degree or to a very high temperature; specif., to heat (a liquid) above its boiling-point without producing vaporization; also, to heat (a gas, as steam not in contact with water) to such a degree that its temperature may be lowered or its pressure increased without the conversion of any of the gas into the liquid form.—**su'per-heat**, *n.* The state of being superheated; the amount of superheating.—**su-per-heat'er**, *n.* A device for superheating steam.

su-per-het-er-o-dyne (sū-pėr-het'ẹ-rọ-dīn), *a.* [See *super-*.] In *wireless teleg.* and *teleph.*: **I.** *a.* Noting or pertaining to a method of receiving radio signals by which the incoming wave is changed by the heterodyne process to a lower frequency (the 'intermediate frequency,' which is inaudible and above the frequency of the ordinary heterodyne beats) and then submitted to a number of stages of radio-frequency amplification with subsequent detection and audio-frequency amplification. **II.** *n.* A superheterodyne receiver.

su-per-hu-man (sū-pėr-hū'mạn), *a.* [See *super-*.] Above or beyond what is human; having a higher nature or greater powers than man has (as, *superhuman* beings; "that *superhuman* man-eating monster supposed to be the guardian of the forest," W. H. Hudson's "Green Mansions," xxii.); exceeding what belongs or is possible to man, as power, actions, etc.; also, exceeding ordinary human power, achievement, experience, etc. (as, "By a *superhuman* effort I succeeded in keeping my eyes fixed on Ghyrkins," F. M. Crawford's "Mr. Isaacs," ix.; "*superhuman* pangs," Tennyson's "St. Simeon Stylites," 11).—**su″per-hu-man'i-ty** (-hụ-man'i-ti), *n.* The character of being superhuman.—**su-per-hu'man-ize**, *v. t.*; *-ized, -izing.* To make superhuman.—**su-per-hu'man-ly**, *adv.*—**su-per-hu'man-ness**, *n.*

su-per-im-pose (sū″pėr-im-pōz'), *v. t.*; *-posed, -posing.* [See *super-*.] To impose, place, or set on something else; fig., to put or join as an addition (with *on* or *upon*).—**su″per-im-po-si'tion** (-pọ-zish'ọn), *n.* The act of superimposing, or the state of being superimposed.

su-per-in-cum-bent (sū″pėr-in-kum'bẹnt), *a.* [L. *superincumbens* (-ent-), ppr. of *superincumbere*, < *super*, over, + *incumbere*, lie on: see *incumbent*.] Lying or resting on something else; situated above, or overhanging; exerted from above, as pressure.—**su″per-in-cum'bence**, *n.*

su-per-in-duce (sū″pėr-in-dūs'), *v. t.*; *-duced, -ducing.* [L. *superinducere*, < *super*, over, + *inducere*, lead in, E. *induce*.] To bring in or introduce in addition to or in the place of another (obs. or archaic); also, to bring in or induce

as an added feature, circumstance, etc.; superimpose.—
su″per-in-duc′tion (-duk′shon), *n.*

su-per-in-tend (sū″pèr-in-tend′), *v. t.* [LL. *superintendere*,
< L. *super*, over, + *intendere*, attend, E. *intend*.] To
oversee and direct (work, processes, affairs, etc.: as, "Marcus
Antoninus provided fourteen governors all at once to *superintend* his son Commodus's education," Sterne's "Tristram
Shandy," vi. 5); exercise supervision over; have the direction or management of (an institution, place, etc.: as, "He
intended to employ Adam in *superintending* the woods,"
George Eliot's "Adam Bede," xxii.).—**su″per-in-tend′-
ence**, *n.* The work or function of superintending: as, "a
treasurer, who acted as a sort of major-domo in the household, having a general *superintendence* over all its concerns"
(Prescott's "Conquest of Mexico," iv. 1).—**su″per-in-tend′-
en-cy**, *n.*; pl. *-cies* (-siz). The position, office, or work of a
superintendent; also, a district under the charge of a superintendent.—**su″per-in-tend′ent. I.** *a.* Superintending.
II. *n.* One who superintends; an official who has the oversight and direction of some work, enterprise, establishment,
or institution, or exercises supervision over some district.—
su″per-in-tend′ent-ship, *n.* The position of superintendent.—**su″per-in-tend′er**, *n.*

su-pe-ri-or (sū-pē′ri-or), *a.* [L., compar. of *superus*, being
above (superl. *supremus*, also *summus*), < *super*, over,
above: see *super-*, and cf. *sum*, *n.*, and *supreme*.] Higher
in place or position (now chiefly in scientific or technical
use); hence, higher in station, rank, degree, or grade (as,
"the middling and *superior* ranks of people," Adam Smith's
"Wealth of Nations," v. 2. 2. 4; a *superior* officer); more
elevated, exalted, or important; more effective or excellent
(as, "The Romans had defeated them, not by *superior*
courage, but by *superior* science": Froude's "Cæsar," xix.);
greater in quantity or amount (as, "The conflict was short,
from the *superior* numbers of the English": Marryat's
"King's Own," xlvi.); of higher grade or quality; hence, of
comparatively high grade, quality, or character; above the
average in excellence, merit, intelligence, culture, etc.; sometimes, showing a consciousness or feeling of being above
others in such respects (as, an oppressively *superior* person;
"She wanted none of Edwin's *superior* airs," Arnold Bennett's "Clayhanger," i. 8); also, of higher status, grade,
quality, etc., as opposed (*to*: as, to prove *superior* to all
others); hence, not yielding or susceptible (*to*: as, to be
superior to temptation or flattery); in *bot.*, situated above
some other organ; of a calyx, seeming to originate from the
top of the ovary; of an ovary, free from the calyx; in *printing*, higher than the main line of type, as algebraic exponents.
—**superior planets.** See under *planet.*—**su-pe′ri-or**, *n.*
One superior to another or others, as in rank, merit, or some
specified particular (as, "Oppressed by the exactions of their
superiors, they had recourse to arms," Hallam's "Europe
during the Middle Ages," ii. 2; "He was . . . his wife's
intellectual *superior*," Lytton Strachey's "Queen Victoria,"
iv.); *eccles.*, the head of a monastery, convent, or the like;
in *printing*, a superior letter or figure.—**su-pe′ri-or-ess**, *n.*
A female superior; a woman who is the head of a convent or
order of nuns.—**su-pe-ri-or′i-ty** (-or′i-ti), *n.* The state or
quality of being superior: as, "In discipline and equipments
the *superiority* was entirely with their enemies" (Cooper's
"Spy," xxxiii.); "a smile of intellectual *superiority*" (Dickens's "Pickwick Papers," li.).—**su-pe′ri-or-ly**, *adv.* In a
superior position, degree, or manner.

su-per-ja-cent (sū-pèr-jā′sent), *a.* [L. *superjacens* (-ent-),
ppr. of *superjacere*, lie over, < *super*, over, + *jacere*, lie.]
Lying above or upon something else; superincumbent.

su-per-la-tive (sū-pèr′la-tiv), *a.* [OF. F. *superlatif*, < LL.
superlativus, < L. *superlatus*, used as pp. of *superferre*,
carry over or beyond.] **I.** *a.* Of the highest kind or order,
or surpassing all other or others (as, *superlative* excellence or
wisdom; a *superlative* success; "the *superlative* social event
of the afternoon," Arnold Bennett's "Pretty Lady," xxiii.);
supreme; extreme (as, "Our loyal laymen can be at times
quite *superlative* bores": H. G. Wells's "Soul of a Bishop,"
vi.); in *gram.*, expressing the greatest degree of the quality
or manner denoted by a positive adjective or adverb (cf.
positive, *a.*). **II.** *n.* Something superlative; a superlative
example (as, "The animal [a bull-terrier] was a *superlative*

of forbidding ugliness": Arnold Bennett's "Old Wives'
Tale," ii. 4); the utmost degree; in *gram.*, the superlative
degree, or that form of an adjective or adverb expressing it.
—**su-per′la-tive-ly**, *adv.*—**su-per′la-tive-ness**, *n.*

su-per-lu-na-ry (sū-pèr-lū′na-ri), *a.* [L. *super*, over,
beyond, + *luna*, moon.] Situated above or beyond the
moon; hence, celestial, rather than earthly. Also **su-per-
lu′nar.**

su-per-man (sū′pèr-man), *n.*; pl. *-men.* [Tr. G. *übermensch*: see *super-*, and cf. *overman*, *n.*] An ideal superior
being conceived by the German philosopher Nietzsche
(1844–1900) as the product of human evolution, being in
effect a ruthless egoist of superior strength, cunning, and
force of will (cf. *the blond beast*, under *blond*, *a.*); hence, a
man who prevails by virtue of such characteristics; also, in a
favorable sense, a man of more than human powers (as,
"Roosevelt . . . a man . . . qualified to play a man's
part (not a *superman's*) in the manifold kinds of progress
upon which the hearts of thousands besides himself were set":
Charnwood's "Theodore Roosevelt," iv.).

su-per-mun-dane (sū-pèr-mun′dān), *a.* [ML. *supermun-
danus*, < L. *super*, over, + *mundus*, world.] Being above
the world; belonging to a region above the world.

su-per-nac-u-lum (sū-pèr-nak′ū-lum). [NL. *super nacu-
lum*, for G. *auf den nagel*, 'on the nail.'] **I.** *adv.* Until
no more liquor remains than will rest on the thumb-nail:
as, to drink *supernaculum* (a phrase having reference to the
custom of turning up the emptied cup or glass on one's
thumb-nail to show how little liquor remained). **II.** *n.*
Wine or other liquor good enough to be drunk to the last
drop; fine liquor; also, a draft that empties the cup or glass
to the last drop; also, a full cup or glass; a bumper. Also
fig.

su-per-nal (sū-pèr′nal), *a.* [OF. *supernal*, < L. *supernus*,
being above or on high, < *super*, over: see *super-*.] Being
on high or in the sky or visible heavens; also, being in or
belonging to a higher world or the heaven of divine or immortal beings; heavenly, celestial, or divine (as, "that
supernal judge, that stirs good thoughts," Shakspere's
"King John," ii. 1. 112; "*Supernal* grace contending With
sinfulness of men," Milton's "Paradise Lost," xi. 359);
also, lofty; elevated or exalted; of more than earthly or
human excellence, powers, etc. (as, "A few [married Amer-
icans] underrate their wives, but the rest think them *supernal*
in intelligence and capability": Howells's "Rise of Silas
Lapham," i.). [Now chiefly poetic or rhetorical.]—**su-
per′nal-ly**, *adv.*

su-per-na-tant (sū-pèr-nā′tant), *a.* [L. *supernatans* (-ant-),
ppr. of *supernatare*, < *super*, over, + *natare*, swim, float.]
Floating above, or on the surface, as a lighter liquid on a
heavier.

su-per-nat-u-ral (sū-pèr-nat′ū-ral). [ML. *supernaturalis*,
< L. *super*, over, beyond, + *natura*, E. *nature*.] **I.** *a.*
Being above or beyond what is natural, or transcending the
powers or the ordinary course of nature (as, *supernatural*
beings or agencies; *supernatural* phenomena; "He recounts
the visions and ecstasies during which a *supernatural* illumination had been conveyed to him," Hallam's "Literature
of Europe," iii. 3. § 20); sometimes, abnormal or extraordinary (as, "The thought of my daughter gave *supernatural* vigour to my arm," Jane Porter's "Scottish Chiefs,"
ii.; to display *supernatural* intelligence); also, of or pertaining to the supernatural. **II.** *n.* That which is supernatural, or the body or the subject of supernatural things
(with *the*); *pl.*, supernatural things; *sing.*, a supernatural being.—**su-per-nat′u-ral-ism**, *n.* Supernatural character or
agency; also, belief in the supernatural, or the doctrine of
supernatural (divine) agency as manifested in the world, or
in human events, religious revelation, etc. (as, "Their [Chris-
tians'] whole conception of human history was based upon
a far more fundamental and thorough *supernaturalism* than
we find among the Greeks and Romans": J. H. Robinson's
"Mind in the Making," v. 11).—**su-per-nat′u-ral-ist**, *n.*
One who believes in the supernatural or in supernaturalism.
—**su-per-nat″u-ral-is′tic**, *a.*—**su-per-nat′u-ral-ly**, *adv.*—
su-per-nat′u-ral-ness, *n.*

su-per-nor-mal (sū-pèr-nôr′mal), *a.* [See *super-*.] Above
or beyond what is normal: as, "You are faced with facts that

have no material explanation. They are supernatural, or *supernormal*, if you prefer the word" (Eden Phillpotts's "Grey Room," v.).—**su-per-nor′mal-ly**, *adv.*

su-per-nu-mer-a-ry (sū-pėr-nū′mẹ-rā-ri). [LL. *supernumerarius*, < L. *super*, over, + *numerus*, number.] **I.** *a.* Being in excess of the usual, proper, or prescribed number; additional; extra; esp., associated with a regular body or staff of persons in order to act as an assistant or substitute in case of necessity, as an official or employee (as, "a *supernumerary* official . . . aboard a packet-ship": Hawthorne's "House of the Seven Gables," xii.); also, superfluous or unnecessary (obs. or rare). **II.** *n.*; pl. *-ries* (-riz). A supernumerary or extra person or thing; esp., a supernumerary official or employee; in *theatrical use*, one not belonging to the regular company, who appears on the stage but has no lines to speak.

su-per-or-der (sū′pėr-ôr″dėr), *n.* [See *super-*.] In *zoöl.* and *bot.*, a group or category ranking above an order.—**su-per-or′di-nal** (-di-nạl), *a.*

su-per-or-di-na-ry (sū-pėr-ôr′di-nạ-ri), *a.* [See *super-*.] Above or beyond the ordinary.

su-per-or-gan-ic (sū″pėr-ôr-gan′ik), *a.* [See *super-*.] Above or beyond what is organic; independent of the physical organism.

su-per-os-cu-late (sū-pėr-os′kū-lāt), *v. t.*; *-lated, -lating.* [See *super-*.] In *geom.*, to osculate at more consecutive points than usually suffice to determine the locus. Cf. *osculate*, *v. t.*—**su-per-os-cu-la′tion** (-lā′shọn), *n.*

su-per-phos-phate (sū-pėr-fos′fāt), *n.* [See *super-*.] In *chem.*, an acid phosphate; in *com.*, any of various fertilizing materials composed chiefly of soluble phosphates.

su-per-phys-i-cal (sū-pėr-fiz′i-kạl), *a.* [See *super-*.] Above or beyond what is physical; hyperphysical.

su-per-pose (sū-pėr-pōz′), *v. t.*; *-posed, -posing.* [F. *superposer*, < L. *super*, over, + F. *poser*, put; in use associated with *superposition* (of different origin): see *pose*[1].] To place above or upon something else, or one upon another; in *physics*, etc., to bring (one thing) into the same space with another, so that they coincide or blend; in *geom.*, to place (one figure) ideally in the space occupied by another, so that the two figures coincide throughout their whole extent. —**su-per-pos′a-ble** (-pō′zạ-bl), *a.*

su-per-po-si-tion (sū″pėr-pọ-zish′ọn), *n.* [F. *superposition*, < LL. *superpositio(n-)*, < L. *superponere*, place over, < *super*, over, + *ponere*, place, put: cf. *superpose*.] The act of placing one thing above or upon another, or the resulting state; a superposing, or a superposed condition; also, something placed upon another thing; a series of things placed one upon another.

su-per-pow-er (sū′pėr-pou″ėr). [See *super-*.] **I.** *n.* Power, esp. mechanical power, on an extraordinary or extensive scale; specif., electric power on an extraordinary scale secured by the linking together of a number of separate power systems, with a view to more efficient and economical generation and distribution. **II.** *a.* Of or pertaining to superpower: as, *superpower* development; a *superpower* system.

su-per-ra-tion-al (sū-pėr-rash′ọn-ạl), *a.* [See *super-*.] Above or beyond what is rational; transcending reason.— **su-per-ra′tion-al-ly**, *adv.*

su-per-re-gen-er-a-tion (sū″pėr-rẹ-jen-ẹ-rā′shọn), *n.* [See *super-*.] In *wireless teleg.* and *teleph.*, a method of effecting an abnormally great regeneration. See *regeneration.*— **su″per-re-gen′er-a-tive** (-ẹ-rā-tiv), *a.*

su-per-salt (sū′pėr-sâlt), *n.* [See *super-*.] In *chem.*, an acid salt.

su-per-sat-u-rate (sū-pėr-saṭ′ū-rāt), *v. t.*; *-rated, -rating.* [See *super-*.] To add to beyond saturation; saturate abnormally: as, a *supersaturated* solution (a solution in which more of a substance is dissolved than the solvent will normally hold under the conditions, and which is thus in an unstable state).—**su-per-sat-u-ra′tion** (-rā′shọn), *n.*

su-per-scribe (sū-pėr-skrīb′), *v. t.*; *-scribed, -scribing.* [L. *superscribere* (pp. *superscriptus*), < *super*, over, + *scribere*, write.] To write (words, letters, one's name, etc.) above or on something; also, to inscribe or mark (something) with writing at the top or on the outside or surface; put an inscription above or on; address (a letter, etc.), as to a person,

by writing the name, place, etc., on the outside or cover.— **su′per-script** (-skript). [L. *superscriptus*, pp.] **I.** *a.* Written above, as a diacritical mark or a correction of a word. Cf. *subscript.* **II.**† *n.* A superscription, as of a letter.— **su-per-scrip′tion** (-skrip′shọn), *n.* [LL. *superscriptio(n-)*.] The act of superscribing; also, that which is superscribed, or written above or on a thing; an inscription over or on something; an address on a letter or the like; in *phar.*, the Latin word *recipe* ('take'), or the symbol ℞, at the head of a prescription.

su-per-sede (sū-pėr-sēd′), *v. t.*; *-seded, -seding.* [L. *supersedere* (pp. *supersessus*), sit above, be superior to, desist, ML. stay, postpone, < L. *super*, over, + *sedere*, sit: cf. also ML. *supercedere*, succeed.] To desist from†; also, to suspend† or stay†; postpone†; also, to set aside as void, useless, or obsolete, now usually in favor of something mentioned (as, "The municipalities *supersede* the orders of the assembly": Burke's "Revolution in France," 312); also, to replace in power, authority, effectiveness, acceptance, use, etc., as by another person or thing (as, "He soon received such accounts of troubles . . . from the exactions and negligence of the new governor, that he resolved to *supersede* him": Prescott's "Conquest of Mexico," iv. 4); displace in office or promotion by another; also, to take the place of, in power, acceptance, use, etc. (as, "In our island the Latin appears never to have *superseded* the old Gaelic speech": Macaulay's "Hist. of Eng.," i.); succeed to the position, function, office, etc., of; supplant.—**su-per-se′de-as** (-sē′dẹ-as), *n.* [ML., 'thou shalt stay.'] In *law*, a writ having in general the effect of a command to stay, on good cause shown, some ordinary proceedings which ought otherwise to have proceeded; hence, fig., a stay, stop, or check.—**su-per-sed′ence** (-sē′dẹns), *n.* Supersedure.—**su-per-sed′er**, *n.*—**su-per-se′dure** (-dụr), *n.* The act of superseding, or the state of being superseded; supersession; supersedure.

su-per-sen-si-ble (sū-pėr-sen′si-bl), *a.* [See *super-*.] Above or beyond what is sensible; beyond the reach of the senses. —**su-per-sen′si-bly**, *adv.*

su-per-sen-si-tive (sū-pėr-sen′si-tiv), *a.* [See *super-*.] Extremely, excessively, or morbidly sensitive.—**su-per-sen′si-tive-ly**, *adv.*—**su-per-sen′si-tive-ness**, *n.*

su-per-sen-so-ry (sū-pėr-sen′sọ-ri), *a.* [See *super-*.] Beyond, or independent of, the organs of sense.

su-per-sen-su-al (sū-pėr-sen′shū-ạl), *a.* [See *super-*.] Above or beyond the field or range of the senses; transcending sense; sometimes, spiritual; also, extremely sensual.—**su-per-sen′su-al-ly**, *adv.*

su-per-sen-su-ous (sū-pėr-sen′shū-us), *a.* [See *super-*.] Above or beyond what is sensuous; supersensual.—**su-per-sen′su-ous-ness**, *n.*

su-per-ser-vice-a-ble (sū-pėr-sėr′vis-ạ-bl), *a.* [See *super-*.] Too serviceable, that is, too disposed to be of service; officious: as, "a . . . *superserviceable*, finical rogue" (Shakspere's "King Lear," ii. 2. 19).—**su-per-ser′vice-a-ble-ness**, *n.*

su-per-ses-sion (sū-pėr-sesh′ọn), *n.* [ML. *supersessio(n-)*, < L. *supersedere*, E. *supersede*.] Supersedure.—**su-per-ses′sive** (-ses′iv), *a.* Superseding.—**su-per-ses′sor**, *n.* One who supersedes.—**su-per-ses′so-ry** (-ses′ọ-ri), *a.*

su-per-son-ic (sū-pėr-son′ik), *a.* [*super-* + *sonic*.] Pertaining to or adapted for speeds greater than that of sound: as, a *supersonic* airplane.

su-per-state (sū′pėr-stāt), *n.* [See *super-*.] A state or a governing power presiding over states subordinated to it.

su-per-sti-tion (sū-pėr-stish′ọn), *n.* [OF. F. *superstition*, < L. *superstitio(n-)*, appar. orig. a standing still over a thing, as in wonder or awe, < *superstare*, stand over or upon, < *super*, over, + *stare*, stand.] Irrational fear of what is unknown or mysterious, esp. in connection with religion; religious belief or practice founded on irrational fear or credulity (as, "We have already got rid of a vast amount of *superstition* and ignorance, and are learning what Christianity really is": Mallock's "New Republic," i. 3); a particular instance or form of such belief or practice; a religious belief or practice, or a religious system, regarded as founded on mere ignorant credulity; also, a belief or notion entertained, either popularly or by an individual, regardless of reason or knowledge, of the ominous significance (for evil or good, or neutrally) of a particular thing, circumstance, occurrence, proceeding, or the like (as, the *superstitions* about Friday, the number 13, a black cat, a four-leaved clover, breaking a mirror, or walking under a ladder; "over the door a couple of horseshoes nailed for luck — a *superstition* yet lingering in the by-ways of the woods and hills," Jefferies's "Gamekeeper at Home," i.); in general, any blindly accepted belief or notion (as, the *superstition* of the divine right of kings).—**su-per-sti'tious** (-stish'us), *a.* [OF. F. *superstitieux*, < L. *superstitiosus*.] Full of or addicted to superstition (as, a *superstitious* sect; "Gamblers and adventurers are generally *superstitious*," Bret Harte's "Luck of Roaring Camp"); of the nature of, characterized by, or proceeding from superstition (as, *superstitious* fears or beliefs; *superstitious* practices; pertaining to or connected with superstition (as, "These *superstitious* legends had invested the mountain with a mysterious horror": Prescott's "Conquest of Mexico," iii. 8); also, extraordinary† or excessive†; also, scrupulous†, punctilious†, or meticulous†.—**su-per-sti'tious-ly**, *adv.*—**su-per-sti'tious-ness**, *n.*

su-per-stra-tum (sū-pėr-strā'tum), *n.*; pl. *-ta* (-tä) or *-tums.* [NL., prop. neut. of L. *superstratus*, pp. of *supersternere*, spread over, < *super*, over, + *sternere*, spread out: cf. *stratum.*] An overlying stratum or layer.

su-per-struct (sū-pėr-strukt'), *v. t.* [L. *superstructus*, pp. of *superstruere*, < *super*, over, + *struere*, build.] To build upon something else; erect as a superstructure.—**su-per-struc'tive** (-struk'tiv), *a.*

su-per-struc-ture (sū'pėr-struk″ṭūr), *n.* [From *super-* + *structure.*] Any structure built on something else, esp. all of an edifice above the basement or foundation; hence, anything erected on a foundation or basis (often fig.: as, "He [Descartes] has destroyed too much of his foundations to render his *superstructure* stable," Hallam's "Literature of Europe," iii. 3. § 93); in *railroad engin.*, the sleepers, rails, and fastenings of a railroad, in contradistinction to the road-bed; *naut.*, the parts of a vessel, as a war-ship, built above the main deck.—**su-per-struc'tur-al**, *a.*

su-per-sub-ma-rine (sū'pėr-sub″ma̱-rēn), *n.* [See *super-.*] A large and powerful type of submarine.

su-per-sub-tle (sū-pėr-sut'l), *a.* [See *super-.*] Extremely or excessively subtle; oversubtle.—**su-per-sub'tle-ty** (-ti), *n.*

su-per-tax (sū'pėr-taks), *n.* [See *super-.*] A tax in addition to a normal tax, as one upon income above a certain amount.

su-per-ton-ic (sū-pėr-ton'ik), *n.* [See *super-.*] In *music*, the second tone of a scale, being the next above the tonic.

su-per-vene (sū-pėr-vēn'), *v. i.*; *-vened, -vening.* [L. *supervenire* (pp. *superventus*), < *super*, over, + *venire*, come.] To come as something additional or extraneous (sometimes with *on* or *upon*); occur or follow as an additional circumstance; ensue.—**su-per-ve'nient** (-vē'ni̱ent), *a.* [L. *superveniens* (-ent-), ppr.] Supervening; coming or occurring in addition or subsequently.—**su-per-ven'tion** (-ven'shon), *n.* [LL. *superventio(n-).*] The act or fact of supervening.

su-per-vi-sal (sū-pėr-vī'za̱l), *n.* Supervision.

su-per-vise (sū-pėr-vīz'), *v. t.*; *-vised, -vising.* [ML. *supervisus*, pp. of *supervidere*, < L. *super*, over, + *videre*, see: cf. *survey.*] To look over†; survey†, or view†; peruse† or read†; revise†; also, to oversee (a process, work, workers, etc.) during execution or performance; superintend; have the oversight and direction of.—**su-per-vi'sion** (-vizh'on), *n.* [ML. *supervisio(n-).*] The act or function of supervising; oversight; superintendence.—**su-per-vi'sor** (-vī'zọr), *n.* [ML.] One who supervises; an onlooker† or observer†; a reviser†; an overseer; a superintendent; in some States of the U. S., an elected officer who has charge, either alone or with others, of the administrative business of a township or other district, all such officers in a county sometimes forming a county board, charged with the administrative business of the county.—**su-per-vi'sor-ship**, *n.*—**su-per-vi'so-ry** (-zọ-ri), *a.* Pertaining to or having supervision.

su-pi-nate (sū'pi-nāt), *v.*; *-nated, -nating.* [L. *supinatus*, pp. of *supinare*, bend backward, lay on the back, < *supinus*, E. *supine, a.*] **I.** *tr.* To render supine; rotate or place (the hand or fore limb) so that the palmar surface is upward when the limb is stretched forward horizontally. Cf. *pronate.*

II. *intr.* To become supinated.—**su-pi-na'tion** (-nā'shon), *n.*—**su'pi-na-tor**, *n.*

su-pine (sū-pīn' or sū'pīn), *a.* [L. *supinus*, bent backward, lying on the back, inactive, indolent.] Lying on the back, or with the face or front upward; having the palm upward, as the hand; fig., inactive; passive; inert; esp., inactive or passive from indolence or indifference (as, "No other colony showed such *supine*, selfish helplessness in allowing her own border citizens to be mercilessly harried": Roosevelt's "Winning of the West," i. 4).—**su'pine**, *n.* [LL. *supinum*, prop. neut. of L. *supinus.*] In *gram.*, a part of the Latin verb, really a verbal noun, with two forms, one ('first supine') ending in *-um*, an accusative, used with verbs of motion (as in 'abiit *deambulatum*,' he has gone a-walking), and the other ('second supine') ending in *-u*, an ablative or dative (locative), used with adjectives or substantives (as in 'facile *dictu*,' easy in the telling, or easy to be told); also, an analogous form in some other language.—**su-pine'ly**, *adv.*—**su-pine'ness**, *n.*

sup-per (sup'ėr), *n.* [OF. *soper* (F. *souper*), noun use of inf.: see *sup*[2].] The evening meal; the last meal of the day, taken in the evening (early or late, according to the time of dinner, the preceding meal); any evening repast, often one forming a social entertainment.—**Last Supper.** See under *last*[4], *a.*—**Lord's Supper.** See under *lord*, *n.*—**sup'per**, *v.* **I.** *tr.* To give supper to; entertain at supper. **II.** *intr.* To take supper; sup.—**sup'per-less**, *a.* Without supper.

sup-plant (su-plant'), *v. t.* [L. *supplantare*, trip up, overthrow, < *sub*, under, + *planta*, sole of the foot.] To trip up†; overthrow†, or cause the downfall of†; also, to turn out or displace (a person), esp. by treacherous or underhand means, in order to take his place; take the place of (another), as in office or favor, through scheming, strategy, or the like (as, "The rivalling poor Jones, and *supplanting* him in her affections, added another spur to his pursuit": Fielding's "Tom Jones," vii. 6); also, to displace or supersede, as one thing does another (as, "The steam engine began to *supplant* the muscular power of men and animals": J. H. Robinson's "Mind in the Making," vi. 13); replace (one thing) by something else; also, to remove† or oust†; get rid of†; root out†.—**sup-plan-ta-tion** (sup-lan-tā'shon), *n.* [LL. *supplantatio(n-).*] The act of supplanting, or the state of being supplanted.—**sup-plant'er**, *n.*—**sup-plant'ment**, *n.*

sup-ple (sup'l), *a.*; compar. *suppler*, superl. *supplest.* [OF. F. *souple*, < L. *supplex* (*supplic-*), suppliant, lit. 'bending under' (as in kneeling), < *sub*, under, + *-plex*, akin to *plicare*, fold: cf. *supplicate.*] Bending readily without breaking or deformation (as, a *supple* rod or switch; *supple* leather); pliant; flexible; also, characterized by ease in bending (as, *supple* joints; a *supple* body or person; *supple* movements); limber; lithe; fig., characterized by ease and adaptability in mental action (as, "his mind, at once *supple* and copious," Lytton Strachey's "Queen Victoria," iii.; "a brilliant French book . . . dealing with certain points . . . in a manner so interesting, *supple*, and apparently impartial," Mrs. H. Ward's "Lady Rose's Daughter," ix.); esp., conforming readily to circumstances or to the will or humor of others; compliant or yielding; obsequious; servilely or unscrupulously accommodating or complaisant (as, "The burgomaster . . . long the *supple* slave of Alva and the Blood-Council, fled": Motley's "Dutch Republic," iii. 7).—**sup'ple**, *v. t.* or *i.*; *-pled, -pling.* To make or become supple.—**sup'ple-jack**, *n.* A strong, pliant cane or walking-stick; also, any of various climbing shrubs with strong stems suitable for making walking-sticks.—**sup'-ple-ly**, *adv.*

sup-ple-ment (sup'le̱-me̱nt), *n.* [L. *supplementum*, < *supplere*, fill up: see *supply.*] Something added to complete a thing, supply a deficiency, or reinforce or extend a whole; a completing or effective addition; esp., a part added to a book, document, or the like to supply deficiencies or correct errors (cf. *appendix*); also, a part, usually of special character, issued as an additional feature of a newspaper or other periodical; in *math.*, the quantity by which an angle or an arc falls short of 180° or a semicircle.—**sup'ple-ment** (-ment), *v. t.* To ment and *BCD* is complete, add to, or extend by a supple-

Supplement. — *BCE* is the supplement and *BCD* is the complement of the angle *BCA*.

ment; form a supplement or addition to (as, "Her father . . . gave her occasional presents to *supplement* her wages": Archibald Marshall's "Anthony Dare," xi.); supply (a deficiency); also, to add as a supplementary remark.—**sup-ple-men'tal** (-men'tạl), *a.* Supplementary.—**sup-ple-men'ta-ry** (-tạ-ri), *a.* Of the nature of or forming a supplement; additional: as, "He had come upon *supplementary* sources of income" (Gissing's "New Grub Street," x.).—**sup-ple-men'ta-ri-ly** (-ri-li), *adv.*—**sup″ple-men-ta'tion** (-tā'shọn), *n.* The act of supplementing; also, something added as a supplement.—**sup'ple-ment-er,** *n.*

sup-ple-ness (sup'l-nes), *n.* The quality of being supple.

sup-plete (su-plēt'), *v. t.*; -pleted, -pleting. [L. *suppletus,* pp. of *supplere,* fill up: see *supply.*] To supplement. [Obs. or rare.]—**sup-ple'tive** (-plē'tiv), *a.* Suppletory.—**sup-ple-to-ry** (sup'lẹ-tọ-ri), *a.* Supplying a deficiency; supplementary.

sup-pli-ance[1] (sup'li-ạns), *n.* The position, condition, or action of a suppliant; supplication.

sup-pli-ance[2] (su-pli'ạns), *n.* The act of supplying; also, something that supplies a want (as, "A violet . . . sweet, not lasting, The perfume and *suppliance* of a minute": Shakspere's "Hamlet," i. 3. 9). [Now rare.]

sup-pli-ant (sup'li-ạnt). [F. *suppliant,* ppr. of *supplier,* < L. *supplicare:* see *supplicate.*] **I.** *a.* Supplicating; humbly entreating or petitioning, as persons; expressive of supplication, as words, actions, etc. **II.** *n.* One who supplicates; a humble petitioner: as, "You would not offer injury to one who sought you as a *suppliant* in her utmost need" (Scott's "Black Dwarf," xvi.).—**sup'pli-ant-ly,** *adv.*—**sup'pli-ant-ness,** *n.*

sup-pli-cant (sup'li-kạnt). [L. *supplicans* (-ant-), ppr.] **I.** *a.* Supplicating; suppliant. **II.** *n.* A suppliant.—**sup'pli-cant-ly,** *adv.*

sup-pli-cate (sup'li-kāt), *v.*; -cated, -cating. [L. *supplicatus,* pp. of *supplicare,* beg or pray humbly, orig. bend or kneel down, < *sub,* under, + *plicare,* fold: cf. *supple.*] **I.** *intr.* To pray humbly; make humble and earnest entreaty or petition: as, "Mary of Burgundy, with streaming eyes . . . *supplicating* . . . for the lives of her treacherous ambassadors" (Motley's "Dutch Republic," i. 3). **II.** *tr.* To pray humbly to, or entreat or petition humbly (as, "*supplicating* God for mercy," H. Melville's "Moby-Dick," ix.; "On my knees I *supplicate* you to forbear," Walpole's "Castle of Otranto," iv.); also, to seek by humble entreaty or petition (as, "Once more subdued, the Saxons met him . . . *supplicating* peace and pardon": G. P. R. James's "Hist. of Charlemagne," iv.).—**sup'pli-cat-ing-ly** (-kā-ting-li), *adv.*—**sup-pli-ca'tion** (-kā'shọn), *n.* [L. *supplicatio*(n-).] The act of supplicating; humble prayer, entreaty, or petition; a prayer or petition (as, "Hear my prayer, O Lord, give ear to my *supplications*": Ps. cxliii. 1); esp., one of a series of petitions in a litany that supplicate special benefits.—**sup'pli-ca-tor,** *n.*—**sup'pli-ca-to-ry** (-kạ-tọ-ri), *a.* Making or expressing supplication: as, "By *supplicatory* letters to the archbishop, they begged his pardon" (Strype's "Memorials of Cranmer," i. 27).

sup-pli-er (su-pli'ẹr), *n.* One who or that which supplies.

sup-ply (su-pli'), *v.*; -plied, -plying. [OF. *supplier, soupleier* (F. *suppléer*), < L. *supplere* (pp. *suppletus*), fill up, complete, supply, < *sub,* under, + *plere,* fill: cf. *supplete.*] **I.** *tr.* To fill up or complete by adding what is wanting†; make up a deficiency in†; supplement†; reinforce†; aid†; also, to furnish (a person, establishment, place, etc.) with what is wanting or requisite (as, "If yourself, too scantily *supplied,* Need help, let honest industry provide," Cowper's "Progress of Error," 251; a power-station for *supplying* a community); furnish or provide (*with:* as, to *supply* a person with money, food, or clothing; "Where'd the farmers be without the town? . . . why, we *supply* them with everything!" Sinclair Lewis's "Main Street," v.); also, to furnish or provide (something wanting or requisite: as, "Water and power were *supplied* to it [a laboratory] . . . by means of pipes and cables," H. G. Wells's "Men Like Gods," ii. 2); afford; also, to make up (a deficiency); make up for or compensate for (a loss, lack, absence, etc.); satisfy (a want, need, demand, etc.); fill (a place, vacancy, etc.: as,

"raw, unpractised lads, in whom genius did not come to *supply* the place of experience," Motley's "Dutch Republic," v. 4); occupy (a pulpit, etc.) as a substitute; discharge (an office, etc.)†; also, to make up for the want of, take the place of, or serve as a substitute for (now rare). **II.** *intr.* To fill the place of another, esp. the minister of a church, as a substitute or temporarily.—**sup-ply',** *n.*; pl. *-plies* (-plīz'). The act of supplying, furnishing, providing, satisfying, etc.; also, that which is supplied; a supplement† or addition†; reinforcements†; aid†; a quantity of something provided or on hand, as for use; a stock or store; a provision, stock, or store of food or other things necessary for maintenance (now usually in *pl.*: as, *supplies* for an army; household or office *supplies*); a sum of money provided by a national legislature to meet the expenses of government (usually in *pl.*: as, "The Commons . . . declared that no more *supplies* should be granted for the war," Macaulay's "Hist. of Eng.," ii.); also, one who supplies a vacancy or takes the place of another, esp. temporarily; a clergyman who officiates in a vacant charge, or in the temporary absence of the pastor; in *polit. econ.,* the quantity of a commodity, etc., that is in the market and available for purchase, or that is available for purchase at a particular price (cf. *demand, n.*).—**sup-ply'=train,** *n.* *Milit.,* a train of vehicles, etc., for carrying supplies. See *train*[2], *n.*

sup-port (su-pōrt'), *v. t.* [OF. F. *supporter,* < L. *supportare,* < *sub,* under, + *portare,* carry.] To bear or hold up (a load, mass, structure, part, etc.); keep from falling or sinking; sustain or withstand (weight, etc.) without giving way; fig., to undergo or endure without giving way, or bear with fortitude (as, anguish too great to be *supported*; "How shall I *support* your frowns without reinforcing my strength?" Scott's "Guy Mannering," xlix.); endure with patience or submission (as, "These things his high spirit could not *support*": Evelyn's "Diary," July 25, 1673); put up with, or tolerate; also, to sustain (a person, the mind, spirits, courage, etc.) under trial or affliction; keep from giving way, weakening, despondency, etc.; keep (life, combustion, or any process) from failing or ceasing; maintain (a person, family, establishment, institution, etc.) by supplying with things necessary to existence; provide for, as by furnishing means or funds; also, to uphold (a person, cause, policy, etc.) by aid or countenance (as, "the policy of Cromwell, who *supported* the growing power of France against the declining power of Spain": Lecky's "Hist. of Eng. in the 18th Century," iii.); back; second (efforts, aims, etc.); maintain or advocate (a theory, etc.); corroborate (a statement, etc.); assist or be in readiness to assist (a force engaged in battle), as troops, artillery, etc.; attend (an official, etc.) on a public occasion as an honorary aid; act with or second (a leading actor), as on a stage; assist in any performance; also, to sustain or act (a part, rôle, or character: often fig.).—**to support arms,** *milit.,* in former use, to carry the rifle (or other weapon) vertically against the left shoulder, with the hammer resting on the left forearm held horizontally across the breast.—**sup-port',** *n.* The act of supporting, or keeping from falling, sinking, giving way, failing, ceasing, etc., or the state of being supported; maintenance, as of a person, family, etc., with necessaries, means, or funds; upholding, backing, or seconding; advocacy; corroboration; aid or assistance; also, a thing or a person that supports; a prop, base, or other piece or thing that supports a load or weight; fig., anything that sustains morally; a stay or reliance (as, "justice, as my prime *support*": Cowper's "Hope," 377); a means or source of maintenance or subsistence (as, "To which title A thousand pound a year, annual *support* . . . he adds": Shakspere's "Henry VIII.," ii. 3. 64); a thing or a person that gives aid or assistance; a body of supporting troops, as in battle; an actor or a body of actors supporting the leading actor or actors of a company; an assistant or a body of assistants in any performance.

sup-port-a-ble (su-pōr'tạ-bl), *a.* Capable of being supported; bearable or endurable; sustainable; maintainable.—**sup-port'a-ble-ness,** *n.*—**sup-port'a-bly,** *adv.*

sup-port-er (su-pōr'tẹr), *n.* One who or that which supports; esp., a thing or device for holding up something (as, hose-*supporters*; an abdominal *supporter*); also, an upholder, backer, or advocate; in *her.,* a figure (often one of a pair), as of an animal or a man, represented as holding up an escutcheon or standing beside it.

sup-port-ing (su-pōr'ting), *p. a.* That supports; sustaining; giving support.—**sup-port'ing-ly**, *adv.*

sup-port-less (su-pōrt'les), *a.* Having no support.

sup-port-ress (su-pōr'tres), *n.* A female supporter.

sup-pos-a-ble (su-pō'zạ-bl), *a.* That may be supposed.— **sup-pos'a-bly**, *adv.*

sup-po-sal (su-pō'zạl), *n.* The act of supposing; a supposition.

sup-pose (su-pōz'), *v.; -posed, -posing.* [OF. F. *supposer*, < L. *sub*, under, + OF. F. *poser*, put (see *pose*[1]), but associated with derivatives of L. *supponere*: see *supposition.*] **I.** *tr.* To assume (something), without reference to its being true or false, for the sake of argument or for the purpose of tracing the consequences (as, let us *suppose* a rate of ten miles per hour; *suppose* the distance to be, or *suppose* that the distance is, one mile); consider as a possibility suggested or an idea or plan proposed (used in the imperative: as, *suppose* that you fail, what then? *suppose* we wait till to-morrow); also, to assume as true, or believe, in the absence of positive knowledge or of evidence to the contrary (as, it is *supposed* that the occurrence was an accident; most authorities *suppose* the document to be authentic); often, to take for granted, assume, or presume, without especial thought of possible error (as, I *supposed* that you had gone; "They *supposed* he had come in search of distinction," Irving's "Conquest of Granada," ii.); presume the existence of (as, "She had surveyed life with prejudice, and *supposed* misery where she did not find it": Johnson's "Rasselas," xxvii.); think, with reference to mere opinion (as, what do you *suppose* he will do?); sometimes, formerly (without qualification), to believe†, think†, deem†, or hold† (as, "I *supposed* it necessary to send to you Epaphroditus . . . For he longed after you all," Phil. ii. 25; "Say, gentle princess, would you not *suppose* Your bondage happy, to be made a queen?" Shakspere's "1 Henry VI.," v. 3. 110); expect†; also, of a proposition, theory, etc., to make or involve the assumption of (as, this theory *supposes* the existence of a world-soul); of facts, circumstances, etc., to require logically (as, possession does not necessarily *suppose* ownership); imply; presuppose; also, to conceive† or imagine†; also, to feign† or pretend†; also, to put by fraud in the place of another† (cf. *supposititious*). **II.** *intr.* To suppose or assume something; presume; think.—**sup-pose'**, *n.* Supposition.—**supposed'**, *p. a.* Assumed as true, regardless of fact, or hypothetical (as, take a *supposed* case); also, accepted or received as true, without positive knowledge and perhaps erroneously (as, the *supposed* site of an ancient temple); hence, merely thought to be such (as, to sacrifice real for *supposed* advantages); also, feigned† or pretended†.—**sup-pos'ed-ly** (-pō'zed-li), *adv.*—**sup-pos'er**, *n.*

sup-po-si-tion (sup-ō-zish'ǫn), *n.* [OF. F. *supposition*, < ML. *suppositio(n-)*, supposition, hypothesis, L. a putting under, substitution, < L. *supponere* (pp. *suppositus*), put under, substitute, < *sub*, under, + *ponere*, put: cf. *suppose.*] The act of supposing; also, that which is supposed; an assumption; a hypothesis; a presumption; a belief, notion, or opinion entertained without positive knowledge or without especial thought of error.—**sup-po-si'tion-al**, *a.* Pertaining to, of the nature of, or based on supposition; hypothetical; supposed.—**sup-po-si'tion-al-ly**, *adv.*

sup-po-si-tious (sup-ō-zish'us), *a.* [Contr. of *supposititious*, with sense in part from *supposition.*] Suppositious, fraudulently substituted, or false; also, based on or involving supposition; suppositional.—**sup-po-si'tious-ly**, *adv.*

sup-pos-i-ti-tious (su-poz-i-tish'us), *a.* [L. *supposititius*, substituted, false, < *supponere* (pp. *suppositus*): see *supposition.*] Put by fraud in the place of another, or fraudulently substituted or pretended (as, a *supposititious* son or heir; "Very many believed the Prince of Wales to be a *supposititious* child," Macaulay's "Hist. of Eng.," ix.); spurious, false, or not genuine (as, a *supposititious* passage in a text; a *supposititious* document); also, suppositional, hypothetical, or supposed (as, "It was the fashion of the Calvinistic preaching . . . to exercise the conscience with most severe *supposititious* tests": Mrs. Stowe's "Oldtown Folks," v.).—**sup-pos-i-ti'tious-ly**, *adv.*—**sup-pos-i-ti'tious-ness**, *n.*

sup-pos-i-tive (su-poz'i-tiv). [ML. *suppositivus*, < L. *supponere* (pp. *suppositus*): see *supposition.*] **I.** *a.* Of the nature of or involving supposition; suppositional; also, supposititious or false; in *gram.*, expressing supposition, as the words *if, granting,* or *provided.* **II.** *n.* In *gram.*, a suppositive word.—**sup-pos'i-tive-ly**, *adv.*

sup-pos-i-to-ry (su-poz'i-tō-ri), *n.; pl. -ries* (-riz). [ML. *suppositorium*, prop. neut. of LL. *suppositorius*, placed under, < L. *supponere* (pp. *suppositus*): see *supposition.*] In *med.*, a mass or piece of some prepared substance, usually in the form of a cone or cylinder, for introduction into the rectum, the vagina, etc., to be dissolved there.

sup-press (su-pres'), *v. t.* [L. *suppressus*, pp. of *supprimere*, < *sub*, under, + *premere*, press.] To put down (a proceeding, attempt, outbreak, etc.) by or as by force; quell; crush; vanquish or subdue (an enemy, rebel, etc.)†; put an end to the activities of (a person, body of persons, etc.); do away with by or as by authority (as, to *suppress* an office or a newspaper; Henry VIII. *suppressed* the monasteries of England); abolish; stop (a practice, etc.: as, "Cock-fighting was *suppressed*," Morley's "Oliver Cromwell," v. 1; to *suppress* vice or waste); arrest (a flow, hemorrhage, etc.); also, to keep in or repress (a feeling, thought, smile, groan, utterance, etc.: as, "I *suppress* for a moment my indignation," Burke's "American Taxation"); also, to withhold from disclosure or publication (truth, facts, evidence, names, etc.: as, "What is told in the fullest and most accurate annals bears an infinitely small proportion to what is *suppressed*," Macaulay's "Essays," History).—**sup-press'er**, *n.* —**sup-press'i-ble**, *a.* That may be suppressed.—**sup-pres'sion** (-presh'ǫn), *n.* [L. *suppressio(n-).*] The act of suppressing, or the state of being suppressed; a putting down by or as by force or authority; abolition; stoppage; repression; withholding from disclosure or knowledge.— **sup-pres'sive** (-pres'iv), *a.* Tending to suppress.—**sup-pres'sor**, *n.*

sup-pu-rant (sup'ū-rạnt), *a. and n.* Same as *suppurative.*

sup-pu-rate (sup'ū-rāt), *v. i.; -rated, -rating.* [L. *suppuratus*, pp. of *suppurare*, < *sub*, under, + *pus* (pur-), pus.] To produce or discharge pus, as a wound; maturate.— **sup-pu-ra'tion** (-rā'shǫn), *n.* [L. *suppuratio(n-).*] The process of suppurating; maturation; also, the matter produced by suppuration.—**sup'pu-ra-tive** (-rạ-tiv). **I.** *a.* Promoting suppuration; also, suppurating, or characterized by suppuration. **II.** *n.* A medicine or application that promotes suppuration.

su-pra (sū'prä), *adv.* [L., adv. and prep., above, beyond, related to *super*, over, above, beyond: see *super-.*] Above: esp. used in making reference to parts of a text. Cf. *infra.* See also *supra protest*, in alphabetical place.

supra-. [L. *supra-*, repr. *supra*, adv. and prep.: see *supra.*] A prefix meaning 'above,' 'beyond,' 'exceedingly,' used like (sometimes interchangeably with) the related *super-*, but occurring esp. in scientific words, as *supra-axillary* (above the axilla or axil), *suprahyoid* (above the hyoid bone), *supra-orbital, supraspinal, supratemporal,* etc. Cf. *super-, infra-,* and *sub-.*

su-pra-lim-i-nal (sū-prä-lim'i-nạl), *a.* [L. *supra*, above, + *limen (limin-),* threshold.] In *psychol.*, above the limen or threshold of consciousness; of or in consciousness. Cf. *subliminal.*

su-pra-max-il-la (sū″prä-mak-sil'ä), *n.; pl. -maxillæ* (-ē). [NL.: see *supra-* and *maxilla.*] In *anat.* and *zoöl.*, the upper jaw or upper jaw-bone.—**su-pra-max'il-la-ry** (-mak'-si-lạ-ri). In *anat.*: **I.** *a.* Of or pertaining to the upper jaw or upper jaw-bone. **II.** *n.; pl. -ries* (-riz). The upper jaw-bone.

su-pra-mo-lec-u-lar (sū″prä-mō-lek'ū-lạr), *a.* [See *supra-.*] Above the molecule; of greater complexity than a molecule; composed of an aggregation of molecules.

su-pra-mun-dane (sū-prä-mun'dān), *a.* Same as *supermundane.*

su-pra pro-test (sū'prä prō'test). [NL. *supra protestum*, for It. *sopra protesto*, upon protest.] Upon or after protest: a phrase used with reference to an acceptance or a payment of a bill by a third person for the honor of the drawer after protest for non-acceptance or non-payment by the drawee.

—su·pra·pro′test, n. An acceptance or a payment of a bill supra protest.

su·pra·re·nal (sū-prā-rē′nạl). [NL. suprarenalis, < L. supra, above, + ren, kidney.] In anat.: **I.** a. Situated above or on the kidney (as, a suprarenal body, capsule, or gland, a ductless gland situated in man at the upper end, and in most vertebrates at the anterior end, of each kidney, and furnishing an important secretion); adrenal; also, pertaining to or connected with a suprarenal. **II.** n. A suprarenal body, capsule, or gland.

su·prem·a·cy (sụ-prem′ạ-si), n. The state of being supreme; supreme authority or power.

su·preme (sụ-prēm′), a. [L. supremus, highest, superl. of superus, being above: see superior.] Highest in place (now only poetic: as, "Blanc, supreme above his earth-brood," Browning's "La Saisiaz")· also, highest in rank or authority (as, a supreme ruler, council, or court; supreme power; "the great man who held the supreme command," Macaulay's "Hist. of Eng.." ii.); paramount; sovereign; chief; also, of the highest quality, character, importance, etc. (as, supreme art; supreme courage; a supreme hour); highest in degree, greatest, utmost, or extreme (as, "the supreme imbecility of a civil war," H. G. Wells's "Mr. Britling," ii. 4. § 15; supreme disgust); also, last (with reference to the end of life: as, the supreme moment).—**the Supreme Being,** the most exalted of beings; the sovereign of the universe; God.—**the supreme sacrifice,** the greatest or utmost sacrifice; the sacrifice of one's own life: as, to make the supreme sacrifice (to give one's life, or die, as for one's country or for any cause).—**su·preme′,** n. The supreme ruler or head†; [cap.] with the, the Supreme Being; also [l. c.], the highest degree (as, "the supreme of power": Keats's "Sleep and Poetry"); the height of something.—**su·preme′ly,** adv.—**su·preme′ness,** n.

sur-. [OF. F. sur- (prep. sur), < L. super-: see super-.] A prefix meaning 'over,' 'above,' 'beyond,' 'exceedingly,' an equivalent of super- occurring in words from the French, and used also to some extent as an English formative, chiefly in legal, scientific, or technical terms, as surbase, surrebut, surrejoin, surroyal.

su·ra (sö′rä), n.; pl. suras (-räz). [Ar. sūrah, row, step, degree.] One of the chapters of the Koran.

su·rah (sö′rä), n. [Appar. < Surat, city and district of northern Bombay, India.] A soft twilled silk fabric.

su·ral (sū′rạl), a. [L. sura, calf of the leg.] In anat., of or pertaining to the calf of the leg.

sur·base (sėr′bās), n. [See sur-.] In arch., a molding above a base, as that immediately above the baseboard of a room; the crowning molding or cornice of a pedestal, etc.—**sur′-based**[1], a. In arch., having a surbase.

sur·based[2] (sėr-bāst′), a. [F. surbaissé, < sur- (see sur-) + baissé, pp. of baisser, lower, < LL. bassus, low, E. base[1].] In arch., of an arch or vault, having a rise that is less than half the span.—**sur·base′ment,** n. In arch., the condition of being surbased.

sur·cease (sėr-sēs′), v.; -ceased, -ceasing. [OF. F. sursis, pp. of surseoir, < L. supersedere, desist: see supersede.] **I.** intr. To cease from some action, or desist (as, "Nor from that task . . . Surcease they": Cary's tr. Dante's "Purgatory," xxv. 131); also, to come to an end. [Archaic.] **II.** tr. To cease from; leave off: as, "The hobby-horse surceased his capering" (Scott's "Abbot," xiv.). [Archaic.] —**sur·cease′,** n. Cessation; end: as, "Vainly I had sought to borrow From my books surcease of sorrow" (Poe's "Raven"). [Archaic.]

sur·charge (sėr-chärj′), v. t.; -charged, -charging. [OF. F. surcharger, < sur- (see sur-) + charger, E. charge, v.] To put an additional or excessive charge, load, or burden upon; overload; overburden; oppress or overwhelm, as with grief; also, to subject to an additional or extra charge (for payment); overcharge, or charge with an excessive or exorbitant price; overburden with expense, exactions, etc.; also, to print officially an additional mark on the face of (a postage-stamp, etc.), as for the purpose of changing the value or status; print (an additional mark) on a postage-stamp, etc.; in law, to overstock (a common, etc.) by putting more cattle into it than the person has a right to put, or more than the herbage will sustain; also, to show an omission in (an

account) of something that operates as a charge against the accounting party; also, to charge (an official, etc.) for an amount improperly paid by him; hence, to disallow (an item of expenditure).—**sur·charge** (sėr′chärj or sėr-chärj′), n. [F. surcharge.] An additional or excessive charge, load, burden, etc.; also, an additional or extra pecuniary charge; an excessive sum or price charged; also, an additional mark officially printed on the face of a postage-stamp, etc., as for the purpose of changing the value or status; also, the act of surcharging, or putting an additional or excessive charge or load upon, or the resulting state; in law, the act or an act of surcharging (see surcharge, v. t.).—**sur·char′ger,** n.

sur·cin·gle (sėr′sing-gl), n. [OF. sorcengle, < L. super, over, + cingula, girdle, < cingere, gird.] A girth for a horse or other animal, esp. a large girth passing over and keeping in place a blanket, pack, or the like; also, a girdle with which a garment, esp. a cassock, is fastened.

sur·coat (sėr′kōt), n. [OF. surcot, surcote: see sur- and coat.] An outer coat or garment; specif., such a garment worn by medieval knights over their armor, and often embroidered with heraldic arms.

sur·cu·lose (sėr′kụ-lōs), a. [L. surculosus, < surculus, shoot, sprout, sucker.] In bot., producing suckers.

Surcoats.—a, 15th century; b, late 13th century.

surd (sėrd). [L. surdus, deaf, dull, indistinct, silent.] **I.** a. Deaf†; also, lacking sense or perception†; senseless, stupid, or irrational; in math., of a quantity, not capable of being expressed in rational numbers; irrational; of an expression, etc., containing or involving a surd quantity; in phonetics, uttered with breath and not with voice, as the sounds p, s, f, etc. (opposed to sonant). **II.** n. In math., a surd quantity; in phonetics, a surd speech-sound.

sure (shör), a.; compar. surer, superl. surest. [OF. seur (F. sûr), < L. securus: see secure.] Free from apprehension or doubt as to the reliability, character, action, etc., of something (often with of: as, to be sure of one's friends; sure of one's self, or of one's position; sure of one's dates or figures); confident, as of something expected (as, sure of ultimate success); convinced, fully persuaded, or positive, as of something firmly believed (as, sure of a person's guilt; sure that one is right); assured or certain beyond question, as of something that cannot be otherwise (as, man is sure of death but of little else); also, worthy of confidence, or reliable (as, a sure messenger); firm or stable (as, to stand on sure ground); unfailing, or never disappointing expectations (as, a sure method, means, or cure); unerring, or never missing, slipping, etc. (as, a sure aim; a sure touch; sure-footed); admitting of no doubt or question (as, sure proof; to make one's case sure); inevitable (as, death is sure); destined, bound inevitably, or certain (to do or be as specified: as, he is sure to come, to win, or to be right; "Any step of Theobald's was sure to be objectionable in his father's eyes," S. Butler's "Way of All Flesh," xii.); bound by alliance, friendship, betrothal, etc. (commonly with to)†; also, secure or safe (obs. or archaic: as, "The forest is not three leagues off; If we recover that, we are sure enough," Shakspere's "Two Gentlemen of Verona," v. 1. 12); involving no risk†; unable or unlikely to do harm†.—**be sure,** be certain or careful (to do or be as specified: as, be sure to close the windows); do not fail; take care (that).—**for sure,** as a certainty; surely: as, "Now, now, for sure, deliverance is at hand" (Milton's "Paradise Regained," ii. 35).—**to be sure,** surely; certainly; without doubt: as, "To be sure, what you say is very reasonable" (Sheridan's "School for Scandal," iv. 3).—**to make sure,** to make matters certain; ensure certainty, as of something desired (with of or that:

as, "Every man emptied his piece each morning so as to *make sure* of having a dry priming," Conan Doyle's "Exploits of Brigadier Gerard," iii.); also, to get sure knowledge (*of* or *that*: as, "She had looked to *make sure* that everything was ready before she descended," H. G. Wells's "Bealby," iii.); also, to feel sure, confident, or convinced, with or without warrant (*of* or *that*: as, "He . . . would push me so close that I *made sure* he must run me through the body," Stevenson's "Kidnapped," xxi.).—**sure,** *adv.* Surely, undoubtedly, or certainly (now chiefly prov. or colloq.: as, " 'Am I meant to tell you the truth?' 'Sure!' " L. Merrick's "House of Lynch," i.); inevitably or without fail (as, it will come as *sure* as fate; I'll do it, *sure*); also, securely or safely (obs. or archaic).

sure=foot-ed (shōr′fut′ed), *a.* Sure of foot (as, "Never was there a more steady, *sure-footed* beast": W. H. Hudson's "Purple Land," xxvii.); not liable to stumble, slip, or fall; fig., proceeding surely; unerring.—**sure′=foot′ed-ness,** *n.*

sure-ly (shōr′li), *adv.* In a sure manner; confidently (archaic: as, "as if they *surely* knew their sovran Lord was by," Milton's "On the Morning of Christ's Nativity," 60); firmly, unerringly, or without missing, slipping, etc.; undoubtedly, assuredly, or certainly (as, the results are *surely* encouraging); often (in emphatic utterances that are not necessarily sustained by fact), assuredly, as must be believed (as, *surely* you are mistaken; you *surely* will not do that!); inevitably or without fail (as, slowly but *surely* the end approached); securely or safely (obs. or archaic).—**sure′-ness,** *n.*

sure-ty (shōr′ti), *n.*; pl. *-ties* (-tiz). [OF. *seurte* (F. *sûreté*), < L. *securitas*, < *securus*: see *sure* and *secure*, and cf. *security*.] The state or quality of being sure (now rare); esp., certainty (archaic: as, "She saw it [state of affairs] with bitter *surety*," Galsworthy's "Saint's Progress," iii. 12); security† or safety†; also, something that is sure, as a fact (obs. or archaic: as, "Who can tell that for a *surety?*" Stevenson's "Kidnapped," i.); also, that which makes sure; ground of confidence or safety; security against loss or damage; security for the fulfilment of an obligation, the payment of a debt, etc.; a pledge, guaranty, or bond; also, one who has made himself responsible for another; specif., in *law*, one who has bound himself with or for another who remains primarily liable; one who has contracted that he will be answerable for the debt, default, or miscarriage of another; *eccles.*, a sponsor at baptism.—**sure′-ty-ship,** *n.*

surf (sėrf), *n.* [Earlier *suff*; origin uncertain.] The swell of the sea which breaks upon a shore or upon shoals; the mass or line of foamy water caused by the breaking of the sea upon a shore, etc.: as, "He was washed out where there is a great *surf* on the white rocks" (Synge's "Riders to the Sea"); "the noise of the white *surf* along the coast" (J. Conrad's "Lord Jim," xxii.).

sur-face (sėr′fās). [F. *surface*, < *sur-*, over (see *sur-*), + *face*, E. *face*: cf. *superficies*.] **I.** *n.* The outer face, or outside, of a thing; the superficies; the part of a body which comes into immediate contact with other bodies or with the air or empty space; any face of a body or thing (as, the six *surfaces* of a cube; the inner *surface* of a tube or a bottle; the under *surface* of cloth); a face, area, or ground with reference to special use or treatment (as, a prepared *surface* for painting); also, extent or area of outer face; superficial area; also, fig., the outward appearance, esp. as distinguished from the inner nature (as, to look below the *surface* of a matter; "The unanimity which had appeared in the Senate's final determination was on the *surface* only," Froude's "Cæsar," xx.); what appears on a casual view or consideration; specif., in *geom.*, an extension having only two dimensions; the boundary between two solid spaces not adjacent to a third space; the boundary of a solid. **II.** *a.* Of, on, or pertaining to the surface; superficial; external; apparent, rather than real.—**sur′face,** *v. t.*; *-faced*, *-facing.* To finish as to surface; give a particular kind of surface to; make even or smooth.—**sur′faced,** *a.* Having a surface (as specified): as, smooth-*surfaced.*—**sur′face=plate,** *n.* In *mech.*, a flat plate used by mechanics for testing surfaces which are to be made perfectly flat.—**sur′fa-cer** (-fā-sėr), *n.* One who finishes surfaces; a machine for finishing surfaces.—**sur′face=ten″sion,** *n.* In *physics*, the tension of the surface film of a liquid, dependent on molecular forces, and associated with the phenomena of capillary action: as, "In the case of a thin soap-film, sudden extension of any part . . . alters the *surface tension* . . . this change must be an increase of tension, and constitutes a species of elasticity in the film" (Encyc. Brit., 11th ed., IX. 396).

surf=bird (sėrf′bėrd), *n.* A plover-like bird, *Aphriza virgata*, of the Pacific coast of America, allied to the turnstones.

Surf-bird.

surf=boat (sėrf′bōt), *n.* A boat of a strong and buoyant type, adapted for passing safely through surf.—**surf′=boat″-man** (-man), *n.*; pl. *-men.*

surf=duck (sėrf′duk), *n.* A scoter, esp. the surf-scoter.

sur-feit (sėr′fit), *n.* [OF. *surfait, sorfait,* < *surfaire, sorfaire,* lit. 'overdo,' < *sur-* (see *sur-*) + *faire,* < L. *facere,* do.] Excess; an excessive amount; specif., excess in eating or drinking; an excessive indulgence in food or drink by which the stomach is overloaded and the system disordered; oppression or disorder of the system due to excessive eating or drinking; in general, disgust caused by excess, or satiety (as, "Why, sir, 'tis enough to give them a *surfeit* of religion, at first hearing": Defoe's "Robinson Crusoe," ii. 6).—**sur′feit,** *v.* **I.** *tr.* To bring to a state of surfeit by excess of food or drink; sicken by overfeeding; supply with anything to excess or satiety; satiate to the point of disgust (as, "*surfeited* with classical beauty": Du Maurier's "Trilby," i.). **II.** *intr.* To eat or drink to excess; suffer from the effects of overfeeding; indulge to excess in anything; become disgusted by excess.—**sur′feit-er,** *n.*

surf=fish (sėrf′fish), *n.* Any of the small to medium-sized viviparous fishes constituting the family *Embiotocidæ,* mostly inhabiting the shallow waters of the Pacific coast of North America.

White Surf-fish (*Phanerodon furcatus*).

surf-man (sėrf′man), *n.*; pl. *-men.* A man skilled in handling boats in surf, esp. one employed in the life-saving service.—**surf′man-ship,** *n.*

surf=sco-ter (sėrf′skō″tėr), *n.* A large scoter, *Œdemia perspicillata,* common in North America, the adult male of which has an entirely black plumage except for white areas on the head and neck.

surf-y (sėr′fi), *a.* Abounding with surf; forming or resembling surf.

surge (sėrj), *v.*; *surged, surging.* [L. *surgere, surrigere* (pp. *surrectus*), rise, < *sub,* under, + *regere,* direct.] **I.** *intr.* To rise and fall, or move along, on the waves, as a ship (as, to *surge* at anchor; "The schooner *surged* slowly forward," Kipling's "Captains Courageous," iii.); rise or roll in

Surf-scoter.

waves, or like waves (as, "We feel the floods *surging* over us," H. Melville's "Moby-Dick," ix.; smoke *surges* from a burning building; a crowd *surges* about a spot); rise as if by a heaving or swelling force (as, blood *surges* to the face; indignation *surges* up within one); swell, well, or sweep tempestuously; in *elect.*, to increase suddenly, as a current; oscillate violently; *naut.*, to slip back, as a rope. **II.** *tr.* To cause to surge or roll in or as in waves (as, "Great organs *surged* through arches dim Their jubilant floods in praise of him": Lowell's "Parable"); heave or sway with a waving motion (as, "A heavy wind seemed to *surge* the branches of the funeral pines": Bret Harte's "Mliss," i.); *naut.*, to slacken (a rope).—**surge,** *n.* A swelling wave, or billow (as, "Many an isle whose coral feet The *surges* of that ocean beat": Whittier's "Daniel Wheeler"); the swelling and rolling sea (as, "roll'd to starboard, roll'd to larboard, when the *surge* was seething free": Tennyson's "Choric Song," viii.); the rolling swell of the sea; also, a surging, wave-like volume or body of something (as, a *surge* of smoke, fire, or sound; "A *surge* of individuals vowed to death will perish to the last man," Buchan's "Hist. of the Great War," liii.); a surging movement, rush, or sweep, like that of swelling or rolling waves (lit. or fig.: as, the onward *surge* of an angry mob; the *surge* of thoughts or feelings to the mind); also, a spring of water†; in *elect.*, a sudden rush of current, a violent oscillatory disturbance, or the like; *naut.*, a surging, or slipping back, as of a rope; also, the tapered part of a capstan or the like, on which the rope may slip back.

sur-geon (sėr′jǫn), *n.* [AF. *surgien,* for OF. *serurgien, cirurgien* (F. *chirurgien*): see *chirurgeon.*] One who practises surgery (as distinguished from a physician); a medical officer in the army or navy, or in a military hospital; in Great Britain (esp. formerly), a general practitioner in medicine; in *zoöl.*, a surgeon-fish.—**sur′geon-cy** (-si), *n.;* pl. *-cies* (-siz). The office or position of a surgeon, as in the army or navy.—**sur′geon=fish,** *n.* Any of the tropical acanthopterygian fishes constituting the family *Teuthididæ,* having one or more lancet-like spines on each side of the base of the tail.—**sur′geon=gen′er-al,** *n.;* pl. *surgeons-general* or *surgeon-generals.* A medical officer of high rank in the army or navy service of a country; in the U. S. army, the chief of the Medical Department; in the U. S. navy, the chief of the Bureau of Medicine and Surgery.

sur-ger-y (sėr′jėr-i), *n.;* pl. *-ies* (-iz). [OF. *surgerie,* for *cirurgerie:* cf. *chirurgery.*] The art, practice, or work of treating diseases, injuries, or deformities by manual operation or instrumental appliances; the branch of medicine that is concerned with such treatment; also, a room or place where surgical operations are performed; in Great Britain, the consulting-office and dispensary of a general medical practitioner (as, "The doctor was due to be entering his *surgery* for the **afternoon session**": Arnold Bennett's "Riceyman Steps," iv. 2).

sur-gi-cal (sėr′ji-kạl), *a.* [Cf. *chirurgical.*] Of, pertaining to, or **involving** surgery; used in surgery.—**sur′gi-cal-ly,** *adv.*

sur-gy (sėr′ji), *a.* Full of surges, or billowy, as the sea; surging or swelling; produced by surges (as, "the *surgy* murmurs of the lonely sea": Keats's "Endymion," i.).

su-ri-cate, su-ri-cat (sō′ri-kăt, -kat), *n.* [F. *surikate;* prob. of South African origin.] A small burrowing mammal, *Suricata tetra-dactyla,* of South Africa, of a grayish color with dark bands across the back, belonging to the civet family.

Suricate.

Su-ri-nam (sō-ri-năm′) **toad.** [From *Surinam,* or Dutch Guiana.] An aquatic toad, *Pipa americana,* of northern South America, notable for the manner in which the eggs, distributed by the male over the back of the female, are retained there, in cells of the skin which form about them, until fully developed into young. See cut in next column.

sur-loin (sėr′loin), *n.* See *sirloin.*

sur-ly (sėr′li), *a.;* compar. *surlier,* superl. *surliest.* [For earlier *sirly,* lordly, < *sir.*] Lordly†, arrogant†, or domineering†; hence, churlishly rude or ill-humored, as a person or the manner, tone, expression, etc. (as, "He seems to be *surly,* vulgar, and disagreeable," Miss Burney's "Evelina,"

Surinam Toad, female.

xii.; "a *surly* and even savage scowl," Scott's "Guy Mannering," iv.); uncivil and morose; of an animal, ill-tempered and unfriendly (as, "On attempting to stroke one of these *surly* brutes [dogs] on the head, he displayed his teeth and growled savagely": W. H. Hudson's "Purple Land," ii.); fig., rough, inclement, or stormy, as weather, the sea, etc. (as, "chill November's *surly* blast": Burns's "Man Was Made to Mourn," 1); gloomy or dismal (as, "You shall hear the *surly* sullen bell Give warning . . . that I am fled From this vile world," Shakspere's "Sonnets," lxxi.; "The drawbridge dropped with a *surly* clang," Lowell's "Vision of Sir Launfal," i. 3); also, refractory, as soil.—**sur′li-ly,** *adv.*—**sur′li-ness,** *n.*

sur-mise (sėr-mīz′), *n.* [OF. *surmise,* accusation, < *surmettre,* put upon, charge, < L. *supermittere,* put upon, < *super,* over, + *mittere,* send.] A formal allegation†; a charge† or imputation†; also, a suspicion†; also, an idea or thought of something as being possible or likely, although without any certain or strong evidence (as, "Many *surmises* of evil alarm the hearts of the people," Longfellow's "Evangeline," i. 2; "If our *surmise* be true, the point . . . ought to lie west of the axis of the glacier," Tyndall's "Forms of Water," § 24); a conjecture; conjecture or surmising (as, the actual cause is wholly a matter of *surmise*; "Silent we with blind *surmise* Regarding, while she read," Tennyson's "Princess," iv. 362); a matter of conjecture (as, "We see how much of that which we would most gladly know in the distant past must ever remain a *surmise*": Morley's "Oliver Cromwell," iv. 6); also, mental conception†; imagination†.—**sur-mise′,** *v.;* -mised, -mising. **I.** *tr.* To allege or charge in accusation† (as, "most slanderous accusations, and untrue matters *surmised* against them to the queen and realm": Strype's "Memorials of Cranmer," iii. 8); also, to suspect†; also, to form a surmise of, conjecture, or guess (as, "Mr. Satterlee might perhaps *surmise* the truth": W. Churchill's "Coniston," ii. 12); think or infer without certain or strong evidence (as, "I had some right to *surmise* that my illness may have been merely the effect of the hot wind": Kinglake's "Eothen," xviii.); also, to conceive†, imagine†, or suppose†. **II.** *intr.* To surmise something; conjecture.—**sur-mis′er** (-mī′zėr), *n.*

sur-mount (sėr-mount′), *v. t.* [OF. F. *surmonter,* < *sur-,* above (see *sur-*), + *monter,* E. *mount*[2].] To mount or rise above; reach or extend above; fig., to surpass† or excel†; exceed in amount†; prevail over (as, "Her sisterly tenderness could not but *surmount* other feelings at this moment": George Eliot's "Middlemarch," v.); also, to mount upon, or get on the top of; esp., to mount upon and cross over (as, to *surmount* a hill; "The mountain tribes . . . could not even delay his march. In seven days he had *surmounted* the passes," Froude's "Cæsar," xiv.); get over or across (barriers, obstacles, etc., lit. or fig.: as, "It was impossible for cowards to *surmount* the barriers of unknown seas and hostile Barbarians," Gibbon's "Decline and Fall of the Roman Empire," xli.; "difficulties which I almost despair of *surmounting*," Miss Burney's "Evelina," xxviii.); also, to be or rest on the top of or above (as, a statue *surmounting* a column; "a man . . . with an enormous black turban *surmounting* a dark face," J. Conrad's "Rescue," iv. 5); furnish with something placed on the top or above (as, to *surmount* a tower with a spire).—**sur-mount'a-ble**, *a.* That may be surmounted.—**sur-mount'er**, *n.*

sur-mul-let (sêr-mul'et), *n.* [F. *surmulet*, OF. *sormulet*: cf. *sore*[1] and *mullet*[1].] Any fish of the family *Mullidæ*, comprising the red mullets. See *mullet*[1].

Surmullet, or Red Mullet (*Mullus barbatus*).

sur-name (sêr'-nām), *n.* [From *sur-* + *name*, after OF. F. *surnom*, surname: see *sur-* and *noun*.] A name added to a person's name or names, as from his place of birth or abode or from some characteristic or achievement (as, "Simeon of the pillar, by *surname* Stylites," Tennyson's "St. Simeon Stylites," 158; William II. of England received the *surname* of Rufus, 'red'); also, the name which a person has in common with the other members of his family, as distinguished from his Christian or given name; a family name.—**sur-name**, *v. t.*; *-named*, *-naming.* To give a surname to; call by a surname: as, "Philip III. (*surnamed* the Bold)" (Hallam's "Europe during the Middle Ages," i. 1); "And Simon he *surnamed* Peter" (Mark, iii. 16).

sur-pass (sêr-pás'), *v. t.* [F. *surpasser*, < *sur-*, beyond (see *sur-*), + *passer*, E. *pass*.] To pass or go beyond (a limit, etc.: obs. or archaic as, "Nor let the sea *Surpass* his bounds," Milton's "Paradise Lost," xi. 894); fig., to go beyond in amount, extent, or degree, be greater than, or exceed (as, "an agility *surpassing* that of a wild cat": W. H. Hudson's "Purple Land," xiii.); go beyond in excellence or achievement, be superior to, or excel (as, "Charles Townshend . . . *surpassed* as a debater only by Murray and Pitt": Bancroft's "Hist. of the U. S.," Amer. Revolution, i. 2); also, to be beyond the range or capacity of, or transcend (as, misery that *surpasses* description; "Men are fond . . . of appearing to understand what *surpasses* the comprehension of ordinary people," Adam Smith's "Wealth of Nations," iv. 9).—**sur-pass'a-ble**, *a.* That may be surpassed.—**sur-pass'er**, *n.*—**sur-pass'ing**, *p. a.* That surpasses, exceeds, or excels; much greater than or superior to the ordinary; extraordinary: as, "structures of *surpassing* magnificence" (Amelia B. Edwards's "Thousand Miles up the Nile," xv.).—**sur-pass'ing-ly**, *adv.*—**sur-pass'ing-ness**, *n.*

sur-plice (sêr'plis), *n.* [OF. *surpliz*, *surpeliz* (F. *surplis*), < ML. *superpellicium* (so called because worn over the fur garments worn for warmth in church), < L. *super*, over, + ML. *pellicia*, fur garment: see *pelisse*.] A loose-fitting, broad-sleeved white vestment, properly of linen, worn over the cassock by clergymen and choristers; also, an arrangement of the material at the front of a woman's bodice in folds descending from each shoulder and crossing on the breast (also used attributively: as, a *surplice* blouse; a *surplice* front).—**sur'pliced** (-plist), *a.* Wearing a surplice.

sur-plus (sêr'plus). [OF. F. *surplus*, < ML. *superplus*, < L. *super*, over, + *plus*, more.] **I.** *n.* That which remains above what is used or needed; an amount in excess of what is required; esp., an amount of assets in excess of what is requisite to meet liabilities. **II.** *a.* Being a surplus; being in excess of what is required: as, "the *surplus* produce of America, imported into Europe" (Adam Smith's "Wealth of Nations," iv. 7. 3).—**sur'plus-age** (-āj), *n.* Surplus; excess; sometimes, an excess of words; in *law*, superfluous matter in a pleading.

sur-print (sêr'print), *v. t.* [See *sur-*.] To print over with additional marks or matter; overprint; also, to print (additional marks, etc.) over something already printed.

Anglican Surplice.

sur-pri-sal (sêr-prī'zal), *n.* The act of surprising, or the state of being surprised; a surprise.

sur-prise (sêr-prīz'), *v. t.*; *-prised*, *-prising.* [OF. F. *surpris*, pp. of *surprendre*, < ML. *superprendere*, < L. *super*, over, + *prendere*, *prehendere*, seize, take.] To seize or capture by a sudden, unexpected attack†; capture in any way†; now, to assail or attack suddenly or without warning, as an army, fort, or person that is unprepared (as, "The Sioux *surprised* and killed five men in a log station": Roosevelt's "Hunting Trips of a Ranchman," i.); also, to come upon suddenly and unexpectedly; take unawares; catch (a person, etc.) in the act of doing something; discover (a thing) suddenly; also, to lead or bring (a person, etc.) unawares, as into doing something not intended (as, "if by chance he has been *surprised* into a short nap at sermon": Addison, in "Spectator," 112); also, to seize or affect suddenly and unexpectedly† (as, "Fearfulness hath *surprised* the hypocrites": Isa. xxxiii. 14); also, to strike with a sudden feeling of wonder that arrests the thoughts, as at something unexpected or extraordinary (as, "I am *surprised* that this doctrine should come from some of the law servants of the Crown": Burke's "Conciliation with the Colonies").—**sur-prise'**, *n.* [OF. F. *surprise*, orig. fem. of *surpris*, pp.] The act of surprising; sudden assault or attack; a coming upon unexpectedly or taking unawares; also, the state or feeling of being surprised as by something unexpected; a feeling of wonder, arresting the thoughts, which is caused by something unexpected or extraordinary; also, something that excites this feeling, as an unexpected or extraordinary occurrence (as, "Life is a series of *surprises*": Emerson's "Essays," Experience).—**surprise party**, a body of troops for making an unexpected attack; also, a social gathering of persons who assemble by agreement, but without invitation, at the house of a common friend, usually bringing with them provisions for a repast.—**sur-pris'ed-ly** (-prī'zed-li), *adv.*—**sur-pris'er**, *n.*—**sur-pris'ing**, *p. a.* That surprises; esp., exciting surprise; astonishing.—**sur-pris'ing-ly**, *adv.*—**sur-pris'ing-ness**, *n.*

sur-re-al-ism (sêr-rē'al-izm), *n.* [F. *surréalisme*: see *sur-*.] A recent movement in literature and art (influenced by Freudism), based on the expression of thought uncontrolled by reason, and seeking to suggest the activities of the subconscious mind whether in dreams or during waking hours.—**sur-re'al-ist. I.** *n.* An adherent of surrealism. **II.** *a.* Pertaining to surrealism.—**sur-re-al-is'tic**, *a.*

sur-re-but (sur-ē-but'), *v. i.*; *-butted*, *-butting.* [See *sur-*.] In *law*, of a plaintiff, to reply to a defendant's rebutter.—**sur-re-but'tal**, *n.* In *law*, the giving of evidence to meet a defendant's rebuttal.—**sur-re-but'ter**, *n.* In *law*, a plaintiff's reply to a defendant's rebutter.

sur-re-join (sur-ē-join'), *v. i.* [See *sur-*.] In *law*, of a plaintiff, to reply to a defendant's rejoinder.—**sur-re-join'der**, *n.* In *law*, a plaintiff's reply to a defendant's rejoinder.

sur-ren-der (su-ren'dér), *v.* [OF. *surrendre*, < *sur-*, over (see *sur-*), + *rendre*, E. *render*[2].] **I.** *tr.* To yield (something) to the possession or power of another; deliver up possession of (something) upon demand or compulsion (as, to *surrender* a fort or a ship); give (one's self) up, esp. as a prisoner; give (one's self) over to some dominating influence or the like (as, "She *surrendered* herself to a certain tranquil gayety": H. James's "Europeans," i.); yield or resign (an office, privilege, etc.) in favor of another; give up, abandon, or relinquish (comfort, hope, etc.); specif., in *law*, to yield up (an estate) to one who has it in reversion or remainder; also, of a bail, to deliver up (his principal) into lawful custody. **II.** *intr.* To give one's self up, as into the power of another; submit or yield (as, "one who is gripped by two strong emotions, and longs to *surrender* to one or to the other": Galsworthy's "Saint's Progress," ii. 6).—**sur-ren'der**, *n.* The act or an act of surrendering; also, the deed by which a legal surrendering is made; in *insurance*, the abandonment of a policy by the party insured, for a consideration, the amount receivable (the 'surrender value') depending on the number of years elapsed from the commencement of the risk.—**sur-ren'der-er**, *n.*

sur-rep-ti-tious (sur-ep-tish'us), *a.* [L. *surrepticius*, *subrepticius*, < *surripere*, *subripere*, take secretly, < *sub*, under, + *rapere*, seize: see *rape*[1], and cf. *subreption* and *subreptitious*.] Obtained, done, made, etc., by stealth (as, "the *surreptitious* discharge of prisoners," Blackstone's "Commentaries," III. 130; "a *surreptitious* glance," Arnold Bennett's "Clayhanger," i. 8); secret and unauthorized; clandestine; also, acting in a stealthy way; also, obtained by subreption; subreptitious.—**sur-rep-ti′tious-ly,** *adv.*—**sur-rep-ti′tious-ness,** *n.*

sur-rey (sur′i), *n.*; pl. *surreys* (-iz). [From *Surrey*, county in southeastern England.] A light, four-wheeled, two-seated carriage with or without a top, and accommodating four persons.

sur-ro-gate (sur′ō-gāt), *v. t.*; *-gated, -gating.* [L. *surrogatus*, pp. of *surrogare, subrogare*, put in another's place, < *sub*, under, + *rogare*, ask: cf. *subrogate*.] To put into the place of another as a successor, substitute, or deputy; substitute for another; specif., to subrogate.—**sur′ro-gate,** *n.* One appointed to act for another; a substitute; a deputy; the deputy of an ecclesiastical judge, esp. of a bishop or his chancellor; a judicial officer having jurisdiction over the probate of wills, the administration of estates, etc. (local, U. S.); also, a thing substituted for another thing; a material used in place of another material.—**sur′ro-gate-ship,** *n.*

sur-round (su-round′), *v. t.* [OF. *suronder, surunder*, < LL. *superundare*, overflow, < L. *super*, over, + *undare*, rise in waves, < *unda*, a wave.] To overflow†, inundate†, or submerge†; also, to inclose on all sides, or encompass; form an inclosure round, or encircle; specif., to inclose, as a body of troops, so as to cut off communication or retreat; invest, as a fortified place; also, to make the circuit of† (as, "Our men began to range over the island, if it was such (for we never *surrounded* it)": Defoe's "Captain Singleton," xv.).—**sur-round′,** *n.* The act or an act of surrounding; specif., the process of hunting some animals, as buffaloes, by surrounding them and driving them into a place from which they cannot escape; also, a cordon of hunters hunting in this manner; also, a border or edging of some material surrounding a central piece.—**sur-round′er,** *n.*—**sur-round′ing,** *n.* That which surrounds; *pl.*, the things that surround or environ anything; environing circumstances, conditions, etc. (as, "She could not all at once undo the effect of such *surroundings* as the boy had had at Battersby": S. Butler's "Way of All Flesh," xxxv.); environment; *sing.*, a body of surrounding or attending persons; entourage; *pl.*, persons surrounding or attending upon one.

sur-roy-al (sėr′roi″al), *n.* [See *sur-.*] A crown-antler (above the royal antler).

sur-tax (sėr′taks), *n.* [F. *surtaxe*, < *sur-*, over (see *sur-*), + *taxe*, tax.] An additional or extra tax on something already taxed; esp., one of a graded series of taxes, in addition to the normal tax, levied on incomes exceeding a certain amount (as, "A system of *surtaxes* was evolved in order to make the man of large income pay more proportionally than the smaller taxpayer": A. W. Mellon's "Taxation," i.).—**sur-tax** (sėr′taks or sėr-taks′), *v. t.* To put an additional or extra tax on; charge with a surtax.

sur-tout (sėr-töt′ or -tö′, F. sür-tö), *n.* [F., < *sur-*, over (see *sur-*), + *tout*, < L. *totus*, all.] A man's overcoat.

sur-veil-lance (sėr-vāl′ans or -vāl′yans), *n.* [F., < *surveiller*, watch over, < *sur-*, over (see *sur-*), + *veiller*, < L. *vigilare*, watch.] Watch kept over a person, etc., esp. over a suspect, a prisoner, or the like; sometimes, spying; also, supervision or superintendence.—**sur-veil′lant.** [F., ppr. of *surveiller*.] **I.** *a.* Exercising surveillance. **II.** *n.* One who exercises surveillance: as, "His mixed character of ambassador and of political *surveillant* . . . gave him a real weight in the Tartar councils" (De Quincey's "Revolt of the Tartars").

sur-vey (sėr-vā′), *v.* [AF. *surveer*, OF. *surveeir, sorveeir*, < ML. *supervidere*, oversee: see *supervise*, and cf. *purvey*.] **I.** *tr.* To look over or upon, as from above (as, "I am monarch of all I *survey*, My right there is none to dispute": Cowper's "Alexander Selkirk," 1); take a general or comprehensive view of (as, "Strickland looked away and idly *surveyed* the ceiling": Maugham's "Moon and Sixpence," xxvi.); consider or contemplate as a whole (as, "When all thy mercies, O my God, My rising soul *surveys*": Addison, in "Spectator," 453); also, to view in detail; scrutinize, inspect, or examine; esp., to inspect or examine formally or officially in order to ascertain condition, value, etc. (as, to *survey* an estate or a building; to *survey* merchandise); specif., to determine the form, boundaries, position, extent, etc., of, as a part of the earth's surface, by means of linear and angular measurements and the application of the principles of geometry and trigonometry; ascertain the form and dimensions of, as a tract of ground, a coast, a harbor, etc., by such means, in order to represent the details by a map, plan, or the like; also, to see† or perceive†. **II.** *intr.* To survey land, etc.; practise surveying.—**sur-vey** (sėr′vā or sėr-vā′), *n.* The act or an act of surveying; a comprehensive view (lit. or fig.: as, "a moment's *survey* of her face," Dickens's "Dombey and Son," liii.; "to avoid any *survey* of the past," Jane Austen's "Sense and Sensibility," xlvii.); an inspection or examination; esp., a formal or official examination of the particulars of something, made in order to ascertain condition, character, etc.; a statement or description embodying the result of this; a body of persons engaged in such an examination; specif., a determining of form, boundaries, position, extent, etc., as of a part of the earth's surface, by linear and angular measurements, etc.; the measured plan or a description of such an operation; a body of persons, or a government department or bureau, engaged in such work; also, a district for the collection of the customs, under the inspection and authority of a particular officer (U. S.).—**sur-vey′a-ble,** *a.* Capable of being surveyed.—**sur-vey′ance,** *n.* The act of surveying; survey.—**sur-vey′ing,** *n.* The act of one who surveys; specif., the process, occupation, or art of making surveys of land, etc.

sur-vey-or (sėr-vā′or), *n.* One who surveys; an overseer or supervisor; one who designs, and superintends the construction of, a building (Eng.); one who inspects or examines something formally or officially for the purpose of ascertaining condition, value, etc.; a customs officer whose duty it is to ascertain the quantity and value of imported merchandise (U. S.); specif., one whose business it is to survey land, etc.; one who practises surveying.—**surveyors′ measure,** a system of units of length used in surveying land: 7.92 inches (or 12 inches) = 1 link; 100 links = 1 chain (66 feet, or 100 feet). See *chain, n.*—**sur-vey′or=gen′er-al,** *n.*; pl. *surveyors-.* A principal or head surveyor; specif., an officer of the U. S. government who supervises the surveys of public lands.—**sur-vey′or-ship,** *n.*

sur-view (sėr-vū′), *n.* [OF. *surveue*, < *surveeir*, E. *survey*.] A view, esp. a mental view, of something; a survey. [Archaic.]

sur-vi-val (sėr-vī′val), *n.* The act or fact of surviving; also, one who or that which survives; a surviving remnant; a surviving custom, observance, belief, or the like.—**survival of the fittest,** in *biol.*, the fact or principle of the survival or continued existence of those forms of animal and vegetable life which are best fitted for the existing conditions, while related but less fit forms become extinct. Cf. *natural selection*, at *selection*.

sur-vive (sėr-vīv′), *v.*; *-vived, -viving.* [OF. F. *survivre*, < L. *supervivere*, < *super*, over, beyond, + *vivere*, live.] **I.** *intr.* To remain alive after the death of some one or after the cessation of something or the occurrence of some event (as, his wife died last winter, and he did not long *survive*); continue to live; hence, to remain in existence after some person, thing, or event (as, "Yea, though I die, the scandal will *survive*": Shakspere's "Lucrece," 204); continue to exist. **II.** *tr.* To continue to live or exist after the death, cessation, or occurrence of; outlive; outlast: as, "No male issue *survived* Robert" (Hallam's "Europe during the Middle Ages," iii. 2); "Sir Dugald is supposed to have *survived* the Revolution" (Scott's "Legend of Montrose," xxiii.); "These frail fragments of papyrus have *survived* the wreck of ages" (Amelia B. Edwards's "Thousand Miles up the Nile," xv.).—

sur-vi-vor (-vī′vor), *n.* One who or that which survives; in *law*, that one of two or more designated persons, as joint tenants or others having a joint interest, who outlives the other or others.—**sur-vi′vor-ship,** *n.* The condition of being a survivor; the state of surviving; in *law*, a right depending on survival; the right of the survivor or survivors of two or more joint tenants or others having a joint interest, to take the whole upon the death of the other or others; the right of future succession, in case of survival, to some office not vacant at the time of the grant.

(variable) đ as d or j, ş as s or sh, ţ as t or ch, ẓ as z or zh; *o*, F. *cloche*; ü, F. *menu*; ċh, Sc. *loch*; ṅ, F. *bonbon*; ′, primary accent; ″, secondary accent; †, obsolete; <, from; +, and; =, equals. See also lists at beginning of book.

sus-cept-ance (su-sep'tạns), *n.* [L. *susceptus*, pp.: see *susception*.] In *elect.*, in alternating-current circuits, the wattless component of admittance.

sus-cep-ti-bil-i-ty (su-sep-ti-bil'i-ti), *n.*; pl. *-ties* (-tiz). The state or character of being susceptible; capability of receiving, admitting, undergoing, or being affected by, something (with *of* or, now more usually, *to*): liability (*to*: as, *susceptibility* to injury, or to a disease); sensitiveness (*to*: as, "her quick and ready *susceptibility* to Svengali's hypnotic influence," Du Maurier's "Trilby," ii.); without an adjunct, capability of being affected, esp. easily; capacity for receiving mental or moral impressions; tendency to be emotionally affected; sensibility; sometimes, sentimental impressibility; *pl.*, capacities for emotion (as, "Blunt *susceptibilities* are very consistent with strong propensities": C. Brontë's "Professor," x.); sensitive feelings (as, "The party with whom he was sailing had offended his *susceptibilities*," Archibald Marshall's "Anthony Dare," xi.); sensibilities; specif., *sing.*, in *elect.*, the ratio of the magnetization produced in a piece of iron or the like to the magnetizing force.

sus-cep-ti-ble (su-sep'ti-bl), *a.* [LL. *susceptibilis*, < L. *suscipere*: see *susception*.] Capable of receiving, admitting, undergoing, or being affected by, something (with *of* or *to*); admitting or capable (*of*: as, *susceptible* of a high polish, of change, of fusion, or of various interpretations); open to the influence (*of*: as, *susceptible* of enthusiasm, or of pity); accessible or especially liable (*to*: as, *susceptible* to attack, to injury, or to a disease); sensitive or especially open (*to*: as, *susceptible* to impressions, to influences, or to flattery); also (without an adjunct), capable of being affected, esp. easily; subject to mental or emotional impressions, readily impressed, or impressionable (as, "Their *susceptible* hearts soon melted at the beautiful music": Du Maurier's "Trilby," iii.); often, sentimentally impressible, or especially sensitive to the charms or allurements of the opposite sex (as, "the fair slave of a notoriously *susceptible* old warrior": G. Meredith's "Lord Ormont and His Aminta," xv.).—**sus-cep'ti-ble-ness,** *n.*—**sus-cep'ti-bly,** *adv.*

sus-cep-tion (su-sep'shọn), *n.* [L. *susceptio(n-)*, < *suscipere* (pp. *susceptus*), undertake, assume, undergo, receive, < *sus-*, for *sub*, under, + *capere*, take.] The act of taking up, assuming, or receiving†; also, merely passive mental reception (rare).

sus-cep-tive (su-sep'tiv), *a.* [ML. *susceptivus*, < L. *suscipere*: see *susception*.] Characterized by taking or receiving; receptive; esp., readily affected by impressions; susceptible; also, susceptible (*of*); admitting or capable (*of*); open to the influence (*of*).—**sus-cep'tive-ness, sus-cep-tiv-i-ty** (sus-ep-tiv'i-ti), *n.*

sus-lik (sus'lik), *n.* [Russ.] A common ground-squirrel or spermophile, *Citellus* (or *Spermophilus*) *citillus*, of Europe and Asia; also, some related species.

Suslik (*Citellus citillus*).

sus-pect (sus-pekt'), *v.* [L. *suspectus*, pp. of *suspicere*, look up to, look at secretly, suspect, < *sub*, under, + *specere*, look at.] **I.** *tr.* To doubt the innocence, uprightness, truth, sincerity, or the like, of (persons), or the honesty, genuineness, desirable quality, soundness, or the like, of (things), on slight evidence or without evidence; imagine to be guilty, false, counterfeit, undesirable, defective, bad, etc., with insufficient proof or with no proof; also, to imagine or believe to be rightly chargeable with something stated, usually something wrong or something considered as undesirable, on little or no evidence (as, to *suspect* a person of murder, of dishonesty, of socialistic tendencies, or of having been deceived; to *suspect* a bill to be a counterfeit; to *suspect* a man of being, or to be, the donor of an anonymous gift); also, to imagine to be the case or to be likely (as, to *suspect* treachery; to *suspect* a man's preference for a particular candidate; to *suspect* that a person is guilty, is not well, or is going to win; "I *suspect* his knowledge did not amount to much," Lamb's "Old Benchers of the Inner Temple"); have a vague notion of; surmise. **II.** *intr.* To imagine something, esp. something evil, wrong, or undesirable, to be the case; have suspicion.—**sus-pect** (sus-pekt' or sus'pekt), *n.* [= F. *suspect*, < L. *suspectus*, pp.] One suspected; a person suspected of a crime, offense, or the like: as, "The arrests and executions of *suspects* were going on now as briskly as ever" (H. G. Wells's "Outline of History," xxxvii. § 11).—**sus-pect'a-ble,** *a.* That may be suspected; open to suspicion.—**sus-pect'er,** *n.*—**sus-pect'ful,** *a.* Inclined to suspect (obs. or rare); also, causing suspicion†.

sus-pend (sus-pend'), *v.* [OF. F. *suspendre*, < L. *suspendere* (pp. *suspensus*), hang up, support, keep undetermined or uncertain, stay, suspend, < *sus-*, for *sub*, under, + *pendere*, hang.] **I.** *tr.* To hang by attachment to something above (as, to *suspend* a lamp from the ceiling); attach so as to allow free movement, as on a hinge; keep from falling or sinking, as if by hanging (as, solid particles *suspended* in a liquid); also, to cause to depend, or be conditioned or contingent, on something (now rare: as, "It is dangerous for a man and woman to *suspend* their fate upon each other, at a time when opinions are fixed," Johnson's "Rasselas," xxix.); also, to hold or keep undetermined, or refrain from forming or concluding definitely (as, to *suspend* one's judgment or opinion); keep in a state of uncertainty or suspense†; keep in a state of fixed attention† (as, "The village-matron, round the blazing hearth, *Suspends* the infant audience with her tales": Akenside's "Pleasures of Imagination," i. 257); also, to defer or postpone, as sentence on a convicted person; also, to cause to cease, or bring to a stop or stay, usually for a time (as, "While these prayers and exhortations are going on, every employment in the camp is *suspended*," Irving's "Captain Bonneville," xlv.; to *suspend* payment, to cease meeting financial obligations because of inability, or become insolvent); cause to cease for a time from operation or effect, as a law, rule, privilege, or the like; also, to debar, usually for a time, from the exercise of an office or function or the enjoyment of a privilege (as, a student is *suspended* for a breach of discipline); also, in *music*, to prolong (a tone in a chord) into the following chord, thus holding back the progression of the part in which it occurs, usually so as to produce a temporary discord. **II.** *intr.* To come to a stop or stay, usually a temporary one; cease from operation for a time; specif., to stop payment, or be unable to meet financial obligations.—**sus-pend'er,** *n.* One who or that which suspends; esp., *pl.*, the pair of straps or bands worn over the shoulders for holding up the trousers.

sus-pense (sus-pens'), *n.* [OF. F. *suspens*, adj. (in phrase *en suspens*, in suspense), < L. *suspensus*, undetermined, uncertain, pp. of *suspendere*, E. *suspend*.] The state of being suspended, or kept undetermined (as, to hold one's judgment in *suspense*); sometimes, the act of suspending, or keeping undetermined; also, a state of mental uncertainty, as in awaiting a decision or outcome, usually with more or less apprehension or anxiety (as, "Mrs. Bagot looked up into her face, herself breathless with keen *suspense* and cruel anxiety—almost imploring": Du Maurier's "Trilby," iv.); sometimes, a state of mental indecision; also, undecided or doubtful condition, as of affairs (as, "leaving this in *suspense* as a thing not altogether certainly known," Hooker's "Ecclesiastical Polity," v. 72. 8; "For a few days matters hung in *suspense*," Froude's "Cæsar," xi.); also, deferment† or postponement†; also, temporary cessation†; abeyance†.

sus-pen-sion (sus-pen'shọn), *n.* [L. *suspensio(n-)*, < *suspendere*, E. *suspend*.] The act of suspending, or the state of being suspended; the act or state of hanging from a support; the condition of being kept from falling or sinking, as of solid particles in a liquid; a keeping or being kept undetermined, as of judgment or opinion; a keeping or being kept in doubt or suspense (now rare); deferment or postponement; cessation or stoppage, esp. for a time (as, "a temporary *suspension* of labor": Cooper's "Prairie," xxxii.); temporary abrogation, as of a law or privilege; stoppage of payment of debts or claims because of financial inability, or insolvency; debarment, esp. for a time, as from a function, office, or privilege; also, something suspended, as from a support; matter suspended in a liquid or other medium; also, something on or by which something else is suspended or hung; also, in *music*, a holding back of the progression of a part in harmony by prolonging a tone in one chord into the following chord, usually producing a temporary discord; the tone so prolonged.—**sus-pen'sion=bridge'**, *n.* A bridge in which the roadway is suspended from ropes, chains, or wire cables, usually hung between massive towers of masonry or steel, and securely fastened at the extremities.—**sus-pen'sion=vase'**, *n.* A vase with a handle or handles by which it may be suspended without spilling the contents.

Suspension-vases.

sus-pen-sive (sus-pen'siv), *a.* [ML. *suspensivus*, < L. *suspendere*, E. *suspend*.] Pertaining to or characterized by suspension, as from a support; also, inclined to suspend the judgment; undecided in mind; pertaining to or characterized by suspense, or mental uncertainty or apprehension; of words, phrases, etc., keeping one in suspense; also, having the effect of suspending or temporarily stopping the operation of something (as, a *suspensive* veto).—**sus-pen'sive-ly**, *adv.*—**sus-pen'sive-ness**, *n.*

sus-pen-sor (sus-pen'sor), *n.* [ML., < L. *suspendere*, E. *suspend*.] That by which something is suspended; a suspensory ligament, bandage, etc.—**sus-pen'so-ry** (-sō-ri). **I.** *a.* Serving or fitted to suspend or hold up, as a ligament, muscle, bandage, etc.; also, suspending the operation of something. **II.** *n.*; pl. *-ries* (-riz). A suspensory ligament, muscle, or the like; a suspensory bandage or the like, as for the scrotum.

sus-pi-cion (sus-pish'ọn), *n.* [Orig. < OF. *sospeçon* (F. *soupçon*), < ML. *suspectio(n-)*, suspicion, < L. *suspicere*, suspect; influenced later by OF. F. *suspicion*, < L. *suspicio(n-)*, suspicion, < *suspicere*: see *suspect*, *v.*] The act of suspecting; imagination of the existence of guilt, fault, falsity, defect, or the like, on slight evidence or without evidence; apprehension of something evil or wrong, on slight grounds or without proof (as, "Dark and threatening hints began to throw *suspicion* around his movements": Cooper's "Spy," iii.); the state of mind or feeling of one who suspects; an instance of suspecting something evil or wrong; more broadly, imagination of anything to be the case or to be likely; a vague notion of something (as, "I never had a *suspicion* that you loved me": W. H. Hudson's "Purple Land," xxvii.); also, a slight trace, a very small amount, or a suggestion (as, "a *suspicion* of a smile," W. Churchill's "Coniston," i. 10; "flip . . . made with beer and sugar, and a certain *suspicion* of strong waters," Holmes's "Elsie Venner," v.).—**sus-pi'cion**, *v. t.* To suspect: as, "Won't he *suspicion* what we're up to?" (Mark Twain's "Huckleberry Finn," xiii.). [Now colloq. or prov.]—**sus-pi'cion-al**, *a.* Of or pertaining to suspicion; esp., pertaining to or characterized by morbid or insane suspicions.

sus-pi-cious (sus-pish'us), *a.* [OF. *suspicieux*, < L. *suspiciosus*, < *suspicio(n-)*: see *suspicion*.] Full of or feeling suspicion (as, "I . . . began to be *suspicious* that I had caught a fearful cold": Hawthorne's "Blithedale Romance," ii.); also, inclined to suspect; esp., inclined to suspect evil; distrustful; also, expressing or indicating suspicion (as, *suspicious* glances); also, liable to cause suspicion, such as to excite suspicion, or questionable (as, "I was a vagabond and a *suspicious* person," Godwin's "Caleb Williams," xxxii. "All divergence from the customary is *suspicious* and repugnant," J. H. Robinson's "Mind in the Making," v. 11).—**sus-pi'cious-ly**, *adv.*—**sus-pi'cious-ness**, *n.*

sus-pire (sus-pīr'), *v.*; *-pired*, *-piring*. [L. *suspirare*, < *sub*, under, + *spirare*, breathe.] **I.** *intr.* To sigh; also, to breathe. [Now chiefly poetic.] **II.** *tr.* To utter with sighs; also, to breathe forth. [Now chiefly poetic.]—**sus-pi-ra'tion** (-pi-rā'shọn), *n.*

Sus-sex (sus'eks) **man.** Same as *Piltdown man.*

sus-tain (sus-tān'), *v. t.* [OF. *sustenir* (F. *soutenir*), < L. *sustinere* (pp. *sustentus*), < *sus-*, for *sub*, under, + *tenere*, hold.] To hold or bear up from below; bear the weight of; be the support of, as in a structure; keep from falling or sinking by supporting in any way, as by suspension from something above; bear or withstand (weight or pressure); also, to bear (a burden, charge, etc.); support or act (a part, rôle, etc.); undergo, experience, or suffer (injury, loss, etc.); endure without giving way or yielding, bear up against, or stand (as, to *sustain* a shock or a siege; "He is far too weak to *sustain* the rawness of the atmosphere," Mrs. Shelley's "Frankenstein," letter iv.); keep (a person, the mind, the spirits, etc.) from giving way, as under trial or affliction (as, "*Sustained* and soothed By an unfaltering trust, approach thy grave": Bryant's "Thanatopsis"); keep in due condition, force, etc., as one's reputation, the laws, etc.; keep up or keep going, as an action or process (as, "the free and unembarrassed manner in which the Portuguese peasantry *sustain* a conversation": Borrow's "Bible in Spain," i.); prolong, as a sound; supply with food and drink, or the necessaries of life, as persons; provide for by furnishing means or funds, as an institution; support by aid or countenance, as a person or cause; maintain or advocate, as a contention or theory; uphold as valid, just, or correct, as a claim or the person making it; confirm or corroborate, as a statement.—**sus-tain'a-ble**, *a.* Capable of being sustained.—**sus-tained'**, *p. a.* Kept up without intermission or flagging (as, "*sustained* industry": Charnwood's "Abraham Lincoln," i.); maintained uniformly, esp. at a high pitch or level (as, "the best *sustained* character in the masquerade": Hawthorne's "Twice-Told Tales," Howe's Masquerade); specif., in *music*, of a tone or note, held to its full time-value; also, maintained for several beats or measures in a middle voice-part while the other parts progress.—**sus-tain'ed-ly**, *adv.*—**sus-tain'er**, *n.*—**sus-tain'ment**, *n.* The act of sustaining, or the state of being sustained; also, one who or that which sustains; means of support; sustenance.

sus-te-nance (sus'tẹ-nạns), *n.* [OF. *sustenance* (F. *soutenance*), < *sustenir*, E. *sustain*.] The process of sustaining, or the state of being sustained, as with food and drink or the necessaries of life; also, means of sustaining life, food, or nourishment; means of living, or livelihood.

sus-ten-tac-u-lar (sus-ten-tak'ụ-lär), *a.* [L. *sustentaculum*, a support, < *sustentare*: see *sustentation*.] Pertaining to or of the nature of a support; supporting.

sus-ten-ta-tion (sus-ten-tā'shọn), *n.* [L. *sustentatio(n-)*, < *sustentare*, support, freq. of *sustinere*, E. *sustain*.] The act of sustaining, or the state of being sustained; a holding up or keeping from falling; maintenance in being or activity, or in due condition, or at a proper level or degree; the sustaining of life through the vital processes within an organism; a providing with the necessaries of life; provision with means or funds for upkeep; also, means of sustaining life; sustenance; food; nourishment.—**sus-ten'ta-tive** (-tạ-tiv), *a.* Tending or serving to sustain; of or pertaining to sustentation, as through the vital processes of an organism.

sus-ten-tion (sus-ten'shọn), *n.* [L. *sustinere* (pp. *sustentus*), E. *sustain*.] The act of sustaining, or the state or quality of being sustained.—**sus-ten'tive** (-tiv), *a.* Tending or serving to sustain.

su-sur-rant (sū-sur'ạnt), *a.* [L. *susurrans* (-ant-), ppr. of *susurrare*, murmur, whisper, < *susurrus*: see *susurrus*.] Softly murmuring; whispering.—**su-sur-ra-tion** (sū-su-rā'shọn), *n.* [LL. *susurratio(n-)*.] A soft murmuring; a whispering; a rustling.—**su-sur'rous**, *a.* Susurrant.

su-sur-rus (sū-sur'us), *n.* [L., a murmur, hum, whisper: cf. Skt. *svar-*, sound, Gr. σῦριγξ, pipe.] A soft murmuring sound; a whisper; a rustle: as, "the soft *susurrus* and sighs of the branches" (Longfellow's "Evangeline," ii. 4).

sut-ler (sut'lér), *n.* [MD. *soeteler* (D. *zoetelaar*), < *soetelen*, do dirty or mean work, peddle, tr. soil, sully: cf. G. *sudeln*, soil, daub.] A person who follows an army or lives in a garrison town, and sells provisions, etc., to the soldiers.—**sut'ler-ship**, *n.*

su-tra (sö'trä), *n.*; pl. *-tras* (-träz). [Skt. *sūtra*, orig. thread, string, < *siv*, sew: see *sew*.] [Also *cap.*] In *Sanskrit lit.*, one of a body of aphoristic rules, or one of a class of treatises consisting of such rules, forming a link between the Vedic and the later Sanskrit literature.

sut-tee (su-tē′), *n.* [Skt. *satī*, a true or good wife, prop. fem. of *sant*, being, existing, real, true, good, ppr. of *as-*, be: see *sooth*.] A Hindu widow who immolates herself on the funeral pile of her husband; also, the self-immolation of a Hindu widow in this manner (a practice now abolished in British India).—**sut-tee′ism**, *n.*

su-tur-al (sū′ṭūr-ạl), *a.* Of, pertaining to, or situated in a suture.—**su′tur-al-ly**, *adv.*

su-ture (sū′ṭūr), *n.* [L. *sutura*, a seam, suture, < *suere*, sew: see *sew*.] A seam as formed in sewing; a line of junction between two parts; also, a sewing together, or a joining as by sewing; specif., in *surg.*, a joining of the lips or edges of a wound or the like by stitching or some similar process; a particular method of doing this; one of the stitches or fastenings employed; in *anat.*, the line of junction of two bones, esp. of the skull, in an immovable articulation, or the articulation itself; in *zoöl.* and *bot.*, the line of junction, or the junction, of contiguous parts, as the line of closure between the valves of a bivalve shell, a seam where carpels of a pericarp join, or a line of dehiscence.—**su′ture**, *v. t.*; *-tured, -turing.* To unite by or as by a suture.

su-ze-rain (sū′zẹ-rạn), *n.* [F. *suzerain*, appar. formed, in imitation of *souverain*, E. *sovereign*, < *sus*, above, < L. *susum*, *sursum*, from below, upward, above, < *sub*, under, + *versus*, pp. of *vertere*, turn.] A feudal overlord (as, "The owner had been compelled to acknowledge himself the man or vassal of a *suzerain*": Hallam's "Europe during the Middle Ages," ii. 1); also, a sovereign or a state exercising political control over a dependent state.—**su′ze-rain-ty** (-ti), *n.* The position or authority of a suzerain.

svelte (svelt), *a.* [F., < It. *svelto*, pp. of *svellere*, < L. *ex-*, out, + *vellere*, pluck.] Slender, esp. gracefully slender in figure; lithe.

swab (swob), *n.* [Cf. Sw. *svabb*, a mop, *svabba*, to mop, MLG. *swabben*, splash in water or mud, also D. *zwabber*, swabber.] A large mop used on shipboard for cleaning decks, etc.; also, anything used for mopping; any mass of material used to take up or to apply moisture; a bit of sponge, cloth, or the like, for cleansing the mouth of a sick person, or for applying medicaments, giving nourishment, etc.; also, a cleaner for the bore of a cannon; a soft brush used to wet molds in founding; also, an epaulet of a naval officer (slang); also, an awkward or unmannerly fellow (slang).—**swab**, *v. t.*; *swabbed*, *swabbing.* To clean with or as with a swab (as, "The planks, which had not been *swabbed* since the mutiny, bore the print of many feet": Stevenson's "Treasure Island," xxv.); apply a swab to, as for cleaning, wetting, etc.; also, to take up, or apply, as moisture, with or as with a swab; also, to pass (a swab, etc.) over a surface.—**swab′ber**, *n.* [D. *zwabber*.] One who uses a swab; one of a ship's crew charged with swabbing the decks, etc.; a petty officer in charge of the swabbing of the decks, etc.; also (in contempt), a person fit only for menial work; an awkward or unmannerly fellow; also, a swab or mop; also, *pl.*, certain cards which formerly in the game of whist entitled the holder to a part of the stakes (used in 'whisk and swabbers,' the name of the form of whist in which these cards were so used: see *whist*[2], etym.).

Swa-bi-an (swä′bi-ạn). **I.** *a.* Of or pertaining to Swabia (Schwaben), an early duchy of Germany, corresponding in general to Württemberg, Baden, and southwestern Bavaria; also, of or pertaining to the modern Swabia, an administrative district in southwestern Bavaria. **II.** *n.* A native or inhabitant of Swabia.

swad-dle (swod′l), *v. t.*; *-dled, -dling.* [ME., in *suadiling band*, swaddling-band; related to *swathe*[2].] To bind (an infant, esp. a new-born infant) with long, narrow strips of cloth to prevent free movement of the limbs; wrap tightly with clothes; fig., to restrict the action of as if by such binding or wrapping; also, to wrap (anything) round with bandages; envelop with wrappings (as, "The pulpit . . . was *swaddled* in black": Barrie's "Auld Licht Idylls," iii.); also, to beat† or cudgel† (as, "I know the place where he my loins did *swaddle*": Beaumont and Fletcher's "Knight of the Burning Pestle," ii.).—**swad′dle**, *n.* A long, narrow strip of cloth used for swaddling an infant, or for bandaging in any similar manner; a swaddling-band; a bandage.—**swad′-**

dling=band, *n.* [ME.: see *swaddle*, *v.*] A band, as of linen, for swaddling an infant, esp. a new-born infant.—**swad′dling=clothes**, *n. pl.* Clothes consisting of swaddling-bands; also, long clothes for an infant. Also fig.

swag (swag), *v.*; *swagged*, *swagging.* [Prob. from Scand.: cf. Norw. *svaga*, sway, also E. *sway* and *swagger*.] **I.** *intr.* To move heavily or unsteadily from side to side or up and down; sway; also, to hang loosely and heavily; sink down; sag; also, to travel about carrying one's 'swag,' or bundle of personal belongings (Australia). **II.** *tr.* To cause to swag (sway, or sink or sag).—**swag**, *n.* A swagging, swaying, or lurching movement; a sinking down or sagging; a heavy fall or drop (prov. Eng.); also, a festoon, as of flowers or foliage; also, a depression in the ground (prov. or local); also, plunder or booty (slang: as, "What'll we do with what little *swag* we've got left?" Mark Twain's "Tom Sawyer," xxvi.); also, a great quantity of something, as a large draft of liquor (prov.); also, a bundle or roll carried across the shoulders or otherwise, and containing the personal belongings of a traveler through the bush, a miner, or the like (Australia, etc.: as, "a '*swag*' in front of F——'s saddle; that is, a long narrow bundle, in this instance enclosed in a neat waterproof case," Lady Barker's "Station Life in New Zealand," xiii.).

swage (swāj), *n.* [OF. *souage* (F. *suage*); origin uncertain.] An ornamental molding or border on a candlestick, vessel, or the like; also, a tool for bending cold metal to a required shape; also, a tool, die, or stamp for giving a particular shape to metal on an anvil, in a stamping-press, etc.—**swage**, *v. t.*; *swaged, swaging.* To bend or shape by means of a swage.—**swage′=block**, *n.* A heavy iron block containing holes and grooves of various sizes, used for heading bolts and shaping or swaging objects not easily worked on an anvil.

Swage-block.

swag-ger (swag′ėr), *v.* [Prob. freq. of *swag*.] **I.** *intr.* To walk or strut with a defiant or insolent air, or with an obtrusive affectation of superiority; behave in an arrogant or vainglorious way; also, to talk in a blustering manner; boast or brag noisily. **II.** *tr.* To bring, drive, force, etc., by blustering.—**swag′ger**. **I.** *n.* The act or behavior of one who swaggers; swaggering gait, bearing, or air; arrogant or vainglorious show of affected superiority: as, "He . . . moved with a dignified *swagger* as became a pirate who felt that the public eye was on him" (Mark Twain's "Tom Sawyer," xviii.). **II.** *a.* Smart in bearing, appearance, etc.; fashionable; 'swell.' [Slang.]—**swag′ger=cane**, *n.* A swagger-stick.—**swag′ger-er**, *n.*—**swag′ger-ing-ly**, *adv.*—**swag′ger=stick**, *n.* A short stick or cane sometimes carried by army officers, soldiers, and others.

Swa-hi-li (swä-hē′lē), *n.*; pl. *-li* or *-lis* (-lēz). A member of a Bantu (negro) people with a large infusion of Arab blood, which inhabits Zanzibar and the neighboring coast of Africa; also, the language of this people.

swain (swān), *n.* [Late AS. *swein*, from Scand.: cf. Icel. *sveinn*, Sw. *sven*, Dan. *svend*, boy, servant; = AS. *swān*, swineherd.] A young man in attendance on a knight†; a male servant or attendant†; a boy†, youth†, or man†; a countryman employed in husbandry, a shepherd, or a rustic (archaic: as, "where health and plenty cheer'd the labouring *swain*," Goldsmith's "Deserted Village," 2); a country gallant or lover; hence, a male lover or sweetheart generally.—**swain′ish**, *a.* Pertaining to or resembling a swain or rustic; rustic; boorish; also, pertaining to or resembling a rustic lover.—**swain′ish-ness**, *n.*

swale[1] (swāl), *n.* [Origin obscure.] A low place in the surface of the ground; a slight depression in a tract of land, usually moister and often having a ranker vegetation than the adjacent higher land. [Prov. or local.]

swale[2] (swāl), *v.* See *sweal*.

swal-low[1] (swol′ō), *n.* [AS. *swealwe* = D. *zwaluw* = G. *schwalbe* = Icel. and Sw. *svala*, swallow.] Any of the small, long-winged passerine birds with a deeply forked tail constituting the genus *Hirundo* (family *Hirundinidæ*), notable for their swift, curving flight and for the extent and regularity of their migratory movements (see *barn-swallow* and *chimney-*

swallow); any bird of the family *Hirundinidæ*, as a martin; also, any of various similar birds not of this family, as a chimney-swift.

swal-low² (swol'ō), *v.* [AS. *swelgan* = D. *zwelgen* = OHG. *swelgan* (G. *schwelgen*) = Icel. *svelgja*, swallow.] **I.** *tr.* To take into the stomach through the throat or gullet (esophagus), as food, drink, or other substances; fig., to take in so as to envelop, withdraw from sight, assimilate, or consume (often with *up*: as, "I expected every wave would

White-bellied Swallow (*Iridoprocne bicolor*, family *Hirundinidæ*).

have *swallowed* us up," Defoe's "Robinson Crusoe," i. 1; to be *swallowed* up by the darkness; "the big Powers of the world, having *swallowed* up all the small ones," Chesterton's "Napoleon of Notting Hill," iii. 2); engulf; absorb; appropriate; devour; often, to take into the mind readily or credulously, or accept without question or suspicion (as, "He would *swallow* almost anything as a truth—a humour which many made use of to impose upon him": Fielding's "Tom Jones," viii. 14); also, to accept without opposition or demur, as something that might be deemed objectionable (as, "She had to make him *swallow* the butler, and the page, and the other servants, and the grand piano": Arnold Bennett's "Helen with the High Hand," xxvii.); take patiently or meekly, or put up with (as, to *swallow* an affront; "Did you think I had *swallowed* my defeat indeed?" Stevenson's "Master of Ballantrae," x.); also, to suppress (emotion, a laugh, sob, etc.) as if by drawing it down one's throat; also, to take back or retract (one's words, etc.). **II.** *intr.* To take food, drink, etc., into the stomach through the throat or gullet; perform the muscular act of deglutition, as in swallowing saliva or in an instinctive effort to suppress emotion.—**swal'low²**, *n.* The passage through which food, drink, etc., pass from the mouth to the stomach; the throat or gullet; the organs of deglutition collectively; hence, capacity for swallowing (also fig.: as, "No tale was too gross or monstrous for his capacious *swallow*," Irving's "Sketch-Book," Sleepy Hollow"); also, an act of swallowing; also, a quantity swallowed at one time; a mouthful; also, a gulf or abyss (archaic); a deep hollow in the ground, rock, etc., as in limestone regions, through which water descends to an underground passage (also called *swallow-hole* and *sink-hole*); also, the space in a block between the groove of the sheave and the shell, through which the rope runs.—**swal'low-a-ble**, *a.* That may be swallowed.—**swal'low-er**, *n.*—**swal'low=hole**, *n.* A swallow or sink-hole. See *swallow²*, *n.*

swal-low-tail (swol'ō-tāl). **I.** *n.* A swallow's tail, or a deeply forked tail like that of a swallow; also, any of various animals having a deeply forked tail or tail-like part; esp., any of various butterflies of the genus *Papilio* and allied genera, having the hind wings prolonged so as to suggest the forked tail of a swallow; also, a thing shaped, or having a part shaped, like a swallow's tail; a broad or barbed arrowhead, or an arrow with such a head; the cleft or

Swallowtail (*Papilio turnus*), one half natural size.

forked end of a flag, or a flag with such an end; a swallow-tailed coat, or dress-coat (colloq.). **II.** *a.* Swallow-tailed. —**swal'low=tailed**, *a.* Having a deeply forked tail like that of a swallow, as various birds; having prolongations of the hind wings that suggest a swallow's tail (as, a *swallow-tailed*

butterfly, a swallowtail); having an end or part suggesting a swallow's tail (as, a *swallow-tailed* pennant, a pennant ending in two tapering points with a cleft between them; a *swallow-tailed* coat, a dress-coat, or coat having the lower part cut away over the hips and descending in a pair of tapering skirts behind).

swal-low-wort (swol'ō-wèrt), *n.* Any of various asclepiadaceous plants; esp., an herb, *Vincetoxicum officinale* (or *Cynanchum vincetoxicum*), of Europe, with pods suggesting a flying swallow and an emetic root formerly esteemed as a counterpoison; also, the greater celandine, *Chelidonium majus*.

swam (swam). Preterit of *swim¹*, *swim²*.

swa-mi (swä'mē), *n.*; pl. -*mis* (-mēz). [Hind. *swāmī*, < Skt. *svāmin*, owner, master, lord.] A Hindu idol; also, a title for a Hindu religious teacher.

swamp (swomp), *n.* [Prob. related to *sump*.] A piece or tract of wet, spongy land; a marsh; marshy ground; sometimes, a tract of soft, wet ground having a growth of certain kinds of trees, but unfit for cultivation.—**swamp**, *v.* **I.** *tr.* To plunge or sink in or as in a swamp; submerge or sink in water (as, "As the river was high and the horses were weak, we came within an ace of being *swamped* at one crossing," Roosevelt's "Ranch Life and the Hunting-Trail," x.; too heavy a load may *swamp* a boat); flood or drench with water or the like (as, "the deluge of hot water, with which, having filled the teapot, he proceeded to *swamp* everything else upon the tray": Lever's "Harry Lorrequer," xiii.); fig., to plunge into inextricable difficulties, overwhelm, or render helpless (as, "Rousseau's tremendous vogue did much to *swamp* the harder, clearer thinkers of this time": H. G. Wells's "Outline of History," xxxvii. § 7); often, to overwhelm by great numbers or excessive quantity (as, to be *swamped* with applications; "Sid Dallam is *swamped* with business, and wants me in New York," W. Churchill's "Modern Chronicle," ii. 1); in *logging*, to clear the ground for (a road) by removing underbrush, fallen trees, etc. **II.** *intr.* To sink or stick in or as in a swamp; fill with water and sink, as a boat; fig., to be plunged into or overwhelmed with difficulties, etc.—**swamp'=cab″bage**, *n.* The skunk-cabbage, *Spathyema fœtida*.—**swamp'er**, *n.* One who swamps; one who cuts trees in a swamp; in *logging*, one who works at clearing the ground of underbrush, fallen trees, etc., as in making roads.—**swamp'=hare**, *n.* A large, long-limbed hare or rabbit, *Lepus aquaticus*, inhabiting the fresh-water swamps of the southern Mississippi valley, etc. —**swamp'ish**, *a.* Swampy, as land: as, "when all this flat central country was *swampish* and hadn't been drained off yet" (Tarkington's "Alice Adams," i.).—**swamp'=ore**, *n.* Bog-ore, a variety of limonite.—**swamp'y**, *a.* Of the nature of or resembling a swamp (as, *swampy* ground; "a devilish wet, *swampy* country," Sterne's "Tristram Shandy," v. 40); also, pertaining to or found in swamps (as, "a marshy tract full of . . . odd, outlandish,

Swamp-hare.

European White Swan (*Cygnus olor*).

swan   **1914**   **swarmer**

swampy trees," Stevenson's "Treasure Island," xiv.; "As we lay moored . . . the darkness brought a thousand *swampy* things to life," H. G. Wells's "Tono-Bungay," iii. 4. § 4).

swan[1] (swon), *n.* [AS. *swan* = D. *zwaan* = G. *schwan* = Icel. *svanr*, swan; perhaps akin to L. *sonus*, E. *sound*[5], *n.*] Any of the large swimming birds (genus *Cygnus*, etc.) constituting the subfamily *Cygninæ* of the duck family, which have a long, slender, flexible, gracefully curving neck, and in most species a pure white plumage in the adult, and which are noted for their graceful and stately movements when swimming, and are fabled to sing melodiously when dying (see cut on preceding page); fig., a person or thing of unusual beauty, excellence, purity, or the like; also, a sweet singer, or poet, of a particular locality (as, Shakspere, the *swan* of Avon; Virgil, the Mantuan *swan*); also [*cap.*], in *astron.*, the northern constellation Cygnus.

swan[2] (swon), *v.* A euphemistic substitute for *swear*, in the expression 'I swan' (I swear, or I declare) used in asseveration or as a mere ejaculation of surprise or the like: as, "Wouldn't a-knowed you, I *swan*, I wouldn't" (W. Churchill's "Coniston," ii. 4). [Prov., U. S.]

swang (swang). Archaic or prov. preterit of *swing*.

swan-herd (swon'hėrd), *n.* One who tends swans; an official who has charge of swans.

swank[1] (swangk), *a.* [Cf. AS. *swancor*, pliant, supple, agile, MLG. *swank*, G. *schwank*, pliant.] Supple; agile; active. [Sc. and north. Eng.]

swank[2] (swangk), *v. i.* [Origin uncertain; orig. prov. Eng.: cf. *swank*[1].] To move or go in a swaggering manner, or strut (as, "There was that in his voice which sent Martin *swanking* down the corridor": Sinclair Lewis's "Arrowsmith," xxviii.); swagger in behavior, or behave ostentatiously; make a vainglorious show of superiority (as, "When you've had a West End run, you'll *swank* over better men than yourself": L. Merrick's "Position of Peggy Harper," ii. 1); also, to make pretense. [Slang.]—**swank**[2], *n.* The action or manner of one who swanks; swagger; ostentatious or vainglorious behavior (as, "More than one German on the bayonet at a time is an incumbrance. And it would be *swank*—a thing we detest in the army": H. G. Wells's "Mr. Britling," ii. 4. § 1); also, dashing smartness, as in bearing, appearance, etc.; style; also, pretense. [Slang.] —**swank'er**, *n.*—**swank'y**, *a.* Swanking; swaggering; 'swagger' or smart. [Slang.]

swan=maid-en (swon'mā"dn), *n.* One of a class of fabulous maidens, in many Indo-European tales, possessing the power of transforming themselves into swans, as by means of a robe or shift of swan's feathers or a magic ring or chain.

swan-neck (swon'nek), *n.* A neck like that of a swan, as in length, slenderness, whiteness, etc.; also, something shaped like or suggesting the neck of a swan, as a curved section of a pipe.—**swan'=necked**, *a.* Having a neck like that of a swan, as in length, slenderness, etc.; also, shaped or curved like the neck of a swan.

swan-ner-y (swon'ėr-i), *n.*; pl. -ies (-iz). A place where swans are kept and reared.

swan's=down (swonz'doun), *n.* The down or under plumage of a swan, used for trimming, powder-puffs, etc.; also, a fine, soft, thick woolen cloth; also, Canton flannel (see *flannel*).

swan-skin (swon'skin), *n.* The skin of a swan, with the feathers on; also, a kind of fine twilled flannel; also, a kind of woolen blanketing used by printers and engravers.

swan=song (swon'sông), *n.* A song of extraordinary sweetness fabled to be sung by the swan when dying; hence, the last work, or a final and supreme work, of a poet, a composer, or other person, produced shortly before his death; in general, a final and notable utterance, production, or achievement.

swan=up-ping (swon'up"ing), *n.* In England, the taking up of young swans in order to mark them with nicks on the beak for the owners; an annual expedition for this purpose on the river Thames.—**swan'=up"per**, *n.*

swap (swop), *v.*; *swapped*, *swapping.* [ME. *swappen*, strike; perhaps imit.] **I.** *tr.* To strike† or smite†; chop or cut (archaic or prov.); cast violently, or slam (obs. or prov.); also, to strike (a bargain: obs. or prov.); exchange,

barter, or trade, as one thing for another (now colloq. or prov.: as, "It's herself, I'm thinking, is after *swapping* the tin can for a pint," Synge's "Tinker's Wedding," ii.); also, to dismiss from employment (slang, Eng.: as, "The junior clerk scrutinised his visage . . . '*Swapped!*' said Kipps," H. G. Wells's "Kipps," i. 5). **II.** *intr.* To strike†; dash, rush, or fall violently or suddenly (obs. or prov.); also, to make an exchange (now colloq. or prov.).—**swap**, *n.* A stroke or blow (obs. or prov.); also, an exchange, as of one thing for another (now colloq. or prov.); also, with *the*, dismissal from employment (slang, Eng.).—**swap'per**, *n.*

swa-raj (swä-räj'). [For Hind. *swarāj*, < Skt. *sva*, own, + *rāj-*, rule.] **I.** *n.* Self-government; [also *cap.*] the government of India by its own people, either as a part of the British Empire, or, esp., in later use, with complete independence of British control, as a political principle advocated by natives of India. Cf. *non-coöperation.* **II.** *a.* Pertaining to swaraj: as, the *swaraj* principle or movement; the *Swaraj* party.—**swa-raj'ism**, *n.* The swaraj principle or movement.—**swa-raj'ist**, *n.* [Also *cap.*] An advocate of swaraj; a member of the Swaraj party.

sward (swârd), *n.* [AS. *sweard* = D. *zwoord* = G. *schwarte* = Icel. *svördhr*, skin, sward.] Skin or rind, esp. the rind of pork or bacon (now prov. Eng.); also, the surface layer of the soil, filled with roots of grass, etc., forming a kind of mat; the grassy surface of land; turf; also, a stretch of turf (as, "We entered upon a green *sward*, round which there ran an arcade or cloister": S. Butler's "Erewhon," xv.); a growth of grass.—**sward**, *v.* **I.** *tr.* To cover with sward or turf. **II.** *intr.* To become covered with sward.—**sward'y**, *a.* Covered with sward or turf.

sware (swâr). Archaic preterit of *swear*.

swarf (swârf or swärf), *n.* [Cf. AS. *geswearf*, filings, and *sweorfan*, file, E. *swerve*.] The wet or greasy grit, mixed with particles of iron or steel, abraded from a grindstone or the like; the scrapings and chippings from iron castings, esp. as used as a reducing agent in the manufacture of aniline, etc.

swarm[1] (swârm), *v. i.* or *t.* [Origin uncertain.] To climb (a tree, pole, or the like) by clasping it with the hands or arms and legs and drawing one's self up; shin: as, "They fright me, when the beech is green, By *swarming* up its stem for eggs" (Calverley's "Fly Leaves," Changed).

swarm[2] (swârm), *n.* [AS. *swearm* = MLG. *swarm* = G. *schwarm*, swarm, = Icel. *svarmr*, tumult.] A body of honey-bees which emigrate from a hive and fly off together, under the direction of a queen, to start a new colony; a body of bees settled together, as in a hive; a large assemblage of insects or other small creatures, esp. flying or moving about in a confused mass; in general, a great number of things or persons, esp. in motion (as, a *swarm* of motes in a sunbeam; "the *swarms* of refugees, who fled eastward over Germany as the French power advanced," Lytton Strachey's "Queen Victoria," i.); a crowd, throng, or multitude; in *biol.*, a group or aggregation of free-floating or free-swimming cells or unicellular organisms, as zoöspores.—**swarm**[2], *v.* **I.** *intr.* To fly off together in a body from a hive to start a new colony, as bees; fly or move about in a swarm, as insects or other small creatures (as, "He ate with his eyes fixed upon his plate, about which the flies *swarmed* furiously": L. Merrick's "Worldlings," i.); move about, along, forth, etc., in great numbers, as things or persons (as, "Sherman with ten thousand of his destroyers *swarmed* out of Vicksburg on his great raid to Meridian": G. W. Cable's "Cavalier," lxiv.); congregate or occur in swarms or multitudes (as, "Faces, faces—they *swarmed* about him": Mrs. Wharton's "Son at the Front," ix.); be exceedingly numerous, as in a place or area (as, "Roman Catholics already *swarmed* in every department of the public service": Macaulay's "Hist. of Eng.," vii.); of a place, to be thronged or overrun (*with*: as, "They beheld the great plain below absolutely *swarming* with buffalo," Irving's "Captain Bonneville," xvii.); abound or teem (*with*: as, "The beds *swarmed* with daffodils and narcissi," H. G. Wells's "Tono-Bungay," iv. 1. § 2); in *biol.*, to move or swim about in a swarm, as zoöspores, etc. **II.** *tr.* To swarm about, over, or in (as, "Cowled and barefoot beggars *swarmed* the way": Bryant's "The Ages," xx.); throng; overrun; also, to produce a swarm of.— **swarm'er**, *n.* One of a number that swarm; one of a

fat, fāte, fär, fåll, åsk, fåre; net, mē, hėr; pin, pīne; not, nōte, mŏve, nôr; up, lūte, půll; oi, oil; ou, out; (lightened) aviăry, ĕlect, agŏny, intŏ, ūnite; (obscured) errănt, operä, ardĕnt, actŏr, natŭre; ch, chip; g, go; th, thin; ᵺ, then; y, you;

swarm; in *biol.*, a swarm-spore.—**swarm'=spore**, *n*. In *biol.*, any minute motile spore produced in great numbers or occurring in groups or aggregations; a zoöspore.

swart (swârt), *a*. [AS. *sweart* = D. *zwart* = G. *schwarz* = Icel. *svartr* = Goth. *swarts*, black.] Of a black, blackish, or dark color (as, "The air *Swart* as the smoke from raging furnace": Scott's "Vision of Don Roderick," liii.); swarthy, as the skin, complexion, etc., or the person (as, "Strange men *Swart* from great suns": Swinburne's "Chastelard," v. 1); producing a swarthy complexion, as the sun; fig., sinister; evil; malignant. [Now literary or prov.]

swarth[1] (swârth), *n*. [AS. *swearth*.] Same as *sward*. [Now chiefly prov.]

swarth[2] (swârth), *n*. Same as *swath*. [Now chiefly prov.]

swarth[3] (swârth), *a*. Same as *swart*. [Archaic or prov.]

swarth-y (swâr'thi or -ꞯHi), *a*.; compar. *swarthier*, superl. *swarthiest*. [Var. of earlier *swarty*, < *swart*.] Of a swart or blackish color or hue; dark-colored, now esp. as the skin, complexion, face, etc., or the person: as, "The door was opened by a *swarthy* foreign-looking maid . . . whom he vaguely fancied to be Sicilian" (Mrs. Wharton's "Age of Innocence," ix.).—**swarth'i-ly**, *adv*.—**swarth'i-ness**, *n*.

swart-ness (swârt'nes), *n*. The state or fact of being swart.

swash[1] (swosh), *v*. [Prob. imit.] **I.** *tr*. To strike violently or noisily (cf. *swashbuckler*); dash or cast violently; esp., to dash (water, etc.) about, down, etc. (as, "I *swashed* down . . . showers on the top of the flames": Moir's "Mansie Wauch," xix.); dash water, etc., upon or against (something); of water, etc., to dash upon or against (something). **II.** *intr*. To deal violent strokes, or lash out, as with a weapon; hence, to behave as a swaggering bully, or swashbuckler; swagger; also, to dash about, as things in violent motion (as, "a jolting trot that set the oats *swashing* in the pocket of my coat": Stevenson's "Travels with a Donkey," v. 1); splash, as things in water, or as water does (as, "How the sea rolls *swashing* 'gainst the side!" H. Melville's "Moby-Dick," xl.). —**swash**[1], *n*. A swashing blow, stroke, or movement, or the sound of it; hence, swashbuckling, swaggering, or swagger; a swashbuckler or swaggering fellow; also, the dashing of water, waves, etc., or the sound of it; ground over which water washes; a channel of water through or behind a sand-bank (cf. *swatch*[2]); liquid refuse, or wash, as for hogs (sometimes fig.).

swash[2] (swosh), *a*. [Origin uncertain.] In *turnery*, noting or pertaining to turning in which the cuttings are inclined to the axis of the cylinder which is being worked; in *printing*, noting or pertaining to italic capital letters of the old style with flourished projections serving to fill up unsightly gaps between letters.—**swash**[2], *n*. In *turnery*, an ornament or the like made by swash turning; in *printing*, a flourished projection on a swash letter.

swash-buck-ler (swosh'buk″lẻr), *n*. [With reference to the striking of swords against bucklers or shields: see *swash*[1], *v*.] A swaggering swordsman or bully; one given to warlike swagger: as, "He had a garrison after his own heart . . . guzzling, deep-drinking *swashbucklers*" (Irving's "Knickerbocker's New York," vi. 1).—**swash'buck″ler-ing**, *n*. and *a*. Same as *swashbuckling*.—**swash'buck″ling**. **I.** *n*. The action or behavior of a swashbuckler. **II.** *a*. Acting like, characteristic of, or befitting a swashbuckler.

swash-er (swosh'ẻr), *n*. One who swashes; a swaggering bully; a swashbuckler.—**swash'ing**, *p. a*. That swashes; striking violently, or slashing, as a weapon or a blow; swashbuckling, as a person; swaggering; dashing.— **swash'ing-ly**, *adv*.

swash=let-ters (swosh'let″ẻrz), *n. pl*. See *swash*[2].

swash=plate (swosh'plāt), *n*. In *mach*., a disk fixed in an inclined position on a rotating axis, for the purpose of communicating a reciprocating motion to a bar in the direction of its length.

swas-ti-ka (swas'ti-kạ or swos'-), *n*. [Skt. *svastika*, < *svasti*, well-being,

Swash-plate.—*A*, shaft; *B*, swash-plate; *C*, rod working in guide *D* and having wheel *E* pivoted to its lower end. Rotation of *A* and *B* causes *C* to rise and descend alternately, the descent being effected by its own gravity or the action of a spring not shown.

luck.] A figure used as a symbol or an ornament in the Old World and in America since prehistoric times, consisting of a cross with arms of equal length, each arm having a continuation at right angles, and all four continuations turning the same way. Also called *fylfot*. Cf. *gammadion*.

Swastikas.

swat[1] (swot), *v. t*.; *swatted*, *swatting*. [Imit.] To hit with a smart or violent blow. [Colloq.]—**swat**[1], *n*. A smart or violent blow. [Colloq.]

swat[2] (swot), etc. See *swot*[2], etc.

swatch[1] (swoch), *n*. [Origin obscure.] A tally or piece of wood attached to cloth to be dyed, as a means of identification†; a sample of cloth or other material (prov. or trade use); a specimen of anything (Sc. and north. Eng.).

swatch[2] (swoch), *n*. [Cf. *swash*[1], *n*.] A channel of water extending through a sand-bank or lying between a sand-bank and the shore; a swash.

swath (swâth or swoth), *n*. [AS. *swæth*, *swathu*, track, trace, = D. *zwad*, G. *schwad*, swath.] The space covered by the stroke of a scythe or the cut of a mowing-machine; the piece or strip so cut (as, to cut a wide *swath*, often fig., as in slang use, to make a pretentious display, or 'splurge'); hence, a strip, belt, or long and relatively narrow extent of anything; also, a line or ridge of grass, grain, or the like, cut and thrown together by a scythe or mowing-machine (also fig.: as, "The rearguard as it fled, Mown down in the bloody *swath* Of the battle's aftermath," Longfellow's "Scanderbeg," 19); also, a crop of grass, grain, or the like, ready for mowing or reaping.

swathe[1] (swāth or swāꞯH), *n*. Same as *swath*.

swathe[2] (swāꞯH), *n*. [AS., in *swathum*, dat. pl.: cf. *swaddle*.] A band of linen or other material in which something is wrapped; a wrapping; a bandage; a single fold or winding of a wrapping. Also fig.—**swathe**[2], *v. t*.; *swathed*, *swathing*. [AS. *swathian*.] To wrap with swathes of some material; wrap up closely or fully (as, "a figure *swathed* in an ulster": Arnold Bennett's "Old Wives' Tale," i. 5); also, to infold or envelop, as wrappings do (as, "the immense masses of clothes that *swathe* his limbs": Kinglake's "Eothen," ii.); also, to wrap round something as or like a swathe (as, "Old Marheyo . . . *swathed* the calico about his loins": H. Melville's "Typee," xv.).—**swath-er** (swā'ꞯHẻr), *n*.—**swath'ing**, *n*. The act of one who or that which swathes; also, that with which something is swathed (usually in *pl*.: as, "Lady Frensham had arrived . . . by automobile; she appeared in veils and *swathings*," H. G. Wells's "Mr. Britling," i. 2. § 4).

swat-ter (swot'ẻr), *n*. One who or that which swats; something to swat with (as, a *swatter* for flies). [Colloq.]

sway (swā), *v*. [ME. *sweyen*, move: cf. Icel. *sveigja*, bend, swing, sway, LG. *swajen*, D. *zwaaien*, swing, sway.] **I.** *intr*. To move† or go†; also, to move to and fro, as something fixed at one end or resting on a support (as, "thousands of the little yellow blossoms all *swaying* to the light wind": W. H. Hudson's "Far Away and Long Ago," xii.); swing to and fro; incline first to one side and then to the other; fig., to fluctuate or vacillate, as in opinion; also, to move or incline to one side or in a particular direction; fig., to incline in opinion, sympathy, tendency, etc.; also, to wield power, exercise rule, or bear sway (also fig.: as, "Lawless feasters in thy palace *sway*," Pope's tr. Homer's "Odyssey," iii.). **II.** *tr*. To cause to move to and fro, as something fixed at one end or resting on a support; swing; cause to incline from side to side; fig., to cause to fluctuate or vacillate (as, "I was *swayed* to and fro by the motions of a spiritual power": G. MacDonald's "Annals of a Quiet Neighbourhood," xv.); also, to cause to move or incline to one side or in a particular direction; fig., to cause (the mind, etc., or the person) to incline or turn in a specified way (as, "Who is there alive that will not be *swayed* by his bias and partiality to the place of his birth?" Swift's "Gulliver's Travels," iv. 7); cause to swerve, as from a purpose or a course of action (as, "No touch either of love or hate *swayed* him from his course": Green's "Short Hist. of the Eng. People," vi. 6); also, to strain, as a horse's back†; also, to wield (a weapon or instrument, esp. the scepter: archaic or poetic: as, "hands, that the rod of empire might have *sway'd*," Gray's "Elegy,"

---

xii.); exercise rule or sovereignty over (archaic or poetic); dominate, control, direct, or influence (as, "The will of man is by his reason *sway'd*": Shakspere's "Midsummer Night's Dream," ii. 2. 115); *naut.*, to hoist or raise, as a yard or topmast (usually with *up*).—**sway**, *n.* The act of swaying; swaying movement; swing, or curving sweep, as of a weapon; rotating movement, as of a wheel†; inclination† or bias†; also, force or pressure that sways or inclines†; also, rule, dominion, or sovereignty (as, to bear or hold *sway*: often fig.); dominating power or influence (as, "They bent before the *sway* of his vehement and impetuous will": J. F. Kirk's "Charles the Bold," iii. 1).—**sway'=backed**, *a.* Of horses, etc., strained in the back, as by overwork; also, having the back sagged or hollowed to an unusual degree.—**swayed**†, *p. a.* Of a horse's back, strained, as by overwork; of a horse, strained in the back.—**sway'er**, *n.*—**sway'ing-ly**, *adv.*

sweal, swale² (swēl, swāl), *v.* [AS. *swǣlan*, tr., *swelan*, intr., burn, akin to G. *schwelen*, burn slowly, G. *schwül*, D. *zwoel*, sultry: cf. *swelt*.] **I.** *tr.* To burn; singe; scorch; cause to melt and gutter, as a candle, instead of feeding the flame; fig., to waste. [Now prov. Eng. and Sc.] **II.** *intr.* To undergo burning; burn; become scorched; of a candle, to melt and gutter; fig., to waste away. [Now prov. Eng. and Sc.]

swear (swār), *v. i.*; pret. *swore* (archaic *sware*), pp. *sworn*, ppr. *swearing.* [AS. *swerian* (pret. *swōr*, pp. *sworen*) = D. *zweren* = G. *schwören* = Icel. *sverja*, swear: cf. *answer*.] To make a solemn declaration with an appeal to God or some superhuman being in confirmation of what is declared; make affirmation in a solemn manner by some sacred being or object, as the Deity or the Bible, or by anything regarded as of binding influence; engage or promise on oath or in a solemn manner; vow; bind one's self by oath (*to*: as, "to *swear* to the performance of them [articles]," Swift's "Gulliver's Travels," i. 3); give evidence or make any statement on oath or by solemn declaration; make oath or testify solemnly or positively (*to*: as, "He could *swear* to it [something asserted] but not on the Bible," G. Meredith's "Ordeal of Richard Feverel," xi.); also, to use profane oaths or language, as in imprecation or anger or for mere emphasis. **—to swear at**, to curse as with an oath; assail with profane language; fig., to clash, or be strikingly incongruous or inharmonious, with (as, colors that *swear at* each other: colloq., from a French use).—**to swear by**, to name (some sacred being or thing, etc.) as one's witness or guarantee in swearing; fig., to rely upon as of the highest authority (colloq.).—**to swear off**, to swear to leave off or give up something, esp. intoxicating drink. [Colloq.]—**swear**, *v. t.* To declare or affirm by swearing by a deity, some sacred object, etc.; affirm with solemn earnestness or great emphasis; promise or undertake on oath or in a solemn manner (as, "Then *swear* allegiance to his majesty": Shakspere's "1 Henry VI.," v. 4. 169); vow; testify or state on oath or by solemn declaration; make oath to (something stated or alleged); take (an oath), as in order to give solemnity or force to a declaration, promise, etc.; bring, get, take, etc., by swearing or oath-taking (as, to *swear* out a warrant for a person's arrest; to *swear* a person's life away); also, to administer an oath to; bind by an oath (*to*: as, "I've *sworn* the lady to secrecy," Arnold Bennett's "These Twain," v.); admit to office or service by administering an oath (often with *in*); also, to invoke or name (a deity, etc.) in swearing†; also, to utter (a profane oath, etc.).—**swear**, *n.* A solemn oath; also, a profane oath or utterance; a fit of profane swearing. [Colloq.]—**swear'er**, *n.*—**swear'=word**, *n.* A word used in profane swearing. [Colloq.]

sweat (swet), *v.*; sweat or sweated, sweating. [AS. *swǣtan*, < *swāt* = D. *zweet* = G. *schweiss* = Icel. *sveiti*, sweat, perspiration; akin to L. *sudor*, Gr. ἶδος, ἱδρώς, sweat, Skt. *svid-*, to sweat.] **I.** *intr.* To excrete watery fluid through the pores of the skin, as from heat, exertion, perturbation, disease, drugs, etc.; perspire, esp. freely or profusely; exude moisture, as green plants piled in a heap; gather moisture from the surrounding air by condensation (as, a pitcher of ice-water *sweats*); of liquid matter, to ooze out or exude like sweat; also, fig., to exert one's self strenuously; work hard, labor, or toil; suffer severely, as for something one has done (now colloq.); fume, as with impatience or vexation (now colloq.). **II.** *tr.* To emit (watery fluid, blood, etc.) through the pores of the skin; exude (moisture, etc.) in drops or small particles; send forth or get rid of with or like sweat (often with *out* or *off*); wet or stain with sweat (as, to *sweat* one's collar; "I must tie up the letters in oilcloth . . . else they will get all *sweated*," Kipling's "Kim," xiv.); also, to cause (a person, a horse, etc.) to sweat, as from exertion; cause (a person) to sweat profusely, as by means of drugs, vapor-baths, etc., in medical or other special treatment; cause (substances, etc.) to exude moisture, esp. as a step in some industrial process of treating or preparing; also, fig., to cause (persons, etc.) to work hard; employ (workers) at low wages during overlong hours or under other unfavorable conditions (see *sweating system*, below); deprive (a person) of money, etc., as by exaction (slang); subject (a person) to severe questioning in order to extract information, as for police purposes (slang); also, to remove part of the metal from (coins, esp. gold coins) by friction, as by shaking them in a bag; also, to heat (solder or the like) until it melts; join (metal parts) by heating, esp. after applying solder; in *metal.*, to heat (metal) to partial fusion in order to remove an easily fusible constituent.—**sweating system**, a general term for the industrial methods involved in employing workers at low wages, during overlong hours, under unsanitary or otherwise unfavorable conditions: often with reference to work let out by contract to middlemen, to be done in inadequate workshops or at the homes of the workers.—**sweat**, *n.* The watery fluid excreted through the pores of the skin in sweating; perspiration; moisture or liquid matter exuded from something or gathered on a surface in drops or small particles; also, a fit of sweating or perspiring, or a sweating condition, as from heat, exertion, perturbation, disease, etc. (as, "an ague very violent . . . cold fit, and hot, with faint *sweats* after it": Defoe's "Robinson Crusoe," i. 6); the sweating-sickness†; a process of inducing sweating or perspiration, or of being sweated, as in medical or other special treatment; a run given to a horse for exercise, as before a race; an exuding of moisture by a substance, etc., or an inducing of such exudation, as in some industrial process; also, fig., strenuous exertion, hard work, labor, or toil (archaic); a state of perturbation, anxiety, or impatience (colloq.: as, "He was in a *sweat* to get to the Indian Ocean right off," Mark Twain's "Huckleberry Finn," xx.).

sweat=band (swet'band), *n.* A band of leather or other material fastened within a hat or cap to protect it against the sweat of the head.

sweat-er (swet'ėr), *n.* One who or that which sweats; esp., an employer who sweats workers, or employs them under the sweating system (see phrase under *sweat*, *v. t.*); also, a kind of jacket or jersey, usually of wool, worn (orig. to induce sweating and reduce weight) by men during athletic exercise, or for warmth after it, or otherwise; also, a garment of the same type, but often lighter and finer (sometimes of silk), worn by women and girls.

sweat-ful (swet'fúl), *a.* Abounding in, attended with, or inducing sweat; toilsome.

sweat=gland (swet'gland), *n.* In *anat.*, one of the minute, coiled, tubular glands of the skin that secrete sweat; a sudoriparous gland.

sweat-i-ly (swet'i-li), *adv.* In a sweaty manner; with sweat.—**sweat'i-ness**, *n.*

sweat-ing=sick-ness (swet'ing-sik″nes), *n.* A febrile epidemic disease which appeared in England in the 15th and 16th centuries, at times spreading to the Continent, characterized by profuse sweating, and frequently fatal in a few hours.

sweat=shop (swet'shop), *n.* A shop in which workers are employed under the sweating system. See phrase under *sweat*, *v. t.*

sweat-y (swet'i), *a.* Covered, moist, or stained with sweat; exuding sweat or moisture; of or like sweat; also, attended with or causing sweat; oppressively hot; laborious or toilsome.

Swede (swēd), *n.* A native or inhabitant of Sweden; [*cap.* or *l. c.*] a Swedish turnip, or rutabaga.

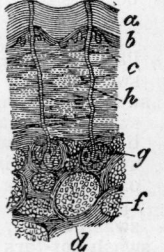

Section of Skin, showing two Sweat-glands.—*a*, epidermis; *b*, its deeper layer; *c* to *d*, corium, derma, or true skin; *f*, fat-cells; *g*, coiled end of a sweat-gland; *h*, its duct, opening on the surface at *i*.

Swe-den-bor-gi-an (swē-dn-bôr′ji-ạn). **I.** *a.* Pertaining to Emanuel Swedenborg (1688-1772), a Swedish scientific and religious writer, or to his religious doctrines, or to the body of followers adhering to these doctrines and constituting the Church of the New Jerusalem, or New Church. **II.** *n.* A believer in the religious doctrines of Swedenborg.—**Swe-den-bor′gi-an-ism,** *n.*

Swed-ish (swē′dish). **I.** *a.* Of or pertaining to Sweden or its inhabitants (as, the *Swedish* turnip, the yellow turnip, or rutabaga; *Swedish* movements or gymnastics, a system of muscular exercises for hygienic or therapeutic purposes); also, of or pertaining to the language of the Swedes. **II.** *n.* The Swedish language, a Scandinavian tongue.

swee-ny (swē′ni), *n.* [Origin uncertain.] Atrophy of the shoulder muscles in the horse.

sweep (swēp), *v.*; swept, sweeping. [ME. *swepen,* for earlier *swopen,* < AS. *swāpan* (pret. *swēop*) = OFries. *swēpa* = OHG. *sweifan* (G. *schweifen*) = Icel. *sveipa,* sweep: cf. *swoop, swipe,* and *swift*[1].] **I.** *tr.* To move, drive, or bring by passing a broom, brush, or the like over the surface occupied, or as the broom or other object does (as, to *sweep* dust away, off, out, up, together, into a heap, etc.); hence, in general, to move, bring, take, etc., by or as by a steady, driving stroke or with continuous, forcible action (as, the wind *sweeps* the snow into drifts; the boat was *swept* on the rocks; the panic *swept* his fortune away; popular enthusiasm *swept* all before it; "He was certainly not a man to *sweep* a young girl off her feet," W. Churchill's "Coniston," i. 13); also. to pass or draw (something) over a surface, or about, along, etc., with a steady, continuous stroke or movement (as, to *sweep* a brush or the arm over a table, or the fingers over a key-board; "'Aye, aye, sir,' cheerily cried little King-Post, *sweeping* round his great steering oar," H. Melville's "Moby-Dick," xlviii.); trail (garments, etc.); also, to clear or clean (a floor, street-crossing, room, chimney, etc.) of dirt, litter, etc., by means of a broom or the like, or as a broom does; make (a path, etc.) by clearing a space with a broom or the like; clear (a surface, place, etc.) of something on or in it (as, to *sweep* the board in gaming, by taking all the stakes; "He showed how his Huguenot sailors would *sweep* the sea of Spanish men-of-war," Besant's "Coligny," ix.); clear or search (water, etc.) by dragging or the like (as, to *sweep* a harbor of or for submarine mines; to *sweep* the water for a lost anchor); also, to brush or rub against (as, garments that *sweep* the ground); also, to pass over (a surface, region, etc.) with a steady, driving movement or unimpeded course, as winds, floods, invaders, pestilence, a popular movement, etc.; pass the fingers or bow over (a musical instrument, its strings or keys, etc.) as in playing, or bring forth (music) thus (chiefly poetic); direct the gaze over (a region, etc.) with the unaided eye or with a telescope or the like; survey with a continuous view over the whole extent (as, "She *swept* him from head to foot with a glance": Howells's "Foregone Conclusion," v.); assail (a whole area, etc.) with gun-fire, or have (an area) within range of fire, as guns do when suitably placed; also, to execute with a sweeping movement of the hand, body, etc., as a bow or curtsy. **II.** *intr.* To sweep a floor, room, etc., as with a broom, or as a broom does (as, a new broom *sweeps* clean); also, to drag water, etc., as for submarine mines, a lost anchor, or the like; also, to move steadily and strongly or swiftly (along, by, down, over, etc.: as, "Four or five riders . . . *swept* at full gallop down the slope," Stevenson's "Treasure Island," v.); pass with unimpeded or resistless course, as wind, floods, fire, a spirit of revolt, etc.; pass in a stately manner, as a person, a funeral cortège, etc.; walk in long, trailing garments; trail, as garments, etc.; move or pass in a continuous course, esp. a wide curve or circuit (as, his glance *swept* about the room); extend in a continuous or curving stretch, as a road, a shore, fields, etc. (as, "Round about them orchards *sweep*": Whittier's "Barbara Frietchie").—**sweep,** *n.* The act or an act of sweeping; esp., a moving, removing, clearing, etc., by or as by the use of a broom (often fig.: as, to make a clean *sweep* of incompetence; to abolish all class distinctions at one *sweep*); the steady, driving motion or swift onward course of something moving with force or unimpeded (as, the *sweep* of the wind or waves; the *sweep* of a pestilence over a region; fig., the *sweep,* or strong rhythmic flow, of verse); a trailing move-

ment, as of garments; a swinging or curving movement or stroke, as of the arm or a weapon, oar, etc.; reach, range, or compass, as of something sweeping about (lit. or fig.: as, within the *sweep* of a scythe, a telescope, the eye, the mind, or one's power); a curving course, or circuit (as, the *sweep* of a road about a marsh); also, a continuous extent or stretch, often curving, as of road, shore, or surrounding country (as, "The tide is out now, and a broad *sweep* of wet sand stretches before her": Whyte-Melville's "Katerfelto," xiv.); a curving, esp. widely or gently curving, line, form, part, or mass; a curving carriage-drive, as before a house (as, "The palace steps descend to a broad gravel *sweep*": Trollope's "Barchester Towers," v.); also, matter removed or gathered by sweeping; specif., the metal-yielding sweepings of an establishment where precious metals are worked (commonly in *pl.*); also, one who sweeps, esp. a chimney-sweeper; a worthless, contemptible, or disreputable person (colloq.: as, "They're a drunken set of *sweeps,*" Buchan's "Three Hostages," v.); also, something that sweeps, or has a sweeping motion; a lever-like device for raising or lowering a bucket in a well, consisting essentially of a long pole pivoted on an upright post; a large oar used in small vessels, sometimes to assist the rudder in turning the vessel but usually to propel the craft; also, a sweepstakes contest (as, "We had a *sweep* on the beast's [a stag's] weight, which Mary won": Buchan's "Three Hostages," xx.); in *card-playing,* in the game of whist, the winning of all the tricks in a hand; in casino, a pairing or combining, and hence taking, of all the cards on the board.

sweep-er (swē′pėr), *n.* One who or that which sweeps; a person whose work it is to sweep (as, a chimney-*sweeper*; a crossing-*sweeper*); a machine, apparatus, vessel, or other means for carrying on some process of sweeping (as, a carpet-*sweeper*; a mine-*sweeper*).

sweep-ing (swē′ping), *n.* The act of one who or that which sweeps; *pl.,* matter swept out or up, as dust, scraps, refuse, etc. (often fig., as of persons).—**sweep′ing,** *p. a.* That sweeps; moving, driving, or passing steadily and forcibly on; brushing or trailing, as over a surface or along the ground; moving or passing about over an area or in a wide curve or circuit (as, a *sweeping* glance, stroke of the pen, gesture of the hand, or bow); extending in a long stretch or wide curve (as, *sweeping* fields or shores); of wide range or scope (as, a *sweeping* victory); widely inclusive (as, a *sweeping* statement or generalization; "Uncle Billy included the whole party in one *sweeping* anathema," Bret Harte's "Outcasts of Poker Flat").—**sweep′ing-ly,** *adv.*—**sweep′ing-ness,** *n.*

sweep-stake (swēp′stāk), *n.* One who wins all the stakes in a game†; fig., one who takes all or everything†; also, a sweeping in or winning of all the stakes in a game†; fig., any total removal or clearance†; also, a sweepstakes.—**sweep′stakes,** *n.* One who wins all the stakes, or takes all or everything†; also, a prize in a race or other contest, consisting of the stakes contributed by the various competitors, and taken all by the winner or divided among a certain number of winners; also, the race or contest itself; also, a gambling transaction, as on the outcome of a race or other contest, in which each of a number of persons contributes a stake, and the stakes are taken by the winner or divided among several winners.

sweep-y (swē′pi), *a.* Sweeping. [Chiefly poetic.]

sweet (swēt), *a.* [AS. *swēte* = D. zoet = G. *süss* = Icel. *sætr* (*sætr*), sweet, akin to Goth. *suts,* also to L. *suavis,* Gr. ἡδύς, Skt. *svādu,* sweet.] Pleasing to the taste; esp., having the pleasant taste or flavor characteristic of sugar, honey, etc.; also, pleasing to the smell, fragrant, or perfumed (as, "The wind of May Is *sweet* with breath of orchards": Bryant's "Among the Trees"); also, free from offensive taste or smell; being in a sound or wholesome state; not putrid, rancid, or stale; fresh; sometimes, fresh as opposed to salt, as water; also, pleasing to the ear; making a pleasant or agreeable sound; musical; melodious; harmonious; in general, pleasing or agreeable, yielding pleasure or enjoyment, or delightful (as, "There's nothing half so *sweet* in life As love's young dream": T. Moore's "Love's Young Dream"); often, of pleasing appearance, attractive, or charming (as, "I went to see the palace and gardens of Chevereux, a *sweet* place," Evelyn's "Diary," June 28, 1644; "How *sweet* you look in that coral!" W. Churchill's "Modern Chronicle," ii. 5); also, free from objectionable qualities, as soil; easily managed, working easily or smoothly, or done or effected without effort (as, a *sweet* ship, engine, or cut); also, pleasant in disposition or manners, or as the disposition, manners, etc. (as, "All young ladies are either very pretty or very clever or very *sweet*," S. Butler's "Way of All Flesh," xlviii.; a naturally *sweet* temper); amiable; kind or gracious, as a person, action, etc. (as, "They were terribly *sweet* to me," Sinclair Lewis's "Main Street," iv.; "Thank you . . . for having me; it's been most awfully *sweet* of you," Galsworthy's "Saint's Progress," ii. 10); also, dear, beloved, or precious (as, "Thy life to me is *sweet*," Shakspere's "1 Henry VI.," iv. 6. 55; "my own *sweet* Alice," Tennyson's "Miller's Daughter," 18); sometimes, dear or precious to the one referred to (usually sarcastic, as in 'at one's own sweet will,' that is, just as one pleases or likes); also, fond of sweet things (as, to have a *sweet* tooth).—**sweet alyssum.** See under *alyssum*.—**sweet basil.** See *basil*[1].—**sweet cicely.** See *cicely*.—**sweet clover**, melilot.—**sweet corn**, a variety of maize, or Indian corn, of a sweet flavor, preferred for eating green.—**sweet marjoram.** See *marjoram*.—**sweet pea.** See *pea*.—**sweet potato.** See *potato*.—**to be sweet on**, to have a sentimental tenderness for (a person); be enamoured of. [Colloq.]—**sweet**, *n.* Sweet taste or flavor; sweet smell; sweetness; also, that which is sweet; a sweet food or drink; a sweet dish, as a pudding or tart (chiefly in *pl.*: esp. Eng.); a sweetmeat or bonbon (chiefly in *pl.*); something having a sweet smell; a perfume; something pleasant to the mind or feelings, or yielding pleasure or enjoyment; the pleasant part of anything (as, "the *sweet* o' the year": Shakspere's "Winter's Tale," iv. 3. 3); *pl.*, the pleasures of something (as, "Never did man feel more vividly . . . the *sweets* of liberty": Godwin's "Caleb Williams," xxvii.); *sing.*, a beloved person, darling, or sweetheart (as, "*Sweet*, do not scorn her so": Shakspere's "Midsummer Night's Dream," iii. 2. 247).—**sweet**, *adv.* In a sweet manner; sweetly.

sweet=bay (swēt′bā), *n.* The bay, or European laurel, *Laurus nobilis*; also, an American magnolia, *Magnolia virginiana*, with fragrant, white, globular flowers, common along the Atlantic coast from Massachusetts southward.

sweet-bread (swēt′bred), *n.* The pancreas ('stomach-sweetbread') of an animal, esp. a calf or a lamb, used for food; also, the thymus gland ('neck-sweetbread' or 'throat-sweetbread'), likewise so used.

sweet-bri-er (swēt′brī′ėr), *n.* A rose, *Rosa rubiginosa*, a native of Europe and central Asia, with a tall stem, stout, hooked prickles often mixed with bristles, and single pink flowers; the eglantine.

Sweetbrier.

sweet-en (swē′tn), *v. t.* or *i.* To make or become sweet.—**sweet′en-er**, *n.*—**sweet′en-ing**, *n.* Something that sweetens food, etc.

sweet=fern (swēt′fėrn′), *n.* A small North American shrub, *Comptonia peregrina* (or *asplenifolia*), with aromatic fern-like leaves. See cut in next column.

sweet=flag (swēt′flag′), *n.* An araceous plant, *Acorus calamus*, with long, sword-shaped leaves and a pungent, aromatic rootstock. Cf. *flag*[3].

sweet=gale (swēt′gāl), *n.* See *gale*[2].

sweet=gum (swēt′gum), *n.* The American liquidambar, *Liquidambar styraciflua*, or the balsamic liquid exuded by it.

sweet-heart (swēt′härt), *n.* A beloved person (often used in affectionate address); esp., one of a pair of lovers with relation to the other, sometimes esp. the girl or woman.

sweet-ie (swē′ti), *n.* [Dim. of *sweet*: orig. Sc.] A sweetmeat, sweet cake, or the like (commonly in *pl.*, and chiefly British: as, "our pockets full of oranges and *sweeties*," S. Butler's "Way of All Flesh," lxxiv.); also, a sweetheart (often used as a term of endearment: as, "He called the coat-girl '*Sweetie*,'" Sinclair Lewis's "Arrowsmith," ix.). [Colloq.]

sweet-ing (swē′ting), *n.* A sweet-flavored variety of apple; also, a beloved person, darling, or sweetheart (archaic).

sweet-ish (swē′tish), *a.* Somewhat sweet.

sweet-ly (swēt′li), *adv.* In a sweet manner.

sweet-meat (swēt′mēt), *n.* A sweet dainty, prepared with sugar, honey, or the like, as preserves, candy, or formerly cakes or pastry; now, esp., any sweet dainty of the confectionery or candy kind, as candied fruit, sugar-covered nuts, sugar-plums, bonbons, balls or sticks of candy, etc.: commonly in *pl.*

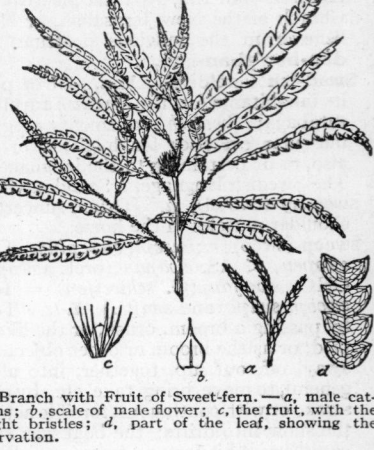
Branch with Fruit of Sweet-fern.—*a*, male catkins; *b*, scale of male flower; *c*, the fruit, with the eight bristles; *d*, part of the leaf, showing the nervation.

sweet-ness (swēt′nes), *n.* The quality of being sweet; also, something sweet.

sweet=oil (swēt′oil), *n.* Olive-oil.

sweet-root (swēt′rōt), *n.* The licorice, *Glycyrrhiza glabra*; also, the sweet-flag.

sweet=sop (swēt′sop), *n.* [Cf. *sour-sop*.] A sweet, pulpy fruit with a thick, scaly rind, borne by an anonaceous tree or shrub, *Anona squamosa*, native in tropical America; also, the tree or shrub.

sweet=wil-liam (swēt′wil′yam), *n.* A kind of pink, *Dianthus barbatus*, common in old-fashioned gardens, bearing small flowers of various colors (often party-colored) in dense clusters.

sweet-wood (swēt′wud), *n.* Any of various chiefly lauraceous trees and shrubs (genus *Ocotea*, etc.) of the West Indies and tropical America; also, the wood of such a tree or shrub.

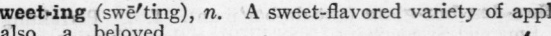
Sweet-sop.

sweet-y (swē′ti), *n.* See *sweetie*.

swell (swel), *v.*; pret. *swelled*, pp. *swelled* or *swollen*, ppr. *swelling*. [AS. *swellan* = D. *zwellen* = G. *schwellen* = Icel. *svella*, swell: cf. Goth. *ufswalleins*, a swelling up.] **I.** *intr.* To grow in bulk, as by absorption of moisture, by inflation or distention, by addition of material in the process of growth, or the like (as, "when beechen buds begin to *swell*": Bryant's "Yellow Violet"); undergo abnormal or morbid increase of size as from infection or injury; rise above the ordinary or general level, as a river or a wave; rise in waves, as the sea; well up, as a spring or as tears (as, "Tears *swelled* into her eyes": Mrs. Radcliffe's "Romance of the Forest," viii.); bulge out or be protuberant, as a sail; be larger, higher, or thicker at a particular part, as a cask in the middle; project gradually above the general level, as a hill; grow in amount, degree, force, or the like (as, "Our two hundred pounds may *swell* into a fortune": Bulwer-Lytton's "Pelham," xxv.); increase gradually in volume or intensity, as sound; give forth an increasing or great volume of sound (as, "Once again the organ *swells*": Whittier's "Sumner"); fig., to arise and grow within one, as a feeling or emotion (as, pride *swelled* in his heart); be affected with such a feeling or emotion (as, "My heart . . . *swelled* with something like joy": Mrs. Shelley's "Frankenstein," x.); become puffed up with pride; behave or talk arrogantly or pretentiously; swagger (as, "He would come home and *swell* around the town in his blackest and greasiest clothes": Mark Twain's "Life on the Mississippi," iv.). **II.** *tr.* To cause to swell or grow in bulk, as by absorption of moisture, by inflation or distention, or by addition of material; enlarge abnormally or morbidly, as a part of the body; cause (a river, the sea, etc.) to rise above the ordinary level or in waves (as, "The stream, *swollen* by the rains, was wide, deep, and rapid": Parkman's "Oregon Trail," v.); cause (a thing) to bulge out or be protuberant; increase in amount, degree, force, etc. (as, daily arrivals were *swelling* their numbers; "If thoughts like these had any share, They only *swell'd* his rage and pain," Coleridge's "Christabel," ii.); increase gradually in loudness, as a musical tone; fig., to affect with swelling emotion (as, "A senseless anger *swelled* the young man's breast": Mrs. Wharton's "Age of Innocence," x.); puff up with pride or self-importance.—**swell. I.** *n.* The act of swelling, or the condition of being swollen; increase in bulk; inflation or distention; a bulging out, or a protuberant part; a rising of water above the ordinary or general level, esp. in long, rolling waves (as, "The *swell* was exceeding great; the motion of the ship beyond description": Stevenson's " Master of Ballantrae," iii.); a wave, esp. when long and unbroken, or such waves collectively; a gradually rising elevation of the land (as, "the prairie's sea-like *swells*": Whittier's "Panorama"); increase in amount, degree, force, etc.; gradual increase in loudness of sound, esp. musical sound; a sound or succession of sounds so increasing; a gradual increase (crescendo) followed by a gradual decrease (diminuendo) in loudness or force of musical sound, or the sign ($<>$) for indicating this; a contrivance, as in an organ, by which the loudness of tones may be varied (cf. *swell-box*); fig., a swelling of emotion within one; also, arrogant or pretentious air or behavior, or swagger (now rare); also (colloq.), a fashionably dressed person; a person of distinguished appearance or bearing; a person of high social standing (as, "What a regular *swell* that Newcome has become! . . . I saw him riding in the Park with the Earl of Kew": Thackeray's "Newcomes," xxii.); a person of distinction or eminence in some field (as, "He would dislike the literary and scientific *swells* if he were to come to know them": S. Butler's "Way of All Flesh," lxxxvi.). **II.** *a.* Of persons, fashionably dressed; of distinguished appearance; of high standing, esp. socially; of things, stylish, elegant, grand, or fine (as, *swell* clothes; a *swell* carriage; a *swell* hotel; "We'll have a *swell* dinner somewhere before I go back," L. Merrick's "Worldlings," iv.); in general, first-rate, or particularly good (as, "The woman is a lot better. That was *swell* medicine you gave her": Sinclair Lewis's "Main Street," xxv.). [Colloq. or slang.]

swell=box (swel'boks), *n.* A box or chamber containing a set of pipes in a pipe-organ or of reeds in a harmonium, and having movable slats or shutters which can be opened or closed by a pedal or a knee-lever to increase or diminish the loudness of the tones.

swelled (sweld), *p. a.* Swollen; esp., morbidly enlarged (as, a *swelled* face or ankle; a *swelled* head, fig., in colloquial use, an overdeveloped sense of one's own importance or merits).

swell=fish (swel'fish), *n.* Any of various fishes capable of swelling out or inflating the body.

swell-ing (swel'ing), *n.* The act of one who or that which swells; the condition of being swol-

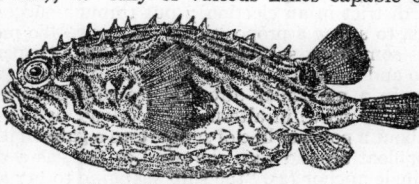

Swell-fish (*Chilomycterus schœpfi*).

len; also, a swollen part; a protuberance or prominence; in *pathol.*, an abnormal or morbid enlargement or protuberance.—**swell'ing,** *p. a.* That swells; growing in bulk; rising in level or in waves; bulging or protuberant; increasing in amount, volume, etc.; fig., arising and growing within one, as emotion; becoming inflated with pride, arrogance,

or the like; of language, elevated, high-flown, turgid, or bombastic.—**swell'ing-ly,** *adv.*

swelt (swelt), *v.* [AS. *sweltan* = OHG. *swelzan* = Icel. *svelta* = Goth. *swiltan*, die; perhaps from the root of E. *sweal*: cf. *swelter*.] **I.** *intr.* To die; also, to faint or swoon; also, to languish or swelter with oppressive heat. [Now prov. Eng. and Sc.] **II.** *tr.* To oppress or overcome with heat; cause to swelter. [Now prov. Eng. and Sc.]

swel-ter (swel'ter), *v.* [Freq. of *swelt*.] **I.** *intr.* To suffer or languish with oppressive heat; perspire profusely from heat: as, "We *sweltered* side by side in the stagnant superheated air" (J. Conrad's "Lord Jim," xxxv.). **II.** *tr.* To oppress, or cause to languish, with heat; also, to exude like sweat, as venom (see Shakspere's "Macbeth," iv. 1. 8).—**swel'ter,** *n.* A sweltering condition.—**swel'ter-ing,** *p. a.* Suffering or languishing with oppressive heat; also, characterized by oppressive heat, as a place, the weather, etc.; sultry; of heat, oppressive or overpowering (as, "The heat was *sweltering*, and he became very tired": Galsworthy's "Saint's Progress," iii. 7).—**swel'ter-ing-ly,** *adv.*—**swel'try** (-tri), *a.* [Cf. *sultry*.] Sweltering; oppressively hot; sultry. [Archaic or prov.]

swept (swept). Preterit and past participle of *sweep*.

swerve (swerv), *v.*; *swerved*, *swerving*. [ME. *swerven*, turn aside, < AS. *sweorfan*, rub, file, = D. *zwerven*, swerve, wander, = OHG. *swerban*, wipe, move about, = Icel. *sverfa*, file, = Goth. -*swairban*, wipe: cf. *swarf*.] **I.** *intr.* To turn aside in movement or direction (as, "The omnibus *swerved* into a dark road and stopped," Arnold Bennett's "Book of Carlotta," i. 5; "His eyes never *swerved* for a moment from Lingard's face," J. Conrad's "Rescue," i. 2; the road here *swerves* to the right); deviate from the straight or direct course; also, to depart from a course of action, line of conduct, etc. (as, "The world has *swerved* from truth and right": W. Morris's "Jason," xvii. 1281); also, to stray† or rove†; also, to swarm or climb upward†. **II.** *tr.* To cause to swerve, or turn aside.—**swerve,** *n.* The act or an act of swerving; a turning aside; a deviation.—**swerve'-less,** *a.* Unswerving: as, "His gaze at the preacher had become *swerveless*" (Wister's "Virginian," xxi.).—**swerv'er,** *n.*

swift[1] (swift). [AS. *swift*, akin to *swāpan*, sweep: see *sweep*.] **I.** *a.* Moving with great speed or velocity, or fleet or rapid (as, "his *swift* pursuers," Milton's "Paradise Lost," i. 326; "the *swift* ships," Job, ix. 26; *swift* of foot); made or done at high speed (as, *swift* movements); coming, happening, or performed quickly or without delay (as, "He watched the *swift* coming of the dawn," J. Conrad's "Lord Jim," xxvii.; "the sin and the *swift* retribution," Longfellow's "Courtship of Miles Standish," iii.); quick or prompt to act, etc. (as, *swift* to hear or to suspect); passing quickly, or brief (chiefly poetic: as, "*Swift* Summer into the Autumn flowed," Shelley's "Sensitive Plant," iii. 22). **II.** *n.* Any of the small, long-winged birds constituting the family *Cypselidæ,* notable for their rapid flight (allied to the humming-birds, but superficially resembling the swallows); also, any of various small lizards, esp. of the genus *Sceloporus,* which run with great swiftness; also, any of the swiftly flying moths constituting the family *Epialidæ* (or *Hepialidæ*); also, an adjustable device upon which yarn, silk, or the like is placed in order that it may be wound off; also, a cylinder covered with wire teeth, used in machines for carding flax, etc.—**swift**[1], *adv.* Swiftly.

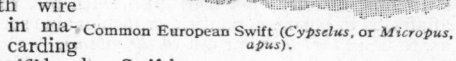

Common European Swift (*Cypselus*, or *Micropus, apus*).

swift[2] (swift), *v. t.* [Cf. Icel. *svipta*, reef (sails).] *Naut.*, to tighten, secure, confine, or fasten together, by means of a rope or ropes.

swift-en (swif'tn), *v. t.* or *i.* To make or become swift or swifter; hasten.

swift-er (swif'tėr), *n.* [See *swift*[2].] *Naut.*, the forward shroud of the lower rigging on either side of a mast; also, a small line joining the outer ends of the bars of a capstan to confine them to their sockets while the capstan is being turned; also, a rope used to encircle a boat lengthwise in order to strengthen and defend its sides. — **swift'er,** *v. t.* *Naut.*, to tighten, secure, or the like, with a swifter; swift.

swift-let (swift'let), *n.* A little swift; any of various small swifts, as those of the genus *Collocalia* (the nests of which are used esp. by the Chinese for making soup: cf. *bird's-nest*).

swift-ly (swift'li), *adv.* In a swift manner; with great speed; without delay. — **swift'ness,** *n.*

swig (swig), *v. t.* or *i.*; *swigged, swigging.* [Origin uncertain.] To drink heartily or greedily. [Colloq.] — **swig,** *n.* A large or deep draft, as of liquor: as, "He . . . took another *swig* from his bottle" (W. H. Hudson's "Purple Land," xxix.). [Colloq.]

swill (swil), *v.* [AS. *swillan, swilian*, wash.] **I.** *tr.* To wash or rinse, or cleanse by flooding or overflowing with water (now chiefly prov. Eng.); also, to drink greedily or to excess, or guzzle (as, "I see a number of well-dressed people . . . devouring sliced beef, and *swilling* port": Smollett's "Humphry Clinker," May 29); also, to fill with drink (as, "to *swill* my belly with wine": Stevenson's "Master of Ballantrae," xi.). **II.** *intr.* To dash or flow forcibly, as water (as, "gutters for any rubbish to *swill* through": George Eliot's "Adam Bede," xxi.); also, to drink greedily or excessively. — **swill,** *n.* Liquid or partly liquid food for animals, esp. kitchen refuse given to swine; hogwash; kitchen refuse in general; garbage; also, any liquid matter; slop; also, liquor, esp. as drunk to excess; a deep draft of liquor; heavy drinking. — **swill'er,** *n.*

swim[1] (swim), *n.* [Appar. (through influence of *swim*[2]) for earlier *swime*, < AS. *swīma* = D. *zwijm* = G. dial. *schweim*, giddiness, swoon.] A state or fit of dizziness or giddiness (as, my head was in a *swim*); a swoon or faint (prov. Eng. and Sc.). — **swim**[1], *v. i.*; pret. *swam* or *swum*, pp. *swum*, ppr. *swimming.* To be dizzy or giddy; have a whirling sensation; seem to whirl: as, "He danced about in a way that made my head *swim*" (Blackmore's "Lorna Doone," ii.).

swim[2] (swim), *v.*; pret. *swam* or *swum*, pp. *swum*, ppr. *swimming.* [AS. *swimman* = D. *zwemmen* = G. *schwimmen* = Icel. *svimma*, swim.] **I.** *intr.* To move along on or in water by movements of the limbs, fins, tail, etc.; move on or in water or other liquid in any way, esp. on the surface; float on the surface of water or other liquid (as, "The brig was so full of water that she could not *swim* many minutes longer," Marryat's "Peter Simple," xxxiii.: often contrasted with *sink*); hence, to move, rest, or be suspended in air or the like, as if swimming in water (as, "High up the vapours fold and *swim*": Tennyson's "Two Voices," 262); also, to move or flow, as water or other liquid (as, "She could feel the tears suddenly *swim* in her eyes": Arnold Bennett's "Hilda Lessways," vi. 3); move, glide, or go smoothly over a surface (as, "The peacock . . . *swims* in radiant majesty along": Thomson's "Seasons," Spring, 785); also, to be immersed or steeped in, or overflowed or flooded with, a liquid (often fig.). **II.** *tr.* To move along on or in by swimming; float on or in; cross by swimming, as a stream; also, to perform by or in swimming, as a stroke; also, to cause to swim (as, to *swim* a horse across a stream); cause to float, as on a stream; furnish with sufficient depth of water to swim or float (as, "not enough water to *swim* a London wherry": Defoe's "Captain Singleton," v.); also, to immerse in liquid, as in order to cause lighter parts to float. — **swim**[2], *n.* An act or period of swimming (as, to take a *swim*); also, a motion as of swimming; a smooth, gliding movement; also, a piece of water to be crossed by swimming; a part of a stream, or any piece of water, much frequented by fish; also, the swimming-bladder of a fish; also, with *the*, the current of affairs, as in business, politics, or fashionable society (colloq.: as, to be in *the swim*, or out of *the swim*).

swim-mer (swim'ėr), *n.* One who or that which swims.

swim-mer-et (swim'ėr-et), *n.* [From *swimmer* + -*et*.] In *zoöl.*, one of a number of abdominal limbs or appendages, in many crustaceans, usually adapted for swimming, and thus distinguished from other limbs adapted for walking or seizing.

swim-ming (swim'ing), *p. a.* That swims; capable of or habituated to swimming (as, a *swimming* bird, a natatorial web-footed or fin-footed bird); floating on or in water, as plants; moving or progressing smoothly as if in swimming; immersed in or overflowing with liquid, as the eyes with tears. — **swim'ming=blad″der,** *n.* In fishes, a sac containing air or gas and serving as an organ of flotation: a structure homologous with the lungs of air-breathing animals. — **swim'ming=hole,** *n.* A pool, as in a small stream, with sufficient depth of water to swim in. — **swim'ming-ly,** *adv.* In a swimming manner; with a smooth, gliding movement, as if swimming; esp., without impediment or difficulty, with great success, or prosperously (as, "I found the association went on *swimmingly*": B. Franklin's "Autobiography," xii.).

swin-dle (swin'dl), *v.*; -*dled*, -*dling*. [Back-formation from *swindler*.] **I.** *intr.* To act as a swindler; put forward plausible schemes or use unscrupulous artifice in order to defraud others. **II.** *tr.* To cheat (a person), as out of money, as a swindler does; also, to get by swindling. — **swin'-dle,** *n.* An act of swindling; a fraudulent transaction or scheme; a cheat; also, anything deceptive; a fraud.

swin-dler (swin'dlėr), *n.* [G. *schwindler*, extravagant projector, swindler, < *schwindeln*, be giddy, swindle.] One who puts forward plausible schemes or makes use of unscrupulous artifice in order to defraud others; a cheat.

swine (swin), *n.*; pl. *swine*. [AS. *swīn* = D. *zwijn* = G. *schwein* = Icel. *svīn* = Goth. *swein*, a swine; all orig. adjectival forms from the noun stem represented by E. *sow*[2].] Any of a group (family *Suidæ*) of non-ruminant ungulate mammals including the wild boar, *Sus scrofa*, and its supposed derivatives the domestic hogs, characterized typically by a stout body, short legs, and an elongated mobile snout (now commonly in *pl.*, often as a collective term for the domesticated forms); fig., a coarse, gross, or brutishly sensual person. — **swine'herd,** *n.* One who herds or tends swine. — **swine'=pox,** *n.* A variety of chicken-pox.

swing (swing), *v.*; pret. *swung* (archaic or prov. *swang*), pp. *swung*, ppr. *swinging*. [AS. *swingan*, strike, beat, whip, fly, = OS. *swingan* = OFries. *swinga* = OHG. *swingan* (G. *schwingen*): cf. *swinge, swingle,* and *swink*.] **I.** *tr.* To strike†, beat†, or whip†; also, to fling† or hurl†; also, to cause to move to and fro, sway, or oscillate, as something suspended from above (as, "Down the steps come two ladies, *swinging* their parasols": Hawthorne's "Twice-Told Tales," Sights from a Steeple); cause (a person) to move to and fro in a swing or the like; cause to move or sway to one side or in a particular direction, as something suspended from above; cause to move in alternate directions, or in either direction, about a fixed point or line of support, as a door on its hinges (as, "The door was *swung* wide open": Longfellow's "Kavanagh," ii.); move (something held or grasped) with an oscillating or rotatory movement (as, to *swing* a club about one's head); transport by or as if by movement in suspension from or in rotation about a point of support (as, to *swing* a stone with a crane); cause to move in a curve as if about a central point (as, to *swing* one's automobile around a corner); suspend so as to hang freely, as a hammock or a door; in fig. use, to sway or influence as desired (colloq.: as, to *swing* a district in an election); put through successfully (colloq.: as, to *swing* a proposition). **II.** *intr.* To move to and fro, as something suspended from above, as a pendulum; move to and fro in a swing, as for sport; move or sway to one side or in a particular direction, as something suspended from above; move in alternate directions, or in either direction, about a point or line of support, as a gate on its hinges; move or float around with the wind or tide, as a ship riding at a single anchor (as, "the ship *swinging* to her anchor with the flood-tide": H. Melville's "Moby-Dick," xvi.); move in a curve as if about a central point, as around a corner; move with a free, swaying motion, as soldiers on the march (as, "The battalion came *swinging* out of the market place," A. S. M. Hutchinson's "If Winter Comes," iii. 5; "Senhouse . . . *swung* forward with his hand out," M. Hewlett's "Open Country," xxvi.); be suspended so as to hang freely, as a bell, etc. (as, "From the shoulder *swung* a short green furred cloak": Chesterton's "Napoleon of Notting Hill," i. 2); suffer death by hanging (colloq.: as, "I will save you from his vengeance, though I *swing* for it," Whyte-Melville's "Katerfelto," ix.).—**swing**, *n.* The act or the manner of swinging; movement in alternate directions, or in a particular direction, as in suspension from above, or as about a fixed point or line of support; the amount of such movement; the swinging, or a swinging movement, of something held or grasped; a curving movement or course; a moving of the body with a free, swaying motion, as in walking; a steady, marked rhythm or movement, as of verse or music (as, "His poetry lacked the *swing* . . . of Kipling": Sinclair Lewis's "Arrowsmith," xix.); a shift or period of work (colloq.); also, sway†, rule†, or control†; freedom of action (as, to have full *swing*, or free *swing*, in a matter); active operation (chiefly in 'in full swing': as, "The game was in full *swing*," W. Churchill's "Coniston," ii. 2); also, something that is swung or that swings; a contrivance consisting of a seat suspended from above as in a loop of rope or between ropes or rods, in which one may sit and swing to and fro for sport; a rope or chain reaching forward from the end of the tongue of a wagon, along which the horses in front of the wheelers are hitched; the position of these horses; hence, the horses; also, dance music characterized by ingenious modern interpretations and played in a stimulating rhythm, tempo, etc.

Ancient Swing, from a Greek red-figured hydria of the 4th century B.C.

swing=bridge (swing′brij), *n.* A form of drawbridge of which the whole or a part may be moved aside horizontally by swinging on a pivot or pivots.

swing=door (swing′dōr′), *n.* A door constructed to swing to or shut of itself, one that opens in either direction.

swinge (swinj), *v. t.*; *swinged, swingeing.* [For earlier *swenge*, shake, smite, dash, fling, < AS. *swengan*, shake, dash, causative of *swingan*, E. *swing.*] To beat, whip, or thrash (archaic or prov.); inflict punishment upon†; also, to swing, as a lash†; brandish or flourish, as a weapon†.—**swinge′ing**, *p. a.* That swinges or thrashes (rare); fig., very forcible, great, or large (colloq. or prov.: as, a *swingeing* blow, price, or load).—**swinge′ing-ly**, *adv.*—**swin-ger**[1] (swin′jér), *n.* A powerful or vigorous fellow†; something very forcible, great, or large of the kind, as a blow, a lie, or a snake (colloq. or prov.).

swing-er[2] (swing′ér), *n.* One who or that which swings.—**swing′ing**, *p. a.* That swings; oscillating; swaying; moving freely in either direction upon a fixed center or axis, as a stool or a door; moving or proceeding with a swing, as a pace or gait, or a rhythm in verse or music.—**swing′ing-ly**, *adv.*

swin-gle (swing′gl), *n.* [AS. *swingel*, stroke, beating, rod, whip, < *swingan*, E. *swing.*] A wooden instrument shaped like a large knife, for beating flax or hemp and scraping from it the woody or coarse portions; also, the swipple of a flail.—**swin′gle**, *v. t.*; *-gled, -gling.* To clean (flax or hemp) by beating and scraping with a swingle.—**swin′gle=bar**, *n.* A swingletree.—**swin′gle-tree**, *n.* A cross-bar, pivoted at the middle, to which the traces of the harness are fastened in a cart, carriage, plow, etc.; a whiffletree or whippletree.

swing-tree (swing′trē), *n.* A swingletree.

swin-ish (swī′nish), *a.* Like or befitting swine; hoggish; brutishly gross or sensual; beastly.—**swin′ish-ly**, *adv.*—**swin′ish-ness**, *n.*

swink (swingk), *v.* [AS. *swincan*, akin to *swingan*, E. *swing.*] **I.** *intr.* To labor; toil. [Archaic or prov. Eng. and Sc.] **II.** *tr.* To cause to toil†; weary with toil (obs. or archaic: see *swinked*).—**swink**, *n.* Labor; toil. [Archaic or prov. Eng. and Sc.]—**swinked**, *p. a.* Wearied with toil: as, "The *swink'd* hedger at his supper sat" (Milton's "Comus," 293). [Archaic.]—**swink′er**, *n.*

swipe (swīp), *n.* [Akin to *sweep.*] A lever-like device for raising or lowering a weight, esp. a bucket in a well; a sweep; also (colloq.), a sweeping stroke; a stroke with full swing of the arms, as in cricket or golf; a hard blow.—**swipe**, *v.*; *swiped, swiping.* **I.** *intr.* To make a sweeping stroke; aim a blow with full swing of the arms. [Colloq.] **II.** *tr.* To strike with a sweeping blow (colloq.); also, to steal (slang).—**swip-er** (swī′pér), *n.*—**swipes**, *n.* Poor, washy beer; small beer; hence, malt liquor in general. [Slang or colloq., Eng.]

swip-ple (swip′l), *n.* [ME. *swipyl, swepyl*: cf. ME. *swippen*, strike, AS. *swipu*, a whip, akin to E. *sweep.*] The freely swinging part (stick or bar) of a flail, which falls upon the grain in threshing; a swingle. Also **swip-le** (swip′l).

swirl (swérl), *v.* [Orig. Sc.: cf. *whirl*, also Norw. *svirla*, whirl.] **I.** *tr.* To drive about or along with a whirling motion; whirl; also, to form into a twist; arrange in a twist about something; also, to encircle with something arranged in a twist. **II.** *intr.* To move about or along with a whirling motion, or whirl or eddy (as, "The dust was *swirling* in the gutters," Buchan's "Three Hostages," vi.; "the river, which *swirls* under the bridges," Vernon Lee's "Genius Loci," Fribourg); also, to be dizzy or giddy, or swim, as the head (as, "My head *swirls* with complaints": L. Merrick's "House of Lynch," xiii.).—**swirl**, *n.* A swirling movement; a whirl; an eddy; also, a curl, as in the grain of wood; a twist, as of hair about the head or of velvet or other trimming about a hat.—**swirl′y**, *a.* Swirling, whirling, or eddying; having swirls, as wood; twisted.

swish (swish), *v.* [Imit.] **I.** *intr.* To move with or make a sibilant sound, as a slender rod or a bullet cutting sharply through the air, or as small waves washing on the shore or an object passing swiftly in contact with water (as, "The rod was raised and it descended *swishing*," Arnold Bennett's "Clayhanger," i. 5; "The bullets *swish* from 'ill to 'ill Like scythes among the 'ay," Kipling's "Piet"); rustle, as silk. **II.** *tr.* To cause to swish; flourish, whisk, etc., with a swishing movement or sound, as a man does a cane or an animal its tail; bring, take, etc., with or as with such a movement or sound (as, to *swish* off the tops of plants with a cane); also, to flog or whip.—**swish**, *n.* A swishing movement or sound (as, "the only sound excepting the *swish* of the sea against the bows": Stevenson's "Treasure Island," x.); also, a short-handled broom, as of twigs bunched together, used for various purposes; also, a stick or rod for flogging, or a stroke given with this (as, "a man who has not . . . become acquainted with the *swish* in boyhood": G. Meredith's "Diana of the Crossways," xxvi.).

Swiss (swis). [F. *Suisse*, < MHG. *Swiz.*] **I.** *n.*; pl. *Swiss.* A native or inhabitant of Switzerland; also [commonly *l. c.*; pl. *swisses*], Swiss muslin (as, dotted *swiss*: see *Swiss*, *a.*). **II.** *a.* Of or pertaining to Switzerland or the Swiss; derived from or associated with Switzerland: as, *Swiss* cheese (a firm, pale-yellow or whitish cheese containing many holes, made usually from cows' milk half skimmed); *Swiss* muslin (a light, sheer muslin, often having a simple pattern of dots, sprigs, stripes, or the like, used for dresses, curtains, etc.); *Swiss* guards or guard (a body of Swiss retained as household guards, as formerly by the kings of France, and still by the Pope).

switch (swich), *n.* [Origin uncertain; prob. from LG.] A slender riding-whip; a slender, flexible shoot, or piece of plant-stem, as of willow, birch, or ratan, used in whipping, beating, etc.; a slender growing shoot, as of a plant (cf. *switch-plant*); also, a separate bunch or tress of long hair (or some substitute) fastened together at one end, worn by women to supplement the hair actually growing on the head; also, the act or an act of switching; a stroke, lash, or whisking movement, as of something long and slender;

Uniform of Papal Swiss Guard about 1800.

a turning, shifting, or changing (as, a *switch* of votes to another candidate); also, a mechanical device for altering the direction of something, making or breaking a connection, or some similar purpose; in *railroading*, a device for shifting a moving train, car, etc., from one track to another, commonly consisting of a pair of movable rails; in *elect.*, a device for turning on, turning off, or directing an electric current, or making or breaking a circuit.—**switch**, *v.* **I.** *tr.* To whip or beat with a switch or the like; strike or lash with something long and slender; drive with or as with a switch; move, swing, or whisk (a cane, an angler's line, etc.) like a switch, or with a swift, lashing stroke (as, "Those good old horses *switch* their tails at flies no more": Tarkington's "Magnificent Ambersons," i.); drive, send, or jerk suddenly (as, the wind *switched* the hat from his head); also, to cut off projecting shoots from (hedges, trees, etc.); also, to turn, shift, or divert (as, to *switch* conversation from a painful subject; to *switch* votes to a stronger candidate); esp., to shift, turn, etc., by a switch; in *railroading*, to shift or transfer (a train, car, etc.) by means of a switch; in *elect.*, to turn, direct, shift, etc., by operating a switch (as, "He *switched* on a light, which lit the first landing of the staircase": Buchan's "Three Hostages," v.). **II.** *intr.* To strike with or as with a switch; also, to change direction or course; turn, shift, or change; esp., to be shifted, turned, etc., by means of a switch.

switch-back (swich′bak), *n.* A railroad in which an easy grade up a steep acclivity is obtained by means of a track that turns alternately in opposite directions in making a gradual ascent; also, a railroad which operates partly or wholly by gravity, as one with steep ascents and descents at a pleasure-resort.

switch-board (swich′bōrd), *n.* A board or device containing a number of switches or plugs by means of which numerous electrical circuits are made, broken, or combined.

switch-er (swich′ẽr), *n.* One who or that which switches.

switch-man (swich′man), *n.*; pl. -*men.* One who has charge of a switch or switches on a railroad.

switch=plant (swich′plant), *n.* In *bot.*, a plant that bears slender green shoots or rod-like branches with leaves small or absent.

Switz-er (swit′sẽr), *n.* [MHG. *Switzer.*] A Swiss.

swiv-el (swiv′l), *n.* [ME. *swyvel*, < AS. *swīfan*, move.] A fastening device which allows the thing fastened to turn round freely upon it; such a consisting of two parts, each of which turns round independently, as a compound link of a chain one part of which turns freely in the other by means of a headed pin or the like; esp., a pivoted support for allowing a gun to turn round in a horizontal plane; also, a gun mounted on such a support (called in full 'swivel-gun').—**swiv′el**, *v.*; -*eled* or -*elled*, -*eling* or -*elling*. **I.** *tr.* To turn on or as on a swivel; fasten by a swivel; furnish with a swivel. **II.** *intr.* To turn on a swivel, pivot, or the like.—**swiv′el=chair′**, *n.* A chair whose seat turns round horizontally on a swivel.

Swivel.—*a*, swivel; *b*, hook, turning freely in *a*; *c*, chain.

swiv-et (swiv′et), *n.* [Origin obscure.] A state of excitement; a hurry. [Prov. Eng. and U. S.]

swiz-zle (swiz′l), *n.* [Origin unknown.] Any of various mixed intoxicating drinks.

swob (swob), etc. See *swab*, etc.

swol-len (swōl′n). Past participle of *swell.*—**swol′len**, *p. a.* Swelled; enlarged by or as by swelling; puffed up; tumid; turgid or bombastic. Also (archaic) **swoln** (swōln).

swoon (swōn), *v. i.* [ME. *swonen, swounen, swownen,* to swoon, < *swoune, iswowen, iswogen,* < AS. *geswōgen,* having swooned, in a swoon.] To fall into a state of syncope; faint; lose consciousness as from physical weakness (as, "After I had bled some time I *swooned*, and they all believed I was dead": Defoe's "Robinson Crusoe," ii. 8); fig., to sink or lie as in a swoon; fail, fade, or pass gradually; die away.—**swoon**, *n.* The act of swooning, or the state of one who has swooned; syncope; a faint or fainting-fit.—**swoon′-ing-ly**, *adv.*

swoop (swōp), *v.* [ME. *swopen*, sweep: see *sweep.*] **I.** *tr.* To sweep, or remove as by a sweeping stroke (obs. or prov.); take at one stroke†; also, to seize as a bird of prey does its victim†; pounce upon†. **II.** *intr.* To sweep along, as with

trailing garments†; trail†; also, to sweep through the air, as a bird or a bat; esp., to sweep rapidly down upon prey, as a hawk does; in general, to come down in a sudden, swift attack, as upon a place, etc. (often with *down* and *on* or *upon*: as, an army *swoops* down upon a region: also fig.).—**swoop**, *n.* The act or an act of swooping; esp., the rapid downward sweep of a flying bird of prey upon its victim; in general, a sudden, swift hostile descent, as of an attacking force (also fig.).—**at one** (**a single**, etc.) **swoop**, at one descent, as of a flying bird of prey; hence, at one blow or stroke (as, "Charles . . . had silently and cautiously raised it [army] to nearly ten thousand men; James raised it *at one swoop* to twenty thousand": Green's "Short Hist. of the Eng. People," ix. 6).—**swoop′er**, *n.*

swop (swop), etc. See *swap*, etc.

sword (sōrd), *n.* [AS. *sweord* = D. *zwaard* = G. *schwert* = Icel. *sverdh*, sword.] A weapon having various forms but consisting typically of a long, straight or slightly curved blade, sharp-edged on one side or both sides, with one end pointed and the other fixed in a hilt or handle, the weapon being commonly carried in a scabbard or sheath attached to a belt; often, this weapon as the symbol of warfare, military power, punitive justice, authority, rank, honor, etc.; fig., the cause of death or destruction (as, "This avarice . . . hath been The *sword* of our slain kings": Shakspere's "Macbeth," iv. 3. 87); war, combat, or slaughter; military force or power; the military profession; one's services as a swordsman or a soldier (as, "Some of the exiles offered their *swords* to William of Orange": Macaulay's "Hist. of Eng.," vi.); less frequently, power or authority to inflict punishment or do justice, or to govern or rule; also, some object or part resembling a sword (weapon) in form or use, as a swingle for dressing flax, a piece in a loom, or the projecting upper jaw of a swordfish.—**at swords′ points**, with swords ready for mutual attack; in the position or relation of active enemies.—**sword of Damocles.** See *Damoclean.*—**to draw** (or **sheathe**) **the sword**, fig., to begin (or end) a war.—**to put to the sword**, to kill by the sword; slay, as those conquered or taken in war.—**sword**, *v. t.* To strike, wound, or kill with a sword.

Sword with Belt, for mounted man-at-arms, 13th century.

sword=arm (sōrd′ärm), *n.* The arm, usually the right arm, with which the sword is wielded. Also fig.

sword=bay-o-net (sōrd′bā″o̯-net), *n.* A kind of short sword for attaching to the muzzle of a gun, to be used as a bayonet.

sword=cane (sōrd′kān), *n.* A hollow cane or walking-stick containing a steel blade like that of a sword or dagger, which may be drawn out as from a sheath or shot out by means of a spring.

sword=craft (sōrd′kráft), *n.* Knowledge of, or skill in the use of, the sword; also, military skill or power.

sword=dance (sōrd′dȧns), *n.* Any of various dances performed with the use of naked swords, as when brandished, raised overhead, or fixed upright in or laid on the ground.

sword-ed (sōr′ded), *a.* Armed with a sword.

sword-fish (sōrd′fish), *n.* A large marine food-fish, *Xiphias gladius,* with the upper jaw elongated into a sword-like weapon; also, any of certain allied fishes.

Swordfish (*Xiphias gladius*).

sword=grass (sōrd′grȧs), *n.* Any of various grasses or plants with sword-like or sharp leaves, as the sword-lily.

sword=knot (sōrd′not), *n.* A looped strap, ribbon, or the like attached to the hilt of a sword, serving as a means of supporting it from the wrist or as an ornament.

sword-less (sōrd′les), *a.* Without a sword: as, "His hand fell upon his *swordless* belt" (W. Morris's "Jason," ii. 140).

sword=lil-y (sōrd′lil″i), *n.* A gladiolus.

---

fat, fāte, fär, fåll, àsk, fåre; net, mē, hėr; pin, pīne; not, nōte, mȯve, nȯr; up, lūte, pὑll; oi, oil; ou, out; (lightened) avīȧry, ĕlect, agŏny, intŏ, ūnite; (obscured) errȧnt, operȧ, ardᶒnt, actᴏr, natūre; ch, chip; g, go; th, thin; ᴛʜ, then; y, you;

sword-man (sōrd′man), *n.*; pl. *-men.* Same as *swordsman.* [Obs. or archaic.]

sword=play (sōrd′plā), *n.* The action, practice, or art of wielding a sword; fencing; also, a sword-dance.

sword=shaped (sōrd′shāpt), *a.* Long and narrow, with tapering point, as a leaf; ensiform; xiphoid.

swords-man (sōrdz′man), *n.*; pl. *-men.* One who uses, or is skilled in the use of, a sword.—**swords′man-ship,** *n.* The art or skill of a swordsman.

swore (swōr). Preterit of *swear.*

sworn (swôrn). Past participle of *swear.*—**sworn,** *p. a.* Having taken an oath; bound by or as by an oath; also, affirmed, promised, etc., on oath.—**sworn brother,** one of two (or more) companions in arms who, according to the laws of chivalry, took an oath to share each other's fortunes; hence, a close or intimate friend or companion.—**sworn enemy,** one who has sworn perpetual enmity against another; hence, an avowed or irreconcilable enemy.

swot[1] (swot), *v.* and *n.* See *swat*[1].

swot[2] (swot), *n.* [Prov. var. of *sweat.*] Hard study at school or college; in general, labor or toil; also, one who studies hard. [Slang, Eng.]—**swot**[2], *v. i.*; *swotted, swotting.* To study or work hard. [Slang, Eng.]—**swot′ter,** *n.*

swound (swound), *v.* and *n.* Same as *swoon.* [Archaic or prov.]

swounds† (swoundz), *interj.* Same as *zounds.*

swum (swum). Pret. and pp. of *swim*[1], *swim*[2].

swung (swung). Pret. and pp. of *swing.*

Syb-a-rite (sib′a-rīt), *n.* [L. *Sybarita,* < Gr. Σνβαρίτης, < Σύβαρις, Sybaris.] An inhabitant of Sybaris, an ancient Greek city of southern Italy, proverbial for its luxury; hence [commonly *l. c.*], one devoted to luxury and pleasure; an effeminate voluptuary.—**Syb-a-rit′ic** (-rit′ik), *a.* Of or pertaining to the Sybarites; [*l. c.*] devoted to or characterized by excessive or effeminate luxury; luxurious; voluptuous.—**syb-a-rit′i-cal-ly,** *adv.*—**syb′a-rit-ism** (-rī-tizm), *n.* Sybaritic life, practices, or luxury: as, "the complex *sybaritism* of European capitals" (Arnold Bennett's "Truth about an Author," xiii.).

syc-a-mine (sik′a-min or -mīn), *n.* [L. *sycaminus,* < Gr. σνκάμινος.] A mulberry (tree), probably the black mulberry. See Luke, xvii. 6.

syc-a-more (sik′a-mōr), *n.* [Also *sycomore*; L. *sycomorus,* < Gr. σνκόμορος, < σῦκον, fig + μόρον, mulberry.] A tree, *Ficus sycomorus,* of Syria, Egypt, etc., allied to the common fig, which bears an edible fruit and is useful for shade; in England, a maple, *Acer pseudo-platanus,* grown as a shady ornamental tree and for its wood; in the U. S., a plane-tree, esp. the buttonwood.

Sycamore (*Ficus sycomorus*).— 1, branch with leaves; 2, the fruits.

syce (sīs), *n.* See *sais.*

sy-cee (sī-sē′), *n.* [From Chinese name meaning 'fine silk'; so called because when pure it may be drawn out, with heat, into fine threads.] Fine uncoined silver in lumps of various sizes, usually bearing a banker's or assayer's stamp or mark, used in China as a medium of exchange. Also **sy-cee′=sil′ver.**

sych-no-car-pous (sik-nō-kär′pus), *a.* [Gr. σνχνός, long, many, + καρπός, fruit.] In *bot.,* capable of bearing fruit many times without perishing, as a tree.

sy-co-ni-um (sī-kō′ni-um), *n.*; pl. *-nia* (-ni-ä). [NL., < Gr. σῦκον, fig.] In *bot.,* a multiple fruit developed from a hollow fleshy receptacle containing numerous flowers, as in the fig. Also (NL.) **sy-co′nus** (-nus); pl. *-ni* (-nī).

syc-o-phan-cy (sik′ō-fan-si), *n.*; pl. *-cies* (-siz). The character or conduct of a sycophant; self-seeking or servile flattery; an instance of this.

syc-o-phant (sik′ō-fant), *n.* [L. *sycophanta,* < Gr. σνκοφάντης, false accuser, slanderer, false adviser, appar. < σῦκον, fig, + φαίνειν, show; the original application of the term being in dispute.] One of a class of informers in ancient Athens; hence, in general, a malicious or false accuser†; also, a self-seeking flatterer (as, "the cowardly *sycophants* who usually rise by the favour of weak princes": Hallam's "Europe during the Middle Ages," iv.); a fawning or servile adulator or parasite.—**syc-o-phan′tic** (-fan′tik), *a.* Pertaining to, characteristic of, or acting as a sycophant; servilely flattering or adulatory.—**syc-o-phan′ti-cal-ly,** *adv.*

sy-co-sis (sī-kō′sis), *n.* [NL., < Gr. σύκωσις, < σῦκον, fig.] In *pathol.,* an inflammatory disease of the hair-follicles, esp. of the bearded part of the face, marked by a pustular eruption.

sy-e-nite (sī′ę-nīt), *n.* [L. (*lapis*) *Syenites,* (stone) of *Syene,* a town (now *Assuan*) in Upper Egypt.] A granular igneous rock consisting typically of feldspar (orthoclase) and hornblende.—**sy-e-nit′ic** (-nit′ik), *a.*

syl-la-ba-ri-um (sil-a-bā′ri-um), *n.*; pl. *-ria* (-ri-ä). [NL.] Same as *syllabary.*

syl-la-ba-ry (sil′a-bā-ri), *n.*; pl. *-ries* (-riz). [= NL. *syllabarium,* < L. *syllaba*: see *syllable.*] A list or catalogue of syllables; a list of characters representing syllables, used (like an alphabet) in certain languages, as the Japanese.

syl-la-bi (sil′a-bī), *n.* Plural of *syllabus.*

syl-lab-ic (si-lab′ik). [Gr. σνλλαβικός, < σνλλαβή: see *syllable.*] **I.** *a.* Of, pertaining to, or consisting of a syllable or syllables (as, a *syllabic* augment, in *gram.,* an augment, as in some Indo-European verb-forms, consisting of an additional syllable prefixed, as ἐ- in Greek or *a-* in Sanskrit); representing a syllable, as a written character, or written in or employing such characters, as writing (cf. *syllabary*); also, pronounced with careful distinction of syllables; of singing, etc., having each syllable sung to one note only. **II.** *n.* A sound capable of forming a syllable; also, a character representing a syllable.—**syl-lab′i-cal-ly,** *adv.*

syl-lab-i-cate (si-lab′i-kāt), *v. t.*; *-cated, -cating.* [ML. *syllabicatus,* pp. of *syllabicare,* < L. *syllaba*: see *syllable.*] To form or divide into syllables: as, to *syllabicate* a word by means of hyphens, as in indicating pronunciation or in order to suggest a mode of dividing the word if necessary at the end of a line.—**syl-lab-i-ca′tion** (-kā′shon), *n.*

syl-lab-i-fy (si-lab′i-fī), *v. t.*; *-fied, -fying.* [L. *syllaba,* syllable, + E. *-fy.*] To syllabicate.—**syl-lab″i-fi-ca′tion** (-fi-kā′shon), *n.*

syl-la-bism (sil′a-bizm), *n.* [NL. *syllaba*: see *syllable.*] The use of syllabic characters, as in writing; also, division into syllables.

syl-la-bize (sil′a-bīz), *v. t.*; *-bized, -bizing.* [ML. *syllabizare,* < Gr. σνλλαβίζειν, < σνλλαβή: see *syllable.*] To form or divide into syllables; syllabicate; also, to utter with careful distinction of syllables.

syl-la-ble (sil′a-bl), *n.* [AF. *sillable,* for OF. *sillabe* (F. *syllabe*), < L. *syllaba,* < Gr. σνλλαβή, syllable, < σνλλαμβάνειν, take together, < σύν, with, + λαμβάνειν, take.] The smallest separately articulated element in human speech, consisting of a vowel either alone or together with one or more consonants, and constituting a word or a part of a word; also, a character or a set of characters representing (more or less exactly) such an element of speech, as in writing or printing; also, the least portion or amount of speech or writing, or the least mention of something (as, "Having attempted in vain to catch a *syllable* of the discourse, he knocked violently at the door," Peacock's "Nightmare Abbey," xiii.; do not breathe a *syllable* of all this).—**syl′la-ble,** *v.*; *-bled, -bling.* **I.** *tr.* To utter in syllables; articulate; also, to read syllable by syllable; also, to represent by syllables. **II.** *intr.* To utter syllables; speak.—**syl′la-bled,** *a.* Consisting of a syllable or syllables: as, one-*syllabled.*

syl-la-bub (sil′a-bub), *n.* See *sillabub.*

syl-la-bus (sil′a-bus), *n.*; pl. *-buses* or *-bi* (-bī). [NL., appar. erron. for L. *sittybus,* a strip of parchment attached to a book and bearing the title and the author's name: cf. Gr. σίττνβον, piece of leather.] A tabular or other brief statement of the heads or main points of a discourse, the subjects of a course of lectures or study, the contents of a treatise, or the like; an abstract, summary, or synopsis.

---

syl-lep-sis (si-lep′sis), n. [LL., < Gr. σύλληψις, < συλλαμ-βάνειν, take together: see *syllable*.] In *gram*. and *rhet*., the use of one word in a sentence to serve two or more purposes without equal appropriateness, as in 'neither he nor we *are* willing,' or to express more than one sense, as in 'he fought *with* desperation and a stout club.'—**syl-lep′tic**, a.

syl-lo-gism (sil′ō-jizm), n. [OF. *sillogisme* (F. *syllogisme*), < L. *syllogismus*, < Gr. συλλογισμός, reasoning, syllogism, < συλλογίζεσθαι: see *syllogize*.] A logical formula, or form of argument, consisting of two premises and a conclusion which follows, or is alleged to follow, from them, as, 'All men are mortal' (major premise), 'I am a man' (minor premise), 'therefore, I am mortal' (conclusion); also, argumentation or reasoning in this form (as, "*Syllogism* may . . . be defined as the act of thought by which from two given propositions we proceed to a third proposition": Jevons's "Elementary Lessons in Logic," xv.); deductive reasoning.—**syl-lo-gis′tic** (-jis′tik). [L. *syllogisticus*, < Gr. συλλογιστικός, < συλλογίζεσθαι.] **I.** a. Of, pertaining to, or of the nature of a syllogism; proceeding by or employing syllogisms, as reasoning. **II.** n. Syllogistic reasoning; the department of logic that deals with syllogisms.—**syl-lo-gis′ti-cal-ly**, adv.

syl-lo-gize (sil′ō-jīz), v.; -gized, -gizing. [OF. *sillogiser*, < LL. *syllogizare*, < Gr. συλλογίζεσθαι, sum up, conclude, infer, < σύν, with, + λογίζεσθαι, calculate, infer, < λόγος, reckoning, reason.] **I.** intr. To argue or reason by syllogisms. **II.** tr. To deduce by syllogisms.—**syl″lo-gi-za′tion** (-ji-zā′shon), n.—**syl′lo-giz-er** (-jī-zėr), n.

sylph (silf), n. [= F. *sylphe*, < NL. *sylphes*, *sylphi*, pl. (used by Paracelsus); origin uncertain: cf. *gnome*[1].] One of a race of imaginary beings supposed (orig. in the system of Paracelsus) to inhabit the air; hence, any slender, graceful, lightly moving creature, esp. a woman or girl.—**syl-phid** (sil′fid), n. [F. *sylphide*, fem. of *sylphe*.] A female sylph; less properly, a little or young sylph.—**syl′phi-dine** (-fi-din), a. Like a sylphid.—**sylph′=like**, a. Like or suggesting a sylph, as in figure or movement; slender; graceful: as, "On one side of the old man was a *sylph-like* form—a young woman of about seventeen" (Scott's "Guy Mannering," xiii.).

syl-va, sil-va (sil′vạ), n.; pl. -vas (-vạz), L. -væ (-vē). [L. *silva*, less correctly *sylva*, wood, forest.] The aggregate of the species of forest-trees of a given region; also, a description of them.

syl-van, sil-van (sil′vạn). [L. *silvanus*, *sylvanus* (as n., *Silvanus*, god of the woods, *silvani*, pl. masc., and *silvanæ*, pl. fem., woodland deities), < *silva*, *sylva*: see *sylva*.] **I.** a. Of, pertaining to, or inhabiting the woods; consisting of or abounding in woods or trees; woodland; wooded; woody: as, "*sylvan* solitude" (Mrs. Wharton's "Age of Innocence," vii.); *sylvan* deities; "vast *sylvan* tracts wherein Norman kings once hunted" (Disraeli's "Coningsby," iii. 1). **II.** n. A fabled deity or spirit of the woods; a person dwelling in a woodland region; an animal, esp. a bird, inhabiting or frequenting woods.

syl-van-ite (sil′vạn-īt), n. [From (*Tran*)*sylvan*(*ia*), where it was found.] A mineral consisting of a telluride of gold and silver, often occurring in crystals so arranged as to resemble written characters.

syl-ves-tral (sil-ves′trạl), a. [L. *silvestris*, *sylvestris*, < *silva*, *sylva*: see *sylva*.] Belonging to or growing in woods.

syl-vi-cul-ture (sil′vi-kul-tụr), n. [L. *sylva*, wood (see *sylva*), + *cultura*, culture.] The cultivation of forest-trees. —**syl-vi-cul′tur-ist**, n.

syl-vine, syl-vi-nite (sil′vin, sil′vi-nīt), n. Same as *sylvite*.

syl-vite (sil′vīt), n. [NL. (*sal digestivus*) *Sylvii*, 'digestive salt' of Sylvius,' an old name of potassium chloride.] A mineral consisting of potassium chloride, usually colorless, and crystallizing in cubes and octahedrons.

sym-. A form of *syn-* used before *b*, *m*, and *p*.

sym-bi-ont (sim′bi-ont, sim′bī-), n. [Gr. συμβιῶν (συμβιουντ-), ppr. of συμβιοῦν: see *symbiosis*.] In *biol*., an organism living in a state of symbiosis.

sym-bi-o-sis (sim-bi-ō′sis or sim-bī-), n. [NL., < Gr. συμβίωσις, a living together, < συμβιοῦν, live with, < σύν, with, + βιοῦν, live.] In *biol*., the living together or union of two unlike organisms: a term usually restricted to cases in which the union of the two animals or plants is advanta-

geous or necessary to one or both, as the case of the fungus and alga which together make up the lichen.—**sym-bi-ot′ic** (-ot′ik), a. Pertaining to, of the nature of, or characterized by symbiosis.—**sym-bi-ot′i-cal-ly**, adv.

sym-bol (sim′bọl), n. [L. *symbolus*, *symbolum*, < Gr. σύμβολον, sign, token, tally, ticket, < συμβάλλειν, put together, compare, < σύν, with, + βάλλειν, throw.] Something used or regarded as standing for or representing something else, esp. a material object that serves to represent something immaterial (as, the lion is the *symbol* of courage, the lamb of meekness, the olive-branch of peace, and the scepter of power); an emblem, token, or sign; also, a letter, figure, or other character or mark, or a combination of letters or the like, used to represent something (as, the algebraic *symbol* x, for an unknown quantity; the chemical *symbol* Au, for aurum or gold; the *symbols* for the signs of the zodiac, see note under *zodiac*); in *numis*., a small device on a coin in addition to the principal device, as the mark on an ancient Greek coin of the magistrate responsible for its issue; in *theol*., a summary of religious doctrine accepted as an authoritative and official statement of the belief of the Christian church or of one of its denominations; a creed.—**sym′bol**, v. t.; -boled or -bolled, -boling or -bolling. To symbolize.

sym-bo-læ-og-ra-phy (sim″bọ-lē-og′rạ-fi), n. [Gr. συμβόλαιον, a contract (< συμβάλλειν: see *symbol*), + -γραφία, < γράφειν, write.] The art of drawing up legal documents.

sym-bol-a-try (sim-bol′ạ-tri), n. A contracted form of *symbololatry*.

sym-bol-ic (sim-bol′ik). [LL. *symbolicus*, < Gr. συμβολικός, < σύμβολον, E. *symbol*.] **I.** a. Of, pertaining to, or expressed by a symbol; characterized by or involving the use of symbols (as, *symbolic* language; *symbolic* writing); serving as a symbol of something (often with *of*); in *gram*., of words, having a merely formal or relational value without presenting any object or conception directly to the mind (opposed to *presentive*); in *theol*., of or pertaining to symbols or creeds. **II.** n. In *gram*., a symbolic word.—**sym-bol′i-cal**, a. Symbolic.—**sym-bol′i-cal-ly**, adv.—**sym-bol′i-cal-ness**, n.—**sym-bol′ics**, n. The branch of theology that treats of the history and matter of Christian creeds and confessions of faith.

sym-bol-ism (sim′bọl-izm), n. The practice of representing things by symbols, or of investing things with a symbolic meaning or character; the use of symbols; a set or system of symbols; symbolic meaning or character; specif., the principles and practice of symbolists in art or literature.—**sym′-bol-ist**, n. One who uses symbols or symbolism; one versed in the study or interpretation of symbols; in *art*, an artist who seeks to symbolize or suggest particular ideas by the objects represented, the colors used, etc.; in *literature*, a writer who seeks to express or suggest ideas, emotions, etc., by means of symbols, as by the mention or introduction of things or the use of words and even word-sounds (as vowels) intended to convey a particular symbolic meaning, often with mystical or vague effect; esp., a member of a group of French and Belgian poets characterized by such procedure (including Verlaine, Mallarmé, and Maeterlinck), which arose during the latter part of the 19th century.—**sym-bol-is′tic**, a. Of or pertaining to symbolists; characterized by symbolism; specif., pertaining to or characteristic of symbolists in art or literature.—**sym-bol-is′ti-cal-ly**, adv.

sym-bol-ize (sim′bọl-īz), v.; -ized, -izing. [F. *symboliser*, < ML. *symbolizare*, < L. *symbolum*, E. *symbol*.] **I.** intr. To agree or accord (obs. or archaic); also, to use symbols. **II.** tr. To represent by a symbol or symbols; also, to be a symbol of; stand for or represent, as a symbol does (as, "To some it [a simple funeral service] would *symbolise* an absolute disbelief in any life beyond": Mallock's "New Republic," v. 1); also, to regard or treat as symbolic.—**sym″bol-i-za′tion** (-i-zā′shon), n.—**sym′bol-iz-er** (-ī-zėr), n.

sym-bol-o-gy (sim-bol′ō-ji), n. [See *symbol* and -*logy*.] The study of symbols; also, the use of symbols; symbolism.

sym-bo-lol-a-try (sim-bọ-lol′ạ-tri), n. [Gr. σύμβολον, E. *symbol*, + λατρεία, worship.] Worship of or excessive reverence for symbols.

sym-met-al-lism (sim-met′ạl-izm), n. [See *sym-* and *syn-*.] The use of two (or more) metals, as gold and silver, combined in assigned proportions as the monetary standard.

sym-met-ri-cal, sym-met-ric (si-met′ri-kal, -rik), *a.* Characterized by or exhibiting symmetry; well-proportioned, as a body or whole; exhibiting symmetry in the size, form, and arrangement of parts on opposite sides of a plane, line, or point, as a whole, or its form or arrangement, or its parts as corresponding one with another; regular in form or arrangement of corresponding parts; well-balanced in the combination of parts or elements (often fig.); in *pathol.*, affecting corresponding parts simultaneously, as certain diseases; in *bot.*, having the same number of parts in each whorl, as a flower with five sepals, five petals, five stamens (or ten stamens, in two rows), and five carpels.—**sym-met′-ri-cal-ly**, *adv.*—**sym-met′ri-cal-ness**, *n.*

sym-me-trist (sim′e-trist), *n.* One who is studious of or favors symmetry.

sym-me-trize (sim′e-trīz), *v. t.; -trized, -trizing.* To reduce to symmetry; make symmetrical.—**sym″me-tri-za′tion** (-tri-zā′shon), *n.*

sym-me-try (sim′e-tri), *n.* [L. *symmetria*, < Gr. συμμετρία, < σύμμετρος, commensurate, < σύν, with, + μέτρον, measure.] The proper or due proportion of the parts of a body or whole to one another with regard to size and form; excellence of proportion; also, the correspondence, in size, form, and arrangement, of parts on opposite sides of a plane, line, or point, each part on one side having its counterpart (in reverse order) on the other side; more generally, regularity of form or arrangement with reference to corresponding parts; well-balanced combination of parts or elements in a unitary whole (often fig., as with reference to a literary work); also, correspondence, conformity, or consonance, as of one thing with another (obs. or rare); in *bot.*, symmetrical condition, as of a flower.

sym-pa-thet-ic (sim-pa-thet′ik), *a.* [Gr. συμπαθητικός.] Characterized by, proceeding from, exhibiting, or feeling sympathy, as with another person (as, "Her tone was exceedingly *sympathetic* and comprehending," Arnold Bennett's "Helen with the High Hand," xii.; "He, whose *sympathetic* mind Exults in all the good of all mankind," Goldsmith's "Traveller," 43); congenial; sympathizing; compassionate; also, expressing sympathy or approval (as, a *sympathetic* strike: see phrase below); also, acting or affected by, of the nature of, or pertaining to a special natural sympathy, relation, or affinity as between things (as, *sympathetic* ink: see phrase below); also, agreeing, consonant, or in accord (as, "Now o'er the soothed accordant heart we feel A *sympathetic* twilight slowly steal": Wordsworth's "Evening Walk," 316); in *physiol.* and *pathol.*, pertaining to or induced by sympathy between parts, organs, or persons; in *anat.* and *zoöl.*, acting by or effecting sympathy between parts, as a system of nerves (see *sympathetic nervous system*, at *nervous system*), or pertaining to this system; in *physics*, pertaining or due to sympathy between sound-producing bodies; of vibrations, sounds, etc., produced by vibrations conveyed through the air (or other medium) from a body already in vibration (cf. *resonance*).—**sympathetic ink**, a kind of ink or fluid for producing writing that remains invisible until brought out by means of heat, lemon-juice, chemicals, or the like.—**sympathetic strike**, a strike by a body of workers, not because of grievances against their own employer, but by way of indorsing and aiding another body of workers who are on strike or have been locked out.—**sym-pa-thet′i-cal-ly**, *adv.*

sym-pa-thize (sim′pa-thīz), *v.; -thized, -thizing.* [F. *sympathiser*, < *sympathie*, < L. *sympathia*, E. *sympathy*.] **I.** *intr.* To be in sympathy, or agreement of feeling, as one person with another; share in a feeling or feelings (*with*); share with another in his feelings over what affects him, esp. his sufferings or troubles; feel a compassionate sympathy (*with*: as, "We may with patience bear our mod′rate ills, And *sympathise* with others, suff′ring more," Cowper's "Task," iv. 340); express sympathy or condole (*with*); also, to be in approving accord, as with a person, party, cause, policy, etc. (as, to *sympathize* with a person's aims); also, to have a special natural sympathy, relation, or affinity as one thing with another; exhibit such a sympathy (*with*), as by some responsive action; also, to agree, correspond, or accord (as,

"Nature, in awe to him, Had doff'd her gaudy trim, With her great Master so to *sympathise*": Milton's "On the Morning of Christ's Nativity," 34); in *pathol.*, to exhibit a sympathetic affection. **II.†** *tr.* To feel sympathy with or for; also, to agree or accord with; also, to frame, express, or represent with due accord.—**sym′pa-thiz-er** (-thī-zėr), *n.* One who or that which sympathizes; esp., one who sympathizes approvingly with a person, party, cause, etc.—**sym′-pa-thiz-ing-ly**, *adv.*

sym-pa-thy (sim′pa-thi), *n.; pl. -thies* (-thiz). [L. *sympathia*, < Gr. συμπάθεια, < συμπαθής, having like feelings, < σύν, with, + παθεῖν, suffer.] Community of or agreement in feeling, as between persons or on the part of one person with respect to another (as, "There was the most perfect *sympathy* and understanding between us," S. Butler's "Way of All Flesh," xviii.; I was in complete *sympathy* with him on this point); the community of feeling naturally existing between persons of like tastes or opinions or of congenial dispositions; also, the sharing of the feelings of another with respect to what affects the latter; the fact or the power of entering into the feelings of another, esp. in sorrow or trouble; fellow-feeling, compassion, or commiseration (as, "They had little *sympathy* to spare for their unfortunate enemies": Prescott's "Conquest of Mexico," iii. 7); *pl.*, feelings or impulses of compassion (as, "an affecting appeal to his human *sympathies*": Kingsley's "Yeast," x.); also, *sing.*, favorable or approving accord (as, to be in *sympathy* with one's aims); favor or approval (as, to have no *sympathy* for a policy or its advocates; to enlist the *sympathy*, or *sympathies*, of the public in behalf of a cause); also, a special natural relation or affinity between things, as between the lodestone and iron; also, agreement, consonance, or accord (as, "The day was a glorious one, and the whole camp seemed lively and animated in *sympathy*": Parkman's "Oregon Trail," xii.); in *physiol.* and *pathol.*, the relation between parts or organs of a living body whereby a condition, affection, or disorder of one part induces some effect in another; a similar relation between persons whereby the condition of one induces a responsive condition in another; in *physics*, the relation between two bodies whereby vibrations in one produce responsive vibrations in the other.

sym-pel-mous (sim-pel′mus), *a.* [Gr. συν-, together, + πέλμα, sole of the foot.] In *ornith.*, having the two deep flexor tendons of the toes blended into one before dividing to proceed to the digits.

sym-pet-a-lous (sim-pet′a-lus), *a.* [See *sym-* and *syn-*.] In *bot.*, gamopetalous.

sym-phon-ic (sim-fon′ik), *a.* [See *symphony.*] Of or pertaining to symphony, or harmony of sounds; characterized by similarity of sound, as words; in *music*, of, pertaining to, or having the character of a symphony.—**symphonic poem**, in *music*, an orchestral work of symphonic dimensions and character but free in form, based on a specified poetic theme: an elaborate form of program music.

sym-pho-ni-ous (sim-fō′ni-us), *a.* [L. *symphonia*: see *symphony.*] Characterized by symphony, or harmony of sounds; in general, harmonious; in harmonious agreement or accord.—**sym-pho′ni-ous-ly**, *adv.*

sym-pho-nist (sim′fō-nist), *n.* A composer of symphonies.

sym-pho-ny (sim′fō-ni), *n.; pl. -nies* (-niz). [OF. F. *symphonie*, < L. *symphonia*, < Gr. συμφωνία, < σύμφωνος, agreeing in sound, < σύν, with, + φωνή, sound.] Harmony of sounds, esp. musical sounds (obs. or archaic); harmony in general, or harmonious agreement (obs. or archaic); harmonious or concerted music, or an instance of such music (as, "Ne'er to *symphony* more sweet Gave mountain echoes answer meet," Scott's "Lord of the Isles," i. 1: also fig.); anything characterized by a harmonious combination of elements; esp., a picture, scene, costume, or the like presenting an effective combination of colors (as, "to execute what some of our young painters would now-a-days call a *Sym-*

flh — fpd

Sympelmous Foot, showing the two tendons (*flh* and *fpd*) with a large sesamoid (*s*) at their point of union.

phony in Yellow": Amelia B. Edwards's "Thousand Miles up the Nile," xvi.); in *music*, an instrumental passage occurring in a vocal composition, or between vocal movements in a composition; also, an instrumental piece, often in several movements, forming the overture to an opera or the like; hence, an elaborate instrumental composition in three or more movements, similar in form to a sonata but written for an orchestra, and usually of far grander proportions and more varied elements; also, in medieval and later use, any of several distinct instruments, as the bagpipe, drum, and hurdy-gurdy.

sym-phy-sis (sim′fi-sis), *n.*; pl. *-physes* (-fi-sēz). [NL., < Gr. σύμφυσις, < συμφύειν, cause to grow together, < σύν, with, + φύειν, produce.] In *anat.* and *zoöl.*, the growing together, or the fixed or movable union, of bones in the middle line of the body, as that of the two halves of the human lower jaw, or that of the two human pubic bones at the lower anterior point of the abdomen; a line of junction or articulation so formed; a growing together, union, articulation, or the like, of bones not in the middle line of the body; a union, line of junction, or the like, of other parts, as nerves; in *bot.*, a coalescence or growing together of parts.—**sym-phys′i-al** (-fiz′i-ạl), *a.*

sym-pi-e-som-e-ter (sim″pi-e-som′e-tėr), *n.* [Gr. συμπίεσις, compression (< συμπιέζειν, compress, < σύν, with, + πιέζειν, press), + μέτρον, measure: cf. *piezometer.*] An instrument for measuring the pressure of a current of water; also, a form of barometer in which the pressure of the atmosphere is balanced partly by a column of liquid and partly by the pressure of a confined gas above it.

sym-po-di-um (sim-pō′di-um), *n.*; pl. *-dia* (-di-ạ). [NL., < Gr. σύμπους (συμποδ-), having the feet together, < σύν, with, + πούς (ποδ-), foot.] In *bot.*, an axis or stem which simulates a simple stem but is made up of the bases of a number of axes which arise successively as branches one from another, as in the grape-vine; a pseudaxis. Cf. *monopodium.*—**sym-po′di-al**, *a.*

sym-po-si-ac (sim-pō′zi-ak). [L. *symposiacus*, < Gr. συμποσιακός, < συμπόσιον, E. *symposium.*] **I.** *a.* Of or pertaining to a symposium; suitable for a symposium; of the nature of a symposium. **II.** *n.* A symposiac meeting, or the conversation at it; an account of such a meeting or conversation.

sym-po-si-arch (sim-pō′zi-ärk), *n.* [Gr. συμποσίαρχος, < συμπόσιον, E. *symposium*, + ἄρχειν, lead, rule.] The president, director, or master of a symposium; the leading spirit of a convivial gathering; the toast-master at a banquet.

sym-po-si-ast (sim-pō′zi-ast), *n.* One who takes part in a symposium; a member of a drinking-party or convivial gathering; a contributor to a symposium on some subject.—**sym-po-si-as′tic**, *a.*

sym-po-si-um (sim-pō′zi-um), *n.*; pl. *-sia* (-zi-ạ) or *-siums*. [L., < Gr. συμπόσιον, a drinking-party, < σύν, with, + -ποσιον, related to πόσις, a drinking, and πίνειν, drink.] A drinking-party; among the ancient Greeks, a convivial meeting, usually following a dinner, for drinking, conversation, and intellectual entertainment; an account of such a meeting or of the conversation at it; hence, any similar convivial gathering; also, a meeting or conference for discussion of some subject; also, a collection of opinions expressed, or a series of articles contributed, by several persons on a given subject or topic.

symp-tom (simp′tọm), *n.* [ML. *symptoma*, < Gr. σύμπτωμα, < συμπίπτειν, fall together, befall, happen, < σύν, with, + πίπτειν, fall.] In *pathol.*, a phenomenon or circumstance constituting a departure from normal bodily condition or function, which arises from and accompanies a particular disease or disorder and serves as an indication of it; hence, in general, any phenomenon or circumstance accompanying something and serving as evidence of it; a sign or indication of something (as, "the gale having rather increased than shown any *symptoms* of abating": Marryat's "King's Own," li.).—**symp-to-mat′ic** (-tọ-mat′ik), *a.* Pertaining to a symptom or symptoms; of the nature of or constituting a symptom; indicative (*of*); specif., in *pathol.*, of a disease, secondary, or arising from and accompanying a primary disease; not idiopathic.—**symp-to-mat′i-cal-ly**, *adv.*—**symp″to-ma-tol′o-gy** (-mạ-tol′ọ-ji), *n.* [See *-logy.*] That

branch of medical science which deals with symptoms.—**symp′tom-less**, *a.* Without symptoms; not attended with the usual symptoms, as an attack of disease.

syn-. [Gr. συν- (also συγ-, συλ-, συμ-, συσ-, etc.), repr. σύν, prep., with, as adv. together.] A prefix meaning 'with,' 'together,' 'jointly,' 'at the same time,' occurring in words from the Greek, and used also as a modern formative, chiefly in scientific terms.

syn-ac-tic (si-nak′tik), *a.* [Gr. συνακτικός, able to bring together, < συνάγειν: see *synagogue.*] Working together; coöperating; synergetic.

syn-ær-e-sis (si-ner′e-sis), *n.* See *syneresis.*

syn-æs-the-sia (sin-es-thē′ziä), *n.* [NL.: see *syn-* and *æsthesia.*] Sensation produced in one part of the body when a stimulus is applied to another part; also, the bringing about, through a sensation produced by something of one kind, of a mental image corresponding to something of an entirely different kind, as when the hearing of a certain sound induces the visualization of a certain color.

syn-a-gogue (sin′ạ-gog), *n.* [OF. *sinagoge* (F. *synagogue*), < LL. *synagoga*, < Gr. συναγωγή, a bringing together, assembly, synagogue, < συνάγειν, bring together, < σύν, with, + ἄγειν, lead.] An assembly or congregation of the Jews for the purposes of religious instruction and worship apart from the service of the temple, constituting, since the destruction of the temple and the dispersion of the Jews, the customary Jewish form of worship; the religious organization of the Jews as typified by this assembly; a building or place of assembly where Jewish religious instruction and worship are maintained; also, any assembly or congregation (now rare); any place of worship†.—**the Great Synagogue**, a Jewish assembly or council of 120 members said to have been founded and presided over by Ezra after the return from the Babylonian captivity.—**syn′a-gog-al** (-gog-ạl), **syn-a-gog′i-cal** (-goj′i-kạl), *a.*

syn-a-lœ-pha, syn-a-lœ-phe (sin-ạ-lē′fä, -fē), *n.* [L., < Gr. συναλοιφή, < συναλείφειν, smear together, < σύν, with, + ἀλείφειν, anoint.] The blending of two successive vowels into one; esp., the coalescence of two vowels, one at the end of a word and the other at the beginning of the next word, by obscuration of the first one, as in *th' enemy* for *the enemy*, or, loosely, by elision of the first one, as in French *l'ami* for *le ami*. Also **syn-a-le′pha** (-lē′fä), **syn-a-le′phe** (-lē′fē).

syn-an-ther-ous (si-nan′thėr-us), *a.* [See *syn-.*] In *bot.*, characterized by stamens that are coalescent by means of their anthers, as a composite plant.

syn-an-thous (si-nan′thus), *a.* [Gr. συν-, together, + ἄνθος, flower.] In *bot.*, having flowers and leaves which appear at the same time; also, characterized by the abnormal union of two or more flowers.—**syn-an′thy** (-thi), *n.* In *bot.*, the abnormal union of two or more flowers.

syn-ar-thro-di-a (sin-är-thrō′di-ạ), *n.*; pl. *-diæ* (-di-ē). [NL., < Gr. σύν, with, + ἀρθρωδία, kind of articulation, < ἄρθρον, a joint, + εἶδος, form.] Synarthrosis.—**syn-ar-thro′di-al**, *a.* Pertaining to or of the nature of a synarthrosis.—**syn-ar-thro′di-al-ly**, *adv.*

syn-ar-thro-sis (sin-är-thrō′sis), *n.*; pl. *-throses* (-thrō′sēz). [NL., < Gr. συνάρθρωσις: see *syn-* and *arthrosis.*] In *anat.*, immovable articulation; a fixed or immovable joint; a suture.

syn-carp (sin′kärp), *n.* [Gr. συν-, together, + καρπός, fruit.] In *bot.*, an aggregate fruit; also, a collective fruit.—**syn-car′pous** (-kär′pus), *a.* In *bot.*, of the nature of or pertaining to a syncarp; also, composed of or having united carpels.—**syn′car-py** (-pi), *n.* In *bot.*, the state of having united carpels; also, the abnormal union of two or more fruits.

syn-cat-e-gor-e-mat-ic (sin-kat″ē-gọr-e-mat′ik), *a.* [Gr. συγκατηγορηματικός: see *syn-* and *categorematic.*] In *logic*, noting or pertaining to words which cannot singly express a term, but only a part of a term, as adverbs and prepositions.

syn-chro-nal, syn-chron-ic (sing′krō-nạl, sin-kron′ik), *a.* [See *synchronous.*] Coinciding or agreeing in time; synchronous.—**syn-chro-ni-ci-ty** (sing-krō-nis′i-ti), *n.* Synchronism.

syn-chro-nism (sing′krō-nizm), *n.* [Gr. συγχρονισμός, < συγχρονίζειν, E. *synchronize.*] The state of being synchronous; coincidence in time; contemporaneousness; simultaneousness; also, the arrangement or treatment of synchronous things or events in conjunction, as in a history (as, "The laws of *synchronism* . . . bring strange partners together, and we may pass at once from Luther to Ariosto": Hallam's "Literature of Europe," i. 4. § 62); a statement that two or more things or events are synchronous; a comparison between or a description of different things or events belonging to the same period; a tabular arrangement of historical events or personages, grouped together according to their dates; also, the bringing together of events, etc., of different times, as into one picture; also, recurrence together at the same successive instants of time; the fact of going on at the same rate and exactly together; in *physics*, *elect.*, etc., the state of being synchronous.—**syn-chro-nis′tic**, *a.* Pertaining to or exhibiting synchronism; synchronous.—**syn-chro-nis′ti-cal-ly**, *adv.*

syn-chro-nize (sing′krō-nīz), *v.*; -nized, -nizing. [Gr. συγχρονίζειν, be synchronous, < σύγχρονος, E. *synchronous*.] **I.** *intr.* To occur at the same time, or coincide or agree in time (as, "The first shooting-party of the season . . . had been . . . made to *synchronise* with the last Newmarket Meeting": Galsworthy's "Country House," i. 1); also, to recur together at the same successive instants of time; go on at the same rate and exactly together. **II.** *tr.* To cause to agree in time of occurrence; assign to the same time or period; bring together as belonging to the same period, as in a history; also, to cause to go on at the same rate and exactly together; also, to cause to indicate the same time, as one timepiece with another.—**syn″chro-ni-za′tion** (-ni-zā′shon), *n.*—**syn′chro-niz-er** (-nī-zėr), *n.*

syn-chron-o-scope (sin-kron′ō-skōp), *n.* [Gr. σύγχρονος, E. *synchronous*: see *-scope*.] In *elect.*, an apparatus for indicating synchronism between two alternating-current machines and also for showing the relative speeds.

syn-chro-nous (sing′krō-nus), *a.* [LL, *synchronus*, < Gr. σύγχρονος, being together in time, < σύν, with, + χρόνος, time.] Occurring at the same time; coinciding in time; contemporaneous; simultaneous; of or pertaining to things or events belonging to the same time (as, a *synchronous* history of two countries); also, recurring together at the same successive instants of time; going on at the same rate and exactly together; in *physics*, *elect.*, etc., having the same frequency, or the same frequency and phase.—**syn′chro-nous-ly**, *adv.*—**syn′chro-nous-ness**, *n.*—**syn′chro-ny** (-ni), *n.* Coincidence or agreement in time; synchronism.

syn-clas-tic (sin-klas′tik), *a.* [Gr. σύν-, together, + κλαστός, adj. < κλᾶν, break, deflect.] Noting or pertaining to a surface (such as that of a sphere) which is curved similarly (that is, either convexly or concavely) in all directions: opposed to *anticlastic*.

syn-cli-nal (sin-klī′nal), *a.* [Gr. συγκλίνειν, incline together, < σύν, with, + κλίνειν, incline.] In *geol.*, inclining upward on both sides from a median line or axis, as a downward fold of rock-strata; pertaining to such a fold.—**syn-cline** (sing′klīn), *n.* In *geol.*, a synclinal fold.—**syn-cli-no-ri-um** (sing-kli-nō′ri-um), *n.*; pl. *-ria* (-ri-ä) or *-riums.* [NL., < Gr. συγκλίνειν + ὄρος, mountain.] In *geol.*, a compound syncline, consisting of a series of subordinate synclines and anticlines, the whole formation having the general contour of an inverted arch: opposed to *anticlinorium.*

Synclinal Fold.

syn-co-pal (sing′kō-pal), *a.* In *pathol.*, pertaining to or marked by syncope.

syn-co-pate (sing′kō-pāt), *v. t.*; -pated, -pating. [ML. *syncopatus*, pp. of *syncopare*, < LL. *syncope*: see *syncope*.] In *gram.*, to contract (a word) by taking one or more letters or syllables from the middle, as in reducing *Gloucester* to *Gloster*; in *music*, to begin (a tone) on an unaccented beat and sustain it into an accented one, which is thus apparently shifted back; also, to employ tones so affected in (a passage, piece, etc.).—**syn′co-pat-er** (-pā-tėr), *n.* See *syncopator.*—**syn-co-pa′tion** (-pā′shon), *n.* [ML. *syncopatio(n-).*] The act of syncopating, or the state of being syncopated.—

syn′co-pa-tor, *n.* One who syncopates; a member of a jazz band; one devoted to jazz.

syn-co-pe (sing′kō-pē), *n.* [LL., < Gr. συγκοπή, < συγκόπτειν, cut up, cut short, < σύν, with, + κόπτειν, cut.] A cutting short; abbreviation; sudden cessation or interruption; in *gram.*, the contraction of a word by taking one or more letters or syllables from the middle, as in the reduction of *never* to *ne'er*; syncopation; in *pathol.*, a temporary diminution or suspension of the heart's action, characterized chiefly by loss of consciousness; fainting.—**syn-cop-ic**, **syn-cop-tic** (sin-kop′ik, -tik), *a.*

syn-cre-tism (sing′krē-tism), *n.* [Gr. συγκρητισμός, < συγκρητίζειν, E. *syncretize.*] The attempted reconciliation or union of different or opposing principles, practices, or parties, as in philosophy or religion (as, "this *syncretism* . . . of the material and immaterial hypotheses": Hallam's "Literature of Europe," iii. 3. § 96); specif., the doctrines of the Lutheran theologian Georg Calixtus (1586–1656) and his followers, who aimed at a union of all Protestants and ultimately of all Christian bodies.—**syn′cre-tist**, *n.* One who practises or favors syncretism.—**syn-cre-tis′tic**, *a.*

syn-cre-tize (sing′krē-tīz), *v.*; -tized, -tizing. [Gr. συγκρητίζειν, combine, as two parties against a common enemy (according to one explanation, in the manner of the Cretans, Gr. Κρῆτες).] **I.** *intr.* To attempt to reconcile or unite different or opposing principles, parties, etc.; practise syncretism. **II.** *tr.* To attempt to combine, as different or opposing principles, parties, etc.

syn-cri-sis (sing′kri-sis), *n.* [NL., < Gr. σύγκρισις, < συγκρίνειν, compare, < σύν, with, + κρίνειν, judge.] Comparison; in *rhet.*, a figure by which opposite things or persons are compared.

syn-dac-tyl (sin-dak′til). [Gr. συν-, together, + δάκτυλος, finger or toe.] **I.** *a.* Having certain digits more or less united, as the kingfisher and the kangaroo, or as a monstrosity of the human species. **II.** *n.* A syndactyl animal, or a syndactyl monstrosity of the human species.—**syn-dac′tyl-ism**, *n.* Syndactyl character or condition.—**syn-dac′ty-lous**, *a.* Syndactyl.

Syndactyl Foot of Kingfisher. — 1, hallux, or hind toe; 2, inner toe; 3, middle toe, which is extensively coherent with 4, outer toe.

syn-des-mo-sis (sin-des-mō′sis), *n.*; pl. *-moses* (-mō′sēz). [NL., < Gr. σύνδεσμος, fastening, ligament, < συνδεῖν: see *syndetic.*] In *anat.*, a connection of bones by ligaments, fasciæ, or membranes other than those of the joints.—**syn-des-mot′ic** (-mot′ik), *a.*

syn-det-ic (sin-det′ik), *a.* [Gr. συνδετικός, < συνδεῖν, bind together, < σύν, with, + δεῖν, bind.] Serving to unite or connect; connective; copulative.—**syn-det′i-cal-ly**, *adv.*

syn-dic (sin′dik), *n.* [F. *syndic*, < LL. *syndicus*, < Gr. σύνδικος, advocate, < σύν, with, + δίκη, right, justice.] A civil magistrate having different powers in different countries; also, a person chosen to represent and transact business for a corporation or the like, as a university.

syn-di-cal (sin′di-kal), *a.* [F. *syndical*, < *syndic*, E. *syndic.*] Noting or pertaining to a union, for the protection of their interests, of persons engaged in a particular trade; also, of or pertaining to syndicalism.—**syn′di-cal-ism**, *n.* [F. *syndicalisme.*] A form or development of trade-unionism, originating in France, which aims at the possession of the means of production and distribution, and ultimately at the control of society and government, by the federated bodies of industrial workers, and which seeks to realize its purposes through the agency of general strikes and of terrorism, sabotage, violence, or other criminal means.—**syn′di-cal-ist**, *n.* An adherent or advocate of syndicalism.—**syn″di-cal-is′tic**, *a.*

syn-di-cate (sin′di-kat), *n.* [F. *syndicat*, < *syndic*, E. *syndic.*] The office or jurisdiction of a syndic; a council or body of syndics; a meeting of such a body; also, a combination of bankers or capitalists formed for the purpose of carrying out some project requiring large resources of capital, as the underwriting of an issue of stock or bonds; hence, any combination of persons, companies, or the like, resembling this; esp., an association of publishers of newspapers or other periodicals in different places, for purchasing articles, stories, etc., and publishing them simultaneously; also, any agency which supplies articles, stories, etc., for simultaneous publication in a number of newspapers or other periodicals in different places (as, "I [editor] found it convenient . . . to buy all my fiction from a large and powerful *syndicate*": Arnold Bennett's "Truth about an Author," xii.).—**syn′di-cate** (-kāt), *v. t.*; *-cated, -cating.* To combine into a syndicate; also, to handle, manage, or effect through a syndicate, or as a syndicate does; also, to publish simultaneously, or supply for simultaneous publication, in a number of newspapers or other periodicals in different places (as, "His exclamatory assertions were *syndicated* in the press," Sinclair Lewis's "Arrowsmith," xvi.; "Edward . . . saw the possibility of *syndicating* this item as a woman's letter from New York," Bok's "Americanization of Edward Bok," x.). —**syn-di-ca′tion** (-kā′shon), *n.* The act or process of syndicating, or the state of being syndicated.—**syn′di-ca-tor,** *n.*

syn-dro-me (sin′drō-mē), *n.* [NL., < Gr. συνδρομή, < σύν, with, + δραμεῖν, run.] Concurrence†; in *pathol.*, the combination of symptoms in a disease; a number of symptoms occurring together.—**syn-drom′ic** (-drom′ik), *a.*

syn-dy-o-ce-ras (sin-dī-os′e̱-ras), *n.* [NL., < Gr. σύν-, together, + δύο, two, + κέρας, horn.] An extinct ungulate mammal of the genus *Syndyoceras*, probably allied to the deer family (*Cervidæ*), having two pairs of curving horns on the skull: found in the Miocene beds of Nebraska. Cf. *protoceras.*

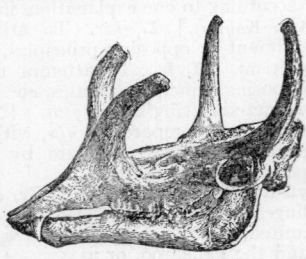

Skull of Syndyoceras, one ninth natural size.

syne (sīn), *adv., prep.,* and *conj.* [Cf. *sin²*.] Since. [Sc. and prov. Eng.]— **auld lang syne.** See under *auld.*

syn-ec-do-che (si-nek′dō-kē), *n.* [L., < Gr. συνεκδοχή, < συνεκδέχεσθαι, understand with something else, < σύν, with, + ἐκδέχεσθαι, take, understand, < ἐκ, out of, + δέχεσθαι, receive.] In *rhet.*, a figure of speech by which a part is put for the whole, or the whole for a part, the special for the general, or the general for the special, or the like, as in 'a fleet of ten *sail*' (for *ships*), or 'to eat of the *tree*' (for *fruit*: see Gen. ii. 17), or 'a *Crœsus*' (for a *rich man*), or 'a *marble* on its pedestal' (for a *statue*).—**syn-ec-doch-ic, syn-ec-doch-i-cal** (sin-ek-dok′ik, -i-kạl), *a.*—**syn-ec-doch′i-cal-ly,** *adv.*

syn-e-cious (si-nē′shus), *a.* See *synæcious.*

syn-e-dral, syn-e-drous (si-nē′drạl, -drus), *a.* [Gr. σύνεδρος, sitting with, < σύν, with, + ἕδρα, seat.] In *bot.*, growing on an angle of a stem.

syn-er-e-sis, syn-ær-e-sis (si-ner′e-sis), *n.* [LL. *synæresis*, < Gr. συναίρεσις, < συναιρεῖν, take together, contract, < σύν, with, + αἱρεῖν, take.] In *gram.*, the contraction of two syllables or two vowels into one; esp. the contraction of two vowels so as to form a diphthong.

syn-er-get-ic (sin-èr-jet′ik), *a.* [Gr. συνεργητικός, < συνεργεῖν, work together, < συνεργός: see *synergy*.] Working together; coöperative; synergic.—**syn-er-get′i-cal-ly,** *adv.*

syn-er-gic (si-nèr′jik), *a.* Of, pertaining to, or involving synergy; coöperative: as, *synergic* action of muscles.— **syn-er′gi-cal-ly,** *adv.*

syn-er-gism (sin′èr-jizm), *n.* [Gr. συνεργία: see *synergy*.] In *theol.*, the doctrine that the human will coöperates with the divine Spirit in the work of regeneration.—**syn′er-gist,** *n.* In *theol.*, one who holds the doctrine of synergism; in *physiol.* and *med.*, a bodily organ or a medicine, etc., that coöperates with another or others.—**syn-er-gis′tic,** *a.* Of or pertaining to synergism; also, working together; synergetic.— **syn-er-gis′ti-cal-ly,** *adv.*

syn-er-gy (sin′èr-ji), *n.*; pl. *-gies* (-jiz). [Gr. συνεργία, coöperation, < συνεργός, working together, < σύν, with, + -εργός, working: cf. *energy*.] Combined action; esp., the coöperative action of two or more bodily organs or the like.

syn-e-sis (sin′e-sis), *n.* [NL., < Gr. σύνεσις, understanding, < συνιέναι, put together, understand, < σύν, with, + ἱέναι, send.] In *gram.*, construction according to the sense, in violation of strict syntax.

syn-es-the-sia, *n.* See *synæsthesia.*

syn-gen-e-sis (sin-jen′e-sis), *n.* [See *syn-* and *genesis*.] In *biol.*, reproduction in which the substance of the embryo is actually derived from both parents, the male furnishing the spermatozoa and the female the ovum; also, the theory that every germ contains the germs of all generations to come.—**syn-ge-net′ic** (-je̱-net′ik), *a.*

syn-i-ze-sis (sin-i-zē′sis), *n.* [LL., < Gr. συνίζησις, < συνιζάνειν, sink in, collapse, < συν-, together, + ἰζάνειν, settle down, < ἵζειν, seat, sit.] In *gram.*, the combination into one syllable of two vowels (or of a vowel and a diphthong) that would not form a diphthong; in *pathol.*, closure or obliteration of the pupil of the eye.

syn-od (sin′od), *n.* [LL. *synodus*, < Gr. σύνοδος, assembly, meeting, < συν-, together, + ὁδός, way.] An assembly of ecclesiastics or other church delegates duly convoked, pursuant to the law of the church, for the discussion and decision of ecclesiastical affairs; an ecclesiastical council; in Presbyterian churches, a court which ranks above the presbytery, and either is subordinate to a general assembly or is itself the supreme court of the church; in general, an assembly, convention, or council of any kind (as, "We could not have had a better dinner, had there been a *Synod* of Cooks": Johnson, in Boswell's "Johnson," Aug. 5, 1763); in *astron.*, conjunction.—**syn′od-al,** *a.*—**syn-od-ic, syn-od-i-cal** (si-nod′ik, -i-kạl), *a.* [LL. *synodicus*, < Gr. συνοδικός.] Of or pertaining to, done or made by, or proceeding from a synod; in *astron.*, pertaining to a conjunction, or to two successive conjunctions of the same bodies.—**synodical month.** See *month*.—**syn-od′i-cal-ly,** *adv.*

syn-œ-cious, syn-e-cious (si-nē′shus), *a.* [Gr. συν-, together, + οἶκος, house.] In *bot.*, having male and female flowers in one head, as in many composite plants; also, having antheridia and archegonia in the same receptacle.

syn-o-nym (sin′ō-nim), *n.* [= F. *synonyme*, < L. *synonymum*, < Gr. συνώνυμον, prop. neut. of συνώνυμος, synonymous, < σύν, with, + ὄνυμα, name.] A word that has the same meaning, or the same general meaning, as a particular word (usually one in the same language), or is in some applications a more or less satisfactory equivalent for it (as, 'joyful,' 'happy,' 'elated,' and 'delighted' are *synonyms* of 'glad': opposed to *antonym*); also, a word or expression accepted as another name for something, or as denoting or implying something (as, 'Arcadia' has become a *synonym* for pastoral simplicity and contentment); also, in *bot.* and *zoöl.*, an alternative but less approved scientific name, as for a species or genus. Also **syn′o-nyme** (-nim).—**syn-o-nym′ic, syn-o-nym′i-cal,** *a.* Of or pertaining to synonyms.—**syn-o-nym′i-cal-ly,** *adv.*—**syn-on-y-mist** (si-non′i-mist), *n.* One who compiles a list or book of synonyms.—**syn-o-nym′i-ty** (-i-ti), *n.* The character or fact of being synonymous.—**syn-on′y-mize,** *v. t.; -mized, -mizing.* To give synonyms for (a word, name, etc.); furnish with synonyms.—**syn-on′y-mous,** *a.* [Gr. συνώνυμος.] Having the character of synonyms or a synonym; of the same meaning, as words, or as one word with another; equivalent in meaning; expressing or implying the same idea (as, "Being good was . . . represented to me as *synonymous* with keeping silence": Mrs. Stowe's "Oldtown Folks," v.).— **syn-on′y-mous-ly,** *adv.*—**syn-on′y-mous-ness,** *n.*—**syn-on′y-my** (-mi), *n.*; pl. *-mies* (-miz). [LL. *synonymia*, < Gr. συνωνυμία.] The character of being synonymous; equivalence in meaning; also, the use or coupling of synonyms in discourse, as for emphasis or rhetorical amplification; also, the study of synonyms; a set, list, or system of synonyms; in *bot.* and *zoöl.*, a list of the alternative scientific names used for a particular species or other group, or for various species, etc., with discriminations or explanatory matter.

syn-op-sis (si-nop′sis), *n.*; pl. *synopses* (-sēz). [LL., < Gr. σύνοψις, < συν-, together, + ὀπ-, see: see *optic*.] A brief or condensed statement giving a general view of some subject; a compendium of heads or short paragraphs so arranged as to afford a view of the whole or of the principal

parts of a matter under consideration; a conspectus.—
syn-op′tic. [Gr. συνοπτικός.] **I.** *a.* Pertaining to or constituting a synopsis; affording or taking a general view of the whole or of the principal parts of a subject; also [often *cap.*], taking a common view (applied distinctively to the first three Gospels — Matthew, Mark, and Luke — from their similarity in contents, order, and statement); pertaining to the synoptic Gospels. **II.** *n.* Any one of the synoptic Gospels, or of their authors.—**syn-op′ti-cal,** *a.* Synoptic.—**syn-op′ti-cal-ly,** *adv.*—**syn-op′tist,** *n.* Any one of the writers of the synoptic Gospels.—**syn-op-tis′ti-cal-ly,** *adv.*

syn-os-to-sis (sin-os-tō′sis), *n.*; pl. *-toses* (-tō′sēz). [NL., < Gr. σύν-, together, + ὀστέον, bone.] In *anat.*, union by means of ossified cartilage or bone; ankylosis. Also **syn-os-te-o-sis** (si-nos-tē-ō′sis).—**syn-os-tot′ic** (-tot′ik), *a.*

syn-ou-si-acs (si-nö′si-aks), *n.* [Gr. συνουσία, a being together, society, < συνών, fem. συνοῦσα, ppr. of συνεῖναι, be with, < σύν, with, + εἶναι, be.] The branch of knowledge which deals with societies.

sy-no-vi-a (si-nō′vi-ạ), *n.* [NL.; a word coined by Paracelsus, of uncertain elements.] In *physiol.*, a lubricating liquid resembling the white of an egg, secreted by certain membranes, as those of the joints.—**sy-no′vi-al,** *a.* Pertaining to, consisting of, or containing synovia; noting or pertaining to any of various membranes which secrete synovia, as those lining the joints.—**sy-no′vi-al-ly,** *adv.*—**syn-o-vi-tis** (sin-ō-vī′tis), *n.* [NL.] In *pathol.*, inflammation of a synovial membrane.

syn-pel-mous (sin-pel′mus), *a.* See *sympelmous.*

syn-sep-a-lous (sin-sep′ạ-lus), *a.* [See *syn-*.] In *bot.*, gamosepalous.

syn-sper-my (sin-sper′mi), *n.* [Gr. σύν-, together, + σπέρμα, seed.] In *bot.*, union or coalescence of two or more seeds.—**syn-sper′mous,** *a.*

syn-tac-tic (sin-tak′tik), *a.* [Gr. συντακτικός.] In *gram.*, of or pertaining to syntax; in accordance with the rules of syntax. Also **syn-tac′ti-cal.—syn-tac′ti-cal-ly,** *adv.*

syn-tax (sin′taks), *n.* [LL. *syntaxis,* < Gr. σύνταξις, < συντάσσειν, arrange together, < σύν, with, + τάσσειν, arrange.] Systematic arrangement†; a system†; in *gram.*, the construction of sentences; the arrangement of the words of sentences in their proper forms and relations according to established usage; the part of grammar that treats of the construction of sentences.

syn-the-sis (sin′the-sis), *n.*; pl. *-theses* (-the-sēz). [L., < Gr. σύνθεσις, a putting together, composition, < συντιθέναι, put together, < σύν, with, + τιθέναι, set, put.] The combination of parts or elements, as material substances or objects of thought, into a complex whole (opposed to *analysis*); a complex whole made up of parts or elements combined; also, a process of reasoning which consists in advancing in a direct manner from principles established or assumed, and propositions already proved, to the conclusion; in *surg.*, an operation by which divided parts are united; in *chem.*, the forming or building up of a complex substance or compound by the union of elements or the combination of simpler compounds or radicals.—**syn′the-sist,** *n.* One who employs synthesis, or who follows synthetic methods.—**syn′the-size** (-sīz), *v. t.*; *-sized, -sizing.* To combine into a complex whole; treat synthetically; also, to make up by combining parts or elements (as, "Gottlieb's . . . effort to *synthesize* antitoxin": Sinclair Lewis's "Arrowsmith," ii.).

syn-thet-ic (sin-thet′ik), *a.* [Gr. συνθετικός.] Of, pertaining to, proceeding by, or involving synthesis (opposed to *analytic*); in *chem.*, pertaining to or formed by synthesis; specif., noting or pertaining to compounds formed by chemical reaction in a laboratory as opposed to those of natural origin; in *biol.*, combining in one organism characters which become specialized in several different organisms in the course of evolution; in *philol.*, characterized by the combination of word-elements or words into composite forms, rather than by the use of separate words to express the same idea, as some languages, expressions, etc. (opposed to *analytic*: thus, the inflected forms 'man's,' 'higher,' and 'loved' are *synthetic*, while 'of man,' 'more high,' and 'did love' are *analytic*).—**synthetic philosophy,** the philosophy

of Herbert Spencer (1820–1903): so called by himself as bringing the various sciences into a systematic whole. Also **syn-thet′i-cal.—syn-thet′i-cal-ly,** *adv.*—**syn-thet′i-cism** (-sizm), *n.* Synthetic methods or procedure.—**syn′the-tist** (-the-tist), *n.* A synthesist.—**syn′the-tize,** *v. t.*; *-tized, -tizing.* To synthesize.—**syn-thet′o-graph** (-ō-gràf), *n.* [See *-graph.*] A composite drawing, as from two or more specimens of a new species.

syn-ton-ic (sin-ton′ik), *a.* [Gr. σύν-, together, + τόνος, E. tone.] In *elect.*, adjusted to oscillations of the same or a particular frequency; characterized by such adjustment, as a system of wireless telegraphy in which the transmitting and receiving instruments are so adjusted that the latter will respond only to oscillations of the particular frequency of those produced by the former.—**syn-ton′i-cal-ly,** *adv.*—**syn′to-nism** (-tō-nizm), *n.* The state of being syntonic; syntony.—**syn′to-nize** (-nīz), *v. t.*; *-nized, -nizing.* To render syntonic.—**syn″to-ni-za′tion** (-ni-zā′shọn), *n.*—**syn′to-niz-er** (-nī-zėr), *n.*—**syn′to-ny** (-ni), *n.* In *elect.*, the state or condition of being syntonic; adjustment to oscillations of the same or a particular frequency.

syn-u-ra (si-nū′rä), *n.*; pl. *-ræ* (-rē) or *-ras* (-räz). [NL., < Gr. σύν-, together, + οὐρά, tail.] A flagellate protozoan (sometimes classed as an alga) of the genus *Synura,* which comprises fresh-water infusorians occurring in radially arranged globose clusters in pools, swamp-waters, etc., and sometimes in reservoirs, and giving off an oily matter of cucumber-like or fishy flavor, which, though harmless, may render the water unpleasant for drinking. Also called *oil-bug.*

sy-pher (sī′fėr), *v. t.* [Var. of *cipher.*] In *carp.*, to overlap the chamfered edges of (boards, etc.) to form a joint with a plane surface.—**sy′pher-joint,** *n.* In *carp.*, a joint in which the edges of the boards overlap so as to leave a plane surface.

syph-i-lide (sif′i-lid), *n.* In *pathol.*, a syphilitic skin eruption.

syph-i-lis (sif′i-lis), *n.* [NL., first used in a Latin poem (published 1530) by Girolamo Fracastoro, entitled "Syphilis, sive Morbus Gallicus" ("Syphilis, or the French Disease"), being the story of *Syphilus,* a shepherd infected with the disease.] In *pathol.*, a chronic, infectious venereal disease, caused by the micro-organism *Spirochæta pallida,* or *Treponema pallidum* (see *spirochæte*), and communicated by contact or heredity, usually having three stages, the first ('primary syphilis'), in which a hard chancre forms at the point of inoculation, the second ('secondary syphilis'), characterized by skin affections and constitutional disturbances, and the third ('tertiary syphilis'), characterized by affections of the bones, muscles, viscera, etc.—**syph-i-lit′ic** (-lit′ik). **I.** *a.* Pertaining to or affected with syphilis. **II.** *n.* One affected with syphilis.—**syph′i-loid,** *a.* Resembling syphilis.—**syph-i-lol′o-gy** (-lol′ọ-ji), *n.* [See *-logy.*] The sum of scientific knowledge concerning syphilis.—**syph-i-lol′o-gist,** *n.*

sy-phon (sī′fọn), etc. See *siphon,* etc.

sy-ren (sī′ren), *n.* and *a.* See *siren.*

Syr-i-ac (sir′i-ak). [L. *Syriacus,* < Gr. Συριακός.] **I.** *a.* Of or pertaining to Syria, esp. with reference to language (see *Syriac, n.*); pertaining to or written or writing in Syriac. **II.** *n.* The ancient (Semitic) language of Syria; Aramaic; esp., the eastern dialect of Aramaic, which during the early centuries of the Christian era prevailed in Mesopotamia and neighboring regions (cf. *Peshitta*).

Syr-i-an (sir′i-ạn). [L. *Syrius,* < Gr. Σύριος.] **I.** *a.* Of or pertaining to Syria (a region of western Asia lying southeast of Asia Minor and immediately east of the Mediterranean) or its inhabitants. **II.** *n.* A native or inhabitant of Syria.

sy-rin-ga (si-ring′gä), *n.* [NL., < Gr. σῦριγξ (συριγγ-), pipe; from the use of the plant-stems for pipe-stems.] Any of the shrubs constituting the genus *Philadelphus,* including species cultivated for ornament, esp. *P. coronarius,* a familiar cultivated species with fragrant white flowers (see cut on following page); also, a lilac (genus *Syringa*).

syr-inge (sir′inj), *n.* [= F. *seringue,* < ML. *syringa,* for LL. *syrinx* (pl. *syringes*), < Gr. σῦριγξ, pipe: see *syrinx.*] A small, portable device for drawing in a quantity of a fluid and ejecting it in a stream, used for cleansing wounds, inject-

---

ing fluids into the body, etc., and commonly consisting of a tube fitted with a piston or a rubber bulb and narrowed at its outlet, but sometimes of an apparatus using the force of gravity, as a rubber bag opening at its base into a long rubber tube ending in a nozzle (in this last case often called 'fountain-syringe'); any of various similar pump-like devices, as for spraying plants, exhausting air from a closed vessel, etc.—**syr′inge**, *v. t.*; *-inged*, *-inging*. To cleanse, wash, inject, etc., by means of a syringe.

Flowering Branch of Syringa or Mock-orange (*Philadelphus coronarius*).—*a*, the fruit.

sy-rin-ge-al (si-rin′jē-al), *a.* In *ornith.*, of, pertaining to, or connected with the syrinx.

syr-inx (sir′ingks), *n.*; pl. *syringes* (si-rin′jēz) or *syrinxes*. [LL., < Gr. σῦριγξ, pipe, tube, passage, tunnel: cf. *susurrus*.] Same as *Pan's pipes* (see under *Pan²*); in *archæol.*, a narrow channel or tunnel cut in the rock, as in the burial vaults of ancient Egypt; in *anat.*, the Eustachian tube; in *ornith.*, the vocal organ of birds, situated at or near the bifurcation of the trachea into the bronchi.

Sy-ro- (sī′rō-). Form of Gr. Σῦρος, Syrian, used in combination, as in *Syro-Arabian*, *Syro-Chaldaic*, *Syro-Hebraic*.

syr-phid (sėr′fid), *n.* [NL. *Syrphidæ*, pl., < *Syrphus*, the typical genus, < Gr. σύρφος, gnat.] Any of the *Syrphidæ*, a family of dipterous insects or flies, some of which are beneficial, their larvæ feeding on plant-lice. See cut below. Also **syr-phus=fly** (sėr′fus-flī).

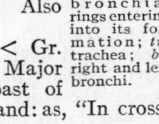

Syrinx of Raven.— *a, b, c,* modified tracheal and bronchial rings entering into its formation; *tr,* trachea; *br,* right and left bronchi.

syr-tis (sėr′tis), *n.*; pl. *-tes* (-tēz). [L., < Gr. Σύρτις, either of two quicksands (Syrtis Major and Syrtis Minor) off the northern coast of Africa, < σύρειν, draw, drag.] A quicksand: as, "In crossing these treacherous *syrtes* with a guide, we perceived a drowned horse" (Smollett's "Humphry Clinker," Sept. 12).—**syr′tic**, *a.*

Syrphid, natural size.

syr-up, sir-up (sir′up), *n.* [OF. F. *sirop*, < Ar. *sharāb*, drink, beverage, syrup: cf. *shrub¹* and *sherbet*.] Any of various sweet, more or less viscid liquids, as preparations of water or fruit-juices boiled with sugar, the solutions of sugar used in pharmacy, the liquid yielding, or that separated from, crystallized sugar in the process of refining, and various liquids prepared for table use from molasses, glucose, etc.—**syr′up, sir′up**, *v. t.*; *-uped*, *-uping*. To cover, fill, or sweeten with syrup; also, to bring to the form or consistence of syrup.—**syr′up-y, sir′up-y**, *a.* Pertaining to or of the nature of syrup; resembling or suggesting syrup, as in consistence or sweetness.

sys-tal-tic (sis-tal′tik), *a.* [LL. *systalticus*, < Gr. συσταλτικός, contracting, < συστέλλειν: see *systole*.] In *physiol.*, contracting; of the nature of contraction; characterized by alternate contraction (systole) and dilatation (diastole), as the action of the heart.

sys-tem (sis′tem), *n.* [LL. *systema*, < Gr. σύστημα, an organized or complex whole, < συνιστάναι, set together, combine, < σύν, with, + ἱστάναι, cause to stand.] An assemblage or combination of things or parts forming a complex or unitary whole (as, a mountain *system*; a *system* of rivers or canals; a railroad *system*; a *system* of pulleys); a number of heavenly bodies associated and acting together according to certain natural laws (as, the *system* of Jupiter and his satellites; the solar *system*, see under *solar*); sometimes, the world or universe; in general, any assemblage or set of correlated members (as, a *system* of weights, measures, or currency; a *system* of shorthand characters); also, an ordered and comprehensive assemblage of facts, principles, doctrines, or the like in a particular field of knowledge or thought (as, a *system* of geology, philosophy, or theology);

also, a coördinated body of methods, or a complex scheme or plan of procedure (as, a *system* of government, education, or taxation; a penal *system*); any formulated, regular, or special method or plan of procedure (as, a *system* of marking, numbering, or measuring; the Bertillon *system* of identification, see the entry; the point *system* in printing, see under *point, n.*; "She informed him that she . . . had won twenty pounds at the tables; she had a *system*," L. Merrick's "Worldlings," xiv.); hence, due method, or orderly manner of arrangement or procedure (as, to have or observe *system* in work or business; work that shows *system*; "Of generalship, of strategic *system* . . . there was little or none," Morley's "Oliver Cromwell," ii. 1); in *biol.*, etc., an assemblage of parts or organs of the same or similar tissues, or concerned with the same function (as, the nervous *system*; the digestive *system*); also, the entire human or animal body as a physiological unity or anatomical whole (as, to expel poison from the *system*); in *geol.*, a division in the classification of stratified deposits, usually comprising those of a given geological period; in *phys. chem.*, any substance or group of substances considered apart from the surroundings; in *music*, a series of tones, as a mode or scale, serving as a basis for musical composition; also, a set of two or more staves connected together for concerted music; in *astron.*, a hypothesis or theory of the disposition and arrangements of the heavenly bodies by which their phenomena, motions, changes, etc., are explained (as, the Ptolemaic *system*; the Copernican *system*); in *nat. hist.*, a method or scheme of classification (as, the Linnean *system* of plants); in *crystal.*, any of the six general modes of crystallization (as, the isometric, tetragonal, hexagonal, orthorhombic, monoclinic, or triclinic *system*).—**sys-te-mat′ic** (-te-mat′ik), *a.* [Gr. συστηματικός.] Arranged in or comprising an ordered system (as, *systematic* theology; a *systematic* treatise); having, showing, or involving a system, method, or plan (as, a *systematic* course of reading; *systematic* efforts to obstruct legislation); characterized by system or method, or methodical (as, a *systematic* person; *systematic* habits); in *nat. hist.*, pertaining to, based on, or in accordance with a system of classification (as, the *systematic* names of plants or animals); concerned with classification (as, *systematic* botany or zoölogy).—**sys-te-mat′i-cal-ly**, *adv.*—**sys-te-mat′ics**, *n.* The study of systems, or of classification.—**sys′te-ma-tism** (-ma-tizm), *n.* The practice of systematizing; also, adherence to system.—**sys′te-ma-tist**, *n.* One who constructs a system, or classifies according to a system; also, one who adheres to system.—**sys′te-ma-tize** (-tīz), *v. t.*; *-tized*, *-tizing*. To arrange in or according to a system; reduce to a system; make systematic.—**sys″te-ma-ti-za′tion** (-ti-zā′shon), *n.*—**sys′te-ma-tiz-er** (-tī-zėr), *n.*—**sys″te-ma-tol′o-gy** (-tol′ọ-ji), *n.* [See *-logy*.] The science of systems or their formation.—**sys-tem′ic**, *a.* Of or pertaining to a system; esp., in *physiol.* and *pathol.*, pertaining to a particular system of parts or organs of the body; also, pertaining to or affecting the entire bodily system, or the body as a whole.—**sys-tem′i-cal-ly**, *adv.*—**sys′tem-ize**, *v. t.*; *-ized*, *-izing*. Same as *systematize*.—**sys′tem-less**, *a.* Without system.

sys-to-le (sis′tọ-lē), *n.* [NL., < Gr. συστολή, contraction, shortening, < συστέλλειν, draw together, < σύν, with, + στέλλειν, set, place, send.] In *physiol.*, etc., the normal rhythmical contraction of the heart, esp. that of the ventricles which drives the blood into the aorta and the pulmonary artery (cf. *diastole*); any of various other rhythmical contractions; in *anc. pros.*, the shortening of a syllable regularly long.—**sys-tol′ic** (-tol′ik), *a.* Pertaining to or characterized by systole.

sy-zyg-i-al (si-zij′i-al), *a.* Pertaining to or of the nature of a syzygy.

syz-y-gy (siz′i-ji), *n.*; pl. *-gies* (-jiz). [LL. *syzygia*, < Gr. συζυγία, < σύζυγος, yoked together, < σύν, with, + ζευγνύναι, yoke, join.] A pair or couple, as of connected or correlated things; a joining or conjunction of two things; in *anc. pros.*, a group or combination of two feet (by some restricted to a combination of two feet of different kinds); in *astron.*, the conjunction or opposition of two heavenly bodies; a point in the orbit of a body, as the moon, at which it is in conjunction with or in opposition to the sun.

T

T¹, t¹ (tē); pl. *T's, t's* (tēz). A consonant, the 20th letter of the English alphabet.—**to a T,** exactly; perfectly; to a nicety: as, that suits me *to a T.*

T² (tē), *n.*; pl. *T's* (tēz). Something having a shape like that of the letter T, as a form of pipe-connection.

taal, *n.* [D., speech, language: see *tale.*] The dialect or patois of Dutch spoken in South Africa.

tab (tab), *n.* [Origin uncertain.] A small flap, strap, loop, or similar appendage, as on a garment, etc.; a tag or label; also, check or account (colloq.: as, to keep *tab* on one).— **tab,** *v. t.*; *tabbed, tabbing.* To furnish or ornament with a tab or tabs.

tab-ard (tab′ärd), *n.* [OF. *tabarde, tabart*; origin unknown.] A kind of coarse, heavy, short coat with or without sleeves, formerly in use as an outdoor garment; also, a loose outer garment with short sleeves, or without sleeves, formerly worn by knights over their armor, and generally emblazoned with the arms of the wearer; also, a similar garment emblazoned with the arms of the sovereign, forming the official dress of heralds and pursuivants.

ta-bas-co (tạ-bas′kō), *n.* [From *Tabasco*, state of southeastern Mexico.] A pungent condiment sauce prepared from the fruit of a variety of capsicum. [Proprietary name.]

tab-a-sheer, tab-a-shir (tabạ-shēr′), *n.* [Ar., Pers., and Hind. *tabāshīr.*] A siliceous concretion formed in the joints of the bamboo, used in the East as a medicine.

English Heralds' Tabards of the 17th century. (From a drawing by Van Dyck.)

ta-ba-tière (tȧ-bȧ-tyär′), *n.* [F., < *tabac*, tobacco.] A snuff-box.

tab-by (tab′i). [F. *tabis*, earlier *atabis*, silk fabric; from Ar., and named from a quarter of Bagdad where it was manufactured.] **I.** *n.*; pl. *tabbies* (-iz). A watered silk fabric; some other watered material, as moreen; a cat with a striped or brindled coat; also, a female cat; also, an old maid; a spinster; also, any spiteful female gossip or tattler (as, "a lot of old *tabbies* always busy criticizing": Sinclair Lewis's "Main Street," viii.). **II.**

Tabernacle of Orcagna, in Or San Michele, Florence.

a. Made of or resembling tabby; also, striped or brindled. —**tab′by,** *v. t.*; *-bied, -bying.* To give a wavy or watered appearance to (silk, etc.).

tab-e-fac-tion (tab-ē-fak′shon), *n.* [LL. *tabefacere* (pp. *tabefactus*), melt, dissolve, < L. *tabere*, melt, waste, + *facere*, make.] A wasting away or consumption of the body by disease; emaciation; tabes.

tab-er-na-cle (tab′ẽr-nạ-kl), *n.* [OF. F. *tabernacle*, < L. *tabernaculum*, tent, dim. of *taberna*, hut, shop: see *tavern.*] A temporary habitation, as a tent or hut; hence, a dwelling-place; also, the human body as the temporary abode of the soul (as, "True image of the Father . . . enshrined In fleshly *tabernacle*, and human form": Milton's "Paradise Regained," iv. 599); also, the tent used by the Jews as a portable sanctuary before their final settlement in Palestine; hence, the Jewish temple; also, any place or house of worship, esp. one designed for a large audience; in *arch.*, an ornate canopied structure, as a tomb or shrine (see cut in preceding column); a canopied niche or recess, as for an image; an ornamental canopy over a tomb, stall, etc.; *eccles.*, an ornamental receptacle for the pyx containing the reserved eucharist; *naut.*, an elevated socket for a river-boat's mast, or a post to which a mast may be hinged when fitted for lowering to pass beneath bridges.—**tab′er-na-cle,** *v. i.* or *t.*; *-cled, -cling.* To dwell or place in or as in a tabernacle. —**tab′er-na-cle=work,** *n.* In *arch.*, ornamental work or tracery as used in tabernacles or canopies over tombs, stalls, etc., and in the carved screens of churches; also, work in which tabernacles form the characteristic feature.—

tab-er-nac′u-lar (-nak′ụlär), *a.* Pertaining to, characteristic of, or resembling a tabernacle.

ta-bes (tā′bēz), *n.* [L., < *tabere*, melt, waste: cf.

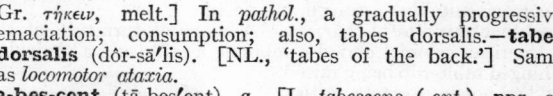

Tabernacle-work. — Church of Santa Maria della Spina, Pisa; 13th century.

Gr. τήκειν, melt.] In *pathol.*, a gradually progressive emaciation; consumption; also, tabes dorsalis.—**tabes dorsalis** (dôr-sā′lis). [NL., 'tabes of the back.'] Same as *locomotor ataxia.*

ta-bes-cent (tạ-bes′ẹnt), *a.* [L. *tabescens* (-ent-), ppr. of *tabescere*, waste, < *tabere*: see *tabes.*] Wasting away.— **ta-bes′cence,** *n.*

ta-bet-ic (tạ-bet′ik or -bē′tik). **I.** *a.* Pertaining to or affected with tabes. **II.** *n.* One affected with tabes.

tab-id (tab′id), *a.* [L. *tabidus*, < *tabere*: see *tabes.*] Wasting; tabetic.

tab-la-ture (tab′lạ-tụr), *n.* [F. *tablature*, < L. *tabula*, E. *table.*] A tabular space, surface, or structure (archaic); also, musical notation†, or a particular form of it†; also, a painting† or design†; fig., a mental picture; a graphic description.

ta-ble (tā′bl), *n.* [OF. F. *table*, < L. *tabula*, board, plank, tablet, writing, list, picture, prob. akin to *taberna*, hut, shop: see *tavern.*] A flat and relatively thin piece of wood, stone, metal, or other hard substance, esp. one artificially shaped for a particular purpose; a smooth, flat board or slab on which inscriptions, etc., may be put; also, *pl.*, the tablets on which certain collections of laws were anciently inscribed (see phrases below); hence, the laws themselves; also, *sing.*, a backgammon-board, or either of its two parts (as, to turn the *tables*, fig., to bring about a complete reversal of circumstances or relations between two persons or parties); *pl.*, the game of backgammon†; also, *sing.*, an article of furniture consisting of a flat top resting on legs or on a pillar, on which to serve meals, play games, perform work, set ornaments, etc.; the board at or round which persons sit at meals; the food placed on a table to be eaten (as, "boats that had an established reputation for setting good *tables*": Mark Twain's "Life on the Mississippi," vii.); a company of persons at a table, as for a meal, game, or business transaction (as, "your flashes of merriment, that were wont to set the *table* on a roar": Shakspere's "Hamlet," v. 1. 211); also, a flat or plane surface; a level area; also, a table-land or plateau; also, an arrangement of words, numbers, or signs, or combinations of them, as in parallel columns, to exhibit a set of facts or relations in a definite, compact, and comprehensive form; a synoptical statement; a list of items or particulars; a synopsis or scheme; in *gem-cutting*, the upper horizontal surface of a faceted gem, esp. a brilliant; a gem with such a surface; in *arch.*, a flat, vertical, usually rectangular surface forming a distinct feature in a wall and often ornamental; also, a string-course or other horizontal band of some size and weight. — **the tables of the law**, or **the two**

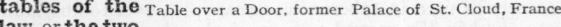

Table over a Door, former Palace of St. Cloud, France.

tables, the stone slabs on which the ten commandments were inscribed; hence, the decalogue. — **the Twelve Tables**, the tablets on which were engraved short statements of those rules of Roman law most important in the affairs of daily life, drawn up by the decemvirs in 451 and 450 B.C. — **to lay on the table.** See under *lay*[1], *v. t.* — **ta′ble**, *v.*; -*bled*, -*bling.* **I.** *tr.* To entertain at table or meals (now rare); also, to place (money, a card, etc.) upon a table; place (a proposal, resolution, etc.) on the table of an assembly for discussion, or, as in the U. S. Congress, by way of postponing or shelving it; also, to enter in or form into a table or list; in *carp.*, to fit together by alternate seams and projections. **II.** *intr.* To have a meal, or dine; take one's meals, or board. [Now rare.]

tab-leau (tab′lō, F. tȧ-blō′), *n.*; pl. **tableaux** (tab′lōz, F. tȧ-blō′). [F., picture, dim. of *table*, E. *table*.] A picture, as of a scene; also, a graphic description; also, a picturesque grouping of persons or objects; a striking scene; also, a tableau vivant; also, a table, schedule, or list. — **tableau vivant** (tȧ-blō vē-väṅ). [F., 'living picture.'] A representation of a picture, statue, scene, etc., by one or more persons suitably costumed and posed.

ta-ble=chair (tā′bl-chār), *n.* A piece of furniture of the American colonial period combining a table and a chair, the hinged table-top being raised, when not in use, to a vertical position at the back of the chair.

ta-ble=cloth (tā′bl-klôth), *n.* A cloth for covering the top of a table, esp. one spread upon a table in preparation for serving a meal.

ta-ble d'hôte (tȧ-bl dōt). [F., 'host's table.'] A common table, or a meal of prearranged courses served at a fixed time and price, for guests at a hotel or restaurant. Cf. *à la carte.*

ta-ble=land (tā′bl-land), *n.* An elevated and generally level region of considerable extent; a plateau.

Table-chair.

ta-ble-spoon (tā′bl-spōn), *n.* A spoon larger than a teaspoon and a dessert-spoon, used in the service of the table. — **ta′ble-spoon″ful** (-fúl), *n.*; pl. -*fuls.* As much as a tablespoon can hold, about half a fluid ounce.

tab-let (tab′let), *n.* [OF. *tablete* (F. *tablette*), dim. of *table*, E. *table*.] A small, flat slab or surface, esp. one bearing or intended to bear an inscription, carving, or the like; also, a leaf or sheet of some inflexible material for writing or marking on, esp. one of a pair or set hinged or otherwise fastened together; *pl.*, the set as a whole; also, *sing.*, a number of sheets of writing-paper or the like fastened together at the edge; a pad; also, a small, flat or flattish cake or piece of some solid or solidified substance, as a drug, chemical, or the like. — **tab′let**, *v. t.*; -*leted*, -*leting.* To provide with or inscribe on a tablet.

Tablet beneath Cinerary Urn. — Columbarium near gate of St. Sebastian, Rome.

ta-ble=talk (tā′bl-tȧk), *n.* Talk at table or meals.

ta-ble-ware (tā′bl-wār), *n.* Dishes, utensils, etc., used at table or meals.

ta-bli-er (tȧ-blē-ā), *n.* [F., < *table*, E. *table*.] An apron; an apron-like piece in a woman's dress; a panel.

tab-loid (tab′loid). [Prop. a trade-mark name for compressed drugs, etc.: cf. *tablet* and *-oid*.] **I.** *n.* A compressed portion of various drugs, chemicals, etc. (see etym.); hence, anything in tabloid form, as a newspaper. **II.** *a.* Compressed in or as in a tabloid; condensed; in small form: as, a *tabloid* drama; a *tabloid* newspaper.

ta-boo, ta-bu (tȧ-bö′). [Polynesian *tabu* (in Tonga Islands), also *tapu*.] **I.** *a.* Among the Polynesians and other races of the southern Pacific Ocean, separated or set apart as sacred; forbidden to general use; placed under a prohibition or ban; hence, in general, forbidden, as by social usage, or interdicted (as, "She could not have outside employment. To the village doctor's wife it was *taboo*": Sinclair Lewis's "Main Street," vii.). **II.** *n.*; pl. -*boos*, -*bus* (-böz′). Among the Polynesians, etc., the system or practice, or an act, whereby things are set apart as sacred, forbidden to general use, or placed under a prohibition or interdiction (as, "the sacred protection of an express edict of the *Taboo*, declaring his person inviolable for ever": H. Melville's "Omoo," vii.); the fact of being so set apart, forbidden, or placed; hence, in general, a prohibition or interdiction of anything; exclusion from use or practice; exclusion from social intercourse; ostracism. — **ta-boo′, ta-bu′**, *v. t.*; -*booed*, -*bued*, -*booing*, -*buing.* To put under a taboo; prohibit or forbid (as, "Political questions . . . were *tabooed* by the well-meaning chaplain": Kingsley's "Alton Locke," xxx.); ostracize, as a person.

ta-bor, ta-bour (tā′bor), *n.* [OF. *tabor*, *tabour* (F. *tambour*), drum; prob. from Ar. or Pers.] A small kind of drum formerly in use, used esp. as an accompaniment to a pipe or fife. — **ta′bor, ta′bour**, *v. i.* To play upon or as upon a tabor; drum. — **ta′bor-er, ta′bour-er**, *n.*

tab-o-ret, tab-ou-ret (tab′ō-ret, -ö-ret), *n.* [F. *tabouret*, orig. dim. of OF. *tabour*, E. *tabor*.] A low seat without back or arms, for one person; a stool; also, a small, low stand of similar form; also, a frame for embroidery; also, a tabret.

tab-o-rine, tab-ou-rine (tab′ō-rin, -ö-rin), *n.* [OF. *tabourin* (F. *tambourin*), < *tabour*, E. *tabor*.] A small drum; also, a tambourine.

tab-ret (tab′ret), *n.* [Dim. of *tabor*.] A small tabor.

ta-bu (tȧ-bö′), *a.*, *n.*, and *v.* See *taboo.*

tab-u-la (tab′ū-lä), n.; pl. -læ (-lē). [L.: see *table*.] In *Rom. antiq.*, a table or tablet, esp. a writing-tablet; a writing or document; a legal instrument or record; *eccles.*, a wooden or metal frontal.

tab-u-lar (tab′ū-lär), a. [L. *tabularis*, < *tabula*: see *table*.] Having the form of a table, tablet, or tablature; flat and expansive; also, pertaining to or of the nature of a table or tabulated arrangement; ascertained from or computed by the use of tables.—**tab′u-lar-ize** (-īz), v. t.; -ized, -izing. To make tabular; put into tabular form; tabulate.—**tab″u-lar-i-za′tion** (-i-zā′shon), n.—**tab′u-lar-ly**, adv. In tabular form.

tab-u-late (tab′ū-lāt), v. t.; -lated, -lating. [L. *tabula*, board, plank, tablet; list: see *table*.] To give a flat surface to; make tabular; also, to put or form into a table, scheme, or synopsis; formulate tabularly.—**tab′u-late**, a. [NL. *tabulatus*, table-shaped, L. boarded, floored, < L. *tabula*.] Shaped like a table or tablet; tabular; also, having transverse dissepiments, as certain corals.—**tab-u-la′tion** (-lā′shon), n. The act or process of tabulating, or the state of being tabulated; arrangement in tabular form, or in the form of a table, scheme, or synopsis.—**tab′u-la-tor**, n. One who or that which tabulates; an attachment to a typewriter, for tabulating accounts, etc.

tac-a-ma-hac (tak′ä-mä-hak), n. [Mex.] Any of certain resinous substances used in incenses, ointments, etc., as the gum obtained from *Terebinthus tomentosa* (a tropical American balsameaceous tree), the aromatic product obtained from *Calophyllum inophyllum* (an East Indian clusiaceous tree), and the resin derived from the buds of *Populus balsamifera* (the balsam-poplar); also, any tree yielding such a product, esp., in North America, the balsam-poplar. Also **tac″a-ma-hac′a** (-ä).

Tacamahac. — Branch of *Calophyllum inophyllum*, which yields the East Indian resin; *a*, lengthwise section of ripe fruit.

ta-cet (tā′set), n. [L., 'it is silent.'] In *music*, an indication that an instrument or voice is to be silent for a time.

tach, tache (tach), n. [OF. *tache*, a fastening, clasp, nail: see *tack*[1].] A contrivance, as a hook, catch, or clasp, for attaching or fastening something. [Now rare.]

tach-e-om-e-ter (tak-ē-om′e-tėr), n. Same as *tachometer* and *tachymeter*.

ta-chis-to-scope (ta-kis′tō-skōp), n. [Gr. τάχιστος, superl. of ταχύς, swift: see -*scope*.] An apparatus which exposes to view, for a selected brief period of time, an object or group of objects, as letters, words, etc.: used in experimental psychology.—**ta-chis-to-scop′ic** (-skop′ik), a.

tach-o-graph (tak′ō-gräf), n. [Gr. τάχος, swiftness, speed: see -*graph*.] A recording tachometer for registering the speed of shafting or wheels; also, a record made by such an instrument.

ta-chom-e-ter (ta-kom′e-tėr), n. [Gr. τάχος, swiftness, speed: see -*meter*.] Any of various instruments for measuring or indicating velocity or speed, as of a machine, a river, the blood, etc.—**ta-chom′e-try**, n.

tachy-. Form of Gr. ταχύς, swift, used in combination.—**tach-y-car-di-a** (tak-i-kär′di-ä), n. [NL. (Gr. καρδία, heart).] In *pathol.*, excessively rapid heart-action.—**tach′y-graph** (-gräf), n. [Gr. ταχυγράφος, swift writer: see -*graph*.] A writer of shorthand; a stenographer; also, a tachygraphic writing.—**ta-chyg-ra-phy** (ta-kig′rä-fi), n.

[+ -*graphy*.] The act or practice of writing quickly, esp. by shorthand; stenography.—**ta-chyg′ra-pher** (-fėr), n.—**tach-y-graph′ic, tach-y-graph′i-cal** (-graf′ik, -i-kąl), a.

tach-y-lyte (tak′i-līt), n. [G. *tachylyt*, < Gr. ταχύς, swift, + λυτός, soluble, < λύειν, loose; named from its fusibility.] A glassy form of basalt, readily fusible and of a black color. — **tach-y-lyt′ic** (-lit′ik), a.

ta-chym-e-ter (ta-kim′e-tėr), n. [See *tachy-* and -*meter*.] A surveying-instrument combining the powers of the transit and the stadia, used for the rapid determination of points in a survey; also, a tachometer.—**tach-y-met-ric** (tak-i-met′rik), a.—**ta-chym′e-try**, n.

tach-yp-nœ-a (tak-ip-nē′ä), n. [NL., < Gr. ταχύς, swift, + πνεῖν, blow, breathe.] Excessively rapid respiration.

ta-cit (tas′it), a. [L. *tacitus*, pp. of *tacere*, be silent, pass over in silence.] Silent, or saying nothing, as a person; unspoken (as, a *tacit* prayer); giving forth no sound, or noiseless (as, "no wind that cared trouble the *tacit* woods": Browning's "Sordello," iii.); also, not openly expressed, but implied (as, "A *tacit* strife had been growing up between father and son," Thackeray's "Newcomes," lxiv.; "The principles he declared were a *tacit* reproach on their proceedings," Jane Porter's "Scottish Chiefs," i.); understood or inferred; in *law*, arising by operation of law, without the intervention of the parties (as, a *tacit* mortgage).—**ta′cit-ly**, adv.—**ta′cit-ness**, n.

ta-ci-turn (tas′i-tėrn), a. [L. *taciturnus*, < *tacitus*, E. *tacit*.] Inclined to silence, or reserved in speech (as, "At the Council board he was *taciturn*; and in the House of Lords he never opened his lips": Macaulay's "Hist. of Eng.," ii.); characterized by or showing such inclination (as, "We are each of an unsocial, *taciturn* disposition": Jane Austen's "Pride and Prejudice," xviii.).—**ta-ci-tur′ni-ty** (-tėr′ni-ti), n.—**ta′ci-turn-ly**, adv.

tack[1] (tak), n. [ME. *tak, takke*, from a var. of OF. *tache*, a fastening, clasp, nail (see *tach*), akin to -*tachier*, fasten (see *attach, detach*, and cf. *attack*); origin uncertain.] A short, sharp-pointed nail or pin, usually with a flat and comparatively large head, used as a fastener by being driven or thrust through the material to be fastened into the substance to which it is to be fixed; also, a stitch, esp. a long stitch used in fastening seams, etc., preparatory to a more thorough sewing; also, a tacking or fastening, esp. in a temporary manner; also, something tacked on or attached to something else as an addition or supplement; *naut.*, a rope which confines the foremost or weather lower corner of a course on a square-rigged ship; the part of a sail to which such a rope is fastened; the lower corner of the luff of a fore-and-aft sail; also, an act of tacking; the direction or course of a ship in relation to the position of her sails (as, the starboard *tack*, when close-hauled with the wind on the starboard; the port *tack*, when close-hauled with the wind on the port); a course obliquely against the wind; one of the series of straight runs which make up the zigzag course of a ship proceeding to the windward; fig., one of the movements of a zigzag course on land; also, a determinate course, or course differing from some preceding or other course, in action or conduct (as, "The president was a wise man, and took another *tack*": W. Churchill's "Mr. Crewe's Career," i.).—**tack**[1], v. **I.** tr. To fasten by a tack or tacks (as, to *tack* down a carpet); also, to fasten or attach with slight stitches; secure by some slight or temporary fastening; hence, to join together; bring into connection; unite or combine; often, to attach as something supplementary, or append or annex (as, "You would be doing a real charity if you *tacked* on his name to the people you expect at Pangbourne": L. Merrick's "Worldlings," xvii.); *naut.*, to change the course of (a ship) to the opposite tack; navigate (a ship) by a series of tacks. **II.** intr. Naut., to change the course of a ship when close-hauled, by bringing her head into the wind and then causing it to fall off on the other side until it is at about the same angle to the wind as before; change its course in this way, as a ship; sail a course obliquely against the wind; proceed to the windward by a series of such courses; fig., to change one's course of action or conduct.

tack[2] (tak), n. [Perhaps another use of *tack*[1].] Food; fare. Cf. *hardtack*.

tack-er (tak′ėr), n. One who or that which tacks.

tack-le (tak′l), *n.* [ME. *takel* = MLG., D., and G. *takel*.] Equipment, apparatus, or gear in general; a combination of appliances; specif., the equipment of a horse, or harness; apparatus for fishing ('fishing-tackle': as, "He had with him all the *tackle* necessary for spooning pike," Mrs. H. Ward's "Robert Elsmere," xxvii.); the rigging of a ship, esp. that used in working the sails, etc.; a mechanism or apparatus, as a rope and block or a combination of ropes and blocks, for hoisting, lowering, and shifting objects or materials; sometimes, food or victuals (slang); also, an act of tackling, as in football; a seizing or grasping; also, either of two players in football, stationed next to the ends in the forward line.—**tack′le**, *v.*; *-led, -ling.* **I.** *tr.* To furnish with tackle or equipment†; harness (a horse: as, "Go out and *tackle* the old mare, and have our wagon round to the house," Mrs. Stowe's "Oldtown Folks," xxviii.); also (colloq.), to lay hold upon, attack, or encounter (as, "I would rather *tackle* the Gætulian lion in his den than embark on such an enterprise": Stevenson's "Travels with a Donkey," iii. 3); approach (a person) on some subject (as, "I *tackled* one of my guides in this matter": H. G. Wells's "Italy, France, and Britain at War," iv. 4); undertake to deal with, master, solve, etc. (as, "I don't see how anyone can be expected to *tackle* a case like this," Maugham's "Moon and Sixpence," x.; "The problem has to be *tackled*," J. H. Robinson's "Mind in the Making," viii. 17); in *football*, to seize and stop (an opponent having the ball). **II.** *intr.* In *football*, to seize and stop an opponent having the ball.— **tack′ler**, *n.*—**tack′ling**, *n.* Equipment, apparatus, or gear; tackle. [Now rare.]

tack-y[1] (tak′i), *a.* [From *tack*[1].] Adhesive; sticky.

tack-y[2] (tak′i). [Origin obscure.] **I.** *n.*; pl. *tackies* (-iz). A wretched, poor, or inferior horse; also, a poor, degraded person. [Southern U. S.] **II.** *a.* Wretched; sorry; poor; shabby; dowdy. [Colloq., U. S.]

tact (takt), *n.* [L. *tactus*, a touching, touch, < *tangere* (pp. *tactus*), touch: cf. *tangent*.] Touch; the sense of touch; also, nice discernment as to what is fitting or expedient in dealing with others, so as to win good-will or avoid giving offense (as, "He had a certain *tact* in avoiding all the sharp corners and angles of her character," Mrs. Stowe's "Oldtown Folks," xxi.; "He had . . . a *tact* that would preserve him from flagrant error in any society," Parkman's "Oregon Trail," ii.); skill in dealing with difficult or delicate situations.—**tact′ful**, *a.* Having or manifesting tact: as, a *tactful* person; a *tactful* speech or reply.—**tact′ful-ly**, *adv.*—**tact′ful-ness**, *n.*

tac-tic (tak′tik). [NL. *tacticus*, < Gr. τακτικός, pertaining to arrangement, esp. in war, < τάσσειν, arrange; as n., NL. *tactica*, < Gr. τακτική, the art of arranging, tactics, prop. fem. of τακτικός.] **I.** *a.* Of or pertaining to arrangement or order; tactical; also, of or pertaining to tactics†. **II.** *n.* A system of tactics (as, the *tactic* of an army); a piece of tactics, or a tactical procedure (as, "She suspected that, had she not adopted this *tactic*, she might have melted before him in gratitude": Arnold Bennett's "Hilda Lessways," ii. 6).— **tac′ti-cal**, *a.* Of or pertaining to arrangement or order; also, of or pertaining to military or naval tactics; pertaining to tactics in general; characterized by skilful tactics or adroit maneuvering or procedure (as, *tactical* movements or efforts; a *tactical* leader).—**tactical unit**, a subdivision of an army which is made the basis of tactical instruction, as a battalion of infantry, a squadron of cavalry, or a battery of artillery. —**tac′ti-cal-ly**, *adv.*—**tac-ti′cian** (-tish′an), *n.* One versed in tactics.—**tac′tics**, *n.* The art or science of disposing military or naval forces in order for battle, and performing military or naval maneuvers or evolutions; the maneuvers or evolutions themselves (construed as *pl.*); hence, in general, mode of procedure with a view to gaining advantage or success (as, "In Parliament, the *tactics* of the Opposition is to resist every step of the Government by a pitiless attack": Emerson's "English Traits," v.); expedients for effecting any purpose (construed as *pl.*). Cf. *strategy*.

tac-tile (tak′til), *a.* [L. *tactilis*, < *tangere*, touch.] Of or pertaining to the organs or sense of touch; endowed with the sense of touch; also, perceptible to the touch; tangible. —**tactile bud** or **corpuscle**, any of numerous minute oval bodies occurring in sensitive parts of the skin, supposed to be concerned with the sense of touch.—**tac′tile**, *n.* In *psychol.*, one in whose mind tactual images are predominant or especially distinct.—**tac-til′i-ty** (-til′i-ti), *n.*

tac-tion (tak′shon), *n.* [L. *tactio(n-)*, < *tangere*, touch.] The act of touching, or the state of being touched; touch; contact: as, "They neither can speak, nor attend to the discourses of others, without being roused by some external *taction* upon the organs of speech and hearing" (Swift's "Gulliver's Travels," iii. 2).

tact-less (takt′les), *a.* Destitute of tact; characterized by want of tact: as, a *tactless* person; a *tactless* reply.—**tact′-less-ly**, *adv.*—**tact′less-ness**, *n.*

tac-tom-e-ter (tak-tom′e-tėr), *n.* [L. *tactus*, touch: see *-meter*.] An instrument for determining the acuteness of the sense of touch.

tac-tu-al (tak′tū-al), *a.* [L. *tactus*, touch: see *tact*.] Of or pertaining to touch; communicating or imparting the sensation of contact; arising from or due to touch.—**tac′tu-al-ly**, *adv.*

tad (tad), *n.* [Prob. for *tadpole*.] A small child, esp. a boy; a little fellow. [Colloq., U. S.]

tad-pole (tad′pōl), *n.* [ME. *tadpolle*, < *tadde*, toad, + *polle*, head, E. *poll*[1].] The aquatic larva or immature form of frogs, toads, etc., esp. after the loss of the external gills and before the appearance of the fore limbs and the resorption of the tail.

Tadpoles.—*A, B*, with gills; *C*, more advanced: *a*, eye; *o*, ear; *m*, mouth; *n*, nasal sacs; *d*, opercular fold; *kb, ki*, gills; *ks*, a single branchial aperture; *z*, horny jaws; *s*, suckers; *y*, rudiment of hind limb.

tae (tā), *prep.* Scotch form of *to*.

tael (tāl), *n.* [Pg. *tael*, < Malay *tāhil*.] A weight of eastern Asia, equal by treaty to 1⅓ ounces avoirdupois; also, a Chinese money of account, being the value of this weight of standard silver.

ta'en (tān), *pp.* Taken. [Prov. or poetic.]

tæ-ni-a (tē′ni-ä), *n.*; pl. *-niæ* (-ni-ē). [L., < Gr. ταινία, band, ribbon, fillet, also tapeworm.] In *archæol.*, a headband or fillet; in *arch.*, the fillet or band on the Doric architrave, which separates it from the frieze; in *anat.*, a ribbon-like structure, as certain bands of white nerve-fibers in the brain or the longitudinal muscles of the colon; in *zoöl.*, a tapeworm.—**tæ-ni-a-sis** (tē-nī′a-sis), *n.* [NL.] In *pathol.*, a diseased condition due to the presence of tæniæ or tapeworms.—**tæ′ni-cide** (-sīd), *n.* [See *-cide*.] An agent that destroys tapeworms.—**tæ′ni-fuge** (-fūj). [See *-fuge*.] **I.** *n.* An agent or medicine to expel tapeworms from the body. **II.** *a.* Expelling tapeworms, as a medicine.— **tæ′ni-oid**, *a.* [See *-oid*.] Of a ribbon-like shape; like a tapeworm; related to the tapeworms.

taf-fer-el (taf′e-rel), *n.* Earlier form of *taffrail*.

taf-fe-ta (taf′e-tä), *n.* [OF. F. *taffetas* = It. *taffettà*, < Pers. *tāftah*, prop. pp. of *tāftan*, twist, spin, weave.] A light-weight, plain-woven, glossy silk fabric; also, any of various other fabrics of silk, linen, wool, etc., in use at different periods.

taff-rail (taf′rāl), *n.* [Earlier *tafferel*, < D. *tafereel*, panel, taffrail, dim. of *tafel*, < L. *tabula*, E. *table*.] *Naut.*, the upper part of the stern of a vessel; also, the rail across the stern.

taf-fy[1] (taf′i), *n.* [Origin uncertain: cf. *toffee*.] A candy made of sugar or molasses boiled down, often with butter, nuts, etc.; also, crude compliment or flattery (colloq.).

Taf-fy[2] (taf′i), *n.*; pl. *Taffies* (-iz). [Said to represent a Welsh pron. of *Davy*, for David, man's name.] A familiar name for a Welshman.

taf-i-a (taf′i-ä), *n.* [F.; appar. of W. Ind. origin.] A kind of rum obtained from the lower grades of molasses, refuse sugar, etc.

tag[1] (tag), *n.* [ME. *tagge*: cf. Sw. *tagg*, prickle, spine, point, tooth.] One of the narrow, often pointed, pendent pieces made by slashing the border of a garment; any small hanging or loosely attached part or piece; a loose end or tatter; also, the tail of an animal, or the tip of the tail; the tail-end or concluding part, as of a course or proceeding; also, something appended, as by way of ornament or addition; a pendant; an appendage; an addition to a speech or writing, as the moral of a fable; a quotation added for special effect (as, "The old man had written his Greek *tags* in shakily resolute capitals. It was his custom always to quote the Greek Testament in his letters": H. G. Wells's "Soul of a Bishop," vi.); any quotation, or bit of literary matter or the like (as, "He knew some of the common *tags* of Greek and Roman history": Morley's "Oliver Cromwell," i. 1); a common phrase or expression (as, "Theobald said he was 'willing to hope' — this was one of his *tags* . . . 'only too ready' — this was another *tag*": S. Butler's "Way of All Flesh," xlv.); the refrain of a song or poem; also, the last words of a speech in a play, etc.; an actor's cue; also, a piece or strip of strong paper, leather, or the like, for attaching by one end to something as a mark or label; also, a point or binding of metal or other hard substance at the end of a cord, lace, or the like (as, "a broken, brown boot lace with a brass *tag*": Eden Phillpotts's "Red Redmaynes," iii.); an aglet; also, the rabble†.—**tag and rag,** or **tag, rag, and bobtail,** the riffraff or rabble. Cf. *tag-rag* and *rag-tag.*—**tag**[1], *v.*; *tagged*, *tagging.* **I.** *tr.* To furnish with a tag or tags; append a tag or tags to; esp., to attach a tag or label to (as, "He was not one who *tagged* and prettily classified bacteria and protozoa": Sinclair Lewis's "Arrowsmith," xii.); also, to append as a tag to something else (as, "I have no other moral than this to *tag* to the present story of 'Vanity Fair' ": Thackeray's "Vanity Fair," Before the Curtain); also, to follow closely (colloq.). **II.** *intr.* To follow closely; go along or about as a follower: as, "He *tagged* after Leora" (Sinclair Lewis's "Arrowsmith," ix.).—**tagged atoms,** atoms made artificially radioactive and used in experimental biology to observe their passage through several generations.

tag[2] (tag), *n.* [Origin uncertain.] A children's game in which one player chases the others till he touches one of them, who then takes his place as pursuer.—**tag**[2], *v. t.*; *tagged*, *tagging.* To touch in or as in the game of tag.

Ta-gal, Ta-ga-log (tä-gäl′, tä-gä′log), *n.* A member of a numerous Malayan race native in the Philippines; also, the Malayo-Polynesian language of this race.

tag=day (tag′dā), *n.* A day on which contributions to a fund or the like are solicited from the public in general, each contributor receiving a tag or other distinguishing mark.

tagged (tagd), *a.* Having a tag or tags.

tag-ger (tag′ėr), *n.* One who or that which tags; also, *pl.*, iron in very thin sheets, either coated or not coated with tin.

tag=rag (tag′rag), *n.* [Cf. *rag-tag.*] A fluttering rag; a tatter; also, the riffraff; the rabble.

ta-ha (tä′hä), *n.* [Native name.] A South African weaver-bird, *Pyromelana taha*, the male of which has a yellow and black plumage; also, any of various related species.

Taha (*Pyromelana taha*).

Ta-hi-ti-an (tä-hē′ti-an). **I.** *a.* Of or pertaining to the island of Tahiti (in the Society Islands), its inhabitants, or their language. **II.** *n.* A native or inhabitant of Tahiti, esp. a member of the native Polynesian race; also, the language of this race.

tahr (tär), *n.* [Native name.] A wild goat, *Hemitragus jemlaicus*, of the Himalayas, having brown, shaggy hair, and small, black horns curving directly backward.

Ta-ic (tä′ik). **I.** *a.* Of or pertaining to the Tai race, the principal race of people in Indo-China, including the Siamese and others. **II.** *n.* The group of languages or dialects spoken by the Tai race.

tail[1] (tāl), *n.* [OF. F. *taille*, a cutting, cut, division, assessment, tax, < OF. *taillier* (F. *tailler*), cut, shape, fix, < ML. *taliare*, cut, < L. *talea*, rod, stick, twig, cutting (for planting): cf. *tally.*] In *law*, the limitation of an estate to a person and the heirs of his body, or some particular class of such heirs.—**tail**[1], *a.* [OF. *taillie*, pp. of *taillier.*] In *law*, limited to a specified line of heirs; being in tail.

tail[2] (tāl), *n.* [AS. *tægel, tægl,* = OHG. *zagel* = Icel. *tagl,* tail, = Goth. *tagl,* hair.] The posterior extremity of an animal, esp. when forming a distinct flexible appendage to the trunk; also, something resembling or suggesting this in shape or position (as, the *tail* of a kite; the *tail* of a coat); the luminous train extending from the head of a comet; the slender part of a muscle at its insertion; a long braid or tress of hair; a line of persons awaiting their turns; also, the hinder, bottom, or concluding part of anything; the back; the rear; the conclusion; specif., the hind part of a cart, plow, etc. (as, "Men, and even women, were still whipped publicly at the *tail* of a cart through the streets": Lecky's "Hist. of Eng. in the 18th Century," iii.); the lower part of a pool or stream; the reverse of a coin (see *head*); the outer corner of the eye (as, "He looked at me with the *tail* of his eye": Galt's "Annals of the Parish," xlvii.); also, a train of followers or attendants; a retinue; also, the inferior or refuse part of anything; also, formerly, in Turkey, a horsetail borne before a pasha as a mark of relative rank (as, a pasha of one, two, or three *tails*); in *aëronautics*, the after portion, or the rear plane or planes, of an aëroplane or the like.—**tail**[2], *v.* **I.** *tr.* To form or furnish with a tail; also, to grasp or pull by the tail; also, to form or constitute the tail or end of (a procession, etc.); terminate; follow like a tail; also, to join or attach (one thing) at the tail or end of another; in *building*, to fasten (a beam, etc.) by one of its ends (*in, into,* etc.). **II.** *intr.* To form, or move or pass in, a line or continuation suggestive of a tail; also, of a boat, etc., to have or take a position with the tail or rear in a particular direction; in *building*, of a beam, etc., to be fastened by the end (*in, into,* etc.).—**tail′=bay,** *n.* The narrow waterway just below the lower gates of a canal-lock, which opens out into the canal; in *carp.*, a division of a roof adjoining the end-wall or gable, comprising a principal rafter with the purlins, etc., between it and the end-wall, or a corresponding division of a floor adjoining the end-wall (cf. *case-bay*).—**tail′=board,** *n.* The board at the hinder end of a cart, etc., which can usually be removed or let down for convenience in loading and unloading.—**tail′=cov″erts,** *n. pl.* In *ornith.*, the feathers which cover the bases of the quill-feathers of the tail in birds. —**tailed,** *a.* Having a tail.—**tail′=end′,** *n.* The hindmost, lowest, or concluding part of anything; also, the end or tip of a tail.—**tail′=gate,** *n.* The down-stream or lower gate of a canal-lock.—**tail′ing,** *n.* The part of a projecting stone or brick tailed or inserted in a wall; also, *pl.*, the residue of any product; leavings; remainders.—**tail′less,** *a.* Having no tail.—**tail′=light,** *n.* A light carried at the rear of a train, motor-car, etc.

tai-lor (tā′lọr), *n.* [OF. *tailleor* (F. *tailleur*), lit. 'cutter,' < *taillier,* cut: see *tail*[1].] One whose business it is to make outer garments for men or boys or for women. Cf. *merchant tailor.* under *merchant, a.* —**tai′lor,** *v.* **I.** *intr.* To do the work of a tailor. **II.** *tr.* To make by tailor's work (cf. *tailor-made*); also, to fit or furnish with clothing.—

Tailor-bird of Java (*Orthotomus sepium*).

tai'lor=bird, *n.* Any of various small Asiatic and African passerine birds which stitch leaves together to form and hide their nests. See cut on preceding page.—**tai'lor-ess**, *n.* A woman tailor.—**tai'lor-ing**, *n.* The business or work of a tailor.—**tai'lor=made**, *a.* Made by or as by a tailor: applied to women's garments made of the more substantial fabrics or with plainness of cut and finish.

tail=piece (tāl'pēs), *n.* A piece forming a tail or end; a piece added at the end; an appendage; specif., a small decorative engraving placed at the end of a chapter, etc.; in musical instruments of the viol class, a triangular piece of wood, usually of ebony, to which the lower ends of the strings are fastened; in *building*, a relatively short beam or rafter inserted in a wall by tailing and supported by a header.

tail=plane (tāl'plān), *n.* In *aëronautics*, the horizontal supporting plane of the tail of an aëroplane.

tail=race (tāl'rās), *n.* The race, flume, or channel which conducts the water away from a water-wheel or the like (cf. *headrace*); in *mining*, the channel for conducting tailings or refuse away in water.

tail=skid (tāl'skid), *n.* In *aëronautics*, a runner or the like under the tail of an aëroplane, which slides along the ground when alighting, etc.

tail=slide (tāl'slīd), *n.* In *aëronautics*, a rearward motion which an aëroplane may be made to take after having been brought into a stalling position.

tail=spin (tāl'spin), *n.* In *aëronautics*, a downward movement of an aëroplane nose foremost, with the tail whirling in a circle above, whether performed as a 'stunt' or occurring as an accident, as when the aëroplane is out of control from stalling.

tail=stock (tāl'stok), *n.* In a lathe, the movable or sliding frame supporting the dead spindle.

taint (tānt), *v.* [OF. F. *teint*, pp. of *teindre*, dye, color, < L. *tingere* (pp. *tinctus*), wet, dye, tinge; the E. word being in part confused with *attaint*.] **I.** *tr.* To color† or tinge†; also, to modify as by a touch of something offensive or deleterious; affect with incipient putrefaction; infect, contaminate, or corrupt (as, "He would spare no one — neither wife nor mother nor brothers, should they be *tainted* with heresy": Besant's "Coligny," vi.); sully or tarnish; also, to touch or hit, esp. in tilting†. **II.** *intr.* To become affected with incipient putrefaction.—**taint**, *n.* [OF. F. *teint*, *teinte*.] Color† or tinge†; also, a touch of something offensive or deleterious; a trace of infection, contamination, or the like; a touch of dishonor or discredit (as, "I hate ingratitude more in a man Than . . . any *taint* of vice": Shakspere's "Twelfth Night," iii. 4. 390); also, a hit in tilting†.—**taint'less**, *a.* Free from taint; pure; clean.—**tain-ture** (tān'tūr), *n.* Tainting; taint. [Obs. or rare.]

Tai=ping (tī'ping'). [Chinese, lit. 'great peace.'] **I.** *a.* Designating or pertaining to a proposed purely native dynasty in China, which a certain Hung Siu-tsuan claimed he was divinely commissioned to set up in place of the ruling Manchu dynasty, and which he attempted to establish by means of a great rebellion ('Tai-ping Rebellion') begun in 1850 and suppressed, largely with the aid of a mixed force under C. G. Gordon ("Chinese Gordon"), in 1864. **II.** *n.* A supporter or adherent of the Tai-ping dynasty.

taj (täj), *n.* [Pers.] A crown or diadem; the conical cap of a Mohammedan dervish; [*cap.*] a white marble mausoleum (called in full *Taj Mahal*, 'crown of buildings') built at Agra, India, by the Mogul emperor Shah Jehan (flourished 1628–58) for his favorite wife.

The Taj Mahal, Agra, India.

take (tāk), *v. t.*; pret. *took*, pp. *taken*, ppr. *taking*. [Late AS. *tacan*, from Scand.; = Icel. *taka* = Sw. *taga* = Dan. *tage*, seize, take, akin to Goth. *tēkan*, touch.] To touch†; also, to lay hold on, or get into one's hands or possession by force or artifice; seize, catch, or capture; grasp, grip, or embrace (as, "He *took* me by the hand": Addison and Steele, in "Tatler," 114); strike or hit (as, the blow *took* him in the head); attack or affect, as a disease does (often in the passive: as, to be *taken* with a fit); come upon suddenly (as, "a man that . . . lodgeth wheresoever the night *taketh* him": Ecclus. xxxvi. 26); catch or detect, as in wrong-doing; captivate or charm (as, a thing *takes* one's fancy; "His lordship was deeply *taken* with Miss Portman," Maria Edgeworth's "Belinda," xvi.); attract and hold (as, a thing *takes* one's eye or attention); also, to get into one's hold, possession, control, etc., by one's own action but without force or artifice (as, to *take* one's pen in hand); receive into the body or system, as by swallowing or inhaling (as, to *take* food; to *take* snuff); expose one's self to (as, to *take* the air); receive or adopt (a person) into some specified or implied relation (as, to *take* one in marriage; to *take* lodgers); secure beforehand, as by payment or contract (as, to *take* a house); secure regularly by payment (as, to *take* a magazine); assume (a form, character, etc.); assume or adopt (a symbol, badge, or the like: as, to *take* the habit, to become a monk; to *take* the veil, to become a nun); assume or undertake (a function, duty, responsibility, etc.: as, to *take* charge; to *take* service; to *take* the blame); assume the obligation of (a vow, pledge, etc.); perform or discharge (a part, service, etc.); assume or adopt as one's own (a part or side in a contest, etc.); assume or appropriate as if by right (as, to *take* the credit for something; to *take* a liberty); have by usage, either as part of itself or with it in construction (a particular form, accent, etc., or a case, mode, etc.), as a word or the like; also, to pick from a number, select, or choose (as, *take* whichever you wish); employ for some specified or implied purpose (as, to *take* measures to check an evil); avail one's self of (an opportunity, etc.); have recourse to (a vehicle, etc.) as a means of progression or travel (as, to *take* a car to the ferry); go into or enter (as, to *take* the field); adopt and enter upon (a way, course, etc.); proceed to deal with in some manner (as, to *take* a matter under consideration); proceed to occupy (as, to *take* a seat); occupy, use up, or consume (space, material, time, etc.); require (as, "It *takes* some pluck to face a mob of angry women": J. Conrad's "Rover," iv.); also, to get or obtain from a source, or derive (as, to *take* pattern from a person); ascertain by inquiry, examination, measurement, scientific observation, etc. (as, "Their herdsman . . . *Takes* of his muster'd flocks a just account," Dryden's tr. Virgil's "Georgics," iv. 626; "For he, by geometric scale, Could *take* the size of pots of ale," Butler's "Hudibras," i. 1); make or perform (a measurement, observation, etc.); write down (notes, a copy, etc.); take a record of (a speech, etc.); make (a reproduction, picture, or photograph of something); make a figure or picture, esp. a photograph, of (a person or thing); also, to receive, or be the recipient of (something bestowed, administered, etc.: as, to *take* a degree; to *take* first prize); suffer or undergo (as, "She [Austria] had been compelled to *take* the first shock of each Russian offensive": Buchan's "Hist. of the Great War," lxxxiii.); enter into the enjoyment of (recreation, a holiday, etc.); receive by way of payment or charge (as, he will not *take* a cent less); obtain or exact (satisfaction or reparation); receive or accept willingly (as, "I will *take* no refusal": Smollett's "Humphry Clinker," Oct. 14); accept and comply with (advice, etc.); accept as true or correct (as, "I would not *take* this from report": Shakspere's "King Lear," iv. 6. 144); receive in a specified manner (as, to *take* a thing ill or kindly); attempt to get over, through, round, etc. (something that presents itself), or succeed in doing this (as, the horse *took* the hedge with an easy jump); receive, admit, or let in (as, a boat that *takes* water); contract (disease, etc.); absorb or become impregnated with (a color, etc.); become affected by (as, a stone which will *take* a high polish); also, to grasp or apprehend mentally, understand, or comprehend (as, to *take* a person's meaning); understand in a specified way (as, how do you *take* this?); assume as a fact (as, I *take* it that you will be there); regard or consider (as, he was *taken* to be wealthy;

"Do you *take* me for a fool?" Stevenson's "Master of Ballantrae," x.); begin to have (a certain feeling or state of mind: as, to *take* a dislike to a thing); experience or feel (delight, pride, etc.); form and hold in the mind (as, to *take* a resolution; to *take* a certain view); form in the mind and show in action (as, to *take* courage; "And never a saint *took* pity on My soul in agony," Coleridge's "Ancient Mariner," iv.); also, to do, perform, execute, etc. (as, to *take* a walk); make, put forth, etc. (as, to *take* exception); also, to carry or convey (as, to *take* one's lunch along with one); conduct or escort (as, "*Take* the stranger to my house": Shakspere's "Comedy of Errors," iv. 1. 36); lead (as, where will this road *take* me?); carry off or remove (with *away*, etc.); remove by death (as, "*Take* me from the world," Shakspere's "3 Henry VI.," i. 4. 167; "In the fulness of years, M. de Bassompierre was *taken*," C. Brontë's "Villette," xxxvii.); subtract or deduct (as, to *take* 2 from 6); devote or apply (one's self), as to some pursuit or action; betake (one's self: as, "Until eleven, When he will *take* himself to bed," Byron's "Werner," i.). —**to take a leaf out of,** or **from, the book of.** See under *leaf, n.*—**to take down,** to pull down; remove by pulling or taking apart; also, to swallow; also, to put in writing; write down; also, to lower in power, strength, etc.; abate; lower the pride or arrogance of, or humble or humiliate (as, "I am obliged to *take* the young man *down* from time to time": Thackeray's "Newcomes," iv.).—**to take in,** fig., to deceive, trick, or cheat: as, "He . . . *took in* my father once, by dressing himself up as a lady" (Mrs. Gaskell's "Cranford," vi.). [Colloq.]—**to take off,** to remove; lead off or away; withdraw, as from service (as, a railroad *takes off* a train); remove by death; also, to imitate or mimic, esp. in ridicule (colloq.).—**to take on,** to engage or hire; also, to undertake to handle or deal with.—**to take stock.** See under *stock, n.*—**to take to task.** See under *task, n.*—**take,** *v. i.* To catch or engage, as a mechanical device; strike root, or begin to grow, as a plant; adhere, as ink, etc.; win favor or acceptance, as a play (as, "I suppose if it [a play] *takes*, you'll be making a lot o' money": L. Merrick's "Actor-Manager," vi.); have the intended result or effect, as a medicine, inoculation, etc.; also, to enter into possession, as of an estate; also, to detract (*from*: as, an imperfection that *takes* from the value of a thing); also, to apply, devote, or addict one's self (see *to take to*, below); make one's way, proceed, or go (as, to *take* across a field: see *to take to*, below); also, to be taken, or become (sick or ill); become affected in a desired way (as, he was vaccinated, but did not *take*); admit of being photographed (*well, badly*, etc.); admit of being taken (*out, apart*, etc.).—**to take after,** to follow the example of; also, to resemble (a parent, etc.) in character, appearance, etc.—**to take off,** to set off; take one's departure; esp., to start to leap, as a horse in taking a fence; leave the ground, as an aëroplane in beginning a flight.—**to take on,** to be greatly agitated; display great excitement, grief, or other emotion: as, "She *took on* sadly about her husband. He has been buried to-day" (Thackeray's "Henry Esmond," ii. 1). [Colloq.]—**to take to,** to apply, devote, or addict one's self to (as, to *take to* rising early; to *take to* drink); also, to be disposed (*kindly*, etc.) to; conceive a liking or affection for (as, "Riceyman *took to* him, seeing in the young man a resemblance to himself": Arnold Bennett's "Riceyman Steps," i. 3); also, to make one's way to, or betake one's self to (as, "She had positively refused to *take to* her bed": Dickens's "Hard Times," ii. 9); resort to, or have recourse to (as, to *take to* one's heels).—**to take up with,** to begin to associate with; consort with.—**take,** *n.* The act or an act of taking; also, that which is taken; the quantity of fish, etc., taken at one time; the portion of copy taken at one time by a compositor to be set into type.

take=down (tāk′doun), *a.* Made or constructed so as to be easily taken down or apart.

take=in (tāk′in), *n.* A deception, fraud, or imposition; something that deceives or imposes on one. [Colloq.]

take=off (tāk′ôf), *n.* An imitating or mimicking, caricature, or burlesque (colloq.); also, a taking or setting off; the leaving of the ground in leaping or in beginning a flight in an aëroplane; the place or point at which one takes off.

tak-er (tā′kẽr), *n.* One who or that which takes.

tak-ing (tā′king), *n.* The act of one who or that which

takes; the state of being taken; specif., a state of agitation or distress (now colloq. or prov.: as, "The Major is in a sad *taking* because of the Captain's being killed," Cooper's "Spy," viii.); also, that which is taken; *pl.*, receipts (colloq.). —**tak′ing,** *p. a.* Captivating, winning, or pleasing (now colloq.: as, "They have a free way with them that is very *taking*," G. B. Shaw's "You Never Can Tell," ii.); also, infectious or contagious (colloq.); also, blighting† or blasting†. —**tak′ing-ly,** *adv.*—**tak′ing-ness,** *n.*

ta-la-ri-a (ta̤-lā′ri-ä̤), *n. pl.* [L., prop. neut. pl. of *talaris*, pertaining to the ankles, < *talus*, ankle.] In *class. myth.*, the winged sandals, or small wings fastened to the ankles, of Hermes (or Mercury) and other divinities.

tal-bot (tâl′bọt), *n.* [Prob. < *Talbot*, Eng. family name.] One of an extinct breed of large dogs with broad mouth, long, pendulous ears, and great powers of scent, and usually white in color.

Tal-bot (tâl′bọt) **House.** See *Toc H.*

tal-bo-type (tâl′bọ-tīp), *n.* [From W. H. F. *Talbot*, the inventor: see -*type*.] Same as *calotype*.

Figure of Iris, wearing Talaria: from a Greek red-figured vase.

talc (talk), *n.* [F. *talc* = ML. *talcus*, *talcum*; from Ar.] A soft mineral, a silicate of magnesium, unctuous to the touch, and usually consisting of broad, flat, smooth laminæ or plates: used in making lubricants, toilet-powder, etc. Cf. *soapstone*, and *French chalk* (under *French, a.*).—**talc,** *v. t.*; **talcked** or *talced*, **talcking** or *talcing*. To treat or rub with talc, as a photographic plate when it is desired to prevent the adherence of a film.—**tal-cose** (tal′kōs), *a.* Containing, or composed largely of, talc. Also **tal′cous.**—**tal′cum** (-kum), *n.* [ML.] Talc.

tale (tāl), *n.* [AS. *talu*, a telling, speech, statement, enumeration, = D. *taal*, speech, = G. *zahl*, number, = Icel. *tala*, speech, account, number: see *tell²*.] The act of telling†; talk† or discourse†; also, that which is told; a relation, account, or narrative; a story; often, a story told idly or maliciously or in violation of confidence (as, to tell or carry *tales* about a person; to tell *tales* out of school, see under *tell², v. t.*); a narrative purporting to relate the facts or occurrences in connection with some event, incident, or case, real or imaginary, whether for the purpose of preserving the history or transmitting the traditions, or merely to please or instruct (as, "Each to each amid the wine-cups told Unwritten, half-forgotten *tales* of old": W. Morris's "Jason," xi. 464); a literary composition having the form of such a narrative (as, Chaucer's "Canterbury *Tales*"; Kipling's "Plain *Tales* from the Hills"; Maria Edgeworth's "Moral *Tales* for Young People"); a mere fictitious story, or a fiction or falsehood; a mere matter of history or tradition, or a thing of the past; also, enumeration, numbering, or counting (as, "Silver and gold were not very scarce . . . but they passed more by weight than by *tale* [as when coined]": Hallam's "Europe during the Middle Ages," ii. 2); the number or count in a particular case, or the amount counted off or to be made up (as, "a deficiency in the quality or the *tale* of the cloth he wove for them": George Eliot's "Silas Marner," i.); the full number or amount, or the total or aggregate, of anything (as, "Though the *tale* of his riches commanded respect, he had never won affection": Arnold Bennett's "Riceyman Steps," v. 13).

tale-bear-er (tāl′bãr″ẽr), *n.* One who officiously carries tales or gossip likely to breed mischief: as, "Where there is no *talebearer*, the strife ceaseth" (Prov. xxvi. 20).—**tale′-bear″ing,** *n.* and *a.*

tal-ent (tal′ẹnt), *n.* [OF. F. *talent*, < L. *talentum*, talent (weight, money), < Gr. τάλαντον, a balance, weight, sum of money, akin to τλῆναι, bear: see *thole¹*.] An ancient unit of weight, varying with time and place, the later Attic talent being estimated at about 57 pounds avoirdupois; this weight of gold, silver, or the like as a monetary unit, the value of the Hebrew gold unit being estimated at about $30,000, that of the Hebrew silver unit at about $2,000, and that of the later Attic silver unit at about $1,000 or $1,200; hence, wealth† or riches†; also, inclination† or disposition†; also, a power or ability of mind or body considered as committed to one for use and improvement (from the parable in Mat. xxv. 14–30); a special natural ability or aptitude (as, "Jack is a universal genius; his *talents* are really astonishing," Smollett's "Humphry Clinker," Oct. 11; "He has a natural *talent* for learning," Ian Maclaren's "Beside the Bonnie Brier Bush," i. 2); a capacity for achievement or success in something; natural ability, gifts, or cleverness (as, young men of *talent*; "But still, they said, she [a dancer] had *talent*, but no genius," Barrie's "Sentimental Tommy," iv.); also, persons or (rarely) a person of ability; specif., the backers of or betters on horses, as distinguished from the book-makers (colloq.).—**tal′ent-ed**, *a.* Having talent or talents; gifted.—**tal′ent-less**, *a.* Without talent.

ta-les (tā′lēz), *n.* [ML. *tales* (*de circumstantibus*), 'such (of the bystanders)': a phrase in an order for summoning such persons.] In *law*, orig. as *pl.*, persons chosen from among the bystanders or those present in court to serve on a jury when the original panel has become deficient in number; as *sing.*, a supply of men, or a man, so chosen; also, the order or writ summoning them.—**tales-man** (tālz′man), *n.*; pl. *-men.* In *law*, a person summoned as one of the tales.

tale-tell-er (tāl′tel″ėr), *n.* One who tells tales or stories; esp., one who carries tales or gossip; a talebearer.—**tale′-tell″ing**, *n.* and *a.*

tal-i-on (tal′i-on), *n.* [OF. F. *talion*, < L. *talio*(*n-*), < *talis*, such: cf. *retaliate.*] Retaliation as authorized by law, esp. when the punishment inflicted corresponds in kind and degree to the injury, as "eye for eye, tooth for tooth" (Lev. xxiv. 20); hence, in general, retaliation or revenge.—**tal-i-on′ic** (-on′ik), *a.*

tal-i-ped (tal′i-ped). [See *talipes.*] **I.** *a.* Of a foot, twisted or distorted out of shape or position; of a person, clubfooted; in *zoöl.*, having the feet twisted into an unusual position, as a sloth. **II.** *n.* A taliped person or animal.

tal-i-pes (tal′i-pēz), *n.* [NL., < L. *talus*, ankle, + *pes* (*ped-*), foot.] A clubfoot; the condition of being clubfooted; in *zoöl.*, a natural formation of the feet by which they are twisted into an unusual position, as in the sloths.

tal-i-pot (tal′i-pot), *n.* [E. Ind.] A tall palm, *Corypha umbraculifera*, of Ceylon, the Malabar Coast, etc., whose large leaves are much used for making fans and umbrellas, for covering houses, and in the place of writing-paper.

tal-is-man (tal′is-man or tal′iz-), *n.*; pl. *-mans* (-manz). [= F. and Sp. *talisman*, < Ar. *tilsam*, < LGr. τέλεσμα, talisman, earlier a religious rite, Gr. payment, < Gr. τελεῖν, complete, fulfil, pay, < τέλος, completion, end.] A stone, ring, or other object engraved with figures or characters under certain superstitious observances of the heavens, which is supposed to possess occult powers, and is worn

Talipot.

as an amulet or charm; any amulet or charm; anything of almost magic power (as, "that dear *talisman*, a mother's name": Lowell's "Threnodia," 28).—**tal-is-man′ic** (-man′ik), *a.* Pertaining to or serving as a talisman.—**tal-is-man′i-cal-ly**, *adv.*

talk (tâk), *v.* [ME. *talken, talkien*, prob. < AS. *talu*, E. *tale.*] **I.** *intr.* To make known or interchange ideas, information, etc., by means of spoken words; speak; converse; consult or confer; speak (*of*, as something under consideration: as, he *talks* of going next week); speak (*to*) in admonition or reproof; make gossiping remarks, or gossip (as, "You say people will '*talk*' about my . . . being pleasant to

an old friend!" Tarkington's "Magnificent Ambersons," xi.); chatter or prate; also, to communicate ideas by other means than speech, as by writing, signs, or signals (as, "Men think that it is essential that the Nation have commerce . . . and *talk* through a telegraph": Thoreau's "Walden," ii.); also, to imitate the sound of spoken words, as certain birds and mechanical contrivances; make sounds suggestive of speech (as, "The ship was *talking*, as sailors say, loudly, treading the innumerable ripples with an incessant weltering splash": Stevenson's "Treasure Island," xxiii.). **II.** *tr.* To express in words; utter (as, to *talk* sense; to *talk* treason); also, to use as a spoken language (as, "I can *talk* three languages besides English": Margaret Kennedy's "Constant Nymph," xviii.); also, to speak or converse about, or discuss (as, "Angus was ready to *talk* deer till all hours," Buchan's "Three Hostages," xx.; to *talk* politics; to *talk* shop, see *shop, n.*); also, to bring, put, drive, influence, etc., by talk (as, to *talk* a person to sleep or to death; to *talk* a reluctant person over, or into consenting); pass or while (*away*) with talk, as time.—**talk**, *n.* The act of talking; speech; conversation, esp. of a familiar kind; an informal discourse; a conference; report or rumor; gossip; mere empty speech; also, a subject or occasion of talking, esp. of public talking, or gossip (as, "A most ridiculous adventure, by making me the town *talk*, obliged me to leave the place": Smollett's "Humphry Clinker," July 4); also, a way of talking (as, baby-*talk*); language, dialect, or lingo.—**talk-a-tive** (tâ′ka-tiv). **I.** *a.* Inclined to talk, loquacious, or garrulous (as, "They became *talkative*, loud, and even clamorous in their mirth": Scott's "Black Dwarf," xiii.); characterized by or showing an inclination to talk (as, a *talkative* mood). **II.** *n.* A talkative person: as, "Those old fools, Exhausted *talkatives* whose blood is still" (Masefield's "Daffodil Fields," ii.).—**talk′a-tive-ly**, *adv.*—**talk′a-tive-ness**, *n.*—**talk′er**, *n.*—**talk′ie**, *n.* In *pl.* (*talkies*), talking pictures; in *sing.* (*talkie*), a talking picture. [Colloq.]—**talk′ing=ma-chine″**, *n.* A machine which reproduces mechanically the sound of the human voice, instrumental music, etc., as a phonograph, a graphophone, or a gramophone.—**talk′ing pic′ture.** In *pl.* (*talking pictures*), moving pictures with accompanying synchronized speech, singing, etc.; in *sing.* (*talking picture*), a moving picture or photoplay with such accompaniment.—**talk′ing=to**, *n.* An admonishing or reproving talk addressed directly to a person; a 'lecture'; a reprimand. [Colloq.]—**talk′y**, *a.* Abounding in talk; disposed to talk; loquacious. [Colloq.]

tall (tâl), *a.* [ME. *talle*: cf. AS. *getæl*, quick, prompt.] Proper† or seemly†; comely† or handsome†; goodly†, excellent†, or fine†; bold† or valiant†; also, having a relatively great stature, as a person or animal (as, a *tall* man; "mounted on a *tall*, meagre . . . shambling gray gelding," Smollett's "Humphry Clinker," July 15); of more than average height, or length from bottom to top (as, a *tall* shrub; *tall* grass; a *tall* goblet; a *tall* hat; a *tall* book); of notable or imposing height, or lofty (as, a *tall* column or tower; *tall* mountains); also, having stature or height as specified (as, a man six feet *tall*; "Mesty . . . strutted about at least three inches *taller* than he was before," Marryat's "Mr. Midshipman Easy," xvii.); also, high, great, or large in amount (colloq.: as, "a *tall* price," Hugh Walpole's "Wooden Horse," xi.); extravagant (colloq.: as, a *tall* statement; "He cajoled them into a bout of *tall* stories," Wister's "Virginian," xix.); high-flown or grandiloquent (colloq.: as, "You have been white once, for all your *tall* talk of this being your own people," J. Conrad's "Lord Jim," xli.).

tal-lage (tal′āj), *n.* [OF. *taillage*, < *taillier*: see *tail¹.*] Orig., a compulsory aid or tax levied by the Norman and early Angevin kings of England upon the demesne lands of the crown and upon all royal towns; hence, a tax, toll, or levy.—**tal′lage**, *v. t.*; *-laged, -laging.* To impose tallage upon; tax.

tall=boy (tâl′boi), *n.* A tall-stemmed glass for wine, etc.; also, a high-boy, or tall chest of drawers; also, a kind of tall chimney-pot.

tall-ish (tâl′ish), *a.* Rather tall.

tal-lith (tal′ith), *n.* [Heb.] A mantle or a scarf-like garment with fringes at the four corners, worn by Jews at prayer.

tall-ness (tâl′nes), *n.* The quality of being tall.

tal-low (tal′ō), *n.* [ME. *talowe, talgh, talg,* = D. *talk* = MLG. *talch* = G., Sw., and Dan. *talg,* tallow.] The fatty tissue or suet of animals; more commonly, the harder fat of sheep, oxen, etc., separated by melting from the fibrous and membranous matter naturally mixed with it, and used in making candles, soap, etc.; also, any of various similar fatty substances (as, vegetable *tallow,* derived from various plants; mineral *tallow,* hatchettin).—**tal′low,** *v. t.* To smear with tallow; also, to fatten (sheep, etc.).—**tal′low=chan″-dler,** *n.* A maker of or dealer in tallow candles.—**tal′low=y,** *a.* Of the nature of or resembling tallow; abounding in tallow.

tal-ly (tal′i), *n.*; pl. *tallies* (-iz). [AF. *tallie* = F. *taille,* < L. *talea,* rod, stick: cf. *tail*[1].] In old-time use, a stick of wood, usually squared, with notches cut transversely to indicate the amount of a debt or payment, and often cleft lengthwise across the notches, the debtor retaining one piece and the creditor the other; anything on which a score or account is kept; also, a score kept upon a notched stick or by other means; an account or reckoning; a record of debit and credit, of the score of a game, or the like; also, a notch or mark made on or in a tally; a mark made to register a certain number of objects in keeping account, as, for instance, a group of five; a number of objects serving as a unit of computation; a number or group of objects recorded; also, a ticket, label, or mark used as a means of identification, etc., as when attached to a plant or tree; also, anything corresponding to another thing as a counterpart or duplicate; correspondence or agreement.—**tal′ly,** *v.*; *-lied, -lying.* **I.** *tr.* To mark or enter on a tally; register; record; also, to count or reckon up; also, to furnish with a tally or identifying label; also, to cause to correspond or agree†. **II.** *intr.* To correspond, as one part of a tally with the other; hence, in general, to accord or agree (as, "It is hard that a man's exterior should *tally* so little sometimes with his soul": Maugham's "Moon and Sixpence," xxxi.).

tal-ly=ho (tal′i-hō′). [Prob. < F. *taïaut,* earlier *thialau, taho,* hunter's cry.] **I.** *interj.* A huntsman's cry on catching sight of the fox. **II.** *n.*; pl. *-hos* (-hōz′). A cry of 'tally-ho'; also, a mail-coach or a four-in-hand pleasure-coach.—**tal′ly=ho′,** *v.*; *-hoed* or *-ho′d, -hoing.* **I.** *tr.* To make known the presence of (a fox) by the cry of 'tally-ho.' **II.** *intr.* To utter a cry of 'tally-ho' or the like.

tal-ly-man (tal′i-man), *n.*; pl. *-men.* One who keeps a tally, score, or account; also, one who sells goods on credit, to be paid for by instalments (Eng.).

tal-ma (tal′mä), *n.* [From F. J. *Talma* (1763—1826), French tragedian.] A kind of cape or cloak formerly worn by men or women.

Tal-mud (tal′mud), *n.* [Aram. *talmūd,* teaching, learning.] In *Jewish lit.,* the body of traditional Jewish law, consisting of the Mishnah and its commentary, the Gemara; sometimes, the Gemara alone.—**Tal-mud′ic,** *a.*—**Tal′mud-ist,** *n.* One of the writers or compilers of the Talmud; also, one who accepts the doctrines of the Talmud; also, one versed in the Talmud.—**Tal-mud-is′tic,** *a.*

tal-on (tal′on), *n.* [OF. F. *talon,* < ML. *talo*(n-), heel, < L. *talus,* ankle, heel.] The heel, esp. in certain quadrupeds†; also, a claw, esp. of a bird of prey; also, in *arch.,* an ogee molding.—**tal′oned,** *a.* Having talons.

tal-pine (tal′pin), *a.* [LL. *talpinus,* < L. *talpa,* mole.] Pertaining or allied to the mole (animal); mole-like.

ta-luk (ta-lök′), *n.* [Hind.] In India, a hereditary estate belonging to a native proprietor; also, a subdivision of a revenue district, placed under a native collector.—**ta-luk′dar** (-där), *n.* [Hind.] In India, the native holder of a hereditary estate; also, the revenue collector in a taluk.

ta-lus[1] (tā′lus), *n.*; pl. *-li* (-li). [L., ankle, heel.] In *anat.,* the ankle or ankle-joint; also, the ankle-bone or astragalus.

ta-lus[2] (tā′lus), *n.* [F. *talus,* OF. *talu,* ult. < L. *talus:* see *talus*[1].] A slope; in *fort.,* the sloping side or face of a wall, rampart, parapet, or the like; in *geol.,* a sloping mass of rocky fragments lying at the base of a cliff or the like.

tam (tam), *n.* Shortened form of *tam-o′-shanter.*

tam-a-ble (tā′ma-bl), *a.* That may be tamed.

ta-mal (ta-mäl′), *n.*; pl. *tamales* (ta-mä′lēz, Sp. tä-mä′läs). [Mex. Sp.] A Mexican dish made of crushed Indian corn and minced meat, seasoned with red peppers, etc., wrapped in husks and roasted or steamed.

ta-ma-le (ta-mä′lē), *n.* [Erron. taken as sing. of *tamales,* pl. of *tamal.*] Same as *tamal.*

tam-a-du-a (ta-man′dū-ä), *n.* [Brazilian.] The four-toed ant-eater, *Tamandua tetra-dactyla,* an arboreal species of the forests of tropical America.

Tamandua.

tam-a-noir (tam′a-nwor), *n.* [F., = *tamandua.*] The ant-bear, or great ant-eater. See *ant-bear.*

tam-a-rack (tam′a-rak), *n.* [N. Amer. Ind.] An American larch, *Larix laricina,* yielding a useful timber (see cut at *larch*); the hackmatack; also, any of several related or similar trees.

ta-ma-ra-o, ta-ma-rau (tä-mä-rä′ō, -rou′), *n.* Same as *timarau.*

tam-a-rin (tam′a-rin), *n.* [From native name in Cayenne.] Any of various South American marmosets of the genus *Midas.*

tam-a-rind (tam′a-rind), *n.* [ML. *tamarindus,* < Ar. *tamr hindī,* 'Indian date.'] The fruit of a large cæsalpiniaceous tropical tree, *Tamarindus indica,* a pod containing seeds inclosed in a juicy acid pulp that is used in beverages and food, and is also exported for medicinal use as a laxative and refrigerant; also, the tree, cultivated throughout the tropics for its fruit, fragrant flowers, shade, and timber.

Tamarin.

tam-a-risk (tam′a-risk), *n.* [LL. *tamariscus,* L. *tamarix.*] A plant of the old-world tropical genus *Tamarix,* esp. *T. gallica,* native in the Mediterranean region, an ornamental shrub or small tree with slender, feathery branches.

ta-ma-sha (ta-mä′shä), *n.* [Hind.] In the East Indies, a show or spectacle; an entertainment.

tam-bo (tam′bō), *n.*; pl. *-bos* (-bōz). [Abbr. of *tam-bourine.*] An end-man in a minstrel-troupe who plays on the tambourine.

Flowering Branch of Tamarisk (*Tamarix gallica*). — *a,* a flower; *b,* pistil; *c,* branch showing the scale-like leaves.

tam-bour (tam′-bör or -bor), *n.* [F.: see *tabor.*] A drum, esp. the bass drum; also, something resembling or suggesting a drum; specif., a circular frame consisting of two hoops, one fitting within the other, or a frame of some other form, on which cloth or other material is stretched for embroidering; hence, embroidery done on this; in *arch.*, the more or less drum-like or bell-like core or central portion of a Corinthian or similar capital; also, the circular or polygonal, vertical supporting wall of a cupola; in *fort.*, a defensive work of palisades or the like, for defending a road or entrance.— **tam′bour,** *v. t.* or *i.* To embroider, or do embroidery, on a tambour.

tam-bou-rine (tam-bö-rēn′), *n.* [F. *tambourin*: see *taborine*.] A small drum formed of a wooden ring or hoop with skin or parchment stretched over one end or side and pairs of loose metal disks or jingles placed in slots around the circumference, played by striking with the knuckles, shaking, etc.

Spanish Tambourine.

tame (tām), *a.*; compar. *tamer*, superl. *tamest.* [AS. *tam* = D. *tam* = G. *zahm* = Icel. *tamr*, tame; akin to L. *domare*, Gr. δαμᾶν, Skt. *dam-*, to tame, conquer.] Reclaimed from the wild or savage state, as an animal or a person (as, a *tame* bear; "a *tame* black lad, that they employed about the place," H. Kingsley's "Geoffry Hamlyn," xl.); domesticated; sometimes, cultivated, or improved by cultivation, rather than wild, as a plant or its fruit, etc. (as, "just as a wild fruit has a sharper taste than that of the *tame* product": Galsworthy's "Saint's Progress," iii. 12); also, gentle, fearless, or without shyness, as if domesticated, as an animal (as, "All our wild birds were if anything too *tame*": W. H. Hudson's "Far Away and Long Ago," xxi.); tractable, docile, or submissive, as a person, the disposition, etc.; subdued in feeling (as, "Such glee was ours . . . till we came Homeward, which always makes the spirit *tame*": Shelley's "Julian and Maddalo," 33); spiritless or pusillanimous; also, lacking in ardor or animation; sluggish or languid; dull or insipid (as, a *tame* book or affair; a *tame* existence); without striking features (as, "The valley . . . is *tame* and featureless": Mrs. H. Ward's "Robert Elsmere," i.).— **tame,** *v.*; tamed, taming. **I.** *tr.* To make tame; reclaim from the wild state; domesticate; make tractable; subdue (as, "Disastrous war and alien domination had *tamed* the spirit of the people": Macaulay's "Hist. of Eng.," ii.); deprive of courage, ardor, interest, etc.; soften, or tone down. **II.** *intr.* To become tame: sometimes with *down*. — **tame′less,** *a.* That has never been or cannot be tamed; untamable: as, "The leopardess is *tameless*" (C. Brontë's "Shirley," xxxvi.).— **tame′less-ness,** *n.*—**tame′ly,** *adv.*— **tame′ness,** *n.*—**tam-er** (tā′mėr), *n.*

Tam-il (tam′il). **I.** *n.* A member of a people of Dravidian stock of southern India and Ceylon; also, the language of this people. **II.** *a.* Of or pertaining to the Tamils or their language.—**Ta-mil-i-an** (ta-mil′i-an), *a.*

Tam-muz (tam′uz), *n.* [Heb.] In the Jewish calendar, the tenth month (29 days) of the civil year and the fourth of the ecclesiastical year, beginning in the latter part of June or the first part of July.

tam-my[1] (tam′i), *n.*; pl. *tammies* (-iz). [Cf. *etamine*.] A thin woolen, or woolen and cotton, fabric, often highly glazed.

tam-my[2] (tam′i), *n.*; pl. *tammies* (-iz). [F. *tamis*, sieve; perhaps from Teut.] A sieve; a strainer.

tam-o′-shan-ter (tam′ō-shan′tėr), *n.* [From *Tam o'*

Shanter in Burns's poem of that name.] A cap, of Scotch origin, with a flat crown larger in diameter than the headband.

tamp (tamp), *v. t.* [Appar. < *tampion*.] In blasting, to fill (the hole made by the drill) with earth, etc., after the powder or explosive has been introduced; also, in general, to force in or down by repeated, somewhat light strokes.—**tamp′er**[1], *n.*

tam-per[2] (tam′pėr), *v. i.* [Var. of *temper*: cf. *meddle*, orig. 'mix.'] To busy one's self or engage secretly or improperly in something (as, "Porcaro . . . *tampering* in a fresh conspiracy, was put to death": Hallam's "Europe during the Middle Ages," iii. 2); meddle (*with*); esp., to meddle (*with*) improperly for the purpose of altering, damaging, misusing, etc. (as, to *tamper* with a will; to *tamper* with a lock; to *tamper* with the mails or with ballot-boxes); undertake underhand or corrupt dealings (*with*), as in order to influence improperly (as, to *tamper* with a witness; "He began another practice, to *tamper* with the justices," Strype's "Memorials of Cranmer," i. 26).—**tam′per-er,** *n.*

tam-pi-on (tam′pi-on), *n.* [OF. F. *tampon*, var. of *tapon*, < *tape*, plug, stopper; from Teut., and akin to E. *tap*[1].] A wooden plug or stopper placed in the muzzle of a piece of ordnance when not in use, to keep out dampness and dust.

tam-pon (tam′pon), *n.* [F.: see *tampion*.] In *surg.*, a plug of cotton or the like inserted into an orifice, wound, etc., as to stop hemorrhage.—**tam′pon,** *v. t.* To fill or plug with a tampon.

tam=tam (tom′tom or tum′tum), *n.* and *v.* See *tom-tom*.

tan (tan), *v.*; tanned, tanning. [AS. *tannian*, appar. from a noun (prob. of Celtic origin) not recorded in AS. but represented by ML. *tannum*, OF. F. *tan*, tan-bark, E. *tan*, *n.*] **I.** *tr.* To convert (a hide, etc.) into leather, esp. by soaking or steeping in a bath prepared from oak-bark or the like; also, to make brown, as a person, the face, etc., by exposure to the sun or open air (as, "Goodly made as such wild folk may be, But *tanned* with sun and wind": W. Morris's "Jason," x. 384); also, to beat or thrash (colloq.: as, "I used to be scared of him . . . he *tanned* me so much," Mark Twain's "Huckleberry Finn," v.). **II.** *intr.* To become tanned: as, "Cover his face lest it freckle and *tan*" (Holmes's "Sweet Little Man").—**tan.** [= F. *tan*: see *tan, v.*] **I.** *n.* The bark of the oak, hemlock, etc., bruised and broken by a mill, and used for tanning hides; the spent bark of the tanning process, used for covering walks, riding-tracks, circus-rings, etc.; also, a yellowish-brown color, like that of tan; also, the brown color imparted to the skin by exposure to the sun or open air. **II.** *a.* Of the color of tan; yellowish-brown.

tan-a-ger (tan′a-jėr), *n.* [NL. *Tanagra*, genus-name; from native Brazilian name.] Any of the small, usually brilliantly colored, American oscine birds constituting the family *Tanagridæ*, as *Piranga rubra* (the 'summer tanager'), and *Piranga erythromelas* (the 'scarlet tanager').

Tan-a-gra (tan′a-grä) **fig-u-rine′.** See *figurine.*

tan-a-grine (tan′a-grin), *a.* Of or pertaining to the tanagers; belonging to the tanager family.

tan=bark (tan′bärk), *n.* The bark used in tanning; tan.

Summer Tanager (*Piranga rubra*), male.

tan-dem (tan′dem). [L., at length (in time), humorously used with reference to spatial length.] **I.** *adv.* One behind another; in single file: as, to drive horses *tandem*. **II.** *n.* A carriage drawn by two or more horses harnessed tandem; a team of horses so harnessed; also, a tandem bicycle or the like, or a tandem engine (see *tandem, a.*). **III.** *a.* Having animals, seats, parts, etc., arranged tandem, or one behind another: as, a *tandem* team; a *tandem* bicycle (with two seats, one behind another); a *tandem* engine (having two cylinders in line); a *tandem* aëroplane (with two or more main planes, or main sets of planes, placed one behind another).

tang[1] (tang), *n.* [ME. *tange, tongge,* prob. from Scand.: cf. Icel. *tangi,* projecting point, spit of land, tang of a knife, also E. *tongs.*] A projecting point, or projection; a long and slender projecting strip, tongue, or prong forming part of an object, as a chisel, file, knife, etc., and serving as a means of attachment for another part, as a handle or stock; also, a strong taste or flavor; a taste of something extraneous to the thing itself; a pungent or distinctive odor (as, "A faint *tang* of autumn smoke was in the air": W. Churchill's "Mr. Crewe's Career," viii.); fig., a smack, touch, or suggestion of something; the distinctive flavor or quality of a thing.—
tang[1], *v. t.* To furnish with a tang.

tang[2] (tang), *n.* [From Scand.: cf. Norw. and Dan. *tang,* Icel. *thang,* seaweed, and E. *tangle*[1].] Any of various large, coarse seaweeds of the genus *Fucus* and allied genera. [Sc. and north. Eng.]

tang[3] (tang), *v.* [Imit.: cf. *twang*[1].] **I.** *tr.* To strike (a bell, etc.) so as to cause a sharp, ringing sound; also, to utter with a ringing sound. **II.** *intr.* To emit a sharp, ringing sound.—**tang**[3], *n.* A sharp, ringing sound; a ring.

tan-ga-lung (tang′ga-lung), *n.* [Malay.] A civet-cat, *Viverra tangalunga,* of Sumatra and Java.

tan-ge-lo (tan′je-lō), *n.;* pl. *-los* (-lōz). [From *tang*(*erine*), *n.,* + (*pom*)-*elo.*] A hybrid of the tangerine orange and the pomelo or grape-fruit.

Tangalung.

tan-gent (tan′jent). [L. *tangens* (*tangent-*), ppr. of *tangere,* touch: cf. *tact, tangible, attain, contingent,* and *intact.*] **I.** *a.* Touching; in *geom.,* touching at one point only (and not intersecting), as a straight line in relation to a curve or surface, or one curve in relation to another, or a plane in relation to a sphere; passing through two (or more) consecutive points of a curve or surface (see *consecutive*); also, in contact along a single line or element, as a plane with a cylinder; also, fig., flying off at a tangent (see phrase under *tangent, n.*). **II.** *n.* In *geom.,* a tangent line or plane; in *trigon.,* orig., a straight line perpendicular to the radius of a circle at one end of an arc and extending from this point to the produced radius which cuts off the arc at its other end; now, the ratio of the length of this line to that of the radius of the circle; hence, of an acute angle of a right-angled triangle, a trigonometric function equal to the ratio of the length of the side opposite the angle to that of the side opposite the other acute angle.—**to fly** (or **go**) **off at a tangent,** fig., to go or pass with sudden divergence from one line of movement, course of action, or train of thought to another: as, "After having twelve times described this circle, he lately *flew off at a tangent* to visit some trees at his country-house in England" (Smollett's "Humphry Clinker," July 4); "Then his mind *went off at a tangent* in another direction" (H. G. Wells's "Men Like Gods," i. 8).—**tan′gen-cy,** *n.*—**tan-gen′tial** (-jen′shal), *a.* Pertaining to or of the nature of a tangent; being or moving in the direction of a tangent; fig., merely touching; slightly connected; divergent or digressive.—**tan-gen-ti-al′i-ty** (-shi-al′i-ti), *n.*—**tan-gen′tial-ly,** *adv.*

Tan-ger-ine (tan′je-rēn). **I.** *a.* Of or pertaining to Tangier, an important seaport of Morocco, on the Strait of Gibraltar; [*l. c.*] noting a small variety of orange derived from the mandarin and of the same type. **II.** *n.* [*l. c.*] A tangerine orange; also, a deep orange color.

tan-ghin (tan′gin), *n.* [Malagasy.] A powerful poison obtained from the fruit of an apocynaceous tree, *Tanghinia venenifera,* of Madagascar, formerly much used by the natives in a form of ordeal to determine guilt or innocence; also, the tree (see cut in next column).

tan-gi-ble (tan′ji-bl), *a.* [LL. *tangibilis,* < L. *tangere,*

touch: cf. *tangent.*] Capable of being touched, or discernible by the touch (as, *tangible* bodies; a mere apparition, without *tangible* form); affecting the sense of touch; hence, such as to be felt physically (as, "There is more torture in the lingering existence of a criminal . . . than in the *tangible* misery of whips and racks": Godwin's "Caleb Williams," xxiii.); material or substantial (as, "For most men . . . pleasure—*tangible* material prosperity in this world—is the safest test of virtue," S. Butler's "Way of All Flesh," xix.; "any man or woman who would give thought and labour without much hope of *tangible* rewards," H. G. Wells's

Tanghin.

"Men Like Gods," i. 5); real or actual, rather than imaginary or visionary (as, "What now appeared certain and *tangible* happiness, might soon dissipate into an airy dream": Mrs. Shelley's "Frankenstein," xxii.); also, capable of being clearly grasped by the mind, definite, or not vague or elusive (as, *tangible* distinctions; to have no *tangible* grounds for dissatisfaction or suspicion).—**tan-gi-bil′i-ty** (-bil′i-ti), **tan′gi-ble-ness,** *n.*—**tan′gi-bly,** *adv.*

tan-gle[1] (tang′gl), *n.* [From Scand.: cf. Icel. *thöngull, thang,* and E. *tang*[2].] Either of two large seaweeds, *Laminaria digitata* and *L. saccharina;* also, any of certain large seaweeds of the genus *Fucus* and allied genera.

tan-gle[2] (tang′gl), *v.;* *-gled, -gling.* [ME. *tangil,* var. of *tagil,* entangle; appar. from Scand.] **I.** *tr.* To involve in something that hampers, obstructs, or overgrows (as, "*Tangled* in the fold Of dire necessity," Milton's "Samson Agonistes," 1665; bushes *tangled* with vines); catch and hold in or as in a net or snare (as, "Look, how a bird lies *tangled* in a net": Shakspere's "Venus and Adonis," 67); fig., to bewilder or confuse (as, "Her turns and sudden contradictions left him *tangled* in a maze," Tarkington's "Gentleman from Indiana," xvi.; "A gray mist [on a river] would *tangle* the head of the oldest man that ever lived," Mark Twain's "Life on the Mississippi," viii.); also, to bring together into a mass of confusedly interlaced or intertwisted threads, strands, or other like parts (as, to *tangle* embroidery silks; to *tangle* the hair; "They [snakes] hibernated there, *tangled* together in a cluster no doubt," W. H. Hudson's "Far Away and Long Ago," xv.); put or get into a tangle (lit. or fig.); snarl. **II.** *intr.* To be or become tangled.—**tan′gle**[2], *n.* A tangled condition (lit. or fig.: as, to get threads into a *tangle;* affairs are in a sad *tangle;* to straighten out a *tangle* in accounts); a snarl; also, a tangled or confused mass or assemblage of something (as, a *tangle* of threads; a *tangle* of vines or vegetation; "Fricourt is a *tangle* of German dug-outs," H. G. Wells's "Italy, France, and Britain at War," iii. 1); fig., a confused jumble (as, a *tangle* of facts or contradictory statements); a complication.—**tan′gle-ber″ry,** *n.* A huckleberry, *Gaylussacia frondosa,* of the eastern U. S.—**tan′gle-foot,** *n.* Something that tangles or entangles the foot; fig., an intoxicating beverage, esp. whisky (slang, U. S.).—**tan′gle-ment,** *n.*—**tan′gler,** *n.*—**tan′gly,** *a.* Full of tangles; tangled.

tan-go (tang′gō), *n.;* pl. *-gos* (-gōz). [Sp.] A round dance, of Spanish-American origin, danced by couples to special music, and having many and varied steps, figures, and poses.—**tan′go,** *v. i.;* *-goed, -going.* To dance the tango.

tan-gram (tang′gram), *n.* [Origin obscure: cf. *trangam.*] A Chinese puzzle consisting of a square cut into five triangles, a square, and a rhomboid, which can be combined so as to form a great variety of other figures.

tan-ist (tan′ist), *n.* [Ir. and Gael. *tanaiste.*] The successor apparent to a Celtic chief, usually the oldest or worthiest of his kin, chosen by election among the tribe during the chief's lifetime.—**tan′ist-ry,** *n.* The system among various Celtic tribes by which the chief's successor (see *tanist*) was chosen by election among the tribe, usually during the chief's lifetime.

tank (tangk), *n.* [Prob. < Pg. *tanque*, pond, tank, = Sp. *estanque* = F. *étang*, < L. *stagnum*, pool, pond: cf. *stagnate*.] A natural or artificial pool, pond, or lake (now chiefly prov., except in India); also, a large receptacle or structure for holding water or other liquid or a gas (as, a water-*tank* for supplying a building; a swimming-*tank*; *tanks* for storing petroleum; gas-*tanks*); a chamber or reservoir on a locomotive or other engine or apparatus, for holding water, oil, or other fluid used in operation (as, "It [a motor-car] had been carefully oiled and the petrol *tank* was full": H. G. Wells's "Men Like Gods," iii. 4); *milit.*, a powerful and formidable self-propelled engine of war, operated by a crew, and consisting of a bullet-proof structure containing a cannon or machine-guns and moving by means of a caterpillar device which permits traveling over rough ground, obstructions, etc.; hence, any of various similar engines of war, as a kind of armored aëroplane ('flying tank').—**tank,** *v. t.* To put or store in a tank.—**tank′age** (-āj), *n.* Tanks collectively; a system of storage-tanks; the capacity of a tank or tanks; also, the act or process of storing liquid in a tank; the price charged for this; also, the residue from tanks in which fat or the like has been rendered, much used as a fertilizer.

tan-kard (tang′kärd), *n.* [ME. *tankard* = MD. *tanckaert* = OF. *tanquart*; origin unknown.] A large drinking-vessel, now usually with a handle and a hinged cover: as, "A massive silver *tankard* . . . held the beverage he was to drink during the night" (Cooper's "Spy," ix.); "He was dealing strenuously with a pile of sandwiches . . . and a *tankard* of ale from the tavern" (Chesterton's "Napoleon of Notting Hill," iii. 2).

tank=car (tangk′kär), *n.* A railroad platform-car carrying a long, commonly cylindrical, closed iron tank for transporting petroleum or the like.

Tankard.

tank-er (tang′kėr), *n.* A tank-ship; also, one of the crew of a military tank.

tank=ship (tangk′ship), *n.* A ship having its hold arranged to carry oil or other liquid in bulk.

tank=sta-tion (tangk′stā″shọn), *n.* A station or place with a tank or tanks for storing water, oil, etc.; esp., a stopping-place on a railroad, with a tank for supplying locomotives with water.

tank=town (tangk′toun), *n.* A town which serves as a tank-station, or at which trains stop chiefly to be supplied with water; hence, any small or unimportant town.

tan-ling (tan′ling), *n.* One tanned or browned by the sun: as, "hot summer's *tanlings*" (Shakspere's "Cymbeline," iv. 4. 29). [Poetic.]

tan-nage (tan′āj), *n.* [= F. *tannage*.] The act or process of tanning: also, the product of tanning; also, the bark or other material used in tanning.

tan-nate (tan′āt), *n.* In *chem.*, a salt of tannic acid.

tan-ner (tan′ėr), *n.* One whose occupation it is to tan hides. —**tan′ner-y** (-i), *n.*; pl. *-ies* (-iz). A place where tanning is carried on; also, the process or work of tanning.

tan-nic (tan′ik), *a.* [F. *tannique,* < *tan,* tan.] In *chem.*, pertaining to, derived from, or related to tan or its tanning principle; as, *tannic* acid (any of the tannins, esp. that obtained from nutgalls).

tan-nif-er-ous (ta-nif′ẹ-rus), *a.* [From *tannin* + *-ferous*.] Yielding tannin.

tan-nin (tan′in), *n.* [F. *tanin, tannin,* < *tan,* tan.] In *chem.*, any of a group of astringent vegetable principles or compounds, as the reddish compound which gives the tanning properties to oak-bark or tan, or the whitish compound (the common tannin, or tannic acid) which occurs in large quantities in nutgalls.

tan-ning (tan′ing), *n.* The process or art of converting hides or skins into leather; also, a making brown, as by exposure to the sun; also, a thrashing (colloq.: as, "They parleyed a minute, the farmer to inquire if they [boys] had had a mortal good *tanning* and were satisfied," G. Meredith's "Ordeal of Richard Feverel," ii.).

tan-rec (tan′rek), *n.* Same as *tenrec.*

tan-sy (tan′zi), *n.*; pl. *-sies* (-ziz). [OF. *tanesie* (F. *tanaisie*), < ML. *athanasia*, tansy, < Gr. ἀθανασία, immortality: see *athanasia*.] Any plant of the asteraceous genus *Tanacetum,* esp. *T. vulgare,* a coarse, strong-scented herb with toothed pinnate leaves and corymbs of yellow flowers, native in the Old World and now a common weed in North America, and formerly much used in cookery and in medicine; also, any of various allied or similar plants.

tan-ta-late (tan′tạ-lāt), *n.* [See *tantalum.*] In *chem.,* a salt of tantalic acid.—**tan-tal′ic** (-tal′ik), *a.* Of or pertaining to tantalum.—**tan′ta-lite** (-līt), *n.* A tantalate of iron occurring as a heavy black mineral, crystallized and massive.

tan-ta-lize (tan′tạ-līz), *v. t.*; *-lized, -lizing.* [From *Tantalus:* see *Tantalus.*] To torment with or as with the sight of something desired but out of reach; tease by arousing expectations that are repeatedly disappointed: as, "I will *tantalize* her: keep her with me, expecting, doubting" (C. Brontë's "Shirley," xxix.).—**tan″-ta-li-za′tion** (-li-zā′shọn), *n.*—**tan′ta-liz-er** (-lī-zėr), *n.*—**tan′ta-liz-ing-ly,** *adv.*

tan-ta-lum (tan′tạ-lum), *n.* [NL., < L. *Tantalus,* Tantalus: cf. *niobium.*] Chem. sym., Ta; at. wt., 181.5; sp. gr., 16.64. A rare element usually associated with niobium.

Tan-ta-lus (tan′tạ-lus), *n.* [L., < Gr. Τάνταλος.] In *Gr. myth.,* a king, son of Zeus and father of Pelops and Niobe, condemned for revealing the secrets of the gods, or for some other offense, to stand in Tartarus up to his chin in water, under branches laden with fruit, the water or fruit receding whenever he sought to satisfy thirst or hunger; hence [*l. c.*], something suggesting this punishment; a stand containing decanters which, though in plain sight, are secured by a lock.

tan-ta-mount (tan′tạ-mount), *a.* [Appar. < F. *tant* (< L. *tantum*), so much, + E. *amount*.] Equivalent, as in value, force, effect, or signification: as, "Damages *tantamount* to a sentence of perpetual imprisonment were demanded by the plaintiff" (Macaulay's "Hist. of Eng.," ii.).

tan-tar-a (tan-tar′ạ), *n.* [Imit.] A blast of a trumpet or horn; also, any similar sound.

tan-tiv-y (tan-tiv′i). [Appar. imit.] **I.** *adv.* At full gallop; at full speed: as, to ride *tantivy.* Sometimes used interjectionally. **II.** *n.*; pl. *-ies* (-iz). A gallop; a rush; a rapid movement; also, a High-church Tory of about the time of James II. **III.** *a.* Swift; rapid; also, pertaining to the tantivies (High-church Tories).

tan-tra (tan′trạ), *n.* [Skt., thread, warp, fundamental doctrine, < *tan-,* stretch: see *tend¹.*] [Often *cap.*] One of a class of Hindu religious works in Sanskrit, of comparatively late date, related to the puranas, in which mysticism and magic play a great part; also, one of a class of Buddhist works of a somewhat similar character.

tan-trum (tan′trum), *n.*; pl. *-trums.* [Origin obscure.] A burst of ill humor; a fit of ill temper or passion: as, "the *tantrums* of a spoiled child" (W. Churchill's "Modern Chronicle," ii. 11); "Only that wench in one of her *tantrums!*" (S. J. Weyman's "Gentleman of France," ix.). [Colloq.]

tan=yard (tan′yärd), *n.* A yard or inclosure where tanning is carried on.

Ta-o-ism (tä′ō-izm), *n.* [Chinese *tao,* 'the way.'] A religious system considered to be founded on the doctrines of an ancient Chinese philosopher, Lao-tsze (born about 604 B.C.), generally ranked with Confucianism and Buddhism as one

Tansy (*Tanacetum vulgare*).— *a,* a disk-flower; *b,* a ray-flower; *c,* an achene.

of the three religions of China.—**Ta′o-ist**, *n.* An adherent of Taoism.—**Ta-o-is′tic**, *a.*

tap¹ (tap), *n.* [AS. *tæppa* = D. *tap* = G. *zapfen* = Icel. *tappi*, tap: cf. *tampion*.] A cylindrical stick, long plug, or stopper for closing an opening through which liquid is drawn, as in a cask; a spigot; also, a faucet or cock; also, the liquor drawn through a particular tap (colloq.); a particular kind or quality of drink (colloq.); a tap-house or tap-room (colloq.); also, something resembling a tap in shape, as a tap-root; an instrument for cutting the thread of an internal screw; also, the act of tapping; a hole made in tapping, as one in a pipe to furnish connection for a branch pipe; a branch pipe, branch line, etc., by which something is tapped.—**on tap**, ready to be drawn off and served, as liquor in a cask; on draught; fig., ready for immediate use; also, furnished with a tap or cock, as a barrel containing liquor.—**tap¹**, *v. t.*; *tapped, tapping.* [AS. *tæppian.*] To furnish (a cask, etc.) with a tap; draw the tap or plug from (a cask, etc.); pierce (a cask, tree, etc.) so as to let out a contained liquid (as, "If there were any sugar maples accessible, they were *tapped* every year": Roosevelt's "Winning of the West," i. 5); draw liquid from (any vessel or reservoir); hence, to penetrate, reach, etc. (anything), for the purpose of drawing something off (as, to *tap* an electric wire, as for the purpose of taking off a telegraphic message); open up (anything) so as to let out or draw off something from it; also, to draw off (liquid) by drawing out or opening a tap, or by piercing the container; draw off from any source; also, to cut an internal screw-thread in (a hole, etc.) with a tap.

tap² (tap), *v.*; *tapped, tapping.* [ME. *tappen*; of imit. origin: cf. OF. F. *taper*, strike, slap.] **I.** *tr.* To strike lightly but audibly, or strike with slight blows (as, "He was . . . gently *tapping* the window-pane with his well-kept finger-nails," Galsworthy's "Dark Flower," i. 2; "Sarah . . . *tapped* the tiles of the floor with the tip of her sunshade," Arnold Bennett's "Helen with the High Hand," ix.); also, to sound or indicate by such blows (as, "She *tapped* time with her fan to the waltz": L. Merrick's "House of Lynch," i.); make, put, etc., by tapping (as, "Jimmy Fort *tapped* out his pipe": Galsworthy's "Saint's Progress," i. 8); also, to strike (the hand, foot, etc.) lightly upon or against something; also, to add a thickness of leather to the sole or heel of (a boot or shoe), as in repairing. **II.** *intr.* To strike lightly but audibly, as to attract attention (as, "Some one *tapped* at the door": Peacock's "Nightmare Abbey," xiii.); strike light blows.—**tap²**, *n.* A light but audible blow (as, "The invalid . . . gave three shaky *taps* on the white post": W. B. Maxwell's "In Cotton Wool," i.); the sound made by this (as, "I hear the *tap* of the elder's cane": Whittier's "Prophecy of Samuel Sewall"); also, a thickness of leather added to the sole or heel of a boot or shoe, as in repairing; *pl.*, *milit.* and *naval*, a signal on a drum, bugle, or trumpet, about fifteen minutes after tattoo, at which all lights in the soldiers' or sailors' quarters must be extinguished.

ta-pa (tä′pä), *n.* [Polynesian.] An unwoven cloth of the Pacific islands, made by steeping and beating the inner bark of a moraceous tree, *Papyrius papyrifera.*

tap-a-de-ra (tap-a-dā′rä), *n.*; *pl.* -*ras* (-räz). [Sp., a cover, < *tapar*, stop up, cover.] A heavy leather housing for the front of a stirrup of a Mexican saddle, to keep the foot from slipping forward and to protect it against thorny underbrush. See cut at *stirrup* (fig. 4). Also **tap-a-de′ro** (-rō); *pl.* -*ros* (-rōz).

tape (tāp), *n.* [AS. *tæppe.*] A long, narrow strip of linen, cotton, or the like, used for tying garments, papers, etc., and for various other purposes; woven material in such strips; also, a string stretched across the finishing-line in a race and broken by the first contestant to cross the line; also, a long, narrow, flexible strip of metal or the like; the strip or ribbon of paper used in a printing telegraph-instrument; also, a tape-measure or tape-line; also, red tape (see under *red²*, *a.*); also, spirituous liquor (slang).—**tape**, *v. t.*; *taped, taping.* To furnish with a tape or tapes; tie up with tape; wind with tape.—**tape′-line**, *n.* A line of tape; esp., a long strip or ribbon, as of linen or steel, marked with subdivisions of the foot or meter for measuring, and sometimes coiled in a case.—**tape′-meas″ure**, *n.* A piece of tape marked with

subdivisions of the foot or meter, esp. one used by tailors, dressmakers, etc.

ta-per (tā′pėr), *n.* [AS. *tapor*, candle. Later senses are perhaps from the verb.] A candle, esp. a very slender one; a long wick coated with wax, tallow, or the like, as for use in lighting candles or gas; also, a spire or slender pyramid; anything having a tapering form; also, gradual diminution of width or thickness in an elongated object; fig., gradual decrease of force, capacity, etc.—**ta′per**, *a.* Long and gradually narrowed toward a point; becoming smaller toward one end; tapering: as, "her *taper* fingers" (Cooper's "Spy," xiii.); "the tall and *taper* spars of a Yankee frigate" (Lever's "Harry Lorrequer," xlv.).—**ta′per**, *v.* **I.** *intr.* To rise like a taper; become gradually slenderer toward one end; grow gradually less. **II.** *tr.* To cause to taper; make gradually smaller toward one end; reduce gradually.—**ta′per-ing-ly**, *adv.*—**ta′per-ness**, *n.*

tap-es-try (tap′es-tri), *n.*; *pl.* -*tries* (-triz). [OF. F. *tapisserie*, < *tapissier*, maker of tapestry, < *tapis*: see *tapis*.] A fabric consisting of a warp upon which colored threads are worked by hand to produce a design, often pictorial, and used for wall-hangings, furniture-coverings, etc. (as, "a curtain of old *tapestry*": George Eliot's "Adam Bede," xliii.); a piece or hanging of this fabric (as, "The heavy *tapestries* and shadowy corners of the huge apartment may be dimly made out": W. Churchill's "Inside of the Cup," vi.); also, a machine-made fabric of similar appearance.—**tapestry carpet**, a carpet resembling Brussels, of which the covering yarns are dyed before weaving so as to produce the intended design in the finished product.—**tap′es-try**, *v. t.*; -*tried*, -*trying.* To furnish, cover, or adorn with or as with tapestry; also, to depict in tapestry.

tap-e-ti (tap′e-ti), *n.* [Brazilian.] A small South American rabbit, *Lepus brasiliensis.*

ta-pe-tum (ta-pē′-tum), *n.*; *pl.* -*ta* (-tä). [NL., < L. *tapete*, < Gr. τάπης (ταπητ-), carpet: cf. *tapis.*] In *bot.*, a layer of cells often investing the archespore in a developing sporangium and absorbed as the spores mature; in *anat.* and *zoöl.*, any of certain membranous layers or the like, as in the choroid or retina.

Tapeti.

tape-worm (tāp′wėrm), *n.* Any of various flat or tape-like cestode worms (genus *Tænia* and allied genera) parasitic when adult in the alimentary canal of man and other vertebrates: usually characterized by having the larval and adult stages in different hosts. Cf. *hydatid* and *measle.*

tap-house (tap′hous), *n.* A house where liquor is kept on tap for sale; a drinking-house; also, a tap-room.

tap-i-o-ca (tap-i-ō′kä), *n.* [Sp. and Pg. *tapioca*, of Brazilian origin.] A granular, farinaceous food-substance prepared from cassava starch by drying while moist on heated plates: used for making puddings, thickening soups, etc.

ta-pir (tā′pėr), *n.* [Brazilian.] Any of various stout-bodied ungulate mammals (family *Tapiridæ*), mostly of tropical America, resembling swine and having a flexible snout or proboscis. See cut on following page.

tap-is (tap′is, F. tȧ-pē′), *n.* [OF. F. *tapis*, < ML. *tapetium*, < Gr. τάπητιον, dim. of τάπης (ταπητ-), carpet, rug, cloth covering: cf. *tapestry* and *tapetum.*] A covering of carpet, tapestry, or other heavy material, as for a floor, wall, or table.—**on the tapis** (tr.

Tapeworm, in several sections, with intervening joints omitted. — *a*, several segments, enlarged; *h*, head, enlarged.

(variable) ḍ as d or j, ṣ as s or sh, ṭ as t or ch, ẓ as z or zh; *o*, F. cloche; ü, F. menu; ċh, Sc. loch; ṅ, F. bonbon; **′**, primary accent; **″**, secondary accent; †, obsolete; <, from; +, and; =, equals. See also lists at beginning of book.

F. *sur le tapis*), on the table-cloth or table, or under discussion or consideration.

tap-per[1] (tap′ẽr), *n.* One who or that which taps, as trees for the sap or juice.

tap-per[2] (tap′ẽr), *n.* One who or that which taps or strikes lightly.

tap-pet (tap′et), *n.* [Cf. *tap*[2].] In *mach.*, a projection, cam, or the like which intermittently

American Tapir (*Tapirus americanus*).

comes in contact with another part to which it communicates or from which it receives an intermittent motion. —**tap′pet=rod**, *n.* In *mach.*, a longitudinally reciprocating rod bearing a tappet or tappets.

tap-ping[1] (tap′ing), *n.* The act of one who or that which taps casks, etc.; that which is drawn by tapping; a hole or outlet made in or as in tapping.

tap-ping[2] (tap′ing), *n.* The act of one who or that which taps or strikes lightly; the sound so made (as, "A furtive *tapping* was heard at the door": Barrie's "Sentimental Tommy," xvii.).

tap-poon (ta-pön′), *n.* [Sp. *tapón*, stopper, plug.] A portable dam of wood, metal, or the like, for temporarily damming the water in an irrigation ditch so that it will overflow the adjacent fields.

tap=room (tap′röm), *n.* A room, as in a tavern, in which liquor is kept on tap.

tap=root (tap′röt), *n.* In *bot.*, a main root descending downward from the radicle and giving off small lateral roots.

tap-ster (tap′stẽr), *n.* [AS. *tæppestre*, fem.] A person, orig. a woman, employed in a tavern to tap or draw the liquor to be served to guests.

tar[1] (tär), *n.* [AS. *teru, teoru*, = D. and G. *teer* = Icel. *tjara*, Sw. *tjära*, Dan. *tjære*, tar; prob. ult. akin to E. *tree*.] A dark-colored viscid product obtained by the destructive distillation of certain organic substances, as coal, wood, etc.; coal-tar or wood-tar (see these words); also, coal-tar pitch. — **tar**[1], *v. t.; tarred, tarring*. To smear or cover with or as with tar. — **to tar and feather a person**, to pour heated tar over him and then cover him with feathers: a punishment sometimes inflicted upon an obnoxious person, as by a mob.

tar[2] (tär), *v. t.; tarred, tarring*. [ME. *terren*: cf. AS. *tergan, tyrgan*, irritate, vex.] To vex or provoke; incite. [Now archaic or prov.]

tar[3] (tär), *n.* [Appar. < *tarpaulin*.] A sailor.

tar′a-did-dle, *n.* See *tarradiddle*.

tar-an-tass (tar-ạn-tas′), *n.* [Russ. *tarantas*.] A large four-wheeled Russian carriage with a covered boat-shaped body fixed to two parallel longitudinal wooden bars.

tar-an-tel-la (tar-ạn-tel′ä),

Tarantass.

n. [It., < *Taranto* (L. *Tarentum*), town in southeastern Italy; traditionally associated with the tarantula and tarantism.] A rapid, whirling southern Italian dance in very quick sextuple (orig. quadruple) rhythm, usually performed by a single couple, and formerly supposed to be a remedy for tarantism; also, a piece of music for this dance or in its rhythm.

tar-an-tism (tar′ạn-tizm), *n.* [From *Taranto*, in Italy: see *tarantella*.] A nervous affection characterized by an uncontrollable impulse to dance; esp., that prevalent in southern Italy from the 15th to the 17th century and popularly attributed to the bite of the tarantula.

ta-ran-tu-la (tạ-ran′tū̇-lä), *n.* [ML., < It. *tarantola*, < *Taranto*, in Italy: see *tarantella*.] A large spider of southern Europe, *Lycosa tarantula*, whose bite was fabled to cause tarantism; any of various related spiders; also, any of various large, hairy spiders of the family *Theraphosidæ*, of the warmer parts of America, as *Eurypelma hentzi*, a common species of the southwestern U. S., whose bite is painful if not dangerous.

ta-rax-a-cum (tạ-rak′sạ-kum), *n.* [NL.; through Ar. from Pers.] Any of the composite plants, mostly stemless herbs, constituting the cichoriaceous genus *Taraxacum*, as the dandelion; also, the root of the dandelion, used in medicine as a tonic, diuretic, and aperient, and esteemed in affections of the liver.

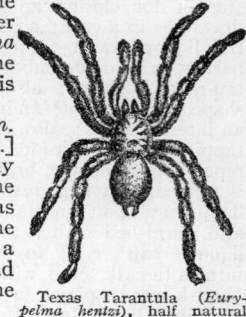

Texas Tarantula (*Eurypelma hentzi*), half natural size.

tar-boosh (tär-bösh′), *n.*¹ [Ar. *tarbūsh*.] A cap of cloth or felt (nearly always red) having a tassel (usually of dark-blue silk) at the crown, worn by Mohammedan men either by itself or as the inner part of the turban. Cf. *fez*.

tar=brush (tär′brush), *n.* A brush for applying tar. — **a dash** (or **a touch**) **of the tar=brush**, a dash of negro or Indian blood in one's veins, showing in the complexion.

Tarboosh.

tar-di-grade (tär′di-grād). [L. *tardigradus*, < *tardus*, slow, + *gradi*, walk, go.] **I.** *a.* Slow in pace or movement; in *zoöl.*, belonging to the *Tardigrada*, an old division of mammals including the sloths; also, belonging to the *Tardigrada*, a group of aquatic animalcules, sometimes considered as an order of arachnids and sometimes as a class of arthropods. **II.** *n.* A tardigrade animal.

tar-di-ly (tär′di-li), *adv.* In a tardy manner; slowly; also, after the proper or expected time; late; sometimes, with delay and reluctance. — **tar′di-ness**, *n.*

tar-do (tär′dō), *a.* [It., < L. *tardus*, slow.] In *music*, slow; noting a passage to be rendered slowly.

tar-dy (tär′di), *a.; compar. tardier; superl. tardiest*. [OF. F. *tardif*, < L. *tardus*, slow.] Moving or acting slowly, slow, or sluggish (as, "Some *tardy* cripple bore the countermand," Shakspere's "Richard III.," ii. 1. 89; "the *tardy* conveyance of ships and chariots," Johnson's "Rasselas," vi.); also, late or behindhand (as, to be *tardy* in one's payments); sometimes, delaying through reluctance.

tare[1] (tär). Archaic preterit of *tear*[1].

tare[2] (tär), *n.* [ME. *tare*; origin uncertain.] Any of various vetches, esp. *Vicia sativa*; also, the seed of a vetch; also, in Biblical use, some injurious weed, possibly the darnel (often fig.).

tare[3] (tär), *n.* [OF. F. *tare* = It. and Sp. *tara*, < Ar. *taraha*, reject.] The weight of the wrapping, receptacle, or conveyance containing goods; a deduction from the gross weight to allow for this; also, of a motor-vehicle, the weight without cargo and passengers, or without these and the fuel-supply and other necessary equipment. — **tare**[3], *v. t.; tared, taring*. To ascertain, note, or allow for, the tare of.

targe[1] (tärj), *n.* [OF. F. *targe*; from Teut.] A shield or buckler: as, "From the walls the attendant band Snatch'd sword and *targe*, with hurried hand" (Scott's "Lady of the Lake," iii. 18). [Archaic.]

targe[2] (tärj), *v. t.; targed, targing*. [Origin uncertain.] To question closely; keep under strict discipline; reprimand or scold; beat or thrash. [Sc.]

tar-get (tär′get), *n.* [OF. *targuete*, var. of *targete*, dim. of *targe*, E. *targe*[1].] A small, round shield or buckler (as, "The plebeian [fought] on foot, with his club and *target*," Hallam's "Europe during the Middle Ages," ii. 2: now hist.: see cut on following page); also, a device marked with concentric circles, set up to be aimed at in shooting practice or contests; any object used for this purpose; anything fired at; fig., anything aimed at; esp., an object of abuse, scorn, derision, etc. (as, "Henslowe had made him the *target* of a vulgar and embittered hostility": Mrs. H. Ward's "Robert Elsmere," xxiii.); a butt; also, a shooting-match; the score made at it; also, a disk-shaped signal, as at a railroad-switch; also, the sliding sight on a leveling-rod.—**tar-get-eer'** (-ge-tēr'), *n.* A soldier armed with a target or shield.

Target.— *a*, Highland target of wood and leather; *b*, back of target, with leather sleeve and handle; *c*, target in profile, showing long protruding spike.

Tar-gum (tär'gum), *n.*; pl. *-gums* (-gumz). [Aram. *targūm*, 'interpretation.'] Each of a number of translations or paraphrases of the various divisions of the Hebrew Old Testament in the Aramaic language or dialect, dating from the time when Aramaic superseded Hebrew as the spoken language of the Jews.—**Tar'gum-ist**, *n.* One of the translators and commentators who prepared the Targums; also, one versed in the language and literature of the Targums.—**Tar'gum-is'tic**, *a.*

tar-heel (tär'hēl), *n.* A native or inhabitant of North Carolina: in allusion to tar as one of the principal products of the State. [Colloq.]

tar-iff (tar'if), *n.* [= F. *tarif*, < It. *tariffa*, < Ar. *ta'rīf*, notification, information.] An official list or table showing the duties or customs imposed by a government on exports or, esp., imports; the system of duties so imposed; any duty in such a list or system; hence, any table or scale of charges, as of a hotel (as, "Upon no consideration did you ask for the *tariff*. It was not good form to mention prices at the Grand Babylon": Arnold Bennett's "Grand Babylon Hotel," i.).— **tar'iff**, *v. t.* To subject to a tariff or a tariff-duty; also, to put a valuation upon according to a tariff.

tar-la-tan (tär'la-tan), *n.* [F. *tarlatane*, earlier *tarnatane*; appar. of East Indian origin.] A thin, transparent, wiry muslin of very open texture.

tarn (tärn), *n.* [ME. *tarne, terne*; from Scand.] A small mountain lake or pool (orig. north. Eng. and Sc.: as, "He did a lot of trout fishing in the *tarns* high up in the hills," Buchan's "Three Hostages," xi.); in general, a pool, lake, or lake-like body of water (prov. or literary).

tar-nish (tär'nish), *v.* [F. *ternir* (terniss-), < *terne*, dull; origin uncertain.] **I.** *tr.* To dull the luster of (esp. a metallic surface by oxidation, etc.); discolor; cause to fade; also, to alter the luster or surface-color of (esp. a metallic mineral); fig., to diminish or destroy the purity of, cast a stain upon, or sully (as, "He reminded them how their conduct was *tarnishing* the glory which they had acquired": Motley's "Dutch Republic," iv. 4). **II.** *intr.* To grow dull or discolored; lose or change luster; fig., to become dim or sullied. —**tar'nish**, *n.* The condition of being tarnished; loss of brightness; discoloration; alteration of the luster or surface-color; stain or blemish; also, a tarnished coating.—**tar'nish-a-ble**, *a.* Liable to tarnish.

ta-ro (tä'rō), *n.*; pl. *-ros* (-rōz). [Polynesian.] A stemless araceous plant, *Caladium colocasia*, cultivated in tropical regions, in the Pacific islands and elsewhere, for its tuberous, starchy, edible root; also, the root. Cf. *caladium, dasheen, eddoes*, and *poi*.

tar-pau-lin (tär-pâ'lin), *n.* [Said to be < *tar*[1] + *pall*[1], *v.*] A covering or sheet of canvas, or sometimes of other material, waterproofed with tar, paint, or the like, used to protect something exposed to the weather or the wet; canvas or other material so waterproofed; a sailor's hat made of or covered with such material; also, a sailor (as, "bandy-legged *tarpaulins*," Stevenson's "David Balfour," xxx.: now rare).— **tar-pau'lin**, *v. t.* To cover with tarpaulin.

tar-pau-ling (tär-pâ'ling), *n.* Same as *tarpaulin*.

Tar-pe-ian (tär-pē'an), *a.* [L. *Tarpeius*.] Noting or pertaining to a rock on the Capitoline Hill at Rome from which persons convicted of treason to the state were hurled.

tar-pon (tär'pon), *n.*; pl. *tarpons* or (esp. collectively)

tarpon. [Origin uncertain.] A large fish, *Tarpon atlanticus*, of the warmer waters of the Atlantic, with an elongate compressed body. Also **tar'pum** (-pum).

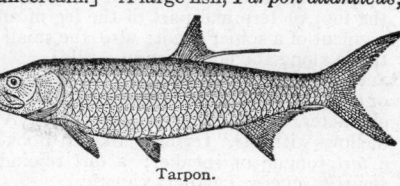

Tarpon.

tar-ra-did-dle (tar'a-did-l or tar-a-did'l), *n.* [Cf. *diddle*[2].] A petty falsehood; a fib; a lie: as, "'You didn't tell such *tarradiddles* once,' she urged" (L. Merrick's "Conrad in Quest of His Youth," x.). [Colloq., Eng.]

tar-ra-gon (tar'a-gon), *n.* [Obs. F. *targon* (mod. F. *estragon*); from Ar., and perhaps ult. < Gr. δράκων, E. *dragon*.] An old-world asteraceous plant, *Artemisia dracunculus*, whose aromatic leaves are used for flavoring.

tar-ri-ance (tar'i-ans), *n.* Tarrying; delay; stay: as, "I must have your Highness back to your tent, and that without further *tarriance*" (Scott's "Talisman," xi.).

tar-ri-er (tar'i-ėr), *n.* One who tarries, delays, or stays.

tar-ry[1] (tär'i), *a.* Of or like tar; smeared with tar (as, "a bit of *tarry* string": Stevenson's "Treasure Island," iv.).

tar-ry[2] (tar'i), *v.*; *-ried, -rying*. [ME. *tarien*; origin obscure.] **I.** *tr.* To delay†; also, to wait for, or await (archaic: as, "He plodded on his way, *tarrying* no further question," Scott's "Guy Mannering," viii.). **II.** *intr.* To delay or be tardy in acting, starting, coming, etc. (as, "Why *tarriest* thou? arise, and be baptized," Acts, xxii. 16; "She was not anxious but puzzled that her husband *tarried*," Eden Phillpotts's "Grey Room," iii.); linger or loiter; also, to wait (as, "Let trouble have rest, Knowing I *tarry* for thee": Tennyson's "Maud," iii. 1); also, to remain or stay, as in a place (as, "I have *tarried* here to enjoy the ministry of that worthy man": Scott's "Abbot," ii.); sojourn.—**tar'ry**[2], *n.* Delay†; also, a stay or sojourn (archaic).

tar-sal (tär'sal), *a.* [NL. *tarsalis*.] Of or pertaining to the tarsus of the foot or leg; also, pertaining to the tarsi of the eyelids.—**tarsal joint**, a joint of the tarsus; specif., in man, the joint between the tibia and fibula and the astragalus or tarsus; a corresponding joint in other vertebrates; in birds, the joint between the tibia and the metatarsus, or, strictly, between the tarsal elements of the tibia and the tarsal elements of the metatarsus.—**tar'sal**, *n.* A tarsal bone, joint, or the like.

tar-si-er (tär'si-ėr), *n.* [F., < *tarse*, < NL. *tarsus*: see *tarsus*.] A small, nocturnal, arboreal lemuroid quadruped, *Tarsius spectrum*, of the East Indies, in which the tarsus is extremely long.

tar-sus (tär'sus), *n.*; pl. *-si* (-sī). [NL., < Gr. ταρσός, flat surface, flat of the foot, edge of the eyelid.] In *anat.* and *zoöl.*, the proximal portion or segment of the foot; the collection of bones between the tibia and the metatarsus, entering into the construction of the ankle-joint, and into that part of the foot known in man as the instep; the part of the leg (properly of the foot) of a bird between the bases of the toes and the first joint above, the bone of this section consisting

Tarsier.

of both tarsal and metatarsal elements (also called *shank*); the foot or terminal part of the leg of an insect; the distal segment of a spider's foot; also, the small plate of connective tissue along the border of an eyelid.

tart[1] (tärt), *a.* [AS. *teart*, severe.] Sharp to the taste, sour, or acid (as, *tart* apples; an agreeably *tart* flavor); fig., sharp in character, spirit, or expression (as, "A *tart* temper never mellows with age," Irving's "Sketch-Book," "Rip Van Winkle; a *tart* tongue or speaker; a *tart* rejoinder); pungently or smartly severe; cutting; caustic.

tart[2] (tärt), *n.* [OF. F. *tarte*; origin uncertain.] A shell or form of pastry, commonly small and saucer-shaped, filled with cooked fruit or other sweetened preparation, and having no crust, or only narrow strips of pastry, over the top; also, a covered pie containing fruit or the like.

tar-tan[1] (tär'tan). [Appar. < OF. F. *tiretaine*, linsey-woolsey.] **I.** *n.* A woolen or worsted cloth woven with lines or stripes of different colors crossing at right angles so as to form a definite pattern, worn chiefly by the Scottish Highlanders, each clan having its distinctive pattern; also, the pattern or design itself; also, any fabric having a similar pattern. **II.** *a.* Made of tartan (as, "the ... *tartan* mantle of the Highlands": Scott's "Castle Dangerous," ii.); of, pertaining to, or resembling tartan (as, *tartan* patterns; *tartan* silks).

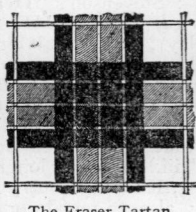

The Fraser Tartan.   The Macpherson Tartan.

tar-tan[2] (tär'tan), *n.* [F. *tartane*, < It. *tartana*; perhaps from Ar.] A single-masted vessel with a lateen sail and a jib, used in the Mediterranean.

tar-tar[1] (tär'tär), *n.* [OF. F. *tartre*, < ML. *tartarum*; perhaps from Ar.] The potassium bitartrate deposited from wines; specif., the partially purified product midway between the crude form or 'argol' and the further purified form or 'cream of tartar' (see under *cream*, *n.*); also, a hard substance deposited on the teeth by the saliva, consisting of calcium phosphate, mucus, etc.—**tartar emetic**, potassium antimonyl tartrate, a poisonous salt with a sweetish metallic taste, occurring in white crystals or as a white granular powder: used in medicine as an emetic, expectorant, and diaphoretic, and in dyeing as a mordant.

Tartan.

Tar-tar[2] (tär'tär). [= *Tatar*. *Tartar* is the common and long-established form in literary and general use; *Tatar*, a more recent form, with more precise ethnological application.] **I.** *n.* A Tatar (as, "They . . . sacked and plundered everything, as completely as a horde of *Tartars* would have done": Defoe's "Robinson Crusoe," ii. 3); [*cap.* or *l. c.*] a savage, intractable person; a person of irritable temper; as applied to a woman, a shrew or vixen; also, one who when attacked or roused proves unexpectedly troublesome to deal with (commonly in the phrase 'to catch a Tartar': as, "He had caught more of a spiritual *Tartar* than he had expected," S. Butler's "Way of All Flesh," lviii.). **II.** *a.* Tatar.

Tar-tar[3]† (tär'tär), *n.* Tartarus.—**Tar-ta're-an** (-tā'rē-an), *a.* Of or pertaining to Tartarus; infernal.

tar-ta-re-ous (tär-tā'rē-us), *a.* Of the nature of tartar; tartar-like; in *bot.*, having a rough, crumbling surface, as the thallus of certain lichens.

Tar-ta-ri-an (tär-tā'ri-an), *a.* [See *Tartar*[2], and cf. *Tata-*

rian.] Of or pertaining to the Tartars or Tatars; Tatar.—**Tartarian lamb.** Same as *Scythian lamb* (see under *Scythian*, *a.*).—**Tar-ta'ri-an**, *n.* A Tartar or Tatar.

tar-tar-ic (tär-tar'ik), *a.* Pertaining to or derived from tartar: as, *tartaric* acid (an organic acid, $C_4H_6O_6$, having several isomeric modifications, the common or dextrorotatory form being a colorless crystalline compound obtained from grapes, etc.).

tar-tar-ize (tär'tär-īz), *v. t.*; *-ized*, *-izing*. In *chem.*, to impregnate, combine, or treat with tartar, or potassium bitartrate.—**tar''tar-i-za'tion** (-i-zā'shon), *n.*

tar-tar-ous (tär'ta-rus), *a.* Consisting of or containing tartar.

Tar-ta-rus (tär'ta-rus), *n.* [L., < Gr. Τάρταρος.] A deep and sunless abyss, described by Homer as being as far below Hades as earth is below heaven, and by later poets as the place of punishment for the spirits of the wicked; also, Hades, or the lower world in general.

tar-tine (tär-tēn'), *n.* [F., < *tarte*, E. *tart*[2].] A slice of bread spread with jam, honey, or the like, or with butter.

tart-let (tärt'let), *n.* A small tart.

tart-ly (tärt'li), *adv.* In a tart manner; acidly; sharply.—**tart'ness**, *n.*

tar-trate (tär'trāt), *n.* In *chem.*, a salt of tartaric acid.—**tar'trat-ed** (-trā-ted), *a.* Formed into a tartrate; combined with tartaric acid.

Tar-tuffe, Tar-tufe (tär-túf', F. tär-tüf), *n.* [From the principal character in Molière's comedy of that name.] A hypocritical pretender to piety.

ta-sim-e-ter (ta-sim'e-tėr), *n.* [Gr. τάσις, stretching, tension: see *-meter*.] An electrical device (invented by Thomas A. Edison) for determining minute changes in temperature, etc., by means of the changes in pressure caused by an expanding or contracting solid.—**tas-i-met'ric** (tas-i-met'rik), *a.*—**ta-sim'e-try**, *n.*

task (tåsk), *n.* [OF. *tasque*, *tasche* (F. *tâche*), < ML. *tasca*, for *taxa*, tax, imposition, < L. *taxare*, E. *tax*.] A tax† or impost†; also, a definite amount of work or labor imposed on or exacted from a person (as, "Ye shall not minish ought from your bricks of your daily *task*": Ex. v. 19); a piece of work assigned or falling to a person or necessary to be done, or a duty (as, "In every house . . . the morning *tasks* were early done": G. W. Cable's "Bonaventure," ii. 10); specif., a portion of study imposed by a teacher, or a lesson to be learned (archaic); in general, any piece of work for doing (as, "An easy *task* it is to win our own," Shakspere's "Richard II.," iii. 2. 191; "How oft in pleasing *tasks* we wear the day!" Pope's "To Mr. Jervas," 17); a matter of considerable labor or difficulty (as, "What to shun will no great knowledge need, But what to follow, is a *task* indeed": Pope's "Moral Essays," iii. 200).—**to take to task**, to call to account, as for fault; deal plainly with in blame or censure: as, "He *took* himself *to task* for his bad sympathies in reference to Roger Chillingworth" (Hawthorne's "Scarlet Letter," xi.).—**task**, *v. t.* To tax†; also, to impose a task on; assign a definite amount of work to; also, to subject to severe or excessive labor or exertion (as, "He . . . *tasked* and strained his brain with night studies till his health sank under it": Mrs. Stowe's "Oldtown Folks," ii.); put a strain upon (powers, resources, etc.: as, "They had to *task* their ingenuity to provide shelter and keep from freezing," Irving's "Captain Bonneville," xvi.); also, to take to task†, or censure†.—**task'er**, *n.*—**task'mas''ter**, *n.* One whose function it is to assign tasks to others; an overseer; in general, one who imposes tasks, or burdens with labor.—**task'mis''tress**, *n.*—**task'=work**, *n.* Work imposed or performed as a task; also, piece-work.

Tas-ma-ni-an (taz-mā'ni-an), *a.* Of or pertaining to Tasmania, an island south of Australia.—**Tasmanian devil**, a fero-

Tasmanian Devil.

cious, burrowing, carnivorous marsupial, *Sarcophilus ursinus*, of Tasmania, about the size of a badger; the ursine dasyure.— **Tasmanian wolf.** Same as *thylacine*.

tass (tas), *n.* [OF. F. *tasse*, prob. from Ar.: cf. *demi-tasse*.] A drinking-cup; a small goblet; also, its contents. [Now chiefly Sc.]

tas-sel¹ (tas′l), *n.* Same as *tercel*. [Obs. or archaic.]

tas-sel² (tas′l), *n.* [OF. *tassel*, a fastening (as for a cloak); origin uncertain.] A pendent ornament consisting commonly of a bunch of threads, small cords, or strands hanging from a roundish knob or head; also, something resembling this, as the inflorescence of certain plants, esp. that at the summit of the stalk of Indian corn.— **tas′sel²**, *v.*; -seled or -selled, -seling or -selling. **I.** *tr.* To furnish or adorn with or as with tassels (as, "the slender twigs of the maple, then *tasseled* with their clusters of small red flowers": Parkman's "Oregon Trail," xxvii.); also, to form into a tassel or tassels; also, to remove the tassel from (growing Indian corn), as in order to improve the crop. **II.** *intr.* Of Indian corn, etc., to put forth tassels.

tass-es (tas′ez), *n. pl.* [Cf. OF. F. *tassette*, piece of armor for the thigh, orig. dim. of OF. *tasse*, pouch, purse; from Teut.] In *armor*, a series of articulated, slightly overlapping plates or splints depending from the cuirass and forming a protection for the thighs and the lower part of the trunk. Also **tas′sets.**

tast-a-ble (tās′ta̤-bl), *a.* That may be tasted.

taste (tāst), *v.*; tasted, tasting. [OF. *taster* (F. *tâter*), try by touching, try, taste, appar. from a freq. of L. *taxare*, touch sharply: see *tax*.] **I.** *tr.* To touch†; examine by touch†; feel† or handle†; test† or try†; also, to try the flavor or quality of (something) by means of the sense of taste, as by taking a little into the mouth (as, to *taste* food in cooking, in order to judge of the seasoning; to *taste* teas for the market);

Corselet with Tasses; 16th century.

try by eating or drinking a little, or eat or drink a little of (as, they barely *tasted* the dishes before them; "Darius, who had not *tasted* food all day, could not eat," Arnold Bennett's "Clayhanger," i. 5); eat or drink (a small quantity: as, "I have not *tasted* a morsel these two days past," H. Mackenzie's "Man of Feeling," xxvi.); also, to perceive or distinguish the flavor of by the sense of taste (as, to *taste* the wine in a sauce; with this cold I cannot *taste* anything); hence, to perceive by some other sense, esp. smell (now poetic or prov.); also, to have or get experience, esp. a slight experience, of (as, "*Taste* the joy That springs from labor," Longfellow's "Masque of Pandora," vi.; "Directly I came into the London atmosphere, *tasting* freedom, *tasting* irresponsibility . . . my discipline fell from me," H. G. Wells's "Tono-Bungay," ii. 1. § 2); have carnal knowledge of†; also, to relish, enjoy, or appreciate (archaic or prov.: as, "He *tasted* the merits of the work like the connoisseur he was," Stevenson's "Master of Ballantrae," ix.); also, to impart a flavor to (now rare). **II.** *intr.* To feel, as by touch†; also, to try the flavor or quality of something by the sense of taste; take a taste, as of food, drink, etc.; eat or drink a little (*of*); also, to perceive or distinguish the flavor or taste of anything; also, to have experience, or make trial in experience, of something (as, "Have you ever *tasted* of prison, Peyrol?" J. Conrad's "Rover," vi.); also, to have a particular flavor or taste (as, the milk *tastes* sour; this wine *tastes* of the cask); fig., to smack or savor (esp. with *of*).— **taste,** *n.* Touch†; test† or trial†; also, the act or an act of tasting food or the like; also, the sense by which the flavor or savor of things is perceived when they are brought into contact with special organs of the mouth (see *gustatory bud*, under *gustatory*); a particular sensation excited in these organs by something (as, dentifrice that leaves a pleasant *taste* in the mouth); the flavor or quality of a thing as perceived by these organs (as, "The *taste* of this strange fruit was by no means so pleasant as the appearance": Borrow's "Lavengro," ii.); also, a small quantity of something tasted, eaten, or drunk; a morsel, bit, or sip; also, a slight experience or a sample of something (as, "This was but a *taste* of the misery I was to go through," Defoe's "Robinson Crusoe," i. 2; "For a *taste* take this that follows," Strype's

"Memorials of Cranmer," i. 24); also, a relish, liking, or predilection for something (as, a *taste* for music or books; persons of congenial *tastes*; "There's no accounting for *tastes*, you know," Du Maurier's "Trilby," vi.); also, the sense of what is fitting, harmonious, or beautiful; the perception and enjoyment of what is beautiful; appreciation of what constitutes excellence in the fine arts, literature, etc.; also, manner, style, or general character as showing perception, or lack of perception, of what is fitting or beautiful; characteristic or prevailing style.— **to one's taste,** to one's liking; agreeable or pleasing to one: as, a book quite *to one's taste*; "I don't say there are not worse men. He isn't *to my taste*" (Howells's "Rise of Silas Lapham," v.).— **taste′=bud,** *n.* A gustatory bud. See under *gustatory*.— **taste′ed** (tās′ted), *a.* Having a (specified) taste: as, ill-*tasted*; sour-*tasted*.— **taste′ful,** *a.* Having an agreeable taste (now rare): also, having, displaying, or in accordance with, good taste.— **taste′ful-ly,** *adv.*— **taste′ful-ness,** *n.*— **taste′less,** *a.* Lacking the sense of taste (now rare); also, having no taste or flavor; insipid; fig., dull or uninteresting; also, lacking in good taste; showing want of good taste.— **taste′less-ly,** *adv.*— **taste′less-ness,** *n.*— **tast′er,** *n.*— **tast′y,** *a.* Pleasing to the taste, savory, or appetizing (as, "a *tasty* supper": Arnold Bennett's "Helen with the High Hand," xvii.); also, agreeable or pleasing (as, "Madeline Fox had hinted that it would be a *tasty* thing to go to the Grand, Zenith's most resplendent hotel": Sinclair Lewis's "Arrowsmith," vi.); also, having or showing good taste. [Now colloq. or prov.]— **tast′i-ly,** *adv.*— **tast′i-ness,** *n.*

tat¹ (tat), *v. i.* or *t.*; tatted, tatting. [Origin obscure; first recorded in *tatting*.] To do, or make by, tatting. See *tatting.*

tat² (tat), *n.* Same as *tattoo³*.

ta-ta (tä′tä′), *interj.* [Also *ta, ta*; a nursery word.] Good-by: as, "*Ta, ta*, dear boy!" (L. Merrick's "Actor-Manager," xi.).

Ta-tar (tä′tär). [Of Tatar origin: see *Tartar²*.] **I.** *n.* A member of any of a mingled host of Mongolian, Turkish, and other tribes, who under the leadership of Jenghis Khan (1162–1227) overran Asia and eastern Europe during the middle ages; a member of the descendants of this people variously intermingled with other races and tribes, now inhabiting parts of Russia and central and western Asia; also, their speech or languages, belonging to the Ural-Altaic family. **II.** *a.* Of or pertaining to the Tatars or their languages.— **Ta-ta′ri-an, Ta-tar′ic** (-tä′ri-a̤n, -tar′ik), *a.* Of or pertaining to the Tatars.

ta-tou, ta-tu (tä-tö′ or tä′tö), *n.* [Brazilian.] An armadillo.

tat-ou-ay (tat′ö-ā), *n.* [Brazilian: cf. *tatou*.] A large armadillo, *Tatoua* (*Cabassous*, or *Xenurus*) *unicinctus*, of tropical South America.

ta-tou-pe-ba (tä-tö′pē′bä̤), *n.* Same as *peba*.

tat-ter (tat′ėr), *n.* [ME. *tater*; from Scand.] A torn piece hanging loose from the main part, as of a garment, etc. (as, "His garments were coarse, but there were no *tatters* anywhere," G. W. Cable's "Bonaventure," iii. 1; "The remains of tapestry hung in *tatters* upon the walls," Mrs. Radcliffe's "Romance of the Forest," ii.); sometimes, a separate torn piece; also, *pl.*, torn or ragged clothing.— **tat′ter,** *v. t.* To tear into tatters; wear to tatters.— **tat′ter-de-ma′lion** (-de̤-māl′yo̤n), *n.* [Formation obscure.] A person in tattered clothing; a ragged fellow.— **tat′tered,** *p. a.* Torn to tatters, or ragged (as, "a *tattered* cloak": Gibbon's "Decline and Fall of the Roman Empire," xl.); wearing ragged clothing (as, "a *tattered* negro mounted on a . . . mule": G. W. Cable's "Bonaventure," ii. 1); also, battered† or dilapidated† (as, "ruined, *tattered* cottages": Jane Austen's "Sense and Sensibility," xviii.).

tat-ting (tat′ing), *n.* [Cf. *tat¹*.] The process or work of making a kind of knotted lace of cotton or linen thread with a shuttle ; also, such lace (see cut on following page).

tat-tle (tat′l), *v.*; -tled, -tling. [Cf. LG. *tateln*, gabble, D. *tateren*, stammer.] **I.** *intr.* To talk idly; chatter; prate; gossip; also, to let out secrets; tell tales. **II.** *tr.* To utter idly; disclose by tattling.— **tat′tle,** *n.* The act of tattling; idle or frivolous talk; chatter; gossip.— **tat′tler,** *n.* One who tattles; an idle talker; a telltale; also, any of various limicoline birds of the snipe family (genus *Totanus* and allied genera), noted for their vociferous cries. — **tat′tling-ly**, *adv.*

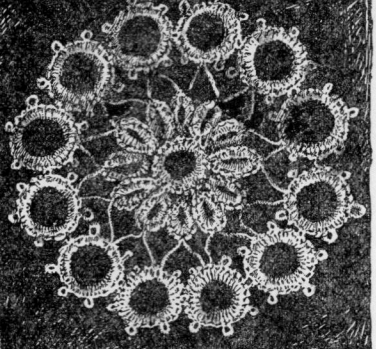

Tatting.

tat-too[1] (ta-tö′), *n.*; pl. *-toos* (-töz′). [D. *taptoe*, lit. 'tap to,' with reference to the turning off of taps of casks, as in the closing of public houses for the night.] A signal on a drum, bugle, or trumpet at night, for soldiers or sailors to repair to their quarters; also, a military entertainment consisting of music and exercises by troops, generally held at night by torch-light or other artificial light; also, in general, a beating of a drum; any beating or pulsation like the beating of a drum (as, the devil's *tattoo*: see under *devil*, *n.*). — **tat-too′**[1], *v. i.*; *-tooed, -tooing.* To beat a tattoo.

tat-too[2] (ta-tö′), *n.*; pl. *-toos* (-töz′). [Polynesian.] The act or practice of marking the skin with indelible patterns, pictures, legends, etc., by making punctures in it and inserting pigments; also, a pattern, picture, legend, etc., so made. — **tat-too′**[2], *v. t.*; *-tooed, -tooing.* To mark (the skin, arms, etc.) with tattoos; also, to put (tattoos) on the skin; fig., to mark, spot, or stain.

tat-too[3] (tat′ö), *n.*; pl. *tattoos* (-öz). [Hind.] An East Indian pony.

tat-too-er (ta-tö′ėr), *n.* One who marks the skin with tattoos. — **tat-too′ing**, *n.* The act, practice, or art of marking the skin with tattoos; the marks or pattern so produced (as, "The elegance of one's *tattooing* was [in the Marquesas Islands] in most cases a sure indication of birth and riches": H. Melville's "Omoo," viii.).

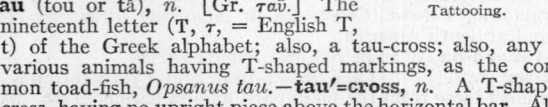

Tattooing.

tat-ty (tat′i), *n.*; pl. *tatties* (-iz). [Hind.] In the East Indies, a screen or mat, esp. of cuscus, hung in a window or door and kept wet to cool and perfume the air.

ta-tu′, *n.* See *tatou*.

tau (tou or tâ), *n.* [Gr. *ταῦ.*] The nineteenth letter (T, *τ*, = English T, t) of the Greek alphabet; also, a tau-cross; also, any of various animals having T-shaped markings, as the common toad-fish, *Opsanus tau.* — **tau′=cross**, *n.* A T-shaped cross, having no upright piece above the horizontal bar. Also called *St. Anthony's cross.*

taught (tât). Preterit and past participle of *teach.*

taunt[1] (tânt), *a.* [Cf. *ataunt.*] *Naut.*, unusually high or tall, as a mast.

taunt[2] (tânt or tänt), *n.* [Origin uncertain: cf. F. *tant pour tant*, 'so much for so much,' one for another.] A smart retort†; also, an insulting gibe or sarcasm; a mocking or scornful reproach or challenge; also, an object of insulting gibes or scornful reproaches† (as, "I will deliver them . . . to be a reproach and a proverb, a *taunt* and a curse": Jer. xxiv. 9). — **taunt**[2], *v.* **I.** *tr.* To make a smart retort to†; banter† or chaff†; also, to reproach in a sarcastic or insulting manner, as with reference to some action or circumstance (as, "The Indians, when fighting, are prone to *taunt* and revile each other," Irving's "Captain Bonneville," vi.; "His partner . . . had *taunted* him with hiding his whereabouts," Maugham's "Moon and Sixpence," x.); twit derisively; invite or urge with taunts (as, "They paraded the ramparts daily . . . *taunting* the besiegers to renewed attempts": Motley's "Dutch Republic," iii. 8); provoke or drive by taunts (as, "The Blackfeet were not to be *taunted* out of their safe shelter": Irving's "Captain Bonneville," xlix.). **II.** *intr.* To utter taunts or scornful reproaches: as, "to

taunt at the ignorance or error of priests" (Strype's "Memorials of Cranmer," i. 30). — **taunt′er**, *n.* — **taunt′ing-ly**, *adv.*

taupe (töp), *n.* [F., < L. *talpa*, mole.] A dark gray with a purplish or brownish tinge.

tau-pie (tâ′pi), *n.* See *tawpie.*

tau-ri-form (tâ′ri-fôrm), *a.* [L. *tauriformis*, < *taurus*, bull, + *forma*, form.] Having the form of a bull; also, shaped like the horns of a bull.

tau-rin, tau-rine[1] (tâ′rin), *n.* [G. *taurin* (first found in ox-bile), < L. *taurus*, bull, ox.] In *chem.*, a neutral crystalline substance obtained from the bile of oxen and other animals, and from muscles, lung-tissue, etc., or as a decomposition product of taurocholic acid.

tau-rine[2] (tâ′rin), *a.* [L. *taurinus*, < *taurus*, bull.] Of, pertaining to, or resembling a bull; bovine; also, pertaining to the zodiacal sign Taurus.

tau-ro-chol-ic (tâ-rō-kol′ik), *a.* [Gr. *ταῦρος*, bull, + *χολή*, gall, bile.] In *chem.*, noting or pertaining to a deliquescent acid occurring as a sodium salt in the bile of oxen, etc.

tau-rom-a-chy (tâ-rom′a-ki), *n.*; pl. *-chies* (-kiz). [Gr. *ταυρομαχία*, < *ταῦρος*, bull, + *μάχεσθαι*, fight.] Bull-fighting; also, a bull-fight.

Tau-rus (tâ′rus), *n.* [L., = Gr. *ταῦρος*, bull.] The Bull, a zodiacal constellation; also, the second sign of the zodiac. See *zodiac.*

taut (tât), *a.* [ME. *touht, toght*, tense, tight: cf. *tight.*] Tightly drawn, or tense (as, "the *taut* rigging of the brig," J. Conrad's "Rescue," i. 3; "clay drums, with heads of *taut* deer-hide," Roosevelt's "Winning of the West," i. 3); not slack; also, in good order or condition; tidy; neat. [Chiefly nautical.] — **taut′en**, *v. t.* or *i.* To make or become taut. — **taut′ly**, *adv.* — **taut′ness**, *n.*

tauto-. Form of Gr. *ταὐτό*, contraction of *τὸ αὐτό*, the same, used in combination.

tau-tog (tâ-tog′), *n.* [N. Amer. Ind., pl. of *taut*, name of the fish.] A food-fish, *Tautoga onitis*, common on the Atlantic coast of the U. S. Also called *blackfish.*

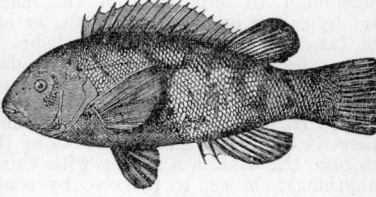

Tautog.

tau-to-log-i-cal (tâ-tō-loj′i-kal), *a.* Pertaining to, characterized by, or using tautology. — **tau-to-log′i-cal-ly**, *adv.*

tau-tol-o-gize (tâ-tol′ō-jīz), *v. i.*; *-gized, -gizing.* To use tautology. — **tau-tol′o-gist**, *n.*

tau-tol-o-gy (tâ-tol′ō-ji), *n.*; pl. *-gies* (-jiz). [LL. *tautologia*, < Gr. *ταυτολογία*, < *ταυτολόγος*, saying the same thing, < *ταὐτό* (see *tauto-*) + *λέγειν*, speak.] The saying of a thing over again, esp. in other words, in the immediate context, without imparting additional force or clearness; a needless repetition in the expression of ideas, as in 'an empty barrel with nothing in it.'

tau-tom-er-ism (tâ-tom′e-rizm), *n.* [Gr. *ταὐτό*, the same (see *tauto-*), + *μέρος*, part.] In *chem.*, the phenomenon exhibited by certain compounds of reacting as if each possessed two or more different structural formulas. — **tau-to-mer′ic** (-tō-mer′ik), *a.*

tau-to-nym (tâ′tō-nim), *n.* [Gr. *ταυτώνυμος*, of the same name, < *ταὐτό* (see *tauto-*) + *ὄνυμα*, name.] In *bot.* and *zoöl.*, a scientific name in which the generic and the specific name are the same, as *Brosme brosme* (the cusk). — **tau-to-nym′ic**, *a.*

tau-toph-o-ny (tâ-tof′ō-ni), *n.* [Gr. *ταυτοφωνία*, < *ταυτόφωνος*, of the same sound, < *ταὐτό* (see *tauto-*) + *φωνή*, sound.] Repetition of the same sound.

tav-ern (tav′ėrn), *n.* [OF. F. *taverne*, < L. *taberna*, hut, shop, tavern: cf. *tabernacle* and *table.*] A place where liquors are sold to be drunk on the premises (as, "some poor, idle, loafing, shiftless object who staggered past her house from the *tavern*": Mrs. Stowe's "Oldtown Folks," iii.); also, a public house for the entertainment of travelers and others; an inn. — **tav′ern-er**, *n.* [OF. F. *tavernier.*] The keeper of a tavern (archaic); also, a frequenter of taverns†.

---

fāt, fāte, fär, fåll, ȧsk, fāre; net, mē, hėr; pin, pīne; not, nōte, mōve, nôr; up, lūte, pùll; oi, oil; ou, out; (lightened) aviȧry, ēlect, agȯny, intȯ, ūnite; (obscured) errȧnt, operȧ, ardẹnt, actọr, natụre; ch, chip; g, go; th, thin; ᴛʜ, then; y, you;

taw[1] (tâ), *v. t.* [AS. *tāwian* = D. *touwen*: see *tool*.] To prepare or dress (some raw material) for use or for further manipulation; soften (skins) by beating; hackle (hemp); specif., to make (skins) into leather by soaking, after preliminary preparation, in a solution of alum and salt; also, to vex† or torment†; also, to beat† or thrash†.

taw[2] (tâ), *n.* [Origin obscure.] A choice or fancy playing-marble with which to shoot; an alley; also, a game at marbles (as, "To kneel and draw The chalky ring, and knuckle down at *taw*": Cowper's "Tirocinium," 307); also, the line from which the players shoot in playing the game.

taw-dry (tâ′dri). [From St. *Audrey* (or *Etheldreda*), patron saint of Ely, in England, reputed to have died from a throat tumor which she took as a judgment upon her for wearing necklaces in her youth.] **I.** *a.* Orig. (in *tawdry lace*), designating a kind of neck-ornament for women sold at the fair held at the shrine of St. Audrey†; hence, of finery, etc., gaudy; showy and cheap; in general, of a pretentious but cheap and tasteless kind (as, "His *tawdry* lampoons are called satires": Goldsmith's "Traveller," Dedication). **II.** *n.* A tawdry lace† (see adj.); also, tawdry finery.—**taw′dri-ly,** *adv.*—**taw′dri-ness,** *n.*

taw-er (tâ′ėr), *n.* One who taws skins.

taw-ny (tâ′ni). [OF. *tané* (F. *tanné*), pp. of *taner* (F. *tanner*), tan.] **I.** *a.* Of a dark-yellowish or dull-yellowish color; tan-colored: as, "A lion's *tawny* skin Around him wrapp'd" (Cowper's tr. Homer's "Iliad," x. 211). **II.** *n.* Tawny color.—**taw′ni-ness,** *n.*

taw-pie, taw-py (tâ′pi), *n.* [Prob. from Scand.] A foolish or thoughtless girl or woman: as, "that *tawpy* the wife of Thomas Wilson" (Galt's "Annals of the Parish," xviii.). [Sc.]

taws, tawse (tâz), *n. pl.* or *sing.* [Appar. < *taw*[1].] A leather strap, usually divided at the end into narrow strips, used as an instrument of punishment by schoolmasters and others: as, "At times a boy got the *tawse* for his negligence, but never a girl" (Ian Maclaren's "Beside the Bonnie Brier Bush," i. 1). [Chiefly Sc.]

tax (taks), *v. t.* [OF. F. *taxer*, tax, < L. *taxare*, touch sharply, handle, rate, appraise, charge, censure, freq. of *tangere*, touch: see *tangent*, and cf. *task* and *taste*.] To estimate or determine the amount or value of (now only in legal use, with reference to assessing costs, etc., judicially); also, to levy or exact contributions of money, etc., from, for the support of the government and for the public needs; impose a tax on; sometimes, to charge (a person) as to amount, for a thing (colloq.); fig., to lay a burden on, or make serious demands on (as, "a process which *taxed* her strength," Galsworthy's "Saint's Progress," ii. 1; "The plays that come here *tax* your patience more than your intellect," L. Merrick's "Position of Peggy Harper," ii. 7); also, to take to task; censure; reprove; charge or accuse (as, "None could *tax* Abner Gale with want of promptitude or decision in an emergency": Whyte-Melville's "Katerfelto," xxix.).—**tax,** *n.* An enforced, usually proportional, contribution, esp. of money, levied on persons, income, land, commodities, etc., for the support of the government and for the public needs; sometimes, a charge, as for a thing (colloq.); fig., a burdensome charge, obligation, or duty; a heavy or oppressive demand.—**direct tax,** a tax demanded from the very persons who will bear the burden of it (not reimbursing themselves at the expense of others), as a poll-tax or an income tax. Cf. *indirect tax*, below.—**income tax.** See under *income*.—**indirect tax,** a tax demanded from persons who, as a general thing, will reimburse themselves at the expense of others, the tax being levied on commodities before they reach the consumer and paid ultimately as part of the market price of these. Cf. *direct tax*, above.—**single tax.** See under *single, a.*

tax-a-ble (tak′sạ-bl), *a.* That may be taxed; subject or liable to taxation.—**tax-a-bil′i-ty** (-bil′i-ti), **tax′a-ble-ness,** *n.*—**tax′a-bly,** *adv.*

tax-a-ceous (tak-sā′shius), *a.* [L. *taxus*, yew.] Belonging to the *Taxaceæ*, or yew family of trees and shrubs.

tax-am-e-ter (tak-sam′e-tėr), *n.* [G.] Same as *taximeter*.

tax-a-tion (tak-sā′shọn), *n.* [OF. F. *taxation*, < L. *taxatio(n-)*.] The act of taxing, or the fact of being taxed; the levying of taxes for the support of the government and for the public needs (as, "*Taxation* . . . is not a means of confiscat-

ing wealth but of raising necessary revenues for the Government": A. W. Mellon's "Taxation," iv.); a tax imposed, or the revenue raised by taxes; also, censure† or reproof†; accusation†.

tax-er (tak′sėr), *n.* One who taxes.

tax-i (tak′si), *n.*; pl. *taxis* (-siz). Shortened form of *taxicab*. [Colloq.]—**tax′i,** *v.; taxied, taxiing.* **I.** *intr.* To ride or travel in a taxicab; also, of an aëroplane or a hydro-aëroplane or seaplane, to move over the surface of the ground or the water under its own power. **II.** *tr.* To cause (an aëroplane or hydro-aëroplane) to taxi. [Colloq.]

tax-i-arch (tak′si-ärk), *n.* [Gr. ταξίαρχος, < τάξις, arrangement, division of troops, + ἄρχειν, lead, rule.] In ancient Greece, a military officer commanding a body of troops varying in size, corresponding to a company or battalion, or to a larger division of an army.

tax-i-cab (tak′si-kab), *n.* [For *taximeter cab*.] A public cab, esp. an automobile cab, fitted with a taximeter.—**tax′i-cab,** *v. i.; -cabbed, -cabbing.* To ride in a taxicab.

tax-i-der-my (tak′si-dėr-mi), *n.* [Gr. τάξις, arrangement, + δέρμα, skin.] The art of preparing and preserving the skins of animals, and stuffing and mounting them in lifelike form.—**tax-i-der′mal, tax-i-der′mic,** *a.*—**tax′i-der-mist,** *n.*

tax-i-me-ter (tak′si-mē-tėr or tak-sim′e-tėr), *n.* [F. *taximètre*, < *taxe*, tax, charge, + Gr. μέτρον, measure: cf. G. *taxameter*.] A device, fitted to a public cab or other vehicle, for automatically computing and indicating the fare due at any moment, in accordance with a fixed tariff of charges; also, a taxicab.

tax-in-o-my (tak-sin′ọ-mi), etc. Same as *taxonomy*, etc.

tax-is (tak′sis), *n.* [NL., < Gr. τάξις, arrangement, order, position, < τάσσειν, arrange.] In *surg.*, the replacing of a displaced part, or the reducing of a hernial tumor or the like, by manipulation; in *biol.*, the exhibition by a cell or organism of movement in a particular direction in relation to an external stimulus.

-taxis, -taxy. Noun terminations from Gr. τάξις, arrangement, order, position, as in *anthotaxis* or *anthotaxy*, *biotaxy*, *chemotaxis*, *phototaxis.*

tax-ite (tak′sīt), *n.* [Gr. τάξις, arrangement.] In *petrog.*, a lava appearing to be formed from fragments, because of its parts having different colors, textures, etc.—**tax-it-ic** (tak-sit′ik), *a.*

tax-on-o-my (tak-son′ọ-mi), *n.* [F. *taxonomie*, < Gr. τάξις, arrangement, + -νομία, < νέμειν, deal out, distribute.] Classification, esp. in relation to its principles or laws; that department of science, or of a particular science, which deals with classification.—**tax-o-nom-ic, tax-o-nom-i-cal** (tak-sọ-nom′ik, -i-kạl), *a.*—**tax-on′o-mist,** *n.*

tax-pay-er (taks′pā″ėr), *n.* One who pays a tax; one liable to taxation.

-taxy. See *-taxis.*

taz-za (tät′sä), *n.*; pl. *-zas* (-säz), It. *-ze* (-sä). [It., = F. *tasse*, E. *tass*.] A shallow, saucer-like ornamental bowl or vase, esp. one having a foot.

T=bar (tē′bär), *n.* A bar of metal having a cross-section like the capital letter T.

T=cart (tē′kärt), *n.* An open, four-wheeled carriage with two seats, having its body resembling the capital letter T.

tchick (chik), *n.* [Imit.] A sound produced by pressing the tongue against the palate and suddenly withdrawing it with suction or sucking out the air at one side, esp. as used to start or quicken the pace of a horse.—**tchick,** *v. i.* To make the sound 'tchick.'

tea (tē), *n.* [= F. *thé*, G. *thee*, NL. *thea*, < Chinese *te*, for *ch'a*, *ts'a*, tea.] The dried and prepared leaves of the shrub *Thea sinensis*, from which a somewhat bitter, aromatic beverage is prepared by infusion in hot water; the beverage so prepared; the shrub itself, *Thea sinensis* (sometimes classed in the genus *Camellia*, and occurring in several varieties which have frequently been classed as separate species), which is extensively cultivated in China, Japan, India, etc., and which has fragrant white flowers (see cut on next page); also, a meal (other than dinner) in the late afternoon or the evening, at which tea is commonly served (cf. *high tea*, under *high, a.*); a service of tea, with or without other food, in the late afternoon; an afternoon reception at which tea is served; also, any of various infusions prepared from the leaves, flowers, etc., of other plants, and used as beverages or medicines; any kind of leaves, flowers, etc., so used, or any plant yielding them; also, an infusion or aqueous extract of beef, of stimulating virtue ('beef-tea').—**black tea**, a tea which has been allowed to wither and ferment in the air for some time, before being subjected to a heating process.—**green tea**, a tea which has been subjected to a heating process without previous special withering and fermenting.—**tea'=ball**, n. A perforated ball, usually of silver, in which tea-leaves are placed to be immersed in hot water to make tea.—**tea'=**

Branch with Flowers of Tea (*Thea sinensis*, var. *bohea*). — *a*, leaf, showing the nervation.

ber"ry, n. The spicy red fruit of the American wintergreen, *Gaultheria procumbens*; also, the plant itself.—**tea'=cad"dy**, n. A caddy, or small box or can, for holding tea.—**tea'=cake**, n. A light, simple cake for serving at tea.

teach (tēch), v.; *taught*, *teaching*. [AS. *tǣcan*, *tǣcean*, show, teach, akin to *tācn*, E. *token*, also G. *zeigen*, show, L. *dicere*, say: see *diction*.] **I.** *tr.* To show†, or point out† or indicate†; direct†, conduct†, or guide†; also, to impart knowledge of or skill in (a thing); give lessons or instruction in (as, he *teaches* mathematics); also, to impart knowledge or skill to (a person, etc.); give instruction to (as, he *teaches* a large class): often used with two objects (indirect and direct) or with an indirect object followed by an infinitive or clause expressing the thing taught (as, he *taught* me physics; John *taught* his brother to swim; experience *teaches* you when to be silent). **II.** *intr.* To impart knowledge or skill; give instruction; act as a teacher.—**teach'a-ble**, *a.* Capable of being taught, as a subject; that may be imparted by instruction; also, capable of being taught or instructed, as a person (as, "teaching half a dozen *teachable* boys to love study for its own sake": Gissing's "Private Papers of Henry Ryecroft," iv. 25); apt or ready to learn; docile.—**teach-a-bil'i-ty, teach'a-ble-ness**, *n.*—**teach'a-bly**, *adv.*—**teach'er**, *n.* One who or that which teaches or instructs; esp., one whose business or occupation it is to instruct others; an instructor.—**teach'er-age** (-āj), *n.* A house provided as a residence for a school-teacher, as in certain rural districts of the U. S.—**teach'er-ship**, *n.*—**teach'ing**, *n.* The act of one who or that which teaches; the work or profession of a teacher; also, that which is taught; instruction; a doctrine or precept.

tea=co-zy, tea=co-sy (tē'kō"zi), *n.* A cozy or covering for a tea-pot, to keep it hot.

tea=cup (tē'kup), *n.* A cup in which tea is served, usually of small or moderate size; also, a teacupful.—**tea'cup-ful** (-fŭl), *n.*; *-fuls*. As much as a tea-cup will hold: sometimes taken as about four fluid ounces, or one gill.

tea=fight (tē'fīt), *n.* A tea-party. [Slang.]

tea=gar-den (tē'gär"dn), *n.* A garden or open-air inclosure where tea and other refreshments are served to customers; also, a plantation where tea-plants are grown.

tea=gown (tē'goun), *n.* A woman's loose gown of effective style and material, for wearing at afternoon tea at home or for négligé.

Teague (tāg or tēg), *n.* [From Ir. proper name.] A nickname for an Irishman. [Now rare.]

tea=house (tē'hous), *n.* A house of entertainment where tea and other light refreshments are served, esp. in China and Japan.

teak (tēk), *n.* [E. Ind. (Dravidian).] A large East Indian verbenaceous tree, *Tectona grandis*, with

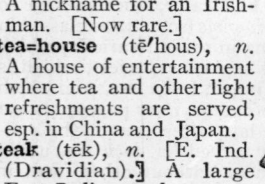

Teak (*Tectona grandis*).

a hard, durable, yellowish-brown, resinous wood valuable for ship-building, etc.; also, the wood; also, any of various similar trees or woods.

tea=ket-tle (tē'ket"l), *n.* A portable kettle with a cover, a spout, and a handle, in which to boil water for making tea and for other uses.

teal (tēl), *n.*; pl. *teals* or (esp. collectively) *teal*. [ME. *tele*: cf. D. *taling*, *teling*, teal.] Any of various small freshwater ducks, esp. of the genera *Nettion* and *Querquedula*, as *Q. carolinensis* (or *N. carolinense*) and *Q. discors* (the 'green-winged teal' and the 'blue-winged teal' respectively) of North America.

tea=leaf (tē'lēf), *n.*; pl. *-leaves* (-lēvz). The leaf of the tea-plant; esp., *pl.*, such leaves after having been infused to make the beverage.

team (tēm), *n.* [AS. *tēam*, progeny, family, team, from the root of *tēon*, draw, *togian*, drag, E. *tow*³.] Off-

Blue-winged Teal (*Querquedula discors*), male.

spring† or progeny†; race† or lineage†; a family or brood of young animals, as a litter of pigs or a brood of ducks (now prov.); also, two or more horses, oxen, or other animals harnessed together to draw a vehicle, plow, or the like; two or more draft-animals, or one such animal, together with the harness and the vehicle drawn; a number of persons associated in some joint action or endeavor, esp. one of the sides or contending parties in a match (as, a *team* of baseball or football players); a flock of birds, as wild ducks, flying in a line.—**team**, *v.* **I.** *tr.* To join together in a team; also, to convey or transport by means of a team. **II.** *intr.* To drive a team; act as a teamster.—**team'ster** (-stėr), *n.* One who drives a team, esp. as an occupation: as, "It needs . . . a good *teamster*, to take a wagon through the Bad Lands" (Roosevelt's "Hunting Trips of a Ranchman," v.).—**team'=work**, *n.* Work done with a team; also, the work of a team or number of persons acting together, esp. with reference to coördination of effort and to collective efficiency (as, "a natural sense of *team-work* and a spirit of comradeship that made for successful co-operation": Bok's "Americanization of Edward Bok," xii.).

tea=par-ty (tē'pär"ti), *n.*; pl. *-ties* (-tiz). A party or entertainment at which tea and other refreshments are served; also, the persons assembled at such an entertainment; also, an occurrence or proceeding marked by commotion or disturbance (colloq.).

tea=pot (tē'pot), *n.* A vessel with a lid, a spout, and a handle, in which tea is made and from which it is poured into tea-cups.

tea=poy (tē'poi), *n.* [Hind. *tipāī*, three-legged table: cf. *charpoy*.] A small three-legged table or stand; also, a small table for use in serving tea; also, a contrivance consisting of a hammock or a seat attached to a pole or poles carried by bearers, used as a means of conveyance in Africa.

tear¹ (tār), *v.*; pret. *tore* (archaic *tare*), pp. *torn*, ppr. *tearing*. [AS. *teran*, tear, = D. *teren*, G. *zehren*, consume, = Goth. *-tairan*, tear, rend; akin to Gr. δέρειν, flay, Skt. *dar-*, burst, split.] **I.** *tr.* To pull apart or in pieces by force, esp. so as to leave ragged or irregular edges (as, "She *tore* the letter in shreds": Mrs. Wharton's "Ethan Frome," ix.); rend; produce or effect by rending (as, to *tear* a hole in one's coat); also, to break violently or shatter (now prov.); also, to wound or injure by or as by rending, or lacerate (as, "Their defenseless limbs the brambles *tear*": Dryden's tr. Virgil's "Georgics," iii. 678); also, fig., to rend or divide (as, "The state was *torn*, first by factions, and at length by civil war": Macaulay's "Hist. of Eng.," i.); distress greatly (as, a heart *torn* with anguish); also, to pull or pluck violently or with force (*off, down, up, out*, etc.: as, "rocks and stones . . . which have been plainly *torn* from the mountain sides," Tyndall's

"Forms of Water," § 18); fig., to remove by force (as, "I could not *tear* myself from the spot": Bulwer-Lytton's "Pelham," xix.). **II.** *intr.* To make a tear or rent; also, to become torn (as, "The roots *tear* up bodily from the thin soil": Jefferies's "Game-keeper at Home," iv.); also, to move or go with violence or great haste (colloq.: as, "*tearing* along in a leather coat and goggles . . . at sixty miles an hour," G. B. Shaw's "Man and Superman," ii.).—**tear**[1], *n.* The act or an act of tearing; a rent or fissure; a rushing movement (colloq.); a spree (slang).

tear[2] (tēr), *n.* [AS. *tēar* = OHG. *zahar* (G. *zähre*) = Icel. *tār* = Goth. *tagr*, a tear; akin to Gr. δάκρυ, L. *lacrima*, a tear: see *lacrymal*.] A drop of the limpid fluid secreted by the lacrymal gland, appearing in or flowing from the eye, chiefly as the result of emotion, esp. of grief; also, something resembling or suggesting a tear, as a drop of a liquid or a tear-like mass of a solid substance.—**crocodile tears.** See under *crocodile*.—**in tears,** weeping.—**tear′=bot″tle,** *n.* A lacrymatory.—**tear′drop,** *n.* A tear.

tear-er (tār′ėr), *n.* One who or that which tears or rends; a mechanical device for tearing.

tear-ful (tēr′fúl), *a.* Full of tears; weeping; also, causing tears (as, "Then war was *tearful* to our foe, But now to me": Chapman's tr. Homer's "Iliad," xix.).—**tear′ful-ly,** *adv.* —**tear′ful-ness,** *n.*

tear=gas (tēr′gas), *n.* A gas used in modern warfare, which makes the eyes smart and water, thus producing a temporary blindness.

tear-ing (tār′ing), *p. a.* That tears, rends, or lacerates; moving with violence or great haste (colloq.); great or tremendous (slang).

tear-less (tēr′les), *a.* Free from tears.

tea=room (tē′rȯȯm), *n.* A room or shop where tea and other refreshments are served to customers.

tea=rose (tē′rōz), *n.* Any of several varieties of cultivated rose having a scent supposed to resemble that of tea.

tear=shell (tēr′shel), *n.* A shell or projectile which upon bursting produces tear-gas.

tear-y (tēr′i), *a.* Tearful; of or like tears.

tease (tēz), *v.*; *teased, teasing.* [AS. *tǣsan* = D. *teezen* = MLG. *tēsen* = MHG. *zeisen*, tease (wool).] **I.** *tr.* To pull apart or separate the adhering fibers of, as in combing or carding wool, or in preparing a specimen for microscopical examination; comb or card (wool, etc.); shred; also, to raise a nap on (cloth) with teazels or the like; teazel; also, to worry or irritate by persistent petty requests, trifling, raillery, or other annoyance; disturb by persistent petty annoyance, for mere sport. **II.** *intr.* To worry or disturb a person, etc., by importunity or persistent petty annoyance. —**tease,** *n.* The act of teasing, or the state of being teased; also, one who or that which teases or annoys (colloq.).

tea-sel (tē′zl), etc. See *teazel*, etc.

teas-er (tē′zėr), *n.* One who or that which teases.

tea=set (tē′set), *n.* A set of articles used in serving tea, as tea-pot, sugar-bowl, cream-pitcher, and sometimes cups, saucers, etc.

tea-spoon (tē′spȯȯn), *n.* The small spoon commonly used to stir tea, coffee, etc.—**tea′spoon-ful** (-fúl), *n.*; pl. *-fuls.* As much as a teaspoon can hold, about one fluid dram.

teat (tēt), *n.* [OF. *iete* (F. *tette*);[*] from Teut., and akin to AS. *tit*, E. *tit*[1].] The protuberance on the breast or udder in female mammals (except the monotremes), where the milk-ducts discharge (now used chiefly with reference to quadrupeds); a nipple or mammilla; sometimes, the breast or udder; also, something resembling a teat.

tea=ta-ble (tē′tā″bl), *n.* A table at which tea is taken, or on which things are placed for tea; also, the persons assembled at tea.

tea=tast-er (tē′tās″tėr), *n.* One whose business it is to test the quality of teas by tasting samples: a tea-expert.

tea=tree (tē′trē), *n.* The shrub or low tree which yields the tea of commerce (see *tea*); also, in Australia, Tasmania, and New Zealand, any of various shrubs or trees, esp. of the myrtaceous genera *Leptospermum* and *Melaleuca*, whose leaves have been used as a substitute for tea.

tea=wag-on (tē′wag″ọn), *n.* A small stand or table on wheels for carrying articles for use in serving tea.

tea-zel (tē′zl), *n.* [AS. *tǣsel*, < *tǣsan*, E. *tease*.] Any of

the herbs with prickly leaves and flower-heads constituting the dipsacaceous genus *Dipsacus*, esp. *D. fullonum* ('fullers' teazel') whose flower-head is covered with stiff, hooked bracts; the dried flower-head or bur of this plant, used for teasing or teazeling cloth; any mechanical contrivance used for the same purpose.—**tea′zel,** *v. t.*; *-zeled* or *-zelled, -zeling* or *-zelling.* To raise a nap on (cloth) with teazels or the like; dress by means of teazels. —**tea′zel-er, tea′zel-ler,** *n.*

Te-bet (te-bet′), *n.* [Heb.] In the Jewish calendar, the fourth month (29 days) of the civil year and the tenth of the ecclesiastical year, beginning in December or in the first part of January. Also **Te-beth′** (-beth′).

Fullers' Teazel (*Dipsacus fullonum*).— *a*, scale of the receptacle; *b*, corolla.

tech-i-ly, tech-i-ness (tech′i-li, -nes). See *tetchily, tetchiness.*

tech-nic (tek′nik). [= F. *technique*, adj. and n., < Gr. τεχνικός, pertaining to art, skilful, technical, < τέχνη, art, workmanly skill.] **I.** *a.* Technical. **II.** *n.* A technical detail; a technical term or expression; a technicality; also, the method of performance in any art; technical skill; technique; also, the study or science of an art or of arts in general; technics.—**tech′ni-cal** (-ni-kạl), *a.* Belonging or pertaining to an art or arts (as, a *technical* dictionary; *technical* skill); peculiar to or characteristic of a particular art, science, profession, trade, etc. (as, *technical* details; a *technical* term; to use a word in a *technical* sense); using technical terms, or treating a subject technically, as a writer or a book; skilled in, or familiar in a practical way with, a particular art, trade, etc., as a person; so considered from a technical point of view (as, a military engagement ending in a *technical* defeat); also, often, pertaining to or connected with the mechanical or industrial arts and the applied sciences (as, a *technical* school).— **tech-ni-cal′i-ty** (-kal′i-ti), *n.*; pl. *-ties* (-tiz). Technical character; the use of technical methods or terms; also, something that is technical, or peculiar to an art, science, profession, trade, etc.; a technical point or detail; a technical term or expression.—**tech′ni-cal-ly,** *adv.* In a technical manner or respect; in relation to a particular art or the like, or to the arts and applied sciences; in accordance with technical methods; in technical terms; in a technical sense (as, a procedure not *technically* legal).—**tech′ni-cal-ness,** *n.*—**tech-ni′cian** (-nish′ạn), *n.* One versed in the technicalities of a subject; also, one skilled in the technique of an art, as music or painting.—**tech′ni-cist** (-sist), *n.* A technical expert; a technician.—**tech′nics,** *n.* The study or science of an art or of arts in general, esp. of the mechanical or industrial arts; also, technic or technique.

tech-nique (tek-nēk′), *n.* [F.: see *technic.*] Technic, or method of performance, esp. in artistic work; technical skill, esp. mechanical skill in artistic work.

tech-noc-ra-cy (tek-nok′rạ-si), *n.* [Gr. τέχνη, art: see *-cracy.*] A theory and movement (prominent in 1932) advocating control and management of industrial resources, together with reorganization of the social system, for the common good, based on the findings of technologists and engineers.—**tech′no-crat** (-nọ-krat), *n.* An advocate of technocracy.—**tech-no-crat′ic,** *a.*

tech-no-lith-ic (tek-nọ-lith′ik), *a.* [Gr. τέχνη, art, + λίθος, stone.] In *anthropol.*, noting or pertaining to stone implements shaped by the operator in accordance with definite designs. Cf. *protolithic.*

tech-nol-o-gy (tek-nol′ọ-ji), *n.* [Gr. τέχνη, art: see *-logy.*] The branch of knowledge that deals with the industrial arts; the science of the industrial arts; also, the terminology of an art, science, etc.; technical nomenclature.—**tech-no-log′i-cal** (-nọ-loj′i-kạl), *a.*—**tech-nol′o-gist,** *n.*

-techny. Noun termination from Gr. τέχνη, art, as in *agrotechny, pyrotechny, zoötechny.*

tech-y (tech′i), *a.* See *tetchy.*

tec-ti-form (tek′ti-fôrm), *a.* [L. *tectum*, roof, + *forma*, form.] Roof-shaped; ridged in the middle and sloping down on each side; also, serving as a covering or lid.

---

tec-tol-o-gy (tek-tol′ō-ji), n. [G. tektologie, < Gr. τέκτων, builder, + -λογία, < λέγειν, speak.] In biol., that branch of morphology which regards an organism as composed of morphons of different orders.—**tec-to-log′i-cal** (-tō-loj′i-kạl), a.

tec-ton-ic (tek-ton′ik), a. [LL. tectonicus, < Gr. τεκτονικός, < τέκτων, carpenter, builder, workman, maker.] Of or pertaining to building or construction; constructive; architectural; in geol., pertaining to the structure of the earth's crust; noting valleys or the like due chiefly to elevation, etc., of portions of the earth's crust, rather than to erosion.—**tec-ton′i-cal-ly**, adv.—**tec-ton′ics**, n. The science or art of assembling, shaping, or ornamenting materials in construction; the constructive arts in general.

ted (ted), v. t.; tedded, tedding. [ME.: cf. Icel. tedhja, spread with manure.] To spread out for drying, as newly mown hay.—**ted′der**, n.

Ted-dy=bear (ted′i-bār′), n. [Named from 'Teddy' (Theodore) Roosevelt, from his well-known interest in hunting and animals.] A stuffed figure of a bear, used as a toy.

Te De-um (tē dē′um). [L.; from the first words, Te Deum laudamus, 'thee, God, we praise.'] An ancient Latin hymn, in the form of a psalm, sung regularly at matins in the Roman Catholic Church and (in an English translation) at morning prayer in the Anglican Church, and also on special occasions as a service of thanksgiving; also, a musical setting of the hymn; also, a service of thanksgiving in which this hymn forms a prominent part.

te-dious (tē′dius or -dyus), a. [LL. tædiosus, < L. tædium, E. tedium.] Marked by tedium; long and tiresome, as a task, journey, etc. (as, "a tedious siege": Froude's "Cæsar," xix.); prolix so as to cause weariness, as a speaker (as, "I overflow with talk, and yet am never tedious": Hawthorne's "Twice-Told Tales," The Village Uncle); also, troublesome or disagreeable (now prov.); also, slow, dilatory, or late (now prov.).—**te′dious-ly**, adv.—**te′dious-ness**, n.

te-di-um (tē′di-um), n. [L. tædium, < tædet, it disgusts, it wearies.] The state of being wearisome; irksomeness; tediousness: as, "the tedium of captivity" (Prescott's "Conquest of Mexico," iv. 4).

tee[1] (tē), n. [Origin uncertain.] The mark aimed at in various games, as curling; in golf, the starting-place, usually a slight heap of earth or sand, from which the ball is driven at the beginning of play for each hole.—**tee**[1], v.; teed, teeing. In golf. **I.** tr. To place (the ball) on a tee. **II.** intr. With off, to play the ball from a tee.

tee[2] (tē), n. The letter T, t; also, something shaped like a T, as a pipe-joint or the like; a metal beam or bar which in section is like the letter T.

teem[1] (tēm), v. [ME. temen; from Scand.; akin to E. toom.] **I.** tr. To empty (a vessel, etc.); also, to empty or pour out; discharge. **II.** intr. To flow in a stream; pour: as, "We look towards the iceberg and see water teeming from its sides" (Tyndall's "Forms of Water," § 50).

teem[2] (tēm), v. [AS. tēman, tȳman, < tēam, progeny: see team.] **I.** tr. To bring forth or produce (offspring). Also fig. [Obs. or archaic.] **II.** intr. To bring forth young; be or become pregnant; fig., to be full, as if ready to give birth; be prolific or fertile (with: as, "His mind teemed with large schemes," Lecky's "Hist. of Eng. in the 18th Century," iii.); abound or swarm (with: as, "Their sea teems with amazing quantities of the finest fish in the world," Smollett's "Humphry Clinker," Sept. 3).—**teem′ing**, p. a. Pregnant; fig., prolific or fertile; abounding or swarming with something, as with people (as, "teeming centers of the modern world": W. Churchill's "Inside of the Cup," i.); hence, existing in swarms or great numbers (as, "the teeming myriads of human beings around him": Dickens's "Hard Times," i. 15).—**teem′ing-ly**, adv.

teen (tēn), n. [AS. tēona, injury.] Harm†, injury†, or damage†; vexation, anger, or wrath (obs. or Sc.); trouble, sorrow, or grief (archaic or Sc.).

-teen. [AS. -tȳne, -tēne, repr. tȳn, tēn, E. ten.] A termination forming the cardinal numerals from thirteen to nineteen.

teens (tēnz), n. pl. [See -teen.] The years of one's age (from thirteen to nineteen inclusive) of which the numbers end in -teen: as, "Abraham Lincoln in his teens grew very fast" (Charnwood's "Abraham Lincoln," i.).

tee-ny (tē′ni), a. Colloq. or prov. variant of tiny: as, "just a teeny bit of cake" (W. Churchill's "Mr. Crewe's Career," viii.).

tee-pee (tē′pē), n. See tepee.

tee-tee (tē-tē′), n. See titi[1].

tee-ter (tē′tèr), v. [Var. of titter[1].] **I.** intr. To seesaw; move like a seesaw; move unsteadily. [Colloq. or prov.] **II.** tr. To move (anything) with a seesaw motion. [Colloq. or prov.]—**tee′ter**, n. A seesaw; a seesaw motion. [Colloq. or prov.]

teeth (tēth), n. Plural of tooth.

teethe (tēꞙ), v.; teethed, teething. [From teeth.] **I.** intr. To grow teeth; cut one's teeth. **II.** tr. To furnish with teeth.—**teeth-ing** (tē′ꞙing), n. The growing or cutting of teeth; dentition.

tee-to-tal (tē-tō′tạl), a. [Extended form of total, appar. for emphasis.] Of or pertaining to, advocating, or pledged to total abstinence from intoxicating drink; also, absolute, complete, or entire (colloq.).—**tee-to′tal-er, tee-to′tal-ler**, n. One who abstains totally from intoxicating drink.—**tee-to′tal-ism**, n. The principle or practice of total abstinence from intoxicating drink.—**tee-to′tal-ly**, adv. Completely or entirely. [Colloq.]

tee-to-tum (tē-tō′tum), n. [Orig. T totum, that is, L. totum, 'the whole,' preceded by its initial letter, T, this letter, representing L. totum, being inscribed on one side of the toy.] Orig., a kind of top having four sides, each marked with a different initial letter, spun with the fingers in an old game of chance; now, also, any small top spun with the fingers.

teff (tef), n. [Native name.] A cereal grass, Eragrostis (or Poa) abyssinica, of Abyssinia, bearing minute grains which yield a flour of good quality.

teg-men (teg′men), n.; pl. -mina (-mi-nä). [L., a covering, < tegere, cover.] A cover, covering, or integument; in entom., one of the fore wings of an insect (esp. an orthopterous insect) when they form a protective covering for the posterior wings; in bot., the delicate inner integument or coat of a seed (cf. testa).

teg-men-tum (teg-men′tum), n.; pl. -ta (-tä). [L., var. of tegumentum, E. tegument.] In bot., the scaly coat which covers a leaf-bud; also, one of the scales of such a coat. —**teg-men′tal**, a.

teg-u-lar (teg′ū-lär), a. [L. tegula, a tile: see tile.] Pertaining to or resembling a tile; consisting of or arranged like tiles.—**teg′u-lar-ly**, adv.

teg-u-ment (teg′ū-ment), n. [L. tegumentum, < tegere, cover.] A covering or investment; an integument.—**teg-u-men′tal** (-men′t·l), **teg-u-men′ta-ry** (-tạ-ri), a.

te-hee (tē′hē′). [Imit.] **I.** interj. A word representing the sound of a tittering laugh. **II.** n. A titter; a snicker.—**te′hee′**, v. i.; -heed, -heeing. To utter a tehee; titter; snicker.

Te I-gi-tur (tē ij′i-tèr). [L., 'thee therefore': the opening words.] Eccles., the first paragraph of the canon in the Roman and some other Latin liturgies.

teil (tēl), n. [OF. teil, til, masc. of tille, < L. tilia, linden.] The linden or lime-tree; also (in the Bible), the terebinth (see Isa. vi. 13).

teind (tēnd), n. [= tenth.] A tithe. [Sc.]

tel-æs-the-sia (tel-es-thē′żiä), n. [NL.: see tele- and æsthesia.] Sensation or perception received at a distance without the normal operation of the recognized organs of sense.

tel-a-mon (tel′ạ-mon), n.; pl. telamones (tel-ạ-mō′nēz). [L. telamon, telamo, < Gr. τελαμών, from the root of τλῆναι, bear: cf. Atlas and atlantes.] In arch., a figure of a man used like a supporting column; an atlas. Cf. caryatid.

te-lan-gi-ec-ta-sis (te-lan-ji-ek′tạ-sis), n. [NL., < Gr. τέλος, end, + ἀγγεῖον, vessel, + ἔκτασις, extension.] In pathol., dilatation of the capillaries and other small blood-vessels, producing a form of angioma.—**te-lan″gi-ec-tat′ic** (-tat′ik), a.

tel-au-to-gram (tel-â′tō-gram), n. The facsimile record, as a written message, produced by a telautograph.

tel-au-to-graph (tel-â′tō-gräf), n. [See tele- and autograph.] A form of telegraph for reproducing handwriting, drawings, etc., the movements of a pen or pencil at one end of the line being reproduced in a pen or pencil at the other end by a system of electromagnets.—**tel-au-to-graph′ic** (-graf′ik), *a.* —**tel-au-tog′ra-phy** (-tog′ra-fi), *n.*

tele-, tel-. Forms of Gr. τῆλε, far off, afar, used in combination, esp. in words denoting instruments, appliances, forces, etc., operating over long distances, or having reference to action or effects taking place at a distance from the cause, as in *telautograph, telegraph, telelectric, telepathy, teleseism.*

tel-e-chi-ro-graph (tel-ē-kī′rō-gráf), *n.* [See *tele-, chiro-,* and *-graph.*] A form of telegraph for transmitting messages in handwriting.

tel-e-du (tel′ē-dö), *n.* [Javanese.] The stinking badger, *Mydaus meliceps,* of the mountains of Java, Sumatra, etc., which (like the skunk) ejects a fetid secretion.

Teledu.

te-le-ga (te-lä′gä or -le′gä), *n.* [Russ. *telyega.*] A Russian cart of rude construction, having four wheels and no springs.

East Siberian Telega.

te-leg-o-ny (tē-leg′ō-ni), *n.* [See *tele-* and *-gony.*] In *biol.,* the supposed influence of a previous sire upon the progeny subsequently borne by the same mother to other sires.—**tel-e-gon-ic** (tel-ē-gon′ik), *a.*

tel-e-gram (tel′ē-gram), *n.* [See *tele-* and *-gram.*] A communication sent by telegraph; a telegraphic message.—**tel-e-gram′mic,** *a.*

tel-e-graph (tel′ē-gráf), *n.* [See *tele-* and *-graph.*] An apparatus, system, or process for transmitting messages or signals to a distance, esp. by means of a modern electrical device consisting essentially of a transmitting or sending instrument and a distant receiving instrument connected by a conducting wire, the making and breaking of the circuit at the sending end causing a corresponding effect, as on an electromagnet, at the receiving end; a similar communicating device or system in which there are no connecting wires, as in wireless telegraphy (see *wireless, a.*).—**tel′e-graph,** *v.* **I.** *tr.* To transmit or send (a message, etc.) by telegraph; also, to send a message to (a person) by telegraph. Also fig. **II.** *intr.* To send a message by telegraph. Also fig.—**te-leg-ra-pher** (tē-leg′ra-fér or tel′ē-gráf-ér), *n.* One whose occupation it is to operate telegraphic instruments; also, a person who sends a telegram.—**tel-e-graph′ic** (-graf′ik), *a.* —**tel-e-graph′i-cal-ly,** *adv.*—**te-leg′ra-phist,** *n.* A telegrapher, or telegraphic operator.

te-leg-ra-phone (tē-leg′ra-fōn), *n.* [See *tele-, -graph,* and *-phone.*] An apparatus devised by Valdemar Poulsen, of Copenhagen, for the recording and subsequent reproduction of speech, etc., transmitted through a telephone, the records being made by the local magnetization of a steel tape, wire, or the like.

tel-e-graph-o-scope (tel-ē-graf′ō-skōp), *n.* [See *telegraph* and *-scope.*] A telegraphic device by means of which a picture may be reproduced at a distance.

tel-e-graph=plant (tel′ē-gráf-plant), *n.* An East Indian plant, *Meibomia gyrans,* a species of tick-trefoil, remarkable for the spontaneous jerking motions of its leaflets, suggesting signaling.

Telegraph-plant.

te-leg-ra-phy (tē-leg′ra-fi or tel′ē-graf-i), *n.* [See *tele-* and *-graphy.*] The art or practice of constructing or operating telegraphs.

tel-e-ki-ne-sis (tel″ē-ki-nē′sis), *n.* [NL., < Gr. τῆλε, afar, + κίνησις, movement.] The production of motion in objects at a distance by the exercise of some non-physical or psychic power.—**tel″e-ki-net′ic** (-net′ik), *a.*

tel-e-lec-tric (tel-ē-lek′trik), *a.* [See *tele-* and *electric.*] Noting or pertaining to any of various devices for producing mechanical effects, etc., at a distance by electrical means.—**tel-e-lec′tro-scope** (-trō-skōp), *n.* [See *-scope.*] Any device by which an image of an object can be transmitted to a distance by electrical means.

te-lem-e-ter (tē-lem′e-tèr), *n.* [See *tele-* and *-meter.*] Any of certain devices or attachments for determining distances, as in artillery practice; also, an apparatus for recording at a distance the indications of a meteorological or other instrument.—**tel-e-met-ric, tel-e-met-ri-cal** (tel-ē-met′rik, -ri-kal), *a.*—**te-lem′e-try,** *n.*

tel-e-mi-cro-scope (tel-ē-mī′krō-skōp), *n.* [See *tele-* and *microscope.*] A magnifying instrument for observing small objects, as insects, from a distance.

tel-e-mo-tor (tel-ē-mō′tor), *n.* [See *tele-* and *motor.*] A device which is connected with a ship's steering-wheel when it is at some distance from the tiller, and which, by electric, hydraulic, or other means, causes the movements of the steering-wheel to be reproduced by the apparatus or engine connected directly with the tiller.

tel-e-o-log-i-cal (tel″ē-ō-loj′i-kal or tē″lē-), *a.* Of or pertaining to teleology; relating to final causes; pertaining to design or purpose in nature.—**tel″e-o-log′i-cal-ly,** *adv.*

tel-e-ol-o-gy (tel-ē-ol′ō-ji or tē-lē-), *n.* [NL. *teleologia,* < Gr. τέλος (gen. τέλεος), end, + -λογία, < λέγειν, speak.] The doctrine of final causes; the study of the evidences of design or purpose in nature; such design or purpose (as, "Either the world shows a *teleology* or it does not": W. R. Inge's "Outspoken Essays," i. 11).—**tel-e-ol′o-gist,** *n.*

tel-e-ost (tel′ē-ost), *n.* [NL. *Teleostei,* pl., complete, + ὀστέον, bone.] **I.** *n.* Any of the *Teleostei,* a group of fishes having a more or less completely ossified skeleton, as the salmon, flounder, mackerel, etc. **II.** *a.* Belonging or pertaining to the *Teleostei.*—**tel-e-os′te-an** (-os′tē-an), *a.* and *n.*

tel-e-o-stome (tel′ē-ō-stōm), *n.* [NL. *Teleostomi,* pl., < Gr. τέλεος, complete, + στόμα, mouth.] Any of the *Teleostomi,* a group of fishes (including the teleosts and ganoids) characterized chiefly by the occurrence of membrane-bones in the cranium, etc., the upper and lower jaws being bounded by such bones, and by the presence of specialized bones forming the arch of the upper jaw.—**tel-e-os′to-mous** (-os′tō-mus), *a.*

tel-e-path (tel′ē-path), *n.* [See *telepathy.*] A telepathist.—**tel′e-path,** *v.* **I.** *tr.* To transmit or convey (a message, thought, etc.) by telepathy. **II.** *intr.* To hold telepathic communication; practise telepathy.—**tel-e-path′ic,** *a.* Of, pertaining to, or of the nature of telepathy; communicated by telepathy (as, "As if in obedience to a *telepathic* command of his master, Pepper [a horse] stopped": W. Churchill's "Mr. Crewe's Career," iv.).—**tel-e-path′i-cal-ly,** *adv.*—**te-lep-a-thist** (tē-lep′a-thist), *n.* A student of or believer in telepathy; also, one who possesses telepathic power.

te-lep-a-thy (tē-lep′a-thi), *n.* [See *tele-* and *-pathy.*] Communication of one mind with another by some means beyond what is ordinary or normal.

tel-e-phone (tel′ē-fōn), *n.* [See *tele-* and *-phone.*] An apparatus, system, or process for the transmission of sound or speech to a distant point, esp. by an electrical device consisting essentially of a transmitter, a conducting wire, and a receiver, the vibrations imparted by the voice to a thin diaphragm in the transmitter being reproduced in a similar diaphragm in the receiver at the other end; a similar communicating device or system in which there are no connecting wires (see *wireless, a.*).—**tel′e-phone,** *v.;* -*phoned,* -*phoning.* **I.** *tr.* To send (a message, etc.) by telephone; also, to speak to (a person) by means of a telephone (as, "He decided . . . to *telephone* her and free himself from the engagement": Sinclair Lewis's "Arrowsmith," vi.); summon by telephone (as, "I am going to *telephone* Dr.

Jarvis . . . and then I shall come back, in order to be here when he arrives": W. Churchill's "Inside of the Cup," x.); also, to provide with telephones. **II.** *intr.* To send a message by telephone: as, "We can *telephone* to your mother for a car" (Galsworthy's "Patrician," ii. 4).—**tel′e-phon-er** (-fō-nèr), *n.*—**tel-e-phon′ic** (-fon′ik), *a.*—**tel-e-phon′i-cal-ly,** *adv.*—**tel-e-pho′no-graph** (-fō′nǫ-gràf), *n.* [Cf. *phonograph.*] A combination of telephone and phonograph, for the recording and subsequent reproduction of transmitted messages; specif., the telegraphone of Poulsen.—**te-leph-o-ny** (tẹ-lef′ǫ-ni or tel′ẹ-fō-ni), *n.* The art or practice of constructing or operating telephones.

tel-e-phote (tel′ẹ-fōt), *n.* [Gr. τῆλε, afar, + φῶs (φωτ-), light.] An electrical device for reproducing at a distance pictures or images of visible objects.

tel-e-pho-to (tel-ẹ-fō′tō), *a.* Shortened form of *telephotographic.*

tel-e-pho-to-graph (tel-ẹ-fō′tǫ-gràf), *n.* [See *tele-*.] A photograph or picture made by telephotography.—**tel-e-pho′to-graph,** *v. t.* To photograph by telephotography; reproduce or send by telephotography.—**tel″e-pho-to-graph′ic** (-graf′ik), *a.* Of, pertaining to, or used in telephotography.—**tel″e-pho-tog′ra-phy** (-fǫ-tog′rà-fi), *n.* The art of photographing objects too distant for the ordinary camera, by the use of telescopic lenses and a special camera; also, the art of electrically reproducing photographs or pictures at a distance by a special telegraphic process.

tel-e-scope (tel′ẹ-skōp). [NL. *telescopium,* < Gr. τηλεσκόπos, far-seeing: see *tele-* and *-scope.*] **I.** *n.* An optical instrument used for making distant objects appear nearer and larger, of which there are two principal forms, one ('refracting telescope') consisting essentially of a lens or object-glass for forming an image of the object and an eyepiece or combination of lenses for magnifying this image, and the other ('reflecting telescope') having a similar arrangement, but containing a concave mirror or speculum instead of an object-glass. **II.** *a.* Consisting of parts which fit and slide one within another, like the tubes of a jointed telescope, so as to be capable of being extended or shortened.—**tel′e-scope,** *v.; -scoped, -scoping.* **I.** *tr.* To force together, one into another, or force into something else, after the manner of the sliding tubes of a jointed telescope. **II.** *intr.* To slide together, or into something else, after the manner of the tubes of a jointed telescope; be driven one into another, as railroad-cars in collision.—**tel′e-scope=carp,** *n.* A variety of the goldfish, *Carassius auratus,* with protruding eyes and a double caudal fin. Also **tel′e-scope=fish.**—**tel′e-scope=sight,** *n.* A telescope used for aiming a gun.—**tel-e-scop′ic** (-skop′ik), *a.* Of, pertaining

Telescope-carp, two thirds natural size.

to, or of the nature of a telescope; also, obtained by means of a telescope (as, a *telescopic* view of the moon); also, seen by means of a telescope; visible only through a telescope; also, far-seeing (as, a *telescopic* eye); also, consisting of parts which slide one within another like the tubes of a jointed telescope, and thus capable of being extended or shortened.—**tel-e-scop′i-cal-ly,** *adv.*—**te-les-co-pist** (tẹ-les′kǫ-pist or tel′ẹ-skō-pist), *n.* One skilled in telescopy, or the use of the telescope.—**te-les-co-py** (tẹ-les′kǫ-pi or tel′ẹ-skō-pi), *n.* [See *-scopy.*] The art of constructing or of using telescopes.

tel-e-seism (tel′ẹ-sīsm or -sīzm), *n.* [Gr. τῆλε, afar, + σεισμόs, earthquake.] An earth-tremor remote from a place where it is recorded or indicated by a seismograph or the like.

tel-e-spec-tro-scope (tel-ẹ-spek′trǫ-skōp), *n.* [See *tele-*.] An instrument consisting of an astronomical telescope with a spectroscope attached.

tel-e-ster-e-o-scope (tel-ẹ-ster′ẹ-ō-skōp), *n.* [See *tele-*.] An optical instrument of the stereoscopic type, used for

viewing distant objects, in which it produces an appearance of relief.

tel-es-the′sia, *n.* See *telæsthesia.*

tel-e-stich (tel′ẹ-stik or tẹ-les′tik), *n.* [Gr. τέλos (gen. τέλεos), end, + στίχos, row, line.] A poem or the like in which the final letters of the lines, in order, spell a word or words.

tel-e-ther-mo-graph (tel-ẹ-thèr′mǫ-gràf), *n.* [See *tele-*.] A telethermometer which automatically records changes in temperature; also, a record made by such a device.

tel-e-ther-mom-e-ter (tel″ẹ-thèr-mom′e-tèr), *n.* [See *tele-*.] Any of various thermometers that indicate or record their temperatures at a distance, as by means of an electric current.—**tel″e-ther-mom′e-try,** *n.*

tel-e-type (tel′ẹ-tīp), *n.* [See *tele-* and *type.*] A type-printing telegraphic apparatus; specif., a radiotelegraphic apparatus by which signals are sent by striking the letters of the keyboard of an instrument resembling a typewriter, and are received by a similar instrument which automatically prints them in types corresponding to the letters struck (proprietary name).

te-leu-to-spore (tẹ-lū′tǫ-spōr), *n.* [Gr. τελευτή, completion, + σπορά, E. *spore.*] In *bot.,* one of the thick-walled spores in fungi of the family *Uredineæ,* formed usually toward the end of fructification.—**te-leu-to-spor′ic** (-spor′ik), *a.*

tel-e-vise (tel′ẹ-vīz), *v.t.; -vised, -vising.* To transmit by television.

tel-e-vi-sion (tel-ẹ-vizh′ǫn or tel′ẹ-vizh-ǫn), *n.* [See *tele-*.] Vision or sight of objects at a distance as made possible by an apparatus reproducing an image of them by electrical or other means; also, the process employed.

tel′fer, etc. See *telpher,* etc.

tel-ford-ize (tel′fǫrd-īz), *v. t.; -ized, -izing.* To construct a Telford pavement on (a road).

Tel-ford (tel′fǫrd) **pave′ment.** A form of pavement devised by the Scotch engineer Thomas Telford (1757–1834), consisting of layers of stones of particular sizes compacted by rolling, the foundation being large stones with smaller pieces packed in tightly between them.

tel-ic (tel′ik), *a.* [Gr. τελικόs, final, < τέλos, end.] Expressing end or purpose, as a clause (cf. *ecbatic*); also, tending to a definite end.—**tel′ics,** *n.* A branch of sociology dealing with consciously planned and directed progress.

tell[1] (tel), *n.* [Ar.] A hill or mound: common in Oriental place-names.

tell[2] (tel), *v. t.; told, telling.* [AS. *tellan* (pret. *tealde*), state, recount, enumerate, reckon, = D. *tellen,* G. *zählen,* reckon, count, = Icel. *telja;* recount, say, speak, count; from the noun represented by E. *tale.*] To give an account or narrative of, or narrate (as, to *tell* one's experiences); relate (a story, tale, etc.); also, to make known by speech or writing (a fact, news, information, etc.); communicate; announce or proclaim; utter (the truth, a lie, etc.); express in words (thoughts, feelings, etc.); reveal or divulge (something secret or private); say plainly or positively (as, I cannot *tell* just what was done); hence, to discern so as to be able to say (as, can you *tell* who that is over there?); recognize or distinguish (as, I couldn't *tell* in the dark which man it was; you could hardly *tell* the difference between them; "I . . . could rattle off my catechism that fast, as you couldn't *tell* one word from another," Stevenson's "Treasure Island," xv.); also, to inform or apprise (a person, etc.) of something; with double object, to inform (a person, etc.) of (something: as, *tell* me your name); often, to assure emphatically (as, I won't, I *tell* you!); bid, order, or command (as, do as I *tell* you; *tell* him to stop); also, to mention one after another, as in enumerating; reckon or count; count or set (*off, out, down,* etc.) one by one or in exact amount (as, to *tell* off five yards in measuring; to *tell* out or *tell* down money due; to *tell* off ten men as a detachment for special duty).—**tell that to the marines.** See under *marine,* *n.*—**to tell (one's) beads,** to tell off the beads of a rosary as prayer after prayer is said: as, "She passed the *beads* which she was *telling* from one finger to the other" (Marryat's "King's Own," lx.).—**to tell tales out of school,** fig., to tell in public what concerns only a limited number of persons; reveal confidential matters.—**tell**[2], *v. i.* To give an account; make report; give evidence or be an indication (*of*); also, to talk or chat (prov. Eng.); also, to disclose something secret or private; play the informer (on); also, to count, have force or effect, or operate effectively (as, a contest in which every stroke *tells*; "On the plains of Brabant the Prince's superiority in cavalry was sure to *tell*," Motley's "Dutch Republic," iii. 4); produce a marked or severe effect (as, the strain was *telling* on his health).—**tell′a·ble,** *a.* Capable or worthy of being told.—**tell′er,** *n.* One who or that which tells, relates, or communicates; a narrator; also, one who tells, counts, or enumerates, as one appointed to count votes in a legislative body, or one employed in a bank to receive or pay out money over the counter.—**tell′er-ship,** *n.*—**tell′ing,** *p. a.* That tells; having force or effect; effective; striking: as, to strike a *telling* blow; to bring out a *telling* point in a speech; "the salient and *telling* prominence that is reserved for party questions" (Morley's "Oliver Cromwell," ii. 3).—**tell′ing-ly,** *adv.*

tell-tale (tel′tāl). **I.** *n.* One who tells tales, or heedlessly or maliciously reveals private, secret, or confidential matters; a tattler; a talebearer; also, a thing serving to reveal or disclose something; specif., any of various indicating or registering devices; a row of cords or strips hung over a track to warn brakemen on freight-trains when they are approaching a low bridge or the like; an indicator showing the position of a ship's tiller; also, a tattler (bird). **II.** *a.* That tells tales, or reveals or betrays what is not intended to be known (often fig.: as, a *telltale* blush; "I watched her eyes for some *tell-tale* flash, some hint of dismay or bitterness," Maugham's "Moon and Sixpence," xxxii.); also, giving notice or warning of something, as a mechanical device.

tell=truth (tel′trŏth), *n.* One who tells the truth; a truthful or candid person: as, "I belong to the unpopular family of *Tell-truths*, and would not flatter Apollo for his lyre" (Scott's "Rob Roy," xvi.).

tel-lu-rate (tel′ū-rāt), *n.* In *chem.,* a salt of telluric acid.

tel-lu-ret (tel′lu-ret), *n.* In *chem.,* a telluride.—**tel′lu-ret-ed, tel′lu-ret-ted,** *a.* In *chem.,* combined with tellurium.

tel-lu-ri-an (te-lū′ri-an). [L. *tellus* (*tellur-*), the earth.] **I.** *a.* Of, pertaining to, or characteristic of the earth or an inhabitant of the earth. **II.** *n.* An inhabitant of the earth; also, a tellurion.

tel-lu-ric[1] (te-lū′rik), *a.* [L. *tellus* (*tellur-*), the earth.] Of or pertaining to the earth; terrestrial; also, of or proceeding from the earth or soil.

tel-lu-ric[2] (te-lū′rik), *a.* [See *tellurium*.] In *chem.,* of or containing tellurium (see *tellurous*): as, *telluric* acid (H_2TeO_4).—**tel-lu-ride** (tel′ū-rīd or -rid), *n.* In *chem.,* a compound of tellurium with an electropositive element or a radical.—**tel-lu-rif′er-ous** (-rif′e-rus), *a.* [See *-ferous*.] Containing or yielding tellurium.

tel-lu-ri-on (te-lū′ri-on), *n.* [L. *tellus* (*tellur-*), the earth.] An apparatus for showing how the diurnal rotation and annual revolution of the earth and the obliquity of its axis produce the alternation of day and night and the changes of the seasons.

tel-lu-rite (tel′ū-rīt), *n.* A mineral consisting of tellurium dioxide, occurring usually in white or yellowish crystals; in *chem.,* a salt of tellurous acid.

tel-lu-ri-um (te-lū′ri-um), *n.* [NL., < L. *tellus* (*tellur-*), the earth.] Chem. sym., Te; at. wt., 127.5; sp. gr., 6.2. A rare silver-white element resembling sulphur in its chemical properties, and usually occurring in nature combined with gold, silver, or other metals.—**tel-lu-rize** (tel′ū-rīz), *v. t.*; *-rized, -rizing.* In *chem.,* to mix or cause to combine with tellurium: as, *tellurized* ores (ores containing tellurium compounds).—**tel′lu-rous,** *a.* In *chem.,* containing tellurium (in larger proportion than a corresponding telluric compound): as, *tellurous* acid (H_2TeO_3).

tel-ma-tol-o-gy (tel-ma-tol′ō-ji), *n.* [Gr. τέλμα (τελματ-), marsh: see *-logy*.] The science that deals with the formation and contents of peat-bogs.

tel-o-dy-nam-ic (tel″ō-dī-nam′ik), *a.* [Gr. τηλο-, afar (= τῆλε: see *tele-*), + E. *dynamic*.] Pertaining to the transmission of power over considerable distances, as by means of endless wire ropes on pulleys.

tel-pher (tel′fėr). [Gr. τῆλε, afar, + φέρειν, bear.] **I.** *a.* Of or pertaining to a system of telpherage: as, a *telpher* railway; *telpher* transport. **II.** *n.* A traveling unit, car, or carrier in a telpherage system; also, a telpherage system.—**tel′pher-age** (-āj), *n.* Transportation effected automatically by the aid of electricity; specif., a system in which motor-bearing cars or carriers are suspended from and run on wire cables or the like, the electric current being taken from the cables or adjacent conductors; hence, any more or less similar system of trans-

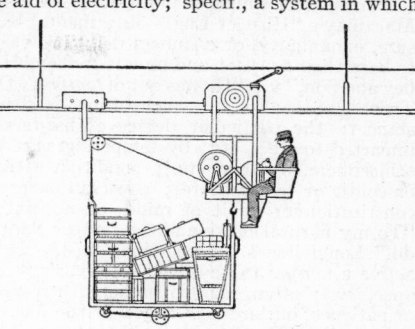

Telpherage Line, with operator.

portation, operated by electricity or otherwise, as one in which cars or carriers fixed to a moving endless cable, and suspended from, and running on small wheels on, a fixed cable, are conveyed up and down a mountainside.

tel-son (tel′son), *n.* [NL., < Gr. τέλσον, boundary, limit.] In *zoöl.,* the last segment, or an appendage of the last segment, of certain crustaceans and arachnidans, as the middle flipper of a lobster's tail or the sting of a scorpion.

Tel-u-gu (tel′ö-gö). **I.** *n.* A Dravidian language spoken in India, in the region north of Madras; also, one of the people or race speaking this language. **II.** *a.* Of or pertaining to Telugu or the Telugus.

tem-blor (tem-blôr′), *n.* [Sp.] A tremor; an earthquake.

tem-e-ra-ri-ous (tem-e-rā′ri-us), *a.* [L. *temerarius,* < *temere*: see *temerity*.] Heedless of consequences; reckless; rash; characterized by temerity: as, "the *temerarious* use of Christian names" (H. G. Wells's "Kipps," i. 2). [Archaic.]—**tem-e-ra′ri-ous-ly,** *adv.*

te-mer-i-ty (tē-mer′i-ti), *n.* [L. *temeritas,* < *temere,* adv., blindly, heedlessly, rashly: cf. Skt. *tamas,* darkness.] Reckless boldness or presumption; rashness: as, "a man brave to *temerity*" (Motley's "Dutch Republic," ii. 3); "When I look round me at this glittering semicircle [audience], I begin . . . to repent of my own *temerity*" (Mallock's "New Republic," v. 1).

tem-e-rous (tem′e-rus), *a.* Same as *temerarious.* [Archaic.]

tem-per (tem′pėr), *v.* [AS. *temprian,* < L. *temperare* (pp. *temperatus*), tr. divide or proportion duly, mingle in due proportion, combine properly, qualify, regulate, intr. observe proper measure, be moderate, perhaps < *tempus,* time: cf. *tamper*[2].] **I.** *tr.* To combine or blend in due proportions (archaic); also, to make or prepare by due combination or blending (archaic); also, to bring to a proper, suitable, or desirable state by or as by blending or mingling with something else; modify by or as by blending or admixture (as, to *temper* justice with mercy; "His animosity appeared to be still *tempered* with the remains of humanity," Godwin's "Caleb Williams," xxxviii.); moderate or mitigate (as, "God *tempers* the wind . . . to the shorn lamb": Sterne's "Sentimental Journey," Maria); soften or tone down; also, to mollify or pacify (obs. or archaic); persuade or dispose (obs. or archaic); also, in specific use, to moisten, mix, and work up into proper consistence, as clay or mortar; prepare (colors) by mixing with oil, etc.; bring to a proper degree of hardness and elasticity, as steel; also, to melt†, or soften by heating†; also, to adjust the pitch of (a musical instrument)†; tune (a pianoforte, organ, etc.) so as to make the tones available in different keys or tonalities (cf. *temperament*); attune†, or bring into harmony† (as, "Meanwhile the rural ditties were not mute, *Temper'd* to the oaten flute": Milton's "Lycidas," 33); also, to regulate, control, or govern (now only prov.); keep within due limits or bounds; restrain, check, or curb (as, "Since they are tumultuous, Let them be *temper'd,* yet not roughly": Byron's "Sardanapalus," i. 2). **II.** *intr.* To be or become tempered.—**tem′per,** *n.* The combination of different ingredients or qualities, esp. in due proportions (obs. or rare); proportionate arrangement or adjustment of parts (archaic); a middle course, or compromise (archaic: as, "Virtue is nothing but a just *temper* between propensities any one of which, if indulged to excess, becomes vice," Macaulay's "Hist. of Eng.," ii.); mental balance or composure, equanimity, or calmness (as, "It's very easy for some to keep their *tempers*, and be soft-spoken," Dickens's "Dombey and Son," v.; "He was out of *temper*," Dickens's "Oliver Twist," xi.); also, the constitution or character of a substance†; the particular degree of hardness and elasticity imparted to steel, etc., by tempering; the condition of the atmosphere, weather, etc.†; condition with respect to heat or cold†, or temperature†; constitution or habit of body†; constitution or habit of mind, or natural disposition (as, "To my natural make and my *temper* Painful the task is I do," Longfellow's "Evangeline," i. 4; "He was of far too active a *temper* to be quiet," Howells's "Chance Acquaintance," v.); often, habit of mind with respect to irritability or patience, outbursts of anger, or the like (as, "My *temper* is hasty," F. M. Crawford's "Mr. Isaacs," ii.; "Mrs. Mackenzie has rather a short *temper*," Thackeray's "Newcomes," lxxii.); the particular state of mind or feelings, frame of mind, or humor (as, "The nation was in such a *temper* that the smallest spark might raise a flame": Macaulay's "Hist. of Eng.," ii.); heat of mind or passion, shown in outbursts of anger, resentment, etc. (as, "an unseemly outbreak of *temper*": Hawthorne's "Scarlet Letter," x.); also, a substance added to something to modify its properties or qualities.

tem-pe-ra (tem′pe-rä), *n.* [It., < *temperare*, < L. *temperare*, E. *temper*.] In *painting*, distemper.

tem-per-a-ble (tem′pėr-ạ-bl), *a.* Capable of being tempered.

tem-per-a-ment (tem′pėr-ạ-ment), *n.* [L. *temperamentum*, < *temperare*, E. *temper*.] The state in which constituents are combined in due proportions†; state or condition with respect to the relative proportion of ingredients or qualities†; in the old physiology, the combination of the four cardinal humors (see *humor*, *n.*) the relative proportions of which were supposed to determine physical and mental constitution; the bodily habit attributed to this (as, a sanguine, choleric, phlegmatic, or melancholy *temperament*); also, that individual peculiarity of physical organization by which the manner of thinking, feeling, and acting of every person is permanently affected (as, "There is the same type of frame and the same keen activity of *temperament* in mother and son," George Eliot's "Adam Bede," iv.; "Her highly strung *temperament* made her uncertain . . . capricious . . . enchanting," G. B. Shaw's "Man and Superman," iii.); natural disposition; sometimes, unusual personal make-up manifested by peculiarities of feeling, temper, action, etc., with disinclination to submit to ordinary rules or restraints, often regarded as a common accompaniment of genius or artistic ability (as, "I tremble for her. I am afraid she has that terrible thing which is called *temperament*": W. Churchill's "Modern Chronicle," i. 4); also, the act of tempering or moderating (obs. or archaic); adjustment or compromise (obs. or archaic); a middle course (obs. or archaic); also, climate†; temperature†; in *music*, the tuning of pianofortes, organs, or the like, so that the tones are available in different keys or tonalities; a particular system of doing this.—**tem″-per-a-men′tal** (-men′tạl), *a.* Of or pertaining to temperament; constitutional; also, having or exhibiting a strongly marked individual temperament; dominated by temperament, as in feeling or action.—**tem″per-a-men′tal-ly**, *adv.*

tem-per-ance (tem′pėr-ạns), *n.* [L. *temperantia*, < *temperans*, observing moderation, temperate, ppr. of *temperare*, E. *temper*.] Moderation or self-restraint in action, statement, etc.; self-control; restraint; esp., habitual moderation in the indulgence of a natural appetite or passion; specif., moderation in the use of alcoholic liquors; also, the principle and practice of total abstinence from alcoholic liquors (often used attributively: as, a *temperance* society; a *temperance* hotel); also, mildness of weather or climate†; also, the act of tempering†; tempered state†.

tem-per-ate (tem′pėr-ạt), *a.* [L. *temperatus*, tempered, moderate, pp. of *temperare*, E. *temper*.] Moderate or self-

restrained; not swayed by passion; not extreme in opinion, etc.; esp., moderate as regards indulgence of appetite or passion; specif., moderate or abstemious in the use of alcoholic liquors; also, not excessive in degree, as things, qualities, etc.; specif., moderate in respect of temperature (as, the *temperate* zones, the parts of the earth's surface lying between the tropics and the polar circles).—**tem′per-ate-ly**, *adv.*—**tem′per-ate-ness**, *n.*

tem-per-a-ture (tem′pėr-ạ-ṭūr), *n.* [L. *temperatura*, < *temperare*, E. *temper*.] The act of tempering†, or the fact or state of being tempered†; a mixture† or compound†; constitution† or temperament†; freedom from excess†, or moderation†; mildness, as of the weather or climate†; also, the state of a substance with regard to sensible heat; the degree or intensity of the sensible heat of a body, the lowest degree being −273° C., or absolute zero, where theoretically all heat vanishes, and very high degrees being, for example, that of the sun, commonly regarded as over 6,000° C., and that of certain stars, sometimes thought to be as high as 28,000° C. (see *absolute temperature* and *absolute zero*, under *absolute, a.*); in *physiol.* and *pathol.*, the degree of heat of a living body, esp. the human body; also, loosely, the excess of this above the normal (which in the adult human being is about 98.6° F., or about 37° C.).

tem-pered (tem′pėrd), *a.* Having a temper or disposition (as specified): as, good-*tempered*.

tem-per-er (tem′pėr-ėr), *n.* One who or that which tempers.

tem-pest (tem′pest), *n.* [OF. *tempeste* (F. *tempête*), < L. *tempestas*, a time, season, weather, storm, < *tempus*, time.] An extensive current of wind rushing with great velocity and violence, esp. one attended with rain, hail, or snow; a violent storm (as, "The icy winds . . . brought with them a *tempest* of arrowy sleet and snow": Prescott's "Conquest of Mexico," iii. 8); violently stormy weather (as, "He looked like a harbinger of *tempest*, a shipmate of the Flying Dutchman": Hawthorne's "Twice-Told Tales," The Village Uncle); fig., a violent commotion, disturbance, or tumult (as, a political *tempest*; a *tempest* in the mind or breast); a violent outburst (of emotion, tears, etc.).—**tempest in a tea-pot**, a great disturbance in a small place or over a small matter.—**tempest**, *v.* **I.** *tr.* To affect by or as by a tempest; disturb violently: as, "He [Boreas] *tempests* Apenninus and the gray Ship-shaking Ocean" (Wiffen's tr. Tasso's "Jerusalem Delivered," iii. 2). **II.** *intr.* To be tempestuous; storm; rage. [Obs. or rare.]—**tem-pes′tu-ous** (-pes′ṭū-us), *a.* [LL. *tempestuosus*.] Characterized by or subject to tempests or violent storms (as, *tempestuous* weather; a *tempestuous* night; the *tempestuous* ocean); of the nature of or resembling a tempest (as, a *tempestuous* wind); violently stormy; fig., characterized by violent commotions or disturbances (as, a *tempestuous* period); tumultuous; turbulent; passionate; also, agitated as by a tempest (as, "A winning wave, deserving note, In the *tempestuous* petticoat": Herrick's "Delight in Disorder").—**tem-pes′tu-ous-ly**, *adv.*—**tem-pes′tu-ous-ness**, *n.*

Tem-plar (tem′plär), *n.* [OF. F. *templier*, < ML. *templarius*, < L. *templum*, E. *temple*³.] A member of a religious and military order, also called Knights Templars, Knights of the Temple, and Poor Soldiers of the Temple, founded at Jerusalem about 1118, chiefly for the protection of the Holy Sepulcher and of pilgrims to the Holy Land, and suppressed by the Council of Vienne in 1312 (so called from the early headquarters of the order on or near the site of the temple of Solomon at Jerusalem); also, a member of an order of freemasons in the U. S., calling themselves Knights Templars and claiming descent from the medieval order; also [sometimes *l. c.*], a student of the law or a barrister occupying chambers in the Inner Temple or the Middle Temple in London (see *temple*³, *n.*).

tem-plate (tem′plāt), *n.* Same as *templet.*

tem-ple¹ (tem′pl), *n.* [OF. *temple* (F. *tempe*), < L. *tempora*, pl. of *tempus*, temple, head, face.] The flattened region on either side of the human forehead; a corresponding region in lower animals; also, either of the side-pieces of a pair of spectacles, extending back above the ears of the wearer.

tem-ple² (tem′pl), *n.* [F. *temple*, also *tempia*: cf. It. *tempia*, temple of the head, *tempiale*, temple of a loom.] In a loom, a device for keeping the cloth stretched to the proper width during the process of weaving.

tem-ple[3] (tem′pl), *n.* [AS. *templ, tempel,* < L. *templum,* consecrated place, sanctuary, temple, orig. open space for augurial observations: cf. *contemplate.*] An edifice or place dedicated to the service or worship of a deity or deities; [also *cap.*] any of the three successive buildings, or groups of buildings, in ancient Jerusalem which were devoted to the worship of Jehovah, the first built by Solomon and destroyed about 586 B.C., the second built by the Jews on their return from the Exile (about 536 B.C.), and the third begun by Herod the Great and destroyed at the capture of Jerusalem by the Romans (A.D. 70); [*l. c.*] an edifice erected as a place of public worship; a church, esp. a large or imposing one; sometimes, a Protestant church, as distinguished from a Roman Catholic church; fig., any place or object regarded as occupied by the divine presence, as the body of a Christian (see 1 Cor. vi. 19); in general, a building, usually large or pretentious, devoted to some public use (as, a *temple* of music; a *temple* of fame); also [*cap.*], either of two establishments of the medieval Templars, one in London and the other in Paris; either of two groups of buildings ('Inner Temple' and 'Middle Temple') on the site of the Templars' former establishment in London, occupied by two of the Inns of Court; [*l. c.*] a building of the order of freemasons known as Knights Templars.—**tem′ple**[3], *v. t.;* -pled, -pling. To provide with a temple; inclose in or as in a temple.—**tem′-pled,** *a.* Having a temple or temples.—**tem′ple-less,** *a.* Destitute of temples.

tem-plet (tem′plet), *n.* [Origin uncertain: cf. F. *templet,* temple of a loom, also L. *templum,* small timber.] A pattern, mold, or the like, usually consisting of a thin plate of wood or metal, serving as a gage or guide in mechanical work; in *building,* a horizontal piece of timber, stone, or the like, in a wall, to receive and distribute the pressure of a girder, beam, etc.; also, a similar piece spanning a doorway or other opening and supporting joists, etc.; in *ship-building,* either of two wedges in each of the temporary blocks forming the support for the keel of a ship while building.

Templet for a Baluster.

tem-po (tem′pō), *n.;* pl. *-pos* (-pōz), It. *-pi* (-pē). [It., < L. *tempus,* time.] In *music,* relative rapidity or rate of movement (usually indicated by such terms as *adagio, allegro,* etc., or by reference to the metronome); also, the proper or characteristic speed or movement of a particular kind of piece, as a dance-tune.

tem-po-ral[1] (tem′pō-ral). [LL. *temporalis,* < L. *tempora:* see *temple*[1].] **I.** *a.* Of or pertaining to the temple or temples (of the head); in *anat.,* noting or pertaining to either of a pair of complex bones which form part of the sides and base of the skull (represented in many vertebrates by several distinct and independent bones). **II.** *n.* In *anat.,* a temporal bone.

tem-po-ral[2] (tem′pō-ral). [L. *temporalis,* < *tempus* (*tempor-*), time, period, season.] **I.** *a.* Of or pertaining to time; enduring for a time only (as, "The things which are seen are *temporal;* but the things which are not seen are eternal": 2 Cor. iv. 18); temporary; transitory; also, pertaining to or concerned with the present life or this world, or worldly (as, *temporal* interests or welfare; "I die thankful for an extraordinary portion of *temporal* mercies," Galt's "Annals of the Parish," xl.); also, secular, lay, or civil, as opposed to *spiritual* or *ecclesiastical* (as, lords *temporal,* in the British House of Lords, the members other than the ecclesiastics or lords spiritual; "All the *temporal* lands which men devout By testament have given to the church," Shakspere's "Henry V.," i. 1. 9; "the establishment of a vast *temporal* power acting in harmony with Rome and imposing laws upon Europe," J. F. Kirk's "Charles the Bold," iv. 1); in *gram.,* of, pertaining to, or expressing time (as, a *temporal* adverb); also, of or pertaining to the tenses of a verb; also, pertaining to or depending on the quantity of syllables (as, a *temporal* augment, an augment, as in some Greek verb-forms, consisting of a lengthening of an initial vowel). **II.** *n.* That which is temporal; a temporal matter or affair (chiefly in *pl.*); also, a temporal possession, estate, or the like (chiefly in *pl.*); a temporality.—**tem-po-ral′i-ty** (-ral′i-

ti), *n.;* pl. *-ties* (-tiz). Temporal character or nature; temporariness; also, something temporal; temporal or secular power or jurisdiction†; a temporal matter or affair (chiefly in *pl.*: as, "The meeting of the church court charged with the *temporalities* had not passed off well," S. R. Crockett's "Stickit Minister," xii.); a temporal possession, revenue, or the like, as of the church or clergy (chiefly in *pl.*); also, the body of secular persons, or the laity (as, "There were none, neither of the *temporality* nor spirituality, but that had either spoke or writ against the Pope's supremacy": Strype's "Memorials of Cranmer," iii. 7).—**tem′po-ral-ly,** *adv.*—**tem′po-ral-ty** (-ti), *n.;* pl. *-ties* (-tiz). Temporal power, jurisdiction, or affairs†; also, a temporal possession or revenue, as of the church or clergy (chiefly in *pl.*); a temporality; also, the body of secular persons, or the laity.

tem-po-ra-ry (tem′pō-rā-ri), *a.* [L. *temporarius,* < *tempus* (*tempor-*), time.] Lasting, existing, or effective for a time only (as, a *temporary* stay in a place; a *temporary* calm; a *temporary* need, relief, or loan); serving for the time being (as, a *temporary* substitute; a *temporary* shelter); transient; not permanent; also, belonging or adapted to the time or period†; also, belonging to the present life or this world†.—**tem′po-ra-ri-ly,** *adv.*—**tem′po-ra-ri-ness,** *n.*

tem-po-rize (tem′pō-rīz), *v. i.;* -rized, -rizing. [F. *temporiser,* < L. *tempus* (*tempor-*), time.] To comply with the time or occasion, or yield temporarily or ostensibly to the current of opinion or circumstances (as, "Though the court of Avignon could not approve of such an usurpation, it *temporized* enough not directly to oppose it": Hallam's "Europe during the Middle Ages," iii. 2); also, to act indecisively or use evasive means in order to gain time or delay matters (as, "I *temporised* and raised obstacles, and quieted him from time to time," S. Butler's "Way of All Flesh," lxxxi.; "Mr. Britling *temporised* by saying he would 'make inquiries,' and put Mr. Van der Pant off for two days," H. G. Wells's "Mr. Britling," ii. 2. § 8); treat or parley (*with*) so as to gain time; also, to come to terms (*with*); effect a compromise (*between*).—**tem″po-ri-za′tion** (-ri-zā′shon), *n.*—**tem′po-riz-er** (-rī-zèr), *n.*—**tem′po-riz-ing-ly,** *adv.*

tempt (tempt), *v. t.* [OF. *tempter,* also *tenter* (F. *tenter*), < L. *temptare,* later *tentare,* touch, feel, try, test, attempt.] To try† or test†; hence, to put to the test or proof in a venturesome way (as, to *tempt* fortune or one's fate); act presumptuously toward, risk provoking, or provoke (as, "They *tempted* God in their heart by asking meat for their lust": Ps. lxxviii. 18); risk the perils of (the sea, storm, etc.: chiefly poetic); also, to try† or attempt†; make an attempt upon†; also, to try to dispose or incite, or assail with enticements, esp. to evil (as, "*Tempt* me no more to folly," Shakspere's "Troilus and Cressida," v. 2. 18; "in all points *tempted* like as we are, yet without sin," Heb. iv. 15); hence, to allure, appeal strongly to, or invite, as something pleasing does (as, the prospect or the offer *tempts* me; a dish *tempts* the appetite; "Green covered places *tempted* the foot," Blackmore's "Lorna Doone," lix.); affect with a strong inclination, or render strongly disposed (to do something): as, "He is *tempted* to palter with the right," Hawthorne's "Blithedale Romance," xv.; I felt *tempted* to tell him what I thought); also, to induce or persuade by enticement or allurement (as, "Not a man was *tempted* to desert the standard of the Gothic king": Gibbon's "Decline and Fall of the Roman Empire," xliii.); bring or draw (*away, off, out,* etc.) by enticement or allurement (as, "Neither prayers, nor defiance . . . could *tempt* the Gothic king beyond the fortifications of Ravenna," Gibbon's "Decline and Fall of the Roman Empire," xli.; the pleasant weather *tempted* them out of doors); also, to try to lead (a person) to contradict or commit himself (obs. or archaic: as, "This they said, *tempting* him, that they might have to accuse him," John, viii. 6).—**tempt′a-ble,** *a.* That may be tempted.—**temp-ta-tion** (temp-tā′shon), *n.* [OF. *temptation* (F. *tentation*), < L. *temptatio*(*n-*), *tentatio*(*n-*).] The act of tempting, or the fact or state of being tempted, esp. to evil (as, "When the devil had ended all the *temptation,* he departed," Luke, iv. 13; "Lead us not into *temptation,*" Mat. vi. 13); enticement or allurement, or an instance of it (as, "He rejected these *temptations* a long while, but at last was overcome and yielded," Strype's "Memorials of Cranmer," iii. 21; "I couldn't resist the *temptation* to see your garden," W. Churchill's "Modern Chronicle," i. 7); also, something that tempts, entices, or allures (as, "Your money's a *temptation* to the evilly disposed": Bret Harte's "Tennessee's Partner"); a tempting object or inducement.—**tempt'er**, *n.* One who or that which tempts, esp. to evil; [sometimes *cap.*] with *the*, the devil.—**tempt'ing**, *p. a.* That tempts; enticing, alluring, or inviting: as, a *tempting* bait; "Never did I see anything so *tempting* as that armchair" (Mrs. H. Ward's "Robert Elsmere," xxi.).—**tempt'ing-ly**, *adv.*—**tempt'ing-ness**, *n.*—**tempt'ress**, *n.* A female tempter.

tem-u-lent (tem'ū-lent), *a.* [L. *temulentus*, drunken: cf. *temetum*, strong drink, and E. *abstemious*.] Drunken; intoxicated; proceeding from drink; also, intoxicating. [Now rare.]—**tem'u-len-cy** (-len-si), *n.*

ten (ten). [AS. *tēn*, *tien*, *tyn* = D. *tien* = G. *zehn* = Icel. *tīu* = Goth. *taihun*, ten; akin to L. *decem*, Gr. δέκα, Skt. *daça*, ten: cf. *-teen* and *-ty*.] **I.** *a.* One more than nine. **II.** *n.* A number composed of ten units, or a symbol, as 10 or x, representing it; a set of ten persons or things; a playing-card with ten pips.

ten-a-ble (ten'a-bl), *a.* [F. *tenable*, < *tenir*, < L. *tenere*, hold.] Capable of being held, maintained, or defended, as against attack (lit. or fig.): as, "There were no *tenable* defences with the exception of a castle" (J. F. Kirk's "Charles the Bold," iii. 2); a theory no longer *tenable*.—**ten-a-bil'i-ty** (-bil'i-ti), **ten'a-ble-ness**, *n.*—**ten'a-bly**, *adv.*

ten-ace (ten'ās), *n.* [F. *tenace*, a tenace, orig. adj., 'tenacious': cf. F. *demeurer tenace*, 'remain tenacious,' hold a tenace.] In *whist*, a combination of the best and third best cards of a suit ('major tenace'), or of the second and fourth best cards ('minor tenace'), esp. when held by the fourth hand.

te-na-cious (tē-nā'shus), *a.* [L. *tenax* (*tenac-*), < *tenere*, hold.] Holding fast, or characterized by keeping a firm hold (as, *tenacious* jaws; *tenacious* vines; a *tenacious* grip; "The hunter has need of a *tenacious* seat in the saddle," Parkman's "Oregon Trail," xxiv.); fig., clinging or adhering persistently to something (often with *of*: as, to be *tenacious* of one's opinions; "The Catalans were *tenacious* of their ancient usages," Hallam's "Europe during the Middle Ages," iv.); highly retentive (as, a *tenacious* memory; a mind *tenacious* of facts); pertinacious, persistent, stubborn, or obstinate (as, "Sir John de Walton . . . was *tenacious* in upholding strict discipline," Scott's "Castle Dangerous," v.; "A sufficiently *tenacious* defense might well wear down the patience of the North," Charnwood's "Abraham Lincoln," vii.); also, adhesive or sticky; viscous or glutinous; also, holding together; cohesive; not easily pulled asunder; tough.—**te-na'cious-ly**, *adv.*—**te-na'cious-ness**, *n.*—**te-na'ci-ty** (-nas'i-ti), *n.* The quality or property of being tenacious; firmness in holding fast (lit. or fig.); retentiveness; pertinacity, persistence, or obstinacy (as, "The Scots fought with desperate *tenacity*": Morley's "Oliver Cromwell," iv. 4); adhesiveness; viscosity; cohesiveness; toughness.

te-nac-u-lum (tē-nak'ū-lum), *n.*; pl. *-la* (-lä). [LL., instrument for holding, < L. *tenere*, hold.] In *surg.*, a small, sharp-pointed hook set in a handle, used for picking up arteries, etc., in operations and dissections.

te-naille, te-nail (tē-nāl'), *n.* [F. *tenaille*, lit. 'pincers,' 'tongs,' < ML. *tenacula*, prop. pl. of LL. *tenaculum*: see *tenaculum*.] In *fort.*, an outwork containing one or two reëntering angles, raised in the main ditch immediately in front of a curtain, between two bastions.—**te-nailled', te-nailed'** (-nāld'), *a.* Furnished with tenailles.

ten-an-cy (ten'an-si), *n.*; pl. *-cies* (-siz). The state of being a tenant; a holding, as of lands, by any kind of title; tenure; specif., occupancy of land, a house, or the like, under a lease or on payment of rent; also, the period of a tenant's occupancy; also, a holding, or piece of land held by a tenant (as, "To successfully work a *tenancy* of such narrow limits . . . the occupier should himself labour in the field": Jefferies's "Gamekeeper at Home," ii.).

ten-ant (ten'ant), *n.* [OF. F. *tenant*, ppr. of *tenir*, < L. *tenere*, hold.] In *law*, one who holds or possesses lands, tenements, or sometimes personalty, by any kind of title; also, one who holds land, a house, or the like of another (the

landlord) for a period of time, as a lessee or occupant for rent (as, "He sympathised with the difficulties of careless *tenants* in a harsh world of landlords": Arnold Bennett's "Clayhanger," iv. 6); hence, in general use, an occupant, inhabitant, or denizen of any place (as, "The grave . . . was instantly made to receive its miserable *tenant*," Cooper's "Prairie," xxxii.; "the wild cattle, the most formidable of all the *tenants* of the ancient Caledonian forest," Scott's "Castle Dangerous," vii.).—**ten'ant**, *v.* **I.** *tr.* To hold or occupy as a tenant (lit. or fig.); dwell in; inhabit: as, "A solitary woman . . . *tenanted* a chamber in this house" (Godwin's "Caleb Williams," xxxiv.); "All sorts of fancies, bright and dark, *tenanted* my mind" (C. Brontë's "Jane Eyre," xii.). **II.** *intr.* To dwell or live (*in*).—**ten'ant-a-ble**, *a.* Fit for being tenanted or occupied.—**ten'ant-less**, *a.* Without a tenant; vacant: as, "a dreary and *tenantless* mansion" (Longfellow's "Courtship of Miles Standish," iii.).—**ten'ant=right**, *n.* A right that a person has as a tenant, as the right to receive, if turned off, a compensation from the landlord for crops left in the ground, labor in preparing the soil for the next crop, produce left on the farm, and unexhausted or permanent improvements.—**ten'ant-ry** (-ri), *n.*; pl. *-ries* (-riz). The state or condition of being a tenant; also, land let out to tenants, or the profits derived from it; also, tenants collectively; the body of tenants on an estate (as, "The old Squire's visits to his *tenantry* were rare": George Eliot's "Adam Bede," xxxii.).—**ten'ant-ship**, *n.*

tench (tench), *n.*; pl. *tenches* or (esp. collectively) *tench*. [OF. *tenche* (F. *tanche*), < LL. *tinca*.] A fresh-water cyprinoid fish, *Tinca tinca* (or *vulgaris*), of Europe, so tenacious of life that it may be conveyed alive in damp weeds for long distances.

Tench.

tend¹ (tend), *v. i.* [OF. F. *tendre*, < L. *tendere* (pp. *tentus*, also *tensus*), tr. stretch, extend, intr. direct the course, go, strive, tend, akin to Gr. τείνειν, Skt. *tan-*, stretch: see *thin*.] To direct the course, or proceed, esp. toward some point (obs. or archaic: as, "I descry this way Some other *tending*," Milton's "Samson Agonistes," 1302); be directed or lead (*to*, *toward*, etc.), as a journey, course, road, etc.; also, to be naturally disposed or impelled to move in a particular direction (as, "The single atoms each to other *tend*," Pope's "Essay on Man," iii. 10; by centrifugal force a body revolving about a center *tends* away from that center); fig., to incline or have a bent or drift in a particular direction, as in a course of progress, change, or action (as, governments are *tending* toward democracy; modern methods are *tending* away from many old-time ideals; all these petitions *tended* to the same end; "The disconsolate archbishop perceived to what this *tended*," Strype's "Memorials of Cranmer," iii. 21); incline in operation or effect, lead, or conduce, as to some result (as, measures *tending* to improved working conditions; exercise *tends* to health); be disposed or inclined in action, operation, or effect (to do something): as, the particles *tend* to unite; "The monopoly . . . *tends* rather to diminish than to increase the sum total of the revenue," Adam Smith's "Wealth of Nations," iv. 7. 3).

tend² (tend), *v.* [For *attend*.] **I.** *tr.* To give heed to†; also, to attend to by work or services, care, etc. (as, to *tend* a fire; to *tend* a machine; "The Painted Lady . . . pretended to be *tending* her plants," Barrie's "Sentimental Tommy," xvi.; "She assisted me cheerfully in my business, folding and stitching pamphlets, *tending* shop," B. Franklin's "Autobiography," v.); look after (a flock or herd, etc.); watch over and care for (an infant, a sick or wounded person, etc.); minister to or wait on (a person, etc.) with service (as, "Dry fuel on the fire he laid, And bade the Saxon share his plaid. He *tended* him like welcome guest": Scott's "Lady of the Lake," iv. 31); attend on for service or escort (obs. or prov.); also, to attend (a meeting, church, etc.), as by being present (now prov.); also, to await†. **II.** *intr.* To give heed (*to*)†; also, to attend (*to*) by action, care, etc. (now prov.: as, "if Pa and you would *tend* to things instead of standing around fussing," Sinclair Lewis's "Arrowsmith," ix.); attend or wait (*on* or *upon*) with ministration or service (as, "Were you sick, ourself Would *tend* upon you": Tennyson's "Princess," iii. 304); also, to wait, as in expectation or readiness†.— **tend'ance**, *n.* Attention or care; ministration, as to the weak or sick; also, attendants collectively.

tend-en-cy (ten'dẹn-si), *n.*; pl. *-cies* (-siz). [ML. *tendentia*, < L. *tendens*, ppr. of *tendere*, E. *tend*[1].] Direction, as of movement or travel† (as, "There is only one condition . . . that you follow my footsteps without any questions asked as to the *tendency* of our journey": Scott's "Castle Dangerous," xiv.); also, natural or prevailing disposition to move, proceed, or act in some direction or toward some point, end, or result (as, the *tendency* of falling bodies toward the earth); an inclination, bent, or predisposition to something (as, "an aged lady with rheumatic *tendencies*": Pinero's "Wife without a Smile," i.); drift or trend, as of discourse; sometimes, special and definite purpose in a novel or other literary work (from German use).—**ten-den'tial** (-den'shạl), *a.* Pertaining to, of the nature of, or marked by a tendency; also, tendentious.—**ten-den'tious** (-shus), *a.* [After G. *tendenziös*.] Having an intended tendency or purpose; exhibiting a definite tendency, aim, or bias.—**ten-den'-tious-ly**, *adv.*—**ten-den'tious-ness**, *n.*

tend-er[1] (ten'dẹr), *n.* [See *tend*[2].] One who tends; one who attends to or takes charge of something (as, a bar-*tender*); also, a vessel employed to attend one or more larger vessels, as for supplying provisions; also, a rowboat or motor-boat carried or towed by a yacht or other vessel, and used for landing persons, etc.; also, a car attached to a locomotive on a railroad, for carrying coal, water, etc.

ten-der[2] (ten'dẹr). [OF. F. *tendre*, < L. *tener*, soft, delicate, tender: cf. L. *tenuis*, thin, fine.] **I.** *a.* Soft or delicate in substance, or not hard or tough (as, *tender* meat; vegetables boiled until *tender*; "the *tender* young grass on the hill-sides," H. Kingsley's "Geoffry Hamlyn," vi.); yielding readily to force or pressure; easily broken; fragile; also, weak or delicate in constitution; not strong or hardy; unable to endure fatigue, hardship, rough treatment, etc.; also, having the weakness and delicacy of youth (as, *tender* babes); young or immature (as, "Being as yet a youth . . . men said . . . that he was over *tender* for marriage": Kipling's "Kim," i.); marked by the weakness of early childhood or youth (as, the *tender* years of infancy; children of *tender* age); also, delicate or soft in quality (as, a *tender* blue or green; "a flood of *tender* light," Bryant's "Waning Moon"; "A small bird had broken out in song, a clear, *tender* melody," W. H. Hudson's "Green Mansions," xvii.); also, delicate, soft, or gentle, as the touch, the hand in touching, etc.; also, soft or soft-hearted, easily touched, feeling, or sympathetic, as the heart, a person, the feelings, etc. (as, "She had a *tender*, human heart, which was easily moved," W. H. Hudson's "Green Mansions," viii.; "Mrs. Hale, *tender* soul, had pictured me as lost," Mrs. Wharton's "Ethan Frome," Conclusion); kind, compassionate, or pitiful; affectionate or loving (as, "His *tender* and social nature had already overflowed in attachments to everything about him," Hawthorne's "Twice-Told Tales," The Gentle Boy; "the *tender* solicitude of a parent," Lytton Strachey's "Queen Victoria," iii.); sentimental or amatory (as, *tender* passages between lovers; the *tender* passion, sexual love); fond (*of*: as, "She was soon reconciled, and by degrees grew extremely *tender* of me," Swift's "Gulliver's Travels," ii. 1); considerate or careful (*of*: as. to be *tender* of a person's feelings or reputation); chary or reluctant (with *of*: as, "I felt *tender* of hurting his feelings," C. Brontë's "Villette," xxxvi.); also, dear† or precious†; also, acutely or painfully sensitive (as, "His vanity was wounded in its *tenderest* point," Froude's "Cæsar," xii.; "He went slowly, for his feet were growing *tender*," G. W. Cable's "John March, Southerner," viii.); readily made uneasy, as the conscience; of a delicate or ticklish nature, or requiring careful or tactful handling, as a matter or subject; also, of a ship, apt to lean over; somewhat crank. **II.**† *n.* Tender state; also, tender feeling or regard.—**ten'der**[2], *v. t.* To make tender; also, to regard or

treat with tenderness; have regard or consideration for (as, "Winchester . . . *tendered* not so much the king's cause as his own": Strype's "Memorials of Cranmer," i. 8). [Archaic or prov.]

ten-der[3] (ten'dẹr), *v.* [F. *tendre*, stretch, extend: see *tend*[1].] **I.** *tr.* To present formally for acceptance (as, to *tender* an oath to a person; to *tender* one's resignation; to *tender* one's thanks); make formal offer of; in general, to offer or proffer; in *law*, to offer, as money or goods, in payment of a debt or other obligation, esp. in exact accordance with the terms of the law and of the obligation. **II.** *intr.* To make a tender or offer.—**ten'der**[3], *n.* The act of tendering; an offer of something for acceptance (as, "He would immediately demand permission . . . to make Liddy a *tender* of his hand and fortune": Smollett's "Humphry Clinker," June 10); also, that which is tendered or offered (as, legal *tender*, money or currency which may legally be tendered in payment of a money obligation); in *law*, an offer, as of money or goods, in payment or satisfaction of a debt or other obligation, esp. in exact accordance with the terms of the law and of the obligation; in *com.*, an offer made in writing by one party to another to execute certain work, supply certain commodities, etc., at a given cost.—**ten'der-a-ble**, *a.* That may be tendered.—**ten'der-er**, *n.*

ten-der-foot (ten'dẹr-fût), *n.*; pl. *-foots* or *-feet* (-fēt). Orig., a new-comer in the ranching and mining regions of the western U. S., unused to the hardships of pioneer life; hence, a raw, inexperienced person; a greenhorn; a novice. [Colloq.]

ten-der=heart-ed (ten'dẹr-här'ted), *a.* Having a tender heart; soft-hearted; feeling; sympathetic.—**ten'der=heart'ed-ness**, *n.*

ten-der-loin (ten'dẹr-loin), *n.* A strip of tender meat forming part of the loin of beef, pork, etc., lying under the short ribs and consisting of the psoas muscle; sometimes, a cut of beef lying between the sirloin and ribs; also [*cap.*], a district in New York City including the great mass of theaters and other places of amusement, hotels, etc., and also haunts of vice, and forming the center of night life (colloq.); a similar district in other cities (colloq., U. S.).

ten-der-ly (ten'dẹr-li), *adv.* In a tender manner; gently; kindly; fondly; with tender feeling.—**ten'der-ness**, *n.* The quality or state of being tender; also, a tender feeling or regard, as for a person or thing.

ten-di-nous (ten'di-nus), *a.* [F. *tendineux*, < ML. *tendo* (*tendin-*), E. *tendon*.] Of the nature of or resembling a tendon; consisting of tendons.

ten-don (ten'dọn), *n.* [= F. *tendon*, < ML. *tendo* (*tendon-* or *tendin-*), appar. formed < L. *tendere*, stretch, to parallel Gr. τένων, sinew, tendon, < τείνειν, stretch: see *tend*[1].] In *anat.*, a cord or band of dense, tough, inelastic, white fibrous tissue, serving to connect a muscle with a bone or other part; a sinew.—**tendon of Achilles**, in *anat.*, the strong tendon which serves to connect the muscles of the calf of the leg with the bone of the heel and forms the principal extensor of the foot: so called because, according to legend, when Achilles' mother dipped him in the Styx to render him invulnerable, she held him by the heel, which thus escaped dipping and remained vulnerable.

ten-dresse (toṅ-dres), *n.* [F.] Tenderness; tender regard.

ten-dril (ten'dril), *n.* [Cf. obs. F. *tendrillon*, dim. of *tendron*, shoot, sprout, < *tendre*, E. *tender*[2].] In *bot.*, a filiform leafless organ of climbing plants, often growing in spiral form, which attaches itself to or twines round some other body, so as to support the plant; hence, something resembling a curl or ringlet of hair.—**ten'driled**, **ten'drilled**, *a.*

Ten-e-bræ (ten'ẹ-brē), *n.*, pl., darkness.] In the *Rom. Cath. Ch.*, the office of matins

Tendril. — Branch of passion-flower.

and lauds for Thursday, Friday, and Saturday of Holy Week, sung respectively on the afternoon or evening of Wednesday, Thursday, and Friday of that week, at which lighted candles are gradually extinguished until but one is left burning, that one being then hidden and brought out again at the end of the office.

ten-e-brif-ic (ten-ē-brif′ik), *a.* [L. *tenebræ*, darkness, + *facere*, make.] Producing darkness.

te-neb-ri-ous (tē-neb′ri-us), *a.* Same as *tenebrous*.

ten-e-brous, ten-e-brose (ten′ē-brus, -brōs), *a.* [L. *tenebrosus*, < *tenebræ*, darkness.] Dark; gloomy; obscure: as, "*tenebrous* night" (Galsworthy's "Dark Flower," iii. 11).

ten-e-ment (ten′ē-ment), *n.* [OF. *tenement*, F. *tènement*, < ML. *tenementum*, a holding, < L. *tenere*, hold.] In legal use, the holding of land or other real property as a possession†; also, any species of permanent property, as lands, houses, rents, an office, a franchise, etc., that may be held of another; specif., *pl.*, freehold interests in things immovable considered as subjects of property (esp. in the phrase 'lands and tenements,' that is, lands and all other freehold interests); also, in general use, any house or building to live in, or a dwelling-house (as, "the fat meadow-lands, the rich fields of wheat . . . which surrounded the warm *tenement* of Van Tassel": Irving's "Sketch-Book," Sleepy Hollow); hence, any habitation, abode, or dwelling-place (as, "the little wagon, which had so long been the *tenement* of Inez": Cooper's "Prairie," xxxii.); sometimes, the body as the abode of the soul (as, "The spirit had . . . departed, and there was nothing remaining but the clay *tenement*": Galt's "Annals of the Parish," xl.); also, a portion of a house or building occupied by a tenant as a separate dwelling; also, a tenement-house.—**dominant tenement.** See under *dominant, a.*—**servient tenement.** See under *servient.*—**ten-e-men′tal** (-men′tạl), **ten-e-men′ta-ry** (-tạ-ri), *a.*—**ten′e-ment=house,** *n.* A house or building divided into sets of rooms tenanted by separate families; esp., such a building occupied by families of the poorer class in crowded parts of large cities.

ten-et (ten′et), *n.* [L., 'he holds,' 3d pers. sing. pres. ind. of *tenere*, hold, maintain.] Any opinion, principle, doctrine, dogma, or the like held as true: as, political or religious *tenets*.

ten-fold (ten′fōld). **I.** *a.* Comprising ten parts or members; ten times as great or as much. **II.** *n.* Ten times as much. **III.** *adv.* In tenfold measure.

te-ni-a (tē′ni-ạ), etc. See *tænia*, etc.

ten-ner (ten′ẹr), *n.* A ten-dollar bill or a ten-pound note (as, "That fellow Soames . . . would have a fit if you tried to borrow a *tenner* from him": Galsworthy's "Man of Property," xvi.); anything that counts as ten. [Colloq.]

ten-nis (ten′is), *n.* [ME. *tenetz, teneys*; origin uncertain; referred by some to OF. *tenez*, impv. of *tenir*, hold (cf. *tenon*), as if a call to an opponent to take or receive the ball.] An old and complicated game in which a ball is struck with a racket (orig. with the palm of the hand) and driven back and forth over a net, usually by two players, in a specially constructed inclosed oblong court (also called 'royal tennis' and, in America, 'court-tennis'); also, lawn-tennis.—**ten′nis= court,** *n.* The oblong inclosed area or edifice in which the old game of tennis is played; also, the plot of ground prepared and marked out for lawn-tennis.

ten-on (ten′ọn), *n.* [OF. F. *tenon*, < *tenir*, < L. *tenere*, hold.] A projection fashioned on an end or side of a piece of wood, etc., for insertion in a corresponding cavity (*mortise*) in another piece, so as to form a joint. See cut at *mortise*.—**ten′on,** *v. t.* To furnish with a tenon; also, to fit together with tenon and mortise; fig., to join securely.

ten-on-ti-tis (ten-ọn-tī′tis), *n.* [NL., < Gr. τένων (τενοντ-), sinew, tendon: cf. *tendon*.] In *pathol.*, inflammation of a tendon.

ten-or (ten′ọr). [OF. *tenor, tenour* (F. *teneur*), < L. *tenor*, a holding on, uninterrupted course, sense, tenor, < *tenere*, hold; in music, OF. *tenor* (F. *ténor*), < It. *tenore*, < ML. *tenor* (so called as orig. sustaining the principal part, or melody).] **I.** *n.* Continuance† or duration†; continuous course, progress, or movement (as, "Along the cool sequester'd vale of life They kept the noiseless *tenor* of their way," Gray's "Elegy," xix.; "His conduct was . . . uniform and unvarying in its *tenor,*" Marryat's "Mr. Midshipman Easy," v.); also, quality†, character†, or condition†; habitual condition, as of mind (now rare); also, the course of thought or meaning which runs through something written or spoken (as, "notions . . . contrary to the whole general *tenor* of Scripture": J. Butler's "Analogy of Religion," ii. 1); general purport or drift; substance or import; also, a transcript or exact copy of a document; in *music*, the adult male voice intermediate between the bass and the alto or countertenor; a part sung by or written for such a voice; a singer with such a voice; an instrument corresponding in compass to this voice, specif. the viola; in *change-ringing*, the lowest-toned bell of a peal. **II.** *a.* In *music*, of, pertaining to, or having the compass of a tenor.

te-nor-rha-phy (tē-nor′ạ-fi), *n.* [Gr. τένων, tendon, + ῥαφή, a sewing.] In *surg.*, suture of a tendon.

te-not-o-my (tē-not′ō-mi), *n.* [F. *ténotomie*, < Gr. τένων, tendon, + -τομία, < τέμνειν, cut.] In *surg.*, the cutting or division of a tendon.

ten-pence (ten′pens), *n.* A sum of money of the value of ten English pennies, or about 20 U. S. cents.—**ten′pen-ny** (-pẹ-ni), *a.* Of the amount or value of tenpence.

ten-pins (ten′pinz), *n.* A game, similar to ninepins, played with ten wooden pins at which a ball is bowled to knock them down, esp. a form of game played in the U. S. and Canada, and known also as 'American bowling' (see *bowling*) (construed as *sing.*); also, the pins used in such a game (construed as *pl.*).

ten-rec (ten′rek), *n.* [F. *tenrec, tanrec*; from Malagasy.] Any of several insectivorous mammals of Madagascar, which superficially resemble the European hedgehog and which constitute the family *Centetidæ*; esp., a common tailless species, *Centetes ecaudatus*.

Tenrec (*Centetes ecaudatus*).

tense[1] (tens), *n.* [OF. *tens* (F. *temps*), < L. *tempus*, time, also *tense*.] Time†; in *gram.*, one of the forms, or sets of forms, which a verb takes in order to indicate the time (present, past, or future) of the action or state denoted by it, and also, by extension, the nature of such action or state as continuing (imperfect), completed (perfect), or the like; in the abstract, modification of the form of a verb to indicate such differences of time, etc.

tense[2] (tens), *a.*; compar. *tenser*, superl. *tensest*. [L. *tensus*, pp. of *tendere*, stretch, extend, E. *tend*[1].] Stretched tight, as a cord, fiber, etc.; drawn taut; strained to stiffness; rigid; fig., in a state of mental or nervous strain, as a person; highly strung; keenly sensitive; characterized by a strain upon the nerves or feelings (as, "that *tense* moment of expectation": Arnold Bennett's "Hilda Lessways," ii. 6).

tense[2], *v. t. or i.*; tensed, tensing. To make or become tense.—**tense′ly,** *adv.*—**tense′ness,** *n.*

ten-si-ble (ten′si-bl), *a.* [ML. *tensibilis*, < L. *tendere*: see *tension*.] Capable of being stretched; tensile.

ten-sile (ten′sil), *a.* [NL. *tensilis*, < L. *tendere*: see *tension*.] Capable of being stretched or drawn out; ductile; also, of or pertaining to tension (as, *tensile* strain).—**tensile strength,** in *physics*, the resistance offered by a given material to tension or rupture; specif., the load necessary to produce rupture in a given material when pulled in the direction of length, commonly given in pounds per square inch.—**ten-sil′i-ty** (-sil′i-ti), *n.*

ten-sim-e-ter (ten-sim′e-tẹr), *n.* [From *tension* + *-meter*.] An instrument for determining vapor pressure or tension.

ten-sion (ten′shọn), *n.* [L. *tensio(n-)*, < *tendere*, stretch, extend, E. *tend*[1].] The act of stretching or straining, or the state of being stretched or strained (as, "The Mad Wolf drew his bow to its utmost *tension*": Parkman's "Oregon Trail," xvi.); often, fig., a straining, or strained condition, of the mind, feelings, or nerves; strong or severe intellectual effort; intense suppressed excitement (as, "The *tension* in Mr. Barnstaple's mind had become intolerable": H. G. Wells's "Men Like Gods," i. 5); a strained state of mutual relations (as, "Disputes about the border strongholds . . . worked with the standing international jealousy to produce a *tension* [between the English and the Scots] that had long been dangerous": Morley's "Oliver Cromwell," iii. 1); in *mech.*, a stress which tends to pull farther apart the particles of the body acted upon; specif., a force tending to elongate a body; in *mach.*, a device for stretching or pulling something; in *physics*, loosely, pressure (as, vapor *tension*, vapor pressure); in *elect.*, the condition of a dielectric body when its opposite surfaces are oppositely electrified; the quality which tends to produce electric discharge; also, electromotive force; potential.—**ten′sion,** *v. t.* To subject ·to tension; make tense.—**ten′sion-al,** *a.*

ten-si-ty (ten′si-ti), *n.* The state of being tense.

ten-sive (ten′siv), *a.* [F. *tensif*, < L. *tendere*: see *tension*.] Stretching or straining; in *pathol.*, noting a sensation of tension or tightness.

ten-son (ten′son, F. toṅ-sôṅ), *n.* [F. *tenson* = Pr. *tenso* = It. *tenzone*, contention, contest, < L. *tendere*, stretch, strive, contend: cf. *tension*.] A contest in verse between rival troubadours; also, a piece of verse composed for or sung at such a contest.

ten-sor (ten′sor), *n.* [NL., < L. *tendere*: see *tension*.] In *anat.*, a muscle that stretches or tightens some part of the body.

ten=strike (ten′strīk), *n.* A stroke which knocks down all the ten pins in the game of tenpins; fig., any stroke or act which is completely successful (as, "She decorated only one room. The rest, Kennicott hinted, she'd better leave till he 'made a *ten-strike*' ": Sinclair Lewis's "Main Street," vi.).

tent[1] (tent), *n.* [OF. F. *tente*, < ML. *tenta*, < L. *tendere*, stretch, extend, E. *tend*[1].] A portable shelter or lodge of skins, coarse cloth, or, esp., canvas, supported by means of one or more poles, and usually extended and secured by ropes fastened to pegs driven into the ground; hence, something like or likened to such a shelter; fig., an abode, habitation, or dwelling-place; also, a form of portable, open-air pulpit (Sc.).—**tent**[1], *v.* **I.** *intr.* To live in or as in a tent; encamp. **II.** *tr.* To provide with or lodge in tents; cover as with a tent.

Tent of form shown in manuscripts of 11th and 12th centuries.

tent[2] (tent), *n.* [OF. F. *tente*, < *tenter*, try: see *tempt*.] In *surg.*, a probe†; also, a roll or pledget, usually of soft absorbent material, as lint or gauze, for dilating an orifice, keeping open a wound, etc.—**tent**[2], *v. t.* In *surg.*, to probe†; also, to apply a tent or pledget to; keep open with a tent, as a wound.

tent[3] (tent), *v. t.* [Cf. *tend*[2].] To pay attention or give heed to; attend to or look after; observe, or take note of. [Now Sc. and north. Eng.]—**tent**[3], *n.* Attention; heed; care. [Now Sc. and north. Eng.]

tent[4] (tent), *n.* [Sp. *tinto*, deep-colored, < L. *tinctus*, pp. of *tingere*, E. *tinge*.] A deep-red Spanish wine, much used as a sacramental wine.

ten-ta-cle (ten′tạ-kl), *n.* [NL. *tentaculum*, < L. *tentare*, touch, feel: see *tempt*.] In *zoöl.*, any of various slender, flexible processes or appendages in animals, esp. invertebrates, which serve as organs of touch, prehension, etc.; a feeler; in *bot.*, a sensitive filament or process, as one of the glandular hairs of the sundew.—**ten′ta-cled,** *a.* Having tentacles.—**ten-tac′u-lar** (-tak′ụ-lär), *a.* Of, forming, or resembling tentacles.—**ten-tac′u-late** (-lāt), *a.* Tentacled.

tent-age (ten′tāj), *n.* Tents collectively; equipment or supply of tents.

ten-ta-tion (ten-tā′shọn), *n.* [L. *tentatio(n-)*, a trying, < *tentare*, try: see *tempt*.] A method of making mechanical adjustments or the like by experiment or a succession of trials.

ten-ta-tive (ten′tạ-tiv). [ML. *tentativus*, < L. *tentare*, try: see *tempt*.] **I.** *a.* Of the nature of, or made or done as, a trial, experiment, or attempt; experimental: as, "He had formed an ideal . . . and was trying in a feeble *tentative* way to realise it" (S. Butler's "Way of All Flesh," lv.). **II.** *n.* A trial or experiment; an essay or attempt: as, "I had even made some *tentatives* for return, for a reconciliation" (H. G. Wells's "Tono-Bungay," ii. 4. § 10).—**ten′ta-tive-ly,** *adv.*—**ten′ta-tive-ness,** *n.*

tent=cat-er-pil-lar (tent′kat″ẽr-pil-ạr), *n.* Any of several caterpillars or larvæ of moths of the genus *Malacosoma*, as *M. americana*, which spin tent-like silken webs in which they live gregariously.

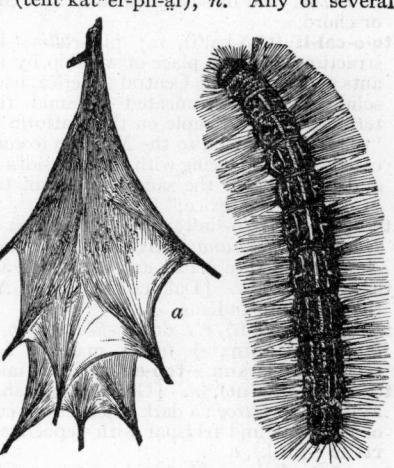

Tent-caterpillar (*Malacosoma americana*). — *a*, tent, one third of natural size.

tent-ed (ten′ted), *a.* Provided or covered with tents; also, tent-like (as, "yon *tented* sky": Wm. Collins's "Ode on the Poetical Character," 26).

tent-er[1] (ten′tẽr), *n.* One who lives in a tent.

tent-er[2] (ten′tẽr), *n.* [See *tent*[3].] One who tends, or has the care of, something, esp. a machine in a factory.

ten-ter[3] (ten′tẽr), *n.* [ME. *teyntur, tenture, tentowre,* ult. < L. *tendere* (pp. *tentus*), stretch, E. *tend*[1].] In the manufacture of cloth, a framework or the like on which the cloth is stretched so that it may set or dry evenly and without shrinking; also, a tenter-hook†.—**ten′ter**[3], *v. t.* To stretch (cloth) on a tenter or tenters.—**ten′ter=hook,** *n.* One of the hooks or bent nails which hold the cloth stretched on a tenter; fig., that on which anything is stretched or strained; a cause of suffering or painful suspense.—**on tenter=hooks,** fig., in a state of painful suspense: as, "Mr. Heath was *on tenter-hooks* all the while lest she should demand explanations" (W. De Morgan's "Alice-for-Short," iv.).

tenth (tenth), *a.* [ME. *tenthe*, < *ten*, E. *ten*: cf. *tithe*.] Next after the ninth; also, being one of ten equal parts.—**tenth Muse.** See under *Muse*[1].—**tenth,** *n.* The tenth member of a series; also, a tenth part; also, a contribution or tax of a tenth part; a tithe; in *music*, a tone distant from another tone by an interval of an octave and a third; the interval between such tones; the harmonic combination of such tones.—**tenth′ly,** *adv.*

ten-u-i-ros-tral (ten″ụ-i-ros′trạl), *a.* [L. *tenuis*, thin, + *rostrum*, beak.] Of birds, slender-billed.

ten-u-is (ten′ụ-is), *n.*; pl. *tenues* (-ēz) [L., thin, used to render Gr. ψιλός, bare, not aspirated.] In *gram.*, any of the three Greek surd mutes, κ, τ, π, or any of their equivalents, as *k, t, p*, in other languages.

te-nu-i-ty (te-nū′i-ti), *n.* The state of being tenuous; slenderness; thinness of consistence; rarefied condition; slightness.

ten-u-ous (ten′ụ-us), *a.* [L. *tenuis*, thin, slender, fine: see *thin*.] Thin or slender in form; slim; also, thin in consistence; rare or rarefied; fig., of slight importance or significance; unsubstantial.—**ten′u-ous-ly,** *adv.*—**ten′u-ous-ness,** *n.*

ten-ure (ten′ụr), *n.* [OF. F. *tenure*, < *tenir*, < L. *tenere*, hold.] The holding of property, esp. real property, originally of a superior; in general, the holding or possessing of anything (as, the *tenure* of an office or a right); the term or period of holding something, as an office; also, the manner of holding property or lands, etc., of a superior, as on particular conditions of service or payment (as, "The military *tenure* of land had been originally created as a means of national defence": Macaulay's "Hist. of Eng.," ii.); the relations, duties, and rights of the tenant with respect to the landlord; the nature of the right or title by which property is held; in general, the manner or terms of holding anything; also, something held, as of another (now rare: as, "These families were beginning to regard their *tenures* as their private property," Froude's "Cæsar," ii.).—**te-nu-ri-al** (te-nū′ri-al), *a.* Of, pertaining to, or of the nature of a tenure (of land, etc.).—**te-nu′ri-al-ly**, *adv.*

te-nu-to (tā-nö′tō), *a.* [It., pp. of *tenere*, < L. *tenere*, hold.] In *music*, held or sustained to its full time-value, as a tone or chord.

te-o-cal-li (tē-ọ-kal′i), *n.*; pl. *-callis* (-kal′iz). [Mex.] A structure used as a place of worship by the ancient inhabitants of Mexico and Central America, usually consisting of a solid four-sided truncated pyramid rising in successive terraces, with a temple on the platform at the summit: as, "the form common to the Mexican *teocallis*, that of a truncated pyramid, facing with its four sides the cardinal points, and divided into the same number of terraces" (Prescott's "Conquest of Mexico," iii. 6).

te-o-sin-te (tē-ọ-ọ-sin′tẹ), *n.* [Mex.] A tall annual grass, *Euchlæna mexicana*, native in Mexico and Central America, closely related to maize, and cultivated as a fodder-plant.

te-pee (tē′pē), *n.* [Dakota Ind. *tipi*.] A tent or wigwam of the American Indians.

tep-e-fy (tep′ẹ-fī), *v. t.* or *i.*; *-fied, -fying.* [L. *tepefacere*, < *tepere*, be warm, + *facere*, make.] To make or become tepid or lukewarm.—**tep-e-fac′tion** (-fak′shọn), *n.*

teph-rite (tef′rīt), *n.* [Gr. τεφρός, ash-colored, < τέφρα, ashes.] In *petrog.*, a dark igneous rock consisting essentially of pyroxene and feldspar with nepheline or leucite.—**teph-rit′ic** (-rit′ik), *a.*

tep-id (tep′id), *a.* [L. *tepidus*, < *tepere*, be warm.] Moderately warm; lukewarm; fig., having or showing little ardor or zeal (as, "He had been in love in a *tepid* fashion": Eden Phillpotts's "Children of Men," Prologue, iii.).—**tep-i-da-ri-um** (tep-i-dā′ri-um), *n.*; pl. *-ria* (-ri-ạ). [L., prop. neut. of *tepidarius*, of tepid water, < *tepidus*.] A warm room in the ancient Roman thermæ, situated between the frigidarium and the caldarium.—**te-pid-i-ty** (te-pid′i-ti), **tep′id-ness**, *n.* —**tep′id-ly**, *adv.*

ter-. [L. *ter*, adv., thrice: cf. *tri*-.] A combining-form or prefix meaning 'thrice,' 'three times,' as in *tercentenary*.

ter-aph (ter′af), *n.* Occasional singular of *teraphim*.

ter-a-phim (ter′ạ-fim), *n. pl.* [Heb.] Idols or images reverenced by the ancient Hebrews and kindred peoples, apparently as household gods; also (construed as *sing.*), an idol or image of this kind.

ter-a-to-gen-e-sis (ter″ạ-tọ-jen′e-sis), *n.* [Gr. τέρας (τερατ-), monster, + γένεσις, genesis.] In *biol.*, the production or formation of monsters. Also **ter-a-tog′e-ny** (-toj′e-ni).—**ter″a-to-ge-net′ic** (-jẹ-net′ik), **ter″a-to-gen′ic** (-jen′ik), *a.*

ter-a-toid (ter′ạ-toid), *a.* [Gr. τέρας (τερατ-), monster: see *-oid.*] In *biol.*, resembling a monster.

ter-a-tol-o-gy (ter-ạ-tol′ọ-ji), *n.*; pl. *-gies* (-jiz). [Gr. τερατολογία, < τερατολόγος, a teller of marvels, < τέρας (τερατ-), marvel, prodigy, monster, + λέγειν, speak.] A discourse or narrative dealing with prodigies; in *biol.*, the science or study of monstrosities or abnormal formations in animals or plants.—**ter″a-to-log′i-cal** (-tọ-loj′i-kạl), *a.* —**ter-a-tol′o-gist** (-jist), *n.*

ter-bi-um (ter′bi-um), *n.* [NL.; named from (*Yt*)*terby*, in Sweden: see *ytterbium.*] Chem. sym., Tb or Tr; at. wt., 159.2. A rare metallic element present in certain minerals, and yielding colorless salts.—**ter′bic**, *a.*

terce (ters), *n.* [= *tierce.*] A third†, or third part†; *eccles.*, the third of the seven canonical hours, or the service for it, orig. fixed for the third hour of the day (or 9 A.M.).

ter-cel (ter′sel), *n.* [OF. *tercel*, < ML. *tertiolus*, dim. < L. *tertius*, third.] A male falcon or goshawk; esp., the male of the peregrine falcon. Also **terce-let** (ters′let).

ter-cen-te-na-ry (ter-sen′te-nạ-ri). [See *ter-.*] **I.** *a.* Pertaining to three hundred or a period of three hundred years; marking the completion of three hundred years. **II.** *n.*;

pl. *-ries* (-riz). A period of three hundred years; also, a three-hundredth anniversary, or its celebration.

ter-cen-ten-ni-al (ter-sen-ten′i-ạl), *a.* and *n.* [See *ter-.*] Same as *tercentenary.*

ter-cet (ter′set), *n.* [F. *tercet*, < It. *terzetto*, dim. < *terzo*, < L. *tertius*, third.] In *pros.*, a group of three lines riming together, or connected by rime with the adjacent group or groups of three lines; in *music*, a triplet.

te-reb-ic (tẹ-reb′ik), *a.* [From *tereb*(*inth*).] In *chem.*, noting or pertaining to an organic acid formed by the action of nitric acid on oil of turpentine.

ter-e-binth (ter′ẹ-binth), *n.* [L. *terebinthus*, < Gr. τερέβινθος, earlier τέρμινθος, terebinth.] A moderate-sized anacardiaceous tree, *Pistacia terebinthus*, of the Mediterranean regions, having pinnate leaves and panicles of inconspicuous flowers, and yielding Chian turpentine (see *turpentine*).—**ter-e-bin′thi-na** (-bin′thi-nạ), *n.* [ML.] In *phar.*, turpentine.—**ter-e-bin′thi-nat-ed** (-nā-ted), *a.* Impregnated with or containing turpentine.—**ter-e-bin′thine** (-thin), *a.* [L. *terebinthinus*, < Gr. τερεβίνθινος.] Of or pertaining to the terebinth; also, of, pertaining to, consisting of, or resembling turpentine.

ter-e-brate (ter′ẹ-brāt), *v. t.* or *i.*; *-brated, -brating.* [L. *terebratus*, pp. of *terebrare*, < *terebra*, instrument for boring, < *terere*, rub: see *trite.*] To bore or perforate.—**ter-e-bra′tion** (-brā′shọn), *n.*

te-re-do (te-rē′dō), *n.*; pl. *-dos* (-dōz), L. *teredines* (te-red′i-nēz). [L., < Gr. τερηδών, < τείρειν, rub: see *trite.*] A ship-worm (genus *Teredo*).

ter-ek (ter′ek), *n.* [From the river *Terek*, in the Caucasus.] An old-world sandpiper, *Terekia cinerea*, with recurved bill, breeding in the high latitudes of Asia and Europe and traveling far southward in its migrations.

te-rel-la (te-rel′ä), *n.* See *terrella.*

te-rete (te-rēt′), *a.* [L. *teres* (*teret-*), rounded, < *terere*, rub: see *trite.*] Rounded and smooth; commonly, slender and smooth, with a circular transverse section; cylindrical or slightly tapering.

Terek.

ter-gal (ter′gạl), *a.* In *zoöl.*, of or pertaining to the tergum.

ter-gi-ver-sate (ter′ji-ver-sāt), *v. i.*; *-sated, -sating.* [L. *tergiversatus*, pp. of *tergiversari*, < *tergum*, the back, + *versare*, turn, twist, freq. of *vertere*, turn.] To change one's attitude or opinions with respect to a cause or subject, esp. repeatedly; turn renegade; shift or shuffle; practise evasion. —**ter″gi-ver-sa′tion** (-sā′shọn), *n.*—**ter′gi-ver-sa″tor**, *n.*

ter-gum (ter′gum), *n.*; pl. *-ga* (-gä). [L., the back.] In *zoöl.*, the back or dorsum, esp. of an arthropod.

term (term), *n.* [OF. F. *terme*, < L. *terminus*, boundary, limit, end, ML. fixed time, also term, word, akin to Gr. τέρμα, τέρμων, boundary, end, and E. *thrum*[1]: cf. *terminus.*] A boundary or limit (now rare or archaic); end, conclusion, or termination (as, "So now my yeare drawes to his latter *terme*," Spenser's "Shepheardes Calender," Dec., 127: now rare or archaic); that to which anything tends or is directed, or that from which it begins or proceeds (now rare or archaic); also, an appointed or set time or date, as for the payment of rent, interest, wages, etc.; hence, a space or period of time to which limits have been set (as, elected for a *term* of four years); the time or period through which something lasts or is intended to last (as, "The pageant of the summer ran its *term*": Masefield's "Daffodil Fields," iv.); each of certain stated periods during which instruction is regularly given to students or pupils in universities, colleges, and schools; each of the periods during which certain courts of law hold their sessions; also, the completion of the period of pregnancy; also, *pl.*, conditions or stipulations limiting what is proposed to be granted or done (as, the *terms* of a treaty; "Jugurtha wanted *terms*, and the consul demanded unconditional surrender," Froude's "Cæsar," iv.; to come to *terms*, that is, to come to an agreement, or agree upon conditions); conditions with regard to payment, price, charge, rates, wages, etc. (as, reasonable *terms*; "the authors' *terms* upon which books were published," Bok's "Americanization of Edward Bok," x.; "The hands had accepted the *terms* of the employers and had gone to work again," John Hay's "Bread-Winners," xv.); footing or standing (as, on equal *terms*; to be on good *terms* with a person; "Lady Delacour is not upon speaking *terms* with this Mrs. Margaret Delacour," Maria Edgeworth's "Belinda," xii.); sometimes, friendly relations (as, "So far the two men had kept outwardly on *terms*": Mrs. H. Ward's "Robert Elsmere," xix.); equal footing (as in sporting use); state†, situation†, or circumstances† (as, "driven into desperate *terms*": Shakspere's "Hamlet," iv. 7. 26); also, *sing.*, a word or phrase used in a recognized and definite sense in some particular subject, science, or art; any word or group of words expressing a notion or conception or denoting an object of thought; *pl.*, words or expressions generally, language, or way of speaking (as, "She in mild *terms* begg'd my patience": Shakspere's "Midsummer Night's Dream," iv. 1. 63); also, *sing.*, in *law*, an estate or interest in land, etc., to be enjoyed for a fixed period; in *geom.*, an extreme of a magnitude, or that which limits or bounds its extent (as, the *terms* of a line are points); in *alg.*, *arith.*, etc., each of the members of which an expression, a series of quantities, or the like, is composed, as one of the two or more parts of an algebraic expression joined to one another by signs of addition or subtraction, or either of the two quantities in a ratio; in *logic*, each of the two things or notions which are compared, or between which a relation is perceived, in a judgment; each of the words or phrases denoting these in a proposition; any of the three such words or phrases constituting the elements of a categorical syllogism; also, in *arch.*, etc., a statue or bust like those of the Roman god Terminus (see *terminus*); a terminal figure; also, the pillar or pedestal bearing such a figure.—**term**, *v. t.* To apply a particular term or name to; name; call; designate: as, "features, which, though of a stern and sinister expression, might well be *termed* handsome" (Scott's "Black Dwarf," xiii.).

ter-ma-gant (tèr′ma-gant). [OF. *Tervagant* = It. *Trivagante*, mythical deity of the Saracens; origin unknown.] **I.** *n.* [*cap.*] A mythical deity held in the middle ages to be worshiped by the Mohammedans, and represented in moralities, etc., as a violent, overbearing personage (obs. or archaic); also [*l. c.*], a violent, brawling person, male or female†; now, a violent, turbulent, or brawling woman (as, "Tom's wife was a tall *termagant*, fierce of temper, loud of tongue, and strong of arm": Irving's "Tales of a Traveler," iv. 3); a virago; a shrew. **II.** *a.* Of the nature of or characteristic of a termagant; violent; turbulent; brawling; shrewish: as, "a *termagant* wife" (Irving's "Sketch-Book," Rip Van Winkle); "He had patiently endured the *termagant* passions of Barbara Palmer" (Macaulay's "Hist. of Eng.," ii.).— **ter′ma-gan-cy** (-gan-si), *n.*

term=day (tèrm′dā), *n.* A fixed or appointed day, as for the payment of money due; a quarter-day.

term-er (tèr′mèr), *n.* One who resorted to London at the time of a term of a court of law, either for business or for amusement, intrigue, etc. (now only hist.); also, one who is serving a term, esp. in prison (as, a first *termer*, second *termer*, etc.); in *law*, same as *termor*.

ter-mi-na-ble (tèr′mi-na-bl), *a.* That may be terminated; of an annuity, coming to an end after a certain term.— **ter″mi-na-bil′i-ty** (-bil′i-ti), **ter′mi-na-ble-ness**, *n.*

ter-mi-nal (tèr′mi-nal). [L. *terminalis*, < *terminus*: see *term* and *terminus*.] **I.** *a.* Pertaining to or placed at a boundary, as a landmark; also, situated at or forming the end or extremity of something; growing at the end of a branch or stem, as a bud, inflorescence, etc.; pertaining to, situated at, or forming the terminus of a railroad; also, occurring at or forming the end of a series, succession, or the like; closing; concluding; also, pertaining to or lasting for a term or definite period; occurring at fixed terms or in every term; in *arch.*, etc., designating a figure of the form of a term or terminus (statue or bust terminating below in a

rectangular pillar or pedestal), its pillar or pedestal alone, or, sometimes, any pedestal which narrows toward the base. **II.** *n.* A terminal part or structure; the end or extremity; a final letter, syllable, or word; a terminus, as of a railroad; a station, or a city or town, at a terminus; a charge made by a railroad for the use of a terminal or other station, and for the handling of freight there; in *elect.*, either of the two ends of an open circuit, as the poles of a battery; a point of attachment where a current enters or leaves an apparatus; in *arch.*, etc., a terminal figure (see *terminal*, *a.*); also, a carving or the like at the end of something, as a finial.

Terminal Pedestal.

Ter-mi-na-li-a (tèr-mi-nā′li-ä), *n. pl.* [L.] An ancient Roman festival celebrated annually on Feb. 23 in honor of Terminus, the god of boundaries.

ter-mi-nal-ly (tèr′mi-nal-i), *adv.* At the end or extremity; also, in every term; once a term.

ter-mi-nate (tèr′mi-nāt), *v.*; *-nated*, *-nating*. [L. *terminatus*, pp. of *terminare*, bound, limit, determine, end, < *terminus*: see *term* and *terminus*.] **I.** *tr.* To direct (an action) to some end or object (with *to*, *upon*, etc.: obs. or rare); also, to bound or limit spatially; form the end or extremity of; be situated at the extremity of; also, to bring to an end, or put an end to (as, "A fever *terminated* the life of Henry Pelham": Bancroft's "Hist. of the U. S.," Amer. Revolution, i. 7); occur at or form the conclusion of; also, to finish or complete (rare). **II.** *intr.* To be directed to some end or object; also, to come to an end (often with *at*, *in*, or *with*: as, "the small street which *terminates* at Sadler's Wells Theatre," Dickens's "Oliver Twist," viii.; "a spacious gravel walk *terminating* in a grotto," Evelyn's "Diary," Feb. 27, 1644); end, conclude, or cease (as, "So *terminated* my adventures at dear Paris": Bulwer-Lytton's "Pelham," xxxi.); issue or result in something.—**ter-mi-na′tion** (-nā′shon), *n.* [L. *terminatio(n-).*] The act of terminating, or the fact of being terminated; also, the place at which or the part in which anything terminates; a bound or limit; an end or extremity; close or conclusion; issue or result; in *gram.*, the ending of a word, as the final syllable or letter; esp., the part annexed to a root or stem in inflection.— **ter-mi-na′tion-al**, *a.*—**ter′mi-na-tive** (-nā-tiv), *a.* Tending or serving to terminate; terminating.—**ter′mi-na-tive-ly**, *adv.*—**ter′mi-na-tor** (-nā-tor), *n.* [LL.] One who or that which terminates; in *astron.*, the dividing line between the illuminated and the unilluminated part of a heavenly body, esp. the moon.

ter-mi-ner (tèr′mi-nèr), *n.* [AF., noun use of OF. *terminer*, inf., determine, < L. *terminare*: see *terminate*.] In *law*, a determining. See *oyer*.

ter-mi-ni (tèr′mi-nī), *n.* Plural of *terminus*.

ter-mi-nism (tèr′mi-nizm), *n.* [L. *terminus*: see *term*.] The philosophical doctrine of nominalism; also, the theological doctrine that God has assigned to every one a definite term for repentance, after which all opportunity for salvation is lost.—**ter′mi-nist**, *n.*

ter-mi-nol-o-gy (tèr-mi-nol′o-ji), *n.*; pl. *-gies* (-jiz). [G. *terminologie*, < ML. *terminus*, term, + Gr. -λογία, < λέγειν, speak.] The science of terms, as in particular sciences or arts; usually, the system of terms belonging to a science, art, or subject (as, the *terminology* of botany); nomenclature; technical terms collectively.—**ter″mi-no-log′i-cal** (-no-loj′i-kal), *a.*—**ter″mi-no-log′i-cal-ly**, *adv.*— **ter-mi-nol′o-gist**, *n.*

ter-mi-nus (tèr′mi-nus), *n.*; pl. *-ni* (-nī). [L., boundary, limit, end, *Terminus*, the god of boundaries: see *term*.] A boundary or limit; also [*cap.*], the Roman god of boundaries; the deity who presided over boundaries and landmarks; [*l. c.*] a figure of this god, representing more or less of the upper part of the body, sometimes without the arms, and terminating below in a rectangular pillar, sometimes tapering toward the base, which serves as a pedestal, and out of which the figure appears to spring; any similar figure; the pillar or pedestal of such a figure; sometimes, a boundary post or stone; also, the point to which anything tends; a goal or end; sometimes, the point from which anything starts; a starting-point; also, either end of a railroad-line, etc.; the station, or the city or town, located there; in general, the end or extremity of anything.

ter-mi-ta-ri-um (tėr-mi-tā'ri-um), n.; pl. *-ria* (-ri-ä). [NL.] A termites' nest; also, a cage or vessel for studying termites. Also **ter'mi-ta-ry** (-tạ-ri); pl. *-ries* (-riz).

ter-mite (tėr'mīt), n. [NL. *termes* (*termit-*), white ant, LL. wood-worm, from the root of L. *terere*, rub: see *trite*.] Any of the pale-colored, soft-bodied, mainly tropical, social insects constituting the family *Termitidæ*, very destructive to buildings, furniture, household stores, etc.; a white ant. — **ter-mit'ic** (-mit'ik), a.

term-less (tėrm'les), a. Having no term or limit; boundless; endless; also, not limited by terms or conditions; unconditional; also, indescribable (poetic and rare: as, "Down . . . Like unshorn velvet on that *termless* skin," Shakspere's "Lover's Complaint," 94).

Termite (*Termes flavipes*).— *a*, larva; *b*, winged male; *c*, worker; *d*, soldier; *e*, large female; *f*, nymph. (Lines show natural sizes.)

term-ly (tėrm'li). **I.** a. Occurring at fixed terms or in every term; periodical. **II.** adv. At fixed terms; in every term; periodically.

term-or (tėr'mọr), n. In *law*, one who has an estate for a term of years or for life.

tern¹ (tėrn), n. [From Scand.: cf. Dan. *terne*, Sw. *tärna*, tern.] Any bird of the subfamily *Sterninæ* (family *Laridæ*), comprising numerous aquatic species which are allied to the gulls, but which have usually a slenderer body and bill, smaller feet, a long and deeply forked tail, and a more graceful flight; esp., any of those constituting the genus *Sterna*, as *S. hirundo*, the common species of Europe and America, and *S. fuliginosa* ('sooty tern').

tern² (tėrn), n. [F. *terne*, < It. *terno*, < L. *terni*, three each, distributive of *tres*, three.] A set of three; three winning numbers drawn together in a lottery; a prize won by drawing these; a group of three stanzas; also, a three-masted schooner (local, New Eng.).

Common Tern (*Sterna hirundo*).

ter-na-ry (tėr'nạ-ri). [L. *ternarius*, < *terni*: see *tern²*.] **I.** a. Consisting of or involving three; threefold; triple; also, being the last of each successive group of three; also, third in order or rank; in *chem.*, formerly, consisting of three atoms; now, consisting of three different elements or radicals; in *metal.*, of an alloy, having three constituents; in *math.*, having three variables; also, based on the number three. **II.** n.; pl. *-ries* (-riz). A group of three.

ter-nate (tėr'nāt), a. [NL. *ternatus*, < L. *terni*: see *tern²*.] Consisting of three; arranged in threes; in *bot.*, consisting of three leaflets, as a compound leaf; also, having leaves arranged in whorls of three, as a plant. — **ter'nate-ly**, adv.

terne=plate (tėrn'plāt), n. [F. *terne*, dull: cf. *tarnish*.] An inferior kind of tin-plate, in which the tin used is alloyed with a large percentage of lead.

ter-ni-on (tėr'ni-ọn), n. [L. *ternio(n-)*, < *terni*: see *tern²*.] A set or group of three; a triad.

Ternate Leaves.— 1, of laburnum (*Laburnum laburnum*); 2, of rosinweed (*Silphium trifoliatum*).

ter-pene (tėr'pēn), n. [G. *terpen*, < *terpentin*, turpentine.] In *chem.*, any of certain hydrocarbons with the formula $C_{10}H_{16}$, occurring in essential or volatile oils; also, any of various analogous or related compounds.

ter-pin (tėr'pin), n. [G. *terpin*, < *terpentin*, turpentine.] In *chem.*, a compound, $C_{10}H_{18}(OH)_2$, of the alcohol type, whose hydrate ('terpin hydrate') is prepared from oil of turpentine and used in medicine; also, a compound isomeric with it. — **ter-pin'e-ol** (-ẹ-ol or -ẹ-ōl), n. In *chem.*, a compound, $C_{10}H_{17}(OH)$, occurring in several isomeric forms, prepared from terpin hydrate, etc., and used in the manufacture of perfumes; also, loosely, a liquid consisting of a crude mixture of these isomers. — **ter'pin-ol** (-pi-nol or -pi-nōl), n. A crude liquid mixture of the isomeric forms of terpineol.

Terp-sich-o-re (tėrp-sik'ō-rē), n. [L., < Gr. Τερψιχόρη, 'delighting in the dance,' < τέρπειν, please, delight, + χορός, dance.] The Muse of dancing and choral song. — **Terp"si-cho-re'an** (-si-kō-rē'ạn). **I.** a. Of or pertaining to Terpsichore; [l. c.] pertaining to dancing. **II.** n. [l. c.] A dancer. [Colloq.]

ter-ra (ter'ä, It. ter'rä), n. [L. and It.] The earth; land; ground; soil; earth. — **terra alba** (al'bä). [L., 'white earth.'] Any of various white, earthy or powdery substances, as pipe-clay, gypsum, kaolin, or magnesia. — **terra firma** (fėr'mä). [L.] Firm or solid earth; dry land, as opposed to water (as, "In maritime life, far more than in that of *terra firma*, wild rumors abound": H. Melville's "Moby-Dick," xli.); also, mainland, as opposed to islands or peninsulas†. — **terra incognita** (in-kog'ni-tä); pl. *terræ incognitæ* (ter'ē in-kog'ni-tē). [L.] An unknown or unexplored land or region: as, "The great western plains . . . remained almost a *terra incognita* to the American trapper" (Irving's "Captain Bonneville," i.). — **terra Japonica** (jạ-pon'i-kä). [NL., 'Japanese earth.'] Gambier or catechu: formerly supposed to be an earth from Japan. — **terra sigillata** (sij-i-lā'tä). [NL., 'sigillated (or sealed) earth.'] Lemnian earth (see under *Lemnian*): so called from its being made into cakes or tablets stamped with a seal. Also called *sigillated earth* and *sphragide*. — **terra verde** (ver'dā). [It., 'green earth.'] Any of certain earthy mineral substances, found native in various places, used as green pigments in painting.

ter-race (ter'ạs), n. [OF. *terrace* (F. *terrasse*), < L. *terra*, earth.] A raised level with a vertical or sloping front or sides faced with masonry, turf, or the like; one of a series of levels with vertical or sloping front, rising one above another (as, "From the high ground on which it [a house] stood a series of *terraces* bordered by balustrades and urns descended . . . to a small irregular lake": Mrs. Wharton's "Age of Innocence," xv.); a natural formation resembling such a level; a nearly level strip of land with a more or less abrupt descent along the margin of the sea, a lake, or a river; also, a row of houses running along the face or top of a slope, or a street with such a row or rows (as, "a *terrace* of small semi-detached houses with little front gardens," L. Merrick's "Conrad in Quest of His Youth," iv.: often applied arbitrarily to ordinary rows of houses or streets); also, the flat roof of a house, esp. of an Oriental or Spanish house. — **ter'race**, v. t.; *-raced*, *-racing*. To form into or furnish with a terrace or terraces.

ter-ra=cot-ta (ter'ä-kot'ä), n. [It., 'baked earth.'] A hard, usually unglazed earthenware of fine quality, used for architectural decorations, statuettes or figurines, vases, etc.; something made of this, esp. a work of art; also, the color of this earthenware, a dull brownish red.

ter-rain (te-rān' or ter'ān), n. [F. *terrain*, < L. *terra*, earth.] A tract of land, esp. as considered with reference to its natural features, military advantages, etc.; in *geol.*, a terrane.

ter-rane (te-rān' or ter'ān), n. [= *terrain*.] In *geol.*, a formation.

ter-ra-pin (ter'a-pin), n.; pl. *terrapins* or (esp. collectively) *terrapin*. [N. Amer. Ind.] Any of various edible North American fresh-water or tide-water tortoises of the family *Emydidæ*, esp. any of those constituting the genus *Malaclemmys* ('diamond-back terrapins') of the Atlantic and Gulf coasts of the U. S.; also, any of various similar tortoises.—**red=bellied terrapin.** See *slider*.

ter-ra-que-ous (te-rā'kwē-us), a. [L. *terra*, land, + *aqua*, water.] Consisting of land and water, as the earth (as, "earth's *terraqueous* ball": Wiffen's tr. Tasso's "Jerusalem Delivered," i. 7); occurring on land and in water, as a plant; extending over land and water, as a journey.

Diamond-back Terrapin (*Malaclemmys concentrica*).

ter-ra-ri-um (te-rā'ri-um), n.; pl. *-riums* or *-ria* (-ri-ä). [NL., < L. *terra*, earth.] A vivarium for land animals (distinguished from *aquarium*); esp., a case or vessel for use in studying small land animals.

ter-rel-la (te-rel'ä), n. [NL., dim. of L. *terra*, earth.] A magnetized globe of steel, spherical lodestone, or the like, with poles diametrically opposite each other, used to represent in miniature the distribution of terrestrial magnetism.

ter-rene (te-rēn'). [L. *terrenus*, < *terra*, earth.] **I.** a. Of or pertaining to the earth (as, the *terrene* globe); also, pertaining to or of the nature of earth; earthy; also, occurring on or inhabiting the land as distinct from the water; also, belonging to the earth or this world; earthly; worldly. **II.** n. The earth; also, a land or region.

terre-plein (tār'plān), n. [F. *terre-plein* = It. *terrapieno*, < L. *terra*, earth, + *plenus*, full.] In *fort.*, the top, platform, or horizontal surface of a rampart, on which the cannon are placed; sometimes, the plane of site or level surface around a field-work, or any plane on which a battery is placed in a field fortification.

ter-res-tri-al (te-res'tri-al). [L. *terrestris*, < *terra*, earth.] **I.** a. Pertaining to, consisting of, or representing the earth (as, *terrestrial* magnetism, the magnetic properties possessed by the earth as a whole; this *terrestrial* sphere; a *terrestrial* globe, see *globe*, n.); also, of or pertaining to the land as distinct from the water; also, of or pertaining to the earth or this world (as, "A genius bright and base, Of tow'ring talents and *terrestrial* aims": Young's "Night Thoughts," vi. 267); earthly; worldly; mundane; in *zoöl.*, living on the ground; not aquatic, arboreal, or aërial; in *bot.*, growing on land; not aquatic; also, growing in the ground; not epiphytic or aërial. **II.** n. An inhabitant of the earth; esp., a human being.—**ter-res'tri-al-ly,** adv.

ter-ret (ter'et), n. [ME. *tyret, turet, toret*, < OF. *toret*, dim. of *tor, tour*, E. *tour*.] One of the round loops or rings on the saddle of a harness, through which the driving-reins pass.

terre=ten-ant (tār'ten"ant), n. [AF., < OF. *terre* (< L. *terra*), land, + *tenant*: see *tenant*.] In *law*, one who has the actual possession of land; the occupant of land.

terre verte (tār vārt). [F., 'green earth.'] Same as *terra verde*, under *terra*.

ter-ri-ble (ter'i-bl), a. [OF. F. *terrible*, < L. *terribilis*, < *terrere*, frighten.] Exciting or fitted to excite terror or great fear (as, "those swift-footed, unspeakably *terrible* hunting-leopards, from which every living thing in the forest flies with shrieks of consternation": W. H. Hudson's "Green Mansions," iii.); dreadful; awful; hence, distressing,

severely trying, or severe (as, a *terrible* experience; a *terrible* winter); extremely unpleasant or bad (colloq.: as, a *terrible* performance); exceedingly or excessively great (colloq.: as, a *terrible* appetite; a *terrible* price).—**ter'ri-ble-ness,** n.—**ter'ri-bly,** adv.

ter-ric-o-lous (te-rik'ō-lus), a. [L. *terra*, earth, + *colere*, inhabit.] Living on or in the ground, as a plant or animal; not aquatic or aërial; specif., belonging to the *Terricolæ*, a group of annelids including the common earthworm and related forms.

ter-ri-er[1] (ter'i-ėr), n. [F. *terrier*, terrier (cf. F. *terrier*, burrow of an animal), orig. adj., pertaining to the earth: see *terrier*[2].] A typically small, active, intelligent, and courageous variety of dog, named from its propensity to pursue prey, as the fox, badger, etc., into its burrow: occurring in numerous breeds which are divided into two classes, one short-haired and the other shaggy. See *Airedale terrier, Dandie Dinmont, fox-terrier, Irish terrier, Scotch terrier, Sealyham terrier, Skye terrier.*

ter-ri-er[2] (ter'i-ėr), n. [OF. F. *terrier*, orig. adj., pertaining to the earth or to land, < ML. *terrarius*, < L. *terra*, earth, land.] In *law*, formerly, a register of landed property including lists of vassals and tenants, with particulars of their holdings, services, and rents; now, a book or roll in which the lands of private persons or corporations are described by their site, boundaries, acreage, etc.

ter-rif-ic (te-rif'ik), a. [L. *terrificus*, < *terrere*, frighten, + *facere*, make.] Causing terror; terrifying; dreadful; hence, terrifyingly or extremely severe (as, a *terrific* storm; a *terrific* earthquake-shock; blows of *terrific* force); extraordinarily great, intense, etc. (colloq.: as, *terrific* applause; *terrific* speed).—**ter-rif'i-cal-ly,** adv.

ter-ri-fy (ter'i-fī), v. t.; *-fied, -fying*. [L. *terrificare*, < *terrificus*: see *terrific*.] To fill with terror, or make greatly afraid (as, "The regulars, *terrified* by the yells of the Indians . . . gathered themselves into a body": Bancroft's "Hist. of the U. S.," Amer. Revolution, i. 8); also, to drive, force, etc., by inspiring terror (as, "I am *terrified* out of my senses": Walpole's "Castle of Otranto," v.).—**ter'ri-fied-ly** (-fīd-li), adv.—**ter'ri-fi-er** (-fī-ėr), n.—**ter'ri-fy-ing-ly,** adv.

ter-rig-e-nous (te-rij'e-nus), a. [L. *terrigenus, terrigena*, < *terra*, earth, + *gen-*, beget, produce: see *genius*.] Earth-born; produced by the earth; in *geol.*, noting or pertaining to sediments on the sea-bottom derived directly from the neighboring land.

ter-rine (te-rēn'), n. [F. *terrine*, < OF. *terrin*, of earth, < L. *terra*, earth: cf. *tureen*.] An earthenware dish or vessel, as for cooking, for holding potted meat, etc., or for other purposes; also, a preparation of food in such a dish.

ter-ri-to-ri-al (ter-i-tō'ri-al), a. [L. *territorialis*.] Of or pertaining to territory or land; also, pertaining or belonging to the territory of a state, sovereign, or ruler; also, of, pertaining to, associated with, or restricted to a particular territory or district; local; also [cap.], of or pertaining to a Territory of the U. S., or any similar district; also [cap.], *milit.*, designating an army or force in the British military system, which is organized on a local basis for home defense, but whose members may volunteer for service abroad in war if called upon.—**territorial system.** *Eccles.*, same as *territorialism*.—**Ter-ri-to'ri-al,** n. A member of the British Territorial Army.—**ter-ri-to'ri-al-ism,** n. A territorial system; the principle of the predominance of the landed classes; a Jewish movement to secure a separate, autonomous territory for the Jews; *eccles.*, the theory of church polity according to which the supreme ecclesiastical authority is vested in the civil power.—**ter-ri-to'ri-al-ist,** n.—**ter-ri-to'ri-al'i-ty** (-al'i-ti), n. Territorial quality, condition, or status.—**ter-ri-to'ri-al-ize** (-īz), v. t.; *-ized, -izing*. To make territorial; put upon a territorial basis; associate with or restrict to a particular territory or particular territories.—**ter-ri-to"ri-al-i-za'tion** (-i-zā'shon), n.—**ter-ri-to'ri-al-ly,** adv. In respect to territory; as to territory.

ter-ri-to-ry (ter'i-tō-ri), n.; pl. *-ries* (-riz). [L. *territorium*, the land around a town, domain, district, territory, < *terra*, earth, land.] The land or district around a town†; also, the land and waters belonging to or under the jurisdiction of a state, sovereign, etc.; any separate tract of land belonging to a state; also, land, esp. as subject to ownership or control (as, "a war . . . for *territory*": Bancroft's "Hist. of the U. S.," Amer. Revolution, i. 3); any tract of land, region, or district; often, the region or district assigned to a representative, agent, or the like, to carry on work in, as in soliciting and making sales, etc.; fig., the field of action, thought, etc., or domain or province, of something; also [*cap.*], in the government of the U. S., a region or district not admitted to the Union as a State but having its own legislature, with a governor and other officers appointed by the President and Senate; also, some similar district elsewhere, as in Canada and Australia.

ter-ror (ter′ọr), *n.* [OF. F. *terreur*, < L. *terror*, < *terrere*, frighten.] Intense, sharp, overmastering fear, or a feeling or instance of this (as, "The man seemed frantic with *terror*," Borrow's "Bible in Spain," iii.; "Trembling with a nameless *terror*, she knew not what to dread," Jane Porter's "Scottish Chiefs," i.; distracted by *terrors*); intense fright, alarm, or dread; intense fear caused for the purpose of coercing or subduing (as, to rule by *terror*); also, a cause of intense fear (as, to be a *terror* to evil-doers; "Their sails were long the *terror* of both coasts of the Channel," Macaulay's "Hist. of Eng.," i.); often, a person or thing that is especially 'dreadful' or unpleasant (colloq.: as, "Oh! isn't she a *terror* since the moon did change?" Synge's "Tinker's Wedding," ii.; "What an awful person! She must be a Holy *Terror* to live with!" Sinclair Lewis's "Main Street," xx.); also [*cap.*], with *the*, the Reign of Terror (see under *reign*, *n.*).—**ter′ror-ism**, *n.* The use of terrorizing methods, or the state of fear and submission produced.—**ter′ror-ist**, *n.* One who uses or favors terrorizing methods; specif., an agent or partizan of the revolutionary tribunal during the Reign of Terror in France; in Russia, formerly, a member of a political party aiming at the demoralization of the government by terror (cf. *nihilism*).—**ter-ror-is′tic**, *a.*—**ter′ror-ize** (-īz), *v.*; *-ized*, *-izing*. **I.** *tr.* To fill or overcome with terror (as, "He was *terrorised* as he looked at that ugly and dark countenance": Arnold Bennett's "Clayhanger," i. 17); esp., to dominate, coerce, or subdue by inspiring terror (as, "secret organizations, which control and *terrorize* a district until overthrown by force," Roosevelt's "Ranch Life and the Hunting-Trail," vi.; "premeditated and systematized *terrorizing* of the civil populations," Mrs. Wharton's "Son at the Front," x.). **II.** *intr.* To prevail or rule by inspiring terror.—**ter′ror-i-za′tion** (-i-zā′shọn), *n.*—**ter′ror-iz-er** (-ī-zẽr), *n.*—**ter′ror-less**, *a.* Free from terror; also, without terrors or causes of terror.—**ter′ror=strick″en**, *a.* Terrified.

ter-ry (ter′i). [Origin obscure.] **I.** *n.*; pl. *terries* (-iz). The loop formed by the pile of a fabric when left uncut; also, any of various fabrics with uncut pile-loops. **II.** *a.* Having the pile-loops uncut: as, *terry* velvet.

terse (tẽrs), *a.*; compar. *terser*, superl. *tersest*. [L. *tersus*, wiped off, clean, neat, pp. of *tergere*, wipe.] Clean or smooth as if from wiping or rubbing†; fig., polished†, refined†, or elegant†; also, neatly or effectively concise, succinct, or brief and pithy, as language, expression, a writer or speaker, etc. (as, "Cromwell's own account of Naseby is the *tersest* bulletin on record": Morley's "Oliver Cromwell," ii. 5).—**terse′ly**, *adv.*—**terse′ness**, *n.*

ter-tial (tẽr′shạl). [L. *tertius*, third.] In *ornith.*: **I.** *a.* Noting or pertaining to any of a set of flight-feathers situated on the basal segment (that corresponding to the upper arm in higher vertebrates) of a bird's wing. Cf. *primary*, *a.*, and *secondary*, *a.* **II.** *n.* A tertial feather.

ter-tian (tẽr′shạn). [L. *tertianus*, < *tertius*, third.] **I.** *a.* Of a fever, ague, etc., characterized by paroxysms which recur every third day, both days of consecutive occurrence being counted. **II.** *n.* A tertian fever or ague.

ter-ti-a-ry (tẽr′shi-ạ-ri). [L. *tertiarius*, < *tertius*, third.] **I.** *a.* Of the third order, rank, formation, etc.; third; [*l. c.* or *cap.*] *eccles.*, noting or pertaining to a branch ('third order') of certain religious orders which consists of lay members living in community ('regular tertiaries') or living in the world ('secular tertiaries'); [*l. c.*] in *ornith.*, tertial; [*cap.*] in *geol.*, noting or pertaining to a geological period or a system of rocks which precedes the Quaternary and constitutes the earlier principal division of the Cenozoic. **II.** *n.*;

pl. *-ries* (-riz). [*l. c.* or *cap.*] *Eccles.*, a member of a tertiary branch of a religious order; [*l. c.*] in *ornith.*, a tertial feather; [*cap.*] in *geol.*, the Tertiary period or system.

ter-ti-um quid (tẽr′shi-um kwid). [L., 'third something.'] Something related in some way to two things, but distinct from both; something intermediate between two things.

ter-va-lent (tẽr-vā′lẹnt), *a.* Same as *trivalent*.

ter-za=ri-ma (ter′tsạ-rē′mạ), *n.* [It. *terza rima*, 'third rime.'] In *pros.*, an Italian form of iambic verse consisting of ten-syllable or eleven-syllable lines arranged in tercets, the middle line of each tercet riming with the first and third lines of the following tercet.

ter-zet-to (ter-tset′tō), *n.*; pl. *-ti* (-tē). [It.: see *tercet*.] In *music*, a trio; esp., a vocal trio.

tes-sel-la (te-sel′ạ), *n.*; pl. *tessellæ* (-ē). [L., dim. of *tessera*: see *tessera*.] A small tessera or block, as in a mosaic.—**tes′sel-late** (tes′e-lāt), *a.* [L. *tessellatus*, < *tessella*.] Tessellated.—**tes′sel-late**, *v. t.*; *-lated*, *-lating*. To form of small squares or blocks, as floors, pavements, etc.; form or arrange in a checkered or mosaic pattern.—**tes-sel-la′tion** (-lā′shọn), *n.* The act or art of tessellating; tessellated form or arrangement; also, tessellated work.

tes-se-ra (tes′ẹ-rạ), *n.*; pl. *-ræ* (-rē). [L., square piece, block, tablet, die, connected with Gr. τέσσαρες, four: see *tetra*-.] A small square of bone, wood, or the like anciently used as a token, tally, ticket, die, etc.; fig., a distinguishing sign or token; a watchword; a password; also, each of the small, generally square pieces of marble, glass, or the like used in mosaic work.

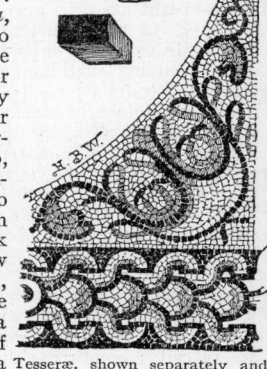

Tesseræ, shown separately and combined in mosaic.

test[1] (test), *n.* [OF. *test* (F. *test*, *têt*), cupel, < L. *testu*, *testum*, earthen vessel, akin to *testa*, piece of earthenware: see *test*[2].] A cupel for assaying or refining metals; hence, that by which the presence, quality, or genuineness of anything is determined; a means of trial; also, the trial or proving of the quality of something (as, to put to the *test*; "Frailest where I seem the best, Only strong for lack of *test*," Whittier's "Andrew Rykman's Prayer"); in *chem.*, the process of detecting the presence of an ingredient in a compound or the like, or of determining the nature of a substance, commonly by the addition of a reagent; a particular process or method of doing this; also, the reagent used; also, an indication or evidence of the presence of an ingredient, or of the nature of a substance, obtained by such means.—**test**[1], *v. t.* To assay or refine in a test or cupel; also, to put to the proof; subject to a test of any kind; try; in *chem.*, to subject to a chemical test.

test[2] (test), *n.* [L. *testa*, piece of baked earthenware, tile, pot, potsherd, shell of animal, ML. skull, head: cf. *test*[1], *tester*[2], and *teston*.] A potsherd†; in *zoöl.*, the hard covering of certain invertebrates, as mollusks, arthropods, etc.; a shell; a lorica; in *bot.*, a testa.

tes-ta (tes′tạ), *n.*; pl. *-tæ* (-tē). [L.: see *test*[2].] In *zoöl.*, a test; in *bot.*, the outer, usually hard, integument or coat of a seed (cf. *tegmen*).

tes-ta-cean (tes-tā′shiạn). [NL. *Testacea*, prop. neut. pl. of L. *testaceus*, E. *testaceous*.] **I.** *a.* Belonging or pertaining to the *Testacea*, any of several former groups of shell-covered invertebrates, esp. the shell-bearing mollusks. **II.** *n.* A testacean animal.

tes-ta-ceous (tes-tā′shius), *a.* [L. *testaceus*, < *testa*, shell: see *test*[2].] Pertaining to or of the nature of a shell or shells; prepared from animal shells; having a shell, as an animal; in *bot.* and *zoöl.*, of a brick-red, brownish-red, or brownish-yellow color.

tes-ta-cy (tes′tạ-si), *n.* The state of being testate.

tes-ta-ment (tes′tạ-mẹnt), *n.* [L. *testamentum*, a will; testament (in LL., eccles., used to render Gr. διαθήκη, covenant), < *testari*: see *testate*.] A formal declaration, usually in writing, of a person's wishes as to the disposition of his property or rights after his death (as, "I, Sir Wycherly Wychecombe . . . do make and declare this to be my last will and *testament*": Cooper's "Two Admirals," xii.); a will; also, a covenant, esp. between God and man; specif., the Mosaic or old covenant or dispensation or the Christian or new covenant or dispensation; [*cap.*] either of two collections of books, one ('Old Testament') containing the records of the Mosaic covenant, and the other ('New Testament') those of the Christian covenant, the two together forming the Christian Bible; also, the New Testament as distinct from the Old Testament; a copy of the New Testament.—

tes-ta-men'ta-ry (-men'ta̤-ri), *a.* [L. *testamentarius.*] Of, pertaining to, or of the nature of a testament or will; given, bequeathed, done, or appointed by will; set forth or contained in a will; also [*cap.* or *l. c.*], of or pertaining to the Old Testament or the New Testament.—**tes-ta-men'ta-ri-ly,** *adv.*

tes-tate (tes'tāt). [L. *testatus,* pp. of *testari,* bear witness, make a will, < *testis,* a witness.] **I.** *a.* Having made and left a valid will. **II.** *n.* One who at death has left a valid will.—**tes-ta'tor,** *n.* [L., < *testari.*] One who makes a will; esp., one who has died leaving a valid will.—**tes-ta'trix** (-triks), *n.* [LL.] A female testator.

tes-te (tes'tē), *n.* [L., abl. (in absolute construction) of *testis,* a witness.] The witness being (a person or authority specified): as, *teste* St. Paul.

test-er[1] (tes'tėr), *n.* One who or that which tests.

tes-ter[2] (tes'tėr), *n.* [ME. *tester, testour:* cf. OF. *testre,* headboard of a bed, *testiere,* head-covering, < *teste* (F. *tête*), head, < ML. *testa:* see *test*[2].] A canopy, as over a bed or a pulpit: as, "a bed of ancient damask, with a *tester* sufficiently lofty to grace a couch of state" (Irving's "Tales of a Traveler," i. 7).

tes-ter[3] (tes'tėr), *n.* [For *teston.*] The teston of Henry VIII.; hence, a sixpence (colloq.: as, "It mattered not the toss of a silver *tester* whether I was drowned," Stevenson's "Master of Ballantrae," ix.).

tes-tes (tes'tēz), *n.* Plural of *testis.*

tes-ti-cle (tes'ti-kl), *n.* [L. *testiculus,* dim. of *testis,* a testicle.] In *anat.* and *zoöl.,* one of the (usually two) glands in the male which secrete the spermatozoa and some of the fluid elements of the semen; a testis.—**tes-tic'u-lar** (-tik'ū-lär), *a.*

tes-ti-fi-ca-tion (tes″ti-fi-kā'shon), *n.* [L. *testificatio(n-).*] The act of testifying; also, testimony; evidence. [Now rare.]

tes-ti-fy (tes'ti-fī), *v.;* -fied, -fying. [L. *testificari,* < *testis,* a witness, + *facere,* make.] **I.** *tr.* To bear witness to (as, "We . . . *testify* that we have seen; and ye receive not our witness": John, iii. 11); affirm as fact or truth; hence, to give or afford evidence of in any manner (as, "He . . . adjured them to *testify* their acceptance to the peace offered by repeating the words . . . 'God save the King!'" Motley's "Dutch Republic," ii. 9; "This [account] will *testify* for me that I was not idle," Defoe's "Robinson Crusoe," i. 11); manifest or evince (archaic: as, "Dr. John, I thought, *testified* a certain gratification at this mark of confidence," C. Brontë's "Villette," xi.); also, to declare, profess, or acknowledge openly (as, "the ministry, which I have received of the Lord Jesus, to *testify* the gospel of the grace of God," Acts, xx. 24; to *testify* one's faith); in *law,* to state or declare under oath or affirmation. **II.** *intr.* To bear witness; give or afford evidence; also, to make solemn declaration; in *law,* to give testimony under oath or solemn affirmation.—**tes-ti-fi-er** (-fī-ėr), *n.*

tes-ti-ly (tes'ti-li), *adv.* In a testy manner.

tes-ti-mo-ni-al (tes-ti-mō'ni-al). [LL. *testimonialis.*] **I.** *a.* Pertaining to or serving as testimony. **II.** *n.* Testimony†, evidence†, or proof†; something serving as proof†; a certificate as to the truth of something†; also, a writing certifying to a person's character, conduct, or qualifications, or to a thing's value, excellence, etc. (as, "He exposed the *testimonials* to patent medicines from senators and congressmen": Bok's "Americanization of Edward Bok," xxx.); a letter or written statement of recommendation; also, something given or done as an expression of esteem, admira-

tion, gratitude, etc.—**tes-ti-mo'ni-al-ize,** *v. t.;* -ized, -izing. To furnish with a testimonial, or letter of recommendation; also, to honor with a testimonial, or expression of esteem, gratitude, etc.

tes-ti-mo-ny (tes'ti-mō-ni), *n.;* pl. -nies (-niz). [L. *testimonium,* < *testari,* bear witness: see *testate.*] Witness or evidence given in support of a fact or statement; any kind of evidence or proof; anything serving as proof; in Biblical use, the decalogue as inscribed on the two tables of the law, or the ark in which the tables were kept (see Ex. xxv. 16, xvi. 34); *pl.,* the precepts of God (as, "My soul hath kept thy *testimonies*": Ps. cxix. 167); also, *sing.,* open declaration or profession, as of faith (obs. or archaic); also, a declaration or expression of disapproval, or a protest (as, "Shake off the very dust from your feet for a *testimony* against them": Luke, ix. 5); in *law,* the statement or declaration of a witness under oath or affirmation.

tes-ti-ness (tes'ti-nes), *n.* The state of being testy.

tes-tis (tes'tis), *n.;* pl. -tes (-tēz). [L.] In *anat.* and *zoöl.,* a testicle.

tes-ton (tes'ton), *n.* [F. *teston,* < It. *testone,* aug. of *testa,* head, < ML. *testa:* see *test*[2].] Any of various silver coins formerly current, with a head or portrait on the obverse, as, in England, the shilling of Henry VII., Henry VIII., or Edward VI., which became reduced in value successively to tenpence, ninepence, and sixpence; also, any of various other silver coins formerly current, without a portrait. Also **tes-toon'** (-tön').

test-pa-per (test'pā″pėr), *n.* In *chem.,* paper impregnated with a reagent, as litmus (see *litmus-paper*), which changes color when acted upon by certain substances, thus indicating their presence.

test-tube (test'tūb), *n.* In *chem.,* a hollow cylinder of thin glass with one end closed, used in testing liquids, etc.

tes-tu-di-nate (tes-tū'di-nāt). [L. *testudinatus,* < *testudo:* see *testudo.*] **I.** *a.* Formed like the carapace of a tortoise; arched; vaulted; in *zoöl.,* belonging to the *Testudinata* (or *Chelonia*), an order or group of reptiles comprising the tortoises and turtles; chelonian. **II.** *n.* In *zoöl.,* a testudinate reptile; a chelonian.

tes-tu-do (tes-tū'dō), *n.;* pl. -dines (-di-nēz). [L., tortoise, tortoise-shell, arch, vault, shelter, < *testa,* E. *test*[2].] Among the ancient Romans, a movable shelter with a strong and usually fireproof arched roof, used for protection in siege operations; also, a shelter formed by a body of troops overlapping their oblong shields above their heads; also, in later times, some other sheltering contrivance, as for protecting miners; in *pathol.,* an encysted tumor.

tes-ty (tes'ti), *a.;* compar. *testier,* superl. *testiest.* [ME. *testif:* cf. OF. *testu* (F. *têtu*), headstrong, < *teste,* head, < ML. *testa:* see *test*[2].] Headstrong†; also, prone to impatience and irritation, or irritably impatient of contradiction or opposition (as, "He was now *testy* and middle-aged": Sinclair Lewis's "Arrowsmith," ii.); characterized

Testudo of Roman Soldiers. — Column of Trajan, Rome.

by or showing impatience and irritability (as, "Must I stand and crouch Under your *testy* humour?" Shakspere's "Julius Cæsar," iv. 3. 46; a *testy* manner; a *testy* speech).

te-tan-ic (tẹ-tan'ik). **I.** *a.* Pertaining to, of the nature of, or characterized by tetanus. **II.** *n.* In *med.*, a remedy which acts on the nerves and through them on the muscles, and which, if taken in overdoses, causes tetanic spasms of the muscles, and death.

tet-a-nize (tet'ạ-nīz), *v. t.*; *-nized, -nizing.* In *physiol.*, to induce a condition of tetanus in (a muscle).—**tet″a-ni-za′tion** (-ni-zā′shọn), *n.*

tet-a-nus (tet'ạ-nus), *n.* [L., < Gr. τέτανος, < τείνειν, stretch.] In *pathol.*, an infectious, often fatal disease, due to a specific micro-organism which gains entrance to the body through wounds, characterized by more or less violent tonic spasm and rigidity of many or all the voluntary muscles, esp. those of the neck and lower jaw (cf. *lockjaw*); in *physiol.*, the condition of prolonged contraction which a muscle assumes under rapidly repeated stimuli.

tet-a-ny (tet'ạ-ni), *n.* [F. *tétanie*, < L. *tetanus*: see *tetanus*.] In *pathol.*, a disease characterized by irregularly intermittent muscular spasms, esp. in the extremities, usually unaccompanied by fever.

te-tar-to-he-dral (tẹ-tär-tọ-hē′drạl), *a.* [Gr. τέταρτος, fourth, + ἕδρα, seat, base.] Of a crystal, having one fourth the planes or faces required by the maximum symmetry.—**te-tar-to-he′drism,** *n.*

tetch-y (tech'i), *a.* [Also *techy* and (now prov.) *teachy*; origin uncertain: cf. *touchy.*] Easily irritated; irritable; touchy.—**tetch′i-ly,** *adv.*—**tetch′i-ness,** *n.*

tête-à-tête (tāt′ạ-tāt′, F. tet-ȧ-tet′). [F. *tête à tête*, 'head to head.'] **I.** *adv.* Together face to face, without the presence of a third person; together in private (of two persons): as, to sit, converse, or dine *tête-à-tête.* **II.** *a.* Of, between, or for two persons together, without others: as, a *tête-à-tête* conversation; a *tête-à-tête* seat. **III.** *n.*; pl. *-têtes* (-tāts′). A tête-à-tête conversation or interview; a period of, or the position of, being tête-à-tête, or together without others (as, "I suppose you asked him on board to break our *tête-à-tête* which must have grown wearisome to you," J. Conrad's "Rescue," v. 1; to dine in *tête-à-tête*); a party of two; also, a form of sofa or seat for two persons, esp. one so shaped that the persons are able to converse more or less face to face.

tête=de=nègre (tät-dẹ-nägr), *n.* [F., 'head of negro': cf. *niggerhead.*] Woolen cloth with a curled or knotted surface finish; also, a dark brown.

tête=de=pont (tät-dẹ-pôṅ), *n.*; pl. *têtes-de-pont* (tät-). [F., 'head of bridge.'] In *fort.*, a bridge-head.

teth-er (teᴛʜ′ẽr), *n.* [ME. *tethir, tedyr*; prob. from Scand.: cf. Icel. *tjōdhr*, tether.] A rope, chain, or the like by which an animal is fastened, as to a stake, so that its range of movement is limited; also, a rope or the like for some other purpose, as a halter for hanging; often, fig., the utmost length to which one can go in action, or the utmost extent or limit of ability or resources (as, "If Robert Redmayne is breaking into houses for food he must be at the end of his *tether*": Eden Phillpotts's "Red Redmaynes," vi.); sometimes, a confining tie or bond (as, "weary of the matrimonial *tether*": Byron's "Beppo," xviii.).—**teth′er,** *v. t.* To fasten or confine with or as with a tether: as, "The horses were *tethered* with tough bark ropes" (Roosevelt's "Winning of the West," i. 3).

tetra-. [Gr. τετρα-, repr. τέτταρες, τέσσαρες, four: see *four.*] A combining-form or prefix meaning 'four.' See *mono-.*

tet-ra-ba-sic (tet-rạ-bā′sik), *a.* [See *tetra-*.] In *chem.*, of an acid, having four atoms of hydrogen replaceable by basic atoms or radicals.

tet-ra-bran-chi-ate (tet-rạ-brang′ki-āt). [NL. *Tetrabranchiata*, pl., < Gr. τετρα-, four, + βράγχια, gills.] **I.** *a.* Belonging to the *Tetrabranchiata*, a subclass of cephalopods with four gills, including the pearly nautilus. **II.** *n.* A tetrabranchiate cephalopod.

tet-ra-car-pel-la-ry (tet-rạ-kär′pe-lạ-ri), *a.* [See *tetra-*.] In *bot.*, having four carpels.

tet-ra-chord (tet′rạ-kôrd), *n.* [Gr. τετράχορδος, four-stringed, < τετρα-, four, + χορδή, string.] In *music*, an instrument with four strings; also, a diatonic series of four

tones, the first and last of which are separated by a perfect fourth; also, the interval of a perfect fourth.

te-tra-cid (te-tras′id), *a.* [See *tetra-*.] In *chem.*, capable of combining with four molecules of a monobasic acid.

tet-rad (tet′rad), *n.* [LL. *tetras* (*tetrad-*), < Gr. τετράς (τετραδ-), < τέτταρες, four: cf. *tetra-*.] The number four; also, a group of four; in *chem.*, a tetravalent or quadrivalent element, atom, or radical.—**te-trad-ic** (te-trad′ik), *a.*

te-trad-y-mite (te-trad′i-mīt), *n.* [G. *tetradymit*, < Gr. τετράδυμος, fourfold.] A mineral consisting essentially of bismuth telluride, usually occurring in foliated masses of a pale steel-gray color and a brilliant metallic luster: so called because the crystals are twinned together in groups of four.

tet-ra-gon (tet′rạ-gon), *n.* [LL. *tetragonum*, < Gr. τετράγωνος, quadrangular, square, < τετρα-, four, + γωνία, angle.] In *geom.*, a figure having four angles; a quadrangle; a quadrilateral.—**te-trag-o-nal** (te-trag′ọ-nạl), *a.* Pertaining to a tetragon; in *crystal.*, noting or pertaining to a system of crystallization in which all three axes are at right angles to one another, and the two equal lateral axes differ in length from the vertical axis.—**te-trag′o-nal-ly,** *adv.*

tet-ra-gram (tet′rạ-gram), *n.* [Gr. τετράγραμμον: cf. *tetragrammaton.*] A word of four letters.

tet-ra-gram-ma-ton (tet-rạ-gram′ạ-ton), *n.*; pl. *-ta* (-tạ). [Gr. τετραγράμματον, < τετρα-, four, + γράμμα (γραμματ-), character, letter, < γράφειν, write.] A word of four letters; specif. [*cap.*], the Hebrew word written JHVH (or YHWH), representing, without vowels, Hebrew *Jahweh* (or *Yahweh*), the 'ineffable name,' commonly rendered in English by *Jehovah* (see *Jehovah*); [*l. c.*] any word of four letters used as a symbol.

tet-ra-he-dral (tet-rạ-hē′drạl), *a.* Pertaining to or having the form of a tetrahedron; also, having four lateral planes or four sides in addition to the top and bottom (as, a *tetrahedral* prism).—**tet-ra-he′dral-ly,** *adv.*

tet-ra-he-drite (tet-rạ-hē′drīt), *n.* [See *tetrahedron.*] A steel-gray or blackish mineral with a brilliant metallic luster, consisting essentially of copper, antimony, and sulphur, but often containing other elements, as silver, etc., occurring in tetrahedral crystals and massive, and forming an important ore of copper and sometimes of silver.

tet-ra-he-dron (tet-rạ-hē′drọn), *n.*; pl. *-drons* or *-dra* (-drä). [LGr. τετράεδρον, < Gr. τετρα-, four, + ἕδρα, seat, base.] In *geom.*, a solid contained by four plane faces; esp., a triangular pyramid whose base and three sides are equilateral triangles.

te-tral-o-gy (te-tral′ọ-ji), *n.*; pl. *-gies* (-jiz). [Gr. τετραλογία, < τετρα-, four, + λόγος, speech, discourse, story.] A group of four dramas, three tragic and one satyric, exhibited consecutively at the festival of Dionysus in ancient Athens; hence, any series of four related dramas, operas, etc.

te-tram-er-ous (te-tram′ẹ-rus), *a.* [Gr. τετραμερής, < τετρα-, four, + μέρος, part.] Consisting of or divided into four parts; in *bot.*, of flowers, having four members in each whorl.

te-tram-e-ter (te-tram′e-tẽr). [LL. *tetrametrus*, < Gr. τετράμετρος, < τετρα-, four, + μέτρον, measure.] In *pros.*: **I.** *a.* Having four measures. **II.** *n.* A tetrameter verse or period, consisting of four dipodies (eight feet) in trochaic, iambic, or anapæstic meter, and of four feet in other rhythms.

tet-ra-morph (tet′rạ-môrf), *n.* [Gr. τετράμορφος, of four forms, < τετρα-, four, + μορφή, form.] In *Christian art*, a composite figure combining the symbols of the four evangelists: represented as having wings covered with eyes, and standing on winged, fiery wheels.

tet-ra-on-id (tet-rạ-on′id). [NL. *Tetraonidæ*, pl., < L. *tetrao*(*n*-), < Gr. τετράων, grouse.] **I.** *a.* Belonging to the *Tetraonidæ*, a family of gallinaceous birds including the grouse and allied forms. **II.** *n.* A tetraonid bird.

tet-ra-pet-a-lous (tet-rạ-pet′ạ-lus), *a.* [See *tetra-*.] In *bot.*, having four petals.

tet-ra-phyl-lous (tet-rạ-fil′us), *a.* [Gr. τετρα-, four, + φύλλον, leaf.] In *bot.*, having four leaves or leaflets.

tet-ra-pod (tet′rạ-pod). [Gr. τετράπους (τετραποδ-), having four feet, < τετρα-, four, + πούς (ποδ-), foot.] **I.** *a.* Having four feet; four-footed; in *entom.*, belonging to the *Tetrapoda*, a division of butterflies having only four perfect legs, with an anterior pair unfitted for walking. **II.** *n.* A tetrapod animal.

te-trap-o-dy (te-trap′ọ̄-di), *n.*; pl. *-dies* (-diz). [Gr. τετραποδία.] In *pros.*, a group of four feet.

te-trap-o-lis (te-trap′ọ̄-lis), *n.* [Gr. τετράπολις, < τετρα-, four, + πόλις, city.] A group of four cities or towns; a political division consisting of four cities.—**tet-ra-pol-i-tan** (tet-rạ-pol′i-tạn), *a.* Of or pertaining to a tetrapolis, or group of four cities: as, the *Tetrapolitan* Confession (a confession of faith presented at the Diet of Augsburg in 1530 by the representatives of the four cities of Constance, Lindau, Memmingen, and Strasburg).

te-trap-ter-ous (te-trap′tẹ-rus), *a.* [Gr. τετράπτερος, < τετρα-, four, + πτερόν, wing.] Having four wings or wing-like appendages: as, a *tetrapterous* insect; a *tetrapterous* fruit.

tet-rarch (tet′rärk or tē′trärk), *n.* [LL. *tetrarcha*, L. *tetrarches*, < Gr. τετράρχης, < τετρα-, four, + ἄρχειν, lead, rule.] In the ancient Roman Empire, the ruler of the fourth part of a country or province, or later, esp. in the East, any subordinate ruler; hence, any ruler of a fourth part, division, etc.; a subordinate ruler generally; one of four joint rulers or chiefs; also, the commander of a subdivision of an ancient Greek phalanx.—**tet′rar-chate** (-rär-kāt), *n.* The office, jurisdiction, or territory of a tetrarch.—**te-trar-chic** (te-trär′kik), *a.* —**tet′rar-chy** (-ki), *n.*; pl. *-chies* (-kiz). [L. *tetrarchia*, < Gr. τετραρχία.] The government or jurisdiction of a tetrarch; the territory governed by a tetrarch; also, a government by four persons; a set of four rulers; a country divided into four governments.

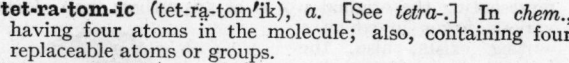

Tetrapterous Fruit.— 1, of silverbell-tree (*Mohrodendron carolinum*); 2, same, cut transversely.

tet-ra-sep-a-lous (tet-rạ-sep′ạ-lus), *a.* [See *tetra-.*] In *bot.*, having four sepals.

tet-ra-sper-mous (tet-rạ-spėr′mus), *a.* [See *tetra-* and *-spermous.*] In *bot.*, four-seeded.

tet-ra-stich (tet′rạ-stik), *n.* [L. *tetrastichon*, < Gr. τετράστιχος, of four rows or lines, < τετρα-, four, + στίχος, row, line.] In *pros.*, a strophe, stanza, or poem consisting of four lines or verses.—**tet-ra-stich′ic**, *a.*

te-tras-ti-chous (te-tras′ti-kus), *a.* [Gr. τετράστιχος: see *tetrastich.*] Disposed in or having four rows; in *bot.*, arranged in a spike of four vertical rows, as flowers; having four such rows of flowers, as a spike.

tet-ra-style (tet′rạ-stīl), *a.* [L. *tetrastylos*, < Gr. τετράστυλος, < τετρα-, four, + στῦλος, pillar, column.] **I.** *a.* Having four columns in front, as a temple or a portico. **II.** *n.* A tetrastyle structure.

tet-ra-syl-la-ble (tet-rạ-sil′ạ-bl), *n.* [Gr. τετρασύλλαβος, of four syllables, < τετρα-, four, + συλλαβή: see *syllable.*] A word of four syllables.—**tet″ra-syl-lab′ic** (-si-lab′ik), *a.*

Tetrastyle Portico. — North porch of the Erechtheum, Athens.

tet-ra-tom-ic (tet-rạ-tom′ik), *a.* [See *tetra-.*] In *chem.*, having four atoms in the molecule; also, containing four replaceable atoms or groups.

tet-ra-va-lent (tet-rạ-vā′lẹnt or te-trav′ạ-lẹnt), *a.* [See *tetra-* and *-valent.*] Same as *quadrivalent.*

te-trox-ide (te-trok′sīd or -sid), *n.* [See *tetra-.*] In *chem.*, an oxide which contains in its molecule four atoms of oxygen.

tet-ter (tet′ėr), *n.* [AS. *teter.*] Any of various cutaneous diseases, as herpes, eczema, impetigo, etc.; also, a cutaneous disease of animals, esp. horses, causing a troublesome itching.

Teu-cri-an (tū′kri-ạn). [L. *Teucrius*, < *Teucri*, pl., the Trojans; so named from *Teucer*, first king of Troy.] **I.** *a.* Of or pertaining to the ancient Trojans. **II.** *n.* One of the ancient Trojans.

Teu-to-, Teu-ton-o- (tū′tọ̄-, tū′tọn-ọ̄-). Form of *Teuton* or *Teutonic* used in combination, as in *Teuto-Celtic* or *Teutono-Celtic* (both Teutonic and Celtic).

Teu-ton (tū′tọn). [L. *Teutoni*, *Teutones*, pl., the ancient Teutons.] **I.** *n.* Orig., a member of a people of unknown race first mentioned in the 4th century B.C., and supposed to have dwelt in Jutland; now, a native of Germany or a person of German race; also, a member of the northern European race including the German, Dutch, Scandinavian, and related peoples. **II.** *a.* Teutonic.—**Teu-ton′ic** (-ton′ik), *a.* [L. *Teutonicus.*] Of or pertaining to the ancient Teutons; also, of or pertaining to the Teutons or Germans; German; also, noting or pertaining to the northern European race which includes the German, Dutch, Scandinavian, and related peoples, or the group of Indo-European languages (including German, Dutch, Anglo-Saxon, Gothic, the Scandinavian tongues, etc.) spoken by them; Germanic.—**Teutonic Knights**, the knights of the Teutonic Order.—**Teutonic Order**, a military and religious order of German knights founded (1190–91) at Acre, in Palestine, for service in the Holy Land, which later became a great power in Europe through its conquests of the heathen nations of Prussia, etc., continuing to exist with decreasing influence until suppressed in 1809 (and since resuscitated in a minor form in Austria). —**Teu-ton′ic**, *n.* The group of Indo-European languages of the Teutonic or Germanic peoples.—**Teu-ton′i-cism** (-i-sizm), *n.* The character or spirit of the Teutons, esp. the Germans; a Teutonic or German characteristic; an idiom or expression peculiar to the Teutonic peoples, esp. the Germans.—**Teu′ton-ism**, *n.*—**Teu′ton-ize** (-īz), *v. t.* or *i.*; *-ized*, *-izing.* To make or become Teutonic.—**Teu″ton-i-za′tion** (-i-zā′shọn), *n.*

Teu′ton-o-. See *Teuto-.*

Teu-to-phil, Teu-to-phile (tū′tọ̄-fil). [See *Teuto-* and *-phil.*] **I.** *a.* Friendly to the Teutons or Germans. **II.** *n.* One who favors or admires the Teutons or Germans.

Teu-to-phobe (tū′tọ̄-fōb), *n.* [See *Teuto-* and *-phobe.*] One who fears or hates the Teutons or Germans.—**Teu-to-pho′bi-a** (-fō′bi-ä), *n.*

tew (tū), *v.* [Var. of *taw¹.*] **I.** *tr.* To taw, as skins; prepare by beating, etc.; beat, drub, or thrash; shake, toss, or pull about; fatigue with hard work. [Obs. or prov.] **II.** *intr.* To work; keep busy; bustle. [Prov.]

tex-as (tek′sạs), *n.* [From the State of *Texas.*] A structure on the hurricane-deck of a steamboat, containing officers' cabins, etc., and having the pilot-house in front or on top: as, "He took me in the *texas* to the officers' lunch" (Mark Twain's "Huckleberry Finn," xxxii.). [Western U. S.]

Tex-as (tek′sạs) **fe′ver.** An infectious disease of cattle in the southern U. S. and elsewhere, due to the parasitic protozoan *Pyrosoma* (or *Piroplasma*) *bigeminum*, which is transmitted from sick to healthy animals by the tick *Ixodes bovis* (or *Margaropus annulatus*), and which multiplies in the blood and destroys the red blood-corpuscles.

Tex-as (tek′sạs) **Lea′guer.** [In allusion to the *Texas League* of baseball clubs.] In *baseball*, a ball that falls midway between infielders and outfielders.

Tex-as (tek′sạs) **spar′row.** A fringilline bird, *Embernagra rufovirgata*, of the lower Rio Grande valley, dull olive-green above with yellow on the wings and rufous stripes on the head. See cut on following page.

text (tekst), *n.* [OF. F. *texte*, < L. *textus*, texture, structure, context, < *texere*, weave.] The actual wording of anything written or printed; the wording adopted by an editor as

---

representing the original words of an author; any of the various forms in which a writing exists; also, the original words of an author in distinction from a translation, paraphrase, commentary, or the like; the main body of matter in a book or manuscript, as distinguished from notes, appendixes, etc.; letterpress, as distinguished from illustrations, margins, etc.; also, the letter of the Holy Scripture, or the Scriptures themselves; a book of the Scriptures, esp. a volume containing the Gospels (now only hist.); also, a short passage of Scripture, esp. one chosen in proof of a doctrine, as the subject of a sermon, etc.; hence, any theme or topic (as, "the incident . . . which furnished the *text* for this reverie upon Sudden Death": De Quincey's "English Mail-Coach," ii.); also, a formal style of handwriting; any form of old English or black-letter type; also, the words of a song or the like.—**text′book,** *n.* A book used by students as a standard work for a particular branch of study; a manual of instruction.

Texas Sparrow.

tex-tile (teks′til). [L. *textilis,* < *texere,* weave.] **I.** *a.* Woven, or capable of being woven (as, *textile* fabrics; *textile* materials); also, of or pertaining to weaving (as, the *textile* art). **II.** *n.* A woven fabric; also, a material suitable for weaving.

tex-tu-al (teks′tū-al), *a.* [L. *textus:* see *text.*] Of or pertaining to the text (as, *textual* criticism; *textual* emendations; *textual* errors); based on or conforming to the text, as of the Scriptures; also, of or pertaining to textbooks.—**tex′tu-al-ism,** *n.* Strict adherence to the text, esp. of the Scriptures; also, textual criticism, esp. of the Bible.—**tex′tu-al-ist,** *n.* One who is well versed in the text of the Scriptures; also, one who adheres closely to the text, esp. of the Scriptures.—**tex′tu-al-ly,** *adv.*

tex-tu-a-ry (teks′tū-ā-ri). [L. *textus:* see *text.*] **I.** *a.* Of or pertaining to the text; textual. **II.** *n.*; pl. *-ries* (-riz). A textualist.

tex-tur-al (teks′tūr-al), *a.* Of or pertaining to texture.—**tex′tur-al-ly,** *adv.*

tex-ture (teks′tūr), *n.* [L. *textura,* < *texere,* weave.] The art or process of weaving†; also, anything produced by weaving; a woven fabric; hence, any structure appearing as if woven; also, the characteristic disposition of the interwoven or intertwined threads, strands, or the like which make up a textile fabric (as, a cloth of a loose *texture;* "cotton . . . of a fine *texture,*" Prescott's "Conquest of Mexico," iv. 2); hence, the characteristic disposition of the constituent parts of any body; structure or constitution in general; in the *fine arts,* the representation of the surface structure of an object, esp. the skin.—**tex′tured,** *a.* Having a texture (as specified): as, open-*textured.*—**tex′ture-less,** *a.* Having no discernible texture or structure.

-th¹. [AS. and ME. *-th.*] A suffix forming nouns of state, quality, action, process, etc., as *bath, depth, health, mirth, tilth, warmth.*

-th². [AS. *-tha, -otha,* also *-ta.*] A suffix forming ordinal numerals, as *fourth, fortieth, fifth, fiftieth, sixth, seventh, eighth,* etc.

-th³. See *-eth.*

thal-a-men-ceph-a-lon (thal″a-men-sef′a-lon), *n.*; pl. *-la* (-lä). [NL.: see *thalamus* and *encephalon.*] In *anat.,* the segment of the brain behind the prosencephalon, consisting of the optic thalami, the pineal gland, etc.; the betweenbrain. —**thal″a-men-ce-phal′ic** (-se-fal′ik), *a.*

thal-a-mus (thal′a-mus), *n.*; pl. *-mi* (-mī). [L., < Gr. θάλαμος, inner chamber.] In *anat.,* a part of the brain where a nerve emerges or appears to emerge (as, an optic *thalamus,* either of two large oblong masses of gray matter forming a part of the thalamencephalon, and giving origin to some of the

fibers of the optic nerve); specif., an optic thalamus; in *bot.,* a receptacle or torus; also, a thallus.—**tha-lam-ic** (tha-lam′ik), *a.*

tha-las-si-an (tha-las′i-an). [Gr. θάλασσα, sea.] **I.** *a.* Of or pertaining to the sea; marine. **II.** *n.* Any sea-turtle.— **tha-las′sic** (-las′ik), *a.* Of or pertaining to the sea; growing, living, or found in the sea; pelagic; marine; sometimes, of or pertaining to the smaller bodies of water called seas, as distinguished from *oceanic.*—**tha-las′so-crat** (-las′ō-krat), *n.* [See *-crat.*] A ruler or master of the sea.—**thal-as-soc-ra-cy** (thal-a-sok′ra-si), *n.*—**thal-as-sog′ra-phy** (-sog′ra-fi), *n.* [See *-graphy.*] The science of the ocean; oceanography.

tha-ler (tä′lėr), *n.*; pl. *thaler.* [G.: see *dollar.*] Any of certain large silver coins of varying value formerly issued in Germany, esp. one of the value of 3 marks, or about 71½ U. S. cents.

Tha-li-a (tha-lī′a), *n.* [L., < Gr. Θάλεια, lit. 'blooming.'] The Muse of comedy and idyllic poetry.

Obverse.

tha-lic-trum (tha-lik′trum), *n.* [L., < Gr. θάλικτρον, meadow-rue.] Any plant of the ranunculaceous genus *Thalictrum;* a meadow-rue.

thal-lic (thal′ik), *a.* In *chem.,* of or containing thallium. See *thallous.*

thal-line (thal′in), *n.* [Gr. θαλλός, young shoot.] In *chem.,* a white crystalline base belonging to the quinoline class, and yielding salts used as antipyretics.

thal-li-ous (thal′i-us), *a.* Same as *thallous.*

thal-li-um (thal′i-um), *n.* [NL., < Gr. θαλλός, young (green) shoot; from the green line in its spectrum.] Chem. sym., Tl; at. wt., 204.0; sp. gr., 11.8. A soft, malleable rare metallic element.

Reverse.

Thaler of Lüneburg, 1547.—British Museum.

thal-lo-gen (thal′ō-jen), *n.* [See *thallus* and *-gen.*] Same as *thallophyte.*

thal-loid (thal′oid), *a.* [See *-oid.*] In *bot.,* resembling or consisting of a thallus.

thal-lo-phyte (thal′ō-fīt), *n.* [NL. *Thallophyta,* pl., < Gr. θαλλός, young shoot, + φυτόν, plant.] In *bot.,* any of the *Thallophyta,* a primary division or group of plants in which the vegetative body is typically a thallus, and which includes the algæ, fungi, and lichens.—**thal-lo-phyt′ic** (-fit′ik), *a.*

thal-lous (thal′us), *a.* In *chem.,* containing thallium (in larger proportion than a corresponding thallic compound).

thal-lus (thal′us), *n.*; pl. *thalli* (-ī). [NL., < Gr. θαλλός, young shoot, young branch.] In *bot.,* a vegetative body undifferentiated into true leaves, stem, and root: the plant body of typical thallophytes.

thal-weg (täl′väch), *n.* [G., < *thal,* valley, + *weg,* way.] In *phys. geog.,* the line of greatest slope along the bottom of a valley, forming the natural direction of a watercourse.

Tham-muz (tham′uz), *n.* Same as *Tammuz.*

than (ᴛʜan), *conj.* [AS. *thanne, thonne, thænne,* than, orig. *then:* see *then.*] A particle used after comparative adjectives and adverbs and certain other words, such as *other, otherwise, else,* etc., to introduce the second member of a comparison: as, this train is faster *than* that one; it was no sooner said *than* done; it was no other *than* he; how else can I come *than* by train? *Than,* as a conjunction, has the same case (usually the nominative) after it as before it (as, he is taller *than I* [am]; I am richer *than he* [is]; they like you better *than* [they like] *me*); but it is sometimes used as if a preposition and followed by a pronoun in the objective case (as, "He was a good bit older *than me*," Lamb's "Dream-Children": a use now considered incorrect except in the expression *than whom*, which is now universally used in place of *than who*, as, "Beëlzebub . . . *than whom*, Satan except, none higher sat," Milton's "Paradise Lost," ii. 299).

than-age (thā'nāj), *n.* The tenure by which lands were held by a thane; the lands so held; also, the office, rank, or jurisdiction of a thane. [Now only hist.]

than-a-tism (than'a-tizm), *n.* [Gr. θάνατος, death.] The belief that at death the human soul ceases to exist. — **than'a-tist,** *n.*

thanato-. Form of Gr. θάνατος, death, used in combination. — **than-a-tol-o-gy** (than-a-tol'ō-ji), *n.* [+ *-logy*.] The scientific study of death and its causes and phenomena. — **than-a-top'sis** (-top'sis), *n.* [+ Gr. ὄψις, sight, view.] A view or contemplation of death: used in the title of Bryant's famous poem "Thanatopsis."

thane (thān), *n.* [ME. *thane,* northern (Sc.) form of *thain, thein,* < AS. *thegn, thegen,* servant, retainer, soldier, thane, = OHG. *degan,* boy, servant, soldier, = Icel. *thegn,* liegeman: cf. Gr. τέκνον, child.] A servant†; an attendant†; a retainer†; in *early Eng. hist.,* a member of any of several classes of men ranking between earls and ordinary freemen, and holding lands of the king or lord by military service; in *Sc. hist.,* a person, ranking with an earl's son, holding lands of the king; the chief of a clan, who became one of the king's barons. — **thane'ship,** *n.*

thank (thangk), *n.* [AS. *thanc, thonc,* thought, favor, liking, thanks, = D. and G. *dank,* thanks, = Icel. *thökk,* liking, thanks; akin to E. *think*[2].] Thought†; favorable thought† or good-will†; feeling of gratitude for a benefit or favor received†; now, *pl.* (formerly also *sing.*), the expression of grateful feeling, or grateful acknowledgment of a benefit or favor by words or otherwise (as, a speech or a smile of *thanks*; to give *thanks* to God for one's blessings; to return a borrowed book with *thanks*). — **thanks,** a common elliptical expression used in acknowledging a favor, service, courtesy, or the like: as, " 'How are you?' she asked . . . 'I'm all right, *thanks*,' said Hilda" (Arnold Bennett's "Hilda Lessways," ii. 1). — **thanks to,** thanks be given to; also, owing to, or as a result or consequence of (as, *thanks to* errors of their opponents, they managed to win). — **thank,** *v. t.* [AS. *thancian, thoncian.*] To give thanks to; express gratitude to. — **to have one's self to thank for,** to owe (a thing) to one's own action; be one's self responsible or at fault for. — **thank'er,** *n.* — **thank'ful,** *a.* [AS. *thancfull.*] Feeling, expressing, or betokening gratitude; grateful: as, "Be *thankful* unto him, and bless his name" (Ps. c. 4); "a *thankful* acknowledgment of His liberality and goodness" (Hooker's "Ecclesiastical Polity," ii. 3). — **thank'ful-ly,** *adv.* — **thank'ful-ness,** *n.* — **thank'less,** *a.* Not feeling or expressing gratitude; ungrateful; also, not such as to be rewarded with thanks (as, "a laborious, perhaps a *thankless* enterprise," Carlyle's "Sartor Resartus," iii. 12; a *thankless* task); not acceptable, or not appreciated. — **thank'less-ly,** *adv.* — **thank'less-ness,** *n.* — **thank'=of"fer-ing,** *n.* An offering made according to the Levitical law as an expression of gratitude to God; hence, any offering made by way of thanks or grateful acknowledgment. — **thanks-giv-er** (thangks'giv"ėr or thangks-giv'ėr), *n.* One who gives thanks. — **thanks-giv'ing,** *n.* The act of giving thanks; grateful acknowledgment of benefits or favors; esp., the act of giving thanks to God; a public celebration in acknowledgment of divine favor; a day set apart for this purpose; [*cap.*] in the U. S., Thanksgiving Day; also [*l. c.*], an act or expression of thanks; esp., a form of words expressive of thanks to God. — **Thanksgiving Day,** in the U. S., an annual festival in acknowledgment of divine favor, first celebrated in Plymouth Colony in 1621, and now appointed by proclamation of the President and the State governors and held on the last Thursday of November. — **thank'-wor"thy** (-wėr"THi), *a.* Worthy of thanks; deserving gratitude. — **thank'=you-ma:am,** *n.* A ridge or hollow in a road causing persons riding over it in a vehicle to nod the head suddenly as if making a bow of acknowledgment; esp., such a ridge or hollow in a road on the face of a hill, designed to throw to one side descending rain-water. [Colloq., U. S.]

tha-ros (thā'ros), *n.* [NL.] A small North American butterfly, *Phyciodes tharos,* with black, orange, and white coloration.

that (ᴛHat), *pron.* and *a.* [AS. *thæt,* neut. nom. and acc. sing. of the demonstrative (and relative) pronoun which came to be used also as the definite article: see *the*[1].] **A.** *demonst. pron.* or *a.*; pl. *those* (ᴛHōz). A demonstrative term indicating: (1) a person, thing, idea, etc., as pointed out or present, as before mentioned, or supposed to be understood, or by way of emphasis; (2) one of two persons, things, etc., already mentioned, either referring to the one more remote in place, time, or thought, or implying mere contradistinction (opposed to *this*). **B.** *rel. pron.* A relative pronoun used: (1) as the subject or object of a relative clause, esp. one defining or restricting the antecedent (sometimes replaceable by *who, whom,* or *which*); (2) as the object of a preposition, the preposition standing at the end of the relative clause (as, the man *that* I spoke of); (3) in various special or elliptical constructions (as, fool *that* he is; the day *that* he was born). — **that,** *adv.* To that extent; to such a degree; so: used with adjectives and adverbs of quantity or extent (as, *that* much; *that* far; *that* high), and also (now only prov. or colloq.) with other adjectives and adverbs (as, he was *that* weak he could hardly stand; "You were *that* cool! *That* quick!" Wister's "Virginian," xxxv.). — **that,** *conj.* A conjunction used: (1) to introduce a clause as the subject or object of the principal verb or as the necessary complement to a statement made, or a clause expressing cause or reason, purpose or aim, result or consequence, etc. (as, *that* he will come is certain; I know *that* he will come; you gave permission *that* I should go; we are sure *that* you will like it; he was surprised *that* I should wish to go; he did it *that* he might save time; she was so ill *that* she had to go home); (2) elliptically, to introduce a sentence or clause expressing desire, surprise, indignation, etc. (as, "O, *that* you bore The mind that I do!" Shakspere's "Tempest," ii. 1. 267; "*That* a brother should Be so perfidious!" Shakspere's "Tempest," i. 2. 67); (3) in place of another conjunction, to avoid repetition (archaic: as, "If it seem good unto you, and *that* it be of the Lord our God, let us send abroad unto our brethren," 1 Chron. xiii. 2).

thatch (thach), *n.* [Assibilated form of (now prov.) *thack,* < AS. *thæc* = D. *dak* = G. *dach* = Icel. *thak,* roof; akin to L. *tegere,* cover, Gr. τέγος, στέγος, roof, στέγειν, cover.] A material, as straw, rushes, leaves, or the like, used to cover roofs, grain-stacks, etc.; a covering of such a material; also, sometimes, a thatched dwelling; also, fig., covering, often the hair covering the head (as, "His dark-brown hair . . . retained its original thickness of *thatch*": Besant's "All Sorts and Conditions of Men," Prologue, ii.); also, any of various palms the leaves of which are used for thatching. — **thatch,** *v. t.* [AS. *theccan.*] To cover with or as with thatch: as, "a long low house, *thatched* with rushes" (W. H. Hudson's "Far Away and Long Ago," xiii.). — **thatch'er,** *n.* — **thatch'ing,** *n.* The act of covering roofs, etc., with thatch; also, the material used for this purpose; thatch; a covering of such material (as, "A light *thatching* of bleached palmetto-leaves hung over it [an edifice]": H. Melville's "Typee," xxiii.). — **thatch'y,** *a.* Composed of, abounding in, or resembling thatch.

thau-ma-tol-o-gy (thâ-ma-tol'ō-ji), *n.* [Gr. θαῦμα (θαυματ-), a wonder: see *-logy*.] The study or description of miracles.

thau-ma-trope (thâ'ma-trōp), *n.* [Gr. θαῦμα, a wonder: see *-trope*.] A card or disk with different pictures or designs on the opposite sides (as a horse on one side and a rider on the other), which, when twirled rapidly about one of its diameters, causes the pictures to appear as if combined, thus illustrating the persistence of visual impressions; also, a phenakistoscope or similar device.

thau-ma-turge (thâ'ma-tėrj), *n.* [ML. *thaumaturgus,* < Gr. θαυματουργός, wonder-working, < θαῦμα (θαυματ-), a wonder, + -εργός, working.] A worker of wonders or miracles; a wonder-worker. — **thau-ma-tur'gic, thau-ma-**

tur′gi-cal (-tẽr′jik, -ji-kạl), a. Pertaining to a thaumaturge or to thaumaturgy; having the powers of a thaumaturge.—thau′ma-tur-gist, n. A thaumaturge.—thau′ma-tur′gus (-gus), n.; pl. -gi (-jī). [ML.] A thaumaturge.—thau′ma-tur′gy (-ji), n. [Gr. θαυματουργία, < θαυματουργός.] The working of wonders or miracles; magic.

thaw (thâ), v. [AS. thāwian = MLG. doien = D. dooien = Icel. theyja, thaw.] I. tr. To reduce from a frozen to a liquid state; melt; also, to melt the frozen liquid contained in (a non-liquid substance rigid with frost); free from the physical effect of frost or extreme cold (as, "snakes in frosty mornings in my path with portions of their bodies still numb and inflexible, waiting for the sun to thaw them": Thoreau's "Walden," i.); fig., to render less cold, formal, or reserved; make genial. II. intr. To pass from a frozen to a liquid or semiliquid state; melt; also, to have the contained frozen liquid melted by heat; be freed from the physical effect of frost or extreme cold; also, to become so warm as to melt ice and snow (used impersonally, with reference to the weather: as, it will probably thaw to-day); also, fig., to become less cold, formal, or reserved (as, "The short, shy manner of their white-haired host thawed under the influence of Mrs. Elsmere's racy, unaffected ways": Mrs. H. Ward's "Robert Elsmere," iv.); become genial.—thaw, n. The act or process of thawing; a condition of the weather caused by the rise of the temperature above the freezing-point; fig., a becoming less cold, formal, or reserved (as, "the partial thaw in Redworth's bearing toward him": G. Meredith's "Diana of the Crossways," xxxvii.).—thaw′er, n.—thaw′less, a. Without thawing.—thaw′y, a. Characterized by thawing.

the[1] (тнē, тнẹ, or тнẻ), def. art. [AS. the (for earlier se, fem. sēo, neut. thæt), art., orig. demonstrative pronoun, from a stem occurring also in OS. the, OFries. thi, D. de, OHG. G. der, Icel. that, Goth. thata, also in L. iste, that, Gr. τό, the, Skt. tat, it, that: cf. that, the[2], then, thence, there, they, this, thither, and thus.] A word used, esp. before nouns, with a specifying or particularizing effect, as opposed to the indefinite or generalizing force of the indefinite article a or an: as, I prize the book that you gave me. Various special uses are: (1) to mark a noun as indicating something well-known or unique (as, the prodigal son; the Alps); (2) with, or as part of, a title (as, the Duke of Wellington; the Reverend John Smith); (3) to mark a noun as indicating the best-known, most approved, or most important of its kind (as, the watering-place of the U. S.); (4) to mark a noun as being used generically (as, the dog is a quadruped); (5) in place of a possessive pronoun, to denote a part of the body or a personal belonging (as, to hang the head and weep; to take one by the sleeve); (6) before adjectives used substantively, and denoting an individual, a class or number of individuals, or an abstract notion (as, to visit the sick; the beautiful); (7) distributively, to denote any one separately, where a or an is more commonly employed (as, at one dollar the pound).

the[2] (тнē, тнẹ, or тнẻ), adv. [AS. thē, thȳ, instrumental case of se: see the[1].] A word used to modify an adjective or adverb in the comparative degree: (a) signifying 'in or by that,' 'on that account,' 'in or by so much,' or 'in some or any degree': as, he is taking more care of himself, and looks the better; if you start now, you will be back the sooner; a garment the worse, or none the worse, for wear; (b) used correlatively, in one instance with relative force and in the other with demonstrative force, and signifying 'by how much . . . by so much' or 'in what degree . . . in that degree': as, the more the merrier; the sooner the better.

the-a-ceous (thẹ-ā′shius), a. [NL. Thea, the typical genus, = E. tea.] Belonging to the Theaceæ, or tea family of plants.

the-an-throp-ic (thē-an-throp′ik), a. [LGr. θεάνθρωπος, 'god-man,' < Gr. θεός, god, + ἄνθρωπος, man.] Of, pertaining to, or of the nature of both God and man; both divine and human.—the-an-thro-pism (thẹ-an′thrọ-pizm), n. The doctrine of the union of the divine and human natures, or of the manifestation of God as man in Christ; in myth., the attribution of human nature to the gods.—the-an′thro-pist, n.

the-ar-chy (thē′är-ki), n.; pl. -chies (-kiz). [LGr. θεαρχία,

< Gr. θεός, god, + ἄρχειν, lead, rule.] The rule or government of God or of a god; also, an order or system of divine rulers or of deities.—the-ar-chic (thẹ-är′kik), a.

the-a-ter, the-a-tre (thē′ạ-tẽr), n. [OF. theatre (F. théâtre), < L. theatrum, < Gr. θέατρον, < θεᾶσθαι, look at, view: cf. theory.] Among the ancient Greeks and Romans, an open-air structure in the form of a segment of a circle, for the presentation of dramatic and other spectacles, the auditorium usually being excavated from a hillside, with the seats ar-

Interior of Roman Theater of Aspendos, Asia Minor.

ranged in tiers behind and above one another; hence, a natural formation rising by steps or gradations like the seats of such a structure; also, in modern use, a specially constructed edifice, formerly only partially roofed, but now entirely under cover, for dramatic performances, etc.; hence, the audience at a performance there; also, dramatic performances as a branch of art, or the drama; dramatic works collectively, as of a literature, a nation, or an author; also, a temporary platform or the like for a public ceremony (as, "Here a large scaffolding or theatre had been erected . . . A throne . . . was arranged in the most elevated position for the Duke": Motley's "Dutch Republic," iii. 5); a room or hall fitted with tiers of seats rising like steps, used for lectures, anatomical demonstrations, surgical operations before a class, etc.; also, fig., a locality or scene where a series of events takes place or may be observed (as, "The watery expanse between Harlem and Amsterdam would be the principal theatre of the operations about to commence": Motley's "Dutch Republic," iii. 8); a place of action; a field of operations.—the′a-ter-go″er, n. One who goes to the theater, esp. habitually.—the′a-ter-go″ing, n. and a.—the-at-ric (thẹ-at′rik), a. [LL. theatricus, < Gr. θεατρικός.] Theatrical.—the-at′ri-cal. I. a. Of or pertaining to the theater, or dramatic or scenic representations (as, theatrical performances; a theatrical company); also, suggestive of the theater or of acting, or artificial (as, "How far the character in which he [Byron] exhibited himself was genuine, and how far theatrical, it would probably have puzzled himself to say": Macaulay's "Essays," Moore's Byron); often, affected, pompous, spectacular, or extravagantly histrionic, in a way often seen on the stage (as, theatrical behavior; a theatrical manner or tone; a theatrical display of feeling); stagy; of persons, behaving, or given to behaving, as if acting on the stage or as if for display or effect before an audience (as, "He is . . . sometimes a little theatrical": H. G. Wells's "Mr. Britling," i. 5. § 1). II. n. Pl., dramatic performances, now esp. as given by amateurs (as, "There were . . . private theatricals in Mrs. Dwyer's new house": W. Churchill's "Modern Chronicle," i. 6); matters pertaining to the stage and acting; also, actions of a theatrical character; sing., a professional actor.—the-at′ri-cal-ism, n. The theory and methods of scenic representations; also, theatrical practice, style, or character; staginess. —the-at-ri-cal′i-ty (-kal′i-ti), the-at′ri-cal-ness, n.—the-at′ri-cal-ize (-īz), v. t.; -ized, -izing. To render theatrical.—the-at″ri-cal-i-za′tion (-i-zā″shọn), n.—the-at′ri-cal-ly, adv.—the-a-tro-ma-ni-a (thē″ạ-trọ-mā′ni-ạ), n. [NL.] A mania or excessive fondness for theater-going.

The-ba-ic (thẹ-bā′ik), a. [L. Thebaicus.] Of or pertaining to Thebes, an ancient city on the Nile and formerly a center of Egyptian civilization.

the-ba-ine (thē′bạ-in), n. [Named from Thebes, Egypt, with allusion to Egyptian opium.] In chem., a white crystalline poisonous alkaloid present in opium in small quantities.

The-ban (thē′bạn). [L. Thebanus.] I. a. Of or pertaining to Thebes, the chief city of ancient Bœotia, in Greece; also,

Thebaic. II. *n.* A native or inhabitant of Thebes in Bœotia.

the-ca (thē′kä), *n.*; pl. *thecæ* (-sē). [L., < Gr. θήκη, case, box, sheath, < τιθέναι, set, put.] A case or receptacle; in *bot.*, a sac, cell, or capsule; a spore-case; specif., in mosses, the spore-bearing sac of the sporophyte or asexual generation; in *anat.* and *zoöl.*, a case or sheath inclosing an organ, etc., as the horny covering of an insect-pupa.—**the′cal** (-kạl), *a.* Pertaining to or of the nature of a theca.—**the′cate** (-kāt), *a.* Having, or contained in, a theca.

thee (ᴛʜē), *pron.* [AS. *thē*, dat. and acc. of *thū*, E. *thou*.] Objective case of *thou*. See *thou*.—**thee**, *v. t.* or *i.*; *thee′d*, *theeing*. To address as 'thee,' or use 'thee' in discourse. Cf. *thou*, *v.*

theft (theft), *n.* [AS. *thēoft, thīefth*, < *thēof*, E. *thief*.] The action of a thief; the act or an instance of stealing; specif., the wrongful taking and carrying away of the personal goods of another; larceny; also, something stolen (now rare).—**thef-tu-ous** (thef′tū-us), *a.* Thievish. [Orig. Sc.]

thegn (thān), *n.* Anglo-Saxon form of *thane*.

the-ine (thē′in), *n.* [NL. *theina*, < *thea*, tea.] Caffeine: so called because found in tea.

their (ᴛʜār), *pron.* [From Scand.: cf. Icel. *theira*, gen. of *their*, they: see *they*.] The possessive form of *they* used before a noun.—**theirs** (ᴛʜārz), *pron.* Form of *their* used predicatively or without a noun following: as, it is *theirs*; bring me *theirs*.

the-ism¹ (thē′izm), *n.* [NL. *thea*, tea.] A morbid condition due to immoderate tea-drinking.

the-ism² (thē′izm), *n.* [Gr. θεός, god.] Orig., belief in the existence of a God or of gods (opposed to *atheism*); now, esp., belief in one God as the creator and ruler of the universe, without rejection of revelation (distinguished from *deism*).—**the′ist**, *n.* One who holds the doctrine of theism.—**the-is-tic** (thē-is′tik), *a.*—**the-is′ti-cal-ly**, *adv.*

Thel-e-mite (thel′ē-mīt), *n.* [F. *thélémite*, < *Thélème*, < Gr. θέλημα, will.] An inmate of the abbey of Thélème (Thelema), in Rabelais's "Gargantua," where the law of the order was "Do what thou wilt." Also fig.

the-li-tis (thē-lī′tis), *n.* [NL., < Gr. θηλή, nipple.] In *pathol.*, inflammation of the nipple.

them (ᴛʜem), *pron.* [Prob. < AS. *thǣm*, dat. pl. of *se*: see *the¹* and *they*.] Objective case of *they*.

the-mat-ic (thē-mat′ik), *a.* [Gr. θεματικός.] Of or pertaining to a theme.—**the-mat′i-cal-ly**, *adv.*

theme (thēm), *n.* [L. *thema*, < Gr. θέμα, something laid down, proposition, theme, < τιθέναι, set, put: see *thesis*.] A subject of discourse, discussion, meditation, or composition, or a topic (as, "Montrose, whose exploits and fate are the *theme* of history": Scott's "Legend of Montrose," xxiii.); in general, a subject, matter, or occasion (obs. or rare: as, "I will fight with him upon this *theme*," Shakspere's "Hamlet," v. 1. 289; "the terrible champion, whose name had been so long the *theme* of her anxiety," Scott's "Castle Dangerous," xv.); also, a short dissertation or essay, esp. a school composition; also, each of the twenty-nine provinces into which the Byzantine Empire was divided; in *philol.*, the part of a word to which inflectional endings are added; a stem; in *music*, the or a principal melody in a musical composition; also, a short melody from which variations are developed.

The-mis (thē′mis), *n.* [L., < Θέμις, personification of θέμις, law, right, < τιθέναι: see *theme*.] The ancient Greek goddess of law, order, and abstract right; hence, law or justice personified.

them-selves (ᴛʜem-selvz′), *pron. pl.* An emphatic form of *them* or *they*; also, a reflexive form of *them*.

then (ᴛʜen), *adv.* [AS. *thanne, thonne, thænne*, then, also *than*, = D. *dan*, then, than, = G. *dann*, then, *denn*, then, than; from the stem represented by E. *the¹*.] At that time (as, prices were *then* lower; come in next week, if you should *then* be in town); also, immediately or soon afterward (as, he stopped, and *then* began again); next in order of time (as, "first the blade, *then* the ear, after that the full corn in the ear": Mark, iv. 28); also, at another time (as, "Sometime the flood prevails, and *then* the wind; Now one time better, *then* another best": Shakspere's "3 Henry VI.," ii. 5. 9); also, in the next place, in addition, or besides (as, "Had

he not been . . . Senior Wrangler, First Chancellor's Medallist and I do not know how many more things besides? And *then*, he was such a wonderful speaker": S. Butler's "Way of All Flesh," xxvii.); also, in that case, or in those circumstances (as, "If there be not a God for whose glory we can live . . . what *then?*" Mallock's "New Republic," i. 4); since that is so, therefore, or consequently (as, " 'Ha!' said the countess, hastily; 'that rumour *then* is true, Janet' ": Scott's "Kenilworth," xx.).—**but then**, but at the same time; but on the other hand: as, he knows little about the subject, *but then* it is not in his field.—**now and then.** See under *now*, *adv.*—**then**, *n.* That time: as, by *then*; till *then*.—**then**, *a.* Being, or being such, then; then existing: as, "the *then* state of the political world" (Kinglake's "Eothen," xviii.); "the *then* prime minister" (Trollope's "Barchester Towers," i.).

the-nar (thē′när). [NL., < Gr. θέναρ.] In *anat.*: **I.** *n.* The prominence or ball of muscle at the base of the thumb; also, the palm of the hand; also, the sole of the foot. **II.** *a.* Of or pertaining to the thenar.

thence (ᴛʜens), *adv.* [ME. *thennes* (with adverbial suffix *-s*), < *thenne*, < AS. *thanone, thanon*, thence; from the stem represented by E. *the¹*.] From that place (as, "When ye depart *thence*, shake off the dust under your feet": Mark, vi. 11); also, from that time, or thenceforth (as, "There shall be no more *thence* an infant of days": Isa. lxv. 20); also, from that source or origin; from that fact or circumstance; as an inference from that fact or those data, or therefrom (as, it would *thence* follow that . . .); also, at a place distant or away from there (as, a few miles *thence* is a wide river; "They prosper best of all when I am *thence*," Shakspere's "3 Henry VI.," ii. 5. 18); distant; absent.—**from thence**, thence: a pleonasm.—**thence′forth′**, *adv.* From that time forward or onward (as, "*Thenceforth* he was considered all right by everybody": W. B. Maxwell's "In Cotton Wool," v.); sometimes, from that place or point onward.—**thence′for′ward**, *adv.* Thenceforth.—**thence′from′**, *adv.* From that place or source.

theo-. Form of Gr. θεός, god, used in combination.

the-o-bro-mine (thē-ọ-brō′min), *n.* [NL. *Theobroma*, the cacao genus, < Gr. θεός, god, + βρῶμα, food.] In *chem.*, a bitter, volatile, white crystalline alkaloid, closely related to caffeine, contained in cacao-seeds, kola-nuts, etc., and also prepared artificially.

the-o-cen-tric (thē-ọ-sen′trik), *a.* [See *theo-*.] Having or regarding God as the center of all things: as, *theocentric* doctrines.

the-oc-ra-cy (thē-ok′rạ-si), *n.*; pl. *-cies* (-siz). [Gr. θεοκρατία, < θεός, god, + κρατεῖν, rule.] A form of government in which God or a deity is recognized as the supreme civil ruler, and his laws are taken as the statute-book of the state, or as the foundation of the established polity (as, "With the death of Cromwell the brief life of Puritan *theocracy* in England expired": Morley's "Oliver Cromwell," v. 10); hence, a system of government by priests claiming a divine commission; also, a state or commonwealth under any such form or system of government (as, the Jewish *theocracy*, instituted by Moses and continuing until the establishment of the monarchy under Saul; "In the little *theocracy* which the Pilgrims established . . . the ministry was the only order of nobility," Mrs. Stowe's "Oldtown Folks," i.).—**the-o-crat** (thē′ọ-krat), *n.* [See *-crat*.] The ruler, or a member of a governing body, in a theocracy; also, one who favors theocracy.—**the-o-crat′ic**, *a.* Of or pertaining to theocracy. Also **the-o-crat′i-cal.**—**the-o-crat′i-cal-ly**, *adv.*

the-od-i-cy (thē-od′i-si), *n.*; pl. *-cies* (-siz). [F. *théodicée* (used in the title of a work by Leibnitz, in 1710), < Gr. θεός, god, + δίκη, right, justice.] A vindication of the divine attributes, particularly holiness and justice, in respect to the existence of physical and moral evil; any writing or theory intended as such a vindication.

the-o-di-dact (thē′ọ-di-dakt″). [Gr. θεοδίδακτος, < θεός, god, + διδάσκειν, teach.] **I.** *a.* Taught by God. **II.** *n.* One taught by God.

the-od-o-lite (thē-od′ọ-līt), *n.* [First as *theodelitus*; origin unknown.] In *surv.*, an instrument for measuring horizontal angles, usually consisting essentially of a mounted horizontal telescope which rotates on its vertical axis, the angles being measured on a graduated horizontal circle; also, an instrument of this kind with other attachments, as for measuring vertical angles (cf. *transit*).—**the-od-o-lit'ic** (-lit'ik), *a.*

the-og-o-ny (thē-og'ọ-ni), *n.*; pl. *-nies* (-niz). [Gr. θεογονία, < θεός, god, + γεν-, bear, produce: see

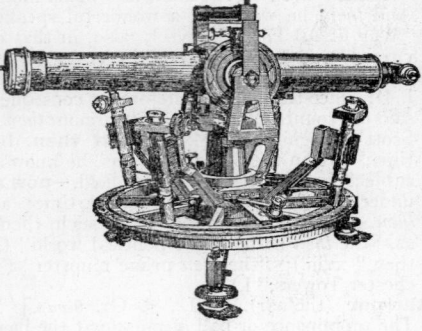

Theodolite.

genius.] The origin of the gods, or an account of this; a genealogical account of the gods: as, the ancient Greek *theogony* of Hesiod.—**the-o-gon-ic** (thē-ọ-gon'ik), *a.*—**the-og'o-nist**, *n.*

the-ol-o-gas-ter (thē-ol'ọ-gas-tèr), *n.* [NL.: see *theologue* and *-aster*.] A shallow theologian; a pretender in theology.

the-o-lo-gian (thē-ọ-lō'jịan), *n.* One versed in theology, esp. Christian theology; one who makes a profession of theology; a divine.

the-o-log-ic (thē-ọ-loj'ik), *a.* [LL. *theologicus*, < Gr θεολογικός.] Theological: as, "*theologic* doctrine" (Morley's "Oliver Cromwell," ii. 3).—**the-o-log'i-cal**, *a.* Of, pertaining to, or connected with theology; also, based upon the nature and will of God as revealed to man (as, the *theological* virtues: see *virtue*).—**the-o-log'i-cal-ly**, *adv.*

the-ol-o-gist (thē-ol'ọ-jist), *n.* A theologian: as, "the Rev. Mr. M'Corkendale, and all the *theologists* and saints of that persuasion" (Smollett's "Humphry Clinker," Sept. 3). [Now rare.]

the-ol-o-gize (thē-ol'ọ-jīz), *v.*; *-gized, -gizing.* **I.** *intr.* To theorize or speculate upon theological subjects. **II.** *tr.* To render theological; treat theologically.

the-o-logue (thē'ọ-log), *n.* [L. *theologus*, < Gr. θεολόγος, < θεός, god, + λέγειν, speak.] A theologian (now rare); also, a theological student (colloq.).

the-ol-o-gy (thē-ol'ọ-ji), *n.*; pl. *-gies* (-jiz). [L. *theologia*, < Gr. θεολογία, < θεολόγος, theologian, E. *theologue*.] The science which treats of God, his attributes, and his relations to the universe; the science or study of divine things or religious truth; divinity; also, a particular form, system, or branch of this science or study (as, the Christian, the Jewish, or the Mohammedan *theology*; dogmatic, homiletic, or historical *theology*).

the-om-a-chy (thē-om'ạ-ki), *n.*; pl. *-chies* (-kiz). [Gr. θεομαχία, < θεός, god, + μάχεσθαι, fight.] A striving against God or his will†; also, a battle or strife among the gods.

the-o-mor-phic (thē-ọ-môr'fik), *a.* [Gr. θεόμορφος, < θεός, god, + μορφή, form.] Having the form or likeness of God; characterized by or pertaining to theomorphism.—**the-o-mor'phism**, *n.* The conception of man as made in the form or likeness of God.

the-op-a-thy (thē-op'ạ-thi), *n.* [Gr. θεός, god, + -πάθεια, suffering, feeling: see *-pathy*.] Emotion excited by the contemplation of God; sensitiveness to divine influence; pious sentiment.—**the-o-pa-thet-ic** (thē''ọ-pạ-thet'ik), **the-o-path'ic** (-path'ik), *a.*

the-oph-a-ny (thē-of'ạ-ni), *n.*; pl. *-nies* (-niz). [LL. *theophania*, < Gr. θεοφάνεια, < θεός, god, + φαίνειν, show.] A manifestation or appearance of God or a god to man.

the-or-bo (thē-ôr'bō), *n.*; pl. *-bos* (-bōz). [F. *théorbe, téorbe*, < It. *tiorba*.] An obsolete musical instrument of the lute class, having two necks, one above the other, the lower bearing the melody strings, which were stretched over a fretted finger-board, and the upper bearing the accompaniment strings, which were deeper in pitch, and were played without being stopped.

the-o-rem (thē'ọ-rem), *n.* [L. *theorema*, < Gr. θεώρημα, < θεωρεῖν, look at, view, < θεωρός, spectator: see *theory*.] A

universal or general proposition or statement which is not self-evident but is demonstrable by argument; in *math.*, a demonstrable theoretical proposition; a statement embodying something to be proved; also, a rule or law, esp. one expressed by an equation or formula.—**the''o-re-mat'ic** (-re-mat'ik), *a.*

the-o-ret-ic, the-o-ret-i-cal (thē-ọ-ret'ik, -i-kạl), *a.* [LL. *theoreticus*, < Gr. θεωρητικός, contemplative, speculative, < θεωρεῖν, look at, view: see *theorem*.] Contemplative†; also, of, pertaining to, or consisting in theory (opposed to *practical*); also, being such according to theory; existing only in theory; ideal; hypothetical; also, given to, forming, or dealing with theories; speculative.—**the-o-ret'i-cal-ly**, *adv.*—**the''o-re-ti'cian** (-re-tish'ạn), *n.* One who deals with or is versed in the theoretical side of a subject.—**the-o-ret'ics**, *n.* The theoretical or speculative parts of a science or subject.

the-o-ric† (thē'ọ-rik), *n.* [OF. *theorique*.] Theory.

the-o-rist (thē'ọ-rist), *n.* One who deals with or is versed in the theory of a subject, as distinct from the practice of it; also, one who theorizes; one given to theory or speculation (often implying a lack of practical capacity).

the-o-rize (thē'ọ-rīz), *v. i.*; *-rized, -rizing.* To form a theory or theories; form opinions solely by theory; speculate.—**the''o-ri-za'tion** (-ri-zā'shọn), *n.*—**the'o-riz-er** (-rī-zèr), *n.*

the-o-ry (thē'ọ-ri), *n.*; pl. *-ries* (-riz). [LL. *theoria*, < Gr. θεωρία, a viewing, sight, contemplation, speculation, theory, < θεωρός, spectator, < θεᾶσθαι, look at, view: cf. *theater*.] Contemplation† or mental view†; also, a particular conception or view of something to be done or of the method of doing it; a system of rules or principles to be followed; also, a particular view or doctrine put forth or held as an explanation of some fact or set of facts, or in connection with some subject (as, "The Greeks and Romans had various *theories* of the origin of things, all vague and admittedly conjectural," J. H. Robinson's "Mind in the Making," v. 11; "By animism I do not mean the *theory* of a soul in nature," W. H. Hudson's "Far Away and Long Ago," xvii.); a formulated statement or hypothesis, based on observation and reasoning, presenting the laws or principles believed to underlie facts or phenomena (as, the *theory* of evolution; Einstein's *theory* of relativity); also, that department of a science or art which deals with its principles or methods, as distinguished from the practice of it; in the abstract, knowledge or statement of principles; abstract knowledge, or the formulation of it; loosely, a mere hypothesis, speculation, or conjecture; an individual view or notion; in *math.*, a body of principles, theorems, or the like, belonging to one subject.

the-o-soph (thē'ọ-sof), *n.* [ML. *theosophus*, < LGr. θεόσοφος, wise in divine things, < Gr. θεός, god, + σοφός, wise.] A theosophist.

the-o-soph-ic, the-o-soph-i-cal (thē-ọ-sof'ik, -i-kạl), *a.* Of or pertaining to theosophy.—**the-o-soph'i-cal-ly**, *adv.*

the-os-o-phism (thē-os'ọ-fizm), *n.* Belief in or adherence to theosophy.—**the-os'o-phist** (-fist), *n.* A believer in or adherent of theosophy.

the-os-o-phy (thē-os'ọ-fi), *n.* [ML. *theosophia*, < LGr. θεοσοφία, knowledge of divine things, < θεόσοφος: see *theosoph*.] Any of various forms of philosophical or religious thought in which claim is made to a special insight into the divine nature, or to a special divine revelation; in recent times, the system of belief and doctrine, based largely on Brahmanic and Buddhistic ideas, of the Theosophical Society, a body founded in New York in 1875, with branches or derived bodies in various parts of the world, and, for its main objects, seeking to form the nucleus of a universal brotherhood of humanity, to promote the study of comparative religion and philosophy, and to investigate the secrets of nature and develop the divine powers latent in man.

the-o-tech-ny (thē'ọ-tek-ni), *n.* [Gr. θεός, god, + τέχνη, art.] The introduction of divine or supernatural beings into a literary composition; also, such beings collectively.—**the-o-tech'nic**, *a.*

ther-a-peu-tic (ther-ạ-pū'tik), *a.* [NL. *therapeuticus*, < Gr. θεραπευτικός, < θεραπεύειν, serve, care for, treat medically, < θέραψ (θεραπ-), an attendant: cf. *therapy*.] Pertaining to the treating or curing of disease; curative.

Also **ther-a-peu′ti-cal.—ther-a-peu′ti-cal-ly,** adv.—**ther-a-peu′tics,** n. The branch of medicine concerned with the remedial treatment of disease; the science or art of healing.—**ther-a-peu′tist,** n. One versed in therapeutics.

ther-a-py (ther′ạ-pi), n. [Gr. θεραπεία, service, care, medical treatment, < θεραπεύειν: see *therapeutic.*] The treatment of disease, as by some remedial or curative process. Much used in compounds: as, balneo*therapy;* hydro*therapy;* serum*therapy.*—**ther′a-pist,** n.

-there, -therium. [NL. *-therium,* < Gr. θηρίον, wild beast: see *theriac.*] Noun terminations occurring in names of extinct mammals, as *dinothere, dinotherium, megathere, megatherium.*

there (ŦHär), adv. [AS. *thær, thār,* = D. *daar* = G. *da* (dar-) = Icel. and Goth. *thar,* there; from the stem represented by E. *the*[1].] In or at that place (as, he was in Paris while I was *there;* "Stand you *there,* or sit here under my footstool," Jas. ii. 3); sometimes, appended to the name of a person or thing indicated (as, "I would have peace and quietness, but the fool will not: he *there,*" Shakspere's "Troilus and Cressida," ii. 1. 91; that man *there;* hence, in illiterate use, appended emphatically to the demonstrative adjective *that,* as in 'that *there* man'); also, at that point in an action, speech, etc. (as, you have done enough, you may stop *there*); also, in that matter, particular, or respect (as, "Thy Juliet is alive . . . *There* art thou happy": Shakspere's "Romeo and Juliet," iii. 3. 137); also, into or to that place, or thither (as, I will go *there* to-morrow). Often used less definitely, and also unemphatically, as: (1) by way of calling the attention to something (as, *there* they go; *there* goes the bell); (2) in interjectional phrases (as, *there*'s a good boy!); (3) in a sentence or clause in which the verb comes before its subject (as, *there* is no hope; is *there* a performance to-night?).—**here and there, neither here nor there.** See under *here,* adv.—**there,** n. That place; the or a place yonder: as, we go to London first, and from *there* to Paris.—**there,** interj. An exclamation used to express satisfaction, triumph, dismay, encouragement, consolation, etc.: as, " '*There!*' said James Ollerenshaw. 'You've done it!' " (Arnold Bennett's "Helen with the High Hand," vi.); *there, there!* don't worry. —**there′a-bout,** adv. About or near that place (as, "Then the heart of me'll know I'm there or *thereabout*": Masefield's "Wanderer's Song"); also, about or near that time or date; about that number, amount, etc.; also, about or concerning that matter or business (archaic or rare: as, "They were much perplexed *thereabout,*" Luke, xxiv. 4).—**there′a-bouts′,** adv. Thereabout.—**there-af′ter,** adv. After that in time or sequence; afterwards; also, according to that†; accordingly†.—**there′a-gainst′,** adv. Against, or in opposition to, that; also, in pressure or impact against that. [Archaic.]—**there′a-mong′,** adv. Among that, those, or them. [Now rare.]—**there′a-nent′,** adv. Anent or concerning that; relating thereto. [Chiefly Sc.]—**there-at′,** adv. At that place, etc.; there; also, on the occasion or occurrence of that; by reason of that; also, at, or in connection with, that matter or business. [Archaic.]—**there′a-way″,** adv. Away thither†; in that direction†; also, in that region; in those parts; also, about that time, amount, etc. (as, "for five or six months or *thereaway*": Scott's "Redgauntlet," ch. xi.). [Now prov. or colloq.]—**there-by′,** adv. By that, by means of that, or in consequence of that (as, "We should . . . walk abroad into other parts, and *thereby* enlarge our sphere of observation": Galt's "Annals of the Parish," xxxii.); also, in connection with or relation to that (now chiefly or only in 'thereby hangs a tale': see Shakspere's "Merry Wives of Windsor," i. 4. 159, "As You Like It," ii. 7. 28, etc.); also, by or near that place (archaic or prov.); also, about that number, quantity, or degree (Sc.: as, "There was one maiden of fifteen or *thereby,*" Scott's "Kenilworth," x.).—**there-for′** (-fôr′), adv. For that or this; for it: as, the building and as much land as shall be necessary *therefor.* —**there′fore** (-fōr), adv. Therefor (obs. or archaic); also, in consequence of that; as a result of what has been stated; consequently.—**there-from′,** adv. From that; from that place, thing, etc.—**there-in′,** adv. In that place or thing; also, in that matter, circumstance, etc.; also, thereinto.— **there-in-af′ter,** adv. Afterward in that document, statement, etc.—**there-in″be-fore′,** adv. Before in that docu-

ment, statement, etc.—**there-in′to,** adv. Into that place, thing, matter, etc.—**there-of′,** adv. Of that or it (as, "In the day that thou eatest *thereof* thou shalt surely die," Gen. ii. 17; "there having been no exact story *thereof* anywhere given," Strype's "Memorials of Cranmer," i. 21); also, from or out of that as a source or origin (as, "Much more good *thereof* shall spring": Milton's "Paradise Lost," xii. 476).—**there-on′,** adv. On or upon that or it; also, immediately after that; thereupon.—**there-out′,** adv. Outside of that place, etc. (now rare); out of doors (now Sc.); also, forth from that place, etc. (now Sc.); also, from or out of that as a source or origin (archaic: as, "the divine instinct of freedom, and all the self-help and energy which spring *thereout,*" Kingsley's "Hereward," ix.).—**there-o′ver,** adv. Over or above that. [Archaic.]—**there-through′,** adv. Through that, it, etc.; also, by means of that; thereby. [Archaic.]—**there-to′,** adv. To that place, thing, matter, etc.; also, in addition to that (archaic or poetic: as, "I would have paid her kiss for kiss, With usury *thereto,*" Tennyson's "Talking Oak," 196). —**there′to-fore′** (-tọ-fōr′), adv. Before that time; previously to that time.—**there-un′der,** adv. Under or beneath that; also, under the authority of, or in accordance with, that.—**there-un-to** (ŦHär-un′tọ or -un-tō′), adv. Unto or to that: as, "He . . . desired the forementioned persons to be witnesses *thereunto*" (Strype's "Memorials of Cranmer," i. 4).—**there-up-on′,** adv. Upon that or it; also, with reference to that; also, immediately following that (as, "*Thereupon* I told him what had passed": Stevenson's "Master of Ballantrae," iv.); also, in consequence of that (as, "I was ta'en for me, And *thereupon* these errors are arose": Shakspere's "Comedy of Errors," v. 1. 388).—**there-with′** (-wiŦH′ or -with′), adv. With that; also, in addition to that; also, following upon that, or thereupon (as, "*Therewith* before his eyes a cloud there came": W. Morris's "Jason," ii. 103).—**there-with-al′** (-âl′), adv. Along or together with that; in addition to that; also, following upon that, or therewith (as, "*Therewithal* A faithful slave unto him did he call": W. Morris's "Jason," i. 37). [Archaic.]

the-ri-ac (thē′ri-ak), n. [L. *theriaca,* < Gr. θηριακή, prop. fem. of θηριακός, adj. < θηρίον, wild beast, animal, reptile, dim. of θήρ, wild beast: cf. *treacle.*] An antidote for poisonous bites or for poisons; esp., a particular old-time remedy ('Venice treacle'), in the form of an electuary, containing sixty or more ingredients. Also (L.) **the-ri-a-ca** (thē-rī′ạ-kạ).—**the-ri′a-cal,** a.

the-ri-an-throp-ic (thē″ri-an-throp′ik), a. [Gr. θηρίον, wild beast, + ἄνθρωπος, man.] Being partly bestial and partly human in form; also, of or pertaining to deities conceived or represented as combining the forms of beasts and men.— **the-ri-an′thro-pism** (-thrọ-pizm), n.

the-ri-o-mor-phic (thē″ri-ọ-môr′fik), a. [Gr. θηριόμορφος, < θηρίον, wild beast, + μορφή, form.] Having the form of a beast; also, of or pertaining to deities conceived or represented as having the form of beasts. Also **the″ri-o-mor′phous.**

-therium. See *-there.*

therm (thėrm), n. [Gr. θέρμη, heat, < θερμός, hot, warm, < θέρειν, make hot: see *warm.*] In *physics,* a unit of heat or thermal capacity; a thermal unit, as the small calory, or the large calory, or a unit equal to 1,000 large calories; sometimes, a unit equal to 100,000 British thermal units (see under *thermal*), esp. as a unit of charge for gas supplied (Eng.).

ther-mæ (thėr′mē), n. pl. [L., hot springs, hot baths, < Gr. θέρμαι, pl. of θέρμη, heat: see *therm.*] Hot springs; hot baths; esp., a public bathing-establishment of the ancient Greeks or Romans.

therm-æs-the-sia (thėrm-es-thē″ziạ), n. [NL., < Gr. θέρμη, heat, + NL. *æsthesia:* see *æsthesia.*] In *physiol.,* ability to feel heat; sensitiveness to heat.

ther-mal (thėr′mạl), a. [Partly < L. *thermæ,* hot springs or baths (see *thermæ*), partly < Gr. θέρμη, heat (see *therm*).] Of, pertaining to, or of the nature of thermæ, or hot springs or baths; also, of or pertaining to heat (as, *thermal* capacity or conductivity; the *thermal* value of a combustible).— **thermal unit,** a unit of measurement or estimation for heat: as, the British *thermal unit* (the quantity of heat required to raise the temperature of one pound of water one degree Fahrenheit).—**ther′mal-ly,** *adv.*

therm-an-æs-the-sia (thẻrm″an-es-thē′ẕiä), *n.* [NL., < Gr. θέρμη, heat, + NL. *anæsthesia*: see *anæsthesia*.] In *pathol.*, absence or loss of ability to feel heat; insensibility to heat.

ther-man-ti-dote (thẻr-man′ti-dōt), *n.* [Gr. θέρμη, heat, + E. *antidote*.] A rotating wheel-like apparatus, usually inclosed in wet tatties, fixed in a window, and used in India to cool the air: as, "Will you bring me to book on the Mountains, or where the *thermantidotes* play?" (Kipling's "To the Unknown Goddess").

ther-mic (thẻr′mik), *a.* [Gr. θέρμη, heat: see *therm*.] Of, pertaining to, or of the nature of heat.—**ther′mi-cal-ly,** *adv.*

Ther-mi-dor (thẻr′mi-dôr, F. ter-mē-dôr), *n.* [F. *thermidor*, < Gr. θέρμη, heat, + δῶρον, gift.] In the calendar of the first French republic, the eleventh month of the year, extending from July 19 to Aug. 17.—**Ther-mi-do′ri-an** (-dō′ri-an), *n.* [F. *thermidorien*.] In *Fr. hist.*, a member of or sympathizer with the more moderate party which overthrew Robespierre and his adherents on the 9th Thermidor (July 27), 1794, thus ending the Reign of Terror.

therm-i-on (thẻrm′ī″ọn), *n.* [Gr. θέρμη, heat, + E. *ion*.] In *physics* and *chem.*, any of a class of electrically charged particles emitted by incandescent metals, etc., and supposed to be ions, charged atoms, or the like.—**therm-i-on′ic** (-on′ik), *a.*

ther-mit (thẻr′mit), *n.* [G. *thermit*, < Gr. θέρμη, heat: see *therm*.] A mixture of finely divided metallic aluminium and one or more oxides, as of iron, producing when ignited an extremely high temperature as the result of the union of the aluminium with the oxygen of the oxide: used in welding, etc. [Proprietary name.]

thermo-. Form of Gr. θερμός, hot, or θέρμη, heat, used in combination: sometimes used also to represent *thermo-electric*.

ther-mo-bar-o-graph (thẻr-mọ-bar′ọ-gräf), *n.* [See *thermo-*.] An apparatus combining a thermograph and a barograph in one instrument.

ther-mo-ba-rom-e-ter (thẻr″mọ-bạ-rom′e-tẻr), *n.* [See *thermo-*.] A thermometer used for measuring the pressure of the atmosphere, and hence altitude, by determining the boiling-point of water; also, a form of barometer which in a reversed position may be used as a thermometer.

ther-mo=bat-ter-y (thẻr″mọ-bat′ẻr-i), *n.*; pl. *-ies* (-iz). [See *thermo-*.] A thermopile.

ther-mo-cau-ter-y (thẻr-mọ-kâ′tẻr-i), *n.*; pl. *-ies* (-iz). [See *thermo-*.] A cautery, or cauterizing device, with which heat is used, specif. one consisting essentially of a hollow platinum point kept hot by injected benzine-vapor; also, cauterizing by means of heat.

ther-mo-chem-is-try (thẻr-mọ-kem′is-tri), *n.* [See *thermo-*.] The branch of chemistry that treats of the relations between chemical action and heat.—**ther-mo-chem′i-cal,** *a.*—**ther-mo-chem′ist,** *n.*

ther-mo=coup-le (thẻr′mọ-kup″l), *n.* [See *thermo-*.] A thermo-electric couple.

ther-mo-dy-nam-ic (thẻr″mọ-dī-nam′ik), *a.* [See *thermo-*.] Pertaining to or operated by force due to heat or to the conversion of heat into mechanical energy; of or pertaining to thermodynamics.—**ther″mo-dy-nam′i-cal-ly,** *adv.*—**ther″mo-dy-nam′ics,** *n.* The science concerned with the relations between heat and mechanical energy or work, and the conversion of one into the other.

ther-mo=e-lec-tric (thẻr″mọ-ẹ-lek′trik), *a.* [See *thermo-*.] Of or pertaining to thermo-electricity (as, a *thermo-electric* current; a *thermo-electric* couple, the two dissimilar conductors whose junction is heated in producing thermo-electricity); also, noting or pertaining to any of various devices in the operation of which heat and electricity are both involved, as an electric alarm working in connection with a thermostat.—**ther″mo= e-lec′tri-cal-ly,** *adv.*—**ther″mo=e-lec-tri′ci-ty,** *n.* Electricity produced directly from heat, as that generated (in

Thermo-electric Couple.

the form of a current) when the ends of two dissimilar metallic conductors, as an iron and a copper wire, are joined to form a closed circuit and one of the junctions is heated; also, the branch of electrical science concerned with such phenomena.—**ther″mo=e-lec-trom′e-ter,** *n.* An instrument for ascertaining the heating power of an electric current, or for determining the strength of a current by the heat it produces.—**ther″mo=e-lec-tro-mo′tive,** *a.* Noting or pertaining to electromotive force produced by heat, as with a thermo-electric couple.

ther-mo-gal-va-nom-e-ter (thẻr″mọ-gal-vạ-nom′e-tẻr), *n.* [See *thermo-*.] A thermo-electric device for measuring small electric currents, or for determining small changes in temperature.

ther-mo-gen-e-sis (thẻr-mọ-jen′e-sis), *n.* [See *thermo-*.] The production of heat, esp. in an animal body by physiological processes. Also **ther-mog′e-ny** (-moj′e-ni).—**ther″mo-ge-net′ic** (-jẹ-net′ik), **ther-mo-gen′ic** (-jen′ik), *a.*

ther-mo-graph (thẻr′mọ-gräf), *n.* [See *thermo-* and *-graph*.] A self-registering thermometer.

ther-mo-la-bile (thẻr-mọ-lā′bil or -lab′il), *a.* [See *thermo-* and *labile*.] In *physiol. chem.*, subject to destruction or loss of characteristic properties through the action of moderate heat, as certain toxins and ferments: opposed to *thermostable*.

ther-mol-y-sis (thẻr-mol′i-sis), *n.* [See *thermo-* and *-lysis*.] In *chem.*, dissociation by heat; in *physiol.*, the dispersion of heat from the body.—**ther-mo-lyt′ic** (-mọ-lit′ik). **I.** *a.* Of, pertaining to, or causing thermolysis. **II.** *n.* A thermolytic substance or agent.—**ther′mo-lyze** (-līz), *v. t.*; *-lyzed*, *-lyzing*. [See *-lyze*.] To subject to thermolysis.

ther-mom-e-ter (thẻr-mom′e-tẻr), *n.* [See *thermo-* and *-meter*.] An instrument for measuring temperature, as by means of the expansion and contraction of mercury or alcohol in a capillary tube and bulb. See *centigrade, Fahrenheit*, and *Réaumur*.—**ther-mo-met′ric, ther-mo-met′ri-cal** (-mọ-met′rik, -ri-kạl), *a.*—**ther-mom′e-try,** *n.* The measurement of temperature; the art of using the thermometer; the science of the construction of thermometers.

ther-mo-mo-tive (thẻr-mọ-mō′tiv), *a.* [See *thermo-*.] Pertaining to motion produced by heat; pertaining to a thermomotor, esp. one using the expansive force of heated air.—**ther-mo-mo′tor,** *n.* An engine operated by heat, esp. an engine driven by the expansive force of heated air.

ther-mo-pile (thẻr′mọ-pīl), *n.* [See *thermo-* and *pile*[2].] A number of thermo-electric couples joined so as to produce a combined effect: used for generating currents or for measuring small differences in temperature.

ther-mo-plas-tic (thẻr-mọ-plas′tik), *n.* [See *thermo-* and *plastic*.] A plastic that can be shaped when hot.

ther-mos (thẻr′mos), *a.* [Gr., θερμός, hot.] Designating a bottle or the like (introduced by Sir James Dewar, 1842–1923) so made that the interior vessel is protected by a vacuum jacket, which prevents the escape of heat from a contained hot liquid, etc., thus keeping it hot, or which, reversely, keeps a cold contents cold. [Trade-mark.]

ther-mo-scope (thẻr′mọ-skōp), *n.* [NL. *thermoscopium*: see *thermo-* and *-scope*.] A device for indicating variations in temperature, usually without measuring their amount.

ther-mo-si-phon (thẻr-mọ-sī′fọn), *n.* [See *thermo-*.] An arrangement of siphon-tubes serving to induce circulation of water in a heating apparatus.

ther-mo-sta-ble (thẻr-mọ-stā′bl), *a.* [See *thermo-*.] In *physiol. chem.*, capable of being subjected to a moderate degree of heat without loss of characteristic properties, as certain toxins and ferments: opposed to *thermolabile*.

ther-mo-stat (thẻr′mọ-stat), *n.* [See *thermo-* and *-stat*.] An automatic device for regulating temperature, as one in which the expansion of a piece of metal by heat closes an electric circuit, which in turn causes a ventilator or the like to open; a similar device for indicating a change in temperature, as by sounding an alarm.—**ther-mo-stat′ic,** *a.*

ther-mo-stat-ics (thẻr-mọ-stat′iks), *n.* [See *thermo-* and *static*.] The science concerned with the equilibrium of heat.

ther-mo-tank (thẻr′mọ-tangk), *n.* [See *thermo-*.] A heating or cooling device which consists essentially of a tank or inclosure containing pipes through which steam, water, or the like circulates.

POTTERY AND PORCELAIN

1. Crown Derby fruit-dish, England (1780-1830). 2. Capodimonte tea-pot, Italy (1780). 3. Spanish plate, Valencia (17th century). 4. Dresden or Meissen tea-caddy, Saxony (1763-1774). 5. Crown Derby plate, England (19th century). 6. Sèvres dish, France (18th century). 7. Dresden or Meissen group, Saxony (18th century). 8. Derby-Chelsea tea-pot, England (18th century). 9. Dish, Bernard Palissy, France (16th century). 10. Chinese (so-called Lowestoft) cup and saucer (late 18th century). 11. Spode cup and saucer, England (1800-1830). 12. Staffordshire plate, "Landing of the Pilgrims," made by Enoch Wood, Burslem, England (19th century). 13. Wedgwood vase on stand, Etruria, England (about 1785-1790). 14. Turkish or Rhodian ewer (16th century). 15. Castel Durante sweetmeat-dish, Italy (second quarter of 16th century). 16. Delft platter, Holland (probably 18th century). 17. Berlin sweetmeat-dish, Prussia (about 1825-1830). 18. Urbino plate with Gubbio luster, Italy (16th century). 19. Crown Derby tureen with platter, England (19th century). 20. Leeds coffee-pot England (1760-1790).

ther-mo-tax-is (thĕr-mọ-tak'sis), *n.* [See *thermo-* and *-taxis*.] In *physiol.*, the regulation of the bodily temperature; in *biol.*, the property in a cell or organism of exhibiting attraction or repulsion in relation to heat.—**ther-mo-tax'ic,** *a.*

ther-mo-ten-sile (thĕr-mọ-ten'sil), *a.* [See *thermo-*.] Pertaining to tensile strength as affected by changes of temperature.

ther-mo-ther-a-py (thĕr-mọ-ther'ạ-pi), *n.* [See *thermo-* and *therapy*.] Treatment of disease by means of heat, either moist or dry.

ther-mot-ic (thĕr-mot'ik), *a.* [Gr. θερμωτικός, < θερμοῦν, make hot, < θερμός, hot.] Of or pertaining to heat; also, of or pertaining to thermotics.—**ther-mot'ics,** *n.* The science of heat.

ther-mot-o-nus (thĕr-mot'ọ-nus), *n.* [NL., < *thermo-* (see *thermo-*) + Gr. τόνος, tension.] In *plant physiol.*, the relation between temperature and irritability or movement; responsiveness to heat.

ther-mot-ro-pism (thĕr-mot'rọ-pizm), *n.* [See *thermo-* and *-tropism*.] In *biol.*, the property in plant or other organisms of turning or bending (toward or away), as in growth, under the influence of heat.—**ther-mo-trop'ic** (-mọ-trop'ik), *a.*

the-rol-o-gy (thẹ-rol'ọ-ji), *n.* [Gr. θήρ, wild beast: see *-logy*.] The science of mammals; mammalogy.

ther-sit-i-cal (thĕr-sit'i-kạl), *a.* [From *Thersites*, a scurrilous Greek at the siege of Troy.] Scurrilous; foul-mouthed; grossly abusive.

the-sau-rus (thẹ-sâ'rus), *n.*; pl. *-ri* (-rī). [L., < Gr. θησαυρός, a store laid up, treasure, treasury: cf. *treasure*.] A treasury; hence, a storehouse or repository, as of words or knowledge; a dictionary, encyclopedia, or the like.

these (ᵺēz), *pron.* and *a.* [ME. *these, thes,* < AS. *thǣs,* var. of *thās* (see *those*), pl. of *thes,* E. *this*.] Plural of *this*.

The-se-um, The-sei-on (thẹ-sē'um, -sī'on), *n.* [NL., < Gr. Θησεῖον, < Θησεύς, Theseus.] A temple or shrine dedicated to Theseus, the legendary hero and king of Athens; specif., a so-called temple of Theseus (now regarded as a temple of Hephæstus) at Athens, a beautiful Doric structure of Pentelic marble and the best preserved of the Greek temples.

the-sis (thē'sis), *n.*; pl. *theses* (-sēz). [L., < Gr. θέσις, a setting or laying down, something laid down, thesis, < τιθέναι, set, put; akin to E. *do*[1].] Orig. the accented, later the unaccented, part of a foot in verse (opposed to *arsis*); also, a proposition laid down or stated, esp. one to be discussed and proved or to be maintained against objections; a statement or assertion; a subject propounded for a school or college composition or essay; the composition or essay itself; a dissertation, as one presented by a candidate for a diploma or degree.

Thes-pi-an (thes'pi-ạn). **I.** *a.* Of or pertaining to Thespis (flourished 6th century B.C.), a Greek tragic poet and the traditional founder of Greek tragedy; hence, pertaining to tragedy or to the dramatic art in general; tragic; dramatic. **II.** *n.* A tragedian; an actor or actress.

Thes-sa-lian (the-sā'liạn). **I.** *a.* Of or pertaining to Thessaly, a district of northern Greece. **II.** *n.* A native or inhabitant of Thessaly.

Thes-sa-lo-ni-an (thes-ạ-lō'ni-ạn). **I.** *a.* Of or pertaining to Thessalonica, an important city of ancient Macedonia. **II.** *n.* A native or inhabitant of Thessalonica; *pl.*, the two books or epistles of the New Testament addressed by St. Paul to the Thessalonians.

The so-called Theseum, at Athens, from the southwest.

the-ta (thē'tạ or thā'tạ), *n.* [L., < Gr. θῆτα.] The eighth letter (Θ, θ, = English th) of the Greek alphabet.

thet-ic (thet'ik), *a.* [Gr. θετικός, < τιθέναι: see *thesis*.] Positive; dogmatic. Also **thet'i-cal.—thet'i-cal-ly,** *adv.*

the-ur-gic (thẹ-ẽr'jik), *a.* Of or pertaining to theurgy: as, "a most zealous old lady, in high repute . . . for her *theurgic* knowledge" (J. H. Newman's "Callista," xiii.). Also **the-ur'gi-cal.—the-ur'gi-cal-ly,** *adv.*

the-ur-gy (thē'ẽr-ji), *n.* [LL. *theurgia,* < LGr. θεουργία, divine work, miracle, theurgy, < θεουργός, divinely working, < Gr. θεός, god, + -εργός, working.] A system of magic practised by the Egyptian Platonists and others professing to have communication with and aid from beneficent deities; any magical art professedly based on aid from beneficent divine or supernatural agencies; also, the working of some divine or supernatural agency in human affairs; the effects brought about among men by such agency.—**the'ur-gist,** *n.*

thew (thū), *n.* [AS. *thēaw,* custom, usage.] A custom† or habit†; *pl.*, physical qualities, features, or endowments†; hence, the bodily powers of a man; bodily proportions as indicating physical strength; muscular development; muscles or sinews (as, "The long walks and our work as cragsmen hardened our *thews*": Roosevelt's "Ranch Life and the Hunting-Trail," xii.).—**thewed,** *a.* Having thews; muscled: as, "A goodly man, *Thewed* mightily" (Swinburne's "Chastelard," v. 3).—**thew'less,** *a.* Without physical vigor or energy; inactive; spiritless.

they (ᵺhā), *pron.*; nom. *they,* poss. *their* or *theirs,* obj. *them.* [From Scand.: cf. Icel. *their* (gen. *theira*: see *their*) = AS. *thā* (dat. *thǣm*: see *them*), pl. of the demonstrative *se*: see *the*[1].] Nominative plural of *he, she,* and *it*: often used to denote persons (or, loosely, a person) indefinitely or people in general (as, *they* say he beats his wife).

thi-al-dine (thī-al'din), *n.* [From *thio-* + *ald(ehyde)* + *-ine*[2].] In *chem.*, a white basic compound, $C_6H_{13}NS_2$, having a powerful action on the heart.

thi-am-ide (thī-am'īd or -id), *n.* [From *thio-* + *amide*.] In *chem.*, any of a class of compounds formed by replacing the oxygen of an amide by sulphur.

thi-am-in (thī'ạ-min), *n.* [*thi(o)-* + *amin(e)*.] In *chem.*, a compound whose chloride is vitamin B_1; also, vitamin B_1.

Thian=shan (tiän'shän') **sheep.** See *Tian-shan sheep*.

thi-az-in, thi-az-ine (thī-az'in), *n.* [From *thio-* + *azin*.] In *chem.*, any of a class of compounds containing a ring composed of one atom each of sulphur and nitrogen and four atoms of carbon, and serving as the parent substances of certain dyestuffs.

thi-az-ole (thī-az'ōl), *n.* [From *thio-* + *azole*.] In *chem.*, a colorless liquid, C_3H_3NS, with a pungent odor, serving as the parent substance of important substantive cotton dyestuffs; also, any of various derivatives of this substance.

thib-et (tib'et or ti-bet'), **Thib-et-an** (tib'e-tạn or ti-bet'ạn). See *tibet, Tibetan*.

thick (thik). [AS. *thicce* = D. *dik* = G. *dick* = Icel. *thykkr,* thick.] **I.** *a.* Having relatively great extent from one surface or side to its opposite (as, a *thick* slice or layer; a *thick* wall; *thick* cloth or paper); not thin; of considerable extent through, or stout in form or build (as, a *thick* club; "a *thick* squat fellow," Smollett's "Humphry Clinker," June 12); measuring as specified between opposite surfaces, or in depth, or in a direction perpendicular to that of the length and breadth (as, a board one inch *thick*; "The snow lay six feet *thick* on the mountains," Froude's "Cæsar," xix.; a block of stone five feet long, three feet wide, and one foot *thick*); also, having numerous parts or individuals set close together or so as to form a dense assemblage or mass (as, a *thick* bush; a *thick* forest; *thick* hair); numerous and close together, as parts or individuals (as, the branch where the leaves are *thickest*; missiles *thick* as hail); in general, numerous, abundant, or plentiful; filled, covered, or abounding (*with*: as, the air was *thick* with flying missiles; tables *thick* with dust; "Her fingers were *thick* with jewels," Hugh Walpole's "Wooden Horse," ii.; "the mother-city *thick* with towers," Tennyson's "Princess," i. 111); also, fig., close in friendship, or intimate (colloq.: as, "They say she's *thick* with Percy Dacier at present," G. Meredith's "Diana of the Crossways," xvii.; "There's Sarah Swetnam. You're as *thick* as thieves," Arnold Bennett's "Helen with the High

---

Hand," xxii.); also, having relatively great consistence (as, a *thick* syrup); containing much solid matter in suspension or solution; of mist, smoke, etc., having the component particles densely aggregated; of the weather, etc., foggy, misty, or hazy (as, "the weather so *thick* that we could not see the ice with which we were surrounded": Dana's "Two Years before the Mast," xxxi.); of darkness, etc., dense, deep, or profound; also, husky, hoarse, muffled, or not clear in sound (as, a *thick* voice); dull of sense-perception (now prov.: as, *thick* of hearing); slow of mental apprehension (as, a *thick* head); also, excessive in a disagreeable way, or too much to tolerate (slang: as, "This is a bit *thick*, this is!" Arnold Bennett's "The Old Adam," i.). **II.** *n.* That which is thick; the thickest part of anything; the densest or most crowded part; the place, time, stage, etc., of greatest activity or intensity (as, in the *thick* of the fight); a thick-headed or stupid person (slang); also, a thicket (now rare).—**through thick and thin**, through everything encountered; under all circumstances; unwaveringly: as, "They stuck to him *through thick and thin*" (Du Maurier's "Trilby," iii.).—**thick,** *adv.* In a thick manner; so as to be thick; to a great depth; closely or densely; in great numbers or abundance (as, "They came into the Marshalsea *thick* and threefold for religion," Strype's "Memorials of Cranmer," iii. 2; honors came *thick* upon him); frequently or fast; with thick consistence (as, the syrup runs *thick*); huskily or hoarsely.—**thick,** *v. t.* or *i.* [AS. *thiccian.*] To thicken: as, "The night-mare Life-in-Death was she, Who *thicks* man's blood with cold" (Coleridge's "Ancient Mariner," iii.). [Archaic.]

thick-en (thik'n), *v.* **I.** *tr.* To make thick or thicker: as, "Twilight and snow-flakes together *thickened* the air" (C. Brontë's "Jane Eyre," xiii.). **II.** *intr.* To become thick or thicker: as, "The trees *thickened* and became a wood" (Borrow's "Bible in Spain," ii.); "The night *thickened* and the fog grew more dense" (Bret Harte's "Princess Bob and Her Friends").—**thick'en-er,** *n.*—**thick'en-ing,** *n.* A making or becoming thick; also, a thickened part or area; also, something used to thicken (as, a *thickening* for gravy).

thick-et (thik'et), *n.* [AS. *thiccet,* < *thicce,* E. *thick.*] A thick or dense growth of shrubs, bushes, or small trees; a thick coppice: as, "No branchy *thicket* shelter yields" (Tennyson's "Sir Galahad," 58).—**thick'et-ed, thick'et-y,** *a.*

thick-head (thik'hed), *n.* A stupid person; a blockhead.—**thick'=head'ed,** *a.* Having a thick head; dull-witted; stupid: as, "They're so narrow — narrow isn't the word! *Thick-headed's* the word. Stupid!" (Arnold Bennett's "Hilda Lessways," iii. 2).—**thick'=head'ed-ness,** *n.*

thick-ish (thik'ish), *a.* Somewhat thick: as, "a faded woman and *thickish*" (Sinclair Lewis's "Arrowsmith," xix.).

thick-knee (thik'nē), *n.* Any of the plover-like birds of the family *Œdicnemidæ,* as *Œdicnemus crepitans,* a common European species.

thick-leaf (thik'lēf), *n.* Any of the succulent herbs or shrubs constituting the genus *Crassula,* various species of which are cultivated in beds or in greenhouses.

Thickknee (*Œdicnemus crepitans*).

thick-ly (thik'li), *adv.* In a thick manner; so as to be thick; closely or densely; abundantly; frequently; with thick consistence; huskily or hoarsely.

thick-ness (thik'nes), *n.* The state or quality of being thick; also, the extent to which a thing is thick; the third (and usually least) dimension of a solid, distinct from length and breadth; also, that which is thick; the thick part, or body, of something (as, "The chambers were in the *thickness* of the wall of the court": Ezek. xlii. 10); a layer, as of cloth or paper.

thick=set (thik'set'), *a.* Set thickly or in close arrangement (as, "dead and broken trees, *thick-set* as a military abatis": Parkman's "Oregon Trail," i.); composed of parts or things in close arrangement, or dense (as, a *thick-set* hedge); set,

studded, or furnished thickly with something (as, a sky *thick-set* with stars); also, of thick form or build, as a person, the bodily frame, etc.; heavily or solidly built; stocky.—**thick=set, thick'set,** *n.* A thickly set growth of shrubs, etc.; a thick hedge; a thick growth of underwood; a thicket.

thick-skin (thik'skin), *n.* A person with a thick skin; esp., fig., one who is not sensitive in feeling, as to criticism, rebuff, etc.—**thick'=skinned',** *a.* Having a thick skin; fig., dull of feeling; stolid; not sensitive to criticism, reproach, rebuff, or the like.

thick=skulled (thik'skuld'), *a.* Having a thick skull; fig., dull of apprehension; stupid.

thick=wit-ted (thik'wit'ed), *a.* Dull of wit or intelligence: as, "I ask myself if I was *thick-witted* not to see that there was in Charles Strickland . . . something out of the common" (Maugham's "Moon and Sixpence," viii.).

thief (thēf), *n.;* pl. **thieves** (thēvz). [AS. *thēof* = D. *dief* = G. *dieb* = Icel. *thjōfr* = Goth. *thiufs,* thief.] One who steals (lit. or fig.: as, "The *thief* cometh not, but for to steal," John, x. 10; "Procrastination is the *thief* of time," Young's "Night Thoughts," i. 393); esp., one who steals secretly or without open force; one guilty of theft or larceny; also, an evil-doer or scoundrel (now prov.).—**thieve** (thēv), *v.;* **thieved, thieving.** [AS. *thēofian.*] **I.** *intr.* To act as a thief; commit theft; steal: as, "'I did not *thieve,*' protested Kim" (Kipling's "Kim," v.). **II.** *tr.* To take by theft; steal.—**thiev'er-y,** *n.;* pl. **-ies** (-iz). The act or practice of thieving; theft; also, something taken by theft.—**thiev'ish,** *a.* Given to thieving or stealing; also, of, pertaining to, or characteristic of a thief or thieves; stealthy; furtive; sly; also, infested or frequented by thieves†.—**thiev'ish-ly,** *adv.*—**thiev'ish-ness,** *n.*

thig (thig), *v. t.* or *i.;* **thigged, thigging.** [Prob. from Scand.: cf. Icel. *thiggja,* receive, get.] To beg (alms, food, etc.); solicit (gifts). [Sc.]—**thig'ger,** *n.*

thigh (thī), *n.* [AS. *thēoh* = D. *dij* = OHG. *dioh* = Icel. *thjō,* thigh.] That part of the leg between the hip and the knee in man, or a homologous or apparently corresponding part of the hind limb of other animals; the region of the femur; in birds, the true femoral region, buried in the general integument of the body, or, loosely, the segment below, containing the fibula and tibia; in *entom.,* the femur.—**thigh'bone,** *n.* The femur.—**thighed,** *a.* Having thighs.

thig-mo-tax-is (thig-mō-tak'sis), *n.* [NL., < Gr. θίγμα, touch, + τάξις, arrangement.] In *biol.,* the property in a cell or organism of exhibiting attraction or repulsion in relation to the stimulus of mechanical contact.—**thig-mo-tac'tic** (-tak'tik), *a.*

thig-mot-ro-pism (thig-mot'rō-pizm), *n.* [Gr. θίγμα, touch: see *-tropism.*] In *biol.,* the property in plant or other organisms of turning or bending (toward or away), as in growth, under the influence of mechanical contact.

thill (thil), *n.* [Cf. AS. *thille,* plank, flooring.] Either of the pair of shafts between which a single animal drawing a vehicle is placed.

thim-ble (thim'bl), *n.* [AS. *thȳmel,* < *thūma,* E. thumb.] A device, usually bell-shaped and of metal, worn on the finger to push the needle in sewing; in *mech.,* any of various devices or attachments likened to a thimble, as a sleeve, tube, or bushing for joining the ends of pipes, etc.; *naut.,* a metal ring with a concave groove on the outside, used to line the inside of a ring of rope forming an eye.—**thim'ble-ber''ry,** *n.* Any of several American raspberries with a thimble-shaped fruit; esp., the black raspberry, *Rubus occidentalis.*—**thim'bled,** *a.* Wearing a thimble: as, "a *thimbled* finger" (Arnold Bennett's "Old Wives' Tale," i. 3).—**thim'ble-fish,** *n.* A jellyfish of the genus *Linerges,* of tropical or warm seas: named from its shape.—**thim'ble-ful** (-ful), *n.;* pl. **-fuls.** As much as a thimble will hold; a small quantity, esp. of liquor: as, "Could I trouble you for another *thimbleful* of brandy?" (H. G. Wells's "Bealby," v.).—**thim'ble-rig,** *n.* A swindling game in which the operator apparently covers a small ball or pea with one of three thimble-like cups, and then, moving the cups about, offers to bet

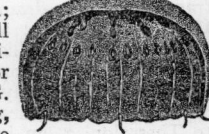

Thimblefish (*Linerges mercurius*).

that no one can tell under which cup the ball or pea lies.—
thim′ble-rig, *v. i.* or *t.*; *-rigged, -rigging.* To cheat by or as by the thimblerig; manipulate (a thing) in the manner of the operator of the thimblerig.—**thim′ble-rig″ger,** *n.*—**thim′ble-weed,** *n.* Any of various plants with a thimble-shaped fruiting head, as the anemone *Anemone virginiana* and the rudbeckia *Rudbeckia laciniata.*

thin (thin). [AS. *thynne* = D. *dun* = G. *dünn* = Icel. *thunnr,* thin; akin to L. *tenuis,* Skt. *tanu,* thin, L. *tendere,* Gr. τείνειν, Skt. *tan-,* stretch: cf. *tend*[1] and *tone.*] **I.** *a.*; compar. *thinner,* superl. *thinnest.* Having relatively little extent from one surface or side to its opposite, or not thick (as, *thin* ice; *thin* paper; a *thin* film or layer); of small cross-section in comparison with the length, or slender (as, a *thin* stem; a *thin* wire); having little flesh, spare, or lean (as, "His whole figure was *thin,* to a degree that suggested the idea . . . of a skeleton": Godwin's "Caleb Williams," xxxviii.); readily penetrated by light or vision (as, a *thin* veil); easily seen through, transparent, or flimsy (as, "He is the *thinnest* kind of an impostor," Mark Twain's "Huckleberry Finn," xxv.; a *thin* pretense; a *thin* excuse); also, having the constituent parts or individuals relatively few and not close together (as, *thin* vegetation; *thin* hair; "He watched the *thin* and the hesitating stream of people," W. Churchill's "Coniston," ii. 15); not dense; sparse; scanty; having scanty attendance (as, "The Senate was convened . . . The house was *thin,* but those present were cold and hostile": Froude's "Cæsar," xxii.); also, having relatively slight consistence, as a liquid; fluid; rare or rarefied, as air, etc. (as, "All day thy wings have fanned, At that far height, the cold, *thin* atmosphere": Bryant's "To a Waterfowl"); without solidity or substance, or unsubstantial (as, "Vain fantasy, Which is as *thin* of substance as the air": Shakspere's "Romeo and Juliet," i. 4. 99); wanting depth or intensity, as color; wanting fullness or volume, as sound; sometimes, weak and shrill; in general, faint, slight, poor, or feeble (as, "He . . . had . . . a ghostly *thin* resemblance to her uncle Bob," Galsworthy's "Saint's Progress," i. 6; "*thin* jokes," G. W. Curtis's "Prue and I," iv.); meager or scanty, as diet, etc.; lacking body, richness, or strength, or of low alcoholic content, as a liquor; in *photog.,* of a developed negative, lacking in opaqueness, and yielding prints without strong contrasts of light and shade. **II.** *n.* That which is thin; the thin part of anything.—**thin,** *adv.* In a thin manner; so as to be thin; thinly.—**thin,** *v.*; *thinned, thinning.* [AS. *thynnian.*] **I.** *tr.* To make thin or thinner (as, "The larger nuts, *thinned* and polished, furnish him with a beautiful goblet," H. Melville's "Omoo," lxix.; "The deer . . . are much *thinned* and reduced by the night hunters," G. White's "Nat. Hist. of Selborne," i. 9); reduce in thickness, density, numbers, consistence, etc. (often with *down, out,* etc.). **II.** *intr.* To become thin or thinner (as, the woods *thin* toward the edge; the hair *thins* with time; the crowd was *thinning*); become reduced or diminished, go, pass, etc. (with *down, off, away,* etc.: as, "The rush of the first few days was *thinning* down," A. S. M. Hutchinson's "If Winter Comes," iii. 5; "The . . . smoke-clouds were *thinning* away," Kipling's "Light That Failed," vi.).

thine (ᴛʜīn), *pron.* [AS. *thīn,* possessive adj., also gen. of *thū,* E. *thou.*] The possessive form of *thou* used predicatively or without a noun following, or before a noun beginning with a vowel or *h.* Cf. *thy.*

thing[1] (thing), *n.* [AS. *thing,* thing, object, matter, affair, cause, assembly, = OS. and OFries. *thing* = D. *ding* = OHG. G. *ding* = Icel. *thing* (see *thing*[2]); akin to Goth. *theihs,* time.] That which is or may become an object of thought, whether material or ideal, animate or inanimate, actual, possible, or imaginary; that which exists individually, whether in fact or in idea; a separate or individual entity; in a more limited sense, some entity, object, or creature which is not or cannot be specifically designated or precisely described, or a something (as, the stick had a brass *thing* on it; "What, has this *thing* appear'd again to-night?" Shakspere's "Hamlet," i. 1. 21); that which is signified or represented, as distinguished from a word, symbol, or idea representing it; a material object without life or consciousness, or an inanimate object; a living being or creature (as applied to a person, now used only in contempt, pity, kindly

feeling, etc.: as, "a poor virgin, sir, an ill-favoured *thing,*" Shakspere's "As You Like It," v. 4. 60; the poor *thing* was in despair; she is a pretty little *thing*); some object not precisely designated but more or less clearly understood (as, "Who first saw the holy *thing* to-day?" Tennyson's "Holy Grail," 67); anything that may be the subject of a property right; *pl.,* personal possessions or belongings, often (colloq.) such as one carries along on a journey (as, "He said I could go 'long with him; so I jest put my *things* together": Mrs. Stowe's "Uncle Tom's Cabin," xxi.); clothes or apparel, esp. articles of dress added to the ordinary clothing when going out of doors (as, "She does wear the most bewitching *things!*" Tarkington's "Magnificent Ambersons," vii.; do take off your *things* and spend the evening); implements, utensils, or other articles for service (colloq.: as, "I help Esther wash up the breakfast *things,*" Mrs. Stowe's "Old-town Folks," xxxii.); *sing.,* a piece of literary or musical composition, artistic work, or the like (as, a little *thing* written for the occasion); also, a matter or affair (as, *things* are going well now); an action, deed, or performance (as, to do great *things*; "A sorry *thing* to hide my head In castle . . . When such a field is near!" Scott's "Marmion," v. 34); a fact or circumstance (as, "It is a curious *thing* that people . . . were so little alive to what was going on": Morley's "Oliver Cromwell," i. 4); an occurrence (as, many *things* have happened since); a particular or respect (as, perfect in all *things*).—**the thing,** the proper, correct, or fashionable thing (as, "It was 'not *the thing*' to arrive early at the opera": Mrs. Wharton's "Age of Innocence," i.); also, the important or necessary thing (as, *the thing* is to raise the money); also, in good physical condition (as, I'm not quite *the thing* to-day). [Colloq.]—**thing in itself** (in *philos.*). See *noumenon.*—**to know a thing or two.** See under *know, v. t.*

thing[2], **ting**[1] (ting), *n.* [Scand.: Icel. *thing,* Dan. and Norw. *thing, ting,* Sw. *ting,* assembly, = AS. *thing,* E. *thing*[1].] In Scandinavian countries, a public meeting or assembly, esp. a legislative assembly or a court of law.

thing-um-bob (thing′um-bob), *n.* [A humorous formation < *thing*[1].] An indefinite name for a thing or person which a speaker or writer is not able, or does not care, to designate more precisely. [Colloq.] Also **thing′um-a-jig″** (-a̤-jig″) and **thing′um-my** (-um-i).

think[1] (thingk), *v. i.*; *thought, thinking.* [AS. *thyncan* (pret. *thūhte*) = OS. *thunkian* = OHG. *dunchan* (G. *dünken*) = Icel. *thykkja* = Goth. *thugkjan,* seem, appear: see *think*[2].] To seem or appear: usually impersonal, with indirect object, as, "Me *thinketh* the running of the foremost is like the running of Ahimaaz" (2 Sam. xviii. 27): now only in *methinks* and *methought* (see *methinks*).

think[2] (thingk), *v. t.*; *thought, thinking.* [AS. *thencan* (pret. *thōhte*) = OS. *thenkian* = OHG. *denchan* (G. *denken*), think, = Icel. *thekkja,* perceive, = Goth. *thagkjan,* think; orig. causative, from the same source as E. *think*[1].] To form or conceive (a thought, etc.) in the mind; have (something) in the mind as an idea, conception, or the like; also, to conceive or feel (an emotion, as scorn, shame, etc.: archaic or prov.: as, "'*Think* shame to yourself,' said I," Stevenson's "Master of Ballantrae," xi.); also, to turn over in the mind, meditate, or ponder (as, he was *thinking* what it could mean: see *to think over,* below); have the mind full of (a particular subject or the like); also, to form or have an idea or conception of, or picture in the mind (a thing, fact, circumstance, etc.: as, you can't *think* how surprised I was); also, to call to mind, recollect, or remember (as, "I am afraid to *think* what I have done": Shakspere's "Macbeth," ii. 2. 51); also, to plan, devise, or contrive (as, "It was this lady's disposition to *think* kindnesses," Thackeray's "Henry Esmond," i. 9: see *to think out,* below); also, to have in mind, intend, or purpose (as, "You *thought* to break a country heart For pastime": Tennyson's "Lady Clara Vere de Vere"); also, to hold as a belief or opinion, believe, or suppose (as, they *thought* that the earth was flat); also, to consider or hold (something) to be (as specified: as, he *thought* the lecture very interesting; "There be . . . some that have the ambition to be *thought* eloquent," Hobbes's "Leviathan," xxv.); also, to suspect (as, *thinking* no harm); anticipate or expect (as, I did not *think* to find you here); also, to bring by thinking, or in thought (as, "Meditation here May *think* down hours to moments": Cowper's "Task," vi. 85).—**to think out**, to think to the end; finish or complete in thought; also, to gain a clear conception or understanding of, by following a line of thought; solve by process of thought; also, to devise or contrive by thinking.—**to think over**, to give continued thought to; apply the mind steadily to, as in order to reach a decision: as, to *think* a matter *over*.—**think**[2], *v. i.* To exercise the mind, esp. the intellect; exercise the cognitive faculties in any way not involving mere perception of external things or passive reception of ideas; cogitate or meditate; also, to form or have an idea or mental image (with *of*: as, "Just *think* of him penning a sonnet with a fist like that!" Hawthorne's "Blithedale Romance," viii.); also, to reflect upon the matter in question (as, *think* carefully before you begin); bethink one's self or remember (usually with *of*: as, I can't *think* of his name); also, to have consideration or regard (usually with *of*: as, to *think* of others first); also, to make mental discovery, or form a plan (usually with *of*: as, he *thought* of it first; try all the ways you can *think* of); also, to have a notion or plan (usually with *of*: as, he *thinks* of selling his house); also, to have a belief or opinion as indicated (as, "*Jul.* I fear me, it will make me scandalized. *Luc.* If you *think* so, then stay at home": Shakspere's "Two Gentlemen of Verona," ii. 7. 62); also, to have a high, low, or other opinion of a person or thing (with *of*: as, to *think* well of a person); also, to have an anticipation or expectation (with *of*: as, "He little *thought* of this divided friendship," Shakspere's "Richard III.," i. 4. 244).—**to think better of**, to think more favorably or highly of (a person, a plan, etc.), as upon further knowledge; also, to think more wisely or sensibly of, as by a change of mind on reconsideration (as, they began an attack, but *thought better* of it and stopped).—**to think for**, to expect or suppose: as, it will be better than you *think for*.—**think**[2], *n.* An act of thinking; a meditation (as, "I . . . had a long *think* about it": Mark Twain's "Huckleberry Finn," iii.); sometimes, an idea or thought; also, what one thinks about something; an opinion. [Colloq.]—**think′a·ble**, *a.* Capable of being thought; conceivable.—**think′er**, *n.* One who thinks; esp., one who has exercised or cultivated his powers of thinking to an unusual degree; also, sometimes, the thinking organ or faculty; the mind.—**think′ing**, *p. a.* That thinks; having or exercising the faculty of thought; reasoning; also, given to thinking, or thoughtful or reflective (as, "Truly a *Thinking* Man is the worst enemy the Prince of Darkness can have": Carlyle's "Sartor Resartus," ii. 4). —**think′ing·ly**, *adv.*

thin·ly (thin′li), *adv.* In a thin manner; with little thickness or depth; sparsely; not substantially.

thin·ner (thin′ėr), *n.* One who or that which thins; specif., a liquid used to thin paint.

thin·ness (thin′nes), *n.* The state or quality of being thin.

thin·nish (thin′ish), *a.* Somewhat thin.

thin-skinned (thin′skind′), *a.* Having a thin skin; fig., sensitive to criticism, reproach, rebuff, or the like; easily hurt or offended; touchy.—**thin′-skinned′ness**, *n.*

thio-. Form of Gr. θεῖον, sulphur, used in combination, esp. in the names of chemical compounds in which sulphur may be viewed as replacing oxygen.—**thi·o·a·cid** (thī-ō-as′id), *n.* In *chem.*, an acid in which sulphur partly or wholly takes the place of oxygen.—**thi·o·al′co·hol**, *n.* In *chem.*, any of the mercaptans, which are regarded as alcohols in which the oxygen has been replaced by sulphur.—**thi·o·al′de·hyde**, *n.* In *chem.*, any of a class of compounds formed by the action of hydrogen sulphide on aldehydes, and regarded as aldehydes with the oxygen replaced by sulphur.

thi·on·ic (thī-on′ik), *a.* [Gr. θεῖον, sulphur.] In *chem.*, of or pertaining to sulphur: used specifically to indicate that in the molecule of the original substance oxygen has been replaced by sulphur.—**thi′o·nine** (-ō-nin), *n.* In *chem.*, a derivative of thiazin, occurring in dark crystalline plates, used as a violet dye, as in staining microscopic objects; also, any of various related dyes.—**thi′o·nyl** (-nil), *n.* [See -*yl*.] In *chem.*, a bivalent radical consisting of a single atom each of sulphur and oxygen.

thi·o·phene (thī′ō-fēn), *n.* [G. *thiophen*: see *thio-* and *phen-*.] In *chem.*, a colorless liquid, C_4H_4S, with an odor like that of benzene, occurring in crude coal-tar benzene and prepared in various ways.—**thi·o·phe′nic** (-fē′nik), *a.*

thi·o·phe·nol (thī-ō-fē′nol or -nōl), *n.* [See *thio-*.] In *chem.*, a colorless mobile liquid, C_6H_5SH, with the odor of garlic: regarded as phenol with the oxygen replaced by sulphur.

thi·o·sin·am·ine (thī″ō-sin-am′in), *n.* [From *thio-* + L. *sinapi*, mustard, + E. *amine*.] In *chem.*, a colorless crystalline compound, $C_4H_8N_2S$, with bitter taste and feeble garlic-like odor, obtained by the action of ammonia on a sulphur compound present in mustard-oil.

thi·o·sul·phate (thī-ō-sul′fāt), *n.* [See *thio-*.] In *chem.*, a salt of thiosulphuric acid. Cf. *hyposulphite*.—**thi″o·sul·phu′ric** (-fū′rik), *a.* In *chem.*, noting or pertaining to an acid, $H_2S_2O_3$, which may be regarded as sulphuric acid with one oxygen atom replaced by sulphur. Cf. *hyposulphurous*.

thi·o·u·re·a (thī-ō-ū′rē-ä), *n.* [See *thio-*.] In *chem.*, a colorless crystalline substance, $CS(NH_2)_2$, with a bitter taste, regarded as urea with the oxygen replaced by sulphur.

third (thėrd), *a.* [AS. *thridda*, ordinal of *thrī*, E. *three*.] Next after the second; also, being one of three equal parts. —**third degree**, the degree of master mason in freemasonry, demanding of the initiate an elaborate and rigid test of proficiency; hence (colloq.), the use of severe measures by the police (or others) in examining a person in order to extort information or a confession.—**third estate**, the commons. See *estate*, *n.*—**third eyelid**, the nictitating membrane.—**third order** (*eccles.*). See *tertiary*, *a.*—**third rail**, a conductor in the form of a supplementary rail, laid beside the rails of the track of an electric railroad, to carry the current, which is taken off by means of a sliding shoe or contact: used as a substitute for a trolley-wire.—**third**, *n.* The third member of a series; also, a third part; in *music*, a tone on the third degree from a given tone (counted as the first); the interval between such tones; the harmonic combination of such tones; in a scale, the mediant; in *law*, usually *pl.*, the third part of the personal property of a deceased husband, which under certain circumstances goes absolutely to the widow; loosely, a widow's dower.

third-bor·ough (thėrd′bur″ō), *n.* [ME. *thridborro*, prob. by corruption from AS. *frithborg*, security for peace: cf. *headborough*.] In England, formerly, the head of a frankpledge or tithing; hence, the peace-officer of a tithing; the petty constable of a township or manor. [Obs. or hist.]

third=class (thėrd′klas′), *a.* Of or belonging to the class next after the second; pertaining to the third grade of conveyances or accommodations for travel (as, "a *third-class* traveller": G. Meredith's "Diana of the Crossways," xx.).

third·ly (thėrd′li), *adv.* In the third place.

third=rate (thėrd′rāt′), *a.* Of the third rate or class; hence, distinctly inferior (as, "After the grandeur of the promenade, the street appeared shabby and *third-rate*": Arnold Bennett's "Hilda Lessways," iii. 3).

thirl[1] (thėrl), *n.* [AS. *thyrel*, < *thurh*, E. *through*.] A hole or aperture. [Prov. Eng. and Sc.]—**thirl**[1], *v. t.* or *i.* [AS. *thyrlian*, < *thyrel*.] To pierce; penetrate; also, to thrill. [Prov. Eng. and Sc.]

thirl[2] (thėrl), *v. t.* [Akin to *thrall*.] To reduce to thraldom or bondage†; restrict (a person) to one particular party for trade, etc.; bind, confine, or restrict in service or action (as, *thirled* to one's duties); in *Sc. law*, to bind or astrict (lands or tenants), esp. to a particular mill for the grinding of their grain. [Chiefly Sc.]—**thirl·age** (thėr′lāj), *n.* Thraldom† or bondage†; in *Sc. law*, a servitude or obligation requiring the tenants of certain lands, or the dwellers in certain districts, to restrict their custom to a particular mill, or formerly also to a particular forge, etc.; also, the proportion of grain, or the dues in lieu of this, paid for grinding at the mill.

thirst (thėrst), *n.* [AS. *thurst* = D. *dorst* = G. *durst*, thirst; akin to Goth. *thaurstei*, thirst, *thaursus*, dry, withered, also L. *torrere*, to dry, parch, Gr. τέρσεσθαι, become dry.] The uneasy or painful sensation of dryness in the mouth and throat caused by want of drink; the physical condition resulting from this want; also, fig., strong or eager desire (as, "his *thirst* for information," H. G. Wells's "Mr. Britling," i. 5. § 1; "Our mind can satisfy her *thirst* to know," Cary's tr. Dante's "Paradise," iv. 121); a craving.—**thirst**, *v.* [AS. *thyrstan*.] **I.** *intr.* To feel thirst; be thirsty; fig., to have a strong desire (as, "He will *thirst* for some appointed field for action": Ruskin's "Crown of Wild Olive," iii.). **II.†** *tr.* To desire vehemently.—**thirst′er**, *n.*—**thirst′y**, *a.*; compar. *thirstier*, superl. *thirstiest*. [AS. *thurstig*.] Having thirst; craving drink; hence, wanting moisture, as land or plants (as, "*thirsty* leaves": Kingsley's "Yeast," ii.); dry, parched, or arid; also, fig., eagerly desirous, or eager (as, "The fellow was evidently *thirsty* for my blood": W. H. Hudson's "Purple Land," xx.); also, causing thirst (now colloq.: as, *thirsty* work).—**thirst′i-ly**, *adv.*—**thirst′i-ness**, *n.*

thir-teen (thėr′tēn′). [AS. *thrēotȳne*.] **I.** *a.* Three more than ten. **II.** *n.* A number composed of thirteen units, or a symbol, as 13 or xiii, representing it.—**thir′teenth′**. **I.** *a.* Next after the twelfth; also, being one of thirteen equal parts. **II.** *n.* The thirteenth member of a series; also, a thirteenth part.

thir-ti-eth (thėr′ti-eth). [AS. *thrītigotha*.] **I.** *a.* Next after the twenty-ninth; also, being one of thirty equal parts. **II.** *n.* The thirtieth member of a series; also, a thirtieth part.

thir-ty (thėr′ti), *a.* [AS. *thrītig*.] Three times ten.—**Thirty Years' War**, a series of European wars, primarily between Protestants and Catholics of the Holy Roman Empire, but with Denmark, Sweden, France, etc., involved, carried on from 1618 to 1648, and causing general desolation in German territory.—**thir′ty**, *n.*; pl. *-ties* (-tiz). A number composed of thirty units, or a symbol, as 30 or xxx, representing it.

this (ᴛʜis), *pron.* and *a.*; pl. *these* (ᴛʜēz). [AS. *thes*, masc., *thēos*, fem., *this*, neut. (pl. *thās*, also *thǣs*: see *those* and *these*), from the stem of *the* (see *the*[1]), with suffix *-s* (earlier *-se*, *-si*) perhaps identical with Goth. *sai*, see, behold.] A demonstrative term indicating: (1) a person, thing, idea, etc., as pointed out, present, or near, as before mentioned, or supposed to be understood, or as about to be mentioned, or by way of emphasis; (2) one of two persons, things, etc., already mentioned, either referring to the one nearer in place, time, or thought, or implying mere contradistinction (opposed to *that*).—**this**, *adv.* In this manner†; also, to this extent or degree (in later use employed chiefly or only to modify adjectives and adverbs of quantity or extent: as, *this* much; *this* far; *this* early).

this-tle (this′l), *n.* [AS. *thistel* = D. and G. *distel* = Icel. *thistill*, thistle.] Any of various prickly asteraceous plants of the genus *Carduus* and allied genera, as *C. lanceolatus*, a stout herb with handsome purple flower-heads, taken as the national emblem of Scotland, or *C. arvensis* (the 'Canada thistle'), an old-world herb with small purple or white flower-heads, which has spread to America and is one of the most troublesome of weeds; also, any of various other prickly plants; also, a thistle as part of the insignia of the Order of the Thistle, a Scottish order of knighthood conferred on noblemen of Scotland; [*cap.*] the order itself.—**this′-tle=down**, *n.* The downy pappus of the thistle.—**this-tly** (this′li), *a.* Of the nature of a thistle or thistles; thistle-like; prickly; also, abounding in thistles.

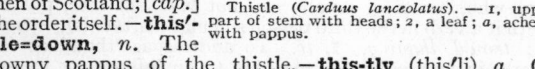

Thistle (*Carduus lanceolatus*). — 1, upper part of stem with heads; 2, a leaf; *a*, achene with pappus.

thith-er (ᴛʜiᴛʜ′ėr or thiᴛʜ′ėr). [AS. *thider*; from the stem represented by E. *the*[1].] **I.** *adv.* To or toward that place or point: as, "Manfred . . . had gone directly to the apartment of his wife, concluding the princess had retired *thither*" (Walpole's "Castle of Otranto," i.). **II.** *a.* On the side or in the direction away from the person speaking; farther; more remote.—**thith-er-to′** (-tö′), *adv.* Up to that time;

until then. [Now rare.]—**thith′er-ward, thith′er-wards** (-wärd, -wärdz), *adv.* [AS. *thiderweard, thiderweardes*.] Toward that place; in that direction; thither: as, "He . . . Bends *thitherward* his way" (Southey's "Thalaba," x. 7).

tho, tho' (ᴛʜō), *conj.* and *adv.* See *though*.

thole[1] (thōl), *v. t.*; *tholed, tholing*. [AS. *tholian*, akin to G. *dulden*, endure, L. *tolerare*, Gr. τλῆναι, bear.] To suffer; bear; endure; tolerate; permit. [Prov. Eng. and Sc.]

thole[2] (thōl), *n.* [AS. *thol* = D. *dol* = Icel. *thollr*, thole.] A pin inserted in a boat's gunwale or the like, to act as a fulcrum for the oar in rowing, or either of two such pins between which the oar works; also, any pin or peg, as the nib of a scythe. Also **thole′=pin**.

Thole.

thol-o-bate (thol′ō-bāt), *n.* [Gr. θόλος, circular building, + -βάτης as in στυλοβάτης, E. *stylobate*.] In *arch.*, the substructure supporting a dome or cupola.

Thom-as (tom′ąs), *n.* [LL., < Gr. Θωμᾶς; from Aram., and meaning 'twin.'] A common masculine name.—**doubting Thomas**, one who refuses to believe without proof: in allusion to the apostle Thomas (see John, xx. 24–29).—**Thomas Atkins**, the typical private soldier in the British army: so called from the use of this name in specimen forms given in army regulations.

Tho-mism (tō′mizm), *n.* The doctrines of St. Thomas Aquinas (1225?–74), the scholastic theologian.—**Tho′mist**, *n.*

thong (thŏng), *n.* [AS. *thwang*.] A narrow strip of hide or leather, used as a fastening, as the lash of a whip, etc.; also, a similar strip of some other material.—**thong**, *v. t.* To furnish with a thong or thongs; fasten or bind with a thong or thongs; lash or flog with a thong.

tho-öid (thō′oid), *a.* [Gr. θώς (gen. θωός), animal of the wolf kind: see *-oid*.] Wolf-like; of the wolf kind; specif., belonging to that group of canine quadrupeds including the wolf, dog, and jackal.

Thor (thôr), *n.* [Icel. *Thōrr*, Thor, = AS. *thunor*, E. *thunder*.] The ancient Scandinavian god of thunder, represented as wielding a mighty hammer. Also fig.

tho-ra-cic (thọ-ras′ik), *a.* Of or pertaining to the thorax.—**thoracic duct**, in *anat.*, the main trunk of the lymphatic system, lying along the front of the spinal column and passing through the thoracic cavity, and conveying the great mass of lymph and chyle into the venous circulation.

tho-rax (thō′raks), *n.*; pl. *thoraxes*, L. *thoraces* (thọ-rā′sēz). [L., < Gr. θώραξ, breastplate, breast, chest.] In man and the higher vertebrates, the part of the trunk between the neck and the abdomen, containing the cavity (inclosed by the ribs, etc.) in which the heart, lungs, etc., are situated; the chest; a corresponding part in other animals; in insects, the portion of the body between the head and the abdomen (cf. *prothorax*, *mesothorax*, and *metathorax*); also, a breast-plate or cuirass, esp. of the ancient Greeks.

tho-ri-a (thō′ri-ą), *n.* [See *thorium*.] In *chem.*, an oxide of thorium, ThO_2, a white powder: used in making incandescent mantles for gas-burners.—**tho′ri-a-nite** (-ą-nīt), *n.* A rare mineral occurring in small black cubic crystals, and consisting largely of thorium oxide, but containing also the oxides of uranium, cerium, etc.: notable for its radioactivity. —**tho′ric**, *a.* Of or containing thorium.—**tho′rite** (-rīt), *n.* A mineral consisting essentially of a silicate of thorium.

tho-ri-um (thō′ri-um), *n.* [NL.; named from the Scandinavian god *Thor*, because found in a mineral from Norway.] Chem. sym., Th; at. wt., 232.4; sp. gr., 11.1. A radioactive metallic element present in certain rare minerals. Cf. *thoria*.

thorn (thôrn), *n.* [AS. *thorn* = D. *doorn* = G. *dorn* = Icel. *thorn* = Goth. *thaurnus*, thorn.] A sharp excrescence on a plant, esp. a sharp-pointed aborted branch; a spine; a prickle; also, a similar process on an animal; also, fig., something that wounds, or causes discomfort or annoyance (as, "the man in whose side he now became a perpetual *thorn*": Motley's "Dutch Republic," ii. 3); also, any of various thorny shrubs or trees, esp. of the genus *Cratægus*, as *C. oxyacantha* ('white thorn,' the common hawthorn), *C. coccinea* ('scarlet thorn,' the scarlet haw), and *C. cordata* ('Washington thorn,' of the southern U. S., planted for hedges or ornament about Washington, D. C., and elsewhere: see cut on next page); also, the Anglo-Saxon letter þ, capital form þ, equivalent to the English *th* (cf. *edh*, also *y²*); in modern phonetic systems, a symbol representing the sound of *th* in *thin*. — **thorn,** *v. t.* To prick with or as with a thorn; vex.

thorn=ap-ple (thôrn′-ap″l), *n.* Any of the poisonous solanaceous plants constituting the genus *Datura*, the species of which bear capsules covered with prickly spines; esp., the jimson-weed, *D. stramonium.*

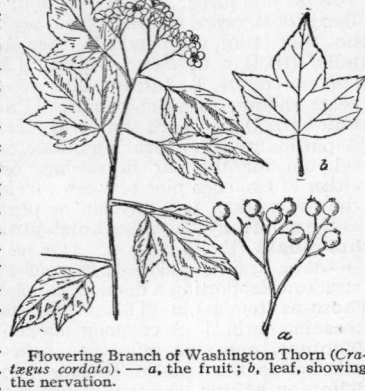

Flowering Branch of Washington Thorn (*Cratægus cordata*). — *a*, the fruit; *b*, leaf, showing the nervation.

thorn-back (thôrn′-bak), *n.* A European ray (fish), *Raia clavata*, with short spines on the back and tail; also, a large crab, *Maia squinado*, of Europe.

thorned (thôrnd), *a.* Having thorns.

thorn-i-ly (thôr′ni-li), *adv.* In a thorny manner. — **thorn′i-ness,** *n.*

thorn-less (thôrn′les), *a.* Without thorns.

thorn-y (thôr′ni), *a.*; compar. *thornier*, superl. *thorniest.* Abounding in or characterized by thorns; spiny; prickly; thornlike; overgrown with thorns or brambles; fig., pricking or piercing to the mind; painful; vexatious; also, full of points of dispute or difficulty (as, a *thorny* question); difficult.

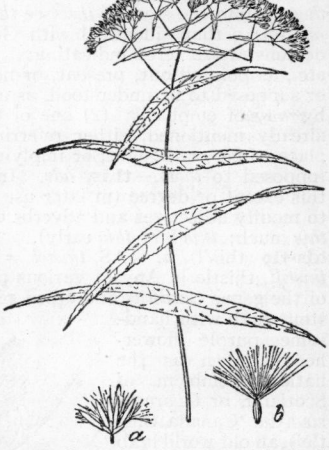

Thornback (*Raia clavata*).

thor-o (thur′ọ), etc. Simplified spelling of *thorough*, etc.

thor-ough (thur′ọ). [AS. *thuruh*, *thurh*: see *through*.] **I.** *prep.* Through: as, "Over hill, over dale, *Thorough* bush, *thorough* brier" (Shakspere's "Midsummer Night's Dream," ii. 1. 3). [Obs. or archaic.] **II.** *adv.* Through; also, thoroughly. [Archaic or prov.] — **thor′ough. I.** *a.* Going, passing, or extending through (now only in special applications); hence, carried out through the whole of something, or fully executed (as, a *thorough* search); being such fully or completely, or complete or perfect (as, "a *thorough* knowledge of the world": Goldsmith's "Vicar of Wakefield," xxv.); of persons, being fully or completely what is expressed by the noun (as, "a *thorough* aristocrat": Bulwer-Lytton's "Pelham," xii.); also, thoroughgoing in action or procedure, leaving nothing undone, or slighting nothing (as, "The Germans . . . are . . . a *thorough* people": H. G. Wells's "Italy, France, and Britain at War," i.). **II.** *n.* Thoroughgoing action, procedure, or policy: applied specif. [*cap.*] in *Eng. hist.* to the policy of Strafford and Laud in the reign of Charles I. (as, "Both the system of government and its temper were designated by Strafford and Laud under the cant watchword of *Thorough*": Morley's "Oliver Cromwell," i. 4). — **thor′ough=bass** (-bās), *n.* In *music*, a bass part written out in full throughout an entire piece, and accompanied by figures which indicate the successive chords of the harmony; the science or method of indicating harmonies by such figures; loosely, harmonic composition in general; also, erroneously, a loud or deep bass. — **thor′ough=brace,** *n.* Either of two strong braces or bands of leather supporting the body of a coach or other vehicle. — **thor′ough=bred. I.** *a.* Of pure or unmixed breed, stock, or race, as a horse or other animal; bred from the purest and best blood; specif., having the pedigree officially recorded in the stud-book for a given number of generations, as a race-horse; hence, having qualities characteristic of pure breeding; high-spirited; mettlesome; elegant or graceful in form or bearing; also, thoroughly educated or trained; thoroughly accomplished; hence,

complete; thorough. **II.** *n.* A thoroughbred animal, esp. a horse; also, a well-bred or thoroughly trained person (colloq.). — **thor′ough-fare** (-fâr), *n.* A passage or way through (as, no *thoroughfare*); also, a road, street, or the like; a public way unobstructed and open at both ends; esp., a main road, or a highway (as, "A great *thoroughfare* was to be driven through three boroughs": Chesterton's "Napoleon of Notting Hill," ii. 2); also, a strait, river, or the like, affording passage for ships, etc. — **thor′ough-go″ing,** *a.* Going through the full length, or doing things thoroughly, as a person; carried out to the full extent, as an action (as, "subjecting traditional ideas and rules to a *thoroughgoing* reconsideration": J. H. Robinson's "Mind in the Making," viii. 16); complete, out-and-out, or unqualified (as, "A *thorough-going* friend that understands more than a million!" Scott's "Legend of Montrose," xiii.; *thoroughgoing* madness). — **thor′ough-ly,** *adv.* In a thorough manner or degree; fully; completely. — **thor′ough-ness,** *n.* — **thor′ough=paced** (-pāst), *a.* Trained to go through all the possible paces, as a horse; fig., thoroughly trained or accomplished (as, "a *thorough-paced* divine": Strype's "Memorials of Cranmer," iii. 23); hence, thoroughgoing, complete, or perfect (as, "a hearty, *thorough-paced* liar": Lamb's "Old Margate Hoy"). — **thor′ough=pin,** *n.* A morbid swelling just above the hock of a horse, usually appearing on both sides of the leg so as to resemble a pin passing through, and sometimes causing lameness. — **thor′ough-wort** (-wẽrt), *n.* A medicinal asteraceous herb, *Eupatorium perfoliatum*, with opposite leaves united at the base, the stem thus passing through the blade; boneset.

thorp (thôrp), *n.* [AS. *thorp* = D. *dorp* = G. *dorf* = Icel. *thorp*, village, = Goth. *thaurp*, field.] A hamlet, village, or small town: as, "through field and forest, through *thorp* and town" (Longfellow's "Saga of King Olaf," iii.). [Archaic, or in place-names.]

those (ᴛʜōz), *pron.* and *a.* [ME. *those, thos*, < AS. *thās*, pl. of *thes*, E. *this.*] Plural (historically of *this*) associated with *that.*

thou (ᴛʜou), *pron.*; nom. *thou*, poss. *thy* or *thine*, obj. *thee*, pl. nom. *ye* or *you*, poss. *your* or *yours*, obj. *you.* [AS. *thū* = OS. *thū* = OHG. *dū* (G. *du*) = Icel. *thū* = Goth. *thu*, thou; akin to L. *tu*, Gr. σύ, τύ, Skt. *tvam*, thou.] The personal pronoun of the second person, in the singular number and nominative case, used to denote the person (or thing) spoken to: formerly in general use, often as indicating (1) equality, familiarity, or intimacy, (2) superiority on the part of the speaker, (3) contempt or scorn for the person addressed; but now little used (being regularly replaced by *you*, which is properly plural, and takes a plural verb) except provincially, archaically, in poetry or elevated prose, in addressing the Deity, and by the Friends or Quakers, who, however, usually say not *thou* but *thee*, putting with it a verb in the third person singular (as, *thee* is). — **thou,** *v.*; *thou'd*, *thouing*. **I.** *tr.* To address as 'thou,' as formerly in familiarity, in speaking to an inferior, or in contempt or scorn, or as in the usage of the Friends. **II.** *intr.* To use 'thou' in discourse.

though (ᴛʜō). [ME. *thoh*, from Scand.: cf. Icel. *thō*, also AS. *thēah*, *thēh* (ME. *theih*, *thaih*), Goth. *thauh*, though, and D. and G. *doch*, yet, however.] **I.** *conj.* Notwithstanding that, or in spite of the fact that (introducing a subordinate clause, which is often marked by ellipsis: as, "The Grand Babylon . . . *though* it never advertised itself . . . stood an easy first among the hotels of Europe," Arnold Bennett's

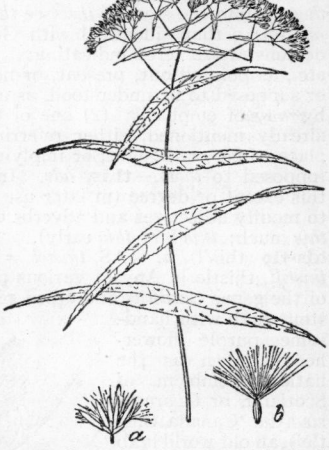

Thoroughwort. — *a*, a mature head; *b*, achene with pappus.

"Grand Babylon Hotel," i.; he continued, *though* tired); also, even if, or granting that (as, "*Though* he slay me, yet will I trust in him": Job, xiii. 15); also, yet, still, or nevertheless (introducing an additional statement restricting or modifying a principal one: as, I will go—*though* I fear it will be useless); also, in a weakened sense, if (usually in 'as though': as, "No marvel then, *though* I mistake my view," Shakspere's "Sonnets," cxlviii.; "'We must have light,' said Mr. Henry, as *though* there had been no interruption," Stevenson's "Master of Ballantrae," v.). **II.** *adv.* For all that; however: as, "I'll shut up now and henceforth. Can't prevent me thinking, *though*" (J. Conrad's "Lord Jim," xvii.).

thought¹ (thôt). Pret. and pp. of *think¹*, *think²*.

thought² (thôt), *n.* [AS. *thôht, gethôht,* < *thencan,* E. *think².*] The act or process of thinking; mental activity, esp. of the intellect; also, the capacity or faculty of thinking; also, the product of mental action, or that which one thinks (as, "Thou understandest my *thought* afar off": Ps. cxxxix. 2); also, the intellectual activity or the ideas, opinions, etc., characteristic of a particular place, class, or time (as, Greek *thought*); also, a single act or product of thinking; an idea or notion (as, to collect one's *thoughts*); a consideration or reflection (as, "In this *thought* they find a kind of ease": Shakspere's "Richard II.," v. 5. 28); also, often, consideration, attention, care, or regard (as, "Catherine . . . never took any *thought* for her appearance": Mrs. H. Ward's "Robert Elsmere," i.); meditation (as, lost in *thought*); intention, design, or purpose, or an intention or design, esp. a half-formed or imperfect intention (as, his *thought* was to avoid controversy; we had some *thoughts* of going); anticipation or expectation (as, I had no *thought* of seeing you here); a judgment, opinion, or belief (as, "What . . . are thy *thoughts* of the emperor?" Scott's "Count Robert of Paris," xxvii.); also, anxiety, trouble, or sorrow (obs. or prov.); also, a very small amount, or a trifle (as, "We're a *thought* before time," Eden Phillpotts's "Children of Men," Prologue, i.; "William de la Marck has been a *thought* too rough," Scott's "Quentin Durward," xxiii.).—**thought′ed,** *a.* Having thoughts (as specified): as, "solemn-*thoughted* Plato" (Whittier's "Questions of Life").—**thought′ful,** *a.* Occupied with or given to thought, as a person; contemplative; meditative; reflective; also, characterized by or manifesting thought (as, a *thoughtful* essay); also, careful, heedful, or mindful (as, to be *thoughtful* of one's safety); also, showing thought or consideration for others; considerate; also, full of anxiety or care†.—**thought′ful-ly,** *adv.*—**thought′ful-ness,** *n.*—**thought′less,** *a.* Devoid of or lacking capacity for thought; also, not taking thought, or unthinking, careless, or heedless (as, "Many a giddy and *thoughtless* boy has become a good bishop": Ruskin's "Crown of Wild Olive," iii.); characterized by or showing lack of thought or reflection (as, "the *thoughtless* vivacity of his character": Scott's "Black Dwarf," xiii.); also, wanting in thought or consideration for others, or inconsiderate (as, "You must be fatigued; it is *thoughtless* of me to keep you standing here so long": W. H. Hudson's "Green Mansions," vii.).—**thought′less-ly,** *adv.*—**thought′less-ness,** *n.*—**thought′=read″ing,** *n.* Same as *mind-reading.*—**thought′=trans″fer-ence,** *n.* Same as *telepathy.*

thou-sand (thou′zand), *n.*; pl. *thousands* or (as after a numeral) *thousand.* [AS. *thûsend* = D. *duizend* = G. *tausend* = Icel. *thûsund* = Goth. *thûsundi,* thousand.] A number composed of ten hundred units, or a symbol, as 1000 (1,000) or M, representing it; indefinitely, a great number. Also used as a quasi-adjective, by omission of *of* before a noun following: as, a *thousand* (of) ways; seven *thousand* (of) men.—**thou′sand-fold** (-fōld). **I.** *a.* Comprising a thousand parts; a thousand times as great or as much. **II.** *n.* A thousand times as much.—**thou′sand=legs,** *n.* A myriapod, esp. a chilopod or centipede, as *Scutigera forceps,* a species common in the southern U. S., which infests houses and preys upon household insects (see cut in next column). —**thou′sandth. I.** *a.* Last in order of a series of a thousand; also, being one of a thousand equal parts. **II.** *n.* The thousandth member of a series; also, a thousandth part.

thow-less (thou′les), *a.* Same as *thewless.* [Sc.]

Thra-cian (thrā′shan). **I.** *a.* Of or pertaining to ancient

Thrace, a region in the eastern part of the Balkan Peninsula, whose boundaries varied at different periods. **II.** *n.* A native or inhabitant of ancient Thrace.

thral-dom (thrâl′dom), *n.* The state or condition of being a thrall; bondage; servitude: as, "The laboring classes worked . . . because they were defenseless and could not escape from *thraldom*" (J. H. Robinson's "Mind in the Making," vi. 13).

thrall (thrâl). [AS. *thrēl,* from Scand.: cf. Icel. *thrēll,* Dan. *trēl,* Sw. *träl,* thrall, bondman.] **I.** *n.* One in bondage to a lord or master; a bondman or slave; hence, a servant; also, a captive; fig., one who is in bondage to some power, influence, or the like (as, "the veriest *thrall* to sympathies, apathies, antipathies": Lamb's "Imperfect Sympathies"); also, thraldom or bondage (lit. or fig.: as, "For them I battle till the end, To save from shame and *thrall*," Tennyson's "Sir Galahad," 16; "Take Godfrey in the *thrall* Of thy sweet looks," Wiffen's tr. Tasso's "Jerusalem Delivered," iv. 26). **II.** *a.* In bondage; enslaved; captive; subject: as, "He was especially *thrall* to the contralto" (Du Maurier's "Trilby," ii.). [Archaic.]—**thrall,** *v. t.* To put or hold in thraldom or bondage; enslave. [Archaic.]—**thrall′dom,** *n.* See *thraldom.*

thrang (thrang), *n., v.,* and *a.* Prov. form of *throng.*

thrap-ple (thrap′l), *n.* See *thropple.*

thrash (thrash), *v.* [= *thresh.*] **I.** *tr.* To thresh (wheat, grain, etc.: see *thresh, v. t.*); also, to beat soundly by way of punishment (as, "Vigors has been *thrashing* me with a rope's end": Marryat's "Mr. Midshipman Easy," xii.); administer a beating to; also, to beat completely; defeat thoroughly; also, *naut.,* to force (a ship) forward against the wind, etc. **II.** *intr.* To thresh (see *thresh, v. i.*); also, to beat, toss, or plunge wildly or violently about (as, "the wash of the waves buffeting the little craft . . . and the continuous *thrashing* of its foresail": J. Conrad's "Rover," xvi.); also, *naut.,* to make way against the wind, tide, etc.; beat.—**thrash,** *n.* The action or an act of thrashing; a beating; a blow; *naut.,* a making way against the wind, etc.—**thrash′er¹,** *n.* One who or that which thrashes or threshes; specif., a large shark, *Alopias vulpes,* having a long tail with which it threshes the water in order to drive together the small fish on which it feeds.

thrash-er² (thrash′ėr), *n.* [Also *thrusher:* cf. *thrush¹.*] Any of various long-tailed thrush-like birds (esp. of the genus *Harporhynchus* or *Toxostoma*) allied to the mockingbird, as *H. rufus* ('brown thrasher'), an American songbird common in shrubbery.

thra-son-ic, thra-son-i-cal (thrā-son′ik, -i-kal), *a.* [From *Thraso,* a bragging soldier in Terence's "Eunuchus."] Boastful; vainglorious.—**thra-son′i-cal-ly,** *adv.*

thraw (thrâ), *v.* [= *throw.*] **I.** *tr.* To turn; twist; set awry; also, to wrest; strain; distort; also, to cross or thwart.

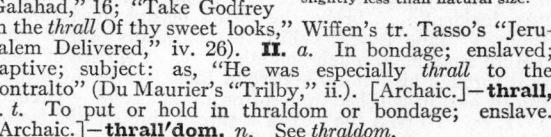
Thousand-legs (*Scutigera forceps*), slightly less than natural size.

Brown Thrasher (*Harporhynchus rufus*).

[Sc.] **II.** *intr.* To turn, twist, or writhe; also, to be perverse; dispute. [Sc.]—**thrawn,** *p. a.* Twisted; crooked; also, perverse; cross-grained. [Sc.]

thread (thred), *n.* [AS. *thrēd* = D. *draad* = G. *draht* = Icel. *thrādhr,* thread, lit. 'something twisted'; from the verb represented by E. *throw.*] A fine cord of flax, cotton, or other fibrous material spun out to considerable length; specif., such a cord composed of two or more filaments twisted together; esp., such a cord of flax or linen, as distinguished from one of cotton, etc.; also, a filament of glass, metal, etc.; also, one of the lengths of yarn forming the warp and woof of a woven fabric; fig., a single interwoven element in anything composite; also, fine cords of flax, cotton, or other fibrous material, or fine filaments of metal, etc., as a material (as, linen *thread*); specif., linen thread, as distinguished from cotton or silk thread; also, something having the fineness or slenderness of a thread, as a thin continuous stream of liquid, a fine line of color, or a thin seam or vein of ore (as, "the little stream, the *thread* of clear water which runs along the glaciers": Vernon Lee's "Genius Loci," High Up); the helical ridge of a screw (see *screw-thread*); also, in fig. use, something conceived as being spun or continuously drawn out, as the continued course of life as fabled to be spun and cut by the Fates; that which guides through a maze, difficulty, etc., in the manner of the clue in the Cretan labyrinth; that which runs through the whole course of something, connecting successive parts, as the sequence of events or ideas continuing through a narrative, train of thought, or the like (as, "I return to the *thread* of my story," Bulwer-Lytton's "Caxtons," xvi. 7; "An incident . . . broke the *thread* of my musings," C. Brontë's "Jane Eyre," xviii.); a continuous or persistent feature running through something (as, a *thread* of piety runs through his letters).—**thread lace,** lace made of linen thread, as distinguished from cotton and silk laces. —**thread,** *v.* **I.** *tr.* To pass the end of a thread through the eye or hole in (a needle or the like); also, to fix (beads, etc.) upon a thread or string that is passed through; string on a thread; also, to cause (something) to pass through something else as a thread through the eye of a needle; also, to pass like a continuous thread through the whole course of (something); pervade; also, to make one's way through (a narrow passage, a forest, a crowd, etc.: as, "He *threaded* the dark passages easily," Hugh Walpole's "Wooden Horse," i.; "I continued to *thread* the tall woods," Stevenson's "Treasure Island," xxii.); make (one's way, etc.) thus (as, "cautiously *threading* her way through the undergrowth": W. H. Hudson's "Green Mansions," xxi.); also, to stretch threads over or across; also, to form a thread on (a screw or the like). **II.** *intr.* To thread one's way, as through a passage or between obstacles (as, "She rose and *threaded* between chairs and tables to the sofa": Arnold Bennett's "Clayhanger," iv. 5); also, to move in a thread-like course; wind or twine.—

thread'bare, *a.* Having the nap worn off so as to lay bare the threads of the warp and woof, as a fabric, garment, etc. (as, "a *threadbare* cloak": Scott's "Quentin Durward," xxvi.); much worn or used; fig., hackneyed or trite (as, "*threadbare* arguments": Motley's "Dutch Republic," ii. 10); meager, scanty, or poor; also, wearing threadbare clothes; shabby; impecunious.—**thread'bare-ness,** *n.*—**thread'en,** *a.* Made of thread. [Archaic or prov.] —**thread'er,** *n.*—**thread'fin,** *n.* Any of the acanthopterygian fishes constituting the family *Polynemidæ,* as the barbudo: so called because the lower part of the pectoral fin is composed of numerous separate slender filaments. — **thread'worm,** *n.* Any of various nematoid

Threadfin.

worms, esp. a pinworm.—**thread'y,** *a.* Consisting of or resembling a thread or threads; fibrous; filamentous; stringy or viscid, as a liquid; of the pulse, thin and feeble; of the voice, etc., lacking in fullness.

threap (thrēp), *v.* [AS. *thrēapian,* rebuke.] **I.** *tr.* To reproach or scold; also, to affirm or aver obstinately; also, to urge, thrust, or force (a thing) on one; also, to bear (*down*) by insistence. [Prov. Eng. and Sc.] **II.** *intr.* To argue; dispute; wrangle. [Prov. Eng. and Sc.]

threat (thret), *n.* [AS. *thrēat,* crowd, pressure, oppression, threat, akin to *thrēotan,* Goth. -*thriutan,* G. (*ver*)*driessen,* trouble, vex: cf. L. *trudere,* thrust, push.] A throng† or crowd†; also, painful pressure†, torment†, or misery†; also, a denunciation of ill to befall some one; a declaration of an intention or determination to inflict punishment, pain, or loss on some one in retaliation for, or conditionally upon, some action or course; a menace; fig., an indication of probable evil to come; something that gives indication of causing evil or harm (as, "Germany had been a *threat,* a menace": H. G. Wells's "Mr. Britling," iii. 2. § 5).— **threat,** *v. t.* or *i.* [AS. *thrēatian.*] To threaten. [Archaic or prov.]

threat-en (thret'n), *v.* [AS. *thrēatnian,* < *thrēat,* E. *threat.*] **I.** *tr.* To utter a threat against; menace; fig., to be a menace or source of danger to (as, "the fell disease which was . . . *threatening* her sister," Mrs. Gaskell's "Cranford," ii.; "The heretics were persecuted . . . because their beliefs *threatened* the vested interests of that day," J. H. Robinson's "Mind in the Making," v. 11); also, to offer (a punishment, injury, etc.) by way of a threat (as, "Who in the breath Wherein thou prayest help still *threatenest* death," W. Morris's "Jason," xv. 534; "upon the point of *threatening* to break off diplomatic relations," Lytton Strachey's "Queen Victoria," v.); fig., to give an ominous indication of (as, the clouds *threaten* rain; "a crack that *threatened* to become a split," Tarkington's "Alice Adams," iii.); presage; portend. **II.** *intr.* To utter or use threats (as, "Harvey expostulated, *threatened,* whimpered, and at last wept outright": Kipling's "Captains Courageous," ii.); fig., to give indication of impending evil or mischief (as, "The clouds . . . had been *threatening* all day": Dickens's "Oliver Twist," xxxviii.).—**threat'en-er,** *n.*—**threat'en-ing-ly,** *adv.*

three (thrē), *a.* [AS. *thrī, thrēo,* = D. *drie* = G. *drei* = Icel. *thrīr* = Goth. *thrija* (neut.), three; akin to L. *tres,* Gr. τρεῖς, Skt. *tri,* three.] One more than two.—**the three R's,** a humorous expression for reading, 'riting, and 'rithmetic, regarded as the fundamentals of education: said to have originated with Sir William Curtis (1752–1829), a lord mayor of London, who proposed it as a toast.—**three,** *n.* A number composed of three units, or a symbol, as 3 or iii, representing it; a set of three persons or things; a playing-card, etc., with three pips.—**Big Three,** U. S., Gt. Brit., and Russia.—**three'-col'or,** *a.* Having, or characterized by the use of, three colors; specif., noting or pertaining to a photomechanical process for making reproductions of paintings, etc., usually carried out by making three plates or printing-surfaces, each corresponding to a primary color, by the half-tone process, and taking superimposed impressions from these plates in three correspondingly colored inks.—**three'=deck'er,** *n.* Formerly, one of a class of war-vessels which carried guns on three decks; now, any vessel, etc., having three decks, tiers, stories, or the like; something with three parts, as a three-volume novel.—**three=dimensional sound,** sound by stereophonic reproduction.—**three'fold** (-fōld). [AS. *thrīfeald.*] **I.** *a.* Comprising three parts or members; three times as great or as much; treble. **II.** *adv.* In threefold manner or measure; trebly.—**three'=mast'er,** *n.* A ship having three masts.—**three'=mile',** *a.* Extending for or pertaining to three miles: as, the *three-mile* limit (the limit of the marine belt which, according to international law, is included within the jurisdiction of the state possessing the coast).—**three'ness,** *n.* The fact or condition of being three or threefold.

threep (thrēp), *v.* See *threap.*

three-pence (thrip'ens or threp'-), *n.* A sum of money of the value of three English pennies, or about 6 U. S. cents; also, a British silver coin of this value (see cut on next page).—**three-pen-ny** (thrip'ę-ni or threp'-), *a.* Of the amount or value of threepence; hence, of little worth; cheap; paltry.

three=phase (thrē′fāz), *a.* Having three phases; noting or pertaining to a system combining three alternating electric currents which differ from one another in phase.

Obverse.   Reverse.
Threepence of Elizabeth. — British Museum.

three=ply (thrē′plī), *a.* Consisting of three thicknesses, layers, strands, or the like.

three=port (thrē′pōrt), *a.* Having three ports; specif., noting or pertaining to a type of two-cycle internal-combustion engine in which the piston opens and closes three ports, namely, an inlet port (through which the fuel mixture from the crank-case enters the cylinder), an exhaust port (for the escape of exhaust gases), and a crank-case admission port (through which the fuel mixture from the carbureter enters and passes to the tightly constructed crank-case).

three=quar-ter (thrē′kwâr′tėr), *a.* Consisting of or involving three quarters of a whole: as, a *three-quarter* portrait (orig. one on a canvas measuring 30 by 25 inches, or of a size about three quarters of the kit-cat, but now usually one showing three quarters of the figure).

three-score (thrē′skōr), *a.* Thrice twenty; sixty.

three-some (thrē′sum). **I.** *a.* Consisting of three; threefold; performed or played by three persons. **II.** *n.* Three forming a group; something in which three persons participate; in *golf*, a match in which one player, playing his own ball, plays against two opponents with one ball, the latter playing alternate strokes.

three=square (thrē′skwär), *a.* Having three equal sides; having an equilateral triangular cross-section, as certain files.

threm-ma-tol-o-gy (threm-a-tol′ọ-ji), *n.* [Gr. θρέμμα (θρεμματ-), nursling: see *-logy*.] In *biol.*, the science of breeding or propagating animals and plants under domestication.

threne (thrēn), *n.* [LL. *threnus*, < Gr. θρῆνος, dirge, lament, < θρεῖσθαι, cry aloud.] A threnody. [Obs. or archaic.]—**thre-net-ic, thre-net-i-cal** (thrē-net′ik, -i-kạl), *a.* [Gr. θρηνητικός.] Pertaining to a threnody; mournful.

thre-node (thrē′nōd or thren′ōd), *n.* [See *threnody*.] A threnody.—**thre-no-di-al, thre-nod′ic** (-nod′ik), *a.* Pertaining to or of the nature of a threnody.—**thren-o-dist** (thren′ọ-dist), *n.* The composer of a threnody.

thren-o-dy (thren′ọ-di), *n.*; pl. *-dies* (-diz). [Gr. θρηνῳδία, < θρῆνος, dirge, lament (see *threne*), + ἀείδειν, sing.] A song of lamentation; esp., a lament for the dead; a dirge or funeral song.

thresh (thresh), *v.* [AS. *therscan* = D. *dorschen* = G. *dreschen* = Icel. *threskja* = Goth. *thriskan*, thresh.] **I.** *tr.* To separate the grain or seeds from (a cereal plant, etc.) by some mechanical means, as by beating with a flail or by the action of a thresher; separate (the grain or seeds) thus; fig. (usually with *out*), to discuss (a matter) exhaustively; get at the truth of by discussion, argument, etc. (as, "I cannot turn my back upon Chadlands till the mystery is *threshed* out to the bottom": Eden Phillpotts's "Grey Room," iv.); also, to beat as if with a flail. See also *thrash, v. t.* **II.** *intr.* To thresh wheat, grain, etc.; also, to deliver blows as if with a flail. See also *thrash, v. i.*—**thresh,** *n.* The action or an act of threshing or thrashing.—**thresh′er**[1], *n.* One who or that which threshes; one who separates grain or seeds from wheat, etc., by beating with a flail or otherwise; a device or machine for this purpose; also, a thrasher (shark).

thresh-er[2] (thresh′ėr), *n.* Same as *thrasher*[2].

thresh-old (thresh′ōld), *n.* [AS. *threscold, therscold*, appar. connected with *therscan*, E. *thresh*.] The piece of timber or stone which lies beneath the bottom of a door; the sill of a doorway; hence, the entrance to a house or building; also, any place or point of entering or beginning (as, "I was on the *threshold* of a surprising adventure": Maugham's "Moon and Sixpence," xlii.); a border or limit, as of a region (as, "The dread strangers were on their march across the Valley,

the very *threshold* of his capital": Prescott's "Conquest of Mexico," iii. 8); in *psychol.*, the limit below which a given stimulus, or the difference between two stimuli, ceases to be perceptible (called in the former case 'threshold of consciousness,' and in the latter case 'threshold of discrimination'); the limen.

threw (thrö). Preterit of *throw*.

thrice (thrīs), *adv.* [ME. *thries* (with adverbial suffix *-s*), < *thrie*, < AS. *thrīwa*, thrice, < *thrī*, E. *three*.] Three times, as in succession (as, "The Lady Baussiere coughed *thrice*": Sterne's "Tristram Shandy," v. 1); on three occasions; also, in threefold quantity or degree (as, "an arm that was *thrice* as strong as Barnes's own": Thackeray's "Newcomes," lviii.); also, very, greatly, or extremely (as, "*thrice* happy isles": Milton's "Paradise Lost," iii. 570).

thrid (thrid), *v. t.* or *i.*; *thridded, thridding*. [Var. of *thread*.] To thread. [Archaic or prov.]

thrift (thrift), *n.* [Cf. Icel. *thrift* and E. *thrive*.] The condition of one who thrives or prospers†; prosperity†; also, industry, labor, or employment (now prov.); also, earnings, savings, or profit (archaic); also, economical management, good husbandry, economy, or frugality (as, "By *thrift* and management, I might reasonably expect . . . to be the wealthiest man in the kingdom": Swift's "Gulliver's Travels," iii. 10); also, vigorous growth, as of a plant; also, an alpine and maritime plumbaginaceous plant, *Statice armeria*, with pink or white flowers, notable for its vigorous growth; any of various allied plants.—**thrift′i-ly**, *adv.* In a thrifty manner.—**thrift′i-ness,** *n.*—**thrift′less,** *a.* Not thriving†; also, unprofitable or worthless (now rare); also, lacking thrift; improvident; wasteful.—**thrift′less-ly,** *adv.*—**thrift′less-ness,** *n.*—**thrift′y,** *a.*; compar. *thriftier*, superl. *thriftiest*. Thriving, prosperous, or successful; also, using, or characterized by, thrift or frugality (as, "Memories of her early straits had made her excessively *thrifty*," Mrs. Wharton's "Age of Innocence," ii.; "the . . . *thrifty* and laudable idea of wearing out our old clothes," Hawthorne's "Blithedale Romance," viii.); careful of expenditure; provident; also, thriving physically, growing vigorously, or flourishing (as, "a *thrifty* growth of the sugar-cane, just ripening": H. Melville's "Omoo," lii.).

thrill (thril), *v.* [Transposed form of *thirl*[1], *v.*] **I.** *tr.* To pierce† or penetrate†; also, to affect with a sudden wave of keen emotion, so as to produce a tremor or tingling sensation through the body (as, "She gave him a quick, tender look that *thrilled* him from head to foot," G. W. Cable's "Bonaventure," i. 6; "I stood *thrilled* with terror," W. H. Hudson's "Far Away and Long Ago," xvi.); also, to cause to vibrate or quiver; utter or send forth tremulously, as a melody. **II.** *intr.* To affect one with a wave of emotion; produce a thrill; pass with a thrill (as, "It *thrilled* through him that she was moving to his side": L. Merrick's "Conrad in Quest of His Youth," ix.); also, to be stirred by a thrill of emotion (as, "His slight, graceful frame *thrilled* with the earnestness of his emotion": G. W. Curtis's "Prue and I," v.); also, to move tremulously, vibrate, or quiver (as, "the great valley of purple heath *thrilling* silently in the sun," Hardy's "Return of the Native," iv. 6; "shrieks and imprecations, that *thrilled* wildly along the waste heath," Scott's "Black Dwarf," iii.).—**thrill,** *n.* A tremor or tingling sensation passing through the body as the result of sudden keen emotion; a penetrating influx of feeling; also, thrilling property or quality, as of a play or story; also, a vibration or quivering; in *pathol.*, an abnormal tremor or vibration, as in the respiratory system.—**thrill′er,** *n.* One who or that which thrills; esp., a sensational play or story (colloq.).—**thrill′ing,** *p. a.* Piercing† or penetrating†; also, affecting with a thrill of emotion (as, "wild *thrilling* sounds": H. Melville's "Moby-Dick," cxxvi.); also, vibrating or quivering.—**thrill′ing-ly,** *adv.*—**thrill′ing-ness,** *n.*

thrips (thrips), *n.* [L., < Gr. θρίψ, a wood-worm.] Any of numerous small insects (family *Thripidæ*) characterized by long, narrow wings fringed with hairs, certain species of which are destructive to plants.

thrive (thrīv), *v. i.*; pret. *throve* or *thrived*, pp. *thriven* (thriv′n) or *thrived*, ppr. *thriving*. [From Scand.: cf. Icel. *thrīfa*, clutch, grasp, *thrīfask*, refl., thrive.] To prosper; be fortunate or successful; of persons, communities, etc., to increase in property or wealth; grow richer or rich; also, to grow or develop vigorously, or flourish (as, "flowers that have not found a climate in which they can *thrive* properly": Mallock's "New Republic," iv. 1).—**thrive′less**, *a.* Not thriving; unsuccessful.—**thriv-er** (thrī′vėr), *n.*—**thriv′-ing-ly**, *adv.*

thro' (thrö), *prep.* and *adv.* See *through.*

throat (thrōt), *n.* [AS. *throtu* = OHG. *drozza*, throat (whence G. *drossel*, throat): cf. *throttle.*] The front of the neck below the chin and above the collar-bones; also, the passage from the mouth to the stomach or to the lungs; the fauces, pharynx, and esophagus; the larynx and trachea; also, some analogous or similar narrowed part or passage; in *bot.*, the orifice of a gamopetalous corolla; *naut.*, the end of a gaff nearest the mast; also, the upper front corner of

Throat of Corolla, of (1) genus *Gerardia* and (2) genus *Acanthus.*

a fore-and-aft sail.—**throat′ed**, *a.* Having a throat (as, white-*throated*); also, channeled or grooved.—**throat′i-ly**, *adv.* In a throaty manner.—**throat′i-ness**, *n.*—**throat′-latch**, *n.* A strap which passes under a horse's throat and helps to hold a bridle or halter in place.—**throat′y**, *a.* Produced or modified in the throat, as sounds; guttural; also, having a prominent throat or capacious swallow, as a dog.

throb (throb), *v. i.*; throbbed, throbbing. [ME. *throbben*; perhaps imit.] To beat with increased force or rapidity, as the heart under the influence of emotion or excitement (as, "His lonely heart *throbbed* at the warm, firm grasp of this friend's hand": Wister's "Virginian," xxxv.); palpitate; exhibit the effect of throbs of the heart, as the pulse, temples, etc. (as, "Although her temples *throbbed*, she tried to analyze the letter": W. Churchill's "Coniston," ii. 19); feel or exhibit emotion, as a person; be experienced as if in throbs, as emotion (as, "the simple affections of human nature *throbbing* under the ermine": Irving's "Sketch-Book," A Royal Poet); also, in general, to pulsate; vibrate.—**throb**, *n.* An act of throbbing; a violent beat or pulsation, as of the heart; a pulsation or vibration in general.—**throb′-bing-ly**, *adv.*—**throb′less**, *a.* Not throbbing; without pulsation.

throe (thrō), *n.* [ME. *throwe*, *thrawe*: cf. AS. *thrawu*, *thrēa*, oppression, affliction, *thrōwian*, suffer, also *thrāwan*, twist, rack, E. *throw.*] A violent spasm or pang; a paroxysm; also, a sharp attack of emotion; *pl.*, the pains of childbirth; also, the agony of death; fig., any violent convulsion or struggle (as, "the *throes* of a revolution": Charnwood's "Abraham Lincoln," vii.).—**throe**, *v. t.* or *i.*; throed, throeing. To subject to or suffer throes; agonize. [Rare.]

throm-base, **throm-bin** (throm′bās, -bin), *n.* [Gr. θρόμβος, lump, clot.] In *physiol. chem.*, the substance or ferment which causes the coagulation of blood.

throm-bo-sis (throm-bō′sis), *n.* [NL., < Gr. θρόμβωσις, a curdling, < θρόμβος, E. *thrombus.*] In *pathol.*, a coagulation of the blood in a blood-vessel or in the heart during life; the formation or existence of a thrombus.—**throm-bot′ic** (-bot′ik), *a.*

throm-bus (throm′bus), *n.*; pl. -bi (-bī). [NL., < Gr. θρόμβος, lump, clot, curd.] In *pathol.*, a fibrinous clot which forms in and obstructs a blood-vessel.

throne (thrōn), *n.* [OF. *trone* (F. *trône*), < L. *thronus*, < Gr. θρόνος, seat, throne.] The chair or seat occupied by a sovereign, bishop, or other exalted personage on occasions

Bishop's Throne. — Basilica of Torcello, near Venice.

of state; esp., the seat occupied by a sovereign on ceremonial occasions, being usually more or less ornate and raised on a dais and covered with a canopy; also, the office or dignity of a sovereign (as, "to wade through slaughter to a *throne*": Gray's "Elegy," xvii.); sovereign power or authority; also, episcopal office or authority; also, the occupant of a throne; a sovereign; also, *pl.*, an order of angels (see *angel*).—**throne**, *v. t.* or *i.*; throned, throning. To set or sit on or as on a throne.—**throne′less**, *a.* Without a throne; dethroned.

throng (thrŏng), *n.* [AS. *thrang*, *gethrang*, crowd, < *thringan* = D. and G. *dringen* = Icel. *thryngva*, press.] Pressing or crowding of people (as, "Went the summons forth Into all quarters, and the *throng* began": Cowper's tr. Homer's "Iliad," ii. 63); crowded condition; also, a multitude of people crowded or assembled together, or a crowd (as, "The streets were filled with *throngs* of people": Dickens's "Old Curiosity Shop," xix.); also, a great number of things crowded or considered together; also, pressure, as of work or affairs (now prov.); also, oppression or trouble (obs. or prov.).—**throng**, *v.* **I.** *tr.* To compress violently†; also, to crowd or press upon; jostle; also, to bring or drive together into a crowd (as, "a beautiful Spanish dancer who had been delighting *thronged* audiences": Mrs. Wharton's "Age of Innocence," i.); also, to fill or occupy with or as with a crowd (as, "The streets were *thronged* with men, horses, and mules": Parkman's "Oregon Trail," i.); fill by crowding or pressing into (as, "Busy politicians *thronged* the coffee-houses": Bancroft's "Hist. of the U. S.," Amer. Revolution, ii. 1); crowd; fill. **II.** *intr.* To force one's way, as through a crowd†; also, to assemble or collect in large numbers; crowd; go in a crowd (as, "They came *thronging* up the steps": Miss Mulock's "John Halifax," viii.).—**throng**, *a.* [Cf. Icel. *thröngr*, narrow, tight, crowded, from the same root as E. *throng*, *n.*] Pressed closely together; also, crowded with people, etc.; thronged; also, busy, as a season; busily engaged, as a person (as, "Mr. Shaw . . . said he was rather *throng* just now, but . . . he should be very glad of a talk with him": S. Butler's "Way of All Flesh," lix.). [Now Sc. and north. Eng.]—**throng′er**, *n.*

throp-ple, **thrap-ple** (throp′l, thrap′l), *n.* [Cf. AS. *throtbolla*, gullet, windpipe.] The throat; the gullet; the windpipe. [Sc. and prov. Eng.]

thros-tle (thros′l), *n.* [AS. *throstle.*] A thrush, esp. the song-thrush (archaic or prov.); also, a machine for spinning wool, cotton, etc., in which the twisting and winding are simultaneous and continuous (so called from its singing noise).

throt-tle (throt′l), *v.*; -tled, -tling. [ME. *throtelen*, appar. < *throte*, E. *throat.*] **I.** *tr.* To stop the breath of by compressing the throat; strangle; sometimes, to choke or suffocate in any way; also, to compress by fastening something tightly about; also, to silence or check as if by choking; in *engin.*, to obstruct the flow of (steam, etc.) by means of a throttle-valve or otherwise; check the supply of steam, etc., to (an engine) in this way. **II.** *intr.* To undergo suffocation; choke.—**throt′tle**, *n.* The throat, gullet, or windpipe (now chiefly prov.); also, a throttle-valve, or a lever or the like which works it.—**throt′tler**, *n.*—**throt′tle=valve**, *n.* In *engin.*, a valve for regulating the supply of a gaseous fluid, as one for controlling the flow of steam to the cylinder of a steam-engine, or one for enlarging and contracting the area of the passage which conducts the fuel mixture from the carbureter to the cylinder of an internal-combustion engine.

through (thrö). [AS. *thurh*, *thuruh*, = OS. *thurh* = OHG. *duruh* (G. *durch*), through, akin to Goth. *thairh*, through: cf. *thirl*[1] and *thorough.*] **I.** *prep.* In at one end, side, or surface, and out at the other, of (as, to pass *through* a doorway); from one end, side, etc., to the other, of (as, to bore a hole *through* a board); also, with passage or course within the limits of, or between or among the individual members or parts of (as, *through* the water, trees, or grass); also, here and there, or everywhere, over the surface or within the limits of (as, to travel *through* a country; matter diffused *through* the atmosphere); also, during the whole period of (as, to enjoy health *through* life); also, from the beginning to the end of, or along the whole course of (as, *through* an action, discourse, book, etc.); also, having reached the farther end or the conclusion of (as, to be *through* one's work);

having finished successfully (as, to get *through* an examination); also, by the means or instrumentality of (as, it was *through* him they found out); also, by reason of or in consequence of (as, to run away *through* fear). **II.** *adv.* In at one end, side, or surface and out at the other (as, an apple with a knife stuck *through*); from one end, side, etc., of a thing to the other (as, a tunnel runs *through*; to cut a thing *through*); also, all the way, or along the whole distance (as, this train goes *through* to Boston); also, through the whole extent, thickness, or substance, or throughout (as, chilled *through*; wet *through*); hence, thoroughly†; also, from the beginning to the end (as, to read a letter *through*); also, to the end or the purposed conclusion (as, to carry a matter *through*); to a favorable or successful conclusion (as, to pull *through*); also, having reached the farther end (as, a few minutes after the train enters the tunnel, it is *through*); having completed an action, process, etc. (as, he has worked all day, but is not yet *through*); also, being completed or finished, as an action, etc. (as, "We had just so much work to do, and when that was *through*, the time was our own": Dana's "Two Years before the Mast," xix.).—**through and through**, with repeated penetration; through the whole extent or substance; from beginning to end; hence, in all respects, or thoroughly (as, "He knew the man *through and through*": W. Churchill's "Coniston," ii. 2).—**through with**, finished or done with (as, let me know when you are *through with* that book; "It's well we're *through with* Easter," H. G. Wells's "Soul of a Bishop," viii.); also, at an end of all relations or dealings with (as, he behaved badly, and they are *through with* him).—**through**, *a.* Passing or extending from one end, side, or surface to the other, as a bolt; also, that extends, goes, or conveys through the whole of a long distance with no or but little interruption (as, a *through* line, train, or ticket).—**through'ly**, *adv.* Thoroughly; fully; completely; also, through the whole extent or substance. [Archaic.]—**through-out'. I.** *adv.* So as to penetrate completely†; also, through the whole of a thing (as, "The coat was without seam, woven from the top *throughout*": John, xix. 23); in or to every part; also, through the whole of a period of time or a course of action (as, "He has deceived you *throughout* in every step of his career": Stevenson's "Master of Ballantrae," v.); at every moment or point. **II.** *prep.* Through, and out at the other side of†; also, in or to every part of (as, "There was much joy *throughout* the town": Hawthorne's "Scarlet Letter," ix.); everywhere in; also, from the beginning to the end of (as, "*Throughout* lunch she had scarcely spoken": Arnold Bennett's "Hilda Lessways," ii. 2).

throve (thrōv). Preterit of *thrive*.

throw (thrō), *v. t.;* pret. *threw*, pp. *thrown*, ppr. *throwing*. [AS. *thrāwan*, twist, turn, rack, = D. *draaien* = G. *drehen*, turn: cf. *thread*.] To turn or twist (now chiefly Sc.: see *thraw, v. t.*); shape or fashion in a lathe; shape (vessels, clay, etc.) on a potters' wheel; twist (raw silk) into thread, as for the loom; also, to project or propel forcibly through the air by a sudden jerk or straightening of the arm; cast; fling; toss; hurl; propel or cast in any way; cast (dice) from a dice-box; or make (a cast) at dice; play (a card) in card-playing; hurl or project (a missile), as a gun does; drive or impel (something) with violence, as the sea or the wind does; project or cast (light, a shadow, etc.); direct (words, a glance, etc.); perform (a somersault, etc.); also, to cause to fall to the ground; bring to the ground, as an opponent in wrestling; defeat, as in a contest; of a horse, etc., to cause (a rider) to fall off; of a serpent, etc., to shed or lose (the skin, etc.); of domestic animals, to bring forth (young); also, to cause to go or come into some place, position, condition, etc., as if by throwing (as, to *throw* a man into prison; to *throw* a bridge across a river; to *throw* troops into action); put hastily (as, to *throw* a shawl over one's shoulders); put or convert into a particular form (as, to *throw* a message into cipher); also, to permit an opponent to win (a race, contest, or the like) unnecessarily or in accordance with a previous agreement (colloq.); in *mech.*, to move (a lever, etc.) in order to connect or disconnect parts of an apparatus or mechanism; connect, engage, disconnect, or disengage by such a procedure.—**to throw cold water on**, fig., to discourage by objection, disapproval, or the like:

as, to *throw cold water on* a project.—**to throw dust in one's eyes,** fig., to confuse, mislead, or deceive one.—**to throw in,** to put in as an addition; add, esp. without charge, as in a sale or bargain.—**to throw over,** to cast off, as from relations: as, to *throw over* a lover or an associate.—**to throw up,** to vomit; also, to erect or construct, esp. rapidly; also, to relinquish, abandon, or give up (as, "He had felt tempted to *throw up* public life in disgust": Froude's "Cæsar," xv.).—**to throw up the sponge,** in *pugilism*, of the attendants or seconds of a fighter, to toss up the sponge used to bathe or freshen him, in acknowledgment of his defeat; hence, in general, to give up a struggle or contest, or acknowledge defeat (colloq.: as, "You mustn't ask me to *throw up the sponge* to your sudden intuition of danger," Eden Phillpotts's "Grey Room," ii.).—**throw,** *v. i.* To turn, twist, or writhe (now chiefly Sc.: see *thraw, v. i.*); also, to cast, fling, or hurl a missile, etc.; cast dice.—**to throw back,** to revert to an ancestral type or character; exhibit atavism. Also fig.: as, "He and his ideas *throw back* to the Middle Ages" (Galsworthy's "Patrician," ii. 1).—**to throw up,** to vomit.—**throw,** *n.* A turn or twist (chiefly Sc.); a lathe, a potters' wheel, or the like; also, an act of throwing or casting; a cast or fling; the distance to which anything is or may be thrown (cf. *a stone's throw*, under *stone, n.*); a cast at dice, or the number thrown (as, "the hazard of a dicer's *throw*": De Quincey's "Revolt of the Tartars"); hence, a venture (as, "It was her last *throw*; and she knew it": Galsworthy's "Saint's Progress," iii. 12); also, a light scarf for draping a picture-frame, etc. (as, "*throws*' which they had the courage to drape upon horsehair sofas": Tarkington's "Magnificent Ambersons," i.); a woman's scarf, boa, or the like; in *mech.,* the movement of a reciprocating part or the like from its central position to its extreme position in either direction, or the distance traversed (equivalent to one half the *travel* or *stroke*); hence, the arm or the radius of a crank or the like; the eccentricity of an eccentric, or the radius of a crank to which an eccentric is equivalent, being equal to the distance between the center of the disk and the center of the shaft; also, the complete movement of a reciprocating part or the like in one direction, or the distance traversed (equivalent to the *travel* or *stroke*); in *geol.* and *mining,* the amount of vertical displacement produced by a fault.

throw-a-way (thrō'ạ-wā''), *n.* A handbill or the like intended to be thrown away after it has been read.

throw-back (thrō'bak), *n.* An act of throwing back; also, a setback or check; also, reversion to an ancestral type or character; an example of this.

throw-er (thrō'ėr), *n.* One who or that which throws.

thrown (thrōn), *p. a.* Of silk, twisted into thread, as for the loom. Cf. *organzine*.

throw-ster (thrō'stėr), *n.* One who throws silk, orig. a woman who did this; also, one who throws dice†.

thru (thrö), etc. Simplified spelling of *through*, etc.

thrum[1] (thrum), *n.* [ME. *throm* = D. *drom* = G. *trumm*, thrum: see *term*.] One of the ends of the warp-threads in a loom, left unwoven and remaining attached to a loom when the web is cut off; *pl.*, the row or fringe of such threads; also, *sing.*, any short piece of waste thread or yarn; a tuft, tassel, or fringe of threads, as at the edge of a piece of cloth; also, *pl.* or *sing.*, *naut.*, short bits of rope-yarn used for mops, etc.—**thrum**[1], *v. t.;* *thrummed, thrumming.* To furnish or cover with thrums, ends of thread, or tufts (now prov.); also, *naut.*, to insert short pieces of rope-yarn through (a piece of canvas) and thus give it a rough surface, as in order that it may be wrapped about a part to prevent chafing.

thrum[2] (thrum), *v.;* *thrummed, thrumming.* [Imit.] **I.** *intr.* To play on a stringed instrument, as a guitar, by plucking the strings, esp. in an idle, monotonous, or unskilful manner; also, to sound when thrummed on, as a guitar, etc.; also, to drum or tap idly with the fingers. **II.** *tr.* To play (a stringed instrument, or a melody on it) by plucking the strings, esp. in an idle, monotonous, or unskilful manner; also, to recite or tell in a monotonous way; also, to drum or tap idly on.—**thrum**[2], *n.* The act or sound of thrumming; any dull, monotonous sound.—**thrum'mer,** *n.*

thrush[1] (thrush), *n.* [AS. *thrysce*.] A common European song-bird, *Turdus musicus* ('song-thrush': see cut on next page); any bird belonging to the same family, *Turdidæ* ('thrush family'), esp. those of the subfamily *Turdinæ*, which are mostly moderate-sized migratory songsters; any of various similar birds of other families. See *hermit-thrush, missel-thrush, wood-thrush, ouzel, redwing, robin,* etc.

thrush² (thrush), *n.* [Cf. Dan. *tröske,* Sw. *torsk,* thrush.] A disease, esp. in children, characterized by whitish spots and ulcers on the membranes of the mouth, fauces, etc., due to a parasitic fungus, *Saccharomyces albicans;* also, in horses, a diseased condition of the frog.

Song-thrush (*Turdus musicus*).

thrust (thrust), *v. t.;* thrusting. [ME. *thrusten, thristen,* from Scand.: cf. Icel. *thrȳsta,* thrust, press.] To push forcibly; shove or drive; impel; put or drive with force, as into some thing or opening (as, to *thrust* a knife into an apple; to *thrust* one's hand into one's pocket); put forth or extend in some direction (as, "The lion dying *thrusteth* forth his paw": Shakspere's "Richard II.," v. 1. 29); put forcibly into some position, condition, etc. (as, to *thrust* one's self into danger); also, to stab or pierce, as with a sword (as, "to . . . *thrust* him through with a spear": W. H. Hudson's "Far Away and Long Ago," xxiii.).—**to thrust in one's oar.** See under *oar, n.*—**thrust,** *v. i.* To push against something; also, to push or force one's way, as against obstacles, through a crowd, or between persons (as, "She *thrust* in between them": Scott's "Fair Maid of Perth," xii.); also, to make a thrust, lunge, or stab at something. —**thrust,** *n.* An act of thrusting; a forcible push or drive; a lunge or stab (lit. or fig.: as, "The man replied with a *thrust* of his sword," Froude's "Cæsar," v.; "a sarcastic *thrust* at a prevailing foible," Howells's "Rise of Silas Lapham," iii.); in *mech., arch.,* etc., a pushing force or pressure exerted by a thing or part against a contiguous one; specif., the force exerted in a lateral direction by an arch, and tending to overturn the abutments.—**thrust′er,** *n.*

thru-way (thrö′wā), *n.* A highly modern motor highway.

thud (thud), *v. i.* or *t.;* thudded, thudding. [Appar. imit.: cf. AS. *thyddan,* strike, thrust.] To beat or strike with a dull sound of heavy impact.—**thud,** *n.* A dull sound, as of a heavy blow or fall (as, "He brought his long arms to his sides with a *thud,*" Arnold Bennett's "Grand Babylon Hotel," xiv.; "The bird . . . fell headlong into the grass sods with a *thud,*" Galsworthy's "Country House," i. 2); also, a blow causing such a sound.

thug (thug), *n.* [Hind. *thag,* cheat, robber, thug.] [Also *cap.*] One of a former body of professional robbers and murderers in India, who strangled their victims; hence [*l. c.*], a cutthroat; a ruffian; a rough.—**thug-gee** (thug′ē), *n.* [Hind. *thagī.*] [Also *cap.*] The system or practices of the thugs.—**thug′ger-y, thug′gism,** *n.*

thu-ja (thū′jȧ), *n.* [NL. *Thuja, Thuya,* < Gr. θυία, θύα, kind of African tree.] Any of the evergreen pinaceous trees constituting the genus *Thuja,* esp. *T. occidentalis,* the common arbor-vitæ, which yields an aromatic oil.

Thu-le (thū′lē), *n.* [L., < Gr. Θούλη, Θύλη.] The ancient Greek and Latin name for an island or region (variously identified as one of the Shetland Islands, Iceland, Norway, etc.), first described by the Greek navigator Pytheas (flourished 4th century B.C.) as lying a six days' sail north of Britain, and supposed to be the most northerly region of the world; hence (chiefly in the Latin phrase *ultima Thule,* 'farthest Thule'), the farthest north; the farthest limit or point possible; the uttermost degree attainable.

thu-li-a (thū′li-ȧ), *n.* [NL.] In *chem.,* the oxide of thulium.

thu-li-um (thū′li-um), *n.* [NL., < L. *Thule,* Thule.] Chem. sym., Tm; at. wt., 168.5. A rare metallic element.

thumb (thum), *n.* [AS. *thūma* = D. *duim* = G. *daumen,* thumb; prob. meaning orig. 'big or thick (finger),' and akin to L. *tumere,* swell.] The short, thick inner digit of the human hand, next to the forefinger, or the corresponding digit in other animals; the pollex; also, that part of a glove, etc., which covers this; in *ornith.,* the movable radial digit of a bird's wing, supposed to correspond to the human thumb, but more probably the homologue of the forefinger; also, the hind toe of a bird.—**under the thumb of,** under the power or influence of; completely subservient to: as, "Her son-in-law . . . was *under the thumb of* his women-folk" (Kipling's "Kim," xii.).—**thumb,** *v. t.* To feel with or as with the thumb; handle; also, to handle, play, or perform clumsily, as if with the thumbs, as a musical instrument or a tune; also, to soil or wear with the thumbs in handling, as the pages of a book (as, "the volume of philosophy, well *thumbed* and hard used as a priest's breviary": F. M. Crawford's "Mr. Isaacs," xi.); hence, to read much or often; also, to press, spread, work, etc., with the thumb (as, "Ere God inspired Himself Into the clay thing *Thumbed* to His image": Henley's "Song of the Sword").—**thumb′kins,** *n. pl.* A thumb-screw (instrument of torture).—**thumb′=nail. I.** *n.* The nail of the thumb; also, anything of the size of a thumbnail, or quite small or brief, as a drawing, a short essay, etc. **II.** *a.* Of the size of a thumb-nail; hence, quite small. —**thumb′=screw,** *n.* A screw whose head is so constructed that it may be turned easily with the thumb and a finger; also, an old instrument of torture by which one or both thumbs were compressed.—**thumb′= stall,** *n.* A device resembling a thimble worn over the thumb by shoemakers, etc., for pushing a needle; also, a protective sheath, as of leather, worn over an injured thumb.— **thumb′=tack,** *n.* A tack with a large, flat head, designed to be thrust in by the pressure of the thumb or a finger.

Thumb-screw (in 2d sense).

Thum-mim (thum′im), *n. pl.* [Heb. *thummīm.*] See *Urim.*

thump (thump), *v.* [Imit.] **I.** *tr.* To strike or beat with something thick and heavy, so as to produce a dull sound; pound; drive or force (*down, off,* etc.) by such action; of an object, to strike against (something) heavily and noisily (as, "He . . . heard . . . many feete fast *thumping* th' hollow ground": Spenser's "Faerie Queene," vi. 10. 10); also, to bring (a thing) with a thump against something else (as, "Mr. Peake slowly and regularly *thumped* one fist on the bench": Arnold Bennett's "Clayhanger," i. 10); also, to thrash severely (colloq.). **II.** *intr.* To strike or beat heavily, with a dull sound (as, "Taffy knocked and *thumped* till the door was opened": Du Maurier's "Trilby," vii.); knock with force; pound; also, to walk with heavy, sounding steps; move with thumps; beat violently, as the heart (as, "She flashed a look at him that made his heart *thump*": W. Churchill's "Coniston," i. 14).—**thump,** *n.* A blow with something thick and heavy, producing a dull sound; a heavy knock; the sound made by such a blow; also, a knocking or pounding of machinery due to slackness at a joint; also, *pl.,* a beating of the chest in horses due to spasmodic contractions of the diaphragm, resembling hiccups in man. —**thump′er,** *n.*—**thump′ing,** *p. a.* That thumps; beating; throbbing; also, of exceptional size, extent, etc. (colloq.).

thun-der (thun′dėr), *n.* [AS. *thunor* = D. *donder* = G. *donner,* thunder, = Icel. *Thōrr,* Thor (god of thunder); akin to L. *tonitrus,* Skt. *tanyatu,* thunder, Skt. *tan-,* resound.] The loud noise which accompanies (but apparently follows) a flash of lightning, due to violent disturbance of the air by a discharge of electricity; the destructive agent in a thunderstorm (now chiefly poetic); a peal of thunder (now chiefly poetic); a thunder-storm (obs. or prov.); also, any loud, resounding noise (as, "Heavy waves beat below them in hollow *thunder*," Eden Phillpotts's "Red Redmaynes," v.; *thunders* of applause); also, a threatening or startling utterance, denunciation, or the like (as, "They heard the chaplain launch his *thunders* at the head of the unpopular favourite": Scott's "Abbot," iv.); vehement or powerful eloquence;

also, used vaguely in exclamations and expletive phrases (as, by *thunder!* what in *thunder* does it mean?).—**to steal one's thunder.** See under *steal, v. t.*—**thun'der,** *v.* [AS. *thunrian*.] **I.** *intr.* To give forth thunder (often with impersonal *it* as subject: as, it *thundered* last night); also, to make a loud, resounding noise like thunder (as, "A footman knocked, or rather *thundered*, at the door": Fielding's "Tom Jones," xiii. 4); move with such noise (as, "The ice avalanches . . . sometimes *thunder* down the slopes": Tyndall's "Forms of Water," § 14); also, to utter loud or vehement denunciations, threats, or the like; speak in a very loud tone. **II.** *tr.* To strike or beat, drive or force, deal or inflict, give forth, etc., with loud noise or violent action suggesting thunder; also, to utter or issue by way of a vehement denunciation or the like (as, "Respectable newspapers *thundered* out their grave invectives": Lytton Strachey's "Queen Victoria," v.); utter loudly.—**thun'der-bolt,** *n.* An imaginary bolt or dart conceived as the material destructive agent cast to earth in a flash of lightning; a flash of lightning with the accompanying thunder; also, any of various fossils, stones, or mineral concretions formerly and still popularly supposed to have been cast to earth with the lightning; also, fig., something very destructive or terrible; a severe denunciation, threat, or the like, as from one in high authority; a sudden or unexpected and startling event, piece of news, etc.; also, one who acts with fury and with sudden and resistless force. —**Thunderbolt.** A U. S. swift, maneuverable fighter plane (Republic).—**thun'der-clap,** *n.* A crash of thunder. Also fig.

Jupiter holding a Thunderbolt in his right hand. (From a Pompeian wall-painting.)

—**thun'der=cloud,** *n.* An electrically charged cloud producing lightning and thunder. —**thun'der-er,** *n.*—**thun'der=head,** *n.* One of the round swelling masses of cumulus cloud appearing above the horizon when conditions are right for thunder-storms, and frequently developing into thunder-clouds.—**thun'der-ing,** *p. a.* That thunders; producing a noise or effect like thunder; also, extraordinary, tremendous, or very great (colloq.). —**thun'der-less,** *a.* Without thunder.—**thun'der-ous,** *a.* Full of or characterized by thunder; also, making a loud noise like thunder; also, violent, destructive, or terrifying like thunder.—**thun'der-ous-ly,** *adv.*—**thun'der=show"er,** *n.* A shower accompanied by thunder and lightning.—**thun'der=stone,** *n.* A thunderbolt; esp., one of the fossils, stones, etc., popularly identified as thunderbolts. [Archaic or prov.]—**thun'der=storm,** *n.* A storm of thunder and lightning, and usually rain.—**thun'der-strike,** *v. t.*; pret. *-struck,* pp. *-struck* or *-stricken,* ppr. *-striking.* To strike with or as with a thunderbolt; render thunderstruck.—**thun'der-struck,** *a.* Struck as by a thunderbolt; esp., overcome with consternation, confounded, or astounded (as, "I was quite *thunderstruck* at this abrupt and unexpected declaration": Miss Burney's "Evelina," xxi.).—**thun'der-y,** *a.* Thunderous: as, "sultry *thundery* weather" (G. White's "Nat. Hist. of Selborne," ii. 21).— **thun'drous,** *a.* Same as *thunderous.*

thu-ri-ble (thū'ri-bl), *n.* [L. *thuribulum,* < *thus* (*thur-*), *tus* (*tur-*), frankincense: cf. Gr. *θύος,* an offering, incense.] A censer.

thu-ri-fer (thū'ri-fèr), *n.* [L. *thurifer,* incense-bearing, < *thus* (see *thurible*) + *ferre,* bear.] One who carries the thurible in religious ceremonies.—**thu-rif'er-ous** (thū-rif'e-rus), *a.* Producing or bearing frankincense.

thu-ri-fy (thū'ri-fī), *v. t.*; *-fied, -fying.* [OF. *thurifier,* < LL. *thurificare,* < L. *thus* (see *thurible*) + *facere,* make.] To burn incense before or about; perfume with incense; cense.—**thu"ri-fi-ca'tion** (-fi-kā'shon), *n.*

Thu-rin-gi-an (thū-rin'ji-an), *n.* **I.** *a.* Of or pertaining to Thuringia, a region in central Germany. **II.** *n.* A native or inhabitant of Thuringia.

Thurs-day (thèrz'dā), *n.* [AS. *Thüresdæg,* also *Thunres-*

dæg, = Icel. *Thōrsdagr,* 'Thor's day': cf. *Thor* and *thunder.*] The fifth day of the week, following Wednesday.—**Holy Thursday.** See under *holy, a.*

thus (ᴛʜus), *adv.* [AS. *thus* = OS. and OFries. *thus* = D. *dus,* thus; appar. from the stem represented by E. *the¹.*] In the manner just indicated or exemplified; in the manner now being indicated or exemplified; in the following manner; also, in accordance with this (as, *thus* we conclude that he was mistaken); accordingly; consequently; also, to this extent or degree (as, *thus* far; *thus* much).—**thus'ly,** *adv.* Thus. [Colloq. or humorous.]—**thus'ness,** *n.* The state of being thus. [Colloq. or humorous.]—**thus'wise,** *adv.* Thus.

thwack (thwak), *v. t.* [Cf. AS. *thaccian,* slap, pat, also E. *whack.*] To strike or beat vigorously, as with a stick or something flat; whack; also, to drive or force by or as by thwacking.—**thwack,** *n.* A sharp stroke or blow, as with a stick or something flat; a whack: as, "The man . . . with his open palm gave the animal a resounding *thwack*" (J. Conrad's "Rover," xvi.).—**thwack'er,** *n.*

thwart¹ (thwârt). [ME. *thwert,* from Scand.: cf. Icel. *thvert,* neut. of *thverr,* adj., cross, transverse, = AS. *thweorh,* cross, perverse, = G. *zwerch-,* cross, Goth. *thwairhs,* angry: cf. L. *torquere,* twist.] **I.** *adv.* Crosswise or transversely; across, or from one side to the other. [Archaic.] **II.** *prep.* So as to cross or intersect; transversely over; from side to side of. [Chiefly archaic.]—**thwart¹,** *a.* Passing or lying crosswise or across; cross; transverse; fig., inclined to resist or obstruct; perverse; obstinate; also, adverse or unfavorable.—**thwart¹,** *v.* **I.** *tr.* To place crosswise†; also, to cross (something) with a line, etc. (now rare); also, to cross the course or direction of (archaic: as, "The lizard seems A flash of lightning, if he *thwart* the road," Cary's tr. Dante's "Inferno," xxv. 72); pass or extend across from side to side of (archaic); also, to obstruct or block with something placed across (now rare: as, "They sometimes speed, but often *thwart* our course," Crabbe's "Parish Register," ii.); also, to act in opposition to (now rare); also, to oppose successfully, or prevent from accomplishing a purpose (as, "He was *thwarted* at every step by political obstacles": Lecky's "Hist. of Eng. in the 18th Century," i.); frustrate (a purpose, etc.); baffle. **II.** *intr.* To pass or extend across (archaic); also, to be adverse, in opposition, or at variance (now rare). —**thwart¹,** *n.* An act of thwarting; hindrance; a check. [Now rare.]

thwart² (thwârt), *n.* [Appar. a var. (due to association with *thwart¹*) of obs. or prov. *thought,* for earlier *thoft,* < AS. *thofte,* rower's bench.] A seat across a boat, on which a rower sits.

thwart-er (thwâr'tèr), *n.* One who or that which thwarts.

thy (ᴛʜī), *pron.* [ME. *thi,* reduced form of *thin,* < AS. *thīn,* E. *thine.*] The possessive form corresponding to *thou* and *thee,* used before a noun. Cf. *thine.*

Thy-es-te-an (thī-es'tē-an), *a.* Of or pertaining to Thyestes, in Greek legend, who was caused to eat unwittingly of the flesh of his sons at a banquet.

thy-ine (thī'in), *a.* [LL. *thyinus,* < Gr. *θύϊνος,* < *θυία,* kind of African tree: cf. *thuja.*] Noting a precious wood mentioned in Rev. xviii. 12: supposed to be that of the sandarac-tree, *Callitris quadrivalvis.*

thy-la-cine (thī'la-sin), *n.* [NL. *Thylacinus,* < Gr. *θύλακος,* pouch.] A carnivorous wolf-like marsupial, *Thylacinus cynocephalus,* of Tasmania. Also called *Tasmanian wolf.*

thyme (tīm), *n.* [OF. *tym* (F. *thym*), < L. *thymum,* < Gr. *θύμον,* thyme.] Any of the menthaceous plants constituting the genus *Thymus,* as *T. vulgaris,* a low shrub with aromatic leaves

Thylacine.

used for seasoning, or *T. serpyllum*, a wild creeping species (as, "I know a bank where the wild *thyme* blows": Shakspere's "Midsummer Night's Dream," ii. 1. 249); also, any of various other plants.

thym-e-læ-a-ceous (thim″e-lę-ā′shius), *a.* [L. *thymelæa*, < Gr. θυμελαία, kind of plant.] Belonging to the *Thymelæaceæ*, a family of chiefly old-world trees, shrubs, and herbs including the mezereon, leatherwood, etc.

thy-mic[1] (thī′mik), *a.* Pertaining to or derived from thyme.

thy-mic[2] (thī′mik), *a.* Of or pertaining to the thymus: as, *thymic* acid (a colorless acid obtained from the thymus).

thy-min (thī′min), *n.* In *physiol. chem.*, a colorless crystalline substance, $C_5H_6N_2O_2$, derived from the thymus, etc., and also obtained synthetically.

thy-mol (thī′mol or -mōl, or thī′-), *n.* In *chem.*, a crystalline phenol, $C_{10}H_{13}.OH$, present in an oil obtained from thyme: used as an antiseptic, etc.

thy-mus (thī′mus), *n.* [NL., < Gr. θύμος, warty excrescence, thymus.] In *anat.*, a glandular body or ductless gland of uncertain function found in vertebrate animals, in man lying in the thorax near the base of the neck and becoming vestigial in the adult: when of an animal and used as food, called *sweetbread*. Also called *thymus gland* and *thymus body*.

thym-y (thī′mi), *a.* Pertaining to or resembling thyme; abounding in thyme (as, "*thymy* hills": Jane Porter's "Scottish Chiefs," lvii.).

thy-roid (thī′roid). [Prop. *thyreoid*, < Gr. θυρεοειδής, shield-shaped, < θυρεός, oblong shield, + εἶδος, form.] **I.** *a.* Shield-shaped; in *anat.*, noting or pertaining to the principal cartilage of the larynx, forming the projection known in men as 'Adam's apple'; also, noting or pertaining to a ductless gland adjacent to the larynx and upper trachea, and furnishing an important secretion. **II.** *n.* In *anat.*, the thyroid cartilage; the thyroid gland; an artery, vein, or the like, of the thyroid region.—**thy-roi′dal** (-roi′dạl), *a.* —**thy-roi-dec′to-my** (-dek′tō-mi), *n.* [+ Gr. ἐκ, out of, + -τομία, E. *-tomy*.] In *surg.*, excision of the whole or a part of the thyroid gland.—**thy-roi-di′tis** (-dī′tis), *n.* [NL.] In *pathol.*, inflammation of the thyroid gland.

thyrse (thèrs), *n.* Same as *thyrsus*.

thyr-soid, thyr-soi-dal (thèr′soid, thèr-soi′dạl), *a.* [See *-oid*.] In *bot.*, having somewhat the form of a thyrsus.

thyr-sus (thèr′sus), *n.*; pl. *-si* (-sī). [L., < Gr. θύρσος, the Bacchic thyrsus.] A staff or spear tipped with an ornament like a pine-cone and sometimes wrapped round with ivy and vine-branches, borne by Dionysus (Bacchus) and his votaries; in *bot.*, a form of mixed inflorescence, as in the lilac, in which the primary ramification is centripetal or indeterminate, and the secondary and successive ramifications are centrifugal or determinate.

thys-a-nu-ran (this-ạ-nū′rạn). [NL. *Thysanura*, pl., < Gr. θύσανος, tassel, + οὐρά, tail.] **I.** *a.* Belonging to the *Thysanura*, an order of wingless insects with long filamentous caudal appendages, comprising the bristletails and springtails, or, according to some authorities, the bristletails only. **II.** *n.* A thysanuran insect. —**thys-a-nu′rous**, *a.*

thy-self (ᵵHī-self′), *pron.* An emphatic form of *thou* or *thee*; also, a reflexive form of *thee*.

Tian-shan (tiän′shän′) **sheep.** [Also *Thian-shan* or *Tien-shan sheep*; so called from a range of mountains in East Turkestan and Turkestan.] A large wild sheep, *Ovis poli*, of high plateaus or mountain regions in central Asia, notable for the great size and spread of the horns of the male. Also called *Pamir sheep* and *Kashgar sheep*; and often spoken of by its Latin scientific name, *Ovis poli* ('sheep of Polo,' from Marco Polo, the 13th century Venetian traveler, in the account of whose travels the animal is described). See cut in next column.

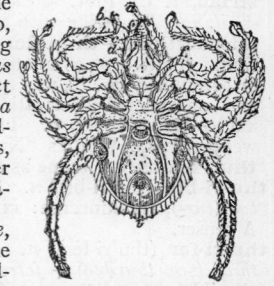

Thyrsus. — From cast of a vase with reliefs, in the Museum of Fine Arts, Boston.

ti-ar (tī′är), *n.* A tiara. [Poetic.]

ti-a-ra (tī-ā′rạ or tę-ā′rạ), *n.*; pl. *-ras* (-rạz). [L., < Gr. τιάρα, Persian tiara.] A raised head-dress or turban worn by the ancient Persians and others; also, a high cylindrical or dome-shaped diadem worn by the Pope, surmounted by the mound (or orb) and cross of sovereignty, and surrounded with three crowns; hence, the papal position or dignity; also, any ornamental coronet or head-band; esp., in modern use, a jeweled ornamental coronet worn by women.—**ti-a′raed** (-rạd), *a.* Adorned with a tiara.

Tian-shan Sheep (*Ovis poli*).

tib-et, thib-et (tib′et or ti-bet′), *n.* [From *Tibet*, in Asia.] A soft, smooth, twilled woolen cloth. Also called *Tibet* (or *Thibet*) *cloth*.

Tib-et-an, Thib-et-an (tib′e-tạn or ti-bet′ạn). **I.** *a.* Of or pertaining to Tibet (in Asia, north of India), its inhabitants, or their language. **II.** *n.* A member of the native (Mongoloid) race of Tibet; also, the (Indo-Chinese) language of Tibet.

tib-i-a (tib′i-ạ), *n.*; pl. *tibiæ* (-ē). [L.] In man, the inner of the two bones of the lower leg, extending from the knee to the ankle, and articulating with the femur and the astragalus; a corresponding bone in the hind limb of other animals; in birds, a bone with tarsal elements at its base, extending from the femur or true thigh to the metatarsus or so-called tarsus; the part of a bird's leg corresponding to the extent of this bone; in insects, the fourth segment or joint of the leg (counting from the proximal end), situated between the femur and the tarsus; also, an ancient variety of flute or flageolet.—**tib′i-al**, *a.*

tic (tik), *n.* [F.: origin uncertain.] In *pathol.*, a local and habitual spasmodic contraction of certain muscles, esp. of the face; esp., tic-douloureux.—**tic=dou-lou-reux** (tik″dö-lö-rö′, F. tēk-dö-lö-rė), *n.* [F. *tic douloureux*, 'painful tic.'] In *pathol.*, severe facial neuralgia accompanied by convulsive twitchings of the facial muscles.

tick[1] (tik), *n.* [ME. *tyke, teke*, akin to D. *teek, tiek*, and G. *zecke*, tick.] Any of various mites or acarids which are parasitic on animals, as those of the genus *Ixodes*, which bury the head in the skin of the host and suck the blood; also, any of various blood-sucking dipters, as *Melophagus ovinus* ('sheep-tick'), a wingless insect infesting sheep, *Hippobosca equina* ('horse-tick'), a blood-sucking fly troublesome to horses, and *Olfersia americana* and other species ('bird-ticks'), flies parasitic on birds.

tick[2] (tik), *n.* [ME. *tykke, teke*, < L. *theca*, case: see *theca*.] The cover or case of a mattress, pillow, etc., containing the hair, feathers, or the like; also, ticking.

tick[3] (tik), *n.* [Abbr. of *ticket*.] Credit or trust (as, to buy on *tick*); also, a score or account. [Colloq.]

tick[4] (tik), *n.* [ME. *tek*, light touch; = D. *tik*, touch, pat, tick (of watch); appar. imit.] A light, quick touch or tap (obs. or prov.); the children's game of tag (now prov.); also, a slight, sharp sound, as that made by a small, hard

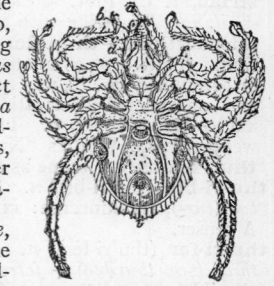

A Tick (*Ixodes ricinus*, female), infesting dogs. — *a*, mandibular hooks; *c*, hooks of sternal surface of proboscis; *b, d, e*, fourth, third, and second joints of the palp; *f*, base of the suctorial proboscis; *g*, stigma; *h*, genital aperture; *i*, anal valves.

body striking upon a hard surface; a recurring click or beat, as of a clock; a moment or instant (colloq.); also, a small dot or mark serving as a check or the like (as, "A tick [was] made against each subscriber in the column for the week": Arnold Bennett's "Clayhanger," i. 13).—**tick**[4], *v.* **I.** *intr.* To touch or tap something lightly (obs. or prov.); also, to emit or produce a tick, like that of a clock; pass as with ticks of a clock (as, "As the hours *ticked* by, the tension increased": L. Merrick's "House of Lynch," xv.). **II.** *tr.* To sound or announce by a tick or ticks; announce or accompany the passing of with ticks (as, "The dark, dreadful minutes *ticked* themselves off": Arnold Bennett's "Old Wives' Tale," ii. 5); also, to mark, note, or check with a tick or ticks (as, "It is a joy to go through booksellers' catalogues, *ticking* here and there a possible purchase": Gissing's "Private Papers of Henry Ryecroft," i. 17).—**tick′er**, *n.* One who or that which ticks; a watch (slang); a telegraphic instrument which automatically prints stock and market reports, etc., on a narrow tape.

tick-et (tik′et), *n.* [F. *étiquette*, ticket, label: see *etiquette*.] A short writing or notice, or a memorandum (now rare); a notice for public information, as a placard (now rare); a written or printed slip of paper, cardboard, etc., affixed to something to indicate its nature, price, or the like; a label or tag; also, a visiting-card (now prov.); also, a slip, usually of paper or cardboard, serving as evidence or token of the holder's title to some service, right, or the like (as, a railroad-*ticket*; an admission-*ticket*); also, an acknowledgment of indebtedness†; a debit account†; also, a list of candidates nominated or put forward by a political party, faction, etc., to be voted for (U. S.); also, with *the*, the correct or proper thing (colloq.: as, that's the *ticket*).—**ticket of leave**, in British use, a permit or license giving a convict his liberty, subject to certain restrictions, before his sentence has expired.—**tick′et**, *v. t.* To attach a ticket to; distinguish by means of a ticket; label; also, to furnish with a ticket, as for travel on a railroad.—**tick′et=chop″per**, *n.* A machine for chopping or mutilating tickets deposited in it, as by passengers entering the gate to a railroad-platform; also, an attendant who operates such a machine. [Colloq.]—**tick′et-er**, *n.*

tick-ing (tik′ing), *n.* A stout cotton or linen fabric, usually twilled, with colored (often blue) stripes, used for bedticks, pillow-coverings, awnings, tents, etc.

tick-le (tik′l), *v.;* -led, -ling. [ME. *tiklen, tikelen,* intr. and tr.: cf. *kittle, v.*] **I.** *intr.* To be affected with a tingling or itching sensation, as from light touches or strokes; also, to be excited agreeably†, or thrill with gratification†; also, to have an impatient or uneasy desire (now rare); also, to produce the sensation of titillation. **II.** *tr.* To touch or stroke lightly, as with the fingers, a feather, etc., so as to excite a tingling or itching sensation (pleasurable or otherwise) in; titillate; poke in some sensitive part of the body so as to excite spasmodic laughter (as, "He would *tickle* him so masterfully under the ribs that the creature howled and became quite hysterical": Du Maurier's "Trilby," ii.); also, to excite agreeably or gratify (as, "a habit of *tickling* thy palate with something strong," R. Graves's "Spiritual Quixote," ii. 5; "He knows how to *tickle* her vanity," Eden Phillpotts's "Red Redmaynes," vi.); excite amusement in (as, "Thinking it was easy to *tickle* him while he continued in this mood, I began making any number of feeble jokes": W. H. Hudson's "Green Mansions," iv.); also, to touch or stir lightly, as a stringed instrument, etc.; sometimes, to beat or chastise; also, to get, move, etc., by or as by tickling.—**tick′le**, *n.* An act of tickling; a tickling sensation; also, a narrow strait, passage, or inlet on the coast of Newfoundland or Labrador. —**tick′le**, *a.* [Cf. *kittle, a.*] Easily affected; uncertain or unreliable; insecure; risky or dangerous (as, "a hornet, *tickle* to the touch": Browning's "Ring and the Book," iv.); delicate, critical, or precarious; fastidious; difficult. [Now chiefly prov.]—**tick′ler**, *n.* One who or that which tickles; a small feather brush used to tickle the faces of others, as at a carnival, etc.; a memorandum-book or the like kept to tickle or jog the memory, as with reference to engagements, payments due, etc.; in *wireless teleg.* and *teleph.*, a tickler-coil.—**tick′ler=coil**, *n.* In *wireless teleg.* and *teleph.*, the coil by which the plate circuit of a vacuum-tube is induc-

tively coupled with the grid circuit in the process of regeneration (see *regeneration*).—**tick′lish**, *a.* Sensitive to tickling; also, unstable or easily upset, as a boat (as, "A canoe is the most *ticklish* of navigable things": H. Melville's "Omoo," xli.); unsteady; also, unsettled or uncertain; also, easily offended; touchy; also, requiring careful handling or action (as, "It's a *ticklish* business, and I must walk very warily": Buchan's "Three Hostages," ix.); delicate; risky or hazardous; difficult.—**tick′lish-ly**, *adv.*—**tick′lish-ness**, *n.*—**tick′ly**, *a.* Ticklish.

tick-seed (tik′sēd), *n.* [See *tick*[1].] Any of various plants having seeds resembling ticks, as a coreopsis or the bug-seed; also, tick-trefoil.—**tickseed sunflower**, any of various species of bur-marigold, esp. *Bidens trichosperma* and *B. coronata*, with conspicuous yellow rays.

tick-tack (tik′tak), *n.* [Imit.: cf. *tick*[4].] An alternating ticking sound, as that made by a clock; the sound of the heart-beat; also, a device for making a ticking or tapping sound, as against a window in playing a practical joke.—**tick=tack=toe′** (-tō′), *n.* A children's game consisting of trying, with the eyes shut, to bring a pencil down upon one of a set of numbers, as on a slate, the number hit being scored; also, the children's game of crisscross (see *crisscross, n.*); also, the practical joke of using a tick-tack.

tick=tre-foil (tik′trē″foil), *n.* [See *tick*[1].] Any of the plants constituting the fabaceous genus *Meibomia*, having trifoliolate leaves and jointed pods with hooked hairs by which they adhere to objects.

tic-po-lon-ga (tik-pō-long′gä), *n.* [E. Ind.] A venomous serpent, *Daboia russelli*, of India and Ceylon.

ti-dal (tī′dal), *a.* Of or pertaining to tides; characterized by tides; flowing and ebbing periodically; hence, periodic or intermittent; alternating or varying; also, dependent on the state of the tide (as, a *tidal* steamer, one whose departure is regulated by the state of the tide).—**tidal wave**, either of the two great wave-like swellings of the ocean surface (due to the attraction of the moon and sun) which move around the globe on opposite sides and give rise to the phenomenon called tide; also, a large destructive ocean wave produced by an earthquake or the like; fig., any widespread or great movement or manifestation of feeling, opinion, or the like (as, a *tidal wave* of popular indignation).—**ti′dal-ly**, *adv.*

tid-bit (tid′bit), *n.* Same as *titbit.*

tide (tīd), *n.* [AS. *tīd*, time, = D. *tijd* = G. *zeit* = Icel. *tīdh*, time: cf. MLG. *getīde, tīde*, time, tide (of the sea), D. *tij*, tide: cf. *time*.] An extent of time, a period, or a season (obs. or prov.); also, a particular point in time (archaic); a suitable or fit time, or the right moment or occasion (archaic or prov.); also, a more or less definite season or period in the course of the year, day, etc. (now chiefly in compounds: as, winter*tide*; noon*tide*); also, an anniversary or festival of the church (chiefly in compounds: as, Christmas*tide*; Whitsun-*tide*); also, time indefinitely (archaic or prov.: chiefly in the alliterative phrase 'time and tide'); also, the periodical rise and fall of the waters of the ocean and its arms, about every 12 hours and 26 minutes, due to the attraction of the moon and sun (see *spring-tide*; *neap*[1], *a.*; *high tide*, under *high, a.*; *low tide*, under *low*[4], *a.*); the inflow, outflow, or current of water resulting from this in any given place; sometimes, the flood-tide; also, any alternate rise and fall, increase and decrease, etc.; fig., something resembling the tide of the sea, as in rising and falling (as, "There is a *tide* in the affairs of men, Which, taken at the flood, leads on to fortune," Shakspere's "Julius Cæsar," iv. 3. 218; "The appearance of Joan of Arc turned the *tide* of war," Hallam's "Europe during the Middle Ages," i. 2); also, a stream or current (lit. or fig.: as, "The front ranges stopped the *tide* of squatters for some little time," S. Butler's "Erewhon," i.); also, the water of the sea (poetic).—**tide**, *v.; tided, tiding.* [Partly < AS. *tīdan*, happen (< *tīd*, time), partly < E. *tide, n.*] **I.** *intr.* To happen or befall (archaic); also, to flow as the tide; flow to and fro; also, to float or drift with the tide; fig., to get (*over*) by some temporary aid or expedient (as, "He struggled to find words to *tide* over what he felt was an awkward moment": W. Churchill's "Coniston," ii. 4); *naut.*, to navigate a ship by taking advantage of the tide and anchoring when it becomes adverse. **II.** *tr.* To carry, as the tide does; carry (a person, etc.) over a difficulty, a period of distress, or the like, as a temporary aid or expedient does (as, "She suggested that she should bring one of her own servants to '*tide* Constance over' Christmas": Arnold Bennett's "Old Wives' Tale," ii. 2).—**tid-ed** (tī′ded), *a.* Having tides: as, "I see . . . The *tided* oceans ebb and flow" (Whittier's "Questions of Life").—**tide′=less**, *a.* Having no tide; without flow and ebb.—**tide′=rip**, *n.* [See *rip*³.] A heavy wave or current in water, due to opposing tides or currents.—**tide′wait″er**, *n.* Formerly, a customs officer who awaited the arrival of ships (coming in with the tide) and boarded them to prevent violation of the customs regulations.—**tide′=wa″ter**, *n.* Water affected by the ordinary flow and ebb of the tide.—**tide′way**, *n.* A channel in which a tidal current runs; also, a current running in such a channel.

ti-di-er (tī′di-ėr), *n.* One who tidies: as, "a most serviceable cleaner and *tidier* of things" (H. G. Wells's "Bealby," iii.).

ti-di-ly (tī′di-li), *adv.* In a tidy manner.—**ti′di-ness**, *n.*

ti-ding (tī′ding), *n.* [AS. *tīdung*, prob. from Scand.: cf. Icel. *tīdhindi*, pl., happenings, tidings, news, also E. *tide*, *v.*] An event or occurrence (archaic); also, in *sing.*, the announcement of an event or occurrence not previously made known (archaic); in *pl.* (sometimes construed as *sing.*), news, information, or intelligence (as, "The *tidings* were communicated to Mrs. Rainscourt," Marryat's "King's Own," xxxix.; "The *tidings* comes that they are all arrived," Shakspere's "King John," iv. 2. 115).

ti-dy (tī′di). [From *tide*, *n.*] **I.** *a.*; compar. *tidier*, superl. *tidiest.* Timely† or seasonable†; also, in good condition, or of good appearance (now prov.); also, good† or excellent†; moderately or fairly satisfactory (colloq.); considerable (colloq.: as, a *tidy* sum; "It's a *tidy* bit draughty here," Arnold Bennett's "Helen with the High Hand," xiv.); also, given to keeping things or the dress, etc., neat and in order (as, a *tidy* woman); in neat condition, neat, or trim (as, a *tidy* room; *tidy* dress; "When she saw me come in *tidy* and well-dressed, she even smiled," C. Brontë's "Jane Eyre," xxix.). **II.** *n.*; pl. *-dies* (-diz). Any of various articles for keeping things tidy; esp., a more or less ornamental covering for protecting the back of a chair, etc.—**ti′dy**, *v. t.* or *i.*; *tidied*, *tidying.* To make (a room, the hair or dress, one's self, etc.) tidy or neat: often with *up*: as, "Bessie faithfully *tidied* up the studio" (Kipling's "Light That Failed," xi.); "He would have liked to linger on, watching her *tidy* up" (Mrs. Wharton's "Ethan Frome," iv.).

tie (tī), *v. t.*; *tied*, *tying.* [AS. *tīgan*, < *tēag*, band, rope, from the root of *tēon*, draw: see *tow*⁴.] To bind or make fast with a cord, string, or the like drawn together and knotted, as one thing to another or two things together; draw together the parts of with a knotted string or the like (as, to *tie* a bundle); fasten by tightening and knotting the string or strings of (as, to *tie* one's shoes); also, to draw together into a knot, as a cord; form by looping and interlacing, as a knot; also, to fasten, join, or connect in any way; bind or join closely or firmly; unite in marriage (colloq.); also, to restrain or constrain; confine, restrict, or limit (as, "He would not like to be *tied* to a single locality": S. Butler's "Way of All Flesh," lxxxvi.); bind or oblige, as to do something; also, to make the same score as, or equal in a contest (as, Harvard *tied* Yale in football); in *surg.*, to bind and constrict (an artery or vein) with a ligature; in *building*, to bind together or connect by means of a piece of timber or metal; in *music*, to connect (notes) by the curved line called a 'tie'; in *railroading*, to furnish (a road-bed, etc.) with ties or sleepers.— **to tie down**, to fasten down by tying; fig., to hinder from free action; confine stringently, as to some thing or action (as, "if I were to be *tied down* to one word for my impression of this war": H. G. Wells's "Italy, France, and Britain at War," i.).—**to tie up**, to fasten securely by tying; bind or wrap up; fig., to hinder from free action; bring to a stop or pause, as industry or traffic; often, to invest or place (money) in such a way as to render unavailable; place (property) under such conditions or restrictions as to prevent sale or alienation.—**tie**, *v. i.* To make a tie, bond, or connection; attach one's self to something (as, "He's one I'd like to *tie* to": W. Churchill's "Mr. Crewe's Career," viii.); also, to become tied; also, to make the same score; be equal in a contest.—**tie**, *n.* That with which anything is tied; a cord,

string, or the like, used for tying or fastening something; also, a knot composed of one or more loops of cord, string, etc.; an ornamental knot, as of ribbon; also, a necktie or cravat; also, a low shoe fastened with a lace (as, Oxford *ties*); also, anything, as a beam, rod, etc., connecting or holding together two or more things or parts; also, fig., anything that makes fast or secures; any uniting principle or bond of union (as, a *tie* of blood); a link or connection; a restraint or constraint; also, the act or method of tying, or the state of being tied; also, a state of equality in points, votes, etc., as among competitors (as, the match or the vote ended in a *tie*); a match or contest in which this occurs; in *music*, a curved line placed above or below two notes on the same degree to indicate that the sound is to be sustained, not repeated; in *railroading*, one of the transverse beams, commonly of wood, to which the rails that form a railroad-track are fastened; a sleeper.—**tie′=beam**, *n.* A timber or piece serving as a tie; esp., a horizontal beam connecting the lower ends of two opposite principal rafters, thus forming the base of a roof-truss.

tie-mann-ite (tē′man-īt), *n.* [G. *tiemannit*; named from W. *Tiemann*, who discovered it.] A mineral, a native selenide of mercury, HgSe, occurring usually in dark-gray masses of metallic luster.

Tien=shan (tien′shän′) **sheep.** See *Tian-shan* sheep.

ti-er¹ (tī′ėr), *n.* One who or that which ties; something used for tying; also, a child's apron or pinafore (U. S.).

tier² (tēr), *n.* [F. *tire*, a drawing, pull, continuous stretch, row, < *tirer*, draw: see *tire*¹, *v.*, and cf. *tire*¹, *n.*] A row, range, or rank; esp., one of a series of rows or ranks rising one behind or above another, as of seats in an amphitheater, of boxes in a theater, of guns in a man-of-war, or of oars in an ancient galley; one of a number of galleries, as in a theater. —**tier**², *v.* **I.** *tr.* To arrange in tiers. **II.** *intr.* To rise in tiers: as, "You'll see her *tiering* canvas in sheeted silver spread" (Kipling's "Three-Decker").

tierce (tērs), *n.* [OF. F. *tierce*, fem. of *tiers*, third, < L. *tertius*, third, ordinal of *tres*, three.] A third† or third part†; also, an old measure of capacity equivalent to one third of a pipe, or 42 wine-gallons; a cask or vessel holding this quantity; *eccles.*, same as *terce*; in *fencing*, the third of a series of eight parries (as, "the secret *tierce* of Coulon, the fencing-master": Bulwer-Lytton's "Caxtons," viii. 2); in *card-playing*, a sequence of three cards.

tiered (tērd), *a.* Arranged in tiers: as, "a three-*tiered* cake-stand displaying assorted cakes" (H. G. Wells's "Tono-Bungay," ii. 2. § 6).

tiers é-tat (tyär-zā-tä). [F.] The third estate; the commons, esp. of France before the Revolution.

tie=up (tī′up), *n.* A stoppage of business, transportation, etc., on account of a strike, storm, accident, etc.

tiff¹ (tif), *n.* [Origin obscure.] Liquor, esp. when poor or weak; a small draft of liquor. [Colloq. or prov.]—**tiff**¹, *v. t.* To drink, esp. in small portions. [Colloq. or prov.]

tiff² (tif), *n.* [Origin obscure.] A slight fit of ill humor; also, a slight or petty quarrel (as, "a boy and a girl . . . having a bit of a *tiff*": Arnold Bennett's "Roll-Call," vii.).— **tiff**², *v. i.* To be in a tiff; also, to have a petty quarrel.

tif-fa-ny (tif′a-ni), *n.*; pl. *-nies* (-niz). [Appar. < OF. *Tiphanie*, the Epiphany, < LL. *theophania*, E. *theophany*.] A thin, transparent silk fabric formerly in use; also, a gauzy muslin.

tif-fin (tif′in), *n.* [Appar. for *tiffing*, < *tiff*¹.] Luncheon; a lunch. [Anglo-Ind.]

tig (tig), *v.*; *tigged, tigging.* [Cf. *tick*⁴.] **I.** *intr.* To give light or playful touches; trifle or dally; also, to interfere or meddle. [Sc. and north. Eng.] **II.** *tr.* To touch in the game of tig or tag.—**tig**, *n.* A touch or tap (Sc. and north. Eng.); also, the children's game of tag.

ti-ger (tī′gėr), *n.* [OF. F. *tigre*, < L. *tigris*, < Gr. τίγρις, tiger.] A large, carnivorous feline quadruped, *Felis tigris*, of Asia, of a tawny color striped with black (see cut on next page); also, one who or that which resembles or suggests a tiger, as in fierceness, courage, etc. (as, Clemenceau, the *Tiger* of France); also, a boy in smart livery acting as groom or footman (colloq.); also, an additional cheer or cry (often the word *tiger*) at the end of a round of cheering (colloq., U. S.: as, three cheers and a *tiger*).—**blind tiger.** See under *blind, a.*—**ti′ger=cat,** *n.* Any of various feline quadrupeds smaller than the tiger, but resembling it in markings or ferocity, as the margay, ocelot, etc.—**ti′ger= eye,** *n.* Same as *tiger′s- eye.*—**ti′- ger=flow″er,** *n.* Any of the plants consti- tuting the iridaceous genus *Tigri- dia,* as *T. pavonia,* a showy-flow- ered garden- plant: so named from the spotted or variegated flowers.—**ti′- ger-ish,** *a.* Tiger-like; fiercely cruel; bloodthirsty;

Tiger.

relentless.—**ti′ger=lil″y,** *n.* A lily, *Lilium tigrinum,* with flowers of a dull-orange color spotted with black, and small bulbs or bulbils in the axils of the leaves.—**ti′ger=moth,** *n.* Any of a group of moths (family *Arctiidæ*), many of which have conspicuously spotted or striped wings.—**ti′ger′s=eye,** *n.* A golden-brown chatoyant stone used for ornament, formed by the alteration of crocidolite, and consisting essen- tially of quartz colored by iron oxide.

tight (tīt), *a.* [ME. *tight,* appar. a var. of *thight, thyht,* dense, solid, prob. from Scand.: cf. Icel. *thèttr,* tight, water-tight, close, Sw. *tät,* Dan. *tæt,* also D. and G. *dicht,* tight, close, dense.] Of such close or compacted texture, or fitted to- gether so closely, as to be impervious to water, air, steam, etc. (often in comp.: as, water-*tight*; air-*tight*); specif., well- calked, as a ship; also, competent, capable, or skilful, as a person (now prov.); neat, tidy, or trim, or neatly or well built or made (archaic or prov.: as, "She's a *tight,* hardy girl," Synge's "Tinker's Wedding," ii.); also, firmly or closely fixed in place, not easily moved, or secure (as, a *tight* bolt; a *tight* knot); drawn or stretched so as to be tense, or taut (as, a *tight* rope, on which acrobats perform feats of balancing at a distance above the ground); fitting closely, esp. too closely (as, "*tight* trousers," W. De Morgan's "Alice-for- Short," viii.; "The *tight* dress gave her a side-ache," Louisa M. Alcott's "Little Women," i. 9); difficult to deal with or manage (as, to be in a *tight* place); close, or nearly even (colloq.: as, a *tight* race); close-fisted, stingy, or parsimoni- ous (colloq.); drunk or tipsy (slang: as, "Abner hasn't been *tight* since last 'lection," Bret Harte's "Idyl of Red Gulch"); in *com.,* of a commodity, difficult to obtain; much in demand; of the market, characterized by scarcity or eager demand.— **tight,** *adv.* In a tight manner; closely; firmly; securely; tensely: as, "the child had taken the silver coin . . . clasp- ing it *tight*" (W. B. Maxwell's "In Cotton Wool," v.); "He . . . shut his lips *tight*" (J. Conrad's "Lord Jim," xiv.).— **to sit tight.** See under *sit, v. i.*—**tight′en,** *v. t.* or *i.* To make or become tight or tighter.—**tight′en-er,** *n.*—**tight′= fist′ed,** *a.* Close-fisted; parsimonious: as, "too *tight- fisted* to spend a few dollars" (Sinclair Lewis's "Main Street," xi.).—**tight′=laced,** *a.* Tightly laced; strait- laced.—**tight′ly,** *adv.*—**tight′ness,** *n.*—**tights,** *n. pl.* A garment of close-fitting elastic material covering the lower part of the body and the legs, or sometimes the whole body, worn esp. by dancers, acrobats, gymnasts, etc., as for per- mitting free movement or displaying the form.—**tight′wad,** *n.* One who holds tightly to his 'wad' or money; a close- fisted or stingy person: as, "I don't want to be a *tightwad*

but after all, a dollar is a dollar" (Sinclair Lewis's "Arrow- smith," xiv.). [Slang.]

tig-lic (tig′lik), *a.* [NL. *tiglium* in *Croton tiglium,* the croton-oil plant.] In *chem.,* noting or pertaining to a crystal- line organic acid obtained from croton-oil, etc. Also **tig- lin′ic** (-lin′ik).

ti-gress (tī′gres), *n.* A female tiger.

ti-grine (tī′grin), *a.* [L. *tigrinus.*] Tiger-like, esp. in color- ing or marking.

ti-grish (tī′grish), *a.* Same as *tigerish.*

tike, tyke (tīk), *n.* [Cf. Icel. *tīk,* bitch.] A dog, esp. a low- bred dog or a cur; also, a low, contemptible fellow; a boor; also, a mischievous or troublesome child. [Now chiefly prov.]

til (til or tēl), *n.* [Hind.] The plant sesame.

til-bu-ry (til′bẹ-ri), *n.*; pl. *-ries* (-riz). [From the name of the inventor.] A light two-wheeled carriage without a top or cover.

til-de (til′de, Sp. tēl′dā), *n.* [Sp., < ML. *titulus:* see *title*[1].] A diacritical mark (~) placed over the letter *n* in Spanish, to indicate the mouillé sound of *n* (or that of *n* followed by *y*), as in *cañón* (pronounced kä-nyōn′).

tile (tīl), *n.* [AS. *tigele, tigule,* < L. *tegula,* tile, < *tegere,* cover: see *thatch.*] A thin slab, plate, or shaped piece of baked clay, sometimes glazed and ornamented, used for covering roofs, lining walls, pav- ing floors, draining land, in or- namental work, etc.; any of vari- ous similar slabs or pieces, as of stone or metal; also, the material of which clay tiles are made; tiles collec- tively; also, a hat, esp. a stiff hat or a high silk hat (slang). —**tile,** *v. t.; tiled, tiling.* To cover with or as with tiles

Figured Tiles as applied to a Fireplace.

(as, "the *tiled* hall": Archibald Marshall's "Anthony Dare," ii.); also (often spelled *tyle*), to guard (a masonic lodge or meeting) from intrusion, so as to keep the proceedings secret; hence, to bind to strict secrecy; keep strictly secret.—**tile′= fish,** *n.* A large, brilliantly colored food-fish, *Lopholati- lus chamæleonticeps,* of the Atlantic.— **til-er** (tī′lẽr), *n.* One who makes or lays tiles; also (often spelled *tyler*), the doorkeeper of a ma- sonic lodge.—**til′er-y** (-i), *n.*; pl. *-ies* (-iz). A place where tiles are made.

Tile-fish.

til-i-a-ceous (til-i-ā′shius), *a.* [LL. *tiliaceus,* < L. *tilia,* linden.] Belonging to the *Tiliaceæ,* or linden family of plants.

til-ing (tī′ling), *n.* The operation of covering with or as with tiles; also, work consisting of tiles; tiles collectively.

till[1] (til). [AS. (Northumbrian) *til,* from Scand.: cf. Icel. *til,* Sw. *till,* Norw. and Dan. *til,* to, till, also G. *ziel,* limit, end, goal, *zielen,* to aim, and E. *till*[4].] **I.** *prep.* To or unto (now only Sc. and north. Eng.); also, onward to (a specified time: as, "*Till* evening, the wind whistled above our heads," Gissing's "Private Papers of Henry Ryecroft," iii. 3); up to the time of, or until (as, "Fight *till* the last gasp": Shakspere's "1 Henry VI.," i. 2. 127); with negatives, before (as, he did not come *till* evening). **II.** *conj.* To the time that or when, or until (as, "I stay here *till* all my horses are sold": Kipling's "Kim," x.); with negatives, before (as, "The brig . . . did not appear in sight of the shallows *till* the morning was far advanced": J. Conrad's "Rescue," ii. 1).

till² (til), *n.* [ME. *tylle*; origin uncertain.] A compartment in the form of a drawer, tray, or the like, as in a cabinet or chest, for keeping valuables, etc. (as, "When I came to the *till* in the chest, I found there three great bags of pieces of eight": Defoe's "Robinson Crusoe," i. 13); now, specif., a drawer or the like under the back of a counter, as in a shop, in which cash for daily transactions is kept.

till³ (til), *n.* [Origin obscure.] A stiff clay; in *geol.*, glacial drift consisting of clay, gravel, and boulders.

till⁴ (til), *v.* [AS. *tilian*, strive for, labor on, till, = D. *telen*, cultivate, breed, = G. *zielen*, aim: cf. *till¹*.] **I.** *tr.* To labor for†; procure by exertion†; obtain†; also, to bestow labor, as plowing, harrowing, etc., upon (land) for the raising of crops; cultivate; specif., to plow; also, to set or prepare, as a trap (now only prov.). **II.** *intr.* To strive† or labor†; also, to cultivate the soil.—**till'a-ble,** *a.* Capable of being tilled; arable.—**till'age** (-āj), *n.* The operation, practice, or art of tilling land; the state of being tilled; also, tilled land, or the crops growing on it.

til-land-si-a (ti-land'zi-ä), *n.* [NL.; named from E. *Tillands*, 17th century botanist in Finland.] Any of the tropical and subtropical American plants constituting the bromeliaceous genus *Tillandsia*, most of which are epiphytic on trees, as Florida moss, *T. usneoides*, which hangs from the branches of trees in long tufts.

till-er¹ (til'ér), *n.* One who tills; a husbandman.

til-ler² (til'ér), *n.* [OF. *telier*, tiller of a crossbow, orig. weaver's beam, < ML. *telarium*, < L. *tela*, web: see *toil¹*.] The stock of a crossbow†; *naut.*, a bar or lever fitted to the head of a rudder, to turn the rudder in steering.

til-ler³ (til'ér), *n.* [Cf. AS. *telgor*, shoot, twig, *telga*, branch, bough.] A shoot of a plant which springs from the root or bottom of the original stalk; also, a sapling.—**til'ler³,** *v. i.* Of a plant, to put forth new shoots from the root, or round the bottom of the original stalk.

til-ly=seed (til'i-sēd), *n.* [F. *tilli*, < NL. *tiglium*: see *tiglic*.] The seed of the croton-oil plant, *Croton tiglium*.

til-ly=val-ly (til'i-val'i), *interj.* [Origin obscure.] Nonsense! bosh! [Obs. or archaic.]

tilt¹ (tilt), *n.* [ME. *telt, teld,* < AS. *teld* = G. *zelt*, tent.] A cover of coarse cloth, canvas, etc., as for a cart or wagon; an awning; a tent or booth; a hut.—**tilt¹,** *v. t.* To furnish with a tilt, cover, or awning.

tilt² (tilt), *v.* [ME. *tylten,* < AS. *tealt,* unsteady.] **I.** *tr.* To cause to fall†; also, to cause to lean or incline from the vertical or horizontal (as, "Peyrol laughed quite loud, *tilting* his head back": J. Conrad's "Rover," xiv.); to pour or slant; also, to cause (contents) to flow out or to one side by inclining a vessel; also, to hold poised for attack, as a lance; also, to rush at or charge, as in a just; also, to hammer or forge with a tilt-hammer. **II.** *intr.* To move unsteadily up and down, as a ship or waves; also, to move into or assume a sloping position or direction (as, "Parker *tilted* far back in his chair": Tarkington's "Gentleman from Indiana," xiii.); also, to engage in a just, tournament, or similar contest; hence, in general, to engage in a contest; combat; contend; also, to strike, thrust, or charge (*at*) with or as if with a lance or the like; also, to rush (*in, out, along,* etc.): colloq.: as, "this butcher's boy, *tilting* along through the crowd with a half-staggering run," Howells's "Chance Acquaintance," iv.).—**tilt²,** *n.* The act of tilting, or the state of being tilted; a sloping position; a slope; also, a tilt-hammer; also, a just, or some similar contest; also, the exercise of riding with a lance or the like at a mark; also, any encounter, combat, or contest; a dispute; also, a thrust of a weapon, as at a tilt or just (often fig.); also, a place for holding tilts or justs.—**full tilt,** at full speed and with direct thrust; with direct and full force.—**tilt'=cart,** *n.* A tipcart.—**tilt'er,** *n.*

tilth (tilth), *n.* [AS. *tilth,* < *tilian,* E. *till⁴*.] The act or operation of tilling; tillage; cultivation; the state of being tilled (as, land in good or bad *tilth*); also, tilled land; land under cultivation; also, the depth of soil turned by the plow or spade in cultivation; also, crop† or produce†.

tilt=ham-mer (tilt'ham"ér), *n.* [See *tilt²*.] A hammer used in forging, etc., consisting of a heavy head at one end of a pivoted lever, the lever and head being tilted up by power and allowed to drop alternately.

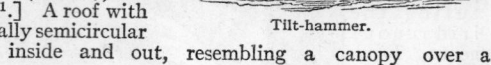

Tilt-hammer.

tilt=roof (tilt'röf), *n.* [See *tilt¹*.] A roof with a generally semicircular section inside and out, resembling a canopy over a wagon.

tilt=yard (tilt'yärd), *n.* A yard or inclosed space for tilting.

ti-ma-rau (tē-mä-rou'), *n.* [Philippine.] A small, sturdy buffalo, *Bos mindorensis,* of the island of Mindoro, one of the Philippine Islands, having thick brown hair and short, massive horns.

tim-bal (tim'bạl), *n.* [F. *timbale,* for earlier *attabale,* Moorish drum, = E. *atabal.*] A kettledrum; in *entom.,* a vibrating membrane, resembling a drumhead, in certain insects, as the cicada, by means of which a shrill chirring sound is produced.

tim-bale (taṅ-bál), *n.* [F., lit. 'kettledrum': see *timbal.*] A preparation of minced meat, fish, or other food, often inclosed in paste, cooked in a mold.

tim-ber¹ (tim'bér), *n.*; pl. *timbers* or (as after a numeral) *timber.* [OF. F. *timbre,* appar. from LG., and perhaps the same word as E. *timber²,* with reference orig. to the boards between which skins were put up in packages.] A certain number of fur-skins, being 40 of some animals, as martens, sables, and ermines, and 120 of others.

tim-ber² (tim'bér). [AS. *timber,* a building, edifice, building material, timber, = MLG. *timber,* timber, = D. *timmer,* G. *zimmer,* room, = Icel. *timbr,* timber, akin to Goth. *timrjan,* build, L. *domus,* build, Gr. δόμος, Skt. *dama,* house, Gr. δέμειν, build.] **I.** *n.* A building†; also, building material†; now, wood suitable for building houses, ships, etc., or for use in carpentry, joinery, etc.; wood in general, esp. after it has been suitably trimmed or prepared for use; also, the wood of growing trees suitable for structural uses; growing trees themselves (as, "a well-watered land of small *timber*": Roosevelt's "Winning of the West," i. 3); hence, wooded land; also, something composed wholly or chiefly of wood, as a wicket in cricket; also, a single beam or piece of wood forming, or capable of forming, part of a structure; also, fig., bodily structure or build; personal character or quality; *naut.,* in a ship's frame, one of the curved pieces of wood which spring upward and outward from the keel; a rib. **II.** *a.* Made or consisting of wood; wooden.—**tim'ber²,** *v. t.* [AS. *timbran, timbrian.*] To build (obs. or archaic); also, to furnish with timber; support with timber.—**tim'ber=cruis"er,** *n.* In *forestry,* one who cruises timber. See *cruise, v.*—**tim'bered,** *p. a.* Built or formed (obs. or archaic); also, made of or furnished with timber; also, covered with growing trees, or wooded (as, "the *timbered* slopes of the Rockies": Roosevelt's "Ranch Life and the Hunting-Trail," xii.).—**tim'ber=head,** *n. Naut.,* the top end of a timber, rising above the deck, and serving for belaying ropes, etc.—**tim'ber=hitch,** *n. Naut.,* a kind of hitch by which a rope is fastened round a spar.—**tim'ber-ing,** *n.* Building material of wood; timbers collectively; timber-work.—**tim'ber=line,** *n.* The elevation above sealevel at which timber ceases to grow.—**tim'ber=tree,** *n.* A tree yielding timber, or wood suitable for building or construction.—**tim'ber=wolf,** *n.* The ordinary large gray or brindled wolf, *Canis lupus occidentalis* (or *Canis occidentalis*), of western North America.—**tim'ber=work,** *n.* Work formed of timbers.

tim-bre (tim'bér, F. taṅbr), *n.* [F., bell sounded by stroke of hammer, quality of sound, OF. kind of tambourine, < L. *tympanum:* see *tympanum.*] In *acoustics,* that characteristic quality of sounds produced from some particular source, as from a voice or an instrument, by which they are distinguished from sounds from other sources, as from other voices or other instruments.

tim-brel (tim′brel), *n.* [Dim. of ME. *timbre*, < OF. *timbre*, kind of tambourine: see *timbre*.] A tambourine or similar instrument.—**tim′brel**, *v. t.*; *-breled* or *-brelled*, *-breling* or *-brelling.* To accompany with a timbrel.

time (tīm), *n.* [AS. *tīma* = Icel. *tīmi*, time, = Sw. *timme*, Dan. *time*, hour; akin to E. *tide*.] The system of those relations which any event has to any other as past, present, or future; indefinite continuous duration regarded as that in which events succeed one another; [*cap.*] the personification of time as an old man, bald-headed but having a forelock, and carrying a scythe and an hour-glass (also called 'Father Time'); also [*l. c.*], duration regarded as belonging to the present life as distinct from the life to come, or from eternity; also, a system or method of measuring or reckoning the passage of time (see phrases below); also, a limited extent of time, as between two successive events (as, a long *time*; a short *time*); a particular period considered as distinct from other periods (as, for the *time* being); a period in the history of the world, or contemporary with the life or activities of a notable person (often in *pl.*: as, in ancient *times*; in the *times* of the Stuarts); the period or era now (or then) present (often in *pl.*: as, "the baser tendencies of the *time*," Gissing's "Private Papers of Henry Ryecroft," iv. 13; "the faithless coldness of the *times*," Tennyson's "In Memoriam," cvi.); a period considered with reference to its events or prevailing conditions, tendencies, ideas, etc. (often in *pl.*: as, "A new *time* is coming . . . Those popular commotions are all over," J. H. Newman's "Callista," xxii.; hard *times*: *times* have changed); a period with reference to personal experience of a specified kind (as, to have a good *time*); a prescribed or allotted term or period, as of one's life, of apprenticeship, etc. (as, "One man in his *time* plays many parts," Shakspere's "As You Like It," ii. 7. 142; to serve one's *time* at a trade); a term of imprisonment (colloq.: as, to do *time*); the period necessary for or occupied by something (as, to ask for *time* to consider); leisure or spare time (as, to have no *time*); a period allowed, as for payment; a period of work of an employee, or the pay for it (as, "Pay was due him — '*time*,' as it was called": Wister's "Virginian," xvii.); also, a particular or definite point in time (as, what *time* is it?); a particular part of a year, day, etc. (as, spring*time*; bed*time*); an appointed, fit, due, or proper time (as, an hour behind *time*; there is a *time* for everything); the right moment, occasion, or opportunity (as, to watch one's *time*); also, each occasion of a recurring action or event (as, "an utter aversion to speaking to more than one man at a *time*," Steele, in "Spectator," 422; to do a thing five *times*); also, used as a multiplicative word in phrasal combinations expressing how many instances of a quantity or factor are taken together (as, four *times* five; six *times* as many; many *times* as much); in *music*, etc., the arrangement of the successive beats or uniform time-units of a piece of music into equal bars or measures, each kind of measure employed in music containing a certain number of these beats or time-units (aliquot parts of a semibreve), as two ('duple time'), three ('triple time'), four ('quadruple time,' a compound form of duple time), six ('sextuple time,' a compound form of duple or of triple time), etc. (the varieties with two or, esp., four such units to the measure, and esp. that with four crotchets to the measure, being called 'common time'); the movement of a dance or the like to music so arranged; also, the metrical duration of a note or rest; also, tempo, or relative rapidity of movement; proper or characteristic tempo; hence, the general movement of a particular kind of musical composition with reference to its rhythm, metrical structure, and tempo; in *pros.*, a unit or a group of units in the measurement of meter; *milit.*, rate of marching, calculated on the number of paces taken per minute (as, double *time*: see under *double, a.*).—**apparent solar time,** the measure of the day by the apparent positions of the sun, usually determined by the apparent noon, or the instant of passage of the sun's center over the meridian.—**apparent time,** apparent solar time.—**astronomical time.** See under *astronomical.*—**at times,** at intervals; occasionally.—

central time, eastern time. See *standard time*, under *standard, a.*—**from time to time,** at intervals; now and then; occasionally.—**in time,** soon or early enough; not too late; also, in the course of events; eventually.—**mean solar time,** time measured by the mean sun; a system of reckoning time such that all the days and their like subdivisions are of equal length, the day being the mean interval between the two successive passages of the sun over the meridian of any place.—**mean time,** mean solar time.—**mountain time.** See *standard time*, under *standard, a.*—**on time,** punctually or punctual.—**Pacific time.** See *standard time*, under *standard, a.*—**sidereal time.** See *sidereal.*—**standard time.** See under *standard, a.*—**time and again,** with frequent recurrence; repeatedly.—**time immemorial,** a time extending or dating back beyond memory or record, in *law*, beyond legal memory, fixed by English statute as beyond the beginning of the reign of Richard I. (1189).—**time measure,** a system of units used in measuring time: commonly, 60 seconds = 1 minute; 60 minutes = 1 hour; 24 hours = 1 day; 7 days = 1 week; 4 weeks, 30 days, or 28, 29, 30, or 31 days = 1 month; 12 months, or 365 or 366 days = 1 year; 100 years = 1 century.—**time out of mind,** during a period or since a time beyond memory, or beyond record: as, "The barber's shop in a country town has been, *time out of mind*, the grand office of intelligence" (R. Graves's "Spiritual Quixote," iii. 3). Cf. *time immemorial*, above.—**to keep time.** See under *keep, v. t.*—**time, v.**; *timed, timing.* **I.** *tr.* To appoint the time of, or choose the moment or occasion for (as, "He had *timed* all his treacheries so well that . . . his fortunes had constantly been rising": Macaulay's "Hist. of Eng.," ii.); also, to regulate as to time, as a train, a clock, etc.; also, to mark the rhythm or measure of, as in music; also, to fix the duration of (as, to *time* an exposure in photography); also, to ascertain or record the time, duration, or rate of (as, to *time* a race). **II.** *intr.* To keep time; sound or move in unison or harmony.

time=clock (tīm′klok), *n.* A clock with an attachment by which a record may be made of the time of something, as of the arrival and departure of employees.

time=hon-ored (tīm′on″ọrd), *a.* Honored by reason of length of time; revered or respected because of antiquity and long continuance: as, a *time-honored* custom; "the *time-honoured* pretensions of priest-craft" (W. R. Inge's "Outspoken Essays," i. 11).

time-keep-er (tīm′kē″pėr), *n.* One who or that which keeps time; one who records time of occurrence or time occupied; a person employed to keep account of the hours of work done by others; one who beats time in music; a timepiece.

time-less (tīm′les), *a.* Untimely or unseasonable (archaic); also, not subject to time, eternal, or unending (as, "*timeless* night and chaos": Young's "Night Thoughts," ii. 222); also, referring to no particular time.

time-lock (tīm′lok), *n.* A lock controlled by clockwork so that when locked it cannot be unlocked before the expiration of a certain interval of time.

time-ly (tīm′li), *a.*; compar. *timelier*, superl. *timeliest.* Being in good time, or early (now rare); also, occurring at a fitting or suitable time, or seasonable, opportune, or well-timed (as, "a *timely* warning," J. Conrad's "Lord Jim," xxxviii.; "a *timely* escape," Jane Porter's "Scottish Chiefs," liv.).—**time′li-ness,** *n.*—**time′ly,** *adv.* Early or soon (now rare); also, seasonably or opportunely.

time-ous, tim-ous (tī′mus), *a.* [From *time* + *-ous.*] Early; also, seasonable; timely. [Chiefly Sc.]

time-piece (tīm′pēs), *n.* An apparatus for measuring and recording the progress of time; a chronometer; a clock or a watch.

time=pleas-er (tīm′plē″zėr), *n.* A time-server.

tim-er (tī′mėr), *n.* One who or that which times; esp., one who measures or records time; a timekeeper; a device for indicating or recording time or intervals of time, as a stop-watch; in an internal-combustion engine, an automatic device which causes the spark for igniting the charge to occur at the instant required.

time=serv-er (tīm′sėr″vėr), *n.* One who adapts his conduct to the time or season; esp., one who meanly and for selfish ends shapes his conduct to conform with the opinions of the time or of persons in power (as, "the Puritan . . . deserted by all the *timeservers* who, in his prosperity, had claimed brotherhood with him": Macaulay's "Hist. of Eng.," ii.). —**time′=serv″ing**, *n.* and *a.*

time=spir-it (tīm′spir″it), *n.* [Tr. G. *zeitgeist*.] The spirit of the time or period; the zeitgeist.

time=ta-ble (tīm′tā″bl), *n.* A table or schedule showing the times at which or within which certain things are to be done or to take place; esp., one showing the times at which the trains on a railroad arrive at and depart from the stations.

time=worn (tīm′wôrn), *a.* Worn or impaired by time; showing the ravages or adverse effects of time: as, *time-worn* buildings; "his large, handsome and yet *time-worn* face" (Arnold Bennett's "Hilda Lessways," v. 1).

tim-id (tim′id), *a.* [L. *timidus*, < *timere*, to fear.] Subject to fear, as a person, etc.; easily alarmed; timorous; shy; characterized by or indicating fear (as, "the *timid* advances of a vagabond yellow dog": Bret Harte's "Romance of Madroño Hollow").—**ti-mid-i-ty** (ti-mid′i-ti), **tim′id-ness**, *n.*—**tim′id-ly**, *adv.*

tim-ist (tī′mist), *n.* A time-server†; in *music*, a performer considered with reference to his ability to keep correct time.

ti-moc-ra-cy (tī-mok′ra̤-si), *n.*: pl. *-cies* (-siz). [= F. *timocratie*, < Gr. τιμοκρατία, < τιμή, honor, valuation, + κρατεῖν, rule.] A form of government in which love of honor is the dominant motive of the rulers; also, a form of government in which a certain amount of property is requisite as a qualification for office.—**ti-mo-crat′ic** (-mō-krat′ik), *a.*

Ti-mon (tī′mọn), *n.* [From *Timon* of Athens, in Shakspere's play of that name.] A misanthrope.

tim-o-rous (tim′ọ-rus), *a.* [ML. *timorosus*, < L. *timor*, fear, < *timere*, to fear.] Full of fear, or fearful (as, "He . . . was rather *timorous* of venturing on Joe": Dickens's "Barnaby Rudge," lxxii.); subject to fear, or timid (as, "I am such a faint-hearted, *timorous* creature!" Smollett's "Humphry Clinker," Oct. 4); characterized by or indicating fear (as, "George Cannon had an overwhelming answer to all *timorous* objections": Arnold Bennett's "Hilda Lessways," i. 11).—**tim′o-rous-ly**, *adv.*—**tim′o-rous-ness**, *n.*

tim-o-thy (tim′ọ-thi), *n.* [From *Timothy* Hanson, who is said to have carried the seed from New York to the Carolinas about 1720.] A coarse grass, *Phleum pratense*, with cylindrical spikes, valuable as fodder. Also **tim′o-thy=grass.**

tim-ous (tī′mus), *a.* See *timeous*.

tim-pa-no (tim′pa̤-nō), *n.*; pl. *-ni* (-nē). [It., < L. *tympanum*: see *tympanum*.] An orchestral kettledrum: usually in *pl.*

tin (tin). [AS. *tin* = D. *tin* = G. *zinn* = Icel. and Dan. *tin* = Sw. *tenn*, tin.] **I.** *n.* Chem. sym., Sn (see *stannum*); at. wt., 118.7; sp. gr., 7.3. A metallic element nearly approaching silver in color and luster, used in making alloys and in plating; also, tin-plate; also, a pot, pan, can, box, or other vessel made of tin or (usually) of tin-plate (as, cooking *tins*; "a *tin* of sardines," J. H. Patterson's "Man-Eaters of Tsavo," xxii.); also, money (slang: as, "And the world was more than kin while he held the ready *tin*," Kipling's "Gentlemen-Rankers"). **II.** *a.* Made or consisting of tin or tin-plate; fig., mean; worthless; counterfeit.—**tin hat**, a steel helmet worn by soldiers. [Colloq.]—**tin spirit**, any of various solutions of compounds of tin in strong acid, used as mordants in dyeing.—**tin**, *v. t.*; *tinned*, *tinning*. To cover or coat with a thin deposit of tin; overlay with tin; also, to put up, pack, or preserve in tins, as foodstuffs; can.

tin-a-mou (tin′a̤-mö), *n.* [F.; from S. Amer. name.] Any of a group of birds (family *Tinamidæ*), mostly of South America, somewhat resembling the gallinaceous birds and hunted as game. See cut in next column.

Timothy.—*1*, flowering plant; *2*, the spicate inflorescence; *a*, the empty glumes; *b*, a floret.

tin-cal (ting′kạl), *n.* [Malay *tingkal*.] The crude native borax found in the East Indies, Tibet, etc.

tinct (tingkt), *a.* [L. *tinctus*, pp. of *tingere*: see *tinge*.] Tinged; colored; flavored. [Obs. or poetic.]—**tinct**, *n.* [L. *tinctus*, n., < *tingere*.] Tint, tinge, or coloring (obs. or poetic); in *alchemy*, a transmuting elixir†.

tinc-to-ri-al (tingk-tō′ri-ạl), *a.* [L. *tinctorius*, < *tinctor*, a dyer, < *tingere*: see *tinge*.] Pertaining to coloring or dyeing.—**tinc-to′ri-al-ly**, *adv.*

Tinamou (*Rhynchotus rufescens*).

tinc-ture (tingk′tūr), *n.* [L. *tinctura*, < *tingere*: see *tinge*.] A dye† or pigment†; also, hue or color (now rare); a tinge or tint (now rare); also, an imparted or derived quality or character†; also, a slight infusion, as of some element or quality; a trace (as, "I perceived the faintest *tincture* of dismay in the features of Judge Henry's . . . foreman": Wister's "Virginian," xxi.); a smack or smattering (as, "This honest worthy gentleman . . . had some *tincture* of learning": Swift's "Gulliver's Travels," ii. 8); in *her.*, any of the metals, colors, or furs used in coats of arms, etc.; in *phar.*, a solution of a medicinal substance in alcohol (or sometimes in a mixture of alcohol and ammonia or ether), prepared by maceration, digestion, or percolation.—**tinc′-ture**, *v. t.*; *-tured*, *-turing*. To impart a tincture or color to; tinge; also, to imbue or impregnate with something (as, "His words were *tinctured* with an uncommon infusion of piety": Walpole's "Castle of Otranto," ii.).

tind (tind), *v. t.* or *i.* [Akin to *tinder*.] To kindle; light. [Now prov. Eng. and Sc.]

tin-der (tin′dėr), *n.* [AS. *tynder*, akin to D. *tonder*, G. *zunder*, Icel. *tundr*, tinder: cf. *tind*.] Any dry substance that readily takes fire from a spark; esp., a material or preparation formerly used for catching the spark from a flint and steel struck together for fire or light.—**tin′der-box**, *n.* A box for holding tinder, usually fitted with a flint and steel; fig., a thing or person likened to a tinder-box, as being very inflammable, excitable, or the like.—**tin′der-y**, *a.* Tinder-like; inflammable.

tine¹ (tīn), *v.* Same as *tind*. [Now prov.]

tine² (tīn), *n.* [AS. *tind* = Icel. *tindr*.] A sharp projecting point or prong, as in a fork, a deer's antler or horn, etc.

tin-e-a (tin′ē-ä), *n.* [L., a gnawing worm.] In *pathol.*, any of various contagious skin-diseases, esp. ringworm.

tined (tīnd), *a.* Having tines: as, two-*tined*.

tin=foil (tin′foil′), *n.* Tin, or an alloy of tin and lead, in the form of a thin sheet, much used as a wrapping for drugs, confectionery, tobacco, etc.—**tin′=foil′**, *v. t.* To cover or coat with tin-foil; wrap in tin-foil.

ting¹ (ting), *n.* See *thing²*.

ting² (ting), *v. t.* or *i.* [Late ME.; imit.] To cause to make, or to make, a clear, ringing sound.—**ting²**, *n.* A tinging sound: as, "She rang the bell cautiously. She heard the distant *ting*" (Arnold Bennett's "Lion's Share," xxxvii.).—**ting′=a=ling′** (-ạ-ling′), *n.* A clear, ringing sound, as of a small bell.

tinge (tinj), *v.*; *tinged*, *tingeing* or *tinging*. [L. *tingere* (pp. *tinctus*), wet, moisten, dye, color, tinge.] **I.** *tr.* To impart a trace or slight degree of some color to; tint; modify the tint or hue of; hence, to impart a slight taste or smell to; fig., to modify by imparting a touch or trace of something (as, "gaiety of spirit *tinged* with a tender melancholy": W. H. Hudson's "Green Mansions," Prologue). **II.** *intr.* To become tinged.—**tinge**, *n.* A slight degree of coloration (as, "The faintest *tinge* of blood coloured his pale cheek": F. M. Crawford's "Mr. Isaacs," vii.); a modifying shade or tint; fig., a slight admixture, as of some qualifying property or characteristic (as, "There was always a *tinge* of cynicism in Miss Pole's remarks": Mrs. Gaskell's "Cranford," x.).— **tin-ger** (tin'jėr), *n.*—**tin'gi-ble** (-ji-bl), *a.*　Capable of being tinged or colored.

tin-gis=fly (tin'jis-flī), *n.*; pl. *-flies* (-flīz).　[NL. *Tingis*, the typical genus.]　Any of the *Tingitidæ*, a family of small, delicate heteropterous insects having the wings and body covered with a lacy network of lines.

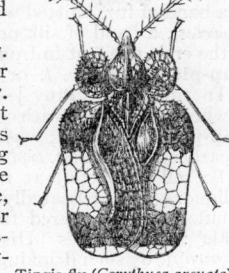

Tingis-fly (*Corythuca arcuata*), enlarged about ten times.

tin-gle (ting'gl), *v.*: *-gled*, *-gling.*　[Prob. orig. a var. of *tinkle*, later associated with *ting*².]　**I.** *intr.* To have a sensation of slight thrills or prickly pains, as the ears upon hearing something shocking to the mind or at a shrill sound, the cheeks under the influence of shame, or the body from a sharp blow or from cold (as, "Harvey's ears *tingled* at the comments on his rowing": Kipling's "Captains Courageous," viii.); also, to cause such a sensation (as, "Hereward . . . felt the lust of battle *tingling* in him from head to heel": Kingsley's "Hereward," vii.); pass with a thrill; also, to make a continued light, ringing sound; tinkle.　**II.** *tr.* To cause to tingle (as, "breasting together the brave wind, and feeling it *tingle* our cheeks": Watts-Dunton's "Aylwin," i. 5); also, to cause to tinkle.—**tin'gle**, *n.*　A tingling sensation; the tingling action of cold, etc.; also, a tingling or tinkling sound.—**tin'gler**, *n.*—**tin'gling-ly**, *adv.*

tin=horn (tin'hôrn').　**I.** *a.*　Noisy or pretentious, with little or no money or small actual resources: as, a *tin-horn* gambler; a *tin-horn* sport.　[Slang.]　**II.** *n.*　A person of the tin-horn kind: as, "I'll bet I make a whole lot more money than some of those *tin-horns* that spend all they got on dress-suits and haven't got a decent suit of underwear to their name!" (Sinclair Lewis's "Babbitt," ii.).　[Slang.]

tink (tingk), *v. i.*　[ME. *tynken*; imit.]　To make a short, light, metallic sound; clink.—**tink**, *n.*　A tinking sound.

tin-ker (ting'kėr), *n.*　[ME. *tinkere*; origin uncertain.]　A mender of pots, kettles, pans, and other metal household articles, esp. an itinerant mender of such articles; hence, a gipsy (prov.); an unskilful or clumsy mender or worker; a bungler; also, one skilled in various minor kinds of mechanical work; a jack of all trades; also, an act or instance of tinkering; a tinkering attempt at something; also, any of various fishes, birds, etc., as a small or young mackerel or the razor-billed auk.—**tinker's damn**, a tinker's curse or oath (in allusion to the reputed addiction of tinkers to swearing): often taken as a type of something worthless (as, not to care a *tinker's damn*).　[Colloq.]—**tin'ker**, *v.* **I.** *intr.*　To do the work of a tinker; mend kettles, pans, etc.; also, to work unskilfully or clumsily at anything; hence, to busy one's self with a thing without useful results.　**II.** *tr.*　To mend as a tinker; also, to repair in an unskilful, clumsy, or makeshift way (as, "This is an old Tudor place, and has been *tinkered* and altered in successive generations": Eden Phillpotts's "Grey Room," i.).

tin-kle (ting'kl), *v.*: *-kled*, *-kling.*　[ME. *tynclen*, tingle (as ears), tinkle (as cymbals): cf. AS. *tinclian*, tickle, also E. *tink.*]　**I.** *intr.*　To tingle, as the ears (now rare); also, to give forth or make a succession of short, light, ringing sounds (as, "a small silver bell that *tinkled* spasmodically": F. M. Crawford's "Mr. Isaacs," iv.); move with such sounds; also, to talk idly; prate.　**II.** *tr.*　To cause to tinkle or jingle (as, "Groups of kine *tinkled* their soft bells": Howells's "Chance Acquaintance," ii.); also, to make known or call attention to by tinkling; attract or summon by tinkling.—**tin'kle**, *n.*　The act of tinkling; a tinkling sound (as, "the dull *tinkle* of a cracked bell on the neck of some wandering cow": J. Conrad's "Rover," vi.).—**tin'kler**¹, *n.*

tin-kler² (ting'klėr), *n.*　[Appar. var. of *tinker.*]　A tinker; a vagabond; a gipsy.　[Sc. and prov. Eng.]

tin-kly (ting'kli), *a.*　Characterized by tinkling: as, "the *tinkly* temple-bells" (Kipling's "Mandalay").

tin-man (tin'man), *n.*; pl. *-men.*　A man who works in or with tin; a tinsmith; also, a dealer in tinware.

tinned (tind), *p. a.*　Covered or coated with tin; also, put up or preserved in tins, or canned (as, "one of those jolly holiday meals of *tinned* provisions": Archibald Marshall's "Anthony Dare," xi.).

tin-ner (tin'ėr), *n.*　One who works in a tin-mine; also, one who works in or with tin; a tinsmith; also, one who tins foodstuffs, etc.; a canner.

tin-ni-tus (ti-nī'tus), *n.*　[L., < *tinnire*, ring.]　In *pathol.*, a ringing or similar sensation of sound in the ears, due to disease of the auditory nerve, etc.

tin-ny (tin'i), *a.*　Of or like tin; containing tin; characteristic of tin, as sounds.

tin-plate (tin'plāt'), *n.*　Thin sheet-iron or sheet-steel coated with tin.

tin-sel (tin'sẹl).　[F. *étincelle*, a spark, flash, < L. *scintilla*: see *scintilla*.]　**I.** *n.*　A fabric of silk or wool interwoven with threads of gold or silver, or later of copper†; also, a glittering metallic substance, as copper, brass, etc., in thin sheets, used in pieces, strips, threads, etc., to produce a sparkling effect without much cost; hence, anything showy or attractive with little or no real worth; showy pretense.　**II.** *a.*　Consisting of or containing tinsel; hence, showy, with little or no real worth; tawdry.—**tin'sel**, *v. t.*; *-seled* or *-selled*, *-seling* or *-selling.*　To adorn with tinsel; adorn with anything glittering; hence, to make showy or gaudy.—**tin'sel-ly**, *a.*　Of the nature of or characterized by tinsel; hence, showy without real worth; tawdry.

tin-smith (tin'smith), *n.*　One who works in or with tin; a maker of tinware.—**tin'smith″ing**, *n.*　The work or trade of a tinsmith.

tin-stone (tin'stōn), *n.*　Same as *cassiterite.*

tint (tint), *n.*　[Prob. < It. *tinta*, tint, color, < L. *tincta*, pp. fem. of *tingere*: see *tinge*, and cf. *tinct*, *n.*]　Color, or a variety of a color; hue; specif., a delicate or pale color; also, a variety of a color produced by mixing it with white; in *engraving*, a uniform shading, as that produced by a series of fine parallel lines; in *printing*, a faintly or lightly colored background upon which an illustration or the like is to be printed.—**tint**, *v. t.*　To apply a tint or tints to; color slightly or delicately; tinge: as, "The sun at length *tinted* the eastern clouds and the tops of the highest hills" (Mrs. Radcliffe's "Romance of the Forest," i.).—**tint'er**, *n.*

tin-tin-nab-u-lar (tin-ti-nab'ū-lär), *a.*　[L. *tintinnabulum*, bell, < *tintinnare*, ring, jingle, redupl. of *tinnire*, ring: cf. *tinnitus.*]　Of or pertaining to bells or bell-ringing: as, "a brisk . . . kind of *tintinnabular* alarum at the great gate" (Bulwer-Lytton's "Caxtons," xi. 7).　Also **tin-tin-nab'u-la-ry** (-lā-ri).—**tin-tin-nab-u-la'tion** (-lā'shọn), *n.*　The ringing or sound of bells: as, "The *tintinnabulation* that so musically wells From the bells" (Poe's "Bells," i.).—**tin-tin-nab'u-lous**, *a.*　Tintinnabular.

tin-tom-e-ter (tin-tom'e-tėr), *n.*　[See *tint* and *-meter.*]　An instrument or apparatus for the exact determination of tints or colors.

tint-y (tin'ti), *a.*　Full of tints; having the tints inharmoniously combined.

tin-type (tin'tīp), *n.*　[See *-type.*]　A photograph (in the form of a positive) taken on a sensitized sheet of enameled tin or iron; a ferrotype.

tin-ware (tin'wār), *n.*　Ware of tin; articles made of tin-plate.

ti-ny (tī'ni), *a.*　[ME. *tine*, *tyne*; origin unknown.]　**I.** *a.*; compar. *tinier*, superl. *tiniest.*　Very small; minute; wee: as, "from the hugest nebula to the *tiniest* atom" (J. H. Robinson's "Mind in the Making," i. 1); "She settled in two *tiny* rooms" (Maugham's "Moon and Sixpence," xvi.).　**II.** *n.*; pl. *tinies* (-niz).　Something tiny; a tiny child: as, "just like when you were a *tiny*" (Galsworthy's "Saint's Progress," iii. 7).

-tion.　[F. *-tion*, < L. *-tio(n-)*, form of *-io(n-)* preceded by *t* of pp. stem: see *-ion.*]　A suffix of nouns (orig. formed from verbs) denoting action or process, a resulting state, condition, product, etc., as in *action*, *ambition*, *conception*, *motion*, *section*, *solution.*　See *-ion* and *-ation.*

tip¹ (tip), *n.*　[ME. *tippe* = MLG. and D. *tip* = Sw. *tipp* = Dan. *tip* = MHG. *zipf*, tip: cf. G. *zipfel*.]　A slender extremity, esp. the pointed or rounded end of anything long and slender, or tapering, or gradually narrowing (as, the *tips* of a crescent; the *tips* of the fingers or toes; the *tip* of the tongue or nose); the top, summit, or apex; also, a small piece or part, as of metal or leather, forming the extremity of something; the topmost section of a jointed fishing-rod; also, a kind of brush or instrument used in laying on gold-leaf. —**tip**[1], *v. t.*; *tipped, tipping.* To furnish with a tip (as, "Cortés ordered . . . lances to be made for him, and to be *tipped* with copper": Prescott's "Conquest of Mexico," iv. 6); also, to serve as or form the tip of; also, to mark or adorn the tip of (as, the sunlight *tips* a spire).

tip[2] (tip), *v.*; *tipped, tipping.* [ME. *tipen, typen*; origin uncertain.] **I.** *tr.* To overthrow, overturn, or upset (often with *over*); also, to cause to assume a slanting or sloping position; incline; tilt; also, to take off (the hat) in salutation; also, to empty out, as a cart or its contents, by tilting; dump. **II.** *intr.* To be overturned or upset; tumble or topple (*over*); also, to assume a slanting or sloping position; incline; tilt up at one end and down at the other.—**tip**[2], *n.* The act of tipping, or the state of being tipped; also, a place or structure where loaded carts, cars, etc., are tipped to discharge their contents; a cart or the like from which coal or other matter is tipped; also, a place or receptacle into which refuse or the like is tipped; a dump.

tip[3] (tip), *v.*; *tipped, tipping.* [Cf. LG. *tippen*, Sw. *tippa*, strike lightly, tap, also E. *tap*[2].] **I.** *tr.* To strike or hit with a light, smart blow; tap; also, to give, pass, or let have (slang, orig. rogues' slang: often with indirect personal object: as, to *tip* one a copper; "He . . . *tipped* me an impudent wink," Irving's "Tales of a Traveler," ii. 4; "*Tip* us none of your palaver," Godwin's "Caleb Williams," xxvii.); hence, to give a small present of money to (colloq.: as, "Remember how happy such benefactions made you . . . and *tip* your nephew at school!" Thackeray's "Newcomes," xvi.); give a gratuity or fee to (a servant, employee, inferior, etc.: colloq.: as, "He [gamekeeper] is one of those fortunate individuals whom all the world *tips*," Jefferies's "Gamekeeper at Home," i.); also, to give private or secret information about (something), as for use in betting, speculation, or other action (colloq., and often with *off*: as, to *tip* a horse as winner in a race; to *tip* off a plot to the authorities); give such information to (colloq., and often with *off*: as, to *tip* off the police as to a projected crime). **II.** *intr.* To step lightly; trip; also, to give a gratuity or fee (colloq.); also, to furnish private or secret information, as for use in betting, speculation, etc. (colloq.).—**tip**[3], *n.* A light, smart blow; a tap; also, a small present of money (colloq.: as, "What money is better bestowed than that of a schoolboy's *tip?*" Thackeray's "Newcomes," xvi.); a gratuity or fee (colloq.: as, "Edgar's companion . . . gave a *tip* which caused the porter to salute extravagantly," Arnold Bennett's "Pretty Lady," xxi.); also, a piece of private or secret information, as for use in betting, speculation, or other action (colloq.: as, "If anything's up, give me the *tip*," W. Churchill's "Mr. Crewe's Career," xi."); hence, in general, a useful hint, suggestion, or idea (colloq.: as, "The French . . . have taken a *tip* from the colouration of animals in this matter [camouflage]," H. G. Wells's "Italy, France, and Britain at War," iii. 3).

tip=cart (tip′kärt), *n.* A cart with a body that can be tipped or tilted to discharge the contents.

tip=cat (tip′kat), *n.* A short piece of wood tapering at both ends (the 'cat'), used in a game in which it is struck lightly at one end with a stick so as to spring up, and while in the air is struck again so as to be driven as far as possible; also, the game itself.

tiph-i-a (tif′i-ạ), *n.* [NL. *Tiphia*, < Gr. τίφη, kind of insect.] A digger-wasp of the genus *Tiphia*, as *T. inornata*, a species common in the eastern U. S.

tipped (tipt), *a.* Having a tip, end, or endpiece: as, pink-*tipped*; gold-*tipped*; cork-*tipped*.

Tiphia (*Tiphia inornata*).— *a*, perfect wasp; *b*, head of larva, enlarged; *c*, larva, ventral view; *d*, cocoon, cut open.

tip-per (tip′ẹr), *n.* One who or that which tips. See *tip*[1], *tip*[2], *tip*[3].

tip-pet (tip′et), *n.* [ME. *tipet*, perhaps < *tippe*, E. *tip*[1].] A long, narrow, pendent part of the dress, as part of a hood or sleeve, or as a scarf (now only hist.); also, an article of dress, usually of fur or wool, for covering the neck, or the neck and shoulders, and having ends hanging down in front; a band of fur, knitted wool, or the like worn about the neck; *eccles.*, a band of silk or the like worn round the neck with the ends pendent in front.

tip-ple[1] (tip′l), *v. t.* or *i.*; *-pled, -pling.* [Freq. of *tip*[2].] To tip over. [Prov.]—**tip′ple**[1], *n.* A place or structure where cars loaded with coal or the like are emptied by tipping.

tip-ple[2] (tip′l), *v.*; *-pled, -pling.* [Cf. *tippler* (recorded earlier), also Norw. *tipla*, drip, drink little and often.] **I.** *tr.* To sell (ale, etc.) at retail†; also, to drink (intoxicating liquor), esp. repeatedly, in small quantities (as, "A mad tailor . . . wandered from pothouse to pothouse, *tippling* ale": Macaulay's "Hist. of Eng.," ii.); drive, pass, etc. (*away*), by such drinking (as, "I took to the bottle, and tried to *tipple* away my cares": Irving's "Tales of a Traveler," ii. 10). **II.** *intr.* To sell liquor at retail†; also, to drink intoxicating liquor, esp. repeatedly or habitually and to some excess.—**tip′ple**[2], *n.* Intoxicating liquor; drink.—**tip′pler**, *n.* [ME. *tipeler*.] A retailer of ale or other strong drink†; also, a habitual drinker of intoxicating liquor (as, "You know the illusion habitual *tipplers* are subject to, that each appeal to the bottle is an exceptional occurrence": W. De Morgan's "Alice-for-Short," ii.).

tip-py[1] (tip′i), *a.* [See *tip*[1].] In the height of fashion (colloq. or prov.); also, neat, smart, or clever (colloq.); also, of tea, consisting largely of the tips or leaf-buds of the shoots.

tip-py[2] (tip′i), *a.* [See *tip*[2].] Liable to tip, upset, or tilt: as, a *tippy* canoe; a *tippy* table. [Colloq.]

tip-si-ly (tip′si-li), *adv.* In a tipsy manner.—**tip′si-ness**, *n.*

tip-staff (tip′stȧf), *n.*; pl. *-staffs* or *-staves* (-stāvz). [For *tipped staff*.] A staff tipped or capped with metal, formerly carried as a badge of office by certain officials, as a constable or sheriff's officer; hence, any of certain officials who formerly carried such a staff; an attendant or crier in a court of law.

tip-ster (tip′stẹr), *n.* One who makes a business of furnishing tips, or private or secret information, as for use in betting, speculation, etc. [Colloq.]

tip-sy (tip′si), *a.* [Appar. < *tip*[2].] Affected by liquor so as to stagger slightly or be without full control of the movements and faculties (as, "I . . . watched him drink . . . until he was so *tipsy* that he wept upon my shoulder": Stevenson's "Kidnapped," xv.); intoxicated, but not to complete drunkenness or stupor; characterized by or due to intoxication (as, a *tipsy* condition; a *tipsy* lurch or laugh); also, tipping, unsteady, or tilted, as if from intoxication (as, a *tipsy* boat, table, or chair; a *tipsy* row of pictures on a wall).—**tip′sy=cake**, *n.* Cake saturated with wine and served with custard sauce.

tip=ta-ble (tip′tā″bl), *n.* A small table with a hinged top that may be tipped vertically when the table is put aside, out of use.

tip-toe (tip′tō). **I.** *n.* The tip or end of a toe; the tips of the toes collectively: commonly in the phrase 'on tiptoe,' expressive of straining upward, eager expectation, cautious or stealthy movement, etc.: as, "The 'boys of Kilkenny' were on *tiptoe* in expectation of my arrival" (Lever's "Harry Lorrequer," xii.); "Mr. Asterias stole out of the library on *tiptoe*" (Peacock's "Nightmare Abbey," vii.). **II.** *a.* Characterized by standing or walking on tiptoe; straining upward; eagerly expectant; cautious or stealthy. **III.** *adv.* On tiptoe: as, "hordes of hungry troopers *tip-toe* for the signal to the buffet" (G. Meredith's "Diana of the Crossways," ii.).—**tip′toe**, *v. i.*; *-toed, -toeing.* To raise one's self or stand on tiptoe, as in trying to reach something or to see over a barrier; also, to move or go on tiptoe, as with caution or stealth (as, "He *tiptoed* over the traitorous boards of the landing": Arnold Bennett's "Hilda Lessways," iii. 4).

tip-top (tip′top′). **I.** *n.* The extreme top or summit; fig., the highest point or degree, as of excellence. [Colloq.] **II.** *a.* Situated at the very top; fig., of the highest quality or excellence, or first-rate (as, "He is a *tiptop* man, and may

be a bishop": George Eliot's "Middlemarch," iv.). [Colloq.]
–tip′top′per, *n.* A tiptop person or thing: as, "Dryden . . . has shown himself such a *tip-topper.* I didn't think he had such grit in him" (W. B. Maxwell's "In Cotton Wool," vi.). [Colloq.]

ti-rade (ti-rād′ or tī′rād), *n.* [F. *tirade*, a pull, passage (of prose or verse), tirade, < It. *tirata*, a drawing or pulling, < *tirare*, draw, = F. *tirer*, E. *tire*[1].] A long, vehement speech on some subject (as, "She listened . . . to her guide's *tirade* in praise of liberty": Scott's "Quentin Durward," xxiii.); esp., a prolonged outburst of denunciation or railing (as, "Mr. Barnstaple launched out into a long and loud *tirade* against the suppression and falsifications of earthly newspapers": H. G. Wells's "Men Like Gods," iii. 2); also, in *lit.*, a passage of varying length dealing with a single theme or idea, as in poetry.**–ti-rade′,** *v. i.*; *tiraded, tirading.* To deliver a tirade; inveigh.

ti-rage (tē-räzh′), *n.* [F., < *tirer*: see *tire*[1].] A printing or impression of a book.

ti-rail-leur (tē-rä-yėr′), *n.* [F., < *tirailler*, fire at will as a sharpshooter, < *tirer*: see *tire*[1].] A skirmisher; a sharpshooter.

tire[1] (tīr), *v.*; *tired, tiring.* [OF. F. *tirer*, draw, pull, shoot; origin uncertain.] **I.**† *tr.* To draw or pull; tear at. **II.** *intr.* To pull, tug, or tear, as falcons at their prey; feed greedily (*on* or *upon*); fig., to be engaged or intent (*on* or *upon*: as, "Upon that were my thoughts *tiring*, when we encountered," Shakspere's "Timon of Athens," iii. 6. 5). [Obs. or archaic.]
–tire[1]†, *n.* [OF. F. *tire*, row, *tir*, shooting, < *tirer*: cf. *tier*[2] and *attire*.] A row, as of guns; also, a discharge of guns; a volley.

tire[2] (tīr), *v. t.*; *tired, tiring.* [For *attire*.] To equip, as with arms†; also, to attire or array (archaic); dress (the head or hair), esp. with a head-dress (archaic: as, "Jezebel . . . painted her face, and *tired* her head," 2 Kings, ix. 30). **–tire**[2], *n.* Equipment†; apparatus†; attire or dress (archaic); a head-dress (archaic: as, "She . . . braided the hair of her head, and put on a *tire* upon it," Judith, x. 3).

tire[3] (tīr), *n.* [Prob. another use of *tire*[2], *n.*] A continuous band of metal, an endless inflated rubber tube, or the like, placed around a wheel of a vehicle to form the tread.**–tire**[3], *v. t.*; *tired, tiring.* To furnish with a tire or tires.

tire[4] (tīr), *v.*; *tired, tiring.* [AS. *tīorian, tēorian*; origin and connections uncertain.] **I.** *intr.* To have the strength reduced or exhausted, as by labor or exertion; become fatigued; also, to have one's appreciation, interest, patience, etc., exhausted, as by excess; become or be weary (*of*: as, "You think I shall *tire* of her!" G. B. Shaw's "Man and Superman," ii.). **II.** *tr.* To reduce or exhaust the strength of, as by exertion; make weary; fatigue; also, to exhaust the interest, patience, etc., of, as by long continuance or by dullness (as, "I have indeed *tired* you by a long discourse": Burke's "Conciliation with the Colonies"); make weary (*of*: as, "Ten years had not *tired* the King of his joke," Chesterton's "Napoleon of Notting Hill," ii. 2).**–tire**[4], *n.* The state of being tired; fatigue. [Prov. or colloq.]

tired[1] (tīrd), *a.* [See *tire*[3].] Having a tire or tires: as, a rubber-*tired* wheel or vehicle.

tired[2] (tīrd), *p. a.* [See *tire*[4].] Exhausted, as by exertion; fatigued; also, weary (*of*: as, "I am heartily *tired* of this itinerant way of life," Smollett's "Humphry Clinker," Oct. 4); impatient or disgusted (colloq.: as, "Oh, you make me *tired!*" Sinclair Lewis's "Babbitt," xxxii.); also, habitually lazy (slang).**–tired′ly,** *adv.***–tired′ness,** *n.*

tire-less (tīr′les), *a.* Untiring; indefatigable: as, a *tireless* worker; *tireless* efforts or zeal.**–tire′less-ly,** *adv.***–tire′-less-ness,** *n.*

tire-some (tīr′sum), *a.* Such as to tire one; tiring or fatiguing; wearisome or tedious; annoying or vexatious (colloq.: as, "Freddie says that I've got to meet him at that *tiresome* Foreign Office," Mrs. H. Ward's "Lady Rose's Daughter," i.).**–tire′some-ly,** *adv.***–tire′some-ness,** *n.*

tire-wom-an (tīr′wŭm″an), *n.*; pl. *-women* (-wim″en). [See *tire*[2].] A woman who assists at a lady's toilet; a lady's-maid. [Archaic.]

tir-ing-glass (tīr′ing-glås), *n.* [See *tire*[2].] A mirror used in dressing or in making the toilet. [Archaic.]**–tir′ing-room,** *n.* A dressing-room, esp. in a theater. [Archaic.]

ti-ro (tī′rō), *n.* See *tyro.*

Ti-ro-ni-an (tī-rō′ni-an), *a.* Of or pertaining to Tiro, the learned freedman and amanuensis of Cicero: as, *Tironian* notes (a system of shorthand used by the ancient Romans, said to have been introduced by Tiro).

'tis (tiz). Contraction of *it is.*

ti-sane (tē-zàn′), *n.* [F.: see *ptisan.*] A nourishing or slightly medicinal decoction; a ptisan.

Tish-ri (tish′rē), *n.* [Heb. *tishrī.*] In the Jewish calendar, the first month (30 days) of the civil year and the seventh of the ecclesiastical year, beginning in September or in the first part of October.

tis-sue (tish′ọ), *n.* [OF. F. *tissu*, orig. pp. of OF. *tistre* (later *tître*), < L. *texere*, weave.] A rich cloth, often interwoven with threads of gold or silver†; now, any of various fabrics of light or gauzy texture; any woven or textile fabric; fig., an interwoven or interconnected series or mass (as, a *tissue* of falsehoods; "Henceforth his political life was a wretched *tissue* of disappointed hopes," Lecky's "Hist. of Eng. in the 18th Century," iii.); also, tissue-paper; in *biol.*, the substance of which an organism or part is composed; an aggregate of cells and cell-products forming a definite kind of structural material in an animal or plant (as, muscular *tissue*; connective *tissue*, see *connective, a.*).**–tis′sue,** *v. t.*; *-sued, -suing.* To weave with threads of gold or silver†; also, to make into a tissue; weave; also, to clothe or adorn with tissue.**–tis′sue=pa′per,** *n.* A very thin, soft paper used for wrapping delicate articles, covering illustrations in books, copying letters, etc.

tit[1] (tit), *n.* [AS. *tit*: see *teat.*] A teat. [Prov. or colloq.]

tit[2] (tit), *n.* [Appar. meaning orig. 'something small': cf. the compounds *titlark, titmouse*, also Icel. *tittr*, Norw. *tita*, little bird, and E. *tit*[3].] A small or poor horse (now chiefly prov.); also, a girl or young woman (archaic or prov.).

tit[3] (tit), *n.* [Prob. detached from *titmouse* (recorded much earlier): cf. *tit*[2].] Any of various small birds; esp., a titmouse, as *Parus cæruleus* of Europe ('blue tit' or 'blue titmouse') and *Psaltri-parus melanotis* of the southwestern U. S. and Mexico ('black-eared bush-tit').

tit[4] (tit), *n.* [Cf. *tip*[3].] In the phrase *tit for tat,* blow for blow; one blow or the like in return for another; an equivalent given in return, as in retaliation, repartee, etc.: as, "She hasn't the courage to give him *tit for tat*" (Maria Edgeworth's "Belinda," xvii.).

Black-eared Bush-tit (*Psaltriparus melanotis*).

Ti-tan (tī′tan), *n.* [L., < Gr. Τιτάν.] **I.** *n.* One of a family of primordial deities in Greek legend, the children of Uranus (Heaven) and Gæa (Earth) (or of their son, Titan), conceived as lawless beings of gigantic size and enormous strength, who overthrew Uranus, the ruler of the world, and raised Cronus, one of their number, to the throne, but were themselves overcome and cast into Tartarus by Zeus, the son of Cronus; also, the sun-god, Helios (Sol), son of the Titan Hyperion; also, a person or thing of enormous size, strength, etc. **II.** *a.* Titanic; gigantic.

ti-ta-nate (tī′ta-nāt), *n.* In *chem.*, a salt of titanic acid.

Ti-tan-esque (tī-tan-esk′), *a.* [See *-esque.*] Titan-like; Titanic.

Ti-tan-ess (tī′tan-es), *n.* A female Titan.

Ti-tan-ic[1] (tī-tan′ik), *a.* Of, pertaining to, or characteristic of the Titans (as, the *Titanic* presumption and audacity of challenging to single combat the sovereign of the world": J. H. Newman's "Callista," xxii.); hence [often *l. c.*], Titan-like; of enormous size, strength, etc.; gigantic, colossal, huge, or vast (as, "The whole scene . . . is on a scale so

Titanic in its massive length and breadth and depth": F. M. Crawford's "Mr. Isaacs," xii.).

ti-tan-ic² (tī-tan′ik), *a.* In *chem.*, of or containing titanium. See *titanous.*—**titanic acid,** titanic oxide, or any of various acids derived from it.—**titanic oxide,** the dioxide of titanium, TiO₂.

ti-ta-nif-er-ous (tī-tạ-nif′ẹ-rus), *a.* [See *-ferous.*] Containing or yielding titanium.

ti-ta-nite (tī′tạ-nīt), *n.* [G. *titanit,* < NL. *titanium.*] A mineral consisting of a combined silicate and titanate of calcium. Cf. *sphene.*—**ti-ta-nit′ic** (-nit′ik), *a.*

ti-ta-ni-um (tī-tā′ni-um), *n.* [NL., < L. *Titan,* Titan.] Chem. sym., Ti; at. wt., 48.1. A metallic element occurring combined in various minerals, and isolated as a dark-gray powder with a metallic luster and an iron-like appearance.

ti-ta-no-there (tī′tạ-nọ-thēr or tī-tā′nọ-), *n.* [NL. *titanotherium:* see *Titan* and *-there.*] Any of the extinct rhinoceros-like animals of the genus *Titanotherium* or family *Titanotheriidæ,* whose remains are found in the Tertiary formations, esp. of North America. Also **ti″ta-no-the′ri-um** (-thē′ri-um).

Titanothere. — From a sketch, based on mounted skeleton and skulls, in the American Museum of Natural History, New York.

ti-ta-nous (tī′tạ-nus), *a.* In *chem.,* containing titanium (in larger proportion than a corresponding titanic compound).

tit-bit (tit′bit), *n.* [Earlier *tidbit:* cf. prov. Eng. *tid,* fond, tender, nice.] A delicate bit of food; a toothsome morsel; hence, a choice or pleasing bit of anything, as news.

ti-ter, ti-tre (tē′tėr), *n.* [F. *titre,* title, fineness, strength, < L. *titulus,* E. *title.*] In *chem.,* the strength of a standard solution used in titration.

tith-a-ble (tī′ᴛʜạ-bl), *a.* Liable to be tithed; subject to the payment of tithes.

tithe (tīᴛʜ). [AS. *teogotha, teotha,* tenth, akin to *tēn, tīen,* E. *ten.*] **I.** *a.* Tenth: as, "every *tithe* soul" (Shakspere's "Troilus and Cressida," ii. 2. 19); not the *tithe* part of them. [Archaic.] **II.** *n.* The tenth part of the annual produce of agriculture, etc., due or paid as a tax for the support of the priesthood, religious institutions, etc. (often in *pl.:* as, "the *tithes* of the corn, the new wine, and the oil, which was commanded to be given to the Levites," Neh. xiii. 5; "We have . . . a nominal religion, to which we pay *tithes* of property and sevenths of time," Ruskin's "Crown of Wild Olive," ii.); hence, any tax, levy, or the like of one tenth; also, a tenth part, or any indefinitely small part, of anything (as, not one *tithe* of the sum was recovered; "if we can believe a *tithe* of Cicero's invective," Froude's "Cæsar," xiii.).—**tithe,** *v. t.; tithed, tithing.* [AS. *teogothian, teothian.*] To give or pay a tithe or tenth of (produce, earnings, etc.), as for the support of the church; pay tithes on; also, to exact a tithe from (a person, etc.); levy a tithe on (produce, goods, etc.).—**tithe′=pig,** *n.* A pig due or given as a tithe.—**tith-er** (tī′ᴛʜėr), *n.* One who tithes; a payer or a receiver of tithes; also, a supporter of the system of ecclesiastical tithes.—**tith′ing,** *n.* [AS. *tēothung.*] One tenth given to the church; a tithe; also, a company of householders, orig. ten in number, in the old English system of frank-pledge; hence, a rural division in England, orig. regarded as one tenth of a hundred, descended from this system.—**tith′ing=man** (-man), *n.; pl. -men.* In England, orig., the chief man of a tithing; a headborough; later, a parish peace-officer; a petty constable; in New England and Maryland, formerly,

an elective town officer with functions derived from those of the English peace-officer (as, "The *tithing-men* must take heed that she go both to school and to meeting": Hawthorne's "Scarlet Letter," viii.).

ti-ti¹ (tē-tē′), *n.; pl. titis* (-tēz′). [S. Amer.] Any of various small monkeys of the genus *Callithrix* (or *Callicebus*), of South America.

ti-ti² (tē′tē), *n.; pl. titis* (-tēz). [Origin uncertain.] Any of several shrubs or small trees, as *Cliftonia monophylla* ('black titi') and *Cyrilla racemiflora* ('white titi'), of the southern U. S., with glossy leaves and racemes of white flowers.

tit-il-late (tit′i-lāt), *v. t.; -lated, -lating.* [L. *titillatus,* pp. of *titillare,* tickle.] To tickle; excite a tingling or itching sensation (pleasurable or otherwise) in, as by touching or stroking lightly; excite agreeably (as, to *titillate* the fancy).—**tit-il-la′tion** (-lā′shọn), *n.* [L. *titillatio(n-).*] The act of titillating, or the state of being titillated; a titillating or tickling sensation; any pleasing excitation, as of the mind.—**tit′il-la-tor,** *n.*

tit-i-vate, tit-ti-vate (tit′i-vāt), *v.; -vated, -vating.* [Also sometimes *tiddivate* (perhaps associated with *tidy*); appar. a made word, in imitation of verbs ending in *-ate.*] **I.** *tr.* To make smart or spruce; spruce up: as, to *titivate* one's self. [Colloq.] **II.** *intr.* To make one's self smart or spruce. [Colloq.]—**tit-i-va′tion, tit-ti-va′tion** (-vā′shọn), *n.*—**tit′i-va-tor, tit′ti-va-tor,** *n.*

tit-lark (tit′lärk), *n.* [See *tit².*] Any of various small lark-like birds, esp. of the genus *Anthus,* as *A. ludovicianus,* a migratory bird of North America; a pipit.

ti-tle (tī′tl), *n.* [OF. *title* (F. *titre*), < L. *titulus,* inscription, label, notice, title, appellation, sign, ML. mark over a letter or word: see *tittle¹.*] An inscription placed on or near something to name or describe it†;

Titlark (*Anthus ludovicianus*).

also, the distinguishing name of a book, poem, piece of music, picture, or the like; a descriptive heading or caption, as of a chapter, section, or other part of a book; a division of a statute, law-book, etc., esp. one larger than an article or section; all the matter on a title-page, or the title-page itself; the panel on the back of a book, giving its name; also, any descriptive or distinctive appellation; a distinguishing appellation belonging to a person by right of rank, office, attainment, etc., or assigned as a mark of respect or courtesy; specif., an appellation indicating social rank as in the nobility or peerage; also, established or recognized right to something (as, to have no *title* to obedience or gratitude; "Some of the creditors disputed his *title* to retain so large a part of the purchase-money," Scott's "Guy Mannering," xix.); ground for a claim (as, "a little contemptible varlet, without the least *title* to birth . . . wit, or common sense": Swift's "Gulliver's Travels," ii. 5); anything affording ground for a claim (as, Gray's "Elegy" is his chief *title* to fame); in *law,* legal right to the possession of property, esp. real property; the ground or evidence of such right; the instrument constituting evidence of such right; *eccles.,* a fixed sphere of work and source of income, required as a condition of ordination; also, any of certain churches in Rome the nominal incumbents of which are cardinals.—**ti′tle,** *v. t.; titled, titling.* To furnish with a title; designate by an appellation; call or style; entitle.—**ti′tled,** *a.* Having a title, esp. of nobility.—**ti′tle=deed,** *n.* A deed or document containing or constituting evidence of ownership.—**ti′tle=page,** *n.* The page, at or near the beginning of a book, which contains its full title, usually with particulars as to its authorship, publication, etc.

tit-mouse (tit′mous), *n.; pl. -mice* (-mīs). [ME. *titmose, tytmase,* < *tit* (appar. = *tit²*) + AS. *māse,* titmouse.] Any of various small birds constituting the family *Paridæ,* as

Parus atricapillus ('black-capped titmouse'), a small American bird notable for its tameness and its peculiar notes (cf. *chickadee*), or *P. cæruleus*, a European species ('blue titmouse,' also called *bluebonnet* and *nun*); also, the reedling ('bearded titmouse').

Black-capped Titmouse (*Parus atricapillus*).

ti-trate (tī′trāt or tit′rāt), *v. t.* or *i.*; *-trated, -trating.* [F. *titrer*, < *titre*, fineness, strength: see *titer*.] In *chem.*, to ascertain the quantity of a given constituent present in (a compound or mixture) by accurately measuring the volume of a liquid reagent of known strength (called a *standard solution*) necessary to convert the constituent into another form, the close of the reaction being marked by some definite phenomenon, as a change of color.—**ti-tra-tion** (tī-trā′shọn or ti-), *n.*

ti-tre (tē′tèr), *n.* See *titer.*

tit=tat=toe (tit-tat-tō′), *n.* Same as *tick-tack-toe.*

tit-ter[1] (tit′èr), *v. i.* [ME., = Icel. *titra*, shake: cf. *teeter.*] To shake; totter; sway; seesaw. [Now prov.]

tit-ter[2] (tit′èr), *v. i.* [Perhaps imit.] To laugh in a low, half-restrained way, as from nervousness or silly levity or in ill-suppressed amusement or derision: as, "The gentlemen burst into a roar of laughter, and all the ladies *tittered*" (Borrow's "Romany Rye," vii.); "A few aristocrats might sniff or *titter*; but with the nation at large the Queen was . . . extremely popular" (Lytton Strachey's "Queen Victoria," iv.).—**tit′ter**[2], *n.* A tittering laugh: as, "An audible *titter* ran through the audience" (W. Churchill's "Coniston," ii. 15); "dead silences, worse for me to bear than *titters* and faces" (G. Meredith's "Lord Ormont and His Aminta," xv.).—**tit′ter-er,** *n.*—**tit′ter-ing-ly,** *adv.*

tit-ter=tot-ter (tit′ėr-tot′ėr), *n.* [Cf. *titter*[1] and *totter.*] The sport of seesaw; a seesaw. [Now prov.]

tit-ti-vate (tit′i-vāt), *etc.* See *titivate,* etc.

tit-tle[1] (tit′l), *n.* [ML. *titulus,* mark over a letter or word, L. inscription, label, sign: see *title,* and cf. *tilde.*] A small stroke or mark in writing or printing, as the dot over the letter *i,* a diacritical mark, a vowel point, or the like; hence, a very small part or quantity, orig. of something written (as, "One jot or one *tittle* shall in no wise pass from the law," Mat. v. 18: cf. *jot*[2], *n.*); a particle, jot, or whit; any least particular or respect (as, "a description of his person, which . . . appeared . . . to tally to the minutest *tittle,*" Godwin's "Caleb Williams," xxxii.; to a *tittle,* to the smallest particular, or exactly).

tit-tle[2] (tit′l), *v. i.* or *t.*; *-tled, -tling.* [ME. *tytyll*; appar. imit.: cf. *tattle* (recorded later).] To whisper; tattle. [Now prov. Eng. and Sc.]

tit-tle=tat-tle (tit′l-tat′l), *n.* [Varied redupl. of *tattle.*] Idle, trifling talk; petty gossip: as, "highly-educated women who scorn *tittle-tattle*" (Arnold Bennett's "Helen with the High Hand," x.); "ill-natured *tittle-tattle*" (Lytton Strachey's "Queen Victoria," iii.).—**tit′tle=tat′tle,** *v. i.*; *-tled, -tling.* To talk tittle-tattle; gossip.—**tit′tle=tat′tler,** *n.*

tit-tup (tit′up), *n.* [Appar. imit.] A canter or easy gallop, as of a horse; also, a prancing movement; a curvet.—**tit′-tup,** *v. i.*; *-tuped* or *-tupped, -tuping* or *-tupping.* To go at a canter or easy gallop, as a horse or the rider (as, "'Twas General Bangs, with Aide and Staff, who *tittupped* on the way": Kipling's "Code of Morals"); hence, to go with an up-and-down movement suggesting this, as a boat on the waves or a person walking in an affected manner; also, to prance; spring; caper; also, to shake, be unsteady, or tip readily (chiefly prov. Eng.).—**tit′tup-y,** *a.* Tittuping, prancing, or lively; also, shaky or unsteady, as furniture (chiefly prov. Eng.).

tit-u-bate (tit′ū-bāt), *v. i.*; *-bated, -bating.* [L. *titubatus,* pp. of *titubare,* stagger.] To stagger; totter; stumble; fig., to falter in speaking; stammer.—**tit-u-ba′tion** (-bā′-shọn), *n.* The act of titubating; in *pathol.,* a staggering or stumbling gait associated with spinal and cerebral disorders.

tit-u-lar (tit′ū-lȧr). [L. *titulus,* title: see *title.*] **I.** *a.* Of, pertaining to, or of the nature of a title or name; also, pertaining to or of the nature of a title of rank or dignity; having or bearing such a title; also, existing or being such in title or name only (as, *titular* sovereignty; a *titular* prince); also, from whom or which a title or name is taken; noting or pertaining to the Roman churches called titles. **II.** *n.* One who bears a title; also, one from whom or that from which a title or name, specif. of a church, is taken.—**tit′u-lar-ly,** *adv.* In a titular manner or respect; with respect to title; nominally.—**tit′u-la-ry** (-lạ-ri), *a.* and *n.* Same as *titular.*

tme-sis (tmē′sis), *n.* [LL., < Gr. τμῆσις, a cutting, < τέμνειν, cut.] In *gram.,* the separation of a compound word by the interposition of one or more words between the parts of it, as in "to us-ward" (2 Peter, iii. 9) for "toward us."

TNT (tē en tē). Abbreviation of *trinitrotoluene* or *trinitrotoluol.* Also **T. N. T.**

to (tö). [AS. *tō* = OS. and OFries. *tō* = D. *toe* = OHG. *zō, zuo* (G. *zu*), to: for the equivalent Scand. word, see *till*[1].] **I.** *prep.* A particle serving to specify a point approached and reached (as, come *to* the house; go *to* him), and hence used (1) to express motion or direction toward something (as, from north *to* south); limit of movement or extension (as, rotten *to* the core); contact or contiguity (as, apply varnish *to* the surface); a point or limit in time (as, *to* this day); aim, purpose, or intention (as, going *to* the rescue); destination, or appointed end (as, sentenced *to* death); result or consequence (as, *to* his dismay); resulting state or condition (as, he tore it *to* pieces); the object of inclination or desire, or of a right or claim (as, they drank *to* his health; claimants *to* an estate); limit in degree or amount (as, punctual *to* the minute; goods *to* the value of $1,000); addition or accompaniment (as, he added insult *to* injury; they danced *to* music); attachment or adherence (as, he held *to* his opinion); comparison or opposition (as, one man's wealth is nothing *to* another's; the score was 9 *to* 5); agreement or accordance (as, a position *to* one's liking); reference or relation (as, what will he say *to* this?); also used (2) to supply the place of the dative in other languages, connecting transitive verbs with their indirect or distant objects, and adjectives, nouns, and intransitive or passive verbs with a following noun which limits their action or application; and (3) as the ordinary sign or accompaniment of the infinitive (expressing orig. motion, direction, purpose, etc., as in the ordinary uses with a substantive object, but now appearing in many cases as a mere meaningless sign). **II.** *adv.* Toward a person, thing, or point implied or understood; also, to a point of contact, or a closed position (now colloq.: as, pull the shutters *to*; "The staircase door had slammed *to* behind her," J. Conrad's "Rover," xv.); also, to a matter, or to action or work (as, fall or set *to*; "We turned *to* with a will," Aldrich's "Story of a Bad Boy," xvii.); also, to consciousness, or to one's senses (as, after he came *to*).—**to and fro,** to and from some place or thing; hence, in opposite or different directions alternately; hither and thither.—**to,** *conj.* Till; until. [Obs. or prov.]

to-. [AS. *to-* = OS. and OFries. *ti-* = OHG. *zi-, zir-* (G. *zer-*), asunder: cf. *dis-* and *dys-*.] A prefix meaning 'asunder,' 'to pieces,' 'away,' or having an intensive force, formerly much used in combination with verbs, as in *to-break*: sometimes written apart from the verb, esp. after *all,* *adv.,* as in *all to break* for *all tobreak* (see Judges, ix. 53), or even (improperly) joined to *all,* as in *all-to break,* the combination *all-to* being taken as an adverb qualifying the verb.

toad (tōd), *n.* [AS. *tādige, tādie,* toad; origin unknown.] Any of various tailless amphibians (order *Anura*), esp. the clumsy terrestrial species of the genus *Bufo* and allied genera (see cut on following page), but sometimes including certain aquatic species which are more commonly called *frogs*; also, any of various other animals, as certain lizards (see *horned toad,* under *horned, a.*); also, a person or thing as an object of disgust or aversion (as, "You spiteful little *toad!*" Pinero's "Wife without a Smile," iii.).

toad=eat-er (tōd′ē″tèr), *n.* One who eats toads; a mountebank's boy who ate, or pretended to eat, toads (supposed to be poisonous), so that his master might show his skill in expelling poison; fig., a mean sycophant; a fawning flatterer. — **toad′= eat″ing,** *n.* and *a.*

Common American Toad (*Bufo lentiginosus*).

toad=fish (tōd′fish), *n.* Any of the thick-headed, wide-mouthed fishes constituting the family *Batrachoididæ,* as *Opsanus tau* of the Atlantic coast of the U.S.; also, any of various rious fishes of other families.

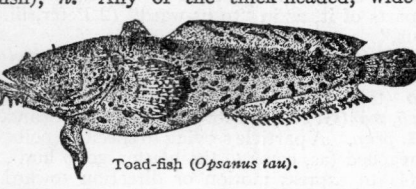

Toad-fish (*Opsanus tau*).

toad=flax (tōd′flaks), *n.* A common European scrophulariaceous plant, *Linaria linaria,* having showy yellow-and-orange flowers, naturalized as a weed in the U. S.; any plant of the same genus.

toad=spit, toad=spit-tle (tōd′spit, -spit″l), *n.* Cuckoo-spit (the secretion).

toad-stone (tōd′stōn), *n.* Any of various stones or stone-like objects resembling a toad in shape or color, or supposed to have been formed in the head or body of a toad, and formerly worn as jewels or amulets.

toad-stool (tōd′stōl), *n.* Any of various fungi having a stalk with an umbrella-like cap, esp., in popular use, those that are poisonous, as distinguished from the edible forms (cf. *mushroom*); also, any of various other fungi, as the puffballs.

toad-y (tō′di), *n.*; pl. *toadies* (-diz). An obsequious sycophant; a fawning flatterer; a toad-eater. — **toad′y,** *v.*; *toadied, toadying.* **I.** *tr.* To play the toady to; treat with flattering servility. **II.** *intr.* To play the toady; act with flattering servility: as, "The Habsburgs, who had *toadied* to his [Napoleon's] success, had taken away his Habsburg empress" (H. G. Wells's "Outline of History," xxxviii. § 5). — **toad′y-ish,** *a.* Resembling, or characteristic of, a toady. — **toad′y-ism,** *n.* The action or behavior of a toady; interested flattery; mean servility.

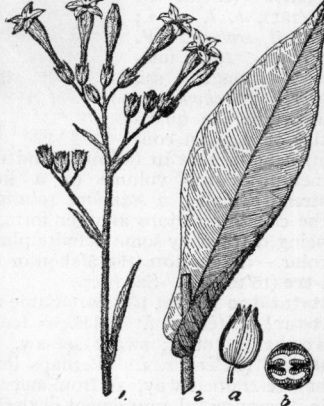

Toad-flax (*Linaria linaria*). — *a,* a flower, longitudinal section; *b,* the fruit; *c,* the seed.

toast[1] (tōst), *v.* [OF. *toster,* < L. *torrere* (pp. *tostus*), dry, parch, scorch: see *thirst.*] **I.** *tr.* To brown, as bread or cheese, by exposure to the heat of a fire; hence, to heat or warm thoroughly at a fire. **II.** *intr.* To become toasted. — **toast**[1], *n.* Bread in slices superficially browned by the fire; also, formerly, a slice or piece of bread so browned.

toast[2] (tōst), *n.* [Another use of *toast*[1], *n.,* with reference to a piece of toast put into a beverage to flavor it.] A person whose health is proposed and drunk; also, an event, sentiment, or the like, to which one drinks; also, a call on another or others to drink to some person or thing, or the act of thus drinking. — **toast**[2], *v.* **I.** *tr.* To propose as a toast; drink to the health of or in honor of: as, "He would . . . *toast* me at his wine" (Whittier's "Maud Muller"). **II.** *intr.* To propose or drink a toast.

toast-er[1] (tōs′tèr), *n.* One who toasts something, as bread or cheese; an instrument for toasting bread, cheese, etc.; also, something to be toasted.

toast-er[2] (tōs′tèr), *n.* One who proposes, or joins in, a toast or health.

toast=mas-ter (tōst′màs″tèr), *n.* One who is appointed to propose or announce the toasts at a public dinner or the like; one who presides at a dinner and introduces the after-dinner speakers.

to-bac-co (tọ-bak′ō), *n.*; pl. *tobaccos* (-ōz). [Sp. *tabaco,* from a West Indian name variously explained as meaning orig. a kind of pipe used in smoking, a roll of leaves smoked, or the plant.] Any plant of the solanaceous genus *Nicotiana,* esp. one of those species, as *N. tabacum,* whose leaves are prepared for smoking or chewing or as snuff; the leaves so prepared; also, any of various more or less similar plants of other genera. — **to-bac′- co=heart′,** *n.* In *pathol.,* a functional disorder of the heart, characterized by a rapid and often irregular pulse, due to excessive use of tobacco. — **to-bac′co-nist,** *n.* A dealer in or manufacturer of tobacco. — **to-bac′co=worm,** *n.* The larva of a sphinx-moth, *Phlegethontius carolina,* or some other species, which feeds on the leaves of the growing tobacco-plant in the U. S.

Tobacco (*Nicotiana tabacum*). — 1, flowering branch; 2, a leaf from the stem; *a,* the fruit; *b,* transverse section of a fruit.

to-bog-gan (tọ-bog′an), *n.* [N. Amer. Ind.: cf. *pung.*] A long, narrow, flat-bottomed sled made of a thin board curved upward and backward at the front end; a similar light sled with low runners, used in the sport of coasting. — **to-bog′gan,** *v. i.* To use a toboggan; coast on a toboggan. — **to-bog′gan-er, to-bog′gan-ist,** *n.*

to-break† (tọ-brāk′), *v. t.* or *i.*; pret. *-broke* or *-brake,* pp. *-broken* or *-broke.* [AS. *tobrecan:* see *to-* and *break.*] To break to pieces.

to-by[1] (tō′bi), *n.*; pl. *-bies* (-biz). [From *Toby,* for *Tobiah* or *Tobias,* man's name.] [Also *cap.*] A small jug or mug in the form of a stout old man wearing a three-cornered hat.

to-by[2] (tō′bi), *n.*; pl. *-bies* (-biz). [Cf. *toby*[1].] A kind of long, slender, cheap cigar. [U. S.]

toc-ca-ta (tok-kä′tä), *n.* [It., orig. pp. fem. of *toccare,* touch.] In *music,* a composition in the style of an improvisation, for the pianoforte, organ, or other keyboard instrument: intended to exhibit the player's technique.

Toc H (tok äch). [From *T* (called *toc,* in order to distinguish it from letters of similar sound, as *P, B,* and *D,* by signalers in the British army) and *H,* the initials of Talbot House, the first headquarters of the organization, in Poperinghe, near Ypres, Belgium, which was named in commemoration of Gilbert Talbot (youngest son of the Right Rev. E. S. Talbot, Bishop of Winchester), who was killed in Belgium in 1915, while serving with the British forces.] An organization, beginning as a club for British soldiers and officers established by the Rev. P. T. B. Clayton and others in Poperinghe, Belgium, in 1915 (see etym.), and refounded by him in England in 1920, and now having branches through-

Toby of English Pottery, 18th century.

out the British dominions and elsewhere. The motto over the door of the chaplain's room at Talbot House in Poperinghe was "All rank abandon, ye who enter here," the aim of the club being to break down the barriers of rank and class; and since the World War the organization has become the instrument of a movement to promote in the younger generation a spirit of reconciliation between classes and of unselfish service.

toch-er (tŏch′ėr), n. [OGael. tochar.] The dowry which a wife brings to her husband. [Sc. and north. Eng.]

to-col-o-gy (tŏ-kol′ō-ji), n. [Gr. τόκος, birth, offspring: see -logy.] The branch of medicine that treats of parturition; obstetrics.

toc-sin (tok′sin), n. [F. tocsin, < Pr. tocar, touch, strike, + senh, sign, signal, bell, < L. signum, sign, ML. bell.] A signal, esp. of alarm, sounded on a bell or bells; also, a bell used to sound an alarm.

tod¹ (tod), n. [ME. todde, weight of wool; perhaps from LG.] An English unit of weight, chiefly for wool, commonly equal to 28 pounds, but varying locally (as, "a tax of five . . . shillings upon the exportation of every tod of wool": Adam Smith's "Wealth of Nations," iv. 8); also, a load; also, a bushy mass, esp. of ivy.

tod² (tod), n. [Origin unknown.] A fox; fig., a crafty person. [Sc. and north. Eng.]

to=day, to-day (tŏ-dā′). [AS. tō dæg: see to, prep., and day.] **I.** adv. On this present day; also, at the present time; in these days. **II.** n. This present day; also, this present time or age.

tod-dle (tod′l), v. i.; -dled, -dling. [Origin uncertain.] To go with short, unsteady steps, as a child or an old person (as, "I had a baby sister who could just toddle about on two legs": W. H. Hudson's "Far Away and Long Ago," xvi.); also, to stroll or saunter, or to walk or go in general colloq.: as, "Toddle up the valley and have dinner with us," Eden Phillpotts's "Children of Men," i. 5).—**tod′dle**, n. The act or an act of toddling; an unsteady gait; a stroll or walk (colloq.).—**tod′dler**, n.

tod-dy (tod′i), n.; pl. toddies (-iz). [From Hind. name.] The drawn sap, esp. when fermented, of various species of palm, used as a drink; also, a drink made of spirits and hot water and sweetened.—**tod′dy=palm**, n. Any palm that yields toddy.

to=do (tŏ-dö′), n. [Orig. inf., to do: cf. ado.] Activity; bustle; fuss; commotion; ado: as, "in spite of all the to-do they make about their idols" (S. Butler's "Erewhon," xvii.). [Colloq.]

to-dy (tŏ′di), n.; pl. -dies (-diz). [Cf. F. todier and NL. Todus, < L. todi, pl., kind of small birds.] Any of the small insectivorous West Indian birds constituting the subfamily Todinæ (family Momotidæ), or, according to some authorities, constituting the family Todidæ, related to the motmots and kingfishers, and having a brightly colored plumage; also, any of various other small, brightly colored birds.

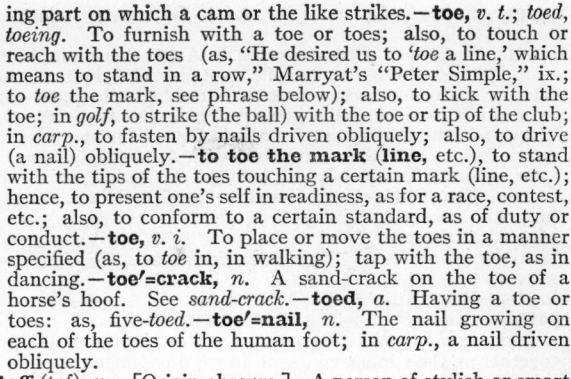

toe (tō), n. [AS. tā = MLG. tē = OHG. zēha (G. zehe) = Icel. tā, toe.] One of the terminal members

Green Tody (Todus viridis), about two thirds natural size. — a, outline of bill from above, slightly reduced.

or digits of the foot in man (as, the great toe, the toe on the inner side of the foot, corresponding to the thumb; the little toe, the outermost and smallest toe of the foot); an analogous part in other animals; the fore part of the foot or hoof of a horse or the like; also, a part, as of a stocking or shoe, to cover the toes; also, a part resembling a toe or the toes in shape or position; in mach., a journal or part placed vertically in a bearing, as the lower end of a vertical shaft; also, an arm or project-

ing part on which a cam or the like strikes.—**toe**, v. t.; toed, toeing. To furnish with a toe or toes; also, to touch or reach with the toes (as, "He desired us to 'toe a line,' which means to stand in a row," Marryat's "Peter Simple," ix.; to toe the mark, see phrase below); also, to kick with the toe; in golf, to strike (the ball) with the toe or tip of the club; in carp., to fasten by nails driven obliquely; also, to drive (a nail) obliquely.—**to toe the mark** (**line**, etc.), to stand with the tips of the toes touching a certain mark (line, etc.); hence, to present one's self in readiness, as for a race, contest, etc.; also, to conform to a certain standard, as of duty or conduct.—**toe**, v. i. To place or move the toes in a manner specified (as, to toe in, in walking); tap with the toe, as in dancing.—**toe′=crack**, n. A sand-crack on the toe of a horse's hoof. See sand-crack.—**toed**, a. Having a toe or toes: as, five-toed.—**toe′=nail**, n. The nail growing on each of the toes of the human foot; in carp., a nail driven obliquely.

toff (tof), n. [Origin obscure.] A person of stylish or smart appearance; a swell; sometimes, in compliment, a good fellow; a 'brick.' [Slang, Eng.]

tof-fee, tof-fy (tof′i), n. Same as taffy¹. [Eng.]

toft (tôft), n. [Late AS. toft; from Scand.] A homestead or messuage; the site of a house and its outbuildings; also, a knoll or hillock. [Now chiefly prov.]

tog (tog), n. [Origin obscure; first in vagabonds' and thieves' slang.] A garment; usually, in pl., clothes. [Colloq.]—**tog**, v. t.; togged, togging. To clothe; dress: often with out or up. [Colloq.]

to-ga (tŏ′gä), n.; pl. -gas (-gäz), L. -gæ (-jē). [L., akin to tegere, cover.] The loose outer garment of the citizens of ancient Rome when appearing in public in time of peace; hence, a robe of office, a professional gown, or some other distinctive garment.—**toga virilis** (vi-ri′lis). [L., 'manly toga.'] The 'manly toga' assumed by Roman youths when they attained the age of fourteen.—**to′gaed** (-gäd), a. Clad in a toga; togated.—**to′gat-ed** (-gā-ted), a. [L. togatus.] Clad in a toga; hence, peaceful; also, stately or majestic.

Roman Toga. — Statue of the Emperor Tiberius.

to-geth-er (tŏ-geTH′ėr), adv. [AS. tōgædere, tōgadore, < tō, to, + gador, geador, together: see gather.] Into or in one gathering, company, mass, or body (as, to call the people together; to consider a number of cases together); into or in union, proximity, contact, or collision, as two or more things (as, to tie or sew things together; the trains came together with a crash; two fields which lie together); into or in relationship, association, business or friendly relations, etc., as two or more persons (as, to bring strangers or estranged persons together; so long as we were together in the enterprise); taken or considered collectively or conjointly (as, this one cost more than all the others together); also, of a single thing, into or in a condition of unity or compactness, or so as to form a connected whole or a compact body (as, to squeeze a thing together; the argument does not hang together well); also, at the same time, or simultaneously (as, "While he and I live together, I shall not be thought the worst poet of the age," Dryden's "Fables," Preface; you cannot have both together); also, without intermission or interruption, continuously, or uninterruptedly (as, for days together); also, in coöperation, with united action, or conjointly (as, two men undertake a task together); also, with mutual action, with one another, mutually, or reciprocally (as, to confer together; to get along together); to multiply two numbers together).—**together with**, along with, or in combination with; in company, association, or coöperation with; simultaneously with.

tog-ger-y (tog'ẽr-i), *n.* [See *tog.*] Garments; clothes; togs. [Colloq.]

tog-gle (tog'l), *n.* [Origin obscure.] A transverse pin, bolt, or rod placed through an eye of a rope, link of a chain, or the like, for various purposes, as to fit into a bight, loop, or ring in another rope or chain, thus fastening the two ropes or chains together, or to serve as a hold for the fingers; also, a toggle-joint, or a device furnished with one. — **tog'gle**, *v. t.*; -*gled*, -*gling.* To furnish with a toggle or toggles; secure or fasten with a toggle or toggles. — **tog'gle=i″ron**, *n.* A harpoon having a pivoted crosspiece near the point, instead of fixed barbs. — **tog'gle=joint**, *n.* In *mech.*,

Toggle-iron.

a device consisting of two arms or pieces pivoted or hinged together at their inner ends and pivoted or hinged to other parts at their outer ends: utilized in printing-presses, etc., for the sake of the pressure caused at the outer ends when the arms are made to open out into a position more or less approaching a straight line by force applied at the bend between them.

Toggle-joint.

togs (togz), *n. pl.* See *tog, n.*

to-hu-bo-hu (tō′hö-bō′hö), *n.* [F.; from the Heb. words in Gen. i. 2, translated "without form, and void."] Chaos; confusion.

toil[1] (toil), *n.* [OF. F. *toile*, cloth, web, < L. *tela*, web, < *texere*, weave.] A net or nets set about a space into which game is driven or within which it is known to be (now usually in *pl.*, and often fig.: as, "I was like a wild beast that had broken the *toils*," Mrs. Shelley's "Frankenstein," xvi.; "The wily old Jew had the boy in his *toils*," Dickens's "Oliver Twist," xviii.); also, any snare or trap for wild beasts†.

toil[2] (toil), *v.* [AF. *toiler*, dispute, contend, OF. F. *touiller*, stir, mix, < L. *tudiculare*, stir, < *tudicula*, dim. of *tudes*, hammer, mallet, akin to *tundere*, beat.] **I.** *intr.* To contend, as in argument, litigation, or battle†; also, to engage in severe and continuous work or exertion (as, "The girls in our workshops *toil* for long hours and little pay": Besant's "All Sorts and Conditions of Men," ix.); labor arduously; also, to move or travel with difficulty, weariness, or pain (as, "He painfully *toiled* up the ascent": J. H. Newman's "Callista," xii.). **II.** *tr.* To weary or exhaust by toil (now rare); also, to bring or effect by toil. — **toil**[2], *n.* Dispute† or controversy†; battle or strife, or a struggle in battle (archaic); also, any struggle with difficulties (as, "the coming *toils* of their remaining route to China": De Quincey's "Revolt of the Tartars"); hence, a spell of arduous labor (as, "the faithful partners of my *toils*": Lamb's "Superannuated Man"); a laborious task; also, hard and continuous work or exertion; exhausting labor or effort; also, something produced or accomplished by toil (as, "How is the *toil* of fate, the work of ages, The Roman empire fallen!" Addison's "Cato," iv. 4). — **toil'er**, *n.*

toi-let (toi'let), *n.* [F. *toilette*, dim. of *toile*, cloth: see *toil*[1].] A piece of cloth for wrapping clothing†; a cloth to be thrown over the shoulders during hair-dressing†; also, a cloth cover for a dressing-table; also, the articles used in dressing, etc., as mirror, brush, comb, etc.; also, a dressing-table; also, the act or process of dressing, including bathing, arranging the hair, etc. (as, "He would complete his *toilet* and take an austere breakfast": H. G. Wells's "Kipps," i. 2); also, formerly, the later stages of this process, including the dressing and powdering of the hair, during which women of fashion received callers; also, the dress or costume of a person; any particular costume (as, a *toilet* of white silk); also, a dressing-room, esp. one with a bath; in a restricted sense, a bathroom or a water-closet; in *surg.*, the cleansing of the part after an operation, esp. in the peritoneal cavity. Also **toi-lette** (as F., two-let). — **toi'let=wa″ter**, *n.* A perfumed liquid for the toilet.

toil-ful (toil'fúl), *a.* Characterized by or involving toil; laborious; toilsome; also, toiling (as, "the *toylefull* Oxe": Spenser's "Hymne of Heavenly Love," 227). — **toil'ful-ly**, *adv.*

toil-less (toil'les), *a.* Free from toil.

toil-some (toil'sum), *a.* Characterized by or involving toil, or laborious or fatiguing (as, "Their journey became *toilsome* in the extreme": Irving's "Captain Bonneville," iv.); also, toiling (as, "the *toilsome* seeker after fame": W. Morris's "Jason," v. 314). — **toil'some-ly**, *adv.* — **toil'some-ness**, *n.*

toil=worn (toil'wôrn), *a.* Worn by toil; showing the effects of toil: as, "my *toil-worn* body" (W. Morris's "Jason," xv. 458).

toise (toiz), *n.* [F., < L. *tensa*, pp. neut. pl. (with reference to the outstretched arms) of *tendere*, stretch, E. *tend*[1].] An old French linear measure equivalent to 1.949 meters or 6.395 English feet.

To-kay (tō-kā′), *n.* [From *Tokay* (or *Tokaj*), town in Hungary.] A rich, sweet, aromatic wine made near Tokay, in Hungary; a California wine made in imitation of it; also, the variety of grape from which it is made.

to-ken (tō′kn), *n.* [AS. *tācn*, *tācen*, = D. *teeken* = G. *zeichen* = Icel. *teikn*, token: see *teach.*] Something serving to represent or indicate some fact, event, feeling, etc. (as, to wear black as a *token* of mourning; to shake hands as a *token* of reconciliation); a sign; a symbol; a characteristic mark or indication (as, the *tokens* of a disease); also, something given as an expression of affection or esteem, or to be kept as a memorial; a memento; a keepsake; also, a signal made, as to attract attention or give notice (as, "I gave *tokens* to let them know that they might do with me what they pleased," Swift's "Gulliver's Travels," i. 1: now rare or obs.); also, something serving as a proof of a fact, statement, etc.; an evidence; also, something used to indicate authenticity, as a material object, a sign, or a password; also, something given as evidence of a right or privilege, upon the presentation of which the right or privilege may be exercised; specif., a stamped piece of lead, a card, or the like, given and presented as a voucher of fitness to receive the communion (now esp. Sc.: as, "Without a *token*, which was a metal lozenge, no one could take the sacrament on the coming Sabbath," Barrie's "Auld Licht Idylls," iii.); also, a stamped piece of metal issued as a medium of exchange, usually by private persons, at a nominal value much greater than its real value; anything of only nominal value similarly used, as a piece of paper currency; in *printing*, a quantity of paper sufficient for 250 impressions (reckoned as one hour's work on the hand-press); also, a measure or quantity of presswork on one form, usually 250 or 500 impressions. — **in token of**, as a token, sign, or evidence of: as, "He sits down *in token* of submission" (G. B. Shaw's "You Never Can Tell," iv.). — **to'ken**, *v. t.* [AS. *tācnian.*] To be a token or sign of; betoken; also, to be a symbol or emblem of; symbolize; typify.

Obverse.   Reverse.
Token of R. Cottam of Reading, Berkshire, England, 1669. — British Museum.

to-kol-o-gy (tō-kol′ọ-ji), *n.* See *tocology.*

tol'booth, *n.* See *tollbooth.*

told (tōld). Preterit and past participle of *tell*[2].

tole (tōl), *v. t.* See *toll*[1].

To-le-do (tọ-lē′dō), *n.*; pl. -*dos* (-dōz). A sword or sword-blade made, or supposed to be made, at Toledo, in Spain, long famous for the manufacture of sword-blades of fine temper.

tol-er-a-ble (tol′ẹ-rạ-bl), *a.* [L. *tolerabilis.*] That may be tolerated; endurable; sufferable or allowable; also, moderate in degree or character (as, "I have seen valor enough in a little fiery-hearted French dwarf to have furnished out a *tolerable* giant": Irving's "Tales of a Traveler," i. 3); now, esp., moderately good or agreeable; fairly good; not bad; also, in fair health (colloq.: as, "We're *tolerable*, sir, I thank you," C. Brontë's "Jane Eyre," xxvi.). — **tol'er-a-ble-ness**, *n.* — **tol'er-a-bly**, *adv.*

tol-er-ance (tol′ẹ-rạns), *n.* [L. *tolerantia.*] The state or fact of being tolerant; the disposition to be patient and indulgent toward those whose opinions or practices differ from one's own; freedom from bigotry or severity in judging the opinions or conduct of others; the action of tolerating, or toleration; also, in *minting*, a legally permissible deviation in the weight and fineness of coins; in *mech.*, an allowable variation in the dimensions of a machine or part; also, in general, the action or capacity of enduring something (obs. or rare); in *med.*, the power of enduring or resisting the action of a drug, poison, etc.

tol-er-ant (tol′ẹ-rạnt). [L. *tolerans* (-*ant*-), ppr.] **I.** *a.* Inclined or disposed to tolerate, or showing forbearance (as, "a sensible and candid man, firm in his own religious opinions, and *tolerant* towards those of others": Macaulay's "Essays," Milton); forbearing; favoring toleration; also, in *med.*, able to endure or resist the action of a drug, poison, etc. **II.** *n.* One who tolerates opinions or practices differing from his own; one who is free from bigotry.—**tol′er-ant-ly**, *adv.*

tol-er-ate (tol′ẹ-rāt), *v. t.*; -ated, -ating. [L. *toleratus*, pp. of *tolerare*, bear, support, endure: see *thole*1.] To endure or sustain, as pain or hardship†; specif., to endure or resist the action of (a drug, poison, etc.); also, to bear without repugnance, or put up with (as, "The great Whig aristocrats . . . only *tolerated* him as an unpleasant necessity thrust upon them by fate": Lytton Strachey's "Queen Victoria," v.); also, to suffer to be, or to be practised or done, without prohibition or hindrance (as, "The law *tolerated* only the Protestant worship": Bancroft's "Hist. of the U. S.," Amer. Revolution, ii. 2); allow or permit by not preventing.— **tol-er-a′tion** (-ẹ-rā′shọn), *n.* [L. *toleratio*(n-).] The act of tolerating; esp., the tolerating or allowing of what is not actually approved; forbearance; sufferance; tolerance; specif., allowance, by a government, of the exercise of religions other than the religion which is officially established or recognized; recognition of the right of private judgment in matters of faith and worship.—**tol′er-a-tor**, *n.*

tol-i-dine (tol′i-din), *n.* [From *toluene.*] In *chem.*, any of several isomeric basic derivatives of toluene, one of which is used in making dyes.

toll1 (tōl), *v. t.* [ME. *tollen, tullen,* akin to AS. *-tyllan* in *fortyllan,* draw away, seduce.] To attract, allure, or entice (now prov.); specif., to lure or decoy (game) by arousing curiosity.

toll2 (tōl), *v.* [Appar. another use of *toll*1.] **I.** *tr.* To cause (a large bell) to sound by pulling the rope (archaic); specif., to cause (a large bell) to sound with single strokes slowly and regularly repeated, as for summoning a congregation to church, or, esp., for announcing a death or on the occasion of a funeral; also, to sound (a knell, etc.), or strike (the hour), by such strokes (as, "the strokes of many bells *tolling* midnight": Mrs. H. Ward's "Lady Rose's Daughter," v.); also, to announce (a death, etc.) by this means; ring a toll for (a dying or dead person); also, to summon or dismiss by tolling. **II.** *intr.* To sound with single strokes slowly and regularly repeated, as a bell.—**toll**2, *n.* The act of tolling a bell, or the sound made; a single stroke made in tolling a bell, or the sound made.

toll3 (tōl), *v. t.* [AF. *toler,* < L. *tollere,* raise, take away.] In *law,* to take away; vacate; annul.

toll4 (tōl), *n.* [AS. *toll, toln,* < LL. *toloneum,* for *telonium,* < Gr. τελώνιον, tollhouse, < τελώνης, collector of taxes, < τέλος, tax, toll.] A payment exacted by a ruler or lord by virtue of sovereignty or lordship or in return for some right or privilege†; hence, a payment exacted by the state, the local authorities, etc., for some right or privilege, esp. for the right of passage along a road, over a bridge, or the like (as, "The carriages which pass over a highway or a bridge, and the lighters which sail upon a navigable canal, pay *toll*": Adam Smith's "Wealth of Nations," v. 1. 3. 1); sometimes, a compensation for services rendered, as for grinding corn or for transportation or transmission; sometimes, in general or fig., a tax, duty, or tribute (as, "Every advance has paid a heavy *toll* to the machine gun": H. G. Wells's "Italy, France, and Britain at War," iii. 5); also, formerly, in England, the right to take toll.—**toll**4, *v.* **I.** *intr.* To take or collect toll; exact or levy toll; also, to pay toll†. **II.** *tr.* To take a portion of (something) by way of toll; also, to exact toll from (a person); also, to collect (something) as toll.—**toll′a-ble**, *a.* Subject to the payment of toll. —**toll-age** (tō′lāj), *n.* The exaction or the payment of toll; also, the amount so exacted or paid.—**toll′=bar,** *n.* A barrier, esp. a gate, across a road or bridge, where toll is

taken.—**toll′booth, tol′booth** (-bȯ͟th or -bōth), *n.* A booth, stall, or office where tolls, taxes, or duties are collected†; also, a town hall or gildhall; also, a town prison; a jail. [Chiefly Sc.]—**toll′=bridge,** *n.* A bridge at which toll is charged for passing over.

toll-er1 (tō′lėr), *n.* One who or that which tolls or decoys; esp., a small kind of dog trained to decoy ducks.

toll-er2 (tō′lėr), *n.* One who tolls a bell.

toll-er3 (tō′lėr), *n.* One who collects tolls, as at a toll-gate.

toll=gate (tōl′gāt), *n.* A gate where toll is taken.

toll-house (tōl′hous), *n.* A house beside a road near a toll-gate, or at the end of a toll-bridge, occupied by the toll-collector.

toll-man (tōl′mạn), *n.;* pl. -men. A man who collects tolls; the keeper of a toll-gate.

Tol-tec (tol′tek). **I.** *n.* A member of an Indian people who flourished in central Mexico previous to the advent of the Aztecs, and who were, according to tradition, the source of Aztec culture. **II.** *a.* Of or pertaining to the Toltecs.— **Tol′tec-an,** *a.*

to-lu (tọ-lū′), *n.* [From *Tolú* (or Santiago de *Tolú*), seaport of Colombia.] A fragrant yellowish-brown balsam obtained from a South American tree, *Toluifera balsamum:* used in medicine as a stomachic and expectorant, and in perfumery.— **tol-u-ate** (tol′ū-āt), *n.* In *chem.,* a salt of toluic acid.—**tol′u-ene** (-ēn), *n.* In *chem.,* a colorless, mobile liquid hydrocarbon, $C_6H_5.CH_3$, obtained from tolu, coal-tar, etc.: used in making dyes, etc.—**to-lu-ic** (tọ-lū′ik), *a.* In *chem.,* noting or pertaining to any of several isomeric acids, C_7H_7COOH, which are derivatives of toluene.—**tol′u-ide** (-īd or -id), *n.* In *chem.,* an amide which contains a tolyl radical united to the nitrogen.—**to-lu′-i-dine** (-i-din), *n.* In *chem.,* any of three isomeric amines, $C_6H_4CH_3.NH_2$, derived from toluene.—**tol′u-ol** (-ol or -ōl), *n.* [See -*ol.*] In *chem.,* toluene.—**tol′u-yl** (-il), *n.* [See -*yl.*] In *chem.,* a univalent radical, C_7H_7CO, present in toluic acids.—**tol′yl,** *n.* [See -*yl.*] In *chem.,* a univalent hydrocarbon radical, $CH_3C_6H_4$, of which toluene is the hydride.

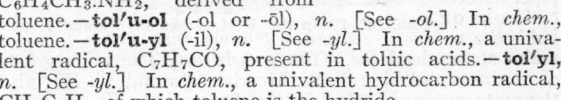
Tree yielding Tolu.

Tom (tom), *n.* A familiar form of the Christian name *Thomas* (as, peeping *Tom,* see under *peeping; Tom* Fool, see *tomfool*); hence, a name given to various things (as, *Tom* of Lincoln, the great bell of the cathedral of Lincoln, England; long *Tom,* a long gun carried on shipboard; old *Tom,* a strong kind of gin); [*l. c.*] a long trough formerly used in gold-washing (also called *long tom*); also, the male of various animals (often used in composition: as, *tom*-cat; "our old *tom*-turkey," Mrs. Stowe's "Oldtown Folks," xxvii.); esp., a tom-cat.—**Tom, Dick, and Harry,** men or persons indiscriminately, esp. of the ordinary run or common herd: as, to refuse to open private grounds to *Tom, Dick, and Harry;* every *Tom, Dick, and Harry* is trying to imitate them.—**Tom Thumb,** a diminutive personage or hero of popular story; hence, in general, a diminutive male person; a dwarf; something small of its kind; also, a petty or insignificant fellow.

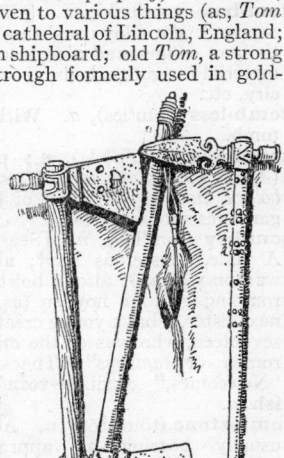
Indian Tomahawks.

tom-a-hawk (tom′ạ-hâk), *n.* [N. Amer. Ind.] A light ax used by the North American Indians as a weapon and a tool, and serving as a token of war (see *hatchet*, with phrases, and cf. *peace-pipe*); hence, any of various similar weapons or implements; in Australia, a hatchet.—**tom′a-hawk**, *v. t.* To strike, cut, or kill with a tomahawk (as, "the very children . . . being held up by their fathers to *tomahawk* the dying victims at the stake": Roosevelt's "Winning of the West," i. 4); also, to cut (sheep) in shearing (Australia: as, "Shearers were very scarce, and the poor sheep got fearfully '*tomahawked*' by the new hands," H. Kingsley's "Geoffry Hamlyn," xx.).

to-mal-ley (to-mal′i), *n.* [Carib.] The soft substance called the liver of the lobster, which becomes green when cooked.

to-man (tō-män′), *n.* [Pers.] In Persia and Turkey, the number or sum of ten thousand; a military division of 10,000 men; also, a Persian gold coin, not now in circulation, nominally equivalent to 10 krans or 10,000 dinars, but actually worth about $1.72; a Persian money of account equivalent to 10 krans, or approximately 80 U. S. cents.

to-ma-to (tō-mä′tō or tō-mā′tō), *n.*; pl. *-toes* (-tōz). [Sp. *tomate*, < Mex. *tomatl*, tomato.] A widely cultivated sola-naceous plant, *Lycopersicon lycopersicum*, bearing a slightly acid, pulpy fruit, commonly red, sometimes yellow, used as a vegetable; the fruit itself; also, any plant of the same genus, or its fruit.

tomb (tōm), *n.* [OF. F. *tombe*, < LL. *tumba*, < Gr. τύμβος, sepulchral mound, tomb: cf. *tumulus*.] An excavation in earth or rock for the reception of a dead body; a grave; also, a chamber or vault wholly or partly in the earth, or wholly above ground, for the reception of the dead; a mausoleum; any sepulchral structure; sometimes, a cenotaph; in general, any place that receives or holds the re-

Tomb of Philip the Bold, Duke of Burgundy (died 1404).— Museum, Dijon, France.

mains of the dead (as, "The greedy sea, The mighty *tomb* of mariners and kings": W. Morris's "Jason," vi. 17); also, the state of death; also, in the *Rom. Cath. Ch.*, a cavity within an altar for containing relics.—**tomb**, *v. t.* To place in or as in a tomb; bury; also, to serve as a tomb for.

tom-bac (tom′bak), *n.* [F. *tombac*, < Malay *tambāga*, copper.] An alloy consisting essentially of copper and zinc, used as a material for gongs, bells, cheap jewelry, etc.

tomb-less (tōm′les), *a.* Without a tomb.

tom-bo-la (tom′bō-lä), *n.*; pl. *-las* (-läz). [F. < It. *tombola*, < *tombolare*, tumble.] A kind of lottery game resembling lotto.

tom-boy (tom′boi), *n.* [See *Tom*.] A rude, boisterous boy†; also, a wanton woman†; also, a boisterous, romping girl, or hoyden (as, "her next sister, a brisk young creature of seventeen, who was of the order of romps or *tomboys*": Thackeray's "Newcomes," xxxii.).—**tom′boy**-ish, *a.*

tomb-stone (tōm′stōn), *n.* A stone, usually bearing an appropriate inscription and sometimes a decorative design, set to mark a tomb or grave: as, "mossy, tumble-down *tombstones*, one with a skull and cross-bones upon it" (H. G. Wells's "Mr. Britling," i. 2. § 2).

Tombstone, 13th century. — Church of St. Martin, Laon, France.

tom=cat (tom′kat′), *n.* [See *Tom*.] A male cat.

tom-cod (tom′kod), *n.* [Perhaps from N. Amer. Ind.] A small gadoid fish, *Microgadus tomcod*, of the Atlantic coast of the U. S. (also called *frost-fish*); also, any of various similar fishes.

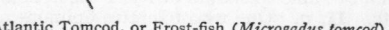

Atlantic Tomcod, or Frost-fish (*Microgadus tomcod*).

tome (tōm), *n.* [F. *tome*, < L. *tomus*, < Gr. τόμος, volume, orig. a cut, piece, section, < τέμνειν, cut.] A volume forming a part of a larger work; hence, any volume, esp. a ponderous one (as, "A volume old and brown, A huge *tome*, bound In brass and wild-boar's hide": Longfellow's "Golden Legend," ii. 113).

-tome. [Gr. -τόμος, cutting, < τέμνειν, cut: cf. *-tomy*.] A noun termination used esp. in names of surgical and other cutting instruments, as *bronchotome*, *microtome*, *osteotome*.

to-men-tose (tō-men′tōs), *a.* [See *tomentum*.] In *bot.* and *entom.*, closely covered with down or matted hair; in *anat.*, fleecy; flocculent.

to-men-tum (tō-men′tum), *n.*; pl. *-ta* (-tä). [L., a stuffing of wool, etc., for cushions.] In *bot.*, pubescence consisting of longish, soft, entangled hairs pressed close to the surface.

tom-fool (tom′föl′), *n.* [From *Tom Fool*, used as a name for a half-witted person.] One who plays the part of a fool in the drama or the like, or a buffoon (as, "They [morris-dancers] are usually attended with one character called the *tom fool*, who . . . seems to be a burlesque upon all the rest": R. Graves's "Spiritual Quixote," ii. 15); also, a grossly foolish person; a silly fool.—**tom′fool′**, *v. i.* To play the tomfool; indulge in senseless or silly foolery.—**tom′fool′er-y** (-föl′èr-i), *n.*; pl. *-ies* (-iz). The action or behavior of a tomfool; senseless or silly foolery; a silly performance, matter, or thing (as, "you whose English Government has so often fought for *tomfooleries*": Chesterton's "Napoleon of Notting Hill," ii. 3).

Tom-my (tom′i), *n.*; pl. *Tommies* (-iz). [Familiar dim. of *Tom*, for *Thomas*, man's name.] Short for *Tommy Atkins*, a nickname for the British private soldier (see *Thomas Atkins*, under *Thomas*); hence, a British private soldier (as, "They [German prisoners] work better than the *Tommies* we put at the same job": H. G. Wells's "Italy, France, and Britain at War," iii. 3); also [*cap.* or *l. c.*], a fool or simpleton (prov. Eng.).—**tom-my-rot′**, *n.* Foolish or silly 'rot,' rubbish, or nonsense: as, "They agreed . . . that this vers libre was *tommyrot*" (Sinclair Lewis's "Babbitt," xvii.). [Slang.]

to-mor-row, to-mor-row (tō-mor′ō), *n.* [ME. *to morwe*: see *to*, *prep.*, and *morrow*.] **I.** *adv.* On the morrow; on the day after this day: as, come *to-morrow*. **II.** *n.* The morrow, or the day after this day (as, *to-morrow* will be fair); also, a day immediately following or succeeding another day (as, "Every day had a *to-morrow* now," J. Conrad's "Rover," x.; "Wait a few years, wait till the *to-morrows* begin to look scantier and scantier," Whyte-Melville's "Katerfelto," xiv.).

tom-pi-on (tom′pi-on), *n.* Same as *tampion*.

Tom-toms.

tom-tit (tom′tit′), *n.* [See *Tom* and *tit*[3].] A titmouse; also, any of various other small birds.

fat, fāte, fär, fåll, åsk, fāre; net, mē, hèr; pin, pīne; not, nōte, möve, nôr; up, lūte, pùll; oi, oil; ou, out; (lightened) aviǎry, ēlect, agŏny, intŏ, ūnite; (obscured) errǎnt, operǎ, ardĕnt, actŏr, natūre; ch, chip; g, go; th, thin; ŦH, then; y, you;

tom=tom (tom'tom), *n.* [Also *tam-tam*; E. Ind.] A native East Indian drum, used by musicians, public criers, etc. (see cut on preceding page); hence, any native drum, as among African peoples; also, a Chinese gong.—**tom'=tom**, *v. i.* or *t.*; *-tommed*, *-tomming.* To beat on or as on a tom-tom.—**tom'=tom''mer**, *n.*

-tomy. [Gr. -τομία, < -τόμος, cutting, -τομος, being cut, < τέμνειν, cut: cf. *-tome*.] A noun termination meaning 'a cutting,' esp. as a surgical operation, as in *appendectomy*, *lithotomy*, *phlebotomy*, or sometimes 'a being cut,' 'division,' as in *dichotomy*.

ton[1] (tun), *n.* [Var. of *tun*.] A tun†; also, a unit of internal capacity of ships, equal to 100 cubic feet; a unit of volume for freight, varying with the different kinds, as 40 cubic feet of oak timber, 20 bushels of wheat, etc.; a unit of volume used in transportation by sea, commonly 40 cubic feet ('shipping ton'); a unit of displacement of ships, equal to 35 cubic feet; also, a unit of weight, now usually 20 hundredweight, commonly equivalent to 2,000 pounds avoirdupois ('short ton') in the U. S., and 2,240 pounds avoirdupois ('long ton') in England; in the *metric system*, a unit of weight equal to 1,000 kilograms, or 2,204.6 pounds avoirdupois ('metric ton,' or millier).

ton[2] (tôn), *n.* [F.: see *tone*.] Fashion; style: as, "He must be a man of *ton*, or he was an atom, a nonentity" (Bulwer-Lytton's "Pelham," iii.).

to-nal (tō'nạl), *a.* [ML. *tonalis*.] Of or pertaining to tones or tone.—**to'nal-ist,** *n.* In *painting*, one who aims at a prevailing tone of color, or a harmonious color-scheme, produced by effects of light and shade in their relation to the principal light rather than by contrasts of color.

to-nal-ite (tō'nạl-īt), *n.* [Named from *Tonale*, in Tyrol.] In *petrog.*, a granular igneous rock, a variety of diorite containing quartz and biotite.

to-nal-i-ty (tō-nal'i-ti), *n.* Tonal character or quality; in *music*, the sum of relations, melodic and harmonic, existing between the tones of a scale or musical system; key; also, a particular scale or system of tones; a key; in *painting*, etc., the system of tones or tints, or the color-scheme, of a picture, etc.

to-nal-ly (tō'nạl-i), *adv.* With respect to tone.

to=name (tō'nām), *n.* [AS. *tōnama*: see *to*, *prep.*, and *name, n.*] A name added to another name; a surname; a nickname; specif., a name added to a Christian name and surname to distinguish a person from others of the same name. [Chiefly Sc.]

tone (tōn), *n.* [OF. F. *ton*, < L. *tonus*, < Gr. τόνος, a stretching, tension, pitch, tone, key, exertion, energy, intensity, < τείνειν, stretch: see *thin*.] Any sound considered with reference to its quality, pitch, strength, source, etc. (as, sweet, shrill, or loud *tones*; "the clear sonorous *tones* of the archdeacon," Trollope's "Warden," vi.; "The *tones* of a distant church bell were borne to them on the valley breeze," W. Churchill's "Modern Chronicle," i. 11); quality or character of sound (as, a voice silvery in *tone*); also, a musical sound, or a sound of definite pitch and character employable in harmonic relations (usually consisting of several relatively simple constituents called 'partial tones,' the lowest of which is called the 'fundamental tone' and the others 'harmonics' or 'overtones'); also, one of the larger intervals of the modern musical scale (also called *whole tone*, as distinguished from *half-tone* or *semitone*); a whole step; also, any of the nine melodies or tunes in Gregorian music, to which the psalms are sung (called 'Gregorian tones'); also, a particular quality, way of sounding, modulation, or intonation of the voice, as expressive of some meaning, feeling, spirit, etc. (as, to speak in a peculiar, mysterious, suspicious, or surly *tone*; a *tone* of approval or command); a characteristic mode of sounding words in speech, or an accent, peculiar to a person, people, locality, etc.; an artificial or affected intonation, as in speaking, recitation, or reading; an inflection of the voice serving to distinguish one word from another that is otherwise of the same sound, as in Chinese; stress of voice on a syllable of a word; a stressed or accented syllable; also, the state of tension or firmness proper to the organs or tissues of the body (as, "Every sinew had its full *tone* and elasticity": Parkman's "Oregon Trail," viii.); that state of the body, or of an organ,

in which all its animal functions are performed with healthy vigor (as, "Mr. Pontifex is not well enough . . . We must wait till he has recovered *tone* a little more": S. Butler's "Way of All Flesh," lxxix.); hence, normal healthy condition of the mind; a particular state or temper of the mind; also, spirit, character, or tenor (as, "The conversation took a higher *tone*, one fine thought called forth another": Carlyle's "Sartor Resartus," ii. 5); prevailing character or style, as of manners or morals; also, style, distinction, or elegance; also, the prevailing effect of color and of light and shade in a painting, etc.; also, hue, or the distinctive quality of color, by which red, yellow, green, blue, etc., differ one from another ('color tone'); loosely, variety of color; a tint; a shade.—**tone,** *v. t.*; *toned, toning.* To sound with a particular tone; intone (as, "The boy . . . commenced *toning* a psalm-tune through his nose": Mrs. Stowe's "Uncle Tom's Cabin," i.); give the proper tone to (a musical instrument); also, to give physical or mental tone to; also, to modify the tone or character of; often, to modify the tone or general coloring of; render (as specified) in tone or coloring (as, "The other side [of blocks of marble] is *toned* and stained a golden rosy flesh colour": Vernon Lee's "Genius Loci," Among the Marble Mountains); give the desired tone to (a painting, etc.).—**to tone down,** to lower the tone, strength, intensity, etc., of; soften; moderate: as, "The more superstitious elements of religious systems are *toned down*" (Lecky's "Hist. of Eng. in the 18th Century," ii.).—**to tone up,** to give a higher or stronger tone to: as, to *tone up* the system. —**tone,** *v. i.* To take on a particular tone; assume color or tint; also, to harmonize in tone or color (*with,* or *in with*).—**to tone down,** to become softened or moderated: as, "His exterior oddities never seem to have *toned down* much" (Charnwood's "Abraham Lincoln," iv.).—**to tone up,** to gain in tone or strength.—**toned,** *a.* Having a tone (as specified): as, sweet-*toned*.—**tone'less,** *a.* Without tone; soundless or mute; without modulation or expression; without vigor; listless.—**tone'=po''em,** *n.* In *music*, an instrumental composition intended to suggest a train of images or sentiments such as are contained in a poem.—**ton-er** (tō'nėr), *n.*

tong[1] (tông), *v.* [See *tongs*.] **I.** *tr.* To seize, gather, hold, or handle with tongs, as oysters or logs. **II.** *intr.* To use, or work with, tongs.

tong[2] (tông), *n.* [Chinese.] Among the Chinese, an association or society.

ton-ga (tong'gä), *n.* [Hind. *tāngā.*] A kind of light two-wheeled vehicle used in India.

tongs (tôngz), *n. pl.* or *sing.* [AS. *tang, tange,* = D. *tang* = G. *zange* = Icel. *töng,* tongs: cf. *tang*[1].] Any of various implements consisting of two arms or limbs hinged, pivoted, or otherwise fastened together, for seizing, holding, or lifting something (as, "Seizing it [hot iron] with the *tongs*, I laid it on my anvil": Borrow's "Romany Rye," i.); also, an implement of a similar kind for curling the hair, etc. Often called *pair of tongs.*

tongue (tung), *n.* [AS. *tunge* = D. *tong* = G. *zunge* = Icel. *tunga* = Goth. *tuggō*, tongue; akin to OL. *dingua*, L. *lingua*, tongue: see *lingual*.] An organ in man and most vertebrates occupying the floor of the mouth and often protrusible and freely movable, being the principal organ of taste and, in man, of articulate speech; a similar or analogous organ or process in invertebrates; often, the human tongue as the organ of speech (as, "On this point of Taxes the ablest pens, and most eloquent *tongues*, have been exercised": Burke's "Conciliation with the Colonies"); hence, the faculty or power of speech (as, "Sanchia, having found her *tongue*, was quickly kindled to eloquence": M. Hewlett's "Open Country," xi.); speech or talk, sometimes mere glib or empty talk; manner or character of speech (as, a smooth or flattering *tongue*; "this young dandy of twenty-three with the airy and cynical *tongue*," Arnold Bennett's "Hilda Lessways," ii. 4); also, the speech or language of a particular people, race, country, or locality (as, the Hebrew *tongue*; the many *tongues* of India; the old Cornish *tongue*); a dialect; a people as distinguished by its language (a Biblical use: as, "I will gather all nations and *tongues*," Isa. lxvi. 18); also, the voice of a hound or other dog; also, the tongue of an animal, as an ox or sheep, as used for food, often prepared by smoking or pickling; also, something resembling or suggesting an animal's tongue in shape, position, or function; a projecting and tapering or elongated part or object; a narrow strip of land running out into a body of water; a tapering jet of flame; the pin of a buckle, brooch, etc.; the pole of a carriage or other vehicle, extending between the animals drawing it; a projecting strip along the edge of a board, for fitting into a groove in another board; the pointer or indicator of a balance, dial, etc.; a movable piece suspended inside of a bell and producing a ringing sound on striking against the side of the bell; a vibrating reed or the like in a musical instrument; the short movable rail of a railroad-switch, by which the wheels are directed to one or the other line of rails; a strip of leather under the lacing or fastening of a shoe.—**at one's tongue's end,** in readiness for saying or reciting at any time: as, to have names or dates *at one's tongue's end.*—**on one's tongue,** on the verge of being uttered: as, "The words had been *on his tongue* all the evening" (Mrs. Wharton's "Ethan Frome," v.). Often, also, *on the tip of one's tongue.*—**to give tongue,** of hounds, etc., to bark, esp. when in pursuit of a quarry. Also fig., of persons.—**to hold one's tongue,** to refrain from speech; be silent.—**with one's tongue in one's cheek,** mockingly; insincerely.—**tongue,** *v.*; *tongued, tonguing.* **I.** *tr.* To speak or utter (archaic); articulate or pronounce (prov.); reproach or scold; talk about injuriously; also, to touch with the tongue; modify (the tones of a flute, cornet, etc.) by strokes of the tongue; also, to furnish with a tongue; cut a tongue on (a board); join or fit together by a tongue and groove. **II.** *intr.* To use the tongue; talk; prate; also, to tongue the tones of a flute, etc.; also, to project as or like a tongue or tongues.—**tongued,** *a.* Having a tongue or tongues: as, many-*tongued.*—**tongue'less,** *a.* Having no tongue; also, speechless; mute.—**tongue'let,** *n.* A little tongue.—**tongue'ster** (-stėr), *n.* A talker; a gossip.—**tongue=tie,** *n.* Impeded motion of the tongue caused esp. by shortness of the frenum which binds down its under side. —**tongue=tie,** *v. t.*; *-tied, -tying.* To render tongue-tied. —**tongue'=tied,** *a.* Affected with tongue-tie; also, unable to speak freely, or speechless or mute, from any cause, as from shyness or embarrassment (as, "He stood looking at her, *tongue-tied* and miserable": Margaret Kennedy's "Constant Nymph," xxiv.); sometimes, reticent or reserved. —**ton-guey** (tung'i), *a.* Talkative, loquacious, or garrulous (now colloq.); also, of the nature of a tongue; produced by the tongue; lingual.

ton-ic (ton'ik), *a.* [F. *tonique,* < Gr. τονικός, < τόνος: see *tone.*] Of or pertaining to a tone or tones in music; specif., pertaining to or founded on the key-note, or first tone, of a musical scale (as, a *tonic* chord, a chord having the key-note for its root); also, pertaining to tone or accent in speech; in *physiol.* and *pathol.,* pertaining to tension, as of the muscles; marked by continued muscular contraction (as, a *tonic* spasm); in *med.,* etc., pertaining to, maintaining, increasing, or restoring the tone or healthy condition of the system or organs, as a medicine; invigorating or bracing to the physical system, or, fig., to the mind, moral nature, etc. (as, "The air, with or without any medicinal virtue blown from the cinchona trees . . . was *tonic,*" W. H. Hudson's "Green Mansions," i.; a *tonic* influence or experience).— **tonic accent,** vocal accent, or syllabic stress, in pronunciation or speaking.—**tonic sol=fa system,** a system of teaching music, esp. singing, in which tonality or key-relationship is emphasized, the usual staff-notation is discarded, and the tones are indicated by the initial letters of the syllables *do, re, mi, fa, sol, la,* and *ti* (for *si*), with *do* always denoting the tonic or key-note. See *sol-fa, n.*—**ton'ic,** *n.* The key-note, or first tone, of a musical scale; sometimes, the final tone of a scale (as, the upper *tonic,* the eighth tone counting from the first upward, itself constituting the beginning of another scale); in *med.,* a tonic agent or remedy; in general, anything invigorating or bracing, physically, mentally, or morally (as, "Sport . . . is of great value . . . as a kind of mental *tonic*": Mallock's "New Republic," iv. 2).—**ton'i-cal-ly,** *adv.*—**to-ni-ci-ty** (tō-nis'i-ti), *n.* Tonic quality or condition; the property of possessing bodily tone; the normal elastic tension of living muscles, arteries, etc., by which the tone of the system is maintained.

to=night, to-night (tö-nīt'). [AS. *tō niht:* see *to,* prep., and *night.*] **I.** *adv.* On this present night; on the night of this present day; also, last night (as, "I dream'd a dream *to-night,*" Shakspere's "Romeo and Juliet," i. 4. 50: obs. or prov.). **II.** *n.* This present or coming night; the night of this present day.

to-nite (tō'nīt), *n.* [L. *tonare,* thunder.] An explosive used in blasting, consisting of guncotton and barium nitrate.

ton-ka=bean (tong'kä-bēn'), *n.* [Guiana negro *tonca.*] The fragrant, black, almond-shaped seed of a tall leguminous tree, *Coumarouna odorata,* of tropical South America, used in perfumes and snuff; also, the tree itself.

ton=mile (tun'mīl), *n.* A unit in railroad accounts, representing the transportation of one ton of freight for the distance of one mile.

ton-nage (tun'āj), *n.* A duty formerly levied in England on wine imported in tuns; also, a duty on ships or boats at so much per ton of cargo or freight, or according to the capacity in tons; also, the carrying capacity of a vessel expressed in tons of 100 cubic feet; also, ships collectively considered with reference to their carrying capacity or together with their cargoes.

ton-neau (to-nō' or tu-nō'), *n.*; pl. *tonneaux* (-nōz'). [F., lit. 'cask,' dim. of *tonne,* tun: see *tun.*] A rear body or compartment of an automobile, with seats for passengers, orig. of rounded form and having a door at the back, but later having a door on each side; also, a complete automobile body having such a rear part; in the *metric system,* a metric ton, or millier.—**ton-neaued'** (-nōd'), *a.* Having a tonneau.

to-no-graph (tō'nọ-gráf or ton'ọ-), *n.* [Gr. τόνος, tension, tone: see *-graph.*] A recording tonometer.

to-nom-e-ter (tō-nom'e-tėr), *n.* [Gr. τόνος, tension, tone: see *-meter.*] An instrument for measuring the pitch of tones; esp., a tuning-fork, or a graduated set of tuning-forks, whose pitch has been exactly determined; also, any of various physiological instruments, as for measuring the tension of the eyeball, or for determining blood-pressure within the vessels; also, an instrument for measuring strains within a liquid.—**to-nom'e-try,** *n.* [See *-metry.*] The process or art of measuring with a tonometer.—**to-no-met-ric** (tō-nọ-met'rik or ton-ọ-), *a.*

ton-qua=bean (tong'kä-bēn'), *n.* See *tonka-bean.*

ton-sil (ton'sil), *n.* [L. *tonsillæ,* pl.] In *anat.,* either of two prominent oval masses of lymphoid tissue situated one on each side of the fauces.—**ton'sil-lar** (-si-lạr), *a.* [NL. *tonsillaris.*] Of or pertaining to the tonsils.—**ton-sil-lec'-to-my** (-si-lek'tọ-mi), *n.* [+ Gr. ἐκ, out of, + -τομία, E. *-tomy.*] In *surg.,* the excision of a tonsil or the tonsils.—**ton-sil-li'tis** (-lī'tis), *n.* [NL.] In *pathol.,* inflammation of a tonsil or the tonsils. Cf. *quinsy.*—**ton-sil-lit'ic** (-lit'ik), *a.*—**ton-sil'lo-scope** (-sil'ọ-skōp), *n.* [See *-scope.*] An instrument for inspecting the tonsils.—**ton-sil-lo-scop'ic** (-skop'ik), *a.*—**ton-sil-lot'o-my** (-si-lot'ọ-mi), *n.* [See *-tomy.*] In *surg.,* the operation of excising a tonsil or the tonsils, wholly or in part.

Tonsil.—*a,* uvula; *b,* pharynx; *c,* tongue; *d,* palate; *e,* posterior, and *f,* anterior, pillar of the fauces, between which is *g,* the tonsil.

ton-so-ri-al (ton-sō'ri-ạl), *a.* [L. *tonsorius,* < *tonsor,* shearer, barber, < *tondere:* see *tonsure.*] Of or pertaining to a barber or his work. [Often humorous.]

ton-sure (ton'shụr), *n.* [OF. F. *tonsure,* < L. *tonsura,* a shearing, ML. eccles. tonsure, < L. *tondere* (pp. *tonsus*), shear, clip, shave.] The act of clipping the hair or shaving the head, or the state of being shorn; specif., the shaving of the head, or of some part of it, as a religious practice or rite, esp. in preparation for entering the priesthood or a monastic order; also, the part of a cleric's head left bare by shaving the hair.—**ton'sure,** *v. t.*; *-sured, -suring.* To subject to tonsure; specif., to confer the ecclesiastical tonsure upon.—

ton′sured, *p. a.* Having undergone tonsure; specif., having received the ecclesiastical tonsure.

ton-tine (ton-tēn′). [F.; named from Lorenzo *Tonti*, a Neapolitan banker who proposed the method in France in 1653.] **I.** *n.* A proceeding or scheme in which subscribers to a loan or common fund share an annuity with the benefit of survivorship, the shares of the survivors being increased as the subscribers die, until the whole goes to the last survivor; also, the annuity shared, the share of each subscriber, or the number who share; also, some more or less similar proceeding or scheme; any of various forms of life-insurance in which the chief benefits accrue to participants who are alive and whose policies are in force at the end of a specified period (called the 'tontine period'). **II.** *a.* Designating, pertaining to, or involving the principle of the tontine: as, *tontine* funds; *tontine* insurance; a *tontine* policy.

to-nus (tō′nus), *n.* [L.: see *tone*.] In *physiol.*, bodily tone; in *pathol.*, tonic spasm.

to-ny (tō′ni), *a.* High-toned; fashionable; stylish. [Slang.]

too (tö), *adv.* [AS. *tō*, *adv.*, the same word as *tō*, *prep.*: see *to*.] In addition, or also (as, John and James, and Henry *too*; young, clever, and rich *too*); furthermore or moreover (as, a great victory, achieved *too* with slight losses; and then *too* we distrusted the others); likewise (as, "This [decayed state] *too* is pretty much the case with Stirling [as with Linlithgow]": Smollett's "Humphry Clinker," Sept. 3); at the same time (as, "He was not sailorly, and yet he had a smack of the sea about him *too*": Stevenson's "Treasure Island," ii.); also, to an excessive extent or degree, or beyond what is desirable, fitting, or right (as, *too* long; *too* much; *too* quickly; *too* good to be true; *too* soon for news); more (as specified) than should be; hence, as an intensive, excessively, exceedingly, or extremely (as, that is *too* good of you; "Only *too* glad to help you in any little way," Dunsany's "If," i. 4).

took (tuk). Preterit of *take.*

tool (töl), *n.* [AS. *tōl*, tool, instrument, = Icel. *tōl*, pl., tools; akin to E. *taw*[1].] Any instrument of manual operation; an instrument, esp. one held in the hand, for performing or facilitating mechanical operations, as a hammer, saw, file, etc.; that part of a lathe, planer, drill, or similar machine, which does the cutting, boring, etc., or the machine itself; specif., a small stamp or roller used by bookbinders for impressing a figure or ornament upon book-covers; the figure or ornament so impressed; also, a weapon, esp. a sword (archaic: as, "Draw thy tool, man, and after him," Scott's "Kenilworth," iv.); also, fig., anything used like a tool to do work or effect some result (as, literary *tools*, that is, books, etc.; "They . . . make use of similitudes, metaphors, examples, and other *tools* of oratory," Hobbes's "Leviathan," xxv.); often, a person used by another for his own ends (as, "The great chief of the Aztec empire was but a convenient *tool* in his hands for accomplishing his purposes": Prescott's "Conquest of Mexico," iv. 4); a cat's-paw.—**tool,** *v.* **I.** *tr.* To work or shape with a tool; specif., to ornament with a bookbinders' tool, as book-covers or their edges; also, to drive (a coach, etc.: colloq.). **II.** *intr.* To work with a tool or tools; also, to drive or ride in a vehicle (colloq.).—

tool′er, *n.*—**tool′ing,** *n.* The act of one who or that which tools; also, work done with a tool; ornamentation on book-covers produced with small stamps or tools.

toom (töm), *a.* [AS. *tōm* = Icel. *tōmr*, empty: cf. *teem*[1].] Empty. [Now Sc. and north. Eng.]—**toom,** *v. t.* To empty. [Sc. and north. Eng.]

toon (tön), *n.* [Hind. *tūn*.] A meliaceous tree, *Toona* (or *Cedrela*) *toona*, of the East Indies and Australia, yielding a red wood resembling mahogany, but

Toon.

softer, and extensively used for furniture, carving, etc.; also, the wood.

toot (töt), *v.* [Cf. MLG. and G. *tuten*, D. *tuiten*, *toeten*, blow a horn; prob. orig. imit.] **I.** *intr.* To sound or blow a horn or other wind-instrument; of such an instrument, to give forth its characteristic sound; also, to make a sound resembling that of a horn or the like; specif., of grouse, to give forth the characteristic cry or call. **II.** *tr.* To cause (a horn, etc.) to sound by blowing it; sound (notes, etc.) on a horn or the like; also, to cry (something) aloud.—**toot,** *n.* An act or sound of tooting.—**toot′er,** *n.*

tooth (töth), *n.*; pl. **teeth** (tēth). [AS. *tōth* (pl. *tēth*) = D. *tand* = G. *zahn* = Icel. *tönn* = Goth. *tunthus*, tooth; akin to L. *dens* (*dent-*), Gr. ὀδούς (ὀδοντ-), Skt. *dant-*, tooth.] In most vertebrates, one of the hard bodies or processes, usually attached in a row to each jaw, serving for the prehension and mastication of food, as weapons of attack or defense, etc., and in mammals typically composed chiefly of dentin surrounding a sensitive pulp and covered on the crown with enamel; in invertebrates, any of various similar or analogous processes occurring in the mouth or alimentary canal; hence, any projection resembling or suggesting a tooth; one of the projections of a comb, rake, saw, etc.; one of a series of projections (cogs) on the edge of a wheel, etc., which engage with corresponding parts of another wheel or body; also, a roughened surface, as of paper; also, in fig. use, a sharp, distressing, or destructive attribute or agency (as, "Jealousy with rankling *tooth*": Gray's "On a Distant Prospect of Eton College"); also, taste, relish, or liking (as, "These are not dishes for thy dainty *tooth*": Dryden's tr. Persius's "Satires," iii. 229).—**first, temporary,** or **deciduous tooth,** one of the temporary mammalian teeth of early life. Also called *milk-tooth.*—**in the teeth,** or **in one's teeth,** in direct opposition or conflict; also, to one's face, or openly (as, "Dost thou jeer and flout me *in the teeth?*" Shakspere's "Comedy of Errors," ii. 2. 22).—**in the teeth of,** so as to face or confront, or straight against (as, "They came on *in the teeth of* our men, fearless of danger," Defoe's "Robinson Crusoe," ii. 5; "a great American ship . . . steaming *in the teeth of* the wind," H. Kingsley's "Geoffry Hamlyn," xlviii.); also, in defiance of, or in spite of (as, to persist *in the teeth of* warnings); also, in the face or presence of (as, "They were . . . *in the* very *teeth of* starvation": Lamb's "Barbara S ———").—**second** or **permanent tooth,** one of the permanent mammalian teeth of later life, which replace the first or temporary teeth.—**tooth and nail,** by or as by biting and scratching; fiercely; vigorously; with all one's might: as, "The Swedes followed up their fire by . . . falling *tooth and nail* upon the foe" (Irving's "Knickerbocker's New York," vi. 8).—**to show one's teeth,** fig., to show hostility; act in a threatening manner.—**to the teeth,** so as to be fully equipped: as, armed *to the teeth.*—**tooth,** *v.* **I.** *intr.* To teethe†; also, to interlock, as cog-wheels. **II.** *tr.* To furnish with teeth; cut teeth upon; also, to bite or gnaw; taste; also, to fix into something by means of or in the manner of teeth.

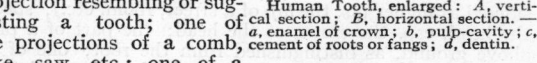

Human Tooth, enlarged: *A*, vertical section; *B*, horizontal section. — *a*, enamel of crown; *b*, pulp-cavity; *c*, cement of roots or fangs; *d*, dentin.

tooth-ache (töth′āk), *n.* Pain in a tooth or the teeth.

tooth-brush (töth′brush), *n.* A small brush with a long handle, for cleaning the teeth.

toothed (töth), *a.* Having teeth; dentate; jagged; notched.

tooth-less (töth′les), *a.* Without teeth.

tooth=or-na-ment (töth′ôr″na-ment), *n.* In *arch.*, a projecting ornament of a pyramidal or flower-like form, often repeated in a series in a hollow molding. Cf. *dog-tooth.*

Tooth-ornament. — Lincoln Cathedral, England.

tooth-pick (tŏth'pĭk), *n.* An implement, usually a sharpened quill or a small pointed piece of wood, for freeing the teeth from substances lodged between them.

tooth=shell (tŏth'shel), *n.* The long, tubular tooth-like shell of any of the mollusks constituting the genus *Dentalium* and allied genera; also, any of these mollusks; also, any of certain similar shells or mollusks.

tooth-some (tŏth'sum), *a.* Pleasing to the taste; palatable; also, fond of savory food. — **tooth'-some-ly**, *adv.* — **tooth'some-ness**, *n.*

tooth-wort (tŏth'wėrt), *n.* A European orobanchaceous plant, *Lathræa squamaria*, having a rootstock covered with tooth-like scales; also, any plant of the brassicaceous genus *Dentaria*, having tooth-like projections upon the creeping rootstock.

Tooth-shell.

too-tle (tŏ'tl), *v. i.; -tled, -tling.* [Freq. or dim. of *toot.*] To toot gently or repeatedly; produce a succession of light modulated sounds on a flute or the like.

top¹ (top), *n.* [AS. *top* = D. *top* = G. *zopf* = Icel. *toppr*, top.] A crowning tuft or crest, as on the head of a person or animal (now prov.); the hair of the head (now Sc.); also, a bunch of hair, fibers, etc.; the portion of flax or tow put on the distaff; a bundle of combed wool ready for the spinner; also, the highest point or part of anything; the apex; the summit; the uppermost or upper part, surface, etc., of anything; the higher end of anything on a slope; a part considered as higher (as, the *top* of a street, room, etc.); specif., the head, esp. the crown of the head; the part of a plant above ground, as distinguished from the root; one of the tender tips of the branches or shoots of plants (chiefly in *pl.*); the top part of a shoe or boot, above the upper; a top-boot (chiefly in *pl.*: colloq.); a platform surrounding the head of a lower mast on a ship, and serving as a foothold, a means of extending the upper rigging, etc.; the cover of a carriage; also, that part of anything which is first or foremost; the beginning; the highest or leading place, position, rank, etc. (as, he is at the *top* of his class); one who or that which occupies the highest or leading position; the highest point, pitch, or degree (as, "He . . . talks at the *top* of his voice": Mrs. Wharton's "Age of Innocence," vii.); the most perfect example, type, etc. (as, the *top* of all honors or blessings); the best or choicest part (as, the *top* of all creation); also, in *golf*, a stroke above the center of the ball; also, the forward spin given to the ball by such a stroke. — **big top,** the large or main tent of a circus. [Colloq.] — **on top,** fig., successful; victorious; dominant: as, the opposite faction came out *on top*. — **on top of,** above and resting on; upon; close upon; following upon. — **over the top.** See under *over, prep.* — **the top of the morning,** a phrase used in forms of greeting, esp. by the Irish: as, " *The top of the morning* to you, Father M'Grath," says she" (Marryat's "Peter Simple," xxxvi.). — **top¹,** *a.* Pertaining to, situated at, or forming the top; highest; uppermost; upper; also, foremost, chief, or principal (as, "the *top* gentry of the country": Godwin's "Caleb Williams," xxxix.); also, highest in degree, or greatest (as, "Off he set again at his *top* speed": Stevenson's "Kidnapped," xxii.). — **top hole,** fig., the 'top notch,' or highest point: often used as an adjective (commonly with a hyphen) in the sense of 'first-rate' (as, "He's absolutely *top hole* at this sort of thing": Eden Phillpotts's "Grey Room," iv.). [Slang, Eng.] — **top notch,** fig., the highest point or degree attainable (as, the *top notch* of efficiency): sometimes used as an adjective (commonly with a hyphen) in the sense of 'first-rate' (as, a *top-notch* performance). [Colloq.] — **top¹,** *v.; topped, topping.* **I.** *tr.* To remove the top of; crop; prune; also, to furnish with a top; put a top on; surmount with something specified; also, to be at or constitute the top of (as, "the decent church that *topp'd* the neighbouring hill": Goldsmith's "Deserted Village," 12); sometimes, to complete by or as by putting the top on or constituting the top of (as, "They finished the meal in silence . . . and Kim *topped* it with a native-made cigarette": Kipling's "Kim," iv.); finish *(off:* colloq.); also, specif., to put the best part of (fruit, etc.) on top (colloq.); top-dress (land); stain the tips of the hair of (fur, etc.); also, to reach the top of (as, "Already they have

topped the Appalachian mountains": Burke's "Conciliation with the Colonies"); rise above (as, "The sun had *topped* the horizon behind me": Roosevelt's "Ranch Life and the Hunting-Trail," xi.); get or leap over the top of (a fence, etc.); also, to exceed in height; hence, to exceed in amount, number, etc.; surpass, excel, or outdo (as, "*topping* all others in boasting": Shakspere's "Coriolanus," ii. 1. 23); also, to come up to or go beyond the requirements of (a part or character); in *dyeing*, to cover with the final color; in *golf*, to hit (the ball) above the center; also, to make (a stroke, etc.) by hitting the ball in this way. **II.** *intr.* To rise aloft; tower; also, to excel; in *golf*, to hit the ball above the center.

top² (top), *v.; topped, topping.* [Origin uncertain: cf. *top¹.*] **I.** *tr. Naut.*, to elevate one end of (a yard or boom). **II.** *intr.* To fall or incline with the top foremost; topple; *naut.*, to rise at one end, as a yard.

top³ (top), *n.* [AS. *top.*] A child's toy of various shapes, often inversely conical, with a tapering point on which it is made to spin, as by the rapid unwinding of a string wound about it, or by lashing it with a whip. — **to sleep like a top,** to sleep soundly: in allusion to the smooth, quiet motion of a spinning top when the axis of rotation is vertical.

to-parch (tō'pärk or top'ärk), *n.* [LL. *toparcha*, < Gr. τοπάρχης, < τόπος, place, district, + ἄρχειν, rule.] The ruler of a small district or petty state. — **to'par-chy** (-pär-ki), *n.; pl. -chies* (-kiz). [L. *toparchia*, < Gr. τοπαρχία.] The territory ruled by a toparch.

to-paz (tō'paz), *n.* [OF. F. *topaze*, < L. *topazus*, < Gr. τόπαζος, topaz: cf. Skt. *tapas*, heat, fire.] A mineral generally regarded as a fluosilicate of aluminium, usually occurring in prismatic crystals of various colors, and used as a gem ('true topaz' or 'occidental topaz'); also, a yellow variety of sapphire ('oriental topaz'); also, a yellow variety of quartz ('false topaz').

top=boot (top'bŏt), *n.* A high boot having the upper part of a different material from the rest and separate from it, as if turned over, or designed to be turned over; also, any boot with a high top. — **top'=boot''ed,** *a.*

top=coat (top'kōt), *n.* An outer coat; an overcoat; specif., a light-weight overcoat.

top=dress (top'dres), *v. t.* To manure (land, etc.) on the surface. — **top'=dress''ing,** *n.* A dressing of manure on the surface of land.

tope¹ (tōp), *n.* [Origin uncertain.] A small shark, *Galeorhinus* (or *Galeus*) *galeus*, found along the European coast; also, any of various related sharks of small size.

European Tope (*Galeorhinus galeus*).

tope² (tōp), *n.* [Hind. *tōp.*] In Buddhist countries, a dome-shaped monumental structure for the preservation of relics or the commemoration of some event; a dagoba or a stupa.

tope³ (tōp), *n.* [Tamil *tōppu*, Telugu *tōpu.*] In India, a clump, grove, or plantation of trees.

tope⁴ (tōp), *v. t. or i.; toped, toping.* [Cf. obs. *tope*, interj., an exclamation (appar. of pledging) used among drinkers, < F. *toper*, accept a wager in dicing, < Sp. *topar*, orig. strike against, meet.] To drink (alcoholic liquors), esp. to excess and habitually.

Great Tope at Sanchi, near Bhilsa, in Bhopal, Central India.

to-pee (tō-pē' or tō'pē), *n.* See *topi.*

to-pek (tō'pek), *n.* Same as *tupik.*

top-er (tō'pėr), *n.* One who topes; a hard drinker; a drunkard.

top=full (top'fúl'), *a.* Full to the brim; brim-full. [Now rare.]

top-gal-lant (top-gal'ant, naut. to-gal'ant). [From *top*[1] + *gallant*.] *Naut.:* **I.** *n.* A top or platform at the head of a topmast of a ship†; also, a topgallantmast or topgallant-sail; fig., the highest part; the summit. **II.** *a.* Pertaining to the topgallantmast.—**top-gal′lant-mast** (-màst, naut. -mast), *n. Naut.,* the mast next above the topmast.—**top-gal′lant=sail** (-sāl, naut. -sl), **top-gal′lant=yard**, *n. Naut.,* the sail or the yard belonging to the topgallantmast.

top=ham-per (top'ham″pèr), *n. Naut.,* any unnecessary weight, either aloft or about the upper decks; also, the light upper sails and their gear.

top=hat (top'hat'), *n.* A man's tall silk hat; any hat of similar shape. [Colloq.]

top=heav-y (top'hev″i), *a.* Having the top disproportionately heavy; liable to fall or fail as from too great weight above.—**top′=heav″i-ness**, *n.*

To-phet (tō'fet), *n.* [Heb. *tōpheth.*] A place in the valley of Hinnom, near Jerusalem, where the Jews made human sacrifices, esp. to Moloch, later used as a dumping-ground for refuse and regarded as symbolic of the place of torment in a future life; hence, the place of punishment for the wicked after death, or Gehenna or hell (as, "I fear that this burden . . . will sink me lower than the grave, and I shall fall into *Tophet*": Bunyan's "Pilgrim's Progress," i.); also, some place, condition, etc., likened to hell.

to-phus (tō'fus), *n.; pl. -phi* (-fī). [L. *tophus, tofus,* tufa.] In *pathol.,* a calcareous concretion formed about the joints, the teeth, the pinna of the ear, etc., esp. in gout; a gouty deposit.

to-pi (tō-pē' or tō'pē), *n.* [Hind.] In India, a hat or cap; esp., a helmet or sun-hat made of sola pith.

to-pi-a-ri-an (tō-pi-ā'ri-an), *a.* Topiary.

to-pi-a-ry (tō'pi-ā-ri), *a.* [L. *topiarius,* pertaining to ornamental gardening, < *topia,* landscape painting, ornamental gardening, < Gr. τόπος, place.] In *gardening:* **I.** *a.* Clipped or trimmed into ornamental shapes; of or pertaining to such trimming. **II.** *n.* Topiary work; the topiary art.

top-ic (top'ik). [As adj., LL. *topicus,* < Gr. τοπικός, pertaining to a place, local, pertaining to commonplaces, < τόπος, place; as n., L. *topica,* pl., < Gr. τοπικά, commonplaces (in title of a work of Aristotle), prop. neut. pl. of τοπικός.] **I.** *a.* Topical. [Obs. or rare.] **II.** *n.* An idea or consideration of general application or reference; a general rule or maxim; a consideration affording a ground of argument; also, the subject of a discourse, argument, or literary composition, or of any distinct part of one; in general, a subject of speech or writing (as, "There was no common *topic* about which we could speak," Kingsley's "Alton Locke," v.; "Hugh's letters divided themselves pretty fairly between two main *topics*," H. G. Wells's "Mr. Britling," ii. 4. § 10; *topics* of public interest).—**top′i-cal**, *a.* Of or pertaining to a place or locality; local; also, pertaining to a topic or general maxim; also, of or pertaining to the subject of a discourse, composition, or the like, or any topic of speech or writing; often, pertaining to or dealing with topics or matters of current or local interest (as, a *topical* song); in *med.,* pertaining or applied to a particular part of the body.—**top′i-cal-ly**, *adv.*

top-in-am-bour (top-in-am'bor), *n.* [F., for *topinambou,* orig. name of a native race of Brazil.] The Jerusalem artichoke.

top-knot (top'not), *n.* A knot or bow of ribbon worn on the top of the head; a knot of hair so worn in some styles of hairdressing; a tuft of hair growing on the top of the head; a tuft or crest of feathers on the head of a bird.—**top′knot″ted**, *a.*

top-less (top'les), *a.* Having no top; hence, immeasurably high, or lofty (as, "the *topless* towers of Ilium": Marlowe's "Doctor Faustus," xiv.).

top-loft-y (top'lóf″ti), *a.* Lofty in character or manner; haughty; pompous; pretentious. [Colloq.]—**top′loft″i-ness**, *n.*

top-man (top'man), *n.; pl. -men. Naut.,* a man stationed for duty in a top.

top-mast (top'màst), *n. Naut.,* the second section of mast

above the deck, being that just above the lower mast or first section.

top-most (top'mōst), *a. superl.* Highest; uppermost: as, "the *topmost* branch" (Dryden's tr. Virgil's "Æneid," vii. 99); "the *topmost* letter of the packet" (Tarkington's "Alice Adams," ix.).

to-pog-ra-pher (tō-pog'ra-fèr), *n.* [Gr. τοπογράφος, < τόπος, place, + γράφειν, write.] One skilled in topography.

top-o-graph-ic, top-o-graph-i-cal (top-ō-graf'ik, -i-kal), *a.* [Gr. τοπογραφικός.] Of or pertaining to topography.—**top-o-graph′i-cal-ly**, *adv.*

to-pog-ra-phy (tō-pog'ra-fi), *n.; pl. -phies* (-fiz). [LL. *topographia,* < Gr. τοπογραφία, < τοπογράφος, a topographer: see *topographer.*] The accurate and detailed description of particular localities, as cities, towns, estates, etc.; the accurate and detailed description of any region; a delineation of the features of a locality or region; also, the features of a locality or region collectively (as, "It was necessary to make himself personally acquainted with the *topography* and local advantages of the capital": Prescott's "Conquest of Mexico," iii. 9); also, local distribution, as of an industry, or the study of this.

top-o-nym (top'ō-nim), *n.* [Gr. τόπος, place, + ὄνυμα, name.] A place-name; a regional name; a name derived from the name of a place or location.—**to-pon-y-my** (tō-pon'i-mi), *n.; pl. -mies* (-miz). A system of place-names; the study of such names; also, the use of toponyms.—**to-pon′y-mal, top-o-nym′ic**, *a.*

top-o-phone (top'ō-fōn), *n.* [Gr. τόπος, place, + φωνή, sound.] An instrument for ascertaining the direction from which any sound proceeds.

topped (topt), *a.* Having a top (as specified): as, "a white-*topped* wagon" (Roosevelt's "Hunting Trips of a Ranchman," vi.).

top-per (top'èr), *n.* One who or that which tops; anything surpassing or excellent (colloq.); also, a top-hat (colloq.).

top-ping (top'ing), *n.* The act of one who or that which tops; also, a distinct part forming a top to something; something put on a thing at the top to complete it; also, *pl.,* that which is removed in topping or cropping plants, as branches.—**top′ping**, *p. a.* Rising aloft; rising above something else, or overtopping; hence, surpassing; preëminent; very high in rank, degree, etc.; also, excellent or first-rate (colloq.: as, "absolutely *topping* weather," A. S. M. Hutchinson's "If Winter Comes," iv. 3); also, assuming or pretentious (colloq., U. S.: as, "She'd bring me down, and have me know . . . that I wasn't going to be so *topping* as I had been," Mrs. Stowe's "Uncle Tom's Cabin," xxix.).

top-ple (top'l), *v.; -pled, -pling.* [Cf. *top*[1] and *top*[2].] **I.** *intr.* To fall top foremost; fall forward as having too heavy a top; pitch or tumble down (as, "The tiles and chimneys began to *topple* into the streets": Motley's "Dutch Republic," ii. 10); also, to lean over or jut, as if threatening to fall (as, "the *toppling* crags": Tennyson's "Ode on the Death of the Duke of Wellington," viii.). **II.** *tr.* To cause to pitch or tumble down; throw headlong; overturn.

top-sail (top'sāl, naut. -sl), *n. Naut.,* a square sail (or either of two square sails) next above the lowest or chief square sail on a mast of a square-rigged vessel, or next above a chief fore-and-aft sail on certain schooners, etc.; also, a fore-and-aft sail next above a mainsail or other chief fore-and-aft sail.

top=saw-yer (top'sâ″yèr), *n.* The sawyer who works the upper handle of a pit-saw; hence, one who holds a higher position than another (colloq.); a person of consequence or importance (colloq.).

top=shell (top'shel), *n.* [See *top*[3].] Any of the marine mollusks constituting the family *Trochidæ,* having a spiral, usually regularly conical shell.

top-side (top'sīd), *n.* The upper side; specif., the upper part of a boat's or ship's side (usually in *pl.*).

top=soil (top'soil), *n.* The surface or upper part of the soil.—**top′=soil**, *v. t.* To remove the top-soil from (land).

Top-shell (*Trochus niloticus*).

---

top-sy-tur-vy (top′si-tėr′vi). [Prob. < *top*[1] (or pl. *tops*) + ME. *terven*, *tirven*, turn, overturn; with second syllable (-*sy*) possibly representing *so*.] **I.** *adv.* With the top where the bottom should be, or upside down (as, "He . . . would frighten them . . . with the alarming fact that the world did absolutely turn round, and that they were half the time *topsy-turvy!*" Irving's "Sketch-Book," Sleepy Hollow); in or into a reversed condition or order; hence, in or into a state of confusion or disorder (as, "A lively child is a godsend, even if she turns the whole house *topsy-turvy*": Mrs. Stowe's "Oldtown Folks," xviii.). **II.** *a.* Turned upside down; inverted; reversed; hence, confused or disorderly (as, "the . . . *topsy-turvy* bed-rooms": C. Brontë's "Jane Eyre," xvii.). **III.** *n.* The act of turning or the fact of being turned upside down; inversion of the natural order; a state of confusion or disorder.—**top′sy-tur′vi-ly**, *adv.*—**top′sy-tur′vi-ness**, *n.*—**top′sy-tur′vy-dom** (-dǫm), *n.* A state of affairs or a region in which everything is topsyturvy.

toque (tōk), *n.* [F.] A kind of cap or hat with little or no brim, or with the brim turned up against the crown, and often with a soft or full crown, worn by women and formerly also by men.

tor (tôr), *n.* [AS. *torr*.] A rocky eminence; a hill. [Eng.]

to-rah (tō′rä), *n.* [Heb. *tōrāh*.] In *Jewish lit.*, instruction; doctrine; law; specif. [*cap*.], the Mosaic law; hence, the Pentateuch.

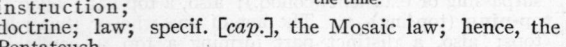
Women's Toques of the 16th century, from portraits of the time.

tor-bern-ite (tôr′bėrn-īt), *n.* [G. *torbernit*; named from *Torbern* Bergman (1735–84), Swedish chemist.] A mineral, a hydrous phosphate of uranium and copper, occurring in square tabular crystals of a bright-green color, pearly luster, and micaceous cleavage.

torch (tôrch), *n.* [OF. F. *torche*, through ML. or LL. < L. *torquere*, twist.] A light to be carried in the hand, consisting of some combustible substance, as resinous wood, or of twisted flax or the like soaked with tallow or other inflammable substance; fig., something considered as a source of illumination, enlightenment, guidance, etc. (as, the *torch* of learning); also, a lamp borne on a pole or other appliance; a portable electric light ('electric torch': as, "Taking from his pocket the electric *torch* which had lately come into fashion, he examined the road for his stick," Arnold Bennett's "Pretty Lady," xxx.); also, any of various lamp-like devices which produce a hot flame, and are used for soldering, burning off paint, etc.—**torched**, *a.* Furnished with or lighted by torches.—**torch′-fish**, *n.* A deep-sea fish, *Linophryne lucifer*, with a dorsal spine carrying a luminous or phosphorescent bulb like a torch above the head.—**torch′-light**, *n.* The light of a torch or torches.

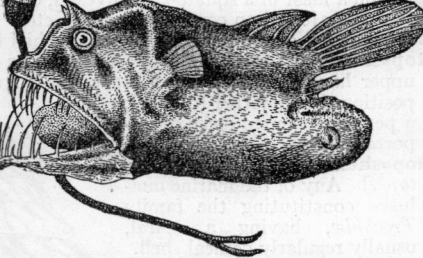
Torch-fish. — From a drawing by R. W. Shufeldt.

tor-chon (tôr′shǫn) **lace.** [F. *torchon*, dish-cloth, duster, < *torcher*, wipe.] A bobbin-made linen lace with loosely twisted threads in simple, open patterns; also, a machine-made imitation of this, in linen or cotton.

torch-wood (tôrch′wúd), *n.* Any of various resinous woods suitable for making torches, as the wood of the rutaceous

tree *Amyris balsamifera*, of Florida, the West Indies, etc.; also, any of the trees yielding these woods.

tore[1] (tōr). Preterit of *tear*[1].

tore[2] (tōr), *n.* [F. *tore*, < L. *torus*: see *torus*.] In *arch.*, a torus; in *geom.*, a surface generated by the revolution of a conic (esp. a circle) about an axis lying in its plane; also, the solid inclosed by such a surface.

tor-e-a-dor (tor″ē-a-dôr′ or tor′ē-a-dôr), *n.* [Sp., < *torear*, fight bulls, < *toro*, < L. *taurus*, bull.] A Spanish bull-fighter, esp. one who fights on horseback.

to-reu-tic (tō-rö′tik), *a.* [Gr. τορευτικός, < τορεύειν, bore, chase, emboss.] Noting or pertaining to the art, esp. the ancient art, of working in metals, ivory, or the like, including embossing, work in relief, chasing, etc.—**to-reu′tics**, *n.* The toreutic art.

to-ri (tō′rī), *n.* Plural of *torus*.

tor-ic (tor′ik), *a.* Of or pertaining to a tore (geometrical surface or solid); specif., noting or pertaining to a lens with a surface forming a portion of a tore, for eye-glasses or spectacles.

to-ri-i (tō′rē-ē), *n.* [Jap.] A form of decorative gateway or portal in Japan, consisting of two upright wooden posts connected at the top by two horizontal crosspieces, and commonly found at the entrance to Shinto temples.

Torii.

tor-ment (tôr′ment), *n.* [OF. *torment* (F. *tourment*), < L. *tormentum*, engine of war, instrument of torture, torture, anguish, < *torquere*, twist: cf. *torture*.] An engine of war worked by torsion, for hurling stones, darts, etc.†; also, an instrument of torture, as the rack or the thumb-screw; hence, the infliction of torture by means of such an instrument; the torture inflicted (as, "the most horrible *torments* which could be inflicted by boot and thumbscrew": Macaulay's "Hist. of Eng.," ix.); also, a state of great suffering, bodily or mental; agony; misery; also, something that causes great pain or suffering of body or mind (as, "the gout, and divers other *torments* of soul and body": Hawthorne's "Twice-Told Tales," Dr. Heidegger's Experiment); a source of pain, anguish, or trouble, or, sometimes, of worry or annoyance; also, a violent storm†; a tempest†.—**tor-ment′**, *v. t.* [OF. *tormenter* (F. *tourmenter*).] To put to torment or torture; also, to afflict with great suffering, bodily or mental (as, "Mrs. Milvain, *tormented* by a familiar headache, kept her room," Gissing's "New Grub Street," iii.; "He . . . was not *tormented* with unsatisfied desires," C. B. Brown's "Wieland," i.); pain; distress; plague; sometimes, to worry or annoy excessively (as, "*Torment* me no more with questions, complaints, or thanks": Scott's "Black Dwarf," viii.); also, to throw into commotion, stir up, or disturb (as, "The murmur of the beach, *Tormented* by the changeful dashing seas": W. Morris's "Jason," xii. 119); fig., to twist or distort (sense, etc.).—**tor-ment′er**, *n.*

tor-men-til (tôr′men-til), *n.* [ML. *tormentilla*, dim. < L. *tormentum*, E. *torment*; from its use medicinally to allay pain.] A low rosaceous herb, *Potentilla tormentilla*, of Europe, with small bright-yellow flowers, and a strongly astringent root which is used in medicine and also in tanning and dyeing. Also **tor-men-til′la** (-til′ä).

tor-ment-ing (tôr-men′ting), *p. a.* That torments.—**tor-ment′ing-ly**, *adv.*—**tor-ment′ing-ness**, *n.*

tor-men-tor (tôr-men′tǫr), *n.* One who or that which torments.—**tor-men′tress**, *n.* A female tormentor.

Tormentil.

torn (tôrn). Past participle of *tear*[1].

tor-na-do (tôr-nā'dō), *n.*; pl. *-does* (-dōz). [Appar. an altered form, by association with Sp. *tornar*, turn, of Sp. *tronada*, thunder-storm, < *tronar*, < L. *tonare*, thunder.] A violent thunder-storm (now rare); also, a violent squall or whirlwind of small extent, as those occurring during the summer months on the west coast of Africa; specif., a destructive rotatory storm of the middle U. S., usually appearing as a whirling, advancing funnel pendent from a mass of black cloud (cf. *cyclone*); also, fig., a violent outburst, as of activity or emotion (as, "In the fifteenth century a last *tornado* of nomadism arose in Western Turkestan," H. G. Wells's "Outline of History," xxxiv. § 5D; "In a *tornado* of rage and mortification, she called for her carriage," Lytton Strachey's "Queen Victoria," ii.).

to-roid (tō'roid), *n.* [See *tore*[2] and *-oid*.] In *geom.*, a surface generated by the revolution of any closed plane curve or contour about an axis lying in its plane; also, the solid inclosed by such a surface.

to-rose (tō'rōs or tō-rōs'), *a.* [L. *torosus*, < *torus*, a bulge, protuberance: cf. *torus*.] Bulging; protuberant; knobbed; in *bot.*, cylindrical, with swellings or constrictions at intervals. Also **to'rous.**

tor-pe-do (tôr-pē'dō), *n.*; pl. *-does* (-dōz). [L. *torpedo*, numbness, torpidity, torpedo (fish), < *torpere*, be numb: cf. *torpid*.] An electric ray (fish: see *ray*[2]); also, any of various submarine explosive devices for destroying hostile ships, as a mine or, esp., a self-propelled cigar-shaped missile containing explosives which is launched from a tube in a torpedo-boat or the like and explodes upon impact with the ship fired at; also, an explosive shell or the like buried in the ground for destructive purposes; also, any of various other explosive devices, as a firework which consists of an explosive wrapped up with gravel in a piece of tissue-paper, and which detonates when thrown forcibly on the ground or against a hard surface; a detonating device employed on a railroad as a signal, being placed on a rail and exploded by the wheels of a passing locomotive; a cartridge of gunpowder, dynamite, or the like, exploded in an oil-well to start or increase the flow of oil, or elsewhere for other purposes.—**torpedo body,** a form of automobile body more or less resembling the cigar-shaped submarine torpedo: used esp. for racing and sport cars.—**tor-pe'do,** *v.*; *-doed, -doing.* **I.** *tr.* To attack, hit, damage, or destroy with a torpedo or torpedoes; also, to lay (a channel, etc.) with torpedoes or submarine mines, as against enemy ships; also, to explode a torpedo in (an oil-well) to start or increase the flow of oil. **II.** *intr.* To use, discharge, or explode torpedoes.—**tor-pe'do=boat,** *n.* A boat for discharging torpedoes, esp. a war-vessel of small size and high speed used exclusively for this purpose.—**torpedo=boat destroyer,** a vessel somewhat larger than the ordinary torpedo-boat, used for destroying torpedo-boats or as a more powerful form of torpedo-boat.—**tor-pe'do-plane** (-plān), *n.* An aëroplane designed and fitted to carry and release self-propelled torpedoes, launching them with the same effect as a torpedo-boat destroyer: invented and patented by Rear-Admiral Bradley A. Fiske in 1912.—**tor-pe'do=tube,** *n.* A tube through which a torpedo-boat or the like launches a self-propelled torpedo, usually by the explosion of a charge of powder.

tor-pid (tôr'pid). [L. *torpidus*, < *torpere*, be numb.] **I.** *a.* Benumbed; in a state in which the physical powers, processes, activities, etc., are suspended (as, "November dark Checks vegetation in the *torpid* plant Expos'd to his cold breath": Cowper's "Task," iii. 468); dormant, as a hibernating or estivating animal; sluggish in action, as a bodily organ; in general, inactive, sluggish, slow, or dull (as, "Wholly untaught, with faculties quite *torpid*, they seemed to me hopelessly dull": C. Brontë's "Jane Eyre," xxxii.); apathetic; stupid. **II.** *n.* At the University of Oxford, England, an eight-oared clincher-built boat in which the Lent races are rowed (as, "He took up rowing; and . . . secured himself a place in his College '*torpid*'": Galsworthy's "Patrician," i. 5); also, one of the crew; also, *pl.*, the races themselves.—**tor-pid'i-ty** (-i-ti), **tor'pid-ness,** *n.*—**tor'pid-ly,** *adv.*

tor-por (tôr'pọr), *n.* [L., < *torpere*, be numb.] Torpid condition; a state of suspended physical powers and activi-ties; dormancy, as of a hibernating animal; sluggish inactivity or inertia; lethargic dullness or indifference, or apathy (as, "My calmness was the *torpor* of despair": C. B. Brown's "Wieland," xiv.).—**tor-po-rif'ic** (-pọ-rif'ik), *a.* [See *-fic*.] Causing torpor.

tor-quate (tôr'kwāt), *a.* [L. *torquatus*, wearing a torque, < *torques*: see *torque*.] In *zoöl.*, ringed about the neck, as with feathers or a color; collared.

torque (tôrk), *n.* [In part, < L. *torques, torquis*, a twisted neck-ring, < *torquere*, twist; in part, < L. *torquere*.] A collar, necklace, or similar ornament consisting of a twisted narrow band, usually of precious metal, worn esp. by the ancient Gauls and Britons; in *mech.*, that which produces or tends to produce torsion or rotation; the moment of a system of forces which tends to cause rotation.—**torqued,** *a.* Twisted; convoluted; formed like a torque.

tor-ques (tôr'kwēz), *n.* [L.: see *torque*.] In *zoöl.*, a ring-like band or for-

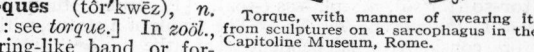

Torque, with manner of wearing it, from sculptures on a sarcophagus in the Capitoline Museum, Rome.

mation about the neck, as of feathers, hair, or integument of distinctive color or appearance; a collar.

tor-re-fy (tor'ē-fī), *v. t.*; *-fied, -fying.* [F. *torréfier*, < L. *torrefacere*, < *torrere*, dry, parch, + *facere*, make.] To dry or parch with heat, as drugs, etc.; roast, as metallic ores.—**tor-re-fac'tion** (-fak'shọn), *n.*

tor-rent (tor'ẹnt). [F. *torrent*, < L. *torrens* (torrent-), a torrent, prop. p. a., burning, boiling, rushing, < *torrere*: see *torrid*.] **I.** *n.* A stream of water flowing with great rapidity and violence (as, a mountain *torrent*; "At times the whole river-bed must be covered with a roaring *torrent* . . . of ungovernable fury," S. Butler's "Erewhon," iii.); hence, a rushing, violent, or abundant and unceasing stream of anything (as, a *torrent* of lava, of missiles, or of assailants; "the endless *torrent* of supplies that pour into France," H. G. Wells's "Italy, France, and Britain at War," iv. 4); a violent downpour of rain (as, "days of rain, real drenching *torrents*": Buchan's "Three Hostages," xx.); fig., a violent, tumultuous, or overwhelming flow (of words, feelings, etc.: as, a *torrent* of abuse; a *torrent* of questions; "The first *torrent* of passion must be allowed to subside," Smollett's "Humphry Clinker," Oct. 26). **II.** *a.* Rushing like a torrent: as, "waves of *torrent* fire" (Milton's "Paradise Lost," ii. 581).—

tor-ren-tial (to-ren'shạl), *a.* Of, pertaining to, or of the nature of a torrent; resembling a torrent in rapidity or violence; falling in torrents (as, "the *torrential* summer rain": Arnold Bennett's "Buried Alive," v.); produced by the action of a torrent; fig., violent, vehement, or impassioned; overwhelming; extraordinarily copious. —**tor-ren'tial-ly,** *adv.*

Tor-ri-cel-li-an (tor-i-sel'i-ạn or -chel'i-ạn), *a.* Pertaining to Evangelista Torricelli (1608–47), an Italian physicist and mathematician, who discovered the principle on which the barometer is constructed, by means of an experiment ('Torricellian experiment') in which a glass tube ('Torricellian tube') closed at one end was filled with mercury and then inverted in a vessel of mercury, the mercury in the tube descending to about 30 inches above the level of the mercury in the vessel, thus leaving a vacuum ('Torricellian vacuum') in the upper part of the tube, the column of mercury in the tube being supported by the pressure of the atmosphere acting on the surface of the mercury in the vessel, and the height of the column corresponding exactly to the atmospheric pressure.

tor-rid (tor'id), *a.* [L. *torridus*, < *torrere*, dry, parch, scorch, burn: see *thirst*.] Subject to parching or burning heat, esp. of the sun, as regions, etc. (as, *torrid* deserts; the *torrid* zone, the part of

Apparatus for Torricellian Experiment.

the earth's surface between the tropics); also, parching or burning (as, "*torrid* heat": Milton's "Paradise Lost," xii. 634); oppressively hot, as climate, weather, air, etc. (as, "The day was too *torrid* for intelligent sight-seeing": Margaret Kennedy's "Constant Nymph," xi.); fig., characterized by great heat of feeling; hotly ardent; passionate.—**tor-rid-i-ty** (to-rid'i-ti), **tor'rid-ness**, *n.*—**tor'-rid-ly**, *adv.*

tor-sade (tôr-sād'), *n.* [F.] A twisted cord; any ornamental twist, as of velvet.

torse (tôrs), *n.* Same as *torso.*

tor-si-bil-i-ty (tôr-si-bil'i-ti), *n.* [L. *torquere* (pp. *tortus*, later *torsus*), twist: cf. *torsion.*] Capability of being twisted.

tor-sion (tôr'shon), *n.* [F. *torsion*, < LL. *torsio*(n-), *tortio*(n-), < L. *torquere*, twist.] The act of twisting, or the resulting state; in *mech.*, the twisting of a body by two equal and opposite couples.—**torsion balance**, an instrument for measuring small forces (as electrical attraction or repulsion) by determining the amount of torsion or twisting they cause in a slender wire or filament.—**tor'sion-al**, *a.* Of, pertaining to, or resulting from torsion.—**tor'sion-al-ly**, *adv.*—**tor'sion-less**, *a.* Free from torsion.

torsk (tôrsk), *n.* [Norw. and Dan. *torsk* = Icel. *thorskr.*] The cusk (fish), *Brosme brosme.*

tor-so (tôr'sō), *n.*; pl. -*sos* (-sōz). [It., trunk, stump, stalk, < L. *thyrsus*, E. *thyrsus.* The trunk of a statue, without, or considered independently of, the head and limbs; also, the trunk of the human body; fig., something mutilated or incomplete.

tort[1] (tôrt), *n.* [OF. F. *tort*, < ML. *tortum*, wrong, injustice, prop. neut. of L. *tortus*, twisted, crooked, pp. of *torquere*, twist.] Wrong†, injustice† or harm†; in *law*, a wrong (other than a breach of contract) such as the law requires compensation for in damages.

tort[2] (tôrt), *a.* Erroneous form of *taut*: as, "Yet holds he them with *tortest* rein" (Emerson's "Initial Love").

tor-te (tôr'tè), *n.*; pl. -*ten* (-ten). [G., < LL. *torta*, cake.] A cake; also, a tart.

Torso of Hercules. Vatican Museum. Rome.

tor-ti-col-lis (tôr-ti-kol'is), *n.* [NL., < L. *tortu*, twisted (see *tort*[1]), + *collum*, neck.] In *pathol.*, an affection in which the neck is twisted and the head inclined to one side, due to muscular contraction or to rheumatism; wryneck.—**torti-col'lar**, *a.*

tor-tile (tôr'til), *a.* [L. *tortilis*, < *torquere*, twist.] Twisted; coiled; also, capable of being twisted.

tor-til-la (tôr-tēl'yä), *n.*; pl. -*las* (-yäz). [Sp., dim. of *torta*, < LL. *torta*, cake.] In Mexico, etc., a thin, round cake prepared from maize, baked on a flat plate of iron, earthenware, or the like, and eaten hot.

tor-tious (tôr'shus), *a.* [See *tort*[1].] Wrongful†; harmful†; in *law*, of the nature of or pertaining to a tort.—**tor'tious-ly**, *adv.*

tor-tive (tôr'tiv), *a.* [L. *tortivus*, < *torquere*, twist.] Twisting; twisted; tortuous: as, "As knots . . . Infect the sound pine and divert his grain *Tortive* and errant from his course of growth" (Shakspere's "Troilus and Cressida," i. 3. 9). [Obs. or archaic.]

tor-toise (tôr'tus or -tis), *n.* [ME. *tortuce*, < ML. *tortuca*, tortoise, said to be named from its crooked feet, < L. *tortus*, twisted, crooked, pp. of *torquere*, twist.] A turtle (see *turtle*[2], *n.*); often, esp., a terrestrial turtle as distinguished from the aquatic species; also, a testudo, movable shelter, or sheltering arrangement of shields.—**tor'-toise=shell. I.** *n.* The shell, or outer shell, of a tortoise; esp., the horny substance, with a mottled or clouded yellow and brown

Common European Tortoise (*Testudo græca*).

coloration, composing the plates or scales that cover the carapace of certain marine turtles, as the hawkbill, used for making combs and other articles, inlaying, etc.; also, a tortoise-shell cat, horse, or other animal (as, "Horses of this colour [yellow] have . . . the muzzle, fetlocks, mane . . . black. I do not know if he ever succeeded in breeding a *tortoiseshell*": W. H. Hudson's "Far Away and Long Ago," xi.). **II.** *a.* Yielding tortoise-shell, as a turtle; also, made of tortoise-shell; also, mottled or variegated like tortoise-shell, esp. with yellow and black and sometimes other color (as, a *tortoise-shell* cat; *tortoise-shell* butterflies, esp. of the genus *Vanessa*; *tortoise-shell* ware, a fine pottery with mottled coloration).

tor-tri-cid (tôr'tri-sid). [NL. *Tortricidæ*, pl., < *Tortrix*, the typical genus, < L. *torquere*, twist.] **I.** *n.* Any of the *Tortricidæ*, a family of small, stout-bodied moths with wide oblong wings. **II.** *a.* Belonging or pertaining to the *Tortricidæ*.

tor-tu-os-i-ty (tôr-ṭu-os'i-ti), *n.*; pl. -*ties* (-tiz). The state of being tortuous; twisted form or course; crookedness; also, a twist, bend, or crook, as in the course of something; a twisting or crooked part, passage, or thing (as, "the labyrinthic *tortuosities* and covered-ways of said citadel": Carlyle's "Sartor Resartus," ii. 10).

tor-tu-ous (tôr'ṭu-us), *a.* [OF. *tortuous* (F. *tortueux*), < L. *tortuosus*, < *tortus*, a twisting, winding, < *torquere*, twist.] Full of twists, turns, or bends (as, "We wind through *tortuous* ravines," Tyndall's "Forms of Water," § 14; "merry-makers homeward bound, many of them following a *tortuous* course," Barrie's "Sentimental Tommy," xviii.); twisting, winding, or crooked; fig., not direct or straightforward, as in a line or course of procedure, thought, speech, or writing (as, "I don't intend to write down here the *tortuous* financial history of Moggs' Limited," H. G. Wells's "Tono-Bungay," iii. 1. § 2; *tortuous* reasoning); often, deceitfully indirect or devious, or morally crooked; as proceedings, methods, policy, etc.; of persons, pursuing an indirect or devious course or policy (as, "a *tortuous* and indirect person playing a hidden game": Kipling's "Kim," vii.); in *geom.*, not in one plane, as a curve of which no two successive portions lie in one plane.—**tor'tu-ous-ly**, *adv.*—**tor'tu-ous-ness**, *n.*

tor-ture (tôr'ṭur), *n.* [F. *torture*, < LL. *tortura*, a twisting, torture, < L. *torquere*, twist: cf. *torment.*] The act of inflicting excruciating pain from sheer cruelty or in hatred, revenge, or the like; specif., the infliction of such pain by judicial or quasi-judicial authority, esp. in order to extort a confession or as a part of punishment ('judicial torture'); a method of inflicting such pain; an instrument for inflicting it†; also, in general, subjection to any excruciating or severe pain, physical or mental; the pain or suffering caused or undergone (in *sing.* or *pl.*: as, "She constantly suffered physical *torture*. She had . . . rheumatism, sciatica, and neuritis," Arnold Bennett's "Hilda Lessways," iv. 1; the *tortures* of suspense or remorse); extreme anguish of body or mind; agony; torment; also, a cause of severe pain or anguish (as, the sight was *torture* to him); also, violent distortion or perversion, as of language.—**tor'ture**, *v. t.*; -*tured*, -*turing.* To subject to torture (as, "Known to be affluent, he was *tortured* by exposing the soles of his feet to a fire": Motley's "Dutch Republic," iii. 8); specif., to subject to judicial torture; in general, to afflict with severe pain of body or mind (as, *tortured* by burns; "She could not express the anxiety and doubt *torturing* her soul," Galsworthy's "Country House," ii. 1); torment; also, to twist, force, or bring into some unnatural position or form (as, trees *tortured* by storms; to *torture* the hair; "an early Victorian room . . . full . . . of twisted and *tortured* mahogany," Arnold Bennett's "Book of Carlotta," i. 1); wrest, distort, or pervert (language, etc.).—**tor'tur-er**, *n.*—**tor'tur-ing-ly**, *adv.*—**tor'tur-ous**, *a.* Full of, involving, or causing torture.

to-rus (tō'rus), *n.*; pl. -*ri* (-rī). [L., a bulge, protuberance, raised ornament, torus (molding), cushion, bed.] In *arch.*, a large convex molding, more or less semicircular in profile, commonly forming the lowest member of the base of a column, or that directly above the plinth (when present), and sometimes occurring as one of a pair separated by a scotia and fillets (see cut on following page); in *bot.*, the receptacle of a flower; in *anat.*, etc., a rounded ridge; a protuberant part; in *geom.*, a tore.

to-ry (tō′ri). [Ir. *toiridhe*, pursuer.] **I.** *n.*; pl. *-ries* (-riz). In the 17th century, one of a class of dispossessed Irish, nominally royalists, who became outlaws and were noted for

Torus. — The upper convex molding is a decorated torus, the hollow molding next below a scotia, and the lower convex molding a plain torus.

their outrages and cruelties; [*cap.*] a member of a great political party in Great Britain, in general favoring conservation of the existing order of things in state and church, and more recently known as the 'Conservative party' (cf. *whig²*); [*cap.*] in *Amer. hist.*, a member of the British party during the Revolutionary period; one who adhered to the crown; a loyalist; [*cap.* or *l. c.*] in general, one advocating conservative principles; one opposed to reform or radicalism. **II.** *a.* [*cap.*] Being a Tory; of, pertaining to, or characteristic of the Tories; [*cap.* or *l. c.*] conservative.—**to′ry-ism,** *n.*

tosh (tosh), *n.* [Origin obscure.] Bosh; nonsense; trash; rubbish: as, "And there was Tracey Wynne, the literary stylist, who ejaculated '*Tosh!*'" (L. Merrick's "House of Lynch," vi.). [Slang, Eng.]

toss (tos), *v. t.* [Origin uncertain: cf. Norw. *tossa*, strew, scatter.] To throw or pitch about, up and down, or here and there with irregular or careless motions (as, a ship *tossed* by the waves or tempests; "He . . . closed his door noisily; and then he could be heard *tossing* things about," Tarkington's "Magnificent Ambersons," xiii.); heave, shake, or stir with irregular, forcible motions, or fling or jerk about (as, a tree *tosses* its branches in the wind; "The other adventurers had *tossed* their limbs in feverish wakefulness," Hawthorne's "Twice-Told Tales," The Great Carbuncle); fig., to agitate, disturb, or disquiet; also, to throw, pitch, or fling in some direction, esp. with the palm of the hand upward; throw lightly or carelessly (as, to *toss* a paper into the waste-basket; "Campton *tossed* the card away," Mrs. Wharton's "Son at the Front," xvii.); throw or send (a ball, etc.) from one to another, as in play; fig., to bandy or pass from one to another in talk or discussion (as, to *toss* one's name about); talk about or discuss freely or openly (as, "Now the matter of sermons chiefly consisted in *tossing* about the king's marriage with the Lady Ann": Strype's "Memorials of Cranmer," i. 5); also, to throw upward or up (once or repeatedly: as, to be *tossed* by a bull; to *toss* a person in a blanket, see phrase below); throw (a coin, etc.) into the air in order to decide something by the side turned up when it falls (often with *up*); raise or jerk upward suddenly (as, to *toss* the head in impatience or disdain).—**to toss in a blanket,** to toss (a person) repeatedly upward from a blanket held slackly at the corners and edges and jerked vigorously up and down: a mode of hazing or rough treatment.—**to toss oars,** to bring them to the perpendicular, with blades uppermost and handles resting on the bottom of the boat, as a salute: as, "The boats' crews *tossed* their *oars* while the cheers were given" (Marryat's "King's Own," xxx.).—**to toss off,** to drink at a draft, or quickly and completely (as, "He *tossed off* a glass of brandy": Thackeray's "Newcomes," xiii.); also, to dispose of, despatch, do, or make quickly and easily (as, "Archer . . . usually *tossed off* half a dozen papers with his morning coffee," Mrs. Wharton's "Age of Innocence," vii.; to *toss off* work; to *toss off* impromptu verses).—**toss,** *v. i.* To pitch, rock, sway, or move irregularly, as a ship on a rough sea, or a flag or plumes in the breeze; fling or jerk one's self or move restlessly about, esp. on a bed or couch (as, to *toss* in one's sleep; "Far into the night Fin Cooper *tossed* and turned . . . restless and sleepless," Whyte-Melville's "Katerfelto," xii.); also, to

throw something; throw a coin or other object into the air in order to decide something by the way it falls (often with *up*); also, to go with a fling of the body, or flounce (as, to *toss* out of a room).—**toss,** *n.* The act or an act of tossing; a pitching about or up and down; a throw or pitch, or the distance to which something is or may be thrown; a tossing of a coin or the like to decide something, or a toss-up; a sudden fling or jerk of the body, esp. a quick upward or backward movement of the head.—**toss′er,** *n.*—**toss′-pot,** *n.* A habitual drinker; a toper.—**toss′-up,** *n.* The tossing up of a coin or the like in order to decide something by its fall; hence (colloq.), an even chance.

tot¹ (tot), *n.* [Cf. Icel. *tottr*, nickname for a dwarfish person.] A small child (as, "What a funny little *tot* it is!" W. De Morgan's "Alice-for-Short," viii.); also, a small drinking-vessel (chiefly prov.); hence, a small portion of drink, or a dram (as, a *tot* of rum; "Our sick, in addition to what they took medicinally, often came in for their respective '*tots*' convivially," H. Melville's "Omoo," xii.); a small quantity of anything.

tot² (tot), *n.* [Appar. an abbr. of *total*: cf. L. *tot*, so many, so much.] The total of an addition; also, the act of totting or adding; an exercise in addition. [Colloq.]—**tot²,** *v. t.*; *totted*, *totting*. To find the total or sum of; add: often with *up*. [Colloq.]

to-tal (tō′tal), *a.* [OF. F. *total*, < ML. *totalis*, < L. *totus*, all, whole, entire.] Of or pertaining to the whole of something (as, a *total* eclipse); also, constituting or comprising the whole, entire, or whole (as, the *total* amount expended; the *total* yield for the year; "the *total* grist unsifted, husks and all," Cowper's "Task," vi. 108); also, complete in extent or degree, absolute, unqualified, or utter (as, a *total* failure; *total* darkness; *total* indifference).—**total abstinence,** complete abstinence from the use of alcoholic beverages.—**total depravity,** in *theol.*, the absolute unfitness of man, due to original sin, for the moral purposes of his being, until born again through the influence of the Spirit of God.—**total heat,** in *physics*, the quantity of heat required to raise a unit mass of a liquid from a standard or convenient temperature, usually its freezing-point, to a given temperature, and then to turn it into vapor at that temperature under constant pressure.—**to′tal,** *n.* The total amount, sum, or aggregate (as, add the several items to find the *total*); the whole; a whole or aggregate (as, the costs reached a *total* of $200).—**to′tal,** *v.*; *-taled* or *-talled*, *-taling* or *-talling*. **I.** *tr.* To bring to a total; add up; also, to reach a total of, or amount to (as, "The yearly correspondence *totalled* nearly a million letters": Bok's "Americanization of Edward Bok," xvi.). **II.** *intr.* To amount (to).—**to-tal-i-ta-ri-an** (tō-tal-i-tā′ri-an). **I.** *a.* Of or pertaining to a centralized form of government in which those in control grant neither recognition nor tolerance to parties of differing opinion. **II.** *n.* An adherent of totalitarian principles.—**to-tal-i-ta′ri-an-ism,** *n.*—**to-tal-i-ty** (tō-tal′i-ti), *n.*; pl. *-ties* (-tiz). The state or character of being total; entirety; specif., total obscuration in an eclipse; also, that which is total; the total amount or aggregate; a total or whole.—**to-tal-i-za-tion** (tō′tal-i-zā′shon), *n.* The act or process of totalizing, or the state of being totalized.—**to′tal-i-za″tor,** *n.* [F. *totalisateur*.] An apparatus for registering and indicating the total of operations, measurements, etc.; specif., an apparatus used at horse-races which registers and indicates the number of tickets sold to betters on each horse.—**to′tal-ize** (-īz), *v. t.*; *-ized*, *-izing*. [= F. *totaliser*.] To make total; combine into a total.—**to′tal-iz-er** (-ī-zèr), *n.* A totalizator.—**to′tal-ly,** *adv.* In a total manner or degree; wholly; entirely; completely; utterly.

to-ta-ra (tō′ta-rā or tō-tä′rä), *n.* [Maori.] A valuable taxaceous timber-tree, *Nageia* (or *Podocarpus*) *totara*, of New Zealand, with reddish wood.

tote (tōt), *v. t.*; *toted*, *toting*. [Origin unknown.] To carry or bear, as on the back or in the arms or hands, as a burden or load (as, "I'd better *tote* you on my back": G. W. Cable's "John March, Southerner," xxii.); also, to carry or have on the person, as for use (as, to *tote* a gun); also, to transport or convey, as in a vehicle or boat (as, to *tote* supplies to a logging-camp; "Will you wait to be *toted* down the river, where they kill niggers with hard work?" Mrs. Stowe's

"Uncle Tom's Cabin," v.). [Colloq. or prov., U. S., orig. southern.]—**tote**, *n.* An act or course of toting, carrying, or transporting. [Colloq. or prov., U. S.]

to-tem (tō′tem), *n.* [Algonquian.] Among the Indians of North America, an object or thing in nature, often an animal, assumed as the token or emblem of a clan, family, or related group (as, "The high chief . . . was elected . . . from some one powerful family — as . . . the families having for their *totems* the wind or the eagle": Roosevelt's "Winning of the West," i. 3); a representation of such an object serving as the distinctive mark of the clan or group; a clan or group having a particular emblem or distinctive mark; also, among other uncivilized peoples, some emblem or mark of like significance, or a clan or group having it.—**to-tem-ic** (tō-tem′ik), *a.* Of, pertaining to, or of the nature of a totem; characterized by having a totem or totems.—**to-tem′i-cal-ly**, *adv.*—**to-tem-ism** (tō′tem-izm), *n.* The practice of having totems; the system of tribal division according to totems.—**to′tem-ist**, *n.* A member of a clan or the like distinguished by a totem. —**to-tem-is′tic**, *a.*— **to′tem=pole**, *n.* A pole or post carved and painted with totemic figures, erected by Indians of the northwest coast of North America, esp. in front of their houses.

toth-er (tuTH′ėr), *a.* and *pron.* [ME. *the tother*, for *thet other*, 'that other,' 'the other.'] The other. [Now prov. or colloq.]

Totem-poles, Canadian Pacific coast.

to-ti-pal-mate (tō-ti-pal′māt), *a.* [NL. *totipalmatus*, < L. *totus*, all, whole, + *palma*, palm, sole.] Having all four toes fully webbed; steganopodous; belonging to the *Totipalmatæ*, a group of birds comprising the steganopods. Cf. *semipalmate.*—**to″ti-pal-ma′tion** (-mā′shon), *n.* Totipalmate condition or formation.

Totipalmate Foot of Pelican.

to-tip-o-tent (tō-tip′ō-tent), *a.* [L. *totus*, all, whole, + *potens* (*potent*-), E. *potent*.] In *biol.*, of a cell, etc., capable of developing into a complete organism.—**to-tip′o-tence,** *n.*

tot-ter (tot′ėr), *v.* [ME. *toteren*: cf. D. *touteren*, swing, AS. *tealtrian*, be unsteady.] **I.** *intr.* To swing to and fro, as at the end of a rope†; swing from the gallows†; also, to sway or rock on the base or ground, as if about to fall, as a tower, wall, pole, tree, etc. (also fig., as of institutions, governments, the reason, etc.); also, to sway, falter, or stagger in standing or walking, as if about to fall (as, "She did not fall, or *totter*, but stood motionless," Wister's "Virginian," xxxv.; "old men *tottering* with infirmity," Prescott's "Conquest of Mexico," iii. 6; to *totter* under a heavy burden); walk or go with faltering steps, as if from extreme weakness (as, "Mrs. Rainscourt . . . *tottered* in, and sunk exhausted on the sofa": Marryat's "King's Own," xxxix.); also, to shake or tremble (as, "He . . . filled himself a glass of wine, but with a hand so *tottering* that he spilled the half": Stevenson's "Master of Ballantrae," viii.). **II.**† *tr.* To cause to totter; bring to a tottering or ruinous condition.—**tot′ter**, *n.* The

or an act of tottering; an unsteady movement or gait: as, "Thou mightst have tracked every reel and *totter* of my footsteps by the blood that followed" (Hawthorne's "Twice-Told Tales," The Gentle Boy).—**tot′ter-er**, *n.*—**tot′ter-ing-ly**, *adv.*—**tot′ter-y**, *a.* Tottering; shaky.

tot-ty (tot′i), *a.* [Cf. *totter*.] Shaky or unsteady; dizzy or dazed; fuddled. [Now prov.]

tou-can (tö-kän′ or tö′kạn), *n.* [F.; from Brazilian name.] Any of various fruit-eating birds (family *Rhamphastidæ*), of tropical America, with an enormous beak and usually a striking coloration.

Toucan (*Rhamphastos ariel*).

touch (tuch), *v. t.* [OF. *tochier*, *tuchier* (F. *toucher*), = Sp. and Pg. *tocar* = It. *toccare*, touch, strike; origin uncertain; commonly explained as from Teut. and akin to G. *zucken*, pluck, jerk, twitch, *ziehen*, draw, and E. *tow*[3].] To put the hand, finger, etc., on, or into contact with (something), so as to feel or perceive it; come into contact with and perceive (something), as the hand or the like does; bring (the hand, finger, etc., or something held) into contact with something; lay the hand or finger on (a person) for the cure of a disease, esp. the king's evil (scrofula); also, to give a slight tap or pat to with the hand, finger, etc.; strike or hit gently or lightly; strike the strings, keys, etc., of (a musical instrument) so as to cause it to sound; sound (a bell, etc.) by striking; play or perform, as an air; mark by strokes of the brush, pencil, or the like; modify or improve (a picture, etc.) by adding a stroke here and there (often with *up*); mark or relieve slightly, as with color (as, "a grey dress . . . *touched* with blue": H. G. Wells's "Soul of a Bishop," vi.); also, to come into or be in contact with; be adjacent to, adjoin, or border on (as, "a part of the road where it *touched* the river": Dickens's "Our Mutual Friend," iii. 8); come up to, reach, or attain (as, "I have *touch'd* the highest point of all my greatness," Shakspere's "Henry VIII.," iii. 2. 223; "The circulation . . . had now *touched* a million and three-quarters," Bok's "Americanization of Edward Bok," xxxiii.); attain equality with, or compare with (usually with a negative: colloq.: as, "There's nothing elsewhere to *touch* this," Arnold Bennett's "Clayhanger," i. 14); stop at, or visit in passing (a place), as a ship or those on board; also, to treat or affect in some way by contact (as, "I'll *touch* my point With this contagion, that, if I gall him slightly, It may be death," Shakspere's "Hamlet," iv. 7. 147; a metal so hard that a file will not *touch* it); also, to affect as if by contact; tinge or imbue (as, "High nature amorous of the good, But *touch'd* with no ascetic gloom": Tennyson's "In Memoriam," cix.); also, to affect with some feeling or emotion (as, "These common things *touch* me with more of admiration and of wonder each time I behold them," Gissing's "Private Papers of Henry Ryecroft," i. 25; "She *touched* my heart with a sudden delight," Blackmore's "Lorna Doone," viii.); esp., to affect with a tender feeling, as of pity, gratitude, etc. (as, "His kind heart was . . . *touched* by the sufferings of the poor girl": Irving's "Captain Bonneville," xxxiii.); have an effect upon as feelings do (as, "if ever yet soft pity *touch'd* thy mind": Pope's tr. Homer's "Iliad," xxi.); also, to wound the feelings of (as, "Telling a man he lies, is *touching* him in the most sensible part of honour": Addison, in "Spectator," 99); also, to affect injuriously, esp. in a slight degree (as, plants *touched* with frost; a horse *touched* in the wind or breathing); infect or taint, as with disease; derange mentally in a slight degree (as, "He was *touched* in the head": J. H. Newman's "Callista," xiii.); also, to test by or as by contact with a touchstone; stamp (tested metal) as being of standard purity, etc.; also, to handle, use, or have to do with (something) in any way (usually with a negative: as, "He says, that he will never *touch* another card," Bulwer-Lytton's "Pelham," xxi.; "I have never *touched* a drop of anything stronger than water," Kingsley's "Alton Locke," iii.; "He says he wouldn't *touch* our money," L. Merrick's "House of Lynch," iii.); meddle with; hurt or injure in the least degree (as, "The lion will not *touch* the true prince": Shakspere's "1 Henry IV.," ii. 4. 300); take or taste, as food or drink; also, to take or get (money), sometimes by underhand means (now colloq.: as, "She never made another will. I proved the one I had recovered at Doctors' Commons, and *touched* the whole of her money," Marryat's "Peter Simple," xxxii.); also, to apply to for money, or succeed in getting money from (slang); also, to deal with or treat in speech or writing; now, esp., to refer or allude to (as, "He never again *touched* or came near the subject that was on his mind": Wister's "Virginian," xxxii.); also, to pertain or relate to (as, "He was . . . a most inexorable critic in all affairs *touching* the kitchen": Trollope's "Barchester Towers," ix.); concern (as, "The quarrel *toucheth* none but us alone": Shakspere's "1 Henry VI.," iv. 1. 118); be a matter of importance to, or make a difference to; in *geom.*, of a line or surface, to be tangent to. — **to touch off**, to represent exactly or aptly, as if by touches of a brush or pencil; also, to fire off or discharge (a cannon, etc.). — **to touch up**, to modify or improve by or as if by slight touches; also, to arouse or stimulate by or as if by touching or striking lightly (as, "The judge *touched up* his colts to a sharper gait," Tarkington's "Gentleman from Indiana," iv.; to *touch up* a person's memory). — **to touch wood**, to touch something made of wood: orig. done by a player in a certain children's game to render himself safe from being caught, and hence adopted generally as a playful or superstitious measure for warding off misfortune, esp. after some mention of good fortune or favorable prospects. — **touch,** *v. i.* To place the hand, finger, etc., on or in contact with something; lay the hand or finger on a person to cure a disease, esp. the king's evil (scrofula); also, to come into or be in contact; make a stop or a short call at a place, as a ship or those on board (usually with *at*: as, "Almost all the ships . . . that sail between Europe and China *touch* at Batavia," Adam Smith's "Wealth of Nations," iv. 7. 3); also, to speak or write briefly or casually (*on* or *upon*) in the course of a discourse, etc. (as, "In a chronicle of war domestic politics are only to be *touched* on in so far as they have a bearing on the campaign": Buchan's "Hist. of the Great War," liv.). — **touch,** *n.* [OF. F. *touche*.] The act or an act of touching; the state or fact of being touched; that sense by which anything material is perceived by means of the contact with it of some part of the body; the sensation or effect caused by touching something, regarded as a quality of the thing (as, an object with a slimy *touch*); a coming into or being in contact; a close relation of communication, agreement, sympathy, or the like (as, to be in *touch* with public opinion; "He had lost *touch* with his surroundings," Galsworthy's "Dark Flower," i. 14); a slight stroke or blow; a slight attack, as of illness or disease (as, "a *touch* of rheumatism": Ian Maclaren's "Beside the Bonnie Brier Bush," vii. 1); also, the act or manner of touching or fingering a musical instrument, esp. a keyboard instrument, so as to bring out its tones; the mode of action of the keys of an instrument; a note or brief strain of instrumental music; also, an act of touching a surface with the proper tool in painting, drawing, etc.; a stroke or dash, as with a brush, pencil, or pen; a dash or stroke of color, as in a picture; a detail in any artistic work (as, "The finest imaginative *touch* in the whole of English poetry . . . he considered to be Panthea's words in the 'Prometheus' [of Shelley]": M. Hewlett's "Open Country," v.); a slight added action or effort in doing or completing any piece of work; manner of execution in artistic work; also, a slight amount of some quality, attribute, etc. (as, "He was free from any *touch* of charlatanry," Froude's "Cæsar," viii.; "She could not help perceiving the slight *touch* of sarcasm in his tone," John Hay's "Bread-Winners," xiv.); a slight quantity or degree (as, "There was a *touch* of frost towards dusk": W. B. Maxwell's "In Cotton Wool," vii.); a distinguishing characteristic or trait (as, to lack most *touches* of humanity); a mention, reference, or brief statement (obs. or rare); also, the act of testing the quality of gold or silver by rubbing it upon a touchstone; an official

mark or stamp put upon gold, silver, etc., after testing, to indicate standard fineness; a die, stamp, or the like for impressing such a mark; the quality or fineness of gold or silver as tested with the touchstone and indicated by the official mark; quality or kind in general; the act of testing anything, or something that serves as a test (as, to put to the *touch*); also, an applying to a person for money, as a gift or a loan, or an obtaining money thus, or the money obtained (slang); an act of stealing, or a sum gained by it (slang); a thing that will move purchasers to the expenditure of a particular sum (colloq. or slang: as, a penny *touch*); also, a kind of black durable stone used in fine monumental work† (cf. *touch-stone*); in *change-ringing*, a partial series of changes on a peal of bells.

touch-a-ble (tuch′a-bl), *a.* Capable of being touched.

touch=and=go (tuch′and-gō′). **I.** *n.* The act of touching for an instant and leaving at once (as, "The racers would stop only at the largest towns, and then it would be only '*touch and go*'": Mark Twain's "Life on the Mississippi," xvi.); something done very quickly; also, an uncertain, precarious, or ticklish state of affairs; a narrow escape. **II.** *a.* Characterized by rapid, or slight or superficial, execution; instantaneous or expeditious; hasty, sketchy, or desultory; also, risky; of the nature of a narrow escape.

touch-back (tuch′bak), *n.* In *football*, the act of a player in touching the ball to the ground on or behind his own goal-line when it has been driven there by the opposing side.

touch-down (tuch′doun), *n.* In *football*, the act of a player in touching the ball down to the ground behind the opponent's goal-line; the play by which this is done; the score made by this play; also, a safety ('safety touchdown').

touch-er (tuch′ėr), *n.* One who or that which touches.

touch-hole (tuch′hōl), *n.* A small tubular opening in the breech of an old-time firearm, through which fire was communicated to the charge within.

touch-i-ly (tuch′i-li), *adv.* In a touchy manner. — **touch′i-ness,** *n.*

touch-ing (tuch′ing), *p. a.* That touches; esp., affecting; moving; pathetic. — **touch′ing,** *prep.* [Orig. ppr.] In reference or relation to; respecting; regarding; concerning; about: as, "Members of the House of Commons were questioned . . . *touching* their parliamentary conduct" (Macaulay's "Hist. of Eng.," i.); often preceded by *as* (as, "*as touching* things offered unto idols": 1 Cor. viii. 1). — **touch′-ing-ly,** *adv.* — **touch′ing-ness,** *n.*

touch-less (tuch′les), *a.* Lacking the sense of touch; also, intangible.

touch=me=not (tuch′mē-not), *n.* In *bot.*, a yellow-flowered balsaminaceous plant, *Impatiens noli-tangere*, whose ripe seed-vessels burst open when touched; any of various other species of the same genus; in *pathol.*, noli-me-tangere.

touch-piece (tuch′pēs), *n.* A coin or medal presented by the sovereign of England to a person touched for the king's evil.

Obverse.   Reverse.
Gold Touchpiece, James II.

touch-stone (tuch′stōn), *n.* A black siliceous stone used to test the purity of gold and silver by the color of the streak produced on it by rubbing it with the metals; basanite; fig., any test or criterion by which the qualities of a thing are tried (as, "an era . . . in which success is the only *touchstone* of merit": Trollope's "Barchester Towers," xiii.); also, any of various other dark-colored stones, as black marble (cf. *touch.*).

touch-wood (tuch′wùd), *n.* Wood converted into an easily ignitible substance by the action of certain fungi, and used as tinder; punk; also, amadou.

touch-y (tuch′i), *a.*; compar. *touchier*, superl. *touchiest.* [Appar. orig. a var. of *tetchy*, with form and later senses due to *touch*.] Apt to take offense on slight provocation (as, "Roland was exceedingly *touchy* on all things connected with his ancestors": Bulwer-Lytton's "Caxtons," iii. 3); irritable; tetchy; also, sensitive to touch; also, easily ignited, as tinder; also, precarious, risky, or ticklish, as a subject; also, in *painting, drawing*, etc., characterized by or composed of distinct touches, dots, or short strokes.

---

tough (tuf). [AS. *tōh*, akin to D. *taai*, G. *zähe*, tough.] **I.** *a.* Of a strongly cohesive substance; not easily broken or cut; not brittle or tender; difficult to masticate, as food; also, of viscous consistence, as liquid or semiliquid matter; also, capable of great endurance, sturdy, or hardy (as, "We . . . again saddled the *tough* little ponies we had ridden all day": Roosevelt's "Hunting Trips of a Ranchman," iv.); also, not easily influenced, as a person; stubborn, hardened, or incorrigible; also, difficult to perform, accomplish, or deal with, or hard, trying, or troublesome (colloq.: as, "It's *tough* work fagging away at a language with no master but a lexicon," C. Brontë's "Jane Eyre," xxviii.; "You're probably about the *toughest* hypnotic proposition in the world, Dick," Buchan's "Three Hostages," vi.); hard to bear or endure (colloq.: as, it's pretty *tough* to be treated so); also, vigorous, severe, or violent (now colloq.: as, "a *tough* struggle," Kinglake's "Eothen," xvi.; "a good, *tough* effort," Stevenson's "Treasure Island," xxiii.); also, rough, disorderly, or rowdyish (colloq., U. S.: as, "a boy of fourteen . . . the most brazen member of the *toughest* gang in Boytown," Sinclair Lewis's "Main Street," vi.; "*tough* neighborhoods," Tarkington's "Gentleman from Indiana," iv.). **II.** *n.* A ruffian; a rowdy. [Colloq., U. S.]—**tough′en**, *v. t.* or *i.* To make or become tough or tougher.—**tough′ish**, *a.* Somewhat tough.—**tough′ly**, *adv.*—**tough′ness**, *n.*

tou-pee (tö-pē′), *n.* [F. *toupet*, dim. of OF. *toup*, *top*, tuft of hair; from Teut., and akin to E. *top*[1].] A curl or an artificial lock of hair on the top of the head, esp. as a crowning feature of a periwig; a periwig with the front hair combed up into a curl or topknot; also, a patch of false hair or a partial wig worn to cover a bald spot. Also **tou-pet** (tö-pā′).

tour (tör), *n.* [OF. F. *tour*, turn, circuit, tour (senses prob. due to *tourner*, E. *turn*, *v.*), orig. a machine for turning, lathe, < L. *tornus*: see *turn*.] A turn to do something, or a shift of work or duty (chiefly *milit.*); also, a turning round† or revolution†; a circular or circuitous movement† (as, "He made so many *tours*, such meanders, and led us by such winding ways": Defoe's "Robinson Crusoe," i. 19); also, a going or traveling around from place to place (as, "He had made the *tour* of the boat, and seen all his fellow-passengers": Howells's "Chance Acquaintance," i.); a journey including the visiting of a number of places in a circuit or in sequence (as, "Miss Fanshawe is gone on a *tour* with the Cholmondeleys," C. Brontë's "Villette," xvii.; a wedding *tour*; "a *tour* of the waterways of France in a barge," H. G. Wells's "Italy, France, and Britain at War," i.); specif., a journey of a theatrical company from town to town to fulfil engagements (as, "The piece'll be going out in the autumn; she wants me to get her into the *tour*": L. Merrick's "Position of Peggy Harper," iii. 6).—**on tour**, on a prolonged journey in which a number of places are visited, as to keep engagements; on the road, as a theatrical company (as, "In the companies *on tour* one is buried": L. Merrick's "Actor-Manager," i.).—**the grand tour**, an extended tour on the Continent of Europe, through France, Switzerland, Italy, etc., esp. as formerly considered essential as the finishing course in the education of British young men of good family: as, "When I was a young man, and had just left Oxford, I was sent on *the grand tour* to finish my education" (Irving's "Tales of a Traveler," i. 8).—**tour**, *v.* **I.** *intr.* To make a tour, or travel about (as, "The *touring* cyclist has caused the revival of wayside inns," Gissing's "Private Papers of Henry Ryecroft," ii. 16; "Mobile batteries *toured* along their [the Germans'] front," Buchan's "Hist. of the Great War," liii.); go on tour (as, "A *touring* actor's world moves with him on Sunday": L. Merrick's "Actor-Manager," ix.). **II.** *tr.* To make a tour of or through (as, "I have never yet *toured* Europe": Sinclair Lewis's "Babbitt," xiv.); also, to take on tour, as a play.

tou-ra-cou (tö′ṟạ-kö), *n.* See *turakoo.*

tou-relle (tö-rel′), *n.* [F., dim. of *tour*, tower: see *tower*[2].] A turret.

tour-er (tör′ėr), *n.* One who tours; also, a touring-car.

tour-ing=car (tör′ing-kär), *n.* An automobile with a body of the tonneau type, designed for five or more passengers.

tour-ist (tör′ist), *n.* One who makes a tour; esp., one who travels for pleasure, stopping at a number of places for the purpose of seeing the sights, scenery, etc.

tour-ma-lin, tour-ma-line (tör′mạ-lin), *n.* [F. *tourmaline*; from Singhalese.] A mineral, essentially a complex silicate containing boron, aluminium, etc., occurring in various colors (black being common: see *schorl*), the transparent varieties (red, pink, green, blue, and yellow) being used in jewelry.

tour-na-ment (tör′nạ-ment or tėr′-), *n.* [OF. *torneiement*, < *torneier*, E. *tourney*.] In the middle ages, orig., a contest or martial sport in which two opposing parties of mounted and armored combatants fought for a prize, with blunted weapons and in accordance with certain rules; later, a meeting at an appointed time and place for the performance of knightly exercises and sports; hence, in modern times, a meeting for contests in athletic or other sports; a trial of skill in some game, in which a number of competitors play a series of contests (as, a chess *tournament*); fig., any contest of strength or skill.

Armor and Adornments of a Knight equipped for the Tournament.

tour-ney (tör′ni or tėr′-), *v. i.*; *-neyed*, *-neying.* [OF. *torneier*, lit. 'make turns' (perform evolutions), < *tor*, *tour*, turn: see *tour*.] To contend or engage in a tournament.—**tour′ney**, *n.*; pl. *-neys* (-niz). [OF. *tornei*.] A tournament.

tour-ni-quet (tör′ni-ket), *n.* [F., < *tourner*, turn: see *turn*.] In *surg.*, any of various devices for arresting bleeding by forcibly compressing a blood-vessel, as a pad pressed down by a screw, a bandage tightened by twisting, etc.; also, a turnstile (rare).

tour-nure (tör-nür′, F. tör-nür), *n.* [F., < *tourner*, turn: see *turn*.] Turn, contour, or form; figure; appearance; bearing.

touse (touz), *v. t.*; *toused*, *tousing.* [ME. *tousen* and *tusen* (recorded in compounds), = G. *zausen*, touse: cf. *tease*.] To pull about roughly; handle roughly; also, to disorder or dishevel; rumple. [Now chiefly prov.]—**touse**, *n.* A pulling about roughly; also, a commotion or uproar: a fuss or disturbance. [Chiefly prov.]—**tous′er**, *n.*

tou-sle (tou′zl), *v. t.*; *-sled*, *-sling.* [Freq. of *touse*.] To pull about or handle roughly or rudely; also, to disorder or dishevel (as, "His hair was *tousled*": F. H. Smith's "Colonel Carter of Cartersville," ix.).

tout (tout), *v.* [ME. *tuten*, var. of *toten*, peep, peer, < AS. *tōtian*, peep out (to sight), protrude.] **I.** *intr.* To peep or look out†; keep a sharp lookout†; esp., to spy on a racehorse, etc., to obtain information for betting purposes; act as a tout; also, to solicit custom, employment, votes, etc., importunately (as, "The free-lance is a tramp *touting* for odd jobs": Arnold Bennett's "Truth about an Author," v.). [Now colloq. or slang.] **II.** *tr.* To watch, or spy on; esp., to spy on (a race-horse, etc.) in order to gain information for betting purposes; also, to give a tip on (a race-horse, etc.), esp. in order to indicate a probable winner; also, to solicit support for importunately; praise highly and insistently (as, "You're always *touting* these Greek dancers": Sinclair Lewis's "Main Street," xvi.); praise or proclaim as being what is specified (as, a politician *touted* as the friend of the people). [Colloq. or slang.]—**tout**, *n.* A thieves' scout or lookout; also, one who spies on race-horses, etc., to gain information for betting purposes, or who gives tips on race-horses, etc., as a business (as, "The man had the brazen demeanour of a racecourse *tout*": Arnold Bennett's "Pretty Lady," xxxv.); also, one who solicits custom, employment, support, etc., importunately (as, "a motor-car *tout* working on commission," Arnold Bennett's "Mr. Prohack," viii.; "a small fat person who looked like a lawyer's *tout*," Kipling's "Kim," xii.). [Colloq. or slang.]

tout en-semble (tö-toṅ-soṅbl). [F.] All together; the assemblage of parts or details, as in a work of art, considered as forming a whole; the ensemble.

tout-er (tou′tẽr), *n.* One who touts; a tout. [Colloq. or slang.]

touze, etc., **tou′zle.** See *touse,* etc., *tousle.*

tow[1] (tō), *n.* [ME. *tow:* cf. AS. *towlíc,* of spinning, *towhūs,* spinning-house, Icel. *tō,* tuft of wool.] The fiber of flax, hemp, or jute prepared for spinning by scutching; more strictly, the coarse and broken parts of flax or hemp separated from the finer parts in hackling.

tow[2] (tou), *n.* [Cf. Icel. *tog, taug,* rope, cord, akin to E. *tie* and *tow*[3].] A rope; a halter. [Sc.]

tow[3] (tō), *v.* [AS. *togian,* drag, secondary form of *tēon* = OHG. *ziohan* (G. *ziehen*) = Goth. *tiuhan,* draw; akin to L. *ducere,* lead: cf. *team, tie, touch, tow*[2], and *tug.*] I. *tr.* To drag† or draw†; esp., to drag or pull (a boat, etc.) through the water by means of a rope or chain (as, "A steam-tug on the river hooted as she *towed* her barges to wharf": Kipling's "Light That Failed," viii.). II. *intr.* To tow a boat, etc.; advance by being towed (as, "The yacht's gig was *towing* easily at the end of the long scope of line": J. Conrad's "Rescue," i. 3).—**tow**[3], *n.* The act of towing, or the state of being towed (chiefly in 'in tow': see phrase below); also, a rope or chain for towing; also, a boat, or a string of boats, being towed.—**in tow,** in the condition of being towed (as, "We all went on shore in the quarter-boat, with the long-boat *in tow*": Dana's "Two Years before the Mast," xviii.); fig., under guidance, or in charge (as, "Theobald had . . . been taken *in tow* by Mrs. Cowey from the beginning of his University career": S. Butler's "Way of All Flesh," x.).—

tow′age (-āj), *n.* The act of towing, or the state of being towed; also, a charge for towing.

to-ward (tō′ård or tōrd). [AS. *tōweard,* coming, approaching, imminent, < *tō,* to, + *-weard:* see *-ward.*] I. *a.* That is to come†; imminent† or impending†; also, going on, or in progress (as, "when there is work *toward*": Kipling's "Light That Failed," xv.); also, promising, hopeful, or apt, as a young person (obs. or archaic); also, compliant or docile (obs. or archaic: as, "Miss hath hitherto been very tractable and *toward,*" Steele, in "Guardian," 142); also, favorable or propitious; also, left, as opposed to right (prov.). II. *adv.* In the direction of one's self or of something indicated. [Obs. or archaic.]—**to-ward** (tō′ård or tōrd, also tö-wård′), *prep.* [AS. *tōweard.*] In the direction of (with reference to either motion or position, lit. or fig.: as, to walk *toward* the north; a village five miles *toward* the south; his back *toward* the wall; to work *toward* an end); also, with respect to, or as regards (as, one's attitude *toward* a proposition); also, nearly as late as, or shortly before (as, *toward* two o'clock); also, nearly as much as; also, as a help or contribution to (as, to give money *toward* a person's expenses).—**to-ward-ly** (tō′ård-li), *a.* Promising or apt (as, "My son Johnny . . . was at the Grammar School, and a *towardly* child": Swift's "Gulliver's Travels," i. 8); also, tractable or docile; friendly or affable; also, favorable or propitious; seasonable or suitable.—**to′ward-li-ness,** *n.*—**to′ward-ly,** *adv.*—**to′ward-ness,** *n.*—**to-wards** (tō′årdz or tōrdz, also, as prep., tö-wårdz′), *adv.* and *prep.* [AS. *tōweardes.*] Same as *toward.*

tow-boat (tō′bōt), *n.* A boat for towing other boats or vessels; a tugboat.

tow-el (tou′el), *n.* [OF. *toaille* (F. *touaille*); from Teut.] A cloth for wiping and drying something wet, esp. one for drying the hands, face, or body after washing or bathing.—**tow′el,** *v. t.;* *-eled* or *-elled, -eling* or *-elling.* To apply a towel to; rub or dry with a towel; also, to beat or thrash (slang).—**tow′el-ing, tow′el-ling,** *n.* Cloth for towels.

tow-er[1] (tō′ẽr), *n.* One who tows.

tow-er[2] (tou′ẽr), *n.* [AS. *torr, tūr,* also OF. *tor, tour* (F. *tour*), < L. *turris,* tower.] A building or structure lofty in proportion to its lateral dimensions, either isolated (see cut in next column) or forming part of a church, castle, or other edifice; such a structure used as or intended for a stronghold, fortress, prison, etc.; specif. [*cap.*], with *the,* orig. a tower or keep and fortress, now a large assemblage of buildings, on the north bank of the Thames in London, formerly used as a royal palace, later as a state prison, and now as an arsenal, a garrison station, and a repository

of various objects of public interest (called in full 'the Tower of London'); also [*l. c.*], fig., a means of defense or protection (as, "Thou hast been a shelter for me, and a strong *tower* from the enemy," Ps. lxi. 3; "The king's name is a *tower* of strength," Shakspere's "Richard III.," v. 3. 12); also, any of various tower-like structures, contrivances, or objects; a tall, movable structure used in ancient and medieval warfare in storming a fortified place; a very high headdress worn by women in the reigns of William

Leaning Tower. — Campanile of the Duomo in Pisa, Italy.

III. and Anne, and built up of pasteboard, ribbons, and lace.—**tower of ivory** [tr. F. *tour d'ivoire*], fig., a position or attitude of delicate or fastidious aloofness or reserve: a phrase used esp. in literary criticism, of the attitude of some writers, orig. (in the French form) by Sainte-Beuve in the poem "A M. Villemain," in his "Pensées d'Août" (1837), in a comment on Alfred de Vigny as contrasted with Victor Hugo.—**tower of silence,** a kind of stone tower on the top of which the Parsees expose the bodies of their dead to be stripped of flesh by birds, the bones then falling through a grating into a pit beneath, from which they are removed for burial.—

tow′er[2], *v. i.* To rise or extend far upward like a tower (as, "the tall Lombardy poplar . . . *towering* high above all

Tower of Silence.

other trees": W. H. Hudson's "Far Away and Long Ago," ix.); rise aloft; also, to soar aloft, as a bird; rise vertically, as a wounded bird; in *falconry,* to mount up, as a hawk, so as to be able to swoop down on the quarry.—**tow′ered,** *a.* Having a tower or towers; adorned or defended with towers; rising like a tower.—**tow′er-ing,** *p. a.* That towers; very lofty or tall (as, "a *towering* oak": Longfellow's "Evangeline," ii. 4); soaring high, as a bird; fig., eminent; exalted; soaring (as, "the *towering* ambition . . . of the son of Pepin": Hallam's "Europe during the Middle Ages," i. 1); also, rising to an extreme degree of violence or intensity (as, "She left me in a *towering* rage": W. H. Hudson's "Purple Land," xi.).—**tow′er-ing-ly,** *adv.*—**tow′er-y,** *a.* Having towers; adorned or defended with towers; also, towering; lofty.

tow-head (tō′hed), *n.* [See *tow*[1].] A head of flaxen or light-colored hair, or a person with such hair; also, a head of, or a person with, rumpled or tousled hair; also, a sand-bar, shoal, or newly formed island in a stream (local, U. S.: as, "A *towhead* is a sand-bar that has cottonwoods on it as thick as harrow-teeth," Mark Twain's "Huckleberry Finn," xii.;

"a large town which lay shut in behind a *tow-head* (i.e., new island)," Mark Twain's "Life on the Mississippi," xxiii.).— **tow′=head″ed**, *a.*

≈ow-hee (tou′hē), *n.* [Imit. of its note.] The chewink, *Pipilo erythrophthalmus*; also, any other bird of the genus *Pipilo*.

tow=line (tō′līn), *n.* A line, hawser, or the like, by which anything is or may be towed.

≈own (toun). [AS. *tūn*, inclosure, yard, manor, village, town, = Icel. *tūn*, inclosure, homestead, house, = D. *tuin*, garden, fence, = G. *zaun*, fence, hedge: cf. Celtic *dūn*, appearing as *-dunum* in Latinized place-names, as L. *Lugdunum*, Lyons.] **I.** *n.* An inclosed piece of ground†; the inclosed land surrounding or belonging to a dwelling†; a house, or a collection of houses or buildings, upon an inclosed piece of land, or a homestead or farmstead (now chiefly Sc.); also, a village or hamlet (now prov. Eng.); a collection of inhabited houses larger than a village and having more complete local government; in a general sense, a city or borough; also, the particular town or city under consideration, or that in or near which the speaker or writer is, or the chief town or city of a district or country (regularly without the article: as, to be out of *town*; to go to *town*); also, in some States of the U. S., as in New England, a municipal corporation with less elaborate organization and powers than a city; in other States, an administrative district consisting of a division of a county; a township; also, the body of inhabitants of a town; the townspeople; sometimes, the qualified voters of a town; also, town-talk, or gossip (Sc.: as, "What a *town* there'll be about that letter!" Barrie's "Sentimental Tommy," xi.). **II.** *a.* Of or pertaining to a town; characteristic of a town.—**town clerk**, a clerk or official who keeps the records of a town.—**town crier**, the public crier of a town.—**town hall**, a hall or building belonging to a town, used for the transaction of the town's business, etc., and often also as a place of public assembly.—**town house**, a town hall; also, a town prison; also, a town poorhouse; also, a house or mansion in town, as distinguished from a country residence.—**town meeting**, a general meeting of the inhabitants of a town; specif., a meeting of the qualified voters of a town for the transaction of public business.—**town′let**, *n.* A little town.—**towns′folk**, *n.* Townspeople.—**town′ship**, *n.* [AS. *tūnscipe*.] The inhabitants of a manor, parish, or the like, or the manor, parish, etc., itself (now chiefly hist.); in England, one of the local divisions or districts of a large parish, each containing a village or small town, usually with a church of its own; in the U. S. and Canada, an administrative division of a county, with varying corporate powers; in U. S. surveys of public land, a region or district 6 miles square, containing 36 sections (cf. *range*, *n.*); in Australia, a village or hamlet. —**towns′man** (-man), *n.*; pl. *-men*. An inhabitant of a town; also, an inhabitant of one's own or the same town, or a fellow-townsman (as, "My *townsmen* would not . . . admit me into the list of town officers": Thoreau's "Walden," i.); also, an ordinary resident of a university town as distinguished from a gownsman, or member of the university; also, in New England, a selectman.—**towns′peo″ple**, *n.* The inhabitants collectively of a town; townsfolk.—**town′= talk′**, *n.* The common talk or gossip of a town; the subject of common conversation or gossip.—**town′ward** (-ward), *adv.* and *a.* Toward the town.—**town′wards**, *adv.*

tow=path (tō′pȧth), *n.* A path along the bank of a canal or river, for use in towing boats.

tow=rope (tō′rōp), *n.* A rope, hawser, or the like, used in towing boats.

towse (touz), *v.* and *n.* See *touse*.

Tows-er (tou′zėr), *n.* [= *touser*.] A common name for a dog, esp. a large, rough animal; [*l. c.*] a large dog.

tow-y (tō′i), *a.* Of the nature of or resembling tow.

tox-e-mi-a, tox-æ-mi-a (tok-sē′mi-ä), *n.* [NL., < Gr. τοξικόν (see *toxic*) + αἷμα, blood.] In *pathol.*, a form of blood-poisoning, esp. one in which the toxins produced by certain micro-organisms enter the blood.—**tox-e-mic, tox-æ-mic** (tok-sē′mik or tok-sem′ik), *a.*

tox-ic (tok′sik), *a.* [ML. *toxicus*, < L. *toxicum*, poison, < Gr. τοξικόν, adj. (with φάρμακον, drug, poison), in τοξικὸν φάρμακον, poison for arrows, hence any poison: τοξικόν,

neut. of τοξικός, of or for the bow, < τόξον, bow.] Of, pertaining to, or caused by a toxin or poison; of the nature of a poison; poisonous. Also **tox′i-cal.—tox′i-cant. I.** *a.* Poisonous; toxic. **II.** *n.* A poison.—**tox-i-ca-tion** (tok-si-kā′shon), *n.* Poisoning.—**tox-i-ci-ty** (tok-sis′i-ti), *n.* Toxic quality; poisonousness.

tox-i-co-gen-ic (tok″si-kō-jen′ik), *a.* [Gr. τοξικόν (see *toxic*) + γεν-, bear, produce: see *-genic*.] Generating or producing toxic products or poisons.

tox-i-col-o-gy (tok-si-kol′ọ-ji), *n.* [Gr. τοξικόν (see *toxic*) + -λογία: see *-logy*.] The science of poisons, their effects, antidotes, detection, etc.—**tox″i-co-log′i-cal** (-kọ-loj′i-kạl), *a.*—**tox-i-col′o-gist**, *n.*

tox-i-co-sis (tok-si-kō′sis), *n.*; pl. *-coses* (-kō′sēz). [NL., < Gr. τοξικόν: see *toxic*.] In *pathol.*, a morbid condition produced by the action of a poison.

tox-in (tok′sin), *n.* [See *toxic*.] Any of various organic poisons produced in living or dead organisms or their products, as a venom, ptomaine, etc.; esp., any of the specific poisonous products generated by pathogenic micro-organisms, and constituting the causative agents in various diseases, as tetanus, diphtheria, etc. Cf. *antitoxin*.

tox-i-pho-bi-a (tok-si-fō′bi-ä), *n.* [NL., < Gr. τοξικόν (see *toxic*) + -φοβία: see *-phobia*.] A morbid fear of being poisoned.

tox-oph-i-lite (tok-sof′i-līt), *n.* [Gr. τόξον, bow, + φίλος, loving.] A devotee of archery; an archer.

toy (toi). [ME. *toye*, toying, play; origin uncertain.] **I.** *n.* Amorous sport† or dallying†; a light caress†; also, an antic† or trick†; also, a trifling story, or literary trifle (archaic); also, a whim† or caprice†; also, a thing or matter of little or no value or importance, or a trifle (as, "a *toy*, a thing of no regard": Shakspere's "1 Henry VI.," iv. 1. 145); also, something intended for amusement rather than practical use (as, a philosophical *toy*, a device of no practical use, as the Cartesian devil, which serves to illustrate in an entertaining way some fact or principle of natural science); esp., an object, often a small imitation of some familiar thing, for children or others to play with (as, "Men deal with life as children with their play, Who first misuse, then cast their *toys* away": Cowper's "Hope," 128); a plaything; also, a small article of little real value, but prized for some reason; a knickknack; a trinket; also, something diminutive like a plaything; often, a toy dog; also, a close linen or woolen cap, with flaps coming down to the shoulders, formerly worn by women of the lower classes in Scotland. **II.** *a.* That is a toy, as for children or others to play with; being a small imitation of some familiar object, used as a plaything; hence, of petty character or diminutive size (as, "No *toy* miniature pistol would she carry, but a full-sized, heavy 'six-shooter' ": F. M. Crawford's "Mr. Isaacs," ix.).—**toy dog**, any dog of unusually small size kept as a pet; esp., any of certain very small breeds of spaniels and terriers.—**toy spaniel.** *spaniel*.—**toy**, *v. i.* To dally amorously; flirt; also, to act idly or without seriousness; trifle; also, to amuse one's self; play; sport; play (*with*) by handling or fingering (as, to *toy* with one's watch-chain; "She *toyed* with her whip," G. W. Cable's "John March, Southerner," x.).

toy-er (toi′ėr), *n.* One who toys.

to-yon (tō′yọn), *n.* [Amer. Sp. *tollon*.] An evergreen malaceous shrub or small tree, *Heteromeles* (or *Photinia*) *arbutifolia*, of the Pacific coast of North America, with white flowers and bright-red berries.

tra-be-ate, tra-be-at-ed (trā′bẹ-āt, -ā-ted), *a.* [L. *trabs*, beam.] In *arch.*, constructed with horizontal beams, as a flat, unvaulted ceiling, or with a lintel or entablature, as an unarched doorway; pertaining to such construction, as distinct from the vaulted or arched kind.—**tra-be-a′tion** (-ā′shọn), *n.* In *arch.*, trabeated construction; a trabeated structure.

tra-bec-u-la (trạ-bek′ụ-lä), *n.*; pl. *-læ* (-lē). [L., dim. of *trabs*, beam.] In *anat.*, *bot.*, etc., a structural part resembling a small beam or cross-bar.—**tra-bec′u-lar**, *a.*

trace[1] (trās), *n.* [ME. *trais*, *trays*, pl., < OF. *trais*, pl. of *trait*, a drawing, line, trace: see *trait*.] Each of the two straps, ropes, or chains by which a carriage, wagon, or the like is drawn by a harnessed horse or other draft-animal.

trace² (trās), v.; traced, tracing. [OF. tracier (F. tracer), through ML. < L. trahere (pp. tractus), draw.] **I.** intr. To take one's course†; make one's way†; go†; also, to step in dancing†; also, to trace one's or its history; go back in time. **II.** tr. To pass along or over†; tread† or traverse†; also, to follow the footprints, track, or traces of (as, "I could trace neither of them any further than the inn": H. Mackenzie's "Man of Feeling," xxix.); hence, to follow the course, development, or history of (as, to trace a political movement); also, to follow or make out the course or line of (as, "Let us trace a river to its source," Tyndall's "Forms of Water," § 1; to trace the walls of a ruined city); make out or decipher (writing); also, to follow (footprints, traces, the history of something, the course or line of something, etc.); also, to ascertain by investigation, find out, or discover (as, "We must take instant measures for tracing the place of her retreat": Scott's "Castle Dangerous," xiii.); discover evidences or proofs of (as, "I could never trace in her one spark of jealousy": Stevenson's "Master of Ballantrae," vi.); also, to make a plan, diagram, or map of; mark out the course or lines of (a road, building, etc.); fig., to map out (a plan, etc.); also, to draw (a line, outline, figure, etc.); also, to put down in writing (as, "The old man seized the pen and traced his name": F. M. Crawford's "Mr. Isaacs," v.); also, to copy (a drawing, plan, etc.) by following the lines of the original on a superimposed transparent sheet; also, to make marks upon; mark or ornament with lines, figures, etc.—**trace²,** n. [OF. F. trace.] The path or way which anything takes†; a course of action or procedure†; also, a line or train of persons†; also, the track made or left by the passage of a person, animal, or thing; the marks which indicate the course pursued by any moving thing; a single such mark (esp. in pl.); sometimes, a beaten track, or trail, as through wild country (U. S.: as, "marching in single file along a most narrow trace," Bancroft's "Hist. of the U. S.," Amer. Revolution, i. 5); also, a mark, token, or evidence of the former presence, existence, or action of something; a vestige; in general, a mark, indication, or evidence (as, "Save for a slight but hardly unnatural pallor, not a trace of death marked the poor little creature": Eden Phillpotts's "Grey Room," i.); also, a scarcely discernible quantity of something; a very small amount; a small quantity or insignificant proportion of a constituent present in a substance; also, a line or figure drawn; a drawing or sketch of a thing; a record traced by a self-registering instrument; in fort., the ground-plan of a work.—**to keep trace of,** to follow the traces or movements of; keep track of.

trace-a-ble (trā'sạ-bl), a. Capable of being traced.—**trace-a-bil'i-ty** (-bil'i-ti), **trace'a-ble-ness,** n.—**trace'a-bly,** adv.

trace-less (trās'les), a. Leaving or showing no traces.—**trace'less-ly,** adv.

tra-cer (trā'sėr), n. One who or that which traces; one whose business is the tracing of missing property, parcels, etc.; an inquiry form sent from point to point to trace a missing shipment, parcel, or the like, as in a transportation system; any of various devices for tracing drawings, plans, etc.

tra-cer-ied (trā'sėr-id), a. Ornamented with tracery.

tra-cer-y (trā'sėr-i), n.; pl. -ies (-iz). Ornamental work consisting of intersecting or ramified ribs, bars, or the like, as in the upper part of a Gothic window, or in panels, screens, etc.; also, any delicate interlacing work of lines, threads, etc., as in carving, embroidery, etc.; network.

trace=tug (trās'tug), n. A strap supporting a trace of a harness.

Tracery. — Window-head of the church of St. Urbain, Troyes, France.

tra-che-a (trạ-kē'ạ, commonly trā'kē-ạ), n.; pl. tracheæ (-ē). [ML., for LL. trachia, < Gr. τραχεία, windpipe, lit. 'rough (artery),' prop. fem. of τραχύς, rough.] In air-breathing vertebrates, the tube extending from the larynx to the bronchi, serving as the principal passage for conveying air to and from the lungs; the windpipe; in insects and other arthropods, one of the air-conveying tubes of the respiratory system; in bot., a duct or vessel formed by a row of cells that have lost their intervening partitions.—**tra-che-al** (trā'kē-ạl), a. [NL. trachealis.] In anat. and zoöl., of, pertaining to, or connected with the trachea or tracheæ; in bot., of the nature of or composed of tracheæ.—**tra'che-id,** n. [G. tracheïde.] In bot., one of the vascular cells with a pitted, lignified wall, in which the end-walls are not absorbed, characteristic of the wood of conifers, etc.—**tra-che-i'tis** (-ī'tis), n. [NL.] In pathol., inflammation of the trachea.

trach-e-late (trak'ē-lāt), a. [Gr. τράχηλος, neck.] In entom., having or forming a neck-like constriction.

tra-che-os-co-py (trā-kē-os'kō-pi), n. [See trachea and -scopy.] In med., examination of the interior of the trachea, as with a laryngoscope.—**tra"che-o-scop'ic** (-ō-skop'ik), a.—**tra-che-os'co-pist,** n.

tra-che-ot-o-my (trā-kē-ot'ō-mi), n. [See trachea and -tomy.] In surg., the operation of cutting into the trachea. —**tracheotomy tube,** the tube used after tracheotomy for insertion into the opening made in the trachea, to facilitate breathing.—**tra-che-ot'o-mist,** n.

tra-cho-ma (trạ-kō'mä), n. [NL., < Gr. τράχωμα, roughness, < τραχύς, rough.] In pathol., a contagious inflammation of the conjunctiva of the eyelids, characterized by the formation of granulations or papillary growths.—**tra-chom'a-tous** (-kom'ạ-tus), a.

tra-chyte (trā'kīt or trak'īt), n. [F. trachyte, < Gr. τραχύς, rough.] An igneous rock, commonly of porphyritic texture, consisting essentially of feldspar and one or more subordinate minerals, as hornblende, mica, etc.—**tra-chyt-ic** (trạ-kit'ik), a.

tra-cing (trā'sing), n. The act of one who or that which traces; also, that which is produced by tracing, marking, or drawing; the record traced by a self-registering instrument; a copy of a drawing, etc., made by tracing.

track¹ (trak), v. [Appar. < D. trekken, draw, pull, tow: cf. trek.] **I.** tr. To tow (a boat), esp. by a line reaching from the boat to the bank or shore. **II.** intr. To tow a boat; advance by being towed.

track² (trak), n. [OF. F. trac, track, trace; perhaps from Teut. and akin to D. trekken: see track¹.] The mark, or series of marks, left by anything that has passed along; a wheel-rut; the wake of a ship; a series of footprints or other marks left by an animal or a person; the scent followed by hounds; a single footprint (esp. in pl.); a fossil footprint of an animal; also, a way made or beaten by the feet of men or animals; a path; also, a line of travel or motion (as, the track of a bird; "We were just in the track of the tremendous hurricane of 1830," Dana's "Two Years before the Mast," xxxiv.); a course followed; fig., a course of action or conduct, or a method of proceeding (as, to go on in the same track year after year); also, a path or course made or laid out for some particular purpose; a course laid out for running or racing; a metal path or way for wheeled vehicles; one or more pairs of parallel lines of rails with their ties, etc., for railroad or railway vehicles; also, the act of tracking, trailing, or tracing.—**to keep track of,** to follow the course or progress of; keep sight or knowledge of; keep under one's attention: as, to keep track of a friend; to keep track of a number of things at once.—**to make tracks,** to make off; decamp: as, "Tom, why don't you make tracks for Canada?" (Mrs. Stowe's "Uncle Tom's Cabin," i.).—**track²,** v. **I.** tr. To follow up the track, traces, or footprints of; trace or pursue by or as by the track left; also, to follow (a track, course, etc.); also, to mark out (a path, etc.: as, "Ranald acted as their guide, going before them with a select party, to track out the way," Scott's "Legend of Montrose," xvii.); mark out (a way) by repeatedly traversing it; also, to make one's way through; traverse; also, to make a track of footprints upon (a floor, etc.: as, "He never tracked Aunt Lois's newly scoured floor with the traces of unwiped shoes," Mrs.

Stowe's "Oldtown Folks," xxi.); make a track with (dirt, snow, etc.) carried on the feet in walking; also, to furnish with a track or tracks, as for railroad vehicles. **II.** *intr.* To follow up a track or trail; also, to make one's or its way; also, to run in the same track, as the wheels of a vehicle; be in alinement, as one gear-wheel with another.—**track'age** (-ăj), *n.* The tracks, collectively, of a railroad or railway; also, the right of one railroad company to use the tracks of another company.—**track'er,** *n.*—**track'=lay"er,** *n.* A workman employed in laying and repairing railroad-tracks; also, a truck equipped for use in laying railroad-tracks.—**track'=lay"ing,** *n.* and *a.*—**track'less,** *a.* Without a track or tracks; untrodden; pathless; also, leaving no track or trace; also, not running on a track, or lines of rails.—**track'less-ly,** *adv.*—**track'man** (-măn), *n.*; pl. -*men.* In *railroading,* a man engaged in work on the track; esp., a track-walker.—**track'=walk"er,** *n.* In *railroading,* a man employed to walk over and inspect a certain section of track at regular intervals.

tract[1] (trakt), *n.* [L. *tractus,* a drawing, train, course, stretch, extent, tract, < *trahere,* draw: cf. *trait.*] Duration, lapse, or course (of time)†; also, a space or extent of time; a period; also, the continuance of some action or state (obs. or rare); also, a stretch or extent of land, water, etc. (as, "a beautiful and fertile *tract* of country," Bancroft's "Hist. of the U. S.," Amer. Revolution, i. 8; "a wide *tract* of black moss," Scott's "Guy Mannering," i.); a region; also, a track, path, way, or course (obs. or rare); also, a track, trail, or trace (obs. or rare: as, "I fell into a beaten road, where I saw many *tracts* of human feet," Swift's "Gulliver's Travels," iv. 1); in *anat.,* a definite region or area of the body; esp., a group, series, or system of related parts or organs (as, the digestive *tract*).

tract[2] (trakt), *n.* [Appar. < L. *tractatus:* see *tractate.*] A treatise or written or printed discourse on some particular topic; now, esp., a brief treatise or pamphlet suitable for general distribution, usually one dealing with some topic of practical religion.

tract[3] (trakt), *n.* [ML. *tractus* (so called because sung through without break for response), a particular use of L. *tractus,* a drawing, stretch: see *tract*[1].] In the *Rom. Cath. Ch.,* an anthem consisting of verses of Scripture, usually from the Psalms, sung after the gradual in the mass from Septuagesima until the day before Easter and on certain occasions outside of that period, taking the place of the alleluias and the verse which ordinarily accompany the gradual.

trac-ta-ble (trak'tạ-bl), *a.* [L. *tractabilis,* < *tractare,* handle, manage: see *treat.*] That may be easily handled or dealt with, as things; readily wrought, as metal; also, easily managed, or docile, as persons or animals, their dispositions, etc. (as, "a very *tractable* boy," Marryat's "Mr. Midshipman Easy," vi.; "the natives . . . being . . . of an intelligent *tractable* disposition," S. Butler's "Erewhon," i.).—**trac-ta-bil'i-ty** (-bil'i-ti), **trac'ta-ble-ness,** *n.*—**trac'ta-bly,** *adv.*

Trac-ta-ri-an (trak-tā'ri-ạn). **I.** *n.* One of the promoters or adherents of the doctrines promulgated within the Church of England in "Tracts for the Times," a series of tracts or treatises published at Oxford, England, from 1833 to 1841, forming a prominent feature of the Oxford movement. See *Oxford movement,* and cf. *Puseyism.* **II.** *a.* Of or pertaining to the Tractarians.—**Trac-ta'ri-an-ism,** *n.*

trac-tate (trak'tāt), *n.* [L. *tractatus,* a handling, treatment, treatise, < *tractare:* see *treat.*] A treatise; a tract: as, "Religious toleration was no novelty either in great books or in the *tractates* of a day" (Morley's "Oliver Cromwell," ii. 3).

trac-tile (trak'til), *a.* [L. *trahere* (pp. *tractus*), draw.] Capable of being drawn; also, that may be drawn out in length; ductile.—**trac-til'i-ty** (-til'i-ti), *n.*

trac-tion (trak'shọn), *n.* [ML. *tractio(n-),* < L. *trahere,* draw.] The act of drawing or pulling, or the state of being drawn; the contraction of a muscle, organ, or the like; the drawing of a body, vehicle, train, or the like along a surface, road, track, railway, waterway, etc.; transportation by means of railroads, esp. street railways; the adhesive friction of a body, as of a wheel on a rail; fig., attracting power or influence.—**trac'tion-al,** *a.*—**trac'tion=en"gine,** *n.* A self-propelled steam-engine of the locomotive type, used for drawing heavy loads along an ordinary road, etc., or for operating threshing machinery or the like after arriving at its destination; a similar engine or motor using gasoline or the like instead of steam.

trac-tive (trak'tiv), *a.* [L. *trahere* (pp. *tractus*), draw.] Serving to draw; drawing.

trac-tor (trak'tọr), *n.* [ML., < L. *trahere,* draw.] One who or that which draws or pulls; something used for drawing or pulling; specif., a self-propelled vehicle for pulling other vehicles or the like; a traction-engine; also, a propeller mounted at the front of an aëroplane or the like instead of at the rear, thus exerting a pull instead of a push ('tractor propeller' or 'tractor screw'); an aëroplane or the like with a propeller so mounted ('tractor machine').

tra-dal (trā'dạl), *a.* Of or pertaining to trade; commercial.

trade (trād), *n.* [ME. *trade,* < MLG. *trade,* track; akin to E. *tread.*] A track† or trail†; a path†, way†, or course†; also, a regular course or direction of movement† (chiefly in the phrase 'to blow trade,' said of winds: as, "The winds generally blow *trade* from the S. and the S.S.E. from May to September," Defoe's "Captain Singleton," xii.: see *trade-wind*); a trade-wind (commonly in *pl.*: as, "We caught the south-east *trades,* and turn before them for nearly three weeks," Dana's "Two Years before the Mast," viii.); also, a course of action or procedure, or a practice or custom (obs. or prov. Eng.); also, a line of work or form of occupation pursued as a business or calling, as for a livelihood or for profit; esp., some line of skilled mechanical work, learned by apprenticeship or otherwise, as distinguished from mercantile, professional, or agricultural occupations or from unskilled labor (as, the *trade* of a carpenter, mason, plumber, or printer; the *trade* of a tailor or shoemaker); often, a profession or non-mechanical calling regarded as involving training or practice, skill, practical work, etc. (as, "With a courteous authority and tact worthy of his *trade,* the old diplomat began," Mrs. H. Ward's "Lady Rose's Daughter," iv.; "the *trade* of a soldier," Froude's "Cæsar," xiv.; the *trade* of authorship); anything practised as a means of getting a living, money, booty, etc. (as, the *trade* of begging; the pirate's *trade*); also, a line of mercantile or commercial business, as the traffic in a particular commodity or class of commodities (as, the silk *trade*; "the agent of an extensive house in the needle *trade,*" Longfellow's "Kavanagh," v.; the grocery *trade*; the slave-*trade*); those engaged in a particular line of business (with *the*: as, to sell books to the *trade*; matters of special interest to the *trade*); mercantile or commercial business in general, or the buying and selling, or exchanging, of commodities, either by wholesale or by retail, within a country or between countries (as, to engage in *trade*; domestic or foreign *trade*; *trade* with South America); business patronage, or custom; a particular commercial or business transaction; a purchase, sale, or exchange; a bargain; a political arrangement or deal (U. S.); also, commodities for use in bartering with savages; native produce for barter; goods or materials (now prov.); rubbish or trash (prov.); also, passage to and fro (now prov. Eng.); passage or resort to a place for commercial purposes†; intercourse† or dealings†.—**balance of trade.** See under *balance, n.* —**trade acceptance.** See *acceptance.*—**trade dollar.** See under *dollar.*—**trade,** *v.*; *traded, trading.* **I.** *tr.* To tread† or traverse†; follow†, pursue†, or practise†; also, to accustom†, habituate†, or train†; also, to frequent for purposes of trade†: also, to buy and sell, barter, or traffic in (as, "They *traded* in thy market wheat . . . and honey, and oil, and balm": Ezek. xxvii. 17); dispose of by sale or barter (with *away*); in general, to exchange, or give in exchange (as, to *trade* marbles; to *trade* seats with a person; to *trade* one thing for another). **II.** *intr.* To tread† or go†; go or resort for purposes of trade, as to a place; hence, to carry on trade (as, to *trade* with the Indians); traffic (*in*: as, to *trade* in wheat); make an exchange (as, if you don't like your book I'll *trade* with you); also, to have dealings or intercourse†; occupy one's self or deal, as in a matter or subject (obs. or archaic).—**to trade on** or **upon,** to act in full reliance on (some fact, circumstance, etc.) in pursuing one's own advantage or ends: as, "Granvelle grew enormously rich . . . by *trading on* the imperial favor" (Motley's "Dutch Republic," i. 1); "Do you suppose he would not *trade upon* the knowledge?" (Stevenson's "Master of Ballantrae," vi.).

trade=mark (trād'märk), *n.* A mark, device, or name used by a trader or manufacturer to distinguish his goods, as from goods of other firms, and now secured by legal registration and protected as his property.

trade=name (trād'nām), *n.* A name invented or adopted as the distinctive name of some article of commerce; also, the name by which an article or substance is known to the trade; also, the name or style under which a firm does business.

trad-er (trā'dėr), *n.* One who trades; one who carries on trade or business dealings, or a particular kind of trade (as, "Your master never deals with those southern *traders*," Mrs. Stowe's "Uncle Tom's Cabin," i.; "these great inland expeditions of the fur *traders*," Irving's "Captain Bonneville," ii.); also, a vessel employed in trade (as, "a Dutch ship from Batavia . . . a coaster, not an European *trader*": Defoe's "Robinson Crusoe," ii. 10).

trad-es-can-tia (trad-es-kan'shiä), *n.* [NL.; named from John *Tradescant* (died about 1638), gardener to Charles I.] Any plant of the genus *Tradescantia.* See *spiderwort.*

trade=school (trād'sköl), *n.* A school for giving instruction in a trade or trades.

trades-folk (trādz'fōk), *n.* Tradespeople.

trades-man (trādz'man), *n.*; pl. *-men.* A man skilled in a trade or craft (now prov.); also, a man engaged in trade; esp., a shopkeeper.

trades-peo-ple (trādz'pē″pl), *n.* People engaged in trade; shopkeepers collectively.

trades=u-nion (trādz'ū″nyon), etc. Same as *trade-union,* etc.

trades-wom-an (trādz'wŭm″an), *n.*; pl. *-women* (-wim″en). A woman engaged in trade.

trade=u-nion (trād'ū″nyon), *n.* An association of the workers in any trade, or in several allied trades, for the promotion of their interests with regard to wages, hours of work, etc., and for the furnishing of aid out of a common fund to members during strikes, unemployment, sickness, or the like. —**trade′=u″nion-ism,** *n.* The system, methods, or practice of trade-unions; also, trade-unions collectively.— **trade′=u″nion-ist,** *n.*

trade=wind (trād'wind), *n.* [Cf. the obs. phrase *to blow trade,* of the wind, to blow in one regular course.] A wind that blows in one regular 'trade' or course, or continually in the same direction; specif., one of the winds prevailing over the oceans from about 30° north latitude to about 30° south latitude, and blowing from northeast to southwest in the northern hemisphere, and from southeast to northwest in the southern hemisphere, toward the equator. Cf. *anti-trade.*

trad-ing (trā'ding), *n.* The process of carrying on trade; buying and selling; commercial dealing; trade.—**trad′ing,** *p. a.* Carrying on or engaged in trade; commercial: as, "England . . . was a great *trading* country" (Adam Smith's "Wealth of Nations," iv. 7. 3).—**trad′ing=post,** *n.* A post or station established for carrying on trade in an unsettled or thinly settled region: as, "Fort Wallah-Wallah is a *trading post* of the Hudson's Bay Company" (Irving's "Captain Bonneville," xxxiv.).—**trad′ing=stamp,** *n.* A stamp with a certain value given as a premium by a dealer to a customer, specified quantities of these stamps being exchangeable for various articles when presented to the issuers of the stamps.

tra-di-tion (tra-dish'on), *n.* [OF. *tradicion* (F. *tradition*), < L. *traditio(n-),* a giving over, delivery, tradition, < *tradere* (pp. *traditus*), give over, deliver, surrender, betray, transmit, < *trans,* across, + *dare,* give: cf. *extradition, traitor, treason.*] The act of handing over something to another, esp. in a formal legal manner; delivery; transfer; also, delivery, esp. oral delivery, of information or instruction (now rare); also, the handing down of statements, beliefs, opinions, customs, etc., from generation to generation, esp. by word of mouth or by practice (as, a story that has come down to us by popular *tradition*); that which is so handed down; a statement, story, or legend transmitted, esp. orally, from earlier times (as, "The causes of their [Northmen's]

sudden appearance . . . could only be sought in the ancient *traditions* of Scandinavia": Hallam's "Europe during the Middle Ages," i. 1); a belief, opinion, custom, or usage coming down from ancestors or predecessors (as, "She has been bred up . . . by a very worldly family, and taught their *traditions*," Thackeray's "Newcomes," xlv.; an action in keeping with the highest *traditions* of the service); transmitted or inherited way of thinking or acting (as, "In a new country one gets to looking at people a little out of our *tradition*," Howells's "Rise of Silas Lapham," v. ; "You could not quite rely on what he might do, having no *tradition* in his blood," Galsworthy's "Dark Flower," ii. 7); in *theol.,* among the Jews, an unwritten body of laws and doctrines, or any one of them, held to have been received from Moses, and handed down orally from generation to generation (see Mat. xv. 2, 3, 6, and Gal. i. 14: cf. *mishnah*); in the Christian Church, a body of teachings, or any one of them, held to have been delivered by Christ and his apostles but not committed to writing.—**tra-di′tion-al,** *a.* Of or pertaining to tradition; handed down by tradition (as, "Look now at the wondrous *traditional* story of how this island was settled by the red-men": H. Melville's "Moby-Dick," xiv.); in accordance with tradition or long-established belief, opinion, custom, etc. (as, " 'Not the *traditional* haunt of spooks, certainly,' said Peter Hardcastle as they entered the bright and cheerful chamber," Eden Phillpotts's "Grey Room," v.; the *traditional* Thanksgiving dinner); being such according to tradition (as, the *traditional* site of the garden of Eden); also, observant of or governed by tradition†.—**tra-di′tion-al-ism,** *n.* Adherence to tradition as authority, esp. in matters of religion; specif., a system of philosophy according to which all knowledge of religious truth is derived from divine revelation and received by traditional instruction.—**tra-di′tion-al-ist,** *n.*—**tra-di″tion-al-is′tic,** *a.*—**tra-di′tion-al-ly,** *adv.* —**tra-di′tion-a-ry** (-ā-ri), *a.* Traditional.—**tra-di′tion-ist,** *n.* One who adheres to tradition; also, one who transmits, preserves, or records traditions.

trad-i-tive (trad'i-tiv), *a.* [Obs. F. *traditif,* < L. *tradere:* see *tradition.*] Of, pertaining to, or based on tradition; traditional.

tra-duce (tra-dūs'), *v. t.; -duced, -ducing.* [L. *traducere* (pp. *traductus*), lead across, bring over, lead along as a spectacle, disgrace, < *trans,* across, + *ducere,* lead.] To bring over†, transfer†, or transmit†; translate, as into another language (obs. or rare); derive†; also, to expose to contempt or disgrace†; now, to speak evil of maliciously and falsely, slander, calumniate, or malign (as, "My character was *traduced* by Captain Hawkins . . . so much so, that even the ship's company cried out shame": Marryat's "Peter Simple," lxii.).—**tra-duce′ment,** *n.*—**tra-du′cer** (-dū′sėr), *n.*

tra-du-cian-ism (tra-dū″shian-izm), *n.* [LL. *traducianus,* < L. *tradux* (*traduc-*), a vine-branch trained for propagation, < *traducere:* see *traduce.*] The doctrine that the human soul is propagated along with the body. Cf. *creationism* and *infusionism.*—**tra-du′cian-ist,** *n.*

tra-duc-tion (tra-duk'shon), *n.* [L. *traductio(n-),* < *traducere:* see *traduce.*] A bringing over†, transferring†, or transmitting†; translation, as into another language (obs. or rare); transmission by generation (obs. or rare); also, the act of traducing or maligning (rare); in *logic,* transfer or transition from one classification or order of reasoning to another.

traf-fic (traf'ik), *n.* [F. *trafic,* < It. *traffico,* traffic; origin obscure.] The transportation of goods for the purpose of trade, by sea or land (as, ships of *traffic*); hence, trade between different countries or places, or commerce; in general, trade, buying and selling, or commercial dealings (as, the chief center of *traffic* in a region; "The war did not interfere with the *traffic* of the pedler," Cooper's "Spy," iii.); trade or dealing in some commodity or thing, often trade of an illicit kind, or concerned with something that should not be traded in (as, "They . . . depend for their livelihood on an extensive *traffic* in stolen goods," Borrow's "Bible in Spain," v.; *traffic* in public offices; the white slave *traffic,* see *white slave,* under *white, a.*); also, intercourse or dealings (now chiefly Sc.: as, "We . . . had little *traffic* beyond formal salutations," Stevenson's "Master of Ballantrae," xi.); also, goods or commodities of trade†; also, the business done by a railroad or other carrier in the transportation of freight or passengers, or the amount of freight or number of passengers carried (as, "There was an old saying that a railroad freight rate should be 'what the *traffic* will bear'; that is, the highest rate at which the largest quantity of freight would move": A. W. Mellon's "Taxation," i.); also, the coming and going of persons, vehicles, vessels, etc., along a way of passage or travel (as, times of heavy *traffic* on a street, bridge, or canal; "Duck Square . . . had no *traffic* across it," Arnold Bennett's "Clayhanger," i. 3); the persons, vehicles, etc., going along such a way (as, "great staggering horse omnibuses in a heaving jumble of *traffic*": H. G. Wells's "Tono-Bungay," i. 3. § 6).—**traf′fic**, *v.*; *-ficked*, *-ficking*. [F. *trafiquer*, < It. *trafficare*.] **I.** *intr.* To carry on traffic, trade, or commercial dealings (as, "We . . . *trafficked* with the natives for some good beef": Defoe's "Captain Singleton," xii.); often, to carry on dealings of an illicit or improper kind (as, to *traffic* in prohibited liquors; to *traffic* in public offices; to *traffic* with the enemy); also, to have intercourse or personal dealings (now chiefly Sc.). **II.** *tr.* To deal in, or exchange in traffic (now rare: as, "Hither also repair the Indian tribes accustomed to *traffic* their peltries with the company," Irving's "Captain Bonneville," i.); trade or barter (*away*: as, "precious woods and fruits and fragrant gums that would never be *trafficked* away," W. H. Hudson's "Green Mansions," v.).—**traf′fick-er**, *n.*

trag-a-canth (trag′a-kanth), *n.* [F. *tragacanthe*, the gum (now usually *adragant*, *adragante*), also the plant yielding it, < L. *tragacantha*, < Gr. τραγάκανθα, the plant, < τράγος, goat, + ἄκανθα, thorn.] A mucilaginous substance derived from various low, spiny Asiatic shrubs of the genus *Astragalus*: used to impart firmness to pills and lozenges, stiffen calicoes, etc. Also called *gum tragacanth*.

tra-ge-di-an (tra-jē′di-an), *n.* [OF. *tragedien* (F. *tragédien*), < *tragedie*, E. *tragedy*.] An actor of tragedy; also, a writer of tragedy.—**tra-gé-dienne** (trà-zhā-dyen), *n.* [F., fem. of *tragédien*.] A female actor of tragedy; a tragic actress.

trag-e-dy (traj′e-di), *n.*; pl. *-dies* (-diz). [OF. *tragedie* (F. *tragédie*), < L. *tragœdia*, < Gr. τραγῳδία, tragedy, < τραγῳδός, tragic singer or actor, appar. lit. 'goat-singer,' < τράγος, goat, + ἀείδειν, sing; perhaps referring to a chorus representing satyrs, clad in goatskins.] A dramatic composition of serious or somber character, with an unhappy ending (as, Shakspere's *tragedy* of "Hamlet"); that branch of the drama which is concerned with this form of composition, dealing with lamentable or dreadful events in a characteristically grave and dignified style; the tragic element of drama, of literature generally, or of life; any literary composition, as a novel, dealing with a somber theme carried to a tragic conclusion; also, a lamentable, dreadful, or fatal event or affair (as, "That [Napoleon's Russian] retreat is one of the great *tragedies* of history," H. G. Wells's "Outline of History," xxxviii. § 4; his failure was a *tragedy* to him); a disaster or calamity.

trag-ic (traj′ik). [L. *tragicus*, < Gr. τραγικός, pertaining to tragedy, lit. pertaining to a goat, < τράγος, goat: see *tragedy*.] **I.** *a.* Of, pertaining to, or of the nature of tragedy (as, the *tragic* drama); also, acting in or composing tragedy (as, a *tragic* actor; a *tragic* poet); also, characteristic or suggestive of tragedy (as, *tragic* solemnity; a *tragic* tone or gesture; "She could not indulge in *tragic* strides," John Hay's "Bread-Winners," i.); mournful, melancholy, or pathetic in the extreme (as, "Her face had taken on a look of . . . *tragic* courage": Mrs. Wharton's "Age of Innocence," xvi.); dreadful, calamitous, disastrous, or fatal (as, a *tragic* death or fate; a *tragic* event; *tragic* consequences). **II.** *n.* A tragic actor or writer.—**trag′i-cal**, *a.* Tragic.—**trag′i-cal-ly**, *adv.*—**trag′i-cal-ness**, *n.*

trag-i-com-e-dy (traj-i-kom′e-di), *n.*; pl. *-dies* (-diz). [F. *tragi-comédie*, < LL. *tragicomœdia*, for L. *tragicocomœdia*, < *tragicus*, E. *tragic*, + *comœdia*, E. *comedy*.] A dramatic

or other literary composition combining elements of both tragedy and comedy; esp., a composition of tragic nature in which the ending is not unhappy; fig., an incident or series of incidents of mixed tragic and comic character.—**trag-i-com′ic**, **trag-i-com′i-cal**, *a.* [= F. *tragi-comique*.] Pertaining to or of the nature of a tragicomedy; combining tragic and comic elements: as, "In viewing this monstrous *tragicomic* scene, the most opposite passions necessarily succeed" (Burke's "Revolution in France," 11).—**trag-i-com′i-cal-ly**, *adv.*

trag-o-pan (trag′ō-pan), *n.* [L., < Gr. τραγόπαν, a fabulous Ethiopian bird, < τράγος, goat, + Πάν, Pan.] Any of the Asiatic pheasants constituting the genus *Ceriornis* (or *Tragopan*), characterized by two fleshy erectile horns on the head.

Crimson Tragopan (*Ceriornis satyra*).

tra-gus (trā′gus), *n.*; pl. *-gi* (-jī). [NL., < Gr. τράγος, tragus, lit. 'goat': so named from the hairs upon it.] In *anat.*, a fleshy prominence at the external opening of the ear, projecting backward from the anterior edge of the orifice, and partly closing it. Cf. *antitragus*.

trail (trāl), *v.* [AF. *trailler*, trail (cf. *trailbaston*), OF. *tow* (a boat), prob. ult. < L. *trahere*, draw: cf. *train²*.] **I.** *tr.* To draw or drag along behind (as, "Heavy barges *trail'd* By slow horses": Tennyson's "Lady of Shalott," i.); drag or let drag along the ground or other surface (as, "Mrs. Archer and Janey *trailed* their long silk draperies up to the drawing-room": Mrs. Wharton's "Age of Innocence," v.); draw (the limbs, body, etc.) along with effort or difficulty, as from weakness or exhaustion, in walking or going; bring or have floating after itself (as, a carriage *trailing* streamers of ribbon; to *trail* clouds of dust or smoke); also, to draw out or protract; utter slowly, or drawl; also, to draw out maliciously in conversation, so as to make ridiculous (colloq.: as, "She was (what is vernacularly termed) *trailing* Mrs. Dent; that is, playing on her ignorance," C. Brontë's "Jane Eyre," xvii.); also, to follow the track or trail of; track; follow along behind (another or others), as in a race (colloq.); also, to mark out, as a track; beat down or make a path or way through (grass, etc.); *milit.*, orig., to carry (a pike, firearm, etc.) in the right hand in an oblique position, with the head or muzzle forward and the lower end or butt near the ground; now, specif., to carry (a firearm) with the muzzle inclined slightly forward and the breech near the ground (the piece being usually held in the right hand), or to carry (a firearm) in a horizontal position with the muzzle forward, the piece being held near the middle and the arm holding it (usually the right arm) being extended downward; *naut.*, to let (oars) trail in the water alongside the boat, as by throwing them out of the rowlocks and allowing them to be pulled along by attached ropes. **II.** *intr.* To be drawn or dragged along the ground or some other surface, as when hanging from something moving (as, long garments *trail* over the floor; "A long straight sword . . . *trailed* and clattered along the pavement," Chesterton's "Napoleon of Notting Hill," i. 2); move with long garments, etc., hanging and dragging (as, "a neat grass plot, across which . . . two youngish women were *trailing* in long morning-gowns": Howells's "Chance Acquaintance," xiii.); also, to hang down loosely from something (as, "Her yeolow locks . . . About her shoulders careleslie downe *trailing*," Spenser's "Ruines of Time," 11; a rope *trailing* from a balloon); stream or float from and after something moving, as dust, smoke, sparks, etc., do; also, to go slowly, lazily, or wearily along; follow as if drawn along (as, "eight or ten young maidens *trailing* round at the skirts of one old maiden": Galsworthy's "Dark Flower," iii. 4); creep or crawl, as a serpent; pass or extend

Astragalus gummifer, a plant yielding Tragacanth.

in a straggling line; of a plant, to extend itself in growth along the ground and over objects encountered, resting on these for support rather than taking root (see *creep, v. i.*) or clinging by tendrils, etc. (see *climb, v. i.*); also, to pass (*off*) by gradual change, as into silence, as the voice or the speaker (as, "Her voice *trailed* off," A. S. M. Hutchinson's "If Winter Comes," iii. 5; "He *trailed* off into silence," Archibald Marshall's "Anthony Dare," viii.); also, to follow a track or scent, as of game; also, to fish by trailing a line from a moving vessel or boat.—**trail,** *n.* Something that is trailed or that trails behind; a train of a skirt or robe; a stream of dust, smoke, light, etc., behind something moving (as, "the smoke *trail* of an ocean tramp," W. De Morgan's "Alice-for-Short," xiii.; the *trail* of a meteor); a line or succession of persons, vehicles, or the like trailing or following after; also, a spray or branch of a trailing plant, a vine, or the like; a running or wreathed ornament of leaves, flowers, etc., as in carved work; also, a mark or track left where something has been trailed or has passed along; the track, scent, or the like left by an animal or a person, esp. as followed by a hunter, hound, or other pursuer (as, "We came across the recent *trails* of but two of the animals we were after": Roosevelt's "Ranch Life and the Hunting-Trail," xii.); also, a path or track made across a wild region, over rough or mountainous country, or the like, by the passage of men or animals (as, to follow or lose the *trail*; "The only outlet was a steep *trail* over the summit of a hill," Bret Harte's "Luck of Roaring Camp"); a primitive path or route of travel (as, the Santa Fé *trail* and the Oregon *trail*, old overland routes of pioneers, traders, emigrants, etc., from Missouri to Santa Fé and Oregon respectively); also, a woman who trails her dress along the ground, or a slattern (Sc.); also, the act of trailing; in *artillery*, that part of a gun-carriage which rests on the ground when the piece is unlimbered.

trail-bas-ton (trāl′bas″tọn), *n.* [AF. *traillebaston*, 'trail-cudgel.'] In *Eng. hist.*, one of a class of lawless ruffians against whom special ordinances were issued in the 14th century.

trail=board (trāl′bōrd), *n.* Either of two curved pieces, one on each side, on the prow of a ship, extending to the figurehead.

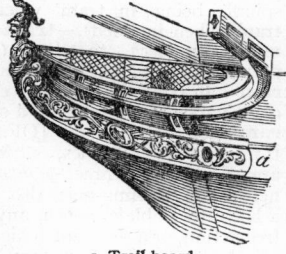

a, Trail-board.

trail-er (trā′lẻr), *n.* One who or that which trails; a person or an animal that follows a trail, or a tracker (as, "They clapped their *trailers* on us To spy the road we went": Kipling's "Broken Men"); a trailing plant; also, a vehicle drawn by another vehicle, as an extra car attached to a street-railway car, or a cart or the like attached to an automobile.

trail=hand-spike (trāl′hand″spīk), *n.* A wooden or metal lever used to move the trail of a gun-carriage in pointing the gun.

trail-ing (trā′ling), *p. a.* That trails; hanging down and dragging along the ground, as garments, etc.; streaming after, as smoke, etc.; extending in growth over the ground, etc., as plants (see *trail, v. i.*).—**trailing arbutus.** See *arbutus.*—**trail′ing-ly,** *adv.*

trail=rope (trāl′rōp), *n.* A prolonge; also, a guide-rope on a balloon.

trail=spade (trāl′spād), *n.* A projection at the lower end of the trail of a gun-carriage, which is driven into the ground by the recoil and thus serves to check it.

train¹† (trān), *n.* [OF. *traine*, < *trair* (F. *trahir*), < L. *tradere*, betray: see *tradition.*] Treachery or trickery; a trick, artifice, or wile (as, "Devilish Macbeth By many of these *trains* hath sought to win me Into his power": Shakspere's "Macbeth," iv. 3. 118); also, a trap or snare; a lure or decoy.

train² (trān), *v.* [OF. *trainer, trahiner* (F. *traîner*), prob. ult. < L. *trahere,* draw: cf. *trail.*] **I.** *tr.* To draw or pull along after one (obs. or archaic); draw out or protract (obs. or archaic); fig., to draw by artifice, entice, or decoy (ar-

chaic: as, "Thou hast been *trained* from thy post by some deep guile," Scott's "Talisman," xv.); also, to treat or manipulate so as to bring into some desired form, position, direction, etc. (as, "Why will she *train* that winter curl In such a spring-like way?" Holmes's "My Aunt"); also, to subject to discipline and instruction; educate, rear, or bring up (as, "You have *trained* me like a peasant," Shakspere's "As You Like It," i. 1. 71; "*Train* up a child in the way he should go," Prov. xxii. 6); make proficient by instruction and practice, as in some art, profession, or work (as, to *train* soldiers; to *train* women as nurses; "She would be compelled . . . to *train* the new servant," Arnold Bennett's "Old Wives' Tale," ii. 1); discipline and instruct (an animal), as in the performance of tasks or tricks; make (a person, etc.) fit by proper exercise, diet, etc., as for some athletic feat or contest; also, to bring to bear on some object, or point, aim, or direct, as a firearm, a camera, a telescope, the glance, etc.; in *hort.*, to bring (a plant, branch, etc.) into a particular shape or position, by bending, pruning, or the like; dispose so as to grow on something (as, to *train* vines on a trellis; to *train* fruit-trees on espaliers). **II.** *intr.* To hang down and drag, or trail, as a garment (now rare); also, to give the discipline and instruction, drill, practice, etc., designed to impart proficiency or efficiency; also, to undergo discipline and instruction, drill, etc.; get one's self into condition by exercise, etc.; also, to travel by train or railroad (colloq.); also, to consort or associate familiarly (*with*: slang, U. S.: as, "We don't *train* with this millionaire outfit," Sinclair Lewis's "Babbitt," ii.); also, to romp, or carry on (colloq., U. S.: as, "Got enough on my hands now, without havin' a boy *trainin'* round my house, and upsettin' all creation," Mrs. Stowe's "Oldtown Folks," viii.).—**train²,** *n.* [OF. *traine*, also *train* (F. *traîne, train*).] Something that is drawn along or trailed after a person or thing; a trailing part; an elongated part of a skirt or robe trailing behind on the ground; the tail or tail-feathers of a bird, esp. when long and trailing, as in the peacock; the tail of a comet or meteor; a trail or stream of something from a moving object (as, "From the torches *trains* of sparkles flew": W. Morris's "Jason," xi. 84); the flowing water of a stream or river (poetic: as, "Like streamlet . . . Now winding slow its silver *train*," Scott's "Marmion," iii., Introd.); also, a line or succession of persons or things following after (lit. or fig.: as, "A long *train* of her once bitter persecutors followed her . . . to her place," Hawthorne's "Twice-Told Tales," The Gentle Boy; an action which brought on a long *train* of consequences; "Learning followed in the *train* of Christianity," Macaulay's "Hist. of Eng.," i.); a body of followers or attendants, or a retinue or suite (as, "six ambassadors, with a *train* of about five hundred persons": Swift's "Gulliver's Travels," i. 5); also, a line or procession of persons, vehicles, animals, etc., traveling together (as, "While I was in the town, a *train* of emigrant wagons . . . passed through," Parkman's "Oregon Trail," i.; a camel *train* on the desert); a succession or series of proceedings, events, circumstances, etc.; a succession of connected ideas, or a continuous course of thought or reasoning; order, esp. proper order, for proceeding (as, "Matters were in good *train*," Kipling's "Kim," xii.; "I was also laying matters in *train* for my escape," S. Butler's "Erewhon," xxviii.); also, a line of combustible material, as gunpowder, for leading fire to an explosive charge; also, a series or row of objects or parts; also, a connected series of cars, etc., for moving together on a railroad or the like; *milit.,* an aggregation of vehicles, animals, and men accompanying an army to carry supplies, baggage, ammunition, or any equipment or materials; in *physics*, a group or series of successive waves, oscillations, or the like; in *mach.*, a series of connected parts, as wheels and pinions, through which motion is transmitted.

train-a-ble (trā′nạ-bl), *a.* Capable of being trained.

train=band (trān′band), *n.* [For *trained band.*] In *Eng. hist.*, one of the trained bands or forces of citizen soldiery organized in London and elsewhere in the 16th, 17th, and 18th centuries.

trained (trānd), *p. a.* [See *train², v.*] Having undergone discipline and instruction; educated; practised; made proficient by training: as, a *trained* observer; a *trained* eye or ear; a *trained* nurse.—**trained,** *a.* [See *train²*, *n.*] Having a train, as a skirt.

train-ee (trā-nē′), *n.* A person or an animal that undergoes training; specif., one receiving vocational training by special governmental provision, as a disabled or retired soldier or a dependent of a dead soldier.

train-er (trā′nėr), *n.* One who or that which trains; esp., one who trains or prepares men, horses, etc., for feats or contests requiring physical fitness; *naval,* a member of a gun's crew who brings the gun or turret laterally to the correct direction.

train-ing (trā′ning), *n.* The act or process of one who or that which trains, or the resulting condition; practical education in some art, profession, or the like; instruction coupled with practice in the use of one's own powers; military drill; the developing of physical strength and endurance, as for some athletic feat or contest, or the resulting physical fitness. —**train′ing=school,** *n.* A school for giving training in some art, profession, or line of work: as, a *training-school* for teachers or for nurses; a *training-school* for manual crafts and arts.—**train′ing=ship,** *n.* A ship equipped for training boys in seamanship, as for naval service.

train-man (trān′man), *n.*; pl. -men. A man employed on a railroad-train; esp., a brakeman.

train=oil (trān′oil), *n.* [MLG. *trān* = D. *traan* = G. *thran,* train-oil.] Oil obtained by boiling from the blubber of whales, esp. of the right whale, or from seals, fishes, etc.

train=shed (trān′shed), *n.* A large, more or less open structure for sheltering railroad-trains, esp. one covering the tracks, adjacent platforms, etc., at a station or terminus.

traipse (trāps), *v.* and *n.* See *trapes.*

trait (trāt, Brit. also trā), *n.* [OF. F. *trait,* a drawing, stroke, line, trait, < L. *tractus:* see *tract¹.*] A stroke made with a pen or pencil; a touch, as in a picture; also, a line of the face; a lineament; also, fig., a stroke, dash, or touch (of something: as, "He fell From talk of war to *traits* of pleasantry," Tennyson's "Lancelot and Elaine," 319; "What distinguished the physician's ecstasy from Satan's was the *trait* of wonder in it," Hawthorne's "Scarlet Letter," x.); a distinguishing feature or quality, or a characteristic (as, good and bad *traits* of character; "This reliance on authority is a fundamental primitive *trait,*" J. H. Robinson's "Mind in the Making," v. 11).

trai-tor (trā′tọr), *n.* [OF. *traitor, traitre* (F. *traître*), < L. *traditor,* betrayer, < *tradere,* betray: see *tradition.*] One who betrays a person, a cause, or any trust (as, "Judas Iscariot, which also was the *traitor*": Luke, vi. 16); specif., one who betrays his country by violating his allegiance; one guilty of treason.—**trai′tor-ous,** *a.* Having the character of a traitor; treacherous; perfidious; faithless; also, characteristic of a traitor; of the nature of treachery or treason.— **trai′tor-ous-ly,** *adv.*—**trai′tor-ous-ness,** *n.*—**trai′tress,** *n.* A female traitor.

tra-ject (trạ-jekt′), *v. t.* [L. *trajectus,* pp. of *trajicere, traicere,* throw across, also go across, < *trans,* across, + *jacere,* throw.] To throw or cast over; transport; transmit. [Now rare.]—**traj-ect** (traj′ekt), *n.* [L. *trajectus,* n.: cf. F. *trajet.*] A passing or crossing over; also, a way or place for passing over; a passage or crossing.—**tra-jec′tion** (-jek′shọn), *n.* [L. *trajectio*(n-).] The act of trajecting; transmission; also, transposition.—**tra-jec′to-ry** (-tọ-ri), *n.*; pl. -ries (-riz). The path described by a body moving under the action of given forces; the curve described by a projectile in its flight through the air; in *geom.,* a curve or surface which cuts all the curves or surfaces of a given system at a constant angle.

tra-la-la (trä-lä-lä′), *interj.* An utterance sung as a musical phrase, or representing a short instrumental flourish, of gay or joyous character. Also **tra-la′.**

tral-a-ti-tious (tral-ạ-tish′us), *a.* [L. *tralatitius, tralaticius,* for *translaticius,* < *translatus,* pp.: see *translate.*] Characterized by transference; transferred; metaphorical or figurative, as words, etc.; repeated by one person from another, as a statement; handed down from one generation to another.

Tral-li-an (tral′i-ạn), *a.* Of or pertaining to the ancient Greek city of Tralles, in Asia Minor, or its inhabitants: as, the *Trallian* school of sculpture. See cut in next column.

tram¹ (tram), *n.* [F. *trame,* < L. *trama,* weft.] Silk thread, consisting of two or more loosely twisted single strands, used for the weft or filling of silks, velvets, etc.

tram² (tram), *n.* [Cf. MLG. *trame,* crossbar, rung, LG. *traam,* G. *tram,* beam.] Either of the two shafts of a cart, wheelbarrow, or other vehicle (Sc.); also, a framework, sledge, or wheeled truck or car on which loads are transported in coalmines; also, either of the

Trallian School of Sculpture. — The group called the Farnese Bull, in the Museo Nazionale, Naples.

two parallel lines of beams, stones, or rails forming a tramroad or tramway; also, a tramroad or tramway; also, in British use, a tram-car or street-car (as, "Eliza Brating said she must go at once in order not to miss the last *tram* home": Arnold Bennett's "Mr. Prohack," viii.).—**tram²,** *v. i.* or *t.*; *trammed, tramming.* To travel or convey by tram.

tram³ (tram), *n.* [For *trammel.*] A trammel, or instrument for describing ellipses; also, in *mech.,* correct position or adjustment (as when the spindle in a grinding-mill is perpendicular to the face of the stationary lower millstone, the spindle being 'in tram' when perpendicular, and 'out of tram' when inclined).—**tram³,** *v. t.* or *i.*; *trammed, tramming.* In *mech.,* to adjust (something) correctly, as in a perpendicular or a parallel position.

tram=car (tram′kär), *n.* A car used on a tramway for the conveyance of passengers; a street-car. [British.]

tram-mel (tram′el), *n.* [OF. *tramail* (F. *trémail*), net with three layers of meshes, < ML. *tramaculum, tremaculum,* appar. < L. *tres,* three, + *macula,* mesh.] A kind of fishing-net; also, a fowling-net; also, a shackle, esp. one for teaching a horse to amble†; hence, anything that impedes or hinders free action, or a restraint (chiefly in *pl.,* and fig.: as, to throw off the *trammels* of custom or etiquette; "An hereditary prince could never have remained quiet in such *trammels* as were imposed upon the Doge of Venice," Hallam's "Europe during the Middle Ages," iii. 2); also, a contrivance hung in a fireplace to support pots, kettles, etc., over the fire (as, "the great black crane . . . with its multiplicity of pothooks and *trammels*": Mrs. Stowe's "Oldtown Folks," vi.); also, an instrument for describing ellipses; also, a beam-compass.—**tram′mel,** *v. t.*; -meled or -melled, -meling or -melling. To catch or entangle in or as in a trammel or net; also, to shackle or hobble (a horse's legs, etc.)†; hence, to subject to trammels or restraints upon action; involve or hold in trammels; hamper; restrain.—**tram′mel-er, tram′mel-ler,** *n.*

tra-mon-ta-na (trä-mọn-tä′nä), *n.* [It.: see *tramontane.*] The north wind, as blowing over Italy (from across the Alps) or the Mediterranean.

tra-mon-tane (trạ-mon′tān or tram′ọn-tān). [It. *tramontano* (as n., *tramontana,* north wind), < L. *transmontanus,* < *trans,* across, + *mons* (*mont-*), mountain.] **I.** *a.* Being or situated beyond the mountains, orig. beyond the Alps as viewed from Italy; pertaining to the other side of the mountains; hence, foreign; barbarous; also, of a wind, coming from beyond the mountains, esp. blowing over Italy, etc., from beyond the Alps; also, going or passing across the mountains (as, "these *tramontane* expeditions": Irving's "Captain Bonneville," i.). **II.** *n.* One who lives beyond the mountains (orig. applied by the Italians to the peoples beyond the Alps, and by the latter to the Italians); hence, a foreigner; an outsider; a barbarian; also, in Italy and the Mediterranean, the north wind; hence, any cold wind from a mountain-range.

tramp (tramp), *v.* [ME. *trampen* = MLG. and G. *trampen*, tramp, stamp: cf. Goth. *anatrimpan*, tread or press upon.] **I.** *intr.* To tread or walk with a firm, heavy, resounding step (as, "Jim's footsteps had a fateful sound as he *tramped* by . . . in his heavy laced boots": J. Conrad's "Lord Jim," xxxiv.); also, to tread heavily or trample (*on* or *upon*: as, to *tramp* on a person's toes); also, to walk heavily or steadily, march, or trudge (as, "Not a few of the gallant warriors *tramped* barefoot from Wales into Yorkshire": Morley's "Oliver Cromwell," iii. 5); travel on foot; go on a walking excursion or expedition; also, to go about as a vagabond or tramp; also, to make a voyage on a tramp steamer. **II.** *tr.* To tread or trample underfoot; also, to tramp or walk heavily or steadily through or over (as, "I've *tramped* the streets, and worn out my boots": L. Merrick's "Actor-Manager," iv.); traverse on foot; travel over as a tramp; also, to run (a vessel) as a tramp.—**tramp**, *n.* The act of tramping; a firm, heavy, resounding tread, or the sound made (as, "The heavy *tramp* of a war-horse was not to be mistaken by the ear of a warrior": Scott's "Castle Dangerous," ix.); a long, steady walk, or trudge; a walking excursion or expedition (as, "the pleasure of long *tramps* in the brown forest": Tarkington's "Magnificent Ambersons," xx.); also, a person who tramps, or travels about on foot, from place to place; esp., a vagabond who wanders about the country living on occasional gifts of money or food or other casual means of subsistence (as, "The idle *tramps* always felt sure they could get a copper from Seth": George Eliot's "Adam Bede," i.); also, a freight-vessel which does not run regularly between fixed ports, but takes a cargo wherever shippers desire (also called *ocean tramp, tramp vessel,* or *tramp steamer*).—**tramp'er**, *n.*

tram-ple (tram'pl), *v.*; -pled, -pling. [Freq. of *tramp*.] **I.** *intr.* To tread or step heavily and noisily, or stamp (as, "At length the *trampling* of horses and the sound of wheels were heard": Scott's "Guy Mannering," xx.); also, to tread heavily, roughly, or crushingly (*on, upon,* etc.), esp. repeatedly (as, "The horse would . . . move with the greatest caution . . . lest he should *trample* on his diminutive companion [a hen]," G. White's "Nat. Hist. of Selborne," ii. 24; to *trample* over young plants); fig., to act in a harsh, domineering, or cruel way as if treading roughly (*on, upon,* etc.: as, to *trample* on an oppressed people or their rights; "He wished to *trample* on her feelings," Arnold Bennett's "Clayhanger," ii. 12). **II.** *tr.* To tread heavily, roughly, or carelessly on or over (as, "It will be well if you and your friends do not *trample* this wreckage": H. G. Wells's "Men Like Gods," i. 3); tread (underfoot, etc., lit. or fig.: as, "*trampling* the golden leaves underfoot," Longfellow's "Kavanagh," xxv.; "to *trample* justice under foot for a bribe," Froude's "Cæsar," xii.); fig., to trample on, domineer harshly over, or crush (as, to *trample* law and order); also, to put, force, reduce, etc., by trampling (as, to *trample* out a fire; to *trample* down a fleeing enemy; "I will *trample* you into atoms," Godwin's "Caleb Williams," i.).—**tram'ple**, *n.* The act or sound of trampling.—**tram'pler**, *n.*

tram-road (tram'rōd), *n.* [See *tram*², *n.*] A road or track, orig. in mining districts, formed of parallel lines of wooden beams, lengths of stone, iron plates, or rails, for wheeled conveyances.

tram-way (tram'wā), *n.* A tramroad; now, esp., in British use, a street-railway.

trance (trảns), *n.* [OF. F. *transe*, orig. passage, esp. from life to death, hence deadly suspense or fear, < *transir*, < L. *transire*, go across, pass over: see *transit*.] A sleep-like state in which formerly the soul was thought to have withdrawn temporarily from the body; an unconscious, cataleptic, or hypnotic condition; also, a half-conscious state, as between sleeping and waking; a dazed or bewildered condition (as, "She lay stone-still in a *trance* of terror": G.

Meredith's "Ordeal of Richard Feverel," i.); a fit of complete mental absorption or deep musing (as, "The Queen immersed in such a *trance*, And moving thro' the past unconsciously": Tennyson's "Guinevere," 398); a state of mental or spiritual withdrawal from mundane things, as to the contemplation of heavenly things (as, "He fell into a *trance*, And saw heaven opened," Acts, x. 10; "The brightness of Faith's holy *trance* Gathered upon thy countenance [in prayer]," Whittier's "Daniel Wheeler"); an ecstasy; in spiritualistic use, a temporary state in which a medium, with suspension of personal consciousness, is controlled by an intelligence from without and used as a means of communication, as from the dead to the living.—**trance**, *v. t.*; **tranced**, **trancing**. To throw into or hold in a trance; entrance: as, "I trod as one *tranced* in some rapturous vision" (Shelley's "Revolt of Islam," v. 17).—**tran-ced-ly** (trȧn'sed-li), *adv.*

tran-gam† (trang'gam), *n.* [Origin obscure.] An intricate or odd contrivance; a puzzle; a toy; a gimcrack.

tran-quil (trang'kwil), *a.* [L. *tranquillus*, tranquil, quiet.] Free from commotion or storm, or calm, as the sea, air, etc. (as, "cruising over the *tranquil* Pacific," H. Melville's "Omoo," lx.; "The smoke rose slowly, slowly, Through the *tranquil* air of morning," Longfellow's "Hiawatha," i. 33); also, free from disturbance or tumult, peaceful, or quiet (as, a *tranquil* retreat; a *tranquil* period; "He was sure matters would not remain *tranquil* at Lisbon," Borrow's "Bible in Spain," i.); serene or placid, as a landscape, etc. (as, "The whole landscape of swelling plains and scattered groves was softened into a *tranquil* beauty": Parkman's "Oregon Trail," xi.); untroubled, as rest, enjoyment, etc.; also, free from or unaffected by disturbing emotions, composed, or unruffled, as a person, the mind, the countenance or bearing, etc. (as, "He was too *tranquil* of nature to be hurried, by passion, into a grave political step," Motley's "Dutch Republic," ii. 4; "a *tranquil* dignity of demeanor," H. Melville's "Typee," xvi.).—**tran'quil-ize, tran'quil-lize,** *v.*; -ized, -lized, -izing, -lizing. **I.** *tr.* To make tranquil; calm; quiet; compose. **II.** *intr.* To become tranquil.—**tran″quil-i-za'tion, tran″quil-li-za'tion** (-kwil-i-zā'shọn), *n.*—**tran'quil-iz-er, tran'quil-liz-er** (-kwil-ī-zėr), *n.*—**tran-quil'li-ty** (-kwil'i-ti), *n.* [L. *tranquillitas*.] The state of being tranquil; calmness; peacefulness; quiet; serenity; composure.—**tran'quil-ly,** *adv.*—**tran'quil-ness,** *n.*

trans- (trans- or tranz-). [L. *trans-*, repr. *trans*, prep.] A prefix meaning 'across,' 'over,' 'through,' 'beyond,' 'on the other side of,' occurring orig. in words from the Latin, but now freely used as an English formative, as in *trans-Appalachian, trans-Mississippi, trans-Siberian,* such words tending, with frequent use, to lose hyphen and capital, as in *transsiberian:* sometimes opposed to *cis-.*

trans-act (trans-akt' or tranz-), *v.* [L. *transactus*, pp. of *transigere*, < *trans*, across, through, + *agere*, drive, do.] **I.** *tr.* To carry through (affairs, business, etc.) to a conclusion or settlement, by such action, arrangements, or negotiations as may be necessary. **II.** *intr.* To carry through affairs or negotiations; transact business. [Now rare.]—**trans-ac'tion** (-ak'shọn), *n.* [LL. *transactio(n-)*.] The act of transacting, or the fact of being transacted; an instance or process of transacting something, or that which is transacted; an affair; a piece of business; *pl.*, records of the doings of a learned society or the like, or, sometimes, reports of papers read, addresses delivered, discussions, etc., at the meetings (cf. *proceeding, n.*).—**trans-ac'tor,** *n.*

trans-al-pine (trans-al'pin or -pīn, or tranz-). [L. *transalpinus*, < *trans*, across, + *Alpes*, the Alps.] **I.** *a.* Across or beyond the Alps, esp. as viewed from Rome or Italy. **II.** *n.* A native or inhabitant of a country beyond the Alps.

trans-an-de-an (trans-an'dē-ạn or tranz-), *a.* [See *trans-*.] Across or beyond the Andes.

trans-at-lan-tic (trans-at-lan'tik or tranz-), *a.* [See *trans-*.] Passing or extending across the Atlantic (as, a *transatlantic* liner; a *transatlantic* cable); also, beyond, or on the other side of, the Atlantic, as viewed from either side; esp., in European use, American.

trans-ca-lent (trans-kā'lẹnt), *a.* [L. *trans*, across, through, + *calens* (*calent-*), ppr. of *calere*, be hot.] Pervious to heat; permitting the passage of heat.—**trans-ca'len-cy,** *n.*

---

trans-cau-ca-sian (trans-kâ-kash′ạn), *a.* [See *trans-*.] Across or beyond the Caucasus Mountains; [*cap.*] of or pertaining to Transcaucasia, the southern portion of Caucasia (between the Black Sea and the Caspian Sea).

tran-scend (tran-send′), *v.* [L. *transcendere*, < *trans*, across, over, + *scandere*, climb.] **I.** *tr.* To climb, get, or pass across or over (a mountain, barrier, etc.)†; fig., to go or be above or beyond (a limit, something with limits, etc.: as, fancy *transcending* the bounds of knowledge; "a world *transcending* the range of the senses," Tyndall's "Forms of Water," § 47; "postulates and axioms which *transcend* demonstration," S. Butler's "Way of All Flesh," lxv.); overpass or exceed; also, to go beyond in elevation, excellence, extent, degree, etc., or be higher or greater than (as, "enthusiasms and passions . . . which far *transcend* the selfish personal infatuations . . . of romance," G. B. Shaw's "You Never Can Tell," iii.; "this sorrow *transcending* all sorrows, darker than death," W. H. Hudson's "Green Mansions," xxi.); surpass, excel, or exceed; in *theol.*, of the Deity, to be above and independent of (the universe). **II.** *intr.* To be transcendent; excel. [Archaic.] —**tran-scend′ence**, **tran-scend′en-cy**, *n.* The state, quality, or fact of being transcendent; transcendent character. —**tran-scend′ent**, *a.* [L. *transcendens* (-*ent*-)′, ppr.] Transcending; going beyond ordinary limits; surpassing or extraordinary (as, "In debate his *transcendent* eloquence . . . enabled him . . . to crush opposition": Lecky's "Hist. of Eng. in the 18th Century," viii.); superior or supreme; of the Deity, transcending the material universe; in the scholastic philosophy, transcending the categories; in the Kantian philosophy, transcending experience; not realizable in human experience. —**tran-scen-den′tal** (-sen-den′tạl), *a.* Transcendent, surpassing, or superior (as, "The new system was to be derived from the *transcendental* power of the British parliament": Bancroft's "Hist. of the U. S.," Amer. Revolution, ii. 3); in the Aristotelian philosophy, transcending the bounds of any single category; in the Kantian philosophy, of, pertaining to, based upon, or concerned with a priori elements in experience; in later use, of certain theories, etc., explaining what is objective as the product of the subjective mind; also, in general, transcending ordinary or common experience, thought, or belief; extraordinary; supernatural; abstract or metaphysical; idealistic, lofty, or extravagant (as, "embellished with those *transcendental* sentiments . . . with which chivalry has invested them": J. H. Newman's "Callista," xi.); in *math.*, not producible by the algebraic operations of addition, subtraction, multiplication, division, and the extraction of roots, each repeated only a finite number of times. —**tran-scen-den′tal-ism**, *n.* Transcendental character, thought, or language; also, transcendental philosophy (see *transcendental*); any philosophy based upon the doctrine that the principles of reality are to be discovered by the study of the processes of thought, or emphasizing the intuitive and spiritual above the empirical. —**tran-scen-den′tal-ist**, *n.* An adherent of some form of transcendentalism. —**tran-scen-den′tal-ize**, *v. t.*; -ized, -izing. To render transcendental; idealize (as, "Not Dante himself *transcendentalised* his Beatrice to more ethereal substance than he his Sanchia": M. Hewlett's "Open Country," xvi.). —**tran-scen-den′tal-ly**, *adv.* —**tran-scend′ent-ly**, *adv.* —**tran-scend′ent-ness**, *n.*

trans-con-ti-nen-tal (trans-kon-ti-nen′tạl), *a.* [See *trans-*.] Passing or extending across a continent (as, a *transcontinental* railroad); also, on the other side of a continent.

tran-scribe (tran-skrīb′), *v. t.*; -scribed, -scribing. [L. *transcribere* (pp. *transcriptus*), < *trans*, across, over, + *scribere*, write.] To make a copy of in writing (as, to *transcribe* the text of a document); write as a copy (as, a few passages remain, *transcribed* from the lost manuscript); also, to reproduce more or less exactly in one writing or book, as matter taken from another (now rare); also, to reproduce in writing or print as from speech (as, "A part of that gentleman's conversation . . . was faithfully *transcribed* [in a letter]," W. Churchill's "Modern Chronicle," i. 9; "I will not . . . shock my readers by *transcribing* the term in which he expressed his feeling," Trollope's "Barchester Towers," vi.); also, to write out in other characters (as, to *transcribe* one's shorthand notes); transliterate; sometimes, to translate;

in *music*, to arrange (a composition) for a voice or instrument other than that for which it was originally written. —**tran-scrib′er** (-skrī′bėr), *n.* —**tran′script** (-skript), *n.* [ML. *transcriptum*, prop. neut. of L. *transcriptus*, pp.] Something transcribed, or made by transcribing; a written copy; a reproduction in writing or print; a form of something as rendered from one alphabet or language into another (as, "on the subject of my spelling — in a *transcript* from the Greek . . . — Greek names . . . precisely as does the Greek author": Browning's "Agamemnon of Æschylus," Preface); in general, a copy or reproduction of anything; an imitation. —**tran-scrip′tion** (-skrip′shọn), *n.* [L. *transcriptio*(*n*-).] The act of transcribing; also, a transcript; a copy; in *music*, the arrangement of a composition for a voice or instrument other than that for which it was originally written; a composition so arranged. —**tran-scrip′tive** (-tiv), *a.* Characterized by or connected with transcribing, copying, or reproducing; of the nature of a transcript.

trans-cur-rent (trans-kur′ẹnt), *a.* [L. *transcurrens* (-*ent*-), ppr. of *transcurrere*, < *trans*, across, + *currere*, run.] Running or extending across or transversely. —**trans-cur′-rent-ly**, *adv.*

tran-sect (tran-sekt′), *v. t.* [L. *trans*, across, + *sectus*, pp. of *secare*, cut.] To cut across; divide by passing across; dissect transversely. —**tran-sec′tion** (-sek′shọn), *n.*

tran-sen-na (tran-sen′ạ), *n.*; pl. *transennæ* (-ē). [L., net, lattice.] In *Christian antiq.*, an openwork screen of marble, silver, or the like before a shrine, as

Transenna in Church at the entrance of the Catacombs of St. Alexander, Rome.

of a martyr.

tran-sept (tran′sept), *n.* [AL. *transeptum*, < L. *trans*, across, + *sæptum*, inclosure: see *septum*.] In *arch.*, the transverse portion of a cruciform church, or sometimes one of two such portions; also, either of the two arm-like divisions of this, one on each side of the nave (as, "the beautiful English window in the south *transept* of the church": W. Churchill's "Inside of the Cup," ii.). —**tran-sep′tal** (-sep′tạl), *a.*

Salisbury Cathedral, England, from the northeast, showing the two Transepts.

tran-se-unt (tran′sē-unt), *a.* [L. *transeunt-*, in oblique cases of *transiens*, E. *transient*.] Passing outward, producing an effect outside, or transient: as, a *transeunt* action. See *transient, a.*

trans-fer (trans-fėr′), *v.*; -ferred, -ferring. [L. *transferre*, bear across, bring over, transfer, translate, < *trans*, across, + *ferre*, bear: cf. *translate*.] **I.** *tr.* To convey or remove from one place, person, etc., to another; pass or hand over from one to another; specif., to make over the possession or control of (as, to *transfer* a title to land); sell or give; also, to convey (a drawing, design, pattern, etc.) from one surface to another. **II.** *intr.* To transfer one's self; be transferred; esp., to change from one conveyance, railway-line, or the like, to another, as on a transfer.—**trans′fer,** *n.* The act of transferring, or the fact of being transferred; also, that which is transferred, as a drawing, pattern, etc.; also, a point or place for transferring; a means or system of transferring; a ticket, issued with or without extra charge, entitling a passenger to continue his journey on another conveyance, railway-line, or the like.—**trans′fer-a-ble** (-fẹ-rạ-bl), *a.* [Cf. *transferrable.*] Capable of being transferred; specif., capable legally of being made over to another; negotiable.—**trans-fer-ee′** (-fẹ-rē′), *n.* One to whom a transfer is made, as of property; also, one who is transferred or removed, as from one place to another.—**trans′fer-ence** (-fẹ-rẹns), *n.* The act or process of transferring, or the fact of being transferred; transfer.—**trans-fer-en′tial** (-fẹ-ren′shạl), *a.* Pertaining to or involving transference.—**trans-fer′or** (-fér′ọr), *n.* One who makes a transfer, as of property.—**trans′fer=pa″per,** *n.* Any of various kinds of specially prepared paper by means of which drawings, impressions, designs, etc., are transferred.—**trans-fer′ra-ble, trans-fer′ri-ble,** *a.* Transferable.—**trans-fer′ral,** *n.* Transference; transfer.—**trans-fer′rer,** *n.* One who or that which transfers.

trans-fig-u-ra-tion (trans-fig-ū-rā′shọn), *n.* [L. *transfiguratio(n-).*] The act of transfiguring, or the state of being transfigured; esp., the change in the appearance of Christ on the mountain (see Mat. xvii. 1–9); [*cap.*] the church festival commemorating this, observed on Aug. 6.

trans-fig-ure (trans-fig′ūr), *v. t.*; -*ured,* -*uring.* [L. *transfigurare* (pp. *transfiguratus*), < *trans,* across, over, + *figurare,* form, E. *figure, v.*] To change in outward form or appearance (as, "My lady was quite *transfigured* into the matron," Stevenson's "Master of Ballantrae," viii.; "He claps on the false nose, and is again grotesquely *transfigured,*" G. B. Shaw's "You Never Can Tell," iv.); in general, to transform, change, or alter (as, "When you think it [madness] fled, it may have but become *transfigured* into some still subtler form," H. Melville's "Moby-Dick," xli.; "all their minds *transfigured* so together," Shakspere's "Midsummer Night's Dream," v. 1. 24); esp., to invest with a radiant or shining appearance (first in New Testament use: as, "Jesus . . . was *transfigured* before them: and his face did shine as the sun, and his raiment was white as the light," Mat. xvii. 2; "His face seemed *transfigured* with a glory," F. M. Crawford's "Mr. Isaacs," v.); fig., to change so as to glorify, exalt, or idealize (as, "dreams . . . of a world *transfigured* to harmony and beauty": H. G. Wells's "Men Like Gods," iii. 2).—**trans-fig′ure-ment,** *n.*

trans-fix (trans-fiks′), *v. t.* [L. *transfixus,* pp. of *transfigere,* < *trans,* across, through, + *figere,* fix, pierce.] To pierce through, as with a pointed weapon, or as the weapon does (as, to *transfix* a person with a spear or dart; "An arrow . . . *transfixed* him," Scott's "Legend of Montrose," xiv.); fix fast with or on something sharp thrust through; fig., to pierce with pain, grief, etc.; render motionless with amazement, terror, etc. (as, "I stood *transfixed* at her astonishing beauty": Watts-Dunton's "Aylwin," i. 2); pierce with the eye or glance, or hold helpless with one's glance.—**trans-fix′ion** (-fik′shọn), *n.*

trans-flu-ent (trans′flŏ-ẹnt), *a.* [L. *transfluens* (-ent-), ppr. of *transfluere,* < *trans,* across, through, + *fluere,* flow.] Flowing or running across or through.

trans-flux (trans′fluks), *n.* [L. *trans,* across, through, + *fluxus,* a flowing, E. *flux.*] A flowing across, through, or beyond.

trans-form (trans-fôrm′), *v.* [L. *transformare* (pp. *transformatus*), < *trans,* across, over, + *formare,* E. *form, v.*] **I.** *tr.* To change in form, change to something of a different form, or metamorphose (as, the enchantress Circe *transformed* men into swine; the tadpole becomes *transformed* into a frog); hence, in general, to change in appearance, condition, nature, or character (as, "A back attic . . . was now *transformed* into a studio," Arnold Bennett's "Old Wives' Tale," ii. 8; "The little man was glowing with enthusiasm and pride; he was *transformed,*" Besant's "All Sorts and Conditions of Men," xxii.; to *transform* hatred

into love); change into another substance, or transmute (as, "The victor sees his fairy gold, *Transformed,* when won, to drossy mold": Scott's "Rokeby," i. 31); in *math.,* to change the form of (a figure, expression, etc.) without changing the value; in *physics,* to change (one form of energy) into another; in *elect.,* to change (a current) in potential or in type. **II.** *intr.* To change in form, appearance, or character; become transformed.—**trans-form′a-ble,** *a.* Capable of being transformed.—**trans-for-ma′tion** (-fôr-mā′shọn), *n.* [LL. *transformatio(n-).*] The act of transforming, or the state of being transformed; change in form, or metamorphosis; change in appearance, nature, or character; also, a transformation-scene; also, an artificial covering of hair, waved or curled and dressed, worn by women over the natural hair or to conceal the lack of it.—**trans-for-ma′tion=scene,** *n. Theat.,* a scene which changes before the eyes of the audience; specif., formerly, in a pantomime, a scene in which the principal characters were transformed into characters in the ensuing harlequinade.—**trans-for′ma-tive** (-mạ-tiv), *a.* Tending or serving to transform.—**trans-form′er,** *n.* One who or that which transforms; in *elect.,* a device for changing the form or potential of a current, esp. one for transforming a comparatively small alternating current of higher voltage into a larger current of lower voltage ('step-down transformer'), or, reversely, a current of lower voltage into one of higher voltage ('step-up transformer').—**trans-form′ism,** *n.* In *biol.,* the doctrine of the gradual transformation of one species into another by descent with modification through many generations; such transformation itself; any doctrine or instance of evolution.—**trans-form′ist,** *n.*

trans-fuse (trans-fūz′), *v. t.*; -*fused,* -*fusing.* [L. *transfusus,* pp. of *transfundere,* < *trans,* across, through, + *fundere,* pour.] To pour from one vessel into another; hence, to transfer or transmit as if by pouring; diffuse through something; infuse (as, "Into thee such virtue and grace Immense I have *transfused*": Milton's "Paradise Lost," vi. 704); in *med.,* to transfer (blood) from the veins or arteries of one person or animal (the *donor*) into those of another; also, to inject, as a saline solution, into a blood-vessel.—**trans-fus′er** (-fū′zèr), *n.*—**trans-fus′i-ble,** *a.* Capable of being transfused.—**trans-fu′sion** (-fū′zhọn), *n.* [L. *transfusio(n-).*] The act or process of transfusing; transference or transmission as if by pouring; in *med.,* the transferring of blood from one person or animal to another, as in order to renew a depleted blood-supply or to give strength to an exhausted subject; also, the injecting of some other liquid into the veins.—**trans-fu′sive** (-siv), *a.* Tending to transfuse or be transfused.

trans-gress (trans-gres′), *v.* [L. *transgressus,* pp. of *transgredi,* step across, overstep, exceed, LL. transgress, < L. *trans,* across, + *gradi,* walk, go.] **I.** *tr.* To pass over or go beyond (a limit, etc.: often fig.: as, to *transgress* the bounds of prudence or reason); also, to go beyond the limits imposed by (a law, command, etc.: as, "They *transgressed* . . . the rules of behavior that were binding on all others," Hawthorne's "Scarlet Letter," xxi.; "The question . . . was . . . whether I should not to some extent *transgress* my instructions," S. Butler's "Way of All Flesh," lxvi.); violate, infringe, or break. **II.** *intr.* To violate a law, command, etc.; offend or sin (*against:* as, "They *transgressed* against the God of their fathers," 1 Chron. v. 25).—**trans-gres′sion** (-gresh′ọn), *n.* [L. *transgressio(n-).*] The act of transgressing; violation of a law, command, etc.; a trespass or sin (as, "Remember not the sins of my youth, nor my *transgressions*": Ps. xxv. 7).—**trans-gres′sive** (-gres′iv), *a.* Transgressing, or inclined to transgress; involving transgression.—**trans-gres′sive-ly,** *adv.*—**trans-gres′sor,** *n.* [LL.] One who transgresses; an offender; a sinner: as, "The way of *transgressors* is hard" (Prov. xiii. 15).

tran-ship (tran-ship′), *v.*; -*shipped,* -*shipping.* [For *trans-ship*: see *trans-.*] **I.** *tr.* To transfer from one ship, car, or other conveyance to another. **II.** *intr.* To change from one ship or other conveyance to another.—**tran-ship′ment,** *n.*

tran-sient (tran′shẹnt). [L. *transiens* (*transeunt-*): see *transeunt*), ppr. of *transire,* go across or through, pass over, pass by: see *transit.*] **I.** *a.* Passing over, as from one person or thing to another (now rare); also, passing outward, or producing an effect outside of the agent or of the mind of the subject (as, a *transient*, or transeunt, action: opposed to *immanent*); also, passing through a place and not staying long; remaining only for a short time, as a guest at a hotel; also, passing with time, not lasting or enduring, or transitory (as, "this *transient* world," Milton's "Paradise Lost," xii. 554; "Pleasure . . . may become mischievous by endearing us to a state which we know to be *transient*," Johnson's "Rasselas," xlvii.); lasting but for a time, or temporary (as, a *transient* stay in a place; *transient* authority); passing, esp. soon or quickly (as, *transient* showers; "The moods were many and *transient*," W. H. Hudson's "Green Mansions," vi.); brief, momentary, or fleeting; in *music*, introduced in passing, as a note, chord, etc., which serves as a connective, but is unessential to the harmony. **II.** *n.* One who or that which is transient; a transient guest, boarder, or the like.—**tran′sience, tran′sien-cy,** *n.*—**tran′sient-ly,** *adv.*—**tran′sient-ness,** *n.*

tran-sil-i-ent (tran-sil′i-ent), *a.* [L. *transiliens* (*-ent-*), ppr. of *transilire*, < *trans*, across, + *salire*, leap.] Leaping or passing from one thing or state to another.

trans-il-lu-mi-nate (trans-i-lū′mi-nāt or tranz-), *v. t.*; *-nated*, *-nating*. [See *trans-*.] To cause light to pass through; in *med.*, to throw a strong light through (an organ or part) as a means of diagnosis.—**trans-il-lu-mi-na′tion** (-nā′shon), *n.*

trans-isth-mi-an (trans-is′mi-an or trans-ist′-, or tranz-), *a.* [See *trans-*.] Passing or extending across an isthmus, esp. the Isthmus of Panama.

tran-sit (tran′sit), *n.* [L. *transitus*, < *transire*, go across or through, pass over, pass by, < *trans*, across, through, + *ire*, go.] The act or fact of passing across or through; passage from one place to another; conveyance from one place to another, as of persons or goods (as, the problem of rapid *transit* in cities, as by street-railways, subways, etc.; "The motor-car had been chosen as a means of *transit*," Arnold Bennett's "Lion's Share," xxiii.); a line of passage or conveyance across, or from place to place; also, fig., a passing or changing from one state, stage, form, etc., to another; the passage from this life to the next by death; a transition or change; in *astron.*, the passage of an inferior planet (Mercury or Venus) across the sun's disk, or of a satellite or its shadow across the face of its primary; also, the passage of a heavenly body across the meridian of a place or through the field of a telescope; also, a transit-instrument; in *surv.*, a theodolite whose telescope can be transited; an instrument of the theodolite kind, adapted for measuring horizontal and vertical angles, and usually having other attachments, as a compass, cross-hairs for stadia measurements, etc.—**tran′sit,** *v. t.*; *-sited*, *-siting*. To pass across or through; in *surv.*, to turn (the telescope of a surveyor's transit) about its horizontal transverse axis so as to make it point in the opposite direction.—**tran′sit-a-ble,** *a.* Admitting of transit or passage.—**tran′sit=in″stru-ment,** *n.* In *astron.*, an instrument consisting essentially of a telescope mounted on a horizontal transverse axis which is adjusted so as to be perpendicular to the plane of the meridian of a place, used for observing the passage of a celestial body across the meridian, esp. with respect to the time of transit.

tran-si-tion (tran-sish′on, -zish′on, or -sizh′on), *n.* [L. *transitio(n-)*, < *transire*, pass over: see *transit*.] Passage from one place, position, or state to another, or a passage of this kind (as, "Without any sense of *transition* the bishop found himself seated in the little North Library," H. G. Wells's "Soul of a Bishop," vi.; "the rapid and perpetual *transitions* from the cottage to the throne," Gibbon's "Decline and Fall of the Roman Empire," x.; "an instant *transition* from death to life," C. B. Brown's "Wieland," xiv.); often, passage or change from one stage, form, style, or character to another, or a change of this kind (as, "We are living . . . in an age of *transition*," S. Butler's "Way of All Flesh," lvi.; a period of *transition* in architecture; "Man . . . may pass by an easy *transition* into a more powerful brute," Froude's "Cæsar," ii.); also, change, or a change, from one action or proceeding to another (as, "He now practised one of his *transitions*; and . . . shifted from or-

dinary civil talk into a stream of insult": Stevenson's "Master of Ballantrae," v.); also, change, or a change, from one subject of discourse or thought to another (as, "Here the archangel paused . . . Then, with *transition* sweet, new speech resumes," Milton's "Paradise Lost," xii. 2; a narrative broken by abrupt *transitions*); in *music*, a passing from one key to another; modulation.—**tran-si′tion-al,** *a.* Of, pertaining to, characterized by, or involving transition; intermediate.—**tran-si′tion-al-ly,** *adv.*—**tran-si′tion-a-ry** (-a̱-ri), *a.* Transitional.

tran-si-tive (tran′si-tiv). [LL. *transitivus*, < L. *transire*, pass over: see *transit*.] **I.** *a.* Passing over to or affecting something else; transient or transeunt; also, characterized by or involving transition; transitional; intermediate; in *gram.*, of verbs, constructions, etc., expressing an action which passes over to an object; taking a direct object. **II.** *n.* In *gram.*, a transitive verb.—**tran′si-tive-ly,** *adv.*

tran-si-to-ry (tran′si-tō-ri), *a.* [LL. *transitorius*, < L. *transire*, pass by: see *transit*.] Passing away, or not lasting, enduring, permanent, or eternal (as, this *transitory* life; "Let pass, as they are *transitory*, The kingdoms of this world," Milton's "Paradise Regained," iv. 209); lasting but a short time, soon passing, or brief (as, "This [civil tumult] was a *transitory* ebullition," Hallam's "Europe during the Middle Ages," iii. 1; "His pleasure was only *transitory*," Thackeray's "Newcomes," lxix.); short-lived; transient.—**tran′si-to-ri-ly,** *adv.*—**tran′si-to-ri-ness,** *n.*

trans-lat-a-ble (trans-lā′ta̱-bl), *a.* Capable of being translated.—**trans-lat′a-ble-ness,** *n.*

trans-late (trans-lāt′), *v.*; *-lated*, *-lating*. [L. *translatus*, pp. of *transferre*, bear across, bring over, transfer, translate: see *transfer*.] **I.** *tr.* To bear, carry, or remove from one place, position, condition, etc., to another; transfer; specif., to remove (a bishop) from one see to another, or (a see) from one place to another; also, to convey or remove to heaven without death (as, "By faith Enoch was *translated* that he should not see death": Heb. xi. 5); exalt in spiritual ecstasy or rapture (as, "lifted or *translated* into a purely spiritual atmosphere and . . . in communion and one with the unseen world," W. H. Hudson's "Far Away and Long Ago," xxiii.; "Their souls, with devotion *translated*, Rose on the ardor of prayer," Longfellow's "Evangeline," i. 4); also, to turn (something written or spoken) from one language into another; render into another language (as, to *translate* English books into Spanish); render into a language understood (as, "Miss Westonhaugh did not understand the language, and Isaacs would have been the last person to *translate* such a speech": F. M. Crawford's "Mr. Isaacs," xi.); also, to express in other terms; paraphrase; explain or interpret; also, to change into another form, transform, or convert (as, "It only meant *translating* into action what had been carefully thought out": Galsworthy's "Dark Flower," ii. 19); in *mech.*, to cause (a body) to move without rotation; subject to translation; in *teleg.*, to retransmit or forward (a message), as by a relay. **II.** *intr.* To practise translation; also, to admit of translation (as, the book *translates* well).—**trans-la′tion** (-lā′shon), *n.* [L. *translatio(n-)*.] The act of translating, or the state of being translated; esp., the rendering of something into another language; the result of this; a version in a different language (as, an English *translation* of Homer; "Tindal revised his *translation* of the New Testament . . . and caused it again to be printed about . . . 1530," Strype's "Memorials of Cranmer," i. 21); in *mech.*, motion in which there is no rotation; onward movement which is not rotary or reciprocating. —**trans-la′tion-al,** *a.*—**trans-la′tor,** *n.* One who or that which translates; esp., one who translates from one language into another.—**trans-la′tress,** *n.* A female translator.

Trans-lei-than (trans-lī′than), *a.* [See *trans-*.] Beyond the river Leitha (between Austria and Hungary): applied to the division of the former Austro-Hungarian Empire having its seat in Budapest.

trans-lit-er-ate (trans-lit′e̱-rāt), *v. t.*; *-ated*, *-ating*. [L. *trans*, across, over, + *litera*, *littera*, letter.] To change (letters, words, etc.) into corresponding characters of another alphabet or language: as, to *transliterate* the Greek χ as ch; to *transliterate* Arabic or Chinese words into English characters.—**trans-lit-er-a'tion** (-ẹ-rā'shọn), n.—**trans-lit'-er-a-tor,** n.

trans-lo-cate (trans-lō'kāt), v. t.; -cated, -cating. [See trans-.] To remove from one place to another; cause to change place; displace; dislocate.—**trans-lo-ca'tion** (-lọ-kā'shọn), n.

trans-lu-cent (trans-lū'sẹnt), a. [L. translucens (-ent-), ppr. of translucere, < trans, across, through, + lucere, shine.] Transparent or clear (as, "As through pure water or translucent glass The sunbeam darts, yet leaves the crystal sound": Wiffen's tr. Tasso's "Jerusalem Delivered," iv. 32); now, esp., transmitting light diffusely or imperfectly, or semitransparent (as, "plates of thin translucent horn," Jefferies's "Gamekeeper at Home," v.; "translucent paper windows," H. G. Wells's "Soul of a Bishop," vii.).—**trans-lu'cence, trans-lu'cen-cy,** n.—**trans-lu'cent-ly,** adv.

trans-lu-cid (trans-lū'sid), a. [L. translucidus.] Translucent: as, "Schuylkill was here a pure and translucid current" (C. B. Brown's "Wieland," v.).

trans-lu-na-ry (trans'lū-nā-ri), a. [L. trans, across, beyond, + luna, moon.] Situated beyond or above the moon; superlunary; fig., celestial, rather than earthly; ideal; visionary.

trans-ma-rine (trans-mạ-rēn'), a. [L. transmarinus, < trans, across, beyond, + mare, sea.] Across or beyond the sea; oversea.

trans-me-rid-i-o-nal (trans-mẹ-rid'i-ọ-nạl), a. [See trans-.] Crossing the meridional lines, or meridians; running east and west.

trans-mi-grant (trans'mi-grạnt). I. a. Transmigrating. II. n. One who or that which transmigrates; specif., a person passing through a country or place on his way from his own country to a country in which he intends to settle.

trans-mi-grate (trans'mi-grāt), v.; -grated, -grating. [L. transmigratus, pp. of transmigrare, < trans, across, over, + migrare, migrate.] I. intr. To remove or pass from one place to another; migrate from one country to another in order to settle there; of the soul, to pass at death into another (living) body. II. tr. To cause to transmigrate, as a soul. —**trans-mi-gra'tion** (-grā'shọn), n. [LL. transmigratio(n-).] The act of transmigrating; migration from one country to another; esp., the passage of a soul at death into another (living) body; metempsychosis.—**trans'mi-gra-tor,** n.—**trans-mi'gra-to-ry** (-mī'grạ-tọ-ri), a. Transmigrating; pertaining to transmigration.

trans-mis-si-ble (trans-mis'i-bl), a. Capable of being transmitted.—**trans-mis-si-bil'i-ty** (-bil'i-ti), n.

trans-mis-sion (trans-mish'ọn), n. [L. transmissio(n-).] The act of transmitting, or the fact of being transmitted; transference; in mach., the transmitting or transferring of motive force; also, a device for this purpose; the mechanism or gearing for transmitting the revolutions of the motor-shaft in an automobile to the driving-wheels, or for varying the speed.—**trans-mis'sion=gear,** n. A mechanism for transferring motive force; esp., the transmission of an automobile.

trans-mis-sive (trans-mis'iv), a. Transmitting; pertaining to transmission; also, obtained by transmission; transmitted; derived.

trans-mit (trans-mit'), v. t.; -mitted, -mitting. [L. transmittere (pp. transmissus), < trans, across, over, + mittere, send.] To send over or along, as to a recipient or destination (as, to transmit despatches; to transmit money by special messenger; "Please transmit th' enclosèd letter," Burns's "Captain Grose," 21); forward, despatch, or convey; communicate, as information, news, etc.; pass on or hand down, as to heirs, successors, or posterity (as, "He was to transmit the dignities to his children": Motley's "Dutch Republic," vi. 5); also, to convey or pass along (an impulse, force, motion, etc.); also, to cause (light, heat, sound, etc.) to pass through a medium; of a medium, to suffer (light, heat, etc.) to pass through (as, glass transmits light).—**trans-mit'ta-ble,** a. Transmissible.—**trans-mit'tal,** n. Transmission.—**trans-mit'ter,** n. One who or that which transmits; specif., that part of a telegraphic or telephonic apparatus by which messages are transmitted.

trans-mog-ri-fy (trans-mog'ri-fī), v. t.; -fied, -fying. [Appar. a humorous made word: cf. transmigrate.] To change the form or appearance of, as by magic; transform, esp. in a surprising or grotesque manner. [Humorous.]—**trans-mog'ri-fi-ca'tion** (-fi-kā'shọn), n.

trans-mon-tane (trans-mon'tān), a. [L. transmontanus: see tramontane.] Across or beyond a mountain or mountains; esp., as viewed from Rome or Italy, beyond, or north of, the Alps.

trans-mun-dane (trans-mun'dān), a. [L. trans, across, beyond, + mundus, world.] Beyond the (or this) world.

trans-mu-ta-ble (trans-mū'tạ-bl), a. Capable of being transmuted.—**trans-mu-ta-bil'i-ty** (-bil'i-ti), n.

trans-mu-ta-tion (trans-mū-tā'shọn), n. [L. transmutatio(n-).] The act of transmuting, or the fact or state of being transmuted; change into another nature, substance, or form; sometimes, change of condition, esp. alternating change; in alchemy, the (attempted) conversion of baser metals into metals of greater value, esp. into gold or silver; in biol., the transformation of one species into another; transformism.—**trans-mu-ta'tion-ist,** n. One who believes in a theory of transmutation, esp. of species in natural history.

trans-mu-ta-tive (trans-mū'tạ-tiv), a. Serving to transmute.

trans-mute (trans-mūt'), v. t.; -muted, -muting. [L. transmutare (pp. transmutatus), < trans, across, over, + mutare, change.] To change from one nature, substance, or form into another; transform.—**trans-mut'er** (-mū'tẹr), n.

trans-nep-tu-ni-an (trans-nep-tū'ni-ạn), a. [See trans-.] In astron., beyond the planet Neptune.

trans-nor-mal (trans-nôr'mạl), a. [See trans-.] Beyond what is normal; supernormal.

trans-o-ce-an-ic (trans-ō-shẹ-an'ik or tranz-), a. [See trans-.] Across or beyond the ocean.

tran-som (tran'sọm), n. [Prob. < L. transtrum, cross-beam, akin to trans, across.] A horizontal transverse beam or bar; a lintel; also, a cross-bar, as of wood or stone, dividing a window horizontally; a window so divided; also, a crosspiece separating a door or the like from a window or fan-light above it; a window above such a crosspiece; also, any of several transverse beams or timbers fixed across the stern-post of a ship, to strengthen and give shape to the after part; also, a couch or seat with storage room beneath, built along the side of a ship's cabin.—**tran'somed,** a.—**tran'som=win'dow,** n. A window divided by a transom; also, a window over the transom of a door.

Transoms and Frame of Ship, inside of Stern.— 1, main transom; 2, 2, half transoms; 3, transom; 4, 4, transom-knees; 5, stern-post.

trans-pa-cif-ic (trans-pạ-sif'ik), a. [See trans-.] Passing or extending across the Pacific (as, a transpacific cable); also, beyond, or on the other side of, the Pacific.

trans-pa-dane (trans-pā'dān or trans'pạ-dān), a. [L. transpadanus, < trans, across, beyond, + Padus, the Po.] On the farther (or north) side of the river Po (from Rome).

trans-par-ence (trans-pār'ẹns or trans-par'-), n. Transparency.

trans-par-en-cy (trans-pār'ẹn-si or trans-par'-), n.; pl. -cies (-siz). [ML. transparentia.] The property or quality of being transparent; also, something which is transparent; a picture, design, or the like on glass or some translucent substance, made visible by light shining through from behind: a fixed or portable sign painted on muslin or the like, mounted on a framework and lighted from behind, or the sign with its framework, etc. (as, "The Harkless Club . . . wheeled into Main Street, two hundred strong, with their banners and transparencies": Tarkington's "Gentleman from Indiana," xix.).

trans-par-ent (trans-pār'ẹnt or trans-par'-), a. [ML. transparens (-ent-), ppr. of transparere, be transparent, < L. trans, across, through, + parere, come forth, appear.] Having the property of transmitting rays of light through its substance so that bodies situated beyond or behind can be distinctly seen (as, transparent glass; "This steam is transparent and invisible," Tyndall's "Forms of Water," § 1:

(variable) ḍ as d or j, ṣ as s or sh, ṭ as t or ch, ẓ as z or zh; o, F. cloche; ü, F. menu; čh, Sc. loch; ṅ, F. bonbon; ', primary accent; ", secondary accent; †, obsolete; <, from; +, and; =, equals. See also lists at beginning of book.

opposed to *opaque*, and usually distinguished from *translucent*); pervious to light; diaphanous; sometimes, admitting the passage of light through interstices; loosely, semitransparent or translucent (as, "*transparent* macintoshes of pink, yellow or green": Arnold Bennett's "Pretty Lady," xli.); also, shining through, as light†; also, fig., open, frank, or candid (as, "the man's *transparent* earnestness": Charnwood's "Abraham Lincoln," v.); easily seen through or understood (as, "Oliver Dromore began to haunt the house . . . on very *transparent* excuses": Galsworthy's "Dark Flower," iii. 6); manifest or obvious (as, "Theobald's impatience became more and more *transparent* daily": S. Butler's "Way of All Flesh," lxxxiii.).—**trans-par′ent-ly**, *adv.* —**trans-par′ent-ness**, *n.*

tran-spic-u-ous (tran-spik′ū-us), *a.* [NL. *transpicuus*, < L. *trans*, across, through, + *specere*, look at.] Transparent; pervious to light; also, easy to be understood; perspicuous; manifest.

trans-pierce (trans-pērs′), *v. t.*; *-pierced, -piercing*. [F. *transpercer*: see *trans-* and *pierce*.] To pierce through; penetrate; pass through.

tran-spire (tran-spīr′), *v.*; *-spired, -spiring*. [F. *transpirer*, < L. *trans*, across, through, + *spirare*, breathe.] **I.** *tr.* To emit or send off in the form of vapor through the walls or surface of a body; give off (waste matter, watery vapor, an odor, etc.) through the surface, as of the body, of leaves, etc. **II.** *intr.* To give off moisture through the skin†, or perspire† (as, "The day was not oppressively hot, yet I saw that the doctor was *transpiring* profusely": Kinglake's "Eothen," xviii.); give off watery vapor from the surface of leaves, etc., as plants; also, to pass off through the walls or surface of a body in the form of vapor; escape as through pores, as moisture, odor, etc.; also, fig., to escape from secrecy, leak out, or become known (as, "He did his best . . . to prevent the fact from *transpiring*," Arnold Bennett's "Clayhanger," ii. 7; "The events of the duel did not *transpire* till the next morning," Marryat's "Mr. Midshipman Easy," xviii.); also, erroneously, to occur, happen, or take place (as, "I did not follow, but I heard afterwards . . . what *transpired*": Miss Mulock's "John Halifax," xiii.).—**tran-spi-ra′-tion** (-spi-rā′shọn), *n.*

trans-plant (trans-plant′), *v.* [LL. *transplantare* (pp. *transplantatus*), < L. *trans*, across, over, + *plantare*, E. *plant, v.*] **I.** *tr.* To remove (a plant) from one place and plant it in another; in general, to remove from one place to another; esp., to bring (a colony, etc.) from one country to another for settlement; in *surg.*, to transfer, as an organ or a portion of tissue, from one part of the body to another or from one person or animal to another. **II.** *intr.* To undergo transplanting, esp. in a manner specified.—**trans-plant** (trans-plant′ or trans′plant), *n.* A transplanting; also, something transplanted; in *forestry*, a seedling which has been transplanted once or several times.—**trans-plant′a-ble**, *a.* That may be transplanted.—**trans-plan-ta′tion** (-plan-tā′shọn), *n.* The act of transplanting; also, something that has been transplanted.—**transplant′er**, *n.* One who transplants; also, a tool, machine, or apparatus for use in transplanting.

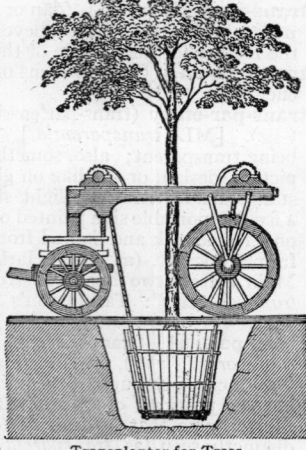
Transplanter for Trees.

trans-po-lar (trans-pō′lär), *a.* [See *trans-*.] Across the (north or south) pole or polar region: as, a *transpolar* flight of an aircraft.

trans-pon-tine (transpon′tin), *a.* [L. *trans*, across, + *pons* (*pont-*), bridge.] Across or beyond a bridge; esp., on the southern side of the Thames in London (as, "the *transpontine* . . . regions of Rotherhithe and Cherry Garden Pier": W. De Morgan's "Somehow Good," i.).

trans-port (trans-pōrt′), *v. t.* [OF. F. *transporter*, < L. *transportare* (pp. *transportatus*), < *trans*, across, over, + *portare*, carry.] To carry or convey from one place to another; also, to remove from this world†; kill†; also, to carry into banishment, as a criminal to a penal colony (as, "I was *transported*, sir, for poaching": H. Kingsley's "Geoffry Hamlyn," xxvi.); fig., to carry away by strong emotion (as, "Ferdinand had been *transported* with joy at hearing of the capture of the Moorish monarch," Irving's "Conquest of Granada," xix.; "Her gentle voice would soothe me when *transported* by passion," Mrs. Shelley's "Frankenstein," xxii.); carry out of one's self; render beside one's self.—**trans′port**, *n.* [OF. F. *transport*.] The act of transporting or conveying; conveyance; also, a means of transporting or conveying; a vessel employed for transporting soldiers or military stores, or convicts; the animals and vehicles used for transporting the supplies of an army (sometimes including the things transported); also, a convict transported, or sentenced to be transported; also, the state of being carried away by some strong emotion, as joy, rage, etc. (as, "A general murmur of applause and involuntary *transport* burst forth from every one present": Godwin's "Caleb Williams," xii.); a fit of strong emotion (as, "a *transport* of enthusiasm," Dickens's "Dombey and Son," vi.; "Lord Dorking . . . speaks of him with *transports* of indignation," Thackeray's "Newcomes," xxxii.); an ecstatic utterance.—**trans-port′a-ble**, *a.* Capable of being transported; also, involving or liable to punishment by transportation.—**trans-por-ta′tion** (-pōr-tā′shọn), *n.* [L. *transportatio(n-).*] The act of transporting, or the state of being transported; banishment, as of a criminal to a penal colony, or deportation (as, "a set of rascals and rebels whom *transportation* is too good for": Dickens's "Hard Times," ii. 5); also, means of transport or conveyance; also, cost of transport or travel by public conveyance; also, tickets or permits for transport or travel.—**trans-por′ta-tive** (-pōr′ta-tiv), **trans-por′tive**, *a.* Serving to transport.—**trans-port′er**, *n.*

trans-pos-a-ble (trans-pō′zạ-bl), *a.* That may be transposed.—**trans-pos-a-bil′i-ty** (-bil′i-ti), *n.*

trans-po-sal (trans-pō′zạl), *n.* Transposition.

trans-pose (trans-pōz′), *v. t.*; *-posed, -posing*. [OF. F. *transposer*, < *trans-* (< L. *trans*), over, + *poser*, put (see *pose*¹), but associated with derivatives of L. *transponere*: see *transposition*.] To transfer or transport (now rare); also, to alter the relative position or order of (a thing in a series, or a series of things); cause (two or more things) to change places; interchange; esp., to alter the order of (letters in a word, or words in a sentence); also, to change the purport, application, or use of†; also, to translate†; adapt†; also, to transform†, transmute†, or convert†; in *alg.*, to bring (a term) from one side of an equation to the other, with change of the plus or minus sign; in *music*, to alter the key of (as, "She had *transposed* 'Angels ever bright and fair' into a lower key, so as to make it suit her voice": S. Butler's "Way of All Flesh," xi.).—**trans-pos′er** (-pō′zėr), *n.*

trans-po-si-tion (trans-pọ-zish′ọn), *n.* [F. *transposition*, < ML. *transpositio(n-)*, < L. *transponere*, transfer, < *trans*, over, + *ponere*, place, put: cf. *transpose*.] The act of transposing, or the state of being transposed; also, the result of transposing; a transposed form of something; a transposed piece of music.—**trans-po-si′tion-al**, *a.*—**transpos′i-tive** (-poz′i-tiv), *a.* Characterized by transposition.

trans-rhe-nane (trans-rē′nān), *a.* [L. *transrhenanus*, < *trans*, beyond, + *Rhenus*, the Rhine.] On the other (the eastern) side of the river Rhine: as, "the *transrhenane* dominions of the Franks" (G. P. R. James's "Hist. of Charlemagne," iii.).

trans-shape (trans-shāp′), *v. t.*; *-shaped, -shaping*. [See *trans-*.] To change into another shape or form; transform. [Now rare.]

trans-ship (trans-ship′), etc. Same as *tranship*, etc.

tran-sub-stan-ti-ate (tran-sub-stan′shi-āt), *v. t.*; *-ated, -ating*. [ML. *transubstantiatus*, pp. of *transubstantiare*, < L. *trans*, across, over, + *substantia*, E. *substance*.] To change from one substance into another; transmute; specif., in *theol.*, to change from bread and wine into the body and blood of Christ.—**tran-sub-stan-ti-a′tion** (-ā′shọn), *n.* [ML. *transubstantiatio(n-).*] The changing of one substance into another; in *theol.*, the conversion, in the eucharist, of the whole substance of the bread into the body, and of the whole substance of the wine into the blood, of Christ, only the appearance of bread and wine remaining (the doctrine of the Roman Catholic Church). Cf. *consubstantiation* and *impanation.*

tran-su-date (tran-sū′dāt), *n.* A substance which has transuded.

tran-su-da-tion (tran-sū-dā′shon), *n.* The act or process of transuding; also, a substance which has transuded.—**tran-su′da-to-ry** (-sū′dạ-tọ-ri), *a.* Transuding; characterized by transudation.

tran-sude (tran-sūd′), *v.*; *-suded, -suding.* [L. *trans*, across, through, + *sudare*, sweat.] **I.** *intr.* To pass or ooze through pores or interstices, as a fluid. **II.** *tr.* To pass or ooze through (something); also, to cause to transude.

trans-val-ue (trans-val′ū), *v. t.*; *-valued, -valuing.* [See *trans-*.] To change the value of.—**trans-val-u-a′tion** (-ū-ā′shon), *n.*

trans-vase (trans-vās′), *v.t.*; *-vased, -vasing.* [F. *transvaser*, < L. *trans*, across, + *vas*, vessel.] To pour from one vessel into another. Also fig.

trans-ver-sal (trans-vėr′sal). [ML. *transversalis.*] **I.** *a.* Transverse. **II.** *n.* In *geom.*, a line intersecting two or more lines.—**trans-ver′sal-ly**, *adv.*

trans-verse (trans-vėrs′), *a.* [L. *transversus*, pp. of *transvertere*, turn or direct across, < *trans*, across, + *vertere*, turn.] Lying or being across or in a cross direction; being or extending across the length of something, esp. at right angles; cross; thwart; in *geom.*, noting that axis of a conic section which passes through the foci.—**transverse colon**, in *anat.*, the upper part of the colon, which extends across the body from right to left, as distinguished from the ascending and descending parts on the right and left sides of the body respectively.—**trans-verse′**, *n.* Something which is transverse; in *geom.*, a transverse axis.—**trans-verse′**, *v. t.*; *-versed, -versing.* To lie or pass across or athwart; also, to turn upside down or backward; turn topsyturvy; alter or transform. [Now rare.]—**trans-verse′ly**, *adv.*

trans-vert-er (trans-vėr′tèr), *n.* [See *transformer* and *converter.*] In *elect.*, a device for changing alternating current of low voltage into direct current of high voltage (functioning as a step-up transformer and a converter), or for changing direct current of high voltage into alternating current of low voltage.

trap¹ (trap), *n.* [AS. *træppe* (recorded in composition), *treppe*, trap: cf. ML. *trappa*, OF. *trape*, F. *trappe*, trap, from Teut.] A contrivance used for taking game, noxious animals, etc., as a pitfall, a mechanical device that shuts suddenly by means of a spring, or a snare; a gin; hence, any device, stratagem, or the like for catching one unawares; also, a movable covering of a pit, or of an opening in a floor, made to fall by the release of a spring or the like, as when stepped upon; hence, a door or movable piece flush, or nearly so, with the surface of a floor, a ceiling, the top of a cab, or the like, and covering an opening, or the opening itself (as, "The fare . . . speaks through the little *trap* to his Jehu": W. De Morgan's "Somehow Good," i.); also, the piece of wood, shaped somewhat like a shoe hollowed at the heel, and moving on a pivot, used in playing the game of trap-ball; the game itself; also, a device for suddenly releasing or tossing into the air objects to be shot at, as pigeons or clay targets; also, trickery or fraud (slang: as, "He was a clever, ready-witted fellow, up to all sorts of *trap*," Lover's "Handy Andy," ii.); also, a detective, policeman, or the like (slang); also, a carriage, esp. a light two-wheeled carriage (colloq.); also, a device in a pipe, as

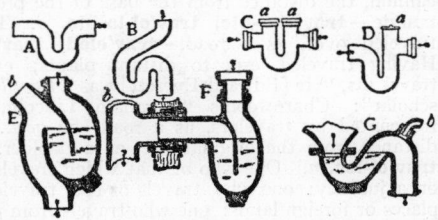

Trap in Pipe.—*A, B,* common traps; *C, D,* modifications of *A* and *B*—screw-caps, as shown at *a,* being added for cleaning out the traps; *E, F, G,* ventilating traps with air-pipes at *b* leading to the exterior of a building.

a double curve or a U-shaped section in which liquid remains and forms a seal, for preventing the passage or escape of air or gases through the pipe from behind or below (see cut in preceding column); any of various contrivances for preventing the passage of steam, water, etc.—**trap¹**, *v.*; *trapped, trapping.* **I.** *tr.* To catch in a trap; hence, to catch as if in a trap; take by stratagem; lead by artifice or wiles (as, "She wanted to *trap* him into damaging revealments": Mark Twain's "Tom Sawyer," i.); also, to furnish or set with traps; trap animals in (as, "A range of country is *trapped* by small detachments from a main body": Irving's "Captain Bonneville," xliv.); also, to provide (a drain, etc.) with a trap; also, to stop and hold by or as by a trap, as air or gas in a pipe. **II.** *intr.* To set traps for game; practise catching animals in traps for their furs; also, to work the trap in trap-shooting.

trap² (trap), *n.* [Sw. *trapp*, < *trappa*, a stair: from the appearance often presented by such rocks.] In *geol.*, any of various fine-grained dark-colored igneous rocks having a more or less columnar structure, esp. some form of basalt.

trap³ (trap), *n.* [ME. *trappe*, prob. from an OF. var. of OF. F. *drap*, cloth: see *drape.*] A cloth or covering for a horse†; also, *pl.*, appurtenances, belongings, or baggage (colloq.: as, "There . . . is an old guitar or something of the kind among my *traps*," F. M. Crawford's "Mr. Isaacs," ix.; "A couple of horses carry us and our *traps*," Thackeray's "Newcomes," xxx.).—**trap³**, *v. t.*; *trapped, trapping.* To furnish with trappings; caparison.

tra-pan (trạ-pan′), *n. and v.* Same as *trepan².*

trap=ball (trap′hâl), *n.* An old game in which a ball placed on the hollowed end of a trap (see *trap¹, n.*) is thrown into the air by striking the other end of the trap with a bat, and then driven to a distance with the bat; also, the ball used in this game.

trap=door (trap′dōr′), *n.* A door flush, or nearly so, with the surface of a floor, ceiling, roof, or the like, or the opening which it covers: as, "He followed, mounting by a ladder, through a *trap-door* on to the roof" (Galsworthy's "Saint's Progress," ii. 1).

trapes (trāps), *v.*; *trapesed, trapesing.* [Origin obscure.] **I.** *intr.* To walk in a slovenly manner, esp. with the dress trailing or draggled; walk aimlessly or idly about; gad: as, "You go *trapesin'* about the fields like a mad woman" (George Eliot's "Adam Bede," xxxvii.); "She didn't think it looked well . . . to go *trapesing* about the country on Sundays" (H. G. Wells's "Mr. Polly," vii.). [Colloq.] **II.** *tr.* To walk or tramp over or through. [Colloq.]—**trapes**, *n.* A slovenly woman or girl; a slattern; also, a tiring or dirty walk; a long tramp. [Colloq.]

tra-peze (trạ-pēz′), *n.* [F. *trapèze*, < NL. *trapezium*: see *trapezium.*] An apparatus consisting of a short horizontal bar suspended at some distance above the ground by two ropes, one at each end, fixed above: used in performing various gymnastic exercises and feats.—**tra-pez′ist** (-pē′zist), *n.* A performer on the trapeze.

tra-pe-zi-um (trạ-pē′zi-um), *n.*; pl. *-ziums* or *-zia* (-zi-ạ). [NL., < Gr. τραπέζιον, dim. of τράπεζα, table: cf. τετράπεζος, four-footed.] In *geom.*, as orig. used by Euclid, any rectilinear quadrilateral plane figure not a parallelogram; now, specif., a quadrilateral plane figure of which no two sides are parallel (usually so called in the U. S., but in England often called *trapezoid*); also, a quadrilateral plane figure having two parallel and two non-parallel sides (often so called in England, but in the U. S. usually called *trapezoid*); in *anat.*, a bone of the carpus articulating with the metacarpal bone of the thumb.

Trapezium.

tra-pe-zi-us (trạ-pē′zi-us), *n.*; pl. *-zii* (-zi-ī). [NL., < *trapezium*: see *trapezium.*] In *anat.*, each of a pair of large flat triangular muscles of the back of the neck and adjacent parts, together forming a somewhat diamond-shaped figure.

trap-e-zo-he-dron (trap″ē-zō-hē′dron), *n.*; pl. *-drons* or *-dra* (-drạ). [Gr. τραπέζιον, trapezium, + ἕδρα, seat, base.] A solid whose faces are all trapeziums or trapezoids.—**trap″e-zo-he′dral**, *a.*

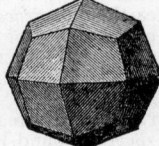

Trapezohedron.

trap-e-zoid (trap′ē-zoid), *n.* [Gr. τραπεζοειδής, table-like, < τράπεζα, table, + εἶδος, form.] In *geom.*, a quadrilateral plane figure having two parallel and two non-parallel sides (usually so called in the U. S., but in England often called *trapezium*); also, a quadrilateral plane figure of which no two sides are parallel (often so called in England, but in the U. S. usually called *trapezium*); in *anat.*, a bone of the carpus articulating with the metacarpal bone of the index-finger.—**trap-e-zoi′dal**, *a.*

trap-pe-an (trap′ē-an), *a.* Of, pertaining to, or of the nature of trap (rock).

trap-per (trap′ėr), *n.* One who traps; esp., one who makes a business of trapping wild animals for their furs.

trap-ping (trap′ing), *n.* [See *trap*³.] A cloth or covering for a horse, etc., esp. when ornamental in character, or a caparison (usually in *pl.*: as, "a numerous train of horses, with their rich *trappings*," Gibbon's "Decline and Fall of the Roman Empire," xl.); hence, in general, *pl.*, articles of equipment or dress, esp. of an ornamental character (as, "indifferent to the gaudy *trappings* and ornaments of his companions": Parkman's "Oregon Trail," xi.); conventional or characteristic articles of dress or adornment (lit. or fig.: as, "the *trappings* . . . of woe," Shakspere's "Hamlet," i. 2. 86; "the *trappings* of chivalry, perhaps without its spirit," Hallam's "Europe during the Middle Ages," i. 2).

Trap-pist (trap′ist). [F. *trappiste*.] **I.** *n.* A member of a monastic body, a branch of the Cistercian order, observing the extremely austere reformed rule established at the abbey of La Trappe, in Normandy, in 1664. **II.** *a.* Of or pertaining to the Trappists.

trap-pose, trap-pous (trap′ōs, -us), *a.* Same as *trappean.*

trap-py (trap′i), *a.* Of the nature of a trap; treacherous; tricky. [Colloq.]

trap=rock (trap′rok′), *n.* Same as *trap*².

trap=shoot-ing (trap′shö″ting), *n.* The sport of shooting at live pigeons released from a trap, or at clay targets, etc., thrown into the air by a trap.—**trap′=shoot″er**, *n.*

trash¹ (trash), *v.* [Prob. from Scand.] **I.** *intr.* To tramp about; trudge; plod. [Now prov.] **II.** *tr.* To fatigue with tramping or exertion; weary; wear out. [Now prov.]

trash² (trash), *n.* [Cf. *trace*¹.] A leash for a dog. [Now prov. Eng.]—**trash**², *v. t.* To check by or as by a trash or leash; hence, to hold back, hinder, or encumber. [Now rare.]

trash³ (trash), *n.* [Cf. Icel. *tros*, rubbish, fallen leaves and twigs, Sw. *trasa*, rag, tatter.] That which is broken or lopped off from anything in preparing it for use; broken or torn bits, as twigs, splinters, rags, or the like; also, the refuse of sugar-cane after the juice has been expressed; also, anything worthless or useless, or rubbish (as, "Who steals my purse steals *trash*," Shakspere's "Othello," iii. 3. 157; "What poor, mean *trash* this whole business of human virtue is!" Mrs. Stowe's "Uncle Tom's Cabin," xix.); sometimes, foolish notions, talk, or writing, or nonsense (as, "I have quite enough to do without reading tedious *trash*": Gissing's "New Grub Street," vii.); also, a worthless or disreputable person; now, usually, such persons collectively (as, "His father hated his travelling with *trash* like them," Wister's "Virginian," xxvii.; the poor white *trash* of the southern U. S.).—**trash**³, *v. t.* To free from trash or refuse; esp., to remove the outer leaves from (growing sugar-cane); also, to treat or discard as worthless (colloq.).—**trash′er-y**, *n.* Trash collectively; rubbish. —**trash′y**, *a.*; compar. *trashier*, superl. *trashiest.* Of the nature of trash, rubbishy, or worthless (as, "*trashy* novels": W. Churchill's "Coniston," ii. 9); also, encumbered with trash, or the withered growth of the previous season, as a field.—**trash′i-ly**, *adv.*—**trash′i-ness**, *n.*

trass (tras), *n.* [D. *tras* or G. dial. *trass*, ult. < L. *terra*, earth: cf. *terrace*.] A rock common along the Rhine, composed chiefly of comminuted pumice or other volcanic material: used for making hydraulic cement.

trat-to-ri-a (trät-tō-rē′ä), *n.* [It.] An Italian eating-house.

trau-ma (trâ′mä), *n.*; pl. *-mata* (-mạ-tä). [NL., < Gr. τραῦμα, wound.] In *pathol.*, a wound; a bodily injury produced by violence; also, the condition produced by this;

traumatism.—trau-mat′ic (-mat′ik), *a.* [LL. *traumaticus*, < Gr. τραυματικός.] Of, pertaining to, or produced by a trauma or wound; also, adapted to the cure of wounds.— **trau′ma-tism** (-mạ-tizm), *n.* In *pathol.*, any morbid condition produced by a trauma; also, the trauma or wound itself.

trav-ail¹ (trav′āl), *v.* [OF. *travaillier* (F. *travailler*), orig. torment, harass, hence exert one's self, labor, be in travail, prob. < LL. *trepalium*, kind of instrument of torture, appar. < L. *tres*, three, + *palus*, stake: cf. *travel*.] **I.** *tr.* To torment; harass; trouble; weary. [Archaic.] **II.** *intr.* To toil, or exert one's self (archaic); also, to suffer the pangs of childbirth; be in labor.—**trav′ail**¹, *n.* [OF. F. *travail*.] Labor, toil, or exertion (archaic); trouble, hardship, or suffering (archaic); also, the labor and pain of childbirth.

tra-vail² (trạ-väi′), *n.*; pl. *-vails.* [Canadian F.] A means of transportation, used esp. by North American Indians, consisting of two long

Travail, as used by the Sioux Indians.

poles harnessed at one end to a horse or dog and trailing on the ground at the other, and bearing cross-bars, a platform, or a net for carrying a load.

trav-el (trav′ẹl), *v.*; *-eled* or *-elled*, *-eling* or *-elling.* [The same word as *travail*¹, but differentiated in sense.] **I.** *intr.* To go from one place to another, whether on foot, on horseback, or in any conveyance, as a carriage, automobile, train, ship, or aircraft; make a journey; often, to go to or visit distant or foreign places (as, to *travel* for one's health, or for pleasure); specif., to go from place to place as a representative or traveler of a commercial house; also, of an animal, to walk or run; move onward while browsing, as a deer; also, in general, to move or go from one place or point to another; proceed or advance in any way; pass, or be transmitted, as light, sound, etc.; move in a fixed course, as a piece of mechanism; also, sometimes, to move with speed (colloq.). **II.** *tr.* To travel, journey, or pass through or over, as a country, district, road, etc.; also, to cause to travel or journey, or move from one place to another.—**trav′el**, *n.* The act of traveling; journeying; often, journeying in distant or foreign places (as, "All the delight I have known in Italian *travel* burned again within my heart": Gissing's "Private Papers of Henry Ryecroft," iii. 19); *pl.*, journeys (as, to start on one's *travels*); journeys as the subject of a written account or literary work, or such an account or work, or such works collectively (as, "*Travels* into Several Remote Nations of the World . . . By Lemuel Gulliver," commonly known as "Gulliver's *Travels*," the title of a book by Jonathan Swift, published in 1726; "There are no books which I more delight in than in *travels*," Addison and Steele, in "Tatler," 254); sometimes, *sing.*, the coming and going of persons or conveyances along a way of passage, or traffic (as, "Each walk as green as is the mantled pool, For want of human *travel*": Hood's "Haunted House," i.); also, movement or passage in general (as, "Th' illustrious stranger [comet] . . . then revisits earth, From the long *travel* of a thousand years": Young's "Night Thoughts," iv. 713); in *mech.*, the complete movement of a moving part (esp. a reciprocating part) in one direction, or the distance traversed; stroke, or length of stroke.—**travel of a projectile**, in ordnance, in a loaded cannon, the distance from the base of the projectile to the muzzle.—**trav′el-a-ble, trav′el-la-ble**, *a.* That may be traveled over, as a road.—**trav′eled, trav′elled**, *p. a.* Having traveled, esp. to distant places; experienced in travel (as, "He [Edward Everett] was a *travelled* man and a scholar": Charnwood's "Abraham Lincoln," v.); also, frequented by travelers, as a road; in *geol.*, moved to a distance from the original site, as a boulder.—**trav′el-er, trav′el-ler**, *n.* One who or that which travels; one who is on a journey; one who travels or has traveled in distant places or foreign lands; one who travels from place to place as the representative of a commercial house, showing samples and soliciting orders ('commercial traveler'); a piece of mechanism constructed to move in a fixed course; *naut.*,

an iron ring or thimble fitted to move freely on a rope, spar, or rod, or the rope, spar, or rod itself; esp., a ring attached to the sheet of a fore-and-aft sail and sliding from side to side on a metal rod fastened to the deck; the rod itself.—
trav'el-er's=joy', *n.* A woody-stemmed European species of clematis, *Clematis vitalba*, often growing over wayside hedges, etc.—
trav'e-logue (-ẹ-log), *n.* [With *-logue* as in *monologue*, *dialogue*.] A lecture describing travel, usually illustrated, as with stereopticon views or moving pictures.

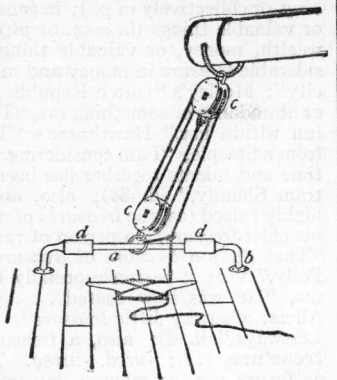

Traveler.— *a*, traveler; *b*, rod on which it travels; *c, c*, blocks; *d, d*, buffers.

trav-ers-a-ble (trav'ẻr-sạ-bl), *a.* Capable of being traversed, or passed across or through; in *law*, capable of being traversed or denied.

trav-erse (trav'ẻrs), *a.* [OF. *travers*, < L. *traversus*, for *transversus*, pp., turned or directed across: see *transverse*.] Lying, extending, or passing across; cross; transverse.—
trav'erse, *n.* [OF. F. *travers*, < L. *traversum*, neut. of *traversus* (see *traverse*, *a*.); also OF. F. *traverse*, partly < L. *traversa*, fem. of *traversus*, partly < OF. F. *traverser*, E. *traverse*, *v*.] Transverse extent or direction; also, something placed or extending across; a crosspiece or cross-bar; a cross-line or transversal; also, the act or an act of traversing, or passing across, over, or through; also, a place where one may traverse or cross; a crossing; also, something that crosses, obstructs, or thwarts (as, "in days of fierce duress, of endless *traverses* and toils": Morley's "Oliver Cromwell," i. 3); an obstacle; a trouble; a mishap; also, a denial; esp., in pleading at law, a formal denial of some matter of fact alleged by the other side; also, a dispute† or controversy†; in *fort.*, a defensive barrier, parapet, or the like placed transversely, esp. one thrown across the terreplein or the covered way of a fortification to protect it from an enfilade; in *surv.*, a single line of survey carried across a region; a tract so surveyed; in *arch.*, a transverse gallery or loft of communication in a church or other large building; in *mountaineering*, a passing transversely across the face of a mountain, or a place where this is done (as, "The descent was very nasty; there was a particularly bad *traverse*": Galsworthy's "Dark Flower," i. 8); *naut.*, the zigzag track of a vessel compelled by contrary winds or currents to sail on different courses; each of the runs in a single direction made in such sailing; in *gun.*, the turning of a gun so as to make it point in any required direction.—
trav-erse† (trav'ẻrs or trạ-vẻrs'), *adv.* Across; crosswise; transversely.—**trav'erse**, *v.*; -ersed, -ersing. [OF. F. *traverser*, < OF. *travers*, n. or *a.*] **I.** *tr.* To lay or place across or crosswise; also, to cross with something else; also, to pass across, over, or through (as, "They had to *traverse* the most dreary and desolate mountains," Irving's "Captain Bonneville," i.; "The ground which they *traversed* was . . . very broken and uneven," Scott's "Castle Dangerous," xvii.); lie or extend across or through (as, "the one good road which *traverses* the hills from south to north": Buchan's "Hist. of the Great War," lxxxvii.); go to and fro over or along, as a place; fig., to go through; pass in review, or survey carefully (as, "It was in the years which we are *traversing* that England became firmly Protestant": Green's "Short Hist. of the Eng. People," vii. 6); also, to cause to move laterally; turn and point (a gun) in any direction; also, to go counter to; obstruct or thwart (as, "She hoped to *traverse* his designs": Jane Porter's "Scottish Chiefs," xxxv.); also, to contradict or deny; deny formally, in pleading at law; *naut.*, to brace (a yard) fore and aft. **II.** *intr.* To pass or go across; cross; cross over; also, to move from side to side or to and fro (archaic); also, to turn freely

from side to side, as a gun; turn about on a pivot; run freely in a channel, socket, ring, etc.; in the *manège*, to move or walk crosswise, as a horse that throws his croup to one side and his head to the other; in *mountaineering*, to pass transversely across the face of a mountain.—**trav'ers-er**, *n.*

trav-er-tin, trav-er-tine (trav'ẻr-tin), *n.* [It. *travertino*, earlier *tivertino*, < L. *Tiburtinus*, of Tibur (an ancient town of Latium, now Tivoli).] A form of limestone deposited by springs, etc.: used in Italy for building purposes.

trav-es-ty (trav'es-ti), *n.*; pl. *-ties* (-tiz). [F. *travesti*, pp. of *travestir*, < It. *travestire*, disguise, < L. *trans*, across, over, + *vestire*, clothe.] A literary composition characterized by burlesque or ludicrous treatment of a serious work or subject; literary composition of this kind; hence, any grotesque or debased likeness or imitation (as, "It's an iniquitous law, a *travesty* of justice": Mrs. Wharton's "Son at the Front," x.).—**trav'es-ty**, *v. t.*; *-tied*, *-tying.* To make a travesty on; turn (a serious work or subject) to ridicule by burlesque imitation or treatment; hence, in general, to imitate grotesquely or absurdly.—**trav'es-ti-er**, *n.*

tra-vois (trạ-voi'), *n.* Same as *travail*[2].

trawl (trâl), *v.* [Origin uncertain.] **I.** *intr.* To fish with a net whose edge is dragged along the sea-bottom to catch the fish living there; also, to drag a seine so as to surround and inclose a school of herring, etc.; also, to fish with a trawl-line. **II.** *tr.* To drag (a trawl-net); also, to catch with a trawl-net or a trawl-line.—**trawl**, *n.* A strong fishing-net ('trawl-net') dragged along the sea-bottom in trawling; also, a buoyed line ('trawl-line') used in sea-fishing, having numerous short lines with baited hooks attached at intervals.—**trawl'er**, *n.* One who trawls; also, a vessel used in trawling; any of various types of vessels used in fishing with a trawl-net.

tray[1] (trā), *n.* See *trey*.

tray[2] (trā), *n.* [AS. *trīg*.] Any of various flat, shallow vessels or receptacles of wood, metal, papier-mâché, etc., having slightly raised edges or a low rim, and used for carrying dishes, glassware, cards, etc., for holding and exhibiting small articles such as jewelry or specimens, and for various other purposes; often, a removable receptacle of this shape in a cabinet, box, trunk, or the like, sometimes forming a drawer.—**tray'ful** (-fúl), *n.*; pl. *-fuls*. As much as a tray holds.

treach-er-ous (trech'ẻr-us), *a.* [OF. *trecherus*, *tricherus*, < *trecheor*, *tricheor*, deceiver, cheater, < *trechier*, *trichier* (F. *tricher*), deceive, cheat, trick: cf. L. *tricari*, trifle, shuffle, play tricks, *tricæ*, trifles, wiles, tricks, also L. *trick*[1].] Deceiving, perfidious, or faithless (as, "a fierce, barbarous, *treacherous* people": Defoe's "Captain Singleton," v.); violating faith or betraying trust; disloyal; traitorous; marked by or showing treachery (as, "She gave the *treacherous* impulse time to subside," H. James's "Portrait of a Lady," xl.; "a foul and *treacherous* murder," H. Kingsley's "Geoffry Hamlyn," vi.); fig., deceptive, untrustworthy, or unreliable (as, "There were some *treacherous* indications of fair weather": Parkman's "Oregon Trail," v.); unstable or insecure (as, "The *treacherous* ice gave an imperfect footing": Prescott's "Conquest of Mexico," iii. 8).—**treach'er-ous-ly**, *adv.*—**treach'er-ous-ness**, *n.*—**treach'er-y** (-i), *n.*; pl. *-ies* (-iz). [OF. *trecherie*, *tricherie* (F. *tricherie*).] Deceit or perfidy; violation of faith; betrayal of trust; treason; also, an act of perfidy or faithlessness (as, "And dead, at end of foiled *treacheries*, There lay his foe": W. Morris's "Jason," xvi. 264).

trea-cle (trē'kl), *n.* [OF. *triacle*, < L. *theriaca*, antidote for poisonous bites or poison: see *theriac*.] Any of various medicinal compounds formerly in repute as antidotes for poisonous bites or for poisons; hence, in general, a sovereign remedy†; also, molasses, esp. that produced during the refining of sugar (Eng.).—**Treacle Bible.** See under *Bible*.—**Venice treacle.** See *theriac*.—**trea'cly**, *a.* Of or like treacle; syrupy; viscous; excessively sweet.

tread (tred), *v.*; pret. *trod* (archaic *trode*), pp. *trodden* or *trod*, ppr. *treading*. [AS. *tredan* = D. *treden* = G. *treten*, akin to Icel. *trodha*, Goth. *trudan*, tread: cf. *trade*.] **I.** *tr.* To step or walk on, about in, or along (as, "Some swift-footed being was *treading* the ground near me," W. H. Hudson's "Green Mansions," iii.; to *tread* the fields, or the desert;

"He speculated, as he *trod* the street," G. Meredith's "Lord Ormont and His Aminta," xxvi.); also, to trample or crush underfoot (as, to *tread* a thing in the mire; to *tread* grapes in pressing out the juice); put into some position or condition by trampling (as, "He caused us to fill this bag with dry sand and *tread* it down," Defoe's "Captain Singleton," viii.; "We *trod* the fire out," Stevenson's "Kidnapped," v.); fig., to trample on; domineer harshly over; crush; also, to press downward with the foot or feet (as, to *tread* water, to move the feet in swimming as if walking upstairs, keeping the body in an erect position and the head above water); also, of male birds, to copulate with (the female); also, to execute by walking or dancing (as, to *tread* a measure); make or form by the action of the feet (as, to *tread* a path). **II.** *intr.* To set down the foot or feet in walking; step; walk; also, to step, walk, or trample (*on* or *upon*); also, of male birds, to copulate.—**tread,** *n.* A footprint (rare); a track† or trail†; a path† or way†; also, a course or manner of action, esp. a habitual course or practice (chiefly Sc.); regular occupation or business (Sc.); also, a treading, stepping, or walking, or the sound of this (as, "They heard the *tread* of a horse behind": Scott's "Guy Mannering," liii.); a single step as in walking; manner of treading or walking; also, any of various things or parts on which a person or thing treads, stands, or moves; the sole of the foot or of a shoe; the horizontal upper surface of a step in a stair, on which the foot is placed, or the width of this from front to back; each of the rungs of a ladder; the top of a banquette of a fortification, on which the soldiers stand to fire over the parapet; the part of a wheel, tire, or runner which bears on the road, rail, etc.; the part of a rail on which the wheels bear; also, the width between the pedals of a bicycle, etc.; in *vet. science,* a wound or bruise on the coronet of a horse's foot, produced by the shoe of either the hind or the fore foot of the opposite side; in *zoöl.,* the cicatricula or the chalaza of a bird's egg.—**tread′er,** *n.*

tread-le (tred′l), *n.* [AS. *tredel,* a step (to mount on), < *tredan,* E. *tread.*] A lever or the like worked by the foot to impart motion to a machine.—**tread′le,** *v.*; *-led, -ling.* **I.** *intr.* To work a treadle. **II.** *tr.* To operate (a machine) by working a treadle.—**tread′ler,** *n.*

tread-mill (tred′mil), *n.* An apparatus for producing rotary motion by the weight of one or more men, or horses or other animals, treading on a succession of moving steps or the like that form a kind of continuous or endless path, as around or connected with the periphery of a horizontal cylinder or similar device; hence, fig., a monotonous or wearisome round, as of work or life.

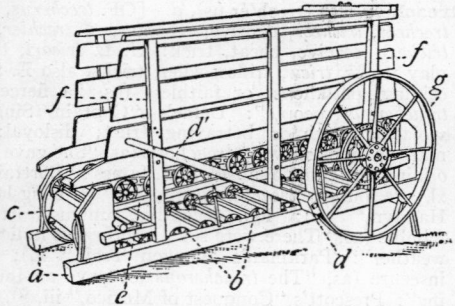

One form of Treadmill.—*a,* bottom timbers of frame; *b,* rollers attached to the treads, one of which is fully shown at *c*; *d, d′,* brake-shoe and brake-lever respectively, used in stopping the machine; *e,* one of the two inclined planes on which the rollers *b* run; *f,* inclosure for horse or mule which operates the machine; *g,* driving-wheel, which in use is belted to the machine to be driven.

trea-son (trē′zn), *n.* [OF. *traisun* (F. *trahison*), < L. *traditio(n-),* a giving over: see *tradition.*] The betrayal of a trust or confidence; breach of faith; treachery; specif., violation by a subject of his allegiance to his sovereign or to the state ('high treason'), in the case of the United States consisting "only in levying war against them, or in adhering to their enemies, giving them aid and comfort" (Constitution of the U. S., iii. 3. 1).—**trea′son-a-ble,** *a.* Of the nature of treason; involving treason; traitorous.—**trea′son-a-ble-ness,** *n.*—**trea′son-a-bly,** *adv.*—**trea′son-ous,** *a.* Treasonable.

treas-ure (trezh′ŭr), *n.* [OF. *tresor* (F. *trésor*), < L. *thesaurus:* see *thesaurus.*] Wealth or riches stored or accu-

mulated, esp. in the form of precious metals or money (in *sing.* or collectively in *pl.*); in general, wealth, rich materials, or valuable things (in *sing.* or *pl.*); also, a store or stock of wealth, money, or valuable things (as, "There was a considerable *treasure* in money and merchandise shut up in that city": Motley's "Dutch Republic," iv. 1); also, a rich store or abundance of something (as, "There is a *treasure* of gentle fun within her," Hawthorne's "Twice-Told Tales," Sights from a Steeple; "I am considering what a *treasure* of precious time and talents together has been wasted," Sterne's "Tristram Shandy," iii. 34); also, anything greatly valued or highly prized (as, the *treasures* of a household; this book was his chief *treasure*); a person of rare worth or excellence (as, "That girl's a *treasure* of *treasures*": H. G. Wells's "Mr. Polly," vi.); a person especially beloved, dear, or precious (as, "He was now seated . . . with the youngest child, Alicia, a gawky little *treasure*": Arnold Bennett's "Hilda Lessways," ii. 4); also, a treasure-house† or treasury†.—**treas′ure,** *v. t.*; *-urcd, -uring.* To put away for security or future use, as money; lay up in store; fig., to retain carefully or keep in store, as in the mind (as, "He would be sure to *treasure* the offence in his remembrance": Scott's "Legend of Montrose," viii.); also, to regard as precious; prize; cherish; also, to furnish with treasures†.—**treas′ure-house,** *n.* A house, chamber, or the like in which treasure is kept; a treasury.—**treas′ur-er,** *n.* One who is in charge of treasure or a treasury; an officer of a state, city, etc., intrusted with the receipt, care, and disbursement of public money; one who has charge of the funds of a corporation, private society, or the like; fig., one intrusted with the keeping of anything valuable or precious (as, "the secrets of which thou seemest to be a too faithful *treasurer*": Scott's "Castle Dangerous," viii.).—**treas′ur-er-ship,** *n.*—**treas′ure=trove′** (-trōv′), *n.* [AF. *tresor trové,* 'treasure found': *trové,* pp. of AF. and OF. *trover,* find: see *trover.*] Anything of the nature of treasure which one finds; in *Eng. law,* any money, bullion, or the like, of unknown ownership, found hidden in the earth or any other place.—**treas′ur-y** (-i), *n.*; *pl. -ies* (-iz). [OF. *tresorie.*] A building, room, chest, or other place for the preservation of treasure or valuable objects; esp., a place where public revenues, or the funds of a corporation, etc., are deposited, kept, and disbursed; also, the funds or revenue of a state or a public or private corporation, etc.; also, the department of government which has control over the collection, management, and disbursement of the public revenue; also, a repository or a collection of treasures of any kind (as, Palgrave's "The Golden *Treasury,* Selected from the Best Songs and Lyrical Poems in the English Language"); a thesaurus; also, treasure†.—**treasury note,** a note or bill issued by the Treasury Department of the U. S., and receivable as legal tender for all debts, public and private, except as otherwise expressly provided.

treat (trēt), *v.* [OF. *tretier, traitier* (F. *traiter*), < L. *tractare,* drag, handle, manage, treat, freq. of *trahere,* draw.] **I.** *tr.* To handle or discuss (an affair, etc.) with a view to settlement†; negotiate†; also, to deal with in speech or writing; discuss; also, to deal with, develop, or represent artistically, esp. in some specified manner or style (as, to *treat* a theme realistically); also, to deal with (a disease, patient, etc.) in order to relieve or cure; also, to subject to some agent or action in order to bring about a particular result (as, to *treat* a substance with an acid); also, to act or behave toward in some specified way (as, "You should be *treated* with respect": H. James's "Portrait of a Lady," lii.); use (well, badly, etc.); also, to look upon, consider, or regard in a specified aspect and deal with accordingly (as, to *treat* a matter as unimportant); also, to entertain with food, drink, amusement, etc. (as, "My uncle . . . talks of *treating* us with a jaunt to London": Smollett's "Humphry Clinker," May 6); regale at one's own expense, as in compliment or in expression of friendly regard. **II.** *intr.* To carry on negotiations with a view to a settlement, discuss terms of settlement, or negotiate (as, "Commissioners . . . came to *treat* for the recognition of the Confederacy": Charnwood's "Abraham Lincoln," vi.); also, to deal with a subject in speech or writing, or discourse (as, "These learned men *treated* of this point of confirmation": Strype's "Memorials of Cranmer," i. 20); also, to give, or bear the expense of, a

---

fat, fāte, fär, fåll, ȧsk, fāre; net, mē, hėr; pin, pīne; not, nōte, mŏve, nôr; up, lūte, půll; oi, oil; ou, out; (lightened) aviȧry, ĕlect, agŏny, intŏ, ūnite; (obscured) errȧnt, operä, ardẹnt, actọr, natụre; ch, chip; g, go; th, thin; ŦH, then; y, you;

treat (as, "The ladies *treat* with tea in their turns": Smollett's "Humphry Clinker," June 23).—**treat,** *n.* Negotiation† or parley†; also, treatment†; also, an entertainment of food, drink, amusement, etc., given by way of compliment or as an expression of friendly regard; a pleasure-party, as for children; an act of treating, or one's turn to treat, as to drink; also, anything that affords particular pleasure or enjoyment (colloq.: as, "I should have deemed it a *treat* to spend the evenings quietly with her," C. Brontë's "Jane Eyre," iv.; this book is a *treat*).—**treat'a·ble,** *a.* Tractable (archaic); also, capable of or suitable for being treated.—**treat'er,** *n.*

trea·tise (trē'tis), *n.* [AF. *tretiz*, < OF. *tretier, traitier*, E. *treat*.] A book or writing treating of some particular subject, esp. one containing a formal or methodical exposition of the principles of the subject: as, "The metaphysical philosophy of Hobbes was promulgated in his *treatise* on Human Nature" (Hallam's "Literature of Europe," iii. 3. § 113).

treat·ment (trēt'ment), *n.* The act or manner of treating; management; literary or artistic handling, esp. with reference to style; management in the application of medicines, surgery, etc.; subjection to some agent or action; action or behavior toward a person, etc.

trea·ty (trē'ti), *n.*; pl. *-ties* (-tiz). [OF. *traitie, traitiet* (F. *traité*), < L. *tractatus*, a handling, treatment, discussion, < *tractare*: see *treat*, and cf. *tractate*.] Negotiation with a view to settlement (now rare: as, "a mere farmer in *treaty* for the Chase Farm," George Eliot's "Adam Bede," xxxii.); also, an agreement or compact; specif., a contract between two or more states or sovereigns in reference to peace, alliance, commerce, or other international relation (as, the *Treaty* of Paris, 1783, the *Treaty* of Ghent, 1814, the *Treaty* of Guadalupe Hidalgo, 1848, and the *Treaty* of Paris, 1898, after the Revolutionary War, the War of 1812, the Mexican War, and the Spanish-American War respectively; the *Treaty* of Versailles, 1919, the general treaty between the Allies and Germany made after the World War, separate treaties between the U. S. and Austria and the U. S. and Germany being made and ratified in 1921); the formally signed and ratified document embodying such a contract; also, treatment in speech or writing†; also, a treatise†; also, entreaty†.

treb·le (treb'l). [OF. *treble*, < L. *triplus*, threefold: see *triple*.] **I.** *a.* Threefold; triple; also, in *music*, of or pertaining to the highest part in harmonized music; soprano; of the highest pitch or range, as a voice-part, voice, singer, or instrument; hence, in general, high in pitch; shrill. **II.** *n.* Something treble or threefold; an amount or number three times as great as another; also, in *music*, the treble or soprano part; a treble voice, singer, or instrument; in *change-ringing*, the highest-pitched bell of a peal; in general, a high or shrill voice or sound.—**treb'le,** *v. t.* or *i.*; *-led, -ling.* To make or become three times as much or as many; triple.—**treb'·ling,** *n. Naut.*, planking fixed on a vessel's bow to strengthen it against the pressure of ice.—**treb'ly,** *adv.*

treb·u·chet (treb'ū-shet, F. trä-bü-shā), *n.* [OF. *trebuchet, trebuket*, engine of war, trap (F. *trébuchet*, trap, balance), < OF. *trebuchier*, overturn (F. *trébucher*, stumble, trip), < L. *trans*, over, + OF. *buc*, trunk of the body (from Teut.), and akin to G. *bauch*, belly).] A medieval military engine for hurling stones and other missiles; also, a kind of balance or scales used in weighing coins, etc.; also, a cucking-stool.

tre·cen·to (trā-chen'tō), *n.* [It., three hundred, short for *mille trecento*, one thousand three hundred.] The 14th century, with reference to Italy, and esp. to the Italian art or literature of that period.—**tre·cen'tist,** *n.*

tree (trē), *n.* [AS. *trēo, trēow*, = OS. *treo* = Icel. *trē* = Goth. *triu*, tree, wood; akin to Gr. δρῦς, tree, oak, δόρυ, tree, shaft,

Trebling.

spear, Skt. *dru*, wood, *dāru*, wood, log.] A perennial plant having a permanent, woody, self-supporting main stem or trunk, ordinarily growing to a considerable height, and usually developing branches at some distance from the ground; any of various shrubs, bushes, and herbaceous plants, as the banana, resembling a tree in form or size; also, wood or timber (obs. or archaic); also, a piece of wood, or a pole, post, beam, bar, or the like, as one forming part of some structure (chiefly in composition, as in *swingletree, roof-tree, axletree*, etc.); a staff or cudgel (now only Sc.); the wooden handle of an implement, etc. (now prov.); the cross on which Christ was crucified (archaic or poetic); a gallows or gibbet; a saddletree; a boot-tree; a wooden vessel, barrel, or cask (Sc.); also, a diagram in the outline form of a tree, indicating the source, main stem, and branches of a family ('family tree' or 'genealogical tree'); hence, a family, race, or stock; also, anything resembling a tree with its branches; a tree-like group of crystals, as one forming in an electrolytic cell.—**tree of heaven,** an Asiatic simarubaceous tree, *Ailantus glandulosa*, bearing ill-scented flowers, and frequently planted as a shade-tree.—**tree of knowledge of good and evil,** in the Bible, a tree in the midst of the garden of Eden, bearing the forbidden fruit the eating of which destroyed the primal innocence of Adam and Eve (Gen. ii. 9, etc.).—**tree of liberty,** a tree planted or transplanted to commemorate the gaining of political liberty, as in France at the time of the Revolution.—**tree of life,** in the Bible, a tree in the midst of the garden of Eden which afforded food giving everlasting life (Gen. ii. 9; iii. 22); also, a tree in the heavenly Jerusalem with leaves for the healing of the nations (Rev. xxii. 2); also, same as *arborvitæ*.—**up a tree,** cut off from escape; entrapped; in a difficult or awkward position. [Colloq.]—**tree,** *v.*; *treed, treeing.* **I.** *tr.* To drive into or up a tree, as a hunted animal, or a man pursued by an animal (as, "They [bloodhounds] ran across a cougar, and after a sharp chase *treed* him": Roosevelt's "Hunting Trips of a Ranchman," i.); hence, to put into a difficult position (colloq.); also, to furnish with a tree (beam, bar, wooden handle, etc.); stretch or shape on a tree, as a boot. **II.** *intr.* To take refuge in a tree; also, to assume a tree-like or branching form.

tree=asp (trē'asp), *n.* Any of the venomous serpents of the African family *Dendraspididæ*, as the mamba.

tree=fern (trē'fėrn), *n.* Any of various ferns, mostly tropical and chiefly of the family *Cyatheaceæ* (also *Polypodiaceæ*, etc.), which attain the size of trees, sending up a straight trunk-like stem with foliage at the summit.

tree=frog (trē'frog), *n.* Any of various arboreal frogs of the family *Ranidæ*, characterized usually by toes which end in adhesive disks; also, a tree-toad.

tree=heath (trē'hēth), *n.* A shrubby heath, *Erica arborea*, of southern Europe, etc.; brier. Cf. *brier*[2].

tree=hop·per (trē'hop"ėr), *n.* Any of various homopterous insects which frequent trees, esp. those of the family *Membracidæ*, which includes numerous small oddly-shaped leaping species.

Tree-fern (*Cibotium regale*).

tree=less (trē'les), *a.* Without trees.—**tree'less·ness,** *n.*

tree=nail (trē'nāl, commonly tren'l), *n.* A cylindrical pin of hard wood for fastening together timbers in ships, etc.

tree=scape (trē'skāp), *n.* A landscape abounding in trees.

tree=toad (trē'tōd), *n.* Any of various arboreal toads, mostly of the family *Hylidæ*, and usually having adhesive suckers on the ends of the toes. See cut on following page.

tree=top (trē′top), *n.* The top or uppermost part of a tree: as, "The *tree-tops* faintly rustle beneath the breeze's flight" (Bryant's "Waiting by the Gate").

tre-foil (trē′foil), *n.* [AF. *trifoil* = OF. *trefeuil* (F. *trèfle*), < L. *trifolium*, < *tri-*, three, + *folium*, leaf.] Any of the herbs constituting the fabaceous genus *Trifolium*, usually having digitate leaves of three

American Tree-toad (*Hyla versicolor*).

leaflets, and reddish, purple, yellow, or white flower-heads, and including the common clovers; any of various similar plants, as the black medic; also, an ornamental figure or structure resembling a trifoliolate leaf, as an opening divided into three lobes by cusps. — **tre′foiled,** *a.* Furnished with or consisting of a trefoil or trefoils (three-lobed figure).

Trefoils.

treil-lage (trel′āj, F. tre-yäzh′), *n.* [F., < *treille*, arbor, trellis, < L. *trichila*, arbor.] Latticework; a lattice or trellis.

trek (trek), *v.*; *trekked, trekking.* [D. *trekken*, draw, pull, go, travel: cf. *track*[1], *track*[2].] **I.** *tr.* Of a draft-animal, to draw (a vehicle or load). [South Africa.] **II.** *intr.* To travel by ox-wagon; in general, to travel; migrate. [South Africa.]—**trek,** *n.* [D.] The act of trekking; a journey by ox-wagon or otherwise; a migration or expedition, as by ox-wagon; a stage of a journey by ox-wagon or otherwise, between one stopping-place and the next. [South Africa.] —**trek′ker,** *n.*

trel-lis (trel′is), *n.* [OF. F. *treillis*, trellis, lattice (with form and sense prob. affected by *treille*: see *treillage*), orig. adj., OF. *treliz*, < L. *trilix* (*trilic-*), woven with three threads, < *tri-*, three, + *licium*, thread.] A frame or structure of latticework, or of light strips of wood or metal crossing one another at intervals, with open spaces between; a lattice; often, a framework of this kind used for the support of growing vines, etc.—**trel′lis,** *v. t.* To furnish with a trellis; inclose in a

Trellises.— 1, wooden; 2, wire.

trellis; also, to train or support on a trellis (as, "*trellised* vines": H. Kingsley's "Geoffry Hamlyn," i.); also, to form into or like trelliswork.—**trel′lis-work,** *n.* Work of crossed strips with openings between.

trem-a-tode (trem′a-tōd). [NL. *Trematoda*, pl., < Gr. τρηματώδης, having holes, < τρῆμα (τρηματ-), hole, + εἶδος, form.] **I.** *a.* Belonging to the *Trematoda*, a class or group of platyhelminths or flatworms, having two or more suckers, and living as ectoparasites or endoparasites on or in various animals. **II.** *n.* A trematode platyhelminth. Also **trem′a-toid** (-toid), *a.* and *n.*

trem-ble (trem′bl), *v.*; *-bled, -bling.* [OF. F. *trembler*, < ML. *tremulare*, < L. *tremulus*, shaking, E. *tremulous*.] **I.** *intr.* Of persons, the body, etc., to shake involuntarily with quick, short movements, as from fear, excitement, weakness, cold, etc.; quake; quiver; shiver; hence, to be agitated with fear, apprehension, or the like (as, I *tremble* to think what may happen; "Jerome . . . *trembled* for his son's life," Walpole's "Castle of Otranto," iii.); also, of things, to be affected with vibratory motion (as, "The vessels . . . *tremble* with the shock": Dryden's tr. Virgil's "Æneid," x. 419); be tremulous, as light, sound, etc. (as, "As Isaacs answered, his voice *trembled*": F. M. Crawford's "Mr.

Isaacs," vii.); also, to pass tremulously (as, "A teardrop *trembled* from its source": Tennyson's "Talking Oak," 161). **II.** *tr.* To cause to tremble.—**trem′ble,** *n.* The act of trembling; a state or fit of trembling; a tremor or vibration; *pl.,* any condition or disease characterized by continued trembling or shaking, as ague; the tremor of delirium tremens, etc.; also, milk-sickness.—**trem′ble-ment,** *n.* Trembling; also, a tremor.—**trem′bler,** *n.* One who trembles; something that trembles or vibrates; specif., an automatic vibrating device which alternately makes and breaks an electric circuit, as on an induction-coil.—**trem′bling-ly,** *adv.*—**trem′bly,** *a.* Trembling; tremulous.

trem-el-lose (trem′e-lōs), *a.* [L. *tremere*, shake, tremble.] In *bot.,* shaking like jelly; of a gelatinous consistence, as certain fungi.

tre-men-dous (trē-men′dus), *a.* [L. *tremendus*, that is to be trembled at, gerundive of *tremere*, shake, tremble.] That is to be trembled at, or regarded with fear or awe (obs. or archaic: as, "I . . . adjure you by every thing that is sacred, and that is *tremendous*," Godwin's "Caleb Williams," xviii.); hence, dreadful or awful, as in character or effect (as, "The . . . continuity of the land was obliterated by this *tremendous* deluge," Motley's "Dutch Republic," Introd., vi.; "a *tremendous* defeat," Hallam's "Europe during the Middle Ages," iv.); of extraordinary impressiveness, power, or importance (as, a *tremendous* scene; "Her mind was agitated as if his coming . . . had been a *tremendous* occurrence," J. Conrad's "Rescue," iii. 7); extraordinarily great in size, amount, degree, intensity, etc. (as, "These *tremendous* warders [statues] sit sixty-six feet high," Amelia B. Edwards's "Thousand Miles up the Nile," xvi.; "the *tremendous* rains," J. H. Newman's "Callista," xxiii.; "*tremendous* enthusiasm," W. H. Hudson's "Far Away and Long Ago," xviii.; "a sigh of *tremendous* relief," Arnold Bennett's "Buried Alive," ii.); extraordinarily good or fine (colloq.: as, "a *tremendous* fellow at the classics," George Eliot's "Felix Holt," ii.; to have a perfectly *tremendous* time).—**tre-men′dous-ly,** *adv.*—**tre-men′dous-ness,** *n.*

trem-o-lan-do (trem-ō-län′dō), *a.* [It., gerund of *tremolare*, < ML. *tremulare*, E. *tremble*.] In *music,* tremulous; with a tremolo.

trem-o-lite (trem′ō-līt), *n.* [From Val *Tremola*, valley in Switzerland.] A white or grayish variety of amphibole, consisting essentially of a silicate of calcium and magnesium.

trem-o-lo (trem′ō-lō), *n.*; pl. *-los* (-lōz). [It., < L. *tremulus*, E. *tremulous*.] In *music,* a tremulous or vibrating effect produced on certain instruments and in the human voice, as to express emotion; also, a mechanical device in an organ by which such an effect is produced.

trem-or (trem′or or trē′mor), *n.* [L. *tremor*, < *tremere*, shake, tremble, = Gr. τρέμειν, tremble.] Involuntary shaking of the body or limbs, as from fear, weakness, etc.; a fit of trembling; hence, a state of tremulous agitation; a thrill of emotion or excitement (as, "Her fair face reddened, and there went and came Delicious *tremors* through her": W. Morris's "Jason," vii. 93); also, any tremulous or vibratory movement, as of the earth; a vibration; a trembling or quivering effect, as of light, etc.; a tremulous sound or note (as, "with no small *tremor* in his voice": H. Mackenzie's "Man of Feeling," xl.).—**trem′or-less,** *a.* Without a tremor.

trem-u-lant (trem′ū-lant), *a.* Trembling; tremulous.

trem-u-lous (trem′ū-lus), *a.* [L. *tremulus*, < *tremere*, shake, tremble.] Of persons, the body, etc., characterized by trembling, as from fear, nervousness, weakness, etc. (as, "His frame was *tremulous* at intervals with a nervous agitation": Hawthorne's "Twice-Told Tales," The Gentle Boy); hence, fearful; timorous; of writing, etc., done with a trembling hand, or minutely wavy (as, "The signature of approval of the court's finding is *tremulous* and unlike his usual writing": Weir Mitchell's "Hugh Wynne," xxv.); also, of things, characterized by vibration; vibratory or quivering (as, a *tremulous* motion; "the birch-tree's *tremulous* shade," Whittier's "Bridal of Pennacook," v.; "the *tremulous* glitter of diamonds," Hawthorne's "Twice-Told Tales," Dr. Heidegger's Experiment; "the *tremulous* thrill of her song," Blackmore's "Lorna Doone," xvi.); easily caused to vibrate.—**trem′u-lous-ly**, *adv.*—**trem′u-lous-ness**, *n.*

tre′nail, *n.* See *treenail*.

trench (trench), *v.* [OF. *trenchier* (F. *trancher*), cut, through LL. < L. *truncare*, reduce by cutting, cut off, cut apart: see *truncate*. Some E. senses are from *trench*, *n*.] **I.** *tr.* To cut; divide by cutting; sever by cutting; cut into; cut or make a linear depression in; cut a trench or trenches in; also, to form (a furrow, ditch, etc.) by cutting into or through something; also, to set or place in a trench; also, to surround or fortify with a trench or trenches; intrench. **II.** *intr.* To cut; cut into something; also, to dig a trench or trenches; also, to extend, as to a point or person†; enter or penetrate so as to affect intimately (with *into* or *unto*)†; encroach or infringe (*on* or *upon*: as, "His half-breed hunters . . . considered him as *trenching* upon their province," Irving's "Captain Bonneville," xli.; to *trench* upon another's rights); sometimes, to come close or verge (*on* or *upon*: as, a speech which *trenches* on treason).—**trench**, *n.* [OF. *trenche*, *tranche*, a cutting, cut, trench (F. *tranche*, slice).] A narrow excavation of considerable length cut into the ground; a deep furrow; a ditch; also, a cut, scar, or deep wrinkle; *milit.*, a long, narrow excavation in the ground, the earth from which is thrown up in front to serve as a shelter from the enemy's fire, as an obstruction to an advancing force, etc.; *pl.*, a system of such excavations, with their embankments, etc. (as, "We mounted guard in the *trenches* before the gate of St. Nicolas," Sterne's "Tristram Shandy," vi. 6; "Their infantry had penetrated our first-line *trenches*," Buchan's "Hist. of the Great War," liii.).

trench-ant (tren′chạnt), *a.* [OF., ppr. of *trenchier*, cut: see *trench*.] Cutting, sharp, or keen-edged, as a weapon (chiefly archaic or fig.: as, "a *trenchant* blade," W. Morris's "Jason," xv. 984); hence, fig., incisive or keen, as language, or a person speaking or writing (as, "*trenchant* wit," Whittier's "Randolph of Roanoke"; "He is . . . *trenchant* in speech," G. B. Shaw's "You Never Can Tell," i.); thorough-going, vigorous, or effective (as, a *trenchant* policy); also, clearly or sharply defined, as an outline (as, "The peaks . . . stood out in *trenchant* gloom against a cold glitter in the east": Stevenson's "Travels with a Donkey," i. 2); in *zoöl.*, of a tooth, etc., having a cutting edge.—**trench′an-cy**, **trench′ant-ness**, *n.*—**trench′ant-ly**, *adv.*

trench-er[1] (tren′chẻr), *n.* One who trenches; one who makes trenches.

trench-er[2] (tren′chẻr), *n.* [OF. *trencheor*, < *trenchier*, cut: see *trench*.] A square or circular flat piece of wood on which meat was formerly served and carved; such a piece of wood with that which it bears (archaic); hence, a supply of food (archaic); also, any flat board of circular or other shape; also, a trencher-cap.—**trench′er=cap**, *n.* A mortar-board (academic cap).—**trench′er-man** (-mạn), *n.*; *pl.* *-men*. An eater or feeder; esp., one who has a hearty appetite; also, a parasite or hanger-on.

trench=foot (trench′fṳt), *n.* A disease of the feet due to exposure to cold and wet, common among soldiers serving in the trenches.

trend (trend), *v. i.* [AS. *trendan*, turn, roll, akin to MLG. *trent*, ring, circumference, Sw. and Dan. *trind*, round: cf. *trindle* and *trundle*.] To turn round†; rotate†; revolve†; roll†; also, to make a circuit†; direct one's course†; also, of a road, river, valley, mountain-range, coast-line, etc., to turn off in a specified direction; tend to take a particular direction; extend in some direction indicated; fig., to have a general tendency, as events, etc.—**trend**, *n.* The direction in which something trends, or turns off or away; the general direction which a road, river, coast-line, or the like tends to take (as, "the *trend* of the valleys being parallel to the sea-coast": Roosevelt's "Winning of the West," i. 5); fig., the general course, drift, or tendency (as, "the *trend* of events," W. R. Inge's "Outspoken Essays," i. 4; "the *trend* of religious thought in recent times," J. H. Robinson's "Mind in the Making," Appendix).

tren-tal (tren′tạl), *n.* [OF. *trental*, *trentel* (ML. *trentalis*), < *trente*, thirty, < L. *triginta*, thirty.] A service of thirty requiem masses said either on the same day or on different days. [Obs. or hist.]

trente et qua-rante (troṅ-tā-kȧ-räṅt′). [F., 'thirty and forty.'] The gambling-game of rouge et noir (which see): so called because thirty and forty are respectively winning and losing numbers.

tre-pan[1] (trẹ-pan′), *n.* [OF. *trepan* (F. *trépan*), < ML. *trepanum*, < Gr. τρύπανον, boring instrument, trepan, < τρυπᾶν, bore.] A surgical instrument in the form of a crown-saw, for cutting out parts of bones, esp. from the skull; also, a boring-tool for sinking shafts or the like.—**tre-pan′[1]**, *v. t.*; *-panned*, *-panning*. To operate upon with a trepan; perforate by a trepan.

tre-pan[2] (trẹ-pan′), *n.* [Earlier *trapan*: cf. *trap[1]*.] One who insnares or entraps others; one who decoys others into some disadvantageous course or position; also, a stratagem; a trick; a trap. [Obs. or archaic.]—**tre-pan′[2]**, *v. t.*; *-panned*, *-panning*. To insnare or entrap; entice, beguile, or lure; cheat or swindle. [Obs. or archaic.]

trep-a-na-tion (trep-ạ-nā′shọn), *n.* The operation of trepanning; perforation of a bone, esp. of the skull, with a trepan.

tre-pang (trẹ-pang′), *n.* [Malay *trīpang*.] Any of various worm-like holothurians, as *Holothuria edulis*, used as food in China.

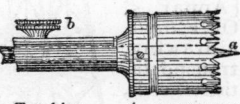

Trepang (*Holothuria edulis*).

tre-phine (trẹ-fīn′ or -fēn′), *n.* [Orig. *trafine*, explained by the inventor as < L. *tres*, three, + *finis*, end.] An improved form of surgical trepan, having a transverse handle, and a sharp steel point (called the *center-pin*) which is fixed in the bone to steady the instrument during operation.—**tre-phine′**, *v. t.*; *-phined*, *-phining*. To operate upon with a trephine.

Trephine. — *A*, crown-saw; *a*, center-pin for guiding the saw; *b*, screw for attachment of the shank to a handle.

trep-id (trep′id), *a.* [L. *trepidus*.] Scared; perturbed; agitated.

trep-i-da-tion (trep-i-dā′shọn), *n.* [L. *trepidatio(n-)*, < *trepidare*, hurry or tremble with alarm, < *trepidus*, E. *trepid*.] Tremulous alarm or agitation, or perturbation (as, "They were . . . full of *trepidation* about things that were never likely to happen": Morley's "Oliver Cromwell," ii. 2); also, trembling of the limbs, as in paralytic affections; also, vibratory movement; a vibration.

tres-pass (tres′pạs), *v.* [OF. *trespasser*, pass over, pass, die, transgress (F. *trépasser*, die), < L. *trans*, across, over, + ML. *passare*, E. *pass*, *v*.] **I.** *intr.* To commit a transgression or offense; transgress; offend; sin; also, to make an improper inroad on a person's presence, time, etc.; encroach or infringe (with *on* or *upon*: as, "I . . . will no longer *trespass* upon your good nature," Bulwer-Lytton's "Pelham," xxxi.); in *law*, to commit a trespass. **II.**† *tr.* To commit (a transgression, etc.); also, to transgress or violate (as, "I stood still an hour, or thereabout, without *trespassing* our orders": Defoe's "Robinson Crusoe," ii. 14). —**tres′pass**, *n.* [OF. *trespas* (F. *trépas*).] A breach of law, duty, etc.; a transgression; an offense, sin, or wrong; also, an encroachment or intrusion; in *law*, any transgression of the law not amounting to treason or felony, or misprision of either; specif., any unlawful act constituting an injury to the person, property, or rights of another, committed with force or violence, actual or implied; esp., a wrongful entry upon the lands of another; also, the action to recover damages for such an injury.—**tres′pass-er**, *n.* One who trespasses; a transgressor; an offender; often, one who trespasses on the lands of another.

tress (tres), *n.* [OF. *trece* (F. *tresse*), < ML. *trecia*, *tricia*, a plait, braid: cf. Gr. τρίχα, threefold.] A plait or braid of the hair of the head; also, any long lock or curl of hair, esp. of a woman, not plaited or braided (usually in *pl.*: as, "her loose falling *tresses*," G. Meredith's "Ordeal of Richard Feverel," xx.); fig., anything braided or plait-like.—**tress**, *v. t.* To arrange (the hair) in tresses.—**tressed**, *a.* Having tresses: as, golden-*tressed*.

tres-sure (tresh′ụr), *n.* [OF. *tresseur*, *treceor*, band for the hair: cf. *tress*.] In *her.*, a bearing resembling the orle, consisting of a narrow band, generally considered as being of half the width of an orle, extending about an escutcheon inside the edge, usually enriched with fleurs-de-lis, and often double.

tres-tle (tres'l), *n.* [OF. *trestel* (F. *tréteau*), dim. < L. *iranstrum*, cross-beam: see *transom*.] A frame used as a support, consisting typically of a horizontal beam or bar fixed at each end to a pair of spreading legs; sometimes, the whole frame which supports the top of a table; in *engin.*, a

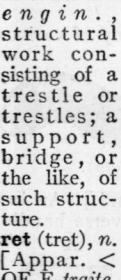

Double Tressure.

supporting framework composed chiefly of vertical or inclined pieces with or without diagonal braces, etc., used for various purposes, as for carrying railroad-tracks across a gap; a bridge or the like of such structure.— **tres'tle-tree**, *n. Naut.*, either of two horizontal fore-and-aft timbers or bars secured to a masthead, one on each side, in order to support the crosstrees.— **tres'tle-work**, *n.* In *engin.*, structural work consisting of a trestle or trestles; a support, bridge, or the like, of such structure.

tret (tret), *n.* [Appar. < OF. F. *traite*, a drawing, transportation of goods, tax on goods transported, < L. *tracta*, pp. fem. of *trahere*, draw.] In *com.*, an allowance formerly

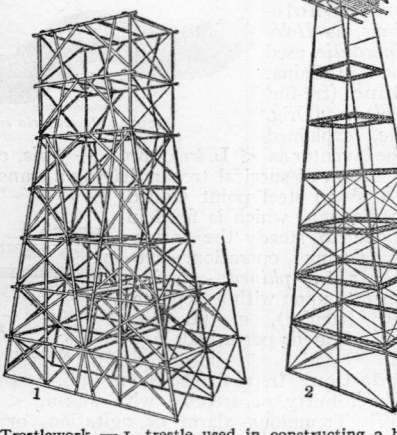

Trestlework. — 1, trestle used in constructing a bridge; 2, section of iron trestle of a viaduct.

granted to a purchaser on goods sold by weight, after deduction for tare.

trews (tröz), *n. pl.* [= *trouse*, pl. *trouses*, later *trousers*: see *trousers*.] Close-fitting trousers, or breeches combined with stockings, formerly worn by Irishmen and Scottish Highlanders, and still by certain Scottish regiments.

trey (trā), *n.* [OF. *treis* (F. *trois*), < L. *tres*, three: see *three*.] In *cards* or *dice*, three; a card, or the side of a die, having three pips.

tri-. [L. *tri-*, repr. *tres*, neut. *tria*, three; also Gr. τρι-, repr. τρεῖς, neut. τρία, three: see *three*.] A combining-form or prefix meaning 'three,' 'threefold,' 'thrice,' occurring orig. in words from the Latin and Greek, but now used freely as a general formative, as in *triatomic, tribasic, tripetalous, triplane*. See *mono-*.

tri-a-ble (trī'a-bl), *a.* [See *try*.] That may be tried; subject or liable to judicial trial.— **tri'a-ble-ness**, *n.*

tri-a-cid (trī-as'id), *a.* [See *tri-*.] In *chem.*, capable of combining with three molecules of a monobasic acid.

tri-ad (trī'ad), *n.* [LL. *trias* (triad-), < Gr. τριάς (τριαδ-), < τρεῖς, three.] The number three; also, a group of three, esp. of three closely related or associated persons or things; in *music*, a chord of three tones, esp. one consisting of a given tone with its major or minor third and its perfect, augmented, or diminished fifth; in *chem.*, an element, atom, or radical having a valence of three; in *Welsh lit.*, an old form of composition characterized by a grouping of three lines, statements, examples, or the like (as, "Thomas of Erceldoun was, according to the Welsh *triads*, one of the three bards of Britain, who never stained a spear with blood": Scott's "Castle Dangerous," v.).— **tri-ad'ic**, *a.*

tri-age (trī'āj, F. trē-äzh'), *n.* [F., < *trier*, pick, cull, sort: see *try*.] The act of sorting, as according to kind or quality; also, something sorted out, as the broken coffee-beans separated from whole coffee in sorting.

tri-al (trī'al). [See *try*.] **I.** *n.* The act of trying or testing, or putting to the proof; test; proof; a testing of qualifications, attainments, or the like; also, the state or position of a person or thing being tried or tested, or probation (as, "We are in a state of *trial* with regard to a future world": J. Butler's "Analogy of Religion," i. 4); also, subjection to suffering or grievous experiences, or affliction (as, comfort in the hour of *trial*); an instance of this, or an affliction or trouble (as, "We had . . . *trials* and tribulations in the days that were past": Galt's "Annals of the Parish," xv.); a trying, distressing, or annoying thing or person (as, "The length of the [church] service was still a *trial* to fidgeting youth," Archibald Marshall's "Anthony Dare," xii.; "You're a *trial*, Maisie!" Kipling's "Light That Failed," vii.); also, tentative or experimental action in order to ascertain results; an experiment; also, an attempt, endeavor, or effort to do something; also, something serving as a proof or sample, as of material, quality, condition, method, skill, etc.; specif., a piece of ceramic material used to try the heat of the kiln and the progress of the firing of its contents; in *law*, the judicial investigation and determination of a cause; the determination of a person's guilt or innocence by due process of law; also, formerly, the determination of guilt or innocence, or of the righteousness of a cause, by a combat, as between one accused and his accuser ('trial by battle' or 'trial by combat'), or the determination of guilt or innocence by ordeal ('trial by ordeal'). **II.** *a.* Of or pertaining to trial; done or used by way of trial, test, proof, or experiment.— **trial jury.** See under *jury*.

tri-al-ism (trī'al-izm), *n.* [L. *tri-*, three: see *tri-*, and cf. *dualism*.] The doctrine that man consists of three essentially different modes of substance, as body, soul, and spirit; also, a union of three countries or states.

tri-an-gle (trī'ang-gl), *n.* [OF. F. *triangle*, < L. *triangulum*, prop. neut. of *triangulus*, having three angles, < *tri-*, three, + *angulus*, E. *angle³*.] A geometrical plane figure formed by three straight lines which meet two by two in three points, thus forming three angles; a similar plane figure in which the three lines are arcs of circles ('circular triangle'), or an analogous figure formed on the surface of a sphere by arcs of great circles ('spherical triangle'); also, any three-cornered or three-sided figure, object, or piece (as, a *triangle* of land); a flat triangular piece of wood, vulcanite, or the like, with straight edges, used in connection with a T-square for drawing perpendicular lines, etc.; also, a group of three, as three characters (two men and one woman, or two women and one man) in a novel or the like, involved in a love entanglement; in *music*, an instrument of percussion, made of a steel rod bent into the form of a triangle open at one of the corners, and sounded by being struck with a small, straight steel rod; [*cap.*] in *astron.*, the northern constellation Triangulum, also, the southern constellation Triangulum Australe ('Southern Triangle').— **triangle spider**, a small American spider, *Hyptiotes cavatus*, which spins on trees a triangular web that it uses as a trap, drawing it taut at the apex and then allowing it to spring back upon the prey.

Triangle Spider. — Spider five times natural size, web one third natural size.

tri-an-gu-lar (trī-ang'gū-lär), *a.* [LL. *triangularis*.] Of, pertaining to, or having the form of a triangle; three-cornered; also, pertaining to or involving a group of three, as three persons, parties, or things (as, "I talked to her, or I talked to him, but the conversation never got *triangular*," A. S. M. Hutchinson's "If Winter Comes," iv. 1; a *triangular* treaty); comprising three parts or elements, or triple.— **tri-an'gu-lar-ly**, *adv.*

tri-an-gu-late (trī-ang′gū-lāt), *v. t.*; *-lated, -lating.* [L. *triangulus*: see *triangle.*] To make triangular; also, to divide into triangles; esp., to survey or map out (a region, etc.) by dividing into triangles and measuring their angles, etc.; also, to determine trigonometrically (as, to *triangulate* the height of a mountain).—**tri-an′gu-late**, *a.* Triangular; also, composed of or marked with triangles.—**tri-an-gu-la′tion** (-lā′shọn), *n.*

tri-ap-sal, tri-ap-si-dal (trī-ap′sạl, -si-dạl), *a.* [See *tri-.*] In *arch.*, having three apses.

tri-ar-chy (trī′är-ki), *n.*; pl. *-chies* (-kiz). [Gr. τριαρχία, < τρι-, three, + ἄρχειν, rule.] Government by three persons; a set of three joint rulers; a triumvirate; also, a country divided into three governments, or a group of three countries or districts each under its own ruler.

tri-as (trī′as), *n.* [LL.: see *triad.*] A triad, or group of three; [*cap.*] in *geol.*, the Triassic system (so named as having, esp. in Germany, three divisions of strata); also, the Triassic period.—**Tri-as′sic. I.** *a.* Noting or pertaining to a geological period or a system of rocks which precedes the Jurassic and constitutes the earliest principal division of the Mesozoic. **II.** *n.* The Triassic period or system.

tri-at-ic (trī-at′ik), *a.* [Origin obscure: cf. *tri-.*] *Naut.*, a term used only in the phrase *triatic stay,* denoting a device consisting usually of two depending ropes lashed one to each of two adjacent masts near the top, and used for attaching tackles for hoisting boats or other heavy weights in or out.

tri-a-tom-ic (trī-ạ-tom′ik), *a.* [See *tri-.*] In *chem.*, having three atoms in the molecule; also, containing three replaceable atoms or groups.

tri-ax-i-al (trī-ak′si-ạl), *a.* [See *tri-.*] Having three axes.

tri-bal (trī′bạl), *a.* Of, pertaining to, or characteristic of a tribe or tribes.—**tri′bal-ism**, *n.* The condition of existing as a separate tribe or in separate tribes; the tribal relation or system.—**tri′bal-ly**, *adv.*

tri-ba-sic (trī-bā′sik), *a.* [See *tri-.*] In *chem.*, of an acid, having three atoms of hydrogen replaceable by basic atoms or radicals.

tribe (trīb), *n.* [L. *tribus,* a tribe, orig. one of the three divisions of the early Roman people, appar. < *tri-*, three: see *tri-.*] Orig., in ancient Rome, in early times, any one of three divisions of the people, the Ramnes, Tities, and Luceres, representing respectively the Latin, Sabine, and Etruscan settlements; later, one of 30 (afterward 35) political divisions of the Roman people; also, in ancient Greece, a phyle; also, any of the twelve divisions of ancient Israel, claiming descent from the twelve sons of Jacob, ten of these being known as the 'ten lost tribes' from their disappearance from history after their deportation by Shalmaneser, king of Assyria; also, a division of some other people or race, esp. a local division of a primitive or barbarous people (as, "the rude *tribes* of Germany," Gibbon's "Decline and Fall of the Roman Empire," ix.; the Berber *tribes*; North American Indian *tribes*); any aggregate of people united by ties of race and blood (as by descent from a common ancestor), community of customs and traditions, adherence to the same chiefs or leaders, etc.; a family (now chiefly humorous or contemptuous); a class or set of persons (now chiefly humorous or contemptuous: as, the scribbling *tribe*; the whole *tribe* of gossips and scandal-mongers); a class, kind, or sort of animals, plants, articles, or other things (as, the feathered *tribe*; "the kindred *tribes* of weeds and flow'rs," Cowper's "Hope," 289; an implement of the knife *tribe*; the various *tribes* of diseases); a company, troop, or number of persons or animals (as, "There flutter'd in . . . A *tribe* of women, dress'd in many hues": Tennyson's "Geraint and Enid," 597); in *zoöl.* and *bot.*, a classificatory group of animals or plants, ranking variously, as between an order and a family, or between a family and a genus; loosely, any group of plants or animals; in *stock-breeding*, a group of animals descended through the female line from a common female ancestor.—**tribe′let**, *n.* A small tribe.—**tribe′ship**, *n.* The condition of being a tribe; also, the territory of a tribe. —**tribes-man** (trībz′man), *n.*; pl. *-men.* A man belonging to a tribe; a member of a tribe: as, "a mob of Arab *tribesmen*" (Buchan's "Hist. of the Great War," lxxxvii.).

tri-bom-e-ter (trī-bom′e-tėr), *n.* [F. *tribomètre*, < Gr. τρίβειν, rub, + μέτρον, measure.] An apparatus for measuring the force of friction in sliding surfaces.

tri-brach (trī′brak), *n.* [L. *tribrachys*, < Gr. τρίβραχυς, of three short syllables, < τρι-, three, + βραχύς, short.] In *pros.*, a foot of three short syllables.—**tri-brach′ic**, *a.*

trib-u-la-tion (trib-ū-lā′shọn), *n.* [OF. F. *tribulation*, < LL. *tribulatio(n-)*, < *tribulare*, oppress, afflict, L. press, < L. *tribulum*, a threshing-sledge.] Affliction, grievous trouble, or severe trial or experience (as, "patient in *tribulation*," Rom. xii. 12; "the fiery furnace of domestic *tribulation*," Irving's "Sketch-Book," Rip Van Winkle); an instance of this, or an affliction, trouble, or trial (as, "your God, who himself saved you out of all your adversities and your *tribulations*": 1 Sam. x. 19); also, something troublesome or trying, as a troublesome person.

tri-bu-nal (trī-bū′nạl or tri-), *n.* [= Sp. *tribunal*, < L. *tribunal*, < *tribunus*, E. *tribune*[1].] A raised platform for the seats of magistrates, orig. in a Roman basilica or hall of justice; a place or seat of judgment (lit. or fig.: as, "They summoned him with their last words to appear before the *tribunal* of God in thirty days," Hallam's "Europe during the Middle Ages," iv.); also, a court of justice (lit. or fig.: as, "He should leave the determination of his dispute to the authorized *tribunals*," Prescott's "Conquest of Mexico," iv. 6; the *tribunal* of public opinion); also (Sp., pron. trē-bö-näl′), in villages in the Philippines, a kind of town hall or municipal building, used for meetings, etc.

trib-u-nate (trib′ū-nāt), *n.* [L. *tribunatus.*] The office of tribune (as, "He had not aspired to the *tribunate*": Froude's "Cæsar," xi.); also, a body of tribunes.

trib-une[1] (trib′ūn), *n.* [L. *tribunus*, orig. chief of a tribe, < *tribus*, E. *tribe*.] In ancient Rome, any of various administrative officers, esp. one of two (later five, then ten) officers ('tribunes of the people') appointed to protect the interests and rights of the plebeians from the patricians; also, an officer holding some similar position elsewhere; hence, a person who upholds or defends popular rights; a champion of the people.

trib-une[2] (trib′ūn), *n.* [F. *tribune*, < It. and ML. *tribuna*, for L. *tribunal*, E. *tribunal*.] Orig., the tribunal or raised platform for magistrates in a Roman basilica, commonly occupying a semicircular recess at one end of the hall; hence, in a Christian basilica, the bishop's throne in a corresponding recess, or apse, or the apse itself; also, in general, a raised platform, or dais; a rostrum or pulpit; a raised part, or gallery, with seats, as in a church (as, "The church was crowded; not a chair nor a *tribune* vacant": Disraeli's "Lothair," lxvi.).

trib-une-ship (trib′ūn-ship), *n.* The office, or term of office, of a tribune.

trib-u-ni-cial, trib-u-ni-tial (trib-ū-nish′ạl), *a.* [L. *tribunicius, tribunitius*.] Of, pertaining to, or characteristic of a tribune or his office or function. Also **tri-bu-ni′cian, tri-bu-ni′tian** (-nish′ạn).

trib-u-ta-ry (trib′ū-tā-ri), *n.* [L. *tributarius*.] **I.** *a.* Paying or required to pay tribute; hence, furnishing subsidiary aid; contributory; auxiliary; of a stream, flowing into a larger stream or other body of water; also, paid as tribute; of the nature of tribute. **II.** *n.*; pl. *-ries* (-riz). One who pays tribute; hence, one who or that which furnishes supplies or aid; a stream contributing its flow to a larger stream or other body of water.—**trib′u-ta-ri-ly**, *adv.*

trib-ute (trib′ūt), *n.* [L. *tributum*, prop. neut. of *tributus*, pp. of *tribuere*, assign, grant, give, pay.] A stated sum or other valuable consideration paid by one sovereign or state to another in acknowledgment of submission or as the price of peace, security, protection, or the like; a rent, tax, or the like, as that paid by a subject to a sovereign; anything paid as under exaction or by enforced contribution (as, to pay *tribute* to bandits; to pay *tribute* for police protection: also fig.); also, the state of being liable to any such payment; the obligation of making such payment; also, a personal offering, testimonial, compliment, or the like given as if due, or in acknowledgment of gratitude, esteem, or regard (as, "orchids and azaleas which the young man recognised as *tributes* from the Beaufort hot-houses," Mrs. Wharton's "Age of Innocence," xii.; "Surely a more touching *tribute* was never engraved on a tombstone," Aldrich's "Story of a Bad Boy," iii.).

tri-car-pel-la-ry (trī-kär′pe-lā̱-ri), *a.* [See *tri-.*] In *bot.*, having three carpels.

trice[1] (trīs), *v. t.*; *triced, tricing.* [MD. *trīsen* (D. *trijsen*) hoist.] To pull†, pluck†, or snatch†; also, to pull or haul with a rope; *naut.*, to haul up and fasten with a rope (usually with *up*).

trice[2] (trīs), *n.* [First in ME. *at a tryse,* appar. lit. 'at one pull, or jerk': cf. *trice*[1].] A very short time; a moment; an instant: now only in 'in a trice': as, "In a *trice* I was back in the chimney" (Buchan's "Three Hostages," xxi.).

tri-cen-ni-al (trī-sen′i-ạl), *a.* [LL. *tricennium,* period of thirty years, < L. *triceni,* thirty each, + *annus,* year.] Of or pertaining to thirty years; occurring every thirty years.

tri-cen-te-na-ry (trī-sen′te-nạ-ri), *a.* and *n.* [See *tri-.*] Same as *tercentenary.* Also **tri-cen-ten′ni-al** (-ten′i-ạl), *a.* and *n.*

tri-ceps (trī′seps). [L. *triceps,* three-headed, threefold, < *tri-,* three, + *caput,* head.] **I.** *a.* Having three heads, or points of origin, as certain muscles. **II.** *n.* A triceps muscle, esp. one extending along the humerus at the back of the upper arm.

tri-cer-a-tops (trī-ser′ạ-tops), *n.* [NL., < Gr. τρι-, three, + κέρας (κερατ-), horn, + ὤψ, eye, face.] A dinosaur of the genus *Triceratops,* with a large horn above each eye, a smaller horn on the nose, and a kind of large, bony collar extending from the skull behind: found in the Cretaceous strata of Montana, Wyoming, and Colorado.

Triceratops. (After a restoration by C. R. Knight.)

tri-chi-na (tri-kī′nạ), *n.*; pl. *-næ* (-nē). [NL., < Gr. τρίχινος, of hair, < θρίξ (τριχ-), hair.] Any of the nematode worms constituting the genus *Trichina* (or *Trichinella*), esp. *T. spiralis,* a parasite sometimes present as an encysted larva in the muscular tissues of man and certain animals (the development of such larvæ into adults taking place only when the flesh of the animal infected is eaten by man or another animal and brought to the intestinal tract, where they mature and produce embryos which in turn find their way to the muscular tissues to form encysted larvæ). —**trich-i-nize** (trik′i-nīz), *v. t.*; *-nized, -nizing.* To infect with trichinæ.—**trich″i-ni-za′tion** (-ni-zā′shọn), *n.*— **trich′i-nosed** (-nōzd), *a.* Affected with trichinosis; infected with trichinæ.—**trich-i-no′sis** (-nō′sis), *n.* [NL.] In *pathol.*, a disease due to the presence of the trichina, *Trichina spiralis,* in the intestines and muscular tissues.— **trich-i-not′ic** (-not′ik), *a.*—**trich′i-nous,** *a.* Infected with trichinæ; pertaining to or of the nature of trichinosis.

trich-ite (trik′īt), *n.* [G. *trichit,* < Gr. θρίξ (τριχ-), hair.] In *petrog.,* any of various minute hair-like mineral bodies occurring in certain vitreous igneous rocks, esp. obsidian.

tri-chlo-ride (trī-klō′rīd or -rid), *n.* [See *tri-.*] In *chem.,* a chloride having three atoms of chlorine.

tricho-. Form of Gr. θρίξ (τριχ-), hair, used in combination.—**trich-o-car-pous** (trik-ō-kär′pus), *a.* [+ *-carpous.*] In *bot.*, having hairy fruit.—**trich′o-cyst** (-sist), *n.* [See *cyst.*] In *zoöl.,* an organ of offense and defense embedded in the outer protoplasm of many infusorians, consisting of a small elongated sac containing a fine, hair-like filament capable of being ejected and of causing a sting.

trich-oid (trik′oid), *a.* [Gr. τριχοειδής, < θρίξ (τριχ-), hair, + εἶδος, form.] Hair-like; capillary.

tri-chol-o-gy (tri-kol′ọ-ji), *n.* [See *tricho-* and *-logy.*] The science of the hair and its diseases.—**tri-chol′o-gist,** *n.*

tri-chome (trī′kōm or trik′ōm), *n.* [Gr. τρίχωμα, a growth

of hair, < θρίξ (τριχ-), hair.] In *bot.,* an outgrowth from the epidermis of plants, as a hair or bristle.

tri-chop-ter-ous (trī-kop′te-rus), *a.* [Gr. θρίξ (τριχ-), hair, + πτερόν, wing.] Having hairy wings; belonging to the *Trichoptera,* a group of insects comprising the caddis-flies, regarded as a suborder of neuropters or as a separate order.

tri-chord (trī′kôrd), *n.* [Gr. τρίχορδος, three-stringed, < τρι-, three, + χορδή, string.] A musical instrument with three strings, as a form of lyre or lute.

tri-cho-sis (tri-kō′sis), *n.* [NL., < Gr. θρίξ (τριχ-), hair.] In *pathol.,* any disease of the hair.

tri-chot-o-mous (trī-kot′ọ-mus), *a.* [Gr. τρίχα, in three parts, + -τομος, < τέμνειν, cut: cf. *dichotomous.*] Divided or dividing into three parts; branching into three parts; giving off shoots by threes.—**tri-chot′o-my,** *n.* Division into three parts; arrangement in three divisions.

tri-chro-ic (trī-krō′ik), *a.* [Gr. τρίχροος, < τρι-, three, + χρόα, color.] Having or exhibiting three colors; of a crystal exhibiting different colors in three different directions when viewed by transmitted light.—**tri′chro-ism** (-krō-izm), *n.* The property of being trichroic.

tri-chro-mat-ic (trī-krō-mat′ik), *a.* [Gr. τριχρώματος, < τρι-, three, + χρῶμα (χρωματ-), color.] Pertaining to, characterized by, or involving three colors; trichromic; specif., pertaining to the use or combination of three different colors, as in printing or in photography in natural colors.—**tri-chro′ma-tism** (-krō′mạ-tizm), *n.* Trichromatic condition; the use or combination of three different colors.

tri-chro-mic (trī-krō′mik), *a.* [Gr. τρίχρωμος, < τρι-, three, + χρῶμα, color.] Pertaining to or involving three colors; trichromatic.

trick[1] (trik), *n.* [OF. *trique,* var. of *triche,* deceit, < *trichier* (F. *tricher*), deceive, cheat, trick: see *treacherous.*] A crafty or fraudulent device, expedient, or proceeding (as, "The native boys . . . had all sorts of *tricks* to prevent us from winning [in racing]," W. H. Hudson's "Far Away and Long Ago," xx.; "knowing their *tricks,* and suspecting they would publish his disputation unfairly," Strype's "Memorials of Cranmer," iii. 10); an artifice, stratagem, ruse, or wile; also, a deceptive or illusory appearance, or mere semblance (as, "And all her love of God . . . A *trick* upon the canvas, painted flame": Cowper's "Conversation," 782); also, a roguish or mischievous performance, or prank (as, to play *tricks*; "Come, I'll question you Of my lord's *tricks* and yours when you were boys," Shakspere's "Winter's Tale," i. 2. 61); a practical joke (as, to play a *trick* on a person); a hoax; also, a foolish, disgraceful, or mean performance or action (as, "Didst thou ever see me do such a *trick?*" Shakspere's "Two Gentlemen of Verona," iv. 4. 43); also, a clever device or expedient, ingenious shift, or 'dodge' (as, a rhetorical *trick;* "one of those fellows who have the *tricks* of their trade at their finger-tips," Pinero's "Wife without a Smile," iii.); the art or knack of doing something (as, to learn or get the *trick* of using a tool; to have the *trick* of handling customers); a clever or dexterous feat, as for exhibition or entertainment (as, *tricks* in horsemanship or diving; "the same happy backwardness . . . which is observed in old dogs — 'of not learning new *tricks,*'" Sterne's "Tristram Shandy," iii. 34); often, a feat of jugglery or legerdemain (as, "He [a conjurer] has to make up new *tricks,* new patter, new nonsense": Chesterton's "Magic," ii.); also, a peculiar habit, practice, or way of acting (as, "She hath an awkward *trick* (to say no worse of it) of reading in company": Lamb's "Mackery End"); a peculiar quality, feature, or trait, or a characteristic (as, to recognize a speaker by a *trick* of the voice; "He had got hold of the English *trick* of not knowing when he was beaten," G. Meredith's "Lord Ormont and His Aminta," i.); also, the mode of operation of a piece of mechanism or the like, or the principle upon which it is constructed; also, a toy, trinket, or knickknack (obs. or archaic); any small or trifling article or belonging (often in *pl.,* collectively: colloq., U. S.); a child or young girl (often with *little*: as, she's a cute little *trick*: colloq., U. S., esp. southern); also, *naut.,* the period of duty of a man at the helm; a spell or turn of duty (sometimes fig.: as, "All I ask is a merry yarn . . . And quiet sleep and a sweet dream when the long *trick*'s over," Masefield's "Sea-Fever"); also, in *card-playing*, the cards collectively which are played and won in one round.—**trick**[1], *v. t.* **I.** *tr.* To deceive by trickery; cheat; often, to cheat or swindle (*out of*); also, to beguile (*into*) by trickery. **II.** *intr.* To practise trickery or deception; cheat; also, to play tricks, trifle, or play (*with*).

trick[2] (trik), *v. t.* [Origin uncertain: cf. *trick*[1].] To dress, array, or deck (often with *out* or *up*: as, "The Indian warriors ... *tricked* themselves out in ... laced hats and bright apparel," Bancroft's "Hist. of the U. S.," Amer. Revolution, i. 8; "You have been *tricked* up with fine garments," Scott's "Abbot," v.: also fig.); also, to arrange† or adjust†.

trick[3] (trik), *v. t.* [Origin uncertain: cf. *trick*[1].] To sketch or draw in outline; in *her.*, to draw (a coat of arms, etc.) in outline, without the use of color but with the tinctures indicated.—**trick**[3], *n.* In *her.*, a tricked sketch of a coat of arms, etc.

trick-er (trik′ėr), *n.* One who tricks or cheats.

trick-er-y (trik′ėr-i), *n.*; pl. *-ies* (-iz). The use or practice of tricks; artifice; a trick or deception.

trick-i-ly (trik′i-li), *adv.* In a tricky manner.—**trick′i-ness**, *n.*

trick-ish (trik′ish), *a.* Tricky.—**trick′ish-ness**, *n.*

trick-le (trik′l), *v.*; *-led, -ling*. [ME. *triklen*; origin uncertain.] **I.** *intr.* To flow or fall by drops, or in a small, broken or gentle stream (as, tears *trickle* down the cheeks; blood *trickles* from a wound; sand *trickles* through a crevice; a brook *trickles* through a valley); fig., to come, go, pass, or proceed as if by drops or in a small stream (as, subscriptions are *trickling* in; "The man's disreputable secret *trickled* out," Stevenson's "Master of Ballantrae," iv.; conversation *trickles* along); also, to shed or let fall drops or a small stream, as of a liquid (as, "Mine eye *trickleth* down," Lam. iii. 49; a hand *trickling* with blood). **II.** *tr.* To let flow or fall by drops or in a gentle stream; pour little by little.—**trick′le**, *n.* A trickling flow or stream (as, "the blue *trickles* of water in the stony river bed": H. G. Wells's "Italy, France, and Britain at War," ii. 1); fig., a quantity of anything coming, going, or proceeding as if by drops or in a small stream (as, a *trickle* of visitors to a house; a thin *trickle* of conversation); also, a trickling movement or course (as, to watch the *trickle* of the raindrops on a window-pane).—**trick′let**, *n.* A little trickle; a small trickling stream.

trick-si-ly (trik′si-li), *adv.* In a tricksy manner.—**trick′si-ness**, *n.*

trick-some (trik′sum), *a.* Full of tricks; mischievous; frolicsome; playful.

trick-ster (trik′stėr), *n.* One who practises tricks; a deceiver; a cheat.

trick-sy (trik′si), *a.* Tricky, crafty, or wily (as, "I still continued *tricksy* and cunning": Goldsmith's "Vicar of Wakefield," xxvi.); also, mischievous, frolicsome, or playful (as, "a very frolicsome and *tricksy* creature, full of wild fantastic humours": W. H. Hudson's "Green Mansions," iv.); whimsical (as, "a rich, idiomatic diction, picturesque allusions ... or quaint *tricksy* turns": Carlyle's "Sartor Resartus," i. 4); also, deceptive, uncertain, or ticklish; also, trim, spruce, or fine.

trick=track (trik′trak), *n.* [F. *trictrac*; imit. of the sound made by the pieces in play.] A variety of backgammon.

trick-y (trik′i), *a.*; compar. *trickier*; superl. *trickiest*. Given to or characterized by deceitful tricks; crafty; wily; also, skilled in clever tricks or 'dodges'; also, deceptive, uncertain, or ticklish to deal with or handle (as, "The lock's a bit *tricky*," H. G. Wells's "Kipps," i. 4; "Revolvers are *tricky* things for young hands to deal with," Kipling's "Light That Failed," i.).

tri-clin-ic (trī-klin′ik), *a.* [Gr. τρι-, three, + κλίνειν, incline.] In *crystal.*, noting or pertaining to a system of crystallization in which the three axes are unequal and intersect at oblique angles.

tri-clin-i-um (trī-klin′i-um), *n.*; pl. *-ia* (-i-ą). [L., < Gr. τρικλίνιον, < τρι-, three, + κλίνη, bed.] In *Rom. antiq.*, a couch extending along three sides of a table, for reclining on at meals; also, a room containing such a couch, or a dining-room (as, "They enter the *triclinium* in the midst of the banquet": J. H. Newman's "Callista," xv.).

tri-col-or (trī′kul-or). [= F. *tricolore*, < LL. *tricolor*, three-colored, < L. *tri-*, three, + *color*, E. *color*.] **I.** *a.* Having three colors. **II.** *n.* A tricolor flag, cockade, or the like; esp., the national flag of France, adopted during the Revolution, consisting of three equal vertical stripes of blue (next the pole), white, and red (as, "The *tricolor* also, and the stars and stripes, distinguish the residences of the other consuls": H. Melville's "Omoo," xxvii.).—**tri′col-ored**, *a.*

tri-corn (trī′kôrn). [= F. *tricorne*, < L. *tricornis*, three-horned, < *tri-*, three, + *cornu*, horn.] **I.** *a.* Having three horns or horn-like projections, as a hat with the brim turned up on three sides. **II.** *n.* An imaginary creature with three horns; also, a tricorn hat.

tri-cor-po-rate (trī-kôr′pō-rāt), *a.* [L. *tricorpor*, < *tri-*, three, + *corpus* (*corpor-*), body.] Having three bodies: specif. in *her.*

tri-cot (trē′kō), *n.* [F., < *tricoter*, knit; origin uncertain.] A knitted fabric made by hand or machine; also, a kind of woolen cloth.

tric-o-tine (trik-ō-tēn′ or trē-kō-), *n.* [F., < *tricot*: see *tricot*.] A kind of woolen cloth with a twilled face.

Lion Tricorporate.

tri-crot-ic (trī-krot′ik), *a.* [Gr. τρι-, three, + κρότος, beat: cf. *dicrotic*.] Having a threefold beat, as shown by the form of the sphygmographic tracing, as certain pulses; pertaining to such a pulse.—**tri′cro-tism** (-krō-tizm), *n.* Tricrotic condition.

tri-cus-pid (trī-kus′pid). [L. *tricuspis* (*tricuspid-*), three-pointed, < *tri-*, three, + *cuspis*, point, E. *cusp*.] **I.** *a.* Having three cusps or points, as a tooth; specif., in *anat.*, noting or pertaining to a valve of three segments, or a set of three valves, guarding the opening from the right auricle into the right ventricle of the heart. **II.** *n.* A tricuspid tooth; also, a tricuspid valve.—**tri-cus′pi-dal, tri-cus′pi-date** (-dāt), *a.*

tri-cy-cle (trī′si-kl), *n.* [F. *tricycle*, < Gr. τρι-, three, + κύκλος, circle, wheel.] A velocipede with three wheels (usually one in front and one on each side behind) propelled by pedals or hand-levers; also, a three-wheeled motorcycle.—**tri′cy-cle**, *v. i.*; *-cled, -cling*. To ride a tricycle.—**tri′cy-cler, tri′cy-clist**, *n.*

tri-dac-tyl (trī-dak′til), *a.* [Gr. τριδάκτυλος, < τρι-, three, + δάκτυλος, finger or toe.] In *zoöl.*, having three fingers, claws, or toes to a limb. Also **tri-dac′ty-lous** (-ti-lus).

tri-dec-ane (trī-dek′ān), *n.* [Gr. τρι-, three, + δέκα, ten; with reference to the thirteen atoms of carbon.] In *chem.*, any of several isomeric, colorless, liquid hydrocarbons of the methane series, with the formula $C_{13}H_{28}$.

tri-dent (trī′dęnt). [L. *tridens* (*trident-*), with three teeth, < *tri-*, three, + *dens* (*dent-*), tooth.] **I.** *a.* Having three prongs or tines. **II.** *n.* A three-pronged instrument or weapon; specif., the three-pronged spear forming a characteristic attribute of the sea-god Poseidon, or Neptune; fig., rule over the sea or ocean; in *Rom. antiq.*, a three-pronged spear used by the retiarius in gladiatorial combats.

tri-den-tate (trī-den′tāt), *a.* [L. *tri-*, three, + *dens* (*dent-*), tooth.] Having three teeth or tooth-like processes.

Tri-den-tine (trī-den′tin). [ML. *Tridentum*, Trent.] **I.** *a.* Pertaining to the city of Trent, in Tyrol, or to the ecumenical council of the Roman Catholic Church held there (1545-63); pertaining to the Council of Trent, or conforming to its decrees and doctrines. **II.** *n.* One who accepts and conforms to the decrees and doctrines of the Council of Trent; an orthodox Roman Catholic.

trid-u-um (trid′ū-um), *n.* [L., < *tri-*, three, + *dies*, day.] A period of three days; in the *Rom. Cath. Ch.*, a three days' period of prayer or devotion, usually preceding some feast.

Neptune with Trident.

tri-e-cious (trī-ē'shus), *a.* See *triæcious*.

tried (trīd), *p. a.* [See *try*.] Tested; proved; having sustained the tests of experience: as, "Jefferson Davis, a *tried* political leader" (Charnwood's "Abraham Lincoln," vii.); *tried* friends or friendship.

tri-en-ni-al (trī-en'i-al). [L. *triennis*, < *tri-*, three, + *annus*, year.] **I.** *a.* Lasting three years; also, occurring every three years. **II.** *n.* A period of three years; also, something that occurs every three years; also, a third anniversary.—**tri-en'ni-al-ly**, *adv.*—**tri-en'ni-um** (-um), *n.*; pl. *-niums* or *-nia* (-ä). [L.] A period of three years.

tri-er (trī'ėr), *n.* [See *try*.] One who or that which tries.

tri-er-arch (trī'ę-rärk), *n.* [L. *trierarchus*, < Gr. τριήραρχος, < τριήρης, trireme, + ἄρχειν, lead, rule.] In *Gr. antiq.*, the commander of a trireme; also, in Athens, a citizen who, singly, or jointly with other citizens, was required to fit out a trireme for the public service.—**tri-er-ar'chic** (-ę-rär'kik), *a.*—**tri'er-ar-chy** (-ki), *n.*; pl. *-chies* (-kiz). [Gr. τριηραρχία.] In *Gr. antiq.*, the office of a trierarch; also, in Athens, the duty of fitting out or furnishing triremes for the public service; also, trierarchs collectively.

tri-e-ter-ic (trī-e-ter'ik). [L. *trietericus*, < Gr. τριετηρικός, < τριετηρίς, period of three years, < τρι-, three, + ἔτος, year.] In *Gr. antiq.*: **I.** *a.* Occurring or held every third year, that is, in the ancient reckoning, every alternate year, as certain festivals. **II.** *n.* A trieteric festival.

tri-fa-cial (trī-fā'shal). [See *tri-*.] In *anat.*: **I.** *a.* Noting or pertaining to either of a pair of double-rooted cranial nerves, each dividing into three main branches to supply the face, etc. **II.** *n.* A trifacial nerve.

tri-fa-ri-ous (trī-fā'ri-us), *a.* [L. *trifarius*: see *tri-* and *-farious*.] Threefold; triple; in three rows.

tri-fid (trī'fid), *a.* [L. *trifidus*: see *tri-* and *-fid*.] Cleft into three parts or lobes.

tri-fi-lar (trī-fī'lär), *a.* [L. *tri-*, three, + *filum*, thread.] Consisting of or furnished with three filaments or threads.

tri-fle (trī'fl), *n.* [OF. *trufle*, *truffle*, for *trufe*, mockery, deception; origin uncertain.] A false or idle tale†; a lying story†; a jest†; also, a matter of slight importance, or a trivial or insignificant affair or circumstance (as, "Some *trifle* took them into the flower-garden," H. Kingsley's "Geoffry Hamlyn," iii.; "They permitted *trifles* to annoy them," Arnold Bennett's "Riceyman Steps," i. 11); also, an article or thing of small value (as, "offering his petty *trifles* of merchandise": Hawthorne's "Blithedale Romance," xxi.); a toy, trinket, or knickknack; also, a literary work, musical composition, or the like of light or trivial character; also, a small, inconsiderable, or trifling sum of money (as, "The thieves are willing to dispose of it [tea] for a *trifle*": Borrow's "Bible in Spain," v.); a small quantity or amount of anything; a little (in the phrase 'a trifle,' used adverbially: as, "Yet am I tremulous and a *trifle* sick," Henley's "In Hospital," iv.); also, a dish consisting of whipped cream or some substitute, as beaten whites of eggs, and usually containing cake soaked in wine or liqueur, and jam, fruit, or the like; also, a kind of pewter of medium hardness; *pl.*, articles made of this.—**tri'fle**, *v.*; *-fled*, *-fling*. [OF. *truffler*, for *trufer*.] **I.** *intr.* To say what is untrue†; jest†; also, to deal lightly or without due seriousness or respect (*with*: as, he was in no mood to be *trifled* with; "I should *trifle* with my conscience if I pretended . . . ," Stevenson's "David Balfour," xiv.); amuse one's self or play (*with*) for mere diversion or in idle dalliance (as, "He's been *trifling* with you, and making a plaything of you": George Eliot's "Adam Bede," xxx.); play or toy (*with*) by handling or fingering (as, "She . . . sat *trifling* with a pen": Gissing's "New Grub Street," vii.); also, to act or talk in an idle or frivolous way; pass time idly or frivolously; waste time; idle. **II.** *tr.* To mock† or befool†; also, to utter lightly or idly (as, "She used him for her sport . . . to *trifle* a leisure sentence or two with": Lamb's "On Some of the Old Actors"); also, to pass (time, etc.) idly or frivolously (now usually with *away*); also, to make a trifle of†, or render trivial† (rare: as, "This sore night Hath *trifled* former knowings," Shakspere's "Macbeth," ii. 4. 4).—**tri'fler**, *n.*—**tri'fling**, *p. a.* That trifles; acting idly or frivolously; frivolous, shallow, or light (as, "'Rasselas' looked dull to my *trifling* taste": C. Brontë's "Jane Eyre," v.); also, of slight importance, trivial, or insignificant (as, a *trifling* matter; *trifling* discomforts; a few *trifling* changes); of small value, cost, or amount (as, a few *trifling* gifts or purchases; a *trifling* sum); inconsiderable; small; paltry; also, mean, worthless, or good-for-nothing (local, U. S.).—**tri'fling-ly**, *adv.*—**tri'fling-ness**, *n.*

tri-fold (trī'fōld), *a.* [See *tri-*.] Threefold; triple.

tri-fo-li-ate (trī-fō'li-āt), *a.* [L. *tri-*, three, + *folium*, leaf.] Having three leaves, leaf-like parts or lobes, or foils; in *bot.*, having three leaves or (commonly) leaflets; trifoliolate. Also **tri-fo'li-at-ed** (-ā-ted).—**tri-fo'li-o-late** (-ō-lāt), *a.* In *bot.*, having three leaflets, as a compound leaf; having leaves with three leaflets, as a plant.

tri-fo-ri-um (trī-fō'ri-um), *n.*; pl. *-ria* (-ri-ä). [AL.; origin uncertain.] In *arch.*, a gallery or arcade between the vaulting or ceiling and the roof of an aisle of a church, at the side of the nave, the choir, or a transept.

Triforium, 13th century, at St. Leu d'Esserent, France.

tri-form (trī'fôrm), *a.* [L. *triformis*, < *tri-*, three, + *forma*, form.] Existing or appearing in three different forms; also, combining three different forms; also, formed of three parts, or in three divisions. Also **tri'formed**.

tri-fur-cate (trī-fėr'kāt), *v. t.* or *i.*; *-cated*, *-cating*. [L. *trifurcus*, three-forked, < *tri-*, three, + *furca*, fork.] To divide into three forks or branches.—**tri-fur'cate**, **tri-fur'cat-ed** (-kā-ted), *a.* Divided into three forks or branches.—**tri-fur-ca'tion** (-kā'shon), *n.*

trig¹ (trig), *a.* [From Scand.: cf. Icel. *tryggr*, trusty, faithful, true, and E. *true*.] True, faithful, or trustworthy (now north. Eng.); also, in good physical condition; sound; well; also, alert, brisk, or nimble (chiefly Sc.); also, neat, trim, smart, or spruce (as, "a *trig* and orderly appearance [of fields]," Galt's "Annals of the Parish," vi.; "Everything was trim and *trig* and bright along the 'coast,'" Mark Twain's "Life on the Mississippi," xl.; "the *trig* corporal, with the little visorless cap worn so jauntily," Howells's "Chance Acquaintance," iv.).—**trig¹**, *v. t.*; *trigged*, *trigging*. To make trig, trim, or smart (as, "He has rigged and *trigged* her with paint and spar": Kipling's "Rhyme of the Three Sealers"); deck or trick (*out*). [Chiefly prov.]

trig² (trig), *v.*; *trigged*, *trigging*. [Origin uncertain.] **I.** *tr.* To stop or prevent the moving of (wheels, etc.), esp. by means of a wedge, block, or other obstacle set beneath; also, to support or prop, as with a wedge. **II.** *intr.* To act as a check on the moving of wheels, vehicles, etc.—**trig²**, *n.* A wedge or block used to prevent a wheel, cask, or the like from rolling; a brake for a wheel; any material placed on a slippery declivity on a road to check the motion of a sled passing over it.

trig-a-mous (trig'a-mus), *a.* [Gr. τρίγαμος, thrice married, < τρι-, three, + γάμος, marriage.] Having three wives or husbands at the same time; guilty of or involving trigamy; in *bot.*, having male, female, and hermaphrodite flowers in the same head.—**trig'a-my**, *n.* [LL. *trigamia*, < Gr. τριγαμία.] The state or offense of having three wives or husbands at the same time.

tri-gas-tric (trī-gas'trik), *a.* [Gr. τρι-, three, + γαστήρ, belly.] In *anat.*, having three fleshy bellies, as certain muscles.

tri-gem-i-nal (trī-jem'i-nal). [L. *trigeminus*, born three at a birth, < *tri-*, three, + *geminus*, twin.] In *anat.*: **I.** *a.*

Same as *trifacial*, *a.* **II.** *n.* A trigeminal or trifacial nerve.

trig-ger (trig'ėr), *n.* [Earlier *tricker*, < D. *trekker*, trigger, < *trekken*, draw, pull: cf. *trek*.] A device, as a lever, the pulling or pressing of which releases a detent or spring; in firearms, a small projecting tongue which when pressed by the finger liberates the hammer of the lock; in crossbows, etc., a lever which when pressed liberates the string of the bow.

trig-ger=fish (trig'ėr-fish), *n.* Any of various moderately compressed, deep-bodied fishes of the genus *Balistes* and allied genera, chiefly of tropical seas, having an anterior dorsal fin with two or three stout spines, the first of which cannot be pressed down until the second is depressed.

Trigger-fish (*Balistes carolinensis*).

tri-glot (trī'glot). [Gr. τρι-, three, + γλῶττα, γλῶσσα, tongue.] **I.** *a.* Using or containing three languages; trilingual. **II.** *n.* A triglot book or edition.

trig-ly (trig'li), *adv.* In a trig manner; trimly.

tri-glyph (trī'glif), *n.* [L. *triglyphus*, < Gr. τρίγλυφος, < τρι-, three, + γλύφειν, carve.] In *arch.*, a structural member of a Doric frieze, separating two consecutive metopes, and consisting typically of a rectangular block with two vertical grooves or glyphs, and two chamfers or half-grooves at the sides, together counting as a third glyph. — **tri-glyph'ic**, *a.* Pertaining to or consisting of a triglyph or triglyphs; also, containing three sets of characters or sculptures.

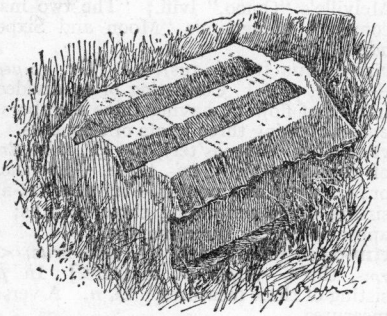
A Triglyph of the Parthenon, Athens, showing the groove in one side of the block into which the metope was slid.

trig-ness (trig'nes), *n.* Trig state or appearance.

tri-gon (trī'gon), *n.* [L. *trigonum*, < Gr. τρίγωνον, triangle, prop. neut. of τρίγωνος, triangular, < τρι-, three, + γωνία, angle.] A triangle; in *astrol.*, a set of three signs of the zodiac, in which the first point of each sign is distant 120° from the first point of each of the other signs, there being four trigons, the 'fiery trigon' (Aries, Leo, and Sagittarius), the 'earthy trigon' (Taurus, Virgo, and Capricornus), the 'airy trigon' (Gemini, Libra, and Aquarius), and the 'watery trigon' (Cancer, Scorpio, and Pisces); also, the aspect of two planets distant 120° from each other. — **trig-o-nal** (trig'ọ-nạl), *a.* Of, pertaining to, or having the form of a trigon; triangular.

trig-o-nom-e-ter[1] (trig-ọ-nom'e-tėr), *n.* [Gr. τρίγωνον, triangle: see -*meter*.] An instrument for solving plane right-angled triangles by inspection.

trig-o-nom-e-ter[2] (trig-ọ-nom'e-tėr), *n.* [From *trigonometry*, after *geometer*.] One skilled in trigonometry or in trigonometrical surveying.

trig-o-no-met-ric, trig-o-no-met-ri-cal (trig″ọ-nọ-met'rik, -ri-kạl), *a.* Of or pertaining to trigonometry; performed by or according to the rules of trigonometry. — **trig″o-no-met'ri-cal-ly**, *adv.*

trig-o-nom-e-try (trig-ọ-nom'e-tri), *n.* [NL. *trigonometria*, < Gr. τρίγωνον, triangle, + -μετρία, measurement: see -*metry*.] The branch of mathematics that deals with the relations between the sides and angles of triangles (plane or spherical), and the calculations, etc., based on these.

trig-o-nous (trig'ọ-nus), *a.* [L. *trigonus*, < Gr. τρίγωνος,

triangular: see *trigon*.] Having three angles or corners; triangular: specif. in *bot.*, of stems, seeds, etc.

tri-graph (trī'gráf), *n.* [Gr. τρι-, three, + γραφή, writing.] A group of three letters representing a single speech-sound, as *eau* in *beau*.

tri-he-dral (trī-hē'drạl), *a.* [Gr. τρι-, three, + ἕδρα, seat, base.] In *geom.*, having, or formed by, three planes meeting in a point (as, a *trihedral* angle), or three lateral planes (as, a *trihedral* prism, which is triangular in section). — **tri-he'dron** (-drọn), *n.*; pl. -*drons* or -*dra* (-drä). In *geom.*, the figure determined by three planes meeting in a point.

tri-ju-gate (trī'jọ-gāt), *a.* [L. *tri-*, three, + *jugum*, yoke.] In *bot.*, having three pairs of leaflets. Also **tri'ju-gous**.

tri-lat-er-al (trī-lat'e-rạl), *a.* [L. *trilaterus*, < *tri-*, three, + *latus* (*later-*), side.] Having three sides. — **tri-lat'er-al-ly**, *adv.*

tri-lem-ma (trī-lem'ä), *n.* [From *tri-* + -*lemma* as in *dilemma*.] A form of argument resembling the dilemma, but involving three alternatives instead of two; hence, a situation requiring a choice of some one out of three alternatives.

tri-lin-e-ar (trī-lin'ē-ạr), *a.* [L. *tri-*, three, + *linea*, line.] Of, pertaining to, or involving three lines.

tri-lin-gual (trī-ling'gwạl), *a.* [L. *trilinguis*, < *tri-*, three, + *lingua*, tongue.] Using or involving three languages.

tri-lit-er-al (trī-lit'e-rạl). [L. *tri-*, three, + *litera*, letter.] **I.** *a.* Consisting of three letters, as a word; specif., consisting of three consonants, as most Semitic roots (cf. *quadriliteral*). **II.** *n.* A triliteral word or root. — **tri-lit'er-al-ism**, *n.* The use of triliteral roots, as in the Semitic languages.

tri-lith (trī'lith), *n.* [Gr. τρίλιθον, neut. of τρίλιθος, of three stones, < τρι-, three, + λίθος, stone.] A prehistoric structure or monument consisting of two large upright stones with another stone resting upon them like a lintel. — **tri-lith'ic**, *a.* Pertaining to or of the nature of a trilith. — **tri'li-thon** (-li-thon), *n.* A trilith.

Triliths. — Stonehenge, England.

trill[1] (tril), *v.* [ME. *trillen*, turn, roll: cf. Sw. *trilla*, Dan. *trille*, *trilde*, roll.] **I.** *tr.* To turn round rapidly; twirl or whirl; also, to roll or bowl; also, to cause to roll down or flow. [Archaic or prov.] **II.** *intr.* To roll; also, to trickle or flow, as water (as, "a little dell, through which *trilled* a small rivulet": Scott's "Guy Mannering," xxii.). [Archaic.]

trill[2] (tril), *v.* [It. *trillare*; perhaps imit.] **I.** *intr.* To sing with a vibratory effect of voice, esp. by a rapid alternation of two consecutive tones, as a person; execute a shake or trill, with the voice or on a musical instrument; hence, to utter, give forth, or make a sound or a succession of sounds more or less resembling such singing, as a bird, a frog, a grasshopper, a person laughing, etc. (as, "The birds were twittering and *trilling* in the tall leafy boughs," George Eliot's "Adam Bede," iv.; "The child burst in, *trilling* with laughter," Kipling's "Kim," ix.); resound vibrantly, or with a rapid succession of sounds, as the voice, song, laughter, etc. **II.** *tr.* To sing with a vibratory effect of voice, esp. in the manner of a shake or trill, or play with like effect on an instrument (as, to *trill* a note); hence, of birds, etc., to sing or give forth in a succession of rapidly alternating or changing sounds (as, "The night-sparrow *trills* her song": Bryant's "Hunter's Serenade"); also, to pronounce with a quick vibration of the tongue or other vocal organ, as the consonant *r*. — **trill**[2], *n.* The act or sound of trilling; a trilled sound, or a rapid alternation of two consecutive tones, in singing or in instrumental music; a shake; hence, a similar sound, or succession of sounds, uttered or made by a bird, an insect, a person laughing, etc. (as, "the faint melancholy *trill* of one small night-singing cicada," W. H. Hudson's "Purple Land," xxiii.; a *trill* of laughter); in *phonetics*, the pronunciation of a consonant, as *r*, with a vibratory sound; a consonant so pronounced.

tril-lion (tril′yọn), *n.* [F. *trillion*, < L. *tri-*, three, + F. (*m*)*illion*, million.] In Great Britain, the third power of a million, represented by 1 followed by 18 ciphers; in France and the U. S., a thousand billions, represented by 1 followed by 12 ciphers. — **tril′lionth**, *a.* and *n.*

tril-li-um (tril′i-um), *n.* [NL., < L. *tri-*, three.] Any of the herbs constituting the convallariaceous genus *Trillium*, characterized by a whorl of three leaves from the center of which rises a solitary flower. See cut at *sessile*.

tri-lo-bate (trī-lō′bāt), *a.* [See *tri-*.] Having three lobes. Also **tri′lobed** (-lōbd).

tri-lo-bite (trī′lọ-bīt), *n.* [NL. *Trilobita*, pl., < Gr. τρι-, three, + λοβός, lobe: with reference to the three lobes or divisions into which the body is divided by longitudinal dorsal furrows.] Any of the *Trilobita*, a group of extinct arthropods variously classed with the crusta-

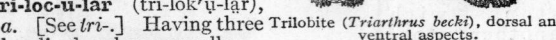

Trilobate Leaf.

ceans or the arachnidans or as intermediate between these, with a flattened oval body varying in length from an inch or less to two feet: their remains being found widely distributed in strata of the Paleozoic era, and important as being among the earliest known fossils. — **tri-lo-bit′ic** (-bit′ik), *a.*

tri-loc-u-lar (trī-lok′ū-lạr), *a.* [See *tri-*.] Having three loculi, chambers, or cells.

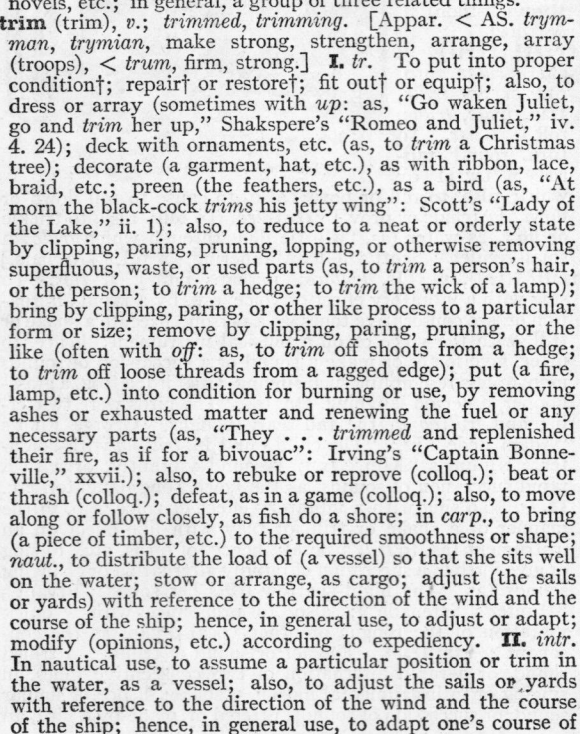

Trilobite (*Triarthrus becki*), dorsal and ventral aspects.

tril-o-gy (tril′ọ-ji), *n.*; pl. *-gies* (-jiz). [Gr. τριλογία, < τρι-, three, + λόγος, speech, discourse, story.] A series of three complete and usually related tragedies performed in ancient Athens at the festival of Dionysus (cf. *tetralogy*); hence, any series or group of three related dramas, operas, novels, etc.; in general, a group of three related things.

trim (trim), *v.*; *trimmed*, *trimming*. [Appar. < AS. *tryman*, *trymian*, make strong, strengthen, arrange, array (troops), < *trum*, firm, strong.] **I.** *tr.* To put into proper condition†; repair† or restore†; fit out† or equip†; also, to dress or array (sometimes with *up*: as, "Go waken Juliet, go and *trim* her up," Shakspere's "Romeo and Juliet," iv. 4. 24); deck with ornaments, etc. (as, to *trim* a Christmas tree); decorate (a garment, hat, etc.), as with ribbon, lace, braid, etc.; preen (the feathers, etc.), as a bird (as, "At morn the black-cock *trims* his jetty wing": Scott's "Lady of the Lake," ii. 1); also, to reduce to a neat or orderly state by clipping, paring, pruning, lopping, or otherwise removing superfluous, waste, or used parts (as, to *trim* a person's hair, or the person; to *trim* a hedge; to *trim* the wick of a lamp); bring by clipping, paring, or other like process to a particular form or size; remove by clipping, paring, pruning, or the like (often with *off*: as, to *trim* off shoots from a hedge; to *trim* off loose threads from a ragged edge); put (a fire, lamp, etc.) into condition for burning or use, by removing ashes or exhausted matter and renewing the fuel or any necessary parts (as, "They . . . *trimmed* and replenished their fire, as if for a bivouac": Irving's "Captain Bonneville," xxvii.); also, to rebuke or reprove (colloq.); beat or thrash (colloq.); defeat, as in a game (colloq.); also, to move along or follow closely, as fish do a shore; in *carp.*, to bring (a piece of timber, etc.) to the required smoothness or shape; *naut.*, to distribute the load of (a vessel) so that she sits well on the water; stow or arrange, as cargo; adjust (the sails or yards) with reference to the direction of the wind and the course of the ship; hence, in general use, to adjust or adapt; modify (opinions, etc.) according to expediency. **II.** *intr.* In nautical use, to assume a particular position or trim in the water, as a vessel; also, to adjust the sails or yards with reference to the direction of the wind and the course of the ship; hence, in general use, to adapt one's course of

action in order to get on under conflicting conditions or to stand well with both or all parties; pursue a neutral, cautious, or time-serving course or policy between parties (as, "He [Pompey] had *trimmed* between the two factions, and was distrusted and hated by them both": Froude's "Cæsar," viii.); follow a middle course (as, "Everything good, he [Lord Halifax] said, *trims* between extremes": Macaulay's "Hist. of Eng." ii.). — **trim**, *n.* Proper condition or order (as, to find everything in *trim*, or out of *trim*; to get into *trim* for a contest); condition or order of any kind (as, the house was in poor *trim*); nature or character; disposition or humor; also, dress, array, or equipment (as, in one's Sunday *trim*); hence, appearance or guise; also, decorative trimming, or a style of trimming, as on dress (as, a military *trim*); also, a trimming by cutting, clipping, or the like (as, "He went to the Pompeian for his fortnightly hair-*trim*": Sinclair Lewis's "Babbitt," xxiv.); in *carp.*, the visible woodwork of the interior of a building; *naut.*, the set of a ship in the water, esp. the most advantageous one; the condition of a ship when properly balanced; the difference between the draft at the bow of a vessel and that at the stern; the adjustment of the sails, etc., with reference to the direction of the wind and the course of the ship; the condition of a ship with reference to her fitness for sailing. — **trim**, *a.*; compar. *trimmer*, superl. *trimmest*. In good condition or order; properly prepared or equipped; hence, good, excellent, or fine (obs. or archaic: as, "*trim* sport," Shakspere's "Titus Andronicus," v. 1. 96); now, esp., pleasingly neat or smart in appearance, or as the appearance, dress, etc. (as, *trim* lawns; *trim* villages; "A *trim* little sail-boat was dancing out at her moorings," H. Melville's "Omoo," lviii.; "The two maids were *trim* and comely," Maugham's "Moon and Sixpence," v.). — **trim**, *adv.* Trimly.

trim-er-ous (trim′ẹ-rus), *a.* [Gr. τριμερής, < τρι-, three, + μέρος, part.] Consisting of or divided into three parts; in *bot.*, of flowers, having three members in each whorl; in *entom.*, having three joints or segments.

tri-mes-ter (trī-mes′tẹr), *n.* [F. *trimestre*, < L. *trimestris*, of three months, < *tri-*, three, + *mensis*, month.] A term or period of three months. — **tri-mes′tri-al** (-tri-ạl), *a.* Consisting of or containing three months; also, occurring or appearing every three months.

trim-e-ter (trim′e-tẹr), *n.* [L. *trimetrus*, < Gr. τρίμετρος, < τρι-, three, + μέτρον, measure.] In *pros.*: **I.** *a.* Consisting of three measures. **II.** *n.* A verse or period of three measures.

tri-met-ric (trī-met′rik), *a.* [Gr. τρι-, three, + μέτρον, measure.] In *crystal.*, orthorhombic.

trim-ly (trim′li), *adv.* In a trim manner; neatly; smartly.

trim-mer (trim′ẹr), *n.* One who or that which trims (in any sense); a tool or machine for trimming or clipping, paring, or pruning; a machine for trimming lumber; an apparatus for stowing, arranging, or shifting cargo, coal, or the like; specif., a person who trims in his course of action, as in politics; one who pursues a cautious policy between parties, accommodating himself to one side or another as expediency may dictate; a time-server; in *building*, a timber or beam into which one of the ends of a header is fitted in the framing about an opening, a chimney, etc.

trim-ming (trim′ing), *n.* The act of one who or that which trims; a rebuking or reproving, a beating or thrashing, or a defeat (colloq.); also, anything used or serving to trim or decorate (as, the *trimmings* of a Christmas tree; *trimming* or *trimmings* for dresses, hats, etc.; upholstery *trimmings*); a decorative fitting or finish; a garnish; *pl.*, agreeable accompaniments or additions to plain or simple dishes or food (colloq.: as, a leg of mutton and *trimmings*; "We'd ought to have more *trimmings*, though [at a barbecue]. We're shy on ducks," Wister's "Virginian," x.); also, *pl.*, pieces cut off in trimming, clipping, paring, or pruning.

trim-ness (trim′nes), *n.* Trim state or appearance.

tri-morph (trī′môrf), *n.* [Gr. τρίμορφος, having three forms, < τρι-, three, + μορφή, form.] In *crystal.*, a substance existing in three distinct forms; a trimorphous substance; also, any one of the three forms. — **tri-mor′phic** (-môr′fik), *a.* Trimorphous. — **tri-mor′phism**, *n.* Trimorphous property or condition; in *crystal.*, the property of some substances of crystallizing in three distinct forms;

---

in *bot.*, the occurrence of three different forms of flowers, leaves, etc., on the same plant or on distinct plants of the same species; in *zoöl.*, the occurrence of three forms distinct in structure, coloration, etc., among animals of the same species.—**tri-mor′-phous**, *a.* [Gr. τρίμορφος.] Existing in or assuming three distinct forms; exhibiting trimorphism.

Tri-mur-ti (tri-mör′ti), *n.* [Skt. *trimūrti*, < *tri*, three, + *mūrti*, shape.] The Hindu triad or trinity, Brahma, Vishnu, and Siva (regarded respectively as the creative, the preserving, and the destroying principle), viewed as an inseparable unity, and represented symbolically as one body with three heads.

Trimorphism in Flowers of Purple Loosestrife (*Lythrum salicaria*).—*a*, the long-styled form; *b*, the intermediate form; *c*, the short-styled form; *s*, style. The calyx and corolla have been removed.

Trimurti.

Tri-na-cri-an (tri-nā′kri-an), *a.* [L. *Trinacria*, < Gr. Τρινακρία, Sicily, orig. Θρινακίη, < θρῖναξ (θρινακ-), trident.] Of or pertaining to Trinacria or Sicily; Sicilian. [Poetic or literary.]

tri-nal (trī′nal), *a.* [LL. *trinalis*, < L. *trinus*: see *trine*.] Threefold; triple; trine.

trin-dle (trin′dl), *n.* [ME. *trindel*, *trendel*, < AS. *trendel*, ring, circle, disk, akin to *trendan*, turn, roll: see *trend*, and cf. *trundle*.] A wheel, esp. of a wheelbarrow; a trundle. [Now prov.]—**trin′dle**, *v.*; -dled, -dling. **I.** *tr.* To roll along; trundle. [Now prov.] **II.** *intr.* To roll. [Now prov.]

trine (trīn), *a.* [L. *trinus*, threefold, pl. *trini*, three each, < *tres* (*tri*-), three.] **I.** *a.* Threefold; triple; in *astrol.*, noting or pertaining to the (favorable) aspect of two planets distant from each other 120°, or the third part of the zodiac. **II.** *n.* A set or group of three; a triad; [*cap.*] the Trinity; [*l. c.*] in *astrol.*, the trine aspect of two planets.

trin-gle (tring′gl), *n.* [F.; origin uncertain.] A curtain-rod; any long, slender rod; in *arch.*, a narrow, straight molding.

Trin-i-ta-ri-an (trin-i-tā′ri-an). [NL. *trinitarius*, < LL. *trinitas*, E. *trinity*.] **I.** *a.* Of or pertaining to the Trinity; believing in the doctrine of the Trinity; pertaining to Trinitarians, or believers in the doctrine of the Trinity; also, belonging or pertaining to the religious order of Trinitarians; also [*l. c.*], forming a trinity; threefold; triple. **II.** *n.* [*cap.*] One who believes in the doctrine of the Trinity; also, a member of a religious order (Order of the Holy Trinity) founded in 1198 to redeem Christian captives from Mohammedans.—**Trin-i-ta′ri-an-ism**, *n.*

tri-ni-tro-tol-u-ene (trī-nī-trō-tol′ū-ēn), *n.* [From *tri-* + *nitro-* + *toluene*.] A high explosive (a nitro derivative of toluene) used in modern warfare, etc.: unaffected by ordinary friction or shock. Abbreviated *TNT* and *T. N. T.*—**tri-ni-tro-tol′u-ol** (-ol or -ōl), *n.* Trinitrotoluene.

trin-i-ty (trin′i-ti), *n.*; pl. -ties (-tiz). [OF. *trinite* (F. *trinité*), < LL. *trinitas*, < L. *trinus*, threefold: see *trine*.] The state of being threefold or triple; threeness; also, a group of three; a triad; [*cap.*] the union of three persons (Father, Son, and Holy Ghost) in one Godhead, or the threefold personality of the one Divine Being (often called 'the Holy Trinity' or 'the Blessed Trinity'); also, Trinity Sunday (as, the second Sunday after *Trinity*).—**Trinity Sunday,** the Sunday next after Pentecost or Whitsunday, observed as a festival in honor of the Trinity.

Trinity, late 13th century.— Church of St. Urbain, Troyes, France.

trin-ket (tring′ket), *n.* [Origin uncertain.] Any small article forming part of an outfit† (esp. in *pl.*); an implement† or tool†; also, any small fancy article, bit of jewelry, or

the like (as, "A soldier purloined some *trinkets* of gold from the treasure," Prescott's "Conquest of Mexico," iv. 4; "A cross is the last thing I would wear as a *trinket*," George Eliot's "Middlemarch," i.); also, anything considered trivial or vain†.—**trin′ket-ry** (-ri), *n.* Trinkets collectively: as, "a young Blackfoot beauty, arrayed in the trappings and *trinketry* of a free trapper's bride" (Irving's "Captain Bonneville," xlviii.).

tri-no-dal (trī-nō′dal), *a.* [L. *trinodis*, having three knots, < *tri-*, three, + *nodus*, knot, E. *node*.] In *bot.*, etc., having three nodes or joints.

tri-no-mi-al (trī-nō′mi-al). [From *tri-* + -*nomial* as in *binomial*.] **I.** *a.* In *alg.*, consisting of or pertaining to three terms connected by the sign +, the sign −, or both of these; in *zoöl.* and *bot.*, noting a name comprising three terms (as of genus, species, and subspecies or variety), or characterized by the use of such names. **II.** *n.* In *alg.*, a trinomial expression (as $a + b - c$); in *zoöl.* and *bot.*, a trinomial name (as, *Cannabis sativa indica*, Indian hemp).— **tri-no′mi-al-ism**, *n.* In *zoöl.* and *bot.*, the trinomial system of nomenclature; the use of trinomial names.— **tri-no′mi-al-ly**, *adv.*

tri-o (trē′ō or trī′ō), *n.*; pl. -os (-ōz). [F., < It. *trio*, < L. *tres* (*tri*-), three.] A musical composition for three voices or instruments; also, a subordinate division of a minuet, scherzo, march, etc., usually in a contrasted key and style (perhaps orig. written for three instruments or in three parts); also, a company of three singers or players; also, any group of three persons or things (as, "bicycles gliding by in pairs and *trios*": Tarkington's "Magnificent Ambersons," xviii.).

tri-ode (trī′ōd), *n.* [See *tri-* and *electrode*.] In *wireless teleg.* and *teleph.*, a three-electrode vacuum-tube.

tri-œ-cious, tri-e-cious (trī-ē′shus), *a.* [Gr. τρι-, three, + οἶκος, house.] In *bot.*, having male, female, and hermaphrodite flowers on different plants.

tri-o-let (trī′ọ-let or trē′-), *n.* [F.: cf. *trio*.] A short poem of fixed form, consisting of eight lines on two rimes, the first, third, fourth, fifth, and seventh lines on one, and the rest on the other, and having the first line repeated as the fourth and seventh, and the second as the eighth.

tri-o-nal (trī′ọ-nal), *n.* [From *tri-* + (*sulph*)*onal*; from its containing three ethyl groups.] In *phar.*, a hypnotic resembling sulphonal, but acting more rapidly, and less likely to cause chronic poisoning.

tri-ose (trī′ōs), *n.* [See *tri-* and -*ose*².] In *chem.*, any of a class of sugars containing three atoms of carbon, and produced from glycerin by oxidation.

tri-ox-ide (trī-ok′sīd or -sid), *n.* [See *tri-*.] In *chem.*, an oxide containing three oxygen atoms.

trip (trip), *v.*; tripped, tripping. [OF. *tripper*, *triper*, *treper*, strike the ground, etc., with the foot, skip, dance; from Teut., and akin to D. *trippen*, *trippelen*, G. *trippeln*, trip.] **I.** *intr.* To step lightly or nimbly, skip, or dance (as, "On the tawny sands . . . *Trip* the pert faeries and the dapper elves": Milton's "Comus," 118); go with a light, quick tread (as, "He *tripped* down the gangway like a boy": Arnold Bennett's "Lion's Share," xxx.); also, to make a journey, excursion, or trip (Eng.: as, "This tripper was more moved by the prospect than if he had *tripped* for 'a week in Gay Ostend,'" L. Merrick's "Position of Peggy Harper," ii. 5); also, to strike the foot against something, or have the foot suddenly impeded or caught, so as to stagger or fall (as, to *trip* over a rope; "Old Lord Rolle *tripped* up in his mantle and fell down the steps," Lytton Strachey's "Queen Victoria," iii.); stumble; fig., to make a slip or mistake, as in a statement; make a wrong step in conduct (as, "ill-wishers . . . who might be glad to catch them *tripping*, and make a case against them at Rome": J. H. Newman's "Callista," xiii.); commit a fault or moral error; also, to tip or tilt. **II.** *tr.* To perform with a light or tripping step, as a dance; dance upon (ground, etc.); also, to cause to trip, stumble, or fall by suddenly impeding or catching the foot (as, "Then *trip* him, that his heels may kick at heaven," Shakspere's "Hamlet," iii. 3. 93: often with *up*); cause to lose the footing, or upset; fig., to overthrow, or bring to confusion (as, "The common arts of attack would have *tripped* him with a quick-witted woman": G. Meredith's "Diana of the Crossways," xxv.); cause to make a slip or error (as, to *trip*, or *trip* up, a witness by artful questions); catch in a slip or error (as, "What she confess'd I will report . . . these her women Can *trip* me, if I err": Shakspere's "Cymbeline," v. 5. 35); also, to tip or tilt; *naut.*, to lift (an anchor) clear of the bottom; lift (an upper mast) before lowering; also, to tip or turn (a yard) from a horizontal to a vertical position; in *mach.*, to release or operate suddenly (a catch, clutch, etc.); operate, start, or set free (a mechanism, weight, etc.) by suddenly releasing a catch, clutch, or the like.—**trip,** *n.* The act of tripping or stepping lightly; a light or nimble movement of the feet; a light, quick tread; also, a journey or voyage (as, "He spoke . . . of a *trip* to India": Stevenson's "Master of Ballantrae," iv.); a journey, voyage, or run made by a boat, train, or the like between two points, or from one point to another and back again ('round trip'); often, a journey, jaunt, or excursion for pleasure or health; also, a tripping, stumbling, or loss of footing suffered (as, to make a *trip* over a footstool in the dark); a sudden impeding or catching of a person's foot so as to throw him down (specif. in wrestling); fig., a slip, mistake, or blunder; a wrong step in conduct (as, "I must now represent him [Cranmer, in recanting] making a great *trip* and a sad fall": Strype's "Memorials of Cranmer," iii. 21); in *mach.*, a projecting part, catch, or the like for starting or checking some movement.

tri-part-ed (trī'pär-ted), *a.* [See *tri-*.] Divided into three parts.

tri-par-tite (trī-pär'tīt), *a.* [L. *tripartitus*, < *tri-*, three, + *partitus*, pp. of *partire*, divide.] Divided into or consisting of three parts; also, being in three corresponding parts or copies, as a contract; also, participated in by three parties, as a treaty; in *bot.*, divided into three parts by incisions which extend nearly to the base, as a leaf.—**tri-par'tite-ly,** *adv.*—**tri-par-ti'tion** (-tish'ọn), *n.* [LL. *tripartitio(n-).*] Division into three parts.

tripe (trīp), *n.* [OF. F. *tripe*; origin uncertain.] The first and second divisions of the stomach of a ruminant, esp. of the ox kind, prepared for use as food; also, the intestines or bowels, or the paunch or belly (usually in *pl.*: now low); also, anything poor or worthless (slang).

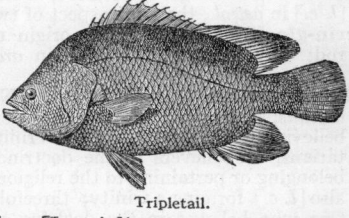 *Tripartite Leaf.*

trip-e-dal (trip'ē-dạl or trī'ped-ạl), *a.* [L. *tripedalis*, < *tri-*, three, + *pes* (*ped-*), foot.] Having three feet.

tripe=de=roche (trēp-dē-rosh'), *n.* [F., 'tripe of rock.'] Any of various edible lichens of arctic and subarctic regions, species of the genera *Gyrophora* and *Umbilicaria*.

tri-per-son-al (trī-pėr'sọn-ạl), *a.* [See *tri-*.] Consisting of or existing in three persons, as the Godhead.

tri-pet-a-lous (trī-pet'ạ-lus), *a.* [See *tri-*.] In *bot.*, having three petals.

trip=ham-mer (trip'ham″ėr), *n.* In *mach.*, a heavy hammer raised and then let fall by means of some tripping device, as a cam.

triph-thong (trif'thông), *n.* [Gr. τρι-, three, + φθόγγος, sound.] A union of three vowel sounds pronounced in one syllable; less properly, a trigraph.—**triph-thon'gal** (-thông'gạl), *a.*

triph-y-line (trif'i-lin), *n.* Same as *triphylite*.

triph-y-lite (trif'i-līt), *n.* [Gr. τρι-, three, + φυλή, tribe; from the three metallic bases.] A mineral, a phosphate of lithium, iron, and manganese, usually occurring in masses of a bluish or greenish color.

tri-phyl-lous (trī-fil'us), *a.* [Gr. τρίφυλλος, < τρι-, three, + φύλλον, leaf.] In *bot.*, having three leaves.

tri-pin-nate (trī-pin'āt), *a.* [See *tri-*.] In *bot.*, bipinnate, as a leaf, with the divisions also pinnate.—**tri-pin-nat'i-fid** (-pi-nat'i-fid), *a.* In *bot.*, bipinnatifid, as a leaf, with the divisions also pinnatifid.

tri-plane (trī'plān), *n.* [See *tri-*.] An aëroplane with three supporting planes, one above another.

trip-le (trip'l), *a.* [F. *triple*, < L. *triplus*, < *tri-*, three, + *-plus*: see *double*.] Threefold; consisting of three parts (as, a *triple* knot; a *triple* window, see cut in next column); of three kinds; three times as great; also, being one of three†; third†.—**triple alliance,** any of various alliances between three nations or powers; esp. [*caps.*], the alliance between Germany, Austria-Hungary, and Italy 1882-1915 (see *dreibund*).—**Triple Entente,** an under-

standing or informal alliance entered into 1904-07 by Great Britain, France, and Russia, as a counterbalance to the Dreibund, and terminating when the Bolsheviki came into control in Russia in 1917. Cf. *Dual Alliance.*—**triple time** or **rhythm,** in *music*, time or rhythm characterized by three beats to the measure.—**triple tree,** the gallows: with allusion to the two posts and cross-beam of which it is often composed. [Archaic.]—**trip'le,** *n.* Something triple or threefold; a triad; an amount, number, etc., three times as great as another.—**trip'le,** *v. t.* or *i.*; *-led, -ling.* To make or become triple; treble. —**trip'le=ex-pan'sion,** *a.* Noting or pertaining to a steam-engine in which the steam is expanded in three cylinders in succession, the exhaust steam from the first cylinder being the driving steam for the second, and so on.

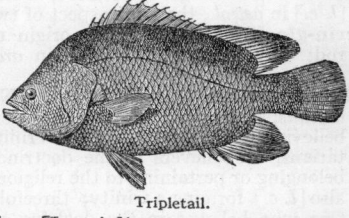 Triple Window. — Lincoln Cathedral, England.

trip-let (trip'let), *n.* [From *triple*.] Any group or combination of three; also, one of three children born at a birth; in *poetry*, three successive verses or lines, esp. when riming and of the same length; in *music*, a group of three notes to be performed in the time of two ordinary notes of the same kind.

trip-le-tail (trip'l-tāl), *n.* A large food-fish, *Lobotes surinamensis*, of warm seas, whose dorsal and anal fins extend backward so that with the caudal fin it appears to have a three-lobed tail.

tri-plex (trī'pleks). [L. *triplex*, < *tri-*, three, + *-plex*: see *duplex*.] **I.** *a.* Threefold; triple. **II.** *n.* Something triple.

Tripletail.

trip-li-cate (trip'li-kāt), *v. t.*; *-cated, -cating.* [L. *triplicatus*, pp. of *triplicare*, < *triplex*: see *triplex*.] To make threefold; triple; make or produce a third time or in a third instance.—**trip'li-cate** (-kạt). **I.** *a.* Threefold; triple; tripartite. **II.** *n.* One of three things, esp. three copies of a document, exactly alike.—**in triplicate,** in three copies, exactly alike.—**trip-li-ca'tion** (-kā'shọn), *n.* [LL. *triplicatio(n-).*] The act of triplicating, or the state of being triplicated; also, something triplicated or threefold.

tri-plic-i-ty (trī-plis'i-ti or tri-), *n.*; pl. *-ties* (-tiz). [ML. *triplicitas*, < L. *triplex*: see *triplex*.] The state of being triple; triple character; also, a group or combination of three; a triad; in *astrol.*, a trigon, or set of three signs of the zodiac (see *trigon*).

trip-lite (trip'līt), *n.* [G. *triplit*, < Gr. τριπλόος, threefold; from its three cleavages.] A mineral, essentially a phosphate of iron and manganese containing fluorine, occurring in dark-brown or blackish masses.

trip-ly (trip'li), *adv.* In a triple manner, measure, or degree.

tri-pod (trī'pod), *n.* [L. *tripus* (*tripod-*), < Gr. τρίπους (τριποδ-), tripod, orig. adj., three-footed, < τρι-, three, + πούς (ποδ-), foot.] A vessel, as a pot, caldron, or vase, with three feet or legs; also, a stool or the like with three legs; a three-legged frame or stand of any kind, as one for supporting a camera; specif., in *Gr. antiq.*, the three-legged seat from which the priestess of Apollo at Delphi delivered the oracles (see *Pythia*) (see cut on following page).—**trip-o-dal** (trip'ọ-dạl), *a.* Pertaining to or having the form of a tripod; having three feet or legs.—**tri-pod-ic** (trī-pod'ik), *a.* Having or using three feet or legs.

trip-o-dy (trip'ọ-di), *n.*; pl. *-dies* (-diz). [From *tri-* + *-pody* as in *dipody*.] In *pros.*, a group or verse of three feet.

trip-o-li (trĭp'ọ̄-li), *n.* [From *Tripoli*, in Africa.] Any of several siliceous substances, as rottenstone and infusorial earth, used in polishing, etc.

tri-pos (trī'pos), *n.*; pl. *triposes.* [Cf. Gr. τρίπος, poetic var. of τρίπους, tripod: see *tripod.*] A tripod†; also, at Cambridge University, England, any of various final honors examinations, orig. in mathematics, but now also in other subjects.

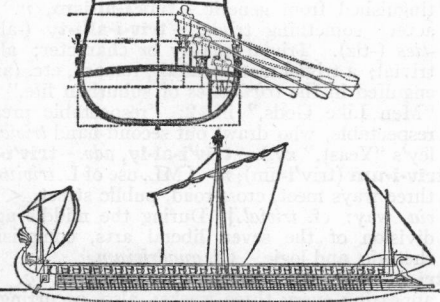

Tripod of the Delphian Apollo. — From a Greek red-figured hydria, in the Vatican.

trip-per (trip'ėr), *n.* One who or that which trips; one who goes on a pleasure-trip or excursion, or an excursionist (colloq., Eng.: as, "The town isn't . . . big enough to put up all the *trippers* that burden it in the summer," Hugh Walpole's "Wooden Horse," ii.); in *mach.*, a tripping device; a trip.

trip-pet (trip'et), *n.* [From *trip.*] In *mach.*, a projection, cam, or the like, for striking some other part at regular intervals.

trip-ping (trip'ing), *p. a.* That trips; stepping lightly or nimbly; light and quick, as the step, pace, etc.; proceeding with a light, easy movement or rhythm, as verse, meters, tunes, etc.; also, stumbling; erring.

trip-ping=line (trip'ing-lin), *n.* *Naut.*, a rope which leads from the deck to the snotter of a light yard and which, when pulled, trips the yard, causes the snotter to pull off the lift and brace, and guides the yard as it is lowered to the deck.

trip-ping-ly (trip'ing-li), *adv.* In a tripping manner.

trip-tych (trip'tik), *n.* [Gr. τρίπτυχος, threefold, < τρι-, three, + πτυχή, a fold.] A hinged or folding three-leaved tablet for writing on; also, a set of three panels or compartments side by side, bearing pictures, carvings, or the like.

tri-quet-rous (trī-kwet'rus), *a.* [L. *triquetrus*, < *tri-*, three.] Three-sided; triangular; having a triangular cross-section: specif. in *bot.*, *zoöl.*, etc.

tri-ra-di-ate, tri-ra-di-at-ed (trī-rā'di-āt, -ā-ted), *a.* [See *tri-*.] Having, or consisting of, three rays; branching in three directions.—**tri-ra'di-ate-ly**, *adv.*

tri-reme (trī'rēm), *n.* [L. *triremis*, < *tri-*, three, + *remus*, oar.] In *class. antiq.*, a galley with three rows or tiers of oars on each side, one above another, used chiefly as a ship of war.

tri-sect (trī-sekt'), *v. t.* [L. *tri-*, three, + *sectus*, pp. of *secare*, cut.] To divide into three parts, esp. into three equal parts.—**tri-sec'tion** (-sek'shon), *n.*

Diagram and cross-section of an Athenian Trireme.

tri-seme (trī'sēm). [LL. *trisemus*, < Gr. τρίσημος, < τρι-, three, + σῆμα, sign.] In *pros.*: **I.** *a.* Containing, consisting of, or equal to three moræ or short syllables, as a metrical foot. **II.** *n.* A triseme foot.—**tri-se'mic** (-sē'mik), *a.*

tri-sep-a-lous (trī-sep'ạ-lus), *a.* [See *tri-*.] In *bot.*, having three sepals.

tri-se-ri-al (trī-sē'ri-ạl), *a.* [See *tri-*.] Arranged in three series or rows. Also **tri-se'ri-ate** (-āt).

tris-kele (tris'kēl), *n.* Same as *triskelion.*

tris-kel-i-on (tris-kel'i-on), *n.*; pl. *-ia* (-i-ạ). [NL., < Gr. τρισκελής, three-legged, < τρι-, three, + σκέλος, leg.] A symbolic figure consisting of three legs, arms, or branches radiating from a common center.

Triskelion.

tris-oc-ta-he-dron (tris-ok-tạ-hē'dron), *n.*; pl. *-drons* or *-dra* (-drạ). [Gr. τρίς, thrice, + E. *octahedron.*] A solid bounded by twenty-four equal faces, three corresponding to each face of an octahedron: called 'trigonal trisoctahedron' when the faces are triangles, and 'tetragonal trisoctahedron' when the faces are quadrilaterals.

Trigonal Trisoctahedron.

tri-sper-mous (trī-spėr'mus), *a.* [See *tri-* and *-spermous.*] In *bot.*, three-seeded.

trist (trist), *a.* [OF. F. *triste*, < L. *tristis.*] Sad; sorrowful; melancholy. [Archaic.] Also (F.) **triste** (trēst).—**trist'ful**, *a.* Same as *trist.* [Archaic.]

tris-tich (tris'tik), *n.* [Gr. τρι-, three, + στίχος, row, line.] In *pros.*, a group of three lines of verse; a stanza of three lines.

tris-ti-chous (tris'ti-kus), *a.* [Gr. τρίστιχος, < τρι-, three, + στίχος, row, line.] Disposed in three rows; in *bot.*, arranged in or characterized by three vertical rows.

tri-sul-cate (trī-sul'kāt), *a.* [See *tri-*.] In *bot.*, having three sulci or grooves; in *zoöl.*, divided into three digits, as a foot.

tri-sul-phide (trī-sul'fīd or -fid), *n.* [See *tri-*.] In *chem.*, a sulphide containing three sulphur atoms.

tri-syl-la-ble (trī-sil'ạ-bl or tri-), *n.* [L. *trisyllabus*, < Gr. τρισύλλαβος, of three syllables, < τρι-, three, + συλλαβή: see *syllable.*] A word of three syllables, as *telephone.*—**tris-yl-lab-ic** (tris-i-lab'ik), *a.*

tri-tag-o-nist (trī-tag'ọ-nist or tri-), *n.* [Gr. τριταγωνιστής, < τρίτος, third, + ἀγωνιστής, contender, actor, E. *agonist.*] In the ancient Greek drama, the third actor, or character of third importance (after the *protagonist* and *deuteragonist*).

trite (trīt), *a.*; compar. *triter*, superl. *tritest.* [L. *tritus*, pp. of *terere*, rub, grind, wear away, akin to Gr. τείρειν, rub: cf. *teredo*, *termite*, and *turn.*] Rubbed or worn by use (archaic); also, hackneyed by constant use or repetition (as, a *trite* saying; "You are talking the *tritest* of cant," F. M. Crawford's "Mr. Isaacs," xiii.); devoid of freshness or novelty; stale; commonplace.—**trite'ly**, *adv.*—**trite'ness**, *n.*

tri-the-ism (trī'thē-izm), *n.* [Gr. τρι-, three, + θεός, god.] Belief in three Gods, esp. in the doctrine that the three persons of the Trinity (Father, Son, and Holy Ghost) are three distinct Gods.—**tri'the-ist**, *n.* One who believes in tritheism.—**tri-the-is'tic**, *a.*

tri-thing (trī'ᴛʜing), *n.* Same as *riding¹.* [Obs. or hist.]

Tri-ton (trī'ton), *n.* [L., < Gr. Τρίτων.] In *class. myth.*, a sea-god, son of Poseidon and Amphitrite, represented as

Triton with Nereid. — From an antique sculpture in the Vatican.

having the head and trunk of a man and the tail of a fish, and bearing a conch-shell trumpet which he blows to raise or calm the waves; also, later, one of a race of subordinate sea-deities similarly represented, attendants on the greater sea-gods; [l. c.] in zoöl., any of various marine gastropods constituting the family *Tritonidæ* (esp. of the genus *Triton*), having a large, spiral, often beautifully colored shell; also, the shell; also, an aquatic salamander of the genus *Triton* or some allied genus.

tri-tone (trī'tōn), n. [Gr. τρίτονος, of three tones, < τρι-, three, + τόνος, E. *tone*.] In *music*, an interval consisting of three whole tones.

trit-u-ra-ble (trit'ū-ra̧-bl), a. That may be triturated.

trit-u-rate (trit'ū-rāt), v. t.; -rated, -rating. [LL. *trituratus*, pp. of *triturare*, thresh, < L. *tritura*, a rubbing, threshing, < *terere*, rub.] To reduce to fine particles or powder by rubbing, grinding, bruising, or the like; comminute; pulverize.—**trit'u-rate**, n. A triturated substance; a trituration.—**trit-u-ra'tion** (-rā'shon), n. [LL. *trituratio(n-).*] The act of triturating, or the state of being triturated; comminution; in *phar.*, any triturated substance; esp., a mixture of a medicinal substance with sugar of milk, triturated to an impalpable powder.—**trit'u-ra-tor**, n.

tri-umph (trī'umf), n. [OF. *triumphe* (F. *triomphe*), < L. *triumphus*, triumphal procession, victory: cf. L. *triumpe*, exclamation used in processions of the Arval Brethren, Gr. θρίαμβος, hymn sung in processions in honor of Bacchus.] The ceremonial entrance into ancient Rome of a victorious commander with his army, spoils, captives, etc., authorized by the senate in honor of an important military or naval achievement (as, "Dolabella was a favourite of the Senate; he had been allowed a *triumph* for his services," Froude's "Cæsar," ix.: cf. *ovation*); hence, any triumphal procession†; any public pageant, spectacle, or the like†; also, pomp† or splendor†; also, the action or fact of being victorious, or triumphing (as, "We may win the crown of martyrdom, but not that of earthly *triumph*": Scott's "Abbot," x.); victory; conquest; a signal victory (as, "If the reduction of Harlem were a *triumph*, it was one which the conquerors might well exchange for a defeat," Motley's "Dutch Republic," iii. 8; "a long procession of turf *triumphs*," Galsworthy's "Country House," i. 10); a distinguished success or achievement (as, "'A *triumph* for all concerned,' as the local Advertiser had stated in its criticism [of a play]": L. Merrick's "Position of Peggy Harper," ii. 5); something that is successful (as, "Her [another's] evening dress made Audrey doubt whether after all her own was the genuine *triumph* which she had supposed": Arnold Bennett's "Lion's Share," xix.); also, the exultation of victory; joy over success; elation or exultant gladness (as, "Great *triumph* and rejoicing was in heaven": Milton's "Paradise Lost," vii. 180); also, a triumphal arch†; in *card-playing*, a trump†.—**tri'umph**, v. [OF. *triumpher* (F. *triompher*), < L. *triumphare*, < *triumphus.*] **I.** intr. To celebrate a triumph, as a victorious Roman commander; also, to gain a victory, or be victorious (as, "Various forms of government . . . followed each other as the advocates of the different systems *triumphed* or fell": J. F. Kirk's "Charles the Bold," iv. 2); gain the mastery, or prevail (as, "His sense of duty *triumphed*": Lytton Strachey's "Queen Victoria," iv.); achieve success; also, to exult over victory; rejoice over success; be elated or glad; rejoice proudly, or glory (as, "He . . . exulted and *triumphed* in her beauty": M. Hewlett's "Open Country," iv.). **II.**† tr. To cause to triumph; also, to conquer; triumph over.—**tri-um'phal** (-um'fa̧l), a. [L. *triumphalis.*] Of or pertaining to a triumph; celebrating or commemorating a triumph or victory (as, a *triumphal* arch, one erected to commemorate a victory: see cut in next column).—**tri-um'-phal-ly**, adv.—**tri-um'phant** (-fa̧nt), a. [L. *triumphans* (-ant-), ppr.] Celebrating, or pertaining to, a triumph or victory (as, "the *triumphant* feast . . . after a victory over their enemies," Defoe's "Robinson Crusoe," i. 14: now rare); also, having achieved victory or success; victorious; successful; also, exulting over victory; rejoicing over success; exultant; also, splendid† or magnificent†.—**tri-um'phant-ly**, adv.—**tri'umph-er**, n.

tri-um-vir (trī-um'vėr), n.; pl. -viri (-vi-rī) or -virs. [L., pl. *triumviri*, < *trium virorum*, of three men: *trium*, gen. of

tres, three; *virorum*, gen. pl. of *vir*, man.] In *Rom. hist.*, one of three officers or magistrates united in the same public function; hence, in general use, one of three persons associated in any office. See *triumvirate*.—**tri-um'-vi-ral** (-vi-ra̧l), a.—**tri-um'vi-rate**

Triumphal Arch. — Arch of Constantine, Rome.

(-rāt), n. [L. *triumviratus.*] In *Rom. hist.*, the office or magistracy of a triumvir; the government of three joint officers or magistrates; a coalition of three magistrates for joint administration; esp., either of two coalitions to assume the government of the Roman state, one ('First Triumvirate') of Julius Cæsar, Pompey, and Crassus, in 60 B.C., and the other ('Second Triumvirate') of Octavius, Mark Antony, and Lepidus, in 43 B.C.; hence, in general use, any association of three in office or authority; also, any group or set of three.

tri-une (trī'ūn), a. [L. *tri-*, three, + *unus*, one.] Three in one; constituting a trinity in unity, as the Godhead.—**tri-u-ni-ty** (trī-ū'ni-ti), n.

tri-va-lent (trī-vā'lent or triv'a̧-), a. [See *tri-* and *-valent*.] In *chem.*, having a valence of three.—**tri-va'lence**, n.

triv-et (triv'et), n. [ME. *trevet*, appar. < AS. *trefet*, < L. *tripes* (*triped-*), three-footed, < *tri-*, three, + *pes* (*ped-*), foot.] A three-footed or three-legged stand or support, esp. one of iron placed over a fire to hold cooking-vessels or the like.—**as right as a trivet**, entirely or perfectly right (in allusion to a trivet's standing firm on its three legs): as, "Go home to-morrow and you'll be *as right as a trivet*" (Buchan's "Three Hostages," ix.).

triv-i-al (triv'i-a̧l), a. [L. *trivialis*, lit. 'of the cross-roads, or public streets,' < *trivium*: see *trivium*.] Of or pertaining to the trivium of medieval studies; also, common, commonplace, or ordinary (as, "the *trivial* round, the common task," Keble's "Christian Year," i.: now rare); also, of little importance, trifling, or insignificant (as, "The differences . . . were at first but *trivial*, and such as are not worth relating": Defoe's "Robinson Crusoe," ii. 2); of no great depth or seriousness (as, "It was odd to find Teddy . . . serious and businesslike . . . this young man wasn't as *trivial* as he had thought him," H. G. Wells's "Mr. Britling," ii. 2. § 5; "the danger of living a *trivial* and superficial life," Mrs. Stowe's "Oldtown Folks," xxxi.); also, of names of animals and plants, (a) popular or vernacular, as distinguished from scientific or technical (in Latin), or (b) specific, as distinguished from generic.—**triv'i-al-ism**, n. Trivial character; something trivial.—**triv-i-al'i-ty** (-al'i-ti), n.; pl. -ties (-tiz). Trivial quality or character; also, something trivial; a trivial matter, affair, remark, etc. (as, "completely engulfed in the *trivialities* of suburban life," H. G. Wells's "Men Like Gods," iii. 2; "respectable preachers to the respectable, who drawl out second-hand *trivialities*," Kingsley's "Yeast," xv.).—**triv'i-al-ly**, adv.—**triv'i-al-ness**, n.

triv-i-um (triv'i-um), n. [ML. use of L. *trivium*, place where three ways meet, cross-road, public street, < *tri-*, three, + *via*, way: cf. *trivial*.] During the middle ages, the lower division of the seven liberal arts, comprising grammar, rhetoric, and logic. Cf. *quadrivium*.

tri-week-ly (trī-wēk'li). [See *tri-*.] **I.** a. Occurring or appearing every three weeks; also, occurring or appearing three times a week. **II.** n.; pl. -lies (-liz). A triweekly publication. **III.** adv. Every three weeks; also, three times a week.

tro-car (trō'kär), n. [F. *trocart*, < *trois* (< L. *tres*), three, + *carre*, angle, edge, side.] In *surg.*, an instrument consisting of a perforator or stylet inclosed in a cannula, used for withdrawing fluid from a cavity, etc.

tro-cha-ic (trō-kā′ik). [L. *trochaicus*, < Gr. τροχαϊκός.] In *pros.*: **I.** *a.* Pertaining to the trochee; consisting of or employing a trochee or trochees. **II.** *n.* A trochee; a verse or poem consisting of trochees (usually in *pl.*).

tro-chal (trō′kạl), *a.* [Gr. τροχός, wheel: see *troche*.] In *zoöl.*, resembling a wheel (as, the *trochal* disk, in rotifers, an organ of locomotion consisting of rings of cilia surrounding the mouth); also, having a trochal disk, as a rotifer.

tro-chan-ter (trō-kan′tẽr), *n.* [NL., < Gr. τροχαντήρ, < τρέχειν, run.] In *anat.* and *zoöl.*, in many vertebrates, a prominence or process on the upper part of the femur; in *entom.*, the second segment or joint of an insect's leg (counting from the proximal end), situated between the coxa and the femur.—**tro-chan-ter-ic** (trō-kan-ter′ik), *a.*

tro-char (trō′kär), *n.* See *trocar*.

troche (trōch, also trōk, commonly trō′kẹ), *n.* [For earlier *trochisk* (with var. *trochis*, taken as pl.), < LL. *trochiscus*, < Gr. τροχίσκος, troche, lozenge, dim. of τροχός, round cake, disk, wheel, hoop, < τρέχειν, run.] A small tablet, esp. of circular form, made of some medicinal substance worked into a paste with sugar and mucilage or the like, and dried.

tro-chee (trō′kẹ), *n.* [L. *trochæus*, < Gr. τροχαῖος, prop. adj., 'running,' < τρόχος, a running, < τρέχειν, run.] In *pros.*, a metrical foot of two syllables, a long followed by a short, or an accented followed by an unaccented; a choree.

tro-chil-ic (trō-kil′ik), *a.* [Gr. τροχιλία, sheave, roller, < τρέχειν, run.] Pertaining to or characterized by rotary motion.—**tro-chil′ics**, *n.* The science of rotary motion.

troch-i-lus (trok′i-lus), *n.*; pl. *-li* (-lī). [L., < Gr. τροχίλος, < τρέχειν, run.] A crocodile-bird; also, any of several small old-world warblers, as the kinglet, *Regulus cristatus*; also, a humming-bird.

troch-le-a (trok′lẹ-ạ), *n.*; pl. *-leæ* (-lẹ-ē). [L., pulley, < Gr. τροχιλία, sheave, roller: see *trochilic*.] In *anat.*, a pulley-like structure or arrangement of parts affording a smooth surface upon which another part glides, as the surface of the inner condyle of the humerus, with which the ulna articulates.—**troch′le-ar** (-ạr), *a.* In *anat.*, belonging to or connected with a trochlea; forming a trochlea; pulley-like; in *bot.*, circular and contracted in the middle so as to resemble a pulley.

tro-choid (trō′koid). [Gr. τροχοειδής, < τροχός, wheel, + εἶδος, form.] **I.** *a.* Wheel-like; rotating like a wheel, as a joint; also, top-shaped, as a top-shell. **II.** *n.* In *geom.*, a curve traced by a point rigidly connected with, but not generally on the circumference of, a circle which rolls upon a right line; also, a curve traced by a point rigidly connected with a circle which rolls upon either the interior or the exterior of another circle.—**tro-choi′dal**, *a.* Trochoid; in *geom.*, pertaining to, or having the form of, a trochoid.

trod (trod). Preterit and past participle of *tread*.—**trod′den.** Past participle of *tread*.—**trode** (trōd). Archaic preterit of *tread*.

trog-lo-dyte (trog′lō-dīt), *n.* [L. *troglodyta*, < Gr. τρωγλοδύτης, < τρώγλη, hole, + δύειν, enter.] A cave-man or cave-dweller; hence, a person living in seclusion; one unacquainted with affairs of the world; also, any of certain anthropoid apes, as the gorilla or the chimpanzee.—
trog-lo-dyt′ic (-dit′ik), *a.* [L. *troglodyticus*, < Gr. τρωγλοδυτικός.] Pertaining to or characteristic of a troglodyte; having the habits of a troglodyte.—
trog′lo-dyt-ism (-dīt-izm), *n.* The state or condition of a troglodyte; the habit of living in caves.

tro-gon (trō′gon), *n.* [NL., < Gr. τρώγων, ppr. of τρώγειν, gnaw, nibble.] Any bird of the family *Trogonidæ*, esp. of the genus *Trogon*, of tropical and subtropical regions, notable for brilliant plumage. See *quetzal*.

An African Trogon (*Hapaloderma constantia*).

troi-ka (troi′kạ), *n.* [Russ.] In Russia, a team of three horses abreast; the vehicle drawn by them; the vehicle and horses together.

Tro-jan (trō′jạn). [L. *Trojanus*, < *Troja*, *Troia*, Troy, < *Tros*, < Gr. Τρώς, Tros, the mythical founder of Troy.] **I.** *a.* Of or pertaining to ancient Troy, a celebrated city in northwestern Asia Minor, or its inhabitants: as, the *Trojan* War (in ancient legend, a ten years' war waged by the confederated Greeks, under the Greek king Agamemnon, against the Trojans, to avenge the abduction of Helen, wife of the Greek king Menelaus, by Paris, son of the Trojan king Priam, and ending in the sack and burning of Troy). **II.** *n.* A native or inhabitant of Troy; also, a boon companion, or good fellow; also, one who shows pluck, determination, or energy (colloq.: as, they all worked like *Trojans*).

troll¹ (trōl), *n.* [Icel. and Sw. *troll* = Dan. *trold*.] In Scandinavian folklore, one of a race of supernatural beings formerly conceived as giants, but now as dwarfs, inhabiting caves or subterranean dwellings: as, "the *Troll* who dwelt in Ulshoi hill" (Whittier's "Kallundborg Church").

troll² (trōl), *v.* [ME. *trollen*, roll, ramble, stroll: cf. OF. *traller*, *troller*, ramble, F. *trôler*, ramble, drag about (prob. from Teut. and akin to G. *trollen*, roll).] **I.** *tr.* To move by or as by rolling; roll; turn round and round; move (the tongue) volubly†; also, to pass from one to another, as a bowl of liquor at table†; also, to sing in the manner of a round or catch (as, to *troll* a song); also, to sing or utter in a full, rolling voice (as, "She ran into the house, *trolling* a song": G. W. Cable's "John March, Southerner," xx.); also, to fish for or in by trolling (see *troll²*, *v. i.*); move (the line or bait) in doing this. **II.** *intr.* To roll; turn round and round; move nimbly, as the tongue in speaking†; also, to pass from person to person, as a bowl of liquor at table†; also, to sing with a full, rolling voice (as, "He *trolled* with ample lungs": Stevenson's "Travels with a Donkey," iv. 2); give forth full, rolling tones; be uttered or sound in such tones; also, to fish with a running or moving line, as one worked up and down in fishing for pike with a rod (as where the water is full of weeds), or, esp., one trailed behind a boat near the surface of the water.—**troll²**, *n.* The act of trolling; a moving or going round; routine; also, a song whose parts are sung in succession; a round; also, the method of trolling for fish; also, a lure used in trolling for fish.—**troll′er**, *n.*

trol-ley (trol′i), *n.*; pl. *trolleys* (-iz). [Cf. *troll²*.] Any of various kinds of low carts or vehicles (local, Eng.); a kind of low truck, esp. one for running on a track; also, a pulley or truck traveling on an overhead track, and serving to support and move a suspended object; also, a grooved metallic wheel or pulley carried on the end of a pole ('trolley-pole') by an electric car or locomotive, and held in contact with an overhead conductor, usually a suspended wire ('trolley-wire'), from which it collects the current for the propulsion of the car or locomotive; any of various other devices for collecting current for such a purpose, as a bow-like structure ('bow trolley') sliding along an overhead wire, or a device ('underground trolley') for taking current from the underground wire or conductor employed by some electric railways; also, a trolley-car.—**trol′ley**, *v. t.* or *i.*, *-leyed*, *-leying*. To convey or go by trolley.—**trol′ley-car**, *n.* A street-railway car propelled electrically by current taken from a conductor by means of a trolley.—**trol′ley-man** (-mạn), *n.*; pl. *-men*. A man employed in operating a trolley-car, as a motorman or a conductor.

troll=mad-am† (trōl′mad″ạm), **troll=my=dame†** (trōl′mī-dām), *n.* [F. *trou-madame* (*trou*, hole).] An old game resembling bagatelle, played esp. by ladies.

trol-lop (trol′op), *n.* [Cf. *troll²*.] An untidy or slovenly woman; a slattern; also, a woman who is morally loose; also, anything draggling, or hanging untidily (Sc.).—**trol′lop**, *v. i.* To be slovenly; go about or work in a slovenly manner; also, to gad about idly; also, to draggle, or hang untidily (Sc.).

trol-ly (trol′i), *etc.* See *trolley*, etc.

trom-bone (trom′bōn), *n.* [It. *trombone*, aug. of *tromba*, trumpet, = E. *trump¹*.] A large brass musical instrument of the trumpet class, usually with a long U-shaped sliding piece for varying the length of the tube in order to produce a desired note.

Trombone, with Slide.

—trom'bon-ist (-bọ-nist), n. A player on the trombone.

tro-mom-e-ter (trọ-mom'e-tėr), n. [Gr. τρόμος, a trembling: see *-meter*.] An instrument for measuring or detecting very slight earthquake-tremors.

tro-na (trō'nä), n. [Sw. *trona*, said to be from Ar.: cf. *natron*.] A grayish or yellowish hydrous carbonate of sodium, occurring native in Egypt and elsewhere.

troop (tröp), n. [F. *troupe*, < ML. *troppus*, flock; origin uncertain.] A body of soldiers, or, by extension, of police, etc.; pl., armed forces, or soldiers, collectively (as, "Mercenary *troops* were substituted for the feudal militia": Hallam's "Europe during the Middle Ages," ii. 2); also, *sing.*, an assemblage of persons or things; a company or band; a herd, flock, or swarm (as, "a *troop* of seven or eight deer": W. H. Hudson's "Far Away and Long Ago," vi.); a great number or multitude (as, "His college friends were entering the Church by *troops*": S. R. Crockett's "Stickit Minister," ix.); specif., *milit.*, a cavalry unit consisting of from 60 to 100 men commanded by a captain; also, a particular roll or call on the drum, being a signal to assemble for marching.—**troop**, v. I. *intr.* To gather in a company; flock together; associate or consort (*with*); also, to go or pass in a troop or troops; go or come in great numbers (as, "The children *trooped* around her": W. Churchill's "Coniston," ii. 14); also, to go or pass in rank or order (as, "*trooping* like a colt at his mother's heels": Irving's "Sketch-Book," Rip Van Winkle); also, in general, to walk, go, or go away (as, "She was at last forced to *troop* off": Addison, in "Spectator," 464). II. *tr.* To assemble in, form into, or unite with a troop or troops.—**troop'er**, n. A soldier in a troop of cavalry; also, a horse ridden by such a soldier; also, a mounted policeman; also, a troop-ship.

troop-i-al, troup-i-al (trö'pi-al), n. [F. *troupiale*, < *troupe*, E. *troop*; from the habit of going in flocks.] Any of the birds of the American family *Icteridæ*, including the American blackbirds, American orioles, etc.; esp., one with brilliant plumage.

troop=ship (tröp'ship), n. A ship for the conveyance of troops; a transport.

troost-ite (tröst'īt), n. [From Dr. G. Troost, of Nashville, Tenn.] A reddish variety of willemite, in which the zinc is partly replaced by manganese.

Common Troopial (*Icterus vulgaris*) of tropical America.

tro-pæ-o-lin (trọ-pē'ọ-lin), n. [See *tropæolum*.] In *chem.*, any of a number of orange or yellow dyes of complex composition: so called because they resemble the colors of the flowers of the nasturtium (genus *Tropæolum*).

tro-pæ-o-lum (trọ-pē'ọ-lum), n.; pl. *-lums*, L. *-la* (-lä). [NL., dim. < Gr. τρόπαιον, trophy (see *trophy*); the leaf being likened to a shield, the flower to a helmet.] Any of the pungent herbs constituting the genus *Tropæolum*, native in tropical America, species of which are well known in cultivation under the name of nasturtium.

tro-pa-ri-on (trọ-pā'ri-on), n.; pl. *-ria* (-ri-ä). [LGr. τροπάριον, < Gr. τρόπος, a turn, manner, musical mode, E. *trope*.] In the *Gr. Ch.*, a short hymn, or a stanza of a hymn.

trope (trōp), n. [L. *tropus*, < Gr. τρόπος, a turn, way, manner, mode, trope, < τρέπειν, turn.] In *rhet.*, a figure of speech consisting in the use of a word or phrase in a sense different from that which properly belongs to it; the word or phrase so used; in *liturgics*, a phrase, sentence, or verse formerly interpolated in a liturgical text as an amplification or embellishment.

-trope. [Gr. -τροπος, turned, < τρέπειν, turn.] A noun termination used to form names of optical instruments, toys, or the like, operated by rotating or revolving, as in *chromatrope*, *thaumatrope*, *zoëtrope*.

tro-pe-ine (trō'pē-in), n. [From *tropine*.] In *chem.*, any one of a series of esters of tropine, some of which resemble atropine in physiological action.

tro-pe'o-lin (trō'pē'ọ-lin), n. See *tropæolin*.

troph-ic (trof'ik), a. [Gr. τροφικός, < τροφή, nourishment, < τρέφειν, nourish.] In *physiol.*, of or pertaining to nutrition; concerned in nutritive processes.—**troph'i-cal-ly**, adv.

tro-phied (trō'fid), a. Adorned with trophies.

tropho-. Form of Gr. τροφή, nourishment, used in combination.—**troph-o-blast** (trof'ọ-blast), n. [+ *-blast*.] In *embryol.*, a special epiblastic layer of cells external to the embryo in many mammals, and having to do with its nutrition.—**tro-phol-o-gy** (trọ-fol'ọ-ji), n. [+ *-logy*.] The branch of physiology that deals with nutrition.

Tro-pho-ni-an (trọ-fō'ni-an), a. Of or pertaining to Trophonius, the legendary builder of the original temple of Apollo at Delphi, who after his death was worshiped as a god, and had a famous oracle in a cavern in Bœotia, which was said to affect those who entered with such awe that they never smiled again.

troph-o-plasm (trof'ọ-plazm), n. [See *tropho-* and *-plasm*.] In *biol.*, that kind of protoplasm which is regarded as forming the nutritive part of a cell.

tro-phy (trō'fi), n.; pl. *-phies* (-fiz). [F. *trophée*, < L. *trophæum*, for *tropæum*, < Gr. τρόπαιον, trophy, < τροπή, a turning, rout, < τρέπειν, turn, put to flight, defeat.] A memorial erected by the ancient Greeks or Romans in commemoration of a victory in war, consisting of arms or other spoils taken from the enemy and hung upon a tree, pillar, or the like; a similar memorial erected by others; a carved, painted, or other representation of objects associated with or symbolical of victory or achievement; also, anything taken in war, hunting, etc., esp. when preserved as a memento (as, "All around, the walls to grace, Hung *trophies* of the fight or chase": Scott's "Lady of the Lake," i. 25); a spoil or prize; also, anything serving as a token or evidence of victory, valor, skill, etc.; any memento or memorial.

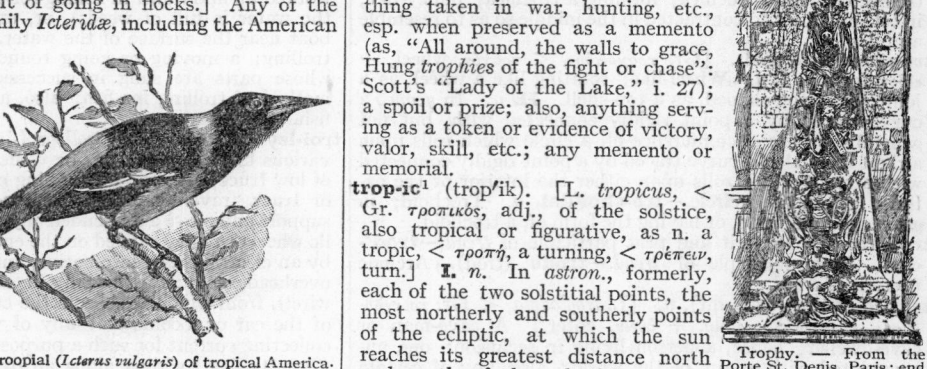

trop-ic[1] (trop'ik). [L. *tropicus*, < Gr. τροπικός, adj., of the solstice, also tropical or figurative, as n. a tropic, < τροπή, a turning, < τρέπειν, turn.] I. n. In *astron.*, formerly, each of the two solstitial points, the most northerly and southerly points of the ecliptic, at which the sun reaches its greatest distance north and south of the celestial equator,

Trophy. — From the Porte St. Denis, Paris; end of 17th century.

and turns toward it again; now, either of two circles on the celestial sphere, parallel to the celestial equator, one ('tropic of Cancer') about 23½° north of it, and the other ('tropic of Capricorn') about 23½° south of it, touching the ecliptic at the solstitial points; in *geog.*, either of two corresponding parallels of latitude on the terrestrial globe, one ('tropic of Cancer') about 23½° north, and the other ('tropic of Capricorn') about 23½° south, of the equator, being the boundaries of the torrid zone; pl., with *the*, the regions lying between and near these parallels of latitude; the torrid zone and neighboring regions. II. a. Pertaining to the tropics; tropical: as, "the unwarning *tropic* gale" (Whittier's "Daniel Wheeler").

trop-ic[2] (trop'ik), a. [From (a)*trop(ine)* + *-ic*: cf. *tropine*.] In *chem.*, noting or pertaining to a colorless, optically inactive crystalline acid derived from atropine; also, noting or pertaining to either of two optically active isomers of this acid.

-tropic, -tropous. [Gr. -τροπος, -τροπος.] Adjective terminations meaning 'turned,' 'turning,' 'characterized by turning,' as in *æolotropic*, *anatropous*, *geotropic*, *orthotropic*, *orthotropous*.

trop-i-cal (trop'i-kạl), *a.* Of or pertaining to the astronomical tropics, or either one of them (as, the *tropical* year: see *year*); also, pertaining to, characteristic of, occurring in, or inhabiting the tropics or the torrid zone (as, "*tropical* flowers," J. Conrad's "Lord Jim," xviii.; "*tropical* oceanic islands," A. R. Wallace's "Darwinism," xii.); hence, very hot or ardent (as, "the *tropical* fervor of his soul": Irving's "Knickerbocker's New York," iv. 1); also, pertaining to, characterized by, or of the nature of a trope or tropes; metaphorical; figurative.—**trop'i-cal-ly**, *adv.*

trop-ic=bird (trop'ik-bėrd), *n.* Any of the totipalmate sea-birds constituting the genus *Phaëthon* (or family *Phaëthontidæ*), rapid in flight, of varied coloration, and having a pair of greatly elongated central tail-feathers: found chiefly in tropical regions.

tro-pine (trō'pin), *n.* [From *atropine*.] In *chem.*, a white crystalline, hygroscopic basic compound formed by the hydrolysis of atropine.

Tropic-bird (*Phaëthon æthereus*). — *a*, the totipalmate foot.

tro-pism (trō'pizm), *n.* [Detached from words ending in *-tropism*.] In *biol.*, the property of a plant or other organism of turning or tending (toward or away), as in growth, under the influence of external stimuli.

-tropism, -tropy. Noun terminations corresponding to *-tropic* or *-tropous* in adjectives.

trop-ist (trop'ist), *n.* One who deals in tropes; also, one who explains Scripture, or a Scripture text, in the way of tropes or a trope.

tro-pol-o-gy (trō-pol'ō-ji), *n.*; pl. *-gies* (-jiz). [LL. *tropologia*, < Gr. τροπολογία, < τρόπος, trope, + -λογία, < λέγειν, speak.] The use of tropes or a trope in speech or writing; also, a treatise on tropes; also, figurative interpretation; the use of a Scripture text to give it a moral interpretation or significance apart from its direct meaning.—**trop-o-log-i-cal** (trop-ō-loj'i-kạl), *a.*

tro-poph-i-lous (trō-pof'i-lus), *a.* [Gr. τροπή, a turning, change, + φίλος, loving.] In *bot.*, adapted to a climate which is alternately dry and moist or cold and hot, as a plant.

trop-o-phyte (trop'ō-fīt), *n.* [Gr. τροπή, a turning, change, + φυτόν, plant.] In *bot.*, a plant adapted to a climate alternately dry and moist or cold and hot.—**trop-o-phyt'ic** (-fit'ik), *a.*

trop-o-sphere (trop'ō-sfėr), *n.* [Gr. τροπή, a turning, change, + σφαῖρα, E. *sphere*.] The layer of the atmosphere between the earth and the stratosphere, within which there is a steady fall of temperature with increasing altitude.

-tropous. See *-tropic*.

trop-po (trop'pō), *adv.* [It.] In *music*, too much: used esp. in directions, as (It.) 'allegro, ma non troppo' (quickly, but not too much so).

-tropy. See *-tropism*.

trot[1] (trot), *v.*; *trotted, trotting.* [OF. *troter* (F. *trotter*); origin uncertain.] **I.** *intr.* Of a horse, etc., to go at a gait between a walk and a run, in which the legs move in diagonal pairs, but not quite simultaneously, so that when the movement is slow one foot at least is always on the ground, and when fast all four feet are momentarily off the ground at once; hence, in general, to go at a similar gait; go at a quick, steady gait; move briskly, bustle, or hurry (as, "The porters and chairmen *trot* with their burdens": Smollett's "Humphry Clinker," May 29). **II.** *tr.* To trot upon†; also, to execute by trotting; also, to cause to trot; ride at a trot; lead at a trot; also, to bring forward for or as for inspection (with *out*: colloq.: as, "Charles *trots* out his little bit of scientific nomenclature," W. De Morgan's "Alice-for-Short," ix.).—

trot[1], *n.* The gait of a horse, etc., when trotting; in general, a jogging gait between a walk and a run; quick, continuous movement (as, to be on the *trot*); also, a toddling child (colloq.: as, "Ethel romped with the little children — the rosy little *trots*," Thackeray's "Newcomes," x.); also, a crib, or translation or other illicit aid (school and college slang, U. S.).

trot[2] (trot), *n.* [Origin obscure.] An old woman: usually in contempt.

troth (trôth or trōth), *n.* [Var. of *truth*.] Faithfulness, fidelity, or loyalty (often in 'by my troth,' as used in asseveration: as, "By my *troth*, I wish he was alive again!" Stevenson's "Kidnapped," xix.); also, one's word or promise (as, "Will you give me your *troth* . . . that I shall have no more to fear from your attempts?" Stevenson's "Master of Ballantrae," ix.); esp., one's word pledged in engaging one's self to marry; also, truth or verity (often in the phrase 'in troth,' sometimes reduced to 'troth': as, "In *troth*, I think she would," Shakspere's "Coriolanus," i. 3. 118). [Archaic.]—**troth**, *v. t.* To plight one's troth or word to; engage by a contract, esp. of marriage; betroth. [Archaic.]

troth=plight (trôth'plīt), *a.* Engaged by troth or promise, esp. of marriage; betrothed. [Archaic.]—**troth'=plight**, *v. t.* To troth; betroth. [Archaic.]—**troth'=plight**, *n.* A solemn troth or promise, esp. of marriage; betrothal. [Archaic.]

trot-ter (trot'ėr), *n.* An animal which trots; a horse bred and trained to trot; also, one who goes at a similar gait, or who moves about briskly and constantly; also, the foot of an animal, esp. of a sheep or pig as used for food (usually in *pl.*); sometimes, a human foot.

trot-teur (tro-tèr'), *a.* [F. *trotteur*, masc. (*trotteuse*, fem.), 'trotter,' < *trotter*, trot, walk briskly, run about.] For wear or use while walking or on the street: applied to articles of women's dress.

trot-toir (tro-twor'), *n.* [F.] A sidewalk.

trou-ba-dour (trö'bạ-dör), *n.* [F., < Pr. *trobador*, < *trobar*, find, invent, compose in verse, = OF. *trover*: see *trover* and *trouvère*.] One of a class of lyric poets who flourished in southern France, eastern Spain, and northern Italy from the 11th century to the 13th century, and wrote in Provençal, chiefly on chivalric love and gallantry. Also fig. Cf. *trouvère*.

trou-ble (trub'l), *v.*; *-led, -ling.* [OF. *trubler, turbler* (F. *troubler*), ult. < L. *turba*, disorder, tumult, disturbance: cf. *turbid*.] **I.** *tr.* To disturb or agitate, or stir up so as to make turbid, as water, etc. (as, "An angel went down . . . and *troubled* the water," John, v. 4: now chiefly in the phrase 'troubled waters,' often fig.); also, to interfere with, interrupt, or hinder (archaic: as, "We should come like ghosts to *trouble* joy," Tennyson's "Choric Song," vi.); molest or harass; cause bodily pain or inconvenience to, as a disease or ailment does (as, "Being *troubled* with a raging tooth, I could not sleep": Shakspere's "Othello," iii. 3. 414); also, to disturb in mind, distress, or worry (as, "Thou didst hide thy face, and I was *troubled*": Ps. xxx. 7); also, to annoy, vex, or bother (as, "Your town is *troubled* with unruly boys": Shakspere's "Comedy of Errors," iii. 1. 62); also, to put to inconvenience, exertion, pains, or the like (as, "I will not *trouble* you with more letters at this time," Steele, in "Spectator," 142: much used in phrases of courteous request, as, may I *trouble* you to shut the door?). **II.** *intr.* To become turbid, as water†; also, to worry; also, to put one's self to inconvenience.—**trou'ble**, *n.* [OF. *truble* (F. *trouble*).] Disturbance or disorder, or an instance of this (as, political *troubles*); also, molestation, harassment, annoyance, or difficulty (as, the bandits gave *trouble* constantly; to make *trouble* for a hated employer); unfortunate position or circumstances, or an instance of this (as, to find one's self in *trouble*; to get into *trouble* with the authorities; a long succession of business *troubles*); also, physical derangement or disorder, or an instance or form of this (as, heart *trouble* or *troubles*; "A *trouble* of the eyes all but drove me mad with fear of blindness," Gissing's "Private Papers of Henry Ryecroft," iii. 5); also, disturbance of mind, distress, or worry, or an instance of this (as, "Incline thine ear unto my cry; For my soul is full of *troubles*": Ps. lxxxviii. 3); also, inconvenience endured, or exertion or pains taken, in some cause or in order to accomplish something (as, "There was no *trouble* he would not take to give pleasure to the humblest": Du Maurier's "Trilby," iv.); also, something that troubles; a cause or source of annoyance, difficulty, distress, or the like (as, "Your appointed feasts . . . are a *trouble* unto me," Isa. i. 14; the boy was a great *trouble* to them).—**troub'ler**, n.—**troub'le-some** (-sum), a. Full of disturbance or disorder† (as, "these *troublesome* times": Strype's "Memorials of Cranmer," i. 21); also, full of distress or affliction (archaic); also, causing trouble or annoyance (as, "*troublesome* neighbors": J. F. Kirk's "Charles the Bold," iii. 1); vexatious; also, involving exertion or effort; laborious; difficult.—**troub'le-some-ly**, adv.—**troub'le-some-ness**, n.—**troub'lous**, a. [OF. *troubleus*.] Characterized by trouble or disturbance; disturbed; unsettled; also, causing disturbance; turbulent; restless; also, causing trouble or annoyance; troublesome.

trou=de=loup (trö-dĕ-lö), n.; pl. *trous-de-loup* (trö-). [F. *trou de loup*, 'hole of wolf.'] *Milit.*, a conical or pyramidal pit with a pointed stake fixed vertically in the center, rows of which are dug before a work to hinder an enemy's approach.

trough (trôf), n. [AS. *trog* = D. and G. *trog* = Icel. *trog* = Dan. *trug*, trough; akin to E. *tree*.] An open, box-like, usually long and narrow receptacle or vessel, as for containing water or food for animals, or for any of various other purposes; any receptacle of similar shape; also, a channel or conduit for conveying water, as under the eaves of a building; also, any long depression or hollow, as between two ridges or waves.

trounce (trouns), v. t.; *trounced*, *trouncing*. [Origin uncertain.] To trouble†, distress†, or harass†; also, to beat or thrash severely; inflict chastisement upon, or punish; punish by legal action, or sue at law (now prov.); attack with rebuke or abuse; also, to defeat, as in a contest (colloq.).

troupe (tröp), n. [F.: see *troop*.] A troop, company, or band, esp. of players, singers, or the like: as, "a *troupe* of strolling actors" (H. James's "Europeans," v.).

troup-i-al (trö'pi-al), n. See *troopial*.

trou-ser (trou'zėr), n. Singular of *trousers*, used chiefly in composition.—**trou'sered**, a. Wearing trousers.—**trou'ser-ing**, n. Cloth for trousers.

trou-sers (trou'zėrz), n. pl. [For *trouses*, pl. of obs. or archaic *trouse*, first used of garments worn by the Irish, and appar. from Celtic: cf. Ir. *trius*, Gael. *triubhas*, and E. *trews*.] Orig., trews; now, a loose-fitting outer garment for men, covering the lower part of the trunk and each leg separately, and extending to the ankles; also, a shorter garment of this kind, reaching to the knees, esp. as worn by boys ('short trousers'); also, the long, loose drawers worn by Mohammedans; also, the long, white, frilled or trimmed drawers reaching to the ankles, formerly worn by women, girls, and young boys.

trousse (trös), n. [F., bundle, case of instruments; = E. *truss*, n.] A number of small implements carried together, as in a receptacle or case; a receptacle containing such implements: as, a surgeon's *trousse*.

trous-seau (trö-sō'), n.; pl. *-seaux* (-sōz'). [F., dim. of *trousse*, bundle, = E. *truss*, n.] A bundle†; also, a bride's outfit of clothes, linen, etc., which she brings with her at marriage.

Trousse (a), from a French illumination of 1350.

trout (trout), n.; pl. *trouts* or (esp. collectively) *trout*. [AS. *truht*, < L. *tructa*, *tructus*, trout, = Gr. τρώκτης, kind of sea-fish, < τρώγειν, gnaw, nibble.] A food-fish, *Salmo fario*, of the salmon family (*Salmonidæ*), common in the colder fresh waters of Europe; any of various other fishes of this genus, as the salmon-trout, or as *S. clarki* ('laketrout,' or 'Rocky Mountain brook-trout'), a common American species; any of various other fishes of the salmon family of the genus *Salvelinus* and the genus *Cristivomer* (commonly regarded as a section of *Salvelinus*), noted for their

gameness and prized as food, and including many common American species, as the brook-trout; any of various similar fishes not of the salmon family. Cf. *salmon-trout*, *lake-trout*, *brook-trout*, and *char*[3].—**trout'let**, **trout'ling**, n. A little trout.—**trout'=perch**, n. Any of the small freshwater fishes of the family *Percopsidæ*, of the cooler parts of North America, as *Percopsis guttatus* of the U. S. and Canada.

Trout-perch (*Percopsis guttatus*).

trou-vère (trö-vâr'), n. [F. *trouvère*, OF. *trovere, troveor*, < *trover*, find, invent, compose in verse: see *trover*, and cf. *troubadour*.] One of a class of poets who flourished in northern France during the 12th and 13th centuries, and whose works were chiefly narrative and epic in character. Cf. *troubadour*. Also **trou-veur'** (-vėr').

trove (trōv), n. [For *treasure-trove*.] Something of value found; a find: as, "delighted as a child at each new *trove*" (Kipling's "Kim," i.).

tro-ver (trō'vėr), n. [Noun use of OF. *trover*, find, invent, compose (F. *trouver*, find); origin uncertain: cf. *troubadour* and *trouvère*.] In *law*, the finding and the assuming possession of any personal property; hence, an action at law ('action of trover') for the recovery of the value of personal property illegally converted by another to his own use.

trow (trō), v. [AS. *trēowian*, *trūwian*, = G. *trauen*, trust, believe; akin to E. *true*.] **I.** *tr.* To trust†, or have confidence in†; also, to believe, or give credence to (a statement, etc.: archaic); also, to believe or think (archaic: as, "I *trow* that lad and I will ken each other when we meet again," Scott's "Legend of Montrose," iv.); suppose (archaic). **II.** *intr.* To believe (*in* or *on*)†; also, to believe, think, or suppose (archaic).

trow-el (trou'el), n. [OF. *truele* (F. *truelle*), < ML. *truella*, for L. *trulla*, dim. of *trua*, skimmer, ladle.] Any of various tools consisting of a plate of metal or other material, usually flat, fitted into a short handle, used for spreading, shaping, or smoothing plaster or the like; a similar tool with a curved, scoop-like blade, used in gardening for taking up plants, etc.—**to lay on with a trowel**, to lay on thickly or coarsely; hence, to express fully or thoroughly (as, "Well said: that was *laid on with a trowel*": Shakspere's "As You Like It," i. 2. 112); esp., to apply (*it*, that is, flattery) fulsomely or to gross excess.—**trow'el**, v. t.; *-eled* or *-elled*, *-eling* or *-elling*. To apply, shape, or smooth with or as with a trowel.—**trow'el=bay'o-net**, n. A bayonet with a short and broad but sharp-pointed trowel-like blade, intended to serve also as an intrenching tool.—**trow'el-beak**, n. A broad-beaked bird, or broadbill, *Corydon sumatranus* (family *Eurylæmidæ*), of Sumatra.

troy (troi), a. In or by troy weight.

troy weight (troi wāt). [From *Troyes*, in France.] A system of weights in use for precious metals and gems (formerly also for bread, etc.): 24 grains = 1 pennyweight; 20 pennyweights = 1 ounce; 12 ounces = 1 pound. The grain, ounce, and pound are the same as in apothecaries' weight, the grain alone being the same as in avoirdupois weight.

Trowelbeak, with outline of beak from above.

truancy   2055   true=love

tru-an-cy (trö′an-si), *n.*; pl. *-cies* (-siz). The act or an act of playing truant; truant conduct or habit.

tru-ant (trö′ant). [OF. *truant* (F. *truand*), vagabond, beggar; prob. from Celtic.] **I.** *n.* A vagabond† or beggar†; also, a lazy or idle person; one who shirks or neglects his duty; esp., a child who stays away from school without leave. **II.** *a.* Lazy, idle, or loitering; wandering or straying; esp., staying away from school without leave, as a child (as, "a sullen and *truant* schoolboy": Scott's "Talisman," xix.); also, pertaining to or characteristic of a truant (as, "a *truant* disposition": Shakspere's "Hamlet," i. 2. 169). —**tru′ant,** *v. i.* To idle; wander or stray; play truant: as, "His charges all would stray *Truanting* in every lane" (Henley's "Ballade of Truisms"). —**tru′ant-ly,** *adv.* —**tru′ant-ry** (-ri), *n.*; pl. *-ries* (-riz). Same as *truancy.*

truce (trös), *n.* [ME. *trewes,* pl. of *trewe,* < AS. *trēow,* truth, good faith, engagement, = OHG. *triuwa* (G. *treue*), truth, faith, = Goth. *triggwa,* covenant; akin to E. *true.*] A suspension of hostilities, as between armies, for a specified period, by agreement; an armistice; an agreement or treaty establishing this; sometimes, absence of hostilities; peace; also, respite, intermission, or freedom, as from trouble, pain, etc. —(a) **truce to** or (a) **truce with,** enough of; have done with: as, "*A truce to* your ill-timed mirth, Mr. Mareschal" (Scott's "Black Dwarf," xiii.); "*Truce with* your impertinence, Jeckols!" (Godwin's "Caleb Williams," xxviii.). [Archaic.] —**flag of truce.** See under *flag*[2], *n.* —**truce of God,** in the middle ages, a suspension of hostilities between armies, or of private feuds, ordered by the Church during Lent, on certain festivals, etc. —**truce′less,** *a.* Without truce; unceasing in hostility.

truck[1] (truk), *v.* [OF. F. *troquer;* origin unknown.] **I.** *tr.* To exchange; trade; barter; peddle or hawk. **II.** *intr.* To exchange commodities; barter; bargain or negotiate; traffic; have dealings. —**truck**[1], *n.* The act or practice of trucking or bartering; barter; a trade; a bargain or deal; also, the payment of wages in goods, etc., instead of money; the system of such payment ('truck system'); also, intercourse or dealings; also, commodities for barter or trade (obs. in general sense); vegetables, etc., raised for the market (U. S.: as, "vegetables from the '*truck* patch,' where squashes, melons, beans, and the like were grown," Roosevelt's "Winning of the West," i. 5); also, articles of miscellaneous character; odds and ends; trash or rubbish (as, "I can't smoke the *truck* the steward sells": Kipling's "Captains Courageous," i.).

truck[2] (truk), *n.* [Perhaps < *truckle.*] A small (wooden) wheel, cylinder, or roller, as on certain old-style gun-carriages; also, any of various wheeled frames or conveyances for moving heavy articles, as a barrow with two very low front wheels, on which sacks, bales, boxes, etc., are tilted to be moved, or a low rectangular frame on which heavy boxes, etc., are moved, or a low, flat car (of various types) for moving goods or the like; any of various strongly built carts, wagons, automobiles, etc., for transporting heavy loads; also, a group of two or more pairs of wheels in one frame, for supporting one end of a railway-car, locomotive, etc.; also, a circular or square piece of wood fixed on the head of a mast or the top of a flagstaff, and usually containing small holes for halyards. —**truck**[2], *v.* **I.** *tr.* To put on a truck; transport by a truck or trucks. **II.** *intr.* To convey articles or goods on a truck; drive a truck. —**truck′age** (-āj), *n.* Conveyance by a truck or trucks; also, the charge for this.

truck-er[1] (truk′ėr), *n.* One who trucks or barters; also, one who grows vegetables, etc., for the market (U. S.).

truck-er[2] (truk′ėr), *n.* One who conveys articles or goods on a truck or trucks.

truck=farm (truk′färm), *n.* A farm devoted to the growing of vegetables, etc., for the market. [U. S.] —**truck′=farm″er,** *n.* —**truck″=farm″ing,** *n.*

truck-ing[1] (truk′ing), *n.* The growing of vegetables, etc., for the market. [U. S.]

truck-ing[2] (truk′ing), *n.* The act or business of conveying articles or goods on trucks.

truck-le (truk′l), *n.* [L. *trochlea,* pulley: see *trochlea.*] A small wheel with a groove in the circumference; a pulley; also, a caster for setting under a piece of furniture, etc. (now

prov.); also, a truckle-bed. —**truck′le,** *v. i.*; *-led, -ling.* To occupy a truckle-bed†; hence, to take an inferior position†; also, to submit with servile complaisance; yield obsequiously or tamely (*to*); act with servility, as for some object sought. —**truck′le=bed,** *n.* A low bed moving on truckles or casters, usually pushed under another bed when not in use; a trundle-bed. —**truck′ler,** *n.* —**truck′ling-ly,** *adv.*

truck-man[1] (truk′man), *n.*; pl. *-men.* A man who grows vegetables, etc., for the market. [U. S.]

truck-man[2] (truk′man), *n.*; pl. *-men.* A man who conveys articles or goods on a truck or trucks; a truck-driver.

truc-u-lent (truk′ū-lent or trū′kū-), *a.* [L. *truculentus,* < *trux (truc-),* rough, harsh, fierce.] Fierce and cruel; savage; savagely threatening or bullying; brutally harsh: as, "*truculent* tyrants" (Scott's "Abbot," xiv.); "an arrogant, but not *truculent,* mood" (W. R. Inge's "Outspoken Essays," i. 4). —**truc′u-lence, truc′u-len-cy,** *n.* —**truc′u-lent-ly,** *adv.*

trudge (truj), *v. i.*; *trudged, trudging.* [Origin obscure.] To make one's way on foot; walk; esp., to walk laboriously or wearily (as, "Let's . . . shoulder our bundles and *trudge* along": Louisa M. Alcott's "Little Women," i. 4). —**trudge,** *n.* An act of trudging; a laborious walk (as, "It was a slow *trudge* home through the heavy fields": Mrs. Wharton's "Ethan Frome," iii.); also, one who trudges.

trudg-en (truj′en), *n.* [From J. *Trudgen,* English swimmer, who learned the stroke in South America.] A stroke in swimming, in which a double overarm motion is used. Also called *trudgen stroke.*

trudg-eon (truj′en), *n.* Erroneous form of *trudgen.*

true (trö), *a.*; compar. *truer,* superl. *truest.* [AS. *trēowe, trȳwe,* = D. *trouw* = G. *treu* = Icel. *tryggr* = Goth. *triggws,* true, faithful: cf. *trow, truce,* and *trust.*] Steadfast in adherence, as to a friend, a cause, or a promise; firm in allegiance; loyal; faithful; trusty; also, honest, honorable, or upright (archaic: as, "Rich preys make *true* men thieves," Shakspere's "Venus and Adonis," 724); free from deceit, or sincere (as, to have a *true* interest in a person's welfare); also, telling the truth, veracious, or truthful (archaic: as, "We know that thou art *true,* and teachest the way of God in truth," Mat. xxii. 16); also, being in accordance with the actual state of things (as, a *true* story); conforming to fact; not false; also, agreeing with a standard, pattern, rule, or the like (as, a *true* copy); exact, correct, or accurate (as, a *true* balance); exactly or accurately shaped, formed, fitted, or placed, as a surface, an instrument, or a part of a mechanism; reliable, unfailing, or sure (as, a *true* sign or indication); of the right kind, such as it should be, or proper (as, to arrange things in their *true* order); legitimate or rightful (as, the *true* heir to a title); also, real or genuine (as, *true* gold); properly so called, or rightly answering to a description (as, "Grenville wanted the elements of *true* statesmanship": Bancroft's "Hist. of the U. S.," Amer. Revolution, ii. 3); in *biol.,* conformable to the type or the accepted character of a class, genus, or the like (as, an amœba is a *true* animal); also, not hybrid or mongrel (as, a *true* Jersey cow). —**true bill,** in *law,* a bill of indictment indorsed by a grand jury, after investigation, as being sufficiently supported by evidence to justify a hearing of the case. —**true discount.** See *discount, n.* —**true,** *n.* That which is true (with *the*); exact or accurate formation, position, or adjustment (as, to be out of *true*). —**true,** *adv.* In a true manner; truly or truthfully; exactly or accurately (as, "One man . . . levelled his piece so *true* that the shot went through the fellow's head": Defoe's "Captain Singleton," xv.); in agreement with the ancestral type (as, to breed *true*). —**true,** *v. t.*; *trued, truing.* To make true; shape, adjust, or place exactly or accurately; make perfectly straight, level, square, or the like. —**true′=blue′. I.** *a.* Unchanging (perhaps with reference to a fast blue dye); unwavering; stanch; true: as, "Tom's *true-blue* . . . He won't desert" (Mark Twain's "Tom Sawyer," xv.). **II.** *n.* One who is true-blue. —**true′=born,** *a.* Born of a pure stock; having the qualities associated with such birth; legitimately born. —**true′=heart′ed,** *a.* Having a true heart; faithful or loyal; honest or sincere. —**true′=love,** *n.* One truly loving or loved; one whose love is pledged; a sweetheart; also, the herb-paris, *Paris quadrifolia,* which has a whorl of four leaves with a single flower or

---

(variable) ḓ as d or j, ṣ as s or sh, ṭ as t or ch, ẕ as z or zh; o, F. *cloche;* ü, F. *menu;* ch, Sc. *loch;* ṅ, F. *bonbon;* ′, primary accent; ″, secondary accent; †, obsolete; <, from; +, and; =, equals. See also lists at beginning of book.

berry in the center suggesting a true-love knot. — **true=love knot,** an ornamental knot, esp. a kind of bow-knot, used as an emblem of true love or interwoven affections. Also called *true-lovers' knot.* — **true′ness,** *n.* — **true′pen″ny,** *n.* A trusty person; an honest fellow. [Archaic.]

truf-fle (truf′l or trŏ′fl), *n.* [F. *truffle, trufle,* obs. var. of *truffe,* truffle, perhaps < L. *tuber:* see *tuber.*] Any of various subterranean edible fungi of the ascomycetous genus *Tuber,* commonly with a black warty exterior; any of various similar edible fungi of other genera. — **truf′fled,** *a.* Furnished, cooked, or stuffed with truffles.

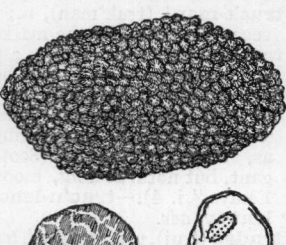

Truffle (*Tuber melanosporum*). — *a,* section, showing the interior structure; *b,* an ascus.

tru-ism (trŏ′izm), *n.* A self-evident truth; a truth so obvious that it might go without saying: as, "The original thought of one age becomes the *truism* of the next" (Hallam's "Literature of Europe," iii. 3. § 107). — **tru-is′tic,** *a.*

trull (trul), *n.* [Cf. G. *trolle, trulle,* trull, trollop.] A low prostitute; a strumpet.

tru-ly (trŏ′li), *adv.* [AS. *trēowlíce.*] In a true manner; faithfully; in accordance with fact or truth; exactly or accurately; rightly or duly; legitimately; really or genuinely; also, indeed or forsooth (as, a great story, *truly!*).

tru-meau (trü-mō′), *n.;* pl. *-meaux* (-mōz, F. -mō). [F.; origin uncertain.] A portion of wall between two openings, as doors or windows; sometimes, a central pier dividing a wide doorway, as in medieval churches; also, a mirror or any piece of decorative work covering the space between two openings or above a mantelpiece or the like.

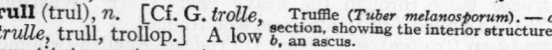

Trumeau, 13th century. — At Villeneuve-le-Comte, France.

trump[1] (trump), *n.* [OF. F. *trompe;* origin uncertain.] A trumpet, or its sound (archaic or poetic); hence, some similar sound (as, "The shore rang with the *trump* of bull-frogs": Thoreau's "Walden," iv.); also, fig., one who or that which sounds, proclaims, etc., loudly like a trumpet (archaic or poetic); also, a jews'-harp (chiefly Sc.). — **trump**[1], *v.* **I.** *intr.* To blow or sound a trumpet (obs. or rare); hence, to give forth a trumpet-like sound (as, "The bullfrogs *trump* to usher in the night": Thoreau's "Walden," v.). **II.** *tr.* To proclaim, etc., by or as by the sound of a trumpet. [Now rare.]

trump[2] (trump), *v. t.* [OF. F. *tromper,* deceive; origin uncertain.] To deceive† or cheat†; also, with *up,* to get up or devise deceitfully or unfairly, as a charge, etc. (as, "if . . . those servants could *trump* up such accusations": Godwin's "Caleb Williams," xxxvii.); fabricate.

trump[3] (trump), *n.* [Corruption of *triumph* (as used in card-playing).] Any playing-card of a suit that for the time outranks the other suits, such a card being able to take any card of another suit; *pl.* or *sing.,* the suit itself; also, *sing.,* an act of trumping; also, a person on whom one can depend, a person of great excellence, or a good fellow (colloq.: as,

"Give me your hand — you are a real *trump,*" Lever's "Harry Lorrequer," xvi.). — **to put to one's trumps,** to oblige (a card-player) to play his trumps; fig., to put (one) to his last resource or expedient (as, "I have been *put* incessantly *to my trumps* to keep thee safe and sound": Irving's "Knickerbocker's New York," vii. 4). — **trump**[3], *v.* **I.** *tr.* To put a trump upon; take with a trump. **II.** *intr.* To play a trump; take a trick with a trump.

trump-er-y (trum′pėr-i). [OF. F. *tromperie,* deceit, < *tromper,* E. *trump*[2].] **I.** *n.;* pl. *-ies* (-iz). Deceit† or fraud†; also, something showy but of little intrinsic value; worthless finery; useless stuff; rubbish; trash; nonsensical or idle belief, practice, discourse, etc., or nonsense (as, "the fairies and fairy *trumpery* of legendary fabling": Lamb's "Old Benchers of the Inner Temple"). **II.** *a.* Showy but unsubstantial or useless; of little or no value; trifling; paltry; rubbishy: as, "To her own eyes his *trumpery* gift looked intrinsically important" (L. Merrick's "Position of Peggy Harper," i. 7).

trum-pet (trum′pet), *n.* [OF. F. *trompette,* dim. of *trompe,* E. *trump*[1].] Any of a class of musical wind-instruments with a penetrating, powerful tone, consisting of a long tube, now usually metallic, and commonly once or twice curved round upon itself, having a cup-shaped mouthpiece at one end and a flaring bell at the other; also, an organ-stop having a tone resembling that of a trumpet; also, a trumpeter; also, a sound like that of a trumpet; the loud cry of the elephant or some other animal; also, any of various trumpet-shaped articles or devices; such a device for directing, intensifying, or collecting sound, as for speaking through, or for listening through when the hearing is defective; also, *pl.,* a pitcher-plant, *Sarracenia flava.* — **trum′pet,** *v.* **I.** *intr.* To blow or sound a trumpet; hence, to emit a sound like that of a trumpet, as an elephant. **II.** *tr.* To sound on a trumpet; utter with a sound like that of a trumpet; fig., to proclaim loudly or widely (as, "He never wearied of *trumpeting* forth the glories of the new knowledge": J. H. Robinson's "Mind in the Making," vi. 12); noise abroad.

Cavalry-trumpet.

trum-pet=creep-er (trum′pet-krē″pėr), *n.* Any of the climbing plants of the bignoniaceous genus *Tecoma,* esp. *T. radicans,* a native of the southern U. S., with large red trumpet-shaped flowers. Also called *trumpet-flower* and *trumpet-vine.*

trum-pet-er (trum′pet-ėr), *n.* One who sounds or plays a trumpet; fig., one who proclaims or announces something loudly or widely; also, one of a breed of domestic pigeons; also, any of the large South American birds constituting the genus *Psophia,* esp. the agami, *P. crepitans* ('golden-breasted trumpeter'), which is notable for its trumpet-like cry; also, a large North American wild swan, *Olor buccinator,* having a sonorous cry.

Trumpet-creeper (*Tecoma radicans*), with opened follicle showing seeds.

trum-pet= flow-er (trum′pet-flou″ėr), *n.* The trumpet-creeper.

Trumpeter (*Olor buccinator*).

trum-pet=hon-ey-suck-le (trum′pet-hun″i-suk″l), *n.* An American honeysuckle, *Lonicera sempervirens*, with large tubular flowers deep red outside and yellow within.

trum-pet=shaped (trum′pet-shāpt), *a.* Tubular, with one end dilated.

trum-pet=tree (trum′pet-trē), *n.* The trumpetwood.

trum-pet=vine (trum′pet-vīn), *n.* The trumpet-creeper.

trum-pet=weed (trum′pet-wēd), *n.* The joepye-weed, *Eupatorium purpureum*.

trum-pet=wood (trum′pet-wùd), *n.* A tropical American moraceous tree, *Cecropia peltata*, with large peltate leaves, and hollow stems which are used for musical instruments.

trun-cate (trung′kāt), *v. t.*; -cated, -cating. [L. *truncatus*, pp. of *truncare*, reduce by cutting, cut off, < *truncus*, E. *trunk*.] To shorten by cutting off a part; cut short; mutilate.—**trun′cate**, *a.* Truncated; in *bot.*, appearing as if cut short at the tip by a transverse line, as certain leaves; in *zoöl.* and *anat.*, square or broad at the end, as if cut off transversely; lacking the apex, as certain spiral shells.—**trun′cat-ed** (-kā-ted), *p. a.* Shortened by the cutting off of a part, or appearing as if so shortened; specif., of a geometrical figure or solid, having the apex, vertex, or end cut off by a plane (as, a *truncated* cone or pyramid); of a crystal, etc., having angles or edges cut off or replaced by planes; of one of the angles or edges, cut off or replaced by a plane; in *bot.*, truncate; in *zoöl.* and *anat.*, truncate.—**trun′cate-ly**, *adv.*—**trun-ca′tion** (-kā′shọn), *n.* [LL. *truncatio(n-)*.] The act of truncating, or the resulting state.

Truncate Leaf.

Cube with Truncated Edges.

trun-cheon (trun′chọn), *n.* [OF. *tronchon* (F. *tronçon*), broken piece, < L. *truncus*, E. *trunk*.] A piece broken off, esp. from a spear or lance (obs. or archaic); the shaft of a spear (obs. or archaic); a length cut from a plant, as for planting or grafting (now rare); a club or cudgel, now esp. a club carried by a policeman; a baton, or staff of office or authority (as, "the *truncheon* of a Marshal [of France": Macaulay's "Hist. of Eng.," ix.).—**trun′cheon**, *v. t.* To beat with a truncheon or club.

trun-dle (trun′dl), *n.* [Var. of *trindle*.] A small wheel, roller, or the like; esp., a small wheel adapted to support a heavy weight, as the wheel of a caster; also, a lantern-wheel, or each of the bars of a lantern-wheel; also, a truck or carriage on low wheels (now rare); also, a quill of gold thread for use by an embroiderer, esp. such a quill as a charge in heraldry; also, an act of trundling or rolling (as, "Our caboose took up again its easy *trundle*": Wister's "Virginian," xvi.); the impulse which causes something to roll.—**trun′dle**, *v.*; -dled, -dling. **I.** *tr.* To cause (a ball, hoop, etc.) to roll along; roll; also, to cause to rotate; twirl; whirl; also, to draw or push along on a wheel or wheels (as, "Uncle Venner, *trundling* a wheelbarrow": Hawthorne's "House of the Seven Gables," xix.); also, to convey in a wheeled vehicle (as, "She followed the porter who *trundled* her luggage": Arnold Bennett's "Helen with the High Hand," xviii.). **II.** *intr.* To roll along (as, "Occasionally a hat or wig . . . came spinning and *trundling* past him": Dickens's "Barnaby Rudge," v.); also, to move or run on a wheel or wheels (as, "This 'bus . . . *trundled* through Sandgate": H. G. Wells's "Kipps," i. 6); also, to go in a wheeled vehicle; also, fig., to go or run easily or rapidly; go away; also, to walk with a rolling or unsteady gait.—**trun′dle=bed**, *n.* A low bed, usually on trundles or casters, which can be pushed under a high bed when not in use; a truckle-bed.—**trun′dle=tail**, *n.* A curled or curly tail; also, a dog with such a tail; a low-bred dog; a cur. [Obs. or archaic.]

trunk (trungk). [OF. F. *tronc*, < L. *truncus*, trunk (of tree, body, etc.), stock, shaft, < *truncus*, mutilated, deprived of parts.] **I.** *n.* The main stem of a tree, as distinct from the branches and roots; the shaft of a column; the dado or die of a pedestal; the body of a human being or of an animal, without the head and limbs, or the head, limbs, and tail, or considered apart from these; the thorax of an insect; the main body of an artery, nerve, or the like, as distinct from its branches; the main line of a river, railroad, canal, telegraph-line, or the like; also, a box, chest, or case, now one for holding clothes and other articles, as for use on a journey; a perforated floating box in which live fish are kept; also, a box-like passage, usually made of boards, for light, air, water, grain, etc.; a shaft; a chute; a large inclosed passage through the decks or bulkheads of a vessel, for coaling, ventilation, or the like; any of various water-tight casings in a vessel, as the vertical one above the slot for a center-board in the bottom of a boat; the tube or hollow cylinder replacing the piston-rod in a trunk-engine; any of various pipes or tubes, as a speaking-tube, a blow-gun, or a telescope†; the long, flexible, cylindrical nasal appendage of the elephant, having the nostrils at the extremity; a proboscis; a long snout; also, *pl.*, trunk-hose†; short, tight-fitting breeches or drawers, as worn over tights in theatrical use, or as worn by athletes, swimmers, etc. **II.** *a.* Noting or pertaining to the main line, as of a railroad.

trunked (trungkt), *a.* Having a trunk.

trunk=en-gine (trungk′en″jin), *n.* A steam-engine, internal-combustion engine, or the like, which has, instead of a piston-rod, a tube or hollow cylinder (the *trunk*) attached to and moving with the piston, and of sufficient diameter to contain the connecting-rod and allow it to be coupled directly to the piston.

trunk=fish (trungk′fish), *n.* Any of the plectognath fishes constituting the family *Ostraciontidæ* (or *Ostraciidæ*), which inhabit warm seas, and have a box-like body incased in bony polygonal plates.

trunk=ful (trungk′fùl), *n.*; pl. -fuls. As much as a trunk will hold.

trunk=hose (trungk′hōz), *n. pl.* Full, bag-like breeches covering the person from the waist to the middle of the thigh or lower, worn in the 16th and 17th centuries.

trun-nel (trun′l), *n.* Corruption of *treenail*.

trun-nion (trun′yọn), *n.* [F. *trognon*, core, stump; origin uncertain.] Either of the two cylindrical projections on a cannon, one on each side, which support it on its carriage; hence, any of various similar supports, gudgeons, or pivots.—**trun′nioned**, *a.* Provided with trunnions.

Trunk-hose. — 1, Charles IX. of France (1550-74); 2, Robert Carr, Earl of Somerset (died 1645).

tru-queur (trü-kèr′), *n.* [F., < *truquer*, prepare alleged antiques, < *truc*, stroke, artful expedient, trick (of a trade).] One who prepares alleged antiques for sale.

truss (trus), *v. t.* [OF. *trusser*, *trosser*, *torser* (F. *trousser*); origin uncertain.] To tie in a bundle, or pack closely in a receptacle (now rare); tie, bind, or fasten, as with a cord or the like (now rare); draw tight and tie, as laces, or draw tight and tie the laces of (now rare); confine or inclose, as the body, by something fastened closely around; adjust and draw closely the garments of (a person); fasten up (the hair); make fast with skewers or the like, as the wings of a fowl preparatory to cooking; hang (a person) as a criminal (usually with *up*); of a bird of prey, to seize and hold firmly (the prey) in the talons; seize and carry off; in *building*, etc., to furnish or support with a truss or trusses.—**truss**, *n.* [OF. F. *trousse*.] A collection of things tied together or packed in a receptacle; a bundle; a pack; a bundle of hay or straw, now usually, in England, one containing 56 pounds of old hay, 60 pounds of new hay, or 36 pounds of straw; in *hort.*, a compact terminal cluster or head of flowers growing upon one stalk; in *surg.*, an appliance, usually consisting of a pad with a belt or a spring, serving for support in hernia, etc.; in *building*, etc., a combination of members, as beams, bars, ties, or the like, so arranged, usually in a triangle or a collection of triangles, as to form a rigid framework, and used in bridges ('bridge-truss'), roofs ('roof-truss'), etc., to give support and rigidity to the whole or a part of the structure; also, a projection from the face of a wall, as for supporting a cornice or the like; *naut.*, an iron fitting by which a lower yard is secured to the mast. —**truss′er**, *n.*—**truss′ing**, *n.* In *building*, etc., the members which form a truss; a structure consisting of trusses; trusses collectively.

trust (trust). [ME. *trust, trost*, from Scand.: cf. Icel. *traust, trust*, confidence; akin to E. *true*.] **I.** *n.* Reliance on the integrity, justice, etc., of a person, or on some quality or attribute of a thing; confidence; that on which one relies (as, "Blessed is that man that maketh the Lord his *trust*": Ps. xl. 4); also, confident expectation of something, or hope (as, "His *trust* was with the Eternal to be deem'd Equal in strength": Milton's "Paradise Lost," ii. 46); also, confidence in the ability or intention of a person to pay at some future time for goods, etc., not paid for when supplied; credit; also, the quality of being trustworthy, or reliability (now rare: as, "There's no *trust*, No faith, no honesty in men," Shakspere's "Romeo and Juliet," iii. 2. 85); also, the state of being relied on, or the state of one to whom something is intrusted (as, "Keep that which is committed to thy *trust*": 1 Tim. vi. 20); the obligation or responsibility imposed on one in whom confidence or authority is placed (as, a position of *trust*; a breach of *trust*); also, the state of being confided to another's care or guard (as, "his seal'd commission, left in *trust* with me": Shakspere's "Pericles," i. 3. 13); also, something committed or intrusted to one, as an office, duty, etc. (as, "the English doctrine that all power is a *trust* for the public good": Macaulay's "Essays," Horace Walpole); in *law*, a confidence reposed in a person by making him the nominal owner of property which he is to hold, use, or dispose of for the benefit of another; an estate, etc., committed to a trustee or trustees; a trustee, or a body of trustees; also, the right of a person to enjoy the use or profits of property held in trust, or to require a disposal of it for his benefit; in *com.*, orig., a combination of industrial or commercial companies having a central committee or board of trustees controlling a majority or the whole of the stock of each of the constituent companies, thus making it possible to manage the concerns so as to economize expenses, regulate production, defeat competition, etc.; popularly, any similar combination of producers in the same line of business, esp. for defeating competition. **II.** *a.* Of or pertaining to trust or a trust; held in trust (as, a *trust* fund).—**trust company,** a company or corporation organized to exercise the functions of a trustee, but usually occupied also with banking and other financial activities.—**trust,** *v. i.* [Cf. Icel. *treysta*, refl., trust, rely.] To have or place trust or reliance (as, "*Trust* in the Lord": Ps. xxxvii. 3); have faith or confidence; also, to look or hope (*for*); also, to sell goods on trust or credit (as, "He kept his shop miserably . . . and often *trusted* without keeping accounts": B. Franklin's "Autobiography," iv.).—**to trust to,** to rely or depend on: as, "The old man *trusts* wholly *to* slow contrivance and gradual progression" (Johnson's "Rasselas," xxvi.).—**trust,** *v. t.* To have trust or confidence in; rely or depend on; also, to give credence to, or believe (as, "if he . . . *trust* my tale": Shakspere's "Taming of the Shrew," iv. 2. 67); also, to expect confidently, or hope (with a clause or an infinitive: as, "Oh yet *we trust* that somehow good Will be the final goal of ill," Tennyson's "In Memoriam," liv.; "They *trusted* to be off and away, before any prowlers could reach the place," Irving's "Captain Bonneville," xxvii.); also, to commit or consign with trust or confidence (as, "The Jewish maiden will rather *trust* her soul with God, than her honour to the Templar!" Scott's "Ivanhoe," xxiv.); permit to be in some place, position, etc., or to do something, without fear of consequences (as, he will not *trust* it out of his sight; "I don't think I could *trust* myself to speak to him about it," Tarkington's "Magnificent Ambersons," xvi.); also, to invest with a trust, or intrust with something (as, "those that had *trusted* him with the government," Hobbes's "Leviathan," xix.; "She *trusted* me with all her secrets," Mrs. H. Ward's "Lady Rose's Daughter," iv.); also, to give credit to (a person) for goods, etc., supplied.

trust-a-ble (trus′tạ-bl), *a.* That may be trusted.

trust=bust-er (trust′bus″tẽr), *n.* One who breaks up trusts, or combinations of industrial or commercial companies in restraint of competition. [Slang, U. S.]—**trust′=bust″-ing,** *n.*

trust-ee (trus-tē′), *n.* One to whom property or funds have been legally intrusted to be administered for the benefit of another; by extension, a person, usually one of a body of persons, appointed to administer the affairs of a company, institution, etc.—**trustee process,** in *law*, the attachment of property, etc., by garnishment. [U. S.]—**trust-ee′,** *v. t.*; *trusteed, trusteeing.* To place in the hands of a trustee or trustees; in *law*, to attach by trustee process (U. S.).—**trust-ee′ship,** *n.*

trust-er (trus′tẽr), *n.* One who trusts.

trust-ful (trust′fúl), *a.* Full of trust; trusting; confiding. —**trust′ful-ly,** *adv.*—**trust′ful-ness,** *n.*

trust-i-ly (trus′ti-li), *adv.* In a trusty manner.—**trust′i-ness,** *n.*

trust-ing (trus′ting), *p. a.* That trusts; confiding; trustful. —**trust′ing-ly,** *adv.*—**trust′ing-ness,** *n.*

trust-less (trust′les), *a.* Not to be trusted; untrustworthy; also, having no trust; distrustful.

trust-wor-thy (trust′wẽr″ᵺi), *a.* Worthy of trust or confidence; reliable: as, "a most *trustworthy* and unexaggerating historian" (H. Melville's "Moby-Dick," xlv.); "So far the report is *trustworthy*" (G. Meredith's "Lord Ormont and His Aminta," ii.).—**trust′wor″thi-ly,** *adv.*—**trust′wor″-thi-ness,** *n.*

trust-y (trus′ti). **I.** *a.*; compar. *trustier*, superl. *trustiest.* Trusting or trustful (now rare); also, that may be trusted, or relied on, or trustworthy or reliable (as, "these excellent and *trusty* servants of the King," Burke's "American Taxation"; "his *trusty* sword," Longfellow's "Courtship of Miles Standish," i). **II.** *n.*; pl. *trusties* (-tiz). One who or that which is trusty or trusted; specif., a well-behaved and trustworthy convict to whom special privileges are granted.

truth (trŏth), *n.*; pl. *truths* (trŏᵺz or trŏths). [AS. *trēowth*, < *trēowe*, E. *true*.] The state or character of being true; fidelity or constancy (archaic); pledged word† or troth†; honesty, uprightness, or integrity; disposition to act without deceit, or sincerity; disposition to speak truly, or veracity; conformity with fact or reality, or verity (as, the *truth* of a statement or a surmise); accuracy of representation or delineation in literature or art (as, "imitations of birds, insects, or flowers, executed with uncommon *truth* and delicacy": Prescott's "Conquest of Mexico," iv. 5); avoidance of deceit and imitation in architectural construction and decoration; agreement with a standard, rule, or the like; accuracy, as of position or adjustment; genuineness, reality, or actual existence (as, "she, having the *truth* of honour in her": Shakspere's "Measure for Measure," iii. 1. 166); also, that which is true; the true or actual facts of a case (as, to tell the *truth*; to perceive, learn, or seek the *truth*; "He is not far off the *truth*," J. Conrad's "Rescue," iv. 4); true religious belief or doctrine; spiritual reality; also, a verified or indisputable fact, proposition, principle, or the like (as, mathematical *truths*; the *truths* of religion; "Shams and delusions are esteemed for soundest *truths*," Thoreau's "Walden," ii.).—**in truth,** in fact; in reality; truly.—**truth′ful,** *a.* Telling the truth, esp. habitually, as a person; conforming to truth, as a statement; corresponding with fact or reality, as a representation (as, "a portrait of her father, villainously *truthful* after the manner of such works": H. G. Wells's "Tono-Bungay," ii. 1. § 5).—**truth′ful-ly,** *adv.*—**truth′ful-ness,** *n.*—**truth′less,** *a.* Unfaithful (obs. or archaic); untruthful or mendacious, as a person; untrue or false, as a statement.

try (trī), *v. t.*; *tried, trying.* [OF. F. *trier*, pick, cull, sort; origin uncertain.] To separate, as one thing from another†; also, to separate by sifting or straining†; sift† or strain†; also, to separate (metal) from the ore or dross by melting†; refine by fire†; also, to extract by heat, as oil from fat or blubber (usually with *out*); melt (fat, etc.) to obtain the oil (usually with *out*); render; also, to ascertain by search or examination† (usually with *out*: as, "He bent himself to *try* out the truth herein," Strype's "Memorials of Cranmer," i. 1); ascertain the truth or right of (a matter, etc.) by test (as, "The rushing winds . . . With equal rage their airy quarrel *try*," Pope's tr. Statius's "Thebais," i. 490: sometimes with *out*: now rare); also, to put to the proof or test; subject to experimental treatment in order to determine the quality, value, fitness, accuracy, etc., of (as, to *try* a new invention); to *try* weights or measures); attempt to open (a door, window, etc.) in order to find out whether it is locked or fastened (as, "The driver got down and *tried* the gate": Bret Harte's "Miggles"); test the effect or result of. or apply or practise tentatively (as, to *try* an experiment, to *try* a new method); endeavor to ascertain by experiment (as, to *try* one's luck or fortune; "I determined . . . to *try* the effect of absence on her," W. H. Hudson's "Green Mansions," x.; to *try* what one can do); sometimes, to experiment upon, as with something; also, to show or prove by test or experience (obs. or rare: as, "He hath still been *tried* a holy man," Shakspere's "Romeo and Juliet," iv. 3. 29); also, to have experience of†; undergo†; also, to attempt to do or accomplish, or essay (as, it seems easy until you *try* it; "I'll couch me here till evening grey, Then darkling *try* my dangerous way," Scott's "Lady of the Lake," iv. 28); also, to incite to wrong, tempt, or solicit; also, to put to a severe test; strain the endurance, patience, etc., of (as, to *try* one's eyes; to *try* one's temper; "The ass, though naturally a good-tempered beast, had been most sadly *tried*," J. H. Newman's "Callista," xx.); subject to grievous experiences, affliction, or trouble; in *law*, to examine and determine judicially, as a cause; determine judicially the guilt or innocence of (a person).—**to try on**, to put on, as a garment, in order to test the fit, etc.—**to try out**, see definitions above; also, to test the value, worth, or fitness of (colloq.); make trial or experiment of (colloq.: as, "She's always *trying out* the latest stunt," Sinclair Lewis's "Arrowsmith," xiv.).—**to try over**, to go through (a performance, etc.) by way of experiment.—**try**, *v. i.* To make trial or experiment; make an attempt or effort (as, *try* harder next time; "There can be no reason why you should not *try* for him," Jane Austen's "Sense and Sensibility," xxxiii.); *naut.*, of a vessel, to lie to†. —**try**, *n.*; pl. **tries** (trīz). An act of trying; an attempt, endeavor, or effort: as, "I suppose we shall all have a *try* at it" (Mrs. H. Ward's "Robert Elsmere," xxxi.). [Chiefly colloq.]—**try′ing**, *p. a.* That tries, or tests severely; hard to endure; annoying; distressing: as, "Sophia's attitude was really very *trying*" (Arnold Bennett's "Old Wives' Tale," i. 3); "their hard and *trying* position" (De Quincey's "Revolt of the Tartars").—**try′ing-ly**, *adv.*—**try′ing=ness**, *n.*

try-ma (trī′mä), *n.*; pl. **-mata** (-mạ-tä). [NL., < Gr. τρῦμα, hole, < τρύειν, rub down, wear out.] In *bot.*, a drupaceous nut having a fibrous or fleshy exocarp which is ultimately dehiscent, as in the walnut and hickory.

try-out (trī′out), *n.* A trial or test made to ascertain the fitness of a person or thing for a particular purpose. [Colloq.]

tryp-a-no-some (trip′ạ-nō-sōm), *n.* [NL. *Trypanosoma*, < Gr. τρύπανον, boring instrument (see *trepan*[1]), + σῶμα, body.] Any of the minute flagellate protozoans constituting the genus *Trypanosoma*, parasitic in the blood of man and other vertebrates, and often causing serious diseases, as sleeping-sickness (due to *T. gambiense*) and tsetse-fly disease (due to *T. brucei*), the infection being usually transferred by the bite of an insect, as a tsetse-fly; any of various related protozoans. Also **tryp″a-no-so′ma** (-sō′mä).—**tryp″a-no-so′mal**, **tryp″a-no-so-mat′ic** (-sō-mat′ik), *a.*—**tryp″a-no-so-mi′a-sis** (-mī′ạ-sis), *n.* [NL.] In *pathol.*, any disease, as sleeping-sickness, due to infection with trypanosomes.

tryp-sin (trip′sin), *n.* [Appar. formed, after *pepsin*, < Gr. τρύειν, rub down, wear out.] In *chem.*, a proteolytic enzyme of the pancreatic juice, capable of converting proteids into peptone.—**tryp′tic**, *a.* Pertaining to, produced by, or of the nature of trypsin.

try-sail (trī′sāl, naut. -sl), *n. Naut.*, a small fore-and-aft sail set with a gaff, and sometimes with a boom, on the foremast or mainmast of a ship, or on a small mast ('trysail-mast') abaft the foremast or mainmast: used esp. for heavy weather.

try=square (trī′skwår), *n.* A square for laying off right angles or for testing the squareness of anything.

tryst (trīst or trist), *n.* [OF. *triste*, *tristre*, an appointed station in hunting; origin uncertain.] An appointment to meet at a certain time and place; also, an appointed meeting; also, an appointed place of meeting; also, a market or fair, esp. for cattle (Sc. and north. Eng.).—**tryst**, *v.* **I.** *tr.* To make an engagement with (a person) for a meeting; also, to engage (a person) to do something; also, to appoint (a time, etc.); also, to arrange for or order (a thing) in advance; also, to betroth or affiance; also, to visit, as with misfortune. [Chiefly Sc.] **II.** *intr.* To make an engagement, as for a meeting or to do something; also, to meet at an appointed time and place. [Chiefly Sc.]—**tryst′er**, *n.*—**tryst′ing=place**, *n.* An appointed meeting-place; a place where a tryst is to be kept.

tsar (tsär), etc. See *czar*, etc.

tset-se (tset′sẹ), *n.* [S. Afr.] Any of the blood-sucking dipterous insects, of Africa, constituting the genus *Glossina*, as *G. palpalis*, which disseminates sleeping-sickness, and *G. morsitans*, which disseminates tsetse-fly disease (cf. *trypanosome*). Also **tset′se=fly.**—**tsetse=fly disease,** a serious disease of animals, common in certain parts of Africa, caused by a parasitic protozoan, *Trypanosoma brucei*, the infection being transferred from one animal to another through the bites of a tsetse-fly, *Glossina morsitans*.

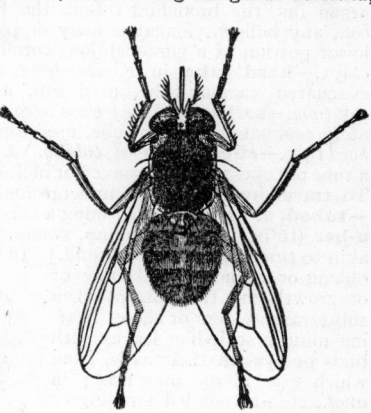

Tsetse (*Glossina morsitans*), four times natural size.

T=square (tē′skwår), *n.* A T-shaped ruler used in mechanical drawing for making parallel lines, etc., the shorter arm, or crosspiece, sliding along the edge of the drawing-board, which serves as a guide.

tub (tub), *n.* [ME. *tubbe* = MLG. *tubbe* = D. *tobbe*, tub.] A round, open wooden vessel, broad in proportion to height, usually made of staves held together by hoops and fitted around a flat bottom; also, as much as a tub will hold; also, any of various vessels resembling or suggesting a tub; a bucket, box, or the like in which material is brought up from or conveyed in a mine; a slow, clumsy ship or boat (colloq.: as, "the second officer of this old *tub*," Stevenson's "Kidnapped," vii.); esp., a vessel or receptacle for bathing in; a bathtub; hence, the act or practice of bathing in a tub, or a bath in a tub (colloq.).—**tub**, *v.*; **tubbed**, **tubbing.** **I.** *tr.* To put or set in a tub; also, to wash or bathe in a tub or bath (colloq.). **II.** *intr.* To wash one's self in a tub or bath; also, to undergo washing in a tub, esp. without damage, as a fabric. [Colloq.]

tu-ba[1] (tū′bä), *n.*; pl. **-bas** (-bạz). [L., trumpet, akin to *tubus*, E. *tube*.] A valved musical instrument of the trumpet class, of very large size and low pitch.

tu-ba[2] (tö′bä), *n.* [Malay.] A beverage consisting of the sap obtained from the immature inflorescence of various palms, as the cocoa-palm; also, a strongly alcoholic liquor distilled from this.

tu-bal (tū′bạl), *a.* Of or pertaining to a tube or tubes; tubular.

tu-bate (tū′bāt), *a.* Forming or having a tube or tubes.

tub-by (tub′i), *a.* Tub-shaped; round like a tub; of a person, corpulent; also, having a sound like that of an empty tub when struck; having a dull sound; without resonance.—**tub′bi-ness**, *n.*

Tuba.

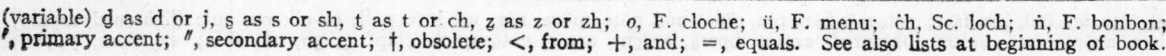

tube (tūb), *n.* [F. *tube*, < L. *tubus*, tube, pipe: cf. *tuba¹*.] A hollow, usually cylindrical body of metal, glass, rubber, or other material, with a relatively small diameter, used for conveying or containing fluids and for other purposes; also, material of tubular form; also, any tube-like instrument, piece, part, organ, etc.; a test-tube; a small, collapsible metal cylinder closed at one end and having the open end provided with a cap, for holding paint, tooth-paste, or other semiliquid substance to be squeezed out by pressure; a telescope (archaic); a tubular channel for the transmission of letters, parcels, etc., by pressure or exhaustion of air; the tubular tunnel in which an underground railway runs, or the railway itself (colloq.: as, "They went back in the *tube* to their modest Bloomsbury hotel," H. G. Wells's "Soul of a Bishop," ix.); in *anat.* and *zoöl.*, any hollow, cylindrical vessel or organ (as, the bronchial *tubes*; the Eustachian *tube*); in *bot.*, any hollow, elongated body or part; esp., the united lower portion of a gamopetalous corolla or a gamosepalous calyx.—**hard tube,** in *wireless teleg.* and *teleph.*, a highly evacuated vacuum-tube, used esp. as an amplifier. Cf. *soft tube.*—**soft tube,** in *wireless teleg.* and *teleph.*, a moderately evacuated vacuum-tube, used esp. as a detector. Cf. *hard tube.*—**tube,** *v.*; *tubed, tubing.* **I.** *tr.* To furnish with a tube or tubes; also, to convey or inclose in a tube. **II.** *intr.* To travel by a tube, or underground railway. [Colloq.]
—**tubed,** *a.* Having or forming a tube: as, a *tubed* corolla.

tu-ber (tū′bėr), *n.* [L., hump, swelling, knob, truffle, prob. akin to *tumere*, swell: see *tumid*.] In *bot.*, a fleshy, usually oblong or rounded thickening or outgrowth (as the potato) of a subterranean stem or shoot, bearing minute scale-like leaves with buds or eyes in their axils, from which new plants may arise; in *anat.*, etc., a rounded swelling or protuberance; a tuberosity; a tubercle.

Tuber of Potato (*Solanum tuberosum*).

tu-ber-cle (tū′bėr-kl), *n.* [L. *tuberculum*, dim. of *tuber*: see *tuber*.] A small rounded projection or excrescence, as on a bone, on the surface of the body in various animals, or on a plant; in *pathol.*, a small, firm, rounded nodule or swelling; specif., the characteristic lesion of tuberculosis.—**tubercle bacillus,** a short, slender, rod-like, often slightly curved or bent micro-organism, *Bacillus tuberculosis*, the cause of tuberculosis: discovered by Robert Koch in 1882.—**tu′ber-cled,** *a.* Characterized by or affected with tubercles.—**tu-ber-cu-lar** (tū-bėr′kū-lär), *a.* Of, pertaining to, or of the nature of a tubercle or tubercles; characterized by tubercles; in *pathol.*, pertaining to or characterized by small rounded nodules or tubercles; sometimes, specif., pertaining to

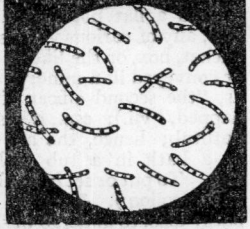

Tubercle Bacillus, very highly magnified.

tuberculosis; tuberculous.—**tu-ber′cu-lar-ly,** *adv.*—**tu-ber′cu-late, tu-ber′cu-lat-ed** (-lāt, -lā-ted), *a.* Having tubercles; tubercled; tubercular.—**tu-ber-cu-la′tion** (-lā′shọn), *n.* The formation of tubercles; the disposition or arrangement of tubercles; a growth or set of tubercles.

tu-ber-cu-lin (tū-bėr′kū-lin), *n.* [G. *tuberkulin*, < L. *tuberculum*, E. *tubercle*.] A sterile liquid prepared from cultures of the tubercle bacillus, used in the diagnosis and treatment of tuberculosis.

tu-ber-cu-lize (tū-bėr′kū-līz), *v. t.*; *-lized, -lizing.* To affect with tubercles; infect with tuberculosis; make tuberculous; also, to treat with tuberculin.—**tu-ber″cu-li-za′tion** (-li-zā′shọn), *n.*

tu-ber-cu-loid (tū-bėr′kū-loid), *a.* Resembling a tubercle.

tu-ber-cu-lo-sis (tū-bėr-kū-lō′sis), *n.* [NL., < L. *tuberculum*, E. *tubercle*.] In *pathol.*, an infectious disease affecting any of various tissues of the body, due to the tubercle bacillus, and characterized by the production of tubercles; esp., this disease when affecting the lungs; pulmonary phthisis; consumption.

tu-ber-cu-lous (tū-bėr′kū-lus), *a.* Tubercular; in *pathol.*,

pertaining to or of the nature of tuberculosis; affected with tuberculosis.

tu-ber-ose¹ (tū′bėr-ōs), *a.* [L. *tuberosus*.] Same as *tuberous*.

tube-rose² (tūb′rōz, properly tū′bėr-ōs), *n.* [L. *tuberosa*, fem. of *tuberosus*, E. *tuberose¹*, *tuberous*.] A bulbous amaryllidaceous plant, *Polianthes tuberosa*, cultivated for its spike of fragrant, creamy-white lily-like flowers.

tu-ber-os-i-ty (tū-bėr-os′i-ti), *n.*; pl. *-ties* (-tiz). The state of being tuberous; also, a swelling or prominence; specif., a rough projection or protuberance of a bone, as for the attachment of a muscle.

tu-ber-ous (tū′bėr-us), *a.* [F. *tubéreux*, < L. *tuberosus*, having lumps or protuberances, < *tuber*, E. *tuber*.] Covered with or characterized by rounded or wart-like prominences or tubers; of the nature of such a prominence; in *bot.*, bearing tubers; of the nature of or resembling a tuber (as, a *tuberous* root, a true root so thickened as to resemble a tuber, but bearing no buds or eyes).

tu-bic-o-lous (tū-bik′ọ-lus), *a.* [L. *tubus*, tube, + *colere*, inhabit.] In *zoöl.*, inhabiting a tube, as a mollusk with a tubular shell, an annelid with a tubular case, or a spider which spins a tubular web.

tu-bi-corn (tū′bi-kôrn), *a.* [L. *tubus*, tube, + *cornu*, horn.] Hollow-horned; cavicorn.

tu-bi-form (tū′bi-fôrm), *a.* [L. *tubus*, tube, + *forma*, form.] Having the form of a tube; tubular.

tub-ing (tū′bing), *n.* Material in the form of a tube; tubes collectively; a piece of tube.

tu-bu-lar (tū′bū-lär), *a.* [L. *tubulus*, E. *tubule*.] Of or pertaining to a tube or tubes; noting a respiratory sound resembling that produced by a current of air passing through a tube; also, characterized by or consisting of tubes; also, of the nature or form of a tube; tube-shaped; in *bot.*, having a tube, or consisting chiefly of a tube, as a corolla, calyx, or flower.—**tu′bu-lar-ly,** *adv.*

Tubicolous Annelid (*Euchone elegans*).

tu-bu-late (tū′bū-lāt), *a.* [L. *tubulatus*, < *tubulus*, E. *tubule*.] Formed into or like a tube; tubular.—**tu′bu-late,** *v. t.*; *-lated, -lating.* To form into a tube; also, to furnish with a tube.—**tu′bu-lat-ed** (-lā-ted), *p. a.* Tubulate; tubular; also, furnished with a tube.—**tu-bu-la′tion** (-lā′shọn), *n.* [L. *tubulatio(n-)*.] The formation of a tube or tubule; the disposition or arrangement of a set of tubes.

tu-bule (tū′būl), *n.* [L. *tubulus*, dim. of *tubus*, E. *tube*.] A small tube; a minute tubular structure.

tu-bu-li-flo-rous (tū″bū-li-flō′rus), *a.* [L. *tubulus*, tubule, + *flos* (*flor-*), flower.] In *bot.*, having the corolla tubular in all the perfect flowers of a head, as certain composite plants.

tu-bu-lose (tū′bū-lōs), *a.* [L. *tubulus*, E. *tubule*.] Having the form of a tube; tubular.—**tu′bu-lous,** *a.* Having the form of a tube; tubular; also, containing or composed of tubes.

tu-bu-lure (tū′bū-lūr), *n.* [F., < L. *tubulus*, E. *tubule*.] A short tubular opening, as in a glass jar or at the top of a retort.

tuck¹ (tuk), *v.* [ME. *tukken*, pull, pluck, tuck up, = MLG. *tucken* = G. *zucken*, pluck, jerk: see *touch*.] **I.** *tr.* To pull† or pluck†; also, to finish (cloth) by stretching, fulling, etc. (now prov. Eng.); also, to draw up in folds or a folded arrangement (as, "Mr. Polly's legs . . . had been *tucked* up . . . under his chair": H. G. Wells's "Mr. Polly," ii.); esp., to draw (*up*) and make fast (cloth, a garment, etc.), often by thrusting one part tightly between other parts or things (as, "He *tucked* up his sleeves": Dickens's "Old Curiosity Shop," iii.); hence, to fasten up the garments of (a person) thus (usually with *up*); also, to thrust the edge or end of (a garment, covering, etc.) closely into place between retaining parts or things (usually with *in*, *up*, etc.: as, "He

. . . bent over to *tuck* the rug about her," Mrs. Wharton's "Ethan Frome," ix.; "with his napkin *tucked* under his chin," W. Churchill's "Coniston," ii. 7); "with his napkin *tucked* under his chin," W. Churchill's "Coniston," ii. 7); hence, to cover snugly in or as in this manner (as, to *tuck* one up in bed); also, to thrust into some narrow space or close or retired place (as, to *tuck* a book under one's arm; *tuck* this in your pocket; "a little shop *tucked* away in Cornhill," W. Churchill's "Coniston," ii. 7); also, to eat or drink (with *in*, *away*, etc.: slang: as, "*Tuck* in as big a supper as you possibly can," Du Maurier's "Trilby," iii.); also, to hang (a criminal: usually with *up*: slang: as, "The assizes . . . will do him justice by *tucking* up the robber," Scott's "Guy Mannering," xvi.); in *needlework*, to sew tucks in. **II.** *intr.* To draw together; contract; pucker; also, to eat or drink heartily or greedily (with *in*, *away*, etc.: slang: as, "You needn't talk while you're *tucking* in," Archibald Marshall's "Anthony Dare," iii.); in *needlework*, to make tucks.—**tuck**[1], *n.* An act of tucking; a pull or twitch (now prov.: cf. *nip and tuck*, under *nip*[1], *n.*); also, a tucked piece or part; a flap on one side of a cover of a book, which folds over the other side and is tucked into a strap or the like, to keep the book closed; also, a hearty meal (slang); food or eatables, esp. sweets or pastry (slang); in *needlework*, a fold, or one of a series of folds, made by doubling cloth or the like upon itself, stitching parallel with the edge of the fold, and laying flat; *naut.*, that part of a vessel where the after ends of the outside planking or plating unite at the stern-post.

tuck[2] (tuk), *n.* [Appar. < F. *estoc*, < It. *stocco*, rapier: see *stoccado*.] A rapier. [Archaic.]

tuck[3] (tuk), *v.* [OF. *toquer*, var. of *tochier*, E. *touch*.] **I.** *tr.* To beat (a drum); blow (a trumpet). [Obs. or Sc.] **II.** *intr.* To sound, as a drum or a trumpet. [Obs. or Sc.] —**tuck**[3], *n.* A blow, stroke, or tap, as on a drum: as, "The heroes who, at *tuck* of drum, Salute thy staff" (Whittier's "Panorama"). [Chiefly Sc.]

tuck-a-hoe (tuk′a̱-hō), *n.* [N. Amer. Ind.] An edible underground fungus, *Pachyma cocos*, consisting chiefly of pectose, occurring in tuber-like masses on the roots of trees in the southern U. S.

tucked (tukt), *p. a.* Drawn up, as in folds; sewed in or ornamented with tucks; also, with *up*, cramped, as in position, space, etc. (colloq. or prov.); wearied or exhausted (colloq. or prov.: as, "You're looking *tucked* up,' he concluded," Kipling's "Light That Failed," iii.: cf. *tucker*[2].)

Tuckahoe. — *a*, a root with growth of tuckahoe; *b*, mass of tuckahoe; *c*, microscopic section of the same.

tuck-er[1] (tuk′ẽr), *n.* One who or that which tucks; a device in a sewing-machine for making tucks; also, a piece of linen, muslin, or the like, worn by women to fill in the space about the neck above a low-cut bodice; also, food (slang).

tuck-er[2] (tuk′ẽr), *v. t.* [Cf. *tucked*.] To weary; tire; exhaust: often with *out*: as, "She's clean *tuckered* out, and kind o' discouraged" (Mrs. Stowe's "Oldtown Folks," xliii.). [Colloq., U. S.]

tuck-et (tuk′et), *n.* [Connected with *tuck*[3].] A flourish on a trumpet; a fanfare. [Archaic.]

-tude. [F. *-tude*, < L. *-tudo*.] A suffix of nouns denoting

Tucker, 18th century.

quality, state, etc., as *amplitude*, *fortitude*, *latitude*, *solitude*.

Tu-dor (tū′dor), *a.* Of or pertaining to the line of English sovereigns (Henry VII., Henry VIII., Edward VI., Mary, and Elizabeth) which reigned from 1485 to 1603, and which was descended from Owen Tudor of Wales, who married Catharine, the widowed queen of Henry V.; in *arch.*, noting or pertaining to a style of architecture, the last phase of the perpendicular English Gothic, which prevailed during the reigns of the Tudors, and was characterized by flat arches, shallow moldings, a profusion of paneling, etc.

Tues-day (tūz′dā), *n.* [AS. *Tīwesdæg*, Tuesday, the day of *Tiw*, ancient Teutonic god of war: see *deity*.] The third day of the week, following Monday.

Tudor Architecture. — Hengrave Hall, Suffolk, England, 1538.

tu-fa (tö′fä), *n.* [It. *tufa*, *tufo*, < L. *tofus*, *tophus*.] Any of various porous rocks; esp., a form of limestone ('calcareous tufa') deposited by springs, etc.; also, volcanic tuff.—**tu-fa-ceous** (tö-fā′shius), *a.* Of the nature of or resembling tufa.

tuff (tuf), *n.* [F. *tuf*, < It. *tufo*: see *tufa*.] Any of various porous rocks, as calcareous tufa; esp., a fragmental rock consisting of the smaller kinds of volcanic detritus ('volcanic tuff'), usually more or less stratified.—**tuf-fa-ceous** (tu-fā′shius), *a.* Of the nature of or resembling tuff.

tuft (tuft), *n.* [Appar. < OF. *tuffe*, *toffe* (F. *touffe*), tuft, prob. from Teut. and akin to E. *top*[1].] A bunch of small, usually soft and flexible things, as feathers, hairs, etc., fixed at the base with the upper part loose; a small patch of hair on the head or chin (as, "a portly person with a *tuft* of yellow beard on his chin": W. Churchill's "Coniston," ii. 2); a cluster of short-stalked flowers, leaves, etc., growing from a common point; also, a small clump of bushes, trees, etc. (as, "a *tuft* of wind-warped trees": Vernon Lee's "Enchanted Woods," The Forest of the Antonines); also, an ornamental tassel on a cap; specif., a gold tassel on the cap formerly worn at English universities by titled undergraduates; an undergraduate who wore such a tassel. —**tuft**, *v.* **I.** *tr.* To furnish with a tuft or tufts; arrange in a tuft or tufts; in *upholstery*, to draw together (a cushion, etc.) by passing a thread through at regular intervals, the depressions thus produced being usually ornamented with tufts or buttons. **II.** *intr.* To form a tuft or tufts; grow in tufts.—**tuft′ed**, *p. a.* Furnished with a tuft or tufts; formed into a tuft or tufts.—**tufted duck**, an old-world crested duck, *Fuligula cristata*, the male of which has the plumage mostly black. — **tuft′=hunt″er**, *n.* One who meanly or obsequiously courts the acquaintance of titled

Tufted Duck (*Fuligula cristata*).

persons or celebrities; hence, any toady or sycophant. —**tuft′=hunt″ing,** *n.* and *a.*—**tuft′y,** *a.* Abounding in tufts; covered or adorned with tufts; also, forming a tuft or tufts.

tug (tug), *v.*; *tugged, tugging.* [ME. *tuggen, toggen*; akin to E. *tow*³.] **I.** *tr.* To pull at with force or effort (as, "Captives may have *tugged* the oars of the galleys": H. G. Wells's "Outline of History," xx. § 2); also, to move by pulling forcibly; drag or haul; sometimes, to tow (a vessel, etc.) by means of a tugboat, or as a tugboat does; also, to pull about roughly† (as, "weary with disasters, *tugg′d* with fortune": Shakspere's "Macbeth," iii. 1. 112). **II.** *intr.* To pull with force or effort (as, to *tug* at an oar); also, to strive hard, labor, or toil, as in the effort to do something; go laboriously; struggle in fighting or wrestling.—**tug,** *n.* The act of tugging; a strong pull; a struggle; a strenuous contest; also, that by which something is tugged; a trace of a harness; sometimes, any of various other pulling or supporting parts of a harness; also, a tugboat.—**tug of war,** a severe or critical struggle, as between contending forces; also, an athletic contest between two teams pulling at the opposite ends of a rope, each team endeavoring to drag the other over a line marked between them.—**tug′boat,** *n.* A small, strongly built, and powerful steamboat for towing other vessels.—**tug′ger,** *n.*—**tug′ging-ly,** *adv.*

tuille (twēl), *n.* [OF. *tieule* (F. *tuile*), tile, < L. *tegula,* E. *tile.*] In *armor,* one of two or more plates of steel hanging below the tasses, or forming the lowermost division of these.

tu-i-tion (tū-ish′on), *n.* [L. *tuitio(n-),* < *tueri* (pp. *tuitus*), look at, look after, guard, keep: cf. *tutor.*] Guardianship† or custody†; also, teaching or instruction, as of pupils; also, the charge or fee for instruction.—**tu-i′tion-al, tu-i′tion-a-ry** (-ā-ri), *a.*

tu-la-re-mi-a, tu-la-ræ-mi-a (tö-lạ-rē′mi-ä), *n.* [NL., < E. *Tulare,* county in California, + Gr. αἷμα, blood.] A disease of rabbits, squirrels, etc., caused by a bacterium, *Pasteurella tularensis* (or *Bacterium tularense*), transmitted to man by insects or by the handling of infected animals, and resembling the plague and taking the form in man of an irregular fever lasting several weeks.

tu-la=work (tö′lạ-wėrk), *n.* [From *Tula,* city and government in central Russia.] Niello-work.

tu-le (tö′lạ), *n.* [Mex.] Either of two large bulrushes, *Scirpus lacustris* and *S. californicus,* which in California and adjacent regions occupy overflowed land and marshes.

tu-lip (tū′lip), *n.* [= F. *tulipe,* earlier *tulipan,* < Turk. *tulband,* for Pers. *dulband,* turban (cf. *turban*); from the shape of the flower.] Any of the liliaceous plants constituting the genus *Tulipa,* cultivated in many varieties, and having large, showy, usually erect, cup-shaped or bell-shaped flowers of various colors; also, a flower or bulb of such a plant.—**tu′lip=ear,** *n.* An erect or pricked ear in dogs. —**tu′lip=eared,** *a.*—**tu-li-po-ma-ni-a** (tū″li-pọ-mā′ni-ä), *n.* [NL.] A mania or craze for the cultivation or acquisition of tulips, as that which arose in Holland about 1634. —**tu″li-po-ma′ni-ac** (-ak), *n.*—**tu′lip=tree,** *n.* A North American magnoliaceous tree, *Liriodendron tulipifera,* with tulip-like flowers and a wood that is used in cabinet-work, etc.; yellow poplar; also, any of various other trees with tulip-like flowers.—**tu′lip=wood,** *n.* The wood of the tulip-tree, *Liriodendron tulipifera;* whitewood; also, any of various striped or variegated woods of other trees; any of these trees.

tulle (töl, F. tül), *n.* [From *Tulle,* town in south-central France.] A thin, fine silk net, plain, dotted, or figured, used in millinery, dressmaking, etc.

Tu-lu (tö′lö), *n.* A Dravidian language spoken in southwestern India.

Tulip-tree (*Liriodendron tulipifera*). — *a,* a stamen; *b,* fruit; *c,* a carpel.

tul-war (tul′wär), *n.* [Hind. *talwār.*] A kind of saber used by the peoples of northern India.

tum-ble (tum′bl), *v. i.*; *-bled, -bling.* [ME. *tumblen,* freq. < AS. *tumbian,* dance, tumble: cf. OF. *tumber,* let fall, overturn, F. *tomber,* fall (from LG.).] To perform leaps, springs, somersaults, or other feats of bodily agility, as for exhibition or sport; also, to roll about by turning one way and another (as, to toss and *tumble* restlessly in sleep; the *tumbling* sea); pitch about; toss; wallow, as an animal; also, to roll or fall over or down as by losing footing, support, or equilibrium (as, to *tumble* off a horse; to *tumble* down the stairs); fall headlong or precipitately; stumble or fall (over: as, "'A lanky, gawky fellow,' said Crawley, '*tumbles* over everybody,'" Thackeray's "Vanity Fair," xiv.); fall in breaking down or collapsing (as, "roses overblown and about to *tumble* to pieces," Arnold Bennett's "Lion's Share," xxxix.; *tumbling* walls); fig., to fall rapidly in amount, value, or cost, as prices, stocks, etc.; also, to go, come, get, etc., in a precipitate or hasty way (as, "All hands, ahoy! *tumble* up here and take in sail," Dana's "Two Years before the Mast," ii.; to *tumble* out at an alarm of fire); also, to come by chance (*into, on,* etc.); also, to become suddenly alive to some fact, circumstance, or the like (often with *to:* slang: as, "A girl may be dull without *tumbling* to it," Pinero's "Wife without a Smile," iii.).—**to tumble home,** or **to tumble in,** *naut.,* same as *to fall home,* under *fall, v. i.*—**tum′ble,** *v. t.* To move or toss about, or turn over, as in handling, searching, etc. (as, "She employed herself in *tumbling* over the contents of her work-basket": Cooper's "Spy," i.); disorder by or as by tossing about (as, to *tumble* bedclothes or a bed; to *tumble* the hair); rumple (as, "You run the risk of *tumbling* her expansive skirt," G. W. Curtis's "Prue and I," i.; "The napkins were *tumbled,*" L. Merrick's "House of Lynch," viii.; "a letter . . . sorely *tumbled,* damp, and covered with . . . mould," H. Melville's "Moby-Dick," lxxi.); also, to send tumbling or falling, or throw over or down (as, to *tumble* a screen over; to *tumble* a person down; "Some antagonist . . . *tumbles* into ruins the whole magnificent structure," W. D. Whitney's "Life and Growth of Language," ii.); overthrow; also, to throw, cast, put, send, etc., in a precipitate, hasty, or rough manner (as, "I was whipped and *tumbled* off to bed": Mrs. Stowe's "Uncle Tom's Cabin," ix.); also, to subject to the action of a tumbling-box.—**tum′ble,** *n.* An act of tumbling; a fall; a downfall; also, tumbled condition; disorder or confusion; a confused heap.—**to take a tumble,** to become suddenly alive, as to something: as, "She'll *take a tumble* to herself" (Sinclair Lewis's "Main Street," xxxix.). [Slang.]

tum-ble=bug (tum′bl-bug), *n.* Any of various dung-beetles (genera *Scarabæus, Copris, Canthon,* etc.) which roll up globular masses of dung in which they deposit their eggs and in which the larvæ develop.

tum-ble=down (tum′bl-doun), *a.* In a tumbling or falling condition; dilapidated; ruinous: as, "The parsonage here's a *tumble-down* place, sir, not fit for gentry to live in" (George Eliot's "Adam Bede," ii.).

tum-bler (tum′blėr), *n.* One who or that which tumbles; one who performs leaps, somersaults, and other bodily feats; one of a breed of dogs resembling small greyhounds, formerly used in hunting rabbits (so named in allusion to their characteristic motions); one of a breed of domestic pigeons having the habit of turning over and over backward in their flight; also, a drinking-vessel, orig. one with a rounded or pointed bottom so that it could not be set down before being emptied, now one of glass with a flat bottom and without a stem or handle; also, a toy, usually representing a fat, squat-

Tumble-bug (*Canthon lævis*). — Upper figure male, lower female, the former pulling and the latter pushing the ball in which are the eggs, and which is thus tumbled into a hole in the ground. (About natural size.)

ting figure, with a heavy or weighted and rounded base, so as to rock when touched; also, a tumbrel (cart) (Sc. and prov. Eng.); also, a tumbling-box; also, in a lock, any locking or checking part which, when in the proper position, prevents the movement of the bolt, and which, when lifted or released by the action of a key or the like, allows the bolt to move; in a gun-lock, a lever-like piece which by the action of a spring forces the hammer forward when released by the trigger.—**tum′bler-ful** (-fúl), *n.*; *pl.* *-fuls.* A quantity sufficient to fill a tumbler.

tum-ble-weed (tum′bl-wēd), *n.* In the western U. S., any of various plants (as an amaranth, *Amarantus græcizans*) whose branching upper part in autumn becomes detached from the roots and is driven about, as a light, rounded mass, by the wind.

tum-bling=box (tum′bling-boks), *n.* An apparatus consisting of a box or cylindrical vessel pivoted at each end or at two corners, so that it can be made to revolve: used for various purposes, as for polishing objects by allowing them to tumble about in the box with an abrasive substance, or for mixing materials.

tum-brel (tum′brel), *n.* [OF. *tumberel* (F. *tombereau*), tip-cart, < *tumber*, let fall, overturn: cf. *tumble.*] A tip-cart or dump-cart, esp. one for carrying dung or manure; also, one of the carts used during the French Revolution to convey victims to the guillotine; also, a two-wheeled covered cart accompanying artillery in order to carry tools, ammunition, etc.; also, a former instrument of punishment, usually identified with the cucking-stool. Also **tum′bril** (-bril).

tu-me-fa-cient (tū-mē-fā′shent), *a.* [L. *tumefaciens* (-ent-), ppr. of *tumefacere*: see *tumefy.*] Tumefying; swelling.

tu-me-fac-tion (tū-mē-fak′shon), *n.* [F. *tuméfaction.*] The act of tumefying or swelling, or the state of being tumefied; also, a swollen part; a swelling.

tu-me-fy (tū′mē-fī), *v. t.* or *i.*; *-fied, -fying.* [F. *tuméfier*, < L. *tumefacere*, < *tumere*, swell, + *facere*, make.] To render or become swollen or tumid.

tu-mes-cent (tū-mes′ent), *a.* [L. *tumescens* (-ent-), ppr. of *tumescere*, begin to swell, < *tumere*, swell.] Becoming swollen; swelling; slightly tumid.—**tu-mes′cence,** *n.*

tu-mid (tū′mid), *a.* [L. *tumidus*, < *tumere*, swell: cf. *tumor, tumult, tumulus, tuber,* and *thumb.*] Swollen; affected with swelling, as a part of the body; of a swollen or protuberant form (as, "round, *tumid*, rosy cheeks": Motley's "Dutch Republic," i. 1); fig., inflated, turgid, or bombastic, as language, literary style, etc. (as, "His letters . . . were *tumid*, formal, and affected": Lecky's "Hist. of Eng. in the 18th Century," viii.).—**tu-mid-i-ty** (tū-mid′i-ti), **tu′mid-ness,** *n.*—**tu′mid-ly,** *adv.*

tu-mor (tū′mor), *n.* [L. *tumor*, < *tumere*, swell: cf. *tumid.*] Swollen condition†; fig., inflated or bombastic character†; also, a swollen part; a swelling or protuberance; in *pathol.*, an abnormal or morbid swelling in any part of the body; esp., a more or less circumscribed morbid growth of new tissue, not due to inflammation, and differing in structure from the part in which it grows.—**tu′mor-ous,** *a.*

tu′mour, *n.* British preferred form of *tumor.*

tump (tump), *n.* [Cf. W. *twmp*, round mass, hillock.] A hillock; a mound; a heap; also, a clump, as of trees. [Prov.]

tump=line (tump′lin), *n.* [With *tump-* prob. of Algonquian origin.] A strap for passing across the forehead (or breast) and supporting a pack carried on the back: much used by Indians and whites in Canada and the northern U. S.

tu-mu-lar (tū′mū-lạr), *a.* Pertaining to or of the nature of a tumulus or mound.

tu-mu-la-ry (tū′mū-lạ-ri), *a.* [Cf. F. *tumulaire*, sepulchral.] Tumular; also, pertaining to a tomb (as, a *tumulary* stone); sepulchral.

tu-mult (tū′mult), *n.* [L. *tumultus*, akin to *tumere*, swell: cf. *tumid.*] The commotion or disturbance of a multitude, usually with noise (as, "scenes of *tumult* and bloodshed": Hallam's "Europe during the Middle Ages," i. 1); an uproar (as, "A *tumult* of war-cries, the vibrating clang of gongs . . . made an awful din": J. Conrad's "Lord Jim," xxxviii.); a popular outbreak or uprising (as, "There is much bloodshedding in Spain . . . and violent wars and *tumults*": Borrow's "Bible in Spain," v.); in general, commotion,

disturbance, or violent disorder (as, "Thy nod can . . . still the *tumult* of the raging sea": Burns's "Stanzas in the Prospect of Death," 22); agitation of mind, or a mental or emotional disturbance (as, "Her breath, in the first *tumult* of her thought, came and went deeply," W. Churchill's "Modern Chronicle," ii. 10; a *tumult* of conflicting feelings).—**tu-mul-tu-a-ry** (tū-mul′tū-ā-ri), *a.* [L. *tumultuarius.*] Tumultuous; disorderly; confused; irregular.—**tu-mul′tu-ous,** *a.* [F. *tumultueux*, < L. *tumultuosus.*] Full of or marked by tumult, violent disorder, or uproar (as, "The assaults became even more *tumultuous* and murderous," De Quincey's "Revolt of the Tartars"; "I wish . . . that these *tumultuous* elections were well over," Galt's "Ayrshire Legatees," vii.); making a tumult or uproar, or disorderly or noisy, as persons, etc.; turbulent or riotous; loud and confused, as sounds, cries, etc.; rough or tempestuous, as waters, winds, etc.; disturbed or agitated, as the mind, thoughts, feelings, etc. (as, "He . . . found his thoughts *tumultuous*; his mind run upon men fighting": Defoe's "Robinson Crusoe," ii. 3).—**tu-mul′tu-ous-ly,** *adv.*—**tu-mul′tu-ous-ness,** *n.*

tu-mu-lus (tū′mū-lus), *n.*; *pl.* *-luses* or *-li* (-lī). [L., mound, esp. sepulchral mound, < *tumere*, swell: cf. *tumid* and *tomb.*] A mound or elevation of earth, etc., esp. of artificial origin and more or less antiquity; specif., such a mound, sometimes of considerable size, raised over or inclosing a tomb or sepulchral chamber; a barrow.

tun (tun), *n.* [AS. *tunne* = D. *ton* = G. *tonne*, tun: cf. OF. F. *tonne*, tun, and E. *tunnel.*] A large cask for holding liquids, etc., esp. wine, ale, or beer; also, a measure of capacity for wine, etc., usually equivalent to 252 wine-gallons; also, any large vessel†.—**tun,** *v. t.*; *tunned, tunning.* To put into or store in a tun or tuns.

tu-na[1] (tö′nä), *n.* [Cf. *tunny.*] The tunny (fish); esp., the great tunny.

tu-na[2] (tö′nä), *n.* [Sp.; from Haitian.] Any of various prickly-pears; esp., an erect, tree-like species, *Opuntia tuna*, a native of Mexico and the West Indies, bearing a sweet, edible fruit; also, the fruit.

tun-a-ble (tū′nạ-bl), *a.* Capable of being tuned; also, in tune; harmonious; tuneful.—**tun′a-ble-ness,** *n.*—**tun′a-bly,** *adv.*

tun=dish (tun′dish), *n.* A funnel. [Now prov. Eng.]

tun-dra (tùn′drä or tun′-), *n.* [Russ.] One of the vast, nearly level, treeless plains of the arctic regions of Europe, Asia, and North America, having the ground frozen beneath the surface even in summer.

tune (tūn), *n.* [ME. *tune*, var. of *tone*, E. *tone.*] A tone† or sound†, esp. a musical tone†; also, a pleasing rhythmical succession of musical sounds; an air or melody, with or without the harmony accompanying it; a musical setting of a hymn or psalm, usually in four-part harmony, intended for use in public worship; also, the state of being in the proper pitch (esp. in the phrases 'in tune' and 'out of tune': as, "She was quite tone-deaf, and couldn't sing one single note in *tune*," Du Maurier's "Trilby," viii.); agreement in pitch, or unison or harmony (as, many voices or instruments sounding in *tune*; one instrument out of *tune* with others); fig., due condition (as, to keep the mind or the body in *tune*); accord or harmony (as, "Such things make one out of *tune* with Providence. They oughtn't to happen": Eden Phillpotts's "Grey Room," iii.); also, due agreement, as of wireless instruments or circuits with respect to frequency; also, frame of mind, or mood or humor (as, "Ye'll find me in a better *tune*": Burns's "Epistle to Hugh Parker," 42).—**to the tune of,** fig., to the sum or amount of. [Colloq.]—**tune,** *v. t.*; *tuned, tuning.* To adjust the tones of (a musical instrument) to a correct or given standard of pitch; put in tune; adapt (the voice, song, etc.) to a particular tone, or to the expression of a particular feeling or the like (as, "Now to sorrow must I *tune* my song": Milton's "Passion," ii.); fig., to put into a proper or a particular condition, mood, etc.; bring into harmony; attune; also, to utter, sound, or express musically (poetic: as, to *tune* one's song or lay; "the little birds that *tune* their morning's joy," Shakspere's "Lucrece," 1107); also, to play upon (a lyre, etc.: poetic); also, to adapt or adjust (mechanisms, etc.) in due agreement; in *wireless teleg.* and *teleph.*, to adjust (a circuit, etc.) so as to bring into resonance with another circuit, a given frequency, or the like.—**to tune in,** in *wire-less teleg.* and *teleph.,* to adjust (a receiving apparatus) so as to accord in frequency with a sending apparatus whose signals are to be received; also, to adjust a receiving apparatus so as to receive (the signals of a sending station).—**to tune out,** in *wireless teleg.* and *teleph.,* to shut out (the signals of a sending station) by altering the frequency of the circuit or circuits of a receiving apparatus.—**to tune up,** to bring (a musical instrument) to the proper pitch; put in tune; also, to put (a machine, etc.) into the proper working condition (as, "a garage, and a yard where chauffeurs were accustomed to '*tune up*' their engines": H. G. Wells's "Soul of a Bishop," ix.).—**tuned radio=frequency ampli-fication,** in *wireless teleg.* and *teleph.,* radio-frequency ampli-fication in which tuning is employed in each stage.—**tune,** *v. i.* To put a musical instrument, etc., in tune; also, to sound or be in harmony; also, to give forth a musical sound. —**to tune in,** in *wireless teleg.* and *teleph.,* to tune in a receiving apparatus. See *to tune in,* under *tune, v. t.*—**to tune out,** in *wireless teleg.* and *teleph.,* to tune out the signals of a sending station. See *to tune out,* under *tune, v. t.*—**to tune up,** to bring a musical instrument to the proper pitch for playing; also, to put a machine or the like into working order; also, to raise the voice in song, etc. (as, "Often a song-bird *tuned up* and fell to singing": Mark Twain's "Life on the Mississippi," li.).—**tune′a-ble,** etc. See *tunable,* etc.—**tune′ful,** *a.* Full of tune or melody; sweet of sound; melodious; also, producing musical sounds; making melody; also, pertaining or adapted to music.—**tune′ful-ly,** *adv.*—**tune′ful-ness,** *n.*—**tune′less,** *a.* With-out tune or melody; unmelodious; unmusical; also, making or giving no music; silent.—**tun-er** (tū′nèr), *n.*

tung-state (tung′stāt), *n.* In *chem.,* a salt of tungstic acid.

tung-sten (tung′sten), *n.* [Sw. *tungsten,* < *tung,* heavy, + *sten,* stone.] Chem. sym., W (see *wolframium*) or Tu; at. wt., 184; sp. gr., 18.7. A rare metallic element having a bright gray color, a metallic luster, and a high melting-point, found in wolframite, tungstite, and other minerals, and used in the manufacture of steel, for making electric lamp filaments, etc.—**tungsten lamp,** an incandescent electric lamp in which the filament is made of tungsten.—**tungsten steel,** a hard special steel containing tungsten: used for making lathe-tools, etc.—**tung-sten′ic,** *a.*—**tung′-stic,** *a.* Of or containing tungsten.—**tung′stite** (-stīt), *n.* Native tungsten trioxide, WO_3, a yellow or yellowish-green mineral occurring usually in a pulverulent form.

Tun-gus (tŏng-gŏz′), *n.*; pl. *-guses* or *-gus.* A member of a Mongolian people comprising a group of tribes dwelling chiefly in central and eastern Siberia; also, the language of this people.—**Tun-gu′si-an** (-gŏ′zi-ạn), *a.*—**Tun-gu′sic.** **I.** *a.* Of or pertaining to the Tunguses; also, noting or per-taining to a division of the Ural-Altaic family of lan-guages containing Tungus, Manchu, and related lan-guages. **II.** *n.* The lan-guage of the Tunguses; also, the Tungusic division of the Ural-Altaic family of lan-guages.

tu-nic (tū′nik), *n.* [L. *tu-nica,* undergarment, integu-ment, membrane.] A gar-ment like a shirt or gown, worn by both sexes among the ancient Greeks and Ro-mans; hence, in later use, a loosely fitting body-garment extending from the neck (commonly) to some distance above the knee; specif., a woman's garment, either loose or close-fitting, extending more or less below the waist and over the skirt; also, a body-coat worn as part of a military or other uniform; *eccles.,* a

Tunic or Chiton of Ionian form (over which is girded the Dionysiac fawn-skin).—From a Greek amphora of the 4th century B.C.

tunicle; in *anat.* and *zoöl.,* any covering or investing mem-brane or part, as of an organ; in *bot.,* a natural integument; esp., any loose membranous skin not formed from the epider-mis.

tu-ni-ca (tū′ni-kạ), *n.*; pl. *-cæ* (-sē). [L.: see *tunic.*] In *anat., zoöl.,* and *bot.,* a tunic.

tu-ni-cate (tū′ni-kāt). [L. *tunicatus,* pp. of *tunicare,* clothe with a tunic, < *tunica,* E. *tunic.*] **I.** *a.* Invested with or having a tunic or covering; in *bot.,* having, or consisting of, a series of concentric layers, as a bulb; in *zoöl.,* belonging to the *Tunicata* or *Ascidia* (see *ascidian*). **II.** *n.* In *zoöl.,* a tunicate animal; an ascidian.—**tu′ni-cat-ed** (-kā-ted), *a.* Having a tunic or covering; tunicate.

tu-ni-cle (tū′ni-kl), *n.* [L. *tunicula,* dim. of *tunica,* E. *tunic.*] A small tunic†; also, an inclosing membrane or integument; *eccles.,* a vestment worn over the alb by subdeacons, as at the celebration of the mass, and also by bishops.

tun-ing=fork (tū′ning-fôrk), *n.* A small steel instrument consisting of two prongs on a stem, designed to produce, when struck, a musical tone of a definite, constant pitch, and thus serving as a stan-dard for tuning musical in-struments, etc.

Tuning-fork.

tun-nel (tun′el), *n.* [OF. F. *tonnelle,* arbor, semicircular vault, < *tonne,* tun, large cask, akin to E. *tun.*] The flue of a chimney†; also, a funnel (now prov.); also, a sub-terranean passage; a roadway, as for a railroad, etc., beneath the ground, through a hill or mountain, or under the bed of a stream; an approximately horizontal passage in a mine; also, the burrow of an animal (as, "His [the rabbit's] round *tunnel* bored in a sandy bank is largest at the opening": Jefferies's "Gamekeeper at Home," v.); one of the long holes made in wood or other substances by ship-worms or the like. —**tun′nel,** *v.*; *-neled* or *-nelled, -neling* or *-nelling.* **I.** *tr.* To make or form as or like a tunnel (as, to *tunnel* a passage under a river; "narrow pathways fairly *tunnelled* through masses of foliage," H. Melville's "Omoo," lii.); also, to make or form a tunnel through or under (as, to *tunnel* a hill or a river; "As rush the waters through a cave That *tunnels* half a sea-girt lonely rock," W. Morris's "Jason," ix. 411); perforate as with tunnels (as, wood *tunneled* by ship-worms). **II.** *intr.* To make a tunnel or tunnels: as, to *tunnel* through the Alps; to *tunnel* under the Hudson River.—**tun′nel-er, tun′nel-ler,** *n.*

tun-ny (tun′i), *n.*; pl. *tunnies* (-iz). [F. *thon,* < Pr. *ton,* < L. *thunnus, thynnus,* < Gr. θύννος, tunny.] A widely dis-tributed ma-rine food-fish, *Thun-nus thynnus* (the 'com-mon tunny' or 'great tunny'), of the mackerel family, some-times grow-ing to a length of ten feet or more (also called *horse-mack-erel* and *tuna*); also, any of va-rious related scombroid fishes, as the albacore, *Germo ala-longa* (the 'long-finned tunny').

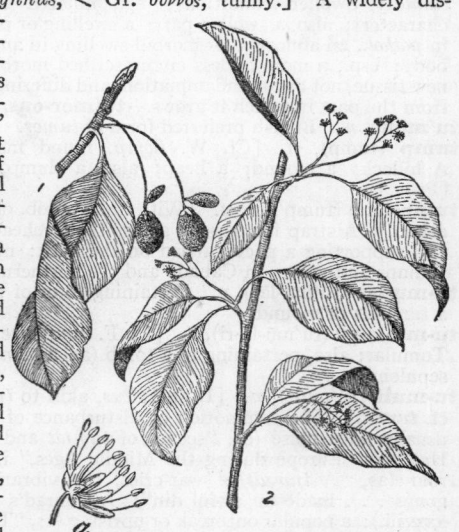

Tupelo (*Nyssa sylvatica*). — 1, branch with fruits; 2, branch with male flowers; *a,* a male flower.

tup (tup), *n.* [ME. *tuppe, tupe;* origin uncertain.] The male of the sheep; a ram.—**tup,** *v. t.; tupped, tupping.* Of the ram, to copulate with (the ewe).

tu-pe-lo (tū′pē-lō), *n.;* pl. *-los* (-lōz). [N. Amer. Ind.] Any of several trees of the cornaceous genus *Nyssa,* esp. *N. sylvatica,* the black-gum or sour-gum, a large North American tree with a strong, tough wood. See cut on preceding page.

Tu-pi (tö′pē), *n.;* pl. *-pis* (-pēz). A member of a tribe, or of a widespread group of tribes, of South American Indians of a distinct linguistic stock, believed to have lived originally along the lower Amazon, but afterward extending southward along the Brazilian coast and through Brazil, Paraguay, and Uruguay; also, the language of these Indians.—**Tu′pi-an** (-pi-an), *a.*

tu-pik (tö′pik), *n.* [Eskimo.] A hut or tent of skins used as a summer dwelling by the Eskimos.

tuque (tūk), *n.* [Canadian F., for F. *toque.*] A kind of knitted cap worn in Canada.

tu quo-que (tū kwō′kwē). [L., 'thou too.'] A retort charging an accuser with the very fault he alleges.

Tuque. — *a,* folded to fit the head; *b,* as knitted.

tu-ra-koo (tö′ra̤-kö), *n.* [= F. *touraco;* said to be imit. of its cry.] Any of the African birds constituting the family *Musophagidæ* (genera *Turacus, Musophaga,* etc.), notable for their large size, brilliant plumage, and helmet-like crest.

Tu-ra-ni-an (tū-rā′ni-an). [Pers. *Tūrān,* name of a region of Asia northeast of Iran (Persia).] **I.** *a.* In loose, indefinite use, belonging or pertaining to a group of Asiatic peoples or languages comprising all or nearly all those which are neither Aryan nor Semitic; in a more restricted sense, Ural-Altaic. **II.** *n.* A member of any of the races speaking a Turanian (esp. a Ural-Altaic) language.

Giant Turakoo (*Corythæola cristata*).

tur-ban (tėr′ban), *n.* [F. *turban,* < Turk. *tulband, dulbend,* < Pers. *dulband,* turban: cf. *tulip.*] A form of head-dress of Mohammedan origin worn by men of Eastern nations, consisting of a scarf of silk, linen, cotton, or the like, wound directly around the head or around a cap (cf. *tarboosh*); also, some head-dress resembling this; a modification of the Oriental turban worn at various periods by women in Europe and America, a bright-colored cloth worn as a head-dress by negroes, esp. women, in the southern U. S. and the West Indies; also, a small hat, either brimless or with the brim turned up close against the crown, worn by women and children. —**tur′baned,** *a.* Wearing a turban.

Oriental Turbans.

tur-ba-ry (tėr′ba̤-ri), *n.;* pl. *-ries* (-riz). [ML. *turbaria,* < *turba,* turf, peat; from Teut., and akin to E. *turf.*] Land, or a piece of land, where turf or peat may be dug or cut; in *law,* the right to cut turf or peat on a common or on another person's land.

tur-bel-la-ri-an (tėr-be-lā′ri-an). [NL. *Turbellaria,* pl., < L. *turbella,* bustle, stir, dim. of *turba,* disorder, tumult; from the currents produced in water by their vibratile cilia.] **I.** *a.* Belonging to the *Turbellaria,* a class or group of platyhelminths or flatworms, mostly aquatic, and characterized by cilia whose motions produce small currents or vortexes in water. **II.** *n.* A turbellarian platyhelminth.

tur-bid (tėr′bid), *a.* [L. *turbidus,* < *turbare,* disturb, < *turba,* disorder, tumult, disturbance.] Of liquids, opaque or muddy with particles of extraneous matter (as, "though their stream is loaded with sand and *turbid* with alluvial waste": Holmes's "Autocrat of the Breakfast-Table," iii.); in general, not clear or transparent; thick, as smoke or clouds; dense; fig., disturbed; confused; muddled.—**tur-bid′i-ty, tur′bid-ness,** *n.*—**tur′bid-ly,** *adv.*

tur-bi-nal (tėr′bi-na̤l). [L. *turbo* (*turbin-*), top: see *turbine.*] **I.** *a.* Top-shaped; spiral; scroll-like; turbinate. **II.** *n.* In *anat.,* a turbinate bone.

tur-bi-nate (tėr′bi-nāt). [L. *turbinatus,* < *turbo:* see *turbine.*] **I.** *a.* Shaped like a spinning-top; inversely conical; spiral, as some shells; scroll-like or whorled; in *anat.,* noting or pertaining to certain scroll-like spongy bones of the nasal passages in the higher vertebrates. **II.** *n.* A turbinate shell; in *anat.,* a turbinate bone.—**tur′bi-nat-ed** (-nā-ted), *a.*—**tur-bi-na′tion** (-nā′shon), *n.* A turbinate formation.

tur-bine (tėr′bin, also -bīn), *n.* [F. *turbine,* < L. *turbo* (*turbin-*), something that whirls, whirlwind, top, spindle, < *turbare,* disturb: see *turbid.*] Any of a class of motors in which a vaned wheel or its equivalent is made to revolve, usually in a horizontal plane, by the impinging force of a jet or jets of water ('impulse turbine' or 'action turbine'), or by the reaction of the water which more or less completely fills and passes through the motor ('pressure turbine' or 'reaction turbine'), or by both; hence, any of certain analogous motors using other fluids, as steam ('steam-turbine') or air ('air-turbine').

tur-bit (tėr′bit), *n.* [Origin unknown.] One of a breed of domestic pigeons with a stout, roundish body, a short head and beak, and a ruffled breast and neck.

tur-bith (tėr′bith), *n.* Same as *turpeth.*

tur-bo- (tėr′bō-). Form used for *turbine* in combination, as in *turbo-generator* (a turbine-driven electric generator), *turbo-motor, turbo-pump.*

tur-bot (tėr′bot), *n.;* pl. *turbots* or (esp. collectively) *turbot.* [OF. *tourbout* (F. *turbot*); origin uncertain.] A large European flatfish, *Scophthalmus maximus* (or *Rhombus maximus,* or *Psetta maxima*), much esteemed as food; also, any of various similar fishes, as certain flounders.

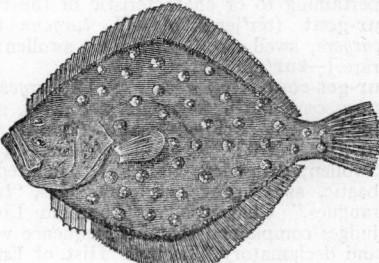

Turbot (*Scophthalmus maximus*).

tur-bu-lent (tėr′bū-lent), *a.* [L. *turbulentus,* < *turba,* disorder, tumult, disturbance: cf. *trouble* and *turbid.*] Disposed or given to disturbances, disorder, or insubordination, or obstreperous or unruly (as, "The Scottish people had always been singularly *turbulent* and ungovernable": Macaulay's "Hist. of Eng.," i.); marked by or showing a spirit of disorder or insubordination (as, *turbulent* outbreaks; "a *turbulent* period . . . when anarchy and stiff-necked opposition reigned rampant," Irving's "Knickerbocker's New York," v. 1); also, disturbed, in commotion, or tumultuous (as, "The prairie was like a *turbulent* ocean, suddenly congealed when its waves were at the highest": Parkman's "Oregon Trail," xiii.); stormy or tempestuous (archaic).—**tur′bu-lence,** *n.* A turbulent state; in *meteor.,* irregular motion of the atmosphere, as that indicated by gusts and lulls in the wind. —**tur′bu-len-cy,** *n.*—**tur′bu-lent-ly,** *adv.*

Tur-co (tėr′kō), *n.*; pl. *-cos* (-kōz). [F., < It. *Turco*, Turk (Algeria having formerly been under Turkish rule).] One of a body of light infantry raised among the natives of Algeria for service in the French army.

Tur-co- (tėr′kọ-). Form of ML. *Turcus*, Turk, used in combination, as in *Turco-Bulgarian* (of Turks and Bulgarians), *Turco-Greek*, *Turco-Italian*.

Tur-co-man (tėr′kọ-man), *n.* See *Turkoman*.

Tur-co-phil, Tur-co-phile (tėr′kọ-fil). [See *Turco-* and *-phil*.] **I.** *a.* Friendly to or favoring the Turks. **II.** *n.* One who favors the Turks.

Tur-co-phobe (tėr′kọ-fōb), *n.* [See *Turco-* and *-phobe*.] One who fears or dislikes the Turks.

tur-di-form (tėr′di-fôrm), *a.* [NL. *turdiformis*, < L. *turdus*, thrush, + *forma*, form.] Having the form of a thrush; thrush-like, as birds.

tur-dine (tėr′din), *a.* [L. *turdus*, thrush.] Belonging or pertaining to the thrushes, esp. the true thrushes, or birds of the subfamily *Turdinæ*.

tu-reen (tụ-rēn′), *n.* [F. *terrine*, earthenware dish: see *terrine*.] A deep dish with a cover, for holding soup, etc., at table.

turf (tėrf), *n.*; pl. *turfs*, also (esp. formerly) *turves* (tėrvz). [AS. *turf* = D. *turf* = OHG. *zurf* = Icel. *torf*, turf, peat: cf. *turbary*.] A piece cut or torn from the surface of grassland, with the grass, etc., growing on it; a sod; also, the covering of grass, etc., with its matted roots, forming the surface of grassland; often, the grassy covering of a grave (as, "When they wha would hae starved thy life Thy senseless *turf* adorn": Burns's "On a Certain Commemoration," 4); also, a block or piece of peat dug for fuel; peat as a substance or fuel (as, "a large sparkling fire of *turf* and bog-wood": Scott's "Black Dwarf," iii.); also, with *the*, the grassy course or other track over which horse-races are run; hence, the practice or institution of racing horses.—**turf**, *v. t.* To cover with turf or sod (as, to *turf* a grave); also, to lay under the turf, or bury; cover as turf or turfy ground does (as, "As vast a mound As after furious battle *turfs* the slain On some wild down": Tennyson's "Merlin and Vivien," 655); also, to dig up for peat.—**turfed**, *a.* Having turf: as, "short-*turfed* prairies" (G. W. Cable's "Bonaventure," i. 1).—**turf′en**, *a.* Consisting or made of turf; covered with turf; turfy.—**turf′ite** (-īt), *n.* A frequenter of the turf or of horse-races; a turfman. [Colloq.]—**turf′less**, *a.* Without turf, as ground.—**turf′man** (-man), *n.*; pl. *-men*. A man interested in or devoted to the turf or horse-racing. —**turf′y**, *a.* Covered with or consisting of grassy turf (as, a *turfy* hillside; a *turfy* covering); turfen; turf-like; also, abounding in, or of the nature of, turf or peat; also, pertaining to or characteristic of the turf or horse-racing.

tur-gent (tėr′jẹnt), *a.* [L. *turgens* (*turgent*-), ppr. of *turgere*, swell out.] Swelling; swollen; turgid. [Obs. or rare.]—**tur′gen-cy**, *n.*

tur-ges-cent (tėr-jes′ẹnt), *a.* [L. *turgescens* (-ent-), ppr. of *turgescere*, begin to swell, < *turgere*, swell out.] Becoming swollen; swelling.—**tur-ges′cence**, *n.*

tur-gid (tėr′jid), *a.* [L. *turgidus*, < *turgere*, swell out.] Swollen; distended; tumid; fig., inflated, pompous, or bombastic, as language, style, etc. (as, "*turgid*, scholarly harangues," Charnwood's "Abraham Lincoln," v.; "Good judges complained that his eloquence was somewhat *turgid* and declamatory," Lecky's "Hist. of Eng. in the 18th Century," iii.).—**tur-gid′i-ty**, **tur′gid-ness**, *n.*—**tur′gid-ly**, *adv.*

tur-gite (tėr′jīt), *n.* [Named from the *Turginsk* copper-mine, in the Ural Mountains.] An iron ore, a hydrated ferric oxide, related to limonite but containing less water.

tur-gor (tėr′gọr), *n.* [LL., < L. *turgere*, swell out.] The state of being swelled or filled out; in *plant physiol.*, the normal distention or rigidity of plant-cells, resulting from the pressure exerted from within by the watery contents against the cell-walls.

tu-ri-on (tū′ri-ọn), *n.* [L. *turio(n-)*, a shoot, sprout.] In *bot.*, a scaly shoot growing from a subterranean bud and becoming a new stem, as in the asparagus.

Turk (tėrk), *n.* [= OF. F. *Turc* = ML. *Turcus* = LGr. Τοῦρκος = Pers. *Turk*, Turk.] A member of any of various peoples of Asia and Europe speaking languages which form the Turkic or Tataric division of the Ural-Altaic family; esp., a member of the dominant race in Turkey; a native or inhabitant of Turkey, esp. a Mohammedan; sometimes, any Mohammedan; also, a person having qualities attributed to the Turks; a cruel, barbarous, or tyrannical person (as, "Nobody in this world was ever such a *Turk* to me as you are!" C. Brontë's "Villette," xxvii.); also, a Turkish horse.—**the Turk**, the people or government of Turkey; also, the Sultan ('the Grand Turk').

tur-key (tėr′ki), *n.*; pl. *-keys* (-kiz). [From *Turkey cock* and *Turkey hen*, formerly, the cock and the hen of the guinea-fowl, supposed to come from Turkey.] A guinea-fowl†; also, either of two large American gallinaceous birds constituting the genus *Meleagris*, esp. *M. gallopavo*, which is domesticated in most parts of the world, and esteemed for eating; the flesh of this bird; also, any of various more or less similar birds; also, a bag holding the personal belongings, carried by lumberjacks and others (U. S. and Canada).

The Wild Turkey of the United States (*Meleagris gallopavo*), male.

tur-key=buz-zard (tėr′ki-buz′ärd), *n.* A vulture, *Cathartes aura*, common in South and Central America and the southern U. S., having a bare reddish head and a dark plumage.

Turkey-buzzard.

tur-key=cock (tėr′ki-kok), *n.* The male of the turkey: sometimes taken as a type of swelling or strutting self-importance.

Tur-key (tėr′ki) **red.** A bright red produced in fabrics by means of madder or alizarin; hence, cotton cloth of this color.

tur-key=trot (tėr′ki-trot), *n.* A round dance, danced by couples, properly to rag-time, the step being a springy walk with little or no bending of the knees, and accompanied by a swinging motion of the body with shoulder movements up and down.

Tur-ki (tör′kē), *a.* [Pers. *Turkī*, < *Turk*, Turk.] Turkish; esp., of or pertaining to two typical groups of Turkic languages ('East Turki' and 'West Turki') spoken in west-central Asia, Persia, Turkey, etc.; also, of or pertaining to the peoples speaking them.

Turk-ic (tėr′kik), *a.* Noting or pertaining to a division of the Ural-Altaic family of languages including the languages of the Turks (in a broad sense), esp. the two typical Turki groups of this division; also, noting or pertaining to the peoples using the Turkic languages.

Turk-i-fy (tėr′ki-fī), *v. t.*; *-fied*, *-fying*. [See *-fy*.] To render Turkish; bring into conformity with Turkish standards or ideas.—**Turk″i-fi-ca′tion** (-fi-kā′shọn), *n.*

tur-kis (tėr′kis), *n.* Same as *turquoise*. [Archaic.]

Turk-ish (tėr′kish), *a.* Of, pertaining to, or derived from the Turks or Turkey; also, of or pertaining to the language of the Turks.—**Turkish bath**, a kind of bath introduced from the East, in which, after a copious perspiration in a heated room, the body is soaped, washed, kneaded, etc.— **Turkish towel, Turkish toweling,** a kind of thick cotton towel or toweling with a long nap which is usually composed of uncut loops.—**Turk′ish,** n. The language spoken by the Turks; esp., Osmanli.

Tur′ko-. Same as *Turco-*.

Tur-ko-man (tẽr′kō-mạn), n.; pl. *-mans* (-mạnz). [Pers. *Turkumān*, one resembling a Turk.] A member of a Turkish people consisting of a group of tribes which inhabit the region about the Aral Sea and parts of Persia and Afghanistan; also, the language of this people.

Turk′s=cap (tẽrks′kap) **lil′y.** Either of two lilies, *Lilium martagon* and *L. superbum*, having nodding flowers with the perianth segments strongly revolute: the former an old-world species much cultivated in Europe, with purple, red, or otherwise colored flowers, the latter common as a wild plant in eastern North America, with dark-spotted orange-colored flowers.

Turk′s=head (tẽrks′hed), n. *Naut.*, a form of knot made by weaving turns of small cord round a larger rope.

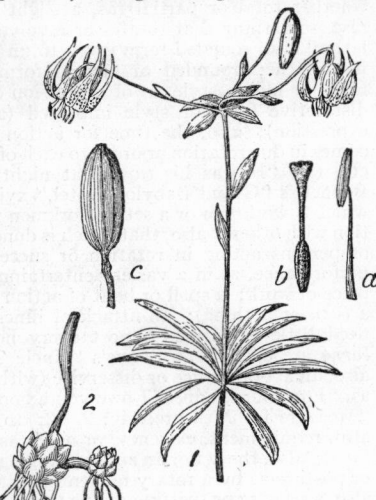

Turk's-cap Lily (*Lilium superbum*). — 1, upper part of plant with flowers; 2, lower part of plant with bulbs; *a*, stamen; *b*, pistil; *c*, fruit.

turm (tẽrm), n. [L. *turma*.] A troop or squadron, as of horsemen (as, "legions and cohorts, *turms* of horse and wings": Milton's "Paradise Regained," iv. 66); a company or band. [Archaic.]

tur-mer-ic (tẽr′mẹ-rik). [Origin obscure: cf. F. *terremérite*, NL. *terra merita*, powdered turmeric, appar. corruptions (simulating F. *terre*, L. *terra*, earth) of some Oriental name.] **I.** *n.* The aromatic rhizome of *Curcuma longa*, an East Indian zingiberaceous plant, or a powder prepared from it, used as a condiment (esp. in curry-powder), a yellow dye, a medicine, etc.; also, the plant itself; also, any of various similar substances or plants. **II.** *a.* Pertaining to or derived from turmeric: as, *turmeric* paper (paper treated with turmeric: used to indicate the presence of alkalis, which turn it brown, or of boric acid, which turns it reddish-brown).

tur-moil (tẽr′moil), n. [Origin uncertain.] A state of commotion or disturbance; tumult; agitation; disquiet: as, "The Settlement was . . . in . . . a *turmoil*" (J. Conrad's "Rescue," vi. 4); "My mind was in a fine *turmoil*" (Buchan's "Three Hostages," viii.).—**tur′moil,** v. t. To disturb, agitate, or disquiet; trouble: as, "Haughty Juno, who, with endless broils, Earth, seas, and heav'n, and Jove himself *turmoils*" (Dryden's tr. Virgil's "Æneid," i. 381).

turn (tẽrn), v. t. [AS. *tyrnan, turnian,* also OF. *torner, tourner* (F. *tourner*), < L. *tornare*, turn in a lathe, round off, < *tornus*, lathe, < Gr. τόρνος, turner's chisel, akin to τείρειν, rub: see *trite*.] To shape (a piece of wood, etc.) into rounded form with a cutting instrument while rotating in a lathe; make by means of a lathe; bring into a rounded or curved form in any way; shape artistically or gracefully, esp. in rounded form (as, a hand beautifully *turned*); form or express gracefully (as, to *turn* a sentence); also, to cause to move round on an axis or about a center (as, to *turn* a wheel); cause to rotate; cause to move round or partly round, as for the purpose of opening or closing something (as, to *turn* a key or a door-knob); execute, as a somersault, by rotating or revolving; also, to change the position of, by or as by rotating (as, "When she [hen] has laid her

eggs . . . what care does she take in *turning* them frequently": Addison, in "Spectator," 120); move into a different position; revolve in the mind (often with *over*); also, to curve, bend, or twist (as, "a bonnet . . . encircled with a gold chain *turned* three times round it": Scott's "Kenilworth," xiv.); bend back or blunt (the edge of a knife, etc.); also, to reverse the position or posture of; move into the opposite position, so that the upper side becomes the under, the front side the back, etc. (as, to *turn* an hour-glass; to *turn* a page); bring the under parts of (sod, soil, etc.) to the surface, as in plowing or digging; reverse (a garment, etc.) so that the inner side becomes the outer; remake (a garment) by putting the inner side outward; also, to cause (the stomach) to reject food or anything swallowed; also, to change or reverse the course of (as, "With shield and blade Horatius Right deftly *turned* the blow": Macaulay's "Horatius," xlvi.); divert; deflect; also, to go or pass round or to the other side of (as, "Alma . . . watched him till he *turned* the corner of the street," L. Merrick's "Actor-Manager," xv.; to *turn* the enemy's flank, to pass round his forces so as to be able to attack him on the flank or from the rear); get beyond or pass (a certain age, time, amount, etc.: as, "a man just *turning* thirty-three," Bok's "Americanization of Edward Bok," xii.); also, to direct (the eyes, face, etc.) another way; sometimes, to avert (the eyes, face, etc.); direct, aim, or set going toward or away from a specified person or thing, or in a specified direction (as, to *turn* a hose on a burning building; to *turn* one's steps toward the north); cause to go, or send or drive (as, to *turn* a person from one's door); direct (thought, desire, etc.) toward or away from something (as, "We . . . *turned* our attention to poor Tom": Stevenson's "Treasure Island," xviii.); also, to cause to change to another religious party, opinion, etc.†; convert†; sometimes, to pervert†; also, to put or apply to some use or purpose (as, to *turn* a thing to good use); also, to change or alter the nature, character, or appearance of (as, "Some dear friend dead; else nothing in the world Could *turn* so much the constitution Of any constant man": Shakspere's "Merchant of Venice," iii. 2. 249); change or convert (*into* or *to*: as, to *turn* water into ice; to *turn* securities into cash; to *turn* friendship to hate); render or make by some change (as, "It almost *turns* my dangerous nature mild": Shakspere's "Timon of Athens," iv. 3. 499); bring (a person) to trouble or harm† (as, "A word or two; The which shall *turn* you to no further harm Than so much loss of time": Shakspere's "Coriolanus," iii. 1. 284); change from one language or form of expression to another (as, to *turn* Virgil into English heroics; to *turn* verse into prose); disturb the mental balance of, or make mad, distract, or infatuate (as, "Your plays and romances have positively *turned* your brain": Scott's "Black Dwarf," v.); cause to become sour, ferment, or the like (as, warm weather *turns* milk); change the color of (leaves, etc.); also, in *cookery*, to pare off the rind of (an orange, lemon, etc.) round and round in a long, narrow, thin strip.—**to turn an honest penny,** to earn or gain a penny, or small amount of money, by honest means.—**to turn down,** to fold or double down; bend downward; also, to turn upside down; invert; place with the face downward, as a playing-card; also, to refuse the request, offer, etc., of (a person, etc.: slang); refuse or reject (a request, proposition, etc.: slang); also, to lower the flame of (a lamp, etc.) by turning a handle or the like.— **to turn into** (or **to**) **ridicule** (**sport,** etc.), to turn into, or take as a matter for, ridicule (sport, etc.).—**to turn off,** to deflect or divert; also, to stop the flow of (water, gas, etc.), as by closing a stop-cock; put out (a light); also, to send away or dismiss; discharge; also, to hang on a gallows (now rare); hence, to dispose of (a person or a couple) by the ceremony of marriage (humorous).—**to turn on,** to bring on the flow of (water, gas, etc.), as by opening a stop-cock.— **to turn one's coat,** fig., to change one's party or principles: as, "Shall I *turn my coat,* and join the victors?" (Froude's "Cæsar," xxi.). Cf. *turncoat.*—**to turn one's hand to,** to turn one's energies to; set to work at: as, "He can *turn his hand to* anything" (Eden Phillpotts's "Red Redmaynes," v.).—**to turn out,** to extinguish or put out (a light, etc.), as by closing a stop-cock; also, to drive out; send away, dismiss, or discharge; also, to produce as the result of labor, etc.; also, to equip; fit out.—**to turn over,** to turn (a thing) from its position so that another side or face is uppermost; also, to hand over; transfer; convert to a different use; also, in *com.*, to invest and get back again (capital) in some transaction or in the course of business; purchase and then sell (goods or commodities) in some transaction or in the course of business; also, to do business, or sell goods, to the amount of (a sum specified).—**to turn over a new leaf,** fig., to adopt a different and a better line of conduct.—**to turn tail,** to turn the back and run away; flee.—**to turn the scale,** to cause one scale of a balance to descend, as by an excess of weight; hence, fig., to turn the fortune of some doubtful matter in favor of, or against, one of the opposing parties or sides.—**to turn the tables.** See *table, n.*—**to turn turtle,** to capsize or overturn completely, so that the bottom is upward: said usually of boats, but also of automobiles, aëroplanes, etc.—**to turn up,** to fold up or over, esp. so as to shorten, as a garment; also, to give an upward turn or direction to (as, to *turn up* one's nose in contempt); also, to turn so as to bring the under side upward; invert; place with the face upward, as a playing-card; bring the under parts of (sod, soil, etc.) to the surface; also, to make the flame of (a lamp, etc.) higher or brighter by turning a handle or the like.—**turn,** *v. i.* To shape material into rounded form in a lathe; also, to take form in a lathe, as material; also, to move round on an axis or about a center; rotate; move partly round in this manner, as a door on a hinge; have a sensation as of whirling, or be affected with giddiness, as the head; hinge or depend (*on* or *upon*: as, the question *turns* on this point); rest (*on* or *upon*: as, "The play *turned* upon a typical French situation," Mrs. H. Ward's "Robert Elsmere," xii.); also, to change or reverse position or posture as by a rotary motion; shift the body about as if on an axis (as, to *turn* on one's side in sleeping); also, to assume a curved form; bend; also, to be affected with nausea, as the stomach; also, to change or reverse the course so as to go in a different or the opposite direction (as, to *turn* to the right; the tide *turns*); put about or tack, as a ship; go or come back†, or return† (as, "ere from this war thou *turn* a conqueror": Shakspere's "Richard III.," iv. 4. 184); also, to change position so as to face in a different or the opposite direction (as, "Seeing me, she *turn'd*": Milton's "Paradise Lost," viii. 507); direct the face or gaze, or the course, toward or away from something, or in a particular direction (as, "He *turned* to me with a singular furtive smile," Stevenson's "Master of Ballantrae," vi.; "Where'er she *turns* the Graces homage pay," Gray's "Progress of Poesy," i. 3); direct one's thought, attention, desire, etc., toward or away from something (as, "Where'er I roam . . . My heart, untravell'd, fondly *turns* to thee": Goldsmith's "Traveller," 8); also, to adopt a different religion, manner of life, etc.; go over or desert, as to another side or party (archaic); also, to change one's position in order to resist or attack (as, the worm will *turn*); take up an attitude or policy of hostility or opposition (as, to *turn* against a person; to *turn* on or upon a person); also, to change or alter, as in nature, character, or appearance; be changed, transformed, or converted (*into* or *to*: as, "Thy mirth shall *turn* to moan," Shakspere's "1 Henry VI.," ii. 3. 44); change so as to be, or become (as, "Sophia *turned* pale at these words," Fielding's "Tom Jones," vii. 7; hair *turns* gray; "We would leave off being pirates and *turn* merchants," Defoe's "Captain Singleton," xiv.); become sour, fermented, or the like, as milk, etc.; become of a different color, as leaves, etc.—**to turn in,** to turn and go in; also, to go to bed (colloq.: as, "It's getting late . . . and you'd better all *turn in*," Bret Harte's "Miggles"); also, to have an inward direction, or point inward, as the toes.—**to turn out,** to turn and go out; go out on strike, as workers; go out for some public or formal assemblage, muster, spectacle, or other like occasion (as, the militia *turned out* in full force; many failed to *turn out* to vote); also, to get out of bed (colloq.); also, to have an outward direction, or point outward, as the toes; also, to result or issue (as, "Things never *turn out* either so well or so badly as they logically ought to do": W. R. Inge's "Outspoken Essays," i. 4); come to be, or become ultimately (as, a bad boy often *turns out* a good man); be found or known, or prove (as,

"a tall figure which immediately *turned out* to be that of an old gentleman": W. Churchill's "Inside of the Cup," xi.).—**to turn to,** to apply one's self to some task, etc.; set to work: as, "After the war he wants to *turn to* and make automobiles again" (H. G. Wells's "Italy, France, and Britain at War," iii. 4).—**to turn up,** to turn and go up; also, to be directed upward; also, to make one's or its appearance (as, "Prince Eugen and his suite, who were expected here for dinner, fail to *turn up*," Arnold Bennett's "Grand Babylon Hotel," vi.; "The expected hamper had not *turned up*," Du Maurier's "Trilby," iv.).—**turn,** *n.* The action of turning about an axis or center; rotation; revolution; a single revolution, as of a wheel; a movement of rotation, whether total or partial (as, a slight *turn* of the handle); also, something that rotates or revolves, as a watchmaker's lathe; also, rounded form given to an object as by rotation in a lathe; rounded or curved form in general; shape, form, or mold; style, as of expression or language; often, a distinctive form or style imparted (as, a happy *turn* of expression); also, the time for action or proceeding which comes in due rotation or order to each of a number of persons, etc. (as, "It was his *turn* that night to watch": Arnold Bennett's "Grand Babylon Hotel," xviii.); the time during which a workman or a set of workmen is at work in alternation with others; also, that which is done by each of a number of persons acting in rotation or succession; an individual performance, as in a variety entertainment; also, a spell or piece of work; a spell or bout of action (as, to take, or have, a *turn* at a thing); an attack of illness or the like (as, "I need little attentions almost every hour, when my worst *turns* are on": Mrs. Stowe's "Uncle Tom's Cabin," xvi.); also, an act of service or disservice (with *good, bad, kind,* etc.: as, "For your kindness I owe you a good *turn*," Shakspere's "Measure for Measure," iv. 2. 62; to do one an ill *turn*); also, requirement, exigency, or need (as, this will serve your *turn*); also, the act or an act of changing or reversing position or posture as by a rotary movement (as, a *turn* of the dice); also, a passing or twisting of one thing round another, as of a rope round a mast; the condition or manner of being twisted; a single round, as of a wound or coiled rope; also, the act or an act of changing or reversing the course (as, to make a *turn* to the right); also, a place or point at which such a change occurs; a place where a road, river, or the like turns; also, a short walk, ride, or the like which includes a going and a returning, esp. by different routes (as, "Rochfort proposed that they should take a *turn* in the park," Maria Edgeworth's "Belinda," vii.; "I am off for a *turn* in the car," G. B. Shaw's "Man and Superman," ii.); also, the act or an act of turning so as to face or go in a different direction (as, "She . . . made a sudden *turn* As if to speak": Tennyson's "Princess," iv. 375); also, direction, drift, or trend (as, "She . . . evidently enjoyed the *turn* the conversation was taking": John Hay's "Bread-Winners," i.); natural inclination, bent, tendency, or aptitude (as, "The North Corkians were of a most hospitable *turn*," Lever's "Harry Lorrequer," vi.; "The child will have a *turn* for mechanics," Bulwer-Lytton's "Caxtons," i. 6); also, change or a change in nature, character, condition, circumstances, etc. (as, "Some *turn* this sickness yet might take": Tennyson's "Two Voices," 55); hence, the point or time of change (as, "It was just past the *turn* of the day," Cooper's "Two Admirals," xvii.; "We can mark time . . . till the *turn* of the year," Eden Phillpotts's "Red Redmaynes," v.); also, a nervous shock, as from fright or astonishment (colloq.: as, "What a *turn* you have given me!" Dickens's "Dombey and Son," vi.); in *music,* a melodic embellishment or grace, commonly consisting of a principal tone with two auxiliary tones, one above and the other below it.—**by turns,** one after another, alternately or in rotation: as, "He coaxed and blustered *by turns*" (H. Melville's "Typee," xxix.).—**in turn,** in due order of succession: as, "Each of these families had, *in turn,* become great by the absorption of other families" (J. F. Kirk's "Charles the Bold," iv. 2).—**on the turn,** at the turning-point; on the point of, or in process of, change or reversal.—**to a turn,** to just the proper degree; to a nicety: orig. in reference to the turns of a revolving spit holding roasting meat.—**turn about,** or **turn and turn about,** by turns; alternately.

turn-a-bout (tĕrn′a̱-bout″), *n.* The act or an act of turning about; a turning so as to face the other way; also, one who or that which turns about; a merry-go-round.

turn-buck-le (tĕrn′buk″l), *n.* A link or sleeve with a swivel at one end and an internal screw-thread at the other, or with an internal screw-thread at each end, used as a means of uniting or coupling, and of tightening, two

Open Turnbuckle.

parts, as the ends of two rods; also, a flat piece of metal, pivoted above its center of gravity to a wall, and serving to fasten back a shutter opened against the wall.

turn-coat (tĕrn′kōt), *n.* One who changes his party or principles; a renegade.

turn=down (tĕrn′doun), *a.* That is or may be turned down; folded or doubled down (as, a *turn-down* collar).

turn-er[1] (tĕr′nẽr), *n.* One who or that which turns; esp., one who fashions objects on a lathe.

turn-er[2] (tĕr′nẽr, G. tûr′nẽr), *n.* [G., < *turnen*, perform gymnastic exercises, < F. *tourner*, turn: see *turn*.] A member of any of the gymnastic societies common among the Germans, first instituted in Berlin in 1811 by F. L. Jahn.

turn-er-y (tĕr′nẽr-i), *n.*; pl. *-ies* (-iz). The art or work of a turner; the forming of objects on a lathe; also, articles fashioned on a lathe; also, a place where articles are turned.

turn-hall (tĕrn′hâl), *n.* [G. *turnhalle*: cf. *turner*[2].] A hall or building in which turners or gymnasts practise or perform.

turn-ing (tĕr′ning), *n.* The act of one who or that which turns (in any sense); esp., the forming of objects on a lathe; also, a place or point where anything turns.—**turn′ing-point**, *n.* A point at which something turns; fig., a point at which a decisive change takes place (as, "As for Elsmere, that hour and a half . . . represented the *turning-point* of life": Mrs. H. Ward's "Robert Elsmere," xxiv.); a critical point; a crisis.

tur-nip (tĕr′nip), *n.* [Formerly *turnepe*, < *tur-* (possibly for *turn*, as suggesting roundness) + *nepe*, *neep*, turnip: see *neep*.] The thick, fleshy edible root of various cultivated varieties of the cruciferous plant *Brassica campestris* (the 'wild turnip,' or navew), including the common 'white turnip,' and the 'yellow turnip,' 'Swedish turnip,' or rutabaga; the plant itself; also, any of various similar roots or plants; also, a thick, old-fashioned watch, or any watch (humorous). See under *Indian*, *a.*—**Indian turnip**.

tur-nix (tĕr′niks), *n.* [NL., < L. *coturnix*, quail.] Any of the small, three-toed, quail-like birds constituting the genus *Turnix*, inhabiting the warmer parts of the Old World.

turn-key (tĕrn′kē), *n.*; pl. *-keys* (-kēz). One who has charge of the keys of a prison; a prison keeper.

turn-out (tĕrn′out), *n.* The act or an act of turning out; a strike of workmen, or one of the strikers (chiefly Eng.); the body of persons who turn out for an assemblage, muster, spectacle, or the like (as, "The attendance in the forenoon amounted to seven . . . but in the afternoon there was a *turn-out* of upwards of fifty": Barrie's "Auld Licht Idylls," ii.); also, a short side track or passage, or a part of a passage wider than the rest, which enables vehicles, etc., to pass one another; a place where animals may be turned out to pasture; also, the quantity of anything turned out or produced; output; also, the manner or style in which anything is turned out or equipped; get-up; also, an equipment or outfit; a driving equipage.

turn-o-ver (tĕrn′ō″vẽr). **I.** *n.* The act or result of turning over; a transfer, as of votes from one party to another; the conversion of something to a different use; the act of going over or changing from one position or engagement, tenancy, or the like to another (as, a movement to reduce labor *turnover*); also, that which is turned over, as the flap of an envelop; an apprentice whose indentures have been turned over or transferred to a new employer (now prov.); a semicircular pie made by turning over one half of a circular crust upon the other; in *com.*, the turning over of the capital or stock of goods involved in a particular transaction or course of business (see *to turn over*, under *turn*, *v. t.*); also, the total amount of business done in a given time. **II.** *a.* Turned over, or that may be turned over; having a part that turns over, as a collar.

turn-pike (tĕrn′pīk), *n.* [From *turn* + *pike*[1].] A defensive barrier of bars with pointed ends fixed in or across a road or passage (now hist.); also, a turnstile to exclude horses, cattle, etc.†; also, a barrier, orig. like a turnstile, later in the form of a gate or gates, set across a road to stop passage until toll is paid; a toll-gate; also, a turnpike road.— **turnpike road**, a road on which turnpikes are, or were formerly, erected for the collection of tolls.

turn=plate (tĕrn′plāt), *n.* A railroad or railway turn-table. [Eng.]

turn-sole (tĕrn′sōl), *n.* [OF. F. *tournesol*, < It. *tornasole*, < *tornare* (< L. *tornare*), turn, + *sole* (< L. *sol*), sun.] Any of various plants regarded as turning with the movement of the sun, as the heliotrope, the sunflower, or *Tournesol tinctorium* (or *Chrozophora tinctoria*), a euphorbiaceous plant of the Mediterranean region; also, a purple dye obtained from the juice of *Tournesol tinctorium*, formerly much used for coloring wines, jellies, etc.

turn-spit (tĕrn′spit), *n.* A person employed to turn a roasting-spit; also, a dog used to turn a spit by working a kind of treadmill-wheel connected with it, esp. a dog of a breed with long body and short legs and resembling the dachshund.

turn-stile (tĕrn′stîl), *n.* A structure consisting of two crossed bars turning horizontally on a vertical post, set in a gateway or opening to prevent the passage of cattle, horses, etc., but permitting that of persons; some similar device set up in an entrance or opening to bar passage until a toll or other charge is paid, to record the number of persons passing through, etc.

turn-stone (tĕrn′stōn), *n.* Any of the small, migratory, limicoline shore-birds constituting the genus *Arenaria* (or *Strepsilas*), notable for their habit of turning over stones in search of food, esp. *A. interpres*, common in North America.

Turnstone (*Arenaria interpres*), in full summer plumage.

turn=ta-ble (tĕrn′tā″bl), *n.* A rotating, track-bearing circular platform used for turning locomotives, etc., around; also, any of various other turning devices.

turn=up (tĕrn′up). **I.** *n.* The act or fact of turning up; also, that which is turned up or which turns up; the turned-up part of anything; also, a fight, or a row or disturbance (colloq.: as, "a possible *turn-up* or set-to between Dr. Hillyer and Mr. Knowles," W. De Morgan's "Joseph Vance," xvi.). **II.** *a.* That is or may be turned up.

turn-ver-ein (tûrn′fer-īn″), *n.* [G., < *turnen*, perform gymnastic exercises, + *verein*, union, society: cf. *turner*[2].] An association of turners or gymnasts. See *turner*[2].

tur-pen-tine (tĕr′pen-tīn), *n.* [OF. *terbentine* (F. *térébenthine*), < ML. *terebinthina*, prop. fem. of L. *terebinthinus*, of or from the terebinth, E. *terebinthine*.] Orig., an oleoresin exuding from the terebinth, *Pistacia terebinthus* (called esp. 'Chian turpentine'); now, esp., any of various oleoresins derived from various coniferous trees, and yielding a volatile

One method of Turpentine-gathering.

(variable) d̦ as d or j, ș as s or sh, ț as t or ch, z̦ as z or zh; o, F. cloche; ü, F. menu; c̆h, Sc. loch; n̦, F. bonbon; ′, primary accent; ″, secondary accent; †, obsolete; <, from; +, and; =, equals. See also lists at beginning of book.

oil (*oil of turpentine*) and a resin (*rosin* or *colophony*) when distilled; also, popularly and commonly, oil of turpentine. — **oil of turpentine**, a colorless, inflammable, volatile oil obtained by distilling the oleoresin turpentine of coniferous trees, having a peculiar, penetrating odor and a pungent, bitterish taste, and consisting of a mixture of terpenes: used in the preparation of paints, varnishes, and the like, and in medicine as a stimulant, diuretic, rubefacient, etc. Also called *spirit* (or *spirits*) *of turpentine.* — **tur′pen-tine,** *v.*; *-tined, -tining.* **I.** *tr.* To treat with turpentine; apply turpentine to. **II.** *intr.* To gather or take crude turpentine from trees.

tur-peth (tėr′peth), *n.* [OF. *turbit* (F. *turbith*) = ML. *turpethum*, < Ar. and Pers. *turbid*.] A drug obtained from the roots of a convolvulaceous plant, *Ipomœa turpethum*, of the East Indies, formerly used as a purgative; the plant itself, or its root; also, a heavy lemon-yellow powder, a basic mercuric sulphate ('turpeth mineral'), sometimes used as a purgative.

tur-pi-tude (tėr′pi-tūd), *n.* [OF. F. *turpitude.* < L. *turpitudo*, < *turpis*, ugly, foul, base, shameful.] Base or shameful character (as, "He could laugh over the story of some ingenious fraud . . . and seem insensible to its *turpitude*": Bulwer-Lytton's "Caxtons," viii. 4); baseness, depravity, or wickedness; also, a base or shameful act (as, "They were not his misdeeds, his *turpitudes*": H. James's "Portrait of a Lady," xlii.).

tur-quoise (tėr′kwoiz or tėr′koiz), *n.* [F. *turquoise*, OF. *turquoyse*, orig. adj., 'Turkish' (stone); because first brought from (or through) Turkey.] A sky-blue or greenish-blue mineral, essentially a hydrous phosphate of aluminium containing a little copper and iron, much used in jewelry; also, a light-blue color, sometimes with a greenish tinge.

tur-ret (tur′et), *n.* [OF. *tourete*, dim. of *tour*, tower: see *tower*².] A small tower, usually one forming part of a larger structure; often, a small tower at an angle of a building, frequently beginning some distance above the ground; also, a tall structure, usually moved on wheels, formerly employed in breaching or scaling a fortified place, a wall, or the like, and carrying soldiers, ladders, etc.; *naval* and *milit.*, a low, tower-like, heavily armored structure, usually revolving horizontally, within which guns are mounted; in *mach.*, an attachment on a lathe, etc., for holding a number of tools, each of which can be brought to the work by a simple rotation or other movement. — **tur′ret-ed,** *a.* Furnished with a turret or turrets; having a turret-like part or parts; in *zoöl.*, having whorls in the form of a long or towering spiral, as certain shells. — **tur′ret=head,** *n.* In *mach.*, the turret of a lathe, etc.

Turrets, 13th century. — Main entrance to the Abbey of Mont St. Michel, Normandy.

tur-ric-u-late (tu-rik′ū-lāt), *a.* [L. *turricula*, dim. of *turris*, E. *tower*².] Furnished with or resembling a turret or turrets; in *zoöl.*, turreted, as a shell. Also **tur-ric′u-lat-ed** (-lā-ted).

tur-ri-lite (tur′i-līt), *n.* [NL. *Turrilites*, < L. *turris*, tower, + Gr. λίθος, stone.] Any of the cephalopod mollusks, with a spiral, turreted shell, which constitute the extinct genus *Turrilites*, and which occur as fossils in Cretaceous formations.

Turreted Shell.

tur-tle¹ (tėr′tl), *n.* [AS. *turtla, turtle,* < L. *turtur*, turtle-dove.] A turtle-dove: as, "Those two cooing *turtles* were caged for life" (Smollett's "Humphry Clinker," Nov. 8).

tur-tle² (tėr′tl), *n.*; pl. *turtles* or (esp. collectively) *turtle*. [Appar. a corruption of obs. *tortue*, < F. *tortue*, < ML. *tortuca*, E. *tortoise*.] Any of the *Chelonia*, an order or group of reptiles having the body inclosed in a shell consisting of a carapace and a plastron, from between which the head, tail, and four legs protrude; often, esp., an aquatic species, as distinguished from a tortoise, or terrestrial species; also, the flesh of some edible species of turtle used or prepared for food (cf. *mock turtle*, under *mock*, *a.*). — **green turtle**, a large marine turtle, *Chelone midas*, with a greenish shell, the female of which is much esteemed for food purposes, esp. for making a choice kind of soup. — **to turn turtle.** See under *turn*, *v. t.* — **tur′tle**², *v. i.*; *-tled, -tling.* To catch turtles; make a practice or business of catching turtles. — **tur′tle-back,** *n.*

Green Turtle (*Chelone midas*).

The back of a turtle; also, an arched protection erected over the deck of a steamer at the bow, and often at the stern also, to guard against damage from heavy seas; in *archæol.*, a rude stone implement having one or both faces slightly convex.

tur-tle=dove (tėr′tl-duv′), *n.* [See *turtle*¹.] Any of various old-world doves, esp. of the genus *Turtur*, as *T. vulgaris* (or *communis*), a common European species having a characteristic plaintive note and notable for the affection existing between mates; also, the mourning-dove (local, U. S.); also, fig., a loving mate.

Turtle-dove (*Turtur vulgaris*).

tur-tle-head (tėr′tl-hed), *n.* [See *turtle*².] Any of the North American herbs constituting the scrophulariaceous genus *Chelone*, having large white, red, or purple flowers with an inflated, arched, nearly closed corolla resembling the head of a turtle.

tur-tler (tėr′tlėr), *n.* A person or a vessel engaged in catching turtles.

Tus-can (tus′kạn). **I.** *a.* Of or pertaining to Tuscany, formerly a grand duchy with Florence as its capital, now a part of the kingdom of Italy, corresponding generally to the ancient Etruria; in *arch.*, noting or pertaining to a classical (Roman) order of architecture distinguished

Tuscan Order.

by a plain (not fluted) column and the absence of decorative detail. **II.** *n.* A native or inhabitant of Tuscany; also, the form of the Italian language spoken in Tuscany, regarded as the standard form of Italian.

Tus-cu-lan (tus′kū-lan), *a.* Of or pertaining to Tusculum, an ancient city about 13 miles southeast of Rome, near the site of the modern Frascati, and near which Cicero had a villa.

tush[1] (tush), *n.* Same as *tusk.* [Now chiefly prov.]

tush[2] (tush). **I.** *interj.* An exclamation expressing impatience, contempt, etc.: as, *"Tush!* we have nothing to fear" (Hawthorne's "Twice-Told Tales," Howe's Masquerade). [Chiefly archaic.] **II.** *n.* An exclamation of 'tush!' [Chiefly archaic.]—**tush**[2], *v. i.* To say 'tush': as, "Shalford never pished and *tushed* with Minton" (H. G. Wells's "Kipps," i. 2). [Chiefly archaic.]—**tush′er-y**, *n.* [A word coined by Robert Louis Stevenson.] The style of romance characterized by much use of 'tush' and like expressions.

tusk (tusk), *n.* [ME. *tuske,* also *tusche,* < AS. *tux, tusc,* = OFries. *tusk, tusch.*] A long, pointed or protruding tooth, esp. of an animal; specif., in certain animals, a tooth developed to great length, usually as one of a pair, as in the elephant, walrus, wild boar, etc., but singly in the narwhal; also, a projecting part resembling the tusk of an animal; in *carp.,* a shoulder or step on a tenon to give it additional strength.

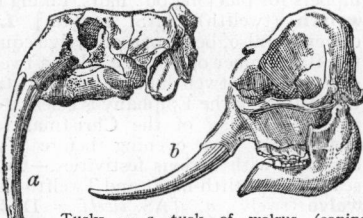

Tusks. — *a,* tusk of walrus (canine tooth); *b,* tusk of elephant (incisor tooth).

—**tusk,** *v.* **I.** *tr.* To dig, tear, or gore with the tusks or tusk; also, to furnish with tusks or tusk-like projections. **II.** *intr.* To thrust or root with the tusks.—**tusked,** *a.* Having tusks: as, *"tusked* boars" (W. Morris's "Jason," xiii. 78).—**tusk′er,** *n.* An animal with tusks, as an elephant or a wild boar.—**tusk′-less,** *a.* Having no tusks.—**tusk′=ten″on,** *n.* In *carp.,* a tenon strengthened by having one or more shoulders or steps (tusks) on the lower side.—**tusk′y,** *a.* Having tusks, as an animal.

tus-sah (tus′ä), *n.* Same as *tussur.*

tus-sal (tus′al), *a.* Pertaining to tussis or cough.

tus′ser, *n.* See *tussur.*

tus-sis (tus′is), *n.* [L.] In *pathol.,* a cough.—**tus-sive** (tus′iv), *a.* Of or pertaining to a cough.

tus-sle (tus′l), *v.;* -sled, -sling. [= *tousle.*] **I.** *tr.* To pull about roughly; struggle or fight roughly with. [Now rare.] **II.** *intr.* To struggle or fight roughly or vigorously; wrestle confusedly; scuffle; hence, to labor strenuously (as, "Still I *tussled* with the rails [of a fence]": G. W. Cable's "Cavalier," xxvi.).—**tus′sle,** *n.* A rough struggle as in fighting or wrestling; a scuffle; any vigorous conflict or contest (as, "the ancient *tussle* of Pope and Emperor for ascendancy," H. G. Wells's "Outline of History," xxxiii. § 7; "a sharp *tussle* with a temptation," S. Butler's "Way of All Flesh," xlv.); hence, an exercise or period of strenuous effort, as with something troublesome or difficult (as, a *tussle* with a hard problem).

tus-sock (tus′ok), *n.* [Origin uncertain.] A bunch or tuft of hair (now rare); also, a tuft or clump of growing grass or the like (as, "The solitary hill was covered with short *tussocks* of yellow, wiry grass": W. H. Hudson's "Purple Land," xxii.); also, a tussock-moth.—**tus′sock=moth,** *n.* Any of various dull-colored moths, as of the genus *Orgyia,* whose larvæ have long tufts of hair.—**tus′sock-y,** *a.* Abounding in tussocks; also, forming tussocks.

tus-sore (tus′ōr), *n.* Same as *tussur.*

tus-sur (tus′er), *n.* [Hind. *tasar,* shuttle; perhaps from the form of the cocoon.] A coarse brown silk obtained from the cocoon of various undomesticated Asiatic silkworms (larvæ of *Antheræa mylitta* and other moths); a fabric made from this; also, the silkworm itself, or its moth.

tut (tut). **I.** *interj.* An exclamation expressing impatience, contempt, etc.: as, " *'Tut, tut,* boy,' said Sir Jeremy testily" (Hugh Walpole's "Wooden Horse," i.). **II.** *n.* An exclamation of 'tut!'—**tut,** *v. i.;* *tutted, tutting.* To say 'tut': as, "The Member of Parliament was pishing and *tutting* over the Globe or the Sun" (Bulwer-Lytton's "Caxtons," viii. 3).

tu-te-lage (tū′te-lāj), *n.* [L. *tutela,* guardianship, < *tueri:* see *tutor.*] The office or function of a guardian; guardianship or protection; also, tuition or instruction (as, "Under Stockmar's *tutelage* he was constantly engaged in enlarging his outlook": Lytton Strachey's "Queen Victoria," v.); also, the state of being under a guardian or a tutor.

tu-te-lar (tū′te-lär), *a.* and *n.* [LL. *tutelaris.*] Same as *tutelary.*

tu-te-la-ry (tū′te-lā-ri). [L. *tutelarius,* < *tutela:* see *tutelage.*] **I.** *a.* Having the position of guardian or protector of a person, place, or thing (as, *tutelary* divinities; a *tutelary* saint); also, of or pertaining to guardianship or a guardian. **II.** *n.;* pl. *-ries* (-riz). A tutelary divinity, saint, spirit, or the like.

tu-te-nag (tū′te-nag), *n.* [E. Ind.] A whitish alloy containing much zinc; also, crude zinc.

tu-tor (tū′tor), *n.* [OF. *tutour* (F. *tuteur*), < L. *tutor,* guardian, < *tueri,* look at, look after, guard, keep.] A guardian†; a protector†; also, one employed to instruct another privately in some branch or branches of learning; a private instructor; also, one of a class of officers in a university or college, as at Oxford and Cambridge, England, having immediate supervision, in studies or otherwise, of undergraduates assigned to them; a teacher subordinate to a professor in some American universities and colleges; in *civil* and *Sc. law,* the guardian of a boy or girl in pupillarity. —**tu′tor,** *v.* **I.** *tr.* To act as a tutor to; teach or instruct, esp. privately; hence, to train, school, or discipline (as, "The servants, even the women, had been *tutored* into silence": Peacock's "Nightmare Abbey," ii.); admonish or reprove (as, "My uncle . . . reprimanded me . . . Thus *tutored,* I asked pardon of the knight": Smollett's "Humphry Clinker," April 24); instruct as to what to do or say; sometimes, to instruct secretly or improperly on such points (as, to *tutor* a witness as to evidence to be given). **II.** *intr.* To act as a tutor or private instructor; also, to study under a tutor.—**tu′tor-age** (-āj), *n.* The office, authority, or care of a tutor; instruction; also, the charge for instruction by a tutor.—**tu′tor-ess,** *n.* A female tutor.—**tu-to-ri-al** (tū-tō′ri-al), *a.* Of, pertaining to, or exercised by a tutor: as, *tutorial* functions or authority.—**tu-to′ri-al-ly,** *adv.*—**tu′tor-ship,** *n.* The office or position of a tutor.

tut-ti (töt′tē). [It., pl. of *tutto,* < L. *totus,* all.] In *music:* **I.** *a.* All, that is, all the voices or instruments together (used as a direction); also, intended for or performed by all (or most of) the voices or instruments together, as a passage or movement in concerted music. Cf. *solo, a.* **II.** *n.;* pl. *-tis* (-tēz). A tutti passage or movement.

tut-ti=frut-ti (töt′i-fröt′i), *n.* [It., 'all fruits.'] A preserve of mixed fruits; also, ice-cream or some other confection containing a variety of fruits (usually candied and minced) or of fruit flavorings.

tut-ty (tut′i), *n.* [OF. F. *tutie,* < Ar. and Pers. *tūtiyā.*] An impure oxide of zinc obtained from the flues of smelting-furnaces, or a similar substance occurring as a native mineral: used chiefly as a polishing-powder.

tu-um (tū′um), *pron.* [L., 'thine.'] See *meum.*

tu=whit, tu=whoo (tö-hwit′, -hwö′), *interj.* and *n.* Words imitative of cries of the owl.—**tu=whit′, tu=whoo′,** *v. i.;* *-whitted, -whitting, -whooed, -whooing.* To cry 'tu-whit' or 'tu-whoo'; hoot as an owl.

tux-e-do (tuk-sē′dō), *n.;* pl. *-dos* (-dōz). [For *Tuxedo coat,* named from a country club at *Tuxedo* Park, N. Y.] A kind of dress-coat for evening wear, made without skirts or tails.

tuy-ère (twē-âr′), *n.* [F.] A tube or pipe through which the blast of air enters a blast-furnace, forge, or the like.

twa (twä), *a.* and *n.* Scotch form of *two.*

Twad-dell (twod′l), *n.* [From the name of the inventor.] A hydrometer used for densities greater than that of water, the excess of density above unity being found by multiplying the number of divisions (degrees) of the scale by 5 and dividing by 1,000.

Tusk-tenon. — *A,* tenon; *B,* tusk.

---

twad-dle (twod'l), v.; -dled, -dling. [Var. of *twattle*.] **I.** *intr.* To talk in a trivial, feeble, or silly and tedious manner (as, "Lord Bletchworth *twaddled* ponderously. He considered there was a lot of disgraceful bosh being printed": L. Merrick's "Conrad in Quest of His Youth," xi.); prate in a weak, prosy way; utter or write twaddle. **II.** *tr.* To utter as twaddle; pour (*out*) in twaddle; also, to pass (*away*) in twaddle, as time. — **twad'dle,** *n.* Trivial, feeble, or silly and tedious talk or writing: as, "garrulous *twaddle* of old men on club sofas" (W. B. Maxwell's "In Cotton Wool," vii.); sentimental *twaddle*. — **twad'dler,** *n.* — **twad'dly,** *a.* Twaddling; characterized by twaddle.

twain (twān), *a.* and *n.* [AS. *twēgen*, masc.: see *two*.] Two: as, sisters *twain*; we *twain*; "a day or *twain* before" (Tennyson's "Pelleas and Ettarre," 19); "With the fall of that city the province would be cut in *twain*" (Motley's "Dutch Republic," iii. 8). [Archaic.] — **to be twain**, to be separate, disunited, or at variance: as, "Thou and I long since *are twain*" (Milton's "Samson Agonistes," 929). [Archaic.]

twang[1] (twang), v. [Imit.] **I.** *intr.* To give out a sharp, ringing sound, as the string of a musical instrument when plucked, a bowstring or bow in shooting, or sometimes a horn; produce such a sound by or as by plucking a string or a stringed instrument; hence, to play on a stringed musical instrument; also, to have a sharp, nasal tone, as the human voice; speak with such a tone; also, to shoot with a bow; of an arrow, to leave the bowstring with a twang. **II.** *tr.* To cause to make a sharp, ringing sound, as a string of a musical instrument; play on (a stringed instrument: as, "Apollo *twanged* his lute," Motley's "Dutch Republic," iv. 2); play (a melody, etc.) on a stringed instrument; sound forth with a twang; also, to utter or pronounce with a sharp, nasal tone; also, to pluck (the bowstring) in shooting; shoot with (a bow); discharge (an arrow). — **twang**[1], *n.* The sharp, ringing sound produced by plucking or suddenly releasing a tense string; a sound resembling this; also, a sharp, nasal tone, as of the human voice; a nasal intonation; also, a manner of intonation or pronunciation peculiar to an individual or to a district or locality (as, "He did speak with an accent — a *twang*": J. Conrad's "Lord Jim," xxiii.).

twang[2] (twang), *n.* [Var. of *tang*[1].] A tang; a flavor; a trace.

twan-gle (twang'gl), v. *i.* or *t.*; -gled, -gling. [Freq. of *twang*[1].] To twang lightly or frequently. — **twan'gle,** *n.* A twangling sound.

'twas (twoz). Contraction of *it was.*

twat-tle (twot'l), v.; -tled, -tling. [Appar. a var. of *tattle*.] **I.** *intr.* To talk idly or foolishly; chatter; tattle. [Obs. or prov.] **II.** *tr.* To utter or tell idly. [Obs. or prov.] — **twat'tle,** *n.* Idle or foolish talk; chatter; tattle. [Obs. or prov.]

tway (twā), *a.* and *n.* [AS. *twēge*, for *twēgen*, E. *twain*.] Two. [Archaic or Sc.]

tway-blade (twā'blād), *n.* [See *tway*.] Any of various orchidaceous plants, esp. of the genera *Ophrys* (or *Listera*) and *Liparis*, characterized by two nearly opposite broad leaves.

tweak (twēk), v. *t.* [Cf. *twitch*.] To seize and pull with a sharp jerk and twist (as, to *tweak* one's ear; "He had got his face slapped and his nose *tweaked* by Taffy," Du Maurier's "Trilby," vii.); twitch smartly; also, to pull (*off*, etc.) by a twitch (as, "Poll had *tweaked* his wig off": Louisa M. Alcott's "Little Women," i. 5). — **tweak,** *n.* An act of tweaking; a sharp pull and twist; a smart twitch: as, "a sly *tweak* at the cat's tail" (Mrs. Stowe's "Oldtown Folks," vi.).

Twayblade (*Liparis liliifolia*). — *a*, flower.

tweed (twēd), *n.* [Said to be due to a misreading of *tweel*, Sc. form of *twill*.] A twilled fabric of wool (or wool and cotton), having an unfinished surface, and usually two or more colors combined in the yarn, used esp. for men's wear; *pl.*, garments made of this fabric (as, "an Englishman in a country costume of golfing *tweeds*": H. G. Wells's "Mr. Britling," i. 1. § 3).

twee-dle (twē'dl), v. *i.*; -dled, -dling. [Appar. imit.] To produce thin or shrill, modulated sounds by playing on a fiddle, bagpipe, or the like; also, to pipe or whistle, as a bird. [Now chiefly prov. Eng. and Sc.] — **twee'dle-dee'** (-dē'), **twee'dle-dum'** (-dum'), *n.* Words imitative of the sound of a fiddle or of some similar musical sound: often used together to represent things nominally different but practically the same: as, "We knew precisely every shade of difference between *tweedle-dum* and *tweedle-dee* which the different metaphysicians had invented" (Mrs. Stowe's "Oldtown Folks," xxxiv.).

'tween (twēn), *prep.* Between. [Poetic or colloq.]

tweet (twēt), *interj.* and *n.* A word imitative of the note of a small bird. — **tweet,** v. *i.* To utter a tweet or tweets: as, "The birds on the walls outside were audible, *tweeting*, chirping" (G. Meredith's "Diana of the Crossways," xx.).

twee-zers (twē'zėrz), *n. pl.* [Earlier *tweezes*, ult. < *etui*.] A set or case of small instruments†; also, small pincers or nippers for plucking out hairs, taking up small objects, etc.

twelfth (twelfth). [AS. *twelfta*.] **I.** *a.* Next after the eleventh; also, being one of twelve equal parts. **II.** *n.* The twelfth member of a series; also, a twelfth part. — **Twelfth'=day,** *n.* The twelfth day after Christmas; Jan. 6, on which the festival of the Epiphany is celebrated: formerly observed as the last day of the Christmas festivities. — **Twelfth'=night,** *n.* The evening before Twelfth-day: formerly observed with various festivities. — **Twelfth'=tide,** *n.* The season of Twelfth-night and Twelfth-day.

twelve (twelv), *a.* [AS. *twelf* = D. *twaalf* = G. *zwölf* = Icel. *tólf* = Goth. *twalif*, twelve; from the Teut. stem represented by E. *two*, with a termination occurring also in E. *eleven*.] One more than eleven. — **the Twelve Tables.** See under *table*, *n.* — **twelve,** *n.* A number composed of twelve units, or a symbol, as 12 or xii, representing it; a set of twelve persons or things. — **the Twelve**, the twelve apostles chosen by Christ. See Mark, iii. 14. — **to strike twelve.** See under *strike*, v. *t.* — **twelve'mo** (-mō), *n.* and *a.* [See *-mo*.] Same as *duodecimo*. — **twelve'month**, *n.* A period of twelve months; a year: as, "New Year comes but once a *twelvemonth*" (Henley's "In Hospital," xvii.).

twen-ti-eth (twen'ti-eth). [AS. *twentigotha*.] **I.** *a.* Next after the nineteenth; also, being one of twenty equal parts. **II.** *n.* The twentieth member of a series; also, a twentieth part.

twen-ty (twen'ti). [AS. *twentig*.] **I.** *a.* One more than nineteen; twice ten; indefinitely, many. **II.** *n.*; pl. -ties (-tiz). A number composed of twenty units, or a symbol, as 20 or xx, representing it; a score of persons or things. — **twen'ty-fold** (-fōld), *a.* and *adv.*

'twere (twėr). Contraction of *it were.*

twi-, twy-. [AS. *twi-*, two, twice, = D. *twee-* = OHG. *zwi-* (G. *zwie-*) = Icel. *tvī-*, akin to AS. *twā*, E. *two*: see *bi-*.] A prefix meaning 'two,' 'twofold,' 'twice,' used in *twibill* or *twybill*, *twifold*, *twilight*, and other words, now mostly archaic or poetic.

twi-bill, twy-bill (twī'bil), *n.* [AS. *twibil*: see *twi-* and *bill*[2].] A kind of ax with two cutting edges†; also, a mattock with one arm like that of an adz and the other like that of an ax; also, a reaping-hook, esp. one used for cutting beans; also, a double-bladed battle-ax (archaic).

twice (twīs), *adv.* [AS. *twiges* (with adverbial suffix -*es*), < *twiga*, *twiwa*, twice, < *twi-*, two: see *twi-*.] Two times, as in succession (as, to write *twice* a week; "God speaketh once, yea *twice*," Job, xxxiii. 14); on two occasions; in two instances; also, in twofold quantity or degree, or doubly (as, *twice* as much or as fast). — **twice'=told,** *a.* Told or related twice; that has been told before: as, "Life is as tedious as a *twice-told* tale Vexing the dull ear of a drowsy man" (Shakspere's "King John," iii. 4. 108).

twid-dle (twid'l), v. *t.*; -dled, -dling. [Origin obscure: cf. *twirl* and *fiddle*.] To turn round and round, esp. with the fingers (as, "Kim, tongue-tied, *twiddled* the brass betel-box in his hands": Kipling's "Kim," ix.); twirl; play with idly; also, to put or bring, as into some position, by twirling or light touches (as, "They *twiddled* the brass thumb-screws to the right focus": Sinclair Lewis's "Arrowsmith," iv.).—**to twiddle one's thumbs** or **fingers**, to keep turning one's thumbs or fingers idly about each other (as, "The bishop was sitting in his easy chair *twiddling his thumbs*": Trollope's "Barchester Towers," xxvi.); fig., to do nothing; be idle.—**twid'dle**, *v. i.* To play with something idly, as by touching or handling; also, to turn round and round; twirl.—**twid'dle**, *n.* The act or an act of twiddling; a twirl; also, a twirled mark or sign.

twi-fold, twy-fold (twī'fōld), *a.* [AS. *twifeald*: see *twi-* and *-fold*.] Twofold; double. [Archaic.]

twi-form, twy-form (twī'fôrm), *a.* [See *twi-*.] Having or combining two forms; biform. Also **twi'formed, twy'formed.** [Archaic.]

twig[1] (twig), *v.*; *twigged, twigging*. [Origin uncertain.] **I.** *tr.* To look at, or observe (as, "Pat . . . was '*twigging*' the enormous hats": H. Melville's "Omoo," xxxvii.); also, to catch sight of; perceive; recognize; fig., to understand or comprehend. [Slang.] **II.** *intr.* To understand: as, "I *twigged* in a minute" (W. B. Maxwell's "In Cotton Wool," viii.). [Slang.]

twig[2] (twig), *n.* [AS. *twigge, twig*, akin to D. *twijg*, G. *zweig*, twig, branch.] A slender shoot of a tree or other plant (as, "Just as the *twig* is bent, the tree's inclined": Pope's "Moral Essays," i. 150); a small offshoot from a branch or stem; often, a small dry, woody piece fallen from a branch (as, a fire of *twigs*; a bird's nest made of *twigs*); also, a stout stick (prov. Eng.); a divining-rod (prov. Eng.); in *anat.*, one of the minute branches of a blood-vessel or nerve.—**twigged**, *a.* Having twigs.—**twig'gen**, *a.* Made of or covered with twigs or osiers. [Archaic or prov. Eng.]—**twig'gy**, *a.* Abounding in twigs; consisting of twigs; twig-like.—**twig'less**, *a.* Without twigs.

twi-light (twī'līt), *n.* [ME. *twylyghte*: see *twi-* and *light*[1], *n.*] **I.** *n.* The light from the sky when the sun is below the horizon in the morning and, esp., in the evening (as, "Now came still evening on, and *twilight* gray Had in her sober livery all things clad": Milton's "Paradise Lost," iv. 598); the time during which this light prevails (as, "accomplished within the narrow space of an April *twilight*": Motley's "Dutch Republic," iii. 1); any dim light or partial illumination (as, the *twilight* of an eclipse of the sun; "The oak and birch, with mingled shade, At noontide there a *twilight* made," Scott's "Lady of the Lake," iii. 26); fig., a condition or period preceding or succeeding full development, glory, etc. (as, "the expiring gleam and late *twilight* of ancestral splendors": G. W. Curtis's "Prue and I," iv.); a condition of imperfect mental illumination or enlightenment. **II.** *a.* Of, pertaining to, or resembling twilight (as, the *twilight* hour; *twilight* shade); seen or done in the twilight; crepuscular, as a bat or moth; also, lighted by or as by twilight, or twilit (as, "arched walks of *twilight* groves": Milton's "Il Penseroso," 133); shadowy; dim; obscure.—**twilight sleep**, a state of semiconsciousness produced by the hypodermic injection of scopolamine and morphine, in order to effect relatively painless childbirth.—**twi'light**, *v. t.* To light by or as by twilight; illuminate dimly: usually in *twilighted* or *twilit*, *pp.*: as, "the silent *twilit* moor" (Hugh Walpole's "Wooden Horse," ii.).

twill (twil), *n.* [ME. *twyll, twylle*, < AS. *twili*, woven with two threads, < *twi-*: two: cf. AS. *thrili*, also L. *trilix*, woven with three threads (see *trellis*).] A fabric woven with the weft-threads so crossing the warp as to produce an effect of parallel diagonal lines, as in serge; also, the characteristic weave of such fabrics, or the diagonal line or pattern formed.—**twill**, *v. t.* To weave in the manner of a twill.

'twill (twil). Contraction of *it will.*

twin (twin). [AS. *twinn, getwinn*, adj., *getwinn*, n., < *twi-*: two: see *twi-*.] **I.** *a.* Twofold† or double†; also, being two, or one of two, children or animals born at the same birth (as, *twin* sisters; his *twin* sister); also, being two persons or things closely related or associated or much alike, or forming a pair or couple (as, "a narrow entrance, flanked . . . by two small *twin* islets," H. Melville's "Typee," iii.; *twin* screws or screw-propellers, see *twin-screw*); being one of two such persons or things, or forming one of a couple or pair (as, a *twin* peak; a *twin* volume; "The frequent curse, and its *twin* sound The cheek-distending oath," Cowper's "Task," iv. 487); also, consisting of two similar parts or elements joined or connected (as, a *twin* vase; "A *twin* earthquake has two maxima of intensity proceeding from two foci," Encyc. Brit., 11th ed., VIII. 819); in *crystal.*, of the nature of a twin (see *twin, n.*); in *bot.* and *zoöl.*, occurring in pairs; didymous. **II.** *n.* *Pl.*, two children or animals brought forth at a birth; *sing.*, one of two such children or animals; also, *pl.*, two persons or things closely related or connected or closely resembling each other; *sing.*, either of two such persons or things; *pl.* [*cap.*], in *astron.*, the zodiacal constellation or sign Gemini; *sing.* [*l. c.*], in *crystal.*, a compound crystal consisting of two parts or two crystals, one of which is in a reversed position with respect to the other; hence, a compound crystal consisting of more than two parts or crystals.—**twin**, *v.*; *twinned, twinning.* **I.** *tr.* To conceive or bring forth as twins or as a twin; also, to pair or couple; unite; combine; also, to furnish a counterpart to; in *crystal.*, to form (crystals or crystal forms) into a twin. **II.** *intr.* To bring forth twins; also, to be twin-born; also, to be paired or coupled.—**twin'ber''ry**, *n.* The partridge-berry, *Mitchella repens.*—**twin'=born**, *a.* Born at the same birth; born along with another.

twine (twīn), *n.* [AS. *twīn*, a double thread, < *twi-*, two: see *twi-*, and cf. *twist*.] Strong thread or string composed of two or more strands twisted together, now made esp. of hemp, manila, or the like; also, the act or an act of twining, or the state of being twined; a twined or twisted thing or part; a fold, convolution, or coil (as, "Typhon huge ending in snaky *twine*": Milton's "On the Morning of Christ's Nativity," 226); a twist or turn; a knot or tangle.—**twine**, *v.*; *twined, twining.* **I.** *tr.* To twist together, as two or more strands to form a thread or string; interwind; intertwine; also, to form by or as by twisting strands (as, to *twine* a wreath); also, to twist (one strand, thread, or thing) with another (often fig.: as, one person's life is *twined* with that of another); bring (*in, into*, etc.) by or as by twisting or winding (as, "A wild grape vine . . . had *twined* and twisted itself up into the tree," Hawthorne's "Blithedale Romance," xii.; "It is strange how inanimate objects will *twine* themselves into our affections," H. Melville's "Typee," xxxii.); put or dispose (*about, around,* etc.) by or as by winding (as, to *twine* ivy about the head; the fingers *twine* themselves around an object); also, to encircle or wreathe with something wound about (as, to *twine* a statue with garlands); infold, as something wound or disposed about does (as, "Let wreaths of triumph now my temples *twine*": Pope's "Rape of the Lock," iii. 161); also, to turn, twist, or wring (now prov.). **II.** *intr.* To become twined or twisted together, as two things, or as one thing with another; also, to wind itself (*about, around*, etc.: as, "By what . . . arts The serpent error *twines* round human hearts," Cowper's "Progress of Error," 4); esp., of plants, stems, etc., to grow in convolutions about a support; also, to wind in a sinuous or meandering course (as, "Dark ravines . . . Where *twined* the path . . . Round many a rocky pyramid": Scott's "Lady of the Lake," i. 11); also, to writhe or squirm (now prov.).—**twin-er** (twī'nėr), *n.*

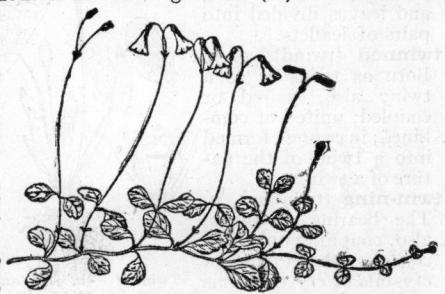

Twining Stems. — 1, bindweed (*Convolvulus sepium*); 2, hop (*Humulus lupulus*).

Flowering Plant of Twin-flower (*Linnæa americana*).

twin=flow-er (twin′flou″ẽr), *n.* A slender, creeping, evergreen caprifoliaceous plant, *Linnæa borealis*, of Europe, or an American variety or species, *L. americana*, with pink or purplish nodding flowers borne in pairs on thread-like peduncles. See cut on preceding page.

twinge (twinj), *v.;* *twinged, twinging.* [AS. *twengan*, pinch.] **I.** *tr.* To pinch or tweak (now prov.); also, to affect with sudden, sharp pain or pains (in body or mind: as, a wound *twinges* one; a thought *twinges* the conscience); give (a person, etc.) a twinge or twinges. **II.** *intr.* To have or feel a twinge or twinges.—**twinge,** *n.* A pinch† or tweak†; also, a sudden, sharp pain (in body or mind: as, a *twinge* of rheumatism; a *twinge* of remorse; "We are apt to feel *twinges* of doubt afterwards as to our own generosity," George Eliot's "Adam Bede," xviii.).

twink (twingk), *v. i.* [ME. *twinken* = G. *zwinken*, wink: cf. *twinkle.*] To wink† or blink†; also, to twinkle or sparkle.—**twink,** *n.* A wink of the eye; the time required for a wink, or a twinkling (as, "In a *twink* she won me to her love": Shakespere's "Taming of the Shrew," ii. 1. 312); also, a twinkle or sparkle.

twin-kle (twing′kl), *v.;* *-kled, -kling.* [AS. *twinclian*, shine, freq. from a stem represented by ME. *twinken*, E. *twink.*] **I.** *intr.* To shine with slight, quick gleams or flashes of light, as stars, distant lights, a lighted place, etc. (as, "a few stars, *twinkling* faintly in the deep blue of the night sky," Hugh Walpole's "Wooden Horse," i.; "Below me was the city already *twinkling* with lights," S. Butler's "Erewhon," xxviii.); sparkle in the light (as, "All the haft [of a sword] *twinkled* with diamond sparks," Tennyson's "Passing of Arthur," 224; dewdrops *twinkling* in the sunlight); often, of the eyes, to be bright with little gleams or flashes, as with amusement, pleasure, etc. (as, "He gave a short laugh. His eyes *twinkled*": Maugham's "Moon and Sixpence," xx.); also, to appear or move as if with little flashes of light (as, "He ran towards me . . . his feet, shod in dirty white shoes, *twinkled* on the dark earth": J. Conrad's "Lord Jim," xxxiv.); also, to close and open the eye or eyes quickly, wink, or blink (archaic: as, "He was observed to *twinkle* with his eyelids," Scott's "Guy Mannering," lv.); of the eyes, to close and open quickly (archaic). **II.** *tr.* To emit (light) in little gleams or flashes; communicate by flashes of light; light or guide by twinkling (poetic); also, to wink (the eyes, etc.: archaic).—**twin′kle,** *n.* A twinkling with light, or shining with little gleams or flashes (as, "the tiny *twinkle* of a votive lamp": Howells's "Chance Acquaintance," vi.); a twinkling brightness in the eyes (as, "A sardonic *twinkle* lit up his eyes": Maugham's "Moon and Sixpence," xxi.); also, a wink of the eye (archaic); the time required for a wink, or a twinkling.—**twin′kler,** *n.*—**twin′kling,** *n.* The act of shining with little gleams or flashes of light; gleaming; sparkling; flashing; also, winking, or a wink, as of the eyes (archaic); also, the time required for a wink, or an instant (as, "We shall all be changed, In a moment, in the *twinkling* of an eye," 1 Cor. xv. 52; "She is off in a *twinkling*," W. De Morgan's "Somehow Good," xxiii.). — **twin′kling-ly,** *adv.*

twin-leaf (twin′lēf), *n.* A berberidaceous plant, *Jeffersonia diphylla*, of the eastern U. S., with solitary white flowers, and leaves divided into pairs of leaflets.

twinned (twind), *p. a.* Born as twins or as a twin; also, paired or coupled; united or combined; in *crystal.*, formed into a twin; of the nature of a twin.

twin-ning (twin′ing), *n.* The bearing of twins; also, coupling; union; in *crystal.*, the union of crystals or crystal forms to form a twin.

Twinleaf.— *a*, pistil and stamens; *b*, ripe fruit; *c*, full-grown leaf, showing nervation.

twin=screw (twin′skrö′), *a.* Of a vessel, having two screw-propellers, which revolve in opposite directions.

twirl (twẽrl), *v.* [Perhaps a var. of obs. or prov. *tirl*, transposed form of *trill*¹.] **I.** *tr.* To cause to rotate rapidly; spin; whirl; swing circularly (as, "He was *twirling* a pair of Indian clubs round his head": Du Maurier's "Trilby," i.); often, to turn round and round in an idle or purposeless way; twiddle (as, "I . . . sit and *twirl* my thumbs": Stevenson's "Kidnapped," xxiii.); wind idly about something (as, "Frome saw her *twirl* the end of her scarf irresolutely about her fingers": Mrs. Wharton's "Ethan Frome," ii.); also, to twist, now esp. idly (as, "Lord Steepleton Kildare sauntered round and *twirled* his big moustache": F. M. Crawford's "Mr. Isaacs," x.). **II.** *intr.* To rotate rapidly; whirl (as, "to see the old woman . . . *twirl* about as some flute girl at a banquet": J. H. Newman's "Callista," vii.); turn quickly so as to face or point another way; also, to twine, curl, or coil.—**twirl,** *n.* A twirling or a being twirled; a spin; a whirl; a twist (as, "I . . . looked him up and down, with a *twirl* of my moustache": Conan Doyle's "Exploits of Brigadier Gerard," iv.); also, something twirled; a curl or convolution; a curling line, or curlicue, as in writing. —**twirl′er,** *n.* One who or that which twirls; a pitcher in baseball (colloq.).

twist (twist), *v. t.* [ME. *twisten*, < AS. *twi-*, two: see *twi-*, and cf. *twine.*] To combine, as two or more strands or threads, by winding together; intertwine; fig., to combine or associate intimately like strands in a cord; also, to entangle; confuse; also, to form by or as by winding strands together; fabricate or compose; also, to entwine (one thing) with or in another; wind or twine (something) about a thing (as, "Green, slender, leaf-clad holly-boughs Were *twisted*, gracefu', round her brows": Burns's "Vision," 50); encircle (a thing) with something wound about; also, to alter in shape, as by turning the ends in opposite directions, so that parts previously in the same straight line and plane are located in a spiral curve; wring out of shape or place; force awry; contort or distort; fig., to wrest from the proper form or meaning, or pervert (as, "She said of course I could *twist* her words to mean anything I liked": W. De Morgan's "Joseph Vance," x.); also, to force (*down, into, off, out*, etc.) by a turning movement or strain (as, "He *twisted* the corkscrew into the cork of the bottle": Arnold Bennett's "Clayhanger," ii. 8); also, to bend spirally, or bring to or shape in a spiral form (as, "a vertical orange-yellow glass vase, *twisted* to a spiral": W. De Morgan's "Somehow Good," iii.); form into a coil, knot, or the like by winding, rolling, etc. (as, to *twist* the hair into a knot); curve or bend in any way; bend tortuously; also, to turn as on an axis (as, to *twist* a ring on the finger); turn so as to face in another direction (as, to *twist* the head in order to look to one side); also, to cause to move with a rotary motion, as a ball pitched in a curve.— **to twist round,** or **around** or **about, one's (little) finger,** fig., to influence or sway at one's will; have completely under one's influence: as, "Sophia . . . could simply *twist* him *round her little finger*" (Arnold Bennett's "Old Wives' Tale," iv. 3); "It had remained for a young girl . . . to *twist* Jethro *around her finger*" (W. Churchill's "Coniston," ii. 14).—**to twist the lion's tail,** fig., to say or do something intended to excite the resentment of the government or people of Great Britain, as in order to please the enemies of that country. See *lion.*—**twist,** *v. i.* To twist something; make movements serving to twist something; also, to be or become intertwined; wind or twine about something; also, to change shape with a spiral or screwing movement of parts; become bent or turned awry; take a contorted form (as, "roots which curl and *twist* in fantastic shapes": Jefferies's "Gamekeeper at Home," iv.); writhe or squirm; also, to take a spiral form or course; wind, curve, or bend; wind tortuously, or meander, as a stream; also, to turn or rotate, as on an axis; revolve, as about something; turn so as to face in another direction; also, to move with a progressive rotary motion, as a ball pitched in a curve.—**twist,** *n.* Thread, cord, or the like made of two or more strands twisted together; a kind of strong twisted silk thread, heavier than ordinary sewing-silk, used for working buttonholes and for other purposes; a kind of cotton yarn of several varieties; also, anything formed by or as oy twisting or twining parts together; a kind of tobacco manufactured in the form of a rope or thick cord; a loaf or roll of dough twisted and baked; also, the act or the manner of twisting strands together, as in thread, yarn, or rope; also, the altering of the shape of anything by or as by turning the ends in opposite directions, or the resulting state; a twisting action, force, or stress; a wrench; a twisting awry; fig., a wresting or perverting, as of meaning; also, spiral disposition, arrangement, or form; spiral movement or course; the spiral formed by a groove in a rifled firearm; a curve, bend, or turn; often, an irregular bend; a crook or kink; fig., a peculiar turn, bent, bias, or the like, as in the mind or nature (as, "He'd done what this *twist* in his brain drove him to do," Eden Phillpotts's "Red Redmaynes," iv.; "a well-intentioned man with a queer regrettable *twist* in his composition," Arnold Bennett's "Mr. Prohack," iii.); also, a turning or rotating as on an axis; rotary motion; spin; a spin given to a ball in pitching, etc., in baseball, cricket, etc.; a ball having such a spin.

twist-a-ble (twis′ta̤-bl), *a.* Capable of being twisted.

twist=drill (twist′dril), *n.* A drill with one or more deep spiral grooves in the body.

twist-ed (twis′ted), *p. a.* Formed by or as by twisting strands together (as, a *twisted* cord; *twisted* columns); also, bent by twisting; forced awry; distorted; also, bent spirally; spiral. — **twist′ed-ly**, *adv.*

twist-er (twis′tẽr), *n.* One who or that which twists; a ball pitched or moving with a spinning motion; a whirlwind or tornado (western U. S.).

twist-ing (twis′ting), *p. a.* That twists; turning; winding. — **twist′ing-ly**, *adv.*

twit (twit), *v.t.*; twitted, twitting. [Earlier *twite*, for obs. *atwite*, < AS. *ætwītan*, < *æt*, at, + *wītan*, reproach, blame.] To reproach or upbraid, esp. in a derisive or annoying manner, as with some fault, error, or folly (as, "We . . . shall be *twitted* with an unseemly apathy": Trollope's "Barchester Towers," xxi.); taunt, gibe at, or banter by references to anything mortifying or embarrassing (as, "The school master was *twitted* about the lady who threw him over," Barrie's "Auld Licht Idylls," ii.; "The foreigners . . . *twitted* him about his hopeful protégés of the Calabooza [jail]," H. Melville's "Omoo," xxxix.); also, to censure or rebuke (an act, etc.: now rare). — **twit**, *n.* An act of twitting; a derisive reproach; a taunt; a gibe.

twitch (twich), *v.* [ME. *twicchen*, akin to AS. *twiccian*, pluck, twitch, and G. *zwicken*, pinch, nip, tweak: cf. *tweak*.] **I.** *tr.* To give a short, sudden pull or tug at, or jerk (as, "His . . . guide suddenly *twitched* him by the skirt of his jerkin": Scott's "Legend of Montrose," xii.); pull or draw with a hasty jerk (as, "I *twitched* the curtain aside with some violence": S. J. Weyman's "Gentleman of France," xxiii.); also, to move (a part of the body) with a quick or spasmodic jerk (as, to *twitch* the ears; "The Mahratta *twitched* his fingers with pain," Kipling's "Kim," xi.); also, to pinch and pull sharply; nip; affect with twitches or twinges; also, to draw or tie tightly (now prov. Eng. and Sc.). **II.** *intr.* To give a short, sudden pull or tug (*at*); tug; also, to move suddenly, as if jerked (as, "Dan's lines [in fishing] *twitched* on the scored and scarred rail": Kipling's "Captains Courageous," iii.); esp., to move or be moved in a quick, jerky way involuntarily or spasmodically, as a person or animal, or the body or a part of it (as, "I could see him all trembling and *twitching*, like a man with palsy," Stevenson's "Kidnapped," iii.; "His mouth *twitched* with repressed laughter," Mrs. H. Ward's "Lady Rose's Daughter," ix.). — **twitch**, *n.* An act or movement of twitching; a short, sudden pull or tug; a jerk; a quick, jerky movement of the body, or of some part of it, occurring involuntarily or spasmodically (as, "Her hands moved with convulsive *twitches*": Maria Edgeworth's "Belinda," x.); a pinch or nip; a twinge or pang (of body or mind: as, "It would be a good thing . . . if somebody had

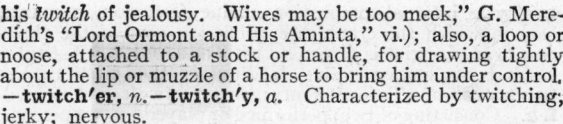
Twisted Columns. — Cloisters of St. John Lateran, Rome.

his *twitch* of jealousy. Wives may be too meek," G. Meredith's "Lord Ormont and His Aminta," vi.); also, a loop or noose, attached to a stock or handle, for drawing tightly about the lip or muzzle of a horse to bring him under control. — **twitch′er**, *n.* — **twitch′y**, *a.* Characterized by twitching; jerky; nervous.

twit-ter[1] (twit′ẽr), *v.* [ME. *twiteren*; imit.] **I.** *intr.* To utter a succession of small, tremulous sounds, as a bird (as, "Swallows and martins skimmed *twittering* about the eaves": Irving's "Sketch-Book," Sleepy Hollow); chirp repeatedly; also, to sing or talk in a manner suggestive of chirping, as a person; also, to titter or giggle (prov.); also, to move tremulously, shake, or tremble (as, "I was . . . *twittering* with cold": Stevenson's "Inland Voyage," xi.); tremble with excitement or the like, or be in a flutter (as, "One of the lads was *twittering* with excitement": M. Hewlett's "Open Country," iii.). **II.** *tr.* To express or utter by twittering: as, "The swallows *twittered* a cheery anthem" (Hawthorne's "Blithedale Romance," xiv.); "She *twittered*, 'You're perfectly right'" (Sinclair Lewis's "Main Street," vii.). — **twit′ter**[1], *n.* The act or an act of twittering; a twittering sound; a titter or giggle (prov.); also, a state of tremulous excitement (as, "Beth hurried on in a *twitter* of suspense": Louisa M. Alcott's "Little Women," i. 6).

twit-ter[2] (twit′ẽr), *n.* One who twits.

twit-ter-er (twit′ẽr-ẽr), *n.* A bird that twitters; also, a person who twitters.

twit-ter-y (twit′ẽr-i), *a.* Given to or characterized by twittering; tremulous; shaky; in a twitter.

'twixt (twikst), *prep.* Betwixt: as, "a tower . . . 'twixt two portals rear'd" (Wiffen's tr. Tasso's "Jerusalem Delivered," iii. 12). [Archaic or prov.]

two (tö), *a.* [AS. *twā*, fem. and neut., *tū*, neut., *twēgen*, masc. (see *twain*). = D. *twee* = G. *zwei* = Icel. *tveir* = Goth. *twai*, two; akin to L. *duo*, Gr. δύο, Skt. *dva*, two.] One more than one; twice one. — **in two**, into or in two parts or pieces: as, to cut a thing *in two*. — **two**, *n.*; pl. *twos* (töz). A number composed of two units, or a symbol, as 2 or ii, representing it; a set of two persons or things; a playing-card, die-face, etc., with two pips. — **to put two and two together**, fig., to bring two or more facts into association in thought and form an opinion thereon; draw a conclusion from certain circumstances. — **two′=cy″cle**, *n.* In an internal-combustion engine, a cycle in which one piston stroke out of every two is a working stroke. — **two′=edged** (-ejd or -ej″ed), *a.* Having two edges, as a sword; hence, cutting or effective both ways. — **two′=faced**, *a.* Having two faces; hence, practising duplicity; deceitful; hypocritical. — **two′=faced-ness**, *n.* — **two′=fist″ed**, *a.* Awkward with the hands, or clumsy (prov.); also, having two fists and able to use them, or strong and vigorous (colloq.: as, "You tell him that no *two-fisted* enterprising Westerner would have New York for a gift!" Sinclair Lewis's "Main Street," xxxv.). — **two′fold** (-fōld). **I.** *a.* Comprising two parts or members; twice as great or as much; double. **II.** *adv.* In twofold measure; doubly. — **two′=hand″ed**, *a.* Having two hands; also, using both hands equally well; ambidextrous; also, involving the use of both hands; requiring both hands to wield or manage (as, a *two-handed* sword); also, requiring the hands of two persons to operate (as, a *two-handed* saw); engaged in by two persons (as, a *two-handed* game). — **two′ness**, *n.* The quality of being two; duality; doubleness. — **two-pence** (tup′ẹns), *n.* A sum of money of the value of two British pennies, or about 4 U. S. cents; also, a British silver coin of this value (since 1662 coined only as maundy money); a British copper coin of this value, issued in the reign of George III.; hence, any very small amount; a trifle; also, something of very little worth or consequence. — **two-pen-ny** (tup′ẹ-ni), *a.* Of the amount or value of twopence; involving an outlay of twopence; hence, of very little value; trifling; worthless. — **two′=phase**, *a.* Same as *diphase*. — **two′=ply**, *a.* Consisting of two thicknesses, layers, strands, or the like. — **two′=port**, *a.* Having two ports; specif., noting or pertaining to a type of

Obverse. Reverse.
Twopence, Maundy Money. — British Museum.

two-cycle internal-combustion engine (common in marine use) in which the crank-case admission port of the three-port type of engine is dispensed with, and for it is substituted a kind of suction valve leading to the crank-case.—
two′score, *a.* Twice twenty; forty.—**two′some** (-sum).
I. *a.* Consisting of two; performed or played by two persons.
II. *n.* Two together or in company; a match, as in golf, between two persons.—**two′=step**, *n.* A round dance in duple rhythm, characterized by sliding steps; also, a piece of music for, or in the rhythm of, this dance.—**two′=way**, *a.* Having two ways or passages (as, a *two-way* cock, a cock by which a fluid may be distributed to both or either of two branches, or be entirely shut off); in *math.*, having a double mode of variation.

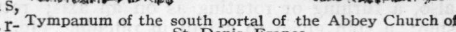

′twould (twŭd). Contraction of *it would.*
twy-, twy′bill, etc. See *twi-, twibill*, etc.
twy-er (twī′ėr), *n.* Same as *tuyère.*

Two-way Cock.— *a*, position which distributes water to two branches; *b*, *c*, positions in which the water is passed through only one branch; *d*, position for stopping flow.

-ty¹. [AS. *-tig* = Icel. *tigr*, Goth. *tigus*, decade; akin to E. *ten*.] A suffix of numerals denoting multiples of ten, as *twenty, thirty, forty.*
-ty². [OF. *-tet, -te* (F. *-té*), < L. *-tat-*, nom. *-tas.*] A suffix of nouns denoting quality, state, etc., as *beauty, liberty, plenty, purity, quality, unity.*
ty-coon (tī-kön′), *n.* [Jap. *taikun*, 'great prince': from Chinese.] A title used to describe the shogun of Japan to foreigners.
ty-ing (tī′ing), *ppr.* and *n.* See *tie.*
tyke (tīk), *n.* See *tike.*
tyle (tīl), **tyl-er** (tī′lėr). Archaic forms of *tile, tiler.*
tym-bal (tim′bạl), *n.* See *timbal.*
tymp (timp), *n.* [Appar. an abbr. of *tympan.*] In some blast-furnaces, the top portion or crown of the opening in front of the hearth.
tym-pan (tim′pạn), *n.* [OF. F. *tympan*, < L. *tympanum*: see *tympanum.*] A drum or drum-like instrument (archaic); a stretched membrane, or a sheet or plate of some thin material, in an apparatus; in *arch.*, a tympanum; in *printing*, a pad-like device interposed between the platen or its equivalent and the sheet to be printed, in order to soften and equalize the pressure.
tym-pan-ic (tim-pan′ik), *a.* Of or pertaining to a tympanum, esp. the tympanum of the ear.—**tympanic bone**, in *anat.* and *zoöl.*, in mammals, a bone of the skull, supporting the tympanic membrane and inclosing part of the tympanum or middle ear.—**tympanic membrane**, in *anat.* and *zoöl.*, a membrane separating the tympanum or middle ear from the passage of the external ear; the eardrum.
tym-pa-nism (tim′pạ-nizm), *n.* Same as *tympanites.*
tym-pa-ni-tes (tim-pạ-nī′tēz), *n.* [LL., < Gr. τυμπανίτης, < τύμπανον, kettledrum: see *tympanum.*] In *pathol.*, distention of the abdomen caused by the presence of air or gas, as in the intestine or in the cavity of the peritoneum.—
tym-pa-nit′ic (-nit′ik), *a.* Pertaining to or characteristic of tympanites: as, *tympanitic* resonance (such as is produced by percussion over the abdomen in cases of tympanites).
tym-pa-ni-tis (tim-pạ-nī′tis), *n.* [NL., < ML. *tympanum*: see *tympanum.*] In *pathol.*, inflammation of the lining membrane of the tympanum or middle ear.
tym-pa-num (tim′pạ-num), *n.*; pl. *-nums*, L. *-na* (-nä). [L., drum, drum-like part, tympanum of a pediment, ML. drum of the ear, < Gr. τύμπανον, orig. kettledrum, < τύπτειν, strike.] A drum or similar instrument; also, the stretched membrane forming a drumhead, or any similar membrane or thin sheet or plate; in *anat.* and *zoöl.*, the middle ear, comprising that part of the ear situated in a recess of the temporal bone; also, the tympanic membrane; in *arch.*, the recessed, usually triangular space inclosed between the horizontal and sloping cornices of a pediment, often adorned with sculpture; also, a similar space between an arch and the horizontal head of a door or window below (see cut in next column); in *elect.*, the diaphragm of a telephone.
ty-pal (tī′pạl), *a.* Pertaining to or forming a type.

type (tīp), *n.* [L. *typus*, < Gr. τύπος, impression, image, figure, form, model, type, < τύπτειν, strike.] An image or figure produced by impressing or stamping, as the principal figure or device on either side of a coin or medal; also, a symbol or emblem (as, "the recognizances of military chieftains, their war-cries, emblems, and other *types* by which they distinguished themselves in battle": Scott's "Castle Dangerous," xix.); specif., a prefiguring symbol, as an Old Testament event prefiguring an event in the New Testament (cf. *antitype*); also, the pattern or model from which something is made (as, "Not that Tom was moulded on the spooney *type* of the Industrious Apprentice": George Eliot's "Mill on the Floss," v. 2); also, a distinguishing mark or sign (rare); also, the general form, style, or character distinguishing a particular kind, class, or group (as, "She was absolutely different in *type* from any of the Clayhangers": Arnold Bennett's "Clayhanger," ii. 7); hence, a kind, class, or group as distinguished by a particular character; also, a person or thing embodying the characteristic qualities of a kind, class, or group; a representative or typical specimen of something (as, "She regarded Spenser as the purest *type* of her country's literature in this line": Trollope's "Barchester Towers," xxii.); sometimes, the perfect specimen of something; in *biol.*, the general form or plan of structure common to a group of animals, plants, etc.; a group or division of animals, etc., as a genus or species, having certain common characteristics; a genus, species, etc., which most nearly exemplifies the essential characteristics of a higher group and usually gives it its name; in *math.*, a succession of symbols susceptible of + and − signs; in *printing*, a rectangular piece or block, now usually of metal, having on its upper surface a letter or character in relief for use in printing; such pieces or blocks collectively; a similar piece in a typewriter or the like, or such pieces collectively; a printed character or printed characters (as, a head-line in large *type*).
**Printing-types are variously named with reference to relative width of face, to style, and to size. For example:

Tympanum of the south portal of the Abbey Church of St. Denis, France.

Type.— *a*, stem or thick stroke; *b*, serif; *c*, depressions in face; *d*, hairline; *e*, beard or neck; *f*, shoulder; *g*, mark made by pin which dislodges type from mold; *h*, nicks; *i*, groove; *j*, feet. The top is known as the face; the part between shoulder and feet is the body or shank.

Widths of Type.

AMO	AMO	AMO	AMO
Standard width.	Condensed.	Expanded.	Extended.

Styles of Type.

Antique.	German Text.
Black-letter.	Gothic.
Bold-face.	Ionic.
Church Text.	Script.
Clarendon.	

This is Caslon old style. This is Elzevir old style.

Sizes of Type.

Name.	Specimen.	Em Quad.	Point.
Brilliant.	abcdefghijklmnopqrstuvwxyz	■	3½
Diamond.	abcdefghijklmnopqrstuvwxyz	■	4½
Pearl.	abcdefghijklmnopqrstuvwxyz	■	5
Agate.	abcdefghijklmnopqrstuvwxyz	■	5½
Nonpareil.	abcdefghijklmnopqrstuvwxyz	■	6
Minion.	abcdefghijklmnopqrstuvwxyz		7
Brevier.	abcdefghijklmnopqrstuvwxyz		8
Bourgeois.	abcdefghijklmnopqrstuvwxyz		9
Long primer.	abcdefghijklmnopqrstuvw	■	10
Small pica.	abcdefghijklmnopqrstuv	■	11
Pica.	abcdefghijklmnopqrst	■	12
English.	abcdefghijklmnopq	■	14
Great primer.	abcdefghijklm	■	18

(Columbian, or 16 point, is of a size between English and great primer.)

—**type,** *a.* Pertaining to a type or to type; forming a type (as, a *type* specimen). —**type genus,** in *biol.*, that genus which is typical of the family or other higher group to which it belongs, or which is formally taken and held to be such.—**type,** *v.*; typed, typing. **I.** *tr.* To be a type or symbol of; represent by a symbol; symbolize; specif., to prefigure or foreshadow as a symbol; also, to constitute the pattern or model for; also, to serve as an example or specimen of; also, to reproduce in type or in print; also, to typewrite. **II.** *intr.* To use a typewriter; typewrite: as, "He's sitting in the office trying to *type*" (Arnold Bennett's "Riceyman Steps," iv. 1).

-**type.** [Gr. -τυπος, struck, formed, < τύπτειν, strike; sometimes, Gr. τύπος: see *type.*] A termination of nouns denoting something formed (orig. as by striking), esp. as a model or pattern, as in *archetype, prototype,* or as a reproduction, impression, print, picture, or the like, as in *antitype, ectype, ferrotype, platinotype.*

type=found-er (tīp′foun″dėr), *n.* One engaged in the founding or making of printers' metallic types (including the cutting of punches, the making of molds, the casting of the types, etc.).—**type′=found″ing,** *n.*—**type′=foun″dry,** *n.*

type=high (tīp′hī′), *a.* In *printing,* of the same height as type.

type=met-al (tīp′met″al), *n.* An alloy for making printing-types, etc., consisting chiefly of lead and antimony, and sometimes small quantities of tin, copper, etc.

typ-er (tī′pėr), *n.* One who or that which types; one who does typewriting; also, a typewriter (machine).

type-script (tīp′skript), *n.* [With -script as in *manuscript.*] A typewritten copy of a literary composition, a document, or the like (as, "a *typescript* of my sermon to-morrow": Arnold Bennett's "Buried Alive," iii.); also, typewritten material, as distinguished from handwriting or print (as, "when I open the parcel of *typescript*": Arnold Bennett's "Truth about an Author," xiv.).

type=set-ter (tīp′set″ėr), *n.* One who sets or composes type; a compositor; also, a type-setting machine.—**type′=set″ting,** *n.*

type-write (tīp′rīt), *v. t.* or *i.*; pret. -wrote, pp. -written, ppr. -writing. [Back-formation from *typewriter.*] To write or print by means of a typewriter; type.

type-writ-er (tīp′rī″tėr), *n.* A machine for writing mechanically in letters and characters like those produced by printers' types; also, one who does typewriting, esp. as a regular occupation; a typist.—**type′writ″ing,** *n.* The act or art of using a typewriter; also, work done on a typewriter.

typh-li-tis (tif-lī′tis), *n.* [NL., < Gr. τυφλός, blind, closed (as the cæcum).] In *pathol.*, inflammation of the cæcum.—**typh-lit′ic** (-lit′ik), *a.*

typh-lol-o-gy (tif-lol′ō-ji), *n.* [Gr. τυφλός, blind: see *-logy.*] The sum of scientific knowledge concerning blindness.

typho-. Form of *typhus* or *typhoid* used in combination.

ty-pho-gen-ic (tī-fō-jen′ik), *a.* [From *typho-* + *-genic.*] In *pathol.*, producing typhus or typhoid fever.

ty-phoid (tī′foid), *a.* [See *typhus* and *-oid.*] In *pathol.*, resembling typhus (as, *typhoid* fever: see below); also, of or pertaining to typhoid fever.—**typhoid fever,** an infectious, often fatal, febrile disease, characterized by intestinal inflammation and ulceration, due to a specific bacillus which is usually introduced with food or drink: formerly regarded as a variety of typhus.—**ty′phoid,** *n.* Typhoid fever.

ty-pho-ma-la-ri-al (tī″fō-ma-lā′ri-al), *a.* [See *typho-.*] Having the character of both typhoid fever and malaria, as a fever.

ty-phoon (tī-fön′), *n.* [Pg. *tufão,* < Ar. *tūfān,* tempest, hurricane; perhaps also, in part, Chinese *t'ai fung,* 'great wind.'] A violent storm or tempest occurring in India; also, a violent hurricane occurring in the China seas and their environs, chiefly during the months of July, August, September, and October.

ty-phus (tī′fus), *n.* [NL., < Gr. τῦφος, smoke, vapor, stupor from fever, < τύφειν, smoke, smolder.] In *pathol.*, an acute infectious disease characterized by great prostration, severe nervous symptoms, and a peculiar eruption of reddish spots on the body; ship-fever; jail-fever: now regarded as due to a specific micro-organism which is transmitted through the agency of fleas, etc. Also called *typhus fever.*—**ty′phous,** *a.*

typ-ic (tip′ik), *a.* [F. *typique,* < LL. *typicus,* < Gr. τυπικός.] Pertaining to or serving as a type; typical; of a fever, conforming to a particular type.—**typ′i-cal,** *a.* [LL. *typicalis.*] Pertaining to, of the nature of, or serving as a type or emblem, or symbolic (as, "It [appearance in the sky] was universally considered *typical* of the anticipated battle between Count Louis and the Spaniards": Motley's "Dutch Republic," iv. 1); also, of the nature of or serving as a type or representative specimen (as, "He looks cool enough . . . the *typical* don with his nose in the air!" Mrs. H. Ward's "Robert Elsmere," xviii.); conforming to the type; specif., exemplifying most nearly the essential characteristics of a higher group in natural history, and forming the type (as, the *typical* genus of a family); also, of or pertaining to a representative specimen; characteristic or distinctive (as, "She has all the *typical* points of her mother's race": Mrs. H. Ward's "Lady Rose's Daughter," i.); also, of or pertaining to printers' type (now rare).—**typ′i-cal-ly,** *adv.*—**typ′i-cal-ness,** *n.*

typ-i-fy (tip′i-fī), *v. t.*; -fied, -fying. [See *type* and *-fy.*] To represent by a type or symbol; serve as a symbol or emblem of; symbolize; prefigure; also, to serve as the typical specimen of; embody the typical characteristics of; exemplify.—**typ″i-fi-ca′tion** (-fi-kā′shon), *n.*—**typ′i-fi-er** (-fī-ėr), *n.*

typ-ist (tī′pist), *n.* An operator of a typewriter.

typo-. Form of Gr. τύπος, impression, image, form, model, type, used in combination, sometimes as if meaning 'printers' type.'

typo (tī′pō), *n.*; pl. -pos (-pōz). [Short for *typographer.*] A printer; a compositor. [Colloq.]

ty-pog-ra-pher (tī-pog′ra-fėr or ti-), *n.* One skilled or engaged in typography; a printer.

ty-po-graph-ic, ty-po-graph-i-cal (tī-pō-graf′ik, -i-kal, or tip-ō-), *a.* Of or pertaining to typography.—**ty-po-graph′i-cal-ly,** *adv.*

ty-pog-ra-phy (tī-pog′ra-fi or ti-), *n.* [F. *typographie,* < NL. *typographia,* < Gr. τύπος, impression (see *typo-*), + -γραφία, < γράφειν, write.] The art or process of printing with types; the work of setting and arranging types and of printing from them; also, the general character or appearance of printed matter.

ty-pol-o-gy (tī-pol′ō-ji or ti-), *n.* [See *typo-* and *-logy.*] The doctrine or study of types or symbols, esp. those of Scripture; also, symbolic significance or representation.

ty-po-script (tī′pō-skript), *n.* Same as *typescript.*

ty-poth-e-tæ (tī-poth′ē-tē), *n. pl.* [NL., < Gr. τύπος, impression (see *typo-*), + θέτης, one who places, < τιθέναι, set, put.] Printers: used in the names of associations of master printers.

ty-ran-nic (tī-ran′ik or ti-), *a.* [L. *tyrannicus,* < Gr. τυραννικός, < τύραννος, E. *tyrant.*] Tyrannical.—**ty-ran′ni-cal,** *a.* Of, pertaining to, or befitting a tyrant, as rule or actions; arbitrary or despotic; despotically cruel

---

(variable) đ as d or j, ş as s or sh, ţ as t or ch, ẓ as z or zh; o, F. cloche; ü, F. menu; ċh, Sc. loch; ṅ, F. bonbon; ′, primary accent; ″, secondary accent; †, obsolete; <, from; +, and; =, equals. See also lists at beginning of book.

or harsh; severely oppressive; also, having the character of a tyrant; despotic or unjustly severe in rule or procedure (as, "He was insupportably arrogant, *tyrannical* to his inferiors": Godwin's "Caleb Williams," iii.).—**ty-ran′ni-cal-ly**, *adv.*—**ty-ran′ni-cal-ness**, *n.*

ty-ran-ni-cide (tī-ran′i-sīd or ti-), *n.* [F. *tyrannicide*, < L. *tyrannicida* (killer), *tyrannicidium* (killing), < *tyrannus*, tyrant, + *cædere*, kill.] One who kills a tyrant; also, the act of killing a tyrant.—**ty-ran′ni-ci-dal** (-sī-dạl), *a.*

tyr-an-nize (tir′ạ-nīz), *v.*; *-nized, -nizing.* [F. *tyranniser*, < *tyran*: see *tyrant*.] **I.** *intr.* To reign as a tyrant; also, to rule despotically or cruelly; hence, to exercise power or control cruelly or oppressively (as, "that restless spirit . . . of *tyrannising* over weaker neighbours": Hallam's "Europe during the Middle Ages," iii. 1). **II.** *tr.* To rule or treat tyrannically; act the tyrant to or over.—**tyr′an-niz-er** (-nī-zėr), *n.*—**tyr′an-niz-ing-ly**, *adv.*

ty-ran-no-sau-rus (tī-ran-ọ-sâ′rus), *n.* [NL., < Gr. τύραννος, absolute ruler, tyrant, + σαῦρος, lizard.] A great carnivorous dinosaur (genus *Tyrannosaurus*) of the later Cretaceous period in North America, which walked erect on its powerful hind limbs.

tyr-an-nous (tir′ạ-nus), *a.* [L. *tyrannus*, E. *tyrant*.] Tyrannical.—**tyr′an-nous-ly**, *adv.*—**tyr′an-nous-ness**, *n.*

tyr-an-ny (tir′ạ-ni), *n.*; *pl. -nies* (-niz). [OF. *tirannie* (F. *tyrannie*), < ML. *tyrannia*, < Gr. τυραννία, < τύραννος, E. *tyrant*.] The government or rule of a tyrant or absolute ruler; also, a state ruled by a tyrant or absolute ruler; also, oppressive or unjustly severe government on the part of any ruler; hence, arbitrary or unrestrained exercise of power; despotic abuse of authority; undue severity or harshness; also, a tyrannical act or proceeding.

ty-rant (tī′rạnt), *n.* [OF. *tyrant* (F. *tyran*), < L. *tyrannus*, < Gr. τύραννος, absolute ruler, despot, tyrant.] An absolute ruler, as in ancient Greece, owing his office to usurpation; also, a king or ruler who uses his power oppressively or unjustly; hence, any person who exercises power or authority despotically or oppressively; an autocratic oppressor; a cruel master; also, a tyrannical or compulsory influence (as, "Public opinion is a weak *tyrant* compared with our own private opinion": Thoreau's "Walden," i.); an overruling power. —**ty′rant=bird**, *n.* A tyrant-flycatcher.—**ty′rant=fly′catch″er**, *n.* Any bird of the American family *Tyrannidæ*, as the kingbird, pewee, phœbe, scissortail, and numerous species of South and Central America.

tyre (tīr), *n.* and *v.* Variant spelling of *tire*[3]. [Eng.]

Tyr-i-an (tir′i-ạn), *a.* Of or pertaining to ancient Tyre, in Phenicia, on the coast of Syria (as, *Tyrian* purple: see below); also, of the color of the dye called Tyrian purple.—**Tyrian purple**, a 'purple' dye (probably crimson) used by the ancient Greeks and Romans, prepared at Tyre from certain mollusks. See *murex.*—**Tyr′i-an**, *n.* A native or inhabitant of ancient Tyre.

ty-ro (tī′rō), *n.*; *pl. -ros* (-rōz). [Better *tiro*, < L. *tiro* (ML. also *tyro*), recruit, young soldier, beginner.] A beginner in learning anything; one who is employed in learning or who has mastered the rudiments only of any branch of knowledge; a novice: as, "I was no more than a *tyro* among a troop of veterans" (Smollett's "Humphry Clinker," Aug. 8).

Tyr-o-lese (tir-ọ-lēs′ or -lēz′). **I.** *a.* Of or pertaining to Tyrol or its inhabitants: as, "a . . . young woman in *Tyrolese* costume" (Lever's "Harry Lorrequer," xlix.). **II.** *n.*; *pl. -lese.* A native of Tyrol.

Tyr-rhe-ni-an (ti-rē′ni-ạn), *a.* [L. *Tyrrhenus*, < Gr. Τυρρηνός, Etruscan.] Of or pertaining to the ancient Etruscans or their country, Etruria; Etruscan.—**Tyrrhenian Sea**, that part of the Mediterranean which lies between the mainland of Italy and the islands of Corsica, Sardinia, and Sicily.

tzar (tsär), etc. See *czar*, etc.

tzet-ze (tset′sẹ), *n.* See *tsetse*.

Tzig-a-ny (tsig′ạ-ni). [Hung.] **I.** *n.* A Hungarian Gipsy. **II.** *a.* Of or pertaining to the Hungarian Gipsies: as, *Tzigany* music.

U

U, u (ū); *pl. U's, u's* (ūz). A vowel, the 21st letter of the English alphabet.

u-bi-ca-tion (ū-bi-kā′shọn), *n.* [= Sp. *ubicación*, < L. *ubi*, where.] The state of having place or local relation; location.

u-bi-e-ty (ū-bī′ẹ-ti), *n.* [NL. *ubietas*, < L. *ubi*, where.] The state of being in a definite place; condition with respect to place; local relation.

u-bi-qui-tous (ū-bik′wi-tus), *a.* Characterized by ubiquity; being everywhere at the same time; present everywhere; omnipresent: as, "So *ubiquitous* are they [locusts] when they have alighted on the earth, that they simply cover or clothe its surface" (J. H. Newman's "Callista," xv.); "the two *ubiquitous* young Cratchits" (Dickens's "Christmas Carol," iii.). [Often humorous.]—**u-bi′qui-tous-ly**, *adv.*—**u-bi′qui-tous-ness**, *n.*

u-bi-qui-ty (ū-bik′wi-ti), *n.* [F. *ubiquité*, < NL. *ubiquitas*, < L. *ubique*, everywhere, < *ubi*, where.] The state or capacity of being everywhere, or in an indefinite number of places, at the same time; omnipresence; also, a locality† or neighborhood†.

U=boat (ū′bōt), *n.* [For G. *unterseeboot*, undersea boat, submarine.] A German (or other) submarine.

U=bolt (ū′bōlt), *n.* A bar of iron bent into the form of the letter U, fitted with a screw and nut at each end.

ud-der (ud′ėr), *n.* [AS. *úder* = OHG. *útar* (G. *euter*), akin to L. *uber*, Gr. οὖθαρ, Skt. *údhar*, udder.] A mamma or mammary gland, esp. when baggy and with more than one teat, as in cows.—**ud′dered**, *a.* Having an udder or udders: as, "the heavy-*uddered* cows" (W. Morris's "Jason," xvi. 422).

u-do (ö′dō), *n.* [Jap.] A plant, *Aralia cordata*, cultivated in Japan, China, and elsewhere for its edible shoots, which are used like asparagus and celery, and grown also for ornament.

u-dom-e-ter (ū-dom′e-tėr), *n.* [L. *udus*, for *uvidus*, wet, moist: see *-meter*.] A rain-gage; a pluviometer.—**u-do-met-ric** (ū-dọ-met′rik), *a.*—**u-dom′e-try**, *n.*

u-dom-o-graph (ū-dom′ọ-gráf), *n.* [From *udom(eter)* + *-graph*.] A recording udometer or rain-gage.

ugh (uh or úch), *interj.* An exclamation expressing disgust, aversion, horror, or the like: usually accompanied by a shudder: as, "*Ugh!* When I thought of what they did in Malta to poor old Jim" (Dunsany's "Night at an Inn").

ug-li-fy (ug′li-fī), *v. t.*; *-fied, -fying.* [See *-fy*.] To make ugly.—**ug″li-fi-ca′tion** (-fi-kā′shọn), *n.*

ug-ly (ug′li), *a.*; compar. *uglier*, superl. *ugliest.* [ME. *ugly*, *uglike*, from Scand.: cf. Icel. *uggligr*, fearful, dreadful, *ugga*, to fear.] Fearful† or frightful†; also, repulsive or displeasing in appearance; offensive to the sense of beauty (as, "The furniture was *ugly* and solid": Eden Phillpotts's "Children of Men," Prologue, i.); also, morally revolting (as, an *ugly* sin; "That was an *ugly* fault in Arthur's life," George Eliot's "Adam Bede," xliv.); base; vile; also, offensive to the smell or taste; nasty; also, in general, disagreeable, unpleasant, or objectionable (as, an *ugly* task; "Reality's played him . . . *ugly* tricks," Eden Phillpotts's "Grey Room," vi.); of a discreditable or disgraceful nature (as, "an *ugly* story about some royal warrants that were never served": Whyte-Melville's "Katerfelto," xx.); of a troublesome nature (as, an *ugly* wound); threatening disadvantage or danger (as, an *ugly* omen; *ugly* symptoms); unpleasantly or dangerously rough (as, *ugly* weather); ill-natured, quarrelsome, or vicious (colloq.: as, an *ugly* disposition; to turn *ugly*).—**ugly duckling**, an unattractive or unpromising child who grows up to be a beautiful or much-admired person: in allusion to the despised young bird among a brood of ducklings, in Hans Christian Andersen's tale, that turned out to be a swan.—**ug'li-ly**, *adv.*—**ug'li-ness**, *n.*

U-gri-an (ō'gri-an or ū'-). [From *Ugria* or *Ugra*, district about the Ural Mountains.] **I.** *a.* Noting or pertaining to a race or ethnological group including the Magyars and related peoples of western Siberia and west-central Asia; also, noting or pertaining to the languages of these peoples. Cf. *Finno-Ugrian*. **II.** *n.* A member of any of the Ugrian peoples.—**U'gric** (-grik), *a.* Same as *Ugrian*.

uh-lan, u-lan (ö'län, G. ö-län'), *n.* [G. *uhlan*, now *ulan*, < Pol. *ulan, hulan*, < Turk. *oghlān*, boy, lad; from Tatar.] One of a body of mounted soldiers of a type first known in Europe in Poland, and usually carrying lances; esp., one of such a body in the German army, classed as heavy cavalry.

u-in-tah-ite, u-in-ta-ite (ū-in'tä-īt), *n.* [From the *Uintah* or *Uinta* Mountains, in Utah.] A very pure variety of asphalt found in considerable deposits in Utah. Also called *gilsonite*.

uit-land-er (oit'län-der), *n.* [D., 'outlander.'] An outlander; a foreigner. [South Africa.]

u-ji-fly (ö'ji-flī), *n.*; pl. *-flies* (-flīz). [Jap. *uji*, maggot.] A dipterous insect, *Ujimyia sericaria* (family *Tachinidæ*), whose larva is the silkworm parasite of Japan, causing disease.

Uji-fly, natural size.

u-kase (ū-kās'), ' *n.* [Russ. *ukaz*.] An edict or order of the emperor or government of Russia, having the force of law; hence, any official proclamation.

U-krain-i-an (ū-krā'ni-an). **I.** *a.* Of or pertaining to the Ukraine (a district in southwestern European Russia, in 1920 recognized as a republic). **II.** *n.* A native or inhabitant of the Ukraine.

u-ku-le-le (ö-kö-lā'lä or yö-), *n.* [Hawaiian, lit. 'flea.'] A small musical instrument of the guitar kind, much used in the Hawaiian Islands.

u-lan (ö'län, G. ö-län'), *n.* See *uhlan*.

ul-cer (ul'sėr), *n.* [OF. *ulcere* (F. *ulcère*), < L. *ulcus* (*ulcer-*), akin to Gr. ἕλκος, wound, sore, ulcer.] A sore open either to the surface of the body or to a natural cavity, and accompanied by the disintegration of tissue and the formation of pus, etc.; fig., an evil, as a moral blemish or a corrupting influence, likened to an open sore.—**ul'cer**, *v. t.* or *i.* To ulcerate.—**ul'cer-ate** (-āt), *v. t.* or *i.*; *-ated, -ating.* [L. *ulceratus*, pp. of *ulcerare*, < *ulcus*.] To affect or be affected with an ulcer; make or become ulcerous.—**ul-cer-a'tion** (-ā'shon), *n.* [L. *ulceratio(n-)*.] The action or process of ulcerating, or the state of being ulcerated; also, an ulcer or a group of ulcers.—**ul'cer-a-tive** (-a-tiv), *a.* Causing ulceration; pertaining to, or of the nature of, or characterized by ulceration.—**ul'cered**, *p. a.* Ulcerated.—**ul'cer-ous**, *a.* Pertaining to or of the nature of an ulcer or ulcers; characterized by the formation of ulcers; affected with an ulcer or ulcers.—**ul'cer-ous-ly**, *adv.*—**ul'cer-ous-ness**, *n.*

-ule. [F. *-ule*, < L. *-ulus, -ula, -ulum*.] A diminutive suffix of nouns, as in *globule, nodule, plumule.* Cf. *-cule*.

u-le-ma (ö-lē-mä'), *n. pl.* [Ar. '*ulamā*, pl. of '*ālim*, learned, scholar.] The Moslem doctors of religion and sacred law, esp. in Turkey; a council of such doctors in a Moslem state.

u-lig-i-nose (ū-lij'i-nōs), *a.* [L. *uliginosus*, moist, marshy, < *uligo*, moisture, marshy quality.] Marshy; muddy; oozy; also, of animals and plants, living or growing in muddy places. Also **u-lig'i-nous.**

ul-lage (ul'āj), *n.* [OF. F. *ouillage*, < OF. *aoillier*, fill up (a cask), < *a* (< L. *ad*), to, + *oil* (< L. *oculus*), eye, bunghole.] The amount that a cask or the like lacks of being full; wantage.

ul-ma-ceous (ul-mā'shius), *a.* [L. *ulmus*, elm.] Belonging to the *Ulmaceæ*, or elm family of trees and shrubs.

ul-na (ul'nä), *n.*; pl. *-næ* (-nē). [NL. use of L. *ulna*, elbow, arm: see *ell*[1].] In *anat.*, in man, that one of the two bones of the forearm which is on the side opposite to the thumb; a corresponding bone in the fore limb of other vertebrates. —**ul'nar** (-när), *a.*

u-loid (ū'loid), *a.* [Gr. οὐλή, scar: see *-oid*.] Scar-like.

u-lot-ri-chous (ū-lot'ri-kus), *a.* [Gr. οὐλόθριξ (οὐλοτριχ-), < οὖλος, woolly, + θρίξ (τριχ-), hair.] Having woolly hair.

ul-ster (ul'stėr), *n.* [From *Ulster*, in Ireland.] A long, loose, heavy overcoat, worn by both men and women, orig. made of Irish frieze.

ul-te-ri-or (ul-tē'ri-or), *a.* [L., compar. adj. (superl. *ultimus*), connected with *ultra*, beyond: cf. *ultra* and *ultima*.] Being or situated beyond, or on the farther side (as, "The Rocky Mountains and the *ulterior* regions . . . have been traversed": Irving's "Captain Bonneville," i.); also, being beyond what is immediate or present, or coming at a subsequent time or stage (as, what *ulterior* action will be taken is uncertain); specif., being beyond what is seen or avowed, or intentionally kept concealed (as, *ulterior* motives).—**ul-te'ri-or-ly**, *adv.*

ul-ti-ma (ul'ti-mä), *n.* [L., fem. of *ultimus*, farthest, last, superl. of *ulterior*: see *ulterior*.] The last syllable of a word.

ul-ti-ma-cy (ul'ti-mä-si), *n.* The state or character of being ultimate.

ul-ti-mate (ul'ti-māt), *a.* [ML. *ultimatus*, < L. *ultimus*, farthest, last: see *ultima* and *ulterior*.] Farthest or most remote; extreme; also, last, as in a series; in general, coming at the end, as of a course of action, a process, etc. (as, "his *ultimate* lot in life": Archibald Marshall's "Anthony Dare," iv.); coming as a final result (as, "the *ultimate* effect of this": A. W. Mellon's "Taxation," vi.); final and decisive (as, an *ultimate* check to progress); also, forming the final aim or object (as, his *ultimate* goal or purpose); also, beyond which it is impossible to proceed, as by investigation or analysis (as, *ultimate* principles; "the *ultimate* source . . . of this increased authority," Hallam's "Europe during the Middle Ages," ii. 2; the *ultimate* constituents of a substance); fundamental; elemental.—**ultimate analysis**, in *chem.*, a form of analysis in which the elements are determined. Cf. *proximate analysis*.—**ultimate strength**, in *mech.*, the inherent resistance in a piece of material equal but opposed to the ultimate stress; also, the load necessary to produce fracture.—**ultimate stress**, in *mech.*, the stress necessary to break or crush a piece of material.—**ul'ti-mate**, *n.* The final point; the final result; the conclusion; also, a fundamental fact or principle.—**ul'ti-mate-ly**, *adv.* —**ul'ti-mate-ness**, *n.*

ul-ti-ma Thu-le (ul'ti-mä thū'lē). [L.] See *Thule*.

ul-ti-ma-tum (ul-ti-mā'tum), *n.*; pl. *-tums*, L. *-ta* (-tä). [NL., prop. neut. of ML. *ultimatus*, E. *ultimate*.] A final proposal or statement of conditions; specif., the final terms of one of the parties in a diplomatic negotiation, the rejection of which by the other party may involve a rupture of diplomatic relations or lead to a declaration of war; also, the final point; the extreme limit; also, an ultimate aim; also, something fundamental; a primary element.

ul-ti-mo (ul'ti-mō), *adv.* [L., 'in the last (month),' abl. of *ultimus*: see *ultima*.] In or of the last month, that is, the month preceding the present: as, on the 12th *ultimo*. Abbreviated *ult.* Cf. *proximo*.

ul-ti-mo-gen-i-ture (ul"ti-mō-jen'i-ṭūr), *n.* [L. *ultimus*, last, + E. *-geniture* as in *primogeniture*.] The right or principle of inheritance or succession by the youngest son: opposed to *primogeniture*.

ul-tra (ul'trä). [L., adv. and prep., beyond: cf. *ulterior*.] **I.** *a.* Going beyond what is usual or ordinary (as, "the *ultra* zeal of his countrymen": Irving's "Tales of a Traveler," iii. 4); immoderate; excessive; extreme; holding extreme views, as a person or party. **II.** *n.*; pl. *-tras* (-träz). One who goes to extremes, as of fashion, etc.; esp., one who holds extreme views or advocates extreme measures (as, "In Scotland Hamilton had got the best of Argyll and the Covenanting *Ultras*": Morley's "Oliver Cromwell," iii. 4); an extremist.

ultra-. [L. *ultra-*, repr. *ultra*, adv. and prep., beyond.] A prefix of Latin origin meaning 'beyond,' much used as an English formative, often in the sense of 'beyond the region, limits, or scope of,' as in *ultraplanetary, ultrasurgical, ultraterrestrial*, or 'beyond what is usual, natural, or reasonable,' 'extremely,' 'exceedingly,' 'excessively,' as in *ultraconventional, ultrafashionable, ultrapacifist, ultrapartizan.* Cf. *cis-*.

ul-tra-con-ser-va-tive (ul″trä-kọn-sėr′vạ-tiv). [See *ultra-.*] **I.** *a.* Conservative in the extreme; excessively conservative. **II.** *n.* One who is extremely conservative.—**ul″tra-con-ser′va-tism,** *n.*

ul-tra-gas-e-ous (ul-trä-gas′ē-us), *a.* [See *ultra-.*] In *physics,* of matter, being in the form of a highly rarefied gas with peculiar electrical and other properties, as that in a vacuum-tube exhausted to one millionth of an atmosphere; of or pertaining to such matter (as, "the most rarefied form of matter — an *ultra-gaseous* condition of it": W. R. Inge's "Outspoken Essays," i. 11).

ul-tra-ism (ul′trä-izm), *n.* The principles or procedure of ultras; extremism; also, an extreme view or act.—**ul′tra-ist,** *n.*

ul-tra-ma-rine (ul″trä-mạ-rēn′). [ML. *ultramarinus,* < L. *ultra,* beyond, + *mare,* sea.] **I.** *a.* Situated beyond the sea; also, of the color called ultramarine. **II.** *n.* A blue pigment consisting of powdered lapis lazuli (the name 'ultramarine' referring to its being brought from 'beyond the sea'); a similar blue pigment artificially prepared; also, any of various other pigments; also, a deep-blue color.

ul-tra-mi-cro-scope (ul-trä-mī′krọ-skōp), *n.* [See *ultra-.*] An instrument for rendering visible, by means of diffractive effects, objects too small to be seen by the ordinary microscope.—**ul″tra-mi-cro-scop′ic, ul″tra-mi-cro-scop′i-cal** (-skop′ik, -i-kạl), *a.* Beyond the power of a microscope to make visible; too small to be seen with a microscope; also, of or pertaining to an ultramicroscope.—**ul″tra-mi-cros′-co-py** (-kros′kọ-pi), *n.* The use of the ultramicroscope.

ul-tra-mon-tane (ul-trä-mon′tān). [ML. *ultramontanus,* < L. *ultra,* beyond, + *mons* (*mont-*), mountain.] **I.** *a.* Situated beyond, or pertaining to the farther side of, the mountains; esp., formerly, of or belonging to, or connected with, the countries north of the Alps; tramontane; noting or pertaining to a party in the Roman Catholic Church maintaining the rights of the northern churches and opposing the claims of absolute supremacy put forth for the popes; now, usually, of or belonging to, or connected with, the country south of the Alps; Italian; noting or pertaining to a party in the Roman Catholic Church supporting the absolute supremacy of the popes. **II.** *n.* One who lives beyond the mountains; esp., formerly, one living to the north of the Alps; a member of a party in the Roman Catholic Church opposing the claims of absolute supremacy put forth for the popes; now, usually, one living south of the Alps; a member of a party in the Roman Catholic Church supporting the absolute supremacy of the popes.—**ul-tra-mon′tan-ism** (-tạ-nizm), *n.* The doctrines of the ultramontanes; esp., the principles of the party in the Roman Catholic Church which claims that the Pope is absolutely supreme in matters of faith and discipline and superior to general councils.—**ul-tra-mon′tan-ist,** *n.*

ul-tra-mun-dane (ul-trä-mun′dān), *a.* [L. *ultramundanus,* < *ultra,* beyond, + *mundus,* world.] Beyond the world; beyond the limits of the universe as known to us; also, beyond this world or the present life.

ul-tra-phys-i-cal (ul-trä-fiz′i-kạl), *a.* [See *ultra-.*] Beyond or transcending what is physical.

ul-tra-rad-i-cal (ul-trä-rad′i-kạl), *a.* [See *ultra-.*] **I.** *a.* Extremely radical, as in politics. **II.** *n.* One who is extremely radical.—**ul-tra-rad′i-cal-ism,** *n.*

ul-tra-stel-lar (ul-trä-stel′ạr), *a.* [See *ultra-.*] Beyond the stars.

ul-tra-trop-i-cal (ul-trä-trop′i-kạl), *a.* [See *ultra-.*] Beyond or outside of the tropics; also, exceeding that of the tropics; warmer than the tropics.

ul-tra=vi-o-let (ul″trä-vī′ọ-lėt), *a.* [See *ultra-.*] Beyond the violet, as the invisible rays of the spectrum lying outside the violet end of the visible spectrum; pertaining to these rays.

u-lu (ö′lö), *n.* [Eskimo.] A kind of knife used by Eskimo women. See cut in next column.

ul-u-lant (ul′ū-lạnt), *a.* Ululating; howling.

ul-u-late (ul′ū-lāt), *v. i.; -lated, -lating.* [L. *ululatus,* pp. of *ululare,* howl, shriek: cf. L. *ulula,* screech-owl, and E. *owl.*] To howl, as a dog or a wolf; utter some similar sound; lament loudly.—**ul-u-la′tion** (-lā′shọn), *n.*

U-lys-se-an (ū-lis′ē-ạn), *a.* [L. *Ulysses,* for *Ulixes,* = Gr. Ὀδυσσεύς, Odysseus.] Of, pertaining to, or characteristic of Ulysses (or Odysseus), legendary king of Ithaca and hero of Homer's "Odyssey"; resembling Ulysses, as in craft or deceit, or in extensive wanderings. See *Odyssey.*

Forms of Ulu.

um-bel (um′bel), *n.* [NL. *umbella,* umbel, L. sun-shade: see *umbrella.*] In *bot.,* an inflorescence in which a number of flower-stalks or pedicels, nearly equal in length, spread from a common center: called a *simple umbel* when each pedicel is terminated by a single flower, and a *compound umbel* when each pedicel bears a secondary umbel.—**um′-bel-lar** (-be-lạr), *a.* Pertaining to or forming an umbel; umbellate.—**um′bel-late** (-lāt), *a.* Having or forming an umbel or umbels; umbel-like.—**um′bel-late-ly,** *adv.*—**um′bel-let,** *n.* A little umbel; an umbellule.—**um-bel-lif′er-ous** (-lif′ẹ-rus), *a.* [See *-ferous.*] Bearing an umbel or umbels; specif., belonging or pertaining to the *Umbelliferæ* (or *Apiaceæ*), a family of plants containing many important umbel-bearing herbs, as the parsley, carrot, etc. (in this sense equivalent to *apiaceous*).—**um-bel′lu-late** (-bel′ū-lāt), *a.* Having or forming umbellules.—**um-bel′-lule** (-bel′ūl), *n.* [NL. *umbellula,* dim. of *umbella.*] One of the secondary umbels in a compound umbel.

um-ber[1] (um′bėr), *n.* [OF. F. *ombre,* < L. *umbra,* shade, shadow.] Shade; shadow. [Now prov. Eng.]

um-ber[2] (um′bėr). [F. *ombre,* for *terre d'ombre,* lit. 'earth of Umbria' (F. *Ombrie*), in Italy.] **I.** *n.* An earth consisting chiefly of a hydrated oxide of iron and some oxide of manganese, used in its natural state ('raw umber') as a brown pigment, or after heating ('burnt umber') as a reddish-brown pigment; also, the color of such a pigment. **II.** *a.* Of the color of umber; dark-brown; dusky or dark.—**um′ber**[2], *v. t.* To color with or as with umber.

um-ber=bird (um′bėr-bėrd), *n.* The umbrette.

um-ber-y (um′bėr-i), *a.* [See *umber*[2].] Of or pertaining to umber; of the color of umber; dark-brown.

um-bil-i-cal (um-bil′i-kạl), *a.* Of or pertaining to the umbilicus or the umbilical cord; hence, formed or placed like a navel; central; also, connected through the female line of descent.—**umbilical cord,** in *anat.,* a cord or funicle connecting the umbilicus of an embryo or fetus with the placenta of the mother, and serving for the transmission of nourishment from the mother.

um-bil-i-cate (um-bil′i-kāt), *a.* [L. *umbilicatus.*] Having the form of an umbilicus or navel; navel-shaped; also, having an umbilicus; pitted.—**um-bil-i-ca′tion** (-kā′shọn), *n.* Umbilicate state or formation; also, a central navel-like depression.

um-bi-li-ci-form, um-bil-i-form (um-bi-lis′i-fôrm, -bil′i-fôrm), *a.* [From *umbilicus* + *-form.*] Having the form of an umbilicus or navel; navel-like.

um-bi-li-cus (um-bi-lī′kus, commonly um-bil′i-), *n.; pl. -ci* (-sī). [L., akin to Gr. ὀμφαλός, navel: see *navel.*] In *anat.,* the navel, or depression on the middle of the abdomen indicating the point of attachment of the cord connecting an embryo or fetus with the mother (see *umbilical cord*); in *bot., zoöl.,* etc., a navel-like formation, as the hilum of a seed, or the pit or hollow around which the whorls of a spiral shell coil.

Umbilicus (*a*) of Snail-shell.

um-bil′i-form, *a.* See *umbiliciform.*

um-bles (um′blz), *n. pl.* Same as *numbles.* [Archaic.]

um-bo (um′bō), *n.; pl. umbones* (um-bō′nēz). [L. *umbo*(*n-*), boss, knob.] The boss, knob, or projection at or near the center of a shield (see cut on next page); hence, any similar boss or protuberance.—**um′bo-nal** (-bō-nạl), *a.*—**um′bo-nate** (-nāt), *a.* Having an umbo or boss; also, boss-like. Also **um′bo-nat-ed** (-nā-ted).—**um-bo-na′tion** (-nā′shọn), *n.* Umbonate formation; an umbo.

um-bra (um′brä), *n.*; pl. *-bræ* (-brē). [L., shade, shadow.] Shade; shadow; specif., the complete or perfect shadow of an opaque body, as a planet, where the light from the source of illumination is wholly cut off (cf. *penumbra*, and see cut at *penumbra*); also, the dark central portion of a sunspot; also, an uninvited person accompanying an invited guest, as at an ancient Roman feast; also, the shade of a deceased person; a ghost.

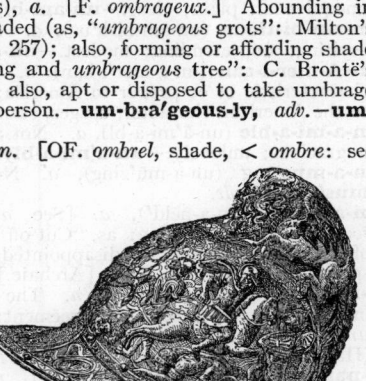

Umbo (*a*) on Shield of the Carolingian period.

um-brage (um′brāj), *n.* [OF. F. *ombrage*, shade, distrust, < L. *umbraticus*, of or in the shade, < *umbra*, shade, shadow.] Shade or shadow, as that cast by trees, etc.; also, the foliage of trees, etc., affording shade (as, "Even starlight was excluded by the *umbrage*": C. B. Brown's "Wieland," vii.); also, a shadowy appearance or semblance of something (now rare); also, offense given or taken, or resentful displeasure (as, "which dispensation . . . gave *umbrage* . . . to every good Protestant," Evelyn's "Diary," May 5, 1686; to take *umbrage* at a person's tone; "He . . . to avoid all cause of *umbrage*, had left a great part of his forces without the walls," Prescott's "Conquest of Mexico," iii. 7).—**um-bra′geous** (-brā′jus), *a.* [F. *ombrageux*.] Abounding in shade, shady, or shaded (as, "*umbrageous* grots": Milton's "Paradise Lost," iv. 257); also, forming or affording shade (as, "a low-spreading and *umbrageous* tree": C. Brontë's "Villette," xxxvii.); also, apt or disposed to take umbrage or offense, as a person.—**um-bra′geous-ly**, *adv.*—**um-bra′geous-ness**, *n.*

um-brel (um′brel), *n.* [OF. *ombrel*, shade, < *ombre*: see *umber*[1].] A piece attached to a helmet to shade or protect the face; a vizor. [Obs. or hist.]

um-brel-la (um-brel′ä), *n.* [It. *ombrella*, < *ombra*, < L. *umbra*, shade: cf. L. *umbella*, sunshade, dim. of *umbra*, and E. *umbel*.] A portable shade or screen for protection from sunlight, rain, etc., in its modern form consisting of a light circular canopy of silk, cotton,

Helmet with Umbrel, 16th century.

or other material extended on a folding frame of radiating bars or strips of steel, cane, etc., sliding on a rod or stick; in *zoöl.*, the umbrella-like gelatinous structure which in most jellyfishes constitutes the largest part of the body.

um-brel-la=bird (um-brel′ä-bėrd), *n.* A South American bird, *Cephalopterus ornatus*, which has a radiating umbrella-like crest above the head; also, any of certain other birds of this genus.

Umbrella-bird (*Cephalopterus ornatus*).

um-brel-la=leaf (um-brel′ä-lēf), *n.* A North American berberidaceous herb, *Diphylleia cymosa*, bearing either a large peltate, umbrella-like, lobed, basal leaf, or two smaller similar leaves on a flowering stem.

um-brel-la=tree (um-brel′ä-trē), *n.* An American magnolia, *Magnolia tripetala*, a tree with large leaves in umbrella-like clusters; also, any of various other trees in some way suggesting an umbrella.

um-brel-la-wort (um-brel′ä-wėrt), *n.* Any of the herbs, chiefly American, constituting the nyctaginaceous genus *Allionia*, having opposite leaves, and flower-containing involucres in loose terminal panicles.

um-brette (um-bret′), *n.* [NL. *umbretta* (F. *ombrette*), < L. *umbra*, E. *umber*[1].] A dusky-brown African wading-bird, *Scopus umbretta*, allied to the storks and herons; the shadow-bird or umber-bird.

Umbrette.

Um-bri-an (um′bri-an). **I.** *a.* Of or pertaining to Umbria, a district in central Italy, or its inhabitants: as, the *Umbrian* school of painting (to which Perugino, Pinturicchio, and Raphael belonged: notable during the 15th and 16th centuries). **II.** *n.* A native or inhabitant of Umbria; also, a member of a race which inhabited Umbria in ancient times; also, the language of this race, allied to Oscan and more distantly to Latin.

um-brif-er-ous (um-brif′e-rus), *a.* [L. *umbrifer*, < *umbra*, shade, + *ferre*, bear.] Casting or making shade.—**um-brif′er-ous-ly**, *adv.*

u-mi-ak (ö′mi-ak), *n.* [Eskimo.] An Eskimo boat consisting of a wooden frame covered with skins and provided with several seats, and worked with paddles, esp. by women. Cf. *kayak*.

um-laut (ŭm′lout), *n.* [G., < *um*, about (implying change), + *laut*, sound.] In *phonetics*, in the Germanic (or other) languages, a vowel-change brought about by the influence of a vowel, as *u* or, esp., *i*, in the following syllable, the modifying vowel being now usually lost or altered; also, the sign (two dots over the vowel modified) used to indicate this, as in G. *männer*, plural of *mann*, man, *füsse*, plural of *fuss*, foot, etc. (such words being also written *maenner*, *fuesse*, etc.).—**um′laut**, *v. t.* In *phonetics*, to form with umlaut; modify by umlaut.

umph (umf or mf), *interj.* and *n.* Same as *humph*: as, "Giving a contemptuous *umph*, he walked on" (Mrs. Stowe's "Uncle Tom's Cabin," xxx.).

um-pir-age (um′pīr-āj), *n.* The office or decision of an umpire; arbitrament.

um-pire (um′pīr), *n.* [ME. *oumpere*, for *noumpere* (a *noumpere* being taken as *an oumpere*), < OF. *nomper*, *nonper*, uneven, odd, < *non* (< L. *non*), not, + *per*, E. *peer*[2].] A person to whose sole decision a controversy or question between parties is referred; an arbiter or referee; esp., a person selected to rule on the plays in a game (cf. *referee*).—**um′pire**, *v.*; *-pired*, *-piring*. **I.** *tr.* To decide or settle (a controversy, etc.) as umpire; also, to act as umpire in (a game). **II.** *intr.* To act as umpire. —**um′pire-ship**, *n.*

un-[1]. [AS. *un-*, *on-*, akin to G. *un-*, L. *in-* (see *in-*[2]), Gr. ἀν-, ἀ- (see *a-*[1] and *an-*[1]).] A prefix of Anglo-Saxon origin, meaning 'not,' freely used as an English formative, giving a negative or opposite force, in adjectives (including participial adjectives) and their derivative adverbs and nouns (as *unfair*, *unfairly*, *unfairness*; *unfelt*, *unseen*, *unfitting*, *unformed*, *unheard-of*, *un-get-at-able*), and less freely in certain other nouns (as *unfaith*, *unrest*, *unemployment*).

While the corresponding prefix *in-²*, of Latin origin, is combined especially with words or stems from the Latin, and *an-*, of Greek origin, with elements from the Greek, *un-¹* may be prefixed to words from any source, esp. to any adjective or participle, thus affording a very great number of adjectives in particular (with possible derivatives), either actually recorded, or in known spoken use, or available at need as new coinages, restricted only by the clumsiness or other defects of a new formation or the fact that a better word for the sense already exists. Of the words in *un-¹* only a selected number are separately entered below, since in most formations of this class the meaning, spelling, and pronunciation may readily be determined by reference to the simple word from which each is formed. Cf. *non-*.

un-². [AS. *un-*, *on-*, < *and-*, back, against, akin to G. *ent-*, and to L. *ante*, before, Gr. ἀντί, opposite to, against: see *anti-*.] A prefix of Anglo-Saxon origin, freely used in English to form verbs expressing a reversal of some action or state, or removal, deprivation, release, etc., as in *unbar*, *unbend*, *uncork*, *unfasten*, *unhand*, *unmask*, *unscrew*, or to intensify the force of a verb already having such a meaning, as in *unloose*.

un-a-bashed (un-ạ-basht′), *a.* Not abashed; unembarrassed by awe or shame.

un-a-bat-ed (un-ạ-bā′ted), *a.* Not abated or lessened.

un-a-ble (un-ā′bl), *a.* Not able; lacking ability or power (*to:* as, "Many men . . . become *unable* to maintain themselves by their labour," Hobbes's "Leviathan," xxx.); also, infirm or feeble (as, "weak *unable* limbs," Shakspere's "1 Henry VI.," iv. 5. 4: now only Sc.).

un-a-bridged (un-ạ-brijd′), *a.* Not abridged or shortened, as a book.

un-ac-a-dem-ic (un-ak-ạ-dem′ik), *a.* Not academic; unconventional, as in literature or art.

un-ac-cent-ed (un-ak-sen′ted), *a.* Not accented.

un-ac-cept-a-ble (un-ak-sep′tạ-bl), *a.* Not acceptable; unsatisfactory; displeasing; not welcome.—**un-ac-cept′a-ble-ness**, *n.*—**un-ac-cept′a-bly**, *adv.*

un-ac-com-mo-dat-ed (un-ạ-kom′ọ-dā-ted), *a.* Not accommodated; not adapted or adjusted; also, not having accommodations; not supplied with necessary provisions or conveniences.—**un-ac-com′mo-dat-ing**, *a.* Not accommodating or obliging.

un-ac-com-pa-nied (un-ạ-kum′pạ-nid), *a.* Not accompanied; in *music*, without an accompaniment.

un-ac-com-plished (un-ạ-kom′plisht), *a.* Not accomplished; incomplete; without accomplishments.

un-ac-count-a-ble (un-ạ-koun′tạ-bl), *a.* Not accountable or answerable; irresponsible; also, not to be accounted for or explained (as, "He had an *unaccountable* foreboding that all was not right": Marryat's "King's Own," xxxii.); inexplicable; strange.—**un-ac-count′a-ble-ness**, *n.*—**un-ac-count′a-bly**, *adv.*

un-ac-cus-tomed (un-ạ-kus′tọmd), *a.* Not accustomed; unusual or unfamiliar (as, "the *unaccustomed* warmth": W. H. Hudson's "Green Mansions," xvi.); not habituated (as, music strange to an *unaccustomed* ear; to be *unaccustomed* to hardships).—**un-ac-cus′tomed-ness**, *n.*

un-ac-knowl-edged (un-ak-nol′ejd), *a.* Not acknowledged; unrecognized; unavowed; unnoticed.

un-ac-quaint-ed (un-ạ-kwān′ted), *a.* Not acquainted.—**un-ac-quaint′ance**, **un-ac-quaint′ed-ness**, *n.*

un-ac-quir-a-ble (un-ạ-kwir′ạ-bl), *a.* Not acquirable; not to be acquired or gained.—**un-ac-quir′a-ble-ness**, *n.* —**un-ac-quired′**, *a.* Not acquired; sometimes, naturally belonging; innate.

un-a-dapt-a-ble (un-ạ-dap′tạ-bl), *a.* Not adaptable.—**un-a-dapt′ed**, *a.* Not adapted; unsuited; unfitted.—**un-a-dapt′ed-ness**, *n.*

un-ad-dressed (un-ạ-drest′), *a.* Not addressed; bearing no address, as a letter.

un-a-dorned (un-ạ-dôrnd′), *a.* Not adorned; without ornament or embellishment; plain: as, "Loveliness Needs not the foreign aid of ornament, But is when *unadorned* adorned the most" (Thomson's "Seasons," Autumn, 206).

un-a-dul-ter-at-ed (un-ạ-dul′tėr-ā-ted), *a.* Not adulterated; pure.

un-ad-vised (un-ad-vīzd′), *a.* Not advised; not guided by forethought or judgment; imprudent; indiscreet; rash.—**un-ad-vis′ed-ly** (-vī′zed-li), *adv.*—**un-ad-vis′ed-ness**, *n.*

un-af-fect-ed¹ (un-ạ-fek′ted), *a.* Not affected, acted upon, or influenced: as, "Many of these birds seem *unaffected* by climate" (A. R. Wallace's "Darwinism," xii.).

un-af-fect-ed² (un-ạ-fek′ted), *a.* Not affected, assumed, or pretended; sincere or genuine (as, "The grand prior . . . seems to have felt a warm and *unaffected* friendship for Egmont": Motley's "Dutch Republic," iii. 1); also, free from affectation, natural, or simple (as, "easy, *unaffected* manners," Jane Austen's "Pride and Prejudice," iii.; an *unaffected* person).—**un-af-fect′ed-ly**, *adv.*—**un-af-fect′ed-ness**, *n.*

un-a-fraid (un-ạ-frād′), *a.* Not afraid; fearless: as, "The menace of the years Finds, and shall find, me *unafraid*" (Henley's "Echoes," iv.).

un-aid-ed (un-ā′ded), *a.* Not aided; without aid.

un-al-lied (un-ạ-līd′), *a.* Not allied; unrelated.

un-al-loyed (un-ạ-loid′), *a.* Not alloyed; pure: as, "some years of *unalloyed* happiness" (Marryat's "King's Own," l.).

un-al-ter-a-ble (un-âl′tėr-ạ-bl), *a.* Not alterable; unchangeable; immutable; fixed.—**un-al′ter-a-bly**, *adv.*—**un-al′tered**, *a.* Not altered; unchanged.

un-am-big-u-ous (un-am-big′ū-us), *a.* Not ambiguous; unequivocal; plain; clear.—**un-am-big′u-ous-ly**, *adv.*

un-am-bi-tious (un-am-bish′us), *a.* Not ambitious; unaspiring; unpretending; modest.—**un-am-bi′tious-ly**, *adv.*

un=A-mer-i-can (un-ạ-mer′i-kạn), *a.* Not American; not characteristic of or proper to America; foreign or opposed to the American character, usages, standards, etc.

un-a-mi-a-ble (un-ā′mi-ạ-bl), *a.* Not amiable; ill-natured; ungracious; unlovely.—**un-a′mi-a-bly**, *adv.*

un-a-mus-ing (un-ạ-mū′zing), *a.* Not amusing.—**un-a-mus′ing-ly**, *adv.*

un-a-neled (un-ạ-nēld′), *a.* [See *anele*.] Not having received extreme unction: as, "Cut off even in the blossoms of my sin, Unhousel'd, disappointed, *unaneled*" (Shakspere's "Hamlet," i. 5. 77). [Archaic.]

u-na-nim-i-ty (ū-nạ-nim′i-ti), *n.* The state of being unanimous; complete accord or agreement: as, "this transient *unanimity* in a people so distracted by internal faction" (Hallam's "Europe during the Middle Ages," iii. 1).

u-nan-i-mous (ū-nan′i-mus), *a.* [L. *unanimus*, < *unus*, one, + *animus*, mind.] Being of one mind, in complete accord, or agreed (as, "We were *unanimous* in our resolutions to go to this place": Defoe's "Robinson Crusoe," ii. 12); characterized by or showing complete accord (as, a *unanimous* vote).—**u-nan′i-mous-ly**, *adv.*—**u-nan′i-mous-ness**, *n.*

un-an-swer-a-ble (un-ȧn′sėr-ạ-bl), *a.* That cannot be answered; not admitting of any answer or reply: as, an *unanswerable* argument; "What remarks he could have made, — sarcastic, bitter, *unanswerable!*" (Arnold Bennett's "Roll-Call," vii.).—**un-an′swer-a-ble-ness**, *n.*—**un-an′swer-a-bly**, *adv.*—**un-an′swered**, *a.* Not answered.

un-ap-peal-a-ble (un-ạ-pē′lạ-bl), *a.* Not appealable; that cannot be carried to a higher court by appeal, as a cause; not to be appealed from, as a judgment or a judge.

un-ap-peas-a-ble (un-ạ-pē′zạ-bl), *a.* Not to be appeased; implacable; insatiable.—**un-ap-peas′a-bly**, *adv.*—**un-ap-peased′**, *a.* Not appeased.

un-ap-pe-tiz-ing (un-ap′ẹ-tī-zing), *a.* Not appetizing.—**un-ap′pe-tiz-ing-ly**, *adv.*

un-ap-pre-ci-at-ed (un-ạ-prē′shi-ā-ted), *a.* Not appreciated; not properly valued or esteemed.—**un-ap-pre′ci-at-ing**, *a.* Not appreciating; unappreciative: as, "drudging at low rates for *unappreciating* booksellers" (Lamb's "Oxford in the Vacation").—**un-ap-pre′ci-a-tive** (-ạ-tiv), *a.* Not appreciative; wanting in appreciation; inappreciative: as, "He was a cold-blooded, *unappreciative* stick" (L. Merrick's "Conrad in Quest of His Youth," x.).

un-ap-proach-a-ble (un-ạ-prō′chạ-bl), *a.* Not to be approached; inaccessible; distant; unrivaled.—**un-ap-proach′a-ble-ness**, *n.*—**un-ap-proach′a-bly**, *adv.* —**un-ap-proached′**, *a.* Not approached; unrivaled.

un-ap-pro-pri-at-ed (un-ạ-prō′pri-ā-ted), *a.* Not appropriated; not taken possession of; not assigned or allotted.

un-ap-proved (un-ạ prövd′), *a.* Not approved; not having received approval or sanction.

un-apt (un-apt′), *a.* Not apt; unfitted or unsuited; not disposed, likely, or liable; not quick to learn; inapt.—**un-apt′ly,** *adv.*—**un-apt′ness,** *n.*

un-ar-gued (un-är′gūd), *a.* Not argued or debated; also, not argued against; undisputed.

un-arm (un-ärm′), *v.* **I.** *tr.* To divest or relieve of armor (as, "Sweet Helen, I must woo you To help *unarm* our Hector": Shakspere's "Troilus and Cressida," iii. 1. 163); also, to deprive of arms†, or disarm†. **II.** *intr.* To take or put off one's armor.

un-armed (un-ärmd′), *a.* Not armed; without arms or armor; not furnished with claws, prickles, scales, or other armature, as animals and plants.

un-ar-mored (un-är′mọrd), *a.* Not armored: as, an *unarmored* cruiser.

un-as-cer-tain-a-ble (un-as-ėr-tā′nạ-bl), *a.* Not ascertainable; that cannot be certainly known, found out, or determined.—**un-as-cer-tained′,** *a.* Not ascertained; not certainly known or determined.

un-a-shamed (un-ạ-shāmd′), *a.* Not ashamed; devoid of shame.—**un-a-sham′ed-ly** (-shā′med-li), *adv.*

un-asked (un-áskt′), *a.* Not asked; unsolicited.

un-as-pi-rat-ed (un-as′pi-rā-ted), *a.* Not aspirated; pronounced without an aspirate.

un-a-spir-ing (un-ạ-spīr′ing), *a.* Not aspiring; unambitious. —**un-a-spir′ing-ly,** *adv.*—**un-a-spir′ing-ness,** *n.*

un-as-sail-a-ble (un-ạ-sā′lạ-bl), *a.* Not assailable; safe from attack; incontestable.—**un-as-sailed′,** *a.* Not assailed or attacked.

un-as-sign-a-ble (un-ạ-sī′nạ-bl), *a.* Not assignable.—**un-as-signed′,** *a.* Not assigned.

un-as-sist-ed (un-ạ-sis′ted), *a.* Not assisted; unaided.

un-as-sum-ing (un-ạ-sū′ming), *a.* Not assuming; unpretending; modest: as, "a simple *unassuming* air" (Arnold Bennett's "Grand Babylon Hotel," xi.).—**un-as-sum′-ing-ly,** *adv.*—**un-as-sum′ing-ness,** *n.*

un-as-sured (un-ạ-shörd′), *a.* Not assured; not sure, confident, or certain; not securely or safely established; not insured, as against loss.

un-at-tached (un-ạ-tacht′), *a.* Not attached; not connected or associated with any particular body, group, organization, or the like; independent; not engaged or married.

un-at-tain-a-ble (un-ạ-tā′nạ-bl), *a.* Not attainable; beyond the possibility of attainment; never to be attained or reached: as, "visions of remote *unattainable* truth" (J. Conrad's "Lord Jim," xxxiv.).—**un-at-tain′a-ble-ness,** *n.*—**un-at-tain′a-bly,** *adv.*—**un-at-tained′,** *a.* Not attained or reached.

un-at-taint-ed (un-ạ-tān′ted), *a.* Not attainted legally; also, unsullied, unblemished, or without defect (obs. or archaic).

un-at-tempt-ed (un-ạ-temp′ted), *a.* Not attempted; not tried or essayed; not subjected to any attempt.

un-at-tend-ed (un-ạ-ten′ded), *a.* Not attended; unaccompanied; also, not attended (*to*: as, so long as the matter remains *unattended to*).—**un-at-tend′ing,** *a.* Not attending or giving heed; inattentive.

un-at-test-ed (un-ạ-tes′ted), *a.* Not attested; not confirmed by witness or testimony.

un-at-trac-tive (un-ạ-trak′tiv), *a.* Not attractive; not such as to attract. — **un-at-trac′tive-ly,** *adv.* —**un-at-trac′-tive-ness,** *n.*

u-nau (ū′nä or ö-nou′), *n.* [S. Amer.] A South American two-toed sloth, *Cholopus didactylus.* See *sloth.*

Unau.

un-aus-pi-cious (un-âs-pish′us), *a.* Inauspicious.

un-au-then-tic (un-â-then′tik), *a.* Not authentic, reliable, or genuine.—**un-au-then′ti-cat-ed** (-ti-kā-ted), *a.* Not authenticated; not established as authentic.—**un″au-then-ti′ci-ty** (-tis′i-ti), *n.* Unauthentic character; want of authenticity.

un-au-thor-i-ta-tive (un-â-thor′i-tạ-tiv), *a.* Not authoritative; lacking authority.—**un-au-thor′i-ta-tive-ly,** *adv.* —**un-au-thor′i-ta-tive-ness,** *n.*

un-au-thor-ized (un-â′thọr-īzd), *a.* Not authorized; not duly commissioned; not warranted by proper authority.

un-a-vail-a-ble (un-ạ-vā′lạ-bl), *a.* Not available; of no avail; ineffectual; not suitable or ready for use.—**un-a-vail′a-ble-ness,** *n.*—**un-a-vail′ing,** *a.* Not availing; ineffectual; useless: as, "regardless of the tears, and *unavailing* pray'rs" (Burns's "Winter Night," 69).—**un-a-vail′ing-ly,** *adv.*

un-a-venged (un-ạ-venjd′), *a.* Not avenged.

un-a-void-a-ble (un-ạ-voi′dạ-bl), *a.* Not to be avoided; inevitable: as, an *unavoidable* accident; "unless an *unavoidable* necessity forced them to it" (Defoe's "Robinson Crusoe," ii. 16).—**un-a-void′a-ble-ness,** *n.*—**un-a-void′-a-bly,** *adv.*

un-a-vowed (un-ạ-voud′), *a.* Not avowed; secret.—**un-a-vow′ed-ly,** *adv.*

un-a-wak-ened (un-ạ-wā′knd), *a.* Not awakened.—**un-a-wak′en-ing,** *a.* Having no awakening: as, "stretched out . . . in eternal, *unawakening* sleep" (W. H. Hudson's "Green Mansions," xvii.).

un-a-ware (un-ạ-wär′). **I.** *a.* Not aware; unconscious, as of something: as, to be *unaware* of any change. **II.** *adv.* Unawares.—**un-a-wares′,** *adv.* While not aware or conscious of a thing one's self (as, "Be not forgetful to entertain strangers: for thereby some have entertained angels *unawares*": Heb. xiii. 2); unknowingly or inadvertently; also, while another is not aware, or unexpectedly (as, "You come upon one so *unawares*, and on a sudden": Fielding's "Tom Jones," vi. 5).

un-backed (un-bakt′), *a.* Not backed; without backing or support; not indorsed; never having been mounted by a rider, as a horse.

un-bag (un-bag′), *v. t.*; *-bagged, -bagging.* To let or pour out of a bag; take from or as from a bag.

un-bail-a-ble (un-bā′lạ-bl), *a.* Not bailable; not admitting of bail, as an offense.

un-baked (un-bākt′), *a.* Not baked; fig., crude; immature. Cf. *half-baked.*

un-bal-ance[1] (un-bal′ạns), *n.* Want of balance; unbalanced condition.

un-bal-ance[2] (un-bal′ạns), *v. t.* To throw out of balance; disorder or derange, as the mind.

un-bal-anced (un-bal′ạnst), *a.* Not balanced, or not properly balanced; lacking due mental balance or steadiness and soundness of judgment; mentally disordered or deranged; of an account, not adjusted; not brought to an equality of debits and credits.

un-bal-last-ed (un-bal′ạs-ted), *a.* Not ballasted; hence, not properly steadied or regulated.

un-bap-tized (un-bap-tīzd′), *a.* Not baptized.

un-bar (un-bär′), *v. t.*; *-barred, -barring.* To remove a bar or bars from; open; unlock.

un-barbed (un-bärbd′), *a.* Not shaved, sheared, or mowed†; also, not having a barb or barbs.

un-bat-ed (un-bā′ted), *a.* Not bated or lessened; also, not blunted, as a sword without a button†.

un-bear (un-bār′), *v. t.*; pret. *-bore,* pp. *-borne,* ppr. *-bearing.* To remove or relax the bearing-rein of (a horse).

un-bear-a-ble (un-bār′ạ-bl), *a.* Not bearable; unendurable; intolerable: as, "If the distress became *unbearable* he would raise the siege" (Froude's "Cæsar," xix.).—**un-bear′a-ble-ness,** *n.*—**un-bear′a-bly,** *adv.*

un-beat-en (un-bē′tn), *a.* Not beaten; not struck or pounded; untrodden (as, *unbeaten* paths); not defeated or surpassed (as, an *unbeaten* competitor).

un-beau-ti-ful (un-bū′ti-fůl), *a.* Not beautiful; plain; ugly.

un-be-com-ing (un-bē-kum′ing), *a.* Not becoming; unbefitting or unbeseeming (as, "Some work . . . Not *un-*

becoming men that strove with Gods": Tennyson's "Ulysses," 53); improper or unseemly (as, "Besides, miss, it is very *unbecoming* in you to want to have the last word with your mamma": Sheridan's "St. Patrick's Day," i. 2); unsuited in appearance, or unfitted to give a pleasing appearance, as clothes. colors, etc., to the wearer (as, "Her style of dress was not *unbecoming*": Marryat's "Mr. Midshipman Easy," xxiii.).—**un-be-com′ing-ly**, *adv.*—**un-be-com′ing-ness**, *n.*

un-be-fit-ting (un-bē-fit′ing), *a.* Not befitting; unbecoming; unseemly.—**un-be-fit′ting-ly**, *adv.*—**un-be-fit′ting-ness**, *n.*

un-be-got-ten (un-bē-got′n), *a.* Not yet begotten or generated; also, having never been generated; self-existent.

un-be-known (un-bē-nōn′), *a.* Unknown; unperceived; without a person's knowledge: often with *to*, and often used adverbially: as, "I was there . . . *unbeknown* to Mrs. Bardell" (Dickens's "Pickwick Papers," xxxiv.). Also **un-be-knownst′** (-nōnst′). [Colloq. or prov.]

un-be-lief (un-bē-lēf′), *n.* Want of belief (as, "The dissidents . . . have nothing to say in defense of their *unbelief*": W. D. Whitney's "Life and Growth of Language," x.); incredulity; disbelief: in religious use, want of belief, or disbelief, in divine revelation or in the truth of the gospel (as, "For what if some did not believe? shall their *unbelief* make the faith of God without effect?" Rom. iii. 3).—**un-be-liev′a-ble** (-lē′va-bl), *a.* Not believable; incredible.—**un-be-liev′a-bly**, *adv.*—**un-be-liev′er**, *n.* One who does not believe; an incredulous person; often, one who does not accept any, or some particular, religious belief; an infidel.—**un-be-liev′ing**, *a.* Not believing; incredulous; skeptical; often, not accepting any, or some particular, religious belief.—**un-be-liev′ing-ly**, *adv.*—**un-be-liev′ing-ness**, *n.*

un-belt (un-belt′), *v. t.* To remove the belt from; ungird; also, to remove by undoing a supporting belt, as a sword.

un-bend (un-bend′), *v.*; *-bent* or *-bended*, *-bending*. **I.** *tr.* To release from tension, as a bow; fig., to relax, as from the strain of effort or close application (as, "an assembly of learned men, who met . . . to *unbend* their minds, and compare their opinions": Johnson's "Rasselas," xxii.); relax (one's self) by laying aside formality or ceremony (as, "a small man, with an . . . expressionless face, who never was known to *unbend* himself to a human being": H. Kingsley's "Geoffry Hamlyn," xiii.); also, to straighten from a bent form or position (as, to *unbend* the fingers); *naut.*, to unfasten from the spars or stays, as sails; also, to cast loose or untie, as a rope. **II.** *intr.* To become unbent; esp., fig., to relax the strictness of formality or ceremony, or act in an easy, genial manner (as, "Dignity must *unbend* now and then," Jefferies's "Gamekeeper at Home," i.; "The great man *unbent*. His face beamed," S. Butler's "Way of All Flesh," xxvii.).

un-bend-ing (un-ben′ding), *a.* Not bending; rigid; unyielding; inflexible.—**un-bend′ing-ly**, *adv.*—**un-bend′-ing-ness**, *n.*

un-bent (un-bent′), *a.* Not bent; unbowed; fig., not forced to yield or submit (as, "her *unbent* will's majestic pride": Whittier's "Snow-Bound").

un-be-seem-ing (un-bē-sē′ming), *a.* Not beseeming; unbecoming.

un-bi-ased, un-bi-assed (un-bī′ast), *a.* Not biased; unprejudiced; impartial.

un-bid (un-bid′), *a.* Unbidden.

un-bid-den (un-bid′n), *a.* Not bidden; uninvited; not commanded.

un-bind (un-bīnd′), *v. t.*; *-bound*, *-binding*. [AS. *unbindan*.] To release from bands or restraint, as a prisoner; free; also, to unfasten or loose, as a band or tie.

un-bit-ted (un-bit′ed), *a.* Not bitted or bridled; uncontrolled.

un-blam-a-ble (un-blā′ma-bl), *a.* Not blamable; blameless.—**un-blam′a-ble-ness**, *n.*—**un-blam′a-bly**, *adv.*

un-bleached (un-blēcht′), *a.* Not bleached, as cloth.

un-blem-ished (un-blem′isht), *a.* Not blemished; without blemish; flawless; spotless; unsullied.

un-blenched† (un-blencht′), *a.* Not 'blenched' or disconcerted; undaunted.

un-blessed (un-blest′ or -bles′ed), *a.* Not blessed; excluded from a blessing; unhallowed, unholy, or evil; unhappy or wretched. Also **un-blest′**.

un-blush-ing (un-blush′ing), *a.* Not blushing; not showing any shame; hence, shameless.—**un-blush′ing-ly**, *adv.*

un-bod-ied (un-bod′id), *a.* Having no body; incorporeal; also, disembodied.

un-bolt (un-bōlt′), *v. t.* To withdraw the bolt of (a door, etc.).

un-bolt-ed[1] (un-bōl′ted), *a.* Not bolted or fastened, as a door.

un-bolt-ed[2] (un-bōl′ted), *a.* Not bolted or sifted, as ground grain.

un-bon-net (un-bon′et), *v.* **I.** *intr.* To take off the bonnet; uncover the head, as in respect. **II.** *tr.* To take off the bonnet from.

un-bon-net-ed (un-bon′et-ed), *a.* Wearing no bonnet; bareheaded.

un-book-ish (un-buk′ish), *a.* Not bookish; not given to reading; also, unlearned.

un-born (un-bôrn′), *a.* Not born (as, "O miserable mankind . . . Better end here *unborn*": Milton's "Paradise Lost," xi. 502); not yet born (as, "Nations *unborn* your mighty names shall sound": Pope's "Essay on Criticism," 193); hence, in general, not yet existing; yet to come, or future (as, ages *unborn*).

un-bos-om (un-buz′om), *v.* **I.** *tr.* To give forth as from the bosom or breast, or disclose, esp. in confidence (one's thoughts, feelings, etc.); unburden (one's self) of one's thoughts, feelings, etc., by disclosure to another (as, "He never sought to *unbosom* himself to me," Irving's "Tales of a Traveler," i. 8; "The indignant Duchess *unbosomed* herself in, her . . . letters . . . of the rage . . . hitherto partially suppressed," Motley's "Dutch Republic," iii. 1); also, to reveal to sight (poetic: as, "Fair-handed Spring *unbosoms* every grace," Thomson's "Seasons," Spring, 529). **II.** *intr.* To unbosom one's self; disclose one's thoughts, feelings, secrets, etc.: as, "Ralph *unbosomed*. His name was down for the army" (G. Meredith's "Ordeal of Richard Feverel," xiv.).—**un-bos′om-er**, *n.*

un-bot-tomed (un-bot′omd), *a.* Bottomless: as, "the dark *unbottom'd* infinite abyss" (Milton's "Paradise Lost," ii. 405).

un-bought (un-bôt′), *a.* Not bought; not acquired by purchase; not hired or bribed.

un-bound[1] (un-bound′). Pret. and pp. of *unbind*.

un-bound[2] (un-bound′), *a.* Not bound, as a book.

un-bound-ed (un-boun′ded), *a.* Not bounded or limited; unlimited, boundless, or very great (as, "men of *unbounded* wealth": Marryat's "King's Own," xlv.); also, not kept within limits; unrestrained or uncontrolled.—**un-bound′-ed-ly**, *adv.*—**un-bound′ed-ness**, *n.*

un-bowed (un-boud′), *a.* Not bowed or bent (as, with *unbowed* head); fig., not forced to yield or submit.

un-brace (un-brās′), *v. t.* To remove the braces of; unfasten, loosen, or relax; free from tension; fig., to lower the tone of, or weaken.

un-braid (un-brād′), *v. t.* To bring out of a braided state; separate (anything braided, as hair) into the several strands.

un-break-a-ble (un-brā′ka-bl), *a.* Not breakable.

un-breathed (un-brēтнd′), *a.* Not breathed (as, air *unbreathed*); also, not exercised or practised†.

un-breeched (un-brēcht′), *a.* Not breeched; wearing no breeches (as, "a parcel of *unbreeched* heathen": H. Melville's "Typee," v.); not yet wearing breeches, as a young boy.

un-brib-a-ble (un-brī′ba-bl), *a.* Not bribable.

un-bri-dle (un-brī′dl), *v. t.* To remove the bridle from (a horse, etc.); hence, to let loose; free from restraint.

un-bri-dled (un-brī′dld), *a.* Not having a bridle on, as a horse; hence, unrestrained or uncontrolled (as, *unbridled* passions; "*unbridled* impulses," Parkman's "Oregon Trail," xviii.).

un-brok-en (un-brō′kn), *a.* Not broken; whole or intact; uninterrupted or continuous; undisturbed; unimpaired; unsubdued; not tamed or rendered tractable.—**un-brok′-en-ly**, *adv.*—**un-brok′en-ness**, *n.*

un-buck-le (un-buk′l), *v. t.* To unfasten the buckle or buckles of.

---

un-build (un-bild′), v. t.; -built, -building. To demolish (something built); raze.

un-built (un-bilt′), a. Not yet or ever built.

un-bur-den (un-bẽr′dn), v. t. To free from or as from a burden; disburden; often, to relieve (one's mind, conscience, etc., or one's self) by disclosure or confession of something (as, "To-morrow I die, and to-day I would unburden my soul," Poe's "Black Cat"; "For some time she was mysterious, but at last she unburdened herself," Hugh Walpole's "Wooden Horse," ix.); also, to cast off or get rid of, as a burden or something burdensome; relieve one's self of, or give vent to (as, "He had retired to unburden his grief": Jane Porter's "Scottish Chiefs," lxxviii.); disclose, reveal, or confess.—**un-bur′den-ment**, n.

un-bur-ied (un-ber′id), a. Not buried.

un-bur-y (un-ber′i), v. t.; -buried, -burying. To take out of the place of burial; disinter; exhume. Also fig.

un-busi-ness-like (un-biz′nes-līk), a. Not businesslike; without the shrewdness, care, system, etc., requisite in business: as, "I can only be sorry I trusted a lady with the originals, which was an unbusinesslike proceeding" (Stevenson's "Master of Ballantrae," vi.).

un-but-ton (un-but′n), v. t. To unfasten the button or buttons of (a garment, etc., or a person); also, to unfasten (a button).

un-cage (un-kāj′), v. t. To release from or as from a cage.

un-called (un-kâld′), a. Not called; not summoned or invited: as, to come uncalled.—**un-called′=for**, a. Not called for or required; unnecessary and improper; unwarranted: as, an uncalled-for remark or proceeding.

un-can-celed, un-can-celled (un-kan′sęld), a. Not canceled.

un-can-did (un-kan′did), a. Not candid; disingenuous.—**un-can′did-ly**, adv.—**un-can′dor**, n. Lack of candor.

un-can-ny (un-kan′i), a. Not canny; unsafe to have dealings with, or to be dreaded, because of supernatural powers or character (as, an old woman reputed to be uncanny; "I felt . . . superstitious — as if I were sitting in the room with something uncanny," C. Brontë's "Jane Eyre," xxxiv.); mysteriously alarming, as if being of supernatural character (as, "The queer stumps and snags had uncanny shapes, as of monstrous creatures, whose eyes seemed to peer out at you," Galsworthy's "Dark Flower," ii. 18; "Doubtless, with my drawn sword, and the blood dripping from my chin . . . I looked fierce and uncanny enough," S. J. Weyman's "Gentleman of France," x.); weird; mysterious; unnaturally strange; such as to arouse superstitious uneasiness; also, superstitiously uneasy or fearful (as, "I feel a little bit uncanny, — and eerie, as the Scotch say," Mrs. Stowe's "Oldtown Folks," xlv.; "I could never overcome a curious shrinking, an almost uncanny feeling, in his presence," W. H. Hudson's "Far Away and Long Ago," xix.); also, ominous or unlucky (as, "It was thought uncanny to have a dead corpse in the house on the new-year's day": Galt's "Annals of the Parish," iv.). [Orig. Sc.]—**un-can′ni-ly**, adv.—**un-can′ni-ness**, n.

un-ca-non-i-cal (un-kạ-non′i-kạl), a. Not canonical; not in accordance with canons or rules; not belonging to the canon of Scripture.—**un-ca-non′i-cal-ly**, adv.

un-cap (un-kap′), v.; -capped, -capping. I. tr. To remove the cap from (the head or a person); also, to remove a cap or cover, or a percussion-cap, from. II. intr. To remove the cap from the head, as in respect.

un-cap-a-ble† (un-kā′pạ-bl), a. Incapable.

un-cared=for (un-kārd′fôr), a. Not cared for or looked after; neglected.

un-car-pet-ed (un-kär′pet-ed), a. Not carpeted.

un-cart (un-kärt′), v. t. To remove or unload from a cart.

un-case (un-kās′), v. t. To take out of a case; remove the case or covering from; strip; uncover; lay bare; disclose or reveal.

un-cat-a-logued (un-kat′ạ-logd), a. Not catalogued.

un-cate (ung′kāt), a. [LL. uncatus, < L. uncus, a hook.] Hooked; uncinate.

un-caused (un-kâzd′), a. Not caused; self-existent.

un-ceas-ing (un-sē′sing), a. Not or never ceasing; incessant; ceaseless; continual.—**un-ceas′ing-ly**, adv.

un-cer-e-mo-ni-ous (un-ser-ē-mō′ni-us), a. Not ceremonious; informal; abrupt.—**un-cer-e-mo′ni-ous-ly**, adv.—**un-cer-e-mo′ni-ous-ness**, n.

un-cer-tain (un-sẽr′tạn), a. Not certain; not fixed or determined (as, the date or the amount was left uncertain); not definitely or surely known (as, the result of the election is still uncertain; a person of uncertain age); doubtful; vague or indistinct (as, "Enoch seem'd to them Uncertain as a vision or a dream": Tennyson's "Enoch Arden," 353); not to be depended on, or not of assured reliability (as, uncertain promises or prospects); dependent on chance; subject to change, variable, or capricious (as, to have an uncertain temper; "O, woman! in our hours of ease, Uncertain, coy, and hard to please," Scott's "Marmion," vi. 30); unsteady or fitful, as light; not sure in mind, or not confident, assured, or decided (as, to be uncertain of the facts; uncertain of one's welcome; uncertain whether to go or stay).—**un-cer′tain-ly**, adv.—**un-cer′tain-ness**, n.—**un-cer′tain-ty** (-ti), n.; pl. -ties (-tiz). The state of being uncertain; also, something uncertain; a doubtful point or matter.

un-cer-ti-fied (un-sẽr′ti-fīd), a. Not certified; without certification.

un-chain (un-chān′), v. t. To free from or as from chains; let loose; set free: as, "Until the spring Unchains the streams" (W. Morris's "Jason," xi. 354).

un-chain-a-ble (un-chā′nạ-bl), a. Incapable of being chained or held in restraint: as, "We . . . abide Unchainable as the dim tide" (W. B. Yeats's "Wanderings of Oisin," i.).—**un-chained′**, a. Not chained; unfettered; free.

un-chal-lenged (un-chal′enjd), a. Not challenged; not called in question; not called to account.

un-chan-cy (un-chän′si), a. [Cf. chancy.] Unlucky or ill-omened; also, unsafe to meddle with; dangerous; risky; also, inconvenient. [Chiefly Sc.]

un-change-a-ble (un-chān′jạ-bl), a. Not changeable; immutable; not subject to variation.—**un-change′a-ble-ness**, n.—**un-change′a-bly**, adv.—**un-changed′**, a. Not changed; unaltered; unvaried.—**un-chan′ging** (-chān′jing), a. Not changing; always the same.—**un-chan′ging-ly**, adv.

un-chap-e-roned (un-shap′ẹ-rōnd), a. Not chaperoned; without a chaperon.

un-char-ac-ter-is-tic (un-kar″ạk-tẽr-is′tik), a. Not characteristic; not typical, natural, or usual in the particular instance.—**un-char″ac-ter-is′ti-cal-ly**, adv.

un-charge (un-chärj′), v. t. To free from or as from a charge or load; unload; also, to free from blame, or acquit (obs. or archaic).

un-char-i-ta-ble (un-char′i-tạ-bl), a. Not charitable; harsh; censorious: as, "I hated them with the bitter uncharitable condemnation of boyhood" (H. G. Wells's "Tono-Bungay," i. 2. § 1).—**un-char′i-ta-ble-ness**, n.—**un-char′i-ta-bly**, adv.—**un-char′i-ty** (-ti), n. Want of charity; uncharitable feeling: as, "I . . . Fought with what seem'd my own uncharity" (Tennyson's "Sea Dreams," 73).

un-char-tered (un-chär′tẽrd), a. Not chartered; without a charter (as, an unchartered company); fig., without license or regulation (as, "Me this unchartered freedom tires": Wordsworth's "Ode to Duty," 37).

un-chaste (un-chāst′), a. Not chaste or virtuous; lewd; also, not marked by purity of taste.—**un-chaste′ly**, adv.—**un-chas′ti-ty** (-chas′ti-ti), n. Want of chastity; unchaste character; lewdness.

un-checked (un-chekt′), a. Not checked; unrestrained; uncontradicted, as a report†.

un-chiv-al-rous (un-shiv′ạl-rus), a. Not chivalrous; ungallant.—**un-chiv′al-rous-ly**, adv.

un-chris-tian (un-kris′chạn), a. Not Christian; not of the Christian faith; opposed to the Christian belief, teachings, spirit, or character (as, an unchristian doctrine, feeling, or act; "In a formal petition to Parliament they [Lollards, in 1395] mingled denunciations . . . with . . . a demand . . . that war might be declared unchristian," Green's "Short Hist. of the Eng. People," v. 5); unworthy of Christians; hence, in general, unseemly, indecent, or reprehensible (as, to rouse a household at an unchristian hour; "He . . . sat biting his fingers and staring on the ground, a most *unchristian* object," Stevenson's "Master of Ballantrae," iii.).—**un-chris-ti-an′i-ty** (-ṭi-an′i-ti), *n.* Want of Christianity.—**un-chris′tian-ly**, *adv.*

un-church (un-chẽrch′), *v. t.* To expel from a church; excommunicate; also, to deprive of the character and rights of a church.

un-cial (un′shial). [L. *uncialis*, of an inch, < *uncia*, twelfth part, inch, ounce: cf. *inch* and *ounce*[1].] **I.** *a.* Designating, written in, or pertaining to a variety of ancient majuscule letters distinguished from capital majuscules by relatively greater roundness, inclination, and inequality in height. **II.**

INFEREN ƆUMAƆQUEAR CENƆUMBELLUNINEƆU IPSEIERRESIRIPERHIS PANIAMCALLIAMSQUE IIINEREIIAIIAMPETE

Latin Uncials, from a manuscript of the 8th century.

n. An uncial letter; uncial writing; a manuscript written in uncials.—**un′cial-ly**, *adv.*

un-ci-form (un′si-fôrm). [L. *uncus*, hook: see *-form*.] **I.** *a.* Having the form of a hook; hook-shaped; in *anat.*, noting a bone of the carpus with a hook-like process projecting from the palmar surface; noting the hook-like process of this bone, or a hook-like process of some other bone, as the ethmoid. **II.** *n.* In *anat.*, the unciform bone of the carpus.

un-ci-nal (un′si-nal), *a.* Same as *uncinate*.

un-ci-na-ri-a-sis (un″si-na-rī′a-sis), *n.* [NL., < *Uncinaria*, genus of hookworms; < L. *uncinus*, hook: see *uncinate*.] Hookworm disease. See *hookworm*.

un-ci-nate (un′si-nāt), *a.* [L. *uncinatus*, < *uncinus*, hook, barb, < *uncus*, hook.] Hooked; bent at the end like a hook: specif. in *anat.*, *zoöl.*, and *bot.* Also **un′ci-nat-ed** (-nā-ted).

un-cir-cum-cised (un-sẽr′kum-sīzd), *a.* Not circumcised; hence, not Jewish; Gentile; also, heathen; unregenerate.—**un-cir-cum-ci′sion** (-sizh′ọn), *n.* Absence of circumcision; the condition of being uncircumcised; also, those who are not circumcised; the Gentiles.

un-civ-il (un-siv′il), *a.* Not civil; uncivilized or barbarous (as, "Man cannot enjoy the rights of an *uncivil* and of a civil state together": Burke's "Revolution in France," 88); without good manners, unmannerly, or rude; impolite or discourteous (as, "I hope it's not *uncivil* to say that you ... ought to be in gaol": Chesterton's "Napoleon of Notting Hill," iii. 3).

un-civ-il-ized (un-siv′i-līzd), *a.* Not civilized; barbarous; unenlightened.

un-civ-il-ly (un-siv′i-li), *adv.* In an uncivil manner.—**un-civ′il-ness**, *n.*

un-clad[1] (un-klad′). Pret. and pp. of *unclothe*.

un-clad[2] (un-klad′), *a.* Not clad; unclothed.

un-claimed (un-klāmd′), *a.* Not claimed.

un-clasp (un-klàsp′), *v.* **I.** *tr.* To undo the clasp or clasps of, or unfasten (as, "He *unclasped* his shackles": Prescott's "Conquest of Mexico," iv. 3); also, to release from the clasp or grasp, as something held; also, to bring out of a clasped position or state (as, "She clasped and *unclasped* her fingers": W. H. Hudson's "Green Mansions," xi.); also, fig., to lay open† or reveal†. **II.** *intr.* To become unclasped, as the hands, etc.; relax the clasp or grasp.

un-clas-si-fi-a-ble (un-klas′i-fī-a-bl), *a.* Not classifiable.—**un-clas′si-fied** (-fīd), *a.* Not classified.

un-cle (ung′kl), *n.* [OF. *uncle* (F. *oncle*), < L. *avunculus*, uncle, dim. of *avus*, grandfather: cf. *avuncular*.] A brother of one's father or mother; also, an aunt's husband; also, a familiar title applied to any elderly man; also, a pawnbroker (slang).—**Uncle Sam,** the government or the people of the United States: a humorous extension of the initials U. S.

un-clean (un-klēn′), *a.* Not clean; dirty, foul, or filthy; morally impure or defiled; unchaste; evil; vile; ceremonially impure.—**un-cleaned′**, *a.* Not cleaned.—**un-clean′ly** (-klēn′li), *adv.* In an unclean manner.—**un-clean′ly** (-klēn′li), *a.* Not cleanly; unclean.—**un-clean′li-ness** (-klen′li-nes), *n.*—**un-clean′ness** (-klēn′nes), *n.*

un-clear (un-klēr′), *a.* Not clear; clouded; obscure; indistinct; uncertain.—**un-cleared′**, *a.* Not cleared.

un-clench (un-klench′), *v. t.* or *i.* To open or become opened from a clenched state: as, "I saw her hands clench and *unclench* spasmodically" (Maugham's "Moon and Sixpence," x.).

un-cloak (un-klōk′), *v.* **I.** *tr.* To remove the cloak from; fig., to reveal; expose. **II.** *intr.* To take off the cloak, or the outer garments generally.

un-clog (un-klog′), *v. t.*; *-clogged, -clogging.* To free from a clog or from anything that clogs: as, "We should sometimes increase the motion of the machine to *unclog* the wheels of life" (Smollett's "Humphry Clinker," Oct. 26).

un-close (un-klōz′), *v. t.* or *i.* To bring or come out of a closed state; open.

un-clothe (un-klōꝥ′), *v. t.*; *-clothed* or *-clad, -clothing.* To strip of clothes; hence, to strip of anything; divest; uncover; lay bare.

un-clothed (un-klōꝥd′), *a.* Not clothed; naked; bare.

un-cloud-ed (un-klou′ded), *a.* Not clouded; free from clouds; clear.—**un-cloud′ed-ness**, *n.*

un-co (ung′kō). [= *uncouth*.] **I.** *a.* Unknown, strange, or unusual; also, uncanny; also, remarkable, extraordinary, or great. [Sc.] **II.** *adv.* Remarkably; extremely; very: as, "Address to the *Unco* Guid, or the Rigidly Righteous" (title of a poem by Burns). [Sc.] **III.** *n.*; pl. *-cos* (-kọz). A stranger†; also, something extraordinary, or a wonder (as, "Mrs. Macadam being considered a great *unco* among them for all manner of ladylike ornaments," Galt's "Annals of the Parish," xxv.: often in *pl.*); *pl.*, news. [Sc.]

un-cock (un-kok′), *v. t.* To let down the hammer of (a firearm) gently from the position of cock, so as not to explode the charge.

un-coil (un-koil′), *v.* **I.** *tr.* To bring out of a coiled form or state; unwind. **II.** *intr.* To uncoil itself.

un-coined (un-koind′), *a.* Not coined; not minted.

un-col-ored, un-col-oured (un-kul′ọrd), *a.* Not colored; fig., not made to appear different from the reality; open or undisguised; truthful or unbiased, as a statement or account; not influenced or affected by something; also, plain or unadorned.

un-com-bined (un-kọm-bīnd′), *a.* Not combined; separate.

un-com-fort-a-ble (un-kum′fọr-ta-bl), *a.* Not comfortable; causing discomfort; disquieting; also, in a state of discomfort; uneasy; ill at ease.—**un-com′fort-a-ble-ness**, *n.* —**un-com′fort-a-bly**, *adv.*

un-com-mer-cial (un-kọ-mẽr′shal), *a.* Not commercial; not engaged in or connected with commerce; not in accordance with the principles or methods of commerce.

un-com-mit-ted (un-kọ-mit′ed), *a.* Not committed; esp., not bound by pledge or assurance, as to a particular course.

un-com-mon (un-kom′ọn), *a.* Not common; unusual or rare; unusual in amount or degree; of an unusual character or an exceptional kind.—**un-com′mon-ly**, *adv.* Rarely or infrequently; also, in an uncommon or unusual degree; remarkably.—**un-com′mon-ness**, *n.*

un-com-mu-ni-ca-tive (un-kọ-mū′ni-ka-tiv), *a.* Not communicative; parsimonious†; not disposed to impart information, opinions, etc.; reserved; taciturn.—**un-com-mu′ni-ca-tive-ly**, *adv.*—**un-com-mu′ni-ca-tive-ness**, *n.*

un-com-plain-ing (un-kọm-plā′ning), *a.* Not complaining; not disposed to murmur; submissive.—**un-com-plain′-ing-ly**, *adv.*

un-com-plet-ed (un-kọm-plē′ted), *a.* Not completed; unfinished.

un-com-pli-men-ta-ry (un-kom-pli-men′ṭa-ri), *a.* Not complimentary; unflattering; disparaging; derogatory.

un-com-pre-hend-ing (un-kom-prẹ-hen′ding), *a.* Not comprehending or understanding.—**un-com-pre-hend′ing-ly**, *adv.*

un-com-pro-mis-ing (un-kom′prọ-mī-zing), *a.* Not compromising, or not admitting of compromise; unyielding; inflexible.—**un-com′pro-mis-ing-ly**, *adv.*

un-con-cealed (un-kọn-sēld′), *a.* Not concealed; openly shown; manifest.

un-con-cern (un-kọn-sẽrn′), *n.* Lack of concern; freedom from interest, solicitude, or anxiety; indifference: as, "Cynthia accepted the present ... with ... magnificent unconcern" (W. Churchill's "Coniston," ii. 9).—**un-con-cerned'**, a. Not concerned; not occupied with or involved in something; disinterested; devoid of concern or interest; free from solicitude or anxiety.—**un-con-cern'ed-ly**, adv.—**un-con-cern'ed-ness**, n.

un-con-di-tion-al (un-kon-dish'on-al), a. Not conditional; absolute: as, an unconditional surrender; an unconditional promise.—**un-con-di'tion-al-ly**, adv.—**un-con-di'tion-al-ness**, n.—**un-con-di'tioned**, a. Not conditioned; not subject to conditions; absolute.

un-con-fined (un-kon-fīnd'), a. Not confined; unrestricted; broad; unrestrained; free.

un-con-firmed (un-kon-fèrmd'), a. Not confirmed; without confirmation.

un-con-form-a-ble (un-kon-fôr'ma-bl), a. Not conformable; not conforming.—**un-con-form'a-bly**, adv.

un-con-for-mi-ty (un-kon-fôr'mi-ti), n. Lack of conformity; incongruity; inconsistency.

un-con-geal (un-kon-jēl'), v. i. To thaw; melt.

un-con-ge-nial (un-kon-jē'nial), a. Not congenial.

un-con-nect-ed (un-ko-nek'ted), a. Not connected; separate; distinct; disconnected; incoherent.

un-con-quer-a-ble (un-kong'kèr-a-bl), a. Not conquerable; invincible; indomitable; incapable of being mastered or brought under control (as, an unconquerable temper).—**un-con'quer-a-ble-ness**, n.—**un-con'quer-a-bly**, adv.—**un-con'quered**, a. Not conquered; not vanquished or subdued.

un-con-scion-a-ble (un-kon'shon-a-bl), a. Not conscionable; not guided by conscience, or unscrupulous (as, "Your friend is an unconscionable dog": Sheridan's "School for Scandal," iii. 1); showing no regard for conscience, or not in accordance with what is just or reasonable (as, unconscionable behavior); unreasonably great, or inordinate, immoderate, or excessive (as, "the unconscionable height of the houses," Smollett's "Humphry Clinker," July 18; "I have paid you an unconscionable visit," Mrs. H. Ward's "Robert Elsmere," vi.).—**un-con'scion-a-ble-ness**, n.—**un-con'scion-a-bly**, adv.

un-con-scious (un-kon'shus), a. Not conscious; not aware of something (as, "I am unconscious of any circumstance . . . that can authorise such a suspicion": Scott's "Black Dwarf," xii.); not endowed with consciousness, or knowledge of one's own existence, etc.; temporarily devoid of consciousness, or not having the mental faculties awake; not known to or perceived by one's self (as, an unconscious mistake); unintentional (as, an unconscious slight).—**un-con'scious-ly**, adv.—**un-con'scious-ness**, n.

un-con-se-crat-ed (un-kon'sē-krā-ted), a. Not consecrated.

un-con-sid-ered (un-kon-sid'èrd), a. Not considered; not reflected on; not taken into consideration; not esteemed; also, unaccompanied by consideration or intention (as, "his own act of cool, nonchalant, unconsidered courage in a crisis": Arnold Bennett's "Clayhanger," i. 13).

un-con-stant (un-kon'stant), a. Inconstant.

un-con-sti-tu-tion-al (un-kon-sti-tū'shon-al), a. Not constitutional; unauthorized by or inconsistent with the constitution, as of a country.—**un-con-sti-tu-tion-al'i-ty** (-al'i-ti), n.—**un-con-sti-tu'tion-al-ly**, adv.

un-con-strained (un-kon-strānd'), a. Not constrained; not acting or done under compulsion; not subject to restraint (as, unconstrained freedom); free from constraint or embarrassment, or easy or unembarrassed (as, "Maggie's manner . . . had been as unconstrained and indifferent as ever": George Eliot's "Mill on the Floss," v. 4).—**un-con-strain'ed-ly**, adv.—**un-con-straint'**, n. Freedom from constraint; ease.

un-con-test-ed (un-kon-tes'ted), a. Not contested or disputed; hence, indisputable; evident.

un-con-tra-dict-ed (un-kon-tra-dik'ted), a. Not contradicted or denied.

un-con-trol-la-ble (un-kon-trō'la-bl), a. Not controllable; ungovernable.—**un-con-trol'la-ble-ness**, n.—**un-con-trol'la-bly**, adv.—**un-con-trolled'**, a. Not controlled, checked, or governed.—**un-con-trol'led-ly** (-trō'led-li), adv.

un-con-ven-tion-al (un-kon-ven'shon-al), a. Not conventional; not bound by or conforming to convention, rule, or precedent; free from conventionality.—**un-con-ven-tion-al'i-ty** (-al'i-ti), n.; pl. -ties (-tiz). The character of being unconventional; freedom from rules and precedents; originality; also, something unconventional; an unconventional act (as, "a girl . . . who would shrink from no unconventionality in the pursuit of truth": Arnold Bennett's "Clayhanger," ii. 9).—**un-con-ven'tion-al-ly**, adv.

un-con-vert-ed (un-kon-vèr'ted), a. Not converted.

un-con-vin-cing (un-kon-vin'sing), a. Not convincing.—**un-con-vin'cing-ly**, adv.

un-cooked (un-kūkt'), a. Not cooked; raw.

un-cork (un-kôrk'), v. t. To draw the cork from.

un-cor-rect-ed (un-ko-rek'ted), a. Not corrected.

un-cor-rob-o-rat-ed (un-ko-rob'ō-rā-ted), a. Not corroborated; unconfirmed.

un-count-ed (un-koun'ted), a. Not counted; hence, innumerable.

un-coup-le (un-kup'l), v. t. To undo the coupling of; disconnect.

un-cour-te-ous (un-kèr'tē-us or, chiefly Brit., -kôr'tyus), a. Not courteous; uncivil; discourteous.—**un-cour'te-ous-ly**, adv.

un-court-ly (un-kôrt'li), a. Not courtly; rude.—**un-court'li-ness**, n.

un-couth (un-kōth'), a. [AS. uncúth, < un- (see un-¹) + cúth, known: see couth.] Unknown†; unfamiliar, unaccustomed, or unfrequented, as a path, place, etc. (now rare); also, unusual or strange; esp., unusual and unpleasant, as sights, sounds, occurrences, etc. (as, "shrill, uncouth, and dissonant tones": Scott's "Black Dwarf," iii.); strange and alarming, or uncanny (as, "How often did he . . . dread to look over his shoulder, lest he should behold some uncouth being tramping close behind him!" Irving's "Sketch-Book," Sleepy Hollow); also, wild, rough, or desolate (as, "this uncouth forest," Shakspere's "As You Like It," ii. 6. 6; uncouth mountains or deserts); also, of a strange and ungraceful or clumsy appearance, form, or kind (as, uncouth armor or dress; "Jethro Bass, rugged, uncouth, in rawhide boots and swallowtail and coonskin cap," W. Churchill's "Coniston," ii. 2; "His face . . . was uncouth and coarse," Maugham's "Moon and Sixpence," xii.); awkward, clumsy, or unmannerly, as persons, behavior, actions, etc. (as, "a raw, uncouth sort of young man," Bulwer-Lytton's "Pelham," iii.; "Cromwell . . . played uncouth practical jokes with them," Morley's "Oliver Cromwell," iii. 2); also, crude, rude, or inelegant, as language, etc. (as, uncouth rimes; "Her Merrimacs and Agiochooks And many a name uncouth," Lowell's "To Whittier").—**un-couth'ly**, adv.—**un-couth'ness**, n.

un-cov-e-nant-ed (un-kuv'ē-nan-ted), a. Not covenanted; not agreed to or promised by covenant; also, not having joined in a covenant.

un-cov-er (un-kuv'èr), v. I. tr. To remove the cover or covering from; divest of the hat or other head-covering; fig., to lay bare; disclose; reveal. II. intr. To remove a cover or covering; take off one's hat or other head-covering, as in respect.

un-cov-ered (un-kuv'èrd), a. Not covered; having no cover or covering; having the head bare; not protected by security, as a note.

un-cre-ate (un-krē-āt'), v. t. To undo the creation of; deprive of existence.

un-cre-at-ed (un-krē-ā'ted), a. Not created; not brought into existence; also, existing without having been created; self-existent.

un-crit-i-cal (un-krit'i-kal), a. Not critical; not in accordance with the rules of just criticism (as, an uncritical estimate); lacking in acuteness of judgment or critical analysis (as, an uncritical audience; an uncritical reader).—**un-crit'i-cal-ly**, adv.

un-cross (un-krôs'), v. t. To change from a crossed position: as, "He uncrossed his legs" (C. Brontë's "Jane Eyre," xxxiii.).

un-crown (un-kroun'), v. t. To deprive or divest of a crown; degrade from royal dignity; reduce from any high dignity or preëminence.

un-crowned (un-kround'), a. Not crowned; not having yet assumed the crown; also, having royal rank or power without occupying the royal office.

unc-tion (ungk'shọn), *n.* [= F. *onction*, < L. *unctio(n-)*, an anointing, an ointment, < *ungere*, *unguere*, smear, anoint: cf. *unguent* and *ointment*.] The act of anointing, esp. for medical purposes or as a religious rite (as, "the *unction* which had been instituted for the kings of Israel": G. P. R. James's "Hist. of Charlemagne," i.); fig., the shedding of a divine or spiritual influence upon a person, or the influence shed; also, that which is applied or used in anointing; an unguent or ointment (as, "greasy *unctions*, which . . . saturated the pores of the skin": Sterne's "Tristram Shandy," v. 35); the oil used in religious rites, as in anointing the sick or dying (as, "The priests . . . had just anointed his dying head with the sacred *unction*": Jane Porter's "Scottish Chiefs," lv.); fig., something soothing or comforting, as a soothing thought (as, "Lay not that flattering *unction* to your soul, That not your trespass, but my madness speaks": Shakspere's "Hamlet," iii. 4. 145); also, a soothing, sympathetic, and persuasive quality in discourse, esp. on religious subjects; moving or appealing force in public delivery; often, a professional, conventional, or affected earnestness or fervor in utterance (as, "a voice to whose natural heavy resonance professional duty had added a certain *unction*," Galsworthy's "Saint's Progress," iii. 6; "Mrs. Fleming . . . read, with the emphasis and the *unction* peculiar to a certain type of revivalism," Mrs. H. Ward's "Robert Elsmere," vi.); in general, fervor or gusto in speech or statement (as, "Other historians of equal veracity, but less *unction*, agree . . . ," Irving's "Conquest of Granada," xxvi.; "I have heard you . . . describe the scene with comic *unction*," Scott's "Guy Mannering," xvi.).—**extreme unction**, in the *Rom. Cath. Ch.*, a sacrament administered by a priest, in which a person who is dangerously sick or injured is anointed with oil.

unc-tu-ous (ungk'tū-us), *a.* [= F. *onctueux*, < ML. *unctuosus*, < L. *unctum*, ointment, < *ungere*: see *unction*.] Of the nature of, resembling, or characteristic of an unguent or ointment; oily; greasy; having an oily or soapy feel, as certain minerals; fig., characterized by religious unction or fervor, esp. of a merely professional or affected kind (as, an *unctuous* preacher); smug; excessively smooth, suave, or bland.—**unc-tu-os'i-ty** (-os'i-ti), **unc'tu-ous-ness**, *n.*—**unc'tu-ous-ly**, *adv.*

un-cul-ti-vat-ed (un-kul'ti-vā-ted), *a.* Not cultivated; fallow; wild; unrefined; rude; undeveloped.

un-cul-tured (un-kul'tụrd), *a.* Not cultured.

un-curl (un-kėrl'), *v. t.* or *i.* To change from a curled condition or form; straighten out, as something curled.

un-cus (ung'kus), *n.*; pl. *-ci* (-sī). [L., hook.] In *zoöl.*, *bot.*, etc., a hook-like part or process.

un-cut (un-kut'), *a.* Not cut; esp., of books, not having the leaves cut open; also, specif., not having the margins cut down.

un-dam-aged (un-dam'ājd), *a.* Not damaged.

un-damped (un-dampt'), *a.* Not damped; not moistened; not deadened; not checked or retarded in action; not depressed or discouraged; in *elect.*, etc., not reduced gradually in amplitude, as oscillations or waves (see phrases following, and cf. *damped*).—**undamped oscillations**, in *elect.*, oscillations (consecutive flows of electricity first in one direction and then in the other) which are not damped, or not broken up into trains of damped oscillations. Such oscillations include those of the ordinary alternating current and follow one another without any interval of time between, and when occurring in the antenna of a wireless transmitting apparatus give rise to continuous waves in the ether. See *continuous waves*, under *continuous*.—**undamped waves**, in *wireless teleg.* and *teleph.*, electric waves which are not damped, or not broken up into damped wave-trains; continuous waves. See *continuous waves*, under *continuous*, and cf. *damped wave-train*, under *damped*.

un-date (un'dāt), *a.* [L. *undatus*, pp. of *undare*, wave, < *unda*, a wave.] In *bot.*, waved; undulate.

un-dat-ed (un-dā'ted), *a.* Not dated; not marked with a date, as a letter.

un-daunt-ed (un-dân'ted or -dän'ted), *a.* Not daunted; not intimidated or discouraged; fearless; intrepid; undismayed: as, an *undaunted* leader; *undaunted* courage.—**un-daunt'ed-ly**, *adv.*—**un-daunt'ed-ness**, *n.*

un-dé (un'dā), *a.* [F. *ondé*, < L. *undatus*, pp.: see *undate*.] In *her.*, wavy.

un-dec-a-gon (un-dek'ạ-gon), *n.* [Irreg. < L. *undecim*, eleven, + Gr. γωνία, angle.] A plane figure having eleven angles and eleven sides.

A Fesse Undé.

un-de-ceive (un-dē-sēv'), *v. t.* To free from deception, fallacy, or mistake.

un-de-cen-na-ry (un-dē-sen'ạ-ri), *a.* Same as *undecennial*.

un-de-cen-ni-al (un-dē-sen'i-al), *a.* [L. *undecim*, eleven, + *annus*, year: cf. *decennial*.] Of or pertaining to a period of eleven years; occurring or observed every eleven years.

un-de-cid-ed (un-dē-sī'ded), *a.* Not decided or determined; not settled; also, not having one's mind made up or one's purpose fixed; irresolute.—**un-de-cid'ed-ly**, *adv.*—**un-de-cid'ed-ness**, *n.*

un-de-ci-pher-a-ble (un-dē-sī'fẻr-ạ-bl), *a.* Indecipherable.

un-de-fend-ed (un-dē-fen'ded), *a.* Not defended; unprotected; not assisted by legal defense, as a prisoner; not contested, as a suit at law.

un-de-filed (un-dē-fīld'), *a.* Not defiled or polluted.

un-de-fin-a-ble (un-dē-fī'nạ-bl), *a.* Indefinable.—**un-de-fined'**, *a.* Not defined; not definitely limited; indefinite; not described by definition or explanation; not explained.

un-dem-o-crat-ic (un-dem-ọ-krat'ik), *a.* Not democratic; not in accordance with the principles of democracy.

un-de-mon-stra-tive (un-dē-mon'strā-tiv), *a.* Not demonstrative; not given to or characterized by open display or expression of the feelings, etc.; reserved.—**un-de-mon'-stra-tive-ly**, *adv.*—**un-de-mon'stra-tive-ness**, *n.*

un-de-ni-a-ble (un-dē-nī'ạ-bl), *a.* Not to be denied or refuted; indisputable (as, "I seem to see an *undeniable* vestige of truth in that exaggerated view": J. Conrad's "Lord Jim," xiv.); also, that cannot be refused; admitting of or accepting no denial; also, undeniably or unquestionably good; unexceptionable.—**un-de-ni'a-ble-ness**, *n.*—**un-de-ni'a-bly**, *adv.*

un-de-nom-i-na-tion-al (un-dē-nom-i-nā'shọn-ạl), *a.* Not denominational; not connected with or restricted to a particular denomination or group of denominations.

un-de-pend-a-ble (un-dē-pen'dạ-bl), *a.* Not dependable; unreliable; untrustworthy.—**un-de-pend-a-bil'i-ty** (-bil'i-ti), **un-de-pend'a-ble-ness**, *n.*

un-der (un'dẻr), *prep.* [AS. *under* = D. *onder* = G. *unter* = Icel. *undir* = Goth. *undar*, under: cf. Skt. *adhara*, lower, *adhas*, below, L. *inferior*, lower, *infra*, below.] Beneath and covered by, whether in immediate contact or not (as, *under* a paper-weight; *under* a table or a tree); below the surface of (as, *under* the ground; *under* water); at a point or position lower than or further down than (as, to hit a man *under* the belt); in the position or state of bearing or supporting, or of sustaining, undergoing, or the like (as, to sink *under* a load; to be *under* heavy expense; *under* fire of the enemy; a matter *under* consideration); beneath (a head, heading, or the like), as in classification; as designated, indicated, or represented by (as, *under* a new name; *under* false colors; *under* the guise of friendship; *under* a show or pretense of submission); below in degree, amount, price, etc., or less than (as, *under* age; *under* 10 pounds; *under* $20); below in rank, dignity, or the like (as, any nobleman *under* a duke); subject to the rule, direction, guidance, etc., of (as, France *under* Napoleon; to serve *under* Wellington; *under* supervision or surveillance; *under* orders); subject to the influence, conditioning force, etc., of (as, *under* an impression; *under* promise of secrecy; *under* these circumstances); with the favor or aid of (as, *under* protection); authorized, warranted, or attested by (as, *under* one's hand or seal); in accordance with (as, *under* the provisions of a legislative act).—**under one's nose.** See under *nose*, *n.*—**under the rose.** See under *rose*[2], *n.*—**under the sun.** See under *sun*[2], *n.*—**under the thumb of.** See under *thumb*, *n.*—**under way.** See under *way*[2].—**un'der**, *adv.* Under or beneath something; beneath the surface, as of the water (as, to go *under*, fig., to fail, or succumb in a struggle); in a lower place; in a lower degree, amount, etc.; in a subordinate position or condition; in or into subjection or submission (as, "I keep *under* my body, and bring it into subjection": 1 Cor. ix. 27).—**un'der**, *a.* Situated beneath (as, "a species of tyrant-bird . . . with a brown back and sulphur-yellow *under* parts": W. H. Hudson's "Far Away and Long Ago," viii.); lower in position; also, lower in degree, amount, etc.; also, lower in rank or condition (as, "I lived along with the Champernownes as *under* house-maid": Eden Phillpotts's "Children of Men," i. 6); subordinate; inferior.—**the under dog,** the dog borne down by an adversary in a dog-fight; fig., one borne down or worsted in any struggle; the downtrodden victim of oppression. [Colloq.]

under-. Prefixal use of *under, prep., adv.,* or *a.,* in various senses, as to indicate situation or place below or beneath, as in *underbrush, underclothes, underlie, undertow,* lower grade or rank, as in *under-bailiff, under-butler, understudy, undertenant,* or lesser degree, extent, or amount, as in *underproof, undersell, undersized,* and hence insufficiency, as in *underfeed, understock, undervalue.* Cf. *over-.*

un-der-act (un-dėr-akt′), *v. t.* or *i.* To act or perform inadequately, or without sufficient energy or force: as, "The play was so *under-acted* by the people engaged in it, that it broke down under their weight": Macready's "Diaries," Nov. 22, 1847, in his "Reminiscences").

un-der-arm (un′dėr-ärm), *a.* Under the arm (as, an *under-arm* seam of a garment); in *cricket,* etc., executed or delivered with the hand below the shoulder; using underhand bowling.

un-der-bid (un-dėr-bid′), *v. t.;* pret. *-bid,* pp. *-bidden* or *-bid,* ppr. *-bidding.* To make a lower bid than (another), as in seeking a contract to be awarded to the lowest bidder.

un-der-bill (un-dėr-bil′), *v. t.* To bill at less than the actual amount or value.

un-der-bod-ice (un′dėr-bod″is), *n.* A bodice worn under an outer bodice.

un-der-bred (un-dėr-bred′), *a.* Of inferior breeding or manners (as, "a pert little obtrusive, *under-bred* creature": Thackeray's "Newcomes," xxiii.); vulgar; showing lack of good breeding, as manners or conduct; also, not of pure breed, as a horse or a dog.

un-der-brush (un′dėr-brush), *n.* Shrubs, small trees, etc., growing under large trees in a wood or forest.

un-der-buy (un-dėr-bī′), *v. t.; -bought, -buying.* To buy at less than the actual value; also, to buy more cheaply than (another).

un-der-car-riage (un′dėr-kar″āj), *n.* The supporting framework beneath the body of a carriage, etc.; in *aëronautics,* the portions of an aëroplane beneath the body, serving as a support when on the ground or water or when alighting.

un-der-charge (un-dėr-chärj′), *v. t.* To put an insufficient charge or load into; also, to charge (a person, etc.) less than the proper price or a fair price; charge (so much) less than such a price.—**un′der-charge,** *n.* An insufficient charge or load; also, a charge or price less than is proper or fair.

un-der-clothes (un′dėr-klōꬸz), *n. pl.* Clothes worn under outer clothes, esp. those worn next the skin. Also **un′der-cloth″ing** (-klō″ꬸing).

un-der-croft (un′dėr-krôft), *n.* [From *under-* + archaic *croft,* vault, < L. *crypta,* E. *crypt.*] A vault or chamber under the ground; the crypt of a church.

un-der-cur-rent (un′dėr-kur″ent), *n.* A current below the upper or superficial currents, or below the surface, of a body of water, air, etc.; fig., an underlying tendency more or less different from what is visible or apparent (as, "a man in whom the habitual *undercurrent* of thought was melancholy": Charnwood's "Abraham Lincoln," iv.).

un-der-cut (un-dėr-kut′), *v. t.; -cut, -cutting.* To cut under or beneath; cut away material from so as to leave a portion overhanging, as in carving or sculpture.—**un′der-cut,** *p. a.* Cut away underneath.—**un′der-cut,** *n.* A cut, or a cutting away, underneath; a notch cut in a tree to determine the direction in which the tree is to fall and to prevent splitting; also, the tenderloin or fillet of beef.

un-der-do (un-dėr-dö′), *v. t.* or *i.;* pret. *-did,* pp. *-done,* ppr. *-doing.* To do less thoroughly, or do less, than is usual or requisite.—**un-der-done** (un-dėr-dun′ or un′dėr-dun), *p. a.* Of food, not thoroughly cooked.

un-der-dose (un′dėr-dōs), *n.* An insufficient dose.—**un-der-dose′,** *v. t.* To dose insufficiently; give too small a dose to.

un-der-drain (un-dėr-drān′), *v. t.* To drain by means of

drains placed under the ground.—**un′der-drain,** *n.* A drain placed under the ground.—**un′der-drain″age** (-āj), *n.*

un-der-dress (un′dėr-dres), *n.* A plain dress worn under an overdress or outer drapery; a slip.

un-der-driv-en (un′dėr-driv″n), *a.* In *mach.,* noting or pertaining to a driving mechanism in which the power is applied below the place where the work is done. Cf. *overdriven.*

un-der-es-ti-mate (un-dėr-es′ti-māt), *v. t.* To estimate at too low a value, amount, rate, or the like: as, "In the latter half of the nineteenth century . . . there was a tendency to *underestimate* the power of human endurance" (Buchan's "Hist. of the Great War," liii.).—**un-der-es′ti-mate** (-māt), *n.* An estimate that is too low.—**un″der-es-ti-ma′tion** (-mā′shon), *n.*

un-der-ex-pose (un″dėr-eks-pōz′), *v. t.* To expose to light for too short a time, as in photography.—**un″der-ex-po′sure** (-pō′zhụr), *n.*

un-der-feed (un-dėr-fēd′), *v. t.* or *i.; -fed, -feeding.* To feed insufficiently: as, "An *under-fed* nation is incapable of the endurance required of first-class soldiers" (W. R. Inge's "Outspoken Essays," i. 4).

un-der-foot (un-dėr-fut′), *adv.* Under the foot or feet; on the ground; underneath or below.—**un′der-foot′,** *a.* Lying under the foot or feet; hence, abject or downtrodden (as, "my Schoolmaster, a downbent, brokenhearted, *underfoot* martyr": Carlyle's "Sartor Resartus," ii. 3).

un-der-fur (un′dėr-fėr), *n.* The fur, or fine, soft, thick, hairy coating, underlying the longer and coarser outer hair in certain animals, as seals, otters, and beavers.

un-der-gar-ment (un′dėr-gär″ment), *n.* A garment worn under another garment, esp. next the skin.

un-der-gird (un-dėr-gėrd′), *v. t.* To support or secure by a rope or the like passed beneath. See Acts, xxvii. 17.

un-der-glaze (un′dėr-glāz), *a.* In *ceram.,* applied before the glaze is put on, as decoration or colors in porcelain painting.

un-der-go (un-dėr-gō′), *v. t.;* pret. *-went,* pp. *-gone,* ppr. *-going.* [AS. *undergān.*] To go or pass under or beneath† (as, "Better my shoulders *underwent* the earth, than thy decease": Chapman's tr. Homer's "Iliad," vi.); also, to be subjected to (as, "My uncle's correspondence *underwent* an exhaustive process of pruning and digestion before it reached him": H. G. Wells's "Tono-Bungay," iii. 1. § 3); experience; pass through (as, "The bounties upon the importation of tar, pitch, and turpentine *underwent* . . . several alterations": Adam Smith's "Wealth of Nations," iv. 8); endure, sustain, or suffer (as, "the irritation which my nerves had *undergone*": G. MacDonald's "Annals of a Quiet Neighbourhood," v.); also, to enjoy† (as, "to *undergo* such ample grace and honour": Shakspere's "Measure for Measure," i. 1. 24); also, to undertake† (as, "to *undergo* . . . an enterprise": Shakspere's "Julius Cæsar," i. 3. 123); perform† or discharge†.

un-der-grad-u-ate (un-dėr-grad′ū-āt). **I.** *n.* A member of a university or college who has not taken his first degree; a student in any school who has not completed his course. **II.** *a.* Having the standing of an undergraduate; also, pertaining to an undergraduate or undergraduates; characteristic of undergraduates; consisting of undergraduates.— **un-der-grad′u-ate-ship,** *n.*

un-der-ground (un-dėr-ground′), *adv.* Beneath the surface of the ground; fig., in concealment or secrecy; not openly.— **un′der-ground,** *a.* Existing, situated, operating, or taking place beneath the surface of the ground; used, or for use, underground; fig., hidden or secret; not open.—**underground railroad,** a railroad running through a continuous tunnel, as under the streets of a city (also called *underground railway*); also, in *U. S. hist.,* before the abolition of slavery, a secret arrangement among certain opponents of slavery for helping fugitive slaves to escape into Canada or some other place of safety.—**un′der-ground,** *n.* The place or region beneath the surface of the ground; the lower world; also, an underground space or passage; also, an underground railroad.

un-der-grown (un′dėr-grōn′), *a.* Not fully grown; of low stature.

un-der-growth (un′dėr-grōth), *n.* That which grows under; short, fine hair underlying longer outer hair on a skin; esp., shrubs or small trees growing beneath or among large trees; also, the condition of being undergrown or undersized.

un-der-hand (un'dėr-hand). **I.** *adv.* With the hand under the object; with the knuckles downward; also, with the hand below the shoulder, as in pitching or bowling a ball; also, secretly; stealthily; slyly; not openly or aboveboard. **II.** *a.* Done or delivered underhand (as, *underhand* pitching or bowling); using underhand bowling; also, secret or covert; not open; esp., secret and crafty or dishonorable.— **un-der-hand′ed**, *a.* Underhand; also, short-handed.— **un-der-hand′ed-ly**, *adv.*—**un-der-hand′ed-ness**, *n.*

un-der-hung (un'dėr-hung), *a.* Resting on a track beneath, instead of being overhung, as a sliding door; also, of the under jaw, projecting beyond the upper jaw; having the under jaw so projecting (as, "His mouth was *underhung*, giving him a pugnacious . . . appearance," Eden Phillpotts's "Red Redmaynes," iv.: cf. *undershot*).

un-der-lay (un-dėr-lā′), *v. t.*; *-laid, -laying.* To lay (one thing) under or beneath another; also, to provide with something laid underneath; raise or support with something laid underneath.— **un'der-lay**, *n.* Something underlaid; in *printing*, a piece or pieces of paper put under types, etc., to bring them to the proper height for printing.

un-der-lease (un'dėr-lēs), *n.* A lease granted by a lessee, esp. for a shorter term than he himself holds, or, sometimes, for only a part of the premises.

un-der-let (un-dėr-let′), *v. t.*; *-let, -letting.* To let below the true value; also, to grant an underlease of; sublet.

un-der-lie (un-dėr-lī′), *v. t.*; pret. *-lay,* pp. *-lain,* ppr. *-lying.* To lie under or beneath; be situated under; hence, to be at the basis of; form the foundation of; also, to be subjected to; undergo.

un-der-line (un-dėr-līn′), *v. t.* To mark with a line or lines underneath, as words in a manuscript; underscore.

un-der-lin-en (un'dėr-lin″en), *n.* Linen (or cotton) undergarments.

un-der-ling (un'dėr-ling), *n.* [Late AS. *underling.*] A subordinate (esp. in disparagement); an understrapper; an inferior (as, "The fault . . . is . . . in ourselves, that we are *underlings*": Shakspere's "Julius Cæsar," i. 2. 141).

un-der-load (un-dėr-lōd′), *v. t.* To put an insufficient load on or in.

un-der-ly-ing (un-dėr-lī′ing), *p. a.* Lying under or beneath; supporting; fundamental; also, of a mortgage, etc., anterior and prior in claim to another one.

un-der-man (un-dėr-man′), *v. t.*; *-manned, -manning.* To furnish with an insufficient number of men: as, "Our merchant ships are always *under-manned*" (Dana's "Two Years before the Mast," xxxi.).

un-der-mine (un-dėr-mīn′), *v. t.* To form a mine or passage under, as in military operations; sap; make an excavation under; work a way under and wear away the foundations of (as, a river *undermines* its banks; "the waves having so far *undermined* the cliff, as to leave a projection," Cooper's "Two Admirals," ii.); render unstable by digging into or wearing away the foundations; also, fig., to affect injuriously or weaken by secret or underhand means (as, to *undermine* one's credit); weaken or destroy insidiously or gradually (as, "Years advancing *undermined* his health": Crabbe's "Tales," ii.).— **un-der-min′er** (-mī′nėr), *n.*

un-der-most (un'dėr-mōst), *a.* and *adv. superl.* Lowest.

un-der-neath (un-dėr-nēth′). [AS. *underneothan,* < *under,* under, + *neothan,* below: see *beneath.*] **I.** *adv.* Beneath; below: as, "as if something was pushing *underneath*" (Jefferies's "Gamekeeper at Home," v.). **II.** *prep.* Under; beneath: as, "The strawberry grows *underneath* the nettle" (Shakspere's "Henry V.," i. 60).

un-der-of-fi-cer (un-dėr-of′i-sėr), *v. t.* To furnish inadequately with officers.

un-der-pass (un'dėr-pås), *n.* A passage running underneath; esp., a passage for pedestrians or vehicles, or both, crossing under a railway, road, etc.

un-der-pay (un-dėr-pā′), *v. t.*; *-paid, -paying.* To pay insufficiently.

un-der-pin (un-dėr-pin′), *v. t.*; *-pinned, -pinning.* To pin or support underneath; place something under for support or foundation; support with masonry, stones, etc., as a building; in general, to support; prop.— **un'der-pin″ning**, *n.*

A support or structure used to underpin a building, etc.; esp., a temporary or permanent structure introduced for support beneath a wall, etc., previously constructed.

un-der-plant (un-dėr-plant′), *v. t.* In *forestry,* to plant (young trees) under an existing stand of trees.

un-der-plot (un'dėr-plot), *n.* A plot subordinate to another plot, as in a play or novel; also, an underhand scheme; a trick.

un-der-pop-u-lat-ed (un-dėr-pop′ū-lā-ted), *a.* Not sufficiently or well populated; having too small a population: as, "England was for a short time *under-populated*" (W. R. Inge's "Outspoken Essays," i. 4).

un-der-pro-duc-tion (un″dėr-prọ-duk′shọn), *n.* Production that is less than normal, or inadequate to the demand.

un-der-proof (un'dėr-pröf), *a.* Containing a smaller proportion of alcohol than proof-spirit does.

un-der-prop (un-dėr-prop′), *v. t.*; *-propped, -propping.* To prop underneath; support; uphold.

un-der-quote (un-dėr-kwōt′), *v. t.* To quote at a price below another price or the market price; also, to quote lower prices than (another).

un-der-rate (un-dėr-rāt′), *v. t.* To rate too low; underestimate: as, "You *underrate* . . . your own powers" (Kingsley's "Alton Locke," xl.).

un-der-run (un-dėr-run′), *v. t.*; pret. *-ran,* pp. *-run,* ppr. *-running.* To run, pass, or go under (something): as, to *underrun* a cable (to pass under it in a boat, as for the purpose of examining it); "*Underrunning* a trawl means pulling it in on one side of the dory, picking off the fish, rebaiting the hooks, and passing them back to the sea again" (Kipling's "Captains Courageous," iv.).— **un'der-run**, *n.* That which runs or passes underneath, as an undercurrent.

un-der-score (un-dėr-skōr′), *v. t.* To mark with a line or lines underneath; underline.— **un'der-score**, *n.* A line drawn beneath something written or printed, as for emphasis.

un-der-sea (un'dėr-sē), *a.* Submarine: as, an *undersea* boat. Also **un'der-seas.**

un-der-sec-re-ta-ry (un'dėr-sek′rẹ-tạ-ri), *n.* A secretary subordinate to a principal secretary.— **un'der-sec′re-ta-ry-ship,** *n.*

un-der-sell (un-dėr-sel′), *v. t.*; *-sold, -selling.* To sell for less than the actual value (obs. or rare); also, to sell things at a lower price than (as, "There are too many people in trade . . . they are all trying to *undersell* each other": Besant's "All Sorts and Conditions of Men," vii.).— **un-der-sell′er,** *n.*

un-der-set (un-dėr-set′), *v. t.*; *-set, -setting.* To provide or support with something set beneath; underpin; prop; also, to set (a thing) under something else.— **un'der-set,** *n. Naut.,* an undercurrent.— **un-der-set′ter,** *n.*

un-der-shap-en (un'dėr-shā″pn), *a.* Undersized; dwarfish. See Tennyson's "Marriage of Geraint," 412. [Poetic.]

un-der-sher-iff (un'dėr-sher′if), *n.* A sheriff's deputy; esp., a deputy on whom the sheriff's duties devolve when the sheriff is incapacitated or when the office is vacant.

un-der-shirt (un'dėr-shėrt), *n.* An inner shirt, worn next to the skin.

un-der-shot (un'dėr-shot), *a.* Having the lower incisor teeth projecting beyond the upper ones when the mouth is closed, as a dog; underhung; also, driven by water passing beneath, as a kind of vertical water-wheel.

un-der-shrub (un'dėr-shrub), *n.* A low shrub.

un-der-sign (un-dėr-sīn′), *v. t.* To sign one's name under, or at the end of (a letter or document); affix one's signature to.— **un'der-signed,** *a.* Signed, as a name, or having signed, as a person, at the end of a letter or document.— **the undersigned,** the person or persons undersigning a letter or document.

un-der-sized (un'dėr-sīzd), *a.* Below the usual size: as, "pallid, *undersized* men" (George Eliot's "Silas Marner," i.).

un-der-skirt (un'dėr-skėrt), *n.* A skirt worn under an outer skirt or under an overskirt or drapery.

un-der-sleeve (un'dėr-slēv), *n.* A sleeve worn under an outer sleeve; esp., an ornamental inner sleeve extending below the outer sleeve.

un-der-soil (un'dėr-soil), *n.* Subsoil.

un-der-song (un'dėr-sông), *n.* The accompaniment of a song; a subordinate strain; fig., an underlying meaning.

---

fat, fāte, fär, fåll, åsk, fāre; net, mē, hèr; pin, pīne; not, nōte, mȯve, nȯr; up, lūte, pu̇ll; oi, oil; ou, out; (lightened) aviạry, ẹlect, agọny, intọ, ụnite; (obscured) errạnt, oper␣, ardẹnt, actọr, natụre; ch, chip; g, go; th, thin; ᴛH, then; y, you;

un-der-stand (un-dėr-stand′), v.; -stood (archaic pp. also -standed), -standing. [AS. understandan.] **I.** tr. To perceive the meaning of, grasp the idea of, or comprehend (as, "Now clear I understand What oft my steadiest thoughts have search'd in vain": Milton's "Paradise Lost," xii. 376); be thoroughly acquainted or familiar with, as a subject, art, etc.; apprehend clearly the character or nature of, as a person; comprehend by knowing the meaning of the words employed, as a language; grasp the meaning of (a person), as by knowing the significance of the words used (as, "Their speech had differing dialects, so that they did not understand one another": Defoe's "Captain Singleton," v.); also, to grasp clearly as a fact, or realize (as, "They understood not that he spake to them of the Father": John, viii. 27); also, to take as a fact, or as settled (as, it is understood between us that you will come); also, to get knowledge of; come to know; learn or hear; also, to accept as a fact, or believe (as, "It was pretty well understood that the outgoing premier had made his selection": Trollope's "Barchester Towers," i.); also, to conceive the meaning of in a particular way (as, you are to understand the phrase literally); take in a particular sense; also, to take as meant (as, "What must we understand by this?" Shakspere's "As You Like It," iv. 3. 95); also, to recognize as meant although not expressed; supply mentally, as a word necessary to complete sense; also, to stand under or support (humorous: as, "My legs do better understand me, sir, than I understand what you mean," Shakspere's "Twelfth Night," iii. 1. 89). **II.** intr. To have the use of the intellectual faculties; also, to perceive what is meant (as, "He smiled and left his sentence unfinished, and she smiled back at him to show she understood": H. G. Wells's "Soul of a Bishop," viii.); also, to have information or knowledge about something (as, to understand about a matter); also, to be informed; believe. —**un-der-stand′a-ble,** a. That may be understood.— **un-der-stand′ing,** n. The act of one who understands; comprehension; personal interpretation; also, the knowing power, in general; intelligence; wit; often, superior intelligence, or superior power of recognizing truth (as, men of understanding); also, in philosophical use, the power of abstract thought; the logical power; also, a mutual comprehension of each other's meaning, thoughts, etc. (as, you and I must have an understanding before going any further); a state of (good or friendly) relations between persons; a mutual agreement of a private or unannounced kind.— **un-der-stand′ing,** p. a. That understands; possessing or showing intelligence or understanding.—**un-der-stand′-ing-ly,** adv.
un-der-state (un-dėr-stāt′), v. t. To state or represent less strongly than the truth will admit; state too low.—**un-der-state′ment,** n.
un-der-stock (un-dėr-stok′), v. t. To supply insufficiently with stock.
un-der-stood (un-dėr-stůd′). Pret. and pp. of understand.
un-der-strap-per (un′dėr-strap″ėr), n. An inferior agent or assistant; an underling.
un-der-stra-tum (un′dėr-strā″tum), n.; pl. -ta (-tä) or -tums. A substratum.
un-der-stud-y (un′dėr-stud″i), v. t. To study (a part) in order to replace the regular actor or actress when necessary; also, to act as understudy to (an actor or actress: as, "I understudied Mrs. Margetson," L. Merrick's "Actor-Manager," i.).—**un′der-stud″y,** n. One trained and retained to act as substitute for an actor or actress.
un-der-take (un-dėr-tāk′), v.; pret. -took, pp. -taken, ppr. -taking. **I.** tr. To take on one's self (some task, performance, etc.); take in hand; essay; attempt; also, to take on one's self by formal promise or agreement; lay one's self under obligation to perform or execute; also, to warrant or guarantee (with a clause: as, "I will undertake you shall be happy," Fielding's "Tom Jones," vi. 5); also, to take in charge, or assume the duty of attending to (a person); also, to engage with, as in a duel†; also, to assume†, or take to one's self† (as, "You are like to Sir Vincentio. His name and credit shall you undertake": Shakspere's "Taming of the Shrew," iv. 2. 106). **II.** intr. To take on one's self any task or responsibility; also, to engage one's self by a promise (for: as, "Labienus had undertaken for his comrades,"

Froude's "Cæsar," xx.); give a guarantee, or become surety (for: as, "On mine honour dare I undertake For good Lord Titus' innocence in all," Shakspere's "Titus Andronicus," i. 1. 436); also, to act as an undertaker or funeral director (colloq.).—**un-der-tak′er** (-tā′kėr), n. One who undertakes something; also (pron. un′dėr-tā-kėr), one whose business it is to prepare the dead for burial and to take charge of funerals.—**un-der-tak′ing,** n. The act of one who undertakes any task or responsibility; also, the business of an undertaker or funeral director; also, a task, enterprise, etc., undertaken (as, "My uncle engaged afterward in more prosperous undertakings": C. Brontë's "Jane Eyre," xxx.); also, a promise; a pledge; a guarantee.
un-der-ten-ant (un′dėr-ten″ant), n. A subtenant.
un-der-things (un′dėr-thingz), n. pl. Underclothes.
un-der-tone (un′dėr-tōn), n. A low or subdued tone, as of utterance (as, "He dropped his voice to a confidential undertone," H. G. Wells's "Mr. Britling," i. 1. § 9; "Some of the women . . . chatted in undertones," L. Merrick's "Actor-Manager," iii.); fig., an underlying quality or element, or an undercurrent; also, a subdued tone of color; a color seen through and giving character to some other color or colors.
un-der-took (un-dėr-tůk′). Preterit of undertake.
un-der-tow (un′dėr-tō), n. Any strong current below the surface of a body of water, moving in a direction different from that of the surface-current; specif., the backward flow or draft of the water, below the surface, from waves breaking on a beach.
un-der-trump (un-dėr-trump′), v. t. In card-playing, to trump with a lower trump than has already been played; play a lower trump than.
un-der-val-ue (un-dėr-val′ū), v. t. To value below the real worth; put too low a value on; sometimes, to diminish in value; make of less value; also, to esteem too low (as, "The Prince never committed the error of undervaluing the talents of his great adversary": Motley's "Dutch Republic," ii. 4); esteem lightly; hold in mean estimation.—**un″der-val-u-a′tion** (-ā′shọn), n.
un-der-vest (un′dėr-vest), n. An undershirt.
un-der-waist (un′dėr-wāst), n. A waist worn under another waist.
un-der-wa-ter (un′dėr-wậ″tėr), a. Being or occurring under water; designed to be used under water (as, an underwater boat, a submarine).
un-der-wear (un′dėr-wār), n. Underclothes.
un-der-went (un-dėr-went′). Preterit of undergo.
un-der-wood (un′dėr-wůd), n. Shrubs or small trees growing under larger trees (as, "The boughs of the tall trees met closely above, and the underwood filled up each interval between their trunks below": Scott's "Black Dwarf," xi.); underbrush; sometimes, a growth of underbrush.
un-der-work (un′dėr-wėrk), n. Subordinate or inferior work; also, secret or underhand work; also, a structure placed under something; a substructure.—**un-der-work′,** v.; -worked or -wrought, -working. **I.** tr. To injure or weaken by secret or insidious means†; undermine†; also, to put insufficient work or labor on (something); also, to exact insufficient work from; also, to do like work at a less price than (another). **II.** intr. To work secretly or insidiously†; also, to do less work than is required or suitable.
un-der-world (un′dėr-wėrld), n. The world below the skies; the earth; also, the opposite side of the earth or globe; the antipodes; sometimes, the part of the earth below the horizon; also, the place or region below the surface of the earth; often, the lower or nether world; Hades; also, a region or sphere below the ordinary one; esp., the lower, degraded, or criminal part of human society.
un-der-write (un-dėr-rīt′), v.; pret. -wrote, pp. -written, ppr. -writing. **I.** tr. To write (something) under a thing, esp. under other written matter; also, to sign one's name to (a document, etc.); subscribe to (a statement, etc.); specif., to write one's name at the end of (a policy of insurance, orig. marine insurance), thereby becoming liable in case of certain losses specified therein; hence, to insure; also, to assume liability to the extent of (a certain sum) by way of insurance; also, to agree to give or pay (a certain sum of money) by signing one's name; also, to agree to meet the expense of;

undertake to finance; agree to buy; specif., to guarantee the sale of (shares or bonds to be offered to the public for subscription), the guarantors engaging to purchase at a certain price (below the subscription price) any shares or bonds left unsold, and receiving on every share or bond sold the difference between that price and the subscription price. **II.** *intr.* To underwrite something; carry on the business of an underwriter.—**un′der-writ″er** (-rī″tėr), *n.* One who underwrites; specif., one who underwrites policies of insurance, or carries on insurance as a business; also, one who underwrites issues of shares or bonds.

un-der-wrought (un-dėr-rôt′). Preterit and pp. of *underwork.*

un-de-served (un-dē-zėrvd′), *a.* Not deserved or merited: as, "an *undeserved* reputation for wit" (Eden Phillpotts's "Banks of Colne," ix.); "a series of *undeserved* misfortunes" (Sheridan's "School for Scandal," iii. 1).—**un-de-serv′ed-ly,** *adv.*—**un-de-serv′er,** *n.* An undeserving person; an unworthy person.—**un-de-serv′ing,** *a.* Not deserving or meriting.—**un-de-serv′ing-ly,** *adv.*

un-de-signed (un-dē-zīnd′), *a.* Not designed; unintentional.—**un-de-sign′ed-ly,** *adv.*—**un-de-sign′ing,** *a.* Not designing; without underhand or selfish designs.

un-de-sir-a-ble (un-dē-zīr′a-bl). **I.** *a.* Not desirable; objectionable. **II.** *n.* An undesirable person or thing.—**un-de-sired′,** *a.* Not desired; unwelcome.—**un-de-sir′-ous,** *a.* Not desirous.

un-de-tect-ed (un-dē-tek′ted), *a.* Not detected; unperceived.

un-de-ter-mined (un-dē-tėr′mind), *a.* Not determined; not settled or decided; not definitely fixed or ascertained; uncertain; indefinite; indeterminate.

un-de-terred (un-dē-tėrd′), *a.* Not deterred.

un-de-vel-oped (un-dē-vel′ǫpt), *a.* Not developed.

un-de-vi-at-ing (un-dē′vi-ā-ting), *a.* Not deviating; not departing from a line of procedure; unvarying; uniform: as, "a course of *undeviating* rectitude" (Goldsmith's "Vicar of Wakefield," xxii.).—**un-de′vi-at-ing-ly,** *adv.*

un-did (un-did′). Preterit of *undo.*

un-dif-fer-en-ti-at-ed (un-dif-ę-ren′shi-ā-ted), *a.* Not differentiated; without well-marked distinctive characters.

un-di-gest-ed (un-di-jes′ted), *a.* Not digested.—**un-di-gest′i-ble,** *a.* Not digestible; indigestible.

un-dig-ni-fied (un-dig′ni-fīd), *a.* Not dignified; lacking in dignity.—**un-dig′ni-fied-ly,** *adv.*

un-dig-ni-fy (un-dig′ni-fī), *v. t.*; *-fied, -fying.* To deprive of dignity; render undignified.

un-di-lut-ed (un-di-lū′ted), *a.* Not diluted or weakened.—**un-di-lu′tion** (-lū′shǫn), *n.* Undiluted state.

un-di-min-ish-a-ble (un-di-min′ish-a-bl), *a.* Not diminishable; not subject to lessening or decrease: as, "Character is of a stellar and *undiminishable* greatness" (Emerson's "Essays," Character).—**un-di-min′ished,** *a.* Not diminished or lessened; of full size, amount, intensity, etc.; unabated.—**un-di-min′ish-ing,** *a.* Not diminishing.

un-dimmed (un-dimd′), *a.* Not dimmed, as light, the eyes, etc.

un-dine (un′dēn or un-dēn′), *n.* [G. *undine* = F. *ondine*, < L. *unda*, a wave, water: see *water.*] One of a class of fabled water-spirits of the female sex. According to Paracelsus, when an undine married a mortal and bore a child she received a soul.—**un-di-nal** (un-dē′nạl), *a.*

un-dip-lo-mat-ic (un-dip-lǫ-mat′ik), *a.* Not diplomatic; wanting in diplomacy; tactless.—**un-dip-lo-mat′i-cal-ly,** *adv.*

un-di-rect-ed (un-di-rek′ted), *a.* Not directed; not guided; also, unaddressed, as a letter.

un-dis-cerned (un-di-zėrnd′), *a.* Not discerned; unperceived.—**un-dis-cern′i-ble,** *a.* Indiscernible; imperceptible.—**un-dis-cern′ing,** *a.* Not discerning; lacking discernment.—**un-dis-cern′ing-ly,** *adv.*

un-dis-ci-plined (un-dis′i-plind), *a.* Not disciplined; untrained; not subjected to disciplinary direction and control; lacking corrective discipline.

un-dis-cov-er-a-ble (un-dis-kuv′ėr-a-bl), *a.* Not discoverable; not to be discovered, learned, or found out.—**un-dis-cov′er-a-bly,** *adv.*—**un-dis-cov′ered,** *a.* Not discovered; not found or known by discovery: as, "The *undiscover'd*

country from whose bourn No traveller returns" (Shakspere's "Hamlet," iii. 1. 79).

un-dis-crim-i-nat-ing (un-dis-krim′i-nā-ting), *a.* Not discriminating; making no distinctions; lacking discrimination.—**un-dis-crim′i-nat-ing-ly,** *adv.*

un-dis-guised (un-dis-gīzd′), *a.* Not disguised; fig., unconcealed, open, plain, or frank (as, *undisguised* fear; "*undisguised* gratitude and delight," F. M. Crawford's "Mr. Isaacs," vii.).—**un-dis-guis′ed-ly** (-gī′zed-li), *adv.*

un-dis-mayed (un-dis-mād′), *a.* Not dismayed; undaunted.

un-dis-posed (un-dis-pōzd′), *a.* Not disposed (*of*: as, goods remaining *undisposed of*); also, indisposed† or disinclined†.

un-dis-pu-ta-ble (un-dis′pū-tạ-bl or un-dis-pū′-), *a.* Indisputable; incontestable.—**un-dis-put′ed** (-pū′ted), *a.* Not disputed; not called in question: as, "Thou say'st an *undisputed* thing In such a solemn way" (Holmes's "To an Insect").—**un-dis-put′ed-ly,** *adv.*—**un-dis-put′ing,** *a.* Not disputing.

un-dis-solv-a-ble (un-di-zol′va-bl), *a.* Not dissolvable; insoluble; indissoluble.—**un-dis-solved′,** *a.* Not dissolved.—**un-dis-solv′ing,** *a.* Not dissolving.

un-dis-tin-guish-a-ble (un-dis-ting′gwish-a-bl), *a.* Not distinguishable; indistinguishable.—**un-dis-tin′guished,** *a.* Not distinguished.—**un-dis-tin′guish-ing,** *a.* Not distinguishing; undiscriminating.—**un-dis-tin′guish-ing-ly,** *adv.*

un-dis-trib-ut-ed (un-dis-trib′ū-ted), *a.* Not distributed.

un-dis-turbed (un-dis-tėrbd′), *a.* Not disturbed; unmolested; untroubled; unperturbed.—**un-dis-turb′ed-ly,** *adv.*

un-di-ver-si-fied (un-di-vėr′si-fīd), *a.* Not diversified; without variety.

un-di-vest-ed (un-di-ves′ted), *a.* Not divested; not stripped or deprived, as of something.

un-di-vid-ed (un-di-vī′ded), *a.* Not divided; not separated into parts; not separated or parted from each other, or one from another; not portioned out or distributed; in *bot.*, not cleft, lobed, or branched.—**undivided profits,** in *finance*, net profits remaining after the payment of dividends, as by a bank or corporation.—**un-di-vid′ed-ly,** *adv.*—**un-di-vid′-ed-ness,** *n.*

un-do (un-dö′), *v. t.*; pret. *-did*, pp. *-done*, ppr. *-doing.* [AS. *undōn.*] To reverse the doing of, or cause to be as if never done (as, "Unless the king *undid* all that he had done . . . he [the pope] would excommunicate him," Strype's "Memorials of Cranmer," i. 4; "The storm had delayed work in one place and *undone* work in another," G. W. Cable's "Bonaventure," iii. 4); annul; do away with, or remove (as, "If you kill him he can't *undo* the spell": J. H. Newman's "Callista," xx.); bring to naught, or destroy; bring to ruin or disaster (as, "During this time a hundred things might happen, any one of which would *undo* me": S. Butler's "Erewhon," xxviii.); also, to unfasten and open (something locked, barred, etc.: as, to *undo* a door or gate; "I *undid* the shutters of the eastern window," Stevenson's "Master of Ballantrae," viii.); unlock (fetters, etc.); draw out (a bolt, button, etc.); untie or loose (strings, etc.: as, "She . . . *Undid* the bands that bound her yellow hair," W. Morris's "Jason," vii. 141); open out (a knot, etc.); loose or unfold (wrappings, etc.); open (a package, a sealed letter, etc.); unfasten the clothing of (a person); also, to explain, interpret, or solve (obs. or archaic: as, to *undo* a riddle).—**un-do′er,** *n.*—**un-do′ing,** *n.* The reversing of what has been done; annulling; a bringing to destruction, ruin, or disaster; also, a cause of destruction or ruin (as, "The *undoing* of Charles was not merely his turn for intrigue and double-dealing; it was blindness . . .": Morley's "Oliver Cromwell," iii. 1). —**un-done′¹** (-dun′), *p. a.* Brought to destruction or ruin: as, "wringing my hands . . . and crying out, I was *undone, undone*" (Defoe's "Robinson Crusoe," i. 4).

un-done² (-dun′), *a.* Not done; not accomplished, completed, or finished (as, so long as the work remains *undone*); neglected or omitted (as, "These ought ye to have done, and not to leave the other *undone*": Luke, xi. 42).

un-doubt-ed (un-dou′ted), *a.* Not doubted; not called in question; accepted or regarded as beyond doubt or suspicion; undisputed.—**un-doubt′ed-ly,** *adv.* Without doubt or question; indubitably.—**un-doubt′ing,** *a.* Not doubting; assured; confident.—**un-doubt′ing-ly,** *adv.*

---

fat, fāte, fär, fȧll, ȧsk, fāre; net, mē, hėr; pin, pīne; not, nōte, mǫve, nôr; up, lūte, pull; oi, oil; ou, out; (lightened) aviạry, ēlect, agǫny, intǫ, ūnite; (obscured) errạnt, operạ, ardẹnt, actǫr, natūre; ch, chip; g, go; th, thin; ᴛʜ, then; y, you;

un-dra-mat-ic (un-drạ-mat′ik), *a.* Not dramatic; lacking dramatic effectiveness.—**un-dra-mat′i-cal-ly,** *adv.*

un-drape (un-drāp′), *v. t.* To strip of drapery; bare.

un-draped (un-drāpt′), *a.* Not draped; without drapery.

un-draw (un-drâ′), *v.*; pret. *-drew*, pp. *-drawn*, ppr. *-drawing.* **I.** *tr.* To draw back or away: as, "I . . . *undrew* the curtain, noted a star or two" (C. Brontë's "Jane Eyre," x.). **II.** *intr.* To be drawn back or withdrawn: as, "'Good speed!' cried the watch, as the gatebolts *undrew*" (Browning's "How They Brought the Good News from Ghent to Aix," i.).

un-drawn (un-drân′), *a.* Not drawn.

un-dreamed, un-dreamt (un-drēmd′, -dremt′), *a.* Not dreamed; undreamed-of.—**un-dreamed′=of, un-dreamt′= of,** *a.* Not conceived or imagined even in dreams.—**un-dream′ing,** *a.* Not dreaming.

un-dress¹ (un-dres′ or un′dres). **I.** *n.* Ordinary dress, as opposed to full dress; also, loose, informal dress; négligé. **II.** *a.* Of or pertaining to ordinary dress (as, an *undress* uniform); informal as to dress (as, an *undress* occasion).

un-dress² (un-dres′), *v.* **I.** *tr.* To divest of the dress or clothing; take off the clothes of; disrobe; also, to strip of whatever decks or adorns (as, to *undress* a Christmas tree or a shop-window); also, to remove the dressing from (a wound, etc.). **II.** *intr.* To take off one's clothes.

un-dressed (un-drest′), *a.* Not dressed; not specially prepared; of kid, finished without the smooth, glossy surface of glacé kid.

un-drink-a-ble (un-dring′kạ-bl), *a.* Not drinkable; unfit for drinking.

un-due (un-dū′), *a.* Not due; not yet owing or payable; not proper, fitting, or right (as, an *undue* proceeding; to exert *undue* influence on one making a will); not requisite or necessary; esp., excessive, or too great (as, *undue* severity; *undue* haste; an *undue* amount).

un-du-lant (un′dū-lạnt), *a.* Undulating; waving; wavy: as, "*undulant* drapery" (Henley's "In Hospital," xxviii.).—**un′du-lan-cy,** *n.*

un-du-late (un′dū-lāt), *a.* [L. *undulatus*, < *unda*, a wave: cf. *undine*.] Wavy; bending with successive curves in alternate directions; having a waved form, surface, margin, etc.; in *bot.*, repand, as a leaf.—**un′du-late,** *v.*; *-lated, -lating.* **I.** *intr.* To have a wavy motion; rise and fall in waves; move in waves; also, to have a wavy form or surface; bend with successive curves in alternate directions. **II.** *tr.* To cause to move in waves; also, to give a wavy form to.—**un′du-lat-ing** (-lā-ting), *p. a.* That undulates; having a wavy motion; also, having a form or surface resembling a series of waves (as, "The country became more *undulating*": S. Butler's "Erewhon," xxi.).—**un′du-lat-ing-ly,** *adv.*—**un-du-la′tion** (-lā′shọn), *n.* The act of undulating; a waving motion; also, wavy form or outline; one of a series of wave-like bends, curves, or elevations (as, "On the left stretched the prairie, rising into swells and *undulations*": Parkman's "Oregon Trail," iii.); in *physics*, wave-motion; a wave; a vibration.—**un′du-la-tive** (-lā-tiv), *a.* Undulating; undulatory.—**un′du-la-to-ry** (-tō-ri), *a.* Of or pertaining to undulation; moving in or marked by undulations; having the form or appearance of a series of waves.—**undulatory theory of light,** in *physics*, the theory that light is a kind of undulatory or vibrational motion produced in an all-pervading fluid, the luminiferous ether, by a luminous body.

un-du-lous (un′dū-lus), *a.* [Cf. F. *onduleux*.] Characterized by undulations or waves; wavy.

un-du-ly (un-dū′li), *adv.* In an undue manner or degree; improperly; excessively.

un-du-ti-ful (un-dū′ti-ful), *a.* Not dutiful; not properly obedient or submissive.—**un-du′ti-ful-ly,** *adv.*—**un-du′ti-ful-ness,** *n.*

un-dyed (un-dīd′), *a.* Not dyed; of the natural color.

un-dy-ing (un-dī′ing), *a.* Not or never dying; deathless; immortal; unending: as, "He . . . Sang of . . . life *undying* In the Islands of the Blessed" (Longfellow's "Hiawatha," vi. 62).—**un-dy′ing-ly,** *adv.*—**un-dy′ing-ness,** *n.*

un-earned (un-èrnd′), *a.* Not earned; not gained by labor or service, or as a due return.—**unearned increment,** in *polit. econ.*, the increase in the value of land, etc., due to natural causes, as growth of population, rather than to labor or expenditure on the part of the owner. In the view of some economists, it rightfully belongs to the community, and should be taken from the owner by taxation in some form.

un-earth (un-èrth′), *v. t.* To dig or get out of the earth; dig up or exhume; uncover or bring to light by digging or excavation (as, to *unearth* a buried city); in general, to get, find, or find out by searching or discovery (as, "In a lidless trunk in the garret I . . . *unearthed* another motley collection of novels and romances," Aldrich's "Story of a Bad Boy," v.; to *unearth* a plot); also, to draw or force (a fox, etc.) from its earth or burrow.

un-earth-ly (un-èrth′li), *a.* Not earthly; not of this earth or world (as, "spiritually feasting upon some *unearthly* reminiscence": H. Melville's "Moby-Dick," lxxxvii.); esp., not natural to this earth; supernatural or ghostly; weird, unnaturally strange, or wild (as, an *unearthly* glare; "He could hear the *unearthly* scream of some curlew piercing the din," H. Kingsley's "Geoffry Hamlyn," xxxiv.); unnatural or extraordinary (colloq.: as, "He got up at an *unearthly* hour," W. Churchill's "Modern Chronicle," i. 7).—**un-earth′li-ness,** *n.*

un-ease (un-ēz′), *n.* Want of ease; discomfort; unrest. [Archaic or prov.]

un-eas-y (un-ē′zi), *a.* Not easy in body or mind; uncomfortable; restless; disturbed; perturbed; sometimes, not easy in manner; constrained; also, not conducive to ease; causing bodily discomfort (as, "one or two *uneasy* sofas": H. G. Wells's "Tono-Bungay," iii. 1. § 3); mentally disturbing†; also, difficult (obs. or prov.).—**un-eas′i-ly,** *adv.*—**un-eas′i-ness,** *n.*

un-eat-a-ble (un-ē′tạ-bl), *a.* Not eatable; unfit to be eaten.—**un-eat′en** (-ē′tn), *a.* Not eaten.

un-eath (un-ēᴛʜ′ or -ēth′), *a.* [AS. *unēathe*: see *un-*¹ and *eath*.] Not easy; difficult; hard. [Obs. or archaic.]—**un-eath′,** *adv.* [AS. *unēathe*.] Not easily; with difficulty; hence, hardly; scarcely; barely. [Obs. or archaic.]

un-ed-i-fy-ing (un-ed′i-fī-ing), *a.* Not edifying; not elevating or beneficial morally.

un-ed-u-cat-ed (un-ed′ū-kā-ted), *a.* Not educated.

un-em-bar-rassed (un-em-bar′ạst), *a.* Not embarrassed; unimpeded or unhampered; not confused; composed; unabashed.

un-e-mo-tion-al (un-ē-mō′shọn-ạl), *a.* Not emotional; phlegmatic; impassive.—**un-e-mo′tion-al-ly,** *adv.*

un-em-ployed (un-em-ploid′), *a.* Not employed; not in use; not kept busy or at work; out of work; without work or employment.—**un-em-ploy′ment,** *n.* Lack of employment; unemployed condition.

un-en-cum-bered (un-en-kum′bèrd), *a.* Not encumbered; free from encumbrance.

un-end-ing (un-en′ding), *a.* Not ending; having no end; endless; ceaseless; eternal.—**un-end′ing-ly,** *adv.*—**un-end′ing-ness,** *n.*

un-en-dowed (un-en-doud′), *a.* Not endowed; without an endowment.

un-en-dur-a-ble (un-en-dūr′ạ-bl), *a.* Not endurable; unbearable; intolerable; insufferable.—**un-en-dur′a-bly,** *adv.*

un-en-force-a-ble (un-en-fōr′sạ-bl), *a.* Not enforceable; incapable of being enforced.—**un-en-forced′,** *a.* Not enforced.

un=Eng-lish (un-ing′glish), *a.* Not English; foreign or opposed to the English character, spirit, usages, etc.; not in accordance with the usages of the English language.

un-en-light-ened (un-en-lī′tnd), *a.* Not enlightened; without intellectual or moral enlightenment; benighted; ignorant.

un-en-ter-pris-ing (un-en′tèr-prī-zing), *a.* Not enterprising; lacking enterprise.

un-en-thu-si-as-tic (un-en-thū-zi-as′tik), *a.* Not enthusiastic; devoid of enthusiasm.—**un-en-thu-si-as′ti-cal-ly,** *adv.*

un-en-vi-a-ble (un-en′vi-ạ-bl), *a.* Not enviable; not such as to excite envy.—**un-en′vi-a-bly,** *adv.*—**un-en′vied,** *a.* Not envied; exempt from the envy of others.—**un-en′vi-ous,** *a.* Not envious; free from envy.

un-e-qual (un-ē′kwạl). **I.** *a.* Not equal; not of the same quantity, value, rank, ability, merit, etc.; not adequate, as in amount, power, ability, etc. (*to*); not evenly proportioned or balanced; not having the parts alike or symmetrical; not uniform in effect, as a law; inequitable, unfair, or unjust; not even or regular, as motion; uneven of surface, as ground, etc.; uneven or variable in character, quality, etc. (as, "He is the most *unequal* writer breathing": Carlyle's "Sartor Resartus," i. 4). **II.** *n.* One who or that which is unequal.—**un-e′qualed, un-e′qualled,** *a.* Not equaled; unparalleled; matchless.—**un-e′qual-ly,** *adv.*—**un-e′qual-ness,** *n.*

un-e-quiv-o-cal (un-ē-kwiv′ō-kạl), *a.* Not equivocal; not ambiguous or doubtful; clear; plain: as, "asking in very terse and *unequivocal* phrase my intentions regarding his sister-in-law" (Lever's "Harry Lorrequer," xl.).—**un-e-quiv′o-cal-ly,** *adv.*—**un-e-quiv′o-cal-ness,** *n.*

un-err-ing (un-ėr′ing or un-er′-), *a.* Not erring; not going astray or missing the mark; without error or mistake; unfailingly right, exact, or sure.—**un-err′ing-ly,** *adv.*—**un-err′ing-ness,** *n.*

un-es-cap-a-ble (un-es-kā′pạ-bl), *a.* Not escapable; not to be escaped or avoided; inescapable.—**un-es-cap′a-bly,** *adv.*

un-es-sen-tial (un-e-sen′shạl), **I.** *a.* Not essential; inessential or insubstantial; not of prime importance; not indispensable; non-essential. **II.** *n.* An unessential thing; a non-essential.—**un-es-sen′tial-ly,** *adv.*

un-eth-i-cal (un-eth′i-kạl), *a.* Not ethical; not in accordance with the rules for right conduct or practice.—**un-eth′i-cal-ly,** *adv.*

un-e-ven (un-ē′vn), *a.* [AS. *unefen*.] Not even; not level or flat; irregular, varying, or not uniform; not equitable or fair; not equally balanced; not equal; of a number, odd, or not divisible into two equal integers.—**un-e′ven-ly,** *adv.* —**un-e′ven-ness,** *n.*

un-e-vent-ful (un-ē-vent′fúl), *a.* Not eventful; lacking in important or striking occurrences: as, "laborious, *uneventful* years" (H. G. Wells's "Tono-Bungay," i. 3. § 2).—**un-e-vent′ful-ly,** *adv.*—**un-e-vent′ful-ness,** *n.*

un-ex-act-ing (un-eg-zak′ting), *a.* Not exacting; requiring little; easy.

un-ex-am-pled (un-eg-zam′pld), *a.* Having no example or similar case; unprecedented; unparalleled: as, "thanking you for your *unexampled* kindness" (Jane Austen's "Pride and Prejudice," lviii.).

un-ex-celled (un-ek-seld′), *a.* Not excelled; unsurpassed.

un-ex-cep-tion-a-ble (un-ek-sep′shọn-ạ-bl), *a.* Not exceptionable; not open or liable to any exception or objection; beyond criticism; wholly satisfactory or admirable.—**un-ex-cep′tion-a-ble-ness,** *n.*—**un-ex-cep′tion-a-bly,** *adv.*

un-ex-cep-tion-al (un-ek-sep′shọn-ạl), *a.* Not exceptional; not unusual or extraordinary; also, admitting of no exception (as, "The orders . . . were imperative and *unexceptional*": Kinglake's "Eothen," xxix.); sometimes, loosely, unexceptionable.—**un-ex-cep′tion-al-ly,** *adv.*

un-ex-cit-ed (un-ek-sī′ted), *a.* Not excited; calm; tranquil.—**un-ex-cit′ing,** *a.* Not exciting; quiet; tame; dull.

un-ex-pect-ed (un-eks-pek′ted), *a.* Not expected; unforeseen; sudden.—**un-ex-pect′ed-ly,** *adv.*—**un-ex-pect′ed-ness,** *n.*

un-ex-pe-ri-enced (un-eks-pē′ri-ẹnst), *a.* Inexperienced.

un-ex-pert (un-eks-pėrt′), *a.* Inexpert.—**un-ex-pert′ly,** *adv.*

un-ex-pired (un-eks-pīrd′), *a.* Not expired; not having come to an end; having still some time to run, as a lease.

un-ex-plain-a-ble (un-eks-plā′nạ-bl), *a.* Not explainable; inexplicable.—**un-ex-plained′,** *a.* Not explained.

un-ex-plod-ed (un-eks-plō′ded), *a.* Not exploded.

un-ex-plored (un-eks-plōrd′), *a.* Not explored; not yet investigated or traversed in exploration.

un-ex-pressed (un-eks-prest′), *a.* Not expressed; unuttered.—**un-ex-press′i-ble,** *a.* Inexpressible.—**un-ex-pres′sive,** *a.* Not expressive; lacking in expression of meaning, feeling, etc.; not given to expression or utterance (as, "the *unexpressive* man whose life expressed so much": Lowell's "Under the Old Elm," vi. 2); also, inexpressible†.—**un-ex-pres′sive-ly,** *adv.*—**un-ex-pres′sive-ness,** *n.*

un-ex-pur-gat-ed (un-eks′pėr-gā-ted), *a.* Not expurgated.

un-fad-ing (un-fā′ding), *a.* Not or never fading; always fresh or bright.—**un-fad′ing-ly,** *adv.*—**un-fad′ing-ness,** *n.*

un-fail-ing (un-fā′ling), *a.* Not or never failing; inexhaustible; not giving way; never wanting at need.—**un-fail′ing-ly,** *adv.*—**un-fail′ing-ness,** *n.*

un-fair (un-fār′), *a.* Not fair; biased or partial; not just or equitable; unjust.—**un-fair′ly,** *adv.*—**un-fair′ness,** *n.*

un-faith (un-fāth′), *n.* Want of faith: as, "*Unfaith* in aught is want of faith in all" (Tennyson's "Merlin and Vivien," 387).

un-faith-ful (un-fāth′fúl), *a.* Not faithful; unbelieving or infidel (obs. or rare); disloyal, perfidious, or faithless; false to duty or promises; not faithfully accurate or exact.—**un-faith′ful-ly,** *adv.*—**un-faith′ful-ness,** *n.*

un-fal-ter-ing (un-fâl′tėr-ing), *a.* Not faltering; unhesitating; unwavering.—**un-fal′ter-ing-ly,** *adv.*

un-fa-mil-iar (un-fạ-mil′yạr), *a.* Not familiar; not acquainted or conversant (as, to be *unfamiliar* with a subject); not well-known (as, a subject *unfamiliar* to me); unaccustomed, unusual, or strange.—**un-fa-mil-i-ar′i-ty** (-i-ar′i-ti), *n.*—**un-fa-mil′iar-ly,** *adv.*

un-fash-ion-a-ble (un-fash′ọn-ạ-bl), *a.* Not fashionable.—**un-fash′ion-a-ble-ness,** *n.*—**un-fash′ion-a-bly,** *adv.*

un-fas-ten (un-fás′n), *v.* **I.** *tr.* To loose from or as from fastenings; undo or open (a fastening). **II.** *intr.* To become unfastened.

un-fa-thered (un-fä′ᴛʜėrd), *a.* Having no father; fatherless; of unknown paternity; bastard; fig., not ascribable to a particular author or responsible person.—**un-fa′ther-ly,** *a.* Not fatherly; unbefitting a father.

un-fath-om-a-ble (un-faᴛʜ′ọm-ạ-bl), *a.* Not fathomable; incapable of being fathomed or sounded; impenetrable by the mind; inscrutable; incomprehensible.—**un-fath′om-a-ble-ness,** *n.*—**un-fath′om-a-bly,** *adv.*—**un-fath′omed,** *a.* Not fathomed.

un-fa-vor-a-ble (un-fā′vọr-ạ-bl), *a.* Not favorable; unpropitious; disadvantageous; adverse.—**un-fa′vor-a-ble-ness,** *n.*—**un-fa′vor-a-bly,** *adv.*

un-fed (un-fed′), *a.* Not fed; having taken no food.

un-feel-ing (un-fē′ling), *a.* Not feeling; devoid of feeling; insensible or insensate; unsympathetic; callous; hardhearted.—**un-feel′ing-ly,** *adv.*—**un-feel′ing-ness,** *n.*

un-feigned (un-fānd′), *a.* Not feigned; sincere; real.—**un-feign′ed-ly,** *adv.*—**un-feign′ed-ness,** *n.*

un-fel-lowed (un-fel′ōd), *a.* Without a fellow; unmatched; unequaled: as, "In his meed he's *unfellowed*" (Shakspere's "Hamlet," v. 2. 150).

un-felt (un-felt′), *a.* Not felt or perceived.

un-fem-i-nine (un-fem′i-nin), *a.* Not feminine; unwomanly.

un-fer-ment-ed (un-fėr-men′ted), *a.* Not fermented.

un-fer-ti-lized (un-fėr′ti-līzd), *a.* Not fertilized.

un-fet-ter (un-fet′ėr), *v. t.* To free from fetters. Often fig.

un-fet-tered (un-fet′ėrd), *a.* Not fettered; fig., free from restraint.

un-fil-ial (un-fil′yạl), *a.* Not filial; unbecoming from a child to a parent; not observing the obligations of a child to a parent.—**un-fil′ial-ly,** *adv.*

un-fil-tered (un-fil′tėrd), *a.* Not filtered.

un-fin-ished (un-fin′isht), *a.* Not finished; incomplete; lacking some special finish; not sheared, as cloth.

un-fit[1] (un-fit′), *a.* Not fit; not adapted or suited; unsuitable; not deserving or good enough (as, *unfit* to live); unqualified or incompetent; not physically fit or in due condition (as, "Doughty certified me medically *unfit*": Kipling's "Kim," vi.).

un-fit[2] (un-fit′), *v. t.*; *-fitted, -fitting.* To deprive of fitness; render unfit or unsuitable; disqualify.

un-fit-ly (un-fit′li), *adv.* In an unfit manner; unsuitably; improperly.—**un-fit′ness,** *n.*

un-fit-ted (un-fit′ed), *a.* Not fitted; unsuited; unfit.—**un-fit′ted-ness,** *n.*

un-fit-ting (un-fit′ing), *a.* Not fitting; unbecoming.—**un-fit′ting-ly,** *adv.*—**un-fit′ting-ness,** *n.*

un-fix (un-fiks′), *v. t.* To render no longer fixed; unfasten; detach; loosen; unsettle.

un-fixed (un-fikst′), *a.* Not fixed; not firmly set; not settled or determined; variable or uncertain.—**un-fix′ed-ness,** *n.*

un-flag-ging (un-flag′ing), *a.* Not flagging; not drooping or failing: as, "*unflagging* spirits" (Hawthorne's "Blithedale Romance," ii.).—**un-flag′ging-ly,** *adv.*

---

fat, fāte, fär, fȧll, ȧsk, fāre; net, mē, hėr; pin, pīne; not, nōte, möve, nôr; up, lūte, púll; oi, oil; ou, out; (lightened) aviạry, ẹlect, agọny, intọ, ụnite; (obscured) errạnt, operạ, ardẹnt, actọr, natụre; ch, chip; g, go; th, thin; ᴛʜ, then; y, you;

un-flat-ter-ing (un-flat′ẽr-ing), *a.* Not flattering; uncomplimentary.—**un-flat′ter-ing-ly,** *adv.*

un-fledged (un-flejd′), *a.* Not fledged; without feathers sufficiently developed for flight, as a young bird; fig., immature; undeveloped; callow.

un-flesh-ly (un-flesh′li), *a.* Not fleshly; not carnal or corporeal; spiritual.

un-flinch-ing (un-flin′ching), *a.* Not flinching; unshrinking.—**un-flinch′ing-ly,** *adv.*

un-fold (un-fōld′), *v.* [AS. *unfealdan.*] **I.** *tr.* To bring out of a folded state (as, to *unfold* a napkin, a letter, or an umbrella; the rose *unfolds* its petals; to *unfold* the arms or wings); spread or open out; fig., to develop (as, "Nothing *unfolds* a child faster than being thus taken into the companionship of older minds": Mrs. Stowe's "Oldtown Folks," ix.); also, to spread out or lay open to view (as, "From this lofty eminence, a vast and magnificent prospect *unfolds* itself": Irving's "Captain Bonneville," xxxviii.); fig., to reveal or display (as, "the greatness of mind and heart which he [Lincoln] *unfolded* under fierce trial": Charnwood's "Abraham Lincoln," vi.); often, to reveal or disclose in words, set forth, or explain (as, "Briefly and plainly, I *unfolded* what I proposed": S. Butler's "Erewhon," xxviii.). **II.** *intr.* To become unfolded; open out.—**un-fold′er,** *n.*—**un-fold′ment,** *n.*

un-for-bid-den (un-for-bid′n), *a.* Not forbidden.

un-forced (un-fōrst′), *a.* Not forced; not compelled; voluntary.

un-fore-see-a-ble (un-fōr-sē′a-bl), *a.* Not foreseeable; incapable of being foreseen: as, "an old order going down in the *unforeseeable* welter of twentieth-century politics" (Arnold Bennett's "The Old Adam," vi.).—**un-fore-see′a-ble-ness,** *n.*—**un-fore-see′a-bly,** *adv.*—**un-fore-see′ing,** *a.* Not foreseeing; without prevision or foresight.—**un-fore-see′ing-ly,** *adv.*—**un-fore-seen′,** *a.* Not foreseen; unexpected: as, "hoping for some *unforeseen* turn of fortune" (George Eliot's "Silas Marner," ix.).—**un-fore-seen′ness,** *n.*

un-for-get-ta-ble (un-for-get′a-bl), *a.* Not forgettable; never to be forgotten: as, "Bridget's *unforgettable* rolls or hot biscuits" (W. Churchill's "Modern Chronicle," i. 2).—**un-for-get′ta-bly,** *adv.*

un-for-giv-a-ble (un-for-giv′a-bl), *a.* Not forgivable; not to be forgiven; unpardonable.—**un-for-giv′en,** *a.* Not forgiven.—**un-for-giv′ing,** *a.* Not forgiving; not disposed to forgive; implacable.—**un-for-giv′ing-ly,** *adv.*—**un-for-giv′ing-ness,** *n.*

un-for-got-ten (un-for-got′n), *a.* Not forgotten.

un-formed (un-fôrmd′), *a.* Not formed; not definitely shaped (as, an *unformed* mass); shapeless or formless; undeveloped or crude (as, "an *unformed* schoolgirl": Margaret Kennedy's "Constant Nymph," xvii.); not made or created.

un-for-mu-lat-ed (un-fôr′mū-lā-ted), *a.* Not formulated.

un-for-ti-fied (un-fôr′ti-fīd), *a.* Not fortified.

un-for-tu-nate (un-fôr′tū-nāt). **I.** *a.* Not fortunate; not having good fortune; unlucky or unhappy; not attended with good fortune. **II.** *n.* An unfortunate person.—**un-for′tu-nate-ly,** *adv.*—**un-for′tu-nate-ness,** *n.*

un-found-ed (un-foun′ded), *a.* Without foundation; baseless: as, "This objection . . . is utterly *unfounded*" (A. R. Wallace's "Darwinism," iii.).—**un-found′ed-ly,** *adv.*—**un-found′ed-ness,** *n.*

un-fre-quent-ed (un-frē-kwen′ted), *a.* Not frequented, as places; little resorted to or visited; solitary.

un-friend (un-frend′), *n.* One who is not a friend; an enemy.—**un-friend′ed,** *a.* Without friends; friendless: as, "a raw and *unfriended* youth" (Godwin's "Caleb Williams," xiv.).—**un-friend′ed-ness,** *n.*—**un-friend′ly,** *a.* Not friendly; hostile; inimical; unkindly.—**un-friend′li-ness,** *n.*—**un-friend′ly,** *adv.* In an unfriendly manner.

un-frock (un-frok′), *v. t.* To divest or strip of a frock; hence, to deprive of the priestly or clerical office.

un-fruit-ful (un-fröt′fúl), *a.* Not fruitful; unproductive; barren; fruitless.—**un-fruit′ful-ly,** *adv.*—**un-fruit′ful-ness,** *n.*

un-ful-filled (un-fúl-fild′), *a.* Not fulfilled.

un-fund-ed (un-fun′ded), *a.* Not funded, as a debt; floating.

un-furl (un-fẽrl′), *v.* **I.** *tr.* To spread or shake out from a furled state, as a sail or a flag; unfold. **II.** *intr.* To become unfurled.

un-fur-nished (un-fẽr′nisht), *a.* Not furnished; not supplied with furnishings or furniture: as, an *unfurnished* house.

un-gain-ly (un-gān′li), *a.* [See *gainly.*] Not gainly; not graceful or shapely; awkward; clumsy; uncouth: as, "his *ungainly* figure, with long arms and large hands and relatively small development of chest" (Charnwood's "Abraham Lincoln," i.).—**un-gain′li-ness,** *n.*

un-gal-lant (un-gal′ant or -ga-lant′), *a.* Not gallant; uncourtly; unchivalrous.—**un-gal′lant-ly,** *adv.*

un-gear (un-gēr′), *v. t.* To strip of gear; also, to throw out of gear.

un-gen-er-ous (un-jen′e-rus), *a.* Not generous; ignoble; illiberal; mean.—**un-gen′er-ous-ly,** *adv.*

un-gen-tle (un-jen′tl), *a.* Not gentle; harsh; rough.

un-gen-tle-man-ly (un-jen′tl-man-li), *a.* Not gentlemanly; ill-bred; impolite; rude; not befitting a gentleman.—**un-gen′tle-man-li-ness,** *n.*

un-gift-ed (un-gif′ted), *a.* Not gifted; not endowed with natural gifts.

un-gird (un-gẽrd′), *v. t.* To unfasten or take off the girdle or belt of; also, to loosen, or take off, by unfastening a girdle.

un-glazed (un-glāzd′), *a.* Not glazed; not provided with glass, as a window; not coated or covered with a glaze, as earthenware.

un-gloved (un-gluvd′), *a.* Not gloved; without a glove or gloves.

un-glue (un-glö′), *v. t.* To separate or open (something fastened with or as with glue).

un-god-ly (un-god′li), *a.* Not godly; not conforming to God's laws; irreligious; impious; sinful; wicked; also, outrageous (colloq.).—**un-god′li-ly,** *adv.*—**un-god′li-ness,** *n.*

un-gov-ern-a-ble (un-guv′ẽr-na-bl), *a.* That cannot be governed, ruled, or restrained; uncontrollable: as, an *ungovernable* people; *ungovernable* passions.—**un-gov′ern-a-ble-ness,** *n.*—**un-gov′ern-a-bly,** *adv.*—**un-gov′erned,** *a.* Not governed; not brought under government or control; unrestrained or unbridled.

un-gown (un-goun′), *v. t.* To divest or strip of a gown; hence, to deprive of the clerical office.

un-grace-ful (un-grās′fúl), *a.* Not graceful; lacking grace or elegance; clumsy; awkward.—**un-grace′ful-ly,** *adv.*—**un-grace′ful-ness,** *n.*

un-gra-cious (un-grā′shus), *a.* Not gracious; ungraceful or unpleasing (obs. or rare); unacceptable or unwelcome (as, an *ungracious* duty; an *ungracious* task); unfortunate† or unlucky†; lacking in gracious courtesy or affability (as, an *ungracious* person; *ungracious* behavior); graceless† or ungodly†.—**un-gra′cious-ly,** *adv.*—**un-gra′cious-ness,** *n.*

un-grad-ed (un-grā′ded), *a.* Not graded; not arranged in grades or classes (as, an *ungraded* school).

un-gram-mat-i-cal (un-gra-mat′i-kal), *a.* Not grammatical; not in accordance with the rules of grammar.—**un-gram-mat′i-cal-ly,** *adv.*

un-grate-ful (un-grāt′fúl), *a.* Not grateful; unpleasing or disagreeable; not feeling or displaying gratitude; exhibiting ingratitude; giving no return or recompense.—**un-grate′-ful-ly,** *adv.*—**un-grate′ful-ness,** *n.*

un-ground-ed (un-groun′ded), *a.* Not grounded; groundless.

un-grudg-ing (un-gruj′ing), *a.* Not grudging; willing; hearty; liberal.—**un-grudg′ing-ly,** *adv.*

un-gual (ung′gwal), *a.* [L. *unguis,* nail, claw, hoof.] Of or pertaining to, bearing, or shaped like a nail, claw, or hoof.

un-guard-ed (un-gär′ded), *a.* Not guarded; unprotected or undefended; incautious or imprudent; having no guard, screen, or the like.—**un-guard′ed-ly,** *adv.*—**un-guard′ed-ness,** *n.*

un-guent (ung′gwent), *n.* [L. *unguentum,* < *unguere,* smear, anoint.] Any soft preparation or salve, usually of butter-like consistence, applied to sores, etc.; an ointment.—**un′guen-ta-ry** (-gwen-ta-ri), *a.*

un-guic-u-lar (ung-gwik′ū-lär), *a.* [L. *unguiculus,* fingernail, dim. of *unguis,* nail, claw.] Of or pertaining to, or bearing, a nail or claw.—**un-guic′u-late** (-lāt). **I.** *a.* Bearing or resembling a nail or claw; specif., in *zoöl.,* having nails or claws, as distinguished from hoofs; in *bot.,* having a claw-like base, as certain petals. **II.** *n.* An unguiculate animal. — **un-guic′u-lat-ed** (-lā-ted), *a.* Unguiculate.

un-guif-er-ous (ung-gwif′ẹ-rus), *a.* [L. *unguis*, nail, claw, + *ferre*, bear.] Bearing a nail, claw, or unguis.

un-gui-nous (ung′gwi-nus), *a.* [L. *unguinosus*, < *unguen* (*unguin-*), fat, unguent, < *unguere*, smear, anoint.] Consisting of or resembling fat or oil; oily.

un-guis (ung′gwis), *n.*; pl. *-gues* (-gwēz). [L., nail, claw, hoof, akin to Gr. ὄνυξ, nail, claw: see *onyx.*] In *zoöl.*, a nail, claw, or hoof; in *bot.*, the claw-like base of certain petals.

un-gu-la (ung′gū-lä), *n.*; pl. *-læ* (-lē). [L., claw, hoof, < *unguis*: see *unguis.*] In *zoöl.*, a hoof; also, a claw or nail; in *geom.*, a more or less hoof-like part cut off from a cylinder, cone, or the like, by a plane oblique to the base; in *bot.*, an unguis. — **un′gu-lar** (-lär), *a.* Pertaining to or of the nature of an ungula; ungual.

un-gu-late (ung′gū-lāt). [LL. *ungulatus*, having claws or hoofs, < L. *ungula*: see *ungula.*] **I.** *a.* Of the nature of a hoof; hoof-like; also, having hoofs; belonging or pertaining to the *Ungulata*, an order or group of mammals containing the hoofed quadrupeds. **II.** *n.* An ungulate mammal.

un-hack-neyed (un-hak′nid), *a.* Not hackneyed; not rendered trite, commonplace, or stale; not habituated or experienced (as, "one *unhackneyed* in the ways of intrigue": Scott's "Waverley," xxxii.).

un-hair (un-hãr′), *v. t.* or *i.* To free, or become free, from hair.

un-hal-low (un-hal′ō), *v. t.* To desecrate; profane.

un-hal-lowed (un-hal′ōd), *a.* Not hallowed or consecrated; profane; impious or wicked.

un-ham-pered (un-ham′pėrd), *a.* Not hampered; unimpeded.

un-hand (un-hand′), *v. t.* To take the hand or hands from; release from a grasp; let go: as, "*Unhand* that lady, — she is my betrothed" (Bulwer-Lytton's "Caxtons," xv. 1).

un-hand-some (un-han′sum), *a.* Not handsome; unhandy† or inconvenient†; inexpert†; ungracious or discourteous; unseemly or mean (as, "the *unhandsome* practice of eaves-dropping": Scott's "Castle Dangerous," ii.); ungenerous or illiberal; not good-looking or comely; plain or ugly. — **un-hand′some-ly**, *adv.* — **un-hand′some-ness**, *n.*

un-hand-y (un-han′di), *a.* Not handy; not easy to handle or manage, as things; not skilful in using the hands, as persons. — **un-hand′i-ly**, *adv.* — **un-hand′i-ness**, *n.*

un-hap-py (un-hap′i), *a.* Not happy; unfortunate or unlucky (as, "I am a little *unhappy* in the mold of my face," Steele, in "Spectator," 17; "the distracted state of that *unhappy* country," Scott's "Abbot," i.; an *unhappy* accident); unfavorable or inauspicious (as, "wretches borne under *unhappy* starre": Spenser's "Faerie Queene," ii. 6. 44); sad, miserable, or wretched (as, to be most *unhappy*; to lead an *unhappy* life); of wretched character, ill-conditioned, or reprehensible (as, "Beat him well, he's an *unhappy* boy," Beaumont and Fletcher's "Knight of the Burning Pestle," ii.: obs. or rare); infelicitous (as, an *unhappy* remark). — **un-hap′pi-ly**, *adv.* — **un-hap′pi-ness**, *n.*

un-harmed (un-härmd′), *a.* Not harmed; uninjured; scatheless; sound; intact. — **un-harm′ful**, *a.* Not harmful; harmless. — **un-harm′ful-ly**, *adv.*

un-har-ness (un-här′nes), *v.* **I.** *tr.* To strip of harness; divest of armor; free (a horse, etc.) from harness or gear. **II.** *intr.* To remove harness or gear.

un-hasp (un-hásp′), *v. t.* To loose the hasp of.

un-hat (un-hat′), *v.*; *-hatted*, *-hatting*. **I.** *tr.* To remove the hat from. **II.** *intr.* To take off one's hat, as in respect.

un-health (un-helth′), *n.* Ill health. — **un-health′ful**, *a.* Not healthful; not possessing health, or not characteristic of health; now, commonly, injurious to health; insalubrious; unwholesome. — **un-health′ful-ly**, *adv.* — **un-health′ful-ness**, *n.* — **un-health′y**, *a.* Not healthy; not possessing health, or not in a healthy or sound condition (as, an *unhealthy* child; an *unhealthy* plant); characteristic of or resulting from bad health (as, an *unhealthy* appearance); hurtful to health, insalubrious, or unwholesome (as, an *unhealthy* climate). — **un-health′i-ly**, *adv.* — **un-health′i-ness**, *n.*

un-heard (un-hėrd′), *a.* Not heard; not perceived by the ear (as, "Heard melodies are sweet, but those *unheard* Are sweeter": Keats's "Ode on a Grecian Urn"); not given a hearing or audience (as, to condemn a person *unheard*); not heard of, or unknown (as, "Nor was his name *unheard* . . . In ancient Greece": Milton's "Paradise Lost," i. 738). — **un-heard′=of**, *a.* That was never heard of; unknown; such as was never known before; unprecedented.

un-heat-ed (un-hē′ted), *a.* Not heated; without heat.

un-heed-ed (un-hē′ded), *a.* Not heeded; disregarded; unnoticed. — **un-heed′ful**, *a.* Heedless; unmindful. — **un-heed′ing**, *a.* Not heeding; unheedful.

un-helm (un-helm′), *v. t.* To deprive of the helm or helmet. [Archaic.]

un-her-ald-ed (un-her′ạl-ded), *a.* Not heralded; not proclaimed or announced beforehand.

un-hes-i-tat-ing (un-hez′i-tā-ting), *a.* Not hesitating; prompt; ready. — **un-hes′i-tat-ing-ly**, *adv.*

un-hewn (un-hūn′), *a.* Not hewn; not shaped or fashioned by hewing; fig., rough; unpolished.

un-hin-dered (un-hin′dėrd), *a.* Not hindered; unimpeded.

un-hinge (un-hinj′), *v. t.* To take (a door, etc.) off the hinges; remove the hinges from; fig., to detach or separate from something (as, "minds that have been *unhinged* from their old faith": George Eliot's "Silas Marner," ii.); also, to deprive of fixity or stability; throw into confusion or disorder; unbalance (the mind, etc.); upset or discompose (a person); unsettle (opinions, etc.).

un-his-tor-ic (un-his-tor′ik), *a.* Not historic; not in accordance with history; unrecorded in history.

un-hitch (un-hich′), *v. t.* To free from being hitched or fastened; unfasten.

un-hive (un-hīv′), *v. t.* To drive from or as from a hive.

un-ho-ly (un-hō′li), *a.* Not holy; not sacred or hallowed; impious, sinful, or wicked; also, unseemly or reprehensible (colloq.). — **un-ho′li-ly**, *adv.* — **un-ho′li-ness**, *n.*

un-hood (un-húd′), *v. t.* To divest of a hood; often, to remove from (a hawk) the hood used to blind it.

un-hook (un-húk′), *v.* **I.** *tr.* To loose from a hook; also, to open or undo by loosening a hook or hooks. **II.** *intr.* To become unhooked.

un-hoped (un-hōpt′), *a.* Not hoped or looked for. — **un-hoped′=for**, *a.* Not hoped for; unhoped.

un-horse (un-hôrs′), *v. t.* To throw from a horse, as in battle; cause to fall from the saddle; also, to deprive of a horse or horses.

un-house (un-houz′), *v. t.* To drive from a house or habitation; deprive of shelter.

un-housed (un-houzd′), *a.* Not housed; houseless.

un-hou-seled, un-hou-selled (un-hou′zẹld), *a.* [See *housel*, *v.*] Not having received the eucharist. See quotation at *unaneled*. [Archaic.]

un-hur-ried (un-hur′id), *a.* Not hurried; without haste; leisurely.

un-hurt (un-hėrt′), *a.* Not hurt; unharmed; uninjured. — **un-hurt′ful**, *a.* Not hurtful; harmless. — **un-hurt′ful-ly**, *adv.*

un-husk (un-husk′), *v. t.* To free from or as from a husk.

un-hy-gi-en-ic (un-hī-ji-en′ik), *a.* Not hygienic; unhealthful; insanitary.

uni-. [L. *uni-*, repr. *unus*, one: see *one.*] A combining-form or prefix meaning 'one,' 'single,' occurring first in words of Latin origin, but now often used as an English formative, preferably in combination with elements likewise of Latin origin, as in *uniaxial, unicellular, unilocular, unisexual.* Cf. *mono-* (of Greek origin).

U-ni-at (ū′ni-at). [Russ. *uniyat*, < *uniya*, part of a Eastern Christian church in communion with Rome, < L. *unus*, one.] **I.** *n.* A member of any of various communities of Greek and other Eastern Christians which acknowledge the supremacy of the Pope and are in communion with the Church of Rome, but which retain their own liturgy, rites, discipline, etc., to a greater or less extent. **II.** *a.* Of or pertaining to the Uniats. Also **U′ni-ate** (-ạt), *n.* and *a.*

u-ni-ax-i-al (ū-ni-ak′si-ạl), *a.* [See *uni-*.] Having but one axis; of a crystal, having only one line or direction in which no double refraction occurs; in *bot.*, of a plant, having a primary stem which does not branch and which terminates in a flower. — **u-ni-ax′i-al-ly**, *adv.*

u-ni-cam-er-al (ū-ni-kam′ẹ-rạl), *a.* [L. *unus*, one, + ML. *camera*, chamber.] Consisting of or characterized by a single chamber, as a legislative assembly.

u·ni·cel·lu·lar (ū-ni-sel'ū-lär), *a.* [See *uni-*.] Pertaining to or consisting of a single cell: as, a *unicellular* animal.

u·ni·col·or (ū'ni-kul-ǫr), *a.* [L., < *unus*, one, + *color*, color.] Of but one color. Also **u'ni-col-ored, u·ni·col'or·ous.**

u·ni·corn (ū'ni-kôrn), *n.* [OF. F. *unicorne*, < L. *unicornis*, having one horn, < *unus*, one, + *cornu*, horn.] A fabulous animal with a single long horn; also, a heraldic representation of this animal, in the form of a horse with a lion's tail and with a long, straight, and spirally twisted horn growing out of the forehead (used, along with the lion, as a supporter of the British royal arms); also, in the Authorized Version of the Bible (Deut. xxxiii. 17, and elsewhere), used of a two-horned animal now identified with the urus; also, a narwhal ('unicorn whale'); also, a pair of horses harnessed with a third horse in front, or the whole equipage (as, "Mrs. Freke . . . drove in her *unicorn* to Oakly Park, to pay Miss Portman a visit": Maria Edgeworth's "Belinda," xvi.); also, a Scotch gold coin of the 15th and 16th centuries, bearing the figure of a unicorn; also [*cap.*], in *astron.*, the constellation Monoceros.—**u'ni-corn=fish,** *n.* A file-fish, *Alutera scripta*, of West Indian and other warm seas, with a horn-like spine upon the head.

Obverse.   Reverse.
Unicorn, James III. — British Museum.

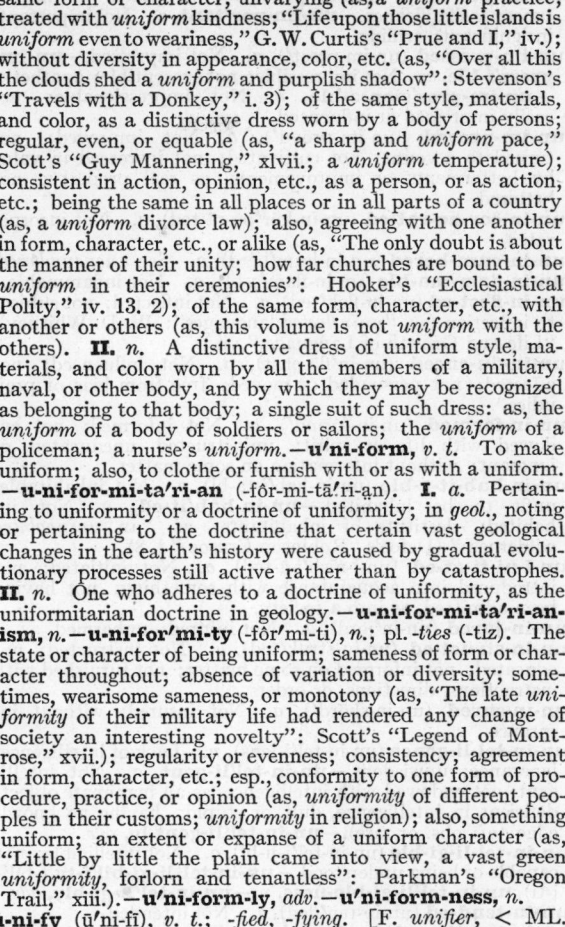

Unicorn-fish.

u·ni·cos·tate (ū-ni-kos'tāt), *a.* [L. *unus*, one, + *costa*, rib.] Having only one costa, rib, or ridge; in *bot.*, of a leaf, having only one primary or prominent rib, the midrib.

u·ni·cus·pid (ū-ni-kus'pid). [See *uni-*.] **I.** *a.* Having only one cusp, as an incisor or canine tooth. **II.** *n.* A unicuspid tooth.

u·ni·cy·cle (ū'ni-sī-kl), *n.* [See *uni-*.] A vehicle with only one wheel.

un·i·den·ti·fied (un-ī-den'ti-fīd), *a.* Not identified.

u·ni·di·rec·tion·al (ū'ni-di-rek'shǫn-al), *a.* [See *uni-*.] Having, or moving in, only one direction: as, a *unidirectional* electric current (a current which flows in only one direction; a direct current).

u·ni·fa·ri·ous (ū-ni-fā'ri-us), *a.* [See *uni-* and *-farious*.] Single; in one row.

u·ni·fi·a·ble (ū'ni-fī-a-bl), *a.* That may be unified.

u·nif·ic (ū-nif'ik), *a.* [L. *unus*, one, + *-ficus*, < *facere*, make.] Making one; forming unity; unifying.

u·ni·fi·ca·tion (ū'ni-fi-kā'shǫn), *n.* The act of unifying, or the state of being unified: as, "a *unification* of command among all the Allies" (Buchan's "Hist. of the Great War," liii.).

u·ni·fi·er (ū'ni-fī-ėr), *n.* One who or that which unifies.

u·ni·fi·lar (ū-ni-fī'lär), *a.* [L. *unus*, one, + *filum*, thread.] **I.** *a.* Having or involving only one thread, wire, or the like: as, a *unifilar* magnetometer (consisting of a magnetic bar suspended by a single thread). **II.** *n.* A unifilar magnetometer.

u·ni·flo·rous (ū-ni-flō'rus), *a.* [L. *unus*, one, + *flos* (*flor-*), flower.] In *bot.*, having or bearing one flower only.

u·ni·fo·li·ate (ū-ni-fō'li-āt), *a.* [L. *unus*, one, + *folium*, leaf.] One-leafed; also, unifoliolate. —**u·ni·fo'li·o·late** (-ǫ-lāt), *a.* In *bot.*, compound in structure yet having but one leaflet, as the leaf of the orange-tree; also, bearing such leaves, as a plant.

Unifoliolate Leaf of Orange-tree (*Citrus aurantium*).

u·ni·form (ū'ni-fôrm). [F. *uniforme*, < L. *uniformis*, having but one form, < *unus*, one, + *forma*, form.] **I.** *a.* Having but one form; having always the same form or character; unvarying (as, a *uniform* practice; treated with *uniform* kindness; "Life upon those little islands is *uniform* even to weariness," G. W. Curtis's "Prue and I," iv.); without diversity in appearance, color, etc. (as, "Over all this the clouds shed a *uniform* and purplish shadow": Stevenson's "Travels with a Donkey," i. 3); of the same style, materials, and color, as a distinctive dress worn by a body of persons; regular, even, or equable (as, "a sharp and *uniform* pace," Scott's "Guy Mannering," xlvii.; a *uniform* temperature); consistent in action, opinion, etc., as a person, or as action, etc.; being the same in all places or in all parts of a country (as, a *uniform* divorce law); also, agreeing with one another in form, character, etc., or alike (as, "The only doubt is about the manner of their unity; how far churches are bound to be *uniform* in their ceremonies": Hooker's "Ecclesiastical Polity," iv. 13. 2); of the same form, character, etc., with another or others (as, this volume is not *uniform* with the others). **II.** *n.* A distinctive dress of uniform style, materials, and color worn by all the members of a military, naval, or other body, and by which they may be recognized as belonging to that body; a single suit of such dress: as, the *uniform* of a body of soldiers or sailors; the *uniform* of a policeman; a nurse's *uniform*.—**u'ni-form,** *v. t.* To make uniform; also, to clothe or furnish with or as with a uniform. —**u·ni·for·mi·ta'ri·an** (-fôr-mi-tā'ri-ạn). **I.** *a.* Pertaining to uniformity or a doctrine of uniformity; in *geol.*, noting or pertaining to the doctrine that certain vast geological changes in the earth's history were caused by gradual evolutionary processes still active rather than by catastrophes. **II.** *n.* One who adheres to a doctrine of uniformity, as the uniformitarian doctrine in geology.—**u·ni·for·mi·ta'ri·an·ism,** *n.*—**u·ni·for'mi·ty** (-fôr'mi-ti), *n.*; pl. *-ties* (-tiz). The state or character of being uniform; sameness of form or character throughout; absence of variation or diversity; sometimes, wearisome sameness, or monotony (as, "The late *uniformity* of their military life had rendered any change of society an interesting novelty": Scott's "Legend of Montrose," xvii.); regularity or evenness; consistency; agreement in form, character, etc.; esp., conformity to one form of procedure, practice, or opinion (as, *uniformity* of different peoples in their customs; *uniformity* in religion); also, something uniform; an extent or expanse of a uniform character (as, "Little by little the plain came into view, a vast green *uniformity*, forlorn and tenantless": Parkman's "Oregon Trail," xiii.).—**u'ni-form-ly,** *adv.*—**u'ni-form-ness,** *n.*

u·ni·fy (ū'ni-fī), *v. t.*; *-fied, -fying*. [F. *unifier*, < ML. *unificare*, < L. *unus*, one, + *facere*, make.] To form into one; make a unit of; reduce to unity.

u·ni·ju·gate (ū-ni-jö'gāt), *a.* [L. *unus*, one, + *jugum*, yoke.] In *bot.*, of a pinnate leaf, having but a single pair of leaflets. Also **u·ni·ju'gous.**

u·ni·lat·er·al (ū-ni-lat'e-ral), *a.* [L. *unus*, one, + *latus* (*later-*), side.] Pertaining to, occurring on, or affecting one side only; also, one-sided; having all the parts disposed on one side of an axis, as an inflorescence; leaning or turned to one side; also, affecting one side, party, or person only; undertaken or performed by one side only; imposing an obligation on one party only, as a contract; also, concerned with or considering but one side of a matter or question.—**u·ni·lat'er·al·ly,** *adv.*

u·ni·lit·er·al (ū-ni-lit'e-ral), *a.* [L. *unus*, one, + *litera*, letter.] Consisting of a single letter.

u·ni·lobed (ū'ni-lōbd), *a.* [See *uni-*.] Having, or consisting of, a single lobe.

u·ni·loc·u·lar (ū-ni-lok'ū-lär), *a.* [See *uni-*.] Having, or consisting of, but one loculus, chamber, or cell.

un·i·mag·i·na·ble (un-i-maj'i-na-bl), *a.* Not imaginable; inconceivable. —**un·i·mag'i·na·tive** (-nạ-tiv), *a.* Not imaginative; literal; prosaic. —**un·i·mag'ined,** *a.* Not imagined; never conceived even in imagination.

un·im·paired (un-im-pärd'), *a.* Not impaired.

un·im·pas·sioned (un-im-pash'ǫnd), *a.* Not impassioned; not influenced by passion; calm; tranquil.

un·im·peach·a·ble (un-im-pē'chạ-bl), *a.* Not impeachable; irreproachable; blameless.—**un·im·peached',** *a.* Not impeached; not called in question.

un·im·ped·ed (un-im-pē'ded), *a.* Not impeded or hindered.

un-im-por-tance (un-im-pôr'tạns), *n.* Lack of importance; insignificance.—**un-im-por'tant**, *a.* Not important; insignificant; trifling.

un-im-pressed (un-im-prest'), *a.* Not impressed.—**un-im-press'i-ble**, *a.* Not impressible; not susceptible; apathetic.—**un-im-pres'sion-a-ble**, *a.* Not impressionable; not easily impressed or influenced.

un-im-proved (un-im-prövd'), *a.* Not improved; not turned to account; not cultivated; not increased in value by betterments or improvements, as real property; not bettered.

un-in-cor-po-rat-ed (un-in-kôr'pọ-rā-ted), *a.* Not incorporated.

un-in-cum-bered (un-in-kum'bėrd), *a.* See *unencumbered.*

un-in-flam-ma-ble (un-in-flam'ạ-bl), *a.* Not inflammable.

un-in-flect-ed (un-in-flek'ted), *a.* Not inflected; not subject to inflection (as, "*uninflected* languages": W. D. Whitney's "Life and Growth of Language," vii.).

un-in-flu-enced (un-in'flö-ẹnst), *a.* Not influenced; not affected; not persuaded or moved; free from bias or prejudice.

un-in-formed (un-in-fôrmd'), *a.* Not informed; not endowed with life or spirit; uninstructed, uneducated, or ignorant; without information on some matter.

un-in-hab-it-a-ble (un-in-hab'i-tạ-bl), *a.* Not inhabitable; unfit to be inhabited.—**un-in-hab'it-ed**, *a.* Not inhabited; destitute of inhabitants: as, "an *uninhabited* wilderness" (Defoe's "Robinson Crusoe," i. 8).

un-i-ni-ti-at-ed (un-i-nish'i-ā-ted), *a.* Not initiated; not introduced into acquaintance with something; not having been admitted, as into a society.

un-in-jured (un-in'jọrd), *a.* Not injured; unharmed.

un-in-struct-ed (un-in-struk'ted), *a.* Not instructed; not educated; not informed on some matter; not furnished with instructions, directions, or orders.

un-in-sured (un-in-shörd'), *a.* Not insured; without insurance.

un-in-tel-li-gence (un-in-tel'i-jẹns), *n.* Lack of intelligence; ignorance; unwisdom.—**un-in-tel'li-gent**, *a.* Not intelligent; not endowed with intelligence, as an inanimate object; deficient in intelligence, dull, or stupid; having no knowledge (*of*: obs. or rare).—**un-in-tel'li-gent-ly**, *adv.*

un-in-tel-li-gi-ble (un-in-tel'i-ji-bl), *a.* Not intelligible; not capable of being understood.—**un-in-tel'li-gi-bil'i-ty** (-bil'i-ti), **un-in-tel'li-gi-ble-ness**, *n.*—**un-in-tel'li-gi-bly**, *adv.*

un-in-tend-ed (un-in-ten'ded), *a.* Not intended.

un-in-ten-tion-al (un-in-ten'shọn-ạl), *a.* Not intentional; not acting with intention; not done purposely, or not designed.—**un-in-ten'tion-al-ly**, *adv.*

un-in-ter-est-ed (un-in'tėr-es-ted), *a.* Not interested; not personally concerned or involved in something; having or showing no feeling of interest (as, an *uninterested* spectator; an *uninterested* tone).—**un-in'ter-est-ing**, *a.* Not interesting; not arousing any feeling of interest.—**un-in'ter-est-ing-ly**, *adv.*—**un-in'ter-est-ing-ness**, *n.*

un-in-ter-mit-ted (un-in-tėr-mit'ed), *a.* Not intermitted; continuous.—**un-in-ter-mit'ting**, *a.* Not intermitting; continuing.—**un-in-ter-mit'ting-ly**, *adv.*

un-in-ter-rupt-ed (un-in-tẹ-rup'ted), *a.* Not interrupted; without interruption; continuous.—**un-in-ter-rupt'ed-ly**, *adv.*

un-in-tox-i-cat-ing (un-in-tok'si-kā-ting), *a.* Not intoxicating.

un-in-vit-ed (un-in-vī'ted), *a.* Not invited.—**un-in-vit'ing**, *a.* Not inviting; unattractive.—**un-in-vit'ing-ly**, *adv.*

u-nion (ū'nyọn), *n.* [F. *union*, < LL. *unio*(n-), the number one, unity, union, L. a single large pearl, a kind of single onion, < L. *unus*, one: cf. *onion.*] The act of uniting two or more things into one, or the state of being so united; junction; combination; a uniting or being united in matrimony, or a marriage (as, "George Cannon, the son of the *union*, had been left early an orphan": Arnold Bennett's "Hilda Lessways," i. 5); a uniting of states or nations into one political body, as that of the American colonies at the time of the Revolution, that of England and Scotland in 1707, or that of Great Britain and Ireland in 1801 (as, "Reflecting men in England dreaded American *union* as the keystone of independence": Bancroft's "Hist. of the U. S.,"

Amer. Revolution, i. 5); the uniting of persons, parties, etc., in general agreement, or the resulting condition; also, something formed by uniting two or more things; a combination; esp., a number of persons, societies, states, or the like, joined or associated together for some common purpose; a number of states united into one political body; specif. [*cap.*], with *the*, the United States of America; [*l. c.*] a number of parishes in England united for the administration of the poor-laws, etc.; a workhouse erected and maintained by such a union (in full, 'union workhouse'); an association of independent churches for purposes of coöperation; a trade-union, or association of workmen; also, a textile fabric of two or more different materials woven together; also, a device emblematic of union, used in a flag or ensign, sometimes occupying the upper corner next to the staff (as in the U. S. ensign, where it indicates the union of the States, or in the British ensign, with reference to the union of England, Scotland, and Ireland), or sometimes occupying the entire field; also [*cap.*], with *the*, any of certain general clubs at different universities, as at Oxford and Cambridge and at Harvard, usually open to all members or all undergraduates of the university; the building or quarters of such a club; also [*l. c.*], something that unites or joins things; any of various contrivances for connecting parts of machinery, etc.; a coupling for pipes or tubes; also, a large, fine pearl† (see Shakspere's "Hamlet," v. 2. 283).—**union down**, of a flag or ensign, displaying the union at the lower corner next to the staff, instead of in its normal position (a flag hoisted in this way forming a signal of distress or of mourning): as, "There was an ensign, *union down*, flying at her main gaff" (J. Conrad's "Lord Jim," xii.).—**u'nion**, *a.* Of or pertaining to union or a union; [*cap.*] pertaining to the United States of America (used particularly with reference to the Civil War period, and opposed to *Confederate*); [*l. c.*] belonging or pertaining to a trade-union; in accordance with the rules of a trade-union; recognizing trade-unions.—**union jack**, a jack consisting of the union of a national flag or ensign; hence, any flag consisting of a union only (see *union*, *n.*).—**union suit**, a suit of underwear (undershirt and drawers) in one piece.

u-ni-on-id (ū-ni-on'id), *n.* [NL. *Unionidæ*, pl., < *Unio*, the typical genus, < L. *unio*, pearl: see *union.*] Any member of the *Unionidæ*, a large and widely distributed family of freshwater mussels, especially numerous in the U.S., species of which produce pearls.

Unionid. — *A*, right valve (genus *Monocondylæa*); *B*, left valve (genus *Unio*).

u-nion-ism (ū'nyọn-izm), *n.* The principle of union; specif., trade-unionism; also, attachment to a union; specif. [*cap.*], loyalty to the federal union of the United States of America, esp. at the time of the Civil War.—**u'nion-ist**, *n.* One who promotes or advocates union; [*cap.*] an adherent of the federal union of the United States of America, esp. at the time of the Civil War; also, in British politics, an upholder of the legislative union of Great Britain and Ireland; an opponent of home rule in Ireland; also [*l. c.*], a member of a trade-union.—**u-nion-is'tic**, *a.*

u-nion-ize (ū'nyọn-īz), *v.*; *-ized, -izing.* **I.** *tr.* To form into a union; esp., to organize into a trade-union; bring into or incorporate in a trade-union; subject to the rules of a trade-union. **II.** *intr.* To form a union; join in a trade-union.—**u''nion-i-za'tion** (-i-zā'shọn), *n.*

u-nip-a-rous (ū-nip'ạ-rus), *a.* [L. *unus*, one, + *parere*, bring forth.] Producing but one at a birth; in *bot.*, of a cyme, producing but one axis at each branching.

u-ni-per-son-al (ū-ni-pėr'sọn-ạl), *a.* [See *uni-.*] Consisting of or existing as but one person (as, a *unipersonal* God); in *gram.*, used in only one person, esp. the third person singular, as certain verbs.

u-ni-pet-a-lous (ū-ni-pet'ạ-lus), *a.* [See *uni-.*] In *bot.*, having only one petal.

u-ni-pla-nar (ū-ni-plā'när), *a.* [See *uni-.*] Lying or taking place in one plane: as, *uniplanar* motion (motion confined to one plane; motion in which the paths described by the particles of the moving body lie in planes parallel to one another).

u-ni-po-lar (ū-ni-pō′lär), a. [See uni-.] Having only one pole; pertaining to or found at one pole only.—**u″ni-po-lar′i-ty** (-pō-lar′i-ti), n.

u-nique (ū-nēk′). [F. unique, < L. unicus, only, single, < unus, one.] **I.** a. Of which there is but one, or sole or only (as, "He despised play. His unique wish was to work": Arnold Bennett's "Clayhanger," i. 12); also, having no like or equal, or standing alone in comparison with others (as, "He admired her passionately and deemed her unique and above all women": Arnold Bennett's "Clayhanger," ii. 19); unparalleled or unequaled; loosely, rare or unusual (as, a most unique specimen or experience). **II.** n. Something unique; something of which there is only one; something without parallel or equal of its kind.—**u-nique′ly**, adv.—**u-nique′ness**, n.

u-ni-sep-tate (ū-ni-sep′tāt), a. [See uni-.] Having only one septum or partition, as a silicle.

u-ni-se-ri-al (ū-ni-sē′ri-al), a. [See uni-.] Arranged in one series or row. Also **u-ni-se′ri-ate** (-āt).

u-ni-sex-u-al (ū-ni-sek′shū-al), a. [See uni-.] Of or pertaining to one sex only; esp., having only male or female organs in one individual, as an animal or a flower; having the two sexes developed in different individuals; not hermaphrodite.

u-ni-son (ū′ni-son or -zon). [F. unisson, unison, < ML. unisonus, having one or the same sound, < L. unus, one, + sonus, sound.] **I.** n. Coincidence in pitch of two or more tones, voices, etc.; the interval between any tone and a tone of exactly the same pitch; also, a sounding together at the same pitch, as of different voices or instruments performing the same part; loosely, a sounding together in octaves, esp. of male and female voices or of higher and lower instruments of the same class; also, fig., accord or agreement (as, "The circumstance was in perfect unison with what she had heard and seen herself": Jane Austen's "Sense and Sensibility," xii.). **II.** a. Of or pertaining to unison; in unison; unisonous.—**u-nis-o-nal** (ū-nis′ō-nal), a. Unisonous.—**u-nis′o-nant**, a. Sounding in unison; unisonous. —**u-nis′o-nance**, n.—**u-nis′o-nous**, a. [ML. unisonus.] According to sound or pitch; being in unison.

u-nit (ū′nit), n. [From unity.] A single thing or person; any group of things or persons regarded as an individual (as, "The efforts of every people to become a political unit have sprung from an original and universal instinct": J. F. Kirk's "Charles the Bold," iv. 2); one of the individuals or groups making up a whole, or into which a whole may be analyzed; also, any magnitude regarded as an independent whole; any standard quantity or amount, as of length, area, volume, force, value, time, etc., by the repetition or division of which any other quantity of the same kind is measured or estimated (sometimes used attributively in unit area, unit mass, etc., to denote an area, mass, etc., to the amount of one unit).—**thermal unit.** See under thermal.

U-ni-ta-ri-an (ū-ni-tā′ri-an), a. [NL. unitarius, < L. unitas, E. unity: cf. Trinitarian.] **I.** n. One who maintains that God is unipersonal, in opposition to the doctrine of the Trinity; specif., a member of a Christian denomination founded upon the doctrine that God is unipersonal; [l. c.] a monotheist; also, a monist; also, one who advocates any unitary system; an advocate of unity or centralization, as in government. **II.** a. [cap.] Pertaining to the Unitarians or their doctrines; accepting Unitarianism; belonging to the Unitarians; [l. c.] pertaining to a unit or unity; unitary.— **U-ni-ta′ri-an-ism**, n. The doctrines of Unitarians; [l. c.] any unitary system, as of government.

u-ni-ta-ry (ū′ni-tā-ri), a. [From unit and unity + -ary.] Of or pertaining to a unit or units; also, pertaining to, characterized by, or based on unity; advocating or directed toward national unity or centralization in government; also, of the nature of a unit; having the individual character of a unit; also, serving as a unit, as of measurement or estimation.

u-nite (ū-nīt′), v.; united, uniting. [L. unitus, pp. of unire, < unus, one.] **I.** tr. To join so as to form one connected whole, as one or more things to or with another or others, or two or more things together; join, combine, or incorporate in one; cause to be one; cause to hold together or adhere (as, to unite bricks or stones by means of cement); join in marriage; associate (persons, etc.) by some bond or tie (as, to unite nations by treaty); join in action, interest, opinion, feeling, etc.; also, to have or exhibit in union or combination (as, a building uniting two different styles of architecture). **II.** intr. To join together so as to form one connected whole; become one; combine; join in marriage; enter into alliance or association; join in action, or act in concert or agreement; become one in opinion or feeling.

u-nit-ed (ū-nī′ted), p. a. Joined together; combined; made one; also, of, or produced by, two or more persons, etc., in combination; formed by the union of two or more things, bodies, etc.—**United Brethren.** See Moravian, n.— **United Greeks,** the members of those Christian communities which retain the liturgy, rites, etc., of the Greek or Eastern Church but are united to or in communion with the Church of Rome. Cf. Uniat.—**United Kingdom,** the kingdom of Great Britain, or esp. (during the period of the legislative union with Ireland, 1801–1922) of Great Britain and Ireland.—**United Nations,** the nations that pledged themselves in Washington (Jan. 2, 1942) to employ full resources against the Axis powers, not to make a separate peace, etc.; also the fifty nations (with subsequent additions) who signed the charter written at the United Nations Conference on International Organization.—**United Nations Conference on International Organization,** a conference held in San Francisco from Apr. 25 to June 26, 1945, to write a charter based on the Dumbarton Oaks proposals. —**United States,** the great federal republic in North America which had its origin in the revolt of 1776 of the thirteen British colonies, and which is called in full 'The United States of America.' As used attributively, of or pertaining to the United States of America: as, the United States army.—**u-nit′ed-ly**, adv.—**u-nit′ed-ness**, n.

u-nit-er (ū-nī′ter), n. One who or that which unites.

u-ni-tion (ū-nish′on), n. [ML. unitio(n-), < L. unire: see unite.] The act of uniting or the resulting state; union.

u-ni-tive (ū′ni-tiv), a. Serving or tending to unite.

u-ni-ty (ū′ni-ti), n.; pl. -ties (-tiz). [OF. unite (F. unité), < L. unitas, < unus, one.] The state or fact of being one; oneness; hence, one single thing; something complete in itself, or regarded as such; also, the oneness of a complex or organic whole or of an interconnected series; a whole or totality as combining all its parts into one; also, the fact or state of being united or combined into one, as of the parts of a whole (as, the national unity of confederated states); a body formed by union; also, freedom from diversity or variety; unvaried or uniform character, as of a plan; also, oneness of mind, feeling, etc., as among a number of persons; concord, harmony, or agreement; in math., the number one; a quantity regarded as one; a quantity which, multiplied by any particular quantity of the system considered, gives that particular quantity as the product; in literature and art, such a relation of all the parts or elements of a work as constitutes a harmonious whole and produces a single general effect; in the drama, any of the three principles of unity of action, unity of time, and unity of place ('the three unities'), derived (by misinterpretation) from Aristotle's "Poetics," and adopted as fundamental rules of dramatic construction by French classical dramatic critics and writers of the 17th century, and in the strictest requirements demanding a single action (with nothing irrelevant admitted) which should occur within a single day and without shifting of the scene from place to place.

u-ni-va-lent (ū-ni-vā′lent or ū-niv′a-), a. [See uni- and -valent.] In chem., having a valence of one.—**u-ni-va′lence**, n.

u-ni-valve (ū′ni-valv). [See uni-.] **I.** a. Having one valve; of numerous mollusks, as the snails, limpets, etc., having a shell consisting of one valve; of a shell, composed of a single valve or piece. **II.** n. A univalve mollusk or

Univalve. — A triton (Triton tritonis).

its shell; a gastropod.—**u′ni-valved, u-ni-val′vu-lar** (-val′-vū-lạr), *a.* Univalve.

u-ni-ver-sal (ū-ni-vẻr′sạl). [L. *universalis*, < *universus*, all together: see *universe*.] **I.** *a.* Of, pertaining to, or characteristic of all or the whole (as, the *universal* experience of mankind; *universal* satisfaction; a *universal* tendency; "With the exceptions noted, the foregoing characters are *universal* among the Rodentia," Huxley's "Anatomy of Vertebrated Animals," viii.); affecting, concerning, or involving all (as, a *universal* rule; "*universal* military service," H. G. Wells's "Mr. Britling," ii. 2. § 3); given or extended to all (as, a *universal* revelation; "You preach of *universal* charity and love," Galsworthy's "Saint's Progress," iii. 10); used or understood by all (as, a *universal* language); existing or prevailing in all parts or everywhere (as, "the *universal* calm of southern seas," G. W. Curtis's "Prue and I," iii.; "*universal* verdure," H. Melville's "Typee," vi.; *universal* stillness); versed in or embracing all subjects, fields, etc. (as, a *universal* genius; *universal* culture or knowledge; a *universal* range of interests or activities); also, comprising all, or whole or entire (archaic: as, the *universal* earth; "The tender grass, whose verdure clad Her [the earth's] *universal* face with pleasant green," Milton's "Paradise Lost," vii. 316); also, of or pertaining to the universe, all nature, or all existing things (as, the doctrine of a *universal* mind; "The *Universal* Cause Acts to one end, but acts by various laws," Pope's "Essay on Man," iii. 1); in *logic*, relating or applicable to all the members of a class or genus (as, a *universal* proposition); also, applicable to many individuals or single cases, or general; in *mech.*, etc., adapted or adaptable for all or various uses, angles, sizes, etc.; as a joint or the like, allowing free movement in all directions within certain limits. **II.** *n.* In *logic*, a universal proposition; also, any of the five Aristotelian predicables (see *predicable, n.*); also, a general term or concept, or the general nature which such a term signifies (see *nominalism, conceptualism,* and *realism*).—**u-ni-ver′sal-ism,** *n.* Universal character; universality; universal range of knowledge, interests, or activities (sometimes opposed to *specialism*); [*cap.*] the doctrine or belief of Universalists.—**u-ni-ver′sal-ist,** *n.* One characterized by universalism, as in knowledge, interests, or activities (sometimes opposed to *specialist*); [*cap.*] one who believes in the doctrine that all men will finally be saved, or brought back to holiness and God; specif., a member of a Christian denomination which holds this doctrine as its distinctive belief.—**u″ni-ver-sal′i-ty** (-sal′i-ti), *n.* The character or state of being universal; relation, extension, or applicability to all; existence or prevalence everywhere; universal character or range of knowledge, interests, etc.; also, the whole number or body of anything, or the whole (archaic: as, the *universality* of the people or nation).—**u-ni-ver′sal-ize** (-sạl-īz), *v. t.;* -ized, -izing. To make universal.—**u-ni-ver″sal-i-za′tion** (-i-zā′shọn), *n.* —**u-ni-ver′sal-ly,** *adv.* In a universal manner; in every instance, part, or place; without exception; generally.—**u-ni-ver′sal-ness,** *n.*

u-ni-verse (ū′ni-vẻrs), *n.* [L. *universum*, the universe, prop. neut. of *universus,* all together, whole, universal, lit. 'turned into one,' < *unus*, one, + *versus*, pp. of *vertere*, turn.] The totality of existing or created things, including the earth (with all on or in it), the heavenly bodies, and all else throughout space (as, "There is but one thought greater than that of the *universe*, and that is the thought of its Maker": J. H. Newman's "Idea of a University," ii. 8); the cosmos or macrocosm; all creation; the whole world; also, a system of heavenly bodies, etc., or an indefinitely great expanse of space, conceived as a single world analogous to the great universe (as, "The stars visible in our telescopes form a *universe* having a more or less defined boundary," Encyc. Brit., 11th ed., XXV. 792; "No cloud above, no earth below, — A *universe* of sky and snow!" Whittier's "Snow-Bound"); fig., a world or sphere in which something exists or prevails (as, "Love's rare *Universe*": Shelley's "Epipsychidion," 589); also, the world or earth (archaic); hence, mankind generally (as, the whole *universe* knows it); in *logic*, the collection of all the objects to which any discourse refers ('universe of discourse').

u-ni-ver-si-ty (ū-ni-vẻr′si-ti), *n.; pl.* -ties (-tiz). [OF. *uni-*

versite (F. *université*), < L. *universitas*, the whole, the universe, a community, society, or corporation, < *universus,* all together: see *universe.*] The whole†; the universe†; also, a collective or corporate body†; also, an institution of learning of the highest grade, having various schools and faculties (as of theology, law, medicine, and the arts), concerned with instruction in all or many of the higher branches of learning and authorized to confer degrees (cf. *college*).— **university extension,** the extending of the advantages of university instruction to others than university students, by means of lectures at convenient centers and sometimes also by class-work, home-work, and correspondence.

un-i-ver-sol-o-gy (ū″ni-vẻr-sol′ọ-ji), *n.* [See *-logy.*] The science of the universe, or of all created things.—**u″ni-ver-sol′o-gist,** *n.*

u-niv-o-cal (ū-niv′ọ-kạl), *a.* [LL. *univocus*, < L. *unus*, one, + *vox* (*voc-*), voice, speech.] Having one meaning only; not equivocal; capable of but one interpretation; of which the meaning is unmistakable.—**u-niv′o-cal-ly,** *adv.*

un-joint (un-joint′), *v. t.* To take apart the joints of; disjoint.

un-just (un-just′), *a.* Not just; not acting justly or fairly, as persons; not in accordance with justice or fairness, as actions; also, unfaithful or dishonest (archaic: as, "the *unjust* steward," Luke, xvi. 8).

un-jus-ti-fi-a-ble (un-jus′ti-fī-ạ-bl), *a.* Not justifiable; indefensible.—**un-jus′ti-fi-a-ble-ness,** *n.*—**un-jus′ti-fi-a-bly,** *adv.*

un-just-ly (un-just′li), *adv.* In an unjust manner.—**un-just′ness,** *n.*

un-kempt (un-kempt′), *a.* [See *kempt.*] Not combed, as the hair (as, "an unwashed brow, an *unkempt* head of hair": Scott's "Castle Dangerous," i.); having the hair not combed or cared for (as, "our wild Seer, shaggy, *unkempt*": Carlyle's "Sartor Resartus," i. 4); in general, in an uncared-for, neglected, or untidy state (as, "The garden became disagreeably *unkempt*," H. G. Wells's "Mr. Britling," ii. 4. § 15; "So foul, draggled, and *unkempt* was every rope and stick aboard," Kipling's "Captains Courageous," iv.); rough. —**un-kempt′ness,** *n.*

un-ken-nel (un-ken′ẹl), *v. t.;* -neled or -nelled, -neling or -nelling. To drive or release from or as from a kennel; dislodge; fig., to bring to light.

un-kind (un-kīnd′), *a.* [Cf. AS. *uncynde, ungecynde,* unnatural.] Not kind; harsh; cruel; unmerciful; unfeeling and distressing: as, an *unkind* stepmother; *unkind* words; "This was the most *unkindest* cut of all" (Shakspere's "Julius Cæsar," iii. 2. 187).—**un-kind′ly,** *a.* Not kindly; ill-natured; unkind; inclement or bleak, as weather, climate, etc.; unfavorable for crops, as soil.—**un-kind′li-ness,** *n.*— **un-kind′ly,** *adv.* In an unkind manner.—**un-kind′ness,** *n.*

un-king-ly (un-king′li), *a.* Not kingly; not befitting a king; not royal.

un-knight-ly (un-nīt′li), *a.* Not knightly; unworthy of a knight; not like a knight.—**un-knight′li-ness,** *n.*—**un-knight′ly,** *adv.*

un-knit (un-nit′), *v. t.;* -knitted or -knit, -knitting. To untie or unfasten (a knot, etc.); also, to ravel out (something knitted); also, to smooth out (something wrinkled: as, "He *unknit* his black brows," C. Brontë's "Jane Eyre," xxiv.).

un-knot (un-not′), *v. t.;* -knotted, -knotting. To bring out of a knotted state; free from knots; untie.

un-know-a-ble (un-nō′ạ-bl). **I.** *a.* Not knowable; incapable of being known; transcending human knowledge. **II.** *n.* Something unknowable; specif., in *philos.*, the (postulated) reality lying behind all phenomena but transcending apprehension by any of the processes by which the mind apprehends its objects (often, 'the Unknowable').— **un-know′a-ble-ness,** *n.*—**un-know′ing,** *a.* Not knowing; ignorant.—**un-know′ing-ly,** *adv.*—**un-know′ing-ness,** *n.* —**un-known′,** *a.* Not known; not within the range of one's knowledge, cognizance, or acquaintance; not ascertained, discovered, or identified; unfamiliar; strange.—**unknown quantity,** in *math.*, a quantity whose value is to be found: in algebra, etc., usually represented by a letter from the last part of the alphabet, as x, y, or z.—**Unknown Soldier,** or **Unknown Warrior,** an unidentified soldier belonging to the army of one of the countries engaged in the World War,

---

fat, fāte, fär, fåll, åsk, fāre; net, mē, hėr; pin, pīne; not, nōte, möve, nȯr; up, lūte, púll; oi, oil; ou, out; (lightened) aviȧry, ęlect, agǫny, intǫ, ụnite; (obscured) errạnt, operạ, ardẹnt, actọr, natụre; ch, chip; g, go; th, thin; ᴛʜ, then; y, you;

killed in the war and buried with honors in a prominent place in his country, his tomb serving as a memorial to all the unidentified dead of the army. The French soldier (F. *Soldat Inconnu*) is buried beneath the Arc de Triomphe de l'Étoile, in Paris; the British soldier (Unknown Warrior), in Westminster Abbey, in London; the Italian soldier (It. *Milite Ignoto*), at the base of the Victor Emmanuel II. Monument, in Rome; the Belgian soldier (F. *Soldat Inconnu*), at the foot of the Colonne du Congrès, in Brussels; the American soldier (Unknown Soldier), in the Arlington National Cemetery, near Washington.—**un-known′**, *n.* One who or that which is unknown (as, the Great *Unknown*, Sir Walter Scott, whose novels were at first published anonymously); an unknown person; in *math.*, an unknown quantity.

un-lace (un-lās′), *v. t.* To undo the lacing of (a garment, etc.); loosen or remove the garments, etc., of by undoing lacing; fig., to expose† or reveal†; undo† or ruin† (as, "What's the matter, That you *unlace* your reputation thus?" Shakspere's "Othello," ii. 3. 194).

un-lade (un-lād′), *v.* **I.** *tr.* To take the lading, load, or cargo from; unload; also, to discharge (the load or cargo). **II.** *intr.* To discharge the load or cargo: as, "I see vessels *unlading* at the wharf" (Hawthorne's "Twice-Told Tales," Sights from a Steeple).

un-la-dy-like (un-lā′di-līk), *a.* Not ladylike; not like or befitting a lady.

un-laid (un-lād′), *p. a.* [See *unlay*.] Untwisted, as a rope.

un-lash (un-lash′), *v. t.* To loose or unfasten, as something lashed or tied fast.

un-latch (un-lach′), *v.* **I.** *tr.* To unfasten or open (a door, etc.) by lifting the latch. **II.** *intr.* To become unlatched; open through the lifting of a latch.

un-laun-dered (un-lân′dėrd), *a.* Not laundered.

un-law-ful (un-lâ′fùl), *a.* Not lawful; contrary to law; illegal; not sanctioned by law; born out of wedlock, or illegitimate.—**unlawful assembly,** in *law*, the meeting of three or more persons to commit an unlawful act, or to carry out some purpose in such manner as to give reasonable ground for apprehending a breach of the peace in consequence of it. Cf. *riot*.—**un-law′ful-ly,** *adv.*—**un-law′ful-ness,** *n.*

un-lay (un-lā′), *v. t.*; -*laid*, -*laying*. To untwist, as a rope.

un-lead-ed (un-led′ed), *a.* Not leaded; not separated or spaced with leads, as lines of type or printed matter.

un-learn (un-lėrn′), *v. t.*; -*learned* or -*learnt*, -*learning*. To put aside from knowledge or memory (something learned); discard or lose knowledge of; forget: as, "Let us *unlearn* our wisdom of the world" (Emerson's "Essays," Spiritual Laws); "The people have long *unlearned* the use of arms" (Macaulay's "Hist. of Eng.," i.).

un-learn-ed (un-lėr′ned), *a.* Not learned; not scholarly or erudite; uneducated; ignorant; devoid of learning; also (pron. un-lėrnd′), not acquired by learning; never learned; sometimes, known without being learned.—**un-learn′ed-ly,** *adv.*

un-leased (un-lēst′), *a.* Not leased.

un-leash (un-lēsh′), *v. t.* To release from or as from a leash; set free to pursue or run at will; let loose: as, to *unleash* dogs in hunting; to *unleash* the passions.

un-leav-ened (un-lev′nd), *a.* Not leavened: as, "the passover, a feast of seven days; *unleavened* bread shall be eaten" (Ezek. xlv. 21).

un-less (un-les′). [For earlier *onlesse*, *on lesse than* (or *that*), 'on less than' (with specification of some condition).] **I.** *conj.* If it be (or were) not that, or if . . . not (as, "The past is not dead *unless* we choose that it shall be so," Mallock's "New Republic," iv. 1; he went once a week, *unless* specially summoned); also, for fear that†, or lest†. **II.** *prep.* Except: as, "Here nothing breeds, *Unless* the nightly owl" (Shakspere's "Titus Andronicus," ii. 3. 97).

un-les-soned (un-les′nd), *a.* Not lessoned; untaught; untutored: as, "an *unlesson'd* girl, unschool'd, unpractised" (Shakspere's "Merchant of Venice," iii. 2. 161).

un-let-tered (un-let′ėrd), *a.* Not lettered; unlearned; uneducated; without knowledge of books.

un-li-censed (un-lī′senst), *a.* Not licensed; having no license; done or undertaken without license; unauthorized.

un-licked (un-likt′), *a.* Not licked; not brought to the proper shape or condition by or as by licking (as, an *unlicked* cub, often fig., a crude or unmannerly young person: see *to lick into shape*, under *lick*, *v. t.*); fig., crude, rough, or unpolished.

un-light-ed (un-lī′ted), *a.* Not lighted; not illuminated; not kindled or ignited.

un-like (un-līk′), *a.* Not like; different or dissimilar; having no resemblance; also, unlikely (archaic or prov.).—**un-like′,** *prep.* Otherwise than like; differently from: as, to act *unlike* others.—**un-like′li-hood** (-li-hùd), *n.* The state of being unlikely; improbability.—**un-like′ly,** *a.* Not likely; improbable; probably not going (to do, be, etc.: as, *unlikely* to do anything; *unlikely* to be found, happen, or succeed); holding out little prospect of success; unpromising.—**un-like′li-ness,** *n.*—**un-like′ly,** *adv.* Improbably.—**un-like′ness,** *n.*

un-lim-ber (un-lim′bėr), *v. t.* or *i.* To detach the limber from (a gun).

un-lim-it-ed (un-lim′i-ted), *a.* Not limited; unrestricted; boundless; limitless.—**un-lim′it-ed-ly,** *adv.*—**un-lim′it-ed-ness,** *n.*

un-link (un-lingk′), *v. t.* To separate the links of (a chain, etc.); also, to separate or detach by or as by undoing a connecting link.

un-li-qui-dat-ed (un-lik′wi-dā-ted), *a.* Not liquidated; not settled: as, *unliquidated* debts or claims.

un-list-ed (un-lis′ted), *a.* Not listed; not entered in a list; in the stock-exchange, of securities, not entered in the regular list of those admitted for dealings.

un-lit (un-lit′), *a.* Not lit; unlighted.

un-live (un-liv′), *v. t.* To deprive of life†; also, to undo or annul (past life, etc.); live so as to undo the consequences of.

un-load (un-lōd′), *v.* **I.** *tr.* To take the load from; remove the burden, cargo, or freight from; relieve of anything burdensome; withdraw the charge from (a firearm); also, to remove or discharge (a load, etc.: as, "lighters . . . with cargoes of merchandise which they *unloaded* into carts," W. H. Hudson's "Far Away and Long Ago," vii.); get rid of (anything burdensome), as by casting upon another; get rid or dispose of (stock, etc.) by sale in large quantities (colloq.). **II.** *intr.* To unload something; remove or discharge a load.—**un-load′er,** *n.*

un-lock (un-lok′), *v.* **I.** *tr.* To undo the lock of; open or release by or as by undoing a lock; in general, to open (anything firmly closed or joined: as, to *unlock* the jaws or the fingers); lay open; disclose. **II.** *intr.* To become unlocked.

un-looked-for (un-lùkt′fôr), *a.* Not looked for; unexpected; unforeseen: as, "this *unlooked-for* danger" (Godwin's "Caleb Williams," xxix.).

un-loose (un-lös′), *v. t.* To set or let loose; release from bonds, fastenings, etc.; set free from restraint (as, "Something . . . seems to have . . . *unloosed* her tongue": J. Conrad's "Rover," xi.); also, to loose or undo (a bond, fastening, knot, etc.); also, to loosen or relax (the grasp, hold, fingers, etc.).

un-loos-en (un-lö′sn), *v. t.* To unloose; loosen.

un-love (un-luv′), *v. t.* To cease to love.

un-love-ly (un-luv′li), *a.* Not lovely; without beauty or charm of appearance, or unpleasing to the eye (as, "the grim, *unlovely* cemetery belonging to the Tower Hamlets": Besant's "All Sorts and Conditions of Men," vii.); unattractive, repellent, or disagreeable in character (as, "Puritanism showed itself to have a most *unlovely* side": Morley's "Oliver Cromwell," ii. 3); unpleasant; objectionable.—**un-love′li-ness,** *n.*

un-lov-ing (un-luv′ing), *a.* Not loving; without love.—**un-lov′ing-ly,** *adv.*—**un-lov′ing-ness,** *n.*

un-luck-y (un-luk′i), *a.* Not lucky; not having good luck; unfortunate or ill-fated; not attended with good luck; also, mischievous or troublesome (archaic or prov.).—**un-luck′i-ly,** *adv.*—**un-luck′i-ness,** *n.*

un-made¹ (un-mād′). Pret. and pp. of *unmake*.

un-made² (un-mād′), *a.* Not, or not yet, made.

un-maid-en-ly (un-mā′dn-li), *a.* Not maidenly; unbefitting a maiden.—**un-maid′en-li-ness,** *n.*

un-mail-a-ble (un-mā′la-bl), *a.* Not mailable; that cannot be mailed.

un-make (un-māk′), *v. t.*; -*made*, -*making*. To cause to be as if never made; reduce to the original matter, elements, or state; take to pieces; destroy; uncreate; ruin or undo (as, "She [Medea] will *unmake* thee [Jason] yet, as she has made": W. Morris's "Jason," xvii. 181); depose from office or authority.—**un-mak′er** (-mā′kẽr), *n.*

un-mal-le-a-ble (un-mal′ē̠-ạ-bl), *a.* Not malleable.—**un-mal″le-a-bil′i-ty** (-bil′i-ti), *n.*

ın-man (un-man′), *v. t.*; *-manned, -manning.* To deprive of the character or qualities of a man or human being; also, to deprive of virility, or emasculate; also, to deprive of manly courage or fortitude, or break down the manly spirit of (as, "This added calamity nearly *unmanned* me": H. Melville's "Typee," xxxi.); also, to deprive of men (as, to *unman* a ship).

un-man-age-a-ble (un-man′ạj-ạ-bl), *a.* Not manageable; intractable; unruly; incapable of being handled.—**un-man′age-a-ble-ness,** *n.*—**un-man′age-a-bly,** *adv.*

un-man-ly (un-man′li), *a.* Not manly; not like or befitting a man; womanish or childish; weak; cowardly.—**un-man′li-ness,** *n.*

un-manned (un-mand′), *a.* Of a hawk, not manned; untamed. Also fig.

un-man-nered (un-man′ẽrd), *a.* Without manners; unmannerly.

un-man-ner-ly (un-man′ẽr-li), *a.* Not mannerly; ill-bred; rude; churlish: as, "How much better to lose a little territory than to be *unmannerly* and unkind" (Dunsany's "Queen's Enemies").—**un-man′ner-li-ness,** *n.*—**un-man′-ner-ly,** *adv.*

un-mar-ket-a-ble (un-mär′ket-ạ-bl), *a.* Not marketable; unsalable.

un-mar-ried (un-mar′id), *a.* Not married; single.

un-mar-ry (un-mar′i), *v.* **I.** *tr.* To dissolve the marriage of; divorce. **II.** *intr.* To become freed from a marriage.

un-mask (un-mȧsk′), *v.* **I.** *tr.* To strip of a mask or disguise; lay open (anything concealed); fig., to expose in the true character (as, to *unmask* a hypocrite; to *unmask* villainy); *milit.*, to reveal the presence of (guns, etc.) by firing (as, "Noircarmes . . . had *unmasked* his batteries, and opened his fire": Motley's "Dutch Republic," ii. 10). **II.** *intr.* To put off a mask or disguise. Also fig.

un-match-a-ble (un-mach′ạ-bl), *a.* Not matchable; not to be matched or equaled.—**un-matched′,** *a.* Not matched; matchless; unequaled.

un-mean-ing (un-mē′ning), *a.* Not meaning anything; without meaning or significance, as words or actions; meaningless; also, expressionless, vacant, or unintelligent, as the face, etc.—**un-mean′ing-ly,** *adv.*—**un-mean′ing-ness,** *n.* —**un-meant′** (-ment′), *a.* Not meant or intended.

un-meas-ured (un-mezh′ụrd), *a.* Not measured; of undetermined or indefinitely great extent or amount; unlimited; measureless; also, unrestrained or intemperate (as, "Lord Melbourne and the Court were attacked by the Tory press in *unmeasured* language": Lytton Strachey's "Queen Victoria," iii.).

un-meet (un-mēt′), *a.* Not meet; unfitting; unbecoming; unseemly.—**un-meet′ly,** *adv.*—**un-meet′ness,** *n.*

un-men-tion-a-ble (un-men′shọn-ạ-bl), *a.* Not mentionable; unworthy or unfit to be mentioned.—**un-men′tion-a-bles,** *n. pl.* Trousers or breeches; also, undergarments. [Humorous.]—**un-men′tioned,** *a.* Not mentioned.

un-mer-chant-a-ble (un-mẽr′chạn-tạ-bl), *a.* Not merchantable; unfit for sale or for the market.

un-mer-ci-ful (un-mẽr′si-fụl), *a.* Not merciful; merciless; pitiless; relentless; unsparing; also, unsparingly great, or unconscionable (as, "a logical and historical argument of *unmerciful* length": Motley's "Dutch Republic," vi. 3).— **un-mer′ci-ful-ly,** *adv.*—**un-mer′ci-ful-ness,** *n.*

un-mer-it-ed (un-mer′i-ted), *a.* Not merited; undeserved. —**un-mer′it-ing,** *a.* Not meriting; undeserving.

un-mew (un-mū′), *v. t.* To set free (something mewed up); release, as from confinement.

un-mind-ful (un-mīnd′fụl), *a.* Not mindful; regardless; heedless; careless.—**un-mind′ful-ly,** *adv.*—**un-mind′ful-ness,** *n.*

un-min-gled (un-ming′gld), *a.* Not mingled; unmixed; pure.

un-mis-tak-a-ble (un-mis-tā′kạ-bl), *a.* Not mistakable; admitting of no mistake; clear; plain; evident.—**un-mis-tak′a-ble-ness,** *n.*—**un-mis-tak′a-bly,** *adv.*

un-mi-ter, un-mi-tre (un-mī′tẽr), *v. t.* To deprive of a miter; depose from the rank of a bishop.

un-mit-i-ga-ble (un-mit′i-gạ-bl), *a.* Not mitigable; not to be softened, lessened, or moderated: as, "*unmitigable* rage" (Shakspere's "Tempest," i. 2. 276).—**un-mit′i-ga-bly,** *adv.*—**un-mit′i-gat-ed** (-gā-ted), *a.* Not mitigated; not softened or lessened (as, *unmitigated* harshness; the *unmitigated* rigor of the law); hence, unqualified or absolute (as, "*unmitigated* frauds," H. G. Wells's "Tono-Bungay," iii. 1. § 3; "You are a most *unmitigated* cad," Maugham's "Moon and Sixpence," xii.).—**un-mit′i-gat-ed-ly,** *adv.*

un-mixed (un-mikst′), *a.* Not mixed; unmingled; pure; unalloyed: as, "Good never comes *unmixed*" (Lowell's "Prometheus," 352).

un-mo-lest-ed (un-mō-les′ted), *a.* Not molested; free from molestation.—**un-mo-lest′ed-ly,** *adv.*

un-moor (un-mör′), *v.* **I.** *tr.* To loose (a ship, etc.) from moorings or from anchorage (also fig.); specif., to bring to the state of riding with a single anchor after having been moored by two or more. **II.** *intr.* To unmoor a ship, etc.; of a ship, etc., to become unmoored.

un-mor-al (un-mor′ạl), *a.* Non-moral; having no moral aspect; neither moral nor immoral.—**un-mo-ral′i-ty** (-mō-ral′i-ti), *n.*

un-mor-tise (un-môr′tis), *v. t.* To unfasten or separate (something mortised). Also fig.

un-mount-ed (un-moun′ted), *a.* Not mounted; not riding or serving on horseback; not fixed on or in a support, backing, setting, or the like.

un-mourned (un-mōrnd′), *a.* Not mourned or lamented.

un-moved (un-mövd′), *a.* Not moved; unshaken; firm; calm; indifferent.—**un-mov′ed-ly** (-mö′ved-li), *adv.*—**un-mov′ing,** *a.* Not moving; motionless.—**un-mov′ing-ly,** *adv.*

un-muf-fle (un-muf′l), *v.* **I.** *tr.* To strip of or free from that which muffles: as, to *unmuffle* the face; "Tell them to open my doors, and *unmuffle* the knocker" (Maria Edgeworth's "Belinda," xi.). **II.** *intr.* To throw off that which muffles: as, "*Unmuffle*, ye faint stars" (Milton's "Comus," 331).

un-mur-mur-ing (un-mẽr′mẽr-ing), *a.* Not murmuring; uncomplaining.—**un-mur′mur-ing-ly,** *adv.*

un-mu-si-cal (un-mū′zi-kạl), *a.* Not musical; not melodious or harmonious; harsh or discordant in sound; not fond of or skilled in music.—**un-mu′si-cal-ly,** *adv.*—**un-mu′si-cal-ness,** *n.*

un-muz-zle (un-muz′l), *v. t.* To remove a muzzle from (a dog, etc.); fig., to free from restraint, as upon speech or expression.

un-muz-zled (un-muz′ld), *a.* Not muzzled; without a muzzle.

un-named (un-nāmd′), *a.* Not named; having no name, or nameless; not called or known by any name; not specified or mentioned by name.

un-nat-u-ral (un-nat′ū-rạl), *a.* Not natural; not proper to the natural constitution or character (as, an *unnatural* flush; a thought or action *unnatural* to him); having or showing a lack of natural or proper instincts, feelings, etc. (as, an *unnatural* parent; "She . . . blamed my lord for his *unnatural* words," Stevenson's "Master of Ballantrae," i.); at variance with or contrary to the nature of things (as, "It seems almost *unnatural* for Scottishmen and English to meet and part without a buffet": Scott's "Castle Dangerous," xix.); at variance with the ordinary course of nature; unusual, strange, or abnormal; artificial or affected; forced or strained.—**un-nat′u-ral-ized,** *a.* Not naturalized.—**un-nat′u-ral-ly,** *adv.*—**un-nat′u-ral-ness,** *n.*

un-nav-i-ga-ble (un-nav′i-gạ-bl), *a.* Not navigable; not admitting of navigation: as, "an *unnavigable* ocean, where ship never sailed" (Defoe's "Robinson Crusoe," ii. 16).— **un-nav″i-ga-bil′i-ty** (-bil′i-ti), *n.*

un-ne-ces-sa-ry (un-nes′e-sạ-ri), *a.* Not necessary; needless.—**un-ne′ces-sa-ri-ly,** *adv.*—**un-ne′ces-sa-ri-ness,** *n.*

un-ne-go-tia-ble (un-nē-gō′shiạ-bl), *a.* Not negotiable.

un-neigh-bor-ly (un-nā′bọr-li), *a.* Not neighborly; not kindly, friendly, or sociable.—**un-neigh′bor-li-ness,** *n.*

un-nerve (un-nẽrv′), *v. t.* To deprive of nerve, strength, or physical or mental firmness; break down the self-control or courage of: as, "The shock of joy . . . was great enough to *unnerve* me, and . . . I stood trembling" (W. H. Hudson's "Green Mansions," xxi.).

un-no-tice-a-ble (un-nō'ti-sạ-bl), *a.* Not noticeable; not such as to attract notice.—**un-no'tice-a-ble-ness,** *n.*—**un-no'tice-a-bly,** *adv.*—**un-no'ticed,** *a.* Not noticed; not observed or heeded; unperceived; not receiving any notice or attention.

un-num-bered (un-num'bèrd), *a.* Not numbered; uncounted; hence, countless; innumerable.

un-ob-jec-tion-a-ble (un-ọb-jek'shọn-ạ-bl), *a.* Not objectionable; not liable to objection.—**un-ob-jec'tion-a-ble-ness,** *n.*—**un-ob-jec'tion-a-bly,** *adv.*

un-ob-ser-vant (un-ọb-zèr'vạnt), *a.* Not observant; not taking notice; not quick to notice or perceive; disregardful, as of rules or customs.—**un-ob-served',** *a.* Not observed; unnoticed; unperceived; disregarded.—**un-ob-serv'ing,** *a.* Not observing; unobservant.

un-ob-struct-ed (un-ọb-struk'ted), *a.* Not obstructed; not blocked, impeded, or hindered; open or clear.—**un-ob-struct'ed-ly,** *adv.*

un-ob-tain-a-ble (un-ọb-tā'nạ-bl), *a.* Not obtainable.

un-ob-tru-sive (un-ọb-trö'siv), *a.* Not obtrusive; modest; inconspicuous.—**un-ob-tru'sive-ly,** *adv.*—**un-ob-tru'sive-ness,** *n.*

un-oc-cu-pied (un-ok'ū-pīd), *a.* Not occupied; not possessed or held; vacant; not employed; idle.

un-of-fend-ing (un-ọ-fen'ding), *a.* Not offending; inoffensive: as, "Who . . . could have thought of harming a creature so simple and so *unoffending?*" (Scott's "Fair Maid of Perth," xix.).

un-of-fi-cial (un-ọ-fish'ạl), *a.* Not official; without official character or authority.—**un-of-fi'cial-ly,** *adv.*

un-o-pened (un-ō'pnd), *a.* Not opened; closed.

un-op-posed (un-ọ-pōzd'), *a.* Not opposed; meeting no opposition.

un-or-gan-ized (un-ôr'gạn-īzd), *a.* Not organized; without organic structure; not being a living organism (as, an *unorganized* ferment, a chemical substance acting as a ferment; an enzyme); not formed into an organized or systematized whole.

un-o-rig-i-nal (un-ọ-rij'i-nạl), *a.* Not original; also, having no origin (rare).

un-or-tho-dox (un-ôr'thọ-doks), *a.* Not orthodox; heterodox; heretical.—**un-or'tho-dox-y,** *n.*

un-os-ten-ta-tious (un-os-ten-tā'shus), *a.* Not ostentatious; not showy or pretentious; without parade; inconspicuous; modest.—**un-os-ten-ta'tious-ly,** *adv.*—**un-os-ten-ta'tious-ness,** *n.*

un-pack (un-pak'), *v.* **I.** *tr.* To undo or take out (something packed); also, to remove the contents packed in (a box, trunk, etc.); also, to remove a pack or load from (a horse, etc.); unload (a vehicle, etc.). **II.** *intr.* To unpack articles, goods, etc.—**un-pack'er,** *n.*

un-paid (un-pād'), *a.* Not paid; not having received payment or pay (as, *unpaid* workmen); serving without pay (as, *unpaid* justices); not discharged (as, an *unpaid* debt); not given in payment (as, sums remaining *unpaid*).—**un-paid'=for,** *a.* Not paid for: as, "rustling in *unpaid-for* silk" (Shakspere's "Cymbeline," iii. 3. 24).

un-pal-at-a-ble (un-pal'ạ-tạ-bl), *a.* Not palatable; not agreeable to the taste; fig., distasteful or unpleasant (as, "*unpalatable* advice": Irving's "Conquest of Granada," lxxxii.).—**un-pal'at-a-ble-ness,** *n.*—**un-pal'at-a-bly,** *adv.*

un-par-al-leled (un-par'ạ-leld), *a.* Not paralleled; having no parallel; unequaled; unmatched.

un-par-don-a-ble (un-pär'dọn-ạ-bl), *a.* Not pardonable; that cannot be pardoned: as, an *unpardonable* offense or mistake; an *unpardonable* offender.—**the unpardonable sin,** the sin of blasphemy against the Holy Ghost (see Mat. xii. 31, 32); hence, in general, the particular sin or offense held by any person or body of persons to be unpardonable.—**un-par'don-a-ble-ness,** *n.*—**un-par'don-a-bly,** *adv.*—**un-par'doned,** *a.* Not pardoned.—**un-par'don-ing,** *a.* Not pardoning.

un-par-lia-men-ta-ry (un-pär-li-men'tạ-ri), *a.* Not parliamentary; not in accordance with parliamentary practice.—**un-par-lia-men'ta-ri-ly,** *adv.*—**un-par-lia-men'ta-ri-ness,** *n.*

un-pat-ent-ed (un-pat'ẹn-ted), *a.* Not patented; not protected by patent.

un-pathed (un-påtht'), *a.* Pathless; trackless: as, "*unpath'd* waters" (Shakspere's "Winter's Tale," iv. 4. 578).

un-pa-tri-ot-ic (un-pā-tri-ot'ik), *a.* Not patriotic.—**un-pa-tri-ot'i-cal-ly,** *adv.*—**un-pa'tri-ot-ism** (-ọt-izm), *n.*

un-paved (un-pāvd'), *a.* Not paved; without pavement.

un-peg (un-peg'), *v. t.*; *-pegged, -pegging.* To remove the peg or pegs from; open, unfasten, or unfix by removing a peg or pegs.

un-pen (un-pen'), *v. t.*; *-penned, -penning.* To release from or as from a pen.

un-peo-ple (un-pē'pl), *v. t.* To deprive of people; depopulate.

un-per-ceiv-a-ble (un-pèr-sē'vạ-bl), *a.* Not perceivable; imperceptible.—**un-per-ceived',** *a.* Not perceived; unnoticed.—**un-per-ceiv'ing,** *a.* Not perceiving.

un-per-turbed (un-pèr-tèrbd'), *a.* Not perturbed; free from perturbation; undisturbed; calm; composed.—**un-per-turb'ed-ness,** *n.*

un-phil-o-soph-i-cal (un-fil-ọ-sof'i-kạl), *a.* Not philosophical.—**un-phil-o-soph'i-cal-ly,** *adv.*

un-pick (un-pik'), *v. t.* To pick or take out (stitches, sewing, etc.); pick out the stitches in (a garment, etc.).

un-pin (un-pin'), *v. t.*; *-pinned, -pinning.* To remove the pin or pins from; unfasten by removing a pin or pins.

un-pit-ied (un-pit'id), *a.* Not pitied.—**un-pit'y-ing,** *a.* Not pitying; devoid of pity: as, "The *unpitying* waters flowed over our prostrate bodies" (H. Melville's "Typee," viii.).—**un-pit'y-ing-ly,** *adv.*

un-plait (un-plāt'), *v. t.* To bring out of a plaited state; unbraid, as hair.

un-pleas-ant (un-plez'ạnt), *a.* Not pleasant; unpleasing; disagreeable: as, "She [wisdom] is very *unpleasant* to the unlearned" (Ecclus. vi. 20); *unpleasant* neighbors; *unpleasant* weather.—**un-pleas'ant-ly,** *adv.*—**un-pleas'ant-ness,** *n.* The quality or state of being unpleasant; also, something unpleasant; an unpleasant state of affairs (as, the late *unpleasantness,* a humorous expression used afterward to designate the American Civil War); a disagreement or quarrel.—**un-pleas'an-try** (-ạn-tri), *n.*; pl. *-tries* (-triz). Unpleasantness or an unpleasantness; an unpleasant circumstance or occurrence.

un-pleas-ing (un-plē'zing), *a.* Not pleasing; not such as to please.—**un-pleas'ing-ly,** *adv.*—**un-pleas'ing-ness,** *n.*

un-plug (un-plug'), *v. t.*; *-plugged, -plugging.* To remove the plug from.

un-plumbed (un-plumd'), *a.* Not plumbed; unfathomed; of unknown depth.

un-po-et-ic (un-pọ-et'ik), *a.* Not poetic; prosaic; matter-of-fact. Also **un-po-et'i-cal.**—**un-po-et'i-cal-ly,** *adv.*

un-pol-ished (un-pol'isht), *a.* Not polished; without polish; rough; unrefined; rude.

un-polled (un-pōld'), *a.* Not polled; esp., not voting or not cast at the polls (as, an *unpolled* voter or vote).

un-pol-lut-ed (un-pọ-lū'ted), *a.* Not polluted; undefiled; clean; pure.

un-pop-u-lar (un-pop'ū-lạr), *a.* Not popular; not liked by the public or by persons generally: as, an *unpopular* law; "a brave, honest, discontented, quarrelsome, *unpopular* man" (Motley's "Dutch Republic," i. 1).—**un-pop-u-lar'i-ty** (-lar'i-ti), *n.*—**un-pop'u-lar-ly,** *adv.*

un-prac-ti-cal (un-prak'ti-kạl), *a.* Not practical; impractical; lacking practical usefulness or wisdom; visionary.—**un-prac-ti-cal'i-ty** (-kal'i-ti), **un-prac'ti-cal-ness,** *n.*—**un-prac'ti-cal-ly,** *adv.*

un-prac-tised (un-prak'tist), *a.* Not practised; not done habitually or as a practice; not trained or skilled; inexpert.

un-prec-e-dent-ed (un-pres'ẹ-den-ted), *a.* Having no precedent or preceding instance; such as was never known before; unexampled: as, "a spectacle altogether *unprecedented* in the history of mankind" (De Quincey's "Revolt of the Tartars"); "*Unprecedented* sums were expended" (Macaulay's "Hist. of Eng.," ii.).—**un-prec'e-dent-ed-ly,** *adv.*

un-pre-cise (un-prẹ-sīs'), *a.* Not precise; lacking precision or definiteness; inexact.—**un-pre-cise'ly,** *adv.*—**un-pre-cise'ness,** *n.*

(variable) ḍ as d or j, ṣ as s or sh, ṭ as t or ch, ẓ as z or zh; *o*, F. cloche; ü, F. menu; ċh, Sc. loch; ṅ, F. bonbon; ', primary accent; ", secondary accent; †, obsolete; <, from; +, and; =, equals. See also lists at beginning of book.

un-prej-u-diced (un-prej′ọ̆-dist), *a.* Not prejudiced; unbiased; impartial; also, not impaired.

un-pre-med-i-tat-ed (un-prē-med′i-tā-ted), *a.* Not premeditated; undesigned.—**un-pre-med′i-tat-ed-ly**, *adv.*—**un-pre-med-i-ta′tion** (-tā′shọn), *n.* Absence of premeditation.

un-pre-pared (un-prē-pārd′), *a.* Not prepared; not made ready; not worked out in advance, as a speech; not ready, or unready, as a person; not prepared for death, as a person. —**un-pre-par′ed-ness** (-pār′ed-nes), *n.*

un-pre-pos-sess-ing (un-prē-pọ-zes′ing), *a.* Not prepossessing; unattractive: as, "*Unprepossessing* . . . in feature, gait and manners . . . these poor fellows formed a class apart" (S. Butler's "Way of All Flesh," xlvii.).—**un-pre-pos-sess′ing-ly**, *adv.*—**un-pre-pos-sess′ing-ness**, *n.*

un-pre-sent-a-ble (un-prē-zen′tạ-bl), *a.* Not presentable; not suitable for being introduced into company; not fit to be seen.

un-pre-tend-ing (un-prē-ten′ding), *a.* Not pretending; unassuming; modest.—**un-pre-tend′ing-ly**, *adv.*

un-pre-ten-tious (un-prē-ten′shus), *a.* Not pretentious; modest; unostentatious.—**un-pre-ten′tious-ly**, *adv.*—**un-pre-ten′tious-ness**, *n.*

un-priced (un-prīst′), *a.* Not priced; having no price set or indicated; also, beyond price; priceless.

un-priest-ly (un-prēst′li), *a.* Not priestly; not befitting a priest.

un-prin-ci-pled (un-prin′si-pld), *a.* Not instructed in the principles of something (with *in*: as, "*unprincipled* in Virtue's book," Milton's "Comus," 367: rare); also, lacking sound moral principles, as a person; showing want of principle, as conduct, etc.—**un-prin′ci-pled-ness**, *n.*

un-print-a-ble (un-prin′tạ-bl), *a.* Not printable; unfit to be printed.—**un-print′ed**, *a.* Not, or not yet, printed.

un-priz-a-ble (un-prī′zạ-bl), *a.* Not worthy to be prized; of little worth; also, beyond price†; priceless†.—**un-prized′**, *a.* Not prized or valued.

un-pro-duc-tive (un-prọ-duk′tiv), *a.* Not productive.—**un-pro-duc′tive-ly**, *adv.*—**un-pro-duc′tive-ness**, **un-pro-duc-tiv′i-ty** (-tiv′i-ti), *n.*

un-pro-fes-sion-al (un-prọ-fesh′ọn-ạl), *a.* Not professional; not pertaining to or connected with a profession; contrary to professional etiquette, or unbecoming in members of a profession; not belonging to a profession.—**un-pro-fes′-sion-al-ly**, *adv.*

un-prof-it-a-ble (un-prof′i-tạ-bl), *a.* Not profitable; producing no gain or advantage.—**un-prof′it-a-ble-ness**, *n.*—**un-prof′it-a-bly**, *adv.*

un-pro-gres-sive (un-prọ-gres′iv), *a.* Not progressive; conservative; backward.—**un-pro-gres′sive-ly**, *adv.*—**un-pro-gres′sive-ness**, *n.*

un-prom-is-ing (un-prom′i-sing), *a.* Not promising; not appearing likely to turn out well.

un-pro-nounce-a-ble (un-prọ-noun′sạ-bl), *a.* Not pronounceable; incapable of being pronounced; difficult to pronounce.—**un-pro-nounced′**, *a.* Not pronounced; not uttered.

un-pro-pi-tious (un-prọ-pish′us), *a.* Not propitious; not favorable; inauspicious.—**un-pro-pi′tious-ly**, *adv.*—**un-pro-pi′tious-ness**, *n.*

un-pros-per-ous (un-pros′pẽr-us), *a.* Not prosperous; unfortunate; unsuccessful.—**un-pros′per-ous-ly**, *adv.*—**un-pros′per-ous-ness**, *n.*

un-pro-tect-ed (un-prọ-tek′ted), *a.* Not protected.—**un-protected cruiser.** See under *cruiser.*—**un-pro-tect′ed-ness**, *n.*

un-proved (un-prōvd′), *a.* Not proved. Also **un-prov′en** (-prō′vn).

un-pro-vid-ed (un-prọ-vī′ded), *a.* Not provided; not furnished or supplied; not furnished or supplied with something (as, "assailants . . . *unprovided* with regular means of attack": Kinglake's "Eothen," viii.).—**un-pro-vid′ed-for**, *a.* Not provided for.

un-pro-voked (un-prọ-vōkt′), *a.* Not provoked; without provocation.—**un-pro-vok′ed-ly** (-vō′ked-li), *adv.*

un-pub-lished (un-pub′lisht), *a.* Not, or not yet, published.

un-puck-er (un-puk′ẽr), *v. t.* To straighten out from a puckered condition.

un-punc-tu-al (un-pungk′tụ-ạl), *a.* Not punctual; tardy.—**un-punc-tu-al′i-ty** (-al′i-ti), *n.*—**un-punc′tu-al-ly**, *adv.*

un-pun-ished (un-pun′isht), *a.* Not punished.

un-qual-i-fied (un-kwol′i-fīd), *a.* Not qualified; not fitted; not having the requisite qualifications; also, not modified, limited, or restricted in any way (as, *unqualified* praise); absolute or out-and-out (as, an *unqualified* failure).—**un-qual′i-fied-ly**, *adv.*—**un-qual′i-fied-ness**, *n.*

un-quench-a-ble (un-kwen′chạ-bl), *a.* Not quenchable; inextinguishable.—**un-quench′a-bly**, *adv.*

un-ques-tion-a-ble (un-kwes′chọn-ạ-bl), *a.* Not questionable; not open to question, or beyond dispute or doubt (as, an *unquestionable* fact); indisputable; indubitable; beyond criticism or unexceptionable (as, "The Governor . . . wished to see the citadel of Antwerp in more *unquestionable* keeping": Motley's "Dutch Republic," v. 3); also, averse to being questioned†.—**un-ques′tion-a-ble-ness**, *n.*—**un-ques′tion-a-bly**, *adv.*—**un-ques′tioned**, *a.* Not questioned; not interrogated; not inquired into; not called in question, or undisputed.—**un-ques′tion-ing**, *a.* Not questioning, disputing, or objecting.—**un-ques′tion-ing-ly**, *adv.*

un-qui-et (un-kwī′et), *a.* Not quiet; restless; turbulent; tumultuous; uneasy or perturbed; agitated or in commotion; not silent or still.—**un-qui′et-ly**, *adv.*—**un-qui′et-ness**, *n.*

un-quot-a-ble (un-kwō′tạ-bl), *a.* Not quotable.

un-rat-i-fied (un-rat′i-fīd), *a.* Not ratified; unsanctioned.

un-rav-el (un-rav′l), *v.*; *-eled* or *-elled*, *-eling* or *-elling.* **I.** *tr.* To free from a raveled or tangled state; disentangle; disengage the threads or fibers of (a woven or knitted fabric, a rope, etc.); separate by unweaving or the like, as threads; fig., to free from complication or difficulty (as, to *unravel* a mystery); make plain or clear; solve; also, to undo† or annul† (as, "All the reformation that was made for twenty years before . . . was *unravelled* in less than a year": Strype's "Memorials of Cranmer," iii. 9). **II.** *intr.* To become unraveled.—**un-rav′el-ment**, *n.*

un-read (un-red′), *a.* Not read or perused, as a book; also, not having gained knowledge by reading.—**un-read′a-ble** (-rē′dạ-bl), *a.* Not readable; illegible; not suitable for reading; not interesting to read.

un-read-y (un-red′i), *a.* Not ready; not made ready, as for action or use; not in a state of readiness or preparation, as a person; not dressed, or not fully dressed (now prov. Eng.); not prompt or quick: in the historical surname of the English king Ethelred II. ('the *Unready*), interpreted to mean 'without rede or counsel' (see *rede, n.*), but usually regarded as meaning 'unprepared' or 'not prompt or quick.'—**un-read′i-ly**, *adv.*—**un-read′i-ness**, *n.*

un-re-al (un-rē′ạl), *a.* Not real; not substantial; imaginary; artificial; unnatural; unpractical or visionary.—**un-re-al′i-ty** (-rẹ-al′i-ti), *n.*; pl. *-ties* (-tiz). Lack of reality; the quality of being unreal; unpractical or visionary character; also, something without reality; something unreal.

un-re-al-iz-a-ble (un-rē′ạl-ī-zạ-bl), *a.* Not realizable.—**un-re′al-ized**, *a.* Not realized.

un-rea-son (un-rē′zn), *n.* Lack of reason; inability or unwillingness to think or act rationally, reasonably, or sensibly (as, "in some mood of cantankerous *unreason*": Gissing's "Private Papers of Henry Ryecroft," i. 1); that which is devoid of or contrary to reason.—**un-rea′son-a-ble**, *a.* Not reasonable; not endowed with reason; not guided by or agreeable to reason or sound judgment; exceeding the bounds of reason; immoderate or exorbitant.—**un-rea′son-a-ble-ness**, *n.*—**un-rea′son-a-bly**, *adv.*—**un-rea′soned**, *a.* Not reasoned or based on reasoning.—**un-rea′son-ing**, *a.* Not reasoning or exercising reason; reasonless.—**un-rea′son-ing-ly**, *adv.*

un-re-ceipt-ed (un-rẹ-sē′ted), *a.* Not receipted.

un-rec-og-niz-a-ble (un-rek′ọg-nī-zạ-bl), *a.* Not recognizable.—**un-rec′og-niz-a-bly**, *adv.*—**un-rec′og-nized**, *a.* Not recognized.

un-rec-om-pensed (un-rek′ọm-penst), *a.* Not recompensed.

un-rec-on-ciled (un-rek′ọn-sīld), *a.* Not reconciled.

un-re-cord-ed (un-rẹ-kôr′ded), *a.* Not recorded.

un-re-deemed (un-rẹ-dēmd′), *a.* Not redeemed; not recalled by payment of what is due, as notes or bonds; not

Water-moccasin
(*Ancistrodon piscivorus*)

Copperhead
(*Ancistrodon contortrix*)

Coral-snake
(*Elaps fulvius*)

Timber Rattlesnake
(*Crotalus horridus*)

Diamond Rattlesnake
(*Crotalus adamanteus*)

Gila Monster
(*Heloderma suspectum*)

POISONOUS REPTILES OF THE UNITED STATES.

taken out of pawn; not fulfilled, as a promise; not ransomed; not delivered or rescued; not saved spiritually; not remedied or relieved by any countervailing quality or feature; unmitigated (as, "*unredeemed* ugliness": Carlyle's "Past and Present," iii. 12).

un-reel (un-rēl′), *v. t.* or *i.* To unwind from a reel.

un-reeve (un-rēv′), *v.*; *-reeved* or *-rove, -reeving.* [See *reeve*[2].] *Naut.*: **I.** *tr.* To withdraw (a rope, etc.) from a block, thimble, etc. **II.** *intr.* To unreeve a rope; of a rope, etc., to become unreeved.

un-re-fined (un-rē-fīnd′), *a.* Not refined; not purified, as substances; not free from coarseness or vulgarity; lacking nice feeling, taste, etc.

un-re-flect-ing (un-rē-flek′ting), *a.* Not reflecting; unthinking; thoughtless.—**un-re-flect′ing-ly,** *adv.*

un-re-gard-ed (un-rē-gär′ded), *a.* Not regarded; unheeded.

un-re-gen-er-ate (un-rē-jen′ē-rāt), *a.* Not regenerate; not born again spiritually; remaining at enmity with God. Also **un-re-gen′er-at-ed** (-ē-rā-ted).—**un-re-gen′er-ate-ly,** *adv.*—**un-re-gen′er-ate-ness,** *n.*

un-reg-is-tered (un-rej′is-tėrd), *a.* Not registered.

un-reg-u-lat-ed (un-reg′ū-lā-ted), *a.* Not regulated.

un-re-lat-ed (un-rē-lā′ted), *a.* Not related.—**un-re-lat′ed-ness,** *n.*

un-re-laxed (un-rē-lakst′), *a.* Not relaxed; not made loose or slack; not slackened or abated.—**un-re-lax′ing,** *a.* Not relaxing or slackening: as, "a time of *unrelaxing* effort" (Morley's "Oliver Cromwell," iv. 2).

un-re-lent-ing (un-rē-len′ting), *a.* Not relenting; not yielding to feelings of kindness or compassion; not slackening in severity or determination.—**un-re-lent′ing-ly,** *adv.*—**un-re-lent′ing-ness,** *n.*

un-re-li-a-ble (un-rē-lī′ạ-bl), *a.* Not reliable; not to be relied or depended on.—**un-re-li′a-ble-ness,** *n.*—**un-re-li′a-bly,** *adv.*

un-re-liev-a-ble (un-rē-lē′vạ-bl), *a.* Not relievable.—**un-re-lieved′,** *a.* Not relieved.—**un-re-liev′ed-ly,** *adv.*

un-re-li-gious (un-rē-lij′us), *a.* Irreligious; also, having no connection with or relation to religion; neither religious nor irreligious.

un-re-mem-bered (un-rē-mem′bėrd), *a.* Not remembered; forgotten.—**un-re-mem′ber-ing,** *a.* Not remembering; having no memory or recollection.

un-re-mit-ted (un-rē-mit′ed), *a.* Not remitted; not pardoned, forgiven, or canceled; not slackened or abated (as, "Our exertions to discover him are *unremitted*": Mrs. Shelley's "Frankenstein," vii.).—**un-re-mit′ting,** *a.* Not remitting or slackening; not abating for a time; incessant: as, "*unremitting* vigilance" (Irving's "Conquest of Granada," iii.); "My lord's first footman . . . was *unremitting* in his attentions" (Whyte-Melville's "Katerfelto," viii.).—**un-re-mit′ting-ly,** *adv.*

un-re-mu-ner-at-ed (un-rē-mū′nē-rā-ted), *a.* Not remunerated; without remuneration.—**un-re-mu′ner-a-tive** (-nē-rạ-tiv), *a.* Not remunerative; not affording remuneration; unprofitable.—**un-re-mu′ner-a-tive-ness,** *n.*

un-rent-ed (un-ren′ted), *a.* Not rented.

un-re-pair (un-rē-pār′), *n.* Want of repair; disrepair; dilapidation.—**un-re-paired′,** *a.* Not repaired.

un-re-peal-a-ble (un-rē-pē′lạ-bl), *a.* Not repealable; irrevocable.—**un-re-pealed′,** *a.* Not repealed.

un-re-pent-ant (un-rē-pen′tạnt), *a.* Not repentant; impenitent.—**un-re-pent′ance,** *n.*

un-re-pin-ing (un-rē-pī′ning), *a.* Not repining; uncomplaining.—**un-re-pin′ing-ly,** *adv.*

un-rep-re-sen-ta-tive (un-rep-rē-zen′tạ-tiv), *a.* Not representative; failing to represent adequately; not typical.

un-re-pressed (un-rē-prest′), *a.* Not repressed; unrestrained.

un-re-quit-ed (un-rē-kwī′ted), *a.* Not requited; without requital or return.

un-re-serve (un-rē-zėrv′), *n.* Absence of reserve; frankness: as, "questions which he will answer with perfect *unreserve*" (S. Butler's "Erewhon," x.).—**un-re-served′,** *a.* Not reserved; without reservation, full, or entire (as, *unreserved* obedience); free from reserve, frank, or open (as, to be *unreserved* in one's speech).—**un-re-serv′ed-ly,** *adv.*—**un-re-serv′ed-ness,** *n.*

un-re-sist-ing (un-rē-zis′ting), *a.* Not resisting; not making resistance; submissive.—**un-re-sist′ing-ly,** *adv.*

un-re-spon-sive (un-rē-spon′siv), *a.* Not responsive or inclined to respond.—**un-re-spon′sive-ness,** *n.*

un-rest (un-rest′), *n.* Lack of rest; restless or uneasy state; inquietude.

un-re-strained (un-rē-strānd′), *a.* Not restrained; unchecked; unrepressed.—**un-re-strain′ed-ly,** *adv.*—**un-re-straint′,** *n.* Absence of or freedom from restraint.

un-re-strict-ed (un-rē-strik′ted), *a.* Not restricted; without limitation.—**un-re-strict′ed-ly,** *adv.*

un-re-vealed (un-rē-vēld′), *a.* Not revealed; not disclosed.

un-re-venged (un-rē-venjd′), *a.* Not revenged.

un-re-ward-ed (un-rē-wâr′ded), *a.* Not rewarded; unrequited.

un-rid-dle (un-rid′l), *v. t.* To read the riddle of; solve (a riddle, mystery, etc.): as, "The riddle . . . was now *unriddled*" (Poe's "Murders in the Rue Morgue").

un-rid-dled (un-rid′ld), *a.* Not solved, as a riddle: as, "the last geographical secret left *unriddled*" (Buchan's "Three Hostages," xviii.).

un-rig (un-rig′), *v. t.*; *-rigged, -rigging.* To strip of rigging, as a ship; hence, to strip of equipment; sometimes, to undress (now colloq.).

un-right-eous (un-rī′chus), *a.* [AS. *unrihtwīs*.] Not righteous; not upright or virtuous; not in accordance with right.—**un-right′eous-ly,** *adv.*—**un-right′eous-ness,** *n.*

un-rip (un-rip′), *v. t.*; *-ripped, -ripping.* To undo by ripping; cut or tear open; rip.

un-ripe (un-rīp′), *a.* [AS. *unrīpe*.] Not ripe; immature; not fully developed: as, "the *unripe* corn" (Galsworthy's "Patrician," ii. 5); "an *unripe* girl" (G. W. Cable's "Bonaventure," iii. 4); an *unripe* scheme.—**un-ripe′ness,** *n.*

un-ri-valed, un-ri-valled (un-rī′vạld), *a.* Having no rival or competitor; having no equal, or peerless (as, "Our higher institutions of learning are *unrivaled*": J. H. Robinson's "Mind in the Making," vii. 15).

un-robe (un-rōb′), *v. t.* or *i.* To disrobe; undress.

un-roll (un-rōl′), *v.* **I.** *tr.* To open or spread out (something rolled, coiled, or folded); hence, to lay open, display, or reveal (as, "The whole state of the case *unrolled* itself to his apprehension": J. H. Newman's "Callista," xxii.); also, to strike from a roll or register (rare). **II.** *intr.* To become unrolled.

un-ro-man-tic (un-rō-man′tik), *a.* Not romantic; prosaic; practical; commonplace.—**un-ro-man′ti-cal-ly,** *adv.*

un-roof (un-röf′), *v. t.* To take the roof off: as, "They . . . *unroofed* a great part of the building" (Kinglake's "Eothen," viii.).

un-root (un-röt′), *v. t.* To uproot.

un-ruf-fled (un-ruf′ld), *a.* Not ruffled; smooth (as, "The broad expanse of ocean . . . was *unruffled*": Marryat's "King's Own," xlv.); calm (as, "with contented mind and *unruffled* spirit": Trollope's "Warden," v.).

un-ruled (un-rōld′), *a.* Not ruled; not marked with lines.

un-ru-ly (un-rö′li), *a.* Not submissive or conforming to rule; ungovernable; turbulent; refractory; lawless.—**un-ru′li-ness,** *n.*

un-sad-dle (un-sad′l), *v.* **I.** *tr.* To take the saddle from (as, "I *unsaddled* and picketed my horses": W. H. Hudson's "Purple Land," xxvi.); also, to cause to fall or dismount from a saddle; unhorse. **II.** *intr.* To take the saddle from a horse.

un-safe (un-sāf′), *a.* Not safe; involving danger or risk; not dependable or trustworthy.—**un-safe′ly,** *adv.*—**un-safe′ness,** *n.*—**un-safe′ty,** *n.* The state of being unsafe; exposure to danger or risk; insecurity.

un-said[1] (un-sed′). Pret. and pp. of *unsay*.

un-said[2] (un-sed′), *a.* Not said or uttered.

un-saint-ly (un-sānt′li), *a.* Not saintly; not like, or not befitting, a saint.

un-sal-a-ble (un-sā′lạ-bl), *a.* Not salable; not meeting a ready sale.—**un-sal′a-ble-ness,** *n.*

un-sal-a-ried (un-sal′ạ-rid), *a.* Not salaried; not paid, or not provided with, a fixed salary.

un-salt-ed (un-sâl′ted), *a.* Not salted; fresh.

un-sanc-ti-fied (un-sangk′ti-fīd), *a.* Not sanctified; unhallowed; unholy; unconsecrated.

(variable) ḍ as d or j, ş as s or sh, ţ as t or ch, ẓ as z or zh; *o*, F. cloche; ü, F. menu; ċh, Sc. loch; ṅ, F. bonbon; ′, primary accent; ″, secondary accent; †, obsolete; <, from; +, and; =, equals. See also lists at beginning of book.

un-sanc-tioned (un-sangk'shǫnd), *a.* Not sanctioned; not ratified; not approved.

un-san-i-ta-ry (un-san'i-tā-ri), *a.* Not sanitary; unhealthful.—**un-san'i-ta-ri-ness**, *n.*

un-sat-is-fac-to-ry (un-sat-is-fak'tō-ri), *a.* Not satisfactory; not satisfying the desires or requirements; inadequate.—**un-sat-is-fac'to-ri-ly**, *adv.*—**un-sat-is-fac'to-ri-ness**, *n.*—**un-sat'is-fied** (-fīd), *a.* Not satisfied; not gratified to the full; not contented.—**un-sat'is-fy-ing** (-fī-ing), *a.* Not satisfying; insufficient to meet the desires; inadequate.—**un-sat'is-fy-ing-ly**, *adv.*—**un-sat'is-fy-ing-ness**, *n.*

un-sat-u-rat-ed (un-sat'ū-rā-ted), *a.* Not saturated; having the power to dissolve still more of a substance; capable of taking on an element, etc., by direct chemical combination without the liberation of other elements or compounds (as, an *unsaturated* compound).

un-sa-vor-y (un-sā'vǫr-i), *a.* Not savory; tasteless or insipid; unpleasant in taste or smell; fig., morally unpleasant or offensive (as, an *unsavory* subject or affair; an *unsavory* reputation).—**un-sa'vor-i-ly**, *adv.*—**un-sa'vor-i-ness**, *n.*

un-say (un-sā'), *v. t.*; *-said, -saying.* To retract (something said): as, "Your daring tongue Scorns to *unsay* what once it hath deliver'd" (Shakspere's "Richard II.," iv. 1. 9).

un-scal-a-ble (un-skā'lạ-bl), *a.* Not scalable; not to be climbed: as, "the *unscalable* side of a mountain" (J. Conrad's "Lord Jim," xl.).

un-scarred (un-skärd'), *a.* Not scarred, as from a wound; having no scars.

un-scathed (un-skāᵵHd'), *a.* Not scathed; unharmed; uninjured.

un-schol-ar-ly (un-skol'ạr-li), *a.* Not scholarly; unbefitting a scholar; lacking scholarly qualities or attainments.—**un-schol'ar-li-ness**, *n.*

un-schooled (un-sköld'), *a.* Not schooled; untaught; undisciplined.

un-sci-en-tif-ic (un-sī-ẹn-tif'ik), *a.* Not scientific; not in accordance with the requirements of science (as, "This assumption is *unscientific*": S. Butler's "Erewhon," xxiv.); not conforming to the principles or methods of science (as, an *unscientific* practitioner).—**un-sci-en-tif'i-cal-ly**, *adv.*

un-scram-ble (un-skram'bl), *v. t.* To bring out of a scrambled condition; reduce from confusion to order. [Colloq.]

un-screw (un-skrö'), *v. t.* To draw the screw or screws from; unfasten by withdrawing screws; also, to loosen or withdraw (a screw, screw-like plug, etc.).

un-scrip-tur-al (un-skrip'tūr-ạl), *a.* Not scriptural; not in accordance with the Scriptures.—**un-scrip'tur-al-ly**, *adv.*

un-scru-pu-lous (un-skrö'pū-lus), *a.* Not scrupulous; untroubled or unrestrained by scruples; conscienceless; unprincipled: as, "a hardy and *unscrupulous* adventurer" (Bulwer-Lytton's "Caxtons," xv. 2).—**un-scru'pu-lous-ly**, *adv.*—**un-scru'pu-lous-ness**, *n.*

un-seal (un-sēl'), *v. t.* To break or remove the seal of (as, to *unseal* a letter; to *unseal* a door); open, as something sealed or firmly closed (lit. or fig.: as, "Grateful smiles my lips *unseal*," Whittier's "To My Old Schoolmaster"; to *unseal* the heart).

un-sealed (un-sēld'), *a.* Not sealed: as, an *unsealed* letter.

un-seam (un-sēm'), *v. t.* To open the seam or seams of; rip apart. See Shakspere's "Macbeth," i. 2. 22.

un-search-a-ble (un-sėr'chạ-bl), *a.* Not searchable; not to be searched into or understood by searching; inscrutable; unfathomable: as, "How *unsearchable* are his judgments, and his ways past finding out!" (Rom. xi. 33).—**un-search'-a-ble-ness**, *n.*—**un-search'a-bly**, *adv.*—**un-searched'**, *a.* Not searched.

un-sea-son-a-ble (un-sē'zn-ạ-bl), *a.* Not seasonable; out of season; untimely; ill-timed; inopportune.—**un-sea'son-a-ble-ness**, *n.*—**un-sea'son-a-bly**, *adv.*

un-sea-soned (un-sē'znd), *a.* Not seasoned; not matured, dried, hardened, or prepared by due seasoning, as things; not inured to a climate, service, work, mode of life, etc., as persons; inexperienced; not tested and approved by time, as securities; not flavored with seasoning, as food; also, unseasonable†.

un-seat (un-sēt'), *v. t.* To displace from a seat; throw from a saddle, as a rider; depose from an official seat or from office (as, "The successful competitors were *unseated* for bribery,"

Froude's "Cæsar," xi.; to *unseat* a member of a legislative body).

un-sea-wor-thy (un-sē'wėr″ᵵHi), *a.* Not seaworthy, as a ship.—**un-sea'wor″thi-ness**, *n.*

un-sec-ta-ri-an (un-sek-tā'ri-ạn), *a.* Not sectarian; not confined to or dominated by any particular sect; free from sectarian character or aims.—**un-sec-ta'ri-an-ism**, *n.*

un-se-cured (un-sẹ-kūrd'), *a.* Not secured; not insured against loss, as by a bond, pledge, etc. (as, *unsecured* debts; *unsecured* creditors).

un-see-ing (un-sē'ing), *a.* Not seeing; not perceiving; unobservant; blind.—**un-see'ing-ly**, *adv.*

un-seem-ly (un-sēm'li), *a.* Not seemly; unfitting; unbecoming; improper; indecorous.—**un-seem'li-ness**, *n.*—**un-seem'ly**, *adv.* In an unseemly manner: as, "Charity . . . Doth not behave itself *unseemly*" (1 Cor. xiii. 5).

un-seen (un-sēn'), *a.* Not seen; unperceived; unobserved; sometimes, invisible (as, "Merlin, who, they say, can walk *Unseen* at pleasure": Tennyson's "Coming of Arthur," 347).

un-seg-ment-ed (un-seg'men-ted), *a.* Not segmented.

un-self-ish (un-sel'fish), *a.* Not selfish; disinterested; altruistic.—**un-self'ish-ly**, *adv.*—**un-self'ish-ness**, *n.*

un-sen-ti-men-tal (un-sen-ti-men'tạl), *a.* Not sentimental; hard-headed; practical; matter-of-fact.—**un-sen-ti-men'-tal-ly**, *adv.*—**un-sen-ti-men'tal-ness**, *n.*

un-ser-vice-a-ble (un-sėr'vis-ạ-bl), *a.* Not serviceable; not satisfactory for service or use; not durable.—**un-ser'-vice-a-ble-ness**, *n.*—**un-ser'vice-a-bly**, *adv.*

un-set (un-set'), *a.* Not set; of gems, unmounted.

un-set-tle (un-set'l), *v. t.* To bring out of a settled state; cause to be no longer firmly fixed or established (as, "This theory, though intended to strengthen the foundations of government, altogether *unsettles* them": Macaulay's "Hist. of Eng.," i.); render unstable; shake or weaken (beliefs, feelings, etc.: as, "a shock which *unsettled*, not his resolution, but his fortitude," J. Conrad's "Rover," xiv.); disturb; disorder; derange (the mind, etc.).

un-set-tled (un-set'ld), *a.* Not settled; not fixed in a place or abode; not populated, as a region; not fixed or stable, as conditions; without established order, as times; liable to change, as weather; wavering or uncertain, as the mind, opinions, etc., or the person; undetermined, as a point at issue; not adjusted, closed, or disposed of finally, as an account or an estate; not paid, as a bill.—**un-set'tled-ness**, *n.*

un-set-tle-ment (un-set'l-mẹnt), *n.* The act of unsettling; also, the state of being unsettled; unsettled or disturbed condition of affairs (as, "The continuing *unsettlement* was a call to him that . . . he had still a portion of the Lord's work to do": Morley's "Oliver Cromwell," iv. 5).

un-sev-ered (un-sev'ėrd), *a.* Not severed; not parted or sundered; not disjoined or separate.

un-sew (un-sō'), *v. t.* To undo (something sewed); rip.

un-sex (un-seks'), *v. t.* To change from the actual sex (as, "Come, you spirits . . . *unsex* me [Lady Macbeth] here": Shakspere's "Macbeth," i. 5. 42); esp., with reference to women, to render (one's self) no longer of the proper sex, as by unnatural conduct (as, "Females who had fought daily in the trenches . . . had *unsexed* themselves in the opinion of those . . .": Motley's "Dutch Republic," vi. 2); of the conduct, life, etc., to deprive (a woman) of womanly character.

un-shack-le (un-shak'l), *v. t.* To free from shackles; unfetter. Also fig.

un-shad-ed (un-shā'ded), *a.* Not shaded; without shade, as of trees; not screened by a shade, as a light; without shades or gradations of light or color, as a picture.

un-shad-owed (un-shad'ōd), *a.* Not shadowed; not darkened or obscured; free from gloom.

un-shak-a-ble (un-shā'kạ-bl), *a.* Not shakable; not to be shaken.—**un-shak'a-bly**, *adv.*—**un-shak'en**, *a.* Not shaken; firm: as, "*unshaken* fidelity to‸his word" (Hallam's "Europe during the Middle Ages," i. 2).—**un-shak'en-ly**, *adv.*

un-shape (un-shāp'), *v. t.* To put out of shape or order; derange: as, "This deed *unshapes* me quite" (Shakspere's "Measure for Measure," iv. 4. 23). [Obs. or archaic.]

---

un-shaped (un-shāpt′), a. Not shaped or definitely formed. See Shakspere's "Hamlet," iv. 5. 8.—**un-shape′ly**, a. Not shapely; unpleasing in shape; ill-formed: as, "a foot, *unshapely* and huge" (C. B. Brown's "Wieland," xxii.).—**un-shape′li-ness**, n.—**un-shap′en** (-shā′pn), a. Not shaped or definitely formed; shapeless; formless; indefinite (as, "this blind trust in some *unshapen* chance": George Eliot's "Adam Bede," xxxv.); also, misshapen or deformed (see Shakspere's "Richard III.," i. 2. 251).

un-shav-en (un-shā′vn), a. Not shaven.

un-sheathe (un-shēᴛʜ′), v. t. To draw from a sheath, as a sword, knife, or the like; bring or put forth from a covering, threateningly or otherwise (as, "people . . . as ready . . . to draw a knife on you as a cat was to *unsheathe* its claws": W. H. Hudson's "Far Away and Long Ago," xix.).

un-shed (un-shed′), a. Not shed: as, *unshed* tears.

un-shell (un-shel′), v. t. To take out of the shell; remove or release as from a shell.

un-shel-tered (un-shel′tėrd), a. Not sheltered; without shelter.

un-ship (un-ship′), v. t.; -shipped, -shipping. To put or take off from a ship, as persons or goods (as, "In the voyage . . . he had had the misfortune to be five times shipped and *unshipped*": Defoe's "Robinson Crusoe," ii. 6); hence, to put or take away, or get rid of (colloq.); also, to remove from the proper place for use, as an oar, tiller, etc.

un-shod (un-shod′), a. Not shod; without shoes.

un-shorn (un-shôrn′), a. Not shorn; not sheared or clipped; unshaven.

un-shrink-a-ble (un-shring′ka-bl), a. Not shrinkable; not liable to shrink: as, "*unshrinkable* flannels" (Arnold Bennett's "Old Wives' Tale," i. 6).—**un-shrink′ing**, a. Not shrinking; not drawing up or contracting; not drawing back or recoiling; unflinching; firm.—**un-shrink′ing-ly**, adv.

un-shroud (un-shroud′), v. t. To remove the shroud from; divest of something that shrouds; uncover; unveil.

un-sift-ed (un-sif′ted), a. Not sifted; fig., not critically examined; untried.

un-sight (un-sīt′), a. [Appar. a contr. of *unsighted*.] In the phrase *unsight, unseen*, without inspection or examination: as, to buy a thing *unsight, unseen* (that is, without seeing it).

un-sight-ed (un-sī′ted), a. Not sighted or seen; also, not furnished with, or not directed by means of, a sight or sights, as a firearm.

un-sight-ly (un-sīt′li), a. Not sightly; not pleasing to the sight; forming an unpleasing sight: as, "A more *unsightly* prospect . . . it would be hard to fancy" (Stevenson's "Travels with a Donkey," ii. 2); "the *unsightly* bareness of the room" (S. J. Weyman's "Gentleman of France," viii.). —**un-sight′li-ness**, n.

un-signed (un-sīnd′), a. Not signed.

un-sing-a-ble (un-sing′a-bl), a. Not singable; not suited or adapted for being sung.

un-sink-a-ble (un-sing′ka-bl), a. Not sinkable.

un-sized (un-sīzd′), a. [See *size*[2].] Not sized; not coated or treated with size.

un-skil-ful (un-skil′fúl), a. Not skilful; inexpert; awkward; bungling; also, undiscerning† (see Shakspere's "Hamlet," iii. 2. 29).—**un-skil′ful-ly**, adv.—**un-skil′ful-ness**, n.— **un-skilled′**, a. Not skilled; untrained; inexpert.

un-slaked (un-slākt′), a. Not slaked, as lime.

un-sling (un-sling′), v. t.; -slung, -slinging. To remove (something) from a position in which it has been slung; naut., to take off the slings of; release from slings.

un-smil-ing (un-smī′ling), a. Not smiling; grave; serious. —**un-smil′ing-ly**, adv.

un-snarl (un-snärl′), v. t. To bring out of a snarled condition; disentangle.

un-so-cia-ble (un-sō′sha-bl), a. Not sociable; having, showing, or marked by a disinclination to friendly intercourse: as, "How reserved and *unsociable* he appeared among us!" (Scott's "Guy Mannering," xxi.); *unsociable* behavior. —**un-so-cia-bil′i-ty** (-bil′i-ti), **un-so′cia-ble-ness**, n.— **un-so′cia-bly**, adv.—**un-so′cial** (-shạl), a. Not social; unsociable: as, "He was now no longer gloomy and *unsocial*" (Johnson's "Rasselas," iv.); "an *unsocial*, taciturn dis-

position" (Jane Austen's "Pride and Prejudice," xviii.).— **un-so′cial-ly**, adv.—**un-so′cial-ness**, n.

un-soft-ened (un-sôf′nd), a. Not softened.

un-soiled (un-soild′), a. Not soiled; not smirched; unsullied; clean.

un-sol-der (un-sod′ėr), v. t. To separate (something soldered); fig., to disunite or dissolve (see Tennyson's "Passing of Arthur," 182).

un-so-li-cit-ed (un-sō-lis′i-ted), a. Not solicited; unasked; unsought.—**un-so-li′ci-tous**, a. Not solicitous; unconcerned; indifferent.—**un-so-li′ci-tous-ness**, n.

un-so-phis-ti-cat-ed (un-sọ-fis′ti-kā-ted), a. Not sophisticated; not falsified; unadulterated, pure, or genuine; simple or artless (as, "this gipsy-girl, an *unsophisticated* child of nature," Whyte-Melville's "Katerfelto," ix.; "that *unsophisticated* little song, which has touched so many simple British hearts," Du Maurier's "Trilby," i.).—**un-so-phis′ti-cat-ed-ness, un-so-phis-ti-ca′tion** (-kā′shọn), n.

un-sought (un-sôt′), a. Not sought; not looked or searched for; not asked for; unsolicited.

un-sound (un-sound′), a. Not sound; diseased, as the body or mind; decayed, as timber or fruit; impaired or defective, as goods; not solid or firm, as foundations; not financially strong or reliable; not well-founded or valid; fallacious; not theologically correct or orthodox (as, "put to recantation for some *unsound* passages they had preached": Strype's "Memorials of Cranmer," i. 23).—**un-sound′ly**, adv.— **un-sound′ness**, n.

un-spar-ing (un-spār′ing), a. Not sparing; liberal or profuse (as, to give with *unsparing* hand); unmerciful (as, *unsparing* criticism or publicity).—**un-spar′ing-ly**, adv.— **un-spar′ing-ness**, n.

un-speak (un-spēk′), v. t.; pret. -spoke, pp. -spoken, ppr. -speaking. To retract (something spoken); unsay. See Shakspere's "Macbeth," iv. 3. 123.

un-speak-a-ble (un-spē′ka-bl), a. Not speakable; that may not be spoken (as, "He was caught up into paradise, and heard *unspeakable* words, which it is not lawful for a man to utter": 2 Cor. xii. 4); exceeding the power of speech, unutterable, or inexpressible (as, *unspeakable* joy; an *unspeakable* loss; "*unspeakable* irreverence," J. Butler's "Analogy of Religion," ii. 1); hence, inexpressibly bad or objectionable (as, "I'm banned. I'm *unspeakable*": A. S. M. Hutchinson's "If Winter Comes," iv. 3); sometimes, unable to speak (rare).—**un-speak′a-bly**, adv.—**un-speak′ing**, a. Not speaking; lacking power of speech: as, "*unspeaking* sots" (Shakspere's "Cymbeline," v. 5. 178).

un-spe-ci-fied (un-spes′i-fīd), a. Not specified; not specifically or definitely named or stated.

un-spent (un-spent′), a. Not spent; not expended; not used up or exhausted; still active or effective.

un-sphere (un-sfēr′), v. t. To remove from its or one's sphere: as, "to *unsphere* the stars" (Shakspere's "Winter's Tale," i. 2. 48); "He . . . Whose soul no siren passion could *unsphere*" (Lowell's "Under the Old Elm," i. 1).

un-spoiled (un-spoild′), a. Not spoiled; not ruined or marred; not impaired in character, or deprived of the original or natural excellences, as by excessive indulgence (as, "Honora Leffingwell is the most natural and *unspoiled* person I know": W. Churchill's "Modern Chronicle," i. 9).

un-spok-en (un-spō′kn), a. Not spoken; unuttered.

un-sport-ing (un-spōr′ting), a. Not sporting; unsportsmanlike: as, "He was not a nice man; he had beaten Inchcape Jones at tennis, with a nasty, *unsporting* serve" (Sinclair Lewis's "Arrowsmith," xxxi.).

un-sports-man-like (un-spōrts′man-līk), a. Not sportsmanlike; unlike or unbefitting a sportsman; not fair or honorable.

un-spot-ted (un-spot′ed), a. Not spotted; free from spot or stain; immaculate; unblemished.

un-squared (un-skwärd′), a. Not squared.

un-sta-ble (un-stā′bl), a. Not stable; not firmly fixed, firm, or steady; liable to fall, change, or cease; unsteadfast, inconstant, or wavering (as, "*Unstable* as water, thou shalt not excel": Gen. xlix. 4).—**un-sta′ble-ness**, n.—**un-sta′bly**, adv.

un-stack (un-stak′), v. t. To bring out of a stacked condition; take down or apart a stack of: as, to *unstack* hay.

---

un-stained (un-stānd′), *a.* Not stained; unsullied; stainless.

un-stamped (un-stampt′), *a.* Not stamped; not bearing a stamp.

un-stan-dard-ized (un-stan′därd-dīzd), *a.* Not standardized.

un-state (un-stāt′), *v. t.* To deprive of state or dignity; also, to deprive of statehood.

un-states-man-like (un-stāts′man-līk), *a.* Not statesmanlike; unlike or unbefitting a statesman.

un-stead-fast (un-sted′fàst), *a.* Not steadfast; not firmly fixed; not firm in purpose, resolution, faith, etc.; inconstant; irresolute.—**un-stead′fast-ly,** *adv.*—**un-stead′fast-ness,** *n.*

un-stead-y (un-sted′i), *a.* Not steady; not firmly fixed; swaying or shaking; faltering; fluctuating or wavering; unsteadfast; irregular in habits.—**un-stead′i-ly,** *adv.*—**un-stead′i-ness,** *n.*

un-steel (un-stēl′), *v. t.* To bring out of a steeled condition; soften.

un-step (un-step′), *v. t.*; -stepped, -stepping. To remove (a mast, etc.) from its step.

un-stint-ed (un-stin′ted), *a.* Not stinted; in generous allowance; plentiful.—**un-stint′ed-ly,** *adv.*

un-stop (un-stop′), *v. t.*; -stopped, -stopping. To remove the stopper from (as, "A phial . . . Which when she had *unstopped,* therefrom she poured . . . A pale green liquor": W. Morris's "Jason," xv. 139); free from any obstruction; open; also, to draw out the stops of (an organ).

un-strained (un-strānd′), *a.* Not strained; not under strain or tension; not forced; natural; not separated or cleared by straining.

un-strat-i-fied (un-strat′i-fīd), *a.* Not stratified; not arranged in strata or layers: as, *unstratified* rocks (such as granite, porphyry, etc., which have not been deposited from water).

un-stressed (un-strest′), *a.* Not stressed; unaccented.

un-stri-at-ed (un-stri′ā-ted), *a.* Not striated; non-striated.

un-string (un-string′), *v. t.*; -strung, -stringing. To deprive of a string or strings; also, to take from a string; also, to loosen the strings of; also, to relax the tension of; relax unduly, or weaken (the nerves); hence, to weaken the nerves of (as, "a man *unstrung* by old sorrows and recent potations," Stevenson's "Master of Ballantrae," xi.; "I'm told getting married *unstrings* some men," Wister's "Virginian," xxxv.).

un-striped (un-strīpt′), *a.* Not striped; non-striated, as muscular tissue.

un-strung (un-strung′), *p. a.* Of the nerves, unduly relaxed, or weakened; hence, having the nerves weakened or in bad condition, as a person.

un-stud-ied (un-stud′id), *a.* Not studied; not premeditated or labored; natural or unaffected (as, "the easy *unstudied* graces of a child of nature": H. Melville's "Typee," x.); sometimes, not having studied; unversed.

un-sub-dued (un-sub-dūd′), *a.* Not subdued; unconquered.

un-sub-mis-sive (un-sub-mis′iv), *a.* Not submissive; refractory; unyielding.—**un-sub-mis′sive-ly,** *adv.*—**un-sub-mis′sive-ness,** *n.*

un-sub-stan-tial (un-sub-stan′shal), *a.* Not substantial; not solid, firm, or strong; flimsy; slight; unreal; insubstantial.—**un-sub-stan′tial-ly,** *adv.*

un-sub-stan-ti-at-ed (un-sub-stan′shi-ā-ted), *a.* Not substantiated; not established by evidence.—**un-sub-stan-ti-a′tion** (-ā′shon), *n.*

un-suc-cess (un-suk-ses′), *n.* Lack of success; failure.—**un-suc-cess′ful,** *a.* Not successful; without success; unfortunate.—**un-suc-cess′ful-ly,** *adv.*—**un-suc-cess′ful-ness,** *n.*

un-suit-a-ble (un-sū′ta-bl), *a.* Not suitable; inappropriate; unfitting; unbecoming.—**un-suit-a-bil′i-ty** (-bil′i-ti), **un-suit′a-ble-ness,** *n.*—**un-suit′a-bly,** *adv.*—**un-suit′ed,** *a.* Not suited; not adapted or suitable; not accommodated or satisfactorily supplied.

un-sul-lied (un-sul′id), *a.* Not sullied; unsoiled; spotless; stainless; untarnished.

un-sung (un-sung′), *a.* Not sung; not uttered or rendered by singing; not framed or told in verse (as, "Half yet remains

unsung": Milton's "Paradise Lost," vii. 21); not celebrated in song or verse (as, "*unsung* beauty": Whittier's "Songs of Labor," Dedication).

un-sup-port-a-ble (un-su-pōr′ta-bl), *a.* Insupportable.

un-sure (un-shōr′), *a.* Not sure; uncertain.—**un-sure′ly,** *adv.*—**un-sure′ness,** *n.*

un-sur-pass-a-ble (un-sėr-pàs′a-bl), *a.* Not surpassable; that cannot be surpassed.—**un-sur-pass′a-bly,** *adv.*—**un-sur-passed′,** *a.* Not or never surpassed; unexcelled.

un-sus-cep-ti-ble (un-su-sep′ti-bl), *a.* Not susceptible; unimpressionable.

un-sus-pect-ed (un-sus-pek′ted), *a.* Not suspected; clear of or not under suspicion (as, "an imperious old dame, not *unsuspected* of witchcraft": Hawthorne's "Twice-Told Tales," The Prophetic Pictures); not imagined to exist (as, an *unsuspected* danger); not surmised.—**un-sus-pect′ed-ly,** *adv.*—**un-sus-pect′ing,** *a.* Not suspecting; having no suspicion; unsuspicious.—**un-sus-pect′ing-ly,** *adv.*—**un-sus-pect′ing-ness,** *n.*

un-sus-pi-cious (un-sus-pish′us), *a.* Not suspicious; without suspicion, or unsuspecting (as, "to visit them openly, as if *unsuspicious* of any hostile design": Parkman's "Oregon Trail," xxiii.); not inclined to suspicion or distrust (as, an *unsuspicious* nature); not such as to excite suspicion (as, a seemingly *unsuspicious* proceeding).—**un-sus-pi′cious-ly,** *adv.*—**un-sus-pi′cious-ness,** *n.*

un-sus-tain-a-ble (un-sus-tā′na-bl), *a.* Not sustainable; not to be supported, maintained, upheld, or corroborated.—**un-sus-tained′,** *a.* Not sustained; not maintained; not upheld.

un-swathe (un-swāᴛʜ′), *v. t.* To free from that which swathes; take the wrappings from.

un-sway-a-ble (un-swā′a-bl), *a.* Not to be swayed or influenced.—**un-swayed′,** *a.* Not swayed or influenced.

un-swear (un-swār′), *v. t.*; pret. -swore, pp. -sworn, ppr. -swearing. To retract (something sworn, or sworn to); recant by a subsequent oath; abjure.

un-sweet-ened (un-swē′tnd), *a.* Not sweetened.

un-swept (un-swept′), *a.* Not swept.

un-swerv-ing (un-swėr′ving), *a.* Not swerving; undeviating; unwavering; firm.—**un-swerv′ing-ly,** *adv.*

un-sym-met-ri-cal (un-si-met′ri-kal), *a.* Not symmetrical; lacking symmetry; asymmetrical.—**un-sym-met′ri-cal-ly,** *adv.*—**un-sym′me-try** (-sim′e-tri), *n.* Lack of symmetry.

un-sym-pa-thet-ic (un-sim-pa-thet′ik), *a.* Not sympathetic; devoid of sympathy.—**un-sym-pa-thet′i-cal-ly,** *adv.*—**un-sym′pa-thiz-ing** (-thī-zing), *a.* Not sympathizing; unsympathetic.—**un-sym′pa-thy** (-thi), *n.* Lack of sympathy.

un-sys-te-mat-ic (un-sis-te-mat′ik), *a.* Not systematic; without system; not methodical.—**un-sys-te-mat′i-cal-ly,** *adv.*

un-tack (un-tak′), *v. t.* To unfasten (something tacked); loose or detach by removing a tack or tacks.

un-taint-ed (un-tān′ted), *a.* Not tainted; free from taint.

un-tam-a-ble (un-tā′ma-bl), *a.* Not tamable; tameless.—**un-tam′a-ble-ness,** *n.*—**un-tamed′,** *a.* Not tamed; not domesticated; unsubdued.

un-tan-gle (un-tang′gl), *v. t.* To bring out of a tangled state; disentangle; unsnarl; straighten out or clear up (anything confused or perplexing).

un-tanned (un-tand′), *a.* Not tanned.

un-tar-nished (un-tär′nisht), *a.* Not tarnished; of unimpaired luster; unstained or unsullied.

un-tast-ed (un-tās′ted), *a.* Not tasted.

un-taught (un-tât′), *a.* Not taught; not communicated by teaching; not instructed or educated; ignorant.

un-taxed (un-takst′), *a.* Not taxed; exempt from taxation.

un-teach (un-tēch′), *v. t.*; -taught, -teaching. To cause to be forgotten or disbelieved as by contrary teaching; also, to cause to forget or disbelieve something previously taught.

un-teach-a-ble (un-tē′cha-bl), *a.* Not teachable; indocile.—**un-teach′a-ble-ness,** *n.*

un-tech-ni-cal (un-tek′ni-kal), *a.* Not technical.

un-tem-pered (un-tem′pėrd), *a.* Not tempered.

un-ten-a-ble (un-ten′a-bl), *a.* Not tenable; indefensible: as, "Fort Sumter became *untenable* on the next day" (Charnwood's "Abraham Lincoln," vi.); "the *untenable* proposition that London is as hot as Calcutta" (Thackeray's "Newcomes," xiii.).—**un-ten′a-ble-ness**, *n*.

un-ten-ant-ed (un-ten′ạn-ted), *a*. Not tenanted; not occupied by a tenant.

un-ten-der (un-ten′dėr), *a*. Not tender; unfeeling.

un-tent-ed (un-ten′ted), *a*. Not treated by tenting or with a tent, as a wound (see *tent*²). See Shakspere's "King Lear," i. 4. 322.

un-test-ed (un-tes′ted), *a*. Not tested; untried.

un-teth-er (un-teᴛн′ėr), *v. t.* To loose from a tether.

un-thank-ful (un-thangk′fûl), *a*. Not thankful; ungrateful; also, not repaid with thanks; thankless.—**un-thank′-ful-ly**, *adv*.—**un-thank′ful-ness**, *n*.

un-think (un-thingk′), *v. t.*; *-thought, -thinking*. To retract in thought; change one's mind about: as, "To *unthink* your speaking And to say so no more" (Shakspere's "Henry VIII.," ii. 4. 104).

un-think-a-ble (un-thing′kạ-bl), *a*. Not thinkable; inconceivable (as, "the *unthinkable* infinitude of time": G. B. Shaw's "Man and Superman," iii.); not to be thought of or considered (as, "All wars are really *unthinkable* till you're in the middle of them": Buchan's "Three Hostages," xviii.). —**un-think′er**, *n*. One who does not think, or is not given to thinking.—**un-think′ing**, *a*. Not thinking; thoughtless; heedless; also, indicating lack of thought or reflection (as, "In a mechanical, *unthinking* way Racksole lighted them [candles]": Arnold Bennett's "Grand Babylon Hotel," xvii.).—**un-think′ing-ly**, *adv*.

un-thought (un-thôt′), *a*. Not thought; not conceived or considered.—**un-thought′-of**, *a*. Not conceived, imagined, or considered in thought; that has not occurred to the mind: as, "For surely now if death be near, *Unthought-of* is it" (W. Morris's "Jason," xii. 401).

un-thread (un-thred′), *v. t.* To draw out or take out the thread from (as, to *unthread* a needle); also, to thread one's way out of (as, to *unthread* a labyrinth).

un-thrift (un-thrift′). **I.** *n*. Lack of thrift; also, a thriftless person. **II.** *a*. Unthrifty: see Shakspere's "Timon of Athens," iv. 3. 311; "this mad, *unthrift* world" (Lowell's "Columbus," 29). [Obs. or archaic.]—**un-thrift′y**, *a*. Not thrifty; not thriving (as, "a border of *unthrifty* grass": Hawthorne's "Scarlet Letter," The Custom House); thriftless, improvident, or prodigal.—**un-thrift′i-ly**, *adv*.—**un-thrift′i-ness**, *n*.

un-throne (un-thrōn′), *v. t.* To dethrone.

un-ti-dy (un-tī′di), *a*. Not tidy or neat; slovenly; disordered: as, an *untidy* person; "The kitchen . . . was . . . *untidy* with clothes and other objects out of place" (George Eliot's "Adam Bede," x.).—**un-ti′di-ly**, *adv*.—**un-ti′di-ness**, *n*.

un-tie (un-tī′), *v.*; *-tied, -tying*. **I.** *tr*. To loose or unfasten (anything tied); let or set loose by undoing a knot; undo the string or cords of; undo, as a cord or a knot; unknot; hence, in general, to let or set loose; free from restraint; resolve, as perplexities. **II.** *intr*. To become untied.

un-til (un-til′). [ME. *until*, < *un-* (see *unto*) + *til*, E. *till*¹.] **I.** *prep*. To or unto (now Sc. and north. Eng.: as, "the Laird of Killancureit, who has devoted his leisure *untill* tillage," Scott's "Waverley," x.); also, onward to, or till (a specified time); up to the time of (some occurrence); with negatives, before (as, he did not go *until* night). **II.** *conj*. Up to the time that or when, or till (as, "He went to his organ and improvised . . . *until* the sounds . . . brought some solace to his heart": Lytton Strachey's "Queen Victoria," iv.); with negatives, before (as, he did not come *until* the meeting was half over).

un-tilled (un-tild′), *a*. Not tilled or cultivated.

un-time-ly (un-tīm′li), *a*. Not timely; not occurring at a suitable time or season; ill-timed or inopportune (as, "He kindles anger by *untimely* jokes": Crabbe's "Tales," i.); often, premature (as, "This great . . . labour . . . came to no effect by reason of the king's *untimely* death": Strype's "Memorials of Cranmer," i. 30).—**un-time′li-ness**, *n*.—**un-time′ly**, *adv*. Unseasonably.

un-time-ous, un-tim-ous (un-tī′mus), *a*. [See *timeous*.] Untimely; unseasonable; premature: as, "He came to some *untimeous* end" (Moir's "Mansie Wauch," xiii.). [Chiefly Sc.]

un-tir-ing (un-tīr′ing), *a*. Not tiring; unwearying; indefatigable: as, "My father was a person of *untiring* energy" (Aldrich's "Story of a Bad Boy," xv.).—**un-tir′-ing-ly**, *adv*.

un-ti-tled (un-tī′tld), *a*. Not titled; without a title; having no title of nobility; having no right or claim (as, "an *untitled* tyrant": Shakspere's "Macbeth," iv. 3. 104).

un-to (un′tö), *prep*. [ME. *unto*, < *un-* (= OS. *und*, OHG. *unz*, Goth. *und*), to, until, + *to*, E. *to*: cf. *until*.] To (in its various uses, except as the accompaniment of the infinitive: as, "Come *unto* me, all ye that labour," Mat. xi. 28; "Be not ye . . . like *unto* them," Mat. vi. 8; "Let the North *unto* the South Speak the word befitting both," Whittier's "Texas"); sometimes, until or till (as, "He shall abide in it [city] *unto* the death of the high priest": Num. xxxv. 25). [Archaic.]

un-told (un-tōld′), *a*. Not told; not related; not revealed; also, not numbered or enumerated; uncounted (as, "In the number let me pass *untold*": Shakspere's "Sonnets," cxxxvi.); hence, countless or incalculable (as, ages *untold*; *untold* wealth; *untold* harm).

un-touched (un-tucht′), *a*. Not touched; left intact; not affected with feeling or emotion; not mentioned or treated.

un-to-ward (un-tō′ạrd), *a*. Not toward; froward or perverse (archaic: as, "this *untoward* generation," Acts, ii. 40); unfavorable or unfortunate (as, an *untoward* wind; an *untoward* accident; "He hurried to get early to his church and see that nothing *untoward* had happened to it," Galsworthy's "Saint's Progress," ii. 1).—**un-to′ward-ly**, *adv*.—**un-to′ward-ness**, *n*.

un-trained (un-trānd′), *a*. Not trained; not disciplined; uneducated; uninstructed; not made fit by training.

un-tram-meled, un-tram-melled (un-tram′ęld), *a*. Not trammeled, hampered, or restrained.

un-trans-lat-a-ble (un-trans-lā′tạ-bl), *a*. Not capable of being translated; also, not fit to be translated.—**un-trans-lat′ed**, *a*. Not translated.

un-trav-eled, un-trav-elled (un-trav′ęld), *a*. Not having traveled, esp. to distant places; not having gained experience by travel (as, "An *untravelled* Englishman cannot relish all the beauties of Italian pictures": Addison, in "Spectator," 407); also, not traveled through or over; not frequented by travelers.

un-trav-ers-a-ble (un-trav′ėr-sạ-bl), *a*. Not traversable. —**un-trav′ersed**, *a*. Not traversed.

un-tried (un-trīd′), *a*. Not tried; not tested or put to the proof; not experimented with; not undergone or experienced; not attempted or essayed; not yet tried at law.

un-trim (un-trim′), *v. t.*; *-trimmed, -trimming*. To deprive of trimming.

un-trimmed (un-trimd′), *a*. Not trimmed; not decorated with trimming; not clipped or pruned (as, "his . . . *untrimmed* hair and beard": Scott's "Talisman," xviii.).

un-trod-den (un-trod′n), *a*. Not trodden.

un-troub-led (un-trub′ld), *a*. Not troubled; undisturbed; tranquil; calm.

un-true (un-trö′), *a*. Not true, as to a person or a cause; not faithful to a fact, or to a standard; unfaithful; false; incorrect or inaccurate.—**un-true′ness**, *n*.—**un-tru′ly** (-trö′li), *adv*.

un-truss (un-trus′), *v. t.* To loose from or as from a truss; unfasten or untie; undress.

un-trust-wor-thy (un-trust′wėr″ᴛнi), *a*. Not trustworthy; unreliable.—**un-trust′wor″thi-ness**, *n*.

un-truth (un-tröth′), *n*. The state or character of being untrue; unfaithfulness or disloyalty (obs. or archaic); want of veracity; divergence from truth; also, something untrue; a falsehood or lie.—**un-truth′ful**, *a*. Not truthful; wanting in veracity; diverging from or contrary to the truth; not corresponding with fact or reality.—**un-truth′ful-ly**, *adv*.—**un-truth′ful-ness**, *n*.

un-tuck (un-tuk′), *v. t.* To release from or bring out of a tucked condition.

un-tuned (un-tūnd′), *a*. Not tuned. See *tune, v. t.*

un-turned (un-tėrnd′), *a*. Not turned.

un-tu-tored (un-tū′tọrd), *a*. Not tutored; untaught; uninstructed: as, "some *untutor′d* youth" (Shakspere's "Sonnets," cxxxviii.).

---

un-twine (un-twīn′), *v. t.* or *i.* To bring or come out of a twined condition.

un-twist (un-twist′), *v. t.* or *i.* To bring or come out of a twisted condition.

un-used (un-ūzd′), *a.* Not used; not put to use; never having been used; not accustomed or habituated (as, hands *unused* to labor).

un-u-su-al (un-ū′zhu̧-ạl), *a.* Not usual, common, or ordinary; uncommon; uncommon in amount or degree; of an exceptional kind.—**un-u′su-al-ly,** *adv.*—**un-u′su-al-ness,** *n.*

un-ut-ter-a-ble (un-ut′ẽr-ạ-bl), *a.* Not utterable; incapable of being uttered or expressed; inexpressible; unspeakable. —**un-ut′ter-a-bly,** *adv.*—**un-ut′tered,** *a.* Not uttered.

un-val-ued (un-val′ūd), *a.* Not valued; not appraised; not esteemed or prized; also, that cannot be valued†, or of inestimable value† (as, "thy *unvalued* book": Milton's "Epitaph on Shakspeare," 11).

un-va-ried (un-vā′rid), *a.* Not varied; not diversified; not changed or altered.

un-var-nished (un-vär′nisht), *a.* Not varnished; fig., not embellished, or plain (as, "a round *unvarnish'd* tale": Shakspere's "Othello," i. 3. 90).

un-va-ry-ing (un-vā′ri-ing), *a.* Not varying or changing; uniform.—**un-va′ry-ing-ly,** *adv.*

un-veil (un-vāl′), *v.* **I.** *tr.* To remove a veil from; disclose to view; reveal. **II.** *intr.* To remove a veil; reveal one's self; become unveiled.

un-ve-ra-cious (un-vẽ-rā′shus), *a.* Not veracious; untruthful.—**un-ve-ra′ci-ty** (-ras′i-ti), *n.*

un-ver-i-fi-a-ble (un-ver′i-fī-ạ-bl), *a.* Not verifiable.—**un-ver′i-fied** (-fīd), *a.* Not verified.

un-versed (un-vẽrst′), *a.* Not versed; unskilled.

un-voiced (un-voist′), *a.* Not voiced; not uttered; in *phonetics,* not uttered with voice or vocal sound as distinguished from breath; voiceless; surd.

un-wa-ri-ly (un-wā′ri-li), *adv.* In an unwary manner; incautiously; unguardedly.—**un-wa′ri-ness,** *n.*

un-warped (un-wârpt′), *a.* Not warped; fig., unbiased; impartial.

un-war-rant-a-ble (un-wor′ạn-tạ-bl), *a.* Not warrantable; unjustifiable (as, "*unwarrantable* prejudices": H. Melville's "Moby-Dick," iii.).—**un-war′rant-a-ble-ness,** *n.*—**un-war′rant-a-bly,** *adv.*—**un-war′rant-ed,** *a.* Not warranted; not assured or certain; not guaranteed, as to fulfilment, reliability, quality, etc.; not authorized or justified (as, *unwarranted* interference).—**un-war′rant-ed-ly,** *adv.*

un-wa-ry (un-wā′ri), *a.* Not wary; not cautious; unguarded.

un-washed (un-wosht′), *a.* Not washed; not cleansed by water; not washed by waves or flowing water.—**the unwashed,** or **the great unwashed,** the lower classes of the people; the rabble.

un-wa-ver-ing (un-wā′vẽr-ing), *a.* Not wavering; steadfast; firm.—**un-wa′ver-ing-ly,** *adv.*

un-wear-ied (un-wēr′id), *a.* Not wearied; not fatigued; indefatigable.—**un-wear′y-ing,** *a.* Not wearying; not growing weary or tired; untiring.—**un-wear′y-ing-ly,** *adv.*

un-weave (un-wēv′), *v. t.;* pret. *-wove,* pp. *-woven,* ppr. *-weaving.* To undo, take apart, or separate (something woven); ravel.

un-wed-ded (un-wed′ed), *a.* Not wedded; unmarried.

un-wel-come (un-wel′kum), *a.* Not welcome; not gladly received: as, an *unwelcome* guest; "*unwelcome* information" (Froude's "Cæsar," xvii.).—**un-wel′come-ly,** *adv.*—**un-wel′come-ness,** *n.*

un-well (un-wel′), *a.* Not well; ailing; ill.

un-wept (un-wept′), *a.* Not wept, or wept for; unmourned; also, not wept or shed, as tears.

un-whole-some (un-hōl′sum), *a.* Not wholesome; unhealthful; deleterious to health or well-being, physically or morally; also, not sound in health; unhealthy, esp. in appearance; suggestive of disease.—**un-whole′some-ly,** *adv.*—**un-whole′some-ness,** *n.*

un-wield-y (un-wēl′di), *a.* Not wieldy; wielded with difficulty; not readily handled or managed in use or action, as from size, shape, or weight: as, "These swords were strange great *unwieldy* things" (Defoe's "Robinson Crusoe," ii. 3);

"He is too fat and *unwieldy* to leap ditches" (Smollett's "Humphry Clinker," June 26).—**un-wield′i-ly,** *adv.*—**un-wield′i-ness,** *n.*

un-willed (un-wild′), *a.* Not willed; involuntary.—**un-will′ing,** *a.* Not willing; loath; reluctant; also, involuntary† or unintentional†.—**un-will′ing-ly,** *adv.*—**un-will′ing-ness,** *n.*

un-wind (un-wīnd′), *v.;* *-wound* (occasionally *-winded*), *-winding.* **I.** *tr.* To undo (something wound); wind off; loose or separate, as what is wound; also, to disentangle. **II.** *intr.* To become unwound.

un-wis-dom (un-wiz′dǫm), *n.* [AS. *unwîsdôm.*] Lack of wisdom; unwise action; folly.

un-wise (un-wīz′), *a.* [AS. *unwîs.*] Not wise; foolish; imprudent; injudicious.—**un-wise′ly,** *adv.*

un-wished (un-wisht′), *a.* Not wished; undesired; unwelcome. Also **un-wished′=for.**

un-wit-ting (un-wit′ing), *a.* Not witting or knowing; ignorant; unaware; unconscious: as, the *unwitting* cause of much controversy.—**un-wit′ting-ly,** *adv.*

un-wom-an-ly (un-wu̇m′ạn-li), *a.* Not womanly; unbecoming in a woman; unfeminine.—**un-wom′an-li-ness,** *n.*

un-wont-ed (un-wun′ted or -wōn′ted). **I.** *a.* Not wonted; unaccustomed or unused (as, a child *unwonted* to strangers); not customary, habitual, or usual (as, "the *unwonted* jollity that brightened the faces of the people": Hawthorne's "Scarlet Letter," xxi.). **II.** *adv.* In an *unwonted* manner or degree: as, "Lenny seemed *unwonted* pale" (W. B. Maxwell's "In Cotton Wool," ix.).—**un-wont′ed-ly,** *adv.* —**un-wont′ed-ness,** *n.*

un-work-a-ble (un-wẽr′kạ-bl), *a.* Not workable; incapable of being worked; unmanageable; impracticable, as a scheme. —**un-worked′,** *a.* Not worked; not developed or exploited, as a field of operations. Cf. *unwrought.*—**un-work′ing,** *a.* Not working; doing no work.—**un-work′man-like,** *a.* Not workmanlike; not like or befitting a workman.

un-world-ly (un-wẽrld′li), *a.* Not worldly; not versed in or devoted to worldly affairs.—**un-world′li-ness,** *n.*

un-worn (un-wôrn′), *a.* Not worn; not impaired by wear.

un-wor-thy (un-wẽr′ŦHi), *a.* Not worthy; lacking worth or excellence; not commendable or creditable (as, "his *unworthy* preference of inglorious ease and material pleasures to the immortality of a hero": Whyte-Melville's "Sarchedon," xiii.); not of adequate merit or character (as, an *unworthy* opponent); of a kind not worthy (with *of,* expressed or understood: as, a speech *unworthy* of the occasion; "a life not *unworthy* such a setting," G. W. Curtis's "Prue and I," ii.); beneath the dignity (*of:* as, conduct *unworthy* of you); undeserved† (as, "Worthy vengeance on thyself, Which didst *unworthy* slaughter upon others": Shakspere's "Richard III.," i. 2. 88); also, undeserving (as, "*Unworthy,* unfit though he were, she loved him," W. Churchill's "Coniston," ii. 12; "These tales were deemed *unworthy* of credit," Hawthorne's "Twice-Told Tales," The Great Carbuncle; "We were *unworthy* to be let into the secret," Burke's "American Taxation").—**un-wor′thi-ly,** *adv.*—**un-wor′thi-ness,** *n.*

un-wound (un-wound′). Pret. and pp. of *unwind.*

un-wound-ed (un-wön′ded), *a.* Not wounded.

un-wrap (un-rap′), *v.;* *-wrapped, -wrapping.* **I.** *tr.* To bring out of a wrapped condition; unfold or open, as something wrapped. **II.** *intr.* To become unwrapped.

un-wreathe (un-rēŦH′), *v. t.* To bring out of a wreathed condition; untwist; untwine.

un-wrin-kle (un-ring′kl), *v. t.* To smooth the wrinkles from.

un-wrin-kled (un-ring′kld), *a.* Not wrinkled; smooth.

un-writ-ten (un-rit′n), *a.* Not written; not reduced to writing; not actually formulated or expressed (as, an *unwritten* rule); also, containing no writing; blank.—**unwritten law,** law which, although it may be reduced to writing, rests for its authority on custom, judicial decision, etc., as distinguished from law originating in written command, statute, or decree; also (preceded by *the*), the principle, popularly accepted as valid, of the right of the individual to avenge wrongs against personal or family honor, esp. in cases involving relations between the sexes (sometimes urged in justification of persons guilty of criminal acts of vengeance under certain circumstances, as when one man kills another to avenge the dishonoring of his wife or any female member of his family).

un-wrought (un-rôt′), *a.* Not wrought; not worked or elaborated into a finished product. Cf. *unworked.*

un-yield-ing (un-yēl′ding), *a.* Not yielding; not giving way; firm; obstinate.—**un-yield′ing-ly**, *adv.*—**un-yield′-ing-ness**, *n.*

un-yoke (un-yōk′), *v.* **I.** *tr.* To free from or as from a yoke; also, to part or disjoin as by removing a yoke. **II.** *intr.* To remove a yoke; hence, fig., to cease work.

up (up), *adv.* [AS. *up, upp,* = OS. *ūp* = OHG. *ūf* (G. *auf*) = Icel. *upp,* akin to Goth. *iup,* up, and prob. ult. to E. *over.*] To, toward, or in a more elevated position (as, to climb *up* to the top of a ladder; *up* in a tree); to or in an erect position (as, to stand *up*); out of bed (as, to get *up*; to sit or stay *up* late); above the horizon (as, the moon is *up*); also, to or at any point that is considered higher (as, *up* north); to or at a source, origin, center, or the like (as, to follow a stream *up* to its head; "There came *up* to London, out of a Northern county, Mr. Thomas Newcome," Thackeray's "Newcomes," ii.); to or at a higher point or degree in a scale, as of rank, size, value, pitch, etc.; also, to or at a point of equal advance, extent, etc. (as, to catch *up* in a race; to keep *up* with the times; to live *up* to one's income); also, having adequate power or ability, or equal (as, to be *up* to the needs of an emergency; to be *up* to a task); well advanced or versed, as in a subject (as, to be *up* in mathematics); also, into or in activity, operation, etc. (as, to set *up* vibrations; to stir *up* rebellion; to be *up* in arms); in process of going on or happening (as, "The woodland rings with laugh and shout, As if a hunt were *up,*" Bryant's "Song of Marion's Men"; what's *up* over there?); into view, prominence, or consideration (as, the lost papers have turned *up*; to bring *up* a new topic); also, into or in a place of safe-keeping, storage, retirement, etc. (as, to lay *up* riches; to put *up* preserves; laid *up* with rheumatism); also, into or in a state of union, contraction, etc. (as, to add *up* a column of figures; to fold or shrivel *up*); also, to the required or final point (as, to pay *up* one's debts; burned or used *up*); to or at an end (as, his hour is *up*; "It's all *up* with your little schemes," H. G. Wells's "Bealby," iii.); in *baseball,* at bat (as, he struck out the second time *up*); in *golf,* ahead of an opponent a specified number of holes (opposed to *down*). Sometimes (by ellipsis of a verb) used as if an imperative: as, *up,* Towser! "*Up* with my tent there!" (Shakspere's "Richard III.," v. 3. 7).—**to be up to a person,** to be before him as a duty; be incumbent on him: as, it *is up to him* to make the next move. [Slang.]—**up against,** confronting or facing, as something to be dealt with: as, "You don't understand the sort of proposition America is *up against*" (H. G. Wells's "Mr. Britling," iii. 1. § 13). [Colloq.]—**up to,** about to do; doing; engaged in: as, to be *up to* mischief; "You little minx . . . What you *up to* now?" (Mrs. Stowe's "Oldtown Folks," x.). [Colloq.] —**up,** *prep.* To, toward, or at a higher place on or in (as, *up* the stairs; *up* a tree); to, toward, near, or at the top of; also, to, toward, or at a point considered as higher (as, *up* the street); toward the source, origin, etc., of (as, *up* the stream); toward or in the interior of (a region, etc.: as, the explorers went *up* country).—**up one's sleeve,** in reserve, for bringing out when new pleases: as, to have several plans *up one's sleeve*; be careful — he has something *up his sleeve*. —**up stage.** See *up-stage, a.*—**up. I.** *a.* Going or directed up; tending upward: as, an *up* train; an *up* grade. **II.** *n.* An upward movement; an ascent; fig., a rise of fortune (as, to have one's *ups* and downs).—**up,** *v.; upped, upping.* **I.** *tr.* To put or take up: as, "We got in the maids and *upped* him, to a room he used to sleep in" (A. S. M. Hutchinson's "If Winter Comes," iv. 1). [Now colloq.] **II.** *intr.* To get or start up; make an upward motion (as, to *up* with one's fist). [Now colloq.]

u-pan-i-shad (ŏ-pan′i-shad), *n.* [Skt.] [Often *cap.*] In *Sanskrit lit.,* one of a class of speculative treatises forming a part of the Vedic literature, and exhibiting the earliest attempts of the Hindu mind to penetrate into the mysteries of creation and existence.

u-pas (ū′pạs), *n.* [Malay *ūpas,* poison.] The poisonous milky sap of *Ipo* (or *Antiaris*) *toxicaria,* a large moraceous tree of Java and neighboring islands, used for arrow-poison; also, the tree; also, the poisonous sap of *Strychnos tieute,* a woody climbing loganiaceous plant of the same region, similarly used; also, the plant.

Flowering Branch of the Upas-tree (*Ipo toxicaria*).

up-bear (up-bãr′), *v. t.*; pret. *-bore,* pp. *-borne,* ppr. *-bearing.* To bear up; raise aloft; support; sustain. — **up-bear′er**, *n.*

up-braid (up-brād′), *v.* [ME. *upbreiden,* < *up,* up, + *breiden,* move quickly, fling, E. *braid*[1].] **I.** *tr.* To reproach for some fault or offense (as, "The archbishop . . . *upbraided* them with their falseness and ingratitude," Strype's "Memorials of Cranmer," i. 27; "Darius Clayhanger *upbraided* him for not having worn his overcoat," Arnold Bennett's "Clayhanger," ii. 18); reprove severely, or chide (as, "We could hear . . . Blake *upbraiding* Egström in an abusive, strained voice": J. Conrad's "Lord Jim," xviii.); sometimes, of things, to bring reproach on; be a reproach to; also, to cast up as a reproach; make a subject of reproach†. **II.** *intr.* To utter reproaches: as, "Mrs. Fitzgerald continued to *upbraid* at the top of her voice" (Lever's "Harry Lorrequer," xviii.).—**up-braid′er**, *n.*—**up-braid′ing-ly**, *adv.*

up-bring-ing (up′bring-ing), *n.* The bringing up or rearing of a person from childhood; care and training devoted to the young while growing up: as, "She had . . . repaid with black ingratitude the love lavished on her *upbringing*" (Galsworthy's "Saint's Progress," iii. 3).

up-build (up-bild′), *v. t.*; *-built, -building.* To build up; establish.

up-burst (up′bērst), *n.* A burst upward; an uprush.

up-cast (up′kạst). **I.** *a.* Cast up; directed upward. **II.** *n.* The act or an act of casting upward; the state of being cast upward; also, something that is cast up; also, a shaft or passage up which air passes, as from a mine.

up-climb (up-klīm′), *v. t.* or *i.* To climb up.

up=coun-try (up′kun′tri). **I.** *adv.* Toward or in the interior of a country. **II.** *a.* Being or living remote from the coast or border; interior: as, an *up-country* village. **III.** *n.* The interior of the country.

up-curl (up-kėrl′), *v. t.* or *i.* To curl upward.

up-end (up-end′), *v.* **I.** *tr.* To set on end, as a barrel. **II.** *intr.* To stand on end.

up-flow (up-flō′), *v. i.* To flow up.—**up′flow,** *n.* An upward flow; also, that which flows up.

up-growth (up′grōth), *n.* The process of growing up; development; also, something that grows up (as, "cartilaginous *upgrowths* . . . in . . . the skull": Huxley's "Anatomy of Vertebrated Animals," i.).

up-gush (up-gush′), *v. i.* To gush up.—**up′gush,** *n.* An upward gush.

up-heav-al (up-hē′vạl), *n.* The act or an act of upheaving, or the state of being upheaved; in *geol.,* a disturbance of a part of the earth's crust, as a result of which certain areas occupy a higher position with reference to adjacent areas than they did before.

up-heave (up-hēv′), *v.* **I.** *tr.* To heave or lift up; raise up or aloft: as, "land . . . *upheaved* by violent volcanic forces" (H. G. Wells's "Outline of History," ii. § 1). **II.** *intr.* To be lifted up; rise as if thrust up: as, "The pavement bursts, the earth *upheaves* Beneath the staggering town!" (Holmes's "Agnes," iv.).

up-held (up-held′). Pret. and pp. of *uphold.*

up-hill (up′hil′), *adv.* Up, or as if up, the slope of a hill; upward: as, "This lane inclined *up-hill* all the way to Hay" (C. Brontë's "Jane Eyre," xii.).—**up′hill,** *a.* Going or tending upward on or as on a hill (as, "a few minutes' *uphill* drive": Amelia B. Edwards's "Thousand Miles up the Nile," ii.); hence, laborious, fatiguing, or difficult (as, "He sat down and tried to seem gay, but it was *up-hill* work": Mark Twain's "Tom Sawyer," x.).

up-hold (up-hōld′), *v. t.*; -*held*, -*holding*. To hold up; raise; also, to keep up, or keep from sinking; support; fig., to sustain; maintain; countenance.—**up-hold′er,** *n.* One who or that which upholds; a supporter; also, a tradesman†; also, an upholsterer†.

up-hol-ster (up-hōl′stèr), *v. t.* [Back-formation from *upholsterer*.] To furnish (rooms, etc.) with hangings, curtains, carpets, or the like; also, to provide (chairs, sofas, etc.) with coverings, cushions, stuffing, springs, etc. (as, "The furniture was *upholstered* in bright blue rep": L. Merrick's "Actor-Manager," ii.).

up-hol-ster-er (up-hōl′stèr-èr), *n.* [For earlier *upholster*, *upholdster*, an upholsterer, for *upholder*: cf. *upholder*.] One whose business it is to furnish and put in place hangings, curtains, carpets, or the like, and to cushion and cover furniture, etc.—**up-hol′ster-er=bee,** *n.* Any of various bees, as those of the genus *Megachile*, which cut small, regularly shaped pieces of leaves or flower-petals to use as a lining for their cells. —**up-hol′ster-y** (-i), *n.*; pl. -*ies* (-iz). The business of an upholsterer; also, the fittings or decorations supplied by an upholsterer, as hangings, curtains, cushions, furniture-coverings, and the like.

Cell of Upholsterer-bee.

u-phroe (ū′frō), *n.* [D. *juffrouw*, lit. 'young lady.'] *Naut.*, an oblong or oval piece of wood perforated with holes through which small lines are rove, forming a crowfoot, from which an awning is suspended. See *crowfoot*.

up-keep (up′kēp), *n.* The process of keeping up or maintaining; the maintenance, or keeping in operation, due condition, and repair, of an establishment, a machine, etc.; also, the cost of this, including operating expenses, cost of renewal or repair, etc.

up-land (up′land). **I.** *n.* Land elevated above other land (as, "that horseshoe of shallow *upland* which separated the Ypres basin from the vale of the Lys": Buchan's "Hist. of the Great War," liii.); the higher ground of a region or district; an elevated region; also, the inland region†; country as distinguished from the neighborhood of towns†. **II.** *a.* Of or pertaining to uplands, or elevated regions (as, "*upland* pastures": Mrs. Gaskell's "Cranford," iv.); found on or frequenting uplands; also, pertaining to the inland region, or the country as distinguished from the neighborhood of towns†.—**upland plover** or **sandpiper,** a large American sandpiper, *Bartramia longicauda*, resembling a plover and valued as a game-bird.—**up′land-er,** *n.* An inhabitant of the uplands; also, the upland plover (local, U. S.).

Upland Plover.

up-lift (up-lift′), *v. t.* To lift up; raise; elevate; fig., to raise socially or morally (as, to *uplift* the masses; to *uplift* the stage); also, to exalt emotionally or spiritually (as, "*uplifted* . . . by the pride of success": S. R. Crockett's "Stickit Minister," xvi.).—**up′lift,** *n.* The act of lifting up or raising; elevation; fig., the process or work of raising socially or morally (as, an apostle of *uplift*; "For several days there was community spirit and much *uplift*," Sinclair Lewis's "Main Street," xx.); also, emotional or spiritual exaltation; in *geol.*, an upheaval.—**up-lift′er,** *n.* One who or that

which uplifts; esp., a person engaged in or devoted to social or moral uplift; an apostle of uplift.—**up-lift′ment,** *n.*

up-most (up′mōst), *a. superl.* Uppermost.

up-on (u-pon′), *prep.* [AS. *uppon, uppan.*] Up and on; upward so as to get or be on (as, "To lift the woman's fallen divinity *Upon* an even pedestal with man": Tennyson's "Princess," iii. 208); in an elevated position on (as, "Three years I lived *upon* a pillar, high Six cubits": Tennyson's "St. Simeon Stylites," 85); hence, on, in any of various senses (used as an equivalent of *on*, with no added idea of ascent or elevation, and preferred in certain cases only for euphonic or metrical reasons: as, "The moon lies fair *Upon* the straits," M. Arnold's "Dover Beach"; "What is Guilt? A stain *upon* the soul," Hawthorne's "Twice-Told Tales," Fancy's Show-Box).

up-per (up′èr), *a.* [Compar. of *up*.] Higher, as in place or position, or in a scale (as, the *upper* lip; the *upper* notes of a singer's voice); superior, as in rank, dignity, or station (as, the *upper* house of a legislature; an *upper* servant; the *upper* classes of society); specif., of places, situated at a higher level, or farther from the sea-level or the sea (as, "Nether Germany was entitled to the same privileges as *Upper* Germany," Motley's "Dutch Republic," iii. 4; *Upper* Egypt); in *geol.*, noting a later division of a period, system, or the like (as, the *Upper* Devonian, *Upper* Cambrian, etc.). —**the upper hand,** fig., the dominating or controlling position; the advantage: as, "I've got *the upper hand* over you, Fagin" (Dickens's "Oliver Twist," xv.).—**upper story,** fig., the head as the seat of the mind or intellect; the brain; the wits: as, "He's not overburthen'd i' th' *upper storey*" (George Eliot's "Amos Barton," i.). [Humorous.]—**upper works,** *naut.*, the parts of a ship which are above the surface of the water when she is loaded for a voyage.—**up′per,** *n.* The upper part of a shoe or boot, above the sole, comprising the vamp and the quarters; *pl.*, cloth gaiters.—**to be on one's uppers,** to have worn out the soles of one's shoes; hence, to be reduced to extreme shabbiness or poverty. [Colloq.]—**up′per=case′,** *a.* In *printing*, pertaining to or belonging in the upper case (see *case²*, *n.*); of a letter, capital (as opposed to *small*).—**up′per-cut,** *n.* In *boxing*, a swinging blow directed upward from beneath, as to an adversary's chin.—**up′per-cut,** *v. t.* or *i.*; -*cut*, -*cutting*. To strike with an uppercut.—**up′per-most. I.** *a. superl.* Highest in place, order, rank, power, etc.; topmost; predominant: as, the *uppermost* rows of seats; the *uppermost* thought in his mind. **II.** *adv. superl.* In the highest or first place.

up-pish (up′ish), *a.* Proud; arrogant; self-assertive; assuming. [Colloq.]—**up′pish-ly,** *adv.*—**up′pish-ness,** *n.*

up-raise (up-rāz′), *v. t.* To raise up: as, "Scarce dare they now *upraise* the abject head" (Wiffen's tr. Tasso's "Jerusalem Delivered," iii. 5).

up-rear (up-rēr′), *v. t.* To rear up; raise.

up-right (up′rīt), *a.* [AS. *upriht*.] Erect or vertical, as in position or posture (as, "*upright* as the palm tree," Jer. x. 5; "She . . . had a thin *upright* body," Archibald Marshall's "Anthony Dare," ii.); raised or directed vertically or upward (as, a dog with ears *upright*); having the longest axis vertical (as, an *upright* boiler); also, adhering to rectitude, or righteous, honest, or just (as, "a valiant and *upright* man": Walpole's "Castle of Otranto," iii.); in accord with what is right (as, "an *upright* life": Shakspere's "Merchant of Venice," iii. 5. 79).—**upright piano.** See under *piano²*, *n.*—**up′right,** *n.* The state of being upright or vertical; also, something standing erect or vertical, as a piece of timber; also, an upright piano.—**up′right,** *adv.* In an upright position or direction (as, "the sand in which their four long lances were planted *upright*": J. Conrad's "Rescue," iv. 3); vertically; also, flat on the back with the face upward†.— **up′right-ly,** *adv.*—**up′right-ness,** *n.*

up-rise (up-rīz′), *v. i.*; pret. -*rose*, pp. -*risen*, ppr. -*rising*. To rise up; get up, as from a lying or sitting posture; rise in revolt; come into being or action; move upward, mount up, or ascend; come above the horizon; slope upward; increase in height or swell up.—**up-rise** (up′rīz or up-rīz′), *n.* The act of rising up.—**up-ris′ing** (-rī′zing), *n.* The act or an act of rising up; esp., an insurrection or revolt; also, an ascent or acclivity.

up-roar (up'rōr), *n.* [D. *oproer* = G. *aufruhr*, tumult, disturbance, revolt; the spelling and sense of the E. word being affected by association with *roar*.] Great tumult, or violent and noisy disturbance, as of a multitude, or an instance or state of this (as, to quell civil *uproar*; the city was in an *uproar*); violent and noisy commotion of any kind (as, "that *uproar* of the elements": Godwin's "Caleb Williams," xvi.); now, often, tumultuous or confused noise or din, or an instance of it (as, "The evening *uproar* of the howling monkeys burst out," W. H. Hudson's "Green Mansions," xii.; "He was dragged to the table, amidst an *uproar* of laughter and shouting," Marryat's "King's Own," xl.; "an *uproar* of guns and shells," H. G. Wells's "Mr. Britling," ii. 3. § 11). —**up-roar'**, *v. t.* To throw into tumult or confusion: as, "I should . . . *Uproar* the universal peace" (Shakspere's "Macbeth," iv. 3. 99). [Obs. or archaic.]—**up-roar'i-ous**, *a.* Characterized by or in a state of uproar; tumultuous; making an uproar, or disorderly and noisy, as an assembly, persons, etc. (as, "The audience was *uproarious* in its approval": Bok's "Americanization of Edward Bok," xxxii.); confused and loud, as sounds, utterances, etc. (as, "*uproarious* laughter," W. Churchill's "Coniston," ii. 2; "*Uproarious* were the 'bravos' which followed the doctor's impromptu," Lover's "Handy Andy," v.); expressed by or producing uproar (as, *uproarious* delight).—**up-roar'i-ous-ly**, *adv.*—**up-roar'i-ous-ness**, *n.*

up-root (up-rōt'), *v. t.* To root up; tear up by the roots; eradicate; remove utterly.

up-rouse (up-rouz'), *v. t.* To rouse up; arouse; awake. See Shakspere's "Romeo and Juliet," ii. 3. 40.

up-rush (up-rush'), *v. i.* To rush upward.—**up'rush**, *n.* An upward rush.

up-set (up-set'), *v.*; *-set, -setting.* **I.** *tr.* To set up†; also, to overturn (as, to *upset* a boat or a carriage; "He had . . . *upset* the ink on the spelling-book," Mark Twain's "Tom Sawyer," xx.); fig., to overthrow or defeat (as, to *upset* a will; "It requires a good deal to *upset* the arguments," S. Butler's "Erewhon," xii.); disturb or derange completely (as, to *upset* a person's plans; "We'll go to London and *upset* the ruby business," Dunsany's "Night at an Inn"); also, to put out of order, or throw into disorder (as, the house, or the room, is *upset*); also, to disturb mentally, or perturb (as, "He had not allowed the letter to *upset* him," Arnold Bennett's "Clayhanger," i. 17; "Poor Ernest came out . . . looking white, frightened and *upset*," S. Butler's "Way of All Flesh," lxx.); also, to shorten and thicken by hammering on the end, as a heated piece of iron; shorten (a tire of a wheel) in resetting it. **II.** *intr.* To become upset or overturned: as, "You'd better look at the reins . . . We almost *upset* just then" (Tarkington's "Magnificent Ambersons," vii.).—**up-set** (up-set' or up'set), *n.* An upsetting or being upset; an overturn (as, "It [boat] capsized . . . that was but the first of some dozens of *upsets*": W. H. Hudson's "Far Away and Long Ago," xii.); fig., an overthrow; often, a defeat of a contestant favored to win (colloq.).—**up'set**, *a.* Set up; fixed; determined: as, the *upset* price (the lowest price at which a thing offered for sale, as at auction, will be sold).—**up-set'ter**, *n.*

up-shoot (up'shöt), *n.* A shooting up; something that shoots up; in *baseball*, a curve which shoots or bends up as it approaches the home base.

up-shot (up'shot), *n.* [Cf. *shot³*.] The final issue, the conclusion, or the result (as, "The *upshot* of the matter . . . was that she showed both of them the door": Stevenson's "Kidnapped," xxviii.); also, the gist, or sum and substance (as, "This was the *upshot* of the document that the body of officers . . . presented to the House of Commons": Morley's "Oliver Cromwell," iii. 5).

up-side (up'sīd), *n.* The upper side or part.—**upside down.** [For earlier *up so down*, 'up as down.'] With the upper part undermost (as, "a burning torch that's turned *upside down*": Shakspere's "Pericles," ii. 2. 32); hence, in complete disorder; topsyturvy.

up-si-lon (ūp'si-lon), *n.* [Gr. *ὖ ψιλόν*, 'simple u.'] The twentieth letter (Υ, υ, = English U, u, or Y, y) of the Greek alphabet.

up-spring (up-spring'), *v. i.*; pret. *-sprang* or *-sprung*, pp. *-sprung*, ppr. *-springing.* To spring up.

up=stage (up'stāj'), *a.* [From the phrase *up stage*, in theatrical use, that is, toward the back of the stage, or back from the audience, as with reference to the position of an actor.] Haughtily aloof; haughty; supercilious. [Slang, orig. theatrical.]

up-stairs (up'stārz'), *adv.* Up the stairs; to or on an upper floor: as, "They went *upstairs*" (Arnold Bennett's "Roll-Call," i.).—**to go upstairs**, to ascend in a plane, esp. to a high altitude. [Colloq.]—**up'stairs**, *a.* Pertaining to or situated on an upper floor: as, "an *upstairs* verandah" (J. Conrad's "Lord Jim," xv.).

up-stand-ing (up-stan'ding), *a.* Standing erect; erect and tall (as, an *upstanding* horse; "some fine, *upstanding* pear trees," Blackmore's "Lorna Doone," xvii.); esp., of persons, erect, well-grown, and vigorous in body or form (as, "two *upstanding*, pleasant children": Maugham's "Moon and Sixpence," vii.); hence, of a fine, vigorous type (as, "the kind of *upstanding*, energetic young man, with a future . . . that we want here": Sinclair Lewis's "Babbitt," vi.); sometimes, upright or honorable.

up-start (up-stärt'), *v. i.* To start up.—**up'start. I.** *n.* One who has risen suddenly from a humble position to wealth or power, or to assumed consequence; a pretentious and objectionable parvenu: as, "Every *upstart* of fortune . . . presents himself at Bath" (Smollett's "Humphry Clinker," April 23). **II.** *a.* Being or resembling an upstart; characteristic of an upstart.

up-surge (up-sėrj'), *v. i.* To surge up.

up-swell (up-swel'), *v. i.* To swell up.

up-swing (up'swing), *n.* An upward swing or swinging movement, as of a pendulum: often fig.: as, an *upswing* in prices or in business.

up-take (up'tāk), *n.* The act of taking up; a lifting; also, apprehension or understanding (Sc. and north. Eng.: as, quick in the *uptake*); also, a pipe or passage leading upward from below, as for conducting smoke, a current of air, or the like.

up-throw (up'thrō), *n.* A throwing up or being thrown up; an upheaval; in *geol.*, an upward displacement of rock on one side of a fault (opposed to *downthrow*).

up-thrust (up'thrust), *n.* A thrust in an upward direction; in *geol.*, an upheaval or uplift.

up-tilt (up-tilt'), *v. t.* To tilt up.

up=to=date (up'tö-dāt'), *a.* Extending to the present time, or including the latest facts (as, an *up-to-date* account or record); in accordance with the latest or newest standards, ideas, or style (as, "*up-to-date* health methods": Sinclair Lewis's "Arrowsmith," xxiii.); of persons, etc., keeping up with the times, as in information, ideas, methods, style, etc. (as, "This new eagerness to be *up-to-date* and modern . . . horrified him": Hugh Walpole's "Wooden Horse," ii.).—**up=to=date'ness**, *n.*

up-town (up'toun), *adv.* To or in the upper part of a town. —**up'town**, *a.* Moving toward, situated in, or pertaining to the upper part of a town.

up-turn (up-tėrn'), *v. t.* or *i.* To turn up.—**up'turn**, *n.* A turning up; esp., an upward turn, or a changing and rising movement, as in prices, business, etc.

u-pu-poid (ū'pū-poid), *a.* [L. *upupa*, hoopoe.] Resembling the hoopoe; belonging or pertaining to the *Upupoideæ*, a superfamily of old-world non-passerine birds including the hoopoes.

up-ward, up-wards (up'wärd, -wärdz), *adv.* [AS. *upweard*, *upweardes*.] Toward a higher place or position (as, "two shallow grooves which pass from below *upward*," Huxley's "Anatomy of Vertebrated Animals," viii.; "The great grating lifts outwards and *upwards*," Dunsany's "Queen's Enemies"); toward a higher or greater rank, degree, age, etc. (as, from ten years *upward*); more (as, "A very foolish fond old man, Fourscore and *upward*": Shakspere's "King Lear," iv. 7. 61); toward the source or origin (as, to trace a stream *upward*); also, in the upper parts, or above (as, "*Upward* man And downward fish": Milton's "Paradise Lost," i. 462).—**upward** or **upwards of**, more than; above: as, "a serene, moderate, quiet man, *upward* of sixty" (Mrs. Stowe's "Oldtown Folks," iii.); "He . . . had the care of *upwards of* one hundred boys" (Marryat's "Mr. Midshipman Easy," v.).—**up'ward**, *a.* Moving or tending upward; directed upward: as, "an *upward* course" (Shakspere's "3 Henry VI.," v. 3. 1).—**up'ward-ly**, *adv.*

up-well (up-wel'), *v. i.* To well up, as water from a fountain.

up-whirl (up-hwerl'), *v. t.* or *i.* To whirl upward.

up-wreathe (up-rēᴛʜ'), *v. i.* To wreathe upward, or rise with a curling motion, as smoke.

u-ræ-mi-a (ū-rē'mi-ä), etc. See *uremia*, etc.

u-ræ-us (ū-rē'us), *n.* [NL., < Egypt. *ouro*, asp (cobra), lit. 'king.'] The sacred asp (a cobra, *Naja haje*) as represented upon the head-dress of divinities and royal personages of ancient Egypt, usually directly over the forehead, as an emblem of supreme power.

U-ral (ū'ral), *a.* Designating a system of mountains on the border between Russia and Siberia, or a river flowing southward from these mountains into the Caspian Sea; of or pertaining to these mountains or this river.

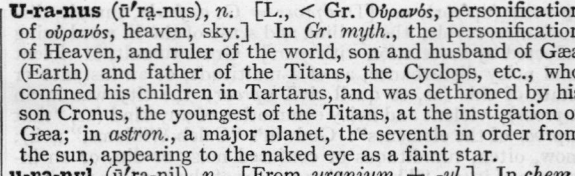
Uræus. — Seti I., father of Rameses II.

U-ral=Al-ta-ic (ū'ral-al-tā'ik), *a.* Of or pertaining to the Ural Mountains, on the border between Russia and Siberia, and the Altai Mountains, in southern Siberia and northwestern Mongolia, or the country or peoples in their neighborhood; esp., noting or pertaining to a large family of agglutinative languages spoken in portions of northern and eastern Europe and nearly the whole of northern and central Asia, containing the Finno-Ugrian, Turkic, Samoyedic, Tungusic, and Mongolian subfamilies or branches; also, noting or pertaining to the peoples using these languages.

u-ral-ite (ū'ral-īt), *n.* [G. *uralit*; named from the Ural Mountains, where it was found.] A pale-green to dark-green, usually fibrous, variety of amphibole, derived from pyroxene by paramorphic change.—**u-ral-it'ic** (-it'ik), *a.*

U-ra-ni-a (ū-rā'ni-ä), *n.* [L., < Gr. Οὐρανία, lit. 'heavenly one,' < οὐρανός, heaven.] The Muse of astronomy; also, a surname of Aphrodite.

u-ran-ic¹ (ū-ran'ik), *a.* [Gr. οὐρανός, heaven.] Of or pertaining to the heavens; celestial; astronomical.

u-ran-ic² (ū-ran'ik), *a.* Of or containing uranium. See *uranous*.

u-ran-i-nite (ū-ran'i-nīt), *n.* A mineral whose chief constituent is uranium, occurring in several varieties and forms, the most important being pitchblende.

u-ra-nite (ū'ra-nīt), *n.* Either of two minerals, a phosphate of uranium and calcium (autunite), and a phosphate of uranium and copper (torbernite).—**u-ra-nit'ic** (-nit'ik), *a.*

u-ra-ni-um (ū-rā'ni-um), *n.* [NL.; named from the planet *Uranus*.] Chem. sym., U; at. wt., 238.2; sp. gr., 18.7. A white, lustrous, radioactive metallic element, having compounds which are used in photography and in coloring glass.

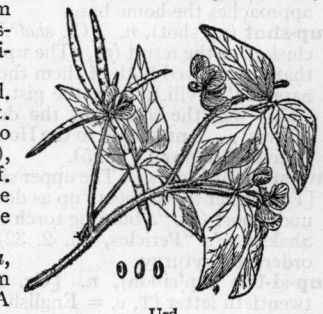
The Muse Urania. — From an antique in the Louvre.

urano-. Form of Gr. οὐρανός, heaven, used in combination. —**u-ra-nog-ra-phy** (ū-ra-nog'ra-fi), *n.* [+ *-graphy*.] The branch of astronomy concerned with the description and mapping of the heavens, and esp. of the fixed stars; descriptive uranology.—**u-ra-nol'o-gy** (-nol'ō-ji), *n.* [+ *-logy*.] The science concerned with the heavens; astronomy.—**u-ra-nom'e-try** (-nom'e-tri), *n.* [+ *-metry*.] The measurement of stellar distances; also, a description of the principal fixed stars arranged in constellations, with their designations, positions, and magnitudes, or a map or chart of the fixed stars showing such details.

u-ra-nous (ū'ra-nus), *a.* Containing uranium (in larger proportion than a corresponding uranic compound).

U-ra-nus (ū'ra-nus), *n.* [L., < Gr. Οὐρανός, personification of οὐρανός, heaven, sky.] In *Gr. myth.*, the personification of Heaven, and ruler of the world, son and husband of Gæa (Earth) and father of the Titans, the Cyclops, etc., who confined his children in Tartarus, and was dethroned by his son Cronus, the youngest of the Titans, at the instigation of Gæa; in *astron.*, a major planet, the seventh in order from the sun, appearing to the naked eye as a faint star.

u-ra-nyl (ū'ra-nil), *n.* [From *uranium* + *-yl*.] In *chem.*, the bivalent radical UO_2, present in many compounds of uranium.

u-rase (ū'rās), *n.* Same as *urease*.

u-rate (ū'rāt), *n.* In *chem.*, a salt of uric acid.

ur-ban (èr'ban), *a.* [L. *urbanus*, belonging to a city, polished, refined, polite, < *urbs*, city: cf. *urbane*.] **I.** *a.* Of, pertaining to, or comprising a city or town (as, "the rising *urban* district of Easewood": H. G. Wells's "Mr. Polly," iv.); living in a city or cities (as, "our *urban* population": W. R. Inge's "Outspoken Essays," i. 4); characteristic of or accustomed to cities, or citified (as, "The clerk was flippant and *urban*. He was a superior person, used to this tumult": Sinclair Lewis's "Main Street," xvii.); also, polite† or urbane†. **II.** *n.* One living, or accustomed to living, in a city: as, "we exiled *urbans*" (H. G. Wells's "Tono-Bungay," i. 3. § 2).

ur-bane (èr-bān'), *a.* [Var. of *urban*: cf. *humane* and *human*.] Urban (obs. or rare); also, courteous or polite, esp. in a refined or elegant way (as, "Lord William was very *urbane*, and . . . accepted men as he found them," M. Hewlett's "Open Country," iv.; "Plato's indecision and *urbane* fair-mindedness," J. H. Robinson's "Mind in the Making," iv. 9); often, in a modified sense, smoothly polite or agreeable, or suave (as, "Mr. Buckingham Smith instantly became the *urbane* and alert showman," Arnold Bennett's "Roll-Call," ii.; "the *urbanest* of head-waiters," L. Merrick's "Conrad in Quest of His Youth," x.).—**ur-bane'ly**, *adv.*—**ur-bane'ness**, *n.*—**ur-ban'i-ty** (-ban'i-ti), *n.*; pl. *-ties* (-tiz). The quality of being urbane; refined or elegant courtesy or politeness (as, "When we think of Athens we think . . . of *urbanity* and clarity and moderation in all things": J. H. Robinson's "Mind in the Making," v. 10); suavity; *pl.*, civilities or amenities (as, "She smiled and murmured *urbanities*," L. Merrick's "Worldlings," xxv.; "the *urbanities* of Winnemac," Sinclair Lewis's "Arrowsmith," ix.); also, *sing.*, polished humor or wit (obs. or archaic).

ur-ban-ize (èr'ban-īz), *v. t.*; *-ized*, *-izing*. To render urban, as in character: as, to *urbanize* a district or its people.—**ur'ban-i-za'tion** (-i-zā'shon), *n.*

ur-ce-o-late (èr'sē-ō-lāt), *a.* [L. *urceolus*, dim. of *urceus*, pitcher.] Shaped like a pitcher; swelling out like the body of a pitcher and contracted at the orifice, as a corolla.

ur-chin (èr'chin), *n.* [OF. *yrechon*, *hirechon*, *hericun* (F. *hérisson*), < L. *ericius*, hedgehog, < *er*, akin to Gr. χήρ, hedgehog.] A hedgehog (archaic or prov.); also, a sea-urchin; also, a kind of elf or mischievous sprite (archaic: as, "*urchins*, ouphes and fairies," Shakspere's "Merry Wives of Windsor," iv. 4. 49); hence, a mischievous boy, or any small boy, or youngster (as, "ragged *urchins* . . . peeping through the railings": Motley's "Dutch Republic," ii. 7).

urd (èrd), *n.* [Hind.] A bean, *Phaseolus mungo radiatus*, a variety of the green gram (see *gram¹*), highly esteemed and largely cultivated throughout India.

Ur-du (ur'dö), *n.* [Hind. *urdū*, Hindustani, lit. 'camp' (with reference to its use as a camp language), < Turki *urdū*, camp: cf. *horde*.] The language called Hindustani. See *Hindustani*, *n.*

Urd.

-ure. [F. *-ure*, < L. *-ura*, suffix forming nouns from the pp. stem of verbs.] A suffix of nouns denoting action or its result, the agents or apparatus, etc., as in *armature*, *capture*, *figure*, *legislature*, *pressure*.

---

u-re-a (ū'rē-ä), *n.* [NL., < Gr. οὖρον, urine.] In *chem.*, a soluble crystalline substance, $CO(NH_2)_2$, present in the urine of mammals.—**u're-al**, *a.*—**u're-ase** (-ās), *n.* In *chem.*, an enzyme which decomposes urea with the formation of ammonium carbonate.

u-re-mi-a, u-ræ-mi-a (ū-rē'mi-ä), *n.* [NL., < Gr. οὖρον, urine, + αἶμα, blood.] In *pathol.*, a morbid condition resulting from the retention in the blood of waste products that should normally be eliminated in the urine.—**u-re'mic, u-ræ'mic**, *a.*

u-re-ter (ū-rē'tèr), *n.* [Gr. οὐρητήρ, < οὐρεῖν, urinate, < οὖρον, urine.] A duct or tube conveying the urine from a kidney to the bladder or cloaca.—**u-re-ter-ic** (ū-rē-ter'ik), *a.*

u-reth-ane (ū-reth'ān), *n.* [From *urea* + *ether* + *-ane.*] In *chem.*, a white crystalline substance, $NH_2CO_2C_2H_5$, obtained by the reaction of ethyl alcohol upon urea or one of its salts, and in other ways: used chiefly as a hypnotic.

u-re-thra (ū-rē'thrä), *n.*; pl. *-thræ* (-thrē). [LL., < Gr. οὐρήθρα, < οὐρεῖν, urinate, < οὖρον, urine.] In most mammals, including man, a complete tube extending from the bladder and serving to convey and discharge urine (and, in the male, semen also); also, a corresponding duct in other animals.—**u-re'thral**, *a.*—**u-re-thri-tis** (ū-rē-thrī'tis), *n.* [NL.] In *pathol.*, inflammation of the urethra.

u-ret-ic (ū-ret'ik), *a.* [LL. *ureticus*, < Gr. οὐρητικός, < οὐρεῖν, urinate, < οὖρον, urine.] In *med.*, of or pertaining to urine; diuretic.

urge (èrj), *v.*; *urged, urging.* [L. *urgere*, press, push, drive, urge: see *wreak.*] **I.** *tr.* To push or force along, or impel with force or vigor (as, "at cricket *urge* the ball," Pope's "Dunciad," iv. 592; "I proceeded to *urge* the canoe along," H. Melville's "Omoo," xli.); drive with incitement to speed or effort, spur, or hurry (as, "He *urged* the dromedary to its speed," Whyte-Melville's "Sarchedon," xxxi.; to *urge* dogs on with shouts); press, push, or hasten (the course, activities, etc.: as, to *urge* one's flight; "Onward . . . the little band *urged* their way," Irving's "Captain Bonneville," xv.; "The work, thus *urged*, went rapidly," Tarkington's "Alice Adams," xviii.; "The peasants *urge* their harvest, ply the fork With double toil," Cowper's "Table Talk," 214); fig., to impel, constrain, or move to some action (as, "What I have done my safety *urged* me to," Shakspere's "1 Henry IV.," v. 5. 11; "*Urged* by an extreme necessity, he had come there to steal food," J. Conrad's "Lord Jim," xxxix.); also, to endeavor to induce or persuade, as by entreaties or earnest recommendations (as, "He *urged* him to take it; but he refused," 2 Kings, v. 16; to *urge* a person to greater caution); entreat or exhort earnestly; also, to press (something) upon the attention (as, to *urge* an argument or a claim; "The thought of Dinah *urged* itself more strongly now," George Eliot's "Adam Bede," xxxvii.); insist on, allege, or assert with earnestness (as, to *urge* the need of haste; to *urge* extenuating circumstances; "He *urged* that times had now changed," S. Butler's "Erewhon," xxvii.); press by persuasion or recommendation, as for acceptance, performance, or use (as, to *urge* a plan or course of action; "These [lozenges and chocolate] we *urged* upon the public for their extraordinary nutritive and recuperative value," H. G. Wells's "Tono-Bungay," ii. 3. § 1); recommend or advocate earnestly; also, to ply hard or assail vigorously in argument†. **II.** *intr.* To exert a driving or impelling force; give an impulse to haste or action (as, when danger or hunger *urges*); also, to make entreaties or earnest recommendations; also, to press arguments or allegations, as against a person.—**urge**, *n.* The act of urging; impelling action, influence, or force; impulse; an involuntary, natural, or instinctive impulse (as, "where the *urge* is to evil," Eden Phillpotts's "Grey Room," iv.; the vital *urge*, see *libido*, and cf. *élan vital*, under *élan*).—**ur-gence** (èr'jens), *n.* Urgent character; urgency; imperativeness: as, "the *urgence* of sleep" (J. H. Robinson's "Mind in the Making," iii. 6).—**ur'gen-cy** (-jen-si), *n.*; pl. *-cies* (-siz). Urgent character; imperativeness; insistence; importunateness; also, *pl.*, urgent requirements or needs (as, "Anxiety to secure the future blunts attention to the *urgencies* of the present": Morley's "Oliver Cromwell," iv. 5); also, *sing.*, in the British Parliament, a formal declaration, by vote, that a matter is urgent and shall take precedence of all other matters.—**ur'gent**, *a.* [F.

urgent, < L. *urgens* (*urgent-*), ppr.] Pressing; compelling or requiring immediate action or attention, or imperative (as, *urgent* necessity; an *urgent* duty; "My business is too *urgent* to waste time on apologies," Buchan's "Three Hostages," ii.); insistent or earnest in solicitation, or importunate, as a person (as, "Mr. Barnstaple . . . was *urgent* to hear more": H. G. Wells's "Men Like Gods," i. 5); expressed with insistence, as requests or appeals.—**ur'gent-ly**, *adv.*—**ur'ger**, *n.*

-uria. [L. *-uria*, < Gr. *-ουρία*, < οὖρον, urine.] A noun termination in pathological terms relating to urine or urination, as in *albuminuria, dysuria, glycosuria, pyuria.*

u-ric (ū'rik), *a.* [Gr. οὖρον, urine.] Pertaining to or obtained from urine: as, *uric* acid (a crystalline acid, $C_5N_4H_4O_3$, present in urine, and also in the blood).—**uric=acid diathesis**, in *pathol.*, a constitution of body predisposing one to gouty and other disturbances, and attributed to excess of uric acid in the blood; a morbid condition in which uric acid is formed in abnormal amount within the body and tends to be deposited in the tissues.

U-rim (ū'rim), *n. pl.* [Heb. *ūrīm*.] Certain objects mentioned in the Old Testament, along with other objects called Thummim (as in Ex. xxviii. 30) or alone (as in Num. xxvii. 21), as connected with the breastplate of the Jewish high priest, or as forming one of the means by which divine communications were obtained. The Urim and Thummim have been regarded by many authorities as forms of lots employed in obtaining oracular answers.

u-ri-nal (ū'ri-nal), *n.* [OF. F. *urinal*, < LL. *urinal*, < L. *urina*, urine.] A vessel for urine; also, a place for urinating.

u-ri-na-ry (ū'ri-nä-ri). [L. *urina*, urine.] **I.** *a.* Of or pertaining to urine (as, a *urinary* calculus, a morbid concretion of crystalline constituents of the urine, often formed in the urinary passages); noting or pertaining to the organs secreting and discharging urine. **II.** *n.*; pl. *-ries* (-riz). A reservoir for the reception of urine, etc., for manure; also, a urinal.

u-ri-nate (ū'ri-nāt), *v. i.*; *-nated, -nating.* [ML. *urinatus*, pp. of *urinare*, < L. *urina*, urine.] To pass or discharge urine; make water.—**u-ri-na'tion** (-nā'shon), *n.* The act of passing urine.—**u'ri-na-tive** (-nä-tiv), *a.*

u-rine (ū'rin), *n.* [OF. F. *urine*, < L. *urina*, akin to Gr. οὖρον, urine: cf. Skt. *vār*, water, AS. *wær*, sea.] The secretion of the kidneys (in mammals, a fluid), which in most mammals is conducted to the bladder by the ureters, and from there to the place of discharge by the urethra.—**u-ri-nif-er-ous** (ū-ri-nif'e-rus), *a.* [See *-ferous.*] Conveying urine.—**u"ri-no-gen'i-tal** (-nō-jen'i-tal), *a.* Same as *urogenital.*—**u-ri-nos'co-py** (-nos'kō-pi), *n.* Same as *uroscopy.*—**u'ri-nose, u'ri-nous** (-nōs, -nus), *a.* Pertaining to, resembling, or containing urine.

urn (èrn), *n.* [L. *urna*.] A kind of vase, of various forms, esp. one with a foot or pedestal; such a vase for holding the ashes of the dead after cremation; hence, any receptacle or place for a dead body or its remains, as a tomb or a grave (as, "Our wasted oil unprofitably burns, Like hidden lamps in old sepulchral *urns*": Cowper's "Conversation," 358); also, a vessel or apparatus with a faucet or cock, used at table for making tea, coffee, etc.—**urn**, *v. t.* To inclose in or as in an urn.

Cinerary Urn.—From a columbarium near Rome.

uro-1. Form of Gr. οὐρά, tail, used in combination.

uro-2. Form of Gr. οὖρον, urine, used in combination.

u-ro-chord (ū'rō-kôrd), *n.* [Gr. οὐρά, tail, + χορδή, string.] In *zoöl.*, the notochord of an ascidian or tunicate, found mostly in the larva, and confined chiefly to the caudal region.

u-rochs (ū'roks), *n.* Same as *aurochs.*

u-ro-dele (ū'rō̆-dēl). [NL. *Urodela*, pl., < Gr. οὐρά, tail, + δῆλος, visible.] **I.** *a.* Belonging to the *Urodela*, an order of amphibians which retain the tail throughout life, including the salamanders, newts, etc. Cf. *anuran.* **II.** *n.* A urodele amphibian.

u-ro-gen-i-tal (ū-rō̆-jen'i-tal), *a.* [See *uro-²* and *genital.*] Noting or pertaining to the urinary and genital organs; genito-urinary.

u-rog-e-nous (ū-roj'e-nus), *a.* [See *uro-²* and *-genous.*] Secreting or producing urine.

u-ro-lith (ū'rō̆-lith), *n.* [See *uro-²* and *-lith.*] In *pathol.*, a urinary calculus. — **u-ro-lith'ic,** *a.*

u-rol-o-gy (ū-rol'ō̆-ji), *n.* [See *uro-²* and *-logy.*] The scientific study of the urine, with special reference to the diagnostic significance of changes in its composition and appearance. — **u-ro-log-i-cal** (ū-rō̆-loj'i-kal), *a.* — **u-rol'o-gist,** *n.*

u-ro-pod (ū'rō̆-pod), *n.* [See *uro-¹* and *-pod.*] An abdominal limb of an arthropod.

u-ro-pyg-i-al (ū-rō̆-pij'i-al), *a.* In *ornith.*, of or pertaining to the uropygium: as, the *uropygial* gland (a large gland opening on the uropygium at the root of the tail in most birds, and secreting an oily fluid used by the bird in preening its feathers).

u-ro-pyg-i-um (ū-rō̆-pij'i-um), *n.*; pl. *-ia* (-i-ä). [NL., < Gr. οὐροπύγιον, for ὀρροπύγιον, < ὄρρος, end of the sacrum, + πυγή, rump.] In *ornith.*, the projecting terminal portion of a bird's body, from which the tail-feathers spring; the pope's-nose.

u-ros-co-py (ū-ros'kō̆-pi), *n.* [See *uro-²* and *-scopy.*] In *med.*, inspection of the urine as a means of diagnosis, etc. — **u-ro-scop-ic** (ū-rō̆-skop'ik), *a.* — **u-ros'co-pist,** *n.*

u-rot-ro-pin, u-rot-ro-pine (ū-rot'rō̆-pin), *n.* [Gr. οὖρον, urine, + -τροπος, turning, < τρέπειν, turn.] In *phar.*, a colorless crystalline substance, $C_6H_{12}N_4$, prepared by the action of ammonia on formaldehyde, and used chiefly as a urinary antiseptic.

Top of Uropygium of a Jäger (*Stercorarius parasiticus*). — *E,* uropygial gland, with circlet of feathers; *C, C,* upper tail-coverts; *R,* quills of two central tail-feathers.

Ur-sa Ma-jor (ėr'sä̇ mā'jọr). [L., 'greater bear': *ursa*, fem. of *ursus*, bear.] The Great Bear, the most prominent constellation in the northern heavens, containing the seven bright stars that form the Dipper, or Charles's Wain. — **Ur'sa Mi-nor** (mī'nọr). [L., 'lesser bear.'] The Little Bear, a northern constellation containing the group of stars forming the Little Dipper, the outermost of which (at the extremity of the tail of the Little Bear) is Polaris, the polestar.

ur-si-form (ėr'si-fôrm), *a.* [L. *ursus*, bear: see *-form.*] Having the form of a bear; bear-like.

ur-sine (ėr'sin), *a.* [L. *ursinus*, < *ursus*, bear.] Of or pertaining to a bear or bears; bear-like; in *entom.*, clothed with bristle-like hairs, as certain caterpillars. — **ursine dasyure,** the Tasmanian devil. See under *Tasmanian.* — **ursine howler,** a howler (monkey), *Mycetes ursinus* (or *Alouatta ursina*), of tropical America.

ur-son (ėr'sọn), *n.* [F.] The Canada porcupine, *Erethizon dorsatus*, of forest regions of eastern North America, a species of large size with short spines and long hairs.

Urson.

Ur-su-line (ėr'sū-lin). [From St. *Ursula*, the patron saint.] **I.** *n.* One of a religious order of Roman Catholic women founded by St. Angela Merici at Brescia, Italy, in 1535, and devoted to the teaching of girls. **II.** *a.* Of or pertaining to the Ursulines.

ur-ti-ca-ceous (ėr-ti-kā'shius), *a.* [L. *urtica*, nettle.] Belonging to the *Urticaceæ*, or nettle family of plants.

ur-ti-ca-ri-a (ėr-ti-kā'ri-ä), *n.* [NL., < L. *urtica*, nettle.] In *pathol.*, an affection of the skin characterized by transient eruptions of itching wheals or pimples, caused chiefly by gastric derangement; nettle-rash; hives. — **ur-ti-ca'ri-al,** *a.*

ur-ti-cate (ėr'ti-kāt), *v.*; *-cated, -cating.* [ML. *urticatus,* pp. of *urticare,* < L. *urtica,* nettle.] **I.** *tr.* To sting with, as with, or like nettles; specif., to whip (a benumbed or paralytic limb) with nettles in order to restore sensation. **II.** *intr.* To sting as or like a nettle; use urtication in treating paralysis, etc. — **ur-ti-ca'tion** (-kā'shọn), *n.* The act of urticating; stinging, as by nettles, or by special organs (nematocysts) of jellyfishes and other cœlenterates; specif., the whipping of a benumbed or paralytic limb with nettles in order to restore sensation.

u-ru-bu (ö-rö̆-bö'), *n.* [Brazilian.] The black vulture, or carrion-crow, *Catharista atrata,* ranging from Argentina to the southern U. S.

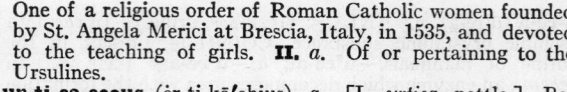

Urubu.

u-rus (ū'rus), *n.* [L., from Teut.: cf. *aurochs.*] A wild ox, *Bos urus* (or *primigenius*), now extinct, but common in Europe at the time of Cæsar.

us (us), *pron.* [AS. *ūs,* pl., dat. and acc. (gen. *ūre*: see *our*), = OS. *ūs* = OHG. G. *uns* = Icel. *oss* = Goth. *uns,* us.] Objective case of *we.*

us-a-ble (ū'za-bl), *a.* That may be used. — **us'a-ble-ness,** *n.*

us-age (ū'zāj or ū'sāj), *n.* [OF. F. *usage,* < *user,* E. *use,* *v.*] The act of using or employing, or use (as, "Nor thou be rageful, like a handled bee, And lose thy life by *usage* of thy sting": Tennyson's "Ancient Sage," 270); also, habitual or customary use, or long-continued practice (as, "a Mohican by blood, consorting with the Delawares by *usage,*" Cooper's "Deerslayer," viii.; to follow the *usage* of the country or the time; immemorial *usage*); customary way of doing; a custom or practice (as, "Neither Bedford, nor Halifax . . . could, of a sudden, overcome the *usages* and policy of more than a half-century": Bancroft's "Hist. of the U. S.," Amer. Revolution, i. 3); often, customary or established mode of employing words as to sense, construction, etc., or a particular instance of this (as, English *usage*; a *usage* borrowed from the French); also, way of using or treating, or treatment (as, dreaded for his *usage* of prisoners; hard or rough *usage*; "You shall have very good *usage* among us," Defoe's "Captain Singleton," x.).

us-ance (ū'zạns), *n.* [OF. F. *usance,* < *user,* E. *use, v.*] Use† or employment†; also, usage† or custom†; also, interest† or usury†; in *polit. econ.*, the income of benefits of every kind derived from the ownership of wealth; in *com.*, the length of time, exclusive of days of grace, allowed by custom or usage for the payment of foreign bills of exchange (it varies between different places).

use (ūs), *n.* [OF. F. *us,* use, usage, < L. *usus,* use, employment, usage, practice, benefit, profit, occasion, need, < *uti,* make use of, employ, practise, enjoy, have; also, in legal use, OF. *ues, oes, oeps,* work, service, benefit, < L. *opus,* work, need; cf. *opus.*] The act of employing or using, or putting into service (as, the *use* of tools, materials, persons, or methods to carry out work; the *use* of the hands, feet, eyes, or brain; "skill in the *use* of the six-shooter," Roosevelt's "Ranch Life and the Hunting-Trail," vi.); the state of being employed or used (as, the book is in *use* just at present; coins or methods long out of *use*); an instance or way of employing or using something (as, each successive *use* of an instrument; a poor *use* of good material); a way of being employed or used, or a purpose for which something is used (as, "Nothing in itself is good or evil, But only in its *use*," Southey's "Thalaba," iv. 15; "The cave contained several apartments appropriated to different *uses*," Johnson's "Rasselas," xxi.); also, the power, right, or privilege of employing or using something (as, to lose the *use* of one eye; to have the *use* of a boat for the season); also, service or advantage in or for being employed or used (as, articles of no practical *use*; the money came too late to be of *use*; "I don't see . . . the *use* of all these new-fangled notions," Mrs. Stowe's "Oldtown Folks," xxv.); utility or usefulness; help, profit, or resulting good (as, what's the *use* of talking?); also, occasion or need, as for something to be employed or used (as, have you any *use* for another calendar? "Here is no *use* for gold," Shakspere's "Timon of Athens," iv. 3. 290); also, continued, habitual, or customary employment or practice (as, "*Use* almost can change the stamp of nature," Shakspere's "Hamlet," iii. 4. 168; to follow the prevailing *use* on such occasions); habit, wont, or usage; a custom, practice, or usage; also, customary or usual experience† (as, "Ghosts did shriek . . . these things are beyond all *use*, And I do fear them": Shakspere's "Julius Cæsar," ii. 2. 25); also, way of using or treating, or treatment (as, rough or harsh *use*); also, interest or usury (archaic or prov.); in *liturgics*, the distinctive form of ritual or of any liturgical observance used in a particular church, diocese, community, etc. (as, Roman *use*; Sarum, or Salisbury, *use*); in *law*, the enjoyment of property, as by the employment, occupation, or exercise of it; also, the benefit or profit of property (lands and tenements) in the possession of another who simply holds them for the beneficiary; the equitable ownership of lands the legal title to which is in another.—**of no use,** or (elliptically) **no use,** of no service, advantage, or help: as, it is *of no use* to complain; "If you agreed with me I should be *no use* here" (G. B. Shaw's "You Never Can Tell," iv.).—**to have no use for,** to have no occasion or need for; also, to have no liking or tolerance for (colloq.: as, "He [Washington] *had no use for* the snob in his fellow man," H. G. Wells's "Outline of History," xxxviii. § 3).—**to make use of,** to employ; put to use; use for one's own purposes or advantage. —**use** (ūz), *v. t.; used, using.* [OF. F. *user*, < ML. *usare,* freq. of L. *uti* (pp. *usus*), make use of, etc.: see *use, n.*] To employ for some purpose, put into service, or make use of (as, to *use* a knife; to *use* spectacles; to *use* a go-between; to *use* the talents of others); avail one's self of; apply to one's own purposes; hence, to expend or consume in use (as, we have *used* most of the amount provided); also, to practise habitually or customarily, or make a practice of (as, "This kind of study he *used* till he was made doctor of divinity": Strype's "Memorials of Cranmer," i. 1); also, to habituate or accustom (except in prov. use, now only in *used, pp.*: as, to be *used* to hardships; "They were *used* to seeing cannibals like him," H. Melville's "Moby-Dick," xiii.); also, to act or behave toward, or treat, in some manner (as, "What a brute am I to *use* her thus!" Sheridan's "Rivals," iii. 2).— **to use up,** to consume entirely by using; use the whole of; also, to exhaust of strength, energy, or the like, as by overwork or strain (colloq.).—**use,** *v. i.* To be accustomed, wont, or customarily found (with an infinitive expressed or understood, and, except in archaic use, now only in the preterit: as, he *used* to go every day; he goes less often than he *used*; the days *used* to seem long; the uniform *used* to be blue); also, to resort, stay, or dwell customarily, or have the customary haunts (archaic or prov.: as, "But we be only sailormen That *use* in London town," Kipling's "Merchant-men").

use′a-ble, etc. See *usable,* etc.

use-ful (ūs′fúl), *a.* Being of use or service; subserving some purpose; serviceable, advantageous, helpful, or of good effect; often, of practical use, as for doing work, producing material results, supplying common needs, etc. (as, *useful* contrivances or gifts; "To advance the *useful* arts is one thing, and to cultivate the mind another," J. H. Newman's "Idea of a University," ii. 1; "She [Nature] calls the *useful* many forth; Plain plodding industry," Burns's "Epistle to Robert Graham," 5).—**use′ful-ly,** *adv.*—**use′ful-ness,** *n.*

use-less (ūs′les), *a.* Of no use; not serving the purpose or any purpose; without useful qualities; of no practical good; unavailing or futile.—**use′less-ly,** *adv.*—**use′less-ness,** *n.*

us-er[1] (ū′zėr), *n.* One who or that which uses.

us-er[2] (ū′zėr), *n.* [OF., noun use of *user,* inf.: see *use, v.*] In *law,* the use or enjoyment of property; the exercise of a right.

ush-er (ush′ér), *n.* [OF. *ussier, uissier* (F. *huissier*), < L. *ostiarius,* doorkeeper: see *ostiary.*] An officer or servant having charge of an entrance-door; a doorkeeper; also, one who escorts persons to seats in a church, theater, etc.; also, an officer whose business it is to introduce strangers or to walk before a person of rank; also, a subordinate teacher or an assistant in a school (Eng.).—**ush′er,** *v. t.* To act as an usher to; conduct or show (*in, into, out,* etc.: as, "They *ushered* the Spaniards into the royal presence," Prescott's "Conquest of Mexico," iii. 9; to *usher* out a visitor; to *usher* persons to seats in a church); fig., to attend or bring at the coming or beginning (as, "The stars that *usher* evening rose," Milton's "Paradise Lost," iv. 355; "the unlucky day that *ushered* in my yachting excursion," Lever's "Harry Lorrequer," xxxiv.).

us-ne-a (us′nē-ä), *n.* [NL.] Any of the lichens of the genus *Usnea,* commonly found as pendulous, grayish or yellowish, moss-like growths on trees or rocks in temperate or cool climates. Cf. *Florida moss.*

us-que-baugh (us′kwē-bâ), *n.* [Gael. and Ir. *uisgebeatha,* lit. 'water of life': cf. *whisky, aqua vitæ* (under *aqua*), and *eau-de-vie.*] In Scotland and Ireland, whisky: as, "a flask of *usquebaugh*" (Stevenson's "David Balfour," xvi.).

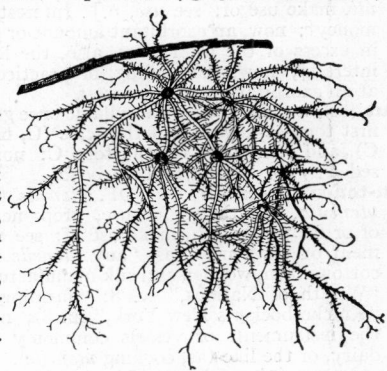

Usnea (*U. barbata*).

us-tu-late (us′tū-lāt), *a.* [L. *ustulatus,* pp. of *ustulare,* scorch, dim. < *urere* (pp. *ustus*), burn.] Colored or blackened as if scorched.—**us-tu-la′tion** (-lā′shon), *n.* The act of scorching or burning; in *phar.,* the roasting or drying of moist substances so as to prepare them for pulverizing; also, the burning of wine.

u-su-al (ū′zhū-ạl), *a.* [LL. *usualis,* < L. *usus,* E. *use, n.*] In common use, or common (as, "Necklaces are quite *usual* now," George Eliot's "Middlemarch," i.; "The parson said the *usual* things about the sea — its blueness . . . its beauty," Du Maurier's "Trilby," v.); habitual or customary (as, "He accomplished his mission with his *usual* adroitness": Froude's "Cæsar," vi.); often, such as is commonly met with or observed in experience, or ordinary (as, the *usual* January weather; the *usual* case of incompatible tempers).—**as usual,** as is (or was) usual; in the usual, customary, or ordinary manner. as, he will come *as usual; as usual,* he was late.—**u′su-al-ly,** *adv.* According to what is usual; commonly; customarily; ordinarily.—**u′su-al-ness,** *n.*

u-su-cap-tion (ū-zū-kap′shon), *n.* [L. *usucapere* (pp. *usucaptus*), acquire ownership of by long use, < *usu,* abl. of *usus,* use, + *capere:* cf. L. *usucapio*(n-), usucaption.] In *civil law,* the acquisition of the title or right to property by the uninterrupted and undisputed possession of it in good faith for a certain term prescribed by law.

u-su-fruct (ū′zū-frukt), *n.* [L. *ususfructus* (abl. *ususfructu*), for *usus et fructus,* 'use and enjoyment': see *use, n.*, and *fruit*.] In *law*, the right of enjoying all the advantages derivable from the use of something which belongs to another so far as is compatible with the substance of the thing not being destroyed or injured.—**u′su-fruct,** *v. t.* To hold in usufruct; make subject to usufruct.—**u-su-fruc′tu-a-ry** (-fruk′tū-ā-ri). [L. *usufructuarius.*] **I.** *a.* Of, pertaining to, or of the nature of a usufruct. **II.** *n.*; pl. *-ries* (-riz). A person who has the usufruct of property.

u-su-rer (ū′zū-rėr), *n.* [OF. F. *usurier,* < ML. *usurarius,* usurer, < L. *usurarius,* adj. < *usura:* see *usury.*] One who lends money at interest†; now, one who lends money at an exorbitant rate of interest.

u-su-ri-ous (ū-zū′ri-us), *a.* Practising usury; taking exorbitant interest for the use of money; also, pertaining to or of the nature of usury (as, *"usurious* interest": Froude's "Cæsar," xxii.).—**u-su′ri-ous-ly,** *adv.*—**u-su′ri-ous-ness,** *n.*

u-surp (ū-zėrp′), *v.* [L. *usurpare* (pp. *usurpatus*), make use of, appropriate, usurp, perhaps < *usus,* use, + *rapere,* seize.] **I.** *tr.* To seize and hold (an office or position, power, etc.) by force or without right: as, "I am the King, and come to claim my own From an impostor, who *usurps* my throne" (Longfellow's "King Robert of Sicily," 78). **II.** *intr.* To commit forcible or illegal seizure of an office, power, etc.; encroach.—**u-sur-pa-tion** (ū-zėr-pā′shọn), *n.* [L. *usurpatio(n-).*] The act of usurping; the seizing and holding of the place, power, or the like of another without right; esp. the wrongful seizure and occupation of a throne (as, "the *usurpation* of the throne of Portugal by Don Miguel": Borrow's "Bible in Spain," ii.).—**u-surp′er,** *n.*—**u-surp′-ing-ly,** *adv.*

u-su-ry (ū′zū-ri), *n.* [ME. *usurie,* for *usure,* < OF. F. *usure,* < L. *usura,* use (as of money lent), interest paid, usury, < *uti,* make use of: see *use, n.*] Interest paid for the use of money†; now, an exorbitant amount or rate of interest, esp. in excess of the legal rate; also, the lending of money at interest†; now, the lending, or practice of lending, money at an exorbitant rate of interest.

ut (öt), *n.* In *music,* the syllable once generally used for the first tone or key-note of the scale (C, in the major scale of C), and sometimes for the tone C: now commonly superseded by *do.* Cf. *do,* and see *sol-fa.*

u-ten-sil (ū-ten′sil), *n.* [OF. *utensile* (F. *ustensile*), < L. *utensilia,* pl., things for use, prop. neut. pl. of *utensilis,* of or for use, < *uti,* make use of: see *use, n.*] An instrument or implement (as, "any *utensils* made use of in the cotton, linen, woollen and silk manufactures," Adam Smith's "Wealth of Nations," iv. 8; "farming *utensils,*" Irving's "Knickerbocker's New York," iii. 8); now, usually, any of the instruments or vessels commonly used in a kitchen, dairy, or the like (as, cooking *utensils*).

u-ter-ine (ū′tẹ-rin), *a.* [LL. *uterinus.*] Of or pertaining to the uterus or womb; also, related as having had the same mother (cf. *consanguineous*).

u-ter-us (ū′tẹ-rus), *n.*; pl. *uteri* (-rī). [L.] In female mammals, the organ which serves as a resting-place for the ovum while it develops into an embryo or fetus; the womb; also, a corresponding part in other animals.

u-til-i-ta-ri-an (ū-til-i-tā′ri-ạn). **I.** *a.* Pertaining to or consisting in utility; having regard to utility or usefulness rather than beauty, ornamentalness, etc. (as, *utilitarian* considerations or purposes); also, of, pertaining to, or adhering to the doctrine of utilitarianism. **II.** *n.* An adherent of the doctrine of utilitarianism.—**u-til-i-ta′ri-an-ism,** *n.* The ethical doctrine that virtue is based on utility, and that conduct should be directed toward promoting the greatest happiness of the greatest number of persons.

u-til-i-ty (ū-til′i-ti), *n.*; pl. *-ties* (-tiz). [OF. *utilite* (F. *utilité*), < L. *utilitas,* < *utilis,* useful, < *uti,* make use of: see *use, n.*] The state or character of being useful (as, "He might now be of very high *utility* in aiding my escape": Stevenson's "Master of Ballantrae," iii.); usefulness; serviceableness; also, something useful; a useful thing; a public service, as a street-car or railroad line, a gas-light or electric-light system, or the like ('public utility'); in *polit. econ.,* the capacity of an object for satisfying a human want.—**u-til′i-ty=man** (-man), *n.*; pl. *-men.* A member of a theatrical company, a baseball team, or the like, who is expected to serve in any capacity when called on; an actor of miscellaneous small parts.

u-ti-liz-a-ble (ū′ti-lī-zạ-bl), *a.* Capable of being utilized.

u-ti-lize (ū′ti-līz), *v. t.*; *-lized, -lizing.* [F. *utiliser,* < L. *utilis,* useful: see *utility.*] To put to use; turn to profitable account: as, to *utilize* a stream for driving machinery.—**u′ti-li-za′tion** (-li-zā′shọn), *n.*—**u′ti-liz-er** (-lī-zėr), *n.*

ut-most (ut′mōst). [AS. *ūtmest,* outmost, extreme, last, superl. of *ūterra,* compar.: see *utter*[1].] **I.** *a.* superl. Being at the furthest point or extremity (as, "the *utmost* boundary of the East": R. W. Gilder's "New Day," Prelude); furthest; extreme; last; also, of the greatest or highest degree, quantity, or the like (as, "What I have to talk to you about is of the *utmost* importance": W. Churchill's "Coniston," i. 12); greatest. **II.** *n.* The extreme limit or extent; the greatest degree or amount; the most possible: as, "Sethos . . . enjoyed many privileges and immunities, of which he availed himself to the *utmost*" (Whyte-Melville's "Sarchedon," vii.).—**to do one's utmost,** to do all one can: as, "He was . . . *doing his utmost* to see the war" (H. G. Wells's "Mr. Britling," ii. 1. § 12).

U-to-pi-a (ū-tō′pi-ạ), *n.* [NL., 'nowhere,' < Gr. οὐ, not, + τόπος, place.] An imaginary island described in Sir Thomas More's "Utopia" (published in Latin in 1516) as enjoying the utmost perfection in law, politics, etc.; hence [often *l. c.*], a place or state of ideal perfection, or any visionary system of political or social perfection (as, "the wildest promises of an earthly *utopia* the day after to-morrow": W. R. Inge's "Outspoken Essays," i. 11); sometimes, any imaginary region.—**U-to′pi-an. I.** *a.* Of, pertaining to, or resembling Utopia; hence [often *l. c.*], founded upon or involving imaginary or ideal perfection (as, *"Utopian* visions of world-wide human order": H. G. Wells's "Outline of History," xxxv. § 9); given to dreams or schemes of such perfection (as, "as not the most *Utopian* of us have hitherto dared to imagine": H. G. Wells's "Italy, France, and Britain at War," iii. 4). **II.** *n.* An inhabitant of Utopia; [often *l. c.*] an ardent but unpractical political or social reformer; a visionary; an idealist.—**u-to′pi-an-ism,** *n.* The characteristic views or habit of mind of a Utopian; impracticable schemes of political or social reform.

u-tri-cle (ū′tri-kl), *n.* [L. *utriculus,* dim. of *uter,* bag or bottle made of skin: cf. L. *utriculus,* dim. of *uterus,* E. *uterus.*] A small sac or bag-like body, as an air-cell in a seaweed; specif., in *bot.,* a thin bladder-like pericarp or seed-vessel; in *anat.,* the larger of two sacs in the membranous labyrinth of the internal ear (cf. *saccule*).—**u-tric′u-lar** (ū-trik′ū-lạr), *a.* Pertaining to or of the nature of a utricle; bag-like; having a utricle or utricles.—**u-tric′u-late** (-lāt), *a.* Having a utricle; utricular; bag-like.—**u-tric′u-lus** (-lus), *n.*; pl. *-li* (-lī). [L.] Same as *utricle.*

ut-ter[1] (ut′ėr), *a.* [AS. *ūterra, ūtera,* outer, compar. adj. (superl. *ūtmest:* see *utmost*) < *ūt,* E. *out.*] Outer† (as, "He brought me forth into the *utter* court": Ezek. xlvi. 21); also, complete, total, or absolute (as, "They were in *utter* amazement," Miss Burney's "Evelina," xxi.; "his *utter* abandonment to his grief," Archibald Marshall's "Anthony Dare," vii.); unconditional or unqualified (as, an *utter* denial).

ut-ter[2] (ut′ėr), *v. t.* [ME. *outren,* appar. for *outen,* E. *out, v.*] To put or send out or forth, expel, or emit (as, "Nicholas Vedder, with his . . . fair long pipe, *uttering* clouds of tobacco-smoke," Irving's "Sketch-Book," Rip Van Winkle: now rare); also, to put forth in trade†, or sell† (as, "Such mortal drugs I have; but Mantua's law Is death to any he that *utters* them": Shakspere's "Romeo and Juliet," v. 1. 67); also, to put into circulation, as coins, notes, etc., esp. counterfeit money, forged checks, etc.; issue in copies made by printing or the like, or publish, as a book (obs. or archaic: as, "an order . . . that the false translation of Tindal, as they called it, should not be *uttered* either by printer or bookseller," Strype's "Memorials of Cranmer," i. 21); also, to make publicly known; publish (as, to *utter* a libel); also, to give audible expression to (as, "Raina stares at him, unable to *utter* her feelings": G. B. Shaw's "Arms and the Man," i.); speak or pronounce (as, "The words were *uttered* in the hearing of Montezuma": Prescott's "Conquest of Mexico," iv. 3); give forth (cries, notes, etc.) with the voice (as, "The

Canon *uttered* a resounding sigh," Galsworthy's "Saint's Progress," iii. 6; "a voice that seemed as if it could never *utter* a false note," Du Maurier's "Trilby," vii.); give forth (a sound) otherwise than with the voice (as, the locomotive *uttered* a shriek); also, to express by written or printed words; sometimes, to express or make known in any manner (as, "the sensibility of the horse, *uttering* itself in the maniac light of his eye": De Quincey's "English Mail-Coach," i.). —**ut′ter-a-ble**, *a.* That may be uttered.—**ut′ter-ance**[1], *n.* The act of uttering; a putting into circulation; vocal expression (as, "The lady stopped for want of breath occasioned by the rapidity of her *utterance*," Marryat's "King's Own," xl.; "A large owl . . . gave *utterance* to a long hiss," W. H. Hudson's "Purple Land," xiii.); manner of speaking; power of speaking; also, something uttered; a word or words uttered; a cry, animal's call, or the like.

ut-ter-ance[2]† (ut′ėr-ạns), *n.* [= *outrance*.] The last or utmost extremity; the bitter end; death: as, "Come fate into the list, And champion me to the *utterance!*" (Shakspere's "Macbeth," iii. 1. 72).

ut-ter-er (ut′ėr-ėr), *n.* One who utters; one who puts into circulation, or publishes, or expresses audibly.

ut-ter-ly (ut′ėr-li), *adv.* In an utter manner; completely; totally; absolutely: as, "I fail *utterly* to see why . . ." (W. Churchill's "Inside of the Cup," v.); "a . . . place . . . *utterly* according to the heart's desire" (Vernon Lee's "Enchanted Woods," Les Charmettes).

ut-ter-most (ut′ėr-mōst). **I.** *a.* *superl.* Utmost, furthest,

or extreme (as, "the *uttermost* parts of the earth": Ps. ii. 8); last (as, "till thou hast paid the *uttermost* farthing": Mat. v. 26); also, of the greatest degree, etc. (as, "*uttermost* distress": Hood's "Midsummer Fairies," xiii.). **II.** *n.* The extreme limit or extent; the utmost.

ut-ter-ness (ut′ėr-nes), *n.* The state of being utter; completeness.

u-var-o-vite (ö-vär′ọ-vīt), *n.* [From Count S. S. *Uvarov* (1785–1855), Russian statesman.] An emerald-green variety of garnet containing chromium, to which the color is due.

u-ve-a (ū′vē̇-ä), *n.* [NL., < L. *uva*, grape.] In *anat.*, the posterior surface of the iris of the eye; also, the middle or vascular tunic of the eye (iris, choroid, etc., taken collectively).—**u′ve-al**, *a.*—**u-ve-i′tis** (-ī′tis), *n.* [NL.] In *pathol.*, inflammation of the uvea.

u-vu-la (ū′vū̇-lä), *n.* [NL., dim. of L. *uva*, grape, cluster of grapes, uvula.] In *anat.*, the small, fleshy, conical body projecting downward from the middle of the soft palate.—**u′vu-lar** (-lär), *a.*—**u-vu-li′tis** (-lī′tis), *n.* [NL.] In *pathol.*, inflammation of the uvula.—**u-vu-lot′o-my** (-lot′ọ-mi), *n.* [See *-tomy.*] In *surg.*, the operation of cutting off the whole or a part of the uvula.

ux-or-i-cide (uk-sor′i-sīd), *n.* [L. *uxor*, wife: see *-cide.*] One who kills his wife; also, the act of killing one's wife.

ux-o-ri-ous (uk-sō′ri-us), *a.* [L. *uxorius*, < *uxor*, wife.] Excessively or foolishly fond of one's wife; doting on a wife: as, "Richard was a fond, almost an *uxorious*, husband" (Scott's "Talisman," xx.).—**ux-o′ri-ous-ly**, *adv.*—**ux-o′ri-ous-ness**, *n.*

V

V[1], **v**[1] (vē); pl. *V's, v's* (vēz). A consonant, the 22d letter of the English alphabet.

V[2] (vē), *n.*; pl. *V's* (vēz). Something shaped like the letter V; a form or outline like that of the letter V (as, a woman's bodice cut in a *V* at the neck); also (from the Roman numeral V, meaning 'five,' on some issues), a five-dollar bill (colloq., U. S.); also, the symbol of British war victory.

va-ca(vä′kä), *n.* [Cuban Sp.] A West Indian fish, *Hypoplectrus unicolor.*

va-can-cy (vā′kạn-si), *n.*; pl. *-cies* (-siz). The state of being vacant; emptiness; unoccupied state; absence of occupation, or idleness or inactivity (as, "much time squandered upon trifles, and more

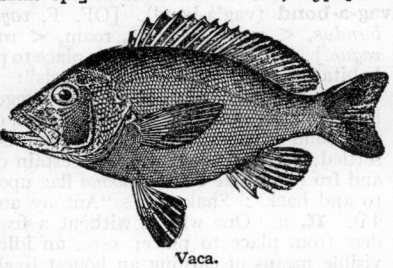

Vaca.

lost in idleness and *vacancy*," Johnson's "Rasselas," xlv.: now rare); lack of thought or intelligence, or vacuity (as, "More absolute *vacancy* I never saw upon the countenances of human beings": S. Butler's "Way of all Flesh," xxiii.); also, something vacant; vacant space (as, "each man gazing into *vacancy*": Ian Maclaren's "Beside the Bonnie Brier Bush," i. 4); a vacant space, or a gap or opening; unoccupied or leisure time†; vacation (archaic); an unoccupied office or position (as, "to fill up *vacancies* by election": Hallam's "Europe during the Middle Ages," ii. 2).

va-cant (vā′kạnt), *a.* [OF. F. *vacant*, < L. *vacans* (*vacant-*), ppr. of *vacare*, be empty: see *vacate.*] Having no contents; empty; void; devoid or destitute (*of*); also, destitute of an occupant (as, "*vacant* chairs": Tarkington's "Alice Adams," viii.); unoccupied; untenanted, as a house, etc. (as, "A small farm of mine in the neighbourhood is now *vacant*": H. Mackenzie's "Man of Feeling," xxxvi.); not in use, as a room; also, not occupied by an incumbent, official, or the like, as a benefice, office, etc.; also, free from work, business, etc., as time (as, "one *vacant* holiday afternoon": C. Brontë's

"Villette," xxvi.); characterized by or proceeding from absence of occupation (as, a *vacant* life; "Every morning waked us to a repetition of toil, but the evening repaid it with *vacant* hilarity," Goldsmith's "Vicar of Wakefield," v.); also, unoccupied with thought or reflection, as the mind; characterized by, showing, or proceeding from lack of thought or intelligence (as, "The childish face rapidly became *vacant* and foolish," Barrie's "Sentimental Tommy," xvi.; "a *vacant* stare," Parkman's "Oregon Trail," xi.); sometimes, wanting in intelligence, as a person (as, "a *vacant* aristocrat, to be depended on for resisting popular demands, but without insight otherwise," Froude's "Cæsar," xii.; "stolid, dull, *vacant* plough-boys," S. Butler's "Way of All Flesh," xiv.).—**va′cant-ly**, *adv.*

va-cate (vā′kāt), *v.*; *-cated, -cating.* [L. *vacatus*, pp. of *vacare*, be empty, be unoccupied, idle, or at leisure.] **I.** *tr.* To make vacant; cause to be empty or unoccupied (as, "a pledge . . . of his elevation to the throne when *vacated* by Frederick's death": J. F. Kirk's "Charles the Bold," iv. 1); quit the occupancy of (as, "Scores of houses were suddenly *vacated* lest they should bury their occupants": Arnold Bennett's "Riceyman Steps," i. 3); give up or relinquish (an office, position, etc.); also, to render inoperative (as, to *vacate* a legal judgment); deprive of validity; annul. **II.** *intr.* To withdraw from occupancy or possession; leave; quit.

va-ca-tion (vạ-kā′shọn), *n.* [OF. F. *vacation*, < L. *vacatio*(*n-*), a being free from duty, etc., exemption, < *vacare*: see *vacate.*] Freedom or release from duty, business, or activity; also, a period of suspension of work or activity; a part of the year when the activities of law-courts or schools are suspended; a holiday period; also, the fact of becoming or being vacant or unoccupied†, or the period of vacancy†; also, the act of vacating; a making or leaving vacant; a making inoperative or of no validity.—**va-ca′tion**, *v. i.* To take a vacation; pass a vacation, as at a place.—**va-ca′tion-er, va-ca′tion-ist**, *n.* One who is taking a vacation or holiday.—**va-ca′tion-less**, *a.* Without a vacation.

vac-ci-nal (vak′si-nạl), *a.* Pertaining or due to vaccine or vaccination.

vac-ci-nate (vak′si-nāt), *v. t.*; *-nated, -nating.* [From *vaccine.*] To inoculate (a person) with vaccine in order to produce a form of cowpox, intended to render the subject immune to smallpox; hence, to inoculate with the modified virus of any of various other diseases, as a preventive measure.—**vac-ci-na′tion** (-nā′shǫn), *n.* The act or practice of vaccinating; inoculation with vaccine.—**vac-ci-na′-tion-ist,** *n.* An advocate of vaccination.—**vac′ci-na-tor,** *n.* One who vaccinates; also, an instrument used in performing vaccination.

vac-cine (vak′sin or -sēn). [L. *vaccinus*, of or from cows, < *vacca*, cow; as n., F. *vaccin*, vaccine virus, < L. *vaccinus*.] **I.** *a.* Of, pertaining to, or derived from cows; also, pertaining to vaccinia or to vaccination. **II.** *n.* The virus of cowpox, obtained from the vesicles of an affected cow or person, and used in vaccination; hence, the modified virus of any of various other diseases, used for preventive inoculation.— **vac′cine=point,** *n.* A thin, pointed, vaccine-coated piece of bone or the like, for use in vaccinating.

vac-cin-i-a (vak-sin′i-ạ), *n.* [NL., < L. *vaccinus*: see *vaccine*.] Cowpox.

vac-cin-i-a-ceous (vak-sin-i-ā′shius), *a.* [L. *vaccinium*, blueberry, whortleberry.] Belonging to the *Vacciniaceæ*, a family of plants containing the blueberry, whortleberry, huckleberry, cranberry, etc.

vac-ci-no-ther-a-py (vak″si-nǭ-ther′ạ-pi), *n.* [See *vaccine* and *therapy*.] Treatment of disease by means of vaccines.

va-cil-lant (vas′i-lạnt), *a.* Vacillating; wavering.

va-cil-late (vas′i-lāt), *v. i.;* *-lated, -lating.* [L. *vacillatus*, pp. of *vacillare*, sway, waver: cf. Skt. *vañc-*, totter, go crookedly.] To sway unsteadily; waver; stagger; fluctuate; also, to waver in mind or opinion; be irresolute or inconstant.— **va′cil-lat-ing** (-lā-ting), *p. a.* That vacillates; wavering; characterized by vacillation.—**va′cil-lat-ing-ly,** *adv.*—**va-cil-la′tion** (-lā′shǫn), *n.* [L. *vacillatio*(n-).] The act of vacillating; unsteady movement; wavering in mind or opinion; irresolution.—**va′cil-la-to-ry** (-lạ-tǭ-ri), *a.*

vac-u-a (vak′ū-ạ), *n.* Latin plural of *vacuum*.

vac-u-ate (vak′ū-āt), *v. t.;* *-ated, -ating.* [L. *vacuatus*, pp. of *vacuare*, < *vacuus*, empty, E. *vacuous*.] To make empty†; specif., to create a vacuum in; also, to annul†; nullify†; also, to clear out† or discharge†.—**vac-u-a′tion** (-ā′shǫn), *n.*

va-cu-i-ty (va-kū′i-ti), *n.;* pl. *-ties* (-tiz). The state of being vacuous or empty; absence of contents; emptiness; the emptiness of a vacuum; also, an empty space; a vacuum; also, absence or lack of something specified; also, vacancy of mind, thought, etc. (as, "a cunning gravity of demeanour, concealing mere *vacuity*": Froude's "Cæsar," xv.); absence of ideas or intelligence; inanity; something inane or senselessly stupid (as, "an undue preoccupation with the *vacuities* which society has invented": Arnold Bennett's "Truth about an Author," xv.).

vac-u-o-lar (vak′ū-ǭ-lạr), *a.* Pertaining to, of the nature of, or resembling a vacuole.

vac-u-o-late, vac-u-o-lat-ed (vak′ū-ǭ-lāt, -lā-ted), *a.* Provided with or containing a vacuole or vacuoles.—**vac″u-o-la′tion** (-lā′shǫn), *n.* The formation of vacuoles; the state of being vacuolate; a system of vacuoles.

vac-u-ole (vak′ū-ōl), *n.* [F. *vacuole*, dim. < L. *vacuum*: see *vacuum*.] A minute cavity or vesicle in organic tissue; a cavity within the protoplasmic mass of cells, containing a watery liquid or secretion.

vac-u-ous (vak′ū-us), *a.* [L. *vacuus*, empty, akin to *vacare*, be empty: see *vacate*.] Empty; without contents; containing a vacuum; fig., empty of ideas or intelligence; stupidly vacant; unintelligent; showing mental vacancy (as, a *vacuous* look).—**vac′u-ous-ly,** *adv.*—**vac′u-ous-ness,** *n.*

vac-u-um (vak′ū-um), *n.;* pl. *-uums,* L. *-ua* (-ū-ạ). [L., an empty space, prop. neut. of *vacuus*, empty, E. *vacuous*.] Empty space; a space void of matter; theoretically, a space entirely void of matter ('absolute vacuum': opposed to *plenum*); hence, practically, an inclosed space from which air (or other gas) has been exhausted to a high degree, as by an air-pump ('partial vacuum'); also, the state or degree of exhaustion in such an inclosed space.—**vacuum method (or system) of ventilation,** a system in which the vitiated air is drawn out of the space to be ventilated, by artificial means, the fresh air coming in from the outside because of the decreased pressure.—**vac′u-um=bot″tle,** *n.* A bottle or flask protected by a vacuum jacket which prevents the escape of heat from hot contents or the entrance of heat from without to cold contents. Cf. *thermos.*—**vac′u-um=clean′er,** *n.* An apparatus for cleaning carpets, floors, etc., by suction.—**vac′u-um=clean′ing,** *n.*—**vac′u-um=fan,** *n.* A fan which ventilates a room or the like by drawing out the vitiated air by suction.—**vac′u-um=flask,** *n.* A vacuum-bottle.—**vac′u-um=gage,** *n.* A device for measuring the amount of vacuum or the internal pressure in the receiver of an air-pump or the like.—**vac′u-um=pump,** *n.* A pump or device by which a partial vacuum can be produced; a pump in which a partial vacuum is utilized in raising water. —**vac′u-um=tube,** *n.* In *elect.*, a sealed glass tube containing a partial vacuum or a highly rarefied gas, in which to observe the effects of a discharge of electricity passed through the tube between electrodes leading into it from the outside (cf. *Crookes tube* and *Geissler's tube*); also, a similar tube more or less resembling an electric-light bulb, used in wireless telegraphy and telephony, etc., to detect or rectify oscillations or radio-frequency currents, to amplify radio-frequency or audio-frequency currents, or to generate oscillations or radio-frequency currents, and fitted, in its most typical form, with three interior elements, the *filament* (which commonly resembles an electric-light filament and is made to glow by means of a battery known as the 'A battery'), the *plate* (a metal plate kept at positive potential by being connected with the positive pole of a battery known as the 'B battery'), and the *grid* (a wire coil, mesh, or the like placed between the filament and the plate, and affecting through its potential the flow of negative electrons from the filament to the plate).—**three=electrode vacuum=tube,** in *wireless teleg.* and *teleph.*, a vacuum-tube with three electrodes, that is, the filament, the grid, and the plate: used as a detector or rectifier, an amplifier, or an oscillator.—**two=electrode vacuum=tube,** in *wireless teleg.* and *teleph.*, a vacuum-tube with only two electrodes, that is, the filament and the plate: used as a detector or rectifier.

va-de=me-cum (vā′dē-mē′kum), *n.* [L. *vade mecum,* 'go with me.'] Anything that a person carries about with him as being of service, esp. a book for ready reference; a manual or handbook.

va-dose (vā′dōs), *a.* [L. *vadosus,* < *vadum,* a shallow.] In *geol.*, noting or pertaining to certain underground waters, springs, etc., situated a comparatively short distance below the surface of the earth, and due to infiltration through the soil and rock.

vag-a-bond (vag′ạ-bond). [OF. F. *vagabond,* < L. *vagabundus,* < *vagari,* wander, roam, < *vagus,* wandering, E. *vague.*] **I.** *a.* Wandering from place to place without settled habitation (as, "*vagabond* minstrels": Scott's "Ivanhoe," xxix.); nomadic; also, leading an irregular or disreputable life; good-for-nothing; worthless; also, of or pertaining to a vagabond or vagrant (as, *vagabond* habits); also, not fixed or settled; moving about without certain direction; driven to and fro (as, "Like to a *vagabond* flag upon the stream, Goes to and back": Shakspere's "Antony and Cleopatra," i. 4. 45). **II.** *n.* One who is without a fixed abode and wanders from place to place; esp., an idle wanderer without visible means of earning an honest livelihood; a tramp or vagrant; also, an idle, worthless fellow; a scamp; a rascal. —**vag′a-bond,** *v. i.* To vagabondize.—**vag′a-bond-age** (-bon-dạj), *n.*—**vag′a-bond-ism,** *n.*—**vag′a-bond-ize,** *v. i.; -ized, -izing.* To wander as or like a vagabond; roam at will.

va-gal (vā′gạl), *a.* Of or pertaining to the vagus.

va-ga-ry (vạ-gā′ri), *n.;* pl. *-ries* (-riz). [Appar. < L. *vagari,* wander, roam: see *vagabond.*] A wandering† or roaming†; also, a wandering of the thoughts; an extravagant idea or notion; also, a wild, capricious, or fantastic action; a freak.—**va-ga′ri-ous** (-gā′ri-us), *a.*

va-gi-na (vạ-jī′nạ), *n.;* pl. *-nas* (-nạz), L. *-næ* (-nē). [L., sheath.] A sheath-like part or organ; specif., in *bot.*, the sheath formed by the basal part of certain leaves where they embrace the stem; in *anat.*, the passage leading from the uterus to the vulva in a female mammal.—**vag-i-nal** (vaj′i-nạl or vạ-jī′-), *a.* Pertaining to or resembling a sheath; in *anat.*, etc., pertaining to the vagina of a female mammal. —**vag′i-nate** (-nāt), *a.* Furnished with a vagina or sheath; sheathed; also, of the nature of a sheath.—**vag-i-ni′tis**

(-nī'tis), *n.* [NL.] In *pathol.*, inflammation of the vagina.

va-gran-cy (vā'grạn-si), *n.*; pl. *-cies* (-siz). Vagrant condition or life; wandering or straying, or an instance of it; specif., the condition, conduct, or practice of a vagrant, idle vagabond, or idle and disorderly person.

va-grant (vā'grạnt). [AF. *vagarant*, appar. an altered form (by association with derivatives of L. *vagari*: see *vagabond*) of OF. *wacrant*, ppr. of *wacrer*, *walcrer*, wander, roam, rove, prob. from Teut.] **I.** *a.* Wandering or roaming from place to place (as, "a purely pastoral and *vagrant* people": De Quincey's "Revolt of the Tartars"); nomadic; straying; specif., wandering about without proper means of livelihood, or living in idle vagabondage (as, "His house was known to all the *vagrant* train": Goldsmith's "Deserted Village," 149); also, of or pertaining to wandering (as, "their *vagrant* propensities": De Quincey's "Revolt of the Tartars"); characteristic of a vagrant (as, a *vagrant* life); also, of plants, straggling in growth (as, "*Vagrant* plants of parasitic breed Had overgrown the Dial": Hood's "Haunted House," i.); of things, not fixed or settled; moving hither and thither; having no certain course, direction, or destination; fig., wandering; inconstant; wayward. **II.** *n.* One who wanders from place to place; a wanderer; a rover; esp., an idle wanderer; a vagabond; a tramp; in *law*, an idle or disorderly person, as a tramp, beggar, unlicensed peddler, prostitute, etc., whose habits of life are inconsistent with the good order of society, and who is liable to arrest and imprisonment.—**va'grant-ly**, *adv.*—**va'grant-ness**, *n.*—**va'grom** (-grọm), *a.* Illiterate corruption of *vagrant*, in Shakspere's "Much Ado about Nothing," iii. 3. 26: hence occasionally used as an archaism by modern writers.

vague (vāg), *a.*; compar. *vaguer*, superl. *vaguest*. [F. *vague*, < L. *vagus*, wandering, roaming, unsettled, indefinite, vague: cf. *vagus* and *vagabond*.] Wandering† or vagrant†; also, not definite in statement or meaning, or not explicit or precise (as, "*vague* promises of assistance": W. H. Hudson's "Purple Land," i.); of an indefinite or indistinct character, as ideas, feelings, etc. (as, "He wandered about at random, with a *vague* notion he was going homewards": J. H. Newman's "Callista," xii.); indistinct to the sight or other sense, or perceptible or recognizable only in an indefinite way (as, *vague* forms seen through mist; *vague* murmurs; "a *vague* smell . . . of drying flowers," Vernon Lee's "Genius Loci," St. Geryon of Cologne); not definitely fixed, determined, or known, or uncertain (as, "The limits of immense provinces . . . uninhabited and even unexplored, were necessarily very *vague*": Lecky's "Hist. of Eng. in the 18th Century," viii.); also, of persons, etc., indefinite in statement; not clear in thought or understanding (as, "Mr. Jeff seems *vague* about the meaning of this phrase": W. De Morgan's "Alice-for-Short," xiv.); of the eyes, expression, etc., showing absence of clear perception or understanding (as, "She . . . laughed gaily into his mild, *vague* old eyes": Tarkington's "Gentleman from Indiana," xiv.).—**vague'ly**, *adv.*—**vague'ness**, *n.*

va-gus (vā'gus), *n.*; pl. *-gi* (-jī). [L., wandering: see *vague*.] In *anat.*, either of a pair of widely distributed cranial nerves extending through the neck and thorax to the upper part of the abdomen; a pneumogastric nerve. Also called *vagus nerve*.

vail[1] (vāl), *v. i.* [For *avail*.] To be of use or value. [Archaic.]—**vail**[1], *n.* Advantage† or profit†; also, an occasional profit or advantage attached to an office or position, or an emolument or fee in addition to salary or wages (usually in *pl.*: now rare); also, a gratuity, as one given to a servant by a visitor on his departure (usually in *pl.*: now rare).

vail[2] (vāl), *v. t.* [For obs. *avale*, < OF. *avaler*, bring or let down, also go down: see *avalanche*.] To cause or allow to descend or sink; lower; also, to take off or doff (a hat, etc.), as in respect or submission. [Archaic.]

vain (vān), *a.* [OF. F. *vain*, < L. *vanus*, empty, unmeaning, fruitless, delusive, vainglorious, perhaps akin to *vacuus*, empty, E. *vacuous*.] Empty† or void†; fig., devoid of real value or importance, or hollow, idle, or worthless (as, "*Vain* pomp and glory of this world, I hate ye," Shakspere's "Henry VIII.," iii. 2. 365; "It is not a *vain* thing for you; because it is your life," Deut. xxxii. 47); also, devoid of force or efficacy,

producing no good result, or unavailing, futile, or useless (as, *vain* entreaties, efforts, or regrets; "We had had a hard, *vain* chase after him," G. W. Cable's "Cavalier," i.); also, false or deceitful (obs. or archaic: as, "Have ye not seen a *vain* vision, and have ye not spoken a lying divination?" Ezek. xiii. 7; "*vain* reasonings," Milton's "Samson Agonistes," 322); also, devoid of sense or wisdom, senseless, or foolish (archaic: as, "unruly and *vain* talkers," Titus, i. 10); also, having an overweening pride in one's own appearance, qualities, gifts, achievements, etc., or conceited (as, "pert, affected, *vain* coquette," Burns's "Epistle from Esopus to Maria," 73; "They were a *vain* and boastful company of heroes," Mark Twain's "Tom Sawyer," xv.); overweeningly proud (*of*: as, "Men of genuine ability are rarely *vain* of what they can do really well," Froude's "Cæsar," xviii.); proceeding from or showing personal vanity (as, *vain* boasts; "I scarce ever heard or saw the introductory words, 'Without vanity I may say,' etc., but some *vain* 'thing immediately followed," B. Franklin's "Autobiography," i.).—**in vain**, without effect or avail; to no purpose: as, to strive or plead *in vain*.—**to take a name in vain**, to use a name, properly God's name, and hence any other entitled to respect, lightly or irreverently: as, "Thou shalt not *take the name* of the Lord thy God *in vain*" (Ex. xx. 7).

vain-glo-ri-ous (vān-glō'ri-us), *a.* Filled with or given to vainglory (as, "the *vainglorious* mighty of the earth": Shelley's "Queen Mab," iii. 139); inordinately proud or boastful; excessively and ostentatiously vain; also, characterized by, showing, or proceeding from vainglory (as, "*vainglorious* pride," Wiffen's tr. Tasso's "Jerusalem Delivered," i. 18; "A *vainglorious* confidence prevailed . . . among the Spanish cavaliers," Irving's "Conquest of Granada," x.).—**vain-glo'ri-ous-ly**, *adv.*—**vain-glo'ri-ous-ness**, *n.*

vain-glo-ry (vān-glō'ri), *n.* [ML. *vana gloria*, vain or empty glory.] Empty or worthless glory; also, inordinate elation or pride over one's achievements, abilities, etc.; boastful vanity; vain pomp or show.—**vain-glo'ry**, *v. i.*; *-ried*, *-rying*. To indulge in vainglory.

vain-ly (vān'li), *adv.* In a vain manner; unavailingly, or in vain; foolishly†; conceitedly.—**vain'ness**, *n.*

vair (vār), *n.* [OF. F. *vair*, < L. *varius*, variegated: see *various*.] A kind of fur much used for lining and trimming garments during the 13th and 14th centuries, and generally assumed to have been the skin of a variety of squirrel with a gray back and white belly (cf. *miniver*); in *her.*, one of the furs, represented by bell-shaped or cup-shaped patches of different tinctures, usually alternately azure and argent, like pieces of skin sewed together.

Vair.

Vais-ya (vīs'yạ), *n.* [Skt. *vāiçya*, < *viç*, settlement, community, people.] A member of the mercantile and agricultural caste among the Hindus.

vai-vode (vā'vōd), *n.* Same as *voivode*.

va-keel, **va-kil** (vạ-kēl'), *n.* [Hind. *vakīl*.] In the East Indies, an agent or representative, esp. of a person of political importance; an ambassador or special commissioner at a court; a native attorney.

val-ance (val'ạns), *n.* [Origin uncertain.] A short curtain or piece of dependent drapery, as at the edge of a canopy or other covering; esp., a short curtain hanging about a bed from the frame on which the mattress rests to the floor.—**val'ance**, *v. t.*; *-anced*, *-ancing*. To furnish or decorate with or as with a valance.

vale[1] (vāl), *n.* [OF. F. *val*, < L. *vallis*, valley.] A valley (now chiefly poetic); often, fig., this world as the place of life, sorrows, etc. (as, "one of his chief consolations in this *vale*," H. G. Wells's "Men Like Gods," i. 1; "my dear friends and brethren in this *vale* of tears," Thackeray's "Newcomes," liii.); also, a small channel or trough.—**the vale of years**, the decline of life. See Shakspere's "Othello," iii. 3. 266.

vale[2] (vāl), *v. t.* See *vail*[2].

va-le[3] (vā'lē), *interj.* [L., impv. of *valere*, be strong, be well.] Farewell.

val-e-dic-tion (val-ē-dik'shọn), *n.* [L. *valedicere* (pp. *valedictus*), say farewell, < *vale* (see *vale*[3]) + *dicere*, say.] A bidding farewell; a leave-taking; an utterance at leave-taking.—**val″e-dic-to′ri-an** (-tō′ri-ạn), *n.* One who delivers a valedictory or farewell address; esp., in American colleges and schools, the student (usually the one who ranks highest in scholarship) who pronounces the valedictory or farewell oration at the graduating exercises of his or her class. —**val-e-dic′to-ry** (-tọ-ri). **I.** *a.* Bidding farewell; farewell; pertaining to an occasion of leave-taking. **II.** *n.*; pl. *-ries* (-riz). A valedictory address or oration; esp., in American colleges and schools, the oration delivered by the valedictorian.

va-lence (vā′lẹns), *n.* [L. *valentia*, strength, < *valens* (*valent*-), ppr. of *valere*, be strong, have force or effect.] In *chem.*, the quality which determines the number of atoms or radicals with which any single atom or radical will unite chemically; the relative combining capacity of an atom or radical compared with the standard hydrogen atom: as, a *valence* of one (the capacity to unite with one atom of hydrogen or its equivalent).

va-len-ci-a (vạ-len′shi-ä), *n.* [Perhaps from *Valencia*, in eastern Spain.] A fabric having a silk or cotton warp and a worsted weft, and often striped, used chiefly for waistcoats.

Val-en-ci-ennes (val″ẹn-si-enz′, F. vȧ-loṅ-syen′) **lace.** A fine bobbin-made lace, orig. made at Valenciennes in northern France, of which the pattern and the net ground are made together, of the same threads; also, some machine-made imitation of it.

va-len-cy (vā′lẹn-si), *n.*; pl. *-cies* (-siz). Same as *valence*.

-valent. [L. *valens* (*valent*-): see *valence*.] An adjective termination used to form chemical terms indicating valence, as in *bivalent, trivalent, quadrivalent*.

val-en-tine (val′ẹn-tīn), *n.* [From St. *Valentine*.] A sweetheart chosen (or drawn by lot) on St. Valentine's Day, Feb. 14; also, an amatory or sentimental (sometimes satirical or burlesque) missive, printed card, or the like, or some token or gift expressive of regard, sent by one person to another on St. Valentine's Day.

Val-en-tin-i-an (val-ẹn-tin′i-ạn), *n.* **I.** *a.* Of or pertaining to Valentinus, a Gnostic leader who taught at Rome in the middle of the 2d century after Christ; noting or belonging to the Gnostic system or sect instituted by him. **II.** *n.* A follower of Valentinus; a Valentinian Gnostic.—**Val-en-tin′i-an-ism**, *n.*

val-er-ate (val′ẹ-rāt), *n.* In *chem.*, a salt of valeric acid.

va-le-ri-an (vạ-lē′ri-ạn), *n.* [OF. *valeriane* (F. *valériane*), < ML. *valeriana*, appar. < L. *Valerianus* or *Valerius*, personal name.] Any of the perennial herbs constituting the genus *Valeriana*, as *V. officinalis*, a plant with white or pink flowers and a medicinal root; also, a drug consisting of or made from this root, used as a nerve-sedative and antispasmodic. — **va-le″ri-a-na′ceous** (-ạ-nā′shius), *a.* Belonging to the *Valerianaceæ*, a family of plants containing valerian, spikenard, etc.— **va-le′ri-an-ate** (-āt), *n.* In *chem.*, a salt of valeric acid.—**va-le-ri-an′ic** (-an′ik), *a.* Same as *valeric*.

va-ler-ic (vạ-ler′ik or -lē′rik), *a.* [From *valerian*.] Pertaining to or derived from valerian; in *chem.*, noting or pertaining to any of several isomeric organic acids, the common one being a liquid of pungent odor obtained from valerian roots.

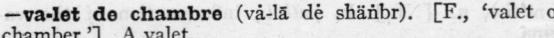

Valerian (*Valeriana officinalis*). — *1*, flowering plant; *2*, the inflorescence; *a*, flower with bract; *b*, section of ovary; *c*, fruit with pappus.

val-et (val′et or val′ä), *n.* [F. *valet*, OF. *vallet, vaslet*, also *varlet* (see *varlet*); akin to E. *vassal*.] A man-servant who is his master's personal attendant for services in the toilet, care of clothing, etc.—**val′et**, *v. t.* or *i.*; *valeted* (val′et-ed or val′ạd), *-eting* (-et-ing or -ạ-ing). To attend or act as valet.

—**va-let de chambre** (vȧ-lā dẹ shäṅbr). [F., 'valet of chamber.'] A valet.

val-e-tu-di-na-ri-an (val-ẹ-tū-di-nā′ri-ạn). [L. *valetudinarius*, < *valetudo* (*valetudin*-), health, poor health, < *valere*, be strong, be well.] **I.** *a.* In poor health; sickly; invalid; leading the life of an invalid; affecting invalidism; also, characterized by or pertaining to invalidism (as, *valetudinarian* retirement; *valetudinarian* habits). **II.** *n.* An invalid (as, "The poor trembling *valetudinarian* is carried in a chair": Smollett's "Humphry Clinker," April 23); often, one who affects invalidism or the condition or habits of an invalid.—**val-e-tu-di-na′ri-an-ism**, *n.* Valetudinarian condition or habits; invalidism.—**val-e-tu′di-na-ry** (-nạ-ri), *a.* and *n.* Same as *valetudinarian*.

val-gus (val′gus), *n.* [L., bow-legged.] In *pathol.*, a form of clubfoot in which the foot is turned outward. Cf. *varus*.

Val-hal-la (val-hal′ä), *n.* [NL., = G. *Walhalla*, < Icel. *Valhöll* (*Valhall*-), lit. 'hall of the slain,' < *valr*, the slain, + *höll*, hall.] In *Scand. myth.*, the hall of immortality into which the souls of heroes slain in battle are received, and from which, each morning, they go forth to fight, returning at night to feast with Odin and the gods.

va-li (vä-lē′), *n.* [Turk. *vālī*, < Ar. *wālī*.] The governor general of a Turkish vilayet.

val-iance (val′yạns), *n.* The quality or fact of being valiant; bravery, courage, or valor (as, "When our affright was over, we . . . set out afresh with double *valiance*": Mrs. Gaskell's "Cranford," x.); also, a valiant deed (obs. or archaic).— **val′ian-cy** (-yạn-si), *n.* The quality of being valiant; valor.

val-iant (val′yạnt), *a.* [OF. *vaillant*, ppr. of *valoir*, < L. *valere*: see *valor*.] Strong† or sturdy†; also, brave, courageous, or stout-hearted, as persons (as, a *valiant* knight; "The *valiant* valet defended himself, tooth and nail," Bulwer-Lytton's "Pelham," xxiv.); marked by or showing bravery or valor, as deeds, attempts, etc.; valorous.—**val′iant-ly**, *adv.*—**val′iant-ness**, *n.*

val-id (val′id), *a.* [L. *validus*, strong, powerful, effective, < *valere*, be strong: cf. *valor*.] Strong, powerful, or vigorous (archaic: as, "Not pitying words, But *valid* actions had thy wrongs redress'd," Wiffen's tr. Tasso's "Jerusalem Delivered," iv. 68); also, in full bodily strength or health, robust, or well (cf. *invalid*[2], *a.*); also, fig., sound, just, or well-founded (as, a *valid* argument or conclusion; a *valid* reason; a *valid* objection); having force, weight, or cogency; authoritative (as, "The authority of the tribunal was founded upon nothing more *valid* than a mere resolution . . . of some fifty members": Morley's "Oliver Cromwell," iii. 7); also, legally sound, effective, or binding; having legal force; sustainable in law.—**val-i-date** (val′i-dāt), *v. t.*; *-dated*, *-dating*. [ML. *validatus*, pp. of *validare*, < L. *validus*.] To make valid; confirm; give legal force to; legalize.— **val-i-da′tion** (-dā′shọn), *n.*—**va-lid′i-ty** (vạ-lid′i-ti), *n.*; pl. *-ties* (-tiz). The state or character of being valid; strength† or robustness†; soundness, as of arguments, conclusions, etc.; legal soundness or force; also, value or worth (obs. or archaic: as, "He had . . . too high an opinion of the *validity* of regular troops," B. Franklin's "Autobiography," xi.).—**val′id-ly**, *adv.*—**val′id-ness**, *n.*

va-lise (vạ-lēs′), *n.* [F. *valise*, < It. *valigia*; origin uncertain.] A traveler's case for holding clothes, toilet articles, etc., now esp. one of leather, of moderate size, for carrying by hand; a traveling-bag.

Val-kyr (val′kir), *n.* [Icel. *Valkyrja*, lit. 'chooser of the slain,' < *valr*, the slain, + *-kyrja*, akin to *kjōsa*, choose.] In *Scand. myth.*, one of the handmaidens of Odin, who ride through the air and hover over fields of battle, choosing the heroes who are to be slain, and afterward conducting them to Valhalla. Also **Val-kyr′ie** (-kir′i or -kī′ri).—**Val-kyr′i-an**, *a.*

val-late (val′āt), *a.* [L. *vallatus*, pp. of *vallare*, surround with a rampart, < *vallum*, palisade, wall, rampart, < *vallus*, stake, pale: cf. *wall*.] Surrounded by a ridge or elevation; having a surrounding ridge or elevation.—**val-lat-ed** (val′ā-ted), *a.* Surrounded with or as with a rampart or wall.— **val-la-tion** (va-lā′shọn), *n.* [LL. *vallatio*(*n*-).] A rampart or intrenchment.

val-lec-u-la (va-lek′ū-lä), *n.*; pl. *-læ* (-lē). [LL., for L. *vallicula*, dim. of *vallis, valles*, valley.] In *anat.* and *bot.*, a furrow or depression.—**val-lec′u-lar** (-lär), *a.* Pertaining to or of the nature of a vallecula.—**val-lec′u-late** (-lāt), *a.* Having a vallecula or valleculæ.

val-ley (val′i), *n.*; pl. *valleys* (-iz). [OF. *valee* (F. *vallée*), < L. *vallis, valles,* valley.] An elongated depression, usually with an outlet, between uplands, hills, or mountains, esp. such a depression following the course of a stream; also, the extensive, more or less flat, and relatively low region drained by a great river-system; hence, any hollow or structure likened to a valley; in *arch.,* a depression or depressed angle formed by the meeting (at its bottom) of two inclined sides of a roof.

val-lis-ne-ri-a-ceous (val-is-nē-ri-ā′shius), *a.* [NL. *Vallisneria,* the typical genus; named from Antonio *Vallisneri* (1661–1730), Italian naturalist.] Belonging to the *Vallisneriaceæ,* a family of aquatic plants containing the frogbit, etc.

val-or (val′ọr), *n.* [OF. *valor, valour* (F. *valeur*), < LL. *valor,* value, worth, ML. valor, < L. *valere,* be strong, have force or effect, be worth: cf. *wield.*] Boldness or firmness in braving danger, or bravery or heroic courage, esp. in battle (as, "The Virginia troops showed great *valor,*" Bancroft's "Hist. of the U. S.," Amer. Revolution, i. 8; "The better part of *valour* is discretion," Shakspere's "1 Henry IV.," v. 4. 121); also, valiant persons, or a valiant person (rare); also, value† or worth†.

val-or-i-za-tion (val″ọr-i-zā′shọn), *n.* [Pg. *valorização.*] The act of valorizing; esp., the fixing of the value or price of a commercial commodity by a government. See *valorize.*

val-or-ize (val′ọr-īz), *v. t.*; *-ized, -izing.* [Pg. *valorizar,* < *valor,* value, < LL. *valor:* see *valor.*] To assign a value to; esp., of a government, to fix the value or price of (a commercial commodity), and make provision for maintaining it against a decline (as to a price below the cost of production), by purchase of the commodity at the fixed price or by other means (used esp. with reference to the action of Brazil in fixing the price of coffee).

val-or-ous (val′ọr-us), *a.* [OF. F. *valeureux.*] Having or displaying valor, valiant, or brave, as persons (as, "that host of *valorous* men who . . . had fought so strenuous a fight for freedom": Morley's "Oliver Cromwell," v. 1); characterized by valor, as actions, etc.; also, valuable†.—**val′or-ous-ly,** *adv.*—**val′or-ous-ness,** *n.*

val′our, *n.* British preferred form of *valor.*

valse (väls), *n.* [F.] A waltz: as, "The newest band was playing the latest *valse*" (L. Merrick's "Worldlings," xv.).

val-u-a-ble (val′ū-ạ-bl). **I.** *a.* Having value or worth; of monetary worth; esp., representing a large market value (as, a *valuable* horse; a *valuable* mineral; *valuable* paintings); of considerable use, service, or importance (as, *valuable* information; *valuable* aid; a *valuable* contribution to knowledge); of persons, estimable† or worthy†; also, capable of having the value estimated. **II.** *n.* A valuable article, as of personal property or of merchandise, esp. one of comparatively small size: commonly in *pl.*: as, "The victors broke into the houses . . . plundering them of whatever *valuables* they contained, plate, jewels . . . wearing-apparel and provisions" (Prescott's "Conquest of Mexico," iii. 7).—**val′u-a-ble-ness,** *n.*—**val′u-a-bly,** *adv.*

val-u-a-tion (val-ū-ā′shọn), *n.* The act of valuing; an estimating or fixing of the value of a thing; also, a value estimated or fixed; estimated worth; also, value† or worth†. —**val-u-a′tion-al,** *a.*

val-u-a-tor (val′ū-ā-tọr), *n.* One who estimates values; an appraiser.

val-ue (val′ū), *n.* [OF. *value,* orig. pp. fem. of *valoir,* be worth, < L. *valere:* see *valor.*] Worth; that property of a thing in virtue of which it is esteemed, desirable, or useful, or the degree of this property possessed (as, a trifling gift may have *value* in the eyes of the recipient; the *value* of education; "the inexpressible *value* of the Bible, the privilege and blessing of it to nations," Defoe's "Robinson Crusoe," ii. 8; "He was very ignorant of the *value* of money," Eden Phillpotts's "Red Redmaynes," iii.); excellence or merit; effective virtue; usefulness or importance; esp., material or monetary worth, as in traffic or sale (as, even the waste has *value*; to insure all articles of *value*); the relative material

or monetary worth of a thing; the worth of a thing as measured by the amount of other things for which it can be exchanged, or as estimated in terms of a medium of exchange; equivalent worth or adequate return (as, for *value* received); estimated or assigned worth, or valuation; also, esteem† or regard† (as, "For Erasmus our archbishop had a great *value,* whose worth and service . . . he well knew": Strype's "Memorials of Cranmer," iii. 23); also, force, import, or significance (as, the *value* of a word or a phrase); also, the number or amount represented by a figure, quantity, etc.; extent or amount (now prov.); in *music,* the relative length or duration of a tone signified by a note; in *painting,* etc., the relative importance or effect of an object, part, spot of color, or the like, as in a picture, esp. with reference to light and shade; also, degree of lightness or darkness.—**val′ue,** *v. t.*; *-ued, -uing.* To estimate the value of; rate at a certain value or price; appraise; also, to consider with respect to worth, excellence, usefulness, or importance; regard (highly or otherwise: as, "The king must take it ill, That he's so slightly *valued* in his messenger," Shakspere's "King Lear," ii. 2. 153); esp., to regard or esteem highly (as, "Nor did Cranmer *value* at all names and titles," Strype's "Memorials of Cranmer," i. 8; "The typical Southern leader *valued* the peculiar form of society under which he lived," Charnwood's "Abraham Lincoln," vi.); think highly of (one's self), as for something (as, "My instructor . . . *valued* himself for his skill": Johnson's "Rasselas," xxxix.); pride (one's self), as on something (as, "the Saxons, a nation *valuing* itself on its populousness and riches": Hallam's "Europe during the Middle Ages," v.); also, to estimate with respect to number or amount†.—**val′ued,** *p. a.* Estimated or appraised; having the value specified, as a policy of insurance; also, highly regarded or esteemed.—**val′ue-less,** *a.* Destitute of value; worthless; also, invaluable or priceless (rare).—**val′ue-less-ness,** *n.*—**val′u-er,** *n.*

val-val, val-var (val′val, -vär), *a.* Pertaining to or of the nature of a valve: as, a *valval* view (in *bot.,* the view of a diatom in which the surface of one of the valves is turned to the observer: cf. *zonal*).

val-vate (val′vāt), *a.* [L. *valvatus,* having folding doors.] Furnished with or opening by a valve or valves; serving as or resembling a valve; in *bot.,* opening by valves, as certain capsules and anthers; also, meeting without overlapping, as the parts of certain buds; composed of or characterized by such parts.

valve (valv), *n.* [L. *valva,* leaf of a door, NL. valve.] One of the halves or leaves of a double or folding door; also, any device for closing or modifying the passage through a pipe, outlet, inlet, or the like, in order to control the flow of liquids, gases, etc.; a hinged lid or other movable part in such a device, which closes or modifies the passage; specif., in musical wind-instruments of the trumpet class, a device for quickly changing the direction and length of the air-column so as to alter the pitch of a tone; in *anat.,* a membranous fold or other structure which controls the flow of a fluid, as one which permits blood to flow through a passage in one direction only; in *bot.,* one of the segments into which a capsule dehisces; also, a flap or lid-like part of certain anthers; also, either half of the silicified shell of a diatom; in *conch.,* one of the two or more separable pieces composing certain shells; also, a shell consisting of a single piece (cf. *univalve*).—**valve,** *v.* **I.** *tr.* To provide with a valve or valves; also, to check or control by a valve; allow to escape by opening a valve, as gas from a balloon. **II.** *intr.* To operate a valve or valves; open a valve, as in order to allow gas to escape from a balloon.—**valved,** *a.* Having a valve or valves.—**valve′less,** *a.* Having no valve.—**valve′let,** *n.* A small valve; a valvule.—**val-vu-lar** (val′vū-lär), *a.* Of or pertaining to a valve or valves, esp. of the heart; also, having the form of a valve; also, furnished with or operating by a valve or valves.—**val′vule** (-vūl), *n.* [NL. *valvula,* dim. of *valva.*] A small valve or valve-like part.—**val-vu-li′tis** (-lī′tis), *n.* [NL.] In *pathol.,* inflammation of a valve, esp. a valve of the heart.

vam-brace (vam′brās), *n.* [ME. *vambras, vantbras,* < OF. *avantbras,* forearm, vambrace, < *avant,* before, + *bras,* arm: cf. *rerebrace.*] A piece of armor for the forearm, from the elbow to the wrist.

---

va-mose, va-moose (vạ-mōs′, -mös′), v.; -mosed, -moosed, -mosing, -moosing. [Sp. vamos, 1st and 2d pers. pl. impv. of ir, go.] **I.** intr. To make off; decamp. [Slang, U. S.] **II.** tr. To decamp from; quit hurriedly. [Slang, U. S.]

vamp[1] (vamp), n. [ME. vampe, vampey, < OF. avanpie (F. avant-pied), < avant, before, + pie, pied, < L. pes (ped-), foot.] The front part of the upper of a shoe or boot, being the part between the sole and the top and in front of a line drawn downward from the ankle-bone or thereabout; also, a piece or patch added to an old thing to give it a new appearance; anything patched up or pieced together; in music, an accompaniment, usually improvised, consisting of a succession of simple chords; also, improvised or other music for filling in time before a singer or other performer is ready to begin.—**vamp**[1], v. **I.** tr. To furnish with a vamp, esp. to repair with a new vamp, as a shoe or boot; hence, to patch up or repair; give an appearance of newness to; make by or as by patching; put together out of old materials; in music, to improvise (an accompaniment or the like). **II.** intr. In music, to improvise an accompaniment, tune, etc. (as, "I got a banjo, you know, and I vamp a bit": H. G. Wells's "Kipps," ii. 1); also, to play improvised or other music to fill in time before a singer or other performer is ready to begin.—**vamp′er**[1], n.

vamp[2] (vamp), n. [Abbr. of vampire.] A female vampire, or a woman or girl who uses her feminine charms or arts to prey upon male victims; a self-seeking or unscrupulous flirt. [Slang.]—**vamp**[2], v. **I.** intr. To act as a vamp. [Slang.] **II.** tr. To act as a vamp toward (a man); use one's feminine charms or arts upon (a man). [Slang.]—**vamp′er**[2], n.

vam-pire (vam′pīr), n. [F. vampire; from Slav.] A preternatural being, in the common belief a reanimated corpse, supposed to suck the blood of sleeping persons at night; hence, one who preys ruthlessly on others; an extortioner; now, esp., a woman who preys on men (see Kipling's poem "The Vampire"); a woman who uses her feminine charms or seductions to extract profit from male victims, or feeds her vanity at their expense; a self-seeking or unscrupulous flirt (cf. vamp[2], n.); also, any of various South and Central American bats which suck blood, or are incorrectly supposed to do so, including Desmodus rufus and Diphylla ecaudata ('true vampires'), which actually suck the blood of animals including man, and Phyllostoma (or Vampyrus) spectrum ('great vampire' or 'false vampire'), which is large but is considered harmless; also, any of various large frugivorous bats of the Old World.—**vampir′ic** (-pir′ik), a.—**vam′pir-ism** (-pīr-izm), n. Belief in the existence of (preternatural) vampires; the supposed existence of vampires; the acts or practices of vampires; hence, the practice of preying on others.

True Vampire (Desmodus rufus).

van[1] (van), n. [Var. of fan[1].] A fan or other contrivance for winnowing grain (obs. or prov.); also, a wing (chiefly poetic: as, "As bats at the wired window of a dairy, They beat their vans," Shelley's "Witch of Atlas," xvi.); also, a sail of a windmill.—**van**[1], v. t.; vanned, vanning. To winnow (grain: obs. or prov.); also, to separate and test (ore) by washing on a shovel.

van[2] (van), n. [Abbr. of vanguard.] The foremost division or the front part of an army, a fleet, or any body of individuals advancing or in order for advancing; the foremost position in such a body; fig., the forefront in any movement, course of progress, or the like; those who are in the forefront of a movement or the like; also, the front part or rank of anything (as, "The divine Litany . . . places such a death in the very van of horrors": De Quincey's "English Mail-Coach," ii.).

van[3] (van), n. [Abbr. of caravan.] A covered wagon, usually of considerable size, for moving furniture, household effects, etc.; a closed vehicle for the conveyance of prisoners (as, "the van which should take him to Coldbath Fields, where he was to serve his term": S. Butler's "Way of All Flesh," lxiv.); a covered railroad-car for baggage, for the accommodation of the guard, etc. (Great Britain).

van-a-date (van′ạ-dāt), n. In chem., a salt of vanadic acid. Also **va-na-di-ate** (vạ-nā′di-āt).

va-nad-ic (vạ-nad′ik), a. In chem., of or containing vanadium. See vanadious.—**vanadic acid**, any of certain acids containing vanadium, esp. one with the formula H_3VO_4.

va-nad-i-nite (vạ-nad′i-nīt), n. A mineral consisting of lead vanadate with a small amount of lead chloride, occurring in yellow, brown, or bright-red crystals.

va-na-di-ous (vạ-nā′di-us), a. In chem., containing vanadium (in larger proportion than a corresponding vanadic compound).

va-na-di-um (vạ-nā′di-um), n. [NL.; from Vanadis, a name of the Scandinavian goddess Freya.] Chem. sym., V; at. wt., 51.0; sp. gr., 5.5. A rare element occurring in certain minerals, and obtained as a light-gray powder with a silvery luster: sometimes used as an ingredient of steel.—**vanadium steel**, a special steel containing a certain amount of vanadium, which tends to increase tensile strength, etc.

Van-dal (van′dạl). [L. Vandali, Vandalii, pl.] **I.** n. One of a Teutonic people which anciently inhabited the regions between the Oder and the Vistula, and which during the 5th century overran Gaul, Spain, northern Africa, etc., sacking Rome in 455 with great destruction to the works of art, literature, etc., accumulated there; hence [often l. c.], one who wilfully or ignorantly destroys artistic or literary treasures, or wantonly attacks or mars anything that is beautiful or venerable. **II.** a. [cap.] Of or pertaining to the Vandals; [often l. c.] imbued with or characterized by vandalism.—**Van-dal′ic** (-dal′ik), a. Pertaining to the Vandals; [often l. c.] characteristic of or befitting the Vandals; wilfully or ignorantly destructive.—**van′dal-ism**, n. Conduct or spirit characteristic of the Vandals; wilful or ignorant destruction of artistic or literary treasures; hostility to or contempt for what is beautiful or venerable; also, a vandalic act (as, "These vandalisms shocked . . . reverential sentiment": Morley's "Oliver Cromwell," i. 6).

Van-dyke (van-dīk′). **I.** a. Of or pertaining to Sir Anthony Van Dyck, or Vandyke (1599–1641), a Flemish painter, for some years in England, or the style of dress, etc., characteristic of his portraits: as, a Vandyke collar (a wide collar of lace or the like with the edge formed into deep points); a Vandyke beard (a short, pointed beard); Vandyke brown (any of several dark-brown pigments). **II.** n. [Usually l. c.] A Vandyke collar; also, one of a series of relatively deep points along an edge, as in lace, cloth, etc., such as are seen in a Vandyke collar; also, a Vandyke beard.—**van-dyke′**, v. t.; -dyked, -dyking. To furnish with or cut into vandykes, or deep points, along the edge.

vane (vān), n. [ME. vane, var. of fane, vane, orig. banner, < AS. fana = OHG. fano, banner: cf. fanon.] A flat piece of metal, or some other device, fixed upon a spire or other elevated object in such a way as to move with the wind and indicate its direction (as, "Doubtfully was shifting every vane On the town spires, with changing gusts of wind": W. Morris's "Jason," i. 374); a weathercock; also, a similar piece, or sail, in the wheel of a windmill, to be moved by the air; any plate, blade, or the like, attached to an axis, and moved by or in air or a liquid (as, a vane of a screw-propeller); in surv., the sliding crosspiece on a leveling-rod; also, a sight on a quadrant or the like; in ornith., the web of a feather.—**vaned**, a. Furnished with a vane or vanes.

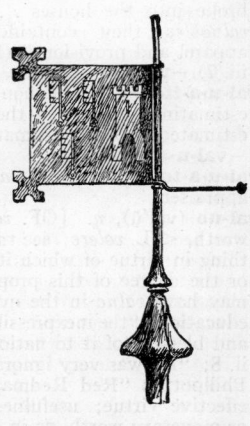

Vane. — From the Hôtel Dieu, Beaune, France, 15th century.

va-nes-sa (vạ-nes'ạ), *n.*; pl. *-sas* (-sạz). [NL.] Any butterfly of the genus *Vanessa*, the members of which have the outer margin of the fore wings more or less notched, as *V. atalanta*, the red admiral.

Vanessa. — Red admiral (*Vanessa atalanta*), right wings reversed: female, natural size.

vang (vang), *n.* [Var. of *fang*.] *Naut.*, either of two ropes extending (one on each side) from the peak of a gaff to the ship's rail: used to steady the gaff.

van-guard (van'gärd), *n.* [OF. *avangarde* (F. *avant-garde*), < *avant*, before, + *garde*, E. *guard*, *n.*] The foremost division or the front part of an army; the van; a part of an army detached from the main body to clear the way and guard against surprise from the front.

va-nil-la (vạ-nil'ạ), *n.* [Sp. *vainilla*, dim. of *vaina*, sheath, pod, < L. *vagina*, sheath.] Any of the tropical climbing orchids constituting the genus *Vanilla*, esp. one, as *V. planifolia*, whose pod-like fruit ('vanilla-bean') yields an extract used in flavoring food, in perfumery, etc.; the fruit or bean itself, or the extract obtained from it.—**va-nil'lic**, *a.* Pertaining to, derived from, or resembling vanilla or vanillin.—**va-nil'lin**, *n.* A white crystalline compound, the active principle of vanilla: now prepared artificially.

Flowering-Branch of Vanilla (*V. planifolia*). — *a*, the fruit.

van-ish (van'ish), *v.* [ME. *vanysshen*, by reduction < OF. *esvanir* (*esvaniss-*), E. *evanish*.] **I.** *intr.* To disappear from sight, or become invisible, esp. quickly (as, "The heavens shall *vanish* away like smoke," Isa. li. 6; "Dropping a small gilded bottle at the witch's feet, the spirit *vanished*," Louisa M. Alcott's "Little Women," i. 2); pass out of view, or go off or away (as, "The moment his visitor had *vanished*, Pierson paced up and down his study": Galsworthy's "Saint's Progress," iii. 7); also, to disappear by ceasing to exist (as, "one of those little old streets, so beautiful, that belonged to a *vanished* London," Galsworthy's "Dark Flower," ii. 9; "a *vanished* race," W. H. Hudson's "Purple Land," xiv.); pass away, as time (as, "His tale was told to *vanished* times": Eden Phillpotts's "Cherry-Stones," Singer Unknown); come to an end, or cease (as, "The pecuniary expense of getting an education would in a great measure *vanish*," Thoreau's "Walden," i.; "In this foreshadowing interval . . . all humor . . . *vanished*," H. Melville's "Moby-Dick," cxxx.); in *math.*, of a number or quantity, to become zero. **II.** *tr.* To cause to vanish or disappear. [Now rare.]—**van'ish**, *n.* In *phonetics*, the brief terminal sound with which a vowel vanishes or ends, usually differing in quality from the main sound.—**van'ish-er**, *n.*—**van'ish-ing-ly**, *adv.*—**van'ish-ing=point**, *n.* In *perspective*, that point toward which receding parallel lines tend to converge. Hence, in general, a point of disappearance.

van-i-ty (van'i-ti), *n.*; pl. *-ties* (-tiz). [OF. *vanite* (F. *vanité*), < L. *vanitas*, < *vanus*, E. *vain*.] Emptiness†; fig., vain or worthless character, want of real value, or hollowness or worthlessness (as, "sermons on the evil and *vanity* of riches": Galt's "Annals of the Parish," xxxii.); something vain or worthless (as, "Every man at his best state is altogether *vanity*," Ps. xxxix. 5; "Nor my wishes More worth than empty *vanities*," Shakspere's "Henry VIII.," ii. 3. 69); vain pleasure or show (as, "that I should renounce . . . the pomps and *vanity* of this wicked world": Book of Common Prayer, Catechism); a form of or a thing for vain pleasure or show (as, "Thus aged men, full loath and slow, The *vanities* of life forego," Scott's "Rokeby," v. 1; "Those toys . . . Riches that vex and *vanities* that tire," Pope's "To Mrs. Martha Blount," 4); also, futility or uselessness (as, "What had he done by fighting? . . . He sickened at the *vanity* of his own rage": George Eliot's "Adam Bede," xxvii.); also, falsehood or deception, or an instance of it (obs. or archaic: as, "The idols have spoken *vanity*, and the diviners have seen a lie," Zech. x. 2; "lying *vanities*," Ps. xxxi. 6); also, foolishness† or folly†; also, the quality of being personally vain; overweening pride in one's own appearance, qualities, gifts, achievements, etc. (as, girlish *vanity*; "I saw myself revered . . . by one whose judgement my *vanity* told me was not likely to err," H. Mackenzie's "Man of Feeling," xxviii.; to speak with the bitterness of wounded *vanity*); excessive admiration for one's self, together with the sense of a right to the admiration of others; conceit; an instance or display of this quality or feeling (as, "In spite of her small *vanities*, Margaret had a sweet . . . nature": Louisa M. Alcott's "Little Women," i. 2); something about which one is vain; also, a vanity-case.—**Vanity Fair**, a fair described in Bunyan's "Pilgrim's Progress," i., as established by Beelzebub, Apollyon, and others in the town of Vanity, in the path of pilgrims to the Celestial City, for the continuous display and sale of all sorts of vanities; hence, any place or scene, as the world, a great city, or the world of fashion, regarded as given over to vain pleasure or empty show.—**van'i-ty=case**, *n.* A small case fitted with a mirror, a powder-puff, etc., carried by women. Similarly, **van'i-ty=bag**, **van'i-ty=box**.

van-ner (van'ėr), *n.* [See *van¹*, *v.*] In *mining*, one who vans ore; also, an apparatus for separating ores.

van-quish (vang'kwish), *v. t.* [OF. *veincre*, *veintre* (pret. *venquis*) (F. *vaincre*), < L. *vincere* (pp. *victus*), conquer: cf. *victor*.] To conquer or defeat in battle or conflict (as, "*Vanquished* . . . in the battle of Poitiers, the Gothic monarchs lost their extensive dominions in Gaul": Hallam's "Europe during the Middle Ages," iv.); reduce to subjection by superior force; also, to defeat in any contest (as, "In arguing too, the parson own'd his skill, For e'en though *vanquish'd*, he could argue still": Goldsmith's "Deserted Village," 212); hence, in general, to overcome or overpower (as, "Sorrow and grief have *vanquish'd* all my powers": Shakspere's "2 Henry VI.," ii. 1. 183); subdue or suppress (as, "to *vanquish* lust, and wear its yoke no more": Cowper's "Expostulation," 411).—**van'quish-a-ble**, *a.* That may be vanquished.—**van'quish-er**, *n.*—**van'quish-ment**, *n.*

van-tage (vȧn'tāj), *n.* [ME. *vantage*, by reduction < OF. *avantage*, E. *advantage*.] Advantage, benefit, or profit (archaic); also, position or condition affording superiority, as for action or defense (as, "Miss Mary . . . taking fresh courage from her *vantage* of distance, asked him . . .": Bret Harte's "Idyl of Red Gulch"); opportunity likely to give superiority; vantage-ground; also, an opportunity† or chance†; in *lawn-tennis*, same as *advantage*.—**van'tage=ground**, *n.* A position which gives one an advantage, as for action or defense; favorable position: as, "No pleasure is comparable to the standing upon the *vantage ground* of truth" (Bacon's "Essays," Of Truth).

van-ward (van'wȧrd), *adv.* and *a.* [See *-ward*.] Toward or in the van or front: opposed to *rearward*.

vap-id (vap'id), *a.* [L. *vapidus*, that has lost life or spirit, flat, akin to *vapor*, E. *vapor*.] Having lost life, sharpness, or flavor, as liquors, beverages, etc. (as, "table-beer, guiltless of hops and malt, *vapid* and nauseous": Smollett's "Humphry Clinker," June 8); insipid; flat, as taste or flavor; also, without strength or vigor, as the blood; also, fig., without animation or spirit, dull, uninteresting, or tedious, as talk, writings, amusements, persons, etc. (as, "My novels seemed *vapid* stuff": Gissing's "New Grub Street," vi.).—**va-pid-i-ty** (va-pid'i-ti), **vap'id-ness**, *n.*—**vap'id-ly**, *adv.*

va-por (vā′por), *n.* [OF. *vapor*, *vapeur* (F. *vapeur*), < L. *vapor*, exhalation, steam, vapor, prob. akin to Gr. καπνός, smoke: cf. *vapid*.] A visible exhalation, as fog, mist, condensed steam coming from a tea-kettle, smoke, atomized medicinal liquid, etc.; an invisible exhalation, as of moisture, noxious gases, etc.; specif., in scientific use, a substance in the gaseous state (sometimes restricted to substances in the gaseous state when below their critical points); a gas; also, fig., something unsubstantial or transitory; also, a fantastic notion†; a foolish boast†; also, *pl.*, injurious exhalations formerly supposed to be produced within the body, esp. the stomach; a morbid condition formerly supposed to be caused by these; hypochondria, morbid low spirits, or the blues (archaic: as, "I had sent for him in a fit of the *vapours*," S. J. Weyman's "Gentleman of France," xx.).—
va′por, *v.* **I.** *intr.* To rise or pass off in the form of vapor; also, to emit vapor or exhalations; also, to talk fantastically or idly; talk grandiloquently or boastfully; bluster; also, to swagger (as, "the robbers *vapouring* about in the court below": Borrow's "Bible in Spain," xl.). **II.** *tr.* To cause to rise or pass off in or as in vapor; also, to dim or obscure with vapor; also, to declare grandiloquently or boastfully; bully or hector; also, to affect with vapors or the blues (archaic).

va-por-a-ble (vā′por-a-bl), *a.* That may be converted into vapor.

va-po-ra-ri-um (vā-pō-rā′ri-um), *n.*; pl. *-riums* or *-ria* (-ri-ä). [NL.: cf. L. *vaporarium*, steam-pipe in a bath.] An apartment or bath equipped for the application of the vapor of water to the body; a vapor-bath.

va-por=bath (vā′por-bȧth), *n.* An application of the vapor of water to the body in a close apartment or place; also, a vaporarium.

va-por-er (vā′por-ėr), *n.* One who vapors; a grandiloquent talker; a braggart; a blusterer.

va-por-es-cence (vā-po-res′ens), *n.* [See *-escence*.] A changing into vapor.—**va-por-es′cent**, *a.*

va-por-if-ic (vā-po-rif′ik), *a.* [See *-fic*.] Producing vapor, or connected with the production of vapor; also, pertaining to or of the nature of vapor.

va-por-im-e-ter (vā-po-rim′e-tėr), *n.* [See *-meter*.] An instrument for measuring the volume or the pressure of a vapor.

va-por-ing (vā′por-ing), *p. a.* That vapors; talking fantastically or grandiloquently; foolishly boastful; blustering. —**va′por-ing-ly**, *adv.*

va-por-ish (vā′por-ish), *a.* Of the nature of vapor; abounding in vapor; also, inclined to or affected by the vapors or low spirits (as, "Lady Lyndon, always *vapourish* and nervous . . . became more agitated than ever": Thackeray's "Barry Lyndon," xix.); pertaining to or connected with low spirits (as, "*vapourish* fears": S. J. Weyman's "Gentleman of France," xxviii.).

va-por-iz-a-ble (vā′por-ī-za-bl), *a.* That may be vaporized.

va-por-ize (vā′por-īz), *v. t.* or *i.*; *-ized*, *-izing*. To convert or be converted into vapor.—**va″por-i-za′tion** (-i-zā′shon), *n.* —**va′por-iz-er** (-ī-zėr), *n.* One who or that which vaporizes; a form of atomizer; a kind of carbureter.

va-por-ole (vā′por-ōl), *n.* A medicinal preparation, as a volatile drug for inhalation, inclosed in a thin glass capsule, to be broken for use. [Proprietary name.]

va-por-ous (vā′por-us), *a.* [L. *vaporosus*.] Full of or abounding in vapor; foggy or misty; dimmed or obscured with vapor; also, exhaling vapor; also, of the form or nature of vapor; hence, unsubstantial; vain or idle (as, "whosoever shall entertain . . . *vaporous* imaginations": Bacon's "Advancement of Learning," ii. 8. 3); given to fanciful or foolish ideas or discourse (as, "the mouth-piece of the debating clubs, noisy, *vaporous*, and democratic": Dana's "Two Years before the Mast," xxviii.).—**va-por-os′i-ty** (-po-ros′i-ti), **va′por-ous-ness**, *n.*—**va′por-ous-ly**, *adv.*

va-por-y (vā′por-i), *a.* Vaporous; vaporish.

va′pour, va′pour-er, va′pour-ing, va′pour-ish, va′pour-y. British preferred forms of *vapor*, etc.

vap-u-la-tion (vap-ū-lā′shon), *n.* [L. *vapulare* (pp. *vapulatus*), be flogged.] A flogging or thrashing. [Obs. or rare.] —**vap′u-la-to-ry** (-la-tō-ri), *a.*

va-que-ro (vä-kā′rō), *n.*; pl. *-ros* (-rōz, Sp. -rōs). [Sp., < *vaca*, < L. *vacca*, cow.] A herdsman or cowboy. [Spanish America and southwestern U. S.]

Va-ran-gi-an (va-ran′ji-an). [ML. *Varangus*, < MGr. Βάραγγος, through Slav. from Scand.: cf. Icel. *Væringi*, a Varangian, lit. 'confederate,' < *várar*, pl., pledge, troth.] **I.** *n.* One of the Northmen who under Rurik established a dynasty in Russia in the 9th century; also, a member of a body-guard of the Byzantine emperors, composed orig. of Northmen, later also of Anglo-Saxons. **II.** *a.* Of or pertaining to the Varangians.

var-gue-ño (vär-gā′nyō), *n.* [Sp.; said to be named from *Vargas*, village near Toledo, Spain.] An antique Spanish type of cabinet or desk, consisting of a box-shaped body mounted on columns or a stand, and having the front hinged at the lower edge so as to afford, when let down, a surface for use in writing. See cut below.

A Vaquero.

va-ri-a-ble (vā′ri-a-bl). [OF. F. *variable*, < L. *variabilis*.] **I.** *a.* Apt or liable to vary or change; changeable; specif., of a wind, tending to change in direction; also, inconstant or fickle, as a person; also, capable of being varied or changed; alterable; in *astron.*, of a star, changing in brightness; in *biol.*, deviating from the strict type, as a species or a specific character; admitting of such deviation. **II.** *n.* Something variable; specif., a shifting wind, esp. as opposed to a trade-wind; *pl.*, a region where such winds occur; *sing.*, in *astron.*, a variable star; in *math.*, a quantity or symbol which has no fixed value, and is considered with reference to its different possible values; in an expression, a quantity whose value may change while one or more other quantities remain constant.—**va″ri-a-bil′i-ty** (-bil′i-ti), **va′ri-a-ble-ness**, *n.*— **va′ri-a-bly**, *adv.*

va-ri-ance (vā′ri-ans), *n.* [OF. *variance*, < L. *variantia*, < *varians*, ppr.: see *variant*.] The state or fact of varying; change or alteration; difference, divergence, or discrepancy; a difference or discrepancy, as between two statements or documents in law which should agree; disagreement, discord, or dissension (as, "Even the virtuous fall sometimes to *variance*": Johnson's "Rasselas," xxvi.); a disagreement, dispute, or quarrel.—**at variance**, in a state of difference, discrepancy, or disagreement, as things (as, "His conduct was not a little *at variance* with his professions": Macaulay's "Hist. of Eng.," ii.); not in agreement or harmony; also, in a state of controversy, or of dissension or enmity, as persons (as, "The wisest heads . . . are irreconcilably *at variance* as to what good really means," W. D. Whitney's "Life and Growth of Language," ii.; "Danger will unite those who are *at variance*," Marryat's "King's Own," xviii.).

va-ri-ant (vā′ri-ant). [OF. F. *variant*, < L. *varians* (*variant-*), ppr. of *variare*, E. *vary*.] **I.** *a.* Varying; exhibiting diversity; characterized by variation or change; tending to change or alter; different or discrepant; being an altered or different form of something (as, a *variant* spelling of a word). **II.** *n.* A variant form; a different form or spelling of the same word (as, 'lanthorn' is an old *variant* of 'lantern'); a different reading of a passage.

Varqueño, 17th century.

va·ri·a·tion (vā-ri-ā′shǫn), *n.* [OF. F. *variation*, < L. *variatio(n-)*, < *variare*, E. *vary*.] The act or process of varying, or the resulting state; diversification; diversity or varied character; alteration or modification; change in condition, character, degree, etc.; amount or rate of change; deviation or divergence; an instance of this, or a point of difference; also, a different form of something; a variant; in *gram.*, inflection; in *music*, the repetition of a melody or theme with changes or elaborations; a varied form of a melody or theme, esp. one of a series of such forms designed to develop the capacities of the subject; in *magnetism*, etc., the declination of the magnetic needle; in *astron.*, any deviation from the mean orbit or mean motion of a heavenly body; in *biol.*, deviation, or a deviation, in the structure, character, or the like, of an organism or a number of organisms from that of others of the same species or group, or that of the parents, esp. as a result of natural selection; an organism exhibiting such deviation.—**va·ri·a′tion·al**, *a.*

var·i·cat·ed (var′i-kā-ted), *a.* In *conch.*, having varices, as a shell.—**var·i·ca′tion** (-kā′shǫn), *n.*

var·i·cel·la (var-i-sel′ä), *n.* [NL., dim. of ML. *variola*, smallpox: see *variola*.] In *pathol.*, chicken-pox.—**var·i·cel′lar** (-sel′är), *a.*

var·i·cel·late (var-i-sel′āt), *a.* [Dim. form < *varix*.] In *conch.*, having small varices, as certain shells.

var·i·cel·loid (var-i-sel′oid), *a.* [See *-oid*.] Resembling varicella: as, *varicelloid* smallpox (varioloid).

var·i·ces (var′i-sēz), *n.* Plural of *varix*.

var·i·co·cele (var′i-kǫ-sēl), *n.* [L. *varix* (*varic-*), varix, + Gr. κήλη, tumor.] In *pathol.*, a varicose condition of the veins of the scrotum or related parts.

var·i·col·ored (vā′ri-kul-ǫrd), *a.* [L. *varius*, various, + *color*, color.] Having various colors; variegated in color; motley.

var·i·cose (var′i-kōs), *a.* [L. *varicosus*, < *varix* (*varic-*), varix.] Abnormally dilated, as a vein or a lymphatic; pertaining to, affected with, or designed to remedy varices or varicose veins, which often affect the superficial portions of the lower limbs.—**var′i·cosed** (-kōst), *a.* Having become varicose.—**var′i·cose-ness**, *n.*

var·i·co·sis (var-i-kō′sis), *n.* [NL., < L. *varix* (*varic-*), varix.] In *pathol.*, the formation of varices; varicosity.

var·i·cos·i·ty (var-i-kos′i-ti), *n.*; pl. *-ties* (-tiz). In *pathol.*, the state or condition of being varicose; also, a varix.

var·i·cot·o·my (var-i-kot′ǫ-mi), *n.* [L. *varix* (*varic-*), varix: see *-tomy*.] In *surg.*, excision of a varicose vein.

va·ried (vā′rid), *p. a.* Made various; diversified, or characterized by variety (as, a *varied* assortment; "The assembly was large and *varied*, containing clergy and laity, men and women," Wiseman's "Fabiola," i. 10); variegated, as in color, as an animal; differing one from another (as, the *varied* interests of a busy man); also, changed or altered (as, a *varied* form of a word).—**va′ried·ly**, *adv.*—**va′ried-ness**, *n.*

va·ri·e·gate (vā′ri-ę-gāt), *v. t.*; *-gated, -gating.* [L. *variegatus*, pp. of *variegare*, < *varius*, various, + *agere*, drive, do.] To give variety to; diversify; esp., to render varied in appearance; mark with different colors, tints, etc.—**va′ri·e·gat·ed** (-gā-ted), *p. a.* Varied; diversified; diverse; esp., varied in appearance or color (as, "a singularly *variegated* landscape": Mrs. Shelley's "Frankenstein," xviii.); marked with patches or spots of different colors.—**va′ri·e·ga′tion** (-gā′shǫn), *n.* The act of variegating, or the state of being variegated; varied coloration.—**va′ri·e·ga·tor**, *n.*

va·ri·er (vā′ri-er), *n.* One who varies.

va·ri·e·tal (vǫ-rī′ę-tǫl), *a.* Of, pertaining to, or characteristic of a variety; constituting a variety.—**va·ri′e·tal·ly**, *adv.*

va·ri·e·ty (vǫ-rī′ę-ti), *n.*; pl. *-ties* (-tiz). [F. *variété* < L. *varietas*, < *varius*, E. *various*.] The state or character of being various or varied; diversity, or absence of uniformity or monotony (as, "*Variety*'s the very spice of life": Cowper's "Task," ii. 606); intermixture of things of different kinds; also, sometimes, difference or discrepancy; also, change† or alteration†; fickleness†; also, a number of things of different kinds (as, "He proceeded to enact a *variety* of laws for the regulation of the barbarous people": G. P. R. James's "Hist. of Charlemagne," v.); a varied assortment of something; also, a different form, condition, or phase of something (as, "He had passed through all *varieties* of fortune,"

Macaulay's "Hist. of Eng.," ii.; "I pictured to myself punishment and humiliation in every *variety* of form," Irving's "Tales of a Traveler," ii. 7); a kind or sort; in *biol.*, a subdivision of a species; a kind of animal or plant which differs, or collectively those individuals which differ, from the rest of its or their species, in certain particulars which are transmissible and fairly constant, yet not distinctive enough to form a new species; a form of plant originating under cultivation ('cultural variety'); a group or race of animals produced by artificial selection; in *theatrical use*, entertainment of a mixed character, consisting of a number of individual performances or 'acts,' as of singing, dancing, acrobatic exhibitions, playlets, etc. (often used attributively, as in 'variety show,' 'variety theater,' and 'variety actor': cf. *vaudeville*).

va·ri·form (vā′ri-fôrm), *a.* [L. *varius*, various, + *forma*, form.] Varied in form; having various forms.

va·ri·o·coup·ler (vā′ri-ǫ-kup″lėr), *n.* [L. *variare*, to vary, + E. *coupler*.] In *wireless teleg.* and *teleph.*, a kind of transformer for coupling one circuit to another, consisting typically of a primary coil within which a secondary coil can be rotated to vary the inductive relation.

va·ri·o·la (vǫ-rī′ǫ-lä), *n.* [ML., < L. *varius*, variegated (spotted), E. *various*.] In *pathol.*, smallpox.—**va·ri′o·lar** (-lär), *a.* Of or pertaining to variola or smallpox.

va·ri·o·late (vā′ri-ǫ-lāt), *v. t.*; *-lated, -lating.* [From *variola*.] To inoculate with the virus of variola or smallpox.—**va″ri·o·la′tion** (-lā′shǫn), *n.*

va·ri·ole (vā′ri-ōl), *n.* [ML. *variola*: see *variola*.] A shallow pit or depression like the mark left by a smallpox pustule; a foveola; in *petrog.*, one of the spherules of variolite.

va·ri·o·lite (vā′ri-ǫ-līt), *n.* [ML. *variola*, smallpox; from the appearance.] In *petrog.*, any of certain basic igneous rocks containing embedded light-colored spherules, which, esp. on weathered surfaces, give them a pock-marked appearance.—**va″ri·o·lit′ic** (-lit′ik), *a.*

va·ri·o·loid (vā′ri-ǫ-loid), *a.* [See *-oid*.] In *pathol.*: **I.** *a.* Resembling variola or smallpox; also, pertaining to varioloid. **II.** *n.* A modified mild form of smallpox, esp. as occurring in persons who have been vaccinated or who have previously had smallpox.

va·ri·o·lous (vǫ-rī′ǫ-lus), *a.* Of or pertaining to variola or smallpox; affected with smallpox; also, having pits like those left by smallpox.

va·ri·om·e·ter (vā-ri-om′e-tėr), *n.* [L. *varius*, various (in second sense, L. *variare*, to vary), + E. *-meter*.] In *elect.*, an instrument for comparing the intensity of magnetic forces, esp. the magnetic force of the earth at different points; in *wireless teleg.* and *teleph.*, an instrument for varying inductance, consisting of a fixed coil and a movable coil connected in series (used as a tuning device).

va·ri·o·rum (vā-ri-ō′rum). [L. (gen. pl. of *varius*, E. *various*), as in *editio cum notis variorum*, edition with notes of various persons.] **I.** *n.*; pl. *-rums*. An edition, esp. of the complete works of an author, in which the notes of various commentators or editors are inserted. **II.** *a.* Of the nature of a variorum (as, a *variorum* edition of Shakspere); pertaining to a variorum; also, obtained from various sources or books.

va·ri·ous (vā′ri-us), *a.* [L. *varius*, diverse, manifold, variegated, various, varying, changeable.] Differing in different parts, or presenting different aspects (as, "A *various* scene the clansmen made, Some sate, some stood, some slowly stray'd," Scott's "Lady of the Lake," iii. 31; "A prospect wide And *various*," Milton's "Paradise Lost," v. 89); exhibiting or possessing different characters or qualities, or varied in nature or character (as, "to show the *various* worth of Catherine Lloyd": Crabbe's "Parish Register," iii.); in general, exhibiting, or marked by, variety or diversity (as, "the completest and most *various* knowledge," G. W. Curtis's "Prue and I," iii.; "A *various* host they came," Scott's "Vision of Don Roderick," lvii.); sometimes, varied in color, or variegated (chiefly poetic: as, "birds of *various* plumage," Longfellow's "Hiawatha," xii. 186); sometimes, versatile or many-sided (obs. or rare: as, "A man so *various*, that he seem'd to be Not one, but all mankind's epitome," Dryden's "Absalom and Achitophel," i. 545); giving attention to many different subjects (as, a *various* reader); also, differing one from another, or being of different kinds, as two or more things (as, "His *various* accomplishments had made him . . . agreeable to his master": Macaulay's "Hist. of Eng.," ii.); hence, divers, several, or many (as, "He heard of the Major's fame from *various* members of his society," Thackeray's "Vanity Fair," lxi.; "in *various* parts of the United States," A. R. Wallace's "Darwinism," ii.); also, exhibiting or undergoing change or alteration† (as, "The servile suitors watch her *various* face, She smiles preferment, or she frowns disgrace," Sheridan's "Rivals," Epilogue; "So *various* is the fate of a people's idol: to-day he is worshipped as a god, to-morrow cast into the fire!" Jane Porter's "Scottish Chiefs," lxxix.); inconstant or fickle, as persons†. **—va′ri-ous-ly**, *adv.* **—va′ri-ous-ness**, *n.*

va-rix (vā′riks), *n.*; pl. *varices* (var′i-sēz). [L., a dilated vein, varix.] In *pathol.*, an abnormal dilatation of a vein (or other vessel of the body), usually accompanied by tortuous development; a varicose vein; in *conch.*, a mark or scar on the surface of a shell denoting a former position of the lip of the aperture.

var-let (vär′let), *n.* [OF. *varlet*, var. of *vallet*, E. *valet*.] A man-servant, valet, or attendant (archaic); specif., an attendant or page attached to a knight (now only hist.); also, a low fellow, a knave, or a rascal (archaic: as, "The king marvellously stormed at the matter, calling Gostwick openly *varlet*," Strype's "Memorials of Cranmer," i. 28).—

var′let-ry (-ri), *n.* Varlets collectively; a number of attendants; the mob or rabble. [Archaic.]

var-mint (vär′mint), *n.* [Var. of *vermin*.] Vermin (prov.); also (prov. or colloq.), a noxious or objectionable animal; an objectionable or troublesome person; a mischievous child.

var-nish (vär′nish), *n.* [OF. *vernis*, *verniz* (F. *vernis*); origin unknown.] A preparation which consists of resinous matter (as copal, lac, etc.) dissolved in an oil ('oil-varnish') or in alcohol ('spirit-varnish') or other volatile liquid, and which when applied to the surface of wood, metal, etc., dries and leaves a hard, more or less glossy, usually transparent coating; in common use, an oil-varnish as distinguished from shellac-varnish (see *shellac*); the sap of certain trees, used for the same purpose ('natural varnish'); any of various other preparations similarly used, as one having india-rubber, pyroxylin, or asphalt for the chief constituent; a coating or surface of varnish; a thin glaze on pottery; also, something resembling a coating of varnish; a gloss; fig., superficial embellishment; a merely external show, or a veneer (as, "in whose demeanour the untamed ferocity of the Scythian might be discerned through a thin *varnish* of French politeness": Macaulay's "Essays," Madame D'Arblay); specious show, or pretense.**—var′nish**, *v. t.* [OF. *vernissier* (F. *vernisser*).] To lay varnish on; hence, to invest with a glossy appearance; fig., to give an improved appearance to; embellish; adorn; also, to cover with a specious or deceptive appearance; gloss over or palliate (as, "Cato's voice was ne'er employed To clear the guilty, and to *varnish* crimes": Addison's "Cato," ii. 2).**—var′nish-er**, *n.*—**var′nish-ing-day**, *n.* A day before the opening of an exhibition of pictures, on which exhibitors have the privilege of retouching and varnishing their pictures already hung.**—var′nish-tree**, *n.* Any of various trees yielding sap or other substance used for varnish, as *Rhus vernicifera* of Japan (see *lacquer*).

var-si-ty (vär′si-ti), *n.* Colloquial reduction of *university*: esp. used with reference to sports.

va-rus (vā′rus), *n.* [L., knock-kneed.] In *pathol.*, a form of clubfoot in which the foot is turned inward. Cf. *valgus.*

va-ry (vā′ri), *v.*; -ried, -rying. [OF. F. *varier*, < L. *variare*, diversify, variegate, change, < *varius*, E. *various*.] **I.** *tr.* To diversify (something); relieve from uniformity or monotony (as, "There were fine open pastures, *varied* by sandy pine barrens": Roosevelt's "Winning of the West," i. 3); also, to cause to be different, one from another; also, to change or alter, as in form, appearance, character, substance, degree, etc.; alter somewhat, or modify; also, to express in different words† (as, "The man hath no wit that cannot . . . *vary* deserved praise on my palfrey": Shakspere's "Henry V.," iii. 7. 35); in *music*, to alter (a melody or theme) by modifications or embellishments, without changing its identity. **II.** *intr.* To be different, or show diversity, in different parts,

specimens, etc., as a thing (as, "The country *varies* in soil and climate," Irving's "Captain Bonneville," xxii.; the color of the ore *varies*); also, to be different, or exhibit divergence, as two or more things, or as one thing from another or others (as, the stars *vary* in brightness; one specimen *varies* from the others); differ; also, to differ in opinion†, or disagree†; also, to undergo change in form, appearance, character, substance, degree, etc. (as, "La Motte's complexion *varied* to every sentence of his speech," Mrs. Radcliffe's "Romance of the Forest," vi.; "animals . . . exposed to a constantly *varying* amount of light and colour," A. R. Wallace's "Darwinism," viii.); become different; undergo a partial change, or be modified; sometimes, to change in succession, follow alternately, or alternate (as, "While fear and anger, with alternate grace, Pant in her breast, and *vary* in her face": Addison's "Cato," iii. 7); also, to make a change, or diverge or depart, as from a rule, practice, or former procedure; in *math.*, to be subject to a continual increase or decrease; change in value according to some law; in *biol.*, to exhibit variation.**—va′ry**†, *n.* Variation.**—va′ry-ing-ly**, *adv.*

vas (vas), *n.*; pl. *vasa* (vā′sä). [L., vessel: cf. *vase*.] In *anat.*, *zoöl.*, and *bot.*, a vessel or duct.**—vas deferens** (def′e-renz); pl. *vasa deferentia* (-ren′shi-ä). [L. *deferens*, ppr., carrying down, E. *deferent*.] In *anat.* and *zoöl.*, the excretory duct of a testicle.**—va-sal** (vā′sal), *a.* Pertaining to a vas, vessel, or duct.

vas-cu-lar (vas′kū-lär), *a.* [L. *vasculum*: see *vasculum*.] In *anat.* and *zoöl.*, pertaining to, composed of, or provided with vessels which convey fluids, as blood or lymph; in *bot.*, pertaining to, composed of, or provided with vessels or ducts which convey fluids, as sap (as, a *vascular* bundle, see *bundle*, *n.*; *vascular* tissue; *vascular* plants, the spermatophytes and the pteridophytes, which contain more or less clearly defined vessels or ducts; *vascular* cryptogams, the pteridophytes).— **vas-cu-lar′i-ty** (-lar′i-ti), *n.*—**vas′cu-lar-ly**, *adv.*

vas-cu-lum (vas′kū-lum), *n.*; pl. *-lums*, L. *-la* (-lä). [L., dim. of *vas*, vessel: cf. *vas*.] A small vessel; a vas; an ascidium; also, a kind of case or box used by botanists for carrying specimens as they are collected.

vase (vās or vāz, F. and Brit. väz), *n.* [F. *vase*, < L. *vas*, vessel: cf. *vas*.] A hollow vessel, generally high in proportion to its horizontal diameter, and now usually decorative in character and purpose; also, some vase-like object, as a calyx of a flower; in *arch.*, the body of the Corinthian or the Composite capital.—**Portland vase**, a famous glass vase or urn of dark blue with cameo-like reliefs in opaque white, found in an ancient Roman tomb, later in the possession of the ducal family of Portland in England, and now in the British Museum. Also called *Barberini vase.*

The Portland Vase. — From photograph of a replica by Wedgwood.

vas-ec-to-my (vas-ek′tō-mi), *n.* [L. *vas*, vessel, + Gr. ἐκ, out of, + -τομία, < τέμνειν, cut.] In *surg.*, excision of the vas deferens, or of a portion of it.

vas-e-line (vas′e-lēn or -lin), *n.* [Irreg. < G. *wasser*, water, + Gr. ἔλαιον, oil.] A translucent, yellow or whitish, semisolid petroleum product (a form of petrolatum) used as a remedial ointment and internal remedy, and in various preparations for medicinal and other purposes. [Proprietary name, registered as a trade-mark.]

vaso-. Form of L. *vas*, vessel, used in combination.**—vas-o-con-stric-tor** (vas″ō-kon-strik′tor), *a.* Serving, when stimulated, to constrict blood-vessels, as certain nerves.—**vas″o-di-la′tor** (-di-lā′tor or -dī-), *a.* Serving, when stimulated, to dilate or relax blood-vessels, as certain nerves.

fat, fāte, fär, fall, åsk, fāre; net, mē, hėr; pin, pīne; not, nōte, mȯve, nȯr; up, lūte, pull; oi, oil; ou, out; (lightened) aviǥry, ēlect, agǫny, intǫ, ūnite; (obscured) errǎnt, operǎ, ardęnt, actǫr, natūre; ch, chip; g, go; th, thin; ᴛʜ, then; y, you;

—**vas-o-mo′tor** (-mō′tor), *a.* Serving to regulate the tension of blood-vessels, as certain nerves.

vas-sal (vas′al). [OF. F. *vassal*, < ML. *vassallus*, < *vassus*, servant, retainer, vassal; from Celtic.] **I.** *n.* In the feudal system, a person holding lands by the obligation to render military service or its equivalent to his superior (as, a great *vassal*, a vassal holding directly from the sovereign; a rear *vassal*, a vassal holding from a higher vassal); a feudatory tenant; hence, a person holding some similar relation to a superior; a subject, follower, or retainer; a servant or slave (lit. or fig.; as, "I was now her Majesty's most humble creature and *vassal*," Swift's "Gulliver's Travels," ii. 3; *vassals* of love); sometimes, in contempt, an abject or base person (archaic). **II.** *a.* Being a vassal or in vassalage; pertaining to or characteristic of a vassal.—**vas′sal-age** (-aj), *n.* The state of being a vassal; the status of a vassal; homage or service due from a vassal to his superior; hence, dependence, subjection, or servitude; also, a territory held by a vassal; also, a body of vassals (as, "What use of the mountains of beef . . . if there is a hungry heart among our *vassalage?*" Scott's "Castle Dangerous," i.); also, conduct befitting a vassal, valorous service, or prowess (obs. or archaic).—**vas′sal-ize**, *v. t.*; *-ized*, *-izing.* To make a vassal or vassals of.—**vas′sal-ry** (-ri), *n.* A body of vassals.

vast (vást). [L. *vastus*, empty, unoccupied, waste, immense, vast.] **I.** *a.* Of very great extent or area, very extensive, or immense (as, a *vast* territory; "a *vast* sheet of water," Bret Harte's "How Santa Claus Came to Simpson's Bar"; "All the land was shrouded in one *vast* forest," Roosevelt's "Winning of the West," i. 5); of very great size or proportions, huge, or enormous (as, "Of creatures, how few *vast* as the whale!" H. Melville's "Moby-Dick," lxviii.; "the *vaster* icebergs of the Northern seas," Tyndall's "Forms of Water," § 50); very great, as extent, area, size, proportions, etc.; fig., of very great range or scope, or on a very large scale (as, "Reforming schemes are none of mine; To mend the world's a *vast* design," M. Green's "The Spleen"; a *vast* enterprise; *vast* powers); also, very great in number, quantity, or amount, or as number, quantity, etc. (as, a *vast* army; a *vast* sum; a *vast* stock of information; "I have a *vast* deal to say," Miss Burney's "Evelina," xi.); sometimes, of very great length or duration (as, "It seemed a *vast* time to Bealby": H. G. Wells's "Bealby," vii.); also, very great in degree, intensity, etc. (as, in *vast* haste; *vast* importance; *vast* satisfaction; "There was a *vast* contempt in his gaze," W. Churchill's "Coniston," ii. 15). **II.** *n.* A vast expanse or space (lit. or fig., and chiefly poetic: as, "through the *vast* of heaven," Milton's "Paradise Lost," vi. 203; "across the *vast* of time," Gissing's "Private Papers of Henry Ryecroft," ii. 27); also, a vast number or amount (Sc. and prov. Eng.: as, "They have heard a *vast* of words," Stevenson's "Master of Ballantrae," xi.; "The waters went forth . . . causing a *vast* of damage," Galt's "Annals of the Parish," xxxvii.).—**vas-ti-tude** (vás′ti-tūd), *n.* [L. *vastitudo*.] The state of being vast; vastness or immensity; vast extent or size; also, a vast expanse or space.—**vast′ly**, *adv.* To a vast extent or degree; immensely; very greatly; exceedingly.—**vast′ness**, *n.*—**vast′y**, *a.* Vast; immense: as, "the *vasty* deep" (Shakspere's "1 Henry IV.," iii. 1. 52). [Archaic.]

vat (vat), *n.* [Var. of *fat*².] A cask, tub, cistern, or other large vessel for holding liquids, esp. liquors in an immature state or liquid preparations used in dyeing, tanning, etc.—**vat**, *v. t.*; *vatted*, *vatting.* To put into or treat in a vat.—**vat′ful** (-fùl), *n.*; pl. *-fuls.* The quantity that a vat will hold.

vat-ic (vat′ik), *a.* [L. *vates*, prophet.] Prophetic.

Vat-i-can (vat′i-kan). [L. *Vaticanus*.] **I.** *a.* Noting or pertaining to a hill in Rome situated on the western bank of the Tiber; also, of or pertaining to the Vatican, or palace of the popes (as, the *Vatican* Council, an ecumenical council of the Church of Rome, held at the Vatican during 1869 and 1870, which promulgated the dogma of papal infallibility). **II.** *n.* The Vatican Hill; also, the palace of the popes, a mass of buildings of vast extent and containing a library, museums of art, etc., of the highest importance, built upon this hill, immediately to the north of the Church of St. Peter; hence, the papal power or government, as distinguished from the Quirinal (representing the Italian royal court or government).—**Vat′i-can-ism**, *n.* The theological and ecclesiastical system based on the dogma of absolute papal infallibility or supremacy as promulgated by the Vatican Council; ultramontanism.—**Vat′i-can-ist**, *n.*

vat-i-cide (vat′i-sīd), *n.* [L. *vates*, prophet: see *-cide*.] The slayer of a prophet; also, the slaying of a prophet.

va-ti-ci-nal (va-tis′i-nal), *a.* [L. *vaticinus*, < *vates*, prophet.] Prophetic.

va-ti-ci-nate (va-tis′i-nāt), *v. i.* or *t.*; *-nated*, *-nating.* [L. *vaticinatus*, pp. of *vaticinari*, < *vates*, prophet.] To prophesy.—**va-ti-ci-na′tion** (-nā′shon), *n.* Prophesying; also, a prophecy (as, "The minstrel proceeded with his explanation of the dubious and imperfect *vaticinations*": Scott's "Castle Dangerous," xviii.).—**va-ti′ci-na-tor**, *n.*

vaude-ville (vâd′vil or vōd′-, F. vōd-vēl), *n.* [F. *vaudeville*, orig. a kind of song, for *chanson du vau de Vire*, 'song of the valley of Vire' (in Normandy).] A light, gay song, frequently embodying satire; a topical song; also, a theatrical piece of light or amusing character, interspersed with songs and dances; now, usually, theatrical entertainment consisting of a number of individual performances, 'acts,' or numbers of mixed character, as of singing, dancing, gymnastic exhibitions, short dramatic sketches, moving pictures, etc. (often used attributively, as in 'vaudeville performance' and 'vaudeville sketch': a more recent and more polite term than *variety*, as if implying a somewhat higher grade of entertainment).

Vau-dois (vō-dwo′), *n. pl.* [F.] The Waldenses.

vault¹ (vâlt), *v.* [OF. *volter*, turn, leap, < It. *voltare*, turn, < L. *volutare*, freq. of *volvere*, roll, turn: cf. *revolt*.] **I.** *intr.* To leap or spring, as to or from a position or over something; esp., to leap with the aid of the hands supported on something, sometimes on a pole: as, to *vault* into the saddle; to *vault* over a fence or a bar (cf. *pole-vault*). **II.** *tr.* To vault over: as, "Georgie immediately *vaulted* the fence" (Tarkington's "Magnificent Ambersons," ii.).—**vault**¹, *n.* The act or an act of vaulting.

vault² (vâlt), *n.* [OF. *volte*, *voute* (F. *voûte*), < ML. *volta*, < L. *volvere* (pp. *volutus*), roll, turn: cf. *volute*.] An arched structure, commonly made of stones or bricks, usually forming a ceiling or roof; something resembling an arched roof (as, the *vault* of heaven); also, an arched space, chamber, or

Vaults. — 1, barrel-vault; 2, intersecting vault; 3, domed vault; 4, stilted vault.

passage, esp. underground (as, "long and spacious *vaults* which had been constructed for the purpose of common sewers": Gibbon's "Decline and Fall of the Roman Empire," xxxix.); an underground chamber, as a cellar or a division of a cellar (as, "He went into the inner *vault* where he kept his choicest wines": S. Butler's "Way of All Flesh," xvii.); a chamber or structure, usually wholly or partly underground, for receiving the bodies of the dead (as, "He will lie in the churchyard of his village — not in the family *vault*": G. Meredith's "Diana of the Crossways," xx.); any room specially constructed (as with steel) for the safe-keeping of things; also, a cavern or natural cavity, as in the earth, a glacier, etc. (as, "A river . . . rushes from a *vault* at the extremity of the Görner glacier": Tyndall's "Forms of Water," § 52); in *anat.*, an arched roof of a cavity.—**vault**², *v. t.* [OF. *volter*, *vouter* (F. *voûter*).] To construct or cover with a vault; also, to make in the form of a vault; arch; also, to set or extend like a vault (as, "Hateful is the dark-blue sky, *Vaulted* o'er the dark-blue sea": Tennyson's "Choric Song," iv.).—**vault′ed**, *p. a.* Constructed or covered with a vault, as a building, chamber, or passage; also, made in or having the form of a vault, as a roof; arched; also, provided with a vault or vaults, as below the surface of the ground.

vault-er (vâl′tèr), *n.* One who or that which vaults or leaps.

vault-ing (vâl'ting), *n.* The act or process of constructing vaults; also, the structure forming a vault or vaults; a vault, vaulted ceiling, or the like, or such structures collectively.

vault-y (vâl'ti), *a.* Like a vault; vaulted; arched.

vaunt (vânt or vänt), *v.* [OF. F. *vanter*, < ML. *vanitare*, < L. *vanus*, E. *vain.*] **I.** *intr.* To talk vaingloriously or boastfully; boast; brag. [Archaic or literary.] **II.** *tr.* To speak vaingloriously or boastfully of (as, "while Mr. Pleydell was thus *vaunting* his knowledge of his profession":Scott's "Guy Mannering," xxxix.); glorify or magnify (one's self: as, "Charity *vaunteth* not itself," 1 Cor. xiii. 4); boast of (one's self) as

Vaulting. — Cathedral of Notre Dame, Paris.

being (as, "a man who could never sufficiently *vaunt* himself a self-made man," Dickens's "Hard Times," i. 4; "He had always *vaunted* himself quite implacable," Stevenson's "Master of Ballantrae," i.); also, to declare boastfully (with a clause as object: as, "She *vaunted* . . . The very train of her worst wearing gown Was better worth than all my father's lands," Shakspere's "2 Henry VI.," i. 3. 87). [Archaic or literary.]—**vaunt,** *n.* Vainglorious or boastful utterance; a boastful assertion, or boast (as, "Cortés, with a politic *vaunt*, assured him 'the Spaniards were never weary' ": Prescott's "Conquest of Mexico," iv. 2); also, a subject or occasion of boasting. [Archaic or literary.]—**vaunt'er,** *n.*

vaunt=cou-ri-er (vânt'kö'ri-ėr), *n.* Same as *avant-courier.* [Archaic.]

vaunt-ing (vân'ting or vän'ting), *p. a.* That vaunts; boasting; bragging; boastful.—**vaunt'ing-ly,** *adv.*

vav-a-sor, vav-a-sour (vav'a-sọr, -sör), *n.* [OF. *vavassor, vavassour* (F. *vavasseur*), perhaps < ML. *vassi vassorum,* 'vassals of vassals': see *vassal.*] In the feudal system, a vassal, or feudal tenant, holding of a great lord (but not of the sovereign), and having other vassals holding of him (as, "*Vavasours* sub-divide again to vassals": Motley's "Dutch Republic," Introd., vi.); in general, a vassal.

Ve-a-dar (vē'a-där), *n.* [Heb., 'second Adar.'] In the Jewish calendar, an intercalary month of 29 days inserted, when required, after Adar.

veal (vēl), *n.* [OF. *veel* (F. *veau*), calf, < L. *vitellus*, dim. of *vitulus*, calf: cf. *vellum* and *wether.*] A calf, esp. as intended or used for food (now rare); also, the flesh of the calf as used for food.—**bob veal.** See *bob*[1], *n.*—**veal'y,** *a.* Like or suggesting veal; having the appearance of veal; immature.

vec-tor (vek'tọr), *n.* [L., carrier, also rider, traveler, < *vehere*: see *vehicle.*] In *math.*, a quantity which, being added to any point of space, gives as the sum that point which is at a certain distance in a certain direction from the first point; a quantity having direction as well as magnitude; also, a radius vector (see under *radius*).

Ve-da (vā'dä or vē'-), *n.* [Skt. *veda*, lit. 'knowledge,' < *vid-*, know: see *wit, v.*] In *Sanskrit lit.*, the sacred scripture of the ancient Hindus, dating in part possibly from before 1500 B.C., and comprising many books, divided into four collections, namely, the *Rig-Veda* or hymns (the oldest and most important collection), the *Sama-Veda* or chants, the *Yajur-Veda* or sacred formulas, and the *Atharva-Veda*, a collection

of later hymns, etc.; also, any of these books, or any of the four collections of them.

Ve-dan-ta (vā-dän'tä or vẹ-dan'-), *n.* [Skt. *vēdānta*, < *veda*, knowledge, Veda, + *anta*, end.] A system of philosophy among the Hindus, founded on the Vedas, and concerned chiefly in the investigation of the Supreme Spirit and the relation in which the universe, and especially the human soul, stands to it.—**Ve-dan'tic,** *a.*—**Ve-dan'tism,** *n.* The doctrines or system of the Vedanta.—**Ve-dan'tist,** *n.*

ve-dette (vẹ-det'), *n.* [F. *vedette*, < It. *vedetta*, < *vedere*, < L. *videre*, see.] A mounted sentry stationed in advance of the outposts of an army; also, a small naval vessel used for scouting ('vedette boat').

Ve-dic (vā'dik or vē'-). **I.** *a.* Of or pertaining to the Veda or the Vedas. **II.** *n.* Vedic Sanskrit, the earliest form of the language preserved.

veer[1] (vēr), *v. t.* [D. *vieren*, let out (a cable, etc.).] *Naut.*, to allow to run out to a greater extent, as a sheet, line, or cable; pay out: usually with *out*: as, "We rode with two anchors ahead, and the cables *veered* out to the better end" (Defoe's "Robinson Crusoe," i. 1).

veer[2] (vēr), *v.* [F. *virer*, turn; origin uncertain: cf. *environ*.] **I.** *intr.* To turn or shift to another direction, or point of the compass, as the wind or anything moving with the wind (as, "the wind *veering* round to the south," W. H. Hudson's "Purple Land," xxix.; a weather-vane *veers* about with the wind); hence, in general, to change direction, or turn about or aside (as, "My dromedary *veered* rather suddenly from her onward course": Kinglake's "Eothen," xxi.); fig., to turn, shift, change, or vary (as, "The talk *veered* into mere profane politics," Arnold Bennett's "Hilda Lessways," ii. 5; "Her ever-*veering* fancy turn'd To Pelleas," Tennyson's "Pelleas and Ettarre," 483); *naut.*, of the wind, to change direction by moving round the points of the compass in the usual manner (as, the wind *veers* in the north temperate regions when it moves clockwise, as from east through south to west: cf. *back*[2], *v. i.*); of a ship, to turn round with the head away from the wind; wear; of the seamen, to cause a ship to do this. **II.** *tr.* To change the direction or course of; turn; shift; *naut.*, to cause (a ship) to veer; wear.—**veer**[2], *n.* An act of veering; a change of direction. Also fig.—**veer'ing-ly,** *adv.*

veer-y (vēr'i), *n.*; pl. *-ies* (-iz). [Perhaps imit.] A thrush, *Turdus* (or *Hylocichla*) *fuscescens*, common in the eastern U. S., of retiring habits and noted for its song.

veg-e-ta-ble (vej'ẹ-ta-bl), *a.* [OF. *vegetable* (F. *végétable*), vegetable, < LL. *vegetabilis*, animating, enlivening, < L. *vegetare*: see *vegetate.*] Having life such as a plant has; also, of the nature of a plant, or consisting of or comprising

Veery.

plants (as, a *vegetable* organism; "one of the *vegetable* wonders of the island, a gigantic oak," Macaulay's "Hist. of Eng.," viii.; the *vegetable* kingdom); pertaining to or characteristic of plants (as, *vegetable* life, growth, or processes); derived from plants or some part of plants (as, *vegetable* fiber; *vegetable* oils; *vegetable* acids, drugs, or poisons); consisting of or containing the substance or remains of plants (as, decomposing *vegetable* matter; *vegetable* mold or soil); also, of, consisting of, or made from edible vegetables (as, a *vegetable* diet; a *vegetable* dinner; "good, steaming *vegetable* curry," Kipling's "Kim," i.).—**vegetable butter,** any of various concrete fixed vegetable oils which are solid at ordinary temperatures.—**vegetable ivory.** See *ivory*.—**vegetable lamb.** Same as *Scythian lamb* (rhizome of fern).—**vegetable marrow,** a kind of gourd or squash of oblong form, the fruit of a variety of *Cucurbita pepo*, used as a vegetable, esp. in England; also, the avocado, or alligator-pear.—**vegetable sponge.** See *sponge, n.*—**vegetable tallow,** any of several tallow-like substances of vegetable origin, used in making candles, soap, etc., and as lubricants.—**vegetable wax,** a wax or wax-like substance obtained from various plants, as the wax-palm.—**veg′e-ta-ble,** *n.* Any member of the vegetable kingdom; a plant; esp., a plant whose fruit, shoots or stems, leaves, roots, or other parts are used for food, as the tomato, cucumber, asparagus, spinach, cabbage, beet, potato, and onion; the edible part of such a plant, as the fruit of the tomato or the tuber of the potato (vegetables, as used in the substantial part of a meal, being commonly distinguished from fruits such as are used for dessert or light refreshment).

veg-e-tal (vej′ē̱-tạl), *a.* [F. *végétal,* < L. *vegetus,* lively, vigorous: see *vegetate.*] Characterized by or pertaining to the series of vital phenomena common to plants and animals, as nutrition, growth, circulation, respiration, etc. (esp. as distinguished from sensation and volition, which are peculiar to animals); also, pertaining to or of the nature of plants or vegetables; vegetable.—**veg-e-tal′i-ty** (-tal′i-ti), *n.*

veg-e-ta-ri-an (vej-ē̱-tā′ri-ạn). [From *veget(able)* + *-arian.*] **I.** *a.* Of or pertaining to the practice or principle of living solely or chiefly on vegetable food; devoted to or advocating this practice; also, consisting of vegetables. **II.** *n.* One who lives solely or chiefly on vegetable food (as, "The flesh of animals . . . was often poisonous, so that practically people were forced . . . to become *vegetarians*": S. Butler's "Erewhon," xxvi.); also, one who on principle lives on vegetable food (refusing meat, etc.), or maintains that vegetables and farinaceous substances constitute the only proper food for man (as, "The Militant *Vegetarians!* . . . Won't obey the law so long as the Government serves out meat": Chesterton's "Magic," ii.).—**veg-e-ta′ri-an-ism,** *n.*

veg-e-tate (vej′ē̱-tāt), *v. i.* *-tated, -tating.* [L. *vegetatus,* pp. of *vegetare,* animate, enliven, quicken, < *vegetus,* lively, active, < *vegere,* move, excite, quicken: cf. *vigor.*] To fulfil vegetable functions; grow in the manner of plants; increase as if by vegetable growth; also, fig., to live like vegetables, in an inactive, passive, or unthinking way (as, "The vast empire of China . . . has *vegetated* through a succession of drowsy ages," Irving's "Knickerbocker's New York," vii. 6; "Unheeding, century after century, the old monks have *vegetated* there," H. Kingsley's "Geoffry Hamlyn," viii.); have a mere physical existence, without mental activities or aspirations; often, to lead a quiet or dull life in some retired place (as, "A man might do worse than settle down to *vegetate* at Porlock for the rest of his life": Whyte-Melville's "Katerfelto," xiv.); in *pathol.,* to grow, or increase by growth, as an excrescence.—**veg-e-ta′tion** (-tā′shọn), *n.* [L. *vegetatio(n-).*] The act or process of vegetating; also, plants collectively as growing, esp. naturally, over an area or region (as, mountaintops bare of *vegetation*; "the delicate green tints of our early spring *vegetation*," A. R. Wallace's "Darwinism," viii.); a growth of plants, or an extent of growing plants (as, "a tangled *vegetation* of trees, bushes, and vines": W. H. Hudson's "Green Mansions," xi.); in *pathol.,* a morbid growth or excrescence.—**veg-e-ta′tion-al,** *a.*—**veg′e-ta-tive** (-tā̱-tiv), *a.* Vegetating; growing or developing as or like plants; also, pertaining to or connected with vegetation or vegetable growth; noting or pertaining to those bodily functions which, being performed unconsciously or involuntarily, are likened to the processes of vegetable growth; hence, characterized by the exercise of the physical functions only; inactive; also, having the power to produce or support growth in plants (as, *vegetative* mold); also, of or pertaining to vegetables or plants.—**veg′e-ta-tive-ly,** *adv.*—**veg′e-ta-tive-ness,** *n.*

ve-he-mence (vē′ē̱-mẹns or vē′hē̱-), *n.* The quality of being vehement. Also **ve′he-men-cy.**

ve-he-ment (vē′ē̱-mẹnt or vē′hē̱-), *a.* [OF. *vehement* (F. *véhément),* < L. *vehemens* (-ent-), very eager, impetuous, violent.] Eager, impetuous, or impassioned, in feeling, action, or speech, as persons (as, "The Duke was more *vehement* than ever in his protestations of loyalty": Motley's "Dutch Republic," vi. 6); characterized by violence of feeling or endeavor (as, *vehement* opposition; "loud and *vehement* quarrels," H. G. Wells's "Kipps," i. 1); passionate, as feeling (as, *vehement* desire; *vehement* dislike); of inani-

mate agencies, natural forces, etc., violent, severe, or intense (archaic).—**ve′he-ment-ly,** *adv.*

ve-hi-cle (vē′i-kl or vē′hi-), *n.* [F. *véhicule,* < L. *vehiculum,* a conveyance, carriage, ship, < *vehere,* carry, convey, also be carried, ride: see *weigh*[2].] Any receptacle, or means of transport, in which something is carried or conveyed, or travels; a receptacle in which something is placed in order to be moved; esp., a carriage or conveyance moving on wheels or runners; in general, a means of conveyance, transmission, or communication (lit. or fig.: as, air is the *vehicle* of sound; "fresh hot toast, which Mrs. Packles . . . made the *vehicle* of much less butter than she took herself," W. De Morgan's "Joseph Vance," i.; "Felix had at all times a brilliant assurance of manner which was simply the *vehicle* of his good spirits," H. James's "Europeans," x.); often, a medium by which ideas are communicated (as, "Language was with him . . . a mere *vehicle* for thought": Miss Mulock's "John Halifax," xii.); specif., in *phar.,* a substance, usually fluid, possessing little or no medicinal action, used as a medium for the administration of active remedies; in *painting,* a liquid, as oil, in which a pigment is applied to a surface.—**ve-hic-u-lar** (vē̱-hik′ū̱-lạr), *a.* Of or pertaining to a vehicle or vehicles; performed, or carried on, by means of a vehicle or vehicles (as, *vehicular* traffic); also, serving as a vehicle.

vehm-ge-richt (fām′ge-richt″), *n.;* pl. *-richte* (-rich″tē). [G., < *vehme,* now *fehme, feme,* criminal tribunal, + *gericht,* court.] Any of a class of irregular tribunals in medieval Germany, esp. in Westphalia, composed of freemen, often meeting in secret, and exercising broad powers, including the power of life and death in case of serious crimes.

veil (vāl), *n.* [OF. *veile, voile* (F. *voile),* < L. *vela,* pl. of *velum,* covering, curtain, veil, sail: cf. *velum* and *voile.*] A piece of cloth or other material used to cover or conceal something; a curtain; a hanging; also, a piece of material, usually light and more or less transparent, worn, esp. by women, over the head or face, as to conceal the face or to protect it from the sun or wind; specif., such a piece of material worn so as to fall over the head and shoulders on each side of the face, forming a part of the head-dress of a nun

Veils.— 1, from statue of Isabeau of Bavaria, queen of France, died 1435 (Abbey Church of St. Denis); 2, as worn in France at the end of the 13th century.

(as, to take the *veil,* to become a nun); also, something resembling or suggesting a veil; the caul which sometimes covers the head of a child at birth (prov.); in *bot., anat.,* and *zoöl.,* a velum; in fig. use, something that covers, screens, or conceals (as, a *veil* of smoke or mist); a mask, disguise, or pretense.—**veil,** *v. t.* [OF. *veler* (F. *voiler),* < L. *velare,* cover, < *velum.*] To cover or conceal with or as with a veil; cover the face of with a veil; cover or conceal as a veil does, or in the manner of a veil (as, "the storms and mists that *veil* the mountains": Blackmore's "Lorna Doone," xx.); fig., to conceal from apprehension or knowledge (as, "She . . . *veiled* her grief, and strove to act the comforter to us all": Mrs. Shelley's "Frankenstein," iii.); hide the real nature of, or mask or disguise (as, "The most barefaced action seeks to *veil* itself under some show of decency": Prescott's "Conquest of Mexico," iv. 3).—**veiled,** *p. a.* Covered with a veil; wearing a veil; covered as with a veil; fig., concealed or hidden; disguised; not openly expressed (as, a *veiled* threat); also, of sound, etc., indistinct or muffled. —**veil′ing,** *n.* The act of one who or that which veils; also, something forming a veil; a veil; material for making veils. Cf. *nun's-veiling.*—**veil′less,** *a.* Without a veil; not covered by a veil.

vein (vān), *n.* [OF. F. *veine*, < L. *vena*, vein.] One of the system of branching vessels or tubes conveying blood from various parts of the body to the heart; loosely, any blood-vessel; also, one of the strands or bundles of vascular tissue forming the principal framework of a leaf; also, a nervure of an insect's wing; also, a small natural channel or water-course within the earth, or the water running through it; also, a body or mass of igneous rock, deposited mineral, or the like, occupying a crevice or fissure in rock; a lode; also, a streak or marking, as of a different shade or color, running through marble, wood, etc.; also, in fig. use, some line, course, or the like suggestive of a vein (as, "In the midst of a *vein* of thought . . . I was interrupted": Irving's "Tales of a Traveler," ii. 4); a strain or intermixture of some quality traceable in character or conduct, writing, etc. (as, "the *vein* of stubbornness in his character": Galsworthy's "Saint's Progress," i. 4); a particular aptitude or capacity, as for literary or artistic work; a particular style of language or expression (as, in a poetic *vein*; "Hereward answered, in his boasting *vein*," Kingsley's "Hereward," xii.); personal character or disposition, or a particular trait of character; a particular state of mind, humor, or mood (as, "I continued, for I was in the talking *vein*": Holmes's "Autocrat of the Breakfast-Table," i.).—**vein,** *v. t.* To furnish with veins; mark with lines or streaks suggesting veins; also, to extend over or through (something) in the manner of veins (as, "All the gold That *veins* the world": Tennyson's "Princess," iv. 522).—**veined,** *a.* Having or showing veins; character-ized by venation; streaked.—**vein'ing,** *n.* An arrange-ment of veins or vein-like markings; a streak or stripe of color, as in a piece of marble.—**vein'let,** *n.* A small vein. —**vein'ous,** *a.* Full of veins; marked with veins; pertain-ing to veins; of blood, venous.—**vein'stone,** *n.* Gangue.— **vein'y,** *a.* Full of veins; veined.

ve-la (vē'lä), *n.* Plural of *velum.*

ve-la-men (vē-lā'men), *n.*; pl. *-lamina* (-lam'i-nä). [L. *velare,* cover, E. *veil, v.*] In *bot.,* the thick, spongy integu-ment or epidermis covering the aërial roots of epiphytic orchids; in *anat.,* a membranous covering; a velum.

ve-lar (vē'lär), *a.* [See *velum.*] Of or pertaining to a velum or veil, esp. that of the palate; in *phonetics,* produced by the aid of the soft palate (as, a *velar* guttural).

ve-la-ri-um (vē-lā'ri-um), *n.*; pl. *-ria* (-ri-ä). [L., < *velum,* E. *veil, n.*] In *Rom. antiq.,* an awning drawn over a theater or amphitheater as a protection from rain or the sun.

ve-late (vē'lāt), *a.* [L. *velatus,* pp. of *velare,* E. *veil, v.*] Veiled; in *bot.* and *zoöl.,* having a velum.—**ve-la-tion** (vē-lā'shon), *n.* The act of covering or the state of being cov-ered with or as with a veil; also, the formation of a velum.

veld, veldt (velt or felt), *n.* [D. *veld:* see *field.*] The open country, bearing grass, bushes, or shrubs, or thinly forested, characteristic of South Africa.

ve-lite (vē'līt), *n.* [L. *veles,* pl. *velites.*] A light-armed ancient Roman soldier.

vel-le-i-ty (ve-lē'i-ti), *n.*; pl. *-ties* (-tiz). [ML. *velleitas,* < L. *velle,* wish, will.] Volition in its weakest form; a mere wish or inclination toward a thing, unaccompanied by an effort to obtain it (as, "He perceived . . . that every wish, every *velleity* of his had only to be expressed to be at once Victoria's": Lytton Strachey's "Queen Victoria," iv.).

vel-li-cate (vel'i-kāt), *v. t.* or *i.*; *-cated, -cating.* [L. *velli-catus,* pp. of *vellicare,* freq. of *vellere,* pluck.] To pluck or twitch.—**vel-li-ca'tion** (-kā'shon), *n.*—**vel'li-ca-tive** (-kā-tiv), *a.*

vel-lum (vel'um), *n.* [OF. *veelin* (F. *vélin*), < *veel,* calf, E. *veal.*] A fine kind of parchment, usually of calfskin, used esp. for writing, printing, painting, and binding; a manu-script or the like on such parchment; also, a kind of paper or of cloth resembling such parchment.

vel-o-cim-e-ter (vel-ō-sim'e-tèr), *n.* [L. *velox* (*veloc-*), swift: see *-meter.*] Any of various devices for measuring velocity or speed, as an instrument for measuring the initial velocity of a projectile, or as a ship's log.

ve-lo-ci-pede (vē-los'i-pēd), *n.* [F. *vélocipède,* < L. *velox* (*veloc-*), swift, + *pes* (*ped-*), foot.] A light vehicle or car-riage, usually with two wheels or three wheels, impelled by the rider, orig. by pushing on the ground with the feet, but afterward by pedals. See cut in next column.

ve-lo-ci-ty (vē-los'i-ti), *n.*; pl. *-ties* (-tiz). [F. *vélocité,* < L. *velocitas,* < *velox* (*veloc-*), swift.] Ra-pidity of mo-tion or opera-tion; swift-ness; celerity; quickness; also, relative

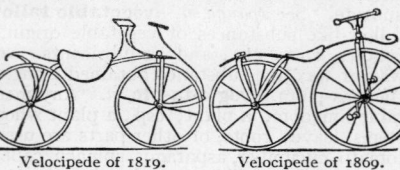

Velocipede of 1819.   Velocipede of 1869.

rapidity; in *physics,* rate of motion; the change of position of a point per unit of time; specif., rate of motion in which direction as well as speed is considered.

vel-o-drome (vel'ō-drōm), *n.* [F. *vélodrome,* < *vélo* (for *vélocipède*), velocipede, bicycle, + Gr. δρόμος, a running, course, race-course.] A place or building having a specially prepared track or race-course for bicycles, motor-cars, etc.

ve-lour', *n.* See *velours* and *velure.*

ve-lours (vē-lör'), *n.* [F. *velours,* OF. *velous,* < L. *villosus,* hairy, shaggy: see *villous,* and cf. *velvet.*] Velvet; any fabric of the velvet kind, of silk, wool, cotton, jute, etc., variously used (according to grade) for clothing, upholstery, etc.; also, a hatters' velure.

ve-lou-té (vè-lö-tā'), *a.* [F.] Velvety: in *cookery,* applied to a smooth white sauce made with chicken or veal stock.

ve-lum (vē'lum), *n.*; pl. *-la* (-lä). [NL. use of L. *velum,* curtain, veil: cf. *veil, n.*] In *bot., anat.,* and *zoöl.,* any of various veil-like or curtain-like membranous coverings or partitions; esp., in *anat.,* the soft palate.

ve-lure (vē-lör'), *n.* [For *velours.*] Velvet† or velours†; also, a hatters' pad of velvet, plush, or the like, for smoothing or dressing silk hats.—**ve-lure,** *v. t.*; *-lured, -luring.* To smooth or dress (a hat) with a velure.

ve-lu-ti-nous (vē-lū'ti-nus), *a.* [NL. *velutinus,* < ML. *velutum,* velvet.] Resembling velvet; having a soft, velvety surface, as certain plants.

vel-vet (vel'vet), *n.* [ME. *velvet, veluett, velwet:* cf. OF. *velve, velvel, veluete* (ML. *velutum*), velvet, *velut, veluveteen, velu, velut,* hairy, shaggy, having the pile of velvet, ult. < L. *villus,* shaggy hair, nap: cf. *velours.*] A fabric of silk, silk and cotton, cotton, etc., with a thick, soft pile formed of warp-thread loops either cut at the outer end (as in or-dinary velvet) or left uncut (as in uncut or terry velvet); also, the soft, deciduous covering of a growing antler (as, "large bucks and very fat, with the *velvet* hanging in shreds from their antlers, for it was late in August": Roosevelt's "Hunting Trips of a Ranchman," v.); also, something likened to the fabric velvet, as in respect of its softness; also, money gained through gambling or speculation (slang); clear gain or profit (slang).—**on velvet,** fig., in a position of ease or prosperity: as, "It might be thought that Lord Woldo was, as they say, *on velvet*" (Arnold Bennett's "The Old Adam," vi.). [Colloq.]—**vel'vet,** *a.* Made of velvet; covered with velvet; also, resembling velvet (as, "Trees . . . dotted a *velvet* lawn": W. Churchill's "Modern Chronicle," i. 7); velvety; smooth and soft.—**velvet scoter,** an old-world scoter, *Œdemia fusca,* or a North American species, *Œdemia* (or *Melanetta*) *vel-vetina* (or *de-glandi*), having a velvety-black plumage with white on the wings and head. —**vel'vet-ed,** *a.* Covered with or clad in velvet. —**vel-vet-een'** (-vè-tēn'), *n.* Cotton or silk-and-cotton vel-vet; *pl.,* trousers

Velvet Scoter (*Œdemia velvetina*), male.

or knickerbockers made of velveteen.—**vel'vet-leaf** (-lēf), *n.* Any of various plants with soft, velvety leaves, as the Indian mallow (*Abutilon abutilon*), the pareira (*Cissampelos pareira*), etc.—**vel'vet-y,** *a.* Like or suggestive of velvet; smooth and soft.

ve-na (vē′näַ), *n.*; pl. *-næ* (-nē). [L.] In *anat.*, a vein.—
vena cava (kā′väַ); pl. *venæ cavæ* (-vē). [L., 'hollow vein.']
In *anat.*, either of two large terminating veins discharging
into the right auricle of the heart.

ve-nal (vē′nạl), *a.* [L. *venalis*, < *venus*, *venum*, sale: cf.
vend[1].] For sale, as merchandise (archaic); hence, purchasable like mere merchandise, as things not properly bought
and sold (as, *venal* offices; *venal* votes); ready to sell one's
services or influence basely or unscrupulously, as a person
(as, "a pack of *venal* and corrupted rascals": Smollett's
"Humphry Clinker," May 19); accessible to bribery; cor-
ruptly mercenary; characterized by venality (as, a *venal*
period; a *venal* agreement).—**ve-nal-i-ty** (vē-nal′i-ti), *n.*
The quality of being venal; venal character or practice;
prostitution of talents or principles for money or reward.
—**ve′nal-ly,** *adv.*

ve-nat-ic (vē-nat′ik), *a.* [L. *venaticus*, < *venatus*, hunting,
< *venari*, hunt.] Of or pertaining to hunting.—**ve-nat′i-
cal-ly,** *adv.*

ve-na-tion (vē-nā′shọn), *n.* [L. *vena*, vein.] The arrangement of veins or nerves, as
in a leaf or an insect's wing;
these veins collectively.—
ve-na′tion-al, *a.*

ven-a-to-ri-al (ven-ạ-tō′-
ri-ạl), *a.* [L. *venatorius*, <
venator, hunter, < *venari*,
hunt.] Of or pertaining to
a hunter or hunting; ve-
natic.

vend[1] (vend), *v.* [F. *vendre*,
< L. *vendere*, sell, < *venum*,
sale, + *dare*, give: cf. *venal*.]
I. *tr.* To dispose of by
sale; sell; trade in as a sell-
er, esp. by hawking, peddling, or the like. **II.** *intr.* To
vend something; also, to be disposed of by sale; find purchasers.

Venation of Wings of a Hymenopterous Insect (genus *Epeolus*), a parasitic bee. (Cross shows natural size.)

vend[2] (vend), *v. t.* [Var. of *vent*[3].] To give utterance to
(an opinion, etc.); put forward.

ven-dace (ven′dās), *n.* [Cf. OF. *vendese*, *vendoise* (F.
vandoise), dace.] A small fresh-water fish, *Coregonus
vandesius*, occurring in Castle Loch, near Lochmaben,
Dumfriesshire, Scotland; also, any of certain closely related
fishes.

Ven-de-an (ven-dē′ạn). [F. *Vendéen*.] **I.** *a.* Of or pertaining to Vendée, a department of western France; also,
belonging to the royalist party (from Vendée and neighboring
departments) that maintained civil war 1793–96 against the
Revolutionary government. **II.** *n.* A native or inhabitant
of Vendée; also, a Vendean royalist.

vend-ee (ven-dē′), *n.* The person to whom a thing is vended
or sold: chiefly in legal use, and opposed to *vendor*.

Ven-dé-miaire (voṅ-dā-myär′), *n.* [F. *vendémiaire*, < L.
vindemia, grape-gathering: see *vintage*.] In the calendar
of the first French republic, the first month of the year, extending from Sept. 22 to Oct. 21.

vend-er (ven′dėr), *n.* One who vends or sells; a seller; often,
one who sells things in the streets; also, a vending-ma-
chine.

ven-det-ta (ven-det′äַ), *n.*; pl. *vendettas* (-äz). [It., < L.
vindicta, vengeance, revenge, < *vindicare*: see *vindicate*.]
A state of private war in which a murdered man's relatives
execute vengeance on the slayer or his relatives; a blood-feud,
esp. as existing in Corsica and parts of Italy.

ven-di-ble (ven′di-bl). [L. *vendibilis*.] **I.** *a.* Capable of
being vended or sold; salable. **II.** *n.* A vendible article.
—**ven-di-bil′i-ty** (-bil′i-ti), **ven′di-ble-ness,** *n.*—**ven′di-
bly,** *adv.*

vend-ing=ma-chine (ven′ding-mạ-shēn″), *n.* A mechanical
device which, upon the dropping of a coin into a slot, delivers
chewing-gum, candy, or other small wares; any slot-ma-
chine.

ven-di-tion (ven-dish′ọn), *n.* [L. *venditio*(n-), < *vendere*,
E. *vend*[1].] The act of vending or selling; sale.

vend-or (ven′dọr), *n.* One who vends, or disposes of a thing
by sale; a seller or vender: chiefly in legal use, and opposed
to *vendee*.

ven-due (ven-dū′), *n.* [= D. *vendu*, < F. (obs. or prov.)
vendue, sale, < *vendre*, E. *vend*[1].] A public auction.

ve-neer (vẹ-nēr′), *v. t.* [G. *furniren*, *fournieren*, < F.
fournir, E. *furnish*.] To overlay or face (wood) with a
thin layer of some finer or more beautiful wood or other fine
material, as ivory, mother-of-pearl, etc.; cover (anything)
with a layer or coating of material giving an appearance of
superior quality; fig., to invest or adorn superficially or speciously (*with*: as, "A rogue in grain *Veneer'd* with sanctimonious theory," Tennyson's "Princess," Prologue, 117);
give a merely superficial fair appearance to (as, "On this
dreadful night who can *veneer* his words?" Stevenson's
"Master of Ballantrae," v.); also, to apply as veneering.—
ve-neer′, *n.* A thin piece of wood of a superior kind, or of
some other fine material, used in veneering; wood or other
material prepared in thin pieces for such use or applied in
veneering; hence, an outer layer or coating of anything (as,
"pavements that had always a thin *veneer* of greasy, slippery
mud": H. G. Wells's "Tono-Bungay," i. 3. § 7); fig., a
merely superficial fair appearance or show (as, a *veneer* of
good manners; "mere savages . . . the old war-paint being
but half disguised under a thin *veneer* of Mohammedanism,"
Amelia B. Edwards's "Thousand Miles up the Nile," xiv.).
—**ve-neer′ing,** *n.* The process, work, or art of applying
veneers; also, material applied as a veneer; fig., a merely
superficial show or specious outward display of something
(as, a *veneering* of civilization).

ven-e-nose, ven-e-nous (ven′ẹ-nōs, -nus), *a.* [L. *venenosus*,
< *venenum*, poison.] Poisonous. [Now rare.]

ven-er-a-ble (ven′ẹ-rạ-bl), *a.* [L. *venerabilis*.] Worthy of
veneration or reverence, as on account of high character or
office (used specif. in the Anglican Church as an epithet of
archdeacons, and in the Roman Catholic Church of those who
have attained the first degree in the process of canonization);
often, commanding respect by reason of age and dignity of
appearance (as, "a *venerable*-looking man, with white hair
and beard and a face of great sagacity": S. Butler's "Erewhon," vii.); arousing such respect (as, "a . . . beggar of
venerable appearance": H. G. Wells's "Christina Alberta's
Father," ii. 2. § 3); aged or old (used in respect or mock
respect, or humorously: as, "a *venerable* lady, known as
Great-Aunt Grantley, who had money to bequeath," G.
Meredith's "Ordeal of Richard Feverel," i.; "such *venerable*
leviathans [whales]," H. Melville's "Moby-Dick," lxxxi.);
also, of places, buildings, etc., hallowed by religious, historic,
or other lofty associations (as, "The capital . . . was even
more *venerable* for the religious traditions which invested it":
Prescott's "Conquest of Mexico," iii. 6); impressive or interesting from age, antique appearance, etc. (as, a *venerable*
castle; a *venerable* ruin; "the *venerable* furniture which had
come from Holland," Irving's "Knickerbocker's New York,"
ii. 7); ancient (as, a *venerable* error).—**ven″er-a-bil′i-ty**
(-bil′i-ti), **ven′er-a-ble-ness,** *n.*—**ven′er-a-bly,** *adv.*

ven-er-ate (ven′ẹ-rāt), *v. t.*; *-ated, -ating.* [L. *veneratus*, pp.
of *venerari*, reverence, venerate.] To regard with reverence,
or revere (as, "an oracle *venerated* throughout many nations
of Asia," De Quincey's "Revolt of the Tartars"; "I *venerate*
the memory of my grandfather," Walpole's "Castle of
Otranto," iii.); also, to treat with reverence; honor by some
act of reverence.—**ven-er-a′tion** (-ẹ-rā′shọn), *n.* [L. *vene-
ratio*(n-).] The act of venerating, or the state of being
venerated; the feeling of one who venerates, or reverence (as,
to regard a person, or a place or thing, with *veneration*;
"*veneration* for learning," R. Graves's "Spiritual Quixote,"
i. 1); the outward expression of reverent feeling, or action
expressive of reverence.—**ven′er-a-tive** (-ẹ-rạ-tiv), *a.*
Characterized by or disposed to veneration.—**ven′er-a-tor**
(-ẹ-rā-tọr), *n.*

ve-ne-re-al (vē-nē′rẹ-ạl), *a.* [L. *venereus*, < *Venus*: see
venery[2].] **I.** *a.* Of or pertaining to venery, or the gratification of sexual desire; also, arising from or connected with
sexual intercourse with an infected person (as, *venereal* diseases); pertaining to diseases so arising; adapted to the
cure of such diseases (as, a *venereal* remedy); infected with
or suffering from venereal disease. **II.** *n.* A person infected
with venereal disease.

ven-er-er (ven′ẹr-ėr), *n.* [From *venery*[1].] A huntsman.
[Pseudo-archaic.]

ven-er-y¹ (ven′ẹ-ri), *n.* [OF. *venerie* (F. *vénerie*), < *vener*, < L. *venari*, hunt.] The practice or sport of hunting; the chase. [Archaic.]

ven-er-y² (ven′ẹ-ri), *n.* [ME. *venerie*, < *Venus* (*Vener*-), Venus (goddess of love), also, sexual love, venery.] The gratification of sexual desire.

ve-ne-sec-tion (vē-nẹ-sek′shọn), *n.* [L. *venæ*, gen. of *vena*, vein, + *sectio*(*n*-), a cutting, E. *section*.] In *med.*, phlebotomy.

Ve-ne-tian (vẹ-nē′shạn), *a.* [ML. *Venetia*, Venice, L. the country of the *Veneti* (an ancient people inhabiting the region).] Of or pertaining to Venice, in Italy.—**Venetian architecture,** the style of medieval architecture elaborated in Venice, combining elements from the Byzantine, Italian, and transalpine European styles, into a new style of high decorative quality and originality.—**Venetian blind,** a blind, as for a window, having overlapping horizontal slats that may be opened or closed, esp. one in which the slats may be raised and drawn together above the window by pulling a cord.—**Venetian red,** a red pigment, orig. prepared from a natural oxide of iron, but now usually made by calcining a mixture of lime and iron sulphate.—**Ve-ne′tian,** *n.* A native or inhabitant of Venice; also [*l. c.*], a Venetian blind; *pl.*, a kind of tape or braid for holding in place the slats of Venetian blinds; *sing.*, a domino

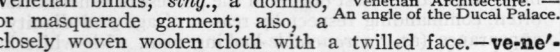
Venetian Architecture.— An angle of the Ducal Palace.

or masquerade garment; also, a closely woven woolen cloth with a twilled face.—**ve-ne′tianed,** *a.* Furnished with Venetian blinds.

Ven-e-zue-lan (ven-ẹ-zwē′lạn). **I.** *a.* Of or pertaining to the South American republic of Venezuela. **II.** *n.* A native or inhabitant of Venezuela.

venge (venj), *v. t.*; *venged, venging.* [OF. *vengier* (F. *venger*), < L. *vindicare*, avenge: see *vindicate*.] To inflict retributive punishment or suffering on behalf of (a person, etc.) or for (a wrong, etc.); avenge; revenge: as, "With this [brand] he cross'd the murderer's path, And *venged* young Allan well!" (Scott's "Lord of the Isles," iii. 29); "I'll *venge* thy death" (Shakspere's "3 Henry VI.," ii. 1. 87). [Archaic.]—**vengeance** (ven′jạns), *n.* [OF. F. *vengeance*.] The avenging of wrong, injury, or the like, or retributive punishment (as, "*Vengeance* is mine; I will repay, saith the Lord," Rom. xii. 19; "The legions burst in . . . furious at . . . the treachery . . . and merciless in their *vengeance*," Froude's "Cæsar," xvi.); infliction of injury or suffering in requital for wrong done or other cause of bitter resentment; an instance or form of retributive punishment or requital (as, "The tortures of hell are too mild a *vengeance* for thy crimes": Mrs. Shelley's "Frankenstein," x.); also, harm or mischief generally† (formerly used in imprecations or for emphasis: as, "What the *vengeance!* Could he not speak 'em fair?" Shakspere's "Coriolanus," iii. 1. 262).—**with a vengeance,** with a mischief invoked†; with a curse†; also, with force or violence; extremely; esp., with surprising or disconcerting force, thoroughness, completeness, etc. (as, "Down had come her house of cards *with a vengeance!*" Galsworthy's "Saint's Progress," ii. 8; "Grey had made him 'earnest' *with a vengeance*," Mrs. H. Ward's "Robert Elsmere," v.).—**venge′ful,** *a.* Desiring or seeking vengeance, as persons; disposed to take vengeance, or vindictive; prompting to vengeance, as feelings, motives, etc.; characterized by or showing a vindictive spirit; also, taking or executing vengeance (as, "a *vengeful* sword": Shakspere's "2 Henry VI.," iii. 2. 198); done in the execution of vengeance (as, a *vengeful* deed; "the *vengeful* massacre of Toulon," J. Conrad's "Rover," vii.); retributive.—**venge′ful-ly,** *adv.*—**venge′ful-ness,** *n.* —**ven′ger,** *n.*

ve-nial (vē′niạl), *a.* [LL. *venialis*, < L. *venia*, indulgence, mercy, pardon.] That may be forgiven or pardoned, as a sin (in *theol.*, opposed to *deadly* or *mortal*); pardonable; not seriously wrong or reprehensible (as, "Horse-stealing and cheating at cards are looked on as *venial* offences," W. H. Hudson's "Purple Land," xv.; a *venial* fault); excusable, as an error or slip; also, permissible†.—**ve-ni-al′i-ty** (-ni-al′i-ti), **ve′nial-ness,** *n.*—**ve′nial-ly,** *adv.*

ve-ni-re (vẹ-nī′rē), *n.* Same as *venire facias.*

ve-ni-re fa-ci-as (vẹ-nī′rē fā′shi-as). [L., 'that you cause to come.'] In *law*, a writ or precept directed to the sheriff, requiring him to summon a jury or a number of jurors to appear in court for the trial of causes.

ven-i-son (ven′i-zọn, Brit. ven′zn), *n.* [OF. *venison, veneson* (F. *venaison*), < L. *venatio*(*n*-), hunting, also game, < *venari*, hunt.] A beast of the chase, esp. one of the deer kind (now rare); such beasts collectively (now rare); also, the flesh of an animal killed in the chase or by hunting; now, usually, the flesh of animals of the deer kind (as, "It would be cruel to kill the poor deer . . . when you don't want their *venison* or their skins": Cooper's "Deerslayer," xxv.).

Ve-ni-te (vẹ-nī′tē), *n.* [L., 2d pers. pl. impv. of *venire*, come: being the first word of the psalm in Latin.] The 95th psalm (94th in the Vulgate), used as a canticle at matins or morning prayer; also, a musical setting of this psalm.

ven-om (ven′ọm), *n.* [OF. *venim, venin* (F. *venin*), < L. *venenum*, poison.] Poison in general (now rare); esp., the poisonous fluid which some animals, as certain serpents, spiders, etc., secrete, and introduce into the bodies of their victims by biting, stinging, etc.; fig., something resembling or suggesting poison in its effect; any noxious or malign influence or effect; spite or malice (as, "She . . . sprang out of reach, her eyes shining with triumph and *venom*": Tarkington's "Gentleman from Indiana," iv.); bitter or virulent language.—**ven′om,** *v. t.* To charge with venom; make venomous; envenom; also, to infect with venom; poison; fig., to charge or infect with some noxious influence.—**ven′om-ous,** *a.* [OF. F. *venimeux*.] Full of venom; poisonous; also, of an animal, having a gland or glands for secreting venom; inflicting a poisoned bite, sting, or wound; also, fig., noxious, baneful, or injurious; spiteful or malignant (as, a *venomous* foe; a *venomous* disposition; a *venomous* attack); also, pertaining to or of the nature of venom.—**ven′om-ous-ly,** *adv.*—**ven′om-ous-ness,** *n.*

ve-nose (vē′nōs), *a.* [L. *venosus*: see *venous*.] Venous; in *bot.*, having many or prominent veins.

ve-nous (vē′nus), *a.* [L. *venosus*, < *vena*, vein.] Full of veins; having veins or nervures, as an insect's wing; also, of, pertaining to, or of the nature of a vein or veins; also, noting or pertaining to the blood of the veins which has given up oxygen and become charged with carbon dioxide, and, in the higher animals, is dark-red in color.—**ve-nos-i-ty** (vẹ-nos′i-ti), *n.*—**ve′nous-ly,** *adv.*

vent¹ (vent), *n.* [Var. of *fent*.] A slit or opening in a garment; a placket.

vent² (vent), *n.* [F. *vente*, < ML. *vendita*, sale, orig. pp. neut. pl. of L. *vendere*, sell, E. *vend¹*.] The act of disposing of goods by sale; opportunity or market for the sale of goods; also, the fact of being disposed of by sale or of finding purchasers. [Now chiefly prov.]—**vent²,** *v. t.* To dispose of by sale; sell; vend. [Now prov.]

vent³ (vent), *v.* [Appar. by reduction < OF. *esventer*, expose or open to the air, let out (water, etc.), divulge (F. *éventer*), < L. *ex*, out of, + *ventus*, wind: see *wind²*.] **I.** *tr.* To furnish (a cask, etc.) with an outlet to the air; unclose, as by opening or making an outlet in; let out or discharge (liquid, smoke, etc.); also, to give free course or expression to (an emotion, passion, etc.: as, "She was jealous . . . and glad of any excuse to *vent* her pique," Bulwer-Lytton's "Pelham," xxii.); pour out or wreak (one's anger, etc.) on or upon some person or thing (as, "Mine hostess . . . *vented* her rage . . . upon Mr. Wildgoose": R. Graves's "Spiritual Quixote," iv. 7); give utterance to (as, "learning by heart scraps of Greek, which she *vents* upon all occasions": Steele, in "Spectator," 278); publish or spread abroad by or as by utterance (as, "the particular matters in these times *vented* and tossed about in the pulpits": Strype's "Memorials of Cranmer," i. 25); also, of a thing, to discharge (itself); of an emotion, etc., to express or show (itself) in something (as, "the . . . hag . . . whose wrath must *vent* itself in impotent curses": Scott's "Ivanhoe," xxvii.); of a person, to relieve (one's self) by giving vent to something (as, "Adams frequently *vented* himself in ejaculations": Fielding's "Joseph Andrews," ii. 10). **II.** *intr.* To have a vent or outlet; also, to escape or pass out through a vent or outlet; issue; also, to give vent to something; of an otter, etc., to rise to the surface of the water in order to breathe.—**vent**³, *n.* The act or fact of venting; emission or discharge; issue; expression or utterance (as, "Many of the audience began to give *vent* to their emotions in tears," C. B. Brown's "Wieland," xvii.; "It was no time to give *vent* to complaints," Scott's "Castle Dangerous," xvii.); also, a means of escaping or passing out, an outlet, as from confinement; an opening or aperture serving for outlet, as of a fluid (as, "The *vent* of the kitchen chimney being foul, the soot took fire": Smollett's "Humphry Clinker," July 1); any aperture or orifice; the small opening at the breech of a gun by which fire is communicated to the charge; in *zoöl.*, the anal or excretory opening of animals, esp. of those below mammals, as birds and reptiles.—**vent-age** (ven′tāj), *n.* A small hole or vent, esp. for the escape or passage of air, as one of the finger-holes of a flute.

ven-tail (ven′tāl), *n.* [OF. *ventaille* (F. *ventail*), < *vent*, wind, air, < L. *ventus*, wind.] The movable front of a helmet.

vent-er¹ (ven′tėr), *n.* One who or that which vents or gives vent; one who utters or publishes a statement, doctrine, etc., esp. of an erroneous or otherwise objectionable nature.

ven-ter² (ven′tėr), *n.* [L., belly, womb; in legal use, through AF. *ventre*.] In *law*, the womb, or a wife or mother as a source of offspring; in *anat.* and *zoöl.*, the abdomen or belly; a belly-like cavity or concavity; a belly-like protuberance.

ven-ti-duct (ven′ti-dukt), *n.* [L. *ventus*, wind, + *ductus*, E. *duct*.] A duct, pipe, or passage for wind or air, as for ventilating apartments.

ven-ti-la-ble (ven′ti-la-bl), *a.* Capable of being ventilated.

ven-ti-late (ven′ti-lāt), *v. t.*; *-lated, -lating.* [L. *ventilatus*, pp. of *ventilare*, fan, winnow, < *ventus*, wind.] To fan or winnow (grain, etc.: now rare); also, to expose (substances, etc.) to the action or free passage of air or wind (as, "thoroughly *ventilating* my garments by shaking and beating them": W. H. Hudson's "Green Mansions," ix.); purify by the action of fresh air (as, the lungs *ventilate* the blood); esp., to provide (a room, mine, etc.) with fresh air in place of air which is vitiated (as, "It was difficult to *ventilate* the nursery without exposing the child to a draught": L. Merrick's "House of Lynch," xv.); produce a current of air in (an inclosed space) so as to maintain a fresh supply; also, to furnish with a vent or opening, as for the escape of air or gas; also, to submit (a question, etc.) to free examination and discussion; bring to public notice or consideration; publish abroad; give utterance or expression to (an opinion, etc.: as, "He was glad of an opportunity of *ventilating* his grievance," W. H. Hudson's "Green Mansions," viii.).—**ven-ti-la′tion** (-lā′shon), *n.* [L. *ventilatio(n-)*.] The act of ventilating, or the state of being ventilated.—**ven′ti-la-tive** (-lā-tiv), *a.* Promoting or producing ventilation; pertaining to ventilation.—**ven′ti-la-tor** (-lā-tor), *n.* One who or that which ventilates; any contrivance for replacing foul or stagnant air by fresh air.

Ven-tôse (voṅ-tōz′), *n.* [F. *ventôse*, < L. *ventosus*, windy, < *ventus*, wind.] In the calendar of the first French republic, the sixth month of the year, extending from Feb. 19 to March 20.

ven-trad (ven′trad), *adv.* [L. *venter* (*ventr*-), belly: see -*ad*.] In *anat.*, toward the belly or ventral side of the body: opposed to *dorsad*.

ven-tral (ven′tral), *a.* [L. *ventralis*, < *venter* (*ventr*-), belly.] Of or pertaining to the venter or belly; abdominal; situated on the abdominal side of the body; hence, of, pertaining to, or situated on the anterior or lower side or surface, as of an organ or part.— **ventral fin**, in fishes, either of a pair of fins situated on the fore part of the lower surface of the body, and corresponding to the hind limbs of higher vertebrates.

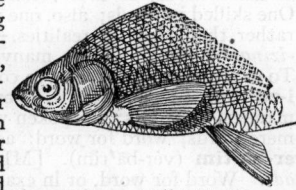
Fish with Ventral Fin behind Pectoral Fin.

Cf. *pectoral fin*, under *pectoral, a.*—**ven′tral,** *n.* A ventral fin.—**ven′tral-ly,** *adv.*

ven-tri-cle (ven′tri-kl), *n.* [L. *ventriculus*, dim. of *venter*, belly.] The belly or stomach (obs. or rare); also, any of various hollow organs or parts in an animal body; esp., one of the two cavities of the heart which receive the blood from the auricles and propel it into the arteries; also, one of a series of connecting cavities of the brain, continuous with the central cavity of the spinal cord.

ven-tri-cose, ven-tri-cous (ven′tri-kōs, -kus), *a.* [NL. *ventricosus*, < L. *venter* (*ventr*-), belly.] Swelling out, esp. on one side or unequally; protuberant; also, having a large abdomen.

ven-tric-u-lar (ven-trik′ū-lär), *a.* Of, pertaining to, or of the nature of a ventricle; also, pertaining to the stomach; also, swelling out; distended.

ven-tril-o-quism (ven-tril′ō-kwizm), *n.* [LL. *ventriloquus*, a ventriloquist, < L. *venter* (*ventr*-), belly, + *loqui*, speak.] The art or practice of speaking or of uttering sounds in such a manner that the voice appears to come, not from the speaker, but from some other source.—**ven-tri-lo′qui-al** (-tri-lō′kwi-al), *a.*—**ven-tril′o-quist** (-kwist), *n.* One who practises or is skilled in ventriloquism.—**ven-tril-o-quis′tic,** *a.*—**ven-tril′o-quize** (-kwīz), *v. i.*; *-quized, -quizing.* To practise ventriloquism; speak or produce sounds in the manner of a ventriloquist.—**ven-tril′o-quous** (-kwus), *a.* Of, pertaining to, resembling, or using ventriloquism.—**ven-tril′o-quy** (-kwi), *n.* Ventriloquism.

ven-ture (ven′tūr), *n.* [ME. *venture*, for *aventure*, E. *adventure*.] Chance†; hazard† or risk†; also, a hazardous or daring undertaking (as, "It was a desperate *venture* for so small a company to cross the most of Scotland unsupported": Stevenson's "Master of Ballantrae," i.); any undertaking or proceeding involving uncertainty as to the outcome; esp., a business enterprise or proceeding in which loss is risked in the hope of profit (as, "Mr. M. was fully able to finance this *venture* [of manufacturing automobiles]": Tarkington's "Magnificent Ambersons," x.); a commercial or other speculation; that on which risk is taken in a business enterprise or speculation, as a ship, cargo, merchandise, etc. (as, "My *ventures* are not in one bottom trusted": Shakspere's "Merchant of Venice," i. 1. 42); also, a venturous experiment at doing something, as if taking a risk (as, "The barefoot children by gradual *ventures* had at length gathered close about": G. W. Cable's "Bonaventure," ii. 3).—**at a venture** (for obs. *at aventure* or *at adventure*), according to mere chance; at random; without any particular aim or purpose: as, "A certain man drew a bow *at a venture*, and smote the king" (1 Kings, xxii. 34); "I ask it quite *at a venture*" (Howells's "Foregone Conclusion," iii.).—**ven′ture,** *v.*; *-tured, -turing.* **I.** *tr.* To put to hazard, or risk (as, "I *venture* my head for your service": Swift's "Gulliver's Travels," i. 7); risk or employ on a business venture (as, "losing the little capital he *ventured*": Gissing's "New Grub Street," v.); take the risk of sending (archaic: as, to *venture* goods to a distant country); also, to take the risk of (as, "I should *venture* purgatory for 't": Shakspere's "Othello," iv. 3. 77); brave the dangers of; dare to undertake or attempt (an action, proceeding, etc.); undertake to utter or express, as if with a sense of daring (as, "I *ventured* a timid inquiry," Mrs. Stowe's "Oldtown Folks," v.; "One or two *ventured* awkward words of condolence," Archibald Marshall's "Anthony Dare," ix.). **II.** *intr.* To make a venture; risk one's self; take the risk of coming, going, or proceeding (as, "I *ventured* out from my hiding-place," W. H. Hudson's "Purple Land," xii.; to *venture* further on a course); dare or presume to enter upon something undertaken or attempted (with *on* or *upon*: as, to *venture* on an ambitious project; to *venture* on making a change in a sentence; "When he *ventured* upon insult, I vowed revenge," Poe's "Cask of Amontillado"); often, to have the daring or presumption (to do, say, etc., as specified: as, they never *ventured* to oppose him; "If I may *venture* to say so, ma'am, I am very glad," G. Meredith's "Diana of the Crossways," xi.).—**ven′tur-er,** *n.*—**ven′ture-some** (-sum), *a.* Having or showing a disposition to venture or take risks, often rashly (as, a *venturesome* lad; a *venturesome* performance); bold; daring; also, attended with risk, or hazardous.—**ven′ture-**

some-ly, *adv.*—**ven'ture-some-ness,** *n.*—**ven'tur-ous,** *a.* Disposed to venture; bold; daring; adventurous; also, hazardous; risky.—**ven'tur-ous-ly,** *adv.*—**ven'tur-ous-ness,** *n.*

ven-ue (ven'ū), *n.* [OF. F. *venue*, a coming, < *venir*, < L. *venire*, come.] A coming†; also, an attack†; a thrust† or lunge†; a match or bout at fencing†; in *law*, the place or neighborhood of a crime or cause of action; the county or place where the jury is gathered and the cause tried; hence, in general use, the scene of any action or event.—**change of venue,** in *law*, change of place of trial, as to ensure fairness.

ven-ule (ven'ūl), *n.* [L. *venula*, dim. of *vena*, vein.] A small vein; in *entom.*, one of the small branches of the veins in an insect's wing.—**ven'u-lose, ven'u-lous** (-ū-lōs, -lus), *a.* Full of venules; having veinlets.

Ve-nus (vē'nus), *n.* [L.] An ancient Italian goddess of gardens and spring, identified by the Romans with the Greek Aphrodite as the goddess of love and beauty; hence, a beautiful woman; also, the most brilliant of the major planets, being the second in order from the sun (cf. *Lucifer* and *Hesper*).—**Ve'nus's comb.** A marine gastropod, *Murex tenuispina*, having a beautiful and delicate shell

Venus (or Aphrodite).—1, the Venus of Medici, in the Uffizi Gallery, Florence; 2, the Venus of Melos (or Milo), in the Louvre, Paris.

with long, slender spines. See *murex.*—**Ve'nus's fly'=trap.** A curious droseraceous plant, *Dionæa muscipula,* a native of North and South Carolina, having leaves with a two-lobed appendage which closes like a trap when certain delicate hairs on it are irritated, as by a fly.—**Ve'nus's hair.** A delicate maidenhair fern, *Adiantum capillus-veneris.*

ve-ra-cious (vē-rā'shus), *a.* [L. *verax* (*verac-*), speaking truly, truthful, < *verus*, true.] Speaking truly, truthful, or habitually observant of truth (as, a *veracious* witness); also, characterized by truthfulness, conforming to truth, or true (as, a *veracious* statement or account; "this *veracious* chronicle," Bret Harte's "Fool of Five Forks").—**ve-ra'cious-ly,** *adv.*—**ve-ra'cious-ness,** *n.*—**ve-ra'ci-ty** (-ras'i-ti),

Venus's Fly-trap.

n.; pl. *-ties* (-tiz). The quality or character of being veracious; truthfulness in speaking or statement (as, "I answered to every question . . . with the same *veracity* that I shall speak now": Walpole's "Castle of Otranto," ii.); habitual observance of truth, or inclination toward or regard for truth (as, men of *veracity*; "Naturally they [mankind] are endued with *veracity*, or a regard to truth in what they say," J. Butler's "Analogy of Religion," ii. 7); conformity to truth or fact, as of statements; sometimes, correctness or accuracy, as of the senses, a scientific instrument, etc.; also, something veracious; a truthful statement; a truth.

ve-ran-da, ve-ran-dah (vē-ran'dä), *n.* [A word introduced from India, < Pg. *varanda*, balcony.] An open portico or gallery, usually roofed and sometimes partly inclosed, attached to the exterior of a house or other building: as, "The house [in India] . . . was surrounded with a wide *verandah*" (Stevenson's "Master of Ballantrae," vii.); "the tavern, with . . . a broad *veranda* in front, with benches" (Mrs. Stowe's "Oldtown Folks," i.). In the U. S. often called *piazza* and *porch.*—**ve-ran'daed, ve-ran'dahed** (-däd), *a.* Furnished with a veranda or verandas: as, "*verandaed* hotels" (Howells's "Rise of Silas Lapham," vi.); "*verandahed* villas" (H. G. Wells's "Mr. Polly," i.).

ve-ra-tric (vē-rā'trik or -rat'rik), *a.* [L. *veratrum*, hellebore.] In *chem.*, noting or pertaining to a white crystalline acid obtained by the decomposition of veratrine and in other ways.

ve-rat-ri-dine (vē-rat'ri-din), *n.* [From *veratrine.*] In *chem.*, an amorphous alkaloid occurring with veratrine in the seeds of a Mexican liliaceous plant, *Schœnocaulon officinale* (or *Asagræa officinalis*).

ve-ra-trine (vē-rā'trin or ver'a-), *n.* [F. *vératrine* (NL. *veratrina*), < L. *veratrum*, hellebore.] In *chem.*, a poisonous alkaloid, or mixture of alkaloids, obtained from the seeds of *Schœnocaulon officinale* (or *Asagræa officinalis*), a liliaceous plant of Mexico sometimes placed in the hellebore genus *Veratrum*: used in medicine, chiefly in the local treatment of rheumatism, neuralgia, etc.—**ve-ra-trize** (vē-rā'trīz or ver'a-), *v. t.*; *-trized, -trizing.* To treat, drug, or poison with veratrine, as animals.

verb (vėrb), *n.* [OF. F. *verbe*, < L. *verbum*, word, verb: see *word.*] In *gram.*, a word that predicates something of a subject, or expresses acting, being, etc., on the part of a subject, as *arise, come, submit, exist, be*, etc.: as, a transitive or intransitive *verb*; a finite *verb*; an auxiliary *verb* (see *auxiliary, n.*).

ver-bal (vėr'bal). [OF. F. *verbal*, < LL. *verbalis*, < L. *verbum*, word, verb: cf. *verb.*] **I.** *a.* Of or pertaining to words (as, *verbal* symbols); consisting of or in the form of words (as, a *verbal* picture of a scene; "This lady very often lied, and she had practised deceptions which were not simply *verbal*," H. James's "Portrait of a Lady," xlii.); often, expressed in spoken words, or oral, rather than written (as, *verbal* tradition; a *verbal* message; "His pension depended only upon a *verbal* promise of the king," Strype's "Memorials of Cranmer," iii. 27); also, pertaining to or concerned with words only, rather than ideas, facts, or realities (as, to make *verbal* changes in an article; *verbal* criticism; "that superstitious reverence for mere *verbal* truth," Kingsley's "Yeast," x.); dealing with mere words (as, a *verbal* critic); also, talkative† or verbose†; also, corresponding word for word (as, a *verbal* translation; a *verbal* copy or quotation); in *gram.*, of or pertaining to a verb; of nouns, derived from a verb and sharing in its senses and constructions, as many English nouns ending in *-ing*. **II.** *n.* In *gram.*, a noun or other part of speech derived from a verb.—**ver'bal-ism,** *n.* A verbal expression; a word or phrase; also, predominance of mere words, as over ideas or realities.—**ver'bal-ist,** *n.* One skilled in words; also, one who deals with words merely, rather than ideas or realities.—**ver'bal-ize** (-īz), *v.*; *-ized, -izing.* **I.** *intr.* To use many words; be verbose. **II.** *tr.* To express in words; also, to convert into a verb.—**ver''bal-i-za'tion** (-i-zā'shon), *n.*—**ver'bal-ly,** *adv.* In a verbal manner; in words; in spoken words, or orally; in, or as to, mere words; word for word; as a verb.

ver-ba-tim (vėr-bā'tim). [ML., < L. *verbum*, word.] **I.** *adv.* Word for word, or in exactly the same words (as, "He saw his remarks reproduced *verbatim* in the papers": Arnold

Bennett's "Pretty Lady," xxxv.); with correspondence word for word, as in translation; also, orally†. **II.** *a.* Corresponding with an original, word for word: as, "a *verbatim* report of the President's speech" (Bok's "Americanization of Edward Bok," iv.).

ver-be-na (vėr-bē'nạ), *n.* [NL. use of L. *verbena*, usually pl., *verbenæ*, leaves or branches used in ceremonies, also plants used as cooling remedies: cf. *vervain*.] Any plant of the genus *Verbena*, comprising species characterized by elongated or flattened spikes of sessile flowers, some of which are much cultivated as garden plants.—**ver-be-na'ceous** (-bē̦-nā'shius), *a.* Belonging to the *Verbenaceæ*, or verbena family of plants, which includes also the lantana, agnus castus, teak, etc.

Verbena (*V. canadensis*).

ver-bi-age (vėr'bi-ạj), *n.* [F. *verbiage*, < L. *verbum*, word.] Abundance of useless words, or of words without force or point, as in writing or speech: as, "Such, in brief, and stripped of its *verbiage*, was this amnesty" (Motley's "Dutch Republic," iii. 5); "long spasms of ungrammatical *verbiage*" (Mallock's "New Republic," iv. 2).

ver-bose (vėr-bōs'), *a.* [L. *verbosus*, < *verbum*, word.] Expressed in, characterized by the use of, or using many or too many words; wordy: as, "some *verbose* Fourth of July oration" (Mrs. Stowe's "Oldtown Folks," xxxiii.); "a natural reserve accentuated by the *verbose* frankness of her husband" (Maugham's "Moon and Sixpence," xxii.); a *verbose* writer or speaker. —**ver-bose'ly**, *adv.*—**ver-bose'ness**, *n.*—**ver-bos'i-ty** (-bos'i-ti), *n.* [LL. *verbositas*.] The quality of being verbose; wordiness; superfluity of words.

ver-bo-ten (fer-bō'tẹn), *pp.* [G., pp. of *verbieten*, forbid.] Forbidden, as by law; prohibited.

ver-dant (vėr'dạnt), *a.* [Appar. < *verdure*.] Of the green color of flourishing vegetation (as, "the grass, now freshly *verdant*": Hawthorne's "House of the Seven Gables," xix.); green; also, green with vegetation (as, "broad and *verdant* valleys": H. Melville's "Typee," iii.); covered with growing plants or grass; also, green in knowledge; inexperienced; unsophisticated.—**ver'dan-cy**, *n.*—**ver'dant-ly**, *adv.*

verd=an-tique (vėrd-an-tēk'), *n.* [F. *verd antique*, now *vert antique*, 'antique green.'] Any of various greenish stones; esp., a green mottled or veined serpentine, much used by the ancient Romans for interior decoration.

ver-der-er (vėr'dėr-ėr), *n.* [AF. *verderer*, for *verder*, OF. *verdier*, < ML. *viridarius*, < L. *viridis*, green.] In *Eng. forest law*, a judicial officer in the royal forests having charge esp. of the vert, or trees and underwood. Also **ver'der-or.**

ver-dict (vėr'dikt), *n.* [AF. *verdit*, OF. *voirdit*, 'a true statement,' < *ver*, *voir* (< L. *verus*), true, + *dit*, pp. of *dire*, < L. *dicere*, say.] In *law*, the answer of a jury given to the court concerning a matter submitted to their judgment; hence, in general, a judgment or decision (as, the *verdict* of the public).

ver-di-gris (vėr'di-grēs), *n.* [OF. *verdegrice*, *vert de Grece* (F. *vert-de-gris*), 'green of Greece.'] A green or bluish-green poisonous compound, a basic acetate of copper, used as a pigment, drug, etc.; also, popularly, a green or bluish coating formed on copper, brass, or bronze surfaces, and consisting of carbonate of copper.—**ver'di-grised**, *a.* Coated with verdigris.

ver-di-ter (vėr'di-tėr), *n.* [OF. *verd* (F. *vert*) *de terre*, 'green of earth.'] Either of two pigments, one green and the other blue, variously prepared, and consisting usually of carbonate of copper.

ver-dure (vėr'dūr), *n.* [OF. F. *verdure*, < OF. *verd* (F. *vert*), < L. *viridis*, green.] Greenness; esp., the fresh green of flourishing vegetation; also, green vegetation; esp., green grass or herbage; hence, freshness in general; flourishing condition.—**ver'dured**, *a.* Covered with verdure or green

vegetation; verdant.—**ver'dure-less**, *a.* Without verdure. —**ver'dur-ous**, *a.* Rich in verdure or fresh greenness, ạ; vegetation; covered with verdure or green vegetation, ạ; places; also, consisting of verdure; also, pertaining to or characteristic of verdure.

ver-e-cund (ver'ē-kund), *a.* [L. *verecundus*, < *vereri*, feel awe of: cf. *revere*.] Bashful; modest. [Now rare.]

ver-ein (fer-īn'), *n.* [G.] A union, association, or society.

verge[1] (vėrj), *n.* [OF. F. *verge*, < L. *virga*, a slender green branch, switch, rod.] A rod, wand, or staff, esp. one carried as an emblem of authority or ensign of office; formerly, a stick or wand held in the hand by a person swearing fealty to the lord on being admitted as a tenant†; also, an area or district subject to a particular jurisdiction; esp., such an area or district in England, being the compass of the jurisdiction of the Marshalsea Court, and embracing the royal palace (now only hist.); also, the precincts or bounds of a place; also, the edge, rim, or margin of something (as, "He stood on the *verge* of the rug," Dickens's "Our Mutual Friend," iii. 1; "A bright streak of clear red sky appeared over the western *verge* of the prairie," Parkman's "Oregon Trail," v.); the utmost limit to which something extends (as, "this warm, still day on the far *verge* of autumn": Gissing's "Private Papers of Henry Ryecroft," iii. 23); sometimes, a limiting belt, strip, or border of something; the grass edging of a bed or border, as in a garden; also, the limit or point beyond which something begins or occurs (as, "The United Provinces . . . had seemed to be on the *verge* of utter ruin," Macaulay's "Hist. of Eng.," ii.; "She was on the *verge* of tears," W. Churchill's "Coniston," i. 11; "a thought which depresses some spirits . . . to the *verge* of melancholia," Vernon Lee's "Genius Loci," Envoy); also, space within boundaries, or room or scope (as, "A great-grandsire and all his descendants might find ample *verge* here [in a large house]": Hawthorne's "Marble Faun," xxiv.); in *watchmaking*, the spindle of a balance-wheel of a watch; in *printing*, a trigger-like device for releasing the matrices of a linotype machine; in *arch.*, the edge of the tiling projecting over the gable of a roof.—**verge**[1], *v.*; verged, verging. **I.** *tr.* To furnish with a verge or border; form the verge or limit of; pass along the verge or edge of. **II.** *intr.* To be on the verge or border, or touch at the border (as, "Forests . . . are of considerable service to neighbourhoods that *verge* upon them": G. White's "Nat. Hist. of Selborne," i. 7); fig., to border (*on* or *upon*: as, "Keep to common sense . . . you are *verging* on nonsense," C. Brontë's "Jane Eyre," xxxv.; "He was already *verging* on old age," W. H. Hudson's "Green Mansions," xv.).

verge[2] (vėrj), *v. i.*; verged, verging. [L. *vergere*, bend, incline.] To incline, turn, or extend in course or direction (as, "Whose rays . . . *Verge* to one point": Shelley's "Queen Mab," ix. 7); fig., to tend (*toward, to*, etc.: as, "He was a tall man, *verging* toward obesity," Arnold Bennett's "Leonora," i.; "Italy . . . was now rapidly *verging* to a great revolution," Hallam's "Europe during the Middle Ages," i. 1); pass gradually (*into*).

ver-ger (vėr'jėr), *n.* [See *verge*[1].] One who carries a verge, or staff of office; an official who carries the verge or other symbol of office before a bishop, dean, or other dignitary; also, an official who takes care of the interior of a church and acts as attendant.—**ver'ger-ship**, *n.*

Ver-gil-i-an (vėr-jil'i-ạn), *a.* See *Virgilian*.

ve-rid-ic, ve-rid-i-cal (vẹ-rid'ik, -i-kạl), *a.* [L. *veridicus*, < *verus*, true, + *dicere*, say.] Truth-telling; truthful; veracious: opposed to *falsidical*.—**ve-rid-i-cal'i-ty** (-kal'i-ti), *n.*—**ve-rid'i-cal-ly**, *adv.*

ver-i-fi-a-ble (ver'i-fī-ạ-bl), *a.* Capable of being verified. —**ver''i-fi-a-bil'i-ty** (-bil'i-ti), **ver'i-fi-a-ble-ness**, *n.*

ver-i-fi-ca-tion (ver''i-fi-kā'shọn), *n.* [F. *vérification*.] The act of verifying, or the state of being verified; confirmation or substantiation; demonstration; formal assertion of the truth of something; ascertainment of correctness, as by examination or comparison; in *law*, a short confirmatory affidavit at the end of a pleading or petition; a formal statement at the end of a plea, to the effect that the pleader is ready to prove his allegations.—**ver'i-fi-ca-tive, ver'i-fi-ca-to-ry** (-kā-tiv, -kā-tọ-ri), *a.* Serving to verify.

(variable) ḏ as d or j, ş as s or sh, ṭ as t or ch, ẓ as z or zh; *o*, F. cloche; ü, F. menu; çh, Sc. loch; ṅ, F. bonbon; ', primary accent; ″, secondary accent; †, obsolete; <, from; +, and; =, equals. See also lists at beginning of book.

ver-i-fy (ver'i-fī), v. t.; -fied, -fying. [OF. verifier (F. vérifier), < ML. verificare, < L. verus, true, + facere, make.] To prove (something) to be true by means of evidence or testimony; confirm or substantiate; serve to prove (something) true, as evidence, facts, subsequent events, etc., do (as, "The judgment of Thucydides . . . has been verified by the experience of all ages," Adam Smith's "Wealth of Nations," v. 1. 1; "In all probability he had seen many visions . . . which were never verified," Smollett's "Humphry Clinker," Sept. 15); fulfil (a prophecy, promise, etc.: as, "The boy . . . seemed destined to verify the prediction," Motley's "Dutch Republic," vi. 1); also, to state to be true, esp., in legal use, formally or upon oath; also, to ascertain the truth or correctness of (as, "The nature of that insult . . . pointed to one conclusion, which I have never verified, and can now never verify until the great assize": Stevenson's "Master of Ballantrae," v.); esp., to ascertain the correctness of by examination or comparison, or to correct where found erroneous upon examination (as, to verify dates, figures, or spelling; to verify a quotation); also, to establish or identify by investigation; also, to give the appearance of truth to†.—**ver'i-fi-er** (-fī-ėr), n.

ver-i-ly (ver'i-li), adv. [From very, a.] In very truth; truly; really; indeed: as, "Verily God hath heard me" (Ps. lxvi. 19); "We . . . began verily to think that the Bermudas were themselves on a cruise" (Marryat's "Peter Simple," xxxiv.). [Archaic.]

ver-i-sim-i-lar (ver-i-sim'i-lär), a. [L. verisimilis, veri similis: veri, gen. of verum, what is true (prop. neut. of verus, true); similis, like.] Like truth or reality; having the appearance or semblance of truth; likely or probable. —**ver-i-sim'i-lar-ly**, adv.—**ver"i-si-mil'i-tude** (-si-mil'i-tūd), n. [L. verisimilitudo.] Likeness to truth or reality; appearance or semblance of truth; probability; also, something having merely the appearance of truth (as, "They [narratives] are . . . but shadows of fact — verisimilitudes, not verities": Lamb's "Old Benchers of the Inner Temple").

ver-i-ta-ble (ver'i-tạ-bl), a. [OF. veritable (F. véritable), < L. veritas, truth, E. verity.] In accordance with truth or fact, or true, as statements, etc.†; truthful or veracious, as persons†; also, being truly such, genuine, or real (as, "the author himself, the veritable and only genuine author," Arnold Bennett's "Great Man," xii.; "Mr. Spence had a veritable triumph," W. Churchill's "Modern Chronicle," i. 8).—**ver'i-ta-ble-ness**, n.—**ver'i-ta-bly**, adv.

ver-i-ty (ver'i-ti), n.; pl. -ties (-tiz). [OF. verite (F. vérité), < L. veritas, < verus, true.] The quality of being true, or in accordance with fact or reality (as, "Some truths there are, the verity whereof time doth alter," Hooker's "Ecclesiastical Polity," ii. 4. 6; "a volume . . . denying the verity of my experiments and of the positions deduced from them," B. Franklin's "Autobiography," xiii.); truth, fact, or reality (as, "a fellow-passenger, whose discourse in verity might have beguiled a longer voyage": Lamb's "Old Margate Hoy"); also, that which is true; the truth, or the true or actual facts, of a case (as, "May I pray thee to use thy scrupulous custom of searching out the verity": Scott's "Castle Dangerous," iv.); religious or spiritual truth (as, "concerning Faith, the principal object whereof is that eternal Verity which hath discovered the treasures of hidden wisdom in Christ": Hooker's "Ecclesiastical Polity," i. 11. 6); a truth, or true statement, principle, belief, idea, or the like (as, "faint and dim because it is deepest seated in the mind among the eternal verities," Emerson's "Nature," viii.; "beliefs that were accepted as eternal verities," J. H. Robinson's "Mind in the Making," iii. 7); a fact or reality; also, truthfulness†, veracity†, or good faith† (as, "The king-becoming graces, As justice, verity, temperance": Shakspere's "Macbeth," iv. 3. 92).

ver-juice (ver'jös). [OF. vert jus (F. verjus), 'green juice.'] **I.** n. An acid liquor made from the sour juice of crab-apples, unripe grapes, etc., formerly much used for culinary and other purposes; hence, sourness, as of temper or expression. **II.** a. Of or pertaining to verjuice; hence, sour in temper, expression, etc.

ver-meil (ver'mil). [OF. F. vermeil, < L. vermiculus, little worm (kermes insect): see vermicule.] **I.** n. Vermilion (now chiefly poetic); also, metal, as silver or bronze, coated with gilt. **II.** a. Of the color vermilion. [Now chiefly poetic.]

ver-mi-an (vėr'mi-ạn), a. [L. vermis (pl. vermes), worm.] Belonging or pertaining to the Vermes, or worms, a (former) primary division of the animal kingdom; worm-like.

ver-mi-cel-li (vėr-mi-sel'i), n. [It., pl. of vermicello, lit. 'little worm,' dim. of verme, < L. vermis, worm.] A kind of paste of Italian origin in the form of long, slender, solid threads (thinner than those known as spaghetti), to be cooked for food. Cf. macaroni.

ver-mi-cide (vėr'mi-sīd), n. [L. vermis, worm: see -cide.] Any agent that kills worms; esp., a drug used to kill parasitic intestinal worms.—**ver'mi-ci-dal** (-sī-dạl), a.

ver-mic-u-lar (vėr-mik'ū-lär), a. [ML. vermicularis, < L. vermiculus: see vermicule.] Of, pertaining to, or characteristic of a worm or worms; of the nature of a worm; resembling a worm in form; like the method of movement of a worm (as, the vermicular, or peristaltic, motion of the intestines); like the sinuous or wavy track of a worm, as a mark; consisting of or characterized by tortuous or wavy outlines or markings, resembling the tracks of worms.

ver-mic-u-late (vėr-mik'ū-lāt), v. t.; -lated, -lating. [L. vermiculatus, pp. of vermiculari, be worm-eaten, < vermiculus: see vermicule.] To work or ornament with winding or wavy outlines or markings, resembling the tracks of worms: chiefly in vermiculated, pp.—**ver-mic'u-late**, a. Worm eaten, or appearing as if worm-eaten; vermiculated; vermicular; sinuous.—**ver-mic-u-la'tion** (-lā'shon), n. [L. vermiculatio(n-).] The condition of being infested with or eaten by worms; also, a sinuous boring or mark made by, or resembling the track of, a worm; marking or ornamentation resembling the tracks of worms; also, vermicular or peristaltic movement, as of the intestines.

Vermicular Ornamental Work in Masonry. — Palace of the Louvre, Paris.

ver-mi-cule (vėr'mi-kūl), n. [L. vermiculus, dim. of vermis, worm.] A little worm; a small worm-like creature or object.

ver-mic-u-lite (vėr-mik'ū-līt), n. [L. vermiculus, little worm (see vermicule); from the worm-like forms produced under the blowpipe.] Any of various micaceous minerals, usually formed by alteration of the common micas.

ver-mi-form (vėr'mi-fôrm), a. [NL. vermiformis, < L. vermis, worm, + forma, form.] Like a worm in form; long and slender; vermicular: as, the vermiform appendix (see under appendix); the vermiform process (in anat., the median lobe or division of the cerebellum).

ver-mi-fuge (vėr'mi-fūj). [F. vermifuge, < L. vermis, worm, + fugare, put to flight.] **I.** a. Serving to expel worms or other animal parasites from the intestines, as a medicine. **II.** n. A vermifuge medicine or agent.—**ver-mif'u-gal** (-mif'ū-gạl), a.

ver-mil-ion (vėr-mil'yon). [OF. vermeillon (F. vermillon), < vermeil: see vermeil.] **I.** n. A bright red pigment consisting of mercuric sulphide, and prepared from the mineral cinnabar or otherwise; also, the color of this; a brilliant red. **II.** a. Of the color of vermilion; of a brilliant red.—**ver-mil'ion**, v. t. To color with or as with vermilion.

ver-min (vėr'min), n. [OF. vermin, vermine (F. vermine), < L. vermis, worm: see worm.] Noxious, troublesome, or objectionable animals collectively, as worms or snakes (now rare), various small wild animals (now chiefly prov.), animals or birds troublesome in game-preserves (chiefly Eng.), or, now esp., troublesome or disgusting insects or other minute animals, more particularly creeping ones parasitic on living animals or plants; a single animal of this kind (obs. or rare); also, objectionable or obnoxious persons collectively; a single person of this kind.—**ver′mi-nate** (-mi-nāt), v. i.; -nated, -nating. [L. verminatus, pp. of verminare, have worms, have crawling pains, < vermis.] To breed vermin; become infested with parasitic vermin.—**ver-mi-na′tion** (-nā′shon), n. [L. verminatio(n-).] The breeding of vermin; the fact of being infested with vermin, esp. parasitic vermin.—**ver′mi-nous**, a. Infested with vermin, esp. parasitic vermin; of the nature of or resembling vermin; pertaining or due to vermin.—**ver′mi-nous-ly**, adv.

ver-miv-o-rous (vėr-miv′ō-rus), a. [L. vermis, worm, + vorare, devour.] Eating worms; feeding on worms, as certain birds.

ver-mouth (vėr′möth), n. [F. vermout, < G. wermut, wermuth, wormwood.] A liqueur consisting of white wine flavored with wormwood and other ingredients. Also **ver′muth** (-möth).

ver-nac-u-lar (vėr-nak′ū-lär). [L. vernaculus, domestic, native, indigenous, < verna, a slave born in the master's house, a native.] **I.** a. Native or originating in the place of its occurrence or use, as language or words (often as opposed to literary or learned language); expressed or written in the native language of a place, as literary works; using such a language, as a speaker or a writer; pertaining to such a language; in general, native or peculiar to a place, as a style of architecture; endemic, as a disease. **II.** n. The native speech or language of a place; also, the language or phraseology peculiar to a class or profession (as, the vernacular of mining).—**ver-nac′u-lar-ism**, n. A vernacular word or expression; also, the use of the vernacular.—**ver-nac′u-lar-ize**, v. t.; -ized, -izing. To make vernacular; express in or translate into the vernacular.—**ver-nac′u-lar-ly**, adv.

ver-nal (vėr′nal), a. [L. vernalis, < vernus, of spring, < ver, spring.] Of or pertaining to spring; appearing or occurring in spring; appropriate to or resembling spring; fig., belonging to youth, the springtime of life.—**ver′nal-ly**, adv.

ver-na-tion (vėr-nā′shon), n. [NL. vernatio(n-), < L. vernare, grow or flourish as in spring, < ver, spring.] In bot., the disposition of the foliage leaves within the bud. Cf. estivation.

ver-ni-cose (vėr′ni-kōs), a. [NL. vernicosus, < ML. vernix, varnish.] In bot., having a shiny surface as if freshly varnished.

ver-ni-er (vėr′ni-ėr), n. [F.; named from Pierre Vernier (1580–1637), who invented it.] A small, movable, graduated scale running parallel with the fixed graduated scale of a sextant, theodolite, barometer, or other graduated instrument, and used for measuring a fractional part of one of the divisions of the fixed scale.

ver-nis Mar-tin (ver-nē mär-taṅ). [F., 'Martin varnish': from a family of French artificers of the 18th century.] A clear, brilliant lacquer used in the decoration of carriages, furniture, snuff-boxes, fans, etc.

ve-ron-i-ca (vē-ron′i-kä), n. [ML. veronica (the cloth), Veronica (the saint), a name identical with L. Berenice, Macedonian Gr. Βερενίκη, for Gr. Φερενίκη, < φέρειν, bear, + νίκη, vic-

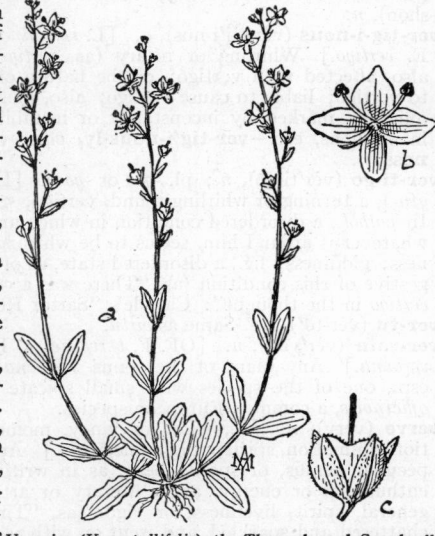

Veronica (V. serpyllifolia), the Thyme-leaved Speedwell. — a, an entire plant; b, a flower; c, fruit.

tory.] The representation of the face of Christ which, according to a legend, was miraculously impressed on a cloth which St. Veronica offered to him to wipe his brow as he carried his cross to Calvary; the cloth itself (cf. sudarium); any similar picture of Christ's face, as on a garment or ornament; also, any plant of the scrophulariaceous genus Veronica, as the speedwell, V. officinalis, the Culver's-root, V. virginica, the brooklime, V. beccabunga, or the thyme-leaved speedwell, V. serpyllifolia (see cut in preceding column).

ver-ru-ca-no (ver-ö-kä′nō), n. [It.; named from La Verruca, a mountain near Pisa.] A conglomerate rock containing rounded fragments of quartz: found in the region of the Alps.

ver-ru-cose, ver-ru-cous (ver′ö-kōs, -kus), a. [L. verrucosus, < verruca, wart.] Studded or covered with wart-like excrescences or elevations.—**ver-ru-cos′i-ty** (-kos′i-ti), n.; pl. -ties (-tiz). The state of being verrucose, or covered with warts; also, a wart.

ver-sant[1] (ver′sant), n. [F., a slope shedding water, < verser, pour, overturn, < L. versare: see versed[2].] A slope of a mountain or mountain-chain; the general slope of a country or region.

ver-sant[2] (ver′sant), a. [L. versans (versant-), ppr. of versari: see versed[2].] Occupied, engaged, or concerned (usually with in or with); also, skilled or versed (in: as, "oaths, a sort of phraseology in which he seemed extremely versant," H. Mackenzie's "Man of Feeling," xxxiii.); conversant or familiar (with).

ver-sa-tile (vėr′sa-til), a. [F. versatile, < L. versatilis, < versare, turn about: see versed[2].] Capable of being turned about or in different directions (as, "a versatile keele [for ships] that should be on hinges," Evelyn's "Diary," Nov. 20, 1661: now chiefly as in bot. and zoöl. below); fig., variable or changeable, esp. in feeling, purpose, policy, etc. (as, "The people of Granada were a versatile, unsteady race," Irving's "Conquest of Granada," xxxi.; "Before the fluctuations of so versatile a mind could fix upon seizing me, I hastened to Highgate," Jane Porter's "Scottish Chiefs," lxxxix.); fickle or inconstant; now, more commonly, capable of or adapted for turning with ease from one to another of various tasks, subjects, etc. (as, "She was so clever, so witty . . . so versatile! why, there's nothing she couldn't do," J. H. Newman's "Callista," xxvi.; "More brilliant, more versatile talent, I never saw," Miss Mulock's "John Halifax," v.); many-sided in abilities (in bot., attached at or near the middle so as to swing or turn freely, as an anther; in zoöl., turning either forward or backward (as, a versatile toe of a bird); moving freely up and down and laterally (as, a versatile antenna).—**ver′sa-tile-ly**, adv.—**ver′sa-tile-ness, ver-sa-til′i-ty** (-til′i-ti), n. The state or quality of being versatile; fig., variableness or inconstancy (as, "Ireland . . . now with strange versatility cursed him as a tyrant": Morley's "Oliver Cromwell," i. 5); esp., facility in doing various things, or many-sided ability (as, "They have observed the versatility of your genius": Marryat's "King's Own," xli.).

verse (vėrs), n. [AS. fers, also OF. F. vers, < L. versus, furrow, line, verse, so called from the turning to begin a new furrow or line, < vertere, turn: see worth[1].] A succession of metrical feet written or printed as one line; one of the lines of a poem; a particular type of metrical line (as, a hexameter verse; a catalectic verse); also, a stanza, or associated group of metrical lines (as, the first verse of a hymn); also, a poem, or piece of poetry; also, metrical composition; poetry, esp. as involving metrical form (as, "who says in verse what others say in prose": Pope's "Satires and Epistles of Horace Imitated," Epistles, ii. 1. 202); a particular type of metrical composition (as, iambic verse; elegiac verse); also, a line of prose, esp. a sentence, or part of a sentence, fitted to be written as one line; a stich; also, a short division of a chapter in the Bible, usually forming one sentence, or part of a long sentence; a similar division in some other book; eccles., a versicle; also, a portion of an anthem to be sung by a single voice or by soloists rather than by the choir.—**verse**, v.; versed, versing. **I.** intr. To compose verses or poetry; versify. **II.** tr. To relate in verse; turn into verse.

versed[1] (vėrst), a. [L. versus, pp. of vertere, turn.] In math., turned.—**versed sine**, in trigon., unity minus the cosine.

versed[2] (vērst), a. [= F. versé, < L. versatus, pp. of versari, occupy or busy one's self, act. versare, turn about, turn over, freq. of vertere, turn.] Experienced; practised; skilled: with in: as, "a person well versed in affairs" (Swift's "Gulliver's Travels," i. 3).

verse-let (vērs'let), n. A little verse; a small or trifling poem.

ver-si-cle (vēr'si-kl), n. [L. versiculus, dim. of versus, E. verse.] A little verse; eccles., one of a series of short sentences, or parts of sentences, usually from the Book of Psalms, said or sung antiphonally in divine service; specif., one said or sung by the officiant, as distinguished from the response of the choir or congregation (cf. response).

ver-si-col-or, ver-si-col-ored (vēr'si-kul-or, -ord), a. [L. versicolor, < vertere (pp. versus), turn, + color, E. color.] Changeable in color; also, of various colors; party-colored.

ver-sic-u-lar (vēr-sik'ū-lär), a. [L. versiculus: see versicle.] Of, pertaining to, or consisting of versicles or verses.

ver-si-fi-ca-tion (vēr″si-fi-kā'shon), n. [L. versificatio(n-).] The act or art of versifying; also, form or style of verse; metrical structure; also, a metrical version of something.

ver-si-fy (vēr'si-fī), v.; -fied, -fying. [OF. F. versifier, < L. versificare, < versus, verse, + facere, make.] I. tr. To relate or describe in verse; treat as the subject of verse; also, to turn into verse or metrical form. II. intr. To compose verses.—**ver'si-fi-er** (-fī-ėr), n.

ver-sion (vēr'shon), n. [F. version, < ML. versio(n-), < L. vertere, turn.] A turning about†; also, conversion or transformation (obs. or rare: as, "the version or conversion of each into other," Emerson's "Representative Men," iii.); also, a translation; esp., a translation of the Bible or a part of it (see phrases below); also, a particular account of some matter, as from one person or source, as contrasted with some other account or accounts (as, "I . . . was determined to . . . give him my version of the affair": W. H. Hudson's "Purple Land," iv.); also, a particular form or variant of anything (as, "a moralised version of the afternoon life of the aristocratic class," H. G. Wells's "Tono-Bungay," iii. 2. § 2; "girls and boys — those who in youth are early versions of their maturity," W. De Morgan's "Joseph Vance," xv.); in med., the act of turning a child in the uterus so as to bring it into a more favorable position for delivery; also, a condition of the uterus in which its axis is turned from the normal position.—**Authorized Version** or **King James Version,** an English translation of the Bible prepared by a special commission of scholars in England under James I., and published in 1611.—**Douay Version,** an English translation of the Bible, from the Latin Vulgate, prepared by Roman Catholic scholars, the Old Testament being published at Douay (Douai) in France, in 1609–10, and the New Testament at Rheims, in 1582.—**Revised Version,** a recension of the Authorized Version of the Bible, prepared by a committee of British and American Protestant scholars, the Old Testament being published in 1885, and the New Testament in 1881.—**ver'sion-al,** a. Of or pertaining to a version.

vers libre (vär lēbr). [F.] Free verse; verse unhampered by fixed metrical forms, in extreme instances consisting of little more than rhythmical prose arranged in lines of irregular length.—**vers=li-brist** (vär'lē'brist), n.

ver-so (vēr'sō), n.; pl. -sos (-sōz). [L., abl. of versus, pp. of vertere, turn.] The reverse, back, or other side of some object; esp., in printing, the back of a leaf, or the left-hand page of an open book (opposed to recto).

verst (vērst), n. [Russ. versta.] A Russian measure of length, equivalent to 3,500 feet (about .6629 mile), or about 1.067 kilometers.

ver-sus (vēr'sus), prep. [ML. versus, against, L. toward, prop. pp. of L. vertere, turn: cf. -ward.] Against: used in legal phraseology to indicate an action brought by one party against another, and in sporting parlance to denote a contest between two teams or players. Abbreviated v. or vs.

vert (vērt), n. [OF. F. vert, < L. viridis, green.] In Eng. forest law, everything bearing green leaves in a forest and capable of serving as cover for deer; also, the right to cut green trees or shrubs in a forest; in her., the tincture green.

ver-te-bra (vēr'tē-brä), n.; pl. -bræ (-brē). [L., joint, vertebra, < vertere, turn.] In anat. and zoöl., any of the bones or segments composing the spinal column: in man and the higher animals consisting typically of a more or less cylindrical body (centrum) and an arch (neural arch) with various processes, forming a foramen through which the spinal cord passes.—**ver'te-bral** (-brạl), a. [NL. vertebralis.] Of or pertaining to a vertebra or the vertebræ; spinal; of the nature of a vertebra; composed of vertebræ (as, the vertebral column, the spinal column); having vertebræ, as an animal.—**ver'te-bral-ly,** adv.—**ver'te-brate** (-brāt). [L. vertebratus.] I. a. Having vertebræ; having a backbone or spinal column (or a notochord); belonging or pertaining to the Vertebrata, a comprehensive division of animals, including all those which have a segmented spinal column (or a notochord); fig., characterized by strength and connectedness, as literary work. II. n. A vertebrate animal.—**ver'te-brat-ed** (-brā-ted), a. Having vertebræ or a spinal column; vertebrate; also, consisting of vertebræ.—**ver-te-bra'tion** (-brā'shon), n. Vertebrate formation.

ver-tex (vēr'teks), n.; pl. -texes or -tices (-ti-sēz). [L. vertex (vertic-), a whirl, whirlpool, vortex, crown of the head (from the disposition of the hair there), pole of the heavens, summit, highest point, < vertere, turn: cf. vortex.] The highest point of something; the apex; the top; the summit; in anat. and zoöl., the crown or top of the head; in astron., etc., the point of the heavens directly overhead; the zenith.—**ver'ti-cal** (-ti-kạl). [F. vertical, < LL. verticalis.] I. a. Of, pertaining to, or situated at the vertex; occupying a position in the zenith or directly overhead (as, "'Tis raging noon; and, vertical, the sun Darts on the head direct his forceful rays": Thomson's "Seasons," Summer, 432); also, being in a position or direction perpendicular to the plane of the horizon (as, "The fine Speke's antelope . . . has pale vertical stripes on the sides": A. R. Wallace's "Darwinism," viii.); upright; plumb; situated or pointing directly upward or downward; in bot., of a leaf, having the blade in a perpendicular plane, so that neither of the surfaces can be called upper or under. II. n. A vertical line, plane, or the like; also, vertical or upright position.—**ver-ti-cal'i-ty** (-kal'i-ti), **ver'ti-cal-ness,** n.—**ver'ti-cal-ly,** adv.

ver-ti-cil (vēr'ti-sil), n. [NL. verticillus, verticil, L. whorl of a spindle, dim. of L. vertex, a whirl: see vertex.] In bot. and zoöl., a whorl or circle, as of leaves, hairs, etc., arranged round a point on an axis.

ver-ti-cil-las-ter (vēr″ti-si-las'tėr), n. [NL., < verticillus, E. verticil.] In bot., an inflorescence in which the flowers are arranged in a seeming whorl, consisting in fact of a pair of opposite axillary, usually sessile, cymes, as in many mints.

ver-ti-cil-late (vēr-tis'i-lāt), a. [NL. verticillatus, < verticillus, E. verticil.] In bot. and zoöl., disposed in or forming verticils or whorls, as flowers, etc.; also, having flowers, etc., so arranged or disposed, as plants. Also **ver-ti'cil-lat-ed** (-lā-ted).—**ver-ti'cil-late-ly,** adv.—**ver-ti-cil-la'tion** (-lā'shon), n.

ver-tig-i-nous (vēr-tij'i-nus), a. [L. vertiginosus, < vertigo, E. vertigo.] Whirling or rotary (as, vertiginous motion); also, affected with vertigo; of the nature of or pertaining to vertigo; liable to cause vertigo; also, fig., apt to change quickly; marked by inconstancy or instability; unsettled in opinions, etc.—**ver-tig'i-nous-ly,** adv.—**ver-tig'i-nous-ness,** n.

ver-ti-go (vēr'ti-gō), n.; pl. -gos or -goes. [L. vertigo (vertigin-), a turning or whirling round, vertigo, < vertere, turn.] In pathol., a disordered condition in which an individual, or whatever is around him, seems to be whirling about; dizziness; giddiness; fig., a disordered state, as of the mind, suggestive of this condition (as, "There was a certain delirious vertigo in the thought": Carlyle's "Sartor Resartus," ii. 5).

ver-tu (vēr-tö'), n. Same as virtu.

ver-vain (vēr'vān), n. [OF. F. verveine, < L. verbena: see verbena.] Any plant of the genus Verbena (see verbena); esp., one of the species with small spicate flowers, as V. officinalis, a common European species.

verve (vērv), n. [F., whim or fancy, momentary inspiration, animation, spirit; origin uncertain.] Animating fancy, peculiar genius, or special bent, as in writing (now rare); enthusiasm or energy, as in literary or artistic work; in general, spirit, liveliness, or vigor (as, "Tina rattled and chattered and sparkled, and went on with verve and gusto": Mrs. Stowe's "Oldtown Folks," xxiii.).

ver-vet (vėr′vet), *n.* [F., < *vert*, green, + (*gri*)*vet*, grivet.] An African monkey, *Cercopithecus pygerythrus*, allied to the green monkey and the grivet, but distinguished by a rusty patch at the root of the tail.

ver-y (ver′i), *a.*; compar. *verier*, superl. *veriest*. [OF. *verai* (F. *vrai*), ult. < L. *verus*, true.] True, genuine, or real (as, the *very* God; a *very* queen); hence, with emphatic or intensive force, being such in the true or full sense of the term (as, the *very* heart of the matter; the *veriest* tyro; "A *verier* monster than on Afric's shore The sun e'er got," Pope's "Satires of Donne," iv. 28); actual (as, caught in the *very* act; "On the *very* morning of the battle the men mutinied for pay," Besant's "Coligny," ix.); precise or identical (as, the *very* thing you should not have done; "The *very* people who reviled him before, now extolled him," Smollett's "Humphry Clinker," June 2); even (what is specified) itself (or himself, themselves, etc.: as, the *very* ground trembled; "The *very* rats . . . were hideous with famine," Dickens's "Oliver Twist," v.; "We grew to dread their *very* names," Du Maurier's "Trilby," iii.); sheer (as, to weep for *very* joy); mere (as, the *very* thought is distressing); also, rightful† or legitimate†; also, truthful† or veracious†.—**ver′y**, *adv.* Truly†; genuinely†; actually†; also, in a high degree, extremely, or exceedingly (used with adverbs and adjectives, also many present and past participles used adjectively: as, *very* soon; *very* glad; *very* pleasing; *very* tiring; *very* tired; with some past participles used adjectively, esp. in America, *much* is usually inserted after *very*, as in 'very much pleased,' rather than 'very pleased,' an expression which is more common in England); also, a mere intensive emphasizing superlatives or stressing identity or oppositeness (as, the *very* best thing to be done; in the *very* same place; the *very* opposite meaning).

ve-si-ca (vẹ-sī′kä), *n.*; pl. *-cæ* (-sē). [L., bladder, blister.] A bladder; a sac; esp., the urinary bladder.—**vesica piscis** (pis′is). [L., 'bladder of a fish.'] A pointed oval figure, formed properly by the intersection of the arcs of two equal circles each of which passes through the center of the other, frequently used in ecclesiastical architecture and art, often to inclose a sacred figure, as that of Christ or the Virgin.—**ves-i-cal** (ves′i-kạl), *a.* Of or pertaining to a vesica or bladder, esp. the urinary bladder.

ves-i-cant (ves′i-kạnt). **I.** *a.* Vesicating; producing a blister or blisters, as a medicinal substance. **II.** *n.* A vesicant agent or substance.

ves-i-cate (ves′i-kāt), *v. t.*; *-cated, -cating*. [NL. *vesicatus*, pp. of *vesicare*, < L. *vesica*, bladder, blister.] To raise vesicles or blisters on; blister.—**ves-i-ca′tion** (-kā′shọn), *n.*—**ves′i-ca-to-ry** (-kạ-tọ-ri), *a.* and *n.* Same as *vesicant*.

ves-i-cle (ves′i-kl), *n.* [L. *vesicula*, dim. of *vesica*, bladder, blister.] A small bladder-like structure, cavity, or the like; a little sac or cyst; a small bubble or hollow sphere; in *anat.* and *zoöl.*, a small bladder-like cavity, esp. one filled with fluid; in *bot.*, a small bladder, or bladder-like air-cavity; in *pathol.*, a circumscribed elevation of the epidermis containing serous fluid; in *geol.*, a small, usually spherical cavity in a rock or mineral, due to gas or vapor.—**ve-sic-u-lar** (vẹ-sik′ū-lär), *a.* Of or pertaining to vesicles; having the form of a vesicle; characterized by or consisting of vesicles.—**ve-sic′u-late** (-lāt), *a.* Characterized by or covered with vesicles; of the nature of a vesicle.—**ve-sic′u-late**, *v. t.* or *i.*; *-lated, -lating.* To make or become vesiculate or vesicular.—**ve-sic-u-la′tion** (-lā′shọn), *n.*—**ve-sic′u-lose** (-lōs), **ve-sic′u-lous**, *a.* [LL. *vesiculosus*.] Full of vesicles; vesiculate.

ves-per (ves′pėr). [L. *vesper*, evening, the evening star, the west, akin to Gr. ἕσπερος, of or at evening, western (see *Hesper*); in part, F. *vespres*, pl., now *vêpres*, < ML. *vesperæ*, pl., vespers, evensong, < L. *vespera*, evening.] **I.** *n.* [*cap.*] The evening star, esp. Venus; Hesper; [*l. c.*] evening (as, "black *vesper's* pageants," Shakspere's "Antony and Cleopatra," iv. 14. 8: now rare; *pl.* (occasionally also *sing.*), the sixth of the seven canonical hours, or the service for it, occurring in the late afternoon or the evening; hence, a religious service held in the late afternoon or the evening; evensong; also, evening devotions (poetic); a song at evening, as of a bird (poetic); *sing.*, the vesper-bell. **II.** *a.* Of, pertaining to, appearing in, or proper to the evening: as, "eve's *vesper* star" (Wiffen's tr. Tasso's "Jerusalem Delivered," iv. 27); "The young men were sitting smoking the *vesper* cigar" (Thackeray's "Newcomes," xxxviii.).— **ves′per=bell′**, *n.* The bell that summons to vespers or evensong.

ves-per-til-i-o-nine (ves-pėr-til′i-ọ-nin), *a.* [L. *vespertilio(n-)*, bat, < *vesper*, evening.] Of or pertaining to the bats of the subfamily *Vespertilioninæ*, of wide distribution and including many well-known species.

ves-per-tine (ves′pėr-tin or -tīn), *a.* [L. *vespertinus*, < *vesper*, evening.] Of, pertaining to, or occurring in the evening; in *bot.*, opening or expanding in the evening, as certain flowers; in *zoöl.*, appearing or flying in the early evening; crepuscular; in *astron.*, descending toward the horizon at sunset, as a star or planet.

ves-pi-a-ry (ves′pi-ạ-ri), *n.*; pl. *-ries* (-riz). [Irreg. (after *apiary*) < L. *vespa*, wasp.] A wasps' nest.

ves-pid (ves′pid). [NL. *Vespidæ*, pl., < L. *vespa*, wasp.] **I.** *n.* Any member of the *Vespidæ*, a widely distributed family of wasps comprising the social wasps (including the hornets), which live like bees in communities composed of males, females, and workers. **II.** *a.* Belonging or pertaining to the *Vespidæ*.

ves-pine (ves′pin), *a.* [L. *vespa*, wasp.] Of or pertaining to wasps; wasp-like.

ves-sel (ves′el), *n.* [OF. *vessel, vaissel* (F. *vaisseau*), < L. *vascellum*, dim. of *vasculum*, small vessel, dim. of *vas*, vessel.] A hollow or concave article, as a cup, bowl, pot, pitcher, vase, bottle, barrel, tub, etc., for holding liquid or other contents (as, a drinking-*vessel*; earthen, china, silver, tin, wooden, or wicker *vessels*; "the Holy *Vessel* of the Grail," Tennyson's "Holy Grail," 837); a receptacle or container; fig., a person regarded as a receptacle or container or as made for some use or end (chiefly in or after Biblical expressions: as, "He is a chosen *vessel* unto me, to bear my name before the Gentiles," Acts, ix. 15; "*vessels* of wrath fitted to destruction," Rom. ix. 22; "giving honour unto the wife, as unto the weaker *vessel*," 1 Pet. iii. 7); also, a ship, boat, or any floating structure for traversing the water and transporting persons or goods; a craft for traveling on water, now esp. one larger than an ordinary rowboat; also, in *anat.* and *zoöl.*, a tube or duct, as an artery, vein, or the like, containing or conveying blood or some other bodily fluid; in *bot.*, a duct formed of connected cells which have lost their intervening partitions, containing or conveying sap, etc.

vest (vest), *n.* [F. *veste*, < It. *veste*, < L. *vestis*, garment, clothing; akin to E. *wear*[2].] An outer garment, robe, or gown (archaic); an ecclesiastical vestment (obs. or rare); dress, apparel, or vesture (poetic); specif., a long garment resembling a cassock, worn by men in the time of Charles II.; also, a waistcoat, or short sleeveless garment worn by men under the coat; a similar garment, or a part or trimming simulating the front of such a garment, worn by women; also, an undervest.—**vest**, *v.* [OF. *vestir* (F. *vêtir*), < L. *vestire*, clothe, < *vestis*.] **I.** *tr.* To clothe, dress, or robe (archaic or poetic in general sense); dress in ecclesiastical vestments; invest formally with a garment or dress; cover or drape (an altar); fig., to cover or surround as if with, or like, a garment; also, to invest or endow (a person, etc.) with something, esp. with powers, functions, etc. (as, "He . . . *vested* me with full authority over his household," Smollett's "Humphry Clinker," Oct. 26; "Halifax . . . was *vested* with the entire patronage and correspondence belonging to American affairs," Bancroft's "Hist. of the U. S.," Amer. Revolution, i. 4); put or establish in the possession of something, or in some office or position; also, to place or settle (something, esp. property, rights, powers, etc.) in the possession or control of a person or persons (usually with *in*: as, to *vest* an estate or a title in a person; "Both house and ground were *vested* in trustees, expressly for the use of any preacher," B. Franklin's "Autobiography," vii.; "The government was *vested* in fifty-six senators," Hallam's "Europe during the Middle Ages," iii. 2); also, to invest (money, etc.: as, "Your fortune is *vested* in the English funds," C. Brontë's "Jane Eyre," xxxiii.: obs. or archaic). **II.** *intr.* To put on vestments; also, to become vested in a person or persons, as a right; pass into possession; devolve upon a person as possessor.

Ves-ta (ves'tȧ), *n.* [L., akin to Gr. Ἐστία (lit. 'hearth'), the Greek goddess Hestia, of like attributes.] Among the ancient Romans, the goddess of the hearth and hearth-fire, worshiped in a temple containing an altar on which a sacred fire was kept burning perpetually under the care of vestal virgins; also [*l. c.*], a short friction-match of wax; also, a similar match of wood.—**ves'tal.** [L. *Vestalis.*] **I.** *a.* Of or pertaining to Vesta (as, a *vestal* virgin, among the ancient Romans, one of four, later six, virgins consecrated to Vesta and to the service of watching the sacred fire kept burning perpetually on her altar); also, pertaining to, characteristic of, or resembling a vestal virgin; virgin; chaste. **II.** *n.* A vestal virgin; also, in general, a virgin; a chaste unmarried woman; sometimes, a nun or religieuse; humorously, an unmarried woman, or maiden (as, "He led the way with another ancient *vestal* in black satin and bugles": Lever's "Harry Lorrequer," xiii.).

The Giustiniani Statue of Vesta (Hestia). — Torlonia Museum, Rome.

vest-ed (ves'ted), *p. a.* Clothed or robed, esp. in ecclesiastical vestments (as, a *vested* choir); also, settled or secured in the possession of a person or persons; so established in the possession of a person or persons as to be regarded, in the contemplation of the law, as a fixed right.

ves-ti-a-ry (ves'ti-ā-ri). [L. *vestiarius*, adj. (as n., *vestiarium*, neut. of *vestiarius*), < *vestis*, garment, clothing.] **I.** *a.* Of or pertaining to garments or dress. **II.** *n.* A room or place for keeping garments or clothes; also, the vestry in a church (now rare).

ves-ti-bule (ves'ti-būl), *n.* [F. *vestibule*, < L. *vestibulum*, entrance-court before a house.] An entrance-court, as before a Roman or Greek building; in modern use, a passage, hall, or antechamber between the outer door and the interior parts of a house or building; also, a covered and inclosed space at the end of a railroad passenger-car, having side doors for entering and leaving the train, and itself affording protected passage to the next car; in *anat.* and *zoöl.*, any of various cavities or hollows regarded as forming an approach or entrance to another cavity or space (as, the *vestibule* of the ear, a cavity in the bony labyrinth between the cochlea and the semicircular canals).—**vestibule school,** a department of an industrial establishment in which new employees are trained for the work they are to perform.—**ves-tib'u-lar** (-tib'ū-lär), *a.*—**ves'ti-bule,** *v. t.*; *-buled, -buling.* To provide with a vestibule or vestibules, as a railroad-car; unite by means of vestibules, as a railroad-train: chiefly in *pp.*

ves-tige (ves'tij), *n.* [F. *vestige*, < L. *vestigium*, footstep, footprint, trace: see *stile.*] A footprint or track (now rare); also, a mark, trace, or visible evidence of something which is no longer present or in existence (as, "I . . . saw the *vestiges* of a fire": Borrow's "Bible in Spain," ii.); a part or piece that remains after the disappearance or destruction of the main portion (as, "long lines of edifices, *vestiges* of whose ruins may still be found": Prescott's "Conquest of Mexico," iv. 1); a surviving evidence or memorial of some condition, practice, etc. (as, "*vestiges* of a very universal custom": Hallam's "Europe during the Middle Ages," ii. 1); also, a very slight trace or amount of something (as, "a hideous desert, where no *vestiges* were seen of vegetation," De Quincey's "Revolt of the Tartars"; "This stranger . . . had no *vestige* of the air of deference proper to a stranger in such a place," Tarkington's "Magnificent Ambersons," v.); in *biol.*, a degenerate or imperfectly developed organ or structure having little or no utility, but which in an earlier stage of the individual or in lower preceding organisms performed a useful function.—**ves-tig'i-al** (-tij'i-al), *a.* Pertaining to or of the nature of a vestige.—**ves-tig'i-al-ly,** *adv.*

vest-ing (ves'ting), *n.* Cloth for making vests or waistcoats.

vest-ment (vest'ment), *n.* [OF. *vestement* (F. *vêtement*), < L. *vestimentum*, clothing, garment, < *vestire*, clothe, E. *vest, v.*] A garment, esp. an outer garment, robe, or gown; often, an official or ceremonial robe; fig., something that clothes or covers like a garment (as, "Great live-oaks stretched their arms clad in green *vestments* and gray drapings": G. W. Cable's "Bonaventure," i. 8); *eccles.*, a garment worn by an ecclesiastic during a service or ceremony; one of the garments worn by the clergy and their assistants, choristers, etc., during divine service and on other occasions; esp., one of the garments worn by the celebrant, deacon, and subdeacon during the celebration of the eucharist.

ves-try (ves'tri), *n.*; pl. *-tries* (-triz). [ME. *vestrye*, for *vestiarie*, E. *vestiary, n.*] A room or place where garments or clothes are kept (now rare); also, a room in or a building attached to a church; in which the vestments, and sometimes also the sacred vessels, etc., are kept; a sacristy; in some churches, a room in or a building attached to a church, used as a chapel, for prayer-meetings, for the Sunday-school, etc.; in parishes of the Church of England, a meeting of all, or of a committee of, the parishioners, held usually in the vestry of the church, for the despatch of the official business of the parish; also, the body of parishioners meeting, constituting a parochial board of management; in the Protestant Episcopal Church in the U. S., a committee, chosen by the members of a congregation, who, in conjunction with the churchwardens, manage the temporal affairs of a church.—**ves'try-man** (-man), *n.*; pl. *-men.* A member of a church vestry.—**ves'try=room,** *n.* A room forming the vestry of a church.

ves-tur-al (ves'tūr-al), *a.* Of or pertaining to vesture or clothing.

ves-ture (ves'tūr), *n.* [OF. *vesture, vesteure,* < *vestir,* E. *vest, v.*] Clothing or apparel, or a garment (as, "Nor on him put The napless *vesture* of humility," Shakspere's "Coriolanus," ii. 1. 250; "Pharaoh . . . arrayed him in *vestures* of fine linen," Gen. xli. 42: archaic or literary); fig., something that covers like a garment, or a covering (archaic or literary); in *law*, everything growing on and covering the land, with the exception of trees; any such product, as grass or wheat.—**ves'ture,** *v. t.*; *-tured, -turing.* To clothe, as with vesture. [Archaic or literary.]

Ve-su-vi-an (vē-sū'vi-an), *a.* Of, pertaining to, or resembling Mount Vesuvius, a volcano near Naples; volcanic.—**ve-su'vi-an**[1], *n.* A kind of match or fusee for lighting cigars, etc.—**ve-su'vi-an**[2], *n.* [G.] Same as *vesuvianite.*—**ve-su'vi-an-ite** (-īt), *n.* [From *vesuvian*[2].] A mineral, a basic silicate of aluminium and calcium, containing small amounts of iron, etc., commonly crystalline in form, and usually of a brown to green color; idocrase: found on Mount Vesuvius.

vet[1] (vet), *n.* A veteran; a veteran soldier. [Colloq.]

vet[2] (vet), *n.* A veterinarian: as, "The doctor . . . ranked below the vicar but above the '*vet*' " (H. G. Wells's "Tono-Bungay," i. 1. § 3). [Colloq.]—**vet**[2], *v. t.*; *vetted, vetting.* To examine or treat as a veterinarian or (humorously) a doctor does: as, "I'd as soon *vet* a hippopotamus for nerves as you" (Buchan's "Three Hostages," vi.). [Colloq.]

ve-tan-da (vē-tan'dȧ), *n. pl.* [L., neut. pl. gerundive of *vetare,* forbid.] Things to be forbidden.

vetch (vech), *n.* [OF. *veche, vece* (F. *vesce*), < L. *vicia,* vetch.] Any of various plants, mostly climbing herbs, of the fabaceous genus *Vicia,* as *V. sativa,* the common tare, which is cultivated for forage; also, any of various allied plants, as the chickling, *Lathyrus sativus,* of Europe, which

Vetch (*Vicia sativa*). — *a,* flower.

is cultivated for its edible seeds and also as a forage-plant; also, the bean-like seed or fruit of any such plant.—**vetch′-ling,** *n.* Any of the plants constituting the fabaceous genus *Lathyrus,* as *L. pratensis* which is common in meadows.

vet-er-an (vet′ẹ-ṛạn). [L. *veteranus,* < *vetus* (*veter*-), old.] **I.** *a.* Grown old in service; having served for a long period; experienced through long service or practice (as, "a *veteran* politician," Hawthorne's "House of the Seven Gables," xviii.; "a *veteran* toper," Whyte-Melville's "Katerfelto," xviii.); esp., of soldiers, having had long service or much experience in warfare (as, "*veteran* troops": Adam Smith's "Wealth of Nations," v. 1. 1); also, of, pertaining to, or characteristic of veterans. **II.** *n.* One who has seen long service in any occupation or office; one who has had much experience in some field; esp., a veteran soldier (as, "He gazed on the lines of his *veterans,* whose weather-beaten visages and battered armor told of battles won and difficulties surmounted": Prescott's "Conquest of Mexico," iii. 8).

vet-er-i-na-ri-an (vet″ẹ-ri-nā′ri-ạn), *n.* One who practises veterinary medicine or surgery.

vet-er-i-na-ry (vet′ẹ-ri-nạ-ri). [L. *veterinarius,* < *veterinus,* belonging or pertaining to cattle.] **I.** *a.* Of or pertaining to the medical or surgical treatment of cattle, horses, and other animals. **II.** *n.*; pl. *-ries* (-riz). A veterinarian.

ve-to (vē′tō), *n.*; pl. *-toes* (-tōz). [L. *veto,* 'I forbid.'] A prohibition directed against some proposed or intended act (as, "On George's intercourse with Amelia he put an instant *veto*": Thackeray's "Vanity Fair," xviii.); the power or right of preventing action by a prohibition; in specific use, the power or right vested in one branch of a government to negative the determinations of another branch; esp., the right of a chief executive, as a president or governor, to reject bills passed by the legislature; the exercise of this right; a document or message by which this right is exercised, in which the executive officially communicates his reasons for rejecting a legislative bill.—**ve′to,** *v. t.*; *-toed, -toing.* To direct a veto against; refuse to consent to; negative or reject, as a legislative bill, by exercising the right of veto. —**ve′to-er,** *n.*

vet-tu-ra (vet-tö′rä), *n.*; pl. *-re* (-rā). [It., < L. *vectura,* < *vehere,* carry: see *vehicle.*] A kind of four-wheeled carriage used in Italy.—**vet-tu-ri′no** (-rē′nō), *n.*; pl. *-ni* (-nē). [It.] In Italy, one who lets out or drives a vettura; also, a vettura.

vex (veks), *v.* [OF. F. *vexer,* < L. *vexare* (pp. *vexatus*), shake, disturb, molest, annoy.] **I.** *tr.* To disturb, molest, or harass, as by aggression or interference (archaic: as, "They [Ammonites] *vexed* and oppressed the children of Israel," Judges, x. 8); trouble or afflict physically (archaic: as, to be *vexed* with the gout or with boils); distress mentally, or grieve (archaic: as, "First hang the child . . . A sight to *vex* the father's soul," Shakspere's "Titus Andronicus," v. 1. 52); torment, plague, or worry (as, "That eternal want of pence Which *vexes* public men," Tennyson's "Will Waterproof's Lyrical Monologue," 44; "Alas, I know not, and in vain *vex* myself to know," Carlyle's "Sartor Resartus," ii. 1); often, to irritate, annoy, provoke, or make angry (as, "Such an injury would *vex* a very saint," Shakspere's "Taming of the Shrew," iii. 2. 28; "It really *vexes* me . . . that Mr. Hollingsworth should be such a laggard," Hawthorne's "Blithedale Romance," iii.; "You stumble . . . and are *vexed* at your own awkwardness," G. W. Curtis's "Prue and I," i.); also, to disturb by motion, stir up, or toss about, or throw into commotion (archaic or poetic: as, storms *vex* the air, water, or trees; "The whole sea was . . . *vexed* by the oars of ships," Irving's "Conquest of Granada," lx.); turn or break up (the soil, etc.) in working (archaic); also, to agitate, discuss, or debate (a subject, etc.) with vigor (as, "The question is everywhere *vexed* . . . whether the man is not better who strives with temptation": Emerson's "Essays," Spiritual Laws). **II.** *intr.* To feel distressed, worried, or annoyed (obs. or archaic); also, to move tumultuously (rare: as, "fragments of broken rocks . . . obstructions to the course of the rapid stream, which *vexed* and fretted about them," H. Melville's "Typee," viii.).—**vex-a-tion** (vek-sā′shọn), *n.* [OF. F. *vexation,* < L. *vexatio*(n-).] The act of vexing, or the state of being vexed; harassment

(archaic); affliction or torment, esp. of mind or spirit (as, "All is vanity and *vexation* of spirit": Eccl. i. 14); irritation or annoyance (as, "He felt no anger, not even *vexation*": Galsworthy's "Saint's Progress," iv. 6); also, something that vexes; an affliction; a trouble; an annoyance (as, "To those who lie out of the road of great afflictions, are assigned petty *vexations*": Scott's "Guy Mannering," v.).—**vex-a′-tious** (-shus), *a.* Causing vexation; vexing; annoying; in *law,* of legal actions, instituted without sufficient grounds, and serving only to cause annoyance to the defendant.— **vex-a′tious-ly,** *adv.*—**vex-a′tious-ness,** *n.*—**vexed,** *p. a.* Disturbed; troubled; annoyed; tossed about, as waves; much discussed or disputed, as a question.—**vex′ed-ly,** *adv.* —**vex′ed-ness,** *n.*—**vex′er,** *n.*

vex-il (vek′sil), *n.* In *bot.,* same as *vexillum.*

vex-il-la (vek-sil′ạ), *n.* Plural of *vexillum.*

vex-il-lar (vek′si-läṛ), *a.* Of or pertaining to a vexillum.

vex-il-la-ry[1] (vek′si-lạ̈-ri), *n.*; pl. *-ries* (-riz). [L. *vexillarius,* < *vexillum,* standard: see *vexillum.*] One who carries a vexillum or standard; also, one of the oldest class of ancient Roman veteran soldiers, who served under a special standard.

vex-il-la-ry[2] (vek′si-lạ̈-ri), *a.* Vexillar.—**vexillary estivation,** in *bot.,* a mode of estivation in which the exterior petal, as in the case of the vexillum, is largest, and incloses and folds over the other petals.

vex-il-late (vek′si-lāt), *a.* Having a vexillum or vexilla.

vex-il-lum (vek-sil′um), *n.*; pl. *vexilla* (-ạ). [L., standard, company, troop, < *vehere,* carry.] A military standard or flag carried by ancient Roman troops; a body of men serving under such a standard; some other standard, banner, or the like; in *bot.,* the large upper petal of a papilionaceous flower; in *ornith.,* the web or vane of a feather.

Pea-blossom, with Vexillum at left.

vex-ing (vek′sing), *p. a.* That vexes; annoying.—**vex′ing-ly,** *adv.*

vi-a[1] (vī′ạ or vē′ạ), *prep.* [L., abl. of *via,* way: see *way*[2].] By way of; by a route that passes through: as, to go to Denver *via* Chicago.

vi-a[2] (vē′ạ or vī′ạ), *interj.* [It., < L. *via,* way: see *via*[1].] Away! off! [Obs. or archaic.]

vi-a-ble (vī′ạ-bl), *a.* [F. *viable,* < *vie,* life, < L. *vita:* see *vital.*] Capable of living; physically fitted to live; of a fetus, having reached such a stage of development as to permit continued existence, under normal conditions, outside of the womb.—**vi-a-bil′i-ty** (-bil′i-ti), *n.*

vi-a-duct (vī′ạ-dukt), *n.* [L. *via,* way, + E. *-duct* as in *aqueduct.*] A bridge consisting of a series of narrow masonry arches with high supporting piers, for carrying a road, railroad, etc., over a valley, ravine, or the like; more broadly, any more or less extensive bridge or elevated roadway.

vi-a-graph (vī′ạ-gräf), *n.* [L. *via,* way: see *-graph.*] An instrument which indicates, and usually records, the resistances (as grades, and inequalities of surface) offered by the roadway to a wheeled vehicle running over it.

Viaduct. — Ancient Roman aqueduct called the Pont du Gard, near Nîmes, France; adapted as a viaduct for the modern highway.

vi-al (vī′ạl), *n.* [ME. *viole,* var. of *fiole,* < OF. F. *fiole,* < L. *phiala,* < Gr. φιάλη, a shallow cup or bowl.] A small vessel for liquids, as one of glass; now, esp., a small glass bottle for holding medicines or the like; fig., *pl.* or *sing.,* a store or accumulation (of wrath, indignation, etc.) poured out upon an offender, victim, or other object (from the seven golden vials full of the wrath of God mentioned in Rev. xv. 7, xvi. 1–17).—**vi′al,** *v. t.*; -aled or -alled, -aling or -alling. To put into or keep in a vial.—**vi′al-ful** (-fúl), *n.*; pl. *-fuls.*

vi-and (vī′ạnd), *n.* [OF. F. *viande*, food, meat, < L. *vivenda*, neut. pl. gerundive of *vivere*, live.] An article of food; commonly, *pl.*, articles or dishes of food, now usually of a choice or delicate kind (as, "All the choicest *viands* that the village could furnish, were served up in rich profusion": Irving's "Captain Bonneville," xxxiii.); also, *sing.*, food or sustenance (archaic).

vi-at-ic (vī-at′ik), *a.* [L. *viaticus*, < *via*, way, road, journey.] Pertaining to a way or road, a journey, or traveling.

vi-at-i-cum (vī-at′i-kum), *n.*; pl. *-ca* (-kạ). [L., neut. of *viaticus*: see *viatic*, and cf. *voyage*.] Among the ancient Romans, a provision or allowance for traveling, orig. of transportation and supplies, later of a sum of money, made to officials sent out on public missions; hence, in general, a supply of money or necessaries for a journey; provisions for use on a journey; *eccles.*, the eucharist or communion as given to a person dying or in danger of death.

vi-brac-u-lum (vī-brak′ū-lum), *n.*; pl. *-la* (-lạ). [NL., < L. *vibrare*, shake, vibrate.] In *zoöl.*, one of the long, tapering, whip-like, movable appendages possessed by certain polyzoans.—**vi-brac′u-lar** (-lạr), *a.*

vi-brant (vī′brạnt), *a.* Vibrating; moving to and fro rapidly; quivering; specif., vibrating so as to produce sound, as a string; also, of sounds, characterized by perceptible vibration, or resonant (as, "the *vibrant* sound of his fiddle": Longfellow's "Evangeline," i. 4).—**vi′bran-cy**, *n.*—**vi′brant-ly,** *adv.*

vi-brate (vī′brāt), *v.*; -brated, -brating. [L. *vibratus*, pp. of *vibrare*, shake, vibrate.] **I.** *tr.* To cause to move to and fro, swing, or oscillate; also, to cause to move to and

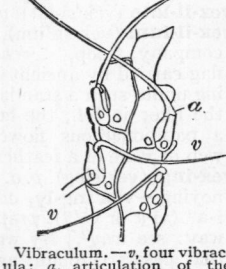

Vibraculum.—*v*, four vibracula; *a*, articulation of the base of one of them. (Magnified.)

fro or up and down quickly and repeatedly; cause to quiver, or shake tremulously; also, to launch or hurl with a tremulous motion (archaic); give forth or emit (sound, etc.) by or as by vibratory motion; also, to measure or indicate by vibration or oscillation (as, a pendulum *vibrating* seconds). **II.** *intr.* To move to and fro, as a pendulum does; oscillate; fig., to move between extremes; fluctuate; vacillate; also, to move to and fro or up and down quickly and repeatedly; quiver; tremble; sometimes, to thrill, as in emotional response (as, "Her being *vibrated* to the mysterious and beautiful romance of existence," Arnold Bennett's "Hilda Lessways," ii. 6; "His whole soul *vibrated* to the appeal," Motley's "Dutch Republic," vi. 6); also, of sounds, to produce or have a quivering or vibratory effect (as, "He hears The clang of tumult *vibrate* on his ears": Byron's "Corsair," i. 16); resound; of other things, to pass or penetrate with a similar effect (as, "Those powers that . . . Catch every nerve and *vibrate* through the frame": Goldsmith's "Traveller," 220).—**vi′bra-tile** (-brạ-til), *a.* Capable of vibrating, or susceptible of being vibrated; having a vibratory motion; also, pertaining to or of the nature of vibration.—**vi-bra-til′i-ty** (-til′i-ti), *n.*—**vi-bra′tion** (-brā′shọn), *n.* [L. *vibratio(n-).*] The act or state of vibrating; oscillation; fluctuation; vacillation; quivering motion; tremulous effect; also, a single vibrating motion; an oscillation; a quiver or tremor; in *physics*, the oscillating, reciprocating, or other stationary motion of a body forced from a position or state of equilibrium; esp., the rapid alternating or like motion of an elastic body whose equilibrium has been disturbed; the vibratory motion of a string or other sonorous body, producing musical sound; the analogous motion of the particles of a mass of air, etc., whose state of equilibrium has been disturbed, as in transmitting sound, etc.; also, a single complete motion of any of these kinds, from the position of equilibrium until the motion begins to repeat itself; sometimes, one half of this complete motion.—**vi-bra′tion-al,** *a.*—**vi-bra′ti-un-cle** (-shi-ung-kl), *n.* [Dim. of *vibration.*] A slight vibration.—**vi′bra-tive** (-brạ-tiv), *a.* Vibratory.—**vi-bra-to** (vē-

brä′tō), *n.* [It., pp. of *vibrare*, vibrate, < L. *vibrare.*] In *music*, a pulsating effect, produced in singing by the rapid reiteration of emphasis on a tone, and on bowed instruments by a rapid change of pitch corresponding to the vocal tremolo.—**vi′bra-tor** (vī′brā-tọr), *n.* One who or that which vibrates; any of various instruments or devices causing or having a vibratory motion or action.—**vi′bra-to-ry** (-brạ-tō-ri), *a.* Producing vibration; vibrating, or admitting of vibration; of the nature of or consisting in vibration; pertaining to vibration.

vib-ri-o (vib′ri-ō), *n.*; pl. *vibrios* (-ōz), L. *vibriones* (vib-ri-ō′nēz). [NL., < L. *vibrare*, vibrate.] Any of the more or less spirally curved motile bacteria constituting the genus *Vibrio*, characterized by a lively motion.—**vib′ri-oid. I.** *a.* Resembling a vibrio: as, a *vibrioid* body (in *bot.*, one of certain vibrio-like cylindrical bodies occurring in the cytoplasm of some algæ and fungi). **II.** *n.* In *bot.*, a vibrioid body.

vi-bris-sa (vī-bris′ạ), *n.*; pl. *vibrissæ* (-ē). [NL., < L. *vibrissæ*, pl., the hairs in the nostrils, < *vibrare*, vibrate.] In *anat.* and *zoöl.*, one of the hairs growing in the nostrils; one of the stiff, bristly hairs growing about the mouth of certain animals, as a whisker of a cat; in *ornith.*, one of the long, slender, bristle-like feathers growing along the side of the mouth in many birds.

vi-bur-num (vī-bėr′num), *n.* [L., the wayfaring-tree.] Any of the shrubs or small trees constituting the caprifoliaceous genus *Viburnum*, species of which, as the cranberry-tree or snowball, *V. opulus*, are cultivated for ornament; also, the dried bark of certain species, used in medicine.

vic-ar (vik′ạr), *n.* [OF. F. *vicaire*, < L. *vicarius*, a substitute, deputy, orig. adj.: see *vicarious.*] One acting in place of another; a person authorized to perform the functions of another; a substitute in office; a deputy; specif., the Pope as representative on earth of God or Christ (chiefly in 'vicar of Christ' or 'vicar of Jesus Christ'); an ecclesiastic representing the Pope or a Roman Catholic bishop; in the Church of England, a per-

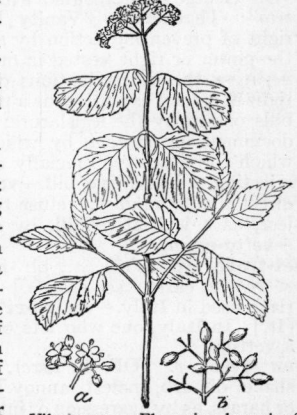

Viburnum. — Flowering branch of *Viburnum dentatum*, an arrow-wood of eastern North America; *a*, flowers; *b*, fruits.

son acting as priest of a parish in place of the rector, or as representative of a religious community to which the tithes belong; the priest of a parish the tithes of which are impropriated, and who receives only the smaller tithes or a salary; in the Protestant Episcopal Church in the U. S., a clergyman whose sole or chief charge is a chapel dependent on the church of a parish, or a bishop's assistant in charge of a church or mission.—**vicar apostolic,** in the *Rom. Cath. Ch.*, formerly, an archbishop, bishop, or other ecclesiastic to whom the Pope delegated a portion of his jurisdiction; now, a missionary or titular bishop stationed either in a country where no episcopal see has yet been established, or in one where the succession of bishops has been interrupted.—**vicar forane.** See *forane.*—**Vicar of Bray,** a person who changes his principles or opinions to suit the time or circumstances: from a 16th century vicar of Bray, in Berkshire, England, who is said to have held his office continuously through alternating periods of Catholic and Protestant ascendancy by corresponding changes in his faith.—**vic′ar-age** (-āj), *n.* The office or duties of a vicar; the benefice of a vicar; the residence of a vicar.—**vic′ar-ess,** *n.* A female vicar or deputy; also, the wife of a vicar.—**vic′ar-gen′er-al,** *n.*; pl. *vicars-general* or *vicar-generals.* A deputy having extensive power or jurisdiction (a title formerly applied to the Pope as vicar of Christ and head of the church, and given to Thomas Cromwell as representative of Henry VIII. in ecclesiastical affairs); in the Roman Catholic Church, a priest deputized by a bishop to assist him in the

---

administration of a diocese; in the Church of England, an ecclesiastical officer, usually a layman, who assists a bishop or an archbishop in the discharge of his office.—**vi-ca-ri-al** (vi-kā′ri-ạl), *a.* Of or pertaining to a vicar or vicars; acting as or holding the office of a vicar; also, delegated or vicarious, as powers.—**vi-ca′ri-ate** (-āt), *n.* The office or authority of a vicar; also, a district under the charge of a vicar.

vi-ca-ri-ous (vī-kā′ri-us), *a.* [L. *vicarius*, substituted, vicarious, < *vicis* (gen.), change, turn, stead: cf. *vice*[3].] Taking the place of another person or thing, or acting or serving as a substitute (as, a *vicarious* agent); performed, exercised, received, or suffered in place of another (as, *vicarious* work or authority; *vicarious* reward or punishment); pertaining to or involving the substitution of one for another; in *physiol.*, noting or pertaining to the performance by one organ or part of the functions normally belonging to another (as, a *vicarious* hemorrhage, one proceeding from another than the usual part).—**vi-ca′ri-ous-ly**, *adv.*—**vi-ca′ri-ous-ness**, *n.*

vic-ar-ship (vik′ạr-ship), *n.* The office of a vicar.

vice[1] (vīs), *n.* [OF. F. *vice*, < L. *vitium*, fault, defect, failing, vice.] A fault, defect, or imperfection (as, a *vice* of method; a *vice* of literary style); a physical defect or infirmity (as, a constitutional *vice*); a bad habit, as in a horse; esp., in persons, an immoral or evil habit or practice (as, the *vice* of drunkenness; "Lord, Lord, how subject we old men are to this *vice* of lying!" Shakspere's "2 Henry IV.," iii. 2. 326); a particular form of depravity (as, a grave moral fault (as, "Obstinacy, Sir, is certainly a great *vice*": Burke's "American Taxation"); also, immoral conduct or life; indulgence in impure or degrading practices or pleasures; [*cap.* or *l. c.*] a character in the old English morality plays, a personification of vice in general or of a particular vice, serving as the buffoon (cf. *morality*).

vice[2] (vīs), *n.* and *v.* See *vise*.

vi-ce[3] (vī′sē), *prep.* [L., abl. of (gen.) *vicis*, change, turn, place, stead: cf. *vicarious*.] Instead of; in the place of: as, A becomes chairman, *vice* B resigned.

vice[4] (vīs), *n.* [Short for words with the prefix *vice-*.] A substitute or deputy official, as a vice-chancellor or vice-consul.

vice- (vīs-). [L. *vice*: see *vice*[3].] A prefix in official titles denoting a substitute, deputy, or subordinate, as in *vice-chairman*, *vice-governor*, *vice-king*, *vice-queen*.—**vice′=ad′-mi-ral**, *n.* A naval officer next in rank below an admiral.—**vice′=ad′mi-ral-ty**, *n.*—**vice′=chan′cel-lor**, *n.* A substitute, deputy, or subordinate chancellor.—**vice′=chan′-cel-lor-ship**, *n.*—**vice′=con′sul**, *n.* A consular officer of a grade below that of consul, often one exercising special functions in a district under the supervision of a consul-general or a consul.—**vice′=con′sul-ship**, *n.*

vice-ge-rent (vīs-jē′rẹnt). [ML. *vicegerens* (-*ent*-), n.: see *vice-* and *gerent*.] **I.** *n.* An officer deputed by a ruler or supreme head to exercise the powers of the ruler or head; in general, one deputed to exercise the powers or authority of another; a deputy. **II.** *a.* Exercising delegated powers; characterized by delegation of powers (as, "Under his [the Son's] great *vicegerent* reign abide United": Milton's "Paradise Lost," v. 609).—**vice-ge′ren-cy** (-rẹn-si), *n.*

vice-less (vīs′les), *a.* Free from vices or vice.

vi-ce-na-ry (vis′e-nạ-ri), *a.* [L. *vicenarius*, < *viceni*, twenty each, distributive of *viginti*, twenty.] Pertaining to or consisting of twenty.

vi-cen-ni-al (vī-sen′i-ạl), *a.* [L. *vicennium*, a period of twenty years, < *vicies*, twenty times, + *annus*, year.] Of or for twenty years; occurring every twenty years.

vice=pres-i-dent (vīs′prez′i-dẹnt), *n.* [See *vice-*.] An officer next in rank to a president (in various senses), whether acting as a deputy or assistant or holding a merely honorary title; in a modern republic, an officer next in rank to a president and taking his place under certain conditions (as, the *Vice-President* of the U. S., who is elected at the same time as the President, and succeeds to the presidential office on the resignation, removal, death, or disability of the President).—**vice′=pres′i-den-cy**, *n.*

vice-re-gal (vīs-rē′gạl), *a.* Of or pertaining to a viceroy.

vice-reine (vīs′rān, F. vēs-rän), *n.* [F. *vice-reine*, < L.

vice (see *vice-*) + F. *reine*, < L. *regina*, queen.] The wife of a viceroy; also, a woman exercising the powers of a viceroy.

vice-roy (vīs′roi), *n.* [F. *vice-roi*, < L. *vice* (see *vice-*) + F. *roi*, < L. *rex*, king.] One appointed to rule a country or province as the deputy of the sovereign (as, the *viceroy* of India); also, a handsome American butterfly, *Basilarchia archippus*, of an orange-red color with black markings.—**vice-roy′al**, *a.*—**vice-roy′al-ty**, *n.*; pl. -ties (-tiz). The dignity, office, or period of office of a viceroy (as, "During his short *viceroyalty* in Ireland he showed very remarkable administrative talents": Lecky's "Hist. of Eng. in the 18th Century," iii.); also, a country or province ruled by a viceroy. —**vice′roy-ship**, *n.*

vi-ce ver-sa (vī′sē vẻr′sạ). [L.: *vice*, abl. of *vicis*, turn, place (see *vice*[3]); *versa*, pp. fem. abl. of *vertere*, turn, turn about.] The order being changed (from that of a preceding statement); so, likewise, with transposition of terms; conversely: as, A distrusts B, and *vice versa* (and B distrusts A).

Vich-y (vish′i, F. vē-shē) **wa′ter.** A natural mineral water from springs at Vichy, in central France, containing sodium bicarbonate and other alkaline salts (also iron, etc.), used in the treatment of digestive disturbances, gout, etc.; hence, some water of similar composition, natural or artificial. Also called *Vichy* or *vichy*.

vi-ci-nage (vis′i-nāj), *n.* [OF. *visenage* (F. *voisinage*), < L. *vicinus*: see *vicinity*.] The region near or about a place (as, "It [a place] lay in the woods . . . in the *vicinage* of the castle": Scott's "Castle Dangerous," xviii.); the neighborhood or vicinity; also, a particular neighborhood or district, or the people belonging to it; also, the state or fact of being near; proximity.

vi-ci-nal (vis′i-nạl), *a.* [L. *vicinalis*, < *vicinus*: see *vicinity*.] Belonging to a neighborhood or district (as, a *vicinal* road, a local road or by-road, as distinguished from a highway; "an old *vicinal* way, which branched from the great western road of the Romans," Hardy's "Return of the Native," i. 1); also, neighboring; adjacent; in *crystal.*, noting planes whose position varies very little from certain prominent fundamental planes which they replace.

vi-cin-i-ty (vi-sin′i-ti), *n.*; pl. -ties (-tiz). [L. *vicinitas*, < *vicinus*, neighboring, < *vicus*, row of houses, quarter, village: see *wick*[2].] The state or fact of being near in place, or proximity or propinquity (as, "The *vicinity* of so remarkable a people [Normans] early began to produce an effect on the public mind of England": Macaulay's "Hist. of Eng.," i.); also, the region near or about a place, or the neighborhood or vicinage (as, "strangers, not only from the *vicinity*, but from many leagues around": Prescott's "Conquest of Mexico," iv. 2); also, close relationship or connection†.

vi-cious (vish′us), *a.* [OF. *vitious* (F. *vicieux*), < L. *vitiosus*, < *vitium*, E. *vice*[1].] Characterized or marred by vices, faults, or defects (as, a *vicious* literary style; *vicious* reasoning; "Oliver's Latin was *vicious* and scanty," Morley's "Oliver Cromwell," i. 1); faulty, defective, or bad; diseased†; morbid, foul, or noxious (obs. or archaic); legally defective, or illegal; of a horse, etc., having vices or bad habits, or an ugly disposition (as, "Some horses . . . are almost incurably *vicious*, and must be conquered by main force": Roosevelt's "Ranch Life and the Hunting-Trail," iii.); of persons, society, the stage, habits, pleasures, etc., addicted to or characterized by vice or immorality, depraved, or profligate (as, "He [Wycherley] appears to have led . . . the life of a *vicious* old boy about town," Macaulay's "Essays," Comic Dramatists of the Restoration; "*Vicious* as the stage was, it only reflected the general vice of the time," Green's "Short Hist. of the Eng. People," ix. 1); less definitely, given or disposed to evil, or bad, as a person (as, "The enemy's mother . . . called Tom a bad, *vicious*, vulgar child," Mark Twain's "Tom Sawyer," i.; "one boy, however, idle and *vicious* as I know him to be," Archibald Marshall's "Anthony Dare," i.); reprehensible, blameworthy, or wrong, as an action, practice, etc.; spiteful or malignant, as persons, actions, spirit, etc. (as, "The people were really mad and *vicious*, and flung dirt upon us," Galt's "Annals of the Parish," i.; a *vicious* attack; *vicious* animosity); hence, unpleasantly severe (colloq.: as, a *vicious* headache; "Both of these [rifles] . . . had a *vicious* recoil," Roosevelt's "Hunting Trips of a Ranchman,"

(variable) ḍ as d or j, ṣ as s or sh, ṭ as t or ch, ẓ as z or zh; o, F. cloche; ü, F. menu; ċh, Sc. loch; ṅ, F. bonbon; ′, primary accent; ″, secondary accent; †, obsolete; <, from; +, and; =, equals. See also lists at beginning of book.

i.).—**vicious circle.** See *circle, n.*—**vi′cious-ly,** *adv.*—**vi′cious-ness,** *n.*

vi-cis-si-tude (vi-sis′i-tūd), *n.* [L. *vicissitudo* (*vicissitudin-*), < *vicis*, change, turn: see *vice*³.] Change, mutation, or mutability (as, "the continual *vicissitude* of circumstances," Hawthorne's "House of the Seven Gables," xxi.; "to see the *vicissitude* of men's minds, and uncertainty of human affairs," Strype's "Memorials of Cranmer," iii. 1); regular change or succession of one state or thing to another (as, the *vicissitude* of the seasons); esp., interchange or alternation, as of states or things (as, the *vicissitude* of day and night; "The moon will come and go With her monotonous *vicissitude*," Lowell's "Prometheus," 321; "In fine *vicissitude*, Beauty alternates with Grandeur," Carlyle's "Sartor Resartus," ii. 6); also, a change or variation, or something different, occurring in the course of a thing (as, "So great a *vicissitude* in his life could not at once be received as real": Hawthorne's "Scarlet Letter," xx.); esp., *pl.*, changes, variations, successive or alternating phases or conditions, etc., in the course of anything (as, "After many *vicissitudes* of fortune . . . his wishes were eventually accomplished," Hallam's "Europe during the Middle Ages," i. 1; "tolerably inured to the *vicissitudes* of traveling," Parkman's "Oregon Trail," ii.).—**vi-cis-si-tu′di-nous** (-tū′di-nus), *a.* Characterized by vicissitudes or changes, esp. in fortune: as, a *vicissitudinous* life.

vi-comte (vē-kôṅt′), *n.* [F.: see *viscount*.] In French use, a viscount.—**vi-com-tesse** (vē-kôṅ-tes′), *n.* [F.] In French use, a viscountess.

vic-tim (vik′tim), *n.* [L. *victima*, beast for sacrifice, victim.] A living creature sacrificed in religious rites (as, "The altars smoked with fresh hecatombs of human *victims*": Prescott's "Conquest of Mexico," iii. 7); hence, a person or animal sacrificed, or regarded as sacrificed, in any undertaking or cause (as, *victims* of militarism; *victims* of vivisection); a sufferer from any destructive, injurious, or adverse action or agency (as, *victims* of disease, of ambition, or of oppression; "the *victim* of a plot," J. Conrad's "Rescue," v. 2); a dupe, as of a swindler.—**vic′tim-iz-a-ble** (-ī-za̤-bl), *a.* Capable of being victimized.—**vic′tim-ize** (-īz), *v. t.*; *-ized, -izing.* To make a victim of; slay as or like a sacrificial victim; put in the position of a victim or sufferer (as, "a fascinating married man, *victimized* by a crazy wife": Mrs. Stowe's "Oldtown Folks," xl.); dupe, swindle, or cheat.—**vic″tim-i-za′tion** (-i-zā′shọn), *n.*—**vic′tim-iz-er** (-ī-zėr), *n.*

vic-tor (vik′tọr), *n.* [L. *victor*, < *vincere* (pp. *victus*), conquer.] **I.** *n.* One who has vanquished or defeated an adversary; a conqueror; a winner in any struggle or contest. **II.** *a.* Victorious: as, "thy *victor* sword" (Shakspere's "King Lear," v. 3. 132).

Vic-to-ri-a (vik-tō′ri-ạ), *n.* [L. *victoria*, E. *victory*.] Queen of Great Britain and Ireland (reigned 1837–1901) and Empress of India (from 1876); [*l. c.*] a low, light, four-wheeled carriage with a calash-top, a seat for two passengers, and a raised seat in front for the driver; also, a kind of touring-car with a folding top, commonly covering only the rear seat; also, a gigantic water-lily, *Victoria regia* (or *amazonica*), a native of still waters from Paraguay to Venezuela, with leaves often over 6 feet in diameter, and white to rose-colored nocturnal flowers from 12 to 18 inches across.—

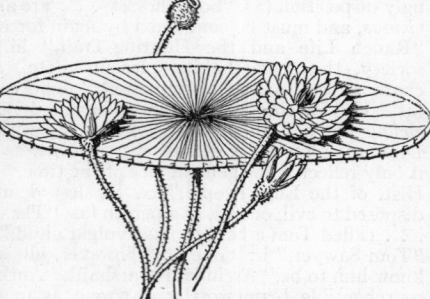
Victoria (*Victoria regia*).

Victoria Cross, a British decoration, a bronze cross bearing the words "For Valour," instituted by Queen Victoria in 1856 and awarded to soldiers and sailors of any grade for acts of conspicuous bravery in the presence of the enemy. See cut in next column. —**Vic-to′ri-an. I.** *a.* Of or pertaining to Queen Victoria or her reign or period: as, the *Victorian* age; *Victorian* poets. **II.** *n.* A person, esp. an author, belonging to the Victorian period in England.—**Vic-to′ri-an-ism,** *n.* The distinctive character, modes of thought, tendencies, etc., of the Victorian period; a characteristic of the Victorian period.

Victoria Cross.

vic-to-ri-ous (vik-tō′ri-us), *a.* [L. *victoriosus*.] Having achieved a victory; characterized by or pertaining to victory; conquering; triumphant.—**vic-to′ri-ous-ly,** *adv.*—**vic-to′ri-ous-ness,** *n.*

vic-to-ry (vik′tọ-ri), *n.*; pl. *-ries* (-riz). [L. *victoria*, < *victor*, E. *victor*.] The position or success of a victor (as, "*Victory* and triumph to the Son of God, Now entering his great duel!" Milton's "Paradise Regained," i. 173); the ultimate and decisive superiority in a battle or any struggle or contest (as, "The ill fate of Labienus [in a battle] decided the *victory*," Froude's "Cæsar," xxv.; "Thanks be to God, which giveth us the *victory*," 1 Cor. xv. 57); a success or triumph won over the enemy in battle or war, or an engagement ending in such a triumph (as, military and naval *victories*; "There has been a great battle in Spain; and it has been a great *victory*," De Quincey's "English Mail-Coach," i.); any success or successful performance achieved over an adversary or opponent, opposition, difficulties, etc. (as, "Peace hath her *victories* No less renown'd than War," Milton's "Sonnets," To the Lord General Cromwell; a *victory* over natural obstacles); also [*cap.*], a female deity of the ancient Romans, or a corresponding deity of the ancient Greeks (by them called Νίκη, Nike), the personification of victory in battle or in any active struggle; a figure, statue, or representation of either deity (as, the Samothracian or Winged *Victory*, a famous statue, now headless, dating from about 306 B.C., representing the winged goddess on the prow of a ship: found in the island of Samothrace, in the northern Ægean Sea, in 1863, and now in the Louvre, in Paris); [*cap.* or *l. c.*] any personage, figure, or representation intended to typify victory.—**Victory Medal,** a bronze medal, bearing on the obverse a winged figure typifying victory, authorized by the U. S. Government in 1919 for presentation to all who served in the army or navy of the country during the World War, and distributed in 1920.—**Victory note,** a note belonging to the issue of notes known as the Victory Liberty Loan, put forth by the U. S. Government in May, 1919, after the cessation of fighting in the World War, to provide funds for meeting obligations connected with the war. Cf. *Liberty bond*, under *liberty*.

Samothracian Victory, in the Louvre, Paris.

vic-tress (vik'tres), *n.* A female victor.

vic-trix (vik'triks), *n.* [L., fem. of *victor*, E. *victor*.] A female victor; a victress.

vict-ual (vit'l), *n.* [OF. *vitaille* (F. *victuaille*), < LL. *victualia*, prop. neut. pl. of L. *victualis*, of or for sustenance, < *victus*, sustenance, food, < *vivere*, live.] Food or provisions, usually for human beings (archaic or prov.: as, "A fair-hair'd youth, that in his hand Bare *victual* for the mowers," Tennyson's "Geraint and Enid," 202; "The farmers . . . had to travel through a heavy road with their *victual*," Galt's "Annals of the Parish," xviii.); *pl.*, supplies or articles of food prepared for use (as, "A plateful of coarse *victuals* was set before him," Dickens's "Oliver Twist," iv.: now chiefly prov. or colloq.).—**vict'ual**, *v.*; -*ualed* or -*ualled*, -*ualing* or -*ualling*. [OF. *vitailler*.] **I.** *tr.* To supply with victuals or provisions; furnish (a ship, troops, etc.) with supplies of food: as, "I *victualled* my ship for the voyage" (Defoe's "Robinson Crusoe," i. 10); "Dalgetty . . . withdrew to *victual* his charger and himself, for the fatigues of his approaching mission" (Scott's "Legend of Montrose," viii.). **II.** *intr.* To take on or obtain victuals or provisions; also, to take food, eat, or feed (archaic: as, "We found Peggy and Smiler [horses] . . . *victualling* where the grass was good," Blackmore's "Lorna Doone," iii.).—**vict'ual-er**, **vict'ual-ler**, *n.* [OF. *vitaillier*.] One who furnishes victuals or provisions; a purveyor; also, a keeper of an eating-house, inn, or tavern (as, a licensed *victualer*, in British use, an innkeeper or keeper of a public house, licensed to sell food or esp. drink, to be consumed on the premises); also, a ship carrying provisions for other ships or for troops, etc. (as, "There were now above 100 sail of *victuallers*, gunboats, and ships of war": Southey's "Life of Nelson," iii.).

vi-cu-gna (vi-kö'nyä), *n.* See *vicuña*.

vi-cu-ña (vi-kö'nyä), *n.*; pl. -*ñas* (-nyäz). [Sp.; from Peruvian.] A wild South American ruminant animal, *Lama* (or *Auchenia*) *vicunia*, related to the guanaco but smaller, and having a soft, delicate wool; also, a fabric made of this wool, or of some substitute, usually twilled and finished with a soft nap.

Vicuña.

vi-dame (vē-däm), *n.* [F., < ML. *vice-dominus*, < L. *vice* (see *vice-*) + *dominus*, lord.] In French feudal use, the deputy or representative of a bishop in temporal affairs, holding a fief from him; hence, a French minor title of nobility.

vi-de (vī'dē). [L.] 'See': esp. used in making reference to parts of a text.—**vide infra** (in'frä). [L.] 'See below.' Cf. *infra*.—**vide supra** (sū'prä). [L.] 'See above.' Cf. *supra*.

vi-del-i-cet (vi-del'i-set), *adv.* [L., for *videre licet*, 'it is permitted to see.'] That is to say; to wit; namely: as, "one of Rob's original profession, *videlicet*, a drover" (Scott's "Rob Roy," Introd.). Abbreviated *viz*.

vi-dette (vi-det'), *n.* Same as *vedette*.

vid-u-ous (vid'ū-us), *a.* [L. *viduus*.] Widowed. [Rare.]

vie (vī), *v.*; *vied*, *vying*. [Ult. < OF. *envier*, invite, challenge, F. increase a stake in gaming, < L. *invitare*, E. *invite*.] **I.** *intr.* In card-playing, to stake a sum on the value of one's hand†; hence, to strive in competition or rivalry with another (as, "The bishops, the higher nobility, the lawyers, *vied* with one another in exalting his prerogatives," Hallam's "Europe during the Middle Ages," iii. 1; "grasses whose verdure *vies* with the emerald," Bancroft's "Hist. of the U. S.," Amer. Revolution, ii. 2); contend for superiority. **II.** *tr.* To stake in card-playing†; put forward or offer in competition

or rivalry (archaic: as, "The roguish eye of J—ll . . . almost invites a stranger to *vie* a repartee with it," Lamb's "Old Benchers of the Inner Temple").

Vi-en-nese (vē-e-nēs' or -nēz'). **I.** *a.* Of or pertaining to Vienna, in Austria. **II.** *n.*; pl. -*nese*. A native or inhabitant of Vienna.

view (vū), *n.* [OF. *veue* (F. *vue*), < *veeir* (F. *voir*), < L. *videre*, see.] A seeing or beholding; an examination by the eye; a survey or inspection; also, sight or vision (as, the field of *view*; exposed or lost to *view*); range of sight or vision (as, objects in *view*, or out of *view*); also, a sight or prospect of some landscape, scene, etc. (as, "The citadel . . . commands a superb *view* of the town": Kinglake's "Eothen," xviii.); a landscape or scene presented to the eye (as, "She gazed at the *view* up and down the valley": Wister's "Virginian," xxii.); a **picture** of a prospect or scene; the aspect, or a particular aspect, of something (as, a front *view*; a profile *view*); also, mental contemplation or examination; a mental survey (as, "Far from deciding on a sudden or partial *view*, I would patiently go round and round the subject": Burke's "Conciliation with the Colonies"); contemplation or consideration of a matter with reference to action (as, a project in *view*); aim, intention, or purpose (as, "cannibals and savages, who would have seized on me with the same *view* as I did of a goat or a turtle": Defoe's "Robinson Crusoe," i. 14); prospect or expectation (as, with no *view* of success); consideration or regard (as, in *view* of the risks); also, a general account or description of a subject (as, Jeremy Collier's "Short *View* of the English Stage"); also, a particular way of regarding something; a conception, notion, or idea of a thing; an opinion; a theory. —**in view**, in sight; within range of vision; also, under consideration; in contemplation or prospect; before one as an end sought.—**in view of**, in sight of; also, in prospect or anticipation of; also, in consideration of (as, "I . . . must take what I can get, *in view of* my age": Galsworthy's "Saint's Progress," iv. 1); on account of.—**on view**, in a situation for public inspection; on exhibition: as, pictures placed *on view*.—**point of view.** See under *point, n.*—**with a view to**, with an aim or intention directed to (as, "He moved towards the staircase door *with a view to* slamming it": H. G. Wells's "Bealby," i.); with an expectation or hope of; also, in consideration of; also, with regard to.—**view**, *v. t.* To see or behold (as, "All the day they [eyes] *view* things unrespected": Shakspere's "Sonnets," xliii.); look at, survey, or inspect (as, "The party *viewed* the scene for a minute or two without speaking," Marryat's "King's Own," xlii.; "She went with him to '*view*' the house," Besant's "All Sorts and Conditions of Men," vi.); also, to contemplate mentally; consider; regard (in a particular light, or as specified: as, "He [man] *viewed* the crocodile as a thing sometimes to worship, but always to run away from," De Quincey's "English Mail-Coach," i; "The first successes of these Norman leaders were *viewed* unfavourably by the popes," Hallam's "Europe during the Middle Ages," iii. 1).—**view'er**, *n.*—**view'=hal-loo** (-ha-lö'), *n.* The shout uttered by a huntsman on seeing a fox break cover.—**view'less**, *a.* That cannot be viewed or seen, or invisible (as, "On the fourth side is the sea, stretching away towards a *viewless* boundary": Hawthorne's "Twice-Told Tales," Sights from a Steeple); also, without views or opinions.—**view'less-ly**, *adv.*—**view'point**, *n.* A point of view. See under *point, n.*—**view'y**, *a.* Given to or full of mere views, notions, or opinions; theorizing; visionary: as, "A mind as keen as his . . . is in danger of getting *viewy*" (Buchan's "Three Hostages," v.).

vi-ges-i-mal (vī-jes'i-mal), *a.* [L. *vigesimus, vicesimus*, twentieth, ordinal of *viginti*, twenty.] Twentieth; pertaining to or based upon twenty; proceeding by twenties.

vi-gi-a (vi-jē'ä), *n.* [Sp. *vigía*, lit. a watch, lookout, < L. *vigilia*: see *vigil*.] An indication given on a hydrographic chart of the presence of a rock, shoal, or the like, dangerous to navigation.

vig-il (vij'il), *n.* [OF. F. *vigile*, < L. *vigilia*, wakefulness, watch, < *vigil*, awake, alert, akin to *vigere*, be lively: see *wake*².] A devotional watching, or keeping awake, during the customary hours of sleep; a nocturnal devotional exercise or service, esp. on the eve of (before) a church festival (often in *pl.*); hence, the eve, or day and night, before a church festival, esp. an eve which is a fast (as, "On the *vigil* of St. Bede, In evil hour, he cross'd the Tweed": Scott's "Marmion," i. 21); in general use, a keeping awake for any purpose during the natural hours of sleep; a watch kept by night or at other times; a course or period of watchful attention; sometimes, a period of wakefulness from inability to sleep.

vig-i-lance (vij′i-lạns), *n.* The quality or fact of being vigilant; watchfulness; also, a watch† or guard†; in *pathol.*, insomnia.—**vigilance committee**, an unauthorized committee of citizens organized for the maintenance of order and the summary punishment of crime in the absence of regular or efficient courts. [U. S.]

vig-i-lant (vij′i-lạnt), *a.* [= Sp. *vigilante*, < L. *vigilans* (-*ant*-), ppr. of *vigilare*, keep awake, watch, < *vigil*, awake: see *vigil*.] Sleeplessly watchful; ever awake and alert; keenly attentive to detect danger; wary: as, a *vigilant* sentry or guardian; *vigilant* attention or care.—**vig-i-lan′te** (-län′tā), *n.* [Sp., 'vigilant.'] A member of a vigilance committee. [U. S.]—**vig′i-lant-ly**, *adv.*—**vig′i-lant-ness**, *n.*

vi-gnette (vin-yet′), *n.* [F., dim. of *vigne*, E. *vine*.] An ornament or decoration representing vine-branches or the like, as in architecture or on a manuscript; a decorative design or small ornamental picture used in printing, as on the title-page of a book or at the beginning or end of a chapter; an engraving, drawing, photograph, or the like that shades off gradually at the edges; any small, pleasing picture or view (as, "sketching fancy *vignettes*, representing any scene that happened momentarily to shape itself in the ever-shifting kaleidoscope of imagination": C. Brontë's "Jane Eyre," xxi.); fig., a small, graceful literary sketch.—**vi-gnette′**, *v. t.*; *vignetted*, *vignetting*. To make a vignette of; finish (a picture, photograph, etc.) in the manner of a vignette.—**vi-gnet′ter**, *n.* A device for producing photographic vignettes.

vig-or (vig′ọr), *n.* [OF. *vigor* (F. *vigueur*), < L. *vigor*, liveliness, activity, vigor, < *vigere*, be lively: see *vigil*.] Active strength or force, as of body or mind; healthy physical or mental energy or power; also, force of healthy growth in any living matter or organism, as a plant; in general, active or effective force (as, "The feudal principle still retained its *vigor*": J. F. Kirk's "Charles the Bold," iii. 2); energy; energetic activity; sometimes, legal force, or validity.—**vig′or-ite** (-īt), *n.* An explosive consisting chiefly of nitroglycerin and potassium chlorate, used in blasting.—**vig′or-ous**, *a.* [OF. *vigorous* (F. *vigoureux*), < ML. *vigorosus*.] Full of or characterized by vigor (as, "a *vigorous* old man, who spent half of his day on horseback," W. H. Hudson's "Far Away and Long Ago," xxiii.; "the time of youth and *vigorous* manhood," Steele, in "Spectator," 260); strong and active; robust; also, growing well, as a plant (as, "*vigorous* and abundant foliage": A. R. Wallace's "Darwinism," xiv.); in general, energetic or forcible (as, "Some measures more *vigorous* . . . seemed necessary to restore the influence of their aristocracy": Hallam's "Europe during the Middle Ages," iii. 2); powerful in action or effect.—**vig′or-ous-ly**, *adv.*—**vig′or-ous-ness**, *n.*

vig′our, *n.* British preferred form of *vigor*.

vi-king (vī′king), *n.* [From Scand.: cf. Icel. *víkingr*, Norw., Dan., and Sw. *viking*, sea-rover, pirate, of uncertain origin; not connected with E. *king*.] A Scandinavian rover or sea-robber of the class that infested the seas about northern and western Europe during the 8th, 9th, and 10th centuries, making raids upon the coasts.

vi-la-yet (vē-lä-yet′), *n.* [Turk. *vilâyet*.] A province, or administrative division of the first class, of Turkey.

vile (vīl), *a.*; compar. *viler*, superl. *vilest*. [OF. F. *vil*, < L. *vilis*, cheap, poor, mean, vile.] Of little value or account, or paltry (as, "I never knew man hold *vile* stuff so dear," Shakspere's "Love's Labour's Lost," iv. 3. 276; "Better to me the meanest weed . . . The *vilest* herb," Tennyson's "Amphion," 95); hence, poor, wretched, or sorry, as in quality or state (as, "a poor man in *vile* raiment": Jas. ii. 2); also, of mean or low condition, as a person (as, "Be he ne'er so *vile*, This day shall gentle his condition": Shakspere's "Henry V.," iv. 3. 62); mean or menial, as tasks, etc. (as, "They . . . with hands unused to service *vile* Lit up the

fire": W. Morris's "Jason," xv. 776); low, degraded, or ignominious, as a condition, etc. (as, *vile* servitude; durance *vile*); also, morally base, depraved, or despicable, as persons or the mind, character, actions, etc. (as, "some of the *vilest* outcasts in the country," Parkman's "Oregon Trail," i.; *vile* thoughts, purposes, endeavors, or arts); despicably or revoltingly bad; foul, as language (as, "the *vilest* abuse, the foulest charges": Mrs. H. Ward's "Robert Elsmere," xxiii.); also, repulsive or disgusting, as to the senses or feelings; highly offensive, obnoxious, or objectionable (often used to express strong personal disapproval: as, reeking with some *vile* perfume; a *vile* creature); in general, and emphatically, wretchedly bad (as, *vile* weather; the coffee was *vile*; "the worst pen and the *vilest* ink," Gissing's "Private Papers of Henry Ryecroft," ii. 16).—**vile′ly**, *adv.*—**vile′ness**, *n.*

vil-i-fi-ca-tion (vil″i-fi-kā′shọn), *n.* The act of vilifying, or the state of being vilified.

vil-i-fy (vil′i-fī), *v. t.*; *-fied*, *-fying*. [LL. *vilificare*, < L. *vilis*, cheap, mean, + *facere*, make.] To make vile, debase, or degrade (obs. or rare); also, to depreciate in speech or writing; speak evil of; defame; traduce.—**vil′i-fi-er** (-fī-ėr), *n.*

vil-i-pend (vil′i-pend), *v. t.* [L. *vilipendere*, < *vilis*, cheap, mean, + *pendere*, weigh, value, regard.] To regard or treat as of little value or account; speak of disparagingly or contemptuously; vilify.—**vil′i-pend-er**, *n.*

vill (vil), *n.* [AF. and OF. *vile* (F. *ville*, town), < L. *villa*: see *villa*.] A village. [Archaic or hist.]

vil-la (vil′ạ), *n.*; pl. *villas* (-ạz). [= It. *villa*, < L. *villa*, country-house, farm, village, appar. a dim. of *vicus*, village: see *vicinity*.] A country residence, usually of some size and pretensions; a country-seat; also, a mansion in the suburbs or at the seashore; a detached or semidetached dwelling-house of the better class (Eng.).

vil-lage (vil′āj), *n.* [OF. F. *village*, < L. *villaticum*, neut. of *villaticus*, belonging to a country-house or farm, E. *villatic*.] A small assemblage of houses in a country district, being larger than a hamlet and smaller than a town, and sometimes (as in parts of the U. S.) incorporated as a municipality; also, the inhabitants collectively (as, "Almost all the *village* had one name": Tennyson's "Aylmer's Field," 35).—**vil-lag-er** (vil′ạ-jėr), *n.* An inhabitant of a village.

vil-lain (vil′ān), *n.* [AF. and OF. *vilain*, *vilein*, < ML. *villanus*, < L. *villa*: see *villa*.] A member of a class of half-free persons under the feudal system who were serfs with respect to their lord but had the rights and privileges of freemen with respect to others (commonly spelled *villein*); hence, a low-born rustic†; a churl†; also, a base or wicked person; an unprincipled person who does or seeks to do wrong or harm; a dangerous scoundrel; often, a character in a play, novel, or the like who constitutes an important evil agency in the plot.—**vil′lain-age** (-āj), *n.* See *villeinage*.—**vil′lain-ess**, *n.* A female villain.—**vil′lain-ous**, *a.* Having the character of a villain; pertaining to or befitting a villain; base; wicked; vile; hence, of things, very bad or unpleasant, or wretched (as, *villainous* weather; "a *villainous* joke," Blackmore's "Lorna Doone," xvii.).—**vil′lain-ous-ly**, *adv.* —**vil′lain-ous-ness**, *n.*—**vil′lain-y** (-i), *n.*; pl. *-ies* (-iz). [OF. *vilanie* (F. *vilenie*).] The condition of a villain or serf†; also, the action or conduct of a villain or scoundrel; a villainous act or deed (as, "An individual who is capable of such baseness would not hesitate at the perpetration of any *villainy*": Borrow's "Bible in Spain," iv.).

vil-la-nel-la (vil-ạ-nel′ä), *n.*; pl. *-nellas* (-nel′äz), It. *-nelle* (-nel′lā). [It., < *villano*, rustic, < ML. *villanus*, E. *villain*.] An Italian rustic part-song without accompaniment.

vil-la-nelle (vil-ạ-nel′), *n.* [F., < It. *villanella*: see *villanella*.] A short poem of fixed form, written in tercets (usually five) with a final quatrain, on two rimes, in the typical form having the first line of the first tercet repeated as the last line of the second and fourth tercets, and the last line of the first tercet as the last line of the third and fifth tercets, with these lines again repeated as the third and fourth lines of the quatrain.

vil′lan-ous, etc., **vil′lan-y**. See *villainous*, etc., *villainy*.

vil-lat-ic (vi-lat′ik), *a.* [L. *villaticus*, belonging to a country-house or farm, < *villa*: see *villa*.] Of or pertaining to a farm; rural.

---

vil-leg-gia-tu-ra (vi-lej-ạ-tö′rä), *n.* [It., < *villeggiare*, stay at a country-house, < *villa*: see *villa*.] A sojourn at a country residence, or in the country, as in summer.

vil-lein (vil′ẹn), *n.* See *villain*.

vil-lein-age, vil-len-age (vil′ẹn-āj), *n.* [See *villain*, def.] The tenure by which a feudal villein held land and tenements; the condition or status of a villein.

vil-li (vil′ī), *n.* Plural of *villus*.

vil-li-form (vil′i-fôrm), *a.* [See *villus* and -*form*.] Having the form of villi; so shaped and closely set as to resemble the pile of velvet, as the teeth of certain fishes.

vil-lose (vil′ōs), *a.* Same as *villous*.

vil-los-i-ty (vi-los′i-ti), *n.*; pl. -*ties* (-tiz). Villous condition; a villous surface or coating; a number of villi together; a villus.

vil-lous (vil′us), *a.* [L. *villosus*, hairy, shaggy, < *villus*: see *villus*, and cf. *velours*.] Covered with or of the nature of villi; abounding in villiform processes; covered with fine hairs; in *bot.*, pubescent with long and soft hairs which are not interwoven.

vil-lus (vil′us), *n.*; pl. *villi* (-ī). [L., shaggy hair, tuft of hair, nap: cf. *velvet*.] In *anat.*, one of the minute, hair-like, vascular processes on certain animal membranes, esp. on the mucous membrane of the small intestine, where they serve in absorbing nutriment; in *bot.*, one of the long, soft, straight hairs covering the fruit, flowers, and other parts of certain plants.

vim (vim), *n.* [L. *vim*, acc. of *vis*, force.] Force; energy; vigor in action: as, "the *vim* with which the little puss went at it" (Mrs. Stowe's "Oldtown Folks," xxxiii.).

vi-ma-na (vi-mä′nä), *n.* [Skt.] In India, a pyramidal tower, built in stories, surmounting the shrine of a temple.

vi-men (vī′men), *n.*; pl. *vimina* (vim′i-nä). [L., pliant twig, withe.] In *bot.*, a long, flexible shoot of a plant. — **vim-i-nal** (vim′i-nal), **vi-min-e-ous** (vi-min′ē-us), *a.*

vi-na (vē′nä), *n.* [Skt. and Hind. *vīnā*.] A Hindu musical instrument of the guitar

Top of Vimana of Great Pagoda, Tanjore, Southern India.

kind, having seven strings stretched over a long bamboo finger-board with movable frets, which rests on two gourds.

vi-na-ceous (vī-nā′shius), *a.* [L. *vinaceus*, < *vinum*, wine.] Of or tending to the color of (red) wine; wine-colored.

vin-ai-grette (vin-ạ-gret′), *n.* [F., < *vinaigre*, E. *vinegar*.] A sauce made of vinegar, oil, herbs, etc., used esp. on cold meats; also, a small ornamental bottle or box for holding aromatic vinegar, smelling-salts, or the like (see cut in next column).

vin-ci-ble (vin′si-bl), *a.* [L. *vincibilis*, < *vincere*, conquer.] Capable of being conquered or overcome. — **vin-ci-bil′i-ty** (-bil′i-ti), *n.*

vin-cu-lum (ving′kū-lum), *n.*; pl. -*la* (-lä). [L., < *vincire*, bind.] A bond of union; a tie; in *math.*, a character in the form of a stroke or brace drawn over a quantity consisting of several members or terms, as $\overline{a+b}$, in order to connect them and show that they are to be considered together.

vin-di-ca-ble (vin′di-kạ-bl), *a.* That may be vindicated.

vin-di-cate (vin′di-kāt), *v. t.*; -*cated*, -*cating*. [L. *vindicatus*, pp. of *vindicare*, lay claim to, appropriate, set free, deliver, defend, avenge, prob. < *vim*, acc. of *vis*, force, power (authority), + *dicere*, say, assert.] To lay claim to, for one's self or another; also, to assert, maintain, or defend (a right, cause, etc.) against opposition (as, "I felt as if I had *vindicated* some right that had been in question": H. G. Wells's "Tono-Bungay," ii. 4. § 7); uphold or justify by argument or evidence (as, "a specious discourse to *vindicate* the justice of his cause":

Vinaigrette of French workmanship.

Gibbon's "Decline and Fall of the Roman Empire," xli.); clear, as from a charge, imputation, suspicion, or the like (as, "His conduct cannot be wholly *vindicated* from the charge of inhumanity": Prescott's "Conquest of Mexico," vi. 6); afford justification for (as, subsequent events *vindicated* this policy, or its author); also, to deliver from something†; also, to avenge†, revenge†, or punish† (as, "A bloody vengeance was instantly prepared, to *vindicate* the insult to the inquisition": Motley's "Dutch Republic," ii. 3). — **vin-di-ca′tion** (-kā′shọn), *n.* [L. *vindicatio(n-)*.] The act of vindicating, or the state of being vindicated; defense; justification; also, something that vindicates; a justifying fact or circumstance. — **vin-dic-a-tive** (vin-dik′ạ-tiv or vin′di-kā-), *a.* [F. *vindicatif*, < L. *vindicare*.] Serving to vindicate; vindicatory; also, vindictive†. — **vin′di-ca-tor** (-kā-tọr), *n.* — **vin′di-ca-to-ry** (-kạ-tō-ri), *a.* Serving to vindicate; justificatory; also, punitive or retributive.

vin-dic-tive (vin-dik′tiv), *a.* [Contr. of *vindicative*.] Disposed or inclined to revenge, or revengeful, as persons or the mind, nature, spirit, etc. (as, "Like many men whose self-love is wounded . . . he felt *vindictive*," G. Meredith's "Ordeal of Richard Feverel," xvi.; "Her fierce and *vindictive* nature was softened," Hawthorne's "Twice-Told Tales," The Gentle Boy); proceeding from or showing a revengeful spirit (as, *vindictive* cruelty; "He seemed to take a *vindictive* pleasure in punishing the least shortcomings," Mark Twain's "Tom Sawyer," xxi.); also, punitive or retributive (now rare). — **vin-dic′tive-ly,** *adv.* — **vin-dic′tive-ness,** *n.*

vine (vīn), *n.* [OF. *vine, vigne* (F. *vigne*), < L. *vinea*, vineyard, vine, < *vinum*, wine, grapes, the vine: see *wine*.] Any of the climbing plants constituting the genus *Vitis*, having a woody stem and bearing grapes, esp. *V. vinifera*, the common European species; a grape-vine; also, any plant with a long, slender stem that trails or creeps on the ground or climbs by winding itself about a support or holding fast with tendrils or claspers; also, the stem of any such plant. — **the vine,** the grape-vine. — **vine′=bor″er,** *n.* The larva of any of certain beetles and moths, which bores into the wood or root of vines and is often very destructive. — **vine′=clad,** *a.* Clad or covered with vines. — **vine′=dress″er,** *n.* One who dresses, trims, or cultivates vines, esp. grape-vines.

vin-e-gar (vin′ē-gär), *n.* [OF. F. *vinaigre*, < *vin* (< L. *vinum*), wine, + *aigre*, sharp, sour, E. *eager²*.] A sour liquid consisting of dilute and impure acetic acid, obtained by acetous fermentation from wine, cider, beer, ale, or the like, and used as a condiment, preservative, etc.; fig., sour or crabbed speech, temper, or countenance; in *phar.*, a solution of a medicinal substance in dilute acetic acid, or vinegar. — **aromatic vinegar,** a solution of various volatile oils, as of lavender, rosemary, juniper, etc., and sometimes camphor, in acetic acid, alcohol, and water: used as a stimulant in fainting, fatigue, and the like. — **Vinegar Bible.** See under *Bible.* — **vin′e-gar,** *v. t.* To add or apply vinegar to; treat or restore with aromatic vinegar (as, "a vast amount of moaning and crying upstairs, and much damping of foreheads, and *vinegaring* of temples": Dickens's "Barnaby Rudge," xix.). — **vin′e-gar=eel,** *n.* A minute nematode worm, *Anguillula aceti*, found in vinegar, sour paste, etc. — **vin″e-gar-oon′** (-ön′), *n.* A large whip-scorpion, *Thelyphonus* *giganteus*, of the southern U. S., etc., which emits a vinegar-like odor when alarmed.—**vin′e-gar-y**, *a.* Of the nature of or resembling vinegar; sour like vinegar. Also fig.

vin-er-y (vī′nẽr-i), *n.*; pl. *-ies* (-iz). A grapery; also, vines collectively.

vine-yard (vin′yärd), *n.* [For earlier *wineyard*, < AS. *win-geard*.] A plantation of grape-vines, for producing grapes for wine-making or for other purposes.—**vine′yard-ed**, *a.* Covered with vineyards; inclosed as or like a vineyard.—**vine′yard-ing**, *n.* The cultivation of vine-yards.—**vine′yard-ist**, *n.*

vingt et un (vaṅ-tā-uṅ). [F., 'twenty and one.'] A gambling-game at cards, played by any number of persons, in which the object of each player is to obtain from the dealer cards whose pips add up to twenty-one, or as near as possible to this number without exceeding it.

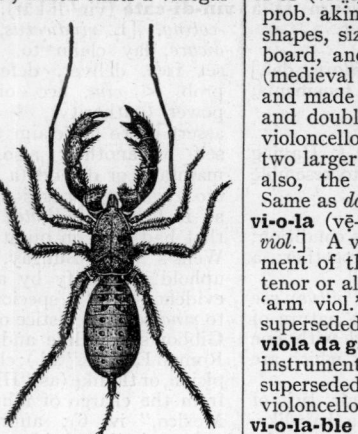
Vinegaroon, about half natural size.

vi-nic (vī′nik), *a.* [L. *vinum*, wine.] Of, pertaining to, found in, or extracted from wine.

vin-i-cul-ture (vin′i-kul-tụr), *n.* [L. *vinum*, wine, grapes, the vine, + *cultura*, culture.] The cultivation of the vine, or of grapes, with especial reference to wine-making. Cf. *viticulture*.—**vin-i-cul′tur-al**, *a.*—**vin-i-cul′tur-ist**, *n.*

vi-nif-er-ous (vī-nif′e-rus), *a.* [LL. *vinifer*, < L. *vinum*, wine, + *ferre*, bear.] Yielding or producing wine.

vin-i-fi-ca-tion (vin″i-fi-kā′shọn), *n.* [F. *vinification*, < L. *vinum*, wine, + *facere*, make.] The process of making wine; conversion of the juice of grapes or the like into wine by fermentation.

vin or-di-naire (vaṅ ôr-dē-nȧr). [F., 'ordinary wine.'] The low-priced wine (usually red) in ordinary use at meals in France and elsewhere.

vi-nous (vī′nus), *a.* [L. *vinosus*, < *vinum*, wine.] Of the nature of or resembling wine; pertaining to or characteristic of wine; produced by, indicative of, or given to, indulgence in wine (as, "*vinous* excitement," Thackeray's "Pendennis," ii. 8; "winking at his cousin with a pair of *vinous* eyes," Thackeray's "Vanity Fair," xxxiv.); also, wine-colored.—**vi-nos′i-ty** (-nos′i-ti), *n.*

vin-tage (vin′tāj), *n.* [OF. F. *vendange*, < L. *vindemia*, grape-gathering, vintage, < *vinum*, wine, grapes, + *demere*, take off, < *de*, from, + *emere*, take.] The act of gathering ripe grapes; the season of gathering grapes, or of wine-making; the annual produce of the grape-harvest, esp. with reference to the wine obtained (as, "Never did . . . the vines yield a more luxuriant *vintage*": Mrs. Shelley's "Frankenstein," iv.); the wine from a particular harvest or crop; esp., an exceptionally fine wine from the grape-crop of a good year, specially designated and sold as the produce of that year (commonly called *vintage wine*); in poetic use, wine, esp. good wine (as, "a draught of *vintage*": Keats's "Ode to a Nightingale"); in colloquial use, the crop or output of anything (as, a hat of last year's *vintage*).—**vin′tage**, *v. t.* *-taged, -taging.* To gather (grapes) in the vintage; produce (wine) from the vintage.—**vin′tag-er** (-tạ-jèr), *n.* One who gathers grapes in the vintage.

vint-ner (vint′nèr), *n.* [Altered form of obs. *vinter*, < OF. *vinetier*, < ML. *vinetarius*, < L. *vinum*, wine.] A dealer in wine; a wine-merchant.

vi-num (vī′num), *n.* [L., wine.] Wine; in *phar.*, a solution of a medicinal substance in wine.

vin-y (vī′ni), *a.* Pertaining to, of the nature of, or resembling vines (as, "*viny* harvests," Pope's tr. Homer's "Iliad," ii.; "her *viny* golden curls," Mrs. Stowe's "Oldtown Folks," xxxiii.); abounding in or producing vines.

vi-nyl (vī′nil), *n.* [L. *vinum*, wine: see *-yl*.] In *chem.*, the univalent radical CH_2CH, present in certain organic compounds.

vi-ol (vī′ọl), *n.* [OF. F. *viole*, < ML. *vitula, vidula*, viol; prob. akin to E. *fiddle*.] A musical instrument, of various shapes, sizes, etc., having a hollow body, a neck, a fingerboard, and strings, and played with a bow; esp., an old (medieval and later) type having from five to seven strings, and made in four principal sizes (treble, tenor or alto, bass, and double-bass) represented by the modern violin, viola, violoncello, and double-bass viol.—**bass viol**, either of the two larger medieval viols (see above); also, the violoncello; also, the modern double-bass viol.—**double=bass viol.** Same as *double-bass*, *n.*

vi-o-la (vẹ-ō′lạ or vī-, It. vē-ō′lä), *n.* [It., = F. *viole*, E. *viol*.] A viol; in modern use, a four-stringed musical instrument of the violin class, slightly larger than the violin; a tenor or alto violin.—**viola da braccio** (dä brät′chō). [It., 'arm viol.'] An old musical instrument of the viol class, superseded by the modern viola; a tenor or alto viol.—**viola da gamba** (gäm′bä). [It., 'leg viol.'] An old musical instrument of the viol class, superseded by the modern violoncello; a bass viol.

Viola da Gamba.

vi-o-la-ble (vī′ọ-lạ-bl), *a.* [L. *violabilis*.] That may be violated.—**vi″o-la-bil′i-ty** (-bil′-i-ti), **vi′o-la-ble-ness**, *n.*—**vi′o-la-bly**, *adv.*

vi-o-la-ceous (vī-ọ-lā′shius), *a.* [L. *violaceus*, < *viola*, violet.] Of a violet color; also, belonging to the *Violaceæ*, or violet family of plants.

vi-o-late (vī′ọ-lāt), *v. t.; -lated, -lating.* [L. *violatus*, pp. of *violare*, treat with violence, injure, outrage, violate, < *vis*, force: cf. *violent*.] To do violence to; deal with or treat in a violent or improper way (as, "We cannot *violate* the lock, nor steal the key": W. Churchill's "Modern Chronicle," i. 3); desecrate or profane (as, to *violate* a temple or an altar: "The sanctity of the spot appeared never to have been *violated*," H. Melville's "Typee," xxiii.); outrage or ravish (a woman); also, to break, infringe, or transgress (a law, rule, agreement, promise, instructions, etc.: as, "He had *violated* every precept of the moral law," R. Graves's "Spiritual Quixote," i. 9; "Thou makest the vestal *violate* her oath," Shakspere's "Lucrece," 883); also, to break in upon or disturb rudely (as, to *violate* privacy, peace, or a peaceful spot; "The dark forests which once clothed those shores had been *violated* by the savage hand of cultivation," Irving's "Knickerbocker's New York," iii. 6); break through or pass by force or without right (as, "collecting all his forces on the frontier he meant to *violate*": G. P. R. James's "Hist. of Charlemagne," v.); also, to damage† or injure†.—**vi-o-la′tion** (-lā′shọn), *n.* [L. *violatio(n-)*.] The act of violating, or the state of being violated; desecration; ravishment or rape; breach, infringement, or transgression, as of a law, promise, etc.—**vi′o-la-tive** (-lạ-tiv), *a.* Tending to violate; causing or involving violation.—**vi′o-la-tor** (-lā-tọr), *n.*

vi-o-lence (vī′ọ-lẹns), *n.* [OF. F. *violence*, < L. *violentia*.] The state or fact of being violent; rough force in action (as, "flinging open the door . . . with much *violence*," Fielding's "Tom Jones," viii. 3; driven along by the *violence* of the wind or waves); rough or injurious action or treatment (as, "If any *violence* is offered them . . . away they run," Defoe's "Robinson Crusoe," ii. 9; to die by *violence*); any unjust or unwarranted exertion of force or power, as against rights, laws, etc.; injury, wrong, or outrage (as, "Any *violence* to the religious sentiment touches all alike": Prescott's "Conquest of Mexico," iv. 5); a violent act or proceeding; distortion of meaning or fact; rough or immoderate vehemence, as of feeling or language; fury; intensity; severity.—**to do violence to**, to do injury or wrong to; outrage; wrest or distort (truth, fact, etc.).

vi-o-lent (vī′ọ-lẹnt), *a.* [OF. F. *violent*, < L. *violentus*, < *vis*, force: cf. *violate*.] Acting with or characterized by uncontrolled, strong, rough force (as, a *violent* assailant, assault, or blow; a *violent* explosive; a *violent* tempest or torrent);

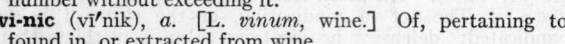

also, acting with, characterized by, or due to injurious or destructive force (as, "The rest prevented Manfred from laying *violent* hands on himself," Walpole's "Castle of Otranto," v.; *violent* measures; a *violent* change of government; a *violent* death); also, roughly or immoderately vehement, ardent, or passionate (as, "a *violent* churchwoman, of the most intolerant zeal," Smollett's "Humphry Clinker," May 6; *violent* feeling, temper, or language; "He made *violent* love . . . and his affection was returned," Eden Phillpotts's "Red Redmaynes," iii.); also, furious in impetuosity, energy, etc. (as, *violent* haste; a *violent* commotion); also, intense in force, effect, character, etc. (as, *violent* heat; a *violent* glare; a *violent* contrast; *violent* pain); severe; acute; extreme.—**vi′o-lent-ly**, *adv.*

vi-o-les-cent (vī-ō-les′ent), *a.* [L. *viola*, violet: see *-escent*.] Tending to a violet color.

vi-o-let (vī′ō-let). [OF. *violete* (F. *violette*), dim. of OF. *viole*, < L. *viola*, violet.] **I.** *n.* Any plant of the genus *Viola*, comprising chiefly low, stemless or leafy-stemmed herbs with purple, blue, yellow, white, or variegated flowers, as *V. cucullata*, a species common in wet woods, *V. odorata* ('English violet' or 'sweet violet'), a fragrant species much cultivated, and *V. tricolor*, the pansy, whose flowers are often variegated in coloring; popularly, any such plant except the pansy; also, any of various similar plants of other genera; also, a bluish-purple color. **II.** *a.* Of the color called violet; bluish-purple.

vi-o-lin (vī-ō-lin′), *n.* [It. *violino*, < *viola*, viol.] The modern treble musical instrument of the viol class, which is held nearly horizontally by the player's arm, with the

Violet.—1, stemmed violet (*Viola tricolor*), *St*, stem; 2, stemless violet (*Viola cucullata*), *s*, scape.

lower part supported against the collar-bone or shoulder, and played with a bow (a development of the medieval treble viol, from which it differs in having but four strings and in various minor particulars); a fiddle; also, any modern instrument of the same general class, as a viola or a violoncello; also, a violinist.—**vi-o-lin′ist**, *n.* A player on the violin.

vi-ol-ist (vī′ol-ist), *n.* A player on the viol.

vi-o-lon-cel-list (vē″ō-lon-chel′ist or vī″ō-lon-sel′ist), *n.* A player on the violoncello: often shortened to *cellist* or *'cellist*.

vi-o-lon-cel-lo (vē″ō-lon-chel′ō or vī″ō-lon-sel′ō), *n.*; pl. *-cellos* (-ōz). [It., dim. of *violone*: see *violone*.] A large modern four-stringed musical instrument of the viol class, which is rested vertically on the floor between the player's knees, and played with a bow (a development of the medieval bass viol, or viola da gamba); a bass violin: often shortened to *cello* or *'cello*.

vi-o-lo-ne (vē-ō-lō′nā), *n.* [It., aug. of *viola*, viol.] The double-bass viol, or contrabass.

vi-per (vī′pėr), *n.* [L. *vipera*.] Any of the old-world venomous snakes of the genus *Vipera* (or *Pelias*); esp., *V.* (or *P.*) *berus*, a small European species that inflicts a severe bite; the adder; also, any of various venomous or supposedly venomous snakes of allied or other genera (as, the horned *viper*, *Cerastes cornutus*, a venomous species of Egypt, Palestine, etc., with a horny process above each eye: cf. *cerastes* and *asp²*); fig., a venomous, malignant, or spiteful person;

Head and Tail of Common Viper (*Vipera berus*).

a false or treacherous person (as, "I had been fostering the *viper* who had assisted to destroy me": Marryat's "Mr. Midshipman Easy," xx.).—**vi′per-ine** (-in), *a.* [L. *viperinus*.] Of, pertaining to, or resembling a viper.—**vi′per-ish**, *a.* Viper-like; viperous.—**vi′per-ous**, *a.* Of the nature of a viper or vipers; viper-like; venomous or malignant; befitting a viper; pertaining to vipers.—**vi′per-ous-ly**, *adv.*—**vi′per′s=bu′gloss**, *n.* Same as *blueweed*.

vi-ra-go (vi-rā′gō or vī-), *n.*; pl. *-goes* (-gōz). [L. *virago* (*viragin-*), manlike woman, < *vir*, man.] A woman of masculine strength or spirit (archaic); hence, a turbulent, violent, or ill-tempered, scolding woman (as, "his wife . . . a *virago* if crossed," Jefferies's "Gamekeeper at Home," ii.; "driven out . . . by the furious ill-temper of the shrill *virago* his wife," Thackeray's "Newcomes," xxxvi.); a termagant.—**vi-rag-i-nous** (vi-raj′i-nus), *a.*

vir-e-lay (vir′e-lā), *n.* [OF. F. *virelai*, earlier *vireli*; origin uncertain.] An old French form of short poem, with short lines running on two rimes, and having the two opening lines recurring at intervals; any of various similar or other forms of poem, as one consisting of stanzas made up of longer and shorter lines, the lines of each kind riming together in each stanza, and having the rime of the shorter lines of one stanza forming the rime of the longer lines of the next stanza.

vir-e-o (vir′e̱-ō), *n.*; pl. *-os* (-ōz). [L., kind of bird.] Any of the small American insectivorous birds constituting the family *Vireonidæ*, having the plumage more or less tinted with olive and green; a greenlet; esp., any such bird of the genus *Vireo*.—**vir′e-o-nine** (-ō-nin), *a.*

vi-res-cent (vī-res′ent), *a.* [L. *virescens* (*-ent-*), ppr. of *virescere*, become green, < *virere*, be green.] Turning green; tending to a green color; greenish.—**vi-res′cence**, *n.*

Red-eyed Vireo (*Vireosylva olivacea*).

vir-gate¹ (vėr′gāt), *a.* [L. *virgatus*, < *virga*, a slender green branch, rod: cf. *verge¹*.] Having the shape of a rod or wand; long, slender, and straight; in *geol.*, noting a system of faults the minor members of which branch from a central fault as twigs from a bough.

vir-gate² (vėr′gāt), *n.* [ML. *virgata*, < *virga*, a measure of land, L. a rod: see *virgate¹*.] An old English measure of land of varying extent, generally regarded as having been equivalent to a quarter of a hide, or about thirty acres.

Vir-gil-i-an (vėr-jil′i-an), *a.* [Also, more properly, *Vergilian*: L. *Vergilianus*, < *Vergilius*, LL. and ML. *Virgilius*, the poet Vergil or Virgil (Publius Vergilius Maro); but the spelling with *i*, if less correct, has long prevailed in English and other languages, and is still the ordinary spelling in general literary (not classical) use.] Of, pertaining to, or suggestive of Virgil (70–19 B.C.), the great Roman poet, or his poetry: as, "the rich *Virgilian* rustic measure" (Tennyson, "Daisy," 75).

vir-gin (vėr′jin). [OF. *virgine*, < L. *virgo* (*virgin-*), maiden, virgin.] **I.** *n.* A woman, esp. a young woman, who has had no sexual intercourse with man; a maid or maiden; in general, a girl, young woman, or unmarried woman (as, "He became enamoured of a fair *virgin*," Walpole's "Castle of Otranto," v.; an elderly *virgin*, an old maid); also, a youth or man who has not had sexual intercourse; any female animal which has not copulated; a parthenogenetic insect; [*cap.*] with *the*, Mary, the mother of Christ (often called 'the Blessed Virgin'); also, the zodiacal constellation or sign Virgo. **II.** *a.* Being a virgin (as, the *Virgin* Mother, Mary the Virgin; the *Virgin* Queen, Queen Elizabeth of England); consisting of virgins (as, a *virgin* band or train); also, pertaining to, characteristic of, or befitting a virgin (as, "Ne'er again . . . The *virgin* snood did Alice wear,"

Scott's "Lady of the Lake," iii. 5; *virgin* innocence or modesty); also, resembling or suggesting a virgin; pure, unsullied, or undefiled (as, *virgin* snow); without admixture, alloy, or modification (as, *virgin* gold; "He preferred it [coffee] in its *virgin* flavor, unimpaired by sugar or cream," Parkman's "Oregon Trail," v.); untouched, untried, or unused (as, *virgin* soil); fresh or new; clear (*of*: as, "Staffordshire rivers have remained *virgin* of keels to this day," Arnold Bennett's "Old Wives' Tale," i. 1); of a fortress, etc., that has never been taken; in *zoöl.*, parthenogenetic.—**vir'gin-al**[1], *a.* [L. *virginalis*.] Of, pertaining to, characteristic of, or befitting a virgin; continuing in a state of virginity; pure or unsullied; untouched; fresh; in *zoöl.*, parthenogenetic.

vir-gin-al[2] (vėr'jin-al), *n.* [Appar. a noun use of *virginal*[1], perhaps as denoting an instrument suitable for virgins or girls.] A spinet, or small harpsichord, usually without legs and set in a box, popular in the 16th and 17th centuries: also *pl.* in same sense, and sometimes called 'a pair of virginals.'

vir-gin-al-ly (vėr'jin-al-i), *adv.* In a virginal manner.—**vir'gin-al-ness,** *n.*

Virginal used by Queen Elizabeth. — Victoria and Albert Museum, London.

vir-gin-hood (vėr'jin-hůd), *n.* Virginity; maidenhood.

Vir-gin-i-a (vėr-jin'i-ä) **creep'er.** A vitaceous climbing plant, *Parthenocissus quinquefolia*, of North America, having palmate leaves, usually with five leaflets, and bluish-black berries. Also called *woodbine* and *American ivy*.

Vir-gin-i-a (vėr-jin'i-ä) **fence.** A snake-fence. Also called *Virginia rail fence*.

Vir-gin-i-an (vėr-jin'i-an), *a.* Of or pertaining to the colony or the State of Virginia.—**Virginian deer**, the common deer, *Cariacus* (or *Odocoileus*) *virginianus*, of eastern North America.—**Virginian trumpet=flower**, the trumpet-creeper.—**Virgin'i-an,** *n.* A native or inhabitant of Virginia.

Virginia Creeper. — *a*, an expanded flower; *b*, diagram of flower.

Vir-gin-i-a (vėr-jin'i-ä) **reel.** An American country-dance in which the partners stand facing each other in two lines.

vir-gin-i-ty (vėr-jin'i-ti), *n.* [OF. *virginite* (F. *virginité*), < L. *virginitas*, < *virgo*, E. *virgin*.] The condition of being a virgin; virginal chastity; maidenhood.

vir-gin's=bow-er (vėr'jinz-bou'ėr), *n.* Any of several climbing varieties of clematis with small white flowers in large panicles, as *Clematis vitalba*, the traveler's-joy of Europe, or *C. virginiana* of the U. S.

Vir-go (vėr'gō), *n.* [L.: see *virgin*.] The Virgin, a zodiacal constellation; also, the sixth sign of the zodiac. See *zodiac*.

vir-gu-late (vėr'gū-lāt), *a.* [L. *virgula*, dim. of *virga*, rod.] Rod-shaped; virgate.

vir-i-des-cent (vir-i-des'ẹnt), *a.* [LL. *viridescens* (-*ent*-), ppr. of *viridescere*, grow green, < L. *viridis*, green.] Somewhat green; greenish.—**vir-i-des'cence,** *n.*

vi-rid-i-an (vi-rid'i-an), *n.* [L. *viridis*, green.] A bluish-green pigment of great permanency, consisting of a hydrated oxide of chromium.

vi-rid-i-ty (vi-rid'i-ti), *n.* [L. *viriditas*, < *viridis*, green, verdant, < *virere*, be green.] Greenness; verdancy; fig., inexperience or simplicity.

vir-ile (vir'il or vī'ril), *a.* [L. *virilis*, < *vir*, man; akin to Skt. *vīra*, Goth. *wair*, AS. *wer*, man: cf. *werwolf*.] Of, pertaining to, or characteristic of a man, as opposed to a woman or a child; masculine or manly; natural to or befitting a man (as, "She showed *virile* force in the contest": C. Brontë's "Jane Eyre," xxvi.); often, having or exhibiting in a marked degree masculine strength, vigor, or forcefulness (as, "when the *virile* figure of Theodore Roosevelt swung down the national highway," Bok's "Americanization of Edward Bok," xxiii.; "a singularly *virile* type of humanity," W. R. Inge's "Outspoken Essays," i. 4); characterized by a vigorous masculine spirit (as, a *virile* literary style; a *virile* tale; a *virile* artistic conception); also, pertaining to or capable of procreation.—**vir'ile-ly,** *adv.*—**vi-ril-i-ty** (vi-ril'i-ti or vī-), *n.* The state or quality of being virile; manhood; masculine or manly character, vigor, or spirit; specif., the power of procreation.

vir-tu (vir-tö' or vėr'tö), *n.* [It. *virtù*, virtue, excellence, < L. *virtus*, E. *virtue*.] Such excellence or merit in objects of art, curios, and the like, as recommends them to the taste of connoisseurs and discriminating collectors (as, articles of *virtu*); also, such objects or articles collectively; also, a taste for or knowledge of such objects.

vir-tu-al (vėr'tū-al), *a.* [ML. *virtualis*, < L. *virtus*, E. *virtue*.] Having virtue or inherent power to produce effects (now rare); also, being such in power, force, or effect, although not actually or expressly such (as, the regent is a *virtual* king; the reply is a *virtual* surrender); in *optics*, noting an image formed by the apparent convergence of rays geometrically (but not actually) prolonged, as the image in a mirror (opposed to *real*); also, noting a focus of a corresponding nature (see *focus*, *n.*).—**vir-tu-al'i-ty** (-al'i-ti), *n.*—**vir'tu-al-ly,** *adv.* In a virtual manner; in effect, if not actually: as, "A penal statute is *virtually* annulled if the penalties which it imposes are regularly remitted" (Macaulay's "Hist. of Eng.," i.).

vir-tue (vėr'tū), *n.* [OF. *virtu, vertu* (F. *vertu*), < L. *virtus*, manly excellence, strength, courage, worth, virtue, < *vir*, man: see *virile*.] Manly excellence, spirit, or valor†; moral excellence or goodness; conformity of life and conduct to moral laws; uprightness; rectitude; chastity, esp. in women; a particular moral excellence (as, the cardinal *virtues*, justice, prudence, temperance, and fortitude; the theological *virtues*, faith, hope, and charity); in general, an excellence, merit, or good quality (as, brevity is often a *virtue*; "I can keep a secret. My enemies will allow me that *virtue*," Fielding's "Tom Jones," viii. 5); also, inherent power to produce effects; potency or efficacy (as, a medicine of sovereign *virtue*); effective force (as, there is no *virtue* in such measures); a power or property of producing a particular effect (as, a healing or a cooling *virtue*; "All the *virtues* of herbs and metals . . . he knew," Whittier's "Cobbler Keezar's Vision"); the power inherent in a supernatural or divine being (obs. or archaic); *pl.*, an order of angels (see *angel*).—**by** or **in virtue of,** by the power or force of; by reason of: as, to act *by virtue of* authority conferred; to speak *in virtue of* one's superior wisdom or experience.—**to make a virtue of necessity,** to accept necessity (however disagreeable) as if it were right or good; submit with a good grace to what cannot be helped.—**vir'tue-less,** *a.* Devoid of virtue; without excellence or merit; bad.

vir-tu-ose (vėr-tū-ōs'), *a.* [It. *virtuoso*.] Having the characteristics of a virtuoso; of or pertaining to virtuosos. Also **vir-tu-o'sic** (-ō'sik).—**vir-tu-os'i-ty** (-os'i-ti), *n.* The character or skill of a virtuoso.

---

vir-tu-o-so (vẽr-ṭụ-ō'sō or vir-tö-), *n.*; pl. *-sos* (-sōz), It. *-si* (-sē). [It., orig. adj., virtuous, excellent, < LL. *virtuosus*, E. *virtuous*.] One who has special interest or knowledge in matters of art and science†; also, one who has a cultivated appreciation of artistic excellence; a connoisseur of works or objects of art; a student or collector of objects of art, curios, antiquities, etc.; also, one who has special knowledge or skill in any field, as in music; one who excels in musical technique or execution.—**vir-tu-o'so-ship**, *n.*

vir-tu-ous (vẽr'ṭụ-us), *a.* [OF. *vertuous* (F. *vertueux*), < LL. *virtuosus*, < L. *virtus*, E. *virtue*.] Possessed of or characterized by virtue; manly† or valiant†; morally excellent or good; conforming or conformed to moral laws; upright; righteous; moral; chaste; having effective virtue, potent, or efficacious (archaic: as, *virtuous* herbs; "a wine of *virtuous* powers," Coleridge's "Christabel," i.).—**vir'tu-ous-ly**, *adv.*—**vir'tu-ous-ness**, *n.*

vir-u-lence (vir'ö-lẹns or vir'ū-), *n.* The quality of being virulent; actively poisonous or malignant quality; fig., venomous hostility (as, "The ill will of Miss Knag had lost nothing of its *virulence*": Dickens's "Nicholas Nickleby," xxi.); intense acrimony. Also **vir'u-len-cy**.

vir-u-lent (vir'ö-lẹnt or vir'ū-), *a.* [L. *virulentus*, poisonous, < *virus*, E. *virus*.] Actively poisonous, malignant, or deadly (as, a *virulent* poison; a *virulent* form of a disease); fig., violently or venomously hostile (as, "The local newspapers were *virulent* in their attacks," Bok's "Americanization of Edward Bok," xxii.; "He had a *virulent* feeling against the respectable shopkeeping class," George Eliot's "Felix Holt," xlvi.); intensely bitter, spiteful, or acrimonious.—**vir'u-lent-ly**, *adv.*

vi-rus (vī'rus), *n.* [L., slimy liquid, poison, venom.] The venom of a poisonous animal; also, a poison produced in the body of one suffering from an infectious or contagious disease, esp. when capable of exciting the same disease in other persons or animals upon introduction by inoculation, etc.; fig., a moral or intellectual poison; a corrupting influence.

vis (vis), *n.*; pl. *vires* (vī'rēz). [L.] Force.—**vis inertiæ** (in-ẽr'shi-ē). [L., 'force of inertia.'] Inertia; fig., indisposition to act; sluggishness.—**vis major** (mā'jọr). [L., 'greater force.'] In *law*, a superior, compelling, or irresistible force which is held to exempt one, barring special contract or fraud, from contract obligation.—**vis mortua** (môr'ṭụ-ạ). [L., 'dead force.'] The so-called 'dead force,' or energy not producing motion.—**vis viva** (vī'vạ). [L., 'living force.'] Orig., the so-called 'living force' of a moving body, being represented by its mass times the square of its velocity; now, usually, the kinetic energy of a moving body, being equal to one half its mass times the square of its velocity.

vi-sa (vē'zạ), *n.* [F., < L. *visa*, pp. fem. of *videre*, see.] Same as *visé*, *n.*—**vi'sa**, *v. t.*; *-saed*, *-saing*. Same as *visé*, *v.*

vis-age (viz'ạj), *n.* [OF. F. *visage*, < L. *visus*, sight, look, appearance, < *videre*, see.] The face, esp. of a human being, and commonly with reference to shape, features, expression, etc.; the countenance; in general, aspect; appearance.—**vis'aged**, *a.* Having a visage (as specified): as, grim-*visaged*.

vis-à-vis (vē'zạ-vē, F. vē-zä-vē). [F., face to face (*vis*, face, < L. *visus*: see *visage*.)] **I.** *adv.* and *a.* Face to face. **II.** *n.* One face to face with, or situated opposite to, another; also, a carriage in which the occupants sit face to face; also, a kind of sofa or double chair in the general shape of the letter S, with seats for two persons thus enabled to face each other. **III.** *prep.* Face to face with; opposite to; hence, in relation to.

Vi-sa-yan (vẹ-sä'yạn), *n.* One of a Malay people, the most numerous native race of the Philippines; also, the language of this people.

vis-ca-cha (vis-kä'chạ), *n.* [Sp. *vizcacha*; from Peruvian.] A burrowing rodent, *Lagostomus trichodactylus*, inhabiting the pampas of South America, and allied

Viscacha (*Lagostomus trichodactylus*).

to the chinchilla but larger; also, a related species, *Lagidium cuvieri*, of the Andes ('alpine viscacha').

vis-ce-ra (vis'ẹ-rạ), *n. pl.* [L., pl. of *viscus*.] The soft interior organs contained in the cavities of the body, including the brain, lungs, heart, stomach, intestines, etc.; esp., such of these as are confined to the abdomen; in popular use, the intestines or bowels.—**vis'ce-ral**, *a.* Of or pertaining to the viscera; affecting the viscera; having the character of viscera.

vis-cid (vis'id), *a.* [LL. *viscidus*, < L. *viscum*, mistletoe, birdlime.] Sticky, adhesive, or glutinous; of a glutinous consistence; viscous.—**vis-cid-i-ty** (vi-sid'i-ti), **vis'cid-ness**, *n.*—**vis'cid-ly**, *adv.*

vis-coid (vis'koid), *a.* [See *-oid*.] Somewhat viscous. Also **vis-coi'dal**.

vis-cose (vis'kōs), *n.* [LL. *viscosus*, E. *viscous*.] A plastic material prepared by treating cellulose with caustic soda and carbon bisulphide: used in manufacturing rayon or artificial silk, in making a product resembling celluloid, and for sizing and other purposes.

vis-cos-i-ty (vis-kos'i-ti), *n.* The state or quality of being viscous; in *physics*, the resistance of a fluid to the motion of its molecules among themselves; also, the capability in a solid of changing shape gradually under the action of gravity or external force.

vis-count (vī'kount), *n.* [OF. *visconte* (F. *vicomte*), < ML. *vicecomes* (*vicecomit-*), < L. *vice-* (see *vice-*) + *comes*, E. *count*[1].] Formerly, a deputy of a count or earl; hence, a sheriff; now, a nobleman ranking next below an earl or count and next above a baron.—**vis'count-cy** (-si), *n.*; pl. *-cies* (-siz). Viscountship.—**vis'count-ess**, *n.* [OF. *viscontesse* (F. *vicomtesse*).] The wife or widow of a viscount; also, a woman holding in her own right a rank equivalent to that of a viscount.—**vis'count-ship**, *n.* The rank or dignity of a viscount.—**vis'count-y** (-koun-ti), *n.*; pl. *viscounties* (-tiz). Viscountship; also, the jurisdiction of a historical viscount, or the territory under his authority.

Coronet of a British Viscount.

vis-cous (vis'kus), *a.* [LL. *viscosus*, < L. *viscum*, mistletoe, birdlime.] Sticky, adhesive, or glutinous; hence, of a glutinous character or consistence; imperfectly fluid; ropy; thick; in *physics*, having the property of viscosity.—**vis'-cous-ly**, *adv.*—**vis'cous-ness**, *n.*

vis-cus (vis'kus), *n.*; pl. *viscera* (vis'ẹ-rạ). [L.] Any one of the viscera. See *viscera*.

vise, vice[2] (vīs), *n.* [OF. F. *vis*, winding stair, screw, < L. *vitis*, vine.] A winding staircase†; also, a screw†; also, any of various devices having two jaws which may be brought together or separated by means of a screw, lever, or the like, used to hold an object firmly while work is being done upon it.—**vise, vice**[2], *v. t.*; *vised*, *viced*, *vising*, *vicing*. To hold, press, or squeeze with or as with a vise.

vi-sé (vē'zā or vē-zā'), *n.* [F., pp. of *viser*, to visé, < *visa*, a word of indorsement, lit. 'seen': see *visa*.] An indorsement made upon a passport or the like by the properly constituted authority, denoting that it has been examined and found correct; a signature of approval placed by an authorized person upon a document requiring to be approved.—**vi'sé**, *v. t.*; *-séed*, *-séing*. To put a visé on; examine and indorse, as a passport.

Vish-nu (vish'nö), *n.* [Skt., < *vish-*, work, be active, accomplish.] In *Hindu religion*, one of the three chief divinities, the second member of the Hindu trinity: known also as 'the Preserver.' See *Trimurti*, and cf. *Brahma*[2] and *Siva*.

Vishnu.

vis-i-bil-i-ty (viz-i-bil'i-ti), *n.*; pl. *-ties* (-tiz). The state or fact of being visible; capability of being seen; specif., the relative capability of being seen under given conditions of distance, light, atmosphere, etc., as of a vessel at sea (as, low or high *visibility*); also, something visible; a visible thing.

vis-i-ble (viz′i-bl). [OF. F. *visible*, < L. *visibilis*, < *videre* (pp. *visus*), see.] **I.** *a.* Capable of being seen; perceptible by the eye; open to sight or view; also, perceptible by the mind (as, "We do not always find *visible* happiness in proportion to *visible* virtue": Johnson's "Rasselas," xxvii.); apparent; manifest; obvious. **II.** *n.* That which is visible; *pl.*, visible things.—**vis′i-ble-ness**, *n.*—**vis′i-bly**, *adv.*

Vis-i-goth (viz′i-goth), *n.* [LL. *Visigothi*, pl., appar. meaning 'west Goths': cf. *Ostrogoth* and *west*.] A member of the westerly division of the Goths, which formed a monarchy about 418, maintaining it in southern France until 507 and in Spain until 711.—**Vis-i-goth′ic**, *a.*

vi-sion (vizh′on), *n.* [OF. F. *vision*, < L. *visio*(n-), < *videre* (pp. *visus*), see: see *wit*.] The act of seeing with the eye; the power, faculty, or sense of sight; also, the act or the power of perceiving what is not actually present to the eye, whether by some supernatural endowment or by natural intellectual acuteness (as, the *vision* of the seer; statesmanly *vision*; to lack *vision* in dealing with momentous issues; "Charles had neither *vision* nor grasp," Morley's "Oliver Cromwell," i. 2); also, something seen; an object of sight; esp., something seen or presented to the mind otherwise than by natural, ordinary sight in the normal waking state; a sight seen in a dream, ecstasy, trance, or the like; a mental view or image, whether of supernatural origin or merely imaginative, of what is not actually present in place or time (as, *visions* of the past or the future; to have a *vision* of probable consequences); a vivid imaginative conception or anticipation (as, *visions* of wealth or glory; "He had no belief in the *visions* of the demagogues," Froude's "Cæsar," v.); also, a sight such as might be seen in a vision, dream, etc. (as, a *vision* of loveliness); a scene, person, etc., of extraordinary beauty.—**vi′sion**, *v. t.* To show, or to see, in or as in a vision.—**vi′sion-al**, *a.* Of or pertaining to visions; belonging to or seen in a vision.—**vi′sion-al-ly**, *adv.*—**vi′-sion-a-ry** (-ā-ri). **I.** *a.* Given to or concerned with seeing visions; given to or characterized by fanciful or unpractical ideas, views, or schemes (as, "The most *visionary* enthusiasts would scarce be capable of proposing such a measure": Adam Smith's "Wealth of Nations," iv. 7. 3); also, belonging to or seen in a vision (as, "the *visionary* pomp of stately phantoms": Whittier's "Tent on the Beach"); proper only to a vision; unreal or imaginary (as, *visionary* evils); purely ideal or speculative, or unpractical (as, "wild and *visionary* notions . . . with little chance of ever arriving to any successful issue": Marryat's "Peter Simple," xlvii.). **II.** *n.*; pl. *-ries* (-riz). One who sees visions; also, one given to unpractical ideas or schemes; an unpractical theorist or enthusiast.—**vi′sion-a-ri-ness**, *n.*—**vi′sioned**, *a.* Endowed with vision; having the power of seeing visions; characterized by visions; pertaining to or seen in a vision.—**vi′sion-ist**, *n.* One who has, or professes to have, visions.—**vi′sion-less**, *a.* Without vision; blind. Also fig.

vis-it (viz′it), *v.* [OF. F. *visiter*, < L. *visitare*, freq. of *visere*, look at, go to see, freq. of *videre*, see.] **I.** *tr.* To go to see (a person, place, etc.) in the way of friendship, ceremony, duty, business, curiosity, or the like; esp., to call upon (a person, family, etc.) for social or other purposes; make a stay or sojourn with as a guest; go to for the purpose of official inspection or examination; inspect or examine; come to in order to comfort or aid; in general, to come or go to; come upon or assail (as, the plague *visited* London in 1665); afflict with suffering, trouble, etc.; inflict punishment for (as, "*visiting* the iniquity of the fathers upon the children": Ex. xxxiv. 7). **II.** *intr.* To make a visit or visits.—**vis′it**, *n.* [F. *visite*.] An act of visiting; a going to see a person, place, etc.; a call paid to a person, family, etc.; a stay or sojourn as a guest; a going to a place to make an official inspection or examination; visitation, as of a neutral vessel by a belligerent (as, the right of *visit* and search: see *visitation*, and cf. *search*, *n.*).—**vis′it-a-ble**, *a.* Capable of or suitable for being visited; also, liable or subject to official visitation.

Vis-i-tan-dine (viz-i-tan′din or -dēn). [F., < L. *visitand-*, gerund stem of *visitare*, E. *visit*.] **I.** *n.* A member of a Roman Catholic order of nuns (Order of the Visitation), founded in 1610 at Annecy, in Savoy, by St. Francis de Sales and St. Jane Frances de Chantal, for the visiting of the sick poor, and largely devoted to the education of girls. **II.** *a.* Belonging or pertaining to the Visitandines.

vis-it-ant (viz′i-tant). **I.** *a.* Visiting; paying a visit. **II.** *n.* A visitor; a guest; a temporary resident; [*cap.*] a Visitandine.

vis-i-ta-tion (viz-i-tā′shon), *n.* [L. *visitatio*(n-).] The act of visiting; a visit; esp., visiting or a visit for the purpose of making an official inspection or examination (as, "The college . . . underwent the archbishop's *visitation*": Strype's "Memorials of Cranmer," i. 23); specif., the visiting of a vessel, as at sea, by an officer of a belligerent state, to ascertain its nationality, the nature of its cargo (whether contraband), etc. (as, the right of *visitation* belongs to belligerents only); [*cap.* or *l. c.*] the visit of the Virgin Mary to her cousin Elisabeth (see Luke, i. 39–56); [*cap.*] a church festival, held on July 2, in commemoration of this visit; also, with *the*, the Order of the Visitation (see *Visitandine*); [*l. c.*] the object or recipient of a visit (poetic and rare); also, a visiting with comfort or aid, or with affliction or punishment, as by God; a special dispensation from heaven, whether of favor or of affliction; any experience or event, esp. an unpleasant one, regarded as occurring by divine dispensation; an affliction or punishment from God; a judgment.—**vis″i-ta-to′ri-al** (-ta-tō′ri-al), *a.* Pertaining to an official visitor or to official visitation (as, "The Queen . . . had over the Church a *visitatorial* power of vast . . . extent": Macaulay's "Hist. of Eng.," i.); also, having the power of visitation.

vis-it-ee (viz-i-tē′), *n.* A person to whom a visit is paid: as, "hoping that she might find her *visitee* out" (Galsworthy's "Patrician," ii. 7).

vis-it-er (viz′i-tèr), *n.* Same as *visitor*. [Now rare.]

vis-it-ing=card (viz′i-ting-kärd), *n.* A card bearing a person's name, and often address, etc., presented or left in paying a visit, sent in polite acknowledgment, or otherwise used.

vis-i-tor (viz′i-tor), *n.* One who visits, or makes a visit, as for friendly, business, official, or other purposes; a visitant. —**vis-i-to′ri-al** (-tō′ri-al), *a.* Of or pertaining to a visitor; visitatorial.—**vis′i-tress**, *n.* A female visitor.

vis-na-ga (vis-nä′gä), *n.* [NL., < Sp. *viznaga*, *biznaga*, through Ar. < L. *pastinaca*, parsnip, carrot.] A carrot-like plant, *Ammi visnaga*, of the Mediterranean region; also, any of various cactaceous plants of Mexico and the southwestern U. S., with spiny cylindrical or globose fleshy stems containing a watery pulp, as species of *Echinocactus* which in desert regions yield a substitute for drinking-water.

vis-or (viz′or or vī′zor), etc. See *vizor*, etc.

vis-ta (vis′tä), *n.* [It., orig. pp. fem. of *vedere*, < L. *videre*, see.] A view or prospect, esp. one seen through a long, narrow avenue or passage, as between rows of trees, houses, or the like (as, "The principal street . . . afforded a noble *vista*, in which the long lines of low stone edifices were broken occasionally by intervening gardens": Prescott's "Conquest of Mexico," iv. 1); also, such an avenue or passage itself (as, "steepled towns through shaded *vistas* seen": Whittier's "Panorama"); sometimes, a long passage in a building affording a continuous view; also, fig., a mental view of a far-reaching kind (as, "*vistas* of thought": Weir Mitchell's "Hugh Wynne," iv.); a mental view extending over an extensive period of time or a long stretch of remembered, imagined, or anticipated experiences, etc. (as, dim *vistas* of the past or the future; "a gloomy *vista* of coming disasters," De Quincey's "English Mail-Coach," ii.).—**vis′taed** (-täd), *a.* Having or forming a vista.

Visnaga (*Echinocactus emoryi*).

vis-u-al (vizh′ū-al), *a.* [F. *visual*, now *visuel*, < LL. *visualis*, < L. *visus*, sight, vision, < *videre*, see.] Of or pertaining to sight; used in sight (as, the *visual* nerve); also, perceptible by the sight; visible; sometimes, perceptible by the mind; of the nature of a mental vision.—**vis-u-al′i-ty**

(-al′i-ti), *n.*; pl. *-ties* (-tiz). Visual or visible character; visibility; also, a view or glimpse; a mental picture.—**vis′u-al-ize** (-īz), *v.*; *-ized, -izing.* **I.** *tr.* To make visual or visible; make perceptible to the mind or imagination; form a mental image or picture of (as, "Her features, which he tried to *visualise*, were misty to him": L. Merrick's "Conrad in Quest of His Youth," ix.). **II.** *intr.* To call up or form mental images or pictures.—**vis″u-al-i-za′tion** (-ī-zā′shon), *n.*—**vis′u-al-i-zer** (-ī-zėr), *n.*—**vis′u-al-ly,** *adv.* In a visual manner or respect; by sight.

vi-ta-ceous (vī-tā′shius), *a.* [NL. *Vitis,* the grape genus, L. *vitis,* vine.] Belonging to the *Vitaceæ,* or grape family of plants, which includes also the ampelopsis, Japanese ivy, Virginia creeper, etc.

vi-tal (vī′tạl), *a.* [OF. F. *vital,* < L. *vitalis,* < *vita,* life, < *vivere,* live: see *quick.*] Of or pertaining to life (as, *vital* functions or processes; *vital* statistics, statistics concerning life or the conditions affecting life and the maintenance of population); also, having life, or living (as, "Spirits that live throughout *Vital* in every part": Milton's "Paradise Lost," vi. 345); capable of living†; also, being the seat or source of life (as, the *vital* parts or organs); necessary to life (as, *vital* air, an old name for oxygen, which is essential to animal life); also, imparting life or vigor, vitalizing, or invigorating (as, "What he admir'd and lov'd, his *vital* smile Unfolded into being": Akenside's "Pleasures of Imagination," i. 72); also, affecting life; destructive to life (as, a *vital* wound); also, fig., necessary to the existence, continuance, or well-being of something (as, a *vital* necessity); indispensable; essential; affecting the existence, well-being, truth, etc., of something (as, a *vital* error); in general (and often with considerable exaggeration), of critical importance (as, *vital* problems; a *vital* contribution to modern thought; a *vital* book).—**vital force,** the animating force in animals and plants.—**vital principle,** the principle upon which, when united with organized matter, the phenomena peculiar to life are supposed to depend.—**vi′tal-ism,** *n.* In *biol.,* the doctrine that ascribes the functions of a living organism to a vital principle distinct from chemical and other forces.—**vi′tal-ist,** *n.* An adherent of the doctrine of vitalism.—**vi-tal-is′tic,** *a.*—**vi-tal′i-ty** (-tal′i-ti), *n.*; pl. *-ties* (-tiz). Vital force; the principle of life; also, power to live, or physical strength as a condition of life (as, "some secret disease that drained his *vitality* away": H. G. Wells's "Tono-Bungay," i. 2. § 1); loosely, exuberant physical vigor (as, "She was a woman of terrific *vitality*": Arnold Bennett's "Clayhanger," i. 7); fig., power of continued existence, as of an institution, a book, etc.; also, something having vital force; *pl.,* vital powers or energies (as, "He may lose the powers of self-guidance, and in a wrong course his very *vitalities* hurry him to perdition": G. Meredith's "Ordeal of Richard Feverel," xvi.).—**vi′tal-ize** (-īz), *v. t.*; *-ized, -izing.* To make vital or living, or give life to; fig., to give vitality or vigor to; animate.—**vi″tal-i-za′tion** (-ī-zā′shon), *n.* —**vi′tal-iz-er** (-ī-zėr), *n.*—**vi′tal-ly,** *adv.* In a vital manner; with life; so as to affect the life; fig., so as to affect the existence, well-being, etc., of something (as, *vitally* important).—**vi′tal-ness,** *n.*—**vi′tals,** *n. pl.* Those bodily organs which are essential to life, as the brain, heart, lungs, and stomach; fig., the essential parts of anything.

vi-ta-min, vi-ta-mine (vī′tạ-min), *n.* [L. *vita,* life, + E. *amine.*] In *chem.,* any of a class of organic compounds which are found in foods and are necessary for proper nourishment, their absence causing such diseases as beriberi, scurvy, etc.: as, *vitamin* A (combating infection); *vitamin* B_1 (thiamin chloride, the 'morale vitamin'); *vitamin* B_2 (riboflavin); *vitamin* C (preventing scurvy); *vitamin* D (preventing rickets); *vitamin* E (preventing sterility); *vitamin* K (preventing hemorrhage).—**vitamin B complex,** an important group of vitamins containing vitamin B_1, vitamin B_2, etc.—**vi-ta-min′ic** (-min′ik), *a.*

vi-ta-phone (vī′tạ-fōn), *n.* [L. *vita,* life: see *-phone.*] An equipment for recording and reproducing speech, music, etc., to supplement moving pictures. [Proprietary name.]

vi-ta-scope (vī′tạ-skōp), *n.* [L. *vita,* life: see *-scope.*] A cinematograph.

vi-ta-tive-ness (vī′tạ-tiv-nes), *n.* [L. *vita,* life.] In *phren.,* love of life.

vi-tel-lin (vī-tel′in or vi-), *n.* [From *vitellus.*] In *physiol. chem.,* a protein contained in the yolk of eggs; also, any of certain proteins in the seeds of plants, etc.

vi-tel-lus (vī-tel′us or vi-), *n.* [L., yolk of an egg.] The yolk of an egg.—**vi-tel′line** (-tel′in), *a.*

vi-ti-ate (vish′i-āt), *v. t.*; *-ated, -ating.* [L. *vitiatus,* pp. of *vitiare,* < *vitium,* fault, defect, E. *vice¹.*] To impair the quality of; make faulty; mar; contaminate; corrupt; spoil; also, to make legally defective, or invalid; invalidate.—**vi-ti-a′tion** (-ā′shon), *n.*—**vi′ti-a-tor,** *n.*

vi-tic-o-lous (vī-tik′ọ-lus), *a.* [L. *vitis,* vine, + *colere,* inhabit.] In *bot.* and *zoöl.,* growing or living upon the grape-vine, as certain fungi and insects.

vit-i-cul-ture (vit′i-kul-ṭūr), *n.* [L. *vitis,* vine, + *cultura,* E. *culture.*] The culture or cultivation of the grape-vine; grape-growing. Cf. *viniculture.*—**vit-i-cul′tur-al,** *a.*—**vit-i-cul′tur-ist,** *n.*

vit-i-li-go (vit-i-lī′gō), *n.* [L., tetter.] In *pathol.,* a disease, most common in negroes, in which smooth white patches are formed on various parts of the body, owing to loss of the natural pigment.

vit-re-ous (vit′rẹ-us), *a.* [L. *vitreus,* < *vitrum,* glass.] Of the nature of glass; resembling glass, as in transparency, brittleness, hardness, etc.; glassy; also, of or pertaining to glass; obtained from glass.—**vitreous humor,** in *anat.,* the transparent gelatinous substance filling the body of the eyeball behind the crystalline lens.—**vit′re-ous-ly,** *adv.*—**vit′re-ous-ness,** *n.*

vi-tres-cent (vi-tres′ẹnt), *a.* [L. *vitrum,* glass: see *-escent.*] Turning into glass; tending to become glass; capable of being formed into glass.—**vi-tres′cence,** *n.*

vit-ric (vit′rik), *a.* [L. *vitrum,* glass.] Of or pertaining to glass; of the nature of glass; glass-like.—**vit′rics,** *n.* The art of the manufacture and decoration of glass; also (as *pl.*), articles of glassware.

vit-ri-fac-tion (vit-ri-fak′shon), *n.* Same as *vitrification.*

vit-ri-fac-ture (vit-ri-fak′ṭūr), *n.* [L. *vitrum,* glass, + *factura,* a making, < *facere,* make.] The manufacture of glass.

vit-ri-fi-a-ble (vit′ri-fī-ạ-bl), *a.* Capable of being vitrified. —**vit″ri-fi-a-bil′i-ty** (-bil′i-ti), *n.*

vit-ri-fi-ca-tion (vit″ri-fi-kā′shon), *n.* [F. *vitrification.*] The act or process of vitrifying, or the state of being vitrified; also, something vitrified.

vit-ri-form (vit′ri-fôrm), *a.* [L. *vitrum,* glass, + *forma,* form.] Having the form or appearance of glass.

vit-ri-fy (vit′ri-fī), *v. t.* or *i.*; *-fied, -fying.* [F. *vitrifier,* < L. *vitrum,* glass, + *facere,* make.] To convert or be converted into glass; make or become vitreous.

vit-rine (vit′rin), *n.* [F., < *vitre,* pane of glass, < L. *vitrum,* glass.] A glass case or cabinet for displaying articles.

vit-ri-ol (vit′ri-ọl), *n.* [OF. F. *vitriol,* < ML. *vitriolum,* prop. neut. of *vitriolus,* for LL. *vitreolus,* of glass, dim. of L. *vitreus,* E. *vitreous.*] In *chem.,* any of certain metallic sulphates of glassy appearance, as of copper ('blue vitriol'), of iron ('green vitriol'), of zinc ('white vitriol'), etc.; also, sulphuric acid (also called 'oil of vitriol'); in fig. use, something highly caustic, or severe in its effects, as criticism.—**vit′ri-ol,** *v. t.*; *-oled, -oling.* To dip in dilute sulphuric acid, as a metal for the purpose of cleansing; also, to injure or burn with vitriol or sulphuric acid; vitriolize.—**vit′ri-o-late** (-ọ-lāt), *v. t.*; *-lated, -lating.* To convert into a vitriol: as, to *vitriolate* iron sulphide (to convert it into green vitriol).—**vit-ri-ol′ic** (-ol′ik), *a.* Of or pertaining to vitriol; obtained from vitriol; resembling vitriol; fig., severely caustic or scathing (as, *vitriolic* criticism; "He . . . wrote *vitriolic* letters," Sinclair Lewis's "Arrowsmith," xii.).—**vit′ri-ol-ize** (-īz), *v. t.*; *-ized, -izing.* To vitriolate; also, to injure or burn with vitriol or sulphuric acid, as by throwing it in one's face.—**vit″ri-ol-i-za′tion** (-i-zā′shon), *n.*

Vi-tru-vi-an (vi-trö′vi-ạn), *a.* Of or pertaining to

Vitruvian Scroll. — From Palazzo Pesaro, Venice.

Marcus Vitruvius Pollio (1st century B.C.), a Roman architect and engineer, and author of a celebrated treatise on architecture; associated with or named from Vitruvius (as, a *Vitruvian* scroll, an architectural ornament consisting of a series of convoluted curves: see cut on preceding page).

vit-ta (vit′ä), *n.*; pl. *vittæ* (-ē). [L., fillet.] A head-band or fillet; in *bot.*, a tube or receptacle for oil, found in the fruits of most umbelliferous plants; in *zoöl.* and *bot.*, a streak or stripe, as of color. — **vit-tate** (vit′āt), *a.* Provided with or having a vitta or vittæ; specif., striped longitudinally.

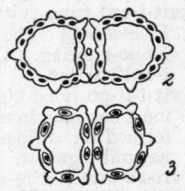

Vitta. — The black spots indicate the vittæ in the transverse sections of the fruits of (1) spotted cowbane (*Cicuta maculata*), (2) celery, and (3) parsley.

vit-u-line (vit′ū-lin), *a.* [L. *vitulinus*, < *vitulus*, calf: cf. *veal*.] Of, pertaining to, or resembling a calf or veal.

vi-tu-per-ate (vī-tū′pe̱-rāt or vi-), *v. t.*; *-ated, -ating.* [L. *vituperatus*, pp. of *vituperare*, censure, blame.] To find fault with abusively; address abusive language to; revile; objurgate. — **vi-tu-per-a′tion** (-pe̱-rā′shon), *n.* [L. *vituperatio(n-)*.] The act of vituperating; verbal abuse; objurgation. — **vi-tu′per-a-tive** (-pe̱-rā-tiv), *a.* Characterized by or of the nature of vituperation; abusive: as, "*vituperative* epithets" (Thackeray's "Newcomes," xxiv.). — **vi-tu′per-a-tive-ly**, *adv.* — **vi-tu′per-a-tor** (-pe̱-rā-tor), *n.*

vi-va (vē′vä). [It.: cf. *vive* and *vivat*.] **I.** *interj.* '(Long) live!' — an Italian word of acclamation. **II.** *n.*; pl. *vivas* (-väz). A shout of 'viva!'

vi-va-ce (vē-vä′chä), *a.* [It.] In *music*, vivacious; lively.

vi-va-cious (vī-vā′shus or vi-), *a.* [L. *vivax* (*vivac-*), < *vivere*, live.] Long-lived, or tenacious of life (archaic); also, lively, animated, or sprightly (as, "a girl so *vivacious*, supple, sparkling, and pretty," Arnold Bennett's "Leonora," iv.; a *vivacious* manner or style; *vivacious* conversation). — **vi-va′cious-ly**, *adv.* — **vi-va′cious-ness**, *n.* — **vi-va′ci-ty** (-vas′i-ti), *n.*; pl. *-ties* (-tiz). The quality of being vivacious; longevity†; liveliness, animation, or sprightliness; also, a vivacious act or speech; a lively sally.

vi-van-dière (vē-vän-dyār′), *n.* [F., < L. *vivenda*: see *viand*.] A woman accompanying a French or other Continental regiment to sell provisions and liquor to the soldiers.

vi-va-ri-um (vī-vā′ri-um), *n.*; pl. *-riums* or *-ria* (-ri-ä). [L., < *vivus*, living, < *vivere*, live.] A place where animals of any kind are kept alive in their natural state. Cf. *terrarium* and *aquarium*.

vi-vat (vī′vat, F. vē-vàt), *interj.* and *n.* [F., < L. *vivat*, '(long) live,' used in phrases of acclamation: cf. *viva* and *vive*.] A shout of acclamation wishing long life, as to a ruler or a popular favorite.

vi-va vo-ce (vī′vä vō′sē). [L., 'with living voice.'] By word of mouth; orally: a phrase also used adjectively, *viva-voce*.

vive (vēv), *v.* or *interj.* [F.: cf. *viva* and *vivat*.] '(Long) live (the person named)!' — used in phrases of acclamation. Cf. *qui vive*.

vi-ver-rine (vī-ver′in or vi-). [L. *viverra*, a ferret.] **I.** *a.* Of or pertaining to the *Viverridæ*, a family of small carnivorous quadrupeds including the civet-cats, palm-cats, etc. **II.** *n.* A viverrine animal.

vi-vers (vē′vėrz), *n. pl.* [F. *vivres*, pl., < *vivre*, inf., < L. *vivere*, live.] Victuals; food. [Sc.]

viv-id (viv′id), *a.* [L. *vividus*, < *vivere*, live.] Lively, or presenting the appearance, freshness, spirit, etc., of life, as a picture (esp., fig., a word-picture, description, or account: as, "*vivid* and invaluable pictures of the half-chaotic scene," Morley's "Oliver Cromwell," iii. 3); also, strikingly alive, or full of life (as, "She had a lovely *vivid* little face," Margaret Kennedy's "Constant Nymph," iii.; a *vivid* personality); vigorous, as activities, etc.; lively or intense, as feelings, etc.; also, strikingly bright, as color, light, objects, etc. (as, a *vivid* green; "the red lightning's *vivid* flash," Wiffen's tr. Tasso's "Jerusalem Delivered," iv. 3; a *vivid* star); clearly perceptible to the eye or mind (as, "On . . . we hurried, and soon the reality of the war was *vivid* to us again": G. W.

Cable's "Cavalier," ix.); strong and distinct, as an impression or recollection; also, forming distinct and striking mental images, as the imagination; lively in operation. — **viv′id-ly**, *adv.* — **viv′id-ness**, *n.*

viv-i-fy (viv′i-fī), *v.*; *-fied, -fying.* [F. *vivifier*, < LL. *vivificare*, < L. *vivus*, alive, + *facere*, make.] **I.** *tr.* To give life to, or quicken; fig., to enliven; render lively or animated; brighten (as, "the sun, whose beams *vivified* every hue of nature": Mrs. Radcliffe's "Romance of the Forest," i.). **II.** *intr.* To become alive. — **viv″i-fi-ca′tion** (-fi-kā′shon), *n.* — **viv′i-fi-er** (-fī-ėr), *n.*

vi-vip-a-rous (vī-vip′a̱-rus), *a.* [L. *viviparus*, < *vivus*, living, + *parere*, bring forth.] In *zoöl.*, bringing forth living young (rather than eggs), as most mammals and some reptiles and fishes. Cf. *oviparous*. — **viv-i-par-i-ty** (viv-i-par′i-ti), **vi-vip′a-rous-ness**, *n.* — **vi-vip′a-rous-ly**, *adv.*

viv-i-sect (viv-i-sekt′), *v.* [Back-formation from *vivisection*.] **I.** *tr.* To dissect the living body of. **II.** *intr.* To practise vivisection.

viv-i-sec-tion (viv-i-sek′shon), *n.* [= F. *vivisection*, < L. *vivus*, living, + *sectio(n-)*, cutting, E. *section*.] The action of cutting into or dissecting a living body, as that of an animal, specif. for purposes of scientific investigation; the practice of subjecting living animals to cutting operations, inoculation experiments, or other experimental treatment, in order to advance physiological and pathological knowledge. — **viv-i-sec′tion-al**, *a.* — **viv-i-sec′tion-ist**, *n.* A vivisector; also, one who favors or defends the practice of vivisection.

viv-i-sec-tor (viv-i-sek′tor), *n.* One who practises vivisection.

vix-en (vik′sn), *n.* [AS. *fyxen*, fem. of *fox*, E. *fox*.] A she-fox (as, "Back to his *vixen* and his young A dog-fox staggered, spent and beat": Eden Phillpotts's "Cherry-Stones," The Last Run); fig., an ill-tempered or quarrelsome woman (as, "An arrant *vixen* of a wife soured his domestic quiet": Fielding's "Tom Jones," viii. 11); a spitfire. — **vix′en-ish**, *a.* Resembling or befitting a vixen: as, "the shrill biting talk of a *vixenish* wife" (George Eliot's "Felix Holt," xi.); "in a . . . *vixenish* mood" (Barrie's "Auld Licht Idylls," ii.). Also **vix′en-ly.**

viz. Abbreviation of *videlicet*.

viz-ard (viz′ärd), *n.* [Var. of *vizor*.] A vizor or mask (lit. or fig.: as, "a little diminutive urchin, wearing a *vizard* with a couple of sprouting horns," Scott's "Kenilworth," xxiv.; "The Spaniards seemed to cast off even the *vizard* of humanity," Motley's "Dutch Republic," iv. 5); also, one wearing a mask. [Obs. or archaic.] — **viz′ard-ed**, *a.*

viz-ca′cha, *n.* See *viscacha*.

vi-zier, vi-zir (vi-zēr′ or viz′yėr, vi-zēr′), *n.* [Turk. *vezir*, < Ar. *wazīr*.] Any of various high officials in Mohammedan countries; a minister of state. — **grand vizier,** the chief officer of state of various Mohammedan countries, as in the former Turkish Empire. — **vi-zier′ate, vi-zir′ate** (-āt), **vi-zier′ship, vi-zir′ship**, *n.*

viz-or, vis-or (viz′or or vī′zọr), *n.* [ME. *viser*, *visere*, < OF. *visiere* (F. *visière*), < *vis*, face, < L. *visus*: see *visage*.] A mask for the face; fig., any disguise or means of concealment; also, the movable front part of a helmet, covering the face, esp. the upper movable part or piece of this; also, the projecting fore piece of a cap, for protecting the eyes. — **viz′ored, vis′-ored**, *a.* Furnished or covered with a vizor. — **viz′or-less, vis′-or-less**, *a.* Having no vizor.

Helmet with Vizor in two parts. — Spanish, 16th century.

vlei (vlī or flī), *n.* [D. *vallei*, valley.] A hollow filled with water by rain; a small lake. [South Africa.]

vly (vlī or flī), *n.* [= *vlei*.] A marsh or pond. [N. Y., etc.]

V.... Mail, a service despatching letters to U. S. armed forces outside continental U. S.: esp. by miniature films.

vo-ca-ble (vō′kạ-bl or vok′ạ-), *n.* [F. *vocable*, < L. *vocabulum*, appellation, name, substantive, ML. word, < L. *vocare*, call.] A word; a term; esp., a word considered merely as composed of certain sounds or letters, without regard to meaning.

vo-cab-u-la-ry (vō-kab′ụ-lạ-ri), *n.*; pl. *-ries* (-riz). [ML. *vocabularium*, < *vocabulum*, word: see *vocable*.] A list or collection of the words of a language, book, author, branch of science, or the like, usually in alphabetical order and defined; a word-book, glossary, dictionary, or lexicon; also, the words of a language; the stock of words used by a people, or by a particular class or person (as, "the ordinary *vocabulary* of the educated," W. D. Whitney's "Life and Growth of Language," ii.; "Her English *vocabulary* was now . . . far above that of most children of her age," Watts-Dunton's "Aylwin," i. 5).

vo-cal (vō′kạl), *a.* [L. *vocalis*, uttering sound, vocal (as n., a vowel), < *vox* (*voc*-), voice: see *voice*, and cf. *vowel*.] Of or pertaining to the voice; uttered with the voice, or oral; rendered by or intended for singing, as music; also, having a voice (as, "*vocal* beings": Pope's "Essay on Man," iii. 156); giving forth sound with or as with a voice; in *phonetics*, voiced; sonant; also, pertaining to or having the character of a vowel.—**vocal cords,** in *anat.*, two pairs of folds of mucous membrane, projecting into the cavity of the larynx, a superior pair ('false vocal cords') not directly concerned in the production of sound, and an inferior pair ('true vocal cords') the edges of which can be drawn tense and approximated together and made to vibrate by the passage of air from the lungs, thus producing vocal sound.—**vo′cal,** *n.* In *phonetics*, a vocal sound; a vowel; also, a vowel-like consonant, as *l* or *r*.—**vo-cal-ic** (vō-kal′ik), *a.* Of, pertaining to, or of the nature of a vowel; vowel-like; containing many vowels.—**vo′cal-ism,** *n.* The use of the voice, as in speech or song; also, a vocalic sound.—**vo′cal-ist,** *n.* A vocal musician; a singer.—**vo-cal-i-ty** (vō-kal′i-ti), *n.* The quality of being vocal.—**vo′cal-ize** (-īz), *v.*; *-ized, -izing.* **I.** *tr.* To make vocal; form into voice; utter or articulate; sing; also, to endow with voice or utterance; also, to utter (speech-sounds) with the voice, and not merely with the breath; make sonant; also, to utter or use as a vowel; also, to furnish with vowels or vowel points. **II.** *intr.* To use the voice, as in speech or song.—**vo″cal-i-za′tion** (-i-zā′shǫn), *n.*—**vo′cal-ly,** *adv.*—**vo′cal-ness,** *n.*

vo-ca-tion (vō-kā′shǫn), *n.* [L. *vocatio*(n-), < *vocare*, call: see *voice*.] A calling or summons, as to a particular activity or career (as, "If he had put off my offer of assistance gayly and with thanks, I should have gone on my way and not felt any *vocation* to renew inquiries": C. Brontë's "Jane Eyre," xii.); designation (by circumstances, necessity, inherent fitness, etc.) for an occupation, business, or profession (as, "an absolute proof that he had no *vocation* for architecture": Arnold Bennett's "Clayhanger," i. 14); sometimes, a divine call to God's service or to the Christian life; also, a particular occupation, business, or profession, or a trade or calling (as, "In this *vocation* of whaling, sinecures are unknown," H. Melville's "Moby-Dick," cx.; "The sole *vocation* conceivable for her was that of teaching," Arnold Bennett's "Hilda Lessways," i. 1); sometimes, a function or station to which one is called by God.—**vo-ca′tion-al,** *a.* Of or pertaining to a vocation or occupation: as, *vocational* schools (schools that train persons for various occupations). —**vo-ca′tion-al-ly,** *adv.*

voc-a-tive (vok′ạ-tiv), *a.* [L. *vocativus*, < *vocare*, call: see *voice*.] **I.** *a.* Pertaining to or used in calling; in *gram.*, designating a person or thing addressed (applied to a case in declension in Latin and some other languages, or to its forms or constructions). **II.** *n.* In *gram.*, the vocative case, or a word in that case.

vo-cif-er-ance (vō-sif′ẹ-rạns), *n.* Vociferant utterance; vociferation.

vo-cif-er-ant (vō-sif′ẹ-rạnt). **I.** *a.* Vociferating. **II.** *n.* One who vociferates.

vo-cif-er-ate (vō-sif′ẹ-rāt), *v. i.* or *t.*; *-ated, -ating.* [L.

vociferatus, pp. of *vociferari,* < *vox* (*voc*-), voice, + *ferre,* bear.] To cry out loudly or noisily; shout; bawl.—**vo-cif-er-a′tion** (-ẹ-rā′shǫn), *n.* [L. *vociferatio*(n-).] The act or an act of vociferating; noisy outcry; a clamor.—**vo-cif′-er-a-tor,** *n.*

vo-cif-er-ous (vō-sif′ẹ-rus), *a.* [L. *vox* (*voc*-), voice, + *ferre,* bear: cf. *vociferate.*] Crying out noisily (as, "Every mouth in the Netherlands became *vociferous* to denounce the hypocrisy": Motley's "Dutch Republic," iii. 5); clamorous; also, of the nature of vociferation, or uttered with clamor (as, "They feel that profanity, unless it be *vociferous*, is almost worthless": Tarkington's "Magnificent Ambersons," i.).—**vo-cif′er-ous-ly,** *adv.*—**vo-cif′er-ous-ness,** *n.*

vod-ka (vod′kä), *n.* [Russ.] A Russian alcoholic liquor, distilled orig. from rye, but now chiefly from potatoes or maize.

voe (vō), *n.* [From Scand.: cf. Icel. *vágr,* bay.] A narrow inlet of the sea: as, "Over headland, ness, and *voe* — The Coastwise Lights of England watch the ships of England go!" (Kipling's "Coastwise Lights"). [Shetland and Orkney Islands.]

vogue (vōg), *n.* [F. *vogue,* vogue, fashion, orig. a rowing, < *voguer,* < It. *vogare,* row (with oars).] The prevailing current of use; the fashion, as at a particular time (as, a style in *vogue* fifty years ago); also, popular currency, acceptance, or favor (as, the book had a great *vogue* in its day; "All these places . . . have their *vogue,* and then the fashion changes," Smollett's "Humphry Clinker," July 4); also, current report or rumor†.

voice (vois), *n.* [OF. *vois, voiz* (F. *voix*), < L. *vox* (*voc*-), voice, sound, word, speech, akin to *vocare,* call, Skt. *vac-,* say, *vacas,* speech, Gr. ἔπος, word, tale (see *epos*).] The sound or sounds uttered by the mouth of living creatures, esp. of human beings in speaking, shouting, singing, etc.; the sounds naturally uttered by a single person (or animal) in speech or vocal utterance, often as characteristic of the utterer (as, "Hoarseness oft invades The singer's *voice,* who sings beneath the shades," Dryden's tr. Virgil's "Pastorals," x. 111; "Lapham had recognised the *voice,*" Howells's "Rise of Silas Lapham," vi.); such sounds considered with reference to their character or quality (as, "You could hear her talking in a very low *voice,*" W. H. Hudson's "Far Away and Long Ago," xiii.; a manly *voice*; a sweet *voice*); the condition of the voice for speaking or singing, esp. effective condition (as, she was in poor *voice,* or not in *voice*); any sound likened to vocal utterance (as, the *voice* of the wind; "The *voice* of a cataract . . . broke upon our ears," H. Melville's "Typee," viii.); anything likened to speech as conveying impressions to the mind (as, the *voice* of nature); also, the faculty of uttering sounds with the mouth, esp. articulate sounds; utterance; speech; also, expression in spoken or written words, or by other means (as, to give *voice* to one's disapproval by a letter, or by withdrawing from a society); also, expressed opinion or choice (as, his *voice* was for compromise; with one *voice,* that is, unanimously); also, the right to express an opinion or choice (as, to have no *voice* in a matter); vote; suffrage; also, expressed wish, or injunction (as, obedient to the *voice* of God); also, report† or rumor†; also, reputation† or fame†; also, the person or other agency by which something is expressed or revealed (as, "I, now the *voice* of the recorded law, Pronounce a sentence": Shakspere's "Measure for Measure," ii. 4. 61); also, a singer; a voice-part; in *phonetics,* sound uttered with resonance of the vocal cords and not by mere emission of breath; sonant utterance; in *gram.,* distinctive form of a verb indicating the relation of the subject to the action expressed by the verb, or any of the groups of forms of a verb serving to indicate this (as, the active, middle, or passive *voice*: see *active, middle,* and *passive*).—**voice,** *v. t.*; *voiced, voicing.* To give voice, utterance, or expression to (an emotion, opinion, etc.: as, to *voice* one's discontent; "Rather assume thy right in silence . . . than *voice* it with claims and challenges," Bacon's "Essays," Of Great Place); express; declare; proclaim; also, to nominate† or elect†; also, to endow with voice or utterance (chiefly poetic); in *music,* to regulate the tone of, as the pipes of an organ; also, to write the voice-parts for (music); in *phonetics,* to utter with voice or vocal sound, as distinguished from breath.—**voiced,**

---

a. Having a voice (as, low-*voiced*); in *phonetics*, uttered with voice or vocal sound (not by mere emission of breath), as the consonants *b*, *d*, and *g*; sonant; vocal.—**voice′ful**, *a.* Having a voice, esp. a loud voice; sounding; sonorous.—**voice′less**, *a.* Having no voice, or mute or dumb; uttering no speech or words, or silent; sometimes, not having a musical voice; also, having no voice or vote; also, unspoken or unuttered (as, "He could not, or he durst not speak, but doom'd To *voiceless* thought his passion": Wiffen's tr. Tasso's "Jerusalem Delivered," ii. 16); characterized by absence or loss of speech (as, "*voiceless* woe": Byron's "Childe Harold," iv. 79); also, characterized by lack of sound, or still (as, "the *voiceless* woods": W. H. Hudson's "Green Mansions," xiii.); in *phonetics*, uttered without voice or vocal sound, as the consonants *p*, *t*, and *k*; surd.—**voice′-less-ly**, *adv.*—**voice′less-ness**, *n.*—**voice′=part**, *n.* In *music*, the melody or succession of tones for one of the voices or instruments in a harmonic or concerted composition.—**voi-cer** (voi′sėr), *n.* One who voices; esp., in *music*, one who voices, or regulates the tone of, organ-pipes.—**voi′cing**, *n.* The act of one who voices; esp., in *music*, the regulation of the tone of organ-pipes so that they shall sound with the proper power, pitch, and quality.

void (void). [OF. *voide*, *vuide* (F. *vide*), prob. ult. < L. *vacuus*, empty, E. *vacuous*.] **I.** *a.* Empty, or without contents, as a receptacle; vacant or unoccupied, as a seat, room, place, space, etc. (as, "The stalls are *void*, the doors are wide," Tennyson's "Sir Galahad," 31; "a pale, *void*, sandy tract," Kinglake's "Eothen," xi.); without an incumbent, as an office (as, "The bishopric of Rochester was *void* three years": Strype's "Memorials of Cranmer," iii. 2); unoccupied with work or business, as time (obs. or rare); empty, devoid, or destitute (*of:* as, "bodies *void* of souls," W. Morris's "Jason," xiii. 216; "He cherished, *void* of selfish ends, The social courtesies," Whittier's "Sumner"); clear (*of:* as, "De Walton was *void* of all censure, having discharged his duty," Scott's "Castle Dangerous," xx.); also, useless, ineffectual, or vain (as, "If they which are of the law be heirs, faith is made *void*, and the promise made of none effect": Rom. iv. 14); in *law*, without legal force or effect; not legally binding or enforceable; less properly, voidable. **II.** *n.* An empty space (as, the *void* of heaven); a place without the usual or desired occupant (as, his death left a *void* among us; an aching *void* within the heart); a gap or opening, as in a wall; also, emptiness or vacancy.—**void**, *v. t.* [OF. *vuidier* (F. *vider*), < *vuide*.] To make empty or vacant, as a vessel, a place, etc. (archaic); clear or rid (*of:* archaic); leave vacant, depart from, or quit, as a place (archaic); also, to empty out or discharge (contents); evacuate (excrement, etc.); also, to render void or of no effect; invalidate; nullify.—**void′a-ble**, *a.* Capable of being voided; in *law*, capable of being made or adjudged void.—**void′ance**, *n.* The act of voiding; ejection from a benefice; vacancy, as of a benefice; annulment, as of a contract.—**void′ed**, *a.* Having a void or opening; in *her.*, cut out (with a narrow rim left) so as to show the field (as, a cross, saltier, or lozenge *voided*).—**void′er**, *n.*—**void′ly**, *adv.*—**void′ness**, *n.*

voile (voil, F. vwol), *n.* [F., veil: see *veil*.] A dress-fabric of wool, silk, or cotton with an open, canvas-like weave.

voir dire (vwor dēr). [OF., 'to say the truth': cf. *verdict*.] In *law*, an oath administered to a proposed witness or juror by which he is sworn to speak the truth in an examination for the purpose of ascertaining his competence; the examination itself.

voi-ture (vwo-tür), *n.* [F., < L. *vectura*: see *vettura*.] In French use, a carriage, wagon, or wheeled vehicle.

voi-vode (voi′vōd), *n.* [Slavic.] Orig., in Slavic countries, the leader of an army; later, the title of various rulers and governing or administrative officials in southeastern Europe, as formerly the princes of Wallachia and Moldavia (now included in Rumania).

vo-lant (vō′lạnt), *a.* [F. *volant*, < L. *volans* (*volant-*), ppr. of *volare*, fly.] Flying; having the power of flight (as, "all *volant* animals": Johnson's "Rasselas," vi.); fig., moving lightly, or nimble (poetic: as, "His *volant* touch . . . pursued transverse the resonant fugue," Milton's "Paradise

Lost," xi. 561); in *her.*, represented as flying, as a bird or a bee.—**vo-lant** (vo-län), *n.* [F.] A flounce, as on a woman's dress.

Bird Volant.

Vo-la-pük (vō-lä-pük′), *n.* [A Volapük word, lit. 'world speech.'] An artificial language for international use, based on English, Latin, German, and other words, invented about 1879 by Johann Martin Schleyer, of Constance, Baden.—**Vo-la-pük′ist**, *n.*

vo-lar (vō′lär), *a.* [L. *vola*, palm of the hand, sole of the foot.] Of or pertaining to the palm of the hand or the sole of the foot.

vol-a-tile (vol′ạ-til), *a.* [F. *volatil*, < L. *volatilis*, flying, winged, fleeting, < *volare*, fly.] Able or accustomed to fly, as winged creatures; also, passing off readily in the form of vapor (as, a *volatile* oil: cf. *essential oil*, under *essential*, *a.*); evaporating rapidly; fig., light and changeable of mind, frivolous, or flighty, as persons (as, "She's *volatile*, she's frivolous, a rattler and gabbler," G. Meredith's "Diana of the Crossways," ii.; "if he is *volatile*, and continually takes things up only to throw them down again," S. Butler's "Way of All Flesh," xxxv.); characterized by levity or flightiness, as the disposition, character, actions, etc.; also, fleeting or transient (as, "Wealth . . . is a highly *volatile* blessing": Kinglake's "Eothen," i.).—**volatile salt**. Same as *sal volatile* (see under *sal*[1]).—**vol′a-tile**, *n.* A flying creature, as a bird; also, a volatile substance or remedy (as, "She . . . by the aid of *volatiles* restored her to recollection": Jane Porter's "Scottish Chiefs," li.).—**vol′a-tile-ness**, **vol-a-til′i-ty** (-til′i-ti), *n.*—**vol′a-til-ize** (-īz), *v.*; *-ized*, *-izing*. **I.** *tr.* To render volatile; cause to pass off in the form of vapor. **II.** *intr.* To become volatile; pass off as vapor.—**vol′a-til-iz-a-ble** (-ī-zạ-bl), *a.*—**vol″a-til-i-za′tion** (-i-zā′shọn), *n.*

vo-la-tion (vō-lā′shọn), *n.* [L. *volare* (pp. *volatus*), fly.] Flying, as of birds.—**vo-la′tion-al**, *a.*

vo-la-tor (vō-lā′tọr), *n.* [NL., < L. *volare*, fly.] A flying-fish.

vol=au=vent (vol-ō-voñ), *n.* [F., for *vole-au-vent*, lit. 'fly-in-the-wind.'] A kind of pie of very light puff-paste filled with a preparation of delicate meat or fish, etc.

vol-can-ic (vol-kan′ik), *a.* Of or pertaining to a volcano or volcanoes (as, "a *volcanic* eruption": A. R. Wallace's "Darwinism," xiii.); discharged from or produced by volcanoes (as, *volcanic* mud); of the nature of a volcano; characterized by the presence of volcanoes; fig., suggestive of a volcano, or its latent force, eruptive violence, etc. (as, "The quiet of this man was *volcanic*": Wister's "Virginian," ii.).—**volcanic glass**, a natural glass produced when molten lava cools very rapidly; obsidian.—**volcanic rock**, in *geol.*, a rock which has been formed by volcanic agency; an igneous rock which has solidified on or near the earth's surface.—**vol-can′i-cal-ly**, *adv.*—**vol-ca-ni′ci-ty** (-kạ-nis′i-ti), *n.* Volcanic state or quality; volcanic activity, or volcanism.

vol-ca-nism (vol′kạ-nizm), *n.* The phenomena connected with volcanoes and volcanic activity.—**vol′ca-nist**, *n.* One versed in the study of the phenomena of volcanoes; also [*cap.*], a Plutonist.

vol-ca-nize (vol′kạ-nīz), *v. t.*; *-nized*, *-nizing*. To subject to or modify by volcanic action.—**vol″ca-ni-za′tion** (-ni-zā′shọn), *n.*

vol-ca-no (vol-kā′nō), *n.*; pl. *-noes* (-nōz). [It. *volcano*, *vulcano*, < L. *Volcanus*, *Vulcanus*, the fire-god Vulcan, or Hephæstus, whose workshop was fabled to be under Mount Etna.] Orig. and popularly, a mountain or hill having an opening or vent through which heated matter is expelled from the interior of the earth; in scientific use, a vent in the earth's crust through which molten rock (lava), steam, ashes, etc., are expelled from within, either continuously or at regular or irregular intervals, gradually forming a conical heap (or in time a mountain), commonly with a cup-shaped hollow (crater) about the vent.—**vol-ca-nol′o-gy** (-kạ-nol′ọ-ji), *n.* [See *-logy*.] The scientific study of volcanoes and volcanic phenomena.—**vol″ca-no-log′i-cal** (-nọ-loj′i-kạl), *a.*—**vol-ca-nol′o-gist**, *n.*

vole[1] (vōl), *n.* [For *vole-mouse* (Norw. *voll*, field).] Any of the rodents of the genus *Microtus* (or *Arvicola*) and allied genera, resembling, and belonging to the same family as, the common rats and mice, and usually of heavy build and having short limbs and tail. See cut on following page.

vole[2] (vōl), *n.* [F.] In *card-playing*, a winning of all the tricks in one deal.

vol-i-tant (vol'i-tant), *a.* [L. *volitans* (*-ant-*), ppr. of *volitare*, fly about, freq. of *volare*, fly.] Flying; having the power of flight; volant.—

vol-i-ta'tion (-tā'shon), *n.* The action or the power of fly-ing; flight.—**vol-i-ta'tion-al**, *a.*

Common European Meadow-vole (*Microtus agrestis*).

vo-li-tient (vō-lish'ent), *a.* [Irreg. < *volition.*] Exercising the will; willing.

vo-li-tion (vō-lish'on), *n.* [F. *volition*, < L. *volo*, I will, inf. *velle*: see *will*[1], *v.*] The act of willing, or exercise of the power of choice to determine action (as, "I shifted my situa-tion with a speed that seemed too swift for *volition*": God-win's "Caleb Williams," xxx.); a determination by the will; also, the power of willing, or will (as, "He perceived . . . that his wife had a genuine individual existence and *volition* of her own": Arnold Bennett's "Mr. Prohack," vii.).—**vo-li'tion-al**, *a.* Of or pertaining to volition.—**vo-li'tion-al-ly**, *adv.*—**vo-li'tion-a-ry** (-ā-ri), *a.* Volitional.—**vol-i-tive** (vol'i-tiv), *a.* Characterized by or pertaining to volition; in *gram.*, expressing a wish or permission (as, a *volitive* proposition).

volks-lied (folks'lēt), *n.*; pl. *-lieder* (-lē''dèr). [G.] A folk-song.

vol-ley (vol'i), *n.*; pl. *volleys* (-iz). [F. *volée*, < *voler*, < L. *volare*, fly.] The flight of a number of missiles together (as, "Stones and brands in rattling *volleys* fly": Dryden's tr. Virgil's "Æneid," i. 215); the discharge of a number of missiles or firearms simultaneously (as, "A *volley* of musketry now rattled in the night wind": Cooper's "Spy," xxii.); hence, a burst or outpouring of many things at once or in quick succession (as, "discharging a furious *volley* of oaths against his mules": Parkman's "Oregon Trail," viii.); in *tennis* and *lawn-tennis*, a flight of a ball in play before strik-ing the ground; also, a return of the ball by the racket before it touches the ground; in *mining*, the explosion of several blasts in the rock at one time.—**vol'ley**, *v.*; *-leyed*, *-leying.* **I.** *tr.* To discharge in or as in a volley; in *tennis*, and *lawn-tennis*, to return (the ball) before it strikes the ground. **II.** *intr.* To fly or be discharged together, as missiles; hence, to move or proceed with great rapidity as in a volley (as, "Sweeping and *volleying*, the wind fought the carriage as the horses ploughed forward": L. Merrick's "House of Lynch," xviii.); also, to fire a volley or sound together, as firearms (as, "Cannon in front of them *Volley'd* and thunder'd": Tennyson's "Charge of the Light Brigade," iii.); emit or produce loud sounds simultaneously or con-tinuously (as, "*volleying* thunders," De Quincey's "Revolt of the Tartars"; "Alan *volleyed* upon the door, and his knocking only roused the echoes of the house," Stevenson's "Kidnapped," xxix.); in *tennis* and *lawn-tennis*, to make a volley.—**vol'ley=ball**, *n.* A game, usually played in a gymnasium, the object of which is to keep a large ball in motion, from side to side over a high net, by striking it with the hands before it touches the ground.

vo-lost (vō'lost), *n.* [Russ.] A small administrative divi-sion in Russia.

vol-plane (vol'plān), *v. i.*; *-planed*, *-planing.* [F. *vol-planer*, < *vol*, flight, + *planer*, float (as a bird) in the air with the outstretched wings apparently motionless.] To glide or descend toward the earth in an aëroplane, without motor power or with the power shut off.—**vol'plane**, *n.* The act or an act of volplaning.

Vol-scian (vol'sian). **I.** *a.* Belonging or pertaining to the Volsci, a people of ancient Italy dwelling southeast of Rome, or to their language. **II.** *n.* One of the Volsci; also, their language, closely allied to Umbrian.

volt[1] (vōlt), *n.* [F. *volte*, < It. *volta*, a turn, < L. *volvere*, roll, turn: cf. *vault*[2].] In the *manège*, a circular or turning movement of a horse; a gait in which a horse going sidewise turns round a center, with the head turned outward; in *fencing*, a sudden movement or leap to avoid a thrust.

volt[2] (vōlt), *n.* [From *Volta*: see *voltaic.*] In *elect.*, the unit of electromotive force, being that electromotive force which will cause a current of one ampere to flow through a resistance of one ohm.

volt-a (vol'tä), *n.*; pl. *-te* (-tā). [It., a turn, time: see *volt*[1].] In *music*, turn; time: used in (It.) phrases, as *una volta*, once; *due volte*, twice; *prima volta*, first time; *seconda volta*, second time.

volt-age (vōl'tāj), *n.* In *elect.*, electromotive force reckoned or expressed in volts.

volt-a-ic (vol-tā'ik), *a.* Of or pertaining to Alessandro Volta (1745–1827), an Italian physicist who made fundamental discoveries dealing with the production of electric currents by chemical action; noting or pertaining to the electricity or electric currents produced by chemical action, or, more broadly, electric currents produced in any way; galvanic.—**voltaic arc**, in *elect.*, an arc.—**voltaic battery.** See *battery.*—**voltaic cell.** See *cell.*—**voltaic couple**, in a voltaic cell, the pair of substances (commonly two metallic plates) placed in the dilute acid or other electrolyte, and giving rise to the electric current.—**voltaic pile.** See *pile*[2], *n.*

vol-ta-ism (vol'tä-izm), *n.* [From *Volta*: see *voltaic.*] The branch of electrical science that deals with the production of electricity or electric currents by chemical action; also, electricity so produced; voltaic electricity.

vol-tam-e-ter (vol-tam'e-tèr), *n.* [From *volta*(*ic*) + *-meter.*] A device for measuring the quantity of electricity passing through a conductor by the amount of electrolytic decompo-sition it produces, or for measuring the strength of a current by the amount of such decomposition in a given time.—**vol-ta-met'ric** (-ta-met'rik), *a.*

volt=am-me-ter (vōlt'am''ē-tèr), *n.* An instrument which can be used for measuring either volts or amperes, and hence watts.

volt=am-pere (vōlt'am-pār''), *n.* An electrical unit equal to the product of one volt and one ampere, which with con-tinuous currents is equivalent to one watt.

Vol-ta's (vol'täz) **pile.** In *elect.*, a voltaic pile.

volte=face (volt-fäs' or vol-tè-fäs'), *n.* [F., for It. *volta-faccia*, lit. 'turn-face.'] A turning so as to face in the oppo-site direction; a complete change of front; a reversal of opinion or policy.

vol-ti (vol'tē), *v.* [It., impv. of *voltare*, turn.] In *music*, turn; turn over: a direction to turn the page.

volt-me-ter (vōlt'mē''tèr), *n.* [See *volt*[2] and *-meter.*] An instrument for measuring the electromotive force or voltage of a circuit.

vol-u-ble (vol'ū-bl), *a.* [L. *volubilis*, < *volvere*, roll, turn: see *volute.*] Characterized by rolling round or along (archaic: as, "Thrice must the *voluble* and restless earth Spin round upon her axle," Cowper's "Task," iii. 490); fig., charac-terized by a ready and continuous flow of words, as a speaker or his tongue or speech (as, a *voluble* talker; "Mr. Reed indeed, from being somewhat silent . . . grew *voluble*," Eden Phillpotts's "Red Redmaynes," iii.; *voluble* protesta-tions); glibly fluent; also, changeable† or mutable†; in *bot.*, of a twining habit.—**vol-u-bil'i-ty** (-bil'i-ti), **vol'u-ble-ness**, *n.*—**vol'u-bly**, *adv.*

vol-u-cra-ry (vol'ū-krā-ri), *n.*; pl. *-ries* (-riz). [= F. *volu-craire*, < L. *volucris*, bird.] A treatise on birds, of a kind written in the middle ages. Cf. *bestiary.*

vol-u-crine (vol'ū-krin), *a.* [L. *volucris*, bird.] Of or per-taining to birds.

vol-ume (vol'ūm), *n.* [OF. F. *volume*, < L. *volumen* (*volu-min-*), a roll (as of manuscript), book, < *volvere*, roll: see *volute.*] Orig., a roll of papyrus, parchment, or the like, or of manuscript, being anciently the usual form of a book (see cut on next page); hence, a collection of written or printed sheets bound together and constituting a book (as, "For him [Cromwell] a single *volume* comprehended all literature, and that *volume* was the Bible": Morley's "Oliver Cromwell," i. 1); often, a book forming one of a related set or series (as, a history in five *volumes*; three bound *volumes* of a magazine);

also, the size of a book† (as, "this book being of a *volume* not large enough": Strype's "Memorials of Cranmer,"i. 21); hence, the size, measure, or amount of anything in three dimensions (as, the *volume* of the sea; the *volume* of a gas; gases expanding to a greater *volume*); cubic magnitude; bulk; in general, amount (as, the *volume* of travel on a railroad for a given period);

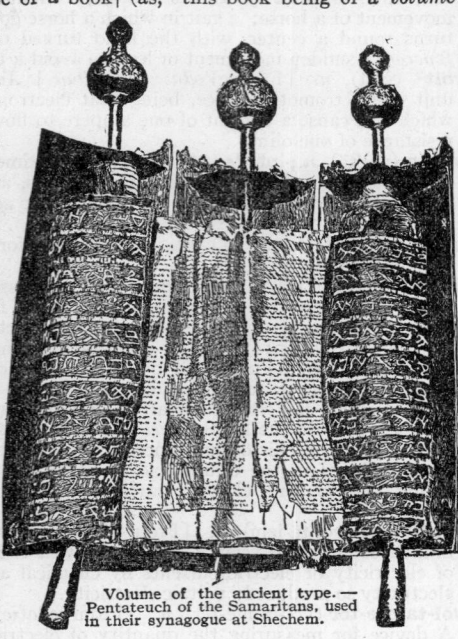

Volume of the ancient type.— Pentateuch of the Samaritans, used in their synagogue at Shechem.

also, a mass or quantity, esp. a large quantity, of anything (as, "The clouds, in lead-colored *volumes* . . . hung sluggishly overhead," Parkman's "Oregon Trail," v.; "an enormous log glowing . . . and sending forth a vast *volume* of light and heat," Irving's "Sketch-Book," Christmas Eve; a *volume* of sound; to pour out *volumes* of abuse); also, a coil, convolution, or winding (archaic: as, the *volumes* of a serpent, or of a meandering stream); in *music*, fullness or roundness of tone or sound.—**to speak volumes**, to express much; convey an abundance of meaning or testimony: as, "Her eyes *spoke volumes*, but her tongue was silent" (Cooper's "Spy," vi.); "This solitary fact [polyandry] *speaks volumes* for the gentle disposition of the male population" (H. Melville's "Typee," xxv.).—**vol′ume**, *v*.; -umed, -uming. **I.** *tr.* To send up or forth in a volume or volumes, as smoke, sound, etc. **II.** *intr.* To roll or rise in a volume or volumes: as, "shutting the registers, through which a welding heat came *voluming* up from the furnace" (Howells's "Rise of Silas Lapham," ii.).—**vol′umed**, *a.* Consisting of a volume or volumes (as, a one-*volumed* book; a ten-*volumed* work); also, in volumes or rolling or rounded masses, as smoke.

vo-lu-me-ter (vō-lū′me-tėr), *n.* [From *volume* + -*meter*: cf. F. *volumètre*.] Any of various instruments or devices for measuring volume, as of gases, liquids, or solids.

vol-u-met-ric (vol-ū-met′rik), *a.* [From *volume* + -*metric* as in *hydrometric*, etc.: cf. F. *volumétrique*.] In *chem.* and *physics*, noting, pertaining to, or depending upon measurement by volume: as, *volumetric* analysis (chemical analysis by volume; specif., chemical analysis by titration). Also **vol-u-met′ri-cal.—vol-u-met′ri-cal-ly**, *adv.*

vo-lu-mi-nal (vō-lū′mi-nạl), *a.* [L. *volumen* (*volumin-*), E. *volume*.] Pertaining to volume or cubic magnitude.

vo-lu-mi-nous (vō-lū′mi-nus), *a.* [LL. *voluminosus*, < L. *volumen* (*volumin-*), E. *volume*.] Having many coils, convolutions, or windings (obs. or archaic); also, forming, filling, or writing a large volume or book, or many volumes (as, a *voluminous* literary work; "the *voluminous* writings of comparative anatomists," A. R. Wallace's "Darwinism," iii.; a *voluminous* author); sufficient to fill a volume or volumes (as, a *voluminous* collection of documents; "I carried on a *voluminous* correspondence with Pepper Whitcomb," Aldrich's "Story of a Bad Boy," xxii.); copious or abundant; also, of great volume, size, or extent, or in great volumes or masses (as, a *voluminous* flow of lava; "Dark and *voluminous* the vapours rise," Cowper's "Heroism," 15; "The booming of a big clock . . . rolled past in *volu-*

minous, austere bursts of sound," J. Conrad's "Lord Jim," xxxvi.); large or swelling; great; often, of ample size, extent, or fullness, as garments, draperies, etc. (as, a *voluminous* cloak, turban, or scarf; "the rich and *voluminous* folds of the silken curtain," Hawthorne's "Twice-Told Tales," The Prophetic Pictures); clothed in ample garments (as, "a *voluminous* damsel, arrayed in a dozen of petticoats": Irving's "Knickerbocker's New York," iii. 4).—**vo-lu-mi-nos′i-ty** (-nos′i-ti), **vo-lu′mi-nous-ness**, *n.*—**vo-lu′mi-nous-ly**, *adv.*

vol-un-ta-ri-ly (vol′un-tạ-ri-li), *adv.* In a voluntary manner; of one's own accord.—**vol′un-ta-ri-ness**, *n.*

vol-un-ta-rism (vol′un-tạ-rizm), *n.* In *philos.*, any theory that regards the will (rather than the intellect) as the fundamental agency or principle.—**vol′un-ta-rist**, *n.*—**vol″un-ta-ris′tic**, *a.*

vol-un-ta-ry (vol′un-tạ-ri). [L. *voluntarius*, acting or done of one's own will, < *voluntas*, will, choice, < *volo*, I will, inf. *velle*: see *will*[1], *v.*] **I.** *a.* Acting of one's own will or choice (as, a *voluntary* substitute); having the power of willing or choosing (as, a *voluntary* agent); resulting from one's own will or choice, and not from constraint (as, "No action is properly termed good or evil unless it be *voluntary*," Hooker's "Ecclesiastical Polity," ii. 8. 1; a *voluntary* contribution, confession, or surrender); done, made, brought about, undertaken, etc., of one's own accord or by free choice; sometimes, proceeding from a natural impulse, or spontaneous (as, "a *voluntary* zeal," Shakspere's "King John," v. 2. 10; a *voluntary* faith); also, done by intention, and not by accident (as, *voluntary* manslaughter); intentional; also, subject to or controlled by the will (as, *voluntary* movements; *voluntary* muscles); also, pertaining to or depending on voluntary action (as, *voluntary* schools, in England and Wales, schools supported by voluntary contributions); in *law*, acting or done without compulsion or obligation; also, made without valuable consideration (as, a *voluntary* conveyance or settlement). **II.** *n.*; pl. -ries (-riz). A volunteer†; also, something done voluntarily; also, an advocate of a church, or of schools, etc., independent of the state and supported by voluntary contributions (Great Britain); in *church music*, a piece of organ (or other) music performed as a prelude to, or during or after, a service.—**vol′un-ta-ry-ism**, *n.* The principle or system of supporting churches, schools, etc., by voluntary contributions or aid, independently of the state; in general, the principle or method of voluntary service (as, military *voluntaryism*).—**vol′un-ta-ry-ist**, *n.*

vol-un-teer (vol-un-tēr′), *n.* [F. *volontaire*, orig. adj., < L. *voluntarius*, E. *voluntary*.] One who enters into any service of his own free will, or who offers himself for any service or undertaking; *milit.*, one who enters the service voluntarily (rather than through conscription or draft), specif. for special or temporary service (rather than as a member of the regular or permanent army); in *agric.*, a volunteer plant; in *law*, one to whom a voluntary conveyance is made.—**Volunteers of America**, a religious reform and relief organization, similar to the Salvation Army, founded in New York City in 1896, by Ballington Booth, son of the founder of the Salvation Army, William Booth.—**vol-un-teer′**, *a.* Entering voluntarily into any service; being a volunteer; consisting of volunteers; in *agric.*, springing up spontaneously, or without being planted (as, a *volunteer* plant, tree, growth, or crop).—**vol-un-teer′**, *v.* **I.** *intr.* To enter service or enlist as a volunteer (as, "He *volunteered* in the English army," Mrs. Wharton's "Son at the Front," xiii.; "The orphan . . . *volunteered* as a boy on board one of the ships of the Republic," J. Conrad's "Rover," vi.); offer one's self for some service or undertaking; make an offer or attempt to do something (as, "I gave them a chance to answer, but none *volunteered*": Stevenson's "David Balfour," xvii.). **II.** *tr.* To offer (one's services, etc., or one's self) for some duty or purpose; offer to undertake or undergo (as, to *volunteer* a dangerous duty; "Who ever was fool enough to *volunteer* a trial?" Godwin's "Caleb Williams," xxix.); offer to give, or give, bestow, show, etc., voluntarily (as, "He was the first to *volunteer* a song (without being asked)," Du Maurier's "Trilby," iv.; "She *volunteered* no friendliness until Dick had taken the first steps," Kipling's "Light That Failed," i.); often, to offer in speech, or communicate, tell, or say voluntarily (as, to *volunteer* a statement, explanation, or remark; "She did not *volunteer* the reason which he seemed to hope for," Hardy's "Return of the Native," ii. 6).

vo-lup-tu-a-ry (vō-lup′tū-ā-ri). [L. *voluptuarius*, for *voluptarius*, < *voluptas*, pleasure, enjoyment.] **I.** *a.* Pertaining to or characterized by luxurious or sensuous pleasures: as, a *voluptuary* life; *voluptuary* habits. **II.** *n.*; pl. *-ries* (-riz). One given up to luxurious or sensuous pleasures: as, "His pleasures were those of a lettered *voluptuary* . . . more in place under Augustus or the Antonines" (Mallock's "New Republic," i. 1).

vo-lup-tu-ous (vō-lup′tū-us), *a.* [OF. F. *voluptueux*, < L. *voluptuosus*, < *voluptas*: see *voluptuary*.] Full of, characterized by, or ministering to pleasure or luxurious or sensuous enjoyment (as, a *voluptuous* life; "Lucullus . . . returned to Rome to lounge away the remainder of his days in *voluptuous* magnificence," Froude's "Cæsar," ix.; "the *voluptuous* precincts of an Eastern harem," Prescott's "Conquest of Mexico," iii. 9); derived from luxurious or full gratification of the senses, as pleasure; directed toward luxurious or sensuous enjoyment, as the desires, inclinations, etc.; also, given or inclined to luxurious enjoyment or the pleasures of the senses (as, "a *voluptuous*, idle woman": Hardy's "Return of the Native," iii. 5); suggestive of an inclination to sensuous pleasure (as, "a tall woman with . . . large *voluptuous* mouth": W. H. Hudson's "Far Away and Long Ago," xiii.); also, sensuously pleasing or delightful (as, *voluptuous* beauty; *voluptuous* music; "the *voluptuous* climates of the south," Irving's "Captain Bonneville," xxxviii.).—**vo-lup′tu-ous-ly**, *adv.*—**vo-lup′tu-ous-ness**, *n.*

vo-lute (vō-lūt′), *a.* [L. *volutus*, pp. of *volvere*, roll, turn; akin to E. *wallow*.] Rolled up; having the form of a volute; voluted.—**vo-lute′**, *n.* [F. *volute*, < L. *voluta*, prop. fem. of *volutus*, pp.] A spiral or twisted formation or object; in *arch.*, a spiral scroll-like ornament, esp. one forming the distinctive feature of the Ionic capital or a more or less important

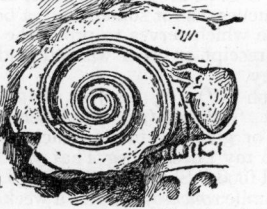

Volute. — 1, Ionic: Temple of Artemis, Ephesus. 2, Composite: Baths of Caracalla, Rome.

part of the Corinthian and Composite capitals; in *zoöl.*, a turn or whorl of a spiral shell; also, any of the *Volutidæ*, a family of marine gastropods of tropical seas, many of the species of which have shells prized for their beauty (cf. *music-shell* and *melon-shell*).—**vo-lut′ed** (-lū′ted), *a.* Having a volute, spiral scroll, or whorl.—**vo-lute′-spring**, *n.* A metal spring resembling a volute, commonly one consisting of a flat bar or ribbon coiled in a conical helix so as to be compressible in the direction of the axis about which it is coiled.—**vo-lu′tion** (-lū′shon), *n.* A rolling or winding; a twist; a convolution; a spiral turn; a whorl; a set of whorls, as of a spiral shell.

Imperial Volute (*Voluta imperialis*).

vol-vu-lus (vol′vū-lus), *n.* [NL., < L. *volvere*, roll, turn.] In *pathol.*, a torsion or twisting of the intestine causing intestinal obstruction.

vo-mer (vō′mėr), *n.* [NL. use of L. *vomer*, plowshare.] In *anat.*, a particular bone of the skull in most vertebrates, in man being shaped like a plowshare, and forming a large part of the nasal septum, or partition between the right and left nasal cavities.—**vo′mer-ine** (-in), *a.*

vom-i-ca (vom′i-kä), *n.*; pl. *-cæ* (-sē). [L., abscess, < *vomere*, vomit, discharge.] In *pathol.*, a cavity in the lungs, containing pus.

vom-it (vom′it), *v.* [L. *vomitus*, pp. of *vomere*, vomit, discharge, akin to Gr. ἐμεῖν, vomit: see *emesis*.] **I.** *intr.* To eject the contents of the stomach by the mouth; spew; also, to be ejected or come out with force or violence. **II.** *tr.* To throw up or eject from the stomach through the mouth; spew; hence, to cast out or eject as if in vomiting; utter (abuse, etc.); discharge or send out with force or copiously (as, "the French troops . . . *vomiting* incessant fire": Marryat's "King's Own," xvi.); also, to cause (a person) to vomit.—**vom′it**, *n.* [L. *vomitus*, n., < *vomere*.] The act or an act of vomiting; also, matter ejected in vomiting; also, something that induces vomiting; an emetic.—**black vomit**. See under *black*, *a.*—**vom′i-tive** (-i-tiv), *a.* [F. *vomitif*.] Emetic; vomitory.—**vom-i-to** (vom′i-tō, Sp. vō′mē-tō), *n.* [Sp.] In *pathol.*, yellow fever in its worst form, usually attended with black vomit (see under *black*, *a.*).—**vom′i-to-ry** (-tō-ri). [L. *vomitorius*, adj. (as n., *vomitorium*, prop. neut. of *vomitorius*), < *vomere*.] **I.** *a.* Inducing vomiting; emetic; also, pertaining to vomiting. **II.** *n.*; pl. *-ries* (-riz). An emetic; also, an opening through which something is ejected or discharged; in *arch.*, one of the openings or passages arranged to give egress from and ingress to the various parts of an ancient Roman theater or amphitheater or some similar building.—**vom″i-tu-ri′tion** (-tū-rish′on), *n.* Ineffectual efforts to vomit; also, the vomiting of but little matter; also, vomiting with little effort.

Amphitheater at Verona, showing a Main Entrance (arched) and Vomitories (small square openings).

von (fon), *prep.* [G.] From; of: much used in German personal names, orig. before names of places or estates, and later before family names, as an indication of nobility or rank, as in 'Herzog von Sachsen' (Duke of Saxony), 'Fürst (Prince) von Bismarck,' 'Graf (Count) von Bernstorff,' 'Freiherr (Baron) von Bunsen,' and 'August Karl von Goeben.' Cf. *de*.

voo-doo (vö′dö or vö-dö′). [Creole F. *vaudou*, prob. of African origin.] **I.** *n.*; pl. *-doos* (-döz). A class of mysterious rites or practices, of the nature of sorcery, witchcraft, or conjuration, prevalent among the negroes of the West Indies and the southern U. S., and probably of African origin; also, one who practises such rites. **II.** *a.* Pertaining to, associated with, or practising voodoo or voodooism.—**voo′doo**, *v. t.* To affect by voodoo sorcery or conjuration.—**voo′doo-ism**, *n.* The voodoo rites or practices; voodoo sorcery; the voodoo superstition.

voor-trek-ker (fōr′trek″ėr), *n.* [S. Afr. D., lit. 'one who treks before'.] A pioneer, as in a new region; specif., one of the Dutch who emigrated from the Cape of Good Hope region into the lands north of the Orange River about 1835–40. [South Africa.]

vo-ra-cious (vō-rā′shus), *a.* [L. *vorax* (*vorac-*), < *vorare*, swallow, devour.] Devouring or craving food in large quantities (as, a *voracious* animal; a *voracious* appetite); greedy in eating; ravenous. Also fig.: as, "The wild *voracious* Ocean, which devours Not fleets alone, but realms" (Wiffen's tr. Tasso's "Jerusalem Delivered," i. 43).—**vo-ra′cious-ly**, *adv.*—**vo-ra′cious-ness**, **vo-ra′ci-ty** (-ras′i-ti), *n.*

-vore. [F. *-vore*, < L. *-vorus*, E. *-vorous*.] A termination of nouns denoting an eater of or feeder on something specified, as in *carnivore*, *insectivore*.

-vorous. [L. -vorus, < vorare, swallow, devour.] An adjective termination meaning 'eating,' 'feeding on,' as in carnivorous, herbivorous, lignivorous, omnivorous.

vor-spiel (fōr'shpēl), n. [G.] A prelude or overture.

vor-tex (vôr'teks), n.; pl. -texes or -tices (-ti-sēz). [L. vortex (vortic-), var. of vertex, a whirl, whirlpool, vortex, also summit: see vertex.] A whirling movement of particles of matter about a center or axis, or the mass of matter itself; specif., in old theories, as in the Cartesian philosophy, a rapid rotatory movement of cosmic matter about a center, regarded as accounting for the origin or phenomena of bodies or systems of bodies in space; a mass of such matter; in more general use, a whirling mass of fire or flame; a whirling movement or mass of air, as a whirlwind; a whirling movement or mass of water, as a whirlpool; fig., a state of affairs likened to a whirlpool for violent activity, irresistible force, etc. (as, "To Peace, however, in this vortex of existence, can the Son of Time not pretend": Carlyle's "Sartor Resartus," ii. 6); something looked upon as drawing into its powerful whirl or current everything that is near it (as, "They continued to be sucked deeper and deeper into the vortex of extravagance and dissipation": Smollett's "Humphry Clinker," Sept. 30).—**vor'ti-cal** (-ti-kạl), a. Of or pertaining to a vortex; resembling a vortex; moving in a vortex. —**vor'ti-cal-ly,** adv.—**vor'ti-cism** (-sizm), n. An eccentric movement of revolt in art and literature, originating in England about 1914 and following upon futurism, which defines a 'vortex' as a 'point of maximum energy,' and seeks to 'get a vortex into,' or make a vortex of, each artistic or literary production, and which requires the abandonment of traditional usage and insists on the utmost simplicity of method. —**vor'ti-cist** (-sist), n. An adherent of vorticism.— **vor'ti-cose** (-kōs), a. [L. vorticosus.] Vortical; whirling. —**vor'ti-cose-ly,** adv.

vor-tig-i-nous (vôr-tij'i-nus), a. [Var. of vertiginous, after vortex.] Whirling; vortical.

vo-ta-ress (vō'tạ-res), n. A female votary.

vo-ta-rist (vō'tạ-rist), n. A votary.

vo-ta-ry (vō'tạ-ri), n.; pl. -ries (-riz). [L. votum, a vow: see vote.] One who is bound by a vow; esp., one bound by vows to a religious life; a monk or a nun; also, a devoted worshiper, as of God, a saint, etc.; a devotee of some form of religious worship; hence, one devoted to some pursuit, study, etc. (as, "the cultured votary of science": F. M. Crawford's "Mr. Isaacs," xii.); a devoted follower or admirer, as of some person, etc.

vote (vōt), n. [L. votum, a vow, wish, desire, < vovere, promise solemnly, vow: cf. vow, n.] A vow†; also, an ardent wish or prayer†; also, a formal expression of will, wish, or choice in some matter, whether of a single individual, as one of a number interested in common, or of a body of individuals, signified by voice, by holding up the hand, by standing up, by ballot, etc.; the right to such expression (as, "Until a man has education, a vote is a useless and dangerous thing for him to possess," H. G. Wells's "Outline of History," xxxv. § 1; women now have the vote); also, the means by which such expression is made, as a ballot, ticket, etc.; also, the decision reached by voting, as by a majority of ballots cast (as, "Marlborough was . . . charged with peculation, and condemned as guilty by a vote of the House of Commons": Green's "Short Hist. of the Eng. People," ix. 9); also, an award, grant, or the like, voted (as, a vote of $1,000,000 for a new building); also, a number of votes (or expressions of will) collectively (as, the labor vote; a light vote was polled).—**casting vote.** See casting, p. a.—**vote,** v.; voted, voting. **I.** intr. To express or signify the will or choice in a matter undergoing decision, as by voice, ballot, or otherwise; give or cast a vote or votes: as, "Longfellow gave up a visit to Europe to vote for Frémont as President" (Charnwood's "Abraham Lincoln," v.). **II.** tr. To enact, establish, or determine by vote; bring or put (in, out, down, etc.) by vote; grant by vote, as an appropriation (as, "The supplies voted by the British parliament . . . amounted to seventy millions of dollars": Bancroft's "Hist. of the U. S.," Amer. Revolution, ii. 3); support by one's vote (as, to vote the Republican ticket); advocate by or as by one's vote (as, to vote that the report be accepted; I vote that we go); also, to declare by general consent (as, they voted the trip a

success).—**vote'less,** a. Having no vote; not entitled to vote.—**vot-er** (vō'tẽr), n. One who votes; one who has a right to vote; an elector.

vo-tive (vō'tiv), a. [L. votivus, < votum, a vow, wish: see vote.] Offered, given, dedicated, etc., in accordance with a vow (as, a votive offering; "to honor the memory of saints by votive lights burnt before their pictures," Irving's "Sketch-Book," The Boar's Head Tavern; a votive church); performed, undertaken, etc., in consequence of a vow; also, of the nature of or expressive of a wish or desire; in the Rom. Cath. Ch., optional, or not prescribed (as, a votive mass, a mass which does not correspond with the office of the day, but is said at the choice of the priest).—**vo'tive-ly,** adv.— **vo'tive-ness,** n.

vo-tress (vō'tres), n. Same as votaress.

vouch (vouch), v. [OF. vochier, call, invoke, declare, < L. vocare, call: cf. avouch.] **I.** tr. To call or summon (a person) into court to make good a warranty of title (obs. or hist., in legal use); also, to call or take to witness, as a person (archaic); cite in warrant or justification, as authority, instances, facts, etc.; adduce or quote in support, as extracts from a book or author; also, to warrant, attest, or confirm (as, "We here receive it [report] A certainty, vouch'd from our cousin Austria": Shakspere's "All's Well," i. 2. 5); affirm or declare as with warrant; vouch for; also, to sustain or uphold by some practical proof or demonstration, or as such proof (as, "such bold words vouch'd with a deed so bold": Milton's "Paradise Lost," v. 66); also, to support or authenticate with vouchers. **II.** intr. To give warrant or attestation; give one's own assurance, as surety or sponsor (for: as, "His character was open for investigation. Judge Henry would vouch for him," Wister's "Virginian," xxix.); in general, to answer (for) as being true, certain, reliable, justly asserted, etc. (as, "Gallant swine they are . . . for the excellence of their flesh I can vouch": Borrow's "Bible in Spain," ii.).—**vouch,** n. A vouching; a supporting warrant or attestation. [Obs. or archaic.]—**vouch'er,** n. One who or that which vouches, as for something; a book, document, stamp, or the like which serves to prove the truth of something; specif., a receipt or other written evidence, as of the payment of money.

vouch-safe (vouch-sāf'), v.; -safed, -safing. [Orig. two words, vouch safe, 'warrant (as) safe,' hence grant, allow.] **I.** tr. To grant or give, by favor, graciousness, or condescension (as, "On my knees I beg That you'll vouchsafe me raiment, bed, and food," Shakspere's "King Lear," ii. 4. 158; "Can I live on a smile vouchsafed twice a week?" Thackeray's "Newcomes," xlvii.; to vouchsafe a reply); deign to bestow; also, to allow or permit, by favor or graciousness (as, "If Brutus will vouchsafe that Antony May safely come to him": Shakspere's "Julius Cæsar," iii. 1. 130); also, to deign to accept†. **II.** intr. To condescend; deign; have the graciousness (to do something: as, "My landlady herself vouchsafed to pay him a visit," Fielding's "Tom Jones," viii. 2).—**vouch-safe'ment,** n. The act of vouchsafing; also, something vouchsafed.

vou-dou (vö'dö or vö-dö'), etc. See voodoo, etc.

vouge (vözh), n. [Also voulge: OF. vouge, voulge (F. vouge); from Celtic.] A long-handled weapon with a kind of ax-blade prolonged to a point at the top, used by foot-soldiers in the 14th century and later.

vous-soir (vö'swor), n. [F., ult. < L. volvere, roll, turn.] In arch., any of the pieces, in the shape of a truncated wedge, which form an arch or vault.

vow (vou), n. [OF. vou, veu (F. vœu), < L. votum, a vow: see vote.] A solemn, religiously binding promise made to God or to any deity or saint, as to perform some act, make some offering or gift, or enter some service or condition (as, "Israel vowed a vow unto the Lord," Num. xxi. 2; "I

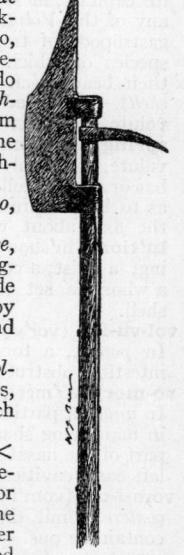

Vouge of the end of the 14th century.

myself remember the canon Robersart who had taken the *vows*, and afterwards broke out of cloister," Scott's "Quentin Durward," v.; solemn and simple *vows*, see *solemn*); hence, any solemn promise, pledge, or personal engagement (as, marriage *vows*; *vows* of amendment; a *vow* of secrecy; *vows* of eternal friendship or love); also, a solemn or earnest declaration†; also, an earnest wish or desire (esp. expressed), or a prayer (obs. or archaic); also, a votive offering†.— **vow,** *v.* [OF. *voer* (F. *vouer*), < ML. *votare*, < L. *votum*.] **I.** *tr.* To make a vow of; promise by a vow, as to God or a saint (as, to *vow* a crusade or a pilgrimage); pledge one's self to do, make, give, observe, etc.; make a solemn threat or resolution of (vengeance, etc.: as, "When he ventured upon insult, I *vowed* revenge," Poe's "Cask of Amontillado"); also, to dedicate or devote by a vow (as, to *vow* one's self to the service of God); also, to make (a vow); also, to declare solemnly or earnestly, assert emphatically, or asseverate (often with a clause as object: as, "She *vowed* she would sooner go to law," Miss Burney's "Evelina," xxii.). **II.** *intr.* To make a vow or solemn promise; also, to make a solemn or earnest declaration.

vow-el (vou′el), *n.* [OF. *vouel, voyeul* (F. *voyelle*), < L. *vocalis*, lit. 'vocal (letter)': see *vocal*.] One of the more open and more resonant speech-sounds, used alone or in combination with consonants to form syllables; also, a letter or character representing such a sound, as, in English, *a, e, i, o,* and *u,* and sometimes *w* and *y.* Cf. *consonant, n.*— **vowel point,** in Hebrew and other Eastern languages, any of certain marks placed above or below consonants, or attached to them, to represent vowel sounds.—**vow′el,** *v. t.*; *-eled* or *-elled, -eling* or *-elling.* To provide or complete with vowels; insert vowel symbols in.—**vow′el-ize,** *v. t.*; *-ized, -izing.* To insert vowels or vowel symbols in; provide with vowel points, as a Hebrew text.—**vow′el-less,** *a.* Without vowels.

vow-er (vou′ėr), *n.* One who vows.

vox (voks), *n.*; pl. *voces* (vō′sēz). [L.: see *voice*.] Voice; sound; word; expression.—**vox angelica** (an-jel′i-kä). [L., 'angelic voice.'] In *music*, an organ-stop producing delicate tones, and having two pipes for each digital, one of which is tuned slightly sharp, so that by their dissonance a wavy effect is produced.—**vox barbara** (bär′ba-rä). [L.] A barbarous word or term, as many 'New Latin' botanical and zoölogical names formed from elements that are not Latin (or Greek).—**vox cælestis** (sē-les′tis). [L., 'heavenly voice.'] Same as *vox angelica.*—**vox humana** (hū-mä′nä). [L., 'human voice.'] In *music*, an organ-stop designed to produce tones resembling those of the human voice.—**vox populi** (pop′ū-lī). [L.] The voice of the people; the expression of the popular will.

voy-age (voi′āj), *n.* [OF. *voiage, veage* (F. *voyage*), < LL. *viaticum*, a journey, L. money or other provision for a journey: see *viaticum*.] Formerly, a journey or passage from one place to another, by land or by sea or water; now, a passage, or course of travel, by sea or water, esp. to a distant place (cf. *journey*); sometimes, a flight through air or space, as a journey in an airship; also, a voyage as the subject of a written account, or the account itself (often in *pl.*); also, a military expedition†; also, an enterprise† or undertaking†. —**voy′age,** *v.*; *-aged, -aging.* [OF. F. *voyager*.] **I.** *intr.* To make or take a voyage; travel by sea or water (as, "There was now no one on board . . . that had ever *voyaged* on the Missouri": Irving's "Captain Bonneville," xli.). **II.** *tr.* To traverse by a voyage: as, "*voyaging* the deeps" (Pope's tr. Homer's "Odyssey," v.).—**voy′age-a-ble,** *a.* Capable of being voyaged over; navigable.—**voy′ag-er,** *n.* One who voyages.—**voy-a-geur** (vwo-yȧ-zhėr′), *n.*; pl. *-geurs* (F. -zhėr). [F., 'traveler.'] In Canada, one of a class of men, chiefly French Canadians or half-breeds, accustomed to traveling through unsettled regions, esp. by canoe on inland waters. Such men were formerly employed by the great fur companies to transport men and goods and maintain communication with their various stations.

vrai-sem-blance (vre-soṅ-bläṅs), *n.* [F.] Appearance of truth; verisimilitude.

vug (vug), *n.* [Cornish.] In *mining*, a small hollow or cavity in a rock or lode, often lined with crystals.—**vug′gy,** *a.* Containing vugs; of the nature of a vug.

Vul-can (vul′kạn), *n.* [L. *Vulcanus, Volcanus*: cf. *volcano*.] The Roman god of fire and metal-working. Cf. *Hephæstus.* —**Vul-ca′ni-an** (-kā′ni-ạn), *a.* Pertaining to or associated with Vulcan; [*l. c.*] volcanic; [*cap.*] of or pertaining to Plutonism.

vul-ca-ni-ci-ty (vul-kạ-nis′i-ti), *n.* Same as *volcanicity.*

vul-ca-nism (vul′kạ-nizm), etc. Same as *volcanism*, etc.

vul-can-ite (vul′kạn-īt), *n.* [See *vulcanize*.] A hard form of rubber, capable of being cut readily and polished, and used for making combs, buttons, etc., and as material for electric insulation, obtained by vulcanizing india-rubber with a large amount of sulphur; ebonite.

vul-can-ize (vul′kạn-īz), *v. t.*; *-ized, -izing.* [From *Vulcan*.] To treat (india-rubber) with sulphur or some compound of sulphur, and subject to a moderate heat, in order to render non-plastic and give greater elasticity, durability, etc., or, when a large amount of sulphur and a more extensive heat treatment are employed, in order to make very hard, as in the case of vulcanite; treat (india-rubber) similarly with sulphur or sulphur compounds, but without the action of heat, in which case the effects are only superficial; hence, to subject (substances other than india-rubber) to some analogous process, as to harden.—**vul″can-i-za′tion** (-i-zā′shọn), *n.*—**vul″can-iz-er** (-ī-zėr), *n.*

vul-ca-nol-o-gy (vul-kạ-nol′ọ-ji), etc. Same as *volcanology*, etc.

vul-gar (vul′gär). [L. *vulgaris*, < *vulgus*, the multitude, the common people.] **I.** *a.* Of, pertaining to, or current among the multitude or general mass of the people (as, *vulgar* errors or superstitions; "There was a *vulgar* tradition . . . that . . . the god would send forth an inundation to overwhelm his enemies," Prescott's "Conquest of Mexico," iii. 7); spoken by, or being in the language spoken by, the people generally, or vernacular (as, "a Bible in the *vulgar* tongue," Borrow's "Lavengro," i.; "The first reformers found the Greek text of the New Testament . . . more favourable to their opinions than the *vulgar* translation," Adam Smith's "Wealth of Nations," v. 1. 3. 2); common or ordinary (as, the *vulgar* era, the Christian era, see under *Christian, a.*; a *vulgar* fraction, see *fraction, n.*); commonplace (as, "Taught on the wings of Truth to fly Above the reach of *vulgar* song": Pope's "Imitations of Horace," Odes, iv. 9); also, belonging to or constituting the common people or the ordinary, plebeian class of society (as, "*Vulgar* people know nothing of the necessaries required in good society," Bulwer-Lytton's "Pelham," i.; the *vulgar* herd); hence, in disparagement, having or showing an inferiority of breeding, manners, taste, etc., supposed to characterize the common people as distinguished from the upper classes of society; underbred or crudely unrefined, as persons (as, "At least I shall be among gentlefolks, and not with *vulgar* city people," Thackeray's "Vanity Fair," vii.; "Mr. Jerrythought was . . . very *vulgar*, and was never without a pipe in his mouth," W. De Morgan's "Alice-for-Short," i.); marked by ignorance of or want of good breeding or taste, as manners, actions, language, dress, display, etc. (as, "Teresa was blowing on her tea to cool it in a *vulgar* way," Margaret Kennedy's "Constant Nymph," xviii.; "Her costume, though *vulgar* and very ill-made, was effective at a little distance," Arnold Bennett's "Hilda Lessways," iv. 3); coarse; low. **II.** *n.* The vulgar tongue, or vernacular (obs. or archaic); also, the common people (archaic: as, "Demons and Angels such as the *vulgar* had once believed in," Carlyle's "Sartor Resartus," ii. 5).—**vul-ga′ri-an** (-gā′ri-ạn), *n.* A vulgar or underbred person, esp. one whose vulgarity is the more conspicuous for his wealth, prominence, or pretensions to good breeding. —**vul′gar-ism,** *n.* Vulgar character or action; vulgarity; also, a vulgar expression; a word or phrase used only in common colloquial, and esp. in coarse, speech.—**vul-gar′i-ty** (-gar′i-ti), *n.*; pl. *-ties* (-tiz). The state or quality of being vulgar; commonness; plebeian character; want of good breeding, manners, or taste; coarseness; also, something vulgar; a vulgar act or speech (as, "She . . . disdained to return any answer to this low *vulgarity*": Godwin's "Caleb Williams," viii.); a vulgar expression, or vulgarism (as, "The uncultivated have current in their dialect a host of inaccuracies . . . slang words, *vulgarities*": W. D. Whitney's "Life and Growth of Language," ix.).—**vul′gar-ize** (-īz), *v. t.*;

(variable) ḍ as d or j, ș as s or sh, ṭ as t or ch, ẓ as z or zh; *o,* F. *cloche*; ü, F. *menu*; c̱h, Sc. *loch*; ṅ, F. *bonbon*; ′, primary accent; ″, secondary accent; †, obsolete; <, from; +, and; =, equals. See also lists at beginning of book.

-ized, -izing. To make vulgar, common, or commonplace; lower; debase: as, to *vulgarize* manners or taste; "the bohemian painter who has done his best to cheapen and *vulgarise* our name" (Watts-Dunton's "Aylwin," ii. 13).—**vul″gar-i-za′tion** (-i-zā′shọn), *n.*—**vul′gar-ly,** *adv.*—**vul′gar-ness,** *n.*

vul-gate (vul′gāt). [L. *vulgatus,* common, ordinary, pp. of *vulgare,* spread among the multitude, make common, < *vulgus,* the multitude: cf. *vulgar.*] **I.** *a.* Common, or in common use (as, a *vulgate* text or version); [*cap.*] of or pertaining to the Vulgate. **II.** *n.* [*cap.*] The Latin version of the Scriptures prepared by Jerome about the close of the 4th century, accepted as the authorized version of the Roman Catholic Church; [*l. c.*] any vulgate text or version.

vul-ner-a-ble (vul′nẹ-rạ-bl), *a.* [LL. *vulnerabilis,* wounding, injurious, < L. *vulnerare,* to wound, < *vulnus* (*vulner-*), a wound.] Capable of wounding†; also, susceptible of being wounded, or liable to physical hurt (as, "Like Achilles, the crocodile has but one *vulnerable* spot": Amelia B. Edwards's "Thousand Miles up the Nile," xvii.); fig., not proof against moral attacks, as of criticism or calumny, or against temptations, influences, etc. (as, "Pierce him on the side of his ambition; there he is *vulnerable*": Jane Porter's "Scottish Chiefs," lvii.); of a place, fortress, etc., open to attack or assault, or weak in the matter of defense (as, "The fortifications of Syria were neglected on the most *vulnerable* side": Gibbon's "Decline and Fall of the Roman Empire," xl.).—**vul″ner-a-bil′i-ty** (-bil′i-ti), **vul′ner-a-ble-ness,** *n.*—**vul′ner-a-bly,** *adv.*

vul-ner-a-ry (vul′nẹ-rạ-ri). [L. *vulnerarius,* < *vulnus* (*vulner-*), a wound.] **I.** *a.* Used or useful for healing wounds, as plants or remedies; also, causing wounds†. **II.** *n.;* pl. *-ries* (-riz). A remedy for wounds.

vul-pec-u-lar (vul-pek′ū-lạr), *a.* [L. *vulpecula,* dim. of *vulpes,* fox.] Pertaining to or of the nature of a young fox or any fox; vulpine.

vul-pine (vul′pin or -pīn), *a.* [L. *vulpinus,* < *vulpes,* fox.] Pertaining to or characteristic of a fox; of the nature of a fox; resembling a fox.

vul-pi-nite (vul′pi-nīt), *n.* [G. *vulpinit;* from *Vulpino* (*Volpino*), in Lombardy, Italy.] A scaly granular variety of the mineral anhydrite.

vul-ture (vul′tụ̄r), *n.* [OF. *voltour* (F. *vautour*), < L. *vulturius, vultur,* vulture.] Any of certain large raptorial birds of the Old World belonging to the family *Falconidæ* (or constituting a separate family *Vulturidæ*) or any of the similar birds of the New World constituting the family *Cathartidæ,* allied to the eagles, hawks, and falcons, which feed chiefly or wholly on carrion, and which have the head and neck more or less bare

Cinereous Vulture (*Vultur monachus*), of the Old World.

of feathers and the beak and claws less powerful than in most birds of prey; fig., a person or thing that preys ravenously and ruthlessly; [*cap.*] in *astron.,* the constellation Aquila.—**vul′tur-ine** (-in or -īn), *a.* [L. *vulturinus.*] Pertaining to or characteristic of a vulture; of the nature of a vulture; resembling a vulture.—**vul′tur-ous,** *a.* Characteristic of or resembling a vulture.

vul-va (vul′vạ), *n.* [L. *vulva, volva,* wrapper, covering, womb, < *volvere,* roll.] In *anat.,* the external genital organs of the female; esp., the orifice of these.—**vul′var** (-vạr), *a.*

vy-ing (vī′ing), *p. a.* That vies; competing.—**vy′ing-ly,** *adv.*

W

W, w (dub′l-ū); pl. *W's, w's* (dub′l-ūz). A consonant and vowel (or semivowel), the 23d letter of the English alphabet.

wab-ble, wob-ble (wob′l), *v.; -bled, -bling.* [Cf. LG. *wabbeln, quabbeln,* wabble, shake.] **I.** *intr.* To incline to one side and to the other alternately, as a wheel, top, or other rotating body when not properly balanced; move unsteadily from side to side (as, "The table *wobbled* under his hand . . . persistently escaping from the wads of paper that he placed beneath its legs": L. Merrick's "Position of Peggy Harper," i. 6); hence, to show unsteadiness, tremble, or quaver, as the voice (colloq.); vacillate or waver, as a person (colloq.: as, "However you may change you mustn't *wobble,*" Galsworthy's "Patrician," ii. 4). **II.** *tr.* To cause to wabble. [Colloq.]—**wab′ble, wob′ble,** *n.* The act or fact of wabbling; a wabbling motion; a vacillating or wavering (colloq.).—**wab′bler, wob′bler,** *n.*—**wab′bling-ly, wob′bling-ly,** *adv.*—**wab′bly¹, wob′bly¹,** *a.* Inclined to wabble; unsteady; shaky.

wab′bly², *n.* See *wobbly².*

WAC. Women's Army Corps.

wack-e (wak′ẹ), *n.* [G.] A soft rock of the texture of sandstone, derived from disintegrated eruptive rocks.

wad¹ (wod), *n.* [Cf. Sw. *vadd,* D. and G. *watte,* F. *ouate,* wadding.] A bundle, esp. a small one, of hay, straw, or the like (now prov. Eng.); also, a small mass of cotton, wool, or other fibrous or soft material, used for stuffing, padding, packing, etc.; a plug of cloth, tow, paper, or the like, used to hold the powder or shot, or both, in place in a gun or cartridge; also, a small mass or lump of anything soft; a ball or mass of something squeezed together (as, "Kim flipped the *wad* of folded paper into the air": Kipling's "Kim," ii.); a roll, as of paper money (as, "He . . . handed her a *wad* of greenbacks": G. W. Cable's "Cavalier," lxiii.); hence, one's stock of money (slang: as, "if we got sick and didn't have a good fat *wad* salted away," Sinclair Lewis's "Main Street," xiv.).—**wad¹,** *v. t.; wadded, wadding.* To form into a wad; also, to fill out with or as with wadding; stuff; pad; line with wadding, as a garment; pack with or as with wadding; put a wad into (a gun, etc.); hold in place by a wad, as powder or shot; also, to force in as a wad.

wad² (wod). Scotch form of *would.*

wad³ (wod), *n.* [Origin obscure.] An impure earthy ore of manganese, which contains manganese dioxide, and is used as a pigment, etc.

wad-a-ble (wā′dạ-bl), *a.* That may be waded.

wad-ding (wod′ing), *n.* Any fibrous or soft material for stuffing, padding, packing, etc.; esp., carded cotton in specially prepared sheets for padding garments, etc.; also, material for wads for guns, etc., or a wad.

wad-dle (wod′l), *v. i.; -dled, -dling.* [Freq. of *wade.*] To walk with short steps, and swaying or rocking from side to side, as a duck, or a fat person with short legs.—**wad′dle,** *n.* The act of waddling; a waddling gait.—**wad′dler,** *n.*—**wad′dling-ly,** *adv.*

wad-dy (wod′i), *n.;* pl. *waddies* (-iz). [Appar. native Australian.] A war-club of heavy wood, used by the Australian aborigines; also, a walking-stick (Australia).

wade (wād), *v.*; *waded, wading*. [AS. *wadan* = D. *waden* = G. *waten* = Icel. *vadha*, wade; akin to L. *vadere*, go, *vadum*, ford.] **I.** *intr.* To go† or proceed†; enter† or penetrate†; also, to walk through any substance, as water, snow, sand, etc., that impedes free motion (as, "I . . . saw . . . the inhabitants *wading* in mud while purchasing their provisions," B. Franklin's "Autobiography," x.; "They walked on . . . *wading* through higher grass as they began to climb a slope," Chesterton's "Napoleon of Notting Hill," i. 3); fig., to make one's way with labor or difficulty (as, to *wade* through an uninteresting book); of the sun or moon, to move through clouds, mist, etc. (prov. or literary: as, "The moon . . . was, in the phrase of that country, *wading* or struggling with clouds," Scott's "Black Dwarf," iii.; "Across the Rhine the sun came *wading* through the reddish vapors," Longfellow's "Hyperion," ii.). **II.** *tr.* To pass through or cross by wading; ford: as, to *wade* a stream.—**wade,** *n.* An act of wading.—**wad-er** (wā′dėr), *n.* One who or that which wades; specif., any of various long-legged birds, as the cranes, herons, storks, sandpipers, plovers, etc., that wade about in water in search of food; also, *pl.*, high waterproof boots for wading.

wa-di, wa-dy (wä′di), *n.*; pl. *-dis, -dies* (-diz). [Ar. *wādī*.] In Arabia, Syria, northern Africa, etc., a valley or ravine through which a stream flows during the rainy season; the channel of a watercourse which is dry except in the rainy season; the stream or watercourse itself.

wad-ing (wā′ding), *p. a.* That wades: as, a *wading* bird (a wader).

wae (wā), *n.* Sc. and north. Eng. form of *woe.*

wa-fer (wā′fėr), *n.* [OF. *waufre* (F. *gaufre*); from LG., and akin to E. *waffle.*] A thin cake or biscuit, variously made, and often sweetened and flavored; a thin disk of unleavened bread, used in the eucharist, as in the Roman Catholic Church; a thin, flat cake of chocolate or the like; also, any of various other thin, flat cakes, sheets, or the like; a thin disk of dried paste, gelatin, or the like, or of paper coated on one side with an adhesive substance, used when moistened for sealing letters, fastening or attaching papers, etc. (as, "The letters of Mrs. Jenkyns and her mother were fastened with a great round red *wafer*," Mrs. Gaskell's "Cranford," v.); a thin, flat cake of compressed material to be dissolved in water and used as a photographic developer; in *med.*, a thin, circular sheet of dry paste or the like, or a pair of such sheets, used upon moistening to wrap about or inclose a powder to be swallowed.—**wa′fer,** *v. t.* To seal, close, or attach by means of a wafer or wafers: as, to *wafer* a letter; "Placards *wafered* in the windows announced that the old house was to let" (Thackeray's "Newcomes," xlviii.).—**wa′fer-y,** *a.* Wafer-like.

waf-fle (wof′l), *n.* [D. *wafel* = LG. *wafel* = G. *waffel*, akin to G. *wabe*, honeycomb: cf. *wafer.*] A kind of indented batter-cake baked in a waffle-iron and served hot.—**waf′fle=i″ron,** *n.* An iron utensil with two hinged parts for baking waffles.

WAFS. Women's Auxiliary Ferrying Squadron.

waft (wȧft), *v.* [Appar. orig. from obs. *wafter*, late ME. *waughter*, an armed convoying vessel or escort (cf. MLG. *wachter*, a watchman, guard, *wachten*, to watch, guard); with later senses derived from *wave* and perhaps still other words.] **I.** *tr.* To convoy (ships, persons, etc.) on the way at sea†; also, to convey or transport over or on the water, as a person, a boat, or the like does (as, "He had the other canoe in the creek . . . so he *wafted* me over," Defoe's "Robinson Crusoe," i. 16; "Yon little bark . . . *Wafting* the stranger on his way," Scott's "Lady of the Lake," ii. 1: now chiefly poetic); bear, carry, or propel over the water, as the waves, wind, etc., do (as, "remnants of icebergs . . . in part *wafted* thither by the wind, but in part slowly borne by the water," Tyndall's "Forms of Water," §50: now chiefly poetic); also, to carry or send (sounds, odors, smoke, dust, etc.) through the air (as, "Now and then the gentle breeze *wafted* the sound of voices": Mrs. Shelley's "Frankenstein," xx.); bear or transport in flight through the air (as, "swift as her pinions *waft* the dove away," Cowper's

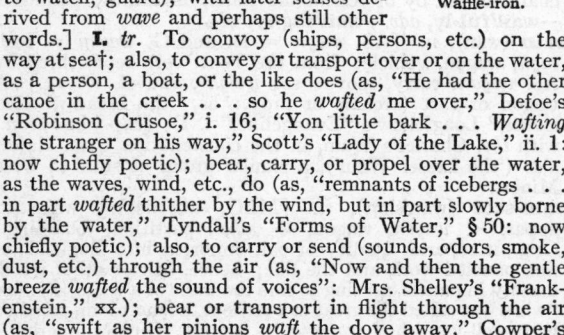
Waffle-iron.

tr. Homer's "Iliad," v. 925; to be *wafted* to heaven by angels); hence, to bear or convey lightly as if in flight (as, "I shall *waft* you away at once to town": C. Brontë's "Jane Eyre," xxiv.); also, to wave (the hand, etc.), as for a signal†; signal to, summon, or direct by waving† (as, "One . . . Whom Fortune with her ivory hand *wafts* to her": Shakspere's "Timon of Athens," i. 1. 70); also, to turn (the eyes) away† (as, "He, *Wafting* his eyes to the contrary . . . speeds from me": Shakspere's "Winter's Tale," i. 2. 372). **II.** *intr.* To move or travel on water†; also, to float or be carried through the air.—**waft,** *n.* The act or an act of wafting, or something wafted; a conveying or passage by water†; a wafting movement, or a current or gust, of wind, air, etc. (as, "A *waft* of wind came sweeping down the laurel-walk": C. Brontë's "Jane Eyre," xxiii.); a sound, odor, puff of smoke, or the like, carried through the air (as, "Upon a light gust came a *waft* of bells," Masefield's "Daffodil Fields," vii.; "*wafts* of the country coming in at the windows," Buchan's "Three Hostages," ii.); fig., a light, transient sensation or experience, as of peace or joy; a waving movement, as of a wing in flying (as, "The lonely seabird crosses With one *waft* of the wing": Tennyson's "Captain")· *naut.*, a signaling, or a signal given, by displaying a flag rolled and stopped or fastened.—**waft-age** (wȧf′tȧj), *n.* The act of wafting, or the state of being wafted; conveyance over water; carrying or propulsion, or floating or passage, through the air. [Archaic.]—**waft′er,** *n.*—**waf-ture** (wȧf′tur), *n.* The act of wafting; the wafting action of the waves, wind, etc., or something wafted; a waving movement, or wave, of something (as, "You . . . with an angry *wafture* of your hand, Gave sign for me to leave you": Shakspere's "Julius Cæsar," ii. 1. 246). [Archaic.]

wag[1] (wag), *v.*; *wagged, wagging.* [ME. *waggen*, akin to AS. *wagian*, move, *wegan*, carry, move: see *weigh*[2].] **I.** *tr.* To set in motion†; move (a limb, finger, etc.: now colloq.); stir† or shake†; now, commonly, to move from side to side, forward and backward, or up and down, esp. rapidly and repeatedly; move (the head) from side to side; move (the tail) from side to side, as a dog does; move (the tongue) in talking (as, "He . . . can still *wag* his tongue with great volubility": Smollett's "Humphry Clinker," June 23). **II.** *intr.* To be in motion†; stir† or move†; move one's limbs (now colloq.); shake or sway (obs. or rare); now, commonly, to be moved from side to side or one way and the other, esp. rapidly and repeatedly, as the head, the tail, or the tongue; also, to depart or be off (as, "Come, neighbours, we must *wag*," Cowper's "Yearly Distress," 50: now colloq.); travel, go, or proceed (as, "They made a pretty good shift to *wag* along," Bunyan's "Pilgrim's Progress," ii.; " 'Thus we may see,' quoth he, 'how the world *wags*,' " Shakspere's "As You Like It," ii. 7. 23).—**wag**[1], *n.* The act or an act of wagging.

wag[2] (wag), *n.* [Perhaps for obs. *wag-halter*, gallows-bird, rogue (used humorously), < *wag*[1], *v.*, + *halter*[1] (hangman's rope).] A roguish or mischievous boy (obs. or archaic, and often used playfully: as, "Was not my lord The verier *wag* o' the two [boys]?" Shakspere's "Winter's Tale," i. 2. 66); hence, a youth or fellow (obs. or archaic: as, "Let us see what the learned *wag* maintains With such a prodigal waste of brains," Longfellow's "Golden Legend," vi. 145); also, a droll, humorous, or facetious person (as, "a loud peal of laughter . . . then another peal, as if a prime *wag* were telling a story": Irving's "Tales of a Traveler," ii. 3).

wage (wāj), *n.* [OF. *wage, guage* (F. *gage*), pledge, security; from Teut., and akin to E. *wed*: cf. *gage*[1].] A gage†, pledge†, or security†; also, in the plural form *wages* (sometimes construed as *sing.*) or, less commonly, in the singular form *wage*, that which is paid for work or services, esp. for work of a manual, mechanical, or menial kind, and usually at short stated intervals, as by the day or week (cf. *salary*); hire; pay; hence, fig., that which is given in recompense or requital (as, "The *wages* of sin is death": Rom. vi. 23); also, in the plural form *wages*, in *polit. econ.*, the share of the products of industry received by labor for its work, as distinct from the share going to capital.—**nominal wages,** in *polit. econ.*, wages estimated in money.—**real wages,** in *polit. econ.*, wages estimated not in money but in their purchasing power with relation to commodities in general; the articles or services which the money wages will purchase.—**wage**, v.; *waged, waging*. [OF. *wagier* (F. *gager*).] **I.** *tr.* To give as a pledge or security†; also, to stake† or wager†; also, in old-time use, to pledge one's self to (battle) for the decision of a case, as in 'wager of battle' (see *wager, n.*); hence, to carry on (a battle, war, conflict, etc.: as, to *wage* war against a nation; to *wage* wars of aggression; "nobles . . . *waging* inherited quarrels among themselves," J. F. Kirk's "Charles the Bold," iv. 1); also, formerly, to pledge one's self for (one's law), by the old legal method of 'wager of law' (see *wager, n.*); hence, to go to (law)† or carry on (a lawsuit)†; also, to engage for pay or wages, or hire (obs. or prov. Eng.); also, to pay wages to (obs. or rare: as, "to *wage* his soldiers out of other men's purses," Scott's "Quentin Durward," v.). **II.**† *intr.* To contend (as, "I abjure all roofs, and choose To *wage* against the enmity o' the air": Shakspere's "King Lear," ii. 4. 212); also, to match or correspond (as, "The commodity *wages* not with the danger": Shakspere's "Pericles," iv. 2. 34).

wa-ger (wā′jėr), *n.* [OF. *wageure* (F. *gageure*), < *wagier*, E. *wage, v.*] A pledge† or guaranty†; also, a staking or betting, or a bet; the subject of a bet; something staked or hazarded on an uncertain event, or a stake; in *old Eng. law*, the act of pledging one's self to make good one's cause (as, *wager* of battle, a method of deciding a question at issue by personal combat between the parties or their champions; *wager* of law, a method by which a defendant, as in actions of debt and detinue, undertook to clear himself by his own oath supported by the oaths of a certain number of compurgators).—**wa′ger**, v. **I.** *tr.* To hazard (something) on the issue of a contest or of any uncertain event or matter; stake; bet. **II.** *intr.* To make or offer a wager; bet.—**wa′ger-er**, *n.*

wa-ges (wā′jez), *n. pl.* See *wage, n.*

wag-ger (wag′ėr), *n.* One who or that which wags.

wag-ger-y (wag′ėr-i), *n.*; pl. *-ies* (-iz). The action, spirit, or language of a wag; a waggish act or performance; a facetious utterance or remark.

wag-gish (wag′ish), *a.* [See *wag²*.] Roguish or mischievous (obs. or archaic); also, having the character or ways of a humorous wag, or jocular or facetious (as, "Muskrat Castle, as the house had been facetiously named by some *waggish* officer": Cooper's "Deerslayer," ii.); characteristic of or befitting a wag (as, a *waggish* action or remark; *waggish* humor).—**wag′gish-ly**, *adv.*—**wag′gish-ness**, *n.*

wag-gle (wag′l), *v. t.* or *i.*; *-gled, -gling.* [Freq. of *wag¹*.] To wag with short, quick movements; move quickly and repeatedly from side to side or one way and the other.—**wag′gle**, *n.* A waggling motion.

wag-gon (wag′ọn), etc. See *wagon*, etc.

Wag-ne-ri-an (väg-nē′ri-ạn or wag-), *a.* Of or pertaining to Richard Wagner (1813–83), the celebrated German musical composer, or his works; pertaining to or in accordance with the ideas or the method of Wagner.—**Wag′ner-ism** (-nėr-izm), *n.* The art theory of Richard Wagner, requiring the combination of music, poetry, action, and scenic agency as equally important coöperating elements; esp., Wagner's theory or method as exemplified in his music dramas, which, departing from the conventional methods of earlier (esp. Italian) opera, show constant attention to dramatic and emotional effect, secured through means both instrumental and scenic, significance of text, and the abundant use of 'leading motives' (see *leitmotiv*) to reinforce the general effect.

wag-on (wag′ọn), *n.* [D. *wagen*, wagon, = AS. *wægn*, E. *wain*.] Any of various kinds of four-wheeled vehicles, esp. one designed for the transport of heavy loads or heavy articles, or for various purposes of business, as the delivery of goods purchased at a shop or of packages sent by express; also, a chariot†; also, a railroad-car for the conveyance of goods or freight (British); in *mining*, a car or truck for carrying ore, etc.; [*cap.*] in *astron.*, Charles's Wain, or the Dipper.—**wag′on**, *v. t.* To transport or convey by wagon.—**wag′on-age** (-āj), *n.* Transport or conveyance by wagon; also, money paid for this; also, a collection of wagons; wagons collectively.—**wag′on-er**, *n.* One who drives a wagon; also, a charioteer†; [*cap.*] in *astron.*, the northern constellation Auriga.—**wag-on-ette′** (-et′), *n.* A four-

wheeled pleasure vehicle, with or without a top, having in front a seat running crosswise and at the back two seats running lengthwise and facing each other.—**wag′on=head″ed**, *a.* Of the form of a round arch or a semicylinder, like the cover of a wagon when stretched over the bows, as a ceiling, roof, etc.—**wa-gon=lit** (vȧ-gôṅ-lē′), *n.*; pl. *wagons lits* (F. vȧ-gôṅ-lē). [F., 'bed car.'] In French and other Continental use, a sleeping-car.

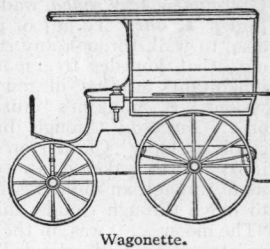

Wagonette.

wag-tail (wag′tāl), *n.* Any of the small, chiefly old-world birds constituting the subfamily *Motacillinæ*, having a slender body with a long, narrow tail which is habitually wagged up and down; also, any of various similar birds, as certain American warblers.

Wa-ha-bi (wȧ-hä′bē), *n.*; pl. *-bis* (-bēz). One of the followers of Abd al-Wahhab (1691?–1787?), a Mohammedan reformer who opposed all practices not sanctioned by the Koran.—**Wa-ha′bi-ism**, *n.*

Pied Wagtail (*Motacilla lugubris*).

wa-hoo (wä-hö′), *n.*; pl. *-hoos* (-höz′). [N. Amer. Ind.] A celastraceous shrub or small tree, *Euonymus atropurpureus*, of North America, with pendulous capsules which in dehiscing reveal the bright-scarlet arils of the seeds; burning-bush; also, any of various other American shrubs or small trees, as an elm, *Ulmus alata*, or a linden, *Tilia heterophylla*.

waif (wāf), *n.* [OF. *waif, gaif*, stray, unclaimed: cf. *waive*.] Something found, of which the owner is not known (esp. in legal use); hence, a stray thing or article (as, "Rolling in his mind Old *waifs* of rhyme": Tennyson's "Brook," 199); a stray animal; esp., a person without home or friends (as, "the great army of *waifs* and strays . . . that marches down, down into all the gutters of the earth": J. Conrad's "Lord Jim," xvi.); often, a homeless or friendless child.

wail (wāl), *v.* [ME. *wailen, weilen*, prob. from Scand.: cf. Icel. *væla*, to wail, *væ, vei*, interj., woe, and E. *woe*.] **I.** *intr.* To utter a prolonged, inarticulate, mournful cry, usually high-pitched or clear-sounding, as in grief or suffering (as, "The women . . . began to *wail* together; they mourned with shrill cries," J. Conrad's "Lord Jim," xlv.; to *wail* with pain; a *wailing* baby); cry piteously; lament or mourn bitterly; hence, to give forth a mournful or plaintive sound suggesting a cry, as musical instruments, the wind, etc.; sound mournfully, as music, etc. **II.** *tr.* To wail over, bewail, or lament (as, to *wail* the dead; to *wail* one's fate); also, to cry or say in lamentation.—**wail**, *n.* The act or sound of wailing; a wailing cry, as of lamentation, grief, or pain; any similar mournful sound (as, "the leisurely *wail* of an old . . . tune": Mrs. Stowe's "Oldtown Folks," iv.). —**wail′er**, *n.*—**wail′ful**, *a.* Full of wailing or lamentation; characterized by or resembling wails; mournful; plaintive. —**wail′ful-ly**, *adv.*—**wail′ing-ly**, *adv.*

wain (wān), *n.* [AS. *wægn* = D. and G. *wagen* = Icel. *vagn*, wagon, vehicle; from the Teut. verb represented by AS. *wegan*, carry, move: see *weigh²*, and cf. *wagon*.] A wagon or cart (archaic or prov.: as, "the broad-wheeled *wains*," Longfellow's "Evangeline," i. 1); [*cap.*] in *astron.*, with *the*, Charles's Wain, in the constellation Ursa Major; also ('the Lesser Wain'), a similar group of stars in Ursa Minor.

wain-scot (wān′skọt), *n.* [MLG. *wagenschot*, wainscot, appar. < *wagen*, wagon, + *schot*, partition, boarding.] Orig., a superior quality of oak imported into England for fine paneled work and the like; hence, oak or other wood, usually in panels, serving to line the walls of a room, etc. (as, "what was called the great oak-parlour, a long room, panelled with well-varnished *wainscot*": Scott's "Guy Mannering," xlii.); a lining or facing of wood on interior walls, etc.; loosely, a dado, or a facing of any material on interior walls, etc.—**wain′scot,** *v. t.*; *-scoted, -scoting* (also *-scotted, -scot-ting*). To line (a room, walls, etc.) with wainscot or wood (as, "a small dark drawing-room . . . *wainscoted* in oak simply carved and panelled": G. MacDonald's "Annals of a Quiet Neighbourhood," vi.); hence, to line or face (walls, etc.) with anything other than wood, as marble, mirrors, etc. —**wain′scot-ing,** *n.* The process or work of lining walls, etc., with wainscot; also, paneling or woodwork with which walls, etc., are wainscoted (as, "The hall was hung round with . . . Thornes . . . by Kneller; each Thorne having been let into a panel in the *wainscoting*": Trollope's "Barchester Towers," xxii.); a lining or facing of wainscot.

wain-wright (wān′rīt), *n.* A wagon-maker.

waist (wāst), *n.* [ME. *wast*, prob. orig. 'growth,' 'size': cf. AS. *wæstm*, growth, stature, form, *weaxan*, grow, E. *wax*[1].] The part of the human body between the ribs and the hips; the contraction marking this; also, a belt† or girdle†; also, the part of a garment covering the waist; also, a garment or a part of a garment covering the body from the neck or shoulders to the waist-line, esp. in women's or children's dress; often, a bodice, blouse, or the like, sepa-rate from the skirt or other garments; also, that part of an object, esp. a central or middle part, which bears some analogy to the human waist (as, the *waist* of a violin, the narrowest part of its body); fig., the middle part of a period of time† (as, "in the dead *waist* [var. *vast*] and middle of the night": Shakspere's "Hamlet," i. 2. 198); *naut.*, the central part of a ship; that part of the deck between the forecastle and the quarter-deck.—**waist′band,** *n.* A band for en-circling the waist, esp. such a band forming part of a skirt, trousers, etc.—**waist′=cloth,** *n.* A loin-cloth.—**waist-coat** (wāst′kōt, colloq. wes′kọt), *n.* A body-garment for men, formerly worn under the doublet; also, a sleeveless body-garment for men, now reaching only a short distance below the waist, worn underneath the coat; a vest; also, a similar garment sometimes worn by women.—**waist′coat-ing,** *n.* Material for making waistcoats.—**waist′ed,** *a.* Having a waist: as, long-*waisted.*—**waist′ing,** *n.* Material for mak-ing waists.—**waist′=line,** *n.* The line of the waist, between the chest and hip portions of the human body.

wait (wāt), *v.* [OF. *waitier, guaitier* (F. *guetter*), watch; from Teut., and akin to *wake*[2] and *watch*.] **I.** *tr.* To watch† or observe†; watch for†; also, to watch with hostile intent†; lie in wait for†; also, to look forward to in expectation; also, to continue stationary or inactive in expectation of (as, "She now *waits* you at the altar," Scott's "Legend of Mont-rose," xxiii.; to *wait* orders; to *wait* one's turn); defer de-parture or action until the arrival or occurrence of; await; of things, to be in readiness for, or be reserved for (as, "Go Where Glory *Waits* Thee," the title of a poem by Thomas Moore); also, to defer or postpone in expectation of the arrival of some one (colloq.: as, "Lady Anne will probably have *waited* dinner for us," Maria Edgeworth's "Belinda," vii.); also, to attend upon† or escort†; also, to attend as an accompaniment or consequence†. **II.** *intr.* To be on the watch†; also, to look expectantly (usually with *for*); also, to stay or rest in expectation (often with *for, till,* or *until*: as, "We came upon our three men *waiting* with the horses," G. W. Cable's "Cavalier," xliii.; "Your father is *waiting* for me to take a walk with him," Tarkington's "Magnificent Ambersons," xiv.); remain in a state of quiescence or inac-tion, as until something expected shall happen; of things, to be in readiness (as, there is a letter *waiting* for you); remain neglected for a time (as, a matter that can *wait*); also, to remain or be in readiness to execute orders; perform the duties of an attendant or servant; esp., to attend upon, or supply the wants of, persons at table.—**to wait on** or **upon,** to watch†; look at or toward†; also, to lie in wait for†; also, to look for† or expect†; also, to await the arrival or convenience of (chiefly prov.); also, to attend on for or with service; act as attendant or servant to; also, to attend to or perform, as a duty†; also, to call upon or visit (a person regarded as or politely implied to be a superior: as, "The general requested permission to return the emperor's visit, by *waiting on* him in his palace," Prescott's "Conquest of Mexico," iii. 9); also, to attend on or accompany for escort

(archaic or prov.: as, "I *waited on* Mr. Mead to the house of Justice Buzzard," Smollett's "Humphry Clinker," June 11; "Major Broad . . . insisted on *waiting on* Miss Mehitable home," Mrs. Stowe's "Oldtown Folks," vi.); also, to attend as an accompaniment or consequence (as, "Now, good digestion *wait on* appetite!" Shakspere's "Macbeth," iii. 4. 38).—**wait,** *n.* [OF. *waite, guaite* (F. *guette*).] A watch-man†; a sentinel†; a scout† or spy†; esp., a watchman or sentinel provided with a horn or trumpet to sound an alarm or signal†; a watchman who by the sound of a trumpet or the like announced the hours†; also, one of a body of musicians in the employ of a city or town, who played on ceremonial and other occasions† (as, "The town-*waits* in the passage below struck up their music": Smollett's "Humphry Clinker," April 24); now, one of a band of singers and mu-sicians who go about the streets by night at Christmas and New Year's singing and playing carols, etc., in order to obtain gratuities (England); also, ambushment or an ambush (as, to lie in *wait*, to lie in ambush, or wait in concealment with hostile intent; to lay *wait*, to set an ambush, or wait in or as in ambush); also, the act of waiting or awaiting; a delay or halt; a period or interval of waiting; in theatrical use, the time between two acts or the like.

wait=a=bit (wāt′a̦-bit), *n.* [Orig. South African, tr. S. Afr. D. *wacht-een-beetje*, name applied to various plants.] Any of various plants bearing thorns or prickly appendages, as a procumbent herb, *Harpagophytum procumbens*, of South Africa, or the greenbrier, *Smilax rotundifolia*.

wait-er (wā′tēr), *n.* A watcher†; also, a watchman†; also, one who waits or awaits; also, an attendant†; now, a man who waits at table, esp. in a hotel or restaurant; also, a tray on which dishes, etc., are carried; a salver; also, a dumb-waiter.

wait-ing (wā′ting), *n.* The act or state of one who or that which waits; staying or resting in expectation; attendance or service.—**in waiting,** in attendance, as upon a king, queen, prince, etc.—**wait′ing=maid,** *n.* A female servant in attendance on a lady; a waiting-woman.—**wait′ing=room,** *n.* A room provided for the use of persons waiting, as in a railroad-station, a physician's office, etc.—**wait′ing=wom″an,** *n.*; pl. *-women* (-wim″en). A woman who waits or attends in service. [Archaic.]

wait-ress (wā′tres), *n.* A woman who waits at table.

waive (wāv), *v. t.*; *waived, waiving.* [AF. *weyver*, OF. *guesver*, relinquish, give over, abandon: cf. *waif*.] To relinquish or forgo (esp. something belonging or due: as, to *waive* powers, privileges, or honors); forbear to insist on (as, to *waive* one's rank; "at once to assert his own vast superi-ority, and to show the generosity and courtesy with which he could *waive* it," Scott's "Guy Mannering," xlii.); also, to refrain from or forbear (as, "He had *waived* noticing the inquiries of Pleyel": C. B. Brown's "Wieland," vii.); dis-pense with (ceremony, etc.); deny to one's self, or go without (as, "We may *waive* just so much care of ourselves as we honestly bestow elsewhere": Thoreau's "Walden," i.); also, to evade or avoid (an action, duty, etc.); also, to put aside or dismiss from consideration or discussion (as, "He ignored or *waived* the poor little attempts I made to ascertain my own position," H. G. Wells's "Tono-Bungay," i. 3. § 3; "Mr. Casaubon mentioned that his young relative had started for the Continent, seeming by this cold vagueness to *waive* inquiry," George Eliot's "Middlemarch," x.); often, to put aside for the time, or defer (as, "But, to *waive* all this for a while, it was in the middle of May . . . that . . .": Defoe's "Robinson Crusoe," i. 13); disregard or ignore; in *law*, to relinquish (a known right, etc.) intentionally.—**waiv′er**[1], *n.* One who waives.—**waiv′er**[2], *n.* [AF. *weyver*, inf., used as noun.] In *law*, the act of waiving some-thing, as a known right; an intentional relinquishment of some right, interest, or the like, or an express or written statement of such relinquishment.

wai-wode (wā′wōd), *n.* Same as *voivode.*

wake[1] (wāk), *n.* [From Scand.: cf. Icel. *vök (vak-)*, hole, opening in ice (affording passage for ships), Sw. *vak*, Dan. *vaage*.] The track left by a ship or other object moving in the water; hence, a track left by anything that has passed; also, the path or course of anything that has passed or pre-ceded (as, wreckage in the *wake* of a storm; "She followed in the *wake* of her mamma," Thackeray's "Newcomes," xliii.).

wake[2] (wāk), *v.*; *waked* or *woke* (pp. sometimes *woken*), *waking*. [AS. *wacan* (pret. *wōc*, pp. *wacen*), wake, arise, also *wacian* (pret. *wacode*, pp. *wacod*), be awake, watch; akin to D. *waken*, G. *wachen*, Icel. *vaka*, Goth. *wakan*, wake, watch, also L. *vigil*, awake, alert: cf. *wait* and *watch*.] **I.** *intr.* To become roused from sleep (often with *up*: as, "She had *woken* up early," Galsworthy's "Dark Flower," i. 15); awake; hence, fig., to become roused from a quiescent or inactive state; become alive, as to something perceived; also, to be or continue awake (as, *waking* or sleeping); remain awake for some purpose, duty, etc. (as, "While the men took rest, their chiefs *waked*, to think for them": Jane Porter's "Scottish Chiefs," lxviii.); revel late at night† (as, "The king doth *wake* to-night and takes his rouse": Shakspere's "Hamlet," i. 4. 8); keep watch or vigil (archaic or prov.); hold a wake over a corpse (prov.). **II.** *tr.* To rouse from sleep (often with *up*); awake; hence, fig., to rouse from quiescence, inactivity, lethargy, unconsciousness, etc.; stir up or excite (activities, feelings, etc.: as, to *wake* strife or controversy; to *wake* ambition); call forth or cause (sounds: as, to *wake* the echoes; "Like an Æolian harp that *wakes* No certain air," Tennyson's "Two Voices," 436); disturb (quiet, etc.: as, "No murmur *waked* the solemn still," Scott's "Lady of the Lake," iii. 26); also, to keep watch or vigil over (archaic or prov.); hold a wake over, as a corpse (prov.: as, "May you die of a good old age . . . and be *waked* handsomely," Marryat's "Peter Simple," li.).—**wake**[2], *n.* The act of waking from sleep†; the state of being awake (as, between sleep and *wake*); also, a watching, or a watch kept, esp. for some solemn or ceremonial purpose; a vigil, as before a church festival; hence, an annual festival held formerly, or now locally, in England in commemoration of the dedication of a parish church, orig. an all-night watch in the church, with the following day kept as a holiday, later becoming a kind of fair with merrymaking and amusements (sometimes in *pl.* with meaning and construction of *sing.*: as, "He had felt much the same as a boy, at Bursley Annual *Wakes* once, on entering a booth which promised horrors and did not supply them," Arnold Bennett's "The Old Adam," iv.); hence, a festivity† or revel†; also, an all-night watch by the body of a dead person before burial, now chiefly among the Irish.—**wake′ful**, *a.* Indisposed or unable to sleep, as a person; characterized by absence of sleep (as, a *wakeful* state; a *wakeful* night); rousing from or as from sleep† (as, "the *wakeful* trump of doom": Milton's "On the Morning of Christ's Nativity," 156); also, sleeplessly alert, watchful, or vigilant (as, "Intermit no watch Against a *wakeful* Foe": Milton's "Paradise Lost," ii. 463).—**wake′ful-ly**, *adv.*—**wake′ful-ness**, *n.*

wak-en (wā′kn), *v.* [AS. *wæcnan*, < *wacan*, wake: see *wake*[2].] **I.** *intr.* To wake, or become awake (lit. or fig.); also, to remain awake; keep vigil. **II.** *tr.* To rouse from sleep; awake; fig., to rouse from inactivity; stir up or excite; arouse.—**wak′en-er**, *n.*

wak-er (wā′kėr), *n.* One who wakes.

wake=rob-in (wāk′rob″in), *n.* The cuckoo-pint, *Arum maculatum*, of Great Britain (see *cuckoo-pint*); any of various other arums or araceous plants, as the jack-in-the-pulpit; also, in the U. S., any of various plants of the convallariaceous genus *Trillium* (see *trillium*), as *T. erectum*, a species with ill-scented purple, pink, or white flowers.

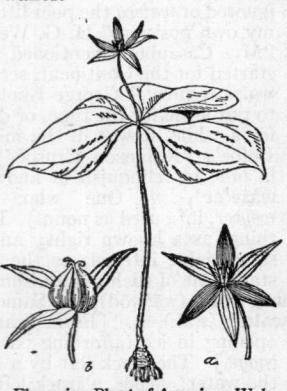

Flowering Plant of American Wake-robin (*Trillium erectum*). — *a*, a flower, laid open; *b*, the fruit, with the persistent sepals.

Wal-den-ses (wol-den′sēz), *n. pl.* [ML.] A Christian sect which arose about 1170 in southern France under the leadership of Pierre Waldo, a merchant of Lyons, and in the 16th cent. joined the Reformation movement.—**Walden′sian** (-sian), *a.* and *n.*

wald-grave (wåld′grāv), *n.* [G. *waldgraf*, 'forest count.'] In the old German Empire, an officer having jurisdiction over a royal forest; also, a nobleman of a certain rank.

wale[1] (wāl), *n.* [ME. *wale, wal*, from Scand.: cf. Icel. *val* = OHG. *wala*, G. *wahl*, choice, from the root of E. *will*[1].] The act or an act of choosing; choice; a number from which to choose; also, that which is chosen; the choicest or best specimen, part, etc. [Sc. and north Eng.]—**wale**[1], *v. t.*; *waled, waling*. To choose; select; pick out. [Sc. and north. Eng.]

wale[2] (wāl), *n.* [AS. *walu*.] A streak, stripe, or ridge produced on the skin by the stroke of a rod or whip; a welt; also, a ridge or raised line formed in the weave of cloth; also, *naut.*, any of certain strakes of thick outside planking on the sides of a wooden ship; sometimes, the gunwale.—**wale**[2], *v. t.*; *waled, waling*. To mark with wales; raise wales on.—**waled**, *a.* Of cloth, woven with a wale: as, wide-*waled* serge.

Wal-er (wā′lėr), *n.* A horse imported from New South Wales, or from Australia. [Anglo-Ind.]

Wal-hal-la (wol-hal′ä, G. väl-häl′ä), *n.* [G.] Same as *Valhalla*.

walk (wåk), *v. i.* [AS. *wealcan*, roll, turn, = OHG. *walchan*, G. *walken*, full (cloth), = Icel. *vālka*, roll.] To roll or toss, as waves†; also, to be in motion or action†, move†, or go† (as, "And ever as she went her toung did *walke*": Spenser's "Faerie Queene," ii. 4. 5); go about or circulate, as reports, etc.† (as, "I . . . now am come to see of whom such noise Hath *walk'd* about": Milton's "Samson Agonistes," 1089); go from place to place†, journey†, or wander†; go forth or about, as in a place or region†; esp., to go or travel on foot at a moderate pace; proceed by steps, or by advancing the feet in turn, at a moderate pace (in bipedal locomotion, so that there is always one foot on the ground, and in quadrupedal locomotion, so that there are always two or more feet on the ground); often, to go about or travel on foot for exercise or pleasure; also, fig., to conduct one's self in a particular manner, or pursue a particular course of life (as, "to *walk* humbly with thy God": Micah, vi. 8); also, to go about on the earth, or appear to living persons, as a ghost; come back as a ghost, as a dead person (as, "an old cottager . . . alleging . . . that my poor brother certainly *walked* after his death": Smollett's "Humphry Clinker," Oct. 11); also, to move off, go away, or depart (now colloq.); also, of things, to move in a manner suggestive of walking, as through repeated vibrations or the effect of alternate expansion and contraction.—**the ghost walks.** See under *ghost, n.*—**to walk out**, to go out from work on a strike. [Colloq.]—**to walk Spanish**, to walk on tiptoe under compulsion, as from the grasp of another on one's collar and the seat of one's trousers; in general, to act under compulsion; also, to walk or proceed gingerly. [Colloq., U. S.]—**walk**, *v. t.* To proceed through, over, or upon by walking (as, "I was *walking* London streets by night": Gissing's "Private Papers of Henry Ryecroft," ii. 26); also, to perform in walking (as, "They *walked* a turn through the hall": Scott's "Ivanhoe," xxxiv.); go through at a walk (as, "They . . . *walk* a quadrille": Bulwer-Lytton's "Pelham," xl.); also, to make, put, drive, etc., by walking (as, "I have *walked* my clothes dry," Scott's "Quentin Durward," iii.; "I've got a headache from travelling; I'm going to *walk* it off," Galsworthy's "Saint's Progress," i. 6); also, to cause to walk; lead, drive, or ride at a walk, as an animal (as, "I was aware of a pair of riders *walking* their horses toward us": F. M. Crawford's "Mr. Isaacs," ii.); force or help to walk, as a person; conduct on a walk (as, "He *walked* the new arrivals about the park and gardens": Thackeray's "Pendennis," ii. 18); also, to move (an object, as a box or a trunk) in a manner suggestive of walking, as by a rocking motion.—**to walk the plank,** to walk along and off a plank extending from a ship's side over the water, under compulsion from those in the ship (a mode of death said to be imposed esp. by pirates); hence, to quit an office or position under compulsion.—**walk**, *n.* An act or course of walking, or going on foot; a spell of walking for exercise or pleasure (as, "Many a ride and *walk* did we take together": Thackeray's "Newcomes," lvi.); a procession (now prov.: as, "There was a 'weavers' *walk*' and five or six others, the 'women's *walk*' being the most picturesque,"

Barrie's "Auld Licht Idylls," ii.); the gait or pace of a person or animal that walks (see *walk, v. i.*); manner of walking (as, "It was impossible to mistake her figure and her *walk*": George Eliot's "Romola," xiii.); fig., manner of behavior, or course of life (as, "Oh! for a closer *walk* with God!" Cowper's "Olney Hymns," Walking with God); also, a department or branch of activity, or a particular line of work (as, "They found every *walk* of life . . . closed against them": Macaulay's "Hist. of Eng.," viii.); hence, a social grade or rank (as, "men in the upper *walks* of life": Trollope's "Barchester Towers," iv.); also, a distance walked or to be walked, often in terms of the time required (as, "her house being a *walke* in the forest, within a little of a quarter mile from Bagshot towne," Evelyn's "Diary," Sept. 15, 1685; a ten minutes' *walk*); also, a customary place of walking†, or a haunt† or resort†; the route of a tradesman, hawker, or the like, or the district traversed (Eng.); also, a course or circuit suitable or chosen for walking (as, a region full of pleasant *walks*); also, a place prepared or set apart for walking; a path in a garden or the like; a way for foot-passengers at the side of a street or road, or a sidewalk; a passage between rows of trees; a public promenade; also, a ropewalk; also, a division of a forest under the charge of a forester or keeper (Eng.); a plantation of coffee or other trees, as in the West Indies; also, an inclosure in which poultry may run about freely; the place where a game-cock is kept; a tract of land for the pasturing of sheep, etc. (cf. *sheepwalk*); a place where puppies are kept and trained for sporting purposes.

walk-er (wâ′kẽr), *n.* One who walks; a pedestrian.

walk-ing (wâ′king), *p. a.* That walks; proceeding on foot at a walk.—**walking delegate**, an official appointed by a trade-union to go from place to place in the interests of the union, as to see that the rules are obeyed, to represent the union in dealings with other organizations and with employers, etc.—**walk′ing=beam**, *n.* In *mach.*, the beam (lever) of a steam-engine. See *beam, n.*—**walk′ing=fern**, *n.* A fern of the polypodiaceous genus *Camptosorus*, with fronds tapering into a slender prolongation which frequently takes root at the apex; esp., *C. rhizophyllus*, a small, hardy species of eastern North America. — **walk′-ing=stick**, *n.* A stick used in walking; a cane; also, a stick-insect.

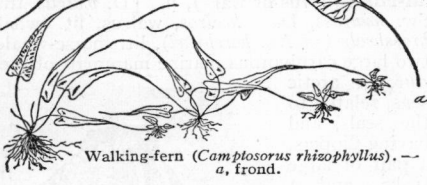
Walking-fern (*Camptosorus rhizophyllus*).— *a*, frond.

walk=out (wâk′out), *n.* A strike of laborers or workers. [Colloq.]

walk=o=ver (wâk′ō″vẽr), *n.* In racing, a going over the course at a walk or otherwise by a contestant who is the only starter; hence, in general, an unopposed or easy victory (colloq.).

Wal-kyr (wol′kir), *n.* [Cf. G. *Walküre*, from Scand., and E. *Valkyr* and *Walkyrie*.] A Valkyr.

Wal-kyr-ie (wol-kir′i), *n.* [Var. of *Valkyrie*, after G. *Walküre* (cf. *Walkyr*): cf. AS. *wælcyrie*, applied to classical Furies, Gorgons, etc., also a sorceress.] A Valkyr.

wall (wâl), *n.* [AS. *weall*, < L. *vallum*, palisade, wall, rampart: see *vallate*.] An upright work or structure of stone, brick, or similar material, serving for inclosure, division, support, protection, etc., as one of the upright inclosing sides of a building or a room, or a solid fence of masonry; specif., a defensive structure inclosing a city, castle, or the like (often in *pl.*); a rampart raised for defensive purposes; also, an inclosing wall, as of a room, considered with reference to its surface (as, "guns, halberts, swords, and pistols . . .

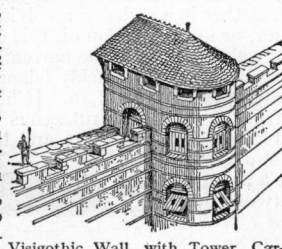
Visigothic Wall, with Tower, Carcassonne, France.

dispos'd upon the *wall*": Cowper's "Charity," 552); also, anything which in its position, function, appearance, or the like, resembles or suggests a wall; a wall-like inclosing part, thing, mass, etc. (as, the *walls* of the chest; a *wall* of fire; a *wall* of troops).—**to drive (push,** etc.) **to the wall,** fig., to drive to the last extremity; force into a position of desperation or helplessness.—**to go to the wall,** fig., to give way or suffer defeat in a conflict or competition (as, "Sam and Mayford are both desperately in love with her, and one must *go to the wall*": H. Kingsley's "Geoffry Hamlyn," xxix.); often, to fail in business, or become bankrupt.—**wall,** *v. t.* To inclose, shut off, divide, protect, etc., with or as with a wall; also, to fill up (a doorway, etc.) with a wall.

wal·la, wal·lah (wol′ä), *n.* [Hind. *-wālā*, adj. suffix.] A person (sometimes a thing) employed at or concerned with a particular thing: used esp. in compounds (as, a punka-*walla*, a man who operates a punka, or fan). [Anglo-Ind.]

wal·la·by (wol′a̱-bi), *n.*; pl. *-bies* (-biz). [Native Australian.] Any of various small and medium-sized kangaroos, esp. of the genera *Halmaturus* and *Petrogale*, some of which are no larger than rabbits.

Wal·la·chi·an (wo-lā′ki-a̱n). **I.** *a.* Of or pertaining to Wallachia, a former principality in southeastern Europe (now a part of Rumania), or its inhabitants or their language. **II.** *n.* A native or inhabitant of Wallachia; also, the language of Wallachia, belonging to the Romance group; Rumanian (which see).

wal′lah, *n.* See *walla*.

wall=board (wâl′bōrd), *n.* An artificially prepared board or sheet-material for use in making or covering walls, ceilings, etc., as a substitute for wooden boards or plaster.

wall=creep-er (wâl′krē″pẽr), *n.* A small old-world bird, *Tichodroma muraria*, which makes its home among precipitous rocks.

walled (wâld), *a.* Having walls: as, high-walled.

wall-er (wâ′lẽr), *n.* One who builds walls.

wal-let (wol′et), *n.* [ME. *walet*, possibly a transposed form of *watel*, basket, bag: cf. *wattle*.] A bag for holding personal necessaries, food, or the like, as for use on a journey, often a long bag with a slit in the middle and closed at each end (archaic: as, "The tried slave stood ready by his lord, With *wallet* on his back," W. Morris's "Jason," i. 108); hence, something hanging loose like a bag†; also, a flat bag or receptacle, usually of leather, having an opening closed by a flap or the like, as for carrying tools; a small kit of tools, supplies, etc., carried by anglers; a pocket-book, esp. one of large size for holding papers, paper money laid flat, etc.— **wal′let-ful** (-fu̇l), *n.*; pl. *-fuls*.

Wall-creeper.

wall=eye (wâl′ī), *n.* [Back-formation from *wall-eyed*.] An eye such as is seen in a wall-eyed person or animal; the condition of being wall-eyed; also, any of various fishes with large, staring eyes, as a pike-perch, *Stizostedion vitreum*.

wall=eyed (wâl′īd), *a.* [From Scand.: cf. Icel. *vagleygr*, wall-eyed, < *vagl*, beam in the eye, + *eygr*, adj. < *auga*, eye.] Having an eye or the eyes presenting little or no color, as the result of a light-colored or white iris or of white opacity of the cornea; having eyes in which there is an abnormal amount of the white showing, because of divergent strabismus; also, having large, staring eyes, as some fishes (as, the *wall-eyed* pike or pike-perch: see *pike-perch*); also, having glaring eyes (as, "*wall-eyed* wrath or staring rage": Shakspere's "King John," iv. 3. 49).

wall=fern (wâl′fẽrn), *n.* The common polypody, *Polypodium vulgare*, which grows on cliffs and walls.

wall-flow-er (wâl′flou″ẽr), *n.* Any plant of the brassicaceous genus *Cheiranthus*; esp., a European perennial, *C. cheiri*, growing wild on old walls, cliffs, etc., and also cultivated in gardens, and having sweet-scented flowers, commonly yellow or orange but in cultivation varying from pale-yellow to brown, red, or purple; also, any of various similar plants; also, a person, esp. a woman, who sits by the wall at a dance and looks on, either from choice or from inability to dance or from failure to obtain a partner (colloq.: as, "He himself stood alone through the dance . . . girl *wallflowers* were sitting near him, waiting to be asked." Sinclair Lewis's "Arrowsmith," vii.).

wall=fruit (wâl′frŏt), *n.* Fruit from trees or other plants trained to grow against a wall, as for protection or warmth.

wall-ing (wâ′ling), *n.* Walls collectively; material for walls.

wall=less (wâl′les), *a.* Having no wall.

Wallflower (*Cheiranthus cheiri*).

Wal-loon (wo-lön′). **I.** *n.* One of a people inhabiting chiefly the southern and southeastern parts of Belgium and adjacent regions in France; also, the language or dialect of the Walloons, related to French. **II.** *a.* Of or pertaining to the Walloons or their language.

wal-lop[1] (wol′ǫp), *v. i.* [OF. *waloper*, var. of *galoper*, E. *gallop*.] To gallop; go with rapid, plunging steps or movements (as, "She [a seal] *walloped* away with all the grace of triumph": Scott's "Antiquary," xxx.); also, to move, plunge, or flop heavily and clumsily about (as, "The dragon *walloped* and hissed, and the hobbyhorse neighed, pranced, and capered": Scott's "Abbot," xiv.); also, to dangle loosely, or flap, as something hanging. [Prov. or colloq.]

wal-lop[2] (wol′ǫp), *v. i.* [Appar. another use of *wallop*[1].] To boil hard, with a noisy bubbling or heaving. [Prov.]

wal-lop[3] (wol′ǫp), *v. t.* [Origin uncertain: cf. *wallop*[1].] To beat soundly; thrash; strike with a vigorous blow; also, to defeat thoroughly, as in a game. [Colloq. or slang.]—

wal′lop[3], *n.* A vigorous blow; also, in boxing, etc., an ability to deliver such blows (as, "the *wallop* in the velvet mitt": Sinclair Lewis's "Babbitt," xvii.). [Colloq. or slang.]—**wal′lop-er**, *n.*—**wal′lop-ing**, *n.* A sound beating or thrashing; also, a thorough defeat. [Colloq. or slang.]—**wal′lop-ing**, *p. a.* Big; strapping; powerful; strong. [Colloq. or slang.]

wal-low (wol′ō), *v.* [AS. *wealwian* = Goth. *walwjan*, roll; akin to L. *volvere*, roll, turn.] **I.** *intr.* To roll or tumble about, as an animal or person on the ground, a vessel on the waves, etc. (as, "The gunboat came out as a long dark shape *wallowing* on the water": H. G. Wells's "Tono-Bungay," iii. 4. § 7); roll or heave in waves (as, "a waste of *wallowing* sea": Kipling's "Captains Courageous," v.); surge up, as smoke, heat, etc.; flounder about or along clumsily or with difficulty; esp., to roll the body about, or lie, in water, snow, mud, dust, or the like, as for refreshment (said commonly of animals: as, "We saw vast great creatures . . . run into the water, *wallowing* and washing themselves for the pleasure of cooling themselves," Defoe's "Robinson Crusoe," i. 2; "the goat having stopped to roll and *wallow* in the dust now and then," Roosevelt's "Ranch Life and the Hunting-Trail," xii.); lie weltering, as in blood; fig., to live contentedly, like animals, in filth, degradation, etc.; live or continue self-indulgently or luxuriously, as in some form of pleasure, manner of life, or the like (now disparaging or humorous: as, to *wallow* in wealth; to *wallow* in sensuality; to *wallow* in sentimentality; "He just loved to stay on and *wallow* in Mrs. Britling's kindness and Mr. Britling's company," H. G. Wells's "Mr. Britling," i. 5. § 7). **II.**† *tr.* To roll about: as, "Gird thee with sackcloth, and *wallow* thyself in ashes" (Jer. vi. 26).—**wal′low**, *n.* The act of wallowing; also, a place where an animal wallows; a place to which animals, as buffaloes, resort to wallow.—**wal′low-er**, *n.*

wall=pa-per (wâl′pā″pèr), *n.* Paper, commonly with printed decorative patterns in color, for pasting on and covering the walls or ceilings of rooms, etc.

wall=plate (wâl′plāt), *n.* In *building*, a plate or timber placed horizontally in or on a wall, under the ends of girders, joists, or other timbers, in order to distribute pressure; in *mach.*, a vertical metal plate secured against a wall or the like, in order to attach a bracket or for some similar purpose.

wall=rock (wâl′rok), *n.* In *mining*, the rock forming the walls of a vein.

wall=rock-et (wâl′rok″et), *n.* A European brassicaceous plant, *Diplotaxis tenuifolia*, growing along old walls, etc.

wall=sid-ed (wâl′sī″ded), *a. Naut.*, having sides nearly perpendicular: said of a ship or vessel.

Wall Street (wâl strēt), *n.* A street in the southern part of the borough of Manhattan, in the city of New York, following the line of the early wall of the city, and now famous as the chief financial center of the U. S.; hence, the money-market or the financiers of the U. S.

wal-nut (wâl′nut), *n.* [AS. *walhhnutu* = Icel. *valhnot*, lit. 'foreign nut' (supposed to have been introduced into Britain by the Romans).] The edible nut of trees of the genus *Juglans*, of the north temperate zone; a tree bearing this nut, as *J. regia* ('English walnut'), which yields the common sweet nut of commerce, or *J. nigra* ('black walnut'), of North America, which yields a valuable timber; the wood of such a tree; also, any of various fruits or trees resembling the walnut; esp., the shagbark (local, U. S.).

Wal-pur-gis (väl-púr′gis) **Night.** The eve of (before) May 1, the feast-day of St. Walpurgis (an English missionary and abbess in Germany, who died about 780), on which, according to German popular superstition, witches ride on broomsticks, he-goats, etc., to some appointed rendezvous, esp. the Brocken, the highest of the Harz Mountains, where they hold revels with their master the devil.

English Walnut (*Juglans regia*).

wal-rus (wol′rus or wâl′-), *n.* [D. *walrus*, from Scand.: cf. Sw. *hvalross*, Dan. *hvalros*, walrus, lit. 'whale-horse,' Icel. *hrosshvalr* (= AS. *horshwæl*), lit. 'horse-whale.')] Either of two large carnivorous marine mammals of the genus *Odobænus*, of arctic seas, related to the seals, and having flippers, a pair of large tusks, and a thick, tough skin; also, a leather prepared from the skin.

wal-ty (wâl′ti), *a.* [Cf. AS. *wealt*, unsteady.] Of a ship, unsteady; crank.

Pacific Walrus (*Odobænus obesus*).

waltz (wâlts), *n.* [= F. *valse*, < G. *walzer*, round dance, waltz, < *walzen*, roll, revolve, waltz; akin to E. *welter*.] A round dance in triple rhythm, danced by couples moving together in a series of revolving steps; also, a piece of music for, or in the rhythm of, this dance.—**waltz**, *v. i.* To dance a waltz; dance in the movement or step of a waltz; also, to move nimbly or quickly (slang).—**waltz′er**, *n.*

wam-pee (wom-pē′), *n.* [Chinese, lit. 'yellow skin.'] The fruit of an Asiatic rutaceous tree, *Clausena wampi*, resembling the grape in size and taste, and growing in clusters; also, the tree.

wam-pum (wom′pum), *n.* [For *wampum-peag.*] Beads

Purple and White Wampum.—From specimen in American Museum of Natural History, New York City.

made from shells, pierced and strung, used by North American Indians as money and for ornament: properly denoting a white variety (see *wampumpeag*), but applied also to a black or dark-purple variety which was commonly considered twice as valuable as the white. Cf. *peag*.

wam-pum-peag (wom′pum-pēg), *n.* [Algonquian *wampompeag*, 'white strings (of shell beads).'] Wampum, properly white wampum. See *wampum*.

wan (won). [AS. *wann*, dark.] **I.** *a.*; compar. *wanner*, superl. *wannest*. Dark or gloomy (archaic or Sc.: as, "They pushed into the waters *wan*," W. Morris's "Jason," v. 126); also, pale in color or hue (as, "cowslips *wan*": Milton's "Lycidas," 147); esp., of an unnatural or sickly pallor, or pallid, as persons, the face, cheeks, etc. (as, "His own *wan* face flushed up": Thackeray's "Newcomes," lxxv.); hence, showing or suggesting ill health, worn condition, unhappiness, etc. (as, a *wan* look; a *wan* smile); also, wanting in brightness, pale, or faint, as stars, light, etc. **II.** *n.* Wan hue or appearance; pallor. [Poetic.]—**wan,** *v. i.* or *t.*; *wanned, wanning.* To become or make wan.

wand (wond), *n.* [ME. *wand*, from Scand.: cf. Icel. *vöndr*, Dan. *vaand*, Goth. *wandus*, rod; from the root of E. *wind*[1].] A slender shoot, stem, or branch of a shrub or tree (as, "as lissome as a hazel *wand*," Tennyson's "Brook," 70; "Between the willow-*wands* there shoots up a thick undergrowth of sedges," Jefferies's "Gamekeeper at Home," iv.); also, a slender stick, or rod (as, "The courier with a red kerchief on a *wand* came galloping round": G. W. Cable's "Bonaventure," i. 3); a rod or staff borne as an ensign of office or authority (as, "The cavalcade arrived. First came two harbingers with *wands*": Walpole's "Castle of Otranto," iii.); a conjurer's or diviner's rod; a baton, as of a musical conductor; also, a switch, stick, or the like, for beating or chastising (as, "Fodder, a *wand*, and burdens, are for the ass," Ecclus. xxxiii. 24: now prov.).

wan-der (won′dėr), *v.* [AS. *wandrian*, akin to G. *wandern*, *wandeln*, wander; a freq. form related to E. *wend*[1].] **I.** *intr.* To ramble without any certain course or object in view (as, "He . . . causeth them to *wander* in a wilderness where there is no way," Job, xii. 24; to *wander* over the earth; to *wander* through a garden or about a house); roam, rove, or stray; go aimlessly or casually (as, "She . . . *wandered* into the adjoining room": H. James's "Portrait of a Lady," xliii.); pass or extend in an irregular course or direction (as, "Through the dark lands of drouth, Far *wanders* ancient Nile," H. Newbolt's "Nile"; "Away off to the south and east and west *wandered* the purple hills," Howells's "Chance Acquaintance," i.); move, pass, or turn idly, at random, or at will, as the hand, the pen, the eyes or glance, etc.; fig., of the mind, thoughts, desires, etc., to take one direction or another without intention or control; also, to stray from a place, companions, etc.; stray from a path or settled course (lit. or fig.); digress, as from a subject; depart, as from a purpose; deviate in conduct, belief, etc. (as, "Let me not *wander* from thy commandments": Ps. cxix. 10); err, or go astray; also, to think or speak confusedly or incoherently (as, "You *wander*; your head becomes confused. I have been too abrupt": C. Brontë's "Jane Eyre," xxxiii.); show loss of the power of coherent thought, recollection, etc., as the mind or a person in illness, exhaustion, or old age; be delirious, or rave. **II.** *tr.* To wander over or through: as, "*wandering* many a famous realm" (Milton's "Paradise Lost," iv. 234).—**wan′der,** *n.* A wandering; a ramble.—**wan′der-er,** *n.*—**wan′der-ing,** *p. a.* That wanders; roaming; roving; straying.—**wandering albatross,** a large albatross, *Diomedea exulans*, of southern waters, having the plumage mostly white with dark markings on the upper parts.—**Wandering Jew,** in medieval legend, a Jew who was condemned by Christ to wander over the earth until Christ's second coming, as a punishment for an insult (according to one version, for refusing to permit Christ to rest before his house on the way to the Crucifixion); also (written *wandering Jew* and *wandering-jew*), any of various trailing or creeping plants, as *Zebrina pendula*, a perennial herb often planted in baskets, etc., from which it spreads in straggling sprays.—**wandering kidney,** in *pathol.*, a floating kidney (see under *floating*).—**wan′der-ing-ly,** *adv.*

wan-der-jahr (vän′dėr-yär), *n.* [G.] A year of wandering

or travel formerly customary in Germany for a journeyman before settling down to his trade. Also fig.

wan-der-lust (vän′dėr-lúst), *n.* [G.] Desire to wander; instinctive impulse to rove or travel about: as, "shabby young men who prowl . . . from state to state . . . in the power of the *Wanderlust*" (Sinclair Lewis's "Arrowsmith," ix.).

wan-de-roo (won-dẹ-rö′), *n.* [Singhalese.] Any of several species of langur, inhabiting Ceylon; commonly, but less properly, a macaque, *Macacus silenus*, of southern India.

Wanderoo (*Macacus silenus*).

wane (wān), *v.i.*; *waned, waning.* [AS. *wanian*, < *wan*, wanting, deficient: see *want*.] To decrease in extent or size, or in quantity (as, "The snow, which had been for some time *waning*, had given way entirely," Scott's "Guy Mannering," xl.: now rare); of the moon, to undergo the periodical decrease in the extent of its illuminated portion after the full (opposed to *wax*); also, to decrease in strength, intensity, etc. (as, "Daylight *waned*, and night came on": M. Arnold's "Balder Dead," ii.); decline in power, importance, prosperity, etc.; also, to draw to a close, or approach an end (as, "When the honeymoon had *waned* . . . the season had opened": L. Merrick's "Worldlings," xiv.).—**wane,** *n.* The act or process of waning; the waning of the moon, or the period of this; gradual decrease or decline in strength, intensity, power, etc., esp. after gradual increase (as, "There were symptoms that Alva's favor was on the *wane*": Motley's "Dutch Republic," iii. 5); the drawing to a close of life, a time, etc., or the period of this (as, "Morning and noon had passed, and the day was on the *wane*," Dickens's "Oliver Twist," xlviii.; "a portly female, considerably in the *wane* of life," Hawthorne's "Twice-Told Tales," Wakefield); also, a beveled edge of a plank or board as sawed from an unsquared log, due to the curvature of the log.—**wan-ey, wan-y** (wā′ni), *a.* Having a wane or natural bevel, as a plank or board; hence, making poor lumber because of irregularities of the surface, as a log.

wan′gan, *n.* See *wanigan*.

wan-gle[1] (wang′gl), *v. i.*; -*gled*, -*gling*. [Cf. *wankle*.] To be unsteady; shake; totter; walk unsteadily. [Prov. Eng.]

wan-gle[2] (wang′gl), *v.*; -*gled*, -*gling*. [Origin obscure: cf. *wangle*[1].] **I.** *tr.* To adjust in a makeshift way; manage (a thing) somehow, as under difficulties; bring about, accomplish, or obtain by contrivance, scheming, or, often, indirect or insidious methods; sometimes, to adjust or manipulate unfairly or dishonestly. [Colloq. or slang, Eng.] **II.** *intr.* To adjust things in a makeshift manner; use contrivance, scheming, or indirect methods to accomplish some end. [Colloq. or slang, Eng.]—**wan′gler,** *n.*

wan-i-gan, wan-gan (won′i-gan, wong′gan), *n.* [N. Amer. Ind.] In lumbering regions, a place or receptacle for small supplies, miscellaneous stores, etc.; also, a kind of boat used by loggers for carrying supplies, tools, etc., and as a house-boat.

Wanigan.

wan-ion† (won′ion), *n.* [ME. *waniand*, the waning moon (regarded as unlucky), prop. ppr. of *wanien*, < AS. *wanian*,

E. *wane*.] A word occurring in certain phrases used in vague imprecation or for emphasis, esp. in *with a wanion* (with ill luck; with mischief befalling one; also, with a vengeance; vigorously; emphatically).

wan-kle (wang'kl), *a.* [AS. *wancol*, unsteady, unstable: cf. *wangle*[1].] Unsteady; shaky; tottering; also, uncertain; precarious. [Now prov. Eng. and Sc.]

wan-ly (wŏn'li), *adv.* In a wan manner.—**wan'ness**, *n.*

wan-nish (wŏn'ish), *a.* Somewhat wan; pallid.

want (wŏnt or wônt), *n.* [ME. *want*, from Scand.: cf. Icel. *vant*, neut. of *vanr*, adj., wanting, lacking, = AS. and OHG. *wan* = Goth. *wans*, wanting: cf. also Skt. *ūna*, lacking, Gr. εὖνις, bereft, and E. *wane* and *wanton*.] Absence or deficiency of something desirable or requisite (as, plants dying for *want* of rain; work showing *want* of care); lack; also, the state of being without something desired or needed (as, to be in *want* of money, a position, or an assistant; "We never . . . know how to value what we enjoy, but by the *want* of it," Defoe's "Robinson Crusoe," i. 10); need; a need or requirement (as, to supply a long-felt *want*; "circumstances of peculiar advantage, adapted to the *wants* of mankind," J. Butler's "Analogy of Religion," ii. 1); also, the state of being without the necessaries of life, or destitution (as, to come to or be in *want*; "age and *want*, oh! ill-match'd pair!" Burns's "Man Was Made to Mourn," 39); need, penury, or extreme and distressing poverty; also, a sense of lack or need of something (as, to feel a vague *want*); also, something lacking but desired or needed; a necessity. —**want**, *v.* [ME.: cf. Icel. *vanta*.] **I.** *intr.* To be lacking or absent, as a part or thing necessary to completeness or full satisfaction (as, "That which *wanteth* in the weight of their speech, is supplied by the aptness of men's minds to accept and believe it," Hooker's "Ecclesiastical Polity," i. 1. 1: see *wanting*, *p. a.*); also, to be deficient by the absence of some part or thing, or fall short (sometimes with *for*: as, "He did not *want* for abilities," Thackeray's "Newcomes," xxviii.: see *wanting*, *p. a.*); also, to have need (as, if you *want* for anything, let him know); esp., to be in want of the necessaries of life; be in a state of destitution. **II.** *tr.* To be without, or be deficient in (as, to *want* judgment or knowledge); lack; fall short by (as, the sum collected *wants* but a few dollars of the desired amount; "He was not of age . . . for he *wanted* nine months," Marryat's "Mr. Midshipman Easy," xxxvii.); also, to do or go without (now prov.); also, to require or need (as, "The choir were *wanting* new hymn-books," Galsworthy's "Saint's Progress," i. 9; "Her pens were uniformly bad and *wanted* fixing," Bret Harte's "Mliss," ii.); also, to feel a need of or a desire for (as, to *want* one's dinner; to be always *wanting* something new; what do you *want?*); wish for; wish or desire (often with an infinitive construction following: as, I *want* to see you; he *wants* to be notified; "I *want* you all to come," Louisa M. Alcott's "Little Women," i. 12); wish to see, or desire the presence of (as, "If he *want* me, let him come to me," Tennyson's "Geraint and Enid," 237; "to apprise Sarchedon he was *wanted* without delay in the royal palace," Whyte-Melville's "Sarchedon," vi.).

wa'n't (wŏnt or wont). Vulgar contraction of *was not*.

want-age (wŏn'tāj or wôn'-), *n.* That which is wanting or lacking; an amount lacking, as the amount that a cask lacks of being full.

want-er (wŏn'tėr or wôn'-), *n.* One who wants; one who wants a wife or a husband (Sc. and prov. Eng.).

want-ing (wŏn'ting or wôn'-), *p. a.* Lacking or absent (as, an apparatus with some of the parts *wanting*); also, deficient in some part, thing, or respect (as, "Thou art weighed in the balances, and art found *wanting*," Dan. v. 27; to be *wanting* in courtesy); defective mentally (prov. or colloq.: as, "Had something given in my brain . . . so that now I was what people call '*wanting*?'" Buchan's "Three Hostages," vi.); also, needy† or destitute†.—**want'ing**, *prep.* [Orig. ppr.] Lacking; without; less; minus: as, a century, *wanting* three years.

wan-ton (wŏn'tọn), *n.* [ME. *wantoun*, *wantowen*, lit. 'lacking proper bringing up,' 'undisciplined,' < AS. *wan-*, prefixal use of *wan*, wanting (see *want*), + *togen*, pp. of *tēon*, draw: see *tow*[3].] **I.** *a.* Undisciplined†, lawless†, or unruly†; spoiled, froward, or bad, as children†; also, lawless or unbridled with

respect to sexual morality, as persons (often women) or the disposition, impulses, behavior, etc.; loose, lascivious, or lewd; also, reckless or disregardful of right, justice, humanity, etc., as persons (as, "I was presented as a *wanton* assailant of my social betters," H. G. Wells's "Tono-Bungay," i. 1. § 9; "He is a *wanton* disturber of men's religious convictions," S. Butler's "Erewhon," xvi.); done, shown, used, etc., maliciously or unjustifiably (as, a *wanton* attack, injury, or affront; *wanton* cruelty); in a milder sense, deliberate and uncalled-for (as, "Why should you break up your life in this *wanton* way?" Mrs. H. Ward's "Robert Elsmere," xxx.); also, sportive or frolicsome, as children, young animals, gambols, etc. (now poetic); fig., having free play, or moving, winding, curling, etc., as if in play or at pleasure (chiefly poetic: as, *wanton* breezes; a *wanton* brook; "*wanton* ringlets," Milton's "Paradise Lost," iv. 306); gay or lively, as music, etc.†; luxurious, as persons, living, dress, etc.†; also, luxuriant, as vegetation (poetic). **II.** *n.* A spoiled child†; a pampered pet†; also, a wanton or lascivious person; often, a wanton woman; also, a sportive child, animal, etc. (obs. or poetic).—**wan'ton**,[*v.* **I.** *intr.* To act or dally in a wanton or lascivious manner; also, to sport, frolic, or play, as a child, an animal, etc. (chiefly poetic); fig., to move, go, wind, wave, etc., as if in play or at pleasure, as a breeze, a rivulet, streamers, etc. (chiefly poetic); revel (*in*: as, "savage tyrants, who *wanton* in cruelty unprovoked," Walpole's "Castle of Otranto," i.); also, to grow or spread luxuriantly, as plants. **II.** *tr.* To squander (*away*), as in pleasure.—**wan'ton-er**, *n.*—**wan'ton-ly**, *adv.*—**wan'ton-ness**, *n.*

wan-y (wā'ni), *a.* See *waney*.

wap[1] (wop), etc. Same as *whop*, etc.

wap[2] (wop), *n.* See *wop*[2].

wap-en-shaw (wop'n-shâ), *n.* [Sc., 'weapon-show.'] A muster or review of persons under arms, formerly held at certain times in the districts of Scotland, for the purpose of satisfying the military chiefs that their men were properly provided with arms.

wap-en-take (wop'n-tāk), *n.* [AS. *wǽpentac*, *wǽpengetæc*, from Scand.: cf. Icel. *vápnatak*, a weapon-touching (symbolic act, as of assent), a vote or resolution passed at a public assembly.] An old (now local) name in certain counties of northern and midland England for a division of the county corresponding to the hundred of other counties.

wap-i-ti (wop'i-ti), *n.*; pl. *wapiti*. [N. Amer. Ind.] A North American species of deer, *Cervus canadensis*, with long, slender antlers: in America often called *elk*. Cf. *elk* and *moose*.

war (wâr), *n.* [Late AS. *werre*, < OF. *werre*, *guerre* (F. *guerre*), = Sp. *guerra* (or *guerrilla*), war; from Teut.: cf. OHG. *werra*, confusion, strife, G. *wirre*, confusion, disorder, disturbance, and E. *worse*.] Conflict carried on by force of arms, as between nations or states ('international war' or 'public war'), or between parties within a state ('civil war'); warfare (by land, by sea, or in the air); also, a contest carried on by force of arms, as in a series of battles or campaigns

Wapiti, or American Elk.

(see phrases below); hence, in general, conflict, or active hostility or contention; a contest, struggle, or contention (as, "a *war* of words": Irving's "Captain Bonneville," xviii.); also, armed fighting as a department of activity, a profession, or an art (as, "*War* is our business": Pope's tr. Homer's "Iliad," xxii.); also, armed soldiers or forces (poetic: as, "They . . . Bear down on England's wearied *war*," Scott's "Lord of the Isles," vi. 30); also, instruments or munitions of war (poetic: as, "Inferior ministers, for Mars, repair His broken axletrees and blunted *war*," Dryden's tr. Virgil's "Æneid," viii. 572).—**Boer War, Civil War, Crimean War,** etc. See first word of phrase.—**Great War, War of the Nations,** or **World War.** See under *world.*—**war baby,** a child born in wartime as the result of marriage, or often of irregular relations, of a woman with a soldier; also, an industry, industrial establishment, or the like, arising from or fostered by wartime needs (colloq.); also, a stock or security issued in connection with such an industry, etc., or which is the object of active speculation in wartime (colloq.).—**war bride,** a woman who marries a soldier in active service, or a man about to be ordered into service as a soldier, in wartime.—**War of 1812,** a war between the United States and Great Britain, during 1812–15. —**Wars of the Roses.** See *rose*[2], *n.*—**war to the knife,** deadly strife; relentless conflict.—**war,** *v.*; *warred, warring.* **I.** *intr.* To make or carry on war; fight; hence, in general, to carry on active hostility or contention (as, "to *war* with evil": Tennyson's "Choric Song," iv.); be in a state of strong opposition (as, *warring* principles). **II.** *tr.* To make war upon†; contend against†; also, to carry on (warfare, etc.: rare).

war-ble[1] (wâr'bl), *n.* [Origin uncertain.] A small, hard tumor on a horse's back, produced by the galling of the saddle; also, a tumor on the back of horses, cattle, etc., caused by the larva of a warble-fly; also, a warble-fly, or its larva.

war-ble[2] (wâr'bl), *v.*; *-bled, -bling.* [OF. *werbler*, from Teut.: cf. G. *wirbeln*, warble, lit. whirl, akin to E. *whirl.*] **I.** *intr.* To sing with trills, quavers, or melodic embellishments (said of persons, also of birds); sing with melodious turns, or in a free, joyous manner; carol; also, to yodel (U. S.); also, to sound with melodious modulations or variations of pitch, as a brook. **II.** *tr.* To sing with trills, quavers, or melodious turns; carol; also, to express or celebrate in song (as, "*warbling* the Grecian woes": Pope's tr. Homer's "Odyssey," i.).—**war'ble**[2], *n.* The act of warbling, or the succession of sounds uttered; a warbled song; any soft, melodious flow of varying sound (as, "the wandering *warble* of a brook": Tennyson's "Last Tournament," 254).

war-ble=fly (wâr'bl-flī), *n.*; pl. *-flies* (-flīz). Any of various flies of the family *Œstridæ*, whose larvæ produce warbles.

war-bler (wâr'blẽr), *n.* One who or that which warbles; specif., any of the small, chiefly old-world, singing birds constituting the family *Sylviidæ*, including the hedge-sparrow, reed-warbler, beccafico, etc.; also, any of the small insectivorous American singing birds constituting the family *Mniotiltidæ* (or *Sylvicolidæ*), as *Dendrœca* (or *Dendroica*) *virens*, common in eastern North America ('black-throated green warbler'), and the myrtle-bird, parula, oven-bird (*Seiurus auricapillus*), etc.

war=club (wâr'-klub), *n.* A club used as a weapon in warfare.

war=cry (wâr'krī), *n.*; pl. *-cries* (-krīz). A battle-cry; a cry, or a word or phrase, shouted in charging or in rallying to attack; hence, a party cry in any contest.

Black-throated Green Warbler (*Dendrœca virens*).

ward (wârd), *n.* [AS. *weard*, masc., a watchman, warder, keeper, *weard*, fem., a keeping watch, guarding; akin to OHG. G. *-wart*, Icel. *vördhr*, Goth. *-wards*, warder, keeper, and E. *guard*; from the root of E. *ware*[2].] A watchman†, guard†, or keeper†; also, a body of persons, as soldiers, whose duty it is to keep guard (obs. or rare); a garrison†; one of the three main divisions, or any large division, of an army†; also, the act of keeping guard or protective watch (archaic: as, "As when a guard Of some proud castle, holding *ward*, Pace forth their nightly round," Scott's "Bridal of Triermain," iii. 10: now chiefly in 'watch and ward,' which see

under *watch, n.*); protection† or defense†; a movement or posture of defense, as in fencing (also fig.); also, the act of keeping restraining watch, as over a prisoner (obs. or archaic); also, keeping, charge, or control by a protector or guardian (now rare); specif., guardianship over a minor or some other person legally incapable of managing his own affairs; in feudal law, the guardianship of an infant heir of a deceased tenant, until of age, with the control and use of the tenant's lands, as vested in the lord or superior; also, the state of being under restraining guard or in custody (as, "He put them in *ward* in the house of the captain of the guard, into the prison," Gen. xl. 3: now rare); also, the state of being under the care or control of a legal guardian; the state of being subject to feudal wardship; also, one who is under the protection or control of another; specif., a person, esp. a minor, who has been legally placed under the care of a guardian or a court; in feudal law, an infant heir of a deceased tenant, whose person and lands were under the control of the superior; also, an open space within walls, or between lines of walls, of a castle or fortified place (as, "Then to the Castle's lower *ward* Sped forty yeomen tall": Scott's "Marmion," i. 4); also, a prison†; each of the separate divisions of a prison; also, a division or apartment of a hospital or the like, as for a number or a particular class of patients (as, a convalescent *ward*; an insane *ward*); also, a division or district of a city or town, as for administrative or representative purposes; one of the administrative districts into which certain English and Scottish counties are divided; a division of a forest†; also, a curved ridge of metal inside a lock, forming an obstacle to the passage of a key which has not a corresponding notch; also, the notch or slot in the bit of a key, into which such a ridge fits when the key is applied.—**ward,** *v. t.* [AS. *weardian* = OS. *wardōn* = OHG. *wartēn*, watch (G. *warten*, wait), = Icel. *vardha*, warrant, guard, defend; from the noun: see *ward, n.*, and cf. *guard, v.*] To keep guard or protective watch over (archaic: as, "Hope Park, a beautiful pleasance . . . *warded* by a keeper," Stevenson's "David Balfour," viii.); keep safe from harm (archaic); defend or protect (*from*: as, "A hand that *warded* him From thousand dangers," Shakspere's "Titus Andronicus," iii. 1. 195: archaic); also, to keep under restraining watch, or in custody or confinement†; also, to parry, repel, or turn aside (a stroke, attack, assailant, missile, etc.: now usually with *off*: as, to *ward* off a blow; "Before Kim could *ward* him off, the Russian struck the old man," Kipling's "Kim," xiii.); avert, or keep off (danger, harm, etc.: often with *off*); also, to place in a ward, as of a hospital.

-ward. [AS. *-weard* = OHG. *-wert* (G. *-wärts*) = Icel. *-verdhr* = Goth. *-wairths*; akin to L. *versus*, toward (see *versus*), and E. *worth*[1].] A suffix indicating direction or tendency, occurring in adjectives and adverbs, as *backward, forward, inward, onward, heavenward, seaward, awkward, froward, wayward*, and also in the preposition *toward.* Cf. *-wards.*

war=dance (wâr'dȧns), *n.* A dance among savages preliminary to a warlike excursion or in celebration of a victory.

war-den[1] (wâr'dn), *n.* [Origin uncertain.] A kind of pear.

war-den[2] (wâr'dn), *n.* [OF. *wardein*, var. of *guardein, gardien*, E. *guardian.*] One who guards, protects, or defends†; also, one charged with the care or custody of something; a keeper; specif., a legal guardian†; a regent or viceroy (obs. or hist.); a governor of a province, district, or the like (obs. or hist.); any of various public officials charged with superintendence of some sort, as over a port, the game of a particular district, etc.; the governor or chief keeper of a prison; a member of the governing body of a gild; a churchwarden; a particular officer of a lodge of freemasons; the head of certain colleges, schools, etc.; in Connecticut, the chief executive officer of a borough.—**war'den-ry** (-ri), *n.*; pl. *-ries* (-riz). The office, jurisdiction, or district of a warden.—**war'den-ship,** *n.* The office of a warden.

ward-er (wâr'dẽr), *n.* One who wards or guards something; a soldier or other person set to guard an entrance; also, an official having charge of prisoners in a jail; also, a truncheon or staff of office or authority formerly carried by a king, commander-in-chief, or the like, and used by him in giving signals.

ward-robe (wârd′rōb), n.   [OF. *warderobe,* var. of *garderobe,* E. *garderobe.*]   A room or place for keeping clothes or costumes in; sometimes, a dressing-room†; also, a piece of furniture for holding clothes, now usually a tall, upright press or case fitted with hooks, shelves, etc.; also, the department of a royal or other great household charged with the care of wearing-apparel; also, a stock of clothes or costumes, as of a person or of a theatrical company.

ward=room (wârd′rŏm), n.   In a war-ship, the apartment constituting the living-quarters of commissioned officers other than the commanding officer.

-wards.   [AS. *-weardes,* < *-weard,* E. *-ward,* + *-es,* adverbial suffix, E. *-s*³.]   Same as *-ward,* originally and chiefly in adverbs, as in *backwards, onwards, seawards, towards.*

ward-ship (wârd′ship), n.   [See *ward, n.*]   Guardianship; custody; specif., guardianship over a minor or ward; in feudal law, the guardianship of an heir of a deceased tenant, until of age, with control of the tenant's lands, as belonging to the lord; also, the state or condition of being a ward, or under a legal or feudal guardian (as, "Three English earls who were in royal *wardship* were wedded by the King to foreigners": Green's "Short Hist. of the Eng. People," iii. 5).

ware¹ (wâr), n.   [AS. *wār.*]   Seaweed (of various kinds).   Cf. *redware* and *seaware.*

ware² (wâr), a.   [AS. *wær* = OS. *war* = Icel. *varr* = Goth. *wars,* wary, cautious: cf. *wary, aware, beware, ward, n.,* and *warn.*]   Watchful, wary, or cautious (archaic: cf. *beware*); also, aware or conscious (archaic: as, "Then was I *ware* of one that on me moved In golden armour," Tennyson's "Holy Grail," 409).—**ware**², v.   [AS. *warian.*]   **I.** *intr.* To be on one's guard; look out; beware: used esp. in the imperative: as, " '*Ware!*' cried Grace . . . the lunatic sprung" (C. Brontë's "Jane Eyre," xxvi.). [Archaic, prov., or colloq.].   **II.** *tr.*   To be on one's guard against; look out for; beware of: used esp. in the imperative: as, *ware* the dog! [Archaic, prov., or colloq.]

ware³ (wâr), n.   [AS. *waru* = D. *waar* = G. *ware* = Icel. *vara,* ware.]   Articles of merchandise or manufacture, or goods (used in *sing.* or, now chiefly, in *pl.*: as, "Hoarse As when a hawker hawks his *wares,*" Tennyson's "Blackbird"); a particular kind or class of articles of merchandise or manufacture (now chiefly in composition, as in *hardware, tinware, silverware, glassware, chinaware, tableware, flat-ware, stem-ware,* except as in the following use); specif., pottery, or a particular kind of pottery (as, "Not yet had Wedgwood fully succeeded in changing . . . tons of clay and flint into brilliantly glazed and durable *ware,*" Bancroft's "Hist. of the U. S.," Amer. Revolution, ii. 1; Delft *ware;* Satsuma *ware;* Spode *ware*).

ware⁴ (wâr), v. t.; *wared, waring.*   [ME.: from Scand.]   To spend (money, time, care, etc.); expend; also, to squander or waste. [Now Sc. and prov. Eng.]

ware-house (wâr′hous), n.   A storehouse for wares or goods; also, a wholesale store, or a large retail store (chiefly Eng.). —**warehouse receipt,** a receipt for goods placed in a warehouse, forming an assignable or transferable instrument. —**ware′house** (-houz), v. t.; *-housed, -housing.*   To deposit or store in a warehouse; esp., to place in a government or bonded warehouse, to be kept until duties are paid.—**ware′-house-man** (-hous-man), n.; pl. *-men.*   One who keeps, or is employed in, a warehouse.

ware-room (wâr′rŏm), n.   A room in which goods are stored or are displayed for sale.

war-fare (wâr′fâr), n.   [See *fare, n.*]   Orig., a warlike or military expedition; hence, military operations against an enemy; military or naval hostilities; the making of war; war.   Also fig.—**chemical warfare.**   See under *chemical, a.*

war=game (wâr′gām), n.   Same as *kriegspiel.*

war=head (wâr′hed), n.   The forward, explosive-containing section of a self-propelled torpedo, which is placed in position only when the torpedo is to be used.

war=horse (wâr′hôrs), n.   A horse used in war; a charger; also, a person who has taken part in many battles, conflicts, controversies, etc. (colloq.).

wa-ri-ly (wā′ri-li or wâr′i-), adv.   In a wary manner.— **wa′ri-ness,** n.

war-i-son (war′i-son), n.   [OF. *warison,* defense, provision,

store, goods, var. of *garison:* see *garrison.*]   Defense†; also, goods† or wealth†; also, a reward†; also, erroneously, a note sounded as a signal for assault (poetic: as, "Or straight they sound their *warison,* And storm and spoil thy garrison," Scott's "Lay of the Last Minstrel," iv. 24).

war-like (wâr′lik), a.   Fit, qualified, or ready for war (as, "deadly fight of *warlick* fleete": Spenser's "Virgil's Gnat," 124); given or inclined to war, martial, or bellicose (as, "predatory and *warlike* tribes": Irving's "Captain Bonneville," xlv.); threatening or betokening war (as, a *warlike* tone); in general, of or pertaining to war (as, a *warlike* expedition; "*warlike* deeds," Cowper's "Task," v. 234); military.—**war′like-ness,** n.

war-lock (wâr′lok), n.   [AS. *wærloga,* traitor, < *wær,* agreement, faith, + *-loga,* akin to *lēogan,* E. *lie*².]   A traitor†; hence, an evil person†; a devil†; a monster†; also, one who practises magic arts by the aid of the devil, or a sorcerer or wizard (esp. Sc., and hence in general literary use: as, "You, deep read in hell's black grammar, *Warlocks* and witches," Burns's "Captain Grose's Peregrinations," 22; "A *warlock,* a wizard is he, And the lord of the wind and sea," Longfellow's "Saga of King Olaf," x.); in a milder sense, a fortune-teller, conjurer, or the like (Sc.: as, "I'm nae *warlock,* to find a fortune for you in the bottom of a parritch [porridge] bowl," Stevenson's "Kidnapped," iii.).

warm (wârm), a.   [AS. *wearm* = D. and G. *warm* = Icel. *varmr,* warm; akin to Goth. *warmjan,* to warm, and perhaps to L. *formus,* warm, Gr. θερμός, warm, hot, Skt. *gharma,* heat.]   Having or communicating a moderate degree of sensible heat; of or at a moderately high temperature; characterized by the prevalence of a comparatively high temperature (as, a *warm* climate; "The air had become *warm* without being oppressively hot," S. Butler's "Erewhon," xxi.); also, having a sensation of bodily heat (as, to be comfortably *warm;* to be *warm* from fast walking); producing such a sensation (as, *warm* clothes); also, characterized by or showing lively feelings, passions, emotions, sympathies, etc. (as, a *warm* heart); ardent, fervent, enthusiastic, or zealous (as, a *warm* admirer or partizan; *warm* interest or support); cordial or hearty (as, a *warm* welcome); strongly attached, or intimate (as, *warm* friends); heated, irritated, or angry (as, to become *warm* when contradicted; "I spoke out pretty straight and we got rather *warm,*" J. Conrad's "Rescue," iii. 8); animated, lively, brisk, or vigorous (as, a *warm* debate; a *warm* contest; "They were received with a *warm* discharge of artillery," Motley's "Dutch Republic," iii. 6); also, uncomfortable or unpleasant (colloq.: as, he found the place too *warm* for him); also, well off, or in easy circumstances (colloq.); also, strong or fresh (as, a *warm* scent); also, of color, effects of color, etc., suggestive of warmth, as from inclining to red or yellow (rather than blue or gray: as, "Not even the mountains [in a painting] . . . were so *warm* with rose and gold," Amelia B. Edwards's "Thousand Miles up the Nile," xvi.).—**warm,** v.   [AS. *wyrman,* tr., *wearmian,* intr.]   **I.** *tr.*   To make warm (in various senses); heat (often with *up:* as, to *warm,* or *warm* up, a room; to *warm* up food, to heat it over again when cold, as when left from a former meal); raise the temperature of; give bodily warmth to; excite ardor, enthusiasm, or animation in; inspire with kindly feeling; affect with lively pleasure (as, "They haven't forgot me. It *warms* my soul": Mrs. Stowe's "Uncle Tom's Cabin," xli.); also, to beat or thrash (colloq.).   **II.** *intr.*   To become warm; warm one's self (as, "There shall not be a coal to *warm* at": Isa. xlvii. 14); become ardent, enthusiastic, animated, etc. (often with *up*); become increasingly ardent in application (*to:* as, "The lama *warmed* to his work," Kipling's "Kim," xiii. "He was now *warming* to his subject," S. Butler's "Erewhon," xxii.); grow kindly, friendly, or sympathetically disposed (often with *to, toward,* or *towards:* as, "He *warmed* and softened to the young man," Howells's "Rise of Silas Lapham," vi.; "I felt my heart *warm* towards him," Conan Doyle's "Exploits of Brigadier Gerard," i.).—**warm,** n.   Warmth† or heat†; also, a warming or heating (colloq.: as, "Sit ye down before the fire, my dear, and have a *warm,*" Dickens's "Christmas Carol," iii.).—**warm′=blood′ed,** a.   Having warm blood; esp., noting or pertaining to animals, as mammals and birds, whose blood ranges in temperature from about 98° to about 112° F., and remains relatively constant irrespective of the temperature of the surrounding medium; fig., ardent, impetuous, or passionate (as, "the young and *warm-blooded* valour of England": Scott's "Castle Dangerous," v.).—**warm′er,** *n.*—**warm′=heart′ed,** *a.* Having or showing warmth of heart, ready sympathies, or an impulsively friendly disposition; cordial; hearty.—**warm′=heart′ed-ness,** *n.*—**warm′ing=pan,** *n.* A long-handled, covered flat vessel, as of brass, for holding hot coals or the like, formerly in common use for warming beds in preparation for being occupied; fig., a person holding a position or office temporarily, until another is ready to take it.—**warm′ly,** *adv.*—**warm′ness,** *n.*

war-mouth (wâr′mouth), *n.* A large-mouthed, voracious fresh-water sunfish, *Chænobryttus gulosus,* of the eastern U. S., esp. west or south of the Alleghany Mountains.

w a r m t h (wârmth), *n.* The state of being warm;

Warmouth.

moderate or gentle heat; the sensation of moderate heat; liveliness of feelings, emotions, or sympathies; ardor or fervor; enthusiasm or zeal; cordiality or heartiness; slight irritation (as, his denial betrayed some *warmth*); in *painting,* a glowing effect arising from the use of warm colors.

warn (wârn), *v.* [AS. *warnian,* take heed, warn, = G. *warnen,* warn; akin to E. *ware*[2].] **I.** *tr.* To give notice or intimation to (a person, etc.) of danger, impending evil, possible harm, or anything unfavorable (as, "Noah, being *warned* of God of things not seen as yet, moved with fear, prepared an ark," Heb. xi. 7; to *warn* a person of a plot against him); hence, to put on one's guard (as, "Our patron, *warned* by this disaster, resolved to take more care of himself for the future": Defoe's "Robinson Crusoe," i. 2); urge or advise to be on one's guard, or caution (as, to *warn* one person against another; to *warn* a foolhardy person in vain); inform or tell (a person, etc.) by way of cautioning (*that:* as, "My father was *warned* by the neighbours that we were in great danger," W. H. Hudson's "Far Away and Long Ago," viii.; "I *warn* you that he is very attractive to women," W. Churchill's "Modern Chronicle," ii. 6); in general, to admonish or exhort as to action or conduct (as, to *warn* a person to be on time; "Ye shall even *warn* them that they trespass not against the Lord," 2 Chron. xix. 10); also, to notify, apprise, or inform (as, to *warn* a person of an intended visit, of a decision made, or of some event; *warn* them that the time has come); give authoritative or formal notice to, order, or summon (as, to *warn* a person to appear in court); give notice to (a person, etc.) to go, stay, or keep (*away, off,* etc.: as, to *warn* trespassers off private grounds). **II.** *intr.* To give warning of danger, impending evil, or the like; also, to give admonition.—**warn′er,** *n.*—**warn′ing,** *n.* The act of giving notice or intimation of danger, impending evil, or the like; notice of this kind given or received (as, death without *warning;* to have no *warning* of an attack); something serving to warn of danger or evil (as, a comet was long regarded as a *warning* of dire events to come); also, the act of cautioning or admonishing; a caution given against something; an admonition as to conduct; something serving to caution or admonish (as, let this experience be a *warning* to you to be more careful hereafter); also, notifying or apprising, as of some fact; notice given of something; specif., notice given of the termination, after a certain time following, of some business relation, as that of master and servant, employer and employee, or landlord and tenant (as, "paying to each [servant] a month's wages in lieu of *warning,*" Smollett's "Humphry Clinker," Oct. 26; to give a tenant two months' *warning*).—**warn′ing-ly,** *adv.*

warp[1] (wârp), *n.* [AS. *wearp,* the warp in weaving, < *weorpan,* throw, cast: see *warp*[2].] In *weaving,* the threads which are extended lengthwise in a loom, and across which

the weft or woof is thrown; the threads crossed by the weft or woof.

warp[2] (wârp), *v.* [AS. *weorpan* = D. *werpen* = G. *werfen* = Icel. *verpa* = Goth. *wairpan,* throw, cast: cf. *warp*[1].] **I.** *tr.* To throw† or cast†; lay (eggs: now prov. Eng.); bring forth (young) prematurely, as cattle, horses, etc. (prov. Eng.); also, to bend or twist out of shape (as, "Confess, or I will *warp* Your limbs with . . . tortures": Shelley's "Cenci," v. 3. 60); esp. to twist or curve from a straight or flat form, as timbers, flooring, pasteboard, etc.; fig., to bend or turn from the natural or true direction or course (as, "Mankind . . . are observed to *warp* their speculative conclusions to the bent of their individual humours": Lamb's "My Relations"); bias or pervert (the mind, judgment, opinions, etc., or a person: as, prejudice *warps* the mind; "a good sort of a man, though most ridiculously *warped* in his political principles," Smollett's "Humphry Clinker," June 2); distort from the truth, fact, true meaning, etc. (as, "scripture *warp'd* from its intent": Cowper's "Progress of Error," 437); set awry (as, "the exquisite cruelty of the order of creation that had *warped* her life": W. De Morgan's "Alice-for-Short," xiii.); in *aëronautics,* to bend (a wing, plane, or aërofoil) at the end or ends, as to promote equilibrium; in *agric.,* to treat (land) by inundation with water that deposits alluvial warp; *naut.,* to move (a ship, etc.) into some desired place or position by hauling on a rope or warp which has been fastened to something fixed, as a buoy, anchor, or the like. **II.** *intr.* To bring forth young prematurely, as cattle, etc. (prov. Eng.); also, to become bent or twisted out of shape, esp. out of a straight or flat form (as, the wood has *warped* in drying); fig., to turn or change from the natural or proper course, state, etc.; *naut.,* to warp a ship or the like along; move by being warped, as a ship; hence, in general use, to make the way slowly or with effort from point to point; fly or float through the air (obs. or archaic: as, "A pitchy cloud Of locusts, *warping* on the eastern wind," Milton's "Paradise Lost," i. 341).—**warp**[2], *n.* A bend or twist in something, as in wood that has dried unevenly; fig., a mental twist or bias; also, alluvial matter deposited by water, esp. water let in to inundate low land for the purpose of enriching it; *naut.,* a rope used in warping or hauling a ship or the like along or into a position.

war=paint (wâr′pānt), *n.* Paint applied to the face and other parts of the body by savages upon going to war; hence (colloq.), official or ceremonial costume; full dress; finery.

war=path (wâr′päth), *n.* The path or course taken by American Indians on a warlike expedition: as, to go on the *war-path* (to go on a hostile expedition, as Indians; fig., to set out on an aggressive campaign or vigorous activities of any kind).

war-plane (wâr′plān), *n.* An aëroplane for use in warfare.

war-rant (wor′ant), *n.* [OF. *warant, guarant,* warrant, security, protection; from Teut., and akin to G. *gewähr,* warrant, guaranty: cf. *guaranty.*] A protector†; a protection† or safeguard†; also, that which serves to give reliable or formal assurance of something; a security or evidence; a guarantee; an assurance, positive declaration, or promise; something having the force of a guarantee or positive assurance of a thing (as, "The cavalry and artillery were . . . reckoned sure *warrants* of success": Scott's "Legend of Montrose," xv.); also, authorization, sanction, or justification; also, a writing or document certifying or authorizing something, as a certificate, receipt, license, or commission; esp., a warehouse receipt (see under *warehouse*); a writing authorizing the payment or receipt of money (as, a treasury *warrant;* a dividend *warrant*); in the army and navy, the certificate of authority or appointment issued to an officer below the rank of a commissioned officer; in *law,* an instrument, issued by a magistrate, authorizing an officer to make an arrest, seize property, make a search, or carry a judgment into execution (cf. *death-warrant*).—**war′rant,** *v. t.* To protect†; keep safe†; also, to give a formal assurance, pledge, or promise of or for (as, to *warrant* payment or safe delivery; to *warrant* the quality of goods; goods *warranted* to wear); guarantee; vouch for; give one's word for (often used with a clause in mere emphatic assertion: as, I'll *warrant* he did!); declare positively; also, to give a formal assurance, or a guarantee or promise, to (as, "I cannot *warrant* you of anything save honourable treatment": Scott's "Castle Dangerous," xiv.); also, to give authority to; authorize; appoint as a warrant-officer; also, to afford warrant or sanction for, or justify (as, the circumstances do not *warrant* such measures; "the general question, how far . . . the end *warrants* the means," Morley's "Oliver Cromwell," iv. 2).—**war′rant-a-ble**, *a.* Capable of being warranted; justifiable; in *hunting*, old enough to be hunted, as deer.—**war′rant-a-ble-ness**, *n.*—**war′rant-a-bly**, *adv.* —**war-rant-ee** (wor-an-tē′), *n.* In *law*, one to whom a warranty is made.—**war′rant-er**, *n.* One who warrants. —**war′rant=of″fi-cer**, *n.* A military or naval officer who has received a warrant of appointment; specif., in the U. S. navy, any of various subordinate officers, as boatswain, gunner, etc., ranking above mates and petty officers; such an officer who, after having served a certain number of years, has been made a commissioned chief boatswain, chief gunner, etc., and given rank with, but after, an ensign ('commissioned warrant-officer'); also, a similar officer in other countries.—**war-ran-tor** (wor′an-tọr or -tôr), *n.* In *law*, one who warrants, or makes a warranty.—**war′ran-ty** (-ti), *n.*; pl. *-ties* (-tiz). [OF. *warantie, guarantie*: cf. *guaranty*.] The act of warranting; warrant; assurance; justification; in *law*, an engagement, express or implied, in assurance of some particular in connection with a contract, as of sale (as, an express *warranty* of the quality of goods; an implied *warranty* of title to goods sold, or of correspondence of goods delivered to samples submitted); in the law of insurance, a statement or promise, made by the party insured, included in a policy as an essential part of the contract, falsity or non-fulfilment of which renders the policy void.

war-ren (wor′en), *n.* [OF. *warenne, guarenne* (F. *garenne*); from Teut.] Formerly, in England, a piece of land privileged for the keeping and breeding of game, esp. of certain animals known as 'beasts and fowls of warren,' including hares, rabbits, partridges, pheasants, etc.; the franchise or privilege of keeping or hunting such animals; now, a piece of land appropriated to the breeding of rabbits; a place where rabbits breed in burrows or abound; sometimes, a place where other animals breed or abound (as, "the vizcachas, the big rodents that make their *warrens* or villages of huge burrows all over the plain": W. H. Hudson's "Far Away and Long Ago," xiv.); hence, a place likened to a rabbit-warren; a habitation having passages like burrows (as, "You are taken down a timbered staircase into its [a dug-out's] *warren* of rooms and passages": H. G. Wells's "Italy, France, and Britain at War," iii. 1); a building or collection of buildings containing many tenants in limited quarters (as, "the 'Amberson Block' — an old-fashioned four-story brick *warren* of lawyers' offices, insurance and real-estate offices . . .": Tarkington's "Magnificent Ambersons," iii.).—**war′ren-er**, *n.* The keeper of a warren.

war-ri-or (wor′i-ẹr or wâr′-), *n.* [ME. *werreour*, from an OF. derivative of *werre, guerre*, E. *war*.] A man engaged or experienced in warfare; a soldier; esp., a brave or veteran soldier. [Now chiefly poetic or rhetorical.]

war′ri-son, *n.* See *warison*.

war-saw (wâr′sâ), *n.* [Sp. *guasa*.] A jewfish, *Promicrops itaiara* (or *guttatus*), of both coasts of tropical America; also, a large grouper, *Garrupa nigrita*, of the southern Atlantic and Gulf coasts of the U. S., etc.

war=ship (wâr′ship), *n.* A ship built or armed for war.

wart (wârt), *n.* [AS. *wearte* = MD. *warte* (D. *wrat*) = G. *warze* = Icel. *varta*, wart: cf. L. *verruca*, wart.] A small, circumscribed, usually hard, abnormal elevation on the skin; also, a protuberance or excrescence on a plant; in general, a small protuberance.

war=tax (wâr′taks), *n.* A tax imposed for the purpose of providing funds to meet expenses incurred in war.

wart-ed (wâr′ted), *a.* Having a wart or warts; verrucose.

wart=hog (wârt′hog), *n.* Either of two wild swine, *Phacochœrus æthiopicus*, of southern Africa, and *P. africanus*, of northern Africa, having large tusks, and warty excrescences on the face. See cut in next column.

war-time (wâr′tīm), *n.* A time or season of war.

wart-y (wâr′ti), *a.*; compar. *wartier*, superl. *wartiest.* Of the nature of or resembling a wart; also, having warts; covered with or as with warts.

warve (wärv), *n.* Same as *wharve*.

war=whoop (wâr′hȫp), *n.* A whoop or yell uttered by American Indians, or others, in attacking, etc.

wa-ry (wā′ri or wär′i), *a.*; compar. *warier*, superl. *wariest.* [Extended form of *ware²*.] Watchful, or on one's guard, esp. habitually, as against danger or deception; on the alert; cautious; careful; also, characterized by caution, as actions, etc. (as, "*wary* walking": Shakspere's "Julius Cæsar," ii. 1. 15).

Wart-hog (*Phacochœrus africanus*).

was (woz), *n.* [AS. *wæs*, inf. *wesan*, be, akin to G. *wesen*, being, Goth. *wisan*, dwell, remain, Skt. *vas-*, dwell.] A verb-form, first and third person singular, preterit indicative, used as a part of *be*.

wash (wosh), *v. t.* [AS. *wascan* = D. *wasschen* = G. *waschen* = Icel. *vaska*, wash; akin to E. *water*.] To apply a liquid, esp. water, to for the purpose of cleansing; cleanse by dipping, rubbing, or scrubbing in water, etc.; cleanse as water does; fig., to free from ceremonial defilement, or from sin, guilt, etc. (as, "*Wash* me thoroughly from mine iniquity": Ps. li. 2); also, to wet with water or other liquid, or as water does (as, "The rose is sweetest *wash'd* with morning dew": Scott's "Lady of the Lake," iv. 1); flow over or against (as, a shore or cliff *washed* by waves; "that part of Europe which is *washed* by the Atlantic ocean," Adam Smith's "Wealth of Nations," iv. 7. 3); also, to wear, as water does by flowing over or against a surface (often with *out* or *away*); form (a channel, etc.), as flowing water does; also, to remove (dirt, stains, paint, or any matter) by or as by the action of water, or as water does (with *out, off*, etc.); carry or bring (*along, up, down*, etc.) with water or any liquid, or as the water or liquid does; also, to cover with a watery or thin coat of color; cover with a broad, thin layer of color rapidly and smoothly applied, as in water-color painting; apply (color) thus; overlay with a thin coat or deposit of metal (as, to *wash* brass with gold); also, to purify (a gas or gaseous mixture) by passage through or over a liquid; in *mining*, etc., to subject (earth, etc.) to the action of water in order to separate valuable material; separate (valuable material, as gold) thus.—**to wash one's hands of,** to renounce all interest in or responsibility for; refuse to have further connection with.—**wash**, *v. i.* To wash one's self (as, "It was time to *wash* for supper": W. Churchill's "Modern Chronicle," i. 2); wash clothes, etc.; cleanse anything with or in water or the like; also, to undergo washing, esp. without injury; fig., to stand being put to the proof (colloq.: as, his patriotism will not *wash*); also, to be worn by the action of water, as a hill or beach (often with *away*); be removed by the action of water (with *out, off*, etc.); be carried or driven (*along, ashore*, etc.) by the action of water; also, to flow or beat with a lapping sound, as waves against a shore; move along in or as in waves, or with a rushing movement, as water.—**wash. I.** *n.* An act of washing with water or other liquid; a washing of one's self, or of one's hands and face; a washing of clothes, household linen, etc. (as, "She may have done a hard day's *wash*": Mrs. Gaskell's "Mary Barton," i.); hence, a quantity of clothes, etc., washed, or to be washed, at one time (as, "A *wash* of sheets and table-cloths tried . . . to get itself dried on a line or two": Dickens's "Little Dorrit," i. 22); also, a liquid with which something is washed, wetted, colored, overspread, etc.; a medicinal lotion; any of various liquids for toilet purposes (as, a tooth-*wash*; a hair-*wash*); a thin coat of color; a broad, thin layer of color applied by a continuous movement of the brush, as in water-color painting; a thin coat of metal applied in liquid form; also, the flow, sweep, dash, or breaking of water; the sound made by this (as, "He lay awake at night and listened to the *wash* of the Atlantic along the beautiful red sandstone coast": Du Maurier's "Trilby," iv.); water moving along in waves or with a rushing movement; the rough or broken water left behind a moving ship, etc.; also, a tract of land washed by the action of the sea or a river, and sometimes overflowed and sometimes left dry; a shallow arm of the sea or a shallow part of a river (as, the *Wash*, a shallow bay of the North Sea, on the Lincolnshire and Norfolk coast of England); a fen, marsh, or bog; a depression or channel formed by flowing water; the dry bed of an intermittent stream (western U. S.: also called *dry wash*); a small stream or shallow pool; also, material deposited by the action of water; alluvial matter transferred and deposited by flowing water; also, liquid refuse; esp., waste liquid matter, refuse food, etc., from the kitchen, as for hogs; hogwash; also, the fermented wort from which the spirit is extracted in distilling; also, washy or weak liquor or liquid food; also, earth, etc., from which gold or the like can be extracted by washing; also, in the stock-exchange, a transaction in washing (see *washing*); a fictitious sale of stock made in order to manipulate the market; a wash sale; in aëronautics, the disturbance in the air left behind by a moving aëroplane or any of its parts. **II.** *a.* Capable of being washed without injury; washable; also, in the stock-exchange, of or pertaining to washing (as, a *wash* sale: see *washing* and *wash, n.*).

wash-a-ble (wosh′ạ-bl), *a.* Capable of being washed, esp. without being injured: as, a *washable* fabric.

wash-board (wosh′bōrd), *n.* A board or frame with a corrugated metallic or other surface, on which clothes are rubbed in the process of washing; also, a baseboard around the walls of a room; *naut.*, a thin board or plank fastened to and projecting above the gunwale or side of a boat to keep out the spray and sea; also, a similar board on the sill of a port.

wash=bottle (wosh′bot″l), *n.* In *chem.*, a glass flask having a stopper which is perforated by tubes so arranged that by blowing in one tube the water or other liquid in the flask may be forced out in a small stream through another tube: used in laboratories, for washing precipitates on filters, etc.

wash=draw-ing (wosh′drâ″ing), *n.* A representation of an object produced by laying in the shades in washes, with merely the outlines and chief details in line; the method of producing such representations.

wash-er (wosh′ėr), *n.* One who or that which washes; a machine or apparatus for washing something, as clothes; also, the outlet valve or outlet of a pipe, basin, cistern, etc.; also, a flat ring or perforated piece of leather, rubber, metal,

Wash-bottle.

etc., used between parts to give tightness to a joint, to prevent leakage (as at a pipe-joint), to distribute pressure (as under the head of a bolt or under a nut), etc.—**wash′er-man** (-man), *n.*; pl. *-men.* A man who washes clothes, etc., for hire.—**wash′er-wom″an**, *n.*; pl. *-women* (-wim″en). A woman who washes clothes, etc., for hire. — **wash′er-y** (-i), *n.*; pl. *-ies* (-iz). A place where something is washed: as, a coal *washery.*

wash-ing (wosh′ing), *n.* The act of one who or that which washes; ablution; the cleansing of clothes, etc., with water; also, clothes, etc., washed or to be washed, esp. a quantity washed at one time; also, *sing.* or *pl.*, liquid that has been used to wash something, or matter removed in washing something; matter carried away or deposited by running or flowing water; material, as gold-dust, obtained by washing earth, etc.; also, *sing.*, a thin coating or covering applied in liquid form; also, in the stock-exchange, the operation of simultaneously buying and selling the same stock in order to manipulate the market.—**wash′ing=bear**, *n.* The racoon: so called from its habit of putting its food into water before eating it.—**wash′ing=bot″tle**, *n.* A washbottle.—**wash′ing=so″da**, *n.* Crystalline sodium carbonate, or sal-soda, used as a cleansing agent.

Wash-ing-ton (wosh′ing-ton) **palm.** A fan-palm, *Neo-*

washingtonia filamentosa, of southern California and adjoining regions.

Wash-ing-ton (wosh′ing-ton) **pie.** A layer-cake with a cream, chocolate, jelly, or other filling.

wash=leath-er (wosh′leᴛн″ėr), *n.* A soft, washable light-yellow or white leather, prepared orig. from the skin of the chamois but later from some substitute: used for gloves, etc.

wash-out (wosh′out), *n.* A washing out of earth, etc., by the action of water, as from an embankment or a roadway by heavy rain or a freshet; the hole or break produced; also, a failure or fiasco (slang, orig. Eng.).

wash=rag (wosh′rag), *n.* A small piece of cloth for use in washing the person.

wash=stand (wosh′stand), *n.* A piece of furniture for holding a basin, a pitcher, and other appurtenances for use in washing the person; also, a permanent fixture having faucets with running water, for the same purpose.

wash=tub (wosh′tub), *n.* A tub for use in washing something, esp. clothes, etc.

wash-wom-an (wosh′wủm″ạn), *n.*; pl. *-women* (-wim″en). Same as *washerwoman.*

wash-y (wosh′i), *a.*; compar. *washier*, superl. *washiest.* Watery†, damp†, or moist†; also, too much diluted, or weak, as a liquid, liquid food, etc. (as, "*washy* coffee": Gissing's "Private Papers of Henry Ryecroft," ii. 16); fig., weak, thin, or poor, as if from watery or excessive dilution (as, *washy* coloring; *washy* poetry; *washy* sentiment; a poor, *washy* creature).

wasp (wosp), *n.* [AS. *wæsp*, *wæfs*, *wæps*, = OHG. *wefsa* (G. *wespe*), wasp; akin to L. *vespa* (see *vespid*).] Any of numerous, usually slender-bodied, hymenopterous insects (comprising true wasps, rubytails, and digger-wasps), the females of which, and in social species also the workers, are provided with a more or less powerful sting; esp., one of the true wasps, constituting the families *Vespidæ* (social species which consist of males, females, and workers or imperfect females) and *Eumenidæ* and *Masaridæ* (solitary species which consist only of males and females), characterized, except in the *Masaridæ*, by a longitudinal folding of the wings when at rest; fig., a waspish person.—**wasp′ish**, *a.* Like or suggesting a wasp; having a very slender waist, like a wasp; of the waist, slender; esp., quick to resent a trifling affront or injury, as persons; irascible; snappish; petulant; showing irascibility or petulance, as an utterance or writing.—**wasp′ish-ly**, *adv.* — **wasp′ish-ness**, *n.* — **wasp′=waist″ed**, *a.* Having a very slender waist; tightly laced.—**wasp′y**, *a.* Wasp-like; waspish.

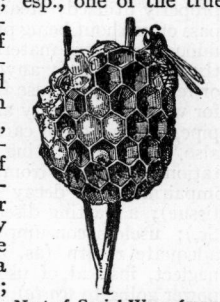

Nest of Social Wasp (genus *Polistes*, family *Vespidæ*).

Nest of Solitary Wasp (genus *Eumenes*, family *Eumenidæ*).

was-sail (wos′l or was′l). [ME. *wæs hæil*, 'be (thou) hale'; from Scand.: cf. *hail²*, *interj.*] **I.** *interj.* A salutation wishing health to a person, used in England in early times when presenting a cup of drink or when drinking to the person: hence used later in rural wassailing (see *wassail, v.*). **II.** *n.* A salutation of 'wassail!' also, a festivity or revel with drinking of healths; also, liquor for drinking healths on festive occasions, esp. spiced ale used by old custom in England on Christmas Eve and Twelfth-night; also, a song sung in health-drinking or wassailing (obs. or prov. Eng.). —**was′sail**, *v.* **I.** *intr.* To drink healths; revel with drinking; also, to go about singing songs of good wishes, soliciting gifts, etc., as children and others at the Christmas season (an old custom in rural England). **II.** *tr.* To drink to the health or success of: as, to *wassail* the apple-trees (an old custom in rural England).—**was′sail-er**, *n.*

wast (wost). Second person sing. of *was*: now only in poetic or solemn use.

wast-age (wās′tāj), *n.* Wasting; loss by use, wear, decay, leakage, or the like.

waste (wāst). [OF. *wast*, also *guast*, *gast*, < L. *vastus*, empty, unoccupied, waste, vast: cf. *vast*.] **I.** *a.* Of land, regions, etc., uninhabited and wild, desolate and barren, or desert (as, "He found him in a desert land, and in the *waste* howling wilderness": Deut. xxxii. 10); also, of regions, towns, habitations, etc., in a state of desolation and ruin, as from devastation or decay (as, to lay *waste* a country invaded in war; "*Waste* are those pleasant farms, and the farmers forever departed!" Longfellow's "Evangeline," 12); also, of land, etc., uncultivated, unused, or unproductive (as, "*waste*, wind-bitten land that no builder had thought it worth his while to defile," Kipling's "Light That Failed," vi.; ground lying *waste*); in general, not used or in use (as, *waste* energy); left over or superfluous (as, *waste* materials; to utilize the *waste* products of manufacture); having served a purpose and no longer of use (as, *waste* steam, exhaust-steam); rejected as useless or worthless, or refuse (as, *waste* paper); also, vain, empty, or futile (archaic or prov. Eng.: as, "vext with *waste* dreams," Tennyson's "Coming of Arthur," 84). **II.** *n.* A tract of uninhabited, wild land, desolate country, or desert (as, "Were I in the wildest *waste*, Sae black and bare," Burns's "O Wert Thou in the Cauld Blast"; "the illimitable *wastes* of the Libyan desert," Amelia B. Edwards's "Thousand Miles up the Nile," xvi.); hence, an empty, desolate, or dreary tract or extent of anything (as, a *waste* of snow, water, or air; "old Ocean's gray and melancholy *waste*," Bryant's "Thanatopsis"; "that endless desolate *waste* of nameless days," W. H. Hudson's "Green Mansions," xxi.); also, a region or place laid waste or in ruins (as, "All the cities thereof shall be perpetual *wastes*": Jer. xlix. 13); also, an uncultivated or unused tract of land; specif., a piece of land lying common, or not belonging to individuals (Eng.); also, anything unused, unproductive, or not properly utilized; steam, heat, water, or the like allowed to pass off without being put to use; anything left over or superfluous, as excess material, by-products, etc., not of use for the work in hand; anything rejected as useless or worthless, or refuse; esp. refuse from the working of cotton, etc., used for wiping machinery and for other purposes; also, a sluice, pipe, or the like for carrying off surplus or waste water, etc.; also, the act of wasting, or the state of being wasted; devastation or ruin, as from war, fire, etc.; gradual destruction, impairment, or decay (as, the *waste* and repair of bodily tissue); a wasting disease, as consumption (prov. Eng. and Sc.); useless consumption or expenditure, or use without adequate return (as, *waste* of material, money, or time); neglect, instead of use (as, *waste* of opportunity; water-power going to *waste*); in *law*, injury to an estate caused by an act or omission on the part of a tenant; in *phys. geog.*, material derived by mechanical and chemical disintegration of rock, as the detritus transported by streams, etc.—**waste**, *v.*; **wasted**, **wasting**. [OF. *waster*, also *gaster*, lay waste (F. *gâter*, spoil), < L. *vastare*, lay waste, < *vastus*.] **I.** *tr.* To lay waste, devastate, or ruin (as, "With fire and sword the country round Was *wasted* far and wide": Southey's "Battle of Blenheim," viii.); also, to destroy or consume gradually, or wear away (as, "and *waste* huge stones with little water-drops": Shakspere's "Lucrece," 959); wear down or reduce in bodily substance, health, or strength, or emaciate or enfeeble (as, to be *wasted* by disease or hunger; "a tall, bent old man, *wasted* almost to a skeleton," W. H. Hudson's "Purple Land," xxii.); also, to consume, spend, or employ uselessly or without adequate return (as, to *waste* ammunition; to *waste* money, time, efforts, or words; to *waste* one's breath in vain importunities); squander; use to no avail; often, to use, bestow, place, etc., where perception or appreciation is lacking (as, to *waste* subtle humor on dull hearers; "Full many a flower is born to blush unseen, And *waste* its sweetness on the desert air," Gray's "Elegy," xiv.; "She esteemed herself a lovable woman, *wasted* and misunderstood," Whyte-Melville's "Katerfelto," vi.); also, to fail or neglect to use, or let go to waste (as, to *waste* an opportunity; to *waste* the natural resources of a district); in *law*, to injure, as an estate, either by damaging it or by allowing to fall into decay. **II.** *intr.* To become gradually consumed, used up, or worn away (as, a candle *wastes* in burning; rocks *waste* under the action of water); become physically wasted, lose flesh or strength, or become emaciated

or enfeebled; pine away; diminish gradually, or dwindle, **as** wealth, power, etc.; pass gradually, as time; also, to go **to** waste, as something not put to use.

waste=bas-ket (wāst′bȧs″ket), *n.* A basket for waste paper, or papers, scraps of paper, etc., to be disposed of as refuse.

waste-ful (wāst′fŭl), *a.* Waste or desolate, as places (archaic); also, devastating or destructive (as, "*wasteful* war": Shakspere's "Sonnets," lv.); wasting the body or strength (now rare); also, given to or characterized by useless consumption or expenditure (as, "the *wasteful* person who lays nothing by," Ruskin's "Crown of Wild Olive," i.; *wasteful* methods, habits, or living); squandering, or grossly extravagant.—**waste′ful-ly**, *adv.*—**waste′ful-ness**, *n.*

waste=pipe (wāst′pīp), *n.* A pipe for conveying away waste water, etc.

wast-er (wās′tėr), *n.* One who or that which wastes; a squanderer; a spendthrift; an idler or good-for-nothing (chiefly Eng.); an animal or person that does not thrive or is wasting away (prov. or colloq.); also, something rejected as useless or defective; an article spoiled in manufacture.

wast-rel (wās′trel), *n.* [From *waste*.] Something waste, unused, or useless; a piece of waste land (prov. Eng.); an article cast aside as useless, inferior, or imperfect; also, an emaciated or unhealthy animal or person (prov. Eng. and Sc.); also, a wasteful person, spendthrift, idler, or good-for-nothing.

wast-y (wās′ti), *a.* Full of waste; containing much waste; also, liable to deteriorate or spoil, as fruit.

watch (woch), *v.* [AS. *wæccan*, wake, watch, = *wacian*, E. *wake*[2], *v.*] **I.** *intr.* To remain awake, esp. for a purpose (as, to *watch* with a sick person, or with the dead); keep vigil, as for devotional purposes; also, to keep awake and on the alert, as against danger, attack, the escape of prisoners, etc.; keep a vigilant watch (*over*), as for protection or safe-keeping; keep guard, or act as watchman, sentinel, or guard (as, "The lieutenant to-night *watches* on the court of guard": Shakspere's "Othello," ii. 1. 219); also, to be on the lookout, look attentively, or be closely observant, as to see what comes, is done, happens, etc. (as, to *watch* while a procession passes or an experiment is performed; be careful — too many eyes are *watching*); look or wait attentively and expectantly (*for*: as, to *watch* for a signal; to *watch* for one's coming; to *watch* for an opportunity). **II.** *tr.* To watch over or guard, for protection or safe-keeping, as persons, places, or property; keep under surveillance or guard, as prisoners; also, to keep under attentive view or observation, as in order to see or learn something (as, "This is no fit place for you and me . . . This is a place they're bound to *watch*," Stevenson's "Kidnapped," xx.; a person who will bear *watching*; to *watch* every move, or every change of expression); view attentively or with interest (a passing or changing scene, etc.: as, to *watch* a play or a game; to *watch* a sunset); contemplate or regard mentally (as, "The aristocracy had *watched* his progress with the bitterest malignity": Froude's "Cæsar," xx.); look or wait attentively and expectantly for (as, to *watch* one's chance or opportunity); in *falconry*, to keep (a hawk) from sleep in order to exhaust and tame it.—**watch**, *n.* [AS. *wæcce*.] A remaining awake†, or wakefulness†; a keeping awake for some special purpose, service, or observance (as, a *watch* beside a sick-bed; a devotional *watch*, or vigil: cf. *watch-night*); also, a keeping awake and on the alert for the purpose of protecting or guarding (as, "He who slumbereth not nor sleepeth His ancient *watch* around us keepeth": Whittier's "Daniel Wheeler"); vigilant guard kept, as for protection, safe-keeping, surveillance, or restraint; also, close, constant observation for the purpose of seeing or discovering something; a lookout, as for something expected (as, to be on the *watch*); also, a person, or a number of persons, charged with watching over persons, property, etc., or formerly with patrolling the streets at night; a watchman, or a body of watchmen; a sentinel; a guard; also, a period of time for watching or keeping guard; one of the periods (in Jewish use three, later four) into which the night was anciently divided (as, "They came . . . in the morning *watch*, and slew the Ammonites," 1 Sam. xi. 11; "in the fourth *watch* of the night," Mat. xiv. 25: see *night-watch*); hence, in general use, a period or portion of the night (usually in *pl.*, and often with implication of wakefulness: as, "Chant no more that dirge of sorrow, through the long and silent *watches* of the night!" Longfellow's "Hyperion," i. 1); also, something that measures and indicates the progress of time; specif., a small timepiece operated by a coiled spring, for carrying on the person; formerly, a clock†; the dial of a clock†; *naut.*, a period of time (usually four hours) during which one part of a ship's crew is on duty, taking turns with another part; also, a certain part (usually a half) of the officers and crew of a vessel who together attend to working it for an allotted period of time.—**watch and ward**, vigilant guard, as over a place, post, or other charge committed: an archaic expression, now chiefly in literary or figurative use.

watch-case (woch′kās), *n.* The case or outer covering for the works of a watch; also, a case or receptacle to keep a watch in.

watch=chain (woch′chān), *n.* A chain for securing a watch when worn on the person.

watch=dog (woch′dog), *n.* A dog kept to watch or guard premises and property; fig., a watchful guardian.

watch-er (woch′ėr), *n.* One who or that which watches.

watch-et (woch′et). [OF. *wachet*; origin obscure.] **I.** *n.* A light-blue color; also, a light-blue fabric. [Archaic.] **II.** *a.* Of the color called watchet; light-blue. [Archaic.]

watch-ful (woch′fúl), *a.* Wakeful or sleepless (archaic); also, vigilant or alert; closely observant.—**watch′ful-ly,** *adv.*—**watch′ful-ness,** *n.*

watch=guard (woch′gärd), *n.* A chain, cord, or ribbon for securing a watch when worn on the person.

watch-mak-er (woch′mā″kėr), *n.* One whose occupation it is to make and repair watches.—**watch″mak″ing,** *n.*

watch-man (woch′man), *n.*; pl. -**men.** A man set to keep watch or guard; a sentinel; a guard; esp., formerly, one who guarded or patrolled the streets at night; now, one who keeps guard over a building at night, to protect it from fire or thieves.

watch=meet-ing (woch′mē″ting), *n.* A religious meeting or service held in Methodist and some other churches on the last night of the year, and terminated on the arrival of the new year.

watch=night (woch′nīt), *n.* The last night of the year, observed in Methodist and some other churches with religious services which last until the arrival of the new year.

watch=tow-er (woch′tou″ėr), *n.* A tower on which a sentinel is placed to watch for enemies, etc.

watch-word (woch′wėrd), *n.* A word or short phrase to be communicated, on challenge, to a sentinel or guard; a password; a countersign; also, a word or phrase expressive of a principle or rule of action (as, "Your English *watchword* is fair-play": Ruskin's "Crown of Wild Olive," i.); a rallying-cry of a party, etc.; a slogan.

wa-ter (wâ′tėr), *n.* [AS. *wæter* = D. *water* = G. *wasser*, akin to Icel. *vatn*, Goth. *watō*, water, also to Gr. ὕδωρ, Skt. *udan*, water, L. *unda*, a wave, water; all from the same root as E. *wet*: cf. *hydra*, *otter*[1], *undine*, and *wash*.] The liquid which in a more or less impure state constitutes rain, oceans, lakes, rivers, etc., and which in a pure state is a transparent, inodorous, tasteless liquid, a compound of hydrogen and oxygen, H_2O, freezing at 32° F. or 0° C., and boiling at 212° F. or 100° C.; a special form or variety of this liquid, as rain, or (often in *pl.*) as the liquid ('mineral water') obtained from a mineral spring (as, "the *waters* of Aix-la-Chapelle": Thackeray's "Newcomes," xxvi.); *pl.*, flowing water, or water moving in waves (as, "the mighty *waters* rolling evermore": Wordsworth's "Intimations of Immortality," ix.); *sing.*, the water of a river, etc., with reference to its relative height, esp. as dependent on tide (as, high *water* or low *water*, the high-*water* mark or low-*water* mark: see under *high*, *a.*, and *low*[4], *a.*); a limited body of water, as a sea, lake, river, or stream (now chiefly prov., except in proper names, as *Derventwater*, the name of a lake in the north of England); also, any liquid or aqueous organic secretion, exudation, humor, or the like, as tears, perspiration, saliva, urine, etc.; also, a liquid solution or preparation (as, toilet-*water*; Cologne *water*, cologne; strong *water*, distilled spirit, also aqua fortis); any of various solutions of volatile or gaseous substances in water (as, ammonia *water*); also, the degree of transparency and brilliancy of a diamond or other precious

stone (as, of the first *water*, of the highest grade, as a diamond: often fig.); also, a kind of wavy, lustrous pattern or marking, as on silk fabrics, metal surfaces, etc.; in *finance*, additional shares or securities created by watering the stock or other securities of a company (see *water*, *v. t.*).—**above water**, above the surface of the water; afloat; fig., out of embarrassment or trouble, esp. of a financial nature.—**to hold water.** See under *hold*[2], *v. t.*—**to make water.** See under *make*[2], *v. t.*—**water of crystallization**, in *chem.*, water of hydration: formerly thought to be necessary to crystallization, but now usually regarded as affecting crystallization only in so far as it forms new molecular combinations.—**water of hydration**, in *chem.*, that portion of a hydrate which is represented as, or can be driven off as, water: now usually regarded as being in true molecular combination with the other atoms of the compound, and not existing in the compound as water.—**wa′ter,** *v.* [AS. *wæterian*.] **I.** *tr.* To sprinkle, moisten, or drench with water (as, to *water* a road or street); supply (land, etc.) with water, as by irrigation; furnish water to (a region, etc.), as streams do (as, "the provinces *watered* by the Rhone and Saône": Hallam's "Europe during the Middle Ages," i. 1); supply (plants) with water to promote growth; supply (animals) with water for drinking (as, "I fed and *watered* my horse": W. H. Hudson's "Purple Land," xx.); furnish with a supply of water, as a ship; also, to produce a wavy, lustrous pattern, marking, or finish on (fabrics, metals, etc.: see *watered*); also, to dilute or adulterate with water (as, to *water* soup; to *water* milk: often with *down*: also fig.); in *finance*, to increase (the stock or other securities of a company) by the issue of additional shares or securities without a corresponding increase in capital or assets. **II.** *intr.* To discharge, fill with, or secrete water or liquid, as the eyes, or as the mouth at the sight or thought of tempting food; also, to drink water, as an animal; take in a supply of water, as a ship.

wa-ter=back (wâ′tėr-bak), *n.* A reservoir, combination of pipes, or the like, at the back of a stove or fireplace, for providing a supply of hot water.

wa-ter=bath (wâ′tėr-bàth), *n.* A bath composed of water, rather than vapor, etc.; in *chem.*, etc., a device for heating or cooling something by means of a surrounding medium of water.

wa-ter=bear-er (wâ′tėr-bār″ėr), *n.* One who carries water; [*cap.*] in *astron.*, the zodiacal constellation or sign Aquarius.

wa-ter=bee-tle (wâ′tėr-bē″tl), *n.* Any of various aquatic beetles (family *Dytiscidæ* and related families) having the hind legs broad and fringed so as to be well adapted for swimming.

wa-ter=bird (wâ′tėr-bėrd), *n.* An aquatic bird, or bird that frequents the water; a swimming or wading bird; a water-fowl.

wa-ter=blink (wâ′tėr-blingk), *n.* A spot of dull or dark color in the sky, due to reflection from open water beneath, seen in arctic regions.

wa-ter=boat-man (wâ′tėr-bōt″man), *n.*; pl. -**men.** Any of various aquatic hemipterous insects of the family *Corixidæ*, which swim on the ventral side of the body, by means of oar-like legs; also, any of various aquatic hemipterous insects of the family *Notonectidæ*, which swim on the back of the body, by means of oar-like hind legs.

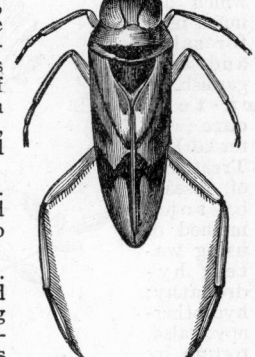

Back-swimming Water-boat-man (*Notonecta undulata*), dorsal view, three times natural size.

wa-ter=borne (wâ′tėr-bôrn), *a.* Supported by the water; carried by the water; conveyed by ship or boat, as goods.

wa-ter=bot-tle (wâ′tėr-bot″l), *n.* A vessel of leather or skin used in some countries for conveying water; also, any bottle for holding water; often, a large glass bottle, without a stopper, for holding drinking-water for use at table, etc.

wa-ter=brain (wâ′tẽr-brān), *n.* The disease gid in sheep, etc.

wa-ter=brash (wâ′tẽr-brash), *n.* In *pathol.*, pyrosis.

wa-ter=buck (wâ′tẽr-buk), *n.* Any of various African antelopes of the genus *Kobus*, etc., frequenting marshes and reedy places, esp. *K. ellipsiprymnus*, a large species of southern and central Africa, which seeks refuge from pursuit in the water.

wa-ter=buf-fa-lo (wâ′tẽr-buf″a̤-lō), *n.* The common buffalo, *Bos bubalus* or *Bubalus buffelus*, of the Old World.

wa-ter=bug (wâ′tẽr-bug), *n.* Any of various aquatic hemipterous insects which live chiefly beneath the surface of the water, as a water-boatman; also, any of various aquatic hemipterous insects of the family *Hydrobatidæ*, etc., which live chiefly on the surface of the water; also, the croton-bug.

wa-ter=chest-nut (wâ′tẽr-ches″nut), *n.* Any of the aquatic plants constituting the genus *Trapa*, bearing an edible, nut-like fruit, esp. *T. natans*, a native of the Old World; also, the fruit.

wa-ter=chin-ka-pin (wâ′tẽr-ching″ka̤-pin), *n.* An American water-lily, *Nelumbo lutea*, with an edible, nut-like seed resembling that of the chinkapin; also, the seed. See cut at *nelumbo*.

wa-ter=clock (wâ′tẽr-klok), *n.* A device, as a clepsydra, for measuring time by the flow of water.

wa-ter=clos-et (wâ′tẽr-kloz″et), *n.* A privy having some contrivance for carrying off the discharges through a waste-pipe below by the agency of water; also, the contrivance; loosely, any privy.

wa-ter=col-or (wâ′tẽr-kul″o̤r), *n.* In *painting*, a pigment for which water and not oil is used as a solvent; the art or method of painting with such pigments; a painting or design executed by this method. — **wa′ter=col″or-ist**, *n.* One who paints in water-colors.

wa-ter=cool (wâ′tẽr-kōl), *v. t.* To cool by means of water, esp. by water circulating in pipes or a jacket. — **wa′ter=cool″er**, *n.* Any device for cooling water, or for cooling something by means of water; esp., a vessel for holding drinking-water, which is cooled by means of ice and drawn off for use by a faucet.

wa-ter=course (wâ′tẽr-kōrs), *n.* A stream of water; a river; a brook; also, a natural channel conveying water; a channel or canal made for the conveyance of water.

wa-ter=crake (wâ′tẽr-krāk), *n.* The spotted crake, *Porzana porzana* (or *maruetta*), a small European rail resembling the American sora, *P. carolina*; also, the water-ouzel, *Cinclus aquaticus*.

wa-ter=cress (wâ′tẽr-kres), *n.* A perennial cress, *Roripa nasturtium*, usually growing in clear, running water, and bearing pungent leaves which are much used for salad and as a garnish.

wa-ter=cure (wâ′tẽr-kūr), *n.* Treatment of disease by some method of using water; hydropathy; hydrotherapy; also, torture by means of forcing water in great quantities into the victim's stomach (colloq.).

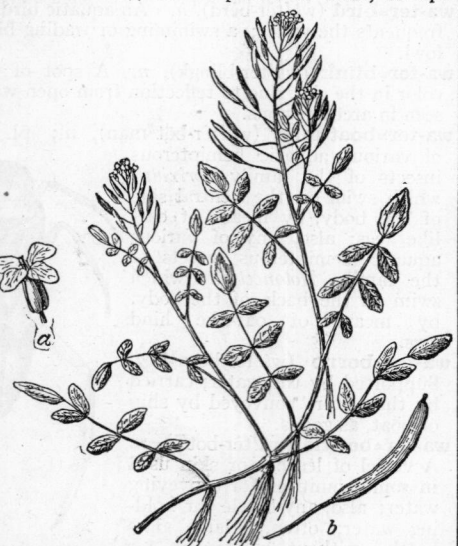

Flowering Plant of Water-cress. — *a*, flower; *b*, pod.

wa-ter=deer (wâ′tẽr-dēr), *n.* A small Chinese deer, *Hydropotes inermis*, without antlers in either sex, but having in the male tusk-like upper canine teeth.

wa-ter=dog (wâ′tẽr-dog), *n.* A dog accustomed to or delighting in the water, or trained to go into the water to retrieve game, as a water-spaniel; also, the mud-puppy (salamander), *Menopoma alleghaniensis*; also, a person at home on or in the water, as a sailor or an experienced swimmer (colloq.).

Water-deer.

wa-tered (wâ′tẽrd), *p. a.* Having a wavy, lustrous pattern or marking, as that produced on a silk fabric by moisture and pressure, or that formed naturally or artificially on the surface of certain steels, etc. Cf. *moire* and *Damascus steel*.

wa-ter-er (wâ′tẽr-ẽr), *n.* One who or that which waters.

wa-ter-fall (wâ′tẽr-fâl), *n.* A steep fall or flow of water from a height (as, "the celebrated *waterfall* of Handeck, where the river Aar plunges into a chasm more than 200 feet deep": Tyndall's "Forms of Water," § 19); a cascade; a cataract; also, a chignon.

wa-ter=flea (wâ′tẽr-flē), *n.* Any of various small or minute crustaceans which skip about in the water like fleas.

wa-ter=fowl (wâ′tẽr-foul), *n.* A water-bird, esp. a swimming bird; also, such birds collectively, esp. swimming game-birds.

wa-ter=front (wâ′tẽr-frunt), *n.* Land abutting on a body of water; esp., a part of a city or town so abutting.

wa-ter=gage (wâ′tẽr-gāj), *n.* A device for indicating the height or quantity of water in a boiler, reservoir, tank, etc.

wa-ter=gap (wâ′tẽr-gap), *n.* A gap in a mountain-ridge, giving passage to a stream.

wa-ter=gas (wâ′tẽr-gas), *n.* A poisonous gas used for illuminating purposes, etc., made by passing steam over incandescent coal or other carbon fuel, and consisting of a mixture of various gases, chiefly carbon monoxide and hydrogen.

wa-ter=gate (wâ′tẽr-gāt), *n.* A gate or gateway through which water passes; also, a gate serving to control the flow of water; a floodgate; also, a gate by which access is gained to a body or supply of water.

wa-ter=glass (wâ′tẽr-glås), *n.* A water-clock or clepsydra; also, a device for observing objects beneath the surface of the water, consisting essentially of an open tube or box with a glass bottom; also, a glass water-gage; also, sodium silicate, esp. a solution of it in water, or a similar preparation of potassium silicate, used to produce a transparent coating on objects in order to protect, preserve, or fireproof them (also called *soluble glass* and *liquid glass*).

wa-ter=gum (wâ′tẽr-gum), *n.* In Australia, any of several myrtaceous trees growing near water; in the U. S., a tupelo, *Nyssa biflora*, of the southern States.

wa-ter=ham-mer (wâ′tẽr-ham″ẽr), *n.* The concussion which results when a moving volume of water in a pipe or passage is suddenly arrested; also, the noise, resembling blows of a hammer, caused in steam-pipes containing water when live steam is admitted.

wa-ter=hem-lock (wâ′tẽr-hem″lok), *n.* Any of the poisonous plants constituting the apiaceous genus *Cicuta*, as *C. virosa*, of Europe, and *C. maculata*, of North America, growing in swamps and marshy places; also, the water-dropwort, *Œnanthe crocata* (see *dropwort*).

wa-ter=hen (wâ′tẽr-hen), *n.* The moor-hen or gallinule, *Gallinula chloropus*, of Europe.

wa-ter=hole (wâ′tẽr-hōl), *n.* A hole or hollow in the ground in which water collects; a natural pool or small pond of water.

Water-gage for Boiler. — *a*, upper cock communicating with steam-space; *a′*, lower cock communicating with water-space; *b*, glass; *c*, water-line.

wa-ter=hy-a-cinth (wâ′tèr-hī″a̤-sinth), *n.* A floating aquatic plant, *Piaropus* (or *Pontederia*) *crassipes*, with violet or blue flowers and ovate leaves with inflated, bladder-like petioles: native in tropical South America, and cultivated elsewhere, but when introduced into inland waters of Florida and Louisiana soon becoming a troublesome weed, seriously impeding navigation.

Water-hyacinth.

wa-ter=ice (wâ′tèr-īs), *n.* A preparation of water, fruit-juice, and sugar, artificially frozen; also, solid ice formed by the direct freezing of fresh or salt water, and not by the compacting of snow (cf. *névé*).

wa-ter=inch (wâ′tèr-inch), *n.* In *hydraulics*, the quantity of water (very nearly 500 cubic feet) discharged in 24 hours through a circular opening of 1 inch diameter leading from a reservoir in which the water is constantly only high enough to cover the orifice.

wa-ter-i-ness (wâ′tèr-i-nes), *n.* Watery state.

wa-ter-ing (wâ′tèr-ing), *n.* The act of one who or that which waters; also, a watered appearance produced on silk, etc.—**wa′ter-ing=cart**, *n.* A cart designed to carry water for watering plants or the streets.—**wa′ter-ing=place**, *n.* A place where water may be obtained, as for drinking, watering cattle, or supplying ships; also, a place of resort for its mineral waters, as a spring or a town; a spa; also, a resort by the sea or other body of water for bathing, boating, etc.—**wa′ter-ing=pot**, *n.* A vessel, esp. a can with a spout having a perforated cap or top, for watering or sprinkling plants, etc.—**wa′ter-ing=trough**, *n.* A trough in which water is provided for domestic animals; in *railroading*, a long, shallow trough parallel to the rails, from which water is scooped by locomotives in passing.

wa-ter-ish (wâ′tèr-ish), *a.* Watery.

wa-ter=jack-et (wâ′tèr-jak″et), *n.* A casing containing water, placed about something to keep it cool or otherwise regulate its temperature.—**wa′ter-jack″et**, *v. t.* To surround or fit with a water-jacket.

wa-ter-leaf (wâ′tèr-lēf), *n.* [Said to be so called from a supposed cavity for water in each leaf.] Any plant of the family *Hydrophyllaceæ*, mostly of North America, with alternate or opposite leaves and a more or less scorpioid inflorescence, as *Hydrophyllum virginicum*, a species with white or purple flowers.

wa-ter-less (wâ′tèr-les), *a.* Without water.

wa-ter=lev-el (wâ′tèr-lev″el), *n.* The surface level of any body of water; also, a leveling instrument employing water instead of spirit, etc.

wa-ter=lil-y (wâ′tèr-lil″i), *n.*; pl. -*ies* (-iz). Any of the aquatic plants constituting the genus *Castalia* (family *Nymphæaceæ*), the species of which have large, disk-like floating leaves and showy, fragrant flowers, esp. *C. odorata* of America or *C. alba* of Europe; any plant of the genus *Nymphæa* of the same family ('yellow water-lily' or 'yellow pond-lily'); in general, any nymphæaceous plant; also, the flower of any such plant.

Waterleaf (*Hydrophyllum virginicum*). — *a*, flower; *b*, fruit.

wa-ter-line (wâ′tèr-līn), *n.* The line in which water at its surface borders upon a floating body; any of several lines marked or indicated on the hull of a ship, showing the depth to which it sinks when unloaded and when partially or fully loaded; in drawings or models of ships, any of a series of lines on the hull, parallel with the surface of the water; also, the surface level of any body of water; the water-level.

wa-ter=logged (wâ′tèr-logd), *a.* [See *logged*.] So filled with water, by leakage or overflow, as to be heavy or unmanageable, as a ship, etc.; also, so saturated with water as to be deprived of buoyancy, as wood, etc.; in general, excessively saturated with water (as, "Our trenches were for the most part in the *water-logged* flats": Buchan's "Hist. of the Great War," liii.).

Wa-ter-loo (wâ-tèr-lö′ or wâ′tèr-lö), *n.* [From the battle near the village of *Waterloo*, in Belgium, in which Napoleon was decisively defeated, June 18, 1815.] A decisive or crushing defeat.

wa-ter=main (wâ′tèr-mān), *n.* A main or principal pipe or conduit in a system for conveying water.

wa-ter=man (wâ′tèr-man), *n.*; pl. -*men*. A mariner† or seaman†; also, a man who manages, or works on, a boat; a boatman; a ferryman; also, a person with reference to his skill in rowing, etc. (as, a good or poor *waterman*); also, a person employed in supplying or distributing water (as, "a . . . city . . . without water-supply beyond that which was sold by *watermen* in buckets": W. H. Hudson's "Far Away and Long Ago," xxii.); an attendant who supplies horses with water for drinking, as at a cab-stand (Eng.).—**wa′ter-man-ship**, *n.* The function or skill of a waterman; skill in rowing, etc.; oarsmanship.

wa-ter=mar-i-gold (wâ′tèr-mar″i-gōld), *n.* An aquatic asteraceous plant, *Bidens beckii*, of North America, having golden-yellow flowers.

wa-ter=mark (wâ′tèr-märk), *n.* A mark indicating the height to which water rises or has risen, as in a river, etc.; also, a faint letter, design, or the like, often marked in the fabric of paper during the process of manufacture by pressure on the moist pulp, usually visible only when the sheet is held against strong light.—**wa′ter-mark**, *v. t.* To mark (paper) with a watermark; also, to impress (a design, etc.) as a watermark.

wa-ter=mel-on (wâ′tèr-mel″on), *n.* The large, roundish or elongated fruit of a trailing cucurbitaceous vine, *Citrullus citrullus*, having a hard, green rind and a (usually) pink or red pulp which abounds in a sweetish, watery juice; also, the plant or vine. Cf. *citron*.

wa-ter=me-ter (wâ′tèr-mē″tèr), *n.* A device for measuring and registering the quantity of water that passes through a pipe or the like.

wa-ter=mil-foil (wâ′tèr-mil″foil), *n.* Any of various aquatic plants, chiefly of the genus *Myriophyllum*, the submersed leaves of which are very finely divided, like the leaves of milfoil or yarrow.

wa-ter=mill (wâ′tèr-mil), *n.* A mill whose machinery is driven by water.

wa-ter=moc-ca-sin (wâ′tèr-mok″a̤-sin), *n.* The venomous moccasin, *Ancistrodon piscivorus* (see *moccasin*); also, any of various similar but harmless water-snakes.

wa-ter=mo-tor (wâ′tèr-mō″tọr), *n.* Any form of prime mover, or motor, that is operated by the kinetic energy, pressure, or weight of water; esp., a small turbine or water-wheel fitted to a pipe supplying water, as for driving sewing-machines or other light machinery.

wa-ter=nymph (wâ′tèr-nimf), *n.* A nymph of the water, as a naiad, a Nereid, or an Oceanid; also, a water-lily; also, any of the aquatic plants constituting the genus *Naias*; also, a dragon-fly.

wa-ter=oak (wâ′tèr-ōk), *n.* An oak, *Quercus nigra*, of the southern U. S., growing chiefly along streams and swamps; also, any of several other American oaks.

wa-ter=ou-zel (wâ′tèr-ö″zl), *n.* Any of several birds of the genus *Cinclus*, allied to the thrushes, esp. *C. aquaticus*, of Europe, and *C. mexicanus*, of western North America, having the habit of diving into streams and moving about under the water in search of food. See cut on following page.

wa-ter=pars-nip (wâ′tèr-pärs″nip), *n.* Any of the herbs of the apiaceous genus *Sium*, growing chiefly in watery places. Cf. *skirret*.

wa-ter=part-ing (wâ′tẽr-pär″ting), *n.* A watershed or divide.

wa-ter=pep-per (wâ′tẽr-pep″ẽr), *n.* Any of various plants of the polygonaceous genus *Polygonum*, growing in wet places, esp. the smartweed, *P. hydropiper*.

wa-ter=pim-per-nel (wâ′tẽr-pim″pẽr-nel), *n.* The brookweed.

wa-ter-plane (wâ′tẽr-plān), *n.* An aëroplane adapted for alighting on, ascending from, and

American Water-ouzel (*Cinclus mexicanus*).

traveling on the water; a hydro-aëroplane; a seaplane.

wa-ter=plan-tain (wâ′tẽr-plan″tān), *n.* Any of the aquatic herbs of the genus *Alisma*, esp. *A. plantago-aquatica*, a species growing in shallow water throughout the temperate regions of the northern hemisphere, and having leaves suggesting those of the common plantain (*Plantago*).

wa-ter=po-lo (wâ′tẽr-pō″lō), *n.* A game played by two teams of swimmers, often in a swimming-tank, with a large inflated ball resembling a football.

wa-ter=pow-er (wâ′tẽr-pou″ẽr), *n.* The power of water used, or capable of being used, to drive machinery, etc.; also, a fall or descent in a stream, capable of being so used.

wa-ter-pox (wâ′tẽr-poks), *n.* In *pathol.*, chicken-pox.

wa-ter-proof (wâ′tẽr-prōf). **I.** *a.* Impervious to water (as, "Their shoes were far from being *waterproof*": Dickens's "Christmas Carol," iii.); rendered impervious to water by some special process, as coating or treating with rubber or the like. **II.** *n.* A waterproof material; a fabric which has been specially treated to render it impervious to water; also, an outer garment of waterproof material.—**wa′ter-proof**, *v. t.* To render waterproof.—**wa′ter-proof″ing**, *n.* The act or process of rendering waterproof; also, a substance, as rubber, oil, etc., used to render something waterproof.

wa-ter=purs-lane (wâ′tẽr-pẽrs″lān), *n.* Any of various marsh-plants somewhat resembling purslane, as a lythraceous plant, *Didiplis diandra*, of North America.

wa-ter=sap-phire (wâ′tẽr-saf″īr), *n.* A deep-blue variety of iolite, found in Ceylon, sometimes used as a gem.

wa-ter-scape (wâ′tẽr-skāp), *n.* [With *-scape* as in *landscape*.] A picture or view of the sea or other body of water. Cf. *landscape*.

wa-ter=scor-pi-on (wâ′tẽr-skôr″pi-ọn), *n.* Any of the aquatic hemipterous insects constituting the family *Nepidæ* (genera *Nepa*, *Ranatra*, etc.), having a tail-like process through which respiration is effected.

wa-ter-shed (wâ′tẽr-shed), *n.* The ridge or line dividing two drainage-areas; a water-parting; a divide; also, the region or area drained by a river, etc.; a drainage-area.

wa-ter-shield (wâ′tẽr-shēld), *n.* Any of the aquatic plants of the nymphæaceous genera *Brasenia* and *Cabomba*, with peltate floating leaves.

wa-ter-side (wâ′tẽr-sīd), *n.* The margin, bank, or shore of the sea, a river, a lake, or some other body of water.

wa-ter-snake (wâ′tẽr-snāk), *n.* Any of various snakes living in or frequenting water; esp., any of the harmless colubrine snakes of the genus *Natrix* (or *Tropidonotus*), found in or near fresh water.

wa-ter-soak (wâ′tẽr-sōk), *v. t.* To soak with water.

wa-ter=span-iel (wâ′tẽr-span″yẹl), *n.* A curly-haired spaniel of either of two varieties which take readily to water and are trained for hunting.

wa-ter-spi-der (wâ′tẽr-spī″dẽr), *n.* Any of various aquatic spiders, as a European fresh-water spider, *Argyroneta aquatica*, which makes a bag-like nest, opening downward, beneath the surface of the water, filling the nest with air brought down in bubbles on the spider's body. See cut in next column.

wa-ter-spout (wâ′tẽr-spout), *n.* A spout, nozzle, or orifice from which water is discharged; a pipe running down the side of a house to take away water from the gutter of the roof; also, a spout or jet of water; sometimes, a sudden and violent downpour of rain; a cloud-burst; in *meteor.*, a tornado-like storm or whirlwind over the ocean or other body of water, which takes the form of a progressive gyrating mass of air laden with mist and spray, presenting the appearance of a solid column of water reaching upward to the clouds.

Water-spider (*Argyroneta aquatica*).

wa-ter=sprite (wâ′tẽr-sprīt), *n.* A sprite or spirit inhabiting the water.

wa-ter=star-wort (wâ′tẽr-stär″wẽrt), *n.* Any plant of the genus *Callitriche*, comprising slender aquatic herbs with minute axillary flowers.

wa-ter=strid-er (wâ′tẽr-strī″dẽr), *n.* Any of the aquatic hemipterous insects constituting the family *Hydrobatidæ*, having long, slender legs, and darting about on the surface of water with great rapidity.

wa-ter=ta-ble (wâ′tẽr-tā″bl), *n.* In *arch.*, a projecting stringcourse or similar member so placed as to throw off water; in *engin.*, etc., the level below which the ground is saturated with water.

wa-ter=thrush (wâ′tẽr-thrush), *n.* Either of two American warblers, *Seiurus nævius* (or *noveboracensis*) and *S. motacilla*, usually found near water; also, the European water-ouzel.

wa-ter=tight (wâ′tẽr-tīt), *a.* Impervious to water.—**wa′ter=tight″ness**, *n.*

wa-ter=tow-er (wâ′tẽr-tou″ẽr), *n.* A stand-pipe; also, a fire-extinguishing apparatus for throwing a stream of water on the upper parts of a tall burning building, consisting of

Water-thrush (*Seiurus nævius*).

a tower-like structure supporting a vertical pipe at the top of which is a movable nozzle from which the water issues.

wa-ter=wag-on (wâ′tẽr-wag″ọn), *n.* A wagon for carrying water, as for sprinkling streets, etc.; hence, the vehicle humorously supposed to carry upon the course through life, and supply the proper refreshment for, those who abstain from or forswear strong drink.

wa-ter-way (wâ′tẽr-wā), *n.* A way or channel for water; also, a river, canal, or other body of water as a way of travel or transport; a route by water; also, the breadth of a navigable water-passage; also, a channel for vessels; esp., the fairway in a harbor, etc.; also, the area of the fully open passage in a cock or valve; in *ship-building*, the thick planking at the outside of the deck, which forms a channel for water to run off the deck.

wa-ter-weed (wâ′tẽr-wēd), *n.* Any wild aquatic plant without special use or beauty; specif., a vallisneriaceous plant, *Philotria canadensis*, native in North America, and common in fresh-water streams and ponds.

wa-ter-wheel (wâ′tẽr-hwēl), *n.* A wheel turned by the action of water and used to perform mechanical work; also, a wheel for raising water, as a noria; also, a paddle-wheel of a vessel†.

wa-ter-white (wâ′tẽr-hwīt), *a.* Colorless and transparent, as water or glass.—**wa′ter=white″ness**, *n.*

wa-ter-work (wâ′tẽr-wẽrk), *n.* A system of apparatus for furnishing a supply of water†; now, *pl.* (often construed as *sing.*), an aggregate of apparatus and structures by which water is collected, preserved, and distributed for domestic and other purposes, as for the use of a city; a building or buildings at a reservoir or the like, with pumping apparatus, etc.; also, *sing.* or *pl.*, an ornamental fountain or the like† (as, "I saw him standing by the wheel, dropping [with water] like a *waterwork*": Smollett's "Humphry Clinker," July 4); also, *pl.*, fig., the source of tears, or tears (colloq.: as, "Sneaking little brute . . . clapping on the *waterworks* just in the hardest place," Hughes's "Tom Brown's School-Days," ii. 5); also, *sing.*, an imitation tapestry painted in distemper or the like†.

wa-ter=worn (wâ′tėr-wôrn), *a.* Worn by the action of water; smoothed by water in motion.

wa-ter-y (wâ′tėr-i), *a.* [AS. *wæterig*.] Full of or abounding in water, as soil, a region, etc.; also, consisting of water (as, "In fourscore barks they plough the *watery* way," Pope's tr. Homer's "Iliad," ii.; a *watery* grave, the place where one lies drowned); of the nature of water (as, *watery* vapor); also, pertaining to or connected with water (as, "*watery* Neptune": Shakspere's "Richard II.," ii. 1. 63); regarded as bringing or portending rain, as heavenly bodies, etc.; also, resembling water in appearance or color; pale as if diluted with water (as, "The *watery* autumn sunlight was failing": Kipling's "Light That Failed," iv.); resembling water in consistence (as, a *watery* fluid); also, containing too much water, as liquid food; containing a large proportion of moisture, as fruits, meat, etc.; fig., weak, thin, washy, vapid, or poor (as, *watery* discourse or writing; "slight Sir Robert with his *watery* smile," Tennyson's "Edwin Morris," 128; a *watery* fool); also, discharging, filled with, or secreting some aqueous organic liquid; tearful, as the eyes; exuding tears as the result of weakness or disease of the lacrymal organs (as, "a middle-aged, lightish-colored man, with weak and *watery* eyes": Jack London's "Call of the Wild," v.).

watt (wot), *n.* [From James *Watt* (1736–1819), British engineer and inventor.] In *elect.*, a unit of power, being the rate of working in a direct-current circuit when the electromotive force is one volt and the current one ampere: equivalent to 10,000,000 ergs per second, or approximately $\frac{1}{746}$ horse-power.—**watt′age** (-äj), *n.* In *elect.*, power in watts; the number of watts required to operate an electrical device.

Wat-teau (wä-tō′, F. vä-tō), *a.* Pertaining to or in the style of the French painter Jean Antoine Watteau (1684–1721) or his paintings: as, a *Watteau* shepherdess; a *Watteau* back (a long, loose, full back of a woman's gown, held in, in folds, only at the neck).

watt=hour (wot′our), *n.* In *elect.*, a unit of energy or work, equal to one watt maintained for one hour.

wat-tle[1] (wot′l), *n.* [AS. *watel*, *watul*, wattle, pl. thatching, roof.] *Pl.* or *sing.*, rods or stakes interwoven with twigs or branches of trees, used for making fences, walls, roofs, etc. (as, "a few large structures of mud, or plastered *wattle*": W. H. Hudson's "Green Mansions," i.); *sing.*, a hurdle (prov. Eng.); also, a twig, wand, stick, or rod (prov. Eng. and Sc.); also, in Australia, etc., any of various acacias whose shoots and branches were much used by the early colonists for wattles, now valued esp. for their bark, which is used in tanning.—**wattle and daub**, stakes interwoven with twigs and plastered with clay or mud, used for building huts, cottages, etc.—**wat′tle**[1], *v. t.*; *-tled*, *-tling*. To construct (a fence, wall, etc.) of rods or stakes interwoven with twigs or branches of trees; also, to interweave (twigs, branches, etc.) in forming wattles (as, "It [a hut] was seen to be constructed of the branches of trees, twisted together or *wattled*, the interstices, or rather the whole surface, being covered with clay": J. H. Newman's "Callista," xxiii.); bind together (stakes, etc.) with interwoven twigs or branches (as, "a long kind of building, made of timber, stuck in the ground, and *wattled* across": Swift's "Gulliver's Travels," iv. 2); also, to surround with wattles or wattle; also, to beat with or as with a switch or rod (Sc. and prov. Eng.).

wat-tle[2] (wot′l), *n.* [Origin obscure.] A fleshy lobe or appendage hanging down from the throat or chin of certain birds, as the domestic fowl, the turkey, etc.; also, a similar fleshy appendage, as at each side of the neck of some swine; also, a barbel of a fish.—**wat′tle=bird**, *n.* Any of several Australian honey-eaters, as *Anthochæra carunculata*, having a pendulous wattle on each side of the throat.—

wat′tled, *a.* Having wattles or a wattle, as a bird.

watt-less (wot′les), *a.* In *elect.*, without watts or power: as, a *wattless* alternating current (one differing in phase by 90 degrees from the electromotive force); a *wattless* electromotive force (one differing in phase by 90 degrees from the current).

watt-me-ter (wot′mē″tėr), *n.* In *elect.*, an instrument for measuring in watts the power developed in an electric circuit.

Wattle-bird (*Anthochæra carunculata*).

waul (wâl), *v. i.* [Imit.: cf. *caterwaul*.] To cry as a cat; squall.

wave (wāv), *v.*; *waved*, *waving*. [AS. *wafian*, wave: cf. Icel. *vafra*, hover about, *vāfa*, swing, vibrate, waver, G. *wabern*, wave, flicker.] **I.** *intr.* To move with advancing swells and depressions of surface, as the sea or a field of grain, or as a flag floating in the breeze (as, "The vast plain *waved* with tall rank grass": Parkman's "Oregon Trail," vii.); undulate; bend or sway up and down or to and fro, as branches or plants in the wind; be moved as a signal, esp. alternately in opposite directions (as, "The lady's handkerchief *waved* in token of encouragement": Bulwer-Lytton's "Pelham," xvii.); be brandished, as a weapon (as, "Now *waved* their fiery swords": Milton's "Paradise Lost," vi. 304); also, to give a signal by waving something (as, "She *waved* to me with her hand": Tennyson's "Maud," ix.); also, to curve alternately in opposite directions; have an undulating form; also, to waver† or vacillate†. **II.** *tr.* To cause to wave; cause to move with advancing swells and depressions (as, "The night wind . . . *waved* the tattered banners": Scott's "Anne of Geierstein," xi.); cause to bend or sway up and down or to and fro; move as a signal, esp. alternately in opposite directions (as, to *wave* the hand); swing or brandish, as a weapon, etc. (as, "my uncle Toby, *waving* his tobacco-pipe, as he would have done his sword at the head of a regiment": Sterne's "Tristram Shandy," v. 32); also, to signal to by waving a flag or the like; direct by a waving movement, as of the hand (as, "She . . . *waved* him away with one hand": Whyte-Melville's "Katerfelto," xxvii.); also, to signify or express by a waving movement (as, "She *waved* a last good-by to John from the window": G. W. Cable's "John March, Southerner," xiii.); also, to give an undulating form to; cause to curve up and down or in and out; also, to give a wavy appearance or pattern to; water, as silk.—**wave**, *n.* A disturbance of the surface of a liquid body, as the sea or a lake, in the form of a ridge or swell which advances or progresses independently of the particles successively composing it; any progressive disturbance or movement resembling a wave of the sea, or any progressing part of a mass or body suggesting such a wave (as, a *wave* of the pulse; a *wave* of contraction, the visible onward contraction of a muscle from a point where it is stimulated; a hot *wave* or a cold *wave*, an advancing layer of hot or cold air extending over a broad extent of country; a *wave* of troops rushing into battle: see also physics def. below); fig., a swell, surge, or rush, as of feeling, excitement, prosperity, etc. (as, "Among the outside public there was a great *wave* of enthusiasm": Lytton Strachey's "Queen Victoria," iii.); an outburst or outbreak (as, a crime *wave*); also, water, a body of water, or the sea (poetic: as, "She thought of Christ, who stilled the *wave*, On the Lake of Galilee," Longfellow's "Wreck of the Hesperus"); also, an outward curve, or one of a series of such curves, in a surface or line; an undulation; a waved, wavy, or undulating line or streak, as of color or luster, as on watered silk or Damascus steel; waved or wavy condition, as of the hair; also, the act or an act of waving; a waving, as in the breeze; a waving of something, as a flag or the hand, as in signaling or gesturing; in *physics*, a progressive vibrational disturbance propagated among the parts or particles of a medium, as air or luminiferous ether, without corresponding progress or advance of the parts or particles themselves, as in the transmission of sound, heat, light, and electricity (see phrases below); the form assumed by the parts or particles of a medium which are out of equilibrium from a single disturbance of this kind.—**continuous waves.** See under *continuous.*—**damped waves.** See *damped.*—**electric wave,** an electromagnetic disturbance or wave produced in the luminiferous ether, serving as a means of transmission in wireless telegraphy and telephony; a Hertzian wave.—**electromagnetic wave,** an electric wave.—**ether wave,** an electric wave.—**Hertzian wave.** See under *Hertzian.*—**undamped.**—**wireless wave,** an electric wave.—**waved,** *a.* Having a wave or waves; also, having a wavy or undulating form or outline; marked with wavy lines; watered, as silk.—**wave′=form,** *n.* The form assumed by a wave; in *elect.*, the shape of the curve obtained by plotting the instantaneous values of an alternating current against time (cf. *oscillograph*).—**wave′=length,** *n.* The distance between the crests of two adjacent waves, or between the lowest parts of the depressions on the sides of a wave; in *physics*, the distance between any particle of a disturbed medium through which waves are passing and the next particle that is in the same phase with it.—**wave′less,** *a.* Free from waves; undisturbed; still.—**wave′let,** *n.* A small wave; a ripple.

wa-vel-lite (wā′vel-īt), *n.* [From Dr. Wm. *Wavell*, who first found it, in Devonshire, England.] A mineral, a hydrous phosphate of aluminium, of a white to yellowish-green or brown color.

wave-me-ter (wāv′mē″tėr), *n.* In *elect.*, an instrument used to measure the wave-length of electric waves.

wave=mo-tion (wāv′mō″shǫn), *n.* Motion like that of waves in water; in *physics*, the motion of waves; progressive undulatory or vibrational motion by which disturbance of equilibrium is transmitted.

wave=of-fer-ing (wāv′of″ėr-ing), *n.* In the Jewish priestly law, an offering which was moved ('waved') from left to right or vice versa by the priest when presented, and became the portion of the priests and their families. See Ex. xxix. 27.

wav-er[1] (wā′vėr), *n.* One who or that which waves.

wa-ver[2] (wā′vėr), *v. i.* [ME. *waveren*, freq. of *waven*, E. *wave.*] To sway to and fro (as, "the foliage of some *wavering* thicket": Carlyle's "Sartor Resartus," ii. 3); flutter or float in the air; also, to sway to and fro as if about to fall; totter; reel; also, to become unsteady, or begin to fail or give way (as, "The Gauls *wavered*, broke, and scattered," Froude's "Cæsar," xix.; "her *wavering* senses," Longfellow's "Evangeline," i. 5); also, to shake or tremble, as the hands, etc. (as, "He stood with *wavering* hands, unable for a moment to begin," H. G. Wells's "Men Like Gods," i. 6; "The voice *wavered*," Mrs. H. Ward's "Lady Rose's Daughter," iv.); flicker or quiver, as light, etc. (as, "thin *wavering* and ascending tongues of flame": W. H. Hudson's "Far Away and Long Ago," v.); also, to feel or show doubt or indecision, or vacillate (as, "I *wavered* in my determination," Borrow's "Romany Rye," xvi.; "After much *wavering*, Charles of France gave his consent," J. F. Kirk's "Charles the Bold," iii. 1); falter in duty, allegiance, etc. (as, "You were . . . men who would never *waver* in your fidelity to me," Conan Doyle's "Exploits of Brigadier Gerard," viii.); of things, to fluctuate or vary.—**wa′ver**[2], *n.* The act or an act of wavering; fluttering; trembling; vacillating.—**wa′ver-er,** *n.*—**wa′ver-ing-ly,** *adv.*—**wa′ver-y,** *a.* Wavering; unsteady.

WAVES. Women's Reserve, U. S. Naval Reserve.

wave=train (wāv′trān), *n.* In *physics*, a group or series of successive waves sent out along the same path or course by a vibrating body, a wireless antenna, or the like.—**damped wave=train.** See under *damped.*

Waved Blade of Malay Creese.

wave=trap (wāv′trap), *n.* In *wireless teleg.* and *teleph.*, a device for eliminating an undesired signal by absorbing it in an extra circuit which can be tuned to the wave-length of the signal.

wav-y (wā′vi), *a.* Abounding in or characterized by waves (as, "the *wavy* sea": W. Morris's "Jason," ix. 166); moving with wave-like motion, as a field of grain; also, resembling or suggesting waves; unsteady; wavering; vibrating or tremulous; also, curving alternately in opposite directions in movement or form (as, a *wavy* course; *wavy* hair); having waved or undulating markings; in *bot.*, bending with successive curves in opposite directions, as a margin; having such a margin, as a leaf.—**wav′i-ly,** *adv.*—**wav′i-ness,** *n.*

wawl (wâl), *v. i.* See *waul.*

wax[1] (waks), *v. i.* [AS. *weaxan* = D. *wassen* = G. *wachsen* = Icel. *vaxa* = Goth. *wahsjan*, grow: cf. Gr. αὐξάνειν, increase.] To increase in extent or size, or in quantity (as, "long ere the flood hath attained this height, and while it is only *waxing*": Blackmore's "Lorna Doone," i.); of the moon, to undergo the periodical increase in the extent of its illuminated portion before the full (opposed to *wane*); also, to increase in strength, intensity, etc. (as, "The discord among the Reformers themselves *waxed* daily," Motley's "Dutch Republic," iv. 4; "The sound of the sea *waxed*," Arnold Bennett's "Clayhanger," iv. 3); increase in power, importance, prosperity, etc. (as, "He was *waxing* yearly. His supremacy as a printer could not be challenged in Bursley": Arnold Bennett's "Clayhanger," i. 17); also, to grow or become (as stated: as, "My bones *waxed* old," Ps. xxxii. 3; "Then *waxed* the heavens black," W. Morris's "Jason," i. 378).

wax[2] (waks), *n.* [AS. *weax* = D. *was* = G. *wachs* = Icel. *vax*, wax.] A solid yellowish substance secreted by bees, plastic when warm and melting at about 145° F., and allied to the fats and oils though containing no glycerin, which is used by bees in constructing their honeycomb, and which is variously employed otherwise, as in making candles, models, casts, ointments, etc.; beeswax; also, any of various similar substances, as spermaceti, the secretions of certain insects (see *wax-insect*), and the secretions of certain plants (see *vegetable wax*, under *vegetable, a.*); also, any of various other substances somewhat resembling beeswax; ear-wax; sealing-wax; ozocerite ('mineral wax'); a resinous substance used by shoemakers for rubbing their thread; also, fig., something suggesting wax as being readily molded, worked upon, handled, managed, etc. (as, "Let me pretend to be helpless *wax* in their hands," Buchan's "Three Hostages," v.; "The Parson was *wax* to my Lord's command," H. Newbolt's "Fidele's Grassy Tomb").—**wax**[2], *v. t.* To rub, smear, stiffen, polish, etc., with wax; treat with wax: as, "Mr. Cyrus Meeker, whose mustaches . . . are *waxed* as tight as ever" (W. Churchill's "Modern Chronicle," i. 4); "The *waxed* floor reflected her dimly" (J. Conrad's "Lord Jim," xxxvii.).—**waxed end,** in *shoemaking*, a thread having its end stiffened with shoemakers' wax, and often pointed with a bristle, for passing through holes made with an awl in sewing shoes.—**wax′=bean,** *n.* Same as *butter-bean.*—**wax′=ber″ry,** *n.* The wax-myrtle, *Myrica cerifera*, or the bayberry, *M. carolinensis*; also, the snowberry, *Symphoricarpos racemosus.*—

wax′bill, *n.* Any of various weaver-birds, esp. of the genus *Estrelda*, having white, pink, or red bills of wax-like appearance, and including many well-known cage-birds, as an African species, *Estrelda astrilda*, and the amadavat, and the Java sparrow.

Waxbill (*Estrelda astrilda*).

wax-en¹ (wak′sn). Obs. or archaic pp. of *wax¹*.

wax-en² (wak′sn), *a*. [AS. *weaxen*.] Made of wax; covered with wax; also, resembling or suggesting wax (as, "Its [a face's] pallor had lost something of its deathly *waxen* appearance": W. H. Hudson's "Green Mansions," xvii.); sometimes, soft, plastic, or impressible.

wax-er (wak′sèr), *n*. One who or that which waxes something, as thread or floors.

wax-i-ness (wak′si-nes), *n*. Waxy quality or character; waxy appearance.

wax=in-sect (waks′in″sekt), *n*. Any of various homopterous insects, as a Chinese scale-insect, *Ericerus pela*, which secrete a wax or wax-like substance sometimes used in making candles, etc.

wax=myr-tle (waks′mèr″tl), *n*. A shrub or tree of the genus *Myrica*, as *M. cerifera*, which bears small berries coated with wax (sometimes used in making candles, etc.), or *M. carolinensis* (see *bayberry*).

wax=palm (waks′päm), *n*. A tall pinnate-leaved palm, *Ceroxylon andicola*, of the Andes, whose stem and leaves yield a resinous wax; also, a palmate-leaved palm, *Copernicia cerifera*, of Brazil, the carnauba, whose young leaves are coated with a hard wax.

Wax-palm (*Ceroxylon andicola*).

wax=plant (waks′-plant), *n*. Any of the climbing or trailing plants of the asclepiadaceous genus *Hoya*, natives of tropical Asia and Australia, having glossy leaves and umbels of pink, white, or yellowish waxy flowers, species of which are familiar in cultivation; also, the Indian-pipe.

wax=tree (waks′trē), *n*. Any of various trees yielding wax, as a sumac, *Rhus succedanea*, of Japan, or the wax-myrtle, *Myrica cerifera*.

wax=weed (waks′wēd), *n*. An American lythraceous herb, *Parsonsia* (or *Cuphea*) *petiolata*, with a viscid pubescence and purple flowers.

wax-wing (waks′wing), *n*. Any bird of the passerine genus *Ampelis*, as *A. garrulus*, of the northern hemisphere, or *A. cedrorum*, the cedar-bird of North America: characterized by a showy crest and a peculiar red, horny appendage resembling sealing-wax at the tip of the shaft of certain wing-feathers and sometimes other feathers.

wax-work (waks′-wèrk), *n*. Work in wax; figures, ornaments, etc., made of wax, or a single such figure; esp., *pl.*, figures, as of real persons, formed partly or wholly of wax for exhibition purposes. — **wax′work″er**, *n*. One who works in wax; a maker of waxwork; also, a bee which produces wax.

Bohemian Waxwing (*Ampelis garrulus*).

wax-y (wak′si), *a.*; compar. *waxier*, superl. *waxiest*. Abounding in, covered with, or made of wax; pertaining to wax; resembling wax, as in substance or appearance; sometimes, fig., pliable, yielding, or impressible.

way¹, **'way** (wā), *adv*. Away. [Colloq.]

way² (wā), *n*. [AS. *weg* = D. and G. *weg* = Icel. *vegr* = Goth. *wigs*, way; akin to L. *via*, way (cf. *via¹*); from the root of E. *weigh²*.] A path or course leading from one place to another; a road, route, passage, or channel (as, a high*way*, rail*way*, water*way*, or tide*way*; an arch*way*; a door*way*); any line of passage or travel used or available (as, to blaze a *way* through dense woods; to find a *way* down a steep mountainside); also, space for passing or advancing (as, to make *way*, see under *make²*, *v. t.*; to give *way*, see under *give*, *v. t.*); also, passage or progress on a course (as, to make one's *way* on foot; to lead the *way*: also fig.); also, distance (as, a long *way* off); also, direction (as, look this *way*); also, fig., course of life, action, or experience (as, "The *way* of the just is uprightness," Isa. xxvi. 7; "The *way* of transgressors is hard," Prov. xiii. 15); calling or business (colloq.: as, in the grocery *way*); condition, as to health, prosperity, etc. (colloq.: as, to be in a bad *way*); also, a course, plan, or means for attaining an end (as, to find a *way* to reduce friction); in general, manner, mode, or fashion (as, a new *way* of looking at a matter; to reply in a polite *way*); often, characteristic or habitual manner (as, that is only his *way*; "All that's madly wild, or oddly gay, We call it only pretty Fanny's *way*," Parnell's "Elegy to an Old Beauty"); a habit or custom (often in *pl.*: as, "I don't like his *ways* at all," Dickens's "Hard Times," ii. 1; "if you will respect our laws and *ways*," H. G. Wells's "Men Like Gods," i. 6); also, one's preferred course or mode of procedure (as, to have one's own *way*); also, range of experience or notice (as, the best device that ever came in my *way*); also, respect or particular (as, a plan defective in several *ways*); *naut.*, movement or passage through the water (as, lee*way*); esp., head-way (as, "The ship . . . gathered fresh *way*": Marryat's "King's Own," liii.); *pl.*, in *ship-building*, the timbers on which a ship is launched; *sing.*, in *law*, a right of way (see under *right*, *n.*). — **by the way**, on the way (as, "If I send them away fasting . . . they will faint by the way": Mark, viii. 3); also, in passing, as something said incidentally (as, "This, however, *by the way*. It was not the chief thing that I wanted to say": Mallock's "New Republic," iii. 3); incidentally speaking (used to introduce an incidental remark or brief digression: as, "*By the way*, I forgot to tell you . . . ," Arnold Bennett's "Hilda Lessways," ii. 7). — **by way of**, by the route of; via; through; also, as a way, method, or means of (as, to number articles *by way of* distinguishing them); as or for (as, to wear a wig *by way of* disguise); also, in the position of, or ostensibly (being, doing, etc.: as, he is *by way of* being an authority on the subject: Eng.). — **covered way.** See under *covered.* — **in a way**, in a manner; after a fashion; to some extent: as, "I was, *in a way*, a sharer in his alarms" (Stevenson's "Treasure Island," i.). — **in the way**, on the way; in one's path, esp. as an obstacle; hence, in a position to hinder, hamper, etc., or being an obstacle, hindrance, or inconvenience (as, "A man . . . is so *in the way* in the house!" Mrs. Gaskell's "Cranford," i.). — **once in a way**, once in a while: occasionally: as, "It did not . . . matter, *once in a way*, if they were tired and inefficient on the morrow" (Arnold Bennett's "These Twain," v.). — **on the way**, on the road taken in traveling; hence, in process of coming, going, or proceeding (as, a letter is now *on the way* to you; a bill *on the way* through the legislature). — **out of the way**, out of the road or path; so as not to obstruct or hinder; off one's hands; also, out of existence (as, to put a person or an animal *out of the way*); also, out of the frequented way or beaten track; apart from what is usual or proper; unusual, improper, or amiss; also, mislaid or lost. Cf. *out-of-the-way*, *a.* — **permanent way.** See under *permanent.* — **right of way.** See under *right*, *n.* — **to take one's way**, to go; proceed. — **under way**, in motion, or moving along, as a ship that has weighed anchor; hence, in progress, as an enterprise. — **way of the cross**, the way or course followed by Christ in going to Calvary to be crucified; hence, *eccles.*, a way or course marked by stations of the cross (see under *station*, *n.*), in commemoration of Christ's course; also, the devotion of the stations of the cross. — **ways and means**, methods and means of accomplishing something; in *legislation*, methods and means of raising revenue for the use of the government (as, the Committee of *Ways and Means* of the U. S. House of Representatives).

-way. A use of *way*[2] in adverbial formations (orig. phrases), as in *alway, anyway, noway, someway.* Cf. *-ways.*

way=bill (wā′bil), *n.* A list of the names of passengers in a public conveyance; also, more commonly, a list of goods sent in the care of a common carrier, as a railroad, with shipping directions for the same.—**way′=bill,** *v. t.* To enter in a way-bill; also, to send accompanied by a way-bill.

way-fare (wā′fār), *v. i.; -fared, -faring.* [Back-formation from *wayfaring.*] To journey or travel, esp. on foot: now only in *wayfaring, ppr.* and *n.*—**way′far″er** (-fār″ėr), *n.* A traveler, esp. on foot.

way-far-ing (wā′fār″ing), *a.* [AS. *wegfarende,* < *weg,* E. *way*[2], + *farende, ppr.* of *faran,* go, E. *fare.*] Journeying or traveling, esp. on foot: as, "An highway shall be there . . . the *wayfaring* men, though fools, shall not err therein" (Isa. xxxv. 8).—**way′far″ing,** *n.* The act of traveling, esp. on foot: as, "At mid-day, after talk and a little *wayfaring,* they slept" (Kipling's "Kim,"xii.).—**way′far″ing-tree,** *n.* A European caprifoliaceous shrub or small tree, *Viburnum lantana,* with dense cymes of small white flowers, common along roadsides; also, the hobble-bush, *V. alnifolium,* a related species of the U. S.

way=go-ing (wā′gō″ing), *a.* [See *way*[1].] Going away, departing, or outgoing (as, a *waygoing* tenant); hence, of or pertaining to one who goes away (as, a *waygoing* crop, a crop sown by a tenant and not ripe until after the expiration of his tenancy, but allowed as his property). [Prov. Eng. and Sc.]

way-lay (wā-lā′ or wā′lā), *v. t.; -laid, -laying.* To lie in wait for (a traveler, passer-by, etc.) on the way; fall upon or assail from ambush, as in order to rob, seize, or slay; less seriously, to await and accost unexpectedly, as in order to obtain some favor, an interview, or the like (as, "If he *waylaid* her on the stairs, he got but little satisfaction": W. Churchill's "Modern Chronicle," i. 10); also, to beset (one's path) by ambushment (rare).—**way-lay′er,** *n.*

way=mark (wā′märk), *n.* A mark or sign set up along a way; a guide-post, milestone, or the like.

-ways. [With adverbial suffix *-s*[3]: cf. *-wards.*] Extended form of *-way,* as in *always, anyways, leastways, noways,* used esp. in adverbs denoting direction or position, as in *edgeways, endways, lengthways, sideways:* many such words having alternative forms in *-wise* (of like meaning but different origin). See *-wise.*

way-side (wā′sīd). **I.** *n.* The side of the way; the border or edge of the road or highway. **II.** *a.* Being, situated, or found at or along the wayside: as, a *wayside* inn; *wayside* flowers or hedges.

way=sta-tion (wā′stā″shǫn), *n.* A station intermediate between principal stations, as on a railroad.

way=train (wā′trān), *n.* A railroad-train which stops at all or most of the stations on its way or route; an accommodation train.

way-ward (wā′wẳrd), *a.* [For obs. *awayward,* turned away, turned from the proper course, wayward, < *away* + *-ward* (cf. *froward*); the sense in later use being colored by association with *way*[2] ('one's own way').] Turned or turning away from what is right or proper, or froward or perverse (as, "A *wayward* son, Spiteful and wrathful": Shakspere's "Macbeth," iii. 5. 11); disposed to turn wilfully from what is proper, reasonable, or expected, in order to follow one's own impulses or whims, or wilfully or capriciously perverse (as, "a lively child, who had been spoiled and indulged, and, therefore, was sometimes *wayward*": C. Brontë's "Jane Eyre," xii.); characterized by or proceeding from perversity or perverse self-will (as, "In the midst of his most *wayward* mood, Richard respected the church," Scott's "Talisman," xviii.; "a scolding for some *wayward* prank," W. Churchill's "Mr. Crewe's Career," i.); also, swayed or prompted by caprice, or capricious (as, "free as the butterfly, going and coming at her *wayward* will," W. H. Hudson's "Green Mansions," viii.; a *wayward* fancy; to yield to a *wayward* impulse); proceeding as if by caprice, turning or changing irregularly, or irregular (as, a *wayward* stream,

path, or breeze; the *wayward* flight of some birds); also, untoward or unfavorable (poetic: as, "Hylas, governed by some *wayward* star, Strayed from them," W. Morris's "Jason," iv. 384).—**way′ward-ly,** *adv.*—**way′ward-ness,** *n.*

way-worn (wā′wŏrn), *a.* Worn or wearied by travel: as, a *wayworn* traveler.

we (wē), *pron.;* nom. *we,* poss. *our* or *ours,* obj. *us.* [AS. *wē* = OS. *wī* = OHG. G. *wir* = Icel. *vēr* = Goth. *weis,* we: cf. Skt. *vayam,* we.] Nominative plural of *I:* specially used by a speaker or writer to denote people in general, including himself, or by a sovereign when alluding to himself in formal speech, or by an editor or other writer to avoid any appearance of egotism from the use of *I.*

weak (wēk), *a.* [ME. *weik, waik:* cf. Icel. *veikr* = OHG. *weih* (G. *weich*) = AS. *wāc,* weak; all from the Teut. verb represented by AS. *wīcan,* G. *weichen,* give way: cf. Gr. εἴκειν, yield, give way, Skt. *vij-,* move suddenly.] Liable to yield, break, or collapse under pressure or strain (as, a *weak* fastening, vessel, barrier, or fortress; a *weak* spot in armor); fragile; frail; not strong; also, deficient in bodily strength or healthy vigor, either constitutionally or from age, sickness, privation, etc. (as, a *weak* old man; *weak* eyes or nerves; "These poor wretches . . . were so *weak* they could hardly sit to their oars," Defoe's "Robinson Crusoe," ii. 2); feeble; infirm; also, deficient in mental power, intelligence, or judgment (as, a *weak* mind, intellect, or head); mentally feeble; silly; foolish; also, deficient in moral strength or firmness, resolution, or force of character, or showing or suggesting such deficiency (as, to prove *weak* under temptation; *weak* compliance; *weak* self-indulgence; "He had pale blue eyes and a *weak* mouth," Maugham's "Moon and Sixpence," viii.); also, deficient in political strength, governing power, or authority (as, a *weak* nation; a *weak* ruler or administration); also, wanting in force, potency, or efficacy (as, *weak* prayers, inducements, or influences); impotent, ineffectual, or inadequate; wanting in logical or legal force or soundness (as, a *weak* argument, case, claim, or title); wanting in rhetorical force or effectiveness (as, a *weak* sentence or conclusion; a *weak* style); also, deficient in the essential or desirable properties or ingredients (as, *weak* tea; a *weak* infusion); diluted; watery; also, deficient in amount, volume, loudness, intensity, etc. (as, *weak* tones; *weak* vibrations; a *weak* current of electricity); faint; slight; also, deficient, wanting, or poor in something specified (as, a hand *weak* in trumps; *weak* in spelling or punctuation); in *gram.,* designating or pertaining to verbs which are inflected without change of the radical vowel, as, in English, verbs which form the preterit and past participle by the addition of *-ed, -d,* or the variant *-t,* to the present, as *work* (*worked*), *spell* (*spelled* or *spelt*), *agree* (*agreed*), *deny* (*denied*) (cf. *strong*); also, designating or pertaining to nouns and adjectives, as in German, etc., inflected with the less marked case-distinctions characteristic of stems in *-n* (cf. *strong*); in *phonetics,* light (as, a *weak* stress); also, unstressed; in *pros.,* noting a verse-ending in which the metrical stress falls on a word or syllable which would not be stressed in natural utterance, as a preposition whose object (by enjambment) is carried over to the next line; in *photog.,* thin; not dense; in *com.,* tending downward in price.—**the weaker vessel,** woman: from the Biblical use, 1 Pet. iii. 7 (see *vessel*). —**weak point,** a point or part liable to give way, be injured, etc.; *fig.,* a point, as in a person's character, particularly susceptible to influences, temptation, etc.—**weak side,** *fig.,* the side of a person's character at which he is most easily influenced or affected.

weak-en (wē′kn), *v. i.* or *t.* To become or make weak or weaker.—**weak′en-er,** *n.*—**weak′en-ing-ly,** *adv.*

weak-fish (wēk′fish), *n.* Any of the sciænoid food-fishes constituting the genus *Cynoscion,* as *C. regalis* (the common weakfish, or squeteague) of the Atlantic and Gulf coasts of the U. S.: so called from the tender mouth, which is easily torn by the hook.

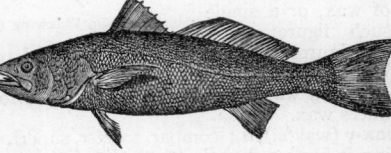

Common Weakfish (*Cynoscion regalis*).

weak=kneed (wēk′nēd), *a.* Having weak knees; fig., yielding readily to opposition, intimidation, etc.; showing lack of moral firmness (as, "a weak-kneed confession of fear": Kipling's "Light That Failed," xiv.).

weak-ling (wēk′ling), *n.* A weak or feeble creature (physically or morally).

weak-ly (wēk′li), *a.*; compar. *weaklier*, superl. *weakliest.* Weak or feeble in constitution; not robust; sickly.—**weak′ly**, *adv.* In a weak manner.

weak=mind-ed (wēk′mīn′ded), *a.* Having or showing a weak mind or feeble intellect; also, having or showing a want of firmness of mind.—**weak′=mind′ed-ness**, *n.*

weak-ness (wēk′nes), *n.* The state or quality of being weak; feebleness; also, a weak point, as in a person's character (as, "He could judge motives . . . and play upon *weaknesses*": W. Churchill's "Mr. Crewe's Career," iv.); a slight fault or defect; a failing or foible; sometimes, a self-indulgent inclination or liking for something; a tenderness.

weal[1] (wēl), *n.* [AS. *wela, weola*, prosperity, riches, akin to *wel*, E. *well*[2].] Well-being, prosperity, or happiness (archaic: as, in *weal* or woe; "intelligent men, zealous only for the public *weal*," W. H. Hudson's "Green Mansions," i.); also, wealth† or riches†; also, the state† or body politic† (cf. *commonweal*).

weal[2] (wēl), *n.* [= *wale*[2].] A wale or welt.

Weald (wēld), *n.* [ME. *wæld*, < AS. *weald*, forest: see *wold*[1].] A district of southeastern England, anciently abounding in forests, comprising parts of the counties of Kent, Surrey, Hampshire, and Sussex; [*l. c.*] an open country (poetic: as, "She . . . Fled all night long by glimmering waste and *weald*," Tennyson's "Guinevere," 127).—**Weald′-en. I.** *a.* Of or pertaining to the Weald, in England; in *geol.*, noting or pertaining to a formation of the Lower Cretaceous, extensively developed in the Weald. **II.** *n.* In *geol.*, the Wealden formation.

wealth (welth), *n.* [ME. *welthe*, < *wele*, E. *weal*[1].] Well-being or prosperity (obs. or archaic: as, "Let no man seek his own, but every man another's *wealth*," 1 Cor. x. 24); also, the state of being rich, or affluence (as, in poverty or in *wealth*; "persons of *wealth* and standing," Parkman's "Oregon Trail," i.); also, great store of valuable possessions or property, or riches (as, "They had amassed *wealth*, and had adopted habits of comparative luxury," Froude's "Cæsar," xiv.; the *wealth* of a temple, of a city, or of the Indies); valuable or valued property (as, "five fine camels, his only *wealth* in this world," Kinglake's "Eöthen," xxiii.; "rough goods, such as make the *wealth* of foresters," Stevenson's "Master of Ballantrae," xii.); rich or valuable contents or produce (as, the *wealth* of the mine, the soil, or the sea); fig., a rich abundance or profusion of anything (as, a *wealth* of golden hair; a *wealth* of imagery); in *polit. econ.*, all things having a value in money, in exchange, or in use; anything having utility and capable of being appropriated or exchanged.—**wealth′y**, *a.*; compar. *wealthier*, superl. *wealthiest.* Of or for well-being or prosperity, or goodly (obs. or archaic: as, "Thou broughtest us out into a *wealthy* place," Ps. lxvi. 12); also, possessed of wealth, or rich (as, a *wealthy* person, family, or nation; "*wealthy* corporations," Roosevelt's "Hunting Trips of a Ranchman," i.); characterized by, pertaining to, or suggestive of wealth (as, persons in *wealthy* circumstances; a *wealthy* appearance); of the nature of wealth, rich, or valuable (as, "swift vessels and their *wealthy* freight": Wiffen's tr. Tasso's "Jerusalem Delivered," i. 79); also, rich or abounding (*with*: as, "Twelve great windows blazon Arthur's wars . . . one . . . *Wealthy* with wandering lines of mount and mere," Tennyson's "Holy Grail," 252); in general, rich in character, quality, or amount; abundant or ample.—**wealth′i-ly**, *adv.*—**wealth′i-ness**, *n.*

wean (wēn), *v. t.* [AS. *wenian*, accustom, wean; akin to E. *won*[1].] To accustom (a child or young animal) to food other than its mother's milk; withdraw in the habit of feeding (*from*: as, to *wean* a child from the breast); fig., to withdraw from any object or form of habit or enjoyment (usually with *from*: as, "Riper years will *wean* him from such toys," Marlowe's "Edward II.," i. 4; to *wean* a person from idle ways or cherished ideas); disengage or alienate in practice, inclination, liking, etc.—**wean**, *n.* An infant; a child.

[Sc. and prov. Eng.]—**wean′er**, *n.* One who or that which weans; a metal guard fixed to the nose of a sucking animal, as a calf, in weaning it.—**wean′ling. I.** *n.* A child or animal newly weaned. **II.** *a.* Newly weaned.

weap-on (wep′on), *n.* [AS. *wǣpen* = D. *wapen* = G. *waffen* (now *waffe*) = Icel. *vāpn* = Goth. *wēpn* (in pl. *wēpna*), weapon: cf. *wapentake*.] Any instrument for use in attack or defense in combat, fighting, or war, as a sword, dagger, spear, arrow, club, rifle, or cannon; anything serving as an instrument for making or repelling an attack (often fig.: as, "Mrs. Heath's deadliest *weapons* were meekness and patience," W. De Morgan's "Alice-for-Short," v.); in *zoöl.*, any part or organ serving for attack or defense, as claws, horns, teeth, stings, etc.—**weap′oned**, *a.* Armed with weapons.—**weap′on-less**, *a.* Without weapons; unarmed.

wear[1] (wēr), *n.* See *weir.*

wear[2] (wār), *v. t.*; pret. *wore*, pp. *worn*, ppr. *wearing.* [AS. *werian*, clothe, wear, = OHG. *werjan* = Icel. *verja* = Goth. *wasjan*, clothe; akin to L. *vestis*, Gr. ἐσθής, clothing, Skt. *vas-*, put on.] To carry or have on the body or about the person as a covering, equipment, ornament, or the like (as, to *wear* a coat, a shawl, a hat, a collar, a ring or a watch, a helmet or a sword; to *wear* a disguise); have or use on the person habitually (as, to *wear* black; to *wear* a beard; "He . . . *wore* his long hair brushed back," J. Conrad's "Lord Jim," xv.); bear or have in the aspect or appearance (as, to *wear* a smile, or an air of triumph; to *wear* one's years well); also, to impair (garments, etc.) by wear (as, gloves *worn* at the finger-tips); in general, to impair, deteriorate, or consume gradually by use or any continued process (as, a well-*worn* volume); weary or exhaust (as, *worn* with toil or care); waste or diminish gradually by rubbing, scraping, washing, etc. (as, rocks *worn* by the waves); make (a hole, channel, way, etc.) by such action; bring, reduce, render, take, etc. (as specified), by wear, use, rubbing, or any gradual change (as, to *wear* clothes to rags, a pencil to a stub, or a person to a shadow; to *wear* a rough surface smooth; to *wear* down sharp edges; to *wear* away the bank of a stream; to *wear* off nap, paint, marks, or impressions); pass (time, etc.) gradually or tediously (commonly with *away* or *out*); *naut.*, to bring (a vessel) on another tack by turning her head away from the wind until the wind is on her stern and then bringing her head up into the wind on the other side.—**to wear one's heart upon one's sleeve**, to expose one's feelings freely, as to a curious or ill-natured world. See Shakspere's "Othello," i. 1. 64.—**to wear out**, to wear or use until no longer fit for use (as, to *wear out* clothes, carpets, or tools); use up; exhaust by continued use, strain, or any gradual process (as, to *wear out* strength or patience; to *wear out* one's welcome, as by too frequent visits); pass (time, etc.) gradually or tediously.—**wear**[2], *v. i.* To be commonly worn or used, as an article that is in the fashion† (as, "like the brooch and the toothpick, which *wear* not now": Shakspere's "All's Well," i. 1. 172); become adjusted or fitted with wear or use, as clothes to the figure; hold out or last under wear, use, or any continued strain (as, materials or colors that will *wear*, or *wear* well; a person who *wears* well, as by retaining youthful appearance or by maintaining good qualities throughout relations with others; "He's a man that'll *wear*," Mrs. Stowe's "Oldtown Folks," xxxvii.); also, to undergo gradual impairment, diminution, reduction, etc., from wear, use, attrition, or other causes (often with *away*, *down*, *out*, or *off*); pass, as time, etc., esp. slowly or tediously (often with *away* or *on*); *naut.*, of a vessel, to come round on another tack by turning away from the wind (cf. *wear*[2], *v. t.*).—**wear**[2], *n.* The act of wearing, or the state of being worn, as on the person; use, as of a garment (as, articles for winter *wear*); clothing, garments, or other articles for wearing (as, under*wear*; neck*wear*; foot*wear*); style of dress, adornment, etc., esp. the proper or the fashionable style (as, "Motley's the only *wear*": Shakspere's "As You Like It," ii. 6. 34); also, gradual impairment, wasting, diminution, etc., as from use, attrition, or other causes (as, the carpet shows *wear*; to be the worse for *wear*; to stand the *wear* and tear of daily use); also, something that has a wearing, impairing, or exhausting effect (as, "sons whose folly or extravagance is a perpetual *wear* and worry to them": S. Butler's "Way of All Flesh," ix.).

wear-a-ble (wăr′a̱-bl). **I.** *a.* Capable of or suitable for being worn. **II.** *n.* Something wearable; an article of apparel: usually in *pl.*—**wear-a-bil′i-ty** (-bil′i-ti), **wear′a-ble-ness,** *n.*

wear-er (wâr′ẽr), *n.* One who or that which wears.

wear-i-ful (wēr′i-fŭl), *a.* Wearisome; tiresome; tedious; dreary. [Chiefly Sc.]—**wear′i-ful-ly,** *adv.*

wear-i-less (wēr′i-les), *a.* Unwearying; tireless.

wear-i-ly (wēr′i-li), *adv.* In a weary manner.—**wear′i-ness,** *n.* The state or feeling of being weary; fatigue; dissatisfaction, as at something tedious.

wear-ing (wâr′ing), *p. a.* That wears; gradually impairing or wasting; wearying or exhausting.—**wear′ing-ly,** *adv.*

wear-i-some (wēr′i-sum), *a.* Causing weariness; fatiguing (as, "a difficult and *wearisome* march": G. P. R. James's "Hist. of Charlemagne," iii.); tiresome or tedious (as, a *wearisome* person, day, or book; "The platitudes you hear about love are so *wearisome*," Eden Phillpotts's "Banks of Colne," xviii.).—**wear′i-some-ly,** *adv.*—**wear′i-some-ness,** *n.*

wear-y (wēr′i), *a.*; compar. *wearier*, superl. *weariest*. [AS. *wērig*, akin to OS. *wōrig*, weary: cf. AS. *wōrian*, wander.] Exhausted physically or mentally by labor, exertion, strain, etc. (as, "The brain benumb'd, As well as the *weary* hand," Hood's "Song of the Shirt"; *weary* eyes, feet, or brain); fatigued; tired; characterized by or causing fatigue (as, a *weary* journey); also, having the patience, tolerance, or liking exhausted by too much of a thing (as, to talk until one's hearers are *weary*); impatient or dissatisfied at excess or overlong continuance (*of*: as, to be *weary* of excuses, monotony, idleness, or pleasure; "I am *weary* of my life," Gen. xxvii. 46); characterized by or causing such impatience or dissatisfaction (as, a *weary* wait; "through *weary* years of separation," Ruskin's "Crown of Wild Olive," iii.); tedious; irksome; dreary.—**wear′y,** *v.*: *wearied, wearying*. [AS. *wērigian*.] **I.** *tr.* To make weary; fatigue or tire; exhaust the patience or liking of by excess, repetition, etc. **II.** *intr.* To become weary; become fatigued or tired; grow impatient or dissatisfied at having too much of something (often with *of*); also, to long impatiently or earnestly (as, "I've been *wearying* to see ye!" Stevenson's "David Balfour," xi.: chiefly prov.).—**wear′y-ing-ly,** *adv.*

wea-sand (wē′za̱nd), *n.* [AS. *wæsend*, *wāsend*.] The windpipe or trachea.

wea-sel (wē′zl), *n.* [AS. *wesle* = D. *wezel* = G. *wiesel* = Icel. *-vīsla*, weasel.] Any of certain small carnivorous mammals of the genus *Putorius* (family *Mustelidæ*), esp. *P. vulgaris*, a common European species with a long, slender body, which feeds on rats, mice, small birds and their eggs, etc., and is noted for wariness and cunning; any

Common Weasel (*Putorius vulgaris*).

of various similar animals of other families; fig., a cunning, sneaking fellow.

weath-er¹ (wĕTH′ẽr), *n.* [AS. *weder* = D. *weder* = G. *wetter* = Icel. *vedhr*, weather; from the same root as E. *wind²*.] The state of the air or atmosphere with respect to wind, temperature, cloudiness, moisture, pressure, etc.; the atmospheric conditions prevailing at a given place and time; also, windy or stormy weather (now prov.); a wind†, storm†, or tempest†; cold and wet (now chiefly prov.: as, to keep out the *weather*).—**under the weather,** indisposed; ill; ailing. [Colloq.]—**Weather Bureau,** a bureau of the U. S. Department of Agriculture, having charge of the gathering of meteorological reports in order to forecast the weather, issue warnings of storms, floods, frost, and the like, prepare statistical records, etc.—**weath′er¹,** *a.* Of or per-

taining to the side or part, as of a ship, that is exposed to the wind (as, the *weather* bow); pertaining to, situated in, or moving toward the quarter or region from which the wind blows (as, a *weather* tide: see phrase below): chiefly *naut.*, and opposed to *lee*.—**to keep one's weather eye open,** to keep a lookout in the direction of possible danger; be on one's guard. [Colloq.]—**weather tide,** a tide running to windward, or in the direction opposite to that in which the wind is blowing.—**weath′er¹,** *v.* **I.** *tr.* To expose to the weather; dry, season, or otherwise affect by exposure to the air or atmosphere; discolor, disintegrate, or affect injuriously, as atmospheric agencies do; also, to bear up against and come safely through (a storm, etc.), as a ship or a mariner (as, "Brave lads, whatever storms may break, We've *weathered* worse of old!" H. Newbolt's "Laudabunt Alii"); fig., to go or come through (danger, trouble, etc.) without permanent damage or loss; *naut.*, of a ship, mariner, etc., to pass or sail to the windward of (as, to *weather* a cape); in *arch.*, to cause to slope, so as to shed water. **II.** *intr.* To undergo change, as discoloration or disintegration, as the result of exposure to atmospheric conditions; also, to endure or resist exposure to the weather; also, to go or come safely through a storm, etc., or, fig., danger or trouble (with *through*: as, "A feeble creature at all times, it seemed almost impossible she could *weather* through," Mrs. H. Ward's "Robert Elsmere," xxi.).

weath-er² (wĕTH′ẽr), *n.* See *wether*.

weath-er=beat-en (wĕTH′ẽr-bē″tn), *a.* Beaten by the weather; bearing evidences of exposure to the weather; seasoned or hardened by exposure to all sorts of weather: as, "a *weather-beaten* cliff" (S. R. Crockett's "Stickit Minister," ix.); "his *weather-beaten* straw hat" (S. R. Crockett's "Stickit Minister," i.); "a bronzed, *weather-beaten* face" (W. H. Hudson's "Purple Land," xv.).

weath-er=board (wĕTH′ẽr-bōrd), *n.* One of a series of thin boards, usually thicker along one edge than along the other, for nailing down on an outside wall or a roof in overlapping fashion so as to form a protective covering which will shed water.—**weath′er=board,** *v. t.* To cover or furnish with weather-boards.—**weath′er=board″ing,** *n.* The covering or facing of weather-boards or the like on a wall, roof, or building; weather-boards collectively.

weath-er=bound (wĕTH′ẽr-bound), *a.* Delayed by bad weather: as, "when their fleet of boats was *weather-bound*" (Hawthorne's "Twice-Told Tales," The Village Uncle).

weath-er=breed-er (wĕTH′ẽr-brē″dẽr), *n.* A fine, clear day, popularly supposed to betoken a coming storm.

weath-er=cock (wĕTH′ẽr-kok), *n.* A weather-vane in the shape of a cock; hence, any weather-vane; fig., any thing or person that is easily and frequently turned or swayed; a fickle or inconstant person.

weath-ered (wĕTH′ẽrd), *p. a.* Seasoned or otherwise affected by exposure to the weather or elements; esp., of wood, discolored or stained by the action of air, rain, etc., or by artificial means; of rocks, worn, disintegrated, or changed in color or composition, by the action of the elements; also, in *arch.*, made sloping or inclined, as a window-sill, to prevent the lodgment of water.

weath-er=gage (wĕTH′ẽr-gāj), *n.* The (advantageous) position of a ship when it is to windward of another ship; fig., the position of advantage; the upper hand.

weath-er=glass (wĕTH′ẽr-glås), *n.* Any of various instruments, as a barometer or a hygroscope, designed to indicate the state of the atmosphere.

weath-er-ly (wĕTH′ẽr-li), *a.* *Naut.*, making very little leeway when close-hauled: said of a boat.—**weath′er-li-ness,** *n.*

weath-er=map (wĕTH′ẽr-map), *n.* A map or chart showing weather conditions over a wide area at a particular time, compiled from simultaneous observations at different places in this area.

weath-er=most (wĕTH′ẽr-mōst), *a.* *superl.* Furthest to windward.

weath-er=proof (wĕTH′ẽr-prōf), *a.* Proof against the weather; able to withstand exposure to all kinds of weather.

weath-er=stain (wĕTH′ẽr-stān), *n.* A stain or discoloration left or produced by the weather: as, "the grey old towers of the ruin . . . bearing the rusty *weather-stains* of ages" (Scott's "Guy Mannering," iii.).—**weath′er=stained,** *a.* Bearing weather-stains.

weath-er=strip (weᴛʜ′ėr-strip), *n.* A narrow strip of material, as india-rubber, adjusted to cover the joint between a door, window-sash, or the like and the jamb, casing, etc., in order to exclude wind, rain, etc.—**weath′er=strip,** *v. t.;* -stripped, -stripping. To fit with weather-strips.

weath-er=vane (weᴛʜ′ėr-vān), *n.* A vane for indicating the direction of the wind; a weathercock.

weath-er=wise (weᴛʜ′ėr-wīz), *a.* Skilful in prognosticating the changes of the weather.

weath-er=worn (weᴛʜ′ėr-wôrn), *a.* Worn by the action of the weather.

weave (wēv), *v.;* pret. *wove* (also *weaved*), pp. *woven* (also *wove, weaved*), ppr. *weaving.* [AS. *wefan* = D. *weven* = G. *weben* = Icel. *vefa*, weave; akin to Gr. ὑφαίνειν, weave.] **I.** *tr.* To form by interlacing threads, yarns, strands, or strips of some material (as, to *weave* a web, fabric, basket, or wreath; to *weave* cloth); interlace (threads, yarns, strips, fibrous material, etc.) so as to form a fabric or texture; fig., to form by combining various elements or details into a connected whole (as, to *weave* a tale or a plot); combine (elements, etc.) into a connected whole (as, to *weave* a series of short stories into a novel); introduce as an element or detail into a connected whole (as, to *weave* an incident into a story; to *weave* a melody into a musical composition). **II.** *intr.* To weave cloth, etc.; compose any connected whole; also, to become woven or interwoven.—**weave,** *n.* The manner of weaving; a particular style of weaving (as, a plain *weave*; a twilled *weave*; a satin *weave*).—**weav′er,** *n.* One who or that which weaves; one whose occupation is the weaving of cloth or the like; also, a weaver-bird.—**weav′er=bird,** *n.* Any of numerous (chiefly African and Asiatic) passerine birds of the family *Ploceidæ*, related to the finches and notable for their elaborately woven nests, and including species ('sociable weaver-birds,' as *Philetærus socius* of South Africa) having the habit of building nests in common (see cuts at *republican* and *hive-nest*).

wea-zen (wē′zn), etc. Same as *wizen*, etc.

web (web), *n.* [AS. *webb* = D. *web* = OHG. *weppi* (cf. G. *gewebe*) = Icel. *vefr*, web; from the verb represented by E. *weave*.] That which is formed by weaving threads, yarns, strips, etc., together; a woven fabric, esp. a whole piece of cloth in the course of being woven or after it comes from the loom; also, webbing, or a woven band or the like; also, the plexus of delicate threads or filaments spun by a spider; a

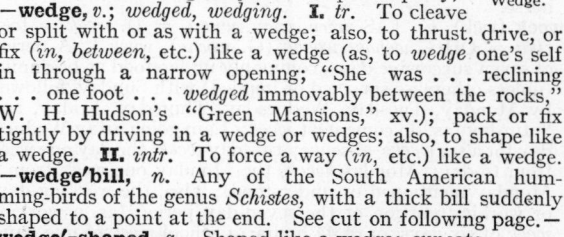

An East Indian Weaver-bird (*Ploceus philippinus*).

cobweb; a similar texture spun by certain insects, usually as a covering or protection; also, fig., something formed as by weaving or interweaving (as, the *web* of life); a tissue (as, a *web* of lies); also, something resembling or suggesting a woven fabric; a long, continuous piece of paper made on the modern paper-making machine, and formed by it into a roll (in which form it is used on a web-press); any of various thin, or sheet-like or plate-like, objects or parts, as the blade of a saw, the part of a steel girder which connects the upper and lower laterally extending portions, the corresponding part between the head and the foot of a rail, etc.; in *ornith.*, the series of barbs on each side of the shaft of a feather; sometimes, the series on both sides, collectively; in *zoöl.*, a membrane which connects the digits of an animal; esp., that which connects the toes of aquatic birds and aquatic mammals.—**webbed,** *a.* Formed like or with a web; having the digits connected by a web, as the foot of a duck (see cut in next column) or a beaver; of the digits, connected thus.—**web′bing,** *n.* Woven material of hemp,

cotton, or the like, in bands of various widths, for use where strength is required; the strip of the plain foundation fabric (without pile or filling) left for protection at the edge of some Eastern rugs, etc.; in *printing*, woven bands used to carry forward paper in a printing-machine, or such bands or leather straps used to move the bed or carriage of a hand-press; a single such band or strap; in *zoöl.*, the membrane forming a web or webs.—**web′by,** *a.* Pertaining to, of the nature of, or resembling a web; having a web or webs.—**web′=foot,** *n.;* pl. -*feet* (-fēt). A foot in which the toes are joined by a web.—**web′=foot″ed,** *a.* Having web-feet.—**web′=press,** *n.* A printing-press which is automatically supplied with its paper from a continuous web in the form of a roll; also, a printing-press in which the paper is carried forward to an impression-cylinder by means of webs, bands, or tapes.—**web′ster** (-stėr), *n.* [AS. *webbestre*, female weaver.] A weaver. [Obs. or prov.]—**web′=winged,** *a.* Having wings consisting of a large web or membrane supported and extended by the fore limbs and four elongated digits: said of bats.—**web′=worm,** *n.* Any of various more or less gregarious caterpillars, as the tent-caterpillar, *Malacosoma americana*, which spin large webs in which they rest and feed.

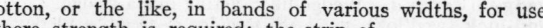

Webbed Foot of a Sea-duck.

wed (wed), *v.;* pret. *wedded*, pp. *wedded* or *wed*, ppr. *wedding.* [AS. *weddian*, < *wedd*, a pledge, = OHG. *wetti* (G. *wette*) = Icel. *vedh* = Goth. *wadi*, akin to L. *vas* (*vad*-), bail, security, also E. *wage* and *gage*[1].] **I.** *tr.* To pledge, stake, or wager (now Sc. and north. Eng.); also, to bind one's self to (a person) in marriage; take for husband or wife; also, to unite (a couple) or join (one person to another) in marriage or wedlock; marry; fig., to bind by close or lasting ties (as, "The latter seemed *wedded* to his profession and his ship": Cooper's "Two Admirals," xi.); attach firmly (as, to be *wedded* to a theory); also, to espouse (a cause)†. **II.** *intr.* To contract marriage; marry; fig., to become united as if in wedlock.—**wed′ding,** *n.* [AS. *weddung*.] The act or ceremony of marrying; marriage; nuptials; also, a celebration of an anniversary of a marriage (as, a paper *wedding*, celebrated on the 1st anniversary with gifts made esp. of paper; similarly, a wooden (5th), tin (10th), crystal (15th), china (20th), silver (25th), golden (50th), or diamond (75th, or 60th) *wedding*).—**wed′ding=cake,** *n.* A cake, usually a dark fruit-cake, distributed in portions to guests at a wedding, pieces being sent to absent friends.—**wed′ding=ring,** *n.* A ring given at a wedding ceremony to one of the couple, esp. the bride, by the other: commonly a plain gold ring, worn constantly on the third finger (ring-finger) of the left hand, and regarded as an indication of marriage.

wedge (wej), *n.* [AS. *wecg* = D. *wig* = Icel. *veggr*, a wedge.] A device (one of the so-called simple machines) consisting of a piece of hard material with two principal faces meeting in a sharply acute angle, thus producing an edge which is used for cleaving, splitting, separating, etc.; hence, a piece of anything of like shape (as, a *wedge* of pie or cheese); also, something that serves to part, divide, etc. (as, this served as an entering *wedge* to disrupt the party).—**wedge,** *v.* **I.** *tr.* To cleave or split with or as with a wedge; also, to thrust, drive, or fix (*in, between*, etc.) like a wedge (as, to *wedge* one's self in through a narrow opening; "She was . . . reclining . . . one foot . . . *wedged* immovably between the rocks," W. H. Hudson's "Green Mansions," xv.); pack or fix tightly by driving in a wedge or wedges; also, to shape like a wedge. **II.** *intr.* To force a way (*in*, etc.) like a wedge.—**wedge′bill,** *n.* Any of the South American humming-birds of the genus *Schistes*, with a thick bill suddenly shaped to a point at the end. See cut on following page.—**wedge′=shaped,** *a.* Shaped like a wedge; cuneate.

Wedge.

Wedg-wood (wej′wud), *a.* Pertaining to, or made or originated by, Josiah Wedgwood (1730–95), the great English potter: as, *Wedgwood* ware (particularly, a type of artistic pottery with tinted ground and white decoration in relief in designs patterned after Greek and Roman models).

wedg-y (wej′i), *a.* Wedge-like; acting like a wedge.

wed-lock (wed′lok), *n.* [AS. *wedlāc*, < *wedd*, a pledge, + *lāc*, a gift.] The state of marriage; matrimony: as, "He mentioneth the king's living in *wedlock* with Queen Katharine twenty years" (Strype's "Memorials of Cranmer," i. 2).

Wedgebill (*Schistes personatus*).

Wednes-day (wenz′dā), *n.* [AS. *Wōdnes dæg*,'Woden's day': cf. *Woden*.] The fourth day of the week, following Tuesday.

wee (wē). [ME. *we*, in *a litill we*, a little bit, appar. orig. 'a little *way*': cf. *way²*.] **I.** *n.* A bit; a short distance; a short space of time. [Now Sc. and prov. Eng.] **II.** *a.* Little; very small: as, "a *wee* little native bear, barely eight inches long" (H. Kingsley's "Geoffry Hamlyn," xxx.). [Orig. Sc. and prov. Eng.]

weed¹ (wēd), *n.* [AS. *wǣd*.] A garment or, *pl.* or *sing.*, clothing or dress (as, "Little Pearl was not clad in rustic *weeds*," Hawthorne's "Scarlet Letter," vi.; "Tired nymphs, stripping the silken *weed* From off their limbs," W. Morris's "Jason," iii. 367: archaic or prov., except as in the following use); *pl.*, mourning garments (as, widow's *weeds*); also, *sing.*, a mourning band of black crape or cloth, as on a man's hat or coat-sleeve.

weed² (wēd), *n.* [AS. *wēod*.] A plant occurring obtrusively in cultivated ground to the exclusion or injury of the desired crop; any useless, troublesome, or noxious plant, esp. one that grows profusely; wild vegetation (archaic: as, "A . . . pard . . . Crouch'd fawning in the *weed*," Tennyson's "Œnone," 197); also, tobacco (with *the*), or a cigar (colloq.); also, a long-limbed, thin, ungainly or weakly person or animal; a sorry animal, esp. a horse unfit for racing or breeding purposes.—**weed²**, *v.* [AS. *wēodian*.] **I.** *tr.* To free from weeds or troublesome plants (as, to *weed* a garden); root out or remove (a plant) as being a weed (often with *out*); fig., to rid of what is undesirable or superfluous (as, "The Senate was at once *weeded* of many of its disreputable members": Froude's "Cæsar," x.); remove as being undesirable or superfluous (often with *out*). **II.** *intr.* To remove weeds or the like.—**weed′ed**, *a.* Overgrown with weeds.—**weed′er**, *n.* One who or that which weeds; any implement or machine for freeing land from weeds.—**weed′less**, *a.* Free from weeds.—**weed′y**, *a.*; compar. *weedier*, superl. *weediest.* Abounding with weeds; consisting of or pertaining to weeds; weed-like; of a poor, straggling growth, as a plant; long-limbed, thin, and ungainly or weakly, as a person or animal; unfit for racing or breeding purposes, as a horse.

week (wēk), *n.* [AS. *wice*, *wicu*, *wucu*, = D. *week* = Icel. *vika* = OHG. *wehha*, *wohha* (G. *woche*), week.] A period of seven successive days, commonly understood as beginning (unless otherwise specified or implied) with Sunday, followed by Monday, Tuesday, Wednesday, Thursday, Friday, and Saturday (as, do come next *week*; I am going away Wednesday for a six *weeks'* absence; this day *week*, the day one week from to-day; Monday *week*, the Monday one week from a Monday mentioned or understood); also, the working-days or working portion of the seven-day period (as, a working *week* of six days, or of 44 hours; a school *week* of five days; to earn $50 a *week*).—**Holy Week.** See under *holy, a.*—**week of Sundays,** a period long enough to include seven Sundays; an indefinitely long time. [Colloq.]—**week′=day.** **I.** *n.* Any day of the week except Sunday. **II.** *a.* Of or on a week-day: as, *week-day* occupations.—**week′=end,** *n.*

The end of the week; the period from Friday night or Saturday to Monday, as a time for recreation, visiting, etc. (orig. Eng.).—**week′=end,** *v. i.* To pass the week-end, as at a place: as, "He . . . *week-ended* at Shonts" (H. G. Wells's "Bealby," v.).—**week′=end-er,** *n.*—**week′ly. I.** *a.* Pertaining to a week, or to each week; also, done, happening, appearing, etc., once a week, or every week; also, continuing for a week. **II.** *n.*; pl. *-lies* (-liz). A periodical appearing once a week. **III.** *adv.* Once a week; by the week.

weel (wēl), *adv.* and *a.* Sc. and north. Eng. form of *well²*.

ween (wēn), *v. t.* or *i.* [AS. *wēnan*, < *wēn*, expectation, belief, = D. *waan*, G. *wahn*, delusion, = Icel. *vān*, Goth. *wēns*, expectation: cf. *overween*.] To expect, think, or suppose: as, "They . . . Stood . . . by force or fraud *Weening* to prosper" (Milton's "Paradise Lost," vi. 795); "Launcelot Far away, I *ween*" (W. Morris's "Chapel in Lyoness," 41). [Archaic.]

weep¹ (wēp), *n.* [Imit. of its note.] The lapwing, *Vanellus cristatus.*

weep² (wēp), *v.*; *wept, weeping.* [AS. *wēpan*, akin to OS. *wōpian*, OHG. *wuofan*, Goth. *wōpjan*, cry aloud.] **I.** *intr.* To manifest grief or anguish, orig. by outcry, now by tears; shed tears, as from sorrow, unhappiness, or any overpowering emotion (as, to *weep* for joy or rage); cry; hence, to let fall drops of water or liquid (as, "His broad felt hat was *weeping* about his ears with the drizzling moisture of the evening": Parkman's "Oregon Trail," vi.); drip; rain; exude water or liquid, as soil, rock, a plant-stem, a sore, etc.; gather moisture from the atmosphere in drops upon the surface, as a glass of ice-water or a cool metal pipe in humid air; of a liquid, to fall or issue in drops; also, of trees, etc., to have drooping branches (see *weeping*). **II.** *tr.* To weep for; mourn with tears or other expression of sorrow (as, "He *wept* the fate of his brother": Gibbon's "Decline and Fall of the Roman Empire," xli.); also, to shed (tears, etc.); let fall or give forth in drops (as, "groves whose rich trees *wept* odorous gums and balm": Milton's "Paradise Lost," iv. 248); also, to pass, bring, put, etc., with the shedding of tears (with *away, out,* etc.: as, to *weep* one's life away; to *weep* one's eyes out; to *weep* one's self to sleep).—**weep²**, *n.* Weeping, or a fit of weeping, or shedding tears; also, exudation of water or liquid.—**weep′er**, *n.* One who weeps, or sheds tears; a hired mourner at a funeral; also, something worn as a badge of mourning, as a widow's long black veil or a long scarf-like hatband formerly worn by men at funerals (colloq. or prov.); also, *pl.*, long side-whiskers (colloq.: as, "He wore an immense pair of drooping auburn whiskers, of the kind that used to be called Piccadilly *weepers*," Du Maurier's "Trilby," i.).—**weep′ing**, *p. a.* That weeps; shedding tears; letting fall or exuding water or liquid; gathering moisture upon the surface; of trees, etc., having slender, drooping branches; of a drooping or pendulous habit. —**weeping sinew,** a gathering of fluid in the synovial sheath of a tendon; a ganglion. [Colloq.]—**weeping willow,** a large willow, *Salix babylonica*, with very long, slender, pendulous branches: taken as an emblem of mourning, and often planted in graveyards.—**weep′ing-ly,** *adv.*—**weep′y,** *a.* Inclined to weep, or tearful (colloq.: as, "The bold dragoon sang . . . with such pathos . . . that his audience felt almost *weepy*," Du Maurier's "Trilby," iv.); also, exuding moisture, oozy, or moist (prov. Eng.).

wee-ver (wē′vér), *n.* [Cf. F. *vive*, weever, for *vivre*, OF. *vivre*, viper: see *wivern*.] Either of two small marine fishes of the genus *Trachinus* (family *Trachinidæ*), *T. draco* ('greaterweever') and *T. vipera* ('lesser weever'), common in British waters, notable for their sharp dorsal and other spines with which they

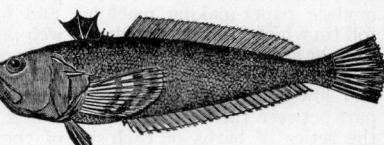
Lesser Weever (*Trachinus vipera*).

are able to inflict painful and serious wounds; also, any fish of the same family.

wee-vil (wē′vl), *n.* [AS. *wifel* = G. *wiebel*.] Any of the numerous, mostly small beetles constituting the group *Rhynchophora*, whose larvæ are destructive to nuts, grain, fruit, the stems of leaves, the pith of trees, etc.; a snout-beetle; also, any of various other similarly destructive beetles (family *Bruchidæ*); also, any of certain moths, etc., destructive to stored grain, etc. — **wee′viled, wee′villed,** *a.* Infested with weevils.   Also **wee′vil-y, wee′vil-ly.**

weft (weft), *n.* [AS. *weft, wefta,* < *wefan,* E. *weave.*] In *weaving,* the threads that run across the web from side to side; the threads that cross the warp; the woof.

wei-ge-la (wī-jē′lä), *n.* [NL. *Weigela,* also *Weigelia;* named from C. E. *Weigel,* German botanist.] Any of various shrubby caprifoliaceous plants, native in eastern Asia, including species or varieties familiar in cultivation, with funnel-shaped white, pink, or crimson flowers: these plants being classed as a separate genus, *Weigela,* or, now more commonly, included in the genus *Diervilla.* Also **wei-ge′li-a** (-li-ä).

weigh¹ (wā), *n.* Erroneous form of *way²,* sometimes used in the phrase *under weigh* (for *under way*): as, "The barque was about to get *under weigh*" (H. Melville's "Typee," xxxiii.).

weigh² (wā), *v.* [AS. *wegan,* carry, move, = D. *wegen,* weigh, = G. *wegen,* move, = Icel. *vega,* carry, move, weigh, = Goth. *-wigan,* move; akin to L. *vehere,* carry, Skt. *vah-,* carry, travel: cf. *vehicle, wain,* and *way².*] **I.** *tr.* To

Weigela (*Diervilla japonica*).

raise or lift (now chiefly in the phrase 'to weigh anchor,' to raise a ship's anchor from the water in order to set out on a voyage); also, to hold up or balance (something), as in the hand, in order to estimate the weight; ascertain the weight of by means of a balance, scale, or other mechanical device (as, to *weigh* gold, sugar, gases, persons, cattle, a load of coal, etc.); measure (a certain quantity of something) according to weight (usually with *out:* as, to *weigh* out five pounds of sugar); also, to bear (*down*) by weight (as, to *weigh* down one arm of a balance; a bough *weighed* down by fruit); fig., to bear (*down*) as with heaviness, oppression, etc. (as, eyelids *weighed* down by sleep; to be *weighed* down with care); also, to balance in the mind (as, to *weigh* one consideration with or against another; "Yet life I hold but idle breath, When love or honour's *weigh'd* with death," Scott's "Lady of the Lake," iv. 17); consider carefully in order to reach an opinion, decision, or choice (as, to *weigh* facts, possibilities, a matter, or a proposal; to *weigh* one's words, to consider and choose them carefully in speaking or writing); also, to regard† or esteem† (as, "My person; which I *weigh* not, Being of those virtues vacant": Shakspere's "Henry VIII.," v. 1. 124). **II.** *intr.* To weigh anchor (see *weigh², v. t.*: as, "The next day we *weighed,* and stood away southerly," Defoe's "Captain Singleton," xiii.); also, to be weighed, or have one's weight ascertained (hence, to *weigh out,* or *in,* of a jockey, to be weighed before, or after, a race); have weight or heaviness (as indicated: as, to *weigh* little or less; to *weigh* a ton); fig., to have importance, moment, or consequence (as, such considerations do not *weigh* with us; his wealth *weighs* little in this case); also, to consider carefully or judicially (as, *weigh* well before deciding); also, to bear down as a weight or burden (as, such responsibility *weighed* upon him; "These letters *weighed* heavily upon Mr. Britling's mind," H. G. Wells's "Mr. Britling," ii. 4. § 15). — **weigh²,** *n.* A particular quantity or measure, estimated by weight. — **weigh′a-ble,** *a.* Capable of being weighed. — **weigh′=bridge,** *n.* A weighing-machine with a platform on which cattle, loaded carts, etc., are weighed. — **weigh′er,** — **weigh′ing=ma-chine″,** *n.* Any of various forms of machine for weighing.

weight (wāt), *n.* [AS. *wiht, gewiht,* akin to D. and G. *gewicht,* Icel. *vætt,* weight; from the root of E. *weigh².*] That property by which a body tends toward the center of the earth; heaviness; ponderousness; amount of heaviness, that is, the measure of a body's tendency toward the center of the earth, being a value which varies with the altitude and latitude of the body, but which is often taken as the measure of mass or quantity of matter, a value which does not so vary; also, a body of determinate mass, as of metal, for using on a balance or scale in measuring the weight or mass of (or weighing) objects, substances, etc.; also, a system of units for expressing weight or mass (as, avoirdupois *weight*); a unit of weight or mass; also, a quantity of a substance determined by weighing (as, a half-ounce *weight* of gold-dust; to measure out small *weights* of sugar or flour); also, any heavy mass or object, esp. an object used because of its heaviness (as, a *weight* of rock; a lead *weight;* the *weights* of a clock); also, fig., pressure or oppressive force, as of something burdensome (as, to sink under the *weight* of cares, sorrows, responsibilities, etc.); a burden, as of care or responsibility (as, "You have . . . removed a *weight* from my mind": Marryat's "King's Own," xxiii.); also, importance, moment, consequence, or effective influence (as, the fact has little *weight* here; an opinion of great *weight;* "The popular faction at Rome . . . was led by men of *weight,*" Froude's "Cæsar," viii.). — **weight,** *v. t.* To add weight to; load with additional weight; attach a weight or weights to; burden with or as with weight (as, to be *weighted* with years); in *dyeing,* to load (fabrics, threads, etc.) with mineral or other matter in order to increase the weight and bulk (as, to *weight* silk). — **weight′i-ly,** *adv.* In a weighty manner; heavily; ponderously; momentously; forcibly. — **weight′i-ness,** *n.* — **weight′less,** *a.* Without weight; light; unimportant. — **weight′y,** *a.;* compar. *weightier,* superl. *weightiest.* Having considerable weight; heavy; ponderous; hence, burdensome or onerous (as, "the *weightier* cares of sovereignty": J. F. Kirk's "Charles the Bold," iv. 1); also, important or momentous (as, "*weighty* negotiations": J. Conrad's "Rescue," vi. 2); influential (as, "a *weighty* merchant and selectman of Boston": Hawthorne's "Twice-Told Tales," The Great Carbuncle); forcible or cogent (as, *weighty* arguments).

weir (wēr), *n.* [AS. *wer* = G. *wehr,* weir, dam; from the root of AS. *werian,* G. *wehren,* defend: cf. *garrison.*] A dam in a river or stream to stop and raise the water, as for conducting it to a mill, for purposes of irrigation, etc.; also, a fence, as of brush or narrow boards, set in a stream, channel, etc., for catching fish; in *engin.,* an obstruction placed across a stream in order to cause the water to pass through a particular opening or notch, in order to measure the quantity flowing or discharging in a given time.

weird (wērd), *n.* [AS. *wyrd,* fate, destiny, < *weorthan,* become, happen: see *worth¹.*] Fate or destiny (archaic or Sc.: as, "Let me spae your *weird* to ye," Stevenson's "David Balfour," iii.; to dree one's *weird,* see *dree¹*); [*cap.*] Fate personified, or one of the Fates (obs. or archaic); also [*l. c.*], a prophecy† or prediction†; a story of the supernatural†. — **weird,** *a.* Concerned with fate or destiny (as, the *weird* sisters, the Fates, also three prophetic witches in Shakspere's "Macbeth"); also, involving or suggesting the supernatural; unearthly or uncanny; unnaturally or mysteriously wild or strange (as, a *weird* scene, light, or sound; "this last, dim, *weird* battle of the west," Tennyson's "Passing of Arthur," 94); also, startlingly or extraordinarily singular, odd, or queer (colloq.: as, a *weird* get-up; *weird* notions of elegance; "These Moncreiffs are rather *weird,*" Arnold Bennett's "Lion's Share," x.). — **weird′ly,** *adv.* — **weird′ness,** *n.*

Weis-mann-ism (vīs′män-izm), *n.* The theories and teachings of the German biologist August Weismann (1834–1914), esp. his theory respecting germ-plasm as the material basis of heredity, with the accompanying doctrine that acquired characters are not and cannot be inherited.

weiss=beer (vīs′bēr), *n.* [G. *weissbier,* 'white beer.'] A light-colored, highly effervescent beer prepared largely from malted wheat.

we-jack (wē′jak), *n.* [N. Amer. Ind.: cf. *woodchuck.*] The fisher, *Mustela pennanti.*

we-ka (wē′kä), *n.* [Maori.] Any of several large flightless New Zealand rails constituting the genus *Ocydromus.* See cut on following page.

welch (welch), etc.   See *welsh²,* etc.

wel-come (wel′kum). [AS. *wilcuma,* a welcome comer, < *wil-,* akin to *willa,* will, pleasure, + *cuma,* one who comes.] **I.** *interj.* A word of kindly greeting as to one whose coming

gives pleasure: as, *welcome*, stranger; *welcome* home.
II. *a.* Gladly received, as one whose coming gives pleasure
(as, a *wel-
come* vis-
itor; to re-
fuse to go
where one
is not *wel-
c o m e*) ;
h e n c e ,
agreeable,
as some-
thing com-
ing, occur-
ring, or ex-
perienced
(as, a *wel-
come* letter;
a *welcome*
opportu-

Weka (*Ocydromus australis*).

nity, change, sight, or rest); also, gladly or freely permitted (to
do something: as, you are *welcome* to take what you need);
given full right (to something) by the cordial consent of
others (as, he is *welcome* to anything he can find); free to
enjoy courtesies, etc., without being under obligation (used
in conventional response to thanks: as, you are quite *welcome*).—**wel′come**, *v. t.*; -comed, -coming. [AS. *wil-
cumian.*] To greet the coming of (a person, etc.) with
pleasure or kindly courtesy; hence, in general, to receive or
regard as welcome (as, to *welcome* a change; to *welcome*
suggestions).—**wel′come**, *n.* The act of welcoming; a
kindly greeting or reception, as of one whose coming gives
pleasure (as, to give one a warm *welcome*).—**wel′come-ly**,
adv.—**wel′come-ness**, *n.*—**wel′com-er**, *n.*

weld[1] (weld), *n.* [ME. *welde*, *wolde*: cf. MLG. *wolde*, D.
wouw, G. *wau.*] A mignonette, *Reseda luteola*, a native of
southern Europe, yielding a yellow dye; also, the dye.
weld[2] (weld), *v.* [Prob. from Scand., and akin to E. *well*[1].]
I. *tr.* To unite or consolidate (pieces of metal, etc.) by hammering, compression, or the like, esp. after rendering soft or
pasty by heat, and sometimes with the addition of fusible
material like or unlike the pieces to be united (as, iron can
be *welded* at a white heat; glass can be *welded* when heated
to stickiness; rails, etc., can be *welded* by means of thermit);
fig., to bring into intimate union (as, "to *weld* together into
one people the representatives of these numerous and widely
different races": Roosevelt's "Winning of the West," i. 5).
II. *intr.* To undergo welding; be capable of being welded.
—**weld**[2], *n.* A welding or being welded; a welded junction or joint.—**weld′a-ble**, *a.* Capable of being welded.—
weld′er, *n.*

wel-fare (wel′fār), *n.* [ME. *welfare*: see *well*[2] and *fare*.]
The state of faring well: well-being (as, to have one's *welfare*
at heart; to labor for the physical or moral *welfare* of
society); also, condition with respect to well-being (as,
"He asked them of their *welfare*, and said, Is your father
well?" Gen. xliii. 27).—**wel′fare=work**, *n.* Work devoted
to the welfare of persons in a community, employees of an
industrial or business establishment, or the like. Cf. *social
work*, under *social*, *a.*—**wel′fare=work″er**, *n.*

wel-i (wel′ē),
n. [A r.
walī.] In
M o h a m -
medan coun-
tries, a saint
o r h o l y
man; hence,
a tomb or
shrine of a
saint, com-
m o n l y a
d o m e d
structure.
welk (welk),
v. i. or *t.*
[ME. *wel-
ken* = D.

Weli.

and G. *welken*, fade, wither: cf. *wilt*[1].] To wilt or wither
(now prov. Eng. and Sc.); also, to decline† or cause to de-
cline†; decrease†.
wel-kin (wel′kin), *n.* [ME. *welkne*, *wolkne*, < AS. *wolcnu*,
clouds, pl. of *wolcen* = D. *wolk* = G. *wolke*, cloud.] The
sky; the vault of heaven: as, "The *welkin* rang with their
shouts" (Irving's "Captain Bonneville," ii.). [Archaic.]
well[1] (wel), *v.* [AS. *wellan*, *wyllan*, secondary form of
weallan = OS. and OHG. *wallan* (G. *wallen*), boil, well up.]
I. *intr.* To rise, spring, or gush from the earth or some
source, as water, etc. (often with *up*, *out*, or *forth*); hence,
to rise or issue as if by a swelling flow (as, tears *well* up to
the eyes; "The generous blood *welled* up under the clear
olive skin," F. M. Crawford's "Mr. Isaacs," iii.; tenderness
wells from the heart; words *well* forth from the lips). **II.** *tr.*
To send welling up or forth: as, "some classic fountain, that
had once *welled* its pure waters in a sacred shade" (Irving's
"Sketch-Book," Roscoe).—**well**[1], *n.* [AS. *wella*, *wylla*.]
A spring or natural source of water; a fountain, fountainhead, or well-spring (often fig.: as, "Dan Chaucer, *well*
of English undefyled," Spenser's "Faerie Queene," iv. 2. 32);
also, a hole, pit, or shaft (often walled or lined) sunk in the
ground, as by digging or boring, in order to obtain a supply
of water, or of other fluid, as brine, petroleum, or natural gas,
from a subterranean source (as, an artesian *well*: see *artesian*); hence, any sunken or deep, inclosed space, as a shaft
for air or light, or for stairs, an elevator, or the like, extending vertically through the floors of a building; a compartment
or inclosure around a ship's pumps to render them easy of
access and protect them from being injured by the cargo;
an inclosed space before the judges' bench in English courts
of law, for the lawyers and their assistants; also, a vessel,
receptacle, or reservoir for a liquid (as, an ink-*well*; a *well*-
platter or *well*-dish, a platter with a hollow for gravy); also,
a whirlpool; a powerful or dangerous eddy in the sea, as
about the Orkney and Shetland Islands.

well[2] (wel), *adv.*; compar. *better*, superl. *best.* [AS. *wel* = D.
wel = Icel. *vel* = OHG. *wela*, later *wola* (G. *wohl*), = Goth.
waila, well, orig. 'as wished': from the root of E. *will*[1].]
In a satisfactory, favorable, or advantageous manner (as,
to fare *well*; affairs are going *well*; to be *well* supplied; *well*
situated); prosperously; beneficially; conveniently; fortunately or happily (as, " 'Ah!' said the strange man, '*well*
met once more!' " Kingsley's "Yeast," xv.); approvingly
or kindly (as, to think or speak *well* of a person; to be *well*
treated); also, in general, in a good manner; commendably,
meritoriously, or excellently (as, to act, write, or reason
well; a good work *well* done); properly or fittingly; admirably or finely; with propriety, justice, or reason (as, I could
not *well* refuse; such may *well* be the case); also, in satisfactory or good measure, adequately, or sufficiently (as,
think *well* before you act); thoroughly or soundly (as, shake
well before using; to rub, knead, or beat *well*); heartily
(as, *well* pleased); also, to a considerable extent or degree
(as, a sum *well* over the amount fixed; the season is *well*
advanced; dilute the acid *well*); considerably; much; very
(see *well-nigh*); also, elliptically (as for 'it is well'), so be it,
or such being the case (as, "He may be a trifle dull. *Well*,
one can't be everything!" Du Maurier's "Trilby," viii.);
also, a mere expletive, often exclamatory, or preliminary to
further speech (as, *well*, so you have come; *well*, *well*! who
would have thought it?). The adverb *well* is much used in
compounds such as *well-bred*, *well-disposed*, *well-doer*, and
many others, mostly self-explanatory, of which only the most
common are separately entered below, many such compounds
being opposed to forms in *ill-*.—**as well, as well as.** See
as well as, under *as*[1], *adv.*—**well off**, in a satisfactory, favorable, or good position or condition (as, to know when one is
well off; "The republic . . . would perhaps be just as *well
off* without your valuable aid," W. H. Hudson's "Purple
Land," x.); esp., in good or easy circumstances as to money
or means; having a comfortable sufficiency of means;
moderately rich.—**well**[2], *a.* (usually *pred. a.*). Satisfactory
or good (as, all is *well* with us; "Striving to better, oft we
mar what's *well*," Shakspere's "King Lear," i. 4. 369); right;
proper or fitting; advisable (as, is it *well* to act so hastily?);
also, in a satisfactory position, or in good case (as, I am very
well as I am); esp., in good health, or sound in body and

mind (in this sense sometimes used attributively: as, a *well* man).

we'll (wēl). Contraction of *we will* or *we shall*.

well-a-day (wel′ạ-dā′), *interj.* Var. of *wellaway*: as, "O, *well-a-day*, that ever I was born!" (Shakspere's "Romeo and Juliet," iv. 5. 15). [Archaic.]

well=ad-vised (wel′ad-vīzd′), *a.* Acting or done with due consideration; judicious; prudent.

well=ap-point-ed (wel′ạ-poin′ted), *a.* Equipped with all due appointments or requisites: as, "remarkably fine and *well-appointed* troops" (Motley's "Dutch Republic," i. 2).

well-a-way (wel′ạ-wā′), *interj.* [ME. *weilawey*, < AS. *wei lā wei, wā lā wā,* 'woe! lo, woe!'] An exclamation of sorrow. [Archaic.]

well=bal-anced (wel′bal′ạnst), *a.* Rightly balanced, adjusted, or regulated; sensible; sane.

well=be-haved (wel′bẹ-hāvd′), *a.* Characterized by good behavior or conduct.

well=be-ing (wel′bē′ing), *n.* Good or satisfactory condition of existence; welfare: as, "A state of physical *well-being* can create a kind of joy" (Hawthorne's "Blithedale Romance," xxiv.).

well=be-lov-ed (wel′bẹ-luv′ed or -luvd′), *a.* Dearly beloved.

well=born (wel′bôrn′), *a.* Of good birth or family.

well=bred (wel′bred′), *a.* Well brought up, as persons; showing good breeding, as behavior, manners, etc.; polite; refined; also, of good breed, as a domestic animal.

well=de-fined (wel′dẹ-fīnd′), *a.* Clearly defined or indicated; distinct.

well=dis-posed (wel′dis-pōzd′), *a.* Rightly or properly disposed; well-meaning; also, favorably or kindly disposed (as, "You lose a thousand *well-disposed* hearts": Shakspere's "Richard II.," ii. 1. 206).

well=do-er (wel′dö′ėr), *n.* One who does well or acts rightly; a doer of good deeds. — **well′=do′ing,** *n.*

well=fa-vored (wel′fā′vọrd), *a.* Of pleasing appearance; good-looking; comely; handsome.

well=formed (wel′fôrmd′), *a.* Rightly or finely formed; shapely.

well=found (wel′found′), *a.* Found or proved to be good†; also, well furnished with supplies, necessaries, etc.

well=found-ed (wel′foun′ded), *a.* Rightly or justly founded, as on good grounds: as, *well-founded* beliefs or suspicions.

well=groomed (wel′grömd′), *a.* Well cared for, as in matters of the toilet: as, "his sleek and *well-groomed* visage" (Mrs. H. Ward's "Lady Rose's Daughter," iii.).

well=ground-ed (wel′groun′ded), *a.* Based on good grounds or reasons; well-founded; also, well or thoroughly instructed in the first or fundamental principles of a subject.

well=grown (wel′grōn′), *a.* Well advanced in growth.

well=head (wel′hed), *n.* A fountainhead; a source: as, "old *well-heads* of haunted rills" (Tennyson's "Eleänore," i.).

well=hole (wel′hōl), *n.* The hole or shaft of a well; a well or shaft in a building, as for a staircase; the open space about which stairs turn; also, an inclosed space within which a balancing weight rises and falls.

well=in-formed (wel′in-fôrmd′), *a.* Having reliable or full information on a subject; also, having information on a wide variety of subjects (as, a *well-informed* man).

Wellington. A British long-range heavy bomber.

well=in-ten-tioned (wel′in-ten′shọnd), *a.* Having or showing good intentions; well-meaning: as, "politicians who were clever and *well-intentioned*" (Charnwood's "Abraham Lincoln," iv.).

well=judged (wel′jujd′), *a.* Done with or resulting from good judgment; judicious.

well=known (wel′nōn′), *a.* Clearly or fully known (as, for reasons *well-known* to you); also, familiarly known, or familiar (as, "Not by the *well-known* stream . . . But unfamiliar Arno": Tennyson's "Brook," 188); also, generally or widely known (as, "Mr. Dolbiac, the *well-known* sculptor": Arnold Bennett's "Great Man," xxvi.).

well=marked (wel′märkt′), *a.* Clearly marked or distinguished; distinct; pronounced.

well=mean-ing (wel′mē′ning), *a.* Meaning or intending well (as, a *well-meaning* but tactless person); also, proceeding from good intentions (as, *well-meaning* attempts or efforts). — **well′=meant′** (-ment′), *a.* Done or proceeding from good

intentions: as, "a cold return for a *well-meant* kindness" (Scott's "Talisman," vii.).

well-ness (wel′nes), *n.* The state of being well.

well=nigh (wel′nī′), *adv.* Very nearly; almost: as, "this peace of *well-nigh* fifty years" (J. H. Newman's "Callista," ii.); "His journey is *well-nigh* over" (H. Kingsley's "Geoffry Hamlyn," xliii.).

well=or-dered (wel′ôr′dėrd), *a.* Ordered or arranged well; well-regulated.

well=read (wel′red′), *a.* Having read much, as in some field of knowledge or interest (as, "He . . . was *well read* in science": W. H. Hudson's "Far Away and Long Ago," xix.); also, having an extensive and intelligent knowledge of books or literature.

well=reg-u-lat-ed (wel′reg′ụ-lā-ted), *a.* Regulated well, kept in due order, or well-ordered (as, a *well-regulated* household, mind, or life; "social virtues not to be disregarded in any *well-regulated* community," Mrs. Stowe's "Oldtown Folks," v.); hence, in general, being what a person or thing should be (as, "He was to return as any respectable, *well-regulated* prodigal ought to return — abject, broken-hearted, asking forgiveness": S. Butler's "Way of All Flesh," lxxxii.).

wells-ite (welz′īt), *n.* [From H. L. *Wells*, American chemist.] A mineral, a hydrous silicate of aluminium, barium, calcium, and potassium, occurring in vitreous, colorless or white crystals.

well=spok-en (wel′spō′kn), *a.* Speaking well, fittingly, or pleasingly; refined, decorous, or polite in speech; fair-spoken; also, spoken well.

well=spring (wel′spring), *n.* A fountainhead: now usually fig.

well=timed (wel′tīmd′), *a.* Fittingly timed; opportune; timely: as, "Wisdom's triumph is *well-timed* retreat" (Pope's "Moral Essays," ii. 225).

well=to-do (wel′tö-dö′), *a.* Having a sufficiency of means for comfortable living, well off, or prosperous (as, "fat, very *well-to-do* folk . . . from outlying farms": S. Butler's "Way of All Flesh," xv.); also, characterized by or showing a comfortable sufficiency of means, or prosperity (as, persons in *well-to-do* circumstances; cottages of *well-to-do* appearance). — **well′=to=do′ness,** *n.*

well=turned (wel′tėrnd′), *a.* Turned or shaped well, as with rounded or curving form (as, a *well-turned* ankle); also, gracefully or happily expressed (as, a *well-turned* compliment; "a few *well-turned* paragraphs . . . in the Bishop's most approved style," Motley's "Dutch Republic," i. 3).

well=wish-er (wel′wish′ėr), *n.* One who wishes well to a person, a cause, etc.: as, "Jones . . . was a hearty *well-wisher* to the glorious cause of liberty" (Fielding's "Tom Jones," vii. 11). — **well′=wish′ing,** *n.*

well=worn (wel′wôrn′), *a.* Much worn or affected by use (as, *well-worn* garments or carpets; a *well-worn* volume); fig., trite, hackneyed, or stale (as, a *well-worn* saying or theme); sometimes, fittingly or becomingly worn or borne (as, "that *well-worn* reserve": Byron's "Lara," i. 27).

Wels-bach (welz′bak, G. vels′bäch) **burn′er.** A gas-burner devised by the Austrian chemist and inventor Karl Auer von Welsbach (born 1858), consisting essentially of a Bunsen burner about the flame of which is placed an incombustible network mantle composed of thoria with a trace of ceria, which becomes incandescent and emits a brilliant light.

Welsh[1] (welsh), *a.* [AS. *wælisc, welisc,* lit. 'foreign,' < *wealh,* a foreigner, esp. a Celt: cf. *walnut.*] Of or pertaining to Wales, its people, or their language. — **Welsh rabbit,** melted cheese, usually mixed with ale or beer, milk, etc., poured over toast. Also (erroneously) *Welsh rarebit.* —

Welsh[1], *n.* The people of Wales; also, the language of Wales, a dialect of Celtic of the Cymric group.

welsh[2] (welsh), *v. t.* or *i.* [Origin uncertain; perhaps from *Welsh,* personal name, or from *Welsh*[1].] To cheat by failing to pay a bet (used of an absconding book-maker or stake-holder at a horse-race); in general, to cheat by evading the payment of a debt or the fulfilment of any obligation. [Slang.] — **welsh′er,** *n.*

Welsh-man (welsh′mạn), *n.; pl.* -men. A man of the Welsh race.

welt (welt), *n.* [ME. *welte,* appar. < *welten,* roll: see *welter*[1].] A strengthening or ornamental hem, binding, or

---

other finish along the edge of a garment, etc.; a strip of material, a covered cord, or the like, sewed in or along a seam; a thickened or raised seam, as one formed by overlapping edges; a strip of leather set in between the edges of the inner sole and upper and the outer sole of a shoe; also, a strip of wood or metal fastened over a butt-joint to strengthen it; also, a ridge or wale on the surface of the body, as from the stroke of a stick or whip, or a stroke of this kind (colloq.).—**welt**, *v. t.* To furnish with a welt or welts; also, to beat soundly, as with a stick or whip (colloq.).

wel-ter[1] (wel'tėr), *v. i.* [ME. *weltren*, freq. of *welten*, < AS. *wyltan*, roll, akin to Icel. *velta*, Goth. *waltjan*, G. *wälzen*, *walzen*, roll: cf. *waltz*.] To roll, toss, or heave, as waves, the sea, etc. (as, "The waves Whelmed the degraded race, and *weltered* o'er their graves": Bryant's "The Ages," xviii.); also, to roll or tumble about, or wallow, as animals (also fig.: as, "Happier are those that *welter* in their sin, Swine in the mud," Tennyson's "Holy Grail," 767); also, to lie bathed or be drenched in something, esp. blood (as, "At his feet lay *weltering* in blood George Singleton": Cooper's "Spy," vii.).—**wel'ter**[1], *n.* The act of weltering; a rolling or tumbling about (as, "In the *welter* of this sea, Nothing stable is but Thee": Whittier's "Andrew Rykman's Prayer"); hence, commotion or turmoil (as, "to get away from the *welter* of our mutable world into a realm of assurance": J. H. Robinson's "Mind in the Making," iv. 8).

wel-ter[2] (wel'tėr), *a.* [From *welter-weight*.] Noting or pertaining to a horse-race in which welter-weights are carried.

wel-ter=weight (wel'tėr-wāt), *n.* [Origin uncertain: cf. *welter*[1].] An extra weight, in addition to the usual weight, carried by horses, as in steeplechases and hurdle-races; also, a boxer or wrestler intermediate in weight between a middle-weight and a light-weight.

welt-po-li-tik (velt'pō-lē-tēk'), *n.* [G., 'world-politics.'] The politics of the world; also, the policy of a nation with respect to the world.

welt-schmerz (velt'shmerts), *n.* [G., 'world-pain.'] Sorrow felt and accepted as the necessary portion of the world; sentimental pessimism.

wen (wen), *n.* [AS. *wenn* = D. *wen*.] In *pathol.*, a benign encysted tumor of the skin, esp. on the scalp, containing sebaceous matter; a sebaceous cyst.

wench (wench), *n.* [ME. *wenche*, for *wenchel*, < AS. *wencel*, child.] A child (of either sex)†; also, a female child, girl, or young woman (archaic or prov. in general sense); specif., a girl or young woman of the rustic, working, or servant class (archaic or prov.: as, "The *wench* in the kitchen sings and scours from morning to night," Steele, in "Tatler," 248); a colored girl or woman (colloq., U. S.); a lewd woman, or strumpet (archaic or prov.).—**wench**, *v. i.* To consort with strumpets.—**wench'er**, *n.*

wend[1] (wend), *v.*; *wended* (formerly also *went*), *wending*. [AS. *wendan*, turn, direct, refl. and intr. go, causative of *windan*, E. *wind*[1].] **I.** *tr.* To turn (obs. or prov. Eng.); also, to direct or pursue (one's way, etc.: now chiefly poetic or literary: as, "He *wended* his way to the riverside," Galsworthy's "Patrician," ii. 6). **II.** *intr.* To turn (obs. or prov. Eng.); also, to direct one's way, proceed, or go (archaic or prov. Eng. and Sc.: as, "I overtook the old man, who was *wending* in the same direction," Borrow's "Lavengro," iv.; "They through the palace courts began to *wend*," W. Morris's "Jason," xvi. 204: cf. *went*).

Wend[2] (wend), *n.* A member of a Slavic people dwelling in Saxony and adjoining parts of Prussia; a Sorb.—**Wend'ic**, **Wend'ish**, *a.*

went (went). Former preterit and past participle of *wend*[1], still used as preterit of *go*.

wen-tle-trap (wen'tl-trap), *n.* [D. *wenteltrap*, a winding staircase.] Any of the handsome, usually white, spiral-shelled marine gastropods constituting the genus *Scalaria* or the family *Scalariidæ*.

wept (wept). Preterit and past participle of *weep*[2].

were (wėr). [AS. *wæron*, ind. pl., Wentletrap (*Scalaria pretiosa*).

wære, subj. sing., *wæren*, subj. pl.] Ind. pl. and subj. sing. and pl. of *was*.

were'wolf, *n.* See werwolf.

wer-gild, **were-gild** (wėr'gild, wėr'-), *n.* [AS. *wergild*, < *wer*, man (see *virile*), + *gild*, *gield*, payment (see *geld*[1]).] In *old Eng. law*, a fine for manslaughter and other crimes against the person, by paying which to the relatives of the deceased in the case of manslaughter, or to the injured person in the case of a wound or the like, the offender freed himself from every further obligation or punishment.

wert (wėrt). [From *were*.] Second person sing. ind. and subj. of *was*: now only in poetic or solemn use.

wer-wolf, **were-wolf** (wėr'wulf, wēr'- or wėr'-), *n.*; pl. *-wolves* (-wulvz). [AS. *werwulf*, < *wer*, man (see *virile*), + *wulf*, wolf.] In old superstition, a human being turned into a wolf, or capable of assuming the form of a wolf, while retaining human intelligence; a lycanthrope; a loup-garou.

Wes-ley-an (wes'li-an, Brit. also wez'-). **I.** *a.* Of or pertaining to the family to which John Wesley (1703–91) and Charles Wesley (1707–88) belonged, or any member of it; esp., of or pertaining to John Wesley, the founder of Methodism; pertaining to Methodism. **II.** *n.* A follower of John Wesley; a member of the denomination founded by him; a Methodist.—**Wes'ley-an-ism**, *n.*

west (west), *adv.* [AS. *west*, adv., akin to D. *west*, adv., G. *west*, n., Icel. *vestr*, n., and perhaps to L. *vesper*, evening, the west, and Gr. ἕσπερος, of or at evening, western: see *vesper* and *Hesper*.] In the direction of the sunset; toward or in the west; also, from the west (as with reference to wind).— **to go west.** See under *go*, *v. i.*—**west**, *n.* A cardinal point of the compass, corresponding to the point where the sun is seen to set at the equinox; the direction in which this point lies; also [*l. c.* or *cap.*], a quarter or territory situated in this direction, as the western part of the U. S. in distinction from the East; [*cap.*] the western part of the world, as distinguished from the East or Orient; the Occident.—**west**, *a.* Lying toward or situated in the west; directed or proceeding toward the west; also, coming from the west, as a wind; *eccles.*, designating, lying toward, or situated in that part of a church opposite to and furthest from the altar.—**West Saxon**, the dialect of Anglo-Saxon which was spoken in the southern and southwestern parts of England, being the form of the language that was dominant for literary purposes from the time of Alfred until the Conquest. Cf. *Anglo-Saxon.*

west-er (wes'tėr), *v. i.* To move or tend toward the west: now chiefly in *westering*, *ppr.*: as, "The sun was *westering*" (Eden Phillpotts's "Banks of Colne," xiii.).

west-er-ly (wes'tėr-li). **I.** *a.* Moving, directed, or situated toward the west; also, coming from the west, as a wind (as, "a *westerly* gale": Marryat's "Mr. Midshipman Easy," xix.). **II.** *adv.* Toward the west (as, "*Westerly* from the city extended a slender strip of land": Motley's "Dutch Republic," iii. 8); also, from the west.

west-ern (wes'tėrn), *a.* [AS. *westerne*.] Lying toward or situated in the west; directed or proceeding toward the west; also, coming from the west, as a wind; also [*l. c.* or *cap.*], of or pertaining to the west (as, the *Western* Church, the *Western* Empire, see phrases below; *Western* churches, the Christian churches making up the Western Church, in its modern sense; a *Western* ranch or cowboy, that is, of the West of the U. S.); [usually *cap.*] Occidental.—**Western Church**, the Christian church in the countries once comprised in the Western Empire and in countries evangelized from these countries, or that part of the Christian church which acknowledged the popes after the schism of the Eastern or Greek Church (cf. *Greek Church*, under *Greek*, *a.*); in modern use, the Roman Catholic Church, sometimes with the Anglican Church, or, more broadly, the Christian churches of western Europe and those churches elsewhere which are connected with or have sprung from them.— **Western Empire**, the western portion of the Roman Empire after its division in A.D. 395, which became extinct in A.D. 476.—**west'ern**, *n.* One living in a western region or country; [*cap.*] a member of the Western Church; also, a Western story or moving picture, that is, dealing with the West of the U. S. (colloq.).—**West'ern-er**, *n.* A person of or from the western U. S.—**west'ern-ism**, *n.* The peculiarities or characteristics of western people; a word, idiom, or practice peculiar to western people, esp. the inhabitants of the western U. S.—**west′ern-ize** (-īz), *v. t.*; *-ized, -izing.* To render western in character, ideas, ways, etc.—**west″ern-i-za′tion** (-i-zā′shǫn), *n.*—**west′ern-most**, *a. superl.* Furthest west.

West In-di-an (west in′di-ạn). **I.** *a.* Of or pertaining to the West Indies, a group of islands in the Atlantic Ocean between Florida and South America. **II.** *n.* A native or inhabitant of the West Indies.

west-ing (wes′ting), *n.* The distance due west made by a ship on any course tending westward; westerly departure; distance westward.

West-pha-li-an (west-fā′li-ạn). **I.** *a.* Of or pertaining to Westphalia, a western province of Prussia (formerly a duchy, later, with larger territory, a Napoleonic kingdom). **II.** *n.* A native or inhabitant of Westphalia.

west-ward (west′wạrd). [AS. *westweard.*] **I.** *adv.* Toward the west; west. **II.** *a.* Moving, bearing, facing, or situated toward the west. **III.** *n.* The westward part, direction, or point: as, "There's some dirty weather to the *westward*" (Lever's "Harry Lorrequer," xxxiii.).—**west′ward-ly. I.** *a.* Having a westward direction or situation; also, coming from the west, as a wind. **II.** *adv.* Toward the west; also, from the west.—**west′wards,** *adv.* Westward.

wet (wet), *a.*; compar. *wetter,* superl. *wettest.* [AS. *wēt* = OFries. *wēt* = Icel. *vātr* = Dan. *vaad,* wet, moist: see *water.*] Covered or charged, wholly or in part, with water or some other liquid (used of things that tend to retain a liquid upon the surface or let it permeate through the substance: as, *wet* hands; *wet* land; a *wet* sponge); overspread, dabbled, soaked, or dripping with water or other liquid; moist, damp, or not dry; also, of a watery or liquid nature; also, characterized by the presence or use of water or other liquid (as, the *wet* way of chemical analysis: see phrase below); also, rainy, as weather, a season, etc. (as, "*wet* October's torrent flood": Milton's "Comus," 930); also, characterized by or favoring allowance of the manufacture and sale of alcoholic liquors for use as beverages.—**wet bargain,** a bargain sealed or ratified by the parties by drinking.—**wet blanket,** a person or thing that dampens ardor or has a discouraging or depressing effect.—**wet plate,** in *photog.,* a glass plate coated with wet sensitized collodion, formerly (and still occasionally) used, like the modern dry plate, for making pictures in a camera, etc.: so called because it must remain wet during the processes of sensitization, exposure, and development.—**wet way,** in *chem.,* the method of analysis in which the reactions are produced mostly in solutions and by the use of liquid reagents.—**wet,** *n.* [AS. *wǣta.*] That which makes wet, as water or other liquid; moisture; often, rain; also, a drink (slang); also, one who favors allowance of the manufacture and sale of alcoholic liquors for use as beverages.—**wet,** *v. t.*; *wetted* or *wet, wetting.* [AS. *wǣtan.*] To make wet; overspread, sprinkle, dabble, soak, or drench with water or other liquid; moisten; also, to seal, inaugurate, celebrate, etc., by drinking (slang: as, to *wet* a bargain; to *wet* a new hat).—**to wet one's whistle,** to take a drink. [Colloq.]

weth-er (weᴛʜ′ẽr), *n.* [AS. *wether* = D. *weer,* = G. *widder* = Icel. *vedhr,* wether, = Goth. *withrus,* lamb: cf. L. *vitulus,* calf, and E. *veal.*] A castrated ram.

wet-ly (wet′li), *adv.* In a wet manner or condition; moistly. —**wet′ness,** *n.*

wet=nurse (wet′nẽrs), *n.* A woman employed to suckle the infant of another.—**wet′=nurse,** *v. t.* To act as wet-nurse to.

wet=shod (wet′shod′), *a.* Having the shoes or feet wet; wearing wet shoes.

wet-ter (wet′ẽr), *n.* One who or that which wets.—**wet′-ting,** *n.* The act of one who or that which wets; a sprinkling, dabbling, or drenching with water (esp. rain) or the like; also, something used to make a thing wet.

wet-tish (wet′ish), *a.* Somewhat wet.

wey (wā), *n.* [AS. *wǣge,* akin to *wegan,* carry: see *weigh*².] A British unit of weight or measure, varying widely according to commodity and locality.

whack (hwak), *v.* [Imit.: cf. *thwack.*] **I.** *tr.* To strike with a smart, resounding blow or blows, esp. with a stick or the like (colloq.: as, "Sid was *whacked,* but . . . it didn't hurt him at all," H. G. Wells's "Kipps," i. 1); also, to divide into or take in shares (slang); also, to beat, outdo, or surpass (prov. Eng. and Sc.). **II.** *intr.* To strike a smart, resounding blow or blows (colloq.); also, to divide or share profits, spoils, etc. (slang: often with *up*).—**whack,** *n.* A smart, resounding blow (colloq.: as, "He fetched the book a *whack* with his hand," Mark Twain's "Huckleberry Finn," v.); also, a trial or attempt (slang: as, to take a *whack* at a job); also, a portion or share (slang); also, condition, esp. good condition (slang: as, "Their stomachs are out of *whack,*" Sinclair Lewis's "Main Street," xxvi.).—**whack′er,** *n.* One who or that which whacks; also, something extraordinary or uncommonly big of its kind. [Colloq.]—**whack′ing,** *p. a.* Extraordinary or uncommonly big of its kind; whopping. [Colloq.]

whale¹ (hwāl), *v.*; *whaled, whaling.* [Cf. *wale*², *v.*] **I.** *tr.* To whip, thrash, or beat soundly: as, "The boy . . . was soundly *whaled* with an old slipper" (W. Churchill's "Mr. Crewe's Career," i.). [Colloq.] **II.** *intr.* To strike vigorous blows (often with *away*: as, to *whale* away at a person); hence, in general, to act vigorously (with *away*). [Colloq.]

whale² (hwāl), *n.* [AS. *hwæl* = Icel. *hvalr* = Sw. and Dan. *hval* = OHG. G. *wāl,* whale: cf. *walrus.*] Any of many marine animals of the order *Cetacea,* the members of which, though of fish-like form, are air-breathing viviparous mammals which suckle their young; a cetacean; esp., one of the larger cetaceans (as distinguished from the smaller ones mostly known as dolphins and porpoises), including the right whales and the other whalebone whales (see below) as well as the larger of the toothed whales; also, any of various other large marine animals; also [*cap.*], in *astron.,* the southern constellation Cetus; also [*l. c.*], something extraordinarily big, great, or fine of its kind (slang: as, "He's been telling me what a *whale* of a lot . . . he knows," Sinclair Lewis's "Arrowsmith," xiv.; "a *whale* of a scholar," Sinclair Lewis's "Main Street," xiv.).—**right whale,** any of the large whales constituting the genus *Balæna,* having no dorsal fin, and comprising the typical whalebone whales. —**whale-bone whale,** any of the large whales which in the adult have whalebone in place of teeth in the upper jaw.

Polar Right Whale (*Balæna mysticetus*).

—**whale's bone**†, ivory from the walrus or some other marine animal confused with the whale: usually in connection with the word *white*: as, "his teeth as white as *whale's bone*" (Shakspere's "Love's Labour's Lost," v. 2. 332).—**whale²,** *v. i.*; *whaled, whaling.* To carry on the work of taking whales.—**whale′back,** *n.* A turtleback, or arched protection over the deck of a vessel; also, a vessel having a rounded deck which meets the sides in a continuous curve, sometimes with upper works, much used on the Great Lakes.—**whale′=boat,** *n.* A long, narrow boat, sharp at both ends, much used in whaling.—**whale′bone,** *n.* An elastic horny substance growing in place of teeth in the upper jaw of certain whales, and forming a series of thin, parallel plates on each side of the palate; baleen; also, a thin strip of this material, used for stiffening corsets or other garments, etc.; a riding-whip made of or containing it. See also *whale's bone,* under *whale²,* *n.*—**whalebone whale.** See under *whale²,* *n.*—**whale′=fish″-ing,** *n.* The work or industry of taking whales; whaling.—**whale′man** (-man), *n.*; pl. *-men.* A man engaged in whaling (as, "a well-to-do, retired *whaleman*": H. Melville's "Moby-Dick," xvi.); also, a vessel engaged in whaling (as, "In most American *whalemen* the mast-heads are manned almost simultaneously with the vessel's leaving her port": H. Melville's "Moby-Dick," xxxv.).—

Four plates of Whale-bone, seen obliquely from within.

whale′=meat, *n.* The flesh of the whale, used for food. **—whal-er** (hwā′lẽr), *n.* A person or a vessel engaged in whaling.—**whal′er-y** (-i), *n.*; pl. *-ies* (-iz). The industry of whaling or whale-fishing; an establishment for carrying on whale-fishing; also, an establishment for canning whale-meat.

whal-ing[1] (hwā′ling), *n.* A sound whipping, thrashing, or beating. [Colloq.]—**whal′ing**[1], *p. a.* Extraordinary or uncommonly big of its kind; whopping. [Colloq.]

whal-ing[2] (hwā′ling), *n.* The work or industry of taking whales; whale-fishing.

whang (hwang), *v. t.* [Imit.] To strike with a resounding blow, or bang (colloq.); also, to throw violently (Sc. and prov. Eng.); also, to slash, chop, or slice (Sc. and prov. Eng.). **—whang,** *n.* A resounding blow, or bang (colloq.); also, a chunk or slice (Sc. and prov. Eng.: as, "a *whang* of bread," Stevenson's "Travels with a Donkey," i. 3).

whap (hwop), etc. See *whop,* etc.

wharf (hwârf), *n.*; pl. **wharves** (hwârvz) or **wharfs.** [AS. *hwearf, hwerf,* bank, embankment, prob. orig. as turning back water, < *hweorfan,* turn: see *wharve.*] A structure built on the shore of, or projecting out into a harbor, stream, etc., so that vessels may be moored alongside to load or unload or to lie at rest (as, "The Patna cast off and backed away from the *wharf*": J. Conrad's "Lord Jim," ii.); a quay; a pier; also, a bank† or shore† (as, "The fat weed That roots itself in ease on Lethe *wharf*": Shakspere's "Hamlet," i. 5. 33).—**wharf,** *v. t.* To provide with a wharf or wharves; also, to place or store on a wharf; also, to bring (a ship) to a wharf.—**wharf-age** (hwâr′fāj), *n.* Accommodation at a wharf; the use of a wharf; storage of goods at a wharf; also, the charge or payment for the use of a wharf (as, "Boats were charged such heavy *wharfage* that they could not afford to land for one or two passengers": Mark Twain's "Life on the Mississippi," xxxv.); also, wharves collectively. **—wharf-in-ger** (hwâr′fin-jẽr), *n.* [For *wharfager,* < *wharfage.*] One who owns, or has charge of, a wharf.— **wharf′-rat,** *n.* The common brown rat, *Mus decumanuṣ,* when living in or about a wharf; fig., a man or boy, without regular or ostensible occupation, who loafs about wharves (colloq.).

wharve (hwärv), *n.* [AS. *hweorfa,* < *hweorfan* = Icel. *hverfa* = OHG. *hwerban* = Goth. *hwairban,* turn, go about: cf. *wharf, whorl,* and *whirl.*] In *spinning,* a wheel or round piece of wood on a spindle, serving as a fly-wheel or as a pulley.

what (hwot), *pron.* (and *a.*); pl. **what.** [AS. *hwæt,* neut. of *hwā,* E. *who.*] **A.** *interrog.* A word (1) asking for the specifying of some thing (not person: as, *what* is your name? *what* did he do?); (2) inquiring as to the nature, character, class, origin, etc., of a thing or person (as, *what* is that animal? *what* is he, by birth, rank, or profession?); (3) inquiring as to the worth, usefulness, force, or importance of something (as, *what* is wealth without health? *what* is their need beside ours?); (4) asking, often elliptically, for repetition or explanation or some word or words used, as by a previous speaker (as, you need five *what?* Mr. *what?* you claim to be *what?*); or (5) used with a general or vague interrogative force, esp. at the end of a sentence (colloq.: as, "a sort of anarchical fellow, *what?*" M. Hewlett's "Open Country," xiii.). Also used adjectively, before a noun (whether thing or person): as, *what* news? *what* price? *what* men? Often used interjectionally to express surprise, disbelief, indignation, etc. (as, "Where did you go last night? *What!* — to Tonans?" G. Meredith's "Diana of the Crossways," xxxiv.), or with intensive force in exclamatory phrases (preceding an indefinite article, if one is used: as, *what* luck! *what* ho! *what* an idea!). Used in various phrases, often elliptical: as, *what* if we do? *what* of it? (what about it? what does it matter?); *what?* for? (for what reason or purpose? why?); toys, pictures, and *what* not (and anything whatever; and anything else that there may be; et cetera). **B.** *rel.* (1) As a compound relative, that which (as, this is *what* he says; I will send *what* was promised); also, the kind of thing or person that, or such as (as, the book is just *what* it professes to be; the old man is not *what* he was); also, anything that, or whatever (as, say *what* you please; come *what* may); also, in parenthetic clauses, something that (as, but he went,

and, *what* is more surprising, gained a hearing); (2) as a simple relative, that, which, or who: now regarded as incorrect or vulgar (as, a bird *what* sings), except in the possessive *whose* (see *whose*) and the phrase *but what* (now colloq.: as, there is no one but *what* is pleased, that is, who is not pleased). Also used adjectively: That or any . . . which; such . . . as: as, take *what* time and *what* assistants you need. **C.** *indef.*† Something; anything; a bit. Cf. *somewhat.*—**what. I.** *adv.* For what reason or purpose†, or why?† (as, "*What* sit we then projecting peace and war?" Milton's "Paradise Lost," ii. 329); also, in what respect, or how? (archaic: as, "*What* are men better than sheep . . . If, knowing God, they lift not hands of prayer?" Tennyson's "Passing of Arthur," 418); also, to what extent or degree, or how much? (as, *what* does it matter? *what* do we care? *what* is he the better for his scheming?); also, in certain expressions, in what or some manner or measure, or partly (as, *what* with storms, *what* with accidents, his return was delayed; *what* with one thing and another he was kept busy). **II.** *conj.* To the extent that, as much as, or so far as (as, he helps me *what* he can: now prov. or colloq.); also, that (in the phrase *but what,* now colloq.: as, I don't know *but what* I will; I can't — not *but what* I'd like to; "There was nothing so humble . . . *but what* his magic could transform it into the rarest beauty," Du Maurier's "Trilby," ii.).—

what-e′er′ (-âr′). Contracted form of *whatever.*—**what-ev′er** (-ev′ẽr). **I.** *pron.* **A.** *interrog.* What ever? what? — used emphatically: as, *whatever* do you mean? [Now colloq.] **B.** *indef. rel.* Anything that (as, do *whatever* you like); also, any amount or measure (of something) that (as, "*whatever* of time or energy or faculty may be mine": Mrs. H. Ward's "Robert Elsmere," xxxii.); also, no matter what (as, do it, *whatever* happens). **II.** *a.* Any . . . that (as, ask *whatever* person you like; *whatever* merit the work has); also, no matter what (as, "He instructed his agent not to quit Guienne, *whatever* rebuffs he might receive": J. F. Kirk's "Charles the Bold," iii. 2); also, being what or who it may be (as, for *whatever* reason, he is unwilling; for no reason *whatever;* any person *whatever*).—**what′=for′** (-fôr′), *n.* [As if in vigorous response to the question 'what for?'] Bodily punishment or chastisement; a severe scolding; any painful lesson or experience: used in the phrases 'to give one what-for,' 'to get what-for,' etc.: as, "His mother . . . was going to give him *what-for*" (W. De Morgan's "Joseph Vance," vi.). [Colloq.]—**what′=not,** *n.* A stand with shelves for bric-à-brac, books, etc.; an étagère.—**what′-so** (-sō), *pron.* and *a.* Whatever: as, "*Whatso* thou wilt do with us, Our end shall not be piteous" (W. Morris's "Jason," iv. 165). [Archaic.]—**what-so-e′er′** (-sō-âr′). Contracted form of *whatsoever.*—**what-so-ev′er,** *pron.* and *a.* Intensive form of *whatever:* as, anything, *whatsoever* it be; in any place *whatsoever.*

whaup (hwâp or hwäp), *n.* [Imit. of its cry.] A curlew. [Sc. and north. Eng.]

wheal (hwēl), *n.* [In part, ME. *whele,* pustule (cf. AS. *hwelian,* suppurate); in part, var. of *weal*[2], *wale*[2].] A pimple† or pustule†; also, a small, burning or itching swelling on the skin, as from a mosquito-bite or from urticaria; also, a ridge raised on the skin by a stroke, as of a rod or whip; a wale.

wheat (hwēt), *n.* [AS. *hwǣte* = Icel. *hveiti* = OHG. *weizzi* (G. *weizen*) = Goth. *hwaiteis,* wheat; akin to E. *white.*] The grain of a widely distributed cereal grass of the genus *Triticum,* esp. *T. sativum* (or *æstivum*), used extensively in the form of flour for making bread, etc.; also, the plant, which bears the grain in dense spikes that sometimes have awns ('bearded wheat') and sometimes do not ('beardless wheat' or 'bald wheat').—**spring** or **summer wheat,** wheat sown in the spring for the crop of the same season.— **winter** or **fall wheat,** wheat sown in the autumn for the crop of the next season.

wheat-ear (hwēt′ẽr), *n.* [Also formerly *wheatears,* prob. equivalent to *white* + *arse,* with reference to the white rump.] A small oscine passerine bird, *Saxicola œnanthe,* found in Europe, Asia, Africa, and North America. See cut on following page.

wheat-en (hwē′tn), *a.* [AS. *hwǣten.*] Of or pertaining to wheat; made of the grain or flour of wheat (as, "*wheaten* bread": George Eliot's "Adam Bede," iv.); made of the stalks or straw of wheat (as, "Peace should still her *wheaten* garland wear": Shakspere's "Hamlet," v. 2. 41). [Now rare.]

wheat-less (whēt′les), *a.* Without wheat; characterized by refraining from the use of wheat (as, *wheatless* days).

Wheatear, adult male.

Wheat-stone (whēt′stọn) **bridge.** [Named from Sir Charles *Wheatstone* (1802–75), English physicist.] In *elect.*, a device for measuring the electrical resistance of a conductor.

wheat=worm (whēt′wėrm), *n.* A small nematode worm, *Tylenchus tritici*, causing the disease ear-cockle in wheat.

whee-dle (whē′dl), *v.*; *-dled, -dling.* [Origin uncertain: cf. AS. *wǣdlian*, be poor, beg.] **I.** *tr.* To endeavor to influence (a person) by smooth, flattering, or beguiling words; influence or persuade thus; coax; cajole; often, to beguile into some condition, action, etc., by artful persuasions (as, "I had . . . been *wheedled* into letting myself be detailed to be a quartermaster's clerk," G. W. Cable's "Cavalier," i.; "I have seen you *wheedle* an angry . . . woman into giving you dates," Kipling's "Light That Failed," xii.); also, to get from a person by artful persuasions (as, "*wheedling* my money from me," Stevenson's "Kidnapped," xxiv.; "I suffered the abbess to *wheedle* the secret out of me," Scott's "Castle Dangerous," xi.). **II.** *intr.* To use beguiling or artful persuasions: as, "Some of 'em — the artful kind — begged and *wheedled* and cried" (John Hay's "Bread-Winners," xv.). —**whee′dler,** *n.* —**whee′dling-ly,** *adv.*

wheel (whēl), *n.* [AS. *hwēol, hweogul,* = D. *wiel* = Icel. *hjōl,* wheel; akin to Gr. κύκλος, ring, circle, wheel, and Skt. *cakra,* wheel: cf. *cycle.*] A circular frame or solid disk arranged to turn on an axis, as in vehicles, machinery, etc.; typically, a frame consisting of a central nave or hub connected by radiating spokes with a circular rim, or felly (sometimes having a tire on the outer face, as in vehicles), and rotating on or with an axle fitted into the nave; also, any instrument, machine, apparatus, etc., shaped like this, or having such a frame or disk as an essential feature (as, a potters' *wheel,* see under *potter*[1]; a spinning-*wheel*); a circular frame with projecting handles and an axle connecting with the rudder, for steering a ship; an old instrument of torture in the form of a circular frame on which the victim was stretched while his limbs were broken with an iron bar; a rotating instrument which Fortune is represented as turning in order to bring about changes or reverses in human affairs; a circular firework which revolves while burning; a bicycle or a tricycle (colloq.); also, anything resembling or suggesting a wheel (in first sense) in shape, movement, etc., as an embroidered decoration with radiating bars, or the trochal disk of a rotifer; also, *pl.,* fig., moving, propelling, or animating agencies (as, the *wheels* of trade, of thought, or of life); also, *sing.,* a wheeling or circular movement (as, "Merrily whirled the *wheels* of the dizzying dances": Longfellow's "Evangeline," i. 4); a movement of troops, ships, etc., drawn up in line, as if turning on a pivot. — **a wheel within a wheel,** one thing involved in another; esp., an obscure or unrecognized factor or complication. Cf. Ezek. i. 16; x. 10. Also *wheels within wheels.* —**fifth wheel.** See under *fifth, a.* —**flat wheel,** or **square wheel.** See under *flat*[2], *a.* —**wheel and axle,** a device (one of the so-called simple machines) consisting, in its typical form, of a cylindrical axle on which a wheel, concentric with the axle, is firmly fastened: used variously, as to lift a weight attached to a rope by causing the rope to wind up on the axle as the wheel is turned. —**wheel,** *v.* **I.** *tr.* To cause to turn, rotate, or revolve, as on an axis; cause to execute a rotating movement, through part or all of a circle, as if turning on a pivot (as, to *wheel* a horse about; to *wheel* a line of troops); direct in a circular or curving course (as, "The sun flies forward to his brother sun; The dark earth follows *wheel'd* in her

ellipse": Tennyson's "Golden Year," 24); perform (a course, flight, etc.) in a circular or curving direction (as, "The silvered kite In many a whistling circle *wheels* her flight": Wordsworth's "Evening Walk," 91); also, to move or roll (a vehicle, piece of furniture, etc.) on wheels, casters, etc. (as, "The servants *wheel* out the card-tables": Longfellow's "Hyperion," iv. 4); convey (a load, goods, persons, etc.) by means of a wheeled vehicle; provide (a vehicle, etc.) with a wheel or wheels; also, to shape (vessels, clay, etc.) with a potters' wheel; also, to treat (hides) with a pinwheel. **II.** *intr.* To turn on or as on an axis or about a center; rotate; revolve; execute a rotating movement, through part or all of a circle, as a line of troops pivoting on one end (as, "The military men . . . are *wheeling* round the corner": Hawthorne's "Twice-Told Tales," Sights from a Steeple); turn or change in procedure or opinion (often with *about* or *around*); move in a circular or curving course (as, "when . . . *wheels* the circled dance," Tennyson's "In Memoriam," xcviii.; "High above the wood some startled pigeons were . . . *wheeling*," Galsworthy's "Country House," i. 2); also, to roll along on wheels; ride on a bicycle or tricycle (colloq.); in general, to travel along smoothly or at a round pace.

wheel=an-i-mal-cule (hwēl′an-i-mal″kūl), *n.* A rotifer.

wheel-bar-row (hwēl′bar″ō), *n.* A frame or box for conveying a load, supported at one end on a wheel on which to run, and having at the other end two legs on which to rest and two shafts by which a person may lift the legs from the ground and push or pull it along; also, some similar vehicle with more than one wheel.

wheel=bug (hwēl′bug), *n.* A large, predaceous hemipterous insect, *Prionidus cristatus*, of North America, which destroys great numbers of other insects: so called from its semi-circular toothed thoracic crest, which resembles a cogged wheel.

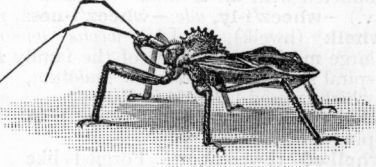

Wheel-bug, female, natural size.

wheeled (hwēld), *a.* Furnished with a wheel or wheels; mounted on wheels.

wheel-er (hwē′lėr), *n.* One who or that which wheels; also, a maker of wheels (now chiefly prov. Eng.); also, something provided with a wheel or wheels (only in composition: as, a side-*wheeler;* a stern-*wheeler*); also, a wheel-horse.

wheel=horse (hwēl′hôrs), *n.* A horse, or one of the horses, harnessed behind others and next to the fore wheels of a vehicle; fig., a plodding worker, esp. one who labors steadily and obediently under the direction of a leader.

wheel=house (hwēl′hous), *n.* The pilot-house of a vessel, which shelters the steering-wheel.

wheel-ing (hwē′ling), *n.* The act of one who or that which wheels; the practice of riding on a bicycle or tricycle (colloq.).

wheel=lock (hwēl′lok), *n.* An old type of gun-lock in which sparks are produced by the friction of a small steel wheel against a piece of iron pyrites or the like.

wheel-man (hwēl′man), *n.;* pl. *-men.* The man at the steering-wheel of a vessel; a steersman; also, a rider of a bicycle, tricycle, or the like.

wheels-man (hwēlz′man), *n.;* pl. *-men.* A wheelman or steersman.

wheel=win-dow (hwēl′win′dō), *n.* An ornamental circular window with radiating tracery or mullions more or less resembling the spokes of a wheel. See cut on following page.

wheel-wright (hwēl′rīt), *n.* One whose trade it is to make or repair wheels, wheeled carriages, etc.

wheen (hwēn), *n.* [Cf. AS. *hwēne,* somewhat.] A few; a number or quantity: often used as a quasi-adjective, by omission of *of* before a noun following (as, a *wheen* (of) things; "He has a *wheen* stout lads at his back," Scott's "Black Dwarf," ii.). [Sc. and north. Eng.]

wheeze (hwēz), *v.;* *wheezed, wheezing.* [AS. *hwēsan.*] **I.** *intr.* To breathe with difficulty and with a whistling sound (as, "Every member waddled home . . . *wheezing* as he went with corpulency and terror": Irving's "Knickerbocker's New York," vii. 9); hence, to make a similar sound. **II.** *tr.* To utter with a sound of wheezing.—**wheeze,** *n.* A wheezing breath or sound; also (slang), a humorous saying or anecdote (orig. prov. Eng.); a theatrical 'gag' (as, "'What I want to know,' grunted the low comedian, 'is 'ow I'm to get that *wheeze* of mine into that song'": L. Merrick's "Conrad in Quest of His Youth," xiv.); in general, a saying, story, or the like (often with implication of

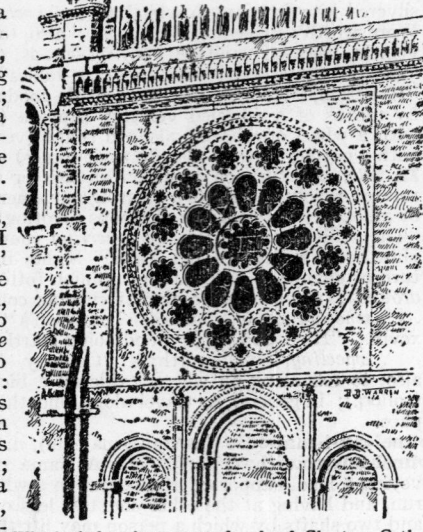

Wheel-window in western façade of Chartres Cathedral, France; end of 12th century.

triteness).—**wheez'er,** *n.*—**wheez'y,** *a.* Affected with or characterized by wheezing: as, "a *wheezy* little pew-opener afflicted with an asthma" (Dickens's "Dombey and Son," v.).—**wheez'i-ly,** *adv.*—**wheez'i-ness,** *n.*

whelk[1] (hwelk), *n.* [AS. *weoloc, wioloc.*] Any of various large marine gastropods of the family *Buccinidæ,* having a spiral shell, esp. *Buccinum undatum,* which is used for food in Europe.

whelk[2] (hwelk), *n.* [AS. *hwylca.*] A pimple or pustule.

whelked (hwelkt), *a.* Formed like a whelk (gastropod); twisted or rigid like the shell of a whelk.

whelm (hwelm), *v. t.* [ME. *whelmen,* akin to *whelven,* roll, AS. *hwylfan,* turn over, AS. *hwealf,* Icel. *hvālf,* a vault, G. *wölben,* to vault, arch.] To overturn (now prov.); turn a hollow vessel, etc.) over a thing so as to cover it (as, "I set down my loaf, or loaves . . . *whelming* down the earthen pot upon them," Defoe's "Robinson Crusoe," i. 9: now prov.); cover with a hollow vessel or the like (now prov.); hence, to cover or

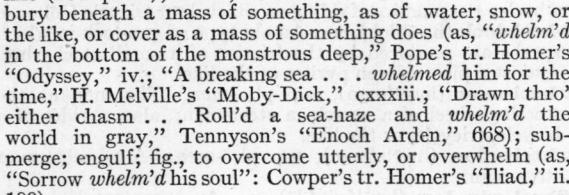

Common Whelk (*Buccinum undatum*).

bury beneath a mass of something, as of water, snow, or the like, or cover as a mass of something does (as, "*whelm'd* in the bottom of the monstrous deep," Pope's tr. Homer's "Odyssey," iv.; "A breaking sea . . . *whelmed* him for the time," H. Melville's "Moby-Dick," cxxxiii.; "Drawn thro' either chasm . . . Roll'd a sea-haze and *whelm'd* the world in gray," Tennyson's "Enoch Arden," 668); submerge; engulf; fig., to overcome utterly, or overwhelm (as, "Sorrow *whelm'd* his soul": Cowper's tr. Homer's "Iliad," ii. 199).

whelp (hwelp), *n.* [AS. *hwelp* = D. *welp* = Icel. *hvelpr* = Dan. *hvalp,* whelp.] The young of the dog, or of the wolf, bear, lion, tiger, seal, etc.; a puppy; a cub; hence, a youth (contemptuous); a contemptible cur; in *mech.,* any of a series of longitudinal projections or ridges of iron or the like on the barrel of a capstan, windlass, etc.; also, one of the teeth of a sprocket-wheel.—**whelp,** *v. i.* or *t.* Of a bitch, lioness, etc., to bring forth (young).

when (hwen). [AS. *hwænne, hwonne,* = OHG. *wanne* (G. *wann*) = Goth. *hvan,* when; from the pronominal stem represented by E. *who.*] **I.** *interrog. adv.* At what time? as, *when* are you coming? *when,* did you say? **II.** *conj.* At what time (as, to know *when* to be silent); also, at the

time that (as, to rise *when* one's name is called; *when* we were young; *when* the noise stopped); also, at any time that, or whenever (as, he is impatient *when* he is kept waiting; I smile *when* I think of those days); also, upon or after which, or and then (as, "The Moors fought valiantly . . . until the alcaydes . . . were slain, *when* they gave way and fled": Irving's "Conquest of Granada," xi.); also, while on the contrary, or whereas (as, "You rub the sóre, *When* you should bring the plaster": Shakspere's "Tempest," ii. 1. 139). **III.** *n.* What time (as, since *when* have you known this? till *when* shall we wait?); also, which time (as, they left on Monday, since *when* we have heard nothing; next week, till *when* adieu); also, the time of anything (as, the *when* and the *where* of an act).—**when-as'** (-az'), *conj.* When; while; whereas. [Archaic.]

whence (hwens). [ME. *whennes* (with adverbial suffix -s), < *whenne,* < AS. *hwanan,* whence, akin to *hwænne,* E. *when.*] **I.** *interrog. adv.* From what place? (as, "*Whence* comest thou?" Judges, xix. 17); hence, from what source or origin? (as, "*Whence* hath this man this wisdom?" Mat. xiii. 54); from what cause? (as, *whence* comes it that he is so favored?); from what fact or circumstance? (as, *whence* do you infer this?). **II.** *conj.* From what place, source, cause, etc. (as, he told *whence* he came; to know *whence* trouble arises); also, from which place, source, cause, etc., or wherefrom (as, the country *whence* we came; the source *whence* the rumors issued).—**from whence,** whence: a pleonasm.—**whence-so-ev'er** (-sọ-ev'ėr), *conj.* From whatsoever place, source, or cause.

when-e'er (hwen-ār'). Contracted form of *whenever.*

when-ev-er (hwen-ev'ėr). **I.** *interrog. adv.* When ever? when? — used emphatically: as, *whenever* did he tell you that? [Now colloq.] **II.** *conj.* At whatever time; at any time when: as, come *whenever* you like.—**when'so** (-sō), *conj.* Whenever. [Archaic.]—**when-so-ev'er** (-sọ-ev'ėr), *conj.* At whatsoever time.

where (hwār). [AS. *hwǣr, hwär,* = OHG. *hwär* (G. *wo*) = Icel. *hvar* = Goth. *hvar,* where; from the pronominal stem represented by E. *who.*] **I.** *interrog. adv.* In or at what place? (as, *where* is he? *where* do you live?); hence, in what part, or at what point? (as, *where* is the pain? *where* did you leave off in your story?); in what position or circumstances? (as, *where* do you stand on this question? without money *where* are you?); in what particular, respect, way, etc.? (as, *where* does this affect us? *where* is the harm of trying?); also, to what place, point, or end, or whither? (as, *where* are you going? *where* is all this tending?); also, from what source, or whence? (as, *where* did you get such a notion? "*Where* have you this [news]? 'tis false," Shakspere's "Antony and Cleopatra," ii. 1. 18). **II.** *conj.* In or at what place, part, point, etc. (as, find *where* he is, or *where* the trouble is); in or at the place, part, point, etc., in or at which (as, the book is *where* you left off; begin *where* you left off); in a position, case, etc., in which (as, "Where ignorance is bliss, 'Tis folly to be wise": Gray's "On a Distant Prospect of Eton College"); in any place, position, case, etc., in which, or wherever (as, "Feed *where* thou wilt, on mountain or in dale," Shakspere's "Venus and Adonis," 232; use the lotion *where* pain is felt); also, to what or whatever place, or to the or any place to which (as, go *where* you will; I will go *where* you go); also, in or at which place, or and there (as, they came to the town, *where* they lodged for the night); also, while on the contrary†, or whereas†. **III.** *n.* What place (as, from *where,* or, commonly, *where* from? *where* to?); also, the place of something (as, the *where* of this occurrence); a place (as, "a better *where* to find," Shakspere's "King Lear," i. 1. 264: cf. *anywhere, nowhere, somewhere,* etc.).—**where'a-bout'. I.** *interrog. adv.* About where? abouts? **II.** *conj.* About what or which.—**where'a-bout**″, *n.* Same as *whereabouts, n.*—**where'a-bouts'. I.** *interrog. adv.* About where? where? **II.** *conj.* Near or in what place: as, "to look out, in hopes of seeing *whereabouts* in the world we were" (Defoe's "Robinson Crusoe," i. 3).—**where'-a-bouts**″, *n.* The place where a person or thing is; the locality of a person or thing: as, "Nor had we enough clue as to his *whereabouts*" (S. Butler's "Way of All Flesh," lxvi.).—**where-as'** (-az'), *conj.* Where (obs. or archaic); also, it being the case that, or considering that (esp. used in formal preambles); also, while on the contrary (as, one came promptly, *whereas* the others hung back).—**where-at′.** **I.** *interrog. adv.* At what? **II.** *conj.* At what or which.—**where-by′. I.** *interrog. adv.* By what? how? **II.** *conj.* By what or which.—**wher-e′er′** (-ār′). Contracted form of *wherever.*—**where′fore** (-fōr). **I.** *interrog. adv.* For what? why? **II.** *conj.* For what or which cause or reason.—**where′fore,** *n.* The cause or reason.—**where-from′,** *conj.* From which; whence.—**where-in′. I.** *interrog. adv.* In what? how? **II.** *conj.* In what or which.—**where-in′so-ev′er** (-sō-ev′ėr), *conj.* In whatsoever place, thing, respect, etc.—**where-in′to. I.** *interrog. adv.* Into what? **II.** *conj.* Into what or which.—**where′ness,** *n.* The state or property of having place or local relation; ubication.—**where-of′. I.** *interrog. adv.* Of what? whence? **II.** *conj.* Of what, which, or whom.—**where-on′. I.** *interrog. adv.* On what? whereupon? **II.** *conj.* On what or which.—**where-out′,** *conj.* Out of which.—**where′so** (-sō), *conj.* Wherever: as, "I will go with thee *Whereso* thou willest" (W. Morris's "Jason," iv. 353). [Archaic.]—**where-so-e′er′** (-sō-ār′). Contracted form of *wheresoever.*—**where-so-ev′er** (-sō-ev′ėr), *conj.* In or to whatsoever place; wherever; also, whenceso-ever†.—**where-through′,** *conj.* Through which.—**where-to′. I.** *interrog. adv.* To what? whither? **II.** *conj.* To what or which.—**where-un′der,** *conj.* Under which.—**where-un-to** (hwär-un′tö̇ or -un-tö̇′), *adv.* and *conj.* Same as *whereto.* [Archaic.]—**where-up-on′. I.** *interrog. adv.* Upon what? whereon? **II.** *conj.* Upon what or which; also, at or after which (as, "Mr. Holt . . . announced a prayer, *whereupon* the family knelt": W. Churchill's "Modern Chronicle," i. 7).—**wher-ev-er** (hwär-ev′ėr). **I.** *interrog. adv.* Where ever? where?—used emphatically: as, *wherever* did you find that? [Now colloq.] **II.** *conj.* In, at, or to whatever place.—**where-with′** (-wiᴛн′ or -wiᴛн′). **I.** *interrog. adv.* With what? **II.** *conj.* With what or which; also, by ellipsis, that with which (as, "So shall I have *wherewith* to answer him that reproacheth me": Ps. cxix. 42). **III.** *n.* Same as *wherewithal,* *n.*—**where-with-al′** (-âl′), *adv.* and *conj.* Same as *wherewith.* [Archaic.]—**where′with-al,** *n.* That wherewith to do something; means or supplies for the purpose or need (as, "Rarely could the inmates . . . boast of having made a full meal, and never of having *wherewithal* for the morrow": Irving's "Captain Bonneville," ix.); esp., with *the,* money (as, "So long should I have the *wherewithal* to pay my rent and buy my food," Gissing's "Private Papers of Henry Ryecroft," i. 2; to be ill supplied with the *wherewithal*).

wher-ry (hwer′i), *n.*; pl. *wherries* (-iz). [Origin unknown.] Any of several kinds of boats; esp., a kind of light rowboat used chiefly in England for carrying passengers and goods on rivers (as, "We embarked at Ranelagh for Vauxhall in a *wherry*": Smollett's "Humphry Clinker," May 31); also, a kind of light rowboat for one person, used for racing, etc.; also, any of certain larger boats (fishing-vessels, barges, etc.) used locally in Great Britain; specif., a kind of broad sail-boat used chiefly for carrying merchandise on rivers, etc., but sometimes for pleasure cruising ('Norfolk wherry': as, "*Wherries* were beginning to be built and elaborately fitted out for nothing but pleasure cruises, but for the most part fittings were adapted to the freight-carriers and taken out when the summer was over," Archibald Marshall's "Anthony Dare," ix.).

wherve (hwėrv), *n.* Same as *wharve.*

whet (hwet), *v. t.*; *whetted* (also, esp. formerly, *whet*), *whetting.* [AS. *hwettan* = D. *wetten* = G. *wetzen,* sharpen, whet; akin to AS. *hwæt,* keen, bold.] To sharpen (a knife, tool, etc.) by grinding or friction; fig., to make keen or eager (as, to *whet* the appetite or the curiosity; "The poor morsel of food only *whetted* desire," Mark Twain's "Tom Sawyer," xxxi.; "sagacity . . . *whetted* and stimulated by a sentiment of vengeance," Godwin's "Caleb Williams," xxxv.); stimulate.—**whet,** *n.* The act of whetting; also, something that whets; a stimulus to the appetite, or an appetizer (as, "I have seen turnips make their appearance . . . by way of hors d'œuvres, or *whets*": Smollett's "Humphry Clinker," Aug. 8); sometimes, an alcoholic appetizer, as a drink of liquor.

wheth-er (hweᴛн′ėr), *pron.* and *a.* [AS. *hwæther* = OHG.

hwedar = Icel. *hvārr* = Goth. *hwathar,* whether; from the pronominal stem represented by E. *who.*] **I.** *interrog.* Which (of two)? as, "*Whether* is greater, the gift, or the altar that sanctifieth the gift?" (Mat. xxiii. 19). [Archaic.] **II.** *rel.* Which (of two); whichever: as, "Before man is life and death; and *whether* him liketh shall be given him" (Ecclus. xv. 17). [Archaic.]—**wheth′er.** [AS. *hwæther.*] **I.** *interrog. adv.* A word introducing a question presenting alternatives (usually with the correlative *or*): as, "*Whether* is it the more mortifying to us, to feel that we are disliked or liked undeservedly?" (Thackeray's "Newcomes," lvi.). [Archaic.] **II.** *conj.* A word introducing, in dependent clauses or the like, the first of two or more alternatives, and sometimes repeated before the second or later alternative (used in correlation with *or*: as, it matters little *whether* we go or stay; *whether* we go or *whether* we stay, the result is the same; violent efforts, *whether* to help or to hinder); also, used to introduce a single alternative (the other being implied or understood), and hence some clause or element not involving alternatives (as, see *whether* he has come [or not]; I doubt *whether* we can do any better).—**whether or no,** whether or not; whether something be done, be true, etc., or not; under whatever circumstances; in any case: as, he threatens to go, *whether or no.*

whet-stone (hwet′stōn), *n.* A stone for sharpening cutlery or tools by friction. Also fig.: as, a *whetstone* for dull wits.

whet-ter (hwet′ėr), *n.* A person or thing that whets.

whew (hwū). **I.** *interj.* A whistling exclamation or sound expressing astonishment, dismay, etc.: as, " '*Whew!*' said the other, lifting his eyebrows" (Mrs. H. Ward's "Robert Elsmere," xiv.). **II.** *n.* An utterance of 'whew!'

whey (hwā), *n.* [AS. *hwæg* = D. *wei,* whey.] The serum of milk, separating as a watery liquid from the curd after co-agulation, as in cheese-making.—**whey′ey** (-i), *a.* Of, like, or containing whey.—**whey′=face,** *n.* A face or a person that is pallid, from fear or other cause.—**whey′=faced,** *a.*—**whey′ish,** *a.* Wheyey.

which (hwich), *pron.* (and *a.*); pl. *which.* [AS. *hwilc, hwylc, hwelc,* = OHG. *hwelīh* (G. *welcher*) = Goth. *hwileiks,* lit. 'of what form or sort'; from the pronominal stem represented by E. *who,* with termination related to E. -*ly*[1] and *like*[1]: cf. *such.*] **A.** *interrog.* What one (of a certain number mentioned or implied)? as, *which* of these, or *which,* do you want? *which* is *which?* (that is, which is the one, which the other?). Also used adjectively: as, *which* way shall we go? **B.** *rel.* (1) As a compound relative, representing both antecedent and consequent (either thing or person), what particular one, or the or any one that (as, choose *which* you like; any one of these men, be it *which* it may); also, in parenthetic clauses, a thing that (as, "And, *which* is worse, all you have done Hath been but for a wayward son": Shakspere's "Macbeth," iii. 5. 10); (2) as a simple relative, with antecedent (thing, body of persons, formerly a single person) expressed, in clauses conveying an additional idea (as, I read the book, *which* was short; they had five sons, of *which* he was the eldest; "Thanks be to God, *which* giveth us the victory," 1 Cor. xv. 57); also, used in clauses defining or restricting the antecedent, regularly after *that* (as, that *which* must be will be), or after a preposition (as, the horse on *which* I rode), or otherwise in place of the restrictive *that* (as, the book *which,* or that, I gave you: cf. *that, rel. pron.*). Also used adjectively: as, be careful *which* way you turn; "In commenting on *which* text Mrs. Western had displayed her eloquence" (Fielding's "Tom Jones," vi. 13). — **every which way,** every way; in every direction; in wild disorder or confusion: as, children with hair and clothes *every which way;* "the Rebs jumpin' and hollerin' around and shoutin' *every which way*" (W. Churchill's "Coniston," ii. 5). [U. S.] —**the which,** which. [Archaic.]—**which-ev′er** (-ev′ėr), *pron.* (and *a.*). Any one (of those in question) that (as, take *whichever* you like); also, no matter which (as, *whichever* you choose, the others will be offended). Also used adjectively: as, *whichever* day; *whichever* person.—**which′so** (-sō), *pron.* Whichever. [Archaic.]—**which-so-ev′er** (-sō-ev′ėr), *pron.* (and *a.*). Intensive form of *whichever.*

whid-ah=bird (hwid′ä-bėrd), *n.* [For *widow-bird* (after Pg. *viuva,* widow-bird, lit. 'widow'), from the black and white plumage of some species.] Any of the small-bodied African

---

(variable) ḍ as d or j, ş as s or sh, ṭ as t or ch, ẓ as z or zh; o, F. cloche; ü, F. menu; ċh, Sc. loch; ṅ, F. bonbon: ′, primary accent; ″, secondary accent; †, obsolete; <, from; +, and; =, equals. See also lists at beginning of book.

birds which constitute the subfamily *Viduinæ*, comprising species of weaver-birds the males of which have enormously elongated drooping tail-feathers.

whiff (hwif), *n.* [ME. *weffe, wef,* whiff, puff; prob. imit.] A slight blast or puff of wind or air (as, "a *whiff* of fresh air": Hugh Walpole's "Wooden Horse," vi.); a puff or waft of air conveying some odor, or a momentary odor or smell (as, "A *whiff* of musk ... caught his

Paradise Whidah-bird (*Vidua,* or *Steganura, paradisea*), male.

opened nostrils," Kipling's "Kim," ix.; "A *whiff* of honeysuckle was borne to us," W. Black's "Strange Adventures of a Phaeton," xiii.); a puff of vapor, smoke, etc., emitted at one blast (as, "a hundred thin *whiffs* of steam," Howells's "Rise of Silas Lapham," iii.; "little *whiffs* of pearl-gray smoke," Bret Harte's "Mliss," ii.); a portion of air, tobacco-smoke, or the like, inhaled or exhaled at one time (as, "She ... lit it [a cigarette] and smoked it, inhaling the smoke in large *whiffs*": Du Maurier's "Trilby," i.); a single inhalation or exhalation of air, tobacco-smoke, or the like (as, "if you'd take two *whiffs* of a cigarette": Pinero's "Wife without a Smile," ii.); also, a puffing sound; also, fig., a slight outburst (as, "This little *whiff* of temper seemed to cool Silver down": Stevenson's "Treasure Island," xx.); also, a glimpse, or momentary view (Sc. and north. Eng.); also, an inkling (prov. or colloq.); also, a flag hoisted as a signal (as, "*Whiffs* ... were seen flying from the mast-heads ... the signals of recall for all boats": Cooper's "Two Admirals," xvi.).—**whiff,** *v.* **I.** *intr.* To blow or come in whiffs or puffs, as wind, smoke, etc.; also, to inhale or exhale whiffs, as in smoking tobacco. **II.** *tr.* To blow or drive with a whiff or puff, as the wind does; also, to inhale or exhale (air, tobacco-smoke, etc.) in whiffs; smoke (a pipe, cigar, etc.).—**whiff'er,** *n.*

whif-fet (hwif'et), *n.* [Dim. of *whiff, n.*: cf. *whippet.*] A little whiff; also, a small dog; also, an insignificant person; a whipper-snapper.

whif-fle (hwif'l), *v.*; *-fled, -fling.* [Freq. of *whiff, v.*] **I.** *intr.* To blow in light or shifting gusts or puffs, as the wind; veer irregularly (*about*); fig., to shift about in thought, opinion, intention, etc.; vacillate; also, to move lightly as if blown by a puff of wind. **II.** *tr.* To blow with light, shifting gusts (as, the wind *whiffles* the leaves about); drive, scatter, or disperse as with a mere puff of air.—**whif'fler**[1], *n.* One who whiffles, or shifts about in thought, opinion, intention, etc.; also, a shifty or evasive person; also, a trifler; an insignificant person.

whif-fler[2] (hwif'ler), *n.* [ME. *wifle,* spear, battle-ax, < AS. *wifel,* javelin, spear.] An attendant armed with a spear, battle-ax, staff, or the like, employed to clear the way, as for a procession; hence, a swaggerer. [Obs. or hist.]

whif-fle-tree (hwif'l-trē), *n.* Same as *whippletree.*

whig[1] (hwig), *v. i.*; *whigged, whigging.* [Origin obscure.] To move at an easy, steady pace; jog along. [Sc.]

whig[2] (hwig). [Appar. < *whiggamore.*] **I.** *n.* In the 17th century, one of the adherents of the Presbyterian cause in Scotland (a name applied in derision); [*cap.*] a member of a great political party in Great Britain, in general holding liberal principles and favoring various reforms, and more recently known as the 'Liberal party' (cf. *tory*); in later use, one of the more conservative members of the Liberal party; [*cap.*] in *Amer. hist.,* a member of the patriotic party during the Revolutionary period; a supporter of the Revolution;

also, a member of a political party which was formed about 1834 in opposition to the Democratic party, and which elected William Henry Harrison (1840) and Zachary Taylor (1848) to the Presidency. **II.** *a.* [*cap.*] Being a Whig; of, pertaining to, or characteristic of the Whigs.

whig-ga-more (hwig'ạ-mōr), *n.* [Origin uncertain; said to be from Gaelic.] [Also *cap.*] One of the people of western Scotland who marched on Edinburgh in 1648, opposed to the engagement entered into with Charles I. of England against the followers of Cromwell; later [*l. c.*], a Scotch Presbyterian.

whig-ger-y (hwig'ėr-i), *n.* The principles or practices of Whigs.

whig-gish (hwig'ish), *a.* Of, pertaining to, or characteristic of Whigs; inclined to whiggism.—**whig'gish-ly,** *adv.*—**whig'-gish-ness,** *n.*

whig-gism (hwig'izm), *n.* The principles of Whigs; whiggery.

while (hwīl), *n.* [AS. *hwīl* = D. *wijl* = G. *weile* = Goth. *hweila,* a while, time, = Icel. *hvíla,* place of rest, bed, = Sw. *hvila,* Dan. *hvile,* rest; perhaps akin to L. *quies,* rest.] A space of time (as, a long *while*; a *while* ago); also, one's time as spent on something (now only in 'worth while,' or 'worth one's while': see under *worth*[2], *a.*); also, a particular time or occasion (as, "There are *whiles* ... when ye are altogether too canny," Stevenson's "Kidnapped," xxii.; at *whiles,* at times: archaic or prov., except in 'between whiles,' which see below).—**between whiles,** between times; at intervals: as, "*Between whiles* Jim had threatening glimpses of the tumbling tide" (J. Conrad's "Lord Jim," i.).—**the while,** during this time (as, "gently stroking *the while* the girl's rough hand which lay on her knee": Mrs. H. Ward's "Robert Elsmere," iii.); also, during the time that (archaic: as, "Beseeching him, *the while* his hand she wrung, To change his purpose," Keats's "Lamia," ii.).—**while,** *conj.* During or in the time that (as, "*While* thus he spake, the angelic squadron bright Turn'd fiery red," Milton's "Paradise Lost," iv. 977; "*While* he was laughing the door opened," Besant's "All Sorts and Conditions of Men," xv.); throughout the time that, or as long as (as, "*While* stands the Coliseum, Rome shall stand": Byron's "Childe Harold," iv. 145); also, at the same time that (implying opposition or contrast: as, "He wonder'd that your lordship Would suffer him to spend his youth at home, *While* other men ... Put forth their sons to seek preferment out," Shakspere's "Two Gentlemen of Verona," i. 3. 6; *while* he appreciated the honor conferred, he could not accept the position); also, until (now prov.).—**while,** *v. t.*; *whiled, whiling.* To cause (time) to pass, esp. in some easy or pleasant manner: usually with *away*: as, "In talk and sport they *whiled* away The morning of that summer day" (Scott's "Lady of the Lake," ii. 27).—**whiles** (hwīlz). **I.** *adv.* At times (as, "Man, I *whiles* wonder at ye": Stevenson's "Kidnapped," xviii.); also, in the meantime. [Archaic or prov.] **II.** *conj.* While: as, "The tiger will be mild *whiles* she doth mourn" (Shakspere's "3 Henry VI.," iii. 1. 39). [Archaic or prov.]

whilk (hwilk), *pron.* and *a.* Obs. or Sc. and north. Eng. form of *which.*

whil-ly=wha, whil-ly=whaw (hwil'i-hwâ), *v. t.* or *i.* [Origin obscure.] To cajole, or use cajolery; wheedle. [Sc.]—**whil'ly=wha, whil'ly=whaw,** *n.* A cajoling speech; also, a cajoler. [Sc.]

whi-lom (hwī'lọm). [AS. *hwīlum,* prop. dat. pl. of *hwīl,* E. *while.*] **I.** *adv.* At times†; also, at one time, formerly, or once (archaic: as, "a celebrated jester, whose adventures, translated into English, were *whilom* extremely popular," Scott's "Abbot," xiv.). **II.** *a.* Former; quondam.

whilst (hwīlst). **I.** *conj.* Same as *while*: as, "Be quiet *whilst* the tempest lasts" (Thackeray's "Vanity Fair," xxv.). [Chiefly British.] **II.** In the phrase 'the whilst,' for 'the while' (see under *while, n.*). [Obs. or archaic.]

whim (hwim), *n.* [Origin uncertain: cf. Icel. *hvima,* wander with the eyes, *vim,* giddiness, Norw. *kvima,* whisk or flutter about, Dan. *vimse,* whisk, bustle, Sw. dial. *hwimsa,* be unsteady or giddy, also E. *whimsy* and *whimwham.*] An odd or fanciful thing†; a gimcrack†; also, an odd or fanciful notion; a freakish or capricious fancy or desire (as, "In manners, he was civil, or rude, familiar, or distant, just as the *whim* seized him": Bulwer-Lytton's "Pelham," xiv.); capricious humor (as, to be swayed by *whim*); also, a device for hoisting a bucket or the like, as from a mine, esp. a vertical drum on which the hoisting-rope winds, usually operated by a horse or horses.

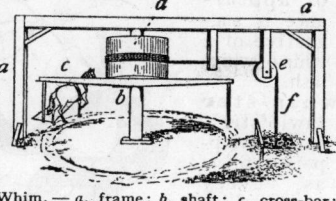

Whim.— *a*, frame; *b*, shaft; *c*, cross-bar; *d*, drum; *e*, pulley; *f*, hoisting-rope.

whim-brel (hwim′brẹl), *n*. [Prob. ult. imit.] A small European curlew, *Numenius phæopus*; any of certain other small curlews.

whim-my (hwim′i), *a*. Full of whims; whimsical; also, of the nature of a whim.

whim-per (hwim′pėr), *v*. [Prob. ult. imit.: cf. G. *wimmern*, whimper.] **I.** *intr.* To cry with low, plaintive, broken sounds, as a child, a grown person, or a dog (as, "The baby *whimpered*," A. S. M. Hutchinson's "If Winter Comes," iv. 2; "The puppies . . . barked and *whimpered*," Eden Phillpotts's "Children of Men," Prologue, iii.); hence, to complain feebly (as, "She is still *whimpering* after that gaby of a husband — dead . . . these fifteen years": Thackeray's "Vanity Fair," lxvii.); also, to make a plaintive murmuring sound (as, "the little brook that *whimpered* by his school-house": Irving's "Sketch-Book," Sleepy Hollow). **II.** *tr.* To utter in a whimper: as, "'Now you see,' *whimpered* Mrs. Gradgrind . . . 'I shall be worrying myself, morning, noon, and night!'" (Dickens's "Hard Times," i. 15).— **whim′per,** *n*. A whimpering cry or sound: as, "The loved caresses of the maid The dogs with crouch and *whimper* paid" (Scott's "Lady of the Lake," ii. 24).— **whim′-per-er,** *n*.— **whim′per-ing-ly,** *adv*.

whim′sey, *n*. See *whimsy*.

whim-si-cal (hwim′zi-kạl), *a*. [From *whimsy*.] Given to or characterized by whimsies or odd notions (as, "the fancies of *whimsical* mystics who held that it was sin to wear garments," Morley's "Oliver Cromwell," iv. 1; a *whimsical* mind or mood); of the nature of or proceeding from a whimsy, as thoughts, actions, etc. (as, "He gave vent to every *whimsical* idea as it rose": Smollett's "Humphry Clinker," May 6); hence, in general, of an odd, queer, quaint, or comical kind (as, "a *whimsical* chayre, which folded into so many varieties as to turn into a bed, a bolster, a table, or a couch," Evelyn's "Diary," Nov. 29, 1644; "the *whimsical* contrast between his military dress and his most unmilitary demeanor," Parkman's "Oregon Trail," xxii.).— **whim-si-cal′i-ty** (-kạl′i-ti), *n*.; pl. *-ties* (-tiz). Whimsical character; also, something whimsical; a whimsical notion, speech, or act (as, "Lady Delacour . . . laughed affectedly at her own *whimsicalities*": Maria Edgeworth's "Belinda," ii.).— **whim′si-cal-ly,** *adv*.— **whim′si-cal-ness,** *n*.

whim-sy (hwim′zi), *n*.; pl. *-sies* (-ziz). [Related to *whim*.] An odd or fanciful notion (as, "Both [the Puritan and the Quaker] had what seemed extravagant *whimsies* about dress, diversions and postures": Macaulay's "Hist. of Eng.," ii.); also, anything odd or fanciful; a product of playful or freakish fancy, as a literary trifle.

whim-wham (hwim′hwam), *n*. [Appar. a varied redupl. of *whim*, although recorded earlier.] Any odd or fanciful object or thing; a gimcrack; a trifle; also, a fanciful notion; an odd fancy. [Archaic or prov.]

whin¹, whin-stone (hwin, hwin′stōn), *n*. [Origin uncertain.] Basaltic rock; any of various other hard rocks; also, a mass or piece of such rock. [Chiefly Sc. and north. Eng.]

whin² (hwin), *n*. [ME. *whynne, quyn*; origin uncertain.] Furze: as, "a vast sheet of purple heath and golden *whin*" (H. Kingsley's "Geoffry Hamlyn," v.).

whin-chat (hwin′chat), *n*. [From *whin²* + *chat* (bird).] A small oscine passerine bird, *Pratincola rubetra*, found in Europe, and in Africa and Asia. See cut in next column.

whine (hwīn), *v*.; *whined, whining.* [AS. *hwīnan*, make a shrill sound, = Icel. *hvína*, Sw. *hvina*, Dan. *hvine*, whiz; prob. ult. imit.] **I.** *intr.* To utter a low, complaining cry or sound, as from uneasiness, discontent, peevishness, etc. (as, "Whip him . . . Till . . . you see him . . . *whine* aloud for mercy," Shakspere's "Antony and Cleopatra," iii. 13. 101; "The yacht's black dog . . . *whined* . . . begging for the charity of human notice," J. Conrad's "Rescue," iv. 4); also, to complain in a feeble, unbecoming way (as, "I don't want to *whine* — I deserved it all right enough": Hugh Walpole's "Wooden Horse," xv.); bemoan one's self weakly. **II.** *tr.* To utter with a whine: sometimes with *out*.— **whine,** *n*. A whining utterance, sound, or tone (as, "'I am afraid I'm going to Hell, Sir,' says the sick woman with a *whine*": S. Butler's "Way of All Flesh," xv.); a feeble, peevish complaint.— **whin-er** (hwī′nėr), *n*.

Whinchat.

whing-er† (hwing′ėr), *n*. Same as *whinyard*. [Chiefly Sc.]

whin-ing-ly (hwī′ning-li), *adv*. In a whining manner.

whin-ny¹ (hwin′i), *v*.; *-nied, -nying.* [Imit.: cf. L. *hinnire*, whinny, also E. *whine*.] **I.** *intr.* Of a horse, to utter its characteristic call or cry (as, "Some wild young colts . . . came galloping and *whinnying* towards him": H. Kingsley's "Geoffry Hamlyn," i.); neigh; sometimes, of other animals, etc., to utter a similar sound (as, "The elk kept up a continual *whinnying* or squealing": Irving's "Captain Bonneville," xli.). **II.** *tr.* To express by whinnying; utter with a whinnying sound.— **whin′ny¹,** *n*.; pl. *whinnies* (-iz). The call or cry of a horse, or a neigh (as, "The horse gave a *whinny*": W. B. Yeats's "Wanderings of Oisin," iii.); some similar sound.

whin-ny² (hwin′i), *a*. Abounding in whin or furze: as, "a fine, large, whinny, undrained, unimproved common" (Sterne's "Tristram Shandy," iv. 31).

whin-stone (hwin′stōn), *n*. See *whin¹*.

whin-yard (hwin′yärd), *n*. [Late ME. *whyneard*; origin obscure.] A kind of short sword. [Obs. or hist.]

whip (hwip), *v*.; *whipped*, also *whipt, whipping.* [ME. *whippen, wippen*: cf. MLG. *wippen*, move up and down, D. *wippen*, swing, leap, Sw. *vippa*, wag, jerk, Dan. *vippe*, bob up and down, rock.] **I.** *tr.* To move quickly and suddenly; pull, jerk, snatch, seize, put, etc., with a sudden movement (with *away, off, out, up, into*, etc.: as, "Aunt Chloe *whipped* the cover off the bake-kettle," Mrs. Stowe's "Uncle Tom's Cabin," iv.; "In an instant he had *whipped* out a knife," W. Churchill's "Mr. Crewe's Career," iii.; "a pie, which she *whipped* into the oven," Arnold Bennett's "Old Wives' Tale," i. 3); also, to strike with quick, repeated strokes of something slender and flexible; lash; beat with a whip or the like, esp. by way of punishment or chastisement; flog; thrash; lash or castigate with words; also, to drive (*on, out, in*, etc.) by strokes or lashes (as, to *whip* a horse on; to *whip* the mischief out of a boy; to *whip* in the hounds, in hunting, to the line of chase); also, to bring (*in, into line, together*, etc.) as a party whip does (from the use in hunting: see preceding def.); also, to strike (a spinning top) with a lash or whip in order to keep it spinning (as, "as young striplings *whip* the top for sport": Dryden's tr. Virgil's "Æneid," vii. 528); beat (eggs, cream, etc.) to a froth with a whisk, fork, or other implement; fish (a stream, etc.) with a rod and line (as, "*whipping* a trout-stream in Wales": Lever's "Harry Lorrequer," xlvii.); also, to beat, outdo, or defeat, as in a contest (colloq.); also, to overlay or cover (cord, etc.) with cord, thread, or the like wound about it; wind (cord, twine, thread, etc.) about something; sew with stitches passing successively over an edge, as a means of joining, finishing, or gathering; also, to hoist or purchase by means of a whip. **II.** *intr.* To move or go quickly and suddenly (*away, off, out, in*, etc.: as, "He *whipped* out of sight in a moment," Stevenson's "Treasure Island," xiii.; "We'll *whip* in at the back door," Mrs. Stowe's "Uncle Tom's Cabin," xxxix.); dart; whisk; beat or lash about,

as a pennant in the wind; also, to fish with a rod and line.—
whip, *n.* [ME. *whippe, wippe,* whip, scourge.] An instrument to strike with, as in driving animals or in punishing, typically consisting of a lash or other flexible part with a more rigid handle; a small instrument with a lash for keeping a top spinning; also, a whipping or lashing stroke or motion; also, one who handles a whip; a driver of horses, a coach, etc. (esp. with reference to skill: as, a good *whip*); one who has charge of the hounds in hunting; hence, in English (and other) political use, a party manager who secures attendance for voting and directs the action of members; also, a call made on members of a party to be in attendance for voting, etc.; also, a dish made of cream or egg-whites whipped to a froth with flavoring, etc., often with fruit-pulp or the like; also, a contrivance for hoisting, consisting essentially of a rope and pulley; also, in certain electrical devices, a vibrating spring for closing an electric circuit.

whip=cord (hwip′kôrd), *n.* A kind of strong, hard-twisted cord, sometimes used for the lashes of whips; also, a worsted fabric with a diagonally ribbed surface.

whip=hand (hwip′hand′), *n.* The hand that holds the whip in driving; hence, the position of control, or the advantage (as, to get the *whip-hand* of a person).

whipped (hwipt), *p. a.* Of cream, etc., beaten to a froth.

whip-per (hwip′ér), *n.* One who or that which whips. Cf. *coal-whipper.*—**whip′per=in′,** *n.*; pl. *whippers-in.* One who whips in hounds in hunting, or keeps them from wandering; hence, one who whips in members of a political party for united action; a party whip.

whip-per=snap-per (hwip′ér-snap″ér), *n.* A petty or insignificant person who affects importance; a shallow, presuming (often young) person.

whip-pet (hwip′et), *n.* [Appar. < *whip,* v. or n.: cf. *whiffet.*] A dog of an English breed, probably a cross between the greyhound and the terrier, used especially in rabbit-coursing and racing; hence, *milit.,* a comparatively light, fast tank.

whip-ping (hwip′ing), *n.* The act of one who or that which whips; a beating administered with a whip or the like, as for punishment; a flogging; also, an arrangement of cord, twine, or the like whipped or wound about a thing, as to bind parts together.—**whip′ping=boy,** *n.* Formerly, a boy educated with a prince, and whipped or punished in his stead.—**whip′ping=post,** *n.* A post to which persons are fastened to undergo whipping as a legal penalty.

whip-ple-tree (hwip′l-trē), *n.* [Also *whiffletree:* cf. *whiffle,* v., also *whip,* v.] A swingletree.

whip-poor-will (hwip′pôr-wil″), *n.* [Imit. of its cry.] A nocturnal goatsucker (bird), *Antrostomus vociferus* (family *Caprimulgidæ* or subfamily *Caprimulginæ*), of the eastern U. S. and Canada, having a variegated plumage of gray, black, white, and tawny. Cf. *goatsucker.*

Whippoorwill.

whip=saw (hwip′sâ), *n.* A saw used for cutting curved kerfs, consisting essentially of a narrow blade stretched in a frame.—**whip′=saw,** *v. t.* To cut with a whip-saw; also, to win two bets from (a person) at one turn or play, as in faro; defeat or worst in two ways at once.

whip=scor-pi-on (hwip′skôr″pi-on), *n.* Any of various arachnids of the genus *Thelyphonus* and allied genera, somewhat resembling the true scorpions of the order *Scorpionida,* and having (in the typical members) an abdomen ending in a slender whip-like part. Cf. *vinegaroon.*

whip=shaped (hwip′shāpt), *a.* Shaped like the lash of a whip; long and slender; flagelliform.

whip=snake (hwip′snāk), *n.* Any of various slender snakes whose form or appearance is suggestive of a whip or whiplash.

whip-ster (hwip′stér), *n.* A whipper-snapper: as, "every puny *whip-ster*" (Shakspere's "Othello," v. 2. 244). [Obs. or archaic.]

whip=stitch (hwip′stich), *v. t.* To sew with stitches passing successively over an edge; whip.—

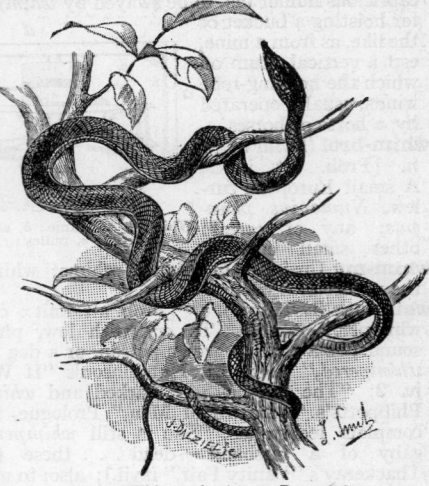

Indian Whip-snake (genus *Passerita*).

whip′=stitch, *n.* A stitch made in whip-stitching; hence (colloq.), a single bit or particle (as, to use up every *w* *stitch*); an instant, or brief space of time (as, I'll be there a *whip-stitch;* to persist in doing a thing every *whip-sti*

whip=stock (hwip′stok), *n.* The handle of a whip.

whip=worm (hwip′wèrm), *n.* Any of certain nema worms of the genus *Trichocephalus,* as *T. dispar,* a sp often found parasitic in the human intestine.

whir, whirr (hwèr), *v.; whirred, whirring.* [Appar. i cf. *whirl.*] **I.** *intr.* To go, fly, dart, revolve, or othe move quickly with a vibratory or buzzing sound (as, grouse *whirrs* away before me," Gissing's "Private I of Henry Ryecroft," iv. 23; a missile *whirs* through th flames *whir* up a chimney); also, to make a vibrato buzzing sound, as of rapid motion, esp. of wings, whee other parts moving rapidly (as, "The motor stopped sno and *whirring*": Vernon Lee's "Enchanted Woods," Motor-Car and the Genius of Places, ii.). **II.** *tr.* To l along or away with a vibratory sound (as, "This world to is like a lasting storm, *Whirring* me from my friends": Shakspere's "Pericles," iv. 1. 21); also, to cause to move or sound with a whir (as, to *whir* the wings).—**whir, whirr,** *n.* The act or sound of whirring: as, the *whir* of wings; "the *whirr* of shafts and wheels" (Dickens's "Hard Times," ii. 1); "the steady *whirr* of the flames" (Galsworthy's "Country House," ii. 5).

whirl (hwèrl), *v.* [ME. *whirlen,* appar. from Scand.: cf. Icel. and Sw. *hvirfla,* Dan. *hvirvle,* whirl, akin to G. *wirbeln,* whirl, and AS. *hweorfan,* turn: see *warble*[2] and *wharve.*] **I.** *intr.* To turn round, spin, or rotate rapidly (as, a *whirling* dervish; "The log was heaved . . . the reel began to *whirl*," H. Melville's "Moby-Dick," cxxv.); move in a circular or curving course (as, dust *whirling* in eddies; "The wind goeth toward the south, and turneth about unto the north; it *whirleth* about continually," Eccl. i. 6); turn about or aside quickly (as, "He [a horse] suddenly *whirled* from the trail": Wister's "Virginian," xxvi.); also, to move, travel, or be carried rapidly along on wheels or otherwise (as, "Soon they were once more *whirling* towards England [on a train]": Galsworthy's "Dark Flower," ii. 8); also, to have the sensation of turning round rapidly (as, "One may gaze and think till the brain *whirls*": Gissing's "Private Papers of Henry Ryecroft," iii. 9). **II.** *tr.* To cause to turn round, spin, or rotate rapidly (as, to *whirl* a wheel or a top); send, drive, or carry in a circular or curving course (as, "He had been as a leaf *whirled* upon a winter torrent": Froude's "Cæsar," xxiii.); swing (a weapon) with a quick, curving movement (as, "As the lad slipped . . . he *whirled* up his sword to finish him": Conan Doyle's "Exploits of Brigadier Gerard," i.); also, to drive or draw rapidly on wheels or otherwise (as, "Edward Henry disappeared within the vehicle, and was *whirled* away": Arnold Bennett's "The Old Adam," vi.); send or carry along with great or dizzying rapidity; also, to cast or throw violently, or hurl (as, "First Sarpedon *whirl'd* his weighty lance": Pope's tr. Homer's "Iliad," xvi.). — **whirl,** *n.* The act of whirling; rapid rotation or gyration; a whirling movement; a quick turn or swing; a rapid passage or course; a short drive, run, walk, or the like, or a spin; also, something that whirls; a whirling current or mass (as, "Upon the *whirl,* where sank the ship, The boat spun round and round," Coleridge's "Ancient Mariner," vii.; *"whirls* and clouds of shining vapour which we call nebulæ," H. G. Wells's "Outline of History," i.); an eddy or vortex; fig., a rapid round of events, affairs, etc. (as, a *whirl* of social festivities; the *whirl* of fashion); also, a mental state suggestive of whirling (as, his brain was in a *whirl*); a state marked by a dizzying succession or mingling of feelings, thoughts, etc. (as, "He parted from her in a *whirl* of variegated ecstasies": Arnold Bennett's "Great Man," xiv.).

whirl-a-bout (hwèrl′a-bout″), *n.* A whirling about; also, something that whirls about; a whirligig.

whirl-blast (hwèrl′blàst), *n.* A whirlwind.

whirl-er (hwèr′lèr), *n.* One who or that which whirls.

whirl-i-gig (hwèr′li-gig), *n.* [See *gig*[1].] A toy for whirling or spinning, as a top; also, a merry-go-round or carrousel; in general, something that whirls, revolves, or goes round; a revolving agency or course (as, "Thus the *whirligig* of time brings in his revenges": Shakspere's "Twelfth Night," v. 1. 385); a continuous round or succession (as, "A merry-go-round of creditors required a corresponding *whirligig* of receipts": G. Meredith's "Diana of the Crossways," xxi.); a giddy or flighty person; also, any of the aquatic beetles of the family *Gyrinidæ,* which are commonly seen circling rapidly about in large numbers on the surface of the water.

whirl-pool (hwèrl′pöl), *n.* A circular eddy or current, as in a river or the sea, produced by the configuration of a channel, by the meeting of opposing currents, by the meeting of winds and tides, etc.; a vortex of water. Also fig.

whirl-wind (hwèrl′wind), *n.* A mass of air rotating rapidly round and toward a more or less vertical axis, and having at the same time a progressive motion over the surface of the land or sea (a term including the eddy-like winds seen circling in dusty streets, the tornadoes, waterspouts, etc., and, according to some authorities, the cyclonic disturbances of large area); fig., any circling rush or violent onward course; anything resembling a whirlwind, as in violent activity (as, "Three horsemen launch in upon them — only three, but those three a *whirlwind*": G. W. Cable's "Bonaventure," i. 4).

Whirligig. (Line shows natural size.)

whirr, *v.* and *n.* See *whir.*

whish (hwish), *v. i.* [Imit.] To make, or move with, the sound of something rushing rapidly through the air; whiz; whistle; swish. — **whish,** *n.* A whishing sound.

whisht (hwisht), *interj.* and *a.* Obs. or prov. form of *whist*[1].

whisk (hwisk), *n.* [Appar. from Scand.: cf. Icel. *visk,* wisp (of hay, etc.), Sw. *viska,* Dan. *viske,* wisp, brush, whisk, OHG. *wisc,* G. *wisch,* brush, duster.] A small bunch of grass, straw, hair, or the like, esp. for use in brushing; a small brush or broom; a whisk-broom; also, an implement, in one form a bunch of loops of wire held together in a handle, for beating or whipping eggs, cream, etc.; also, an act of whisking; a rapid, sweeping stroke; a light, rapid movement. — **whisk,** *v.* **I.** *tr.* To sweep (dust, crumbs, etc., or a surface) with a whisk, brush, or the like; also, to whip (eggs, cream, etc.) to a froth with a whisk or beating implement; also, to move with a rapid, sweeping stroke (as, "The horses . . . *whisked* their tails about in all directions": Dickens's "Pickwick Papers," iv.); draw, snatch, carry, etc., lightly and rapidly (as, "a solitary omnibus, which daily *whisks* a few country people and their parcels down to Uxbridge": W. Black's "Strange Adventures of a Phaeton," ii.). **II.** *intr.* To sweep, pass, or go lightly and rapidly: as, "Nurses *whisked* backward and forward with trays and pails" (Mrs. Wharton's "Son at the Front," xii.).

whisk=broom (hwisk′bröm′), *n.* A small broom for brushing clothes, etc.

whisk-er (hwis′kèr), *n.* One who or that which whisks; also, the hair growing on the side of a man's face, esp. when worn long and with the chin clean-shaven (usually in *pl.*); often, *pl.,* the beard generally; sometimes, the mustache (now prov. or colloq.); *sing.,* a single hair of the beard; also, one of the long, stiff, bristly hairs growing about the mouth of certain animals, as the cat, rat, etc.; a vibrissa; *naut.,* either of two bars of wood or iron projecting laterally one from each side of the bowsprit, to give more spread to the guys which support the jib-boom. — **whisk′ered,** *a.* Having whiskers (as, "a grave *whiskered* young man": Arnold Bennett's "Clayhanger," i. 4); also, in the form of whiskers (as, *"whisker'd* hair": M. Green's "The Spleen").

whis-ky, whis-key (hwis′ki), *n.*; pl. *-kies, -keys* (-kiz). [Gael. and Ir. *uisge,* water, in *uisgebeatha,* 'water of life,' E. *usquebaugh.*] A distilled alcoholic liquor made from grain, as barley, rye, maize, etc., containing commonly from 37 to 47½ per cent by weight of alcohol; also, a similar liquor distilled from potatoes, etc.

whis-ky=jack (hwis′ki-jak), *n.* [For *whisky-john,* a corruption of the Cree Indian name.] A jay, *Perisoreus canadensis,* of (chiefly northern) North America, having a plain grayish plumage.

Whisky-jack.

whis-per (hwis′pèr), *v.* [AS. *hwisprian,* akin to OHG. *hwispalōn,* G. *wispeln, wispern,* D. *wispelen,* whisper; orig. imit.] **I.** *intr.* To speak with soft, low sounds, using the breath, lips, etc., without vibration of the vocal cords; hence, to talk softly and privately (often with implication of gossip, slander, or plotting); fig., of trees, water, breezes, etc., to make a soft, rustling sound (as, "soft zephyrs *whispering* through the trees": Thomson's "Of a Country Life," 5). **II.** *tr.* To utter with soft, low sounds, using the breath, lips, etc.; say or tell in a whisper (sometimes fig., of things: as, "My fear *whispers* that some deed of horror has been perpetrated," C. B. Brown's "Wieland," xxii.); hence, to tell privately (as, "I have heard it *whispered* that her youth was not altogether happy": Cooper's "Spy," xxxv.); repeat as rumor; also, to speak to or tell (a person) in a whisper, or privately. — **whis′per,** *n.* The mode of utterance, or the voice, of one who whispers (as, to speak in a *whisper*); a sound, word, remark, or the like, uttered by whispering (as, low *whispers*); hence, something said or repeated privately; a rumor; fig., a soft, rustling sound, as of leaves moving in the wind. — **whis′per-er,** *n.* — **whis′per-ing=gal″le-ry,** *n.* A gallery, as that in St. Paul's Cathedral, London, so shaped that a whisper uttered at a certain point can be heard (by reflection and concentration of the sound) at a distant point, beyond the range of ordinary hearing; any chamber or hollow place, as a cave, having the same acoustic property. — **whis′per-ing-ly,** *adv.*

whist[1] (hwist), *interj.* [ME. *whist,* a natural utterance calling for silence: cf. *hush, v.,* and *hist.*] Hush! silence! be still! — **whist**[1], *a.* Hushed; silent; still: chiefly used predicatively: as, "The winds are *whist,* and the owl is still" (J. R. Drake's "Culprit Fay," ii.). [Archaic or prov.]

whist[2] (hwist), *n.* [First recorded as *whisk,* explained as referring to the whisking or sweeping of the cards from the table (cf. *whisk and swabbers,* an old name for a particular form of the game); later associated with *whist*[1], as if expressing a call for silence during the game.] A card-game played by four players, two against two, with a pack of 52 cards, all of which are dealt out for each hand or round, partners scoring on every trick they take in excess of six.

whis-tle (hwis'l), v.; -tled, -tling. [AS. hwistlian, akin to Sw. hvissla, Dan. hvisle, whistle, Icel. hvīsla, whisper; orig. imit.] **I.** intr. To make a kind of clear musical sound, or a series of such sounds, by the forcible expulsion of the breath through a small orifice formed by contracting the lips, or through the teeth, together with the aid of the tongue; make such a sound or series of sounds otherwise, as by blowing on a device made for the purpose; produce a more or less similar sound by an instrument operated by steam or the like, or as such an instrument does; emit somewhat similar sounds from the mouth, as birds do (as, "A multitude of quails were plaintively whistling in the woods": Parkman's "Oregon Trail," ii.); sound shrilly, as the wind does (as, "The wind whistled through the cracked walls": Dickens's "Bleak House," viii.); move, go, pass, etc., with a whizzing sound, as a bullet (as, "William . . . was surprised with hearing a musket-shot whistle by him": Defoe's "Captain Singleton," xiii.). **II.** tr. To produce by whistling (as, "The surgeon . . . employed himself in whistling a low air": Cooper's "Spy," xi.); also, to call, direct, or signal by or as by whistling (as, "The under-butler whistled up a hansom for the General": H. G. Wells's "Bealby," viii.); also, to send with a whistling or whizzing sound (as, "sturdy young giants as ever . . . carried bolt to whistle at a chamois": Scott's "Anne of Geierstein," xiii.). —**whis'tle,** n. [AS. hwistle, whistle, pipe.] An instrument for producing whistling sounds, as by the force of the breath, of steam, etc., as a small wooden or tin tube, a small pipe, or any of various larger instruments used on railroad-engines, factories, etc., for giving signals or the like; also, the mouth and throat (colloq.: as, to wet one's whistle, to take a drink); also, a sound produced by or as by whistling (as, "a long-drawn . . . whistle of astonishment," H. Melville's "Moby-Dick," x.; "The whistle of the locomotive penetrates my woods," Thoreau's "Walden," iv.; "The whistle of the wind increased," W. Morris's "Jason," xiv. 443). —**whis'tler,** n. One who or that which whistles; specif., a large marmot, Arctomys pruinosus, of northwestern North America, closely related to the woodchuck; in vet. science, a horse afflicted

Whistler (*Arctomys pruinosus*).

with whistling. —**whis'tling,** n. The act of one who or that which whistles; the sound produced; in vet. science, a form of roaring characterized by a peculiarly shrill sound. —**whis'tling-ly,** adv.

whit (hwit), n. [AS. wiht, thing, creature: see wight[1], and cf. aught[1].] A particle; a bit; a jot: used esp. in negative phrases: as, never a whit; not a whit better.

white (hwīt), a.; compar. whiter, superl. whitest. [AS. hwīt = D. wit = G. weiss = Icel. hvītr = Goth. hweits, white: cf. wheat.] Of the color of pure snow; reflecting sunlight or a similar light without absorbing any of the rays composing it; also, light or comparatively light in color; esp., having a light-colored skin; noting or pertaining to the Caucasian race; also, blond or fair (chiefly poetic: as, "fresh Antigone the whyte," Chaucer's "Troilus and Criseyde," ii. 887); pallid or pale, as from fear or other strong emotion (as, "to turn white and swoon at tragic news": Shakspere's "Lover's Complaint," 308); silvery, gray, or hoary, as hair; also, wearing white clothing (as, a white friar: see phrase below); also, blank, as an unoccupied space in printed matter; of silverware, not burnished; of wines, light-colored or yellowish, as opposed to red (many 'white wines' being of a deep-amber or brownish color); fig., free from spot or stain, or pure or innocent (as, "Calumny The whitest virtue strikes": Shakspere's "Measure for Measure," iii. 2. 198); honorable, trustworthy, or square (slang, orig.

U. S.: as, "You have acted in a way which them that know the facts would call pretty near white," Wister's "Virginian," xxi.; "I'm a white woman all through. Haven't you learnt that yet?" Arnold Bennett's "Lion's Share," xl.); benevolent, beneficent, or good (as, a white witch; white magic); auspicious or fortunate (as, "The Thanksgiving festival of that year is particularly impressed on my mind as a white day": Mrs. Stowe's "Oldtown Folks," xxvii.); also (as opposed to red, or revolutionary), royalist or reactionary. —**the white man's burden,** the duty incumbent upon the white race of caring for and educating ignorant or uncivilized peoples, esp. subject peoples, of other races: from Kipling's poem "The White Man's Burden." —**white alkali,** in com., refined soda-ash. —**white ant,** a termite. —**white bryony,** a species of bryony, Bryonia alba, native in Europe. —**white canon,** a Premonstratensian canon: so called from the white habit. —**white clover,** a clover, Trifolium repens, with white flowers, common in pastures and meadows. —**white coal,** wood used for fuel†; also, water, as of a running stream, used as a source of power. —**white daisy.** See daisy. —**white elephant,** an elephant of an abnormally whitish or pale color; an albino elephant; fig., a possession of great value but entailing even greater expense (in allusion to the white elephants of the East Indies, which are highly prized, and maintained in costly state); anything ostensibly desirable or excellent but exceedingly burdensome or troublesome to have. —**white feather,** a symbol of cowardice: orig. from a white feather in a game-cock's tail taken as a sign of inferior breeding and hence of poor fighting qualities. —**white flag.** See flag[2], n. —**white flax,** the plant gold-of-pleasure. —**white friar,** a Carmelite friar: from the distinctive white cloak. —**white fuel,** water used as a source of power; white coal. —**white heat,** the very high temperature at which iron or the like becomes incandescent and emits a dazzling white light; fig., a stage of intense activity, excitement, feeling, etc. (as, to work at a white heat; "The failure at Gergovia had kindled the enthusiasm of the central districts into white heat," Froude's "Cæsar," xix.). —**white horse,** a white-topped wave; a whitecap: as, "Myriads of white horses curved and tossed and vanished over the shifting colours of the sea" (Hugh Walpole's "Wooden Horse," ix.). —**White House,** the official residence ('Executive Mansion') of the President of the U. S., at Washington, a large two-story freestone building painted white. —**white lead.** See under lead[2], n. —**white leather,** leather prepared by tawing, retaining the natural light color. —**white lie,** a lie uttered from polite, amiable, or pardonable motives; a polite or harmless fib. —**white lily.** See lily, n. —**white lupine.** See lupine[2]. —**white matter,** in anat., nervous tissue, esp. of the brain and spinal cord (of which it constitutes a great part), containing fibers only, and nearly white in color. Cf. gray matter, under gray, a. —**white meat,** any light-colored flesh-meat, as veal, the breast of chicken, etc.; also, food composed of milk, or of cheese, butter, eggs, and the like. —**white metal,** any of various light-colored alloys, as Babbitt metal, Britannia metal, etc. —**white oak,** an oak, Quercus alba, of eastern North America, having a light-gray to white bark and a hard, durable wood; any of several other species of oak, as Q. garryana or Q. oblongifolia of western

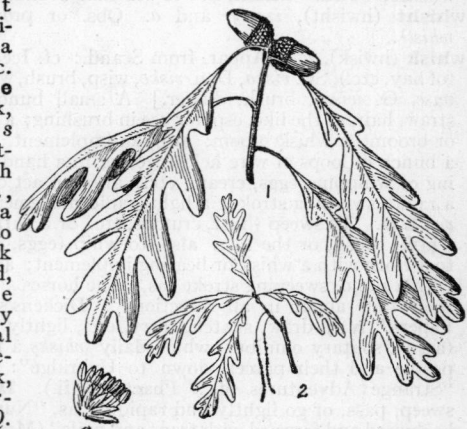

White Oak (*Quercus alba*).— 1, branch with acorns; 2, branch with male catkins; a, a male flower.

North America, or *Q. pedunculata* of Great Britain; also, the wood of any of these trees.—**white pine,** a pine, *Pinus strobus,* of eastern North America, yielding a light-colored, soft, light wood of great commercial importance; the wood itself; also, any of various other species of pine.—**white plague,** tuberculosis, esp. pulmonary tuberculosis.—**white poplar,** an old-world poplar, *Populus alba,* widely cultivated in the U. S., having the under side of the leaves covered with a dense silvery-white down.—**White Russians.** See under *Russian, n.*—**white sauce,** a sauce made of butter, flour, and milk or cream, or sometimes chicken or veal stock.—**white slave,** a white person held as a slave or in some condition resembling slavery; esp., a white woman who is sold or forced to serve as a prostitute.—**white slaver,** a person engaged in the traffic in white slaves.—**white slavery,** the condition of or the traffic in white slaves.—**white squall,** *naut.,* a whirlwind or violent disturbance of small radius, which is not accompanied by the usual clouds, but is indicated merely by the whitecaps and turbulent water beneath it.—**white whale,** the beluga, *Delphinapterus leucas.*—**white,** *n.* White hue or color; also, a white pigment or paint; also, something white, or a white part of something; the albumen of an egg, or the pellucid viscous fluid which surrounds the yolk; the sclerotica, or white part of the eyeball; the central part of the butt in archery, formerly painted white; a blank space in printing (usually in *pl.*); white clothing; also, a member of the white or Caucasian race; also, *pl.,* in *pathol.,* leucorrhea.—**white,** *v. t.*; whited, whiting. [AS. *hwítan.*] To make white; whiten. [Now rare.]—**whited sepulcher,** fig., a person having a fair outward appearance that covers corruption within; a specious hypocrite: from the expression as used in Mat. xxiii. 27.

white-bait (hwīt′bāt), *n.*; pl. -*bait.* A very small, silvery fish, the young of any of various clupeoid fishes, esp. herrings and sprats, prized as a delicacy in England; also, any of various similar fishes.

White-boy (hwīt′boi), *n.* A member of an illegal agrarian association formed in Ireland about 1761, for the redressing of grievances: so called because the members wore white frocks over their other clothes at their nightly meetings and in their raids.

white-cap (hwīt′kap), *n.* A white-capped wave; a wave with a broken, white crest; a white horse; also [*cap.*], a member of a self-constituted committee in a community, who, in undertaking to deal with persons deemed harmful to the community, commit various outrages and lawless acts (so called from the head-coverings worn by some of them: U. S.).

white=col-lar (hwīt′kol′ẹr), *a.* Wearing a white collar; hence, wearing the conventional genteel dress proper to occupations above the grade of manual or mechanical labor (as, clerks, teachers, officials, and others of the *white-collar* class; *white-collar* workers); of or pertaining to those wearing such dress (as, *white-collar* occupations or jobs).

white=eye (hwīt′ī), *n.* Any of certain birds having eyes in which the iris is white or colorless; also, any of the numerous small, old-world, chiefly tropical singing birds constituting the genus *Zos-terops,* most species of which have a ring of white feathers around the eye.

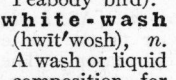

White-eye (*Zosterops cærulescens*).

white=faced (hwīt′fāst), *a.* Having a white or pale face; also, marked with white on the front of the head, as a horse; also, having a white front or surface (as, "that *white-faced* shore": Shakspere's "King John," ii. 1. 23).

white-fish (hwīt′fish), *n.* Any fish of the genus *Coregonus,* of the salmon family, esp. *C. clupeiformis* (the common

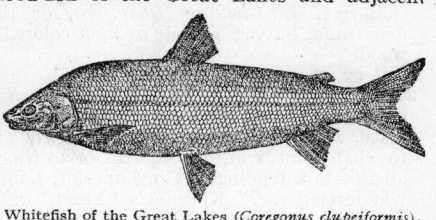

Whitefish of the Great Lakes (*Coregonus clupeiformis*).

whitefish), a food-fish of the Great Lakes and adjacent waters, having an olivaceous color above and white sides; any fish of the related genus *Argyrosomus,* as the black-fin, bloater, cisco, etc.; also, any of various other fishes having a more or less whitish color, as the whiting, menhaden, etc.; also, the beluga (cetacean).

white=gum[1] (hwīt′gum), *n.* Any of various Australian eucalyptuses with a whitish bark; also, the sweet-gum.

white=gum[2] (hwīt′gum), *n.* [Cf. *red-gum*[2].] An eruption of whitish spots affecting infants. See *strophulus.*

white=hot (hwīt′hot′), *a.* Heated to a white heat (see phrase under *white, a.*). Also fig.

white=liv-ered (hwīt′liv″ẽrd), *a.* Having (supposedly) a light-colored liver; pale or unhealthy; cowardly or pusillanimous.

white-ly (hwīt′li), *adv.* With a white hue or color.

whit-en (hwī′tn), *v. t.* or *i.* To make or become white.—**whit′en-er,** *n.*

white-ness (hwīt′nes), *n.* The quality or state of being white.

whites (hwīts), *n. pl.* See *white, n.*

white-smith (hwīt′smith), *n.* [Cf. *blacksmith.*] A tinsmith; also, a worker in iron who finishes or polishes, in distinction from one who forges.

white-ster, whit-ster (hwīt′stẽr, hwīt′-), *n.* A bleacher, as of linen. [Obs. or prov. Eng.]

white-thorn (hwīt′thôrn), *n.* The common hawthorn, *Cratægus oxyacantha.*

white-throat (hwīt′thrōt), *n.* A small old-world warbler, *Sylvia cinerea,* with a whitish throat and belly; any of several other old-world birds of the same genus; also, the Peabody bird.—**white′=throat″ed,** *a.* Having a white throat: as, the *white-throated* sparrow (the Peabody bird).

white-wash (hwīt′wosh), *n.* A wash or liquid composition for whitening something; esp., a composition, as of lime and water or of whiting, size, and water, used for whitening walls, woodwork, etc.; fig., anything used as a means of covering up defects, glossing over faults or errors, rehabilitating reputation, or imparting a specious semblance of respectability, honesty, etc. (as, to reorganize a party with a lavish use of *whitewash*); also, in various games, a defeat in which the loser fails to score (colloq.).—**white′wash,** *v. t.* To whiten with whitewash (as, "a . . . *white-washed* outhouse": H. G. Wells's "Kipps," i. 1); fig., to cover up or gloss over the defects, faults, errors, etc., of by some special means (as, to *whitewash* a person, his reputation or memory, or a questionable transaction; "Wait till you see how the Railroad Commission 'll *whitewash* that case," W. Churchill's "Mr. Crewe's Career," iii.); also, in various games, to subject to a whitewash (colloq.).—**white′wash″er,** *n.*

Common Whitethroat (*Sylvia cinerea*).

white-weed (hwīt′wēd), *n.* The common white daisy, *Chrysanthemum leucanthemum,* of the U. S.

white-wings (hwīt′wingz), *n.*; pl. *white-wings.* One of a body of public street-cleaners, as in New York City, wearing a white uniform.

white-wood (hwīt'wud), *n.* Any of numerous trees, as the tulip-tree, *Liriodendron tulipifera,* or the linden, *Tilia americana,* having a white or light-colored wood; also, the wood.

whit-ey (hwī'ti), *a.* See *whity.*

whith-er (hwiᴛʜ'ėr). [AS. *hwider,* from the pronominal stem represented by E. *who.*] **I.** *interrog. adv.* To what place? (as, "*Whither* goest thou?" Gen. xxxii. 17); hence, to what point, end, course, etc., or to what? (as, *whither* is all this talk tending? "Oh, Lancelot, Lancelot, *whither* are you forcing me?" Kingsley's "Yeast," x.); also, to what extent, or how far?† **II.** *conj.* To what, whatever, or which place, point, end, etc.: as, to go *whither* duty calls one; one final goal, *whither* all our ways lead.—**whith″er-so-ev′er** (-sǫ-ev′ėr), *conj.* To whatsoever place.—**whith′er-ward** (-wärd). **I.** *interrog. adv.* Toward what place? in what direction? whither? [Archaic.] **II.** *conj.* Toward what, whatever, or which place. [Archaic.]

whit-ing[1] (hwī'ting), *n.*; pl. *whitings* or (esp. collectively) *whiting.* [From *white, a.*] A common European gadoid fish, *Merlangus merlangus,* abundant off the coast of Great Britain, and highly esteemed for food; also, the silver hake, *Merlucius bilinearis*; also, the kingfish, *Menticirrus saxatilis,* or a related species; also, any of various other fishes.

Whiting (*Merlangus merlangus*).

whit-ing[2] (hwī'ting), *n.* [From *white, v.*] Pure white chalk (calcium carbonate) which has been ground and washed, used in making putty, whitewash, etc., and for cleaning silver, etc.

whit-ish (hwī'tish), *a.* Somewhat white; tending to white; whity.—**whit′ish-ness,** *n.*

whit-leath-er (hwit'leᴛʜ″ėr), *n.* [= *white leather.*] Same as *white leather* (see under *white, a.*); also, the paxwax.

whit-low (hwit'lō), *n.* [ME. *whitflowe, whitflawe*; appar. = *white* + *flaw*[2].] In *pathol.,* an inflammation of the deeper tissues of a finger or toe, esp. of the terminal phalanx, usually terminating in suppuration.—**whit′low=grass,** *n.* Any of several plants formerly reputed to cure whitlows, as a saxifrage, *Saxifraga tridactylites,* of the Old World, or, esp., an early-blooming brassicaceous herb, *Draba verna,* of Europe and North America ('vernal whitlow-grass').

Whit=Mon-day (hwit'mun'dą), *n.* The Monday following Whitsunday.

whit-ster (hwit'stėr), *n.* See *whitester.*

Whit-sun (hwit'sn), *a.* Of or pertaining to Whitsunday or Whitsuntide.

Whit-sun-day (hwit'sun'dą or hwit'sn-dā), *n.* [AS. *hwīta sunnandæg,* 'white Sunday': said to refer to the white garments of candidates for baptism at that season.] The seventh Sunday after Easter, celebrated as a festival in commemoration of the descent of the Holy Spirit on the day of Pentecost; also, in Scotland, May 15, as one of the quarter-days.—**Whit′sun-tide** (-sn-tīd), *n.* The season of Whitsunday; the week beginning with Whitsunday, esp. the first three days of this week.—**Whit′sun=week′,** *n.* The week beginning with Whitsunday.

whit-tle (hwit'l), *n.* [ME. *thwitel,* < AS. *thwītan,* cut.] A knife, esp. a case-knife or a clasp-knife, or a carving-knife or a butcher's knife (archaic or prov. Eng. and Sc.); also, a whetstone or a steel for sharpening knives, etc. (prov. Eng. and Sc.).—**whit′tle,** *v.*; *-tled, -tling.* **I.** *tr.* To cut, trim, or shape (a stick, piece of wood, etc.) by taking off bits with a knife; cut off (a bit or bits); fig., to cut by way of reducing amount (esp. with *down*: as, to *whittle* down expenses); also, to sharpen (a knife, etc.: prov. Eng. and Sc.); fig., to make tipsy or drunk (obs. or prov. Eng.). **II.** *intr.* To cut bits or chips from wood or the like with a knife, as in shaping something or as a mere aimless diversion.—**whit′-tling,** *n.* The act of one who whittles; also, a bit or chip whittled off (usually in *pl.*: as, "Shavings and *whittlings* strewed the floor," Howells's "Foregone Conclusion," iii.).

Whit=Tues-day (hwit'tūz'dą), *n.* The Tuesday next after Whitsunday.

whit-y (hwī'ti), *a.* Whitish.

whiz, whizz (hwiz), *v.*; *whizzed, whizzing.* [Imit.] **I.** *intr.* To make a humming or hissing sound, as an object passing rapidly through the air; move or rush with such a sound (as, "The shot *whizzed* between the masts": Marryat's "King's Own," xiii.). **II.** *tr.* To cause to whiz; also, to treat with a whizzer.—**whiz, whizz,** *n.* The sound of a whizzing object, or a swift movement producing such a sound: as, "The *whiz* of the arrow over their heads kept the horses in terror" (Morley's "Oliver Cromwell," ii. 1).—**whiz′zer,** *n.* Something that whizzes; specif., a centrifugal machine for drying sugar, grain, clothes, etc. (see *centrifugal, a.*).—**whiz′zing-ly,** *adv.*

who (hö), *pron.*; nom. *who,* poss. *whose,* obj. *whom*; pl. the same. [AS. *hwā* (gen. *hwæs,* dat. *hwǣm, hwām,* acc. *hwone*; neut. *hwæt,* E. *what*), akin to OHG. *hwer* (G. *wer*), Icel. *hverr,* Goth. *hwas,* also to L. *qui, quis,* Skt. *kas,* who: cf. *how*[2], *when, where, whether, which, whither, why,* and *quality*).] **A.** *interrog.* What person? (as, *who* told you so? *whose* book is this? of *whom* are you speaking?); also, of a person, what as to character, origin, position, importance, etc.? (as, "*Who* art thou that judged another?" Jas. iv. 12; *who* is the man in uniform?). **B.** *rel.* (1) As a compound relative, the or any person that (as, "*Who* steals my purse steals trash," Shakspere's "Othello," iii. 3. 157; any person, be it *who* it may); one that (after *as,* in archaic expressions: as, "He nods at us, as *who* should say, I'll be even with you," Shakspere's "2 Henry VI.," iv. 7. 99); (2) as a simple relative, with antecedent (a person, or sometimes an animal or a personified thing) expressed, in clauses conveying an additional idea (as, we saw several men, *who* were at work; "Ye stars, *Who* slowly begin to marshal . . . Your . . . lines," M. Arnold's "Empedocles on Etna," ii.); also, used in clauses defining or restricting the antecedent (as, release all *who* have served their term; one on *whose* word we can rely; the man to *whom* this was told: cf. *that, rel. pron.*).

whoa (hwō), *interj.* [= *ho*[2].] Stop!—used esp. to horses.

who-e′er (hö-ār′). Contracted form of *whoever.*

who-ev-er (hö-ev′ėr), *pron.* **I.** *interrog.* Who ever? who?—used emphatically: as, *whoever* is that? [Colloq.] **II.** *indef. rel.* Whatever person, or any one that (as, *whoever* wants it may have it); also, no matter who (as, "*Whoever* bound him, I will loose his bonds": Shakspere's "Comedy of Errors," v. 1. 339).

whole (hōl), *a.* [AS. *hāl* = D. *heel* = G. *heil* = Icel. *heill* = Goth. *hails,* hale, whole: cf. *hale*[2], *heal,* and *holy.*] In good health or sound physical condition (archaic: as, "They that be *whole* need not a physician, but they that be sick," Mat. ix. 12); also, uninjured, undamaged, or unbroken (as, to get off with a *whole* skin; not a dish was left *whole*); sound; intact; also, undivided, or in one piece (as, to swallow a thing *whole*); integral, or not fractional (as, a *whole* number: see phrase below); also, containing all the elements properly belonging (as, a *whole* set or assortment; *whole* milk, milk not deprived of the cream; *whole* meal, *whole* wheat flour, meal or wheat flour not deprived of the bran); complete; also, comprising the full quantity, amount, extent, number, etc., without diminution or exception (as, a *whole* melon, dollar, mile, year, dozen; the *whole* world; the *whole* subject; one's *whole* heart or strength); entire, full, or total; with a plural, the entire number of, or all (as, "the *whole* inhabitants of the district," Scott's "Castle Dangerous," xx.: now chiefly Sc.); also, being fully or entirely such (as, *whole* brother, *whole* sister, brother or sister by both parents: cf. *half-brother, half-sister*).—**out of whole cloth,** out of materials of fabrication rather than of fact or truth; without foundation in fact: as, a story made *out of whole cloth.*—**whole blood.** See *half blood,* under *blood, n.*—**whole number,** a number consisting of one or more units, as 1 or 119, as distinguished from a fraction or a mixed number; an integer.—**whole,** *n.* The whole assemblage of parts or elements belonging to a thing; the entire quantity, amount, extent, or number; all; also, a thing complete in itself, or comprising all its parts or elements; a complete or total assemblage of parts; a total; also, an assemblage of parts associated or viewed together as one thing; a unitary system.—**com-**

mittee of the whole. See under *committee.*—**on** or **upon the whole,** on consideration of the whole matter, or in view of all the circumstances (as, *on the whole*, the results seemed satisfactory); also, as a whole or in general, without regard to exceptions (as, "The real bulk of the country remained *on the whole* agricultural": Charnwood's "Theodore Roosevelt," iv.).

whole=heart-ed (hōl′här′ted), *a.* Hearty; cordial; earnest; sincere; single-hearted.—**whole′=heart′ed-ly,** *adv.*—**whole′= heart′ed-ness,** *n.*

whole=hoofed (hōl′hōft), *a.* Having the hoof undivided or not cloven, as the horse; solidungulate.

whole-ness (hōl′nes), *n.* The state of being whole; completeness; entireness.

whole=note (hōl′nōt), *n.* In *music*, a semibreve.

whole-sale (hōl′sāl), *n.* The sale of commodities in large quantities, as to retailers or jobbers rather than to consumers directly: opposed to *retail.*—**by wholesale** (or, elliptically, simply **wholesale**), in large quantities, as in the sale of commodities; fig., on a large scale and without discrimination (as, slaughter *by wholesale*).—**whole′sale,** *a.* Of, pertaining to, or engaged in sale by wholesale; fig., extensive and indiscriminate (as, *wholesale* discharge of workers; *wholesale* blame).—**whole′sale,** *v. t.* or *i.*; *-saled, -saling.* To sell by wholesale.—**whole′sal″er** (-sā′lėr), *n.* One who sells by wholesale.

whole-some (hōl′sum), *a.* Conducive to bodily health (as, *wholesome* food, air, or exercise); healthful; salubrious; also, conducive to moral or general well-being (as, *wholesome* advice; a *wholesome* lesson; "a set of just and *wholesome* laws," Strype's "Memorials of Cranmer," i. 30); salutary; beneficial; also, healthy or sound in condition (now chiefly prov.); characteristic of or proper to a healthy or good condition (as, "Exercise develops *wholesome* appetites," Louisa M. Alcott's "Little Women," i. 12; "When shalt thou see thy *wholesome* days again?" Shakspere's "Macbeth," iv. 3. 105); suggestive of health (physical or moral), esp. in appearance (as, "a broad grin on his ugly *wholesome* face": Archibald Marshall's "Anthony Dare," ii.); clean and neat (obs. or prov. Eng.).—**whole′some-ly,** *adv.*—**whole′some-ness,** *n.*

whole=souled (hōl′sōld), *a.* Whole-hearted; hearty: as, "*whole-souled* hospitality" (Roosevelt's "Ranch Life and the Hunting-Trail," i.).

whol-ly (hō′li), *adv.* To the whole amount, extent, etc.; so as to comprise or involve all; entirely; totally; altogether; quite.

whom (hōm), *pron.* [AS. *hwām*, dat. of *hwā*, E. *who.*] Objective case of *who.*—**whom-ev′er** (-ev′ėr), **whom′so** (-sō), **whom-so-ev′er** (-sō-ev′ėr). Objective case of *whoever, whoso, whosoever.*

whoop (hōp), *v.* [OF. F. *houper*, < *houp*, interj. used in shouting.] **I.** *intr.* To utter a loud cry or shout (orig. the syllable *whoop*, or *hoop*), as a call or in enthusiasm, excitement, frenzy, etc. (as, "They [Indians] . . . came down yelling and *whooping* into the plain": Irving's "Captain Bonneville," vi.); also, to cry as an owl, crane, or certain other birds; also, to make the characteristic sound accompanying the deep inspiration after a series of coughs in whooping-cough. **II.** *tr.* To utter with or as with a whoop or whoops; also, to whoop to or at; call, urge, pursue, or drive with whoops (as, to *whoop* dogs on).—**whoop,** *n.* The cry or shout uttered by one who whoops (as, a war-*whoop*; a *whoop* of defiance; a *whoop* of joy); also, the cry of an owl, crane, or the like; also, the whooping sound characteristic of whooping-cough.—**whoop-ee** (hö′pē or hwö′-). **I.** *interj.* A cry of sportive excitement. **II.** *n.* Uproarious festivity: often in 'to make whoopee.' [Slang, U. S.]—**whoop-er** (hö′pėr), *n.* One who or that which whoops; specif., a common old-world swan, *Olor cygnus* or *Cygnus* (or *Olor*) *musicus*, notable for its whooping cry; a hooper.—**whoop′ing=cough,** *n.* An infectious disease of the respiratory mucous membrane, esp. of children, characterized by a series of short, convulsive coughs followed by a deep inspiration accompanied by a whooping sound; pertussis.

whop (hwop), *v.*; *whopped, whopping.* [Also *whap, wap, wop*; ME. *whappen, wappen*; origin obscure.] **I.** *tr.* To throw with force, pitch, or dash; also, to strike forcibly; beat;

flog, or thrash; defeat soundly, as in a contest; surpass completely. [Now prov. or colloq.] **II.** *intr.* To plump suddenly down; flop. [Prov. or colloq.]—**whop,** *n.* A forcible blow or impact, or the sound made by it; a bump; a heavy fall. [Now prov. or colloq.]—**whop′per,** *n.* Something uncommonly large of its kind; esp., a big lie. [Colloq.] —**whop′ping,** *p. a.* Very large of its kind; thumping; huge. [Colloq.]

whore (hōr), *n.* [AS. *hōre* = Icel. *hōra* = OHG. *huora* (G. *hure*), whore: cf. Goth. *hōrs*, masc., adulterer.] A woman who prostitutes her body for hire; a prostitute, harlot, or strumpet; hence, any unchaste woman. Also fig.—**whore,** *v.*; *whored, whoring.* **I.** *intr.* To act as a whore; also, to consort with whores. Also fig. **II.** *tr.* To make a whore of; debauch.—**whore′dom** (-dom), *n.* The prostitution of the body for hire; in general, the practice of unlawful sexual intercourse; in Biblical use, sometimes, idolatry. [Archaic.] —**whore′mas″ter,** *n.* A whoremonger. [Obs. or archaic.] —**whore′mong″er** (-mung″gėr), *n.* One who consorts with whores. [Archaic.]—**whore′son** (-sun). **I.** *n.* A bastard, also, a coarse term of contempt or abuse for a person, sometimes used jocularly. [Obs. or archaic.] **II.** *a.* Being a bastard; also, mean; scurvy. [Obs. or archaic.]—**whor-ish** (hōr′ish), *a.* Having the character of a whore; pertaining to or characteristic of whores; lewd; unchaste. [Obs. or archaic.]

whorl (hwėrl or hwôrl), *n.* [ME. *whorle, wharle, wharwyl*, whorl of a spindle; akin to E. *wharve.*] In *spinning*, the wharve of a spindle; in *bot.*, a circular arrangement of like parts, as leaves, flowers, etc., round a point on an axis; a verticil; in *zoöl.*, one of the turns or volutions of a spiral shell; in *anat.*, one of the turns in the cochlea of the ear.—**whorled,** *a.* Having a whorl or whorls; also, disposed in the form of a whorl, as leaves.

whort (hwėrt), *n.* Same as *whortleberry.*

whor-tle-ber-ry (hwėr″tl-ber″i), *n.*; pl. *-berries* (-iz). [Also *hurtleberry*; first element of uncertain origin.] The edible black berry of a shrub, *Vaccinium myrtillus*, of Europe, Siberia, and northwestern America, used in the Old World as an article of food but of less importance in America; the shrub itself; also, the berry yielded by any of certain related shrubs; any of these shrubs. [A name confined mostly to the Old World.]

Whorls of Ammonite.

whose (hōz), *pron.* [AS. *hwæs*, gen. of *hwā*, E. *who*, and of *hwæt*, E. *what.*] Possessive case of *who*, and historically also of *what*, and hence still used also (as a relative) with a neuter antecedent, although the nominative and the objective *what* in such constructions are now replaced by *which*, *whose* itself becoming interchangeable with *of which*: as, a pen *whose* point is broken, or *of which* the point is broken.— **whose′so** (-sō), **whose-so-ev′er** (-sō-ev′ėr), **whos-ev-er** (hōs-ev′ėr). Possessive case of *whoso, whosoever, whoever.*

who-so (hō′sō), *pron.* Whoever: as, "O Lord, or Prince, or *whoso* thou mayst be" (W. Morris's "Jason," iv. 241). [Archaic.]—**who-so-ev′er** (-sō-ev′ėr), *pron.* Whatsoever person; whoever: as, "*Whosoever* hath, to him shall be given" (Mat. xiii. 12).

why (hwī), [AS. *hwī, hwȳ*, instrumental case of *hwæt*, E. *what.*] **I.** *interrog. adv.* For what? for what cause, reason, or purpose? wherefore? as, *why* did he do it? *why* should you go? and *why* not, pray? **II.** *conj.* For what cause or reason (as, "Nobody . . . could conceive *why* she married him": Scott's "Guy Mannering," ii.); also, for which, or on account of which (after *reason*, etc.: as, the reason *why* he refused); the reason for which (as, "That is *why* I raised this question again": Drinkwater's "Robert E. Lee," vi.).— **why,** *n.*; pl. *whys.* The cause or reason: as, "She was . . . in the dark as to the *whys* and wherefores of her sister's moods" (Mrs. H. Ward's "Robert Elsmere," xxxi.).—**why,** *interj.* An expression of surprise, hesitation, etc., or sometimes a mere expletive: as, *why*, it is all gone; *why*, no, I think not; if we must, *why*, we must.

whyd-ah=bird (hwid′ä-bėrd), *n.* See *whidah-bird.*

-wich. Var. of *-wick* (see *wick*[2]) in place-names, as *Greenwich, Sandwich.*

(variable) ḍ as d or j, ş as s or sh, ţ as t or ch, z as z or zh; o, F. *cloche*; ü, F. *menu*; ċh, Sc. *loch*; ṅ, F. *bonbon*; ′, primary accent; ″, secondary accent; †, obsolete; <, from; +, and; =, equals. See also lists at beginning of book.

wick[1] (wik), *n.* [AS. *wice, weoce.*] A bundle or loose twist or braid of soft threads, or a woven strip or tube, as of cotton, which in a candle, lamp, oil-stove, or the like serves to draw up the melted tallow or wax or the oil or other inflammable liquid to be burned gradually at its own top or end: forming a part of a candle, but inserted as a separate piece in a lamp, etc.

wick[2] (wik), *n.* [AS. *wīc*, dwelling, village, < L. *vicus*, row of houses, quarter, village, akin to Gr. οἶκος, Skt. *veça*, house: cf. *vicinity*.] A town or village (now only in place-names, as *Hampton Wick, Berwick, Warwick*); also, an official district (used in certain compounds, as *bailiwick, sheriffwick*).

wick[3] (wik), *n.* [From Scand.] A small bay or inlet. [Sc. and north. Eng.]

-wick. See *wick*[2].

wick-ed (wik′ed), *a.* [ME. *wicked*, < *wicke*, evil, bad; perhaps related to AS. *wīcan*, give way: see *weak*.] Evil or morally bad in principle or practice (as, *wicked* persons, thoughts, intentions, or deeds; a *wicked* world); iniquitous; sinful; also, ill-natured, savage, or vicious (now chiefly colloq. or prov.: as, a *wicked* horse); also, mischievous or playfully malicious (as, "a parcel of *wicked* hoydens, bent on mischief," H. Melville's "Omoo," lxxi.; a *wicked* smile, glance, or retort); also, pernicious or noxious (archaic: as, "*wicked* dew . . . from unwholesome fen," Shakspere's "Tempest," i. 2. 321); "The *wicked* broth Confused the chemic labour of the blood," Tennyson's "Lucretius," 19); distressingly severe, as cold, pain, wounds, etc. (now colloq.); extremely trying, unpleasant, or troublesome (colloq.).—**Wicked Bible.** See under *Bible.*—**wick′ed-ly,** *adv.*—**wick′ed-ness,** *n.* The quality or state of being wicked; wicked conduct or practices; a wicked act or thing.

wick-er (wik′ėr). [ME. *wyker*; cf. Sw. dial. *vikker, vekker,* Dan. dial. *vigger,* willow, also AS. *wīcan,* give way, and E. *weak.*] **I.** *n.* A slender, pliant twig; an osier; a withe; also, plaited or woven twigs or osiers as the material of baskets, chairs, etc.; wickerwork; also, something made of wickerwork, as a basket. **II.** *a.* Consisting or made of wicker (as, a *wicker* basket, chair, or cradle); also, covered with wicker (as, a *wicker* bottle).—**wick′ered,** *a.* Made of or covered with wicker.—**wick′er-work,** *n.* Work consisting of plaited or woven twigs or osiers; articles made of wicker.

wick-et (wik′et), *n.* [OF. *wiket, wichet, guichet* (F. *guichet*); prob. from Teut.] A small door or gate, esp. one beside, or forming part of, a larger one; hence, a turnstile in an entrance; a small gate by which a canal-lock is emptied; a gate by which a flow of water is regulated, as to a water-wheel; also, a window or opening, often closed by a grating or the like, as in a door, or forming a place of communication in a ticket-office, a teller's cage in a bank, etc. (as, "He was paying teller . . . he stood behind his *wicket* reading a letter": W. Churchill's "Modern Chronicle," i. 1); in *cricket*, either of the two frameworks, each consisting of three stumps with two bails lying in grooves across their tops, at which the bowler aims the ball; also, one batsman's turn at the wicket, or the period during which two men bat together; also, the ground on which the wickets are set; in *croquet*, a hoop or arch.—**wick′et=keep″er,** *n.* In cricket, the player on the fielding side who stands immediately behind the wicket to stop balls that pass it.

wick-ing (wik′ing), *n.* Material for wicks, as for lamps.

wick-i-up (wik′i-up), *n.* [N. Amer. Ind.] An American Indian hut made of brushwood or covered with mats (Nevada, Arizona, etc.); hence, any rude hut (western U. S.).

wic-o-py (wik′ō-pi), *n.*; pl. *-pies* (-piz). [Algonquian.] The leatherwood, *Dirca palustris*; also, any of various willow-herbs, as *Chamænerion angustifolium*.

wid-der-shins, wid-er-shins (wid′ėr-shinz), *adv.* Same as *withershins.* [Sc. and prov. Eng.]

wide (wīd). [AS. *wīd* = D. *wijd* = G. *weit* = Icel. *vīdhr* = Sw. and Dan. *vid*, wide.] **I.** *a.*; compar. *wider*, superl. *widest.* Having considerable, or great extent from side to side (as, "*Wide* is the gate . . . that leadeth to destruction," Mat. vii. 13; a *wide* river); broad; not narrow; of more than a specified, implied, or usual extent from side to side; also, having a certain or specified extent from side to side (as, 3 feet *wide*); also, of great horizontal extent (as, the

wide ocean; "the *wide* plains of South Russia," H. G. Wells's "Outline of History," xxxiv. § 5c); extensive; vast; spacious; also, of great range or scope (as, *wide* culture; *wide* reading; *wide* experience); embracing a great number or variety of subjects, cases, etc.; also, open to the full or a great extent (as, to stare with *wide* eyes, or a *wide* mouth); expanded; distended; also, full, ample, or roomy, as clothing; also, apart or remote from a specified point or object (as, a guess *wide* of the truth); too far or too much to one side (as, a *wide* ball in cricket); in *phonetics*, uttered with a relatively wide opening of the vocal organs; not narrow. **II.** *n.* Width†; a wide space or expanse; also, that which goes wide; in *cricket*, a bowled ball that goes wide of the wicket, and counts as a run to the side that is batting.—

wide, *adv.* [AS. *wīde.*] To a great, or relatively great, extent from side to side; over an extensive space or region, or far abroad (as, "Let Fame from brazen lips blow *wide* Her chosen names," Whittier's "My Namesake": often in the phrase 'far and wide'); also, to the full extent of opening (as, to open the eyes or the mouth *wide*); hence, to the utmost, or fully (as, to be *wide* awake: see *wide-awake, a.*); also, away from or to one side of a point, mark, purpose, or the like (as, the shot went *wide*); aside; astray.

wide=a-wake (wīd′a̲-wāk′), *a.* Fully awake, with the eyes wide open (written with a hyphen when used before a noun, as in 'a wide-awake baby,' but preferably as two words when used predicatively, as in 'the baby was wide awake': cf. *wide, adv.*); hence, fig., alert, keen, or knowing (as, "His parents . . . despite their notion of themselves as *wide-awake* parents were a simple pair": Arnold Bennett's "Old Wives' Tale," ii. 4).—**wide′=a-wake″,** *n.* A soft, low-crowned felt hat.—**wide′=a-wake′ness,** *n.*

wide-ly (wīd′li), *adv.* To a wide extent; over a wide space or area (as, a *widely* distributed plant); throughout a large number of persons (as, a man who is *widely* known); in many or various subjects, cases, etc. (as, to be *widely* read); to the full extent (of opening: as, *widely* opened eyes or doors); so as to leave a wide space or interval (as, "We . . . *widely* shun the Lilybæan strand": Dryden's tr. Virgil's "Æneid," iii. 927); greatly, very much, or very (as, **two** *widely* different accounts of an affair).

wid-en (wī′dn), *v. t.* or *i.* To make or become wide or wider; broaden; expand.

wide-ness (wīd′nes), *n.* The quality or state of being wide.

wide-spread (wīd′spred), *a.* Spread over or occupying a wide space (as, *widespread* wings); also, distributed over a wide region, or occurring in many places or among many persons or individuals (as, "the Danish and Saxon tongues, both dialects of one *widespread* language," Macaulay's "Hist. of Eng.," i.; "*widespread* discontent," J. H. Robinson's "Mind in the Making," viii. 17; "Colours acquired for the purpose of serving as a danger-signal to enemies are very *widespread* in nature," A. R. Wallace's "Darwinism," ix.).

widg-eon (wij′on), *n.*; pl. *widgeons* or (esp. collectively) *widgeon.* [= F. *vigeon, vingeon*; origin uncertain: cf. L. *vipio(n-)*, kind of small crane, also E. and F. *pigeon*, < LL. *pipio(n-)*.] Any of the fresh-water ducks constituting the genus *Mareca*, esp. *M. penelope* of Europe and *M. americana* of North America; also, any of various other wild ducks.

wid-ish (wī′dish), *a.* Rather wide.

wid-ow (wid′ō), *n.* [AS. *widewe, wuduwe,* = D. *weduwe* = G. *witwe* = Goth. *widuwō,* widow; akin to L. *vidua,* Skt.

American Widgeon (*Mareca americana*).

vidhavā, widow, Skt. *vidh-,* be without.] A woman who has lost her husband by death and has not married again; also, a widower (prov. Eng. and Sc.); in *card-playing*, an additional hand or part of a hand, as one dealt to the table.—**college widow.** See under *college.*—**widow bewitched,** a grass-widow. [Colloq.]—**widow's peak,** a point formed by the hair growing down in the middle of a woman's forehead. [Colloq.]—**wid′ow**, *v. t.* To render (one) a widow; bereave of a husband, or sometimes of a wife (chiefly in *pp.*: as, "a *widowed* mother," Mrs. Wharton's "Son at the Front," xii.; "a *widowed* clergyman," John Hay's "Bread-Winners," xi.); fig., to deprive of anything valued, or bereave (as, "Wit, *widow′d* of good sense, is worse than nought": Young's "Night Thoughts," viii. 1264); also, to endow with a widow's right†; also, to survive as the widow of†.—**wid′ow-bird,** *n.* Same as *whidah-bird.*—**wid′ow-er,** *n.* A man who has lost his wife by death and has not married again.—**wid′ow-hood** (-hud), *n.* The state or the period of being a widow (or, sometimes, a widower); also, a widow's right or estate†.

width (width), *n.* [From *wide.*] Extent from side to side; breadth; wideness; also, a breadth, or piece of the full wideness, as of cloth.—**width′wise,** *adv.* In the direction of the width.

wie-gen-lied (vē′gĕn-lēt), *n.*; pl. *-lieder* (-lē″dėr). [G.] A cradle-song; a berceuse; a lullaby.

wield (wēld), *v. t.* [ME. *welden,* < AS. *(ge)wieldan, (ge)wyldan,* < *wealdan* = OHG. *waltan* (G. *walten*) = Icel. *valda* = Goth. *waldan,* wield, rule; akin to L. *valere,* be strong.] To exercise power, rule, or sway over (a country, etc.: obs. or archaic); exercise (power, authority, influence, etc.) as in ruling or dominating; also, to manage (a weapon, instrument, etc.) in use (as, "Well as the sceptre canst thou *wield* the blade," Wiffen's tr. Tasso's "Jerusalem Delivered," ii. 3; to *wield* a club, an ax, or a pen); handle or employ in action; use (anything) with freedom and ease (as, "He [a child] can grasp and *wield* only the grosser elements of speech": W. D. Whitney's "Life and Growth of Language," ii.); also, to have†, possess†, or enjoy†.—**wield′a-ble,** *a.* That may be wielded.—**wield′er,** *n.*—**wield′y,** *a.* Readily wielded or managed, as in use or action. Cf. *unwieldy.*

Wie-ner schnit-zel (vē′nėr shnit′sĕl). [G., 'Vienna cutlet.'] A breaded veal cutlet, variously seasoned or garnished.

wife (wīf), *n.*; pl. *wives* (wīvz). [AS. *wīf* = D. *wijf* = G. *weib* = Icel. *vīf,* woman, wife.] A woman (archaic or prov., except in compounds, as *fishwife, housewife, midwife*); esp., a woman joined in marriage to a man as husband.— **old wives′ tales.** See *old wife,* under *old, a.*—**wife′hood** (-hud), *n.* The position or relation of a wife; wifely character.—**wife′less,** *a.* Destitute or bereft of a wife.— **wife′ly,** *a.* Of, like, or befitting a wife.—**wif-ie** (wī′fi), *n.* Familiar form of *wife.*

wig¹ (wig), *n.* [Abbr. of *periwig.*] An artificial covering of hair for the head, worn to conceal baldness, for disguise or theatrical make-up, as part of the professional costume of a judge or lawyer or of the livery of a servant, or formerly as an ordinary head-covering (cf. *peruke*).—**wigs on the green,** fig., rough disorder or fighting (as if with wigs knocked off or fallen to the ground). [Colloq. or prov.]—**wig¹,** *v. t.*; *wigged, wigging.* To furnish with a wig or wigs.

wig² (wig), *n.* [Origin uncertain; perhaps another use of *wig¹.*] A severe reprimand or reproof; a wigging. [Colloq., Eng.]—**wig²,** *v.*; *wigged, wigging.* **I.** *tr.* To reprimand or reprove severely; scold. [Colloq., Eng.] **II.** *intr.* To scold: as, "Miss Wilson hasn't done anything! What are you *wigging* away at her for?" (W. De Morgan's "Somehow Good," xxv.). [Colloq., Eng.]

wig-an (wig′ạn), *n.* [From *Wigan,* town in Lancashire, England.] A stiff, canvas-like fabric used for stiffening parts of garments.

wig-eon (wij′ọn), *n.* See *widgeon.*

wigged (wigd), *a.* Wearing a wig.

wig-ger-y (wig′ėr-i), *n.*; pl. *-ies* (-iz). Wigs or a wig; false hair.

wig-ging (wig′ing), *n.* [See *wig².*] A severe reprimand or reproof; a scolding: as, "Palmerston was most apologetic . . . must give the clerks a *wigging*" (Lytton Strachey's "Queen Victoria," v.). [Colloq., chiefly Eng.]

wig-gle (wig′l), *v.*; *-gled, -gling.* [ME. *wigelen* = MLG. and D. *wiggelen,* shake, totter; a freq. form akin to E. *wag¹, waggle,* and *weigh².*] **I.** *intr.* To move or go with short, quick, irregular movements from side to side; wriggle: as, "The spider . . . *wiggled* round and round, evidently trying to take hold of his prey" (W. H. Hudson's "Green Mansions," v.). **II.** *tr.* To cause to wiggle; move quickly and irregu-

larly from side to side.—**wig′gle,** *n.* A wiggling movement or course; also, a wiggly line.—**wig′gler,** *n.* One who or that which wiggles; specif., the larva of a mosquito.— **wig′gly,** *a.* Given to wiggling; apt to wiggle; also, having a succession of small irregularities or undulations in form (as, "editorials . . . printed in bold type surrounded by a *wiggly* border": Sinclair Lewis's "Babbitt," xvi.).

wight¹ (wīt), *n.* [AS. *wiht,* thing, creature, = D. *wicht,* child, = G. *wicht,* creature, = Goth. *waihts,* thing, whit: cf. *whit.*] A living being or creature†; also, a supernatural or unearthly being†; also, a human being, or person (archaic or prov.: as, "a worthy *wight* of the name of Ichabod Crane," Irving's "Sketch-Book," Sleepy Hollow); also, a whit†.

wight² (wīt), *a.* [ME. *wight, wiht:* cf. Icel. *vīgr,* in fighting condition, Sw. *vig,* agile, nimble.] Having warlike prowess, strong and brave, or valiant (as, "He would venture his nephew on him [adversary], were he as *wight* as Wallace": Scott's "Quentin Durward," xxxvii.); also, strong, vigorous, or active; nimble or swift. [Archaic or Sc.]

wig-wag (wig′wag), *v. t.* or *i.*; *-wagged, -wagging.* [Varied redupl. of *wag¹.*] To move to and fro; *milit.,* etc., to signal by movements of flags or the like waved by the signaler according to a code.—**wig′wag,** *n.* *Milit.,* etc., wigwagging, or signaling by movements of flags or the like; also, a message so signaled.—**wig′wag″ger,** *n.*

wig-wam (wig′wâm or -wom), *n.* [Algonquian.] An American Indian hut or lodge, usually of rounded or conical shape, formed of poles overlaid with bark, mats, or skins; hence, any similar hut of natives elsewhere; any dwelling or house (humorous); also, a structure, esp. of large size, used for political conventions, etc. (U. S.).

Indian Wigwam.

wik-i-up (wik′i-up), *n.* See *wickiup.*

Wil-bur-ite (wil′bėr-īt), *n.* One of a seceding body of American Quakers, founded by John Wilbur (1774–1856), opposed to evangelicalism.

wild (wīld), *a.* [AS. *wilde* = D. and G. *wild* = Icel. *villr* = Goth. *wiltheis,* wild.] Living in a state of nature, as animals that have not been tamed or domesticated (as, *wild* beasts, birds, or bees); feral; growing or produced without cultivation or the care of man, as plants, flowers, fruit, honey, etc.; uncultivated, uninhabited, or waste, as land; uncivilized or barbarous, as tribes or savages; untrained or artless (as, "Or sweetest Shakspeare . . . Warble his native wood-notes *wild*": Milton's "L'Allegro," 134); shy, as game-birds; also, undisciplined, unruly, lawless, or turbulent (as, *wild* boys; a *wild* crew); disregardful of moral restraints as to pleasurable indulgence (as, he was *wild* in his youth); also, of unrestrained violence, fury, intensity, etc. (as, *wild* strife; *wild* storms; *wild* passions); violent; furious; tempestuous; in general, unrestrained, untrammeled, or unbridled (as, *wild* gaiety; *wild* orgies); often, unrestrained by reason or prudence (as, *wild* schemes or theories; a *wild* venture; *wild* folly); extravagant or fantastic (as, *wild* fancies; a *wild* tale); also, disorderly or disheveled (as, *wild* locks); also, violently excited (as, *wild* with rage, fear, or pain); characterized by or indicating violent excitement, as actions, the appearance, etc. (as, "My aunt made a *wild* rush to rescue them," Weir Mitchell's "Hugh Wynne," xxx.; "Your looks are pale and *wild,*" Shakspere's "Romeo and Juliet," v. 1. 28); frantic; distracted, crazy, or mad (as, "The fictions of Oates had driven the nation *wild*": Macaulay's "Hist. of Eng.," vi.); intensely eager or enthusiastic (chiefly colloq.:

as, "He is *wild* to go," S. J. Weyman's "Gentleman of France," xxvii.; *wild* about baseball); also, wide of the mark (as, a *wild* throw or shot). — **to run wild,** to live as a wild animal, or as an animal escaped from domestication; grow as a wild plant, or with unchecked luxuriance; hence, to go about freely without discipline or restraint. — **wild boar.** See *boar.* — **wild brier,** the dogrose, *Rosa canina;* also, the sweetbrier, *Rosa rubiginosa.* — **wild carrot,** an apiaceous weed, *Daucus carota,* having a thin and woody root, common in fields and waste places: the original of the cultivated carrot. — **wild cat.** See *wildcat.* — **wild dog,** any of various wild canine animals, as *Cyon primævus* of northern India, and the dhole and the dingo. — **wild flax,** gold-of-pleasure. — **wild fowl.** See *wild-fowl.* — **wild goose,** any undomesticated goose, esp. the graylag of Europe or the Canada goose of North America. — **wild= goose chase,** a wild or absurd

Wild Dog (*Cyon primævus*).

chase, as after something as erratic in its course as a wild goose; any senseless pursuit of an object or end. — **wild horse,** an undomesticated horse, or horse living in a state of nature; a domestic horse run wild, or a wild descendant of such a horse. — **Wild Huntsman,** in European (esp. German) legend, a spectral huntsman who, with a phantom host of followers, goes careering over woods, fields, and villages during the night, attended with shouts of huntsmen and baying of hounds. — **wild hyacinth,** a camass, *Quamasia hyacinthina,* of eastern North America; also, the harebell, *Scilla non-scripta,* of Europe. — **wild indigo,** any of the American fabaceous plants constituting the genus *Baptisia,* esp. *B. tinctoria,* a species with yellow flowers. — **wild lettuce,** any of various uncultivated species of lettuce (genus *Lactuca*), growing as weeds in fields and waste places. — **wild mandrake,** the May-apple, *Podophyllum peltatum.* — **wild oat.** See *oat.* — **wild olive.** See *oleaster.* — **wild parsnip,** an apiaceous weed, *Pastinaca sativa,* having an inedible acrid root, common in fields and waste places: the original of the cultivated parsnip. — **wild rye,** any of the grasses of the genus *Elymus,* somewhat resembling rye. — **wild spinach,** any of various plants of the genus *Chenopodium,* sometimes used in place of spinach. — **wild strawberry.** See *potentilla.* — **wild vanilla,** an asteraceous plant, *Trilisa odoratissima,* of the southeastern U. S., bearing leaves with a persistent vanilla-like fragrance. — **wild,** *n.* An uncultivated, uninhabited, or desolate region or tract; a waste; a wilderness; a desert. — **wild,** *adv.* In a wild manner; wildly.

wild-cat (wīld′kat). **I.** *n.* A wild European cat, *Felis catus,* resembling the common domestic cat, but larger and having a shorter and thicker tail; also, any of various other small or medium-sized, wild feline animals, as the lynx, eyra, etc. **II.** *a.* Wild, reckless, or irresponsible (as, *wildcat* schemes or enterprises); esp., characterized by or proceeding from recklessly unsound or unsafe business methods (as, *wildcat* banks, banking, or currency; *wildcat* companies or stocks); also, running without control or regulation, as a locomotive, or apart from the regular schedule, as a train. — **wild′cat,** *v. i.;* *-catted, -catting.* To seek for oil, ore, or the like as an independent prospector, esp. in a region of uncertain resources, and with a view to selling out one's finds to capitalists for development. [Colloq., U. S.] — **wild′cat′ter,** *n.*

Wildcat. A U. S. Navy fighter plane (Grumman).

wil-de-beest (vĭl′dė-bāst), *n.* [S. Afr. D., 'wild beast.'] A gnu.

wil-der (wĭl′dėr), *v.* [Appar. < *wilderness.*] **I.** *tr.* To cause to lose one's way; bewilder or perplex. **II.** *intr.* To lose one's way; go astray; be bewildered. [Archaic.] — **wil′der-ment,** *n.* Bewilderment. [Poetic.]

wil-der-ness (wĭl′dėr-nes), *n.* [ME. *wildernesse,* < AS. *wilder, wilddēor,* wild animal, < *wilde,* E. *wild,* + *dēor,* E. *deer.*] A tract of land inhabited only by wild animals; a wild region, as of forest or desert; a waste; hence, any desolate tract, as of water (as, "environ'd with a *wilderness* of sea": Shakspere's "Titus Andronicus," iii. 1. 94); also, a part of a garden set apart for plants growing with unchecked luxuriance; also, a place wholly given over to something; a bewildering mass or collection (as, "the *wilderness* of masts on the river, and the *wilderness* of steeples on the shore": Dickens's "Little Dorrit," i. 9); also, wildness†.

wild=fire (wīld′fīr), *n.* A highly inflammable composition, as Greek fire, difficult to extinguish when ignited, formerly used in warfare (now referred to chiefly as a type of something that runs or spreads with extraordinary rapidity: as, the news spread like *wild-fire*); also, sheet-lightning, unaccompanied by thunder; also, the will-o'-the-wisp or ignis fatuus; in *pathol.,* erysipelas or some similar disease; in *vet. science,* an inflammatory disease of the skin of sheep.

wild=fowl (wīld′foul), *n.* Collectively, the birds ordinarily pursued as game, esp. ducks, geese, and the like.

wild-ing (wīl′ding). **I.** *n.* Any plant that grows wild, or its fruit; esp., a wild apple-tree or apple; also, an escape (plant); also, a wild animal (as, "*wildings* of the paw and wing": Eden Phillpotts's "Cherry-Stones," Theory and Practice). **II.** *a.* Not cultivated or domesticated; wild. [Chiefly poetic.]

wild-ish (wīl′dish), *a.* Somewhat wild.

wild-ly (wīld′li), *adv.* In a wild manner. — **wild′ness,** *n.*

wild=wood (wīld′wud), *n.* A wood growing in the wild or natural state; a forest.

wile (wīl), *n.* [Late AS. *wīl:* cf. *guile.*] A trick, artifice, or stratagem; an artful or beguiling procedure: as, "He did not fail to see His uncle's cunning *wiles* and treachery" (W. Morris's "Jason," ii. 900); the *wiles* of a coquette. — **wile,** *v. t.;* *wiled, wiling.* [In part prob. due to *while, v.*] To trick† or deceive†; also, to beguile, entice, or lure (*away, from, into,* etc.: as, "Lady Macadam wrote me a very complaining letter, for trying to *wile* away her companion," Galt's "Annals of the Parish," ix.); also, to while (*away*), as time.

wil-ful (wĭl′ful), *a.* Willing† or desirous†; also, willed, voluntary, or intentional (as, *wilful* murder; *wilful* waste); also, self-willed or headstrong (as, a *wilful* man must have his way; "A woman's mind is a *wilful* thing, and not easily turned from its waywardness," Cooper's "Prairie," xxxi.); perversely obstinate or intractable. — **wil′ful-ly,** *adv.* — **wil′ful-ness,** *n.*

wil-i-ly (wī′li-li), *adv.* In a wily manner. — **wil′i-ness,** *n.*

will¹ (wil), *v.;* pres. 1 *will,* 2 *wilt,* 3 *will,* pl. *will;* pret. 1 *would,* 2 *wouldest* or *wouldst,* 3 *would,* pl. *would;* imperative and infinitive lacking. [AS. *willan* (pret. *wolde*) = D. *willen* = OHG. *wellan* (G. *wollen*) = Icel. *vilja* = Goth. *wiljan,* wish, will; akin to L. *velle,* wish, will: cf. *volition* and *voluntary.*] **A.** *tr.* or *intr.* To wish; desire; like: as, "What *wilt* thou?" (Mat. xx. 21); as you *will;* [I] *would* it were true! *will* he, nill he (see *nill*). See *would.* **B.** auxiliary. Am (is, are, etc.) disposed or willing to (as, *will* you go? if you *would* only take my advice); am determined or sure to (used emphatically: as, you *would* do it; people *will* talk); also, am accustomed to, or do usually or often (as, he *would* write for hours at a time); also, am expected or required to (as, "As soon as your uniforms arrive, you *will* repair on board": Marryat's "Peter Simple," iii.); also, may be expected or supposed to (as, you *will* not have forgotten him; this *will* be about right); also, am about or going to (in future constructions, denoting in the first person promise or determination, in the second and third persons mere futurity: see *shall*). See *would.* — **will¹,** *n.* [AS. *willa.*] Wish or desire (as, to have the *will,* but not the power, to do harm; to submit against one's *will*); purpose or determination, often hearty determination (as, to have the *will* to succeed; where there's a *will* there's a way; "I then set to work with a *will,*" Marryat's "Peter Simple," lx.); the wish or purpose as carried out, or to be carried out (as, to work one's *will;* "Thy *will* be done," Mat. vi. 10); discretionary pleasure (as, to wander at *will;* to hold an estate at the *will* of another); disposition (good or ill) toward another; also, the faculty of conscious and esp. of deliberate action (as, the *will* as distinguished from the faculties of knowing and feeling; the freedom of the *will*); power of choosing one's own actions (as, to display strength of *will*; to have a strong or a weak *will*); the process of willing, or volition; in *law*, a legal declaration of a person's wishes as to the disposition of his property, etc., after his death; the document containing such a declaration.

will² (wil), *v.*; *willed, willing* (2 sing. pres. ind. *willest*, 3 *wills* or *willeth*). [In part, < AS. *willian*, a secondary verb related to *willan*, E. *will¹*, *v.*; in part, < *will¹*, *n.*] **I.** *tr.* To wish or desire (archaic: as, "A great party in the state *Wills* me to wed her," Tennyson's "Queen Mary," i. 4. 53); hence, to request† or bid† (as, "They *will'd* me say so": Shakspere's "Henry VIII.," iii. 1. 18); require† (as, "What custom *wills*, in all things should we do 't": Shakspere's "Coriolanus," ii. 3. 125); also, to purpose, determine on, or elect by act of will (as, "He set his hand To do the thing he *will'd*, and bore it thro'," Tennyson's "Enoch Arden," 294; to *will* success); decide by act of will (as, "Fate has *willed* it otherwise": Du Maurier's "Trilby," i.); also, to influence by exerting will-power (as, to *will* one's self or another person into submission; to *will* a hypnotized person to do something); also, to give by will or testament, or bequeath. **II.** *intr.* To wish or desire (archaic: as, "Since thou *willest*, I will go with thee," W. Morris's "Jason," xvii. 580); also, to determine, decide, or ordain, as by act of will (as, "Meanwhile, as nature *wills*, night bids us rest": Milton's "Paradise Lost," iv. 633); exercise the will.

willed (wild), *a.* Having a will: as, strong-*willed*.

wil-lem-ite (wil'em-īt), *n.* [From *Willem* (William) I., king of the Netherlands 1815–40.] A mineral, a native silicate of zinc, occurring in hexagonal prisms, granular masses, etc., and varying much in color. Cf. *troostite*.

will-er (wil'ėr), *n.* One who wills.

wil-let (wil'et), *n.* [Imit. of its cry.] A North American bird, *Symphemia semi-palmata* (or *Catoptro-phorus semipalmatus*), of the snipe family, a large tattler with half-webbed toes.

will'ful, etc. See *wilful*, etc.

will-ing (wil'ing), *a.* [Orig. ppr. of *will¹*, *v.*] Wishing† or desirous† (as, "You will not extort from me what I am *willing* to keep in," Shakspere's "Twelfth Night," ii. 1. 14; "Being *willing* to see the place, I went on shore," Defoe's "Robinson Crusoe," ii. 10); also, disposed or consenting (without being particularly desirous: as, to be *willing* to take what one can get; if you are *willing* to wait; he is *willing* to give you a hearing); also, cheerfully consenting or ready (as, a *willing* mind; a *willing* victim; a *willing* worker; a *willing* horse); done, given, borne, used, etc., with cheerful readiness (as, *willing* service; *willing* obedience; *willing* poverty; *willing* hands).—**will'-ing-ly,** *adv.*—**will'ing-ness,** *n.*

will=less (wil'les), *a.* Lacking will or will-power; also, involuntary.

will=o'=the=wisp (wil'ọ-тне-wisp'), *n.* [Cf. *wisp*, in the sense of 'torch' or 'candle,' also *jack-o'-lantern*.] The ignis fatuus; hence, anything that deludes or misleads as by luring on (as, "You . . . will be misled by a *will-o'-the-wisp*, from one error into another": Smollett's "Humphry Clinker," June 10).

wil-low¹ (wil'ō), *n.* [AS. *welig* = D. *wilg* = LG. *wilge*.] Any of the trees or shrubs constituting the genus *Salix*, many species of which have tough, pliable twigs or branches which are used for wickerwork, etc. (see cut in next column); also, the wood of the willow; also, something made of this, as a baseball bat.—**weeping willow.** See under *weeping*.

wil-low² (wil'ō), *n.* [Said to be named from the use formerly

Willet, in winter plumage.

of *willow* rods (see *willow¹*) to beat the fiber.] A machine consisting essentially of a cylinder armed with spikes revolving within a spiked casing, for opening and cleaning cotton or other fiber.—**wil'low²,** *v. t.* To treat with the willow.—**wil'-low-er,** *n.*

wil-low=herb (wil'ō-ėrb), *n.* An onagraceous plant, *Chamænerion angustifolium*, with narrow willow-like leaves and racemes of purple flowers (see cut below); also, any plant of this genus, or of the related genus *Epilobium*.

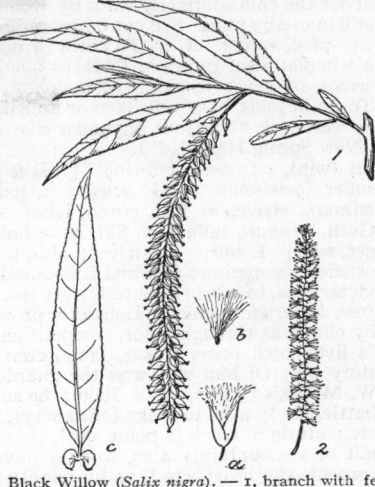

Black Willow (*Salix nigra*).— 1, branch with female ament; 2, male ament; *a*, capsule, opening; *b*, seed; *c*, leaf.

wil-low=oak (wil'-ō-ōk), *n.* An oak, *Quercus phellos*, of the eastern U. S., with narrow entire leaves suggesting those of the willow. See cut at *oak*.

wil-low-y (wil'ō-i), *a.* Abounding with willows; also, willow-like; pliant; lithe; gracefully slender and supple.

wil-ly (wil'i), *n.* and *v. t.* Same as *willow²*.

wil-ly=nil-ly (wil'i-nil'i). [For *will he, nill he*: see *nill*.] **I.** *adv.* Willingly or unwillingly. **II.** *a.* Shilly-shallying; vacillating: as, "thy *willy-nilly* nun" (Tennyson's "Harold," v. 1. 85).

wilt¹ (wilt), *v.* [Altered form of *welk*.] **I.** *intr.* To become limp and drooping, as a fading flower; wither; fig., to lose strength, vigor, assurance, etc. **II.** *tr.* To cause to wilt.

wilt² (wilt). Second person sing. pres. ind. of *will¹*: now only in poetic or solemn use.

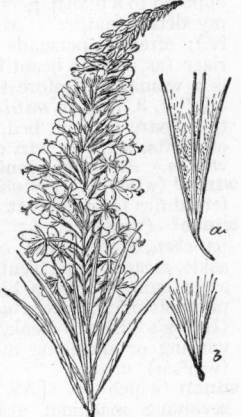

Inflorescence of Willow-herb (*Chamænerion angustifolium*).—*a*, capsule, opening; *b*, seed.

Wil-ton (wil'tọn) **car'pet.** [From *Wilton*, town in southern England, where such carpet was first made.] A kind of carpet woven like Brussels carpet but having the loops cut to form a velvet pile.

wil-y (wī'li), *a.*; compar. *wilier*, superl. *wiliest*. Full of, marked by, or proceeding from wiles; crafty; cunning: as, a *wily* politician; *wily* arts or schemes.

wim-ble (wim'bl), *n.* [ME. *wymble* = MLG. *wimmel*, *wemel*, wimble: cf. *gimlet*.] A gimlet†; also, any of various other instruments for boring, etc.; a marble-workers' brace for drilling; a device used in mining, etc., for extracting the rubbish from a bored hole.—**wim'-ble,** *v. t.*; *-bled, -bling.* To bore or perforate with or as with a wimble.

wim-ple (wim'pl), *n.* [AS. *wimpel* = OHG. *wimpal*, head-cloth (G. *wimpel*, pen-

Wimple, from a statue (of about 1327) of Jeanne d'Évreux, queen of France, consort of Charles IV.

nant): cf. *guimpe*.] A woman's head-cloth drawn in folds about the chin: formerly worn by women out of doors, and still in use by nuns. See cut on preceding page. — **wim'ple**, *v.*; *-pled, -pling*. **I.** *tr.* To cover or muffle with or as with a wimple; also, to lay in folds, as a veil (obs. or archaic); hence, to cause to ripple or undulate, as water. **II.** *intr.* To lie in folds, as a veil (obs. or archaic); hence, to ripple, as water (as, "the trout in yonder *wimpling* burn": Burns's "Now Spring Has Clad").

win (win), *v.*; *won, winning*. [AS. *winnan*, labor, strive, suffer (*gewinnan* = G. *gewinnen*, gain, win), = OHG. *winnan*, strive, = Icel. *vinna*, labor, suffer, gain, win, = Goth. *winnan*, suffer: cf. Skt. *van-*, hold dear, desire, seek, get, win.] **I.** *intr.* To strive†; also, to succeed by striving or effort (sometimes followed colloquially by *out*); gain the victory (as, to *win* in a contest); get (*in, out, through, to*, etc., *free, loose*, etc.: chiefly archaic or prov.). **II.** *tr.* To get by effort, as through labor, competition, or conquest; gain (a livelihood, prize, stakes, fame, etc.: as, "That ancient story . . . Of him who *won* the guarded Fleece of Gold," W. Morris's "Jason," xvii. 1366); be successful in (a game, battle, etc.); also, to make (one's way), as by effort, ability, etc.; attain or reach (a point, goal, etc.: as, to *win* the summit of a mountain); also, to gain (favor, love, sympathy, consent, the heart, etc.), as by qualities or influence; gain the favor, regard, or adherence of (as, "You've quite *won* my uncle": Eden Phillpotts's "Red Redmaynes," v.); bring (*over*) to favor, consent, etc. (as, to *win* over persons opposed to a plan); persuade (as, "You have *won* me to alter my determination": Mrs. Shelley's "Frankenstein," letter iv.); often, to persuade to love or marriage, or gain in marriage (as, "She's beautiful and therefore to be woo'd; She is a woman, therefore to be *won*": Shakspere's "1 Henry VI.," v. 3. 79); in *mining*, to get out (ore, coal, etc.); also, to prepare (a vein, bed, mine, etc.) for working, by means of shafts, etc. — **to win one's spurs.** See under *spur*, *n.* — **win**, *n.* An act of winning; a success; a victory. [Colloq.]

wince¹ (wins), *n.* [= *winch*.] A reel used by dyers to transfer fabrics from one vat to another.

wince² (wins), *v. i.*; *winced, wincing*. [ME. *wincen, winchen*, from a var. of OF. *guenchir* or *guenchier*, turn aside, escape; from Teut., and akin to E. *wink*.] To shrink, as in pain or from a blow; start; flinch: as, "your mere puny stripling, that *winced* at the least flourish of the rod" (Irving's "Sketch-Book," Sleepy Hollow). — **wince²**, *n.* A wincing or shrinking movement; a slight start. — **win-cer** (win'sėr), *n.*

winch (winch), *n.* [AS. *wince*.] The crank or handle of a revolving machine; also, a kind of windlass turned by a crank, for hoisting, etc.

Win-ches-ter (win'ches-tėr) **bush'el.** See *bushel¹*, and *dry measure* (under *dry, a.*).

wind¹ (wīnd), *v. i.*; *wound* (occasionally *winded*), *winding*. [AS. *windan* = D. and G. *winden* = Icel. *vinda* = Goth. *-windan*, wind: cf. *wend¹*.] To change direction; bend; turn; also, to take a frequently bending course, or meander (as, "a little stream, *winding* down the hill": Vernon Lee's "Enchanted Woods," Nymphs and a River God); also, to have a circular or spiral course or direction; coil or twine about something (as, a vine *winds* round a pole); also, to be twisted or warped, as a board; also, fig., to proceed circuitously or indirectly; also, to undergo winding, or winding up (as, a clock which *winds* with a key). — **to wind up,** to wind up or conclude action, speech, etc. (as, a speaker *winds up* with a summary of facts); come to a conclusion, terminate, or end (as, the meeting did not *wind up* till late; he'll *wind up* in the poorhouse). [Chiefly colloq.] — **wind¹**, *v. t.* To bend or turn about (as, to *wind* a ship, to reverse its position, end for end); also, to turn or direct at will†; also, to roll or coil (thread, etc.) into a ball or on a spool or the like; twine, fold, wrap, or place about something; sometimes, to bring out of a rolled or coiled state (with *off*, etc.); also, to encircle or wreathe, as with something twined, wrapped, or placed about; also, to adjust (a mechanism, etc.) for operation by some turning or coiling process (as, to *wind*, or *wind*

Winch.

up, a clock: see phrase *to wind up*, below); also, to haul or hoist by means of a winch, windlass, or the like; also, to make (one's or its way) in a winding or frequently bending course (as, "I gladly *wound* my way from out of the pest-stricken city": Kinglake's "Eothen," xviii.); fig., to make (the way) by indirect or insidious procedure; also, to introduce insidiously; insinuate or worm (as, to *wind* one's self into a man's confidence). — **to wind up,** to roll or coil up; tighten (a lute-string, etc.), put (a clock, etc.) into condition for running, raise (a load), etc., by some process of winding; fig., to bring to a state of great tension; key up; work up or excite; give fresh energy to; also, to adjust or settle (affairs, etc.) finally; conclude (action, speech, etc.), often with something specified (as, to *wind up* an argument). — **wind¹**, *n.* A winding; a bend or turn; a twist producing an uneven surface.

wind² (wind, poetic wīnd), *n.* [AS. *wind* = D. and G. *wind* = Icel. *vindr* = Goth. *winds*, wind; akin to L. *ventus*, Gr. ἀήτης, Skt. *vāta*, wind, Skt. *vā-*, Gr. ἀῆναι, to blow: cf. *air³*, *vent³*, and *weather*.] Air in natural motion, as along the earth's surface; an air-current, breeze, or blast; also, any stream of air, as that produced by a bellows, a fan, or a cannon-ball; the air by which a wind-instrument is sounded; hence, a wind-instrument, or wind-instruments collectively (as, the brass-*winds*, or, collectively, the brass-*wind*, that is, the trumpets, horns, etc., or the wood-*winds*, or, collectively, the wood-*wind*, that is, the flutes, oboes, etc., in an orchestra); also, air impregnated with animal odor, or scent (see phrase *to get wind of*, below); also, breath or breathing; power of breathing freely, as during continued exertion (as, "Their horses are stout, well built ponies, of great *wind*": Irving's "Captain Bonneville," xii.); hence, the region of the stomach, a blow on which checks breathing (slang); also, gas generated in the stomach and bowels; also, empty talk; mere words; also, a point of the compass, esp. a cardinal point (as, "Come from the four *winds*, O breath, and breathe upon these slain," Ezek. xxxvii. 9; "He who divides his purposes scatters his life to the four *winds* of heaven," H. G. Wells's "Bealby," viii.); *naut.*, the point or direction from which the wind blows (see phrases below). — **between wind and water,** in that part of a ship near the water-line or brought above water by rolling, etc. (any breach effected in this part, as by a shot, being peculiarly dangerous); fig., at a vulnerable point. — **by the wind,** *naut.*, pointing as nearly as possible toward the direction from which the wind blows: as, to sail *by the wind* (to sail close-hauled). — **close to the wind.** See under *close²*, *adv.* — **in the eye** (or **teeth**) **of the wind,** directly against the wind. — **in the wind,** going on or impending, though not generally known; afoot: as, "If anything's *in the wind*, I wish you'd let me know" (W. Churchill's "Mr. Crewe's Career," xi.). — **into the wind,** *naut.*, into such a position that the head of a vessel is pointing toward the direction from which the wind blows: as, to come up *into the wind*. — **off the wind,** *naut.*, with the wind abaft the beam: as, to sail *off the wind*. — **on the wind,** *naut.*, close to the wind. — **to get wind of,** to get scent or (fig.) knowledge of: as, "If they once *get wind of* the affair there will be a great deal of talk" (Hugh Walpole's "Wooden Horse," ix.). — **to raise the wind.** See under *raise*, *v.* — **to sail close to the wind,** *naut.*, see *close to the wind*, under *close²*, *adv.*; fig., to manage with close calculation or the utmost economy; often, to come very near to imprudence, dishonesty, indecency, etc. — **to sow the wind.** See under *sow¹*, *v. t.* — **to the wind,** *naut.*, to the point from which the wind blows: as, to sail nearer *to the wind*. — **wind²** (wind), *v. t.*; *winded, winding*. To expose to wind or air; winnow (grain, etc.); also, to perceive by the wind or scent (as, "The rhino *winded* my companion and at once changed its direction and made for him": J. H. Patterson's "Man-Eaters of Tsavo," xxii.); follow by the scent; also, to render short of wind or breath, as by vigorous exercise (as, "By that time they were up the hill and William Wetherell quite *winded*": W. Churchill's "Coniston," i. 13); also, to let recover breath, as by resting after exertion.

wind³ (wīnd), *v. t.*; *winded* (often *wound*), *winding*. [The same word as *wind²*, *v.*, with different sense and pronunciation.] To blow (a horn, a blast, etc.); sound by blowing; also, to signal or direct by blasts of a horn or the like.

wind-age (wind′āj), *n.* The wind or wind-production of a moving missile, wheel, etc.; also, the air-friction of a mechanism in motion; also, the influence of the wind in deflecting a missile; the amount or extent of such deflection; also, the space between the moving part of a mechanism and the inclosing part; also, a difference allowed between the diameter of a projectile and that of the gun-bore, for the escape of gas and the preventing of friction; *naut.*, that portion of a vessel's surface upon which the wind acts.

wind-bag (wind′bag), *n.* A bag full of wind; fig., an empty, voluble, pretentious talker (colloq.: as, "some wordy *wind-bag*," S. Butler's "Erewhon," xiii.).

wind=borne (wind′bôrn), *a.* Carried by the wind, as pollen or seed.

wind=bound (wind′bound), *a.* Detained by contrary winds, as a ship, etc.: as, "We . . . put in at Galway . . . where we lay *wind-bound* two-and-twenty days" (Defoe's "Robinson Crusoe," ii. 1).

wind-break (wind′brāk), *n.* A growth of trees, a structure of boards, or the like, serving as a shelter from the wind; also, a windbreaker.—**wind′break″er,** *n.* A kind of short jacket of suède or chamois leather or the like, with close-fitting elastic hip-band, cuffs, and (often) collar, for sports or other outdoor wear in cold weather by men, women, or children. Also called *windbreak.*

wind=brok-en (wind′brō″kn), *a.* In *vet. science,* of horses, etc., having the power of breathing impaired; affected with heaves.

wind-ed (win′ded), *a.* Having wind or breath (as specified): as, short-*winded.*

wind-er¹ (wīn′dér), *n.* One who or that which winds (bends, turns, etc.) or is wound; a single one of a winding flight of steps; a plant that coils or twines itself about something; an instrument or a machine for winding thread, etc.

wind-er² (wīn′dér), *n.* One who winds a horn, etc.

wind-fall (wind′fâl), *n.* Something blown down by the wind, as fruit; also, an unexpected piece of good fortune, as a legacy.

wind=flow-er (wind′flou″ér), *n.* [Cf. *anemone.*] Any plant of the ranunculaceous genus *Anemone;* an anemone.

wind=gall (wind′gâl), *n.* In *vet. science,* a puffy distention of the synovial bursa at the fetlock-joint.

wind-hov-er (wind′huv″ér), *n.* [From its hovering in the face of the wind.] The kestrel.

wind-i-ly (win′di-li), *adv.* In a windy manner.—**wind′i-ness,** *n.*

wind-ing (wīn′ding), *n.* The act of one who or that which winds; a bend, turn, or flexure; a meander; a coiling, folding, or wrapping, as of one thing about another; also, something that is wound or coiled, or a single round of it.—**wind′ing,** *p. a.* Bending or turning; having a frequently bending course, meandering, or sinuous (as, "the *winding* passes of the mountains": Gibbon's "Decline and Fall of the Roman Empire," xlii.); spiral, as stairs.—**wind′ing-ly,** *adv.* —**wind′ing=sheet,** *n.* A sheet in which a corpse is wrapped for burial; also, a mass of tallow or wax that has run down and hardened on the side of a candle, suggesting drapery and popularly supposed to portend death or misfortune (as, "The candles flickered and guttered down, and made long *winding-sheets*": Dickens's "Barnaby Rudge," lv.).

wind=in-stru-ment (wind′in″strọ-ment), *n.* A musical instrument sounded by wind; specif., one sounded by air or breath from the lungs of the player (see *wind²,* n.).

wind=jam-mer (wind′jam″ér), *n.* A sailing-vessel, or a member of its crew (colloq.); also, a player on a bugle, trumpet, or the like (slang); also, a windy talker (slang).

wind-lass¹† (wind′las), *n.* [Cf. ME. *wanlace,* a circuit in hunting, OF. *wanlace, wenelaz,* deceit, appar. from Teut., and ult. akin to E. *wind¹.*] A circuit made in hunting; any circuit or circuitous course; hence, a roundabout proceeding (see Shakspere's "Hamlet," ii. 1. 65).

wind-lass² (wind′las), *n.* [For ME. *windas* = OF. *windas* (F. *guindas*), from Scand.: cf. Icel. *vindāss,* lit. 'winding-pole,' < *vinda,* wind, + *āss,* pole, beam.] A device used for raising weights, etc., consisting, in its usual form, of a horizontal cylinder or barrel which is turned by a crank, lever, or the like, and upon which a cable or the like winds, the outer end of the cable being attached directly or indirectly to the weight to be raised or the thing to be hauled or pulled. —**wind′lass²,** *v. t.* To raise, haul, or move by means of a windlass.

wind-less (wind′les), *a.* Free from wind; calm; also, out of breath.

win-dle-straw, win-dle-strae (win′dl-strâ, -strā), *n.* [AS. *windelstrēaw,* < *windel,* basket, + *strēaw,* straw.] The dry stalk of any of various grasses; hence, anything weak and slender; sometimes, a thin, weak person. [Prov. Eng. and Sc.]

wind-mill (wind′mil), *n.* A mill or machine, as for grinding or pumping, operated by the wind, usually by the wind acting on a set of arms, vanes, sails, or slats attached to a horizontal axis so as to form a vertical revolving wheel; also, fig., an imaginary opponent, wrong, etc. (as, to fight *windmills:* in allusion to the adventure of Don Quixote, in Cervantes's romance, i. 1. 8, with the windmills which he took for giants); a visionary notion or scheme; in *aëronautics,* a small air-turbine with blades like those of an aëroplane propeller, exposed on a moving aircraft and driven by the force of the air, and used to operate gasoline pumps, wireless apparatus, etc.

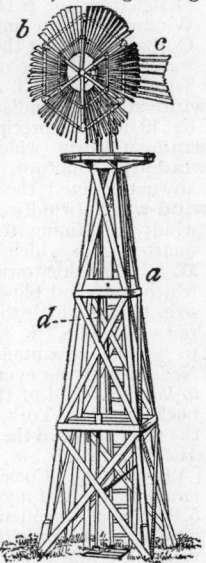

Windmill. — *a,* frame; *b,* sails; *c,* vane to bring wheel into wind; *d,* pump-rod.

wind=mo-tor (wind′mō″tor), *n.* Any prime mover or motor using the force of the wind directly: a term including the ordinary windmills, but applied more especially to apparatuses of other construction.

win-dow (win′dō), *n.* [ME. *windowe, windoge,* from Scand.: cf. Icel. *vindauga,* window, lit. 'wind-eye': see *wind²* and *eye.*] An opening in the wall or roof of a building, the cabin of a boat, etc., for the admission of air or light, or both, commonly fitted with a frame in which are set movable sashes containing panes of glass; such an opening together with the frame, sashes, and panes of glass, or any other device, by which it is closed; the frame, sashes, and panes of glass, or the like, intended to fit such an opening. Also fig.— **win′dow,** *v. t.* To furnish with a window or windows; also, to place at or in a window.—**win′dow=box,** *n.* One of the vertical hollows at the sides of the frame of a window, for the weights counterbalancing a sliding sash; also, a box for growing plants, placed at or in a window.—**win′dow=dress″er,** *n.* A person employed to dress the windows of a store, or arrange in them attractive displays of goods for sale.—**win′dow=dress″ing,** *n.* The action or work of a window-dresser; fig., the arrangement or the presentation of matters for a financial report, as by a bank, so as to appear to good advantage.—**win′dowed,** *a.* Having a window or windows: as, "many-*windowed* . . . houses" (Vernon Lee's "Enchanted Woods," Les Charmettes).—**win′dow-less,** *a.* Without windows: as, "a dead, *windowless* wall" (S. J. Weyman's "Gentleman of France," ix.).—**win′dow=pane,** *n.* One of the panes (plates of glass) used in a window.—**win′dow=seat,** *n.* A seat built within a recessed or other window.—**win′dow=shop″per,** *n.* One who gazes at articles in the windows of shops, instead of going in to do actual shopping.—**win′dow=shop″ping,** *n.* and *a.*— **win′dow=sill,** *n.* The sill beneath a window: as, "There were nasturtiums and mignonette on the outer *window-sill*" (Du Maurier's "Trilby," iii.).

wind-pipe (wind′pīp), *n.* The trachea of an air-breathing vertebrate.

wind-row (wind′rō), *n.* A row or line of hay raked together to dry before being made into cocks or heaps; any similar row, as of sheaves of grain, made for the purpose of drying; also, a row of dry leaves, dust, etc., swept together by the wind.—**wind′row,** *v. t.* To arrange in a windrow or windrows.—**wind′row″er,** *n.* One who or that which windrows, esp. an attachment to a mowing-machine.

wind=shake (wind′shāk), *n.* A flaw in wood supposed to be caused by the action of strong winds upon the trunk of the tree; such flaws collectively; anemosis. — **wind′=shak″en** (-shā″kn), *a.* Shaken by the wind; specif., affected by wind-shake.

wind=shield (wind′shēld), *n.* A shield or protection against the force of the wind, etc., esp. a framed shield of glass, in one or more sections, projecting above the dashboard of an automobile.

Wind-sor (win′zǫr), *a.* [From *Windsor* Castle, in Berkshire, England, the chief residence of the British sovereigns.] Designating, or pertaining to, the British royal house of Windsor (known until 1917 as the house of Saxe-Coburg-Gotha), including the successors of Victoria (whose husband was Albert, Prince of Saxe-Coburg-Gotha), or Victoria and her successors. Cf. *Hanoverian, a.*

wind=storm (wind′stôrm), *n.* A storm with heavy wind, but little or no precipitation.

wind=suck-ing (wind′suk″ing), *n.* Same as *crib-biting.*

wind=up (wīnd′up), *n.* A winding up; the conclusion of any action, etc.; the end or close; a final act or part.

wind=ward (wind′wärd). **I.** *a.* On the side toward the wind; pertaining to, situated in, or moving toward the quarter from which the wind blows: opposed to *leeward.* **II.** *n.* The side toward the wind; the point or quarter from which the wind blows: as, "The brig's head had been laid so as to pass a little to *windward* of the small islands" (J. Conrad's "Rescue," i. 3). — **to get to the windward of,** fig., to get the advantage of: as, "as ready to trade with the Nederlanders as ever — and not a whit more prone to *get to the windward of* them in a bargain" (Irving's "Knickerbocker's New York," iv. 4). — **wind′ward,** *adv.* Toward the wind; toward the point from which the wind blows.

wind-y (win′di), *a.;* compar. *windier,* superl. *windiest.* [AS. *windig.*] Consisting of or resembling wind (as, "the *windy* tempest of my heart": Shakspere's "3 Henry VI.," ii. 5. 86); also, accompanied or characterized by wind (as, *windy* weather; "a *windy* day," H. G. Wells's "Men Like Gods," ii. 1); tempestuous; also, exposed to or swept by the wind (as, "the *windy* pier": Kipling's "Light That Failed," ix.); toward the wind, or windward (as, "the *windy* side of care": Shakspere's "Much Ado about Nothing," ii. 1. 327); also, characterized by or causing flatulence; also, fig., unsubstantial or empty (as, "*windy* joy": Milton's "Samson Agonistes," 1574); also, of the nature of, characterized by, or given to prolonged, empty talk (as, *windy* eloquence; "the *windy* demagogue, who had filled half Flanders with his sound and fury," Motley's "Dutch Republic," vi. 2); voluble; sometimes, boastful (chiefly prov. Eng. and Sc.).

wine (wīn), *n.* [AS. *wīn, <* L. *vinum,* wine, grapes, the vine, akin to Gr. οἶνος, wine, οἴνη, the vine: cf. *vine.*] The fermented juice of the grape, in many varieties (red, white, sweet, dry, still, sparkling, etc.), used as a beverage and in cookery, religious rites, etc. (as, "*wine* that maketh glad the heart of man," Ps. civ. 15; "He pour'd to Bacchus, on the hallow'd ground, Two bowls of sparkling *wine,*" Dryden's tr. Virgil's "Æneid," v. 102); a particular variety of such fermented grape-juice (as, French and Italian *wines;* Rhine *wines;* port and sherry *wines*); loosely, unfermented grape-juice; also, the juice, fermented or unfermented, of various other fruits or plants, used as a beverage, etc. (as, gooseberry *wine;* currant *wine;* palm-*wine*); fig., something that invigorates, cheers, or intoxicates like wine (as, "Joy is the best of *wine,*" George Eliot's "Silas Marner," v.; "The new strong *wine* of love, That made my tongue so stammer and trip," Tennyson's "Maud," i. 6. 9); also, intoxication due to the drinking of wine (as, "Noah awoke from his *wine*": Gen. ix. 24); also, a party for wine-drinking (chiefly Eng.); in *phar.,* same as *vinum.* — **wine,** *v.; wined, wining.* **I.** *tr.* To supply with wine; also, to entertain with wine (as, "I'll bet he *wined* and dined the superintendent": Sinclair Lewis's "Babbitt," xxi.). **II.** *intr.* To drink wine. — **wine′bib″ber,** *n.* [See *bib*[1].] One who drinks much wine: as, "a gluttonous man, and a *winebibber*" (Luke, vii. 34). — **wine′bib″bing,** *n.* and *a.* — **wine′=cel″lar,** *n.* A cellar for the storage of wine; also, the wine stored there; a store or stock of wines. — **wine′=col″or,** *n.* The color of (red) wine; a dark purplish-red color. — **wine′=col″ored,** *a.* Of a

dark purplish-red color. — **wine′=fat,** *n.* [See *fat*[2].] A vat or vessel in which grapes were trodden in making wine. See Isa. lxiii. 2. [Archaic.] — **wine′=gal″lon,** *n.* See *gallon.* — **wine′glass,** *n.* A small drinking-glass for wine. — **wine′glass-ful** (-fūl), *n.;* pl. *-fuls.* — **wine′less,** *a.* Without wine. — **wine′=meas″ure,** *n.* An old English system of measures for wine, etc., in which the gallon ('wine-gallon') was smaller than the gallon for beer, etc.: its gallon is the standard gallon in the U. S. See *gallon.* — **wine′=palm,** *n.* Any of various palms yielding palm-wine; a toddy-palm. — **wine′=press,** *n.* A wine-fat (see Isa. lxiii. 3); also, a machine in which the juice is pressed from grapes for wine. — **win-er-y** (wī′nėr-i), *n.;* pl. *-ies* (-iz). An establishment for making wine. — **wine′sap,** *n.* A highly esteemed red winter apple of the U. S. — **wine′=shop,** *n.* A shop where wine is sold. — **wine′=skin,** *n.* A vessel made of the nearly complete skin of a goat, hog, or the like, used, esp. in the East, for holding wine; fig., one who drinks great or excessive quantities of wine (as, "What! you have been dining with the Teutonic *wine-skin?*" Scott's "Talisman," xi.).

Oriental Wine-skins.

wing (wing), *n.* [ME. *winge, wenge,* prob. from Scand.: cf. Icel. *vœngr,* Sw. and Dan. *vinge,* wing.] Either of the two anterior extremities, or appendages of the scapular arch or shoulder-girdle, of most birds and of bats, which constitute the fore limbs and correspond to the human arms, but are adapted for flight or aërial locomotion; either of two corresponding but rudimentary or functionless parts in certain other birds; any of various analogous but structurally different appendages by means of which insects fly; any of certain other wing-like structures of other animals, as the patagium of a flying-squirrel; a similar structure with which gods, angels, demons, etc., are conceived to be provided for the purpose of flying; also, a foreleg of a quadruped, or an arm of a human being (now chiefly humorous); also, fig., a means or instrument of flight, travel, or progress (as, "Riches . . . make themselves *wings,*" Prov. xxiii. 5; "Fiery expedition be my *wing,*" Shakspere's "Richard III.," iv. 3. 54); protection, care, or patronage (with allusion to the sheltering of the young under the wings of the mother bird: as, to take a person under one's *wing*); also, the act or manner of flying (as, "The crow Makes *wing* to the rooky wood": Shakspere's "Macbeth," iii. 2. 51); flight or, fig., departure (as, to take *wing*); also, something resembling or likened to a wing, as a vane or sail of a windmill, the feather of an arrow, either of the parts of a double door, etc.; in *anat.,* an ala (as, the *wings* of the sphenoid); in *bot.,* any leaf-like expansion, as of a samara; also, one of the two side petals of a papilionaceous flower; in *arch.,* a part of a building projecting on one side of, or subordinate to, a central or main part (as, "The house was of stone, long, low, and with a small *wing* at each extremity": Cooper's "Spy," i.); in *theatrical use,* the platform or space on the right or left of the stage proper; also, one of the long, narrow side pieces of scenery; in *fort.,* either of the longer sides of a crown-work, uniting it to the main work; in *aëronautics,* a wing-like structure, or plane; specif., that portion of a main supporting surface confined to one side of an aëroplane; *milit.* and *naval,* either of the two side portions of an army or fleet when in battle array (usually called *right wing* and *left wing,* and distinguished from the *center*). — **on the wing,** in flight, or flying (as, "The bird That flutters least is longest *on the wing*" Cowper's "Task," vi. 931); hence, in motion; traveling; active. — **wing and wing,** *naut.,* with a sail extended on each side by a boom, as a schooner sailing before the wind with the foresail out on one side and the mainsail out on the other. — **wing,** *v.* **I.** *tr.* To equip with wings; fig., to enable to fly, move rapidly, etc.; lend speed or celerity to; also, to supply with a wing-like part, a side structure, etc.; also, to brush or clean with a wing; also, to transport on or as on wings (as, "I . . . Will *wing* me to some wither'd bough": Shakspere's "Winter's Tale," v. 3. 133); perform or accomplish by means of wings (as, "Wasps . . . frequently *wing* their way at a considerable elevation": Jefferies's "Gamekeeper at Home," iii.); traverse in flight (as, "all that . . . *wing* the sky": Pope's "Essay on Man," iii. 120); also, to wound or disable (a bird, etc.) in the wing; wound (a person) in the arm or some other non-vital part (colloq.); bring down (an aëroplane, etc.) by a shot (colloq.); in *theatrical use*, to perform (a part, etc.) with reliance on prompters in the wings. **II.** *intr.* To travel on or as on wings; fly; soar: as, "In the upper gloom The bat . . . was *winging*" (Hood's "Haunted House," iii.).

wing=bow (wing′bō), *n.* In *ornith.*, the plumage of the bend of a bird's wing when having a distinctive marking or coloration.

wing=case (wing′kās), *n.* An elytrum.

wing=chair (wing′chār), *n.* A form of chair with wing-like parts projecting from the back above the arms.

wing=cov-er (wing′kuv″ėr), *n.* An elytrum.

wing=cov-erts (wing′kuv″ėrts), *n. pl.* In *ornith.*, the feathers which cover the bases of the quill-feathers of the wing in birds.

winged (wingd or wing′ed), *a.* Having wings; also, having a wing-like part or wing-like parts (as, a *winged* bone; a *winged* seed); also, abounding with wings or winged creatures (as, "the *wing'd* air dark'd with plumes": Milton's "Comus," 730); also, moving or passing on or as if on wings (as, *winged* words); rapid or swift (as, "*winged* haste": Shakspere's "1 Henry IV.," iv. 4. 2); elevated or lofty (as, *winged* sentiments); also,

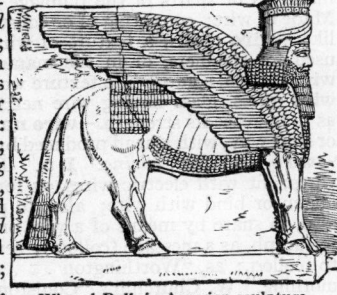

Winged Bull, in Assyrian sculpture.

disabled in the wing, as a bird; of a person, wounded in the arm or some other non-vital part (colloq.).—**Winged Victory.** See *victory*.

wing-er (wing′ėr), *n.* One who or that which wings.

wing=fish (wing′fish), *n.* A flying-fish; esp., a flying-gurnard.

wing=foot-ed (wing′fút″ed), *a.* Having winged feet; hence, rapid; swift.

wing-less (wing′les), *a.* Having no wings; also, having only rudimentary wings, as an apteryx.

wing-let (wing′let), *n.* A little wing; also, an alula.

wing=rail (wing′rāl), *n.* On a railroad-track, an additional rail at a switch, laid so as to prevent the wheels from leaving the track.

wing=shell (wing′shel), *n.* A stromb (so called from the wing-like lip of the aperture); also, any of various bivalves of the family *Aviculidæ*, esp. of the genus *Avicula*, characterized by wing-like expansions of the hinge margin.

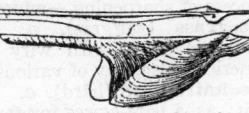

Wing-shell (*Avicula hirundo*).

wink (wingk), *v.* [AS. *wincian*, wink, akin to OHG. *winkan*, move aside, totter, nod, G. *winken*, nod, wink: cf. *wince²*.] **I.** *intr.* To close and open the eyes quickly, or, of the eyes, to close and open thus (as, "His gray eyes, accustomed to the shaded light . . . were *winking* . . . in the unadulterated sunshine": Hawthorne's "Scarlet Letter," iii.); blink; nictitate; also, to close and open one eye quickly as a hint or signal or with some sly meaning (often with *at*: as, "Mr. Merrill *winked* at Jethro, and laughed," W. Churchill's "Coniston," i. 11); also, to close the eyes (obs. or archaic); sleep†; fig., to be purposely blind to a thing, as if to avoid the necessity of taking action (commonly with *at*: as, to *wink* at petty offenses; "The Prince had *winked* at a project which he would not openly approve," Motley's "Dutch Republic," vi. 1); connive; also, to shine with little flashes of light, or twinkle (as, "The lamps were *winking* through the dusk": L. Merrick's "Conrad in Quest of His Youth," iv.). **II.** *tr.* To close and open (the eyes or an eye) quickly; execute or give (a wink: as, "Long Jack *winked* one tremendous wink," Kipling's "Captains Courageous," vi.); also, to drive or force (*away*, *back*, etc.) by winking (as, to *wink* away one's tears); also, to signal or convey by a

wink (as, "Milly glanced coolly at the conductor, who *winked* back his permission": Arnold Bennett's "Leonora," vi.).—

wink, *n.* The act of winking; a winking movement, esp. of one eye as in giving a hint or signal; a hint or signal given by or as by winking (as, "Your reply is a nod and a *wink*": Jefferies's "Gamekeeper at Home," iii.); also, the time required for winking once; an instant or twinkling; a moment of sleep (colloq.: as, I didn't sleep a *wink*; forty *winks*, a short nap); a nap or sleep (now prov.); in general, a bit (colloq.: as, "an old, old sight . . . and not changed a *wink* since I first saw it," H. Melville's "Moby-Dick," cxxxv.); also, a little flash of light, or a twinkle (as, "the red gleam . . . instantly eclipsed like the *wink* of a signalling lantern": J. Conrad's "Rescue," iv. 4).—**wink′er,** *n.* One who or that which winks; an eyelash or an eye (colloq.); also, a blinker or blinder for a horse.

win-kle (wing′kl), *n.* [Appar. an abbr. of *periwinkle²*.] Any of various marine gastropods; a periwinkle.

win-ner (win′ėr), *n.* One who or that which wins; a successful contestant or competitor.

win-ning (win′ing), *n.* The act of one who or that which wins; also, that which is won (chiefly in *pl.*).—**win′ning,** *p. a.* That wins; successful or victorious, as in a contest; taking, engaging, or charming, as a person or the manner, qualities, ways, etc.—**win′ning-ly,** *adv.*—**win′ning=post,** *n.* A post on a race-course, forming the goal of a race.

win-now (win′ō), *v.* [AS. *windwian*, akin to *wind*, E. *wind²*.] **I.** *tr.* To free (grain, etc.) from chaff, refuse particles, etc., by means of wind or driven air; fan; blow upon, as the wind does upon grain in this process; drive or blow (chaff, etc.) away by fanning; fig., to subject to some process of separating or distinguishing (as, to *winnow* a mass of statements); analyze critically; sift; separate or distinguish (as, to *winnow* truth from falsehood, or the false from the true; to *winnow* out the facts in a case); also (chiefly poetic), to fan or stir (the air) as with the wings in flying; move or flap (the wings) in flying; pursue (a course) with flapping wings in flying. **II.** *intr.* To free grain from chaff by wind or driven air; also, to fly with flapping wings; flutter.—**win′-now,** *n.* A device or contrivance for winnowing grain, etc.; also, the act of winnowing; a winnowing movement.—**win′now-er,** *n.*

win-some (win′sum), *a.*; compar. winsomer, superl. winsom-est. [AS. *wynsum*, delightful, < *wynn*, joy: cf. G. *wonne*, joy, delight. In modern E. use commonly associated with *win*.] Delightful, pleasing, or agreeable; now, esp., winning, engaging, or charming (as, a *winsome* young girl; a *winsome* smile); also, cheerful or merry (prov.).—**win′some-ly,** *adv.* —**win′some-ness,** *n.*

win-ter (win′tėr). [AS. *winter* = D. and G. *winter* = Icel. *vittr*, *vetr*, = Sw. and Dan. *vinter* = Goth. *wintrus*, winter.] **I.** *n.* The last and the coldest season of the year, in North America taken as comprising December, January, and February, in Great Britain November, December, and January; also, a whole year as represented by this season (as, a man of sixty *winters*); also, fig., the last or final period, as of life (as, "Father Mapple was in the hardy *winter* of a healthy old age": H. Melville's "Moby-Dick," viii.); a period of decline or decay; a season of inertia or suspended activity; a season of cheerlessness, dreariness, or adversity (as, "The *winter* of sorrow best shows The truth of a friend such as you": Cowper's "Winter Nosegay," 23). **II.** *a.* Of, pertaining to, or characteristic of winter (as, *winter* weather; *winter* clothes; *winter* sports); of fruit and vegetables, of a kind that may be kept for use during the winter (as, a *winter* apple or pear; *winter* squash).—

winter aconite, a small ranunculaceous herb, *Cammarum hyemale*, a native of the Old World, often cultivated for its bright-yellow flowers, which appear very early in the spring.—**winter wheat.** See under *wheat.*—**win′ter,** *v.* **I.** *intr.* To spend or pass the winter: as, "Our present plans are to *winter* in Italy" (Lever's "Harry

Winter Aconite.

(variable) ḍ as d or j, ş as s or sh, t as t or ch, z as z or zh; o, F. cloche; ü, F. menu; ch, Sc. loch; ṅ, F. bonbon; ′, primary accent; ″, secondary accent; †, obsolete; <, from; +, and; =, equals. See also lists at beginning of book.

Lorrequer," xli.); "Some of the young stock which were *wintering* on the range . . . died from the exposure" (Roosevelt's "Hunting Trips of a Ranchman," iv.). **II.** *tr.* To keep, feed, or manage during the winter, as plants or cattle.

win-ter-ber-ry (win′tèr-ber″i), *n.*; pl. *-berries* (-iz). Any of several North American species of holly (genus *Ilex*) with red berries that are persistent through the winter.

win-ter-green (win′tèr-grēn), *n.* A small, creeping, evergreen ericaceous shrub, *Gaultheria procumbens*, common in eastern North America, with white bell-shaped flowers, a bright-red berry-like fruit, and aromatic leaves which yield a volatile oil ('oil of wintergreen'); any of various other plants of the same genus; also, any of various small evergreen herbs of the genera *Pyrola* and *Chimaphila*.

win-ter-kill (win′tèr-kil), *v. t.* or *i.* To kill by or die from exposure to the cold of winter, as wheat. [U.S.]

win-ter-less (win′tèr-les), *a.* Having no winter; without wintry weather.

win-ter-ly (win′tèr-li), *a.* Wintry.

win-ter-tide (win′tèr-tīd), *n.* [AS. *wintertīd.*] Wintertime. [Now poetic.]

win-ter-time (win′tèr-tīm), *n.* The season of winter.

Wintergreen (*Gaultheria procumbens*).—*a*, the fruit.

win-try (win′tri), *a.* Of, pertaining to, or characteristic of winter (as, *wintry* weather, storms, or cold; a *wintry* sky); having the season or cold of winter (as, *wintry* shores; *wintry* lands); suggestive of winter, as in lack of warmth or cheer (as, "a faint, sweet, *wintry* smile": Mrs. Gaskell's "Cranford," ii.).—**win′tri-ness,** *n.*

win-y (wī′ni), *a.* Of the nature of or resembling wine; pertaining to or characteristic of wine; affected by wine.

winze (winz), *n.* [Origin uncertain.] In *mining*, a small shaft, esp. one connecting one level with another, as for ventilation, etc.

wipe (wīp), *v. t.*; *wiped, wiping.* [AS. *wīpian*, wipe: cf. *wisp.*] To rub lightly with a cloth, towel, paper, the hand, etc., in order to clean or dry (as, to *wipe* the face or hands, a dusty table, or weeping eyes; to wash and *wipe* dishes); rub on something in order to clean or dry (as, "You have not *wiped* your shoes properly on the mat": C. Brontë's "Villette," iii.); also, to take (*away, off, out*, etc.) by rubbing with or on something (as, to *wipe* away tears; to *wipe* off dust; to *wipe* out chalk-marks; to *wipe* mud from one's shoes on a door-mat); hence, to remove as if by rubbing (with *away, off*, etc.: as, the rain *wiped* away all footprints; "unless he let all these people be *wiped* off the face of the earth," J. Conrad's "Rescue," iii. 8); often, to blot (*out*), as from existence or memory (as, to *wipe* out a regiment in battle; "I want to *wipe* out all the past," Mrs. Wharton's "Age of Innocence," xii.); also, to rub or draw (something) over a surface, as in cleaning or drying; also, to strike, beat, or whip (now prov. or slang); also, to defraud† or cheat†; in *plumbing*, to apply (solder in a semifluid state) by spreading with a pad of leather or cloth over the part to be soldered; form (a joint between lead pipes) in this manner.—**wipe,** *n.* The act or an act of wiping; a rub, as of one thing over another (as, "a melancholy *wipe* of his sleeve across his brow": George Eliot's "Felix Holt," viii.); a sweeping stroke or blow (now prov. or colloq.: as, "The centre of the storm swept by behind us . . . and we only got a *wipe* from the tail of it," Roosevelt's "Hunting Trips of a Ranchman," iv.; "There's the scar of the *wipe* he got," Kipling's "Light That Failed," vi.); a gibe (now prov. or colloq.); a scar† or brand†; also, a handkerchief (slang); in *mach.*, a wiper.—**wip-er** (wī′pèr), *n.* One who or that which wipes; also, that with which anything is wiped, as a towel or a handkerchief; in *mach.*, a projecting piece, as on a

rotating axis, acting on another part, as a stamper, esp. for the purpose of raising it so that it may fall by its own weight.

wire (wīr). [AS. *wīr* = MLG. *wire* = Icel. *vīrr*, wire.] **I.** *n.* A piece of slender, flexible metal, ranging from a thickness that can be bent by the hand only with some difficulty down to a fine thread, and usually circular in section; such pieces as a material; also, a long wire or cable used in electric transmission, as in electric lighting, or in a telephone, telegraph, or cable system; hence, the telegraphic system (colloq.: as, to send a message by *wire*); a telegram (colloq.: as, "I'll have to send a *wire* to Daddy," Galsworthy's "Saint's Progress," iii. 9); also, a metallic string of a musical instrument (as, "Listening to what unshorn Apollo sings To the touch of golden *wires*": Milton's "At a Vacation Exercise," 38); also, *pl.*, a system of wires by which puppets are moved; fig., secret means of directing or controlling the action of others, as in carrying out schemes (as, to pull *wires* to win a political nomination); also, *sing.*, a cross-wire or cross-hair; in *ornith.*, one of the extremely long, slender, wire-like filaments or shafts of the plumage of various birds. **II.** *a.* Made of wire; consisting of or constructed with wires; wire-like.—**wire cloth,** a texture of wires of moderate fineness, used for strainers, or in the manufacture of paper, etc.—**wire gauze,** a gauze-like texture woven of very fine wires.—**wire glass,** glass having wire netting embedded within it, as to increase its strength.—**wire nail,** a nail made from iron or steel wire, with a head produced by compression of the end.—**wire,** *v.*; *wired, wiring.* **I.** *tr.* To furnish with a wire or wires; fit with electric wires, as for lighting, etc.; also, to fasten or bind with wire; also, to put on a wire, as beads; also, to snare by means of a wire or wires; also, to send by telegraph, as a message (colloq.); send a telegraphic message to (colloq.: as, "Worthington . . . *wired* the President this morning," W. Churchill's "Coniston," ii. 4). **II.** *intr.* To send a telegraphic message; telegraph. [Colloq.]

wired (wīrd), *a.* Having a wire or wires; having wire-like feathers (as, the twelve-*wired* bird of paradise).—**wired wireless.** See under *wireless, n.*

wire-draw (wīr′drâ), *v. t.*; pret. *-drew*, pp. *-drawn*, ppr. *-drawing.* To draw (metal) out into wire, esp. by pulling forcibly through a series of holes gradually decreasing in diameter; hence, to draw out to great length, in quantity or time; stretch out to excess; esp., to spin out (a subject, discourse, argument, etc.) with excessive refinement or subtlety, hair-splitting, etc.; also, to strain unwarrantably, as in meaning; wrest.—**wire′draw″er,** *n.*

wire-edge (wīr′ej), *n.* A thin, wire-like bur or thread of metal often formed at the edge of a cutting-tool during the process of sharpening.—**wire′=edged,** *a.*

wire-grass (wīr′gräs), *n.* An old-world meadow-grass, *Poa compressa*, with wiry culms, naturalized in North America; also, any of various similar grasses.

wire=haired (wīr′hârd), *a.* Having coarse, stiff, wire-like hair: as, a *wire-haired* fox-terrier.

wire-less (wīr′les), *a.* Having no wire; operated without a wire or wires; esp., noting or pertaining to a system of telegraphy in which there are no connecting wires, the signals being transmitted through space by means of the radiated energy of Hertzian waves; also, noting or pertaining to a system of telephony in which Hertzian waves are similarly employed; also, noting or pertaining to any of various devices which are operated with or set in action by Hertzian waves.—**wireless wave.** See under *wave, n.*—**wire′less,** *n.* Wireless telegraphy or telephony; in general, transmission through space, without wires, by means of Hertzian waves; also, a wireless telegraph or telephone; also, a wireless message.—**wired wireless,** a system of telegraphy and telephony similar to ordinary wireless except that the communications are sent along a guiding wire instead of through the air.—**wire′less,** *v. t.* or *i.* To telegraph or telephone by wireless.—**wire′less-ly,** *adv.*

wire-man (wīr′man), *n.*; pl. *-men.* A man who puts in place and looks after wires, as for a telegraph, telephone, electric lighting, or electric power system.

wire=pull-er (wīr′pul″èr), *n.* One who pulls the wires, as of puppets; fig., one who manipulates secret means of directing or controlling the action of others (as, a political *wire-puller*; "the standing alliance between business interests and party wire-pullers," Charnwood's "Theodore Roosevelt," iii.).— **wire'=pull"ing**, n.

wir-er (wīr'er), n. One who wires.

wire-smith (wīr'smith), n. One who makes metal into wire, esp. by beating or hammering.

wire=tap-per (wīr'tap"er), n. One who illicitly taps wires to learn the nature of messages passing over them; also, a swindler who professes to secure by this or some similar means advance information for betting or the like (colloq.). —**wire'=tap"ping**, n.

wire-work (wīr'wèrk), n. Work consisting of wire; fabrics or articles made of wire.—**wire'works**, n. pl. or sing. An establishment where wire is made, or is put to some industrial use.

wire-worm (wīr'wèrm), n. The slender, hard-bodied larva of an elaterid or click-beetle, which in many species lives underground and feeds on the roots of plants, often causing much damage to cereal and other crops; also, any of various small myriapods.

wir-i-ly (wīr'i-li), adv. In a wiry manner.—**wir'i-ness**, n.

wir-ing (wīr'ing), n. The act of one who wires; also, an arrangement, system, or aggregate of wires, as of electric wires in a room, building, or the like.

wir-y (wīr'i), a.; compar. wirier, superl. wiriest. Made of wire; in the form of wire; also, resembling wire, as in form, stiffness, etc. (as, "wiry grass," J. Conrad's "Rover," ii.; "wiry hair," Bulwer-Lytton's "Pelham," xl.); lean and sinewy, as persons, the body, etc. (as, "a little man, with a spare, wiry body": Ian Maclaren's "Beside the Bonnie Brier Bush," iv. 1).

wis (wis), v. [A spurious verb-form corresponding to wist (< wit, v.), due to misunderstanding of iwis, adv.] To know. See iwis. [Archaic.]

wis-dom (wiz'dǫm), n. [AS. wīsdōm: see wise¹ and -dom.] The quality or state of being wise; knowledge of what is true or right coupled with just judgment as to action (as, the infinite wisdom of God; the limits of human wisdom; to gain wisdom with years or experience); sagacity, prudence, or common sense; scholarly knowledge, or learning (as, the wisdom of the schools); knowledge in a specified field or subject (as, worldly wisdom); also, something wise; wise action or conduct; wise sayings or teachings; occasionally, a wise act or saying.—**The Wisdom of Jesus, the Son of Sirach.** See Ecclesiasticus.—**The Wisdom of Solomon,** one of the books of the Apocrypha, the authorship of which is traditionally ascribed to Solomon, treating of wisdom and its relation to righteousness.—**wis'dom=tooth**, n. The back (last molar) tooth on either side of each jaw in man, appearing ordinarily between the ages of 17 and 25 (as if with one's coming to years of wisdom or discretion).

wise¹ (wīz), a.; compar. wiser, superl. wisest. [AS. wīs = D. wijs = G. weise = Icel. vīss = Goth. -weis, wise; from the root of E. wit.] Having the power (whether from experience or by natural endowment) of discerning and judging properly as to what is true or right (as, a wise counselor; a wise father); characterized by or showing such power (as, wise sayings, plans, or actions); sage; sagacious; judicious or prudent; shrewd or astute; also, possessed of or character- ized by scholarly knowledge or learning (as, wise professors; wise treatises); learned; erudite; also, having knowledge of occult or supernatural things (archaic or prov.: as, a wise man or woman, a wizard or witch, a fortune-teller, or the like); also, having knowledge in a specified field or subject (as, wise in the law; weather-wise; worldly-wise); versed; having knowledge or information as to facts, circumstances, etc. (as, we are none the wiser for his explanations); aware or cognizant (used in slang phrases: as, to be wise to a thing, to be aware of it; to put one wise to a secret); also, of sound mind (Sc.).—**wise crack.** See entry in next column.

wise² (wīz), n. [AS. wīse, wīs, = D. wijs = G. weise, way; from the same source as E. wise¹: cf. guise.] Way of pro- ceeding; manner; fashion; also, respect; degree: now usually in composition (see -wise) or in certain phrases (as, in any wise, in any way, respect, or degree; in no wise; in some wise; on this wise, in this way).

-wise. A suffixal use of wise² in adverbs denoting manner, direction, position, etc., as in anywise, edgewise, likewise, sidewise. See -ways.

wise-a-cre (wīz'ā-kèr), n. [MD. wijssegger = G. weissager, prophet: cf. OHG. wīzago, AS. wītega, prophet, and E. witch.] A wise person; one who possesses or affects to possess great wisdom: now used only ironically or humor- ously.

wise crack (wīz krak), **wise-crack** (wīz'krak), n. A smart or facetious remark. [Slang.]—**wise'crack**, v. i. To make wise cracks. [Slang.]—**wise'crack"er**, n.

wise-ly (wīz'li), adv. In a wise manner.—**wise'ness**, n.

wish (wish), v. [AS. wȳscan, akin to D. wenschen, G. wünschen, Icel. æskja, Sw. önska, Dan. önske, wish: cf. Skt. vānch-, wish, van-, hold dear, desire, and E. win.] **I.** intr. To have a distinct mental inclination toward the doing, ob- taining, attaining, or realization (whether by one's self or by another) of a particular thing (often followed by for: as, to wish for a book, for news, or for aid; to wish for another's happiness); have a desire or wish; also, to entertain wishes, favorably or otherwise (with to: as, to wish well to a person or a cause). **II.** tr. To wish for (as, to wish money, aid, or peace; "'Tis a consummation Devoutly to be wish'd," Shakspere's "Hamlet," iii. 1. 64); want; desire (often with an infinitive or a clause as object: as, I wish to see him; I wish him to come; I wish that he would come); desire (a person or thing) to be (as specified: as, to wish one's self elsewhere; we could not wish it more successful); entertain wishes, favorably or otherwise, for (as, to wish one well or ill); desire (good or evil) to come to a person or thing (as, to wish no harm to one, or to wish one no harm); also, to express a desire for (happiness, joy, luck, etc.) to come to a person or thing (as, his letter wished success to the new firm, or wished the new firm success); bid, as in greeting or leave- taking (as, to wish one a good morning; "Belle gave him her hand and wished him farewell," Borrow's "Romany Rye," i.); also, to commend or recommend as to a person†.— **wish,** n. A distinct mental inclination toward the doing, obtaining, attaining, or realization of something; a desire, felt or expressed (as, to inquire one's wishes; to disregard the wishes of others); an expression of a wish, often one of a kindly or courteous nature (as, to send one's best wishes); also, that which is wished (as, to get one's wish; your welfare is our chief wish).—**wish'bone**, n. The forked bone (a united pair of clavicles) in front of the breast-bone in most birds; the furcula.—**wish'er**, n.—**wish'ful**, a. Having or showing a wish; desirous; longing; also, desirable†.— **wish'ful-ly**, adv.—**wish'ful-ness**, n.—**wish'ing=cap**, n. A fabulous cap supposed to ensure fulfilment of any wish made by one wearing it.

wish-y=wash-y (wish'i-wosh"i), a. [Varied redupl. of washy.] Washy or watery, as a liquid; thin and weak; fig., lacking in substantial qualities; without strength or force; weak, feeble, or poor (as, a wishy-washy novel; "your wishywashy fool of a daughter," Sinclair Lewis's "Babbitt," xix.).

wisp (wisp), n. [ME. wisp, wips, wisp (of hay): cf. MLG. wip, bunch of straw, twigs, etc., wisp, Sw. visp, a whisk, and E. wipe.] A handful or small bundle of straw, hay, or the like; hence, a small or thin tuft, lock, mass, or streak of anything (as, a wisp of wool; straggling wisps of hair; "a wisp of smoke," J. Conrad's "Lord Jim," ii.; "They groped downstairs, guided by a wisp of light from Tommy's studio," Arnold Bennett's "Lion's Share," xi.); also, a whisk, or small broom; also, a small bundle of straw or hay, a twisted or folded bit of paper, or the like, used for kindling or lighting; a torch or candle (prov.: cf. will-o'-the-wisp); also, a will- o'-the-wisp, or ignis fatuus (as, "the wisp that flickers where no foot can tread": Tennyson's "Princess," iv. 339); also, an inflammatory and suppurative disease affecting the feet of cattle.—**wisp'ish, wisp'y**, a. Being a wisp or in wisps; wisp-like: as, "the most preposterous wispish beard" (Buchan's "Three Hostages," xi.); "wispy gleams" (J. Conrad's "Rescue," i. 3).

wist (wist). Preterit and past participle of wit.

wis-ta-ri-a (wis-tā'ri-ä), n. [NL., orig. Wisteria (given as genus-name), but prop. Wistaria; in honor of Caspar Wistar (1761–1818), American anatomist.] Any of the climbing shrubs, with handsome pendent racemes of purple flowers, which constitute the fabaceous genus Kraunhia, as K. chinensis ('Chinese wistaria'), much used to cover verandas and walls. Also **wis-te'ri-a** (-tē'ri-ä).

(variable) ḓ as d or j, ş as s or sh, ţ as t or ch, ʓ as z or zh; o, F. cloche; ü, F. menu; ċh, Sc. loch; ṅ, F. bonbon; ', primary accent; ", secondary accent; †, obsolete; <, from; +, and; =, equals. See also lists at beginning of book.

wist-ful (wist'fúl), *a.* [Appar. orig. < *whist*[1], *a.*, with sense later affected by *wishful*.] Hushed† or silent†; also, pensive or melancholy; esp., melancholy and longing; showing a feeling of longing tinged with melancholy (as, *wistful* eyes or faces; a *wistful* expression; "I . . . cast many a *wistful* melancholy look towards the sea," Swift's "Gulliver's Travels," ii. 8; "He looked so *wistful* . . . hearing the frolic, and evidently having none of his own," Louisa M. Alcott's "Little Women," i. 2).—**wist'ful-ly**, *adv.*—**wist'ful-ness**, *n.*

wit (wit), *v. t.* or *i.*; pres. 1 *wot*, 2 *wost*, later *wottest, wotst*, 3 *wot*, later *wotteth*, pl. *wit*; pret. and pp. *wist*; ppr. *witting*. (With the forms *wottest, wotst*, and *wotteth*, cf. *wot*[2], *v.*) [AS. *witan* = OHG. *wizzan* (G. *wissen*) = Icel. *vita* = Goth. *witan*, know; akin to L. *videre*, see, Gr. ἰδεῖν, see, οἶδα, I know (lit. 'I have seen'), Skt. *vid-*, know, perceive: cf. *vision, idea, Veda, wise*[1], and *wise*[2].] To know: as, "Swift-winged with desire to get a grave, As *witting* I no other comfort have" (Shakspere's "1 Henry VI.," ii. 5. 16); "Little *wist* she Maggie's mettle!" (Burns's "Tam o' Shanter," 214); "God *wot*, his shield is blank enough" (Tennyson's "Lancelot and Elaine," 196). [Now chiefly archaic or prov.: cf. *witting* and *unwitting*.]—**had I wist,** had I but known: an old phrase expressive of unavailing regret over something known too late, a lost opportunity, etc.: sometimes used as a noun. [Obs. or archaic.]—**to wit,** that is to say; namely: as, "more worthy men — ourselves, *to wit*" (W. H. Hudson's "Green Mansions," i.); "the limbo of unanswered letters, *to wit* my pocket" (S. Butler's "Way of All Flesh," lxxxvi.). —**wit,** *n.* [AS. *wit, witt*.] Understanding, intelligence, or sagacity (as, "tried men of *wit* and audacity," Strype's "Memorials of Cranmer," i. 27; "*wit* enough to keep himself warm," Shakspere's "Much Ado about Nothing," i. 1. 68); also, the mind (as, "I am . . . a shepherd's daughter, My *wit* untrain'd in any kind of art": Shakspere's "1 Henry VI.," i. 2. 73); *pl.*, mental faculties, or senses (as, to lose or regain one's *wits*; to be out of one's *wits* with fright); mental abilities, or powers of intelligent observation, keen perception, ingenious contrivance, etc. (as, let them use their *wits*; you must have your *wits* about you in dealing with them; adventurers living by their *wits*); also, *sing.*, the keen perception and cleverly apt expression of those connections between ideas which awaken pleasure and especially amusement (as, "His conversation overflowed with thought, fancy, and *wit*": Macaulay's "Hist. of Eng.," ii.); speech or writing showing such perception and expression (as, "True *wit* is nature to advantage dress'd; What oft was thought, but ne'er so well express'd": Pope's "Essay on Criticism," 297); also, a person endowed with or noted for such wit (as, "He's a *wit* and an orator, extremely entertaining": Smollett's "Humphry Clinker," June 5); a witty person.—**at one's wits'** (or **wit's**) **end,** at the end of one's powers of knowing, thinking, etc. (as, "They reel to and fro . . . and are *at their wit's end*": Ps. cvii. 27); utterly at a loss or perplexed (as, "the gesture of a weak man who is *at his wits' end* what to do," Conan Doyle's "Exploits of Brigadier Gerard," vi.; "They . . . were *at their wits' end* to devise some new combination," Irving's "Conquest of Granada," xxxi.).—**the five wits,** the five senses; in general, the mental faculties, considered as five and sometimes enumerated as common wit, imagination, fantasy, estimation, and memory (as, "Alas, sir, how fell you besides your *five wits?*" Shakspere's "Twelfth Night," iv. 2. 93). [Archaic.]

wit-an (wit'an), *n. pl.* [AS., pl. of *wita*, wise man, councilor, < *witan*, know, E. *wit.*] In *Anglo-Saxon hist.*, the members of the national council, or witenagemot; also (construed as *sing.*), the witenagemot.

witch (wich), *n.* [AS. *wicca*, masc., *wicce*, fem.: cf. AS. *witega, witga*, OHG. *wizago*, prophet, Icel. *vitki*, wizard (all akin to AS. *witan*, know, E. *wit, v.*), also E. *wiseacre*.] A person, now esp. a woman, who professes or is supposed to practise magic, esp. black magic or the black art; a sorceress; hence, an ugly or malignant old woman; a hag; also, a bewitching or fascinating woman or girl (as, "one of the prettiest little *witches* in the valley": H. Melville's "Typee," xxv.); also, a mischievous person, esp. a child.—**white witch.** See *white, a.*—**witches' sabbath.** See *Sabbath, n.* —**witch,** *v. t.* To affect by or as by witchcraft; bewitch; charm; also, to bring by or as by witchcraft (with *into, to*,

etc.: as, "Ellery *witched* himself into the good graces of every one," Mrs. Stowe's "Oldtown Folks," xxxviii.). —**witch'=broom,** *n.* Same as *witches'-broom*.—**witch'-craft,** *n.* [AS. *wiccecræft*.] The art or practices of a witch; sorcery; magic; also, magical influence; witchery.—**witch'=doc″tor,** *n.* A medicine-man, esp. among the Kafirs and other African peoples.

witch=elm (wich'elm'), *n.* [Often *wych-elm*; AS. *wice*, kind of tree.] An elm, *Ulmus montana*, of northern and western Europe.

witch-er-y (wich'ėr-i), *n.*; pl. -*ies* (-iz). Witchcraft; magic; also, magical influence; fascination; charm.

witch-es'=be-som (wich'ez-bē′zọm), *n.* Same as *witches'-broom*.

witch-es'=broom (wich'ez-bröm'), *n.* A peculiar, abnormal, broom-like growth on various trees and shrubs, esp. conifers, consisting of a dense mass of branching twigs, due to irritation set up by certain ascomycetous fungi; hexenbesen.

witch=grass (wich'grås), *n.* [Cf. *quitch, quitch-grass.*] Quitch-grass or couch-grass; also, a panic-grass, *Panicum capillare*, with a brush-like compound panicle, common as a weed in North America.

witch=ha-zel (wich'hā'zl), *n.* [Also *wych-hazel*: see *witch-elm*.] The witch-elm; also, a shrub, *Hamamelis virginiana*, of eastern North America, whose bark and leaves afford medicinal preparations used for inflammation, bruises, etc.; also, a liquid medicinal preparation of this kind.

Branch with Fruits of Witch-hazel (*Hamamelis virginiana*). — *a*, male flower; *b*, fruit.

witch=ing (wich'-ing), *p. a.* That witches; bewitching; magical; enchanting.— **witch'ing-ly,** *adv.*

wit-e-na-ge-mot (wit′e-na̤-ge̤-mōt′), *n.* [AS. *witena gemōt*: *witena*, gen. pl. of *wita*, wise man, councilor; *gemōt*, assembly: see *witan* and *gemot*.] In *Anglo-Saxon hist.*, the assembly of the witan; the national council or parliament.

with (wiᴛн or with), *prep.* [AS. *with*, against, toward, to, with (= OS. *with*, Icel. *vidh*), beside *wither*, against, akin to OHG. *widar*, G. *wider*, Icel. *vidhr*, Goth. *withra*, against: cf. *withers, withershins*.] Against, as in opposition or competition (as, to fight or vie *with*); in some particular relation to (esp. implying interaction, company, association, conjunction, or connection: as, to deal, talk, sit, side, or rank *with*; to mix, compare, or agree *with*; "Cnæus Pompey had been born in the same year *with* Cicero," Froude's "Cæsar," viii.); accompanied by or accompanying (as, to come *with* an army; I will go *with* you); characterized by or having (as, a man *with* initiative); in the keeping or service of (as, leave it *with* me; to be *with* an insurance company); in the region, sphere, or view of (as, it is day *with* us while it is night *with* the Chinese; *with* us such things do not matter); in correspondence or proportion to (as, their power increased *with* their number); in regard to (as, to be pleased *with* a thing); of manner, using or showing (as, to work *with* diligence); of an agent, by the action of† (as, "He was torn to pieces *with* a bear": Shakspere's "Winter's Tale," v. 2. 68); of means or instrument, by the use of (as, to line a coat *with* silk; to cut *with* a knife); of cause, owing to (as, to die *with* pneumonia, or *with* thirst; "Your own hands are almost numbed *with* cold," C. Brontë's "Jane Eyre," xi.); of separation, etc., from (as, to part *with* a thing).

with-al (wiᴛн-âl'). **I.** *adv.* With it all; also; as well; besides: as, "one so delicate, so slender and *withal* so beautiful" (Dunsany's "Queen's Enemies"). [Archaic.] **II.** *prep.* With: used after its object: as, "This diamond he greets your wife *withal*" (Shakspere's "Macbeth," ii. 1. 15). [Archaic.]

with-draw (wiᴛʜ-drâ′), v.; pret. -*drew*, pp. -*drawn*, ppr. -*drawing*. [See *with*.] **I.** tr. To draw back or away (as, "She had *withdrawn* her hand in haste," J. Conrad's "Lord Jim," xxxii.; "life's bright promise, just shown and then *withdrawn*," Bryant's "Waiting by the Gate"); take back; remove; also, to retract or recall (as, to *withdraw* a charge). **II.** intr. To retire; retreat; go apart or away: as, "Mr. Beeton *withdrew* and left Dick to himself" (Kipling's "Light That Failed," xiv.).—**with-draw′al**, n. The act of withdrawing.—**with-draw′er**, n.—**with-draw′ing=room**, n. A room for withdrawing or retiring to; a parlor; a drawing-room. [Archaic.]—**with-draw′ment**, n. Withdrawal.

withe (with or wiᴛʜ), n. [AS. *withthe*: see *withy*[1].] A willow twig, or osier; any tough, flexible twig or stem suitable for binding things together; also, an elastic handle for a tool, to lessen shock in using.—**withe**, v. t.; *withed*, *withing*. To bind with withes.

with-er (wiᴛʜ′ėr), v. [ME. *widren*, var. of *wederen* to the weather, < AS. *weder*, E. *weather*[1].] **I.** tr. To make flaccid, shrunken, or dry, as from loss of vegetable or animal moisture; cause to lose freshness, bloom, vigor, etc.; fig., to affect harmfully (as, reputations *withered* by scandal); also, to abash, as by a scathing glance (as, "He scrutinised my face with . . . *withering* contempt": J. Conrad's "Lord Jim," v.). **II.** intr. To become withered; shrivel; fade; decay.—**with′er-ing-ly**, adv.

with-er-ite (wiᴛʜ′ėr-īt), n. [From Dr. W. *Withering*, English scientist, who described it in 1784.] A white to grayish mineral, native barium carbonate, occurring in crystals and in columnar or granular masses.

withe=rod (with′rod or wiᴛʜ′-), n. Either of two North American species of viburnum, *Viburnum cassinoides* and *V. nudum*, having tough, osier-like shoots.

with-ers (wiᴛʜ′ėrz), n. pl. [So called because 'against' or resisting the strain of the collar, < AS. *wither*, against: see *with*.] The highest part of a horse's or other animal's back, behind the neck.

with-er-shins (wiᴛʜ′ėr-shinz), adv. [AS. *withersȳnes*, < *wither*, against: see *with*.] In the reverse or wrong direction; in a direction contrary to the apparent course of the sun. [Sc. and prov. Eng.]

with-hold (wiᴛʜ-hōld′), v.; -*held*, -*holding*. [See *with*.] **I.** tr. To hold back; restrain or check; also, to keep back; refrain from giving or granting (as, to *withhold* payment; to *withhold* assent to something). **II.** intr. To hold back; refrain.—**with-hold′er**, n.—**with-hold′ment**, n.

with-in (wiᴛʜ-in′). [AS. *withinnan*, < *with*, against, + *innan*, in.] **I.** adv. In or into the interior or inner part, or inside; in or into a house, building, etc., or indoors (as, "The house doth keep itself. There's none *within*": Shakspere's "As You Like It," iv. 3. 83); on, or as regards, the inside, or internally; in the mind, heart, or soul, or inwardly (as, "You frame my thoughts, and fashion me *within*": Spenser's "Amoretti," viii.). **II.** prep. In or into the interior of or the parts or space inclosed by (as, *within* a solid or a hollow sphere; *within* the body; *within* a city or its walls); inside of; in; also, in the compass or limits of (as, *within* view, hearing, reach, or range; *within* bounds; to live *within* one's income); not beyond; at or to some point not beyond, as in length or distance (as, *within* a radius of a mile; *within* a mile of, that is, from, the city); not farther than; at or to some amount or degree not exceeding (as, to come *within* a dollar of, that is, from, the full sum; to guess *within* ten pounds of the true weight; *within* two degrees of freezing); in the course or period of, as in time (as, *within* one's lifetime or memory; "He expects to be in action *within* half an hour," Drinkwater's "Robert E. Lee," v.); inside of the limits fixed or required by (as, *within* the law; *within* reason); not transgressing; in the field, sphere, or scope of (as, *within* the family or the profession; *within* one's power).

with-out (wiᴛʜ-out′). [AS. *withūtan*, < *with*, against, + *ūtan*, outside.] **I.** adv. In or into the space without, or outside; outside a house, building, etc. (as, "There's a gentlewoman *without* would speak with your worship": Beaumont and Fletcher's "Knight of the Burning Pestle," iv.); as regards the outside, or externally (as, "Pitch it [the ark]

within and *without*": Gen. vi. 14); as regards external acts, or outwardly; also, without, or lacking, something implied or understood (as, we must take this or go *without*). **II.** prep. At, on, or to the outside of (as, both within and *without* the house or the city); outside of; also, beyond the compass, limits, range, or scope of (now used chiefly in opposition to *within*: as, whether within or *without* the law); also (as opposed to *with*), not with; with no; with absence, omission, or avoidance of; lacking; free from; excluding. **III.** conj. Unless: as, "We should make no mention of what concerns ourselves, *without* it be of matters wherein our friends ought to rejoice" (Steele, in "Spectator," 100). [Archaic, prov., or colloq.]

with-stand (wiᴛʜ-stand′), v.; -*stood*, -*standing*. [AS. *withstandan*, < *with*, against, + *standan*, stand.] **I.** tr. To stand or hold out against; resist; oppose, esp. successfully: as, "Neither the southern provinces, nor Sicily, could have *withstood* his power" (Hallam's "Europe during the Middle Ages," i. 1). **II.** intr. To stand in opposition.

with-y[1] (with′i or wiᴛʜ′i), n.; pl. -*ies* (-iz). [AS. *wīthig*, beside *withthe* (see *withe*), akin to G. *weide*, willow, osier, Icel. *vidh*, *vidhja*, withy: cf. L. *vitis*, vine.] A willow or osier; also, a flexible twig, or withe (as, "huts . . . made of the boughs of trees stuck in the ground, and bound together on the top with *withies*": Defoe's "Captain Singleton," iii.); also, a band or halter made of withes.

with-y[2] (with′i or wī′ᴛʜi), a. Made of withes; also, withe-like, as in slenderness, flexibility, etc.

wit-less (wit′les), a. Devoid of wit or intelligence, or stupid (as, "looking the picture of *witless* incapacity": G. W. Cable's "Bonaventure," i. 4); senseless, foolish, or silly; out of one's wits, or deranged; also, unwitting or ignorant (as, "His pretty pouting mouth, *witless* of speech, Lay halfway open": Hood's "Midsummer Fairies," lxxxi.); also, without any claim to being considered witty (as, "*witless* gibes": Motley's "Dutch Republic," iii. 1).—**wit′less-ly**, adv.—**wit′less-ness**, n.

wit-ling (wit′ling), n. A petty or would-be wit: as, "His bon mots are in every *witling's* mouth" (Smollett's "Humphry Clinker," April 30).

wit-ness (wit′nes), n. [AS. *witnes*, *gewitnes*, < *witan*, know: see *wit*.] Testimony or evidence (as, to bear *witness* to the truth of a statement); also, a person or thing that affords evidence; specif., one who gives sworn testimony, as in a court of law; one who signs a document in attestation of the genuineness of its execution; one who is present at a ceremony, transaction, or the like as a formal observer, in order to be able to testify concerning it; in general, one who, being present, personally sees or perceives a thing; a beholder, spectator, or eye-witness (as, "My father was a *witness* of what passed to-day": G. B. Shaw's "You Never Can Tell," iv.).—**wit′ness**, v. **I.** intr. To bear witness; testify; give or afford evidence (sometimes used in inverted constructions, such as 'he is afraid; *witness* his hesitation,' that is, let his hesitation witness, or afford evidence). **II.** tr. To bear witness to; testify to; give or afford evidence of (as, "Dinmont . . . stared on the whole scene with great round eyes that *witnessed* his amazement": Scott's "Guy Mannering," l.); also, to act as a witness of; sign (a document) as witness; attest by one's signature; be present at (a ceremony, transaction, etc.) as a formal witness; in general, to see or know by personal presence and perception; behold (as, "The natives when they *witnessed* the damage were astonished": Marryat's "King's Own," xliii.).—**wit′ness-er**, n.

wit-ted (wit′ed), a. Having wit or wits (as specified): as, quick-*witted*.

wit-ti-cism (wit′i-sizm), n. A witty remark or sentence.

wit-ti-ly (wit′i-li), adv. In a witty manner.—**wit′ti-ness**, n.

wit-ting (wit′ing), p. a. [See *wit*, v.] Knowing; aware; conscious.—**wit′ting-ly**, adv.

wit-tol (wit′ọl), n. [Var. of *witwall*, *woodwall*: cf. *cuckold*.] A man who knows and tolerates his wife's infidelity. [Obs. or archaic.]

wit-ty (wit′i), a.; compar. *wittier*, superl. *wittiest*. [AS. *wittig*, *witig*, < *wit*, E. *wit*, n.] Wise, intelligent, clever, or ingenious (now prov. Eng. and Sc.); also, possessed of or characterized by wit in speech or writing, as persons, remarks, epigrams, etc.; amusingly clever in perception and expres-

---

(variable) ḏ as d or j, § as s or sh, ṭ as t or ch, ᵹ as z or zh; o, F. *cloche*; ü, F. *menu*; ċh, Sc. *loch*; ṅ, F. *bonbon*; ′, primary accent; ″, secondary accent; †, obsolete; <, from; +, and; =, equals. See also lists at beginning of book.

sion; often, apt at, indulging in, or marked by sharply clever comment or repartee (as, "Will Honeycomb, who was so unmercifully *witty* upon the women": Addison, in "Spectator," 530); smartly or pungently facetious.

wit-wall (wit′wâl), *n.* Same as *woodwall.*

wive (wīv), *v.*; *wived, wiving.* [AS. *wīfian*, < *wīf*, E. *wife.*] **I.** *intr.* To take a wife; marry. **II.** *tr.* To take as wife; marry; also, to provide with a wife.

wi-vern (wī′vèrn), *n.* [OF. *wivre*, viper, < L. *vipera*, E. *viper.*] In *her.*, a two-legged, winged dragon having the hinder part of a serpent with a barbed tail.

Wivern.

wives (wīvz), *n.* Plural of *wife.*

wiz-ard (wiz′ärd). [Earlier *wisard*, ME. *wysard*, appar. < *wys, wis*, E. *wise*[1].] **I.** *n.* A wise man† (as, "From far, upon the eastern road, The star-led *wisards* haste with odours sweet": Milton's "On the Morning of Christ's Nativity," 23); also, one who professes to practise magic, or a magician or sorcerer (as, "spells such as only potent *wizards* know": J. H. Newman's "Callista," xxi.); also, a conjurer or juggler. **II.** *a.* Of or pertaining to a wizard (as, "in his *wizard* habit strange": Scott's "Marmion," iii. 20); hence, magic (as, *wizard* spells; "I hear a *wizard* music roll," Tennyson's "In Memoriam," lxx.).—**wiz′ard-ly**, *a.* Of, like, or befitting a wizard.—**wiz′ard-ry**, *n.* The art or practices of a wizard; sorcery; magic: as, "Of *wizardry* and charms they spoke" (W. Morris's "Jason," xii. 199).

wiz-en (wiz′n), *v. i.* or *t.* [Also *weazen*; AS. *wisnian* = Icel. *visna.*] To wither; shrivel; dry up. [Now Sc. and prov. Eng., except as in *wizened, p. a.*]—**wiz′en**, *a.* [Also *weazen*: cf. Icel. *visinn*, withered.] Wizened: as, "the *wizen* Leprechaun" (Henley's "Arabian Nights' Entertainments"). —**wiz′ened**, *p. a.* [Also *weazened.*] Withered or shriveled as from drying: as, a *wizened* apple; a *wizened* face; "a wrinkled, *wizened* hag" (Synge's "Well of the Saints," i.).—**wiz′en=faced,** *a.*

wo (wō), *interj.* and *n.* See *woe.*

woad (wōd), *n.* [AS. *wād* = D. *weede* = G. *waid*, woad: cf. L. *vitrum*, woad.] A European brassicaceous plant, *Isatis tinctoria*, formerly much cultivated for a blue dye extracted from its leaves; also, the dye.—**woad′ed,** *a.* Dyed or colored blue with woad.

woad-wax-en (wōd′wak″sn), *n.* [Also *woadwax, woodwax*, < AS. *wuduweaxe*, < *wudu*, wood, + *weaxan*, grow, E. *wax*[1].] Dyeweed, *Genista tinctoria.*

Woad.

wob′ble, etc., **wob′bly**[1]. See *wabble*, etc., *wabbly*[1].

wob-bly[2] (wob′li), *n.*; pl. *wobblies* (-liz). [According to an I. W. W. tradition, representing a Chinaman member's attempt to pronounce the *W.* of *I. W. W.*; but otherwise explained as connected with *wabbly*[1], orig. with reference to a want of fixedness of opinion on particular points.] [Also *cap.*] A member of the Industrial Workers of the World (I. W. W.): see under *industrial, a.* [Slang, orig. western U. S.]

wo-be-gone (wō′bē-gòn″), *a.* See *woebegone.*

Wo-den (wō′den), *n.* [AS. *Wōden* = OHG. *Wuotan* (G. *Wodan, Wotan*) = Icel. *Odhinn* (cf. *Odin*); perhaps akin to AS. *wōd*, mad, furious, E. *wood*[1]: cf. *Wednesday.*] An Anglo-Saxon deity identified with the Scandinavian Odin. See *Odin.*

woe (wō). [AS. *wā* = D. *wee* = G. *weh* = Icel. *vei* = Goth. *wai*, interj.: cf. L. *væ*, Gr. *οὐαί.*] **I.** *interj.* An exclamation of grief, distress, or lamentation. **II.** *n.* Grievous distress, affliction, or trouble (often used in opposition to *weal*, also in old phrases of lamentation, denunciation, etc.: as, *woe* is me! *woe* to the vanquished! "*Woe* unto you, scribes and Pharisees, hypocrites!" Mat. xxiii. 13); misery; wretchedness; also, an affliction (as, "solacing his *woes* with tobacco and Shakspere": Parkman's "Oregon Trail," xiv.);

a calamity.—**woe′be-gone″, wo′be-gone″** (-bē-gòn″), *a.* [ME. *wo begon* (pp. of *begon*, surround, beset).] Beset with woe; affected by woe, esp. in appearance (as, "His sorrow . . . made him look . . . haggard and . . . *woe-begone*": Du Maurier's "Trilby," iv.); showing or indicating woe (as, "Sanchia, whose *woe-begone* aspect suggested a crisis": M. Hewlett's "Open Country," xxii.).—**woe′ful, wo′ful,** *a.* Full of woe; affected with, characterized by, or indicating woe (as, "Weep no more, *woful* shepherds," Milton's "Lycidas," 165; "She . . . begins a wailing note And sings . . . a *woeful* ditty," Shakspere's "Venus and Adonis," 836; a *woeful* countenance); wretched; unhappy; also, of wretched quality, sorry, or poor (as, "What *woful* stuff this madrigal would be": Pope's "Essay on Criticism," 418).—**woe′ful-ly, wo′ful-ly,** *adv.*—**woe′ful-ness, wo′ful-ness,** *n.*

woi-wode (woi′wōd), *n.* Same as *voivode.*

woke (wōk). Preterit and past participle of *wake*[2].—**wok-en** (wō′kn). Occasional past participle of *wake*[2].

wold[1] (wōld), *n.* [ME. *wold, wald, wæld*, < AS. *weald, wald*, forest, = D. *woud* = G. *wald*, forest: cf. *Weald*.] An open, elevated tract of country: esp. applied, in *pl.*, to districts in parts of England (as Yorkshire and Lincolnshire) resembling the downs of the southern counties.

wold[2] (wōld), *n.* Same as *weld*[1].

wolf (wulf), *n.*; pl. *wolves* (wulvz). [AS. *wulf* = D. and G. *wolf* = Icel. *ūlfr* = Goth. *wulfs*, wolf; akin to L. *lupus*, Gr. λύκος, wolf.] A large, wild carnivorous quadruped, *Canis lupus*, of Europe, belonging to the dog family, a swift-footed, crafty, rapacious animal, very destructive to game, sheep, etc.; some allied variety or species, as the timber-wolf or the coyote; also, the fur of such an animal; also, some

Common Wolf (*Canis lupus*).

wolf-like animal not of the dog family, as the thylacine ('Tasmanian wolf'); fig., a cruelly rapacious person (as, "their fortunes stolen from them . . . by . . . *wolves* calling themselves Roman senators": Froude's "Cæsar," ix.); in *entom.*, the larva of any of various small insects, infesting granaries; also, the larva of a bot-fly; [*cap.*] in *astron.*, the southern constellation Lupus.—**to cry wolf,** to give a false alarm: in allusion to the shepherd in the fable, who raised the cry of "Wolf!" so often in mere sport that when the wolf really came his cry went unheeded.—**to keep the wolf from the door,** to keep out hunger or want.—**wolf in sheep's clothing,** a hypocrite. Cf. Mat. vii. 15.—**wolf,** *v.* **I.** *intr.* To hunt for wolves. **II.** *tr.* To devour or swallow ravenously: as, "Country boys . . . were *wolfing* sandwiches" (Sinclair Lewis's "Main Street," xxiv.). [Colloq.]—**wolf′ber″ry,** *n.* A caprifoliaceous shrub, *Symphoricarpos occidentalis*, of northern North America, sometimes cultivated for ornament, esp. on account of its white berries.—**wolf′=dog,** *n.* Any of various dogs of different breeds used for hunting wolves (cf. *wolfhound*); also, a cross between a wolf and a domestic dog; also, an Eskimo dog.—**wolf′er,** *n.* One who hunts wolves.

Wolff-i-an (wul′fi-ạn), *a.* Pertaining to Kaspar Friedrich Wolff (1733–94), a German anatomist and physiologist: as, the *Wolffian* body (in *embryol.*, one of a pair of primitive functional renal organs in the embryo of most vertebrates, developing into permanent renal organs in fishes and amphibians, but in other vertebrates replaced by true kidneys).

wolf=fish (wulf′fish), *n.* A large acanthopterygian fish, *Anarrhichas lupus*, of the northern Atlantic, allied to the blenny, and noted for its ferocious

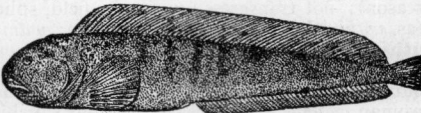

Wolf-fish (*Anarrhichas lupus*).

aspect and habits; also, any of various related fishes.

wolf-hound (wulf′hound), *n.* A hound of any of various breeds used in hunting wolves: as, the Russian *wolfhound* (a large dog of a Russian breed, resembling the deerhound in general build, but having much softer hair).

wolf-ish (wulf′fish), *a.* Resembling a wolf, as in form or characteristics (as, "*wolfish* creatures": Jack London's "Call of the Wild," ii.); characteristic of or befitting a wolf (as, "ferocious barbarians, of a most brutal and *wolfish* aspect," Parkman's "Oregon Trail," xvi.; "a war of *wolfish* malignity," Motley's "Dutch Republic," iii. 8).—**wolf′-ish-ly,** *adv.*

wolf-kin, wolf-ling (wulf′kin, -ling), *n.* A little or young wolf.

wol-fram (wul′fram), *n.* [G., said to be < *wolf*, wolf, + *rahm*, cream, froth.] Wolframite; also, tungsten.

wol-fram-ite (wul′fram-īt), *n.* [G. *wolframit,* < *wolfram*: see *wolfram*.] A mineral consisting of a tungstate of iron and manganese, usually of a brownish or grayish black color, occurring massive and in crystals, and forming a source of tungsten.

wol-fra-mi-um (wul-frā′mi-um), *n.* [NL., < G. *wolfram*: see *wolfram*.] In *chem.*, same as *tungsten*: abbreviated W (no period).

wolf's-bane (wulfs′bān), *n.* A plant of the genus *Aconitum* (see *aconite*), esp. a yellow-flowered species. *A. lycoctonum.*

wolf-skin (wulf′skin), *n.* The skin or pelt of a wolf.

wol-la-ston-ite (wul′a-ston-īt), *n.* [From W. H. *Wollaston* (1766–1828), English chemist and physicist.] A mineral consisting of a silicate of calcium, occurring usually in fibrous masses, but also in monoclinic crystals.

wol-ve-rene, wol-ve-rine (wul-ve-rēn′), *n.* [Appar. < *wolf.*] The glutton, *Gulo luscus,* of America; also, its fur. Also called *carcajou.* See *glutton.*

wolves (wulvz), *n.* Plural of *wolf.*

wolv-ish† (wul′vish), *a.* Same as *wolfish.*

wom-an (wum′an), *n.*; pl. **women** (wim′en). [ME. *woman, wumman, wimman,* < AS. *wīfmann,* woman, female human being, < *wīf,* woman, E. *wife,* + *mann,* human being, E. *man.*] The female human being (distinguished from *man*: as, *woman's* sphere is the home); an adult female person (as, a married *woman;* a single *woman,* a spinster); also, a female attendant on a lady of rank (as, the queen's *women;* "Isabella . . . was carried to her apartment by her *women,*" Scott's "Black Dwarf," x fl.); also, a wife, or, sometimes, a mistress (prov. or vulgar); also, a man who displays characteristics commonly supposed to be feminine (esp. in the phrase 'old woman,' with implication of fussiness, antiquated ideas, maundering talk, etc.); also, feminine nature, characteristics, or feelings (as, this roused the *woman* in her; he has too much of the *woman* in him for such a task).—**woman of the world,** a woman versed in the ways and usages of the world, esp. the world of society.—**woman's rights,** the rights claimed for woman, equal to those of man, with respect to suffrage, property, the professional fields, etc.—**woman suffrage,** the political right of woman to vote; female suffrage.—**wom′an,** *v. t.* To put into the company of a woman; also, to cause to act or yield like a woman; also, to call (one) 'woman,' esp. rudely or condescendingly.—**wom′an=hat″er,** *n.* One who hates or dislikes women; a misogynist.—**wom′an-hood** (-hud), *n.* The state of being a woman; womanly character or qualities; also, women collectively (as, "Life has no greater ornament than cultured *womanhood*": Mallock's "New Republic," iv. 2); womankind.—**wom′an-ish,** *a.* Womanlike or feminine; characteristic of or suitable for women rather than men; often, weakly feminine; effeminate.—**wom′an-kind′,** *n.* Women, as distinguished from men; the female sex.—**wom′an-less,** *a.* Destitute of women.—**wom′an-like,** *a.* Like a woman; womanly.—**wom′an-ly,** *a.* Like or befitting a woman; feminine; not masculine or girlish; being what is proper or becoming in a woman: as, "She's a most *womanly* woman" (Eden Phillpotts's "Banks of Colne," xii.); "The sight . . . filled her with a *womanly* sympathy" (Arnold Bennett's "Old Wives' Tale," iii. 7).—**wom′an-li-ness,** *n.*—**wom′an-ly,** *adv.* In the manner of, or befitting, a woman.

womb (wöm), *n.* [AS. *wamb, womb,* = D. *wam* = G. *wamme* = Icel. *vömb* = Goth. *wamba,* belly: cf. *gambeson.*] The belly†; also, the uterus, as in the human female and

some of the higher mammalian quadrupeds; fig., the place in which anything is formed or produced (as, the *womb* of time); the interior of anything (as, the *womb* of a ship).

wom-bat (wom′bat), *n.* [Native Australian.] An animal of the genus *Phascolomys,* comprising small bear-like burrowing marsupials of the Australian region.

Wombat.

w o m • e n (wim′en), *n.* Plural of *woman.*

won¹ (wun), *v. i.;* **wonned** (formerly *woned, wont*), **wonning.** [AS. *wunian,* dwell, remain, *gewunian,* be accustomed, akin to D. *wonen,* G. *wohnen,* dwell, G. *gewohnen,* become accustomed, also to E. *wean*: cf. *wont, a.*] To dwell, abide, or stay (now archaic or Sc. and north. Eng.: as, "Neither in forest haunts love I to *won,*" Hood's "Midsummer Fairies," lii.; "auld Rob Morris that *wons* in yon glen," Burns's "Auld Rob Morris"); also, to be accustomed†.

won² (wun). Preterit and past participle of *win.*

won-der (wun′dėr), *n.* [AS. *wundor* = D. *wonder* = G. *wunder* = Icel. *undr,* a wonder.] Something strange and surprising; a cause of surprise, astonishment, or admiration (as, to see the *wonders* of a city; "Circe the wise, the *wonder* of all lands," W. Morris's "Jason," x. 61); a marvel; a prodigy; a miracle, or miraculous deed or event (as, "Except ye see signs and *wonders,* ye will not believe": John, iv. 48); a surprising thing, circumstance, or matter (as, it is a *wonder* he declined such an offer; "What *wonder* if his pupil had taken him at his word?" Kingsley's "Yeast," xii.); also, the emotion excited by what is strange and surprising; a feeling of surprised or puzzled interest, sometimes tinged with admiration (as, "In open-mouthed *wonder* the lama turned to this and that": Kipling's "Kim," i.).—**for a wonder,** as a surprising thing or circumstance: as, *for a wonder* everybody was satisfied.—**nine days' wonder,** a subject of general surprise and interest for a short time.—**no wonder,** no marvel or prodigy (as, the lecturer is *no wonder*); also, nothing surprising (as, it is *no wonder* that he resigned, or, elliptically, *no wonder* he resigned; he resigned, and *no wonder*).—**seven wonders of the world,** the seven most remarkable structures of ancient times: as commonly given, the Egyptian pyramids, the Mausoleum erected by Artemisia at Halicarnassus, the temple of Artemis at Ephesus, the walls and hanging gardens of Babylon, the Colossus of Rhodes, the statue of Zeus by Phidias at Olympia, and the Pharos or lighthouse at Alexandria.—**to do wonders,** to do wonderful things; achieve or produce extraordinary results.—**won′der,** *v.* [AS. *wundrian.*] **I.** *intr.* To be affected with wonder (as, to *wonder* at a thing); marvel; be surprised (as, "I shouldn't *wonder* if I got one of those Indians": Wister's "Virginian," xxvii.); also, to think or speculate curiously (as, to *wonder* about a thing). **II.** *tr.* To feel wonder at (as, "Both stood, like old acquaintance . . . Met far from home, *wondering* each other's chance," Shakspere's "Lucrece," 1596: now only with a clause as object, as, I *wonder* that you went); also, to speculate curiously or be curious about (with a clause: as, to *wonder* what happened; I *wonder* why he went); be curious to know.—**won′der-er,** *n.*

won-der-ful (wun′dėr-ful), *a.* [AS. *wundorfull.*] Of a kind to excite wonder; marvelous (as, "things too *wonderful* for me, which I knew not": Job, xlii. 3); extraordinary; remarkable; remarkably fine (as, a *wonderful* collection of paintings; a *wonderful* people; a *wonderful* achievement).—**won′der-ful-ly,** *adv.*—**won′der-ful-ness,** *n.*

won-der-ing-ly (wun′dėr-ing-li), *adv.* In a wondering manner; with wonder.

won-der-land (wun′dėr-land), *n.* A land of wonders or marvels (as, "Alice's Adventures in *Wonderland,*" a children's story, published 1865, by C. L. Dodgson, "Lewis Carroll"); also, a wonderful country or region (as, "All day we walked . . . through a white *wonderland.* On every side the snowy hills . . . stretched away," Roosevelt's "Ranch Life and the Hunting-Trail," xi.; "that wooded *wonderland*," W. H. Hudson's "Far Away and Long Ago," iv.).

won-der-ment (wun′der-ment), *n.* Wondering or wonder; also, a cause or occasion of wonder (as, "That you should have been able to exist in it [solitude] so long is the *wonderment* to me": J. H. Newman's "Callista," xi.).

won-der-strick-en, won-der-struck (wun′der-strik″n, -struk), *a.* Struck or affected with wonder.

won-der-work (wun′der-werk), *n.* [AS. *wundorweorc.*] A wonderful work; a marvel; a miracle.—**won′der=work″er,** *n.* A worker or performer of wonders or marvels.—**won′der=work″ing,** *a.*

won-drous (wun′drus), *a.* [Formerly *wonderous.*] Wonderful; marvelous: as, "*Wondrous* miracle of the unfolding leaf!" (Aldrich's "Story of a Bad Boy," xiv.). [Now chiefly literary.]—**won′drous,** *adv.* In a wonderful or surprising degree; remarkably: as, "It grew *wondrous* cold" (Coleridge's "Ancient Mariner," i.). [Archaic or literary.]—**won′drous-ly,** *adv.*—**won′drous-ness,** *n.*

wont (wunt or wōnt), *a.* [Orig. pp.: see *won*[1].] Accustomed (commonly followed by an infinitive); used: as, as he was *wont* to say; he said, as he was *wont.*—**wont,** *v.* **I.** *tr.* To accustom (a person), as to a thing; also, to render (a thing) customary or usual: commonly in the passive. See *wonted.* **II.** *intr.* To be wont or accustomed: as, "Thou, fair moon, That *wont'st* to love the traveller's benison" (Milton's "Comus," 332). [Poetic.]—**wont,** *n.* Custom; habit; practice: as, he rose early, as was his *wont*; "situations where the use and *wont* of their fathers no longer meets their necessities" (Froude's "Cæsar," ii.).

won't (wōnt or wunt). Colloquial contraction of (obs. or prov.) *woll not* for *will not.*

wont-ed (wun′ted or wōn′ted), *p. a.* Accustomed, as a person to a thing; habituated; used; also, rendered customary, as a thing; habitual or usual (as, "R. was missing from his *wonted* place": Parkman's "Oregon Trail," vi.).—**wont′ed-ness,** *n.*

woo (wö), *v.* [AS. *wōgian.*] **I.** *tr.* To seek the favor, affection, or love of, esp. with a view to marriage (as, "The king . . . would . . . *Woo* me, and win me, and marry me": Tennyson's "Mermaid," iii.); court; fig., to seek to win (as, to *woo* fortune or fame); invite (consequences, good or bad) by one's own action (as, to *woo* one's own destruction); also, to seek to persuade (a person, etc.), as to do something (as, "Mr. Voules *wooed* her to swallow a little drop of liquid refreshment": H. G. Wells's "Mr. Polly," vi.); solicit; importune. **II.** *intr.* To sue in love, or make love (as, "Men are April when they *woo*, December when they wed": Shakspere's "As You Like It," iv. 1. 147); also, to seek; make entreaty.

wood[1] (wud), *a.* [AS. *wōd* = Icel. *ōdhr* = Goth. *wōds,* mad, furious: cf. G. *wut,* fury, rage, also E. *Woden.*] Mad; frantic; furious; wild, as with rage or excitement. [Now prov. Eng. and Sc.]

wood[2] (wud), *n.* [AS. *wudu, widu,* = OHG. *witu* = Icel. *vidhr,* wood.] A large and thick collection of growing trees, or a grove or forest (often in *pl.* in same sense: as, "We will sit down a little way within the *wood,*" Hawthorne's "Scarlet Letter," xvi.; "There is a pleasure in the pathless *woods,*" Byron's "Childe Harold," iv. 178); also, the hard, fibrous substance composing most of the stem and branches of a tree or shrub, and lying beneath the bark; also, the trunks or main stems of trees as suitable for architectural and other purposes; timber or lumber; also, firewood; also, the cask, barrel, or keg, as distinguished from the bottle (as, wine drawn from the *wood*); in *printing,* wood-blocks collectively, or a wood-block; in *music,* a wooden wind-instrument, or such instruments collectively in a band or orchestra.—**out of the woods,** fig., out of a situation of danger or difficulty: as, "When a patient reaches this stage, he is *out of the woods*" (Wister's "Virginian," xxix.).—**wood**[2], *v.* **I.** *tr.* To supply with wood; get supplies of wood for. **II.** *intr.* To take in or get supplies of wood.—**wood′=a″cid,** *n.* Wood-vinegar.—**wood′=al″co-hol,** *n.* Methyl alcohol (see under *methyl*). —**wood′=a-nem″o-ne,** *n.* Any of certain species of anemone, esp. *Anemone nemorosa* of the Old World or *A. quinquefolia* of the U. S.—**wood′=bet″o-ny,** *n.* The

betony, *Betonica officinalis*; also, a scrophulariaceous herb, *Pedicularis canadensis*; lousewort.

wood-bine (wud′bīn), *n.* [Also *woodbind,* < AS. *wudu-binde,* < *wudu,* wood, + *bindan,* bind; with reference to its twining about trees.] The common European honeysuckle, *Lonicera periclymenum,* which is cultivated in the U. S.; any of various other honeysuckles, as *L. caprifolium* ('American woodbine'); also, the Virginia creeper (U. S.).

wood=block (wud′blok), *n.* A block of wood engraved in relief, for printing from; a woodcut; also, a print or impression from such a block.

wood-chuck (wud′chuk), *n.* [N. Amer. Ind.; akin to *wejack.*] A common North American marmot, *Arctomys monax,* of stout, heavy form, which burrows in the ground and hibernates in the winter. Also called *ground-hog.*—**woodchuck day.** Same as *ground-hog day.*

Woodchuck.

wood-coal (wud′kōl), *n.* Charcoal; also, lignite.

wood-cock (wud′kok), *n.*; pl. *woodcocks* or (esp. collectively) *woodcock.* [AS. *wuducoc.*] An old-world limicoline game-bird, *Scolopax rusticula,* with a long bill, short legs, and large eyes, allied to the snipe; also, a similar and closely related but smaller bird, *Philohela minor,* of eastern North America.—**Scotch woodcock.** See under *Scotch*[3], *a.*

European Woodcock (*Scolopax rusticula*).

wood-craft (wud′kraft), *n.* Skill in anything which pertains to the woods or forest, esp. in making one's way through, or providing for one's self in, the woods, or in hunting, trapping, or other pursuits carried on there (as, "They left a trail that only a master in *woodcraft* could follow," Roosevelt's "Winning of the West," i. 4; "game and fish brought in by the united *woodcraft* of the minister and Mr. Rossiter," Mrs. Stowe's "Oldtown Folks," xxxiii.); also, forestry (as, "These hollow trees, according to *woodcraft,* ought to come down by the axe": Jefferies's "Gamekeeper at Home," iv.).

wood-cut (wud′kut), *n.* An engraved block of wood for printing from; also, a print or impression from such a block.

wood-ed (wud′ed), *a.* Covered with or abounding in woods or trees (as, "a *wooded* knoll": Scott's "Lady of the Lake," iii. 19); also, having wood (as specified: as, a hard-*wooded* tree).

wood-en (wud′n), *a.* Consisting or made of wood; fig., stiff, ungainly, or awkward (as, "Kim took a few paces in a stiff, *wooden* style": Kipling's "Kim," iii.); without spirit or animation (as, a *wooden* stare); dull or stupid (as, *wooden* wits).—**wooden horse,** in classical legend, the gigantic, hollow, wooden figure of a horse, filled with armed Greeks, which was introduced into Troy during the siege by a stratagem, these Greeks being liberated in the night by Sinon (see *Sinon*), and then admitting the Greek army to the city and thus ensuring its destruction (see Virgil's "Æneid," ii.); also, a wooden device, sometimes set with sharp points, upon which soldiers were compelled to sit astride as a military punishment†; also, a ship†.—**wooden nutmeg.** See under *nutmeg.*

wood=en-grav-ing (wud′en-grā″ving), *n.* The art or process of cutting designs in relief upon blocks of wood, usually boxwood, so that impressions can be made from them in a printing-press; also, a block of wood so engraved, or a print or impression from it.—**wood'-en-grav″er**, *n.*

wood-en-head (wŭd′n-hed), *n.* A blockhead; a dull or stupid person. [Colloq.]—**wood′en=head′ed**, *a.* Thick-headed; dull; stupid. [Colloq.]—**wood′en=head′ed-ness**, *n.*

wood-en-ly (wŭd′n-li), *adv.* In a wooden manner; stiffly, clumsily, or awkwardly; without spirit; stupidly.—**wood′en-ness**, *n.*

wood-en-ware (wŭd′n-wār), *n.* Vessels, utensils, etc., made of wood, as bowls, pails, tubs, spoons, rolling-pins, and the like.

wood-grouse (wŭd′grous), *n.* The capercaillie; also, any of various other species of grouse, esp. the Canada grouse, *Canace canadensis.*

wood-hen (wŭd′hen), *n.* Same as *weka.*

wood=hoo-poe (wŭd′hö″pö), *n.* Any bird of the irrisor family.

wood-house (wŭd′hous), *n.* A house or shed in which wood is stored.

wood=i-bis (wŭd′ī″bis), *n.* A large wading bird, *Tantalus loculator,* of the stork family, inhabiting the wooded swamps of the southern U. S. and regions southward; any of certain allied birds.

wood-i-ness (wŭd′i-nes), *n.* The state or quality of being woody.

wood-land (wŭd′land). [AS. *wuduland.*] **I.** *n.* Land covered with woods or trees. **II.** *a.* Of, pertaining to, or inhabiting the woods; sylvan.—**wood′land-er,** *n.* An inhabitant of the woods.

wood-lark (wŭd′lärk), *n.* A European lark, *Alauda arborea,* closely related to the skylark, but of more arboreal habits.

wood=louse (wŭd′lous), *n.*; pl. *-lice* (-līs). Any of certain small terrestrial isopods (crustaceans) of the genera *Oniscus* (see *sow-bug*), *Armadillo* (see *pill-bug*), etc., found in decaying wood, damp places, etc., and having a flattened elliptical body which in some species is capable of being rolled up into a ball; also, any of certain small insects of the family *Psocidæ,* found in the woodwork of houses.

Woodlark.

wood-man (wŭd′man), *n.*; pl. *-men.* An officer having charge of the king's woods (Eng.); also, a hunter of forest game†; also, one who dwells in the woods; also, one who fells timber (as, "*Woodman,* Spare That Tree!" — the title of a poem by George Pope Morris).

wood=note (wŭd′nōt), *n.* A wild or natural musical tone, as that of a forest-bird.

wood=nymph (wŭd′nimf), *n.* A nymph of the woods, or a dryad (as, "green forests where the *wood-nymphs* play": W. Morris's "Jason," ii. 669); also, any of several noctuid moths of the genus *Euthysanotia,* some of which are injurious to the grape-vine; also, any of certain butter-flies and humming-birds.

Wood-nymph (*Euthysanotia grata*), natural size.

wood=o-pal (wŭd′ō″pal), *n.* Wood which has become petrified in the form of opal.

wood-peck-er (wŭd′pek″ėr), *n.* Any of the scansorial birds constituting the family *Picidæ,* having a hard, chisel-like bill adapted for boring into wood, as for insects, rigid and acuminate tail-feathers to assist in climbing, and usually a more or less brightly variegated plumage. See cut in next column. Cf. *flicker*[1], *hickwall, piculet, popinjay, sapsucker.*

wood=pe-wee (wŭd′pē″wē), *n.* A small flycatcher, *Contopus virens,* of eastern North America, having a plumage olive-

brown above and greenish-yellow below; also, a similar species, *C. richardsoni,* of western North America.

wood=pi-geon (wŭd′pij″on), *n.* The ring-dove, *Columba palumbus,* of Europe; also, a wild pigeon, *Columba fasciata,* of western North America.

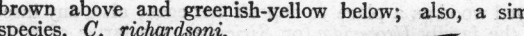

wood-pile (wŭd′pīl), *n.* A pile or stack of wood, esp. wood for fuel.

wood-pitch (wŭd′pich), *n.* See *wood-tar* and *pitch*[2], *n.*

wood-pulp (wŭd′pulp), *n.* Wood reduced to a pulp, used in making paper, etc.

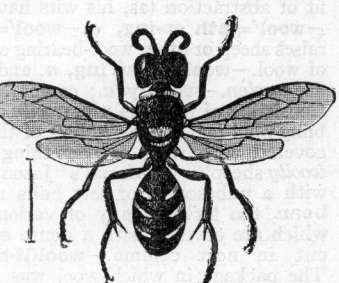

Red-headed Woodpecker (*Melanerpes erythrocephalus*), of North America.

wood-ruff (wŭd′ruf), *n.* [AS. *wudurofe.*] A low, aromatic rubiaceous herb, *Asperula odorata,* of the Old World, having small, sweet-scented white flowers; also, any other plant of the genus *Asperula.*

wood-screw (wŭd′skrö), *n.* See *screw, n.*

wood-shed (wŭd′shed), *n.* A shed for storing wood, esp. firewood.

wood-si-a (wŭd′zi-ą), *n.* [NL.; named from Joseph *Woods* (1776–1864), English botanist.] A fern of the polypodiaceous genus *Woodsia,* comprising small and medium-sized species in temperate and cold regions.

wood-side (wŭd′sīd), *n.* The side or border of woods or a forest: as, "a lonely spot by a *woodside*" (Gissing's "Private Papers of Henry Ryecroft," i. 3).

woods-man (wŭdz′man), *n.*; pl. *-men.* One accustomed to life in the woods and skilled in the arts connected with it, as hunting, fishing, trapping, etc.; also, a lumberman.—**woods′man-ship,** *n.* The condition or the skill of a woodsman; woodcraft.

wood=sor-rel (wŭd′sor″el), *n.* Same as *oxalis.*

wood=spir-it (wŭd′spir″it), *n.* Methyl alcohol (see under *methyl*).

woods-y (wŭd′zi), *a.* Of, like, suggestive of, or associated with the woods: as, a *woodsy* fragrance. [U. S.]

wood=tar (wŭd′tär), *n.* A dark-colored viscid product obtained from wood by distillation or burning slowly without flame: used in its natural state to preserve timber, etc., or subjected to further distillation, when it yields creosote, various oils, and a final residuum called *wood-pitch.*

wood=thrush (wŭd′thrush), *n.* A thrush, *Turdus mustelinus* (or *Hylocichla mustelina*), common in copses and woods in eastern North America.

wood=tick (wŭd′tik), *n.* Any of the ticks (acarids) constituting the family *Ixodidæ,* found frequently in woods; also, a death-watch (insect).

wood=vin-e-gar (wŭd′vin″ẹ-gär), *n.* An impure acetic acid obtained by the distillation of wood; pyroligneous acid.

wood-wall (wŭd′wâl), *n.* [ME. *wodewale*: cf. D. *weduwaal,* MLG. *wedewale,* G. *wittewal,* also E. *witwall* and *wittol.*] The green woodpecker, *Gecinus viridis.* [Prov. Eng.]

wood-ward (wŭd′wârd), *n.* [AS. *wuduweard.*] Formerly, in England, a forest-keeper or forester: as, "The *wood-ward* . . . could claim every tree that the wind blew down" (Green's "Conquest of England," vii.).

wood=wasp (wŭd′wosp), *n.* Any of various wasps that burrow in wood, as species of the family *Crabronidæ,* the female of which excavates a cell in de-

Wood-wasp (genus *Crabro*). (Line shows natural size.)

cayed wood as a place to deposit her eggs; also, any insect of the family *Uroceridæ* (or *Siricidæ*), the larvæ of which burrow in the wood of trees.

wood-wax (wùd′waks), *n.* Same as *woadwaxen.*

wood=wind (wùd′wind), *n.* See *wind²*, *n.*

wood-work (wùd′wėrk), *n.* Work done in or with wood; also, work made of wood; objects or parts made of wood; esp., the interior wooden fittings of a house or the like.—**wood′work″er,** *n.* A worker in wood, as a carpenter, joiner, or cabinet-maker; also, a machine for working in or shaping wood.—**wood′work″ing,** *n.*

wood=worm (wùd′wėrm), *n.* A worm or larva that is bred in or bores in wood.

wood-y (wùd′i), *a.*; compar. *woodier,* superl. *woodiest.* Abounding with woods, or wooded (as, "the *woody* crests of the precipices": Irving's "Sketch-Book," Sleepy Hollow); also, belonging or pertaining to the woods, or sylvan (as, "The Satyres scorne their *woody* kind": Spenser's "Faerie Queene," i. 6. 18); also, consisting of or containing wood (as, "*woody* vegetation": A. R. Wallace's "Darwinism," xii.); resembling wood; ligneous; also, pertaining to or characteristic of wood (as, a *woody* scent or flavor).

woo-er (wö′ėr), *n.* One who woos; a suitor.

woof (wöf), *n.* [ME. *oof,* < AS. *ōwef, ōweb, āweb,* < *ō-, ā-,* + *wefan,* weave: cf. *abb.*] The weft of a web or woven fabric; also, texture; fabric.

woo-ing-ly (wö′ing-li), *adv.* In the manner of wooing; invitingly.

wool (wùl), *n.* [AS. *wull* = D. *wol* = G. *wolle* = Icel. *ull* = Goth. *wulla,* wool: cf. L. *vellus,* fleece, Skt. *ūrnā,* wool.] The fine, soft, curly hair, characterized by minute, overlapping surface-scales (to which its felting property is mainly due), that forms the fleece of sheep and certain other animals, that of sheep constituting one of the most important materials of clothing; also, the thick, soft underfur of animals; also, short, thick, curly or kinky hair on the head of a human being, as a negro; hence, the hair of the head generally (colloq.); also, any coating of short, fine hairs or hair-like processes, as on a caterpillar or a plant; pubescence; also, cotton-wool; also, any finely fibrous or filamentous matter suggestive of the wool of sheep (as, glass *wool*); also, cloth or garments made of the wool of sheep, etc.; also, woolen yarn used for knitting, crocheting, ornamental needlework, etc.; worsted; also, any of various substances used commercially as substitutes for the wool of sheep, etc.; any of certain vegetable fibers, such as cotton, flax, etc., so used, esp. after preparation by special process ('vegetable wool'); a kind of wool-like yarn or material made from cellulose by a process similar to that used in manufacturing rayon or artificial silk.—**to pull the wool over one's eyes,** fig., to deceive or delude one.—**wooled,** *a.* Having wool: as, fine-*wooled.*—**wool′en, wool′len. I.** *a.* Made or consisting of wool (as, *woolen* cloth); also, of or pertaining to wool or woolen fabrics (as, the *woolen* manufacture). **II.** *n.* Cloth or a fabric made of wool: as, "English *woollens*" (Adam Smith's "Wealth of Nations," iv. 6).—**wool′=fat,** *n.* Same as *lanolin.*—**wool′fell,** *n.* [See *fell³.*] The skin of a wool-bearing animal with the fleece still on it.—**wool′=gath″er-ing,** *n.* The gathering of the tufts of wool left caught here and there on bushes, etc., by passing sheep: an occupation popularly attributed to the wits or thoughts of one absorbed in desultory fancies or lost in a fit of abstraction (as, his wits have gone a-*wool-gathering*).—**wool′=gath″er-ing,** *a.*—**wool′=grow″er,** *n.* One who raises sheep or other wool-bearing animals for the production of wool.—**wool′=grow″ing,** *n.* and *a.*—**wool′len,** *a.* and *n.* See *woolen.*—**wool′ly,** *a.*; compar. *woollier,* superl. *woolliest.* Consisting of wool (as, the *woolly* coat of the sheep); resembling wool (as, the *woolly* hair of the negro); also, clothed or covered with wool or something resembling it (as, "the *woolly* sheep": W. Morris's "Jason," ii. 328); in *bot.,* covered with a pubescence of soft hairs resembling wool.—**woolly bear,** the larva of any of various moths, as tiger-moths, which are covered with a dense coat of woolly hairs. See cut in next column.—**wool′li-ness,** *n.*—**wool′pack,** *n.* The package in which wool was formerly done up, as for transportation; specif., a bundle or bale weighing 240 pounds; also, a cumulus cloud of fleecy appearance.—**wool′sack,** *n.*

A sack or bag of wool; also, in the British House of Lords, one of a number of cloth-covered seats or divans stuffed with wool, for the use of judges, esp. one for the lord chancellor.—**wool′=sta″pler,** *n.* A dealer in wool; also, one who sorts wool according to the staple or fiber.—**wool′ward†** (-wärd), *adv.* With wool (of clothing) next the skin, as from absence of underlinen: as, to go *woolward* (as from poverty, or by way of penance: see Shakspere's "Love's Labour's Lost," v. 2. 717).—**wool′=work,** *n.* Needlework done with wool, as on canvas.

woo-ra-li, woo-ra-ri (wö-rä′lẹ, -rẹ̄), *n.* Same as *curare.*

woo-zy (wö′zi), *a.* [Origin obscure.] Muddled, or stupidly confused, as persons, the mind, etc.; also, in a confused or uncertain condition; also, out of sorts physically. [Slang.]

wop¹ (wop), etc. Same as *whop,* etc.

wop² (wop), *n.* [Origin obscure.] An Italian; also, the Italian language (as, "to chatter *Wop* . . . like a regular native": Sinclair Lewis's "Arrowsmith," xvi.). [Slang, U. S.]

Yellow Woolly Bear, larva of the American moth *Spilosoma virginica,* natural size.

word (wėrd), *n.* [AS. *word* = D. *woord* = G. *wort* = Icel. *ordh* = Goth. *waurd,* word; akin to L. *verbum,* word, E. *verb.*] A sound or a combination of sounds, or its written or printed representation, used in any language as the sign of a conception; any single bit of language that forms a grammatical part of speech; a vocable or term; hence, *pl.* or *sing.,* speech or talk (as, "Who is this that darkeneth counsel by *words* without knowledge?" Job, xxxviii. 2; "He's . . . The gentleman in *word* and deed," Burns's "Dedication to Gavin Hamilton," 46); *pl.,* contentious or angry speech (as, "You called him selfish! — You had *words* with him!" Thackeray's "Newcomes," lxxviii.); *sing.,* a short talk or conversation (as, to have a *word* with a person; "The friar and you Must have a *word* anon," Shakspere's "Measure for Measure," v. 1. 364); also, an expression or utterance (as, a *word* of praise or of warning; to speak a *word* in season; to have the last *word* in an argument); an authoritative utterance, or command (as, the father's *word* was law); warrant, assurance, or promise (as, to give one's *word* for a thing); to keep one's *word*; to assert a thing on one's *word* of honor); intelligence or tidings (as, to send or get *word* of an occurrence); also, a verbal signal, as a password, watchword, or countersign; [*cap.*] in *theol.,* the Scriptures, or Bible (often called 'the Word of God'); also, the Logos.—**a man of his word,** a man who keeps his word or promise.—**by word of mouth,** by spoken words; orally.—**in a word,** in a brief statement; in short.—**my word!** upon my word! used as an ejaculation (see *upon my word,* below): as, "My word! . . . What a thing that would be for us!" (Gissing's "New Grub Street," vii.). [Eng.]—**the last word,** fig., the last or latest thing or example in a class or field (as, "Every one thought that . . . you were as safe on *the last word* in liners as in your own bedroom": A. S. M. Hutchinson's "If Winter Comes," ii. 7); sometimes, the final thing or example, beyond which no advance or improvement is possible.—**to be as good as one's word,** to keep one's word or promise; act in accordance with what one has said: as, "Seeing I had offered them so much favour, I would *be as good as my word*" (Defoe's "Robinson Crusoe," i. 18).—**to take one at his word,** to take one's words as spoken seriously, and act accordingly.—**upon my word,** a phrase used in promising or asseveration (as, *upon my word,* I will; "*Upon my word* . . . I believe you are perfectly right," Jane Austen's "Sense and Sensibility," ii.); also, used as a mere ejaculation of surprise or the like (as, well, *upon my word!* what can he be thinking of?).—**word for word,** with each successive word of one series, sentence, etc. (spoken, written, or printed) corresponding to each successive word of another: as, to repeat a message *word for word* (that is, in the exact words of the original); to print a speech *word for word*; to translate a Latin sentence *word for word* (rendering word after word in the order of the original).—**word**, *v.* **I.** *tr.* To express in words, or phrase (as, "The archdeacon wrote a letter to the bishop, strongly *worded*, but still respectful": Trollope's "Barchester Towers," xviii.); also, to ply (a person) with words or cajolery†. **II.** *intr.* To speak. [Archaic.]

word=blind (wėrd′blīnd), *a.* Unable (as from cerebral lesion) to understand written or printed words, even while able to see, write, and speak, and to understand spoken words.—**word″=blind″ness**, *n.*

word=book (wėrd′bŭk), *n.* A book of words, usually with explanations, etc.; a vocabulary or dictionary.

word-i-ly (wėr′di-li), *adv.* In a wordy manner.—**word′i-ness**, *n.*

word-ing (wėr′ding), *n.* The act or the manner of expressing in words; phrasing; the form of words in which a thing is expressed.

word-less (wėrd′les), *a.* Without words or speech; speechless, silent, or mute; also, not put into words; unexpressed.

word=paint-ing (wėrd′pān″ting), *n.* The act of depicting or portraying in words with the effect of painting; graphic, vivid, or colorful description: as, "The Soudan campaign was a picturesque one, and lent itself to vivid *word-painting*" (Kipling's "Light That Failed," ii.).—**word′=paint″er**, *n.*

word=pic-ture (wėrd′pik″tūr), *n.* A picture presented in words; a graphic or vivid description.

word=square (wėrd′skwār), *n.* A set of words such that when arranged one beneath another in the form of a square they read alike horizontally and vertically.

S A T E D
A T O N E
T O A S T
E N S U E
D E T E R

Word-square.

word-y (wėr′di), *a.*; compar. *wordier*, superl. *wordiest.* Full of words; characterized by or given to the use of many, or too many, words (as, a *wordy* speech or speaker); verbose; also, pertaining to or consisting of words; verbal.

wore (wōr). Preterit of *wear²*.

work (wėrk), *n.* [AS. *weorc* = D. and G. *werk* = Icel. *verk*, work; akin to Goth. *waurkjan*, to work, also to Gr. ἔργον, work, ὄργανον, instrument, E. *organ*.] Exertion directed to produce or accomplish something (as, hard *work*; hand-*work*; brain-*work*); labor; toil; employment, as in some form of industry (as, to be out of *work*; to look for *work*); productive or operative activity (as, machine-*work*); also, that on which exertion or labor is expended; something to be made or done; a task or undertaking; materials, things, etc., on which one is working, or is to work; also, the result of exertion, labor, or activity; a deed or performance; *pl.*, in theological use, acts performed in obedience to the law of God, or righteous deeds (as, "Faith, if it hath not *works*, is dead": Jas. ii. 17); *sing.*, a product of exertion, labor, or activity (as, a *work* of art; literary or musical *works*; a piece of needle*work*; lattice*work*; repoussé *work*); sometimes, needlework, embroidery, or other decoration; also, an engineering structure, as a building, bridge, dock, or the like; a building, wall, trench, or the like, constructed or made as a means of fortification (as, an out*work*; earth*work*s); also, now *pl.* (often construed as *sing.*), a place or establishment for carrying on some form of labor or industry (as, gas-*works*, or a gas-*works*; iron-*works*); *pl.*, the working parts of a mechanical contrivance (as, the *works* of a clock or a watch); in *physics*, the transference of energy from one body or system to another; that which is accomplished by a force when it acts through a distance, being equal to the product of the force and the distance through which its point of application moves (as, a force of one dyne acting through a distance of one centimeter does one erg of *work*).—**upper works.** See under *upper*, *a.*—**work**, *v.*; *worked* or *wrought*, *working.* [AS. *wyrcan* (pret. *worhte*).] **I.** *intr.* To do work, or labor (as, "If any would not *work*, neither should he eat," 2 Thes. iii. 10; "He *wrought* doggedly at languages," Gissing's "New Grub Street," vii.); be employed, as in some industry, as a person; be in operation, as a machine; act or operate effectively (as, the pump will not *work*; the plan *works*); have an effect or influence, as on a person or on the mind or feelings; make way with effort or difficulty (as, a ship *works* to windward); get (*up*, *round*, *loose*, etc.), as if by continuous effort; move in agitation, as the features under strong feeling (as, "Her features *worked* in her attempt to conceal her feelings": Hardy's "Return of the Native," iii. 6); ferment, as a liquid (as, "I had . . . no yeast to make it

[beer] *work*": Defoe's "Robinson Crusoe," i. 12); *naut.*, to give slightly at the joints, as a vessel under strain at sea; in *mach.*, to move improperly, as from defective fitting of parts or from wear. **II.** *tr.* To expend work on; manipulate or treat by labor (as, to *work* dough; to *work* butter); operate (a mine, farm, etc.) for productive purposes; carry on operations in (a district or region); also, to use or manage (an apparatus, contrivance, etc.) in operation (as, "He had *worked* a gun at the bombardment of Vera Cruz in the Mexican War": Aldrich's "Story of a Bad Boy," iii.); put into effective operation (as, "He saw the enemies of his country . . . *working* their will, unchecked and undisturbed," Besant's "Coligny," viii.; to *work* a scheme); put into operation or use insidiously or guilefully (slang: as, you can't *work* that game here); keep (a person, a horse, etc.) at work; also, to make, fashion, or execute by work (as, "one of the famous cups of Tours, *wrought* by Martin Domique": Scott's "Quentin Durward," iv.); make or decorate by needlework or embroidery; achieve or win by work or effort (as, to *work* one's passage; "He *worked* his way through the law school," W. Churchill's "Modern Chronicle," i. 3); bring about (any result) by or as by work or effort (as, to *work* a change; to *work* wonders; to *work* mischief); effect, accomplish, cause, or do (as, "All are ready here To . . . *work* all crimes": Southey's "Thalaba," vii. 9); solve (often with *out*: as, to *work*, or *work out*, a problem); find (*out*) by or as by calculation (as, to *work out* a result); bring, put, get, render, etc., by work, effort, or action (with *in*, *off*, *out*, *up*, or other completive words: as, to *work off* a debt; to *work up* a case, as by development or elaboration; to *work* one's hands free, as from bonds); influence or persuade, esp. insidiously (as, to *work* men to one's will); use arts upon (a person) in order to obtain some profit or favor (slang: as, to *work* a friend for a loan); move, stir, or excite in feeling, etc. (often with *up*: as, "*working* himself *up* into a rage," W. H. Hudson's "Far Away and Long Ago," xiv.); also, to cause (a liquid, etc.) to ferment.

work-a-ble (wėr′ka̤-bl), *a.* Capable of or suitable for being worked (as, a *workable* mine); practicable or feasible (as, a *workable* scheme); proper for working (as, children of a *workable* age).—**work-a-bil′i-ty** (-bil′i-ti), **work′a-ble-ness**, *n.*

work-a-day (wėrk′a̤-dā). **I.** *n.* A working-day. [Now prov. Eng.] **II.** *a.* Of or befitting working-days; working; practical; everyday: as, "the *workaday* world" (Gissing's "Private Papers of Henry Ryecroft," ii. 5); "a *workaday* education" (W. B. Maxwell's "In Cotton Wool," iii.).

work=bag (wėrk′bag), *n.* A bag for holding implements and materials for work, esp. needlework. Similarly **work′=bas″ket.**

work=bench (wėrk′bench), *n.* A bench for working at, as in carpentry.

work=box (wėrk′boks), *n.* A box to hold instruments and materials for work, esp. needlework.

work-day (wėrk′dā), *n.* and *a.* Same as *working-day.*

work-er (wėr′kėr), *n.* One who or that which works; in *entom.*, the neuter or undeveloped female of the bee, wasp, ant, or certain other insects, which does work for its community; in *printing*, one of a set of electrotyped plates used to print from, as contrasted with a set of molders (see *molder²*).

work-fel-low (wėrk′fel″ō), *n.* One engaged in the same work with another.

work=folk (wėrk′fōk), *n.* Work-people. Also **work′=folks**, *n. pl.*

work-house (wėrk′hous), *n.* [AS. *weorchūs.*] A workshop; also, a house in which paupers are lodged and set to work; a poorhouse; also, a house of correction (U. S.).

work-ing (wėr′king), *n.* The act of a person or thing that works; operation; action; also, a part of a mine, quarry, or the like, in which work is being or has been carried on (commonly in *pl.*).—**work′ing**, *p. a.* That works (as, a *working* partner; a *working* housekeeper); doing some form of work or labor, esp. manual, mechanical, or industrial work, as for a living (as, the *working* class; *working* people); operating, or producing effects; also, pertaining to, connected with, or used in operating or working (as, *working* expenses or capital); serving for the purposes of working (as, a *working*

---

method, arrangement, or hypothesis).—**working cylinder,** in an internal-combustion engine, a cylinder in which the gas or vapor explodes.—**working drawing,** a drawing, as of the whole or a part of a structure or machine, made to scale and in such detail with regard to dimensions, etc., as to form a guide for the workmen in the construction of the object represented.—**working fluid,** the fluid (as steam, etc.) which operates an engine or other prime mover.—**working stroke,** in engines, that stroke of the piston during which the working fluid performs its useful work, that is, drives the piston outward.—**working substance,** the substance, as a working fluid, which operates a prime mover.—**work′ing= day. I.** *n.* A day ordinarily given to working (opposed to *holiday*); also, the daily period of hours for working. **II.** *a.* Workaday; everyday.—**work′ing=girl,** *n.* A girl of the working class; a girl who earns her living at some form of manual or industrial work.—**work′ing=man** (-man), *n.*; pl. *-men.* A man of the working class; a man (skilled or unskilled) who earns his living at some form of manual or industrial work. Similarly **work′ing=wom″an; pl.** *-women* (-wim″en).

work-man (wêrk′man), *n.*; pl. *-men.* A man employed or skilled in some form of manual, mechanical, or industrial work; in general, a male worker, esp. with reference to his skill.—**work′man-like,** *a.* and *adv.* Same as *workmanly.*—**work′man-ly,** *a.* Like or befitting a workman; skilful; well executed.—**work′man-ly,** *adv.* With skilful workmanship.—**work′man-ship,** *n.* The art or skill of a workman; skill in working or execution; also, quality or mode of execution, as of a thing made (as, "articles . . . more admirable for the *workmanship* than for the value of the materials": Prescott's "Conquest of Mexico," iv. 5); also, the product or result of the labor and skill of a workman; work executed.

work-out (wêrk′out), *n.* A performance for practice or training or as a trial or test; esp., a trial at running, boxing, a game, or the like, preliminary to and in preparation for a contest, exhibition, etc. [Colloq.]

work=peo-ple (wêrk′pē″pl), *n.* People employed at work or labor.

work-room (wêrk′rôm), *n.* A room in which work is carried on.

work-shop (wêrk′shop), *n.* A shop or building in which work, esp. mechanical work, is carried on.

work=ta-ble (wêrk′tā″bl), *n.* A table for working at: often with drawers or receptacles for materials, etc., as for sewing.

work-wom-an (wêrk′wùm″an), *n.*; pl. *-women* (-wim″en). A woman employed or skilled in some manual, mechanical, or industrial work; a female worker.

world (wêrld), *n.* [AS. *woruld, weorold,* = D. *wereld* = OHG. *weralt* (G. *welt*) = Icel. *veröld,* world; a compound word, lit. 'age of man,' from Teut. elements represented by AS. *wer,* man (see *virile*), + *yldu,* age (see *eld*).] An age or period of human life†; a generation†; also, any period, state, or sphere of existence (as, this *world;* the *world* to come; the other *world,* see under *other, a.;* "He . . . Allured to brighter *worlds,* and led the way," Goldsmith's "Deserted Village," 170); also, the entire system of created things; the universe; the macrocosm; any complex whole conceived as resembling the universe (cf. *microcosm*); any indefinitely great expanse (as, "the *world* of waters," Johnson's "Rasselas," ix.; "a *world* of heather," Jean Ingelow's "Divided," i.); also, the earth or globe (as, "We know the merry *world* is round, And we may sail for evermore": Tennyson's "Voyage," xii.); a particular division of the earth (as, the New *World,* America; the Old *World,* Europe, Asia, and Africa); the earth, with its inhabitants, affairs, etc., during a particular period (as, the ancient *world*); also, any heavenly body (as, the starry *worlds*); also, any sphere, realm, or domain, with all that pertains to it (as, woman's *world;* the *world* of dreams; the insect *world*); also, mankind, or the public generally (as, the whole *world* knows it); a particular class of mankind, with common interests, aims, etc. (as, the Christian *world;* the fashionable *world*); the class of persons devoted to the affairs, interests, or pursuits of this life (as, the *world* worships success; a man of the *world,* see under *man*); society; secular, social, or fashionable life, with its ways and interests (as, to withdraw from the *world;* to know the *world;* to have an air of the *world*); also, the

course of affairs or experience (as, to begin the *world;* how goes the *world* with you?); also, a very great quantity or extent (as, "The monks do a *world* of good," Kinglake's "Eothen," x.; a *world* of meaning; clothes a *world* too big).— **all the world and his wife,** everybody, male and female, esp. everybody of any social pretensions: as, "Aunt Charlotte knows *all the world and his wife*" (Mrs. H. Ward's "Robert Elsmere," xxi.).—**for all the world,** for any consideration, no matter how great (as, I wouldn't do it *for all the world*); also, in every respect, or precisely (as, "He was, *for all the world,* like a forked radish": Shakspere's "2 Henry IV.," iii. 2. 333).—**in the world,** in the universe, or on earth; anywhere; hence, at all; ever: much used to add emphasis, often after *where, what, how,* etc.—**lower world.** See under *lower*[2], *a.*—**the world, the flesh, and the devil,** the world with its interests, the flesh with its appetites, and the devil with his evil promptings, as the great sources of temptation and sin for mankind: as, "From all the deceits of *the world, the flesh, and the devil,* Good Lord, deliver us" (Book of Common Prayer, Litany).—**World Court** (properly, Permanent Court of International Justice), an international tribunal, sitting at The Hague, Netherlands, provided for in the establishment of the League of Nations, and itself established on Dec. 16, 1920, by the assembly of that body, and empowered to arbitrate in disputes threatening future war.—**World War I,** the war in Europe, Asia, Africa, and elsewhere, extending from July 28, 1914, to Nov. 11, 1918, between the powers of the Triple Entente (Great Britain, France, and Russia), with their allies and associates (Belgium, Serbia, Montenegro, Japan, Portugal, Italy, Rumania, the United States, Greece, etc.), on the one side, and Germany and Austria-Hungary, with their allies Turkey and Bulgaria, on the other side, which ended with the collapse of the latter group. Also called *Great War* and *War of the Nations.* The United States entered the war on April 6, 1917, when it declared war against Germany. See *Treaty of Versailles.* —**World War II,** the world-wide conflict (1939–45) which involved most of the principal nations of the world.—**world without end,** through all eternity; forever.

world-ed (wêrl′ded), *a.* Containing worlds: as, "yon myriad-*worlded* way" (Tennyson's "Charge of the Heavy Brigade at Balaclava," Epilogue).

world-li-ness (wêrld′li-nes), *n.* The state or character of being worldly; worldly ideas, ways, or conduct.

world-ling (wêrld′ling), *n.* One devoted to the interests and pleasures of this world; a worldly person.

world-ly (wêrld′li), *a.*; compar. *worldlier,* superl. *worldliest.* Of or pertaining to this world or the present state or sphere of existence (as, "The weariest . . . *worldly* life . . . is a paradise To what we fear of death," Shakspere's "Measure for Measure," iii. 1. 129; *worldly* wealth); earthly or mundane (as opposed to *heavenly, spiritual,* etc.: as, "No newspaper ever brought the clash of *worldly* things into its [a house's] heavenward seclusion," H. G. Wells's "Tono-Bungay," i. 2. § 1); secular (as opposed to *ecclesiastical, religious,* etc.: as, *worldly* powers or institutions; members of the *worldly* professions; "Dr. Grantly interfered very little with the *worldly* doings of those . . . subject to him," Trollope's "Barchester Towers," iv.); also, devoted to, directed toward, or connected with the affairs, interests, or pleasures of this world (as, a *worldly* person or mind; *worldly* spirit or ambition; *worldly* considerations).—**world′ly,** *adv.* In a worldly manner.—**world′ly=mind′ed,** *a.* Having or showing a worldly mind, or devotion to the affairs and interests of this world.—**world′ly=mind′ed-ness,** *n.*— **world′ly=wise′,** *a.* Wise as to the affairs of this world.

world=soul (wêrld′sōl), *n.* A (supposed) soul of the world or universe.

world=wear-y (wêrld′wēr″i), *a.* Weary of the world or of existence.

world=wide (wêrld′wīd′), *a.* Extending or spread throughout the world: as, "This man . . . had a *world-wide* reputation as an engineer" (Buchan's "Three Hostages," xi.).— **world′=wide′ly,** *adv.*

worm (wêrm), *n.* [AS. *wyrm, wurm,* = OHG. G. *wurm* = Icel. *ormr* = Goth. *waurms,* akin to L. *vermis,* worm: cf. *vermin.*] In popular language, any of numerous small creeping animals with more or less slender, elongated bodies, and without limbs or with very short ones, including individuals of widely differing kinds, as earthworms, tapeworms, insect larvæ, adult forms of some insects, certain small crustaceans and mollusks, certain lizards, etc.; technically, one of the *Vermes,* a (former) primary division of the animal kingdom, varying according to different authorities, but including the platyhelminths, nemathelminths, annelids, etc.; also, a snake or serpent (obs. or prov.); a dragon or monster (obs. or archaic: as, "Therewith began A fearful battle betwixt *worm* and man," W. Morris's "Jason," x. 258); also, fig., a groveling, abject, or contemptible creature (as, "I am a *worm,* and no man," Ps. xxii. 6; "'Crushed *worm!*' said the Knight, looking down on his miserable adversary," Scott's "Legend of Montrose," xxi.); a downtrodden or miserable person; also, something that penetrates, injures, or consumes slowly or insidiously, like a gnawing worm (as, "He found, conceal'd beneath a fair outside, The . . . *worm* of pride": Cowper's "Expostulation," 90); an agency conceived as continually preying upon and tormenting the wicked in hell (as, "To be cast into hell fire: Where their *worm* dieth not, and the fire is not quenched," Mark, ix. 48; "Rid heaven of these rebell'd . . . driven down, To chains of darkness, and the undying *worm,*" Milton's "Paradise Lost," vi. 739); the torment of conscience, or remorse (as, "The *worm* of conscience still begnaw thy soul!" Shakspere's "Richard III.," i. 3. 222; "a torment like the undying *worm* of conscience," De Quincey's "Revolt of the Tartars"); also, something resembling or suggesting a worm in appearance, movement, etc.; a worm-like bodily part, as the vermiform process of the cerebellum, or the lytta of a dog, etc.; the spiral pipe in a still, in which the vapor is condensed; a screw or screw-thread; an endless screw, or a device in which this is the principal feature; esp., the endless screw (shaft on which a spiral groove is cut) which engages with a worm-wheel or worm-gear; *pl.,* in *pathol.,* any disease or disorder arising from the presence of parasitic worms in the intestines or other tissues.—**worm,** *v.* **I.** *intr.* To move or act like a worm; creep, crawl, or advance slowly or stealthily (as, "He lay close in the grass and *wormed* nearer to the house": Kipling's "Kim," ii.); fig., to get by insidious procedure (*into,* etc.: as, "Already some of these riffraff are *worming* into it [a club]," Tarkington's "Magnificent Ambersons," vii.). **II.** *tr.* To make (one's way) by or as by creeping or crawling, or stealthily (as, "Henry was *worming* his way, lying flat on the ground . . . toward his unsuspecting victims": Parkman's "Oregon Trail," vii.); also, to bring (one's self, the body, etc.) along by creeping or crawling, or by stealthy or devious advances (as, "Belzoni, *worming* himself through the subterranean passages of the Egyptian catacombs," H. Melville's "Typee," viii.; "He *wormed* his small body through the crowd," Mark Twain's "Tom Sawyer," xi.); fig., to bring insidiously, or insinuate (as, "the man's singular dexterity to *worm* himself into our troubles": Stevenson's "Master of Ballantrae," viii.); get by persistent, insidious efforts (esp. with *out* or *from*: as, to *worm* a secret out of a person; "I *wormed* your address from him," L. Merrick's "Conrad in Quest of His Youth," x.); also, to free (a garden, etc.) from worms; also, to remove the worm or lytta from the tongue of (a dog, etc.); *naut.,* to wind yarn or the like spirally round (a rope) so as to fill the spaces between the strands and render the surface smooth.

worm=eat-en (wẽrm′ē″tn), *a.* Eaten into or gnawed by worms (as, *worm-eaten* timbers); hence, impaired by time, decayed, or antiquated.

wormed (wẽrmd), *a.* Damaged by worms; worm-eaten: as, "The manse had fallen into a sore state of decay — the doors were *wormed* on the hinges" (Galt's "Annals of the Parish," xxvii.).

worm=fence (wẽrm′fens′), *n.* A snake-fence.

worm=gear (wẽrm′gēr), *n.* In *mach.,* a gear-wheel which engages with a revolving worm, or endless screw, in order to receive or impart motion; a worm-wheel; also, such a gear-wheel together with the endless screw, forming a device by which the rotary motion of one shaft can be transmitted to another shaft at right angles to it.

worm=hole (wẽrm′hōl), *n.* A hole made by a burrowing or gnawing worm, as in timber, nuts, etc.—**worm′=holed,** *a.* Having worm-holes.

wor-mil, wor-mul (wôr′mil, -mul), *n.* [Cf. *warble*[1].] The larva of a warble-fly, or some other larva which burrows beneath the skin of animals.

worm-seed (wẽrm′sēd), *n.* The dried, unexpanded flower-heads of santonica, *Artemisia pauciflora,* or the fruit of certain goosefoots, esp. *Chenopodium anthelminticum,* used as an anthelmintic drug; also, any of these plants.

worm-shell (wẽrm′shel), *n.* The shell of any of the gastropod mollusks of the family *Vermetidæ,* in the youth of the animal regularly conic and spiral, but having later whorls separate, and often crooked or contorted, with a worm-like appearance; also, the animal itself.

worm-wheel (wẽrm′hwēl), *n.* In *mach.,* a toothed wheel which engages with a revolving worm, or endless screw, in order to receive or impart motion. Cf. *worm-gear.*

Worm-shell (*Vermetus lumbricalis*).

worm-wood (wẽrm′wŭd), *n.* [AS. *wermōd* = OHG. *wermuota* (G. *wermut*): cf. *vermouth.*] A bitter, aromatic asteraceous herb, *Artemisia absinthium,* a native of the Old World, formerly much used as a vermifuge and a tonic, but now chiefly in making absinthe; also, any plant of the genus *Artemisia,* as *A. pauciflora* (santonica), *A. moxa* (moxa), etc.; fig., something bitter, grievous, or extremely unpleasant; bitterness.

worm-y (wẽr′mi), *a.*; compar. *wormier,* superl. *wormiest.* Containing a worm or worms; infested with worms; worm-eaten; also, worm-like; groveling; low.

worn (wôrn). Past participle of *wear*[2].

—worn, *p. a.* Impaired by wear or use (as, *worn* clothing); also, wearied or exhausted; showing the wearing effects of toil, care, suffering, etc. (as, "the *worn* and haggard appearance of the elder men": Kingsley's "Yeast," xiii.).—**worn′=out′,** *a.* Worn or used until no longer fit for use (as, a *worn-out* coat; a *worn-out* pen); exhausted by continued use, strain, etc. (as, a *worn-out* horse; a *worn-out* worker); also, past† or bygone† (as, "this pattern of the *worn-out* age": Shakspere's "Lucrece," 1350).

Wormwood (*Artemisia absinthium*).

wor-ri-er (wur′i-ẽr), *n.* One who or that which worries.

wor-ri-less (wur′i-les), *a.* Free from worry.

wor-ri-ment (wur′i-ment), *n.* Worrying; harassing annoyance; also, worry; anxiety. [Colloq.]

wor-ri-some (wur′i-sum), *a.* Worrying, annoying, or disturbing; causing worry; also, inclined to worry or be anxious. —**wor′ri-some-ly,** *adv.*

wor-rit (wur′it), *v.* and *n.* Prov. form of *worry.*

wor-ry (wur′i), *v.*: -*ried,* -*rying.* [ME. *worowen,* < AS. *wyrgan* = G. *würgen,* strangle.] **I.** *tr.* To strangle, choke, or suffocate (now Sc. and north. Eng.); also, to seize (orig. by the throat) with the teeth and shake or mangle, as one animal does another; harass by repeated biting, snapping, etc.; fig., to harass as by repeated attacks; torment with annoyances, importunities, cares, anxieties, etc.; plague, pester, or bother (as, "Now, Horace, hush your talk, and don't *worry* your mother": Mrs. Stowe's "Oldtown Folks," v.); also, to be a cause of discomfort or anxiety to (as, "It would *worry* her if she thought I was anxious about her": Howells's "Foregone Conclusion," ix.); cause to feel uneasy or anxious; trouble; also, to swallow (prov., except as in the colloquial phrase 'to worry down,' to swallow with an effort, as food). **II.** *intr.* To strangle or choke (now Sc. and north. Eng.); also, to worry an animal, prey, or the like by seizing with the teeth and shaking, mangling, etc.; fig., to torment one's self with or suffer from disturbing thoughts (as, "She *worried* over Miltoun's forlorn case": Galsworthy's "Patrician," ii. 5); dwell uncomfortably on actual or possible troubles; feel uneasy or anxious; fret; also, to get (*along* or *through*) by constant effort, in spite of difficulties or troubles (colloq.: as, "We shall *worry* through all right," L. Merrick's "House of Lynch," xiv.).—**wor′ry,** *n.*; pl. *worries* (-iz). The act of worrying (as, the *worry* of the quarry by hounds);

also, worried condition or feeling; harassing care, uneasiness, or anxiety; a cause of uneasiness or anxiety, or a trouble (as, "I was wrong to grumble to you . . . You have *worries* enough of your own": Hugh Walpole's "Wooden Horse," vii.).—**wor′ry-ing-ly,** *adv.*

worse (wêrs). [AS. *wiersa, wyrsa* (akin to Icel. *verri,* OHG. *wirsiro,* Goth. *wairsiza,* worse), a compar. form, with superl. *wiersta, wyrsta* (see *worst*), associated with *yfel,* E. *evil,* as positive; perhaps from the same root as E. *war.*] **I.** *a.;* compar. of *bad* and *ill.* Bad or ill in a greater or higher degree; inferior in excellence, quality, or character; more faulty, unsatisfactory, or objectionable; more evil or wicked; more unfavorable or injurious; in less good condition; in poorer health. **II.** *n.* That which is worse; a worse thing or state; the disadvantage, or defeat, as in a contest (with *the*: as, to have the *worse*; "Judah was put to the *worse* before Israel; and they fled every man to their tents," 2 Kings, xiv. 12).—**worse,** *adv. compar.* [AS. *wiers, wyrs.*] In a worse manner (as, to go farther and fare *worse*); with greater violence or intensity (as, it is raining *worse* than ever; to hate one *worse* than all others); also, in a lower degree, or less (as, to like one no *worse* for his frankness).—**wors′en,** *v. i.* or *t.* To become or make worse.—**wors′er,** *a.* and *adv.* [A double compar. form: see *-er*[4].] Same as *worse*: as, "I cannot hate thee *worser* than I do" (Shakspere's "Antony and Cleopatra," ii. 5. 90). [Now prov.]

wor-ship (wêr′ship), *n.* [AS. *weorthscipe,* < *weorth,* worthy, honorable (see *worth*[2], *a.*), + *-scipe,* E. *-ship.*] Honorable character or standing, dignity, or credit (archaic: as, men of *worship*); also, honor paid, respect, or deference (as, "Then shalt thou have *worship* in the presence of them that sit at meat with thee," Luke, xiv. 10: archaic, except as in following senses); reverent honor and homage paid to God or a sacred personage, or to any object regarded as sacred (as, idol-*worship*; fire-*worship*); formal or ceremonial rendering of such honor and homage (as, divine *worship*, religious services of praise, prayer, preaching, etc., as in a church; family *worship*, services of prayer, etc., held within a family); adoring reverence or regard felt or shown toward any person or thing (as, hero-*worship*; the *worship* of rank, wealth, or power; "The *worship* of financial success seems to be in every one's blood," W. Churchill's "Modern Chronicle," i. 9); idolatrous devotion; also, the object of adoring reverence or regard (as, "In attitude and aspect formed to be At once the artist's *worship* and despair!" Longfellow's "Michael Angelo," i. 2); also, with *your, his,* etc., a title of honor used in addressing or mentioning certain magistrates and others of rank or station (as, "The thing I hope is, that your *worships* and reverences are not offended": Sterne's "Tristram Shandy," iv. 32).—**wor′ship,** *v.;* *-shiped* or *-shipped, -shiping* or *-shipping.* **I.** *tr.* To hold in or treat with honor or respect (obs. or archaic); also, to render religious reverence and homage to (a deity, sacred personage or object, etc.); pay divine honors to; also, to feel an adoring reverence or regard for (any person or thing: as, "the home where she had been *worshipped,*" W. H. Hudson's "Purple Land," i.; "She had *worshipped* intellect," Kingsley's "Yeast," x.); idolize. **II.** *intr.* To render religious reverence and homage, as to a deity or at a shrine; attend services of divine worship (as, "Still the pair *worshipped* with that . . . denomination": Eden Phillpotts's "Children of Men," i. 1); also, to feel an adoring reverence or regard.—**wor′ship-er, wor′-ship-per,** *n.*—**wor′ship-ful,** *a.* Honorable, or worthy of or regarded with honor (now used chiefly as a respectful epithet applied in Great Britain to certain magistrates and corporate bodies, and employed in freemasonry to indicate a certain official rank or dignity); also, given to the worship of something (as, "They were too *worshipful* of the best London conventions not to regard silence at table as appalling": Arnold Bennett's "Lion's Share," xxiv.).—**wor′ship-ful-ly,** *adv.*—**wor′ship-ful-ness,** *n.*

worst (wêrst). [AS. *wiersta, wyrsta*: see *worse.*] **I.** *a.;* superl. of *bad* and *ill.* Bad or ill in the greatest or highest degree; most faulty, unsatisfactory, or objectionable; most evil or wicked; most unfavorable or injurious; in the poorest condition. **II.** *n.* That which is worst; the worst thing or state; the most disadvantageous part, position, or fate (with *the*: as, to get the *worst* of a bargain or a contest); one's

utmost in the way of what is bad (as, to do one's *worst*).—**if the worst comes to the worst,** if the very worst happens.—**worst,** *adv. superl.* In the worst manner (as, to fare *worst*); with the greatest violence or intensity (as, to hate one *worst* of all); also, least (as, he liked this book *worst* of the three).—**worst,** *v. t.* To give (one) the worst of a contest or struggle; defeat; beat: as, "None had *worsted* me, although . . . I had fought more than threescore battles" (Blackmore's "Lorna Doone," ii.).

wor-sted (wus′ted). [From *Worsted,* now *Worstead,* town in Norfolk, England.] **I.** *n.* Firmly twisted yarn or thread spun from combed long-staple wool, used for weaving, etc.: cloth (of various kinds) woven of such yarn; also, woolen yarn (of various kinds) for knitting, crocheting, ornamental needlework, etc. **II.** *a.* Consisting or made of worsted.

wort[1] (wêrt), *n.* [AS. *wyrt* = OHG. G. *wurz,* plant, root, = Goth. *waurts,* root; akin to E. *root*[2].] A plant; an herb; a vegetable: now chiefly in composition, as in *liverwort, figwort, colewort,* etc.

wort[2] (wêrt), *n.* [AS. *wyrt* (in *mascwyrt,* 'mash-wort'): cf. G. *würze,* Icel. *virtr,* wort in brewing, also E. *wort*[1].] In *brewing* and *distilling,* the unfermented or fermenting infusion of malt which after fermentation becomes beer or wash.

worth[1] (wêrth), *v. i.* [AS. *weorthan,* become, happen, = OHG. *werdan* (G. *werden*) = Icel. *verdha* = Goth. *wairthan,* akin to L. *vertere,* turn: cf. *verse, weird,* and *-ward.*] To become† or come to be†; also, to happen or betide (now only in certain archaic phrases, with indirect object: as, woe *worth* the day, that is, woe betide, or be, to the day: see Ezek. xxx. 2).

worth[2] (wêrth), *a.* [AS. *weorth, wurth* (also *wyrthe*), = OHG. *werd* (G. *wert*) = Icel. *verdhr* = Goth. *wairths,* worth, worthy.] Honorable†, estimable†, or worthy†; also, having worth, merit, usefulness, or importance to an amount indicated (as, books, advice, aid, or efforts *worth* much or little; "You are *worth* twenty of him," Hugh Walpole's "Wooden Horse," x.); good or important enough to justify (what is specified: as, advice *worth* taking; a place *worth* visiting; "small errors . . . not *worth* altering," W. H. Hudson's "Far Away and Long Ago," xxii.); deserving of; also, having a value, of or equal in value to, as in money or in exchange (as, "ambergris, *worth* a gold guinea an ounce," H. Melville's "Moby-Dick," xci.; *worth* two oxen; not *worth* a cent or a straw); having property to the value or amount of (as, "a man *worth* thirty million dollars": Sinclair Lewis's "Arrowsmith," xxvii.).—**worth one's salt,** worth as much, as to an employer, as the value of the salt one consumes: often with a negative: as, "He is not *worth his salt*" (Dickens's "Hard Times," ii. 1).—**worth while,** or **worth one's while,** worth one's time; such as to repay one for the time, or the period of attention, effort, etc., required: as, it is not *worth while* to reply; I will make it *worth your while* to go. Cf. *worth-while, a.*—**worth**[2], *n.* [AS. *weorth, wurth.*] Honor† or dignity†; also, excellence of character or quality as commanding esteem (as, men of *worth*; books of genuine *worth*); merit; effective virtue; usefulness or importance, as to the world, to a person, or for a purpose (as, to demonstrate one's *worth* in a crisis; to reward one according to the *worth* of his services; to test the *worth* of a promise or of an invention); also, value, as in money or any medium of exchange (as, the *worth* of a commodity is usually the price it will bring in the market, but price is not always *worth*; "She had had a good deal more than her money's *worth* for her money," S. Butler's "Way of All Flesh," xxxii.); hence, a quantity of something, of a specified value (as, a dollar's *worth* of sugar); also, property or wealth (obs. or archaic: as, "They are but beggars that can count their *worth,*" Shakspere's "Romeo and Juliet," ii. 6. 32).

wor-thi-ly (wêr′THi-li), *adv.* In a worthy manner; excellently; meritoriously; adequately; deservedly; deservingly.—**wor′thi-ness,** *n.*

worth-less (wêrth′les), *a.* [AS. *weorthlēas.*] Without worth; devoid of excellence or merit; of no use, importance, or value; good-for-nothing; useless; valueless; also, unworthy† (with *of*: as, "a peevish schoolboy, *worthless* of such honour," Shakspere's "Julius Cæsar," v. 1. 61).—**worth′less-ly,** *adv.*—**worth′less-ness,** *n.*

worth=while (wérth′hwĭl′), *a.* That is worth while (see phrase under *worth*[2], *a.*); such as to repay one's time, attention, interest, work, trouble, etc.; of real worth or merit: as, a *worth-while* book; a *worth-while* plan or undertaking; a *worth-while* young fellow. [Colloq.]

wor-thy (wèr′тнi). [AS. *wyrthig.*] **I.** *a.*; compar. *worthier,* superl. *worthiest.* Having worth; estimable, as a person (now often used with a condescending force: as, a very *worthy* fellow); of commendable excellence or merit (as, a *worthy* enterprise; "I have done thee *worthy* service," Shakspere's "Tempest," i. 2. 247); of adequate merit or character (as, a *worthy* adversary); adequate for the requirements (with *of,* expressed or understood: as, a speech *worthy* of, or *worthy,* the occasion); deserved (as, a *worthy* reward or punishment); also, deserving (with *of,* expressed or understood, an infinitive, or occasionally a clause: as, to be *worthy* of, or *worthy,* one's hire; *worthy* to be praised or blamed; not *worthy* that men should revile him). **II.** *n.*; pl. *-thies* (-тнiz). A person of eminent worth or merit, especially in his country or time (as, "The History of the *Worthies* of England," by Thomas Fuller, published in 1662; "I fail to find in any gallery of *worthies* . . . any other man so truly and so incomparably great [as Coligny]," Besant's "Coligny," ix.); a personage (now often humorous: as, "Both of these *worthies* . . . frequented the studios . . . where they adored (and were adored by) the grisettes and models," Du Maurier's "Trilby," iii.).

wost (wost). Second person sing. pres. of *wit.* [Obs. or archaic.]

wot[1] (wot). First and third person sing. pres. of *wit.*

wot[2] (wot), *v. t.* or *i.*; *wotted, wotting.* [Erroneously assumed as an independent verb ('to wot') from *wot*[1], which belongs to *wit*: see *wit, v.*] To know: as, "The two little boys *wotted* little of it as they played together" (S. R. Crockett's "Stickit Minister," v.); "The good man *wots* not . . . of the licence which Magazines have arrived at" (Lamb's "Old Benchers of the Inner Temple"); "in some other dimension of space than those we *wot* of" (H. G. Wells's "Men Like Gods," i. 3). [Now a supposed or intended archaism.]

would (wŭd). Preterit of *will*[1]: specially used in expressing a wish (as, I *would* it were true), and often, in place of *will,* to make a statement or question less direct or blunt (as, that *would* scarcely be fair; *would* you be so kind?). — **would′-be,** *a.* Wishing, aspiring, or pretending to be (as, a *would-be* wit; "the real bad men . . . and the *would-be* 'bad men' who aped them," Charnwood's "Theodore Roosevelt," ii.); also, intended to be (as, *would-be* kindness; *would-be* economy).

Woulfe's (wŭlfs) **bot′tle.** [From Peter *Woulfe* (died 1803), English chemist.] A bottle or jar with two or three necks, used in washing gases, saturating liquids with gases, etc.: a series of such bottles with connecting tubes being called a *Woulfe's apparatus.*

wound[1] (wound). Pret. and pp. of *wind*[1].

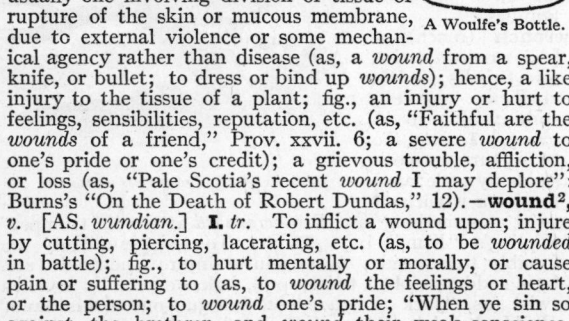

A Woulfe's Bottle.

wound[2] (wŏnd, also wound), *n.* [AS. *wund* = D. *wond* = G. *wunde* = Icel. *und,* a wound; related to adj., AS. *wund,* G. *wund,* Goth. *wunds,* wounded, perhaps orig. pp. from the verb represented by E. *win.*] An injury to the body of a person or animal, usually one involving division of tissue or rupture of the skin or mucous membrane, due to external violence or some mechanical agency rather than disease (as, a *wound* from a spear, knife, or bullet; to dress or bind up *wounds*); hence, a like injury to the tissue of a plant; fig., an injury or hurt to feelings, sensibilities, reputation, etc. (as, "Faithful are the *wounds* of a friend," Prov. xxvii. 6; a severe *wound* to one's pride or one's credit); a grievous trouble, affliction, or loss (as, "Pale Scotia's recent *wound* I may deplore": Burns's "On the Death of Robert Dundas," 12). — **wound**[2], *v.* [AS. *wundian.*] **I.** *tr.* To inflict a wound upon; injure by cutting, piercing, lacerating, etc. (as, to be *wounded* in battle); fig., to hurt mentally or morally, or cause pain or suffering to (as, to *wound* the feelings or heart, or the person; to *wound* one's pride; "When ye sin so against the brethren, and *wound* their weak conscience, ye sin against Christ," 1 Cor. viii. 12). **II.** *intr.* To inflict a wound or wounds; fig., to inflict hurt, as of mind; give pain. — **wound′er,** *n.* — **wound′less,** *a.* Free from wounds; not wounded; also, invulnerable; also, not wounding†.

wove (wōv). Preterit and occasional past participle of *weave.* — **wove,** *p. a.* Of paper, made with a smooth, plain surface, without the parallel markings of laid paper. Cf. *laid, p. a.* — **wov-en** (wō′vn). Past participle of *weave.*

wow (wou). **I.** *interj.* An exclamation of surprise, wonder, pleasure, dismay, etc.: as, "She screwed up her face in torture. 'Oh, *wow!* Isn't it [noise] too awful!'" (A. S. M. Hutchinson's "If Winter Comes," ii. 4). [Colloq. or prov.] **II.** *n.* Something that proves an extraordinary success; an unqualified hit: as, the new play is a *wow.* [Slang.]

wrack[1] (rak), *n.* [See *wreck.*] Wreck or wreckage cast ashore by the sea (obs. or archaic); also, shipwreck (archaic); hence, ruin or destruction (archaic: as, "a world devote to universal *wrack*," Milton's "Paradise Lost," xi. 821: cf. *rack*[4]); also, seaweed or other marine vegetation cast ashore.

wrack[2] (rak), *n.* See *rack*[3].

wraith (rāth), *n.* [Sc.; origin uncertain.] An apparition of a living person, or of one supposed to be living, popularly reputed to portend or indicate his death; in general, a visible spirit; a ghost.

wran-gle (rang′gl), *v.*; *-gled, -gling.* [ME. *wranglen;* akin to E. *wring.*] **I.** *intr.* To argue or dispute, esp. in a noisy or angry manner; carry on an altercation; formerly, at certain universities, to dispute publicly; defend or oppose a thesis by argument. **II.** *tr.* To argue or dispute; also, to tend (horses) as a horse-wrangler does (western U. S.). — **wran′gle,** *n.* A noisy or angry dispute; an altercation. — **wran′gler,** *n.* One who wrangles or disputes; also, at Cambridge University, England, one of those in the first grade of honors in mathematics (cf. *optime*); also, a horse-wrangler (western U. S.).

wrap (rap), *v. t.*; *wrapped* (also *wrapt*), *wrapping.* [ME. *wrappen;* origin uncertain.] To inclose, envelop, or muffle in something wound or folded about (often with *up*: as, to *wrap* one's self in a shawl; to *wrap* up an injured hand); protect with coverings, outer garments, etc. (usually with *up*: as, to be well *wrapped* up against the cold); inclose and make fast (an article, bundle, etc.) within a covering of paper or the like (often with *up*: as, to *wrap* up goods for delivery to purchasers); also, to wind, fold, or bind (something) about as a covering (as, "*Wrapping* the shawl about her, I led her out," W. H. Hudson's "Purple Land," xxvii.; "*wrapping* . . . the handkerchief round his bleeding hand," Chesterton's "Napoleon of Notting Hill," i. 2; to *wrap* paper about a package); also, to fold or roll up†; also, fig., to surround, envelop, shroud, or hide (as, mountain summits *wrapped* in clouds; "The wild landscape was *wrapt* in snow," Irving's "Captain Bonneville," xv.; things *wrapped* in mystery); involve. — **wrapped up in,** fig., involved in or associated with (as, possibilities *wrapped up in* a case); engrossed in (as, *wrapped up in* one's thoughts); bound up in, as in an object of affection (as, a mother *wrapped up in* her children). — **wrap,** *v. i.* To wrap one's self (*up*); also, to become wrapped, as about something; fold. — **wrap,** *n.* Something to be wrapped about the person, esp. in addition to the usual indoor clothing, as a shawl, scarf, or mantle; *pl.,* outdoor garments or coverings, furs, etc. (as, "Followed by the first footman carrying her *wraps* . . . a lady stepped forward": Galsworthy's "Country House," i. 1). — **wrap-page** (rap′āj), *n.* The act of wrapping; also, that in which something is wrapped; a wrapping. — **wrap′per,** *n.* One who or that which wraps; also, that in which something is wrapped; a covering or cover (as, a stamped paper *wrapper* for use in mailing newspapers; a paper *wrapper* or jacket for protecting the binding of a book); the tobacco-leaf used for covering cigars; also, a long, loose outer garment; esp., a woman's loose house-gown, or negligée. — **wrap′ping,** *n.* The act of one who or that which wraps; also, that in which something is wrapped (often in *pl.*).

wrasse (ras), *n.* [Origin uncertain.] Any of various acanthopterygian marine fishes of the family *Labridæ,* esp. of the genus *Labrus,* having thick, fleshy lips, powerful teeth, and usually a brilliant coloration, certain species being valued as food-fishes. See cut on following page.

wrath (råth, Brit. râth), *n.* [AS. *wræththo*, < *wráth*, angry, E. *wroth*.] Strong, stern, or fierce anger (as, "Thou provokedst the Lord thy God to *wrath*," Deut. ix. 7; "We know

A British Wrasse (*Labrus maculatus*).

what was the *wrath* of Juno when her beauty was despised," Trollope's "Barchester Towers," xi.); deeply resentful indignation; ire; also, vengeance or punishment, as the consequence of anger (as, "a revenger to execute *wrath* upon him that doeth evil": Rom. xiii. 4); also, frenzy or fury, as of passion† (as, "They are in the very *wrath* of love": Shakspere's "As You Like It," v. 2. 44).—**wrath,** *a.* Obs. or archaic form of *wroth.*—**wrath′ful,** *a.* Full of wrath, very angry, or ireful, as a person or the mind, mood, etc.; characterized by or showing wrath, as the manner, aspect, actions, words, etc.; also, serving for or connected with the manifestation or execution of wrath (archaic or poetic: as, "we, God's *wrathful* agent," Shakspere's "King John," ii. 1. 87; *wrathful* weapons; "That *wrathful* day, When man to judgment wakes from clay," Scott's "Lay of the Last Minstrel," vi, 31); also, fig., raging or stormy (as, "*wrathful* seas": Tennyson's "Enoch Arden," 91).—**wrath′ful-ly,** *adv.*—**wrath′ful-ness,** *n.*—**wrath′y,** *a.* Wrathful; angry. [Colloq.]—**wrath′i-ly,** *adv.*—**wrath′i-ness,** *n.*

wreak (rēk), *v. t.* [AS. *wrecan,* drive, expel, punish, avenge, = OHG. *rehhan* (G. *rächen*), avenge, = Icel. *reka,* drive, wreak, = Goth. *wrikan,* persecute; akin to L. *urgere,* press, drive: see *urge, wreck,* and *wretch.*] To inflict punishment for, or avenge (a wrong or injury: archaic); also, to take vengeance on behalf of (one's self, another, etc.), as for a wrong sustained (archaic: as, "Grant me some knight to do the battle for me . . . and *wreak* me for my son," Tennyson's "Gareth and Lynette," 355); also, to inflict or execute (vengeance, etc.: as, "So certain was the revenge they *wreaked* upon any who dared to strike a Doone," Blackmore's "Lorna Doone," v.); also, to carry out the promptings of (one's rage, ill humor, will, desire, etc.), as on a victim or object (as, "Timid people always *wreak* their peevishness on the gentle": George Eliot's "Adam Bede," iv.).—**wreak′er,** *n.*

wreath (rēth), *n.*; pl. *wreaths* (rēᴛʜz). [AS. *wræth, wrǽd,* < *wrúhan,* twist, E. *writhe.*] Something twisted or bent into a circular form; a circular band of flowers, foliage, or any ornamental work, for adorning the head or for any decorative purpose (as, "Their casques adorn'd with laurel *wreaths* they wear," Dryden's tr. Virgil's "Æneid," v. 727; a *wreath* of Christmas greens); a garland or chaplet; hence, any ring-like, curving, or curling mass or formation (as, "A delicate *wreath* of smoke curls spirally into the air," H. Melville's "Typee," xiii.; a *wreath* of dancers); also, a drifted mass, as of snow or sand (as, "Thousands [of sheep] are lost under huge *wreaths* of snow," Smollett's "Humphry Clinker," Sept. 15: chiefly Sc.); in *her.,* a twisted, cord-like roll (circular when shown in full), usually combining two colors.—**wreathe** (rēᴛʜ), *v.; wreathed* (archaic pp. *wreathen*), *wreathing.* **I.** *tr.* To encircle or adorn with or as with a wreath or wreaths (as, to *wreathe* one's head with flowers; to *wreathe* a tomb with laurel); also, to dispose in or like a wreath about something (as, to *wreathe* flowers about one's head; "a wild grape vine . . . *wreathing* the entanglement of its tendrils almost around every bough," Hawthorne's "Blithedale Romance," xii.); also, to form as a wreath, by twisting, twining, or otherwise (as, to *wreathe* garlands); also, to form a wreath about (as, flowers *wreathed* the bowl); hence, to surround in ring-like, curving, or curling masses or form (as, mists *wreathed* the hills; "*Wreathed* in smoke the ship stood out to sea," M. Arnold's "Balder Dead," iii.); fig., to envelop (as, a face *wreathed* in smiles); also, to twist up or about (obs. or archaic: as, "The unwieldy elephant . . . *wreathed* his lithe proboscis," Milton's "Paradise

Heraldic Wreath.

Lost," iv. 346); form into a twisted or spiral shape (archaic: as, "two chains of pure gold . . . of *wreathen* work shalt thou make them," Ex. xxviii. 14); twist or twine together (obs. or archaic). **II.** *intr.* To take the form of a wreath or wreaths; move in curving or curling masses, as smoke; swirl or drift, as snow (Sc.); also, to become entwined, as trees (obs. or archaic).—**wreath-er** (rē′ᴛʜėr), *n.*

wreck (rek), *n.* [ME. *wrek, wrak,* appar. from Scand.: cf. Icel. *rek,* a thing drifted ashore, Sw. *vrak,* Dan. *vrag,* wreckage, wreck, refuse, Icel. *reka,* drive, also AS. *wrecan,* drive, *wræc,* exile, misery: see *wreak.*] That which is cast ashore by the sea, as the remains of a ruined vessel or of its cargo; shipwrecked property, or wreckage, cast ashore or (less strictly) floating on the sea; also, a vessel in a state of ruin from disaster at sea, on rocks, etc.; hence, any building, structure, or thing reduced to a state of ruin (often fig.: as, to be the *wreck* of one's former self); also, the ruin or destruction of a vessel in the course of navigation; shipwreck; hence, the ruin or destruction of anything (as, the *wreck* of one's hopes or fortunes).—**wreck,** *v.* **I.** *tr.* To cause the wreck of (a vessel), as in the course of navigation; shipwreck; in general, to cause the ruin or destruction of (as, "The Boers had just *wrecked* a British military train," Arnold Bennett's "Roll-Call," i.; to *wreck* a bank; "That's a small thing to . . . *wreck* a fellow's life," Du Maurier's "Trilby," v.); also, to involve in a wreck (as, *wrecked* sailors; *wrecked* merchandise). **II.** *intr.* To suffer wreck (as, "rocks, whereon greatest men have oftest *wreck′d*": Milton's "Paradise Regained," ii. 228); also, to act as a wrecker; engage in wrecking.—**wreck′age** (-āj), *n.* The act of wrecking, or the state of being wrecked; also, remains or fragments of something that has been wrecked (as, stranded or floating *wreckage*; to remove the *wreckage* after a railroad collision).—**wreck′er,** *n.* One who or that which wrecks; esp., one who causes shipwrecks, as by false lights on shore, in order to secure wreckage, or who makes a business of plundering wrecks or gathering wreckage; also, a person or a vessel employed in recovering wrecked or disabled vessels or their cargoes, etc., as in the interest of the owners or underwriters; also, a person, car, or train employed in removing wreckage, etc., from railroad-tracks; also, one whose business it is to tear down buildings, as in clearing sites for other use.—**wreck′ful,** *a.* Causing or involving wreck, ruin, or destruction. [Archaic.]—**wreck′ing,** *n.* The act of a person or thing that wrecks; the causing of a wreck or wrecks; the gathering of wreckage; the recovering of wrecked or disabled vessels or their cargoes, etc.; also, the removing of wreckage, etc., from railroad-tracks; also, the tearing down of buildings, as in clearing sites.—**wreck′ing=car,** *n.* A car provided with means and appliances for clearing wreckage, etc., from railroad-tracks.

wren (ren), *n.* [AS. *wrenna, wrænna.*] Any of the small oscine passerine birds constituting the family *Troglodytidæ,* as *Troglodytes parvulus,* the common wren of Europe, o. *T. hiemalis,* the 'winter wren' of North America, or *T. aëdon,* the common 'house wren' of North America; also, any of various similar birds of other families.

wrench (rench), *v.* [AS. *wrencan,* twist, use tricks, = G. *renken,* wrench, sprain; akin to E. *wring.*] **I.** *intr.* To twist, turn, or move suddenly aside; also, to give a wrench or

Winter Wren (*Troglodytes hiemalis*).

twist at something (as, "Kim *wrenched* at the tin trumpet": Kipling's "Kim," ix.). **II.** *tr.* To twist suddenly and forcibly to one side; overstrain or injure (the ankle, etc.) by a sudden, violent twist; pull, jerk, or force by a violent twist (as, "Jack . . . *wrenched* his gun out of his hand," H. Mackenzie's "Man of Feeling," xxxiv.; "He *wrenched* off the enormous padlock . . . with a bar of iron," J. Conrad's "Rover," vii.); fig., to affect distressingly as if by a wrench (as, "He was *wrenched* by emotions . . . odd and unaccountable": H. G. Wells's "Mr. Britling," ii. 4. § 22); also, to wrest, as from the right use or meaning (as, to *wrench* facts or statements).—**wrench,** *n.* A wrenching movement; a sudden, violent twist; a painful, straining twist, as of the ankle or wrist (as, "That stupid high heel turned, and gave me a horrid *wrench*": Louisa M. Alcott's "Little Women," i. 3); fig., a sharp, distressing strain, as to the feelings (as, "I am not anxious to leave the old place . . . It will be a *wrench* to me": Arnold Bennett's "Grand Babylon Hotel," iv.); also, a wresting, as of meaning; also, a tool or instrument for catching upon or gripping and turning or twisting the head of a bolt, a nut, a pipe, or the like, commonly consisting of a bar of metal with fixed or adjustable jaws at the end (cf. *monkey-wrench*).

wrest (rest), *v. t.* [AS. *wrǣstan* = Icel. *reista*, wrest; perhaps akin to E. *writhe.*] To twist or turn; esp., to twist or turn from the proper course, application, use, meaning, or the like (as, to *wrest* the law to one's own purposes; to *wrest* facts or words; "So far to extend their speeches is to *wrest* them against their true intent and meaning," Hooker's "Ecclesiastical Polity," ii. 5. 3); also, to pull, jerk, or force by a violent twist (as, "Her husband . . . *wrested* the pistol out of the fellow's hand": Smollett's "Humphry Clinker," June 26); take away by force (as, "He *wrested* from the count of Flanders the Vermandois . . . and . . . the county of Artois": Hallam's "Europe during the Middle Ages," i. 1); get by effort (as, to *wrest* a living from the soil). —**wrest,** *n.* A wresting; a twist or wrench; also, a key or small wrench for tuning stringed musical instruments, as the harp or the piano, by turning the pins to which the strings are fastened.—**wrest′er,** *n.*

wres-tle (res′l), *v.*; *-tled, -tling.* [AS. *wrǣstlian*, freq. of *wrǣstan*, E. *wrest.*] **I.** *intr.* To twist about†; writhe†; also, to struggle in a hand-to-hand contest; specif., to struggle in a contest in which each of two adversaries strives to throw or force his opponent to the ground, esp. as an athletic exercise governed by rules; fig., to contend as in a struggle for mastery (as, "He must . . . *wrestle* with destiny single-handed": W. B. Maxwell's "In Cotton Wool," ix.); struggle with or against a moral foe (as, "We *wrestle* not against flesh and blood, but . . . against spiritual wickedness": Eph. vi. 12); grapple, as with a task or problem; sometimes, to devote one's self earnestly to prayer (cant). **II.** *tr.* To contend with in wrestling (colloq.: as, "Darn' if he didn't *wrestle* a fellow half his age!" Sinclair Lewis's "Arrowsmith," xix.); also, to force by or as if by wrestling (as, "I will *wrestle* down my feelings of rebellious humanity": Scott's "Black Dwarf," vi.); also, to throw (an animal) for the purpose of branding (western U. S.).—**wres′tle,** *n.* An act of or bout at wrestling; a struggle: as, "Hands and his companion locked together in deadly *wrestle*, each with a hand upon the other's throat" (Stevenson's "Treasure Island," xxiii.).—**wres′tler,** *n.*—**wres′tling,** *n.* The act of one who wrestles; specif., an exercise or sport, subject to special rules, in which two persons struggle hand to hand, each striving to throw or force the other to the ground.

wretch (rech), *n.* [AS. *wrecca, wrǣcca*, exile, outcast, wretch, < *wrecan*, drive, expel: see *wreak.*] A deplorably unfortunate or unhappy person (as, "The poor *wretch* was flogged till he was insensible": Froude's "Cæsar," xix.); a miserable or pitiable creature; also, a person of despicable character (as, "All cursed me as a *wretch* who would sell his country for gold": Cooper's "Spy," xxix.); a contemptible or base person; a mean creature (often used playfully).—**wretch′ed,** *a.* Deplorably unfortunate in condition or circumstances (as, *wretched* slaves); miserable; pitiable; characterized by or attended with misery (as, a *wretched* hovel; a *wretched* life); deeply unhappy in mind (as, to be *wretched* over a loss, a failure, or a misunderstanding); in an unsatisfactory physical condition (as, he has been *wretched*, or in *wretched* health, all winter); also, despicable, contemptible, or mean (as, a *wretched* informer); hence, poor, sorry, or pitiful (as, a *wretched* blunderer; a *wretched* daub; *wretched* stuff); paltry; worthless; in general, miserably unsatisfactory or unpleasant (as, "the *wretched* stipend I draw from the

Pall Mall Gazette," Thackeray's "Newcomes," lxiv.; *wretched* cooking; *wretched* weather; to have a *wretched* time).—**wretch′ed-ly,** *adv.*—**wretch′ed-ness,** *n.*

wrick (rik), *v.* [ME. *wrikken*, twist to and fro, = D. *wrikken*, shake, move, = Sw. *vricka*, Dan. *vrikke*, wriggle, sprain: cf. *wrig, wriggle*, and *wry, v.*] **I.**† *intr.* To twist to and fro. **II.** *tr.* To wrench or strain (the neck, back, ankle, etc.) painfully; sprain.—**wrick,** *n.* A wrench, strain, or sprain.

wried (rīd). Preterit and past participle of *wry.*

wri-er, wri-est (rī′ėr, rī′est). Compar. and superl. of *wry, a.*

wrig (rig), *v. i.* or *t.*; *wrigged, wrigging.* [Var. of *wrick.*] To wriggle. [Obs. or prov. Eng.]

wrig-gle (rig′l), *v.*; *-gled, -gling.* [Freq. of *wrig.*] **I.** *intr.* To twist to and fro, writhe, or squirm (as, "Cæsar *wriggled* a little in his chair": Cooper's "Spy," xxviii.); also, to move along by twisting and turning the body, as a worm or a snake does (as, "An animal . . . *wriggled* from its hiding-place under the dead wood": W. H. Hudson's "Green Mansions," xxi.); proceed in a winding or sinuous course (as, "Beside the path gurgled, and *wriggled* on, a tiny brook": Wiseman's "Fabiola," i. 18); hence, to make one's way by shifts or expedients (as, to *wriggle* out of a difficulty; "He had managed to *wriggle* through all the deadly complications," J. Conrad's "Lord Jim," xxix.). **II.** *tr.* To cause to wriggle (as, "Dick . . . *wriggled* his toes inside the soft leather moccasins": Kipling's "Light That Failed," viii.); also, to bring, get, make, etc., by wriggling (as, "Mr. Polly *wriggled* his arm free," H. G. Wells's "Mr. Polly," ix.; to *wriggle* one's way).—**wrig′gle,** *n.* The act or an act of wriggling; a wriggling movement; also, a sinuosity (rare).—**wrig′gler,** *n.* One who or that which wriggles; specif., the larva of a mosquito; a wiggler.—**wrig′gly,** *a.* Characterized by wriggling.

wright (rīt), *n.* [ME. *wrihte, wurhte*, < AS. *wyrhta*, < *wyrcan*, E. *work, v.*] A workman, esp. a constructive workman; a maker; an artificer; a mechanic: now chiefly in composition, as in *wheelwright, millwright, playwright*, etc.

wring (ring), *v.*; *wrung, wringing.* [AS. *wringan* = MLG. and D. *wringen* = OHG. *ringan* (G. *ringen*), wring: cf. *wrangle, wrench*, and *wrong.*] **I.** *tr.* To twist forcibly, as something flexible; twist and compress, or compress without twisting, in order to force out water, etc. (as, to *wring* clothes after washing, whether by hand or in a wringer: often with *out*, as, "She continued to *wring* out a cloth in her pail," Arnold Bennett's "Book of Carlotta," i. 4); clasp tightly with or without twisting (as, to *wring* the hands in pain or distress; to *wring* another's hand in greeting); twist out of place or shape (as, to *wring* a mast); twist from the proper course, application, meaning, etc. (archaic); affect painfully by or as if by some contorting or compressing action (as, a shoe that *wrings* the foot; "The griefs That *wring* my soul," Addison's "Cato," i. 1); pain, distress, or torment; also, to extract or expel by twisting or compression (usually with *out* or *from*: as, to *wring* water from clothes); extract or extort as if by twisting (as, a tale which *wrings* tears from one; "to *wring* from him his consent to laws which he disliked," Macaulay's "Hist. of Eng.," ii.; "money which had been *wrung* from a trusting public by extortion," W. Churchill's "Inside of the Cup," xi.); also, to force (*off*, etc.) by twisting (as, "The priest shall . . . *wring* off his head": Lev. i. 15). **II.** *intr.* To perform the action of wringing something; also, to writhe, as in anguish† (as, "those that *wring* under the load of sorrow": Shakspere's "Much Ado about Nothing," v. 1. 28).—**wring,** *n.* A wringing; a forcible twist or squeeze (as, to give a person's hand a *wring* in greeting); also, a wringer or press (obs. or prov. Eng.).—**wring′er,** *n.* One who or that which wrings; esp., an apparatus or machine which by pressure forces water or the like out of anything wet, as clothes which have been washed. —**wring′ing=wet′,** *a.* So wet that water may be wrung out.

wrin-kle (ring′kl), *n.* [AS. *wincle* = MD. *wrinckel*, wrinkle.] A ridge or furrow on a surface, due to contraction, folding, rumpling, or the like (as, "His troubles had left no *wrinkles* on his smooth forehead," F. M. Crawford's "Mr. Isaacs," iii.; *wrinkles* in a garment); a corrugation; a slight fold; a crease; also (colloq.), an ingenious indirect or artful procedure or method; a novel or clever trick or device (as, "the latest fad and *wrinkle* in science": Sinclair Lewis's "Arrowsmith," xvii.); a useful idea or hint; an individual method or notion.—**wrin′kle**, *v.*; *-kled, -kling.* [AS. *wrin-clian.*] **I.** *tr.* To form a wrinkle or wrinkles in; corrugate; crease: as, "Hilda *wrinkled* her forehead when her parasol would not subside" (Arnold Bennett's "Clayhanger," ii. 10); "a man's face . . . old and *wrinkled*" (Bret Harte's "Miggles"). **II.** *intr.* To become contracted into wrinkles; become wrinkled: as, "The King's brow *wrinkled* thoughtfully" (Chesterton's "Napoleon of Notting Hill," ii. 2).—**wrin′kly**, *a.* Having wrinkles; wrinkled; apt to wrinkle.

wrist (rist), *n.* [AS. *wrist*, wrist, = MLG. *wrist*, G. *rist*, wrist, instep, = Icel. *rist*, Sw. and Dan. *vrist*, instep; perhaps akin to E. *writhe*.] The part of the arm between the forearm and the hand; technically, the carpus; also, the joint between the radius and the carpus ('wrist-joint'); in *mach.*, a wrist-pin.—**wrist-band** (rist′band, commonly riz′band), *n.* The band or part of a sleeve, as of a shirt, which covers the wrist.—**wrist′=drop**, *n.* In *pathol.*, paralysis of the extensor muscles of the hand so that it cannot be extended, due usually to lead-poisoning.—**wrist′let**, *n.* A band worn around the wrist, esp. to protect it from cold; also, a bracelet; also, a handcuff (humorous or slang).—**wrist′=pin**, *n.* In *mach.*, a stud or pin projecting from the side of a crank, wheel, or the like, and forming a means of attachment to a connecting-rod leading to some other part of the mechanism.—**wrist′=watch**, *n.* A watch (timepiece) attached to a strap or band worn about the wrist: as, "noting by her *wrist-watch* that it was four o'clock" (Galsworthy's "Saint's Progress," i. 8).

writ (rit), *n.* [AS. *writ, gewrit.*] Something written, or a writing (as, "Too late I bring this fatal *writ* [a letter]," Shakspere's "Titus Andronicus," ii. 3. 264: obs. or archaic except as in the following uses); [*cap.*] Scripture, or the Bible (as, "That's true as *Writ!*" G. Meredith's "Diana of the Crossways," iii.: usually in 'Holy Writ' or 'Sacred Writ'); [*l. c.*] in *law*, a formal order under seal, issued in the name of a sovereign, government, court, or other competent legal authority, enjoining the officer or other person to whom it is issued or addressed to do or refrain from doing some specified act.

write (rīt), *v. t.*; pret. *wrote* (archaic *writ*), pp. *written* (archaic *writ*), ppr. *writing.* [AS. *wrītan*, cut, engrave, draw, write, = D. *rijten*, tear, = OHG. *rīzan* (G. *reissen*), cut, tear, draw, = Icel. *rīta*, cut, draw, write; akin to Goth. *writs*, stroke of a pen.] To trace or form (characters, letters, words, etc.) on the surface of some material, as with a pen, pencil, or other instrument or means; inscribe; fig., to impress the marks or indications of (as, honesty is *written* in his face; "Is not Destiny *writ* large upon this day's adventure?" H. G. Wells's "Men Like Gods," ii. 2); also, to trace significant characters on, or mark or cover with writing (as, "A roll of a book was therein . . . it was *written* within and without": Ezek. ii. 10); fill in the blank spaces of (a form, etc.) with writing (as, to *write* a check; to *write* an income-tax return); also, to express or communicate in writing (as, to *write* one's observations; to *write* all the news); give a written account of; make a record of; sometimes, to record or set forth as ordained by law, God, fate, etc. (as, "They kept also the feast of tabernacles, as it is *written*," Ezra, iii. 4; "It is *written* that I should live in barracks," G. Meredith's "Diana of the Crossways," iv.); also, to execute or produce by setting down words, etc. (as, to *write* two copies of a letter); also, to compose and produce in words or characters duly set down (as, to *write* a letter to a friend; to *write* a novel; to *write* the music for a song); produce as author or composer; also, to style or entitle in writing (as, to *write* one's self esquire).—**to write down**, to set down in writing (as, to *write down* an address or date); set down in writing as (lit. or fig.: as, "O that he were here to *write* me *down* an ass!" Shakspere's "Much Ado about Nothing," iv. 2. 78); also, to write in depreciation of; injure by writing against.—**to write off**, to cancel, as an entry in an account, as by an offsetting entry; hence, in general, to cancel, or render as if non-existent.—**to write out**, to put into writing (as, to *write out* directions for reaching a place); write in full form (as, to *write out* abbreviated words); write in a complete and finished form, as from notes or a rough draft; also, to exhaust the capacity or resources of by excessive writing (as, an author who has *written* himself *out*).—**to write up**, to bring up to date or to the latest fact or trans-

action in writing; also, to write out in full or in det... sent to public notice in a written description or ... sometimes, to commend to the public by a favorabl... description or account.—**write**, *v. i.* To trace ... characters, words, etc., with a pen, pencil, or othe... ment or means, or as a pen or the like does; also, to ... clerk, amanuensis, or the like; also, to express ideas ... ing; write a letter or letters, or communicate by ... compose or work as a writer or author.—**write**, *n.* W... as, "a well-written letter, in a fair hand of *write*" (... "Annals of the Parish," i.). [Sc.]

writ-er (rī′tėr), *n.* One who writes; a penman; also, ... whose occupation is writing, as a clerk or amanuensis; also, a lawyer or solicitor (Sc.); also, one who expresses ideas in writing; esp., one engaged in literary work; an author; also, a manual for teaching how to write (chiefly in composition: as, a letter-*writer*).—**writers' cramp**, in *pathol.*, a nervous disorder affecting the muscles of the hand of persons who write much: in various forms, marked by spasmodic contractions, trembling, severe pain or other abnormal sensations, or inability to control the hand.—**writer to the signet**, in *Sc. law*, orig., a clerk in the office of the secretary of state, who prepared the writings passing the signet; now, one of a class of law agents corresponding to the English solicitors.

write=up (rīt′up), *n.* The act of writing up; also, a written description or account of something, as in a newspaper or magazine; sometimes, a laudatory description or account of this kind. [Colloq.]

writhe (rīₜн), *v.*; pret. *writhed*, pp. *writhed* (archaic *writhen*), ppr. *writhing.* [AS. *wrīthan* = OHG. *rīdan* = Icel. *rīdha* = Sw. *vrida* = Dan. *vride*, twist: cf. *wreath, wrest, wrist*, and *wroth*.] **I.** *tr.* To twist or bend out of shape or position (as, "He will *writhe* his mouth, and slander thy sayings," Ecclus. xxvii. 23; "the *writhed* lip of scorn," Hawthorne's "Twice-Told Tales," The Haunted Mind); distort; contort; also, to twist (one's self, the body, etc.) about, as in pain (as, "The prisoner *writhed* himself in his chains": Scott's "Legend of Montrose," xiii.); bring, get, set, etc., by twisting movements (as, "She *writhed* her slim body like a snake through tufted grass . . . to a hedge," Whyte-Melville's "Katerfelto," xvii.; "She *writhed* herself free," H. Kingsley's "Geoffry Hamlyn," ix.); make (the way) by twisting movements (as, "a huge serpent *writhing* its way down the gorge": H. G. Wells's "Men Like Gods," ii. 4); also, to wring or extort, as money†; wrest or pervert, as in meaning†. **II.** *intr.* To twist the body about, or squirm, as in pain, violent effort, etc. (as, the wounded man *writhed* in agony; "The tough Punjabi *writhed* and twisted like a cat in my grasp," F. M. Crawford's "Mr. Isaacs," xii.); get (*away*, etc.) by twisting movements (as, "She tried to *writhe* away, but could not": Galsworthy's "Dark Flower," ii. 17); also, fig., to shrink mentally, as in acute discomfort (as, "I *writhed* under the glance of covert scorn," S. J. Weyman's "Gentleman of France," vii.; "He *writhed* under the jokes . . . made at his expense," Maugham's "Moon and Sixpence," xviii.).—**writhe**, *n.* A writhing movement; a twisting of the body, as in pain.—**writh-en** (rīₜн′en), *p. a.* Twisted; contorted: as, "Others [stones] are twisted and *writhen* like the Vesuvian lava of 1871" (Amelia B. Edwards's "Thousand Miles up the Nile," xvii.). [Archaic.]—**writh-ing-ly** (rī′ₜнing-li), *adv.*

writ-ing (rī′ting), *n.* The act of one who or that which writes; the tracing of characters, words, etc., as with a pen, pencil, or the like; the expression of ideas by written words; literary composition or production; also, the state of being written, or written form (as, to obtain a statement in *writing*; to commit one's thoughts to *writing*); also, that which is written; characters or matter written with a pen or the like (as, paper bearing *writing*; two lines of *writing*); such characters or matter with respect to style, kind, quality, etc. (as, an example of ancient Greek *writing*; childish *writing*; clear or good *writing*); an inscription; a letter; any written (or, sometimes, as in law, any printed) paper, document, or the like; literary matter or work, esp. with respect to style, kind, quality, etc. (as, "two kinds of *writing* . . . the mythological and the satirical," J. Butler's "Analogy of Religion," ii. 7; allegorical *writing*; a specimen of

1

2

3

5

4

1. Ghiordes prayer-rug from Asia Minor. The small water-urn depicted at the end of each column supporting the mihrab (niche) is the urn with the aid of which the devout Mohammedan performs his ablutions before entering the mosque.
2. Chinese rug of the Kien-lung period. An example of this period for which conventionalized lotus was used as the key-note.
3. Modern example of fine Czecho-Slovakian chenille rug, reproducing French design of late 18th century.
4. Typical example of hand-hooked rug from the northeastern coast of North America.
5. Kashan rug. One of the finest weaves of modern Persian rugs. Fine all-over designs of conventionalized flowers and elaborate medallions predominate in rich colorings.
Courtesy of W. & J. SLOANE.

clever *writing*); a literary composition or production (as, the *writings* of Thomas Carlyle; novels, poems, and miscellaneous *writings*).—**writ′ing=desk**, *n.* A desk or piece of furniture for use in writing, commonly with drawers, pigeonholes, etc., for holding materials, papers, or the like; also, a portable case for holding materials for writing, and affording when opened a surface to rest the paper on in writing.—**writ′ing=pa″per**, *n.* Paper of suitable kinds and sizes for writing on.

writ-ten (rit′n). Past participle of *write*.

wrong (rông), *a.* [ME. *wrong, wrang*, from Scand.: cf. Icel. *rangr*, awry, wrong, Dan. *vrang*, wrong, akin to E. *wring*.] Twisted† or crooked†; also, out of order, awry, or amiss (as, something is *wrong* with the machine; "What in the world is *wrong* with you?" Tarkington's "Magnificent Ambersons," xxi.); also, not in accordance with what is morally right or good (as, *wrong* courses; "It was *wrong* of Gecko to strike him," Du Maurier's "Trilby," vii.); not just or equitable; also, deviating from truth or fact (as, a *wrong* statement or answer); erroneous; also, not in accordance with intention or purpose (as, to take the *wrong* road; "She . . . put the two letters into the *wrong* envelopes," S. Butler's "Way of All Flesh," lxxxiii.); not proper, or not in accordance with requirements (as, the *wrong* way to hold a golf-club); not suitable or appropriate (as, to say the *wrong* thing; "She placed her affections on the *wrong* person," W. H. Hudson's "Far Away and Long Ago," xiii.; the *wrong* man for the place); less advantageous or desirable (as, to be on the *wrong* side of forty); also, that should be worn or kept inward or under (as, the *wrong* side of a coat or of cloth); also, not correct in action, judgment, opinion, method, etc., as a person (as, "You are *wrong* in affecting contempt of the Press": G. Meredith's "Diana of the Crossways," xxix.); in error.—**in the wrong box**, fig., in the wrong place or position; in an awkward situation; mistaken: as, "I do not know whether it be or no! I am afraid we are *in the wrong box!*" (Godwin's "Caleb Williams," xxxvi.).—**wrong font**, in *printing*, of a type, not of the proper font, or size and style, for its place. Abbreviated *w. f.*—**wrong**, *n.* [Late AS. *wrang*, from Scand.] That which is wrong, or not in accordance with morality, goodness, justice, truth, or the like (as, "A free determination 'Twixt right and *wrong*": Shakspere's "Troilus and Cressida," ii. 2. 171); evil; injustice; also, wrong action or conduct, or a violation of right or duty (as, to do or commit *wrong*, or a *wrong*); also, an injustice or injury inflicted or received (as, to do one a *wrong*; "Men were accustomed to redress their *wrongs* by the strong hand," Macaulay's "Hist. of Eng.," i.); also, the state of being wrong, as in action, judgment, or opinion (as, to be in the *wrong*; to put one in the *wrong*, to show him to be, or cause him to appear to be, wrong); also, in *law*, an invasion of right, to the damage of another person; esp., a tort.—**wrong**, *adv.* In a wrong manner; awry or amiss; ill, badly, or unfavorably; not righteously or uprightly; not equitably; erroneously; incorrectly; improperly.—**to go wrong**, to go in a wrong way; esp., to go or proceed amiss, ill, or badly; proceed or turn out in an unfavorable or unfortunate way (as, "She had a vision of the business *going wrong*, of her investments *going wrong*": Arnold Bennett's "Riceyman Steps," i. 6); also, to take the wrong road or course; also, to deviate from uprightness or virtue.—**wrong**, *v. t.* To do wrong to; treat unfairly or unjustly; injure or harm; sometimes, to impute evil to unjustly (as, "Thou *wrong′st* a gentleman, who is as far From thy report as thou from honour": Shakspere's "Cymbeline," i. 6. 145); sometimes, to dishonor (a woman).—**wrong′=do′er**, *n.* One who does wrong.—**wrong′=do′ing**, *n.*—**wrong′er**, *n.*—**wrong′ful**, *a.* Full of or characterized by wrong, as actions, etc.; unrighteous; unfair; unjust; injurious: as, "I despise thee for thy *wrongful* suit" (Shakspere's "Two Gentlemen of Verona," iv. 2. 102); a *wrongful* taking of property.—**wrong′ful-ly**, *adv.*—**wrong′ful-ness**, *n.*—**wrong′=head′ed**, *a.* Wrong in judgment or opinion; misguided and stubborn; perverse: as, "a *wrong-headed* enthusiast" (Smollett's "Humphry Clinker," June 10); *wrong-headed* distrust.—**wrong′=head′ed-ness**, *n.*—**wrong′ly**, *adv.*—**wrong′ness**, *n.*

wrote (rōt). Preterit of *write*.

wroth (rôth or, esp. Brit., rōth), *a.* [AS. *wrāth* = OS. *wrēth* = Icel. *reidhr* = Sw. and Dan. *vred*, angry; akin to AS. *wrūthan*, twist, E. *writhe*.] Affected with anger; incensed; wrathful: used predicatively: as, "The archdeacon waxed *wroth*, talked big, and looked bigger" (Trollope's "Warden," xx.). [Archaic.]

wrought (rôt), *p. a.* [See *work, v.*] Worked; elaborated; not rough or crude.—**wrought′=i′ron**, *n.* A comparatively pure form of iron (as that produced by puddling pig-iron) which contains practically no carbon, and which is easily forged, welded, etc., and does not harden when suddenly cooled.—**wrought=iron casting**, casting with, or a casting made from, mitis metal.

wrung (rung). Preterit and past participle of *wring*.

wry (rī), *v.*; *wried, wrying*. [ME. *wrien*, < AS. *wrīgian*, turn, tend: cf. Goth. *wraigs*, crooked, also E. *wrick*.] **I.** *intr.* To turn; twist; wind; also, to turn aside from a course; swerve; deviate from the right course; go astray. [Archaic or prov.] **II.** *tr.* To turn aside; also, to give a twist to; distort; make wry; fig., to pervert. [Archaic or prov. Eng. and Sc.]—**wry**, *a.*; compar. *wryer* or *wrier*, superl. *wryest* or *wriest*. Abnormally bent or turned to one side, or twisted or crooked (as, a *wry* nose); also, distorted or perverted, as in meaning; also, devious in course or purpose; misdirected; also, harsh, cross, or disagreeable (prov.: as, "with few words for any man, and *wry* words for none," Stevenson's "Master of Ballantrae," i.; a *wry* name).—**wry face**, or **wry mouth**, a twisted face or mouth; a contortion of the face or mouth indicating displeasure, disgust, pain, or the like; a grimace: as, "to the disgust of Miss Susan Nipper . . . making *wry faces* behind the door" (Dickens's "Dombey and Son," v.); "to . . . die like a man, without making *wry mouths*" (Scott's "Quentin Durward," xxxiv.).—**wry′ly**, *adv.*—**wry′neck**, *n.* In *pathol.*, torticollis; in *ornith.*, any of the scansorial birds constituting the genus *Iynx*, allied to the woodpeckers, and notable for their peculiar manner of twisting the neck and head.—**wry′=necked**, *a.* Having a wry or twisted neck; afflicted with wryneck.—**wry′ness**, *n.*

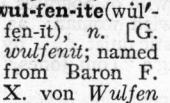

Common Wryneck of Europe (*Iynx torquilla*).

wul-fen-ite (wŭl′fen-īt), *n.* [G. *wulfenit*; named from Baron F. X. von *Wulfen* (1728–1805), Austrian scientist.] A mineral consisting of lead molybdate, occurring usually in tabular crystals, and varying in color from grayish to bright yellow or red.

wur-ley (wèr′li), *n.*; pl. *-leys* (-liz). [Also *wurlie*; native Australian.] In South Australia, a hut of the aborigines; a native hut.

wuth-er (wuᴛʜ′èr), *v. i.* [Also *wudder, whuther, whither*; prob. from Scand.] To blow with a roaring sound, as the wind; bluster; also, to rush noisily; whiz. [North. Eng. and Sc.]—**wuth′er**, *n.* A wuthering sound or movement: as, "the '*wuther*' of wind amongst trees" (C. Brontë's "Villette," xvi.). [North. Eng. and Sc.]

Wy-an-dotte (wī′an-dot), *n.* [From the *Wyandotte*, or *Wyandot*, Indians.] One of an American breed of medium-sized, hardy domestic fowls, valuable for eggs and for the table.

wych′=elm′, wych′=ha′zel. See *witch-elm, witch-hazel*.

Wyc-lif-ite, Wyc-liff-ite (wik′lif-īt). **I.** *n.* A follower of John Wyclif, or Wycliffe (died 1384), the English religious reformer; a Lollard. **II.** *a.* Of or pertaining to Wyclif or the Wyclifites.

wye (wī), *n.* The letter Y, or something having a similar shape.

wynd (wīnd), *n.* [= *wind*[1], *n.*] An alley between houses; a narrow lane or street: as, "It was up a *wynd* off a side street in St. Bride's that Jessie had her lodging" (Stevenson's "Master of Ballantrae," ii.). [Sc. and north. Eng.]

wy-vern (wī′vèrn), *n.* See *wivern*.

X

X[1], x[1] (eks); pl. *X's, x's* (ek'sez). A consonant, the 24th letter of the English alphabet.—**X[1], x[1]**, *n.*; pl. *X's, x's* (ek'sez). A term often used to designate a person, thing, agency, factor, or the like whose true name is unknown or withheld (from the use of *x* in mathematics to denote an unknown quantity); also, an electromagnetic disturbance due to atmospheric electricity, causing a false signal or interference in wireless telegraphy; a static disturbance or interference; also (from the Roman numeral X, meaning 'ten,' on some issues), a ten-dollar bill (colloq., U. S.).

X[2]. A symbol derived from the Greek letter X (see *chi*), usually rendered in English as *Ch*, used in certain abbreviated forms, as *Xmas, Xtian*, for *Christmas, Christian*.

xan-thate (zan'thāt), *n.* In *chem.*, a salt of xanthic acid.

xan-the-in (zan'thē-in), *n.* [See *xanthin.*] That part of the yellow coloring matter in yellow flowers which is soluble in water. Cf. *xanthin.*

Xan-thi-an (zan'thi-an), *a.* Of or pertaining to Xanthus, an ancient town in Asia Minor: as, the *Xanthian* sculptures or marbles (a collection of ancient sculptures, chiefly sepulchral, from the neighborhood of Xanthus, preserved in the British Museum).

xan-thic (zan'thik), *a.* [Gr. ξανθός, yellow.] Yellow (applied esp. to a series of colors in flowers including the yellows and all colors which tend toward yellow); in *chem.*, of or pertaining to xanthine (as, *xanthic* oxide, xanthine); also, noting or pertaining to an organic acid occurring as a colorless, oily liquid with a penetrating smell, and having its copper salt bright yellow.

xan-thin (zan'thin), *n.* [Gr. ξανθός, yellow: cf. *xanthein.*] That part of the yellow coloring matter in yellow flowers which is insoluble in water (cf. *xanthein*); also, a yellow coloring matter contained in madder; in *chem.*, xanthine.

xan-thine (zan'thin), *n.* [Gr. ξανθός, yellow.] In *chem.*, a crystalline nitrogenous compound closely related to uric acid, found in urine, blood, and certain animal and vegetable tissues.

Xan-thip-pe, Xan-tip-pe (zan-thip'ē or -tip'ē, -tip'ē), *n.* [Commonly *Xantippe*; from *Xanthippe*, wife of Socrates.] A scolding or ill-tempered wife; a shrewish woman: as, "An arrant vixen of a wife soured his domestic quiet . . . by this *Xanthippe* he had two sons" (Fielding's "Tom Jones," viii. 11).

xan-tho-chro-ic (zan-thō-krō'ik), *a.* [Gr. ξανθόχροος, yellow-skinned, < ξανθός, yellow, + χρόα, skin, complexion.] Light-colored; belonging or pertaining to the light-complexioned or light-haired peoples of the white race. Cf. *melanochroic.*

xan-thone (zan'thōn), *n.* [Gr. ξανθός, yellow.] In *chem.*, a white crystalline organic compound obtained by heating salicylic acid with acetic anhydride and in other ways, and regarded as the parent substance of various natural coloring matters.

xan-tho-phyl, xan-tho-phyll (zan'thō-fil), *n.* [Gr. ξανθός, yellow, + φύλλον, leaf.] In *bot.*, the peculiar yellow coloring matter left in autumn leaves after the disappearance of the chlorophyl.

xan-thop-si-a (zan-thop'si-ä), *n.* [NL., < Gr. ξανθός, yellow, + ὄψις, sight.] Defective vision in which all objects appear to be tinged with yellow, as after the administration of santonin.

xan-thous (zan'thus), *a.* [Gr. ξανθός, yellow.] Yellow; in *anthropol.*, having yellow or light hair; also, noting or pertaining to the peoples with a yellow complexion (the Mongolians).

Xan-tip-pe (zan-tip'ē), *n.* See *Xanthippe.*

xe-bec (zē'bek), *n.* [= F. *chebec* = It. *sciabecco* = Sp. *xabeque*, now *jabeque*, = Pg. *xaveco*; said to be from Turkish.] A small three-masted vessel of the Mediterranean, formerly much used by corsairs, and now employed to some extent in commerce. See cut in next column.

xe-ni-a (zē'ni-ä), *n.* [NL., < Gr. ξένιος, pertaining to a guest or to hospitality, < ξένος, guest.] In *bot.*, the immediate influence or effect of pollen on the seed or fruit which is pollinated rather than on the seed or fruit of a plant which springs from the pollinated seed.

xe-ni-al (zē'ni-al), *a.* [Gr. ξενία, hospitality, < ξένος, guest.] Pertaining to hospitality, or the relations between a host and his guest, esp. in ancient Greece.

Xebec.

xeno-. Form of Gr. ξένος, guest, stranger, also foreign, strange, used in combination.

xen-o-do-chei-on (zen″ō-dō-kē'on), *n.*; pl. *-cheia* (-kē'ä). [Gr. ξενοδοχεῖον, < ξένος, guest, stranger, + δέχεσθαι, receive.] In Greek use, a lodging-place for strangers; an inn; a hotel.

xe-nog-a-my (zē-nog'a-mi), *n.* [See *xeno-* and *-gamy.*] In *bot.*, fertilization in which the pollination of a flower is effected by pollen from a flower of another plant.—**xe-nog'a-mous,** *a.*

xen-o-gen-e-sis (zen-ō-jen'e-sis), *n.* [See *xeno-* and *genesis.*] In *biol.*, heterogenesis; also, the supposed generation of offspring completely and permanently different from the parent. Also **xe-nog-e-ny** (zē-noj'e-ni).—**xen″o-ge-net'ic** (-jē-net'ik), **xen-o-gen'ic** (-jen'ik), *a.*

xen-o-ma-ni-a (zen-ō-mā'ni-ä), *n.* [NL.: see *xeno-* and *mania.*] A mania or inordinate fondness for what is foreign: as, "a command of pure English, unadulterated by *xenomania*" (Saintsbury's "Hist. of Elizabethan Literature," iv.).—**xen-o-ma'ni-ac** (-ak), *n.*

xen-o-mor-phic (zen-ō-môr'fik), *a.* [See *xeno-* and *-morphic.*] Having a form not properly its own; noting or pertaining to a mineral constituent of a rock, which does not have its own characteristic crystalline form, but a form forced upon it by other constituents of the rock. Cf. *idiomorphic.*—**xen-o-mor'phi-cal-ly,** *adv.*

xen-on (zen'on), *n.* [NL., < Gr. ξένον, neut. of ξένος, foreign, strange.] Chem. sym., Xe (or X); at. wt., 130.2. A heavy, colorless, chemically inactive, monatomic gaseous element present in the atmosphere in very small quantities.

xen-o-pho-bi-a (zen-ō-fō'bi-ä), *n.* [NL.: see *xeno-* and *-phobia.*] Fear or hatred of foreigners.

xe-ro-der-ma (zē-rō-dèr'mä), *n.* [NL., < Gr. ξηρός, dry, + δέρμα, skin.] In *pathol.*, a disease in which the skin becomes dry and hard, and usually scaly.

xe-ro-ma (zē-rō'mä), *n.* [NL., < Gr. ξηρός, dry: see *-oma.*] Same as *xerophthalmia.*

xe-roph-a-gy (zē-rof'a-ji), *n.* [LL. *xerophagia*, < Gr. ξηροφαγία, < ξηρός, dry, + φαγεῖν, eat.] The habit of living on dry food; esp., a form of abstinence, as in the early church, in which only bread, herbs, salt, and water were consumed.

xe-roph-i-lous (zē-rof'i-lus), *a.* [Gr. ξηρός, dry, + φίλος, loving.] Loving dryness; of plants, growing in, or adapted for existence in, dry, esp. dry and hot, regions.

xe-roph-thal-mi-a (zē-rof-thal'mi-ä), *n.* [LL., < Gr. ξηροφθαλμία, < ξηρός, dry, + ὀφθαλμός, eye.] In *pathol.*, abnormal dryness of the eyeball, usually due to long-continued conjunctivitis.

xe-ro-phyte (zē'rō-fīt), *n.* [Gr. ξηρός, dry, + φυτόν, plant.] A plant adapted for growth in very dry ground.—**xe-ro-phyt'ic** (-fit'ik), *a.*

xe-ro-sis (zē-rō'sis), *n.* [NL., < Gr. ξήρωσις, a drying up, < ξηρός, dry.] In *pathol.*, abnormal dryness, as of the skin or the eyeball.—**xe-rot'ic** (-rot'ik), *a.*

---

fat, fāte, fär, fȧll, ȧsk, fãre; net, mē, hėr; pin, pīne; not, nōte, mŏve, nôr; up, lūte, půll; oi, oil; ou, out; (lightened) aviäry, ēlect, agǫny, intǫ, ūnite; (obscured) errạnt, operä, ardẹnt, actǫr, natũre; ch, chip; g, go; th, thin; ᴛʜ, then; y, you;

xi (zī or ksē), n. [Gr. ξῖ.] The fourteenth letter (Ξ, ξ, = English X, x) of the Greek alphabet.

xiph-i-oid (zif′i-oid), a. [Gr. ξιφίας, swordfish (< ξίφος, sword), + εἶδος, form.] Resembling the swordfish; belonging to the *Xiphiidæ*, or swordfish family.

xiph-i-ster-num (zif-i-stėr′num), n.; pl. -na (-nạ). [NL., < Gr. ξίφος, sword, + NL. *sternum*.] The hindmost (or, in man, the lowermost) segment or division of the sternum.

xiph-oid (zif′oid or zī′foid). [Gr. ξιφοειδής, < ξίφος, sword, + εἶδος, form.] **I.** a. Sword-shaped; ensiform: as, the *xiphoid* process (the xiphisternum); the *xiphoid* cartilage (the xiphisternum when wholly or partly cartilaginous). **II.** n. The xiphisternum.—**xi-phoi-dal** (zi-foi′dạl or zī-), a.

xiph-o-phyl-lous (zif-ō-fil′us), a. [Gr. ξίφος, sword, + φύλλον, leaf.] In bot., having sword-shaped or ensiform leaves.

Xmas (kris′mạs, often popularly eks′mạs), n. Abbreviated form of *Christmas*, in which *X* represents the Greek X, usually rendered in English as *Ch*. See *X²*.

X=ray (eks′rā′). [From the mathematical use of *x* for an unknown quantity.] **I.** n. One of the Röntgen rays (usually in pl.: see under *Röntgen*); also, a radiograph made by means of X-rays. **II.** a. Of or pertaining to X-rays, or Röntgen rays: as, an *X-ray* tube (a vacuum-tube in which X-rays are produced); an *X-ray* examination.—**X′=ray′**, v. t. To make an X-ray radiograph of; also, to examine by means of X-rays; also, to treat with X-rays.

xy-lem (zī′lem), n. [G., < Gr. ξύλον, wood.] In bot., that part of a vascular bundle which consists of tracheids and immediately associated cells, forming the woody portion; woody tissue. Cf. *phloëm*.

xy-lene (zī′lēn), n. [Gr. ξύλον, wood.] In chem., any of three isomeric hydrocarbons of the benzene series, occurring as oily, colorless liquids obtained chiefly from coal-tar, and used in the manufacture of dyes, etc.—**xy′lic**, a. In chem., designating or pertaining to any of several isomeric acids which are derivatives of xylene.—**xy′li-dine** (-li-din), n. In chem., any of six isomeric compounds, derivatives of xylene, which resemble aniline; esp., an oily liquid consisting of a mixture of certain of these compounds, used commercially in the manufacture of dyes.

xylo-. Form of Gr. ξύλον, wood, used in combination.—**xy-lo-carp** (zī′lō-kärp), n. [+ -carp.] In bot., a hard and woody fruit.—**xy-lo-car′pous**, a.—**xy′lo-gen** (-jen), n. [+ -gen.] In bot., wood or xylem in a formative state; also, lignin.

xy-log-ly-phy (zī-log′li-fi), n. [Cf. Gr. ξυλογλύφος, carving wood, < ξύλον, wood, + γλύφειν, carve.] The art of carving in wood.

xy-lo-graph (zī′lō-gráf), n. [See *xylo-* and *-graph*.] An engraving on wood, or a print from such an engraving.—**xy-log′ra-pher** (-log′rạ-fėr), n. An engraver on wood.—**xy-log′ra-phy**, n. [See *-graphy*.] The art of engraving on wood, or of printing from such engravings.—**xy-lo-graph′ic**, **xy-lo-graph′i-cal** (-graf′ik, -i-kạl), a.

xy-loid (zī′loid), a. [Gr. ξυλοειδής, < ξύλον, wood, + εἶδος, form.] Resembling wood; of the nature of wood; ligneous.

xy-lol (zī′lol or -lōl), n. Same as *xylene*.

xy-lol-o-gy (zī-lol′ō-ji), n. [See *xylo-* and *-logy*.] The study of the structure of wood.

xy-lo-nite (zī′lō-nīt), n. [Gr. ξύλον, wood.] Celluloid.

xy-loph-a-gous (zī-lof′ạ-gus), a. [Gr. ξυλοφάγος, < ξύλον, wood, + φαγεῖν, eat.] Eating wood, as the larvæ of certain insects; lignivorous; also, perforating or destroying timber, as certain mollusks and crustaceans.

xy-lo-phone (zī′lō-fōn or zil′ō-), n. [See *xylo-* and *-phone*.] A musical instrument consisting of a graduated series of wooden bars, usually sounded by striking with small wooden hammers.—**xy-lo-phon-ist** (zī′lō-fō-nist or zil′ō-), n. One who plays on a xylophone.

xy-lot-o-mist (zī-lot′ō-mist), n. One skilled or versed in xylotomy.

Xylophone.

xy-lot-o-mous (zī-lot′ō-mus), a. [Gr. ξύλον, wood, + -τόμος, cutting, < τέμνειν, cut.] Boring into or cutting wood, as certain insects.

xy-lot-o-my (zī-lot′ō-mi), n. [Gr. ξύλον, wood, + -τομία, a cutting, < τέμνειν, cut.] The art of cutting sections of wood, as with a microtome, for microscopic examination.

xy-lyl (zī′lil), n. [Gr. ξύλον, wood: see *-yl*.] In chem., a univalent radical, C_8H_9, regarded as a part of xylene.—**xy′ly-lene** (-li-lēn), n. In chem., a bivalent radical, C_8H_8, regarded as a part of xylene.

xyst (zist), n. [L. *xystus*, < Gr. ξυστός, prop. adj., smoothed or polished (with reference to the floor), < ξύειν, scrape, smooth.] Among the ancient Greeks, a portico or covered space in a gymnasium, in which athletes exercised in winter or in stormy weather; among the ancient Romans, a walk in a garden, between rows of trees or the like.

xys-ter (zis′tėr), n. [NL., < Gr. ξυστήρ, tool for scraping, < ξύειν, scrape.] A surgical instrument for scraping bones.

xys-tos, xys-tus (zis′tos, -tus), n. Same as *xyst*.

Y

Y¹, y¹ (wī); pl. *Y′s, y′s* (wīz). A consonant and vowel (or semivowel), the 25th letter of the English alphabet.—**Y¹**, n.; pl. *Y′s* (wīz). Something resembling the letter Y in shape, as a forked clamp for holding drills, a forked support for the telescope of a surveyor's level, etc.

y². A symbol derived from the Anglo-Saxon letter þ (see *thorn*), equivalent to *th*, used in certain old word-forms or abbreviations, as *ye* for *the* (see *ye³*), or *yat* or *yt* for *that*.

y-. [ME. *y-*, *i-*, < AS. *ge-*.] A prefix common in Middle English use, esp. in past participles, still seen in a few archaic words, as *yclad*, *ycleped*, and *ywis* (for *iwis*).

-y¹. [AS. *-ig*.] An adjective suffix meaning 'full of,' 'composed of,' 'containing,' 'having,' 'characterized by,' 'like,' etc., as in *dewy, icy, juicy, salty, watery*. Cf. *-ey*.

-y². A diminutive suffix of nouns, as in *baby, deary*, used esp. in familiar forms of personal names, or of names of animals, or in other familiar epithets, as in *Billy, Jacky, doggy, pussy, aunty, blacky, darky*. Cf. *-ie*.

-y³. [F. *-ie*, < L. *-ia*, in part < Gr. *-ία*.] A suffix of nouns (many of which are abstract), as in *family, fury, glory, history, theory*. Cf. *-ery*.

yacht (yot), n. [D. *jacht*, yacht, fast-sailing vessel, also chase, hunting (= G. *jagd*), < *jagen* (= G. *jagen*), drive, chase, hunt: cf. *jäger*.] A boat propelled by sail, engine, or motor, and used for pleasure-trips or private cruising, for racing, or the like.—**yacht**, v. i. To sail, voyage, or race in a yacht.—**yacht′er**, n.—**yacht′ing**, n. The art of navigating a yacht; the practice or sport of sailing or voyaging in a yacht.—**yachts′man** (-mạn), n.; pl. *-men*. One who owns or sails a yacht.—**yachts′man-ship**, n.

yaf-fin-gale (yaf′ing-gāl), n. Same as *yaffle*. [Local, Eng.]

yaf-fle (yaf′l), n. [Imit. of its laughing cry.] The hickwall, or green woodpecker, *Gecinus viridis*: as, "A *yaffle* laughed a field or two away" (Galsworthy's "Country House," ii. 2). [Prov. Eng.]

ya-ger (yā′gėr), n. See *jäger*.

Ya-hoo (yä-hö′), n. In Swift's "Gulliver's Travels," iv., one of a race of brutes having the form of man and all his degrading passions, who are subject to the Houyhnhnms, a race of horses endowed with reason; hence [l. c.], a rough, coarse, or uncouth person (as, "a mere *yahoo* of a stable boy": R. Graves's "Spiritual Quixote," iv. 10); a lout.

(variable) ḍ as d or j, ṣ as s or sh, ṭ as t or ch, ẓ as z or zh; o, F. cloche; ü, F. menu; ċh, Sc. loch; ṅ, F. bonbon; ′, primary accent; ″, secondary accent; †, obsolete; <, from; +, and; =, equals. See also lists at beginning of book.

Yah-weh (yä′wā), n. [Heb.: see *Jehovah*.] A name of God in the Hebrew text of the Old Testament: often used by writers on the religion of the Hebrews. See *Jehovah*.— **Yah′wism**, n. The religion of the ancient Hebrews, as based on the worship of Yahweh as the national deity; also, the use of *Yahweh* as the name of God. — **Yah′wist**, n. The writer (or writers) of certain parts of the Hebrew text of the Hexateuch in which God is spoken of as *Yahweh* (or Jehovah) instead of *Elohim*. Also called *Jehovist*. See *Elohist*.— **Yah-wis′tic**, a. Of or pertaining to the Yahwist; characterized by the use of *Yahweh* (Jehovah) instead of *Elohim*.

yak (yak), n. [Tibetan.] The wild ox, *Bos* (or *Poëphagus*) *grunniens*, of Tibet, etc., with very long hair, or a domesticated variety.— **yak lace**, heavy lace made from yak hair or wool.

Yak.

Yalta Conference. A meeting of President Roosevelt, Prime Minister Churchill, and Marshal Stalin in the town of Yalta, Crimea (8 days in February, 1945).

yam (yam), n. [Pg. *inhame* or Sp. *igname*, *ñame*, = F. *igname*; prob. of African origin.] The starchy, tuberous root of any of various climbing vines of the genus *Dioscorea*, much cultivated for food in the warmer regions of both hemispheres; also, any of these plants; also, the sweet potato (southern U. S.); also, the common white potato (Sc.).

ya-men, ya-mun (yä′men, -mun), n. [Chinese.] The official residence of a Chinese mandarin, including offices, court-rooms, prisons, etc.; the headquarters of any department of the public service in China.

yam-mer (yam′ėr), v. [AS. *gēomerian*, mourn, complain, < *gēomor*, sad, mournful; akin to G. *jammer*, lamentation, misery.] **I.** *intr.* To lament, wail, whine, or complain; make an outcry or clamor; talk loudly and persistently. [Now prov. or colloq.] **II.** *tr.* To utter or say in complaint. [Prov. or colloq.]—**yam′mer**, n. The action or an act of yammering; a lamenting or complaining; outcry; clamor; loud, persistent talk. [Now prov. or colloq.]—**yam′mer-er**, n.

Branch of Female Plant of Yam (*Dioscorea alata*).

yank (yangk), v. t. or i. [Origin obscure.] To pull with a sudden jerking motion; jerk: as, to *yank* the reins; "where a lifting foresail-foot is *yanking* at the sheet" (Masefield's "Wanderer's Song"). [Colloq.]—**yank**, n. A sudden jerking pull; a jerk. [Colloq.]

Yan-kee (yang′kē). [Of disputed origin; commonly referred to an Indian corruption of the word *English*; also conjectured to be from D. *Janke*, dim. of *Jan*, John.] **I.** n. A native or inhabitant of New England; by extension, a native or inhabitant of any of the Northern States; a Federal soldier in the American Civil War; also, any native or inhabitant of the U. S. **II.** a. Of, pertaining to, or characteristic of the Yankees: as, "*Yankee* shrewdness" (Thoreau's "Walden," i.).—**Yan′kee-dom** (-dom), n. The region inhabited by the Yankees; also, Yankees collectively.—**Yan′kee-ism**, n. Yankee character or characteristics; also, a Yankee peculiarity, as of speech.

yap (yap), v.; *yapped*, *yapping*. [Imit.] **I.** *intr.* To yelp (as, "The dog began again to *yap* and moan": Arnold Bennett's "Riceyman Steps," v. 5); bark snappishly; also, to talk snappishly, noisily, or foolishly (as, "Next thing, I suppose you'll be *yapping* about free speech": Sinclair Lewis's "Main Street," xxxvi.); also, to cry, as a child. [Prov. or slang.] **II.** *tr.* To utter by yapping. [Slang.]— **yap**, n. A yelp (as, "Margery's puppies lifted their shrill *yap*": Eden Phillpotts's "Children of Men," Prologue, iii.); a snappish bark; also, snappish, noisy, or foolish talk; an utterance of this kind; also, crying, or a cry, as of a child; also, a yelping dog; a peevish or noisy person; a crying child. [Prov. or slang.]

ya-pok (ya-pok′), n. [From the river *Oyapok*, between French Guiana and Brazil.] A small South and Central American aquatic opossum, *Chironectes variegatus* (or *minimus*), with webbed hind feet and variegated fur.

Yapok.

ya-pon, yau-pon (yâ′pon), n. [N. Amer. Ind.] An aquifoliaceous shrub or small tree, *Ilex vomitoria*, a species of holly, of the southern U. S., with leaves which are sometimes used as a substitute for tea. Cf. *Appalachian tea* and *cassioberry*.

yapp (yap). [From the name of a London bookseller for whom the style was first made.] **I.** a. Designating or pertaining to a style of bookbinding in limp leather or the like with projecting flaps overlapping the edges of the pages: used esp. on Bibles. **II.** n. Yapp binding.—**yapped** (yapt), a. Made in the yapp style.

yard[1] (yärd), n. [AS. *geard* = D. and Dan. *gaard* = Icel. *gardhr*, yard, = Goth. *gards*, house; akin to L. *hortus*, garden, *cohors*, inclosure, Gr. χόρτος, yard: cf. *garth*, *garden*, *court*, and *gird*[1].] A piece of inclosed ground of small or moderate size adjoining or surrounding a house or other building, or surrounded by it; a piece of inclosed ground for use as a garden, for animals, or for some other purpose (as, a kale*yard*; a poultry-*yard*; a grave*yard*); an inclosure within which any work or business is carried on (as, a brick*yard*; a navy-*yard*); a space with tracks, etc., adjacent to a railroad-station or terminus, used for the switching or making up of trains, the accommodation of rolling-stock, etc.; also, the winter pasture or browsing-ground of moose and deer.—

yard[1], v. **I.** *tr.* To put into or inclose in a yard: as, "Well, lad, suppose we *yard* these rams?" (H. Kingsley's "Geoffry Hamlyn," xxxi.). **II.** *intr.* To resort to winter pastures, as moose or deer; also, to shoot moose or deer in their winter pastures.

yard[2] (yärd), n. [AS. *gierd* = OHG. *gerta* (G. *gerte*), rod; akin to E. *gad*[2].] A rod† or stick†; a branch† or twig†; a staff†; a wand of office or authority†; also, a measuring-rod†; a yardstick†; also, a unit of linear measure, equal to 3 feet, or 36 inches (0.9144 meter), used in England, the U. S., etc. (see *long measure*, under *long*[1], a.); also, *naut.*, a long cylindrical spar with a taper toward each end, slung crosswise to a mast and used for suspending a square sail, lateen sail, or the like.

yard-age[1] (yär′dāj), n. The use of a yard or inclosure, as in lading or unlading cattle, etc., at a railroad-station; also, the charge made for such use.

yard-age[2] (yär′dāj), n. Measurement, or the amount measured, in yards.

yard=arm (yärd′ärm), n. *Naut.*, either end of a yard of a square sail.

yard=grass (yärd′gras), n. A coarse annual grass, *Eleusine indica*, a native of the Old World, common in dooryards and fields.

---

fat, fāte, fär, fåll, åsk, fâre; net, mē, hėr; pin, pīne; not, nōte, mŏve, nôr; up, lūte, pull; oi, oil; ou, out; (lightened) aviăry, ēlect, agŏny, intŏ, ŭnite; (obscured) errant, operä, ardent, actor, natŭre; ch, chip; g, go; th, thin; ᴛʜ, then; y, you;

yard-stick (yärd′stik), *n.* A stick a yard long, commonly marked with subdivisions, used to measure with; fig., any standard of measurement. Also (archaic) **yard′=wand.**

yare (yār), *a.* [AS. *gearu* = OS. *garu* = OHG. *garo* (G. *gar*) = Icel. *görr*, ready: see *gear*.] Ready or prepared; prompt; brisk or quick; of a ship, answering quickly to the helm, or swift. [Archaic or prov.]—**yare, yare′ly,** *adv.*

yarn (yärn), *n.* [AS. *gearn* = D. *garen* = G. *garn* = Icel., Sw., and Dan. *garn*, yarn.] Thread spun from wool or other fibrous material, esp. that prepared for weaving or for knitting, etc., as distinguished from sewing-thread; a variety of such thread; also, the thread, in the form of a loosely twisted aggregate of fibers, as of hemp, of which rope is made ('rope-yarn'); one of the aggregates or threads so twisted, of which several twisted together form a strand; also, a story or tale, esp. one fabricated by the teller as he relates it (as, to spin a *yarn* of the sea; sailors' *yarns*); any tale of adventure, extraordinary occurrences, or the like, esp. a tale that is highly improbable.—**yarn,** *v. i.* To spin a yarn; tell stories.

yar-row (yar′ō), *n.* [AS. *gearwe* = D. *gerw* = G. *garbe*, yarrow.] An asteraceous plant, *Achillea millefolium*, of Europe and America, with finely divided leaves and whitish flowers, sometimes used in medicine as a tonic and astringent; milfoil; also, any of various other plants of the genus *Achillea* (cf. *sneezewort*).

yash-mak (yash′mak), *n.* [Ar.] The veil worn by Mohammedan women in public.

yat-a-ghan (yat′ȧ-gan), *n.* [Turk.] A sword used by Mohammedans, peculiar in having no guard

Yarrow (*Achillea millefolium*), upper part of stem with heads.—*a*, head; *b*, disk-flower; *c*, ray-flower.

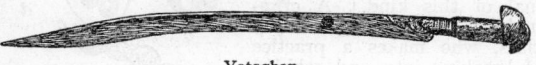
Yataghan.

for the hand and no crosspiece, but usually a large and often decorative pommel.

yaul (yâl), **yaup** (yâp). See *yawl*[1], *yawp*.

yau-pon (yâ′pon), *n.* See *yapon*.

yaw[1] (yâ), *v.* [Cf. Icel. *jaga*, move to and fro.] **I.** *intr.* To deviate temporarily from the straight course, as a vessel (as, "She [a boat] *yawed* sharply and seemed to change her course": Stevenson's "Treasure Island," xxiii.); turn from side to side in the course; in general, to turn from the course or go unsteadily (as, "a peculiar walk in this old man, a certain slight but painful appearing *yawing* in his gait": H. Melville's "Moby-Dick," cxii.); specif., of an aircraft, to have a motion about its vertical axis; of a projectile, to move with a yaw. **II.** *tr.* To cause to yaw.—**yaw**[1], *n.* An act of yawing; a movement of deviation from the direct course, as of a vessel (as, "The schooner in front of me gave a violent *yaw*, turning, perhaps, through twenty degrees": Stevenson's "Treasure Island," xxiii.); specif., a motion of an aircraft about its vertical axis; an angle (to the right or left) between the direction of progress of an aircraft and its (vertical and longitudinal) plane of symmetry; also, an angle between the axis of a projectile and the direction of motion of the center of gravity.

yaw[2] (yâ), *n.* [Back-formation from *yaws*.] In *pathol.*, one of the tubercles or excrescences characteristic of the disease yaws or frambœsia.—**yaw′ey** (-i), *a.*

yawl[1] (yâl), *v. i.* [ME. *yaulen*, also *youlen*; imit.: cf. *yowl* and *yell*.] To yowl or howl, as an animal or a person: as,

"They [savages] all ran screaming and *yawling* away, with a kind of howling noise" (Defoe's "Robinson Crusoe," ii. 5). [Now prov. or colloq.]—**yawl**[1], *n.* A yowl; a howl. [Prov. or colloq.]

yawl[2] (yâl), *n.* [D. *jol*.] A ship's small boat, usually rowed by four or six oars; also, a fore-and-aft rigged vessel with two masts, a large mainmast (nearer the bow) and a much smaller jigger-mast (nearer the stern, and set far aft, usually behind the rudder).

yawn (yân), *v.* [Cf. AS. *geonian*, *ginian*, and *gānian*, yawn, akin to Icel. *gīna*, G. *gähnen*, yawn, gape.] **I.** *intr.* To open the mouth wide, as if to swallow something (obs. or archaic); open wide, as the mouth, jaws, etc.; open wide like a mouth (as, the earth *yawns* in an earthquake; "Graves, *yawn* and yield your dead," Shakspere's "Much Ado about Nothing," v. 3. 19); stand or lie wide open (as, "The big French window . . . *yawned* inviting," H. G. Wells's "Tono-Bungay," iii. 2. § 2; "a *yawning* bag," Arnold Bennett's "Old Wives' Tale," ii. 2; *yawning* wounds); extend or stretch wide, as an open (and usually deep) space (as, a *yawning* gulf, chasm, or abyss); also, specif., to open the mouth involuntarily with a prolonged, deep inspiration, as from drowsiness or weariness (as, "Dick staggered away rubbing his eyes and *yawning*": Kipling's "Light That Failed," vi.); also, to stand or stare open-mouthed, or gape, as in wonder (obs. or prov. Eng.); also, to long hungrily or eagerly†. **II.** *tr.* To open wide, or lay open, as if by yawning (chiefly poetic: as, "None felt stern Nature rocking at his feet, And *yawning* forth a grave," Byron's "Childe Harold," iv. 63); also, to say with a yawn (as, " 'I have had a most refreshing slumber, Mr. Goslett,' he *yawned*": Besant's "All Sorts and Conditions of Men," x.); also, to have or give (a yawn: as, "He . . . *yawned* a long irresistible nervous yawn," J. Conrad's "Rover," xii.); also, to bring, put, pass, etc., by yawning or with yawns (as, to *yawn* a person into silence; to *yawn* the time away).—**yawn,** *n.* The act or an act of yawning; an opening wide; specif., an involuntary opening of the mouth with a prolonged, deep inspiration, as from drowsiness or weariness; also, an opening, open space, or chasm.—**yawn′er,** *n.*—**yawn′-ing-ly,** *adv.*—**yawn′y,** *a.* Disposed to yawn: as, "She felt rather sleepy and *yawny*" (Margaret Kennedy's "Constant Nymph," xx.).

yawp (yâp), *v. i.* [Imit.: cf. *yap* and *yelp*.] To utter a loud, harsh cry or sound; bawl; talk noisily and foolishly. [Prov. or colloq.]—**yawp,** *n.* A yawping cry; hence, any harsh or raucous sound (as, "Schlemihl pressed down the button of the motor horn and held it, producing a demanding, infuriating *yawp*": Sinclair Lewis's "Arrowsmith," xxiv.); a poetic outburst or production untrammeled by conventional usages or restraints (orig. or formerly used humorously of the poetry of Walt Whitman); a noisy, foolish utterance. [Prov. or colloq.]—**yawp′y,** *a.* Given to or characterized by yawping. [Prov. or colloq.]

yaws (yâz), *n.* [Origin obscure; perhaps S. Amer.] In *pathol.*, frambœsia.

y-clad (i-klad′), *pp.* [See *y-* and *clothe*.] Clad; clothed: as, "A grave personage . . . *Yclad* in costly garments" (Spenser's "Faerie Queene," iii. 12. 3). [Archaic.]

y-cleped, y-clept (i-klēpt′, i-klept′), *pp.* [See *y-* and *clepe*.] Called; named; styled: as, "the discomfort of the American purification, *yclep'd* 'a house-cleaning' " (Cooper's "Two Admirals," xi.). [Archaic.]

ye[1] (yē), *pron.*; nom. *ye* (also *you*), poss. *your* or *yours*, obj. *you.* [AS. *gē* = OS. *gī* = OHG. *ir* (G. *ihr*) = Icel. *ēr* = Goth. *jus*, ye; akin to Gr. ύμεῖs, Skt. *yūyam*, ye.] Nominative plural of *thou* (as, "Tarry ye here . . . until we come again unto you," Ex. xxiv. 14: now archaic, chiefly in poetry or the solemn style, or prov.); sometimes, used for the objective *you* (as, "Vain pomp and glory of this world, I hate *ye*," Shakspere's "Henry VIII.," iii. 2. 365: archaic or prov.); sometimes, used for the singular (as, "Sweet mother, do *ye* love the child?" Tennyson's "Gareth and Lynette," 35: archaic or prov.).

ye[2] (yē), *pron.* A colloquial or provincial reduction of *you*: as, how d'*ye* do?

ye[3] (ᵺē, also erron. yē), *def. art.* An archaic written or printed form of *the*[1]. See *y*[2].

yea (yā), *adv.* [AS. *gēa* = OHG. *jā* (G. *ja*) = Icel. *jā* = Goth. *ja*, yes: cf. *yes.*] Yes (used in affirmation or assent); also, indeed or truly (used to introduce a sentence or clause): as, "*Yea*, mistress, are you so peremptory?" Shakspere's "Pericles," ii. 5. 73); also, not only so, but also (used in adding something which intensifies and amplifies: as, "I therein do rejoice, *yea*, and will rejoice," Phil. i. 18). [Chiefly archaic.] —**yea**, *n.* An affirmation; an affirmative reply or vote; also, one who votes in the affirmative.

yean (yēn), *v. t.* or *i.* [Earlier *ean*, < AS. *ēanian*, yean; perhaps akin to E. *ewe.*] To bring forth (young), as a sheep or a goat. —**yean'ling**, *n.* The young of a sheep or a goat; a lamb or a kid. [Archaic.]

year (yēr), *n.* [AS. *gēar* = D. *jaar* = G. *jahr* = Icel. *ār* = Goth. *jēr*, year; akin to Gr. ὥρα, time, season, E. *hour.*] A full round of the seasons; the period of the earth's revolution round the sun; in scientific use, the interval between one vernal equinox and the next, or the period of one complete apparent circuit of the ecliptic by the sun ('tropical year,' 'solar year,' or 'astronomical year': being equal to about 365 days, 5 hours, 48 minutes, 46 seconds); also, the true period of the earth's revolution round the sun, the time it takes for the apparent traveling of the sun from a given star back to it again ('sidereal year': being about 20 minutes longer than the tropical year, which is affected by the precession of the equinoxes); hence, the time in which any planet completes a revolution round the sun (as, the *year* of Jupiter); also, a period consisting of 12 lunar months ('lunar year'); in ordinary use, a period of 365 or 366 days, divided into 12 calendar months, now reckoned as beginning Jan. 1 and ending Dec. 31 (the usual 'calendar year'), or a period of approximately the same length in other calendars; hence, a space of 12 calendar months reckoned from any point (as, he left May 15, to be gone a *year*; a fiscal *year*, a period of 12 months at the end of which the accounts of a government, business, or the like, are balanced; the Christian *year*, or church *year*, beginning with Advent); also, a period out of every 12 months, devoted to a certain pursuit, activity, or the like (as, a school, academic, or college *year*, being usually a period of 8, 9, or 10 months devoted to instruction and study, beginning in the fall, and followed by a summer vacation); also, *pl.*, age (as, large for one's *years*; advanced in *years*); sometimes, old age (as, a man of *years*). —**a year and a day**, a period specified as the limit of time in various legal matters, as in determining a right or a liability, in order to allow for a full year by whatever way of counting. —**year by year**, during or with each succeeding year. —**year in, year out**, from the beginning to the end of each succeeding year; always. —**year'=book**, *n.* A book giving facts about the year, its seasons, festivals, dates, etc.; also, a book published annually, each issue containing new or additional information, of general or special nature, in regard to matters pertaining to the year preceding or the year following publication; also, one of a series of books containing chronological reports of cases adjudged or argued in the courts of England during the reigns of the kings from Edward I. to Henry VIII. —**year'ling. I.** *n.* An animal one year old or in the second year of its age; in *horse-racing*, a horse one year old, dating from Jan. 1 of the year of foaling. **II.** *a.* A year old (as, "a *yearling* goat": Defoe's "Robinson Crusoe," i. 16); also, of a year's duration. —**year'long**, *a.* Lasting for a year, or year after year. —**year'ly**, *a.* [AS. *gēarlīc.*] Pertaining to a year, or to each year; done, made, happening, appearing, coming, etc., once a year, or every year (as, a *yearly* trip; *yearly* interest); annual; also, continuing for a year (as, a *yearly* tenancy); lasting but a year (as, a *yearly* plant); also, comprehending, or accomplished in, a year (as, the *yearly* revolution of the earth round the sun). —**year'ly**, *adv.* [AS. *gēarlīce.*] Once a year; annually; in every year; year by year.

yearn (yėrn), *v.* [AS. *geornian, giernan*, < *georn* = OHG. *gern* = Icel. *gjarn* = Goth. *-gairns*, desirous, eager: cf. G. *gern*, *adv.*, willingly, *gier*, eagerness, *begehren*, long for.] **I.†** *tr.* To desire earnestly; also, to grieve (as, "She laments, sir, for it, that it would *yearn* your heart to see it": Shakspere's "Merry Wives of Windsor," iii. 5. 45). **II.** *intr.* To have an earnest or strong desire, or long (as, "*Yearning* for the large excitement . . . Eager-hearted as a boy": Tenny-

son's "Locksley Hall," 111); esp., to have a strong, deep-seated desire tinged with tenderness or sadness (as, to *yearn* to see one's face again; to *yearn* after home; "She *yearned* for reconciliation," W. H. Hudson's "Purple Land," i.); also, to be moved or attracted tenderly (as, "a young girl . . . towards whom my heart *yearned* greatly": George Eliot's "Adam Bede," viii.); also, to grieve† or sorrow†. —**yearn**, *n.* A yearning. —**yearn'ful**, *a.* Full of yearning or longing; also, sorrowful. —**yearn'ful-ly**, *adv.* —**yearn'ing**, *n.* The feeling of one who yearns; deep longing, esp. when tinged with tenderness or sadness, or an instance of it: as, "Her spirit felt . . . the old half-painful *yearning* for she knew not what" (Galsworthy's "Country House," ii. 1); "There were romantic *yearnings* in his heart" (Lytton Strachey's "Queen Victoria," iii.). —**yearn'ing-ly**, *adv.*

yeast (yēst), *n.* [AS. *gist, gyst*, = D. *gest, gist*, = G. *gäscht, gischt*, = Icel. *jastr*, yeast; akin to Gr. ζεῖν, boil.] A yellowish, somewhat viscid, semifluid substance consisting of the aggregated cells of certain minute fungi (see *yeast-plant*), which appears in saccharine liquids (fruit-juices, malt worts, etc.), rising to the top as a froth ('top yeast' or 'surface yeast') or falling to the bottom as a sediment ('bottom yeast' or 'sediment yeast'), employed to induce fermentation in the manufacture of alcoholic liquors, esp. beer, and as a leaven to render bread, etc., light and spongy, and also used in medicine; also, a yeast-plant; also, fig., spume or foam, or a foaming mass (as, "They melt into thy *yeast* of waves": Byron's "Childe Harold," iv. 181); also, ferment or agitation. —**yeast'=cake**, *n.* A small portion of condensed, dried yeast in the form of a cake, used in making bread, etc. —**yeast'=plant**, *n.* Any of the minute, unicellular ascomycetous fungi constituting the genus *Saccharomyces*, esp. *S. cerevisiæ*, or any of certain related fungi, which produce alcoholic fermentation in saccharine liquids. —**yeast'y**, *a.* Of, containing, or resembling yeast; frothy or foamy (as, *yeasty* waves; "*yeasty* waterfalls," G. W. Cable's "John March, Southerner," viii.); also, light, trifling, or frivolous.

yegg (yeg), *n.* [Said to be so called from John *Yegg*, a criminal of this kind.] A criminal, esp. of the roving or tramp class, who makes a practice of breaking into and robbing safes. Also **yegg'man** (-man); *pl.* **-men**.

yelk (yelk), *n.* Archaic or prov. var. of *yolk.*

Yeast-plant (*Saccharomyces cerevisiæ*).— *a*, showing increase by budding; *b*, a cell, showing the formation of the spores; *c*, a cell, containing four mature spores; *d*, the spores; *e*, germinating spores.

yell (yel), *v.* [AS. *giellan*, yell; akin to *galan*, sing: cf. *nightingale*[1].] **I.** *intr.* To cry out with a strong, loud, clear sound (as, the Indians *yelled* as they charged); scream; sometimes, to scream with pain, fright, etc.; shriek. **II.** *tr.* To utter or tell by yelling: as, "half-clad infants . . . *yelling* the names of newspapers" (Arnold Bennett's "Clayhanger," iv. 3). —**yell**, *n.* A cry uttered by yelling; a loud, clear, vigorously uttered cry, as of fury, rage, terror, pain, enthusiasm, etc., or for any reason (as, "A *yell* of despair arose," Motley's "Dutch Republic," iii. 8; "a loud and shrill *yell* of exultation," Scott's "Legend of Montrose," xiv.); also, a cry or shout of fixed character as to sounds or words, adopted and used by members of a particular college, class, or the like. —**yell'er**, *n.*

yel-low (yel'ō), *a.* [AS. *geolu* = D. *geel* = G. *gelb*, yellow; akin to L. *helvus*, light-bay, Gr. χλωρός, greenish-yellow, green, Skt. *hari*, yellow: cf. *gold.*] Of a bright color like that of gold, butter, lemons, etc.; also, having the yellowish skin characteristic of Mongolians; noting or pertaining to the Mongolian race; also, having the yellowish skin characteristic of mulattoes or dark-skinned quadroons (colloq., U. S.: as, a *yellow* boy; a *yellow* girl); also, jaundiced; hence, jealous; envious; also, cowardly, or mean or con-

---

fat, fāte, fär, fåll, ȧsk, fāre; net, mē, hėr; pin, pīne; not, nōte, mŏve, nôr; up, lūte, půll; oi, oil; ou, out; (lightened) aviȧry, ĕlect, agŏny, intŏ, ŭnite; (obscured) errȧnt, operȧ, ardȩnt, actŏr, natṳre; ch, chip; g, go; th, thin; ŦH, then; y, you;

temptible (slang: as, a man with a *yellow* streak; to be *yellow* clear through); also, of newspapers, etc., sensational, esp. morbidly or offensively sensational (colloq.: as, a *yellow* journal; *yellow* journalism).—**yellow arsenic.** Same as *orpiment.*—**yellow avens.** Same as *herb-bennet.*—**yellow clover,** a hop-clover, *Trifolium agrarium,* with yellow flowers.—**yellow daisy.** See under *daisy.*—**yellow fever,** in *pathol.,* a dangerous, often fatal, infectious febrile disease of warm climates, transmitted by the bite of a mosquito, *Aëdes* (or *Stegomyia*) *calopus,* and characterized by jaundice, vomiting, hemorrhages, etc. Cf. *vomito.*—**yellow flag.** See *flag²,* n.—**yellow jack,** yellow fever; also, the (yellow) flag of quarantine.—**yellow jasmine.** See *jasmine* and *gelsemium.*—**yellow lead ore.** Same as *wulfenite.*—**yellow metal,** a yellow alloy consisting of approximately

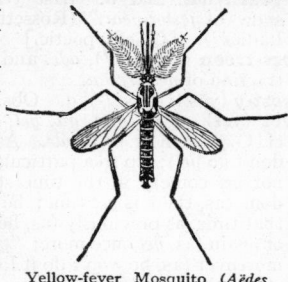
Yellow-fever Mosquito (*Aëdes calopus*).

three parts of copper and two of zinc; also, gold.—**yellow peril,** the danger of a predominance of the yellow race, with its enormous numbers, over the white race and Western civilization generally; also, the yellow race regarded as presenting such a danger.—**yellow pond=lily,** a yellow water-lily (see below).—**yellow poplar,** the tulip-tree, *Liriodendron tulipifera.*—**yellow sapphire,** a transparent yellow variety of sapphire; oriental topaz.—**yellow spot,** in *anat.,* a small, circular yellowish area on the retina, opposite the pupil.—**yellow vision,** xanthopsia.—**yellow warbler,** a small American warbler, *Dendrœca* (or *Dendroica*) *æstiva,* the male of which has a bright-yellow plumage streaked with brown on the under parts.—**yellow water-lily,** a water-lily of the genus *Nymphæa,* usually having yellow flowers.—**yel′low,** *n.* A yellow color; also, a yellow pigment or dye; also, the yolk of an egg. See also *yellows.*

Yellow Warbler, male.

—**yel′low,** *v.* **I.** *tr.* To make yellow: as, "tall trees, whose lightly falling leaves *yellowed* the pavement" (Du Maurier's "Trilby," vi.). **II.** *intr.* To become yellow: as, "the *yellowing* fern" (Mrs. H. Ward's "Robert Elsmère," xix.).

yel-low-bird (yel′ō-bėrd), *n.* Any of various birds of a yellow or golden color, as the golden oriole, *Oriolus galbula,* of Europe, or the yellow warbler, *Dendrœca* (or *Dendroica*) *æstiva,* of America, or a goldfinch, *Chrysomitris* (or *Spinus*) *tristis,* of America.

yel-low=cov-ered (yel′ō-kuv″ėrd), *a.* Covered with yellow; esp., having a yellow paper cover, as a novel; hence (in allusion to the character of many such novels), trashy, as books or fiction.

yel-low-ham-mer (yel′ō-ham″ėr), *n.* [Cf. G. *ammer,* bunting.] A common bunting, *Emberiza citrinella,* of Europe, the male of which is marked with bright yellow; also, the flicker, *Colaptes auratus* (local, U. S.).

yel-low-ish (yel′ō-ish), *a.* Somewhat yellow; tending to yellow.

yel-low=jack-et (yel′ō-jak″et), *n.* Any of several social wasps, or hornets, of the genus *Vespa,* having the body marked with bright yellow.

yel-low-legs (yel′ō-legz), *n.* Either of two American tattlers

(birds), *Totanus flavipes* (the 'lesser yellowlegs') and *T. melanoleucus* (the 'greater yellowlegs'): so called from the color of the legs.

yel-low-ly (yel′ō-li), *adv.* With a yellow color or light.—**yel′low-ness,** *n.*

yel-lows (yel′ōz), *n.* Jaundice, esp. in animals; fig., jealousy†; in *bot.,* a disease of plants, esp. peach-trees, which causes the leaves to turn yellow.

yel-low-tail (yel′ō-tāl), *n.* Any of various fishes with a yellowish tail, as a carangoid fish, *Seriola dorsalis,* of the coast of California, or a rockfish, *Sebastodes flavidus,* also of California, or the menhaden, *Brevoortia tyrannus.*—**yel′low=tailed,** *a.*

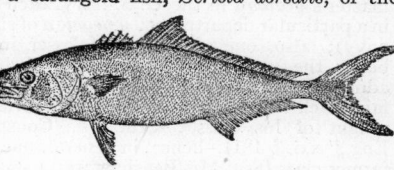
Yellowtail (*Seriola dorsalis*).

yel-low-throat (yel′ō-thrōt), *n.* Any of several American warblers of the genus *Geothlypis,* having a yellow throat, esp. *G. trichas* (the 'Maryland yellowthroat').—**yel′low=throat″ed,** *a.*

yel-low=weed (yel′ō-wēd), *n.* The plant weld; also, any of certain coarse species of goldenrod.

yel-low=wood (yel′ō-wùd), *n.* The hard, yellow wood of *Cladrastis lutea,* a fabaceous tree found locally in the southern U. S., which bears showy white flowers and yields a yellow dye; also, the tree; also, any of various other yellow woods, as that of *Schæfferia frutescens,* a small celastraceous tree of southern Florida and neighboring regions; also, any of the trees yielding these woods.

Yellow-wood (*Cladrastis lutea*). — *a,* pod.

yel-low-y (yel′ō-i), *a.* Yellowish: as, "*yellowy* hair" (Synge's "Well of the Saints," ii.).

yelp (yelp), *v.* [AS. *gielpan,* boast, = Icel. *gjālpa,* yelp: cf. *yap* and *yawp.*] **I.** *intr.* To boast†; also, to give a quick, sharp, shrill cry, as dogs, foxes, etc., and some birds (as, "Some of the dogs . . . were carried down by the current, *yelping* piteously," Parkman's "Oregon Trail," ix.; "Let the wild Leanheaded eagles *yelp* alone," Tennyson's "Princess," vii. 196); bark or cry sharply and shrilly; hence, of persons, to call or cry out sharply; speak or write in spiteful criticism or attack. **II.** *tr.* To utter or express by or as by yelps: as, "Martin *yelped* the last words from the step at the back of the ambulance" (Sinclair Lewis's "Arrowsmith," xi.). —**yelp,** *n.* A boast†; also, a quick, sharp bark or cry, as of a dog; any utterance or sound suggestive of the yelping of a dog.—**yelp′er,** *n.*

yen (yen), *n.*; pl. *yen.* [Jap., < Chinese *yüan,* round, dollar.] The gold monetary unit of Japan, equal to 100 sen, or about 49¼ U. S. cents; also, a silver coin of this value, formerly current.

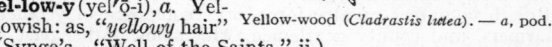

Obverse.

Reverse.
Silver Yen.

yeo-man (yō′man), *n.*; pl. -men. [ME. *yoman, yeman*; origin uncertain: cf. ME. *yong man,* servant, attendant,

---

(variable) d̯ as d or j, s̯ as s or sh, t̯ as t or ch, z̯ as z or zh; *o,* F. cloche; ü, F. menu; c̆h, Sc. loch; n̊, F. bonbon; ′, primary accent; ″, secondary accent; †, obsolete; <, from; +, and; =, equals. See also lists at beginning of book.

lit. 'young man' (AS. *geong man*), also OFries. *gāman*, villager, *gāfolk*, village people, *gā*, *gō*, D. *gouw*, G. *gau*, Goth. *gawi*, district, province, country.] A servant, attendant, or subordinate official in a royal or other great household (archaic or hist.: as, *yeoman* of the buttery, the wardrobe, or the chamber; *yeoman* of the guard, see phrase below); a subordinate or assistant, as of a sheriff or other official or in a craft or trade (archaic or hist.); a petty officer in the navy (as, a ship's *yeoman*, an engineer's *yeoman*, or a paymaster's *yeoman* in the U. S. navy, each in charge of stores in a particular department; a *yeoman* of signals in the British navy); also, one of a class of lesser freeholders (ranking below the gentry) who cultivated their own land, early admitted in England to political rights (as, "It was only the fairly well-to-do *yeoman* who could contribute to the political weight of his class": Stubbs's "Constitutional Hist. of Eng.," xxi. § 481); hence, in general, one of the landowning farmer class (as, "Mr. Benshaw was a small holder, a sturdy English *yeoman* of the new school": H. G. Wells's "Bealby," vii.); sometimes, a tenant farmer; also, one coming from the farming class (as, "the *yeomen* who drew the bow [at Crecy and Poitiers] . . . accustomed to use it in their native fields," Hallam's "Europe during the Middle Ages," i. 2; "The Roman legionaries were no longer *yeomen* taken from the plough," Froude's "Cæsar," xiv.); also, a member of the yeomanry cavalry (Eng.).—**yeoman of the guard**, a member of the body-guard of the English sovereign, instituted in 1485, which now consists of 100 men (with their officers), retaining the picturesque old-time uniform and carrying a halberd, and having duties which are purely ceremonial; sometimes (erroneously), one of the warders of the Tower of London, who wear a similar uniform. Cf. *beef-eater*.—**yeoman's** (or **yeoman**) **service**, good, useful, or substantial service: as, "I once did hold it . . . A baseness to write fair . . . but, sir, now It did me *yeoman's service*" (Shakspere's "Hamlet," v. 2. 36).—**yeo′man-ly**, *a.* Of the condition or rank of a yeoman; pertaining to or befitting a yeoman.—**yeo′man-ly**, *adv.* Like or as befits a yeoman.—**yeo′man-ry**, *n.* Yeomen collectively; hence, a British volunteer cavalry force, orig. composed of yeomen, farmers, and county gentlemen, which now forms part of the British Territorial Army.—**yeo′wom″an**, *n.*; pl. *-women* (-wim″en). A woman enlisted as a yeoman in the U. S. navy.

yer-ba (yer′bä), *n.* [Sp., < L. *herba*, E. *herb*.] An herb or plant (used in various Spanish plant-names); esp. (for *yerba de mate*, 'herb of mate'), the species of holly, *Ilex paraguayensis*, from whose leaves the beverage mate is made (see *mate*³).

yerk (yėrk), *v.* [Cf. *jerk*².] **I.** *tr.* To strike or lash smartly; also, to pull, thrust, or throw suddenly; jerk; also, to bind tightly. [Now prov.] **II.** *intr.* To make a sudden, quick motion; give a jerk. [Now prov.]—**yerk**, *n.* A smart stroke or blow; a kick; a sudden, quick motion; a jerk. [Now prov.]

yes (yes), *adv.* [AS. *gese*, *gise*, appar. < *gēa*, yea, + *swā*, so.] A word used to express affirmation or assent (as, 'Will you go?' '*Yes*.'), or to mark the addition of something emphasizing and amplifying a previous statement (as, it is good, *yes*, very good): opposed to *no*¹.—**yes**, *n.* An utterance of the word 'yes'; an affirmative reply.

yes-ter- (yes′tėr-). [AS. *geostran-*, *giestran-*, akin to D. *gisteren*, *gister*, G. *gestern*, yesterday, also to L. *hesternus*, of yesterday, Gr. χθές, Skt. *hyas*, yesterday.] Being, or belonging to, the day next before the present (as, *yesterday*; *yesternight*); hence, in general, being that preceding the present (as, *yesterweek*; *yesteryear*). Also used occasionally in poetry as a separate word (quasi-adjective): as, *yester* sun (that is, yesterday's sun).—**yes′ter-day** (-dā). [AS. *geostrandæg*.] **I.** *adv.* On the day preceding this day. **II.** *n.* The day preceding this day (sometimes used attributively: as, *yesterday* morning; *yesterday* noon); hence, time in the immediate past (as, fashions of *yesterday*; "They are all moderns, people of *yesterday*," Peacock's "Headlong Hall," xiv.).—**yes′ter-eve′**, **yes′ter-e′ven**, **yes′ter-eve′-ning**, *adv.* and *n.* Yesterday evening: as, "no longer ago than *yester-eve*" (Hawthorne's "Scarlet Letter," xiv.). [Archaic or poetic.]—**yes′ter-morn′**, **yes′ter-morn′ing**, *adv.* and *n.* Yesterday morning: as, "even so late as *yestermorning*" (Stevenson's "David Balfour," i.). [Archaic or poetic.]—**yes′ter-night′**, *adv.* and *n.* Last night: as, "*yesternight*, at supper" (Shakspere's "Julius Cæsar," ii. 1. 238). [Archaic or poetic.]—**yes′ter-noon′**, *adv.* and *n.* Yesterday noon. [Archaic or poetic.]—**yes′ter-week′**, *adv.* and *n.* Last week. [Archaic or poetic.]—**yes′ter-year′**, *adv.* and *n.* Last year: as, "But where are the snows of *yester-year?*" (Rossetti's tr. Villon's "Ballad of Dead Ladies"). [Chiefly poetic.]

yes-treen (yes-trēn′), *adv.* and *n.* Sc. and north. Eng. contraction of *yestereven*.

yest-y (yĕs′ti or yes′-), *a.* Obs. or archaic form of *yeasty*.

yet (yet). [AS. *gīet*, *git*, *get*, = OFries. *ieta*, *eta*, *ita*, yet: cf. G. *jetzt*, now.] **I.** *adv.* As soon as the present time (as, don't go *yet*); up to a particular time, or thus far (as, he had not *yet* come); in the time still remaining, or before all is done (as, there is *yet* time; he will be caught *yet*); at this or that time, as previously (as, he is here *yet*); also, in addition, or again (as, *yet* once more; "*yet* a little sleep," Prov. vi. 10); moreover (as, he won't do it for you nor *yet* for me); even or still (with comparatives: as, a *yet* milder tone; "Another and a *yet* baser traitor was Decimus Brutus," Froude's "Cæsar," xxvi.); also, though the case be such, or nevertheless (as, strange and *yet* true; unpretentious but *yet* excellent). **II.** *conj.* And yet, but yet, or nevertheless: as, a slow *yet* steady gain; it is good, *yet* it could be improved.

yew (yō), *n.* [AS. *īw*, *ēow*, = OHG. *īwa* (G. *eibe*) = Icel. *ȳr*, yew.] An evergreen tree, *Taxus baccata*, of moderate height, a native of the Old World, having a thick, dark foliage and a fine-grained, elastic wood; any tree or shrub of the genus *Taxus*; also, the wood of such a tree; also, a bow for shooting, made of this wood (archaic).

Yid-dish (yid′ish). [G. *jüdisch*, Jewish.] **I.** *n.* A dialect of German containing many Hebrew and Slavic expressions, and written and printed in Hebrew characters: spoken by German and other Jews. **II.** *a.* Of or pertaining to Yiddish; expressed in Yiddish.

Yew (*Taxus baccata*).

yield (yēld), *v.* [AS. *gieldan*, *geldan*, = OHG. *geltan* = Icel. *gjalda* = Goth. *-gildan*, pay, yield: cf. *geld*¹.] **I.** *tr.* To give in payment†; also, to give as due or required (as, to *yield* obedience or thanks; "What token canst thou give me that we should *yield* credence to thee?" Scott's "Quentin Durward," xv.); render; also, to make return for, or requite (an action, etc.)†; also, to give payment or recompense to (archaic: as, "Heaven *yield* her for it," Tennyson's "Gareth and Lynette," 18); also, to give or produce in return for cultivation or labor (as, land *yielding* crops; a mine which *yields* silver; ore *yielding* gold); give forth or produce by a natural process (as, "the fruit of a tree *yielding* seed," Gen. i. 29; "Injurious wasps, to feed on such sweet honey And kill the bees that *yield* it," Shakspere's "Two Gentlemen of Verona," i. 2. 107); in general, to give forth or produce (as, "Air-swept lindens *yield* Their scent": M. Arnold's "Scholar-Gipsy"); furnish or afford (as, "Old wood inflam'd doth *yield* the bravest fire": Sidney's "Arcadia," ii. 1); often, to produce or furnish as payment, profit, or interest (as, "I have sold the things. They have not *yielded* quite as much as they might have done," Dickens's "Old Curiosity Shop," xii.; an investment *yielding* 6 per cent); also, to give, grant, or accord, as in response to a request (as, "Slowly was my mother brought To *yield* consent to my desire": Tennyson's "Miller's Daughter," 138); also, to give up, as to superior power or authority (as, to *yield* a military position to the enemy: often with *up*); surrender; give up or surrender (one's self: as, "He . . . was about to *yield* himself to his enemies," Cooper's "Spy," ix.: often with *up*); in general, to give up or over, relinquish, or resign (as, "Garrett had had to *yield* all hopes of eventual succession": Hugh Walpole's "Wooden Horse," xi.); also, to allow, admit, or concede (now rare: as, "I *yield* it just, said Adam, and submit," Milton's "Paradise Lost," xi. 526). **II.** *intr.* To give a return, as for labor expended (as, a mine which is *yielding* well); produce or bear (as, a tree which *yields* abundantly); also, to surrender or submit, as to superior power (as, "There needed very few arguments to persuade a single man to *yield* when he saw five men upon him": Defoe's "Robinson Crusoe," i. 18); give way or succumb (as, "Oft did the harvest to their sickle *yield*," Gray's "Elegy," vii.; "The child . . . soon *yielded* to the drowsiness," Dickens's "Old Curiosity Shop," xliv.); also, to give place or precedence (with *to*: as, "In that which touches the true advancement of religion, I will *yield* to no man," Motley's "Dutch Republic," vi. 2); resign its place to another, or be inferior (with *to*: as, "Their mutton *yields* to ours, but their beef is excellent," Swift's "Gulliver's Travels," i. 6); also, to give way to force, pressure, etc., so as to move, bend, collapse, or the like (as, "The door was not locked. It *yielded* to my touch," Watts-Dunton's "Aylwin," iii. 2; "The floor might *yield* one day and add . . . all the machinery to the baker's stores below," Arnold Bennett's "Clayhanger," i. 12); give way under any action (as, ice *yields* to heat); prove amenable, as to treatment, as a disease; also, to give way to influence, entreaty, argument, or the like (as, "He was convinced that his father would not *yield*": Arnold Bennett's "Clayhanger," ii. 21); assent; consent.—**yield,** *n.* Payment†; a sum paid†; also, the action of yielding or producing; also, that which is yielded, or the quantity or amount yielded; the return or product from cultivation, natural growth, etc.; the produce resulting from labor; the return from a financial transaction, an investment, or the like; also, the action of yielding or giving way, as under pressure or tension.—**yield′a-ble,** *a.* That may be yielded; also, inclined to yield†; compliant†.—**yield′er,** *n.*—**yield′ing,** *p. a.* That yields; esp., giving way to force, pressure, etc. (as, "paths of *yielding* sand": Watts-Dunton's "Aylwin," i. 5); also, submissive or compliant (as, "She was by nature *yielding* and good tempered": S. Butler's "Way of All Flesh," xi.).—**yield′ing-ly,** *adv.*—**yield′ing-ness,** *n.*—**yield′=point,** *n.* In testing the tensile strength of iron, steel, etc., by pulling in a testing-machine, the point at which the elongation begins to increase very greatly for a slight increase of pull or load, or, from another point of view, the minimum load which produces permanent deformation.

yill (yil), *n.* Scotch form of *ale*.

-yl. Noun termination from Gr. ὕλη, wood, matter, used specifically in names of chemical radicals, as *methyl, nitryl, phenyl.*

y-lang=y-lang (ē′lang-ē′lang), *n.* [Philippine.] An anonaceous tree, *Canangium odoratum* (or *Cananga odorata*), a native of the Philippines, Java, etc., bearing fragrant drooping flowers from which a volatile oil used in perfumery is distilled; also, the oil or perfume.

Y=lev-el (wī′lev″el), *n.* A form of surveyor's level in which the telescope rests on two forked supports (called *Y′s*), one near each end.

yo-del, yo-dle (yō′dl), *v. t. or i.* ; *-deled* or *-delled, -dled, -deling* or *-delling, -dling.* [G. *jodeln*.] To sing with frequent changes from the ordinary voice to falsetto and back again, in the manner of the mountaineers of Switzerland and Tyrol. —**yo′del, yo′dle,** *n.* A song, refrain, or series of meaningless syllables which is yodeled.—**yo′del-er, yo′del-ler, yo′dler,** *n.*

yo-ga (yō′gä), *n.* [Hind. *yoga*, < Skt. *yoga*, union.] In Hindu religious philosophy, the union of the human soul with the universal spirit; a system of ascetic practice which aims at effecting such union through the withdrawal of the senses from all external objects, concentration of the mind on some grand central truth, etc.—**yo-gi** (yō′gē), *n.*; pl. *-gis* (-gēz). [Hind. *yogī*.] One who practises the yoga system; one claiming enhanced susceptibilities and powers, along with a knowledge of the secrets of nature, through the practice of this system.—**yo′gism** (-gizm), *n.* The doctrine or practice of the yogis.

yo-gurt, yo-ghurt (yō′gurt), *n.* [Turk. *yōghurt*.] A kind of thickened fermented liquor made from milk, used by the Turks and others. Cf. *kefir* and *kumiss*.

yo=ho (yō-hō′), *interj.* A sailors' call or shout to attract attention, accompany effort, etc. Also in general use.— **yo=ho′,** *n.* A call or shout of 'yo-ho!'—**yo=ho′,** *v. i.*;

-hoed, -hoing. To shout 'yo-ho!' as, "the men . . . *yo-hoing* at their work" (Stevenson's "Treasure Island," ix.).

yoicks (yoiks), *interj.* [Cf. *hoicks*.] A cry used to urge on the hounds in fox-hunting.

yoke (yōk), *n.* [AS. *geoc* = OHG. *joh* (G. *joch*) = Icel. *ok* = Goth. *juk*, yoke; akin to L. *jugum*, Gr. ζυγόν, Skt. *yuga*, yoke; from a root seen in E. *join*.] A contrivance for joining together a pair of draft-animals, esp. oxen, usually consisting of a cross-piece with two bow-shaped pieces beneath, one at each end, each bow inclosing the head of an animal; also, something resembling a yoke or a bow of a yoke in form or use; a frame fitting the neck and shoulders of a

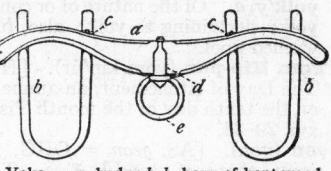

Yoke. — *a*, body; *b, b*, bows of bent wood; *c, c,* keys for fastening bows; *d,* clip; *e,* draft-ring.

person, for carrying a pair of buckets or the like, one at each end; a wooden frame attached to the neck of an animal to prevent it from going under or through a fence or otherwise straying; a neck-yoke for suspending the tongue of a vehicle; a cross-bar or curved piece from which a large bell is hung; a cross-bar on the head of a boat's rudder; any crosspiece connecting two other parts; a shaped piece in a garment, fitted about or below the neck, or about the hips, from which the rest of the garment hangs; also, an emblem or token of subjection, servitude, slavery, etc., as one under which prisoners of war were compelled to pass by the ancient Romans and others; also, fig., any power, rule, or influence entailing subjection or bondage, or regarded as so doing (as, "Pisa fell several times under the *yoke* of usurpers," Hallam's "Europe during the Middle Ages," iii. 2; "The country had thrown off the *yoke* of old England," Irving's "Sketch-Book," Rip Van Winkle; "I had broken the *yoke* of custom and opinion," Kingsley's "Alton Locke," xxxix.); something that couples or binds together, or a bond or tie (as, the *yoke* of matrimony); also, a pair of draft-animals fastened together by a yoke (pl., after a numeral, *yokes* or *yoke*: as, "five *yoke* of oxen," Luke, xiv. 19); a brace or couple; also, the time during which a plowman and his team work at one stretch, a period of steady work, or a part of the working-day in which work is carried on without interruption (prov. Eng. and Sc.).—**yoke,** *v.*; *yoked, yoking.* **I.** *tr.* To put a yoke on (a pair of draft-animals); join or couple by means of a yoke; hence, to attach (a draft-animal) to a plow or vehicle; harness a draft-animal to (a plow or vehicle: as, "These on their horses vault; those *yoke* the car," Dryden's tr. Virgil's "Æneid," xii. 433); also, to put any yoke-like device on; fasten a yoke round the neck of (an animal), as to prevent it from straying; suspend (a bell) by a yoke; also, fig., to bring into subjection or servitude (as, "*yok'd* by despotism's hand": Cowper's "Table Talk," 258); join, couple, link, or unite (as, "the influence which had *yoked* together . . . so many turbulent and ambitious spirits": Macaulay's "Essays," William Pitt, Earl of Chatham); sometimes, to join in marriage (as, "I have the honour to be *yoked* to a young lady": Steele, in "Spectator," 455). **II.** *intr.* To be or become joined, linked, or united (as, "The care That *yokes* with empire": Tennyson's "To the Queen"); become joined in marriage (as, "a man who *yokes* with such a partner for life": Smollett's "Humphry Clinker," Oct. 14).—**yoke′fel″low,** *n.* One associated with another in labor, or in a task or undertaking; also, an intimate associate; a partner; a mate; often, a spouse.

yo-kel (yō′kl), *n.* [Appar. < *yoke*.] A plowboy (north. Eng.); also, a countryman or rustic; a country bumpkin.

yol-dring (yol′dring), *n.* [Akin to *yellow*.] The yellowhammer, *Emberiza citrinella*, of Europe. [Sc. and prov. Eng.]

yolk (yōk, also yōlk), *n.* [AS. *geoloca*, < *geolu*, E. *yellow*.] The yellow and principal substance of an egg, as distinguished from the white; in biological use, that part of the contents of the ovum or egg of an animal which enters into the formation of the embryo ('formative yolk,' or archiblast: constituting the whole or the greater part of the ovum in most mammals, and a very small part of the ovum in birds and

reptiles), together with any material which serves to nourish the embryo during its formation ('nutritive yolk,' deutoplasm, or parablast: constituting a considerable part of the ovum in birds and reptiles), as distinguished from a mass of albumen (the white of the egg) which may surround it, and from the membrane or shell inclosing the whole; also, a natural grease exuded from the skin of sheep; suint.—
yolked, a. Having a yolk: as, a double-yolked egg.—
yolk′y, a. Of the nature of or consisting of yolk; resembling yolk; pertaining to yolk; also, full of yolk or suint, as unwashed wool.

Yom Kip-pur (yom kip′ur). [Heb., 'Day of Atonement.'] The Day of Atonement, an annual Jewish fast-day observed on the tenth day of the month Tishri (see *Tishri*). See Lev. xvi. 29–34.

yon (yon). [AS. *geon* = OHG. *jenēr* (G. *jener*) = Goth. *jains*, that: cf. *yond*.] **I.** a. That or those (referring to something at a distance); yonder: as, "Let us go directly to *yon* light" (Fielding's "Tom Jones," viii. 10); "*yon* dark queens in *yon* black boat" (Tennyson's "Passing of Arthur," 452). [Archaic or prov.] **II.** *pron.* That or those yonder: as, "Was *yon* the messenger?" (Scott's "Peveril of the Peak," xl.). [Now prov.]—**yon,** adv. Yonder; there or thither: as, " 'Missis is up *yon*,' said the servant" (Arnold Bennett's "These Twain," viii.); hither and *yon* (this way and that, or hither and thither). [Now chiefly prov.]

yond (yond). [AS. *geond* (= Goth. *jaind*), < *geon*, E. *yon*.] **I.** adv. Yonder: as, "Say what thou seest *yond*" (Shakspere's "Tempest," i. 2. 409). [Archaic or prov.] **II.** *prep.* Across, along, or through; also, beyond or past. [Now prov.]—**yond,** a. and *pron.* That or those yonder: as, "whether *yond* troops are friend or enemy" (Shakspere's "Julius Cæsar," v. 3. 18). [Now prov.]

yon-der (yon′dėr), adv. [ME. *yonder* (cf. Goth. *jaindrē*); from the stem represented by E. *yon*.] At, in, or to that (more or less distant) place; at, in, or to that place there; over there: as, "Next you'd see a raft sliding by, away off *yonder*" (Mark Twain's "Huckleberry Finn," xix.); "Abide ye here . . . and I and the lad will go *yonder* and worship" (Gen. xxii. 5).—**yon′der,** a. Being in that place or over there, or that or those over there (as, on *yonder* hill; "Look at *yonder* battlements," Scott's "Abbot," xiii.); also, being the more distant, or farther (as, on the *yonder* side of a brook).

yore (yōr), adv. [AS. *gēara*, of old, formerly, orig. gen. pl. of *gēar*, E. *year*.] Of old; years ago; long ago: now only in the phrase 'of yore': as, "the knights-errant *of yore*" (Irving's "Sketch-Book," Sleepy Hollow); "The glorious sounds shall still float on as *of yore*" (Kinglake's "Eothen," xxviii.).

York-ist (yôr′kist). In *Eng. hist.*: **I.** n. An adherent or member of the house of York (see below), esp. in the Wars of the Roses. **II.** a. Of or pertaining to the Yorkists; belonging or pertaining to the English royal house of York, which was descended from Edmund, Duke of York, fifth son of Edward III., and which in the person of his grandson, Richard, Duke of York (1411–60), father of Edward IV. and Richard III., laid claim to the throne in opposition to the last Lancastrian king, Henry VI., and which was represented on the throne by Edward IV., Edward V., and Richard III., who reigned from 1461 to 1485. Cf. *Lancastrian*, a., also *Wars of the Roses* (under *rose²*, n.).

York-shire (yôrk′shėr) **pud′ding.** [From the county of *Yorkshire* in northern England.] A pudding made of batter (unsweetened), baked under meat, so as to catch the drippings.

you (yō), *pron.*; nom. *ye* or *you*, poss. *your* or *yours*, obj. *you*. [AS. *ēow*, dat. and acc. of *gē*, E. *ye¹*.] The ordinary pronoun of the second person, orig. the objective (plural) of *ye*, but now used regularly as either objective or nominative (see *ye¹*), and with either plural or singular meaning (see *thou*), but always, when used as subject, taking a plural verb.

young (yung), a. [AS. *geong* = D. *jong* = G. *jung* = Icel. *ungr* = Goth. *juggs*, young; akin to L. *juvenis*, Skt. *yuvan*, young: cf. *juvenile*.] Being in the first or early stage of life, as a human being or an animal (as, a *young* child; a *young* horse; *young* ones, offspring, also children or youngsters); youthful; not old; also, being in an early stage of growth, as a plant; also, being in an early stage generally, as of exist-

ence, progress, operation, etc. (as, when the world was *young*; a *young* republic; a *young* business or enterprise; the *young* moon); new; early; not far advanced (as, "We've time enough, the day's *young* yet": Lover's "Handy Andy," xviii.); having but newly or recently begun or come, or inexperienced (as, "I was too *young* in the trade to keep any journal of this voyage": Defoe's "Captain Singleton," i.); also, having the appearance, freshness, vigor, or other qualities of youth (as, to remain *young* in looks or feelings); also, not far advanced in years in comparison with another or others (often in the comparative and superlative: as, the *younger* Pliny, nephew of the elder Pliny; a *younger* son or brother; the *youngest* of three old men); often, junior (applied to the younger of two persons of the same name: as, *young* Mr. Jones came with a message from his father; the *Young* Pretender, see *pretender*); also, of or pertaining to youth (as, in one's *young* days); also, representing or advocating recent or progressive tendencies, policies, or the like, esp. in politics (used esp. to designate certain parties, groups, etc.: as, the *Young* Turks); in *phys. geog.*, same as *youthful*.
— **Young Men's Christian Association,** an organization for promoting the spiritual, intellectual, physical, and social well-being of young men, and having many older members, which was founded in London in 1844 by George (afterward Sir George) Williams (1821–1905), and has since spread widely, now comprising allied associations in all parts of the world. Abbreviated *Y. M. C. A.* or simply *Y*.—**Young Men's Hebrew Association,** an organization for the moral, mental, physical, and social improvement of Jewish young men, which was organized in New York City in 1874, and now includes many widely distributed associations. Abbreviated *Y. M. H. A.*—**Young Women's Christian Association,** an organization for promoting the spiritual, intellectual, physical, and social welfare of young women, which originated in England in 1855 (simultaneously in two different bodies, united in 1877), and now consists of allied associations spread all over the world. Abbreviated *Y. W. C. A.*—**young,** n. Young offspring (whether consisting of several or of but one: construed respectively as *pl.* or *sing.*).
—**with young,** pregnant.—**young′ish,** a. Rather young: as, "a variety of young and *youngish* men" (H. G. Wells's "Tono-Bungay," iii. 1. § 3).—**young′ling.** [AS. *geongling*.] **I.** n. A young person, or a child or youth (as, "This *youngling* . . . In days to come a mighty man shall be": W. Morris's "Jason," i. 159); anything young, as an animal, plant, etc.; also, a novice; a beginner. [Archaic.] **II.** a. Young; youthful: as, "the mountain raven's *youngling* brood" (Wordsworth's "Idle Shepherd-Boys," 6). [Archaic.] —**young′ly,** adv. In the manner of young persons; also, in youth.—**young′ness,** n.—**young′ster** (-stėr), n. A young person; a child; often, a boy; a youth or young fellow (as, "Hal was a *youngster* of nineteen or twenty": Jack London's "Call of the Wild," v.); sometimes, a young horse or other animal; also, in the British navy, a midshipman of less than four years' standing.

youn-ker (yung′kėr), n. [D. *jonker, jonkheer*, < *jong*, young, + *heer*, gentleman: cf. *junker*.] A young gentleman or knight†; also, a youngster, lad, or young fellow (archaic: as, "So may the *younkers* of this generation eye you," Lamb's "Old Benchers of the Inner Temple"); also, a novice†, simpleton†, or dupe†.

your (yōr), *pron.* [AS. *ēower*, gen. of *gē*, E. *ye¹*.] The possessive form of *ye, you*, used before a noun. Cf. *yours*. —**yours** (yōrz), *pron.* Form of *your* used predicatively or without a noun following.—**yours truly,** a conventional phrase professing faithfulness or sincerity used at the end of a letter, just before the signature; hence, I, myself, or me (colloq.: as, "It suits the governor . . . but it wouldn't suit *yours truly*," W. B. Maxwell's "In Cotton Wool," v.).— **your-self′,** *pron.*; pl. *-selves* (-selvz′). An emphatic form of *ye* or *you*; also, a reflexive form of *you*.

youth (yōth), n.; pl. *youths* (yō̄ᴛʜz). [AS. *geoguth* = OS. *juguth* = OHG. *jugund* (G. *jugend*), youth; from the Teut. adj. represented by E. *young*.] The condition of being young, or youngness (as, the charm of mere *youth*; his *youth* is in his favor); also, the appearance, freshness, vigor, spirit, etc., characteristic of one that is young (as, to keep one's *youth* well); also, the time of being young (as, "Thou hast taught me from my *youth*," Ps. lxxi. 17; "How bless'd is he who crowns . . . A *youth* of labour with an age of ease," Goldsmith's "Deserted Village," 100); early life; esp., the period of life from puberty to the attainment of full growth; adolescence; in general, the first or early period of anything (as, "tall arrowy white pines, still in their *youth*," Thoreau's "Walden," i.; in the *youth* of the world); also, young persons collectively (as, "Now all the *youth* of England are on fire": Shakspere's "Henry V.," ii., Prologue, 1); a young person, esp. a young man (as, *youths* and maidens; "Pleasant *youth*, young Lennan; hope he won't bore us out there!" Galsworthy's "Dark Flower," i. 3); also, newness† or recentness†. —**youth′=and=old=age′**, *n.* The plant zinnia. —**youth′-ful**, *a.* Characterized by youth; young; also, having the appearance, freshness, vigor, etc., of youth (as, to keep *youthful*); also, early in time (as, "the *youthful* season of the year": Shakspere's "Julius Cæsar," ii. 1. 108); also, of, pertaining to, or befitting youth (as, in one's *youthful* years; *youthful* pastimes); in *phys. geog.*, of topographical features, having advanced in reduction by erosion, etc., to a slight extent only (cf. *mature, a.*, and *old, a.*). —**youth′ful-ly**, *adv.* —**youth′ful-ness**, *n.* —**youth′hood** (-hud), *n.* Youth; youthful state; also, young persons collectively.

yowl (youl), *v. i.* [ME. *youlen*: see *yawl*[1].] To utter a long, distressful or dismal cry, as an animal or a person; howl: as, "He [a dog] *yowls* and shows his teeth" (Eden Phillpotts's "Children of Men," i. 10); "all the suff'ring babes *yowling* for it" (H. G. Wells's "Tono-Bungay," i. 3. § 1). —**yowl**, *n.* A yowling cry; a howl.

Y=track (wī′trak), *n.* A short track laid at right angles to a line of railroad, with which it is connected by two curved branches resembling the branches of the letter Y: used instead of a turn-table for reversing engines or cars.

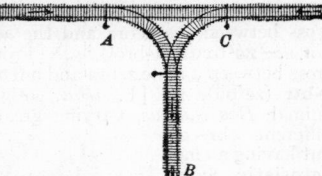

Y-track. — Engine advancing toward *A* is switched at *A* to Y-track *B*, and then backed up over switch *C* to main track again, heading now in reverse direction.

yt-ter-bi-a (i-tèr′bi-ä), *n.* [See *ytterbium*.] In *chem.*, ytterbium oxide, Yb_2O_3, which is white and forms colorless salts. —**yt-ter′bic**, *a.* In *chem.*, of or containing ytterbium. —**yt-ter-bite** (it′èr-bīt), *n.* Gadolinite. —**yt-ter-bi-um** (i-tèr′bi-um), *n.* [NL.; named from *Ytterby*, in Sweden, where gadolinite was found: cf. *erbium, terbium*, and *yttrium*, of like origin.] Chem. sym., Yb; at. wt., 173.5. A rare metallic element found in the mineral gadolinite, and forming compounds resembling those of yttrium.

yt-tri-a (it′ri-ä), *n.* [See *yttrium*.] In *chem.*, the sesquioxide of yttrium, Y_2O_3, obtained as a white powder. —**yt′tric**, *a.* In *chem.*, of or containing yttrium. —**yt-trif-er-ous** (i-trif′e̞-rus), *a.* [See *-ferous*.] Yielding or containing yttrium.

yt-tri-um (it′ri-um), *n.* [NL.; named from *Ytter(by)*, in Sweden: see *ytterbium*.] Chem. sym., Y or Yt; at. wt., 88.7. A rare trivalent metallic element, found in gadolinite and other minerals.

yu-ca (yö′kä), *n.* [Sp.; of W. Ind. origin.] Cassava. [West Indies, etc.]

Yu-ca-tec-an (yö-kạ-tek′ạn). [Sp. *Yucateco*.] **I.** *a.* Belonging or pertaining to Yucatan, a peninsula of southeastern Mexico. **II.** *n.* A native or inhabitant of Yucatan.

yuc-ca (yuk′ä), *n.* [NL., < Sp. *yuca*: see *yuca*.] Any of the plants (including both low forms and trees) constituting the liliaceous genus *Yucca*, natives of the southern U. S., Mexico, and Central America, having a woody stem with long, pointed, and usually rigid leaves, and bearing large, commonly white, pendulous flowers in terminal racemes (see *Adam's needle and thread*, under *Adam*; *bear-grass*; *Joshua-tree*; and *Spanish bayonet*, under *Spanish, a.*); also, yuca or cassava.

Yucca (*Y. gloriosa*).

yu-ga (yu̇′gä), *n.*; pl. *-gas* (-gäz). [Skt., age, orig. yoke: see *yoke*.] In Hindu use, an age of time; esp., one of four ages distinguished in a period of the world's existence, the first being a golden age, with deterioration in those following.

Yu′go-slav, etc. See *Jugoslav*, etc.

yu=kin (yö-kin′), *n.* [Chinese.] A Chinese four-stringed musical instrument with a large circular body and a short neck.

Yule (yöl), *n.* [AS. *gēol* = Icel. *jōl* = Sw. and Dan. *jul*, Yule.] Christmas, or the Christmas season: as, "the merry merry bells of *Yule*" (Tennyson's "In Memoriam," xxviii.). — **Yule log**, a large log of wood which in olden times formed the backlog of the fire at Christmas. — **Yule′tide** (-tīd), *n.* The season of Yule; the Christmas season; Christmastide. — **Yule′=time**, *n.* Yuletide; Christmastide.

Yu-kin. — In Stearns Collection, University of Michigan.

y-wis (i-wis′), *adv.* See *iwis*.

Z

Z, z (zē); pl. *Z's, z's* (zēz). A consonant, the 26th letter of the English alphabet. See *izzard, zed*.

zac-a-ton (zak-ạ-tōn′), *n.* [Amer. Sp. *zacatón*, aug. of *zacate*, grass, hay; from Mex.] Any of various grasses of the southwestern U. S., esp. *Sporobolus wrightii*, which yields a coarse hay.

zaf-fer, zaf-fre (zaf′èr), *n.* [F. *zafre, safre*: cf. *sapphire*.] An impure oxide of cobalt used esp. to produce a blue color in glass and porcelain, and in the manufacture of smalt.

za-mi-a (zā′mi-ạ), *n.* [NL.] Any of the plants constituting the cycadaceous genus *Zamia*, chiefly natives of tropical and subtropical North America, having a short, thick trunk partly or wholly above ground, a crown of palm-like pinnate leaves, and oblong, cylindrical cones. See cut on next page.

za-min-dar (zạ-mēn-där′), *n.* [Hind. and Pers. *zamīndār*, landholder.] In India, orig., under Mogul rule, a farmer of the revenue, required to pay a fixed sum on the tract or district assigned to him; now, a native landlord, or a person recognized as possessing some property in the soil, who is responsible to the British government for the land-tax on the soil under his jurisdiction. — **za-min-da′ri** (-dä′rē), *n.* [Hind. and Pers. *zamīndārī*.] The status, jurisdiction, or territory of a zamindar; the system of landholding and revenue-collection under zamindars.

za-ny (zā′ni), *n.*; pl. *-nies* (-niz). [F. *zani*, < It. *zanni*, zany, orig. a familiar form of *Giovanni*, John.] Orig., a comic performer on the Italian stage who mimicked the actions of the professional clown; in general, a clown's or mountebank's assistant; any apish buffoon; a clown; hence, an attendant, follower, or assistant (in contempt:

archaic); any buffoonish person; a silly person, or simpleton (now chiefly prov. Eng.: as, "What a zany an old chap must be to light a bonfire when there's no youngsters to please!" Hardy's "Return of the Native," i.3).—**za′ny-ism,** n. The action of a zany; buffoonery.

zap-ti-eh (zặp-tē′ė), n. [Turk.] A Turkish policeman.

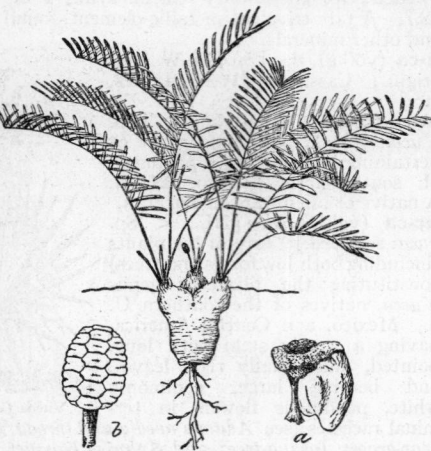

Female Plant of Zamia (Z. pumila), the waved line indicating the surface of the ground.—a, scale with one seed; b, the young female flower.

Zar-a-thus-tri-an (zar-ạ-thös′tri-ạn), a. and n. Same as Zoroastrian.

zar-a-tite (zar′ạ-tīt), n. [Named from Señor Zárate, a Spaniard.] A mineral, a hydrous carbonate of nickel, occurring in emerald-green incrustations and compact masses.

za-re-ba, za-ri-ba (zạ-rē′bạ), n. [Ar. zarībah, inclosure for cattle, etc.] In the Sudan and adjoining regions, an inclosure, as of thorn-bushes or the like, built about a camp or village, for protection against enemies or wild animals; a camp or village with such an inclosure.

zarf (zärf or zėrf), n. [Ar.] A cup-like holder, usually of ornamental metal, for a coffee-cup without a handle, as used in the Levant.

zar-zue-la (thär-thwā′lä), n. [Sp.] A kind of Spanish theatrical entertainment consisting of a combination of drama and music; a Spanish light opera or musical comedy.

zas-tru-ga (zas-trö′gä), n.; pl. -gi (-gē). [Russ.] In Siberia and elsewhere, one of a series of wave-like ridges formed in snow by the action of the wind, and running in the direction of the wind: commonly in pl.

zax (zaks), n. Same as sax.

Z=bar (zē′bär), n. A steel bar used in constructing steel columns for buildings, etc., consisting essentially of a web with two flanges at right angles to it, and having the cross-section somewhat resembling the letter Z.

Z=beam (zē′bēm), n. A metal beam with a cross-section somewhat resembling the letter Z.

zeal (zēl), n. [= OF. zele (F. zèle), < L. zelus, < Gr. ζῆλος, eager rivalry, emulation, jealousy, zeal: cf. jealous.] Passionate ardor in behalf of a person, cause, or object (as, "Had I but served my God with half the zeal I served my king," Shakspere's "Henry VIII.," iii. 2. 455; "his fervent zeal for the interests of the state," Macaulay's "Essays," Warren Hastings); eager desire or endeavor to further aims or accomplish any purpose; enthusiastic diligence; also, strong feeling, as indignation or wrath† (as, "Which thing when Mattathias saw, he was inflamed with zeal . . . neither could he forbear to shew his anger": 1 Mac. ii. 24); ardent affection or attachment† (as, "Methinks my zeal to Valentine is cold, And that I love him not as I was wont": Shakspere's "Two Gentlemen of Verona," ii. 4. 203).—**zeal-ot** (zel′ọt), n. [LL. zelotes, < Gr. ζηλωτής.] One who displays zeal; esp., one carried away by excess of zeal; an immoderate partizan (as, "those furious zealots who blow the bellows of faction until the whole furnace of politics is red-hot": Irving's "Knickerbocker's New York," v. 7); [cap.] one of a fanatical Jewish sect of Palestine under Roman dominion, who were excessively zealous in behalf of the Mosaic law.—**zeal′ot-ry** (-ri), n. The action or methods of a zealot; undue or excessive zeal; fanaticism.—**zeal-ous** (zel′us), a. [ML. zelosus: cf. jealous.] Full of, characterized by, or due to zeal; ardently active, devoted, or diligent: as, "clans . . . which

were peculiarly zealous in the royal cause" (Scott's "Legend of Montrose," xv.); servants zealous to please; a zealous spirit; zealous efforts or aid.—**zeal′ous-ly,** adv.—**zeal′ous-ness,** n.

ze′bec, n. See xebec.

ze-bra (zē′brä), n. [Of African origin.] A wild equine mammal, Equus zebra ('true zebra' or 'mountain zebra'), of southern Africa, very fully and regularly striped with dark bands on a whitish ground; also, either of two similar and closely related species, E. burchelli ('Burchell's zebra,' or the dauw), of southern, central, and eastern Africa, and E. grevyi ('Grévy's zebra'), of northeastern Africa. Cf.

Zebra (Equus zebra).

quagga.—**ze′brass** (-brȧs), n. [From zebra + ass.] A cross between a zebra and an ass.—**ze′bra=wood,** n. The striped hard wood of a tropical American tree, Connarus guianensis, used for cabinet-work, etc.; the tree itself; also, any of various similar woods or trees.—**ze′brine** (-brin), a. Pertaining to or resembling a zebra.—**ze′broid.** I. a. Resembling the zebra. II. n. A zebroid animal; a cross between the zebra and the ass, or the zebra and the horse.—**ze′brule** (-bröl), n. [From zebra + (m)ule.] A cross between a male zebra and a female horse.

ze-bu (zē′bū), n. [F. zébu; origin obscure.] A bovine animal, Bos indicus, varying greatly in size and color in different breeds, but having a characteristic large hump (sometimes double) over the shoulders, and a very large dewlap: widely domesticated in India, China, eastern Africa, etc.

Zebu.

zec-chin (zek′in), n. Same as zecchino.

zec-chi-no (tsek-kē′nō), n.; pl. -ni (-nē). [It.: see sequin.] Same as sequin (coin).

zed (zed), n. [F. zède, < L. zeta, < Gr. ζῆτα, E. zeta.] A name for the letter Z (common in England); also, a Z-bar.

zed-o-a-ry (zed′ọ-ạ-ri), n. [= F. zédoaire, < ML. zedoaria, < Ar. zedwār.] An East Indian drug consisting of the rhizome of either of two species of curcuma, Curcuma zedoaria or C. aromatica, with a bitter, aromatic, camphorous taste: used as a stimulant. See curcuma.

zeit-geist (tsīt′gīst), n. [G., 'time-spirit.'] The spirit of the time: the general drift of thought or feeling characteristic of a particular period of time.

ze-min-dar (zẹ-mēn-där′), etc. Same as zamindar, etc.

zem-stvo (zemst′vō), n.; pl. zemstvos (-vōz). [Russ.] In Russia, an elective assembly of a local district or of a province, having the oversight and regulation of affairs within its territory.

ze-na-na (ze-nä′nạ), n. [Hind. and Pers. zanāna, < Pers. zan, woman.] In India, that part of the house in which the women and girls of a family are secluded; also, its occupants collectively. Cf. harem.

Zend (zend), n. [Pers.] Properly, the translation and exposition, in a later form of Persian (Pahlavi), of the Zoroastrian Avesta; less correctly, the language of the

Avesta; Avestan.—**Zend=A·ves′ta** (-ạ-ves′tä), *n.* The Avesta.

ze·nith (zē′nith, also, esp. Brit., zen′ith), *n.* [OF. *cenith* (F. *zénith*), < Sp. *cenit, zenit*, < Ar. *samt*, way, in *samt-ar-rās*, 'way of the head': cf. *azimuth*.] The point of the celestial sphere vertically above any place or observer, and diametrically opposite to the nadir (as, "The sun wanted but two or three minutes of the *zenith*": Cooper's "Deerslayer," xxvii.); hence, fig., the highest point or state (as, "Chivalry was then in its *zenith*," Hallam's "Europe during the Middle Ages," i. 2; "Mr. Gladstone, at the *zenith* of his strength," Charnwood's "Theodore Roosevelt," iii.); the culmination.—**ze′nith-al**, *a.*

ze·o·lite (zē′ọ̄-līt), *n.* [Sw. *zeolit*, < Gr. ζεῖν, boil, + λίθος, stone; so called from its swelling up under the blowpipe.] Any of a group of hydrated silicates of aluminium with alkali metals or alkaline earth metals or both, closely related to the feldspars, and commonly occurring as secondary minerals in cavities in igneous rocks.—**ze·o·lit′ic** (-lit′ik), *a.*

zeph·yr (zef′ẽr), *n.* [L. *Zephyrus*, < Gr. Ζέφυρος.] [*cap.*] The west wind personified (poetic: as, "*Zephyr*, with Aurora playing, As he met her once a-Maying," Milton's "L'Allegro," 19); [*l. c.*] any soft, mild breeze (as, "The wind drops to a *zephyr*": G. W. Cable's "Cavalier," xlvi.); also, any of various things of fine, light quality, as a fabric (cloth, flannel, etc.), a yarn or worsted for knitting, or a kind of cracker or biscuit.

Zep·pe·lin (zep′ẹ-lin, G. tsep-ė-lēn′), *n.* [From Count F. von *Zeppelin* (1838–1917), German aëronautic inventor.] A large type of dirigible balloon, consisting of a long, cylindrical covered framework containing numerous compartments or cells filled with gas, and of various structures for holding the engines, passengers, etc.: used in transportation and in warfare.—**Zep′pe·lin**, *v. t.* To drop bombs on from a Zeppelin in warfare: as, "They will *Zeppelin* the fleet" (H. G. Wells's "Mr. Britling," i. 5. § 12).

ze·ro (zē′rō), *n.*; pl. *-ros* or *-roes* (-rōz). [F. *zéro*, < It. *zero*, contr. of *zefiro*, < Ar. *çifr*, cipher, lit. 'empty': cf. *cipher*.] The figure or symbol 0, which stands for the absence of quantity in the Arabic notation for numbers; a cipher; hence, naught or nothing; the origin of any kind of measurement; the line or point from which all divisions of a scale (as of a thermometer) are measured in either a positive or a negative direction; in fig. use, something that counts as or amounts to nothing (as, "He . . . swore . . . that he would no longer serve as a shadow, a statue, a *zero*": Motley's "Dutch Republic," vi. 6); a person or thing of no importance; a nonentity; also, the lowest point or degree (as, "My courage sinks to *zero*": Hood's "Desert-Born," 64); the starting-point or beginning; sometimes, zero hour (colloq.).—**zero hour**, in military use, the time set for the beginning of an attack; hence, in general use, the time at which any contemplated move is to begin (colloq.).

Zero. A swift Japanese fighter plane (Mitsubishi).

zest (zest), *n.* [F. *zeste*; origin uncertain.] A piece of orange-peel or lemon-peel, or the oil squeezed from it, used as a flavoring; hence, anything added to impart flavor or cause relish, or an agreeable or piquant flavor imparted (often fig.: as, to add *zest* to a story; to give *zest* to an occasion), piquancy, interest, or charm (as, "His style in conversation had an uncommon *zest*": Godwin's "Caleb Williams," xix.); also, keen relish, hearty enjoyment, or gusto (as, "All the goods of life he tasted with epicurean *zest*," Maria Edgeworth's "Belinda," xvi.; "I returned with a new wonderful *zest* to my old sports," W. H. Hudson's "Far Away and Long Ago," xxiv.).—**zest**, *v. t.* To give zest, relish, or piquancy to.—**zest′ful**, *a.* Full of zest; characterized by keen relish or hearty enjoyment.—**zest′ful-ly**, *adv.*—**zest′ful-ness**, *n.*

ze·ta (zē′tạ or zā′tạ), *n.* [L., < Gr. ζῆτα.] The sixth letter (Z, ζ, = English Z, z) of the Greek alphabet.

ze·tet·ic (zẹ-tet′ik), *a.* [Gr. ζητητικός, < ζητεῖν, seek, inquire.] Pertaining to or proceeding by inquiry or investigation.

zeug·ma (zūg′mä), *n.* [L., < Gr. ζεῦγμα, < ζευγνύναι, yoke, join: see *join*.] In *gram.* and *rhet.*, a figure in which a verb is associated with two subjects or objects, or an adjective with two nouns, although appropriate to but one of the two, as in 'to wage war and peace,' 'swift-rolling chariots and arms.'—**zeug·mat′ic** (-mat′ik), *a.*

Zeus (zūs), *n.* [Gr. Ζεύς: see *deity*.] The chief god of the ancient Greeks, the ruler of the heavens, identified by the Romans with Jupiter.

Zeus.— Bust found at Otricoli, in Umbria, now in the Vatican Museum, at Rome.

zib·e·line (zib′ẹ-lēn), *n.* [F. *zibe-line*, earlier *zibel-line*, < It. *zibel-lina*; of Slavic origin, and akin to E. *sable*.] The sable, *Mustela zibellina*; also, the fur of the sable; also, a woolen cloth with a flattened hairy nap.

zib·et (zib′et), *n.* [= *civet*.] A species of civet-cat, *Viverra zibetha*, of India, the Malay Peninsula, etc. Also **zib′eth** (-eth).

zig·gu·rat (zig′ọ̄-rat), *n.* Same as *zikkurat*.

zig·zag (zig′zag). [F. *zigzag*, perhaps < G. *zickzack*, zigzag: cf. G. *zacke*, a sharp projection.] **I.** *n.* A line, course, or progression characterized by sharp turns first to one side and then to the other; one of a series of such turns, as in a line or a path. **II.** *a.* Proceeding or formed in a zigzag, or with sharp alternating turns from one side to the other: as, "a sort of maze of *zigzag* trenches" (H. G. Wells's "Mr. Britling," ii. 4. § 13). **III.** *adv.* In a zigzag manner; with frequent sharp turns from side to side: as, "A glittering stream ran *zig-zag* through the varied shades of green" (C. Brontë's "Jane Eyre," xxviii.).—**zig′zag**, *v.*; *-zagged, -zagging*. **I.** *intr.* To proceed in a zigzag line or course: as, "the faint track which *zigzagged* up the hill" (S. J. Weyman's "Gentleman of France," xxviii.). **II.** *tr.* To make zigzag, as in form or course; move in a zigzag direction.

Zigzag Molding.— West door, Cathedral of Lincoln, England.

zik·ku·rat (zik′ọ̄-rat), *n.* [Babylonian (Akkadian).] Among the ancient Babylonians and Assyrians, a kind of temple (of Sumerian origin) in the form of a pyramidal tower consisting of a number of stories, and having about the outside a broad ascent winding round and round the structure and presenting the appearance of a series of terraces.

zil·lah (zil′ä), *n.* [Hind.; from Ar.] In British India, an administrative division of a province.

zinc (zingk), *n.* [= F. *zinc*, < G. *zink*, zinc; origin uncertain.] Chem. sym., Zn; at. wt., 65.37; sp. gr., 7. A bluish-white metallic element occurring combined in various minerals, resembling magnesium in its chemical relations, and used in making galvanized iron, alloys, etc., and as an element in voltaic cells, and, when rolled out into sheets, as a protective covering for roofs, etc.; also, a piece of this metal in the form of a rod, plate, or the like, used as an element in a voltaic cell.—**zinc**, *v. t.*; *zincked* or *zinced* (zingkt), *zincking* or *zincing* (zing′king). To coat or cover with zinc.—**zinc-ate** (zing′kāt), *n.* In *chem.*, a compound which may be viewed as resulting from the replacement of the hydrogen in zinc hydroxide by a very strongly electropositive metal such as potassium or sodium.—**zinc′=blende**, *n.* A native zinc sulphide; sphalerite; blende. See *blende.*—**zinc-ic** (zing′-kik), *a.* Pertaining to, consisting of, containing, or resembling zinc.—**zinc-if-er-ous** (zing-kif′e-rus), *a.* [See *-ferous.*] Yielding or containing zinc.—**zinc-i-fy** (zing′ki-fī), *v. t.*; *-fied, -fying.* To cover or impregnate with zinc.—**zinc-i-fi-ca-tion** (zing″ki-fi-kā′shon), *n.*—**zinc-ite** (zing′kīt), *n.* Native zinc oxide, a brittle mineral of deep-red to orange-yellow color, usually occurring massive or granular, and constituting an important ore of zinc.

zinck-en-ite, zink-en-ite (zing′ken-īt), *n.* [G. *zinkenit*; named from J. K. L. *Zincken* (1790–1862), German metallurgist and mining official.] A steel-gray mineral with a metallic luster, consisting of the sulphides of lead and antimony, and occurring in crystals and massive.

zinck′ic, zinck-if′er-ous, etc. See *zincic,* etc.

zinck-y (zing′ki), *a.* Pertaining to, containing, or resembling zinc.

zinco-. Form of *zinc* used in combination.—**zin-co-graph** (zing′kọ-gráf), *n.* [+ *-graph.*] A zinc plate produced by zincography; also, a print from such a plate.—**zin-cog-ra-phy** (zing-kog′ra-fi), *n.* [+ *-graphy.*] The art or process of producing a printing surface on a zinc plate, esp. of producing one in relief by etching away with acid unprotected parts.—**zin-co-graph′ic** (-gráf′ik), *a.*—**zin′co-type** (-tīp), *n.* [+ *-type.*] Same as *zincograph.*

zinc-ous (zing′kus), *a.* Pertaining to zinc; zincic.

zinc-y (zing′ki), *a.* Same as *zincky.*

Zin-ga-ra (zing′ga-rä, It. tseng′gä-rä), *n.*; pl. *-re* (-rä). [It.] A female Gipsy.—**Zin′ga-ro** (-rō), *n.*; pl. *-ri* (-rē). [It.] A Gipsy.

zing-el (tsing′el), *n.* [G.] A small fish, *Zingel zingel,* of the perch family, found in the Danube and its tributaries.

zin-gi-ber-a-ceous (zin″ji-be-rā′-shius), *a.* [L. *zingiber,* < Gr. ζιγγίβερις, ginger.] Belonging to the *Zingiberaceæ,* or ginger family of plants.

Zingel.

zink-en-ite, *n.* See *zinckenite.*

zink′ite, zink′y. See *zincite, zincky.*

zin-ni-a (zin′i-ä), *n.* [NL.; named from J. G. *Zinn* (1727–59), of Göttingen.] Any of the plants constituting the asteraceous genus *Crassina,* natives of Mexico and the southwestern U. S., as *C. elegans,* which is cultivated in many varieties for its showy flowers in a wide range of color.

zin-zi-ber-a-ceous (zin″zi-be-rā′shius), *a.* Zingiberaceous.

Zi-on (zī′ọn), *n.* [LL. *Sion,* < Gr. Σιών, < Heb. *Tsîyôn,* orig. a hill.] A hill or mount of Jerusalem, the center of ancient Hebrew worship; hence, the house or household of God, as consisting of the chosen people; the Israelites; also, the theocracy, or church of God; the church in general; also, heaven as the final gathering-place of true believers; also, a church or chapel of some Christian denominations.—**Zi′on-ism,** *n.* A modern plan or movement to colonize Hebrews in Palestine, the land of Zion; a movement to secure for such Jews as cannot or will not be assimilated in the country of their adoption a national homeland in Palestine.—**Zi′on-ist. I.** *n.* An advocate or adherent of Zionism. **II.** *a.* Of or pertaining to Zionists or Zionism.—**Zi-on-is′tic,** *a.*—**Zi′on-ite** (-īt), *n.* A Zionist.—**Zi′on-ward** (-wärd), *adv.* Toward Zion.

zip (zip), *n.* [Imit.] A sudden, brief, hissing sound, as of a flying bullet; hence, energy or vim. [Colloq.]—**zip,** *v. i.*; *zipped, zipping.* To make a zip (sound); move with a zip; hence, to proceed with energy. [Colloq.]—**zip′per,** *n.* One who or that which zips (colloq.); also, a kind of rubber and fabric boot or overshoe fastened up the leg by a slide-fastening device (proprietary name); hence, any fastener of this type, consisting of an interlocking device set along two edges to unite them (or separate them) when an attached piece sliding between them is pulled, and used in place of buttons, hooks, or the like, on clothing, bags, etc.

zir-con (zėr′kọn), *n.* [= F. *zircon*: cf. Pg. *zarcão, azarcão,* red lead, minium, Ar. *zarqūn,* vermilion, Pers. *āzargūn,* flame-color, also E. *jargon*[2].] A native silicate of zirconium,

occurring in tetragonal crystals of various colors, commonly opaque, but also transparent, and in this latter case used as a gem, the reddish-brown or reddish-orange varieties being known as *jacinth* and *hyacinth,* and the colorless, pale-yellow, or smoky ones from Ceylon as *jargon.*

zir-co-ni-a (zėr-kō′ni-ä), *n.* [See *zirconium.*] In *chem.,* an oxide of zirconium, ZrO_2, notable for its infusibility, and used in making glowers for Nernst lamps.

zir-co-ni-um (zėr-kō′ni-um), *n.* [NL.; named from *zircon.*] Chem. sym., Zr; at. wt., 90.6; sp. gr., 4.25. A metallic element found combined in zircon, etc., and resembling titanium in its chemical relations.—**zir-con′ic** (-kon′ik), *a.*

zith-er (zith′ėr), *n.* [G. *zither,* < L. *cithara,* E. *cithara.*] A musical instrument consisting of a flat sounding-box with from 30 to 40 strings stretched over it, which is placed on a horizontal surface and played with a plectrum and the fingers.—**zith′er-ist,** *n.* A player on the zither.—**zith-ern, zit-tern** (zith′ėrn, zit′ėrn), *n.* Same as *cithern, cittern.*

zi-zith (zē′zith), *n. pl.* [Heb. *tsîtsith.*] The fringes or tassels of entwined blue and white threads at the four corners of the tallith. See *tallith.*

zlot-y (zlot′ę), *n.*; pl. *zlotys* (-ęz). [Pol., orig. adj., golden, < *zloto,* gold.] The gold monetary unit (introduced in 1924), and a silver coin, of Poland, equivalent to the French franc, or to 19.3 U. S. cents.

zo-a (zō′ä), *n.* Plural of *zoön.*

zo-a-ri-um (zō-ā′ri-um), *n.*; pl. *-ria* (-ri-ä). [NL.: see *zoön* and *-arium,* and cf. *polyzoarium.*] In *zoöl.,* the colony or aggregate of individuals of a compound animal.

zo-di-ac (zō′di-ak), *n.* [OF. F. *zodiaque,* < L. *zodiacus,* < Gr. ζωδιακός, zodiac, prop. adj. < ζώδιον, small figure or image (in painting, etc.), sign of the zodiac, dim. of ζῶον, living being, animal, figure or image: see *zoön.*] An imaginary belt encircling the heavens, extending about 8° on each side of the ecliptic, and containing twelve constellations and hence twelve divisions (called *signs*), each division, however, because of the precession of the equinoxes (see under *precession*), now containing the constellation west of the one from which it took its name (see note below, also *sign, n.*); also, a circular or elliptical diagram representing this belt, and usually containing pictures of the animals, etc., which are associated with the constellations and signs; also, *fig.,* a belt or encircling band; a circuit or round.

*⁎⁎*The twelve signs of the zodiac, taken in order from west to east, are as follows: — (1) *Aries,* called in English 'the Ram' (symbol ♈), which the sun enters at the vernal equinox, about March 21; (2) *Taurus,* 'the Bull' (♉), which the sun enters about April 20; (3) *Gemini,* 'the Twins' (♊), which the sun enters about May 20; (4) *Cancer,* 'the Crab' (♋), which the sun enters at the summer solstice, about June 21; (5) *Leo,* 'the Lion' (♌), which the sun enters about July 22; (6) *Virgo,* 'the Virgin' (♍), which the sun enters about Aug. 22; (7) *Libra,* 'the Balance' (♎), which the sun enters at the autumnal equinox, about Sept. 22; (8) *Scorpio,* 'the Scorpion' (♏), which the sun enters about Oct. 23; (9) *Sagittarius,* 'the Archer' (♐), which the sun enters about Nov. 23; (10) *Capricornus,* or *Capricorn,* 'the Goat' (♑), which the sun enters at the winter solstice, about Dec. 22; (11) *Aquarius,* 'the Water-bearer' (♒), which the sun enters about Jan. 21; (12) *Pisces,* 'the Fishes' (♓), which the sun enters about Feb. 19. The sign Aries now contains the constellation Pisces; the sign Taurus, the constellation Aries; the sign Gemini, the constellation Taurus; and so on.

zo-di-a-cal (zō-dī′a-kal), *a.* Of or pertaining to the zodiac.—**zodiacal light,** a luminous triangular tract in the sky, seen near the ecliptic at certain seasons of the year, either in the west after sunset or in the east before sunrise: supposed to be the glow from a cloud of meteoric matter revolving round the sun.

zo-ë-trope (zō′ē-trōp), *n.* [Gr. ζωή, life: see *-trope.*] An optical device by means of which a series of pictures, representing the different attitudes successively assumed by an object in motion, are so viewed that the pictured object appears as if actually in motion: usually consisting of a cylinder open at the top and having the pictures arranged around its interior circumference, the illusion being produced by viewing the pictures through slits in the cylinder when it revolves.—**zo-ë-trop′ic** (-trop′ik), *a.*

---

fat, fāte, fär, fåll, åsk, fāre; net, mē, hėr; pin, pīne; not, nōte, môve, nôr; up, lūte, půll; oi, oil; ou, out; (lightened) aviary, ęlect, agọny, intọ, ụnite; (obscured) errạnt, operạ, ardẹnt, actọr, natụre; ch, chip; g, go; ᵺ, thin; ᴛʜ, then; y, you;

zo-ic (zō′ik), *a.* [Gr. ζωικός, < ζῷον, living being, animal: see *zoön*.] Of or pertaining to living beings or animals; characterized by animal life.

Zo-i-lus (zō′i-lus), *n.* [From *Zoilus*, a Greek grammarian of the 4th century B.C., a severe critic of Homer and others.] A spiteful or malignant critic.

zois-ite (zois′it), *n.* [Named (1805) from Baron von *Zois*, who first observed it.] A mineral consisting of a hydrated silicate of aluminium and calcium, sometimes with iron replacing some of the aluminium, occurring in orthorhombic crystals and massive, and varying in color from gray to brownish, greenish, or rose-red.

Zo-la-ism (zō′lä-izm), *n.* The characteristic qualities of the works of the French novelist Émile Zola (1840–1902), noted for his unreserved realism or naturalism. Cf. *naturalism.*

zoll-ver-ein (tsol′fer-īn″), *n.* [G., < *zoll*, toll, custom, + *verein*, union.] A union of German states for the maintenance of a uniform tariff on imports from other countries, and of free trade among themselves; hence, any similar union or arrangement between a number of states; a customs-union.

zo-nal (zō′nal), *a.* [LL. *zonalis*.] Pertaining to a zone or zones; characterized by zones; of the nature of a zone; in *bot.*, noting that view of a diatom in which the zone or suture of the valves is presented to the eye (cf. *valval*).—**zo′nal-ly,** *adv.*

zo-na-ry (zō′na̤-ri), *a.* [L. *zonarius*.] Zonal.

zo-nate (zō′nāt), *a.* [NL. *zonatus*.] Marked with a zone or zones, as of color, texture, or the like; arranged in a zone or zones.—**zo-na′tion** (-nā′shon), *n.* Zonate state or condition; esp., arrangement or distribution in zones.

zone (zōn), *n.* [F. *zone*, < L. *zona*, < Gr. ζώνη, girdle, belt, zone, < ζωννύναι, gird.] A girdle, belt, or cincture (as, "The alb . . . was confined round the waist by a *zone* or girdle," J. H. Newman's "Callista," xxx.: chiefly poetic); hence, a band encircling an object like a belt or girdle (as, "That milky way, Which nightly, as a circling *zone*, thou seest Powder'd with stars": Milton's "Paradise Lost," vii. 580); any continuous tract or area, whether forming a belt about an object or extending about a point, or forming a straight band or stripe, or having any other shape, which differs in some respect, or is distinguished for some purpose, from adjoining tracts or areas, or within which certain distinguishing circumstances exist or are established (as, a wheat *zone*; a war *zone*; the Canal *Zone*, on the Isthmus of Panama, see *isthmian*, *a.*); specif., a ring-like or surrounding area, or one of a series of such areas, about a particular place, to all points within which a uniform charge is made for transportation or some similar service, as, in the U. S. parcel-post system, such an area to all points within which the same rate of postage prevails for parcel-post shipments from the particular place; also, an area or district in a city or town under special restrictions as to buildings (see *zone, v. t.*); in *geom.*, a part of the surface of a sphere included between two parallel planes; in *geog.*, any of five great divisions of the earth's surface, bounded by lines parallel to the equator, and named according to the prevailing temperature (as, the torrid *zone*, extending from the tropic of Cancer to the tropic of Capricorn; the north temperate *zone*, extending from the tropic of Cancer to the arctic circle; the south temperate *zone*, extending from the tropic of Capricorn to the antarctic circle; the north frigid *zone*, extending from the arctic circle to the north pole; the south frigid *zone*, extending from the antarctic circle to the south pole); in *phytogeog.* and *zoögeog.*, an area or region distinguished by more or less uniform and characteristic plant or animal life. —**zone,** *v.*; zoned, zoning. **I.** *tr.* To encircle with or surround like a zone, girdle, or belt; mark with zones or bands; divide into zones, tracts, or areas, as according to existing characteristics, or as distinguished for some purpose; specif., to divide (a city or town) into areas or districts subject to special restrictions as to buildings, as with respect to their purpose or use (business, industrial, residential, etc.), their maximum height, and the amount of the lot that may be covered. **II.** *intr.* To be formed into a zone or zones.— **zoned,** *a.* Wearing a zone or girdle; also, marked with or having zones; divided into zones.—**zone′less,** *a.* Not confined by or wearing a zone or girdle; also, not marked with or divided into zones.—**zo-nule** (zō′nūl), *n.* [L. *zonula*, dim. of *zona*.] A little zone, belt, or band: as, the *zonule* of Zinn (in *anat.*, the suspensory ligament of the crystalline lens of the eye, named after J. G. Zinn, 1727–59, a German anatomist).

zoo (zö), *n.* A zoölogical garden: as, "monkeys in the *Zoo*" (Sinclair Lewis's "Main Street," xx.). [Colloq.]

zoö-. Form of Gr. ζῷον, living being, animal, used in combination.—**zo-ö-chem-is-try** (zō-ō-kem′is-tri), *n.* The chemistry of the constituents of the animal body; animal chemistry.—**zo-ö-chem′i-cal,** *a.*—**zo″ö-dy-nam′ics** (-dī-nam′iks), *n.* The branch of biology that treats of the vital force or energy of animals; animal physiology.—**zo″ö-dy-nam′ic,** *a.*—**zo-ö-g-a-my** (zō-og′a̤-mi), *n.* [+ -*gamy*.] The coupling, mating, or pairing of animals of opposite sexes for the purpose of reproduction; sexual reproduction of animals.—**zo-ög′e-ny** (-oj′e-ni), *n.* [+ -*geny*.] The origin and development of animals.

zo-ö-ge-og-ra-phy (zō″ō-jē-og′ra̤-fi), *n.* [See *zoö-.*] The science treating of the geographical distribution of animals.— **zo″ö-ge-og′ra-pher,** *n.*—**zo″ö-ge-o-graph′ic, zo″ö-ge-o-graph′i-cal** (-jē-ō-graf′ik, -i-ka̤l), *a.*

zo-ö-glœ-a (zō-ō-glē′ä), *n.* [NL., < Gr. ζῷον, animal, + γλοία, glue.] In *bact.*, a jelly-like mass or aggregate of bacteria formed when the cell-walls swell through absorption of water and become contiguous.—**zo-ö-glœ′ic,** *a.*

zo-ög-ra-phy (zō-og′ra̤-fi), *n.* [See *zoö-* and -*graphy*.] That branch of zoölogy which deals with the description of animals; descriptive zoölogy.—**zo-ög′ra-pher,** *n.*—**zo-ö-graph-ic, zo-ö-graph-i-cal** (zō-ō-graf′ik, -i-ka̤l), *a.*

zo-öid (zō′oid), *n.* [Gr. ζῳοειδής, < ζῷον, animal, + εἶδος, form.] **I.** *a.* Resembling, or of the nature of, an animal. **II.** *n.* In *biol.*, any organic body or cell, whether of animal, vegetable, or equivocal character (as a protozoön, a spermatozoid, a spermatozoön, etc.), which is capable of spontaneous movement and of an existence more or less apart from or independent of the parent organism; in *zoöl.*, any animal organism or individual capable of separate existence, and produced by fission, gemmation, or some method other than direct sexual reproduction; also, one of the individuals, as certain free-swimming medusæ, which intervene in the alternation of generations between the products of proper sexual reproduction; also, any one of the recognizably distinct individuals or elements, as a hydranth or polypite, of a compound or colonial organism, whether detached or detachable or not.—**zo-öi′dal,** *a.*

zo-öl-a-try (zō-ol′a̤-tri), *n.* [See *zoö-* and -*latry*.] The worship of animals.—**zo-öl′a-ter,** *n.*—**zo-öl′a-trous,** *a.*

zo-ö-lite (zō′ō-līt), *n.* [See *zoö-* and -*lite*.] A fossil animal. Also **zo′ö-lith** (-lith).

zo-ö-log-i-cal (zō-ō-loj′i-ka̤l), *a.* [See *zoölogy*.] Of or pertaining to zoölogy; relating to or concerned with animals: as, a *zoölogical* garden (a park or other large inclosure in which live animals are kept for public exhibition). Also **zo-ö-log′ic.**—**zo-ö-log′i-cal-ly,** *adv.*

zo-öl-o-gist (zō-ol′ō-jist), *n.* One versed in zoölogy.

zo-öl-o-gy (zō-ol′ō-ji), *n.*; pl. -*gies* (-giz). [See *zoö-* and -*logy*.] The science that treats of animals or the animal kingdom; also, a treatise on this science.

zoom (zöm), *v.* [Imit.] **I.** *intr.* To make a continuous humming sound; also, to drive an aëroplane suddenly and very sharply upward at great speed for a short distance, as in regaining altitude, clearing an obstacle, signaling, etc.; of an aëroplane, to go upward in this manner. **II.** *tr.* To cause (an aëroplane) to zoom; also, to fly over or surmount (an obstacle) by zooming.—**zoom,** *n.* An act of zooming; a sudden, very sharp upward movement of an aëroplane.

zo-ö-mag-net-ism (zō-ō-mag′net-izm), *n.* [See *zoö-.*] Animal magnetism; mesmerism.

zo-öm-e-try (zō-om′e-tri), *n.* [See *zoö-* and -*metry*.] Measurement of the proportionate lengths or sizes of the parts of animals.

zo-ö-morph (zō′ō-môrf), *n.* [See *zoö-* and -*morph*.] A representation of an animal as in primitive art; a zoömorphic image or design.—**zo-ö-mor′phic,** *a.* Representing or using animal forms (as, *zoömorphic* ornament: see cut on following page); also, ascribing animal form or attributes to beings or things not animal; representing a deity under the

form of an animal; characterized by or involving such ascription or representation.
—**zo-ö-mor′phism**, n. Zoömorphic representation, as in ornament; also, zoömorphic conception, as of a deity.

zo-ön (zō′on), n.; pl. **zoa** (zō′ä). [NL., < Gr. ζῷον, living being, animal, akin to ζωή, life, and ζῆν, live.] In zoöl., any of the individuals of a compound animal.

-zoön. Noun termination from Gr. ζῷον, animal, as in ectozoön, entozoön.

zo-ön-al (zō′ọ-nal), a. Pertaining to or of the nature of a zoön.

zo-ön-o-my (zọ-on′ọ-mi), n. [See zoö- and -nomy.] The science treating of the causes and relations of the phenomena of living animals.

zo-ö-pa-thol-o-gy (zō″ọ-pạ-thol′ọ-ji), n. [See zoö-.] The science treating of the diseases of the lower animals; veterinary pathology.

zo-öph-a-gous (zọ-of′ạ-gus), a. [Gr. ζωοφάγος, < ζῷον, animal, + φαγεῖν, eat.] Feeding on animals; carnivorous.

zo-ö-phile (zō′ọ-fil), n. [See zoö- and -phil.] A lover of animals. Also **zo-öph-i-list** (zọ-of′i-list).—**zo-öph′i-lous**, a. [See -philous.] Loving animals; in bot., adapted to pollination by the agency of animals.

zo-ö-phor-ic (zō-ọ-for′ik), a. [Gr. ζωοφόρος, < ζῷον, living being, animal, + φέρειν, bear.] Bearing a figure of a man or an animal, or more than one such figure: as, a zoöphoric column.

zo-ö-phys-ics (zō-ọ-fiz′iks), n. [See zoö-.] The study of the physical structure of animals; comparative anatomy as a branch of zoölogy.

zo-ö-phyte (zō′ọ-fit), n. [F. zoophyte, < Gr. ζωόφυτον, < ζῷον, animal, + φυτόν, plant.] Any of various animals resembling a plant, as a coral, a sea-anemone, etc.—**zo-ö-phyt′ic** (-fit′ik), a.—**zo-ö-phy-tol′o-gy** (-fī-tol′ọ-ji), n. [See -logy.] The science that treats of zoöphytes.

zo-ö-plas-ty (zō′ọ-plas-ti), n. [See zoö- and -plasty.] In surg., the transplantation of living tissue from a lower animal to the human body.—**zo-ö-plas′tic**, a.

zo-ö-psy-chol-o-gy (zō″ọ-sī-kol′ọ-ji), n. [See zoö-.] The psychology of animals other than man; animal psychology.

zo-ö-sperm (zō′ọ-spèrm), n. [See zoö- and -sperm.] In biol., a spermatozoön; in bot., a zoöspore.—**zo″ö-sper-mat′ic** (-spèr-mat′ik), a.

zo-ö-spo-ran-gi-um (zō″ọ-spọ-ran′ji-um), n.; pl. -gia (-ji-ä). [NL.: see zoö- and sporangium.] In bot., a sporangium or spore-case in which zoöspores are produced.—**zo″ö-spo-ran′gi-al**, a.

zo-ö-spore (zō′ọ-spōr), n. [See zoö- and spore.] In bot., an asexual spore produced by certain algæ and some fungi, capable of moving about by means of cilia or the like; in zoöl., any of the minute motile flagelliform or amœboid bodies which issue from the sporocyst of certain protozoans. —**zo-ö-spor′ic** (-spor′ik), a.—**zo″ö-spo-rif′er-ous** (-spọ-rif′ẹ-rus), a. [See -ferous.] Bearing or producing zoöspores.

zo-ö-tech-ny (zō′ọ-tek-ni), n. [zoö- + -techny.] Keeping and breeding animals in domestication.—**zo-ö-tech′nic**, a.

zo-ö-the-ism (zō′ọ-thē-izm), n. [See zoö- and theism².] The attribution of deity to an animal; the worship of animals or animal forms.—**zo′ö-the-ist**, n.—**zo″ö-the-is′tic**, a.

zo-öt-o-my (zọ-ot′ọ-mi), n. [See zoö- and -tomy.] The dissection or the anatomy of animals.—**zo-ö-tom-ic, zo-ö-tom-i-cal** (zō-ọ-tom′ik, -i-kal), a.—**zo-öt′o-mist**, n.

zo-ö-trope (zō′ọ-trōp), n. Same as zoëtrope.

zoot suit. An extreme suit with big tight-cuffed pants and an over-sized coat: worn by jive enthusiasts. [Slang.]

Zoömorphic Ornament. — Doorway of church of Borgund, Norway.

zor-il (zor′il), n. [F. zorille, < Sp. zorrilla, dim. of zorra, fox.] A South African musteline animal, Zorilla striata (or Ictonyx capensis), resembling a skunk, and capable of emitting a fetid odor; also, any other animal of this genus.

Zoril (Zorilla striata).¹

Zo-ro-as-tri-an (zō-rọ-as′tri-ạn). **I.** a. Pertaining to Zoroaster, or Zarathustra, the Persian religious teacher (of uncertain date; by some placed as early as 1000 B.C.), or to the ancient Persian religion founded by him. **II.** n. One of the followers of Zoroaster, now represented by the Guebers of Persia and the Parsees of India.—**Zo-ro-as′tri-an-ism**, n. The religious system of Zoroaster and his followers, prevalent in Persia till its overthrow by the Mohammedans in the 7th century A.D., and still held by the Guebers and the Parsees. Cf. Avesta, Ormazd, Ahriman, and Magus.

zos-ter (zos′tėr), n. [L., < Gr. ζωστήρ, girdle, < ζωννύναι, gird.] In Gr. antiq., a belt or girdle; in pathol., same as herpes zoster.

Zou-ave (zọ-äv′), n. [F. zouave; from the name of a Kabyle tribe in Algeria. [Also l. c.] One of a body of infantry in the French army, composed orig. of Algerians, distinguished for their dash and hardiness, and wearing a picturesque Oriental uniform; also, a member of any body of soldiers wearing a similar dress.—**Zouave jacket**, a short jacket ending at or above the waist and open or cut away in front.

zounds (zoundz), interj. [Also swounds; reduced form of God's wounds.] A minced oath, often used as a mere emphatic exclamation, as of surprise, indignation, or anger: as, "Zounds! do you intend to kill my friend?" (Fielding's "Tom Jones," ix. 3); "Zounds! . . . that is not to be borne" (S. J. Weyman's "Gentleman of France," xxxii.). [Archaic.]

zuc-chet-to (zọ-ket′ō), n.; pl. zucchettos (-ōz). [It., dim. < zucca, gourd.] A small, round skullcap worn by Roman Catholic ecclesiastics, a priest's being black, a bishop's violet, a cardinal's red, and the Pope's white.

Zu-lu (zō′lö). **I.** n.; pl. -lus (-löz) or -lu. A member of a warlike and superior branch of the Kafir (negroid) race, of southeastern Africa, dwelling in Zululand (Natal) and regions north of it; also, their language. **II.** a. Of or pertaining to the Zulus or their language.

zurf (zėrf), n. See zarf.

zwie-back (tsvē′bäk), n. [G., 'twice-baked': for the meaning, cf. biscuit.] A kind of bread or cake cut into slices and dried in the oven.

Zwing-li-an (tsving′li-ạn or zwing′gli-). **I.** a. Of or pertaining to Ulrich Zwingli (1484–1531), a Swiss religious reformer, or his doctrines, which were characterized esp. by denial of the real presence of the body of Christ in the eucharist. **II.** n. A follower of Zwingli.—**Zwing′li-an-ism**, n.

zy-ga-poph-y-sis (zī-gạ-pof′i-sis or zig-ạ-), n.; pl. -yses (-i-sēz). [See zygo- and apophysis.] In anat., one of the articular processes upon the neural arch of a vertebra, usually occurring in two pairs, one anterior and the other posterior, and serving to interlock each vertebra with the one above and below.

zygo-, zyg-. Forms of Gr. ζυγόν, yoke, used in combination.

zy-go-dac-tyl (zī-gọ-dak′til or zig-ọ-). [NL. zygodactylus, < Gr. ζυγόν, yoke, + δάκτυλος, finger or toe.] In ornith.: **I.** a. Of a bird or a bird's foot, having the toes disposed in pairs, one pair before and one pair behind on each foot. **II.** n. A zygodactyl bird.—**zy-go-dac′tyl-ism**, n.

Zygodactyl Foot of Woodpecker, digits 2 and 3 the pair before, and 4 and 1 the pair behind.

zy-go-ma (zī-gō'mạ or zi-), *n.*; pl. *-mata* (-mạ-tạ̈). [NL., < Gr. ζύγωμα, < ζυγοῦν, to yoke, < ζυγόν, a yoke.] In *anat.*, the bony arch below the orbit of the skull, which is formed by the jugal bone, etc., and serves to connect the bones of the face with those about the ear (also called *zygomatic arch*); also, a process of the temporal bone forming part of this arch (also called *zygomatic process*); also, the jugal bone (rare).—**zy-go-mat-ic** (zī-gō-mat'ik or zig-ọ̄-), *a.* Of, pertaining to, or constituting the zygoma: as, the *zygomatic* arch; the *zygomatic* bone (the jugal bone); the *zygomatic* process (see *zygoma*).

zy-go-mor-phic, zy-go-mor-phous (zī-gō-môr'fik or zig-ọ̄-, -fus), *a.* [See *zygo-*, *-morphic*, and *-morphous*.] In *bot.*, of flowers, etc., divisible into similar or symmetrical halves by one plane only. Cf. *actinomorphic*.

zy-go-phyl-la-ceous (zī''gō-fi-lā'shius or zig''ọ̄-), *a.* [NL. *Zygophyllum*, the typical genus, < Gr. ζυγόν, yoke, + φύλλον, leaf.] Belonging to the *Zygophyllaceæ*, or bean-caper family of plants. See *bean-caper* and *guaiacum*.

zy-go-phyte (zī'gō-fīt or zig'ọ̄-), *n.* [See *zygo-* and *-phyte*.] In *bot.*, a plant which is reproduced by means of zygospores.

zy-go-spore (zī'gō-spōr or zig'ọ̄-), *n.* [See *zygo-* and *spore*.] In *bot.*, a spore formed in the process of reproduction by the union or conjugation of two similar gametes or protoplasmic masses, as in certain algæ and fungi.—**zy-go-spor'ic** (-spor'ik), *a.*

zy-gote (zī'gōt or zig'ōt), *n.* [Gr. ζυγωτός, yoked, < ζυγοῦν, to yoke: see *zygoma*.] In *biol.*, a cell or spore formed by the union of two gametes; a fertilized ovum; sometimes, the organism produced from a fertilized ovum; also, a zygospore.

zylo-, etc. See *xylo-*, etc.

zy-mase (zī'mās), *n.* [Gr. ζύμη, leaven: see *-ase*.] An enzyme in yeast which causes the decomposition of sugar into alcohol and carbon dioxide, and which may be obtained in the form of an extract.

zyme (zīm), *n.* [Gr. ζύμη, leaven.] A ferment or enzyme; in *pathol.*, the specific morbific principle regarded as the cause of a zymotic disease.—**zy-mic** (zī'mik or zim'ik), *a.* Pertaining to, of the nature of, or due to a zyme or ferment.

zymo-, zym-. Forms of Gr. ζύμη, leaven (ferment), used in combination.—**zy-mo-gen** (zī'mō-jen), *n.* [+ *-gen*.] Any of various substances which by some internal change may give rise to an enzyme.—**zy'mo-gene** (-jēn), *n.* In *biol.*, any of various bacterial organisms which produce enzymes.—**zy-mo-gen'ic**, *a.* [+ *-genic*.] Causing fermentation (as, a *zymogenic* organism, any micro-organism causing fermentative processes); also, of or pertaining to a zymogen or a zymogene.—**zy'moid**, *a.* [+ *-oid*.] Resembling a zyme or ferment.—**zy-mol'o-gy** (-mol'ọ̄-ji), *n.* [+ *-logy*.] The science that treats of fermentation.—**zy-mo-log'i-cal** (-loj'i-kạl), *a.*—**zy-mol'y-sis** (-mol'i-sis), *n.* [+ *-lysis*.] Fermentation; specif., digestion by means of enzymes.—**zy-mo-lyt'ic** (-lit'ik), *a.*—**zy-mom'e-ter** (-mom'e-tèr), *n.* [+ *-meter*.] An instrument for ascertaining the degree of fermentation.

zy-mo-sis (zī-mō'sis), *n.*; pl. *zymoses* (-sēz). [NL., < Gr. ζύμωσις, fermentation, < ζυμοῦν, to ferment, < ζύμη, leaven.] Fermentation; in *med.*, a process analogous to fermentation, by which certain infectious and contagious diseases were supposed to be produced; also, an infectious or contagious disease.

zy-mot-ic (zī-mot'ik), *a.* [Gr. ζυμωτικός, < ζυμοῦν, to ferment: see *zymosis*.] Pertaining to or caused by, or as if by, fermentation (as, a *zymotic* disease: see phrase below); also, pertaining to a zymotic disease.—**zymotic disease**, any of various infectious and contagious diseases, as smallpox, typhoid fever, etc., which were regarded as due to the presence in the system of a morbific principle acting in a manner analogous to the process of fermentation; a bacterial disease.—**zy-mot'i-cal-ly**, *adv.*

zy-mur-gy (zī'mėr-ji), *n.* [Gr. ζύμη, leaven, + -εργός, working.] That branch of chemistry which deals with the processes of fermentation, as in wine-making, brewing, distilling, the preparation of yeast, etc.

(variable) ḍ as d or j, ş as s or sh, ṭ as t or ch, ẓ as z or zh; o, F. cloche; ü, F. menu; ċh, Sc. loch; ṅ, F. bonbon; ', primary accent; ", secondary accent; †, obsolete; <, from; +, and; =, equals. See also lists at beginning of book.

SYNONYMS, ANTONYMS, AND DISCRIMINATIONS

COMPILED BY

ALBERT C. BAUGH, Ph.D., AND PAUL C. KITCHEN, Ph.D.

ASSISTANT PROFESSORS OF ENGLISH, UNIVERSITY OF PENNSYLVANIA

A

abandon. Syn.: give up, give over, relinquish, yield, surrender, resign, waive, abdicate; renounce, forswear, discard, repudiate; forsake, desert, leave, quit; desist from, cease. **Ant.:** keep, retain, hold, adhere to, maintain, continue, cherish.

Abandon implies absolute or final giving up, either under the force of circumstances or as a shirking of one's responsibility: as, to *abandon* a sinking ship, a hopeless undertaking, one's offspring. *Desert* always implies the blame or culpability of leaving or quitting in violation of obligation, duty, or oath (except sometimes when used of localities): as, to *desert* one's family, post, colors, regiment; the inhabitants *deserted* the devastated regions; a *deserted* village or camp. *Forsake* chiefly suggests the leaving of a person or thing bound to one by intimate or familiar association or by natural affection: as, to *forsake* one's home, friends, country, or a cause.

abandoned. Syn.: given up, relinquished, forsaken, deserted, friendless, etc. (see **abandon**); profligate, dissolute, depraved, unprincipled, reprobate, corrupt, vicious. See **dissipated.**

abase. Syn.: lower, reduce, cast down, depose, discredit, dishonor, humble, humiliate, disgrace, mortify, shame, degrade, debase (*q. v.*). **Ant.:** raise, elevate, advance, promote, dignify, honor, exalt.

To *abase* is to lower in rank, position, or condition, as by making others believe one to be unworthy of their respect, estimation, or honor. When used reflexively *abase* implies an assumption of complete humility: as, he *abased* himself before his king. To *degrade* is to demote or reduce to a lower rank or position, especially as a punishment: as, to *degrade* an officer. It is also (and more commonly) used to imply the lowering of moral standards and the corrupting of one's character. To *humble* is to lower a person's pride, to make one meek in spirit. To *humiliate* is to humble one painfully, usually before others.

abash. Syn.: embarrass, disconcert, discompose, discomfit, dismay, bewilder, humble, mortify, chagrin, confuse, daunt, confound, subdue, awe, overawe. **Ant.:** compose, calm, encourage.

A person is *abashed* when his self-possession is destroyed because he is in the presence of superiors or is detected in misconduct: as, Satan was *abashed* before God; *awed* by that which is of vast power or dimensions, frequently inspiring fear or dread: as, to be *awed* by some great spectacle of nature; *overawed* by that which restrains or controls by threats, intimidation, or the like; *subdued* when he feels that some one has got so much the better of him that he is temporarily beaten.

abate. Syn.: bring down, lessen, decrease, diminish, curtail, reduce; mitigate, moderate, calm, assuage; remove, abolish, destroy; subside, intermit, slacken, decline, fall away, wane, ebb, sink. **Ant.:** augment, increase, enlarge, extend, develop, magnify, intensify, continue, revive, heighten.

abatement. Syn.: decrease, reduction, diminution, subsidence, etc. (see **abate**); rebate, allowance, deduction, discount.

abbey. Syn.: see **convent.**

abbreviate. Syn.: shorten, curtail, abridge, reduce, contract, compress, condense, epitomize, cut down. **Ant.:** lengthen, extend, expand, prolong, protract.

abdicate. Syn.: see **relinquish.**

aberration. Syn.: wandering, irregularity, deviation, divergence, eccentricity, derangement.

abet. Syn.: support, aid, assist, sanction, back, countenance, stand by, further, uphold, encourage, connive at, incite, egg on, instigate. **Ant.:** deter, dissuade, discourage, hinder, impede, obstruct, counteract, bar, embarrass, balk, baffle, foil, frustrate, defeat.

abetter. Syn.: see **accomplice.**

abhor. Syn.: loathe, abominate, detest, hate, despise, scorn, dislike. **Ant.:** like, approve, admire, esteem, value, prize. See **hate.**

abhorrent. Syn.: loathsome, repulsive, detestable, abominable, odious, repugnant. **Ant.:** attractive, agreeable, pleasing.

abide. Syn.: await, wait for, expect; rest, stop, lodge, tarry, linger, sojourn, remain, stay, reside, dwell, inhabit, live; tolerate, submit to, endure, bear; continue, be stable, stand firm, last. **Ant.:** leave, quit, go away, move, proceed, journey, depart; rove, roam, wander, migrate; retire, withdraw, vacate; waver, vacillate. See **live.**

ability. Syn.: capacity, capability, proficiency, competency, qualification, faculty; power, energy, strength, efficacy, efficiency; skill, expertness, dexterity, cleverness, aptness, readiness, adroitness, adeptness, aptitude, talent. **Ant.:** inability, incapacity, incompetence, inefficiency, clumsiness, awkwardness, unskilfulness, inaptitude. See **genius.**

abject. Syn.: abased, prostrate, groveling, degraded, brought low; low, mean, debased, ignoble, base, vile, contemptible, despicable, beggarly, menial, servile, slavish. **Ant.:** lofty, dignified, exalted, noble, honorable, worthy; haughty, imperious, supercilious; bold, audacious. See **mean.**

abjure. Syn.: see **forswear, renounce.**

able. Syn.: capable, competent, adequate, qualified, fitted, potent; strong, sturdy, vigorous, powerful; effective, efficient, talented, skilled, accomplished, gifted, adapted, clever. **Ant.:** incapable, incompetent, unfitted, inefficient, weak.

Able implies the power (sometimes in a distinguished or remarkable degree) of doing something: as, the child is *able* to read and write; an *able* orator or diplomat; *capable*, the qualifications for meeting or fulfilling the (usually ordinary or expected) requirements or demands: as, he is *capable* of holding a good position; a *capable* teacher or officer.

abnormal. Syn.: irregular, anomalous, unconformable, aberrant, peculiar, exceptional, unusual, odd, strange, extraordinary, unnatural, erratic, eccentric, monstrous. **Ant.:** normal, regular, common, usual, wonted, natural, ordinary, sane. See **irregular.**

abode. Syn.: stay, sojourn; habitation, quarters, dwelling-place, dwelling, lodging, house, domicile, residence, home. See **habitation.**

abolish. Syn.: do away with, destroy, end, annihilate, exterminate, extirpate, obliterate, eradicate, quash, overthrow, stamp out, terminate, abate, suppress, remove, abrogate, nullify, annul, repeal, rescind, revoke, reverse, cancel. **Ant.:** establish, continue, promote, sustain, enact, legalize, revive.

To *abolish* is to do away with completely, often by a summary act, something (usually) long established or deeply rooted, as the institution of slavery or the custom of smoking opium; to *annul* is to render null and void what was before in force, as a marriage or other contract; to *abrogate* is to annul by an authoritative act, such as that of a ruler; to *rescind* is to make inoperative the force of a decision, contract, decree, vote, or the like; to *revoke* is to recall, as a grant or privilege. A legislative body formally *repeals* an existing law; a higher court or authority may *reverse* the decision of a lower.

abominable. Syn.: execrable, loathsome, odious, revolting, intolerable, disgusting, horrible, hateful, shocking, detestable, offensive. **Ant.:** admirable, charming, delightful, pleasant, gratifying, agreeable, engaging, fascinating.

abominate. Syn.: see **hate.**

abomination. Syn.: loathing, disgust, hatred, detestation, aversion; bane, plague, pest.

aboriginal. Syn.: see **primitive.**

above. Syn.: see **over.**

abrade. Syn.: see **scrape.**

abridge. Syn.: cut down, abbreviate, curtail, epitomize, shorten, lessen, diminish, reduce, compress, contract, condense. **Ant.:** expand, lengthen, extend, enlarge, amplify, augment. See **shorten.**

abridgment. Syn.: abbreviation, contraction, etc. (see **abridge**); compendium, epitome, abstract, summary, résumé, synopsis, conspectus, outline, syllabus, digest, brief. **Ant.:** enlargement, expansion, amplification.

An *abridgment* is a work resulting from omitting or condensing the less essential parts of a larger work, the retained parts of which are usually unaltered or practically so: as, an *abridgment* of a dictionary. A *compendium* is a concise but comprehensive view of a subject, branch of science, knowledge, or the like, but unlike an abridgment it is usually not a condensation of a definite larger work: as, a *compendium* of literature or universal history. An *epitome* contains only the most important points of a work or subject, expressed in the smallest compass: as, an *epitome* of the political situation. A *summary* is a brief statement of the main points of a work, treatise, argument, or the like, especially when used as a conclusion or recapitulation: as, a *summary* of the arguments in a case. A *digest* is an orderly and methodical arrangement of the material of a literary, historical, scientific, or legal subject under heads and titles so that it will be in a more convenient or usable shape: as, a *digest* of Roman law. An *abstract* is a concise statement of the principal topics of a discussion: as, an *abstract* of a lecture, historical work, legal decision, etc. A *brief* is a detailed outline, by heads and subheads, forming the skeleton of a discourse to be completed: as, a *brief* for an argument in a debate or trial. A *synopsis* is usually a compressed statement of the plot of a novel, play, etc.: as, a *synopsis* of *Ivanhoe.*

abrogate. Syn.: see **abolish.**

abrupt. Syn.: broken, precipitous, craggy, rugged, steep; disconnected, unexpected, sudden, unceremonious, blunt, brusque, curt. **Ant.:** gradual, gently sloping, even, level; smooth; calm, considerate, courteous, gentle; suave, urbane. See **steep.**

abscond. Syn.: see **flee.**

absent. Syn.: see **abstracted.**

absent-minded. Syn.: see **abstracted.**

absolute. Syn.: unrestricted, unconditioned, uncontrolled, independent; autocratic, despotic; unqualified, unreserved, unequivocal, downright, positive; perfect, consummate, pure, simple, mere, actual, real. **Ant.:** restricted, limited, restrained, qualified, conditional. See **utter,** *a.*

absolution. Syn.: see **forgiveness.**

absolve. Syn.: free, liberate, exempt, release, excuse, forgive; acquit, exculpate, exonerate, clear, pardon, justify, vindicate. **Ant.:** bind, restrict; condemn, convict, doom. See **exculpate.**

absorb. Syn.: swallow up, suck up, drink in, take in, imbibe, assimilate, consume, engulf; engross, engage, occupy, monopolize. **Ant.:** exude, sweat, ooze, effuse, emit, emanate, discharge, eject, expel, cast out, vomit.

abstain. Syn.: refrain, forbear, desist, cease. See **refrain.**

abstemiousness. Syn.: temperateness, moderation, sobriety, temperance, abstinence. **Ant.:** self-indulgence, gluttony, intemperance. See **abstinence.**

abstinence. Syn.: abstention, forbearance, abstemiousness, moderation, temperance, sobriety, self-denial, continence, fasting. **Ant.:** indulgence, excess, dissipation, sensuality, licentiousness, gluttony.

Abstinence is the act or habit of refraining from any indulgence of appetite or passions; *abstemiousness*, habitual moderation in the gratification of appetites and desires. *Temperance* and *sobriety* suggest wise self-control and moderation in the gratification of desires and appetites, the measure of abstention being proportioned to the individual's idea of what is proper. In popular use, however, *abstinence, total abstinence,* and *temperance* especially denote a total abstaining from intoxicating drink.

abstract, *n.* **Syn.:** see **abridgment.**

abstract, *v.* **Syn.:** take away, withdraw, remove, divert, disengage, distract; abridge, epitomize, summarize; appropriate, purloin, steal. **Ant.:** add, affix, attach, increase, restore, replace.

abstracted. Syn.: separated, withdrawn, etc. (see **abstract**); inattentive, preoccupied, absent, absent-minded, absorbed, oblivious, distracted.

Abstracted implies reflection upon subjects so engrossing as to draw the mind away from the immediate present; *absent* or *absent-minded* especially suggests an unconscious or aimless wandering of the mind away from the immediate surroundings, or the present topic demanding attention; *preoccupied,* intense interest or absorption in some previous thought; *distracted,* a mental confusion resulting from emotional strain, or a diffusion of the attention in several directions and a concentration in none. *Distracted* is often used in connection with interruptions which draw one's attention away from the point of previous concentration.

abstruse. Syn.: hidden, obscure, occult, recondite, profound, deep. **Ant.:** plain, simple, evident, clear, obvious. See **obscure.**

absurd. Syn.: irrational, unreasonable, senseless, preposterous, nonsensical, ridiculous, wild. **Ant.:** reasonable, sensible, logical, sane.

That which is *absurd* is glaringly opposed to common sense and reason: as, that a part should be greater than the whole is *absurd.* That which is *preposterous* is at the height of absurdity, and excites amazement that any one should be capable of such an extreme of foolishness: as, it is *preposterous* to pay one's taxes twice. That which is *ridiculous* is so absurd as to be fit only to be laughed at, sometimes contemptuously or derisively: as, a *ridiculous* suggestion; a *ridiculous* alibi.

abundance. Syn.: plenteousness, plentifulness, plenty, copiousness, profusion, exuberance, luxuriance, affluence, wealth. **Ant.:** deficiency, dearth, scarcity, want, poverty, famine. See **plenty.**

abundant. Syn.: abounding, plenteous, plentiful, copious, profuse, overflowing, lavish, ample, rich.

abuse, *n.* **Syn.:** misuse, misapplication, perversion; maltreatment, injury, outrage, profanation; revilement, vilification, vituperation, tirade, invective, scolding, scurrility, billingsgate.

abuse, *v.* **Syn.:** misuse, misapply, misemploy; ill-use, maltreat, molest, injure, oppress; revile, vilify, vituperate, rail at, berate, reproach, upbraid, disparage, malign, slander, calumniate. See **revile.**

abusive. Syn.: reviling, vituperative, railing, reproachful, opprobrious, scurrilous, insolent, insulting.

abutting. Syn.: see **adjacent.**

academic. Syn.: see **formal.**

accede. Syn.: attain, succeed (to); agree, assent, acquiesce, consent, concur, conform, comply, yield. **Ant.:** decline, refuse, oppose. See **assent.**

accelerate. Syn.: see **quicken.**

accent, *n.* **Syn.:** see **inflection.**

accent, *v.* **Syn.:** accentuate, emphasize, stress.

accept. Syn.: see **receive.**

access. Syn.: admission, admittance, entrance, approach, increase, addition.

accession. Syn.: coming, arrival, attainment; adhesion, assent; addition, increase, extension, augmentation, increment. **Ant.:** refusal, rejection; decrease, diminution.

accessory. Syn.: see **accomplice.**

accident. Syn.: chance; mischance, mishap, misfortune, misadventure, casualty, disaster, calamity, catastrophe. **Ant.:** intention, plan, certainty, calculation.

accidental. Syn.: fortuitous, chance, casual, unintended, unpremeditated, unexpected; non-essential, incidental, adventitious, extraneous. **Ant.:** purposed, intentional, planned; important, necessary, indispensable.

Accidental commonly expresses occurrence without design or expectation, and is applied to what happens outside the usual course of things. *Casual* usually adds to accidental the idea of relatively slight importance. *Incidental* describes that which is secondary to the main design: as, by-products are *incidental* to a process of manufacture. *Fortuitous*, a more learned word, is applied to events for which there is no assignable cause: as, a *fortuitous* concourse of atoms.

accommodate. Syn.: fit, suit, adapt, adjust, arrange, conform, reconcile; furnish, supply, provide, equip; serve, aid, assist, oblige, favor. See **adapt, oblige.**

accompaniment. Syn.: concomitant, adjunct, accessory.

An *accompaniment* is something minor that is added to another thing, usually by reason of its fitness or harmoniousness, or because it rounds out or is conducive to completeness. A *concomitant* goes with something else by a natural connection, but in a subordinate way. An *adjunct* is something subordinate joined to another, usually not essential but advantageous to it. An *accessory* contributes to something else in a supplementary way without forming an integral part of it.

accompany. Syn.: associate with, consort with, convoy, escort, attend, conduct, wait on, follow, chaperon. **Ant.:** shun, avoid, desert, leave, quit.

To *accompany* is to go along with some one, especially as his equal and often for the purpose of enjoying his society or friendship or showing him courtesy and honor. To *attend* is to go along with, usually as an inferior or servant, for the purpose of rendering service or discharging duties. To *escort* is to accompany for the purpose of protecting or guarding or of showing civility or courtesy. To *convoy* is to accompany (especially ships) with an armed force for protection.

accomplice. Syn.: supporter, backer, ally, assistant, accessory, abetter, confederate, henchman. **Ant.:** hinderer, adversary, opponent, obstructionist, enemy.

An *accomplice* is either a principal or a subordinate associate in the commission of a crime or offense. A *confederate* is one leagued with another or others, often secretly or surreptitiously, for unlawful or criminal purposes. An *abetter* purposely and intentionally aids, supports, or encourages another, usually in wrong-doing, without taking a principal or direct part in it. An *accessory* assists in a contributory capacity in some misdemeanor or felony, either by instigating or aiding before, or concealing after, its commission.

accomplish. Syn.: complete, finish, perfect, consummate, fulfil, carry out, achieve, perform, execute, effect, do. See **do.**

accomplishment. Syn.: completion, fulfilment, achievement, etc. (see **accomplish**); acquirement, attainment, acquisition, qualification, ability. See **acquirement.**

accord. Syn.: agree, correspond, concur; harmonize, reconcile, adjust, settle; grant, give, concede.

accordance. Syn.: harmony, agreement, unison, accord, concord, unanimity, conformity, concurrence, congruity. **Ant.:** discord, dissension, conflict.

accordingly. Syn.: therefore, wherefore, consequently, hence, thus, then. See **therefore.**

accost. Syn.: address, speak to, greet, salute, hail; hold up, assail.

Accost implies going up and speaking to a person, often with the unceremoniousness or abruptness allowed by familiarity or prompted by necessity or hostile intent. *Greet* suggests the salutations usual upon meeting, but often adds the idea of personal warmth or heartiness of feeling. *Salute* is applied to the expression of respect required by usage or custom upon meeting, or, specifically, to the sign of formal recognition employed in the army or navy. *Address* implies some formality in speaking (sometimes writing) to a person or group. *Hail* implies hearty or demonstrative greeting; it has a specific (nautical) use in reference to calling from a distance to arrest attention.

account. Syn.: reckoning, computation, calculation, enumeration, record; recital, relation, narrative, narration, chronicle, history, story, tale, report, statement, description.

accountable. Syn.: amenable, responsible, answerable, liable. **Ant.:** independent, free, irresponsible, exempt.

Accountable implies liability to be called to account, usually for some specific thing and often to some definite superior; *responsible*, while frequently interchangeable, rather implies general accountability: as, a bank is *accountable* for the money deposited with it, and *responsible* for acts of its employees; a steward is *accountable* to his employer; a sane person is *responsible* for his actions; a *responsible* position. *Answerable* often implies an ethical or legal obligation; *ame-*

nable, submission to authority or legal jurisdiction that has the power to compel submission: as, a father is *answerable* for the acts of a minor son; a man is *answerable* for his sins; one is *amenable* to the law, to rules, discipline, or reason.

accoutre. Syn.: see **equip.**

accredit. Syn.: authorize, sanction, countenance, warrant, credit, attribute.

accrue. Syn.: see **increase.**

accumulate. Syn.: heap up, pile up, amass, hoard, gather, collect, aggregate, increase, accrue. **Ant.:** disperse, divide, parcel out, scatter, spend, waste, dissipate.

Accumulate usually suggests a gradual collecting or piling up; *amass* implies a more rapid heaping up and in larger quantities, especially of money, resources, or what has substantial value; *hoard* suggests a selfish or greedy storing up, especially of money or wealth.

accurate. Syn.: careful, painstaking, particular, precise, exact, correct, unerring, true, just, strict, literal, nice. **Ant.:** inaccurate, approximate, careless, slipshod, incorrect, erroneous, loose.

Accurate implies conformity to fact, truth, or standard, usually as a result of endeavor, care, or pains; *exact*, complete correspondence with a standard, rule, truth, or fact: as, an *accurate* copy; an *exact* reproduction. *Nice* implies (sometimes excessive) attention to fine or minute details: as, a *nice* difference; *precise*, strict (sometimes excessive) conformity to accuracy: as, a *precise* statement, observation, instrument; *correct*, freedom from error, mistakes, or faults: as, a *correct* answer. *Correct* is also used of persons, their possessions, etc., to imply conventionality: as, a *correct* hostess, costume; *correct* taste.

accusation. Syn.: charge, arraignment, indictment, impeachment, incrimination, imputation.

accuse. Syn.: charge, tax, arraign, blame, indict, incriminate, impeach. **Ant.:** absolve, acquit, exonerate.

Accuse is applied to a wide range of offenses extending from a grave crime to a mere social breach: as, to *accuse* one of murder, of trumping his partner's ace; *charge* has nearly the same force, but, except in law, is less commonly used. *Indict* and *arraign* are primarily specific legal terms, *indict* referring to the criminal proceedings by which a grand jury finds a sufficient case against the accused to warrant his being brought to trial; *arraign*, to the actual calling of the accused into court for trial. *Impeach* especially refers to accusing an official (usually one holding a high position) before a competent tribunal for misconduct in office.

accustom. Syn.: habituate, familiarize, inure, harden, train.

accustomed. Syn.: habituated, etc. (see **accustom**); customary, habitual, wonted, usual, ordinary. **Ant.:** unusual, infrequent, extraordinary.

acerbity. Syn.: see **acrimony.**

ache. Syn.: pain, sore, hurt, agony, pang, distress.

achieve. Syn.: consummate, finish, complete, accomplish, effect, execute, do; attain, realize, gain, win. **Ant.:** fail, lose, fall short. See **do.**

achievement. Syn.: accomplishment, etc. (see **achieve**); deed, feat, exploit. See **feat.**

acid. Syn.: see **sour.**

acidulous. Syn.: see **sour.**

acknowledge. Syn.: admit, confess, concede, allow, own, assent to, grant, recognize, accept, avow, profess. **Ant.:** deny, repudiate, disclaim, refute, disown, disavow.

To *acknowledge* is to state, sometimes under pressure or force, that one has knowledge of or is responsible for something, possibly something which one would have preferred to keep unknown or not to admit. *Acknowledge* is frequently used without implication of guilt or wrong-doing: as, to *acknowledge* a payment, favor, the receipt of a letter, etc. To *admit* is especially to assent to under pressure, or to concede or grant for the sake of argument. *Confess* is usually to admit what is detrimental, wrong, or criminal. To *own* is to acknowledge something that has particular reference to oneself.

acknowledgment. Syn.: admission, concession, confession, avowal; recognition, appreciation.

acme. Syn.: top, apex, summit, pinnacle, culmination, climax, zenith. See **top.**

acquaint. Syn.: inform, apprise, tell, familiarize, make conversant. See **inform.**

acquaintance. Syn.: knowledge, association, familiarity, intimacy, fellowship, friendship; friend, companion, comrade. **Ant.:** ignorance, inexperience, estrangement; stranger.

acquiesce. Syn.: see **accede, assent.**

acquiescence. Syn.: assent, consent, agreement, concurrence, compliance, resignation, submission. **Ant.:** refusal, denial, rejection; disagreement, resistance.

acquire. Syn.: get, obtain, procure, secure, gain, win, earn, gather, attain; learn, assimilate. **Ant.:** lose, give up, surrender, forfeit, abandon; forget. See **get.**

acquirement. Syn.: getting, gaining, etc. (see **acquire**); acquisition, attainment, accomplishment, endowment.

Acquirements refer especially to personal attributes acquired by continued effort or cultivation as opposed to natural gifts or talent: as, the ability to swim is a common *acquirement*; *attainments,* to the higher intellectual acquirements and distinguished achievements: as, a man of high *attainments*; *accomplishments,* to those polite and elegant acquirements that particularly fit one for refined society: as, dancing is a familiar social *accomplishment.*

acquisition. Syn.: see **acquirement.**

acquit. Syn.: clear, exculpate, exonerate, discharge, release; conduct, demean, deport. **Ant.:** condemn, convict. See **exculpate.**

acrid. Syn.: see **sour.**

acrimony. Syn.: sharpness, sourness, bitterness, tartness, acerbity, pungency, causticity, crabbedness, asperity, rancor, malignity, virulence, venom, harshness. **Ant.:** amiability, gentleness, good-nature, mildness, meekness, tenderness, kindness.

Acrimony implies biting, caustic, or angry sharpness of disposition, manner, or speech. *Acerbity* and *asperity* differ chiefly in their figurative suggestion. *Acerbity* indicates a sourness to the taste; *asperity,* a roughness painful to the touch. With these implications they are applied to speech, conduct, or manner: as, she spoke with *acerbity, asperity.* In ordinary use one more frequently acts with *acerbity,* speaks with *asperity.*

act, *n.* **Syn.:** action, deed, feat, exploit, achievement, accomplishment, transaction; ordinance, statute, law, edict, decree.

act, *v.* **Syn.:** perform, enact, play; simulate, feign, imitate, personate; do, execute, conduct one's self, behave.

action. Syn.: see **battle.**

active. Syn.: acting, working, operative; vigorous, energetic, strenuous, industrious, indefatigable, busy; alert, agile, nimble, brisk, lively, animated, restless, quick, sprightly. **Ant.:** see **inactive.**

Active implies motion or change, often quick and suggestive of diligence: as, an *active* man; *active* (as opposed to *inert*) gases. *Vigorous* adds the idea of strength to action; *energetic* implies forceful, intense, sometimes nervous activity; *strenuous* implies eager, zealous, sometimes excessively ardent or violent activity; *brisk* suggests quick or spirited movement.

actor, actress. Syn.: player, performer, Thespian, histrion, tragedian, tragédienne, comedian, comédienne, impersonator, mimic, pantomimist, mime, diseur, diseuse, barn-stormer.

actual. Syn.: real, positive, veritable, true, genuine, certain, absolute. See **real.**

actuate. Syn.: move, impel, drive, force, prompt, stir, instigate, promote, incite, excite, induce, urge, persuade, sway, influence. **Ant.:** hinder, restrain, retard, dissuade, deter.

To *actuate* is generally used to refer to a cause of action which lies within oneself: as, the murderer was *actuated* by revenge; to *prompt* may be used in the same sense, but is also used to refer to causes of action relatively minor or slight: as, the criticism *prompted* him to make a reply; to *impel* is to push forward to some action, as by an urgent force: as, he was *impelled* by hunger to take the chance. To *drive* implies greater pressure; *force,* inescapable necessity.

acumen. Syn.: sharpness, keenness, acuteness, penetration, insight, discernment, perspicacity, shrewdness, sagacity, astuteness. **Ant.:** dullness, obtuseness, stupidity. See **discernment.**

acute. Syn.: sharp, keen, shrewd, penetrating, astute, discerning, perspicacious, sagacious, subtle, sharp-witted; intense, poignant, piercing, excruciating. **Ant.:** dull, heavy, stupid.

Acute is used figuratively for sharp or pointed to indicate keen penetration or accurate discrimination: as, an *acute* observation; also to indicate extremity: as, an *acute* situation, *acute* indigestion. *Perspicacious, sagacious, shrewd,* and *astute* are used exclusively to describe qualities of mind. *Perspicacious* implies clear discernment; *sagacious,* acuteness coupled with wise or judicious foresight; *shrewd,* practical wisdom combined with cleverness, and often suggests a willingness to take advantage of one's neighbor; *astute* adds to acute the element of cunning or finesse: as, an *astute* politician.

adage. Syn.: see **proverb.**

adapt. Syn.: fit, adjust, harmonize, accommodate, conform, suit, compose, reconcile.

To *adapt* is to change or modify so as to fit or suit different conditions, requirements, or the like: as, to *adapt* oneself to the ways of a new country. To *adjust* is to arrange one thing in suitable or harmonious relation to another, there being usually some inherent fitness or preconceived relation between them: as, to *adjust* a sail to the wind. To *accommodate* is to bring two things into (often merely temporary or external) harmony or accord, generally by subordinating the one to the demands of the other: as, to *accommodate* one's gait to that of a companion. To *conform* is to cause to agree with the form or requirements of something, usually some model or standard: as, to *conform* one's conduct to the usage of a community.

adapted. Syn.: see **fit.**

add. Syn.: join, append, affix, attach, annex. **Ant.:** subtract, deduct, remove.

addict. Syn.: give over, devote, apply, accustom, habituate; incline.

addition. Syn.: adding, joining, appending, etc. (see **add**); augmentation, increase, enlargement, increment, accession, supplement, annex, adjunct, appendage, postscript, appendix.

address, *n.* **Syn.:** adroitness, dexterity, cleverness, readiness, ingenuity, tact; speech, discourse, oration, lecture, sermon, harangue. See **speech.**

address, *v.* **Syn.:** speak to, accost, salute, hail, greet; inscribe, superscribe. See **accost.**

adduce. Syn.: cite, present, advance, offer, quote, allege.

adept. Syn.: see **expert,** *n.*

adequate. Syn.: equal, commensurate, proportionate, suitable, adapted, fit, satisfactory, sufficient, ample, enough, capable, competent. **Ant.:** see **inadequate.**

That which is *adequate* conforms to a general standard of fitness or suitability; that which is *sufficient* satisfies the demands of a person or a situation; that which is *enough* fulfils a purpose or a desire: as, the information which is *sufficient* to pass an examination is not always an *adequate* preparation; a miser never has *enough.*

adhere. Syn.: cleave, cling, hold, stick, belong.

adherence. Syn.: adhesion; attachment, fidelity.

The following two words are becoming somewhat clearly distinguished in use, *adherence* being limited to figurative and moral senses; *adhesion,* to physical senses: as, *adherence* to a belief, principle, or party; the *adhesion* of putty to glass.

adherent. Syn.: follower, disciple, pupil, supporter, ally, upholder, partizan. **Ant.:** opponent, adversary, antagonist. See **follower.**

adhesion. Syn.: see **adherence.**

adieu. Syn.: see **farewell.**

adjacent. Syn.: adjoining, contiguous, abutting, bordering, neighboring, next, near, close. **Ant.:** distant, remote, separate, detached, disjoined.

Adjacent things lie near to each other, but may or may not be touching: as, *adjacent* angles or villages. Things are *adjoining* which touch either at a single point or along a line: as, *adjoining* fields. That which is *contiguous* usually touches along the whole or a considerable part of one of its boundaries: as, *contiguous* estates.

adjoining. Syn.: see **adjacent.**

adjourn. Syn.: postpone, defer, delay, prorogue, suspend, dissolve, terminate, end.

As applied to legislative or deliberative bodies, to *adjourn* is voluntarily to suspend business, usually for a short time and with the intention of resuming it where it was left off. To *prorogue* is used especially of the British Parliament when the authority which called it together adjourns it without dissolving it; to *dissolve* it is to end completely its existence.

adjournment. Syn.: postponement, prorogation, suspension, dissolution, termination, recess.

adjudge. Syn.: adjudicate, award, assign, decree; sentence, condemn, doom; decide, determine, settle, ordain.

adjure. Syn.: conjure, implore, supplicate, pray, entreat, beseech, beg.

adjust. Syn.: settle, arrange, rectify, reconcile; adapt, accommodate, suit, fit. See **adapt.**

administer. Syn.: manage, conduct, control; dispense, minister, apply, give, deal, distribute.

admirable. Syn.: wonderful, praiseworthy, excellent, fine, good.

admiration. Syn.: approbation, approval, esteem, veneration.

admire. Syn.: wonder at, esteem, revere, venerate. **Ant.:** despise, abhor, detest, contemn.

admissible. Syn.: allowable, permissible.

admission. Syn.: admittance, entrance, access; acknowledgment, allowance, concession.

As far as the following words are differentiated, *admittance* is usually used literally of entrance into a place; *admission*, figuratively of admitting to rights, privileges, or membership, or of admitting the truth or validity of something: as, no *admittance*; *admission* to a society or to the bar; the *admission* (not *admittance*) of guilt. When used literally *admission* is usually less definite with respect to place than *admittance* or implies some special right or privilege of entrance: as, aliens must comply with the immigration laws before *admission* into the country.

admit. Syn.: see **acknowledge.**

admittance. Syn.: see **admission.**

admonish. Syn.: advise, counsel, warn, caution, remind, reprove, rebuke, censure. See **advise.**

admonition. Syn.: advice, counsel, monition, warning, caution, remonstrance, expostulation, reprehension, reproof, censure, reprimand, rebuke, reproach.

ado. Syn.: see **excitement.**

adolescent. Syn: see **young.**

adoration. Syn.: see **worship,** *n.*

adore. Syn.: worship, idolize, reverence, revere, venerate. See **worship,** *v.*

adorn. Syn.: ornament, decorate, embellish, garnish, beautify, deck, bedeck, trim, array. **Ant.:** disfigure, deface, mar.

Adorn implies the addition or possession of that which enhances beauty or attractiveness, especially in a true, noble, or lofty way, and seems to be in complete harmony or unity with that to which it adds grace or loveliness: as, carvings *adorned* the temple; many virtues *adorned* his character. *Ornament* implies the addition of something external which often preserves its separate character: as, to *ornament* a building with statuary. *Decorate* suggests ornamental additions (especially to that which would otherwise be deficient or bare) which usually remain distinctly additional and are often employed for special purposes or occasions: as, to *decorate* the street with flags. *Embellish* suggests the addition of highly ornamental, often adventitious or ostentatious, beauty: as, a style *embellished* with flowery figures of speech. *Beautify* is a general word, applicable to whatever makes more beautiful or fair in any way.

adroit. Syn.: dexterous, skilful, expert, clever, apt, handy, quick, ready, deft; ready-witted, ingenious, sly, artful. See **dexterous.**

adulation. Syn.: flattery, blandishment, sycophancy, fawning, obsequiousness, compliment. **Ant.:** detraction, disparagement, depreciation. See **compliment.**

adulterate. Syn.: alloy, vitiate, contaminate, corrupt, mix.

advance, *n.* **Syn.:** progress, progression, advancement, growth, improvement, promotion; enhancement, preferment, elevation, betterment, amelioration; overture, approach, proposal, offer, proffer, tender.

advance, *v.* **Syn.:** promote, forward, elevate, enhance, aggrandize, dignify, exalt; increase, enlarge, augment, heighten, accelerate; progress, proceed, rise, thrive, prosper; adduce, allege, assign, propound; propose, offer, lend. See **proceed.**

advantage. Syn.: superiority, ascendency, mastery; benefit, profit, gain, help, good.

Advantage is anything that gives one a superiority over, or places him in a better position than, another, especially in coping with competition or difficulties: as, to have the *advantage* of an education; the high ground was an *advantage* to the enemy. *Profit* is any valuable, useful, or helpful gain: as, *profit* from trade or experience. *Benefit* is anything that improves the state of a person or thing: as, the chief *benefit* of exercise is improved health; a *benefit* to society.

advantageous. Syn.: beneficial, profitable, favorable, helpful, serviceable, auspicious.

advent. Syn.: see **arrival.**

adventitious. Syn.: see **extraneous.**

adventurous. Syn.: daring, venturous, venturesome, enterprising, temerarious, foolhardy, reckless, rash. See **bold.**

adversary. Syn.: antagonist, opponent, enemy, foe. See **opponent.**

adverse. Syn.: opposed, contrary, opposing, antagonistic, hostile, inimical; unfavorable, untoward, unfortunate, unlucky, disastrous, calamitous. **Ant.:** accordant, agreeing, sympathetic, friendly; favorable, fortunate, propitious, auspicious.

adversity. Syn.: misfortune, hardship, affliction, trouble, distress, suffering, misery, disaster, calamity, trial. **Ant.:** prosperity, happiness, success. See **misfortune.**

advert. Syn.: see **allude.**

advertise. Syn.: announce, proclaim, promulgate, publish, noise abroad, notify, apprise.

advice. Syn.: counsel, admonition, monition, suggestion, recommendation, instruction, persuasion, exhortation; information, intelligence, tidings, report, notification, word.

advisable. Syn.: expedient, politic, proper, fitting, desirable, prudent, judicious, wise.

advise. Syn.: counsel, admonish, caution, warn; inform, notify, apprise, acquaint, tell; consult, confer. See **inform.**

Advise implies the giving of practical information or direction as to action or conduct, usually by one who has, or affects to have, superior knowledge or experience. *Counsel* suggests advice given on weighty or serious matters, usually after careful deliberation. *Admonish* suggests earnest, authoritative, or gently reproving advice, sometimes with tacit reference to the danger or penalty attending failure to take heed. *Caution*, and the stronger word *warn*, both imply advice against anticipated error or fault or impending trouble or danger.

advocate. Syn.: see **plead.**

affability. Syn.: approachableness, graciousness, complaisance, sociability, amiability, suavity, urbanity.

affable. Syn.: approachable, gracious, complaisant, sociable, friendly, amicable, courteous, urbane. See **civil.**

affect. Syn.: act on, influence, concern, interest; move, touch, soften, melt, subdue. See **pretend.** Cf. **effect,** *v.*

affectation. Syn.: pretense, pretension, airs; foppery, mannerism.

affected. Syn.: assumed, pretended, simulated, feigned, artificial, mannered, foppish, insincere, pretentious, self-conscious.

affecting. Syn.: moving, touching, pathetic, piteous, sad.

affection. Syn.: feeling, disposition, devotion, attachment, fondness, love, endearment, tenderness, partiality. **Ant.:** dislike, aversion, hate. See **love, disease.**

affectionate. Syn.: loving, fond, tender, warm-hearted, attached, devoted.

affinity. Syn.: see **relation.**

affirm. Syn.: see **assert, declare.**

affix. Syn.: see **attach.**

afflict. Syn.: distress, trouble, vex, harass, torment, plague, hurt, pain, grieve, persecute.

affliction. Syn.: distress, trouble, misery, wretchedness, bereavement, tribulation, adversity, sorrow, grief. See **grief.**

Affliction suggests deep and bitter suffering or sorrow, especially as caused by loss or misfortune. *Distress* implies the anxiety, anguish, or acute suffering caused by the pressure of trouble or adversity. *Misery* suggests such great and unremitting pain or wretchedness of body or mind as crushes the spirit. *Tribulation* implies severe and long-continued affliction; it is especially Biblical in its application and suggests some disciplinary purpose of God.

affluence. Syn.: abundance, profusion, plenty, wealth, riches, fortune, opulence. **Ant.:** scantiness, dearth, poverty, indigence, want, penury. See **riches.**

affluent. Syn.: see **rich.**

affray. Syn.: see **quarrel.**

affright. Syn.: see **frighten.**

affront. Syn.: insult, impertinence, rudeness, contumely, slight, indignity, offense, provocation.

Affront implies open disrespect or offense, shown, as it were, to the face; *slight*, sometimes inadvertent indifference or disregard, or ill-concealed contempt for one. *Insult* is a stronger word than affront, and implies such insolence of speech or manner as deeply humiliates or wounds one's feelings and arouses to anger. *Indignity* is especially used of inconsiderate, contemptuous treatment towards one entitled to respect.

afraid. Syn.: frightened, alarmed, scared, fearful, apprehensive, shrinking, timid, pusillanimous, cowardly. **Ant.:** brave, courageous, undaunted, fearless.

after. Syn.: behind, subsequent, following, later. See **behind.**

age. Syn.: oldness, seniority, senescence, longevity, senility, decrepitude, dotage; era, epoch, æon, period, cycle, time.

Age usually refers to a considerable extent of time, especially such as is associated with a dominant personality or his influence, or is marked by some distinctive characteristic or institution: as, the golden *age*; the *age* of Pericles; the *age* of chivalry. *Period* is very indefinite as to extent of time, being either long or short, but usually marked by some characteristic condition or feature: as, the glacial *period*; a *period* of financial depression. *Epoch*, which is properly a point of time and should indicate the beginning of a new and, especially, of a markedly individual period, is now frequently interchanged with *era*, which especially indicates a period characterized by changed conditions, new undertakings, or the like: as, an *epoch* of military aggression; the Christian *era*; an *era* of invention. *Generation* indicates the average period of time that separates the birth of a man from that of his children, generally assumed to be thirty-five years.

aged. Syn.: old, elderly. See **old.**

agent. Syn.: representative, substitute, deputy, factor, middleman, attorney, emissary, envoy; canvasser, solicitor.

aggrandize. Syn.: augment, enhance, elevate, exalt, advance, promote, enrich.

aggravate. Syn.: intensify, heighten, increase, magnify. See **increase,** v.

aggregate, n. **Syn.:** see **sum.**

aggregate, v. **Syn.:** see **accumulate.**

aggregation. Syn.: see **collection.**

aggression. Syn.: attack, assault, offense, encroachment, provocation, invasion, intrusion.

aghast. Syn.: horrified, horror-struck, confounded, amazed, dismayed, terrified, thunderstruck, dumfounded, astounded.

agile. Syn.: active, nimble, sprightly, spry, brisk, supple, lively, quick. See **nimble.**

agitate. Syn.: stir, shake, excite, disturb, perturb, discompose, disconcert, ruffle, unsettle; discuss, debate. **Ant.:** quiet, calm, compose, allay.

agitation. Syn.: commotion, excitement, disturbance, perturbation, trepidation, emotion, turmoil, unrest, tremor, flutter; discussion, debate. See **excitement.**

agnostic. Syn.: see **skeptic.**

agony. Syn.: anguish, distress, torment, torture, throe, paroxysm, suffering, pang, pain, ache. See **pain.**

agree. Syn.: consent, assent, concur, acquiesce, subscribe, accede, comply, promise, contract; accord, harmonize, comport, conform, correspond, coincide, match, tally. **Ant.:** disagree, dissent, differ, dispute, quarrel; conflict, jar, vary.

Agree is a general word to express the absence of conflict between persons or things: as, the committee *agreed* upon a minimum wage; all the reports *agree*. *Correspond* suggests a likeness of essential features in whatever subjects are under consideration: as, the plots of two stories *correspond*; his testimony *corresponds* with yours. *Coincide* implies complete agreement: as, the results of the computations *coincide*.

agreeable. Syn.: see **pleasing.**

agreement. Syn.: see **contract,** n.

agriculture. Syn.: see **farming.**

aid, n. **Syn.:** help, assistance, support, coöperation, succor, relief, subsidy, subvention, patronage; helper, assistant, auxiliary, coadjutor, accessory, accomplice, abetter; aide-de-camp.

aid, v. **Syn.:** help, assist, support, sustain, second, back, abet, serve, succor, befriend, relieve. **Ant.:** hinder, impede, thwart, obstruct. See **help,** v.

ailing. Syn. See **sick.**

ailment. Syn.: sickness, illness, indisposition, malady, disease, disorder, distemper, complaint. See **disease.**

aim. Syn.: intent, intention, purpose, endeavor, aspiration, ambition, determination; mark, goal, object, end.

air. Syn.: atmosphere, breeze, zephyr, wind; look, appearance, aspect, bearing, demeanor, attitude; tune, melody, song, aria.

air-raid. Syn.: see **invasion.**

airy. Syn.: see **ethereal.**

akin. Syn.: related, kindred, consanguineous, cognate, allied, similar, analogous.

alacrity. Syn.: briskness, readiness, promptitude, celerity, willingness, eagerness, animation, liveliness. See **quickness.**

alarm, n. **Syn.:** warning, signal, tocsin; fright, terror, consternation, panic, fear, dread, apprehension. **Ant.:** calmness, composure, tranquillity. See **fear.**

alarm, v. **Syn.:** see **frighten.**

alert. Syn.: vigilant, watchful, wide awake, attentive, heedful, wary; ready, prompt, brisk, lively, quick, active. See **watchful.**

alien, n. **Syn.:** see **foreigner.**

alien, a. **Syn.:** foreign, strange, extraneous, adventitious, remote, distant, unconnected, irrelevant, adverse, opposed, hostile.

alienate. Syn.: transfer, assign; estrange, disaffect, wean.

alike. Syn.: like, similar, resembling, homogeneous, homologous, analogous, equivalent, equal, uniform, akin, same, identical. **Ant.:** unlike, dissimilar, different, various, heterogeneous, discordant.

aliment. Syn.: see **food.**

allay. Syn.: quiet, still, calm, compose, soothe, tranquilize, mollify, appease, pacify, assuage, alleviate, mitigate, soften, moderate, lessen, reduce, relieve, palliate, abate. **Ant.:** agitate, stir up, excite, rouse, kindle, inflame, irritate, aggravate, intensify.

To *alleviate* is, figuratively, to make lighter anything that bears down as a burden; to *mitigate* is to render milder, or less severe, harsh, or violent; to *assuage* is to calm or quiet; to *allay* is, as it were, to lay to rest by reducing or lowering: as, to *alleviate* poverty; *mitigate* punishment; *assuage* anger or pain; *allay* fears or anxiety.

allege. Syn.: assert, declare, state, say, affirm, maintain, claim, asseverate, aver. **Ant.:** deny, contradict, dispute, gainsay.

allegiance. Syn.: fealty, homage, loyalty, fidelity, faithfulness, devotion. **Ant.:** disloyalty, disaffection, treason, sedition, rebellion, mutiny.

Allegiance is used in a restricted sense suggesting the duty of a citizen to his country, and, by extension, one's obligation to support a party, cause, etc. *Fealty*, now a somewhat rare word except in elevated or poetic style, retains most of its original meaning of the obligation of a vassal to his lord. *Homage*, which retains little of its original sense of a vassal's formal acknowledgment of allegiance to his lord, is used of the reverence and honor paid to what is superior in rank, worth, or excellence. *Loyalty* expresses the sentiment and feeling of devotion which one holds for one's family, friends, country, creed. *Fidelity* implies steadfast and noble faithfulness.

allegory. Syn.: see **parable.**

alleviate. Syn.: see **allay.**

alley. Syn.: see **way.**

alliance. Syn.: association, union, coalition, combination, connection, relationship, partnership, affinity; compact, covenant, treaty, marriage; league, federation, confederation, confederacy. **Ant.:** disunion, separation, schism, secession, divorce.

Alliance is applied to the joining of two sovereign states by treaty, as for mutual protection or aid, or of families by marriage, or, less formally, to any connection entered into for mutual benefit. *League* is often used with scarcely any perceptible difference in meaning from alliance, but it may suggest closer combination or a more definite object or purpose. *Confederation* is used of a number of (usually sovereign) states united by treaty or compact into a permanent combination, the purpose of which is to exercise certain governmental functions in common. *Coalition* implies a temporary combination of persons, parties, or states that might be opposed to one another. *Union* implies such close and permanent alliance as to make the separate states or parties to the agreement essentially one.

allot. Syn.: distribute, deal, apportion, portion, parcel, dispense, assign, award, appropriate, destine, mete, divide. See **assign.**

allow. Syn.: assign, grant, give, yield; admit, concede, confess, own, acknowledge; permit, let, suffer, tolerate, sanction. **Ant.:** withhold, refuse; deny, gainsay; disallow, disapprove, prohibit, forbid. See **permit.**

allowance. Syn.: grant, allotment, portion, share, annuity, stipend, alimony; permission, sufferance, tolerance, **sanction,** leave, assent; deduction, discount, rebate.

allude. Syn.: refer, advert, hint. See **refer.**

allure. Syn.: see **lure, attract.**

ally. Syn.: see **associate.**

almsgiving. Syn.: see **charity.**

alone. Syn.: unaccompanied, unattended, companionless, solitary, single, isolated, unaided, unassisted; only, solely. See **solitary.**

also. Syn.: likewise, in addition, besides, further, moreover, too.

alter. Syn.: change, turn, modify, transform, transmute. See **change,** v.

altercation. Syn.: see **dispute,** n., **quarrel,** n.

alternative. Syn.: choice, option, selection, preference, election, pick. See **choice,** n.

although. Syn.: though, notwithstanding, even if, however, nevertheless, yet, still, albeit.

altitude. Syn.: see **height.**

altruistic. Syn.: see **unselfish.**

always. Syn.: perpetually, everlastingly, forever, evermore, ever, unceasingly, continually, constantly.

Always and *ever* are interchangeable in expressing uniform or perpetual continuance; *always* also expresses uniformity of repetition: as, human nature is *always* (or *ever*) the same; he *always* (not *ever*) comes home on Saturday. However, in negative or interrogative sentences, *ever* means at any time: as, did you *ever* see anything like it? I do not think I *ever* did.

amalgamate. Syn.: see **mix, join, unite.**

amass. Syn.: see **accumulate.**

amateur. Syn.: dilettante, novice, tyro, neophyte.

amaze. Syn.: surprise, astonish, astound, dumfound, confound, stupefy, stun. See **surprise,** v.

ambassador. Syn.: see **envoy.**

ambiguous. Syn.: doubtful, indeterminate, uncertain, puzzling, equivocal, amphibolous, enigmatical, obscure, mystifying, vague, indistinct.

That which is *ambiguous* is not clear or definite in meaning and hence leaves the intended sense doubtful; it may not be purposely deceptive. That which is *equivocal* is equally capable of two or more interpretations, and is usually intended to be so for the purpose of mystifying.

ambition. Syn.: aspiration, emulation.

ambitious. Syn.: aspiring, enterprising, emulous; showy, ostentatious. **Ant.:** see **unambitious.**

The *ambitious* man seeks to advance, especially towards worldly success, and puts forth effort to attain his end. The *aspiring* man wishes to rise to a higher level or plane, or to attain some end that he feels to be above his ordinary expectations.

ameliorate. Syn.: see **improve.**

amenable. Syn.: accountable, responsible, answerable; submissive, responsive, tractable, pliant, docile. See **accountable.**

amend. Syn.: emend, rectify, correct, reform, mend, repair, improve, better, ameliorate.

To *amend* is to bring into a more perfect state by removing defects, errors, or faults; *mend* refers especially to the restoring or repairing of that which has become impaired or broken; *emend* is almost limited to the restoring or improving of (usually faulty or imperfect) texts. *Correct* and *rectify* both mean to make right, especially by bringing a thing from an imperfect state into conformity with some standard or rule. *Reform* implies lasting betterment, and is especially used of eradicating defects and abuses from institutions or reclaiming persons from evil.

amends. Syn.: see **reparation.**

amiable. Syn.: friendly, kindly, gracious, obliging, good-natured, agreeable, pleasing, winsome, charming, lovely, sweet. **Ant.:** crabbed, caustic, ill-natured, disagreeable, sullen, surly. See **kind.**

amicable. Syn.: friendly, sociable, neighborly, harmonious, cordial, peaceable. **Ant.:** unfriendly, inimical, antagonistic, hostile, opposed, adverse. See **friendly.**

amid, amidst. Syn.: see **among.**

amiss. Syn.: see **wrong,** a.

amity. Syn.: friendliness, friendship, good-will, harmony, peace.

among. Syn.: amid, amidst, betwixt, between.

Among suggests a mingling with; *amid,* being in a middle

place; *amidst* being surrounded by: as, he disappeared *among* the crowd; *among* my books; *amid* the waves or ruins; he felt safe *amidst* his friends and protectors. *Between* refers to only two objects and should be closely distinguished from *among,* which always refers to more than two: as, he divided his estate *between* two friends and not *among* his relatives. In special instances, however, *between* is occasionally used with more than two objects: as, the center of an equilateral triangle is midway *between* its three points.

amorous. Syn.: loving, ardent, passionate, amatory, erotic, fond, tender.

amount. Syn.: sum, total, aggregate, whole.

ample. Syn.: large, big, full, abundant, plenteous, plentiful, enough, copious, bountiful, liberal, extensive, profuse, overflowing, unrestricted. **Ant.:** small, insufficient, inadequate, sparing, scanty, meager.

Ample implies an excess over what is needed to meet a demand; *copious* an abundance even to apparent inexhaustibility of material or supply.

amplify. Syn.: enlarge, augment, increase, extend, expand, widen; expatiate, dilate. **Ant.:** diminish, curtail, condense, contract, abridge, epitomize.

amulet. Syn.: see **charm,** n.

amuse. Syn.: divert, please, entertain, cheer, beguile, enliven, recreate, disport.

That which *amuses* occupies the mind pleasantly, either by preventing the tedium of idleness or by pleasing the fancy or exciting merriment or laughter. *Divert* implies turning the attention from serious thoughts or pursuits to something light, amusing, or lively. That which *entertains* engages and sustains the attention by being pleasing and sometimes instructive in character, and is usually purposely planned or contrived.

amusement. Syn.: diversion, entertainment, pastime, game, recreation, sport, play, frolic, fun, pleasure, merriment. See **pastime.**

analogous. Syn.: comparable, correspondent, similar, like, parallel.

analogy. Syn.: comparison, similitude, correspondence, agreement, similarity, resemblance, likeness.

analysis. Syn.: outline, synopsis, syllabus, summary; separation, dissection.

anarchy. Syn.: lawlessness, disorder, chaos.

anathema. Syn.: see **curse,** n.

ancestor. Syn.: forefather, forebear, progenitor, primogenitor.

ancestral. Syn.: hereditary, inherited, patrimonial, lineal.

ancestry. Syn.: lineage, descent, extraction, pedigree, stock, parentage, family. See **lineage.**

anchoret. Syn.: see **recluse.**

ancient. Syn.: old, antique, venerable, old-fashioned, antiquated, archaic, obsolescent, obsolete, former, past, bygone, pristine, primitive.

That which is *ancient* existed or occurred in time long past. *Antique* is applied either to that which has come down from antiquity and is (usually) curiously or pleasingly old, or to that which is made in imitation of ancient style. *Antiquated* is applied disparagingly to that which is too old, and has passed out of fashion or use. *Old-fashioned* may be used derogatorily of that which is out of date, or approvingly of that which is regarded with pleasure or affection as belonging to the past. That which is *archaic* is marked by features retained from the past for particular, especially poetical, purposes. *Obsolescent* is applied to what is in the process of becoming *obsolete,* which denotes that which has gone out of general use.

anecdote. Syn.: story, tale, relation, reminiscence. See **story.**

angel. Syn.: archangel, cherub, seraph, spirit.

anger, n. **Syn.:** wrath, ire, displeasure, resentment, indignation, exasperation, irritation, vexation, dudgeon, animosity, choler, spleen, passion, rage, fury, temper. **Ant.:** good humor, amiability, patience, forbearance, self-control.

Anger is a sudden, violent feeling of displeasure at real or supposed wrong or injury, and is usually accompanied by a strongly retaliatory impulse. *Wrath,* and the poetical or rhetorical *ire,* express an angry feeling of great power, especially as manifested by a superior, proud, or imperious person: as, a fit of *anger*; the *wrath* of the gods; the *ire* of Achilles.

anger, v. **Syn.:** vex, irritate, incense, provoke, exasperate, enrage, infuriate, ruffle, displease.

angle. Syn.: see **corner.**

angry. Syn.: wrathful, wroth, irate, ireful, incensed,

enraged, exasperated, infuriated, furious, irritated, vexed, indignant, provoked, piqued.

anguish. Syn.: agony, grief, distress, torment, torture, misery, suffering. See **pain.**

animadversion. Syn.: reflection, observation, comment, remark; stricture, censure, condemnation, blame. **Ant.:** approval, commendation, laudation, praise. See **criticism.**

animal, *n.* **Syn.:** beast, brute.

animal, *a.* **Syn.:** sentient, living, physical; brutish, brutal, beastly; fleshly, carnal.

animate. Syn.: vivify, quicken, vitalize, inspirit, enliven, invigorate, exhilarate, gladden, cheer; rouse, actuate, inspire, stimulate, incite, impel, urge.

animated. Syn.: see **lively.**

animation. Syn.: life, spirit, liveliness, vigor, buoyancy, vivacity, energy, enthusiasm, ardor, sprightliness, gaiety. See **life.**

animosity. Syn.: ill-will, enmity, malice, hostility, hatred, hate, malevolence, malignity, rancor, grudge, spite. **Ant.:** good will, friendliness, love. See **ill-will.**

annals. Syn.: see **history.**

annex. Syn.: attach, append, affix, adjoin, subjoin, join, add. See **attach.**

annihilate. Syn.: see **destroy.**

annotation. Syn.: note, footnote, gloss, scholium, remark, comment.

announce. Syn.: proclaim, declare, blazon, publish, promulgate, herald, advertise, communicate, acquaint, state, report.

To *announce* is to make known in a formal or public way, often something expected or coming in the future: as, to *announce* a book by a new author. To *declare* is to make clear (often emphatically) so there will be no mistake or misunderstanding: as, to *declare* one's independence, belief. To *proclaim* is to announce what is of public interest, with endeavor to make it a matter of general knowledge: as, to *proclaim* a day of thanksgiving. To *publish* is to make public in a formal or official way; in popular usage the word is becoming more and more restricted to issuing through the press: as, to *publish* the bans of marriage, a book. To *promulgate* is to make known with the purpose of spreading or propagating widely: as, to *promulgate* a decree, doctrine, or belief.

annoy. Syn.: vex, irritate, harass, molest, torment, disturb, trouble, bother, pester, plague, heckle. See **vex.**

annoyance. Syn.: torment, trouble, disturbance, vexation, irritation, umbrage, resentment.

Annoyance implies disturbance by slight but repeated irritations. *Vexation* expresses the annoyance and chafing caused by troubles of a teasing or irritating nature, as the crossing of one's will, or the thwarting of one's purposes. *Umbrage*, based on the idea of being thrown in the shade or overshadowed, implies offense or wounded pride because of an injury or slight. *Resentment* implies a reaction of displeasure or anger resulting from injury to feelings or from an affront.

annul. Syn.: nullify, abolish, abrogate, repeal, invalidate, rescind, revoke, recall, cancel, countermand.

anomalous. Syn.: irregular, abnormal, unnatural, aberrant, unusual, singular, peculiar, odd, exceptional, unaccountable. See **irregular.**

answer. Syn.: reply, response, rejoinder, retort, repartee. See **reply.**

answerable. Syn.: see **accountable.**

antagonist. Syn.: opponent, adversary, foe, enemy, rival, assailant. See **opponent.**

antagonistic. Syn.: opposing, hostile, conflicting, contradictory, adverse.

antecedence. Syn.: see **priority.**

antecedent. Syn.: see **previous.**

anterior. Syn.: see **previous.**

anticipate. Syn.: forestall, preclude, obviate, prevent; expect, foresee, await. See **expect.**

Anticipate implies either helpful or hindering action taken in advance; *forestall* refers to such previous action as obstructs, hinders, or renders ineffective: as, to *anticipate* another's wishes or his evil intent; the police *forestalled* a riot by placing guards on the streets.

anticipation. Syn.: see **hope.**

antidote. Syn.: remedy, cure, counterpoison, counteractive, corrective.

antipathy. Syn.: repugnance, aversion, distaste, dislike, abhorrence, detestation, loathing, hatred. **Ant.:** sympathy, congeniality, agreement. See **aversion.**

antiquated. Syn.: see **ancient.**

antique. Syn.: see **ancient.**

anxiety. Syn.: care, concern, solicitude, worry, uneasiness, disquiet, inquietude, apprehension, misgiving, foreboding, fear. **Ant.:** calmness, unconcern, confidence. See **care.**

anxious. Syn.: concerned, solicitous, worried, troubled, disturbed, uneasy, apprehensive; eager.

any. Syn.: see **every.**

apartment. Syn.: see **room.**

apathetic. Syn.: passionless, impassive, unmoved, lethargic, phlegmatic, indifferent, unconcerned. **Ant.:** sensitive, emotional.

apathy. Syn.: impassivity, lethargy, insensibility, indifference, unconcern, stoicism, phlegm. **Ant.:** sensibility, feeling, emotion, sympathy. See **indifference.**

ape. Syn.: see **imitate.**

aperture. Syn.: see **hole.**

aphorism. Syn.: see **proverb.**

aplomb. Syn.: see **assurance.**

apocryphal. Syn.: see **legendary.**

apology. Syn.: defense, justification, plea, excuse, extenuation, explanation, vindication, confession.

Apology usually implies acknowledgment that one has been, at least seemingly, in the wrong; it may aim at setting matters right by either alleging extenuating circumstances, or offering frank acknowledgment of error. *Excuse* implies a fault with an attempt at (at least partial) justification. *Plea* except in law is an excuse or an appeal for help, indulgence, mercy, etc.

apostate. Syn.: deserter, backslider, renegade, turncoat, traitor, pervert. See **traitor.** Cf. **convert,** *n.*

appal. Syn.: see **frighten, terrify.**

apparel, *n.* **Syn.:** clothing, clothes, dress, raiment, robes, vesture, attire, array, garb, costume, habiliments. See **dress.**

apparel, *v.* **Syn.:** see **clothe.**

apparent. Syn.: visible, perceptible; clear, distinct, manifest, patent, plain, obvious, evident, unmistakable, indubitable, certain; seeming, ostensible. See **manifest.**

apparition. Syn.: ghost, specter, phantom. See **ghost.**

appeal. Syn.: petition, suit, prayer, supplication, entreaty, solicitation, application.

appear. Syn.: see **seem.**

appearance. Syn.: appearing, showing, manifestation, apparition; aspect, look, guise, demeanor, mien, air; semblance, show, color, pretense.

appease. Syn.: pacify, mollify, calm, quiet, soothe, lull, quell, allay, assuage, placate, propitiate, conciliate, reconcile.

We *appease*, commonly, by relieving emotions or offering satisfaction or amends; *pacify*, by quieting strife, discord, discontent, etc.; *mollify*, by softening the heart or disposition.

appellation. Syn.: see **name,** *n.*

append. Syn.: see **attach.**

appendage. Syn.: adjunct, annex, addition, supplement, attachment, appurtenance.

appendix. Syn.: see **supplement.**

appertain. Syn.: see **pertain.**

appetite. Syn.: craving, longing, desire, inclination, propensity, appetence, appetency, relish, zest, passion, hunger, thirst, lust.

applaud. Syn.: see **cheer,** *v.*

applause. Syn.: clapping, cheering, cheers, acclamation, acclaim, plaudits, commendation, laudation, praise.

application. Syn.: industry, assiduity, effort; request, solicitation, petition.

apply. Syn.: affix, administer; appropriate, allot, assign; direct, address, devote; request, petition.

appoint. Syn.: ordain, decree, command, prescribe, establish; assign, allot, designate; nominate, commission, authorize, empower, delegate, constitute; equip, supply, furnish. See **equip.**

apportion. Syn.: allot, assign, distribute, dispense, deal, partition, divide. See **assign.**

apposite. Syn.: see **pertinent.**

appreciate. Syn.: appraise, estimate; esteem, prize, value; rise, go up, improve. **Ant.:** undervalue, underrate, despise, depreciate.

To *appreciate* is to set a just value on; the word implies the use of wise judgment and delicate perception, and often the acute ability to see the worth of something likely to be overlooked or underestimated. To *value* is to attach importance to a thing because of its worth. To *prize* is to value highly, usually for other than pecuniary reasons; the word often suggests the notion of reluctance to lose. To *esteem* is to have a highly favorable opinion of; the word implies respect combined with warm and kindly feeling.

apprehend. Syn.: seize, grasp, arrest; perceive, see, conceive, understand, know, comprehend; anticipate, expect, dread, fear.

apprehension. Syn.: seizure, capture, arrest; perception, conception, idea, notion, understanding, comprehension; dread, fear, misgiving, anxiety, uneasiness. See **fear.**

apprise. Syn.: inform, notify, acquaint, advise, tell, warn. See **inform.**

approbation. Syn.: approval, concurrence, commendation, sanction, endorsement, consent. **Ant.:** disapprobation, disapproval, censure.

appropriate. Syn.: fit, befitting, proper, suitable, becoming, apt, meet, felicitous, applicable. **Ant.:** inappropriate, unsuitable, unbecoming. See **fit.**

approval. Syn.: see **approbation.**

approve. Syn.: countenance, uphold, sanction, ratify, authorize, confirm, second, endorse. **Ant.:** disapprove, condemn, nullify.

Approve is active and implies willing and hearty consent; *countenance* is more passive and rather implies lack of opposition, or, sometimes, no more than good-natured tolerance; it is most often applied to persons or their conduct. *Sanction* implies approbation, encouragement, and support, especially such as carries weight or authority; *ratify*, official or authoritative confirmation of that which has been done by a delegate or representative. *Approve, countenance,* and *sanction* may apply to that which is planned or contemplated, *ratify* only to what has already been accomplished.

approximation. Syn.: approach, proximity, nearness, likeness, similarity, resemblance.

appurtenance. Syn.: see **appendage.**

apt. Syn.: fit, suited, suitable, adapted, apposite, pertinent, appropriate, felicitous; disposed, inclined, prone, liable, likely; clever, quick, intelligent, bright, deft.

aptitude. Syn.: inclination, proneness, propensity, proclivity; faculty, capacity, knack, talent, genius. See **genius.**

arbiter. Syn.: arbitrator, umpire, referee, judge, adjudicator. See **judge.**

arbitrary. Syn.: discretionary, voluntary, optional; capricious, wilful, dictatorial, imperious, domineering, autocratic, despotic, tyrannical.

arbitrator. Syn.: see **judge.**

arch. Syn.: see **playful.**

archaic. Syn.: antiquated, obsolescent, obsolete, old-fashioned. See **ancient.**

archives. Syn.: records, registers, chronicles, annals, muniments.

ardent. Syn.: burning, fiery, hot, glowing, fervid, fervent, intense, eager, impetuous, enthusiastic, keen, zealous, impassioned, vehement, earnest. **Ant.:** cold, cool, apathetic, phlegmatic, dispassionate, indifferent.

Ardent implies burning or intense eagerness or zeal; *impetuous*, sudden or rash impulse without reflection or deliberation; *impassioned*, deep and vehement emotion; *earnest*, seriousness and sincerity of intention or purpose.

ardor. Syn.: fervor, fervency, rapture, eagerness, enthusiasm, zeal, passion, vehemence.

Ardor (L. *ardere*, burn) suggests a burning eagerness in the pursuit of an end or desire; *fervor* (L. *fervere*, boil) describes an intensity of feeling, often that associated with religious devotion. *Enthusiasm* suggests a domination of the mind by an interest which often stirs to action. *Zeal* denotes passionate and (usually) sustained earnestness or devotion, sometimes excessively intense or misdirected by poorly balanced judgment.

arduous. Syn.: hard, laborious, toilsome, difficult, onerous, wearisome, exhausting, strenuous, severe. See **hard.**

arena. Syn.: amphitheater, ring, field, stadium, bowl.

argot. Syn.: see **jargon.**

argue. Syn.: dispute, debate, discuss, reason, plead, expostulate, remonstrate; show, indicate, denote, betoken, imply.

To *argue* is to bring forth reasons or proofs to support or refute an assertion, proposition, or principle. To *discuss* is to present varied opinions and views, usually in an informal and amicable way, to find out the truth, the best means of procedure, or the like. To *debate* is to interchange (usually opposing) arguments in a somewhat formal manner, especially for settling questions of public interest. To *dispute* is to put forth antagonistic or contradictory assertions or arguments, often in a vehement, heated, or angry manner.

arid. Syn.: dry, parched; barren, bare, uninteresting, dull, lifeless, pithless. See **dry.**

arise. Syn.: see **rise.**

aristocratic. Syn.: patrician, noble, gentle, lordly, titled.

arms. Syn.: weapons, firearms, guns, artillery, armor.

army. Syn.: soldiery, soldiers, troops, legion, force; multitude, throng, host, array.

aroma. Syn.: see **smell.**

aromatic. Syn.: spicy, savory, fragrant, redolent, balmy.

arouse. Syn.: rouse, wake, awaken; animate, inspirit, incite, stimulate, kindle.

arraign. Syn.: accuse, charge, indict, impeach, denounce, censure. See **accuse.**

arrange. Syn.: range, marshal, dispose, array, classify, group, sort, assort; settle, fix upon, determine, adjust; devise, plan, organize, construct, contrive, concoct. **Ant.:** disarrange, disorder, mix, jumble, scatter.

arrant. Syn.: notorious, rank, unmitigated, downright, consummate, utter, thorough, complete, perfect.

array, *n.* **Syn.:** see **dress.**

array, *v.* **Syn.:** arrange, range, marshal, draw up; adorn, ornament, decorate, deck, attire, dress. See **clothe.**

arrest, *n.* **Syn.:** stoppage, check, halt, stay, interruption; apprehension, seizure, capture, detention, imprisonment, custody.

arrest, *v.* **Syn.:** stop, check, detain, stay, delay, stunt, dwarf; apprehend, seize, capture, imprison. See **stop,** *v.*

arrival. Syn.: advent, coming, landing.

arrogance. Syn.: haughtiness, superciliousness, insolence, disdain.

arrogant. Syn.: assuming, presumptuous, overbearing, overweening, haughty, proud, imperious, supercilious, disdainful, insolent, insulting. See **proud.**

arrogate. Syn.: see **assume.**

art. Syn.: skill, knack, adroitness, dexterity, address, craft, cunning, science; subtlety, astuteness, shrewdness, artifice, deceit, duplicity.

Art is of two kinds: fine art, which seeks to create the beautiful for its own sake; applied art, which seeks to create the useful. In the latter sense *art* is the practical and skilful application of a body of rules (usually based on past experience) that are designed to facilitate work or give it superior excellence. In the former sense *art* is the expression of individual genius, and while it may follow rules, transcends them. *Science* is coördinated and systematized knowledge, reduced by observation, comparison, and generalization to laws, principles, or general truths. *Science* formulates knowledge which the practical arts employ. Pure science like fine art is pursued for its own sake. Titian's *Assumption* is a work of fine art. Chemistry is a science which formulates knowledge that may be applied (applied science) to the manufacture of dyes, and these, in turn, may be skilfully employed in a useful art such as the weaving of textiles.

artful. Syn.: skilful, clever, adept, adroit, cunning, crafty, sly, wily, shrewd, astute, deceitful.

The *artful* man is ingenious and cunning in contriving ways of getting or keeping unfair advantage; he who is *wily* practises subtle stratagems and deceits. One becomes *crafty* by practice or experience in forwarding underhand schemes or knavish tricks. *Sly* implies a combination of cunning and stealth in the doing of dishonorable or evil things. It may also be used inoffensively in the sense of roguish.

articulate. Syn.: enunciate, pronounce; join, unite, connect. See **utter,** *v.*

artifice. Syn.: contrivance, device, shift, dodge, trick, ruse, subterfuge, stratagem, wile; trickery, craft, guile, deception, deceit.

An *artifice* is a skilful and ingenious expedient or contrivance for the accomplishment of an end that cannot be directly reached. A *stratagem* is a carefully prepared maneuver or trick to deceive or discomfit one who is, or bears the relation of, an enemy. A *ruse* is an (often slight or petty) deception by which one's real intentions or purposes are concealed. A *subterfuge* is an artifice or shift by which one evades or escapes something undesired or disagreeable.

artificer. Syn.: see **artist.**

artificial. Syn.: made, manufactured, factitious, imitated, sham; feigned, pretended, assumed, counterfeit, spurious, false; affected, unnatural. See **factitious.**

artisan. Syn.: see **craftsman.**

artist. Syn.: painter, artificer, craftsman.

artless. Syn.: unskilled, rude, inartistic; natural, simple, ingenuous, naïve, unsophisticated, simple-minded; guileless, undesigning, straightforward, sincere. **Ant.:** See **artful.**

Artless implies such sincerity or openness as comes from a lack of experience, worldly knowledge, or ways of evil; *guileless,* lack of cunning or deceit; *unsophisticated,* natural or, sometimes, rude or gullible simplicity; *ingenuous,* straightforward frankness or candidness; *naïve,* a pleasing innocence or unaffected simplicity.

as. Syn.: see **because.**

ascend. Syn.: go up, climb, mount, scale, rise, soar, tower. See **climb.**

ascendancy. Syn.: predominance, superiority, mastery, control, sway, authority, dominion; sovereignty, supremacy. See **authority.**

ascent. Syn.: rise, ascension; hill, eminence.

ascertain. Syn.: see **discover.**

ascetic, *n.* **Syn.:** see **recluse.**

ascetic, *a.* **Syn.:** see **stern.**

asceticism. Syn.: see **self-denial.**

ascribe. Syn.: attribute, refer, impute, assign, charge to.

Ascribe and *attribute* are frequently interchangeable, but *attribute* lays greater emphasis on the factor of individual judgment. *Impute* generally is to ascribe or attribute an evil or unfortunate act or event or censurable motives.

ashamed. Syn.: disconcerted, abashed, confused, mortified.

asinine. Syn.: see **foolish.**

ask. Syn.: inquire, query, question, interrogate, catechize, quiz, interpellate; request, solicit, petition, beg, crave, entreat, beseech, supplicate, sue, implore; demand, claim, require, exact, call for; importune, dun; invite, bid.

Ask is a general word, implying nothing as to the right, feelings, or manner of the asker. We *request* politely or formally, *demand* confidently or authoritatively, *claim* as due, *require* as proper or necessary, *solicit* earnestly, *importune* with persistence, *crave* humbly or apologetically, and *beg, entreat, beseech, supplicate,* and *implore* with increasing degrees of urgency and humility. *Inquire* usually means no more than the simpler term *ask;* but *question* and the more formal *interrogate* commonly imply the asking of a series of questions.

askance. Syn.: sidewise, obliquely, askant, asquint.

askew. Syn.: obliquely, sidelong, awry.

aspect. Syn.: look, appearance, expression, feature, countenance, mien, air; prospect, outlook, view, scene.

asperity. Syn.: roughness, harshness, severity, acrimony, crabbedness, bitterness, sourness. See **acrimony.**

asperse. Syn.: sprinkle, bespatter, besmirch; slander, calumniate, malign, defame, traduce, vilify, libel, slur, backbite, lampoon.

To *asperse* is to bespatter, as it were, a person's character or conduct without necessarily bringing definite charges. To *defame* is to lower one's fame or repute by spreading, more or less publicly, injurious reports or charges. To *traduce* is to misrepresent maliciously, so as to exhibit the character of a person or institution in an odious light. *Malign, slander,* and *calumniate* are not sharply distinguished in meaning. To *malign* is to speak ill of a person, often with malicious intent. To *slander* is to circulate orally, often in a secret or underhand way, false statements or reports such as damage a person's standing in the community. To *calumniate* adds to slander the idea of invention and refers often to persons or institutions in the public eye. To *libel* is to defame in writing by statements which render the defamer liable to be sued for damages.

aspiration. Syn.: see **ambition.**

aspiring. Syn.: see **ambitious.**

assail. Syn.: attack, assault, beset, oppugn. See **attack.**

assassinate. Syn.: see **kill.**

assault. Syn.: attack, onslaught, onset, charge, storming.

assemblage. Syn.: see **meeting.**

assemble. Syn.: gather, collect, convoke, muster; congregate, convene, meet. See **gather.**

assembly. Syn.: assemblage, gathering, concourse, meeting, convention; convocation, congregation, company, crowd, throng, group. See **meeting.**

assent. Syn.: agree, acquiesce, accede, concur, coincide,

consent, subscribe. **Ant.:** dissent, disagree, deny, contradict, contravene, oppose.

To *assent* indicates primarily an intellectual agreement with an assertion or idea; to *consent,* distinctly an act of the will in expressing compliance with another's wish or suggestion. To *concur* implies concord in matters of opinion or judgment, as of minds running along the same channels. *Acquiesce* expresses tacit or limited agreement with something with which one is possibly not in full or hearty accord. To *accede* is to yield to some suggestion, wish, or request.

assert. Syn.: maintain, defend, vindicate; affirm, declare, avouch, asseverate, aver, claim, allege, state, say. See **declare.**

assertion. Syn.: maintenance, vindication; affirmation, allegation, declaration, statement, asseveration, averment.

asseverate. Syn.: see **assert, declare.**

assiduity. Syn.: sedulity, application, attention, diligence, industry, perseverance, persistence, devotion, zeal. **Ant.:** slackness, remissness, negligence, inattentiveness, sloth, indolence, laziness, dawdling.

Assiduity and *sedulity* are often interchangeable, but *assiduity* suggests more active prosecution of an enterprise, *sedulity* more conscientious perseverance in it.

assiduous. Syn.: sedulous, diligent, industrious, persevering, indefatigable, unremitting, untiring, persistent, devoted. **Ant.:** idle, lazy, indolent.

assign. Syn.: allot, apportion, mete out, distribute; ascribe, attribute, refer, allege; designate, specify, show, give, furnish, name, appoint, present, advance.

To *assign* is to give a share, part, or allowance to, especially authoritatively. To *allot,* originally to assign by lot, is to set apart a particular portion or amount, without implication of any other similar distribution. To *apportion* is to set aside one portion (often according to some set standard or fixed rule to obtain uniformity or fairness of division) where a number of similar portions are implied.

assist. Syn.: aid, help, support, sustain, serve, befriend, relieve, further, second, back. See **help,** *v.*

assistance. Syn.: aid, help, support, relief, succor, backing, reinforcement, coöperation, collaboration.

assistant. Syn.: aid, helper, supporter, ally, coöperator, collaborator, auxiliary, coadjutor, adjutant, abetter, accessory, confederate, accomplice.

associate. Syn.: companion, comrade, mate, friend, partner, ally, colleague, coadjutor; confederate, accomplice.

An *associate* is one who is connected with another, possibly by no more than friendly relations, but usually because of some work, enterprise, or pursuit in common. A *partner* is one who takes part with another, especially in business or in any kind of joint undertaking. *Colleague* especially denotes an associate in some office or work, and like *coadjutor,* which is especially used of an ecclesiastical assistant, is applicable only to one engaged in work regarded as dignified. *Ally* is now chiefly used of states or rulers joined by treaty for the sake of common interests, protection, or military undertakings.

association. Syn.: fellowship, companionship, intercourse, familiarity; federation, alliance, combination, union; society, club, lodge, fraternity.

assuage. Syn.: mitigate, abate, relieve, soothe, calm, mollify, pacify, appease, allay.

assume. Syn.: undertake; adopt, appropriate, usurp, arrogate, take; suppose, presuppose, presume, postulate; pretend, simulate, affect, feign, counterfeit.

To *assume* is to take to oneself that to which one has a real or pretended right, often that which is not naturally or truly one's own: as, to *assume* one's proper place in society, an attitude of indifference. *Arrogate* implies assumption in a haughty and overbearing way of something to which one has no right: as, to *arrogate* powers to oneself. *Usurp* implies (forcible) taking possession of what is properly another's, especially office, power, or property.

assumption. Syn.: undertaking; adoption, appropriation, arrogation, usurpation, arrogance, presumption, self-conceit, effrontery, forwardness, officiousness; supposition, conjecture, hypothesis, theory, postulate.

assurance. Syn.: proof, pledge, promise, guaranty, surety; security, certainty, assuredness, confidence, self-confidence, self-reliance, intrepidity, courage, aplomb; presumption, impudence, effrontery, audacity, boldness. See **confidence.**

astonish. Syn.: surprise, amaze, astound, startle, shock. See **surprise,** *v.*

astound. Syn.: see **surprise**, v.

astringent. Syn.: see **sour**.

astute. Syn.: sagacious, shrewd, sharp, penetrating, discerning, knowing, subtle, artful, crafty, cunning, wily, sly. **Ant.:** stupid, dull, shallow, artless, simple, unsophisticated.

asylum. Syn.: see **hospital**.

at. Syn.: in, by.

At Paris, in Paris: here at singles out Paris from other places as a geographical point, while in designates Paris as the area within which, at some point not specified, a thing is situated, has happened, etc. Thus in commonly suggests a place of considerable size.

atheist. Syn.: see **skeptic**.

atom. Syn.: molecule, particle, jot, iota, tittle, scintilla, scrap, grain, bit.

atonement. Syn.: amends, reparation, expiation, propitiation.

atrocious. Syn.: wicked, heinous, villainous, flagitious, monstrous, infamous, outrageous, nefarious, scandalous, shocking, horrible, flagrant, diabolical.

That which is flagrant, literally flaming into notice, is glaring, striking, or notorious in badness. That which is heinous, literally hateful, is hatefully wicked or criminal. That which is flagitious is shamefully or scandalously wicked or vile. Etymologically that which is atrocious is cruel or fierce; that which is nefarious is unspeakably wicked or impious.

attach. Syn.: fasten (to), affix, annex, append, subjoin, conjoin, join, connect, unite, add; assign, attribute, ascribe, associate. **Ant.:** detach, disjoin, disconnect, separate.

To attach is to cause one thing to hold securely to another, usually by a strong fastening or connection which, however, can be easily undone or broken: as, to attach an engine to a train, a bayonet to a gun, a condition to a promise. To affix is usually to fasten or incorporate a minor or subordinate thing (which may or may not be an essential or integral part) to or in something greater or more important: as, to affix a sign to a post, a signature or seal to a document. To append is to hang on or add something supplementary or accessory, which often is or has the effect of an afterthought: as, to append a charm from a chain, a codicil to a will. To annex is to add or join something additional to something larger or more important, usually with the implication that the two parts are united or at least brought into vital relationship: as, to annex a village to a city.

attachment. Syn.: fastening, junction, connection; adherence, affection, regard, love, devotedness, devotion; adjunct, appendage, appurtenance. See **love**.

attack. Syn.: assault, assail, beset, charge, bombard, storm, besiege, waylay; criticize, censure, impugn, abuse.

Attack is the most general of these words and applies to an initiation of hostilities, especially those definitely planned. Assail implies vehement, sudden, and sometimes repeated attack. Beset implies an attack on all sides.

attain. Syn.: reach, arrive at, gain, win, compass, achieve, accomplish, secure, acquire. See **get**.

attainable. Syn.: achievable, obtainable, practical, feasible, possible.

attainment. Syn.: see **acquirement**.

attempt, n. Syn.: undertaking, effort, endeavor, enterprise, experiment, trial.

attempt, v. Syn.: try, essay, undertake, endeavor, strive, seek, aim. See **try**.

attend. Syn.: see **accompany**.

attendant. Syn.: follower, escort, associate, companion, retainer, servant.

attention. Syn.: heed, regard, notice, mindfulness, consideration, application, concentration, care; courtesy, assiduity, civility, devoirs, homage, deference, politeness, respect.

attentive. Syn.: heedful, regardful, mindful, observant, watchful, careful, alert, intent, wary; courteous, assiduous, deferential, considerate.

attest. Syn.: testify to, witness, certify, vouch for, indorse, confirm, declare, authenticate, corroborate, prove.

attire, n. Syn.: dress, clothes, garments, raiment, apparel, garb, array, wardrobe, habiliments, costume, livery. See **dress**.

attire, v. Syn.: see **clothe**.

attitude. Syn.: posture, position, pose. See **position**.

attract. Syn.: draw (to), engage, interest, invite, win, fascinate, allure, charm, entice, decoy.

Attract expresses no more than the exertion of a force that tends to draw towards: as, a magnet attracts steel; flowers attract bees; to attract attention. Allure usually implies subtle or tempting attraction, as that exerted by something charming or enticing or by the prospect of future benefit or delight: as, to allure into speculation or into sin.

attraction. Syn.: attractiveness, fascination, allurement, charm, magnetism, lure.

attractive. Syn.: engaging, inviting, pleasing, taking, winning, alluring, magnetic, seductive, enticing. **Ant.:** unattractive, forbidding, repellent, repulsive.

attribute, n. Syn.: quality, characteristic, feature, property, character. See **quality**.

attribute, v. Syn.: ascribe, assign, impute, refer, charge. See **ascribe**.

audacious. Syn.: bold, daring, intrepid, foolhardy, rash, presumptuous, unabashed, impudent, shameless.

audacity. Syn.: boldness, temerity, daring, hardihood, presumption, effrontery, shamelessness.

Audacity is a bold impetuosity of mind which renders one oblivious of the risks involved in an enterprise; it may also denote defiance of conventionalities and manners. Temerity signifies rashness that underrates or disregards dangers or consequences; effrontery, shameless and brazen-faced audacity.

augment. Syn.: see **increase**, v.

augmentation. Syn.: increase, enlargement, amplification, addition, extension.

augur. Syn.: divine, predict, prognosticate, prophesy, foretell, presage, portend, forebode, foreshadow, betoken, indicate. See **foretell**.

augury. Syn.: divination, prognostication, presage, prophecy; omen, portent, auspice, sign, token, indication.

august. Syn.: majestic, grand, magnificent, stately, imposing, impressive, worshipful, venerable, awful, sublime.

auspice. Syn.: divination, prognostication; omen, portent, sign; patronage, protection, favor, support, care, guidance, authority.

auspicious. Syn.: propitious, favorable, encouraging, promising, fortunate, lucky, bright. **Ant.:** inauspicious, unpropitious, unfavorable, unpromising. See **favorable**.

austere. Syn.: severe, rigid, rigorous, stern, hard, strict, relentless, harsh; grave, sober, serious; unadorned, simple. **Ant.:** mild, gentle, forbearing, tolerant, lenient, indulgent. See **stern**.

authentic. Syn.: reliable, authoritative, trustworthy, credible, genuine, true, correct. **Ant.:** unauthentic, spurious, counterfeit, unreliable, erroneous, false, untrue, fictitious.

A manuscript may be authentic or genuine as the actual work of the reputed author, and at the same time by no means authentic or true as to facts.

authenticate. Syn.: certify, attest, confirm, prove, verify. See **confirm**.

authoritative. Syn.: conclusive, final, unquestioned, sound, weighty, impressive, imposing, magisterial, dogmatic.

Authoritative indicates the finality arising from superior knowledge, judgment, or position. Magisterial usually implies a grandiose and dictatorial bearing or attitude. Dogmatic implies a positive assertion of (alleged) fact or opinion without evidence, and, when applied to persons, suggests stubborn or arrogant insistence upon the correctness of (often narrow or pedantic) opinions.

authority. Syn.: power, right, control, mastery, ascendancy, sway, dominion, jurisdiction, rule, government; influence, weight, importance, credit, prestige; authorization, sanction, warrant, license, permission, permit.

Authority is the power or admitted right to command respect, acquiescence, obedience, etc. Control is complete or successful direction or manipulation of persons or things. Influence is the power exerted by a person upon others through persuasion or personality or because of deference to his ability, character, or station. Ascendancy is overmastering influence, often thought of as undesirable. Mastery is the power completely to command or control, often obtained by victory over others or oneself.

authorize. Syn.: empower, commission, ratify, sanction, approve, confirm.

autobiography. Syn.: see **biography**.

autocrat. Syn.: despot, tyrant, dictator.

An *autocrat* exercises absolute authority, though not necessarily inequitably; a *despot* rules with arbitrary power, usually exercised with severity; a *tyrant* rules in a cruel or oppressive manner; a *dictator* in governing owns no authority except his own wishes and desires.

autocratic. Syn.: absolute, despotic, arbitrary.

auxiliary, *n.* **Syn.:** helper, aid, assistant, ally, confederate.

auxiliary, *a.* **Syn.:** helping, aiding, assisting, supporting; subsidiary, subordinate, ancillary, additional.

Auxiliary and *subsidiary* both denote that which assists or gives aid, but the latter is more likely to imply help from a subordinate source. *Subsidiary* is also used to indicate that which is merely of secondary importance.

avail. Syn.: see **use,** *n.*

avarice. Syn.: cupidity, rapacity, covetousness, greed, miserliness, penuriousness. **Ant.:** liberality, generosity, prodigality, extravagance.

Avarice implies a sordid and selfish desire to gain and possess wealth; *cupidity* stresses the eagerness with which one desires and strives for possession; *covetousness* indicates the sin of wishing to possess that which is properly another's; *rapacity* retains its original force of seizing and carrying off and suggests the ravenous desire to grasp things for oneself.

avaricious. Syn.: covetous, greedy, rapacious, grasping, miserly.

avenge. Syn.: revenge, punish, retaliate.

Avenge is restricted to the infliction of punishment as an act of retributive justice or a vindication of the right; *revenge*, to the infliction of pain or harm to gratify resentful feelings or the desire of retaliation for some real or fancied wrong: as, Hamlet sought to *avenge* the murder of his father; Othello was moved to *revenge* himself upon Iago.

avenue. Syn.: see **way.**

aver. Syn.: assert, affirm, avouch, declare, allege, insist, maintain. See **declare.**

average. Syn.: intermediate, medial, medium, ordinary, usual, mediocre, middling.

averse. Syn.: disinclined, reluctant, unwilling, loath, opposed, hostile, inimical. **Ant.:** inclined, disposed, willing.

Averse implies sustained dislike or unwillingness, though not of a very strong character. *Reluctant* implies some sort of a struggle as between inclination and a sense of duty. *Unwilling*, the most general and the weakest of these words, expresses little more than disinclination. *Loath* suggests disinclination sometimes amounting to repugnance.

aversion. Syn.: repugnance, disgust, distaste, dislike, antipathy, detestation, abhorrence, loathing, hatred.

Aversion is a strong and fixed desire to turn away from or avoid something that displeases, annoys, or offends. *Repugnance* is an instinctive hostility or antagonism against something one feels impelled to do, bear, or be associated with. *Antipathy* is a strong and settled constitutional feeling of dislike or disgust for something.

avert. Syn.: preclude, obviate. See **prevent.**

To *avert* is to turn aside some imminent or potential misfortune or evil: as, to *avert* bankruptcy. To *preclude*, literally to close or debar in advance, is usually to prevent by anticipating what would otherwise happen as a logical or necessary consequence: as, armed guards *precluded* every possibility of escape. To *obviate* is to make possible the avoidance of danger, difficulty, etc., through the interposition of sufficient means: as, the necessity of using trolley wires would be *obviated* by the invention of an adequate storage battery.

avid. Syn.: see **eager.**

avidity. Syn.: eagerness, craving, greediness, cupidity.

avocation. Syn.: see **occupation, vocation.**

avoid. Syn.: shun, eschew, evade, elude, avert, escape.

Avoid expresses no more than keeping away from; *shun* implies persistent or habitual avoidance, as from aversion, scruple, or sense of danger; *eschew*, abstention from, as on the ground of wrong or because of a feeling of distaste or uncongeniality.

avow. Syn.: see **acknowledge.**

awake. Syn.: wake, awaken, arouse, rouse, excite, stir up, stimulate.

aware. Syn.: see **conscious.**

awe. Syn.: reverence, veneration, dread.

awful. Syn.: dreadful, terrible, frightful, horrible, appalling, dire; awe-inspiring, solemn, imposing, majestic, sublime. See **grand, terrible.**

awkward. Syn.: clumsy, bungling, unskilful, unhandy, inexpert, inept; ungraceful, ungainly, gawky, loutish, clownish, lubberly, uncouth; embarrassing, trying. **Ant.:** handy, dexterous, skilful, adroit, apt, deft; courtly, polished, well-bred.

Awkward suggests especially a want of grace, as in action or procedure; *clumsy*, bulkiness of form and want of skill, especially as manifested in movement or performance; *ungainly*, the reverse of a graceful or shapely form; *uncouth*, an unlovely strangeness or oddity, as in appearance or manners.

awry. Syn.: askew, oblique, crooked, distorted, amiss, wrong.

axiom. Syn.: see **proverb.**

aye. Syn.: see **yes.**

B

babble. Syn.: prattle, prate, chatter, gabble, gossip, tattle, blab, gibber, jabber; murmur, purl.

Babble implies foolish or irresponsible talk, sometimes inarticulate or indistinct speech; *prattle*, the innocent, artless, and harmless talk of a child; *chatter*, rapid and high-pitched talk in sounds that seem much alike and often either lack or appear to lack sense; *gabble*, voluble and foolish talk that resembles the sound made by geese; *prate*, idle, purposeless talk, sometimes, presumptuous or boasting talk; *jabber*, the rapid or excited utterance of unintelligible sounds; *gibber*, the senseless speech of an idiot or fool.

babyish. Syn.: see **childish.**

back. Syn.: see **support.**

backbite. Syn.: slander, calumniate, vilify, traduce, defame.

backing. Syn.: aid, support, assistance, coöperation, subsidy, subvention.

backslider. Syn.: see **deserter.**

backward. Syn.: back, rear, reversed, regressive, retrograde, retrogressive, retrospective; late, tardy, delayed, behindhand, undeveloped; slow, sluggish, dull, unprogressive, unadvanced; reluctant, unwilling, disinclined, indisposed, averse, loath, hesitating; bashful, timid, retiring, modest.

bad. Syn.: worthless, poor, inferior, defective, deficient, imperfect, incorrect, faulty; unfavorable, unfortunate, unwelcome, depressing, grievous, adverse, disadvantageous, unprofitable; offensive, disagreeable, hurtful, painful, injurious, distressing, noxious, noisome, pernicious, baneful, baleful, deleterious, unwholesome, ill; evil, wicked, vicious, depraved, corrupt, base, malignant, unprincipled, abandoned, incorrigible, unscrupulous, knavish, licentious, libertine; wrong, sinful, criminal, iniquitous, nefarious, felonious, infamous, villainous, heinous, flagrant, atrocious, flagitious. **Ant.:** see **good.**

Bad in its ethical uses is the broadest and simplest term for that which is wanting in moral qualities, or is actually vicious and reprehensible: as, *bad* habits; a *bad* man. *Evil* is applied to that which violates or leads to the violation of moral law: as, *evil* practices or associations. *Ill* is less emphatic in its implication of evil and especially appears in a number of fixed expressions: as, *ill* repute, *ill*-natured, *ill*-tempered. *Wicked* implies wilful and determined doing of what is very wrong: as, a *wicked* heart; *wicked* designs. That which is *iniquitous* is grossly unjust or wicked: as, the *iniquitous* system of slavery.

badge. Syn.: see **emblem.**

badger. Syn.: see **tease.**

badinage. Syn.: see **banter,** *n.*

baffle. Syn.: see **frustrate.**

bag. Syn.: sack, pouch, purse, wallet, reticule, satchel, valise, portmanteau, knapsack, haversack.

bail. Syn.: see **security.**

bait. Syn.: decoy, lure, allurement, enticement, inducement.

balance, *n.* **Syn.:** counterpoise, equipoise, equilibrium, poise, steadiness, composure; remainder, rest, residue, surplus, excess.

balance, *v.* **Syn.:** weigh, compare, consider, ponder; poise, steady, equalize, adjust, arrange, settle, square; counterbalance, counteract, offset, neutralize.

bald. Syn.: hairless, bare; plain, unadorned, undisguised, unvarnished, unqualified, barefaced.

baleful. Syn.: evil, hurtful, pernicious, disastrous, destructive, ruinous, direful, deadly.

balk. Syn.: see **frustrate.**

balky. Syn.: stubborn, contrary, perverse, headstrong, unruly, refractory, recalcitrant. Ant.: submissive, obedient, tractable, docile.

ball. Syn.: see **globe.**

balm. Syn.: see **ointment.**

balmy. Syn.: aromatic, fragrant, odorous; fair, mild, gentle, temperate, clement; soothing, assuaging, refreshing.

ban, *n.* Syn.: proclamation, edict, notice; curse, anathema, execration, malediction, denunciation; prohibition, proscription, interdiction, excommunication, taboo.

ban, *v.* Syn.: curse, anathematize, execrate; prohibit, proscribe, interdict, forbid, taboo, excommunicate, outlaw.

banal. Syn.: commonplace, hackneyed, trite, trivial, platitudinous. See **trite.**

band. Syn.: company, party, troop, gang, crew, coterie, clique. See **company.**

bandit. Syn.: outlaw, brigand, robber, highwayman, marauder, desperado.

bane. Syn.: poison, scourge, curse, pest.

baneful. Syn.: deadly, evil, pernicious, injurious, harmful, hurtful, mischievous. See **pernicious.**

bang. Syn.: see **thump.**

banish. Syn.: exile, expel, expatriate, outlaw, transport, ostracize.

To *banish* is to expel from a community or country by ban or authoritative edict. To *exile* is likewise to force to leave a native place or country, but in this case the authority may be that of circumstances or one's own will: as, for many years business abroad had *exiled* him from America. *Expatriate* emphasizes more strongly through its etymological force the separation of a person from his native land. *Ostracize* refers to exclusion (often only temporary) from society, frequently because the person involved is discredited or in disgrace.

banishment. Syn.: exile, expatriation, expulsion, proscription, ostracism.

bank. Syn.: embankment, mound, heap, pile, ridge, drift, dike, levee, shore, slope, acclivity; shoal, bar, shallow.

bankrupt. Syn.: insolvent, broken, impoverished, exhausted, depleted.

bankruptcy. Syn.: insolvency, failure, wreck, ruin.

banner. Syn.: see **flag.**

banquet. Syn.: see **feast.**

banter, *n.* Syn.: raillery, joking, jesting, persiflage, badinage, pleasantry, teasing, mockery, ridicule, satire.

Banter is good-humored jesting directed at something pretentious or ridiculous that one has said or done. *Raillery* is often sharp, sarcastic banter; *pleasantry*, delicate and pleasant banter; *badinage*, diverting and purposeless banter; *persiflage*, light, frivolous, or flippant banter.

banter, *v.* Syn.: rally, chaff, joke, quiz, tease.

Banter (often reciprocal) implies mischievous but good-natured jesting at some one's expense. *Chaff* especially emphasizes the trying of one's good nature, temper, or patience by ironical or satirical remarks or questions. To *rally* is to make good-natured thrusts at some specific fault, offense, or weakness.

bar, *n.* Syn.: barrier, counter, obstruction, obstacle, barricade, hindrance, restraint, restriction; shoal, sandbar.

bar, *v.* Syn.: fasten, bolt, barricade, block; prevent, hinder, obstruct, prohibit, except, exclude, keep out.

barbarian. Syn.: foreign, uncivilized, barbarous, barbaric, uncultivated, untutored, unlettered, ignorant, rude, savage.

Barbarian is applied to whatever pertains to the life of an uncivilized people; *barbaric* implies crudeness of taste or practice in uncivilized people, especially as expressed in fondness for rude magnificence, splendor, or noise; *barbarous* emphasizes especially the inhumanity and cruelty of barbarian life and by extension may be applied to whatever is harsh or repellent.

barbarism. Syn.: barbarity, brutality, cruelty, savagery, inhumanity; outrage, atrocity. See **impropriety.**

barbarous. Syn.: foreign, outlandish, bizarre, uncultured, uncivilized, rude, barbarian, barbaric, brutal, fierce, savage, ruthless, truculent, inhuman. Ant.: cultured, refined, polished, kind, tender, merciful, compassionate.

bare, *a.* Syn.: naked, nude, undressed, unclothed, denuded, stripped, exposed; unconcealed, open; napless, threadbare; empty, unfurnished; plain, meager, bald, unadorned, unembellished; mere, sheer. See **mere.**

bare, *v.* Syn.: undress, denude, strip, divest; uncover, unmask, reveal, disclose, expose.

barefaced. Syn.: unmasked, undisguised, open, glaring, shameless, impudent, audacious, brazen.

barely. Syn.: see **hardly.**

bargain. Syn.: agreement, contract, compact, covenant, transaction.

bark. Syn.: yelp, yap, bay.

barn. Syn.: stable, byre, granary.

baron. Syn.: see **noble.**

barrel. Syn.: see **cask.**

barren. Syn.: sterile, unproductive, unfruitful, unprolific, infecund, childless, infertile, desert, effete; fruitless, ineffective; devoid, destitute, bare, lacking, wanting.

barricade, barrier. Syn.: see **bar,** *n.*, **obstacle.**

barter. Syn.: exchange, interchange, traffic, trade, deal.

base, *n.* Syn.: foundation, basis, groundwork, pedestal, support.

base, *a.* Syn.: low, lowly, humble, plebeian, common, vulgar, menial, servile, slavish, ignoble, groveling, abject; degraded, mean, mean-spirited, despicable, contemptible, villainous, infamous, vile. See **mean.**

bashful. Syn.: shy, diffident, modest, retiring, reserved, shamefaced, sheepish, embarrassed, timid. See **shy.**

bashfulness. Syn.: shyness, coyness, diffidence, modesty, timidity.

basis. Syn.: see **base,** *n.*

battle. Syn.: combat, fight, fray, affray, skirmish, onset, attack, encounter, action, engagement, conflict, contest, struggle, strife, warfare, tournament. See **fight.**

Battle is the usual term for a combat (generally of some length and importance) between organized armed forces. *Action* implies minor but often spirited fighting. *Engagement* is a somewhat technical or formal term for battle, but is a less forcible word, and often implies fighting on a less extensive scale. *Encounter* usually suggests an accidental meeting of opposing forces which results in a minor conflict. *Skirmish* implies an irregular or desultory contest between outposts or other small detachments of troops or ships.

bauble. Syn.: see **knickknack.**

bawl. Syn.: see **cry.**

beach. Syn.: shore, margin, strand, shingle, coast, seashore. See **shore.**

beak. Syn.: bill, nib, neb; prow, bow.

Beak is the general term applicable to all birds, but ordinarily it is used of birds of prey, especially when the idea of seizing or rending is referred to; *bill* is used of birds having slender, delicate, or flattened beaks.

beam, *n.* Syn.: see **gleam,** *n.*

beam, *v.* Syn.: see **shine.**

beaming. Syn.: radiant, shining, bright.

bear. Syn.: hold up, support, sustain; carry, fetch, bring, convey, transport, waft; press, push, thrust, drive, force, urge; undergo, endure, abide, stand, suffer, tolerate, brook, submit to; entertain, cherish, harbor; deport, conduct, behave; bring forth, produce, yield.

Bear is the general word for supporting the burden of something distressing, irksome, or painful. *Endure* implies continued resistance and patience in bearing; *suffer*, the allowance of something contrary to one's feelings, judgment, or sense of right, often through good-natured or passive indifference. *Tolerate*, or, more colloquially, *stand*, implies a somewhat unwilling restraint of one's opposition to something offensive or repugnant. *Brook* is a more literary word, and generally is used in the negative.

bearing. Syn.: supporting, sustaining, etc. (see **bear**); carriage, deportment, conduct, behavior, demeanor, port, mien, air, manner.

Bearing denotes the impression one makes upon others, primarily with reference to one's manner of carrying oneself. *Carriage* especially refers to the (often habitual) manner of holding the body, particularly when in motion. *Deportment* refers to one's actions or general behavior as judged by social requirements or standards of conduct. *Demeanor* describes one's manner of conducting oneself as expressing character or one's attitude towards others. *Port* is a literary word, and differs little from bearing in meaning; *mien* refers to a person's air, bearing, or countenance, as expressive of nature or mood. See **behavior.**

beast. Syn.: see **animal,** *n.*

beastly. Syn.: see **bestial.**

beat. Syn.: strike, smite, hit, pound, bang, thump, thwack, pommel, buffet, belabor, drub club, cudgel, maul, baste, thrash, flog, flagellate, whip, scourge, fustigate; overcome, defeat, vanquish, conquer, subdue, surpass, eclipse, outdo.

Beat implies the repeated giving of blows. *Thrash* emphasizes the idea of beating soundly or of punishing by whipping. *Flog* implies severe or brutal thrashing; *pommel*, repeated, often indiscriminate, beating or striking, as with a pommel or the fists. To *belabor* is to beat continuously with all one's might.

beating. Syn.: striking, pounding, hammering, battering, belaboring, thumping, pommeling, drubbing, mauling, thrashing, flogging, castigation; defeat, repulse; throbbing, pulsation.

beatitude. Syn.: see **happiness.**

beau. Syn.: dandy, exquisite, fop, dude, blade; lover, sweetheart, swain, suitor, inamorato.

beautiful. Syn.: beauteous, handsome, pretty, comely, fair, good-looking, lovely, exquisite, graceful, charming, picturesque. **Ant.:** homely, unlovely, ugly, hideous, repulsive, grotesque.

That is *beautiful* which has the excellence and charm of form, tone, movement, color, etc., or the noble or spiritual qualities, which give highest satisfaction to the eye, ear, mind, or soul. *Handsome* often implies the pleasing proportion and symmetry of form or appearance that results from cultivation, training, or the like. *Pretty* implies a moderate but noticeable beauty, especially in things that are comparatively small or of minor importance. *Fair* denotes that superficial beauty which delights the eye by its brightness or freshness, and is used especially of the face or features. *Comely* implies simple and wholesome attractiveness of form or feature. *Good-looking* especially relates to such beauty of countenance as attracts attention and wins approval. That which is *lovely* is so beautiful that it immediately excites admiration and love. *Lovely*, *beautiful*, and *pretty* are not applied to men except contemptuously or sarcastically.

beautify. Syn.: embellish, garnish, ornament, decorate, deck, adorn, grace. See **adorn.**

beauty. Syn.: loveliness, fairness, comeliness, handsomeness, prettiness, exquisiteness, grace, charm, pulchritude.

because. Syn.: as, since, inasmuch as, for.

Because indicates a direct relation of cause and effect: as, ice floats *because* it is lighter than water. *Since* often introduces an antecedent circumstance less directly related to its consequence than is a cause to an effect: as, *since* I am through with my work, I am going home.

becoming. Syn.: fitting, befitting, proper, meet, suitable, appropriate, seemly, comely. **Ant.:** see **unbecoming.** See **fitting.**

bed. Syn.: couch, lounge, cot, pallet, cradle, crib, berth, bunk; plot, layer, stratum, vein.

bedim. Syn.: becloud, befog, obscure, darken, overcast, obfuscate.

bedizen. Syn.: see **deck.**

befall. Syn.: chance, bechance, betide, happen, occur.

befitting. Syn.: fit, fitting, appropriate, proper, suitable, becoming, seemly, meet.

beg. Syn.: entreat, supplicate, pray, importune, sue, crave, implore, beseech, petition, solicit, request. See **ask.**

beget. Syn.: procreate, generate, engender, breed, produce.

beggar. Syn.: mendicant, supplicant, pauper, tramp, vagrant, fakir, schnorrer; wretch, rogue, fellow.

beggary. Syn.: indigence, destitution, poverty, want, pauperism, penury, mendicancy.

begin. Syn.: commence, start, spring, arise, originate, institute, inaugurate, initiate, undertake.

Begin, the common term, and *commence*, the more formal word, are practically interchangeable, but *begin*, the Saxon word, is often preferred. *Inaugurate* implies formal or appropriate beginning; *initiate*, the beginning of something new, as a campaign, plan of procedure, etc.

beginner. Syn.: starter, originator; novice, tyro, neophyte, amateur, understudy, probationer, apprentice, recruit.

beginning. Syn.: commencement, start, initiation, inauguration, inception, incipiency, outset, opening, origin, source, rise.

begrime. Syn.: see **soil.**

beguile. Syn.: deceive, delude, cheat, mislead, befool, lure, inveigle, insnare; entertain, charm, divert, amuse. See **lure.**

behavior. Syn.: conduct, deportment, demeanor, carriage, bearing, manner, manners, actions. See **bearing.**

Behavior refers to one's mode of acting before or towards others. *Conduct* refers to actions viewed collectively, especially to actions considered with reference to an ideal standard of behavior. *Deportment* is behavior as related to a set of rules or to an arbitrary standard by which it can be judged. *Conduct* is governed by principles of ethics, *deportment* by rules of etiquette.

behead. Syn.: decapitate, decollate, guillotine, execute. See **kill.**

behest. Syn.: bidding, injunction, mandate, charge, command, order, precept. See **command,** *n.*

behind. Syn.: after.

Behind relates primarily to position in space, and suggests definite and close relation of one person or thing to another; as, they marched *behind* the band; six cars were *behind* the engine; he stood *behind* the chair. *After* relates primarily to time, but when it does note position in space, it suggests a less exact relationship or a less close proximity than behind and refers almost entirely to bodies in motion: as, rest *after* a hard day's work; they entered the room one *after* another.

behold. Syn.: look, see, observe, contemplate, regard, view, survey, gaze, scan, eye. See **see.**

beholden. Syn.: see **indebted.**

beholder. Syn.: see **spectator.**

belabor. Syn.: see **beat.**

belated. Syn.: see **late.**

belief. Syn.: confidence, trust, reliance, credence; faith, persuasion, doctrine, tenet, creed, dogma, principle, view, conviction, certitude, certainty.

Belief is the acceptance of an alleged fact or body of facts as true without positive knowledge or proof. *Faith* is confidence in a person, or (especially) trust in a doctrine or creed. *Faith* often inspires to action. *Conviction* is settled, profound, or earnest belief. *Certitude* and *certainty* indicate subjective conviction or positiveness that something is true.

belittle. Syn.: depreciate, disparage, decry, underrate, minimize. See **depreciate.**

belles-lettres. Syn.: see **literature.**

bellicose. Syn.: see **belligerent.**

belligerent. Syn.: warring, warlike, hostile, militant, bellicose, pugnacious, fighting, combative, quarrelsome, contentious.

Belligerent applies to the active waging or carrying on of hostilities or to that which is likely to provoke them; *bellicose*, a readiness or strong inclination on the part of nations to wage war, and by extension is applied to a similar attitude in individuals. *Pugnacious* suggests the disposition of one who likes and often goes out of his way to seek a fight; *combative* implies an extreme willingness to take one's own part.

bellow. Syn.: see **cry,** *v.*

belly. Syn.: stomach, paunch, abdomen.

below. Syn.: under, beneath, underneath.

That which is *below* (opposite of *above*) is in a lower plane than something else: as, the sun sinks *below* the horizon; *below* the water line of a ship. That which is *under* (opposite of *over*) is lower in a perpendicular line: as, the plaything is *under* the chair. *Beneath* may have a meaning similar to below (as, the pool *beneath* the falls), but more usually it denotes being under so as to be covered, overhung, or overtopped: as, *beneath* a pile of rubbish; *beneath* the sky.

belt. Syn.: see **zone.**

bemoan. Syn.: see **lament.**

bend, *n.* **Syn.:** curve, crook, flexure, deflection, turn, twist, corner, angle, bight.

bend, *v.* **Syn.:** curve, crook, flex, deflect, turn, twist, warp; bow, stoop, incline; direct, apply. See **lean,** *v.*

beneath. Syn.: see **below.**

benediction. Syn.: see **blessing.**

benefaction. Syn.: beneficence, kindness, charity; benefit, donation, gift, contribution, alms, boon.

beneficence. Syn.: benefaction, kindness, charity, generosity, bounty, liberality, munificence, alms.

beneficent. Syn.: see **kind.**

beneficial. Syn.: advantageous, salutary, wholesome, good, helpful, serviceable, useful, profitable, remunerative. **Ant.:** detrimental, harmful, hurtful, injurious, unprofitable.

benefit, *n.* **Syn.:** kindness, favor, boon, service; advantage, profit, gain, avail, use, good. See **advantage.**

benefit, *v.* **Syn.:** help, advantage, avail, profit.

benevolent. Syn.: kindly, charitable, generous, liberal, bountiful, munificent, philanthropic. **Ant.:** malevolent, unkind, harsh. See **kind.**

benighted. Syn.: see **ignorant.**

benign. Syn.: benignant, kind, gracious, good-natured, favorable, propitious, salutary. **Ant.:** malign, unfavorable, unpropitious. See **kind.**

benignant. Syn.: see **kind.**

bent, *n.* **Syn.:** inclination, leaning, proneness, tendency, turn, propensity, proclivity, predilection, predisposition, bias, penchant. See **inclination.**

bent, *a.* **Syn.:** curved, crooked, hooked; determined, resolved, bound, set.

berate. Syn.: see **scold, revile.**

bereave. Syn.: see **deprive.**

bereft. Syn.: see **destitute.**

beseech. Syn.: beg, entreat, supplicate, implore, pray, adjure, importune, petition, solicit, request. See **ask.**

beset. Syn.: surround, encompass, hem in, harass, attack, assail, besiege, beleaguer. See **attack.**

besides. Syn.: beside, too, also, moreover. See **moreover.**

Beside is almost exclusively used as a preposition meaning 'by the side of'; *besides* is used both as a preposition and an adverb, and means 'in addition to' or 'over and above': as, *beside* the stream; *besides* these honors he received much money.

besiege. Syn.: see **beset.**

bestial. Syn.: beastly, brute, brutish, brutal, animal, degraded, depraved, sensual, carnal.

Brutish implies the qualities of dumb animals, often with a suggestion of stupidity or dullness; *brutal*, cruelty or lack of feeling. *Beastly* expresses that which is altogether unworthy of a man, especially that which is filthy or disgusting in conduct or manners. *Bestial* implies low, lustful desires, or the gratification of carnal instincts.

bestow. Syn.: stow, put, deposit, store; confer, give, grant, present. See **give.**

bet. Syn.: stake, wager, gamble.

betimes. Syn.: see **early.**

betoken. Syn.: indicate, show, denote, signify, foretell, foreshadow, portend, presage, prefigure, bode, augur.

better. Syn.: improve, amend, emend, correct, ameliorate, meliorate, advance, enhance. See **improve.**

between. Syn.: see **among.**

betwixt. Syn.: see **among.**

bevy. Syn.: see **flock.**

bewail. Syn.: see **lament.**

bewilder. Syn.: confuse, perplex, puzzle, mystify, nonplus, confound, daze. See **perplex.**

bewitch. Syn.: enchant, charm, fascinate, captivate, enamour. See **charm,** *v.*

bias. Syn.: leaning, inclination, penchant, bent, turn, proneness, tendency, propensity, prepossession, predisposition, predilection, partiality, prejudice.

Bias denotes a strong, often unreasonable, leaning towards some opinion, belief, or course of action. *Prejudice* almost always denotes unfavorable attitude or opinion, often preconceived without sufficient reason or actual experience to warrant it. *Prepossession* almost always denotes favorable predisposition or natural liking for something.

bicker. Syn.: see **quarrel.**

bid. Syn.: offer, proffer, tender, propose; command, order, direct, charge, enjoin, tell, summon, invite. See **call.**

big. Syn.: large, huge, bulky, massive, capacious, voluminous, extensive, immense; important, consequential, pompous, inflated, arrogant. See **great.**

bigot. Syn.: fanatic, zealot. See **zealot.**

bigoted. Syn.: fanatical, intolerant, illiberal, opinionated, narrow-minded.

bigotry. Syn.: fanaticism, dogmatism, intolerance, narrow-mindedness, prejudice.

bill. Syn.: beak, neb; notice, bulletin, poster, placard, circular, handbill, dodger, broadside; invoice, account. See **beak.**

billow. Syn.: see **wave,** *n.*

bind. Syn.: fasten, tie, fetter, shackle, bandage, swathe, gird; oblige, obligate, constrain, compel.

biography. Syn.: autobiography, memoirs, memoir.

A *biography* is the (written) account of a person's life; an *autobiography* is a biography written by the person whose life it records; *memoirs* are a written (and usually reminiscent) account of matters upon which the writer is specially informed or which are a part of his own life, not necessarily as complete as a biography and more selective as to material.

birth. Syn.: nativity, origin, beginning, genesis, nascency; parentage, extraction, lineage, race, family. See **lineage.**

bit. Syn.: particle, piece, speck, grain, mite, whit, atom, iota, jot, tittle, scintilla, mote, bite, morsel, scrap, crumb, fragment. See **part.**

bite. Syn.: chew, gnaw, nibble, snap, champ. See **eat.**

bitter. Syn.: acrid, biting, piercing, harsh, severe, acrimonious, caustic, poignant, painful, distressing, grievous.

bitterness. Syn.: acridity, acrimony, asperity, harshness, severity, rancor, malice, spite, painfulness, grievousness.

bizarre. Syn.: see **fanciful, grotesque.**

blab. Syn.: see **tattle.**

black. Syn.: sable, ebon, swart, swarthy, nigrescent, dark, dusky, sooty, inky, pitchy, murky, lowering, dismal, gloomy, sullen, forbidding. **Ant.:** see **white.**

blacken. Syn.: darken, sully, besmirch, defame, vilify, slander, calumniate.

blamable. Syn.: blameworthy, censurable, reprehensible, culpable, faulty.

blame, *n.* **Syn.:** censure, reproach, reproof, reprehension, condemnation, stricture; culpability, reprehensibility, guilt.

blame, *v.* **Syn.:** censure, reproach, reprove, chide, rebuke, upbraid, reprehend, reprobate, decry, inculpate, implicate, accuse.

To *blame* is to find fault with as answerable for or guilty of some error, mistake, omission, neglect, or the like. To *reproach* is to censure, often with intense feeling as of anger, indignation, or grief, to make one ashamed of what he has done.

blameless. Syn.: irreproachable, inculpable, innocent, guiltless, unsullied, unblemished, faultless, stainless, spotless. See **innocent.**

bland. Syn.: smooth, suave, urbane, courtly, agreeable, affable, complaisant, soothing; soft, mild, gentle, balmy.

Bland implies mild or soothing assurance in manner, speech, or demeanor; *suave*, smooth and ingratiating manner; *urbane*, agreeable and elegant politeness.

blandishment. Syn.: cajolery, flattery, blandiloquence, wheedling, caress, endearment.

blank. Syn.: white, clean, void, bare, vacant, empty; expressionless, disconcerted, nonplussed, dumfounded. See **empty.**

blasphemous. Syn.: see **profane.**

blasphemy. Syn.: profanity, cursing, swearing, malediction.

blast, *n.* **Syn.:** see **wind,** *n.*

blast, *v.* **Syn.:** blight, destroy, ruin.

blatant. Syn.: clamorous, vociferous, noisy, loud-mouthed, bawling, braying, bellowing. See **loud.**

blaze, *n.* **Syn.:** flame, fire, conflagration; glare, brightness, splendor, effulgence. See **flame.**

blaze, *v.* **Syn.:** see **burn.**

blazon. Syn.: see **publish.**

bleach. Syn.: whiten, blanch, etiolate.

bleak. Syn.: bare, wind-swept, desolate, cheerless, dreary, raw, cold, chill, penetrating, piercing.

blemish, *n.* **Syn.:** defect, flaw, imperfection, disfigurement, blot, spot, stain, fault. See **imperfection.**

blemish, *v.* **Syn.:** damage, impair, deface, disfigure, mar, sully, tarnish, stain.

blench. Syn.: see **shrink.**

blend. Syn.: mix, mingle, combine, coalesce, fuse, assimilate, amalgamate, merge. See **mix.**

blessedness. Syn.: see **bliss.**

blessing. Syn.: prayer, invocation, benediction, benison; favor, gift, boon, benefit.

blind, *n.* **Syn.:** shutter, shade, curtain, screen; blinder, blinker; cover, hiding-place, ambush; subterfuge, pretense, pretext.

blind, *a.* **Syn.:** sightless, purblind, unseeing, undiscerning, undiscriminating, heedless, oblivious, unmindful.

blink. Syn.: see **wink.**

bliss. Syn.: blissfulness, gladness, happiness, joy, ecstasy, rapture, felicity, beatitude, blessedness. See **happiness.**

blithe. Syn.: glad, cheerful, joyous, merry, mirthful, sprightly, light-hearted, buoyant. See **gay.**

block. Syn.: obstruct, hinder, bar, blockade.

blockhead. Syn.: see **dunce.**

blond. Syn.: see **fair.**

bloodshed. Syn.: see **slaughter.**

bloody. Syn.: sanguinary, gory; bloodthirsty, murderous, cruel, truculent.

Bloody refers to the presence of blood or to the shedding of blood: as, a *bloody* dagger or cloak; a *bloody* encounter or deed. *Sanguinary* is applied to what is marked by great bloodshed or to one who eagerly desires bloodshed: as, a *sanguinary* battle or tyrant.

bloom. Syn.: blossom, flower, inflorescence; freshness, glow, flush, prime, heyday; fuzz, down.

blossom. Syn.: see **bloom.**

blot, *n.* Syn.: spot, stain, blur, blotch, splotch; blemish, disgrace.

blot, *v.* Syn.: spot, stain, bespatter, blur, blotch, smear, sully, dishonor, disgrace; cancel, erase, efface, expunge, delete, obliterate, destroy, annihilate.

blow. Syn.: stroke, hit, knock, buffet, thump, thwack, bang, rap, slap, cuff, box; shock, calamity, disaster, reverse.

A *blow* is a sudden and forceful impact of one object upon another, often intentional: as, the *blow* of a sledgehammer. A *stroke* is generally either a sharp blow or a regulated or sustained movement: as, a *stroke* of lightning, of a pen in writing, of a piston.

blue. Syn.: azure, cerulean, sapphire, livid; depressed, despondent, melancholy, dejected, downhearted; dismal, gloomy, unpromising.

bluff. Syn.: steep, precipitous, perpendicular; brusque, blunt, plain-spoken, hearty, frank, unceremonious, abrupt, curt, rude, rough, gruff, surly, crusty, discourteous, impolite. See **blunt.**

blunder. Syn.: mistake, error, slip, oversight, bungle. See **error.**

blunt. Syn.: obtuse, dull; abrupt, unceremonious, downright, plain-spoken, candid, frank, bluff, brusque, curt, rude, unmannerly. See **dull.**

Blunt implies that unceremoniousness of manner or speech that disregards the feelings of others; *bluff*, big-souled roughness which, because of fearless good-nature, rides over the reserves of others; *brusque*, rudeness in manner or disposition and an uncivil abruptness of speech; *curt*, rude shortness or conciseness of speech.

blur. Syn.: blot, smear, stain, disfigure, dim, bedim, obscure.

bluster. Syn.: blast, roar, boisterousness, boasting, bragging, swaggering, bullying.

boast. Syn.: brag, vaunt, gasconade, bluster, flaunt, vapor, crow, blow.

Boast and *brag* agree in the idea of self-praise or self-exaltation, but *brag* is more colloquial and often implies an exaggerated or more reprehensible egotism. *Vaunt* is a more literary word implying proud or vain speech.

boastful. Syn.: bragging, vaunting, vainglorious, thrasonic.

boasting. Syn.: bragging, vaunting, gasconading, vaporing, braggadocio, rodomontade, swaggering, blustering, bravado, parade.

boat. Syn.: vessel, ship, steamship, liner, merchantman, freighter, tanker, whaler, sealer; frigate, cruiser, battle-ship, dreadnought, superdreadnought, torpedo-boat, destroyer, scout, monitor, submarine, transport, receiving-ship, store-ship, school-ship, hospital-ship; schooner, sloop, brig, brigantine, bark, lugger, smack, trawler, junk, lorcha, xebec, felucca, dahabiyeh, galley, galleon, argosy, caravel; cutter, launch, yacht, tug, tender, barge, lighter, scow, hoy; skiff, canoe, rowboat, punt, scull, dory, wherry, dinghy, pinnace, gondola, caïque, sampan; coracle, umiak, kayak, dugout, pirogue, catamaran, raft.

bode. Syn.: foretoken, foreshadow, portend, presage, augur.

bodily. Syn.: corporeal, corporal, physical.

body. Syn.: see **corpse.**

bog. Syn.: see **swamp.**

bogus. Syn.: see **false.**

boil. Syn.: seethe, simmer, well up, effervesce, bubble.

Boil is the general term; *simmer* implies a gentle, usually long-continued boiling; *seethe*, a violent boiling, usually accompanied by a surging up of bubbles or foam.

boisterous. Syn.: rough, turbulent, tempestuous, uproarious, obstreperous, noisy, clamorous, hoydenish.

Boisterous implies noisy roughness in behavior and speech, especially such as results from (often excessive) exuberance of spirits. *Turbulent* implies disorder or disturbance and often disobedience and insubordination. *Obstreperous* implies noisy or clamorous opposition, unruliness, or disapproval.

bold. Syn.: fearless, courageous, brave, gallant, valiant, intrepid, dauntless, daring, audacious, reckless, rash, foolhardy, adventurous, venturesome, enterprising; forward, impudent, malapert, impertinent, saucy, immodest, shameless, brazen; striking, conspicuous, prominent, salient. Ant.: timid, timorous, afraid, cowardly, pusillanimous; modest, retiring. See **immodest.**

The *bold* man disregards danger; the *daring* man courts and defies it. He who is *adventurous* is inclined to incur risks or go in quest of danger, often from love of the novel or the arduous. The *venturesome* boy is often inclined to take heedless, unthinking, or foolish chances or risks. The *enterprising* person is alert to undertake new things or carry out difficult or untried schemes.

boldness. Syn.: courage, bravery, intrepidity, fearlessness, audacity, hardihood, temerity, assurance, impudence, effrontery, brazenness, bravado.

bolster. Syn.: see **cushion.**

bomb. Syn.: grenade, shell, explosive, infernal machine.

bombast. Syn.: grandiloquence, magniloquence, pomposity, fustian, rant.

bombastic. Syn.: high-sounding, high-flown, grandiloquent, magniloquent, grandiose, turgid, tumid, swollen, inflated, stilted.

Bombastic language abounds in extravagance of statement and often exaggeration of fact. *Grandiloquent* and *magniloquent* imply lofty or high-sounding language. A *grandiose* style is affectedly grand or pompous. *Turgid* and *tumid* imply swollen or inflated diction.

bond. Syn.: band, shackle, fetter, manacle, chain; link, tie; compact, agreement, security.

bondage. Syn.: serfdom, thraldom, slavery, servitude, subjection, subjugation, captivity. See **slavery.**

bonus. Syn.: see **reward.**

boon. Syn.: favor, gift, benefit, benefaction, blessing.

boorish. Syn.: clownish, loutish, churlish, rude, uncouth, unmannerly, ill-mannered, ill-bred, surly, sullen, crabbed.

The *boorish* man is low-bred and rude in manner; he who is *churlish* is selfishly ill-natured or uncivil; *surly* denotes a sullen nature or state of mind revealed in sourness and curtness of speech.

bootless. Syn.: profitless, vain, useless, unavailing, futile, ineffectual.

booty. Syn.: spoil(s), plunder, pillage, loot, prize.

Booty is applied to that which is seized and carried off in war or robbery. *Plunder* especially suggests the quantity and value of that which is taken; *spoils*, the great loss to the owner in being stripped or despoiled of his property. The latter is often used of the seizures of war and the fruits of political victory. *Loot* denotes booty taken in pillaging or marauding, especially that gotten wrongfully or illicitly.

booze. Syn.: see **drink.**

border. Syn.: side, edge, margin, rim, brim, brink, verge, boundary, bound, limit, confine, outskirt, frontier, march. See **edge.**

bore. Syn.: pierce, perforate, penetrate, drill; tire, fatigue, weary, annoy.

bother. Syn.: harass, annoy, molest, vex, pester, worry, trouble, plague, tease, discommode, inconvenience. See **tease.**

bothersome. Syn.: troublesome, inconvenient, vexatious, annoying, perplexing.

bottle. Syn.: vial, cruet, flask, canteen, demijohn, flagon, magnum, carafe, costrel, carboy, ampulla.

bottom. Syn.: base, foundation, groundwork, basis, foot, pedestal.

bough. Syn.: branch, limb, sprig, spray, twig.

boulevard. Syn.: see **way.**

bounce. Syn.: spring, bound, leap.

bound, *n.* Syn.: boundary, confine, limit, border; leap, spring, jump, skip.

bound, *v.* Syn.: limit, restrict, circumscribe, inclose, border; leap, spring, jump, skip, rebound, bounce. See **jump.**

boundary. Syn.: see **border.**

bounden. Syn.: see **indebted.**

boundless. Syn.: unbounded, unlimited, immeasurable, illimitable, infinite.

bounteous. Syn.: bountiful, munificent, generous, liberal, plentiful, copious, abundant, ample.

bounty. Syn.: generosity, munificence, liberality, charity, gift, gratuity, premium, bonus, subsidy, reward. See **liberality, reward.**

bow, *n.* **Syn.:** obeisance, curtsy, courtesy, salaam, nod.

bow, *v.* **Syn.:** bend, stoop, incline; yield, submit.

box. Syn.: receptacle, chest, case, coffer, casket, caddy, carton, bandbox, trunk.

boy. Syn.: lad, youngster, youth, stripling, chap, urchin, gamin, hobbledehoy.

boyish. Syn.: youthful, juvenile, childish, puerile, immature. See **young.**

brace. Syn.: see **pair, support,** *n.*

brag. Syn.: see **boast.**

braid. Syn.: plait, plat, interweave, interlace, entwine.

brain. Syn.: see **mind.**

brains. Syn.: see **mind.**

branch. Syn.: see **bough.**

brandish. Syn.: flourish, shake, wave, flaunt, wield.

brave. Syn.: courageous, valiant, valorous, intrepid, fearless, bold, dauntless, undaunted, heroic, plucky, gallant. **Ant.:** cowardly, fearful, pusillanimous, craven.

Brave is the most comprehensive of these words; it is especially used of that confident fortitude or daring that actively faces difficulties or dangers. *Courageous* implies a higher or nobler kind of bravery, especially such as results from that natural or inborn quality of mind or spirit that faces or endures dangers, perils, or difficulties without fear or shrinking. *Valiant* is an elevated or poetic word, and is used especially for bravery in action, as in battle. *Gallant* implies chivalrous, dashing, or showy bravery. *Fearless* implies unflinching spirit in the face of danger; *dauntless*, such courage as cannot be shaken by threats, perils, or misfortunes; *intrepid*, fearlessness that brushes aside danger.

bravery. Syn.: courage, valor, intrepidity, fearlessness, boldness, daring, prowess, heroism, pluck.

Bravery refers to actions or conduct in the midst of danger or difficulty; *courage* to the state of mind which enables one to face peril, endure misfortune, or adhere to a principle or ideal. *Valor* especially refers to bravery in war. *Heroism* indicates courage of an exalted kind, especially such as is characterized by a noble superiority to fear, a high forgetfulness of self, almost superhuman power to dare, achieve, or suffer. *Prowess* implies bravery combined with ability or power to meet a need.

brawl. Syn.: broil, fracas, fray. See **quarrel,** *n.*

A *brawl* is a noisy, unseemly quarrel, usually in a public place. A *broil* is a confused and angry contention, generally involving a number of persons. A *fracas* is a low, disorderly, and indiscriminate fight, among several combatants. A *fray* is a fight producing a public disturbance, sometimes a struggle between armed opponents. A *brawl* or a *broil* may become a *fracas* or a *fray* if it leads to fighting.

brawny. Syn.: muscular, sinewy, strong, powerful.

breach. Syn.: break, fracture, rupture, rift, fissure, crack, rent, cleft, gap, chasm; infraction, infringement, violation; estrangement, alienation, difference, quarrel.

breadth. Syn.: width, latitude, liberality, catholicity, tolerance.

break, *n.* **Syn.:** see **breach.**

break, *v.* **Syn.:** shatter, burst, smash, crush, split, rend, sever, sunder, fracture, splinter, shiver, crack, demolish; infringe, transgress, violate, disobey.

To *break* is to divide into parts by the violence or force of a blow, collision, pull, or the like. To *crush* is to subject to (usually heavy or violent) pressure, so as to press out of shape or reduce to small particles. To *shatter* is to break in a way to cause the pieces to fly in many directions. To *smash* is to break into many pieces, usually with noise and suddenness. To *shiver* is to break into numerous (splinter-like) fragments.

breaker. Syn.: see **wave,** *n.*

breathe. Syn.: respire, inhale, exhale, pant, gasp, wheeze.

breed. Syn.: generate, engender, procreate, propagate; cause, occasion; bring up, rear, raise, educate, school, train.

breeding. Syn.: generation, procreation; upbringing, rearing, raising, training; manners, good manners, refinement, cultivation.

breeze. Syn.: see **wind,** *n.*

brevity. Syn.: shortness, briefness, conciseness, terseness, succinctness, pithiness. **Ant.:** length, diffuseness, amplification, verbosity, loquacity.

bridal. Syn.: hymeneal, nuptial, conjugal.

bridle. Syn.: curb, check, restrain, repress, control, govern, master.

brief, *n.* **Syn.:** see **abridgment.**

brief, *a.* **Syn.:** short, short-lived, fleeting, transitory, ephemeral; concise, succinct, terse, compact; abrupt, curt. See **short.**

brigand. Syn.: see **bandit.**

bright. Syn.: shining, beaming, radiant, gleaming, luminous, effulgent, refulgent, sparkling, scintillating, glittering, glowing, glaring, dazzling, glistening, shimmering, lustrous; brilliant, splendid, resplendent; quick-witted, clever, smart, intelligent, precocious; animated, vivacious, lively, gay, cheerful; favorable, promising, encouraging, auspicious, propitious. **Ant.:** dull, lusterless, dim, dark, gloomy.

Bright is used of that which gives forth, reflects, or is filled with light. *Radiant* implies the pouring forth of steady rays of light, especially such as is agreeable to the eyes. That which is *brilliant* shines with a strong, unusual, or sparkling brightness, often with a changeful or varied play of light which is sometimes too strong to be agreeable. *Effulgent* and *refulgent*, literary words, are used with little difference in meaning, denoting a splendid light that seems to flood every place where it is, but is not necessarily intense or painful. That which is *resplendent* shines with glistening luster or magnificence.

brighten. Syn.: polish, burnish, furbish; cheer, enliven, inspirit.

brilliant. Syn.: see **bright.**

brim. Syn.: see **rim, edge.**

bring. Syn.: fetch, convey, transport, conduct, carry, bear.

To *bring* (opposite to *take*) is to convey or conduct, usually to or towards the place where the speaker is: as, *bring* it to me; *take* it to him. To *fetch* is to go and bring.

brink. Syn.: see **border, edge.**

brisk. Syn.: quick, active, lively, smart, nimble, spry, energetic, prompt, sprightly, vivacious, spirited, animated. See **active.**

brittle. Syn.: breakable, frangible, fragile, friable, crisp, frail.

broad. Syn.: wide, large, extensive, ample, vast; comprehensive, general, full; liberal, tolerant; plain-spoken, coarse, gross, indelicate, indecent. See **wide.**

broil. Syn.: see **quarrel,** *n.*, **brawl.**

broken. Syn.: shattered, smashed, crushed, split, fractured, splintered, cracked, demolished; infringed, violated; interrupted, disconnected, uneven, irregular, rough; subdued, tamed.

broken-hearted. Syn.: see **disconsolate.**

brood. Syn.: see **flock.**

brook, *n.* **Syn.:** rivulet, runlet, runnel, rill, bourn, burn, stream, creek.

brook, *v.* **Syn.:** see **tolerate, bear.**

brotherly. Syn.: fraternal.

Brotherly expresses the more affection; *fraternal* is often more formal or official: as, *brotherly* love; a *fraternal* organization.

browbeat. Syn.: intimidate, bully, cow, hector, domineer, overbear.

Bully, browbeat, and *hector* all indicate attempts at intimidation: *bully*, more by the threat of physical force; *browbeat*, by argumentative attack; *hector*, by blustering words and manner.

bruit. Syn.: see **rumor.**

brush. Syn.: see **conflict.**

brusque. Syn.: see **blunt.**

brutal. Syn.: brutish, animal, inhuman; rude, rough, harsh, savage, truculent, ruthless, merciless; gross, sensual. See **bestial, cruel.**

brutality. Syn.: inhumanity, cruelty, barbarity, savageness, ferocity, truculence.

brute. Syn.: see **animal,** *n.*

brutish. Syn.: see **bestial.**

bucolic. Syn.: see **rural.**

bud. Syn.: sprout, germinate, burgeon, pullulate, blossom.

buffoon. Syn.: see **clown, zany.**

bugbear. Syn.: bugaboo, bogy, hobgoblin, ogre.

build. Syn.: construct, erect, frame, fashion, make, establish, found, base, raise, rear.

building. Syn.: edifice, structure, house, dwelling, barn.

Building is the common term for what is built, generally for use as a house, dwelling, barn, factory, or the like. *Edifice* implies a large, fine, or imposing building. *Structure* emphasizes the size or plan of a building rather than its beauty or purpose.

bulge. Syn.: see **projection.**

bulk. Syn.: mass, volume, magnitude, bigness, largeness, size. See **size.**

bulky. Syn.: massive, ponderous, large, unwieldy, clumsy, burly.

Bulky refers to that which has (often excessive and disproportionate) greatness of size: as, a *bulky* bundle of clothes. *Massive* denotes weight and solidity quite as much as size: as, a *massive* column. *Ponderous* primarily denotes great weight, often combined with considerable size: as, a *ponderous* load. *Unwieldy* implies such size, shape, weight, or other condition as to make moving, handling, or managing difficult: as, an *unwieldy* machine.

bully. Syn.: see **browbeat.**

bulwark. Syn.: see **fortification.**

bumpkin. Syn.: see **clown.**

bunch. Syn.: cluster, tuft, knot.

bundle. Syn.: parcel, package, pack, packet, roll, bale.

A *bundle* is a number of things or an amount of something bound together: as, a *bundle* of sticks, rags, or hay. A *parcel* is usually a small wrapped bundle. A *package* is a quantity of anything or a number of things packed up, especially for carrying or transporting.

bungling. Syn.: clumsy, awkward, unskilful, maladroit.

buoyant. Syn.: see **cheerful.**

burden, *n.* **Syn.:** load, cargo; weight, heaviness, grievousness, oppression, encumbrance, incubus; responsibility, obligation.

burden, *v.* **Syn.:** see **load.**

burdensome. Syn.: weighty, heavy, cumbersome, onerous, oppressive, wearisome, fatiguing, troublesome. See **heavy.**

burial. Syn.: burying, interment, entombment, inhumation, sepulture.

burial-ground. Syn.: graveyard, cemetery, necropolis, churchyard, God's-acre, catacombs.

burlesque. Syn.: travesty, caricature, parody, take-off, extravaganza, mimicry, perversion, mockery.

A *caricature* is a picture, sometimes in language, which makes the original amusing, absurd, or undignified by exaggerating distinguishing characteristics; a *caricature* may be sympathetically conceived and executed. A *burlesque* renders a subject ludicrous by treating it incongruously, as by dealing with a grave subject lightly or frivolously, or a light subject with mock gravity. A *parody* changes the subject matter but imitates (especially) the peculiarities of form, style, or language of a (usually familiar) composition. In a *travesty* the subject matter is retained but the language or style is made absurd. A humorous speech in the style and manner of Mark Antony's oration would be a *parody*; the version of the Declaration of Independence in modern slang is a *travesty.*

burly. Syn.: see **bulky.**

burn. Syn.: blaze, flame, glow, scorch, singe, sear, scald, cauterize, brand, char, incinerate, cremate.

To *burn* is to consume, wholly or in part, or to injure by contact with fire or from excessive heat. *Scorch* implies superficial or slight burning that changes the color or injures the texture; the word often suggests shriveling or curling. *Singe* is especially applied to a superficial burning that takes off the ends (of hair, etc.) or projections of something. *Sear* has reference particularly to the drying or hardening caused by heat. *Char* emphasizes the idea of reducing to carbon or black cinders, especially on the surface.

burnish. Syn.: see **polish.**

burst. Syn.: break, split, crack, explode, rend, tear.

bury. Syn.: inter, entomb, inhume; hide, conceal, secrete, cache.

bush. Syn.: shrub, herb.

business. Syn.: trade, occupation, profession, vocation; pursuit, employment, work, job; traffic, trading, commerce, enterprise, industry. See **occupation.**

bustle. Syn.: stir, commotion, pother, ado.

busy. Syn.: employed, occupied, engaged, engrossed; diligent, industrious, hard-working, assiduous, sedulous; officious, meddlesome, prying, intrusive, intriguing. See **diligent, meddlesome.**

but. Syn.: only, merely, just; except, save; however, still, nevertheless, yet, notwithstanding.

butcher. Syn.: see **kill.**

butchery. Syn.: see **slaughter.**

buttress. Syn.: see **support.**

buzz. Syn.: hum, murmur, bombinate.

by. Syn.: through, with, at, beside, near.

By is the preposition regularly used to designate the agent in passive constructions, and properly governs any noun or pronoun (person or thing) which may be made the subject in the corresponding active construction: as, it is done *by* all (all do it); it was destroyed *by* fire (fire destroyed it); it was done *by* my pen (my pen did it). *With* designates the instrument: as, I did it *with* (rather than *by*) my pen. Either *by* or *with* may specify means: as, to kill *by*, or *with*, kindness. *Through* designates particularly intermediate agency or instrumentality, or reason or motive: as, it was done *through* my aid; he yielded *through* fear; *through* his disregard of precaution he was killed *by* a companion *with* a pistol.

bystander. Syn.: see **spectator.**

C

cabal. Syn.: combination, party, faction, junto, conspiracy, confederacy, league, camarilla, gang. See **party.**

cabalistic. Syn.: see **mysterious.**

cabin. Syn.: hut, cot, shanty, shack. See **cottage.**

caitiff. Syn.: see **wretch.**

cajole. Syn.: beguile, blandish, flatter, wheedle, coax. See **coax.**

calamitous. Syn.: disastrous, ruinous, baleful, dire, ill-starred, deplorable, grievous, distressing, afflictive.

calamity. Syn.: disaster, misfortune, affliction, adversity, reverse, blow, stroke, catastrophe, cataclysm. See **misfortune.**

calculate. Syn.: compute, reckon, count, figure, cast, estimate, weigh.

calculating. Syn.: computing, reckoning, etc. (see **calculate**); scheming, designing, shrewd, sharp, crafty, astute.

calculation. Syn.: computation, reckoning, estimate; forethought, prudence, circumspection, caution, wariness.

call. Syn.: announce, proclaim, shout, cry, clamor, scream, shriek, yell; invite, summon, bid; invoke, appeal, petition; convoke, convene, assemble; name, designate, entitle, term, style, dub.

Call is the general term; *summon* implies an authoritative or formal call, usually to a particular place; *convoke*, the calling of an organized body together; *invite*, a formal or courteous asking that leaves the answer to the will and pleasure of another. *Bid* in the sense of invite is now obsolete or poetic.

caller. Syn.: see **visitor.**

calling. Syn.: see **occupation.**

callous. Syn.: hard, hardened, indurate, unfeeling, insensible, unimpressionable, unsusceptible, indifferent. See **unfeeling.**

callow. Syn.: unfledged, unfeathered; immature, inexperienced, green.

calm, *a.* **Syn.:** still, quiet, motionless, smooth, placid, tranquil, peaceful, serene, undisturbed, unruffled, composed, self-possessed, collected, cool, unmoved, imperturbable, dispassionate. **Ant.:** excited, agitated, ruffled, discomposed, boisterous, stormy, tempestuous, perturbed, impassioned, hysterical.

Calm denotes the absence of agitation, especially under disturbing conditions. One who is *composed* has or has gained control over his emotions. One who is *collected* has complete command or possession of himself. *Cool* implies absence of the heat of strong feeling or excitement, especially in circumstances of danger or strain; *dispassionate*, freedom from passion or prejudice.

calm, *v.* **Syn.:** still, quiet, tranquilize, compose, lull, appease, pacify, allay, assuage, alleviate.

calmness. Syn.: stillness, quietude, placidity, tranquillity, serenity, composure, imperturbability, equanimity.

calumniate. Syn.: see **asperse.**

calumnious. Syn.: see **slanderous.**

calumny. Syn.: slander, defamation, libel, aspersion, backbiting.

can. Syn.: be able, may.

Can denotes ability or power to do something; *may*, probability, possibility, or permission: as, the child *can* read well; he *may* (possibility or probability) play football Saturday if the doctor says that he *may* (permission). The two words are especially confused where *can* is used for *may* in asking permission to do something: as, *may* (not *can*) I have an apple? The negative *cannot*, however, also expresses extreme improbability: as, I *cannot* be mistaken, for I saw it myself.

canard. Syn.: see **fabrication.**

cancel. Syn.: cross out, strike out, expunge, efface, obliterate, eliminate, annul, countermand, revoke, rescind, nullify. See **efface.**

candid. Syn.: frank, truthful, outspoken, straightforward, open, sincere, honest, impartial, fair, just. See **frank.**

candle. Syn.: see **light,** *n.*

candor. Syn.: frankness, sincerity, truthfulness, ingenuousness, openness, naïveté.

candy. Syn.: confectionery, confection, sweetmeat, bonbon, comfit.

canoe. Syn.: see **boat.**

canon. Syn.: rule, regulation, law, principle, standard, criterion. See **rule.**

cañon. Syn.: gorge, gulch, ravine, pass, chasm. See **valley.**

cant. Syn.: jargon, lingo, argot, slang, phraseology, vocabulary; hypocrisy, pretense. See **jargon.**

capability. Syn.: see **ability.**

capable. Syn.: able, competent, efficient, proficient, qualified, fitted. See **able.**

capacious. Syn.: spacious, roomy, large, broad, wide.

capacity. Syn.: volume, tonnage, size; ability, competency, power, faculty; position, character, relation. See **genius.**

caparison. Syn.: trapping, housing, accoutrement, equipment, dress.

caper. Syn.: leap, skip, jump, spring, gambol, frisk, prance, capriole, cavort. See **skip.**

capital. Syn.: principal, foremost, leading, cardinal, chief; excellent, first-rate, splendid.

caprice. Syn.: whim, whimsy, freak, notion, humor, fancy, vagary, crotchet.

Caprice denotes a sudden shift of opinion, intention, or desire without apparent or adequate motive. *Whim* implies an eccentric or fantastic turn of the mind. *Freak* goes so far as to imply peculiarity of conduct or even mental derangement. *Vagary* is applied to thought or action that is unusual or unreasonable because of its departure from the course of conduct demanded by custom or propriety.

capricious. Syn.: whimsical, fanciful, notional, freakish, fitful, changeable, fickle. See **wayward.**

capsize. Syn.: see **overturn.**

captious. Syn.: caviling, carping, faultfinding, hypercritical, censorious, touchy, contentious.

captivate. Syn.: enchant, charm, fascinate, bewitch, entrance, infatuate, enamour. See **charm,** *v.*

captive. Syn.: see **prisoner.**

captivity. Syn.: bondage, servitude, slavery, subjection; imprisonment, incarceration, immurement, confinement.

capture, *n.* Syn.: seizure, arrest, apprehension, catching.

capture, *v.* Syn.: catch, seize, apprehend, arrest, take.

carcass. Syn.: see **corpse.**

cardinal. Syn.: see **principal.**

care. Syn.: anxiety, concern, solicitude; attention, heed, regard, watchfulness, caution; charge, custody, management, tutelage, oversight.

Care suggests that the mind is weighed down by anxiety, apprehension, or the constant pressure of a multiplicity of things to be attended to. *Solicitude* suggests tender regard or desire for the welfare or safety of some person or thing. *Concern* implies agitation or uneasiness of mind, arising from uncertainty as to the well-being of something in which one has a strong interest. *Anxiety* implies a restless dread of some possible future evil.

careful. Syn.: solicitous, attentive, heedful, regardful, mindful, provident, prudent, painstaking, scrupulous, particular; cautious, wary, guarded, chary, circumspect, discreet. See **watchful.**

careless. Syn.: unconcerned, indifferent, regardless, heedless, inattentive, unmindful, improvident, imprudent, inconsiderate, thoughtless, forgetful; inaccurate, negligent, neglectful, remiss, lax, slack, desultory; incautious, unwary, indiscreet, reckless.

caress. Syn.: fondle, pet, coddle, embrace.

cargo. Syn.: lading, freight, load, burden.

caricature. Syn.: see **burlesque.**

carnage. Syn.: see **massacre.**

carnal. Syn.: fleshly, bodily, animal, sensual, lustful, gross, impure, base, worldly.

carousal. Syn.: carouse, drinking-bout, revel, wassail, spree, debauch, orgy, bacchanalia, saturnalia.

carp. Syn.: see **cavil.**

carriage. Syn.: carrying, conveyance, transportation; vehicle, coach, cab, hack, surrey, buggy; bearing, deportment, demeanor. See **bearing.**

carry. Syn.: convey, transport, bring, transfer, waft, bear, support, sustain.

cart. Syn.: see **wagon.**

cascade. Syn.: waterfall, cataract.

A *cascade* is a small and usually beautiful waterfall, often one in a series of descents, and may be either natural or artificial; a *cataract* is a waterfall of considerable size, characterized by a great volume of water and rapidity of descent.

case. Syn.: instance, example; condition, state, situation, plight, predicament, dilemma; covering, sheath, quiver, scabbard, box; action, suit, trial, process; inflection, form.

cash. Syn.: see **money.**

cashier. Syn.: see **dismiss.**

cask. Syn.: barrel, butt, pipe, tierce, hogshead, puncheon, tun, keg.

cast. Syn.: see **throw.**

castigate. Syn.: see **punish.**

castle. Syn.: fortress, citadel, stronghold, fastness, donjon; palace, mansion, château.

casual. Syn.: chance, accidental, fortuitous, unexpected, unforeseen; occasional, incidental, unpremeditated, offhand. See **accidental.**

casualty. Syn.: chance, accident, mishap, injury, death.

cataclysm. Syn.: see **flood.**

catalogue. Syn.: see **list.**

cataract. Syn.: see **cascade.**

catastrophe. Syn.: dénouement, conclusion, finale, end; disaster, blow, calamity, cataclysm. See **misfortune.**

catch. Syn.: capture, apprehend, seize, grip, grasp, clutch, snatch, nab; insnare, entrap, entangle; surprise, detect.

cathedral. Syn.: see **church.**

catholic. Syn.: universal, all-embracing, world-wide, general; broad-minded, liberal, tolerant, unsectarian.

catholicon. Syn.: see **remedy.**

cause, *n.* Syn.: occasion, ground, reason, motive, incentive, incitement, inducement; movement, principle.

cause, *v.* Syn.: occasion, effect, prompt, impel, induce, force, make, create, produce.

caustic. Syn.: burning, stinging, biting, pungent, cutting, sarcastic, satirical, mordacious, mordant.

caution, *n.* Syn.: warning, admonition, counsel, advice; prudence, thought, wariness, circumspectness, watchfulness, heed, care.

caution, *v.* Syn.: see **advise.**

cautious. Syn.: prudent, discreet, guarded, wary, circumspect, careful. Ant.: see **incautious.**

Cautious expresses the character of one who realizes the possibility of danger or evil and is on guard against it. The *guarded* person is careful and restrained because he considers the possible effects of his behavior, speech, or opinions. *Wary* implies great caution or alertness to protect oneself against suspected danger, stratagem, or trickery.

cave. Syn.: cavern, grotto, grot, den.

cavil. Syn.: carp, criticize, find fault.

caviling. Syn.: see **captious.**

cavity. Syn. see **hole.**

cease. Syn.: leave off, desist, discontinue, stop, quit, pause, refrain, abstain. Ant.: continue, prolong, begin, commence, start, initiate.

Cease is generally a more literary and formal word than *stop* and describes the leaving off or coming to an end of that which has had considerable duration. *Stop* is the usual (in most cases the only permissible) word to use of objects in motion or action: as, the storm *ceased*, the clock *stopped*. *Pause* implies the prospect of resumption (usually) after a short interval: as, to *pause* in speaking. *Desist* usually suggests giving up an action or proceeding that is undesirable, unpleasant, or annoying: as, to *desist* from making a noise.

ceaseless. Syn.: unceasing, uninterrupted, incessant, unending, continual, constant.

cede. Syn.: yield, relinquish, surrender, deliver, transfer, convey, grant. See **yield,** *v.*

celebrate. Syn.: solemnize, commemorate, observe, keep; extol, laud, glorify, honor.

To *celebrate* is to signalize with ritual an event or occasion of rejoicing: as, to celebrate mass, Armistice Day. To *commemorate* is to keep in memory by some solemn or public observance or ceremony: as, Decoration Day was set aside to *commemorate* the dead of the Civil War. To *solemnize* is especially to sanction with formal or religious ceremonies: as, to *solemnize* a marriage. To *observe* or, idiomatically, to *keep*, is to pay regard to in an appropriate or reverent way: as, to *observe* the Sabbath; to *keep* Lent.

celebrated. Syn.: famous, renowned, noted, illustrious, eminent, well-known. See **famous.**

celerity. Syn.: see **quickness.**

celestial. Syn.: see **godlike.**

censorious. Syn.: critical, hypercritical, faultfinding, carping, captious, condemnatory.

censure, *n.* **Syn.:** criticism, faultfinding, blame, stricture, reprehension, condemnation, disapproval, reproof, rebuke, reprimand.

censure, *v.* **Syn.:** criticize, blame, reprehend, reprove, rebuke, reprimand, chide, lecture, upbraid. See **reprove.**

center. Syn.: see **middle.**

ceremonious. Syn.: ceremonial, formal, stiff, precise, punctilious. **Ant.:** see **unceremonious.**

ceremony. Syn.: observance, ritual, rite, form, formality, punctilio.

Ceremony is a much broader term than *rite*, being applicable to any of the more or less formal or dignified acts of religious services or public occasions, and may even go so far as to cover mere forms of politeness, while *rite* refers to the established, prescribed, or customary forms of religious or other solemn practice: as, we attended the inaugural *ceremony*; we were allowed to witness the *rites* of the sun-worshipers.

certain. Syn.: fixed, settled, determined, prescribed, specified, definite, particular; trustworthy, unfailing, unerring, infallible, unquestionable, indisputable, undeniable, incontrovertible, irrefutable, incontestable, indubitable; confident, assured, sure, positive, convinced, satisfied. **Ant.:** see **uncertain.** See **sure.**

certainty. Syn.: see **belief.**

certitude. Syn.: see **belief.**

cessation. Syn.: ceasing, discontinuance, pause, stop, stay, postponement, rest, respite, lull, recess, interval, intermission.

chafe. Syn.: rub, wear, abrade, gall, irritate, annoy, vex, exasperate; fret, fume, rage. See **vex.**

chaff. Syn.: see **tease, banter,** *v.*

chagrin. Syn.: vexation, humiliation, mortification, shame, confusion, discomposure, disappointment, dismay. See **mortification.**

challenge. Syn.: object to, question; dare, defy, brave; invite, call, summon.

chamber. Syn.: see **room.**

champion, *n.* **Syn.:** defender, protector, vindicator, combatant, conqueror, hero, winner.

champion, *v.* **Syn.:** defend, maintain, fight for, advocate.

chance, *n.* **Syn.:** uncertainty, hap, fortuity, fortune, luck, accident, contingency; possibility, probability, likelihood, opportunity; risk, hazard.

chance, *a.* **Syn.:** casual, accidental, fortuitous, random, offhand, unexpected.

chance, *v.* **Syn.:** see **happen.**

change, *n.* **Syn.:** exchange, substitution; alteration, mutation, modification, variation, transformation, transition, deviation; variety, diversity, innovation, novelty, vicissitude.

change, *v.* **Syn.:** exchange, substitute, commute; alter, vary, diversify, transmute, transform, transpose, convert, shift, veer, reverse.

To *change* is to make a material difference in a thing so that it is distinctly other than what it was; to *vary* is to change irregularly or intermittently; to *alter* is to change a thing partially, usually preserving its identity: as, to *change* one's opinion; to *vary* the temperature of a room; to *alter* a dress.

changeable. Syn.: alterable, variable, mutable, unstable, uncertain, wavering, vacillating, inconstant, fickle.

changeless. Syn.: unalterable, unvarying, invariable, immutable, undeviating, permanent, steadfast, constant.

channel. Syn.: strait, passage, canal, conduit, gutter; furrow, groove; avenue, route, artery.

chant. Syn.: see **sing.**

chaos. Syn.: confusion, disorder, disorganization, anarchy.

char. Syn.: see **burn.**

character. Syn.: mark, symbol, sign; personality, individuality, nature, temperament, disposition; reputation, repute; person, individual. See **characteristic.**

Character commonly refers to the sum of the qualities that distinguish the possessor, often those that determine the moral nature. *Personality* refers particularly to the combination of qualities that determines the impression a person makes upon others. *Individuality* implies the presence in an individual of one or more peculiarly distinctive characteristics. See **reputation.**

characteristic. Syn.: quality, attribute, property, feature, character, mark, trait, peculiarity, idiosyncrasy.

Characteristic denotes a distinguishing mark or quality. *Character* is used specifically of a determining characteristic of a species or genus. *Trait* implies a well-established, often inborn, quality of nature or disposition. *Feature* indicates an outstanding part that leaves an impression on the mind. A *peculiarity* is that distinct or unusual characteristic which marks off an individual in the class to which it belongs; an *idiosyncrasy* is a personal eccentricity or oddity.

characterize. Syn.: portray, describe; distinguish, mark, stamp.

charge, *n.* **Syn.:** load, weight, burden; duty, responsibility, care, custody, oversight, management; command, injunction, order; accusation, indictment, imputation, allegation, complaint; attack, onset, onslaught, assault. See **command,** *n.,* **price.**

charge, *v.* **Syn.:** load, lade, burden, freight; command, enjoin, exhort, urge, instruct; accuse, indict, arraign; impute, attribute, ascribe; attack, assault. See **accuse.**

charitable. Syn.: kindly, kind, benevolent, benign, beneficent, liberal, generous, bountiful; lenient, tolerant, merciful, compassionate, forgiving. **Ant.:** see **uncharitable.**

charity. Syn.: love, good-will, benevolence, beneficence, bounty, almsgiving, philanthropy, liberality, leniency, indulgence. See **philanthropy.**

charlatan. Syn.: quack, mountebank, empiric, pretender, impostor, cheat, fraud, humbug. See **quack.**

charm, *n.* **Syn.:** incantation, spell, magic, enchantment, witchery, fascination, attractiveness, allurement; amulet, talisman, phylactery, fetish.

An *amulet,* usually worn or carried, is supposed to exert a constant protecting power by warding off evil; a *talisman,* besides averting evil or bringing fortune, is supposed to be able to produce, under special conditions, extraordinary desired results.

charm, *v.* **Syn.:** enchant, bewitch, fascinate, captivate, entrance, enrapture, transport, ravish, delight, allure.

To *charm* is to subdue, soothe, or entice as by beauty or amiability; to *fascinate* is to attract irresistibly, sometimes against one's will; to *captivate* is to capture and hold by very pleasing or winning qualities. *Enchant* and *bewitch* both mean to bring under a spell; but one may be *bewitched* by that which is pleasurable or merely magical whereas one who is *enchanted* is usually thought of as held in the thraldom of pleasure or delight.

charming. Syn.: see **winning.**

chart. Syn.: see **map.**

chary. Syn.: careful, wary, cautious, circumspect, shy; sparing, frugal, saving. See **sparing.**

chase. Syn.: pursue, follow, hunt, drive.

chasm. Syn.: fissure, gorge, cleft, breach, gap, abyss.

chaste. Syn.: pure, undefiled, inviolate, innocent, virtuous, continent, restrained; simple, classic, refined. **Ant.:** see **unchaste.**

chasten. Syn.: discipline, punish, chastise, correct, subdue, restrain; purify, refine. See **punish.**

chastise. Syn.: see **punish.**

chastity. Syn.: see **virtue.**

chat. Syn.: see **talk.**

château. Syn.: see **castle.**

chatter. Syn.: see **talk, babble.**

cheap. Syn.: inexpensive, low-priced; poor, mean, inferior, common, paltry, worthless.

Cheap and *inexpensive* agree in their suggestion of low cost. *Inexpensive* emphasizes lowness of price, generally without implying that the price is less than the article is worth. *Cheap* primarily suggests a discrepancy between price and value which is in favor of the buyer. It may also imply inferiority or showy imitation: as, *cheap* jewelry, *cheap* furniture.

cheat, *n.* **Syn.:** fraud, swindle, imposture, deception, stratagem, finesse, artifice, trick, hoax, humbug, blind; swindler, impostor, deceiver, trickster, sharper, blackleg.

cheat, *v.* **Syn.:** defraud, swindle, deceive, fool, circumvent, hoodwink, trick, beguile, cozen, gull, dupe, chouse, bilk, bamboozle, humbug, hoax.

Cheat implies fraudulent dealings, especially for profit or advantage to oneself; to *trick* means to deceive another by a stratagem, often of a petty, crafty, or dishonorable nature; to *swindle* is to cheat grossly or flagrantly by inspiring false confidence. *Cozen* is a literary word for cheating or beguiling. To *dupe* is to take advantage of another's credulity or gullibility; to *hoax* is to make one the victim of a practical joke by creating in him a false impression or belief.

check, *n.* **Syn.:** rebuff, repulse, reverse, setback, stoppage, obstacle, obstruction, hindrance, restriction, restraint, curb, bridle, damper; ticket, coupon, tag.

check, *v.* **Syn.:** stop, halt, block, obstruct, repress, restrain, curb, bridle, inhibit. See **stop,** *v.*

cheer, *n.* **Syn.:** gladness, joy, gaiety, jollity, animation; fare, viands, food; encouragement, comfort; acclamation, shouting, applause.

cheer, *v.* **Syn.:** gladden, enliven, exhilarate, animate, inspirit, encourage, comfort, console, solace; shout, applaud, acclaim.

Cheer implies the raising of the spirits of one who is downhearted; *gladden,* the making happier of one who may not have been previously unhappy; *enliven,* the imparting of life or gaiety, as to a group of persons or to a social occasion; *exhilarate,* a rousing of the spirits as by producing sensations of lively enjoyment.

cheerful. **Syn.:** cheery, glad, joyous, gay, blithe, buoyant, merry, jolly, jocund, bright, sunny, smiling, sanguine, optimistic; cheering, gladdening, enlivening.

cheerfulness. **Syn.:** see **gladness.**

cheerless. **Syn.:** joyless, gloomy, dismal, somber, drear, dreary, desolate, forlorn, dejected, disconsolate, despairing, hopeless, melancholy, sad.

Cheerless implies lack of cheer, comfort, or enlivenment; *gloomy,* depressing somberness or darkness. *Dreary* suggests that which saddens or depresses through being mournful, tedious, or dull. That which is *dismal* has a disheartening effect on the spirits and often suggests future ill. Thus, a *cheerless* room, a *gloomy* prison, a *dreary* ceremony, a *dismal* day.

cherish. **Syn.:** hold dear, foster, harbor, entertain, retain, treasure.

We *cherish* that which we regard or treat as an object of affection or value; we *foster* that which we sustain and nourish with care, especially to promote, increase, or strengthen it; we *harbor* that which we give shelter to or entertain, especially evil thoughts or intentions: as, to *cherish* a memory or a friendship; to *foster* a hope, ambition, or a feeling of anger; to *harbor* malice or a grudge.

chest. **Syn.:** see **box.**

chew. **Syn.:** masticate, Fletcherize, munch, crunch, champ, ruminate. See **eat.**

chicanery. **Syn.:** chicane, artifice, trickery, deception, quibbling, sophistry.

chide. **Syn.:** scold, rebuke, reprimand, reprove, reproach, upbraid, blame, censure. See **scold.**

chief, *n.* **Syn.:** head, leader, master, commander, chieftain, sachem.

chief, *a.* **Syn.:** leading, foremost, first, principal, capital, head, prime, cardinal, main, essential.

chiefly. **Syn.:** see **especially.**

chieftain. **Syn.:** see **chief,** *n.*

child. **Syn.:** infant, baby, babe, tot, boy, girl, youth, maid, maiden, foundling, waif, brat.

childish. **Syn.:** childlike, infantile, babyish, immature, puerile, weak, silly.

Childlike suggests those qualities that are becoming or pleasing in a child; *childish,* usually those that are natural in a child but inappropriate to a mature person: as, *childlike* innocence; *childish* petulance. *Infantile* is applied especially

to what belongs to or is characteristic of the early stages of childhood: as, *infantile* diseases. The actions of a mature person which resemble those of a baby are *babyish*: as, *babyish* whining.

childlike. **Syn.:** innocent, simple, inexperienced, artless, unsophisticated. See **childish.**

chilly. **Syn.:** chill, cold, raw.

chimerical. **Syn.:** unreal, imaginary, visionary, fanciful, fantastic, wild. See **imaginary.**

chink. **Syn.:** see **crack,** *n.*

chivalrous. **Syn.:** chivalric, knightly, gallant, valorous, courteous, magnanimous.

choice, *n.* **Syn.:** selection, option, alternative, preference, election.

Choice implies the power or opportunity of choosing between two or more things; *option* emphasizes free right or privilege of choosing; *alternative* is especially applied to the (often necessary) choice between two things.

choice, *a.* **Syn.:** select, superior, exquisite, rare, precious. See **fine,** *a.*

choke. **Syn.:** strangle, throttle, stifle, suffocate; stop, obstruct, block, clog, congest.

choler. **Syn.:** see **anger,** *n.*

choleric. **Syn.:** irascible, irritable, touchy, testy, peppery. See **irritable.**

choose. **Syn.:** select, prefer, pick, elect.

Choose expresses the idea of taking one or some where all are not wanted or cannot be had. *Prefer* emphasizes the strong desire for one thing rather than for another or others. A person may *choose* tea though he *prefers* coffee. *Elect* is especially used to express by ballot or otherwise a choice of persons for office, positions, or honors. *Select* implies careful and discriminating choice.

chop. **Syn.:** see **split.**

chronic. **Syn.:** long-continued, continuous, constant, inveterate, habitual, confirmed, hardened.

Chronic suggests that which is more or less permanent or of constant recurrence, and is especially applied to ailments: as, a *chronic* cough. *Confirmed* implies being firm or settled in an opinion, habit, or state: as, a *confirmed* believer in spiritualism; a *confirmed* user of drugs; *confirmed* restlessness. *Hardened* implies callousness of feeling or confirmed tendencies to evil: as, a *hardened* criminal. *Inveterate* denotes that which is firmly established by long continuance or indulgence: as, *inveterate* hatred; *inveterate* smoking.

chronicle. **Syn.:** history, annals, record, register, diary, journal, narrative, story. See **history.**

chuckle. **Syn.:** see **laugh.**

chum. **Syn.:** see **friend.**

church. **Syn.:** cathedral, minster, temple, sanctuary, tabernacle, chapel, meeting-house, bethel, synagogue.

churl. **Syn.:** see **countryman.**

churlish. **Syn.:** see **boorish.**

circle. **Syn.:** circlet, ring. See **coterie.**

circuitous. **Syn.:** roundabout, indirect, devious.

Circuitous implies a circuit or successive circuits in a course; *roundabout,* a going around rather than straight to a point; *devious,* repeated departure from the right way.

circulate. **Syn.:** see **disseminate.**

circumlocution. **Syn.:** see **verbosity.**

circumscribe. **Syn.:** surround, inclose, bound, limit, confine, restrict, restrain.

circumspect. **Syn.:** watchful, vigilant, careful, cautious, wary, prudent, discreet. See **prudent.**

circumstance. **Syn.:** see **event.**

circumstantial. **Syn.:** see **minute.**

circumvent. **Syn.:** see **cheat,** *v.,* **frustrate, overreach.**

citadel. **Syn.:** see **fortification.**

cite. **Syn.:** summon, call; quote, adduce, mention.

citizen. **Syn.:** see **inhabitant.**

civil. **Syn.:** courteous, polite, respectful, deferential, gracious, complaisant, suave, affable, urbane, courtly. **Ant.:** see **uncivil.**

Civil suggests the minimum observance of social conventions which will keep one from being rude. *Polite* implies willing and polished conformity to the demands of social etiquette. *Courteous* connotes that politeness which springs from sincere and thoughtful consideration of others. *Deferential* implies the showing of due respect. *Complaisant* implies acquiescence to a degree greater than established social custom demands. *Affable* suggests ease of approach, often with an implication of condescension.

civility. Syn.: see **complaisance.**

claim. Syn.: demand, assert, maintain. See **ask.**

clamber. Syn.: see **climb.**

clamor. Syn.: outcry, vociferation, shouting, uproar.

clamorous. Syn.: see **loud.**

clan. Syn.: see **tribe.**

clandestine. Syn.: secret, private, concealed, hidden, covert, surreptitious, stealthy, furtive, underhand, sly. See **secret.**

clash. Syn.: collision, conflict, disagreement, opposition. See **conflict.**

clasp. Syn.: fasten, hook; grasp, clutch, embrace, hug.

clean, *a.* **Syn.:** pure, unadulterated, unsoiled, unstained, unsullied, clear, spotless, immaculate, chaste, virtuous. **Ant.:** see **unclean.**

Clean suggests freedom from dirt or anything that soils; *pure*, freedom from any extraneous matter or anything that debases or defiles; *clear*, freedom from anything that clouds, dims, or dulls. *Spotless* and *immaculate* (a more formal or elegant word) suggest the absence of disfiguring or sullying marks or stains.

clean, *v.* **Syn.:** cleanse, scour, scrub, sweep, brush, wipe, mop, dust, wash, rinse, lave.

To *clean* is to remove dirt or impurities; *cleanse*, a stronger or more elevated word, is especially used of cleaning by chemical or other technical process, and figuratively of moral or spiritual purification.

cleanse. Syn.: clean, wash, purge, purify. See **clean,** *v.*

clear. Syn.: unclouded, cloudless; transparent, pellucid, translucent, lucid, limpid, crystalline, diaphanous; evident, obvious, plain, manifest, apparent, patent, intelligible, comprehensible, perspicuous, unmistakable, unambiguous; unobstructed, open; disentangled, disengaged, free. **Ant.:** unclear, cloudy, opaque, muddy, turbid, foggy; obscure, indistinct, abstruse, unintelligible, ambiguous. See **clean,** *a.*

clearly. Syn.: see **distinctly.**

cleave. Syn.: see **split.**

cleft. Syn.: fissure, crevice, rift, crack, chink, cranny.

clemency. Syn.: mildness, gentleness, tenderness, indulgence, leniency, forbearance, mercy, compassion, forgiveness. **Ant.:** severity, harshness, sternness, austerity, relentlessness. See **mercy.**

clergyman. Syn.: minister, divine, preacher, priest, rabbi, ecclesiastic, pastor, parson, rector, curate, vicar, evangelist, chaplain, dominie, sky-pilot.

clever. Syn.: dexterous, deft, skilful, adroit, ingenious, talented, versatile, quick-witted, smart.

Clever implies mental quickness, skilfulness, or adroitness, especially in practical affairs, but often suggests the lack of the larger powers of mind; *ingenious*, inventiveness or resourcefulness in meeting any problem, demand, or exigency. *Versatile* suggests ready facility or adaptability in turning from one thing to another, especially things covering a wide range or variety; *smart*, sharpness or keenness, especially in promoting one's own advantage.

cleverness. Syn.: dexterity, deftness, skill, adroitness, aptness, ingenuity, intelligence.

climax. Syn.: see **culmination.**

climb. Syn.: mount, ascend, scale, clamber, rise.

To *climb* is to go upwards, commonly by using the hands and feet or by continued effort. *Clamber* usually implies hurried or ungraceful climbing; *scale*, difficult or hazardous climbing up or over something either steep or high. *Ascend* especially suggests a gradual or stately upward movement, with or without effort, often to a considerable degree of altitude.

clip. Syn.: see **cut,** *v.*

clique. Syn.: see **coterie.**

cloak. Syn.: see **hide.**

clodhopper. Syn.: see **clown.**

clog. Syn.: impede, encumber, hamper, fetter; obstruct, choke. See **load.**

cloister. Syn.: see **convent.**

close, *n.* **Syn.:** see **end,** *n.*

close, *a.* **Syn.:** closed, inclosed; confined, narrow, cramped; heavy, oppressive, uncomfortable, unventilated, muggy; reticent, uncommunicative, close-mouthed; parsimonious, stingy, niggardly, penurious, miserly, close-fisted; compact, compressed, condensed, dense; near, adjacent; intimate, confidential; strict, minute.

close, *v.* **Syn.:** shut, stop, obstruct; end, conclude, terminate, finish, complete.

To *close* is to stop a hole or opening, or bring into a compact form, especially by bringing the parts together, or, figuratively, to bring to an end: as, to *close* the mouth or eyes; to *close* a book; to *close* a service with a song. To *shut* is to close especially so as to offer obstruction of some kind, particularly hindrance to entrance or exit: as, to *shut* a door or gate; to *shut* a person in a cell.

clothe. Syn.: dress, attire, apparel, array, invest.

Clothe is used of providing or covering with garments; *dress* has reference particularly to the operation of putting on the clothes or to the character or style of clothes worn. *Attire*, *apparel*, and *array* all suggest elegant or pretentious dress or personal adornment.

clothes. Syn.: clothing, dress, attire, apparel, raiment, vesture, costume, garb, garments, vestments, habiliments.

Clothing is the general word for any covering of the body. *Raiment* and *vesture* are now literary or poetic, the former sometimes regarding clothing as a necessity of life; the latter especially being applied to costly garments, often of a flowing character.

clothing. Syn.: see **clothes.**

cloudy. Syn.: overclouded, lowering, overcast, murky, dark, gloomy.

clown. Syn.: peasant, rustic, hind, swain, bumpkin, boor, lout, clodhopper, gawk; buffoon, jester, fool, merry-andrew, zany, mimic.

Clown is applied to the coarse or ill-bred, *lout*, to the awkward or stupid, countryman. *Hind* and *swain* are poetic, *hind* suggesting the simple-minded or illiterate country fellow; *swain*, especially the unsophisticated country lover. *Rustic* suggests the simple, honest dweller in the country. *Bumpkin*, *clodhopper*, and many similar words are used contemptuously, especially by people of the town or city, to express the lack of culture or urbanity of those living in the country.

clownish. Syn.: boorish, loutish, gawky, awkward, clumsy, rude.

cloy. Syn.: surfeit, satiate, sate, pall, glut, gorge. See **satiate.**

club. Syn.: cudgel, bludgeon, bat; society, association, coterie.

clumsy. Syn.: awkward, ungraceful, ungainly, lumbering, lubberly; unwieldy, unhandy, unskilful, maladroit, inexpert, bungling. See **awkward.**

cluster. Syn.: bunch, clump, tuft, group, crowd.

clutch. Syn.: see **seize.**

coadjutor. Syn.: see **associate.**

coagulate. Syn.: curdle, clot, congeal, thicken, concrete.

coalesce. Syn.: unite, combine, consolidate, merge, blend, fuse.

coalition. Syn.: see **alliance.**

coarse. Syn.: common, rough, rude, unsifted, unrefined, vulgar, gross, crass, indelicate, ribald.

coast. Syn.: seashore, seaboard, seaside, shore, strand, beach. See **shore.**

coax. Syn.: wheedle, cajole, beguile, inveigle, persuade.

To *coax* is to appeal to one by reiterated entreaty or by winning arts to persuade him to grant what is desired. To *cajole* is to persuade, or attempt to persuade, by deceptive allurements or flattery. *Wheedle* implies persistent importunities involving artful or even dishonest tricks in getting out of another what one wishes.

coddle. Syn.: humor, indulge. See **fondle.**

coerce. Syn.: constrain, compel, force, intimidate. See **force,** *v.*

coercion. Syn.: see **force,** *n.*

coeval. Syn.: see **contemporary.**

cogent. Syn.: compelling, forcible, powerful, potent, effective, convincing, telling, strong.

cogitate. Syn.: see **reflect.**

cognizant. Syn.: see **conscious.**

cohere. Syn.: stick, cleave, adhere.

coherence. Syn.: cohesion, congruity, consistency.

coin. Syn.: see **money.**

coincide. Syn.: correspond, agree, concur, harmonize, tally. See **agree.**

coincident. Syn.: coinciding, agreeing, concurring, concurrent, contemporary.

cold. Syn.: cool, chill, chilly, chilling, frosty, frigid, freezing, frozen, icy, gelid, wintry; unresponsive, indifferent, apathetic, phlegmatic, passionless. **Ant.:** see **hot.**

colleague. **Syn.:** see **associate.**

collect. **Syn.:** gather, assemble, accumulate, amass, muster, convene. See **gather.**

collected. **Syn.:** gathered, assembled, etc. (see **collect**); self-possessed, composed, calm, cool. See **calm,** *a*.

collection. **Syn.:** assemblage, accumulation, aggregation, agglomeration, group; offering, contribution.

collision. **Syn.:** see **shock.**

colloquial. **Syn.:** conversational, familiar, informal.

collusion. **Syn.:** see **connivance.**

color, *n*. **Syn.:** hue, shade, tint, tinge, tincture; pigment, paint, dye; guise, semblance, pretext.

Color is the general term. *Hue* indicates the distinctive quality of a color, especially the respect in which colors differ though they have the same luminosity and chroma. Strictly speaking *shade* is any variation in one color produced by the admixture of another; *tint* is a variation in depth or intensity of any shade. In popular use *shade* is sometimes loosely employed for *tint*. *Tinge* implies the presence of a color in small amount, whether concentrated or diffused.

color, *v*. **Syn.:** tint, tinge, tincture, paint, dye, stain; flush, blush.

colorable. **Syn.:** see **ostensible.**

colossal. **Syn.:** gigantic, huge, enormous, monstrous, prodigious, vast. **Ant.:** small, diminutive, tiny, minute, microscopic. See **enormous.**

colt. **Syn.:** see **horse.**

column. **Syn.:** pillar, shaft, obelisk, pilaster; file, line, row.

combat, *n*. **Syn.:** fight, struggle, conflict, engagement, duel. See **battle, fight.**

combat, *v*. **Syn.:** fight, battle, struggle, contend, oppose, resist, withstand.

combative. **Syn.:** pugnacious, contentious, disputatious. See **belligerent.**

combination. **Syn.:** see **confederation.**

combine. **Syn.:** unite, join, coalesce, coöperate, merge, mix, blend, compound, amalgamate. See **join.**

comely. **Syn.:** fair, pretty, handsome, beautiful, good-looking, pleasing, personable. **Ant.:** uncomely, homely, plain, ugly. See **beautiful.**

comfort, *n*. **Syn.:** consolation, solace, relief, help, succor, encouragement, ease, contentment.

Comfort implies the bringing of the mind or body into a state of cheer, rest, or ease. *Solace* is applied to that which lessens or removes loneliness, sadness, or sorrow. *Consolation* suggests alleviation of grief or distress. Both *solace* and *consolation* affect only one's state of mind. *Relief* is applied to whatever lightens pain, trouble, discomfort, or hardship.

comfort, *v*. **Syn.:** soothe, console, solace, cheer, gladden, refresh, encourage, inspirit.

comfortless. **Syn.:** inconsolable, disconsolate, cheerless, dejected, desolate, forlorn, miserable.

comic, comical. **Syn.:** see **funny.**

comity. **Syn.:** courtesy, civility, politeness, amenity.

command, *n*. **Syn.:** order, direction, bidding, injunction, charge, precept, commandment, behest, mandate; authority, leadership, control, mastery.

Command implies an authoritative order, usually issued by one of superior station or power; *charge*, a direct, specific, and, often, peremptory order, as to a jury. *Mandate* and *behest* are dignified or poetic words for official or lofty bidding or injunction.

command, *v*. **Syn.:** order, direct, bid, enjoin, charge, instruct; govern, control, rule, lead; exact, compel, secure; overlook, dominate. See **direct,** *v.*, **govern.**

commander. **Syn.:** see **chief,** *n*.

commanding. **Syn.:** controlling, powerful, paramount; authoritative, imperious, imperative; imposing, impressive; overlooking, dominating. See **impressive.**

commemorate. **Syn.:** see **celebrate.**

commence. **Syn.:** see **begin.**

commend. **Syn.:** intrust, deliver, commit, recommend; praise, laud, extol, eulogize. See **commit.**

commendable. **Syn.:** laudable, praiseworthy, creditable.

commendation. **Syn.:** recommendation, approbation, praise, eulogy, encomium.

commensurate. **Syn.:** see **proportionate.**

comment. **Syn.:** annotation, explanation, commentary; remark, observation. See **remark.**

commerce. **Syn.:** traffic, trade, business, intercourse, dealing. See **trade,** *n*.

commercial. **Syn.:** see **mercantile.**

commiserate. **Syn.:** pity, compassionate, sympathize, condole.

commiseration. **Syn.:** see **pity.**

commission. **Syn.:** authorize, empower, delegate, depute, appoint.

commit. **Syn.:** intrust, trust, confide, consign, commend; perpetrate, do.

Commit expresses no more than the delivery of something into the charge or keeping of another. *Consign* implies more or less formality, and, sometimes, finality in the surrender. *Intrust* and *confide* imply committal based upon confidence or belief in another's fidelity or integrity, the latter particularly suggesting closeness or intimacy of relationship. *Commend* is now used especially of reliance upon divine protection.

commodious. **Syn.:** spacious, roomy, comfortable.

commodity. **Syn.:** merchandise, goods.

common. **Syn.:** general, universal, prevalent, popular, public; usual, customary, ordinary, commonplace, plebeian, everyday; mediocre, inferior, mean, low, cheap, coarse, vulgar. **Ant.:** see **uncommon.**

What is *common* is shared by all, and belongs to one as much as to another. What is *general* belongs to or prevails throughout a whole class or body collectively, irrespective of individuals. What is *popular* belongs to or is adapted for or favored by the people or the public generally, rather than a particular (especially a superior) class. What is *vulgar* belongs to or is characteristic of the common people, or those making no pretension to rank or to superior culture or refinement.

commonly. **Syn.:** see **often.**

commonplace, *n*. **Syn.:** see **platitude.**

commonplace, *a*. **Syn.:** ordinary, every-day, trite, hackneyed, banal, platitudinous, prosaic.

commonwealth. **Syn.:** see **state,** *n*.

commotion. **Syn.:** agitation, disturbance, disorder, turmoil, tumult, riot, turbulence.

Commotion, tumult, and *turmoil* all denote disturbance, physical or mental. *Commotion* suggests particularly the idea of confusion; *tumult*, that of disorder with violence or noise; *turmoil*, that of struggling, conflicting efforts, or distressing unrest.

communicate. **Syn.:** impart, transmit, convey, tell. See **impart.**

communication. **Syn.:** imparting, transmission; intercourse, connection; correspondence, letter, message.

communion. **Syn.:** association, intercourse, converse, fellowship, union; eucharist, sacrament, Lord's supper.

communism. **Syn.:** see **socialism.**

compact, *n*. **Syn.:** agreement, covenant, treaty, contract, pact. See **contract,** *n*.

compact, *a*. **Syn.:** packed, dense, solid; concise, succinct, terse, pithy.

companion. **Syn.:** mate, comrade, associate, partner, compeer, chum, crony.

companionable. **Syn.:** see **sociable.**

company. **Syn.:** companionship, fellowship, association, society; party, band, group, circle, coterie, set, troop, squad, crew, gang; assembly, gathering, concourse, crowd; guest, visitor; firm, house, corporation, syndicate. Cf. **coterie.**

A *company* is any group of people formally or informally associated: as, the Standard Oil *Company*; a *company* of pilgrims. *Party*, except when used of a political group, usually implies an indefinite and temporary assemblage of people, as for some common pursuit or for amusement or social pleasure. *Band*, used especially of a *band* of musicians, suggests a relatively small group of persons pursuing the same purpose or sharing a common fate. *Troop*, used specifically of a body of cavalry, usually implies a number of individuals who are organized as a unit. *Crew*, except of sailors, trainmen, electric linemen, etc., indicates a group with common characteristics: as, a merry *crew*. It is often used jocosely or disparagingly. *Gang*, except of a body of workmen, is derogatory, and is especially used to stigmatize dishonest political combinations or bands of robbers, thugs, or criminals.

compare. **Syn.:** see **contrast,** *v*.

comparison. **Syn.:** likening, similitude, parallel, simile, metaphor.

compass, *n*. **Syn.:** circuit, limits, bounds, extent, range, reach, scope. See **range.**

compass, *v*. **Syn.:** encircle, inclose, surround; grasp, attain, obtain, procure, gain, achieve, effect, consummate, accomplish.

compassion. Syn.: pity, ruth, commiseration, sympathy, tenderness, mercy. See **pity.**

compassionate. Syn.: pitying, sympathizing, sympathetic, tender, kind, merciful.

compatible. Syn.: consistent, congruous, reconcilable, congenial, consonant, accordant.

compeer. Syn.: see **companion.**

compel. Syn.: constrain, oblige, coerce, force, drive, make, necessitate. See **force,** v.

compendious. Syn.: concise, summary, succinct, terse, condensed, comprehensive.

compendium. Syn.: summary, epitome, abstract, digest, abridgment. See **abridgment.**

compensate. Syn.: counterbalance, offset; recompense, remunerate, requite, reimburse, indemnify, reward, pay.

Compensate, remunerate, and *recompense* are often used with little difference of meaning. We *compensate* a person by payment or some offsetting consideration for loss or injury, or for services performed; *remunerate* him by some reward or return for his trouble, work, etc.; *recompense* him for his services, pains, sufferings, losses, etc.; *requite* him for his deeds, good or ill; *reimburse* him by repaying what he has expended; and *indemnify* him against risk, and for damage or loss sustained.

compensation. Syn.: recompense, remuneration, reward, payment, amends, reparation.

competent. Syn.: fit, qualified, able, capable, proficient.

competition. Syn.: rivalry, emulation.

Competition is a striving between two or more individuals or groups for the same goal or prize. *Competition* may be between equal or unequal forces and, except in special phrases such as *unfair competition,* implies a friendly or legitimate contest. *Rivalry,* unless qualified by some favorable adjective, suggests keen, selfish, or even hostile competition, generally between more or less evenly matched opponents. *Emulation* implies a desire to equal or surpass the quality, attainment, or achievement of others, arising from admiration, reverence, or a natural love of superiority.

competitor. Syn.: see **rival.**

complacency. Syn.: self-satisfaction, self-approval, self-contentment, smugness. See **vanity.**

complain. Syn.: lament, murmur, repine, grumble, growl, grunt, croak, whine.

To *complain* is to protest against or lament a condition or cause of pain, dissatisfaction, wrong, etc. To *grumble* is to utter half to oneself surly or ill-natured complaint. To *murmur* is to complain in low or suppressed tones. To *repine* is to be fretfully or depressingly dispirited because of regret or disappointment.

complaint. Syn.: lament, murmuring, faultfinding, querulousness; accusation, charge, allegation, grievance; ailment, disorder, sickness, illness. See **disease.**

complaisance. Syn.: obligingness, graciousness, courtesy, politeness, civility, urbanity, suavity, affability.

complaisant. Syn.: obliging, agreeable, gracious, courteous, civil, urbane, compliant, yielding, accommodating. See **civil.**

complement. Syn.: supplement.

complete, a. **Syn.:** whole, entire, full, total, utter, absolute, thorough, perfect, plenary; finished, ended, concluded.

That which is *complete* is an admitted unit which has all its parts and those parts fully developed or perfected (as, a *complete* course of study), and may be a process or purpose carried to fulfilment (as, a *complete* revolution of the earth). That which is *full,* strictly speaking, contains so much that it will hold no more, but *full* is also used to indicate approximate saturation or simply a large quantity: as, a rag *full* of grease; he was *full* of information. *Whole* implies a unit from which no part has been taken or a combination of parts necessary to make up an arbitrary unit: as, a *whole* apple, a *whole* crowd of people. *Entire* agrees with whole in so far as it suggests that which is not divided or separated, and hence has unbroken unity. *Total* refers to the sum or aggregate of parts taken together.

complete, v. **Syn.:** finish, perfect, consummate, fulfil, accomplish, end.

complex. Syn.: compound, composite, complicated, intricate, involved, perplexing.

compliance. acquiescence, yielding, assent, consent, obedience, submission.

compliant. Syn.: complying, yielding, assenting, consenting, pliant, tractable, obedient, submissive, obliging, complaisant.

complicated. Syn.: see **complex.**

compliment. Syn.: commendation, laudation, praise, tribute, encomium, eulogy, panegyric, flattery, adulation.

Compliment implies mild and polite praise which may be either sincere or merely conventional; *flattery,* insincere or excessive praise, especially to gratify vanity or gain favor; *adulation,* servile, hypocritical, or fulsome praise, proceeding from blind worship or from hope of advantage.

comply. Syn.: acquiesce, yield, conform, obey, submit.

component. Syn.: constituent, ingredient, part. See **constituent.**

composed. Syn.: calm, tranquil, serene, quiet, cool, collected, self-possessed. See **calm,** a.

composure. Syn.: calmness, collectedness, equanimity, serenity, tranquillity.

Composure implies recovery or retention of self-control, especially during or in spite of the stress of excitement; *equanimity,* inherent evenness of temper or disposition that withstands elation, depression, anger, etc.; *tranquillity,* freedom of the mind from harassing cares or anxieties; *serenity,* exalted calmness that rises above ordinary storms, stresses, or excitements.

compound, n. **Syn.:** see **mixture.**

compound, v. **Syn.:** see **mix.**

comprehend. Syn.: include, comprise, embrace; conceive, understand, apprehend, grasp, perceive. See **include, know.**

comprehension. Syn.: see **apprehension.**

comprehensive. Syn.: comprehending, inclusive, broad, wide, extensive, full.

compress. Syn.: condense, compact, squeeze, constrict.

comprise. Syn.: comprehend, include, embrace, contain. See **include.**

compulsion. Syn.: constraint, obligation, coercion, force.

compunction. Syn.: see **regret.**

computation. Syn.: calculation, reckoning, figuring, estimate.

compute. Syn.: calculate, reckon, estimate, count, enumerate, figure.

comrade. Syn.: see **companion, friend.**

conceal. Syn.: hide, secrete, screen, cover, cloak. See **hide,** v.

concealment. Syn.: hiding, seclusion, retirement, retreat, privacy, secrecy.

concede. Syn.: see **grant.**

conceit. Syn.: self-esteem, vanity, pride, egotism, complacency; fancy, whim, notion, idea. See **vanity.**

conceited. Syn.: vain, proud, egotistical, self-satisfied, opinionated, priggish.

conceive. Syn.: apprehend, understand, comprehend, imagine, fancy, think, deem.

Conceive and *conceive of* indicate differing mental processes. To *conceive* is to form an image (often of something which may be or is about to be brought into existence), or to gestate an idea or feeling: as, the author *conceived* the first act of his play; he *conceived* a dislike for the East. To *conceive of* is to comprehend through the intellect something which one does not or cannot perceive through the senses: as, Woodrow Wilson *conceived of* a world free from war. To *imagine* is either to *conceive* in the first sense or to *conceive of:* as, *imagine* yourself in Shakspere's London; could you *imagine* a greater pleasure than being there? But *imagine* is not used in the second sense of *conceive.* Thus we say: he *conceived* (not *imagined*) an ambition to be king. To *fancy* is to imagine pleasurably or idly.

concentrate. Syn.: centralize, focus, consolidate, intensify, condense.

conception. Syn.: apprehension, comprehension; concept, idea, notion, impression.

concern, n. **Syn.:** relation, interest, connection; moment, importance, weight, consequence; care, solicitude, uneasiness, anxiety; firm, house, establishment. See **care.**

concern, v. **Syn.:** affect, touch, interest, engage, involve.

conciliate. Syn.: placate, pacify, soothe, appease, propitiate, reconcile. See **pacify.**

concise. Syn.: succinct, condensed, compendious, summary, brief, terse, pithy, laconic, sententious, epigrammatic.

Ant.: diffuse, verbose, prolix, extended, wordy, long-winded.

Concise signifies the expression of much in a few words, as by cutting down to the essentials. *Succinct* is applied to subject matter that is compressed into small compass. *Terse* implies finished, clear-cut, or pointed expression in the smallest possible compass. *Laconic* often suggests extreme or even blunt or curt conciseness or brevity. A *sententious* style is characterized by striking phrases or quotable utterances, and is sometimes rhetorical or inflated. *Pithy* remarks give the gist of a matter in a brief and forcible way.

conclude. Syn.: end, finish, close, terminate; deduce, infer; decide, determine, resolve. See **infer, end.**

conclusion. Syn.: end, ending, close, termination, completion, peroration, finale; result, issue, outcome, upshot, event; deduction, inference, illation.

conclusive. Syn.: decisive, definitive, convincing, unanswerable, irrefutable, indisputable, final.

concoct. Syn.: compound, mix, prepare, brew, combine; devise, contrive, invent, plan, plot. See **prepare.**

concomitant. Syn.: accompanying, attendant, accessory, coincident, concurrent, synchronous.

concur. Syn.: coincide, unite, combine, coöperate; agree, accord, acquiesce, approve. See **assent.**

concurrent. Syn.: coincident, united, conjoined, combined, coördinate, coöperating, agreeing, accordant.

concussion. Syn.: see **shock.**

condemn. Syn.: censure, blame, reprove, denounce, reproach, upbraid; sentence, convict, doom.

condense. Syn.: compact, compress, contract, concentrate, inspissate, boil down, reduce, abridge, shorten, abbreviate, epitomize.

condescend. Syn.: stoop (to), deign, vouchsafe.

Condescend implies a (real or imagined) stooping from the height of one's dignity or pride to the level of an inferior, or the doing of something considered beneath one. *Deign* implies polite or gracious granting of something asked or desired, or, often, in the negative, arrogant refusal to do something which one considers unworthy or distasteful. *Vouchsafe* usually suggests condescension in the granting or bestowal of something.

condign. Syn.: well-deserved, merited, just, fitting, suitable, adequate.

condition. Syn.: stipulation, prerequisite, requirement, provision, proviso, article, term; situation, position, state, plight, predicament, circumstances. See **state.**

conditional. Syn.: dependent, contingent, provisory, subject. **Ant.:** see **unconditional.**

That which is *conditional* is subject to or limited by something else; that which is *contingent* is dependent on future circumstances which are themselves uncertain.

condolence. Syn.: sympathy, commiseration, pity. See **pity.**

condone. Syn.: see **pardon.**

conduce. Syn.: lead (to), tend, contribute, redound.

That which *conduces* leads or tends to a (usually) favorable or desirable end or result; that which *contributes* has an actual share with other contributors in promoting a common end; that which *redounds* has a return effect, creditable or advantageous (less often discreditable or disadvantageous) to a person or thing.

conducive. Syn.: contributive, promotive, helpful.

conduct, *n.* **Syn.:** guidance, escort; management, supervision, administration; behavior, deportment, action. See **behavior.**

conduct, *v.* **Syn.:** lead, guide, escort, pilot, convoy; manage, carry on, superintend, supervise, regulate, direct, control; behave, act. See **guide,** *v.*

confederate. Syn.: see **accomplice.**

confederation. Syn.: confederacy, federation, league, alliance, union, coalition, combination. See **alliance.**

confer. Syn.: bestow, grant, give; consult, deliberate. See **give.**

To *consult* is to seek from a personal or impersonal source advice, information, or opinion; to *confer* is to interchange views for the purpose of illuminating a subject under consideration: as, to *consult* an authority; the partners *conferred* concerning their business policy.

conference. Syn.: see **meeting.**

confess. Syn.: acknowledge, avow, own, admit, concede. See **acknowledge.**

confide. Syn.: see **commit.**

confidence. Syn.: trust, reliance, faith, belief; self-reliance, assurance, aplomb, boldness, hardihood, presumption.

Confidence is a feeling of security in or reliance on oneself whether commendable or objectionable. *Assurance* suggests a feeling of certainty so strong as to preclude doubt: as, the prisoner's *assurance* of acquittal was based on the knowledge of his innocence. In a derogatory sense *assurance* implies self-satisfied or impudent belief in oneself or in one's ability: as, the *assurance* of the criminal angered the judge. *Presumption* suggests arrogant or self-important forwardness; *hardihood*, boldness or audacity, often such as disregards good judgment. See **trust,** *n.*

confident. Syn.: sure, certain, positive, reliant, bold, undaunted, overbold, presumptuous. See **hopeful.**

confidential. Syn.: see **familiar.**

configuration. Syn.: see **form.**

confine, *n.* **Syn.:** see **border.**

confine, *v.* **Syn.:** limit, restrict, shut in, shut up, bound, circumscribe, restrain, imprison, incarcerate, immure.

confinement. Syn.: restraint, imprisonment, incarceration, immurement, durance, duress.

confirm. Syn.: strengthen, settle, establish, assure, prove, verify, corroborate, substantiate, authenticate, sanction, ratify, validate.

To *confirm* is to make more firm or certain; to *corroborate* is to strengthen with supporting testimony; to *authenticate* is to prove true or genuine; to *substantiate* is to establish by proof or valid evidence.

confirmed. Syn.: strengthened, settled, fixed, established, corroborated, sanctioned, upheld, habitual, inveterate, chronic. See **chronic.**

conflagration. Syn.: see **fire.**

conflict. Syn.: collision, clash, strife, struggle, combat, fight, battle, encounter, brush, contention, antagonism, opposition, controversy, variance.

A *conflict* is a collision between parties or forces contending or fighting one against the other. *Struggle* implies vigorous bodily effort or violent exertion; *clash*, a direct and sharp collision between opposing parties, efforts, interests, etc.; *brush*, a brief but smart, and often casual, competition between opponents.

conflicting. Syn.: conflictive, antagonistic, contradictory, contrary, incompatible.

conform. Syn.: adapt, adjust, accommodate, suit; agree, correspond, comply, submit. See **adapt.**

conformable. Syn.: corresponding, harmonizing, consonant, consistent; compliant, acquiescent, submissive, obedient.

conformation. Syn.: see **form.**

confound. Syn.: see **confuse.**

confuse. Syn.: jumble, mix, disorder, disarrange; confound, perplex, bewilder, fluster, nonplus, disconcert, abash, embarrass.

Confuse refers to general bewilderment of mind; *confound*, to confusion that overwhelms the faculties, rendering one incapable, for the moment at least, of knowing what to think or do.

confused. Syn.: jumbled, disordered, deranged, involved, indistinct, indiscriminate; perplexed, bewildered, disconcerted, abashed, embarrassed.

confusion. Syn.: jumble, disorder, disarray, turmoil, tumult, commotion, chaos, babel, pandemonium; perplexity, bewilderment, perturbation, abashment, embarrassment.

confute. Syn.: see **refute.**

congenial. Syn.: kindred, sympathetic, harmonious, companionable; agreeable, pleasing, suitable.

congenital. Syn.: see **inborn.**

congratulate. Syn.: felicitate, compliment.

To *congratulate* is to express a hearty feeling of gratification at another's happiness or good fortune. To *felicitate* is to express to another in a more formal way one's belief that he has reason to be happy.

congregate. Syn.: assemble, collect, gather, meet, convene, throng.

congress. Syn.: assembly, conference, council, convention, conclave, synod, diet, parliament, legislature.

congruous. Syn.: agreeing, corresponding, harmonious, consonant, consistent, appropriate, fitting, proper, meet. **Ant.:** incongruous, disagreeing, inappropriate, discordant, inharmonious.

conjecture, *n.* **Syn.:** surmise, guess, inference, supposition, theory, hypothesis.

conjecture, *v.* **Syn.:** surmise, guess, suppose, presume, imagine, fancy, think.

To *conjecture* is, as it were, to cast the mind upon some hypothetical opinion in the absence of sufficient evidence to establish certainty. *Guess* is to risk an opinion regarding something which one cannot know about; *guess at* implies more haphazard or random guessing. *Guess* sometimes means to arrive wholly or partly by chance at the correct answer to a question: as, he *guessed* the answer to a riddle. *Surmise* implies an intuitive conjecture.

conjoin. **Syn.:** unite, combine, associate, connect, join.

conjugal. **Syn.:** see **matrimonial.**

conjure. **Syn.:** adjure, implore, entreat, pray, beg; charm, bewitch, enchant, invoke, summon.

conjurer. **Syn.:** see **magician.**

connect. **Syn.:** conjoin, join, unite, couple, link, combine, associate, affiliate, relate, correlate. See **join.**

connection. **Syn.:** junction, conjunction, union, affiliation, relationship, alliance, association, combination; bond, tie, link, coupling; relation, relative, kinsman.

connivance. **Syn.:** collusion, fraud, deceit.

Connivance implies pretended ignorance of, or tacit or secret assent to, wrongdoing. *Collusion* implies secret or underhanded coöperation with another for unworthy purposes.

connoisseur. **Syn.:** see **judge,** *n.*

connote. **Syn.:** see **denote.**

connubial. **Syn.:** see **matrimonial.**

conquer. **Syn.:** vanquish, subdue, overpower, overthrow, defeat, beat, crush, rout, subjugate, subject, master, overcome, surmount.

Conquer implies gaining control or a final victory over, usually after a series of efforts or against systematic resistance; *vanquish,* the complete overthrow of another, usually in a single and often personal combat or battle; *overcome,* surmounting difficulties or prevailing over an antagonist. *Defeat* suggests at least a temporary and often a permanent beating or frustrating of an opponent. *Subdue* refers to that which has been so conquered that its spirit of resistance has been broken; *subjugate,* to that which is rendered completely subservient to the will of another.

conqueror. **Syn.:** see **victor.**

conquest. **Syn.:** vanquishment, subjugation, subjection, triumph, victory. **Ant.:** defeat, submission, surrender, failure.

consanguinity. **Syn.:** see **relation.**

conscientious. **Syn.:** scrupulous, just, upright, honest, faithful, careful, particular, painstaking.

conscious. **Syn.:** sensible, sentient, cognizant, aware.

Conscious implies to be awake or awakened to a realization within the mind of a fact, a truth, a condition, etc.; *aware* lays the emphasis on sense perceptions which lead to consciousness; as, he was *conscious* of an extreme weariness; he was *aware* of the odor of tobacco. *Sensible* may be used for either *conscious* or *aware,* but often suggests an added stimulation of the feelings: as, he was *sensible* of the honor paid him. *Cognizant* refers to the active realization which comes from certain knowledge: as, to be *cognizant* of a fact; he was *cognizant* of their attempts to injure his character.

consecrate. **Syn.:** dedicate, devote, ordain, sanctify, hallow. See **devote.**

consecrated. **Syn.:** see **holy.**

consecutive. **Syn.:** see **successive.**

consent, *n.* **Syn.:** assent, agreement, concurrence, compliance, acquiescence, permission, approval.

consent, *v.* **Syn.:** assent, agree, concur, comply, yield, acquiesce. **Ant.:** dissent, disagree, refuse, decline. See **assent.**

consequence. **Syn.:** effect, result, outcome, issue, upshot, sequel, end, eventuality; importance, significance, moment, weight, distinction, influence, note. See **importance, effect,** *n.*

consequently. **Syn.:** see **therefore.**

conserve. **Syn.:** preserve, keep, maintain, save.

consider. **Syn.:** contemplate, meditate, reflect, ponder, deliberate, weigh, revolve, study; regard, respect, esteem.

To *consider* is to fix the mind upon something, generally with a view to some decision or action. *Study* implies an attempt to obtain a grasp of something by methodical or exhaustive thought; *revolve,* a turning of an idea over and over

so as to see it from all sides; *weigh,* deliberate and judicial estimate, as by a balance.

considerate. **Syn.:** thoughtful, deliberate, regardful, mindful, kind.

consideration. **Syn.:** contemplation, deliberation, advisement, attention, thought; regard, respect, thoughtfulness, deference; recompense, compensation, remuneration; importance, consequence, standing.

consign. **Syn.:** commit, deliver, intrust, transfer, assign, relegate. See **commit.**

consistent. **Syn.:** agreeing, compatible, congruous, consonant, harmonious. **Ant.:** see **inconsistent.**

consolation. **Syn.:** comfort, solace, relief, encouragement, cheer. See **comfort.**

console. **Syn.:** comfort, solace, soothe, cheer.

consolidate. **Syn.:** solidify, compact, combine, unite, unify, merge, incorporate. See **join.**

consonance. **Syn.:** see **harmony.**

consonant. **Syn.:** see **consistent.**

conspectus. **Syn.:** see **abridgment.**

conspicuous. **Syn.:** visible, manifest, noticeable, clear, marked, salient, prominent, striking, noteworthy. See **prominent.**

conspiracy. **Syn.:** plot, intrigue, cabal, collusion.

conspire. **Syn.:** plot, complot, intrigue; combine, concur, coöperate. See **plot.**

constancy. **Syn.:** steadfastness, faithfulness, fidelity, fealty, loyalty, firmness, stability; invariableness, unchangeableness, uniformity, regularity.

constant. **Syn.:** steadfast, faithful, loyal, stanch, true, resolute, firm, steady, unwavering, unswerving, unshaken; invariable, unchanging, uniform; continual, incessant, ceaseless, perpetual, unremitting, uninterrupted, persistent, faithful. See **continual.**

consternation. **Syn.:** dismay, bewilderment, amazement, alarm, terror, fear, panic. See **dismay,** *n.*

constituent. **Syn.:** component, ingredient, element.

Element denotes a fundamental, ultimate part, or, in chemistry, one of the simplest, irreducible substances; it always emphasizes the simple or basic nature of the thing. *Constituent* and *component* denote that which goes into the making of a compound and are practically synonymous, *constituent* implying active and necessary participation, *component,* the fact that it is one of a number of parts that make up the compound. *Ingredient* denotes something which enters into a mixture or compound, and which may or may not be essential to it.

constitutional. **Syn.:** see **inborn.**

constrain. **Syn.:** compel, force, drive, oblige, necessitate; restrain, check, bind, confine. See **force,** *v.*

constraint. **Syn.:** compulsion, force, coercion, pressure; restraint, repression, embarrassment, stiffness.

constrict. **Syn.:** compress, cramp, squeeze, bind, contract, tighten.

construct. **Syn.:** build, erect, frame, form, make. See **make.**

construe. **Syn.:** explain, interpret, render, translate.

consult. **Syn.:** see **confer.**

consume. **Syn.:** destroy, devour, burn up, annihilate; use up, exhaust, expend, waste, squander, dissipate. See **eat.**

consummate, *a.* **Syn.:** complete, excellent, perfect, finished, supreme. See **perfect.**

consummate, *v.* **Syn.:** complete, perfect, fulfil, accomplish, achieve.

contagion, contagious. **Syn.:** see **infection, infectious.**

contain. **Syn.:** hold, inclose, include, comprise, embrace; restrain, repress.

contaminate. **Syn.:** defile, pollute, befoul, sully, taint, infect, poison, corrupt. See **taint.**

contemn. **Syn.:** despise, disdain, scorn, spurn, slight. See **despise.**

contemplate. **Syn.:** observe, regard, view; consider, reflect on, meditate on, ponder; intend, purpose, design, plan.

contemplative. **Syn.:** thoughtful, reflective, meditative, musing, dreamy.

contemporaneous. **Syn.:** see **contemporary.**

contemporary. **Syn.:** contemporaneous, coeval, coexistent, synchronous, simultaneous, coincident.

The following three words are not rigidly distinguished, but *contemporary* rather refers to persons, *contemporaneous.* to things, that more or less definitely occupy or belong to the same period of time. *Coeval* emphasizes more definitely extension over the same period of time, generally thought of as remote and of considerable duration.

contempt. Syn.: disdain, scorn, contumely, derision, despite.

Contempt expresses a feeling of disapproval tinged with disgust for what is deemed mean, base, or worthless. *Disdain* expresses a feeling entertained for what is deemed beneath the level of one's own dignity or unworthy of one's notice or acceptance. *Scorn* denotes derisive, open, or undisguised contempt, as for a thing deemed unworthy of considerate treatment.

contemptible. Syn.: despicable, mean, abject, low, base, paltry, sorry, pitiful.

Contemptible is applied to that which is unworthy of notice or is deserving of contempt because of its petty or ignoble nature; *despicable*, a stronger word, to that which is looked down upon because of its baseness or vileness: as, a *contemptible* trick; *despicable* treachery.

contemptuous. Syn.: disdainful, scornful, sneering, insolent, arrogant, supercilious, haughty.

contend. Syn.: struggle, compete, vie, cope, strive, wrestle, grapple, combat, battle, fight; dispute, argue, wrangle; assert, affirm, maintain.

content, *a.* **Syn.:** satisfied, willing.

content, *v.* **Syn.:** satisfy, appease, gratify. See **satisfy.**

contention. Syn.: struggle, strife, conflict, combat, quarrel, disagreement, dissension, dispute, debate, wrangle, controversy, altercation, litigation. See **discord.**

contentious. Syn.: quarrelsome, dissentious, disputatious, wrangling, litigious, polemical, controversial.

contest, *n.* **Syn.:** dispute, controversy, struggle, conflict, combat; competition, rivalry, match, tournament, game.

contest, *v.* **Syn.:** dispute, question, controvert, oppose, challenge; contend, strive, compete, vie.

contiguous. Syn.: see **adjacent.**

contingent. Syn.: chance, casual, fortuitous, accidental; conditional, provisional. See **conditional.**

continual. Syn.: continuous, unceasing, ceaseless, incessant, uninterrupted, unintermitted, unremitting, unbroken, constant, interminable, eternal, endless, everlasting, perpetual, perennial; repeated, frequent.

Continual in present use means habitually or repeatedly recurring. *Continuous* applies to that which extends in space, and, by analogy, in time, without any break or interruption. *Constant* implies steadfast continuance or regular recurrence; *incessant*, persistent or unceasing activity. *Perpetual* may be applied either to that which is eternal or is incessantly recurring. *Unremitting* implies persevering or persistent repetition.

continuance. Syn.: see **continuation.**

continuation. Syn.: continuance, continuity, continuousness, prolongation, protraction, extension.

continue. Syn.: prolong, extend; postpone, adjourn; proceed, advance; last, endure, remain, abide, stay.

Continue implies duration or existence without break or interruption: as, the rain *continued* for two days. *Remain* is especially applied to what continues without change in its essential state: as, he *remained* a bachelor. *Endure* implies persistent continuance against influences that tend to weaken, undermine, or destroy: as, in spite of strained relations peace *endured* between the two nations for many years. *Last* often applies to that which holds out to a desired end, fresh, unimpaired, or unexhausted, sometimes under conditions that tend to produce the opposite effect: as, they had provisions enough to *last* all winter.

continuity. Syn.: see **continuation.**

continuous. Syn.: see **continual.**

continuousness. Syn.: see **continuation.**

contort. Syn.: twist, bend, distort.

contour. Syn.: see **outline.**

contraband. Syn.: prohibited, forbidden, unauthorized, unlawful, illegal, illicit.

contract, *n.* **Syn.:** agreement, bargain, pact, compact, covenant, treaty.

Agreement is the most general word, and refers to any more or less binding arrangement, either formal or informal, made between two or more parties. *Compact* especially refers to solemn international agreements or treaties, but it may be no more than the personal pledging (sometimes of a considerable number) to follow a specified course: as, they made a *compact* to preserve secrecy. *Contract* is especially used in law and business for such agreements as are enforceable by law;

covenant, in legal or religious associations, for such agreements as are made under solemn oath, seal, or divine promise.

contract, *v.* **Syn.:** compress, condense, reduce, shorten, lessen, narrow, shrivel, shrink; agree, covenant, betroth, affiance; incur, acquire. **Ant.:** expand, enlarge, amplify, extend. See **incur, decrease.**

contradict. Syn.: deny, gainsay, impugn, controvert, dispute.

To *contradict* is to state that the opposite or contrary is true; to *deny* is simply to declare that a thing is untrue; to *gainsay* is to oppose in speech either by contradiction, denial, or dispute.

contradictory. Syn.: contrary, opposing, inconsistent, antagonistic, irreconcilable, paradoxical.

contrariety. Syn.: contradictoriness, opposition, inconsistency, disagreement, discrepancy.

contrary. Syn.: contradictory, opposite, opposed, conflicting, discordant, counter, incompatible, inconsistent; perverse, intractable, refractory, obstinate, headstrong, unaccommodating; untoward, unfavorable, adverse. See **opposite.**

contrast, *n.* **Syn.:** unlikeness, difference, dissimilitude, antithesis

contrast, Syn.: compare, differentiate, discriminate, distinguish, oppose.

contravene. Syn.: oppose, transgress, infringe.

contribute. Syn.: see **give, conduce.**

contrite. Syn.: penitent, repentant, humbled, sorrowful. **Ant.:** impenitent, obdurate, stubborn.

contrition. Syn.: penitence, repentance, compunction, regret, self-reproach. See **repentance.**

contrivance. Syn.: plan, scheme, shift, expedient, device, invention, machine. See **means.**

contrive. Syn.: plan, design, devise, invent, plot, frame, concoct, hatch. See **prepare.**

control, *n.* **Syn.:** check, regulation, direction, management, superintendence, charge, authority, government, command, domination, influence, ascendancy, restraint, repression. See **authority.**

control, *v.* **Syn.:** check, regulate, direct, manage, govern, rule, command, dominate, restrain, repress, curb, bridle. See **govern.**

controversy. Syn.: dispute, disputation, debate, contention, disagreement, altercation, quarrel, wrangle. See **dispute,** *n.*

controvert. Syn.: dispute, deny, disprove, oppose, overthrow, debate, discuss.

contumacious. Syn.: stubborn, obstinate, headstrong, wilful, perverse, refractory, intractable, unmanageable, ungovernable, unruly, disobedient.

contumelious. Syn.: insolent, contemptuous, reproachful, disdainful, reviling, abusive, humiliating, opprobrious.

contumely. Syn.: insolence, contemptuousness, disdain, scorn, abuse, insult, obloquy, opprobrium.

conundrum. Syn.: see **puzzle.**

convene. Syn.: congregate, meet, assemble, collect, gather, convoke, summon.

convenient. Syn.: suitable, adapted, fitting, serviceable; accessible, handy.

convent. Syn.: nunnery, monastery, abbey, priory, cloister, friary, hermitage.

While these words are not strictly synonymous, they all denote kinds of religious houses. *Convent*, while formerly used generally of religious houses to which persons went to live in common, is now popularly restricted to such a house for women. *Nunnery*, a house for nuns, is more or less identical with convent. *Monastery*, literally a place for solitude, came to suggest an establishment, often of considerable size, for monks. An *abbey* is so called from being governed by an abbot or abbess; a *priory*, by a prior or prioress. *Cloister* strictly denotes a sheltered walk, surrounding the courtyard of a religious house, used for exercise or meditation, and particularly suggests seclusion or retirement from the world.

convention. Syn.: meeting, assembly, conference, congress, diet, synod, convocation; custom, usage, precedent, conventionality. See **meeting.**

conventional. Syn.: see **formal.**

conversant. Syn.: acquainted, familiar, versed, learned, skilled, practised, well-informed, proficient. See **versed.**

conversation. Syn.: talk, colloquy, converse, chat, causerie, confabulation, interview.

converse, *n.* **Syn.:** intercourse, communion, fellowship; talk, conversation.

converse, *v.* **Syn.:** talk, chat, confabulate, commune.

To *converse* is to exchange ideas in informal talk. To *chat* is to converse in an easy and inconsequential way. To *commune* is to bring oneself close in spirit to another, with uttered or unuttered words, often in a solemn and sacred kinship: as, in solitude he *communed* with God. When used reflexively *commune* means to meditate: as, to *commune* with oneself.

convert, *n.* **Syn.:** proselyte, neophyte, disciple. Cf. **apostate.**

As applied religiously, a *convert* is one who sincerely and unreservedly accepts a belief, sometimes in place of one previously held. *Proselyte* suggests one who has shifted from one faith or creed to another, often by virtue of external influence, sometimes unworthy, rather than through inner conviction.

convert, *v.* **Syn.:** turn, change, transform, transmute.

convey. **Syn.:** carry, transport, transfer, move, bear, transmit, communicate. See **impart.**

convict. **Syn.:** prisoner, felon, criminal, malefactor.

conviction. **Syn.:** see **belief.**

convince. **Syn.:** persuade, satisfy. See **persuade.**

convincing. **Syn.:** persuasive, cogent, conclusive, forceful.

convivial. **Syn.:** see **sociable.**

convocation. **Syn.:** see **meeting.**

convoke. **Syn.:** call together, summon, convene, assemble. See **call.**

convoy. **Syn.:** escort, accompany, attend, conduct. See **accompany.**

convulsion. **Syn.:** agitation, commotion, tumult, disturbance; spasm, fit, paroxysm, throe.

cook. **Syn.:** stew, broil, roast, fry, frizzle, boil, seethe, heat.

cool. **Syn.:** calm, unmoved, composed, collected, self-possessed, undisturbed, unruffled, unexcited, dispassionate, deliberate, imperturbable; indifferent, unconcerned, distant, nonchalant, lukewarm. See **cold, calm,** *a.*

coop. **Syn.:** see **pen.**

copious. **Syn.:** plentiful, abundant, overflowing, profuse, exuberant, ample, full. See **ample.**

copse. **Syn.:** coppice, thicket, brushwood, underwood, boscage, bosk, grove.

copy, *n.* **Syn.:** transcript, reproduction, duplicate, counterpart, imitation, counterfeit, facsimile, replica, apograph. **Ant.:** original, pattern, model, prototype.

A *copy* may be either an exact or approximate reproduction of something else. A *duplicate* is an exact counterpart which serves all the purposes for which the original was intended. A *facsimile* is an exact imitation or likeness of an original, especially in appearance. A *replica* is a work of art made in exact likeness of another, strictly speaking by the artist himself. Thus: a *copy* of a will, of the Parthenon; a *duplicate* of a part for an automobile; a photographic *facsimile* of a manuscript; a *replica* of a medal.

copy, *v.* **Syn.:** transcribe, reproduce, duplicate, trace, imitate, ape. See **imitate.**

coquetry. **Syn.:** see **flirtation.**

cordial. **Syn.:** see **hearty.**

corner. **Syn.:** angle, projection, point, cantle; coign, nook, niche, recess.

corollary. **Syn.:** inference, deduction, consequence, result.

corporal. **Syn.:** see **bodily.**

corpse. **Syn.:** body, corse, cadaver, carcass, remains, clay, ashes, dust.

Body refers to the organized material substance of an individual man or animal, either living or dead. *Corpse* refers only to the dead body of man; *carcass,* only to that of animals except when it is applied to the human body conceived as that of an animal. *Corse* is now archaic or poetic for a dead human body.

corpulent. **Syn.:** see **stout.**

correct, *a.* **Syn.:** right, faultless, perfect, exact, accurate, precise. **Ant.:** incorrect, wrong, erroneous. See **accurate.**

correct, *v.* **Syn.:** rectify, right, emend, amend, reform, remedy; admonish, discipline, punish. See **amend.**

correspond. **Syn.:** agree, harmonize, comport, accord, tally, answer, match, suit; communicate, write.

corroborate. **Syn.:** see **confirm.**

corrode. **Syn.:** gnaw, eat, waste, consume, canker, rust, crumble.

corrupt, *a.* **Syn.:** spoiled, putrid, vitiated, tainted; debased, depraved, dishonest, vicious, venal. See **mercenary.**

Corrupt implies a deterioration from an original condition of soundness or uprightness; *depraved* suggests abnormal degeneration of character, taste, etc.; *vicious,* debased, sometimes dangerous, indulgence in vice or evil.

corrupt, *v.* **Syn.:** spoil, putrefy, rot, vitiate, infect, taint, contaminate, pollute; debase, deprave, demoralize, bribe.

corruption. **Syn.:** putrefaction, decay, foulness, pollution; baseness, depravity, dishonesty, bribery.

corse. **Syn.:** see **corpse.**

coruscate. **Syn.:** sparkle, scintillate, flash, glitter. See **shine,** *v.*

cosmos. **Syn.:** see **universe.**

cost. **Syn.:** price, charge, outlay, expense, expenditure. See **price.**

costly. **Syn.:** expensive, dear, high-priced, precious, valuable, sumptuous, rich.

Expensive is applied to whatever entails (usually considerable) expense; it suggests a price beyond a thing's worth, or beyond what the person can properly afford to pay: as, *expensive* gifts; a poor person should not have *expensive* tastes. *Costly* is applied to that which it takes a large sum of money to purchase, usually on account of its fineness, preciousness, sumptuousness, or the like; it is sometimes used of that which it would take a great deal to rectify or replace: as, a *costly* error or fire. *Dear* is applied to that which is selling beyond its usual or just price: as, fruits are *dear* this year; he is always *dear* in his prices.

costume. **Syn.:** see **clothes, dress.**

cot. **Syn.:** see **cottage.**

coterie. **Syn.:** clique, set, circle, ring.

A *circle* is a group of persons united for a common purpose or associated in some common activity or class. A *coterie* is a small company of persons associated for social, literary, or other purposes. A *clique* is a narrowly exclusive or selfish group, usually suggesting the possibility of intrigue. A *set* (a more colloquial word) is especially a group of persons distinguished by common social characteristics and tendencies. A *ring* is especially a group of persons banded together for the selfish or dishonest control of business or politics. Thus: a sewing *circle,* a *coterie* of artists, a *clique* within a club, a gambling *set,* an anarchist *ring.*

cottage. **Syn.:** cot, cabin, lodge, bungalow, chalet, hut, shack, shanty, hovel.

Cottage refers primarily to the small and simple dwelling of a peasant, fisherman, or other humble person, but in the U. S. is also applied to the summer houses, often elaborate, of wealthier people. *Cot,* chiefly poetical, suggests a humble rural dwelling and, from poems such as *The Cotter's Saturday Night,* the joys and virtues of homely life. *Cabin* implies a temporary or makeshift structure such as a hunter's cabin, sometimes a rude log dwelling used by settlers in a frontier region, or a cheap and often squalid shelter for slaves.

council. **Syn.:** assembly, meeting, conference, consultation, cabinet, synod, board.

counsel, *n.* **Syn.:** consultation, deliberation; advice, admonition, exhortation, recommendation, opinion, warning, counselor, *q. v.*

counsel, *v.* **Syn.:** see **advise.**

counselor. **Syn.:** adviser, admonisher, mentor; advocate, barrister, lawyer, attorney.

count. **Syn.:** number, enumerate, compute, reckon, calculate; consider, deem, regard; depend, rely.

countenance, *n.* **Syn.:** aspect, appearance; face, visage, features; favor, encouragement, support, approval. See **face.**

countenance, *v.* **Syn.:** see **approve.**

counteract. **Syn.:** neutralize, counterbalance, contravene, frustrate, defeat, thwart, check.

counterfeit, *a.* **Syn.:** forged, spurious, false, sham, pretended, feigned, simulated, fraudulent. **Ant.:** genuine, real, sincere, authentic. See **false.**

counterfeit, *v.* **Syn.:** forge, sham, feign, simulate. See **imitate.**

countermand. **Syn.:** revoke, recall, cancel, stop, rescind, annul, void.

countryman. **Syn.:** rustic, farmer, yeoman, husbandman, peasant, hind, churl, boor, clown, bumpkin, yokel, clodhopper, hayseed, hick; compatriot, fellow-citizen.

couple. **Syn.:** pair, brace, team, span, yoke, couplet, two. See **pair.**

couplet. Syn.: see **verse.**

courage. Syn.: bravery, fearlessness, dauntlessness, intrepidity, fortitude, pluck, valor, prowess, heroism, daring, boldness, hardihood. **Ant.:** cowardice, fear, timidity. See **bravery.**

courageous. Syn.: brave, fearless, dauntless, intrepid, plucky, valorous, valiant, heroic, daring, bold, hardy. See **brave.**

course. Syn.: way, route, road, path, track, passage; method, manner, mode; order, series, sequence, succession; progress, procedure, process, career.

court. Syn.: woo; seek, invite, attract, solicit.

Court suggests the systematic attentions paid by a man to a woman in order to win her hand in marriage. The word is often used in other connections. *Woo* now suggests rather a series of tender assiduities associated with a proposal of marriage.

courteous. Syn.: polite, civil, urbane, deferential, obliging, gracious, affable. **Ant.:** discourteous, impolite, disrespectful, rude. See **civil.**

courtesy. Syn.: courteousness, politeness, civility, urbanity, complaisance; favor, indulgence.

courtezan. Syn.: see **prostitute.**

courtly. Syn.: polished, refined, polite, elegant, dignified, ceremonious. **Ant.:** see **uncourtly.**

covenant. Syn.: see **contract.**

cover, *n.* **Syn.:** covering, envelope, wrapper, wrap, vesture, case, sheath, integument, lid; quilt, blanket, counterpane, spread; shelter, protection; screen, cloak, mask, disguise, covert.

cover, *v.* **Syn.:** overlay, overspread, envelop, enwrap, clothe; screen, cloak, hide, conceal; comprise, embrace, include; offset, counterbalance, compensate for.

covert, *n.* **Syn.:** covering, cover, shelter, protection, refuge, retreat, concealment, hiding-place; thicket, underbrush, underwood.

covert, *a.* **Syn.:** covered, sheltered, concealed, hidden, disguised, secret, furtive, clandestine. See **secret.**

covet. Syn.: see **desire,** *v.*

covetous. Syn.: greedy, grasping, rapacious, avaricious.

covetousness. Syn.: greediness, avarice, cupidity. See **avarice.**

covey. Syn.: see **flock.**

cow. Syn.: intimidate, daunt, frighten, scare, overawe.

coward. Syn.: craven, poltroon, dastard, milksop.

Coward is a general word for one who lacks courage to meet danger or difficulty. *Craven, poltroon,* and *dastard,* all very strong words, are not clearly distinguished, but *craven* especially suggests weak-hearted or abject fear; *poltroon,* mean-spirited or contemptible cowardice; *dastard,* base, sneaking cowardice, especially as manifested in malicious acts.

cowardice. Syn.: poltroonery, dastardliness, pusillanimity, timidity.

cowardly. Syn.: craven, poltroon, dastardly, pusillanimous, timorous, faint-hearted, white-livered, chicken-hearted. See **timid.**

cower. Syn.: crouch, squat, quail, cringe. See **crouch.**

coxcomb. Syn.: fop, dude, exquisite, beau, popinjay, jackanapes. See **dandy.**

coy. Syn.: shy, retiring, diffident, bashful, demure, coquettish. See **shy.**

cozen. Syn.: see **cheat,** *v.*

cozy. Syn.: see **snug.**

crabbed. Syn.: see **cross,** *a.*

crack, *n.* **Syn.:** snap, clap, pop, shot, report, explosion; fissure, crevice, cranny, chink, cleft, interstice.

crack, *v.* **Syn.:** see **break.**

craft. Syn.: skill, ingenuity, adroitness, dexterity, knack; craftiness, deceit, guile, subtlety, artifice, stratagem; trade, handicraft; vessel, boat, ship. See **cunning, occupation.**

craftsman. Syn.: artificer, artisan, mechanic, handicraftsman, artist.

crafty. Syn.: cunning, artful, wily, sly, insidious, tricky, designing, scheming, plotting, deceitful. See **artful.**

cragged. Syn.: craggy, jagged, rough, rugged, broken.

cram. Syn.: stuff, crowd, pack, squeeze, compress, overcrowd.

cranky. Syn.: eccentric, queer; crotchety, cantankerous, ill-tempered, cross, perverse, unreasonable; unsteady, shaky.

cranny. Syn.: see **crack.**

crash. Syn.: shattering, smash, destruction, collapse, failure, ruin.

crass. Syn.: thick, coarse, unrefined, crude, gross, stupid, dense, obtuse.

crave. Syn.: beg, beseech, entreat, implore; desire, want, long for, yearn for, hunger for. See **ask.**

craven. Syn.: see **coward.**

craving. Syn.: begging, entreaty, supplication; desire, longing, yearning, hankering, hungering, appetite. See **desire,** *n.*

crawl. Syn.: see **creep.**

craze. Syn.: craziness, insanity; infatuation, passion, mania, rage. See **fashion.**

craziness. Syn.: see **insanity.**

crazy. Syn.: crazed, insane, demented, deranged, delirious, mad, lunatic, distracted, frantic, crack-brained; rickety, dilapidated, shaky, tottering, decrepit, frail.

create. Syn.: produce, originate, invent, cause, occasion, make; appoint, constitute, ordain.

creation. Syn.: see **universe.**

credence. Syn.: belief, credit, confidence, trust, faith.

credential. Syn.: see **testimonial.**

credit, *n.* **Syn.:** belief, trust, confidence; repute, reputation, standing; commendation, honor, esteem; trust, tick.

credit, *v.* **Syn.:** believe, trust; ascribe, attribute.

creditable. Syn.: praiseworthy, meritorious, estimable, honorable, reputable, respectable.

credulous. Syn.: believing, trustful, unsuspecting, gullible.

creed. Syn.: see **belief.**

creek. Syn.: see **brook.**

creep. Syn.: crawl.

Crawl and *creep* are frequently interchangeable, but *crawl* is used of more prostrate movement than *creep.* In their figurative application to human actions, *crawl* expresses cringing or servility; *creep,* slow progress and, frequently, stealth.

crest. Syn.: top, head, crown, summit, peak, ridge.

crevice. Syn.: see **crack,** *n.*

crew. Syn.: band, company, force, gang, crowd, mob, throng. See **company.**

crime. Syn.: felony, offense, trespass, transgression, misdemeanor, outrage, atrocity, wickedness, sin, iniquity. See **offense.**

criminal, *n.* **Syn.:** felon, convict, malefactor, evil-doer, transgressor, culprit.

criminal. *a.* **Syn.:** felonious, unlawful, illegal, guilty, nefarious, flagitious, iniquitous, wicked, sinful, wrong. See **illegal.**

cringe. Syn.: shrink, crouch, cower, fawn, truckle. See **crouch.**

cringing. Syn.: shrinking, cowering, fawning, truckling, obsequious, servile, slavish.

cripple. Syn.: lame, maim, disable, impair.

Cripple suggests injury that deprives of the use of a member, particularly a leg or arm; *disable,* a more general word, implies such injury or impairment as renders a person incapable of engaging in his normal activities. A broken arm *cripples* but does not *disable* a judge. A soldier gassed in war is *disabled,* not *crippled.*

crisis. Syn.: turning-point, climax, juncture, emergency, exigency, strait, pinch. See **emergency.**

crisp. Syn.: curly, crinkled, crimpled, rippled; brittle, friable; fresh, brisk, lively, sharp; pithy, terse, sparkling.

criterion. Syn.: standard, measure, test, rule, law, principle, touchstone. See **standard.**

critic. Syn.: reviewer, censor, judge, connoisseur; censurer, carper, caviler.

critical. Syn.: discriminating, fastidious, nice, exact; captious, censorious, carping, faultfinding, caviling; hazardous, precarious; decisive, crucial, climacteric.

criticism. Syn.: critique, review; censure, faultfinding, stricture, animadversion, reflection.

A *criticism* passes, usually after careful or minute examination, a judgment upon the merits or faults of anything. *Animadversion* suggests remarks less definite than a criticism, usually of a censorious kind. A *stricture* is always adverse criticism or censure, as upon defects, faults, or wrongs.

croak. Syn.: see **grumble.**

crony. Syn.: see **friend.**

crooked. Syn.: bent, curved, winding, devious, sinuous, flexuous, tortuous, spiral, labyrinthine, twisted, askew, awry, deformed, misshapen; dishonest, unscrupulous, knavish, tricky, fraudulent.

crop, *n.* **Syn.:** see **harvest.**

crop, *v.* **Syn.:** cut off, clip, lop, nibble, browse.

cross, *n.* **Syn.:** crucifix, rood.

cross, *a.* **Syn.:** intersecting, transverse; ill-humored, ill-natured, peevish, petulant, fretful, fractious, touchy, irascible, waspish, snappish, crabbed, churlish, sulky, sullen, cantankerous.

cross, *v.* **Syn.:** cancel, mark (out); intersect; oppose, thwart, baffle, frustrate, foil, contradict; interbreed, hybridize.

crotchet. Syn.: see **caprice.**

crouch. Syn.: stoop, squat, cower, cringe.

Crouch describes a posture that affects the whole body, as of a person or animal stooping or sinking toward the ground with knees bent. *Cower* expresses a shrinking movement with head and shoulders bent, as if in fear. To *cringe* is to cower basely through fear or servility.

crow. Syn.: see **boast.**

crowd, *n.* **Syn.:** throng, swarm, multitude, host, horde, mob; populace, commonalty, masses, proletariat, rabble, riffraff. See **multitude.**

crowd, *v.* **Syn.:** push, shove, press, jostle; throng, swarm, troop; compress, pack, cram, squeeze, cramp.

crown. Syn.: wreath, garland, chaplet; diadem, coronet; top, crest, summit, vertex. See **top.**

crucial. Syn.: see **critical.**

crude. Syn.: raw, unfinished, undeveloped, unformed, unpolished, unrefined, uncouth, inexperienced, green, rough, rude, coarse, clumsy.

cruel. Syn.: harsh, savage, brutal, fell, barbarous, bloodthirsty, inhuman, ferocious, ruthless, pitiless, merciless, relentless, implacable. **Ant.:** kind, gentle, merciful, lenient, tender.

Cruel implies the disposition to inflict suffering upon others, or (hard-hearted) indifference to their suffering; *harsh*, severity or rigorousness of treatment; *brutal*, cruelty which takes the form of physical violence; *inhuman*, the lack of feeling, kindness, or pity proper to human nature. *Pitiless*, *merciless*, and *ruthless* imply the relentless disregard for or repudiation of the claims of charity in the pursuit of an end.

cruelty. Syn.: harshness, brutality, ruthlessness, barbarity, inhumanity, atrocity.

crumple. Syn.: rumple, wrinkle, ruck, crush. See **wrinkle,** *v.*

crunch. Syn.: see **chew.**

crush. Syn.: break, shatter, bray, pulverize, mash, demolish; crumple, rumple; quell, subdue, overcome, overwhelm. See **break.**

crusty. Syn.: see **bluff.**

crux. Syn.: see **puzzle.**

cry, *n.* **Syn.:** shout, clamor, outcry, exclamation, ejaculation, roar, scream, shriek, screech, howl, yell, whoop, hoot; hello, call; wail, plaint, lament; appeal, entreaty, supplication; watchword, battle-cry, slogan.

cry, *v.* **Syn.:** shout, clamor, vociferate, exclaim, ejaculate, roar, bawl, bellow, scream, shriek, screech, howl, yell, yowl, squeal, squawk, honk, croak, caw, coo, squeak, peep, pipe, mew, bark, yelp, bay, low, moo, neigh, whinny, bray, bleat, whoop, hoot; wail, bewail, weep, sob, squall, blubber, whimper, mewl, pule; utter, announce, proclaim, hawk.

Cry is the general word. To *shout* is to raise the voice in words or other articulate sounds. *Bellow* especially refers to the loud, deep cry of a bull, moose, etc., or, somewhat in depreciation, to human utterance which suggests such a sound. *Bawl* suggests loud outcry, incoherent in children, coarse and clamorous in adults. *Roar* implies tumultuous volume; *vociferate*, excitement or vehemence.

crying. Syn.: wailing, weeping, etc. (see **cry,** *v.*); flagrant, notorious, urgent.

cryptic. Syn.: see **secret, obscure.**

cuddle. Syn.: hug, embrace, fondle, nestle, snuggle.

cudgel. Syn.: see **club.**

cuff. Syn.: beat, buffet, strike, slap, box.

cull. Syn.: pick, gather, collect, pluck, choose, select.

culmination. Syn.: climax, acme, zenith, peak.

culpable. Syn.: blameworthy, censurable, reprehensible, wrong, sinful.

culprit. Syn.: offender, transgressor, delinquent, malefactor, criminal.

cultivation. Syn.: tillage; training, refinement, culture.

culture. Syn.: cultivation, enlightenment, refinement, education, learning.

Education is the development through study and learning of the special and general abilities of the mind. *Enlightenment* suggests the state of mind, usually resulting from education, characteristic of a person or nation which is liberally informed and therefore disposed to tolerance. *Culture* is a mode of thought and feeling nourished by education and enlightenment, and exalted by a powerful aspiration towards high intellectual and esthetic ideals.

cumbersome. Syn.: burdensome, unwieldy, unmanageable, clumsy, awkward.

cunning, *n.* **Syn.:** ability, skill, expertness; shrewdness, artfulness, craft, craftiness, wiliness, guile, trickery, artifice, finesse, intrigue.

Cunning denotes a shrewd, often instinctive, skill in concealing or disguising the real purposes of one's actions. *Craft* is cunning sharpened by experience or thought and seeking to outwit others by deceptive devices and tricks. *Finesse* suggests agility and subtle precision in handling affairs to one's own advantage.

cunning, *a.* **Syn.:** shrewd, artful, crafty, sly, wily, tricky, sharp, foxy.

cupidity. Syn.: greed, covetousness, avarice. See **avarice.**

curb. Syn.: check, bridle, restrain, repress, control.

curdle. Syn.: curd, coagulate, clabber, congeal.

cure. Syn.: heal, remedy, relieve, restore, eradicate, remove.

While the following two words often replace each other, *cure* is especially applied to the eradication of disease or sickness, and *heal*, to the making whole of wounds, sores, etc.: as, to *cure* consumption or a headache; to *heal* a cut or burn.

curiosity. Syn.: inquisitiveness; curio, rarity, wonder, marvel, phenomenon, freak.

curious. Syn.: inquisitive, prying, meddling, intrusive; strange, odd, unusual, singular, novel, rare.

Curious implies the desire to know, *inquisitive*, the active effort to satisfy that desire. Both *curious* and *inquisitive* are often used to refer to a petty interest in others' affairs.

current, *n.* **Syn.:** see **stream.**

current, *a.* **Syn.:** prevalent, present, circulating, common, general, rife. See **prevalent.**

curse, *n.* **Syn.:** anathema, ban, imprecation, execration, fulmination, malediction, malison; oath, swearing, profanity, blasphemy; bane, scourge, plague, affliction, torment.

Curse is the general word for the heartfelt invocation or violent or angry calling down of evil upon another. An *imprecation* is more superficial and temporary than a *curse*, which springs from the depths of one's emotion and summons a fate which pursues and blights. *Malediction*, a more formal word, pronounces its object worthy of an evil fate. *Execration* is a curse dictated by anger and abhorrence. *Anathema*, strictly speaking, expresses a solemn curse pronounced formally by ecclesiastical authority.

curse, *v.* **Syn.:** damn, anathematize, excommunicate, execrate, imprecate, fulminate; swear, blaspheme.

cursed. Syn.: damned, anathematized; damnable, execrable, abominable, hateful.

cursory. Syn.: hasty, rapid, slight, superficial, careless, passing, desultory. **Ant.:** careful, painstaking, minute, thorough, detailed, exhaustive. See **hasty.**

curt. Syn.: see **blunt.**

curtail. Syn.: shorten, abridge, reduce, lessen, diminish, retrench, dock. See **shorten.**

curtain. Syn.: hanging, drapery, portière, lambrequin, valance; shade, blind.

curve. Syn.: bend, crook, deflect, wind, deviate.

cushion. Syn.: pillow, bolster, pad.

custody. Syn.: keeping, safe-keeping, charge, watch, care, guardianship, confinement, imprisonment, incarceration. See **keeping.**

custom. Syn.: usage, practice, habit, wont, fashion, way, consuetude.

Custom, applied to a community or to an individual, implies a (more or less permanent) continuance of a procedure. *Habit*, applied particularly to an individual, implies such repetition of the same action as to develop a natural, spontaneous, or rooted tendency or inclination to perform it. *Usage* applies to long-established or sanctioned custom. *Wont* is a literary or poetic word for habit. *Practice* applies to the repeated doing of something, especially in a careful, regular, or persistent way.

customary. **Syn.:** usual, habitual, wonted, accustomed, ordinary, common, conventional. See **habitual.**

customer. **Syn.:** patron, buyer, purchaser.

cut, *n.* **Syn.:** gash, slash, slit, incision, wound, notch, groove, furrow, channel; piece, slice.

cut, *v.* **Syn.:** gash, slash, slit, lance, chop, hack, haggle, hew, fell, lop, prune, amputate, detruncate, sever, cleave, sunder, bisect, whittle, shave, pare, slice, clip, snip, nip, crop, trim, prune, shear, dock, carve, chisel, incise, chase, score, mow, reap; cross, intersect; abridge, curtail, lower, diminish, reduce; wound, hurt; slight, ignore.

cutting, *n.* **Syn.:** slashing, slitting, incision; curtailment, reduction; piece, slice, clipping, slip, scion.

cutting, *a.* **Syn.:** penetrating, piercing, sharp, keen, incisive, trenchant, sarcastic, caustic, biting, mordant. See **sharp.**

cynical. **Syn.:** sneering, sarcastic, satirical, pessimistic, misanthropic, morose. See **misanthropic.**

D

dabbler. **Syn.:** dilettante, smatterer, sciolist, amateur.

dagger. **Syn.:** dirk, stiletto, poniard, misericord, skean, creese, barong, anlace, yataghan, bowie-knife.

daily. **Syn.:** diurnal, quotidian.

Daily, the popular word, applies to what happens or occurs every day: as, the *daily* delivery of mail; a *daily* newspaper. *Diurnal,* the scientific or poetic term, is applied to what occupies a day (twenty-four hours), or occurs by day or in the daytime, or, like *daily,* to what occurs every day: as, the *diurnal* motion of the earth upon its axis; the *diurnal* sleep of an owl; a *diurnal* task.

dainty, *n.* **Syn.:** see **delicacy.**

dainty, *a.* **Syn.:** toothsome, delicious, luscious; exquisite, delicate, choice, fine, neat, trim; fastidious, finical, overnice, squeamish. See **particular.**

dale. **Syn.:** see **valley.**

dalliance. **Syn.:** playing, toying, trifling, dawdling, loitering, delay.

dally. **Syn.:** sport, play, toy, coquet, wanton; trifle, dawdle, linger, loiter, idle. See **trifle.**

damage, *n.* **Syn.:** injury, harm, hurt, impairment, detriment, loss. See **injury.**

damage, *v.* **Syn.:** injure, harm, hurt, impair, deface, disfigure, mar, spoil, scathe.

damages. **Syn.:** indemnity, reparation, satisfaction.

damn. **Syn.:** condemn, denounce, imprecate, curse, swear.

damnable. **Syn.:** accursed, execrable, detestable, abominable, outrageous, atrocious, heinous.

damp. **Syn.:** moist, wet, humid, foggy, misty, dank, clammy. See **moist.**

dampen. **Syn.:** moisten, wet, damp; dull, deaden, repress, depress.

dance. **Syn.:** waltz, two-step, one-step, fox-trot, tango, lancers, minuet, gavotte, polonaise, polka, mazurka, schottische, quadrille, cotillion, ballet, fandango, reel, pigeonwing, jig.

dandy. **Syn.:** exquisite, beau, fop, dude, coxcomb, popinjay, jackadandy.

A *dandy* is a man who gives excessive attention to elegance and fashion in dress. An *exquisite* prides himself upon his fastidious and superfine taste in dress, manners, language, etc. A *coxcomb* is a vain, showy fellow, foolishly conceited in regard to his accomplishments, looks, and dress. A *fop* is an affected, silly, and often effeminate man who displays his vanity in extravagant dress and finery, finical tastes, and pertness of manner. A *popinjay* is a vain, chattering fop or dandy, especially one who annoys or disgusts by his excessive or effusive movements. *Dude* is a more colloquial word for dandy

danger. **Syn.:** risk, hazard, jeopardy, peril, imperilment, exposure. **Ant.:** security, safety, protection.

Danger is a general word for exposure to all kinds of injury or evil consequences, which may be either near at hand and certain or remote and doubtful: as, to be in *danger* of catching cold or of being killed. *Peril* usually denotes great and imminent danger: as, the passengers on the disabled ship were in great *peril.* *Jeopardy,* a less common word, has essentially the same meaning as peril, but emphasizes exposure to the hazards and chances of a situation: as, to save his friend he put his life in *jeopardy.*

dangerous. **Syn.:** hazardous, insecure, unsafe, perilous.

dank. **Syn.:** see **moist.**

dapper. **Syn.:** neat, trim, spruce, natty, smart, active, brisk. See **spruce.**

dappled. **Syn.:** spotted, mottled, piebald, pied.

dare. **Syn.:** venture, risk, brave, defy, challenge, stump. See **venture.**

daring. **Syn.:** bold, intrepid, fearless, dauntless, undaunted, venturesome, adventurous, audacious, rash, reckless, daredevil. See **bold.**

dark. **Syn.:** unilluminated, dim, shadowy, murky, tenebrous; dusky, swarthy, swart, black, sable; gloomy, dismal, dreary, somber; sullen, frowning, lowering, threatening, sinister, evil; obscure, mysterious, enigmatical, recondite, abstruse, hidden, secret, inscrutable; unenlightened, ignorant.

Dark implies a more or less complete absence of light; it is used among many other figurative applications of what is perplexing, unintelligible, mysterious, or inscrutable: as, the *dark* ways of fate. *Obscure* suggests indistinctness of outline or detail which is due to an insufficiency of light; figuratively it is applied to what is not clear to the mind, to places hidden or remote, or to persons or things little known: as, an *obscure* paragraph, village, musician. *Dim* implies faintness of light, or indistinctness of form resulting from faintness of light or insufficiency or imperfection of vision. *Murky* implies a thick, cloudy, or misty darkness; *tenebrous* is applied to that which seems full of shadows and gloomy obscurity.

darken. **Syn.:** dim, shade, cloud, becloud, obscure, obfuscate, blind; sully, tarnish.

darkness. **Syn.:** dimness, shadow, gloom, dark, night; duskiness, swarthiness, blackness; obscurity, secrecy; blindness, unenlightenment, ignorance.

dart. **Syn.:** hurl, shoot, launch; dash, spring, bolt, dodge.

dash, *n.* **Syn.:** splash, spot, touch, tinge, tincture, smack; rush, onset, sally, race; impetus, impetuosity, spirit, élan, flourish, display.

dash, *v.* **Syn.:** smash, shatter, shiver, crush; throw, hurl; splash, bespatter, sprinkle; cast down, deject, confound, ruin; rush, dart, spring. See **rush.**

dashing. **Syn.:** rushing, impetuous, spirited, showy, brilliant, stylish.

dastard. **Syn.:** see **coward.**

dastardly. **Syn.:** see **cowardly.**

daub. **Syn.:** smear, bedaub, plaster, soil, sully, defile.

daunt. **Syn.:** intimidate, cow, overawe, discourage, dispirit, dishearten, dismay.

To *daunt* is to shake the courage or confidence of a person, usually so that he is checked or deterred in some action, proceeding, or purpose by a realization of the difficulty, dangerousness, or impossibility of it: as, his spirit was not *daunted* by persecution. To *cow* is to overawe by fear, punishment, or threats so that a person's spirit and resistance are completely broken: as, to *cow* a slave into submission. To *intimidate* is to put into a state of fear, as by threats of force, violence, or dire consequences, usually for the purpose of compelling some action or preventing it: as, to *intimidate* a prospective witness.

dauntless. **Syn.:** fearless, unflinching, intrepid, bold, daring, courageous, valorous, indomitable. See **brave.**

dawdle. **Syn.:** see **trifle.**

dawn. **Syn.:** daybreak, sunrise, aurora, dayspring; advent, beginning, appearance, rise.

daze. **Syn.:** stun, stupefy, benumb, bewilder, confuse, confound.

dazzle. **Syn.:** blind, daze, bewilder, confuse, astonish.

dazzling. **Syn.:** see **bright.**

dead. **Syn.:** lifeless, deceased, defunct, extinct, inanimate; benumbed, numb, insensible; still, motionless, inert, inoperative; unfeeling, indifferent, callous. **Ant.:** alive, living, animate.

Dead is usually applied to that which had life but from which life is now gone; *lifeless,* to what may or may not have had life but which does not have it (or appear to have it) now; *inanimate,* to what never had life: as, they recovered the *dead* bodies; they picked up the *lifeless* form of the child; *inanimate* objects. *Defunct* is applied to something the existence of which has (recently) terminated; *extinct,* especially to a race, species, or the like no member of which is any longer alive.

deaden. **Syn.:** benumb, dull, blunt, impair, weaken, devitalize.

deadly. **Syn.:** fatal, mortal, poisonous, lethal, destructive, internecine; implacable, relentless, unrelenting; deathly.

That which is *deadly* is capable of producing death or is as unrelenting as death; *deathly* is applied to that which suggests death: as, *deadly* poison; a *deadly* foe; a *deathly* paleness. *Mortal* is applied to an action or the result of an action that produces death, or to an individual or feeling deadly in character; *fatal*, to what causes or is attended with death or destruction: as, a *mortal* injury or blow; *mortal* hatred or enmity; a *fatal* shot; a *fatal* mistake.

deal. Syn.: distribute, apportion, allot, mete out, share, dispense, divide; bestow, deliver, inflict, trade, traffic.

dealer. Syn.: trader, tradesman, trafficker, merchant, shopkeeper, jobber.

dear. Syn.: esteemed, valued, beloved, precious; expensive, high-priced. See **costly.**

dearth. Syn.: scarcity, poverty, famine, want, lack. See **scarcity.**

death. Syn.: decease, demise, passing, departure, dissolution, extinction, destruction, bloodshed, murder, plague, epidemic.

Death is the common and general word for the act of dying or the state of being dead, and unlike the other words here discriminated, is applicable not only to persons but also to plants and lower animals. *Decease* is a technical term of law for death and suggests the idea of withdrawing from life and leaving it to those remaining behind; when used in ordinary language for death, it is more formal and less forcible and harsh than death: as, he had been the girl's guardian since the *decease* of her father. *Demise* is used primarily in reference to the death of royal or illustrious persons, which occasions the transmission of estates, possessions, or titles; its use for death apart from this idea is figurative, euphemistic, or stilted: as, at his father's *demise* the son became king. *Passing* is a literary or poetic word for death; as, *The Passing of Arthur*. *Departure*, which suggests the leaving of this life for a future one beyond the grave, is but one of a number of words used to avoid calling up the sorrow and fear associated with death.

deathless. Syn.: undying, immortal, imperishable, unceasing, unending, perpetual.

deathly. Syn.: deadly.

debar. Syn.: exclude, preclude, prohibit, interdict, prevent, hinder. See **exclude.**

debase. Syn.: degrade, lower, vitiate, corrupt, deteriorate, adulterate, alloy.

debatable. Syn.: disputable, contestable, uncertain, controvertible, questionable, moot.

debate, *n.* **Syn.:** discussion, dispute, disputation, argument, argumentation, controversy, contention.

debate, *v.* **Syn.:** discuss, dispute, argue, moot; deliberate, reflect, consider. See **argue.**

debauch, *n.* **Syn.:** see **carousal.**

debauch, *v.* **Syn.:** seduce, corrupt, pollute, deprave, demoralize, pervert.

debauchery. Syn.: dissipation, drunkenness, licentiousness, sensuality.

debilitate. Syn.: enfeeble, weaken, enervate, exhaust. See **weaken.**

debilitated. Syn.: see **weak.**

debility. Syn.: feebleness, weakness, infirmity, languor, exhaustion.

debonair. Syn.: courteous, affable, gracious, urbane, complaisant, gay, light-hearted.

debt. Syn.: liability, obligation, duty, due.

decadence. Syn.: decline, decay, deterioration, degeneration, retrogression. See **decline,** *n.*

decamp. Syn.: see **flee.**

decay, *n.* **Syn.:** deterioration, decline, decadence, impairment, dilapidation, ruin, rotting, decomposition, putrefaction, putrescence, corruption.

decay, *v.* **Syn.:** deteriorate, decline, waste, wither, molder, spoil, rot, decompose, disintegrate, putrefy.

Decay implies either entire or partial dissolution or deterioration by progressive natural changes. *Molder* implies a crumbling, gradual, and often long-continued decay. *Disintegrate* emphasizes the breaking up or wearing away of anything so that its original wholeness is impaired. *Decompose* suggests the reducing of a substance through natural change or human agency to its component elements. *Putrefy* is especially used in reference to foul-smelling, decaying animal matter. *Rot* is a stronger word than decay and is especially applied to decaying vegetable matter, which may or may not emit offensive odors. Teeth *decay*; walls *molder*; rocks *disintegrate*; some chemical compounds *decompose* under the

action of atmospheric moisture; meat *putrefies*; potatoes *rot*.

decease. Syn.: see **die, death.**

deceit. Syn.: deception, deceptiveness, deceitfulness, duplicity, double-dealing, hypocrisy, dissimulation, cunning, craft, guile, wile, wiliness, trickery, chicanery. **Ant.:** sincerity, candor, frankness, openness.

Deceit is the habit or practice of concealing or perverting the truth for the purpose of misleading; the word is also, but more rarely, used to express the act of deceiving. *Duplicity* suggests treachery and faithlessness and describes the practice of speaking or acting in such a way as to mislead regarding one's sentiments or intentions. *Dissimulation* is a method of deceiving which depends upon concealment, hiding the reality or true significance of something under a contrary or otherwise false appearance. *Hypocrisy* is the pretended possession of those qualities which would make others believe in one's sincerity, goodness, devotion, etc.

deceitful. Syn.: hypocritical, insincere, disingenuous, false, hollow.

deceive. Syn.: mislead, delude, beguile, cozen, dupe, fool, gull, hoodwink, trick, defraud, cheat, overreach, outwit, entrap, insnare, betray, bamboozle. See **mislead.**

decency. Syn.: see **propriety.**

decent. Syn.: seemly, proper, decorous, modest, respectable, fitting, appropriate, suitable, becoming; fair, tolerable, passable, moderate.

deception. Syn.: delusion, imposture, cozenage, treachery, subterfuge, artifice, finesse, stratagem, ruse, trick, hoax, fraud, cheat.

Deception is an act or means by which intentionally or unintentionally a false impression is created. A *fraud* is an act or series of acts of intentional and subtle deceit or duplicity by which one attempts to benefit himself at the expense of another. A *trick* is usually an underhand act for the purpose of cheating some one. The word especially emphasizes the ingenuity, cleverness, or dexterity of the agent, and is sometimes used in a lighter sense, where all that is intended is an exhibition of such qualities for the pleasurable deception of the senses: as, a sleight-of-hand *trick*; a card *trick*.

deceptive. Syn.: deceiving, misleading, delusive, illusive, fraudulent, fallacious, specious, false.

decide. Syn.: determine, settle, resolve, conclude, close, terminate.

decided. Syn.: determined, settled; unquestionable, unmistakable, undeniable, indisputable, positive, certain, emphatic, pronounced; decisive, resolute, determined, unwavering, unhesitating.

decipher. Syn.: interpret, translate, make out, unravel, unfold, reveal, explain.

decision. Syn.: determination, judgment, verdict, decree, order; resolution, firmness. **Ant.:** indecision, irresolution, wavering, vacillation.

Decision is the quality or habit of being able to make up one's mind promptly, clearly, and firmly as to what shall be done and the way to do it. *Resolution* is usually a positive and active quality, as firmness of purpose, unyielding resistance, or courage against opposition, temptation, or danger. *Determination* is dogged, sometimes obstinate, sticking to a fixed or settled purpose.

decisive. Syn.: conclusive, final; resolute, determined, positive, decided, prompt, summary, peremptory.

deck. Syn.: bedeck, garnish, trim, array, bedizen. See **adorn.**

To *deck* is to decorate for a social occasion with ornaments that add gaiety or richness of display: as, a ship *decked* with flags; a woman *decked* with jewels. *Garnish* is especially used of such accessories or tasty additions as embellish food. *Trim* suggests the addition of such decorations as will relieve bareness or give an appropriate finish. *Bedizen* suggests an excessive decorating with gay, gaudy, or vulgar clothes or finery.

declaim. Syn.: orate, denounce, inveigh, rail, assail, attack.

Declaim especially implies high-flown or oratorical public speaking; *inveigh*, vehement (often personal) denunciation or rebuke; *rail*, highly reproachful, often opprobrious or scurrilous language.

declaration. Syn.: proclamation, announcement, affirmation, assertion, avowal, statement.

declare. Syn.: proclaim, announce, affirm, assert, aver, asseverate, state, predicate, promulgate.

To *declare* is to make known emphatically, openly, or formally, sometimes in the face of actual or potential contradiction. To *assert* is to state emphatically or boldly, usually without other proof than personal authority or conviction. To *affirm* is to make a statement based upon one's reputation for knowledge or veracity, or so related to a generally recognized truth that denial is not likely. To *aver* is to state confidently from what is within one's own knowledge or from one's deep conviction. To *asseverate* is to declare positively, earnestly, or solemnly, often removing doubt by the very force of manner. See **announce.**

decline, *n.* **Syn.:** slope, declivity; diminution, retrogression, deterioration, degeneration, decay, decadence, failing.

decline, *v.* **Syn.:** refuse, reject, avoid, shun; bend, slope, slant, droop; descend, sink, wane; decrease, diminish, deteriorate, degenerate, decay. See **refuse,** *v.*

Decline implies a progressive diminution in strength, vigor, character, value, or the like; *deterioration* implies an impairment of quality such as to lessen the value of something or render it unfit for the purpose which it should properly serve. *Degeneration* suggests a reduction to a lower type in some scale of being (especially moral); *decadence* implies a state of complete or continuing decay in vigor, standards, moral discipline, etc.

decompose. **Syn.:** see **decay,** *v.*

decorate. **Syn.:** embellish, deck, bedeck, adorn, ornament, trim, garnish, bedizen. See **adorn.**

decoration. **Syn.:** embellishment, adornment, ornamentation, garniture; ornament, medal, badge, trapping, regalia, insignia.

decorous. **Syn.:** proper, seemly, becoming, appropriate, fit, decent, sedate, conventional. See **fitting.**

decorum. **Syn.:** see **propriety.**

decoy. **Syn.:** lure, allure, entice, inveigle, insnare, entrap. See **lure.**

decrease, *n.* **Syn.:** diminution, abatement, subsidence, reduction, decline, depreciation, loss, decrement.

decrease, *v.* **Syn.:** diminish, reduce, lessen, fall off, decline, depreciate, contract, shrink, dwindle, abate, subside, ebb, wane.

Decrease when used intransitively commonly implies a gradual and sustained reduction, especially of bulk, size, volume, or quantity, often from some imperceptible cause or inherent process going on within: as, the swelling *decreased* daily. *Diminish* usually implies the action of some external cause that keeps taking away: as, the number of troops *diminished* steadily from disease and cold. *Dwindle* implies an undesirable reduction by degrees, resulting in attenuation: as, his followers *dwindled* to a mere handful. *Contract* implies a loss in size, bulk, or extent by a drawing together of parts or elements without the loss of constituent substance or parts usually expressed by the first three words: as, the chest expands and *contracts* with breathing. *Shrink* especially implies contraction through an inherent property under specific conditions: as, many fabrics *shrink* when wet.

decree, *n.* **Syn.:** edict, proclamation, order, mandate, fiat, ordinance, decretal. See **proclamation.**

decree, *v.* **Syn.:** ordain, order, adjudge, enact.

decrepit. **Syn.:** see **weak.**

decry. **Syn.:** depreciate, belittle, disparage, discredit, run down, traduce, censure, condemn, denounce. See **depreciate.**

dedicate. **Syn.:** see **devote, consecrate.**

deduce. **Syn.:** see **infer.**

deduct. **Syn.:** subtract, rebate.

Both of the following words express diminution in quantity or sum, but are not always interchangeable in use. To *deduct* is to take away an amount or quantity from an aggregate or total so as to lessen or lower it; to *subtract* is a mathematical process, generally represented by numbers, suggesting the taking of a part from a whole. *Deduct* is always transitive and usually has a concrete and practical application; *subtract* is both transitive and intransitive and in the latter case is sometimes used in a general and figurative sense. Thus, to *deduct* a discount; a merchant *deducts* what is paid from the total of a bill; to *subtract* one number from another; a damaging admission *subtracts* from the force of an argument.

deduction. **Syn.:** subtraction, abatement, diminution; discount, rebate; induction, inference, illation, corollary, conclusion.

In logic and science the following two words denote opposite processes in arriving at truth or fact. *Deduction* is the process of drawing from a general proposition an inference concerning a particular instance which falls under it; it is reasoning from

the general to the particular. *Induction* is the process of deriving a general truth from a number of substantiating instances; it is reasoning from the particular to the general. Thus we reason *deductively* when, knowing that all objects thrown into the air fall to the ground, we say that an apple will do so. We reason *inductively* when, knowing that the Babylonian, Assyrian, Egyptian, Alexandrian, Roman, and other empires in the past have crumbled, we say that all empires eventually crumble. The conclusions of inductive reasoning are always tentative because we cannot be sure our generalization is based upon all possible instances.

deed. **Syn.:** act, action, achievement, exploit, feat. See **feat.**

deem. **Syn.:** judge, think, believe, opine, suppose, regard, consider. See **think.**

deep. **Syn.:** profound, abysmal, unfathomable, recondite, mysterious, dark, abstruse, incomprehensible; heartfelt, intense; penetrating, sagacious, astute; low, guttural.

deface. **Syn.:** disfigure, mar, cancel, obliterate, efface, spoil.

Disfigure covers such changes of external form or surface as injure the appearance or beauty of anything: as, to *disfigure* a statue by breaking off the arms; to *disfigure* one's body by tattoos. *Deface* refers to the (usually superficial) impairing or injuring of the face or surface of something: as, to *deface* a building by marking on it. *Mar* is a more general word for impairment or damage to the character, value, or appearance of any thing: as, to *mar* a tree by cutting initials in it.

defamation. **Syn.:** slander, libel, calumny, aspersion, backbiting, scandal.

defamatory. **Syn.:** slanderous, libelous, calumnious, calumniating, contumelious.

defame. **Syn.:** see **asperse.**

defeat. **Syn.:** overcome, vanquish, conquer, overthrow, overwhelm, rout, beat, checkmate, outwit; frustrate, thwart, baffle, foil, balk, disappoint. See **conquer.**

defect. **Syn.:** lack, want, deficiency, imperfection, blemish, flaw, fault, failing, shortcoming, infirmity. See **imperfection.**

defective. **Syn.:** lacking, wanting, deficient, inadequate, insufficient, incomplete, imperfect, faulty.

That which is *deficient* falls short of a real or ideal completeness; that which is *defective* is imperfect in construction, material, or operation: as, blood *deficient* in red corpuscles; a *defective* bridge, tooth, furnace.

defend. **Syn.:** protect, guard, garrison, fortify, shield, shelter, screen; vindicate, justify, uphold, maintain. See **guard,** *v.*

defense. **Syn.:** protection, guard, safeguard, fortification, bulwark; vindication, justification, plea, apology.

defer. **Syn.:** put off, postpone, delay, suspend, adjourn; wait, procrastinate.

To *defer* a thing is to put it off to some future period: as, to *defer* a decision or payment. To *postpone* a thing is to defer it to (usually) some particular time in the future, with the intention of definitely initiating or resuming it then; the word is especially used of official business, formal meetings, or the like: as, to *postpone* an election. To *delay* is sometimes the equivalent of to *defer*: as, he *delayed* his departure until the first of the month; but usually it is to put off in a dilatory manner till some indefinite time in the future: as, to *delay* answering a letter. To *procrastinate* is to keep putting an action off, literally till to-morrow, because of lack of purpose or resolution, or because of more or less habitual unwillingness to commence action, usually with no assurance that it will ever be taken up.

deference. **Syn.:** respect, regard, consideration, submission, complaisance.

deferential. **Syn.:** see **civil.**

defiant. **Syn.:** disobedient, insubordinate, contumacious, refractory, recalcitrant, rebellious, mutinous, headstrong, insolent. **Ant.:** obedient, submissive, tractable.

deficiency. **Syn.:** incompleteness, imperfection, defect, insufficiency, inadequacy, want, lack, scantiness, meagerness, scarcity, shortage, deficit, dearth.

deficient. **Syn.:** see **defective.**

defile, *n.* **Syn.:** pass, gorge. See **valley.**

defile, *v.* **Syn.:** pollute, befoul, soil, tarnish, sully, violate, debauch, desecrate. See **soil,** *v.*

definite. **Syn.:** definitive, defined, determined, fixed, certain, clear, exact, precise, express. **Ant.:** see **indefinite.**

Definite means clear and explicit; *definitive* means

conclusive, authoritative, and final: as, a *definite* statement; a *definitive* history of the United States, or edition of Shakspere.

definitive. Syn.: see **definite.**

deflect. Syn.: see **bend.**

deformed. Syn.: misshapen, malformed, distorted, disfigured, crippled, crooked, unsightly, ugly.

deformity. Syn.: see **imperfection.**

defraud. Syn.: see **cheat,** *v.*

deft. Syn.: dexterous, nimble, skilful, clever, adroit, apt. See **dexterous.**

defunct. Syn.: see **dead.**

defy. Syn.: challenge, dare, brave, flout, scorn.

degenerate. Syn.: see **deteriorate, degrade.**

degeneration. Syn.: see **deterioration.**

degradation. Syn.: deposition, dismissal, humiliation, disgrace, dishonor, debasement, depravity, degeneration. See **decline,** *n.*

degrade. Syn.: lower, demote, depose, cashier, humiliate, humble, disgrace, dishonor, debase, deprave, degenerate.

Degrade applies primarily to a reduction or lowering in rank, office, or character, resulting from either a single disgraceful act or a long-continued series of such acts; *degenerate*, to a loss of the higher or proper qualities of a kind, type, or race, usually resulting from a gradual decline. Both words suggest a moral decline, but *degenerate* implies indulgence in such insidious vices as lead to moral decay. Cf. **abase.**

deign. Syn.: see **condescend.**

deist. Syn.: see **skeptic.**

dejected. Syn.: depressed, disheartened, discouraged, despondent, dispirited, low-spirited, downhearted, downcast, melancholy, sad, forlorn. See **sad.**

dejection. Syn.: depression, despondency, melancholy, sadness, gloom.

delay, *n.* **Syn.:** deferment, postponement, respite, reprieve; procrastination, lingering, loitering. **Ant.:** promptness, haste, despatch.

delay, *v.* **Syn.:** defer, postpone, adjourn; impede, hinder, retard, detain, stop; procrastinate, tarry, linger, loiter, lag, dally, dawdle. See **defer.**

delectable. Syn.: see **pleasing.**

delectation. Syn.: see **pleasure.**

delegate, *n.* **Syn.:** deputy, commissioner, representative, envoy, legate, proxy, substitute.

delegate, *v.* **Syn.:** depute, commission, empower, commit, intrust.

deleterious. Syn.: injurious, noxious, poisonous, destructive, pernicious, hurtful, harmful, unwholesome. See **pernicious.**

deliberate, *a.* **Syn.:** weighed, considered, studied, intentional, premeditated, prepense; thoughtful, careful, circumspect, cautious, cool, slow, unhurried. See **intentional, slow.**

deliberate, *v.* **Syn.:** weigh, ponder, consider, reflect, meditate, cogitate; consult, confer, debate. See **reflect.**

deliberation. Syn.: consideration, reflection, meditation; consultation, conference, discussion, debate; coolness, leisureliness, slowness.

delicacy. Syn.: tenderness, fragility, weakness; fineness, daintiness, nicety, sensitiveness, refinement, exquisiteness, subtlety; dainty, titbit, sweetmeat, kickshaw, luxury.

A *dainty* is a choice trifle for eating, often a confection. A *delicacy* is some item of food, prized because it is infrequently obtained. A *titbit* is a particularly choice or delicious morsel of food, especially a small quantity taken from a larger on account of its excellence. A *kickshaw* is a fancy dish of food, sometimes an over-elaborate and unsubstantial one.

delicate. Syn.: tender, frail, fragile, weakly, feeble; fine, nice, sensitive, refined, exquisite, subtle, soft, faint; dainty, delicious, choice; exact, precise, accurate; ticklish, critical, precarious.

Delicate implies extreme fineness or niceness of texture, construction, or adjustment, often such as to be easily broken or injured; *tender*, such softness of texture or consistence as to yield readily or be sensitive to force or pressure: as, a *delicate* skin or mechanism; *tender* meat; some horses have very *tender* mouths. *Fragile* is applied to what is easily broken or shattered, or liable to be destroyed; *frail*, to what is extremely weak in texture, or, figuratively, weak in health or moral resistance: as, *fragile* china; a *fragile* flower; a *frail* web; a *frail* constitution.

delicious. Syn.: delightful, luscious, toothsome, dainty, palatable, savory. **Ant.:** distasteful, unpalatable.

That which is *delicious* is highly agreeable to the taste or, sometimes, to the smell or hearing: as, *delicious* food or odors. *Toothsome* is applied to something that is particularly pleasing to the taste, especially because of its delicacy or daintiness: as, a *toothsome* morsel. *Luscious* implies such a luxuriant fullness or ripeness as to make an object sweet and rich, sometimes even to excess: as, *luscious* fruit.

delight. Syn.: pleasure, enjoyment, joy, rapture, transport, ecstasy, delectation, gratification. See **gladness.**

delighted. Syn.: pleased, charmed, enraptured, joyful, glad.

delightful. Syn.: pleasurable, enjoyable, pleasing, charming, enchanting, ravishing, delectable, refreshing, exquisite, delicious.

delineate. Syn.: see **depict.**

delineation. Syn.: drawing, sketch, outline, draft, diagram, portrayal, portrait, description, account.

delinquency. Syn.: shortcoming, failure, fault, misdeed, misdemeanor, offense, wrong, guilt, sin, crime. See **offense.**

delinquent. Syn.: see **culprit.**

delirium. Syn.: see **insanity.**

deliver. Syn.: free, liberate, emancipate, release, redeem, ransom, rescue, save; hand over, transfer, give up, cede, surrender; throw, cast, launch; communicate, impart, utter, pronounce. See **free,** *v.*

dell. Syn.: see **valley.**

delude. Syn.: mislead, deceive, beguile, cozen, dupe, cheat, defraud. See **mislead.**

deluge. Syn.: see **flood.**

delusion. Syn.: see **illusion.**

demand, *n.* **Syn.:** request, claim, requisition, exaction, requirement, need, call, desire.

demand, *v.* **Syn.:** see **ask.**

demeanor. Syn.: conduct, deportment, behavior, bearing, carriage, manner. See **bearing.**

demented. Syn.: see **crazy.**

demerit. Syn.: ill desert, misconduct, misdeed, wrongdoing, delinquency, fault, failure.

demise. Syn.: see **death.**

demolish. Syn.: see **destroy.**

demon, demoniac, demoniacal. Syn.: see **devil, devilish.**

demoralize. Syn.: corrupt, debase, deprave, pervert, vitiate; disorder, disorganize, dishearten.

demur. Syn.: see **hesitate.**

demure. Syn.: sober, serious, grave, sedate, staid, decorous, discreet, modest, coy. See **modest.**

den. Syn.: cave, cavern, lair, retreat, haunt, resort.

denial. Syn.: contradiction, negation, refusal, rejection, disavowal, disclaimer.

denizen. Syn.: see **inhabitant.**

denominate. Syn.: name, call, entitle, style, designate, dub.

denomination. Syn.: see **name.**

denote. Syn.: designate, signify, indicate, betoken, imply, mean, connote.

Denote differs from *connote* as the literal meaning of a word differs from its suggestions and implications. Fifth Avenue in New York *denotes* a street between Fourth Avenue and Sixth; it *connotes* wealth, prosperity, luxury, etc.

dense. Syn.: compact, compressed, close, crowded, thick; thick-headed, obtuse, stupid, dull.

dent. Syn.: dint, indentation. See **hole.**

denude. Syn.: bare, uncover, strip, divest.

denunciation. Syn.: condemnation, censure, accusation, arraignment.

deny. Syn.: contradict, gainsay, forbid, withhold, refuse, reject, renounce, disown, disavow, disclaim, repudiate, abjure. See **contradict.**

depart. Syn.: leave, withdraw, retire, retreat, quit; diverge, deviate, differ, vary.

Depart is a somewhat dignified or literary word, denoting the leaving of a place, sometimes with the implication of a more or less definite destination in view. *Withdraw* suggests departure from some specific place or situation and usually for some definite, often unpleasant, reason. *Retire* emphasizes the reason or purpose for absenting oneself or receding; *retreat* implies a necessary withdrawal, especially as a result of adverse fortune in war. *Retire* may be used as a euphemism for *retreat.*

departure. **Syn.:** see **death.**

dependable. **Syn.:** reliable, trustworthy, trusty.

dependent. **Syn.:** retainer, follower, servant, vassal, minion, satellite.

depict. **Syn.:** portray, picture, delineate, sketch, describe.

All these words express an actual reproduction of an object or scene by colors or lines, or by words. *Depict* emphasizes vividness or detail; *portray*, faithful representation. *Depict* commonly deals with physical realities; *portray* may also reveal feelings and states of mind: as, he *depicted* the confusion of departure, but could not *portray* the anguish of the exiles. *Delineate* suggests sharpness of outline and such attention to detail as to define accurately the contours of a subject. *Sketch* suggests still less fullness of detail, only the outstanding features or fundamental facts being given, often in a preparatory way.

deplorable. **Syn.:** lamentable, grievous, pitiable, miserable, wretched, calamitous.

deplore. **Syn.:** lament, mourn, bemoan, bewail, regret, rue. See **lament.**

deportment. **Syn.:** see **behavior, bearing.**

depose. **Syn.:** see **degrade.**

deposit. **Syn.:** sediment, precipitate, alluvium, alluvion, deposition; pledge, security, payment.

deposition. **Syn.:** deposing, degradation, dethronement; statement, declaration, testimony, evidence; precipitation, sediment, deposit.

depository. **Syn.:** repository, storehouse, warehouse, depot, magazine.

depot. **Syn.:** see **depository.**

depravation. **Syn.:** vitiation, corruption, contamination, deterioration, degeneracy, depravity.

deprave. **Syn.:** vitiate, corrupt, debase, pervert, contaminate.

depraved. **Syn.:** vitiated, corrupted, perverted, wicked, iniquitous, base, profligate, abandoned. See **corrupt,** *a.*

depravity. **Syn.:** corruption, wickedness, baseness, profligacy, degeneracy, viciousness.

depreciate. **Syn.:** lessen, reduce, lower, undervalue, underrate, disparage, belittle, decry, slur.

The following words agree in expressing an effort to lower the esteem in which a person or thing is held. To *depreciate* is primarily to lower the value of, or reduce in reputation by representing a person or thing as of less worth than it really is: as, to *depreciate* currency, a person's efforts. To *disparage* is to (attempt to) reduce in reputation by slighting reference or other indirect means: as, to *disparage* one's success. To *decry* is to cry down or clamor against, by vigorous and open condemnation; unlike the other words *decry* may indicate the purest motives: as, to *decry* certain abuses in politics. To *belittle* is to make smaller or less in importance by underrating or underestimating; to *slur* is to make a person feel inferior or unimportant by slighting, cutting, or haughty speech or manner.

depredation. **Syn.:** pillaging, plundering, sacking, robbery, ravage, rapine, spoliation, waste.

depress. **Syn.:** lower, humble, dispirit, discourage, dishearten, deject, sadden.

depressed. **Syn.:** see **sad.**

depression. **Syn.:** discouragement, dejection, sadness, melancholy, despondency, gloom; dullness, inactivity, exhaustion; indentation, dent, hollow.

deprive. **Syn.:** dispossess, divest, strip, rob, bereave, despoil, debar.

To *deprive* is to take away forcibly or coercively what one has, or to withhold what one might have. To *dispossess* is to deprive of the possession of something, especially to remove a tenant or occupant from the house or premises of another. *Divest* is usually used in an unfavorable sense of depriving of rights, privileges, powers, or the like. To *strip* is to take away violently and completely, so as to leave in a powerless or destitute state.

deputy. **Syn.:** substitute, lieutenant, representative, delegate, proxy.

derange. **Syn.:** disarrange, disorder, displace, disturb, discompose, confuse, unsettle, upset. See **disturb.**

derangement. **Syn.:** disarrangement, disorder, confusion; lunacy, madness, insanity.

derelict. **Syn.:** left, abandoned, deserted, forsaken, lost, adrift; delinquent, unfaithful, neglectful, negligent, careless, remiss.

dereliction. **Syn.:** see **negligence.**

deride. **Syn.:** jeer, scoff, mock, ridicule, taunt, flout, gibe, banter, rally.

derision. **Syn.:** jeering, scoffing, mockery, ridicule, taunting, gibing, scorn.

derive. **Syn.:** draw, take, obtain, deduce, trace, get, receive.

derogatory. **Syn.:** detracting, disparaging, depreciatory, depreciative, unflattering.

descant. **Syn.:** see **expatiate.**

descend. **Syn.:** fall, drop, sink, slope, go down; condescend, stoop. **Ant.:** see **ascend.**

descendant. **Syn.:** see **offspring.**

descent. **Syn.:** falling, sinking; slope, decline, grade, declivity; extraction, lineage, parentage; incursion, attack, raid.

describe. **Syn.:** depict, portray, characterize, explain, narrate, recount, relate.

To *describe* is to convey an image or impression in words designed to reveal the appearance, nature, attributes, etc., of the thing described. The word applies primarily to what exists in space, and by extension to what occurs in time, and often implies the vividness of personal observation: as, to *describe* a view or race. To *narrate* is to recount the occurrence of something, usually by giving the details in the order of their happening. *Narrate* applies only to events, — *i.e.*, to that which happens in time; it may cover a series of events extending over a long period.

description. **Syn.:** depiction, portrayal, delineation, characterization, sketch, narration, account; sort, kind, class, character. See **kind,** *n.*

descry. **Syn.:** espy, perceive, discern, detect, discover, see.

desecrate. **Syn.:** profane, pollute, violate.

desert, *n.* **Syn.:** merit, worthiness, excellence; reward, meed, due. See **merit.**

desert, *a.* **Syn.:** uninhabited, desolate, unproductive, infertile, barren, waste. See **waste.**

desert, *v.* **Syn.:** see **abandon.**

deserter. **Syn.:** turncoat, renegade, apostate, backslider, traitor, rat. See **traitor.**

deserve. **Syn.:** see **merit.**

design, *n.* **Syn.:** intention, purpose, intent, aim, object; plan, scheme, plot; drawing, sketch, outline, plan, draft, pattern, model.

design, *v.* **Syn.:** intend, purpose, mean; contrive, plan, scheme, plot; draw, sketch, outline. See **intend, plan.**

designate. **Syn.:** point out, indicate, show, specify; name, entitle, style, denominate; nominate, appoint, assign, allot.

designation. **Syn.:** see **name.**

designing. **Syn.:** scheming, plotting, intriguing, calculating, artful, cunning, crafty, wily, insidious.

desire, *n.* **Syn.:** wish, longing, yearning, craving, hankering, appetite, appetency, passion, lust, itch; request, petition.

Desire is a strong feeling, worthy or unworthy, that impels to the attainment or possession of something which is, in reality or imagination, within reach: as, a *desire* to be successful. *Wish*, when applied to what is attainable, is a milder word than desire; when applied to the unattainable, *wish* has the strength of desire without its dynamic character: as, a *wish* to be alone; a *wish* to be tall. A *longing* is an intense wish, generally repeated or enduring, for something that is at the moment beyond reach but may be attainable at some future time: as, a *longing* to visit Europe. *Yearning* suggests persistent, uneasy, and sometimes wistful or tender longing: as, a *yearning* for one's native land. *Hankering* is a disturbing and persistent, but fitful longing: as, a *hankering* after notoriety. *Craving* implies a deep and imperative demand for something, especially something to satisfy the appetite or physical needs: as, a *craving* for food or companionship. *Lust* implies an unreasoning and intemperate desire, usually reprehensible: as, *lusts* of the flesh; a *lust* for conquest. *Itch*, a more or less colloquial and contemptuous term, suggests a restless and gnawing desire: as, an *itch* for power.

desire, *v.* **Syn.:** wish, long, yearn, want, crave, covet, desiderate; ask, request, solicit, beg, entreat.

desist. **Syn.:** cease, stop, discontinue, forbear, pause, halt. See **cease.**

desolate, *a.* **Syn.:** forsaken, lonely, solitary, cheerless, forlorn, disconsolate, inconsolable, miserable, wretched, brokenhearted; uninhabited, deserted, barren, waste, wild, dreary, dismal, gloomy; depopulated, ravaged, devastated.

The *desolate* person is, as it were, alone in his sadness or wretchedness; one who is *disconsolate* is unable to be relieved or cheered by consolation or comfort; the *forlorn* person has the feeling of one lost or of one forsaken by his friends.

desolate, *v.* **Syn.:** see **devastate.**

desolation. Syn.: desolateness, loneliness, dreariness, devastation, ruin.

despair. Syn.: hopelessness, desperation, despondency, discouragement.

Despair is a state of mind in which there is a total loss or abandonment of hope. *Despair* may be passive of may drive to desperation. *Desperation*, on the contrary, is usually an active state, resulting from such apparent hopelessness as impels to a furious struggle against adverse circumstances and to utter disregard of consequences.

despairing. Syn.: see **hopeless.**

despatch, *n.* **Syn.:** promptitude, promptness, speed, haste, expedition; telegram, message, letter. See **haste.**

despatch, *v.* **Syn.:** see **kill.**

desperate. Syn.: hopeless, despairing, reckless, furious, violent, frantic, wild; dangerous, critical, serious. See **hopeless.**

desperation. Syn.: hopelessness, despair, recklessness. See **despair.**

despicable. Syn.: contemptible, abject, worthless, base, vile. See **contemptible.**

despise. Syn.: scorn, disdain, contemn, spurn.

To *despise* is to look down upon with strong contempt or disgust: as, to *despise* a coward; to *despise* cheating. To *disdain* is to have high-minded abhorrence of what is base or wrong, or a proud and haughty contempt for what is inferior in comparison with oneself: as, to *disdain* to take a bribe; to *disdain* to notice a poor acquaintance. To *contemn* (primarily a literary word) is to slight or to spurn as unworthy of regard: as, to *contemn* danger or death. To *scorn* is to have an extreme and passionate contempt for: as, to *scorn* a dishonorable proposal.

despite. Syn.: see **notwithstanding,** *prep.*

despoil. Syn.: strip, rob, rifle, plunder, pillage, ravage, devastate.

despondency. Syn.: dejection, depression, discouragement, melancholy, gloom, desperation.

despondent. Syn.: dejected, depressed, discouraged, disheartened, downhearted, melancholy, low-spirited, spiritless. See **sad.**

despot. Syn.: autocrat, dictator, tyrant, oppressor. See **autocrat.**

despotic. Syn.: autocratic, arbitrary, unlimited, absolute, dictatorial, imperious, tyrannical, tyrannous.

despotism. Syn.: autocracy, absolutism, tyranny.

destine. Syn.: foreordain, predetermine, doom, fate; design, intend, dedicate, consecrate.

destiny. Syn.: fate, lot, fortune, doom.

The following three words are frequently interchangeable. *Destiny* emphasizes the idea of predetermined plan or unalterable course of events; *fate* stresses the irrationality of the power which determines events, and, being (apparently) lacking in reason, is often thought of as relentless and cruel. *Doom* especially applies to the final unhappy or terrible ending brought about by destiny or fate: as, Napoleon is called a man of *destiny*; it was his *fate* to be defeated; he met his *doom* bravely.

destitute. Syn.: deprived, bereft, devoid, void, lacking, deficient; needy, poor, indigent, necessitous, penniless, poverty-stricken.

Destitute implies a serious lack of what it is necessary or desirable to possess, especially the ordinary or common requirements of life: as, *destitute* of food or means. *Devoid* implies complete absence and is used with of especially in reference to the lack of qualities or attributes: as, *devoid* of fear, generosity, ideas. *Void* is a somewhat archaic word with much the same meaning as devoid: as, *void* of reason or common sense; unlike *devoid*, however, it can be used absolutely in the sense of empty: as, the contract is null and *void*. *Bereft* usually implies forcible or inevitable deprivation or loss, especially of what was cherished or dear: as, to be *bereft* of a friend by death.

destitution. Syn.: deprivation, lack, want, need, indigence, poverty, penury. See **poverty.**

destroy. Syn.: raze, demolish, ruin, annihilate, extinguish, consume, exterminate, eradicate, extirpate, kill, undo.

To *destroy* is to reduce to naught or take away the powers and functions of something so that restoration is impossible; it is usually violent or sudden, but may be gradual and slow, especially when due to a reversal of natural processes: as, fire *destroyed* the building; disease *destroyed* the tissue. To *demolish* is to destroy an organized body or structural mass by complete separation of parts: as, to *demolish* a fortress. To *raze* is to level down to the ground: as, to *raze* a house. To *exterminate* is to wipe out of existence (generally) insects or other groups of living beings; to *annihilate* is literally to reduce to nothing, or, by extension, to destroy so completely that few or no traces remain: as, to *exterminate* mosquitoes; to *annihilate* an army.

destruction. Syn.: demolition, ruin, annihilation, extinction, extermination, perdition. See **ruin.**

destructive. Syn.: demolishing, ruinous, annihilative, internecine, baleful, fell, pernicious, deleterious, deadly, mortal, fatal.

desultory. Syn.: shifting, wavering, roving, rambling, disconnected, unmethodical, unsystematic, aimless, cursory, random, fitful. See **hasty.**

detach. Syn.: disjoin, disconnect, disunite, unfasten, unhitch, disengage, sever, separate, part, withdraw, isolate, segregate.

detail. Syn.: item, particular, circumstance; squad, detachment, party.

detain. Syn.: keep, withhold, restrain, hinder, retard, delay, arrest, check, stop. See **restrain.**

detect. Syn.: see **discover.**

deter. Syn.: dissuade, discourage, restrain, hinder, prevent, stop.

deteriorate. Syn.: decline, degenerate, retrograde; impair, corrupt.

deterioration. Syn.: decline, degeneration, retrogression, decadence, decay, degradation. See **decline,** *n.*

determination. Syn.: resolve, resolution, firmness. See **decision.**

determine. Syn.: decide, resolve, conclude, settle; ascertain, verify; induce, influence, lead.

determined. Syn.: decided, resolute, firm, stanch, inflexible, unflinching, unfaltering, unwavering.

detest. Syn.: hate, abhor, loathe, abominate, execrate, despise, dislike. See **hate.**

detestable. Syn.: hateful, abhorrent, loathsome, abominable, execrable, odious, vile.

detract. Syn.: derogate, subtract, depreciate, disparage, decry.

detraction. Syn.: depreciation, disparagement, traducement, defamation, aspersion, calumny, slander.

detriment. Syn.: damage, injury, harm, hurt, impairment, deterioration, disadvantage, prejudice. See **injury.**

detrimental. Syn.: injurious, harmful, hurtful, damaging, disadvantageous, prejudicial.

devastate. Syn.: ravage, harry, desolate, waste, pillage, plunder, sack, despoil. See **ravage.**

devastation. Syn.: ravage, desolation, waste, havoc, ruin, destruction.

develop. Syn.: unfold, expand, elaborate, evolve, mature.

development. Syn.: unfolding, expansion, elaboration, evolution, progress, ripening, growth.

deviate. Syn.: swerve, diverge, digress, depart, stray, wander, vary.

To *deviate* is to turn or wander, often by slight degrees, from a path which is considered the most direct or desirable approach to a given physical, intellectual, or moral end: as, fear caused him to *deviate* from the truth. Two paths *diverge* when they proceed from a common point in such directions that the distance between them increases: as, two sides of a triangle *diverge* from their point of junction; or, figuratively, after a time their interests gradually *diverged*. *Digress* applies primarily to a wandering from the main theme or topic in writing or speaking, especially for explanation or illustration: as, some authors are prone to *digress*. *Swerve* especially implies a sudden or sharp turning from a line or course: as, a frightened horse *swerves* from the road; to *swerve* from one's intention.

device. Syn.: plan, scheme, expedient, shift, trick, artifice, stratagem, wile, ruse; invention, contrivance; design, figure, pattern, symbol, emblem, badge, motto, trade-mark. See **means, emblem.**

devil. Syn.: Satan, Lucifer, Apollyon, Beelzebub, Belial, Abaddon, Mephistopheles, Ahriman; deuce, dickens, mischief, old Harry, old Nick, old Scratch, old Bogy, old boy, old gentleman, old one, evil one, tempter, serpent; demon, fiend, imp.

devilish. **Syn.:** diabolical, fiendish, satanic, demoniac, demoniacal, infernal, hellish, impious, wicked, atrocious, nefarious, detestable; terrible, excessive.

Devilish is applied to what is befitting a devil in its evil or wicked qualities; *diabolical*, to what is outrageously wicked or infernal, especially in a methodically malevolent way: as, a *devilish* weapon; a *diabolical* plot. *Demoniacal* suggests such frenzy as might come from one possessed of an evil spirit; *fiendish* emphasizes the exulting pleasure derived from the infliction of cruelty or suffering: as, *demoniacal* shrieks; *fiendish* revenge.

devious. **Syn.:** circuitous, roundabout, winding, tortuous, rambling, swerving, straying, erring, sinful. See **circuitous.**

devise. **Syn.:** plan, invent, contrive, concoct, concert, excogitate. See **prepare.**

devoid. **Syn.:** empty, vacant, void, destitute, lacking. See **destitute.**

devote. **Syn.:** consecrate, dedicate, hallow; appropriate, assign, apply, addict.

To *devote* is to set apart by a solemn act or with firm intention, especially for the worship or service of God: as, to *devote* one's life to the ministry; to *devote* some time each day to prayer. When used in other than a religious connection, *devote* still retains its earnest or serious implication: as, to *devote* oneself to study. To *dedicate* is to declare (usually by formal act or solemn rite) something as belonging literally or figuratively to a chosen person or cause, often sacred: as, to *dedicate* a church, a book to an illustrious person, or one's life to science. To *consecrate* is to surrender or set apart something, often by a religious act or ceremony, as sacred: as, to *consecrate* ground for burial. To *hallow* is to make holy, or to esteem or worship as holy: as, to *hallow* the name of God, the memory of the dead.

devoted. **Syn.:** consecrated, dedicated; ardent, zealous, assiduous, addicted, attached.

devotee. **Syn.:** zealot, enthusiast.

devotion. **Syn.:** consecration, dedication, attachment, fidelity, constancy, devotedness, ardor, zeal; worship, adoration, prayer. See **love.**

devour. **Syn.:** consume, swallow, gulp, engulf, destroy, waste. See **eat.**

devout. **Syn.:** devotional, prayerful, pious, religious, reverential, godly; sincere, earnest, heartfelt. **Ant.:** impious, irreligious, irreverent. See **pious.**

dexterity. **Syn.:** adroitness, deftness, skill, expertness, knack, cleverness, address.

dexterous. **Syn.:** adroit, deft, nimble, skilful, expert, apt, quick, clever.

Dexterous implies either natural or acquired ability to do something requiring agility, precision, or skill with the hands: as, a *dexterous* swordsman. *Deft* implies particular aptness, cleverness, or neatness in action or performance: as, a *deft* surgeon. *Adroit* expresses readiness or skill in action, but is now more usually applied to mental readiness, address, and tact which meets and handles a difficult situation or exigency quickly and aptly: as, an *adroit* movement; an *adroit* diplomat; an *adroit* answer. *Skilful* implies practical knowledge or ability or alert and well-trained faculties for the doing of some particular thing: as, a *skilful* mechanic.

diabolical. **Syn.:** see **devilish.**

diadem. **Syn.:** see **crown.**

dialect. **Syn.:** language, tongue, vernacular, patois. See **language.**

diatribe. **Syn.:** tirade, philippic. See **invective.**

dictate, *n.* **Syn.:** order, command, injunction.

dictate, *v.* **Syn.:** prescribe, order, decree, command, enjoin, pronounce, speak.

dictator. **Syn.:** see **autocrat.**

dictatorial. **Syn.:** imperious, autocratic, arbitrary, magisterial, domineering, overbearing. See **imperative.**

diction. **Syn.:** language, expression, phraseology, wording, style.

Diction refers chiefly to the choice of words and to the force, accuracy, and distinction with which they are used; *phraseology*, more to the manner of combining the words into phrases, clauses, or sentences, especially to the peculiar or distinctive manner in which certain technical, scientific, and professional ideas are expressed: as, poetic *diction*; legal *phraseology*. *Wording* refers to the exact words or phraseology used to convey thought: as, the *wording* of a will. *Style* is the most comprehensive and general term, referring not only to the words and the manner in which they are combined, but to everything that relates to the form in which the thought is expressed, including peculiarities more or less characteristic of the writer or speaker or the age. The word is normally used in dignified connections and of what has artistic merit: as, an ornate or a classic *style*; the *style* of Dickens.

dictionary. **Syn.:** lexicon, word-book, glossary, thesaurus.

dictum. **Syn.:** see **proverb.**

die. **Syn.:** expire, perish, decease; wither, fade, wane, subside, recede, vanish.

To *die* is simply to cease to live, to part with life, to become dead from any cause and under any circumstances. It is the simplest, plainest, and most direct word for this idea, and is used figuratively of anything that displays activity: as, an echo, flame, storm, or rumor *dies*. *Expire*, now a familiar euphemism for die, means strictly to emit the last breath, and is used figuratively of many things which have a fixed term of life: as, an insurance policy or a truce *expires*. *Decease*, a less common word, is, like expire, a euphemism, and may be an affectation: as, old age often finds the friends of youth *deceased*. *Perish* implies death under harsh circumstances such as hunger, cold, neglect, etc.: as, hardship caused many pioneers in America to *perish*. Figuratively *perish* connotes utter extinction: as, Egyptian civilization has *perished*.

diet. **Syn.:** dietary, regimen; food, fare, provision, nourishment, aliment.

differ. **Syn.:** vary, disagree, quarrel.

difference. **Syn.:** variance, variation, discrepancy, disparity, dissimilarity, dissimilitude, unlikeness, diversity, contrast, distinction, discrimination, contrariety, disagreement, controversy, dissension, dispute, quarrel. **Ant.:** similarity, likeness, uniformity, agreement.

Difference implies a complete or partial lack of identity or the degree of unlikeness: as, a *difference* of opinion; a *difference* of six inches. *Dissimilarity* indicates an essential lack of resemblance between things in some respect comparable: as, a *dissimilarity* of dress. *Discrepancy* usually signifies the difference or inconsistency between things that should agree, balance, or harmonize: as, a *discrepancy* between the statements of the two witnesses. *Disparity* implies inequality, often where a greater approximation to equality might reasonably be expected: as, a *disparity* in the ages of a husband and wife.

different. **Syn.:** dissimilar, unlike, altered, changed, diverse, divergent, distinct, separate, opposite, contrary; various, sundry, divers, miscellaneous, unclassified.

Different is applied either to a single thing differing in identity or character from another or to two or more things differing thus from one another. *Diverse* commonly implies a number or assortment of things or parts differing one from another. *Distinct* implies want of connection between things, which, however, may possibly be alike or similar.

differentiate. **Syn.:** see **distinguish.**

difficult. **Syn.:** hard, arduous, laborious, toilsome, onerous, troublesome, trying, perplexing, embarrassing. See **hard.**

difficulty. **Syn.:** arduousness, laboriousness, troublesomeness; perplexity, dilemma, predicament, quandary, trouble, hindrance, obstacle; disagreement, controversy, quarrel.

diffidence. **Syn.:** shyness, bashfulness, timidity, modesty, reluctance, hesitation.

diffident. **Syn.:** shy, bashful, timid, modest, retiring, hesitating, shrinking. See **shy.**

diffuse, *a.* **Syn.:** widespread, scattered, dispersed; verbose, prolix, wordy, rambling, long-winded.

diffuse, *v.* **Syn.:** spread, scatter, disseminate, disperse, circulate.

diffuseness. **Syn.:** see **verbosity.**

digest, *n.* **Syn.:** see **abridgment.**

digest, *v.* **Syn.:** prepare, classify, codify, systematize, methodize; assimilate, comprehend, understand.

dignified. **Syn.:** exalted, honored, elevated, stately, grave, august, majestic, lordly, lofty, imposing. **Ant.:** undignified.

Dignified implies the possession of dignity or proper self-respect, especially as manifested by outward appearance, bearing, or manner: as, a *dignified* man. *Stately* suggests such height and symmetry of form or such easy restraint in motion as to convey the impression of imposing dignity: as, a *stately* palace or ship. *Majestic* suggests the attribute of majesty, particularly such as creates in one the impression of august power and splendor: as, a *majestic* assemblage. *Lordly* refers to a real or assumed loftiness of spirit or manner, sometimes a haughty condescension towards others: as, a *lordly* air.

dignify. Syn.: exalt, honor, ennoble, grace, adorn.

dignity. Syn.: worthiness, worth, nobleness; honor, eminence, rank, station, office, title; stateliness, loftiness, augustness, grandeur.

digress. Syn.: diverge, deviate, wander, stray. See **deviate.**

digression. Syn.: divergence, deviation, excursus.

dilapidated. Syn.: decayed, ruined, ramshackle, disintegrated.

dilate. Syn.: expand, distend, inflate, swell, puff out, stretch, enlarge, amplify, expatiate, descant. See **expand.**

dilatory. Syn.: delaying, procrastinating, lingering, loitering, dawdling, lagging, tardy, slow, behindhand. See **late.**

dilemma. Syn.: perplexity, quandary, predicament, strait. See **predicament.**

dilettante. Syn.: see **amateur.**

diligence. Syn.: industry, assiduity, sedulousness, application, perseverance.

diligent. Syn.: industrious, assiduous, sedulous, painstaking, persevering, indefatigable, busy, untiring, unremitting, constant.

Diligent implies earnest and constant effort or application in accomplishing something, usually some particular or occasional thing, although habitual endeavor may be implied. *Industrious* implies steady or zealous application of oneself to any work, business, or activity, especially as an habitual characteristic. *Diligent* usually suggests fondness for or enjoyment in what one is doing, for its own sake; *industrious*, that the application or endeavor is the result of a natural tendency or is a means to something else: as, a *diligent* student; an *industrious* clerk. *Indefatigable* implies a lack of or indifference to fatigue in the pursuit of a task: as, an *indefatigable* worker. *Busy* implies being actively employed, either temporarily or habitually: as, a *busy* official; a *busy* man. The word sometimes has the unfavorable sense of being fond of employing oneself in the affairs of others, as from curiosity or officiousness: as, a *busy* gossip.

dilute. Syn.: thin, weaken, reduce, attenuate.

dim, *a.* **Syn.:** obscure, shadowy, cloudy, foggy, misty, hazy, vague, blurred, indistinct, faint, lusterless, dull. **Ant.:** bright, clear, vivid. See **dark.**

dim, *v.* **Syn.:** darken, cloud, blur, dull, fade.

diminish. Syn.: lessen, decrease, curtail, abate, reduce, lower, subside, ebb, dwindle, shrink. See **decrease.**

diminution. Syn.: lessening, decrease, abatement, subsidence, reduction, decrement.

diminutive. Syn.: see **small.**

din. Syn.: noise, clamor, hubbub, uproar, racket. See **noise.**

dingy. Syn.: dark, dirty, dull, rusty.

dint. Syn.: see **hole.**

dip. Syn.: plunge, immerse, submerge, souse, douse, duck, dive; lade, ladle; sink, drop, incline, slope.

To *dip* is to put down temporarily into a liquid. *Plunge* adds a suggestion of force or suddenness to the same action. *Duck, douse,* and *souse* are homely terms of like meaning, sometimes with a humorous force as suggesting an unexpected or embarrassing experience for the victim. *Immerse* denotes a lowering into a liquid until covered by it, generally for a moment only (as in one mode of baptism). *Submerge* indicates more especially a descent altogether beneath the surface.

diplomatic. Syn.: see **tactful.**

dire. Syn.: dreadful, awful, direful, fearful, terrible, disastrous, calamitous.

direct, *a.* **Syn.:** straight, undeviating, unswerving, straightforward, unambiguous, plain, downright, positive, absolute. **Ant.:** indirect, devious, circuitous, roundabout.

direct, *v.* **Syn.:** point, aim; guide, conduct, regulate, manage, govern, superintend; command, order, enjoin, instruct; address, superscribe. See **guide,** *v.*

To *direct* is to tell a person to do something in a more or less authoritative manner. To *enjoin* is to direct with urgent admonition. To *instruct* is to direct in detail, usually because of superior knowledge. To *order* and to *command* are to direct imperatively, but the latter often suggests greater formality and a more fixed authority on the part of the one who directs.

direction. Syn.: guidance, management, superintendence, administration, oversight; command, order, instruction; address, superscription; trend, tendency.

Direction is the line along which an object or course of action moves, often toward some set point or intended goal. *Trend* emphasizes movement in a certain direction, although neither the course nor the goal may be very definite. *Tendency* is inclination in a certain direction, and is often the result of inherent qualities, nature, or habit.

directly. Syn.: straight; immediately, straightway, instantly, promptly, presently; straightforwardly, unambiguously. See **immediately.**

direful. Syn.: see **dire.**

dirge. Syn.: requiem, elegy, threnody, coronach, lament.

dirt. Syn.: filth, mud, mire, muck, dust; soil, ground, earth.

dirty. Syn.: soiled, unclean, foul, besmeared, begrimed, grimy, muddy, bedraggled, filthy, squalid; vile, mean, base, scurvy; indecent, obscene, nasty; dark-colored, dingy, dull.

Dirty is applied to what is filled or covered with dirt so that it is unclean or defiled. *Soiled* is especially applied to dirt upon the surface of something, usually comparatively small in amount but enough to spoil its cleanness or freshness. *Foul* usually implies uncleanness that is grossly offensive to the senses. *Filthy* is an emphatic word suggesting that which is offensively defiled or is excessively soiled or dirty. *Squalid* implies dirtiness or uncleanness that results from the slovenly indifference often associated with poverty. *Nasty* in its physical sense indicates that which is disgusting to the senses: as, a *nasty* sight. It is generally used to-day in its figurative sense, where it implies that which is furtive or sinister in its uncleanness, or that which is merely disagreeable or troublesome: as, a *nasty* picture, a *nasty* situation.

disability. Syn.: inability, incapacity, incompetence, unfitness, weakness, impotence, disqualification. See **inability.**

disable. Syn.: incapacitate, maim, paralyze, disqualify. See **cripple.**

disabuse. Syn.: see **undeceive.**

disadvantage. Syn.: detriment, injury, hurt, harm, damage, drawback, inconvenience, hindrance.

disadvantageous. Syn.: detrimental, unfavorable, prejudicial.

disaffection. Syn.: alienation, estrangement, dissatisfaction, discontent, disloyalty.

disagree. Syn.: differ, vary, disaccord, dissent, conflict, bicker, wrangle, squabble, quarrel.

disagreeable. Syn.: unpleasant, unwelcome, distasteful, offensive, obnoxious, repugnant; unamiable, uncongenial, crabbed, cross.

disagreement. Syn.: difference, disaccord, discord, discrepancy, dissension, altercation, controversy, dispute, wrangle, squabble.

disallow. Syn.: prohibit, forbid, reject, disown, disavow, repudiate.

disappear. Syn.: vanish, fade, evanesce, recede.

Disappear is used of whatever suddenly or gradually passes from sight. *Vanish* suggests complete, generally rapid, and often mysterious disappearance; *fade,* a complete or partial disappearance, proceeding gradually and often by means of a blending into something else.

disappointment. Syn.: failure, defeat, frustration, dissatisfaction, mortification, chagrin.

disapproval. Syn.: disapprobation, disfavor, dislike, condemnation, censure.

disarrange. Syn.: see **disorder,** *v.*

disaster. Syn.: mischance, misfortune, misadventure, casualty, calamity, catastrophe, blow, reverse. See **misfortune.**

disastrous. Syn.: unfortunate, calamitous, ruinous.

disavow. Syn.: see **disclaim.**

disband. Syn.: disorganize, demobilize, dissolve, disperse, break up.

disbelief. Syn.: unbelief, incredulity, distrust, skepticism, agnosticism, infidelity.

Disbelief is the active refusal to believe something because of the conviction that it is untrue, untrustworthy, or false, without any implication of wilful or blameworthy disregard of evidence. *Unbelief* is rather the absence of belief or the simple failure to believe because of lack of evidence or knowledge, but its theological use has given it the more active force of wilful opposition to the truth.

disbeliever. Syn.: see **skeptic.**

disburden. Syn.: unburden, unload, disencumber, lighten, free.

disburse. Syn.: see **spend.**

discard. Syn.: cast aside, reject, dismiss, discharge.

discern. Syn.: distinguish, discriminate, perceive, see, descry, espy, detect, discover.

discernible. Syn.: distinguishable, perceptible, visible, apparent, manifest.

discerning. Syn.: discriminating, penetrating, sharp-sighted, acute.

discernment. Syn.: discrimination, perception, penetration, insight, acumen, acuteness, perspicacity, sagacity.

Discernment combines keenness of perception with accuracy of discrimination. *Insight* implies the power of seeing deeply into the heart of a thing which results in a better or more sympathetic understanding of what would otherwise be only partially or imperfectly understood. *Penetration* suggests the keen understanding of insight but implies the power of analysis rather than sympathy. *Acumen* results from the complete coördination of intellectual powers and suggests the high development of insight and penetration.

discharge, *n.* **Syn.:** shot, fusillade, volley, salvo; dismissal, removal; release, acquittal, exoneration; ejection, emission, excretion; payment, settlement; fulfilment, execution, performance.

discharge, *v.* **Syn.:** unload, disburden; fire, shoot; dismiss, cashier; release, free, acquit; eject, expel, emit, excrete, exude; pay, settle, liquidate; fulfil, execute, perform. See **dismiss.**

disciple. Syn.: pupil, follower, adherent, votary. See **pupil.**

discipline, *n.* **Syn.:** instruction, training, drill; correction, chastisement, punishment.

discipline, *v.* **Syn.:** train, drill; correct, chasten, chastise, punish.

disclaim. Syn.: renounce, repudiate, disavow, disown, deny, reject.

Disclaim and *disavow* agree in denying any share in or responsibility for something. *Disclaim* implies more often that what is disclaimed has been attributed or imputed to the disclaimer. Disavowal may proceed from an impulse entirely within the agent and is more frequently associated with a formal and public statement. To *repudiate* is to separate oneself by word or act from something, often an obligation, accusation, temptation, etc., as being burdensome, unjust, or shameful. Thus: to *disclaim* any knowledge of an accident; to *disavow* a faith in democracy; to *repudiate* a debt, a charge, an alliance.

disclose. Syn.: uncover, unveil, expose, reveal, divulge, betray, confess, communicate.

Disclose and *reveal* differ chiefly in their etymological suggestion. To *disclose* is to lay open; to *reveal* is to uncover as if by drawing away a veil. Both words may be used either literally or figuratively: as, to *disclose* the contents of a box, the terms of an agreement; the fog lifted and *revealed* the harbor; to *reveal* an aptitude for music. To *divulge* is to communicate, sometimes to a large number, what was intended to be private, confidential, or secret: as, to *divulge* a confidence.

discomfit. Syn.: rout, vanquish, defeat, frustrate, thwart, baffle, disconcert, confuse, abash. See **embarrass.**

discommode. Syn.: incommode, inconvenience, trouble, annoy, disturb. See **disturb.**

discompose. Syn.: disarrange, disorder, unsettle, disturb, confuse, disconcert, perturb, ruffle, nettle, irritate, agitate, embarrass. See **embarrass.**

disconcert. Syn.: confuse, discompose, embarrass, upset, abash, discomfit. See **embarrass.**

disconnect. Syn.: disunite, disjoin, detach, dissever, separate, sunder, dissociate.

disconnected. Syn.: disunited, disjoined, detached, separate, incoherent, rambling, scattered, broken, desultory.

As applied to thought, speaking, or writing, *disconnected* simply implies lack of connection between the parts, although these within themselves may be connected, consistent, and logical; *incoherent* implies lack of logical cohesion or sense in the ideas themselves as well as in their sequence or continuity, as in the speech of one during excitement, intoxication, or delirium.

disconsolate. Syn.: inconsolable, broken-hearted, forlorn, dejected, sad, melancholy, cheerless, gloomy, woebegone. See **desolate.**

discontent. Syn.: discontentment, dissatisfaction, uneasiness, inquietude, restlessness, displeasure.

discontented. Syn.: dissatisfied, displeased, disgruntled.

discontinuance. Syn.: see **cessation.**

discontinue. Syn.: stop, quit, cease, desist, pause, intermit. See **suspend.**

discord. Syn.: disagreement, variance, dissension, contention, strife; dissonance, jarring, clashing, noise.

Discord indicates a lack of agreement in the units which comprise a whole, often such as to render impossible any concerted or unified action. *Dissension* implies the expressed differences, sometimes violent, resulting from the opposition of feelings, ideas, wills, etc. *Contention* and *strife* imply a more specific contest, *contention* usually expressing itself in heated dispute, *strife* more frequently in actions which may culminate in violence. In elevated use *contention* and *strife* may be applied to contests that in themselves are dignified and often commendable.

discordant. Syn.: disagreeing, incongruous, inconsistent, irreconcilable, opposite, contradictory, contrary; dissonant, inharmonious, unmelodious, jarring, clashing, grating, strident, harsh.

discount. Syn.: see **deduction.**

discourage. Syn.: daunt, dishearten, dispirit, depress, deject; dissuade, deter, hinder.

discouragement. Syn.: depression, dejection, hopelessness; dissuasion, deterrent, damper.

discourse, *n.* **Syn:** talk, conversation, intercourse; speech, address, oration, harangue, sermon, homily, disquisition, dissertation, treatise.

discourse, *v.* **Syn.:** see **speak.**

discourteous. Syn.: impolite, uncivil, disrespectful, unmannerly, rude, boorish.

discover. Syn.: find, detect, espy, descry, discern, ascertain, learn, unearth, ferret out; invent, contrive, devise, originate.

One *discovers* what was unknown to himself and perhaps to every one else; he *detects* what is obscure, secret, or perhaps intentionally or even criminally concealed; he *ascertains* facts by careful inquiry, research, or analysis; he *learns* what is looked upon as being added to his store of knowledge or information.

discovery. Syn.: invention.

A *discovery* is the finding of something already in existence but hitherto unknown; an *invention* is the creation of something new, especially something contrived by original thought, or ingenuity, by which mechanical or other operations can be performed or work done more expeditiously: as, the *discovery* of gold in Alaska; the *invention* of the cotton-gin.

discredit. Syn.: disesteem, dishonor, disrepute, disgrace, reproach.

discreet. Syn.: prudent, judicious, wise, circumspect, careful, cautious, wary. See **prudent.**

discrepancy. Syn.: see **difference.**

discretion. Syn.: choice, liberty, will; judgment, prudence, circumspection, wariness.

discriminate. Syn.: see **distinguish.**

discrimination. Syn.: differentiation, distinction, discernment, penetration, insight, acumen, acuteness. See **judgment.**

discursive. Syn.: rambling, digressive, desultory.

discuss. Syn.: debate, argue, reason, deliberate, moot. See **argue.**

discussion. Syn.: see **debate,** *n.*

disdain, *n.* **Syn.:** contempt, contemptuousness, scorn, haughtiness, arrogance, superciliousness, contumely. See **contempt.**

disdain, *v.* **Syn.:** despise, contemn, scorn, scout, spurn. See **despise.**

disdainful. Syn.: contemptuous, scornful, haughty, supercilious, contumelious. See **proud.**

disease. Syn.: malady, ailment, disorder, complaint, affection, distemper, sickness, illness.

While *disease* is a general word for any deviation of the body or some part or organ of it from the healthy or normal state, it usually implies a serious, active, prolonged, and deep-rooted morbid condition, especially when structural change is involved. *Malady* is applied especially to a lingering, chronic disease, usually painful, and often in the end fatal. *Disorder* usually implies a (frequently slight and transitory) physical or mental derangement, and differs from disease in not being organic or causing structural change. *Affection* is applied to a more seriously abnormal state of the body or mind, especially one that interferes with the functions of one of its organs or systems. *Ailment* and *complaint* are familiar words for illnesses of many kinds. *Distemper,* formerly applied to human beings to denote a morbid state of a part or the whole of the body, and still used of mental ailment, is now in its physical meaning usually restricted to diseases of animals, especially a catarrhal disease of dogs and horses.

disembarrass. Syn.: relieve, rid, clear, extricate, disentangle, disengage, release.

disembodied. Syn.: see **incorporeal.**

disengage. Syn.: free, release, liberate, detach, extricate, disentangle, disembarrass.

To *disengage* is to loosen or free that which has been caught or involved. To *disentangle* is to release, usually by painstaking care, from a condition of being intricately involved. To *extricate* is to get out of a complicated position of difficulty, embarrassment, or danger, either by the exercise of physical force or by mental shrewdness or cleverness.

disentangle. Syn.: untangle, extricate, disengage, loose. See **disengage.**

disfavor. Syn.: disesteem, disapproval, disgrace.

disfigure. Syn.: see **deface.**

disfigurement. Syn.: see **imperfection.**

disgrace, *n.* **Syn.:** dishonor, disrepute, discredit, ignominy, shame, infamy, odium, obloquy, humiliation, stigma.

Disgrace implies disfavor, with a greater or less degree of reproachful disapprobation; it relates to the opinion of others. *Dishonor* involves a stain on honor or honorable reputation; it relates especially to the conduct of the person himself. *Infamy* is shameful notoriety or baseness of action or character; it is widely known and recognized. *Ignominy* is disgrace attended with contempt.

disgrace, *v.* **Syn.:** dishonor, discredit, degrade, sully.

disgraceful. Syn.: dishonorable, disreputable, discreditable, ignominious, shameful, infamous, scandalous.

disguise. Syn.: mask, veil, cloak, shroud, misrepresent, dissemble.

disgust. Syn.: distaste, loathing, aversion, abhorrence, repugnance, repulsion. See **dislike.**

disgusting. Syn.: disgustful, loathsome, offensive, sickening, nauseous, repulsive, revolting.

dishearten. Syn.: see **discourage.**

dishonest. Syn.: unscrupulous, knavish, thievish, corrupt, fraudulent.

dishonesty. Syn.: unscrupulousness, improbity, corruption, fraud, theft, stealing, cheating.

dishonor, *n.* **Syn.:** disgrace, discredit, disrepute, ignominy, shame, infamy. See **disgrace,** *n.*

dishonor, *v.* **Syn.:** disgrace, discredit, humble, humiliate, shame, stain, seduce, ravish, debauch.

dishonorable. Syn.: disgraceful, discreditable, disreputable, ignominious, shameful, infamous, unscrupulous, unprincipled, base.

disillusion. Syn.: disenchant, disabuse, undeceive. See **undeceive.**

disinclination. Syn.: averseness, distaste, dislike, indisposition, unwillingness, reluctance, repugnance.

disingenuous. Syn.: uncandid, insincere, artful, crafty, deceitful.

disintegrate. Syn.: see **decay,** *v.*

disinter. Syn.: exhume, disentomb.

disinterested. Syn.: unselfish, unbiased, impartial, dispassionate, neutral. See **unselfish.**

disjoin. Syn.: see **disconnect.**

disjoint. Syn.: disarticulate, disjoin, disconnect, dislocate, luxate.

disjointed. Syn.: disarticulated, disconnected, broken, incoherent, rambling, loose.

dislike. Syn.: distaste, disrelish, dissatisfaction, disfavor, disinclination, disaffection, antipathy, repugnance, aversion, disgust, hatred.

Dislike is a very general word, expressing a positive, but not necessarily strong, though sometimes inherent or permanent, feeling of antipathy for something. It depends upon its connection for its strength. *Dissatisfaction* usually results from contemplating what falls short of one's wishes or expectations, and is usually only temporary. *Distaste* implies a more or less settled feeling of dislike for what is naturally uncongenial, or has been made so by association. *Disgust,* though etymologically the same as distaste, is a much stronger word, expressing a feeling of loathing for what is offensive to the physical taste or to the feelings or sensibilities.

dislocate. Syn.: see **disjoint.**

disloyal. Syn.: faithless, unfaithful, false, perfidious, treacherous, traitorous, treasonable, recreant, apostate. See **faithless.**

disloyalty. Syn.: faithlessness, unfaithfulness, perfidy, treachery, treason.

Disloyalty implies that one is untrue to the allegiance or obligation to which one is bound by ties of patriotism, friendship, affection, etc. *Perfidy* implies intentional betrayal of acknowledged and accepted obligations, trusts, or even sacred relationships. *Treachery* adds the idea of craftiness, meanness, or deceit, and may be manifested by a betrayal of a confidence or trust reposed in one or by luring another on to harm or ruin by fair appearances. *Treason* is applied specifically to the act of violating one's allegiance to one's country, especially by betraying it or its interests to an enemy.

dismal. Syn.: gloomy, somber, dreary, cheerless, joyless, melancholy, sad, sorrowful, doleful, dolorous, funereal, lugubrious. See **cheerless.**

dismay, *n.* **Syn.:** consternation, terror, panic, horror, fear, apprehension.

Dismay confuses the mental faculties by the prospect of imminent danger or disaster, so that one's courage or spirit is appalled or broken down and action to cope with the difficulty is rendered impossible. *Consternation* overwhelms or paralyzes the reason by the suddenness or the utterly unexpected greatness of the danger so that one is powerless to avert or combat it.

dismay, *v.* **Syn.:** appal, terrify, horrify, frighten, affright, daunt, disconcert.

dismiss. Syn.: discharge, cashier, remove, eject, oust.

Dismiss usually expresses some degree of formality, and sometimes peremptoriness, in the removal from office, service, or employment, and does not necessarily imply that the reason for removal was any delinquency on the part of the person dismissed: as, to curtail expenses he had to *dismiss* his assistants. *Discharge* applies especially to the dismissal of inferior employees, often because of incompetency, insubordination, or other serious fault on the part of the person discharged: as, to *discharge* an inefficient workman or a careless servant. *Cashier* implies dismissal from a place of command or trust, usually with more or less permanent disgrace or ignominy.

disobedient. Syn.: insubmissive, insubordinate, refractory, contumacious, defiant, mutinous, undutiful.

Disobedient may be applied to one who either neglects or refuses to obey the rules, orders, or commands rightly enjoined upon him. *Insubordinate* implies a more or less settled tendency to resist or defy authority. *Undutiful* implies neglect in the performance of such things as duty or obligation requires. *Refractory* adds to disobedience the idea of sullen or perverse resistance to control or a persistent breaking of rules; *contumacious* adds the suggestion of arrogance and contempt.

disobey. Syn.: transgress, violate, disregard, defy.

disorder, *n.* **Syn.:** disarrangement, disarray, jumble, litter, clutter; commotion, disturbance, tumult, riot; confusion, chaos, pandemonium, anarchy; ailment, disease, malady. See **disease.**

disorder, *v.* **Syn.:** disarrange, derange, disorganize, jumble, clutter, tousle.

disorderly. Syn.: disarranged, untidy, jumbled, confused, unsystematic; unruly, turbulent, tumultuous, riotous, unrestrained, lawless.

disorganization. Syn.: disarrangement, disorder, confusion; disbanding, dissolution, demobilization.

disorganize. Syn.: disarrange, disorder; disband, demobilize, disperse.

disown. Syn.: see **disclaim.**

disparage. Syn.: depreciate, belittle, decry, discredit, cheapen, lower, underrate. See **depreciate.**

disparagement. Syn.: depreciation, derogation, detraction, dispraise.

disparity. Syn.: inequality, dissimilarity, difference, disproportion, discrepancy. See **difference.**

dispassionate. Syn.: calm, cool, serene, collected, composed, unruffled, temperate, moderate, impartial, fair. See **calm,** *a.*

dispel. Syn.: scatter, disperse, dissipate, banish, remove.

To *disperse* is to cause (usually), a compact or organized body to separate or scatter in different directions, the parts of which may, however, be brought together again, or at least are generally as real and tangible as they were before they were separated: as, the troops were *dispersed* by the enemy. To *dispel* is to drive away or scatter, usually intangible things, so that they vanish or cease to exist: as, to *dispel* darkness, gloom, fears, doubts, or illusions. To *dissipate* is usually to scatter by dissolving or reducing to small atoms or parts which cannot be brought together again: as, to *dissipate* vapor, clouds, or a fortune.

dispense. Syn.: deal out, distribute, allot, apportion, assign, mete, administer, execute. See **distribute.**

disperse. Syn.: see **dispel.**

dispirit. Syn.: see **discourage.**

displace. Syn.: dislodge, oust, dismiss, discharge, remove.

display, *n.* **Syn.:** exhibit, exhibition, show, ostentation, parade. See **show,** *n.*

display, *v.* **Syn.:** exhibit, show, manifest, evince, flourish, flaunt, parade, air. See **show,** *v.*

displease. Syn.: dissatisfy, annoy, irritate, pique, chafe, fret, vex, provoke, offend, anger, disgust.

displeasure. Syn.: dissatisfaction, annoyance, irritation, vexation, anger, indignation, resentment, umbrage, dudgeon.

disposal. Syn.: disposition, distribution, bestowal; control, ordering, direction.

dispose. Syn.: arrange, range, rank, group; incline, influence, induce.

disposition. Syn.: arrangement, grouping; distribution, bestowal; temperament, nature; inclination, tendency, propensity, proneness; control, regulation, direction. See **mood.**

dispossess. Syn.: dislodge, eject, oust, evict, remove. See **deprive.**

dispraise. Syn.: see **disparagement.**

disprove. Syn.: see **refute.**

disputatious. Syn.: argumentative, controversial, polemical, contentious, quarrelsome.

dispute, *n.* **Syn.:** argumentation, debate, controversy, altercation, wrangle, contention, squabble, quarrel.

A *dispute* is an oral contention, usually of short duration and often of a heated, angry, or undignified character. A *controversy* may also be oral, but is often a clash of contrary opinions in writing, and is therefore naturally of longer duration and of more dignity. An *altercation* is, literally, an alternate expression of sharp, quarrelsome, personal difference of opinion or feeling, usually between two persons or sides, while a dispute or controversy may be among many. A *wrangle* is a persistent, often noisy dispute which threatens and sometimes develops into violence. A *squabble* is an insignificant and unseemly *wrangle*.

dispute, *v.* **Syn.:** argue, contest, debate, wrangle, bicker, squabble, quarrel. See **argue.**

disquiet. Syn.: disturb, excite, agitate, vex, harass.

disregard, *n.* **Syn.:** indifference, inattention, neglect, slight.

disregard, *v.* **Syn.:** overlook, ignore, neglect, slight, disobey.

disrepute. Syn.: ill repute, discredit, disesteem, dishonor, disgrace.

disrespect. Syn.: disesteem, discourtesy, incivility, impoliteness, rudeness.

disrespectful. Syn.: irreverent, contemptuous, discourteous, uncivil, impolite, rude, impudent, insolent, saucy.

dissatisfaction. Syn.: discontent, discontentment, displeasure, disapproval. See **dislike.**

dissemble. Syn.: disguise, mask, cloak, hide, dissimulate, pretend.

Dissemble and *dissimulate* are etymologically related and differ little in meaning; but *dissemble* suggests generally more of concealment, *dissimulate* more of pretense.

dissembler. Syn.: see **hypocrite.**

dissembling. Syn.: see **dissimulation.**

disseminate. Syn.: scatter, sow, broadcast, spread, diffuse, circulate, promulgate, propagate.

To *circulate* a rumor is to set it in motion among people so that it receives more or less general currency. To *disseminate* ideas is, as it were, to sow or scatter them broadcast. To *diffuse* information is, as it were, to pour it out over a large area. To *propagate* a doctrine is to spread it insistently so that it will become deeply and widely established.

dissension. Syn.: disagreement, discord, dispute, contention, strife. See **discord.**

dissent. Syn.: disagreement, dissidence, nonconformity.

dissenter. Syn.: see **heretic.**

dissimilar. Syn.: see **different.**

dissimilarity. Syn.: unlikeness, dissimilitude, difference. See **difference.**

dissimulation. Syn.: dissembling, pretense, hypocrisy, duplicity. See **deceit.**

dissipate. Syn.: scatter, disperse, dispel, squander, waste. See **dispel.**

dissipated. Syn.: intemperate, dissolute, profligate, abandoned.

Dissipated suggests wasted and degenerate physical and mental powers following upon excessive or vicious indulgence in pleasure which leads to vice. *Dissolute*, literally set free or released, describes the character of one who throws off all moral obligation and gives himself over to his indulgence in sensual pleasure. *Profligate* suggests reckless or wanton depravity which throws away both character and means in the pursuit of vice; it is especially used of the extravagant indulgence of the great, powerful, or rich, as a *profligate* monarch, but not a *profligate* peasant. *Abandoned* is applied to one who has voluntarily and hopelessly given himself up to self-indulgence and wickedness.

dissolute. Syn.: profligate, licentious, dissipated, fast, wild. See **dissipated.**

dissolution. Syn.: disintegration, decomposition, decay; dismissal, adjournment, prorogation, recess.

dissolve. Syn.: liquefy, melt, thaw, deliquesce; dismiss, adjourn, disband, disorganize. See **melt.**

dissonant. Syn.: see **discordant.**

dissuade. Syn.: see **deter.**

distant. Syn.: remote, far; aloof, offish, reserved, cold, unfriendly. See **reserved.**

Distant usually implies a definite or indefinite, but often considerable, separation in space, time, connection, relation, etc.: as, the rows are about six feet *distant* from one another; a *distant* view, period, hope, relative. *Remote* implies indefinite and often great separation, especially from a specific starting-point or standard: as, a *remote* country, resemblance, chance to succeed, cause. It often adds the idea of the effect produced by such distance upon the object itself: as, a *remote* spot is likely to be a solitary, possibly an inaccessible or unknown, one. *Far* as an adjective before its noun is more or less literary and is applicable to what is an indefinitely long way off: as, a *far* cry; a *far* country.

distaste. Syn.: dislike, disinclination, aversion, repugnance, disgust. See **dislike.**

distasteful. Syn.: unpalatable, unsavory, displeasing, disagreeable, offensive, repulsive.

distemper. Syn.: see **disease.**

distend. Syn.: see **dilate, expand.**

distinct. Syn.: separate, different, dissimilar; plain, obvious, definite, unmistakable. See **different.**

distinction. Syn.: discrimination, difference; prominence, eminence, repute, note, rank, superiority.

distinctive. Syn.: distinguishing, characteristic, peculiar, unique.

distinctly. Syn.: clearly, definitely, precisely, explicitly, unmistakably.

distinguish. Syn.: discriminate, differentiate, discern, recognize.

To *distinguish* is to pick out something as exhibiting recognizable features or characteristics: as, to *distinguish* a sloop from a yawl. To *discriminate* is to apprehend the particular, nice, or exact differences between things and to determine wherein these differences consist: as, to *discriminate* true from false modesty. To *differentiate* is especially to point out exactly and in detail the differences (usually) between two things: as, the symptoms of some diseases are so similar that it is hard to *differentiate* between them.

distinguished. Syn.: conspicuous, marked, signal, notable, noted, eminent, famous, illustrious, renowned, celebrated. See **eminent.**

distort. Syn.: contort, twist, wrest, pervert, misrepresent, misinterpret, falsify.

distracted. Syn.: disturbed, confused, perplexed, bewildered; crazed, deranged, mad, frantic, frenzied. See **abstracted.**

distraction. Syn.: disturbance, confusion, perplexity, bewilderment; craziness, derangement, madness, frenzy; diversion, amusement, pastime.

distress, *n.* **Syn.:** pain, suffering, grief, agony, anguish, misery, sorrow, trouble, affliction. See **affliction.**

distress, *v.* **Syn.:** pain, grieve, trouble, worry, bother, annoy, harass, afflict.

distribute. Syn.: deal, dispense, mete, allot, apportion; spread, scatter, disperse; classify, sort, assort, group.

Distribute implies apportioned, individualized, and, often, personal giving, especially of something that is definite or limited in amount or number; *dispense* implies indiscriminate, general, and liberal giving, especially of something that is more or less indefinite or unmeasured in amount: as, the king *distributed* the land among his nobles; the will *distributed* the property among the heirs; God *dispenses* blessings to men; nature *dispenses* her bounties. *Mete* is now almost entirely a literary or poetic word, and implies giving out according to (especially a just or righteous) measure.

distribution. **Syn.:** allotment, apportionment, division, partition; scattering, dispersion, diffusion; arrangement, classification, sorting, grouping.

district. **Syn.:** precinct, ward, division, province, locality, quarter, region, country, territory.

distrust. **Syn.:** doubt, suspicion, mistrust. See **suspicion**.

disturb. **Syn.:** agitate, perturb, disquiet, worry, trouble, molest, annoy, vex, plague, discommode, incommode, disarrange, derange.

To *disturb* is to throw out of proper, regular, or natural order or condition: as, to *disturb* the contents of a drawer; to *disturb* one's peace of mind. To *derange* is to disorder what has been systematically or carefully arranged: as, to *derange* plans. To *incommode* or *discommode* is to disturb in such a way as to put to inconvenience or trouble.

disturbance. **Syn.:** agitation, perturbation, disorder, commotion, confusion, tumult, riot.

ditch. **Syn.:** trench, drain, sewer, gutter, channel, waterway, moat, fosse.

ditty. **Syn.:** see **song**.

diurnal. **Syn.:** see **daily**.

diverge. **Syn.:** see **deviate**.

divers, diverse. **Syn.:** see **several, different**.

diversion. **Syn.:** recreation, pastime, entertainment, amusement, play, sport, relaxation; divergence, deviation. See **pastime**.

diversity. **Syn.:** see **difference, variety**.

divert. **Syn.:** see **amuse**.

divest. **Syn.:** disrobe, strip, deprive, dispossess.

divide. **Syn.:** separate, sunder, sever, cleave, split, part; apportion, allot, distribute, share. See **separate**.

divine, *n.* **Syn.:** see **clergyman**.

divine, *a.* **Syn.:** holy, sacred, celestial, heavenly, angelic, godlike, supernatural, superhuman, transcendent. See **godlike**.

divine, *v.* **Syn.:** foresee, foreknow, forebode, presage, surmise, conjecture, guess; prognosticate, prophesy, predict. See **foresee**.

division. **Syn.:** separation, sundering, etc. (see **divide**); apportionment, allotment, distribution, partition; section, segment, portion, part, group; disunion, schism.

divulge. **Syn.:** disclose, reveal, betray, impart, communicate, tell. See **disclose**.

do. **Syn.:** perform, execute, effect, accomplish, fulfil, achieve, finish, complete, consummate; render, pay, show; fare, prosper; transact, discharge; commit, perpetrate; suffice, serve, answer.

Do is the most general word in the language for the idea of bringing something to an (intended) conclusion. *Perform*, while a more formal word, is likewise very general, and is applicable to the ordinary affairs of life that are carried through by simple action or labor; it often, however, implies regular, methodical, or protracted application till the work is completed. *Execute* emphasizes the carrying out to a successful end of something that has been projected or ordered. *Accomplish* usually suggests the fulfilment or completion of some undertaking, plan, or purpose which requires effort and perseverance. *Achieve* suggests resistance overcome in the accomplishing of something that is important, excellent, or great. *Effect* especially views the outcome as a result of what has been done to bring it about.

docile. **Syn.:** teachable, tractable, manageable, obedient, submissive, yielding, compliant, gentle. See **obedient**.

dock. **Syn.:** see **curtail**.

doctor. **Syn.:** sage, savant; physician, surgeon, leech, allopath, homeopath.

doctrine. **Syn.:** teaching, precept, belief, tenet, dogma, principle.

A *doctrine* is any belief or opinion which is taught or advocated by a teacher, sect, or school of thinkers in religion, science, etc. A *precept* is a teaching which points out a mode of conduct: as, the *precepts* of Marcus Aurelius. A *dogma* is a belief or principle established by authority, especially religious; it is now often an opinion set forth in an arbitrary or even dictatorial way. A *tenet* is especially a belief or doctrinal position held and defended as true or right.

dodge. **Syn.:** duck, evade, elude, parry, prevaricate, equivocate, quibble. See **evade**.

dogged. **Syn.:** surly, churlish, sullen, obstinate, stubborn, mulish, headstrong, inflexible, unyielding. See **obstinate**.

doggish. **Syn.:** currish, snarling, snappish, surly, sullen, cynical.

dogma. **Syn.:** see **doctrine**.

dogmatic. **Syn.:** opinionated, positive, arrogant, overbearing, domineering. See **authoritative**.

doleful. **Syn.:** dolorous, sorrowful, mournful, woeful, lugubrious, plaintive, dismal, gloomy. See **mournful**.

dolorous. **Syn.:** see **sad**.

domain. **Syn.:** possession, dominion, sovereignty, rule; realm, territory, province, demesne.

domestic, *n.* **Syn.:** see **servant**.

domestic, *a.* **Syn.:** home, household; native, intestine; tame, domesticated.

domicile. **Syn.:** see **habitation**.

dominant. **Syn.:** ruling, governing, controlling, commanding, prevailing, predominant, paramount, principal, chief.

dominate. **Syn.:** rule, govern, control, sway; overtop, command.

domineer. **Syn.:** tyrannize, lord, swagger, bluster, bully, hector.

domineering. **Syn.:** tyrannical, lordly, overbearing, dictatorial. See **imperative**.

dominion. **Syn.:** sovereignty, lordship, authority, rule, sway, control, mastery, ascendancy, supremacy; domain, realm, kingdom, empire.

donation. **Syn.:** contribution, benefaction, offering, gift, present. See **present**.

doom. **Syn.:** see **destiny**.

dormant. **Syn.:** sleeping, inactive, inoperative, inert, torpid, quiescent, latent, abeyant. See **inactive**.

doting. **Syn.:** silly, weak-minded, senile.

double. **Syn.:** twofold, bifold, duplex, paired, coupled; ambiguous, equivocal, deceitful, hypocritical, insincere.

doubt, *n.* **Syn.:** uncertainty, indecision, irresolution, hesitation, hesitancy, vacillation; distrust, mistrust, misgiving, suspicion, incredulity, disbelief, skepticism. **Ant.:** certainty, assurance, decision, resolution, trust, belief.

Doubt implies lack of certainty or conviction as to the truth of an assertion or the reality of a fact, usually through want of sufficient evidence. *Incredulity* may be applied to the reluctance to believe either what ought to be believed or what ought not to be (readily) believed; it also refers to a generally unbelieving state of mind, therein resembling *skepticism*, which implies a general disposition to doubt or question.

doubt, *v.* **Syn.:** hesitate, waver; distrust, mistrust, suspect, question.

doubtful. **Syn.:** uncertain, undecided, irresolute, hesitating, vacillating; undetermined, unsettled, indefinite, ambiguous, questionable, dubious.

douse. **Syn.:** see **dip**.

dowdy. **Syn.:** ill-dressed, untidy, slovenly, slatternly, frowzy.

downcast. **Syn.:** see **downhearted**.

downfall. **Syn.:** downcome, descent, ruin, overthrow, reverse, humiliation, disgrace.

downhearted. **Syn.:** downcast, dejected, depressed, discouraged, despondent.

downright. **Syn.:** direct, straightforward, unceremonious, plain, blunt, outspoken; thorough, absolute, positive, complete, utter, out-and-out.

downy. **Syn.:** pubescent, flocculent, fluffy, soft, soothing, restful.

doze. **Syn.:** see **sleep**, *v.*

drag. **Syn.:** draw, pull, hale, haul, lug, tug, trail, dredge. See **draw**.

drain. **Syn.:** see **ditch**.

drama. **Syn.:** play, tragedy, comedy, farce, melodrama, mystery, miracle-play, pageant, pantomime, dumb-show, burlesque, travesty, playlet, mime.

dramatic. **Syn.:** melodramatic, theatrical, sensational.

Dramatic describes that which suggests drama, such as a

striking situation involving emotional tension and rising to a climax. That which is *melodramatic* is violently or exaggeratedly dramatic. *Theatrical* implies such connection with or imitation of the theater or stage as makes situations, actions, or speech artificial, affected, or spectacular. That which is *sensational* aims to produce a thrilling impression by exaggerated emotional effects.

draw. **Syn.:** pull, haul, drag, hale, tug, lug, tow; remove, extract, unsheathe; attract, entice, allure; get, obtain, derive, deduce, infer; stretch, lengthen, prolong; trace, sketch, delineate, depict; write, draft, frame, formulate.

To *draw* is to move by an attractive force in the direction from which the force is exerted. To *drag* is to draw against greater resistance than is overcome in drawing, especially such as results from friction between the object drawn and the surface on which it rests. *Haul* especially applies to a heavy object that is slowly transported by mechanical force or sustained effort. *Hale* is now obsolescent except in literary language, and suggests dragging by main force against active resistance and unwillingness.

drawback. **Syn.:** see **disadvantage.**

drawing. **Syn.:** representation, picture, sketch, draft, diagram, plan, design.

dread, *n.* **Syn.:** fear, terror, horror, apprehension, awe, reverence. See **fear.**

dread, *a.* **Syn.:** see **formidable.**

dreadful. **Syn.:** fearful, frightful, terrible, horrible, dire, direful, formidable, awe-inspiring, awful. See **terrible.**

dream. **Syn.:** vision, reverie, fantasy, fancy.

dreary. **Syn.:** gloomy, dismal, drear, cheerless, lonesome, lonely, dull, monotonous, tedious, wearisome. See **cheerless.**

dregs. **Syn.:** see **sediment.**

drench. **Syn.:** see **wet,** *v.*

dress, *n.* **Syn.:** clothing, attire, apparel, array, raiment, vesture, garb, clothes, garments, vestments, accoutrements, habiliments, togs; gown, robe, suit, habit, costume.

Dress is the general term for the outer clothing, especially such as is used not only for covering, but for adornment. *Apparel* suggests dress of a fine or elegant nature; sometimes it regards dress in its commercial aspect: as, rich *apparel*; a sale of ladies' *apparel*. *Attire* likewise suggests elegance, and is especially used of elaborate or official dress: as, court *attire*. *Array*, when not archaic, is now chiefly poetic, and often includes besides dress various articles of adornment disposed in proper and befitting order upon the person: as, he rode forth in fine *array*. *Garb* especially denotes the distinctive dress of some office, profession, rank, or class: as, the *garb* of a judge, hermit. In general use *habit* is archaic except as it is applied to a settled or permanent (usually plain, ample, or flowing) mode of dress among a particular class, especially, a religious order: as, the *habit* of a nun or clergyman. *Costume* is used of the style of dress appropriate to some occasion, purpose, period, or character, especially as used on the stage, at balls, at court, or the like.

dress, *v.* **Syn.:** clothe, attire, apparel, array, robe, drape, deck, trim, adorn, accoutre, equip. See **clothe.**

drift. **Syn.:** impulse, rush, impetus, drive; current, flow, course, direction, aim, tendency, intention, intent, meaning, purport; bank, pile, heap, diluvium. See **meaning.**

drill, *n.* **Syn.:** see **exercise.**

drill, *v.* **Syn.:** see **bore.**

drink, *n.* **Syn.:** draft, potation; potion, dram, beverage, liquor.

drink, *v.* **Syn.:** imbibe, sip, sup, quaff, guzzle, swill, tipple, tope, booze, bouse.

Drink is the general word for the swallowing of a liquid. *Sip* implies drinking little by little at short, succeeding intervals, often in a delicate, toying, or idle manner. *Quaff*, now a literary word with a quaint flavor, implies drinking deeply or copiously, as in hearty enjoyment or good-fellowship. *Imbibe*, a more formal word, particularly emphasizes the taking in of the liquid. *Guzzle* and *swill* both imply greedy or excessive drinking in an offensive or hoggish manner. *Tipple*, *tope*, and *booze* refer only to the drinking of alcoholic liquor, *tipple* emphasizing the frequent and habitual use of liquor in small quantities; *tope*, its habitual and too liberal use; *booze*, the degrading result of excessive drinking.

drip. **Syn.:** see **drop.**

drive. **Syn.:** impel, chase, urge, push, force, compel, constrain, overtask; rush, dash. See **actuate, ride.**

drizzle. **Syn.:** see **fog, mist.**

droll. **Syn.:** waggish, facetious, odd, comical, whimsical, amusing, laughable, funny, ludicrous, ridiculous. See **funny.**

drollery. **Syn.:** waggery, facetiousness, humor, jesting, jest, whimsicality, pleasantry.

drone. **Syn.:** see **idler.**

droop. **Syn.:** bend, sink, flag, fail, decline, languish, fade, wilt, wither.

drop. **Syn.:** drip, trickle, dribble, distil; fall, sink, descend; cease, dismiss, discontinue, discard.

dross. **Syn.:** scum, waste, refuse, recrement, scoria, draff, sediment, lees, dregs, leavings.

droughty. **Syn.:** see **dry.**

drove. **Syn.:** see **flock.**

drowse. **Syn.:** see **sleep,** *v.*

drudge. **Syn.:** toiler, slave, menial, scullion, fag, hack, penny-a-liner.

drudgery. **Syn.:** see **work,** *n.*

drunk. **Syn.:** see **drunken.**

drunkard. **Syn.:** inebriate, toper, sot, dipsomaniac.

drunken. **Syn.:** drunk, intoxicated, inebriated, tipsy, fuddled, maudlin.

Both *drunk*, which is used only predicatively, and *drunken*, which is used attributively, express the condition or character of being overcome by liquor, but *drunken* also often implies habitual intemperateness or addiction to drink and the associations and effects of drinking. *Intoxicated* and *inebriated* are both used euphemistically for *drunk*, the former, however, often being applied to a comparatively slight state of drunkenness and figuratively to a state of intense feeling. There are many words, some euphemistic but most of them humorous or slang terms, to express the idea of drunkenness.

dry. **Syn.:** arid, parched, droughty, evaporated, desiccated, thirsty; uninteresting, dull, tedious, tiresome.

Dry is the general word for the condition of lacking water or being free from moisture: as, a *dry* well, *dry* clothes or land. *Arid* suggests great or intense dryness in a region or climate, especially such as results in bareness or barrenness: as, *arid* tracts of land. *Parched* especially suggests dryness caused by evaporation of moisture from intense or excessive heat; *droughty*, the dryness caused by lack or insufficiency of rain: as, *parched* corn, soil, lips; *droughty* weather or season.

dubious. **Syn.:** see **doubtful.**

duck. **Syn.:** plunge, dive, dip, souse; bob, bow, dodge. See **dip.**

ductile. **Syn.:** see **flexible.**

dude. **Syn.:** see **dandy.**

dudgeon. **Syn.:** see **anger.**

due. **Syn.:** owed, unpaid, payable; appropriate, fitting, proper; regular, appointed; attributable, assignable.

dull. **Syn.:** stupid, doltish, blockish, heavy, sluggish, slow, apathetic, lifeless, spiritless, inactive, drowsy, unfeeling, callous; dismal, gloomy, cheerless, melancholy; uninteresting, wearisome, tedious; blunt, obtuse, pointless; lusterless, clouded, dim; muffled, deadened.

Dull is applied to the edge or point of an instrument, tool, or the like which should possess but lacks or has lost its keenness or sharpness; *blunt* may be similarly applied, but is also used of an edge or point that is not intended to be keen or sharp: as, a *dull* razor or saw; a *blunt* crayon; a *blunt* foil for fencing.

dumb. **Syn.:** mute, speechless, inarticulate, silent, reticent, mum. See **silent.**

dumfound. **Syn.:** confound, stupefy, astound, confuse, amaze, bewilder. See **surprise,** *v.*

dunce. **Syn.:** dullard, dolt, numskull, blockhead, ignoramus, simpleton, nincompoop, ninny, booby, mooncalf.

dupe. **Syn.:** see **cheat.**

duplicate. **Syn.:** see **copy.**

duplicity. **Syn.:** double-dealing, deceitfulness, guile, hypocrisy, deception, dissimulation, falsehood. See **deceit.**

durable. **Syn.:** lasting, enduring, permanent, stable, firm, strong. See **lasting.**

dusk. **Syn.:** see **evening.**

dusky. **Syn.:** dark, swarthy, tawny, fuscous; dim, gloomy.

Dusky and *swarthy* differ more in application than in meaning. *Dusky* suggests half-blackness produced by a veiled or faint light, or by darkness of coloring; *swarthy*, which usually denotes a greater degree of darkness or blackness, is used only of the complexion: as, *dusky* evening shadows; the *dusky* Ethiopian; *swarthy* skin.

dutiful. Syn.: duteous, obedient, submissive, deferential, respectful, docile. See **obedient**.

duty. Syn.: homage, obedience, respect; obligation, responsibility; custom, impost, excise, tax; office, function, service, work, business.

Duty is what one performs in fulfilment of the grave, permanent, and generally accepted dictates of conscience, piety, right, or law; an *obligation* is rather what one is bound to do to fulfil a particular, specific, and often personal promise or agreement, or the dictates of usage, custom, or propriety: as, *duty* to one's country; it is one's *duty* to tell the truth; to raise children properly; financial or social *obligations*.

dwarf, *n.* **Syn.:** pygmy, midget, manikin, homunculus, hop-o'-my-thumb, gnome, runt.

dwarf, *v.* **Syn.:** stunt, atrophy.

dwarfish. Syn.: pygmy, diminutive, tiny, stunted, atrophied, runty.

dwell. Syn.: linger, pause, abide, sojourn, stay, reside, live. See **live**.

dwelling. Syn.: see **habitation**.

dwindle. Syn.: shrink, diminish, decrease, decline, waste, degenerate. See **decrease**.

dye. Syn.: see **color**.

E

each. Syn.: see **every**.

eager. Syn.: keen, ardent, glowing, fervent, fervid, zealous, impetuous, impassioned, vehement, anxious, impatient, avid, ravenous, greedy. **Ant.:** indifferent, uninterested, unconcerned, stolid, phlegmatic, cold, dispassionate.

Eager implies intense desire, keenness, or even impatience, usually in the pursuit or for the attainment of something; *avid*, intense, sometimes too ardent, desire for possession or enjoyment of something; *greedy*, an excessive or selfish desire, especially for food or gain.

eagerness. Syn.: ardor, fervor, zeal, impetuosity, enthusiasm, heartiness, alacrity, vehemence, impatience, avidity. See **ardor**.

early. Syn.: soon, betimes.

Early denotes occurrence in or during the first part of some division of time or before some fixed or usual time: as, he rose *early* may mean either before the day had advanced very far or before his usual time of rising. *Soon* means shortly or in a short time after the present or some fixed point of time: as, write *soon*; he left *soon* after my arrival. *Betimes* is now a somewhat archaic word for early or in good time for all practical purposes: as, he arrived *betimes*.

earn. Syn.: see **get**.

earnest, *n.* **Syn.:** pledge, security, deposit, pawn, gage, handsel, foretaste.

Earnest is generally used figuratively for a part that is paid or given in warrant that more (usually of the same kind) is forthcoming: as, his precocity gave an *earnest* of his genius. *Pledge* is used both literally and figuratively for something (usually of a different nature) given as a security or guarantee for what is promised: as, he gave his watch as a *pledge* of payment, his word as a *pledge* of his support. *Pawn*, now mostly replaced by pledge, is something given or deposited as security, as for money borrowed. *Gage*, now an archaic word, historically denotes a pledge given to assure appearance for combat, usually by throwing down a glove.

earnest, *a.* **Syn.:** serious, sincere, diligent, eager, zealous, ardent, fervent, impassioned, pressing, urgent. See **ardent**.

earnestness. Syn.: seriousness, sincerity, eagerness, zeal, fervency, enthusiasm.

earth. Syn.: globe, world.

Earth is used as the distinctive name of our planet in the solar system: as, Mercury, Venus, *earth*, Mars, etc. It is also used of the planet regarded as material, especially as soil, and frequently to imply a contrast with heaven or hell: as, the surface of the *earth*; the children of *earth*. *World* has especial application to the earth in relation to its inhabitants and their activities, interests, and concerns. The word is more inclusive than earth, and is also used more abstractly: as, the races of the *world* differ greatly; the future of the *world*. *Globe* emphasizes the roundness of the earth: as, to circumnavigate the *globe*.

earthly. Syn.: terrestrial, terrene, mundane, sublunary, worldly; possible, conceivable.

Earthly denotes that which pertains to the earth, and now

almost always implies a contrast to what is heavenly, while *terrestrial*, the dignified Latin equivalent of earthly, applies more to the earth as a planet, or to the land of the earth as opposed to the water, and is contrasted with celestial: as, *earthly* pleasures; *terrestrial* globe. *Worldly* means of the world in fact or in spirit; it is commonly used in the derogatory sense of being devoted to the cares, pleasures, vanities, advantages, or gains of this present life to the exclusion of spiritual interests or the life to come: as, *worldly* success. *Mundane*, the more formal Latin equivalent of *worldly*, especially suggests that which is bound to the earth, is not exalted, and therefore is commonplace: as, *mundane* affairs, pursuits, etc.

earthwork. Syn.: see **fortification**.

ease, *n.* **Syn.:** tranquillity, rest, comfort, contentment, leisure; facility, readiness, knack.

Ease implies the ability or power to do something without seeming effort; *facility*, the ease that comes from some natural gift or endowment or (especially) from practice or skill; *knack*, the peculiar ability or expertness that allows one to do a certain thing with unusual or surprising ease: as, the strings of a banjo may be plucked with *ease*; practice enables one to play with *facility*; many untrained persons have the *knack* of playing music by ear.

ease, *v.* **Syn.:** tranquilize, soothe, relieve, mitigate, alleviate, assuage, allay.

easy. Syn.: tranquil, comfortable, contented; untroubled; complaisant, lenient, indulgent, credulous; smooth, flowing, fluent, facile, unconstrained; mild, moderate, gentle. **Ant.:** see **uneasy**.

eat. Syn.: devour, gulp, bolt, gobble, gorge; consume, waste, destroy, corrode. Cf. **bite**.

Eat is the general word for taking food into the mouth and swallowing it. To *bite* is to set the teeth into so as to cut or pierce. To *chew* is to masticate and grind with the teeth. To *gnaw* is to bite persistently to get off small fragments, usually from a substance that is hard, or bitten with difficulty, or where there is little or nothing to get. To *nibble* is to bite so as to take little pieces of a thing. To *devour* is to eat up eagerly or ravenously; to *gobble* is to eat hurriedly, noisily, or offensively, as in large pieces; to *consume* is to eat up (usually large quantities) completely.

eatable. Syn.: edible, comestible, esculent.

ebb. Syn.: recede, subside, sink, wane, decrease, decline, abate.

ebullition. Syn.: effervescence, fermentation, seething, boiling.

eccentric. Syn.: irregular, erratic, whimsical, peculiar, singular, odd, queer, strange. See **singular**.

eccentricity. Syn.: irregularity, whimsicality, peculiarity, oddity, oddness, freakishness, unconventionality.

echo. Syn.: resound, reverberate; repeat, imitate.

eclipse. Syn.: obscure, darken, overshadow; outshine, excel, surpass. See **excel**.

economical. Syn.: economic, frugal, saving, provident, thrifty.

economize. Syn.: save, husband, retrench.

economy. Syn.: frugality, thriftiness, thrift, saving, retrenchment, parsimony.

Economy implies prudent use of one's resources so as to avoid unnecessary waste or expense. *Frugality* emphasizes the idea of saving, sometimes that of excessive saving, especially in such matters as food, dress, or the like. *Parsimony* is a pinching and narrowing frugality which indicates stinginess. *Thrift* is a stronger word for economy, and adds to it the idea of industry and successful management.

ecstasy. Syn.: rapture, transport, exaltation. See **rapture**.

eddy. Syn.: see **whirlpool**.

edge. Syn.: border, margin, verge, brink, rim, brim, extremity.

Edge is the boundary line, or adjacent part, of a surface or plane (as, the *edge* of a table), or the intersection of two surfaces or planes (as, the *edge* of a box or knife), or the narrowest surface of a three dimensional object (as, the *edge* of a board). *Border* is the boundary of a surface or the strip adjacent to it, inside or out: as, the Canadian *border*, a *border* of lace. *Margin* is a limited strip, generally unoccupied, at the extremity of an area: as, the *margin* of a river or a page. *Rim* is a line or surface bounding a (generally) circular or curved area: as, the *rim* of a wheel. *Brim* is the rim (generally at the top) of a hollow, three dimensional object or a cavity: as, the *brim* of a cup or hat. *Brink* is the edge of a sharp declivity: as, the *brink* of a well. *Verge* refers to the outermost or furthest edge or point: as, the *verge* of the desert. All these words may be used figuratively: as, the *edge* of one's appetite, the *border* of insanity, a *margin* of safety, the *rim* of the universe, a mind filled to the *brim*, the *brink* of destruction, the *verge* of ruin.

edible. **Syn.:** see **eatable.**

edict. **Syn.:** decree, proclamation, manifesto, ordinance, fiat, bull. See **proclamation.**

edifice. **Syn.:** see **building.**

educate. **Syn.:** train, teach, instruct, school, drill, edify, indoctrinate.

educated. **Syn.:** see **learned.**

education. **Syn.:** training, teaching, instruction, tuition, schooling, study, learning, knowledge, enlightenment. See **instruction, culture.**

eerie. **Syn.:** fearful, timid, timorous, uneasy; weird, strange, uncanny. See **weird.**

efface. **Syn.:** rub out, erase, obliterate, expunge, cancel, destroy.

To *efface* is to remove from the face of, as a picture, an inscription, etc. To *obliterate* is to blot out entirely so as to remove all sign or trace of; hence it is more emphatic than *efface.* To *erase* is to remove by scraping or rubbing (usually) writing. To *expunge* is to take out completely, usually something from a record or account. To *cancel* is to cross out something as by running lines through it, so that it loses its force or validity without being removed.

effect, *n.* **Syn.:** result, consequence, outcome, issue, event; force, validity, weight; purport, meaning, intent, significance; accomplishment, realization, fulfilment.

An *effect* is something produced, usually more or less immediately and directly, by an action or cause; a *consequence*, something that follows naturally or logically, as in a train of events or sequence of time, but it is less intimately connected with its cause than an *effect*; a *result* may be near or remote, and often is the sum of effects or consequences as making an end or final outcome: as, the *effect* of morphine is to produce sleep; he who will not obey must take the *consequences*; English is the *result* of the fusion of many different elements.

effect, *v.* **Syn.:** accomplish, achieve, realize, compass, fulfil, effectuate, make, do. See **do.**

Effect and *affect* are sometimes confused. To *effect* is to accomplish or bring about; to *affect* is to stir, change, or influence.

effective. **Syn.:** effectual, efficacious, efficient, capable, competent, potent, cogent, availing.

Effective is applied to that which has the power to or which actually does produce an (often lasting) effect: as, an *effective* action, remedy, or speech. *Efficacious* suggests the capability of achieving a certain end, a capability often manifested only when actually employed: as, an *efficacious* plan. *Effectual* is used especially of that which produces the effect desired or intended or a decisive result: as, an *effectual* bombardment silenced the enemy. *Efficient* is the most active of these words, and implies the use of energy, industry, or skill in accomplishing results: as, *efficient* methods, an *efficient* manager.

effects. **Syn.:** see **property.**

effectual. **Syn.:** see **effective.**

effeminate. **Syn.:** feminine, womanish, unmanly, weak. See **feminine.**

effervescence. **Syn.:** see **ebullition.**

effete. **Syn.:** unproductive, unfruitful, barren, exhausted, spent.

efficacious. **Syn.:** see **effective.**

efficacy. **Syn.:** effectiveness, efficiency, potency, virtue.

efficient. **Syn.:** effective, effectual, competent, capable. See **effective.**

effigy. **Syn.:** see **image.**

effort. **Syn.:** exertion, endeavor, attempt, trial, essay; labor, toil, strain, pains, trouble; achievement, production.

Effort is the expenditure of energy to accomplish some (usually single and definite) action or object: as, he made an *effort* to control himself. *Exertion* is the (vigorous and often strenuous) expenditure of energy, frequently without conscious reference to any definite object: as, to be out of breath from *exertion.* *Endeavor* is usually a continued and sustained series of efforts to achieve some, often worthy and difficult, end: as, a constant *endeavor* to be helpful.

effrontery. **Syn.:** impudence, boldness, audacity, hardi-hood, assurance, presumption, insolence, brass, cheek, gall. See **audacity.**

effulgence. **Syn.:** brilliance, radiance, luster, splendor.

effulgent. **Syn.:** see **bright.**

egg. **Syn.:** see **urge.**

egoism. **Syn.:** see **egotism.**

egotism. **Syn.:** egoism, self-conceit, vanity.

Egotism is the common word for obtrusive and excessive reference to and emphasis upon oneself and one's own importance, in conversation and writing, often to the monopoly of attention and disregard for others' opinion. *Egoism*, a less common word and used especially in philosophy, ethics, or metaphysics, where it emphasizes the importance of self in relation to other things, does not imply such obnoxious parade of self-conceit and boastfulness as egotism.

egotistic. **Syn.:** egoistic, self-conceited, self-important, vain, opinionated.

ejaculation. **Syn.:** see **exclamation.**

eject. **Syn.:** discharge, emit, exude; evict, oust, dislodge, dispossess, expel, dismiss. See **expel.**

elaborate. **Syn.:** detailed, minute, perfected, studied, painstaking, labored.

That which is *elaborate* is characterized by great, sometimes even excessive, nicety or minuteness of detail; that which is *studied* is accomplished with care and deliberation; that which is *labored* is marked by excessive, often forced or uninspired, effort: as, *elaborate* preparations for a banquet; a *studied* pose; a *labored* style of writing.

elastic. **Syn.:** rebounding, resilient, springy, buoyant, flexible.

elated. **Syn.:** exhilarated, exultant, jubilant, overjoyed, triumphant.

Elated implies high spirits, sometimes proudness of spirit, resulting from success or whatever is supremely good or beneficial; *exultant*, great rejoicing or elation, especially as manifested outwardly; *jubilant*, joyful demonstration, as in songs or acclamations; *triumphant*, the pride and glory of victory or achievement.

elder. **Syn.:** see **older.**

elderly. **Syn.:** see **old.**

elect. **Syn.:** pick, select, choose, prefer. See **choose.**

election. **Syn.:** selection, choice, freewill, preference, option, preferment.

electric. **Syn.:** electrical, electrifying, thrilling, stimulating, stirring, galvanizing, magnetic.

electrocute. **Syn.:** see **kill.**

elegance. **Syn.:** fineness, luxuriousness, sumptuousness, beauty, grace, exquisiteness, choiceness.

elegant. **Syn.:** fastidious, nice, fine, luxurious, polished, courtly, refined, polite, graceful, tasteful, exquisite, dainty, choice. **Ant.:** see **inelegant.** See **fine,** *a.*

elegy. **Syn.:** see **dirge.**

element. **Syn.:** see **constituent.**

elemental. **Syn.:** see **elementary.**

elementary. **Syn.:** elemental, rudimentary, primary, initial, simple.

Elementary is applied to what is primary or simple in its nature; *rudimentary*, to what is in an undeveloped or imperfect form or stage: as, *elementary* substances; *elementary* book or school; *rudimentary* gland or organ; even savages have a *rudimentary* form of government.

elevate. **Syn.:** raise, lift, hoist; promote, advance, exalt, ennoble; elate, exhilarate, cheer, inspire. See **raise.**

elevation. **Syn.:** raising, lifting, uplifting; promotion, advancement, exaltation, superiority, dignity, nobleness; loftiness, altitude; eminence, height, hill. See **height.**

elf. **Syn.:** see **fairy.**

elfish. **Syn.:** elfin, mischievous, prankish, impish.

elicit. **Syn.:** draw out, educe, evoke, extract, extort. See **extract.**

eliminate. **Syn.:** exclude, remove, erase, omit, except. See **exclude.**

elocution. **Syn.:** oratory, declamation, eloquence, delivery. See **oratory.**

eloquence. **Syn.:** see **oratory.**

elucidate. **Syn.:** see **explain.**

elude. **Syn.:** evade, avoid, shun, dodge, escape, baffle, foil, frustrate. See **evade.**

emanate. **Syn.:** see **issue.**

emancipate. **Syn.:** liberate, free, release, disenthrall, unfetter, unshackle, manumit, enfranchise. See **free,** *v.*

emancipation. Syn.: liberation, freedom, release, manumission, enfranchisement.

embankment. Syn.: bank, dike, levee, mound.

embarrass. Syn.: impede, hamper, hinder, obstruct; perplex, confuse, discompose, disconcert, discomfit, abash, mortify, chagrin; complicate, involve.

To *embarrass* is to render a person ill at ease or uncomfortable in feeling, so that as a result his usual judgment and presence of mind desert him: as, he was *embarrassed* by his friend's rudeness. To *discompose* is to disturb one's equilibrium as by perplexities, difficulties, disarrangement of plans, irritation, or the like: as, the chairman was *discomposed* by the remarks of the speaker. To *disconcert* is to discompose quickly or violently so that for a time it is difficult for one to collect his thoughts: as, the lecturer was *disconcerted* by the interruptions of the audience. To *discomfit* is to throw into perplexity or distress by foiling a plan or purpose, and usually to create a more or less mortifying sense of defeat: as, to *discomfit* the enemy.

embarrassment. Syn.: hampering, hindrance, entanglement; perplexity, bewilderment, discomposure, disconcertment, abashment, mortification, chagrin.

embellish. Syn.: beautify, ornament, decorate, adorn, garnish, bedeck, embroider. See **adorn.**

embellishment. Syn.: beautification, ornamentation, decoration, adornment, enrichment; ornament, trimming, garnish.

embezzle. Syn.: see **steal.**

emblem. Syn.: symbol, token, sign, figure, image, device, badge, type.

An *emblem* is usually some tangible object which, from some natural resemblance or fitness or from customary association, stands for some abstract quality, state, class of persons, etc.: as, the eagle is the *emblem* of the American spirit. A *symbol* is usually a recognized or conventional sign that represents something else, either with or without natural fitness, and is sometimes entirely arbitrary: as, a mathematical *symbol*; the olive branch is the *symbol* of peace. A *badge* is a distinctive token or mark that is used as a sign of position, authority, membership in a fraternal order, etc.: as, a police officer's *badge*; a Masonic *badge*. A *device* is an emblematic or decorative, often heraldic, representation, often containing a recondite allusion and frequently accompanied by a motto: as, the *device* of Richard the Lion-Hearted.

embody. Syn.: incorporate, combine, compact, comprise, embrace, include.

embrace. Syn.: hug, clasp; accept, adopt, espouse; include, embody, contain, comprise. See **include.**

embroider. Syn.: see **embellish.**

embroil. Syn.: confuse, disorder, disturb, distract, involve, implicate.

embryo. Syn.: fetus, germ, origin, rudiment.

emend. Syn.: see **amend.**

emerge. Syn.: see **issue.**

emergency. Syn.: exigency, crisis, strait, pinch, juncture.

An *emergency* is a sudden necessity for immediate action to avert undesirable consequences. An *exigency* is a difficult and perplexing situation in which something helpful must be done. A *crisis* is a vital, critical, or decisive exigency or turning point in a condition or state of affairs on the outcome of which everything depends. *Strait* suggests a pressing situation, often one of need or want, which usually makes necessary some difficult choice or alternative; *pinch*, the pressure or discomfort of (especially) poverty or deprivation.

emigrant. Syn.: immigrant, migrator.

emigrate. Syn.: see **migrate.**

eminence. Syn.: elevation, height, hill; distinction, prominence, superiority, rank, celebrity, renown.

eminent. Syn.: distinguished, prominent, celebrated, renowned, illustrious, famous, noted, noteworthy, signal.

Eminent suggests high standing in reputation, position, talent, or attainment; *prominent* means standing out conspicuously so as to draw attention to itself; *distinguished* describes that which is acknowledged to be superior to others of its kind.

emissary. Syn.: see **spy.**

emit. Syn.: send out, give forth, vent, belch, breathe out, exhale, exude, expel, eject, vomit.

To *emit* is to send forth or throw out, sometimes with considerable force: as, a volcano *emits* fire and lava. To *vent* is to let out at a (usually small) opening, frequently that

which has been compressed or condensed, or, figuratively, to give forcible expression to feelings, such as joy, anger, etc.: as, to *vent* one's wrath upon an enemy. To *exhale* is usually to give off by a natural or gradual process: as, the lungs *exhale* air; a rose *exhales* fragrance. To *exude* is to discharge, as by drops, through pores or small openings: as, the rocks of the cave *exuded* water.

emolument. Syn.: compensation, remuneration, profit, salary, stipend. See **gain,** n.

emotion. Syn.: see **feeling,** n.

emperor. Syn.: see **ruler.**

emphasis. Syn.: stress, accent, accentuation.

emphatic. Syn.: expressive, positive, earnest, energetic, forcible, striking, pronounced.

empire. Syn.: sovereignty, dominion, rule, sway, power; realm, domain, kingdom.

empiric. Syn.: see **quack.**

employ. Syn.: use, occupy, engage, hire. See **use.**

Employ implies a certain regularity and sometimes dignity in services to be rendered, and usually that they continue for a considerable time; *hire*, commoner or less dignified employment, and especially that the services are rendered for the sake of the pay; to *engage* is to enter into an agreement with a person for some definite and often dignified service: as, the directors *employed* the teacher for three years; he *employs* 3000 men in his factory; he *hired* a boy to show him through the grounds; the movement of labor requires that new men constantly be *hired*; they *engaged* a tutor for their children; to *engage* a nurse.

employment. Syn.: employ, service; occupation, work, trade, business, profession, vocation, function, office.

empower. Syn.: authorize, warrant, commission, license, qualify, enable, permit.

empty, a. **Syn.:** void, vacant, unoccupied, unfilled, blank, depleted, deflated; devoid, destitute; hollow, unsubstantial, meaningless, delusive, vain, vacuous, inane; frivolous, senseless, foolish. Cf. **destitute.**

Empty means that something is devoid of contents, whether intended to be filled or not; *vacant* usually applies to that which has been occupied, or is intended to be: as, an *empty* bottle, drawer, space; a *vacant* chair, throne, apartment; in an *empty* house there are no furnishings; in a *vacant* house no one is living. *Void* is used in a physical sense only in poetic or elevated diction, and conveys the impression of vast emptiness. The expression *void of* means completely lacking in: as, a mind *void of* original ideas. *Blank* especially refers to surfaces that are free from all marks, writing, decorations, or the like, or to surfaces lacking in markings, openings, etc., appropriate to them: as, a *blank* sheet of paper; a *blank* wall; a *blank* check.

empty, v. **Syn.:** discharge, unload, unburden, evacuate, deplete, deflate, disembogue.

emulation. Syn.: competition, rivalry, vying. See **competition.**

enable. Syn.: see **empower.**

enact. Syn.: see **decree.**

enamour. Syn.: charm, captivate, fascinate, bewitch.

enchant. Syn.: bewitch, charm, fascinate, captivate, enrapture, transport, delight. See **charm,** v.

enchantment. Syn.: magic, sorcery, spell, charm, fascination, witchery, ravishment, transport, glamour, illusion.

encircle. Syn.: surround, encompass, environ, gird, infold, inclose, circumscribe.

encomium. Syn.: see **eulogy.**

encompass. Syn.: see **encircle.**

encounter. Syn.: meeting, rencounter, conflict, combat, skirmish, brush. See **battle.**

encourage. Syn.: hearten, inspirit, animate, incite, urge, foment, stimulate, promote, advance.

encroach. Syn.: intrude, trespass, infringe, intrench, trench.

To *encroach* is to creep, as it were, upon territory, rights, or privileges gradually and often stealthily so that a footing is imperceptibly established: as, to *encroach* upon a person's time; the sea slowly *encroached* upon the land. To *infringe* is to break in upon or invade rights, customs, or the like by violating or disregarding them: as, no law should *infringe* upon the liberties of the press; to *infringe* upon a patent. To *trespass* is to pass unlawfully within the boundaries of another's property, or, figuratively, to make an improper or offensive inroad upon what is rightfully another's: as, hunters *trespass* on a farmer's fields; to *trespass* on a friend's leisure. To *intrench*, or more often now *trench*, is to cut, as it were, into another's land, rights, or sphere by pushing forward a trench; unlike *encroach*, it usually suggests what is done openly, decisively, or even presumptuously: as, certain laws *intrench* upon the rights of the individual. To *intrude* is to thrust oneself into the presence of a person or into places or circumstances where one is undesired: as, a reporter often *intrudes* upon people's privacy.

encumber. Syn.: impede, hamper, hinder, obstruct, burden, overload, oppress, embarrass. See **load.**

end, *n.* **Syn.:** extremity, tip, bound, limit, terminus; termination, conclusion, expiration, close, finish, finale, finis, peroration; death, destruction, extermination, annihilation, ruin; issue, outcome, result, consequence; purpose, intention, design, aim, object, goal; remnant, fragment, scrap.

end, *v.* **Syn.:** conclude, complete, finish, terminate, discontinue, stop, cease, close.

To *end* is to stop or discontinue a thing, usually with finality, whether completed or not: as, to *end* a discussion abruptly. To *finish* is to bring to an intended or fitting end, especially by making the last changes in a thing so as to perfect it: as, to *finish* one's toilet. To *terminate* is to bring to an end (especially as that end resembles a limit or boundary), usually something which has been continuous or in process for some time: as, to *terminate* a dispute or one's relations with another. To *conclude* is usually to bring to a formal, desired, or accepted termination: as, to *conclude* a treaty. To *close* is especially to bring to an end as if shutting something that was open: as, the firm *closed* its books at the end of the year.

endanger. Syn.: imperil, jeopard, jeopardize, risk, hazard. See **risk,** *v.*

endeavor, *n.* **Syn.:** effort, exertion, struggle, attempt, essay. See **effort.**

endeavor, *v.* **Syn.:** strive, struggle, labor, try, attempt, essay, undertake, seek, aim. See **try.**

endless. Syn.: boundless, limitless, illimitable, infinite, immeasurable, interminable, unending, incessant, unceasing, continuous, continual, perpetual, everlasting, eternal. **Ant.:** limited, finite, brief, transient, ephemeral, temporary.

endow. Syn.: furnish, equip, invest, clothe, endue.

To *endow* is to furnish or equip with or as with a gift, and is especially used of financial or of bodily or mental gifts: as, to *endow* an institution or a professorship; few men are *endowed* with genius. To *endue* is to invest as with a garment, and is especially used of moral or spiritual qualities: as, he is *endued* with piety and virtue; Iago was *endued* by Shakespeare with a rare villainy.

endowment. Syn.: donation, gift, bequest, fund; capacity, talent, faculty. See **genius.**

endue. Syn.: see **endow.**

endurance. Syn.: fortitude, patience, sufferance, forbearance, toleration, tolerance; continuance, duration, persistence. See **patience.**

endure. Syn.: undergo, suffer, bear, experience, tolerate, brook, stand; continue, abide, remain, last, persist. See **continue, bear.**

enduring. Syn.: abiding, lasting, permanent, unchangeable, imperishable. See **lasting.**

enemy. Syn.: adversary, antagonist, opponent, foe. See **opponent.**

energetic. Syn.: vigorous, strenuous, forcible, active, effective. See **active.**

energy. Syn.: vigor, force, potency, activity, zeal, push.

enervate. Syn.: unnerve, weaken, enfeeble, debilitate, relax. See **weaken.**

enfeeble. Syn.: see **weaken.**

enforce. Syn.: see **execute.**

enfranchise. Syn.: see **emancipate.**

engage. Syn.: pledge, bind, contract, promise, betroth, affiance, plight; hire, employ; involve, attract, occupy, engross.

engagement. Syn.: pledge, contract, agreement, promise, betrothal; encounter, combat, conflict. See **battle.**

engender. Syn.: beget, procreate, generate, breed, produce, cause, create, occasion, excite, stir up.

engrave. Syn.: carve, chisel, cut, impress, imprint.

engross. Syn.: see **absorb.**

enhance. Syn.: raise, heighten, increase, advance, intensify, augment.

enigma. Syn.: see **puzzle.**

enigmatic. Syn.: puzzling, perplexing, ambiguous, obscure, dark, mysterious.

enjoin. Syn.: prescribe, direct, order, command, charge, admonish, bid; prohibit, forbid, restrain. See **direct,** *v.*

enjoyment. Syn.: pleasure, delight, delectation, happiness, felicity, gratification, satisfaction.

enlarge. Syn.: increase, augment, amplify, magnify, broaden, extend, expand, dilate. See **increase,** *v.*

enlighten. Syn.: illumine, edify, instruct, teach, inform.

enlightenment. Syn.: see **culture.**

enlist. Syn.: see **enroll.**

enliven. Syn.: animate, inspirit, vivify, invigorate, stimulate, quicken, exhilarate, gladden, cheer, brighten. See **cheer,** *v.*

enmity. Syn.: hostility, hatred, animosity, ill-will, malevolence, malice, antipathy, antagonism, unfriendliness. See **ill-will.**

ennoble. Syn.: elevate, exalt, dignify, raise.

enormity. Syn.: enormousness.

Enormity is strictly limited to vastness in atrocity, baseness, or wickedness; *enormousness*, to vastness in extent or amount: as, the *enormity* of the crime; the *enormousness* of the ocean, of an undertaking, of an indemnity.

enormous. Syn.: huge, immense, vast, colossal, gigantic, mammoth, monstrous, prodigious, stupendous; outrageous, abominable, atrocious, heinous, flagrant.

Enormous, literally out of rule, is applicable to what exceeds in extent, magnitude, or degree, a norm or standard. *Huge* usually adds to the idea of great size that of massiveness, bulkiness, or even shapelessness. *Immense,* literally not measurable, is particularly applicable to what is exceedingly great without reference to a standard. *Mammoth, gigantic,* and *colossal,* all derived from objects of comparatively great size, are especially used of whatever is physically or metaphorically of extreme magnitude.

enough. Syn.: sufficiency, plenty, abundance. See **adequate.**

enrage. Syn.: infuriate, exasperate, incense, anger. See **irritate.**

enroll. Syn.: enlist, register, record, matriculate.

enslave. Syn.: enthrall, captivate, bewitch, subjugate, overcome.

ensue. Syn.: follow, succeed, result. See **follow.**

entangle. Syn.: tangle, snarl, knot, mat, complicate, enmesh, involve, insnare, embarrass, perplex, bewilder, confuse. See **implicate.**

enterprise. Syn.: project, plan, undertaking, venture; activity, energy, boldness, adventurousness.

enterprising. Syn.: alert, wide-awake, active, energetic, venturesome, adventurous. See **bold.**

entertain. Syn.: amuse, divert, beguile, recreate, delight; consider, harbor, hold, cherish. See **amuse.**

entertainment. Syn.: amusement, diversion, recreation, pastime, play, merriment, fun; hospitality, cheer, banquet, feast, collation.

enthrall. Syn.: see **enslave.**

enthusiasm. Syn: zeal, eagerness, warmth, ardor, fervor, fervency, passion, devotion. **Ant.:** indifference, lukewarmness, apathy, coldness. See **ardor.**

enthusiast. Syn.: zealot, fanatic, devotee, dreamer, visionary. See **zealot.**

enthusiastic. Syn.: zealous, eager, ardent, fervent, passionate, impassioned, devoted.

entice. Syn.: lure, attract, inveigle, decoy, tempt, wheedle, coax. See **lure.**

enticement. Syn.: allurement, inveiglement, beguilement; lure, decoy, bait.

entire. Syn.: whole, complete, full, undivided, continuous, unbroken, intact, unimpaired, undiminished. See **complete,** *a.*

entitle. Syn.: call, name, denominate, style, designate, dub; empower, enable, qualify.

entrance. Syn.: entry, ingress, admission; opening, passage, inlet, gate, gateway, door, doorway, portal, adit.

entrap. Syn.: insnare, catch, entangle, involve.

entreat. Syn.: beseech, supplicate, implore, importune, beg, solicit, request, ask. See **ask.**

entreaty. Syn.: supplication, prayer, appeal, solicitation, request, suit, petition.

enumerate. Syn.: count, number, recapitulate, recount, rehearse, detail, relate.

enunciate. Syn.: enounce, announce, proclaim, declare; utter, pronounce, articulate. See **utter,** *v.*

envelop, *n.* Syn.: see **cover**.

envelop, *v.* Syn.: wrap, infold, surround, cover, encompass, encircle, environ. See **wrap**.

environ. Syn.: see **encircle**.

envoy. Syn.: ambassador, plenipotentiary, legate, delegate, minister, attaché, diplomat, commissioner.

envy. Syn.: jealousy, covetousness.

Envy is a feeling of mortification and resentment because of the superior good fortune of another, which, without having any just claim to it, one desires for oneself. *Jealousy* is a suspicious or malign feeling directed against a rival for his actual or fancied attempt to obtain that which one possesses or desires or regards as one's own.

ephemeral. Syn.: short-lived, transitory, fleeting, evanescent, transient. See **fleeting**.

epicure. Syn.: gastronome, gourmet, gourmand, glutton.

An *epicure* is one who selects his food and drink with fastidious taste, but may freely indulge in that which he likes. A *gourmet* is a connoisseur in food and drink, and eats very daintily. A *gormand*, or *gourmand*, may appreciate fine food but is essentially greedy and intemperate in eating.

episode. Syn.: see **event**.

epistle. Syn.: see **letter**.

epitome. Syn.: see **abridgment**.

epitomize. Syn.: abridge, summarize, condense, reduce.

epoch. Syn.: era, age, period. See **age**.

equable. Syn.: uniform, regular, unvarying, steady, smooth, even, tranquil. See **even**.

equal, *n.* Syn.: peer, compeer, match, mate, equivalent.

equal, *a.* Syn.: equivalent, tantamount, proportionate, commensurate, coördinate, correspondent, adequate, sufficient; even, uniform, regular, unvarying. **Ant.**: see **unequal**.

Equal indicates a correspondence in all respects unless a particular respect (or particular respects) be stated or implied: as, the angles of an equilateral triangle are *equal* (*i.e.*, in all respects); a dime is *equal* to ten cents (*i.e.*, in respect to purchasing power, which is understood). *Equivalent* indicates a correspondence in one or more respects, but not in all: as, it is popularly said that an egg is the *equivalent* of a pound of meat (*i.e.*, in nutritive value). *Tantamount*, a word of limited application, is used especially of immaterial things that are practically identical: as, the prisoner's refusal to answer was *tantamount* to an admission of guilt.

equanimity. Syn.: equability, calmness, composure, self-possession, serenity, tranquillity. See **composure**.

equilibrium. Syn.: equipoise, balance.

equip. Syn.: fit out, furnish, appoint, provide, array, accoutre.

To *equip* is to supply with the necessary materials, appliances, or apparatus for some service, action, or undertaking: as, the vessel is *equipped* for the voyage. To *appoint*, used especially in the past participle, is to equip with all requisites and accessories: as, well-*appointed* lodgings. To *accoutre* is especially to equip with military accessories (except arms and clothing).

equipment. Syn.: outfit, apparatus, paraphernalia, equipage, gear, rigging, furniture, dress, habiliments, accoutrements.

equitable. Syn.: fair, reasonable, just, right, upright. See **fair**.

equity. Syn.: see **justice**.

equivalent. Syn.: see **equal**, *a.*

equivocal. Syn.: ambiguous, uncertain, doubtful, enigmatic, questionable, dubious, suspicious. **Ant.**: unequivocal, unambiguous, certain, evident, manifest, obvious, unquestionable, indisputable. See **ambiguous**.

equivocate. Syn.: prevaricate, quibble, shuffle.

To *equivocate* is consciously to use words in a double and deceptive sense so that either one of two possible meanings may be taken from them or so that the apparent meaning conceals the truth. To *quibble* is to evade the truth or the real point at issue by insisting upon trifling or unimportant distinctions or objections, especially in the meaning of words. To *shuffle* is to answer in an evasive or shifty way, usually to extricate oneself from some unpleasant position or condition. To *prevaricate* is to evade the truth by using loose or indefinite language, or it may be actually to employ untruth.

era. Syn.: see **age**.

eradicate. Syn.: see **exterminate**.

erase. Syn.: rub out, efface, expunge, obliterate, delete, remove. See **efface**.

erect, *a.* Syn.: upright, perpendicular, vertical, standing.

Ant.: horizontal, oblique, recumbent, prone. See **upright**.

erect, *v.* Syn.: upraise, uprear; raise, build, construct, establish, institute, found, form.

err. Syn.: stray, deviate, wander, mistake, blunder, sin.

errand. Syn.: see **mission**.

erratic. Syn.: wandering, deviating, eccentric, queer.

erroneous. Syn.: mistaken, incorrect, inaccurate, wrong, untrue, false. See **wrong**, *a.*

error. Syn.: mistake, blunder, slip, oversight, misapprehension, misconception, incorrectness, inaccuracy; wrongdoing, sin.

Error and *mistake* are frequently interchangeable. An *error* is an unintentional wandering or deviation from accuracy, correctness, truth, or right: as, an *error* of grammar. A *mistake* is a false judgment or a disregard of rule or principle: as, it was a *mistake* to discuss the matter. A *blunder* is a careless, stupid, or gross mistake in action or speech, committed through heedlessness, awkwardness, or ignorance: as, the clerk's *blunder* confused the orders. A *slip* is usually a minor mistake made through haste or carelessness: as, a *slip* of the tongue. An *oversight* is a mistake that results from inadvertently overlooking something: as, not to deduct the discount was an *oversight*.

erudition. Syn.: see **learning**.

escape. Syn.: flee, abscond, decamp, elope; shun, avoid, evade, elude. See **evade**.

eschew. Syn.: see **avoid**.

escort. Syn.: accompany, conduct, usher, attend, guard, convoy. See **accompany**.

esoteric. Syn.: see **obscure**, **secret**.

especial. Syn.: see **special**.

especially. Syn.: specially, particularly, chiefly, principally, primarily, mainly, mostly.

Especially and *particularly* single out the foremost case or example from others of the same class or kind, and are therefore exclusive and superlative in import: as, we ought to be kind to all people, but *especially* to the old; heat is oppressive in the torrid zone, but *particularly* in the desert regions. *Chiefly* and *principally* refer to the majority of cases out of any number, and have a more or less comparative force, *chiefly* being a stronger term than *principally*: as, owls fly *chiefly* at night; crime occurs *principally* in the lower classes of society. *Mainly* and *mostly* have much the same significance as *chiefly* or *principally*, *mainly* being particularizing, *mostly* distributive: as, environment was *mainly* responsible for his crime; the use of tobacco is *mostly* a habit.

espy. Syn.: discern, descry, discover, perceive.

essay, *n.* Syn.: effort, endeavor, attempt; article, treatise, tract, tractate, thesis, dissertation, disquisition.

essay, *v.* Syn.: see **try**.

essential. Syn.: necessary, indispensable, fundamental, requisite, vital. See **necessary**.

establish. Syn.: fix, settle, confirm, strengthen, sanction, ordain; institute, found, form, organize; prove, verify, substantiate. See **fix**.

estate. Syn.: see **property**.

esteem, *n.* Syn.: estimation, favor, regard, respect, admiration, honor, reverence, veneration. **Ant.**: disesteem, disrespect, contempt, odium, unpopularity. See **respect**.

esteem, *v.* Syn.: rate, value, prize, regard, respect, honor, revere; consider, think, deem, hold, account. See **appreciate**, **think**.

estimable. Syn.: calculable, computable; reputable, respectable, worthy, meritorious, excellent.

Estimable is applied in dignified language to persons deemed worthy of esteem. *Reputable* indicates the possession of a reputation generally recognized as good. *Respectable*, formerly in general use to attribute to a person a just title to public respect, now suggests no more than ordinarily fair or decent character. *Worthy*, formerly a term of respectful commendation, now often implies an attitude of condescension on the part of the user.

estimate. Syn.: calculate, compute, count, reckon, judge, gage.

estimation. Syn.: calculation, computation, judgment, opinion; appreciation, regard, respect, esteem, honor, admiration, veneration.

estrange. Syn.: see **alienate**.

eternal. Syn.: everlasting, perpetual, endless, interminable, enduring, imperishable, immortal, deathless, undying, timeless, æonian.

Eternal means primarily without beginning or end in duration, but it especially emphasizes continuance in the future; *everlasting* is frequently interchanged with *eternal*, but particularly means lasting from the present to an endless future. Both words have frequently a sacred association: as, the *eternal* God and His *everlasting* mercy. *Perpetual* points to the future and applies especially to that which though not necessarily continuous is so firmly rooted that it will last forever: as, the *perpetual* wars between nations. However, *perpetual* is used by hyperbole for that which lasts seemingly for an indefinitely long time, in which sense *interminable* is also used with the added idea that the matter described is prolonged to a length that becomes irksome: as, a *perpetual* feud; *interminable* talk or dispute.

ethereal. Syn.: heavenly, celestial, empyreal; airy, aërial, light, tenuous, intangible, impalpable, subtle, delicate, refined, thin, rare. See **spiritual.**

ethical. Syn.: see **moral.**

etiquette. Syn.: see **propriety.**

eulogize. Syn.: praise, laud, extol, panegyrize, commend. See **praise.**

eulogy. Syn.: praise, laudation, panegyric, encomium, commendation.

Eulogy implies warm praise, usually in a more or less set form and often of a deceased person; *panegyric*, formal public praise, often exaggerating or undiscriminating; *encomium*, general praise, applied to either persons or things: as, Everett's *Eulogy* upon the Pilgrim Fathers; a *panegyric* on democracy; to bestow *encomiums* upon a work of art.

evade. Syn.: elude, escape, avoid, shun, dodge, shirk, parry, baffle, foil, prevaricate, equivocate, quibble, tergiversate.

To *evade* is to go out of the reach of a person or thing, usually by dexterity, artifice, or stratagem: as, to *evade* the police, a question. To *elude* is to avoid, often by vigilance, adroitness, dexterity, or slyness, so as to baffle or foil: as, to *elude* a pursuer, justice, or detection. To *dodge* is to get away from by quick movements or shifts, or to deal indirectly or evasively with: as, to *dodge* a blow, the point of a discussion. To *escape* is actually to succeed in evading or eluding danger, pursuit, observation, etc.: as, to *escape* punishment; to *escape* notice.

evanesce. Syn.: see **disappear.**

evanescent. Syn.: disappearing, vanishing, fleeting, transitory, ephemeral.

evasion. Syn.: avoidance, dodging, prevarication, equivocation, shuffling, quibble, shift, subterfuge.

even. Syn.: level, plane, flat, smooth, regular, uniform, unvarying, equable, unruffled. **Ant.:** see **uneven.** See **level,** *a.*

Even implies freedom from inequalities or irregularities; *uniform* emphasizes the idea of sameness or of conformity to a standard; *equable* suggests the inherent quality of regularity or of being well balanced, fair: as, *even* breathing or flow; a *uniform* law, height, or practice; an *equable* temperature or decision.

evening. Syn.: even, eventide, dusk, twilight, gloaming, nightfall, darkness, night.

event. Syn.: occurrence, incident, happening, episode, affair, circumstance, case, chance; outcome, result, consequence, conclusion.

An *event* is usually an important happening, especially one that comes out of and is connected with previous happenings: as, historical *events.* An *occurrence* is something (usually of an ordinary nature) that happens, with no particular connection with or causation from antecedent happenings: as, his arrival was an unexpected *occurrence.* An *incident* is usually an occurrence which takes place in connection with an event or a series of events of greater importance: as, an amusing *incident* in a play. An *episode* is one of a progressive series of happenings, frequently distinct from the main course of events but arising naturally from them, and having a continuity and interest of its own: as, an *episode* in one's life. A *circumstance* is not necessarily anything that happens or takes place, but may be one of the surrounding or accompanying conditions of an event, occurrence, or incident; but it may be a secondary or subordinate happening that is a distinctive accessory to the principal fact, event, or occurrence, to which it may be of very little moment or upon which it may react with great force: as, an unforeseen *circumstance* changed the outcome of the battle.

eventual. Syn.: see **final.**

ever. Syn.: always, forever, eternally, perpetually, constantly, continuously, incessantly. See **always.**

everlasting. Syn.: see **eternal.**

every. Syn.: each, any, either, both, all.

Each and *every* are distributive (as *all* and *both* are collective), but *each* directs attention to the members composing a (usually) definite aggregate, while *every* emphasizes the idea of inclusiveness, or universality, and is generally used of an indefinite number: as, *each* cause (of those considered or enumerated) has its partizans; *every* cause (of all in existence) has its partizans.

evidence. Syn.: information, testimony, proof, exhibit, deposition, affidavit.

Evidence is any information, whether given by witnesses or derived from documents or from any other source, that is furnished in a legal investigation to support a contention. *Testimony* is usually evidence given by witnesses under oath. *Proof* is evidence that is so complete and convincing as to put a conclusion beyond reasonable doubt. An *exhibit* in law is a document or article which is presented in court as evidence.

evident. Syn.: plain, clear, obvious, manifest, apparent, palpable, patent, conspicuous, unmistakable. See **manifest.**

evil, *n.* **Syn.:** harm, mischief, disaster, calamity; wickedness, sin, iniquity, depravity, unrighteousness.

evil, *a.* **Syn.:** bad, harmful, pernicious (see **bad**); wicked, sinful, iniquitous, depraved, vicious, corrupt, immoral, base.

evince. Syn.: see **show,** *v.*

evolution. Syn.: see **development.**

exact, *a.* **Syn.:** precise, accurate, correct, nice, literal, strict, rigid, rigorous, severe, methodical, careful, punctilious. See **accurate.**

exact, *v.* **Syn.:** force, compel, extort, extract, wrest, wring, demand, require. See **extract.**

exaggerate. Syn.: magnify, overstate, stretch, color, caricature.

exaggeration. Syn.: overstatement, hyperbole.

exalt. Syn.: elevate, promote, dignify, ennoble, apotheosize, glorify, extol, laud, praise.

exalted. Syn.: elevated, lofty, sublime, dignified, noble, grand.

examination. Syn.: inspection, scrutiny, investigation, search, research, inquiry, inquisition, inquest, autopsy.

All these words express an active effort to find out that which is unknown. An *examination* is an attempt to obtain greater insight into something, often something open to observation, by the scrutiny of details: as, a physical or a civil service *examination.* An *investigation* is a systematic, minute, and thorough examination, usually formal and often official, which tracks back, as it were, from what is observed or known to what is complex or hidden: as, an *investigation* of a bank failure. An *inquiry* is an examination made by asking questions, or, figuratively, by study or investigation; an *inquisition* is a thorough and searching inquiry, usually legal or ecclesiastical, conducted with vigor, severity, or even persecution. *Research* is careful and sustained investigation, usually into remote recesses of knowledge.

examine. Syn.: inspect, scrutinize, investigate, search, probe, explore, test, interrogate, question, catechize, review, study, consider, canvass, discuss, debate.

example. Syn.: specimen, sample; paragon, pattern, model, archetype, prototype, ideal, standard, type; precedent, instance, illustration, case.

The following words when used of persons or personal conduct imply a standard generally to be followed. An *example* is a person or his action or conduct regarded as worthy of being followed or imitated in a general way, or sometimes, as properly to be avoided: as, an *example* of courage; an *example* of drunkenness. While *pattern* and *model* both refer primarily to some physical shape that is to be closely copied, they likewise refer to examples of conduct or character that are excellent to follow: as, a *pattern* of propriety; a *model* of unselfishness. A *precedent* is an example (especially in law) that may be taken as authority or justification for similar action in a subsequent, analogous case or decision: as, to set a dangerous *precedent.* A *paragon* is a model or pattern of supreme merit or excellence: as, a *paragon* of virtue. An *ideal* is a conception or standard of perfection in a person or conduct, which others emulate, ordinarily imaginary but sometimes, by hyperbole, real: as, the *ideals* of democracy; Sir Philip Sidney was considered the *ideal* of a gentleman.

exasperate. Syn.: exacerbate, irritate, incense, enrage, anger, nettle, chafe, vex, provoke. See **irritate.**

excavation. Syn.: see **hole.**

exceed. Syn.: overstep, transcend, surpass, outdo.

excel. Syn.: surpass, outdo, outstrip, eclipse.

To *excel* is to be superior to others in some (usually) good or desirable quality, attainment, or performance: as, in politeness the French *excel* all other nations. To *surpass* is to go beyond another, especially in a matter of competition or where a definite comparison is suggested: as, he *surpassed* all his associates in a knowledge of corporation law. To *eclipse* is to surpass as if by overshadowing the ability, power, attainment, etc. of another: as, Napoleon *eclipsed* all the other generals of Europe.

excellence. Syn.: superiority, preëminence, transcendence; merit, worth, goodness, virtue.

excellent. Syn.: superior, meritorious, worthy, estimable, good, valuable, choice, select, fine, exquisite, first-rate.

except. Syn.: see **unless.**

exceptionable. Syn.: objectionable, undesirable, displeasing, offensive. Cf. **exceptional.**

exceptional. Syn.: unusual, uncommon, peculiar, singular, extraordinary, superior. Cf. **exceptionable.**

From their similarity of sound the two following words are sometimes confused, but in meaning they are entirely distinct. That is *exceptional* which forms an exception or unusual instance, sometimes to the point of being remarkable; *exceptionable* is that to which exception may be taken, usually on account of its objectionableness or undesirability: as, *exceptional* advantages; an *exceptional* student; there were some *exceptionable* passages in the book.

excess. Syn.: superabundance, exuberance, superfluity, redundancy, immoderation, prodigality, intemperance, dissipation; overplus, surplus, surplusage, waste, residue, remainder. **Ant.:** dearth, deficiency, inadequacy, insufficiency, scantiness, lack, want.

Excess denotes whatever is over and above the normal, needful, or desirable. *Superabundance* usually denotes a satisfactory and pleasing surplus; *superfluity*, a needless, undesirable, or wasteful excess. *Redundancy* is especially applied to speech or writing to denote the use of more words than are necessary or useful.

excessive. Syn.: superabundant, superfluous, extravagant, immoderate, intemperate, extreme, inordinate, exorbitant.

Excessive means going beyond what is requisite or proper; that which is *exorbitant* is usually extortionately excessive, as from a desire to obtain more than is proper or just in charges or demands; *inordinate* denotes that which is not restrained within proper bounds and is used especially of human desires: as, *excessive* praise; *exorbitant* rates of interest; *inordinate* desire for wealth.

exchange, n. Syn.: interchange, commutation, reciprocity, barter, trade, traffic.

exchange, v. Syn.: interchange, commute, barter, trade, traffic, truck, swap, bandy.

Exchange usually implies a single act of giving and receiving reciprocally; *interchange*, a succession or repetition of such acts, often involving more than two persons or things and sometimes suggesting mutual advantage: as, to *exchange* greetings; to *exchange* coupons for a prize; to *interchange* ideas.

excitable. Syn.: emotional, passionate, susceptible, hasty, fiery, irritable, irascible, choleric. **Ant.:** impossible, impassive, imperturbable, calm, serene, tranquil.

excite. Syn.: stir, rouse, arouse, awaken, stimulate, animate, kindle, inflame, agitate, perturb, provoke.

excitement. Syn.: agitation, perturbation, commotion, ado, tumult, sensation.

Excitement implies a highly emotional state or condition, experienced either by a single person or by a group and caused either by agreeable or distressing circumstances. *Agitation* implies a state of mental disturbance, as though caused by a shaking of the emotions, which is usually perceptible in the face or movements of a person. *Perturbation* may be less manifest in visible nervousness, but often involves a more profound disturbance of one's tranquillity.

exclaim. Syn.: cry, shout, ejaculate, vociferate.

exclamation. Syn.: cry, outcry, ejaculation, interjection.

An *exclamation* may be either an emphatic or emotional sentence or a series of connected words with definite meaning, or a mere interjection indicative of surprise, joy, grief, anger, pain, etc., and may be the simultaneous expression of a number of people. An *ejaculation* is a brief and abrupt exclamation uttered by a single person.

exclude. Syn.: shut out, debar, preclude, except, omit, eliminate, reject, eject, expel, extrude, exile.

To *exclude* is to keep from entering; to *debar* is to keep out, especially by authority or force, from a place or from the use or enjoyment of privileges, rights, or the like; to *eliminate* is to put out or remove, especially as irrelevant, unnecessary, or undesirable.

exclusive. Syn.: undivided, single, sole; select, narrow, clannish, snobbish.

excretion. Syn.: discharge, elimination, exudation, secretion.

exculpate. Syn.: exonerate, absolve, acquit, vindicate, pardon, excuse.

To *acquit* is to release or relieve from a specific and usually formal accusation or charge by a decision, especially legal or judicial, either through evidence of innocence or lack of evidence of guilt. To *exculpate* is to prove innocent of a particular crime or fault. To *exonerate* is to disburden a person from the blame, consequences, or obloquy attaching to an act, even when the act is admitted. To *absolve* is to loose or free from sin or guilt or its consequences, especially by divine or ecclesiastical remission, or from such ties or bonds as obligations, oaths, promises, or the like, failure to observe which would imply a grave fault: as, God *absolves* the sins of the repentant; to *absolve* a person from a responsibility.

excursion. Syn.: sally, raid, sortie; expedition, journey, tour, trip, jaunt, ramble; digression, excursus. See **journey.**

excursus. Syn.: see **digression.**

excusable. Syn.: justifiable, pardonable, venial. See **pardonable.**

excuse, n. Syn.: apology, justification, plea, pretext, subterfuge. See **apology.**

excuse, v. Syn.: justify, extenuate, palliate; forgive, pardon, condone, overlook, absolve, exculpate, release, exempt. See **pardon.**

execrable. Syn.: cursed, abominable, detestable, hateful, odious, obnoxious, vile.

execrate. Syn.: curse, anathematize; abominate, detest, abhor.

execration. Syn.: see **curse.**

execute. Syn.: perform, accomplish, fulfil, complete, consummate; administer, enforce; kill, hang, electrocute, behead, guillotine. See **kill, do.**

exemplar. Syn.: see **pattern.**

exemption. Syn.: immunity, impunity, dispensation.

Exemption implies release or privileged safety from sharing with others some (usually arbitrarily imposed) obligation, duty, tax, or penalty: as, *exemption* from an income tax. *Immunity* implies freedom from a penalty or from some natural or common liability, especially one that is disagreeable or threatening: as, *immunity* from punishment, disease, or pain. *Impunity* primarily suggests freedom from punishment: as, the police force was so inadequate that crimes could be committed with *impunity*.

exercise, n. Syn.: use, employment, application, practice, effort, exertion; ceremony, performance; training, discipline, drilling, drill; lesson, task; gymnastics, calisthenics.

Exercise is either physical or mental exertion for the sake of health, training, or enjoyment, and may be more or less irregular in time and varied in kind: as, to take a walk for *exercise* when the weather is pleasant. *Practice* is methodical exercise, usually characterized by much repetition, with a view to becoming perfect in some operation or pursuit: as, even great musicians require constant *practice*. *Drill* is disciplined practice, often of a group, directed by a leader: as, a fire *drill*, military *drill*, grammar *drill*.

exercise, v. Syn.: use, employ, apply, practise, exert, wield; train, develop, discipline, drill; perturb, worry, distress, annoy.

exertion. Syn.: effort, endeavor, struggle, attempt.

exhale. Syn.: see **emit.**

exhaust. Syn.: drain, empty, deplete, use up, consume, spend; tire, fatigue, debilitate, enervate, prostrate.

exhaustion. Syn.: depletion, consumption; fatigue, weariness, lassitude, languor, prostration, collapse.

exhibit, n. Syn.: see **evidence, exhibition.**

exhibit, v. Syn.: show, display, manifest, evince, reveal, disclose, expose. See **show, v.**

exhibition. Syn.: exhibit, show, display, exposition.

An *exhibition* is an array of works of art, natural or manufactured products, etc., for public inspection. An *exhibit* is a small exhibition or a section of an exhibition, usually devoted to some industry or group of products, or it may be an object or group of objects in such a section, sometimes in competition with others of the same class for an award or prize. An *exposition* (borrowed from French usage) is usually a large, national or international exhibition, as a world's fair.

exhilarate. Syn.: cheer, gladden, enliven, animate, inspirit. See **cheer,** *v.*

exhilaration. Syn.: animation, joyousness, gaiety, jollity, hilarity.

exhort. Syn.: urge, advise, admonish, warn, caution, incite, encourage. See **urge.**

exhortation. Syn.: see **sermon.**

exhume. Syn.: see **disinter.**

exigency. Syn.: urgency, need, necessity, pressure, demand, requirement; emergency, crisis, strait, pinch. See **emergency.**

exile, *n.* **Syn.:** banishment, expulsion, expatriation, proscription, ostracism.

exile, *v.* **Syn.:** see **banish.**

exonerate. Syn.: see **exculpate.**

exorbitant. Syn.: inordinate, excessive, extravagant, unreasonable, unconscionable, fabulous. See **excessive.**

expand. Syn.: spread, unfold, unfurl, extend, distend, dilate, swell, enlarge, increase. **Ant.:** see **contract.**

To *expand* is to spread out usually in every direction so as to occupy more space or have a larger capacity: as, steel *expands* when heated; to *expand* a business. To *dilate* is especially to increase the width or circumference, and applies to space enclosed within confines or to hollow bodies: as, his heart *dilated* with pride. To *distend* is especially to stretch or swell out as by inflation, often beyond the point of natural expansion: as, to *distend* an artery, or (figuratively) *distended* credit. The first word often denotes an increase in the substance; the last two usually do not have this suggestion.

expanse. Syn.: see **extent.**

expatiate. Syn.: dilate, descant, enlarge, harp.

The following words have a more or less derogatory implication of unnecessary or excessive amplification. To *expatiate* is to discourse with leisurely fullness; to *dilate* is to discourse expansively, often through vanity; to *descant* is to enlarge or dwell upon a matter in a variety of remarks or comments; to *harp* is to persist in discussing or reverting to a subject, or especially a detail or details, with monotonous or tiresome iteration.

expatriate. Syn.: see **banish.**

expect. Syn.: anticipate, hope.

Expect, anticipate, and *hope* all look forward to something in the future. We *expect* something, either desirable or undesirable, which probability points to; we *anticipate* what we can project ourselves into as though it had happened, so that we can foretaste the pleasure or good that is coming, or can realize the bad beforehand and take measures to meet it; we *hope* for that which directly or indirectly benefits us and which there is some possibility of attaining: as, we *hope* to settle the matter amicably and have *anticipated* some of the difficulties we are likely to meet, and *expect* to have trouble. The use of *expect* for suppose is colloquial, and since *expect* refers to the future, its application to things of the present and past is to be condemned: as, I *expect* he is waiting in the next room; I *expect* he was frightened by the noise.

expectation. Syn.: expectancy, anticipation, hope, trust, presumption.

expedient, *n.* **Syn.:** resort, resource, shift, device, contrivance, means. See **means.**

expedient, *a.* **Syn.:** advantageous, profitable, advisable, wise, desirable, suitable, fit.

expedite. Syn.: hasten, quicken, speed, despatch, push. See **promote.**

expedition. Syn.: promptness, haste, quickness, speed, despatch; journey, voyage, trip, excursion, raid. See **haste, journey.**

expeditious. Syn.: see **prompt.**

expel. Syn.: drive out, banish, exile, expatriate, dislodge, eject, oust, discharge, dismiss.

The idea of exclusion or forcible removal from a place is common to all these words. To *expel,* literally to drive out, is to force out from a country, community, institution, or organization, usually in disgrace. To *eject* is to throw out,

especially from office or occupancy, as an indolent employee, a tenant. *Oust* is a less formal word for eject.

expend. Syn.: see **spend.**

expense. Syn.: expenditure, disbursement, outlay, cost, charge. See **price.**

expensive. Syn.: see **costly.**

experience. Syn.: observation, association, contact; trial, proof, experiment. See **undergo.**

Experience refers to the past and concerns what has befallen us or what we have learned by personal observation or participation. On the other hand, *experiment* looks to the future, and is a test conducted to prove or illustrate the truth or validity of something or an attempt to discover something new. *Observation* is attentive and careful looking at a thing, usually with a view to becoming more closely acquainted with it or deriving some additional information from it.

experienced. Syn.: skilled, expert, practised, veteran.

experiment. Syn.: see **trial, experience.**

expert, *n.* **Syn.:** proficient, adept, connoisseur, master, authority, specialist. **Ant.:** novice, tyro, beginner, amateur, smatterer, bungler.

An *expert* is one whose knowledge, skill, or proficiency in any branch of thought or activity distinguishes him conspicuously above others and often makes him an authority in his field: as, an *expert* in alienism, chemistry, or transportation. A *proficient* is one who is well advanced in any field of knowledge or activity: as, a *proficient* in politics. An *adept* is one who possesses natural as well as acquired aptitude or skill in anything: as, an *adept* in the art of governing, in diplomacy, lying, cajolery, or whist-playing.

expert, *a.* **Syn.:** experienced, practised, skilled, trained, proficient, skilful, dexterous, adroit.

expertness. Syn.: skill, dexterity, adroitness, facility, knack.

expiation. Syn.: see **atonement.**

expire. Syn.: see **die.**

explain. Syn.: elucidate, explicate, expound, analyze, interpret.

To *explain* is to make plain, clear, or intelligible something that is not known or understood: as, to *explain* a theory, problem, or one's reasons for doing a thing. To *interpret* is to give the meaning of something, either by a translation, or by an explanation (sometimes involving one's personal opinion and therefore original), often of a systematic and detailed nature: as, to *interpret* a poem, song, symbol, dream, or a man's actions. To *expound* is to give a methodical, elaborate, or scholarly explanation of something, especially Scriptures, doctrines, or philosophy. To *elucidate* is to throw light upon what before was dark or obscure, usually by illustration and commentary, and sometimes with the same elaborateness suggested in *expound.*

explanation. Syn.: elucidation, explication, exposition, definition, interpretation, solution, key.

explicit. Syn.: express, definite, precise, exact, unequivocal, unambiguous, unmistakable, positive, outspoken. **Ant.:** vague, indefinite, ambiguous, implied.

Explicit (literally unfolded) is applied to what is clear, definite, and so detailed that it cannot fail to be understood: as, *explicit* directions; an *explicit* statement of one's meaning. *Express* combines clearness and definiteness with force or emphasis, so that a thing will not easily be passed over or disregarded: as, an *express* denial or command.

explode. Syn.: burst, detonate; discredit, disprove.

exploit. Syn.: see **feat.**

explore. Syn.: see **search.**

expose. Syn.: subject (to), endanger, imperil, jeopardize; exhibit, show, display; reveal, disclose, uncover, unveil, unmask, denounce. See **show,** *v.*

exposition. Syn.: disclosure, exposure, exposé; display, exhibition, fair, show; explanation, elucidation, commentary. See **exhibition.**

expostulate. Syn.: remonstrate, argue, reason.

exposure. Syn.: disclosure, divulgement, revelation, exposé.

expound. Syn.: see **explain.**

express, *a.* **Syn.:** see **explicit.**

express, *v.* **Syn.:** utter, declare, state, say; signify, indicate, denote, designate, represent, mean.

expression. Syn.: utterance, declaration, assertion, statement; language, diction, phraseology, phrase, term, **word;** manifestation, indication, sign, token; look, aspect, **air,** intonation, modulation. See **word.**

expressive. Syn.: indicative, suggestive, significant, meaning, vivid.

Expressive suggests the conveying of a meaning or thought, by words or otherwise, in an effective or vivid manner: as, an *expressive* phrase; an *expressive* shrug. *Significant* and *meaning* imply an underlying and unexpressed thought whose existence is plainly shown although its precise nature is left to conjecture: as, *significant* or *meaning* glances. *Suggestive* implies an indirect or covert conveying of a meaning, sometimes mentally stimulating, sometimes verging on impropriety or indecency: as, a *suggestive* remark or story.

expunge. Syn.: strike out, cancel, erase, efface, obliterate, annihilate, destroy. See **efface.**

exquisite, *n.* **Syn.:** see **dandy.**

exquisite, *a.* **Syn.:** consummate, perfect, matchless, incomparable; delicate, dainty, fine, beautiful, elegant, rare, discriminating, fastidious, refined; intense, acute, keen, poignant. See **fine,** *a.*

extemporaneous. Syn.: extemporary, extempore, impromptu, improvised, offhand, unpremeditated.

As applied to speech, *extempore, extemporary*, and *extemporaneous* emphasize a lack, total or partial, of preparation. *Impromptu* may have the same meaning, but more often refers to a speech delivered at a moment's notice. *Improvised* suggests a speech fabricated quickly for an occasion and generally implies one that is in part at least made up as the speaker goes along.

extemporary, extempore. Syn.: see **extemporaneous.**

extend. Syn.: stretch out, spread, expand, enlarge, widen, lengthen, prolong, protract, continue; reach, project, jut; give, bestow, impart. See **lengthen.**

extension. Syn.: stretching, expansion, enlargement, prolongation; projection, addition.

extensive. Syn.: extended, broad, large, spacious, comprehensive, ample, vast.

Extensive applies to what stretches over a wide area or is comprehensive in its scope; *spacious* implies largeness and roominess; *vast* suggests immense extent, size, number, etc.: as, *extensive* tracts were flooded by the river; *spacious* halls and corridors; a *vast* empire.

extent. Syn.: magnitude, size, area, length, measure, amount, scope, compass, range, expanse, stretch, reach.

extenuate. Syn.: see **palliate.**

exterior. Syn.: outer, outward, outside, outlying, external, extraneous, extrinsic. See **outer.**

exterminate. Syn.: extirpate, eradicate, abolish, destroy, annihilate. See **destroy.**

Eradicate (literally to pull up by the roots) suggests less violent and more superficial rooting out than *extirpate*, which implies a complete and final removal as though by both roots and stalk: as, to *eradicate* obnoxious weeds or insects; to *eradicate* graft or abuses; to *extirpate* a cancer, a sect.

external. Syn.: see **outer.**

extinct. Syn.: see **dead.**

extirpate. Syn.: see **exterminate.**

extol. Syn.: praise, commend, laud, eulogize, glorify. See **praise.**

extort. Syn.: see **exact.**

extortion. Syn.: exaction, oppression, overcharge.

extortionate. Syn.: oppressive, exorbitant, excessive.

extra. Syn.: additional, supplemental, supplementary, supernumerary.

extract, *n.* **Syn.:** essence, tincture, quintessence; excerpt, citation, quotation, selection, passage.

extract, *v.* **Syn.:** draw out, elicit, exact, extort, wrest, separate, withdraw, distil; derive, obtain, deduce.

To *extract* is to draw forth something as by pulling, importuning, or the like: as, to *extract* a confession by the third degree. To *elicit* is to draw out often something potential or hidden: as, to *elicit* sympathy by a sad story. To *exact* is to impose a penalty, or to obtain by force or authority something to which one lays claim: as, to *exact* tribute, payment, obedience. To *extort* is usually to wring out by intimidation or threats from an unwilling person: as, to *extort* money by blackmail. To *wrest* is to take by force or violence: as, the usurper *wrested* the power from the king.

extraction. Syn.: see **lineage.**

extraneous. Syn.: external, extrinsic, adventitious, foreign, alien.

That which is *extraneous* is outside the proper limits of a thing although sometimes attached to it; that which is *extrinsic*, while it has a connection with and forms a part of something, is not an essential or component part; that which is *adventitious* is or appears to be a more or less casual or accidental addition from without, and hence is often foreign to the thing: as, there are many digressions and other *extraneous* matters in the book; *extrinsic* value or aid; an *adventitious* circumstance.

extraordinary. Syn.: uncommon, unusual, unwonted, egregious, strange, exceptional, singular, rare, unprecedented, remarkable, wonderful, marvelous, phenomenal. See **wonderful.**

extravagance. Syn.: immoderation, excess, lavishness, prodigality, waste, profusion, dissipation. **Ant.:** thrift, economy, frugality, parsimony.

extravagant. Syn.: immoderate, excessive, inordinate, exorbitant, unconscionable; unrestrained, fantastic, wild; lavish, prodigal, wasteful. See **profuse.**

extreme, *n.* **Syn.:** see **extremity.**

extreme, *a.* **Syn.:** outermost, endmost, utmost, farthest, last, final, ultimate; immoderate, excessive, radical, fanatical.

Extreme denotes a going beyond moderation or even to excess in opinion, belief, action, etc.; *radical* emphasizes the idea of going to the root of a matter, and this often seems extreme in its thoroughness or completeness; *fanatical* is applied to a person who has extravagant views, especially in matters of religion or morality, which render him incapable of sound judgments or of tolerance for others: as, *extreme* measures or ideas; *radical* changes or laws; *fanatical* opinions.

extremity. Syn.: end, termination, extreme, verge, border, boundary, limit.

extricate. Syn.: see **disengage.**

extrinsic. Syn.: outward, external, extraneous, foreign, adventitious, unessential. See **extraneous.**

exuberance. Syn.: superabundance, copiousness, profusion, luxuriance, lavishness, excess.

exuberant. Syn.: superabundant, copious, profuse, luxuriant, rank, lavish, effusive. See **luxuriant.**

exude. Syn.: see **emit.**

exultant. Syn.: elated, jubilant, joyous, triumphant. See **elated.**

F

fable. Syn.: story, tale, legend, myth, allegory, parable, apologue; fabrication, fiction, fib. See **legend.**

fabricate. Syn.: make, produce, manufacture; invent, concoct, contrive, devise. See **make.**

fabrication. Syn.: invention, concoction, fable, fiction, figment, falsehood, forgery, canard.

A *fabrication* is a falsely, but often carefully, invented statement or series of statements, sometimes so interwoven with truth that the false and the true are hard to distinguish, the whole usually intended to deceive: as, the accounts of the rich oil discoveries were *fabrications* of the speculators. A *figment* is an imaginary or fictitious idea or statement which may or may not be intended to deceive: as, his influence over others was a *figment* of his own brain. A *fiction* is an invention or exaggeration set forth more often to make an interesting story than culpably to deceive: as, many of his adventures later proved to be good-natured *fictions*. A *canard* is a false and extravagant report circulated as a hoax, or (sometimes) with intent to injure: as, the story of his elopement was a *canard*.

fabulous. Syn.: fabled, legendary, mythical, fictitious, apocryphal, imaginary, incredible, amazing, astonishing, enormous, immense, inordinate, exorbitant. See **legendary.**

face, *n.* **Syn.:** visage, countenance, physiognomy, features; front, exterior, façade; assurance, effrontery, audacity, impudence.

Face is the combination of features composing the front of the (usually human) head. *Countenance* denotes the face as it is affected by or reveals the state of the mind, and hence often signifies the look or expression on the face. *Visage* regards the face as seen in a certain aspect, especially as revealing a seriousness or severity of mood. *Physiognomy* refers to the peculiarities of contour and detail of the face as they are considered to reveal character.

face, *v.* **Syn.:** look, front, confront, meet; brave, defy, oppose; overlay, coat, veneer.

facetious. Syn.: witty, humorous, jocose, jocular, waggish, droll, comical, funny, amusing. See **jocose.**

facilitate. Syn.: see **promote.**

facility. Syn.: ease, easiness, readiness, dexterity, quickness, expertness, knack; aid, convenience, opportunity, resource, means. See **ease.**

facsimile. Syn.: see **copy.**

fact. Syn.: actuality, reality, truth.

faction. Syn.: party, group, clique, cabal; strife, dissension, division. See **party.**

factious. Syn.: dissentious, quarrelsome, turbulent, seditious, rebellious, refractory.

factitious. Syn.: made, artificial, unnatural.

That which is *factitious* is forced or worked up, as contrasted with what comes about naturally: as, *factitious* enthusiasms. That which is *artificial* does not grow or come about naturally, but is either made or done to simulate nature: as, *artificial* respiration. In its figurative use *artificial* is opposed to natural or sincere in respect to manners, conventions, etc.: as, his whole attitude toward life was *artificial*. That which is *unnatural* is abnormal or not to be expected in the course of nature: as, *unnatural* phenomena.

factor. Syn.: see **agent.**

factory. Syn.: manufactory, mill, shop.

factotum. Syn.: see **servant.**

faculty. Syn.: capacity, ability, power, capability, aptitude, aptness, knack, gift, turn, talent, skill, expertness, adroitness, dexterity. See **genius.**

fad. Syn.: fancy, hobby, whim, crotchet, fashion, craze. See **fashion.**

fade. Syn.: wither, droop, languish, decay, die, perish; disappear, evanesce, vanish; blanch, bleach, pale. See **disappear.**

fag. Syn.: see **tire.**

fail. Syn.: fall short, give out, cease, disappear, miscarry; decline, sink, wane, dwindle, deteriorate; disappoint, desert, forsake, neglect.

failing. Syn.: shortcoming, defect, imperfection, vice, weakness, foible, infirmity, fault; decline, deterioration.

A *failing* is usually a more or less permanent or inherent moral shortcoming in some particular: as, procrastination is a common *failing*. A *weakness* is a failing that results from an inability to control a particular impulse or tendency: as, boasting was his greatest *weakness*. An *infirmity* is a weakness inherent in the nature of humanity: as, human *infirmities*. A *foible* is a slight and often amusing weakness, exhibiting itself in eccentricity rather than in wrongdoing: as, the *foibles* of artists. A *fault* is a definite and blameworthy imperfection in one's nature or conduct: as, the *fault* of rudeness. A *vice* is a more or less serious fault: as, the *vice* of gambling.

failure. Syn.: cessation, disappearance, deficiency, lack, want, loss; decline, decay, deterioration; fiasco, fizzle; neglect, omission, dereliction, default; bankruptcy, insolvency, suspension.

faint. Syn.: timid, half-hearted, faltering, irresolute, weak; exhausted, fatigued, wearied, feeble, languid; indistinct, ill-defined, dim, faded, dull. **Ant.:** see **energetic, clear.**

fair. Syn.: beautiful, pretty, comely, attractive; blond, light, white; spotless, pure, untarnished, unsullied; legible, distinct; specious, plausible; impartial, unprejudiced, unbiased, equitable, just, honest; legitimate, honorable; passable, tolerable, average, middling, so-so; promising, favorable, propitious; clear, cloudless, sunny. See **beautiful. Ant.:** see **unfair.**

Fair implies freedom from bias, prejudice, or injustice; *impartial*, the attitude or action of one who does not favor one party or side more than another; *equitable*, conformity to the requirements of equity or fairness; *just*, the rendering to each of that which is his due.

fairly. Syn.: beautifully, handsomely; courteously, civilly, agreeably, pleasantly, kindly; legibly, distinctly, plainly, clearly, evenly; impartially, equitably, justly, honestly; passably, tolerably, moderately, reasonably; favorably, auspiciously; actually, positively, absolutely.

fairy. Syn.: elf, fay, sprite, sylph, pixy, brownie, nix, nixie, gnome, goblin, jinnee, genie, banshee, kobold. Cf. **nymph.**

Fairy is the most general name for a diminutive imaginary being, usually in human form, and either benevolent or malevolent in relation to mankind. *Fay* is a more poetic word for fairy. *Sprite* especially suggests a hostile or impish fairy; *elf*, a young, mischievous, or roguish one. *Goblin* suggests a sprite that is grotesque, ugly, or frightful in appearance, and wicked, or at least mischievous, in disposition. *Gnome* denotes a dwarfish spirit living under the ground and guarding the mines and quarries; gnomes are usually thought of with repugnance and dread.

faith. Syn.: trust, confidence, reliance, dependence, credence; doctrine, tenet, creed, belief, dogma, persuasion, conviction, religion; loyalty, fidelity, constancy, faithfulness. See **belief. Ant.:** see **doubt, disloyalty.**

faithful. Syn.: loyal, true, devoted, stanch, constant; trustworthy, trusty, reliable; accurate, precise, exact.

Faithful implies long-continued and steadfast fidelity to whatever one is bound to by a pledge, duty, or obligation; *loyal*, unswerving allegiance to a person, organization, cause, or idea; *constant*, steadfastness and firmness in attachment; *stanch*, stout adherence to one's affiliations, beliefs, etc.

faithfulness. Syn.: see **constancy.**

faithless. Syn.: unbelieving, doubting, skeptical; disloyal, false, inconstant, fickle, perfidious, treacherous, traitorous; unreliable, delusive, deceptive.

Faithless implies want or violation of faith, as to one's word or to a friend. *Disloyal* implies breach of loyalty, as to a sovereign or government, a cause, or a friend. *Traitorous* suggests the spirit or action of one who betrays the trust reposed in him or proves false to his allegiance. *Inconstant* attributes a want of constancy or steadfast faithfulness; so also *fickle*, which suggests greater readiness to change, with perhaps greater indifference to obligations.

fake. Syn.: see **fraud.**

fall, *n.* **Syn.:** drop, descent, decline, decrease, depreciation, slump, subsidence, ebbing; slope, declivity; surrender, capture, overthrow, downfall, destruction, ruin; waterfall, cascade, cataract.

fall, *v.* **Syn.:** drop, descend, gravitate, sink, slope, decline, decrease, diminish, abate, subside, ebb; stumble, founder, tumble, topple; hang, droop; befall, happen, occur; sin, err; perish, die.

fallacious. Syn.: deceptive, delusive, misleading, sophistical, false, erroneous.

fallacy. Syn.: deceptiveness, delusiveness, erroneousness; deception, delusion, misconception, error, mistake, sophism, paralogism.

fallen. Syn.: dropped, decreased, depreciated; degraded, debased; overthrown, ruined, prostrate, dead.

fallow. Syn.: uncultivated, untilled, dormant, inactive, neglected.

false. Syn.: erroneous, mistaken, incorrect, wrong, untrue, untruthful, lying, mendacious, misleading, deceptive, fallacious, insincere, hypocritical, disingenuous; disloyal, unfaithful, inconstant, recreant, perfidious, treacherous, traitorous; spurious, bogus, forged, counterfeit, sham, artificial, imitative. **Ant.:** see **true, loyal.**

False is applied to whatever does not actually have the nature or character it purports to have, or does not correspond truly to the name it bears: as, *false* diamonds; *false* teeth; *false* modesty. *Spurious* is applied to what is not only false but is put forth intentionally to pass as genuine: as, *spurious* writings. *Counterfeit* things are not only false but are made in careful imitation of that for which they are intended (often for dishonest gain) to be taken: as, *counterfeit* money. *Sham* implies pretense or simulation, sometimes of an innocent or harmless kind: as, a *sham* battle. *Bogus* is applied colloquially to what is spurious or counterfeit: as, *bogus* securities; *bogus* money.

falsehood. Syn.: falsity, falseness, untruthfulness, inveracity, mendacity; lie, untruth, fib. Cf. **fabrication.**

A *falsehood* is a statement that distorts or suppresses the truth, usually intentionally for the purpose of deceiving. An *untruth* is an incorrect statement, either intentionally misleading (in which case it is less harsh than falsehood or lie), or arising from misunderstanding or ignorance. A *lie* is a vicious falsehood intended utterly to deceive. A *fib* denotes a trivial falsehood, and is often used to characterize that which is not strictly true.

falsify. Syn.: misstate, misrepresent, distort, pervert, garble; lie, prevaricate.

falsity. Syn.: untruthfulness, etc. (see **falsehood**); incorrectness, erroneousness, fallaciousness; deceitfulness, perfidy, treachery.

falter. Syn.: stumble, stagger, totter, tremble; stammer, stutter; hesitate, waver, vacillate. See **hesitate.**

fame. Syn.: reputation, repute, notoriety, celebrity, renown, eminence, honor, glory. **Ant.:** obscurity, ingloriousness, oblivion.

Fame is the repute or celebrity given to a person by widespread report. *Honor* is the high esteem accorded to recognized worth, achievement, etc. *Renown* is a widespread and honorable fame. *Glory* is a kind of shining honor or splendid distinction, constituting a superlative reward for noble deeds or signal success.

familiar. Syn.: intimate, confidential, close, friendly, fraternal; unceremonious, informal, unconstrained, free, forward, intrusive; acquainted, conversant, versed; common, well-known, frequent. **Ant.:** unfamiliar, strange, distant, ceremonious, shy.

That is *familiar* which is known through long association, and when applied to the relations between people, the word suggests a freedom from restraint which may become excessive; *intimate* suggests close acquaintance or connection, often based on interest, sympathy, or affection; *confidential* implies intimacy which extends to the sharing of confidences and secrets with another: as, a *familiar* acquaintance; an *intimate* friend; a *confidential* adviser.

familiarity. Syn.: intimacy, sociability, friendship, fellowship; informality, freedom, unconstraint; liberty, unreserve; disrespect; acquaintance, conversance, knowledge.

familiarize. Syn.: see **habituate.**

family. Syn.: household, tribe, clan, race; ancestry, stock, lineage, descent, genealogy.

famine. Syn.: see **scarcity.**

famished. Syn.: see **hungry.**

famous. Syn.: famed, celebrated, renowned, distinguished, noted, notable, illustrious, eminent, remarkable, signal, notorious. **Ant.:** obscure, inglorious, unknown, nameless.

Famous is applied to whatever is widely and usually favorably known. *Noted* is a weaker word, and often means being known by common report for some particular thing. That is *notable* which for any reason is worthy of attention. *Celebrated* was originally applied to what was commemorated in a solemn way and may still occasionally show a trace of this meaning (as, a *celebrated* victory), but is ordinarily applied to whatever is widely talked about for conspicuous merit (or fault), success, talent, services, etc. One becomes *renowned* by being named again and again, as for signal accomplishment, deeds, valor, or the like; *illustrious* suggests a shining out before the world, as for splendid achievement. *Notorious* indicates being publicly or widely known, especially in an unfavorable way.

fanatic. Syn.: see **zealot.**

fanatical. Syn.: fanatic, extreme, extravagant, wild, rabid, bigoted, uncompromising. See **extreme,** *a.*

fanaticism. Syn.: see **bigotry.**

fanciful. Syn.: imaginative, whimsical, capricious, wild, chimerical, visionary, impractical, strange, fantastic, grotesque, bizarre. See **imaginary.**

Fanciful suggests imagination rather than reality and denotes something odd but not beyond the point of pleasing; *fantastic* implies less restraint, suggesting an extravagant and unregulated fancy: as, a *fanciful* picture of an ideal commonwealth; the *fantastic* notions of a lunatic. *Whimsical* describes that which is pleasing because of its capricious, often mildly ironical, humor. The *grotesque* is a vigorous distortion of the real, creating an effect that is unnatural or absurd by striking incongruities. *Bizarre* implies singularity or strangeness in appearance, style, or general character. Thus, a *whimsical* story, a *grotesque* idol, a *bizarre* design.

fancy, *n.* **Syn.:** imagination, fantasy; conception, notion, whim, caprice, vagary; inclination, liking, fondness, taste, penchant, hobby, fad. See **imagination.**

fancy, *a.* **Syn.:** fanciful, capricious, extravagant, exorbitant; fine, elegant, elaborate, ornate, showy.

fancy, *v.* **Syn.:** imagine, conceive, picture; suppose, presume, conjecture. See **like,** *v.,* **conceive.**

fantastic. Syn.: fanciful, whimsical, capricious, freakish, bizarre, grotesque, wild, odd, queer, eccentric, strange. See **fanciful.**

fantasy. Syn.: imagination, fancy; notion, illusion, hallucination, phantasm; whim, caprice, vagary. See **imagination.**

far. Syn.: distant, remote. See **distant.**

farce. Syn.: see **drama.**

farcical. Syn.: see **ludicrous.**

farewell. Syn.: good-by, adieu, valediction, valedictory.

Good-by is the expression generally used at parting. The words *farewell* and *adieu* are no longer in ordinary use as ejaculations, but are still fairly frequent as nouns to designate the interchange of sentiment at leave-taking. *Farewell* is preferred by the Society of Friends to *good-by,* as not involving the careless mention of the name of God.

farmer. Syn.: agriculturist, husbandman, granger, agronomist.

farming. Syn.: agriculture, husbandry, tillage, agronomy, geoponics.

farrago. Syn.: see **mixture.**

fascinate. Syn.: bewitch, charm, enchant, entrance, enrapture, captivate, attract, allure, infatuate, enamour. See **charm,** *v.*

fashion, *n.* **Syn.:** make, shape, form, cut, pattern; style, vogue, fad, rage, craze; mode, manner, way, practice, custom.

Fashion is that which characterizes or distinguishes the habits, manners, dress, etc., of a period or group: as, the *fashions* of the eighteenth century. *Mode* is the French word for the same idea, and by virtue of its origin has perhaps a suggestion of distinctive elegance. *Style* is sometimes the equivalent of fashion, but also denotes the quality that characterizes a person or thing especially in matters of conformance to a prevalent standard: as, a chair in the Queen Anne *style.* *Vogue* suggests the temporary popularity of certain fashions. *Fad* and *craze* both describe something which enjoys wide but temporary popularity, but a *craze* is perhaps the more contagious.

fashion, *v.* **Syn.:** shape, form, frame, construct, mold. See **make.**

fashionable. Syn.: modish, stylish, smart.

fast, *a.* **Syn.:** fixed, firm, immovable, rigid; secure, tight, tenacious, adhesive, attached; loyal, faithful, steadfast, true; permanent, lasting, durable; quick, rapid, swift, fleet, speedy, hasty, hurried, expeditious; dissipated, dissolute, profligate, immoral. See **quick.**

fast, *adv.* **Syn.:** fixedly, firmly, immovably; securely, tenaciously; close, near; quickly, rapidly, swiftly, post-haste.

fasten. Syn.: attach, connect, link, hook, clasp, clinch, rivet, clamp, secure, bind, tie, tether, moor, lock, latch.

fastidious. Syn.: overnice, squeamish, exacting, critical, finical, dainty, punctilious. See **particular.**

fastness. Syn.: fixedness, immovability; quickness, rapidity, swiftness, speed, haste, celerity, expedition; stronghold, citadel, fort, fortress.

fat. Syn.: corpulent, obese, adipose, fleshy, stout, plump, chubby, pursy, pudgy; oily, greasy, unctuous; profitable, lucrative, remunerative; dull, stupid, heavy. See **stout.**

fatal. Syn.: destructive, disastrous, ruinous, mortal. See **deadly.**

fate. Syn.: see **destiny.**

fatherly. Syn.: paternal, parental.

Fatherly suggests an attitude which is kind, tender, or forbearing; *paternal* and *parental* imply a relationship more formal, strict, or official: as, *fatherly* care, interest, letters; *paternal* authority, admonition, estate; *parental* duties.

fatigue, *n.* **Syn.:** weariness, lassitude, languor, exhaustion.

Fatigue is either physical or mental exhaustion due to prolonged or strenuous exertion. *Weariness* is the wearing out of the bodily strength or the flagging of the spirits, often from a continued or repeated cause, as long standing or sitting in one position, importunities from others, delays, etc. *Fatigue* and *weariness* are both natural conditions from which one readily recovers by rest. *Lassitude* and *languor* are more constitutional or lasting. *Lassitude* is a condition in which bodily or mental energy is at a low ebb, as a result of greater fatigue or weariness than one can well bear, or of ill health, etc. *Languor* is a more or less habitual want of energy or alertness, or, sometimes, an affected listlessness.

fatigue, *v.* **Syn.:** weary, tire, fag, jade, exhaust. See **tire.**

fatuous. Syn.: see **foolish.**

fault. Syn.: defect, flaw, blemish, imperfection, failing, shortcoming; error, mistake, misdemeanor, misdeed, slip, lapse, offense, transgression, dereliction; culpability, blame. See **failing.**

faultfinding. Syn.: see **captious.**

faultless. Syn.: perfect, unblemished, flawless, blameless, impeccable.

faulty. Syn.: defective, imperfect, wrong, incomplete; culpable, blamable, blameworthy, reprehensible, censurable. See **wrong,** *a.*

favor, *n.* **Syn.:** good-will, grace, countenance, indulgence, patronage; kindness, gift, present, token.

Favor is kind regard or friendly disposition voluntarily shown by an individual or group; *good-will* is more active than favor and leads often to outward manifestations of kindness. *Grace* is favor extended as a concession to one who is guilty or undeserving. Thus, he soon won the *favor* of his new employers; the audience showed its *good-will* toward the speaker by frequent applause; it is an act of *grace* to pardon a murderer; men are saved by the *grace* of God.

favor, *v.* **Syn.:** approve, commend, encourage, aid, help, support, patronize, befriend.

favorable. Syn.: well-disposed, approving, commendatory, friendly; promising, hopeful, auspicious, propitious; advantageous, helpful, conducive. **Ant.:** see **unfavorable.**

That which is *favorable* tends to further or aid; that which is *auspicious* augurs well for the future; that which is *propitious* is favorably disposed towards something, or actively helpful in bringing about its success. *Favorable* may be used of humanity or nature; *auspicious* refers chiefly to circumstances and never to persons; *propitious* most often applies to natural forces or special conditions.

favoritism. Syn.: partiality, nepotism.

fawn. Syn.: see **cringe.**

fawning. Syn.: see **servile.**

fay. Syn.: see **fairy.**

fealty. Syn.: see **allegiance.**

fear, *n.* **Syn.:** apprehension, dread, consternation, dismay, terror, fright, alarm, panic, trepidation, anxiety, solicitude, concern, misgiving; awe, reverence, veneration.

Fear is a general term for the painful emotion which we experience when confronted by threatening danger or evil. *Apprehension* realizes the possibility or probability of danger and often leads to worry. *Dread*, a stronger word, is the fear, brief or prolonged, with which one contemplates a future danger, or the state of mind with which one looks forward to what is painful or disagreeable. *Alarm* implies an agitation of the feelings caused by the awakening to sudden danger. *Fright* and *terror* imply sudden, startling fear; *fright* (sometimes arising from trivial causes) often being a shock to the nerves and senses which, momentarily at least, makes one lose control of himself; *terror* being an overwhelming fear, causing consternation, even paralysis of the faculties. *Panic* denotes sudden, undefined, and sometimes unaccountable fear, usually affecting a number of persons, and leading to desperate efforts to escape danger.

fear, *v.* **Syn.:** apprehend, dread; revere, venerate.

fearful. Syn.: afraid, apprehensive, frightened, alarmed, timid, timorous, cowardly, craven, pusillanimous; dreadful, awful, frightful, terrible, horrible, appalling, dire, direful, grim, fell. See **terrible.**

fearless. Syn.: unafraid, undaunted, dauntless, intrepid, bold, courageous, daring. See **brave.**

feasible. Syn.: see **practicable.**

feast. Syn.: banquet, repast, regale, festivity, festival.

A *feast* is a meal at which there is an abundance of excellent food and drink, usually partaken of by a large number of persons. A *banquet* is an elaborate feast, especially one attended with the elegance and ceremony appropriate to formal occasions. A *festival* or *festivity* is a joyous, often regularly recurring, celebration of some particular event, or a season of public rejoicing, of which feasting is a frequent but not necessary feature. A *repast* is any kind of meal, whether plain or luxurious.

feat. Syn.: action, deed, achievement, exploit, stunt.

A *feat* is the performance of something unusually difficult, generally demanding strength or skill: as, a *feat* of horsemanship, of diplomacy. A *deed* is a conspicuous or noteworthy act and may be either noble or base: as, a *deed* of kindness, violence, etc. An *exploit* is a feat or enterprise of boldness or bravery, especially in arms, involving more or less of ingenuity: as, the *exploits* of an aviator. An *achievement* is the accomplishment of something great or worthy, for which one has striven often or long in the face of obstacles and discouragements: as, *achievements* in business, science, government, etc. A *stunt* is a feat attempted for the purpose of displaying one's boldness or skill.

feature. Syn.: see **characteristic.**

fecund. Syn.: see **fruitful.**

federation. Syn.: see **confederation.**

fee. Syn.: see **pay.**

feeble. Syn.: weak, infirm, frail, sickly, enervated, doddering; slight, faint. See **weak.**

feeble-minded. Syn.: see **idiotic.**

feed, *n.* **Syn.:** food, fodder, provender, forage.

Feed is a general word for any kind of food for animals, especially animals kept for work or fattening for market. *Fodder* is especially applied to dry or green feed as opposed to pasturage, as used for feed for horses, cattle, etc. *Provender* denotes any kind of dry feed. *Forage* is primarily applied to food obtained for horses in an army by foraging a country.

feed, *v.* **Syn.:** nourish, sustain, supply, gratify; eat, graze.

feel. Syn.: touch, handle, grope; experience, suffer; seem, appear.

feeling, *n.* **Syn.:** sensation, impression, emotion, passion, sentiment, sympathy.

Feeling is the general term for the sensation, pleasurable or painful, experienced when one is stirred, or the ability or readiness to feel sympathy for the misfortunes of others. *Emotion* is an intensified form of certain feelings, such as fear, hate, love, anger, etc. *Passion* is strong or violent emotion, often so overpowering that it masters the mind or judgment.

feeling, *a.* **Syn.:** sentient, sensitive, sympathetic, vivid, earnest.

feign. Syn.: pretend, assume, affect, simulate, sham, counterfeit. See **pretend.**

feint. Syn.: see **pretense.**

felicitate. Syn.: see **congratulate.**

felicitous. Syn.: happy, fortunate, graceful; apt, appropriate, pertinent, apposite, opportune.

felicity. Syn.: happiness, joy, bliss, blessedness; aptness, appropriateness. See **happiness.**

fell, *n.* **Syn.:** see **skin,** *n.*

fell, *a.* **Syn.:** see **fierce.**

fellowship. Syn.: companionship, comradeship, friendship, association, intercourse, communion; company, corporation, gild.

felon. Syn.: criminal, convict, culprit, malefactor, outlaw.

felonious. Syn.: criminal, unlawful, nefarious, infamous, flagitious, heinous. See **illegal.**

felony. Syn.: see **offense.**

female, *n.* **Syn.:** woman, girl, lady.

Woman is the general term for the adult of the human race correlative with man; *lady* implies family or social position, but is very frequently used conventionally or by courtesy for any woman; *female*, which applies to animals and plants as well as to human beings, refers especially to sex, but is sometimes used with a contemptuous implication for woman: as, *women* now do much work formerly done only by men; the demeanor of a *lady*; *ladies'* waiting-room; in the census the *females* outnumbered the males; an irate *female*.

female, *a.* **Syn.:** see **feminine.**

feminine. Syn.: female, womanly, womanish, girlish, maidenly, ladylike; effeminate.

Feminine, matching *masculine*, applies to women and the attributes particularly appropriate to them, especially the softer and more delicate or graceful qualities; it is seldom used merely to denote sex, and as applied to men, suggests the weakness or delicacy of women. *Female*, matching *male*, is the general and scientific word to designate one of the two sexes. *Womanly* is applied to that which is nobly becoming in a woman, especially her maturer and deeper qualities; *ladylike*, to that which is refined or well-bred in a woman, although sometimes used of men to imply daintiness. *Womanish* applies to that which is weak in women or which suggests in a man the weakness of women: as, *womanish* fears. *Effeminate* is applied reproachfully or contemptuously to qualities which, though they might be proper and becoming in a woman, are unmanly and weak in a man.

fen. Syn.: see **swamp.**

fend. Syn.: see **ward.**

fender. Syn.: see **protection.**

fermentation. Syn.: see **ebullition.**

ferocious. Syn.: fierce, savage, cruel, fell, truculent, ruthless, pitiless, merciless, brutal, barbarous, bloodthirsty, murderous. See **fierce.**

fertile. Syn.: fruitful, productive, prolific, fecund, rich. See **fruitful.**

fervent. Syn.: warm, hot, burning, glowing, fervid, fiery, ardent, eager, earnest, zealous, vehement, impassioned, passionate.

Fervent suggests the glowing feeling of one who is carried away by an emotion or cause. *Fervid* implies a flaming excitement of the mind which shows itself in what we think, say, or do: as, *fervent* love, patriotism; *fervid* imagination, denunciation, endeavor.

fervid. Syn.: see **fervent**.

fervor. Syn.: warmth, heat, ardor, intensity, eagerness, zeal, enthusiasm. See **ardor**.

festal. Syn.: festive, gala, holiday.

Festal implies connection with a feast or celebration; *festive*, the character, spirit, or proceedings proper to feasting, celebrations, or merrymaking generally; *gala*, the gay dress, decorations, or pomp customary on festive occasions: as, a *festal* day; a *festive* party; *gala* array.

festival. Syn.: see **feast**.

festive. Syn.: see **festal**.

festivity. Syn.: see **feast**.

fetch. Syn.: see **bring**.

fetter. Syn.: shackle, manacle, chain, bind, confine, hamper, impede.

fetters. Syn.: shackles, manacles, gyves, bonds, chains. See **shackles**.

fetus. Syn.: see **embryo**.

feud. Syn.: hostility, enmity, quarrel, conflict, strife, broil, vendetta.

fewer. Syn.: see **less**.

fiasco. Syn.: see **failure**.

fiat. Syn.: see **decree**.

fib. Syn.: see **falsehood**.

fickle. Syn.: unstable, unsteady, inconstant, changeable, volatile, variable, vacillating, wavering, capricious, fitful. **Ant.:** constant, steadfast, unchanging, faithful. See **faithless**.

fiction. Syn.: story, tale, novel, romance, fable, fabrication, figment, falsehood, fib. See **fabrication**.

fictitious. Syn.: counterfeit, sham, false, pretended, feigned, assumed, imaginary, unreal.

fidelity. Syn.: faithfulness, loyalty, constancy, allegiance, fealty; exactness, accuracy. See **allegiance**.

field. Syn.: meadow, mead, croft, lea, pasture.

fiend. Syn.: devil, demon.

fiendish. Syn.: see **devilish**.

fierce. Syn.: savage, wild, cruel, ferocious, truculent, fell, furious, raging, ravenous, violent, vehement, fiery, ardent. **Ant.:** tame, submissive, gentle, mild, docile.

Fierce suggests violence of temper or savage intensity of feeling or appetite; *savage*, wildness or barbarousness of nature; *ferocious*, fierceness or cruelty, especially of a bloodthirsty kind, in disposition or action; *truculent*, an intimidating or bullying fierceness of manner or conduct; *fell* (an archaic or poetic word), an evil and savage intent.

fiery. Syn.: flaming, glowing, hot, ardent, fervid, fervent, vehement, spirited, impassioned, passionate, irascible.

fight, *n*. Syn.: battle, combat, conflict, encounter, engagement, affray, fray, mêlée, scuffle, tussle, struggle.

Fight denotes conflict between opposing forces, usually of a more or less informal and unregulated kind: as, a street *fight*; a fist *fight*; but the *battle* (not *fight*) of the Marne. *Fight* may also be used of a conflict that does not involve physical encounter: as, a *fight* for social reform. *Combat* is a word of more dignity than *fight*, and is especially used of a struggle between two opponents, whether they be persons, animals, squadrons, or armies. *Mêlée* emphasizes the confusion in which those engaged in a fray or struggle are mingled. *Scuffle* and *tussle* both imply an undignified struggle at close quarters, usually between two; the former emphasizes the scrambling nature of the fight; the latter, its vigor and the desire of each combatant for supremacy. See also *battle*.

fight, *v*. Syn.: battle, combat, contend, struggle, strive.

fighter. Syn.: combatant, belligerent, soldier, warrior, champion, gladiator, pugilist, boxer.

figment. Syn.: see **fabrication**.

figure, *n*. Syn.: form, shape, conformation, outline; likeness, image, effigy, statue, bust; pattern, design, diagram, drawing, illustration, cut; metaphor, trope; emblem, symbol; personage, character; numeral, number, digit. See **form**.

figure, *v*. Syn.: compute, calculate, cipher; scheme, plan, contrive.

filch. Syn.: see **steal**.

file. Syn.: see **row**.

fill. Syn.: inflate, expand, distend; furnish, supply, replenish, stock; hold, occupy; pervade, permeate; satisfy, satiate, sate, glut, cloy, stuff.

filter. Syn.: filtrate, percolate, strain; ooze, seep; purify, clarify, defecate.

filth. Syn.: dirt, muck, squalor, filthiness, foulness, corruption, obscenity.

filthy. Syn.: dirty, squalid, nasty, foul, corrupt, impure, indecent, obscene, ribald, lewd, smutty. See **dirty**.

final. Syn.: last, ultimate, eventual, conclusive, terminal, decisive. See **last**, *a*.

financial. Syn.: see **pecuniary**.

find. Syn.: see **discover**.

fine, *n*. Syn.: mulct, amercement, forfeit, forfeiture.

fine, *a*. Syn.: choice, rare, elegant, exquisite, superior, finished, consummate, perfect, excellent, admirable, splendid; skilled, accomplished; good-looking, handsome, beautiful, attractive, striking, showy; polished, refined, sensitive, nice, dainty, delicate, subtle; small, minute, powdered, pulverized; thin, slender, attenuated, light, filmy, flimsy. **Ant.:** see **coarse**.

Fine is a general term of praise with reference to quality or superiority. *Choice* implies a discerning comparison between things. *Elegant* suggests such a refined and graceful superiority as is quite beyond the common run of things and is generally associated with luxury and a cultivated taste; *exquisite*, an admirable delicacy, finish, or perfection.

finery. Syn.: ornament, decoration, gewgaws, frippery.

finesse. Syn.: fineness, delicacy, subtlety, artfulness, adroitness, craft, strategy, subterfuge, artifice, stratagem, ruse. See **cunning**.

finical. Syn.: overnice, fastidious, particular, dainty, squeamish, finicky. See **particular**.

finish. Syn.: see **complete, end**.

finished. Syn.: see **perfect**.

fire, *n*. Syn.: flame, blaze, burning, combustion, conflagration, holocaust; ardor, fervor, enthusiasm, passion, vehemence.

Fire (as here discriminated) denotes a burning with more or less loss of valuable material, as a building or forest. *Conflagration*, a more impressive word, denotes a fierce and extensive fire, such as consumes a considerable section of a town or city. *Holocaust* implies a terrible fire, especially involving a great sacrifice of life, as when a theater or ship burns.

fire, *v*. Syn.: kindle, ignite, burn; inflame, excite, arouse, animate; shoot, discharge.

firm. Syn.: compact, solid, hard, impenetrable, stiff, rigid; fixed, fast, secure, stable, immovable; strong, stanch, sturdy, unshaken, unwavering, inflexible, constant, steadfast, enduring, resolute, determined, positive.

Firm is applied to substances that do not yield readily to pressure or force, tending to retain their form unaltered; *solid*, to substances that without external support retain their form and resist pressure; the latter word sometimes denotes the opposite of hollow. *Hard* is applied to substances so firm that it is difficult to make any impression upon their surface or to penetrate their interior. *Stiff* implies firmness that resists a bending force.

firmament. Syn.: see **sky**.

firmness. Syn.: compactness, solidity, hardness; constancy, steadfastness, faithfulness, fidelity.

first. Syn.: earliest, original, initial, prime, primal, primary, pristine, primordial, primeval, primitive; foremost, highest, principal, leading, chief.

fiscal. Syn.: see **pecuniary**.

fissure. Syn.: see **cleft**.

fit, *n*. Syn.: spasm, convulsion, paroxysm, access, attack, spell, period.

fit, *a*. Syn.: suitable, appropriate, proper, meet, fitting, befitting, becoming, seemly, adapted, qualified, eligible, competent. **Ant.:** see **unfit**.

Fit is a term of wide range of meaning, signifying having the qualities or qualifications to meet some condition, circumstance, purpose, or demand. *Suitable* suggests that which accords with a person's age, character, occupation, or station, or fits with propriety any purpose, occasion, or condition. *Appropriate* suggests especial fitness, as of that which belongs naturally to something. *Adapted* suggests possession of natural or acquired qualities requisite for some work or purpose, or that something has been rendered useful by alteration. *Meet* is a more or less archaic word, used especially in poetry or for that which is spiritually appropriate. Cf. **fitting**.

fit, *v*. Syn.: befit, become; adapt, adjust, prepare, furnish, provide, equip, qualify.

fitful. Syn.: spasmodic, irregular, variable, changeable, capricious, inconstant, intermittent.

fitting. Syn.: befitting, becoming, beseeming, seemly, proper, decorous, decent. See **fit,** *a.*

That which is *fitting* is nicely adapted to certain requirements or demands: as, *fitting* remarks. That which is *becoming* matches or accords harmoniously so that it creates an (often visual) pleasing impression: as, a *becoming* color; a *becoming* modesty. That which is *seemly* is pleasing, especially to one's sense of what is proper or desirable: as, *seemly* appearance; *seemly* conduct. *Proper* is applied to what is suitable to an occasion, especially to what conforms to moral standards or recognized usage; *decorous*, to what conforms to the accepted or conventional standards of social behavior; *decent*, to what is modest or free from indelicacy.

fix. Syn.: fasten, place, set, establish, implant; settle, determine, confirm; adjust, arrange; repair, mend.

To *fix* is to fasten securely or to make more or less permanent against change, especially something already existing: as, to *fix* a flag-pole in the ground; to *fix* a bayonet on a gun; *fixed* ideas or principles. To *establish* is to make firm or permanent something (usually newly) originated, created, or ordained: as, to *establish* a business, a claim to property, law and order. To *settle* is to establish gradually, permanently, or conclusively: as, the constant rain helped to *settle* the post in the ground; to *settle* oneself in a new home; to *settle* a colony; the court *settled* the case. The use of *fix* in the sense of arrange, adjust, repair, or mend is common in the U. S. but not approved by the best English usage.

fixed. Syn.: fast, firm, stable, stationary, immovable, rigid, set; unchangeable, steadfast; appointed, settled, determined, established, definite.

flabby, flaccid. Syn.: see **limp.**

flag, *n.* **Syn.:** ensign, standard, banner, pennant, pennon, streamer, guidon, vexillum, gonfalon, oriflamme, fanion, banderole, bannerol, colors; Stars and Stripes, Stars and Bars, Old Glory.

flag, *v.* **Syn.:** droop, decline, languish, fail.

flagitious. Syn.: see **atrocious, nefarious.**

flagrant. Syn.: glaring, outrageous, notorious, scandalous. See **atrocious.**

flame. Syn.: blaze, flare, glare, glow, flash, light, flicker.

Flame is the common word for the mingled light and heat given off by visible combustion. *Blaze* usually denotes a quick, hot, bright, and comparatively large flame. *Flare*, a sudden, intense, and fitful flame like that of a gas jet. *Glow* suggests a steady, sometimes intense light, generally accompanied by heat, such as that emanating from a hot or incandescent substance: as, the *glow* of burning coals, a volcano; *flicker*, an unsteady or fluttering flame, especially one that is waning or dying out. As used figuratively, *flame* suggests a burning feeling or passion, as of anger, love, zeal; *blaze*, a fiery, sudden, or uncontrolled outburst of passion; *flare*, a sudden but brief display of feeling; *glow*, warmth and heartiness.

flare. Syn.: see **flame.**

flash. Syn.: see **flame, shine,** *v.*

flashy. Syn.: glittering, dazzling, brilliant; showy, gaudy, tawdry, meretricious. See **gaudy.**

flat. Syn.: level, even, plane, smooth; prostrate, prone, supine; unqualified, downright, absolute, positive, peremptory; dull, monotonous, uninteresting; lifeless, spiritless, insipid, vapid, tasteless, savorless, stale. See **tasteless, level.**

flatter. Syn.: compliment, praise, blandish, cajole, wheedle.

flattery. Syn.: adulation, compliment, blandishment, blandiloquence, cajolery, obsequiousness, sycophancy, blarney, taffy. See **compliment.**

flaunt. Syn.: see **display.**

flavor. Syn.: savor, smack, tang, relish, zest. See **taste.**

flaw. Syn.: crack, chink, breach, rent, rift; defect, imperfection, blemish, fault. See **imperfection.**

flay. Syn.: see **skin,** *v.*

flee. Syn.: run away, abscond, decamp, levant (*colloq.* skip, skedaddle, absquatulate, vamose).

To *flee* is to run away, either for a good or bad reason, but especially from danger. To *decamp* is to leave suddenly, secretly, or unceremoniously, especially to elude detection or pursuit. To *abscond* is to flee secretly and to hide oneself for some discreditable reason, especially because of the theft of money. *Levant* is especially applied among gamblers to one who steals away to avoid paying his debts.

fleer. Syn.: see **scoff.**

fleet, *n.* **Syn.:** squadron, flotilla, armada, **navy.**

fleet, *a.* **Syn.:** see **swift, quick.**

fleeting. Syn.: transitory, temporary, momentary, ephemeral, evanescent. See **transient.**

That which is *fleeting* runs from us so fast that we can perceive it, as it were, but for a moment; that which is *evanescent* disappears in an instant. *Transient* rather marks the fact that a thing soon passes or will pass away; *transitory*, that by its inherent nature it lacks permanence. *Ephemeral* describes that which has so little vitality that its existence is necessarily brief.

fleshly. Syn.: see **carnal.**

fleshy. Syn.: see **stout.**

flexible. Syn.: pliable, pliant, supple, limber, lithe, willowy, lissome, elastic, ductile, compliant, yielding, tractable, manageable. **Ant.:** see **inflexible.**

Flexible and *pliant* agree in the suggestion of that which is capable of being bent, *pliant* stressing the inherent quality, *flexible* adding sometimes the idea of compressibility or expansibility. Figuratively *flexible* is applied to many things and, in the case of persons, to one who can bend his mind so as to adapt it to various necessities, *pliant* to one whose disposition is so easy-going that he can be readily influenced by others. *Supple* denotes easy and ready pliability, as of the joints; figuratively, a yielding nature, even to the point of obsequiousness. *Limber* is especially applied to the body to denote ease of movement; *lithe* adds the suggestion of grace. Besides grace of movement, *willowy* implies tallness and slenderness of stature. *Lissome* is used poetically for lithe(some).

flicker. Syn.: see **flame, flutter.**

flightiness. Syn.: see **levity.**

flimsy. Syn.: frail, unsubstantial, thin, slight, sleazy; trivial, shallow, feeble, weak, frivolous, foolish.

flinch. Syn.: shrink, wince, blench, quail, recoil. See **shrink.**

fling. Syn.: see **throw.**

flippancy. Syn.: see **levity.**

flippant. Syn.: smart, pert, malapert, forward, impertinent, disrespectful, saucy. See **impudent.**

flirtation. Syn.: flirting, coquetry, philandering, dalliance.

flit. Syn.: see **fly.**

float. Syn.: drift, sail, soar, waft.

flock. Syn.: herd, drove, pack, bevy, covey, flight, gaggle, brood, hatch, litter, shoal, school, swarm, group, band, company, crowd, throng, multitude.

Flock is the popular term for a company of birds of any sort or of animals, especially sheep or goats, often under the care or guidance of some one. *Herd* is usually applied to larger animals, especially to cattle, originally under the charge of some one, but, by extension, to other animals feeding or driven together, as buffaloes or elephants; *drove* is especially applied to a number of oxen, sheep, or swine when driven in a body; *pack*, to a number of animals kept together, as hounds, or herding together for offense or defense, as wolves. As applied to crowds of people *herd*, *drove*, and *pack* imply contempt. We speak specifically of a *bevy* of quail, larks, or women, a *covey* of partridges or grouse, a *swarm* of insects or bees, a *shoal* or *school* of fish, porpoises, or whales, a *brood* of chickens, a *litter* of pigs or puppies. *Brood* is especially applied to the young of fowls and birds hatched from eggs at one time and raised under their mother's care; *litter*, to a group of young animals brought forth at a birth.

flog. Syn.: see **whip, beat.**

flood, *n.* **Syn.:** inundation, deluge, cataclysm, freshet.

Flood denotes the rapid sweeping of a great body of water overflowing a normally dry area; *inundation*, a more learned and literary word, suggests the covering of a great area of land by water. *Freshet* especially suggests a small, quick overflow, as that caused by heavy rains; *deluge*, a great downpouring of water, usually with much destruction; *cataclysm*, a sudden and violent flood such as overthrows or destroys all before it, hence any great upheaval or disturbance that affects society.

flood, *v.* **Syn.:** overflow, inundate, deluge, submerge.

florid. Syn.: flowery.

Flowery language is such as is full of ornate and high-sounding words and ornamented figures of speech; *florid* is a stronger word suggesting a more intimate relation between style and matter, and often a greater breach of taste.

flourish. Syn.: thrive, prosper, succeed; brandish, wave. See **thrive.**

flout. Syn.: mock, jeer, scoff, sneer, gibe, taunt. See **scoff.**

flow. Syn.: run, glide, stream; gush, spurt, spout; issue, emanate.

Flow is the generic term. To *gush* is to rush forth copiously in as large a volume as can issue from the cavity as a result of some strong impelling force: as, the water *gushed* from the broken main. To *stream* is to flow freely and continuously, usually in a long narrow course; as, the blood *streamed* down his arm. *Spurt* and *spout* both imply the ejecting of a liquid from a cavity by some internal impetus given to it, *spurt* in a forcible, possibly sudden, spasmodic, or intermittent issue or jet; *spout* in a rather steady, possibly well-defined, jet or stream, not necessarily of long duration but always with considerable force: as, the liquid *spurted* from the bottle; a whale *spouts* water.

flower. **Syn.:** bloom, blossom, bud, blow, floret, floweret; prime, vigor, perfection.

flowery. **Syn.:** see **florid**.

fluctuate. **Syn.:** vary, oscillate, undulate, vacillate, waver.

fluctuation. **Syn.:** variation, oscillation, vacillation, wavering, shifting, change.

fluent. **Syn.:** flowing, smooth, voluble, glib.

As applied to speaking, *fluent* suggests an easy and ready flow of words, and is usually a term of commendation; *voluble*, a copious, even excessive, and often rapid flow of words; *glib*, an excessive fluency that does not proceed from sincerity or depth of thought: as, a *fluent* speaker; a *voluble* politician; a *glib* salesman.

fluid. **Syn.:** liquid, liquor, solution, gas. See **liquid**.

flunky. **Syn.:** see **servant**.

flurry. **Syn.:** see **wind**.

fluster. **Syn.:** excite, confuse, agitate, perturb, disconcert, embarrass, flustrate.

flutter. **Syn.:** hover, flicker, flit; tremble, palpitate, throb. See **fly**.

fly. **Syn.:** soar, wing, flit, flutter, hover; shoot, dart, rush, leap, spring; flee, abscond, decamp.

To *fly* is to move through the air as on wings. To *soar* is to fly upward to a great height usually with little advance in any other direction, or to fly at a lofty height without visible movement of the wings. To *hover* is to linger indecisively in the air or move irresolutely over or about something by the moving of the wings. To *flutter* is to agitate the wings tremulously, either without flying or in flying only short distances. To *flit* is to make short rapid flights from place to place.

foal. **Syn.:** see **horse**.

fodder. **Syn.:** see **feed**, *n*.

foe. **Syn.:** see **opponent**.

fog. **Syn.:** haze, mist, drizzle, vapor, brume.

The size of the constituent particles or globules is a distinguishing characteristic of these words. A *haze* is composed of a countless number of microscopic particles of moisture, smoke, dust, etc., suspended near the earth's surface, causing an obscuration in the transparency of the atmosphere, which sometimes gives a pleasant indistinctness or vagueness to things, as in autumn. A *fog* is composed of particles of moisture less minute, or more compact, but still separately indistinguishable; it varies in density, and is sometimes impenetrable by the sight for any distance. In a *mist* the globules are very fine, but are separately distinguishable and have a visible motion. A *drizzle* is a fine, misty rain.

foible. **Syn.:** weakness, failing, infirmity, imperfection, defect, fault, frailty. See **failing**.

foil. **Syn.:** see **frustrate**.

follow. **Syn.:** come after, succeed; go after, pursue, chase, trail, track, trace; attend, accompany; ensue, result.

To *follow* is to come after, often close upon but without any necessary connection with, what precedes: as, he could not make out the letters that *followed*. To *succeed* is to follow, usually as one of a series, and so to occupy a given place immediately after a predecessor: as, the prince *succeeded* to the throne. To *ensue* is to follow by a necessary connection or as a logical or chronological sequence: as, the motion was seconded and a general discussion *ensued*.

follower. **Syn.:** attendant, retainer, dependent, adherent, disciple, votary, partizan, henchman, supporter, satellite, hanger-on, parasite, sycophant, toady, lickspittle.

A *follower* is one who attends another as a servant, attendant, associate, etc., or follows the leadership of another in regard to his doctrines or opinions. An *adherent* is one who owns allegiance, often openly, to an individual, a group, or a cause. A *partizan* is an adherent who openly champions, sometimes unreasoningly, that to which he adheres.

folly. **Syn.:** foolishness, fatuity, imprudence, indiscretion, unwisdom, absurdity.

Folly is foolish or ridiculous conduct, procedure, or practice, as that resulting from lack of common sense or sound reason; *imprudence*, unwise or incautious conduct or action, as that resulting from heedlessness, rashness, or the like; *indiscretion*, unguarded or injudicious conduct or speech, as that resulting from want of tact or good judgment: as, the *follies* of youth; the *imprudence* of violating the law; the *indiscretion* of betraying a secret.

foment. **Syn.:** encourage, abet, instigate, excite, stir up, foster, promote.

fond. **Syn.:** doting, indulgent, loving, affectionate, amorous, enamoured, attached.

fondle. **Syn.:** caress, pet, coddle, cosset.

fondness. **Syn.:** attachment, affection, devotion; liking, inclination, propensity, predilection, appetite; folly, delusion, doting. See **love**.

food. **Syn.:** aliment, nutriment, nutrition, nourishment, sustenance, pabulum, fare, provisions, rations, viands, refreshments, victuals, eatables, edibles, comestibles. Cf. **feed**, *n*.

Food is a general word for whatever sustains life in any organized body, whether of men, animals, or plants, and is especially applied to human beings, small animals, and household pets. *Victuals*, an old-fashioned word, is used especially of food set out for human consumption. *Nutriment* is often used to denote in a more or less scientific way the elements in food which nourish the body. *Aliment* (*lit.* nourishment) is a less common word for anything that supports the body or, figuratively, sustains the mind. *Pabulum* is especially used figuratively for whatever is food for thought.

fool, *n.* **Syn.:** simpleton, dolt, dunce, blockhead, dullard, numskull, ignoramus, dunderhead, beetlehead, clodpate, clodpoll, oaf, mooncalf, ninny, nincompoop, booby, ass, goose, saphead, sap, silly; jester, buffoon, droll, clown, harlequin, merry-andrew, zany; dupe, butt, victim; idiot, imbecile, natural, defective. See **idiot**.

fool, *v.* **Syn.:** play, trifle, toy, dally, idle, dawdle, loiter, tarry; deceive, delude, hoodwink, trick, dupe, cheat, gull, hoax, cozen, victimize. See **meddle**.

foolhardy. **Syn.:** rash, reckless, daredevil, venturesome. See **rash**.

foolish. **Syn.:** unwise, indiscreet, imprudent, senseless, brainless, witless, stupid, dull, fatuous, asinine; nonsensical, ridiculous, absurd, silly; half-witted, weak-minded, idiotic, imbecile. **Ant.:** see **wise**.

Foolish implies lack of common sense or good judgment, or, sometimes, weakness of mind; *stupid*, natural slowness or dullness of intellect, or, sometimes, a benumbed or dazed state of mind; *silly*, extreme and conspicuous foolishness, senselessness, or empty-headedness, even approaching imbecility; *fatuous*, complacent stupidity or the witlessness of a person in whom one might naturally expect greater intelligence; *asinine*, that complete stupidity that one associates with an ass.

foot. **Syn.:** hoof, paw; bottom, base; extremity, end.

footpad. **Syn.:** see **robber**.

fop. **Syn.:** exquisite, dude, coxcomb, popinjay, jackadandy. See **dandy**.

for. **Syn.:** see **because**.

forage. **Syn.:** see **feed**, *n*.

foray. **Syn.:** see **invasion**.

forbear. **Syn.:** refrain, hold back, abstain, desist, cease, stop.

forbearance. **Syn.:** abstinence, self-restraint; patience, long-suffering, tolerance, lenity, indulgence.

forbid. **Syn.:** prohibit, interdict, proscribe, inhibit, taboo.

Forbid is a common and familiar word, usually designating a direct or personal command to refrain from some action; *prohibit*, a formal or legal word, is usually to forbid by official or authoritative edict, enactment, or the like: as, I *forbid* you to go; opium traffic is *prohibited*. *Interdict* is used of legal or ecclesiastical prohibitions, especially those of a formal or public kind. *Inhibit*, besides indicating ecclesiastical prohibition, implies a checking or hindering, often of desires, impulses, etc., restrained by the mind. *Proscribe* especially implies prohibition of something on the ground that it is morally wrong: as, some religious sects *proscribe* dancing. *Taboo*, primarily associated with primitive superstition, is to prohibit by common disapproval: as, many subjects are *tabooed* in polite conversation.

forbidden. Syn.: prohibited, interdicted, proscribed, taboo, contraband, illicit.

forbidding. Syn.: repellent, repulsive, disagreeable, displeasing, grim.

force, *n.* **Syn.:** strength, power, might, vigor, energy; cogency, potency, validity; compulsion, coercion, violence, constraint; value, significance, meaning, import; troops, army. See **strength.**

force, *v.* **Syn.:** compel, coerce, constrain, necessitate, oblige, make, cause.

To *force* is to bring to a certain course of action or thought, overpowering or nullifying any resistance. To *compel* is to drive irresistibly to some course, often by moral force or necessity. *Constrain,* a less vigorous word, is used especially of the compelling action of circumstances. *Coerce* implies the use of superior power to compel submission or obedience, and now usually suggests an overriding of personal or private rights. See *actuate.*

forced. Syn.: enforced, compulsory, involuntary; strained, unnatural, affected, far-fetched.

forcible. Syn.: strong, powerful, vigorous; effective, convincing, cogent, potent.

forebode. Syn.: foretell, predict; presage, augur, anticipate. See **foresee.**

foreboding. Syn.: presage, presentiment, premonition.

Foreboding suggests a vague, depressing sense of approaching evil; *presentiment,* a feeling of expectation, without definite or assignable cause, of something, not necessarily evil, that is seemingly impending; *premonition,* a mental warning of what is to befall.

forecast. Syn.: see **foretell.**

forefather. Syn.: see **ancestor.**

foregoing. Syn.: see **previous.**

foreign. Syn.: alien, strange, exotic, extraneous, extrinsic, adventitious, irrelevant.

foreigner. Syn.: alien, stranger.

Foreigner refers to a person belonging by birth to another race or national group than one's own; *alien,* to a citizen of another country than that in which he is living. *Foreigner* emphasizes the difference in language, customs, and the like; *alien,* the difference in political allegiance.

foreordain. Syn.: preordain, predetermine, predestine, predestinate, foredoom.

forerunner. Syn.: see **herald,** *n.*

foresee. Syn.: anticipate, divine, forebode.

Foresee simply signifies seeing ahead or beforehand, often with the implication of preparing or providing for what will happen; *divine* implies intuitive or supernatural foreknowledge of what is to come; *forebode,* a vague feeling of evil or impending misfortune.

foreshadow. Syn.: see **portend.**

foresight. Syn.: prevision, prescience, prudence.

Foresight suggests a practical faculty of seeing in advance what is likely to occur. *Prevision,* a more formal term, suggests ability to foresee and to judge of the effect of future contingencies. *Prescience,* literally foreknowledge, suggests a knowledge or anticipatory vision of the future that is beyond ordinary human power.

forest. Syn.: wood, woods, woodland, grove, copse, chase, park.

A *forest* is an extensive area covered with trees, preserving its primitive wildness, and usually having game or wild animals in it. A *wood* is a smaller tract resembling a forest but less wild in its character and in closer proximity to civilization. A *grove* is a group or cluster of trees not sufficiently large to be called a wood.

forestall. Syn.: see **anticipate.**

foretell. Syn.: predict, prophesy, vaticinate, prognosticate, forecast, presage, augur, forebode.

To *foretell* is to tell (usually correctly) beforehand what will happen: as, the soothsayer *foretells* the future. To *predict* is usually to foretell with the precision of calculation, knowledge, or shrewd inference from facts or experience: as, an economist *predicts* high prices from the scarcity of labor. To *prophesy* is to predict with much confidence or to foretell future events as by supernatural or divine inspiration or foreknowledge: as, the coming of Christ was frequently *prophesied.* To *prognosticate* is to foretell by studying signs and symptoms: as, to *prognosticate* bad weather or the course of a disease. To *forecast* is to make a conjecture about the future, usually upon a more or less uncertain ground or basis: as, to *forecast*

snow and a fall in temperature for to-morrow. To *augur* is to divine the future by the interpretation of signs or omens, which usually have well established meanings.

forethought. Syn.: premeditation, foresight, prudence, care.

forever. Syn.: eternally, continually, perpetually, endlessly, everlastingly, always, ever, evermore, aye.

foreword. Syn.: see **introduction.**

forfeit. Syn.: fine, mulct, penalty, amercement.

forfeiture. Syn.: see **loss.**

forge. Syn.: form, make, beat, hammer; fabricate, counterfeit, falsify.

forgetful. Syn.: see **oblivious.**

forgetfulness. Syn.: see **oblivion.**

forgive. Syn.: pardon, excuse, absolve. See **pardon.**

forgiveness. Syn.: pardon, absolution, remission.

forgo. Syn.: surrender, relinquish, waive, renounce, resign, yield.

Forgo implies a voluntary refraining from what one might easily have, especially as a matter of expediency or self-denial; *waive,* a refusal to insist on some claim, right, or prerogative which properly belongs to one: as, to *forgo* rich food for the sake of health; the prosecutor *waived* the privilege of cross-examining the witness.

forlorn. Syn.: abandoned, forsaken, deserted, desolate, friendless, miserable, disconsolate, wretched, abject, woe-begone. See **desolate.**

form, *n.* **Syn.:** shape, figure, configuration, conformation, contour, outline; species, kind, variety; formality, conventionality, ceremony, ritual, rite, observance, formula; mold, pattern, model.

Form, shape, and *figure* are frequently used with little distinction of meaning, but *form* has the widest application, being used of both physical objects and mental images, methods of procedure, etc. They all suggest outline as contrasted with color and material; *form* at times suggests a contrast not only with substance but with spirit. Thus we say, the *form* of a cross, a *form* of ceremony, the *form* of a poem or musical composition. Both *form* and *shape* exist as concepts independent of concrete realities, as in the phrase ' without *shape* or *form,*' but *figure* is always associated with a particular object, as, the *figure* of a man. *Conformation* and *configuration* denote form as it results from the arrangement of the parts of the whole, *conformation* suggesting the proportion and relation of the parts, internal and external, to each other, and often emphasizing arrangement in reference to some particular use.

form, *v.* **Syn.:** shape, fashion, mold, make, construct; arrange, combine, organize; compose, constitute, make up.

formal. Syn.: regular, conventional, academic, ceremonial, ceremonious, stiff, rigid, precise, punctilious, perfunctory, methodical. **Ant.:** see **informal.**

Formal in a favorable sense denotes accordance with proper and usual forms (as, a *formal* notification), but it usually implies excessive emphasis on form, or form for its own sake at the sacrifice of the substance or spirit: as, *formal* prayers. *Conventional* may denote proper and desirable conformity with conventions or customs, but it usually implies arbitrary or superficial conformance at the expense of the natural or spontaneous: as, *conventional* compliments. *Academic* may be applied to whatever pertains to an academy or higher institution of learning, but it often implies conformance to mere rules and theories that have no bearing upon practical affairs or results: as, *academic* discussions.

former. Syn.: prior, earlier, anterior, antecedent, previous, foregoing, preceding, quondam, past, bygone.

formerly. Syn.: previously, anciently, once.

Formerly generally means before the present time, usually an indefinite and often considerable time before; *previously,* before some particular event or time, and generally up to that point: as, the rates of postage were *formerly* much higher than now; they were reduced in 1845, having *previously* been at an average of about 12½ cents. The two words are, however, often interchangeable.

formidable. Syn.: dread, dreadful, fearful, alarming, appalling, threatening, menacing, redoubtable.

Formidable implies strength of a kind to make one hesitate before opposing it; *redoubtable* has much the same meaning, but is now often used humorously, ironically, or contemptuously; that which is *dread* inspires an overwhelming fear or deep reverence, especially by its inherent majesty or contingent possibilities of harm: as, a *formidable* foe; a *redoubtable* hero; the *dread* name of Jehovah.

forsake. **Syn.:** desert, abandon, leave, quit, relinquish, renounce, forswear. See **abandon.**

forswear. **Syn.:** abjure, disavow, recant, retract, repudiate, renounce, reject.

Forswear and its etymological equivalent *abjure* signify to renounce upon oath, and, metaphorically, with protestations and utterly. To *recant* is to make known publicly that we give up as erroneous what we have formerly maintained; to *retract* is to take back as untrue an assertion or accusation.

fortification. **Syn.:** fortress, fort, citadel, stronghold, castle, bulwark, rampart, breastwork, earthwork, field-work, redoubt, redan, trench, rifle-pit.

fortitude. **Syn.:** endurance, patience, firmness, resoluteness, resolution, courage, bravery, hardihood, strength. See **patience.**

fortress. **Syn.:** see **fortification.**

fortuitous. **Syn.:** see **accidental.**

fortunate. **Syn.:** lucky, successful, prosperous, happy, favored; auspicious, advantageous, felicitous, favorable. **Ant.:** see **unfortunate.**

Fortunate implies the receiving of good or the attaining of success by the operation of favorable circumstances or through accident more than by direct effort, and is usually applied to graver or larger matters (especially those happening in the ordinary course of things) than *lucky*, which is a more colloquial word and is applied to things of minor moment that turn out well, but often suddenly or unexpectedly, by chance: as, a *fortunate* investment; a *lucky* speculation; a *fortunate* (but not *lucky*) marriage. *Successful* implies that effective effort has been made in the gaining or achieving of what was sought: as, a *successful* merchant. *Prosperous* has nearly the same meaning as successful, but does not emphasize effort made and is applied especially to a continued enjoyment of good fortune: as, a *prosperous* farmer; a *prosperous* year of trade.

fortune. **Syn.:** chance, hap, luck; fate, destiny, lot; success, prosperity, wealth.

forward, *a.* **Syn.:** fore, front, anterior; advanced, precocious, presumptuous, bold, pert, impertinent, obtrusive.

forward, *v.* **Syn.:** transmit, send, ship, despatch; further, advance, promote, accelerate, expedite, hasten.

forward, *adv.* **Syn.:** onward, ahead. See **onward.**

foster. **Syn.:** nourish, support, rear, harbor, cherish; promote, encourage, further. See **cherish.**

foul, *a.* **Syn.:** filthy, dirty, soiled, polluted, unclean, impure, noisome, offensive, vile, scurrilous. See **dirty.**

foul, *v.* **Syn.:** defile, dirty, soil, pollute.

found. **Syn.:** establish, plant, settle.

foundation. **Syn.:** founding, establishment; base, basis, groundwork, substructure, bottom.

fountain. **Syn.:** fount, spring. See **well.**

fracas. **Syn.:** see **brawl.**

fractious. **Syn.:** refractory, unruly, perverse; cross, peevish, irritable, fretful, snappish.

fracture, *n.* **Syn.:** crack, split, break, breach, rupture.

fracture, *v.* **Syn.:** see **break.**

fragile. **Syn.:** breakable, frangible, brittle, frail, delicate, weak. **Ant.:** tough, elastic, strong. See **delicate.**

fragment. **Syn.:** piece, bit, scrap, chip, remnant. See **part.**

fragrance. **Syn.:** scent, perfume, redolence, aroma, balminess, savor. See **smell.**

fragrant. **Syn.:** sweet-scented, perfumed, odorous, odoriferous, redolent, spicy, aromatic, balmy.

frail. **Syn.:** brittle, delicate, weak, feeble, infirm. See **fragile, delicate.**

frame. **Syn.:** fashion, shape, plan, devise, contrive, concoct, fabricate. See **make.**

frank. **Syn.:** open, ingenuous, artless, sincere, straightforward, direct, plain, candid, plain-spoken, outspoken, unreserved, free. **Ant.:** disingenuous, insincere, hypocritical, deceitful.

Frank is applied to one who is open or unreserved in the expression of his real opinions and sentiments, sometimes to one who is so free or bold in expressing the truth that he disregards conventional reticence; *candid*, to one who is sincere and truthful in his speech, sometimes unpleasantly so, or impartial and fair in his opinions. The *outspoken* man expresses his mind freely, often unceremoniously or bluntly, when reserve or silence might be better.

frantic. **Syn.:** mad, distracted, frenzied, infuriated, raging, raving, wild.

fraternal. **Syn.:** see **brotherly.**

fraternity. **Syn.:** brotherhood, society, association, sodality, league, clan.

fraud. **Syn.:** deceit, trickery, chicanery; swindle, trick, artifice, dodge, sham, fake; impostor, pretender, humbug, cheat. See **deception.**

fraudulent. **Syn.:** deceptive, dishonest, knavish, cheating.

fray. **Syn.:** see **quarrel,** *n.*, **brawl.**

freak. **Syn.:** whim, fancy, vagary, whimsy, crotchet, caprice, antic, caper, prank. See **caprice.**

free, *a.* **Syn.:** independent, unrestrained, released, liberated, freed, emancipated, delivered; exempt, immune; open, unobstructed; loose, movable, unfastened; liberal, generous, bounteous, lavish, open-handed; frank, untrammeled, unconstrained, licentious. **Ant.:** subject, bound, restrained; firm, immovable, fastened, tied; stingy, parsimonious, close-fisted.

free, *v.* **Syn.:** release, liberate, emancipate, manumit, disenthrall, enfranchise, deliver; relieve, exempt; clear, rid; disengage, disentangle, extricate.

To *free* is to release from any kind of entanglement, restraint, imprisonment, or burden; to *liberate*, especially to set free from confinement or subjection; to *emancipate*, to free from slavery or bondage; to *deliver*, to release or rescue from persecution, oppression, danger, or evil of any kind.

freebooter. **Syn.:** see **robber.**

freedom. **Syn.:** independence, liberty; ease, facility; exemption, immunity, privilege, license; frankness, unconstraint, boldness, familiarity.

Freedom, a dignified and exalted word, implies the absence of undue restriction, and usually emphasizes the large opportunity given for the exercise of one's rights, powers, desires, or the like: as, he expressed his views with *freedom*; *freedom* of speech or conscience. *Liberty*, though often interchanged with freedom, is commonly used where reference is made to past or possible restriction, confinement, or subjection: as, the prisoners were set at *liberty*; the statue of *Liberty*. *Independence* indicates that that to which it is applied is not sustained by anything else: as, political or financial *independence*.

freely. **Syn.:** unreservedly, readily, willingly, voluntarily, gratuitously; liberally, bounteously, abundantly, copiously, lavishly.

freethinker. **Syn.:** see **skeptic.**

freight. **Syn.:** cargo, lading, load.

frenzy. **Syn.:** delirium, madness, rage, fury, raving. See **fury.**

frequent. **Syn.:** haunt, infest.

To *frequent* is to visit a place constantly or repeatedly with no sinister design: as, to *frequent* a club or the theater. To *haunt* is to frequent persistently, usually secretly or stealthily, and often for some sinister purpose: as, the slums of a city are often *haunted* by those who fear the law.

frequently. **Syn.:** see **often.**

fresh. **Syn.:** new, recent, novel; additional, further; inexperienced, unsophisticated, artless, untrained, raw, green; cool, refreshing, invigorating, brisk; blooming, ruddy. See **new.**

freshen. **Syn.:** refresh, revive, renew, renovate.

freshet. **Syn.:** see **flood.**

fret. **Syn.:** gnaw, corrode, chafe, abrade, rub, fray; irritate, vex, provoke, worry, harass. See **vex.**

fretful. **Syn.:** irritable, peevish, petulant, querulous, impatient, fractious.

friar. **Syn.:** monk.

friend. **Syn.:** intimate, companion, comrade, chum, crony; favorer, well-wisher, advocate, supporter, patron.

Friend is the most general word for persons who, through community of life, intimacy, mutual attachment, regard, or respect, have kindly feelings towards each other. *Comrade*, commonly applied to men, denotes close friends or companions who share the same fortunes, experiences, occupations, etc., together. *Intimate* implies close association and the sharing of personal and private matters. *Chum* and *crony* are more or less colloquial words, the former suggesting close companionship, especially between young people, as boys or students, the latter, mellow and familiar companionship, especially that of long duration, as between old men.

friendly. **Syn.:** amicable, kind, brotherly, fraternal, companionable, neighborly, hospitable, sociable, amiable, cordial, genial, kindly, favorable, propitious. **Ant.:** see **unfriendly.**

Etymologically *friendly* and *amicable* are equivalent, but *friendly* is positive and ranges in emphasis from the warmth of personal affection or regard to the cordiality of association or esteem: as, *friendly* advice, a *friendly* manner. *Amicable* is often weaker than friendly, and usually refers to formal or conventional friendships, especially those expressed in agreements, arrangements, or relations, in which case it signifies mutual freedom from ill-feeling, disagreement, or quarrels: as, an *amicable* disposition or discussion.

friendship. Syn.: amity, fellowship, liking. **Ant.:** enmity, hostility, estrangement.

fright. Syn.: terror, dismay, consternation, fear. See **alarm, fear.**

frighten. Syn.: affright, scare, alarm, terrify, appal, dismay, daunt, intimidate, browbeat, cow.

To *frighten* is to shock with sudden, startling, but usually short-lived fear, especially that arising from the apprehension of physical harm. To *alarm* is to arouse the feelings through the realization of some imminent or unexpected danger. To *scare* is to frighten into a loss of poise or dignity, often in fun, or to cause to flee or to desist from something: as, a sudden noise may *scare* any one; to *scare* an animal off. To *terrify* is to strike with violent, overwhelming, or paralyzing fear. To *appal* is to overcome or confound by dread, dismay, or horror: as, the suffering caused by the earthquake *appalled* him.

frightful. Syn.: dreadful, terrible, fearful, horrible, awful, hideous, grisly, revolting, shocking. See **terrible.**

frigid. Syn.: see **cold.**

frisk. Syn.: see **skip.**

frisky. Syn.: see **frolicsome.**

frivolity. Syn.: see **levity.**

frivolous. Syn.: trifling, trivial, petty, unimportant, flimsy, childish, puerile, idle, silly, foolish. See **trifling.**

frolic. Syn.: merrymaking, gaiety, fun, play, gambol; prank, escapade, lark.

frolicsome. Syn.: playful, sportive, gamesome, frisky, coltish, prankish, mischievous, lively.

frontier. Syn.: see **border.**

froth. Syn.: foam, spume, lather, suds, scum.

froward. Syn.: perverse, contrary, obstinate, wilful, refractory, disobedient, untoward. See **wayward.**

frown. Syn.: scowl, lower, glower.

To *frown* is to wrinkle the forehead in annoyance or disapproval, or sometimes in deep thought; to *scowl* is to imply by the expression of the countenance sullenness, anger, or malignance; to *glower* is to exhibit in one's looks fierceness or violence of temper; to *lower* is to look darkly, as with a threatening, foreboding, or gloomy aspect.

frowzy. Syn.: see **slovenly.**

frugal. Syn.: economical, saving, sparing, self-denying, thrifty, chary, parsimonious, stingy. **Ant.:** extravagant, wasteful, prodigal, lavish.

frugality. Syn.: see **economy.**

fruitful. Syn.: productive, fecund, prolific, fertile, rich. **Ant.:** see **unfruitful.**

That which is *rich* or *fertile* is capable of producing abundantly by proper husbandry; that which is *fruitful, prolific,* or *productive* does produce abundantly. *Rich* and *fertile* seem to have a primary reference to soil or the earth; *fruitful* originally referred to trees and plants, *prolific* to animals, including man; *productive* has a general application to whatever may be said to produce. All have widely extended figurative uses: as, a *rich* field of investigation; a *fertile* brain; a *fruitful* suggestion; a *prolific* source of mischief.

fruitless. Syn.: unproductive, infecund, infertile, barren, sterile; vain, ineffective, useless, abortive, unprofitable, bootless, futile.

frustrate. Syn.: thwart, baffle, balk, foil, circumvent, outwit, checkmate, defeat, disappoint.

All these words imply prevention or defeat, intentional or fortuitous, and may be used either of persons or their activities. To *frustrate* is to make useless or vain; to *thwart* is to intercept; to *baffle* is to check by confusing; to *balk* is to obstruct; to *foil* is to turn aside. Thus when we *frustrate* a person we defeat (at least temporarily) his hopes or intentions; we *thwart* him by crossing his plans, *baffle* him by bewildering him so that he is at a loss to know how to proceed, *balk* him by stopping him in his course, *foil* him by diverting his progress.

fugitive. Syn.: see **transient.**

fulfil. Syn.: complete, consummate, accomplish, realize; perform, execute, discharge, do; satisfy, answer, meet, fill.

full. Syn.: filled, replete, sated; complete, entire, whole, plenary, comprehensive, extensive, ample, plentiful, copious, large, wide. **Ant.:** see **empty.** Cf. **complete,** *a.*

fully. Syn.: completely, entirely, wholly, perfectly, amply, abundantly, plentifully, copiously.

fulsome. Syn.: excessive, immoderate, offensive, gross.

fume. Syn.: smoke, reek; chafe, fret, rage, storm.

fun. Syn.: sport, merriment, mirth, gaiety, diversion, amusement, enjoyment; drollery, jest, pleasantry, waggery.

function. Syn.: office, capacity, duty, business; party, reception, levee, soirée.

fundamental. Syn.: basic, basal, essential, indispensable, necessary, first, primary, elementary, original.

funereal. Syn.: mournful, gloomy, dismal, lugubrious, sepulchral, solemn, sad.

funny. Syn.: amusing, comic, comical, laughable, ludicrous, farcical, absurd, ridiculous, droll, witty, facetious, waggish; curious, strange, queer, odd. **Ant.:** serious, sober, solemn, sad, sorrowful, melancholy.

Funny and *laughable* are both applied to that which provokes laughter or deserves to be laughed at. From its connection with the drama, *comical* is especially used of something seen or done that produces mirth, as though it were fit for a comedy. That which is *droll* is quietly amusing because of its oddity or quaintness. The *ludicrous* excites laughter by its foolish absurdity; *ridiculous* often adds the idea of contempt for, or discredit attaching to, whatever is involved.

fur. Syn.: see **skin,** *n.*

furbish. Syn.: see **polish.**

furious. Syn.: raging, frantic, furibund; violent, vehement, fierce. **Ant.:** calm, cool, composed, dispassionate, self-possessed. See **vehement.**

furnish. Syn.: provide, supply, equip, appoint; afford, give, yield.

Furnish, supply, and *provide* all denote the getting or making ready of that which is proper or needful; *furnish* is often associated with the idea of adequate and appropriate equipment, *supply* with the filling of a particular want, *provide* with the exercise of care and foresight.

further. Syn.: see **promote.**

furtive. Syn.: see **secret.**

fury. Syn.: furor, rage, frenzy, ire, wrath, anger; violence, vehemence, fierceness.

Fury is violent anger or extreme excitation which sometimes rises almost to madness: as, a *fury* of revenge, the *fury* of battle. *Frenzy* is temporary madness which manifests itself in irrational expression or action: as, the *frenzy* of despair. *Rage* is usually a sudden and vehement outburst of anger, especially as manifested by extravagant expressions and violent, although often ridiculous, actions: as, the *rage* of a spoiled child.

fuse. Syn.: melt, liquefy, dissolve, smelt; blend, amalgamate, unite, merge, coalesce. See **melt.**

fuss. Syn.: bustle, ado, to-do, pother, stir, excitement, commotion.

fustian. Syn.: see **bombast.**

futile. Syn.: ineffectual, unavailing, vain, idle, useless, profitless, unprofitable, bootless; trifling, trivial, frivolous. See **unavailing.**

G

gabble. Syn.: see **babble.**

gag. Syn.: muzzle, muffle, stifle, silence, suppress.

gage. Syn.: see **earnest.**

gaiety. Syn.: merriment, mirth, glee, jollity, joyousness, liveliness, sportiveness, fun, hilarity, festivity, merrymaking. **Ant.:** see **sorrow.**

gain, *n.* **Syn.:** profit, benefit, advantage, lucre, emolument; increase, advance, addition, increment, accretion, acquisition, accession.

Gain is a general term denoting what accrues to one from the advantageous employment of capital or effort. *Profit* is especially gain from trade or dealing. *Emoluments* are gains arising from office, service, or employment. *Lucre,* always used in a disparaging sense, denotes sordid or ill-gotten gain.

gain, *v.* **Syn.:** acquire, earn, obtain, secure, procure, get, win, achieve, attain; profit, benefit. **Ant.:** lose, forfeit, surrender. See **get.**

gainsay. Syn.: deny, contradict, dispute, controvert, oppose. **Ant.:** affirm, assert, aver, prove, verify. See **contradict.**

gala. Syn.: see **festal.**

gale. Syn.: see **wind.**

gall. Syn.: see **vex.**

gallant. Syn.: gay, showy, fine; **brave, valiant, courageous,** heroic; chivalrous, courtly, polite. **Ant.:** cowardly, pusillanimous, craven; discourteous, impolite, rude. See **brave.**

gallantry. Syn.: bravery, valor, heroism; chivalry, courtliness, politeness, deference.

gallop. Syn.: see **run.**

gambol. Syn.: skip, leap, spring, caper, frisk, romp, frolic, play, sport.

game. Syn.: sport, contest, play, amusement, pastime, diversion; project, scheme, artifice, trick, stratagem; prey, quarry. See **play,** *n.*

gang. Syn.: see **company.**

gap. Syn.: see **opening.**

gape. Syn.: see **look, yawn.**

garb. Syn.: dress, costume, attire, apparel, habiliments, garments. See **dress.**

garbage. Syn.: offal, refuse, waste, swill.

garble. Syn.: mutilate, corrupt, falsify, distort, pervert, misrepresent, misstate, misquote.

garish. Syn.: glaring, gaudy, flashy, showy. See **gaudy.**

garland. Syn.: see **wreath.**

garner. Syn.: see **gather.**

garnish. Syn.: decorate, adorn, embellish, ornament, beautify, deck, trim. **Ant.:** denude, strip, dismantle. See **deck.**

garret. Syn.: attic, loft.

garrulous. Syn.: talkative, loquacious, chattering, prattling, babbling, wordy, verbose, diffuse. **Ant.:** silent, taciturn, reticent, laconic. See **talkative.**

gash. Syn.: see **cut.**

gasp. Syn.: pant, puff, blow. See **pant.**

gastronome. Syn.: see **epicure.**

gather. Syn.: assemble, collect, muster; pick, cull, pluck, crop, reap, glean, garner, harvest; accumulate, amass, hoard; pucker, ruffle, shirr; infer, deduce, conclude. **Ant.:** scatter, disperse, separate. See **pick.**

Gather expresses the general notion of bringing or drawing together. To *collect* is to gather with design or choice from different sources, and often adds the idea of accumulating, or of forming an ordered whole. *Assemble* often denotes the gathering together of persons. To *muster* is to assemble formally, as troops for inspection, or to bring together for military or other service; figuratively, also, we *muster* our powers or resources to meet an emergency.

gathering. Syn.: assemblage, assembly, convocation, meeting, congregation, concourse, company, party, crowd, throng; swelling, boil, abscess, carbuncle. See **meeting.**

gaudy. Syn.: showy, flashy, garish, tawdry, meretricious.

That which is *gaudy* challenges the eye, as by brilliant or glaring colors, and is not in good taste. The *tawdry* is a cheap and pretentious imitation of what is rich or costly. *Showy* things are strikingly conspicuous, but not necessarily offensive to good taste: as, *showy* flowers; *showy* dress. *Flashy* suggests insistent and vulgar showiness. *Garish* expresses a glaring brightness, or crude vividness of color.

gaunt. Syn.: thin, lean, spare, emaciated, scrawny, lank, angular, bony, raw-boned, lantern-jawed. See **thin.**

gawk. Syn.: see **lout.**

gay. Syn.: merry, blithe, gleeful, jolly, jovial, glad, joyous, jocund, light-hearted, lively, vivacious, frolicsome, sportive, merry, hilarious, convivial; bright, brilliant, showy, gaudy; loose, dissipated, fast. **Ant.:** see **sad.**

Gay suggests a lightness of heart or a liveliness of mood that is openly manifested; *joyous,* a happy gaiety of heart; *blithe* (now chiefly a provincial or literary word) and *jocund* (now literary), a cheery or sprightly gaiety. *Merry* suggests animated enjoyment, or mirth and laughter. *Jolly* indicates a good-humored, expansive gaiety of mood or disposition; *jovial,* a hearty, joyous humor, or a spirit of good-fellowship. *Hilarious* implies unrestrained or boisterous gaiety or mirth.

gaze. Syn.: see **look.**

gem. Syn.: see **jewel.**

gender. Syn.: sex.

genealogy. Syn.: see **pedigree.**

general. Syn.: common, prevalent, usual, customary, regular, ordinary, universal; indefinite, vague. **Ant.:** uncommon, exceptional, rare, singular; definite, specific, particular. See **common.**

generally. Syn.: commonly, usually, ordinarily, mainly, principally, chiefly. See **often.**

generate. Syn.: procreate, beget, engender; produce, evolve, originate.

generation. Syn.: see **age.**

generosity. Syn.: magnanimity, nobleness; liberality, munificence, beneficence, bounty. See **liberality.**

generous. Syn.: magnanimous, high-minded, noble; liberal, munificent, open-handed, free, bountiful, lavish; ample, plentiful, abundant. **Ant.:** see **ungenerous.**

genial. Syn.: fostering, kindly, bland, warm, cordial, friendly, hearty, pleasant, agreeable, cheerful.

genius. Syn.: abilities, gifts, endowments, talent, parts, aptitude, faculty, capacity, ingenuity, cleverness.

All these words denote special mental qualifications or powers. *Abilities* is a general word for mental powers, native or acquired, enabling one to do something. *Gifts* are regarded as abilities bestowed by God or nature, rather than as acquirements gained by effort. *Endowments* are gifts conceived as conferred as if by some formal act. *Capacity* often means receptive power, ability to take in ideas or knowledge, but is also used in a more active sense: as, *capacity* to rule; *capacity* for self-government; superior mental *capacities.* *Parts,* now a somewhat homely or archaic term, denotes abilities or gifts as belonging to one's make-up: as, a man of *parts*; to possess good natural *parts.* *Aptitude* and *faculty* denote ability for a particular kind of action, and suggest a ready ease due to special fitness, an *aptitude* being either native or acquired, and a *faculty* being often taken as a natural gift. *Talent,* in accordance with its Biblical origin, denotes a mental gift bestowed upon one for use or improvement, a capacity for achievement or success, a native ability or aptitude especially worthy of cultivation; in a more general sense it often implies the ability or aptitude only, apart from any thought of cultivation. *Genius* is a mental power or endowment of an exalted or phenomenal kind, and includes capacity and instinctive aptitude in their highest forms; it is especially the creative power of original conceptions and combinations, as in literature, art, and science; and it is so clearly distinguished from the lower or more ordinary powers or endowments that it is often conceived as proceeding from supernatural inspiration or kindling the mind like a spark of 'divine fire.'

genteel. Syn.: well-bred, refined, elegant, polished, polite. **Ant.:** see **rude.**

Genteel, once in good use in its original sense of gentle or well born, and hence characterized by the breeding, refinement, elegance, or other qualities usually associated with gentle birth, now implies little more than an air of respectability and a disposition to conform in appearance and behavior to the standards of the upper class. The *well-bred* person has had the advantage of training. The *refined* person may be such through a native fineness of feeling or taste, unaided by external advantages. The *polished* person is the product of training and experience that have imparted a superficial finish shown especially in elegance of manners.

gentle. Syn.: well-born, noble, genteel, refined; mild, soft, bland, meek, peaceful, pacific, soothing, kind, tender, humane, lenient, merciful; docile, tame, tractable, subdued. **Ant.:** rough, harsh, severe, rigorous, drastic, cruel, brutal, pitiless, merciless, inhuman; wild, refractory, intractable.

Gentle has reference especially to disposition and behavior, and often suggests a voluntary kindness or forbearance in dealing with others. *Mild* suggests absence of harshness or severity, due rather to natural character or temperament than to conscious choice. *Meek* implies a submissive spirit, and may even indicate undue submission in the face of insult or injustice. *Tame* denotes a still more marked absence of spirit, as of one whose capacity for resistance or even resentment has been extinguished.

gentlemanly. Syn.: see **masculine.**

genuine. Syn.: real, authentic, true, veritable, unadulterated, unalloyed, pure, sterling; sincere, frank, unaffected. **Ant.:** false, counterfeit, spurious, bogus, sham. See **authentic.**

germ. Syn.: see **embryo.**

germane. Syn.: see **pertinent.**

gesticulation. Syn.: see **gesture.**

gesture. Syn.: gesticulation, flourish.

The following words may have the same meaning, but a *gesture* is usually an expressive or illustrative movement, while a *gesticulation* is an animated, excited, or extravagant gesture: as, a *gesture* of impatience; wild *gesticulations*.

get. **Syn.:** acquire, obtain, procure, secure, earn, gain, win, capture, seize, attain, achieve, realize; catch, contract, take; induce, persuade.

Get is the most general term, and means to come into possession of, in any manner, voluntarily or involuntarily. To *acquire* is especially to get by one's own exertions, or by contact or exposure, or as the result of one's own actions or qualities: as, to *acquire* wealth, knowledge, a library; to *acquire* immunity to a disease; to *acquire* a reputation for honesty or dishonesty. To *obtain* is especially to get by effort, request, solicitation, or other deliberate action: as, to *obtain* food, money, aid, votes. To *procure* is especially to get, or to bring about, by some instrumentality: as, to *procure* an introduction; to *procure* a criminal's conviction. *Gain* and *win* include the idea of advantageous or successful achievement; *earn* emphasizes the securing of rewards through labor or desert. To *attain* is to arrive at a point, end, or result, and often implies effort.

gewgaw. **Syn.:** see **knickknack.**

ghastly. **Syn.:** horrible, frightful, shocking, hideous, grisly, gruesome, grim; death-like, deathly, pallid, pale, cadaverous, haggard, wan.

Ghastly is applied especially to whatever excites the kind of horror caused by death: as, *ghastly* wounds; a *ghastly* sight. *Grim* suggests a fierce, stern, or forbidding cast of countenance. *Grisly* is used of what causes a shuddering horror. *Hideous* implies a repulsive or revolting ugliness or a shocking appearance. One shrinks from what is *gruesome* because of its mysterious and sinister possibilities.

ghost. **Syn.:** spirit, specter, apparition, phantom, phantasm, wraith, revenant, shade, spook.

A *ghost* is the disembodied soul of a deceased person which appears or otherwise manifests itself to man. *Spirit* is frequently interchangeable with *ghost*, but it is used also for a supernatural incorporeal being other than a disembodied soul, often with indication of its disposition (benevolent or malevolent) toward man. *Shade* is the term of the ancient classical mythology for the spirit which survives after death, but is found also in general poetic or other literary use. An *apparition* of a person or thing is an immaterial appearance counterfeiting the reality, and is generally sudden or startling in its manifestation. A *specter* is a ghost or apparition of more or less weird, unearthly, or terrifying appearance. Both *phantom* and *phantasm* denote an immaterial appearance of a person or thing, frequently an illusion of the imagination, as in a dream.

giant. **Syn.:** see **monster.**

gibber. **Syn.:** see **babble.**

gibberish. **Syn.:** see **prattle.**

gibe. **Syn.:** sneer, scoff, jeer, fleer, flout, mock, taunt, deride, ridicule. See **scoff.**

giddy. **Syn.:** dizzy, light-headed, vertiginous; frivolous, unstable, volatile, flighty, harebrained.

gift. **Syn.:** present, donation, contribution, offering, benefaction, bounty, boon, largess, alms, gratuity, premium, allowance, subsidy, bequest, legacy; endowment, talent, faculty, aptitude, bent, turn, knack. See **genius, present,** *n.*

gigantic. **Syn.:** huge, enormous, immense, colossal, monstrous, prodigious, herculean, cyclopean, titanic. **Ant.:** small, little, minute, diminutive, tiny, puny. See **enormous.**

giggle. **Syn.:** see **laugh.**

gild. **Syn.:** see **society.**

gimcrack. **Syn.:** see **knickknack.**

girdle. **Syn.:** belt, band, girth, sash, cincture, zone.

girl. **Syn.:** maid, maiden, lass, lassie, damsel, miss, virgin, hoyden, minx, wench, gill; domestic, servant, waitress; sweetheart, lady-love.

gist. **Syn.:** pith, marrow, essence, substance. See **meaning.**

give. **Syn.:** bestow, confer, grant, present, deliver, accord, furnish, provide, supply, donate, contribute; deal, administer; impart, communicate; assign, allot, award; emit, utter, issue; relinquish, surrender, yield, cede.

Give is a general word, and means to transfer from one's own to another's possession. *Bestow* and *grant* emphasize the gratuitousness of the gift, *grant* often presupposing a request and sometimes implying formality in the giving. To *confer* usually expresses the act of a superior giving that which might be withheld: as, to *confer* knighthood, honors, privileges.

Present usually implies formality or ceremony in the giving, and sometimes considerable value in the gift.

glad. **Syn.:** joyful, joyous, happy, merry, cheerful, elated, delighted, gratified, pleased; gladsome, cheering, animating. **Ant.:** sad, sorrowful, depressed, dejected, downhearted, melancholy.

gladden. **Syn.:** cheer, elate, animate, enliven, delight, gratify, please. See **cheer,** *v.*

gladness. **Syn.:** joy, cheerfulness, delight, pleasure, triumph.

Gladness is a strong, cheerful happiness which usually shows itself outwardly. *Joy* is a keener or more lively feeling of happiness than gladness, and is often more demonstrative. *Delight* is a high degree of pleasure or joy, but is usually not of long duration. *Pleasure* represents a wide range of enjoyment, from that coming from indulgence of the appetites to that derived from what is good or admirable. *Cheerfulness* denotes brightness and contentment of mood or disposition. *Triumph* is joy over success, exultation over victory or achievement.

glamour. **Syn.:** magic, enchantment, fascination, witchery, charm, spell.

glance, *n.* **Syn.:** glimpse, peep; gleam, flash.

A *glance* is a brief look at something; a *glimpse* is a momentary or chance sight obtained of something.

glance, *v.* **Syn.:** see **look, shine.**

glare. **Syn.:** see **shine,** *v.*, **look.**

glaring. **Syn.:** dazzling, brilliant, intense; conspicuous, notorious, flagrant.

glass. **Syn.:** tumbler, goblet; looking-glass, mirror, speculum; lens, microscope, telescope, spy-glass, field-glass.

gleam, *n.* **Syn.:** beam, ray, glimmer.

Gleam denotes a not very brilliant, and frequently only transient, stream of light. *Glimmer* indicates a feeble, unsteady light. *Ray* usually implies a smaller amount of light than *beam*, which in scientific use commonly denotes a shaft of light made up of parallel rays.

gleam, *v.* **Syn.:** see **shine,** *v.*

glee. **Syn.:** merriment, mirth, gaiety, jollity, hilarity, joy. See **mirth.**

gleeful. **Syn.:** merry, mirthful, gay, jolly, joyous. **Ant.:** see **sad.**

glen. **Syn.:** see **valley.**

glib. **Syn.:** fluent, voluble, smooth-tongued, bland, oily. See **fluent.**

glide. **Syn.:** see **slide.**

glimmer, *n.* **Syn.:** see **gleam,** *n.*

glimmer, *v.* **Syn.:** see **shine,** *v.*

glimpse. **Syn.:** see **glance.**

glint, glisten, glister, glitter. **Syn.:** see **shine,** *v.*

gloaming. **Syn.:** see **evening.**

gloat. **Syn.:** see **look.**

globe. **Syn.:** sphere, orb, ball. See **earth.**

Globe and *sphere* denote something that is either perfectly or approximately round. *Ball* is a less exact term, and may be applied to any rounded object or part: as, the *ball* of the foot. *Orb*, as denoting something of spherical shape, is applied especially to the heavenly bodies and to the eyeball or eye, and is now found only in elevated or scientific use.

gloom. **Syn.:** melancholy, depression, dejection, sadness, despondency; darkness, obscurity, dimness, shadow, shade.

gloomy. **Syn.:** melancholy, dejected, downcast, downhearted, sad, despondent, morose, pessimistic, glum; dark, dismal, cloudy, shadowy, somber. **Ant.:** happy, joyful, merry, cheerful, gay; light, bright, sunny. See **cheerless.**

glorify. **Syn.:** see **exalt.**

glorious. **Syn.:** illustrious, famous, renowned; splendid, magnificent, grand, brilliant.

glory. **Syn.:** praise, honor, renown, fame, distinction, eminence; splendor, magnificence, grandeur, pomp. **Ant.:** ignominy, dishonor, obscurity. See **fame.**

gloss. **Syn.:** luster, sheen, polish, glaze; commentary, comment, annotation, note. See **polish.**

glossary. **Syn.:** see **vocabulary.**

glossy. **Syn.:** lustrous, shining, polished, glazed, smooth, sleek.

glow, *n.* **Syn.:** see **flame.**

glow, *v.* **Syn.:** see **shine,** *v.*

glower. **Syn.:** see **look, frown.**

glowing. **Syn.:** incandescent, luminous; ardent, impassioned, fervent, fervid.

glum. Syn.: see **sullen.**

glut. Syn.: see **satiate.**

glutton. Syn.: see **epicure.**

gnaw. Syn.: see **bite, eat.**

gnome. Syn.: see **fairy.**

go. Syn.: move, pass, walk, run, ride, travel, proceed, advance, repair, leave, depart; reach, extend.

goad. Syn.: prick, spur, stimulate, urge, incite, instigate, impel, drive.

goal. Syn.: aim, destination, end, bourn.

gobble. Syn.: gulp, bolt, devour. See **eat.**

goblin. Syn.: see **fairy.**

godless. Syn.: ungodly, unrighteous, impious, wicked. See **irreligious.**

godlike. Syn.: divine, heavenly, celestial.

Godlike expresses likeness or appropriateness to a god, or to God. *Divine* is applied to that which is of the nature of or pertains to a god, or God, in distinction to what is human. *Heavenly* is applied to what is proper to or associated with heaven, in distinction to what is earthly, but the word is often used hyperbolically. *Celestial*, having reference originally to the sky or the material heavens, is used also with reference to the spiritual heaven.

godliness. Syn.: see **piety.**

godly. Syn.: pious, devout, religious, righteous, saintly. Ant.: see **ungodly.**

Godly implies obedience or conformity to the laws of God; *righteous*, conformity to the requirements of right as embodied in either the moral law or divine will.

good, *n.* Syn.: goodness, excellence, virtue, value, worth; well-being, welfare, weal, prosperity, advantage, benefit, profit, interest.

good, *a.* Syn.: excellent, commendable, admirable, satisfactory; genuine, sound, valid, honest, sterling, reliable, safe, sure; righteous, holy, pious, devout, pure, moral, virtuous, conscientious, meritorious, worthy, exemplary; well-behaved, decorous; right, proper, fit; gracious, kind, benevolent, humane, merciful, altruistic, philanthropic; honorable, worthy, fair, untarnished; favorable, auspicious, propitious, fortunate, advantageous, beneficial, profitable, useful; cheerful, friendly, pleasant, agreeable; competent, efficient, proficient, capable, skilful, dexterous, adroit, clever, apt; ample, full, adequate, sufficient. Ant.: see **bad.**

good-by. Syn.: see **farewell.**

good-humored. Syn.: see **good-natured.**

good-looking. Syn.: see **beautiful.**

good-natured. Syn.: good-humored, good-tempered, amiable, affable, jovial, genial.

Good-natured indicates a genial, amiable, or complaisant disposition; *good-humored*, a cheerful, pleasant temper or mood; *good-tempered*, serenity of temper, especially as a permanent characteristic.

goodness. Syn.: virtue, morality. See **virtue.**

Goodness is the simple word for the general quality recognized in character or conduct as entitling the possessor to approval and esteem. *Virtue* is a more formal word, and suggests usually goodness that is consciously or steadily maintained, often in spite of temptations or evil influences. *Morality* implies conformity to the recognized standards of right conduct.

goods. Syn.: see **property.**

good-tempered. Syn.: see **good-natured.**

good-will. Syn.: see **favor,** *n.*

gorge, *n.* Syn.: see **valley.**

gorge, *v.* Syn.: glut, satiate, stuff; bolt, gulp, gobble. See **satiate.**

gorgeous. Syn.: splendid, magnificent, sumptuous, costly, rich, superb, grand, brilliant, resplendent. See **magnificent.**

gossip. Syn.: scandal, tattle.

Gossip is light chat or talk about current affairs, and especially about the affairs of others. *Scandal* is rumor or general talk that is damaging to reputation; it is usually more or less malicious. *Tattle* is idle, irresponsible, or silly gossip, especially that which implies tale-bearing.

gourmand, gourmet. Syn.: see **epicure.**

govern. Syn.: rule, command, manage, direct, regulate, conduct, supervise, guide, control, restrain, curb, bridle.

To *govern* is to exercise authoritative guidance or direction over persons or things, especially over the affairs of a province or territorial unit. *Control* implies a firm direction of or check upon persons or things. *Rule* expresses the exercise of authority as by a sovereign. To *command* is to exercise authoritative direction as a military leader does over his men and implies the power to exact obedience. To *regulate* is to order or adjust in accordance with a standard or need. To *manage* is to conduct affairs, or to direct or control people, often by tact, address, or artifice.

government. Syn.: rule, dominion, sway, authority, direction, administration, control.

grab. Syn.: see **seize.**

grace, *n.* Syn.: attractiveness, charm, beauty, gracefulness, ease, elegance, refinement; favor, good-will, kindness, lenity, mercy; excellence, merit, virtue. See **favor,** *n.*

grace, *v.* Syn.: adorn, decorate, embellish, beautify, honor, enhance.

graceful. Syn.: see **elegant.**

gracious. Syn.: kindly, benign, benevolent, complaisant, lenient, merciful, friendly, affable, courteous, civil, condescending. See **kind.**

gradual. Syn.: see **slow.**

grand. Syn.: great, large, lofty, stately, imposing, majestic, palatial, magnificent, superb, elevated, exalted, sublime, awful, pompous, grandiose.

Grand suggests imposing size or appearance, stately or noble dignity, magnificence, or splendor. *Lofty* indicates imposing height, exalted dignity, or elevated character or style. *Sublime* is a strong word, implying a moral or spiritual height so great as to exalt the beholder and seem above comparison or criticism. That which is *awful* inspires one with a reverential dread or fear: as, the *awful* majesty of God.

grandeur. Syn.: greatness, stateliness, majesty, sublimity, pomp, splendor, state.

grandiloquent. Syn.: pompous, grandiose, bombastic, turgid, highfalutin. See **bombastic.**

grandiose. Syn.: see **bombastic.**

grant, *n.* Syn.: gift, present, bounty, allowance, subsidy, concession.

grant, *v.* Syn.: give, bestow, confer, transfer, convey, cede; admit, concede. Ant.: withhold, reserve, deny. See **give.**

graphic. Syn.: picturesque, vivid.

A *graphic* description produces by words the effect of a picture drawn with telling strokes; a *vivid* description presents the facts with such clearness and spirit as to make them live, as it were, once more before the mental view. *Picturesque* description abounds in striking imagery and may at times emphasize effect at the expense of fidelity to fact.

grapple. Syn.: seize, clutch, grasp, grip, clinch; wrestle, struggle, contend.

grasp. Syn.: seize, grip, clutch, grab, snatch; comprehend, understand. See **seize.**

grateful. Syn.: thankful.

Grateful indicates a warm or deep appreciation of kindness shown to one; *thankful*, a disposition to express gratitude by giving thanks, as to a benefactor or to a merciful Providence.

gratification. Syn.: pleasure, delight, delectation, satisfaction.

gratify. Syn.: please, delight, satisfy, indulge, humor.

To *gratify* is to please by satisfying one's likings or desires. *Indulge* denotes a yielding to wishes by way of favor or complaisance rather than in order to satisfy a just claim, and may imply a habitual or excessive yielding to whims. *Humor* denotes a complying with the humor, fancy, or caprice of another, as in order to satisfy, soothe, or manage.

gratuitous. Syn.: free, voluntary, spontaneous; unwarranted, uncalled-for.

That which is *gratuitous* is given freely or without charge on the part of the giver; that which is *voluntary* is given or done by the free will of the agent, without any sort of compulsion. In another and less favorable sense, *gratuitous* is applied to what is not warranted by circumstances or reason or is uncalled-for or unjustifiable: as, a *gratuitous* assumption; a *gratuitous* insult.

gratuity. Syn.: see **present.**

grave. Syn.: weighty, important, momentous; serious, solemn, sober, staid, sedate, dignified, thoughtful, sage. Ant.: unimportant, trivial, immaterial; gay, merry, jolly, lively.

Grave indicates a weighty dignity, or the character, aspect, demeanor, speech, etc., of one conscious of heavy responsibilities or cares or of threatening possibilities. *Serious* indicates earnestness of mood or purpose or an aspect or demeanor betokening deep or anxious thought. *Solemn* implies an impressive seriousness. *Sober*, from its original sense of freedom from intoxication, and hence temperate, staid, sedate, has come to indicate absence of levity, gaiety, or mirth, and thus to be akin to *serious* and *grave*.

gravel. Syn.: see **stone**.

greasy. Syn.: oily, unctuous, oleaginous, fat, slippery.

great. Syn.: large, big, immense, enormous, gigantic; numerous, countless; important, weighty, serious, momentous; distinguished, eminent, renowned, famous, illustrious; lofty, noble, magnanimous; first-rate, excellent, fine. **Ant.:** see **small**.

Great is a very general word, covering size, extent, number, and degree, with both literal and figurative applications, and usually implies something notable, imposing, or surprising about the greatness affirmed (whether sincerely or ironically): as, a *great* oak; *great* mountains, lakes, avalanches; a *great* undertaking; a *great* victory; a *great* sinner; a *great* fool. *Large* commonly expresses a considerable physical magnitude in at least two dimensions, with corresponding figurative applications: as, a *large* area (but not a *large* line); a *large* house; a *large* head; *large*-hearted sympathies; *large* ideas or interests. *Big* is a more colloquial word than either *great* or *large*, and has reference especially to bulk, size, or extent: as, a *big* frame; a *big* boy; the *big* hotels; *big* business.

greed. Syn.: greediness, avidity, avarice, cupidity, covetousness. See **greediness**.

greediness. Syn.: ravenousness, voracity, gluttony; greed, avarice, cupidity.

Greediness is used either literally or figuratively: as, *greediness* for food; *greediness* for gain, praise, or knowledge. *Greed*, unless a different application is indicated, means greediness for gain or wealth.

greedy. Syn.: avid, ravenous, voracious, gluttonous; avaricious, covetous, grasping, rapacious. See **eager**.

green. Syn.: verdant, emerald, viridescent; unripe, immature, unseasoned; untrained, unskilled, inexperienced, raw, unsophisticated, simple, young, callow; ignorant, gullible. **Ant.:** sear, parched, dried; ripe, seasoned; trained, experienced; clever, shrewd, astute.

greet. Syn.: address, salute, welcome, hail, accost. See **accost**.

greeting. Syn.: see **salutation**.

gregarious. Syn.: see **sociable**.

grief. Syn.: sorrow, anguish, heartache, agony, woe, distress, remorse, regret, sadness, melancholy; misfortune, disaster. **Ant.:** joy, gladness, happiness, elation, exultation, gaiety. See **affliction**.

Grief is a feeling of keen distress over trouble or loss, always over something recent or freshly present to the mind and conceived as affecting one directly and personally; it is usually too keen to be long continued, and may be demonstrative. *Sorrow*, though more quiet and perhaps not openly displayed, may be deep and of long continuance. *Grief* and *sorrow* are both due to a particular cause. *Sadness* is a depressed or mournful state of mind; it may be due to a particular circumstance or to the general condition of affairs, or even to a vague sense of regret, disappointment, hopelessness, or the like. *Woe*, a word of elevated or poetical association, implies a condition of intense unhappiness or grief. *Melancholy* implies enduring depression of spirits either induced by grief or arising from a constitutional derangement.

grievance. Syn.: wrong, injustice, injury, hardship.

A *grievance* is a wrong, real or fancied, that is considered a proper matter for complaint or redress. A *hardship* is a condition or circumstance that bears hard upon one, but is thought of as coming in the general course of experience, or by some inevitable fate, rather than as deliberately imposed by an oppressor. Taxes may be a *hardship* to those required to pay them, but the word implies nothing as to the motives of the government imposing the taxes; they may also constitute a *grievance* to the citizens against the government, but without entailing actual *hardship* for any one.

grieve. Syn.: sorrow, mourn, lament, weep.

grievous. Syn.: distressing, afflictive, oppressive, severe; deplorable, lamentable, calamitous; atrocious, heinous, outrageous.

grim. Syn.: fierce, savage, cruel, merciless, relentless, unyielding; stern, severe, harsh, hard, forbidding, repellent. **Ant.:** kind, tender, gentle, mild, pleasing, attractive. See **ghastly**.

grimy. Syn.: see **dirty**.

grin. Syn.: see **laugh**.

grind. Syn.: crush, pulverize, powder, bray, triturate, comminute, levigate, bruise; grit, grate; harass, persecute, oppress.

grip. Syn.: see **seize**.

grisly. Syn.: fear-inspiring, hideous, horrible, frightful, dreadful, gruesome. See **ghastly**.

grit. Syn.: sand, gravel; firmness, resolution, fortitude, courage, pluck.

groan. Syn.: moan.

A *groan* is a deep vocal sound emitted involuntarily under pressure of pain or suffering, or uttered as if involuntarily in expression of strong disapproval or indignation. A *moan* is a prolonged, low, inarticulate sound indicative of suffering, either physical or mental.

groove. Syn.: channel, furrow, rut, rabbet.

gross. Syn.: large, big, bulky; thick, dense, rank, heavy; rude, ignorant, dull, stupid, witless; broad, coarse, indelicate, indecent, low, animal, sensual; glaring, flagrant, shameful, outrageous; whole, entire, total, aggregate.

grotesque. Syn.: fantastic, odd, strange, bizarre, unnatural, ugly, absurd, ludicrous. See **fanciful**.

grotto. Syn.: see **cave**.

ground. Syn.: foundation, basis, premise, reason, motive, inducement; land, earth, soil, mold, loam, dirt.

groundless. Syn.: baseless, unfounded, chimerical.

grounds. Syn.: see **sediment**.

group. Syn.: assemblage, aggregation, cluster, crowd.

grove. Syn.: see **forest**.

grovel. Syn.: crawl, creep, cringe, fawn.

groveling. Syn.: prostrate, prone; abject, base, servile, mean.

grow. Syn.: vegetate, germinate, sprout, bud, burgeon, pullulate; increase, expand, enlarge, wax, develop, mature, flourish, thrive; cultivate, raise, produce.

To *grow* is to develop toward full size or maturity by natural process, as living things do, or by some process analogous to natural growth. To *increase* is to become greater in size, amount, extent, duration, etc., in any manner. Cf. *increase*.

growl. Syn.: see **grumble**.

growth. Syn.: increase, augmentation, expansion, extension, enlargement, development, advancement.

grudge, *n.* **Syn.:** ill-will, resentment, spite. See **malice**.

grudge, *v.* **Syn.:** begrudge, envy.

gruesome. Syn.: see **ghastly**.

gruff. Syn.: rough, harsh, surly, grumpy, brusque, rude, impolite; deep, hoarse, guttural. **Ant.:** pleasant, complaisant, courteous, polite, civil, gracious.

grumble. Syn.: mutter, murmur, growl, croak, complain, repine. See **complain**.

guarantee. Syn.: warrant, security, surety. See **warrant,** *v.*

guard, *n.* **Syn.:** defense, protection, bulwark, shield, safeguard, fender; defender, protector, watch, watchman, guardsman, sentry, sentinel, picket, patrol, escort, convoy.

guard, *v.* **Syn.:** defend, protect, shield, watch, safeguard, preserve, save, fortify.

To *guard* is to watch over in order to keep safe. To *defend* is to strive to keep safe by resisting invasion or attack. To *protect* is to keep safe by interposing a shield or barrier. To *preserve* is to keep safe from impairment or decay, and may refer either to a single action or occasion or to a continuous safe-keeping. To *save* is to rescue or deliver from danger, evil, or destruction.

guarded. Syn.: defended, protected, watched; cautious, circumspect, careful, reserved, non-committal. See **cautious**.

guardian. Syn.: protector, defender, trustee, warden, keeper, guard.

guess, *n.* **Syn.:** estimate, conjecture, surmise, supposition, speculation.

guess, *v.* **Syn.:** estimate, conjecture, surmise, presume, suppose, divine; think, believe, opine. See **conjecture,** *v.*

guest. Syn.: see **visitor**.

guffaw. Syn.: see **laugh**.

guide, *n.* **Syn.:** leader, conductor, director, pilot, cicerone; guide-book, handbook, key.

guide, *v.* **Syn.:** lead, conduct, direct, pilot, steer; regulate, control, manage, govern.

Guide implies continuous presence or agency in showing the way or in indicating or determining the course to be taken: as, to *guide* a traveler; to *guide* a horse, a plow, or a pen. To *lead* is to bring onward in a course, often with implication of guiding by contact or by going in advance, and is hence used figuratively of influencing or inducing to some course of conduct. To *conduct* is to lead or escort to a place, and suggests a degree of ceremony in the process. *Direct* expresses the giving of information for guidance or of instructions or orders for a course of procedure.

guile. **Syn.:** cunning, artfulness, wiliness, trickery, craft, deceit. **Ant.:** see **honesty.**

guileful. **Syn.:** cunning, artful, wily, crafty, deceitful.

guileless. **Syn.:** sincere, honest, truthful, frank, candid, straightforward, ingenuous, artless, unsophisticated. See **artless.**

guillotine. **Syn.:** see **kill.**

guilt. **Syn.:** guiltiness, culpability, criminality, wrongdoing, iniquity.

guiltless. **Syn.:** see **innocent.**

guilty. **Syn.:** culpable, sinful, criminal.

guise. **Syn.:** dress, garb, appearance, semblance, aspect, shape.

gulch. **Syn.:** see **ravine.**

gulf. **Syn.:** bay; chasm, abyss; whirlpool, maelstrom.

gull. **Syn.:** see **cheat.**

gully. **Syn.:** see **ravine.**

gulp. **Syn.:** see **swallow.**

gun. **Syn.:** firearm, shotgun, rifle, musket, flintlock, matchlock, blunderbuss, harquebus, cannon, howitzer, mortar, machine-gun, pistol, revolver, derringer.

gush. **Syn.:** flow, pour, stream, spurt, spout. See **flow.**

gust. **Syn.:** see **wind.**

gusto. **Syn.:** taste, liking, relish, zest, enjoyment, appreciation. See **relish.**

guzzle. **Syn.:** see **drink,** *v.*

gyves. **Syn.:** see **shackles.**

H

habiliment. **Syn.:** dress, clothing, attire, raiment, vesture, apparel, garment.

habit. **Syn.:** practice, usage, use, wont, habitude, consuetude, routine, rule; proclivity, disposition, tendency; attire, apparel, dress, clothing, garb, costume. See **dress,** *n.*

habitation. **Syn.:** abode, dwelling, residence, domicile, quarters, home.

Habitation is a general term for a place inhabited, whether a house, cave, den, or other shelter, or even a spot or region. *Abode* and *dwelling*, also general terms and now found especially in literary use, imply some mention or obvious thought of the occupant or occupants. *Home* is the familiar term for an abode or dwelling-place, whether of a family or household or of an individual, with all the intimate associations connected with domestic life. *Residence* denotes an abode regularly occupied or generally recognized as one's home, and commonly suggests a house of a more or less pretentious kind. *Domicile* is especially a legal term for a permanent or recognized residence, to which one, if absent, intends to return.

habitual. **Syn.:** customary, usual, wonted, ordinary, everyday; confirmed, inveterate. **Ant.:** occasional, unusual, exceptional, rare.

That which is *habitual* has become settled or constant as the result of habit on the part of the individual. That which is *customary* is in accordance with prevailing usage or individual practice. *Usual* indicates that which is to be expected by reason of previous experience, which shows it to occur more often than not.

habituate. **Syn.:** accustom, familiarize, inure, harden, acclimatize, acclimate, naturalize.

hack. **Syn.:** see **cut,** *v.*

hackneyed. **Syn.:** trite, commonplace, stale, threadbare. See **trite.**

haggard. **Syn.:** careworn, gaunt, lean, thin, wasted, emaciated, hollow-eyed.

haggle. **Syn.:** bargain, chaffer, higgle. See **cut,** *v.*

hail. **Syn.:** greet, salute, address, accost, signal. See **accost.**

hairy. **Syn.:** bristly, shaggy, hirsute, pubescent, pilose, villose.

hale, *a.* **Syn.:** sound, healthy, hearty, robust, vigorous. **Ant.:** see **sick.** See **strong.**

hale, *v.* **Syn.:** see **draw.**

half-hearted. **Syn.:** lukewarm, indifferent, perfunctory, faint.

hallow. **Syn.:** consecrate, dedicate, sanctify, bless. See **devote.**

hallowed. **Syn.:** see **holy.**

hallucination. **Syn.:** see **illusion.**

halo. **Syn.:** nimbus, aureola, aureole, glory.

halt. **Syn.:** see **stop,** *v.*

hamlet. **Syn.:** see **town.**

hammer. **Syn.:** mallet, maul, sledge, gavel.

hamper. **Syn.:** impede, obstruct, restrain, hinder, encumber, clog, trammel, shackle, fetter, curb, restrict. See **hinder.**

handbook. **Syn.:** manual, treatise, guide-book, vademecum.

handsome. **Syn.:** see **beautiful.**

handy. **Syn.:** accessible, convenient, ready; dexterous, skilful, deft, adroit. **Ant.:** see **unhandy.**

hang. **Syn.:** suspend; depend, dangle, droop, lean, incline. See **kill.**

hanger-on. **Syn.:** dependent, follower, fawner, minion, sponger, satellite, sycophant, toady, toad-eater, heeler. See **parasite.**

hanging. **Syn.:** suspended, pendent, pendulous, pensile, dangling.

hanker. **Syn.:** see **long.**

hankering. **Syn.:** see **desire,** *n.*

haphazard. **Syn.:** chance, accidental, random, stray, aimless.

hapless. **Syn.:** luckless, unlucky, unfortunate, forlorn.

happen. **Syn.:** occur, take place, chance, befall, betide.

Happen, which originally denoted the occurrence of an event by hap or chance, is now the most general word for coming to pass. *Chance* more than *happen* suggests the fortuitousness of the event: as, to persist, in spite of whatever may *chance*. *Occur* is often interchangeable with *happen*, but is more formal, and is used of more definite or specific events: as, his death *occurred* the following year; the presidential election *occurs* (not *happens*) every four years.

happiness. **Syn.:** fortune, prosperity, blessedness, bliss, beatitude, felicity; joy, gladness, rapture, ecstasy, delight.

Happiness is a state of pleasure or pleasurable content resulting from the possession or attainment of what one considers good. *Felicity* is happiness of an especially fortunate or intense kind. *Bliss* is unalloyed happiness or supreme delight. *Beatitude* suggests the felicity of those who are divinely blessed.

happy. **Syn.:** lucky, fortunate, successful, prosperous; favorable, propitious, auspicious; joyous, joyful, glad, gay, cheerful, elated, rapturous, exultant, delighted, gratified, contented; felicitous, appropriate, fitting, apt. **Ant.:** see **unhappy.**

harangue, *n.* **Syn.:** see **speech.**

harangue, *v.* **Syn.:** see **speak.**

harass. **Syn.:** worry, annoy, molest, trouble, torment, badger, vex, pester, bother, plague, tease, afflict, persecute, harry.

To *harass* is to disturb or torment in a persistent, wearying way, as by attacks, annoyances, or importunities; figuratively it is often used of the action of cares, anxieties, troubles, and the like. To *harry* is to ravage as an army does, or any band of predatory raiders; figuratively it carries the idea of harassing with violence or ruthless cruelty. To *molest* is to interfere with annoyingly or injuriously, so as to disturb one's peace, comfort, or well-being: as, they shall not be *molested* in the exercise of their rights. *Persecute*, to pursue with harassing or oppressive treatment, especially for adherence to religious or other opinions, is used also of any persistent vexation that is peculiarly distressing to the victim.

harbinger. **Syn.:** see **herald,** *n.*

harbor, *n.* **Syn.:** lodging, shelter, refuge, asylum, retreat; haven, port.

A *harbor*, as a place of shelter for ships, may be either natural or artificially constructed or improved. A *haven* is usually a natural harbor which can be utilized by ships as a place of safety; the word is common in poetic use. A *port* is a harbor viewed especially in its commercial relations.

harbor, *v.* **Syn.:** see **cherish.**

hard. **Syn.:** solid, compact, firm, impenetrable, inflexible, rigid, unyielding, resisting, adamantine, flinty; perplexing, puzzling, intricate, knotty, tough; difficult, arduous, onerous, laborious, toilsome, burdensome, tiresome, wearisome, fatiguing, exhausting; harsh, severe, rigorous, oppressive, grinding, cruel, merciless, unsparing; stern, austere, strict, exacting, unfeeling, unsympathetic, callous. **Ant.:** see **soft.** See **firm, harsh.**

Hard is a simple, general word, applicable to whatever resists one's efforts or taxes one's endurance. *Difficult* means not easy, and particularly denotes that which requires special effort or skill. *Arduous* retains something of its original meaning of steep, or difficult to climb, and suggests the need of severe and protracted effort.

harden. Syn.: solidify, indurate, petrify, ossify; inure, accustom, habituate, train, discipline, toughen, season, temper, fortify, steel, brace, nerve.

hardened. Syn.: solidified, indurated, callous; confirmed, inveterate. See **chronic.**

hard-headed. Syn.: see **sensible.**

hard-hearted. Syn.: unfeeling, unsympathetic, callous, stern, cruel, unmerciful, pitiless, ruthless, inhuman. **Ant.:** see **kind.**

hardihood. Syn.: boldness, courage, intrepidity, audacity, effrontery, impudence. See **confidence.**

hardly. Syn.: scarcely, barely.

Hardly and *scarcely* have about the same force, *hardly* emphasizing the idea of the difficulty involved, *scarcely* the idea of an incomplete measure of attainment or a deficiency of ability: as, I can *hardly* do that; he will *scarcely* appreciate it. *Barely* means only just, just but no more: as, we *barely* succeeded.

hardship. Syn.: trial, affliction, privation, want, adversity, oppression. See **grievance.**

hardy. Syn.: bold, courageous, intrepid, daring, resolute; strong, robust, vigorous, sturdy, hale, hearty, lusty.

harebrained. Syn.: giddy, careless, heedless, reckless, rash, wild.

harken. Syn.: see **hear.**

harlot. Syn.: see **prostitute.**

harm. Syn.: see **injury.**

harmful. Syn.: injurious, hurtful, detrimental, mischievous, deleterious, noxious, pernicious, baneful, nocent.

harmless. Syn.: unharmed, uninjured, unhurt, undamaged; inoffensive, unoffending, innoxious, innocuous, peaceable.

harmonious. Syn.: congruous, congruent, consonant, conformable, consistent; melodious, tuneful, symphonious; concordant, amicable, peaceable, cordial. **Ant.:** inharmonious, incongruous, contradictory; discordant, dissonant, harsh, strident, grating; antagonistic, unfriendly, hostile.

harmonize. Syn.: agree, correspond, accord, comport, tally, square, fit, jibe; pacify, reconcile.

harmony. Syn.: agreement, congruity, consonance, conformity, correspondence, consistency; concord, chime, accord, concurrence, unity, amity, peace, friendship. **Ant.:** incongruity, inconsistency; discord, variance, contention, dissension, controversy, conflict. See **melody.**

harry. Syn.: ravage, devastate, plunder, pillage, despoil, strip, rob; harass, torment, molest. See **harass.**

harsh. Syn.: rough, rugged; sour, acrid, astringent, sharp; discordant, dissonant, inharmonious, jarring, grating, rasping, strident, raucous, cacophonous; severe, stern, austere, blunt, brusque, churlish, hard, rigorous, unfeeling, unkind, brutal, cruel. **Ant.:** see **harmonious, kind,** *a.* See **cruel.**

Harsh, originally expressing a disagreeable roughness to the touch, is hence used of qualities or actions that produce a like effect upon the feelings. *Rough,* in addition to its primary idea of a surface so diversified with small projections as to be uneven to the touch, is also used to describe what is rudely disagreeable or even violent. *Severe* suggests something rigorous, unsparing, or harsh, but does not necessarily imply intentional cruelty: as, *severe* penalties; *severe* discipline; *severe* weather. That which is *hard* is unyielding, unfeeling, or devoid of tenderness or leniency: as, a *hard* man; *hard* conditions.

harshness. Syn.: see **acrimony.**

harvest. Syn.: crop, yield, reaping, produce, fruit.

Harvest is the time of reaping or gathering, or the gathering, or that which is gathered, and is a word of many beautiful and poetic applications. *Crop* denotes the produce of the land at one cutting or for a particular season, and is a term common in agricultural and commercial use: as, the wheat *crop*; the bean *crop.* *Yield* denotes what is given by the land in return for the expenditure of time and labor. *Produce* is used to denote especially household vegetables.

haste. Syn.: celerity, swiftness, quickness, speed, rapidity, expedition, despatch; precipitancy, impetuosity, hurry, flurry, bustle.

Haste indicates quick, impetuous, or precipitate movement or action, as from eagerness or from urgency of circumstances. *Hurry* is haste that suggests effort and a degree of excitement or confusion. *Speed* denotes swiftness of movement from one place to another, or rapidity of performance generally. *Expedition* denotes quickness or promptness of procedure; *despatch,* quickness or promptness in accomplishing, settling, or concluding matters.

hasten. Syn.: accelerate, quicken, expedite, festinate, press, urge, precipitate; hurry, hie. See **quicken.**

hasty. Syn.: swift, quick, speedy, rapid, fast; cursory, superficial, desultory; hurried, precipitate, rash, foolhardy, reckless; quick-tempered, irascible, passionate. **Ant.:** slow, dilatory, leisurely, studied, deliberate.

That which is *hasty* is done in haste, or hurriedly; it may have been done too quickly to be thorough, accurate, or reliable. *Cursory,* literally running, suggests a rapid consideration which does not pause to note details; the word is not necessarily depreciatory, since many things require nothing more than a cursory view. *Superficial* is applied to what does not go beneath the surface and therefore lacks depth or thoroughness. *Desultory,* literally leaping from point to point, implies irregularity or disconnectedness in procedure.

hatch. Syn.: incubate, breed; contrive, concoct, scheme, plot.

hate, *n.* **Syn.:** see **ill-will.**

hate, *v.* **Syn.:** detest, abhor, abominate, loathe, execrate, despise, dislike.

To *hate* is to regard with a strong or passionate dislike. To *detest* is to hate intensely or vehemently. *Abominate* indicates a feeling of utter hatred, mingled with repulsion, directed against what is deemed outrageous or intolerable. *Loathe* emphasizes the disgust felt for what is highly offensive to the tastes or feelings. *Abhor,* retaining something of its original sense of shrinking back in horror, is a very strong word, expressing the utmost repugnance or aversion.

hateful. Syn.: detestable, abominable, execrable, odious, abhorrent, repugnant, invidious, obnoxious, loathsome.

hatred. Syn.: hate, detestation, abhorrence, loathing, aversion, animosity, enmity, ill-will, malice, spite. **Ant.:** love, affection, kindliness, friendliness. See **ill-will.**

haughtiness. Syn.: pride, arrogance, hauteur, lordliness, disdain, superciliousness, contemptuousness, contumely.

haughty. Syn.: proud, arrogant, lordly, disdainful, supercilious, contemptuous.

haul. Syn.: see **draw.**

haunt. Syn.: see **frequent.**

have. Syn.: hold, possess, own, occupy.

Have, being the most general word, admits of the widest range of application: as, to *have* money, rights, discretion, a disease, a glimpse, an idea; to *have* a friend's umbrella. To *hold* is to have in one's grasp or one's control, but not necessarily as one's own: as, to *hold* stakes. To *possess* is to have as one's own: as, to *possess* property, faculties, or attributes. To *own* is to have the full rights of property in a thing, which, however, another may be holding or enjoying. To *occupy* is to hold and use, but not necessarily by any right of ownership: as, to *occupy* a chair, a house, a position.

haven. Syn.: see **harbor.**

havoc. Syn.: devastation, destruction, wreck, ruin, damage, waste. See **ruin.**

hazard, *n.* **Syn.:** chance, risk, jeopardy, danger, peril. **Ant.:** certainty, safety, security.

hazard, *v.* **Syn.:** stake, venture, risk, jeopard, endanger, peril, imperil. See **risk,** *v.*

hazardous. Syn.: uncertain, unsafe, precarious, risky, dangerous, perilous.

haze. Syn.: see **fog.**

head, *n.* **Syn.:** poll, noddle, pate; top, summit, crest, pinnacle; headland, promontory, foreland, cape; leader, chief, commander, director; advance, progress; culmination, crisis.

head, *a.* **Syn.:** chief, principal, cardinal, foremost, first.

headlong. Syn.: precipitate, rash, reckless, hasty, impetuous, pell-mell, helter-skelter.

headstrong. Syn.: wilful, perverse, froward, stubborn, unruly, obstinate, ungovernable, intractable, heady. See **obstinate.**

heal. **Syn.:** see **cure.**

healing. **Syn.:** curing, curative, restorative, remedial, medicinal, therapeutic, sanatory, sanative, emollient, soothing.

healthful. **Syn.:** see **healthy.**

healthy. **Syn.:** hale, hearty, robust, vigorous, strong, sound, well; healthful, wholesome, nutritious, nourishing, hygienic, salutary, salubrious, invigorating, bracing. **Ant.:** see **unhealthy.**

Healthy is applied especially to what possesses health but also to what is conducive to health: as, a *healthy* child; a *healthy* climate, sport, or life. *Healthful* is applied chiefly to what is conducive to health: as, *healthful* diet or exercise. That which is *wholesome* tends to keep one in a whole or sound physical condition, or, figuratively, to do one good morally: as, *wholesome* food or air; *wholesome* influences or advice. *Salutary* is applied to what is conducive to health or to well-being generally, especially by counteracting undesirable tendencies or promoting restoration to a sound condition. It is now used chiefly of what is morally wholesome or beneficial: as, a *salutary* fear of consequences; a *salutary* effect. *Salubrious*, applied especially to air, climate, or places, indicates conditions favorable to health.

heap. **Syn.:** mass, pile, stack, cumulation, accumulation.

hear. **Syn.:** listen, harken.

To *hear* is to have perception of sound by the ear; to *listen* is to give attention in order to hear. *Harken* is now chiefly an archaic or poetic equivalent of *listen.*

hearsay. **Syn.:** see **rumor.**

heartless. **Syn.:** see **unfeeling.**

hearty. **Syn.:** whole-souled, sincere, heartfelt, cordial, warm, friendly, genial; healthy, hale, robust, strong, vigorous.

Hearty implies a feeling, supporting or opposed, that proceeds, as it were, straight from the heart, and is expressed with more or less vigor or downrightness. *Cordial* implies a feeling also proceeding from the heart, but less vigorous or more conventional in its expression.

heat. **Syn.:** hotness, warmth, caloric; ardor, fervor, zeal, vehemence, rage, violence.

heath. **Syn.:** moor, moorland, fell.

heathen. **Syn.:** see **pagan.**

heave. **Syn.:** see **raise.**

heaven. **Syn.:** sky, firmament; paradise, Eden, Elysium, Olympus, Valhalla, happy hunting-grounds.

heavenly. **Syn.:** celestial, supernal, sublime, divine, blessed, blissful, beatific. See **godlike.**

heavy. **Syn.:** ponderous, weighty, massive; burdensome, onerous, oppressive, grievous, trying, severe, difficult, hard, momentous; serious, grave, depressed, gloomy, sad; clumsy, lumbering; dull, stupid, slow, sluggish. **Ant.:** see **light.**

Heavy is a general word of many applications, describing not only physical weight but clumsiness, dullness, gloom, depression, sadness, etc., or great amount, force, or intensity. *Burdensome* indicates the heaviness of something wearisome or oppressive; *onerous*, that of a troublesome duty or obligation. *Weighty* commonly indicates great importance; *momentous*, great consequences.

hector. **Syn.:** see **browbeat.**

heed, *n.* **Syn.:** attention, regard, notice, consideration, care.

heed, *v.* **Syn.:** regard, notice, note, observe, mind, consider.

heedful. **Syn.:** attentive, regardful, observant, mindful, careful, watchful, vigilant. **Ant.:** inattentive, careless, negligent.

height. **Syn.:** altitude, elevation, highness, eminence, tallness, stature; top, apex, summit, zenith, culmination; hill, mountain.

Height denotes both extent upward, as from foot to head, bottom to top, or base to summit, and also distance above a particular level, as the level of the ground or of the sea. *Altitude* is applied especially to distance above a given level: as, the *altitude* of a star. *Elevation* is distance above a level.

heighten. **Syn.:** see **raise.**

heinous. **Syn.:** hateful, odious, wicked, infamous, atrocious, nefarious, flagitious, horrible, monstrous. See **atrocious.**

hell. **Syn.:** Hades, inferno, Gehenna, sheol, Abaddon, Tartarus, pandemonium, Avernus.

hellish. **Syn.:** infernal, diabolical, fiendish, malignant, wicked.

help, *n.* **Syn.:** aid, assistance, succor, support, backing; relief, remedy, cure.

help, *v.* **Syn.:** aid, assist, succor, befriend, support, uphold, back, second, encourage, abet; facilitate, further, promote, foster; mitigate, ameliorate, alleviate, relieve, remedy, cure, heal.

Help is the common word for furnishing another with anything that furthers his efforts or relieves his wants or necessities. *Aid* and *assist* are somewhat more formal words, and are used especially to denote a furthering or seconding of another's efforts. To *succor* is to relieve by timely help in difficulty or distress.

helper. **Syn.:** aid, assistant, supporter, backer, auxiliary, ally, associate, colleague, coadjutor, deputy, collaborator, abetter, accessory, confederate, accomplice.

helpful. **Syn.:** serviceable, useful, conducive, instrumental, beneficial, salutary.

herald, *n.* **Syn.:** messenger, forerunner, precursor, harbinger; proclaimer, crier.

Herald, denoting originally a royal or official proclaimer or messenger, carries a suggestion of ceremony or formality in its figurative applications, as to any person or thing conceived as a proclaimer, announcer, or news-bearer. *Harbinger*, applied formerly to one sent in advance to secure lodgings for troops, a royal train, or the like, is now chiefly a figurative and literary term for that which is conceived as signifying the approach of something. *Forerunner* and *precursor*, both having the literal meaning of one who runs before, are applied to any person, circumstance, or occurrence that precedes or foreshadows what is to come.

herald, *v.* **Syn.:** see **proclaim.**

herb. **Syn.:** see **plant,** *n.*

herd. **Syn.:** see **flock.**

here. **Syn.:** hither.

Here indicates place in the immediate vicinity of the speaker and is used with both verbs of rest and verbs of motion: as, the book is *here*; bring the book *here*. *Hither* indicates direction towards the speaker and is used only with verbs of motion: as, "Then Jesus answered . . . bring him *hither* to me." (*Matthew*, xvii. 17.) The word is now confined almost wholly to literary use.

hereditary. **Syn.:** inherited, ancestral, patrimonial.

heresy. **Syn.:** see **heterodoxy.**

heretic. **Syn.:** dissenter, nonconformist, separatist, schismatic, recusant, sectary, sectarian.

A *heretic* maintains religious opinions at variance with the accepted doctrines of the Christian church or of the established or dominant religious system. A *schismatic* promotes or supports schism or division within a religious body. A *sectary* is a member of a particular sect, often a sect that is regarded as outside of, or in some way separated from, the established or orthodox church. *Dissenter* and *nonconformist* are used especially of Protestants in England who do not conform to the ritual or usages of the English church.

heritage. **Syn.:** see **inheritance.**

hermit. **Syn.:** see **recluse.**

heroic. **Syn.:** intrepid, valiant, dauntless, gallant.

heroism. **Syn.:** intrepidity, valor, prowess, gallantry. See **bravery.**

hesitate. **Syn.:** doubt, waver, vacillate, falter, scruple, demur, delay, deliberate; stammer, stutter.

Hesitate, from its etymological sense of sticking fast, means to hold back in doubt or indecision. To *falter* is to become unsteady in gait or action, and hence to halt or hesitate in any procedure as from failure of resolution or of courage. To *waver* is to hesitate between alternatives, or to falter in a course already adopted. To *vacillate* is to swing from one opinion or purpose to another as from lack of conviction or determination. To *scruple* is to hesitate on conscientious grounds to do a thing proposed or under consideration. To *demur* is to make objection or take exception to something.

hesitation. **Syn.:** hesitancy, doubt, indecision, irresolution, vacillation, uncertainty, delay.

heterodoxy. **Syn.:** heresy.

Heterodoxy is deviation from orthodox or generally accepted doctrine. *Heresy* is heterodoxy which threatens to undermine accepted doctrine or the established church.

heterogeneous. **Syn.:** dissimilar, unlike, incongruous, miscellaneous. **Ant.:** homogeneous, similar, like, same.

hew. **Syn.:** see **cut.**

hidden. **Syn.:** concealed, secreted, secret, covert, clandestine, occult, mysterious, recondite, esoteric, obscure, latent, dormant.

hide, *n.* **Syn.:** see **skin,** *n.*

hide, *v.* **Syn.:** conceal, secrete, screen, mask, cloak, veil, shroud, disguise, dissemble, suppress. **Ant.:** uncover, unmask, unveil, expose, disclose, reveal, divulge, confess.

Hide, a common word, is to put something out of sight or in a place where it will not be (easily) found; *conceal,* somewhat more formal, is to cover from sight: as, to *hide* or *conceal* one's money or purpose; a rock *hid* or *concealed* them from view; a dog *hides* a bone. To *secrete* is to hide carefully in order to keep secret: as, the smuggler *secretes* his contraband.

hideous. Syn.: horrible, grisly, grim, ugly, repulsive, revolting, detestable, odious. See **ghastly.**

high. Syn.: lofty, tall, towering; elevated, exalted, eminent, noble.

High is a general term, and denotes either continuous (usually considerable or great) extension upward or position at a considerable height, and is used figuratively of that which is superior, elevated, or exalted. *Tall* is applied either to that which is high in proportion to its breadth, or to anything the height of which is greater than that to which we have become accustomed. *Lofty* denotes imposing height, and is often applied figuratively to what is noble or exalted, or, sometimes, to what is condescending or affectedly superior. *Towering* applies to that which rises to a great or conspicuous height.

high-flown. Syn.: grandiose, grandiloquent, magniloquent, bombastic, inflated, turgid, highfalutin.

high-handed. Syn.: arbitrary, overbearing, autocratic, despotic, tyrannical.

high-minded. Syn.: see **noble.**

highway. Syn.: see **way.**

highwayman. Syn.: see **robber.**

hilarious. Syn.: cheerful, gay, mirthful, merry, rollicking, boisterous. **Ant.:** see **sad.** See **gay.**

hilarity. Syn.: cheerfulness, joy, gaiety, mirth, merriment, glee, jollity, joviality. See **mirth.**

hill. Syn.: elevation, eminence, mound, knoll, hillock, hummock, foothill, monticule, butte, mountain.

hind, *n.* **Syn.:** see **clown.**

hind, hinder, *a.* **Syn.:** see **posterior.**

hinder. Syn.: impede, encumber, retard, delay, hamper, obstruct, trammel, check, block, stop, prevent, thwart. **Ant.:** help, aid, further, facilitate.

To *hinder* is to keep back by delaying or stopping progress or action. To *prevent* is to hinder effectually as by forestalling action and rendering it impossible. To *obstruct* is to block or retard passage or progress as by putting obstacles in the way. To *impede* is to make difficult the movement or progress of anything by interfering with its proper functioning. To *hamper* is to impede as by a clog, entanglement, or any embarrassing restraint. To *trammel* is to hamper or restrain as by something that shackles or binds.

hindrance. Syn.: impediment, encumbrance, obstruction, obstacle, check, restraint.

hint, *n.* **Syn.:** suggestion, intimation, allusion, inkling, reminder, insinuation, innuendo, implication.

hint, *v.* **Syn.:** suggest, intimate, insinuate, imply.

All these words express the conveying of an idea to the mind indirectly or without full or explicit statement. To *hint* is to convey the idea indirectly or covertly but intelligibly, so that one's meaning may be caught by another. To *intimate* is to put one on the track of an idea. To *insinuate* is to hint artfully, often what one would not dare to say directly. *Suggest* is a broader word, denoting both the intentional bringing of an idea to the mind and the unintentional or merely casual effecting of the same result, as through the association of ideas.

hire, *n.* **Syn.:** see **pay,** *n.*

hire, *v.* **Syn.:** engage, employ, bribe; let, lease, rent, charter. See **employ.**

hireling. Syn.: see **mercenary.**

history. Syn.: narrative, account, record, story, chronicle, annals.

History may be used as a general word for any orderly narrative of a train of events, but in its more restricted sense it is a careful recording of ascertainable facts in an attempt to recreate the past vividly and in such a way as to set in proper perspective events and their causes. *Annals* are records of events, year by year, but the word has been extended in meaning to include historical accounts generally; *chronicles* are detailed and continuous records of events in the order of time; both words frequently imply the mere recording of facts, with-

out selection or analysis, and without any particular attempt at literary style.

hit. Syn.: see **strike.**

hitch. Syn.: jerk, twitch; fasten, attach, tie, hook, catch, tether, harness, yoke.

hither. Syn.: see **here.**

hoard. Syn.: amass, accumulate, collect, store, save, treasure. See **accumulate.**

hoarse. Syn.: husky, gruff, harsh, grating, raucous.

hoary. Syn.: hoar, frosty, whitish, white, gray, old, venerable.

hoax. Syn.: see **cheat, deception.**

hobble. Syn.: limp, halt, hop.

hobby. Syn.: avocation. See **vocation.**

hobgoblin. Syn.: see **bugbear.**

hodgepodge. Syn.: see **mixture.**

hoist. Syn.: see **raise.**

hold. Syn.: grasp, grip, seize, arrest, detain, confine; sustain, support, bear, carry; contain; have, possess, own, occupy, keep, retain; defend, uphold, maintain, believe, entertain, cherish; consider, regard, deem, esteem; control, restrain, check. See **have.**

hole. Syn.: hollow, cavity, depression, indentation, dent, dint, cave, cavern, crater, excavation, pit, burrow, mortise; opening, orifice, aperture, interstice, mesh, perforation, puncture, rent, slit, gap, cleft, crack, crevice, fissure, chasm, breach, loophole, hatchway, scuttle, bunghole, bore, eyelet, vent, pore.

Hole is the common word for a hollow place or an opening or perforation in anything. *Cavity* is a more dignified or scientific term for a hollow within a body or substance, whether with or without a passage outward: as, a *cavity* in a tooth; the cranial *cavity.* An *excavation* is an extended hole made by digging out or removing material. A *dent* or *dint* is a depression in a surface, especially one made by a blow. An *indentation* is commonly a notch in a margin.

holiness. Syn.: sanctity, sacredness; godliness, saintliness, piety.

hollow, *n.* **Syn.:** see **hole, valley.**

hollow, *a.* **Syn.:** empty, vacant, void, unfilled, cavernous; worthless, vain; insincere, false, hypocritical, deceitful; concave, depressed, sunken, gaunt. **Ant.:** filled, full, solid; sincere, frank, straightforward; convex, rounded, plump, fleshy.

holocaust. Syn.: see **fire.**

holy. Syn.: consecrated, hallowed, sacred, blessed, divine; godly, saintly, sanctified, devout, pious, pure. **Ant.:** see **unholy.**

Holy is a stronger and more absolute term than any other of similar meaning. That which is *holy* is of a divine character, or has its sanctity directly from God or as connected with him; that which is *sacred,* while sometimes accepted as entitled to religious veneration, may derive its sanction from man; hence we speak of the *Holy* Bible, and of one's *sacred* duty to his country. That which is *consecrated* is specially or formally dedicated to some religious use or service. That which is *hallowed* is made holy, or invested with a sacred character.

homage. Syn.: allegiance, fealty; respect, deference, obeisance, honor, reverence. See **allegiance.**

home. Syn.: dwelling, domicile, residence, abode, hearth, hearthstone, fireside, ingleside. See **habitation.**

homely. Syn.: see **simple, ugly.**

homily. Syn.: see **sermon.**

honest. Syn.: fair, just, upright, incorruptible, chaste, trusty, trustworthy, truthful, straightforward, frank, open, candid, sincere. **Ant.:** see **dishonest.**

honesty. Syn.: fairness, justice, uprightness, integrity, probity, rectitude, honor, trustworthiness, frankness, candor, sincerity. **Ant.:** see **dishonesty.**

Honesty denotes the avoidance of deceit or fraud, especially in business dealings. *Honor* denotes a fine sense of and a strict conformity to what is considered morally right or due. *Integrity* indicates a soundness of moral principle which no power or influence can impair. *Probity* is a moral excellence that is expressed in complete trustworthiness and reliability. *Rectitude* and *uprightness* suggest a moral straightness that will not bend to anything wrong or bad. *Sincerity* implies freedom from dissimulation or deceit.

honor, *n.* **Syn.:** esteem, respect, deference, homage, reverence, veneration; reputation, repute, credit, fame, glory, renown; rank, position, dignity, distinction, eminence;

probity, integrity, uprightness, chastity, virtue, modesty. See **honesty, fame, respect.**

honor, *v.* **Syn.:** esteem, respect, reverence, revere, venerate, adore, worship.

honorable. Syn.: honorary; estimable, reputable, creditable; honest, upright, noble, high-minded, magnanimous. **Ant.:** see **dishonorable.**

Honorary often implies the conferring or enjoying of honor only, in connection with a title or position, without the requirements or the rewards usually attaching in such cases. *Honorable* is applied to what is worthy of honor, fulfils the requirements of honor, or brings honor to the possessor.

honorarium. Syn.: see **pay,** *n.*

honorary. Syn.: see **honorable.**

hoodwink. Syn.: see **cheat,** *v.*

hook. Syn.: see **fasten.**

hooked. Syn.: bent, curved, uncinate, aquiline, hook-nosed.

hoot. Syn.: see **cry.**

hop. Syn.: see **skip.**

hope, *n.* **Syn.:** expectation, anticipation, optimism.

hope, *v.* **Syn.:** see **expect.**

hopeful. Syn.: expectant, sanguine, optimistic, confident.

The *hopeful* man is full of hope of attaining what he desires. The *sanguine* man is naturally hopeful in disposition. The *optimistic* man takes a favorable view of things and is persistently hopeful for the best. He who is *confident* feels sure of realizing his hopes or expectations.

hopeless. Syn.: despairing, desperate, desponding, despondent; irreparable, incurable.

Hopeless expresses absence of hope, where hope may or may not have once existed. *Desperate* implies an extremity which leads one to violent action, especially in a struggle against odds, and a reckless disregard of consequences.

horde. Syn.: see **multitude.**

horizontal. Syn.: see **level,** *a.*

horrible. Syn.: dreadful, terrible, awful, appalling, dire, frightful, hideous, grim, ghastly, shocking, revolting, repulsive, horrid.

Horrible and *horrid* are both applied to what excites horror, but *horrid* is now frequently used as a generally opprobrious term for whatever is regarded as disagreeable or objectionable.

horrid. Syn.: see **horrible.**

horror. Syn.: terror, dread, loathing, abhorrence, aversion.

horse. Syn.: stallion, sire, gelding, mare, dam, pony, colt, foal, filly, steed, charger, mount, palfrey, roadster, cob, sumpter, pad, broncho, mustang, hackney, hack, hobby, nag, jade, plug.

hospital. Syn.: infirmary, sanitarium, sanatorium, retreat, asylum.

A *hospital* is an institution in which sick or injured persons are given medical or surgical treatment. An *infirmary* is a hospital, now often one attached to a school or the like, for the care of its members or inmates. A *sanatorium* or *sanitarium* is an establishment to which persons resort for a course of treatment or a sojourn under especially favorable hygienic conditions, with a view to regaining or fortifying the health. A *retreat* is an establishment affording special seclusion or privacy to insane persons, inebriates, or others received for care or treatment. An *asylum* is an institution for the maintenance and care of a particular class of afflicted or unfortunate persons, as the insane, the blind, deaf-mutes, etc.

host. Syn.: see **multitude.**

hostage. Syn.: see **pledge,** *n.*

hostelry. Syn.: see **inn.**

hostile. Syn.: inimical, warlike, unfriendly, antagonistic, adverse, averse, opposed. **Ant.:** friendly, amicable, cordial, favorable, agreeable.

Hostile implies the spirit, attitude, or action of an enemy; *inimical,* an antagonistic or injurious tendency or influence.

hostility. Syn.: enmity, animosity, ill-will, unfriendliness, antagonism, opposition; war, warfare, fighting. See **ill-will.**

hot. Syn.: warm, heated, burning, scorching, scalding, boiling, torrid, sultry; pungent, biting, peppery; ardent, fervent, fervid, fiery, hot-blooded, passionate, impetuous, vehement, angry. **Ant.:** see **cold.**

hotchpotch. Syn.: see **mixture.**

hotel. Syn.: see **inn.**

house. Syn.: dwelling, domicile, residence, mansion, palace,

castle, château, manse, rectory, cot, cottage, villa, bungalow, lodge, cabin, hovel, hut, shack, shanty, shed. See **inn.**

hover. Syn.: see **fly.**

however. Syn.: see **but.**

howl. Syn.: see **cry.**

hubbub. Syn.: see **noise.**

huckster. Syn.: see **peddler.**

hue. Syn.: see **color,** *n.*

hug. Syn.: see **embrace.**

huge. Syn.: immense, enormous, mammoth, gigantic, colossal, vast, stupendous, bulky. **Ant.:** see **small.** See **enormous.**

hull. Syn.: see **skin,** *n.*

hum. Syn.: drone, buzz, bombinate, murmur, croon.

human. Syn.: humane.

Human denotes the nature or attributes proper to or characteristic of mankind or the activities of mankind; *humane,* possession or manifestation of the benevolent or kindly feelings that should actuate human beings in their treatment of one another or of the lower animals.

humane. Syn.: merciful, kind, kind-hearted, tender, compassionate, sympathetic. **Ant.:** inhuman, cruel, fell, brutal, merciless. See **human.**

humble, *a.* **Syn.:** lowly, meek, submissive, modest, unassuming, unpretentious, plain, common, poor. **Ant.:** proud, haughty, arrogant, lordly, imperious, egotistical.

Humble commonly refers to spirit or feeling; *lowly,* to station or worldly circumstances.

humble, *v.* **Syn.:** see **abase.**

humbug, *n.* **Syn.:** trick, hoax, imposture, deception; pretense, sham; impostor, pretender, cheat, deceiver, charlatan.

humbug, *v.* **Syn.:** see **cheat,** *v.*

humdrum. Syn.: see **monotonous.**

humid. Syn.: see **moist.**

humiliate. Syn.: humble, degrade, debase, dishonor, disgrace, shame, mortify, chagrin. See **abase.**

humiliation. Syn.: see **shame.**

humility. Syn.: lowliness, meekness, modesty. **Ant.:** see **vanity.**

humor, *n.* **Syn.:** disposition, temperament, mood; wit, waggery, pleasantry, facetiousness. See **wit, mood.**

humor, *v.* **Syn.:** see **gratify.**

humorous. Syn.: witty, waggish, droll, facetious, jocose, jocular, funny, comic, comical.

hungry. Syn.: greedy, voracious, ravenous, famishing, famished, starved.

Hungry is a general word, expressing various degrees of eagerness or craving for food. *Famished* denotes the condition of one reduced to actual suffering from want of food. *Starved* denotes a condition resulting from long-continued lack or insufficiency of food, and implies enfeeblement, emaciation, or death.

hunt. Syn.: chase, pursue, follow, track; search, seek, rummage, ransack, scour, ferret.

hurl. Syn.: see **throw.**

hurricane. Syn.: see **wind.**

hurried. Syn.: see **hasty.**

hurry, *n.* **Syn.:** haste, celerity, expedition, despatch, bustle, rush. See **haste.**

hurry, *v.* **Syn.:** hasten, quicken, accelerate, expedite, hustle. See **quicken.**

hurt. Syn.: see **injury.**

hurtful. Syn.: harmful, injurious, destructive, pernicious, noxious, baneful, deleterious, unwholesome, prejudicial, mischievous, detrimental, disadvantageous. **Ant.:** helpful, beneficial, wholesome, salutary.

hushed. Syn.: see **still,** *a.*

husk. Syn.: see **skin,** *n.*

hut. Syn.: see **house.**

hybrid. Syn.: mongrel.

Hybrid is the scientific term for the product that results from crossing two different varieties, species, or genera of animals or plants. *Mongrel,* used originally of dogs and denoting especially the offspring of repeated crossings of different breeds, is now extended to other animals and to plants, but in common language is usually depreciatory, as denoting mixed, nondescript, or degenerate breed or character.

hygienic. Syn.: sanitary.

Hygienic is applied to whatever concerns the care of the body and the promotion of health. *Sanitary* refers more especially to the conditions affecting health, or to measures for guarding against infection or disease.

hymeneal. Syn.: see **matrimonial.**
hyperbole. Syn.: see **exaggeration.**
hypocrisy. Syn.: pretense, cant, Pharisaism. See **deceit.**
hypocrite. Syn.: pretender, dissembler, Pharisee.

A *hypocrite* (a term of opprobrium) makes pretense of piety, virtue, principles, or feelings that he does not possess. A *dissembler* conceals his real character, feelings, or purposes under some false semblance.

hypocritical. Syn.: pretending, feigning, insincere, canting, pharisaical, sanctimonious.
hypothesis. Syn.: see **theory.**

I

icy. Syn.: cold, frosty, frigid, gelid; slippery, glassy.
idea. Syn.: notion, concept, conception, thought, belief, principle, intention, plan.
ideal, *n.* **Syn.:** pattern, model, archetype. See **example.**
ideal, *a.* **Syn.:** perfect, faultless, consummate; imaginary, visionary, chimerical, utopian, fanciful, unreal, quixotic. **Ant.:** imperfect, faulty; real, actual, practical.

That which is *ideal* represents, or conforms to, a standard of perfection. That which is *utopian* suggests or befits an ideal realm, especially one imagined by theorists and too nearly perfect for realization in a world of imperfect human beings. That which is *quixotic* is proper to the dreams of an extravagantly romantic idealist rather than to the prosaic ideas of practical men.

identical. Syn.: see **same.**
identity. Syn.: see **sameness.**
idiocy. Syn.: imbecility, dotage, fatuity, senselessness, foolishness, folly. **Ant.:** sense, intelligence, wisdom, sagacity, astuteness.
idiom. Syn.: see **language.**
idiosyncrasy. Syn.: see **characteristic.**
idiot. Syn.: imbecile, fool, simpleton.

An *idiot* is a person seriously deficient, especially from birth, in the ordinary mental powers. An *imbecile* is one who is feeble-minded, whether from defective development or from loss of faculty; his condition is less extreme than that of the idiot. A *simpleton* is one deficient in intelligence or sense, silly rather than stupid. A *fool* is deficient in judgment, or blindly negligent of the dictates of good sense.

idiotic. Syn.: imbecile, feeble-minded, half-witted, stupid, fatuous, senseless, foolish.
idle. Syn.: vain, futile, unavailing, ineffectual, useless, bootless; trifling, trivial, frivolous, unprofitable; leisure, unoccupied, unemployed, inactive, inert, sluggish, indolent, lazy, slothful, otiose. **Ant.:** availing, useful, serviceable; occupied, busy, active, diligent, industrious.

To be *idle* is to be doing nothing, to be unemployed or not working; the word is not necessarily derogatory, for one may be idle through necessity. The *indolent* person is naturally disposed to avoid exertion. The *lazy* person is averse to exertion or work, and especially to continued application. *Slothful* denotes a reprehensible unwillingness to do such work as is demanded of man.

idleness. Syn.: vanity, futility, uselessness; leisure, inactivity, indolence, laziness, sloth.
idler. Syn.: sluggard, drone, loafer, lounger, dawdler, ne'er-do-well.
idol. Syn.: see **image.**
idolize. Syn.: see **worship,** *v.*
ignite. Syn.: see **kindle.**
ignoble. Syn.: lowly, humble, obscure, plebeian, vulgar; mean, base, degraded, dishonorable, contemptible. **Ant.:** noble, lofty, high-born, aristocratic, patrician; honorable, magnanimous. See **mean.**
ignominious. Syn.: disgraceful, shameful, infamous, humiliating, degrading. See **inglorious.**
ignominy. Syn.: disgrace, dishonor, shame, opprobrium, obloquy, odium, infamy. See **disgrace,** *n.*
ignoramus. Syn.: see **fool,** *n.*
ignorant. Syn.: illiterate, unlettered, unlearned, untaught, untutored, uninstructed, uneducated, uninformed, unenlightened, benighted. **Ant.:** learned, educated, instructed, wise, erudite.

The *ignorant* man does not know what he might reasonably be expected to know. One is *ignorant of* a particular fact or subject concerning which he is not informed. One who is *unlearned* is without learning, either in general or in a particular field. *Unlettered* also denotes want of learning, especially of polite learning or literary culture. *Illiterate* is applied to grossly ignorant persons, especially those unable to read. *Untutored* denotes want of tutoring or instruction, often especially in worldly knowledge or ways. *Uneducated* denotes want of the advantages given by education or systematic instruction; *unenlightened*, want of the intellectual light that dispels ignorance, superstition, prejudice, etc.; *benighted*, a being involved in intellectual or moral darkness.

ignore. Syn.: disregard, overlook, slight, neglect.
ill. Syn.: see **sick, bad.**
illegal. Syn.: unlawful, illicit, illegitimate, unlicensed, prohibited, criminal, felonious.

Illegal is applied to what is contrary to or forbidden by law; *illicit*, to what is not permitted by authority or sanctioned by society, and hence is improper or unlawful. *Illegitimate* denotes what is unjustified and unsanctioned and is used especially of those born out of lawful wedlock. *Criminal* is applied to grave offenses punishable by law; *felonious*, to crimes of the most serious character.

illegitimate. Syn.: unlawful, illegal, illicit, unauthorized, unwarranted, unfair; bastard, adulterine. See **illegal.**
ill-favored. Syn.: see **ugly.**
illiberal. Syn.: unscholarly, vulgar, coarse; niggardly, parsimonious, penurious, miserly, stingy, close-fisted, mean, selfish; narrow-minded, bigoted, intolerant. **Ant.:** see **liberal.**
illicit. Syn.: see **illegal.**
illimitable. Syn.: limitless, boundless, unlimited, unbounded, immeasurable, infinite, vast.
illiterate. Syn.: see **ignorant.**
ill-natured. Syn.: ill-tempered, spiteful, crabbed, cross, surly, churlish, quarrelsome.
illness. Syn.: see **sickness.**
illogical. Syn.: unreasonable, irrational, unsound, fallacious, sophistical, inconclusive.

Illogical is applied to what is contrary to the principles of logic or sound inference; *unreasonable*, to what is contrary to reason or sound judgment; *irrational*, to what exceeds the bounds of reason or escapes from its control.

illusion. Syn.: delusion, hallucination, phantasm, phantom, chimera, mirage, fancy.

A *delusion* is a mental deception, especially a fixed, false view of something which really exists but under conditions other than those attributed to it, and the error in the view is not capable of correction or removal by examination or reasoning: as, the fixed belief that an inanimate object is a living person or that all food offered is poisoned is a *delusion*. *Delusions* are usually disagreeable or repulsive, and sometimes mischievous or harmful, as those of a fanatic or lunatic. *Illusion* signifies a false mental appearance or conception produced by an external cause acting through the senses. Thus, the momentary belief that the reflection in a mirror is a real object is an *illusion*. In contrast to delusion, the falsity of an illusion can usually be readily detected by examination or reasoning; moreover, illusions are often pleasing, harmless, or even useful: as, the *illusions* of fancy, hope, youth. A *hallucination* is a false conception which has nothing but a disordered imagination (that may sometimes go beyond the bounds of sanity) as its cause. It is generally of some degree of permanence, but the central suggestion in the word is the groundlessness of the belief or opinion: as, *hallucinations* caused by shell-shock.

illusory. Syn.: illusive, illusionary, delusive, deceptive, chimerical, unreal.
illustrate. Syn.: explain, elucidate, demonstrate, exemplify, picture, adorn.
illustration. Syn.: explanation, elucidation; picture, drawing, sketch, cartoon; example, instance.
illustrious. Syn.: distinguished, renowned, famed, famous, celebrated, noted, eminent. **Ant.:** unknown, obscure, inglorious, ignoble. See **famous.**
ill-will. Syn.: enmity, hostility, animosity, malice, hatred, hate.

Ill-will is a general word, denoting varying degrees of unfriendly or malevolent feeling. *Enmity* is a strong, settled feeling of ill-will, whether secretly cherished or openly displayed. *Hostility* is (usually) open and active enmity, on the part either of individuals or of bodies, peoples, or nations. *Animosity* is a warmly hostile feeling animating the conduct or tending to display itself in action. *Hatred* is passionate dislike or ill-will; *hate* has the same meaning, but may be even more intense.

image. Syn.: statue, figure, effigy, icon, idol; reproduction, counterpart, copy, likeness.

An *image* is a representation of a person or thing, especially in the solid form (as in a statue or effigy), and is sometimes regarded as an object of worship: as, an *image* of Apollo; graven *images* of false gods. An *idol* is an image worshiped by the heathen or pagan as representing or as being a deity.

imaginary. Syn.: fancied, fanciful, visionary, shadowy, utopian, ideal, chimerical, baseless, unreal.

Imaginary is applied to that which exists only in the imagination, and which is hence unreal; *fanciful*, to what is created or suggested by fancy and is often whimsically pleasing in its deviation from the ordinary or the real; *visionary*, to what is seen in or is proper only to a vision, and is hence unreal or beyond the likelihood of realization; *chimerical*, to any idea, scheme, project, or the like, too fantastic to be taken seriously.

imagination. Syn.: fancy, fantasy.

With reference to literary composition, a distinction is now commonly made between *imagination* and *fancy*. *Imagination* bodies forth mental images consistent with experience, and reveals a hitherto unperceived vision of the realities of life. The creations of *fancy* are lighter and more whimsical than those of imagination and have less of seriousness and profundity. *Fantasy*, formerly used in the general sense of an image-forming faculty, now usually denotes an unrestrained or extravagant fancy, bordering on caprice.

imaginative. Syn.: inventive, creative. **Ant.:** see **unimaginative**.

imagine. Syn.: conceive, fancy; assume, suppose, conjecture, surmise, guess, believe, think. See **conceive**.

imbecile. Syn.: see **idiot**.

imbecility. Syn.: see **idiocy**.

imbibe. Syn.: see **drink**, *v.*

imitate. Syn.: reproduce, copy, counterfeit, mimic, personate, impersonate, simulate, ape, mock, parody, caricature.

Imitate is the general term for the idea, common to all these words, of following or trying to follow an example or pattern. To *copy* is to make a fairly exact imitation or reproduction. To *counterfeit* is to imitate exactly, or as closely as possible, usually with the intent to deceive or defraud. To *mimic* is to imitate in sport or ridicule: as, to *mimic* one's manner, affectations, speech. To *ape* is usually to imitate absurdly or servilely. To *mock* is to deride by imitation.

imitation. Syn.: reproduction, mimicry, impersonation; copy, counterfeit, parody, travesty.

imitator. Syn.: copyist, mimic, impersonator, mime, ape, echo.

immaculate. Syn.: spotless, stainless, pure, clean, unblemished, unsullied, undefiled. See **clean**, *a.*

immaterial. Syn.: incorporeal, spiritual; unimportant, unessential, insignificant. See **incorporeal**.

immature. Syn.: unripe, undeveloped, green, raw, crude.

immediate. Syn.: nearest, next, close; direct, instant, present, instantaneous.

immediately. Syn.: instantly, instantaneously, straightway, forthwith, at once, now, promptly, directly, presently. **Ant.:** later, sometime, hereafter.

Immediately, directly, and *straightway* all indicate absence of delay, *immediately* suggesting without lapse of time, *directly* and *straightway* a procedure that goes straight to its end. *Straightway* is now chiefly a literary word. *Presently,* originally having reference to the time actually present, and hence equivalent to *immediately,* is now commonly used to mean soon, or in a little while. *Directly* and *immediately,* as used in promising action at once, often have little more force than *presently. Instantly* implies action or occurrence on the instant, and hence immediately.

immense. Syn.: immeasurable, boundless, infinite, vast, huge, enormous. See **enormous**.

immerse. Syn.: immerge, submerge, sink, plunge, dip, duck, douse, souse; involve, occupy, absorb, engross. See **dip**.

immigrant, immigrate. Syn.: see **emigrant, migrate**.

imminent. Syn.: impending, overhanging, threatening.

Imminent is applied usually to danger or evil that hangs, as it were, over one's head, ready to fall at any moment; less often to any event that is on the point of happening. *Impending* is similarly used, but with less suggestion of immediateness. *Threatening* is applied to what indicates coming evil or conveys some ominous or unfavorable suggestion: as, a *threatening* frown, outlook; *threatening* weather, sky.

immoderate. Syn.: excessive, extreme, unreasonable, inordinate, intemperate, extravagant, exorbitant.

immodest. Syn.: bold, forward, impudent, shameless; indelicate, indecorous, indecent, lewd, obscene.

Immodest, in indicating a want of modesty, usually refers to indelicacy, or disregard of decency. *Bold,* in its derogatory sense, suggests forwardness, audacity, or even impudence. *Shameless* implies insensibility to shame, or, more actively, brazen defiance of decency.

immolate. Syn.: see **sacrifice**.

immoral. Syn.: unrighteous, unprincipled, sinful, dissolute, profligate, licentious, unchaste.

Immoral indicates want of conformity or obedience to the moral law. *Sinful* implies transgression of the laws of God.

immortal. Syn.: undying, deathless, imperishable, incorruptible, everlasting, perpetual, eternal, endless, sempiternal, unfading, enduring.

immovable. Syn.: stationary, fixed, stable, firm, permanent, steadfast, resolute, unyielding, unalterable, unchangeable.

immunity. Syn.: see **exemption**.

immure, immurement. Syn.: see **imprison, imprisonment**.

immutable. Syn.: unchangeable, unalterable, changeless, constant, permanent, fixed.

imp. Syn.: see **devil**.

impair. Syn.: deteriorate, injure, damage, harm, hurt, mar, weaken, enfeeble.

To *impair* is to make imperfect in any way, often with a suggestion of progressive deterioration and of permanency in the result; to *injure* is to do harm or damage to: as, the constant strain *impaired* his sight; the fall *injured* his spine.

impalpable. Syn.: intangible, insubstantial, imperceptible. See **intangible**.

impart. Syn.: give, bestow, convey, communicate, tell, relate, reveal, disclose, divulge, confide.

Impart and *communicate* denote giving to a person or thing a part or share of something, now usually something immaterial, as knowledge, thoughts, hopes, qualities, or properties. *Impart* usually implies directness of action, *communicate* often an indirect or gradual transmission. *Convey* also sometimes suggests a communicating through some medium of transmission, or a serving as a medium of transmission: as, to *convey* one's meaning by a gesture; his words *conveyed* no meaning to us.

impartial. Syn.: unbiased, unprejudiced, fair, equitable, just. See **fair**.

impassable. Syn.: impenetrable, impervious, impermeable, pathless.

Impassable is applied to what does not admit of passage, as in traversing or traveling; *impenetrable,* to what cannot be penetrated, either literally, as by piercing or passing into interior parts, or figuratively, as by arriving at inner thoughts or meaning. *Impervious,* implying absence of a way through, is often applied to what resists penetration by physical agencies, or is proof against moral agencies or forces: as, *impervious* to heat or moisture; *impervious* to argument, ridicule, or hints. *Impermeable,* implying impossibility of passing through, is applied especially to substances that do not permit passage through their pores or interstices.

impassioned. Syn.: see **passionate, ardent**.

impassive. Syn.: impassible, apathetic, unmoved, passive. See **unemotional**.

impatient. Syn.: irritable, choleric, quick-tempered; uneasy, restless, eager, impetuous. **Ant.:** see **patient**.

impeach. Syn.: see **accuse**.

impeccable. Syn.: see **innocent**.

impecunious. Syn.: see **poor**.

impede. Syn.: obstruct, hinder, retard, delay, hamper, check, clog. See **hinder**.

impediment. Syn.: obstruction, hindrance, encumbrance, obstacle, check, bar, barrier, stumbling-block. **Ant.:** aid, help, assistance, benefit, advantage. See **obstacle**.

impel. Syn.: drive, force, urge, instigate, incite, prompt, move. See **actuate**.

impending. Syn.: see **imminent**.

impenetrable. Syn.: see **impassable.**

imperative. Syn.: peremptory, imperious, dictatorial, domineering, absolute, positive; compulsory, obligatory, binding, urgent.

Imperative is applied to what has the force of a command or calls for compliance or obedience; *peremptory*, to what demands immediate and unqualified compliance; *imperious*, to what is haughtily or arrogantly commanding. *Dictatorial* implies the assumption of a right to dictate the action or opinion of others; *domineering*, the use of an overbearing or bullying tone or attitude toward others.

imperfect. Syn.: incomplete, undeveloped, defective, deficient, faulty.

imperfection. Syn.: incompleteness, defectiveness, deficiency, faultiness; defect, blemish, flaw, disfigurement, deformity, fault, foible, failing, shortcoming, weakness, frailty, vice, infirmity.

Imperfection is a general word for any faulty detail which detracts from perfection. A *defect* implies a lack of something which is essential to perfection or completeness. A *blemish* is commonly an imperfection on the surface which mars the appearance; a *flaw*, an irregularity in texture; a *disfigurement*, an obvious and defacing imperfection. *Deformity* indicates misshapenness or malformation, as of the body.

imperial. Syn.: sovereign, supreme, commanding; regal, royal, kingly, majestic, august, magnificent. See **royal.**

imperil. Syn.: see **endanger, risk,** *v.*

imperious. Syn.: commanding, domineering, overbearing, dictatorial, dogmatic, magisterial, tyrannical, despotic; urgent, pressing, imperative. See **imperative.**

imperishable. Syn.: see **enduring.**

impermeable. Syn.: see **impassable.**

impertinence. Syn.: see **impudence.**

impertinent. Syn.: irrelevant, inapplicable, inapposite, inappropriate; meddlesome, presumptuous, officious, uncivil, rude, saucy, flippant, pert, impudent, insolent.

Impertinent, from its primary meaning of not pertinent, and hence inappropriate or out of place, has come to imply often an unseemly intrusion into what does not concern one, or a presumptuous rudeness toward one entitled to deference or respect. *Impudent* suggests a bold and shameless impertinence; *insolent*, insulting or arrogantly contemptuous behavior.

imperturbable. Syn.: see **calm,** *a.,* **unemotional.**

impervious. Syn.: see **impassable.**

impetuous. Syn.: vehement, furious, headlong, precipitate, hasty, impulsive, passionate. **Ant.:** leisurely, slow, deliberate, careful, calm. See **ardent.**

impetus. Syn.: momentum, force, impulse, stimulus.

impious. Syn.: irreligious, unrighteous, wicked, profane. See **irreligious.**

implacable. Syn.: unappeasable, unforgiving, inexorable, pitiless, relentless. See **inflexible.**

implant. Syn.: ingraft, infix, infuse, instil, inculcate, inspire.

To *implant* is to infix something as by planting, with the implication that it will grow or develop: as, to *implant* ideas. To *ingraft* is to infix something as by grafting, with the implication that it will become united as a part of the whole: as, to *ingraft* new elements. To *infuse* is to put in as by pouring: as, to *infuse* new life or spirit. To *instil* is to introduce, as it were, drop by drop: as, to *instil* virtue. To *inculcate* is to impress on the mind by persistent repetition or emphatic admonition: as, to *inculcate* doctrines or truths.

implement. Syn.: see **tool.**

implicate. Syn.: infold, entwine, entangle, involve.

To *implicate* is to connect a person with something discreditable or wrong though not necessarily deeply: as, to *implicate* one in a charge or a crime. To *involve* is to bring more or less deeply into something, especially of a complicated, embarrassing, or troublesome nature: as, to *involve* one in difficulties, debt, or litigation. To *entangle* is to involve so that extrication is difficult: as, to be *entangled* in sophistry; to avoid *entangling* alliances.

implicit. Syn.: implied, tacit, inferential; unquestioning, undoubting, unhesitating, unreserved.

implore. Syn.: beseech, entreat, supplicate, crave, beg. See **ask.**

imply. Syn.: involve, signify, mean, suggest, insinuate.

To *imply* is to indicate that a thing, although not expressly stated, is fairly to be inferred; to *involve* a thing is to include or entail it as a necessary circumstance or consequence: as, army

enlistment *implies* the necessary legal and physical qualifications; it *involves* the necessity of obeying orders, enduring hardships, and incurring risks.

impolite. Syn.: uncivil, discourteous, disrespectful, rude, impertinent, insolent. **Ant.:** see **polite.**

impolitic. Syn.: inexpedient, injudicious, untactful, unwise, indiscreet.

import, *n.* **Syn.:** significance, meaning, sense, gist, substance, tenor; importance, moment, weight, consequence. See **meaning.**

import, *v.* **Syn.:** signify, denote, betoken, indicate, mean, imply.

importance. Syn.: significance, moment, momentousness, weight, consequence; pretentiousness, pompousness.

Importance, referring originally to the bringing or involving of noteworthy results, is a general term for expressing a quality, character, or standing such as to entitle to attention or consideration. *Consequence* has the same general sense as *importance*, but is a weaker word, less suggestive of seriousness, dignity, or extensiveness: as, fair weather is a matter of *consequence* to the tourist, of *importance* to the farmer. The words are often used interchangeably.

important. Syn.: significant, momentous, weighty, serious, critical, decisive, material, considerable, substantial, influential, prominent; pretentious, pompous. **Ant.:** see **unimportant.**

importune. Syn.: beg, urge, crave, press, dun. See **ask.**

imposing. Syn.: impressive, commanding, stately, majestic, august. See **impressive.**

imposition. Syn.: burden, task, tax; imposture, deception, trick, fraud.

impossible. Syn.: impracticable, unfeasible, unattainable.

impost. Syn.: see **tax.**

impostor. Syn.: pretender, deceiver, cheat, quack.

imposture. Syn.: deception, cheat, trick, fraud, imposition.

impotent. Syn.: powerless, helpless, weak, feeble, infirm, impuissant. See **weak.**

impoverished. Syn.: see **poor.**

imprecation. Syn.: see **malediction.**

impregnable. Syn.: see **invincible.**

impress. Syn.: affect, touch, move, stamp.

To *impress* is to produce an effect upon the mind. *Affect, touch,* and *move* express particularly action upon the feelings, with increasing degrees of force in the successive words.

impressionable. Syn.: see **sensitive.**

impressive. Syn.: imposing, commanding, striking.

That which is *impressive* produces a deep effect on the mind. That which is *imposing* impresses by its size, grandeur, stateliness, or like qualities. That which is *commanding* suggests a dominating superiority, or a title to deference or obedience. That which is *striking* makes a marked impression by its unusualness, vividness, conspicuousness, or the like.

imprison. Syn.: confine, incarcerate, immure.

Imprison is the common word for confining in a prison; *incarcerate*, a literary or rhetorical word with the same meaning. *Immure*, to confine within walls, as in a prison, a fortress, or a cloister, is also a literary word.

imprisonment. Syn.: confinement, incarceration, immurement, durance, duress.

impromptu. Syn.: offhand, extempore, improvised, makeshift. See **extemporaneous.**

improper. Syn.: unsuitable, inappropriate, unfit; unseemly, unbecoming, indecorous, indelicate, indecent. **Ant.:** see **proper.**

Improper is applied to whatever is not of a proper, suitable, or fitting kind or nature, and often specifically to what does not conform to the standards of conventional morality. *Unbecoming* is applied to what is especially unfitting in the person concerned; *unseemly*, to what is unfitting or improper in any person. *Indecorous* is applied to what is contrary to decorum, or to the accepted standards of proper behavior; *indelicate*, to what shows the want of a delicate sense of propriety, or even approaches coarseness or immodesty; *indecent*, to what is offensively contrary to the standards of propriety and especially of modesty.

impropriety. Syn.: unsuitableness, inappropriateness; unseemliness, indecorum, indelicacy; mistake, blunder, slip; barbarism, solecism.

As commonly used in rhetoric, the following three words have special meanings. An *impropriety* is a word or phrase used in a sense not authorized by good usage, as 'learn' for 'teach,' or 'aggravate' for 'annoy.' A *barbarism* is a word or phrase regarded as foreign and unnecessary, or, by reason of its character, recentness, or other circumstances, disapproved as undesirable, as 'distingué' for 'distinguished,' 'burglarize' for 'rob', or 'gent' for 'gentleman.' A *solecism* is a construction at variance with grammatical usage or the approved idiom, as 'Who (for *whom*) did you see?' 'It was *him* (for *he*).'

improve. Syn.: amend, mend, better, ameliorate, correct, rectify, promote, develop, advance; utilize, use.

Improve, to bring into a more profitable or desirable state, and hence, in general, to make better, and *better*, with the same general sense, are alike in not implying that their object, although admitting of being made better, has necessarily been bad. *Ameliorate*, a more formal word, is used especially of action on conditions that need improvement: as, to *ameliorate* the condition of the poor.

improvident. Syn.: thoughtless, careless, heedless, imprudent, shiftless, thriftless, unthrifty, wasteful, prodigal. **Ant.:** see **provident.**

improvised. Syn.: see **extemporaneous.**

imprudence. Syn.: see **folly.**

imprudent. Syn.: indiscreet, injudicious, ill-advised, incautious, heedless, rash.

impudence. Syn.: insolence, impertinence, rudeness, effrontery, sauciness, pertness, boldness, audacity, assurance, presumption, brazenness, face. **Ant.:** modesty, humility, meekness, diffidence, bashfulness.

impudent. Syn.: insolent, impertinent, rude, saucy, pert, malapert, flippant, bold, presumptuous, brazen. See **impertinent.**

Saucy suggests an unchastened, sometimes defiant, impertinence towards one's elders or superiors; *pert* implies a smart forwardness inappropriate to one's years, station, or sex; *flippant* implies an unseemly and disrespectful jocularity.

impulse. Syn.: thrust, push, impulsion, impetus, stimulus. See **motive.**

impulsive. Syn.: quick, hasty, rash, impetuous, passionate.

impunity. Syn.: see **exemption.**

impure. Syn.: adulterated, mixed; unclean, dirty, filthy, foul, ribald, obscene.

imputation. Syn.: see **insinuation.**

impute. Syn. See **ascribe.**

in. Syn.: see **at.**

inability. Syn.: disability, incapacity, incompetence, inefficiency, impotence.

Inability denotes want of ability, usually to do a specified thing; *disability*, some disqualifying deprivation or loss of power, physical or other.

inaccuracy. Syn.: inexactness, incorrectness; error, mistake, blunder, slip.

inaccurate. Syn.: inexact, incorrect, erroneous, wrong, faulty, blundering, loose.

inactive. Syn.: inert, sluggish, dormant, torpid, passive, quiescent, latent, inoperative, motionless, stagnant; idle, indolent, lazy, slothful, dilatory. **Ant.:** see **active.**

Inactive indicates absence of action, or indisposition to activity. *Inert* suggests the condition of dead matter, which has no inherent power of motion or action; *dormant*, the quiescence or inactivity of that which sleeps but may be roused to action; *torpid*, a state of suspended physical powers and activities, as in a hibernating animal. *Sluggish* expresses the slowness of that which tends naturally to inactivity or does not move readily or vigorously: as, a *sluggish* stream, brain.

inadequate. Syn.: insufficient, incommensurate, defective, imperfect, incomplete. **Ant.:** see **adequate.**

inadvertence. Syn.: see **negligence.**

inadvertent. Syn.: inattentive, unobservant, thoughtless, careless, heedless, negligent; unintentional, unconscious, accidental.

inane. Syn.: empty, void; silly, foolish, trifling, puerile, frivolous, senseless. See **vacant.**

inanimate. Syn.: see **lifeless, dead.**

inapplicable. Syn.: unsuitable, inappropriate, inapposite, irrelevant.

inappropriate. Syn.: unsuitable, unfitting, unbecoming.

inapt. Syn.: unsuited, unsuitable, inappropriate, inapplicable, inapposite, irrelevant; unskilful, unhandy, awkward.

inarticulate. Syn.: see **dumb.**

inasmuch. Syn.: see **because.**

inattention. Syn.: heedlessness, carelessness, negligence, disregard.

inattentive. Syn.: heedless, careless, regardless, inadvertent, unmindful, absent-minded, preoccupied.

inaugurate. Syn.: see **begin.**

inauspicious. Syn.: unfavorable, unlucky, unpropitious, unpromising, untoward.

inborn. Syn.: innate, inbred, ingrained, inherent, congenital, constitutional, organic, natural, native, instinctive.

Inborn and *innate* are both applicable to what is born in one, or exists in one from birth, but *inborn* is the simpler word, belonging to ordinary speech and literature, while *innate*, in addition to its general use, is employed as a specific philosophical term: as, an *inborn* sense of justice; *innate* ideas. *Congenital*, born with one, or existing with one from birth, is applied especially to physical peculiarities or defects: as, a *congenital* weakness or deformity; *congenital* blindness. *Constitutional*, inherent in the constitution or make-up of a person, is applied to both physical and mental traits or peculiarities: as, a *constitutional* weakness; a *constitutional* hopefulness.

incapable. Syn.: incompetent, inefficient, unable, unfit.

incapacity. Syn.: inability, incapability, incompetency; disability, disqualification, unfitness.

incarcerate. Syn.: see **imprison.**

incautious. Syn.: heedless, unwary, rash, indiscreet, imprudent, impolitic. **Ant.:** see **cautious.**

incense. Syn.: inflame, exasperate, enrage, madden, provoke, offend, nettle, gall. See **irritate.**

incentive. Syn.: motive, stimulus, spur, incitement, inducement. See **motive.**

inception. Syn.: see **beginning, origin.**

incessant. Syn.: ceaseless, unceasing, unremitting, uninterrupted, continual, continuous, constant, perpetual. See **continual.**

incident, *n.* **Syn.:** occurrence, episode. See **event.**

incident, *a.* **Syn.:** pertaining, belonging, relating, accessory.

incidental. Syn.: occasional, casual, chance, fortuitous, contingent. See **accidental.**

incisive. Syn.: see **sharp.**

incite. Syn.: urge, stimulate, encourage, prompt, instigate, provoke, goad, spur, arouse, fire, induce.

To *incite* is to urge on to some action, either good or bad, as by working on the feelings or passions. To *instigate* is to spur on or incite, often in an underhand way, especially to something evil. To *induce* is to lead or bring to some action, condition, belief, etc., as by persuasion or influence. Cf. *actuate.*

incitement. Syn.: see **incentive.**

incivility. Syn.: discourtesy, disrespect, impoliteness, rudeness.

inclement. Syn.: severe, harsh, cruel; rough, rigorous, stormy, boisterous, tempestuous.

inclination. Syn.: leaning, bending, bowing, nod; slant, slope, declivity, obliquity; tendency, propensity, proclivity, bent, bias, proneness, predilection, preference, liking, desire, turn.

Inclination denotes a mental leaning, more or less decided, toward something; *bent*, a general and natural mental tendency in a particular direction or toward a particular mode of action. *Proclivity* and *propensity* both denote a natural or habitual inclination toward a particular thing, often something reprehensible. *Turn* is a homely word for a natural aptitude for doing a particular thing.

incline. Syn.: lean, bend, slant, slope. See **lean,** *v.*

inclose. Syn.: surround, encircle, environ, encompass.

include. Syn.: comprise, comprehend, embrace, contain.

To *include* is to contain as a part or member, or among the parts or members, of a whole; to *comprise* is to contain, or consist of, as the various parts serving to make up the whole: as, the list *includes* many new names; this genus *comprises* fifty species, *including* several that are sometimes classified otherwise. To *comprehend* is to contain or have within the limits, scope, or range of reference, as either a part or the whole number of the items concerned: as, this case is *comprehended* under the same head; a plan *comprehending* several projects. To *embrace* is also to have within the limits or scope, but emphasizes the extent or assortment of that which is included: as, the report *embraces* all the results of the year's investigations; a curriculum *embracing* a great variety of subjects.

incoherent. Syn.: disconnected, inconsecutive, inconsistent, incongruous. See **disconnected.**

income. Syn.: revenue, proceeds, receipts, profit, interest, salary, wages, annuity.

Income denotes the returns or receipts coming in, for the year or any given period, from one's labor, business, lands, investments, etc. *Interest* is the gain coming from money lent at a fixed rate. *Revenue* is applied especially to the income of a government or state, derived from taxes, customs, and other sources, and used for the payment of public expenses.

incommode. Syn.: discommode, inconvenience, trouble, annoy. See **disturb.**

incomparable. Syn.: matchless, peerless, inimitable, unequaled, unrivaled, unparalleled.

incompatible. Syn.: see **incongruous.**

incompetence. Syn.: see **inability.**

incompetent. Syn.: incapable, unable, unfit, disqualified.

incomplete. Syn.: unfinished, imperfect, defective, deficient, partial.

incongruous. Syn.: inharmonious, inconsonant, inconsistent, incompatible, inapposite, inappropriate, unsuited, absurd.

That which is *incongruous* is inappropriate or out of keeping, often to the point of being ridiculous or absurd; thus the *incongruous* is frequently the basis of comedy and comic effects. That which is *inconsistent* is not in agreement or accord, but involves variance, discrepancy, or even contradiction, especially from the point of view of truth, reason, or logic: as, his actions are *inconsistent* with his professions; statements *inconsistent* with each other and with the facts. *Incompatible* expresses incapability of close association or harmonious relationship, as from differences of nature, character, temperament, etc.: as, *incompatible* qualities, ideas, dispositions; actions *incompatible* with honesty of purpose.

inconsiderable. Syn.: unimportant, insignificant, petty, trifling, slight, small.

inconsistent. Syn.: incongruous, incompatible, discrepant, contradictory, irreconcilable, paradoxical. Ant.: see **consistent.** See **incongruous.**

inconsolable. Syn.: see **disconsolate.**

inconstant. Syn.: changeable, variable, fickle, capricious. See **faithless.**

incontestable. Syn.: incontrovertible, indisputable, undeniable, unquestionable, indubitable, certain. See **indisputable.**

incontrovertible. Syn.: see **indisputable.**

inconvenience. Syn.: incommodiousness, incommodity, troublesomeness, discomfort, disadvantage, difficulty.

inconvenient. Syn.: incommodious, troublesome, embarrassing, inopportune, unseasonable, untoward, unsuitable, unhandy, awkward, cumbersome, unwieldy.

incorporate. Syn.: embody, unite, combine, blend, merge, consolidate.

incorporeal. Syn.: immaterial, insubstantial, spiritual, disembodied, bodiless, ghostly.

That which is *incorporeal* has no body or material form. That which is *disembodied* has been divested of its body. That which is *immaterial* does not consist of matter, but has its existence apart from material substance. *Spiritual*, of the nature of spirit, or existing as spirit, does not imply (though it does not exclude) any connection, present or past, with matter.

incorrect. Syn.: faulty, improper, erroneous, inaccurate, inexact, untrue, wrong, ungrammatical.

incorrigible. Syn.: incurable, irreclaimable, hopeless, hardened.

increase, *n.* Syn.: enlargement, augmentation, extension, expansion; addition, accession, accretion, increment.

increase, *v.* Syn.: grow, wax, multiply; enlarge, amplify, augment, extend, accrue, enhance, intensify, heighten, accelerate, aggravate. See **grow.**

Increase is the general word for becoming or making greater, as in bulk, quantity, extent, etc. *Enlarge*, from its origin, naturally denotes especially an increasing in largeness, size, extent, or range. *Augment*, a more formal word, is to increase or enlarge especially by addition from without. To *intensify* is to make more intense, or increase the degree of force, energy, vividness, violence, etc.; to *aggravate* is to make more serious or less bearable; as, to *intensify* heat, color, ardor, rage; to *intensify*, or *aggravate*, sufferings; to *aggravate* an offense by repetition.

incredulity. Syn.: unbelief, disbelief, distrust, skepticism. See **doubt.**

incriminate. Syn.: see **accuse.**

inculcate. Syn.: see **implant.**

incumbent. Syn.: see **obligatory.**

incur. Syn.: contract.

Incur, literally to run into, denotes a becoming liable or subject to something, usually adverse or unpleasant, entailed as a consequence of one's own action: as, to *incur* danger, suspicion, or reproach. *Contract* is used for the acquiring, often involuntarily, of something undesirable or noxious: as, to *contract* a fever, debts, etc.

incurable. Syn.: irremediable, irrecoverable, fatal, hopeless, incorrigible.

incursion. Syn.: see **invasion.**

indebted. Syn.: obliged, beholden, bounden.

Indebted indicates a being under obligation, as to a person, for some benefit, favor, or service; it is often used in expressions of grateful acknowledgment, as of a favor of implied importance. *Obliged*, with like meaning, is now used chiefly in expressions of gratitude or in conventional acknowledgment of favors or courtesies. *Beholden* and *bounden*, held or bound by obligation, indebted, have now a somewhat archaic or provincial flavor.

indecency. Syn.: see **indecorum.**

indecent. Syn.: unseemly, unbecoming, indecorous, indelicate, immodest, coarse, gross, ribald, obscene. See **improper.**

indecision. Syn.: irresolution, hesitation, vacillation, uncertainty.

indecorous. Syn.: unseemly, unbecoming, unmannerly, improper, rude. See **improper.**

indecorum. Syn.: indecency, indelicacy, impropriety.

indefatigable. Syn.: tireless, untiring, unwearying, unflagging, persevering, persistent, assiduous, indomitable. See **diligent.**

indefensible. Syn.: see **unwarrantable.**

indefinite. Syn.: undefined, undetermined, indeterminate, uncertain, inexplicit, inexact, general, ambiguous, equivocal, vague, obscure. Ant.: see **definite.**

indelible. Syn.: ineffaceable, ingrained, fixed, fast, abiding, permanent.

indelicacy. Syn.: see **indecorum.**

indelicate. Syn.: coarse, vulgar, gross, immodest, indecorous. See **improper.**

indemnify. Syn.: reimburse, compensate, recompense, requite, remunerate. See **compensate.**

indentation. Syn.: see **hole.**

independence. Syn.: see **freedom.**

independent. Syn.: free, uncontrolled, unrestricted, autonomous.

indicate. Syn.: point out, designate, show, signify, denote, betoken, evidence, intimate, disclose, reveal.

indication. Syn.: designation, manifestation, intimation, hint, suggestion, mark, token, sign, symptom.

indict. Syn.: see **accuse.**

indifference. Syn.: impartiality, neutrality; apathy, unconcern, impassibility, insensibility, coolness, coldness, inattention, listlessness, heedlessness, carelessness, nonchalance, stoicism; mediocrity, inferiority.

Indifference denotes an absence of feeling or interest; *unconcern*, an absence of concern or solicitude, a calm or cool indifference in the face of what might be expected to cause uneasiness or apprehension; *listlessness*, an absence of inclination or interest, a languid indifference to what is going on about one; *apathy*, profound indifference suggestive of mental faculties either naturally sluggish or dulled by sickness or grief. *Insensibility* denotes an absence of capacity for feeling, or of susceptibility to emotional influences. *Stoicism* implies a studied repression of all feeling, an austere indifference to pleasure and pain.

indifferent. Syn.: impartial, unbiased, disinterested, fair; apathetic, unconcerned, cool, cold, lukewarm, inattentive, heedless, perfunctory, nonchalant; medium, moderate, mediocre, ordinary, tolerable, passable.

indigence. Syn.: see **poverty.**

indigenous. Syn.: see **native.**

indigent. Syn.: see **poor.**

indignant. Syn.: resentful, displeased, incensed, provoked.

indignation. Syn.: see **anger.**

indignity. Syn.: see **affront.**

indirect. Syn.: circuitous, roundabout, devious, tortuous; unfair, dishonest.

indiscreet. Syn.: injudicious, imprudent, unwise, foolish, hasty, rash.

indiscretion. Syn.: see **folly.**

indiscriminate. Syn.: see **promiscuous.**

indispensable. Syn.: see **necessary.**

indisposed. Syn.: sick, ill, unwell; disinclined, unwilling, reluctant, averse, loath. See **sick.**

indisposition. Syn.: sickness, illness; disinclination, unwillingness, reluctance, averseness.

indisputable. Syn.: incontrovertible, irrefragable, incontestable, unquestionable, undeniable, indubitable, certain, positive, obvious.

What is *indisputable* admits of no dispute as to truth, justice, genuineness, etc.: as, *indisputable* facts, principles, statements, or claims; an *indisputable* success. What is *incontestable* cannot be contested, or made the object of adverse arguments: as, *incontestable* evidence or proofs. What is *incontrovertible* is too evident or certain to be overthrown by argument or debate: as, an *incontrovertible* point; *incontrovertible* reasoning. What is *irrefragable* is not to be gainsaid or refuted: as, *irrefragable* arguments; the *Irrefragable* Doctor (Alexander of Hales). *Unquestionable* is applied to whatever is beyond question as to truth, certainty, or the like; *indubitable*, to what admits of no doubt.

indistinct. Syn.: undefined, indistinguishable, confused, dim, faint, obscure, vague, uncertain.

individual, *n.* **Syn.:** see **person.**

individual, *a.* **Syn.:** see **special.**

individuality. Syn.: see **character.**

indolent. Syn.: lazy, slothful, sluggish, listless, idle, supine. See **idle.**

indomitable. Syn.: unyielding, unconquerable, untamable. See **invincible.**

indubitable. Syn.: see **indisputable.**

induce. Syn.: persuade, influence, incite, impel, lead. See **incite.**

inducement. Syn.: see **motive.**

induction. Syn.: see **deduction.**

indulge. Syn.: gratify, satisfy, humor, pamper, cocker, baby. See **gratify.**

indulgence. Syn.: gratification, humoring, kindness, lenience, forbearance.

industrious. Syn.: industrial; diligent, busy, sedulous, assiduous, active, laborious. See **diligent.**

industry. Syn.: diligence, application, labor, work. See **assiduity.**

inebriated. Syn.: see **drunken.**

ineffable. Syn.: see **inexpressible.**

ineffectual. Syn.: ineffective, unavailing, futile, fruitless, vain. See **useless.**

inefficient. Syn.: incapable, incompetent, ineffective, inefficacious.

inelastic. Syn.: see **inflexible.**

inelegant. Syn.: crude, rough, homely, plain, unpolished, unrefined, ungraceful, awkward, clumsy. **Ant.:** see **elegant.**

inequality. Syn.: disparity, disproportion, diversity, unevenness, irregularity, variableness.

inert. Syn.: see **inactive.**

inestimable. Syn.: incalculable, invaluable, priceless.

inexcusable. Syn.: unpardonable, unjustifiable, unwarrantable, indefensible.

inexorable. Syn.: relentless, unrelenting, implacable, unyielding, immovable. See **inflexible.**

inexpedient. Syn.: inadvisable, impolitic, unwise, unprofitable, disadvantageous.

inexpensive. Syn.: see **cheap.**

inexperienced. Syn.: unpractised, untrained, undisciplined, unskilled, unversed, inexpert, raw, green.

inexplicable. Syn.: unaccountable, incomprehensible, mysterious.

inexpressible. Syn.: unspeakable, unutterable, ineffable, indescribable.

Inexpressible is applied to what cannot be expressed, often because it is too great for expression; *unutterable*, to what cannot be uttered, often because it is too deeply felt for utterance; *unspeakable*, to what exceeds the power of speech, generally to what is too bad or vile to be spoken of or described: as, *unspeakable* conditions; *unspeakable* villainy. *Ineffable* is applied to what transcends expression, or is too great, too wonderful, or too sacred for utterance: as, *ineffable* grandeur, power, beauty.

infallible. Syn.: see **certain, reliable.**

infamous. Syn.: disreputable, notorious, disgraceful, scandalous, nefarious, odious, wicked.

infamy. Syn.: see **disgrace,** *n.*

infant, infantile. Syn.: see **child, childish.**

infatuation. Syn.: see **love.**

infect. Syn.: taint, contaminate, pollute; imbue, impregnate, permeate. See **taint,** *v.*

infection. Syn.: contagion, virus, germ, pest, pestilence; disease, ailment, distemper, poisoning, sepsis.

infectious. Syn.: catching, communicable, contagious, pestiferous, pestilential.

infer. Syn.: deduce, conclude, gather.

Infer, the broadest of these terms, is used for the deriving of a belief or opinion by reasoning from any circumstance, evidence, or premises. To *deduce* is to derive by formal reasoning from what is already known or assumed. To *conclude* is to infer as the final step in a process of reasoning.

inference. Syn.: deduction, conclusion, illation, presumption, assumption, surmise.

infernal. Syn.: see **devilish.**

infest. Syn.: harass, torment, plague, overrun.

infidel. Syn.: see **skeptic.**

infinite. Syn.: unbounded, boundless, unlimited, absolute, illimitable, immeasurable, endless, innumerable, numberless, countless, inexhaustible, immense, vast.

infirm. Syn.: weak, feeble, shaky, decrepit, debilitated, sickly. See **weak.**

infirmary. Syn.: see **hospital.**

infirmity. Syn.: weakness, feebleness, debility; failing, foible, defect. See **failing.** Cf. **disease.**

inflame. Syn.: fire, kindle, arouse, excite, incense, enrage, exasperate. See **kindle.**

inflate. Syn.: distend, swell, expand, enlarge.

inflection. Syn.: modulation, intonation, accent.

Inflection and *modulation* both express change in the pitch or tone of the voice, but *inflection* usually denotes a particular change, which may produce a harsh effect, while *modulation* denotes rather a series of changes, or a regulated variation of pitch or tone, which produces a musical or agreeable effect. *Intonation* is the manner in which the tones of the voice are employed. *Accent* is primarily a special emphasis in utterance by which a syllable is given prominence over others; the word is often used more broadly to indicate differences of pronunciation and modulation peculiar to a race, class, district, or the like.

inflexible. Syn.: unbending, inelastic, rigid, stiff, firm; unyielding, steadfast, dogged, stubborn, obstinate, unrelenting, relentless, implacable, inexorable. **Ant.:** see **flexible.**

Inflexible indicates incapability of being bent or turned from a purpose, as by entreaty or argument; *inexorable,* incapability of being moved by prayer or entreaty; *implacable,* incapability of being placated or appeased. *Unrelenting* and *relentless* indicate the absence of any yielding or softening in the spirit that impels one to carry out a harsh purpose.

influence, *n.* **Syn.:** ascendancy, mastery, control, power, prestige, sway, rule. See **authority.**

influence, *v.* **Syn.:** move, stir, sway, incite, impel, induce, persuade.

inform. Syn.: acquaint, apprise, notify, advise, tell.

Inform, to make cognizant or aware of a thing by imparting knowledge of it, is a formal or dignified word for what in simple language is often expressed by *tell*: as, he *informed* us of his intentions; let me *inform* you that I shall not consent. *Acquaint,* with the same general sense, suggests particularly the imparting of a knowledge of something hitherto unknown or unfamiliar to one. *Apprise,* a formal word, suggests a putting in possession of a knowledge of facts or circumstances likely to be of interest to one. To *notify* is to inform by special notice. To *advise* is to inform by special intelligence, as of action in a business matter.

informal. Syn.: unceremonious, unconventional, natural, easy, unconstrained. **Ant.:** see **formal.**

informant. Syn.: informer.

An *informant* is one who communicates information or intelligence of any sort to another; an *informer* is often one who gives information against another, usually to secure some advantage for himself, as immunity from punishment, or who makes a practice of detecting offenses against the law and presenting to the authorities information against the offenders.

information. Syn.: see **knowledge.**

informer. Syn.: see **informant.**

infringe. Syn.: violate, transgress, break; encroach, trespass, intrude, intrench. See **encroach.**

infringement. Syn.: violation, transgression, infraction, breach; encroachment, trespass, intrusion, intrenchment, invasion.

infuriate. Syn.: see **irritate.**

infuse. Syn.: see **implant.**

ingenious. Syn.: inventive, resourceful, skilful, clever, bright. See **clever;** cf. **ingenuous.**

ingenuous. Syn.: frank, open, candid, naïve, artless, guileless, innocent. Cf. **artless.**

Ingenuous (frank, candid) and *ingenious* (inventive, clever) are distinct words and should not be confused. *Ingenuousness* and *ingenuity,* however, both etymologically associated with *ingenuous,* are now differentiated in use, so that while *ingenuousness* still corresponds in sense to *ingenuous, ingenuity,* having lost almost wholly its original meaning, has now taken on senses conforming to *ingenious.*

inglorious. Syn.: humble, obscure; ignoble, ignominious.

Inglorious indicates the absence of glory, either where glory may have been sought or expected or where, because of obscurity or humbleness, it could not have been looked for. *Ignominious* implies humiliation or disgrace. Both words are often used humorously or derisively.

ingraft. Syn.: see **implant.**

ingrained. Syn.: see **inborn.**

ingredient. Syn.: constituent, component, element, part. See **constituent.**

inhabitant. Syn.: dweller, resident, citizen, denizen.

An *inhabitant* is one who dwells in a place as a permanent resident. A *citizen* is an inhabitant of a city or town who possesses full civic rights and privileges, or a member (native or naturalized, resident or absent) of a state, owing allegiance to, and entitled to the protection of, its government. A *denizen,* originally a dweller in a place or region (now chiefly in figurative and literary uses), is specifically an alien admitted to residence and certain rights in a country.

inherent. Syn.: intrinsic.

That which is *inherent* in a thing is a permanent and inseparable attribute of it: as, an *inherent* weakness; tendencies *inherent* in one's nature. That which is *intrinsic* is in the constitution of a thing (as opposed to what is extrinsic, or comes from without): as, the *intrinsic* value of an honorary medal may be very small in proportion to the esteem in which it is held.

inheritance. Syn.: heritage, patrimony, legacy.

These words all denote something inherited. *Inheritance* is the common term for property or any possession that comes to an heir. *Heritage,* a dignified or literary word, indicates whatever is bequeathed to a subsequent generation by an individual or society: as, our *heritage* from Greece and Rome. *Patrimony* is the property or estate inherited from one's father or ancestors.

inhibit. Syn.: prohibit, forbid, interdict; restrain, repress, check, stop. See **forbid.**

inhuman. Syn.: unfeeling, pitiless, merciless, ruthless, brutal, barbarous, savage, fiendish. See **cruel.**

inimical. Syn.: unfriendly, adverse, opposed, antagonistic, hurtful. See **hostile.**

inimitable. Syn.: see **incomparable.**

iniquitous. Syn.: unjust, unrighteous, wicked, nefarious, heinous. See **bad.**

iniquity. Syn.: see **offense.**

initiate. Syn.: begin, commence, originate, introduce, inaugurate; induct, install, instate. See **begin.**

injudicious. Syn.: see **indiscreet.**

injunction. Syn.: see **command,** *n.*

injure. Syn.: wrong, hurt, harm, wound, maim, maltreat, abuse, impair, damage, disfigure, mar. See **impair.**

injurious. Syn.: wrongful, hurtful, harmful, detrimental, disadvantageous, mischievous, deleterious, pernicious, baneful, destructive, ruinous; abusive, derogatory, defamatory, slanderous.

injury. Syn.: wrong, hurt, wound, harm, scathe, detriment, mischief, damage, injustice, prejudice.

Injury, originally denoting a wrong done or suffered, is hence used for any kind of evil, impairment, or loss, caused or sustained: as, physical or moral *injury;* an *injury* to one's person, reputation, or prospects. *Harm* is a more popular term for injury, physical or moral. *Hurt* suggests especially physical or material injury, often bodily injury attended with pain. *Damage* denotes especially material injury, such as to impair value, usefulness, soundness, appearance, etc. *Mischief* is harm or trouble, especially as due to a particular cause or agent, and often as proceeding from wantonness or malice. *Detriment* is injury or harm, especially slight, to welfare or interests. *Prejudice* is contingent injury, or unfavorable consequence: as, an agreement made without *prejudice* to one's rights.

injustice. Syn.: inequity, unfairness, wrong.

inkling. Syn.: see **hint,** *n.*

inn. Syn.: hotel, hostelry, tavern, public house, house, caravansary, khan.

Inn, for a public house for the lodging and entertainment of travelers and others, is a word not in popular use in the United States to-day, although occasionally used for quaint or archaic effect in names given to such houses. *Hotel* is now the common word; it suggests a more or less commodious or pretentious establishment with up-to-date appointments, whereas *inn* suggests rather a place of homely comfort and old-time appearance or ways. Both words, however, when used in the names given to particular houses, may bear little relation to the character of the places themselves. *Hostelry* is an archaic term for an inn, sometimes used humorously or pedantically for a hotel. *House* is often used in the name of a particular hotel. *Tavern,* usually, like the English *public house,* a house for the sale of liquors for drinking on the premises (although in this sense an archaic or provincial rather than a popular word in the United States), has also been used in the sense of *inn,* and is still found locally in the United States, especially in New England, in the names of inns some of which date back to the colonial days.

innate. Syn.: see **inborn.**

inner. Syn.: inward, interior, inside, internal, intrinsic.

The following words exhibit minor differences, but the distinctions are largely a matter of use. *Inner* (opposed to outer), applicable strictly to what is further within (as *innermost* and *inmost* are to what is furthest within), is also used more generally of what is within, or inside a place, area, thing, the body, the mind, etc. *Inward* (opposed to outward), toward or in the inside, is often used of what exists or goes on within one, or within the mind or soul. *Interior* (opposed to exterior) is used especially of what is situated in or belongs to the inside of a thing: as, *interior* parts or districts; *interior* decorations. *Internal* (opposed to external) is likewise used of what is situated or exists in the interior of a thing, and pertains to the inner parts, nature, relations, etc.: as, *internal* injuries; *internal* evidence; *internal* revenue.

innocent. Syn.: sinless, pure, clean, virtuous, spotless, immaculate, faultless, guiltless, blameless, impeccable, inculpable; simple, naïve, artless, guileless, unsophisticated.

Innocent denotes freedom from the responsibility of having done wrong, either at any time or in a particular instance, or from the very knowledge of evil. *Guiltless* denotes freedom from guilt or responsibility for wrong-doing, usually in a particular instance. *Blameless* denotes freedom from blame, especially moral blame, either in general or in a particular instance. *Impeccable* denotes faultless and irreproachable character or behavior.

innocuous, innoxious. Syn.: see **harmless.**

innuendo. Syn.: see **insinuation.**

innumerable. Syn.: countless, numberless, unnumbered, myriad. See **many.**

inopportune. Syn.: untimely, unseasonable, inappropriate, malapropos.

inordinate. Syn.: see **excessive.**

inquire. Syn.: see **ask.**

inquiry. Syn.: see **examination, question,** *n.*

inquisition. Syn.: see **examination.**

inquisitive. Syn.: inquiring, intrusive, prying, peeping, mousing. Ant.: uninterested, unconcerned, indifferent, apathetic. See **curious.**

inroad. Syn.: see **invasion.**

insane. Syn.: deranged, demented, lunatic, crazed, crazy, mad, maniacal, delirious; foolish, senseless, wild.

insanity. Syn.: derangement, dementia, lunacy, craziness, madness, mania, frenzy, delirium, aberration, alienation.

Insanity is the general and scientific term for unsoundness of mind in various forms; in law, for such mental unsoundness as renders one legally irresponsible. *Lunacy,* applied originally to intermittent insanity as supposed to be connected with the changes of the moon, and now to any form of insanity, is found chiefly in legal and literary use. *Madness*, in literary and general use, often denotes insanity characterized by wild excitement, violence, or raving. *Craziness* is a more popular term for unsoundness of mind, especially such as manifests itself in senseless speech and absurd behavior.

insatiable. Syn.: unappeasable, unquenchable, greedy, voracious, rapacious.

inscrutable. Syn.: impenetrable, unfathomable, incomprehensible, mysterious. See **obscure.**

insecure. Syn.: uncertain, unreliable, precarious, risky, unsafe, unstable, shaky, rickety. See **uncertain.**

insensibility. Syn.: unconsciousness, stupefaction, stupor, torpor, lethargy, coma, numbness. See **indifference.**

insensible. Syn.: imperceptible, inappreciable, slow, gradual; inanimate, insensate, insentient, senseless, unconscious, numb; insensitive, unsusceptible, indifferent, impassive, apathetic, unfeeling, callous, hard.

insert. Syn.: interpolate, intercalate, interject, introduce.

Insert, to put in, is used especially of putting one thing into a hole or space in another thing or between two things: as, to *insert* a key in a lock, a word in a sentence, an advertisement in a newspaper. *Introduce*, to bring or put in, suggests especially the bringing of a thing into a new place, position, or relation, or into first notice, knowledge, or vogue: as, to *introduce* a probe into a wound, or gas into a balloon; to *introduce* American goods into Africa, or an invention to the public; to *introduce* a new subject. *Interject*, to throw in between other things, is used especially of interposing a remark abruptly or as an interruption. *Interpolate*, to introduce as an addition, is often used of the inserting of unauthorized or spurious matter in a text or writing. *Intercalate*, originally to insert as an extra day in the calendar, is sometimes used for the inserting of anything additional or extraneous between successive parts of a whole.

inside. Syn.: interior.

Inside, denoting the inner side or part of a thing or the space within it, is used with reference to things of any size, small or large: as, the *inside* of a pocket or of a shoe; the *inside* of a building. *Interior*, denoting the inner part or the space or regions within, usually suggests considerable size or extent: as, the *interior* of a cathedral; the *interior* of the earth; the *interior* of a country.

insidious. Syn.: sly, crafty, wily, cunning, deceitful, treacherous.

insight. Syn.: see **discernment.**

insignificant. Syn.: unimportant, inconsiderable, slight, trivial, trifling, paltry, petty, little, small.

insincere. Syn.: dissembling, disingenuous, hypocritical, hollow, double-faced. **Ant.:** see **sincere.**

insinuate. Syn.: see **hint.**

insinuation. Syn.: innuendo, imputation, reflection.

An *insinuation* is an indirect or covert suggestion, often of something discreditable to a person; an *innuendo* is an allusive remark intended to convey a meaning indirectly, commonly a derogatory, injurious, or indelicate meaning; both are deliberate, and often more or less malicious. An *imputation* is an attributing of something discreditable, either expressly or by implication. A *reflection* is a remark casting reproach or discredit, or an action or circumstance having the same effect: as, he took this warning as a *reflection* on his discretion.

insipid. Syn.: tasteless, flat, vapid, stale, lifeless; uninteresting, dull, stupid, prosaic. See **tasteless.**

insist. Syn.: press, urge, contend, persist.

insnare. Syn.: entrap, entangle, inveigle.

insolence. Syn.: see **arrogance.**

insolent. Syn.: overbearing, arrogant, contemptuous, contumelious, insulting, impudent, impertinent, rude. See **impertinent.**

insolvency. Syn.: see **failure.**

inspect, inspection. Syn.: see **examine, examination.**

inspire. Syn.: infuse, imbue, impregnate.

inspirit. Syn.: animate, enliven, encourage, cheer, invigorate, rouse, fire.

install. Syn.: see **initiate.**

instance. Syn.: see **example.**

instant. Syn.: see **moment.**

instantaneously, instantly. Syn.: see **immediately.**

instigate. Syn.: spur, incite, provoke, stimulate, goad, foment. See **incite.**

instil. Syn.: see **implant.**

instinctive. Syn.: intuitive, natural, innate, inherent, involuntary, spontaneous, automatic.

institute. Syn.: set up, establish, found, constitute, organize, ordain, inaugurate, start, commence, begin.

instruct. Syn.: teach, tutor, coach, train, drill, discipline, indoctrinate, school, educate, inform, enlighten, edify; order, direct, command. See **direct.**

instruction. Syn.: teaching, tutoring, coaching, training, drill, discipline, indoctrination, schooling, education, tuition, cultivation, nurture; order, direction, command, mandate.

Instruction is the imparting of knowledge, either in general or in a particular branch of study, in a methodical way. *Teaching* is essentially the same as instruction, but the word is less formal and suggests more individual attention to the particular student. *Training* is the development of the body, mind, character, or some particular faculty, by exercise, instruction, or discipline. *Tuition* is the most formal of these words, and suggests the organized instruction for which one pays, as in a university. *Education* denotes the development of the faculties and powers by systematic instruction and training, particularly that given in schools or by professional teachers.

instructor. Syn.: teacher, tutor, governess, schoolmaster, schoolmistress, preceptor, preceptress, professor, pedagogue, coach, trainer.

instrument. Syn.: see **tool.**

insubordinate. Syn.: disobedient, unruly, intractable, mutinous. See **disobedient.**

insufferable. Syn.: see **intolerable.**

insufficient. Syn.: see **inadequate.**

insult. Syn.: see **affront.**

insulting. Syn.: see **insolent.**

insuperable. Syn.: insurmountable, impassable, unconquerable, invincible.

insure. Syn.: assure, guarantee, indemnify, underwrite.

insurgent. Syn.: rebel, revolter, mutineer. Cf. **traitor.**

insurrection. Syn.: rebellion, revolt, revolution, mutiny, riot, uprising, sedition.

An *insurrection* is a rising in active resistance against civil or governmental authority; it may be local or general, and is often unorganized. A *revolt* is a casting off of allegiance or subjection to rulers or authorities; it is usually a vigorous outbreak, whether brief or prolonged, and may arise from general turbulence or from opposition to tyranny or oppression. A *rebellion* is on a larger scale, is generally better organized, and has for its object the securing of independence or the overthrow of the government. A rebellion or any public movement (with or without fighting or bloodshed) that succeeds in overthrowing one government or political system and establishing another is a *revolution*. A *mutiny* is a revolt of persons under discipline against those in authority over them, especially a revolt of soldiers or sailors against their officers. A *riot* is a disorderly public outbreak by a number of persons, usually with violence.

intact. Syn.: see **sound,** *a.*

intangible. Syn.: impalpable, insubstantial, shadowy, vague, dim.

Intangible is applied to what one cannot touch or lay hold of, as anything non-material or incorporeal; *impalpable*, to what cannot be distinguished by feeling, either because it has no material substance or because it is too fine and smooth to impress the sense of touch. Figuratively both words are used of that which lacks definiteness and clarity, but *intangible* especially suggests that which eludes the understanding, *impalpable* that which escapes perception.

integrity. Syn.: wholeness, completeness, entirety; uprightness, rectitude. See **honesty.**

intellect. Syn.: see **mind.**

intellectual. Syn.: see **intelligent.**

intelligence. Syn.: intellect, understanding, discernment, sagacity, insight; information, tidings, advice, notice, notification. See **mind, news.**

intelligent. Syn.: discerning, sagacious, acute, clever, bright, intellectual.

Intelligent often implies a natural quickness of understanding; *intellectual*, a high degree of understanding, a capacity and taste for the higher forms of knowledge.

intelligible. Syn.: understandable, comprehensible, perspicuous, plain, clear.

intemperance. Syn.: excess, immoderation, indulgence, intoxication, drunkenness.

intemperate. Syn.: excessive, extreme, inordinate, immoderate, unrestrained, unbridled.

intend. Syn.: purpose, design, plan, mean, propose, contemplate.

To *intend* is to have in mind as a thing willed to be done or brought about: as, we *intend* to return soon; no offense was *intended*; men are presumed to *intend* the consequences of their actions. *Mean* is a simpler word for the same idea, but suggests perhaps less definite thought or conscious choice. *Purpose* suggests the setting of a thing before oneself for accomplishment; *design*, a planning or studying to effect a particular result.

intensify. Syn.: heighten, increase, aggravate. See **increase**, *v.*

intention. Syn.: intent, purpose, design, plan, aim, object, end.

intentional. Syn.: intended, designed, premeditated, contemplated, studied, deliberate. **Ant.:** see **unintentional.**

Intentional is applied to what is definitely intended, or done on purpose, as opposed to what is accidental; *deliberate*, to what is not done hastily but with full realization of what one is doing; *premeditated*, to what has been planned beforehand.

intently. Syn.: attentively, fixedly, closely, earnestly, eagerly, sedulously.

intercalate. Syn.: see **insert.**

intercede. Syn.: see **interpose.**

interchange. Syn.: see **exchange**, *v.*

intercourse. Syn.: see **communion, fellowship.**

interdict. Syn.: see **forbid.**

interest, *n.* **Syn.:** concern, share, portion, part, participation; profit, advantage, benefit, behoof. See **income.**

interest, *v.* **Syn.:** concern, involve, affect, engage, occupy, hold, entertain.

interfere. Syn.: collide, clash, conflict; intervene, meddle. See **interpose.**

interior, *n.* **Syn.:** see **inside.**

interior, *a.* **Syn.:** see **inner.**

interject. Syn.: see **insert.**

interloper. Syn.: see **intruder.**

intermeddle. Syn.: see **interpose.**

intermediate. Syn.: intervening, interjacent.

Intermediate is applied to what holds a middle place or comes or occurs between other points, stages, grades, parts, or things, as if forming a member of a series: as, a point *intermediate* between extremes; a school divided into the primary, *intermediate*, and grammar grades. *Intervening* also is applied to what comes between, whether in space, time, a series, a course of action, etc., but without necessarily implying a relation to what precedes or what follows, since that which intervenes is often extraneous or of casual occurrence, or is regarded merely as occupying an interval or serving to separate, interrupt, or obstruct: as, *intervening* miles, years, events, or acts; an *intervening* wall or obstacle.

interminable. Syn.: unending, endless, limitless, boundless, infinite. See **eternal.**

intermission. Syn.: cessation, pause, interval, interruption, suspension, respite, rest. See **stop**, *n.*

intermit. Syn.: see **abate, suspend.**

internal. Syn.: see **inner.**

interpolate. Syn.: see **insert.**

interpose. Syn.: intervene, interfere, intermeddle, intercede, mediate.

Interpose, literally to put between, is often used of bringing one's action, words, or influence to bear in a case between parties, with or without authority, but commonly for some good purpose. *Intervene*, literally to come between, is often used of interposing formally in a case, or in the affairs of a country, as for the purpose of adjusting differences, regulating matters, or restoring order. *Mediate*, literally to be in the middle, is the usual term for acting between parties at variance in an effort to bring about a compromise or reconciliation. *Intercede*, literally to go between, is to step in with pleading or argument in order to help another. *Interfere*, literally to strike each other, naturally implies a collision in action, and is hence used particularly of interposing actively in an affair, either with or without right, in order to oppose or thwart another or otherwise to affect action or results. *Intermeddle* is used of meddling or interfering in matters that do not concern one.

interpret. Syn.: expound, elucidate, construe, solve, decipher, unfold, unravel. See **explain, translate.**

interpretation. Syn.: see **translation.**

interrogate. Syn.: see **ask.**

interrogation. Syn.: see **question**, *n.*

interrogatory. Syn.: see **question**, *n.*

intervene. Syn.: see **interpose.**

intervening. Syn.: see **intermediate.**

interview. Syn.: see **meeting.**

intimacy. Syn.: see **acquaintance.**

intimate, *n.* **Syn.:** see **friend.**

intimate, *a.* **Syn.:** see **familiar.**

intimate, *v.* **Syn.:** see **hint**, *v.*

intimation. Syn.: see **hint**, *n.*

intimidate. Syn.: overawe, frighten, cow, deter, dismay, abash. See **daunt.**

intolerable. Syn.: insufferable, unbearable, unendurable.

intolerant. Syn.: illiberal, narrow, bigoted, dogmatic.

intonation. Syn.: see **inflection.**

intoxicated. Syn.: drunk, fuddled, tipsy, boozy, full, tight. See **drunken.**

intoxication. Syn.: drunkenness, inebriety, inebriation.

intractable. Syn.: unmanageable, ungovernable, unruly, refractory, restive, stubborn, perverse, wilful, headstrong. See **unmanageable.**

intrench. Syn.: see **trespass, encroach.**

intrepid. Syn.: fearless, bold, dauntless, undaunted, undismayed, courageous, daring, valiant, brave. See **brave.**

intricate. Syn.: entangled, involved, complicated, complex, compound.

intrigue, *n.* **Syn.:** plot, scheme, machination, cabal, conspiracy; amour, liaison.

intrigue, *v.* **Syn.:** plot, scheme, machinate. See **plot.**

intrinsic. Syn.: inward, innate, inherent, inseparable, essential, genuine, real. See **inherent.**

introduce. Syn.: present. See **insert.**

Introduce is the ordinary term for bringing persons, ostensibly equals, into personal acquaintance with each other, as by announcement of name, etc. *Present*, a more formal term, suggests a degree of ceremony in the process, and implies, if only as a matter of compliment, superior dignity, rank, or importance in the person to whom another is presented.

introduction. Syn.: preface, foreword, preamble, prelude, prologue, prelusion, exordium, proem, prolegomenon.

An *introduction*, strictly speaking, is a preliminary part of a book, writing, or discourse, leading up to the main part and containing explanatory or other useful matter bearing on the subject; a *preface* is a preliminary statement, often brief, by the author or another, dealing usually with the circumstances of the preparation or publication of the work, or of a particular edition, etc.; but each word is occasionally found in the sense more proper to the other. *Foreword*, a modern coinage from English elements of Anglo-Saxon origin, is affected by some writers in preference to *preface* and *introduction*, both of Latin origin, perhaps on the erroneous supposition that *foreword* is the old or historic term and thus able to impart a picturesque or archaic effect.

introductory. Syn.: preparatory, prefatory, proemial. See **preliminary.**

intrude. Syn.: obtrude. See **trespass, encroach.**

intruder. Syn.: interloper, trespasser.

An *intruder* thrusts himself in, perhaps only for a short time, where he has no right to be or where his presence is unwelcome; an *interloper* takes up a position, usually of more or less permanence, in a field or domain (originally that of trade) which others consider to belong solely to themselves.

intrusive. Syn.: see **meddlesome.**

intrust. Syn.: see **commit.**

intuitive. Syn.: see **instinctive.**

inundation. Syn.: see **flood.**

invade. Syn.: see **trespass.**

invalidate. Syn.: see **annul.**

invaluable. Syn.: inestimable, priceless, precious.

invariable. Syn.: unalterable, unchanging, uniform, constant. **Ant.:** see **variable.**

invasion. Syn.: intrusion, encroachment, infringement, intrenchment; irruption, incursion, raid, air-raid, foray, inroad.

An *invasion* is a hostile entering and overrunning of territory by enemy forces, as for conquest or spoliation; it may involve organized military movements on a large scale and through a considerable period of time. An *incursion* is more limited in scope and duration, being a sudden, hasty expedition into a region in order to plunder, waste, or destroy; it is often one of a number or succession of such expeditions. A *raid* is a short, rapid incursion by a hostile troop, especially on horseback and usually for booty or supplies. An *air-raid* is a destructive attack by hostile aircraft. A *foray*, originally a foraging expedition, is much the same as a raid; the word is sometimes applied particularly to the plundering excursions of lawless troops or irregular forces. *Inroad*, denoting an incursion, with reference particularly to the penetrating of territory and the damaging effects, is now a literary rather than a military term, and less common in literal than in figurative use.

invective. Syn.: denunciation, railing, diatribe, tirade, philippic.

All these words indicate a verbal onslaught. An *invective* is violent, but may be dignified; a *diatribe* is violent, bitter, and personal or particular in its application; a *tirade* is vehement, and more or less angry or abusive; a *philippic* (originally used of the orations of Demosthenes against Philip of Macedon) is usually oratorical or formal in style.

inveigh. Syn.: see **declaim.**

inveigle. Syn.: entice, allure, insnare, decoy, beguile, dupe, trick, cajole, wheedle. See **lure.**

invent, invention. Syn.: see **discover, discovery.**

inventory. Syn.: see **list.**

invert. Syn.: see **overturn.**

investigate. Syn.: search, explore, sift, scrutinize, study, probe, overhaul. See **examine.**

investigation. Syn.: see **examination.**

inveterate. Syn.: long-standing, chronic, habitual, confirmed, hardened. See **chronic.**

invidious. Syn.: hateful, odious, offensive, disagreeable, unfair.

invigorate. Syn.: strengthen, brace, refresh, stimulate, animate.

invincible. Syn.: impregnable, indomitable.

Invincible is applied to what cannot be conquered in combat or war, or overcome or subdued in any manner: as, an *invincible* army or navy; *invincible* courage, prejudice, or ignorance. *Impregnable* is applied to a place or position that cannot be taken by assault or siege, and hence to whatever is proof against attack: as, *impregnable* virtue. *Indomitable*, literally not to be tamed or subdued, implies an unyielding spirit or stubborn persistence in the face of opposition or difficulty.

invite. Syn.: ask, bid, request, summon; encourage, incite, attract. See **call.**

invoke. Syn.: supplicate, beseech, solicit, implore.

involuntary. Syn.: unintentional, instinctive, automatic; unwilling, compulsory, forced.

involve. Syn.: infold, envelop, surround; entwine, entangle, complicate, embarrass, embroil; include, contain, embrace, entail. See **implicate, imply.**

inward. Syn.: see **inner.**

iota. Syn.: see **particle.**

irascible. Syn.: choleric, irritable, splenetic, touchy, testy, waspish, snappish, peppery, hasty, fiery, passionate. See **irritable.**

irate, ire. Syn.: see **angry, anger.**

irksome. Syn.: tiresome, tedious, burdensome, troublesome, annoying, vexatious. See **wearisome, tiresome.**

irony. Syn.: sarcasm, satire.

In *irony* the essential feature is the contradiction between the literal and the intended meaning, since one thing is said and another is implied; *irony* attacks or derides, or, often, is merely playful. In *sarcasm* the characteristic feature is the harsh or cutting quality; *sarcasm* is commonly, though not necessarily, ironical. *Satire*, originally applied to a literary composition which attacks by means of irony or sarcasm, denotes also the use of such means, in writing or speaking, in order to deride, whether for some serious purpose (as the exposing or denouncing of abuses) or in a malicious or a merely playful spirit. Literary *satire* commonly implies a light, skilful, or graceful touch in its execution.

irrational. Syn.: unreasonable, illogical, injudicious. See **illogical.**

irrecoverable. Syn.: irretrievable, irreparable, irremediable.

irrefragable. Syn.: see **indisputable.**

irrefutable. Syn.: incontrovertible, indisputable, undeniable, unquestionable, unanswerable, irrefragable.

irregular. Syn.: anomalous, abnormal, unusual, exceptional; unsymmetrical, uneven, variable, changeable; unmethodical, unsystematic, disorderly, capricious, erratic, eccentric, lawless. **Ant.:** see **regular.**

Irregular, not according to rule, is a general term covering any kind of deviation from what is regular, proper, conventional, usual, or natural, as in form, arrangement, quality, character, action, behavior, occurrence, etc.; it may imply such deviation as a mere fact, or as regrettable or even reprehensible. *Abnormal* and *anomalous* both express deviation from the common rule, *abnormal* having regard particularly to the non-typical form or nature of a thing, *anomalous* rather to the unusual or exceptional character of a phenomenon.

irreligious. Syn.: ungodly, godless, unrighteous, impious, blasphemous, sacrilegious, profane, wicked, atheistic.

Irreligious implies usually not a mere absence of religion (as from want of knowledge), but indifference to it, and especially open disregard or defiance of its principles. *Godless* implies especially absence of the belief in or worship of God, or the sinfulness which is regarded as a consequence; *ungodly*, disregard of God's laws. *Impious*, a strong word, indicates a presumptuous irreverence toward God or sacred things.

irremediable, irreparable. Syn.: see **irrecoverable.**

irreproachable. Syn.: blameless, faultless, spotless, immaculate.

irresolute. Syn.: doubtful, undecided, unsettled, hesitating, wavering, vacillating.

irretrievable. Syn.: see **irrecoverable.**

irritable. Syn.: irascible, choleric, touchy, testy.

The *irritable* man, often in consequence of his physical condition or of special circumstances, is easily moved to impatience or angry feeling. The *irascible* man is given to sudden outbursts of anger. The *choleric* man has the temperament associated by the old physiologists with the humor known as choler (bile), and hence is hot-tempered or irascible. The *touchy* man takes offense on slight cause; the *testy* man is irritable, obstinate, and resentful of contradiction or opposition.

irritate. Syn.: provoke, vex, annoy, chafe, fret, gall, nettle, ruffle, pique, incense, anger, exasperate, enrage, infuriate.

To *irritate* is to excite to impatience or angry feeling, often of no great depth or duration. To *provoke* is to stir to a sudden, strong feeling of resentful anger, as by unwarrantable acts or wanton annoyance. To *incense* is to inflame with indignation or anger, as by serious provocation. To *exasperate* is to irritate to a point where self-control is threatened or lost; *enrage* and *infuriate* denote provoking to rage and to fury respectively.

isolate. Syn.: separate, detach, segregate, insulate.

isolation. Syn.: see **solitude.**

issue, *n*. Syn.: egress, exit, outflow; offspring, progeny, descendants; outcome, event, result, upshot, conclusion, termination. See **offspring.**

issue, *v*. Syn.: emerge, emanate, proceed, sally, debouch, spring, gush, disembogue; emit, discharge; publish, print.

Issue, to come forth from a place or source, is used less of individuals than of a number of persons, a mass of matter, or a volume of smoke, sound, or the like, coming forth through any outlet or outlets. *Emerge*, originally to come forth from immersion or submergence as in water, is used of coming forth from something that envelops or incloses, from a place shut off from view, or from concealment, obscurity, retirement, or the like, into sight or notice. *Emanate*, literally to flow forth, is used especially of intangible or immaterial things, as light, vapor, effluvia, influences, ideas, rumors, etc., streaming or issuing from a source.

itch. Syn.: see **desire, *n*.**

J

jabber. Syn.: chatter, gabble, babble, prattle, gibberish. See **babble.**

jade. Syn.: exhaust, fatigue, weary, tire, dull. See **tire.**

jagged. Syn.: jaggy, notched, indented, serrated, craggy.

jail. Syn.: prison, lockup, workhouse, bridewell, calaboose.

jailer. Syn.: warden, turnkey.

jam, *n*. Syn.: crush, crowd, throng.

jam, *v*. Syn.: press, squeeze, wedge, pack, crowd, push, shove, force, thrust, ram.

jangle. Syn.: see **quarrel.**

jape. Syn.: see **joke.**

jar, *n.* **Syn.:** grating, discord; clash, collision, conflict, quarrel, strife, dissension; jolt, shock, vibration.

jar, *v.* **Syn.:** grate, scrape, grind; clash, conflict; shake, jolt, jounce, shock, unsettle, discompose, disturb.

jargon. Syn.: gibberish, babble, nonsense; lingo, cant, argot, slang.

Jargon, first used of the twittering or chattering of birds, is applied more or less contemptuously to any talk or language that seems mere gibberish, or to a barbarous or hybrid language or dialect (as, the Chinook *jargon,* composed of Indian, French, and English words), or to the phraseology of a particular class, profession, science, or the like, which abounds in terms unfamiliar to the general public (as, metaphysical *jargon*; the *jargon* of the law). *Lingo* is a contemptuous designation for a foreign language, or for any speech or phraseology regarded as outlandish or unintelligible. *Cant,* denoting the whining or sing-song speech of beggars, and hence a special language used by vagabonds and thieves, is also applied, like *jargon,* to the phraseology peculiar to any class, viewed, however, less as an unintelligible jargon than as something specially affected by the class; *cant* is also used of affectedly pious language, or of any conventional and insincere use of religious or other forms of speech. *Argot,* the French term for the special language (cant) of vagabonds and thieves, serves also to denote the jargon or phraseology of a particular class. *Slang,* applied first to the language or vocabulary used by vagabonds, criminals, and others of low or disreputable character, and hence to the jargon of any class, is now used particularly to denote language of a markedly colloquial character, regarded as below the standard of cultivated speech. Slang is ordinarily made up of new words, or of ordinary words or phrases employed in special or arbitrary senses; it is in some cases vulgar, pointless, or silly, and often short-lived, in other cases pleasingly or cleverly expressive, in time passing as a useful and generally accepted element into approved speech.

jaunt. Syn.: see **journey.**

jaunty. Syn.: sprightly, airy, gay, smart, showy.

jealous. Syn.: envious, grudging, suspicious, resentful.

jealousy. Syn.: see **envy.**

jeer. Syn.: scoff, mock, taunt, flout, gibe, ridicule, deride, sneer. See **scoff.**

jejune. Syn.: barren, dry, uninteresting, insipid, dull, flat. **Ant.:** interesting, lively, witty.

jeopardize. Syn.: jeopard, hazard, risk, endanger, imperil. See **risk,** *v.*

jeopardy. Syn.: exposure, hazard, risk, peril. See **danger.**

jerk. Syn.: pluck, twitch, tweak, yank, tug, pull. See **pull.**

jest. Syn.: joke.

A *jest* is something said (now seldom something done) in sport or to cause amusement; a *joke,* either something said or something done to cause amusement. A *jest* is more suggestive of wit, sometimes exercised at the expense of another person; a *joke,* of humor, especially humor of a simple or even crude kind, likewise sometimes exercised at the expense of another, as by pranks or tricks (practical jokes).

jester. Syn.: joker, wag; fool, buffoon, clown, merry-andrew, zany.

jet. Syn.: spurt, spout, gush, shoot.

jewel. Syn.: gem, brilliant, trinket, bijou.

Jewel and *gem* are both applied to precious stones, *jewel* usually to a stone set as an ornament, *gem* to one either set or unset, especially when cut and polished.

jibe. Syn.: see **harmonize.**

jiffy. Syn.: see **moment.**

jingle. Syn.: tinkle, clink, ringing; rime, verse, couplet, limerick.

job. Syn.: task, undertaking; position, situation, post.

jocose. Syn.: jocular, jesting, joking, waggish, droll, facetious, witty, humorous, funny, comic, mirthful, merry, playful, sportive. **Ant.:** serious, grave, solemn, dreary, sad, lugubrious.

Jocose and *jocular* are much alike in their suggestion of humor and jest, but *jocose* implies more of merriment, *jocular* more of levity and wit. *Facetious* suggests a desire or attempt to be humorous or witty; *waggish,* the spirit of sly mischief and roguery of the constant joker.

jocular. Syn.: see **jocose.**

jocund. Syn.: cheerful, joyous, blithe, merry, sportive, light-hearted, glad. See **gay.**

jog. Syn.: push, nudge, jolt, jar, shake, jostle, joggle; trot, amble.

join. Syn.: connect, unite, link, couple, fasten, attach, conjoin, combine, associate, consolidate, amalgamate.

Join is a general term for the bringing of things together, either directly, as in contact, or by means of something intervening. *Connect* denotes a joining as by a tie, link, or other intervening part. *Unite* denotes a joining of two or more things to form one, and connotes particularly the coherence of the resulting union. *Combine* expresses a bringing into close or intimate union, sometimes involving coalescence, or loss of distinction between parts; *consolidate,* combination into a solid or compact whole.

joint. Syn.: articulation, juncture, seam, suture, commissure, node, knuckle, hinge.

joke, *n.* **Syn.:** jest, witticism, jape, quip, quirk, sally; jesting, raillery. See **jest.**

joke, *v.* **Syn.:** jest, jape, rally, chaff, banter.

joker. Syn.: see **jester.**

jollity. Syn.: merriment, mirth, hilarity, fun, gaiety, frolic, merrymaking, festivity, revelry.

jolly. Syn.: jovial, jocular, jocose, merry, mirthful, hilarious, joyful, gleeful, gay, sportive, playful, frolicsome, rollicking, festive, convivial, boon. See **gay.**

jolt. Syn.: see **jar.**

jostle. Syn.: see **crowd,** *v.*

jot. Syn.: see **bit.**

journal. Syn.: diary, day-book, register, record; periodical, magazine, newspaper, gazette.

journey. Syn.: trip, excursion, jaunt, junket, tour, voyage, expedition, pilgrimage, peregrination.

Journey and *voyage* both denote a course of travel, usually of considerable length, whether for pleasure, business, or other reasons, *journey* commonly having reference to travel wholly or mainly by land, *voyage* now only to travel by sea or water. *Trip* is the familiar word, especially where the journey or voyage is short or regularly repeated. Among various kinds of journey or voyage, a *tour* covers certain places of interest and generally returns to the starting-point; an *expedition,* made often by an organized company, is designed to accomplish a specific purpose; a *pilgrimage* is made as to a shrine, from motives of piety or veneration. An *excursion* is a short trip, often no more than a day's outing, made for observation, pleasure, etc. *Jaunt* is a familiar term for a short trip, especially for pleasure, or taken as lightly and agreeably as possible; so also *junket,* with its still stronger suggestion of a pleasure-seeking character, and its frequent application to trips, made ostensibly on official business, enjoyed at the public expense.

jovial. Syn.: see **gay.**

joy. Syn.: happiness, gladness, delight, pleasure, rapture, felicity, bliss; mirth, merriment, festivity, glee, exultation, elation. See **gladness.**

joyful. Syn.: joyous, happy, glad, cheerful, blithe, buoyant, elated, jubilant.

joyless. Syn.: sad, cheerless, gloomy, dismal, dreary.

joyous. Syn.: see **gay.**

jubilant. Syn.: rejoicing, joyful, hilarious, exultant, triumphant. See **elated.**

judge, *n.* **Syn.:** justice, magistrate; arbitrator, arbiter, referee, umpire; connoisseur, critic.

Judge, in its legal and other uses, implies particularly the authority or qualification for giving decision in matters at issue. *Arbiter* (now chiefly in literary and figurative use) suggests especially the power to decide matters with finality. An *arbitrator* acts by the choice or agreement of the parties subject to his decision. An *umpire* rules on matters referred to his sole decision, as in the case of a disagreement between arbitrators, or in the settlement of points arising during a game. A *referee* deals with a particular matter, case, contest, or the like, or with particular points, as in a game, referred to him for action or decision.

judge, *v.* **Syn.:** adjudge, adjudicate, arbitrate, decide; consider, deem, regard, esteem. See **think.**

judgment. Syn.: decision, verdict, sentence, decree; opinion, estimation, belief; understanding, discrimination, discernment, sagacity, perspicacity.

Judgment denotes ability to judge wisely or correctly, especially in matters affecting action; *discrimination,* ability to mark differences between things closely allied; *perspicacity,* ability to see through or into things under consideration;

sagacity, keenness of perception or discernment, especially in practical matters.

judicious. Syn.: wise, sensible, discreet, prudent, politic, well-advised, astute. See **sensible.**

juggler. Syn.: see **magician.**

jugglery. Syn.: manipulation, magic, conjuring, legerdemain, prestidigitation; deception, trickery.

juicy. Syn.: luscious, succulent, sappy.

jumble, *n.* **Syn.:** mixture, medley, hodgepodge, farrago, mess, muddle, chaos. See **mixture.**

jumble, *v.* **Syn.:** mix, confuse, disorder, muddle.

jump. Syn.: leap, spring, bound, vault, skip, hop, caper, start, jerk.

Jump and *leap* are often used interchangeably, but *jump* indicates more particularly the springing movement of the feet in leaving the ground or support, *leap* (which formerly also meant to run) the passage by a springing movement from one point or position to another: as, to *jump* for joy; to *leap* across a brook; to *leap* from a horse. *Bound* suggests an elastic, springing movement, as from a surface, or a succession of such movements, as along a course. *Vault* implies leaping over or upon something.

juncture. Syn.: junction, joint, articulation, seam; conjuncture, crisis, exigency, emergency, pass, strait.

junket. Syn.: see **journey.**

junto. Syn.: see **party.**

just. Syn.: righteous, upright, honest; equitable, impartial, fair; rightful, legitimate, due, deserved, merited, condign; right, proper, fitting, correct, true, precise, exact. **Ant.:** see **unjust.** See **fair.**

justice. Syn.: justness (see **just**); right, equity, law; judge, magistrate.

Justice is the principle by which rights and claims are weighed and a balance is arrived at so that fair treatment shall be given to all concerned. *Equity* is especially used of the administration of law in accordance with considerations of inherent right. *Right* is the general word for what ought to be.

justifiable. Syn.: vindicable, defensible, warrantable, excusable.

justify. Syn.: vindicate, defend, uphold, exonerate, exculpate; sustain, warrant. See **vindicate.**

juvenile. Syn.: youthful, boyish, puerile, childish, immature. See **young.**

K

keen. Syn.: eager, ardent, earnest; sharp, acute, cutting, piercing, penetrating, poignant, trenchant, biting, sarcastic, bitter; shrewd, sharp-witted, discerning. **Ant.:** see **dull.** See **sharp.**

keep, *n.* **Syn.:** maintenance, support; stronghold, donjon.

keep, *v.* **Syn.:** observe, celebrate, solemnize, commemorate; fulfil, execute, obey; guard, protect, defend, shield, preserve; maintain, sustain, support; conduct, manage, tend; hold, detain, confine, prevent, restrain, repress, withhold, reserve, retain; continue, remain, stay. See **celebrate.**

Keep (a common word) and *retain* (a more formal one) agree in meaning to continue to hold or have, as opposed to losing, parting with, or giving up. To *reserve* is to keep for some future use, occasion, or recipient, or to hold back for a time. To *withhold* is generally to hold back altogether.

keeper. Syn.: guard, watch, warden, custodian, curator, superintendent, overseer, guardian, protector, defender.

keeping. Syn.: observance, celebration, commemoration; protection, guardianship, charge, custody, care, possession; maintenance, support, keep; agreement, congruity, harmony.

Keeping denotes a having in one's care or charge, as for guarding or preservation; *custody*, a strict keeping, as by a formally authorized and responsible guardian or keeper.

keepsake. Syn.: remembrance, token, memento, souvenir.

A *keepsake* is something, perhaps of little intrinsic value, which is kept, or given to be kept, for the sake of the giver. A *remembrance* is something serving or given to remind one person of another. A *memento* is something serving or kept to remind one of a past occasion, an absent friend, or the like, or sometimes of what the future may bring. A *souvenir* is something, often an article of appropriate character, serving or intended to remind one of a place, occasion, or person.

kick. Syn.: recoil; resist, object, complain.

kickshaw. Syn.: see **delicacy.**

kill. Syn.: slay, slaughter, massacre, murder, butcher, execute, hang, electrocute, behead, guillotine, strangle, garrote, assassinate, lynch, immolate, burke, despatch; deaden, destroy, blast; neutralize, counteract; veto, defeat, suppress.

Kill is the general word, meaning simply to deprive of life, without implication as to the manner of killing, the agent or cause, or the nature of what is killed (whether human being, animal, or plant). *Slay* (now chiefly in literary or rhetorical use) particularly implies killing by smiting with a weapon, and hence by any form of violence. *Murder* is the usual word for the killing of a human being unlawfully, especially with premeditation; *assassinate*, for the killing of a public official or other personage by a sudden or secret murderous assault. *Butcher* and *slaughter*, primarily expressing the killing of cattle and other animals for food, are both used also of the brutal or indiscriminate killing of human beings. *Massacre* indicates a general slaughtering of helpless or unresisting victims. *Execute, hang, behead, guillotine,* and *electrocute* are all used of putting to death in accordance with a legal sentence. *Lynch* is used of the summary putting to death, by private persons (usually a mob), without legal authority, of one charged with some flagrant offense. To *despatch* is to kill with promptness or quickness, and generally in a quiet way.

kin. Syn.: kindred, relatives, relations, family, stock, race.

Kin, denoting the body of persons related to one, or one's kinsfolk or relatives collectively, is also used occasionally in the abstract sense of kinship or relationship (*kindred*); while *kindred*, meaning kinship or relationship, is commonly used in the sense of kinsfolk or relatives collectively (*kin*). Both words have a somewhat archaic flavor.

kind, *n.* **Syn.:** nature, character, type, sort, description, strain, family, breed, stock, race, variety, species, genus.

Kind denotes a class of individuals of the same nature or character; *sort*, a class or assemblage of individuals ranked together as of the same nature or on some other (sometimes vague) principle of association. *Description* is sometimes used to mean a kind or sort as indicated by distinctive characteristics.

kind, *a.* **Syn.:** kindly, kind-hearted, sympathetic, compassionate, merciful, humane, gentle, benign, benignant, charitable, benevolent, beneficent, gracious, amiable, friendly, indulgent, clement, lenient. **Ant.:** see **unkind.**

Kind implies a good-natured or sympathetic readiness to do good or give pleasure to others, either habitually or on a particular occasion, or the manifesting of such readiness in action; *kindly*, a milder word, has reference usually to general disposition, characteristic spirit or manner, etc. *Benevolent*, literally well-wishing, indicates a desire for the good of others or a generous or charitable wish to do good; *beneficent*, literally well-doing, indicates the doing of good, as from benevolent motives. *Benign*, having reference to disposition, aspect, influence, etc., implies kindliness, gentleness, mildness, or favorable character; *benignant*, used chiefly in connection with persons, suggests the kindliness of a benevolent superior or elder. *Gracious* suggests the showing of grace or favor by a superior, or a benevolent civility or sweet-natured condescension. *Amiable* implies a pleasant, kindly disposition, a willingness to please and be pleased.

kindle. Syn.: enkindle, light, ignite, fire, inflame, excite, rouse, awaken, stimulate, inspire.

Kindle is especially to cause something to burn; to *ignite* is to catch fire or set something on fire; *kindle* is often used figuratively, *ignite* seldom: as, to *kindle* a blaze, or the flame of passion; to *ignite* a match. *Inflame*, to set aflame, is now found chiefly in figurative uses, as of the inducing of morbid heat in the body or blood (inflammation) or of exciting the mind by strong passion or emotion.

kindly. Syn.: see **kind.**

kindness. Syn.: kindliness, sympathy, compassion, tenderness, gentleness, benignity, benevolence, generosity; favor, service, good turn.

kindred, *n.* **Syn.:** see **kin.**

kindred, *a.* **Syn.:** related, cognate, allied, congenial.

king. Syn.: see **ruler.**

kingdom. Syn.: monarchy, empire, realm, domain, dominion.

kingly. Syn.: royal, regal, imperial, princely, sovereign, majestic, august, magnificent, exalted, grand. **Ant.:** slavish, servile, abject. See **royal.**

kink. Syn.: see **twist.**

kinship. Syn.: see **relation.**

kiss. Syn.: osculation, smack, buss.

knack. Syn.: readiness, aptitude, aptness, facility, dexterity, adroitness, expertness, skill. See **ease.**

knave. Syn.: rogue, rascal, scoundrel, villain, scamp, scapegrace, sharper, swindler, cheat. See **rogue.**

knavery. Syn.: roguery, rascality, villainy.

knavish. Syn.: rascally, villainous, unprincipled, dishonest, fraudulent.

knickknack. Syn.: trifle, toy, trinket, bauble, gimcrack, gewgaw, kickshaw, curio.

Knickknack is applied to any pleasing or curious trifle, for ornament rather than for use, as, particularly, a bit of bric-a-brac; *trinket*, to any trifling ornament or small fancy article, as, particularly, a bit of jewelry; *gimcrack*, to any showy trifle or trumpery article of no obvious use or value; *gewgaw*, to any trinket or bit of finery regarded as a mere gaudy vanity; *bauble*, to a trinket or other ornamental article regarded as but a toy, fit to please a child.

knightly. Syn.: see **chivalrous.**

knob. Syn.: protuberance, excrescence, lump, knot, knop, boss, stud, tubercle; knoll, hill, hillock, mound.

knock. Syn.: strike, rap, tap, hit, beat, hammer, pound, thump, bump. See **strike.**

knoll. Syn.: see **knob.**

knot. Syn.: tangle, snarl; lump, knob, boss, gnarl, burl, node; tuft, cluster, group, company; bond, link, tie; problem, difficulty, perplexity, puzzle.

knotty. Syn.: knotted, gnarled, rough, rugged; difficult, intricate, complicated, involved, perplexing.

know. Syn.: perceive, apprehend, cognize, understand, comprehend, ascertain, recognize, distinguish.

As here considered, to *know* is to be aware of something as a fact or truth; to *understand* is to grasp its meaning; to *comprehend* is to take it in or understand it fully or adequately.

knowing. Syn.: perceiving, conscious, informed, intelligent, clever, smart, wide-awake, discerning, shrewd, sharp, cunning.

knowledge. Syn.: perception, apprehension, cognizance, understanding, experience; information, learning, lore, erudition, scholarship, wisdom, science.

Knowledge (in one sense) is the sum of what is known, whether on a single point or on all subjects, by individuals or by all mankind; often it is the store of truths accumulated by mankind in the course of time and transmitted to following generations of learners or students. *Information* is knowledge imparted to or acquired by individuals, often the miscellaneous stock of knowledge gathered by a person from observation, reading, study, and practical experience. *Science* is systematized knowledge of subjects of study and investigation, specifically of the facts and laws of the physical universe. *Wisdom*, for the knowledge possessed by the wise, is now chiefly a literary or rhetorical term: as, the *wisdom* of a sage; the *wisdom* of the ancients or of the schools.

L

labor, *n.* **Syn.:** work, toil, exertion, effort; task, achievement; childbirth, travail, parturition. See **work,** *n.*

labor, *v.* **Syn.:** work, toil, strive, struggle, moil, drudge, plod, slave.

labored. Syn.: laborious, elaborate, studied, forced, constrained, unnatural, stiff. See **elaborate.**

laborer. Syn.: see **worker.**

laborious. Syn.: toilsome, arduous, onerous, wearisome, fatiguing; hard-working, diligent, industrious, assiduous, careful, painstaking.

labyrinth. Syn.: maze, windings, involutions, intricacy, complexity.

lacerate. Syn.: tear, rend, mangle, wound, harrow, distress, afflict. See **mutilate.**

lack, *n.* **Syn.:** want, need, deficiency, deficit, dearth, scarcity, paucity.

Lack denotes deficiency or absence of something requisite, desirable, or customary, or at least not unnatural under the circumstances; *want*, a stronger word, denotes a wish for something, the lack of something which one deems valuable, or the thing which one lacks or would like to have; *need* suggests the pressure, created by a deficiency, to obtain something, or the thing to be obtained.

lack, *v.* **Syn.:** want, need, be without.

lackey. Syn.: see **servant.**

laconic. Syn.: brief, short, concise, condensed, terse, succinct, pithy, sententious. See **concise.**

lacrymose. Syn.: see **tearful.**

lading. Syn.: see **load,** *n.*

lady. Syn.: see **female.**

ladylike. Syn.: see **feminine.**

lag. Syn.: loiter, linger, delay, dawdle, idle. See **linger.**

lake. Syn.: pond, lagoon.

lame, *a.* **Syn.:** crippled, maimed, disabled, halt, halting, limping, hobbling, game; imperfect, defective, inconclusive, unconvincing, unsatisfactory, feeble.

lame, *v.* **Syn.:** cripple, maim, disable, hamstring.

lament. Syn.: mourn, grieve, wail, weep, deplore, bemoan, bewail.

To *lament* is commonly to express grief or sorrow by words or cries. To *mourn* is either to feel grief or to express or show it openly, as by lamentation or weeping. Both *bemoan* and *bewail* indicate audible expression of sorrow, the former suggesting plaintiveness, the latter absence of restraint. *Deplore* denotes either the expressing or the feeling of sorrow or regret, as for some loss or misfortune.

lamentable. Syn.: deplorable, pitiable, distressing, sad.

lampoon. Syn.: see **satire.**

lance. Syn.: see **spear.**

land. Syn.: ground, earth, soil, glebe; country, realm, domain, demesne, estate, farm, plantation; continent, island, desert, plateau, plain, headland, cape, peninsula, isthmus, delta.

landscape. Syn.: view, prospect, scene, scenery.

lane. Syn.: see **way.**

language. Syn.: tongue, speech, vernacular, dialect, idiom, lingo, jargon, cant, slang, argot, flash; phraseology, diction, wording, vocabulary.

Language (in one important sense) denotes the aggregate of words used by a people or race to express thoughts or ideas: as, the English *language*; foreign *languages*; the dead *languages*. *Tongue*, with the same sense, is now a literary word rather than a term of ordinary speech. *Dialect* is applied to a particular form or variety of a language, especially one differing from the standard or literary form: as, the negro *dialect*; the Yorkshire *dialect*; also occasionally to a particular member of a family or group of languages: as, French, Italian, and other Romance *dialects*; the Scandinavian *dialects*. The variety of language peculiar to a people or a region is sometimes called the *idiom*; the language or dialect indigenous to a region, or the phraseology peculiar to a class, is called the *vernacular*.

languid. Syn.: drooping, flagging, weak, feeble, weary, fatigued, exhausted, listless, spiritless, lifeless, sluggish, apathetic, lackadaisical.

languish. Syn.: droop, wither, fade, dwindle, pine.

languor. Syn.: weakness, feebleness, enervation, debility, weariness, lassitude, fatigue, exhaustion, listlessness, lifelessness. See **fatigue,** *n.*

lank, lanky. Syn.: see **lean.**

lapse. Syn.: passing, gliding; slip, misstep, mistake, fault, indiscretion, backsliding.

larceny. Syn.: see **theft.**

large. Syn.: big, great, huge, vast, enormous, immense, gigantic, colossal, massive, bulky, capacious, commodious, spacious, extensive, expansive, comprehensive. **Ant.:** see **small.** See **great.**

largess. Syn.: see **gift, present.**

lascivious. Syn.: wanton, lewd, lustful, lecherous, libidinous, licentious, salacious, incontinent.

lash. Syn.: whip, beat, scourge, flog, castigate, flagellate; berate, vituperate, scold, satirize.

lassitude. Syn.: see **fatigue.**

last, *a.* **Syn.:** final, ultimate, concluding, closing, furthest, remotest, hindmost, latest.

That which is *last* comes after all others in a series or succession. That which is *final* comes at the end, or serves to end or terminate, admitting of nothing further. That which is *ultimate* (literally furthest, or most remote) is the last that can be reached, as in progression or regression, experience, or a course of investigation: as, the *ultimate* state of man; *ultimate* sources of energy; *ultimate* truths.

last, *v.* **Syn.:** continue, endure, persist, abide, remain. See **continue.**

lasting. Syn.: enduring, permanent, stable, perpetual,

unending, imperishable, durable. **Ant.:** ephemeral, transient, transitory, fleeting.

Lasting implies continuance for an indefinitely long time, or for all known time; *enduring*, a hardihood capable of withstanding the onslaughts of time and circumstance: as, an *enduring* peace. *Durable* is applied especially to tangible objects that are capable of resisting wear, decay, or any destructive change. What is *permanent* continues indefinitely, without change, cessation, or removal, as opposed to what is temporary; what is *stable* stands firm, without being moved, shaken, or overthrown.

late. Syn.: tardy, slow, dilatory, delayed, belated; recent, new; deceased. **Ant.:** early, timely, seasonable.

Late is applied to what comes after the usual, proper, or set time; *tardy*, to what is late or behindhand, especially from natural slowness or from reluctance or delay. *Dilatory* implies a disposition or tendency to delay. *Belated*, first applied to persons overtaken by lateness or darkness when journeying, implies delay in arriving or appearing.

latent. Syn.: hidden, concealed, dormant, undeveloped, potential.

Latent (generally used of intangible things) is applied to what lies concealed; that which is *potential* exists in an undeveloped state, being capable of coming into full being or activity: as, *latent* qualities or powers; *latent* diseases; *potential* energy; a *potential* hero.

latest. Syn.: see **last.**

laud. Syn.: see **extol, praise.**

laugh. Syn.: smile, grin, chuckle, chortle, cackle, cachinnate, hawhaw, guffaw, roar, giggle, snicker, snigger, titter, tehee, scoff, jeer.

Laugh, a general word, commonly implies an audible manifestation of mirth; *smile*, as also the familiar or humorous *grin*, refers only to the expression of the face. *Chuckle* suggests private amusement or satisfaction; *giggle* and *titter* indicate a half-suppressed or ill-controlled laughter proceeding from thoughtless or silly levity; *snicker*, a half-suppressed laughter that is usually more or less indecorous or disrespectful. *Guffaw* is used of loud or boisterous laughter.

laughable. Syn.: funny, comic, comical, amusing, droll, humorous, ridiculous, ludicrous, farcical. See **funny.**

launch. Syn.: see **start, throw.**

lavish. Syn.: profuse, prodigal, extravagant, wasteful, excessive, unstinted. See **profuse.**

law. Syn.: equity, etc. (see **justice**); principle, rule, regulation, statute, enactment, ordinance, edict, decree, mandate, canon, commandment.

Law is the general term for the body of rules, or a single rule, prescribed by authority or established by custom as binding on a community or state. A *statute* is a law enacted by legislative authority; an *ordinance* is especially a local law or municipal regulation.

lawful. Syn.: legal, legalized, licit, constitutional, legitimate, just, rightful. **Ant.:** see **unlawful.**

Lawful and *legal* are both applied to what is in conformity with or permitted by law, *lawful* suggesting rather the thought of right or propriety, *legal* that of literal or formal correctness: as, a *lawful* enterprise; such acts are not *legal*. *Legitimate*, applied specifically to children born in lawful wedlock, is used of whatever is duly authorized or warranted, as by right, reason, or propriety: as, a *legitimate* successor; a *legitimate* inference; a *legitimate* question. *Licit*, literally permitted, and hence lawful, is used especially with reference to trade, commerce, or personal relations, and is rarely used except in the phrase *licit or illicit.*

lawless. Syn.: unruly, ungovernable, uncontrolled, riotous, licentious, anarchical.

lawlessness. Syn.: see **anarchy.**

lawsuit. Syn.: case, action, litigation.

lawyer. Syn.: attorney, counselor, advocate, solicitor, barrister, pettifogger, shyster.

lax. Syn.: loose, slack, relaxed, flabby; careless, negligent, remiss, easy-going.

lay, *n*. Syn.: see **song.**

lay, *v*. Syn.: place, put, deposit, set; stake, bet, wager, venture; impose, assess; impute, charge, ascribe, attribute. See **put.**

Lay (originally to cause to lie, and hence to put down, etc.), with its parts, *laid, laying*, is often used incorrectly for *lie* (to recline, etc.), with its parts, *lay* (did lie, was lying), *lain, lying*. *Lay* (to put down) naturally requires or implies a grammatical object as necessary to complete the sense; that is, one *lays something*, or *oneself*, down: as, "Now I *lay me* down to sleep." *Lie*, on the other hand, requires no object; that is, one *lies* down (not *lies oneself* down). The misuse of *lay* for *lie* seems to be due to the fact that the preterit of *lie* is identical in form with the present of *lay*, and so *lay* is often heard in expressions without a grammatical object, where *lie* should be used: as, I will *lay* (properly *lie*) down for a while; I *laid* (properly *lay*) down; I had *laid* (properly *lain*) down; I was *laying* (properly *lying*) down; the book *laid* (properly *lay*) on the shelf; the book was *laying* (properly *lying*) open.

lazy. Syn.: indolent, slothful, sluggish, slow, inert, inactive, dilatory, idle. See **idle.**

lead. Syn.: guide, conduct; direct, command, head, precede; persuade, induce, entice, allure, impel, influence. See **guide,** *v*.

leader. Syn.: guide, conductor, director, commander, chief, head, pilot, bell-wether.

leading. Syn.: guiding, directing, chief, foremost, principal, prominent, influential.

league. Syn.: federation, confederacy, union, coalition, association, society, fraternity. See **alliance.**

leak. Syn.: see **ooze, trickle.**

lean, *a*. Syn.: thin, spare, skinny, lank, lanky, emaciated, gaunt; scant, meager, bare, barren, unprofitable, poor. **Ant.:** see **fat.** See **thin.**

lean, *v*. Syn.: incline, bend, slant, slope, tend; depend, rely.

Lean often implies deviation from a vertical position; *incline*, deviation from either the vertical or the horizontal, or from or toward any given line of direction; *bend*, deviation from a straight line. *Slant* implies deviation at an oblique angle from a straight line or course; *slope*, also implying obliqueness, is used especially of ground or surfaces inclining from the horizontal.

leaning. Syn.: inclination, tendency, proneness, propensity, proclivity, bias, bent.

leap. Syn.: jump, spring, bound, vault, skip, caper, gambol, prance, capriole, curvet, cavort, dance, frisk, frolic. See **jump.**

learn. Syn.: see **discover.**

learned. Syn.: educated, lettered, literate, erudite, scholarly.

Learned attributes to a person the possession of learning, or knowledge acquired by systematic study; *scholarly*, the habit of mind, the tastes, or the methods of one given to profound study and investigation, especially of pure science, history, literature, philosophy, etc.

learning. Syn.: education, knowledge, scholarship, erudition, lore, wisdom.

Learning is knowledge acquired by systematic study, as of literature, history, or science. *Scholarship* is learning actively employed by one seeking to master some field of knowledge or extend its bounds. *Erudition* is learning, especially in literature, languages, history, antiquities, etc., rather than in the mathematical and physical sciences; the word commonly suggests scholastic or the more recondite sort of knowledge obtained by profound research. *Lore*, a somewhat poetic word, is accumulated knowledge, especially of a curious, anecdotal, or traditional nature: as, herb *lore*; fairy *lore*; folk*lore*.

leave, *n*. Syn.: permission, consent, sufferance, allowance, liberty, authorization, license, authority, permit.

Leave is generally used for allowance asked for or granted in a familiar or personal way. In the army *leave* is used of formal permission to be absent, as *liberty* is used of shore leave in the navy. In ordinary use *permission* is a more formal word and is the authorization of an act or course of action. *License* implies a privilege granted by constituted authority (as, *license* to drive an automobile, to preach), or in art it may indicate a permission to depart from the ordinary rules of procedure (as, poetic *license*). *Leave* and *permission* imply an arbitrary right to refuse, *license* only a limited or discretionary right. When used without reference to a specific permission, *license* indicates an abuse of liberty, often an undue and excessive casting off of restraint.

leave, *v*. Syn.: bequeath, will, devise, transmit; commit, intrust, refer; quit, withdraw, depart, retire, vacate, abandon, forsake, desert; cease, stop, quit, desist.

leavings. Syn.: see **refuse,** *n*.

lecherous. Syn.: see **lustful.**

lees. Syn.: see **sediment.**

legal. Syn.: see **lawful.**

legate. Syn.: see **envoy.**

legend. Syn.: myth, fable.

Legend, originally denoting a story of the life of a saint, is applied to any non-historical or unverifiable story, sometimes involving the supernatural, handed down by tradition, concerning a person, place, or other subject. A *myth* is one of a class of stories, usually concerning gods, heroes, fabulous animals, alleged events, etc., current among a people from primitive times; by a natural transfer, anything purely fictitious or imaginary may be called a *myth.* A *fable* is a fictitious story, specifically one (often with animals or inanimate things as speakers or actors) designed to inculcate a moral.

legendary. Syn.: mythical, traditional, fabulous, fictitious, doubtful, apocryphal.

What is *legendary,* or found in legend, may relate to real persons or events and yet be in part or wholly fictitious or untrue. What is *mythical* is wholly fictitious, or without foundation in fact. What is *fabulous* goes so far beyond the usual range of fact as to be or seem imaginary or incredible. What is *apocryphal* is spurious, and sometimes makes a false pretense of being genuine or true.

legible. Syn.: readable, decipherable, plain.

legion. Syn.: see **multitude.**

legitimate. Syn.: see **lawful.**

leisure. Syn.: see **ease.**

leisurely. Syn.: see **slow.**

lend. Syn.: see **loan.**

lengthen. Syn.: elongate, extend, stretch, draw out, prolong, protract, amplify.

To *lengthen* is to make longer, either in a material or immaterial sense. To *extend* is to lengthen beyond some original point or so as to reach to a certain point. To *stretch* is primarily to lengthen by drawing or tension. Both *prolong* and *protract* are especially to lengthen in time: to *prolong* is to continue beyond the desired, estimated, or allotted time; to *protract* is to draw out to undue length or to be slow in coming to a conclusion.

lengthy. Syn.: long, extended, protracted, prolix, verbose.

leniency. Syn.: lenity, clemency, mercy, humanity, tenderness, gentleness, mildness, forbearance. See **mercy.**

lenient. Syn.: clement, merciful, compassionate, gentle, mild, forbearing, tolerant.

lenity. Syn.: see **mercy.**

less. Syn.: smaller, fewer, lesser.

Smaller as applied to concrete objects (*smaller* apples, houses, coins) is used with reference to size. Where other attributes (value, degree, etc.) are in question, ambiguity is avoided by the use of *less.* One coin is *less* than another in value; one house is *less* than another in price. A dime is *smaller* than a nickel, but a nickel is *less* than a dime. A sergeant is *less* than a lieutenant. *Less* is used of material in bulk with reference to amount. Amount as an abstraction (or concept) may be either *smaller* or *less. Less* is more frequently used with abstractions, especially where the idea of amount is figuratively present: as, *less* courage, *less* wealth; *smaller* is used when the particular instance suggests size: as, a *smaller* opportunity, a *smaller* satisfaction. *Fewer* refers to number. *Less* is usually considered obsolete with reference to material dimensions and number, and when so used is inelegant or erroneous: as, this apple is *smaller* (not *less*) than that; there are *fewer* (not *less*) people than I expected.

lessen. Syn.: decrease, diminish, contract, shrink, reduce, minimize, lower, mitigate, abate, impair, weaken, depreciate, disparage, degrade.

let. Syn.: see **hire,** *v.,* **permit,** *v.*

lethargy. Syn.: torpor, sluggishness, drowsiness, stupor, unconsciousness, apathy.

letter. Syn.: epistle, missive, note, encyclic.

Letter is the common term for an ordinary written communication. *Epistle* is a more elevated and dignified word, usually denoting a letter that is formal, didactic, literary, dedicatory, or public in its character. *Missive* usually denotes an official letter sent by a superior to those under him, and is used of an ordinary letter only in a playful or high-flown manner. A *note* is a short letter, or a diplomatic communication upon some particular topic.

letters. Syn.: see **literature.**

levant. Syn.: see **flee.**

level, *a.* Syn.: flat, horizontal, plane, plain, even, smooth, uniform; steady, well-balanced. Ant.: uneven, undulating, hilly, rough, craggy.

That which is *level* is parallel to the horizon and may be either a line or a plane: as, a billiard-table must be *level. Flat* is applied to any plane surface free from marked irregularities. With reference to land or country, *flat* implies lowness or unattractiveness, while *level* suggests nothing derogatory. That which is *even* is free from irregularities, though not necessarily level or plane: as, an *even* slope, an *even* curve. *Smooth* suggests a high degree of evenness in any surface, especially to the touch, sometimes to the sight.

level, *v.* Syn.: flatten, smooth, equalize, reduce; raze, destroy, demolish; point, aim, direct.

levity. Syn.: lightness, giddiness, flippancy, frivolity, volatility, flightiness.

Levity denotes want of seriousness, as in treating important matters lightly, or by manifesting ill-timed flippancy or mirth. *Frivolity* implies an inability to care about any but trifling or silly things. *Volatility* denotes an instability of mind and feeling that shows itself in an ebullition of temporary interest or emotion and a lack of continuous concentration. *Flightiness* denotes a lack of mental poise that shows itself in extreme subservience to impulse or in the caprices arising from mental unsoundness or delirium.

lewd. Syn.: wanton, sensual, lustful, lecherous, lascivious, libidinous, licentious, incontinent, unchaste, prurient, ribald, salacious, pornographic.

lexicon. Syn.: see **dictionary.**

liability. Syn.: responsibility, accountability, amenability, obligation, duty.

liable. Syn.: responsible, answerable, accountable, amenable, subject, exposed; apt, likely. Ant.: exempt, immune, free. See **likely, subject,** *a.*

libel, *n.* Syn.: see **defamation.**

libel, *v.* Syn.: see **asperse.**

liberal. Syn.: ample, large, full, plentiful, abundant, unstinted, generous, bountiful, munificent, charitable, broadminded, catholic, tolerant. Ant.: see **illiberal.**

liberality. Syn.: generosity, bounty, munificence.

Liberality denotes giving freely in proportion to one's means or paying amply for services rendered; figuratively the word often denotes broadness or tolerance in respect to views, beliefs, or opinions. *Generosity* adds to the notion of liberality nobleness, heartiness, or self-sacrifice in the nature of the giver, and thus sometimes denotes a kindly and forgiving spirit towards those who are in some way in opposition to one. *Bounty* denotes goodness or graciousness shown in abundant giving, and especially refers to the blessings bestowed by God, or to the gifts of the great or wealthy. *Munificence* indicates princely liberality or lavish generosity in giving, and implies gifts vast in amount.

liberate. Syn.: free, emancipate, manumit, enfranchise, disenthrall, ransom, deliver, discharge, release, disengage. Ant.: enslave, enthrall, subjugate, confine, restrict, bind. See **free,** *v.*

libertine. Syn.: profligate, rake, roué.

liberty. Syn.: freedom, independence, emancipation, franchise, license, privilege, permission, leave. Ant.: slavery, serfdom, bondage, servitude, captivity. See **freedom, leave,** *n.*

libidinous. Syn.: see **lustful.**

license. Syn.: see **leave,** *n.*

licentious. Syn.: unrestrained, unbridled, loose, profligate, libertine, wanton, sensual, immoral, lustful, lascivious, libidinous, lewd. Ant.: continent, chaste, moral, pure.

licit. Syn.: see **lawful.**

lie, *n.* Syn.: falsehood, untruth, fiction, fabrication, fib. See **falsehood.**

lie, *v.* Syn.: recline, repose, rest; occur, be. See **lay,** *v.*

life. Syn.: existence, being, vitality; animation, vivacity, spirit, liveliness, sprightliness; biography, autobiography, memoir. Ant.: see **death.**

Life indicates full vital force in any form of its manifestation: as, his words were instinct with *life;* his delivery lacked *life. Spirit* denotes a vigor of soul, which manifests itself in enthusiasm, zest, steadfastness, courage, etc.: as, the *spirit* of a martyr, a reformer. *Animation* is a brightness or warmth of spirit, looks, etc.; as, she conversed with *animation. Vivacity* is heightened *animation*: as, the *vivacity* of an actress. *Liveliness* implies an overflow of spirit, manifesting itself in quickness of movement, alertness of mind, or freshness of interest: as, the *liveliness* of a dinner-party. *Sprightliness* suggests a brisk and cheerful liveliness: as, *sprightliness* of speech, manner, mind.

lifeless. Syn.: defunct, inanimate, inorganic; dull, heavy, inactive, inert, passive, sluggish, torpid, spiritless, flat. See **dead.**

lift. Syn.: see **raise.**

light, *n.* **Syn.:** illumination, radiance, luminosity, incandescence, brightness, shine, glow, glimmer, gleam, beam, flash, flare, flicker, blaze, flame; daylight, dawn, aurora; candle, taper, lamp, lantern, torch, cresset, flash-light, spotlight, beacon, lighthouse, window.

light, *a.* **Syn.:** weightless, feathery, fleecy, gossamer, unsubstantial, delicate, thin, flimsy, sleazy, spongy, porous; slight, unimportant, inconsiderable, trivial; buoyant, gay, cheerful; agile, nimble, active, spry. **Ant.:** see **heavy.**

light, *v.* **Syn.:** illuminate, illumine, irradiate; kindle, ignite.

like, *a.* **Syn.:** similar, akin, resembling, corresponding, analogous, parallel, equivalent, equal, homogeneous, identical, uniform. **Ant.:** see **unlike.**

like, *v.* **Syn.:** be pleased with, fancy, relish, enjoy, esteem, love; prefer, choose, wish.

To *like* is to feel attraction of various degrees for persons or things; to *love* is to have a deep affection, especially for a person of the opposite sex: as, to *like* books, to *love* a man or woman, one's country. Formal use does not sanction the substitution of *love* for *like* where the object of the verb is of little importance: as, to *love* blue, to *love* candy.

likely. Syn.: probable, liable, apt. **Ant.:** unlikely, improbable.

Likely and *probable* agree in indicating an eventuality which one may reasonably expect: as, it was considered *likely* (or *probable*) that he would be late. *Liable* expresses an unfavorable eventuality: as, he is *liable* to be hurt.

likeness. Syn.: similarity, similitude, resemblance, analogy; semblance, appearance, guise; representation, picture, portrait, image, copy, facsimile, counterpart.

The following words are often interchangeable, but frequently *likeness* implies a general agreement, *similarity* and *resemblance* a partial agreement, the latter having special reference to appearance.

likewise. Syn.: see **also.**

liking. Syn.: preference, inclination, predilection, favor, partiality, fondness, affection, attachment, love. **Ant.:** dislike, antipathy, aversion. See **love,** *n.*

limb. Syn.: see **member.**

limber. Syn.: see **flexible, supple.**

limit. Syn.: bound, boundary, confine, bourn, frontier, border, edge, terminal; restriction, restraint, check, limitation.

limited. Syn.: see **narrow.**

limitless. Syn.: unlimited, illimitable, boundless, infinite.

limp. Syn.: flaccid, flabby, drooping, soft, weak. **Ant.:** see **stiff.**

Limp suggests lack of the customary or proper stiffness, as in a garment or a fabric; *flabby* and *flaccid* (a less popular word), a want of tension or firmness, especially in flesh that droops or hangs loosely as from its own weight.

limpid. Syn.: see **clear.**

line. Syn.: thread, string, cord, rope, cable; mark, stroke, scratch, stripe, streak, score, dash, crease, wrinkle; limit, boundary, outline, contour, lineament; row, rank, file, series; route, course, way.

lineage. Syn.: descent, extraction, birth, ancestry, race, family, stock. See **pedigree.**

Lineage emphasizes one's line of descent, especially when honorable or noble; *ancestry*, one's forebears viewed collectively; *extraction*, derivation from a certain race or stock; *birth*, the lineal advantages with which, or the position in which, one begins life.

linger. Syn.: tarry, loiter, saunter, lag, dawdle, delay, drag.

To *linger* is to remain in or delay departure from a place, especially one to which a person is drawn by sentiment and attachment, or to move away from it wistfully, slowly, or reluctantly. To *loiter* is to move along slowly or idly on one's way, especially when one should be going directly, as on an errand or to school or work. To *saunter* is to walk along leisurely, carelessly, or aimlessly, as though one had no definite object or purpose in view. To *lag* is especially to move more slowly than others or to stop while they are moving forward, as from weariness or unwillingness.

lingo. Syn.: see **language, jargon.**

link. Syn.: see **join.**

liquid. Syn.: fluid, liquor, solution.

Liquid is commonly applied to substances, such as water, oil, alcohol, and the like, which are neither solid nor gaseous; *fluid*, to anything that flows, whether liquid or gaseous.

lissom. Syn.: see **flexible.**

list. Syn.: roll, register, roster, catalogue, inventory, schedule, index.

List, a general word used either of persons or things, denotes a series of names, items, or figures arranged one after another in a row or line. *Roll* indicates a list of names of persons, usually as belonging to some organization or defined group, and is often used to ascertain their presence or absence. *Register* denotes a book or volume in which are formally or officially recorded entries of names or events, considered important enough for preservation or desired for reference: as, a *register* of voters, guests at a hotel, births, etc. *Catalogue* adds to list the idea of alphabetical or other orderly arrangement, and, often, descriptive particulars and details: as, a *catalogue* of the paintings of a gallery, books in a library. An *inventory* is a detailed list of property, stock, goods, or the like, usually with a statement of the nature, value, or price, made for legal or business purposes. A *schedule* is a methodical (especially official) list, arranged for convenient consultation, and often indicating the time or sequence of certain events: as, a train *schedule*, a baseball *schedule*, a *schedule* of import duties.

listen. Syn.: attend, harken, list, heed, eavesdrop, auscultate. See **hear.**

listless. Syn.: careless, indifferent, indolent, spiritless, languid, supine.

listlessness. Syn.: see **indifference.**

literature. Syn.: belles-lettres, books, writings, letters, poetry, prose, drama, novel, essay, history, biography, autobiography, criticism. See **poem, drama, story.**

Literature in the broadest sense includes everything that has been written, but it often denotes what has been written on a given subject: as, the *literature* of medicine, of the French Revolution. In ordinary use, however, *literature* is the body of artistic writings (often) of a country or period, of which the essential characteristics are beauty of expression and form, and permanence and universality of intellectual and emotional appeal. Literature of this type is often designated by the term *belles-lettres*. *Letters* describes literature as a domain of study or creation: as, a man of *letters*, the republic of *letters*.

lithe. Syn.: pliant, flexible, limber, supple, lithesome, lissome, willowy. See **flexible.**

litigious. Syn.: see **contentious.**

litter. Syn.: see **flock.**

little. Syn.: small, minute, tiny, wee, infinitesimal, diminutive, undersized, dwarfish, puny; trivial, insignificant, inconsiderable, petty, mean, contemptible, narrow, illiberal; short, scanty, brief, limited. **Ant.:** see **big.**

Little, which is the opposite of **great** or **much**, is a very general word, covering size, extent, number, quantity, amount, duration, or degree, and in its figurative applications denotes that which is inconsiderable or unimportant. The word sometimes expresses pettiness or meanness in character, sometimes tenderness or endearment: as, a man with a *little* soul; "the *little* old log cabin in the lane." *Small*, which is the opposite of *large*, can many times be used interchangeably with *little*, but it is especially applied to what is limited, or below the average or ordinary in size. Its figurative uses are much the same as those of *little*, denoting that which is insignificant, and sometimes mean or petty. Unlike *little*, *small* seldom expresses tenderness. *Diminutive* denotes (usually physical) size that is much less than the average or ordinary, and frequently disparagingly so. *Minute* suggests that which is so small that it is difficult to discern, or that which implies attention to the smallest details: as, *minute* care, *minute* observation.

live. Syn.: exist, subsist, survive; dwell, reside, sojourn, lodge, abide, stay.

Live is a general and common word for passing one's life more or less permanently at a place, especially one considered as a home. *Dwell* and *abide* are elevated or literary words, usually indicating permanent living at a place which to some extent at least has become one's home. *Reside* denotes having one's usual, settled, or often official or fixed abode at a place, the word carrying with it certain notions of civilization and society, and especially implying dignity or elegance in the place wherein one *resides*; one would not say that savages *resided* on the plains. *Lodge* denotes living temporarily, often for only a night, at a place, such as an inn or lodging-house, for the privilege of which payment is made. *Sojourn*, a less common word, likewise denotes a temporary, often a brief, remaining at a place, and implies the expectation to leave. *Stay* is the most colorless of these words, usually denoting nothing more than a remaining in a place for a longer or shorter period, but it sometimes implies visiting a person as his guest: as, my friend *stayed* with me three weeks.

livelihood. Syn.: see **living,** *n.*

liveliness. Syn.: activity, briskness, animation, sprightliness, vivacity, life, spirit. See **life.**

lively. Syn.: active, brisk, vigorous, energetic, stirring, spirited, animated, sprightly, vivacious, blithe, gay, buoyant, frolicsome, sportive.

living, *n.* **Syn.:** livelihood, subsistence, sustenance, support, maintenance; benefice, cure, curacy.

Living is especially applied to that which one earns in order to keep alive. In this sense the word often implies what is sufficient to live on economically, but not sufficient for luxury. *Livelihood*, a somewhat less common word, denotes a means of maintaining life, especially as earned, gained, or sought. *Support* and *maintenance* denote the providing of oneself or another with the means of living, *support* implying what is sufficient for necessary expenses, *maintenance* often implying more elaborate upkeep. *Subsistence* often and *sustenance* generally refer to food or what is taken directly into the body to maintain life.

living, *a.* **Syn.:** alive, live, quick; lively, active, vigorous.

load, *n.* **Syn.:** burden, weight, cargo, lading, freight, pack, encumbrance, clog, incubus.

load, *v.* **Syn.:** burden, encumber, clog.

To *load* is to place something on a person or animal, or to fill a vehicle, for conveyance. To *burden* is to load a person or animal, either literally or figuratively, with that which is wearisome to bear. To *encumber* is to load with what is awkward or embarrassing so that movement or progress is retarded or stopped. To *clog* is to load or fill up so as to impede or obstruct.

loan. Syn.: lend.

The use of *loan* for *lend*, except in the specific sense of advancing money at interest, is largely limited to the U. S. and is condemned by purists.

loath. Syn.: see **averse.**

loathe. Syn.: abhor, hate, abominate, detest, execrate. See **hate.**

loathsome. Syn.: abhorrent, abominable, detestable, disgusting, repulsive, revolting, sickening, nauseous, odious.

location. Syn.: locality, place, situation, site.

lock. Syn.: bolt, latch, catch, clasp, hasp, hook, bar, fastening; tress, curl, ringlet.

lodge. Syn.: house, quarter, shelter, harbor, entertain; dwell, reside, live, sojourn, abide; place, put, deposit, implant, vest. See **live.**

loftiness. Syn.: height, elevation; sublimity, grandeur; haughtiness, pride, arrogance.

lofty. Syn.: high, elevated, tall, towering; exalted, sublime, stately, majestic, impressive; haughty, proud, magisterial, arrogant. See **grand, high.**

logical. Syn.: consistent, rational, reasonable, sound.

loiter. Syn.: linger, delay, tarry, lag, dawdle, dilly-dally. See **linger.**

lone. Syn.: alone, unaccompanied, companionless, solitary, isolated, unfrequented.

loneliness, lonesomeness. Syn.: see **solitude.**

lonely. Syn.: companionless, solitary, lonesome, forsaken, lorn; unfrequented, secluded, sequestered, desolate. See **solitary.**

lonesome. Syn.: see **solitary.**

long, *a.* **Syn.:** lengthy, extended, prolonged, protracted, lingering, tedious, wearisome, prolix, wordy, diffuse.

long, *v.* **Syn.:** yearn, crave, hanker, lust, desire, wish.

longing. Syn.: yearning, craving, hankering, pining, desire. See **desire,** *n.*

look, *n.* **Syn.:** gaze, stare, glare; glance, glimpse, sight; appearance, semblance, aspect, expression, countenance, mien, air.

look, *v.* **Syn.:** gaze, stare, gape, glare, glower, lower, gloat, ogle, leer, squint, blink, glance, peep, peek, pry, peer, regard, contemplate, view, behold, watch, see, witness, observe, survey, inspect, scrutinize, scan, pore, peruse, con, investigate, examine. See **seem.**

To *look* is to focus the eyes upon something in order to see it. To *gaze* is to look steadily and intently at something, especially that which excites admiration or curiosity. To *stare* is to gaze with the eyes wide open and usually with a blank or vacant expression, as from surprise, wonder, alarm, stupidity, rudeness, or impertinence. To *gape* is to look with open mouth, as from curiosity or ignorant wonder. To *glare* is to look piercingly or angrily. To *glower* is to look fiercely and threateningly as from wrath. To *gloat* is to look with exultation, either literally or figuratively, on something, sometimes with a malicious pleasure: as, a miser *gloats* over his gold; to *gloat* over a fallen enemy. To *glance* is to look briefly or casually at something. To *peep* and to *peek* are usually to look through a narrow aperture or small opening, or over or around something, the former often furtively, slyly, or pryingly, the latter sometimes curiously or playfully. To *peer* is to look narrowly, especially in order to penetrate obscurity or overcome some obstacle in the way of vision.

looker-on. Syn.: see **spectator.**

loose, *a.* **Syn.:** unbound, unfastened, untied, disengaged, detached, unattached, movable; slack, lax, relaxed; rambling, disconnected, indefinite, vague, uncertain, inaccurate, careless, slovenly; incompact, porous; unrestrained, wanton, immoral, unchaste, dissolute.

loose, *v.* **Syn.:** release, unbind, unfasten, untie, undo, disengage, detach, disconnect; slacken, loosen, relax.

loot, *n.* **Syn.:** plunder, booty, spoil, prize. See **booty.**

loot, *v.* **Syn.:** plunder, pillage, sack, rifle, rob. See **rob.**

lop. Syn.: see **cut.**

loquacious. Syn.: see **talkative.**

loquacity. Syn.: talkativeness, garrulity, volubility, glibness, chatter.

lord. Syn.: see **ruler.**

lordly. Syn.: grand, noble, aristocratic, proud, haughty, arrogant, insolent, overbearing, domineering, imperious, despotic. See **dignified.**

lore. Syn.: see **learning.**

loss. Syn.: destruction, ruin, damage, injury, waste; forfeiture, deprivation; detriment, disadvantage. **Ant.:** see **gain.**

lost. Syn.: destroyed, ruined, consumed, wasted, misspent, forfeited; missing, astray, adrift; absorbed, preoccupied, bewildered, dazed.

lot. Syn.: allotment, portion, share, part, parcel; fortune, destiny, fate, doom.

loud. Syn.: noisy, resounding, deafening, resonant, sonorous, stentorian, clamorous, vociferous, blatant; gaudy, flashy, showy.

Loud indicates sound which is great and powerful; *noisy*, that which is unmusically, confusedly, or offensively loud. *Clamorous* suggests an urgent or importunate outcry, usually by a combination of voices, as in demand or protest; *vociferous*, loud and unrestrained talking or shouting. *Blatant* implies the unpleasantness and vulgarity of loud speaking. *Sonorous* describes deep and resonant sound; *stentorian* denotes a voice of great power and volume.

lounge. Syn.: see **recline.**

lout. Syn.: lubber, gawk, lummox. See **clown.**

loutish. Syn.: see **awkward.**

lovable. Syn.: likable, attractive, winning, pleasing, amiable, winsome.

love, *n.* **Syn.:** affection, fondness, regard, partiality, liking, predilection, tenderness, attachment, devotion, passion, infatuation, amorousness.

Love is a word of wide range and of varying degrees of intensity, including the eternal charity of the Creator, the tender and beautiful relation of parent and child, the noble regard of friends for each other, and the strong passionate regard for a person of the opposite sex normally underlying marriage. *Affection* is enduring love of persons or animals without passion. *Attachment* is the sentiment which unites one to another because of association, mutual sympathy, common interests, etc. *Fondness* is the sentiment arising from the pleasure which one receives from the object of regard. *Liking* is a favorable regard or a preference for a person or thing. A *predilection* is a natural liking or inclination towards something. *Devotion* is a sort of consecration or dedication to a cause, or an intense and steadfast loyalty to a person, especially a superior.

love, *v.* **Syn.:** see **like,** *v.*

lovely. Syn.: attractive, beautiful, pretty, handsome,

charming, amiable, delightful. **Ant.**: see **unlovely**. See **beautiful**.

lover. Syn.: suitor, admirer, beau, swain, inamorato, paramour, philanderer. Cf. **sweetheart**.

loving. Syn.: see **fond**.

low. Syn.: lowly, humble, meek, obscure; coarse, vulgar, mean, base, abject, ignoble, degraded, sordid, servile, menial; feeble, weak, depressed, dejected, dispirited; cheap, moderate, reasonable; deep, grave, subdued. See **mean**.

lower. Syn.: drop, reduce, decrease, diminish; descend, sink, fall; humble, humiliate, degrade, dishonor. See **frown**.

Lower and *reduce* are often interchangeable, but *lower* emphasizes a change of level, *reduce* a change of size. *Reduce* in certain uses suggests a change which leads back to a more primitive or elemental condition. Thus we may *lower* or *reduce* prices, *lower* a flag, *reduce* a picture in size, *reduce* wood to pulp for paper-making, *reduce* a child to obedience.

lowly. Syn.: humble, meek, submissive, modest, unassuming, unpretending, rude, inferior. See **humble**.

loyal. Syn.: faithful, true, constant, stanch, devoted, unwavering. **Ant.**: disloyal, faithless, false, treacherous. See **faithful**.

loyalty. Syn.: fidelity, allegiance, fealty, faithfulness, constancy, devotion, homage. See **allegiance**.

lubber. Syn.: lout, dolt, bumpkin, clown, churl, boor.

lubberly. Syn.: see **clumsy**.

lucid. Syn.: see **clear**.

lucidity. Syn.: see **perspicuity**.

luck. Syn.: fortune, chance, hap, hazard, success.

lucky. Syn.: fortunate, happy, auspicious, propitious, favorable. **Ant.**: see **unlucky**. See **fortunate**.

lucrative. Syn.: paying, gainful, profitable, remunerative.

lucre. Syn.: see **gain**, *n*.

ludicrous. Syn.: ridiculous, laughable, droll, comical, funny, absurd, grotesque, farcical, burlesque. See **funny**.

lug. Syn.: see **drag**.

lugubrious. Syn.: mournful, sorrowful, doleful, woeful, melancholy, dismal, sad, funereal. See **mournful**.

lukewarm. Syn.: tepid, cool, indifferent, unconcerned.

lull. Syn.: soothe, calm, quiet, still, hush.

lullaby. Syn.: see **song**.

luminous. Syn.: see **bright**.

lunacy. Syn.: see **insanity**.

lunatic. Syn.: see **madman**.

lunch. Syn.: luncheon, repast, refection, collation, tiffin.

lunge. Syn.: thrust, plunge, lurch.

lurch. Syn.: pitch, stagger, roll, sway, lunge.

lure. Syn.: allure, entice, coax, attract, charm, beguile, captivate, inveigle, decoy, insnare, entrap, seduce. **Ant.**: repel, disgust, offend. Cf. **attract**.

To *lure* is to attract and draw in by exercising a subtle but strong influence upon the mind or senses, especially by appealing to the hope of pleasure or gain. To *inveigle* is to lead one into something, often evil or wrong, by such deception or persuasion as blinds him temporarily to the nature or consequence of his action. To *beguile* is to create an illusion such as to lead one into a pleasurable state of mind or into a course of action which he would not otherwise follow. To *entice* is to allure subtly, artfully, or insidiously; to *decoy* is to allure into a snare by deceptive appearances.

lurk. Syn.: hide, skulk, sneak, slink, prowl.

To *lurk* is to remain in or about a place secretly, sometimes menacingly. To *skulk* is to move about stealthily or sullenly, as if unwilling to be seen. To *slink* is to move or slip away like a whipped cur. To *sneak* is to creep or steal about in a cautious or stealthy manner to avoid being seen, or for some sinister purpose. To *prowl* is to roam about in a quiet or secretive way, especially in search of prey or plunder.

luscious. Syn.: delicious, savory, juicy, sweet, fulsome, cloying. See **delicious**.

lush. Syn.: see **luxuriant**.

lust. Syn.: see **desire**, *n*.

luster. Syn.: sheen, gloss, polish, brightness, brilliance, radiance, glitter; glory, celebrity. See **polish**.

lustful. Syn.: lascivious, libidinous, lecherous, incontinent, licentious, carnal, sensual, fleshy, concupiscent, prurient.

lustrous. Syn.: see **bright**.

lusty. Syn.: healthy, robust, strong, sturdy, vigorous, hearty, strapping. See **strong**.

luxuriance. Syn.: exuberance, profusion, superabundance, richness.

luxuriant. Syn.: exuberant, profuse, superabundant, rank, lush. Cf. **luxurious**.

As applied to vegetation all these words suggest abundant growth. *Luxuriant* emphasizes flourishing condition as manifested by density, richness, or beauty; *exuberant* adds to luxuriant the idea of abounding vitality which may lead to excessive profuseness; *rank* implies coarseness; *lush*, juiciness or succulence: as, *luxuriant* honeysuckle vines; *exuberant* foliage; *rank* and poisonous weeds; *lush* grasses.

luxurious. Syn.: voluptuous, self-indulgent, epicurean, sybaritic.

luxury. Syn.: voluptuousness, self-indulgence, epicurism, sensuality, extravagance; dainty, delicacy.

lying. Syn.: untruthful, false, mendacious, deceptive; reclining, leaning, resting, reposing.

lynch. Syn.: see **kill**.

M

machination. Syn.: see **plot**.

mad. Syn.: insane, crazy, demented, lunatic, deranged, maniacal, rabid, frenzied, delirious; infuriated, furious, enraged, exasperated, angry.

madman. Syn.: maniac, lunatic, bedlamite.

madness. Syn.: see **insanity**.

magic. Syn.: enchantment, sorcery, necromancy, witchcraft, wizardry, conjuring, jugglery, legerdemain, prestidigitation.

Magic denotes the art of producing marvelous effects by the pretended control of supernatural beings or some occult force of nature. *Witchcraft* especially denotes a malignant kind of magic, usually supposed to have been practised by aged and mysterious women. *Sorcery*, which at first denoted divination by lots, and *necromancy*, which pretended to hold converse with the dead, both now denote magic in general.

magician. Syn.: enchanter, sorcerer, necromancer, wizard, conjurer, juggler, thaumaturge.

magisterial. Syn.: authoritative, dictatorial, domineering, peremptory, overbearing, haughty, arrogant, imperious, lordly. **Ant.**: humble, meek, submissive. See **authoritative**.

magnanimous. Syn.: noble, high-minded, great-souled, generous, unselfish. **Ant.**: ignoble, selfish, narrow, illiberal, uncharitable. See **noble**.

magnificence. Syn.: grandeur, splendor, sumptuousness, pomp, state, majesty, sublimity.

magnificent. Syn.: grand, splendid, gorgeous, sumptuous, superb, august, stately, majestic, imposing, sublime.

That which is *magnificent* is beautiful, princely, grand, or ostentatious. That which is *superb* is above others in, or is of the highest degree of, excellence, elegance, imposingness, or grandeur. That which is *splendid* is dazzling or impressive in its brilliance, radiance, or excellence. That which is *gorgeous* moves one to admiration by the richness and (often colorful) variety of its effects. *Sumptuous* chiefly emphasizes costliness. All of these words are often used colloquially in weak hyperbole.

magnify. Syn.: enlarge, augment, increase, amplify; exaggerate, overstate.

magniloquent. Syn.: see **bombastic**.

magnitude. Syn.: greatness, largeness, size, length, area, volume. See **size**.

maid. Syn.: maiden, girl, damsel, virgin.

maim. Syn.: mutilate, cripple, disable. See **mutilate**.

main. Syn.: principal, leading, chief, cardinal, prime, paramount.

mainly. Syn.: see **especially**.

maintain. Syn.: keep up, continue, preserve; support, sustain, provide for; uphold, defend, vindicate; assert, affirm, contend, claim. See **support**, *v*.

maintenance. Syn.: continuance, preservation; support, subsistence, sustenance, livelihood, living. See **living**.

majestic. Syn.: august, regal, royal, imperial, noble, grand, magnificent, imposing, lofty, sublime. See **dignified**.

majesty. Syn.: see **magnificence**.

make. Syn.: form, construct, build, frame, shape, fashion, produce, fabricate, manufacture, forge, create, bring about, compose, prepare, arrange, formulate, design, originate, invent, concoct; get, gain, acquire, obtain; cause, occasion, induce, require, necessitate, oblige, compel, force, constrain; do, perform, execute, effect, accomplish, consummate, achieve; convert, transform, change; arrive at, reach.

Make is the generic term for producing or causing to exist. *Construct* implies the putting of parts together, usually according to some design. *Fashion* implies giving shape to, often according to some model. To *fabricate* is to build or manufacture, or, sometimes, to invent fictitiously. To *frame* is to construct (perhaps tentatively) something intangible, as an argument, a sentence, the terms of a treaty.

malady. **Syn.:** see **disease.**

male. **Syn.:** see **masculine.**

malediction. **Syn.:** execration, imprecation, anathema. See **curse.**

malefactor. **Syn.:** evil-doer, law-breaker, criminal, felon, culprit, offender, convict. See **villain.**

malevolence. **Syn.:** see **malice.**

malevolent. **Syn.:** malicious, malignant, malign, evil-minded, rancorous, spiteful, resentful, hostile, vicious, wicked, bitter. **Ant.:** see **benevolent.**

malice. **Syn.:** maliciousness, ill-will, animosity, malevolence, malignity, rancor, venom, spite, spitefulness, grudge, hatred, enmity.

Malice is the state of mind which delights in doing harm, or seeing harm done, to others, whether expressing itself in an attempt seriously to injure or merely in sardonic humor. *Malevolence* is smouldering ill-will; *malignity* is lasting and corrosive ill-will. *Malignity* is a deep-seated and virulent disposition to injure. *Spite* is petty and often sudden resentment that manifests itself usually in trifling retaliations. A *grudge* is a feeling of resentment harbored because of some real or fancied wrong.

malicious. **Syn.:** see **malevolent.**

malign, *a.* **Syn.:** see **malevolent.**

malign, *v.* **Syn.:** see **asperse.**

malignant. **Syn.:** see **malevolent.**

malignity. **Syn.:** ill-will, enmity, animosity; virulence, destructiveness, deadliness. See **malice.**

malodorous. **Syn.:** ill-smelling, noisome, unsavory, fetid, stinking.

Malodorous is applied to whatever gives off an offensive odor; *noisome,* to that which is extremely offensive to the smell and is unwholesome; *unsavory,* especially to food that is disagreeable to the smell and taste.

maltreat. **Syn.:** see **abuse.**

mammoth. **Syn.:** huge, gigantic, colossal, monstrous, immense. See **enormous.**

man. **Syn.:** being, mortal, person, individual; mankind, humanity; vassal, servant, valet, follower, attendant.

manacles. **Syn.:** see **shackles.**

manage. **Syn.:** handle, wield, manipulate; control, direct, guide, conduct, regulate, administer, superintend, supervise; arrange, contrive, engineer. See **govern.**

manageable. **Syn.:** wieldy, controllable, governable, tractable, docile, sequacious. **Ant.:** see **unmanageable.**

management. **Syn.:** handling, control, direction, guidance, conduct, regulation, administration, superintendence, care, charge.

manager. **Syn.:** director, administrator, executive, superintendent, supervisor, overseer, boss.

mandate. **Syn.:** command, order, injunction, edict, behest. See **command.**

maneuver. **Syn.:** see **stratagem.**

manful. **Syn.:** manly, brave, courageous, intrepid, resolute, strong. See **masculine.**

mangle. **Syn.:** hack, tear, slash, lacerate, mutilate, disfigure, mar, spoil. See **mutilate.**

manhood. **Syn.:** maturity, manliness, virility, courage, bravery, fortitude, resolution.

mania. **Syn.:** see **insanity.**

maniac. **Syn.:** see **madman.**

maniacal. **Syn.:** mad, insane, frenzied, raving, delirious, frantic, wild.

manifest, *a.* **Syn.:** plain, obvious, apparent, clear, evident, patent, distinct, palpable, overt, conspicuous, unmistakable.

That which is *manifest* is immediately clear, as by an intuition, to the understanding. That is *evident* which facts or circumstances make plain. That is *apparent* which can readily be seen or perceived. That which is *patent* is open to view or understanding by all. That which is *palpable* is readily perceptible to the senses. That which is *obvious* lies so directly in the way that one cannot help coming upon it and perceiving it.

manifest, *v.* **Syn.:** show, exhibit, reveal, disclose, evince, evidence. See **show,** *v.*

manifold. **Syn.:** varied, various, diverse, sundry, multifarious, multitudinous, many. See **many.**

manlike. **Syn.:** see **masculine.**

manly. **Syn.:** see **manful, masculine.**

manner. **Syn.:** way, mode, method, fashion, style, habit, custom; bearing, demeanor, air, mien, behavior, deportment, conduct.

The following words are often interchangeable. *Manner* is an indefinite word denoting the qualities which distinguish an action, event, development, etc.: as, an agreeable *manner* of conversing; the *manner* of conducting one's business. *Mode* usually implies a settled, customary, or characteristic manner: as, a new *mode* of disposing of refuse; kangaroos have a peculiar *mode* of carrying their young; savages have many strange *modes* of dressing. *Method* denotes a mode of procedure in the doing of something, usually according to a special, definite, established, logical, or systematic plan: as, the *method* of solving a problem; a *method* of investing money. *Way* is a very general word, in wide popular use for each of the others: as, a child's *way* (*manner*) of staring at people; *way* (*mode*) of holding its pen; *way* (*method*) of counting on its fingers.

mannerism. **Syn.:** affectation, peculiarity, idiosyncrasy.

mannerly. **Syn.:** courteous, polite, civil, well-behaved.

mannish. **Syn.:** see **masculine.**

mansion. **Syn.:** see **house.**

manufacture. **Syn.:** see **make.**

many. **Syn.:** numerous, manifold, multifarious, multitudinous, myriad, innumerable, frequent. **Ant.:** few, scarce, meager, insufficient, scanty.

Many, a popular and common word, and *numerous,* a more dignified word, both denote a large number of units, individuals, or particulars. *Manifold* adds to numerous the idea of variety or complexity and when applied to a singular subject directs attention to the compositeness of the whole; *multifarious* adds the idea of diversity or difference in the kinds, natures, or characteristics of the things considered: as, *manifold* blessings, *manifold* pleasure; *multifarious* activities. *Innumerable* denotes number that is beyond count, or, more loosely, what is extremely difficult to count: as, the *innumerable* stars of the sky; *innumerable* kinds of tropical birds.

map. **Syn.:** chart, atlas.

mar. **Syn.:** spoil, injure, damage, impair, deface, disfigure, blot. See **deface.**

marauder. **Syn.:** see **robber.**

margin. **Syn.:** see **border, edge.**

marine. **Syn.:** see **maritime.**

mariner. **Syn.:** seaman, sailor, tar, salt. See **sailor.**

marital. **Syn.:** see **matrimonial.**

maritime. **Syn.:** marine, nautical, naval, ocean, oceanic.

Maritime refers to the sea especially as a field for human action or as connected with human interests: as, *maritime* nations, laws, trade. *Marine* refers to the sea in its merely physical aspects: as, a *marine* product, *marine* fauna, *marine* deposits.

mark, *n.* **Syn.:** target, bull's-eye, goal, standard; sign, token, symbol, characteristic, feature, trait, property, symptom, indication, manifestation; impress, stamp, print, brand, stigma, bruise, stain, spot, scar, scratch, cut, dent, notch, dot, line, track, trace, vestige; badge, device, label, ticket; note, importance, prominence, distinction, eminence.

Mark is a very general word for an indication of any kind: as, the *mark* of a heel on the ground; *marks* of violence; a *mark* of respect; the *marks* of a criminal. A *sign* is an indication, generally familiar or customary, of the existence of something, and may take the form of a motion or gesture either arbitrary or generally understood: as, the *sign* of the cross, *signs* of the zodiac, to nod the head as a *sign* of assent. *Note* is a mark or sign by which something may be inferred or known, and is especially a peculiar and distinguishing characteristic: as, a *note* of originality in his writing; a *note* of sadness in her voice. *Token* is something that is understood or interpreted as indicating a condition or a state of mind, or, more specifically, something given as an evidence of affection or for remembrance: as, a bow is a *token* of respect; a gift is often a *token* of friendship. A *symptom* in medical science is an indication which knowledge and experience have confirmed as a natural forerunner or concomitant of a disease or sickness.

mark, *v.* **Syn.:** impress, imprint, stamp, brand, stain, spot, trace, label; note, notice, observe, regard, heed, consider, see.

marked. **Syn.:** noticeable, prominent, conspicuous, outstanding, salient.

market. **Syn.:** mart, emporium, exchange, shop.

marketable. **Syn.:** see **salable.**

marriage. **Syn.:** wedlock, matrimony; wedding, nuptials, espousals, spousals, union.

Marriage denotes either the act which unites two persons as husband and wife, or the state or condition of this relation. *Matrimony*, generally a more formal word, denotes the marriage state with its relationships, rights, duties, and obligations. *Wedlock* is now a homely, somewhat archaic word, agreeing with matrimony in meaning, and is the ordinary term in law: as, born in *wedlock*. The word emphasizes the bond of the union: as, joined in holy *wedlock*. *Wedding* denotes the ceremony of marriage, and usually includes the accompanying festivities; *nuptials* is a lofty and formal word for wedding, and usually implies rank, pomp, or grandeur: as, a simple *wedding*; royal *nuptials*.

marry. **Syn.:** wed, espouse, unite.

marsh. **Syn.:** swamp, bog, fen, morass, quagmire, slough. See **swamp.**

marshal. **Syn.:** see **array.**

marshy. **Syn.:** swampy, boggy, fenny, quaggy, muddy, miry.

martial. **Syn.:** warlike, military, soldierly, brave.

Martial refers to what is connected with war, especially as appealing to the eye or ear: as, *martial* music, array; or to that which pertains to the army as an organization: as, *martial* law, court *martial*; or to what is characteristic of or befitting a warrior: as, *martial* bearing, fortitude. *Warlike* applies to natural or ingrained fondness for war, but also to what is like war or naturally goes with war: as, *warlike* tribes; *warlike* preparations, gestures. *Military* refers to what pertains directly to soldiers or the army, and only indirectly to war and the affairs of war: as, *military* dress, parade, discipline, court, tactics.

marvel. **Syn.:** see **wonder.**

marvelous. **Syn.:** wonderful, surprising, astonishing, amazing, extraordinary, stupendous, prodigious, miraculous, incredible. **Ant.:** ordinary, commonplace, usual. See **wonderful.**

masculine. **Syn.:** male, manlike, manly, manful, virile, vigorous, strong, gentlemanly, mannish.

Masculine, matching feminine, applies to men and their attributes, especially the stronger, hardier qualities that distinguish man, and to the corresponding gender; as applied to women it usually suggests harshness or uncouthness, although it may indicate qualities which, though characteristic of man, may also be praiseworthy in woman: as, George Eliot had a *masculine* mind. *Male*, matching female, refers to sex among human beings and animals, and, by extension, among plants. *Manlike* implies distinctive masculine qualities, both good and bad: as, *manlike* courage; *manlike* indifference to household details. *Manful* implies the strength, fearlessness, etc., that become a man, as opposed to that which is weak, cowardly, or supine: as, a *manful* resistance. *Manly*, matching womanly, refers to the qualities in man that are noblest and most worthy of his manhood, especially as opposed to that which is cowardly, fawning, insincere, or underhand. *Virile* has lost much of its literal meaning; it now usually expresses the notion of vigor, force, or strength, especially of mature manhood. *Mannish* is applied to that which is somewhat like a man (as, a boy with a *mannish* voice) and, as applied to a woman, is a derogatory term, expressing the displeasing likeness to a man which arises from ostentatious imitation: as, a *mannish* stride. *Gentlemanly* expresses refinement, both in nature and manners, or it may imply mere external courtesy and politeness.

mash. **Syn.:** see **crush.**

mask, *n.* **Syn.:** covering, disguise, false face, screen, cloak, blind, pretext, subterfuge.

mask, *v.* **Syn.:** cover, disguise, conceal, screen, masquerade.

mass, *n.* **Syn.:** lump, aggregate, aggregation, assemblage, collection, accumulation, heap, pile, conglomeration, congeries; bulk, size, magnitude, bigness, massiveness.

mass, *v.* **Syn.:** amass, assemble, collect, gather, accumulate, conglomerate.

massacre, *n.* **Syn.:** slaughter, butchery, carnage.

All these words denote extensive destruction of life. *Massacre* emphasizes the indiscriminate and ruthless killing of large numbers of human beings, especially through fanaticism or racial hatred. *Butchery*, from its association with animals, suggests fierceness and brutality in the taking of human life. *Slaughter*, as applied to persons, denotes the extensive, though not necessarily wanton, destruction of life, as in battle. *Carnage* views slaughter in retrospect, and thus stresses the result rather than the act.

massacre, *v.* **Syn.:** see **kill.**

massive. **Syn.:** massy, bulky, weighty, heavy, ponderous, huge, immense, imposing. See **bulky.**

master, *n.* **Syn.:** chief, head, leader, ruler, commander, director, manager, employer, teacher; victor, conqueror; adept, expert, proficient, dabster; owner, possessor, proprietor. **Ant.:** servant, vassal, slave, laborer.

master, *v.* **Syn.:** subdue, subjugate, conquer, overpower, overcome, control.

masterful. **Syn.:** controlling, commanding, authoritative, magisterial, lordly, imperious, domineering.

masterly. **Syn.:** skilful, proficient, consummate, finished, excellent.

mastery. **Syn.:** command, control, dominion, rule, sway, authority, ascendancy, supremacy; victory, triumph; skill, knowledge, acquirement, attainment, grasp. See **authority.**

masticate. **Syn.:** see **chew.**

match. **Syn.:** equal, mate, counterpart; contest, competition, game, tournament, tourney; engagement, marriage, alliance.

matchless. **Syn.:** unequaled, unparalleled, unrivaled, peerless, incomparable, surpassing, inimitable.

mate. **Syn.:** associate, companion, comrade, chum, crony, partner, colleague; equal, match.

material, *n.* **Syn.:** matter, substance, stuff, fabric, cloth, goods. See **matter.**

material, *a.* **Syn.:** substantial, physical, corporeal, bodily, worldly, gross; important, essential, necessary, momentous.

maternal. **Syn.:** see **motherly.**

matrimonial. **Syn.:** connubial, conjugal, marital, nuptial, hymeneal.

Matrimonial, like matrimony, refers to the marriage state: as, the *matrimonial* bond; *matrimonial* intentions. *Connubial* and *conjugal* also refer to the state and are often interchangeable, but *conjugal* frequently connotes the rights, duties, and responsibilities of marriage. *Nuptial* is more suggestive of the act and ceremony of marriage or that which is in close connection with it: as, the *nuptial* hour; *nuptial* agreement. *Hymeneal* is a lofty and poetic word, likewise referring to the ceremony of marriage. *Marital* means, specifically, belonging to a husband, but is also used of the marriage state in general: as, *marital* rights or authority; *marital* alliance.

matrimony. **Syn.:** see **marriage.**

matronly. **Syn.:** see **motherly.**

matter. **Syn.:** substance, material, stuff; pus, purulence; ground, occasion, cause, subject, topic, theme, affair, thing; consequence, importance, significance, moment, weight, concern.

Matter, opposed to mind and spirit, is a very broad word for all that can be perceived through the senses and which is regarded as incapable of being produced or destroyed. *Substance* is the matter which composes a thing and in which its essential properties are contained. *Material* usually denotes some definite kind, quality, or quantity of matter for some particular use or of which something is made. *Stuff*, a less scientific word than material, permits of a more free and varied use ranging from homely and colloquial idioms to literary and poetic applications.

matter-of-fact. **Syn.:** see **unimaginative.**

mature. **Syn.:** ripe, mellow, full-grown, developed, finished, perfected, thorough, digested, well-considered. See **ripe.**

maudlin. **Syn.:** sentimental, foolish, fuddled, intoxicated, tipsy.

maul. **Syn.:** see **beat.**

maxim. **Syn.:** see **proverb.**

may. **Syn.:** see **can.**

maze. **Syn.:** bewilderment, perplexity; labyrinth, tangle, entanglement, intricacy.

meadow. **Syn.:** mead, lea, grassland, pasture.

meager. **Syn.:** lean, thin, spare, lank, gaunt, emaciated; poor, scanty, barren, jejune. See **scanty.**

mean, *n.* **Syn.:** middle, medium, average.

mean, *a.* **Syn.:** common, low, humble, plebeian, obscure;

insignificant, petty, paltry, poor, shabby, scurvy; small-minded, contemptible, despicable, base, vile, ignoble, abject, servile, menial, groveling; penurious, miserly, niggardly, stingy, close, sordid; middle, middling, intermediate, average, medium, moderate, mediocre.

Mean suggests pettiness, littleness, or stinginess in character or conduct, such as is worthy of contempt; *low*, coarseness, indecency, vulgarity, or depravity in nature or condition; *base*, selfishness, cowardice, or moral depravity; *vile*, such foulness or baseness as creates disgust. *Sordid* suggests the wretchedness of that which is unclean, sometimes a pursuit of personal gain by means that are morally reprehensible. *Ignoble* denotes meanness or baseness in character, disposition, or aim. *Abject* implies extreme humility or servility of spirit, as produced by misery, superstition, shame, etc.

mean, *v.* **Syn.:** intend, purpose, design, contemplate; signify, import, denote, indicate, betoken, typify. See **intend.**

meander. Syn.: see **wind, saunter.**

meaning, *n.* **Syn.:** signification, significance, import, purport, sense, tenor, gist, drift, explanation, interpretation.

Meaning is a general word, denoting that which is intended to be or actually is expressed or indicated by something: as, the *meaning* of a word, a glance; you do not understand my *meaning*. *Signification*, a less general word, denotes especially that which is indicated by a sign, symbol, word, or the like: as, the *signification* of a chemical formula. *Sense* denotes the meaning, or one of the meanings, of a word or phrase, attached to it by use or recognized acceptation, or it may denote general meaning that can be understood: as, in this passage the word has a peculiar *sense*; I could make some *sense* out of what he had written. *Import* denotes the full force of a word, gesture, statement, etc., and thus includes whatever is suggested as well as what is specifically set forth: as, to grasp the *import* of a person's remarks. *Purport* usually denotes the general meaning, substance, or sense conveyed or intended: as, the *purport* of a letter, a remark. *Gist* indicates the essence or pith of the meaning of something. *Tenor* refers to the underlying meaning or character which runs through a document or speech; *drift*, to the general tendency, aim, or object of it.

meaning, *a.* **Syn.:** see **expressive.**

means. Syn.: agency, instrumentality, device, contrivance, expedient, shift, method, way; resources, funds, income, wealth, property.

Means is a general word for any agency or process by which some end is attained. *Device* implies a studied, often skilful, calculated, sometimes crafty, means for the accomplishing of a purpose. *Contrivance* suggests most of ingenuity and cleverness. *Expedient* is especially used of a more or less irregular or improvised means resorted to in order to achieve a desired result. A *shift* is a temporary, poor, or desperate expedient, sometimes a tricky or fraudulent one by which to evade some difficulty.

measure. Syn.: dimension, size, area, extent, capacity, volume, quantity, amount; rod, rule, tape, gage, meter; procedure, action, step, course.

mechanic. Syn.: see **worker.**

meddle. Syn.: intermeddle, interfere, mix in, tamper, fool, monkey.

To *meddle* is to touch or handle things, particularly those that do not concern or belong to one, or to busy oneself curiously or officiously, or to put oneself forward unwarrantably in the affairs of another. To *tamper* is to meddle with a thing so as to change, alter, or pervert it, or to try to influence a person to do something improper or wrong: as, to *tamper* with a machine; to *tamper* with ballots; to *tamper* with a jury. *Fool* is a homely but expressive word for meddling with something idly or foolishly, often at the risk of detrimental or disastrous results: as, to *fool* with the works of a watch; to *fool* with a gun.

meddlesome. Syn.: meddling, interfering, officious, intrusive, obtrusive, busy, pragmatic(al).

He who is *meddlesome* interferes in the affairs of others, as from curiosity or impertinence. An *intrusive* person is so blind or indifferent to the feelings of others that he forces himself upon them unjustifiably. He has a *busy* disposition who is unduly inquisitive in regard to what concerns others. He who is *officious* is too forward or zealous in offering or undertaking services where they are unasked or undesired by others, or even annoying and irritating to them.

mediate. Syn.: see **interpose.**

mediation. Syn.: intervention, interposition, intercession, conciliation.

mediocre. Syn.: middling, medium, average, commonplace, ordinary, indifferent.

meditate. Syn.: reflect, ponder, muse, ruminate, cogitate, think; contemplate, consider, intend, plan. See **reflect.**

meditation. Syn.: reflection, contemplation, cogitation, thought.

meditative. Syn.: see **thoughtful.**

medium, *n.* **Syn.:** see **mean,** *n.*

medium, *a.* **Syn.:** see **mean,** *a.*

medley. Syn.: see **mixture.**

meed. Syn.: see **reward.**

meek. Syn.: mild, forbearing, patient, submissive, yielding, docile, humble, lowly. **Ant.:** arrogant, haughty, high-spirited, assertive. See **gentle.**

meet, *a.* **Syn.:** fit, befitting, suitable, appropriate, proper, seemly. See **fit.**

meet, *v.* **Syn.:** encounter, find, confront, face; satisfy, settle, discharge, fulfil; gather, assemble, congregate, convene, collect; intersect, converge, collide; undergo, suffer, experience.

meeting. Syn.: gathering, congregation, assembly, assemblage, convention, convocation, conclave, conference, interview; tryst, rendezvous; union, junction, juncture, confluence; encounter, duel.

Meeting is a general word for a coming together, either of two persons or a large number, either accidentally or designedly, and if designedly, for such purposes as conference, recreation, legislation, or worship. *Gathering* suggests a coming together of persons or objects, sometimes fortuitously, often because drawn by common circumstances. *Assembly* usually implies a meeting of persons for a settled or customary purpose, as for discussion, deliberation, or legislation, or for participation in a social function. *Assemblage* may refer to things as well as persons, and suggests a less formal gathering than *assembly*, and one with less definite object or purpose in view. *Convention* signifies a meeting, especially of delegates from different quarters, representing political, ecclesiastical, social, or fraternal organizations, for some common object, as for deliberation or legislation. *Convocation*, literally that which is called together, denotes an assembly (especially ecclesiastical) the members of which are summoned for a specific purpose. *Conference* suggests a meeting for consultation and discussion, especially in connection with problems arising in the conduct of business. *Interview* denotes a meeting granted by one or more persons for some definite purpose, as to adjust disputes or to obtain a statement for publication.

melancholy, *n.* **Syn.:** depression, dejection, despondency, sadness, gloominess, hypochondria. See **grief.**

melancholy, *a.* **Syn.:** depressed, dejected, despondent, disconsolate, downcast, low-spirited, sad, somber, dismal, gloomy, doleful, mournful. See **sad.**

mêlée. Syn.: see **quarrel,** *n.*, **fight,** *n.*

mellow. Syn.: see **ripe.**

melodious. Syn.: melodic, musical, tuneful, harmonious, sweet, dulcet, euphonious, mellifluous.

melodrama. Syn.: see **drama.**

melody. Syn.: music, harmony, rhythm; tune, air, theme, song.

In music, *melody* is the agreeable and rhythmical combination of successive sounds of various pitch, making the tune or air; *harmony* is the agreeable blending of simultaneous sounds of different pitch or quality, making chords: the sounds in either case being from voices or musical instruments.

melt. Syn.: liquefy, dissolve, thaw, fuse, blend, shade, merge; soften, mollify, subdue. **Ant.:** congeal, freeze, harden, solidify.

While *melt* and *dissolve* are sometimes interchangeable, to *melt* is to bring a substance from a solid to a liquid condition by the agency of heat alone; to *dissolve* is to bring about this result by distributing the particles of the substance acted on among the particles of another substance, usually liquid: as, to *melt* ice, butter, sealing-wax; to *dissolve* sugar in water; to *dissolve* iodine. To *thaw* is to reduce a frozen substance, whose ordinary condition is liquid, to a liquid or semiliquid state by raising its temperature above the freezing-point of water. To *fuse* is to reduce a solid substance to a fluid state by subjecting it to a high temperature and is used especially of the melting or blending together of metals: as, bell-metal is made by *fusing* copper and tin.

member. **Syn.:** part, organ, limb, leg, arm; constituent, component.

Member is a general term applied to any integral part or vital organ of an organized animal body performing a definite function, or, more widely, to any integral or distinguishable part of a whole: as, the nose, eyes, ears, tongue, arms, legs are *members* of the body; a *member* of a sentence, equation, family, society, or state. *Limb* is a more precise term, referring to the legs and arms of the human body, and is rarely used for the leg of an animal. The word is used for a large branch of a tree, but in its figurative use it is jocose: as, "a limb of the law," for a lawyer; or "a limb of the devil," for a rogue.

memento. **Syn.:** see **keepsake.**

memoir. **Syn.:** see **biography.**

memorable. **Syn.:** notable, remarkable, extraordinary, signal, famous.

memorial. **Syn.:** monument, remembrance, memento, souvenir, reminder, memorandum.

The following words denote a means of preserving the memory of persons or events, and are often used interchangeably, but *memorial* is more general in its application, including vast and stately commemorative structures, illuminated windows, and the like, for public remembrance, or slight personal tokens for private remembrance, or it may even be an observance or service commemorating a noteworthy event; a *monument* may be any structure erected in memory of a person, action, or event, such as a shaft or column in memory of the dead. A *monument* is always public in its exhibition, and usually more or less so in its appeal to remembrance.

memory. **Syn.:** remembrance, recollection, reminiscence, retrospection, retrospect.

Memory is the faculty for reviving in the mind past thoughts, experiences, and events; it may also indicate that which is remembered. *Recollection* is the exercise, often voluntary, of memory, or is that which is recalled. *Remembrance* is another exercise of memory less voluntary and less detailed than recollection. *Reminiscence* may be the exercise of the faculty of remembering, but is more especially the meditative, wistful, or dreamy recalling of (usually) pleasurable events or personal experiences. *Reminiscence* and *recollection* are higher faculties belonging to man; *memory* belongs to both men and beasts. *Retrospection* is the looking back by aid of the memory upon things of the past, usually in a contemplative way.

menace. **Syn.:** threaten.

mend. **Syn.:** repair, patch, sew; correct, rectify, remedy, improve, better, emend. See **amend.**

mendacious. **Syn.:** lying, untruthful, prevaricating, untrue, false.

mendicant. **Syn.:** see **beggar.**

menial, *n.* **Syn.:** see **servant.**

menial, *a.* **Syn.:** servile, slavish, groveling, low, mean.

mental. **Syn.:** intellectual, subjective.

mentality. **Syn.:** see **mind.**

mercantile. **Syn.:** commercial, business.

Mercantile applies to the actual purchase and sale of goods, or to the transactions of business: as, a *mercantile* house; the *mercantile* class. *Commercial* is a broader term, covering all the activities and relationships of industry and trade: as, *commercial* people, treaties, relations, education, law. In a derogatory sense *commercial* suggests such a preoccupation with the affairs of commerce as results in indifference to other considerations.

mercenary. **Syn.:** hired, hireling, venal, corrupt, sordid, greedy, grasping.

These words suggest readiness to put reward above honor. *Mercenary* implies such greed for gain as leads to the neglect of higher considerations: as, a *mercenary* marriage, a *mercenary* spirit. *Venal* implies sale, or willingness to sell, for a price, at the sacrifice of principles, honor, conscience, character, or independence: as, a *venal* public officer; a *venal* press. *Hireling* denotes serving for hire or pay, usually in such abject or servile manner and often in such mean employment as to sacrifice self-respect and to merit contempt: as, a *hireling* soldier; a *hireling* tool. *Corrupt* in this sense often has especial reference to willingness to accept bribes: as, a *corrupt* politician.

merchandise. **Syn.:** see **property.**

merciful. **Syn.:** compassionate, humane, kind, forgiving, clement, lenient, tender-hearted.

merciless. **Syn.:** unmerciful, pitiless, unfeeling, unsparing, implacable, relentless, ruthless, barbarous, savage.

mercy. **Syn.:** compassion, pity, tenderness, mildness, forgiveness, forbearance, indulgence, clemency, leniency, lenity, grace.

Mercy has a twofold use, expressing forbearance in visiting severity or punishment on an enemy or offender, or great compassion and pity manifested in an attempt to help those in trouble and distress. *Clemency* is mercy shown to offenders by those in exalted places or those with authority to remit or lighten penalty, and is often a natural characteristic of the person granting it. *Leniency* and *lenity,* a less common word, may be practised by any one having authority to lighten or remit penalty or excuse from tasks; they sometimes suggest excessive indulgence where strictness in discipline would be better.

mere. **Syn.:** bare, sheer, simple.

Mere and *bare* are often interchangeable, but *mere* frequently means "no more than," *bare,* "scarcely as much as." Thus, a *mere* livelihood means enough to live on but no more; a *bare* livelihood means scarcely enough to live on.

merge. **Syn.:** sink, immerse, engross, absorb; combine, unite, consolidate, coalesce.

merit, *n.* **Syn.:** desert, worth, worthiness, goodness, excellence.

Merit is usually the excellence of a person, action, or thing which entitles it to praise or recognition. *Desert* is a just reward or the quality which entitles one to it. *Worth* is always used in a favorable sense and signifies inherent value or goodness.

merit, *v.* **Syn.:** deserve, earn.

meritorious. **Syn.:** deserving, worthy, commendable, laudable.

merriment. **Syn.:** mirth, jollity, gaiety, sportiveness, laughter, levity, glee, hilarity, frolic. See **mirth.**

merry. **Syn.:** mirthful, joyous, jolly, gay, sportive, gleeful, jovial, festive, hilarious. **Ant.:** grave, sober, sad, sorrowful. See **gay.**

merry-andrew. **Syn.:** see **zany.**

mesh. **Syn.:** see **net.**

mess. **Syn.:** see **mixture.**

message. **Syn.:** communication, letter, note, despatch, telegram, cablegram.

messenger. **Syn.:** carrier, courier, forerunner, precursor, harbinger, herald.

metamorphose. **Syn.:** see **transform.**

metaphor. **Syn.:** see **comparison.**

mete. **Syn.:** see **distribute.**

method. **Syn.:** mode, manner, way; order, system, plan, design. See **manner.**

methodical. **Syn.:** see **orderly.**

mettle. **Syn.:** spirit, temper, ardor, enthusiasm, courage.

mettlesome. **Syn.:** mettled, spirited, fiery, ardent.

middle, *n.* **Syn.:** center, midst.

Middle denotes the point or part equidistant from or intermediate between extremes or limits: as, the *middle* of the road, of a speech, of a line, of the day. *Center* is a more precise word, ordinarily applied to circular, globular, or regular bodies, but it is used wherever a similar exactness appears to exist: as, the *center* of a dish, the earth, or a field; the *center* of a crowd. *Center* is primarily a point, while *middle* may be a point or a part. *Midst* suggests that a person or thing is surrounded or encompassed on all sides, especially by that which is close upon him or it, or is thick or dense: as, in the *midst* of a forest, a storm, enemies, troubles.

middle, *a.* **Syn.:** intermediate, middling, medial, medium, center, mean.

midst. **Syn.:** see **middle,** *n.*

mien. **Syn.:** air, manner, bearing, demeanor, aspect, appearance. See **bearing.**

might. **Syn.:** strength, power, force, puissance, potency. See **strength.**

mighty. **Syn.:** strong, powerful, puissant, potent, invincible; great, huge, enormous, vast. **Ant.:** weak, feeble, infirm, impotent, puny. See **powerful.**

migrate. **Syn.:** emigrate, immigrate.

To *migrate* is to pass from one part of a country to another, usually considerably distant, or to go from one country to another, often repeatedly, in either case for the purpose of taking up a new abode. The word is also applied to animals that go from one region or habitat to another, especially periodically. To *emigrate* is to leave a country, usually one's own, and take up residence in another. To *immigrate* is to enter and settle in a country not one's own: as, each year many *emigrate* from Europe and *immigrate* to the United States. While *migrate* is applicable to animals, the other terms are generally used of the movements of men.

migratory. Syn.: roving, wandering, nomad, nomadic, unsettled.

mild. Syn.: gentle, tender, soothing, mollifying, conciliatory, bland, soft, pacific, lenient, merciful; temperate, moderate, clement, pleasant. **Ant.:** severe, austere, harsh, acrimonious, rough, drastic, rigorous. See **gentle.**

militant. Syn.: warring, fighting, combative, pugnacious, belligerent, warlike.

military. Syn.: see **martial.**

mimic. Syn.: see **imitate.**

mind. Syn.: intellect, understanding, reason, judgment, sense, intelligence, mentality, brain, brains, faculties, soul, spirit; memory, remembrance, recollection; intention, purpose, will.

Mind is the general word for the center of mental activity: as, a healthy *mind. Intellect* suggests mental processes of a comparatively high order, or the faculty involved: as, a powerful *intellect. Soul* and *spirit* indicate that in man which makes him akin to the divine: as, body and *soul*; a noble *spirit. Mentality* denotes the capacity or ability of the mind; *intelligence*, the quickness with which the mind grasps things, and makes use of them: as, the *mentality* of a child of ten; a man of remarkable *intelligence. Brain* is the physiological term for the organic structure which makes mental activity possible; *brains* is a colloquial word for clear thought, good judgment, and (often) effective action: as, the *brain* is the center of the nervous system; he has *brains.* Most of these words are variously defined technically by psychologists.

mindful. Syn.: heedful, regardful, careful, attentive, observant, cognizant, aware. **Ant.:** see **unmindful.**

mingle. Syn.: see **mix.**

minister, *n.* **Syn.:** see **clergyman, envoy.**

minister, *v.* **Syn.:** serve, attend, aid, help, succor, assist.

minor. Syn.: smaller, lesser, lower, inferior, subordinate, subsidiary, secondary.

minute, *n.* **Syn.:** see **moment.**

minute, *a.* **Syn.:** little, small, diminutive, tiny, microscopic, slender, fine, trifling, trivial; precise, accurate, exact, detailed, particular, circumstantial. **Ant.:** see **large.** See **little.**

A *minute* account treats a matter with painstaking precision even to the smallest details; a *particular* account gives all that is of any importance or interest with accuracy of detail; a *circumstantial* account elaborates the matter with convincing fullness.

minutes. Syn.: memoranda, records, notes, items.

miracle. Syn.: see **wonder.**

miraculous. Syn.: wonderful, marvelous, extraordinary, surprising, incomprehensible, incredible, supernatural, superhuman. See **supernatural.**

mire. Syn.: mud, slush, slime, ooze, dirt, filth.

mirror. Syn.: see **glass.**

mirth. Syn.: merriment, gaiety, jollity, laughter, glee, hilarity.

Mirth suggests gaiety, especially that manifested outwardly and often briefly. *Merriment* suggests more of fun, good spirits, and accompanying noise, as laughter, joking, music, singing, dancing, or the like. *Glee* implies an effervescence of high spirits or exultation, often manifested in ecstatic or playful gestures. *Hilarity* implies noisy and boisterous mirth, often exceeding the strict limits of reason or propriety. All these words express varying degrees of the gaiety or festive spirit which belongs to people in their social intercourse or companionship.

mirthful. Syn.: merry, gay, gleeful, jovial, sportive, playful.

misadventure. Syn.: mishap, mischance, accident, disaster, misfortune.

misanthropic. Syn.: cynical, pessimistic, misogynous.

Misanthropic expresses hatred for mankind as a race, which usually manifests itself in a settled distrust of human character. *Cynical* suggests a tendency to sneer at the sincerity of human motives. *Pessimistic* implies a more or less habitual disposition to look on the dark side of things and to believe that the worst will happen; it is sometimes a philosophical epithet applying to those who hold that no reasoning or faith can ever justify the actualities of life.

misapply, misappropriate. Syn.: see **misuse,** *v.*

miscellaneous. Syn.: mixed, varied, diversified, diverse, promiscuous, indiscriminate, heterogeneous, multifarious.

Miscellaneous suggests that the parts of a whole manifest marked individual differences: as, a *miscellaneous* collection of stamps. *Promiscuous* suggests union or mixture without order or selection: as, a *promiscuous* gathering.

miscellany. Syn.: see **mixture.**

mischance. Syn.: see **misfortune.**

mischief. Syn.: harm, hurt, injury, damage, trouble, vexation, annoyance, mischievousness, playfulness. See **injury.**

mischievous. Syn.: harmful, hurtful, injurious, destructive; teasing, roguish, arch, playful, naughty. See **playful.**

misconceive. Syn.: see **misunderstand.**

misconduct. Syn.: see **misdeed.**

miscreant, *n.* **Syn.:** heretic, infidel; villain, wretch, scoundrel, rascal. See **villain.**

miscreant, *a.* **Syn.:** misbelieving; depraved, villainous, base, vile, detestable.

misdeed. Syn.: misdemeanor, offense, transgression, delinquency, trespass, misconduct, fault. See **offense.**

misdemeanor. Syn.: see **offense.**

misemploy. Syn.: see **misuse.**

miser. Syn.: niggard, skinflint, muckworm, curmudgeon, screw, hunks.

miserable. Syn.: pitiable, deplorable, lamentable, distressing, wretched, unhappy, sorry, abject, forlorn, disconsolate, doleful; contemptible, despicable, mean, sordid, paltry, worthless. See **wretched.**

miserly. Syn.: avaricious, niggardly, stingy, penurious, parsimonious, curmudgeonly, close, sordid. See **stingy.**

misery. Syn.: wretchedness, distress, sorrow, grief, anguish, woe, destitution, privation. See **affliction.**

misfortune. Syn.: mischance, mishap, misadventure, accident, disaster, calamity, catastrophe, adversity, reverse, blow, stroke, trouble. **Ant.:** blessing, boon, success, triumph, prosperity.

A *misfortune* is any adverse event or circumstance which brings about suffering: as, he had the *misfortune* to break his leg. A *mishap* is a slight misfortune; a *mischance* is a fortuitous intervention (or its result) which upsets prearranged plans: as, children have many *mishaps*; by a *mischance* he took the wrong road. A *disaster* is a great and sudden misfortune. A *calamity* is a grave misfortune having widespread public consequences; it can come to an individual only by affecting his welfare largely or by bringing him into deep distress. A *catastrophe* is a great misfortune which brings things to an end with a final crash. *Adversity* is a series of misfortunes, failures, and disappointments, usually long continued.

misgiving. Syn.: doubt, distrust, suspicion, apprehension, qualm.

mishap. Syn.: see **misfortune.**

misinterpret. Syn.: misconstrue, mistranslate, misunderstand, misconceive.

mislead. Syn.: misguide, misdirect, delude, deceive, beguile, dupe.

To *mislead* is to lead wrongly or into error of thought or action, either intentionally or unintentionally. To *deceive* is purposely and designedly to create a false belief. To *delude* is to mislead grossly, generally in connection with the other's interests or intentions and especially by raising false hopes. All three words may be used of circumstances without implication of intent.

misleading. Syn.: see **fallacious.**

misname. Syn.: miscall, misterm.

misshapen. Syn.: deformed, distorted, unshapely, ugly.

missing. Syn.: lacking, wanting, absent, lost, gone.

mission. Syn.: commission, delegation, deputation, embassy; errand, message, office, charge, trust, duty.

missive. Syn.: see **letter.**

misstate. Syn.: misrepresent, distort, falsify.

mist. Syn.: fog, haze, mizzle, drizzle, rain. See **fog.**

mistake. Syn.: misconception, misapprehension, misunderstanding, error, blunder, oversight, slip, fault, impropriety, solecism, bull. See **error.**

mistress. Syn.: matron, dame; sweetheart, ladylove; paramour, concubine.

mistrust. Syn.: distrust, doubt, question, suspect.

misunderstand. Syn.: misapprehend, misconceive, misinterpret, misjudge, mistake.

misunderstanding. Syn.: misapprehension, misconception; variance, disagreement, dissension, dispute, quarrel, spat, tiff.

misuse, *n.* **Syn.:** misapplication, perversion, profanation; abuse, maltreatment.

misuse, *v.* **Syn.:** misapply, misemploy, pervert, profane; abuse, mistreat, maltreat, hurt, harm.

mite. Syn.: see **bit.**

mitigate. Syn.: see **allay.**

mix. Syn.: mingle, blend, fuse, amalgamate, combine, compound, concoct; jumble, confuse, confound; associate, consort, fraternize. **Ant.:** separate, assort, classify, distinguish.

To *mix* is to combine in intimate association two or more things, often so that the units are individually indistinguishable; it may be with or without loss of identity to the parts: as, to *mix* water and milk; to *mix* different sizes of nails. While *mingle* is often synonymous with mix, it usually does not suggest so complete a loss of individuality of the elements or parts: as, flowers and weeds were *mingled* in the garden. As applied to people, *mingle* denotes less closeness and familiarity of association than *mix*: as, he *mingled* with the crowd; he *mixes* with gamblers. Figuratively the participles *mixed* and *mingled* are used frequently with a slight idiomatic distinction. *Mixed* is applied generally to one noun, *mingled* more commonly to two or more: as, *mixed* feelings, *unmixed* pleasure; *mingled* hope and fear. *Blend* suggests the joining of two or more colors, sounds, feelings, etc. so intimately or harmoniously that the identity of the things joined is lost or obscured in a new product, which, however, partakes somewhat of the qualities of each. *Compound* especially suggests mixing in definite proportions, as according to a formula, to form a composite product: as, to *compound* an ointment. *Amalgamate* emphasizes the homogeneity or uniformity in the result of combining two or more substances.

mixed. Syn.: mingled, blended, fused; jumbled, confused, promiscuous, miscellaneous, heterogeneous, conglomerate, indiscriminate, motley.

mixture. Syn.: blend, combination, compound, concoction, conglomeration, miscellany, jumble, medley, mélange, potpourri, olio, olla podrida, farrago, hodgepodge, hotchpotch, mess, gallimaufry, salmagundi.

Mixture is a general term indicating an intermingling of two or more ingredients, more often, but not necessarily, congruous. *Miscellany* denotes a collection of things not closely connected but brought together by some rational design; it specifically denotes a collection of literary pieces on various subjects, with no other unity than their general character. *Medley* suggests a mingled assortment of various unrelated, and often incongruous things; it is used specifically for a song or tune made up of scraps of other songs or tunes, ingeniously or amazingly fitted together. *Farrago* emphasizes the confusion or indiscriminateness of the mixture or collection; it is applied chiefly to printed or spoken discourse. *Hotchpotch*, or its more common variant, *hodgepodge*, expresses still more the confusion of the combination. *Jumble* implies the idea of a heap turned over and over till everything is hopelessly mixed.

moan. Syn.: bemoan, lament, bewail, wail, deplore, groan, complain. See **groan.**

mob. Syn.: crowd, multitude, populace, masses, rabble, riffraff, canaille, hoi polloi.

mobile. Syn.: see **movable.**

mock, *a.* **Syn.:** feigned, pretended, counterfeit, sham, spurious.

mock, *v.* **Syn.:** deride, ridicule, taunt, flout, gibe, scoff, jeer; imitate, mimic, ape; deceive, delude, fool, tantalize. See **imitate, ridicule.**

mockery. Syn.: derision, ridicule, sarcasm; sham, travesty, farce.

mode. Syn.: manner, method, way; style, fashion, vogue. See **manner, fashion.**

model, *n.* **Syn.:** pattern, design, example, exemplar, paragon, prototype, archetype, standard, criterion. See **example.**

model, *v.* **Syn.:** mold, shape, fashion, form, design.

moderate, *a.* **Syn.:** restrained, temperate, mild; medium. **Ant.:** immoderate, intemperate, excessive, extreme.

That which is *moderate* is neither extreme nor excessive; that which is *temperate* keeps within the bounds of some generally recognized standard. *Temperate* almost always implies personal restraint, but is idiomatically used of climate.

moderate, *v.* **Syn.:** reduce, lessen, diminish, abate, mitigate, assuage.

modern. Syn.: see **new.**

modest. Syn.: unassuming, unpretentious, demure, coy, shy, diffident, bashful, humble; decorous, delicate, decent, pure, prudish. **Ant.:** immodest, bold, forward, conceited, egotistical.

Modest, in the sense here discriminated, implies a becoming conformity to propriety and decorum (especially the proprieties of sex), or a distaste for anything approaching coarseness or indecency. *Demure* suggests an arch or playful display of modesty, soberness, or gravity. *Prudish* implies exaggerated modesty or propriety in behavior or conversation.

modesty. Syn.: unassumingness, shyness, diffidence, bashfulness, humility; delicacy, decency.

modification. Syn.: limitation, qualification, alteration, change.

modify. Syn.: moderate, limit, reduce, qualify, alter, change. See **temper,** *v.*

modulation. Syn.: see **inflection.**

moist. Syn.: damp, humid, wet, dank. **Ant.:** dry, arid, parched.

Moist denotes that which is slightly wet, naturally or properly: as, *moist* ground or leather. *Humid* is a literary or scientific term for moist, and is especially applied to that which is so permeated with moisture that the moisture seems a part of it: as, *humid* ground or air, but not a *humid* sponge. *Damp* usually implies slight and extraneous wetness, generally undesirable or unpleasant unless the result of intention: as, a *damp* cellar, clothes, ground; to put a *damp* cloth on a patient's forehead. *Dank* strongly suggests disagreeable, chilling, or unwholesome dampness: as, a *dank* marsh, fog, dungeon.

mold. Syn.: mildew, smut, blight, must, mustiness, decay.

molder. Syn.: see **decay.**

moldy. Syn.: mildewed, musty, fusty, decaying.

molecule. Syn.: see **particle.**

molest. Syn.: see **harass.**

mollify. Syn.: soften, appease, calm, quiet, pacify, soothe, ease, mitigate, moderate. See **appease.**

moment. Syn.: instant, second, minute, trice, twinkling, flash, jiffy; weight, importance, consequence, significance.

Minute, properly denoting sixty seconds, is often used loosely for any very short space of time, but even then it retains a suggestion of its original meaning: as, I'll be ready in a *minute*. *Moment* denotes a shorter and less definite period of time than *minute*; although it has slight duration, it is many times practically the same as *instant*, which has no duration, but is rather a point of time: as, wait a *moment*; come this *instant*; he did not wait a *moment* (or an *instant*) before he shot. *Jiffy* is a colloquial but expressive word, denoting a short period, but it often emphasizes the quickness or speed of the agent rather than the brevity of the time: as, I'll answer these letters in a *jiffy*.

momentary. Syn.: see **fleeting.**

momentous. Syn.: weighty, grave, serious, critical, important. **Ant.:** trifling, trivial, paltry, petty, insignificant. See **heavy.**

momentum. Syn.: impetus, impulse, force, moment.

monarch. Syn.: see **ruler.**

monastery. Syn.: see **convent.**

monetary. Syn.: see **pecuniary.**

money. Syn.: coin, cash, currency, specie, change, banknotes, funds, capital, assets, wealth, lucre, pelf, wherewithal, spondulics, dough.

mongrel. Syn.: see **hybrid.**

monition. Syn.: see **admonition.**

monk. Syn.: see **friar.**

monotonous. Syn.: singsong, unvarying, uniform, tedious, humdrum, uninteresting, dull.

monster. Syn.: monstrosity, prodigy, giant, ogre, dragon; brute, villain.

monstrous. Syn.: abnormal, shocking, horrible, atrocious; huge, enormous, colossal, stupendous, prodigious.

monument. Syn.: see **memorial.**

mood. Syn.: humor, temper, temperament, disposition, vein, inclination.

Mood denotes a more or less temporary state of mind, especially as manifested in the feelings: as, a merry or melancholy *mood*. *Humor* also denotes a temporary state of mind, but suggests greater variability: as, a changeable *humor*. *Disposition* is the natural or prevailing aspect of one's character: as, a sanguine or selfish *disposition*. *Temperament* suggests the delicate balance of one's emotions, the disturbance of which determines one's moods: as, an artistic *temperament*. *Temper* denotes the essential quality of one's nature: as, an even *temper*.

moody. Syn.: melancholy, gloomy, sad, pensive, sullen, ill-humored. See **sullen**.

moor. Syn.: see **heath**.

mopish. Syn.: see **spiritless**.

moral. Syn.: ethical; virtuous, chaste, pure, good, righteous, just.

Moral implies conformity to generally accepted laws of conduct or right living; *ethical*, to formal rules of conduct or practice: as, *moral* restraint, *ethical* standards of the medical profession.

morality. Syn.: ethics, morals, virtue, rectitude. See **goodness**.

morass. Syn.: see **swamp**.

morbid. Syn.: see **sick**.

moreover. Syn.: besides.

Moreover and *besides* both indicate something additional to what has already been stated, but *moreover* is more formal and implies the addition of something particular, emphatic, or important; *besides* often suggests that what is added is in the nature of an afterthought: as, I did not care for the appearance of the house; *moreover*, I did not have the money to buy it. The bill cannot be paid until the first of the month; *besides*, the work is not yet completed.

morning. Syn.: morn, dawn, daybreak, sunrise, dayspring, cockcrow, aurora.

morose. Syn.: sullen, moody, surly, crabbed, crusty, gruff. Ant.: amiable, pleasant, genial. See **sullen**.

morsel. Syn.: see **bit**.

mortal. Syn.: see **deadly**.

mortification. Syn.: humiliation, chagrin, pique, embarrassment, vexation.

Mortification is a feeling of humiliation so great as to seem a death to one's pride or self-respect; *chagrin* is vexation and regret caused especially by what might have been prevented, or resulting from failure after confident expectation of success; *pique* is a sudden and usually transient feeling of irritation or resentment caused by a real or imaginary injury to one's pride or self-love.

mortify. Syn.: humiliate, humble, chagrin, embarrass, shame, abase; repress, restrain, deny.

mostly. Syn.: see **especially**.

motherly. Syn.: maternal, matronly.

Motherly suggests the tenderness, love, solicitude, or kindred feelings of a mother: as *motherly* care, advice. *Maternal* is a colder and more formal word referring to motherhood or kinship: as, *maternal* instinct; a *maternal* uncle. *Matronly* suggests the staidness and stability proper to one who is the mother of a family: as, a *matronly* air.

motion. Syn.: movement, move, change, action, activity, gesture, gesticulation, signal, sign. Ant.: inertia, quiescence, immobility, rest, repose, stillness.

Motion denotes change of position in space, either considered apart from, or as a characteristic of, that which moves, usually the former, in which case it is often a somewhat technical or scientific term: as, the laws of *motion*; rate of *motion*; perpetual *motion*; a *motion* of the sea. *Movement* is always connected with the person or thing moving, and is usually a definite or particular motion: as, the *movements* of a dance; a stealthy *movement*. The chief uses of *move* are founded upon the idea of moving a piece, in chess or a similar game, for winning the game, and hence the word denotes any change of position, condition, or circumstances for the accomplishment of some end: as, it was a wise *move* first to placate his enemies.

motionless. Syn.: inert, stationary, still, quiet, quiescent.

motive. Syn.: inducement, incentive, impulse, incitement, stimulus, reason, object, design, purpose, cause.

A *motive* is that which determines volition or choice and moves to action: as, the *motive* for the crime. A *reason* is that which addresses the rational nature by way of argument as an explanation, ground, or basis for following a course of action or thought. An *inducement* is a prospect of pleasure or profit which leads one to action: as, the low price was an added *inducement*. An *incentive* is something that urges or spurs to action, especially working on the feelings: as, his handicap was an *incentive* to greater effort. An *impulse* is

something that drives one, usually to sudden, sometimes to ill-advised, action: as, the *impulse* to kill is strong in uncivilized peoples.

motley. Syn.: see **variegated**.

mottled. Syn.: see **dappled**.

motto. Syn.: see **proverb**.

mount. Syn.: rise, soar, ascend, climb.

mountain. Syn.: see **hill**.

mountebank. Syn.: see **quack**.

mourn. Syn.: grieve, lament, bewail, bemoan, deplore, sorrow. See **lament**.

mournful. Syn.: sorrowful, doleful, dolorous, lugubrious, plaintive, rueful, melancholy, sad, tearful, lacrymose; grievous, lamentable, deplorable, woeful.

Mournful applies to what causes or expresses sorrow or grief; *doleful*, to what is dismally sad, as a funeral bell or a muffled drum; *lugubrious*, to what is exceedingly or even exaggeratedly sorrowful; *plaintive*, to what is tenderly or pitifully sad; *rueful*, to what invites pity or sorrow, often with a humorous or even ludicrous implication as being self-imposed misery: as, Don Quixote, the knight of the *rueful* countenance.

movable. Syn.: mobile, portable, transportable.

move, *n.* Syn.: see **motion**.

move, *v.* Syn.: remove, transfer, carry, convey, draw, shift; march, walk, pass, go, proceed, advance, migrate, emigrate; actuate, prompt, stimulate, animate, kindle, impel, induce, incite, instigate; influence, affect, touch, agitate. See **impress**.

movement. Syn.: see **motion**.

mud. Syn.: see **mire**.

muddy. Syn.: see **turbid**.

muffle. Syn.: see **gag**.

mulct. Syn.: see **fine**.

multifarious. Syn.: see **many**.

multitude. Syn.: crowd, concourse, throng, swarm, horde, host, legion, army.

Multitude denotes a great number of persons or things, but however great, there is no indication that there is not space enough to give each ample room. *Throng* and *crowd* suggest a smaller number than multitude, but describe people gathered into a close body; *throng* implies a company that presses together or forward, often with some common aim; *crowd*, a jostling, disordered, or uncomfortably close company. *Host* may be applied to any large and indefinite company, at times hostile, though usually not strictly organized as an army. *Horde* is generally used in a disparaging sense for a large and unorganized mass of people, such as suggests savage and nomadic tribes. *Swarm*, as used of people, is usually contemptuous, suggesting a moving, restless, often noisy, crowd: as, a *swarm* of dirty children played in the street.

mumble. Syn.: see **murmur**.

mundane. Syn.: see **earthly**.

munificence. Syn.: see **beneficence, liberality**.

munificent. Syn.: generous, bountiful, bounteous, lavish, liberal.

murder. Syn.: see **kill**.

murderer. Syn.: homicide, manslayer, slayer, cutthroat, assassin, thug.

murderous. Syn.: bloodthirsty, slaughterous, sanguinary, savage, brutal, cruel, fell, destructive.

murky. Syn.: see **dark**.

murmur. Syn.: babble, hum; mutter, mumble, grumble, complain, repine. See **complain**.

To *murmur* is to utter sounds or words in a low, almost inaudible tone, as in expressing blandishments, affection, dissatisfaction, etc. To *mutter* is to utter words in a low, grumbling way, often voicing complaint or discontent not meant to be fully audible. To *mumble* is to utter imperfect or inarticulate sounds with the mouth partly closed, so that the words can be distinguished only with difficulty.

muscle. Syn.: brawn, sinew, thew.

muscular. Syn.: brawny, sinewy, strong, powerful, stalwart, sturdy. Ant.: weak, weakly, feeble.

muse. Syn.: meditate, ponder, reflect, contemplate, ruminate, cogitate, study, brood, mull. See **reflect**.

musical. Syn.: see **melodious**.

must. Syn.: ought, should, shall.

Must expresses necessity, obligation, or compulsion; *ought* and *should* express duty or moral obligation less forcibly and also indicate the weaker relations, — propriety, fitness, expediency, natural expectation, or logical deduction: as, all men *must* die; I *must* answer this letter; soldiers *must* obey orders; one *ought* to (or *should*) love his fellow-men; a person *ought* to (or *should*) dress becomingly; rain *ought* to (or *should*) cause the river to rise.

muster. Syn.: collect, assemble, gather, convene, marshal, array. **Ant.:** disband, disorganize, dissolve. See **gather.**

musty. Syn.: see **moldy.**

mutable. Syn.: changeable, alterable, variable, unstable, inconstant, fickle.

mute. Syn.: see **silent.**

mutilate. Syn.: maim, mangle, dismember, disfigure, lacerate, hack, cripple; garble, misquote.

To *mutilate* is to injure the completeness or beauty of a body, especially by cutting off an important member. To *maim* is to injure by depriving a person of one or more members, or their use. To *mangle* is to crush or rend the body or members by blows or pressure as if caught in machinery. To *lacerate* is to inflict numerous and severe cuts and tears to the skin or flesh, or, figuratively, to distress a person or harrow the feelings.

mutinous. Syn.: rebellious, seditious, insubordinate, refractory, riotous. **Ant.:** obedient, submissive, tractable, dutiful, compliant, subservient.

mutiny. Syn.: see **insurrection.**

mutter. Syn.: see **murmur.**

mutual. Syn.: reciprocal, correlative, joint, interchanged, common.

Mutual indicates an exchange of a feeling, obligation, etc., between two people, or an interchange of some kind between persons or things. *Reciprocal* indicates a relation in which one act, thing, feeling, etc., balances or is in return for another: as, *mutual* esteem, *mutual* dependence; *reciprocal* concessions, *reciprocal* distrust. *Mutual* in the sense of *common,* shared by or pertaining to each of two or more, is not considered good usage, but is nevertheless so used by many writers, especially in the collocation 'a *mutual* friend.'

muzzle. Syn.: see **gag.**

mysterious. Syn.: obscure, inexplicable, inscrutable, unfathomable, recondite, dark, hidden, secret, esoteric, enigmatical, occult, cryptic, mystic, mystical, cabalistic. **Ant.:** clear, plain, evident, manifest, unambiguous. See **obscure,** *a.*

mystery. Syn.: secret, enigma, riddle, puzzle, arcanum.

mystic, mystical. Syn.: see **obscure,** *a.*

mystify. Syn.: confuse, perplex, puzzle, befog, obfuscate, nonplus. See **perplex.**

myth. Syn.: legend, fable, tradition. See **legend.**

mythical. Syn.: legendary, fabled, traditional, fabulous, fictitious, imaginary. See **legendary.**

N

nag. Syn.: annoy, torment, plague, pester, tease. See **tease.**

naïve. Syn.: unaffected, unsophisticated, artless, natural, ingenuous, open, frank, candid, sincere, simple, innocent. See **artless.**

naked. Syn.: unclothed, undressed, uncovered, nude, bare, exposed; unprotected, unguarded, defenseless; unfurnished, unadorned, barren, leafless; mere, plain, simple, unexaggerated.

Naked is the common word applied to that which is without clothing or covering, often with the implication that there should be clothing or covering. *Nude* is used especially as a term of art, or, in general speech, as a more refined substitute for *naked.*

name, *n.* **Syn.:** prænomen, cognomen, agnomen, surname, patronymic, nickname, sobriquet, pseudonym, nom de plume, alias, appellation, style, denomination, designation, title, epithet, term, misnomer; reputation, character; repute, note, renown, eminence, fame.

Name is the simplest and most general word for that by which a person or thing is called. An *appellation* is usually a descriptive term, as of an individual or his characteristics, as, John the Baptist, Charles the Bold. A *title* is an official or honorary appellation, or the specific designation of a book, article, etc., as, reverend, doctor, colonel, *Vanity Fair.* *Style* may be essentially the same as appellation, but it is now generally limited to a name assumed or assigned for public use: as, to do business under the firm *style* of Smith and Company. *Nickname* is applied to a name substituted by way of ridicule,

pleasantry, familiarity, or affection, for the real name. *Sobriquet* denotes a nickname applied because of some outstanding characteristic or foible: as, Jenny Lind was known by the *sobriquet* of the " Swedish Nightingale."

name, *v.* **Syn.:** denominate, entitle, style, call, christen, dub; designate, specify, appoint, nominate.

nap. Syn.: see **sleep,** *v.*

narcotic. Syn.: opiate, soporific, stupefacient, sedative, anodyne, anesthetic.

narrate. Syn.: relate, recount, recite, repeat, rehearse, detail, tell. See **describe.**

narration. Syn.: account, relation, recital, rehearsal; narrative, story, tale, history.

narrow. Syn.: confined, restricted, circumscribed, limited, cramped, strait, straitened; scanty, meager, impoverished; illiberal, prejudiced, bigoted; close, accurate, careful. **Ant.:** see **wide.**

narrow-minded. Syn.: illiberal, intolerant, prejudiced, bigoted, dogmatic.

nasty. Syn.: filthy, dirty, foul, squalid, unclean; indecent, gross, obscene, lewd, ribald, smutty; disagreeable, disgusting, repulsive, sickening, nauseous; ill-natured, mean, hateful. See **dirty.**

natal. Syn.: see **native.**

nation. Syn.: see **people.**

native. Syn.: natal, inborn, innate, inbred, inherent, hereditary, natural, indigenous, aboriginal, autochthonous. **Ant.:** unnatural, acquired, assumed, artificial, foreign, exotic.

Native emphasizes the fact of birth in a certain place, and indicates that which is conferred by birth, or belongs to or is associated with one by birth or origin: as, a *native* inhabitant, *native* courage, *native* country or language. It often implies a contrast to what is acquired or superadded. *Natural* is applied to that which is implanted, formed, or produced by nature, or which results from processes that suggest the inevitability of nature: as, a *natural* talent, waterfall, development, result. *Indigenous* is especially applied to the vegetation or animal life originating in and natural to a region or climate.

natty. Syn.: see **spruce.**

natural. Syn.: native, inborn, innate, inherent, characteristic; easy, spontaneous, artless, unaffected, simple, ingenuous; normal, regular. **Ant.:** see **unnatural.** See **native.**

nature. Syn.: character, kind, class, sort, stock, quality, essence; disposition, temper, mood; universe, creation, cosmos.

naughty. Syn.: bad, mischievous, disobedient, perverse. **Ant.:** good, obedient, dutiful.

nauseous. Syn.: sickening, disgusting, revolting, repulsive, offensive.

nautical. Syn.: naval. Cf. **maritime.**

Nautical, by derivation referring to sailors, is particularly applicable to anything connected with navigation; *naval,* by derivation referring to ships, especially applies to a ship of war or a navy, its crew, equipment, tactics, etc.: as, *nautical* calculations, instruments, almanac, or tables; *naval* officers, heroes, battles, affairs.

naval. Syn.: see **nautical.**

navigate. Syn.: see **sail.**

nay. Syn.: see **no.**

near. Syn.: nigh, close, proximate, neighboring, adjacent, contiguous; imminent, impending; intimate, familiar; short, direct. **Ant.:** see **distant.**

nearest. Syn.: next, closest, proximate.

Nearest and *next* are sometimes synonymous words: as, the *nearest* or *next* of kin. But *nearest* especially denotes closest relative proximity; *next,* the closest in an order or arrangement: as, the *nearest* house; the *next* house.

nearness. Syn.: closeness, proximity, approximation, propinquity, contiguity; intimacy, familiarity, fellowship.

neat. Syn.: clear, pure, undiluted; well-arranged, well-proportioned, pleasing, nice, trim, dapper, natty, tidy, clean, cleanly, orderly; deft, skilful, adroit. **Ant.:** untidy, unkempt, slovenly, slatternly, dowdy, littered, disorderly.

Neat suggests a nice and becoming orderliness; *tidy,* a painstaking or studied orderliness; *trim,* a combination of neatness and smartness.

necessary. Syn.: inevitable, unavoidable; indispensable, essential, requisite, required, needed, needful. **Ant.:** see **unnecessary.**

Necessary and *indispensable* apply to that which is inevitable to the fulfilment of a condition: as, food is *necessary* (or *indispensable*) to life; but *necessary* may also suggest the inevitable consequence to certain causes: as, multiplicity is a *necessary* result of division. That which is *essential* forms a vital part of the constitution or organization of something: as, hydrogen and oxygen are *essential* to water. *Requisite* is applied to that which is deemed necessary: as, recreation is *requisite* to an individual's well-being.

necessitate. Syn.: oblige, require, demand, force, compel.

necessitous. Syn.: see **needy.**

necessity. Syn.: inevitableness, unavoidableness; constraint, compulsion; essential, requisite, requirement, sine qua non; want, need, indigence, exigency.

Necessity expresses logical urgency or imperative demand for something; *need*, lack of something desired, wanted, or required, or, in a narrower sense, such lack as results in poverty: as, a merchant may have *need* of money to enlarge his business, but *necessity* for cash to keep from going into bankruptcy; and if he should lose all his money, he might be in *need*.

necromancer, necromancy. Syn.: see **magician, magic.**

need, *n.* **Syn.:** necessity, obligation; want, destitution, poverty, indigence, privation, strait. See **lack,** *n.*, **necessity, poverty.**

need, *v.* **Syn.:** see **lack,** *v.*

needful. Syn.: necessary, indispensable, requisite, required, essential, vital.

needless. Syn.: unnecessary, useless.

needy. Syn.: necessitous, indigent, pinched, destitute, penniless, impecunious, poor.

nefarious. Syn.: iniquitous, flagitious, heinous, villainous, atrocious, impious, abominable, execrable, infamous, horrible, wicked. See **atrocious.**

neglect, *n.* **Syn.:** negligence, disregard, remissness, dereliction, slight, oversight, default, omission. See **negligence.**

neglect, *v.* **Syn.:** disregard, ignore, slight, overlook, omit.

neglectful. Syn.: see **negligent.**

negligence. Syn.: neglect, neglectfulness, disregard, inattention, indifference, inadvertence, thoughtlessness, carelessness, heedlessness, remissness, dereliction.

Negligence and *neglect* are occasionally interchangeable, but *negligence* commonly expresses the habit or trait, *neglect*, the act, of failing to attend to or perform what is expected or required. *Remissness* implies the omission or the careless or indifferent performance of a duty, task, or the like; *dereliction*, culpable or reprehensible neglect or failure in the performance of duty.

negligent. Syn.: neglectful, regardless, inattentive, indifferent, thoughtless, careless, heedless, remiss, derelict, slack, slothful. **Ant.:** see **careful.**

negotiate. Syn.: see **transact.**

neighborhood. Syn.: vicinity, vicinage, proximity, nearness.

Neighborhood implies a region close to or about a given place, and often the (especially friendly) relationship among those living in it. *Vicinity*, and the less common *vicinage*, indicate only nearness of place.

neighboring. Syn.: adjacent, contiguous, close, near.

neighborly. Syn.: friendly, kindly, considerate, sociable, obliging. **Ant.:** see **unneighborly.**

neophyte. Syn.: see **convert, novice.**

nervous. Syn.: high-strung, excitable, sensitive; vigorous, energetic; apprehensive, anxious, timid.

nestle. Syn.: see **cuddle.**

net. Syn.: netting, network, mesh, reticulation, seine, drag-net, trawl, dredge.

nettle. Syn.: sting, irritate, provoke, vex, exasperate, incense, pique, ruffle. See **vex.**

neutrality. Syn.: impartiality, independence, indifference.

neutralize. Syn.: counteract, counterbalance, countervail, nullify, annul.

nevertheless. Syn.: see **but.**

new. Syn.: late, recent, modern, neoteric; novel, strange, unfamiliar, unaccustomed, untried, unusual, unique, rare; fresh, unused; further, additional. **Ant.:** see **old.**

New is applied to that which has not been long in existence, experience, possession, or use. *Novel* implies an unexpected, strange, or striking, but generally pleasing, newness. *Fresh* implies such newness as is not yet diminished by use or the passage of time. That which is *recent* is separated from the present or the time of action by only a short interval. *Modern* is applied to those things which exist in the present age, espe-

cially in contrast to those of a former age or an age long past; hence the word sometimes has the connotation of up-to-date and, thus, good.

news. Syn.: tidings, advices, report, word, intelligence, information.

News is the most general word for recent intelligence of something that has lately taken place, especially as published in a newspaper. *Tidings* is a more literary word for news, especially when expected or eagerly awaited; *intelligence* is news about a particular matter, often communicated in a formal or official way; *word* in a similar sense carries the suggestion of informality or intimacy.

next. Syn.: see **nearest.**

nibble. Syn.: see **eat.**

nice. Syn.: fastidious, particular, dainty, delicate, finical, squeamish; refined, critical, discriminating, discerning, subtle, precise, accurate, exact, close, careful, minute; neat, finished, exquisite, fine; pleasing, pleasant, enjoyable, gratifying, agreeable, considerate, kind. See **accurate, particular.**

niche. Syn.: recess, nook, cavity, hollow.

nick. Syn.: notch, dent, indentation.

nickname. Syn.: see **name.**

niggardly. Syn.: niggard, miserly, stingy, parsimonious, close-fisted, illiberal, stinting, sparing. **Ant.:** generous, munificent, liberal, free-handed. See **stingy.**

night. Syn.: see **evening.**

nightly. Syn.: nocturnal.

Nightly, the familiar word, tends to limit itself in application to that which happens or occurs every night: as, a *nightly* visit. *Nocturnal*, the more literary or poetic word, applies both to that which belongs to the night, and to that which exists or occurs, however accidentally, in the night: as, the *nocturnal* beauty of the heavens; the *nocturnal* prowlings of an animal.

nimble. Syn.: agile, active, lively, spry, sprightly, quick, brisk, alert. **Ant.:** slow, heavy, clumsy, dull.

Nimble suggests lightness or quickness of motion, especially of the hands and feet; *agile*, flexibility or suppleness, combined with dexterity, in the use of the limbs: as, a *nimble* dancer; an *agile* acrobat. *Spry* suggests an energetic or smart briskness of action: as, a *spry* old lady.

nip. Syn.: pinch, squeeze; clip, cut; bite, sting, chill, kill, blast.

no. Syn.: nay.

Both these words are used to express denial or negative rejoinder. *No* is the common term; *nay* is used in sacred, solemn, or formal style, or in deliberative bodies to express negative vote.

nobility. Syn.: nobleness, rank, greatness, magnanimity, high-mindedness; peerage, aristocracy.

noble, *n.* **Syn.:** nobleman, peer, grandee, prince, duke, marquis, earl, lord, viscount, count, baron, baronet, knight, chevalier.

noble, *a.* **Syn.:** illustrious, famous, renowned, eminent; high-born, aristocratic, patrician; magnanimous, high-minded, honorable, worthy, generous; lofty, exalted, stately, imposing, grand, magnificent, fine.

Noble implies loftiness of character or spirit that scorns the petty, mean, base, or dishonorable; *high-minded*, elevated or lofty principles or sentiments; *magnanimous*, greatness of mind or soul, especially as manifested in generosity or in overlooking or forgetting injuries.

nocturnal. Syn.: see **nightly.**

noise. Syn.: shouting, outcry, clamor, babel, racket, clatter, hubbub, uproar, tumult, blare, din, hullabaloo.

Noise is the general word for any unmusical or confused sound. *Din* suggests a loud, continued, resonant noise; *uproar*, noise created by disturbance, confusion, or the like; *hubbub*, a mingling of noises resulting from animated or excited tones, shouting, cries, or the like.

noiseless. Syn.: see **still,** *a.*

noisome. Syn.: see **noxious, malodorous.**

noisy. Syn.: shouting, clamorous, vociferous, brawling, blatant, uproarious, riotous, boisterous. See **loud.**

nomad. Syn.: see **wanderer.**

nomenclature. Syn.: see **vocabulary.**

nonchalant. Syn.: indifferent, unconcerned, cool, careless.

nonconformist. Syn.: see **heretic.**

nonplus. Syn.: confound, confuse, mystify, bewilder, perplex, puzzle, disconcert, embarrass. See **perplex.**

nonsense. **Syn.:** foolishness, absurdity, twaddle, balderdash, moonshine, rubbish, flummery, fudge, bosh, stuff, rigmarole.

nonsensical. **Syn.:** senseless, foolish, silly, absurd, preposterous, unmeaning, amphigoric.

nook. **Syn.:** see **recess.**

normal. **Syn.:** regular, ordinary, everyday, usual, common, natural. **Ant.:** see **abnormal.**

Normal implies conformity to a standard which represents the average condition or behavior of individual units composing a group: as, the patient's temperature was *normal; normal* breathing. That which is *regular* conforms to rule or habit and is opposed to that which is irregular, fitful, or exceptional: as, *regular* exercise, the *regular* monthly meeting.

northern. **Syn.:** north, northerly, arctic, boreal.

notable. **Syn.:** noteworthy, remarkable, signal, conspicuous, memorable, noted, distinguished, famous, renowned, celebrated, eminent, great, notorious. See **famous.**

notch. **Syn.:** nick, dent, indentation, score, crenature.

notched. **Syn.:** nicked, indented, jagged, toothed, dentate, serrate, emarginate, crenate, incised.

note, *n.* **Syn.:** mark, sign, symbol, character, token; record, memorandum, minute; comment, commentary, annotation, gloss, scholium; billet, letter, communication; notice, heed, observation; consequence, significance, distinction, repute, renown; tone, sound, cry, call. See **letter, mark.**

note, *v.* **Syn.:** notice, mark, perceive, regard, observe; record, jot down; denote, indicate, signify.

noted. **Syn.:** see **famous.**

nothing. **Syn.:** see **zero.**

notice, *n.* **Syn.:** information, intelligence, news; intimation, warning, notification, announcement, statement, bulletin, placard; observation, cognizance, attention, regard, note.

notice, *v.* **Syn.:** see, mark, note, perceive, recognize, heed. **Ant.:** overlook, skip, slight, disregard, ignore. See **see.**

noticeable. **Syn.:** discernible, observable, appreciable; conspicuous, prominent, salient.

notification. **Syn.:** see **notice,** *n.*

notify. **Syn.:** publish, proclaim, announce; acquaint, apprise, inform, tell. See **inform.**

notion. **Syn.:** concept, conception, idea, impression; view, opinion, judgment, belief, theory; inclination, desire, fancy, caprice, whim.

notional. **Syn.:** see **whimsical.**

notorious. **Syn.:** see **famous.**

notwithstanding, *conj.* **Syn.:** see **although.**

notwithstanding, *prep.* **Syn.:** despite, in spite of.

nourish. **Syn.:** feed, nurture, nurse, foster, cherish; support, maintain, encourage, promote. See **nurture,** *v.*

nourishment. **Syn.:** see **food.**

novel, *n.* **Syn.:** romance, story, tale, narrative. See **story.**

novel, *a.* **Syn.:** see **new.**

novelty. **Syn.:** newness, recentness, freshness, strangeness; innovation, rarity, curiosity.

novice. **Syn.:** beginner, tyro, apprentice; probationer, novitiate, neophyte.

A *novice* is an inexperienced beginner in anything. A *tyro* is especially a new learner in some branch of knowledge. A *neophyte* is especially one who is new in the doctrine or duties of a religion.

now. **Syn.:** see **immediately.**

noxious. **Syn.:** hurtful, harmful, injurious, unhealthful, unwholesome, insalubrious, noisome, pernicious, deleterious, poisonous, pestilential, deadly, baneful. **Ant.:** healthful, wholesome, salutary, beneficial. See **pernicious.**

nucleus. **Syn.:** center, core, kernel, heart.

nude. **Syn.:** see **naked.**

nugatory. **Syn.:** see **vain, unavailing.**

nuisance. **Syn.:** annoyance, inconvenience, trouble, plague, bore, pest.

nullify. **Syn.:** annul, abrogate, invalidate, repeal, cancel, countermand.

numb. **Syn.:** benumbed, deadened, paralyzed, insensible.

number, *n.* **Syn.:** numeral, figure, digit, integer; aggregate, total, amount, lot, collection, company, multitude.

number, *v.* **Syn.:** numerate, enumerate, count, calculate, reckon, tell.

numberless. **Syn.:** innumerable, countless, myriad, infinite.

numerous. **Syn.:** see **many.**

nunnery. **Syn.:** see **convent.**

nuptial. **Syn.:** see **matrimonial.**

nuptials. **Syn.:** see **marriage.**

nurse. **Syn.:** suckle, nourish, nurture, cherish, foster, encourage, tend. See **nurture,** *v.*

nurture, *n.* **Syn.:** rearing, upbringing, training, breeding, care, education; nourishment, food, diet.

nurture, *v.* **Syn.:** nourish, sustain, nurse, feed, foster; rear, train, discipline, instruct, educate.

To *nurture* is to bring up or rear, usually with tenderness or solicitude. To *nourish* is to supply what is needful for natural bodily development. To *nurse* is to feed or care for the helpless or incapacitated.

nutriment, nutrition. **Syn.:** see **food.**

nutritious. **Syn.:** nutritive, nourishing, strengthening, invigorating, wholesome.

nymph. **Syn.:** sylph, naiad, oread, dryad, hamadryad, Nereid; maiden, damsel, girl.

O

oath. **Syn.:** vow, promise, pledge, declaration; curse, expletive, malediction, blasphemy, profanity, swearing.

obdurate. **Syn.:** hardened, callous, impenitent; stubborn, obstinate, unyielding, unbending, inflexible, firm, inexorable. See **obstinate.**

obedience. **Syn.:** compliance, submission, subservience, deference. **Ant.:** disobedience, insubordination, defiance.

obedient. **Syn.:** obeying, compliant, submissive, yielding, dutiful, docile, tractable, subservient, obsequious. **Ant.:** disobedient, intractable, refractory, stubborn, contumacious.

Obedient implies (willing) compliance or submission to some superior power or authority; *docile*, tractability or easy management; *dutiful*, that one is conscientious concerning obligations, services, or attentions due to another.

obese. **Syn.:** see **stout.**

object, *n.* **Syn.:** thing, article; purpose, motive, aim, intent, design, goal, end.

object, *v.* **Syn.:** oppose, disapprove, demur, refuse. **Ant.:** approve, accede, comply, concur, consent.

objection. **Syn.:** opposition, disapproval, dislike, exception, scruple.

objectionable. **Syn.:** disagreeable, displeasing, unpleasant, undesirable, unacceptable, offensive, obnoxious. See **odious.**

objectless. **Syn.:** purposeless, aimless, desultory, pointless, indefinite, vague.

objurgate. **Syn.:** see **scold.**

obligation. **Syn.:** engagement, agreement, covenant, contract, bond; duty, responsibility; indebtedness, gratitude. See **duty.**

obligatory. **Syn.:** binding, compulsory, imperative, incumbent.

oblige. **Syn.:** bind, force, compel, constrain, necessitate; accommodate, serve, gratify, please.

Oblige emphasizes the conferring of a favor; *accommodate*, the furnishing of a convenience.

obliged. **Syn.:** see **indebted.**

obliging. **Syn.:** accommodating, helpful, kind, friendly, complaisant, courteous, civil.

obliterate. **Syn.:** blot out, efface, erase, expunge, remove, destroy. See **efface.**

oblivion. **Syn.:** obliviousness, forgetfulness, Lethe, nirvana.

oblivious. **Syn.:** forgetful, unmindful, disregardful, heedless, inattentive.

Forgetful implies a lapse of memory, often habitual; *oblivious*, deep but usually only temporary forgetfulness, as from absent-mindedness, preoccupation, carelessness, or indifference: as, the proverbially *forgetful* professor; he was *oblivious* of his surroundings or of approaching danger.

obloquy. **Syn.:** calumny, slander, defamation, aspersion, censure, blame, reproach, reprehension; shame, disgrace, odium, opprobrium, infamy. See **odium.**

obnoxious. **Syn.:** objectionable, offensive, odious, hateful. See **odious.**

obscene. **Syn.:** impure, indecent, immodest, gross, lewd, ribald, smutty.

obscure, *a.* **Syn.:** darkened, dim, shadowy, dusky, murky, gloomy; hidden, remote, secluded; unknown, undistinguished, humble, lowly, inglorious; doubtful, dubious, ambiguous, indefinite, equivocal, vague, mysterious, mystic, occult, esoteric, enigmatical, involved, complicated, intricate, recondite, abstruse, inscrutable, cryptic, unintelligible, incomprehensible. **Ant.:** see **clear.** See **dark.**

That which is *obscure* is seen or comprehended dimly or with difficulty. That which is *mysterious*, by being unknown or puzzling, excites curiosity, amazement, or awe. That which is *mystic* has a secret significance, such as that attaching to certain signs, rites, etc. The *occult* appears to be impenetrable in its mystery and suggests traffic with supernatural agencies; the *esoteric* denotes that which is known or understood only by the initiated. That is *recondite* which is mentally remote or out of the common course and therefore often not easily discovered; *abstruse* applies to what is difficult to understand because of its remoteness, complexity, or depth; *inscrutable*, to what is so obscure or mysterious that one cannot interpret its significance; *cryptic*, to what is mystifying because capable of more than one interpretation.

obscure, *v.* **Syn.:** darken, dim, obfuscate, eclipse; conceal, hide, disguise.

obscurity. Syn.: darkness, dimness, shade; retirement, seclusion, privacy; ambiguity, vagueness, unintelligibleness.

obsequious. Syn.: compliant, servile, slavish, cringing, fawning, sycophantic. See **servile.**

observance. Syn.: observing, keeping, celebration; custom, practice, ceremony, rite. Cf. **observation.**

observant. Syn.: observing, watching, watchful, heedful, regardful, mindful, attentive.

observation. Syn.: observing, noting, notice; remark, comment, statement. See **remark, experience.** Cf. **observance.**

observe. Syn.: watch, regard, survey, eye, behold, perceive, see; remark, say, mention, comment; conform to, comply with, obey, fulfil; keep, celebrate. See **celebrate, see.**

observer. Syn.: see **spectator.**

obsolescent, obsolete. Syn.: see **ancient.**

obstacle. Syn.: obstruction, barrier, bar, check, impediment, hindrance, difficulty, stumbling-block.

An *obstacle* is something that stands in the way of progress or advance; an *impediment* is something that clogs the feet, as it were, and is likely to continue with one as a hindrance; an *obstruction* blocks the passage and is sometimes put in the way intentionally; a *barrier* is usually a serious and, sometimes, insurmountable obstacle in the way of one's advance, progress, ambition, etc.

obstinacy. Syn.: stubbornness, wilfulness, doggedness, pertinacity, obduracy.

obstinate. Syn.: stubborn, headstrong, wilful, contumacious, opinionated, determined, mulish, dogged, pertinacious, obdurate, unyielding, unbending, inflexible, intractable, refractory, perverse. **Ant.:** compliant, yielding, submissive, tractable, obedient.

Obstinate and *stubborn* both imply resistance to advice, remonstrance, entreaty, or force, but *stubborn* implies more of innate quality and is the more frequent word when referring to inanimate things. One who is *headstrong* is violently, often foolishly or perversely, self-willed. *Dogged* suggests pertinacity in the doing of something, especially in the face of difficulty; *obdurate*, hard-hearted determination in adhering to a purpose, in spite of persuasion or entreaty.

obstreperous. Syn.: noisy, clamorous, vociferous, uproarious, boisterous, tumultuous, turbulent, unruly. See **boisterous.**

obstruct. Syn.: block, stop, close, choke, clog, dam, check, bar, barricade; impede, hinder, delay, retard, arrest, stay, interrupt. **Ant.:** open, clear, free, aid, help, further, promote. See **hinder.**

obstruction. Syn.: see **obstacle.**

obtain. Syn.: get, acquire, procure, secure, gain, earn, achieve, win, attain. See **get.**

obtrusive. Syn.: intrusive, meddlesome, forward, officious.

obtuse. Syn.: see **dull.**

obviate. Syn.: see **avert.**

obvious. Syn.: plain, manifest, evident, patent, palpable, unmistakable. See **manifest.**

occasion, *n.* **Syn.:** juncture, time, instance; opportunity, chance; cause, ground, necessity, need.

occasion, *v.* **Syn.:** cause, produce.

occasional. Syn.: casual, incidental, accidental.

occult. Syn.: hidden, veiled, shrouded, secret, abstruse, recondite, mysterious, mystic, cabalistic, transcendental. See **obscure,** *a.*

occupation. Syn.: occupancy, possession, incumbency, tenure; employment, business, pursuit, office, calling, vocation, profession, trade, craft, work, job, avocation, hobby.

An *occupation* is the activity to which one regularly devotes oneself, especially one's regular work or means of earning a living. *Business* especially suggests a commercial or mercantile occupation; a *trade*, an occupation involving manual training and skill; a *craft*, a trade demanding delicate skill and fine workmanship. *Profession* implies an occupation requiring special knowledge and training in some field of science or learning. *Calling* and *vocation*, somewhat elevated terms, suggest that one is summoned by natural endowment, Providence, or an inward conviction of duty, to follow a particular kind of work. *Pursuit* is applied to the occupation one pursues or follows.

occupy. Syn.: hold, possess, have, fill, use; engage, employ, busy, absorb, engross, monopolize. See **have.**

occur. Syn.: happen, befall. See **happen.**

occurrence. Syn.: see **event.**

ocean. Syn.: see **sea.**

odd. Syn.: uneven, unmatched, unmated, remaining, additional, single, sole; incidental, occasional, casual singular, unique, anomalous, unusual, uncommon, peculiar, strange, queer, quaint, droll, bizarre, grotesque, freakish, eccentric, abnormal, nondescript. See **singular.**

oddity. Syn.: singularity, peculiarity, strangeness; curiosity, freak, wonder, marvel.

odious. Syn.: hateful, detestable, abominable, obnoxious, loathsome, repulsive, disgusting, abhorrent, repellent, offensive, disagreeable, objectionable, unpleasant.

That which is *odious* excites hatred, disgust, or repugnance; the *obnoxious* is highly distasteful or distressing. *Offensive* is especially used of that which is disgusting to the senses, or is morally repulsive. *Objectionable*, a weaker word, is applied to whatever seriously merits disapproval.

odium. Syn.: hatred, detestation, dislike; reproach, opprobrium, obloquy, disgrace, shame, infamy, ignominy, disfavor.

Odium implies general hatred or blame brought upon one by base or culpable action or behavior; *opprobrium*, the reproach or discredit which is a natural consequence of dishonorable conduct; *obloquy*, shame or disgrace associated with public condemnation.

odor. Syn.: smell, scent, fragrance, aroma, redolence, perfume, savor, stench, stink, fetor; repute, esteem, estimation. See **smell.**

odorous. Syn.: odoriferous, fragrant, aromatic, redolent, balmy, perfumed, sweet-scented.

offal. Syn.: see **refuse,** *n.*

offend. Syn.: displease, provoke, vex, annoy, irritate exasperate, affront, insult, wound.

offender. Syn.: see **malefactor.**

offense. Syn.: offending, displeasing, affront, insult; displeasure, resentment, umbrage; misdeed, misdemeanor, trespass, transgression, crime, felony, sin, iniquity, delinquency, peccadillo.

Offense is a very indefinite word for any kind of transgression of what is held to be lawful, right, or for the general good. *Misdemeanor*, *felony*, and *crime*, are used of legal offenses; *sin*, *transgression*, *trespass*, and *iniquity*, of offenses against the moral law. *Misdeed* is applied to any wrong or reprehensible action; *delinquency*, to failure to comply with the demands of law or duty; *peccadillo*, to a trifling or venial offense.

offensive. Syn.: aggressive, attacking, assailing, rude, insolent, insulting; displeasing, disagreeable, distasteful, annoying, disgusting, repulsive, obnoxious, noisome, foul. See **odious.**

offer, *n.* **Syn.:** proffer, tender, overture, proposal, proposition, bid; attempt, endeavor, essay, pretense, show.

offer, *v.* **Syn.:** present, proffer, tender, volunteer, propose, suggest, bid; sacrifice, immolate; attempt, endeavor, try.

Offer is a common word in general use for the presenting of something for acceptance or rejection. *Proffer*, with the same meaning, is now chiefly a literary word. *Tender* is a ceremonious term for a more or less formal or conventional act: as, to *tender* one's resignation; to *tender* one's sympathy or thanks.

offhand. Syn.: unpremeditated, unstudied, improvised, impromptu, extempore, extemporaneous; unceremonious, curt.

office. **Syn.:** service, duty, charge, function; post, place, position, situation.

officious. **Syn.:** busy, meddlesome, meddling, interfering, intrusive, pragmatical, impertinent. See **meddlesome.**

offset. **Syn.:** see **balance.**

offspring. **Syn.:** progeny, issue, descendant, descendants, children, posterity.

Offspring is applied to the young of either man or beast, and usually to the first generation of descendants. *Issue* is almost always a legal or genealogical term, relating to the child or children (usually) of one who has died. *Progeny* applies to one or more generations of descendants; *posterity* usually suggests all future generations.

often. **Syn.:** frequently, repeatedly, commonly, usually, generally.

Often and *frequently* are in most cases used without distinction of meaning, but *often* implies numerous repetitions and, sometimes, regularity of occurrence, *frequently* especially suggests repetition at comparatively short intervals. *Commonly* is applied to what is characteristic of everyday experience, or is prevalent among the majority of people. *Usually* implies occurrence much more often than not. *Generally* suggests a range extending from the merely numerous to the majority of possible instances.

oily. **Syn.:** oleaginous, unctuous, greasy, fat; smooth, bland, suave, glib, tricky, sly.

ointment. **Syn.:** unguent, salve, balm, balsam.

old. **Syn.:** aged, elderly, patriarchal, venerable, veteran, hoary; experienced, practiced, wise, sagacious; feeble, effete, senescent, senile, decrepit, superannuated; dilapidated, shabby, decayed, outworn, disused; long-established, time-honored, familiar, known, traditional, immemorial; ancient, antique, old-fashioned, antiquated, obsolete, archaic; olden, past, early, former, preceding, primitive, primeval, pristine. **Ant.:** see **young, new.**

The person who is *old* has lived for a long time, and has nearly completed the usual period of life; the *elderly* person is somewhat old or is beginning to be old, but usually has the mellowness, satisfactions, and joys of age before him; the *aged* person is very far advanced in years, and usually endures the decay, infirmities, or decrepitude of age.

older. **Syn.:** elder, senior.

Older is the usual form of the comparative of old; *elder*, now greatly restricted in application, is used to indicate priority of birth as between any two people but especially children born of the same parents.

old-fashioned. **Syn.:** see **ancient.**

omen. **Syn.:** augury, portent, auspice, presage, prognostic, foretoken, sign. See **sign.**

ominous. **Syn.:** portentous, inauspicious, threatening, menacing, foreboding, sinister.

omit. **Syn.:** neglect, overlook, miss, ignore, skip, leave out, cancel, delete.

omnipresent. **Syn.:** ubiquitous.

Omnipresent emphasizes the fact of being everywhere present, as though all-enveloping; *ubiquitous*, the fact of appearing in many and all sorts of places.

on. **Syn.:** see **over.**

onerous. **Syn.:** burdensome, oppressive, heavy, weighty, arduous, toilsome, laborious. See **heavy.**

onlooker. **Syn.:** see **spectator.**

only. **Syn.:** see **single.**

onset. **Syn.:** onrush, onslaught, assault, attack, charge; beginning, commencement, start.

onward. **Syn.:** forward.

Onward applies to any movement in continuance of a course; *forward*, to movement toward what is or is conceived to be the front or the goal.

ooze. **Syn.:** exude, percolate, filter, seep, leak, drip.

open, *a.* **Syn.:** unclosed, ajar, uncovered, unsealed, unstopped, unlocked; unprotected, exposed, accessible; unoccupied, unemployed, disengaged, available, free; undecided, unsettled, debatable; liable, subject; frank, candid, plain, overt, unreserved, public; expanded, spread, extended, unfolded, parted, gaping, yawning; liberal, generous, bounteous; perforated, porous; clear, passable.

open, *v.* **Syn.:** unclose, uncover, unseal, unstop, unfasten, unlock, unroll, unfold; disclose, reveal, expose, divulge; spread, expand, extend; start, begin, commence, initiate. **Ant.:** see **close.**

open-handed. **Syn.:** see **generous.**

opening. **Syn.:** start, beginning, commencement, introduction; hole, orifice, aperture, gap, fissure, rift, breach, chasm; vacancy, opportunity.

operate. **Syn.:** work, act, perform; manage, conduct.

opiate. **Syn.:** see **narcotic.**

opine. **Syn.:** see **think.**

opinion. **Syn.:** view, belief, idea, notion, impression, sentiment; judgment, decision, verdict, sentence.

opinionated. **Syn.:** see **obstinate.**

opponent. **Syn.:** opposer, antagonist, enemy, foe, adversary, competitor, rival.

An *opponent* is a person or group that constitutes an opposing force in any contest. An *antagonist* is an active and often formidable opponent. An *adversary* is a person or group hostile in purpose or feeling. An *enemy* may be either one who harbors personal hatred and active desire to injure, or one who is a member of an opposing party or army without a feeling of personal animosity, or, collectively, the opposing party or army itself. *Foe*, a literary word, is synonymous with enemy, but often implies a more hostile spirit.

opportune. **Syn.:** see **timely.**

opportunity. **Syn.:** occasion, chance, opening.

oppose. **Syn.:** confront, withstand, resist, obstruct, hinder, contravene, thwart, combat, counter, defy, contradict, gainsay. **Ant.:** agree, concur, acquiesce, assist, help.

Oppose implies the setting of a conscious, active force against something: as, to *oppose* the passage of a law. *Resist* implies unyielding endurance of or active striving against opposing force: as, to *resist* pressure, an attack, temptation. *Withstand* generally implies successful resistance: as, to *withstand* a blow, a shock, importunities.

opposite. **Syn.:** opposed, reverse, converse, inverse, adverse, contrary, antipodal, antithetic, conflicting, contradictory, inconsistent, incompatible.

Opposite suggests symmetrical antithesis in position, action, or character: as, *opposite* ends of a pole or sides of a road; expansion is the *opposite* of contraction; *opposite* natures. *Contrary* sometimes adds to opposite the idea of conflict or antagonism: as, *contrary* winds or statements. *Reverse* suggests that which faces or moves in the opposite direction: as, the *reverse* side of a coin, a *reverse* gear; a *reverse* decision.

oppress. **Syn.:** weigh down, burden, overburden, crush, subdue, tyrannize over, persecute.

oppression. **Syn.:** tyranny, despotism, persecution; depression, weariness, lassitude.

oppressor. **Syn.:** see **tyrant.**

opprobrious. **Syn.:** see **abusive.**

opprobrium. **Syn.:** disgrace, infamy, odium, reproach, contumely, obloquy. See **odium.**

optic. **Syn.:** optical.

optimistic. **Syn.:** see **hopeful.**

option. **Syn.:** choice, preference, election, alternative, discretion, privilege. See **choice,** *n.*

opulence. **Syn.:** see **riches.**

opulent. **Syn.:** wealthy, rich, affluent; plentiful, abundant, luxuriant, profuse.

oral. **Syn.:** spoken, nuncupative, verbal, vocal.

Oral is properly applied to that which is uttered by word of mouth, as opposed to what is conveyed in writing: as, an *oral* message, recitation, tradition. *Verbal* is often used for oral: as, a *verbal* agreement. Literally, however, *verbal* applies to the words, spoken or written, in which thought or feeling is conveyed: as, a *verbal* picture; *verbal* nicety or criticism.

oration. **Syn.:** see **speech.**

oratory. **Syn.:** elocution, eloquence, rhetoric.

Oratory is the act or the art of making a finished and effective address; *rhetoric*, the theory of the art of composing effective discourse in either spoken or written form. *Elocution* refers to the mode of delivery employed to please and impress an audience, and includes clear and distinct pronunciation, correct inflection, agreeable intonation of the voice, and sometimes appropriate gesture; *eloquence*, to the use of the highest powers of speech, especially to move the feelings or the will.

orb. **Syn.:** see **globe.**

ordain. **Syn.:** decree, order, prescribe, institute, establish, enact, destine, predestine.

ordeal. **Syn.:** trial, test.

order, *n.* **Syn.:** row, line, series; grade, class, degree, rank;

arrangement, system, method; sequence, succession; direction, injunction, command, mandate, decree, regulation.

order, *v.* **Syn.:** arrange, array, regulate, methodize, systematize; direct, enjoin, instruct, command, bid. See **direct,** *v.*

orderly. Syn.: regular, well-regulated, methodical, systematic; peaceable, quiet, harmonious, obedient, well-behaved, law-abiding.

Orderly, methodical, and *systematic* are sometimes used interchangeably, but *orderly* implies neatness of arrangement, *methodical* suggests a logical plan, *systematic* a more extensive and elaborate plan.

ordinance. Syn.: see **law.**

ordinary. Syn.: regular, normal, customary, usual, wonted, habitual; common, commonplace, indifferent, mediocre, inferior, cheap. **Ant.:** see **extraordinary.**

organic. Syn.: innate, inherent, constitutional, structural, fundamental, essential, vital, radical; organized, systematized, systematic.

organize. Syn.: form, arrange, systematize.

orgy. Syn.: see **carousal.**

orifice. Syn.: see **hole.**

origin. Syn.: birth, parentage, ancestry; source, root, beginning, inception, rise, cause, occasion.

original. Syn.: first, primal, initial, pristine, primeval, aboriginal, indigenous, native; novel, new, fresh, striking; inventive, creative, ingenious.

ornament, *n.* **Syn.:** adornment, decoration, embellishment.

ornament, *v.* **Syn.:** see **adorn.**

ornate. Syn.: adorned, ornamented, decorated, embellished, elaborate, florid, flowery.

orthodox. Syn.: conventional, approved, sanctioned, accepted, customary. **Ant.:** heterodox.

oscillate. Syn.: see **fluctuate, swing.**

oscillation. Syn.: see **vibration.**

ostensible. Syn.: apparent, professed, specious, colorable. Cf. **plausible.**

ostentation. Syn.: show, display, parade, pomp, flourish, bravado. **Ant.:** modesty, reserve, retiringness, simplicity. See **show,** *n.*

ostentatious. Syn.: showy, spectacular, pretentious, pompous, flaunting, gaudy.

Ostentatious implies a desire or attempt to make a show or attract public notice; *pretentious,* an endeavor to make others believe our possessions, endowments, etc. are greater than they are; *spectacular,* a striking or sensational display suggestive of a public spectacle.

ostracize. Syn.: see **banish.**

ought. Syn.: see **must.**

oust. Syn.: eject, evict, expel, dislodge, displace, dispossess, depose, remove, dismiss. See **expel.**

outbreak. Syn.: outburst, eruption, uprising, insurrection, riot.

outcast, *n.* **Syn.:** exile, castaway, tramp, vagabond, reprobate, pariah.

outcast, *a.* **Syn.:** expelled, rejected, forsaken, forlorn, miserable.

outcome. Syn.: issue, result, upshot, consequence.

outcry. Syn.: shout, scream, clamor, uproar, noise.

outdo. Syn.: surpass, excel, exceed, outdistance, outstrip, overmatch, overcome.

outer. Syn.: outward, outside, exterior, external, superficial, surface.

The following words exhibit minor differences, but the distinctions are largely a matter of usage. *Outer* (opposed to inner), applicable strictly to what is further without, is also used at times of what is without, or outside a place, area, thing, the body, the mind, etc.: as, the *outer* chamber, garments, influences. *Outward* (opposed to inward), toward the outside, is often used of what exists or goes on outside a person or thing, or outside of the mind or soul, and sometimes denotes the apparent or visible: as, *outward* appearance or display; *outward* pretense of friendship. *Exterior* (opposed to interior) is applied especially to what is situated without or belongs to the outside of a thing: as, an *exterior* scaffolding; *exterior* decoration. *External* (opposed to internal) is likewise used of what is situated or exists on the outside, and pertains to the outer parts, nature, relations, etc.: as, *external* injuries, application. *Superficial* applies to what is on the surface or outside, or does not go beneath the surface: as, *superficial* color or resemblance; a *superficial* investigation.

outgrowth. Syn.: offshoot, process, excrescence; outcome, development, result.

outlandish. Syn.: foreign, unfamiliar, strange, odd, uncouth, bizarre, barbarous.

outlaw. Syn.: bandit, brigand, highwayman, robber, marauder, desperado, freebooter, pirate, buccaneer, criminal, fugitive.

outlet. Syn.: opening, orifice, mouth, vent, exit, passage.

outline. Syn.: contour, profile, delineation, sketch, brief, draft, scenario.

Outline refers to the line which bounds or defines a figure; *contour,* to the form of a body or mass as it is determined by its outline or surface; *profile,* especially to the boundary of the face or figure when seen directly from the side.

outlive. Syn.: survive, outlast.

While *outlive* and *survive* are frequently interchanged, the former means to continue to live after another has died or after a given period or point of time; the latter, besides expressing the same idea more gently, is also used of living beyond an occasion or forces antagonistic or destructive to life: as, he *outlived* his children; to *outlive* one's usefulness; to *survive* one's wife or friend; to *survive* an accident or operation.

outlook. Syn.: lookout, watch; view, prospect, vista, scene.

outlying. Syn.: external, distant, remote, isolated, frontier.

outrage. Syn.: injury, insult, affront, indignity, assault, ravishment.

outrageous. Syn.: excessive, immoderate, unrestrained, violent, monstrous, flagrant, atrocious, heinous, nefarious, villainous, wicked.

outside, *n.* **Syn.:** exterior, surface, superficies.

outside, *a.* **Syn.:** see **outer.**

outskirts. Syn.: border, edge, suburb, purlieu, frontier.

outspoken. Syn.: candid, frank, unreserved, blunt, ingenuous. See **frank.**

outstrip. Syn.: see **outdo.**

outward. Syn.: see **outer.**

outwit. Syn.: circumvent, outgeneral, overreach, foil, frustrate, balk. See **overreach.**

over. Syn.: above, on, upon. **Ant.:** under, below, beneath.

Over denotes more or less vertical superiority in space or that one body more or less completely envelops another: as, to hold an umbrella *over* one; to wear an apron *over* one's dress. That which is *above* is at a greater height or elevation, and need not be in a perpendicular line or near: as, mountain peaks are often *above* the clouds. *On* and *upon* denote that one object or surface is superimposed on another: as, to put wall-paper *on* (*upon*) a ceiling; to hang a coat *on* (*upon*) a hook. The older distinction by which *upon* emphasized motion and *on* rest has practically disappeared in modern use. The two words are now interchangeable except for the demands of emphasis and euphony.

overawe. Syn.: intimidate, cow, daunt.

overbearing. Syn.: domineering, dictatorial, magisterial, imperious, lordly, haughty, arrogant, insolent, overweening, supercilious. **Ant.:** meek, humble, lowly, retiring.

overcome. Syn.: overpower, overwhelm, conquer, vanquish, subdue, master. See **conquer.**

overdo. Syn.: overact, exaggerate; overwork, overtask, overtax, fatigue, exhaust.

overeat. Syn.: surfeit, satiate, glut, gorge.

overestimate. Syn.: see **overvalue.**

overfeed. Syn.: surfeit, gorge, glut, stuff, overload.

overflow, *n.* **Syn.:** inundation, flood, deluge; superfluity, superabundance, excess, profusion, exuberance.

overflow, *v.* **Syn.:** inundate, flood, deluge, overrun.

overlay. Syn.: see **cover.**

overlook. Syn.: overtop, dominate, command; oversee, superintend; inspect, examine, overhaul; disregard, ignore, skip, miss, pass, slight, neglect; excuse, condone, forgive.

overnice. Syn.: fastidious, dainty, finical, squeamish.

overplus. Syn.: see **surplus.**

overpower. Syn.: overcome, subdue, master, defeat, conquer, vanquish, overthrow, overwhelm, crush, subjugate.

overprize. Syn.: see **overvalue.**

overreach. Syn.: outwit, circumvent, dupe, cozen, gull, cheat, defraud, swindle, bamboozle.

To *circumvent* is to get the better of another, not necessarily by unfair means; *outwit,* to do so by superior cleverness, ingenuity, or cunning; *overreach,* by trickery and sharp practice.

overrule. Syn.: disallow, reject, override, annul, abrogate.

overrun. Syn.: overflow, overspread; invade, infest, ravage.

oversee. Syn.: supervise, superintend, examine, inspect.

overseer. Syn.: supervisor, superintendent, foreman, taskmaster, inspector.

oversight. Syn.: inspection, supervision, superintendence, management, direction, care, charge, control; overlooking, inadvertence, omission, error, mistake, blunder, slip. See **error.**

overt. Syn.: plain, manifest, apparent, patent, open, public.

overthrow, *n.* **Syn.:** overturn, subversion, defeat, rout, wreck, demolition, destruction.

overthrow, *v.* **Syn.:** overturn, upset, subvert, overcome, overpower, overwhelm, vanquish, rout, crush, ruin, demolish, prostrate.

overtop. Syn.: overlook, overshadow, transcend, surpass, excel, outstrip.

overture. Syn.: see **proposal, prelude.**

overturn. Syn.: overthrow, upset, capsize, invert, subvert, destroy, ruin, overwhelm.

Overturn usually suggests violence in bringing from a standing or erect position, or any condition of stability, to a prostrate or demoralized one: as, the earthquake *overturned* the houses; to *overturn* a government. *Upset* is more familiar, and is applied to simple, everyday actions: as, to *upset* a table, a basket, or a glass of water. *Capsize* is applied especially to the overturning or upsetting of a boat or vessel: as, to *capsize* a canoe.

overvalue. Syn.: overprize, overestimate, overrate.

overweening. Syn.: see **overbearing.**

overwhelm. Syn.: see **defeat.**

overwork. Syn.: overtask, overtax, overburden, exhaust, fatigue, overdo.

own. Syn.: possess, have, hold; admit, concede, grant, confess. See **have, acknowledge.**

P

pabulum. Syn.: see **food.**

pace. Syn.: step, gait, amble, rack, trot, canter, gallop.

pacific. Syn.: peaceful, peaceable, conciliatory, appeasing, mild, gentle, quiet, calm, still, tranquil, serene, smooth, unruffled, undisturbed, placid.

That which is *pacific* tends toward the making or preserving of peace; that which is *peaceable* desires to be at peace or is free from the disposition to quarrel; that which is *peaceful* is in a state of peace: as, a *pacific* agreement; *peaceable* citizens; a *peaceful* atmosphere.

pacify. Syn.: pacificate, placate, conciliate, propitiate, appease, mollify, tranquilize, quiet, calm, still, soothe. See **appease.**

To *placate* is to pacify and so to remove anger, resentment, or unfriendly feeling; to *propitiate* is to forestall opposition and gain the favor of one who is or may be opposed; to *conciliate* is to seek, especially by concession or compromise, to avoid opposition or to satisfy one who is opposed.

pack, *n.* **Syn.:** bundle, bale; set, lot, company, gang, crew; flock, herd. See **flock.**

pack, *v.* **Syn.:** bundle, roll, truss; press, crowd, cram, stow; fill, load.

package. Syn.: bundle, parcel, packet, truss, pack, bale. See **bundle.**

pact. Syn.: see **compact.**

pad. Syn.: see **cushion.**

pagan. Syn.: heathen, barbarian, gentile.

Pagan and *heathen* are both used to designate peoples who are not Christian, Jewish, or Mahommedan, but *pagan* is often distinctively applied to those nations that, although worshiping false gods, are more cultivated, as the Greeks or Romans, and *heathen*, to unenlightened or barbaric idolaters, as the tribes of Africa.

pageant. Syn.: see **drama.**

pain, *n.* **Syn.:** punishment, penalty; ache, pang, stitch, crick, twinge, smart, cramp, gripe, throe, paroxysm; suffering, distress, torture, misery, grief, anguish, agony, heartache. **Ant.:** ease, comfort, solace, relief.

Pain is the general term for bodily or mental suffering. *Anguish* denotes excruciating or crushing pain, especially of the mind; *agony* implies such extreme bodily pain as to cause struggling; *torture* is by derivation pain that seems to rack or

wrench the body, and often suggests suffering cruelly imposed.

pain, *v.* **Syn.:** hurt, afflict, rack, excruciate, distress, torture, torment, grieve, agonize.

painful. Syn.: afflictive, racking, severe, excruciating, distressing, torturing, agonizing.

painstaking. Syn.: careful, particular, scrupulous, precise.

paint. Syn.: picture, sketch, draw, delineate, depict, portray, describe; color, stain, decorate, ornament, adorn.

pair. Syn.: two, couple, brace, span, yoke.

Pair is used of two things naturally or habitually associated together, mated, or making a set, often necessary to each other for completeness or use: as, a *pair* of gloves, shoes, or oars. It is more loosely used of any two similar things that are put together, or of one thing composed of two similar and complementary parts: as, a *pair* of jacks; a *pair* of scissors, trousers, or spectacles. In *couple* the idea of combination or interdependence is much less marked, and it may be used loosely for two of anything: as, a *couple* of apples. *Brace* is peculiarly a hunter's term, used of a pair of dogs, partridges, ducks, etc., or a pair of pistols or slugs. *Yoke* applies to two animals hitched together for pulling: as, a *yoke* of oxen. *Span* is especially used of a pair of horses driven together.

palace. Syn.: see **castle.**

palaver. Syn.: parley, conference, debate, talk; flattery, cajolery.

pale. Syn.: pallid, wan, colorless, white, whitish, blanched, ashy, ashen, ghastly, cadaverous; dim, faint, indistinct. **Ant.:** ruddy, rosy, flushed, healthy.

Pale implies a faintness or absence of color, which may be natural (as, the *pale* blue of a violet) or, as applied to the human countenance, unnatural and often temporary as arising from sickness or sudden emotion: as, *pale* cheeks; he turned *pale*. *Pallid* and *wan* describe a more permanent lack of color in the face, suggesting a more lasting derangement, and, in the case of *wan*, general lassitude.

pall. Syn.: see **satiate.**

palliate. Syn.: extenuate, mitigate, moderate, lighten, alleviate, lessen, diminish, reduce, excuse, gloss.

To *extenuate* (literally to draw out to thinness or fineness) and *palliate* (to cover as with a cloak) both refer to the effort to make an offense seem less serious by bringing forward considerations tending to excuse it; neither implies an effort to exonerate or exculpate completely. *Palliate* is more likely to be used of a serious offense, and attempts to lessen its gravity; *extenuate* offers in excuse whatever may subtract from the guilt of the offender.

pallid. Syn.: see **pale.**

palpable. Syn.: tangible, perceptible, plain, evident, manifest, obvious, unmistakable. See **manifest.**

palpitate. Syn.: see **throb.**

paltry. Syn.: trashy, worthless, trifling, insignificant, petty, trivial, mean, contemptible. See **trifling.**

pamper. Syn.: indulge, gratify, humor, spoil, cocker, coddle.

pamphlet. Syn.: booklet, brochure, tract.

panacea. Syn.: cure-all, heal-all, catholicon, remedy, solace. See **remedy.**

panegyric. Syn.: see **praise, eulogy.**

pang. Syn.: see **pain,** *n.*

panic. Syn.: see **alarm, fear.**

panic-stricken. Syn.: alarmed, terrified, dismayed, appalled.

pant. Syn.: gasp, puff, blow; long, yearn, thirst, hunger, sigh, crave.

Pant suggests quick, hard breathing, as from violent exertion or excitement; *gasp*, difficult, spasmodic breathing, as from exhaustion or amazement.

pantaloons. Syn.: see **trousers.**

pantry. Syn.: cupboard, larder, buttery.

papal. Syn.: pontifical, popish.

paper. Syn.: essay, article, dissertation; newspaper, journal, periodical, gazette.

parable. Syn.: allegory, fable.

parade, *n.* **Syn.:** show, display, ostentation, pomp; procession, pageant, cavalcade. See **show,** *n.*

parade, *v.* **Syn.:** show off, display, flaunt; march, promenade.

paradise. Syn.: see **heaven.**

paradoxical. Syn.: see **contradictory.**

paragon. Syn.: see **model, example.**

parallel. Syn.: equidistant, corresponding, analogous, correlative, similar, like.

paralyze. Syn.: benumb, deaden, prostrate, stun, stupefy, dumfound, unnerve. See **startle.**

paraphrase. Syn.: restatement, version, translation.

parasite. Syn.: satellite, hanger-on, sycophant, toady. Cf. **hanger-on.**

Parasite, always a term of opprobrium or contempt, describes one who gets a maintenance or a more comfortable maintenance by living upon one who is richer. *Hanger-on* is a familiar or disparaging term for one who follows after or frequents the company of another or others, usually for some advantage he hopes to gain. *Satellite* usually has the derogatory implication of subserviency or obsequiousness on the part of one who attends upon a person of importance, often with no other gain to himself than the gratification of his vanity at being associated with the great. *Sycophant* denotes one who ingratiates himself with the wealthy or powerful, usually by means of servility or flattery, to gain their favor or influence.

parcel. Syn.: see **bundle.**

parch. Syn.: see **scorch.**

parched. Syn.: see **dry.**

pardon, *n.* **Syn.:** forgiveness, absolution, remission, amnesty.

pardon, *v.* **Syn.:** forgive, excuse, absolve, acquit, exculpate, condone, overlook. **Ant.:** convict, condemn, sentence, punish.

Pardon usually expresses a specific act of lenity, kindness, or mercy by an official or superior in remitting all or the remainder of the punishment that belongs to a (usually) serious offense or crime. *Excuse* means to overlook some (usually) slight offense, error, neglect, or breach of etiquette, because of circumstances or personal leniency; the word sometimes expresses no more than a declination, as when one replies to an invitation to go for a walk, "You must *excuse* me this time." *Pardon* is also conventionally used in social intercourse in much the same way as *excuse:* as, "*Pardon* (or *excuse*) me, but I did not understand." *Forgive* implies that the one who has been wronged or offended not only overlooks the offense but harbors no ill feeling against the offender.

pardonable. Syn.: forgivable, excusable, venial. **Ant.:** see **unpardonable.**

Pardonable and *excusable* may both be applied to faults not calling for serious censure. In graver offenses *excusable* suggests mitigating circumstances, *pardonable,* leniency in judgment. *Venial* in Roman Catholic theology describes those sins that are not deadly or mortal, and in general use is applied to transgressions of minor importance.

pare. Syn.: peel, strip, skin, flay, bark, decorticate, shave.

Pare is used of trimming off chips, flakes, or superficial parts from something, or of cutting off the skin or rind of something; *peel* is used of cutting off (in which sense it agrees with *pare*) or of stripping or pulling off (in which sense *pare* is not used) the natural external covering or protection of something: as, to *pare* (not *peel*) the nails or a horse's hoofs; to *pare* or *peel* an apple or potato; to *peel* (not *pare*) an orange or the bark from a tree.

parentage. Syn.: see **ancestry.**

pariah. Syn.: see **wretch.**

park. Syn.: see **forest.**

parody. Syn.: see **burlesque.**

paroxysm. Syn.: convulsion, spasm, fit.

parry. Syn.: ward off, avert, evade, elude, avoid, prevent, stop. See **ward.**

parsimonious. Syn.: sparing, frugal, stinting, stingy, close, close-fisted, penurious, niggardly, miserly. **Ant.:** generous, liberal, free, lavish, munificent.

parsimony. Syn.: sparingness, frugality, economy, stinginess, penuriousness. See **economy.**

parson. Syn.: see **clergyman.**

parsonage. Syn.: rectory, manse.

part, *n.* **Syn.:** portion, share, moiety, allotment, lot, piece, section, division, fraction, fragment, bit, segment, instalment, component, constituent; member, organ; rôle, character; region, quarter, district, place.

Part is the general word for that which is less than the whole. *Portion* is especially the part of anything allotted or assigned to a person, purpose, etc. *Piece* is a part taken from a whole, or an independent unit of well-defined and often standardized form: as, a *piece* of bread; a *piece* of music. A *fragment* is a part broken from a whole or a part of an unfinished whole; a *bit* is an exceedingly small part of something.

part, *v.* **Syn.:** divide, sever, dissever, separate, sunder, disunite, disconnect, disjoin, detach, dismember; apportion, allot, distribute. See **separate,** *v.*

partake. Syn.: participate, share.

To *partake* is to take a part of or possess the qualities of something: as, to *partake* of food; to *partake* of the nature of one's ancestors. To *participate* is especially to enter into some thought, feeling, or action, or to have a part of something: as, to *participate* in a race; to *participate* in the general prosperity. To *share* is to give or receive a part of something, or to enjoy or assume something in common: as, to *share* one's possessions, to *share* another's hospitality, to *share* a room or an obligation.

partaker. Syn.: participator, participant, sharer.

partial. Syn.: incomplete, imperfect, component; biased, prejudiced, warped, one-sided, unfair, unjust.

partiality. Syn.: bias, favoritism, unfairness; preference, predilection, leaning, bent, liking, fondness.

participate. Syn.: see **partake.**

particle. Syn.: atom, molecule, corpuscle, monad, bit, mite, speck, whit, iota, jot, tittle, scintilla, grain, shred, crumb, morsel, bite, scrap.

particular. Syn.: special, individual, specific, characteristic, peculiar, distinctive; singular, unusual, striking, noteworthy; specific, minute, detailed, circumstantial; careful, precise, strict, exact, nice, fastidious, dainty, finical, squeamish. See **minute.**

Particular, in the sense here discriminated, implies care and attention to details; *dainty* and *nice* imply delicate discrimination or taste; *fastidious* implies a tendency towards proud or haughty objection to or rejection of things because of displeasure at small or minor points; *finical,* overnice or extreme fastidiousness; *squeamish* suggests excessive sensibility to what is unpleasant, often resulting in disgust, and generally is applied to a specific thing.

particularly. Syn.: see **especially.**

parting, *n.* **Syn.:** division, separation; leave-taking, departure, farewell.

parting, *a.* **Syn.:** dividing, separating; departing, farewell, valedictory, final.

partition. Syn.: division, apportionment, allotment, distribution.

partizan. Syn.: see **follower.**

partner. Syn.: sharer, partaker, associate, colleague, ally, accessory, confederate, accomplice. See **associate.**

parts. Syn.: see **genius.**

party. Syn.: faction, ring, clique, cabal, junto, coterie, set, circle; company, detachment, squad, band; accessory, participant, participator; reception, soirée, levee, entertainment, assembly, function. See **company.**

A *party* is a more or less permanent organization of individuals formed to promote certain principles or common interests which they consider of fundamental importance. A *faction* is a subdivision of a larger group, whose ends are often selfish or mischievous and pursued so persistently as not to be disregarded. A *cabal* is a small group of persons who intrigue usually for their own personal aggrandizement. *Junto,* once current in the sense of cabal, now suggests more often a self-appointed group or committee formed (especially) for political purposes.

pasquinade. Syn.: see **satire.**

pass, *n.* **Syn.:** thrust, lunge; state, condition, situation, predicament, plight; permit, ticket, passport; passage, passageway, defile.

pass, *v.* **Syn.:** go, move, proceed, advance; elapse, lapse; depart, recede, disappear, vanish; happen, occur; spend, while away, waste; surpass, exceed, excel, transcend, overstep; transfer, transmit, convey, deliver; enact, ratify, sanction, approve; undergo, experience; disregard, overlook, ignore, skip, omit.

passable. Syn.: traversable, navigable, penetrable; acceptable, admissible, tolerable, mediocre, middling, ordinary, fair, so-so.

passage. Syn.: passing, movement, transit, transition, lapse, progress, journey, voyage; enactment, adoption; way, course, avenue, street, alley, lane, path, track, pass, defile, hall, lobby, vestibule, corridor, gangway; verse, sentence, paragraph, section, chapter.

passing, *n.* **Syn.:** see **death.**

passing, *a.* **Syn.:** current, cursory, momentary, transient, transitory, fleeting.

passion. Syn.: suffering, pain, agony; emotion, feeling, anger, rage, wrath, fury, hatred, joy, rapture, transport, love, affection, infatuation, craze, mania. See **feeling,** *n.*

passionate. Syn.: hot-headed, hot, fiery, quick-tempered, irascible, choleric; ardent, fervent, fervid, impassioned, vehement.

passionless. Syn.: dispassionate, unemotional, calm, impassive, phlegmatic, apathetic, stoical.

passive. Syn.: inactive, inert, relaxed, quiet, impassive; receptive, unresisting, submissive, long-suffering, patient.

past. Syn.: bygone, elapsed, preceding, foregoing, earlier.

pastime. Syn.: amusement, diversion, entertainment, recreation, sport, play, fun.

A *pastime* is a means of pleasantly or agreeably passing time. An *amusement* is something that gives pleasure to the mind, often in the form of humorous relaxation. A *diversion* is something that turns one away from serious work or ordinary routine to pleasing or lively entertainment. A *recreation* is that sort of play or agreeable occupation which refreshes a tired person and renews his energies.

pastor. Syn.: see **clergyman.**

pastoral. Syn.: see **rural.**

patch. Syn.: mend, repair, vamp, sew.

patent. Syn.: open, expanded; manifest, plain, obvious, evident, apparent, palpable, public, protected. See **manifest.**

paternal. Syn.: see **fatherly.**

path. Syn.: footway, runway, track, trail, walk, way, course, route, lane, tow-path. See **way.**

pathetic. Syn.: pitiable, piteous, moving, touching, affecting, mournful, plaintive, sad.

pathless. Syn.: trackless, untrodden, unexplored.

patience. Syn.: endurance, long-suffering, forbearance, fortitude, resignation, calmness, composure.

Patience may denote calm, self-possessed, and unrepining bearing of pain, misfortune, annoyance, or delay, or painstaking and untiring industry or application in the doing of something. *Endurance* denotes the ability to bear labor, hardship, or suffering, without implication of the moral qualities required or shown. *Fortitude* implies patient courage in the midst of pain, affliction, or hardship.

patient. Syn.: uncomplaining, long-suffering, forbearing, resigned. **Ant.:** see **impatient.**

patrimony. Syn.: see **inheritance.**

patron. Syn.: protector, guardian, defender, supporter, benefactor.

pattern. Syn.: original, model, design, prototype, archetype, exemplar, ideal. See **example.**

pauper. Syn.: see **beggar.**

pauperism. Syn.: see **poverty.**

pause, *n.* **Syn.:** stop, cessation, interruption, intermission, suspension, break, rest, delay, hesitation.

pause, *v.* **Syn.:** stop, desist, intermit, stay, wait, delay, hesitate, linger, tarry. See **cease.**

pawn. Syn.: see **pledge,** *n.,* **earnest,** *n.*

pay, *n.* **Syn.:** compensation, payment, remuneration, recompense, salary, wages, hire, emolument, stipend, fee, honorarium, allowance, reward, gratuity, tip, perquisite, bonus.

Pay is the general word for compensation given in return for work done or services rendered. *Hire,* except in Biblical or archaic use, now generally has a mercenary association. *Wages* is the word used for pay for manual or mechanical work, and usually implies employment for and payment at short periods, as by the day or week. *Salary* is usually pay for mental or professional work, and implies greater permanence of employment than wages, and payment at longer intervals. *Stipend* is used of the fixed allowance or salary of a clergyman, scientific investigator, or the like. *Honorarium* is especially a sum given for professional services.

pay, *v.* **Syn.:** compensate, remunerate, recompense, requite, reward, fee, reimburse, indemnify; settle, defray, discharge, liquidate, satisfy.

payable. Syn.: due, owing, unpaid, outstanding.

payment. Syn.: compensation, remuneration, recompense, requital, reward, settlement, discharge, liquidation, reparation, amends.

peace. Syn.: concord, harmony, amity; reconciliation, armistice, truce; tranquillity, calmness, quietness, serenity, rest, repose. See **rest.**

peaceable. Syn.: amicable, friendly, mild, quiet. **Ant.:** bellicose, belligerent, quarrelsome, contentious, pugnacious. See **pacific.**

peaceful. Syn.: pacific, mild, tranquil, calm, quiet, undisturbed, placid, serene. See **pacific.**

peacemaker. Syn.: pacificator, conciliator, mediator, arbitrator, intercessor, intermediary.

peak. Syn.: point, top, apex, pinnacle, crest, summit, spire.

peal. Syn.: resound, reverberate, boom.

peasant. Syn.: countryman, tiller, rustic, hind.

peccadillo. Syn.: see **offense.**

peculiar. Syn.: individual, personal, particular, special; singular, uncommon, unusual, unconventional, eccentric, strange, odd, queer, bizarre, grotesque. See **singular.**

peculiarity. Syn.: characteristic, attribute, trait, idiosyncrasy, eccentricity. See **characteristic.**

pecuniary. Syn.: monetary, financial, fiscal.

Pecuniary refers to matters which money enters into; *monetary* relates especially to money as such; *financial* usually refers to money matters or transactions of some size or importance; *fiscal* is used especially in connection with the administering of governmental funds, or those of any organization: as, *pecuniary* obligations or rewards; a *monetary* system or standard; *financial* interests or panic; a *fiscal* agent or year.

pedagogue. Syn.: see **instructor.**

pedant. Syn.: see **scholar.**

pedantic. Syn.: pedagoguish, learned, dogmatic.

peddle. Syn.: hawk, vend, sell, retail.

peddler. Syn.: hawker, vender, huckster, packman, chapman, canvasser, costermonger, cadger.

pedigree. Syn.: genealogy, ancestry, family, race. See **lineage.**

A *pedigree* is a table or chart recording a line of ancestors, either of persons or (more especially) of animals, as horses, cattle, and dogs, in which latter case it is used as proof of superior qualities. A *genealogy* is an account of the descent of a person or family traced through a series of generations, usually from the first known ancestor.

peek. Syn.: see **look.**

peel, *n.* **Syn.:** see **skin,** *n.*

peel, *v.* **Syn.:** see **pare.**

peep. Syn.: cheep, chirp, pipe, squeak; peer, peek, glance. See **look.**

peer, *n.* **Syn.:** equal, mate, match, compeer; nobleman, noble, lord.

peer, *v.* **Syn.:** see **look.**

peerless. Syn.: matchless, unmatched, unequaled, unsurpassed, unrivaled, inimitable, incomparable, nonpareil.

peevish. Syn.: querulous, fretful, petulant, pettish, cross, irritable, ill-humored, spleenful, splenetic, testy, touchy, snappish, waspish. See **petulant.**

pell-mell. Syn.: headlong, helter-skelter, tumultuously, confusedly.

pellucid. Syn.: see **transparent.**

pelt. Syn.: see **skin,** *n.*

pen. Syn.: sty, fold, paddock, corral, pound, hutch, coop, mew, cote, inclosure.

penalty. Syn.: punishment, retribution, forfeiture, fine, mulct.

pendent. Syn.: hanging, suspended, pendulous, pensile, overhanging, projecting.

pending, *a.* **Syn.:** impending, imminent, unsettled, undecided.

pending, *prep.* **Syn.:** during.

pendulous. Syn.: see **pendent.**

penetrate. Syn.: pierce, bore through, permeate, pervade, perforate, transfix; see through, discern, comprehend, understand, fathom.

Penetrate may mean no more than to make entrance into, and that slowly and with difficulty, or it may have the meaning of *pierce,* which is to run through or into something deeply and quickly, as with a sharp or pointed instrument. *Permeate* is to penetrate and spread through, *pervade,* to permeate completely: as, water *permeates* sand; a stillness *pervaded* the room.

penetrating. Syn.: piercing, transfixing; penetrative, penetrant, discerning, keen, sharp, acute, sagacious.

penetration. Syn.: piercing, perforation; discernment, sharpness, acuteness, acumen, shrewdness, insight. See **discernment.**

penitence. **Syn.**: see repentance.

penitent. **Syn.**: repentant, contrite, remorseful.

penitentiary. **Syn.**: see prison.

penman, penmanship. **Syn.**: see writer, writing.

penniless. **Syn.**: destitute, poverty-stricken, poor, impecunious, indigent. See poor.

pensile. **Syn.**: see pendent.

pensive. **Syn.**: thoughtful, meditative, reflective, musing, dreamy, sober, grave, sad, melancholy. See thoughtful.

penurious. **Syn.**: parsimonious, stingy, niggardly, miserly, close, mean, sordid, sparing, saving, grasping, covetous, avaricious. See stingy.

penury. **Syn.**: see poverty.

people, *n.* **Syn.**: tribe, clan, race, folk, nation; persons, subjects, citizens, electorate, inhabitants, population; commonalty, populace, rabble, canaille.

People refers to the body of persons composing a race, nation, tribe, etc. *Race* refers to a large body of people characterized by community of descent. *Nation* considers a body of people as living under an organized government, occupying a fixed area, and dealing as a unit in matters of peace and war with other similar groups.

people, *v.* **Syn.**: populate, inhabit, colonize.

peppery. **Syn.**: pungent, hot; choleric, irascible, hot-tempered.

perceive. **Syn.**: apprehend, see, discern, notice, grasp, gather, discover, learn, comprehend, understand. See see.

perceptible. **Syn.**: perceivable, discernible, visible, sensible, palpable, appreciable, noticeable.

perception. **Syn.**: apprehension, discernment, cognizance, cognition, recognition, comprehension, insight.

percolate. **Syn.**: see filter.

perdition. **Syn.**: destruction, ruin, wreck, Hades. See ruin.

peremptory. **Syn.**: conclusive, final, incontrovertible; positive, express, absolute, authoritative, arbitrary, dogmatic, dictatorial, magisterial, imperious. See imperative.

perennial. **Syn.**: enduring, abiding, lasting, everlasting, perpetual, permanent, undying, imperishable, deathless, immortal.

perfect, *a.* **Syn.**: perfected, finished, complete, whole, entire, full, correct; unblemished, sound; flawless, faultless, blameless, sinless, immaculate, impeccable; consummate, superlative, supreme; unqualified, absolute, downright, utter. **Ant.**: see imperfect.

That which is *perfect* is a whole without fault. *Finished* suggests such excelling execution or workmanship that nothing can or need be done to improve the product; *consummate* implies that the subject under consideration has the highest qualities which it is possible for it to possess. That which is *complete* lays its chief claim to excellence upon the possession of all its parts.

perfect, *v.* **Syn.**: finish, complete, accomplish, consummate, improve, develop, elaborate.

perfection. **Syn.**: completion, consummation, completeness, faultlessness, impeccability, perfectness.

perfidious. **Syn.**: unfaithful, faithless, treacherous, traitorous, treasonable, false-hearted. **Ant.**: faithful, loyal, constant, true.

perfidy. **Syn.**: see disloyalty.

perforate. **Syn.**: see penetrate.

perforation. **Syn.**: see hole.

perform. **Syn.**: execute, accomplish, achieve, effect, fulfil, discharge, do, render, act. See do.

performance. **Syn.**: execution, accomplishment, achievement, fulfilment, completion, consummation, discharge; act, deed, exploit, feat, trick, stunt; production, entertainment.

performer. **Syn.**: actor, player, impersonator, musician, contortionist, juggler, conjurer, magician, prestidigitator, acrobat, tumbler, rope-walker, funambulist.

perfume. **Syn.**: fragrance, redolence, aroma, balminess, scent, odor, smell; essence, incense, frankincense, musk, attar. See smell.

perfunctory. **Syn.**: formal, mechanical, indifferent, half-hearted, superficial, careless, negligent.

perhaps. **Syn.**: perchance, peradventure, possibly, haply, maybe.

peril. **Syn.**: jeopardy, hazard, risk, exposure. See danger.

perilous. **Syn.**: dangerous, hazardous, risky, unsafe, insecure. **Ant.**: safe, secure, impregnable.

period. **Syn.**: time, term, interval, duration, continuance; cycle, era, epoch; point, end, termination. See age.

periphrasis. **Syn.**: see verbosity.

perish. **Syn.**: see die.

perjure. **Syn.**: forswear.

permanent. **Syn.**: lasting, abiding, enduring, durable, unchangeable, immutable, imperishable, indestructible, indelible, stable, steadfast, fixed. **Ant.**: impermanent, ephemeral, evanescent, changing, unstable. See lasting.

permeate. **Syn.**: pervade, penetrate. See penetrate.

permissible. **Syn.**: admissible, allowable, legitimate, lawful, proper.

permission. **Syn.**: allowance, consent, leave, liberty, sanction, sufferance, authorization, license. **Ant.**: refusal, prohibition, denial, objection, opposition. See leave, *n.*

permit, *n.* **Syn.**: license, warrant, leave.

permit, *v.* **Syn.**: allow, let, consent to, suffer, sanction, tolerate, empower, authorize, license.

Permit and *allow* are often interchangeable, but *permit* suggests formal or implied assent or authorization, *allow* is less formal and implies absence of an attempt, or even an intent, to hinder. *Let* is a familiar or conversational word for permit or allow. *Suffer*, now rare or archaic, implies tolerance of or passive consent to something, sometimes against one's feelings, judgment, or sense of right.

pernicious. **Syn.**: destructive, ruinous, injurious, deleterious, noxious, harmful, hurtful, poisonous, baneful, baleful, deadly, fatal.

That which is *pernicious* insidiously destroys: as, *pernicious* habits, *pernicious* anemia; that which is *baneful* is poisonous or deadly: as, a *baneful* drug, a *baneful* influence; that which is *noxious* is dangerously harmful, especially to health: as, *noxious* gases, a *noxious* climate; that which is *deleterious* implies slower and less serious injury: as, *deleterious* ingredients in food, a *deleterious* effect.

perpendicular. **Syn.**: vertical, upright. **Ant.**: horizontal, oblique, slanting. See upright.

perpetual. **Syn.**: everlasting, eternal, endless, perennial, enduring, permanent; continuous, continual, ceaseless, unceasing, incessant, constant, uninterrupted. See continual, eternal.

perplex. **Syn.**: confuse, puzzle, bewilder, nonplus, mystify, embarrass.

To *perplex* is to entangle or baffle one's judgment so that he is at a loss what to think or how to act. *Puzzle* implies less serious mental embarrassment or uncertainty as to opinion or conduct. *Bewilder* suggests that the mind is confused by and lost in a multiplicity of considerations and alternatives; *nonplus*, that it has come to a point where it is temporarily balked at every turn. To *mystify* is to confound the mind by that which apparently defies comprehension.

perplexity. **Syn.**: bewilderment, embarrassment, uncertainty, doubt, dilemma, quandary, difficulty.

persecute. **Syn.**: oppress, harass, worry, torment, dragoon, badger, annoy, vex. See harass.

perseverance. **Syn.**: persistence, persistency, assiduity, indefatigableness, pertinacity, tenacity, industry, sedulousness, application, diligence, constancy, steadfastness.

Perseverance commonly suggests activity maintained in spite of difficulties; *persistence*, unremitting, sometimes annoying perseverance; *pertinacity*, resolute or unyielding adherence to a purpose; *tenacity*, dogged or determined holding on in spite of opposing force or circumstances.

persevere. **Syn.**: persist, continue.

persiflage. **Syn.**: see banter, *n.*

persist. **Syn.**: see persevere.

persistence. **Syn.**: perseverance, assiduity, pertinacity, doggedness, obstinacy. See perseverance.

persistent. **Syn.**: persevering, untiring, indefatigable, insistent, importunate, pertinacious, tenacious; lasting, enduring; repeated, continuous, unremitting.

person. **Syn.**: individual, being, personage, personality; character, part, rôle.

Person is the most general and common word for a human being; *individual* views a person or thing as standing alone or, if used of more than one, each of the group separately; *personage* is used of an outstanding or illustrious person, sometimes ironically.

personage. **Syn.**: see person.

personality. **Syn.**: see character.

perspicacious. **Syn.**: sharp-sighted, keen, shrewd, acute.

perspicacity. Syn.: sagacity, insight, penetration, discernment, acuteness, sharpness, shrewdness. Cf. **judgment, perspicuity.**

perspicuity. Syn.: lucidity, clearness, plainness.

Although completely different in meaning, the following two words, from their similarity of sound, are frequently confused. *Perspicacity* is a combination of insight and good judgment which enables one to penetrate to the hidden aspects of a problem or situation; *perspicuity*, the quality of being clear or lucid in statement or meaning: as, the *perspicacity* of a statesman; the *perspicuity* of an essay.

perspiration. Syn.: sweat.

Perspiration is the more refined and elegant word, and is often used over-fastidiously by those who consider *sweat* coarse, but *sweat* is much stronger and in some cases obviously more appropriate: as, the *sweat* of his brow. *Sweat* is almost always used when referring to animals.

persuade. Syn.: convince, prevail on, influence, induce, impel, incite, move, lead, urge, coax.

Persuade especially refers to inducing the will to a certain action or course of conduct; *convince*, to satisfying the understanding as to a truth or fact.

persuasion. Syn.: inducement, incitement; opinion, belief, conviction, creed, faith.

persuasive. Syn.: winning, moving, cogent.

pert. Syn.: saucy, impudent, impertinent, forward, bold, malapert. **Ant.:** modest, retiring, humble, meek. See **impudent.**

pertain. Syn.: belong, relate, appertain.

pertinacious. Syn.: persistent, determined, unyielding, dogged, stubborn, obstinate.

pertinacity. Syn.: see **perseverance.**

pertinence. Syn.: relevance, appositeness, applicability, aptness, appropriateness, suitableness, propriety.

pertinent. Syn.: relevant, germane, apposite, apt, applicable, appertaining, relating, appropriate.

As applied to remarks, statements, illustrations, or the like, *pertinent* suggests direct and fitting applicability; *relevant*, close and necessary relation to the matter in hand; *apposite*, nice or appropriate adjustment; *germane*, natural connection.

perturb. Syn.: disturb, disquiet, excite, agitate, trouble, distress, discompose.

perturbation. Syn.: disturbance, disorder, disquiet, excitement, agitation, trepidation, worry, distress, discomposure, disconcertment. See **excitement.**

pervade. Syn.: see **penetrate.**

perverse. Syn.: perverted, wicked, erring; obstinate, stubborn, mulish, headstrong, wilful, froward, untoward, contrary, wayward, intractable, ungovernable; fractious, cross, peevish, petulant. See **wayward.**

pervert, n. Syn.: see **apostate.**

pervert, v. Syn.: misapply, misuse, misinterpret, distort, falsify; corrupt, debase, vitiate.

pessimistic. Syn.: see **misanthropic.**

pest. Syn.: pestilence, plague, epidemic; nuisance, annoyance, curse.

pester. Syn.: see **tease.**

pestiferous. Syn.: pestilential, infectious, contagious, noxious, pernicious; mischievous, annoying, troublesome.

pestilence. Syn.: see **pest.**

pestilential. Syn.: pestilent, pestiferous, destructive, deadly, poisonous, noxious, pernicious.

pet. Syn.: fondle, caress, coddle, cosset, pamper, cocker, humor, indulge, baby, spoil.

petition, n. Syn.: entreaty, supplication, prayer, suit, solicitation, request.

petition, v. Syn.: entreat, supplicate, pray, beg, beseech, solicit, request.

petrify. Syn.: lapidify, ossify, fossilize; benumb, deaden, stupefy, paralyze.

pettiness. Syn.: smallness, littleness, triviality, insignificance.

pettish. Syn.: see **petulant.**

petty. Syn.: small, little, trifling, trivial, slight, unimportant, inconsiderable, insignificant, mean; minor, inferior, subordinate. See **trifling.**

petulant. Syn.: peevish, pettish, cross, fretful, choleric, querulous, irritable, ill-humored.

Petulant suggests quick or capricious impatience, often showing itself in small outbursts of feeling or anger; *pettish*, impatience, vexation, or testiness over such small or trivial

matters as render the mood undignified or unworthy; *peevish*, a state of fretful dissatisfaction.

phantasm, phantom. Syn.: see **ghost.**

pharmacist. Syn.: druggist, apothecary, chemist.

phase. Syn.: aspect, appearance, guise.

phenomenal. Syn.: see **wonderful.**

phenomenon. Syn.: manifestation, occurrence, event; prodigy, marvel, wonder; object, thing.

philanthropic. Syn.: benevolent, humane, kind.

philanthropy. Syn.: benevolence, charity, almsgiving.

Philanthropy aims at general human welfare, especially as manifested in preventing or mitigating evil conditions or suffering; *charity* refers especially to the benevolence that gives relief directly to those in need.

philippic. Syn.: see **invective.**

phlegm. Syn.: see **apathy.**

phlegmatic. Syn.: sluggish, apathetic, dull, heavy, impassive, indifferent, unemotional, cool, self-possessed. **Ant.:** energetic, vigorous, active, alert, emotional, excitable. See **unemotional.**

photograph. Syn.: see **picture.**

phrase. Syn.: see **word.**

phraseology. Syn.: see **diction.**

physical. Syn.: material, visible, tangible; bodily, corporal, corporeal.

physician. Syn.: see **doctor.**

physiognomy. Syn.: see **face.**

piazza. Syn.: see **porch.**

pick. Syn.: pluck, gather, collect, cull, glean; choose, select, elect.

Pick emphasizes discrimination in choosing; *pluck*, the pulling off or out, especially from the place of growth; *gather*, the bringing together into a group, collection, or the like.

picket. Syn.: post, stake, pale; sentry, sentinel, guard, watchman.

pictorial. Syn.: picturesque. See **graphic.**

picture, n. Syn.: painting, drawing, engraving, etching, lithograph, chromo, print, cut, photograph, picturization, motion-picture, cinema, film; sketch, illustration, portrait, likeness, miniature, vignette, silhouette, cartoon, caricature; tableau, scene, view, landscape, panorama.

picture, v. Syn.: depict, delineate, portray, sketch, draw, represent, photograph, film, screen, describe.

picturesque. Syn.: see **graphic.**

piebald. Syn.: see **spotted.**

piece, n. Syn.: portion, part, section, slice, morsel, bit, scrap, fragment, chunk, hunk, hunch. See **part.**

piece, v. Syn.: patch, mend, repair; enlarge, augment, extend.

pier. Syn.: wharf, quay, dock, jetty, landing-place.

pierce. Syn.: penetrate, transfix, stab, impale, gore, puncture, prick, perforate, bore, drill. See **penetrate.**

piercing. Syn.: penetrating, cutting, sharp, keen, poignant, shrill.

piety. Syn.: godliness, holiness, sanctity, saintliness, devoutness, devotion, dutifulness, reverence, religion.

Piety particularly suggests acts of reverence and submission rendered to God with constant regularity and devotion; *godliness* refers rather to an inward likeness to God, or to the endeavor to attain such likeness.

pile. Syn.: heap, stack, mass, accumulation.

pilfer. Syn.: steal, purloin, filch, embezzle. See **steal.**

pilferer. Syn.: see **robber.**

pilgrim. Syn.: traveler, wanderer, wayfarer, sojourner, crusader.

pilgrimage. Syn.: see **journey.**

pillage, n. Syn.: plundering, spoliation, rapine; plunder, booty, spoil, loot, prey.

pillage, v. Syn.: plunder, despoil, sack, strip, rob, devastate, foray. See **rob.**

pillar. Syn.: column, pier, post, shaft, monument, obelisk, monolith; supporter, upholder.

pillow. Syn.: see **cushion.**

pilot, n. Syn.: steersman, helmsman, guide, leader, conductor, driver.

pilot, v. Syn.: steer, guide, direct.

pincers. Syn.: tweezers, pliers, forceps, nippers.

pinch, n. Syn.: squeeze, nip, tweak; strait, emergency, pressure, difficulty; hardship; bit, dash, modicum. See **emergency.**

pinch, v. Syn.: squeeze, nip, tweak, gripe; straiten, distress, afflict, cramp.

pine. **Syn.:** waste, languish, droop, flag, grieve; long, yearn.

pinnacle. **Syn.:** peak, apex, top, summit, acme, zenith.

pious. **Syn.:** godly, devout, righteous, religious, reverent, holy, saintly. **Ant.:** impious, irreligious, irreverent, atheistic, wicked.

All the following words may be used to indicate a spirit of reverence toward God. *Pious* suggests sincere and constant discharge of spiritual duties. The word sometimes suggests a conformity which appears to others to be extreme. *Religious*, of wider application, may be used in connection with whatever pertains to faith or worship: as, *religious* books, a *religious* ceremony. *Devout* indicates a fervent spirit in the exercises of religion.

piquancy. **Syn.:** pungency, sharpness, spiciness; cleverness, raciness, liveliness.

piquant. **Syn.:** pungent, sharp, biting, spicy, appetizing; clever, racy, smart, lively, sparkling. See **pungent.**

pique, *n.* **Syn.:** displeasure, resentment, irritation, vexation, umbrage. See **mortification.**

pique, *v.* **Syn.:** offend, displease, irritate, sting, nettle, vex, provoke; stimulate, excite, prick, goad.

pirate. **Syn.:** sea-robber, freebooter, buccaneer, corsair, picaroon, viking.

pit. **Syn.:** hole, cavity, excavation, quarry, abyss; depression, indentation, hollow; pitfall, trap, snare; parquet, orchestra.

pitch. **Syn.:** set, place; throw, toss, hurl, cast, fling, heave; plunge, fall; slope, slant. See **throw.**

piteous. **Syn.:** compassionate, merciful; affecting, distressing, lamentable, woeful, mournful, doleful, sorrowful, sad.

pitfall. **Syn.:** see **trap.**

pith. **Syn.:** marrow, kernel, substance, essence, gist, heart, quintessence; strength, vigor, force; weight, importance, moment.

pithy. **Syn.:** terse, concise, pointed, sententious, laconic. See **concise.**

pitiable. **Syn.:** lamentable, deplorable, sad; contemptible, insignificant.

pitiful. **Syn.:** compassionate, merciful, ruthful, clement, tender-hearted; touching, moving, affecting, distressing, lamentable, woeful, mournful, sorrowful, sad, pathetic; contemptible, insignificant, despicable, paltry, mean. See **wretched.**

pitiless. **Syn.:** merciless, ruthless, hard-hearted. See **cruel.**

pity. **Syn.:** ruth, compassion, commiseration, condolence, sympathy, mercy. **Ant.:** mercilessness, ruthlessness, barbarity, inhumanity.

Pity is the feeling of sorrow which prompts one to relieve the suffering or distress of another, who is often regarded as inferior. *Compassion* is deep tenderness of feeling for one who is suffering. *Sympathy* is a feeling of kinship or equality in the suffering or distress of another. *Commiseration* is, by derivation, sharing another's misery; *condolence* is sharing another's grief.

placard. **Syn.:** poster, bill, notice.

placate. **Syn.:** see **pacify.**

place, *n.* **Syn.:** square, plaza, court; region, locality, site, spot; space, room; stead, lieu; situation, position, appointment, post, office, duty, function, work.

place, *v.* **Syn.:** put, set, lay, deposit, station, locate, establish. See **put.**

placid. **Syn.:** see **calm.**

plague, *n.* **Syn.:** affliction, calamity, evil; pestilence, pest; nuisance, vexation, trouble, bother.

plague, *v.* **Syn.:** afflict, torment, harass, vex, trouble, annoy, worry, tantalize, pester, tease, badger, twit, nag, devil. See **tease.**

plain, *n.* **Syn.:** prairie, heath, moor, steppe, pampas, llano, champaign, tundra, veldt.

plain, *a.* **Syn.:** flat, level, even, smooth; clear, apparent, manifest, evident, obvious, patent, unmistakable, unequivocal, unambiguous; unqualified, downright, absolute, sheer; sincere, unaffected, frank, candid, unreserved, straightforward, blunt; simple, common, ordinary, homely; unembellished, unadorned, ungarnished, untrimmed, unfigured. **Ant.:** see **obscure, ornate.** See **simple, ugly.**

plainness. **Syn.:** see **perspicuity.**

plain-spoken. **Syn.:** see **frank.**

plaintive. **Syn.:** lamenting, repining, complaining, querulous, doleful, lugubrious, mournful, sorrowful, sad, melancholy, whining. See **mournful.**

plan, *n.* **Syn.:** map, chart, diagram, draft, delineation; scheme, project, design, plot, proposal, method.

Plan refers to any formulated method of doing something. *Design* implies art, dexterity, or craft (sometimes evil or selfish) in the elaboration or execution of a plan and often tends to emphasize the purpose in view. A *project* is a proposed or tentative plan; a *scheme* is often either a speculative or impractical plan, or a selfish or dishonest one.

plan, *v.* **Syn.:** design, sketch; scheme, project, devise, contrive, intend, purpose.

plant, *n.* **Syn.:** herb, bush, shrub, tree, vine, vegetable.

plant, *v.* **Syn.:** set, set out, sow, fix, implant, post, station, establish, settle.

plastic. **Syn.:** molding, formative, creative; pliant, flexible, impressionable, fictile.

platform. **Syn.:** stage, dais, rostrum, pulpit.

platitude. **Syn.:** flatness, dullness, insipidity, triteness, banality; truism, commonplace.

A *commonplace* is an idea or remark so lacking in originality that it might be put forth by any one. A *truism* is a statement too obvious to need explanation or proof. A *platitude* is a commonplace grown familiar through frequent repetition and often uttered as if important or novel. *Commonplace* and *platitude* are always derogatory.

platitudinous. **Syn.:** flat, dull, insipid, stale, trite, banal, commonplace.

plausible. **Syn.:** specious.

Plausible is applied to that which strikes the superficial judgment favorably, and may or may not bear severe examination; *specious* relates to what is superficially or deceitfully fair, just, or correct, and is not truly what it seems: as, a *plausible* excuse; *specious* reasoning or argument.

play, *n.* **Syn.:** movement, action, operation, exercise, employment, use; liberty, scope, room, swing; diversion, amusement, recreation, pastime, game, sport, frolic, fun, merrymaking; jest, trifling; performance, drama, tragedy, comedy, farce, melodrama, burlesque.

Play is the general term for any form of diverting activity, often undirected, spontaneous, or random. *Sport* suggests an active, physical, and more often outdoor pastime or contest. *Game* implies a recreational contest, mental or physical, usually governed by set rules.

play, *v.* **Syn.:** flutter, flicker, dance, dart; sport, frolic, gambol, caper, romp, skip, frisk, revel; trifle, toy, dally, wanton; gamble, stake, wager; perform, execute; act, personate, impersonate.

player. **Syn.:** idler, trifler, drone; performer, instrumentalist; actor, Thespian, histrion.

playful. **Syn.:** sportive, frolicsome, wanton, frisky, prankish; mischievous, roguish, waggish, arch; humorous, jocular, bantering, jesting, facetious.

Playful suggests good humor or high spirits; *mischievous*, a disturbance of order sometimes by teasing or annoyance, often with no other intent than to indulge a desire for play. *Roguish* implies sly and sportive teasing. *Arch* implies coy insinuation, especially in women.

plea. **Syn.:** justification, vindication, defense, excuse; pretext, pretense; appeal, entreaty, prayer. See **apology.**

plead. **Syn.:** advocate, defend, champion, argue, reason; entreat, supplicate, implore, beseech, beg.

pleasant. **Syn.:** pleasing, agreeable, delightful, congenial, enjoyable, gratifying; amiable, affable. **Ant.:** see **unpleasant.** See **pleasing.**

pleasantry. **Syn.:** drollery, facetiousness, badinage, banter, raillery, waggery, wit; witticism, jest, joke. See **banter,** *n.*

please. **Syn.:** like, choose, prefer, want; suit, satisfy, content, gratify, delight.

pleasing. **Syn.:** pleasant, pleasurable, agreeable, gratifying, delightful, delectable; amiable, gracious, winning. **Ant.:** see **unpleasant.**

Pleasing and *pleasant* both imply the giving of pleasure, but *pleasant* suggests the effect produced, *pleasing* the power of producing it. That which is *agreeable* pleases because it accords with one's own mood or nature. *Delightful* implies a high degree of pleasure; *delectable*, a more literary word, suggests an epicurean quality in the pleasure given.

pleasure. **Syn.:** gratification, enjoyment, delight, joy, happiness, gladness, delectation; self-indulgence, sensuality, voluptuousness; will, desire, choice, preference. See **gladness.**

plebeian. **Syn.:** common, vulgar, unrefined, coarse, mean.

pledge, *n.* **Syn.:** pawn, stake, gage, earnest, token, security, guarantee, surety, hostage; promise, covenant, vow. See **earnest,** *n.*

pledge, *v.* **Syn.:** pawn, plight, guarantee, hypothecate.

plenipotentiary. Syn.: see **envoy.**

plentiful. Syn.: plenteous, abundant, bounteous, bountiful, copious, lavish, profuse, overflowing, ample, sufficient, adequate. **Ant.:** scarce, scant, scanty, insufficient, inadequate.

plenty. Syn.: plenteousness, abundance, sufficiency, copiousness, profusion, exuberance.

Plenty suggests a full supply, all that can be needed. *Abundance* is a great plenty, as much as can be wanted or more. *Profusion* is such excessive abundance as suggests luxury and extravagance.

pleonasm. Syn.: see **verbosity.**

pliant. Syn.: pliable, flexible, supple, limber, lithesome, lithe; compliant, yielding, facile, adaptable, tractable. **Ant.:** inflexible, rigid, stiff, brittle; resolute, firm, intractable, ungovernable. See **flexible.**

plight, *n.* **Syn.:** condition, state, situation, position, predicament, dilemma, scrape, fix. See **predicament.**

plight, *v.* **Syn.:** pledge, promise, engage, betroth.

plod. Syn.: trudge, tramp, jog; toil, drudge. See **walk,** *v.*

plot, *n.* **Syn.:** tract, patch, parcel; plan, chart, map, diagram; project, scheme, design, machination, intrigue, conspiracy, cabal.

plot, *v.* **Syn.:** map, diagram; plan, devise, scheme, contrive, concoct, machinate, intrigue, conspire, cabal.

To *plot* is to contrive a secret plan of a selfish and often treasonable kind. To *conspire* is to unite with others in an illicit or illegal machination. To *scheme* is to plan ingeniously, subtly, and often craftily for one's own advantage. To *intrigue* is to engage in secret and generally complicated schemes.

pluck, *n.* **Syn.:** pull, tug, jerk, twitch; courage, resolution, stamina, spirit.

pluck, *v.* **Syn.:** pick, gather, cull; pull, tug, jerk, twitch, tweak; strip, fleece, plunder, swindle. See **pick.**

plucky. Syn.: brave, courageous, resolute, unflinching, game.

plug. Syn.: stopper, stopple, cork, bung, spile, tampion, wedge, peg; nag, jade.

plumb. Syn.: see **vertical.**

plump. Syn.: well-rounded, chubby, roly-poly, stout, fleshy, fat, corpulent, obese, pudgy.

Plump suggests fullness, *chubby*, pleasing roundness of form.

plunder, *n.* **Syn.:** pillage, spoliation, rapine, robbery; spoil, booty, loot, prey. See **booty.**

plunder, *v.* **Syn.:** pillage, ravage, despoil, spoil, loot, sack, rifle, rob, steal. See **rob.**

plunge. Syn.: immerse, submerge, dip, duck, douse, souse; dive, leap, rush, pitch. See **dip.**

pocket-book. Syn.: purse, wallet, porte-monnaie.

pod. Syn.: capsule, legume, bur, boll. See **skin,** *n.*

poem. Syn.: epic, lyric, elegy, pastoral, idyl, eclogue, georgic, bucolic, ballad, song, ode, sonnet, rondel, rondeau, roundelay, virelay, madrigal, dithyramb, rhapsody, doggerel, macaronic, limerick, distich, quatrain.

poet. Syn.: bard, singer, laureate, versifier, poetaster, rimester.

poetry. Syn.: verse, poesy, poems.

The difference between *poetry* and *verse* is the difference between substance and form. *Poetry* is lofty thought or impassioned feeling expressed in imaginative words. *Verse* is any expression in words which conforms to accepted metrical rules. In most cases *poetry* is written in *verse.*

poignant. Syn.: pungent, biting, keen, sharp, severe, penetrating, intense, bitter. See **pungent.**

point, *n.* **Syn.:** prick, goad; tip, apex, peak, promontory, cape, headland; dot, period; item, detail, particular; place, location, position, step, stage, degree; gist, meaning, purport; crisis, juncture; characteristic, peculiarity, trait; end, aim, purpose, object; hint, suggestion.

point, *v.* **Syn.:** sharpen, taper; direct, aim, level; indicate, designate, show; punctuate, dot.

point-blank. Syn.: direct, straightforward, plain, explicit, express, unqualified.

pointed. Syn.: sharp, peaked, tapering, conical; epigrammatic, pithy; marked, emphasized, direct.

pointless. Syn.: blunt, dull, witless, inane, insipid.

poise, *n.* **Syn.:** balance, equipoise, equilibrium, equanimity.

poise, *v.* **Syn.:** balance, librate.

poison. Syn.: venom, virus, toxin, toxicant, bane.

Poison is the general word for any substance that destroys or impairs life when absorbed into the system. *Venom* is especially used of the poisons secreted by certain animals; *virus,* of poisons which are produced in the body of a person or animal suffering from some contagious disease, and which are usually capable of producing the same disease in others when transferred to them, as by inoculation. *Toxin* is used in medicine for the albuminous secretion of microbes, which causes certain diseases.

poisonous. Syn.: venomous, toxic, virulent, noxious, baneful, destructive.

poke. Syn.: prod, thrust, push, punch, jog, nudge, dig; pry, search, grope; idle, potter, dawdle.

polar. Syn.: arctic, antarctic.

policy. Syn.: statecraft, polity; prudence, address, shrewdness, expediency; course, system, platform.

polish, *n.* **Syn.:** smoothness, glossiness, gloss, glaze, luster, sheen; refinement, elegance, courtliness.

Polish suggests the smooth and shining quality which is given to a surface by friction. *Luster* denotes the light, often soft and rich, that is reflected from a polished surface. *Sheen,* sometimes poetical, is a glistening brightness such as that reflected from the surface of a piece of silk. *Gloss* suggests a superficial smoothness such as characterizes an oiled or lacquered surface.

polish, *v.* **Syn.:** burnish, furbish, brighten, rub; refine, civilize.

polished. Syn.: burnished, shining, glistening, bright; refined, cultured, elegant, courtly. See **genteel.**

polite. Syn.: polished, refined, cultured, well-bred, courteous, complaisant, civil, urbane, affable, gracious, gentlemanly, ladylike, courtly. **Ant.:** impolite, discourteous, uncivil, rude, impertinent, insolent, impudent. See **civil.**

politic. Syn.: political; sagacious, judicious, wise, discreet, prudent, expedient, diplomatic, shrewd, astute. See **tactful.**

politician. Syn.: statesman, politicaster.

Politician suggests the schemes and devices of one who engages in (especially small) politics for party ends or his own advantage; *statesman,* the eminent ability, foresight, and unselfish devotion to the interests of his country of one dealing with (especially important or great) affairs of state.

polity. Syn.: see **policy.**

pollute. Syn.: defile, befoul, soil, taint, corrupt, deprave, debase, profane, ravish. See **soil,** *v.*

poltroon. Syn.: see **coward.**

pommel. Syn.: see **pound, beat.**

pomp. Syn.: show, display, flourish, splendor, grandeur, magnificence, state, pageantry, parade. See **show,** *n.*

pompous. Syn.: grand, splendid, magnificent, stately, imposing; self-important, pretentious, magisterial, swelling, inflated, grandiose, grandiloquent, bombastic.

pond. Syn.: see **lake.**

ponder. Syn.: consider, deliberate, reflect, cogitate, ruminate, meditate, muse. See **reflect.**

ponderous. Syn.: heavy, weighty, bulky, massive, huge, unwieldy, cumbersome; labored, dull, slow. See **bulky.**

pony. Syn.: see **horse.**

poor. Syn.: needy, indigent, penurious, necessitous, straitened, impoverished, destitute, penniless, poverty-stricken, impecunious; barren, infertile, infecund, effete, exhausted; lean, thin, spare, bony, skinny, scrawny, pinched, meager, haggard, peaked, gaunt, emaciated; scanty, inadequate, insufficient, insignificant, paltry, trifling; weak, feeble, unhealthy; inferior, faulty, defective, worthless, bad; shabby, seedy, sorry, miserable, wretched, sordid; unfavorable, inauspicious, unpropitious, unfortunate. **Ant.:** see **rich.**

Poor is the simple term for expressing the lack of means to procure the comforts of life. *Impoverished* often implies a former state of greater plenty, from which one has been reduced. *Penniless* implies extreme poverty; *impecunious* often suggests habitual lack of means.

popinjay. Syn.: see **dandy.**

popish. Syn.: see **papal.**

populace. Syn.: commonalty, proletariat, multitude, crowd, masses, mob, rabble.

popular. Syn.: common, general, prevailing, current, familiar; favorite, approved, in vogue. See **common.**

porch. Syn.: veranda, piazza, stoop, porte-cochère, portico.

port. **Syn.:** harbor, haven, bay, cove, inlet; bearing, carriage, demeanor, air, mien. See **harbor, bearing.**

portend. **Syn.:** presage, augur, forebode, foreshadow, foretoken, foreshow, bode, betoken, signify, threaten.

Foreshow implies indication or revelation in advance of what will happen; *foreshadow*, vague or imperfect indication, as when an object casts its shadow before it, of coming (often unhappy or inauspicious) events or results. *Presage* is to feel a presentiment of as well as to give an indication of something in the future; *portend* is to signify in advance, and, from association with portent, often implies unfavorable or ominous foreshadowings.

portent. **Syn.:** presage, omen, sign, token. See **sign.**

portentous. **Syn.:** ominous, foreboding, premonitory; monstrous, marvelous, prodigious, wonderful.

portion. **Syn.:** part, section, piece, division, share, quota, contingent, allotment, allowance; lot, fate, destiny; dowry, dot, inheritance. See **part.**

portly. **Syn.:** dignified, stately, imposing; fleshy, stout, corpulent, obese. See **stout.**

portrait. **Syn.:** see **picture,** *n.*

portray. **Syn.:** depict, picture, draw, paint, sketch, delineate, represent, impersonate, act, describe. See **depict.**

portrayal. **Syn.:** depiction, delineation, representation, impersonation, description, account.

pose. **Syn.:** see **position.**

position. **Syn.:** situation, station, place, site, locality, spot; posture, attitude, pose; status, standing, rank; post, office, job.

Position is a general word to indicate the situation, location, or disposal of the body, or any part of it, or of an inanimate object. *Posture* is the arrangement assumed, generally unconsciously, by the body and especially its movable parts in lying, sitting, standing, etc. *Attitude* is often a posture assumed for intentional effect, such as exemplification or imitation, but it may be a posture consciously or unconsciously adopted for a particular purpose, as that of a tight-rope walker or a swordsman. *Pose* is an attitude assumed, in most cases, for artistic effect.

positive. **Syn.:** express, explicit, precise, definite, emphatic, unequivocal, unquestionable, unmistakable, indisputable; confident, certain, sure, assured; over-confident, arbitrary, dogmatic, peremptory, imperative; absolute, downright, unqualified. See **sure.**

possess. **Syn.:** own, have, hold, occupy. See **have.**

possession. **Syn.:** ownership, occupation, tenure, control; property, belonging.

possessor. **Syn.:** owner, proprietor, holder, master, lord.

possible. **Syn.:** see **practicable.**

possibly. **Syn.:** see **perhaps.**

post. **Syn.:** stake, pile, column, pillar, pilaster; office, position, place, employment.

posterior. **Syn.:** hinder, hind, rear, back.

posterity. **Syn.:** see **offspring.**

postpone. **Syn.:** defer, adjourn, prorogue, delay, procrastinate. See **defer.**

postulate. **Syn.:** see **assume.**

posture. **Syn.:** see **position.**

potent. **Syn.:** powerful, mighty, strong, puissant, cogent, convincing, forcible, effective, efficacious. **Ant.:** see **weak.** See **powerful.**

potential. **Syn.:** see **latent.**

potter. **Syn.:** see **trifle,** *v.*

pouch. **Syn.:** see **bag.**

pound. **Syn.:** pulverize, bray, comminute, triturate; beat, strike, thump, thwack, pommel, maul, cudgel, belabor, drub.

poverty. **Syn.:** indigence, penury, impecuniosity, beggary, pauperism, destitution, privation, need, want; dearth, scarcity, paucity, deficiency, lack.

Poverty denotes serious lack of the means for proper existence. *Destitution* implies a state of having absolutely nothing; *indigence*, a state of privation and especially the lack of those things to which one has been used and which befit one's station. *Penury* suggests poverty that is severe to abjectness. *Want* emphasizes the lack of even the necessaries of life; *need*, the necessity of help or relief.

powder. **Syn.:** see **pulverize.**

power. **Syn.:** ability, capability, faculty; strength, might, force, vigor, potency, cogency; authority, command, sway, dominion, control, domination, influence. See **strength.**

powerful. **Syn.:** strong, mighty, potent, puissant; convincing, forcible, cogent.

Powerful suggests capability of exerting great force or overcoming strong resistance. *Mighty*, now chiefly rhetorical, implies uncommon or overwhelming strength or power. *Puissant*, now mostly an archaic word, refers particularly to the power or influence of kingdoms, empires, or those in high places. *Potent*, a dignified word, implies great natural or inherent power.

powerless. **Syn.:** impotent, weak, feeble, helpless.

practicable. **Syn.:** possible, feasible.

Practicable is used of projects that can be accomplished by means that one possesses or can obtain; *feasible*, of what can be readily and successfully done or effected. But the two words are often interchangeable.

practical. **Syn.:** practicable. See **sensible.**

practice, *n.* **Syn.:** usage, habit; exercise, training, drill, experience. See **custom, exercise.**

practise, *v.* **Syn.:** perform, execute, do, apply, pursue; exercise, train, drill, rehearse.

practised. **Syn.:** experienced, skilled, versed, accomplished, proficient, expert.

praise, *n.* **Syn.:** commendation, laudation, eulogy, panegyric, encomium, acclaim, acclamation, plaudit, compliment, flattery, adulation. **Ant.:** condemnation, censure, reproach, disapprobation, disparagement, vilification.

praise, *v.* **Syn.:** commend, extol, laud, applaud, eulogize, panegyrize, glorify, magnify, exalt. **Ant.:** condemn, disparage, depreciate, criticize, reprove, blame.

Praise is the common word to express approbation or commendation. *Laud* implies great, sometimes excessive, praise; *extol*, high and lofty praise; *eulogize*, formal praise, as in a eulogy.

prance. **Syn.:** see **skip.**

prank. **Syn.:** caper, antic, frolic, gambol, vagary, escapade.

prankish. **Syn.:** see **frolicsome.**

prate. **Syn.:** prattle, chatter, babble, gabble. See **babble.**

prattle. **Syn.:** chatter, babble, gabble, twaddle, tattle, gossip, palaver, balderdash, gibberish, jargon, rigmarole. See **babble.**

pray. **Syn.:** supplicate, entreat, implore, importune, beseech, beg, petition.

prayer. **Syn.:** supplication, entreaty, petition, suit, request, appeal, invocation, litany, orison.

preacher. **Syn.:** clergyman, minister, evangelist, revivalist, homilist, predicant, pulpiteer. See **clergyman.**

precarious. **Syn.:** uncertain, doubtful, unstable, insecure, risky, hazardous, dangerous, perilous. **Ant.:** certain, settled, stable, steady, sure, safe, secure. See **uncertain.**

precedence. **Syn.:** see **priority.**

precedent, *n.* **Syn.:** see **example.**

precedent, *a.* **Syn.:** see **previous.**

preceding. **Syn.:** see **previous.**

precept. **Syn.:** commandment, mandate, direction, injunction, instruction, teaching, rule, maxim, axiom, adage. See **doctrine.**

precious. **Syn.:** costly, expensive, valuable; dear, beloved, idolized. See **valuable.**

precipitate. **Syn.:** precipitous, steep, sheer, abrupt.

precipitous. **Syn.:** see **steep.**

precise. **Syn.:** definite, exact, correct, strict, express; punctilious, scrupulous, fastidious, particular, overnice, prim, stiff, formal, ceremonious. See **accurate.**

precision. **Syn.:** preciseness, definiteness, exactness, accuracy, correctness, nicety.

preclude. **Syn.:** exclude, prevent, bar, prohibit, debar. See **avert.**

precursor. **Syn.:** forerunner, predecessor, herald, harbinger. See **herald,** *n.*

predatory. **Syn.:** predacious, marauding, plundering, pillaging, thieving, rapacious.

predestinate. **Syn.:** predestine, predetermine, foreordain, foredoom, decree.

Predestinate is found especially in theological use, with reference to the action of God in foreordaining to a particular end or lot; *predestine*, in more general use, of predetermination as if by fate or destiny.

predestination. **Syn.:** predetermination, foreordination, fate.

predestine. **Syn.:** see **predestinate.**

predicament. **Syn.:** state, condition, situation, case, difficulty, quandary, dilemma, plight, strait, scrape, fix.

A *predicament* is usually an unpleasant, annoying, or dangerous situation. *Plight* is also used in the same sense, but more often indicates a general condition that is serious, though sometimes a situation that is laughable or ridiculous. A *quandary* is a state of mental perplexity and anxiety as to a choice that will avoid disagreeable consequences; a *dilemma* is a situation in which one is confronted by two equally undesirable alternatives.

predicate. Syn.: see **declare.**

predict. Syn.: foretell, prophesy, presage, prognosticate, augur, divine, vaticinate. See **foretell.**

prediction. Syn.: prophecy, prognostication, augury, divination, vaticination.

predilection. Syn.: prepossession, preference, partiality, predisposition, inclination, bent, bias, prejudice. See **love.**

predominance. Syn.: ascendancy, superiority, mastery, dominance, control, prevalence, preponderance. See **priority.**

predominant. Syn.: dominant, ruling, controlling, preponderant, prevailing, prevalent, ascendant, chief, supreme. **Ant.:** subordinate, subsidiary, secondary.

preëminence. Syn.: see **priority.**

preface. Syn.: see **introduction.**

prefatory. Syn.: introductory, preparatory, precursory, preliminary, proemial.

prefer. Syn.: see **choose.**

preference. Syn.: liking, partiality, favor, choice, selection, election, option.

prejudice, *n.* **Syn.:** prepossession, bias; disadvantage, detriment, injury, harm, hurt. See **injury, bias.**

prejudice, *v.* **Syn.:** bias, warp; impair, injure, hurt.

prejudicial. Syn.: disadvantageous, detrimental, hurtful, damaging, deleterious.

preliminary. Syn.: preparatory, introductory, prefatory.

The *preliminary* brings one, as it were, to the threshold of the principal matter; the *introductory* leads one, with natural, logical, or close connection, into the subject of consideration.

prelude. Syn.: overture, voluntary.

premeditated. Syn.: see **intentional.**

premium. Syn.: see **reward,** *n.*

premonition. Syn.: see **foreboding.**

preoccupied. Syn.: see **abstracted.**

preparatory. Syn.: see **preliminary.**

prepare. Syn.: contrive, devise, concoct, get ready, make ready, fit.

To *prepare* is to get things ready beforehand for some approaching need. *Contrive* implies the exercise of ingenuity in achieving one's purpose. *Devise* emphasizes the use of thought and imagination in inventing plans or methods. *Concoct* is colloquially ' to cook up,' and suggests irregularity and often haste in the process.

prepossessing. Syn.: pleasing, charming, winning, taking, attractive.

prepossession. Syn.: see **predilection.**

preposterous. Syn.: irrational, nonsensical, foolish, silly, crazy, wild, ludicrous, ridiculous. See **absurd.**

prerogative. Syn.: see **privilege.**

presage, *n.* **Syn.:** see **omen.**

presage, *v.* **Syn.:** see **foretell, portend.**

prescience. Syn.: see **foresight.**

prescribe. Syn.: ordain, order, command, designate, appoint, establish.

present, *n.* **Syn.:** gift, benefaction, donation, largess, grant, boon, gratuity, tip, fee, douceur.

Present and *gift* are both used of something given as an expression of respect, friendship, interest, or affection, but *gift* (not *present*) is generally used of beneficences to individuals, groups, or institutions: as, a Christmas *gift* or *present*; a *gift* of a million dollars to a university. *Donation* emphasizes the thought of charity in a gift, and is often used of small contributions on particular occasions for some worthy purpose. *Largess* is an old word representing a gift bestowed by a superior, especially one high in authority, and generally shared by a considerable number.

present, *v.* **Syn.:** see **give, introduce.**

presentiment. Syn.: see **foreboding.**

presently. Syn.: see **immediately.**

preserve. Syn.: save, protect, defend, shield, guard, keep, secure, maintain, uphold, conserve. See **guard,** *v.*

press. Syn.: compress, squeeze, push, thrust, crowd; beset, harass; constrain, compel, force; beseech, entreat. See **urge.**

presume. Syn.: see **conjecture.**

presumption. Syn.: presumptuousness, overconfidence, assurance, forwardness, effrontery, arrogance. See **confidence.**

presumptuous. Syn.: presuming, overbold, forward, impudent, impertinent, arrogant. **Ant.:** unassuming, modest, meek, humble.

pretend. Syn.: claim, allege, profess; feign, simulate, sham, counterfeit, affect.

To *pretend* is to create an imaginary reality or character which we believe in or wish others to believe in: as, the child *pretends* to be a man; to *pretend* to be enthusiastic. *Simulate* implies imitation of the character or appearance of something that really does not belong to one: as, to *simulate* grief, love, etc. To *feign*, like *simulate*, stresses, though less strongly, the imitation involved in assuming a character or appearance not one's own: as, to *feign* surprise. To *affect* is to make one's own, at least outwardly, the qualities or appearances which one seeks to exhibit to others: as, to *affect* the manners of the rich. To *profess* is to lay claim to or assert, either rightfully or otherwise, that which one wishes to establish: as, to *profess* to have special information on some subject.

pretense. Syn.: show, feigning, make-believe, sham, deception, hypocrisy, cant, affectation; pretension, ostentation, display; pretext, excuse, disguise, blind, mask, cloak, color, ruse, subterfuge, feint. **Ant.:** actuality, reality, truth, candor, openness, sincerity.

pretentious. Syn.: see **ostentatious.**

preternatural. Syn.: see **supernatural.**

pretext. Syn.: see **pretense.**

pretty. Syn.: fair, comely, good-looking, handsome, beautiful. **Ant.:** see **ugly.** See **beautiful.**

prevailing. Syn.: see **prevalent.**

prevalent. Syn.: prevailing, predominant, ruling, widespread, current, rife, common, general, usual, ordinary, established.

That which is *prevalent* exists or is spread widely; that which is *current* is in general circulation or a matter of common knowledge or acceptance; that which is *rife* is intensely prevalent and is accompanied by excitement: as, a *prevalent* belief; *current* political gossip; wild reports of a massacre were *rife*.

prevaricate. Syn.: equivocate, quibble, shuffle, lie. See **equivocate.**

prevarication. Syn.: see **evasion.**

prevent. Syn.: hinder, restrain, check, stop, bar, debar, preclude, obviate, thwart, avert, parry, frustrate, deter. See **hinder.**

previous. Syn.: prior, earlier, anterior, antecedent, precedent, preceding, foregoing, former.

Previous and *prior* are frequently interchangeable, but *previous* often expresses no connection with what follows, while *prior* often implies that being earlier in time also gives superior claim or right: as, the author's statement here disagrees with a *previous* one; *prior* allegiance. *Preceding* is usually applied to that which goes before (with the indefinite article) or immediately before (with the definite article) in time or place: as, a *preceding* administration; the *preceding* chapter. *Antecedent* may be used generally of what goes before, but may imply a causal relation, especially when used in the appositive or predicate position: as, an *antecedent* offer; the political conditions *antecedent* to the fall of the Roman Empire.

previously. Syn.: see **formerly.**

prevision. Syn.: see **foresight.**

prey. Syn.: spoil, plunder, booty, loot; quarry, victim.

price. Syn.: charge, cost, expense, value, worth.

Price usually represents the amount of money asked for a thing offered for sale; *cost*, the amount a buyer pays for a thing. *Charge* especially refers to cost of personal services; *expense*, to general, and often continued, outlays, as for keeping something up. *Value* and *worth* refer to the inherent utility or desirability that gives something its price.

prick. Syn.: puncture, pierce, sting, hurt, wound; goad, spur, incite, impel.

prickly. Syn.: see **thorny.**

pride. Syn.: self-esteem, vanity, vainglory, arrogance, hauteur, haughtiness, lordliness. **Ant.:** humility, modesty, meekness, lowliness.

priest. Syn.: see **clergyman.**

prim. Syn.: neat, precise, proper, formal, nice, prudish, demure.

primal. Syn.: see **primary.**

primary. Syn.: first, foremost, original, principal, chief, fundamental, prime, primal, pristine, primeval, primordial, primitive.

Primary may mean first in time, or, now especially, first in order of importance; *prime*, especially agrees with the latter meaning of primary; *primitive* suggests the characteristics of the origins or early stages of a development, and, hence, implies the simplicity of original things; *primal* is chiefly poetic for that which is most ancient or original: as, *primary* class; *primary* reason; the *prime* consideration; *prime* minister; *primitive* tribes or customs; the *primal* sin. *Primeval* means belonging to the first or earliest ages; *primordial* pertains to that which goes back to the beginning of things and hence is likely to be rudimentary in character; *pristine* applies to the desirable or unspoiled qualities of that which is early or original: as, *primeval* simplicity or forest; *primordial* instincts; *pristine* splendor or vigor.

prime, primeval. Syn.: see **primary.**

primitive. Syn.: early, pristine, primeval, aboriginal, original, ancient, old, old-fashioned, antique. See **primary.**

primordial. Syn.: see **primary.**

prince. Syn.: see **noble, ruler.**

princely. Syn.: regal, royal, imperial, noble, magnificent, sumptuous.

principal. Syn.: chief, cardinal, first, foremost, prime, paramount, dominant, preëminent, predominant, predominating, leading, main. Ant.: minor, secondary, subordinate, subsidiary, supplemental.

principally. Syn.: see **especially.**

principle. Syn.: law, rule, precept; rectitude, uprightness. See **rule.**

prior. Syn.: see **previous.**

priority. Syn.: antecedence, precedence, preëminence, predominance, superiority, supremacy.

priory. Syn.: see **convent.**

prison. Syn.: penitentiary, jail, lockup, workhouse, bridewell, bastile, clink, quod, calaboose, cooler, jug.

prisoner. Syn.: captive, hostage, jailbird.

pristine. Syn.: see **primary.**

private. Syn.: individual, personal, particular, special; secret, covert, secluded, isolated, sequestered, solitary, retired.

privation. Syn.: deprivation, want, need, destitution.

privilege. Syn.: liberty, license, right, prerogative, immunity, exemption, franchise, grant, advantage, favor.

A *privilege* is a special right or advantage enjoyed by one or more but generally not by all. A *prerogative* is a particular or official privilege, arising from one's character or position: as, the *privilege* of citizenship, the *prerogative* of a king.

prize, n. Syn.: reward, award, guerdon, meed, premium, trophy, laurel, palm. See **reward.**

prize, v. Syn.: see **appreciate.**

probable. Syn.: likely, presumable, credible. See **likely.**

probe. Syn.: see **examine.**

probity. Syn.: uprightness, honesty, integrity, sincerity, trustworthiness, incorruptibility. See **honesty.**

procedure. Syn.: see **process.**

proceed. Syn.: go, advance, progress, continue; issue, emanate, arise, result. Ant.: stop, halt, pause, wait.

Proceed emphasizes movement as from a place, especially movement that is a continuation after a cessation or halt. *Advance* applies to movement forward, especially towards an objective. *Progress* often adds to advance a suggestion of improvement.

proceeding. Syn.: action, doing, performance, transaction, measure, step. See **process.**

process. Syn.: proceeding, procedure, method, formula, operation.

Proceeding applies to what goes on or takes place on a given occasion. *Procedure* usually implies a formal or set way of doing a thing. A *process* is a series of progressive and interdependent steps by which something is accomplished.

procession. Syn.: parade, cavalcade, cortège, train, file.

proclaim. Syn.: declare, promulgate, publish, herald, blazon, trumpet, cry. See **announce.**

proclamation. Syn.: edict, decree, manifesto, bull, banns.

A *proclamation* is a public, official announcement or order, usually for some specific occasion. An *edict* is usually a public command of a sovereign, especially an autocrat, and carries the implication of absolute authority; a *decree* is generally the order of an executive body or court, and carries the implication of obligation to obey. A *manifesto* usually makes public the reason or motives for the actions of a sovereign or government.

proclivity. Syn.: inclination, propensity, tendency, aptitude, predisposition, proneness, bent, bias. See **inclination.**

procrastinate. Syn.: defer, postpone, delay. Ant.: hurry, hasten, quicken. See **defer.**

procure. Syn.: obtain, acquire, get, gain, win, secure, effect, cause. See **get.**

prodigal. Syn.: extravagant, wasteful, lavish, profuse. Ant.: frugal, saving, provident, stingy, close. See **profuse.**

prodigious. Syn.: marvelous, amazing, astonishing, astounding, extraordinary, monstrous, enormous, immense, huge, excessive, extreme. See **wonderful.**

prodigy. Syn.: portent, omen, sign; miracle, wonder, marvel.

produce, n. Syn.: see **harvest.**

produce, v. Syn.: bring forward, exhibit, show; generate, engender, bear, create, yield, furnish, supply, manufacture, make; cause, effect, occasion.

product. Syn.: see **production.**

production. Syn.: produce, product, creation, work.

productive. Syn.: see **fruitful.**

profanation. Syn.: desecration, defilement, debasement, pollution, sacrilege.

profane, a. Syn.: secular, temporal, worldly, unholy, unhallowed, unconsecrated, unsanctified; godless, ungodly, irreligious, irreverent, sacrilegious, impious, blasphemous. Ant.: sacred, holy, consecrated, sanctified; reverent, pious, godly, devout.

Profane, in the sense here discriminated, implies lack of reverence or actual contempt for sacred things; *blasphemous*, especially impious utterance against God or sacred things; *sacrilegious*, an invasion of the rights or sanctity of whatever is consecrated to God's service.

profane, v. Syn.: desecrate, defile, pollute, violate.

profanity. Syn.: see **blasphemy.**

profess. Syn.: declare, aver, avouch, avow, acknowledge, own; claim, assume, pretend. See **pretend.**

profession. Syn.: declaration, avowal, etc. (see **profess**); vocation, calling, occupation, business. See **occupation.**

proffer, n. Syn.: offer, tender, proposal.

proffer, v. Syn.: offer, tender, volunteer, propose. See **offer,** v.

proficiency. Syn.: see **progress,** n.

proficient, n. Syn.: see **expert,** n.

proficient, a. Syn.: skilled, versed, qualified, competent, adept.

profile. Syn.: see **outline.**

profit. Syn.: benefit, good, weal, welfare, behoof, avail; gain, dividend, revenue, proceeds, returns. See **gain,** n., **advantage.**

profitable. Syn.: advantageous, beneficial, useful, gainful, lucrative, remunerative, productive. Ant.: see **unprofitable.**

profligate. Syn.: see **abandoned.**

profound. Syn.: deep, low, abysmal; abstruse, recondite, obscure; thorough, complete, exhaustive; intense, extreme, great. Ant.: see **shallow.**

profuse. Syn.: lavish, extravagant, prodigal, abundant, bountiful, copious, exuberant, overflowing, superabundant.

Profuse implies a generous or abundant pouring forth or giving; *lavish*, unstinted, sometimes excessive expenditure or overflowing liberality; *extravagant*, unreasonable or wasteful expenditure, especially beyond one's means; *prodigal*, reckless or reprehensible waste, especially in unrestrained or riotous living.

profusion. Syn.: see **plenty.**

progenitor. Syn.: see **ancestor.**

progeny. Syn.: see **offspring.**

prognosticate. Syn.: see **foretell.**

prognostication. Syn.: see **prediction.**

progress, n. Syn.: advance, advancement, development, growth, improvement, progression, proficiency.

progress, v. Syn.: proceed, advance, develop, improve, grow. See **proceed.**

prohibit. Syn.: see **forbid.**

prohibition. Syn.: interdiction, inhibition, embargo.

project, n. Syn.: see **plan.**

project, *v.* **Syn.:** protrude, bulge, jut, beetle, overhang; plan, devise, scheme, contrive.

projection. Syn.: protuberance, prominence, bulge, bump.

prolific. Syn.: see **fruitful.**

prolix. Syn.: wordy, verbose, diffuse, long-winded, prolonged, protracted, tedious, tiresome, wearisome. **Ant.:** concise, succinct, terse, brief.

prolixity. Syn.: see **verbosity.**

prologue. Syn.: see **introduction.**

prolong. Syn.: lengthen, protract, stretch, extend, continue, draw out. See **lengthen.**

prominent. Syn.: projecting, jutting, protuberant; conspicuous, salient, marked; eminent, distinguished, leading. See **eminent.**

That is *prominent* which is outstanding; that is *conspicuous* which forcibly strikes the eye or attracts the attention; that which is *salient* juts out, as it were, and is therefore prominent or conspicuous.

promiscuous. Syn.: miscellaneous, indiscriminate, undiscriminating. See **miscellaneous.**

promise, *n.* **Syn.:** assurance, engagement, pledge, covenant, vow, word, parole.

promise, *v.* **Syn.:** assure, engage, pledge, plight, covenant.

promote. Syn.: advance, forward, further, push, encourage, foster, help, assist, facilitate, expedite, raise, prefer, elevate, exalt. **Ant.:** demote, lower, hinder, obstruct, impede.

To *promote* is to help anything forward in improvement, development, etc., or progress toward establishment; to *further* is to move forward or bring nearer to some desired end; to *facilitate* is to promote by making easier; to *expedite* is to hasten by clearing the way.

prompt, *a.* **Syn.:** ready, quick, speedy, swift, expeditious, punctual, immediate, timely, early. **Ant.:** slow, dilatory, behindhand, tardy, late.

Prompt implies quick and unhesitating action in response to a demand; *ready* adds to prompt the idea of natural endowment, preparation, or willingness; *expeditious* implies speedy execution or despatch of what is to be done.

prompt, *v.* **Syn.:** move, induce, incite, impel, instigate. See **actuate.**

promulgate. Syn.: see **announce.**

prone. Syn.: see **prostrate.**

proneness. Syn.: see **bent,** *n.*

pronounce. Syn.: see **enunciate, utter,** *v.*

proof. Syn.: test, trial, essay, demonstration, experiment; verification, corroboration, confirmation, attestation, certification, testimony, evidence. See **trial, evidence.**

prop. Syn.: support, staff, stay, brace, fulcrum, shore, stanchion, buttress.

propagate. Syn.: multiply, generate, breed; increase, extend, spread, diffuse, disseminate, promulgate, circulate, transmit.

propagation. Syn.: generation, reproduction, breeding; diffusion, dissemination.

propensity. Syn.: see **inclination.**

proper. Syn.: peculiar, individual, characteristic; appropriate, suitable, fit, fitting, befitting, becoming, meet, seemly, right, legitimate; decorous, decent, respectable, correct, conventional, formal. **Ant.:** see **improper.** See **fitting.**

property. Syn.: possessions, estate, land, goods, effects, chattels, stock, merchandise, wares, commodities; quality, attribute, characteristic, trait. See **quality.**

Property is the general word for material things which are owned. *Goods* refers to movable property, especially that comprising the stock in trade of a business; *effects*, to personal property, including things even of the least value; *estate*, to property, often landed property, which has been, or is capable of being, handed down to descendants.

prophecy, *n.* **Syn.:** see **prediction.**

prophesy, *v.* **Syn.:** predict, foretell, prognosticate, augur, divine, vaticinate. See **foretell.**

prophet. Syn.: soothsayer, prognosticator, diviner, vaticinator, seer, oracle, sibyl.

propinquity. Syn.: nearness, proximity.

propitiate. Syn.: see **appease, pacify.**

propitiation. Syn.: appeasement, conciliation, reconciliation, atonement, expiation, satisfaction.

propitious. Syn.: gracious, benign, kind, helpful, advantageous, auspicious, favorable, fortunate, promising, opportune, happy, lucky. **Ant.:** unpropitious, inauspicious, unfavorable, forbidding, antagonistic, hostile, adverse. See **favorable.**

proportion. Syn.: see **symmetry.**

proportionate. Syn.: proportional, commensurate.

proposal. Syn.: offer, proposition, overture.

A *proposal* offers something for acceptance or rejection; a *proposition* proposes something to be considered or deliberated upon as to its truth, wisdom, practicability, or the like; an *overture* is an opening move looking toward the settlement of a controversy, or preparing the way for a proposal, etc.

propose. Syn.: propound, offer, present, move, suggest, recommend; purpose, intend, mean.

proposition. Syn.: see **proposal.**

proprietor. Syn.: see **possessor.**

propriety. Syn.: seemliness, decency, modesty, respectability, decorum, etiquette; suitability, fitness, aptness.

Propriety implies conformance to an ethical standard or established convention; *decorum*, conformance to what is seemly, appropriate, or decent in behavior; *etiquette*, observance of the formal or conventional requirements governing behavior in polite society.

prorogue. Syn.: see **adjourn.**

prosaic. Syn.: commonplace, matter-of-fact, prosy, humdrum, uninteresting, dull, stupid, tedious. See **unimaginative.**

proscribe. Syn.: outlaw, exile, banish; interdict, prohibit, forbid. See **forbid.**

proselyte. Syn.: see **convert.**

prospect. Syn.: view, scene, sight; outlook, hope, promise, expectation, anticipation. See **view,** *n.*

prosper. Syn.: see **thrive.**

prosperous. Syn.: successful, thriving, flourishing, well-to-do, rich, wealthy. **Ant.:** unsuccessful, unfortunate, improvident, needy, poor. See **fortunate.**

prostitute. Syn.: harlot, strumpet, whore, bawd, wanton, courtezan, cocotte, lorette, demirep, drab, punk.

prostrate. Syn.: prone, supine, groveling, flat.

prosy. Syn.: see **unimaginative.**

protect. Syn.: defend, guard, shield, shelter, screen, keep, secure, fortify. See **guard,** *v.*

protection. Syn.: defense, guard, security; shield, shelter, safeguard, screen, bulwark, fender, fence.

protector. Syn.: defender, guardian, patron.

protest. Syn.: affirm, assert, aver; remonstrate, object, expostulate.

prototype. Syn.: see **pattern.**

protract. Syn.: see **lengthen.**

protrude. Syn.: see **project,** *v.*

protuberance. Syn.: see **projection.**

proud. Syn.: arrogant, haughty, disdainful, supercilious, overbearing, overweening, vain; dignified, majestic, stately, lofty. **Ant.:** meek, humble, lowly.

Proud implies sensitiveness and a jealous preservation of one's dignity, station, etc., often an unreasonable estimate of one's own superiority in any respect; *haughty*, lofty reserve and confident assumption of superiority over others; *arrogant*, insolent or overbearing behavior arising from an exaggerated belief in one's importance; *supercilious*, a condescending or contemptuous manner towards others; *disdainful*, pride mingled with disregard, aversion, or indignation.

prove. Syn.: test, try; demonstrate, show; verify, corroborate, substantiate, confirm. **Ant.:** disprove, confute, refute.

provender. Syn.: see **feed,** *n.*

proverb. Syn.: adage, axiom, maxim, aphorism, apothegm, saw, saying, truism, dictum, motto, precept.

A *proverb* is a short, pithy saying popularly repeated, usually expressing simply and concretely, although often metaphorically, a truth based on common sense or the practical experience of mankind. *Adage* stresses the traditional quality of a proverb made venerable by age. A *saw* is usually a homely truth that has become trite and wearisome by its reiteration. An *aphorism* is a truth pointedly set forth, relating rather to speculative principles, ethics, or science than to practical matters, and forming a brief and excellent statement of a doctrine: as, "Maladies are cured by nature, not by remedies," or, "Life is short and art is long." An *apothegm* is a terse saying of a sententious character, usually about matters of a common or homely kind: as, "Heaven helps those that help themselves." A *maxim* is a brief statement of a general and practical truth, especially one that serves as a rule for conduct: as, "It is wise to risk no more than one can afford to lose." An *axiom* is a self-evident or universally conceded truth which needs no proof: as, "A straight line is the shortest distance between two points."

provide. **Syn.:** supply, furnish, afford. See **furnish.**

provided. **Syn.:** if, on condition that.

provident. **Syn.:** foreseeing, prudent, careful, economical, frugal. **Ant.:** see **improvident, imprudent.**

provoke. **Syn.:** stir up, stimulate, rouse, incite, kindle, fan, instigate; anger, incense, exasperate, irritate, vex, nettle, chafe, gall, offend, displease. See **irritate.**

prowess. **Syn.:** valor, bravery, courage, intrepidity, daring, gallantry. **Ant.:** cowardice, pusillanimity, fear, timidity. See **bravery.**

prowl. **Syn.:** creep, rove, wander. See **lurk.**

proximate. **Syn.:** see **near.**

proximity. **Syn.:** see **propinquity.**

prudence. **Syn.:** discretion, judiciousness, judgment, foresight, forethought, care, caution, circumspection, wariness.

prudent. **Syn.:** discreet, sagacious, judicious, wise, politic, careful, heedful, cautious, circumspect, wary, provident, economical, prudential. **Ant.:** imprudent, indiscreet, thoughtless, foolish, rash, improvident, wasteful.

The *prudent* man exercises careful judgment in following the most advantageous course; the *circumspect* man looks around warily and with due regard for propriety before taking any step. He who is *discreet* wisely discerns the most expedient or politic way to act; he who is *provident* foresees the future, and takes judicious steps to provide for its demands.

prudish. **Syn.:** see **modest.**

prying. **Syn.:** see **curious.**

public house. **Syn.:** see **inn.**

publish. **Syn.:** proclaim, promulgate, blazon, advertise, disclose, divulge, reveal. **Ant.:** suppress, withhold, conceal, hide. See **announce.**

pucker. **Syn.:** wrinkle, crease, corrugate, cockle, purse.

puerile. **Syn.:** boyish, childish, juvenile, youthful, immature, weak, trivial, foolish, silly. See **young.**

pugnacious. **Syn.:** bellicose, quarrelsome, contentious. See **belligerent.**

puissant. **Syn.:** see **powerful.**

pull. **Syn.:** draw, drag, haul, tow, tug, jerk, twitch; pick, pluck, extract.

To *pull* is to move or endeavor to move something in the direction from which a force is exerted: as, to *pull* a rope or a cart. To *tug* is to pull at persistently or with great effort: as, to *tug* at one's sleeve, to *tug* at a great weight. *Jerk* implies a sudden or abrupt pulling; to *twitch* is to jerk lightly or spasmodically.

pulverize. **Syn.:** powder, bray, triturate, comminute, levigate.

punch. **Syn.:** pierce, puncture, perforate; thump, strike, prod, poke, push, nudge.

punctilious. **Syn.:** particular, precise, scrupulous, exact. **Ant.:** careless, negligent, remiss, lax, loose. See **scrupulous.**

punctual. **Syn.:** see **prompt.**

puncture. **Syn.:** pierce, prick, perforate.

pungent. **Syn.:** sharp, piquant, biting, stinging, spicy, tart, acrid, peppery, lively, caustic, sarcastic, poignant.

That which is *pungent* has a sharp, penetrating taste or smell, such as that of strong spices. That which is *piquant* is agreeably sharp to the taste, or, figuratively, pleasantly stinging or provocative to the mental palate: as, a *piquant* sauce; a *piquant* style of writing. *Poignant* is chiefly used of that which is painfully sharp, as a physical craving, or, especially, emotional distress: as, *poignant* hunger; *poignant* sorrow.

punish. **Syn.:** chastise, chasten, castigate, correct, discipline, scourge, whip, cane, lash, flog, beat, thrash.

To *punish* is chiefly to inflict penalty or pain as a retribution for misdeeds, with little or no notion of correction or improvement. *Chastise* is a dignified word for the infliction of (especially) corporal punishment, combining in some degree the notions of desert and correction. *Chasten* aims primarily at the reformation of the offender and is used especially in a spiritual sense for providential disciplining by God.

punishment. **Syn.:** chastisement, castigation, retribution, visitation.

puny. **Syn.:** undeveloped, undersized, stunted, diminutive, little, small, weak, feeble, petty, insignificant. **Ant.:** large, strong, hardy, robust.

pupil. **Syn.:** scholar, student, disciple, learner.

A *pupil* is one under the close supervision of a teacher, either because of his youth or of specialization in some branch of study: as, a *pupil* in a primary grade, a *pupil* of a famous musician. A *disciple* is one who follows the teachings or doctrines of a person (or school) he considers a master or authority: as, a *disciple* of Swedenborg, of post-impressionism. A *student* is one attending a higher institution of learning, or one who has devoted much attention to a particular problem, or one who by temperament is given to assiduous study: as, a college *student*, a close *student* of economic conditions. A *scholar* is one who attends an elementary school, or one who has acquired wide erudition in some field of learning: as, a youthful *scholar*, a great Sanskrit *scholar*.

pure. **Syn.:** unmixed, unadulterated, unalloyed, unsophisticated; genuine, clear, faultless, perfect, correct; mere, sheer, utter, bare, absolute; virtuous, chaste, virgin, innocent, clean, spotless, undefiled, unpolluted, uncorrupted, unstained, immaculate. **Ant.:** see **impure.** See **clean,** *a.*

purify. **Syn.:** cleanse, purge, expurgate, refine, distil, sublime.

puritan. **Syn.:** puritanic, puritanical, austere, strict, straitlaced.

purloin. **Syn.:** see **steal.**

purport. **Syn.:** import, meaning, sense, gist, signification, tenor, drift, intent. See **meaning.**

purpose, *n.* **Syn.:** intention, intent, design, object, aim, goal, end.

purpose, *v.* **Syn.:** intend, mean, propose, contemplate, design. See **intend.**

pursue. **Syn.:** follow, chase, hunt, track, dog, hound, seek.

pursuit. **Syn.:** pursuance. See **occupation.**

push. **Syn.:** shove, thrust, press, drive, force, impel, compel, propel, crowd, jostle, hustle, elbow; urge, hasten, prosecute, promote.

To *push* is to move or attempt to move something in the direction in which a force is exerted. To *shove*, sometimes a more colloquial word, is to cause to move by sliding, or to push roughly. To *thrust* is a dignified word meaning to push sharply, often with the effect of penetrating through or into something.

pusillanimous. **Syn.:** faint-hearted, timorous, cowardly, spiritless, feeble, weak, effeminate. **Ant.:** brave, valiant, intrepid, courageous, manly. See **timid.**

put. **Syn.:** set, place, lay, deposit; propose, offer, state, express.

Put is a very indefinite word to indicate a change of position or condition. *Set* suggests fixedness, especially of something upright: as, to *set* a pole in the ground; *lay* suggests a horizontal position: as, to *lay* a book on the table. *Place* suggests definiteness of location: as, to *place* one's finger on a sore spot.

putrefy. **Syn.:** decompose, rot. See **decay.**

puzzle, *n.* **Syn.:** bewilderment, maze, quandary; enigma, crux, riddle, conundrum, rebus.

A *puzzle* is a question or problem intricate enough to be perplexing to the mind; it is sometimes a contrivance made purposely perplexing to test one's ingenuity. A *riddle* is an intentionally obscure statement or question, the meaning of or answer to which is to be obtained only by guessing. An *enigma* is a baffling problem which confounds the reason and defies solution.

puzzle, *v.* **Syn.:** perplex, bewilder, mystify, pose, nonplus, confuse. See **perplex.**

pygmy. **Syn.:** see **dwarf.**

Q

quack. **Syn.:** quacksalver, mountebank, charlatan, empiric, impostor, pretender.

A *quack* is an ignorant impostor who pretends to medical knowledge or skill. An *empiric*, originally one ignorant of medical theory who based his practice entirely upon experience, is now one who practises medicine or surgery without being regularly or properly trained for it. A *mountebank*, originally a traveling quack who sold his nostrums with the aid of tricks and chicanery, is now one who goes from place to place obtaining money by jugglery, clownery, or other cheap entertainment. A *charlatan* is an unscrupulous pretender, especially to knowledge or skill which he does not possess.

quaff. **Syn.:** see **drink,** *v.*

quagmire. Syn.: bog, swamp, marsh, fen, morass, slough.

quail. Syn.: shrink, flinch, blench, falter, cower, tremble, quake. See **shrink.**

quaint. Syn.: curious, strange, uncommon, odd, fanciful, whimsical, old-fashioned, antique.

quake. Syn.: shake, shiver, shudder, tremble, quiver, vibrate. See **shiver.**

qualified. Syn.: fitted, fit, capable, competent, eligible; modified, limited, restricted. **Ant.:** see **unqualified.**

qualify. Syn.: fit, prepare, equip, capacitate; modify, limit, restrict, condition; moderate, reduce, diminish, temper, soften, mitigate. See **temper,** v.

quality. Syn.: property, attribute, trait, characteristic, character, feature, accident, predicate, mark, affection, difference; nature, kind, grade.

A *quality* is a characteristic which determines the nature of a person or thing in some particular. A *property* is a peculiar quality belonging to something as distinctly its own. An *attribute* is a quality which one conceives of as fundamental or innate: as, the *attributes* of God are omniscience, omnipotence, etc. An *accident* is an accidental or contingent quality.

qualm. Syn.: misgiving, scruple, compunction, uneasiness.

quandary. Syn.: perplexity, uncertainty, puzzle, dilemma, predicament, difficulty, strait, pickle. See **predicament.**

quantity. Syn.: amount, sum, quantum.

quarrel, n. **Syn.:** dispute, contention, disagreement, controversy, dissension, feud, vendetta, altercation, bickering, wrangle, jangle, squabble, brawl, scuffle, tussle, affray, fray, broil, mêlée, rumpus, fracas, row, fuss, spat, tiff, jar.

A *quarrel* varies in degrees of seriousness from a slight, brief, and petty difference or dispute to an angry, violent altercation or deep-seated hostility, but in either case it is confined to words. A *feud* is an enduring hostility between families or groups (rarely individuals) often resulting in acts of violence and efforts at retaliation and revenge. A *vendetta* is a bloody, murderous, and often treacherous feud, such as is sometimes found in rude and semicivilized society.

quarrel, v. **Syn.:** dispute, disagree, differ, bicker, wrangle, squabble. See **dispute.**

quarrelsome. Syn.: disputatious, contentious, litigious, irascible, choleric. **Ant.:** amiable, friendly, peaceable.

quarry. Syn.: see **prey.**

quay. Syn.: see **pier.**

queer. Syn.: strange, odd, peculiar, singular, unique, curious, quaint, freakish, fantastic, bizarre, grotesque, ludicrous, droll, whimsical, erratic, eccentric. **Ant.:** ordinary, usual, common, customary. See **singular.**

quell. Syn.: suppress, crush, quash, overpower, subdue, extinguish, smother.

quench. Syn.: extinguish, suppress, stifle, check, repress; slake, allay.

querulous. Syn.: complaining, faultfinding, peevish, fretful, petulant, whining, cross.

query. Syn.: see **question,** n.

quest. Syn.: see **search,** n.

question, n. **Syn.:** interrogation, query, interrogatory, inquiry; problem, proposition, subject, theme, topic.

A *question* may be asked either to obtain information desired from another, or to test his knowledge. A *query* is usually a question without force upon some particular matter or point about which one desires to know or on which one has some doubt. An *interrogatory* is an authoritative or searching questioning which must be replied to.

question, v. **Syn.:** ask, interrogate, query, examine, quiz, catechize, pump, heckle; doubt, dispute, challenge, controvert. See **ask.**

questionable. Syn.: debatable, disputable, controvertible, doubtful, dubious, uncertain, ambiguous, suspicious. **Ant.:** see **unquestionable.**

quibble, n. **Syn.:** evasion, prevarication, equivocation, sophism, shift.

quibble, v. **Syn.:** see **equivocate.**

quick. Syn.: living, alive, animate, active; fast, rapid, swift, speedy, fleet, hurried, hasty, precipitate, expeditious, summary, prompt, ready, brisk, nimble, agile; impatient, excitable, irritable, irascible, sharp. **Ant.:** slow, dilatory, sluggish, phlegmatic, deliberate.

Quick, the generic word, implies promptness, or accomplishment in a brief time; *fast* and *rapid* suggest speedy movement; *swift,* great rapidity; *fleet,* a poetic word, suggests light and easy, as well as rapid, movement, especially in the limbs of living creatures.

quicken. Syn.: vivify, animate, stimulate, incite, rouse, accelerate, speed, expedite, despatch, hasten, hurry. **Ant.:** impede, hinder, obstruct, check, retard, delay.

Quicken and its Latin equivalent, *accelerate,* both mean to increase the rate of motion of something. *Hasten* and *hurry* indicate the exercise of personal effort to do something quickly, *hurry* suggesting somewhat more of excitement and confusion.

quickness. Syn.: fastness, rapidity, swiftness, speed, celerity, fleetness, velocity, promptness; despatch, alacrity, agility.

Quickness is the general word for rapidity of action. *Celerity* is applied to the swift voluntary movements of beings, especially to such as accomplish things quickly; *alacrity* adds the idea of a ready willingness to set about some project.

quiescent. Syn.: see **dormant.**

quiet, n. **Syn.:** see **rest,** n.

quiet, a. **Syn.:** see **still,** a.

quiver. Syn.: see **shake.**

quixotic. Syn.: see **ideal,** a.

R

rabble. Syn.: see **mob.**

rabid. Syn.: furious, raging, violent, mad, rampant, fanatical.

race. Syn.: family, tribe, stock, lineage, line, strain. See **people.**

rack. Syn.: torture, stretch, strain, wrench, disjoint, rend, tear. See **torment.**

racket. Syn.: see **noise.**

racy. Syn.: spicy, pungent, piquant, fresh, smart; vigorous, forcible, spirited, lively, sprightly, exhilarating. **Ant.:** tasteless, flavorless, stale, flat, vapid, insipid, dull, prosy.

As applied to literary style both of the following words suggest cleverness and wit. *Racy* implies more of the rapid, provocative, and sarcastic, *spicy,* more of the smart, sensational, and risqué.

radiance. Syn.: brilliance, brilliancy, effulgence, refulgence, luster, brightness, splendor.

radiant. Syn.: see **bright.**

radiate. Syn.: diffuse, shine, gleam, beam.

radical. Syn.: original, inherent, organic, intrinsic, basic, fundamental; extreme, fanatical. See **extreme,** a.

raft. Syn.: see **boat.**

rage, n. **Syn.:** fury, frenzy, passion, anger, indignation, wrath; vogue, fashion, craze, mania. See **fury.**

rage, v. **Syn.:** rave, fume, storm, chafe, fret.

ragged. Syn.: rent, torn, tattered, frayed, frazzled; jagged, craggy, rocky, rough, broken.

raid. Syn.: incursion, invasion, foray, inroad, descent. See **invasion.**

rail. Syn.: scoff, inveigh, upbraid, scold, reproach, abuse. See **declaim.**

raillery. Syn.: banter, pleasantry, jesting, ridicule. See **banter,** n.

raiment. Syn.: see **clothes.**

rain. Syn.: drizzle, mizzle, mist, shower, downpour.

raise. Syn.: lift, uplift, elevate, rear, erect, hoist, heave; rouse, stir, incite; heighten, intensify, increase, augment, advance, enhance, promote, exalt; breed, produce, cultivate, bring up, grow; gather, collect, muster, levy. **Ant.:** see **lower.**

Raise, the most general word, suggests the bringing of something to or towards an upright position with one end resting on the ground, or it may be used like *lift* of moving an object generally a comparatively short distance upward, but breaking completely its physical contact with the place where it was. *Elevate* implies raising to a relatively higher level, position, or state. *Heave* implies lifting with effort or exertion; *hoist,* lifting slowly and gradually something of considerable weight, usually with mechanical help, such as a crane or derrick.

rake. Syn.: rakehell, profligate, libertine, debauchee, roué.

rakish. Syn.: licentious, dissolute; smart, showy, jaunty, dashing.

rally. Syn.: reassemble, collect; revive, rouse, recover, recuperate; banter, tease, joke, quiz. See **banter,** v.

ram. Syn.: butt, batter, strike, thrust, poke; stuff, cram, compress.

ramble. Syn.: wander, roam, rove, stroll, saunter, stray, range, prowl.

Ramble implies pleasant, care-free wandering about with no specific purpose. *Roam* implies rambling over a larger area, especially as prompted by restlessness or curiosity. *Rove* sometimes implies wandering with specific incentive or aim, as an animal for prey. *Range* usually implies wandering over a more or less defined but extensive area in search of something: as, a forester *ranges* the woods.

rambling. Syn.: wandering, roaming, etc. (see **ramble**); disconnected, incoherent, discursive, digressive.

rampant. Syn.: rearing, ramping; violent, raging, furious, unbridled, unrestrained.

rampart. Syn.: bulwark, breastwork, outwork, redan, embankment, mound, elevation, barricade, wall, fortification, defense.

ramshackle. Syn.: loose, shaky, unsteady, disjointed, rickety, dilapidated, tumble-down.

rancor. Syn.: malice, spitefulness, spite, hatred, malevolence, malignity, virulence, animosity, enmity, bitterness, vindictiveness. **Ant.:** love, compassion, forgiveness, pardon. See **malice.**

rancorous. Syn.: malicious, spiteful, malevolent, malignant, virulent, bitter, vindictive.

random. Syn.: haphazard, accidental, chance, casual, stray, aimless.

range, n. Syn.: row, line, tier, chain, series, sequence; scope, compass, reach, sweep, latitude, extent.

Range emphasizes extent and diversity: as, the *range* of his interests was very wide. *Scope* often suggests a proper limit, *compass* a definite limit: as, the *scope* of one's obligations, the *compass* of one's mind.

range, v. Syn.: arrange, array, classify, class, rank; rove, roam, wander, ramble; stretch, extend, run. See **ramble.**

rank, n. Syn.: row, line, range, series; class, order, grade, position, standing, status, station, degree; eminence, distinction.

rank, a. Syn.: exuberant, luxuriant, overgrown, coarse, gross; offensive, tainted, rancid, strong, fetid; foul, indecent, obscene; absolute, downright, utter. See **luxuriant.**

rank, v. Syn.: arrange, classify, class, group, estimate.

ransack. Syn.: rummage, search, overhaul, explore. See **search.**

ransom. Syn.: redeem, deliver, liberate, release. See **redeem.**

rant, n. Syn.: declamation, vociferation, rodomontade, bombast.

rant, v. Syn.: declaim, vociferate, spout, rave. See **speak.**

rap. Syn.: strike, knock, tap, thump, thwack, whack, bang.

rapacious. Syn.: grasping, greedy, avaricious, extortionate, predatory, voracious, ravenous.

rapacity. Syn.: see **avarice.**

rapid. Syn.: swift, fast, fleet, speedy, quick, expeditious, hasty, hurried, cursory. See **quick.**

rapidity. Syn.: swiftness, fleetness, speed, velocity, celerity, expedition, despatch, haste.

rapine. Syn.: robbery, depredation, spoliation, pillage, plunder.

rapt. Syn.: enraptured, transported, ecstatic, fascinated, spellbound, engrossed, absorbed.

rapture. Syn.: transport, ecstasy, exaltation, bliss, delight, joy.

Rapture is mental exaltation from intense joy or delight. *Ecstasy* describes a state of emotion which lifts one out of oneself and beyond the consciousness of one's surroundings. *Transport* implies that one is carried away by the strength of one's feeling.

rare. Syn.: thin, rarefied, tenuous, fine; scarce, infrequent, unusual, uncommon, recherché, unique, unparalleled; excellent, exquisite, valuable, precious.

A thing is *rare* which is seldom to be met with and therefore often sought after; the word often implies exceptional quality or value: as, a *rare* book or print. *Scarce* is applied to that of which there is a deficient supply; it usually implies a previous or usual condition of greater abundance: as, fruit is *scarce* this year.

rascal. Syn.: rogue, knave, scoundrel, villain, miscreant, varlet, caitiff, blackguard, scapegrace, scamp, rapscallion, scalawag. See **rogue.**

rascality. Syn.: knavery, villainy, trickery, chicanery, fraud.

rash. Syn.: hasty, precipitate, headlong, reckless, heedless, incautious, foolhardy, madcap, temerarious, venturesome, adventurous, bold, daring, impulsive, impetuous. **Ant.:** deliberate, cool, calm, cautious, wary, discreet.

The *rash* man hastens to do a thing with little thought of the consequences, often on the spur of the moment; the *reckless* man shows an even greater disregard of consequences; the *foolhardy* man shows such absence of thought or judgment in taking great risks that he seems to have the senselessness of a fool.

rashness. Syn.: hastiness, precipitancy, thoughtlessness, recklessness, temerity, foolhardiness.

rate, n. Syn.: ratio, proportion, degree, quantity, amount; rank, order, class. See **tax,** n.

rate, v. Syn.: reckon, calculate, estimate, appraise, value, assess.

ratify. Syn.: confirm, sanction, authorize, substantiate. See **approve.**

ration. Syn.: allowance, share, portion, allotment.

rational. Syn.: reasonable, sensible, sane, sound, intelligent, wise, judicious, discreet. **Ant.:** irrational, unreasonable, unwise, foolish, crazy, insane. See **reasonable.**

ravage, n. Syn.: devastation, havoc, ruin, waste, damage, harm.

ravage, v. Syn.: devastate, lay waste, waste, despoil, desolate, plunder, pillage, sack, ruin, destroy.

To *ravage* is to despoil and plunder with violence; to *devastate* is to destroy, often wantonly as does an invading army; to *waste* is to leave a trail of desolation and dreariness behind.

rave. Syn.: rage, rant, storm, fume.

ravenous. Syn.: see **voracious.**

ravine. Syn.: glen, gorge, gulch, gully, arroyo, couloir, cañon.

ravish. Syn.: transport, enrapture, entrance, enchant, delight; deflower, violate, rape.

raw. Syn.: uncooked, unprepared, untrained, unwrought, unfinished, unrefined, crude, rude, coarse; inexperienced, unskilled, undisciplined, green; damp, chilly, bleak; galled, abraded, sore.

Raw applies particularly to material not yet changed by a process, manufacture, or preparation for consumption; *crude,* to that which has not been refined; *rude,* to what is still in a condition of rough simplicity: as, *raw* cotton, silk, leather; *crude* petroleum; *rude* agricultural implements.

raw-boned. Syn.: see **gaunt.**

ray. Syn.: beam, gleam. See **gleam,** n.

raze. Syn.: see **destroy.**

reach. Syn.: extend, stretch, hold out; come to, arrive at, attain, gain.

readiness. Syn.: preparedness, fitness; willingness, inclination; promptness, quickness, alacrity, expedition, facility, ease, aptness, dexterity, knack, skill, expertness.

ready. Syn.: prepared, equipped, fitted; willing, disposed; prompt, quick, unhesitating, facile, easy, dexterous, clever; accessible, available, convenient, handy. See **prompt,** a.

real. Syn.: actual, genuine, authentic, true, veritable, substantial, positive, certain. **Ant.:** see **unreal.**

Real is applied to that which has unquestioned existence as opposed to what is imaginary, counterfeit, artificial, feigned, or the like. *Actual* applies to that which is brought to be or to pass, as opposed to what is possible, rumored, believed, likely, hypothetical, etc. But the distinction between the two words is not always sharply maintained.

reality. Syn.: actuality, truth, verity.

realize. Syn.: accomplish, achieve, effectuate; conceive, apprehend, understand.

really. Syn.: actually, truly, veritably, positively, absolutely, indeed.

realm. Syn.: kingdom, dominion, domain, territory, region, province, sphere, department.

rear, a. Syn.: back, hinder, hindmost, last.

rear, v. Syn.: lift, raise, elevate, hoist; erect, build, construct; breed, grow, foster, educate, bring up.

reason, n. Syn.: ground, motive, cause, purpose, object, aim, consideration, inducement; intellect, understanding, rationality, logic, sense. See **motive.**

reason, v. Syn.: ratiocinate, syllogize, argue, debate, deduce, infer, think; expostulate, remonstrate.

reasonable. Syn.: rational, sensible, logical, just; moderate, equitable, fair. **Ant.:** see **unreasonable.**

Reasonable usually refers to the application of sound sense and equable judgment to practical matters; *rational* indicates possessing or exercising the faculty of reason: as, a *reasonable* proposition; man is a *rational* being.

reasoning. Syn.: ratiocination, argumentation, discussion, debate.

rebate. Syn.: deduction, discount, allowance.

rebel, *n.* **Syn.:** revolter, insurgent, insurrectionist, mutineer.

rebel, *v.* **Syn.:** revolt, mutiny.

rebellion. Syn.: revolt, insurrection, mutiny, sedition, revolution, insubordination, disobedience. **Ant.:** see **loyalty, obedience.** See **insurrection.**

rebellious. Syn.: insurgent, insurrectionary, mutinous, seditious, insubordinate, disobedient, intractable, refractory. **Ant.:** loyal, faithful, obedient, submissive, compliant, docile.

rebound. Syn.: recoil, reverberate, ricochet.

rebuff. Syn.: check, repulse, snub, defeat.

rebuke, *n.* **Syn.:** reproof, reprimand, reprehension, censure. See **admonition.**

rebuke, *v.* **Syn.:** reprove, reprimand, reprehend, censure, upbraid, chide. See **reprove.**

recall. Syn.: call back, summon, withdraw, revoke, countermand, cancel, retract, recant, repeal, rescind, annul, abrogate; recollect, remember. See **remember.**

recant. Syn.: retract, disavow, renounce, abjure, forswear. See **forswear.**

recapitulate. Syn.: restate, repeat, recount, rehearse, recite, review, summarize, sum up.

recede. Syn.: withdraw, retreat, retire, retrograde. **Ant.:** advance, progress, increase.

receipt. Syn.: recipe, formula, prescription.

receive. Syn.: accept, take, get; admit, greet, welcome.

That which is *received* has usually been tendered, offered, presented, or sent, but not always with the desire or willingness of the recipient: as, to *receive* a letter, news, an appointment; to *receive* a wound, blow, or insult. *Accept* implies willingness to receive what is offered and abide by the consequences: as, to *accept* an apology, invitation, or contract. One may *take* what has or has not been offered, or what one does or does not desire: as, to *take* a bribe; to *take* another's purse; to *take* credit for something; to *take* offense or a cold.

recent. Syn.: late, new, fresh, modern. See **new.**

receptacle. Syn.: receiver, container, repository.

reception. Syn.: receiving, receipt; greeting, welcome; soirée, levee, assembly, function.

recess. Syn.: intermission, respite, prorogation, dissolution, adjournment; nook, corner, alcove, niche, indentation.

reciprocal. Syn.: mutual, correlative, correspondent, complementary. See **mutual.**

recital. Syn.: recitation, repetition, rehearsal, performance, concert; relation, account, narration, narrative.

recite. Syn.: repeat, rehearse, recount, relate, narrate, enumerate, detail, recapitulate. See **relate.**

reckless. Syn.: careless, heedless, thoughtless, rash, foolhardy, temerarious, hasty. **Ant.:** careful, heedful, deliberate, cautious, wary. See **rash.**

reckon. Syn.: count, enumerate, compute, calculate, cast; regard, consider, esteem, value, account, deem.

reclaim. Syn.: reform, regenerate, redeem, rescue, restore; subdue, tame, domesticate. See **recover.**

recline. Syn.: lean, lie, lounge, loll.

recluse. Syn.: hermit, eremite, ascetic, solitary, anchoret, anchoress, monk, nun.

A *recluse* withdraws from the world, and lives, usually in a single cell, a life devoted to religious meditation; more broadly, the word is used of any one who lives apart because of a desire for solitude. A *hermit* usually withdraws to desert or lonely places for religious solitude, but does not deny himself shelter or occupation. An *anchoret* chooses absolute solitude, and practises excessive austerities and endures great privations.

recoil. Syn.: retreat, shrink, flinch; rebound, react.

recollect. Syn.: see **remember.**

recollection. Syn.: see **memory.**

recommend. Syn.: commend, praise, approve.

recommendation. Syn.: see **testimonial.**

recompense, *n.* **Syn.:** repayment, compensation, requital, remuneration, reward, amends, satisfaction, indemnity. See **reward.**

recompense, *v.* **Syn.:** repay, compensate, requite, remunerate, reward. See **compensate.**

reconcile. Syn.: conciliate, appease, pacify, propitiate; harmonize, adjust, settle. **Ant.:** estrange, alienate, disaffect.

reconciliation. Syn.: reconcilement, appeasement, pacification, propitiation, reunion, atonement.

recondite. Syn.: concealed, hidden, secret, abstruse, obscure, dark, profound, deep, esoteric, occult. See **obscure.**

record, *n.* **Syn.:** register, chronicle, archives, annals, minutes, notes, memorandum, memorial, memoir, diary, account.

record, *v.* **Syn.:** register, chronicle, note, enroll, enlist.

recount. Syn.: tell, narrate, rehearse, recite, repeat, detail. See **relate.**

recover. Syn.: regain, repossess, retake, recapture, reclaim, rescue, retrieve, repair, recoup; rally, recuperate, convalesce.

To *recover* is to obtain again what one has lost possession of; to *reclaim* is to bring back from error or wrong-doing, or from a rude or undeveloped state; to *retrieve* is to bring back, especially something to its former prosperous state: as, to *recover* one's equilibrium, health; to *reclaim* criminals, arid land; to *retrieve* one's fortune, reputation.

recovery. Syn.: repossession, recapture, retrieval, restoration, recuperation, convalescence.

recreant. Syn.: cowardly, craven, pusillanimous; unfaithful, untrue, false, apostate.

recreate. Syn.: revive, refresh, reanimate, enliven, cheer, entertain.

recreation. Syn.: refreshment, relaxation, diversion, amusement, entertainment, pastime, play, sport, fun. See **pastime.**

rectify. Syn.: correct, amend, remedy, redress, adjust, regulate; purify, refine. See **amend.**

rectitude. Syn.: uprightness, integrity, honesty, probity, virtue. See **honesty.**

rector. Syn.: see **clergyman.**

red. Syn.: crimson, scarlet, ruby, auburn, rubescent, bloody, fiery, flaming, florid, rubicund, ruddy, blowzy, blowzed, flushed, blushing.

redeem. Syn.: repurchase, regain, recover, ransom, deliver, liberate, release.

Redeem is wider in its application than *ransom*, and means to buy back or improve the condition of anything, as by money, endeavor, devotion, sacrifice, or the like. To *ransom* is to redeem a person from captivity by paying a stipulated price.

redemption. Syn.: repurchase, ransom, deliverance, salvation.

redolence. Syn.: see **smell.**

redolent. Syn.: see **odorous.**

redoubt. Syn.: see **fortification.**

redoubtable. Syn.: see **formidable.**

redound. Syn.: react, result, contribute, conduce. See **conduce.**

redress. Syn.: reparation, amends, indemnification, compensation, relief. See **reparation.**

reduce. Syn.: diminish, decrease, lessen, lower, abate, shorten, abridge, curtail, retrench; weaken, impair, impoverish, lower, degrade, debase, humble, subdue. See **lower.**

reduction. Syn.: diminution, decrease, lessening, abatement, abridgment, curtailment, contraction, retrenchment; debasement, subjugation, subjection.

redundance. Syn.: see **verbosity.**

redundancy. Syn.: see **excess.**

redundant. Syn.: superfluous, superabundant, exuberant, excessive.

reecho. Syn.: resound, reverberate.

reel. Syn.: stagger, totter, sway, shake, waver.

To *reel* is to sway dizzily and be in imminent danger of falling; to *stagger* is successively to lose and regain one's equilibrium and ability to maintain one's direction, as when carrying a burden too great to be borne steadily. *Totter*, which may apply to inanimate objects, suggests the immediate likelihood of falling from weakness or feebleness, as of an infant or the very aged.

refer. Syn.: attribute, ascribe, assign, impute; relate, advert, allude, hint.

We *refer* to a thing by a clear and direct statement; we *allude* to what is well enough known to make a passing, indirect, sometimes obscure, remark or hint understood or more effective, or to what is a matter of sensitiveness, suspicion, or secrecy, and cannot be spoken of plainly or openly.

referee. Syn.: umpire, arbiter, arbitrator. See **judge.**

refine. Syn.: purify, clarify, defecate, sublimate, sublime, subtilize.

refined. Syn.: purified, clarified; polished, cultured, well-bred, courtly, exquisite, fine; subtle, precise, exact. **Ant.:** see **unrefined.** See **genteel.**

refinement. Syn.: purification, clarification; polish, culture, elegance, politeness.

reflect. Syn.: throw back, mirror; meditate, ruminate, ponder, deliberate, muse, consider, cogitate, think, contemplate.

To *reflect* is to turn the mind back on something in order to think it over carefully. *Meditate* implies quiet and serious contemplation of a matter. To *ponder* is to dwell patiently in thought upon a matter in an effort to consider it from all sides. To *muse* is to lose oneself in reverie. *Ruminate* suggests placidly going over and over a matter in thought; *cogitate*, the active exercise of the thinking faculties; *deliberate*, slow, judicial weighing of all facts and reasons in order to reach a correct conclusion.

reflection. Syn.: image, representation; meditation, rumination, deliberation, cogitation, study; imputation, aspersion, reproach. See **insinuation.**

reflective. Syn.: see **thoughtful.**

reform, *n.* **Syn.:** see **reformation.**

reform, *v.* **Syn.:** improve, better, rectify, correct, reclaim, regenerate, convert. See **amend.**

reformation. Syn.: amendment, improvement, betterment, correction, reform.

refractory. Syn.: stubborn, obstinate, perverse, disobedient, intractable, unruly, contumacious, unmanageable, ungovernable, headstrong, mulish. **Ant.:** obedient, tractable, submissive, docile, meek. See **disobedient.**

refrain. Syn.: forbear, abstain, desist.

Refrain implies a curbing of one's desires, inclinations, or impulses, especially those of a light or passing kind. To *abstain* is to hold oneself off from what is enjoyable or profitable in the belief that it is or may prove harmful or wrong: as, to *refrain* from making an angry reply; to *abstain* from liquor.

refresh. Syn.: freshen, brighten, renovate, renew, restore; reinvigorate, reanimate, revive, recruit, enliven, cheer.

refuge. Syn.: shelter, protection, safety, security; asylum, retreat, sanctuary, harbor, stronghold, covert.

refulgence. Syn.: see **radiance.**

refulgent. Syn.: see **bright.**

refund. Syn.: restore, repay, return.

refusal. Syn.: denial, rejection, dissent.

refuse, *n.* **Syn.:** rubbish, trash, waste, scraps, leavings, offal, garbage, offscouring, scum, dross, recrement, dregs, lees, sediment, draff.

refuse, *v.* **Syn.** decline, deny, reject, repel, rebuff.

Refuse and *decline* both imply determination not to accept what is offered or proposed, but *refuse* is more direct and emphatic, *decline* is milder and more courteous. To *reject* is to cast aside as inappropriate, unsatisfactory, or repugnant.

refute. Syn.: disprove, confute, controvert, rebut, deny, overthrow.

Both *refute* and *confute* refer to proving something to be false or erroneous. *Refute* is the broader term, applying to charges, accusations, or slanders as well as to arguments, opinions, or reasons, to which *confute* especially applies.

regain. Syn.: recover, retrieve, repossess.

regal. Syn.: royal, kingly, majestic, stately, splendid, magnificent. See **royal.**

regale. Syn.: feast, entertain, gratify, delight.

regard, *n.* **Syn.:** look, gaze; heed, attention, consideration, notice, interest, care, concern; esteem, respect, liking, affection, favor; reference, relation; particular, point, matter. See **respect,** *n.*

regard, *v.* **Syn.:** observe, view, contemplate, consider; heed, mind; esteem, respect; account, reckon, deem, hold; relate to, concern.

regardful. Syn.: observant, heedful, attentive, mindful, watchful, careful.

regardless. Syn.: heedless, inattentive, unmindful, careless, negligent, neglectful, indifferent.

region. Syn.: area, space, tract, district, territory, country, clime, locality, neighborhood, vicinity, quarter; sphere, realm, domain.

register, *n.* **Syn.:** record, list, roll, roster, catalogue, schedule, chronicle. See **list.**

register, *v.* **Syn.:** record, enroll.

regret, *n.* **Syn.:** sorrow, grief, remorse, compunction, qualm, penitence, repentance, contrition.

Regret denotes that a person is sorry for what he or some one else has done or left undone or for circumstances or occurrences, sometimes those beyond his control. *Compunction*, literally a pricking, as of the conscience, implies a feeling of self-reproach for what one has done or is about to do, which in the latter case may or may not prove a deterrent. *Remorse*, literally a gnawing, denotes sharp mental distress or grief because of that which one is powerless to undo or remedy.

regret, *v.* **Syn.:** deplore, lament, rue.

regular. Syn.: normal, typical, uniform, unvarying, standard, symmetrical, formal; habitual, usual, constant, steady, stated, periodic, settled, established; methodical, orderly, systematic; perfect, thorough, downright, out-and-out. **Ant.:** irregular, abnormal, exceptional, uncommon, unusual. See **normal.**

regulate. Syn.: rule, direct, manage, order, adjust, arrange. See **govern.**

regulation. Syn.: direction, management, control; rule, order, ordinance, statute. See **law.**

rehearse. Syn.: recite, repeat, relate, narrate, recount, recapitulate, describe, detail. See **relate.**

reign. Syn.: rule, dominion, sovereignty, sway, power, control.

reimburse. Syn.: see **compensate.**

reiterate. Syn.: see **repeat.**

reject. Syn.: refuse, decline, rebuff, repulse, repudiate. See **refuse.**

rejoice. Syn.: gladden, cheer, delight, exhilarate, enrapture; exult, glory.

rejoinder. Syn.: reply, answer, retort. See **reply,** *n.*

relate. Syn.: recount, recite, rehearse, narrate, tell, report, describe; refer, pertain.

To *relate* is to give an account of happenings, events, circumstances, etc. To *recount* is usually to set forth consecutively the details of an occurrence, argument, experience, etc. *Recite* may have approximately the same meaning as recount, but more often applies to the repetition from memory of something which has been learned with verbal exactness. *Rehearse* implies some formality and exactness in telling, sometimes repeated performance as for practice before final delivery.

related. Syn.: narrated, reported; connected, allied, akin, cognate, consanguineous, germane.

relation. Syn.: narration, recital, account, report; relationship, tie, connection, alliance, filiation, affiliation, affinity, kinship, cognation, consanguinity; kinsman, kinswoman, relative; respect, reference.

Relationship can be applied to connection either by blood or by marriage. *Kinship* may be used of both, but generally denotes common descent, and implies a more intimate connection than relationship. *Consanguinity* refers to relationship by blood; *affinity*, by marriage or by inherent attraction of elements.

relative. Syn.: see **relation.**

relax. Syn.: loosen, slacken, unbrace, unbend; reduce, remit, temper, mitigate, abate; ease, relieve, divert, recreate.

relaxation. Syn.: loosening, slackening; relief, rest, diversion, recreation.

release, *n.* **Syn.:** liberation, deliverance, extrication, disengagement, discharge, absolution, acquittal, acquaintance, exemption.

release, *v.* **Syn.:** give up, surrender, relinquish; liberate, free, loose, untie, unfasten, unbind, extricate, disengage, discharge, absolve, acquit, exempt, emancipate. **Ant.:** fasten, bind, fetter, shackle, confine, imprison.

relentless. Syn.: pitiless, ruthless, unmerciful, implacable, inexorable. See **inflexible.**

relevant. Syn.: pertinent, applicable, germane, apposite, appropriate, suitable, fitting. See **pertinent.**

reliable. Syn.: trustworthy, trusty, dependable, infallible. **Ant.:** see **unreliable.**

That which is *reliable* can be depended upon with certainty; that which is *trustworthy* is worthy of confidence or belief; that which is *infallible* is incapable of being in error or of making mistakes. All three words may be applied to both persons and things.

reliance. Syn.: trust, confidence, dependence. See **trust,** *n.*

relic. Syn.: remains.

relief. Syn.: alleviation, mitigation, assuagement, ease, comfort; succor, aid, help, redress, remedy. See **comfort.**

relieve. Syn.: alleviate, mitigate, assuage, allay, lighten; succor, aid, help, remedy, redress.

religion. Syn.: piety, devotion, godliness, righteousness, morality, sanctity, saintliness, holiness, religiosity.

religious. Syn.: see **pious.**

relinquish. Syn.: surrender, yield, cede, waive, forgo, renounce, abandon, resign, abdicate, leave, quit.

To *relinquish* is to give up, usually something desirable or pleasurable, under pressure, compulsion, or necessity. To *resign* is to give up, especially an office, by a formal and deliberate act. To *renounce* is to declare strongly and more or less formally that one gives up some claim, opinion, pursuit, etc., forever. To *abdicate* is to renounce a throne or supreme authority, as does a king or ruler.

relish. Syn.: taste, flavor, savor; trace, touch, smack; zest, gusto; enjoyment, liking, partiality, predilection, propensity.

Relish implies a gratification of taste, *zest*, energetic pursuit, *gusto*, vehement enthusiasm: as, he told the story with evident *relish*, began the task with *zest*, applauded with *gusto*.

reluctance. Syn.: unwillingness, disinclination, dislike, repugnance, aversion.

reluctant. Syn.: unwilling, disinclined, loath, averse, backward, slow. See **averse.**

remain. Syn.: abide, stay, wait, tarry, rest, sojourn, dwell; endure, continue, last. See **continue.**

remainder. Syn.: residue, residuum, remnant, balance, rest, surplus, surplusage.

remark, n. Syn.: utterance, observation, comment, note, commentary.

A *remark* is a brief statement, usually upon matters of present interest, often casual and made without previous thought. An *observation* is a remark made after thought or reflection. A *comment* is especially a remark or observation bearing closely upon some situation, utterance, opinion, etc., often for purposes of criticism or interpretation.

remark, v. Syn.: observe, note, notice, regard; comment, speak.

remarkable. Syn.: notable, noteworthy, noticeable, striking, extraordinary, wonderful, unusual, singular, strange. **Ant.:** commonplace, ordinary, common, usual.

remediless. Syn.: cureless, incurable, irremediable, irrecoverable, irretrievable, irreparable, desperate, hopeless.

remedy, n. Syn.: cure, restorative, corrective, antidote, specific, medicament, panacea, catholicon, elixir, arcanum, nostrum; relief, reparation, redress.

Remedy does not suggest as thorough or complete a removal of disease as *cure*. *Panacea* is used of a medicine reputed to cure any and all diseases, and is often applied contemptuously to idealistic schemes or plans for the abolishment of all evils. *Catholicon*, a more or less archaic word, is also used of so-called universal cures for diseases.

remedy, v. Syn.: cure, heal, restore, relieve, repair, correct, redress.

remember. Syn.: recollect, recall.

Remember implies that a thing exists in the memory, not that it is actually present in the thoughts at the moment, but that it can be called up without effort. *Recollect* implies voluntary effort to remember some definite, desired fact or thing. *Recall* has generally the same meaning as recollect, but usually implies less effort and is more conversational.

remembrance. Syn.: recollection, memory; reminder, memento, token, keepsake, souvenir, trophy. See **keepsake, memory.**

reminiscence. Syn.: see **memory.**

remiss. Syn.: neglectful, negligent, slack, derelict, careless, thoughtless, dilatory.

remission. Syn.: see **pardon.**

remissness. Syn.: see **negligence.**

remit. Syn.: send, transmit, forward; slacken, relax, abate; relinquish, release, forgive, pardon.

remnant. Syn.: remainder, residue, rest, fragment, piece, end.

remonstrance. Syn.: expostulation, protest.

remonstrate. Syn.: expostulate, protest, object, reason.

To *remonstrate* is to endeavor to show another by argument and protest that his opinion is wrong or that his action, either past or contemplated, is blameworthy; to *expostulate* is to plead with another, earnestly and sometimes even vehemently, in an effort to change his views or intended course of action.

remorse. Syn.: regret, compunction, self-reproach, penitence, contrition. See **regret.**

remorseless. Syn.: pitiless, merciless, ruthless, relentless, unrelenting, implacable, cruel.

remote. Syn.: see **distant.**

removal. Syn.: dislodgment, transference, withdrawal, elimination, dismissal, ejection.

remove. Syn.: dislodge, transfer, move, shift, displace, dismiss, discharge, eject, oust.

remunerate. Syn.: repay, recompense, requite, reward. See **compensate.**

remuneration. Syn.: repayment, recompense, compensation, requital, reward.

remunerative. Syn.: profitable, gainful, lucrative, paying.

rencounter. Syn.: see **encounter.**

rend. Syn.: tear, rip, rive, sunder, sever, split, cleave, chop, fracture. See **tear.**

render. Syn.: return, repay, restore, reproduce, interpret, construe, translate; give, supply, furnish, contribute, deliver; extract, clarify.

renegade. Syn.: apostate, backslider, recreant, turncoat, deserter, traitor, rebel, runaway. See **traitor.**

renew. Syn.: restore, repair, renovate, reconstruct, remodel, reëstablish, recreate, revive, rejuvenate, regenerate; resume, recommence.

renounce. Syn.: resign, abandon, forsake, quit, forgo, relinquish, discard, abdicate, repudiate, disown, disclaim, disavow, retract, recant, abjure, forswear, revoke, recall. See **relinquish.**

renown. Syn.: fame, celebrity, glory, distinction, note, repute. See **fame.**

renowned. Syn.: famed, famous, celebrated, illustrious, eminent. **Ant.:** unknown, obscure, inglorious. See **famous.**

rent, n. Syn.: tear, rip, split, breach, break, rift, rupture, crack, fissure.

rent, v. Syn.: let, lease, hire.

renunciation. Syn.: abandonment, relinquishment, surrender, repudiation, disavowal, denial, recantation, abjuration, abnegation, rejection.

repair. Syn.: restore, renew, remodel, renovate, mend, patch, darn, revamp; remedy, redress, retrieve, recruit.

reparation. Syn.: restoration, rehabilitation; redress, indemnification, restitution, amends, atonement, compensation, recompense, requital.

Reparation is used especially of a return made for a loss sustained or an injury suffered; *restitution* refers to the return of something, or an equivalent, of which one has been wrongfully deprived; *redress* emphasizes the idea of justice in setting right or seeking to have set right a wrong done.

repartee. Syn.: retort, rejoinder. See **reply, n.**

repast. Syn.: see **feast.**

repay. Syn.: refund, reimburse, indemnify, restore, requite, recompense.

repeal. Syn.: revoke, rescind, abrogate, annul.

repeat. Syn.: iterate, reiterate, recapitulate; recite, rehearse, recount, relate.

To *repeat* is to do or say something over again. To *reiterate* is to say a thing a second time, or a number of times. To *recapitulate* is to summarize, often by repeating the principal points in a discourse.

repel. Syn.: repulse, parry, ward off, rebuff, reject, decline.

repellent. Syn.: see **repulsive.**

repentance. Syn.: contrition, contriteness, penitence, remorse, sorrow, regret, compunction.

Repentance implies grief over sins committed and a distinct intention to turn to righteousness. *Penitence* implies intense grief for offenses committed, especially against God and right. *Contrition* is a bruising of the soul, resulting in a deep and continued sorrow, chiefly for specific acts.

repentant. Syn.: contrite, penitent, sorrowful. **Ant.:** unrepentant, impenitent, sinful.

repetition. Syn.: iteration, reiteration. See **verbosity.**

repine. Syn.: see **complain.**

replace. Syn.: restore, refund, repay, return, reinstate; supersede, supplant.

replete. Syn.: filled, abounding, full.

repletion. Syn.: fullness, surfeit, superabundance.

replica. Syn.: see **copy, n.**

reply, n. Syn.: answer, response, rejoinder, retort, repartee.

Reply and *answer* denote that which meets and is aroused

by a question, accusation, attack, argument, etc., but *reply* is sometimes more formal and specific. *Response* often suggests an answer to an appeal, exhortation, etc., or an expected or fixed reply, as to one's name on a roll or to chants in a liturgical service. *Rejoinder* is strictly applied to an answer to a reply, but is more loosely used of any short, pointed answer. *Retort* implies a keen, prompt answer, especially one that turns a remark upon the person who makes it; *repartee*, a witty, good-humored answer to a remark of similar character which it is meant to surpass in wittiness.

reply, *v.* **Syn.:** answer, respond, rejoin, retort.

report, *n.* **Syn.:** account, statement, communication, narrative, narration, description; rumor, bruit, gossip, hearsay, talk, tale, story; repute, reputation, fame; noise, detonation, repercussion, reverberation, echo, sound.

report, *v.* **Syn.:** announce, state, tell, communicate, relate, narrate, describe; rumor, bruit, circulate, publish.

repose, *n.* **Syn.:** rest, sleep; quiet, calm, tranquillity. See **rest.**

repose, *v.* **Syn.:** place, deposit; lie, recline, rest, sleep, slumber.

repository. **Syn.:** depository, storehouse, depot, magazine, warehouse.

reprehend. **Syn.:** reprove, reprimand, censure, rebuke, upbraid, blame.

reprehensible. **Syn.:** reprovable, censurable, blamable, blameworthy, culpable.

reprehension. **Syn.:** see **admonition.**

represent. **Syn.:** show, present, portray, depict, delineate; personate, impersonate; typify, symbolize.

representation. **Syn.:** reproduction, protrayal, delineation, picture, portrait, likeness.

representative. **Syn.:** type, example, specimen, exponent; delegate, deputy, agent, substitute, proxy, emissary, envoy.

repress. **Syn.:** check, curb, bridle, restrain, restrict, suppress, subdue, overcome, crush, quell, smother, stifle, muzzle. See **restrain.**

reprieve. **Syn.:** delay, postponement, respite, relief.

reprimand, *n.* **Syn.:** see **admonition.**

reprimand, *v.* **Syn.:** see **censure,** *v.,* **reprove.**

reprisal. **Syn.:** see **revenge,** *n.*

reproach, *n.* **Syn.:** blame, censure, reprehension, invective, abuse; discredit, disgrace, disrepute, shame, odium, infamy.

reproach, *v.* **Syn.:** upbraid, blame, censure, reprove, rebuke, chide, revile, abuse, vilify. See **blame.**

reproachful. **Syn.:** upbraiding, censorious, abusive, contemptuous, opprobrious, contumelious.

reprobate, *n.* **Syn.:** see **villain.**

reprobate, *a.* **Syn.:** abandoned, depraved, corrupt, profligate, base, vile, wicked, vicious.

reprobate, *v.* **Syn.:** condemn, censure, denounce, reject.

reproduce. **Syn.:** generate, beget, propagate; copy, imitate, duplicate, repeat.

reproof. **Syn.:** censure, reprehension, blame, reprimand, rebuke.

reprove. **Syn.:** censure, reprehend, reprimand, admonish, rebuke, reproach, upbraid, chide, berate, scold.

To *reprove* is to admonish with (often gentle) disapprobation. To *censure* is to condemn with adverse opinion, usually for a fault or offense of some gravity. To *reprimand* is to reprove specifically, often formally or officially. To *rebuke* is to reprove sharply or with severity.

repudiate. **Syn.:** reject, disown, disclaim, disavow, renounce, abjure. See **disclaim.**

repugnance. **Syn.:** objection, distaste, aversion, antipathy, dislike, loathing. See **aversion.**

repugnant. **Syn.:** objecting, averse; opposed, contrary, antagonistic; objectionable, distasteful, offensive, disagreeable.

repulse. **Syn.:** drive back, repel; reject, refuse, rebuff, snub.

repulsive. **Syn.:** repellent, forbidding, offensive, disgusting, revolting.

reputable. **Syn.:** respectable, estimable, honorable, creditable. See **estimable.**

reputation. **Syn.:** repute, credit, estimation, esteem, name, fame, distinction, renown. See **character.**

Reputation indicates the position one occupies in the opinion of others in respect to attainments, integrity, etc. *Character* is the combination of moral traits which make a person what he really is.

repute. **Syn.:** see **reputation.**

request, *n.* **Syn.:** solicitation, entreaty, supplication, petition, suit, prayer.

request, *v.* **Syn.:** ask, solicit, beg, beseech, entreat, supplicate, petition, importune. See **ask.**

requiem. **Syn.:** see **dirge.**

require. **Syn.:** demand, exact, claim, prescribe, enjoin, command; want, need, necessitate. See **ask.**

requirement. **Syn.:** demand, claim, command; requisite, need, essential.

A *requirement* is something demanded or imposed; a *requisite* is something absolutely necessary or essential: as, to meet the *requirements* for admission to college; truth is a *requisite* of great literature.

requisite, *n.* **Syn.:** see **requirement.**

requisite, *a.* **Syn.:** required, needful, necessary, essential, indispensable. See **necessary.**

requital. **Syn.:** repayment, reward, recompense, compensation, remuneration, retaliation, punishment, revenge, reprisal, retribution.

requite. **Syn.:** repay, reward, recompense, remunerate, pay off, punish. See **compensate.**

rescind. **Syn.:** abrogate, annul, revoke, repeal, reverse.

rescue, *n.* **Syn.:** liberation, release, deliverance, ransom, redemption.

rescue, *v.* **Syn.:** liberate, release, deliver, save, retake, recapture.

research. **Syn.:** see **examination.**

resemblance. **Syn.:** similarity, similitude, likeness, analogy. See **likeness.**

resentment. **Syn.:** displeasure, indignation, umbrage, rankling, heartburning. See **annoyance.**

reserve, *n.* **Syn.:** store, stock, supply; exception, qualification, limitation, reservation; constraint, reticence, taciturnity, coldness.

reserve, *v.* **Syn.:** keep, retain, preserve, withhold. See **keep,** *v.*

reserved. **Syn.:** withheld, retained, excepted; restrained, distant, unsociable, uncommunicative, reticent, taciturn. **Ant.:** forward, presumptuous, brazen, talkative.

Reserved implies restraint or reticence in social intercourse; *distant*, coldness or haughtiness towards others.

reside. **Syn.:** dwell, live, abide, sojourn, stay, lodge. See **live.**

residence. **Syn.:** domiciliation, inhabitance, sojourn, stay; dwelling, abode, habitation, domicile, mansion, home. See **habitation.**

resident. **Syn.:** inhabitant, inhabiter, dweller, sojourner, denizen.

residue, residuum. **Syn.:** see **remainder.**

resign. **Syn.:** give up, surrender, relinquish, renounce, abdicate; yield, submit. See **relinquish.**

resignation. **Syn.:** surrender, relinquishment, abdication; submission, acquiescence, meekness, patience.

resigned. **Syn.:** submissive, acquiescent, unresisting, uncomplaining, patient.

resist. **Syn.:** withstand, oppose, defy. See **oppose.**

resolute. **Syn.:** determined, firm, constant, steadfast, unshaken, unwavering, unflinching, pertinacious.

resolution. **Syn.:** separation, dissolution; determination, firmness, constancy, steadfastness, pertinacity, persistence; resolve, purpose, intention, design. See **decision.**

resolve. **Syn.:** separate, dissolve, reduce; decide, determine, purpose, intend.

resort. **Syn.:** see **expedient,** *n.*

resound. **Syn.:** reëcho, reverberate, detonate, ring, peal, boom.

resource. **Syn.:** see **expedient,** *n.*

respect, *n.* **Syn.:** regard, reference, relation; particular, detail, point, feature; esteem, estimation, honor, reverence, veneration, homage.

Respect is commonly the result of admiration and approbation; *esteem* adds the idea of deference or affection; *regard* is a mild form of esteem without the element of deference. *Honor* is used of recognition or high respect shown to worth or merit. *Reverence* suggests deep respect often combined with humility and love. *Veneration* is such reverence as we feel for persons or things hallowed by association or age.

respect, *v.* **Syn.:** relate to, concern; esteem, honor, reverence, revere, venerate.

respectable. **Syn.:** reputable, estimable, honorable;

proper, decent; tolerable, fair, moderate, average. See **estimable.**

respectful. Syn.: deferential, courteous, polite.

respite. Syn.: cessation, stop, stay, delay, pause, interval, intermission, relief. See **reprieve.**

resplendent. Syn.: shining, beaming, effulgent, glorious, splendid. See **bright.**

response. Syn.: answer, reply, rejoinder, retort, antiphon. See **reply.**

responsibility. Syn: accountability, amenability; duty, trust, charge.

responsible. Syn.: answerable, accountable, amenable; trustworthy, reliable. **Ant.:** irresponsible, unreliable, careless, negligent.

rest, *n.* **Syn.:** repose, sleep, slumber; quiet, quietude, tranquillity, calm, peace, ease; inactivity, inaction, pause, stop, cessation, intermission; support, brace, stay; remainder, balance, residue, surplus, remnant.

Rest refers to a suspension of activity, as between periods of work, especially for refreshment of the body and mind; *repose,* especially to a state of relaxation, often such as accompanies sleep or a reclining position. *Quiet* refers especially to freedom from movement, noise, or disturbance; *peace,* to freedom of the mind from harassing cares or demands.

rest, *v.* **Syn.:** repose, sleep, slumber; pause, stop, cease, desist; lie, recline, lean, depend; lay, place.

restitution. Syn.: restoration, return, refundment, repayment, indemnification, reparation, amends. See **reparation.**

restive. Syn.: stubborn, balky, intractable, refractory, fractious, fretful, skittish, restless, uneasy, impatient, fidgety.

restless. Syn.: unquiet, uneasy, fidgety, roving, unstable.

Restless suggests that a person is unable or unwilling to remain long in one place or position, especially because of discomfort, nervousness, or simply a desire for change. *Uneasy* especially suggests the restlessness of mind induced by apprehension or worry.

restoration. Syn.: reconstruction, revival, renewal, reëstablishment, reinstatement, rehabilitation, return, restitution, replacement, recovery, recuperation.

restore. Syn.: rebuild, reconstruct, repair, renovate; refresh, revive, renew, reëstablish, reinstate, rehabilitate, repatriate; refund, repay, return, replace, heal, cure, resuscitate, redintegrate. See **return.**

restrain. Syn.: detain, repress, restrict, limit, check, curb, bridle, hinder.

To *restrain* is to curb or put a check upon; to *detain* is to delay or keep from proceeding; to *repress* is to hold back or subdue, sometimes to eliminate entirely; to *restrict* is to keep within certain definite limits.

restraint. Syn.: restriction, limitation, check, curb, hindrance, prohibition; confinement, detention, duress.

restrict. Syn.: limit, confine, curb, circumscribe, abridge. See **restrain.**

result, *n.* **Syn.:** consequence, effect, outcome, issue, product, upshot, conclusion, termination, end. See **effect,** *n.*

result, *v.* **Syn.:** follow, ensue, eventuate, terminate, end.

résumé. Syn.: summary, recapitulation, condensation, abstract.

retain. Syn.: keep, hold, reserve, preserve. See **keep,** *v.*

retaliation. Syn.: see **revenge,** *n.*

retard. Syn.: delay, slow up, impede, hinder, detain.

reticent. Syn.: reserved, taciturn, uncommunicative, silent.

Reticent implies an inclination, often temporary, to be silent or secretive; *uncommunicative,* a disinclination to talk, usually about some particular thing; *taciturn,* a habitual disposition to refrain from speaking.

retinue. Syn.: train, suite, retainers, followers, cortège.

retire. Syn.: withdraw, retreat, recede, depart. See **depart.**

retired. Syn.: withdrawn, secluded, sequestered, unfrequented, out-of-the-way, remote.

retirement. Syn.: withdrawal, privacy, seclusion, retreat.

retiring. Syn.: retreating, departing; reserved, modest, quiet, unobtrusive, bashful, shrinking, shy.

retort. Syn.: see **repartee, reply,** *n.*

retract. Syn.: withdraw, revoke, rescind, recall, recant, disown, disavow, renounce. See **forswear.**

retreat, *n.* **Syn.:** withdrawal, retirement, departure; seclusion, privacy, solitude; refuge, asylum, shelter, haunt, den, fastness. See **hospital.**

retreat, *v.* **Syn.:** withdraw, retire, recede. See **depart.**

retrench. Syn.: reduce, diminish, lessen, curtail, economize.

retrenchment. Syn.: reduction, curtailment, economy.

retribution. Syn.: see **revenge,** *n.*

retrieve. Syn.: see **recover.**

retrograde. Syn.: recede, retire; decline, deteriorate, degenerate.

retrospection. Syn.: see **memory.**

return, *n.* **Syn.:** restoration, restitution, repayment, requital, recompense; reversion, recurrence, reappearance; profit, proceeds, results; reply, response, answer.

return, *v.* **Syn.:** restore, replace, refund, repay, requite, render; go back, revert, recur; reply, respond, rejoin.

The following two words differ in application rather than in meaning. We *return* a thing to its former place; *restore* it to its former condition. We *return* generally what has been given or lent, *restore* what has been stolen, taken, or intrusted.

reveal. Syn.: disclose, divulge, unveil, uncover, impart, show, display, exhibit. See **disclose.**

revel. Syn.: see **carousal.**

revelation. Syn.: disclosure, divulgement, manifestation, apocalypse.

revenge, *n.* **Syn.:** vengeance, retaliation, retribution, reprisal, vindictiveness.

Revenge is the carrying out of a bitter desire to injure another for a wrong done to oneself or those who seem a part of oneself. *Vengeance* is usually wrathful or furious revenge. *Retribution* suggests just or deserved punishment, often without personal actuation, for some evil done. *Retaliation* definitely suggests the infliction of an injury or harm as the equivalent of one received. *Reprisal* is used specifically in warfare for retaliation upon the enemy for his (usually unlawful) actions.

revenge, *v.* **Syn.:** see **avenge.**

revengeful. Syn.: vindictive, resentful, unforgiving, implacable, vengeful, rancorous, spiteful.

Revengeful is a strong word, implying a deep, powerful, and continued intent to repay a wrong; *vindictive* expresses the same kind of emotion but is not so strong a term; *spiteful* implies a mean or malicious desire for (often petty) revenge.

revenue. Syn.: see **income.**

reverberate. Syn.: see **rebound, resound.**

revere. Syn.: reverence, venerate, honor, respect, worship, adore.

reverence, *n.* **Syn.:** veneration, awe, adoration. See **respect.**

reverence, *v.* **Syn.:** revere, venerate, worship, adore.

reverie. Syn.: see **dream.**

reverse, *n.* **Syn.:** opposite, contrary; check, repulse, setback, relapse, defeat, failure, misfortune.

reverse, *a.* **Syn.:** see **opposite.**

reverse, *v.* **Syn.:** turn about, invert; revoke, repeal, annul, rescind, countermand.

review. Syn.: examination, inspection, survey, reconsideration, criticism, critique; journal, magazine, periodical, quarterly, monthly, weekly.

revile. Syn.: abuse, vituperate, berate, rail at, objurgate, upbraid, reproach, vilify, defame, traduce, asperse, calumniate, malign, lampoon.

To *revile* is to attack another with violent and opprobrious language so as to make him seem vile or worthless, either to himself or to others. *Abuse* suggests a vulgar outburst of anger against another in harsh and scathing words. *Berate* implies vehement chiding; *vituperate,* a flood of scurrilous reproach.

revision. Syn.: revisal, recension, correction, review.

revive. Syn.: revivify, resuscitate, reanimate, hearten, cheer, refresh, renew, restore.

revocation. Syn.: withdrawal, recall, repeal, annulment, retraction.

revoke. Syn.: withdraw, repeal, annul, rescind, reverse, countermand, retract.

revolt, *n.* **Syn.:** rebellion, mutiny, uprising, insurrection, sedition, revolution, insubordination, disobedience. See **insurrection.**

revolt, *v.* **Syn.:** rebel, mutiny; repel, disgust, sicken.

revolting. Syn.: rebellious, mutinous; repulsive, abhorrent, offensive, disgusting, sickening, shocking.

revolution. Syn.: see **insurrection.**

revolve. Syn.: rotate, gyrate, turn, whirl, spin; ponder, study, consider. See **consider, turn,** *v.*

reward, *n.* **Syn.:** recompense, requital, compensation, remuneration, guerdon, meed, premium, prize, bonus, honorarium, bounty; retribution, penalty.

A *reward* is usually something given in recognition of past performance or good done. A *recompense* is a return for service rendered or loss suffered. A *prize* is a reward won in competition or rivalry. A *premium* is usually something additional given as an inducement or stimulation to buying, producing, or the like. A *bonus* is a gift over and above what is regularly payable. A *bounty* is public aid or reward for a specific purpose or achievement: as, a *bounty* for settling land or emigrating.

reward, *v.* **Syn.:** recompense, requite, repay, compensate, remunerate.

rhetoric. Syn.: see **oratory.**

ribald. Syn.: coarse, disreputable, indelicate, indecent, gross, obscene, scurrilous, filthy, lewd. See **scurrilous.**

rich. Syn.: wealthy, affluent, opulent, well-to-do, moneyed; valuable, costly, expensive, sumptuous, gorgeous, luxurious; plentiful, abundant, bountiful, copious; fertile, productive, fruitful, fecund. **Ant.:** see **poor.** See **fruitful.**

riches. Syn.: wealth, opulence, affluence.

Riches and *wealth* both imply the possession of abundant property or indicate the property possessed; but *wealth* often suggests more of permanence and stability: as, *riches* amassed by a beggar; the *wealth* of a banker. *Affluence* and *opulence* suggest the condition of one possessing great wealth, *affluence* especially implying the flow of wealth to one from abundant resources and the resulting free expenditure for objects of desire.

rick. Syn.: see **sheaf.**

rickety. Syn.: shaky, tottering, infirm, ramshackle, dilapidated, tumble-down, crazy.

riddle. Syn.: enigma, puzzle, rebus, conundrum, problem. See **puzzle.**

ride. Syn.: drive.

Ride is used of progression on horseback or in a public conveyance, such as a train, street-car, or bus; *drive,* of progression in one's own vehicle, especially when the person in question holds the reins or is steering; but the two words are often used with little distinction: as, to *ride* or *drive* through the country in an automobile.

rider. Syn.: horseman, equestrian, jockey; amendment, addition.

ridicule, *n.* **Syn.:** derision, mockery, raillery, gibes, jeers, sneers, satire, sarcasm.

ridicule, *v.* **Syn.:** deride, mock, banter, rally, quiz, chaff, taunt, twit, satirize, burlesque, scout, flout, scoff.

To *ridicule* is to make game of, either in a sportive, good-humored way or with considerable unkindness and severity. To *deride* is to make one the object of scornful laughter; to *mock* is to ridicule, sometimes playfully, often even insultingly, by imitating and caricaturing the peculiarities of another. To *taunt* is exultingly to press upon a person some annoying or insulting fact concerning himself. To *twit* is to taunt banteringly about small matters.

ridiculous. Syn.: nonsensical, preposterous, ludicrous, laughable, funny. See **funny, absurd.**

rife. Syn.: see **prevalent.**

rifle. Syn.: see **rob.**

rift. Syn.: cleft, break, crack, fissure, crevice, cranny, chink.

right, *n.* **Syn.:** justice, equity, morality, virtue; claim, title; privilege, prerogative, liberty. See **justice.**

right, *a.* **Syn.:** just, equitable, lawful, ethical; correct, accurate, true; proper, fit, fitting, seemly, due, appropriate, suitable, convenient, favorable; principal, front, upper. **Ant.:** see **wrong,** *a.*

right, *v.* **Syn.:** correct, rectify, emend, adjust, alter; vindicate, redress.

righteous. Syn.: upright, virtuous, godly, holy, saintly, pious, devout, religious; rightful, just, equitable. **Ant.:** see **unrighteous.** See **godly.**

rightful. Syn.: equitable, just, lawful, proper, due.

rigid. Syn.: stiff, unyielding, unbending, firm, hard; rigorous, strict, stringent, austere, stern.

Rigid, literally stiff or unbending, applies to that which is (often unnecessarily or narrowly) inflexible; *rigorous,* literally having the same meaning, applies to that which is severe or exacting, especially in action or application: as, *rigid* economy; *rigorous* self-denial. *Strict,* drawn close or tight, implies great exactness, especially in the observance or enforcement of rules; *stringent* applies to what is vigorously exacting: as, *strict* discipline; *stringent* measures to suppress disorder.

rigmarole. Syn.: see **prattle.**

rigor. Syn.: severity, harshness, sternness, austerity, strictness; inclemency, sharpness.

rigorous. Syn.: severe, harsh, stern, austere, strict, exact, precise; inclement, hard, bitter. See **rigid.**

rill. Syn.: see **brook.**

rim. Syn.: brim, brink, edge, border, margin, verge. See **edge.**

rind. Syn.: see **skin,** *n.*

ring, *n.* **Syn.:** circlet, band, circle, hoop; clique, coterie, set.

ring, *v.* **Syn.:** sound, resound, reverberate, peal, clang, chime, ding, tinkle, knell, toll.

ringlet. Syn.: curl, tress, lock.

riot. Syn.: outbreak, tumult, uproar, brawl; luxury, revelry. See **insurrection.**

riotous. Syn.: turbulent, tumultuous; luxurious, wanton, licentious, disorderly.

rip. Syn.: see **rend, tear.**

ripe. Syn.: ripened, mellow, mature, matured, consummate, complete.

Ripe implies completed growth beyond which the processes of decay begin, and hence the end of any period of preparation: as, a *ripe* harvest; a *ripe* scholar; the time was *ripe* for revolt. *Mature,* used literally of both organic and inorganic growth, figuratively has the same meaning as ripe: as, *mature* judgment or consideration. *Mellow* denotes the complete absence of sharpness or asperity, such absence as characterizes ripeness, or age and experience: as, *mellow* fruit, wine, flavor; a genial and *mellow* humor.

ripple. Syn.: see **wave,** *n.*

rise, *n.* **Syn.:** rising, ascension; ascent, elevation, knoll, hill; increase, advance, augmentation; origin, beginning.

rise, *v.* **Syn.:** arise, stand, mount, ascend, levitate; revolt, rebel; swell, increase; appear, emerge, issue.

The confusion between *rise* and *raise* is obviated if it is remembered that *rise* is an intransitive verb and represents a subject as acting, and that *raise* is transitive and represents also an object as acted upon: as, a person *rises* from a chair; a soldier *raises* his hand in salute.

risk, *n.* **Syn.:** hazard, danger, peril, jeopardy, venture.

risk, *v.* **Syn.:** expose, hazard, endanger, imperil, jeopardize, venture, stake.

Risk and *hazard* both suggest exposure to the chances of fate; but *hazard* emphasizes the uncertainty of the outcome, *risk* stresses the possibility of loss or injury though the chance be voluntarily taken. *Jeopardize, endanger,* and *imperil* all indicate exposure to danger; but *jeopardize* suggests more often the risk of loss, *endanger* implies the possibility of harm, *imperil* emphasizes the seriousness of the danger and the urgency of taking steps to meet the situation.

risky. Syn.: hazardous, dangerous, perilous, jeopardous, precarious, unsafe.

rite, ritual. Syn.: see **ceremony.**

rival. Syn.: competitor, contestant, emulator, antagonist.

rivalry. Syn.: competition, emulation, contest. See **competition.**

rive. Syn.: see **split.**

rivulet. Syn.: streamlet, brook, rill, runnel, creek, bourn.

road. Syn.: highway, highroad, roadway, turnpike, thoroughfare, passageway, channel, route, way, course, street, avenue, boulevard, causeway, alley, lane, path. See **way.**

roam. Syn.: ramble, wander, rove, stray, stroll, range. See **ramble.**

roar. Syn.: bellow, bawl, howl, yell; resound, boom, thunder, peal. See **cry,** *v.*

rob. Syn.: plunder, pillage, sack, loot, strip, rifle, fleece, despoil.

Rob is the general word for taking possessions from a person by unlawful force or violence. To *plunder* is to seize and carry off extensive booty, often with violence. To *pillage* is to despoil, as a city or district in war. *Loot* emphasizes the making away with spoils, as in war or through corruption in political office; *sack,* the destruction wrought by the despoilers; *rifle* the thorough search for what is valuable or worth while.

robber. Syn.: highwayman, footpad, bandit, brigand, ladrone, plunderer, pillager, forager, marauder, rifler, pilferer, burglar, thief, pirate, buccaneer, freebooter, raider, corsair, picaroon. See **thief.**

robbery. Syn.: plundering, pillaging, spoliation, theft, larceny, burglary, piracy.

robust. **Syn.:** strong, hardy, sturdy, stalwart, sinewy, muscular, brawny, stout, lusty, vigorous, hale, hearty, sound. See **strong.**

rock, *n.* **Syn.:** boulder, stone, crag, cliff.

rock, *v.* **Syn.:** sway, swing, roll, shake, totter. See **swing.**

rod. **Syn.:** stick, pole, staff, cane, bar, wand, baton, truncheon, scepter, warder, verge.

rogue. **Syn.:** knave, rascal, scoundrel, scamp, cheat, sharper, swindler, miscreant, scapegrace, rapscallion.

A *rogue* is a worthless fellow who is not above dishonesty and who sometimes preys extensively upon the community by fraud. A *scoundrel* is a rogue of the worst sort. *Rascal* suggests shrewdness and trickery in dishonesty. *Knave* emphasizes baseness of nature and intention.

roguery. **Syn.:** knavery, rascality, fraud; mischievousness, waggery.

roguish. **Syn.:** knavish, tricky, fraudulent, dishonest; mischievous, waggish, sportive, playful, arch. See **playful.**

roll, *n.* **Syn.:** scroll, roster, record, list, register, catalogue; cylinder, roller, coil, convolution. See **list.**

roll, *v.* **Syn.:** wheel, trundle, turn, revolve, gyrate; rock, sway, lurch, undulate; curl, coil, convolve.

rolling. **Syn.:** undulating, wavy, hilly.

romance. **Syn.:** see **story.**

romantic. **Syn.:** imaginative, fanciful, fantastic, picturesque, wild, extravagant, sentimental.

room. **Syn.:** space, scope, range, sweep, swing, play, latitude, compass; chamber, apartment, compartment.

roomy. **Syn.:** see **spacious.**

rope. **Syn.:** cord, line, cable, hawser.

rostrum. **Syn.:** platform, stage, dais, pulpit.

rosy. **Syn.:** see **ruddy.**

rot. **Syn.:** decompose, putrefy, corrupt. See **decay.**

rotate. **Syn.:** see **revolve, turn,** *v.*

rotten. **Syn.:** decomposed, decayed, putrefied, putrescent, putrid, malodorous, fetid.

rotund. **Syn.:** see **round,** *a.*

rough. **Syn.:** uneven, irregular, broken, rugged, jagged, craggy, shaggy, bristly; disorderly, turbulent, boisterous, tumultuous, tempestuous, violent, stormy, inclement; rude, uncultivated, unpolished, discourteous, impolite, uncivil, blunt, abrupt, brusque, bluff, gruff, churlish, boorish; harsh, severe, hard, drastic, rigorous; discordant, inharmonious, jarring, grating, raucous; unwrought, unfinished, untrimmed, uncut, crude, coarse; approximate, imperfect, incomplete, preliminary, hasty, cursory. See **harsh.**

round, *n.* **Syn.:** circle, ring; revolution, cycle, series, succession, circuit, beat; rung, rundle, step.

round, *a.* **Syn.:** circular, cylindrical, curved, spherical, globular, orbicular, orbed, discoid, annular; rotund, plump, stout.

roundabout. **Syn.:** see **circuitous.**

rouse. **Syn.:** arouse, stir, excite, animate, kindle, stimulate, awaken.

rout. **Syn.:** see **defeat.**

route. **Syn.:** way, road, path, course, passage.

rove. **Syn.:** wander, roam, ramble, range, stroll. See **ramble.**

row. **Syn.:** line, file, series, rank. See **quarrel,** *n.*

royal. **Syn.:** regal, kingly, imperial, majestic, august, stately, magnificent.

Royal is especially applied to what pertains to or is associated with the person of a monarch; *regal*, to the office or to the external manifestation of kingship, or to what has the attributes worthy of such an office or state: as, the *royal* family, castle, robes, salute; *regal* authority, bearing, munificence; a subject may live in a *regal* (but not a *royal*) residence. What is *kingly* may either belong to a king or be befitting, worthy of, or like a king; as, *kingly* presence; *kingly* grace. *Imperial* suggests power and grandeur; *august*, such impressive magnificence and majesty as inspire respect combined with awe.

rub. **Syn.:** polish, burnish, furbish, scour, scrape, abrade, chafe, fret.

rubbish. **Syn.:** trash, debris, litter, trumpery lumber, refuse, garbage.

rubicund. **Syn.:** see **ruddy.**

ruddy. **Syn.:** red, reddish, rubicund, florid, rosy.

Ruddy indicates a deep and healthy red upon the human skin, such as is associated with life out of doors; *rubicund*, an unnatural red in the face or some part of it, as the cheeks or nose, especially as a result of high living or intemperance in drink; *rosy*, a charming, blooming red, especially on the cheeks.

rude. **Syn.:** unwrought, raw, crude, rough, primitive, uncivilized, unlearned, unpolished, unrefined, coarse, ignorant; uncivil, discourteous, impolite, ill-bred, boorish, surly, saucy, impertinent, impudent; rugged, sturdy, robust, vigorous. See **raw.**

rudeness. **Syn.:** crudeness, roughness, inelegance, simplicity; incivility, discourtesy, impoliteness, surliness, sauciness, impertinence, impudence, effrontery.

rudiment. **Syn.:** see **embryo.**

rudimentary. **Syn.:** elementary, undeveloped, embryonic, vestigial, abortive. See **elementary.**

rue. **Syn.:** see **regret,** *v.*

rueful. **Syn.:** mournful, doleful, woeful, lugubrious, melancholy, sad. See **mournful.**

ruffian. **Syn.:** bully, bravo, rowdy, rough, hoodlum, larrikin, desperado, cutthroat, assassin.

ruffle. **Syn.:** wrinkle, pucker, rumple, roughen, disorder, disarrange; disturb, disquiet, discompose, agitate, annoy, vex.

rugged. **Syn.:** rough, uneven, broken, craggy, scraggy; inclement, severe, austere, harsh, unfeeling, hard; uncultivated, unpolished, homely, rude; vigorous, hardy, sturdy, robust.

ruin, *n.* **Syn.:** downfall, collapse, overthrow, subversion, demolition, destruction, wreck, havoc; dilapidation, decay, ruination, perdition; bankruptcy.

Ruin implies a fallen, decayed, or wrecked state or condition; *destruction* suggests disintegration or annihilation. *Havoc* implies the extensive destruction wrought by combined force and fury, especially such as is found in the wake of a tornado or earthquake. *Perdition* implies loss beyond salvation, as that of a condemned soul.

ruin, *v.* **Syn.:** overthrow, overwhelm, overturn, demolish, destroy, wreck, spoil, undo, impoverish. See **spoil,** *v.*

rule, *n.* **Syn.:** standard, principle, law, regulation, order, precept, maxim, guide, formula, canon; control, direction, authority, government, dominion, sway, mastery, supremacy, domination.

A *rule* is usually something adopted or enacted for regulating or guiding conduct or practice; it is often the specific application of a *principle*, which is a general and basic truth. *Canon* is especially used of an authoritative, ecclesiastical rule.

rule, *v.* **Syn.:** direct, manage, govern, dominate, domineer, sway. See **govern.**

ruler. **Syn.:** sovereign, monarch, potentate, autocrat, dictator, despot, tyrant; king, queen, emperor, empress, kaiser, czar, sultan, mikado, khan, calif, shah, rajah, amir; prince, regent, viceroy, khedive, bey, pasha, satrap, doge; president, governor, magistrate, consul, pretor, prefect; chief, chieftain, lord.

ruling. **Syn.:** reigning, regnant; predominating, prevalent, current.

ruminate. **Syn.:** meditate, muse, ponder, reflect. See **reflect.**

rummage. **Syn.:** see **search,** *v.*

rumor. **Syn.:** report, bruit, talk, gossip, hearsay.

rumple. **Syn.:** crumple, wrinkle, pucker, crease, disorder. See **wrinkle,** *v.*

rumpus. **Syn.:** see **quarrel.**

run. **Syn.:** trip, scamper, scurry, scuttle, sprint, gallop, lope, trot, flee, hie, hasten, hurry, rush, race, speed, scour, scud; creep, trail, twine, climb; flow, proceed; melt, fuse; continue, last; elapse, pass; extend, stretch; pursue, follow, chase; conduct, manage, operate.

runaway. **Syn.:** runagate, deserter, absconder, fugitive, truant.

rupture. **Syn.:** see **fracture, breach.**

rural. **Syn.:** agrarian, rustic, country, pastoral, bucolic, agrestic, countrified.

Rural is used in a favorable sense of the country and that which belongs to it: as, *rural* scenery, pleasures, mails. *Rustic* usually implies a lack of the polish or sophistication of the town or city: as, *rustic* gallantry; *rustic* credulity. *Pastoral* refers to shepherds and to the simplicity of Arcadian life as idealized by poets. *Bucolic* is a term of similar meaning, but sometimes has a slight shade of humor or contempt.

ruse. **Syn.:** trick, stratagem, artifice, dodge, wile. See **artifice.**

rush. **Syn.:** dash, hurry, speed, press, dart.

Rush implies speed and sometimes violence in motion; *dash*, impetuosity or spirited action.

rustic. **Syn.:** see **rural, clown.**

rut. **Syn.:** furrow, groove, track.

ruthless. **Syn.:** merciless, pitiless, fell, hard-hearted, implacable, relentless. See **cruel.**

S

sack. **Syn.:** plunder, pillage, devastate, despoil, ravage, strip, loot. See **rob.**

sacred. **Syn.:** consecrated, hallowed. See **holy.**

sacrifice, *n.* **Syn.:** offering, immolation; surrender, destruction, loss.

sacrifice, *v.* **Syn.:** offer, immolate; surrender, give up, forgo.

sacrilege. **Syn.:** see **profanation.**

sacrilegious. **Syn.:** impious, irreverent, profane, wicked. See **profane.**

sad. **Syn.:** sorrowful, melancholy, unhappy, wretched, miserable, dejected, depressed, despondent, downcast, disconsolate, desolate, doleful, mournful, dolorous, lugubrious, woebegone, woeful, funereal, dreary, dismal, cheerless, somber, gloomy, sober, grave; lamentable, deplorable, grievous, distressing, pitiable, touching, pathetic. **Ant.:** glad, cheerful, happy, merry, jolly, joyous, gay, lively, sportive.

Sad is the general term and varies in its suggestion from slight, momentary unhappiness to deep-felt grief. It often implies nothing more than a vague feeling of low spirits. *Sorrowful* generally indicates sadness arising from some definite cause. *Melancholy* usually denotes a more or less habitual state of sadness, but is sometimes used of a pensively or wistfully sad mood. A *dejected* person is downcast from discouragement or disappointment; a *depressed* person is in low spirits; a *despondent* person has lost hope and courage. *Dolorous* implies mournful, lugubrious sorrow.

sadden. **Syn.:** depress, dishearten, distress, afflict.

sadness. **Syn.:** see **grief.**

safe. **Syn.:** unharmed, unscathed, immune, secure; trustworthy, trusty, reliable, certain, sure. **Ant.:** see **unsafe.**

While *safe* and *secure* are frequently interchangeable, *safe* is rather applied to a person or thing that is out of, or has passed beyond, the reach of danger; *secure*, to that about which there is no need to fear.

safeguard, *n.* **Syn.:** protection, defense, security; convoy, escort, guard.

safeguard, *v.* **Syn.:** guard, protect, defend, shield.

sagacious. **Syn.:** shrewd, keen, sharp-witted, far-sighted, intelligent, discerning, perspicacious, long-headed, astute. **Ant.:** dull, obtuse, stupid, ignorant, senseless, silly.

sagacity. **Syn.:** shrewdness, insight, acumen, perspicacity, penetration, mother-wit. See **judgment.**

sage. **Syn.:** wise, judicious, prudent, knowing, learned. See **wise.**

sail. **Syn.:** navigate, cruise, float.

sailor. **Syn.:** seaman, mariner, navigator, seafarer, salt, tar, tarpaulin, Jacky.

Sailor is a term for any one leading a seafaring life, but, like *seaman*, is usually applied only to those below the rank of officer. *Mariner* is a technical, elevated, or quaint term for a seaman, especially one in command of a ship. *Salt* and *tar* are familiar or colloquial terms for (especially) old and experienced sailors.

saintliness. **Syn.:** see **religion.**

salable. **Syn.:** vendible, marketable, merchantable, purchasable.

salacious. **Syn.:** lustful, lecherous, lascivious, lewd.

salary. **Syn.:** stipend, wages, pay, hire, allowance. See **pay.**

salient. **Syn.:** projecting, prominent, striking, noticeable, conspicuous. See **prominent.**

sally. **Syn.:** rush, dash, sortie, excursion, expedition; witticism, jest.

saloon. **Syn.:** salon, parlor, drawing-room; bar-room, dram-shop, grog-shop, groggery, café.

salt, *n.* **Syn.:** see **sailor.**

salt, *a.* **Syn.:** saltish, salty, saline, briny, brackish.

salubrious. **Syn.:** see **healthy.**

salutary. **Syn.:** healthful, wholesome, beneficial, profitable, advantageous, useful. **Ant.:** insalutary, unwholesome, unhygienic, unsanitary, detrimental, disadvantageous. See **healthy.**

salutation. **Syn.:** greeting, salute.

salute. **Syn.:** greet, welcome, hail, accost, address.

salve. **Syn.:** ointment, unguent, balm, remedy.

same. **Syn.:** identical, very; similar, like, corresponding, interchangeable, equal. **Ant.:** different, dissimilar, unlike, diverse.

Same and *identical* may be interchanged in use: as, this is the *same* (or the *identical*) book I had yesterday. *Same* is more likely to be used than *identical* to express similarity between two things in kind, character, meaning, appearance, shape, amount, or the like, and *identical* where the very thing and no other is meant.

sameness. **Syn.:** identity; similarity, likeness, correspondence, parallelism; monotony, tedium.

sample. **Syn.:** see **specimen.**

sanatorium. **Syn.:** see **hospital.**

sanctify. **Syn.:** hallow, consecrate.

sanction, *n.* **Syn.:** ratification, confirmation, authorization, indorsement, approbation, countenance, permission, support, warrant, authority.

sanction, *v.* **Syn.:** ratify, confirm, countenance, allow, permit. See **approve.**

sanctity. **Syn.:** saintliness, sacredness, holiness, purity, inviolability.

sanctuary. **Syn.:** church, temple, shrine, altar, sanctum, adytum; asylum, refuge.

sane. **Syn.:** sound, rational, sensible. **Ant.:** insane, deranged, demented, crazy, mad.

sanguinary. **Syn.:** see **bloody.**

sanguine. **Syn.:** red, ruddy; hopeful, cheerful, confident, optimistic, enthusiastic, ardent. See **hopeful.**

sanitarium. **Syn.:** see **hospital.**

sanitary. **Syn.:** healthful, hygienic, sanatory. See **hygienic.**

sapient. **Syn.:** see **wise.**

sarcasm. **Syn.:** see **irony.**

sarcastic. **Syn.:** ironical, satirical, taunting, sneering, biting, cutting, mordant, mordacious, bitter, derisive, caustic, sardonic.

Satan. **Syn.:** see **devil.**

satchel. **Syn.:** see **bag.**

sate. **Syn.:** see **satiate.**

satellite. **Syn.:** see **follower, parasite.**

satiate. **Syn.:** sate, surfeit, glut, gorge, cloy, pall, overfeed, stuff.

To *satiate* is to satisfy completely (especially with food) so that one does not desire or could not enjoy any more. *Sate* is the same as satiate, only is less popular and more rhetorical. To *surfeit* is to give a person so much that he is conscious of excess; *cloy* emphasizes the distaste which one feels for something indulged in to excess or possessing some quality, such as sweetness, to excess. To *gorge* is to stuff to the limit of capacity; to *glut* is to overburden with an excess of anything. All these words apply primarily to the consumption of food, but *glut* is often used in the phrase ' to *glut* the market.'

satiety. **Syn.:** satiation, surfeit, repletion.

satire. **Syn.:** lampoon, pasquinade, squib. See **irony.**

satiric. **Syn.:** satirical, sarcastic, ironical, cutting, caustic, bitter, mordant, sneering, derisive.

satisfaction. **Syn.:** gratification, enjoyment, pleasure, contentment, content, complacency; reparation, atonement, expiation, amends, requital, recompense, compensation. **Ant.:** dissatisfaction, discontent, unhappiness.

satisfactory. **Syn.:** satisfying, gratifying, pleasing, adequate, sufficient, convincing, conclusive.

satisfy. **Syn.:** gratify, appease, content; pay, liquidate, discharge, settle, indemnify, requite, recompense, remunerate, compensate.

To *satisfy* is to meet to the full one's desires, wants, expectations, etc.; to *content* is to give enough to keep one from being disposed to find fault or repine.

saturate. **Syn.:** soak, steep, drench, imbue, impregnate. See **wet,** *v.*

saucy. **Syn.:** see **impudent.**

saunter. **Syn.:** stroll, wander, meander, loiter, linger, lounge. See **linger.**

To *saunter* is to go along idly at a slow, easy gait; to *stroll* is to walk as fancy leads, often for the mere pleasure of being abroad; to *meander* is to pursue an indefinite and wandering course.

savage. Syn.: wild, untamed, uncivilized, barbarous; fierce, ferocious, furious, ravenous, murderous, bloody, brutal, cruel, fell, inhuman, truculent, pitiless, merciless. See **fierce.**

save. Syn.: rescue, deliver, redeem; safeguard, shield, protect, preserve, keep; economize, husband, hoard, store; reserve, except, spare. See **guard,** v.

saving. Syn.: redeeming, redemptory, preserving; economical, thrifty, provident, sparing, frugal, parsimonious, chary.

savor. Syn.: taste, flavor, smack, relish; odor, scent, smell. See **taste, smell.**

savory. Syn.: appetizing, palatable, tasty, toothsome, gustable, agreeable, pleasing. **Ant.:** see **unsavory.**

saw. Syn.: see **proverb.**

say. Syn.: utter, express, articulate, enunciate, pronounce, announce, exclaim, tell, declare, state, assert, affirm, allege, aver, asseverate, recite, repeat, rehearse. Cf. **speak, tell.**
Say is the most common word in the language to indicate utterance. *Tell* emphasizes the idea of communicating something. *State* implies setting forth a matter fully or explicitly, and usually with some formality.

saying. Syn.: utterance, statement, declaration, assertion, dictum; adage, axiom, maxim, saw, aphorism, apothegm, proverb, precept, motto.

scalawag. Syn.: see **rascal.**

scale. Syn.: climb, ascend, mount, clamber, escalade. See **climb.**

scamp. Syn.: see **rascal.**

scamper. Syn.: see **run.**

scandal. Syn.: discredit, disrepute, dishonor, disgrace; slander, calumny, defamation, aspersion, detraction, backbiting, gossip. See **gossip.**

scandalous. Syn.: disreputable, disgraceful, shameful, shocking, infamous, opprobrious, wicked; slanderous, defamatory, libelous.

scanty. Syn.: scant, inadequate, insufficient, meager, scrimpy, scarce, sparse, limited, stinted, short, deficient. **Ant.:** ample, abundant, plentiful, copious.
Scanty denotes smallness or insufficiency of quantity, number, supply, etc. *Meager* indicates that something is deficient, poor, and lean. *Sparse* applies particularly to that which is thinly strewn or sown, often over a wide area.

scapegrace. Syn.: see **rogue.**

scar. Syn.: cicatrix, disfigurement, mark, blemish, flaw.

scarce. Syn.: scanty, scant, deficient; rare, infrequent. See **rare.**

scarcely. Syn.: see **hardly.**

scarcity. Syn.: insufficiency, deficiency, paucity, dearth, want, lack, famine; rareness, rarity, infrequency.
Scarcity expresses a scant or inadequate amount of anything, especially of something which might be expected, or is desired, in larger quantities; *dearth* literally suggests such scantiness as renders things dear, but the word often indicates simply any great or serious scarcity.

scare. Syn.: frighten, affright, terrify, alarm, startle, dismay, appal, daunt, terrorize. See **frighten.**

scatter. Syn.: disperse, dispel, dissipate, rout; strew, sow, sprinkle, spread, diffuse.
To *scatter* is to spread or drive in different directions the units which compose a group or mass: as, to *scatter* seeds, pieces of paper, or troops. In the passive *scatter* may simply indicate an irregular distribution without intention or design: as, two-story houses were *scattered* all over the city. *Strew* is to scatter with or without design, especially in such a way as to cover or partially cover a surface: as, to *strew* rushes on the floor. *Sprinkle* is used of scattering in small drops or particles: as, to *sprinkle* water on clothes or powder on plants.

scene. Syn.: view, prospect, landscape. See **view.**

scent. Syn.: see **smell.**

schedule. Syn.: see **list.**

scheme, n. **Syn.:** diagram, map, outline, sketch; plan, design, project, plot, machination. See **plan.**

scheme, v. **Syn.:** plan, design, plot, machinate. See **plot.**

scheming. Syn.: designing, plotting, intriguing, artful, wily, tricky.

schismatic. Syn.: see **heretic.**

scholar. Syn.: pupil, student, learner, disciple; savant, polymath, philomath, sage, pedant, wiseacre. See **pupil.**

scholarly. Syn.: learned, erudite, academic, scholastic. See **learned.**

scholarship. Syn.: learning, erudition, culture, knowledge, education, polymathy. See **learning.**

school. Syn.: academy, seminary, institute, college, university, conservatory, lyceum, gymnasium, kindergarten. See **flock.**

science. Syn.: art. See **knowledge, art.**

scintilla. Syn.: see **bit.**

scintillate. Syn.: sparkle, glitter, gleam, flash, coruscate. See **shine,** v.

scion. Syn.: see **shoot,** n.

scoff. Syn.: jeer, flout, gibe, mock, sneer, fleer.
To *scoff* is to express scornful doubt or derision, openly and emphatically. *Gibe* implies the use of mocking or taunting expressions; to *jeer* is to shout in disapproval or scorn, sometimes to try to raise a laugh by sarcastic language. To *flout* is to treat with contempt or reject disdainfully; to *fleer* is to offer indignity by a derisive laugh or grin. To *sneer* is to express by tone of voice or facial expression contempt or ill-humored detraction.

scold. Syn.: chide, berate, upbraid, reproach, reprove, rebuke, reprimand, reprehend, censure, lecture, rail at, objurgate, vituperate, abuse, revile.
Scold implies cross or ill-tempered, usually sharp-tongued and sometimes nagging, reproof. *Chide* generally implies gentle or refined reproof, as for some minor fault. *Upbraid* suggests sharp or bitter reproach, especially to make the person feel the guilt of his offense and to mend his ways. *Objurgate* applies to severe or vehement reproach, as for some grave matter.

scolding. Syn.: rebuke, reprimand, reprehension, censure.

scope. Syn.: extent, range, compass, purview; room, space, opportunity, liberty. See **range,** n.

scorch. Syn.: parch, sear, singe, char, torrefy. See **burn.**

scorn, n. **Syn.:** contempt, disdain, contumely, derision, mockery. See **contempt.**

scorn, v. **Syn.:** contemn, disdain, despise, spurn, scout, flout, reject, disregard. See **despise.**

scornful. Syn.: contemptuous, disdainful, contumelious, derisive, insolent, defiant.

scoundrel. Syn.: see **villain, rogue.**

scour. Syn.: see **rub, run.**

scout. Syn.: see **scorn.**

scowl. Syn.: frown, lower, glower. See **frown.**

scrap. Syn.: see **bit.**

scrape. Syn.: scratch, abrade, rasp, grate, shave, rub, chafe.

scratch. Syn.: see **scrape.**

scrawny. Syn.: see **gaunt.**

scream. Syn.: shriek, screech, yell, cry, outcry.
To *scream* is to utter a loud, high, piercing cry. *Shriek* usually refers to a sharper and more sudden cry than scream, which when due to fear or pain is indicative of more terror or distress. *Screech* emphasizes the disagreeable shrillness of an outcry, and its lack of dignity in a person.

screech. Syn.: see **scream.**

screen, n. **Syn.:** shield, protection, guard, defense, fender, mask, disguise.

screen, v. **Syn.:** shield, protect, defend, shelter, cover, cloak, hide, conceal, mask, shroud.

scribe. Syn.: see **writer.**

scruple. Syn.: see **hesitate.**

scrupulous. Syn.: conscientious, particular, nice, punctilious, strict, precise, exact. **Ant.:** see **unscrupulous.**
Scrupulous implies conscientious nicety and care, especially in matters of conduct; *punctilious*, strictness and preciseness, especially in the observance of social rules and conventions.

scrutinize. Syn.: see **search,** v.

scrutiny. Syn.: see **examination.**

scuffle. Syn.: struggle, tussle, scrimmage, fray, fight. See **fight,** n., **quarrel,** n.

scurrilous. Syn.: coarse, indecent, vulgar, low, gross, ribald, foul, vile, offensive, abusive, opprobrious.
Scurrilous is applied to low, coarse, and abusive remarks; *ribald*, to that which is wantonly vulgar or indecent.

scurry, scuttle. Syn.: see **run.**

sea. Syn.: ocean, main, deep.

seaman. Syn.: see **sailor.**

sear, a. **Syn.:** dry, withered, dead.

sear, v. **Syn.:** see **burn.**

search, n. **Syn.:** examination, inquiry, investigation, quest, pursuit.

search, *v.* **Syn.**: examine, explore, probe, investigate, scrutinize, hunt, seek, rummage, ransack.

To *search* is to examine closely and thoroughly, as for something hidden, lost, or stolen. *Explore* especially implies a search into an unknown or little known region to gain more complete knowledge of it or to discover something within it. *Rummage* implies a rough upsetting and overhauling of that which is searched; *ransack*, a thorough and complete going through, especially for the purpose of discovering plunder or booty.

seasonable. **Syn.**: opportune, timely, convenient, apropos. **Ant.**: see **unseasonable**. See **timely**.

seat. **Syn.**: chair, stool, bench, settee, sofa, divan, lounge, pew, throne; site, location, locality; abode, residence.

secluded. **Syn.**: withdrawn, isolated, retired, sequestered, lonely.

seclusion. **Syn.**: see **solitude**.

secondary. **Syn.**: subordinate, subsidiary, auxiliary, inferior, minor.

secret. **Syn.**: concealed, hidden, covered, shrouded, veiled, unknown, obscure, recondite, esoteric, covert, latent, occult, mysterious, cryptic; private, privy, retired, secluded, sequestered; surreptitious, clandestine, underhand, stealthy, furtive; uncommunicative, secretive, reticent, close. **Ant.**: unconcealed, open, manifest, clear, apparent, evident, obvious, plain.

Secret is the most general term for that which is concealed. That which is *covert* is covered or disguised, and is the opposite of frank or avowed. *Surreptitious* is used of what is done, as it were, under cover and in a guilty way. *Furtive* suggests nervous shiftiness, as in doing something of which one is ashamed. *Clandestine* is used of studious or artful concealment of objectionable, illicit, or unlawful acts. *Underhand* implies craft and deceit; *stealthy*, slow and careful secrecy of movement.

secretary. **Syn.**: see **writer**.

secrete. **Syn.**: hide, conceal, shroud, cloak, bury. See **hide**, *v.*

secretion. **Syn.**: concealment, hiding. See **excretion**.

secretive. **Syn.**: reticent, reserved, uncommunicative, taciturn, close, silent. **Ant.**: talkative, communicative, prattling.

sectarian, sectary. **Syn.**: see **heretic**.

section. **Syn.**: division, portion, part, segment, piece.

secular. **Syn.**: see **worldly**.

secure, *a.* **Syn.**: confident, overconfident, careless; safe, guarded, protected, impregnable, unassailable; fast, firm, stable, immovable; assured, sure, certain. **Ant.**: insecure, unsafe, hazardous, perilous, exposed, risky. See **safe**.

secure, *v.* **Syn.**: assure, insure, guard, protect, defend, shield; fasten, tie, moor, confine; get, obtain, acquire, procure, gain, win.

security. **Syn.**: confidence, unconcernedness, carelessness; safety, protection, defense, bulwark, shelter; assurance, pledge, guaranty, surety, bond, bail, gage, earnest.

sedate. **Syn.**: composed, quiet, calm, staid, unruffled, imperturbable, sober, serious, demure. See **staid**.

sedative. **Syn.**: see **narcotic**.

sediment. **Syn.**: precipitate, settlings, grounds, dregs, lees, dross, feculence.

Sediment is any insoluble or undissolved solid matter that sinks to the bottom of a liquid. *Dregs* may refer to the worthless matter which is sometimes found in the bottom of a liquid, or, like *lees*, to the sediment from wine or other liquors.

sedition. **Syn.**: rebellion, revolt, insurrection, mutiny, riot, insubordination.

seditious. **Syn.**: rebellious, insurrectionary, insurgent, mutinous, insubordinate.

seduce. **Syn.**: entice, inveigle, tempt, mislead, corrupt, betray. See **tempt**.

sedulity. **Syn.**: see **assiduity**.

sedulous. **Syn.**: diligent, industrious, assiduous, persistent, persevering, unremitting, untiring.

see. **Syn.**: behold, descry, espy, discern, notice, note, perceive, look at, view, watch, observe, witness, regard, scan, scrutinize, inspect; understand, apprehend, comprehend, grasp, ascertain, learn; meet, interview, visit.

See is the general word, and may indicate either a voluntary or an involuntary act. *Perceive*, a more formal word, often implies seeing something intelligently or understandingly. *Behold* refers to seeing something interesting or remarkable, either in a fixed manner or for some time. *Observe* implies close or careful watching, especially to note significant facts or details. *Notice* especially applies to casual, accidental, or involuntary seeing of something. To *witness* is to see an action take place, and hence often to testify to that effect: as, to *witness* a signature.

seem. **Syn.**: appear, look.

Seem is applied to what has the semblance of being true or probable. *Appear* suggests, as it were, coming into view or becoming evident. *Look* more vividly suggests the use of the eye, literally or figuratively.

seemly. **Syn.**: becoming, fitting, befitting, meet, appropriate, suitable, proper, decorous, decent. See **fitting**.

seep. **Syn.**: see **filter**.

seer. **Syn.**: see **prophet**.

seethe. **Syn.**: see **boil**.

segment. **Syn.**: section, portion, division, part, piece.

segregate. **Syn.**: see **separate**.

seize. **Syn.**: take, catch, capture, apprehend, arrest; clutch, grasp, grip, snatch, grab, nab; appropriate, confiscate, usurp.

To *seize* is to fasten upon suddenly or forcibly. *Grasp* implies a firm hold with the hand; *clutch*, a tight or convulsive grasping, sometimes of that of which one seems to be losing hold; *grip*, a strong, secure, often determined grasp; *grab*, a sudden or vigorous, *snatch*, a quick or abrupt, seizure, as in taking something away from another.

select, *a.* **Syn.**: selected, chosen, picked, choice, superior.

select, *v.* **Syn.**: choose, pick, cull, elect, prefer. See **choose**.

self-denial. **Syn.**: abnegation, self-sacrifice, abstemiousness, asceticism, austerity. **Ant.**: self-indulgence, gratification, voluptuousness, sensuality.

self-esteem. **Syn.**: see **vanity**.

self-evident. **Syn.**: obvious, axiomatic.

self-important. **Syn.**: pompous, vain, egotistical, bumptious.

selfish. **Syn.**: self-interested, self-seeking, mercenary, illiberal. **Ant.**: see **unselfish**.

self-possessed. **Syn.**: composed, collected, poised, assured, calm, unruffled.

self-possession. **Syn.**: self-control, self-command, composure, poise, calmness, equanimity, aplomb, assurance.

self-sacrifice. **Syn.**: see **self-denial**.

sell. **Syn.**: vend, barter, trade.

To *sell* is to exchange a commodity or other item of value for money; *vend* applies especially to the selling of small articles, as by peddling or upon the street, and always with direct contact between the seller and buyer.

semblance. **Syn.**: see **likeness**.

send. **Syn.**: despatch, forward, transmit, consign; drive, impel, hurl, throw, cast.

senile. **Syn.**: aged, decrepit, feeble, infirm.

sensation. **Syn.**: see **sense**.

sensational. **Syn.**: exciting, thrilling, melodramatic.

sense. **Syn.**: perception, feeling, sensation, sensibility; apprehension, understanding, wisdom, sagacity, judgment; gist, substance, meaning, signification, import; opinion. See **meaning**.

senseless. **Syn.**: insensate, insensible, unconscious; stupid, foolish, fatuous, silly, nonsensical, absurd, unwise, unreasonable.

sensibility. **Syn.**: sensitiveness, susceptibility, impressibility, delicacy, feeling, emotion. See **sense**.

sensible. **Syn.**: perceptible, appreciable; sentient, cognizant, conscious, aware; wise, judicious, discreet, sagacious, sound, practical, hard-headed. See **sensitive, conscious**.

As applied to persons, *sensible* implies the possession and use of sound reason or common sense; *judicious*, of discreet judgment; *practical* suggests peculiar ability to adopt means for an end, or to turn what is at hand to account.

sensitive. **Syn.**: sensible, impressionable, impressible, susceptible.

As applied to a person's nature or disposition, *sensitive* is used of one easily and acutely affected by external circumstances, especially one too easily hurt by the real or imagined slights of others. *Impressionable* usually refers to the condition of being readily moved or influenced, as by surroundings, appearances, ideas, or the like. The *susceptible* person is subject to, and easily stirred by, emotional impressions.

sensual. **Syn.**: sensuous, voluptuous, self-indulgent, wanton, carnal, fleshly, lecherous, lewd. **Ant.:** virtuous, continent, chaste.

Sensuous refers, favorably or literally, to what is experienced through the senses; *sensual*, unfavorably, to the enjoyments derived from the senses, generally implying grossness or lewdness. *Voluptuous* implies the luxurious or elegant gratification of sensuous or sensual desires.

sensuous. Syn.: see **sensual.**

sententious. Syn.: pithy, terse, concise, compact, laconic, pointed, epigrammatic. See **concise.**

sentient. Syn.: see **sensible.**

sentiment. Syn.: opinion, view, thought; feeling, emotion, sentimentality; maxim, saying, epigram.

Sentiment is an activity of the affections, worthy, refined, and tender; *sentimentality* implies affected, excessive, sometimes mawkish sentiment.

sentimental. Syn.: emotional, gushing, mawkish. See **romantic.**

sentimentality. Syn.: see **sentiment.**

sentinel. Syn.: sentry, picket, guard, watch, vedette.

separate. Syn.: divide, disunite, disjoin, disconnect, dissociate, detach, disengage, sever, sunder, cleave, part, isolate, insulate, segregate, scatter, disperse.

To *separate* is to remove from each other things previously associated, or to keep apart things not to be united. *Divide* implies careful separation according to measurement, rule, or plan. *Part* is nearly identical with *divide* in meaning, but is less common in use. *Sever* refers especially to complete separation, as by cutting off a part from a whole. To *sunder* is now chiefly literary for to *separate*, sometimes with violence.

separation. Syn.: division, disunion, disjunction, disconnection, detachment, severance, parting, isolation, segregation, rupture, divorce.

separatist. Syn.: see **heretic.**

sequel. Syn.: continuation, consequence, result, outcome, issue.

sequence. Syn.: see **series.**

sequestered. Syn.: see **secluded.**

serene. Syn.: clear, calm, tranquil, placid, peaceful, unruffled, undisturbed, untroubled, unperturbed, composed, sedate. **Ant.:** cloudy, stormy, ruffled, excited, agitated, disconcerted.

serenity. Syn.: calmness, tranquillity, placidity, quiet, peace, composure. See **composure.**

serf. Syn.: see **slave.**

serfdom. Syn.: see **slavery.**

series. Syn.: sequence, succession, chain, concatenation, order, line, row.

Series is applied to a number of things of the same kind, usually related to each other, arranged or happening in order: as, a *series* of articles, of baseball games; a mathematical *series*. *Succession* implies that one thing is followed by another (or others in turn) without the necessity of any relation or connection between them: as, a *succession* of calamities; a *succession* of tricks by a magician. *Sequence* stresses continuity in time, thought, cause and effect, etc.: as, the *sequence* of events, a sonnet *sequence*.

serious. Syn.: earnest, grave, solemn, sober, thoughtful, sedate, staid, saturnine; weighty, momentous, important; critical, alarming, dangerous. **Ant.:** gay, light, buoyant, elated, blithe, happy, cheerful, joyous. See **grave.**

sermon. Syn.: homily, exhortation, preachment, discourse.

serrate. Syn.: see **notched.**

servant. Syn.: domestic, servitor, factotum, helper, menial, lackey, flunky, butler, valet, groom, coachman, footman, maid.

A *servant* is one employed to render personal service or do household work; a *domestic* is a servant of the latter kind; *servitor* is a somewhat uncommon word for servant or servile follower; *factotum* denotes one who does all kinds of work; *menial* indicates one performing the humblest and most unpleasant services; *lackey* stresses the servility and complete obedience of a personal servant; *flunky* suggests one who performs petty services with pomp and display.

serve. Syn.: attend, wait upon; promote, advance, subserve; suffice, satisfy, content, answer; deal out, distribute.

servile. Syn.: slavish, cringing, fawning, obsequious, subservient, truckling, groveling, abject, base. **Ant.:** imperious, masterful, commanding, independent.

Servile suggests fawning abasement before authority;

slavish describes one who follows or obeys with abject submission. *Obsequious* implies the ostentatious subordination of oneself to the wishes of another. *Subservient* describes one whom another is able to control in order to further his own ends. *Truckling* implies mean, debasing submission to the will, desires, or whims of another to win or keep his favor.

servitor. Syn.: see **servant.**

servitude. Syn.: see **slavery.**

set, *n.* **Syn.:** series, collection, class, group, company, band, party, clique, coterie, circle; slip, shoot, sprout, scion.

set, *p. a.* **Syn.:** placed, posted, stationed; fixed, established, appointed, prescribed, determined, firm, rigid, immovable, inflexible, unyielding, obstinate; regular, uniform, formal, ceremonious.

set, *v.* **Syn.:** place, put, post, station, locate, plant; fix, establish, appoint, prescribe, ordain, assign, determine, settle, arrange; sink, decline, wane; solidify, stiffen. See **put.** See also **sit.**

setback. Syn.: see **reverse,** *n.*

settle. Syn.: adjust, arrange; balance, pay, discharge, liquidate; compose, calm, quiet, pacify, still, tranquilize; establish, fix, appoint, set, ordain, decide, determine; colonize, people; fall, sink, descend, alight, subside. See **fix.**

settled. Syn.: see **staid.**

sever. Syn.: separate, dissociate, disjoin, disunite, disconnect, divide, part, sunder, tear, cut. See **separate.**

several. Syn.: different, various, manifold, sundry, divers.

Several indicates a small and indefinite number greater than two: as, *several* people, *several* days. *Sundry* emphasizes the miscellaneous character of the units composing a designated group: as, he agitated *sundry* measures at *sundry* times. *Divers*, even more strongly than *sundry*, suggests the idea of variety: as, *divers* colors, *divers* criticisms.

severe. Syn.: serious, earnest, grave, sober; austere, stern, strict, exact, precise, rigid, rigorous, harsh, rough, hard, drastic, cruel, inflexible, inexorable, relentless, unmerciful; plain, unadorned, chaste; sharp, cutting, keen, acute, intense, extreme, distressing, violent; arduous, trying, critical. **Ant.:** gay, buoyant, happy, joyous; kind, tender, gentle, mild, soft, lenient, tractable, yielding, indulgent. See **harsh, stern.**

severity. Syn.: seriousness, gravity; austerity, strictness, exactness, rigidity, rigor, rigorousness, harshness, asperity, cruelty; plainness, simplicity; sharpness, intensity, violence.

sex. Syn.: gender.

shabby. Syn.: see **threadbare.**

shack. Syn.: see **house.**

shackles. Syn.: fetters, manacles, irons, handcuffs, gyves.

The following four words are now somewhat old-fashioned or literary in their use. *Shackles* are rings for the wrists, ankles, or neck, by which a prisoner is chained to the floor or wall. *Manacles* are similar devices for binding the wrists together. *Fetters* are chains for the feet. *Gyves* is a less usual word for manacles or fetters.

shade, *n.* **Syn.:** shadow, darkness, gloom, obscurity; trace, tinge, tint; spirit, phantom, specter, ghost, apparition; curtain, blind, awning, screen. See **ghost, color,** *n.*

Shade indicates the lesser brightness of an area where the direct rays of light do not fall. It differs from *shadow* in that it implies no particular form or definite limit, while a *shadow* represents in form or outline the object which intercepts the light.

shade, *v.* **Syn.:** shadow, darken, dim, cloud, obfuscate, obscure.

shadow. Syn.: see **shade.**

shadowy. Syn.: shady, dark, obscure, gloomy; unsubstantial, unreal, visionary, vague, illusory, chimerical, fleeting.

shaft. Syn.: spear, lance, arrow, missile; pole, stalk, trunk, column, pillar, obelisk, monument; boring, excavation, passage, opening.

shake. Syn.: agitate, quake, shiver, shudder, quiver, quaver, flutter, tremble, vibrate, totter, dodder, sway, swing, rock, jar, jolt, jounce.

To *shake* is to agitate more or less quickly, abruptly, and often unevenly, so as to disturb the poise, stability, or equilibrium of a person or thing: as, to *shake* the contents of a bottle; to *shake* one's head; the buildings *shook* in the earthquake. *Quiver* is to exhibit a slight vibratory motion such as that resulting from disturbed or irregular (surface) tension: as, her lips *quivered*; the surface of the pool *quivered* in the breeze. To *tremble* is to shake so as to suggest instability or a loss of coördination and control: as, to *tremble* from weakness or fright; the house *trembled* whenever a truck passed. To *vibrate* is to exhibit a rapid, rhythmical motion such as that of a violin-string when a bow is drawn across it, or that of a standing automobile when the engine is running.

shall. Syn.: will, must.

The confusion in the use of *shall* and *will* is of long standing and many of the distinctions are breaking down in modern English. It may be generally stated that *shall* in the first person (singular and plural) denotes futurity, and simply foretells or declares what is about to take place: as, I (or we) *shall* go to town to-morrow. Used with the second or third persons *shall* implies authority, command, threat, promise, determination, or inevitability: as, thou *shalt* not steal; you *shall* make amends; they *shall* receive their wages; you *shall* go; it *shall* be as the fates decree. *Will* in the second and third persons denotes simple futurity: as, you *will* know to-morrow; they *will* come by train. With the first person *will* denotes consent, promise, determination, or resolution: as, I *will* take it for you; we *will* meet you at noon; I *will* fight for my rights. Interrogatively, *shall* or *will* is used according as the one or the other would be used in reply. Thus *shall* is usually required for questions in the first person. In the second person, " *Shall* you go?" expects the answer "I *shall* (or *shall* not) go" (simple futurity); " *Will* you go?" expects "I *will* (not)" (promise). In the third person, " *Shall* he go?" anticipates a decision or command, "He *shall* (not);" "*Will* he go?" inquires merely for information about a future event and is answered by "He *will* (not)."

shallow. Syn.: shoal, depthless; slight, superficial.

sham, *n*. Syn.: imitation, make-believe, pretense, simulation, humbug, fraud, imposture.

sham, *a*. Syn.: counterfeit, spurious, false, make-believe, fictitious, factitious, simulated, mock, bogus, fake. See **false.**

sham, *v*. Syn.: pretend, feign, simulate, fake.

shame, *n*. Syn.: disgrace, dishonor, ignominy, humiliation, mortification, abashment.

Shame is a painful feeling caused by the consciousness or exposure of unworthy or indecent conduct or circumstances; *humiliation* is diminished self-esteem resulting from any assault on one's pride.

shame, *v*. Syn.: disgrace, dishonor, discredit, degrade, humiliate, mortify.

shameful. Syn.: disgraceful, dishonorable, ignominious, infamous, scandalous, vile, immodest, indecent.

shameless. Syn.: impudent, unblushing, brazen, barefaced, immodest, indecent. See **immodest.**

shanty. Syn.: see **house.**

shape, *n*. Syn.: form, figure, contour, outline, cut, cast, build; fashion, appearance, guise, state, manner, way. See **form.**

shape, *v*. Syn.: form, mold, fashion, frame, construct, make; adapt, conform, adjust, regulate; contrive, devise, plan, arrange.

shapely. Syn.: well-formed, symmetrical, comely.

share, *n*. Syn.: portion, part, allotment, lot, quota, dole.

share, *v*. Syn.: see **partake.**

sharp. Syn.: keen, acute, pointed, angular; clean-cut, distinct, clear; pungent, acrid, acid, sour, bitter, peppery; shrill, piercing; biting, nipping, pinching, cutting; incisive, trenchant, caustic, sarcastic, acrimonious, tart; poignant, piercing, penetrating, intense, excruciating, distressing, painful; severe, harsh, rigorous, stern; fierce, violent, fiery, eager; vigilant, attentive, alert; quick, discerning, perspicacious, shrewd, cunning, astute. **Ant.:** see **dull.**

Sharp, opposed to *dull* or *blunt*, is the general word and may be used of any cutting edge or penetrating point. *Keen* is especially applied to long edges, as of a dagger, sword, or knife. These words are capable of a variety of figurative uses. As applied to speech or writing, *sharp* implies biting or acrimonious, *keen*, penetrating or satirically clever, expression. Other words with corresponding literal or etymological meanings have similar figurative uses. *Cutting* implies such sharpness as intentionally hurts; *trenchant* implies clean-cut vigor of statement; *incisive* is applied to language that goes clearly and directly to the point.

sharpen. Syn.: point, whet, grind, hone, edge; intensify, quicken.

sharper. Syn.: see **swindler.**

shatter. Syn.: smash, shiver, splinter, crush, demolish, break, disorder, derange. See **break.**

shave. Syn.: see **pare.**

sheaf. Syn.: shock, stack, rick.

sheath. Syn.: see **case.**

shed, *n*. Syn.: see **house.**

shed, *v*. Syn.: cast off, discard, molt, mew, exuviate; emit, diffuse, radiate, spread, scatter, disperse.

sheen. Syn.: see **luster, polish.**

sheer. Syn.: unmixed, undiluted, unadulterated, pure; absolute, utter, downright; abrupt, precipitous, perpendicular. See **utter,** *a*.

shell. Syn.: see **bomb, skin,** *n*.

shelter, *n*. Syn.: protection, safeguard, defense, shield, screen, cover, covert, refuge, asylum, sanctuary, haven, retreat.

shelter, *v*. Syn.: protect, shield, screen, shroud, hide, harbor, house.

shield. Syn.: see **shelter.**

shift, *n*. Syn.: movement, moving, sliding; expedient, device, contrivance, resource, resort; evasion, dodge, trick, artifice, subterfuge, ruse, stratagem; detachment, group, crew, gang. See **means.**

shift, *v*. Syn.: change, alter, move, transfer; vary, veer, turn.

shiftless. Syn.: inefficient, unthrifty, improvident, lazy, slack, lax.

shimmer. Syn.: see **shine.**

shine, *n*. Syn.: gleam, radiance, luster, sheen, shimmer, gloss, polish, glaze.

shine, *v*. Syn.: beam, gleam, glance, glint, glisten, glister, shimmer, glimmer, flicker, twinkle, flash, sparkle, scintillate, coruscate, glitter, glow, glare, flare.

Shine denotes the steady emission or reflection of light. That which *beams* gives forth a radiant or bright light. *Gleam* is used of a distant light, as of the stars; a sudden light, as from a revolving light on a lighthouse; a diffused light, as of a street lamp in a fog. *Glance* refers to light momentarily reflected by a surface, as moonlight reflected by a wave. *Glint* suggests a hard bright gleam or flash of reflected light, as from something polished or burnished. *Glimmer* refers to a faint, unsteady light as of a candle; *shimmer*, to the changing play of light on a (generally moving) surface, as of water or silk. *Glisten*, to a lustrous light, as from something sleek or wet. *Twinkle* suggests a distant, tremulous light, as from a star. To *flash* is to send forth light with a sudden and transient brilliancy. To *sparkle* is to give off sparks or small ignited particles, or to send forth small but brilliant gleams of light as does a diamond. To *scintillate* is to sparkle brilliantly, as white-hot iron. To *glitter* is to catch and reflect (intermittently) flashes of light like bright coins. To *coruscate* is to throw off vivid flashes of light, like those of a sky-rocket.

shining. Syn.: beaming, gleaming, glowing, glistening, radiant, luminous, resplendent, effulgent, refulgent, brilliant, bright, lustrous, glossy, shiny; conspicuous, notable, illustrious.

ship. Syn.: see **boat.**

shirk. Syn.: evade, shun, avoid, neglect.

shiver. Syn.: shatter, splinter, demolish; tremble, quiver, quake, shake, shudder. See **break.**

We *shiver* with cold or a sensation like that of cold; we *shudder* with horror or abhorrence; we *quake* with fear.

shoal. Syn.: see **flock.**

shock, *n*. Syn.: concussion, clash, collision, jolt, jar, blow.

shock, *v*. Syn.: jar, jolt, stun, paralyze, astound, stagger, appal, dismay, terrify, horrify, frighten, startle, scandalize, outrage, disgust, revolt. See **startle.**

shocking. Syn.: appalling, dreadful, terrible, dire, heinous, frightful, scandalous, outrageous, abominable, disgusting, revolting, offensive.

shoe. Syn.: slipper, boot, sandal, pump, moccasin, brogue, brogan, stogy, clog, patten, sabot, bottine, buskin, overshoe, rubber, galosh.

shoot, *n*. Syn.: chute, trough, channel, flume; sprout, offshoot, scion, sucker, tiller, chit.

shoot, *v*. Syn.: dart, dash, rush; sprout, bud, germinate, burgeon; project, protrude, jut, extend; cast, throw, hurl, thrust, eject, emit; discharge, fire; hit, wound, kill.

shore. Syn.: coast, beach, strand, bank, marge, margin, border, brink.

Shore is the land bordering any considerable body of water, as the ocean, a river, or a lake. *Coast* is that part of a continent, country, or division of a country that is contiguous to the sea. *Beach* is the strip along the shore washed by the water, as from tides, and therefore sandy or pebbly. *Strand* is a poetic word for a sandy or gradually sloping shore.

short. **Syn.:** low, small, little; brief, concise, terse, succinct, laconic, pithy, epigrammatic, summary; abrupt, curt, uncivil, crusty, sharp, petulant; limited, scant, deficient, insufficient, inadequate, lacking; friable, brittle, crisp. **Ant.:** see **long,** *a.*

Short and *brief* are opposed to *long,* and indicate slight extent: as, a *short* story; a *brief* treatise; a *short,* or *brief,* interval. But *short* is alone applied to physical distance and certain purely spatial relations: as, a *short* (not *brief*) pole, coat, trolley line.

shortage. **Syn.:** deficiency, insufficiency, inadequacy, deficit, dearth.

shortcoming. **Syn.:** defect, imperfection, fault, foible.

shorten. **Syn.:** abridge, abbreviate, contract, condense, curtail, reduce, diminish, lessen, limit, restrict.

To *shorten* is to make less in extent or duration; to *abridge* is to reduce to smaller compass, especially by condensation and omission; to *curtail* is especially to cut off some part: as, to *shorten* a dress, or a prisoner's sentence; to *abridge* a dictionary; to *curtail* expenses or one's activities.

should. **Syn.:** see **must.**

shout. **Syn.:** see **cry,** *v.*

shove. **Syn.:** push, thrust, jostle, elbow, propel, drive, boost. See **push.**

show, *n.* **Syn.:** exhibition, display, manifestation; pomp, parade, ostentation, ceremony, pageantry, pageant, spectacle, flourish, splurge; appearance, semblance, likeness; pretense, pretext, color, feint; sign, indication, promise.

Show refers to the appearances of things and often indicates a spectacle arranged for the observation of others, sometimes with a view to exalting one's position. *Display* is intentionally conspicuous show; *parade,* pretentious, boastful, often hollow display; *ostentation,* vain, ambitious, or offensive parade. *Pomp* suggests such a show of dignity and authority as characterizes a ceremony of state.

show, *v.* **Syn.:** exhibit, display, present, disclose, reveal, expose, divulge, evince, manifest, indicate; direct, guide, conduct, usher; bestow, confer; demonstrate, prove, explain.

To *show,* in its transitive uses, is to bring something before the view of another for the purpose of having him see it. To *exhibit* is to put forward something for particular observation. To *display* is literally to spread out, so that that which is displayed shall be most completely and favorably seen. To *expose* is to lay open what would otherwise be covered or concealed. To *evince* and *manifest* differ from these in not referring to material things but rather to characteristics, qualities, etc.: as, to *evince* or *manifest* surprise, interest, sympathy.

showy. **Syn.:** gay, gaudy, flashy, garish, striking, brilliant, magnificent, gorgeous, sumptuous, pompous, spectacular. **Ant.:** inconspicuous, unostentatious, quiet, subdued. See **gaudy.**

shred. **Syn.:** rag, tatter, scrap, bit.

shrew. **Syn.:** scold, termagant, virago, vixen.

shrewd. **Syn.:** sagacious, astute, sharp, keen, acute, discerning, long-headed, far-seeing.

shriek. **Syn.:** see **scream.**

shrine. **Syn.:** see **sanctuary.**

shrink. **Syn.:** shrivel, contract, dwindle, decrease; retreat, recoil, flinch, blench, quail, wince.

To *shrink* is to feel an impulse (whether controlled or uncontrolled) to draw back or recoil, as through fear or pain, or to feel an aversion to something, as through revulsion or distaste. To *flinch* is to manifest weakness by shrinking in the face of what demands endurance or courage. To *blench* is to start back or turn aside, as when confronted with something fearful or terrifying. To *wince* is to betray involuntarily a hurt. To *quail* is to give way or cower, as through timidity or fear. See *decrease.*

shrivel. **Syn.:** see **shrink.**

shudder. **Syn.:** see **shiver.**

shuffle. **Syn.:** jumble, mix; equivocate, prevaricate, quibble, shift, dodge. See **equivocate.**

shun. **Syn.:** avoid, eschew, evade, elude. See **avoid.**

shut. **Syn.:** close, bar, block, stop up. See **close.**

shy. **Syn.:** timid, bashful, diffident, retiring, reserved, modest, demure, coy, backward, shamefaced; suspicious, cautious, wary, distrustful, chary. **Ant.:** forward, bold, presumptuous, brazen, impertinent, pert, immodest.

Shy usually implies a constitutional shrinking from the notice of, or contact with, others. *Bashful* implies timidity and a disturbed state of feeling at meeting others or at being brought into prominence or notice. *Diffident* denotes marked unwillingness to put oneself forward, as from fear of failure, censure, or the like. *Coy* implies modest reserve or hesitation, often assumed in teasing playfulness or coquetry.

sick. **Syn.:** ill, unwell, ailing, indisposed, diseased, infirm, morbid, sickly; nauseated, qualmish, queasy.

Sick and *ill* are general words to indicate any departure from a state of health and refer to a condition presumably temporary, however severe. In England *sick* has the specific sense of nauseated. *Unwell* is negative in character, and expresses a less definite condition of bad health. *Indisposed* refers to a slight, temporary illness. *Ailing* implies a somewhat unhealthy condition usually extending over some time; *sickly* suggests a tendency toward ill health arising from constitutional weakness.

sickly. **Syn.:** ailing, unwell, unhealthy, diseased, frail, feeble, weak, languid, puny. **Ant.:** healthy, strong, robust, hale. See **sick.**

sickness. **Syn.:** illness, ailment, indisposition, disorder, nausea, complaint, disease, malady, infirmity.

sift. **Syn.:** screen, bolt, strain, sieve.

sign. **Syn.:** mark, symbol, emblem, indication, manifestation, sympton, token, stigma, signal, gesture, motion; trace, vestige; omen, portent, auspice, presage, prognostic, augury. See **mark.**

Sign is a general word for whatever gives evidence of a past, present, or future event: as, dark clouds are often a *sign* of rain. An *omen* may foretell future events, either good or bad, and often rests upon superstitious practices or beliefs. *Portent* usually refers to some approaching misfortune or calamity.

signal. **Syn.:** conspicuous, eminent, prominent, outstanding, notable, distinguished, extraordinary, remarkable, memorable, striking.

significance. **Syn.:** signification, meaning, sense, import; moment, importance, consequence, gravity.

significant. **Syn.:** meaning, expressive, telling, meaningful, suggestive; important, weighty, momentous. See **expressive.**

signification. **Syn.:** see **meaning.**

signify. **Syn.:** represent, betoken, indicate, denote, import, purport, mean, imply, suggest, connote.

silence, *n.* **Syn.:** muteness, reticence, reserve; stillness, hush, quiet, quietness, noiselessness.

silence, *v.* **Syn.:** still, quiet, hush, lull; repress, suppress, stop, quell.

silent. **Syn.:** speechless, mute, dumb, hushed, tacit, taciturn, reticent, reserved, uncommunicative, mum; still, quiet, noiseless. See **still,** *a.*

Silent denotes the absence of speech or sound, and may indicate either a temporary or permanent condition. *Mute* and *dumb* are frequently interchangeable, but *mute* oftener implies the temporary suspension of speech, as from fear, astonishment, or obstinacy; *dumb,* the lack of the organs or power of speech. *Speechless* means without the power of speech either because of natural incapacity or special circumstance such as surprise, horror, etc. *Tacit* usually refers to that which is silently indicated or implied.

silly. **Syn.:** foolish, senseless, nonsensical, ridiculous, absurd, stupid, fatuous, inane, vacuous, trifling, puerile; feeble-minded, half-witted, simple, imbecile. See **foolish.**

similar. **Syn.:** see **like,** *a.*

similarity. **Syn.:** likeness, similitude, semblance, resemblance, correspondence, analogy, parallelism. See **likeness.**

simile. **Syn.:** see **comparison.**

simmer. **Syn.:** see **boil.**

simper. **Syn.:** smirk.

Both these words describe forms of smiling, *simper* implying a silly primness and affectation, *smirk* suggesting scarcely concealed contempt, or self-satisfaction.

simple. **Syn.:** unmixed, elementary, single; bare, pure, absolute; unadorned, plain, homely, poor, humble, lowly; artless, unstudied, undesigning, sincere, straightforward, open, frank, unaffected, unassuming, unpretentious, naïve, unsophisticated; trifling, unimportant, insignificant; credulous, gullible, stupid, silly, feeble-minded. **Ant.:** elaborate, involved, intricate, complex; artful, designing, wily, crafty, deceitful.

That which is *simple* is not elaborate or complex; that which is *plain* has little or no adornment or embellishment; *homely* suggests the absence of natural beauty, sometimes a wholesome simplicity without artificial refinement or elegance.

simpleton. Syn.: see **idiot.**

simulate. Syn.: feign, pretend, affect, sham, counterfeit, imitate. See **pretend.**

simultaneous. Syn.: coincident, synchronous, contemporaneous.

sin. Syn.: transgression, offense, wrong, crime, evil, vice, immorality, iniquity, wickedness, unrighteousness. **Ant.:** blamelessness, uprightness, integrity, virtue, innocence, purity, morality. See **offense.**

since. Syn.: see **because.**

sincere. Syn.: pure, genuine, true, unfeigned, unaffected, heartfelt, candid, frank, truthful, straightforward, upright, honest. **Ant.:** see **insincere.**

sincerity. Syn.: see **honesty.**

sinew. Syn.: see **muscle.**

sinful. Syn.: wicked, iniquitous, impious, vicious, depraved, immoral, evil, bad, wrong, unholy, unrighteous. See **immoral.**

sing. Syn.: carol, warble, croon, hum, chant, hymn, troll, yodel, twitter, chirp, chirrup.

singe. Syn.: see **burn.**

singer. Syn.: songster, songstress, chorister, vocalist, cantatrice, prima donna, soprano, treble, mezzo-soprano, contralto, alto, tenor, barytone, bass, basso; minstrel, troubadour, trouvère, jongleur, bard, poet.

single. Syn.: solitary, sole, singular, one; individual, particular, only, unique; unmarried, celibate.

Single denotes one, without always implying that others do not exist; *sole* adds to singleness the idea that something is alone of its kind or the only one: as, a *single* tree stood on the summit; God is the *sole* creator of the universe. *Only* may apply to one or more, and is used to mark off an individual or a group from others of the kind: as, the *only* man (or men) who came. A thing is *unique* when no other like it exists: as, a *unique* specimen. Since the idea of unity is present in all these words, there are cases where their differentiation depends largely upon usage.

singular. Syn.: single, sole, unique; exceptional, uncommon, unwonted, unusual, remarkable, strange, extraordinary, unprecedented, unparalleled; curious, odd, peculiar, queer, eccentric.

That which is *singular* stands in some way apart from the usual or general and often has a slight implication of disapprobation: as, a *singular* fellow; a *singular* way to act. That which is *peculiar* mystifies, or exhibits qualities not shared by others. *Strange* implies that the thing or its cause is unknown or unexplained: as, a *strange* insect or phenomenon. That which is *odd* is irregular or unconventional, and sometimes approaches the bizarre: as, an *odd* custom or dress. *Queer* sometimes adds to odd the suggestion of something abnormal: as, *queer* behavior. The above words may often be used with but slight difference of meaning: as, a *singular*, *peculiar*, *strange*, *odd*, or *queer* situation or occurrence. The *eccentric* departs from the ordinary or regular, often in a whimsical or unaccountable manner. It is applied to persons or to their actions, tastes, ideas, etc.

sinister. Syn.: left, left-hand; unlucky, inauspicious, ominous, threatening, malign, evil.

sink. Syn.: subside, descend, fall, drop, settle, decline; slope, slant, droop; diminish, decrease, dwindle, deteriorate; submerge, immerse, engulf.

sinless. Syn.: see **innocent.**

sinuous, *a.* Syn.: winding, meandering, crooked, tortuous, circuitous, serpentine, anfractuous, anfractuose. See **winding.**

sip. Syn.: see **drink,** *v.*

sit. Syn.: rest, repose. Cf. **set,** *v.*

The confusion between *sit* and *set* is obviated if it is remembered that *sit*, being intransitive, takes no object, and that *set* is regularly transitive and represents an object as acted upon: as, to *sit* before the fire; to *set* a dish on the table.

site. Syn.: see **location.**

situation. Syn.: location, site, station, position, place; condition, state, case, circumstances, plight, predicament; post, office, employment, job.

size. Syn.: magnitude, bulk, volume, dimensions, area, extent, length, width, breadth, thickness.

Size is the general word for things large or small; *magnitude* suggests greatness and ordinarily applies to things of considerable size: as, the *size* of an apple, the *magnitude* of Niagara Falls. *Bulk* and *volume*, in contrast to size or magnitude, which may refer to extent or area, are used only of magnitude in three dimensions, *bulk* applying to what has recognizable and often unwieldy shape, *volume* often to what has no particular suggestion of shape: as, the *bulk* of a bale of cotton or of an elephant; a *volume* of smoke.

skeptic. Syn.: doubter, unbeliever, disbeliever, freethinker, atheist, infidel, deist, agnostic.

The *skeptic* doubts through inherent tendency the fundamental doctrines of religion; the *unbeliever* fails to believe, or opposes, Christianity (or some other faith) as a whole. The *agnostic* justifies his unbelief by denying there is any proof of the existence of God or of a future life; an *atheist* denies that there is a God; an *infidel* is a professed and open opponent of Christianity, usually because of adherence to another religion.

skeptical. Syn.: doubting, incredulous, disbelieving, distrustful.

skepticism. Syn.: see **doubt.**

sketch, *n.* **Syn.:** draft, outline, skeleton, design, plot, plan, drawing, delineation, scenario, brief.

sketch, *v.* **Syn.:** outline, draw, delineate, portray, depict. See **depict.**

skilful. Syn.: dexterous, deft, adroit, apt, clever, expert, proficient, skilled, practised, accomplished, experienced. **Ant.:** see **unskilful.** See **dexterous.**

skill. Syn.: dexterity, deftness, adroitness, aptitude, knack, facility, cleverness, expertness, proficiency, ingenuity.

skin, *n.* **Syn.:** epidermis, cuticle, integument, pelt, coat, hide, fell, fur; peel, rind, bark, epicarp, husk, shuck, hull, pod, shell.

Skin is the general word for the outer covering of animals, including man, and the (especially) thin coating of fruits and vegetables. *Hide* applies to the skin of large (especially domesticated) animals, such as cattle, horses, elephants; *pelt*, to the untanned skin of smaller (especially fur-bearing) animals. *Fell* is now a poetic word for the skin or hide of an animal. *Rind* is usually applied to a hard, firm covering, as that of a watermelon or cantaloup; *peel*, to the skin of fruit which has been removed as by peeling off: as, an orange or banana *peel*. We speak of the *husk* of corn; the *hull* of beans or oats; the *pod* of peas; the *shell* of a cocoanut or peanut.

skin, *v.* **Syn.:** flay, excoriate, peel, pare, bark, decorticate.

skip. Syn.: spring, leap, bound, jump, vault, hop, trip, caper, cavort, prance, gambol, frisk, ricochet; omit, disregard.

To *skip* is to spring forward with an easy and graceful movement, as by alternate hops and bounds, often from lightness of spirits or joy. To *hop* is to make a short jump, generally on one foot, sometimes with the feet together. To *caper* is to leap or spring about as in a frolicsome exuberance of spirits or mirth. *Prance* is especially used of the nervous movements of a spirited, excited, or impatient horse.

skirmish. Syn.: see **battle.**

skulk. Syn.: see **lurk.**

sky. Syn.: firmament, heavens, welkin, empyrean, ether.

slack. Syn.: lax, remiss, negligent, careless, indolent, loose, relaxed; slow, dull, inactive.

slacken. Syn.: loosen, relax; retard, slow, reduce, moderate, abate.

slander, *n.* **Syn.:** defamation, traducement, calumny, scandal, libel, backbiting, aspersion, vilification, abuse.

slander, *v.* **Syn.:** defame, traduce, calumniate, libel, backbite, asperse, vilify, malign. See **asperse.**

slanderous. Syn.: defamatory, calumnious, calumniating, libelous.

slang. Syn.: see **jargon.**

slant, *n.* **Syn.:** slope, incline, inclination, pitch, obliquity.

slant, *v.* **Syn.:** see **lean,** *v.*

slash. Syn.: see **cut.**

slatternly. Syn.: see **slovenly.**

slaughter, *n.* **Syn.:** killing, slaying, murder, massacre, bloodshed, carnage, butchery. See **massacre.**

slaughter, *v.* **Syn.:** see **kill.**

slave. Syn.: bond-servant, bondsman, bondman, bondmaid, serf, thrall, helot, peon, drudge.

A *slave* is absolutely the property of his master, and can be sold, given away, or treated like any other personal possession. A *serf* in the Middle Ages was attached to the soil and went with it in all sales or leases, but had a certain interest in the land and certain privileges connected with it. *Thrall* is now chiefly a poetic word for a slave or bondsman.

slavery. Syn.: bondage, serfdom, thraldom, servitude, peonage, subjection.

The following words express involuntary subjection to another. *Slavery* emphasizes the idea of complete ownership and control by a master; *bondage* indicates a state of subjugation or captivity often involving burdensome and degrading labor; *servitude* is compulsory service, often such as is required as a legal penalty.

slavish. Syn.: servile, base, mean, ignoble, cringing, groveling, abject, submissive. See **servile.**

slay. Syn.: see **kill.**

sleek. Syn.: see **smooth.**

sleep, *n.* **Syn.:** slumber, repose, rest, doze, drowse, snooze, nap, siesta, stupor, coma, torpor, lethargy.

sleep, *v.* **Syn.:** slumber, repose, rest, doze, drowse, snooze, nap, nod, hibernate.

To *sleep* is to take rest by a natural suspension of bodily activity and of consciousness. *Slumber,* now an elevated or poetic word for sleep, formerly signified a light sleep. *Doze* implies a fitful sleep that is never far from waking; *nap,* a short sleep, often in the daytime; *drowse,* dulled sensations and sleepiness.

sleepy. Syn.: drowsy, slumberous, somnolent, lethargic, nodding.

slender. Syn.: slim, thin, slight, spare, sparse, lank, lean, spindling; scant, scanty, meager, inadequate.

As applied to the human figure, *slender* implies a generally pleasing, *slim,* lithe or delicate thinness; *slight* often adds the idea of frailness.

slide. Syn.: slip, glide.

Slide suggests the movement of one surface over another in contact with it; to *slip* is to slide smoothly, often in a sudden or accidental way; *glide* suggests a continuous, smooth, easy, and (usually) noiseless motion: as, to *slide* down hill; to *slip* on the ice; a skater *glides* over the ice or a boat through the water.

slight, *n.* **Syn.:** disrespect, snub. See **affront.**

slight, *a.* **Syn.:** slender, slim, thin, frail, flimsy, unsubstantial; meager, scanty, inconsiderable, unimportant, trivial, trifling, superficial, hasty, hurried, cursory. See **slender.**

slight, *v.* **Syn.:** disregard, ignore, overlook, neglect, snub.

slim. Syn.: see **slender.**

slink. Syn.: see **lurk.**

slip, *n.* **Syn.:** see **error.**

slip, *v.* **Syn.:** see **slide.**

slippery. Syn.: see **smooth.**

slop. Syn.: see **spill.**

slope. Syn.: see **lean,** *v.*

sloth. Syn.: sluggishness, laziness, indolence, idleness.

slothful. Syn.: sluggish, lazy, indolent, slack. See **idle.**

slouchy. Syn.: see **slovenly.**

slough. Syn.: see **swamp.**

slovenly. Syn.: untidy, unkempt, slatternly, slipshod, draggletailed, slouchy, dowdy, frowzy, careless.

Slovenly implies negligence or untidiness, especially in matters of dress or personal appearance; *slatternly* is particularly applied to slovenliness in a woman. *Slouchy* denotes an undignified relaxation in posture, suggestive of indifference.

slow. Syn.: sluggish, gradual, lingering, dilatory, delaying, tardy, leisurely, deliberate; dull, uninteresting, wearisome, tiresome. **Ant.:** fast, swift, fleet, speedy, rapid, quick.

That which is *slow* acts or moves without haste or rapidity. *Gradual* suggests the slowness of that which advances one step at a time. That which is *leisurely* moves with the slowness allowed by ample time or the absence of pressure. *Deliberate* implies the slowness which marks careful consideration before and while acting.

sluggish. Syn.: slothful, lazy, indolent, slow, dull, inactive, inert, apathetic. See **inactive.**

slumber. Syn.: see **sleep,** *v.*

slur. Syn.: see **depreciate.**

sly. Syn.: artful, crafty, wily, cunning, subtle; surreptitious, covert, stealthy, furtive; knowing, mischievous, waggish. See **artful.**

smack. Syn.: taste, flavor, savor; trace, touch, dash, tinge, suggestion. See **taste.**

small. Syn.: slender, thin, narrow, little, diminutive, undersized, undeveloped, stunted, puny, tiny, minute, wee, microscopic, infinitesimal; slight, trifling, unimportant, inconsiderable, insignificant, trivial, petty, paltry; ungenerous, selfish, illiberal, stingy, mean. **Ant.:** see **large.** See **little.**

smaller. Syn.: see **less.**

smart. Syn.: stinging, sharp, vigorous, energetic, forceful, brisk, lively; clever, witty, bright, brilliant, precocious, gifted, talented, keen, shrewd; trim, spruce, natty, stylish, fashionable, showy. **Ant.:** dull, stupid, unintelligent; slovenly, slouchy, dowdy. See **clever, spruce.**

smash. Syn.: see **dash, break,** *v.*

smell. Syn.: odor, scent, savor, perfume, fragrance, aroma, redolence, stench, stink, fetor.

Smell, scent, and *odor* may give either a pleasant or unpleasant sensation. *Smell* is the general word for any quality perceived through the olfactory sense; *odor* is little more than a Latin and sometimes daintier substitute for smell; *scent* is a faint and pervasive smell, often distinctive of a particular thing: as, the *scent* of honeysuckle, or burning leaves. *Perfume, fragrance,* and *aroma* express only agreeable odors. *Perfume* often indicates strong, rich smell, natural or manufactured; *fragrance* is best used of fresh, delicate, and delicious odors, especially from growing things; *aroma* is restricted to a somewhat spicy smell: as, the *perfume* of flowers, the *fragrance* of new-mown hay, the *aroma* of coffee. *Stench* and *stink* express only disagreeable odors. They represent a strong, penetrating, and disgusting smell; the latter is not in polite use.

smile. Syn.: see **laugh.**

smirk. Syn.: see **simper.**

smite. Syn.: see **strike.**

smoke. Syn.: fume, reek, vapor; cure; smirch, darken.

smooth. Syn.: even, plain, flat, level, polished, glossy, sleek, slippery; calm, placid, unruffled, undisturbed; fluent, voluble, glib, bland, suave, plausible, flattering, wheedling. **Ant.:** see **rough.** See **level.**

smother. Syn.: suffocate, stifle, choke, strangle, throttle; extinguish, deaden.

smug. Syn.: spruce, nice, proper, complacent, self-satisfied.

snap. Syn.: see **bite.**

snappish. Syn.: testy, crabbed, cross, tart, irascible, crusty, petulant, touchy, snippy.

snare. Syn.: trap, springe, gin, toil, decoy, lure. See **trap,** *n.*

snatch. Syn.: seize, grasp, grab, catch, snap, pluck, wrest. See **seize.**

sneak. Syn.: slink, skulk, lurk, steal. See **lurk.**

sneaking. Syn.: stealthy, furtive, clandestine, underhand, mean, contemptible, hangdog.

sneer. Syn.: scoff, jeer, gibe, scout, flout, mock. See **scoff.**

snicker. Syn.: see **laugh.**

snob. Syn.: upstart, parvenu.

snub. Syn.: see **slight.**

snug. Syn.: close, comfortable, cozy.

Snug suggests a close fit or compact or limited quarters, always with comfortable or agreeable effect. *Cozy* suggests comfortable quarters or conditions, as if sheltered from storm, cold, or anything that might produce discomfort.

snuggle. Syn.: see **cuddle.**

so. Syn.: see **therefore.**

soak. Syn.: see **wet,** *v.*

soar. Syn.: see **fly.**

sob. Syn.: see **weep.**

sober. Syn.: unintoxicated, abstinent, abstemious, temperate; calm, dispassionate, self-controlled, collected, cool, deliberate, sensible, rational, sound, sane; grave, serious, solemn; dignified, sedate, staid; subdued, somber, dull. **Ant.:** intoxicated, drunk, intemperate; passionate, impassioned, unreasonable, extravagant, extreme, crazy; lighthearted, gay, happy, thoughtless, frivolous. See **grave.**

sobriety. Syn.: see **abstinence.**

sobriquet. Syn.: see **name.**

sociable. Syn.: companionable, friendly, social, affable, agreeable, genial, gregarious, convivial. **Ant.:** see **unsociable.**

A *sociable* person takes pleasure in the society of others; *companionable* suggests a capacity for sharing the interests, pleasures, confidences, etc., of another; *gregarious* applies to the natural desire of men to associate or congregate together.

socialism. Syn.: communism, collectivism, Bolshevism.

society. Syn.: companionship, fellowship, company, partnership; association, fraternity, brotherhood, sodality, league, gild, club, lodge.

soft. Syn.: plastic, pliable, flexible, malleable, impressible, mellow; low, subdued, delicate; mild, gentle, tender, sympathetic, lenient, compassionate; compliant, submissive, effeminate, unmanly, weak; impressionable, susceptible, sentimental, silly. **Ant.:** see **hard.**

soften. Syn.: melt, fuse; mollify, mitigate, temper, qualify.

soil, *n.* **Syn.:** earth, ground, mold, humus, loam, clay, dirt.

soil, *v.* **Syn.:** dirty, daub, begrime, besmirch, befoul; stain, tarnish, sully, defile, pollute. Cf. **dirty.**

To *soil* is especially to make the surface of something dirty. To *sully*, little used in a physical application, is especially to besmirch or make morally unclean. To *tarnish* is to alter or dull the luster of, especially the surface of metals by exposure, or, figuratively, to cast a stain upon a person's name, reputation, or the like. To *defile* is to make either physically or morally dirty or foul. To *pollute* is to make, especially a liquid, dirty or unfit, or to render, especially a place, ceremonially unclean.

sojourn. Syn.: see **live.**

solace, *n.* **Syn.:** consolation, comfort, relief, cheer. See **comfort.**

solace, *v.* **Syn.:** console, comfort, soothe, cheer.

soldier. Syn.: warrior, infantryman, cavalryman, artilleryman, marine, sapper, aviator, grenadier, dragoon, chasseur, cuirassier, zouave, uhlan, trooper, gunner, sharpshooter, rifleman, guerrilla, franc-tireur, militiaman, reservist, volunteer, recruit, conscript, veteran, cadet, rookie, dough-boy.

sole. Syn.: see **single.**

solecism. Syn.: See **impropriety.**

solemn. Syn.: formal, ceremonial, ceremonious; impressive, awe-inspiring, venerable, majestic, august; serious, sober, grave. See **grave.**

solemnize. Syn.: see **celebrate.**

solicit. Syn.: ask, request, beg, petition, importune, seek. See **ask.**

solicitude. Syn.: see **care.**

solid. Syn.: compact, dense, firm, hard, rigid, stable, unyielding; substantial, trustworthy, reliable, dependable, stable, sound, genuine, real, valid, weighty; unanimous, united, undivided. **Ant.:** hollow, porous, spongy, soft, plastic, unstable. See **firm.**

solitary. Syn.: alone, lone, unattended, companionless, lonesome, lonely; remote, secluded, unfrequented, deserted, desolate; single, sole, only.

Solitary and *alone* both express the condition of being absolutely by oneself, the former perhaps implying greater removal from, or lack of, companionship or association. The person or place that is *lonely* has or creates a disquieting or sad feeling of isolation or solitariness; the *lonesome* person has an unsatisfied longing for the companionship or society of others.

solitude. Syn.: loneliness, lonesomeness, retirement, seclusion, isolation; wilderness, desert.

somber. Syn.: dark, gloomy, cloudy, murky; dismal, dull, melancholy, depressing.

some. Syn.: any.

somnolent. Syn.: see **sleepy.**

song. Syn.: carol, lay, ditty, lullaby, hymn, canticle, chant, dirge, pæan, catch, round, aria, chanson, lied; lyric, ballad.

sonnet. Syn.: see **poem.**

sonorous. Syn.: see **loud.**

soon. Syn.: shortly, presently, promptly, quickly, speedily. See **early.**

soothe. Syn.: calm, quiet, compose, tranquilize, pacify, mollify, ease, alleviate, mitigate, assuage, allay.

soothsayer. Syn.: diviner, prognosticator, augur, seer, haruspex. See **prophet.**

sophism. Syn.: fallacy, paralogism.

sorcerer. Syn.: conjurer, necromancer, magician, wizard, enchanter, medicine-man, shaman.

sorcery. Syn.: necromancy, magic, wizardry, witchcraft, enchantment. See **magic.**

sordid. Syn.: dirty, filthy, foul, squalid; mean, ignoble, degraded, low, base. See **mean.**

sore. Syn.: painful, aching, ulcerated, festered, cankered, raw, inflamed, galled, irritated; grievous, bitter, severe, oppressive.

sorrow. Syn.: grief, sadness, unhappiness, remorse, contrition, penitence, regret; affliction, trouble, misfortune, woe. See **grief.**

sorrowful. Syn.: sad, unhappy, mournful, woeful, doleful, rueful, disconsolate; distressing, lamentable, pitiable, pathetic. **Ant.:** happy, joyous, merry, cheerful, lighthearted, gay. See **sad.**

sorry. Syn.: sorrowful, sad, unhappy, pained, grieved; contrite, penitent; mean, poor, paltry, pitiful, shabby. See **wretched.**

sort, *n.* **Syn.:** kind, species, class, description, variety. See **kind,** *n.*

sort, *v.* **Syn.:** assort, classify, class, select, cull.

soul. Syn.: see **mind.**

sound, *n.* **Syn.:** noise, tone, note.

sound, *a.* **Syn.:** healthy, hale, uninjured, unhurt, unimpaired, unbroken, whole, entire, intact, flawless, perfect; deep, profound, undisturbed; valid, legal, lawful, orthodox; logical, rational, sensible, sane, clear-minded; trustworthy, solvent, strong. **Ant.:** see **unsound.**

That is *sound* which has not been impaired by injury, disease, defect, deterioration, decay, etc.; that is *whole* which has all of its parts in perfect condition; that which is *intact* is complete or uninjured, especially after the possibility of impairment.

sound, *v.* **Syn.:** fathom, probe, measure; examine, question, interrogate; resound, reverberate, echo.

sour. Syn.: acid, acidulous, subacid, acerb, acrid, tart, astringent, sharp; curdled, turned, fermented, rancid, musty; harsh, acrimonious, bitter, embittered, cynical, misanthropic, morose, crabbed.

That which is *sour* or *acid* has a taste like that of vinegar or lemon-juice; that which is *acidulous* has a slightly acid quality; the *subacid* is moderately acid; that which is *tart* has a (pleasingly) astringent effect on the organs of taste. Figuratively, *sour* implies that one is cross, harsh, or misanthropic; *tart* suggests a quick, keen, and sharp wit, especially as manifested in retort.

source. Syn.: spring, fountainhead, origin, root.

souse. Syn.: see **dip.**

souvenir. Syn.: memento, remembrance, keepsake, reminder, token. See **keepsake.**

sovereign, *n.* **Syn.:** see **ruler.**

sovereign, *a.* **Syn.:** supreme, paramount, chief, predominant, commanding; efficacious, potent, effectual.

sovereignty. Syn.: supremacy, dominion, empire, rule, sway, authority.

spacious. Syn.: wide, broad, extensive, large, roomy, capacious, commodious. **Ant.:** narrow, small, contracted, cramped. See **extensive.**

span. Syn.: see **pair.**

spare. Syn.: superfluous, additional, extra; thin, lean, lank, gaunt; scanty, meager. See **thin.**

sparing. Syn.: chary, parsimonious, stingy. See **frugal.**

The *sparing* person betrays (sometimes undue) economy and frugality; the *chary* person is cautious and not disposed to give more than is necessary: as, to be *chary* of one's praise.

sparkle. Syn.: flash, glitter, scintillate, coruscate, twinkle, glisten. See **shine,** *v.*

sparkling. Syn.: flashing, glittering, scintillating, coruscant, twinkling, brilliant; effervescing, bubbling.

sparse. Syn.: scattered, thin, scanty, meager. See **scanty.**

spasm. Syn.: convulsion, paroxysm, fit, throe.

spasmodic. Syn.: convulsive, jerky, fitful, intermittent.

speak. Syn.: talk, discourse, descant, expatiate, harp, argue, plead, preach, lecture, declaim, harangue, rant, spout; converse, chat, confer, parley, palaver; chatter, babble, prattle, prate, gabble, maunder, mumble, mutter, stammer, stutter, jabber, gibber. Cf. **say, tell.**

To *speak* is to utter one or more words, not necessarily connected; to *talk* is to utter consecutive and related words. *Speak* may, however, apply to the delivery of a formal address before an audience, whereas *talk* implies a conversational manner of speaking. To *discourse* is to speak in an extensive, authoritative, or self-important way to another or others. *Harangue* refers to noisy or vehement speaking; *rant*, to bombastic, unrestrained, or violent declamation.

spear. Syn.: javelin, lance, pike, harpoon, trident, assagai; shoot, spire, blade.

special. Syn.: especial, particular, peculiar, specific, individual; exceptional, uncommon, extraordinary.

Special and the less common form *especial* indicate that which is in some way out of the ordinary. Choice in the use of these words is dependent only on euphony.

specie. Syn.: see **money.**

species. Syn.: class, group, sort, kind, variety.

specific. Syn.: definite, explicit, precise, specified. See **special.**

specify. Syn.: designate, particularize, name.

specimen. Syn.: sample, example, instance, illustration.

A *sample* is a part taken from a quantity or one from a number, and represents the qualities that are to be found in the whole: as, a *sample* of soap, cotton, cloth. A *specimen* is a part of a larger whole employed to exhibit the nature or kind of that of which it forms a part, but, unlike sample, a *specimen* need not be exactly like other individual portions: as, a *specimen* of early handwriting, of Greek architecture, of a rare species.

specious. Syn.: see **ostensible, plausible.**

speck. Syn.: spot, dot, stain; particle, atom, jot, mite. See **bit.**

spectacle. Syn.: show, exhibition, display, parade, pageant.

spectacular. Syn.: see **ostentatious.**

spectator. Syn.: beholder, observer, witness, onlooker, looker-on, bystander.

specter. Syn.: see **ghost.**

speculation. Syn.: see **theory.**

speech. Syn.: talk, discourse, utterance; language, tongue, dialect; saying, remark; oration, address, harangue.

A *speech* represents ideas, arguments, reminiscences, etc. in a more or less dignified way before an audience. An *address* is a more or less formal speech appropriate to a particular subject or occasion. An *oration* is a polished, rhetorical address, that employs eloquence and studied methods of delivery to impress the audience. A *harangue* is a violent and noisy speech, aiming to rouse the crowd to strong feeling or action.

speechless. Syn.: see **silent.**

speed. Syn.: swiftness, rapidity, celerity, velocity, quickness, expedition, despatch, haste. See **haste.**

speedy. Syn.: swift, rapid, quick, fast, fleet, expeditious.

spend. Syn.: expend, disburse, use, squander, waste, exhaust.

Spend is the common word for the paying out of money; *expend* is more formal, and implies spending for some definite and (usually) sensible or worthy object. *Disburse* implies expenditure from a specific source or sum or in definite allotments; *squander*, lavish, wasteful, or foolish expenditure.

sphere. Syn.: globe, ball, orb; position, station, rank; region, domain, realm, field. See **globe.**

spicy. Syn.: aromatic, balsamic, fragrant; pungent, piquant, pointed, racy. See **racy.**

spill. Syn.: scatter, drop, splash, slop.

spin. Syn.: twirl, whirl, rotate, revolve, turn. See **turn,** *v.*

spirit. Syn.: soul, life, intellect, mind; ghost, shade, phantom, specter, apparition, fairy, elf, sprite; animation, liveliness, cheerfulness, vivacity, enthusiasm, ardor, zeal, fire, mettle, courage; temper, humor, mood; meaning, significance, intent. See **ghost, life, mind.**

spirited. Syn.: animated, lively, ardent, fiery, mettlesome.

spiritless. Syn.: lifeless, listless, dull, mopish, languid, depressed, dejected, glum.

spiritual. Syn.: spirituel, ethereal, unearthly. See **incorporeal.**

Spiritual applies to those things which are of a lofty, elevating, or supernatural nature, as suggestive of the soul; *spirituel* refers to refined intellectuality and delicacy; *ethereal* is used of that which is intangible or incorporeal in its nature, as seeming to dwell above the earth.

spirituel. Syn.: see **spiritual.**

spite. Syn.: ill-will, malevolence, malice, grudge, rancor. See **malice.**

spiteful. Syn.: see **revengeful.**

splendid. Syn.: shining, bright, brilliant, dazzling; magnificent, gorgeous, sumptuous, superb, grand; glorious, remarkable, fine. See **magnificent.**

splendor. Syn.: brightness, brilliancy, refulgence; magnificence, grandeur, pomp, glory.

splenetic. Syn.: see **sullen.**

split. Syn.: cleave, rive, rend, crack, sunder, divide, chop, disrupt.

To *split* is primarily to part lengthwise or in the direction of the grain, weave, or line of cleavage. *Cleave* may be a more dignified word for split, or it may express a cutting apart by a straight, heavy stroke. To *rive* is to rend with a tearing of the fibers.

spoil, *n.* **Syn.:** plunder, pillage, booty, loot. See **booty.**

spoil, *v.* **Syn.:** despoil, plunder, pillage, sack, ravage, rob; corrupt, vitiate, demoralize, wreck, ruin, injure, damage, deface, disfigure, mar, undo; deteriorate, decay, rot.

To *spoil* is seriously to impair the value, quality, usefulness, etc., of anything. *Wreck* implies a violent breaking up or demolition; *ruin*, completely destructive or irreparable injury; *undo*, the ruin of a person's morals, reputation, plans, prospects, or accomplishment.

spontaneous. Syn.: voluntary, unforced, unbidden, instinctive, involuntary, automatic. See **voluntary.**

sport. Syn.: amusement, diversion, pastime, recreation, play, game, fun, frolic, merriment, hilarity. See **play.**

sportive. Syn.: see **playful.**

spot, *n.* **Syn.:** stain, blot, blotch, speck, fleck; site, place, locality.

spot, *v.* **Syn.:** stain, blot; sully, tarnish, blemish.

spotless. Syn.: unspotted, stainless, unsullied, untarnished, unblemished, immaculate. See **clean,** *a.*

spotted. Syn.: stained, specked, flecked, dotted, variegated, party-colored, mottled, dappled, piebald, pied, pinto, speckled, freckled.

spout. Syn.: spurt, gush, jet, squirt; declaim, rant, harangue, speechify. See **flow.**

sprain. Syn.: see **strain.**

spread. Syn.: unfold, unroll, unfurl, open, expand, stretch; distribute, disperse, scatter, diffuse, disseminate, circulate.

sprightliness. Syn.: see **life.**

sprightly. Syn.: spirited, animated, lively, vivacious, gay.

spring, *n.* **Syn.:** leap, jump, bound, vault, saltation; elasticity, resiliency, buoyancy, vigor; fountain, source, origin.

spring, *v.* **Syn.:** leap, jump, bound, vault, skip, hop; shoot, rush, dart, fly; rebound, recoil; bend, warp; arise, originate, emerge, emanate, issue, flow.

springy. Syn.: see **elastic.**

sprinkle. Syn.: besprinkle, bespatter, spatter, asperse, bedew, strew, scatter, distribute, disperse. See **scatter.**

sprite. Syn.: see **fairy.**

sprout, *n.* **Syn.:** bud, shoot, sucker, tiller, scion, chit, twig, acrospire, plumule.

sprout, *v.* **Syn.:** bud, germinate, burgeon, pullulate, branch, vegetate, grow, spring.

spruce. Syn.: smart, neat, dapper, natty, jaunty, trim, smug, dandified, foppish, fastidious, finical, fussy.

As applied to appearance or dress, *spruce* implies a too conspicuous trimness for complete reserve; *smart* suggests fashionable up-to-dateness or dash of style; *dapper* suggests finical neatness, especially as combined with briskness of action on the part of a little person; *natty* implies a combination of tidiness with smartness.

spry. Syn.: see **nimble.**

spur. Syn.: see **goad.**

spurious. Syn.: bastard, illegitimate, adulterine; counterfeit, false, sham, adulterated, supposititious, fictitious, unauthentic. See **false.**

spurn. Syn.: repel, reject, scorn, despise, contemn, scout.

spurt. Syn.: gush, spout, jet, squirt. See **flow.**

spy. Syn.: scout, detective, emissary.

squabble. Syn.: see **dispute, quarrel.**

squad. Syn.: see **company.**

squalid. Syn.: see **dirty.**

squall. Syn.: see **wind,** *n.*

squander. Syn.: spend, waste, dissipate, lavish. See **spend.**

square. Syn.: squared, quadrate; true, just, equitable, fair, impartial; even, balanced, settled; absolute, positive, downright; satisfying.

squeamish. Syn.: qualmish, sickish; dainty, fastidious, particular, finical, overnice, prudish. See **particular.**

squeeze. Syn.: compress, gripe, pinch, press, push, crowd, elbow; hug, clasp, embrace; wring, extort, oppress, crush.

squirm. Syn.: see **twist,** *v.*

stab. Syn.: pierce, transfix, gore, wound, injure.

stability. Syn.: fixedness, firmness, steadiness, equilibrium, permanence; steadfastness, constancy.

stable, *n.* **Syn.:** see **barn.**

stable, *a.* **Syn.:** fixed, immovable, firm, steady, established, permanent, durable, lasting; steadfast, constant, resolute, unwavering. **Ant.:** see **unstable.** See **lasting.**

stack. Syn.: pile, heap, rick.

staff. Syn.: see **stick,** *n.*

stage. Syn.: platform, dais, rostrum, scaffold; theater, boards; point, station, step, degree.

stagger. Syn.: see **reel.**

stagnant. Syn.: standing, motionless, quiet, inert, inactive, dull, sluggish, foul.

staid. Syn.: sober, grave, serious, sedate, composed, demure, steady, settled.

Staid indicates an ingrained seriousness and propriety which shows itself in complete decorum. One who is *settled* has become fixed, especially in a sober or determined way, in his manner, judgments, or mode of life. *Sedate* refers to one who is noticeably quiet, composed, and sober in conduct.

stain, *n.* **Syn.:** discoloration, spot, blot, blemish, taint, disgrace, stigma; dye, pigment.

stain, *v.* **Syn.:** discolor, spot, blot, soil, sully, tarnish, defile, disgrace, dishonor; color, dye, tinge, tint.

stake, *n.* **Syn.:** post, pale, picket; bet, wager, pledge; hazard, risk.

stake, *v.* **Syn.:** see **wager.**

stale. Syn.: old, insipid, vapid, flat, dry, musty, sour, spoiled; trite, hackneyed, banal, commonplace.

stalk. Syn.: see **walk,** *v.*

stalwart. Syn.: stout, sturdy, strong, muscular, brawny, sinewy, strapping, powerful; brave, bold, valiant, courageous. See **strong.**

stammer. Syn.: stutter, falter.

Stammer indicates difficulty in uttering a word or syllable, which results in broken or inarticulate sounds that seem to stick in the mouth, and sometimes in complete stoppage of speech; it may be caused by sudden excitement, confusion, embarrassment, or lack of muscular control. *Stutter* indicates rapid, involuntary repetition of a (especially initial) sound or syllable of a word; stuttering, though accentuated by excitement, is more likely than stammering to be an inherent speech defect.

stanch. Syn.: firm, strong, steadfast, loyal, constant, true, faithful, unwavering, unswerving, steady. **Ant.:** vacillating, inconstant, fickle, faithless, false. See **steady, faithful.**

stand, *n.* **Syn.:** stop, halt, pause, stay, rest; position, place, post, station, site, location; rostrum, platform, dais, pulpit; table, trivet, tripod; stall, booth.

stand, *v.* **Syn.:** stop, halt, pause, stay; endure, last, continue, remain; undergo, suffer, endure, bear, tolerate, stomach, brook, weather. See **bear.**

standard. Syn.: criterion, measure, gage, norm, pattern, model, mold, type, prototype. See **flag.**

A *standard* is an authoritative or generally accepted model or measure by comparison with which the quantity, excellence, correctness, etc., of other things may be determined; a *criterion* is a test by which value, suitability, probability, etc., may be judged: as, a *standard* of liquid measure, conduct, workmanship; wealth is no *criterion* of a man's worth; a man's success is a good *criterion* of what may be expected of him.

standing. Syn.: erect, upright, perpendicular; lasting, enduring, permanent.

stanza. Syn.: see **verse.**

stare. Syn.: gaze, glare, glower, gloat, gape. See **look.**

stark. Syn.: see **utter,** *a.*

start. Syn.: jump, spring, leap, dart, rush; set out, embark, leave, go; originate, initiate, commence, begin, institute, launch.

startle. Syn.: scare, frighten, affright, alarm, surprise, shock, stun, paralyze.

Startle implies sharp surprise or sudden fright; *shock* suggests a strong blow, as it were, to one's nerves, sentiments, sense of decency, etc.; *stun* implies such a shock as bewilders or stupefies; *paralyze* is stronger, implying the rendering of one helpless or useless.

starved. Syn.: see **hungry.**

state, *n.* **Syn.:** condition, situation, circumstances, plight, predicament, pass; position, station, standing, status, rank; dignity, pomp, grandeur, magnificence; commonwealth, body politic.

In the singular *state* and *condition,* though both have their idiomatic uses, do not differ in meaning; in the plural *condition* is used of surrounding circumstances: as, he left his affairs in an excellent *state* (or in excellent *condition*); the *conditions* made flying impossible. *Status* is sometimes the equivalent of state or condition but has a particular use with reference to relative rank, position, authority, etc.: as, the *status* of a negotiation; the *status* of an alien; his *status* is that of a sergeant.

state, *v.* **Syn.:** see **tell, say.**

stately. Syn.: majestic, pompous, grand, imposing, dignified, formal, ceremonious. See **dignified.**

statement. Syn.: narrative, account, report, specification, declaration, assertion.

statesman. Syn.: see **politician.**

station. Syn.: place, location, position, situation, post; status, standing, rank; depot.

statue. Syn.: see **image.**

status. Syn.: see **state,** *n.*

statute. Syn.: see **law.**

stave. Syn.: see **verse.**

stay, *n.* **Syn.:** support, prop, brace; stoppage, check, break, cessation, halt, pause; sojourn, abode.

stay, *v.* **Syn.:** support, prop, brace, uphold, strengthen, sustain, steady; hinder, obstruct, impede, retard, detain, check, stop; delay, linger, tarry, wait, rest, remain, sojourn, lodge, abide, reside, dwell. See **live.**

steadfast. Syn.: firm, stable, unyielding, unwavering, unswerving, unflinching, stanch, resolute, constant. See **steady.**

steady. Syn.: stable, firm, fixed; undeviating, invariable, uniform, regular, constant; stanch, steadfast, unwavering, unfaltering, resolute; industrious, sober, reliable. **Ant.:** see **unstable.**

Literally, *steady* is applied to that which is relatively firm in position or continuous in movement or duration; figuratively, it implies sober regularity or persistence. *Steadfast* literally means fixed, but is chiefly used figuratively to indicate undeviating or unswerving constancy or resolution. *Stanch* literally means water-tight, as of a vessel, and therefore strong and firm; figuratively it is used of loyal support that will endure strain: as, *stanch* friendship.

steal. Syn.: purloin, pilfer, filch, embezzle, defalcate, peculate, poach, kidnap, abduct, plagiarize, pirate, crib, swipe, snitch; sneak, skulk, slink.

Steal is the general term for taking things dishonestly; *pilfer* is a more colloquial word especially used of petty theft; to *filch* is to steal in small ways, as by snatching; to *purloin* is improperly to make off with something belonging to another.

stealthy. Syn.: furtive, sneaking, sly, underhand, secretive, secret, clandestine, surreptitious. See **secret.**

steep, *a.* **Syn.:** precipitous, declivitous, abrupt, sharp, sheer.

Steep is used of any incline which rises more or less sharply from a level plane, and often implies difficulty of ascent or descent: as, a *steep* hill, a *steep* flight of steps. *Precipitous* describes a slope almost perpendicular like a precipice, and suggests headlong descent: as, a *precipitous* wall of rock, a *precipitous* fall. *Abrupt* describes that which is sharp, sudden, and sometimes unexpected: as, an *abrupt* rise, turn, stop.

steep, *v.* **Syn.:** see **saturate, wet,** *v.*

steer. Syn.: see **guide.**

stench. Syn.: see **smell.**

stentorian. Syn.: see **loud.**

step. Syn.: pace, gait, stride; measure, action, procedure, expedient.

stereotyped. Syn.: see **trite.**

sterile. Syn.: barren, infertile, infecund, unproductive, unfruitful.

stern. Syn.: severe, austere, ascetic, harsh, rigorous, strict, exacting; grim, forbidding, repelling; firm, rigid, uncompromising, unyielding, inflexible.

Stern implies uncompromising or inflexible firmness, and is especially manifested in aspect or facial expression. *Severe* implies strictness, harshness, and freedom from all that is suggestive of frivolity; *austere,* an unsparing self-restraint in the conduct of one's own life or one's manner toward others. *Ascetic* implies the extreme self-denial or even self-mortification of the religious hermit or recluse.

stick, *n.* **Syn.:** rod, club, cudgel, staff, cane, ruler, ferule, wand, baton, truncheon.

stick, *v.* **Syn.:** pierce, stab, gore, puncture, penetrate; insert, infix, thrust, push, poke; fasten, attach, affix, paste, cement, glue; adhere, cling, cleave; hesitate, scruple, stickle, quibble; puzzle, perplex.

sticky. Syn.: adhesive, viscous, viscid, glutinous, mucilaginous, gluey, clammy.

stiff. Syn.: rigid, firm, inflexible, inelastic, unbending, unyielding, stark; taut, tense; unnatural, stilted, affected, cramped, constrained, ceremonious, formal, precise, prim; obstinate, stubborn, pertinacious; severe, harsh, rigorous; high, immoderate, excessive. **Ant.:** see **limp.** See **firm.**

stifle. Syn.: choke, strangle, suffocate; stop, extinguish, quench; repress, suppress, gag, muzzle, muffle, hush. See **smother.**

stigma. Syn.: see **disgrace,** n.

still, a. **Syn.:** motionless, stationary, stagnant, quiet, calm, peaceful, tranquil, placid, undisturbed, unruffled; silent, noiseless, hushed, mum.

Still indicates the absence of sound or movement: as, the house was *still,* a *still* pool; *quiet* implies relative freedom from noise, activity, disturbance, or excitement: as, a *quiet* engine, a *quiet* sector, a *quiet* vacation. *Silent* means without sound: as, a *silent* benediction, a *silent* cave. *Noiseless* characterizes that which does not reveal its presence or movement by any sound. *Hushed* implies the suppression of sound or noise: as, a *hushed* whisper, the sick-room was *hushed.*

still, v. **Syn.:** quiet, calm, tranquilize, pacify, lull, allay, appease, compose, subdue; silence, hush.

still, conj. **Syn.:** see **but.**

stilted. Syn.: elevated, pompous, grandiose, bombastic, inflated, high-flown, grandiloquent.

stimulate. Syn.: prick, goad, spur, incite, rouse, urge, encourage, whet, impel, provoke, instigate, foment.

stingy. Syn.: parsimonious, miserly, niggardly, illiberal, penurious, close, close-fisted, mean, saving, chary, scanty.

Stingy indicates a grudging, narrow-hearted, or unreasonable parsimony in giving or providing. *Niggardly* especially expresses meanness or stinginess in the treatment of others because of the desire to save. *Miserly* implies an avaricious desire to acquire and retain wealth, especially for its own sake. A *penurious* person saves as closely as though he were in poverty.

stink. Syn.: see **smell.**

stipend. Syn.: see **pay,** n.

stir, n. **Syn.:** movement, motion, activity, hurry, flurry, bustle, commotion, flutter, fuss, pother, ado, to-do.

stir, v. **Syn.:** move, budge; rouse, awaken, animate, excite, disturb, agitate.

stirring. Syn.: active, lively, bustling, brisk, enterprising; animating, stimulating, inspiriting, inspiring.

stock, n. **Syn.:** stalk, stem, trunk; lineage, family, breed, race; capital, fund, supply, store, merchandise, goods, wares.

stock, v. **Syn.:** supply, furnish, store, replenish.

stoicism. Syn.: see **indifference.**

stolid. Syn.: heavy, stodgy, lumpish, impassive, dull, stupid, doltish. See **unemotional.**

stomach. Syn.: abdomen, belly, paunch, maw, crop, craw, gizzard.

stone. Syn.: rock, boulder, pebble, cobblestone, flagstone, gravel, shingle, rubble; flint, granite, marble, adamant, sandstone, quartz, shale, slate; concretion, calculus; gem, jewel; seed, pit, putamen.

stony. Syn.: rocky, flinty, adamantine, petrous; hard, obdurate, pitiless, unrelenting.

stoop. Syn.: bend, bow, incline; deign, condescend, descend.

stop, n. **Syn.:** stoppage, obstruction, hindrance, check, interruption, intermission, suspension, cessation, halt, pause, rest; stay, sojourn.

stop, v. **Syn.:** close, block, plug, cover, barricade; obstruct, hinder, impede, deter, intercept, interrupt, prevent, thwart, check, arrest, halt, suppress, repress, suspend, end; withhold, discontinue, intermit; cease, desist, pause; tarry, stay, remain, lodge. See **cease.**

Stop is the general term for bringing anything in motion or progress to a standstill; *check* implies an abrupt, partial, or temporary stop; *arrest* usually refers to stopping by putting a sudden restraint upon what is in action, motion, or progress; *halt* usually refers to a temporary stop, as on a march, especially one resulting from a command.

store. Syn.: see **stock.**

storehouse. Syn.: see **depository.**

storm, n. **Syn.:** see **wind,** n.

storm, v. **Syn.:** rage, fume, rant; attack, assault, assail.

stormy. Syn.: tempestuous, blustery, windy, gusty, squally, rainy, inclement; violent, wild, furious.

story. Syn.: relation, recital, rehearsal, narrative, record, chronicle, history, anecdote, tale, fable, legend, myth, parable, allegory, novel, romance, yarn; account, statement, report; falsehood, lie, fib, canard.

Story is the general word for a sequence of true or fictitious incidents so arranged and related as to be entertaining. An *anecdote* is a short account of an interesting or amusing incident, reported as true. *Tale* is a word of varied application, but usually refers to a narrative marked by simplicity and directness in which incident is more prominent than character. A *romance* is a story laid especially in remote or unfamiliar times or places, describing unusual adventures and persons of extraordinary prowess or of lofty sentiments and ideals. *Novel* is now the usual word for a comparatively long, fictitious story, picturing in a series of evolving situations characters and actions that are true to life.

stout. Syn.: bold, valiant, brave; resolute, determined, persistent, stubborn; vigorous, sturdy, hardy; strong, durable, tough; stocky, thick-set, plump, portly, corpulent, fleshy, fat, obese. See **strong.**

A *stout* person has a large, thick-set, sometimes bulky, body; a *portly* person is large and suggests weight and solidity but carries himself well. *Corpulent* usually implies an uncomfortable excess of flesh; *obese* describes a person who is extremely corpulent. *Fleshy* and *fat* are familiar words applied to a condition of corpulency.

straight. Syn.: even, direct, undeviating, unswerving, uninterrupted, unbroken; upright, honorable, honest, reliable, square. **Ant.:** crooked, curved, bent, circuitous, circular.

straightforward. Syn.: see **frank.**

straightway. Syn.: see **immediately.**

strain. Syn.: stretch, pull, tighten; wrench, twist, sprain; filter, percolate. See **sift.**

strained. Syn.: stretched, tense; forced, artificial, unnatural, far-fetched.

strait, n. **Syn.:** channel, narrows; difficulty, perplexity, dilemma, pinch. See **emergency.**

strait, a. **Syn.:** see **narrow.**

strand. Syn.: see **shore.**

strange. Syn.: foreign, alien, unfamiliar, unknown, new, novel, unique; odd, queer, fantastic, outlandish, singular, peculiar, unusual, uncommon, unnatural, remarkable, surprising, extraordinary, wonderful. **Ant.:** familiar, commonplace, ordinary, usual, conventional. See **singular.**

strangle. Syn.: choke, throttle, stifle, suffocate, strangulate, garrote. See **smother.**

stratagem. Syn.: artifice, trick, ruse, trap, snare, plot, scheme, contrivance, maneuver. See **artifice.**

stray. Syn.: wander, roam, rove, straggle; deviate, err. See **wander.**

streak, streaked. Syn.: see **stripe, striped.**

stream, n. **Syn.:** current, river, creek, rivulet, streamlet, brook, run, runlet, runnel, rill.

stream, v. **Syn.:** see **flow.**

streamer. Syn.: see **flag.**

street. Syn.: see **road, way.**

strength. Syn.: power, might, force, potency, puissance; robustness, sturdiness, stamina; efficacy, cogency; toughness, durability; intensity, vehemence, violence.

Strength refers especially to inherent or inward capacity to do, endure, or resist: as, the *strength* of a current, *strength* of character, the tensile *strength* of steel; *power* is often identical with strength but tends to be more active in its suggestion: as, the *strength* of a machine; its *power* to do work; *might* implies great strength or power: as, the *might* of an army or ruler; *force* is especially power that seeks to produce motion, or overcome opposition: as, the *force* of gravity or an argument.

strenuous. Syn.: strong, vigorous, energetic, zealous, ardent, earnest. See **active.**

stress. Syn.: strain, tension, pressure, urgency; significance, importance, weight; emphasis, accent, ictus.

stretch. Syn.: extend, lengthen, elongate, expand, spread, distend; overstate, exaggerate, magnify. See **lengthen.**

strew. Syn.: see **scatter.**

strict. Syn.: close, exact, accurate, precise, scrupulous; exacting, austere, stern, rigid, rigorous, stringent, severe, ascetic, strait-laced, puritanical. See **rigid.**

stricture. Syn.: see **animadversion, censure,** n., **criticism.**

stride. Syn.: see **walk,** v.

strident. Syn.: see **harsh.**

strife. Syn.: competition, contention, conflict, struggle, discord, quarrel, fight. See **discord.**

strike. Syn.: smite, hit, beat, buffet, cuff, slap, whack, thump, knock; impress, affect; light upon, find, discover.

Strike describes the action of two bodies coming suddenly in contact with each other; *smite* is now restricted to rhetorical or poetical use; *hit* is less formal than strike and often implies aim; to *knock* is to strike, often with a tendency to displace the object struck. *Knock* is frequently used with prepositions such as *on* or *at*, in which case it emphasizes the sound produced.

striking. Syn.: noticeable, remarkable, impressive, surprising. See **impressive.**

string. Syn.: cord, twine, thread, line, rope, leash; series, succession, row, chain, concatenation.

stringent. Syn.: strict, rigid, rigorous, exacting, binding, severe. See **rigid.**

strip. Syn.: rob, plunder, despoil; deprive, dispossess, divest; skin, peel; undress, disrobe, dismantle. See **deprive.**

stripe. Syn.: streak, band, bar, line, vein, wale, wheal, striation.

striped. Syn.: streaked, barred, striate.

strive. Syn.: endeavor, try, aim, seek; contend, struggle, cope, battle, fight. See **try.**

stroke. Syn.: see **blow.**

stroll. Syn.: saunter, ramble, roam, rove, wander, stray, range, meander. See **saunter.**

strong. Syn.: forceful, forcible, powerful, mighty, potent, puissant; robust, healthy, hardy, hale, sturdy, lusty, stout, muscular, brawny, sinewy, stalwart, athletic, able-bodied; effective, cogent, sound, valid, convincing, conclusive; fortified, impregnable, invincible; impetuous, vehement, violent, irresistible; stable, firm, enduring, durable; urgent, strenuous, drastic; intense, ardent, eager, zealous, determined; vivid, dazzling, glaring; pungent, piquant, concentrated, spirituous, alcoholic, intoxicating; rank, rancid, tainted. **Ant.:** see **weak.**

Strong in the sense here considered is the general term and denotes the power of enduring strain, resisting disease, or exerting great muscular force. *Sturdy* suggests stockiness and solidity, or well-knit strength that is hard to shake or overcome. *Stalwart* suggests tallness or largeness combined with great strength or sturdiness. *Stout* is little different from strong, except that it often adds the implication of strength associated with a thick-set body. *Lusty* is strength that results from abounding health, vigor, or vitality. *Robust* suggests oaken strength, combining toughness of body with perfect health. *Hale* indicates a condition of sound or vigorous health, especially in later life.

stronghold. Syn.: see **fortification.**

structure. Syn.: see **building.**

struggle, n. **Syn.:** endeavor, effort, exertion, pains, labor; contest, conflict, strife. See **conflict.**

struggle, v. **Syn.:** strive, labor, toil, grapple, cope, contend.

strut. Syn.: swagger.

Strut and *swagger* refer especially to carriage in walking, the former implying swelling pride or pompousness, the latter a domineering, sometimes jaunty, superiority or challenge.

stubborn. Syn.: obstinate, unyielding, obdurate, perverse, intractable, refractory, unruly, ungovernable, headstrong, mulish. See **obstinate.**

student. Syn.: see **pupil.**

studied. Syn.: see **elaborate.**

studious. Syn.: earnest, zealous, assiduous, attentive, thoughtful, scholarly.

study, n. **Syn.:** endeavor, application, examination, investigation, reflection, meditation.

study, v. **Syn.:** endeavor, seek; examine, investigate, scrutinize; meditate, ponder, muse, pore; learn, master. See **consider.**

stuff, n. **Syn.:** material, substance, fabric, cloth; goods, things, belongings, possessions, baggage; refuse, rubbish, trash; nonsense, twaddle, balderdash. See **matter.**

stuff, v. **Syn.:** cram, crowd, pack, press, stow, fill.

stumble. Syn.: see **fall,** v.

stun. Syn.: stupefy, benumb, bewilder, dumfound, astound, amaze. See **startle.**

stunt. Syn.: see **feat.**

stunted. Syn.: undeveloped, undersized, dwarfed, atrophied, weazened, puny, runty, scrubby.

stupefy. Syn.: deaden, benumb, dull, blunt, hebetate.

stupid. Syn.: stupefied, lethargic, torpid, comatose, drowsy; dull, heavy, sluggish, lumpish, stolid, dense, obtuse, slow-witted, doltish, sottish, muddle-headed; inane, vapid, flat, uninspiring, foolish, senseless. **Ant.:** shrewd, sharp, discerning, clever, apt; interesting, exciting, lively, spirited. See **foolish.**

stupor. Syn.: lethargy, torpor, torpidity, drowsiness, insensibility, unconsciousness, coma.

sturdy. Syn.: resolute, firm, unyielding; strong, hardy, robust, stout, muscular, brawny, vigorous. See **strong.**

stutter. Syn.: see **stammer.**

style. Syn.: method, manner, mode, way; fashion, vogue; appellation, title. See **diction, fashion, name.**

suave. Syn.: pleasing, agreeable, affable, gracious, courteous, urbane, bland, smooth, unctuous, oily. See **bland.**

subacid. Syn.: see **sour.**

subdue. Syn.: conquer, vanquish, overcome, overpower, crush, quell; lower, reduce, soften, tone down. See **conquer.**

subject, n. **Syn.:** dependent, subordinate; theme, topic, thesis, point, text.

Subject, topic, and *theme* are often interchangeable. *Subject* is a broad word for whatever is treated of in writing, speech, art, etc.; *topic* and *theme* are usually narrower and apply to some limited or specific part of a general subject, a *theme* often being the underlying conception of a discourse or composition.

subject, a. **Syn.:** subjected, exposed, liable, prone; subservient, subordinate, inferior; answerable.

One is *subject* to contingencies that arise from his nature or constitution; one is *liable* to undesirable eventualities, especially those resulting from exposure or risk: as, men are *subject* to disease or temptation; one is *liable* to catch cold from damp clothes.

subject, v. **Syn.:** expose, submit; subdue, subordinate.

subjoin. Syn.: see **attach.**

subjugate. Syn.: see **conquer.**

sublime. Syn.: lofty, exalted, noble, grand, glorious, magnificent, supreme. See **grand.**

submerge. Syn.: inundate, overflow, deluge, flood; plunge, immerse, submerse, sink. See **dip.**

submission. Syn.: compliance, acquiescence, obedience, surrender, resignation.

submissive. Syn.: yielding, compliant, obedient, obsequious, subservient, tractable, docile, humble, patient, passive, resigned. **Ant.:** disobedient, refractory, intractable, rebellious, defiant, belligerent.

submit. Syn.: yield, comply, acquiesce, surrender, succumb, bow; refer, commit. **Ant.:** resist, oppose, defy, disobey, rebel, revolt.

subordinate. Syn.: subservient, subject; secondary, minor, inferior.

subservient. Syn.: see **servile.**

subside. Syn.: sink, fall, abate, decrease, ebb, cease.

subsidiary. Syn.: see **auxiliary,** a.

subsidy. Syn.: subvention, bounty.

Both *subsidy* and *subvention* refer to grants of pecuniary aid, especially governmental, to private undertakings. A *subsidy* is usually given to promote commercial enterprise, especially the development of a mercantile marine; a *subvention* is usually a grant to stimulate enterprises connected with science and the arts.

subsistence. Syn.: see **living,** n.

substance. Syn.: nature, essence; matter, material, stuff; meaning, purport, gist, pith. See **matter.**

substantiate. Syn.: see **verify, confirm.**

substitute. Syn.: deputy, alternate, proxy, understudy, delegate, representative, agent; makeshift, expedient.

subterfuge. Syn.: artifice, ruse, trick, mask, blind, shift. See **artifice.**

subtle. Syn.: subtile, tenuous, thin, rare, fine; discerning, discriminating, refined, acute, keen; sly, crafty, artful, cunning, designing, insinuating.

subtlety. Syn.: fineness, nicety, delicacy, discernment, discrimination, penetration; slyness, craftiness, artfulness, artifice, cunning.

subtract. **Syn.:** see **deduct.**

suburbs. **Syn.:** environs, confines, outskirts, purlieus.

subvention. **Syn.:** see **subsidy.**

subvert. **Syn.:** overthrow, overturn, ruin, destroy; pervert, corrupt.

succeed. **Syn.:** prosper, thrive, flourish, win, prevail. See **follow.**

successful. **Syn.:** prosperous, fortunate, happy, victorious, triumphant. **Ant.:** see **unsuccessful.** See **fortunate.**

succession. **Syn.:** see **series.**

successive. **Syn.:** consecutive, sequent, following, continuous.

Successive and consecutive are applied to things that follow one upon another, but consecutive always denotes a close and uninterrupted sequence, sometimes with the implication of an established order: as, discouraged by successive misfortunes, the army was finally routed by defeats on three consecutive days.

succinct. **Syn.:** compressed, condensed, concise, short, brief, terse, compendious, summary, laconic. See **concise.**

succor. **Syn.:** see **help.**

sudden. **Syn.:** unexpected, unanticipated, unlooked-for, abrupt, hasty, rapid.

suffer. **Syn.:** endure, bear, feel, experience, undergo, sustain; allow, permit, tolerate. See **bear, permit.**

sufferance. **Syn.:** see **permission.**

suffering. **Syn.:** pain, distress, agony, misery, discomfort.

sufficient. **Syn.:** adequate, enough, ample, abundant, satisfactory. See **adequate.**

suffocate. **Syn.:** choke, stifle, asphyxiate, burke. See **smother.**

suggest. **Syn.:** hint, intimate, insinuate; propose, advise, recommend. See **hint,** v.

suggestion. **Syn.:** hint, intimation, allusion, insinuation, trace; proposal, advice, recommendation.

suggestive. **Syn.:** see **expressive.**

suit, n. **Syn.:** solicitation, petition, entreaty, prayer; wooing, courtship, address; suite, train, retinue.

suit, v. **Syn.:** adapt, adjust, accommodate, fit; befit, become; satisfy, gratify, please, content; accord, agree, comport.

suitable. **Syn.:** fitting, appropriate, meet, seemly, proper, becoming. **Ant.:** see **unsuitable.** See **fit.**

sulky. **Syn.:** see **sullen.**

sullen. **Syn.:** morose, churlish, sulky, glum, grum, grumpy, dumpish, moody, saturnine, cynical, splenetic, surly, crabbed, cross, grouchy; gloomy, dismal, somber. **Ant.:** sociable, amiable, friendly, genial, cheerful, happy, joyous.

The sullen person is silently ill-humored or angry; the sulky person displays his ill-humor by childishly obstinate silence and seclusion. He who is moody is unstable in his humor, and given to depression or melancholy. The glum person is, as it were, down in the mouth, and shows his depression by gloomy looks and taciturnity. One is morose who is churlishly sullen or by nature bitter, as though dissatisfied with the world in general.

sully. **Syn.:** see **soil,** v.

sum. **Syn.:** amount, whole, total, aggregate, number, quantity; problem, example.

A sum is a number or amount in which the individual units have been merged: as, a sum of money; the sum of two plus two. Total stresses the wholeness of a result obtained by adding things together: as, the total of a column of figures; the amount collected reached a large total. An aggregate is a collection or assemblage of items or parts considered as a whole or in the gross.

summary, n. **Syn.:** abstract, epitome, digest, compendium, synopsis, résumé, recapitulation. See **abridgment.**

summary, a. **Syn.:** short, brief, concise, terse, succinct, compendious; prompt, rapid.

summit. **Syn.:** top, apex, vertex, pinnacle, zenith, acme, climax. See **top.**

summon. **Syn.:** see **call.**

sumptuous. **Syn.:** costly, expensive, rich, luxurious, magnificent, gorgeous, superb. See **magnificent.**

sunder. **Syn.:** separate, part, divide, sever, disjoin, disconnect, disunite. See **separate.**

sundry. **Syn.:** several, divers, various, numerous, many. See **several.**

sunny. **Syn.:** shining, radiant, bright, cheerful, genial, pleasant.

sunrise. **Syn.:** see **dawn.**

superabundance, superabundant. **Syn.:** see **superfluity, superfluous, excess.**

superb. **Syn.:** grand, magnificent, splendid, elegant, rich, exquisite, beautiful, stately, imposing. See **magnificent.**

supercilious. **Syn.:** proud, haughty, overweening, overbearing, arrogant, contemptuous, disdainful. **Ant.:** humble, lowly, modest, meek. See **proud.**

superciliousness. **Syn.:** see **arrogance.**

superficial. **Syn.:** see **hasty, outer.**

superfluity. **Syn.:** superabundance, redundancy, excess, surplusage, surfeit. See **excess.**

superfluous. **Syn.:** superabundant, redundant, excessive, needless, useless.

superhuman. **Syn.:** see **supernatural.**

superintend. **Syn.:** oversee, supervise, manage, conduct, administer, control.

superintendence. **Syn.:** supervision, management, direction, charge, control, care.

superintendent. **Syn.:** overseer, supervisor, manager, director, controller, warden, principal, curator, custodian.

superior. **Syn.:** higher, greater, better, surpassing, predominant, preëminent, paramount.

superiority. **Syn.:** see **priority.**

supernatural. **Syn.:** superhuman, hyperphysical, miraculous, preternatural, unnatural.

That which is supernatural is above or superior to the beings, powers, or properties of nature; that which is preternatural is outside or in some way beyond the ordinary or usual course or laws of nature; miraculous describes that which transcends human experience and apparently contravenes laws which according to human assumption govern the universe.

supersede. **Syn.:** see **replace.**

superstition. **Syn.:** credulity, fanaticism, bigotry.

supervise, supervision. **Syn.:** see **superintend, superintendence.**

supine. **Syn.:** negligent, careless, heedless, thoughtless, listless, languid, indolent, inert, abject. See **prostrate.**

supplant. **Syn.:** see **replace.**

supple. **Syn.:** pliant, pliable, flexible, lithe, limber, lissome. **Ant.:** see **stiff.** See **flexible.**

supplement. **Syn.:** addition, appendix, postscript, addendum.

A supplement contains additional matter, completing or improving the principal work, especially such as supplies omissions or adds new material at a later time to bring the work up to date; an appendix contains matter related but not essential to the principal work, such as could not be appropriately or conveniently included in the main body of the text.

supplicate. **Syn.:** beg, implore, entreat, crave, beseech, petition, importune. See **ask.**

supplication. **Syn.:** entreaty, solicitation, petition, suit, obsecration. See **prayer.**

supply. **Syn.:** furnish, provide, afford, give, yield; replenish, stock. See **furnish.**

support, n. **Syn.:** prop, brace, stay, strut, shore, fulcrum, bolster, stanchion, pillar, buttress, base, basis, foundation; aid, help, succor, assistance, encouragement, favor, patronage, advocacy, espousal; subsistence, sustenance, maintenance, living, livelihood. See **living.**

support, v. **Syn.:** bear, sustain, uphold, prop, brace, bolster; endure, undergo, suffer, tolerate; aid, help, succor, assist, second, further, forward, encourage, countenance, favor, patronize, back, abet; keep, maintain, provide for; substantiate, verify, confirm, corroborate.

To support is to hold up or add strength to, literally or figuratively. Sustain, a more elevated word, suggests completeness and adequacy in supporting. To maintain is to support so as to preserve intact. Uphold applies especially to supporting or backing another, as in a statement, opinion, or belief.

supporter. **Syn.:** upholder, defender, advocate, adherent, partizan, vindicator.

suppose. **Syn.:** assume, presume, expect, surmise, imagine, believe, think, opine. See **think.**

supposition. **Syn.:** assumption, presumption, surmise, conjecture, inference, hypothesis, postulate.

supposititious. **Syn.:** see **spurious.**

suppress. **Syn.:** subdue, quell, crush; restrain, repress, stop, check, stifle.

supremacy. **Syn.:** predominance, domination, sway, mastery. See **priority.**

supreme. Syn.: highest, greatest, first, chief, best, paramount, superlative, transcendent, utmost, extreme.

sure. Syn.: confident, convinced, assured, positive, certain; reliable, unfailing, trustworthy, unerring, infallible; fixed, firm, stable, steady, secure.

Sure, certain, and *positive* may often be interchanged. *Sure* is the simplest and most general of these words, and denotes absence of doubt; *certain* suggests having been freed from doubt or made fully confident: as, I was *sure* he would come; his letter makes me *certain. Positive* implies emphatic certainty, sometimes overconfidence or dogmatism.

surety. Syn.: security, guaranty, pledge; bondsman, bail, sponsor, hostage.

surf. Syn.: see **wave,** *n.*

surface. Syn.: see **outside.**

surfeit, *n.* **Syn.:** excess, repletion, satiety, plethora.

surfeit, *v.* **Syn.:** overfeed, overload, glut, gorge, satiate, cloy. See **satiate.**

surge. Syn.: see **wave,** *n.*

surly. Syn.: sullen, churlish, ill-natured, cross, crabbed, gruff, crusty, snappish, snarling. **Ant.:** amiable, genial, cordial, friendly, civil, urbane. See **boorish.**

surmise, *n.* **Syn.:** see **inference.**

surmise, *v.* **Syn.:** infer, conjecture, guess, suppose, imagine, fancy, suspect. See **conjecture,** *v.*

surpass. Syn.: exceed, excel, outdo, outstrip, outrun, overtop, eclipse, beat. See **excel.**

surplus. Syn.: surplusage, overplus, excess, residue, remainder.

surprise, *n.* **Syn.:** astonishment, amazement, wonder.

surprise, *v.* **Syn.:** astonish, amaze, astound, dumfound, startle, disconcert.

To *surprise* is to take unawares or to affect with wonder. To *astonish* is to strike with wonder by something unlooked for, startling, or seemingly inexplicable. To *amaze* is to astonish so greatly that one is bewildered, as though in a maze. To *astound* is so to overwhelm with surprise that one is unable to think or act. To *dumfound* is, as it were, to strike dumb, or completely confound or confuse with amazement.

surprising. Syn.: astonishing, amazing, striking, extraordinary, marvelous. See **wonderful.**

surrender. Syn.: yield, relinquish, waive, cede, resign, abandon; capitulate. See **yield,** *v.*

surreptitious. Syn.: see **secret.**

surround. Syn.: inclose, hem in, encompass, environ, encircle, invest.

surveillance. Syn.: oversight, supervision, watch, observation, spying.

survey. Syn.: inspection, examination, view, review, retrospect.

survive. Syn.: see **outlive.**

susceptibility. Syn.: see **sensibility.**

susceptible. Syn.: impressible, impressionable, sensitive, tender. See **sensitive.**

suspect. Syn.: surmise, conjecture, imagine; doubt, mistrust, distrust.

suspend. Syn.: hang, dangle, swing; interrupt, intermit, discontinue, delay, stay, stop; defer, withhold. **Ant.:** keep on, continue, proceed.

To *suspend* is to break off relations, operations, proceedings, privileges, etc., for a longer or shorter period. To *intermit* is to interrupt or divide by an interval or intervals; to *discontinue* is to stop or leave off, often permanently.

suspense. Syn.: uncertainty, indetermination, indecision, irresolution, wavering, hesitation.

suspension. Syn.: cessation, interruption, intermission, delay, stop, postponement, respite. See **failure.**

suspicion. Syn.: doubt, mistrust, distrust, misgiving, fear, jealousy; suggestion, hint; conjecture, surmise, supposition, idea, belief.

Suspicion is the tendency to doubt the trustworthiness of appearances and therefore to believe that one has detected something unreliable, unfavorable, menacing, or the like; *distrust* is a want of trust, faith, or reliance in a person or thing.

suspicious. Syn.: distrustful, mistrustful, jealous; questionable, doubtful, shady.

sustain. Syn.: uphold, support, prop; aid, assist, comfort, relieve; suffer, bear, undergo, stand; prove, confirm, corroborate, sanction, ratify. See **support,** *v.*

sustenance. Syn.: see **living.**

swagger. Syn.: see **strut.**

swain. Syn.: see **clown.**

swallow. Syn.: gulp, bolt, ingurgitate, engulf; accept, believe; bear, tolerate, brook.

swamp. Syn.: marsh, morass, bog, fen, slough, quagmire.

swarm. Syn.: multitude, crowd, throng, cluster. See **flock, multitude.**

swarthy. Syn.: see **black, dusky.**

swathe. Syn.: see **wrap.**

sway, *n.* **Syn.:** inclination, swing; power, dominion, empire, rule, authority, control, influence, weight.

sway, *v.* **Syn.:** incline, lean, bend, move, swing, wave, fluctuate, oscillate, vacillate; wield, brandish, shake; rule, govern, control, guide, direct, influence, prejudice, bias. See **swing.**

swear. Syn.: vow, promise; curse, blaspheme.

sweat. Syn.: see **perspiration.**

sweep. Syn.: see **range,** *n.*

sweet. Syn.: sugary, honeyed, saccharine, ambrosial, nectareous; fragrant, balmy, perfumed; melodious, tuneful, dulcet, mellifluous, musical, harmonious, symphonious; delicious, agreeable, pleasing, winning, lovable, charming; fresh, clean, pure. **Ant.:** sour, acrid, tart, bitter.

sweetheart. Syn.: lover, suitor, beau, swain, spark, flame, lady-love, darling.

swell, *n.* **Syn.:** see **wave,** *n.*

swell, *v.* **Syn.:** inflate, expand, dilate, distend, bulge, bloat, tumefy; rise, increase.

swerve. Syn.: turn aside, deviate, diverge, stray. See **deviate.**

swift. Syn.: fleet, rapid, speedy, fast, quick, expeditious, prompt; short, brief. See **quick.**

swill. Syn.: see **drink,** *v.*

swindle. Syn.: see **cheat.**

swindler. Syn.: cheat, sharper, rogue, crook.

swing. Syn.: sway, brandish, flourish, wave, whirl; oscillate, rock, vibrate.

Swing expresses the comparatively regular motion to and fro of a body supported or held from the end or ends, especially from above or at one side, as a pendulum or door. To *sway* is to swing gently: as, the lantern *swayed* in the breeze; the word also describes the irregular movement of a body supported at the base, such as a flag-pole or carriage. *Rock* expresses the slow and regular movement back and forth of a body as on curved supports (*e.g.,* a cradle or rocking-chair). *Oscillate* refers to the smooth, regular, alternating movement of a body within certain limits.

sword. Syn.: rapier, saber, blade, scimitar.

sycophant. Syn.: parasite, fawner, flatterer, toady, lickspittle. See **parasite.**

syllabus. Syn.: compendium, abstract, synopsis. See **abridgment.**

sylph. Syn.: see **fairy.**

symbol. Syn.: sign, figure, token, type. See **emblem.**

symmetry. Syn.: proportion, balance, shapeliness.

sympathetic. Syn.: compassionate, commiserating, pitiful, tender, kind; harmonious, concordant, congenial.

sympathy. Syn.: fellow-feeling, compassion, commiseration, pity, tenderness, condolence; harmony, agreement, concord, affinity. See **pity.**

symptom. Syn.: sign, token, indication, mark, evidence. See **mark.**

synchronous. Syn.: see **contemporary.**

synopsis. Syn.: summary, compendium, digest, epitome, abstract, conspectus. See **abridgment.**

system. Syn.: plan, method, order, arrangement.

systematic. Syn.: methodical, orderly. **Ant.:** unsystematic, unmethodical, chaotic. See **orderly.**

T

tabernacle. Syn.: see **church.**

table. Syn.: tablet, plate, panel, board, slab; taboret, teapoy, stand, counter; list, schedule, synopsis, index.

taboo. Syn.: see **forbid, forbidden.**

tacit. Syn.: see **silent.**

taciturn. Syn.: silent, reserved, reticent, uncommunicative, close. **Ant.:** talkative, communicative, garrulous, loquacious. See **reticent.**

tact. Syn.: discernment, adroitness, address, diplomacy.

tactful. Syn.: diplomatic, politic, discreet, judicious.

Tactful suggests a nice touch in the handling of delicate matters or situations, especially those in which the feelings or wishes of others are involved. *Diplomatic* suggests the smooth or finished skill of an experienced diplomatist; *politic*, the sagacity or adroitness of one who is accustomed to consider expediency.

taint, *n.* **Syn.:** tinge, trace, touch, infection, contamination, stain, blemish.

taint, *v.* **Syn.:** tinge, imbue, impregnate, infect, poison, contaminate, corrupt, pollute, vitiate, stain, sully, tarnish, besmirch, defile.

To *taint* is to spoil slightly; to *infect* is to affect seriously with corruption, especially with germs of disease; to *contaminate* is to corrupt or defile by impurity or evil that deeply pervades or permeates.

take. Syn.: grasp, seize, clutch, hold, capture, arrest; appropriate, confiscate, usurp, steal; deduct, subtract, abstract, remove; extract, quote; derive, deduce; accept, receive, admit; assume, adopt; select, choose, pick; contract, catch; captivate, charm, please, delight, attract; endure, undergo, bear, experience, feel; acquire, obtain, procure, get, win; need, require, demand; conduct, escort, convey, carry. See **receive.**

tale. Syn.: see **story.**

talent. Syn.: faculty, aptitude, capacity, endowment, gift, knack. See **genius.**

talisman. Syn.: see **charm,** *n.*

talk, *n.* **Syn.:** conversation, converse, colloquy, chat, confabulation, palaver, chatter, babble, twaddle; speech, discourse, lecture, harangue; conference, discussion, parley; report, rumor, gossip; language, parlance, lingo, jargon.

talk, *v.* **Syn.:** converse, chat, chatter, babble, prattle, gabble, jabber, mumble, mutter, tattle, blab, peach, gossip, prate; speak, discourse, expatiate, descant, comment, argue, plead, lecture, preach, declaim, harangue, rant, spout, harp. See **speak.**

talkative. Syn.: communicative, loquacious, garrulous, babbling, chatty, loose-tongued, voluble, fluent, glib. **Ant.:** reserved, taciturn, reticent, silent.

Talkative is a mildly unfavorable word for one who is in the habit of speaking frequently with or without much significance: as, a *talkative* child. A *loqacious* person talks continuously and at length: as, a *loquacious* companion. The *garrulous* person talks with wearisome persistence about personal and trivial things: as, a *garrulous* old woman.

talker. Syn.: conversationalist, chatterer, chatterbox, babbler, gossip; speaker, lecturer.

tall. Syn.: high, lofty, towering. See **high.**

tally. Syn.: mark, record, score, register; correspond, agree, accord, conform, comport, match.

tame, *a.* **Syn.:** domesticated, domestic, gentle, docile; subdued, submissive, meek, spiritless, pusillanimous; dull, insipid, vapid, flat. **Ant.:** see **wild.** See **gentle.**

tame, *v.* **Syn.:** domesticate, break; subdue, subjugate, curb, repress, soften, temper.

tamper. Syn.: see **meddle.**

tang. Syn.: see **taste.**

tangible. Syn.: touchable, palpable, material, real, substantial, perceptible, evident, obvious.

tangle. Syn.: entangle, snarl, interweave, interlace, intertwine, intertwist; entrap, insnare, enmesh, embroil, involve, complicate. **Ant.:** disentangle, unravel, extricate, free.

tantalize. Syn.: tease, torment, plague, vex. See **tease.**

tantamount. Syn.: see **equal,** *a.*

tar. Syn.: see **sailor.**

tardy. Syn.: slow, sluggish; late, behindhand, procrastinating, dilatory, reluctant. See **late.**

tarnish. Syn.: dull, dim, discolor, stain, sully, besmirch, blacken. See **soil,** *v.*

tarry. Syn.: see **delay,** *v.,* **wait,** *v.*

tart. Syn.: see **sour.**

tartness. Syn.: see **acrimony.**

task. Syn.: duty, work, assignment, undertaking, lesson, job, stint.

taste. Syn.: tasting, gustation, degustation; savor, flavor, relish, tang, smack, race; inclination, predilection, liking, fondness, appetite; discernment, discrimination.

Taste is the general word for the quality of a substance that is perceived through the gustatory sense. *Flavor* is a characteristic taste, usually of a pleasing kind: as, vanilla *flavor*. *Savor* implies a slight, suggestive stimulation of the sense of taste or smell. *Smack* and *tang* generally imply a slightly sharp or pungent taste or smell, sometimes one that seems to be added to the thing tasted.

tasteless. Syn.: insipid, flat, vapid.

That which is *tasteless* is without taste or flavor, or excites no sensation of taste. That which is *insipid* is without distinctive taste, or without sufficient taste to be pleasing to the palate; or, figuratively, without distinctive character, or qualities that excite interest or emotion. *Flat* and *vapid* suggest especially a loss or absence of the proper flavor, sharpness, or life, as in stale beverages; both words are often used figuratively.

tattle, *n.* **Syn.:** see **gossip.**

tattle, *v.* **Syn.:** tell tales, blab, gossip.

To *tattle* is to betray in a childish fashion what another would not want revealed. To *blab* is to divulge such a matter more loudly and openly.

taunt. Syn.: deride, ridicule, jeer, mock, flout, chaff, gibe, twit. See **ridicule.**

tautology. Syn.: see **verbosity.**

tavern. Syn.: see **inn.**

tawdry. Syn.: showy, gaudy, flashy, meretricious, tinsel, gingerbread. See **gaudy.**

tawny. Syn.: see **dusky.**

tax, *n.* **Syn.:** assessment, levy, toll, tribute, duty, impost, excise, customs, rate, rates; burden, strain; charge, exaction.

tax, *v.* **Syn.:** assess; burden, strain, task; accuse, charge.

teach, teacher, teaching. Syn.: see **instruct, instructor, instruction.**

team. Syn.: see **couple.**

tear. Syn.: rend, rip, sunder, disrupt, split; lacerate, wound.

To *tear* is to split the fibers of something by pulling apart, usually so as to leave ragged or irregular edges. *Rip* implies more vigorous tearing, especially along a seam or a line. *Rend* implies great force or violence in tearing apart or in pieces.

tearful. Syn.: weeping, lacrymose, maudlin, mournful, melancholy.

tease. Syn.: irritate, vex, worry, annoy, molest, torment, plague, badger, chaff, pester, bother, tantalize, nag, taunt, rally, banter.

Tease implies persistent, petty, sometimes playful, annoyance; *plague* is stronger than tease, and implies constant repetition of what is vexing. *Badger* implies persistence, energy, and some rudeness as in baiting a person; *pester* suggests importunity or a succession of small vexations. That which *bothers* gives trouble or weariness; *worry* suggests wearing or exhausting solicitude. That which *tantalizes* teases or torments by repeatedly arousing and then thwarting expectations. *Nag* implies persistent annoyance by continued faultfinding or urging.

tedious. Syn.: tiresome, wearisome, irksome, humdrum, monotonous, dull, dreary, prolix. See **tiresome.**

tell. Syn.: number, count, reckon; inform, apprise, acquaint, notify, advise; relate, narrate, recount, rehearse, recite, report, enumerate; impart, communicate, mention, disclose, reveal, divulge, betray, blab, tattle; discern, distinguish, recognize; order, direct, request. Cf. **say, speak.**

telling. Syn.: effective, potent, cogent, forcible, striking, impressive, conclusive.

temerity. Syn.: boldness, venturesomeness, rashness, recklessness, foolhardiness, audacity, presumption. **Ant.:** caution, discretion, wariness, prudence. See **audacity.**

temper, *n.* **Syn.:** disposition, mood, humor; passion, anger. See **mood.**

temper, *v.* **Syn.:** soften, qualify, modify, moderate, mitigate, assuage, appease, calm; blend, mix.

To *temper* is to alter the quality of anything, generally so as to diminish its force or harshness; to *modify* is to alter in one or more particulars without changing the fundamental constitution of a thing; the alteration is generally in the direction of leniency, moderation, etc.; to *qualify* is to restrict by exceptions, limitations, conditions, etc.

temperament. Syn.: see **mood.**

temperance. Syn.: moderation, restraint, self-restraint, self-control, abstemiousness, sobriety, teetotalism. See **abstinence.**

temperate. Syn.: moderate, restrained, abstemious, sober; calm, cool, dispassionate. See **moderate.**

tempest. Syn.: see **wind,** *n.*

tempestuous. Syn.: see **stormy.**

temple. Syn.: sanctuary, tabernacle, fane, synagogue, mosque, pagoda, teocalli. See **church.**

temporal. Syn.: temporary, transient; earthly, terrestrial, mundane, secular, lay, political, civil. See **worldly.**

temporary. Syn.: transient, transitory, ephemeral, fleeting, evanescent, brief. **Ant.:** permanent, abiding, lasting, immortal.

tempt. Syn.: attract, allure, lure, entice, inveigle, decoy, seduce, bribe.

To *tempt* is to attract by holding out the probability of gratification or advantage, often in the direction of that which is wrong or unwise. To *seduce* is literally to lead astray, sometimes from that which absorbs one or demands attention, but oftener, in a moral sense, from rectitude, chastity, etc.

temptation. Syn.: attraction, allurement, lure, enticement, inducement, decoy, bait.

tenacious. Syn.: clinging, adhesive, glutinous, sticky; pertinacious, obstinate, stubborn, persistent, unyielding.

tenacity. Syn.: see **perseverance.**

tend. Syn.: incline, lean, verge, trend; contribute, conduce; attend, serve, care for, watch, guard, protect.

tendency. Syn.: inclination, leaning, bias, bent, proneness, propensity, proclivity, drift, trend, direction, course. See **direction.**

tender, n. Syn.: offer, proffer, proposal, overture.

tender, a. Syn.: soft, delicate, fragile, weak, effeminate; young, youthful, immature; gentle, mild, sympathetic, humane, merciful, compassionate, affectionate, loving; sensitive, impressionable; careful, considerate, solicitous. **Ant.:** see **tough, cruel.** See **delicate.**

tender, v. Syn.: offer, proffer, present. See **offer, v.**

tenebrous. Syn.: see **dark.**

tenet. Syn.: see **doctrine.**

tenor. Syn.: see **meaning.**

tense. Syn.: taut, rigid, stretched, strained, intense, intent, rapt. **Ant.:** loose, lax, relaxed.

tent. Syn.: pavilion, marquee, tabernacle, wigwam, tepee.

tenuous. Syn.: see **thin.**

tepid. Syn.: see **warm.**

term. Syn.: space, period, time, duration; word, name, phrase, expression, vocable. See **word.**

terminate. Syn.: end, close, conclude, finish, complete; result, eventuate. See **end.**

termination. Syn.: boundary, bound, limit, extremity, end, terminus, terminal; ending, conclusion, completion, issue, result.

terms. Syn.: conditions, stipulations, provisions, articles; relations, standing, footing.

terrestrial. Syn.: see **earthly.**

terrible. Syn.: dreadful, fearful, frightful, appalling, awful, horrible, shocking, gruesome, dire; violent, severe; extreme, immoderate, excessive, exorbitant.

The following words derive their qualities from the corresponding nouns: that which is *terrible* excites terror; the *dreadful* inspires dread; that which is *fearful* impresses with a sense of fear or danger; that which is *frightful* inspires fright, abhorrence, or almost paralyzing fear; the *awful* impresses with awe or reverential fear. All these words are used colloquially, with little difference of meaning, to intensify unpleasantness, ugliness, greatness, etc.

terrify. Syn.: frighten, scare, alarm, horrify, appal, terrorize, intimidate, dismay, affright, daunt. See **frighten.**

territory. Syn.: district, province, region, domain, land.

terror. Syn.: fear, fright, alarm, panic, consternation, dread. See **fear.**

terse. Syn.: see **concise.**

test, n. Syn.: examination, trial, proof, ordeal; criterion, standard, touchstone, watchword, shibboleth. See **trial.**

test, v. Syn.: examine, try, prove.

testimonial. Syn.: recommendation, credential, certificate, voucher.

A *testimonial* is anything which bears public witness to one's excellence, service, accomplishment, etc. A *recommendation* commends one to another's consideration for acceptance, especially for a position. A *credential* entitles the bearer to credit, confidence, or authority, especially in an official or governmental position.

testimony. Syn.: evidence, witness, proof; attestation, declaration, affirmation, profession, deposition. See **evidence.**

testy. Syn.: irritable, irascible, cross, petulant, peevish, pettish, touchy, snappish, waspish, peppery. See **irritable.**

text. Syn.: see **subject, n.**

thankful. Syn.: see **grateful.**

that. Syn.: see **who.**

thaw. Syn.: see **melt.**

theatrical. Syn.: dramatic, melodramatic, histrionic, sensational; artificial, affected, assumed, stagy; showy, pretentious. See **dramatic.**

theft. Syn.: thievery, stealing, pilfering, shoplifting, larceny, looting, robbery, embezzlement, peculation, cribbing, plagiarism.

theme. Syn.: see **subject, n.**

then. Syn.: see **therefore.**

theory. Syn.: opinion, doctrine, principle, hypothesis, speculation, supposition, conjecture.

A *theory* is a more or less verified or established explanation accounting for known facts or phenomena; a *hypothesis* is a tentative conjecture put forth as a possible explanation of certain phenomena or relations, and serves as a basis of argument or experimentation by which to reach the truth. In colloquial use *theory* is often used of an untested idea or opinion.

there. Syn.: thither.

There indicates place somewhat removed from the speaker and is used with both verbs of rest and verbs of motion: as, the horse is *there*; lead the horse *there*. *Thither* indicates direction toward a place mentioned or indicated and is used with verbs of motion only: as, "And the congregation sent *thither* twelve thousand men" (*Judges*, xxi. 10). The word is now confined almost wholly to literary use.

therefore. Syn.: wherefore, consequently, accordingly, hence, whence, then, so.

All these words draw a conclusion or infer a consequence from what immediately precedes. *Therefore*, for this or that reason, is the most formal, and is especially used in mathematics, logic, or elaborate argument. *Wherefore*, for which reason, has the same meaning as *therefore*, but introduces a clause grammatically dependent upon a preceding clause. *Accordingly* and *consequently* differ from these only in the promptness with which they suggest etymologically their meaning. *Then* and *so* indicate a looser logical relation and are more conversational in tone.

thesis. Syn.: see **subject, n.**

thick. Syn.: dense, close, compact, crowded, numerous, abundant, plentiful; coagulated, inspissated, incrassated, viscid, grumous, turbid, muddy; foggy, misty, hazy; slow, dull, stupid, obtuse, cross; indistinct, inarticulate, muffled; intimate, familiar. **Ant.:** see **thin.**

thicken. Syn.: condense, concrete, congeal, coagulate, inspissate, incrassate, curdle, clot.

thicket. Syn.: brake, copse, coppice, shrubbery, boscage, chaparral, spinney.

thief. Syn.: pilferer, filcher, cutpurse, pickpocket, shoplifter, embezzler, peculator, defaulter, kleptomaniac. See **robber.**

A *thief* takes the goods or property of another by stealth without his knowledge; a *robber* trespasses upon the house, property, or person of another and makes away with things of value even at the cost of violence.

thin, a. Syn.: narrow, slender, slim, attenuated, fine; lean, meager, spare, emaciated, wasted, gaunt, lank, scrawny, skinny, peaked, haggard; transparent, gauzy, gossamer, diaphanous, flimsy, sleazy; rarefied, rare, tenuous, subtile; unsubstantial, shallow, slight, weak, feeble; scanty, sparse, inadequate, insufficient. **Ant.:** see **thick.**

Thin applies to one having little flesh, often to one in an unnaturally reduced state, as from sickness, overwork, lack of food, or the like. *Lean* usually applies to a person or animal that is naturally thin. *Spare* implies a muscular leanness with no diminution of vitality. *Gaunt* suggests the angularity of bones prominently displayed in a thin face and body.

thin, v. Syn.: attenuate, rarefy, subtilize, dilute, reduce.

thing. Syn.: object, article; event, deed.

think. Syn.: conceive, imagine, picture; recollect, recall, remember; plan, devise, intend, purpose, mean; consider, deem, judge, opine, suppose, hold, count, esteem; cogitate, meditate, reflect, ponder, muse, brood, ruminate, speculate, reason.

Think is the general word for forming or having a thought, opinion, notion, or idea in the mind. *Deem* implies holding as an opinion. *Judge* suggests a careful balance of reason and evidence. To *esteem* is to regard in a certain light, especially to value as of worth. To *opine* is to venture an opinion; *suppose* suggests an opinion that is not certain but appears to be justified.

thinkable. **Syn.:** conceivable, imaginable, cogitable.

thinking. **Syn.:** reasoning, ratiocinative, rational, cogitative, reflective, contemplative, thoughtful, pensive.

thither. **Syn.:** see **there.**

thorn. **Syn.:** spine, prickle.

thorny. **Syn.:** spiny, spinose, spinous, prickly, pointed, sharp; painful, vexatious, difficult, troublesome.

thorough. **Syn.:** thoroughgoing, unqualified, complete, out-and-out. **Ant.:** superficial, cursory, hurried, partial.

though. **Syn.:** see **although, while,** *conj.*

thought. **Syn.:** idea, notion, concept, conception, opinion, belief; recollection, memory; intention, purpose, design; cogitation, deliberation, meditation, reflection, musing, study, contemplation, rumination, retrospection, abstraction, preoccupation, reverie; attention, consideration, regard, care, heed.

thoughtful. **Syn.:** reflective, meditative, contemplative, abstracted, preoccupied, pensive; careful, heedful, mindful, provident; attentive, considerate, regardful, kindly.

Thoughtful suggests that a person is engrossed in thought or that he is by nature seriously given to thinking. *Reflective* suggests a tendency or disposition to turn things over in the mind and dwell upon matters of previous experience. *Meditative* implies quiet and sustained reflection; *pensive* adds a tinge of wistfulness or melancholy.

thoughtless. **Syn.:** unthinking, unreflecting, indiscreet, rash, harebrained; careless, remiss, negligent, inconsiderate.

thraldom, thrall. **Syn.:** see **slavery, slave.**

thrash. **Syn.:** see **beat.**

thread. **Syn.:** filament, fiber, pile, warp, woof, stamen, staple, lint, raveling, thrum.

threadbare. **Syn.:** napless, worn, shabby, seedy; hackneyed, trite, stale.

threat. **Syn.:** menace, commination, fulmination, intimidation.

threaten. **Syn.:** menace, intimidate; portend, presage, augur, forebode, foreshadow.

Threaten is the general and familiar word with respect to both great and little things; *menace* is more dignified, and is used of matters of greater moment; as, to be *threatened* with a cold; to *threaten* a person's life; fire *menaced* the lives of all on board the ship; a *menacing* gesture.

threatening. **Syn.:** menacing, minatory; impending, imminent, ominous. See **imminent.**

three. **Syn.:** trio, trinity, triad, triplet, ternion.

thrift. **Syn.:** thriftiness, economy, frugality.

thriftless. **Syn.:** improvident, wasteful, prodigal, extravagant, spendthrift.

thrifty. **Syn.:** thriving, growing, flourishing, prosperous, fortunate, successful, well-to-do; economical, saving, provident, careful, frugal, sparing.

thrill. **Syn.:** pierce, stir, move; quiver, vibrate, throb, tingle.

thrilling. **Syn.:** piercing, penetrating, moving, exciting, sensational.

thrive. **Syn.:** prosper, flourish.

Thrive suggests vigorous growth and development such as results from natural vitality or favorable conditions. To *prosper* is to achieve and enjoy material success. To *flourish* is to give evidence of success or a ripe development of power, reputation, etc.

throb. **Syn.:** beat, pulsate, palpitate, vibrate, quiver, tremble.

throe. **Syn.:** see **pain,** *n.*

throng. **Syn.:** crowd, concourse, host, pack, mass. See **multitude.**

throttle. **Syn.:** strangle, choke. See **smother.**

through. **Syn.:** see **by.**

throw. **Syn.:** fling, cast, hurl, pitch, toss, sling, heave, launch; floor, unhorse.

Throw is the general word for projecting anything through the air; *cast* is used in a number of idiomatic expressions, such as to *cast* a ballot, to *cast* off (a boat), *cast* aside; it is otherwise a more elevated word for throw. *Hurl* suggests throwing with violence or great force; *pitch,* throwing with aim, or the dipping or plunging of a boat descending into the trough of a wave. To *fling* is to throw sharply, as with impatience or contempt. To *toss* is to throw lightly as with an underhand or sidewise motion, or to move irregularly up and down or back and forth like branches *tossing* in the wind.

thrust, *n.* **Syn.:** push, shove, punch, dig, lunge, stab.

thrust, *v.* **Syn.:** push, shove, drive, force, impel; stab, pierce. See **push.**

thud. **Syn.:** see **thump.**

thug. **Syn.:** cutthroat, assassin, ruffian, rough. See **murderer.**

thump. **Syn.:** blow, knock, bang, whack, thwack, thud.

thwart. **Syn.:** obstruct, block, balk, baffle, foil, contravene, defeat. See **frustrate.**

tidings. **Syn.:** see **news.**

tidy. **Syn.:** neat, trim, orderly. **Ant.:** see **untidy.** See **neat.**

tie. **Syn.:** bind, fasten, secure, tether, leash.

tight. **Syn.:** close, compact; close-fitting, snug; fixed, firm, tense, taut; stingy, niggardly, parsimonious.

tilt. **Syn.:** lean, incline, tip, cant, slant, slope.

time. **Syn.:** duration; epoch, era, age, æon, date; term, period, season, while, spell, generation, lifetime, interval, interim; occasion; opportunity, leisure; measure, tempo.

timely. **Syn.:** seasonable, opportune, convenient, appropriate, suitable, fitting.

That which is *timely* occurs or is done at an appropriate time, especially in time to meet some need: as, a *timely* arrival, *timely* intervention. That which is *seasonable* is right or proper for the time or season: as, *seasonable* weather. That which is *opportune* meets exactly the demands of the time or occasion: as, *opportune* evidence.

timepiece. **Syn.:** clock, watch, sun-dial, gnomon, hour-glass, clepsydra, chronometer, chronograph, repeater, stop-watch.

timid. **Syn.:** timorous, fearful, frightened, cowardly, pusillanimous, faint-hearted, shrinking, retiring, diffident, bashful, shy.

A *timid* person is lacking in boldness or self-confidence. *Timorous* implies a shrinking disposition easily frightened. The *cowardly* person is basely timid in the face of risk or danger. *Pusillanimous* implies abject and despicable cowardice.

timidity. **Syn.:** see **bashfulness.**

timorous. **Syn.:** see **timid.**

tincture. **Syn.:** see **color.**

tinge. **Syn.:** see **color.**

tint. **Syn.:** see **color.**

tiny. **Syn.:** see **small.**

tip, *n.* **Syn.:** point, extremity, end, apex, summit, top.

tip, *v.* **Syn.:** overthrow, overturn, upset, capsize; tilt, cant, incline, lean, career, list, dip, slope, slant.

tipple. **Syn.:** see **drink,** *v.*

tirade. **Syn.:** see **invective.**

tire. **Syn.:** exhaust, fatigue, fag, jade, weary, bore, irk, tucker. **Ant.:** refresh, revive, enliven.

To *tire* is to use up a considerable part of the bodily or mental resources. *Fatigue* is the technical word to indicate the consumption of energy to a point where natural repose is demanded. *Weary* suggests protracted exertion or strain gradually wearing out one's strength. *Exhaust* implies a complete draining of one's energy or vitality. *Jade* implies weariness caused by repetition of effort or indulgence. To be *fagged* is to be worn out by unrelieved labor.

tiresome. **Syn.:** exhausting, fatiguing, arduous, wearisome, irksome, tedious, humdrum, dull, prosy.

That which is *tiresome* exhausts either one's physical strength or one's patience. *Wearisome* is more emphatic and suggests the necessity for longer endurance. That is *tedious* which tires by reason of its length and slowness. *Irksome* describes that which frets or is wearing, or a task which one is reluctant to undertake.

titbit. **Syn.:** see **delicacy.**

title. **Syn.:** see **name,** *n.*

titter. **Syn.:** see **laugh.**

toady. **Syn.:** see **sycophant.**

toddle. **Syn.:** see **walk,** *v.*

toil, *n.* **Syn.:** work, labor, travail, drudgery, effort, exertion, pains; snare, trap, gin. See **work,** *n.*

toil, *v.* **Syn.:** work, labor, moil, drudge, slave.

toilsome. **Syn.:** tiring, fatiguing, laborious, onerous, tedious.

token. **Syn.:** sign, symbol, mark, indication, index, evidence; souvenir, memorial, memento, keepsake. See **mark.**

tolerable. **Syn.:** endurable, bearable, sufferable, supportable; passable, mediocre, middling, ordinary, indifferent, so-so.

tolerance. Syn.: toleration, endurance, sufferance, indulgence, liberality, catholicity.

The following two words are frequently interchangeable, but *tolerance* suggests rather a liberal spirit toward the views and actions of others; *toleration* implies the allowance of conduct or procedure with which one is not personally in accord.

tolerate. Syn.: endure, bear, suffer, brook, allow, permit. See **bear.**

toleration. Syn.: see **tolerance.**

toll. Syn.: see **tax,** *n.*

tomb. Syn.: grave, sepulcher, crypt, vault, sarcophagus, mausoleum, charnel-house, ossuary, catacomb.

tone. Syn.: see **sound,** *n.*

tongue. Syn.: see **language.**

too. Syn.: see **besides.**

tool. Syn.: implement, instrument, utensil; cat's-paw, hireling.

A *tool* is a manual contrivance for furthering or facilitating the work of (especially) mechanics or laborers: as, a carpenter's or gardener's *tools*. An *instrument* is anything which is employed in doing a certain work or producing a certain result, especially such as requires delicacy, accuracy, or preciseness: as, surgical, mathematical, or musical *instruments*. Figuratively, of human agency, *tool* is generally used in a dishonorable or contemptuous sense; *instrument*, in a neutral or good sense: as, he is a *tool* of unscrupulous men; he is an *instrument* of Providence. An *implement* is any tool or contrivance designed or used for a particular purpose: as, agricultural or mining *implements*. A *utensil* is especially an article of domestic use: as, kitchen *utensils*.

toothsome. Syn.: see **savory, delicious.**

top, *n.* Syn.: crest, crown, head, apex, vertex, summit, pinnacle, zenith, acme, culmination.

The *top* is the highest point or part of anything, sometimes a removable cover. A *summit* is the topmost part of (especially) something with sloping sides or that is reached by a gradual upward climb. *Crown* applies especially to a rounded top, as that of the head, a hat, or a mountain. *Zenith*, literally referring to the point of the heavens directly overhead, figuratively signifies the highest point in one's fortunes, success, or career, often with the implication of glory, splendor, or spectacular rise to greatness. *Acme* suggests the highest or culminating point of perfection in development or progress, beyond which it is impossible to go.

top, *v.* Syn.: tip, cap, crown; surmount, overtop, exceed, excel, surpass, outdo.

tope. Syn.: see **drink,** *v.*

topic. Syn.: see **subject,** *n.*

torment, *n.* Syn.: torture, agony, anguish, misery, distress, suffering, pain.

torment, *v.* Syn.: torture, rack, persecute, grill, excruciate, distress, pain, afflict; tease, plague, tantalize, worry, trouble, harass, harry.

To *torment* is to harass as by incessant repetition of vexations or annoyances; to *torture* is to afflict with acute and more or less protracted suffering; to *rack* is to affect with such pain as that suffered by one stretched on a rack.

tornado. Syn.: see **wind.**

torpid. Syn.: numb, benumbed, stupefied, insensible, lethargic, comatose, sluggish, apathetic. See **inactive.**

torpor. Syn.: numbness, insensibility, stupor, lethargy, coma, sluggishness, apathy.

torrid. Syn.: see **hot.**

tortuous. Syn.: winding, sinuous, circuitous, serpentine, twisted, crooked, zigzag, irregular, indirect, devious, roundabout. Ant.: straight, direct, undeviating, honest. See **winding.**

torture, *n.* Syn.: see **pain,** *n.*

torture, *v.* Syn.: see **torment,** *v.*

toss. Syn.: see **throw.**

total, *n.* Syn.: see **sum.**

total, *a.* Syn.: see **complete,** *a.*

totter. Syn.: rock, shake, tremble, stagger, wabble. See **reel.**

touch, *n.* Syn.: feel, taction, palpation, contact, tangency; tap, stroke, push; relation, connection, harmony; trace, tinge, shade, smack, dash.

touch, *v.* Syn.: feel, handle; tap, hit, strike; concern, affect; impress, move, soften; adjoin, border, meet, graze. See **impress.**

touching. Syn.: affecting, moving, pathetic, sad.

touchstone. Syn.: see **test,** *n.*

touchy. Syn.: see **irritable.**

tough. Syn.: tenacious, cohesive, firm, strong; hardy, sturdy, stout; unyielding, stubborn; trying, troublesome, difficult, hard, laborious; hardened, incorrigible, vicious. Ant.: see **tender.**

tour. Syn.: see **journey.**

tower. Syn.: spire, steeple, belfry, cupola, campanile, minaret, turret, tourelle, donjon, keep, citadel, fortress, castle.

towering. Syn.: see **high.**

town. Syn.: city, borough, village, hamlet, thorp, dorp, bourg.

toxin. Syn.: see **poison.**

toy. Syn.: trifle, knickknack, gimcrack, trinket, plaything, bauble, gewgaw.

trace. Syn.: track, vestige, mark, sign, token, indication, shade, hint.

Trace, the broader term, denotes any mark or slight indication of something past or present; *vestige* is more limited and refers to some slight, though actual, remains of something that no longer exists: as, a *trace* of footprints, a *trace* of ammonia in water; *vestiges* of a family's former wealth. The words are often interchanged: as, *traces* (or *vestiges*) of former greatness.

track, *n.* Syn.: trace, footmark, footprint; path, trail, way.

track, *v.* Syn.: follow, pursue, trace, trail.

trade, *n.* Syn.: occupation, craft, profession; commerce, business, traffic, barter; transaction, bargain, deal. See **occupation.**

Trade is the general word for the exchanging of commodities for other commodities or for money: as, *trade* is dull; the doctrine of free *trade* versus that of a protective tariff. *Traffic* may refer to a particular kind of trade: as, the liquor or opium *traffic*; but it usually suggests the travel, transportation, and activity associated with or incident to trade: as, the *traffic* on a railroad. *Commerce* applies to trade on a large scale and over an extensive area: as the Department of *Commerce*; the *commerce* of nations.

trade, *v.* Syn.: exchange, barter, swap; deal, traffic.

tradesman. Syn.: merchant, shopkeeper, dealer, trader, trafficker.

traditional. Syn.: see **legendary.**

traduce. Syn.: defame, calumniate, slander, vilify. See **asperse.**

traffic. Syn.: see **commerce, trade,** *n.*

tragedy. Syn.: see **drama.**

trail. Syn.: train, appendage; trace, track, footmark, spoor, clue; path, route, road, way. See **way.**

train, *n.* Syn.: succession, sequence, order, course; series, row, rank, chain, line, file, procession; retinue, suite.

train, *v.* Syn.: educate, teach, instruct, drill, discipline, school, accustom, habituate, inure; point, aim.

training. Syn.: see **instruction.**

trait. Syn.: see **characteristic.**

traitor. Syn.: deserter, turncoat, renegade, apostate. See **insurgent.**

A *traitor* is especially one who breaks faith or trust by betraying his country or by violating his allegiance. A *deserter* is one who forsakes his duty, cause, or party, especially a soldier or sailor who absents himself without leave and without the intention of returning. A *turncoat* is one who turns from one allegiance to another, usually for personal advantage. A *renegade* is one who, presumably without conversion of mind or heart and from sheer self-interest, goes over from one faith or party to another. An *apostate* definitely and completely renounces the faith he formerly professed.

traitorous. Syn.: treacherous, perfidious, treasonable, faithless, disloyal, false. Ant.: faithful, loyal, constant, true. See **faithless.**

trammel. Syn.: see **hinder.**

tramp, *n.* Syn.: see **vagabond.**

tramp, *v.* Syn.: see **walk,** *v.*

tranquil. Syn.: quiet, peaceful, calm, placid, serene, undisturbed, composed.

tranquilize. Syn.: quiet, calm, pacify, compose, allay, soothe, still, lull, hush.

tranquillity. Syn.: quietness, calmness, serenity, stillness, peace. See **composure.**

transact. Syn.: perform, manage, conduct, negotiate.

One *transacts* a piece of business, or carries it through to completion; one *negotiates* a treaty, a loan, etc., by discussing and settling terms with others.

transaction. Syn.: procedure, proceeding, negotiation, deal, matter, affair.

transcend. Syn.: overstep, overpass, exceed, surpass, excel, outdo, outstrip.

transcendent. Syn.: transcendental; excellent, superior, surpassing, unequaled, unrivaled, unparalleled, peerless, preëminent, supreme.

transcript. Syn.: see **copy,** *n.*

transfer. Syn.: transport, convey, carry, transmit, alienate.

transfigure. Syn.: see **transform.**

transfix. Syn.: see **penetrate.**

transform. Syn.: transmute, change, metamorphose, turn, transfigure, convert.

Transform is the most general word, and may refer to change in mere external aspect, or to internal change, whether physical or spiritual: as, different clothes *transform* one's appearance; a tadpole is *transformed* into a frog, a drunkard into a self-controlled man. *Transmute* usually implies a complete change of nature, amounting even to the miraculous or the impossible: as, to *transmute* iron into gold. Except in its scientific uses, *metamorphose* often indicates such a complete change as to suggest the fabulous transformation of men into trees, stones, etc., in Ovid's *Metamorphoses*. *Transfigure*, from its use in connection with the change in the appearance of Jesus Christ, suggests such change as exalts or glorifies.

transgress. Syn.: overpass, overstep, transcend, contravene, disregard, violate, break. See **trespass,** *v.*

transgression. Syn.: trespass, violation, breach, offense, misdeed, fault, sin. See **offense.**

transient. Syn.: transitory, passing, fleeting, fugitive, evanescent, momentary, ephemeral, temporary, brief, short. **Ant.:** abiding, enduring, permanent, everlasting, eternal. See **fleeting.**

transitory. Syn.: see **fleeting.**

translate. Syn.: render, interpret, construe, explain, paraphrase.

translation. Syn.: version, rendering, interpretation, paraphrase.

Translation and *version* are often the same in meaning. A *translation* is a more or less exact turning from one language into another. Different translations of the same thing are often called *versions*; the word is especially used of older translations and translations of the Bible: as, Homer in Pope's *version*; the King James *version* of the Bible. *Version* also has the meaning of a personal account, often with individual differences: as, a witness's *version* of an accident.

translucent. Syn.: see **transparent.**

transmute. Syn.: see **transform.**

transparent. Syn.: clear, limpid, pellucid, lucid, diaphanous, translucent, crystalline, sheer; open, frank, candid; manifest, obvious.

That which is *transparent* allows objects to be clearly seen through it; that which is *translucent* allows the passage of light yet diffuses it, so that objects beyond are not distinctly seen: as, clear water is *transparent*; ground glass or tissue-paper is *translucent*.

transport, *n.* **Syn.:** see **rapture.**

transport, *v.* **Syn.:** see **convey.**

trap, *n.* **Syn.:** snare, toil, springe, gin, pitfall; stratagem, artifice, fraud.

Literally, a *trap* is a mechanical contrivance for catching animals, the main feature of which is usually a spring; a *snare* is a device for entangling with intent to capture; a *pitfall* is a (usually) concealed pit arranged for the capture of animals or men who may fall into it. Figuratively, *trap* suggests the scheme of one person to take another by surprise; *snare* implies enticement and inveiglement; *pitfall*, any concealed danger or source of disaster.

trap, *v.* **Syn.:** entrap, catch, insnare.

trash. Syn.: see **rubbish.**

travel, *n.* **Syn.:** traveling. Cf. **journey.**

travel, *v.* **Syn.:** go, journey, tour, peregrinate.

traveler. Syn.: wayfarer, seafarer, voyager, pilgrim, tourist, itinerant, peregrinator.

travesty. Syn.: see **burlesque.**

treacherous, treasonable. Syn.: see **perfidious.**

treachery. Syn.: see **disloyalty.**

treason. Syn.: see **disloyalty.**

treatise. Syn.: disquisition, dissertation, thesis.

treaty. Syn.: see **contract,** *n.*

tree. Syn.: see **plant.**

tremble. Syn.: shake, shiver, quake, shudder, dodder, totter, quiver, vibrate. See **shake.**

tremendous. Syn.: awful, dreadful, frightful, horrible, terrific; immense, monstrous, marvelous, astounding.

tremor. Syn.: trembling, shaking, quaking, quivering. See **agitation.**

tremulous. Syn.: trembling, shaking, shaky, quivering, vibrating, unsteady, infirm.

trench, *n.* **Syn.:** see **ditch.**

trench, *v.* **Syn.:** see **trespass,** *v.*

trenchant. Syn.: see **sharp.**

trend. Syn.: see **direction, tendency.**

trepidation. Syn.: perturbation, flutter, flurry, fright, tremor, tremulousness. See **agitation.**

trespass, *n.* **Syn.:** encroachment, infringement, infraction, transgression, offense, wrong, sin. See **offense.**

trespass, *v.* **Syn.:** intrude, encroach, invade, infringe, intrench, trench; transgress, sin. See **encroach.**

trial. Syn.: test, proof, experiment, examination, ordeal, competition; attempt, essay, endeavor, effort, exertion; hardship, trouble, misfortune, sorrow, tribulation, affliction.

Trial is the general word for trying anything; *test* is stronger and more specific, and represents a trial under approved and fixed conditions or a trial that is final and decisive: as, articles sent for ten days' free *trial*; the engine stood every *test*. *Proof* applies especially to a process that tends to establish a fact or truth.

tribe. Syn.: race, clan, family. See **people.**

tribulation. Syn.: trial, persecution, oppression, trouble, distress, suffering. See **affliction.**

tribute. Syn.: see **tax.**

trick, *n.* **Syn.:** artifice, stratagem, subterfuge, ruse, fraud, imposture, hoax, joke; feat, exploit, stunt; trait, characteristic, peculiarity, mannerism. See **deception.**

trick, *v.* **Syn.:** deceive, cheat, defraud, cozen, inveigle, beguile, cajole, delude; dress, array, attire, deck. See **cheat,** *v.*

trickery. Syn.: artifice, stratagem, fraud, deception, imposture, chicanery, duplicity.

trickle. Syn.: drip, dribble, percolate, ooze, leak.

trickster. Syn.: deceiver, impostor, cheat, rogue, knave, scoundrel, quack, shyster.

tricky. Syn.: trickish, deceptive, deceitful, artful, crafty, knavish, unprincipled, treacherous, shifty. See **cunning.**

trifle, *n.* **Syn.:** triviality, bagatelle, bit, jot, trinket, knickknack, bauble.

trifle, *v.* **Syn.:** play, toy, fiddle; dally, dawdle, potter, piddle; waste, fritter, idle.

Trifle implies a lack of seriousness or definite purpose; *dally*, indecisive loitering or the sportive delay characteristic of one who is free from care or responsibility; *dawdle*, a frittering away of time through lack of concentrated purpose; *potter*, desultory activity devoted to comparatively unimportant jobs.

trifling. Syn.: frivolous, foolish, shallow, vain, idle; trivial, paltry, petty, small, slight, insignificant, unimportant, worthless, good-for-nothing.

That which is *trifling* is so unimportant as to be practically negligible; that which is *trivial* is small and insignificant; *petty* implies contemptible insignificance and littleness of soul; *paltry* is applied to that which is beneath one's notice; *frivolous* suggests a lack of seriousness in character or intent.

trim, *a.* **Syn.:** neat, tidy, spruce, natty, smart. See **neat.**

trim, *v.* **Syn.:** embellish, garnish, adorn, deck, decorate; cut, clip, pare, prune; beat, thrash, trounce.

trinket. Syn.: see **knickknack.**

trip, *n.* **Syn.:** excursion, tour, voyage, jaunt; misstep, mistake. See **journey.**

trip, *v.* **Syn.:** move, run, skip, caper, prance; stumble, fall.

trite. Syn.: hackneyed, commonplace, stereotyped, banal, threadbare, stale, vapid. **Ant.:** original, new, fresh, vivid, striking.

Trite suggests ideas or utterances that have been worn smooth by use and hence lack any sharpness or emphasis; *hackneyed* suggests expressions that have grown stale with countless repetition; the *banal* is so lacking in individuality as to be flat and insipid; that which is *stereotyped* is limited by a fixed form however often employed.

triumph, *n.* **Syn.:** celebration, ovation, jubilee; victory, conquest, achievement; exultation, elation, joy. See **glad-ness.**

triumph, *v.* **Syn.:** prevail, succeed, conquer; exult, glory, rejoice.

triumphant. Syn.: victorious, successful; exultant, exulting, rejoicing, jubilant. See **elated.**

trivial. Syn.: trifling, insignificant, slight, paltry, small, unimportant. **Ant.:** momentous, important, weighty, serious, grave.

troop. Syn.: company, band, squad, crowd, multitude, throng, troupe. See **company.**

trot. Syn.: see **run.**

trouble, *n.* **Syn.:** distress, grief, worry, anxiety, tribulation, affliction, misfortune, calamity; vexation, annoyance, embarrassment, inconvenience, discomfort; disturbance, disorder, confusion; pains, effort, exertion, labor, toil, care, difficulty; disease, ailment, affection.

trouble, *v.* **Syn.:** disturb, agitate, distress, grieve, worry, harass, afflict; vex, annoy, bother, inconvenience, incommode.

troublesome. Syn.: disturbing, distressing, harassing, vexatious, annoying, bothersome, irksome, burdensome, difficult, trying.

trousers. Syn.: breeches, pantaloons, knickerbockers, knee-breeches, small-clothes, chaparejos, trews, overalls.

truce. Syn.: see **peace.**

truckle. Syn.: yield, submit, knuckle, cringe.

truckling. Syn.: see **servile.**

truculent. Syn.: see **fierce.**

trudge. Syn.: see **walk,** *v.*

true. Syn.: faithful, loyal, stanch, constant; trustworthy, truthful, veracious; exact, accurate, precise, correct; rightful, legitimate; genuine, veritable, real, actual. **Ant.:** see **untrue.** See **authentic.**

truism. Syn.: see **proverb, platitude.**

trumpery. Syn.: see **rubbish.**

trust, *n.* **Syn.:** confidence, belief, credence, reliance, faith, expectation, anticipation, hope; duty, charge, commission, office; custody, care; credit, tick.

Trust and *confidence* are used with little difference in meaning, but *confidence* seems sometimes to rest upon a more rational foundation: as, I would put complete *trust* (or *confidence*) in his word; the *trust* of a child in its parents is different from the *confidence* of a man in his associates. *Reliance* is more or less firm faith, often expressing itself in the form of dependence.

trust, *v.* **Syn.:** rely on, depend on; believe, hope; commit, intrust, confide.

trustful. Syn.: trusting, confiding, credulous, unsuspicious, naïve, innocent, gullible.

trustworthy. Syn.: trusty, reliable, dependable, faithful, honest. See **reliable.**

truth. Syn.: trueness, truthfulness, veracity, honesty; exactness, accuracy, precision, correctness; genuineness, reality, verity, fact.

truthful. Syn.: true, veracious, veridical, sincere, candid, honest; exact, accurate, correct. **Ant.:** see **untrue.**

try. Syn.: attempt, essay, endeavor, strive, seek, strain; test, prove, examine; purify, refine, assay, render; afflict, trouble.

Try is the simplest word for putting forth effort toward a specific end; *attempt* is slightly more formal; *essay*, which occurs chiefly in literary use, often suggests trying in order to see if a thing can be done or attained; *endeavor* suggests resolution and continuous effort, especially in the face of difficulties; *strive*, hard and earnest exertion to accomplish something difficult or arduous.

trying. Syn.: severe, difficult, hard, distressing, afflictive, vexing, vexatious.

tuft. Syn.: see **cluster.**

tug. Syn.: see **pull.**

tuition. Syn.: see **instruction.**

tumble. Syn.: roll, toss, pitch, wallow; topple, fall; disorder, rumple.

tumid. Syn.: see **bombastic.**

tumult. Syn.: commotion, confusion, disorder, turmoil, uproar, noise, hubbub, hurly-burly, disturbance, brawl, mêlée, outbreak, uprising, riot. See **commotion.**

tumultuous. Syn.: disorderly, noisy, boisterous, turbulent, riotous, tempestuous.

tune. Syn.: air, melody, strain; harmony, unison, concord, accord.

tuneful. Syn.: harmonious, melodious, musical, sweet.

turbid. Syn.: muddy, roiled, cloudy, unclear; muddled, confused.

turbulence. Syn.: disorder, commotion, tumult, mutiny, sedition, insurrection, riot.

turbulent. Syn.: disorderly, boisterous, uproarious, obstreperous, unruly, refractory, brawling, mutinous, riotous; tumultuous, violent, stormy, tempestuous. See **boisterous.**

turf. Syn.: sward, greensward, grass, sod, peat.

turgid. Syn.: swollen, tumid, inflated, pompous, bombastic, magniloquent, grandiloquent, grandiose. See **bombastic.**

turmoil. Syn.: confusion, commotion, tumult, uproar. See **commotion.**

turn, *n.* **Syn.:** revolution, rotation; coil, twist; bend, curve, crook, angle, flexure, deflection; change, alteration; turning-point, crisis; spell, while, time; chance, opportunity; tendency, inclination, bias, bent, aptitude, drift, trend; act, deed, favor, kindness, service; convenience, requirement, emergency, need. See **inclination.**

turn, *v.* **Syn.:** revolve, rotate, spin, twirl, whirl; bend, twist; invert, reverse; divert, deflect, shift, veer; direct, aim, devote; change, alter, transform, transmute, translate; hinge, depend; deviate, swerve, digress, stray, avert.

Turn is the general and popular word for motion on an axis or around a center, but it is also used of motion less than a complete circle: as, to *turn* the page of a book. *Revolve* refers especially to movement in an orbit around a center, but is sometimes exchangeable with *rotate*, which refers only to the motion of a body round its own center or axis. *Spin* implies very rapid rotation.

turncoat. Syn.: see **traitor.**

turret. Syn.: see **tower.**

tussle. Syn.: see **fight,** *n.*, **quarrel,** *n.*

tutor. Syn.: see **instructor.**

twaddle. Syn.: see **prattle.**

twig. Syn.: see **bough.**

twilight. Syn.: see **evening.**

twinge. Syn.: see **pain.**

twinkle. Syn.: sparkle, scintillate, flash, glitter, glimmer, shine. See **shine,** *v.*

twirl. Syn.: whirl, twiddle.

twist, *n.* **Syn.:** convolution, curve, bend, flexure, twirl, curl, kink, knot, snarl; distortion, wrench, strain; bent, turn.

twist, *v.* **Syn.:** intertwine, interweave; wreathe, wind, twine, coil; bend, squirm, writhe, wriggle; contort, distort, pervert, warp, wrench, wrest.

twit. Syn.: see **taunt, ridicule.**

twitch. Syn.: see **jerk, pull.**

twitter. Syn.: see **sing.**

two. Syn.: couple, pair, span, brace, doublet, dyad, twain, twins.

type. Syn.: sign, symbol, emblem, token, image; exemplar, pattern, model, prototype, archetype.

typical. Syn.: emblematic, representative, illustrative, indicative, characteristic.

tyrannical. Syn.: despotic, autocratic, arbitrary, absolute, dictatorial, domineering, galling, grinding, oppressive, severe.

tyranny. Syn.: despotism, absolutism; oppression, harshness, severity, rigor.

tyrant. Syn.: despot, autocrat, oppressor, persecutor. See **autocrat.**

tyro. Syn.: see **beginner.**

U

ubiquitous. Syn.: see **omnipresent.**

ugly. Syn.: ill-favored, hard-featured, uncomely, unsightly, repulsive, hideous, homely, plain; base, vile; disagreeable, unpleasant, ill-natured, surly, spiteful. **Ant.:** see **pretty.**

Ugly is applied to what is repulsive to the eye or more or less deeply offends the sense of beauty. *Ill-favored*, an archaic word based upon *favor* in an old sense of appearance or looks, describes what is by nature unpleasing or unprepossessing in appearance. *Unsightly* is applied to what forms an unpleasant sight, often to an object that mars a view or scene. *Plain* indicates absence of any of the features or advantages that go to make up good looks. *Homely*, suggesting a commonplace or ordinary appearance, is often used as a mild substitute for *ugly*.

ultimate. Syn.: see **last,** *a.*

umbrage. Syn.: offense, resentment, displeasure, pique. See **annoyance.**

umpire. Syn.: referee, judge, arbiter, arbitrator. See **judge.**

unable. Syn.: see **incapable.**

unaccountable. Syn.: inexplicable, incomprehensible, inscrutable, mysterious, strange; unanswerable, irresponsible.

unaccustomed. Syn.: unused, unwonted, unfamiliar, uncommon, unusual, strange.

unadulterated. Syn.: see **pure.**

unadvised. Syn.: uninformed, thoughtless, hasty, imprudent, unwise, indiscreet, inconsiderate, rash.

unaffected. Syn.: unmoved, untouched, unimpressed; plain, natural, simple, naïve, sincere, unfeigned.

unambitious. Syn.: unaspiring, unenterprising, indifferent; unpretending, modest. **Ant.:** see **ambitious.**

unamiable. Syn.: ill-natured, ungracious, unlovely, unfriendly, cross, irascible, surly.

unanimity. Syn.: agreement, accord, unison, harmony.

unanswerable. Syn.: irrefutable, irrefragable, incontrovertible, undeniable.

unassuming. Syn.: see **modest.**

unattainable. Syn.: see **impossible.**

unavailing. Syn.: ineffectual, useless, bootless, vain, futile, nugatory, abortive, fruitless.

The following words are differentiated in their application to effort or endeavor. That is *unavailing* which fails to produce the desired or expected result. That which is *useless* is unavailing because of the circumstances of the case or some inherent defect: as, it is *useless* to cry over spilt milk. That is *vain* which is void of accomplishment; *futile* suggests wasted effort and complete failure to attain a desired end; that is *nugatory* which is without force or effect: as, the lawyer's argument was rendered *nugatory* by additional evidence.

unaware. Syn.: unmindful, unconscious, insensible, oblivious, heedless.

unbearable. Syn.: intolerable, insufferable, unendurable.

unbecoming. Syn.: improper, indecorous, unseemly, unsuitable, inappropriate. **Ant.:** see **becoming.** See **improper.**

unbelief. Syn.: see **disbelief.**

unbelievable. Syn.: incredible, implausible, fabulous.

unbeliever. Syn.: see **skeptic.**

unbelieving. Syn.: incredulous, skeptical, doubtful, distrustful, suspicious.

unbending. Syn.: inflexible, unyielding, rigid, firm.

unbiased. Syn.: unprejudiced, impartial, disinterested, fair, neutral.

unbidden. Syn.: spontaneous, voluntary, volitional; uninvited, unasked.

unblemished. Syn.: unstained, spotless, pure.

unbounded. Syn.: boundless, limitless, unlimited, illimitable, immeasurable, infinite, immense, vast.

unbridled. Syn.: uncurbed, unrestrained, unchecked, uncontrolled, immoderate, licentious.

unbroken. Syn.: whole, entire, intact; untamed, wild; undisturbed, profound, sound; regular, even.

uncanny. Syn.: see **weird.**

unceasing. Syn.: ceaseless, continuous, continual, perpetual, incessant, constant, uninterrupted, unremitting.

unceremonious. Syn.: informal, unconstrained, familiar; abrupt, blunt, bluff. **Ant.:** see **ceremonious.**

uncertain. Syn.: doubtful, dubious, distrustful, hesitating; insecure, unreliable, untrustworthy, fallible, precarious; vague, indefinite, problematical, ambiguous, equivocal; inconstant, capricious, fickle, unsteady, variable, fitful. **Ant.:** see **certain.**

That which is *uncertain* often involves danger through an inability to predict or place confidence in the unknown. That which is *insecure* is not firm, stable, or safe, and hence is liable to give way, fail, or be overcome. *Precarious* suggests great liability to failure, or exposure to imminent danger.

unchangeable. Syn.: immutable, unalterable, invariable, permanent, constant. **Ant.:** see **changeable.**

uncharitable. Syn.: ungenerous, illiberal, intolerant, censorious, harsh, severe. **Ant.:** see **charitable.**

unchaste. Syn.: impure, immoral, wanton, incontinent, libidinous, lewd. **Ant.:** see **chaste.**

uncivil. Syn.: discourteous, impolite, unmannerly, ill-mannered, rude, boorish, churlish. **Ant.:** see **civil.**

uncivilized. Syn.: savage, barbarous, unreclaimed, benighted, rude.

unclean. Syn.: dirty, soiled, foul, filthy, impure, polluted, defiled. **Ant.:** see **clean,** *a.*

uncommon. Syn.: unusual, rare, scarce, infrequent, unwonted, exceptional, strange, extraordinary, singular, unique. **Ant.:** see **common.**

uncommunicative. Syn.: reserved, taciturn, reticent, secretive. See **reticent.**

uncomplaining. Syn.: submissive, resigned, forbearing, patient, long-suffering, meek.

uncomplimentary. Syn.: unflattering, disparaging, derogatory.

uncompromising. Syn.: unyielding, inflexible, firm.

unconcern. Syn.: indifference, nonchalance. See **indifference.**

unconcerned. Syn.: indifferent, nonchalant, cool, apathetic.

unconditional. Syn.: unqualified, unrestricted, absolute, unreserved, complete. **Ant.:** see **conditional.**

uncongenial. Syn.: see **unpleasant.**

unconquerable. Syn.: invincible, indomitable, insuperable, impregnable.

unconscious. Syn.: insensible, comatose; unaware, oblivious, heedless, regardless, unmindful.

unconstrained. Syn.: voluntary, spontaneous, free, easy, natural.

uncouple. Syn.: unfasten, disconnect, disjoin, detach, loose.

uncourtly. Syn.: unpolished, inelegant, ungraceful, coarse, uncivil, rude. **Ant.:** see **courtly.**

uncouth. Syn.: ungainly, ungraceful, gawky, awkward, clumsy, loutish, homely, plain, ugly. See **awkward.**

uncover. Syn.: unveil, disclose, reveal, expose, show.

unctuous. Syn.: greasy, oily, smooth, bland, suave.

uncultured. Syn.: uncultivated, unlettered, ignorant, rude, Philistine.

undaunted. Syn.: undismayed, unafraid, unflinching, bold, fearless, intrepid, brave.

undeceive. Syn.: disabuse, disillusion.

To *undeceive* is to free from a false or mistaken belief; to *disabuse* is to use the truth to liberate the mind conceived of as having been tricked by false hopes, beliefs, or ideas; to *disillusion* is to shatter the illusions of youth, inexperience, or overconfidence.

undecided. Syn.: unsettled, pending; irresolute, wavering.

undefined. Syn.: indefinite, vague, dim, obscure.

undemonstrative. Syn.: quiet, staid, sedate, reserved, phlegmatic.

undeniable. Syn.: indisputable, incontestable, incontrovertible, irrefragable, unquestionable, indubitable.

under. Syn.: see **below.**

undergo. Syn.: endure, suffer, bear, sustain, experience.

Undergo usually refers to the bearing or enduring of something hard, difficult, disagreeable, or dangerous; to *experience* is to be affected by what one meets with in life so that one's self to a greater or less degree suffers a change: as, to *undergo* hardship or an operation; to *experience* disappointment, a severe shock, a change of heart.

underhand. Syn.: secret, covert, clandestine, surreptitious, sly, deceitful, fraudulent. See **secret.**

underlying. Syn.: fundamental, basic, essential.

underrate. Syn.: see **undervalue.**

understand. Syn.: comprehend, apprehend, discern, grasp. See **know.**

understanding. Syn.: comprehension, apprehension, discernment; intelligence, wit; agreement, accord, harmony, union.

undertake. Syn.: see **attempt.**

undervalue. Syn.: underrate, underestimate, depreciate, despise, vilipend.

undeserved. Syn.: unmerited, unearned, unjust.

undesigned. Syn.: see **unintentional.**

undesirable. Syn.: inexpedient, objectionable, unacceptable.

undetermined. Syn.: unsettled, indefinite, indeterminate, suspended, abeyant; irresolute, wavering.

undiminished. Syn.: unlessened, unabated.

undisciplined. Syn.: untaught, untrained, undrilled, raw, wild.

undismayed. Syn.: see **undaunted.**

undisturbed. **Syn.:** calm, placid, serene, tranquil, peaceful, quiet, composed, unmoved, unruffled.

undo. **Syn.:** reverse, annul, nullify, invalidate, abrogate; unfasten, untie, unloose, unlace, unhook, unhitch, unlatch, unlock, disconnect, disentangle, untangle, unravel; ruin, spoil. See **spoil,** *v.*

undress. **Syn.:** disrobe, disarray, strip.

undue. **Syn.:** improper, excessive, immoderate, unreasonable, inordinate, exorbitant.

undulate. **Syn.:** see **fluctuate.**

undutiful. **Syn.:** disobedient, unfilial, refractory. See **disobedient.**

undying. **Syn.:** deathless, immortal, imperishable, everlasting, eternal, endless.

unearthly. **Syn.:** otherworldly, supernatural, weird, wild, terrifying, appalling. See **weird.**

uneasy. **Syn.:** unquiet, restless, restive, impatient, uncomfortable, disturbed, perturbed, agitated, anxious. **Ant.:** see **easy.** See **restless.**

uneducated. **Syn.:** illiterate, ignorant, untutored, unenlightened, benighted. See **ignorant.**

unemotional. **Syn.:** unexcitable, imperturbable, impassive, phlegmatic, stolid.

Unemotional implies a nature that is not susceptible to the excitation of the feelings. The *imperturbable* man remains undisturbed by circumstances which tend generally to produce agitation. The *impassive* person does not betray by look or movement the emotion which he may perhaps feel. *Phlegmatic* implies constitutional sluggishness or apathy; *stolid* suggests the insensibility of one thick, heavy, and dull.

unending. **Syn.:** interminable, ceaseless, eternal, everlasting, perpetual.

unendurable. **Syn.:** see **unbearable.**

unenlightened. **Syn.:** see **ignorant.**

unequal. **Syn.:** uneven, unsymmetrical, irregular, disproportionate, disparate; one-sided, unfair, unjust, inequitable, partial; inadequate, insufficient, inferior. **Ant.:** see **equal,** *a.*

unequaled. **Syn.:** unrivaled, unexcelled, unsurpassed, unexampled, unmatched, matchless, peerless, incomparable, unique.

unequivocal. **Syn.:** unambiguous, unmistakable, obvious, plain, downright, emphatic.

unerring. **Syn.:** unfailing, infallible, certain, sure.

uneven. **Syn.:** unequal, rough, rugged, jagged, humpy, hummocky; changeable, jerky. **Ant.:** see **even.**

unexampled. **Syn.:** see **unequaled.**

unexpected. **Syn.:** unforeseen, unanticipated, unlooked-for, sudden, chance.

unfading. **Syn.:** enduring, lasting, permanent, perennial.

unfailing. **Syn.:** sure, certain, inevitable, infallible, inexhaustible, constant, loyal.

unfair. **Syn.:** partial, prejudiced, biased, one-sided, inequitable, unjust, dishonest. **Ant.:** see **fair.**

unfaithful. **Syn.:** faithless, false, perfidious, disloyal, traitorous, treasonable, treacherous, renegade, recreant, apostate, derelict, untrustworthy, inconstant, fickle.

unfaltering. **Syn.:** unhesitating, unwavering, unswerving, steadfast, firm.

unfamiliar. **Syn.:** unknown, strange, novel, unaccustomed, unacquainted.

unfasten. **Syn.:** see **undo.**

unfathomable. **Syn.:** immeasurable, abysmal, inscrutable, bottomless.

unfavorable. **Syn.:** inauspicious, unpropitious, discouraging, adverse, prejudicial, derogatory, hostile, inimical, malign. **Ant.:** see **favorable.**

unfeeling. **Syn.:** insensate, insensible, insentient, apathetic, impassive, stoic; callous, unsympathetic, uncompassionate, unkind, hard-hearted, heartless, stern, brutal, cruel.

Unfeeling implies indifference or coldness to what ordinarily excites pity, sympathy, etc.; *unsympathetic,* a lack of feeling with and for others; *callous,* that the feelings are hardened and insensible by nature or have become so through continued repression and indifference.

unfeigned. **Syn.:** unaffected, unassumed, sincere, genuine, real.

unfit. **Syn.:** unsuitable, inappropriate, improper, unmeet, unbecoming, unqualified, ineligible, incompetent, unworthy.

unfledged. **Syn.:** unfeathered, callow, inexperienced, immature.

unflinching. **Syn.:** see **undaunted.**

unfold. **Syn.:** spread out, expand, unroll, unfurl; disclose, reveal, divulge.

unforced. **Syn.:** unconstrained, spontaneous, voluntary, optional.

unforgiving. **Syn.:** implacable, unrelenting, relentless, hard.

unfortunate. **Syn.:** unlucky, unsuccessful, unhappy, disastrous, calamitous, ill-fated, ill-starred. **Ant.:** see **fortunate.**

unfounded. **Syn.:** baseless, groundless, vain, idle.

unfrequented. **Syn.:** see **lonely.**

unfriendly. **Syn.:** hostile, antagonistic, inimical, cold, distant, alienated, estranged. **Ant.:** see **friendly.**

unfruitful. **Syn.:** unproductive, infecund, unprolific, infertile, barren, sterile, effete. **Ant.:** see **fruitful.**

ungainly. **Syn.:** awkward, clumsy, gawky, uncouth, loutish, lumbering, ungraceful, uncourtly. See **awkward.**

ungenerous. **Syn.:** illiberal, stingy, grudging, miserly, parsimonious, uncharitable, narrow, mean. **Ant.:** see **generous.**

ungodly. **Syn.:** godless, impious, irreverent, profane, unrighteous, wicked, sinful. **Ant.:** see **godly.** See **irreligious.**

ungovernable. **Syn.:** see **unmanageable.**

ungraceful. **Syn.:** see **ungainly.**

unguarded. **Syn.:** unprotected, defenseless; careless, incautious, unwary, negligent.

unhallowed. **Syn.:** see **unholy.**

unhandy. **Syn.:** inconvenient, inaccessible, incommodious; awkward, clumsy, maladroit. **Ant.:** see **handy.**

unhappy. **Syn.:** unlucky, unfortunate, unfavorable, unpropitious, inauspicious; sad, sorrowful, downcast, cheerless, disconsolate, miserable, wretched; infelicitous, inappropriate, inapt. **Ant.:** see **happy.**

unharmed. **Syn.:** unhurt, uninjured, unimpaired, unscathed, inviolate, intact.

unhealthy. **Syn.:** sickly, delicate, frail, weak, ill, diseased; unhealthful, unwholesome, unsanitary, unhygienic, insalutary, insalubrious, pestilent, pestiferous, noxious. **Ant.:** see **healthy.**

unheeded. **Syn.:** unnoticed, disregarded, neglected, ignored.

unholy. **Syn.:** unconsecrated, unhallowed, ungodly, impious, profane, wicked, sinful, evil. **Ant.:** see **holy.**

unhurt. **Syn.:** see **unharmed.**

uniform. **Syn.:** invariable, unvarying, unchanging, equable, regular, undeviating, alike, homogeneous, constant. **Ant.:** variable, changing, diverse, heterogeneous. See **even.**

unify. **Syn.:** see **unite.**

unimaginative. **Syn.:** matter-of-fact, literal, prosaic, prosy, practical, unromantic. **Ant.:** see **imaginative.**

Unimaginative implies lack of imagination, especially such as hinders one from being inventive or creative or enjoying esthetic pleasures. *Matter-of-fact* implies inability to see or enjoy anything except the literal, ordinary, or tangible. The *unromantic* person is little stirred by love, nature, strangeness, or chivalrous adventure. The *prosaic* is uninspired, pedestrian, and commonplace; the *prosy* is dull and tiresome.

unimportant. **Syn.:** insignificant, immaterial, trivial, paltry, trifling, petty. **Ant.:** see **important.**

uninjured. **Syn.:** see **unharmed.**

unintentional. **Syn.:** undesigned, unpremeditated, accidental, fortuitous. **Ant.:** see **intentional.**

uninterested. **Syn.:** unconcerned, uninvolved, apathetic. Cf. **disinterested.**

uninteresting. **Syn.:** dull, tiresome, tedious, wearisome.

uninterrupted. **Syn.:** see **unceasing.**

union. **Syn.:** combination, amalgamation, consolidation, fusion, coalition, confederation, confederacy, league, merger; connection, conjunction, junction; harmony, agreement, concord, unison, unity. See **alliance.**

unique. **Syn.:** single, sole, only; unequaled, unmatched, unexampled, rare. See **single.**

unite. **Syn.:** combine, amalgamate, compound, blend, fuse, weld, incorporate, merge, consolidate, confederate, unify; connect, conjoin, join, couple, link, yoke, attach, annex. **Ant.:** disunite, separate, divide, disintegrate, dissolve, disperse, scatter; disconnect, disjoin, detach, unfasten, sever, sunder. See **join.**

unity. **Syn.:** oneness, singleness; harmony, concord, agreement, unison, concert.

universal. Syn.: see **common.**

universe. Syn.: cosmos, creation, world. See **earth.**

unjust. Syn.: unrighteous, iniquitous; inequitable, partial, unfair; undeserved, unmerited, unjustifiable. Ant.: see **just.**

unjustifiable. Syn.: see **unwarrantable.**

unkind. Syn.: unkindly, unsympathetic, ungracious, harsh, cruel, brutal. Ant.: see **kind,** a.

unknowingly. Syn.: unwittingly, unconsciously, unintentionally, inadvertently, ignorantly.

unknown. Syn.: obscure, nameless, inglorious, undistinguished, unrenowned, unhonored, unsung; incalculable, unascertained, unexplored.

unlawful. Syn.: illegal, illicit, illegitimate, unlicensed, contraband. Ant.: see **lawful.**

unlearned. Syn.: see **ignorant.**

unless. Syn.: except.

Unless and *except* are both used to introduce a qualifying idea. *Except* in older writers is sometimes found where *unless* would be used today: as, "*Except* a man be born again, he cannot see the kingdom of God." *Unless* is always a conjunction, introducing a conditional clause; *except* is now only a preposition and introduces a phrase containing an exception to some general statement.

unlettered. Syn.: see **ignorant.**

unlike. Syn.: dissimilar, different, diverse, variant, heterogeneous. Ant.: see **like,** a.

unlimited. Syn.: limitless, illimitable, boundless, unbounded, infinite; unrestricted, unconfined.

unlock, unloose. Syn.: see **undo.**

unlovely. Syn.: unattractive, homely, plain, unamiable, unpleasant, disagreeable. Ant.: see **lovely.**

unlucky. Syn.: unfortunate, unhappy, inauspicious, unpropitious, unsuccessful, untoward, ill-fated, luckless. Ant.: see **lucky.**

unmanageable. Syn.: refractory, intractable, unruly, fractious, ungovernable, unbridled, rampant, wild.

That is *unmanageable* which proper authority cannot control and direct. The *ungovernable* bursts the bounds of control through impetuosity or rage. *Intractable* applies to that which resists or balks at direction; *unruly*, to that which is hard to keep under restraint or law.

unmanly. Syn.: cowardly, weak, soft, effeminate, womanish, childish.

unmannerly. Syn.: see **uncivil.**

unmarried. Syn.: unwedded, single, celibate, bachelor.

unmeet. Syn.: see **unfit.**

unmerciful. Syn.: pitiless, unrelenting, cruel, inhuman, brutal, ruthless.

unmindful. Syn.: unheedful, heedless, regardless, careless, negligent, inattentive, unobservant, oblivious, forgetful. Ant.: see **mindful.**

unmistakable. Syn.: clear, manifest, obvious, patent, palpable, evident, unambiguous, unequivocal.

unmoved. Syn.: unshaken, firm; unruffled, unstirred, calm, dispassionate, impassive, indifferent, apathetic, stoical.

unnatural. Syn.: abnormal, aberrant, irregular, anomalous, monstrous; affected, assumed, feigned, artificial, forced, strained. Ant.: see **natural.** See **factitious.**

unnecessary. Syn.: dispensable, unessential, needless, useless, superfluous, redundant. Ant.: see **necessary.**

unneighborly. Syn.: unsociable, exclusive, distant, reserved, unaccommodating. Ant.: see **neighborly.**

unnerve. Syn.: weaken, enfeeble; discompose, upset.

unobtrusive. Syn.: see **unpretending.**

unpalatable. Syn.: unappetizing, unsavory, distasteful, disagreeable.

unpardonable. Syn.: unforgivable, inexpiable. Ant.: see **pardonable.**

unpleasant. Syn.: displeasing, disagreeable, unenjoyable, uncongenial, offensive, obnoxious, objectionable, odious, repellent. Ant.: see **pleasant.**

unprecedented. Syn.: unexampled, unequaled, unparalleled, unmatched, novel, new.

unprejudiced. Syn.: unbiased, impartial, fair, open-minded.

unpremeditated. Syn.: undesigned, unstudied, offhand, impromptu, extempore, spontaneous. See **extemporaneous.**

unpretending. Syn.: unpretentious, unassuming, unobtrusive, unostentatious, modest.

unprincipled. Syn.: see **unscrupulous.**

unproductive. Syn.: see **unfruitful.**

unprofitable. Syn.: unremunerative, fruitless, bootless, useless, futile, vain. Ant.: see **profitable.**

unpromising. Syn.: unpropitious, inauspicious, unfavorable, untoward.

unqualified. Syn.: unfit, incompetent, ineligible; absolute, unconditional, out-and-out. Ant.: see **qualified.** See **utter,** a.

unquenchable. Syn.: see **insatiable.**

unquestionable. Syn.: indisputable, incontrovertible, incontestable, indubitable, certain, positive, sure. Ant.: see **questionable.** See **indisputable.**

unravel. Syn.: disentangle, untangle, undo; unriddle, unfold, decipher, solve.

unreal. Syn.: artificial, sham, spurious, fictitious, imaginary, illusive, theoretical, impractical, visionary, ideal. Ant.: see **real.**

unreasonable. Syn.: irrational, senseless, foolish, silly, absurd; excessive, immoderate, exorbitant, unfair, unjust. Ant.: see **reasonable.** See **illogical.**

unrecognized. Syn.: unacknowledged, disregarded, ignored.

unrefined. Syn.: unpurified, crude, coarse; unpolished, uncultured, ill-bred, rude, boorish, vulgar, gross. Ant.: see **refined.**

unrelenting. Syn.: unyielding, obdurate, hard-hearted, harsh, cruel, unmerciful, merciless, pitiless. See **inflexible.**

unreliable. Syn.: untrustworthy, irresponsible, uncertain, fallible. Ant.: see **reliable.**

unremitting. Syn.: unceasing, incessant, constant, continued, persevering, indefatigable. See **continual.**

unreserved. Syn.: unrestricted, unlimited, unconditional, entire; open, frank, candid, outspoken.

unresisting. Syn.: see **passive.**

unrest. Syn.: unquietness, inquietude, restlessness, uneasiness.

unrestrained. Syn.: unrestricted, unconfined, unlimited, uncurbed, unbridled, unchecked.

unrighteous. Syn.: unholy, sinful, evil, wicked, iniquitous, vicious; unjust, inequitable, dishonest. Ant.: see **righteous.**

unrivaled. Syn.: see **unequaled.**

unroll. Syn.: unfold, unfurl, unwind, open.

unromantic. Syn.: see **unimaginative.**

unruly. Syn.: disobedient, refractory, indocile, insubordinate, froward, intractable, ungovernable. Ant.: submissive, obedient, docile, meek. See **unmanageable.**

unsafe. Syn.: insecure, precarious, hazardous, risky, dangerous, perilous. Ant.: see **safe.**

unsavory. Syn.: unpalatable, insipid, tasteless, vapid, stale; disagreeable, offensive. Ant.: see **savory.** See **malodorous.**

unscrupulous. Syn.: unprincipled, unconscientious, dishonest, dishonorable, knavish.

The *unprincipled* man is without principles or ethical standards in his conduct or action; the *unscrupulous* man is without scruples of conscience, and disregards, or has contempt for, such laws of right or justice as should restrain him in his actions.

unseasonable. Syn.: inopportune, untimely, premature, malapropos, inconvenient. Ant.: see **seasonable.**

unseemly. Syn.: see **improper.**

unseen. Syn.: unperceived, unobserved, unnoticed, invisible, concealed, secret.

unselfish. Syn.: disinterested, altruistic, magnanimous, charitable, liberal. Ant.: see **selfish.**

The *unselfish* person is not centered in his own affairs or welfare, and is regardful of others. The *disinterested* person is unbiased by personal interest or desire for personal gain. The *altruistic* person actively concerns himself in what will benefit others.

unsettle. Syn.: disorder, derange, upset, disconcert.

unsettled. Syn.: see **unstable.**

unshapely. Syn.: misshapen, deformed.

unshrinking. Syn.: unflinching, resolute, determined.

unsightly. Syn.: ugly, deformed, offensive, repulsive. See **ugly.**

unskilful. Syn.: awkward, clumsy, bungling, unhandy, maladroit, inexpert, untrained. Ant.: see **skilful.**

unsociable. Syn.: unamiable, uncompanionable, taciturn, morose. Ant.: see **sociable.**

unsophisticated. Syn.: artless, guileless, ingenuous, innocent, simple, gullible; unadulterated, pure, genuine. See **artless.**

unsound. Syn.: unhealthy, infirm, impaired, defective, imperfect; illogical, fallacious, sophistical. **Ant.:** see **sound,** *a.*

unsparing. Syn.: liberal, ungrudging, abundant, profuse; unmerciful, severe.

unspeakable. Syn.: unutterable, inexpressible, ineffable. See **inexpressible.**

unstable. Syn.: unsteady, insecure, unsettled, variable, wavering, vacillating, irresolute, inconstant. **Ant.:** see **steady, stable,** *a.*

That which is *unstable* is easily moved, shaken, or overthrown; that which is *unsteady* is infirm or shaky in position or movement; that which is *unsettled* is not fixed or determined.

unsteady. Syn.: see **unstable.**

unstudied. Syn.: see **unpremeditated.**

unsuccessful. Syn.: unprosperous, unfortunate, unlucky, unavailing, fruitless, futile. **Ant.:** see **successful.**

unsuitable. Syn.: unfit, inappropriate, incongruous, unseemly, improper, unbecoming. **Ant.:** see **suitable.**

unsurpassed. Syn.: see **unequaled.**

unsuspicious. Syn.: unsuspecting, credulous, gullible, unsophisticated.

unsympathetic. Syn.: see **unfeeling.**

unsystematic. Syn.: see **irregular.**

untangle. Syn.: see **unravel.**

untidy. Syn.: disorderly, littered, cluttered, slovenly, slatternly. **Ant.:** see **tidy.**

untie. Syn.: see **undo.**

untimely. Syn.: see **unseasonable.**

untiring. Syn.: tireless, unwearying, indefatigable, unceasing, unremitting.

untoward. Syn.: froward, perverse, wilful, contrary, refractory, intractable; inconvenient, awkward, unfortunate, unlucky. See **wayward.**

untrained. Syn.: see **undisciplined.**

untrue. Syn.: unfaithful, disloyal; untruthful, mendacious, lying, false, inaccurate, incorrect. **Ant.:** see **true, truthful.**

untrustworthy. Syn.: see **unreliable.**

untruth. Syn.: untruthfulness, mendacity; lie, falsehood, fib, equivocation. See **falsehood.**

untutored. Syn.: see **ignorant.**

unused. Syn.: disused, unemployed; unaccustomed, unhabituated, unfamiliar; new, fresh.

unusual. Syn.: uncommon, infrequent, unwonted, strange, singular, rare. **Ant.:** see **usual.**

unutterable. Syn.: see **inexpressible.**

unvarying. Syn.: see **uniform.**

unveil. Syn.: see **uncover.**

unwarrantable. Syn.: unjustifiable, indefensible, unjust, illegal.

That which is *unwarrantable* results from the taking of undue liberty, or lacks the sanction of proper authority; that which is *unjustifiable* cannot be vindicated by principles of right or justice; the *indefensible* is such that no defense or excuse for it can be produced.

unwary. Syn.: incautious, unguarded, careless, indiscreet. **Ant.:** see **wary.**

unwavering. Syn.: see **steadfast.**

unwearying. Syn.: see **untiring.**

unwell. Syn.: see **sick.**

unwholesome. Syn.: see **unhealthy.**

unwieldy. Syn.: unmanageable, cumbersome, ponderous, clumsy. See **bulky.**

unwilling. Syn.: averse, reluctant, disinclined, indisposed, loath. **Ant.:** see **willing.** See **averse.**

unwise. Syn.: injudicious, imprudent, indiscreet, foolish. **Ant.:** see **wise.**

unwittingly. Syn.: see **unknowingly.**

unworthy. Syn.: undeserving, worthless; unbecoming, unsuitable, unfit; discreditable, ignoble, base, mean. **Ant.:** see **worthy.**

unyielding. Syn.: unbending, inflexible, stiff, firm, resolute, obdurate, obstinate. **Ant.:** see **yielding.**

upbraid. Syn.: reproach, reprove, reprehend, censure, blame, chide, scold. See **scold.**

uphold. Syn.: see **support,** *v.*

upon. Syn.: see **over.**

upright. Syn.: erect, vertical, perpendicular, plumb; honest, honorable, straightforward, just, conscientious. See **righteous.**

That which is *upright* is in a position corresponding to that of a man standing up; *erect* emphasizes the straightness of position or posture; *vertical* especially suggests upward direction along the shortest line from the earth to a level above it; *perpendicular,* a frequently interchangeable term, is especially used in mathematics.

uprightness. Syn.: see **honesty.**

uprising. Syn.: see **insurrection.**

uproar. Syn.: tumult, disturbance, commotion, noise, clamor, din, racket, hubbub, hurly-burly. See **noise.**

uproot. Syn.: eradicate, deracinate, extirpate, exterminate.

upset. Syn.: overturn, overthrow, overset, capsize, invert; disarrange, disorder; discompose, disconcert, agitate, excite, perturb, unnerve. See **overturn.**

upshot. Syn.: outcome, issue, result, event, conclusion, consequence, effect.

urbane. Syn.: civil, courteous, suave. See **polite, bland.**

urbanity. Syn.: civility, courtesy, politeness, amenity, complaisance, affability, suavity.

urge. Syn.: press, impel, incite, spur, goad; importune, exhort, egg.

To *urge* is to try to persuade one to do or grant something desired, by argument or inducements; *press* is little different from *urge,* but suggests more of repetition and personal appeal; *exhort* implies earnest entreaty and appeal, often addressed to a large group; *egg,* persistent incitement to some action, especially of a reprehensible nature.

urgent. Syn.: urging, pressing, imperative, necessary; importunate, insistent, vehement.

usage. Syn.: use, treatment; practice, habit. See **custom.**

use, *n.* **Syn.:** employment, application, service, utilization, exploitation; usefulness, utility, avail, advantage, help, profit; necessity, exigency, need; usage, custom, practice, habit.

use, *v.* **Syn.:** employ, apply, utilize, exploit; practise, exercise; accustom, habituate, familiarize, inure; consume, exhaust, expend; treat, behave towards.

Use is the general word for making something serve one's purpose. *Employ* is more dignified, and often implies making definite or specific use of, or hiring for a particular purpose. A further distinction is that what is *used* often has depreciated or been diminished, sometimes completely consumed: as, a *used* automobile, a *used* candle, all the butter has been *used.* As applied to persons, *use* implies some selfish or sinister purpose: as, to *use* another to advance oneself. *Utilize* implies practical or profitable use.

useful. Syn.: serviceable, advantageous, helpful, profitable.

useless. Syn.: unserviceable, unavailing, ineffectual, futile, bootless, fruitless, profitless, unprofitable, valueless, worthless. See **unavailing.**

usual. Syn.: common, ordinary, general, prevailing, prevalent, wonted, accustomed, customary, everyday, conventional. **Ant.:** see **unusual.** See **habitual.**

usually. Syn.: see **often.**

usurp. Syn.: arrogate, appropriate, seize, take, assume. See **assume.**

utensil. Syn.: see **tool.**

utility. Syn.: usefulness, profitableness, service. See **advantage.**

utilize. Syn.: see **use,** *v.*

utmost. Syn.: furthest, extreme, last, uttermost, maximum, greatest.

utopian. Syn.: see **ideal,** *a.*

utter, *a.* **Syn.:** complete, entire, total, unqualified, absolute, sheer, stark, pure.

Utter expresses completeness, totality, or entirety: as, an *utter* stranger, fool, or failure. That which is *unqualified* is without any qualification or reservation: as, an *unqualified* success. That which is *absolute* is unconditioned, unlimited, or final; *sheer* (*literally* pure) and *stark* (*literally* strong) are used in much the same way: as, an *absolute* coward; *sheer* nonsense; *stark* madness.

utter, *v.* **Syn.:** speak, express, deliver, pronounce, articulate, enunciate.

Utter applies to the giving out of any vocal sound, as a sigh, word, shriek, exclamation; to *articulate* is to form by adjustment of the organs of speech intelligible sounds. *Pronounce* applies to units of speech: as, he cannot *pronounce* the letter 'r'; to *pronounce* a certain word; or, often, to solemn and formal utterance: as, to *pronounce* a sentence of death; to *pronounce* a benediction. *Enunciate* expresses careful utterance, in which each sound or word is made completely audible.

utterly. Syn.: completely, entirely, wholly, totally, absolutely, altogether.

V

vacancy. Syn.: emptiness, vacuity, vacuum, void; space, chasm, gap.

vacant. Syn.: empty, unfilled, void, devoid, destitute, uninhabited, unoccupied, untenanted; unemployed, disengaged, free, leisure, idle; blank, vacuous, inane. **Ant.:** filled, full, overflowing, packed, crammed, crowded, inhabited, tenanted; engaged, engrossed, busy.

As here discriminated, *vacant* implies emptiness of expression as from absence of thought or intelligence, which may, however, be but momentary: as, at the question a *vacant* look came over his face. *Vacuous* refers to an expressionless, characterless, or stupid appearance, especially as a natural or permanent characteristic; *inane* applies to what is silly, stupid, flat, or pointless: as, a *vacuous* stare; an *inane* remark. See *empty*.

vacate. Syn.: empty, evacuate, resign, relinquish, abdicate, quit, leave.

vacation. Syn.: intermission, recess, leisure, rest, holiday.

vacillate. Syn.: waver, oscillate, sway, hesitate, falter. See **hesitate.**

vacillation. Syn.: wavering, oscillation, fluctuation, changeableness, irresolution, indecision, uncertainty, inconstancy.

vacuous. Syn.: empty, vacant, void, unfilled; inane, blank, unexpressive, stupid. See **vacant.**

vagabond. Syn.: vagrant, wanderer, nomad, beggar, mendicant, tramp, hobo; rascal, rogue, knave, scamp.

Vagabond and *vagrant* are frequently interchangeable, but the former especially emphasizes the idea of idle or worthless living, often by trickery or disreputable means, whereas the latter suggests the idea of wandering or roving from place to place.

vagary. Syn.: whim, caprice, fancy, freak. See **caprice.**

vagrant. Syn.: see **vagabond.**

vague. Syn.: indefinite, indistinct, obscure, hazy, shadowy, dim, ambiguous, uncertain. **Ant.:** definite, specific, explicit, precise, exact.

vain. Syn.: empty, idle, frivolous, chimerical, delusive; ineffectual, futile, useless, unavailing, abortive, nugatory, fruitless, bootless, profitless, worthless; foolish, silly, trifling, trivial; conceited, egotistical, self-complacent, vainglorious, proud, arrogant, overweening. **Ant.:** real, substantial, sound; effective, useful, availing, potent, profitable; modest, meek, humble. See **unavailing.**

vainglorious. Syn.: boastful, vaunting, overweening, arrogant, pretentious, conceited, egotistical, proud.

vale. Syn.: see **valley.**

valiant. Syn.: valorous, gallant, courageous, dauntless, intrepid, daring, bold, heroic. See **brave.**

valid. Syn.: sound, effective, cogent, binding, legal, just, good.

valley. Syn.: vale, dale, glen, dell, dingle, hollow, ravine, clough, bottom, basin, defile, gorge, cañon.

valor. Syn.: bravery, courage, prowess, intrepidity, gallantry, heroism. See **bravery.**

valorous. Syn.: see **brave.**

valuable. Syn.: costly, expensive, precious, rare; profitable, serviceable, useful; estimable, esteemed, worthy. **Ant.:** valueless, worthless, trashy.

Valuable applies to whatever has value, but especially to what has considerable value, whether pecuniary or because of its usefulness, rarity, etc. That which is *precious* has a very high intrinsic value, or is very dear for its own sake, associations, or the like.

value, n. Syn.: worth, excellence, importance, utility. See **price.**

value, v. Syn.: rate, appraise; regard, esteem, prize. See **appreciate.**

vanish. Syn.: see **disappear.**

vanity. Syn.: emptiness, unreality, sham, folly; conceit, self-esteem, egotism, complacency, vainglory, ostentation. **Ant.:** see **humility.**

Vanity implies admiration for oneself and an excessive desire to be admired by others for one's personal accomplishments, appearance, or advantages. *Conceit* implies an overestimate or exaggeration of one's own abilities or attainments; *self-esteem*, a (sometimes unduly) favorable estimate of oneself. *Complacency* suggests (often annoying) self-satisfaction.

vanquish. Syn.: overcome, overpower, overthrow, defeat, rout, subdue, subjugate, prostrate, crush. See **conquer.**

vapid. Syn.: flat, insipid, tasteless; dull, uninteresting, mawkish. **Ant.:** fresh, sweet, sparkling; interesting, vivid, animated, lively. See **tasteless.**

variable. Syn.: changeable, mutable, unsteady, unstable, wavering, fluctuating, vacillating, fitful, fickle, inconstant. **Ant.:** see **invariable.**

variance. Syn.: variation, change; difference, disagreement, discord, dissension, controversy, dispute.

variegated. Syn.: varicolored, party-colored, polychrome, spotted, speckled, dappled, mottled, motley, checkered, piebald, pied.

variety. Syn.: diversity, multiplicity; assortment, collection, group; kind, sort, class, species.

Variety denotes a succession of changes, or intermixture of different things, and is always used of more than two; *diversity* implies an essential or marked difference, and may be used of two things: as, there was a *variety* of movements in the dance; a *variety* of articles in a show-window; there was considerable *diversity* in the testimony of the two witnesses; the *diversity* in religious beliefs.

various. Syn.: varied, diversified, diverse, different, several, sundry, divers, manifold, numerous, multifarious.

vary. Syn.: change, alter, modify, diversify; differ, disagree, deviate, swerve, depart. See **change,** *v.*

vassal. Syn.: liegeman, liege, feudatory, subject, retainer, dependent, follower, servant, bondman, slave.

vast. Syn.: immense, extensive, immeasurable, enormous, huge, colossal, gigantic, stupendous, tremendous, prodigious. See **extensive.**

vault, n. Syn.: see **tomb.**

vault, v. Syn.: leap, jump, bound, spring. See **jump.**

vaunt. Syn.: see **boast.**

veer. Syn.: see **turn,** *v.*

vegetable. Syn.: legume, plant.

vegetate. Syn.: see **grow.**

vehemence. Syn.: violence, fury, impetuosity, ardor, fervor, fire.

vehement. Syn.: violent, furious, impetuous, passionate, energetic, vigorous, ardent, fervid.

Vehement suggests the impetuosity and intensity of strong enthusiasm or passion; *violent* implies fiery feeling or destructive action; *furious* suggests the fierce violence of anger or rage.

veil. Syn.: cover, conceal, mask, disguise, screen, shroud, cloak.

vein. Syn.: blood-vessel, capillary, artery; lode, seam; streak, stripe, marking; strain, trace, touch, tinge, shade, dash.

velocity. Syn.: see **quickness.**

venal. Syn.: purchasable, mercenary, hireling. See **mercenary.**

vend. Syn.: see **sell.**

vendetta. Syn.: see **quarrel,** *n.*

vendible. Syn.: salable, marketable, merchantable.

venerable. Syn.: see **old.**

venerate. Syn.: revere, reverence, honor, esteem, respect. See **adore.**

veneration. Syn.: see **reverence,** *n.*, **respect,** *n.*

vengeance. Syn.: punishment, retribution, retaliation. See **revenge,** *n.*

venial. Syn.: excusable, pardonable, forgivable, trivial, slight. See **pardonable.**

venom. Syn.: poison, virus; spite, malice, malignity, rancor, hate. See **poison.**

venomous. Syn.: poisonous, baneful, noxious, virulent; spiteful, malignant.

vent, n. Syn.: hole, opening, aperture, air-hole; outlet, exit, passage; utterance, expression, voice.

vent, v. Syn.: emit, utter, express, declare, voice. See **emit.**

venture, n. Syn.: undertaking, enterprise, adventure, speculation, hazard, risk.

venture, *v.* **Syn.:** hazard, risk, stake, dare.

Venture emphasizes the act of doing something which involves risk; *dare,* the state of mind that makes one willing to meet danger: as, he *ventured* into deep water; he *dared* to do what he knew was right.

venturesome. Syn.: adventurous, venturous, daring, bold, fearless, intrepid, hardy, temerarious. **Ant.:** timid, timorous, faint-hearted, cowardly. See **bold.**

veracious, veracity. Syn.: see **truthful, truth.**

verbal. Syn.: spoken, oral, literal. See **oral.**

verbiage. Syn.: see **verbosity.**

verbose. Syn.: wordy, diffuse, prolix, long-winded. **Ant.:** terse, concise, succinct.

verbosity. Syn.: verbiage, wordiness, diffuseness, repetition, prolixity, redundance, redundancy, tautology, pleonasm, circumlocution, periphrasis.

Verbosity denotes a superfluous use of words to express an idea. *Verbiage* implies a minimum of thought and a maximum of words. *Prolixity* implies wearisome length as a result of trivial or needless details. *Tautology* denotes the repetition of the same idea in different words, without added emphasis.

verdant. Syn.: see **green.**

verdict. Syn.: see **decision.**

verge. Syn.: edge, border, margin, brink, boundary, limit. See **rim, edge.**

verify. Syn.: confirm, substantiate, corroborate, authenticate, attest, prove.

verity. Syn.: see **truth.**

vernacular. Syn.: see **language.**

versatile. Syn.: see **clever.**

verse. Syn.: line, stanza, stave, couplet; poetry, versification.

Verse is primarily a single metrical line, but the word is often extended to include a stanza (as, the third and fourth *verses* of a hymn), or a particular variety of metrical arrangement (as, blank *verse*), or the writings of an author in verse (as, the *verses* of Austin Dobson). In the Bible it may indicate a short numbered section, even in prose, printed as a paragraph. A *stanza* is a combination of lines commonly bound together by a particular rime scheme, forming in most cases one of a series which constitutes a poem. *Stave* is a less usual word for a metrical unit or stanza. A *couplet* is two successive lines of verse (usually iambic pentameter) united by rime. See **poetry.**

versed. Syn.: conversant, familiar, acquainted, practised, skilled, proficient.

Versed implies intimate knowledge or a degree of skill, as from long association or experience with something; *conversant* implies less familiarity or acquaintance: as, *versed* in the art of war; to be *conversant* with the facts.

version. Syn.: see **translation.**

vertex. Syn.: apex, top, crown, summit.

vertical. Syn.: perpendicular, upright, plumb. **Ant.:** horizontal, flat, level, oblique. See **upright.**

very. Syn.: extremely, exceedingly, greatly, highly, excessively, surpassingly.

vessel. Syn.: see **boat.**

vestige. Syn.: see **trace.**

vestigial. Syn.: see **rudimentary.**

vesture. Syn.: see **clothes.**

vex. Syn.: annoy, irritate, provoke, harass, nettle, fret, chafe, gall, trouble, bother, plague, tease, torment, tantalize; afflict, distress, grieve.

To *vex* is to cause a feeling approaching anger by small, often repeated, irritations. To *annoy* is to disturb the peace of a person as by unwelcome interruptions or intrusions. That which *nettles* pricks or stings into resentment. That which *frets* gnaws at one's sensibilities. That which *chafes* afflicts as by irritating rubbing. That which *galls* moves to wrath and rebellion.

vexation. Syn.: irritation, exasperation, indignation, chagrin. See **anger, mortification, annoyance.**

vexatious. Syn.: annoying, disturbing, irritating, provoking, troublesome, bothersome, afflictive.

vibrate. Syn.: swing, oscillate, librate; quiver, tremble, shake, throb, thrill; waver, fluctuate, vacillate. See

vibration. Syn.: swinging, oscillation, libration; quiver, tremulousness.

vice. Syn.: sin, iniquity, depravity, corruption, licentiousness, immorality; fault, defect, blemish, imperfection. See **failing.** Cf. **crime.**

vicinage. Syn.: see **neighborhood.**

vicinity. Syn.: see **neighborhood.**

vicious. Syn.: depraved, wicked, licentious, immoral, profligate; pernicious, blameworthy, reprehensible, bad; faulty, defective, imperfect, incorrect; refractory, unruly, unmanageable, ugly. See **corrupt.**

vicissitude. Syn.: see **change,** *n.*

victor. Syn.: conqueror, vanquisher, champion, master, winner.

victory. Syn.: triumph, conquest, success. **Ant.:** defeat, failure, disappointment, retreat, rout.

victuals. Syn.: see **food.**

vie. Syn.: strive, contend, compete.

view, *n.* **Syn.:** sight, look, survey, inspection, examination, scrutiny; scene, prospect, perspective, vista, landscape, scenery, panorama; picture, sketch, photograph; judgment, opinion, impression, conception, notion, theory; purpose, aim, intention, intent.

View is more general than the following words, referring to whatever lies open to sight. *Prospect* suggests a sweeping and often distant view, as from a place of vantage. *Scene* suggests an organic unity in the details such as is to be found in a picture. *Vista* suggests a long narrow view, as along an avenue between rows of trees.

view, *v.* **Syn.:** see, behold, look at, witness, contemplate, survey, scan, inspect, examine, scrutinize; regard, consider.

vigilant. Syn.: wakeful, awake, alert, observant, attentive, circumspect, careful, wary, cautious. **Ant.:** sleepy, drowsy, dull, inattentive, neglectful, negligent, careless, heedless, unwary, incautious. See **watchful.**

vigor. Syn.: strength, health, robustness, bloom, lustiness; energy, force, might, power.

vigorous. Syn.: strong, hale, robust, sturdy, lusty, hardy, hearty, sound; active, energetic, strenuous, vehement. **Ant.:** weak, frail, delicate, infirm, feeble, enervated, potent, sluggish, lazy. See **active.**

vile. Syn.: worthless, mean, ignoble, abject, despicable, miserable, wretched; base, wicked, iniquitous, vicious, villainous; outrageous, atrocious. See **mean.**

vilify. Syn.: depreciate, disparage, traduce, calumniate, malign, vilipend.

villa. Syn.: see **house.**

village. Syn.: see **town.**

villain. Syn.: scoundrel, rascal, malefactor, reprobate, miscreant, blackguard, scamp.

A *villain* is a base man bent on the undoing of others to serve his own ends. A *miscreant* is a vile wretch. A *malefactor* is an evildoer. A *reprobate* is one lost to all good doing.

villainous. Syn.: base, vile, wicked, wretched, infamous.

villainy. Syn.: depravity, infamy, baseness.

vindicate. Syn.: defend, justify, assert.

excellence, merit, worth; goodness, morality, uprightness, rectitude, integrity, probity, purity, chastity, virginity. See **goodness.**

virtuous. Syn.: good, upright, righteous, worthy, exemplary; moral, pure, chaste, continent. **Ant.:** see **immoral.**

virulence. Syn.: poisonousness, venom, deadliness; bitterness, rancor, malignity. See **acrimony.**

virulent. Syn.: poisonous, venomous, noxious; bitter, spiteful, malignant, acrimonious.

virus. Syn.: see **poison.**

visage. Syn.: see **face.**

viscid, viscous. Syn.: see **sticky.**

visible. Syn.: discernible, perceivable, perceptible, apparent, manifest, clear, patent, plain, obvious, evident.

vision. Syn.: seeing, sight; apparition, phantom, phantasm, dream.

visionary, n. **Syn.:** dreamer, enthusiast.

visionary, a. **Syn.:** fanciful, imaginative, unpractical, quixotic; chimerical, utopian, ideal, imaginary, unreal. **Ant.:** unimaginative, matter-of-fact, practical, pragmatical. See **imaginary.**

visit. Syn.: visitation, call, sojourn, stay.

visitant. Syn.: see **visitor.**

visitor. Syn.: visitant, caller, guest.

A *visitor* comes to see a person or stay in a place, often for some time, for the enjoyment of social intercourse, the pursuit of business, sight-seeing, etc. *Visitant*, a somewhat unusual word, except in ornithology, now refers especially to supernatural beings and official, often religious, visitors: as, a ghostly *visitant*; he was sent as a *visitant* to the capitals of Europe. A *caller* comes for a short, often formal visit; a *guest* is any one who enjoys another's hospitality, especially meals and lodging, and so the word is extended to include those who pay for their accommodation at a hotel.

vi... ...rn.: see **view,** n.

...m.: impair, invalidate, spoil, contaminate, pol-...debase, demoralize, deprave. See **taint,** v.

...abuse, rail at, berate, revile, upbraid, ...le.

...see **abuse,** n.

...ive, opprobrious, scurrilous.

..., lively, sprightly, frolicsome,

...life.

..., lively, fresh, striking, ...intense. **Ant.:** spirit-...aded. See **graphic.**

...lexicon, nomen-

...pation.

...profession, ...alled to it ...ike. An ...om his ...is an ...m to ...w,

by itself from the nature of the circumstances or conditions: as, a *voluntary* contribution; *spontaneous* applause.

voluptuous. Syn.: see **sensual.**

voracious. Syn.: ravenous, greedy, avid, insatiable, gluttonous. See **rapacious.**

Voracious means that a person or animal eats, or is disposed to eat, a great deal, without reference to the degree of hunger; *ravenous* implies hunger of an extreme sort, especially as shown in a violent, uncontrollable craving for food: as, a *voracious* child; a *ravenous* beast.

vortex. Syn.: see **whirlpool.**

vouchsafe. Syn.: see **condescend.**

vow. Syn.: see **pledge,** n.

voyage. Syn.: cruise, sail. See **journey.**

vulgar. Syn.: common, ordinary, plebeian, low-born, ignoble; unrefined, inelegant, low, coarse, ribald. **Ant.:** aristocratic, high-born, refined, cultured, polite. See **common.**

vulgarism. Syn.: vulgarity, impropriety.

W

waddle. Syn.: see **walk,** v.

wade. Syn.: ford.

wager. Syn.: stake, bet, hazard, risk, venture.

wages. Syn.: pay, hire, compensation, emolument, earnings. See **pay,** n.

waggery. Syn.: waggishness, jesting, facetiousness, pleasantry, drollery.

waggish. Syn.: frolicsome, sportive, roguish, jocular, jocose, humorous, facetious, droll. See **jocose.**

wagon. Syn.: cart, van, wain, truck, dray, lorry. Cf. **carriage.**

wail. Syn.: see **moan.**

wait, n. **Syn.:** waiting, tarrying, lingering, pause, delay, stop, halt; ambush, ambuscade.

wait, v. **Syn.:** await, stay, tarry, linger, rest, remain, abide.

Wait usually implies staying for a limited time and for a definite purpose, as in expectation of the happening of an event or the arrival of a person. *Tarry* is a somewhat archaic word for wait, but it sometimes suggests lingering or indicates a brief pause in one's journey.

waive. Syn.: relinquish, surrender, forgo, abandon, forsake. See **forgo.**

wake. Syn.: awake, waken, rouse, arouse, revive.

wakeful. Syn.: sleepless, insomnious, restless, vigilant, alert. See **watchful.**

walk, n. **Syn.:** stroll, promenade, march, tramp, hike, constitutional; gait, step, carriage; sidewalk, mall, avenue; range, sphere, province.

walk, v. **Syn.:** step, stride, stroll, saunter, ambulate, perambulate, promenade, pace, march, tramp, hike, plod, trudge, tread, stalk, strut, mince, trip, tiptoe, shuffle, shamble, slouch, toddle, waddle, hobble, limp, hop, halt, reel, stagger, gad, gallivant, trapes.

Walk is the general word; *pace* suggests steady, monotonous, or measured steps as of one completely lost in thought or impelled by some distraction. *Stride* suggests long steps, often with implication of pompousness, eagerness, or impatience; *stalk*, stiff, high steps, and heavy tread, often with implication of haughtiness, disdain, or anger. *Plod* implies a heavy, laborious, weary walk; *trudge* describes a spiritless, but usually steady and doggedly persistent, walk. *Toddle* refers to the short, unsteady steps of a child; *waddle* implies short steps with ungainly or awkward movement of the body from side to side, as of a duck.

...ll. **Syn.:** partition, rampart, battlement, breastwork, ...lwark.

...low. **Syn.:** welter, grovel, flounder, roll.

... **Syn.:** see **pale.**

...d. **Syn.:** see **rod.**

...er. **Syn.:** ramble, roam, rove, range, stray, stroll, ...nder, saunter, straggle, itinerate, peregrinate, migrate; ...t, digress, swerve, diverge, deviate.

...*wander* is to walk or proceed without purpose or re-...; to *stray* is to depart from a prescribed path or region, ...y or figuratively: as, the children *wandered* down the ...d *strayed* into the woods; children sometimes *stray* ...me; to *stray* from the course of honor.

...er. **Syn.:** rover, nomad, pilgrim, wayfarer, itiner-...regrinator, vagrant, vagabond, gipsy, tramp.

se and often desperate person who plots the
to accomplish his own selfish or even criminal
eant is a detestable person inimical to society.
is any one who is guilty of evil or criminal acts.
e is one who has utterly abandoned himself to wrong-

us. **Syn.:** wicked, unprincipled, knavish; mean,
ned, vile. See **nefarious.**

ny. **Syn.:** wickedness, rascality, turpitude, baseness,
my; atrocity, crime.

dicate. **Syn.:** defend, justify, sustain, clear. See
ssert.

Vindicate emphasizes the idea of clearing from accusation,
censure, suspicion, or dishonor; *justify*, of proving a person or
thing to be in accordance with right, justice, or reason.

vindictive. Syn.: revengeful, retaliatory, implacable,
resentful, spiteful, rancorous, malevolent. **Ant.:** forgiving,
merciful, compassionate. See **revengeful.**

violate. Syn.: break, infringe, transgress, contravene, disregard, disobey; desecrate, dishonor, profane, defile, deflower,
debauch, ravish, outrage.

violation. Syn.: infringement, infraction, transgression,
breach; desecration, profanation, ravishment, rape.

violence. Syn.: vehemence, impetuosity, fierceness, fury,
passion, rage; violation, injury, attack, assault.

violent. Syn.: vehement, impetuous, fierce, furious, passionate, turbulent, boisterous; intense, extreme, poignant,
severe, great. See **vehement.**

virago. Syn.: see **shrew.**

virile. Syn.: manly, masterful, forceful, vigorous, strong.
Ant.: womanish, puerile, weak, impotent. See **masculine.**

virtually. Syn.: practically, substantially, essentially,
actually, really.

virtue. Syn.: power, strength, force, potency, efficacy;

vixen. **Syn.:** see **shrew.**

vocabulary. **Syn.:** glossary, dictionary, clature.

vocation. **Syn.:** avocation, hobby. See **occu**

Vocation denotes one's regular occupation or often with the suggestion that one chose it or was c because of special fitness, adaptability, or the l *avocation* is an interest which one pursues apart fr regular vocation, for the pleasure it affords. A *hobby* avocation which so possesses a person as often to cause hi pursue it extravagantly.

vociferate. **Syn.:** clamor, shout, scream, roar, bello bawl. See **cry,** *v.*

vociferous. **Syn.:** clamorous, bawling, blatant, noisy turbulent, obstreperous. See **loud.**

vogue. **Syn.:** see **fashion.**

void, *a.* **Syn.:** empty, vacant, unfilled, unoccupied; destitute, devoid, lacking; ineffectual, invalid, null. See **destitute, empty.**

void, *v.* **Syn.:** vacate, leave, quit; emit, eject, discharge, evacuate, excrete, egest; invalidate, nullify, annul.

volatile. **Syn.:** airy, lively, variable, changeable, unstable, fickle, inconstant, flighty, giddy.

volatility. **Syn.:** lightness, frivolity, instability, fickleness. See **levity.**

volition. **Syn.:** will, choice, preference, determination, decision. See **will,** *n.*

voluble. **Syn.:** see **fluent, talkative.**

volume. **Syn.:** see **size.**

voluntary. **Syn.:** willing, spontaneous, unconstrained, unforced, free, volitional; intentional, deliberate, purposed. See **gratuitous.**

That which is *voluntary* is done by choice and intention, and without compulsion; that which is *spontaneous* arises

wandering. Syn.: rambling, roaming, roving, nomadic, wayfaring, itinerant, migratory, errant; digressive, deviating, devious, excursive.

wane. Syn.: decrease, decline, fall, sink, fade, fail.

want, *n.* **Syn.:** deficiency, lack, dearth, scarcity, scarceness, inadequacy, insufficiency, scantiness, shortness, paucity, absence, default; privation, need, destitution, poverty, penury, indigence, straits; necessity, requirement, desideratum. **Ant.:** abundance, plenty, plenitude, copiousness, wealth, riches, luxury. See **lack, poverty.**

want, *v.* **Syn.:** lack, need, require; desire, crave, long for.

wanting. Syn.: deficient, defective; lacking, missing, absent.

wanton. Syn.: undisciplined, unbridled, unruly, wild; reckless, malicious; luxuriant, exuberant, rank; playful, sportive, frolicsome; dissolute, licentious, immoral, unchaste, lewd.

war. Syn.: warfare, hostilities, strife, conflict, belligerence, militancy.

warble. Syn.: see **sing.**

ward. Syn.: guard, protect, defend, watch; fend, parry, avert, repel.

Ward, parry, and *fend* all indicate a defensive effort, but *ward* more commonly suggests raising an obstruction, *parry* turning aside, especially a thrust, and *fend* interposing interference or maintaining a distance.

warden. Syn.: warder, guardian, guard, custodian, keeper, watchman.

warehouse. Syn.: see **depository.**

wares. Syn.: see **property.**

warfare. Syn.: see **war.**

warlike. Syn.: bellicose, belligerent, hostile, military, soldierly. See **martial.**

warm. Syn.: lukewarm, tepid, heated, hot, incalescent; glowing, flushed, sunny, sultry; affectionate, cordial, hearty, enthusiastic, zealous, fervent, fervid, ardent, passionate, vehement, fiery, peppery; brisk, strenuous, arduous.

warmth. Syn.: heat, glow; cordiality, geniality, heartiness, enthusiasm, zeal, earnestness, fervency, fervor, ardor, passion, vehemence.

warn. Syn.: caution, admonish, apprise, inform, notify. See **advise.**

warning. Syn.: caution, admonition, advice.

warp. Syn.: turn, twist, bend, contort, distort; pervert, bias.

warrant, *n.* **Syn.:** security, surety, guaranty, guarantee, warranty; voucher, commission, license; authority, authorization, sanction, justification, right.

warrant, *v.* **Syn.:** guarantee, insure, assure; affirm, attest, vouch for; authorize, sanction, justify.

Warrant and *guarantee* are etymologically the same, and are frequently interchangeable. To *warrant* is to give a pledge or assurance that something is safe or genuine; to *guarantee* is to make something sure or certain by binding oneself to replace it or refund its price if it is not as represented: as, to *warrant* the soundness of a horse; *warranted* silverware; to *guarantee* a watch.

wary. Syn.: cautious, alert, watchful, vigilant, guarded, circumspect, careful, prudent. **Ant.:** see **unwary.** See **cautious.**

wash. Syn.: cleanse, clean, bathe, lave, rinse, launder, scrub, mop, swab.

Wash is the general word for cleansing by water or other liquid; *bathe* refers especially to washing the body or some part of it; *lave* is now used poetically for wash or bathe.

waspish. Syn.: see **irascible.**

wassail. Syn.: see **carousal.**

waste, *n.* **Syn.:** desert, wilderness, wild; desolation, devastation, destruction; diminution, decay, decline, emaciation, consumption; refuse, rubbish, trash, leavings, remnants, offal, chaff, dross, scum, lees, dregs; squandering, prodigality, dissipation.

waste, *a.* **Syn.:** desert, uninhabited, wild, desolate, devastated, pillaged, ravaged; untilled, unproductive; refuse, rejected, worthless, useless, unused, unnecessary, superfluous.

As applied to land, *waste* implies vast, unproductive, often desolate places; *wild* applies to that which is not cultivated or inhabited, though perhaps luxuriant with vegetation; *desert* implies barrenness accompanied by dryness and heat.

waste, *v.* **Syn.:** devastate, ravage, pillage, sack, plunder, strip, ruin, destroy; squander, misspend, dissipate, fritter away; diminish, impair, consume; decline, decay, pine, wither, dwindle, molder. See **ravage.**

wasteful. Syn.: devastating, destructive, ruinous; squandering, lavish, prodigal, improvident, unthrifty, thriftless. See **extravagant.**

watch. Syn.: wakefulness, vigil; attention, notice, vigilance, outlook; watcher, watchman, sentry, sentinel, guard, guardsman, picket, patrol, vedette.

watchful. Syn.: sleepless, wakeful, vigilant, wide-awake, observant, alert, attentive, heedful, careful, wary, circumspect, cautious.

Watchful implies careful observation and preparedness; *vigilant,* which suggests more of immediate necessity, implies continued, active, and keen watchfulness; *alert* denotes quick, wide-awake, or roused attention.

watchword. Syn.: password, countersign, shibboleth, parole, open sesame.

wave, *n.* **Syn.:** undulation, billow, swell, surge, breaker, surf, ripple, whitecap.

Wave is the general word for a ridge or swell on the surface of the water. *Billow,* often a poetical word, denotes a great, rolling wave; *breaker,* a wave breaking or about to break upon the shore or upon rocks. *Surge* denotes a long sweeping rush of water; *surf* is the collective name for breakers, especially in reference to bathing. *Ripple* applies to the smallest kind of a wave, such as is caused by a stone thrown in a pool.

wave, *v.* **Syn.:** undulate, fluctuate, flutter, float, sway, rock; swing, brandish, flourish.

waver. Syn.: wave, sway, flutter, quiver, flicker, oscillate, vacillate, falter, hesitate. See **hesitate.**

wavy. Syn.: undulating, undulatory, crinkled, curly, kinky.

wax. Syn.: see **grow.**

way. Syn.: course, route, road, roadway, highroad, highway, thoroughfare, street, avenue, boulevard, driveway, bridle-path, pathway, path, track, trail, pass, passage, lane, alley, channel; distance, space, interval; headway, progress, advance; manner, mode, method, fashion, style, custom, practice; respect, point, particular.

Way is the generic word for any kind of a passage or route from one place to another. A *path* is a way for passing on foot. A *trail* is a rough way made or worn through woods, or across mountains, prairies, or other untraveled regions. A *lane* is a narrow way, especially one inclosed between buildings, fences, hedges, trees, etc. A *road* is a (public) way, broad and good enough for vehicles. A *street* is a road in a village, town, or city, especially as lined with houses. An *alley* is a narrow street or footway, especially at the rear of a row of houses. An *avenue* is a prominent street, often one bordered by fine residences and impressive buildings. A *boulevard* is a beautiful broad street, lined with rows of stately trees, especially used as a promenade. A *highway* is a main public road, much traveled as the ordinary route between two cities or great centers of population or industry.

wayfarer. Syn.: see **traveler.**

wayward. Syn.: wilful, untoward, capricious, perverse, contrary, headstrong, stubborn, obstinate, disobedient, froward, unruly, refractory, intractable.

The *wayward* person turns towards ways that suit himself, whether or not they are what others expect or desire of him. *Wilful* suggests a stubborn persistence in doing what one wishes, especially in opposition to those whose wishes ought to be respected or whose commands ought to be obeyed. The *capricious* man follows the whim or preference of the moment. The *perverse* person is unreasonably or obstinately intractable or contrary, often with the intention of being disagreeable. *Froward* is a literary or somewhat archaic word, except as applied to the wilfulness of children.

weak. Syn.: bending, yielding, pliant, pliable, soft, tender, fragile, resistless; frail, delicate, weakly, feeble, infirm, impotent, decrepit, debilitated, enervated, emasculated; vacilating, wavering, unstable, irresolute, weak-kneed; unsound, ineffective, inadequate, illogical, inconclusive, unsustained, unsatisfactory, lame; diluted, thin, insipid. **Ant.:** see **strong.**

Weak denotes the absence of strength in any form: as, a *weak* body, mind, character. *Feeble* indicates a pervading, often lamentable weakness. *Infirm* suggests the unsoundness, in body or mind, of age or disease. *Decrepit* describes the decayed state and faltering weakness of old age. *Impotent* describes one rendered by nature or circumstances powerless or ineffective.

weaken. Syn.: enfeeble, debilitate, enervate, undermine, sap, exhaust, deplete; lessen, diminish, lower, reduce, impair, minimize, invalidate.

To *weaken* is to lessen or reduce in any way the strength, power, influence, or quality of a person or thing: as, to *weaken* the body or mind, a solution, the force of an argument. *Enfeeble, debilitate,* and *enervate* are restricted almost wholly to persons. *Enfeeble* applies especially to the lessening of mental or bodily strength, as by sickness or old age; *debilitate* suggests impairment of health, as from excesses or disease; *enervate* implies a loss of energy or vitality such as is the effect of a hot climate.

weakness. Syn.: fragility, frailness, feebleness, infirmity, debility; peculiarity, idiosyncrasy, foible, defect, deficiency; vacillation, irresolution, indecision. See **failing.**

wealth. Syn.: riches, possessions, assets, goods, property, money, affluence, opulence, fortune, prosperity, plenty, luxury, profusion, abundance. **Ant.:** poverty, indigence, beggary, penury, destitution, need, want, scarcity. See **riches.**

wealthy. Syn.: rich, affluent, opulent, prosperous, well-to-do, moneyed, capitalistic.

weapon. Syn.: firearm, gun, rifle, musket, revolver, pistol, sword, rapier, saber, dagger, stiletto, knife, dirk, spear, lance, javelin, club, cudgel, bludgeon, staff; shield, buckler.

weariness. Syn.: see **fatigue,** *n.*

wearisome. Syn.: fatiguing, tiresome, tedious, irksome, monotonous, humdrum, dull, prosy, prolix. See **tiresome.**

weary, *a.* **Syn.:** wearied, fatigued, tired, exhausted, jaded, fagged, spent, worn, bored, ennuyé.

weary, *v.* **Syn.:** fatigue, tire, exhaust, jade, fag, bore, annoy. See **tire.**

weave. Syn.: interlace, entwine, mat, braid, plait; contrive, fabricate, construct.

wedding, wedlock. Syn.: see **marriage.**

weep. Syn.: sob, cry, bewail, lament.

weigh. Syn.: see **consider.**

weight. Syn.: heaviness, ponderousness, gravity, burden, load; importance, consequence, moment, significance, influence, power.

weighty. Syn.: heavy, ponderous, massive, onerous, burdensome; important, momentous, serious, grave, impressive, influential, authoritative. **Ant.:** light, feathery, buoyant, porous; unimportant, insignificant, trivial, trifling. See **heavy.**

weird. Syn.: uncanny, unearthly, eerie, mysterious, strange.

That is *weird* which is suggestive of the fateful intervention of supernatural influences in human affairs. That is *uncanny* which is mysterious because of its apparent defiance of the laws established by experience. That is *unearthly* which seems by its nature to belong to another world. That is *eerie* which, by suggesting the ghostly, makes one's flesh creep.

welcome, *n.* **Syn.:** greeting, salutation.

welcome, *a.* **Syn.:** agreeable, gratifying, pleasant, acceptable.

welfare. Syn.: prosperity, success, happiness, well-being, weal.

well, *n.* **Syn.:** spring, fountain, cistern.

well, *a.* **Syn.:** healthy, hale, sound, hearty.

well-bred. Syn.: see **genteel.**

welter. Syn.: see **wallow.**

wet, *a.* **Syn.:** moist, damp, humid, rainy, drizzly, soaked, drenched.

wet, *v.* **Syn.:** moisten, dampen, drench, saturate, soak, steep, dip.

To *wet* is to moisten in any manner with water or other liquid. *Drench* suggests wetting completely as by a downpour. *Saturate* implies wetting to the limit of absorption. To *soak* is to keep covered or partially covered by a liquid for a longer or shorter time. To *steep* is to permeate anything with (especially heated) moisture or liquid, for the purpose of imbuing it with or extracting from it certain properties.

wharf. Syn.: see **pier.**

wheedle. Syn.: cajole, flatter, blandish, coax, entice, inveigle. See **coax.**

where. Syn.: whither.

Where is used with both verbs of rest and verbs of motion: as, *where* is the book? *where* are you going? *Whither* is used with verbs of motion only, and is now confined almost wholly to literary use.

wherefore. Syn.: see **therefore.**

whet. Syn.: see **sharpen.**

which. Syn.: see **who.**

while, *v.* **Syn.:** spend, consume, pass, beguile.

while, *conj.* **Syn.:** when, as long as, whilst, whereas, though, although.

whim. Syn.: whimsy, fancy, caprice, vagary, quirk, notion, humor, crotchet, maggot. See **caprice.**

whimper. Syn.: see **whine.**

whimsical. Syn.: capricious, notional, changeable, crotchety, freakish; fanciful, fantastic, grotesque, odd. See **fanciful, eccentric.**

whine. Syn.: whimper, pule, complain.

Whine implies a protracted, plaintive sound expressive of complaint or distress; *whimper,* a low, broken, often gently stifled, whining sound, indicative of the same feeling. *Pule* especially refers to the whining or whimpering of a child.

whip, *n.* **Syn.:** scourge, lash, switch, ratan, cat-o'-nine-tails, horsewhip, crop, quirt, rawhide, knout, kurbash.

whip, *v.* **Syn.:** scourge, lash, flog, flagellate, beat, thrash, trounce, switch, spank, punish, chastise; overcome, conquer, defeat, outdo.

whir. Syn.: buzz, hum, whiz.

whirl. Syn.: rotate, revolve, twirl; spin, gyrate, pirouette.

whirlpool. Syn.: maelstrom, vortex, eddy.

whirlwind. Syn.: see **wind,** *n.*

whit. Syn.: see **bit.**

white. Syn.: snowy, hoary, hoar, bleached, blanched, pallid, pale, ashen. **Ant.:** see **black.**

whiten. Syn.: bleach, blanch, etiolate, decolor, decolorize.

whither. Syn.: see **where.**

whiz. Syn.: see **whir.**

who. Syn.: that, which.

As relative pronouns, *who* is used of persons, though occasionally of the higher animals; *which* is used only of animals or things, except archaically of persons; *that* is used of persons, animals, or things, except after a preposition, where only *who* or *which* can stand. If a relative clause merely adds an idea or incidentally describes, *who* or *which* generally introduces the relative clause, which is set off by commas: as, this man, *who* came to lecture, had had a varied experience; his house, *which* was just built, burned down. If a relative clause limits, restricts, or defines, *who, which,* or (especially) *that* is used, without commas: as, the man *who* (or *that*) came to lecture had had a varied experience; the house *that* is for sale is on this street.

whole, *n.* **Syn.:** entirety, totality, total, aggregate, sum. **Ant.:** part, portion, piece, fraction.

whole, *a.* **Syn.:** hale, healthy, well, sound, healed; unimpaired, uninjured, unbroken, intact, perfect, entire, complete, total, integral. See **sound,** *a.,* **complete,** *a.*

wholesome. Syn.: healthful, salubrious, nourishing, nutritious, invigorating, salutary, beneficial. See **healthy.**

whoop. Syn.: see **cry.**

whore. Syn.: see **prostitute.**

wicked. Syn.: bad, evil, sinful, unrighteous, ungodly, godless, impious, profane, unprincipled, immoral, profligate, corrupt, depraved, iniquitous, heinous, infamous, vicious, vile. See **criminal, bad.**

wickedness. Syn.: evil, sin, immorality, corruption, iniquity, infamy, villainy, rascality, knavery, vice, crime.

wide. Syn.: broad, extensive, spacious, vast, ample, large, comprehensive. **Ant.:** see **narrow.**

Wide and *broad* are very often interchangeable, but *wide* especially applies to that of which the length is much greater than the width, as a ribbon or road, or to that which is to be passed through, as a door or aperture. *Broad* is more emphatic and applies to things of considerable or great width, especially to surfaces or lateral extension: as, *broad* acres of meadow land.

wide-awake. Syn.: see **watchful.**

wiggle. Syn.: wag, waggle, jiggle, shake; wriggle, squirm, twist.

wild. Syn.: undomesticated, untamed, feral, ferine, savage, uncivilized, barbarous; uncultivated, uninhabited, desert, waste; self-willed, ungoverned, unrestrained, riotous, turbulent, wayward, wanton; boisterous, stormy, tempestuous; reckless, rash, extravagant, impracticable; fantastic, queer, grotesque, bizarre; enthusiastic, eager, excited. **Ant.:** see **tame.** See **waste,** *a.*

wilderness. Syn.: desert.

wile. Syn.: trick, stratagem, ruse. See **artifice.**

wilful. Syn.: voluntary, deliberate, intentional; self-willed, headstrong, obstinate, stubborn, perverse, contrary, disobedient, unruly, refractory, intractable. See **wayward.**

will, *n.* **Syn.:** wish, desire, pleasure, inclination, choice, preference; volition, determination, decision, resolution.
Will denotes the power of choice, or the object or course of conduct which as a result of that power is selected or determined upon. *Volition* has much the same meaning as *will*, but stresses the outward manifestation of the faculty.

will, *v.* **Syn.:** wish, desire, want, like; determine, purpose, intend; bequeath, devise, leave. See **shall.**

willing. Syn.: disposed, inclined, minded, ready, desirous. See **voluntary.**

willowy. Syn.: see **flexible, lithe.**

wily. Syn.: crafty, artful, subtle, sly, insidious, designing, intriguing, tricky, foxy. See **cunning, artful.**

win. Syn.: get, gain, obtain, secure, acquire, earn, achieve, attain, reach; succeed, prevail. See **get.**

wince. Syn.: shrink, flinch, recoil, start. See **shrink.**

wind, *n.* **Syn.:** air, breeze, zephyr, draft, flurry, gust, flaw, squall, gale, blast, storm, tempest, whirlwind, hurricane, cyclone, tornado, typhoon, simoon, monsoon.

wind, *v.* **Syn.:** bend, turn, curve, crook, meander; roll, coil, twine, twist, encircle, wreathe; insinuate, worm.

winding. Syn.: curving, meandering, circuitous, serpentine, labyrinthine, sinuous, tortuous, flexuous, twisted, spiral.
Winding suggests that a thing curves continuously, often irregularly: as, a *winding* stairway; a *winding* path. That which is *sinuous* repeatedly bends or turns; as applied to bodily forms the word suggests grace and suppleness. That which is *tortuous* is unpleasantly crooked or full of twists.

wink. Syn.: blink, nictate, nictitate; twinkle, sparkle, flash; connive.

winning. Syn.: getting, gaining, etc. (see **win**); engaging, taking, captivating, charming, attractive, winsome.

wisdom. Syn.: sagacity, prudence, discretion, judgment, knowledge, learning, sapience, erudition. See **knowledge.**

wise. Syn.: sagacious, judicious, prudent, discreet, discerning, sensible, philosophical, learned, sapient, sage, erudite. **Ant.:** see **foolish.**
Wise suggests a balance of the mind and a combination of knowledge, experience, and reflection leading to soundness of judgment; *sage* suggests the wisdom of age and experience; *sapient* is a learned word, and especially suggests the wisdom of learning.

wish. Syn.: see **desire.**

wit. Syn.: wisdom, intelligence, sagacity; mind, intellect, understanding, sense; humor, drollery, facetiousness, waggishness, repartee.
Wit is a purely intellectual though often spontaneous manifestation of cleverness in discovering pleasing but occult or farfetched analogies between things really unlike and expressing them quickly in brief, diverting, and sometimes sharp observations or remarks. *Humor* consists in the bringing together of certain incongruities which arise naturally from situation or character, frequently so as to illustrate some fundamental absurdity in human nature or conduct.

witch. Syn.: sorceress, enchantress, hag, crone.

witchcraft. Syn.: witchery, sorcery, magic, necromancy. See **magic.**

witchery. Syn.: sorcery, magic, enchantment, spell, fascination, charm.

with. Syn.: see **by.**

withdraw. Syn.: pull out, remove, recall, retract, recant, disavow; retire, retreat. See **depart.**

wither. Syn.: shrivel, shrink, dry, fade, decay, decline, languish.

withhold. Syn.: see **keep,** *v.*

withstand. Syn.: see **oppose.**

witness, *n.* **Syn.:** see **spectator.**

witness, *v.* **Syn.:** see **see.**

witty. Syn.: facetious, droll, clever, original, sparkling, brilliant. **Ant.:** dull, uninteresting, commonplace, trite, jejune.

wizard. Syn.: magician, sorcerer, enchanter, necromancer, thaumaturge, conjurer, juggler.

wizardry. Syn.: magic, sorcery, necromancy, thaumaturgy, legerdemain.

woe. Syn.: grief, sorrow, distress, tribulation, wretchedness, misery, affliction, calamity. See **grief.**

woeful. Syn.: sorrowful, mournful, distressed, wretched, miserable, afflicted.

woman. Syn.: see **female,** *n.*

womanish, womanly. Syn.: see **feminine.**

wonder. Syn.: marvel, prodigy, miracle, portent; surprise, astonishment, amazement, bewilderment, admiration, awe.

wonderful. Syn.: wondrous, marvelous, miraculous, portentous, prodigious, surprising, astonishing, amazing, startling, extraordinary, remarkable, phenomenal, unique, curious, strange.
That which is *wonderful* is so above the common or usual as to excite wonder. The *marvelous* is wonderful to such a degree that it baffles understanding. That which is *prodigious* is so great in its size or effect as to astonish and amaze; that which is *phenomenal* is so exceptional as to deserve widespread attention. The *extraordinary* so far exceeds the ordinary as to be surprising and memorable.

wont. Syn.: see **habit, custom.**

woo. Syn.: see **court.**

wood. Syn.: see **forest.**

woodland. Syn.: see **forest.**

woody. Syn.: wooded, sylvan, bosky; wooden, ligneous.

woolly. Syn.: fleecy, downy, nappy, lanate, flocculent, pubescent.

word. Syn.: vocable, term, phrase, expression; utterance, remark, saying; password, watchword, countersign, signal, order, command; warrant, promise, parole; information, intelligence, tidings, news, message, report. See **news.**
Word is generic, and is the spoken or written symbol of an idea, conception, or thing. A *term* is especially a word of exact or specific meaning: as, a medical *term*. A *phrase* is a combination of words, grammatically without a finite verb, and constituting a dependent unit in a sentence: as, a participial or prepositional *phrase*. *Expression* is the general name for the words and form in which an idea is conveyed.

wordiness, wordy. Syn.: see **verbosity, verbose.**

wording. Syn.: see **diction.**

work, *n.* **Syn.:** exertion, effort, labor, toil, drudgery, employment, occupation, business, industry, diligence, assiduity; task, undertaking, enterprise, project, job, deed, product, achievement, feat, performance. **Ant.:** idleness, sloth, trifling, dalliance, relaxation, recreation, leisure, ease, repose, rest, vacation.
Work is the general word for exertion of the body or mind in performing or accomplishing something; it may be either easy or hard. *Labor* especially denotes hard, physical work as in farming or industry. *Toil* suggests wearying or exhausting labor; *drudgery*, unrelieved and dispiriting work, especially of a menial or servile kind.

work, *v.* **Syn.:** labor, toil, strive, drudge, slave, moil, grub; operate, manipulate, manage, handle; make, form, fashion, shape, mold, embroider; do, perform, execute, accomplish, effect, produce; ferment, effervesce.

worker. Syn.: workman, artisan, artificer, craftsman, handicraftsman, journeyman, mechanic, operative, laborer, toiler, drudge, hack, peon, coolie, roustabout. **Ant.:** idler, loafer, shirker, sluggard, drone, truant, dabbler, dilettante.

world. Syn.: universe, cosmos, macrocosm, globe, earth; sphere, realm, domain; mankind, humanity, society. See **earth.**

worldly. Syn.: mundane, earthly, terrestrial, terrene, sublunary, temporal, secular, lay, profane, carnal. See **earthly.**

worry, *n.* **Syn.:** anxiety, apprehension, solicitude, concern.

worry, *v.* **Syn.:** harass, annoy, trouble, vex, torment, plague, pester, tease; fret, fume. See **tease.**

worship, *n.* **Syn.:** honor, homage, reverence, adoration, idolizing, idolatry.

worship, *v.* **Syn.:** honor, venerate, revere, reverence, adore, glorify, idolize, deify.
Worship refers especially to rendering homage to a Divine Being by outward forms or in customary places; it is metaphorically used in reference to persons: as, he *worshiped* the ground she walked on. *Adore* is now little used religiously of veneration for God, but rather expresses great love for persons: as, to *adore* a child. *Idolize*, properly expressing worship of an idol, implies unreasoning or immoderate love, admiration, or veneration: as, to *idolize* a hero; to *idolize* children.

worth. Syn.: worthiness, excellence, merit, usefulness, value. See **merit, price.**

worthless. Syn.: useless, valueless, good-for-nothing, trashy, mean, contemptible, scurvy.

worthy. Syn.: deserving, meritorious, estimable, excellent, exemplary; becoming, suitable, fitting, proper. Ant.: see **unworthy.** See **estimable.**

wound, *n.* Syn.: injury, hurt, cut, stab, laceration, lesion, trauma.

wound, *v.* Syn.: injure, hurt, pain, maim, disable.

wrangle, *n.* Syn.: dispute, altercation, squabble, brawl. See **dispute,** *n.,* **quarrel,** *n.*

wrangle, *v.* Syn.: argue, dispute, bicker, altercate, jangle, squabble, brawl. See **dispute,** *v.,* **quarrel,** *v.*

wrap. Syn.: infold, inclose, envelop, cover, muffle, swathe, swaddle.

Wrap is the common word for inclosing in a covering; *swathe* especially suggests wrapping by winding round and round; *envelop* implies a complete covering, often by mist, fog, flame, etc.

wrath. Syn.: ire, rage, resentment, indignation, dudgeon. See **anger.**

wrathful. Syn.: angry, irate, furious, raging, incensed, resentful, indignant.

wreath. Syn.: garland, chaplet, festoon, crown.

wreck, *n.* Syn.: destruction, ruin, demolition, devastation, havoc, shipwreck, debris.

wreck, *v.* Syn.: destroy, ruin, overthrow, demolish, raze, scatter, strand, shipwreck. See **spoil,** *v.*

wrench. Syn.: wring, twist, wrest, extort; strain, sprain.

wrest. Syn.: see **extract.**

wretch. Syn.: outcast, pariah, caitiff, miscreant, poltroon, rascal, knave, rogue, scoundrel, villain, reprobate.

A *wretch* is a person in a profoundly unhappy or miserable condition, or one addressed or referred to (sometimes jestingly) with condemnation or pity; a *caitiff* is a cowardly, base, and despicable creature; a *pariah* is a degraded and despised outcast.

wretched. Syn.: miserable, dejected, distressed, afflicted, woeful, woebegone, forlorn, unhappy; despicable, contemptible, base, vile, mean, worthless, bad; paltry, sorry, shabby, pitiful.

Wretched refers to a condition of extreme unhappiness, affliction, or distress, especially as outwardly apparent: as, *wretched* hovels. *Miserable* refers more to the inward feeling of unhappiness or distress; *pitiful* to that which excites pity or compassion. All these words have a lighter application to what is unworthy, inadequate, poor, mean, or contemptible, in which they agree with *sorry*: as, a *wretched* performance; a *miserable* failure; a *pitiful* attempt; in a *sorry* plight.

wretchedness. Syn.: see **affliction.**

wriggle. Syn.: see **wiggle.**

wring. Syn.: twist, squeeze, pinch; wrench, wrest, exact, extort.

wrinkle, *n.* Syn.: crease, fold, corrugation, pucker, rumple, crinkle; notion, fancy, device.

wrinkle, *v.* Syn.: crease, fold, corrugate, rumple, crumple, pucker, crinkle, cockle.

To *wrinkle* is to put creases, ridges, or folds in; to *rumple* is to wrinkle through inadvertence, carelessness, or rough treatment; to *crumple* is to wrinkle by crushing together.

write. Syn.: inscribe, superscribe, subscribe, record, scribble, scrawl.

writer. Syn.: penman, copyist, scribe, scrivener, amanuensis, calligrapher, clerk, secretary, correspondent, author, novelist, essayist, biographer, poet, hack.

writing. Syn.: handwriting, penmanship, chirography, calligraphy, hand.

wrong, *n.* Syn.: injustice, injury, hurt, pain, offense, grievance, tort; wrong-doing, misdoing, evil, wickedness, sin, vice, immorality, iniquity, trespass, transgression, misdemeanor, delinquency, dereliction.

wrong, *a.* Syn.: awry, amiss, perverse, faulty, erroneous, inaccurate, inexact, incorrect, false, untrue, mistaken; bad, evil, wicked, sinful, immoral, iniquitous, base, criminal, blameworthy, reprehensible, inequitable, unjust, crooked; improper, inappropriate, unsuitable, unfit; reverse, inside. Ant.: see **right,** *a.*

That which is *wrong* deviates from what is moral, correct, suitable, etc. *Amiss*, used predicatively, is generally a milder word than wrong and indicates that which is wide of the mark set by ideals of conduct, propriety, custom, etc. That which is *faulty* contains defects, blemishes, imperfections, or failings. That which is *erroneous* contains errors or mistakes.

wrong, *v.* Syn.: injure, harm, maltreat, abuse, oppress, cheat, defraud, dishonor.

wrong-doer. Syn.: sinner, transgressor, malefactor, offender, culprit, criminal, crook.

wrought. Syn.: worked, elaborated, finished.

Y

yacht. Syn.: see **boat.**

yard. Syn.: inclosure, court, courtyard, quadrangle, garden, croft, garth, close.

yawn. Syn.: gape.

To *yawn* is to open the mouth wide while taking a deep breath; the action suggests weariness, drowsiness, or a lack of fresh air. To *gape* is sometimes to yawn, sometimes to open the mouth in amazement or vacuity of mind.

yea. Syn.: see **yes.**

yearn. Syn.: see **long.**

yearning. Syn.: see **desire,** *n.*

yell. Syn.: see **cry.**

yellow. Syn.: golden, amber, buff, saffron, écru, fallow, luteous, tawny, fulvous, ocherous, jaundiced, sallow; jealous, envious; cowardly, dishonorable, mean.

yes. Syn.: yea, aye.

All these words express affirmation or assent. *Yes* is the common term; *yea* is used in sacred, solemn, or formal style; *aye* is especially used in deliberative bodies to express affirmative vote.

yet. Syn.: see **but.**

yield, *n.* Syn.: production, produce, crop, harvest, fruit, income, result. See **harvest.**

yield, *v.* Syn.: produce, bear, furnish, supply, render, pay, return; give, afford, confer, grant, allow; relinquish, surrender, cede, waive, resign; submit, succumb, capitulate.

To *yield* is to concede under some degree of pressure, if not absolute compulsion; *surrender* implies the complete abandonment of resistance that has proved futile; *cede* usually refers to the formal transference of territory or rights by treaty, either as a result of force or for a return.

yielding. Syn.: plastic, pliant, flexible; unresisting, compliant, tractable, submissive, docile. Ant.: see **unyielding.**

yoke, *n.* Syn.: see **pair.**

yoke, *v.* Syn.: see **unite.**

young. Syn.: immature, undeveloped, puerile, juvenile, youthful, boyish, adolescent; inexperienced, green. Ant.: see **old.**

Young is the general word for that which is undeveloped and in process of growth: as, a *young* child. *Youthful* is generally used in a good sense suggesting the characteristics of youth, such as vigor, ardor, enthusiasm, or hopefulness: as, *youthful* sports or energy. *Adolescent* applies to the characteristics of the change of life from childhood to maturity. *Juvenile* suggests the immaturity of youth, and if derogatory, it is not strongly so: as, *juvenile* reading; the poem was a *juvenile* performance. *Boyish* is used in a good sense of those to whom it properly belongs, but is used with some deprecation with reference to an adult: as, *boyish* enthusiasm, wonder, or conduct. *Puerile* always expresses marked contempt for what is childish or silly: as, a *puerile* attempt to be funny.

youth. Syn.: youthfulness, youngness, juvenility, adolescence, puberty, nonage, minority, teens; lad, boy, juvenile, youngster, stripling, minor.

youthful. Syn.: young, immature, juvenile, adolescent, girlish, boyish, puerile, childish, callow. Ant.: see **old.** See **young.**

Z

zany. Syn.: merry-andrew, buffoon, mimic. See **clown.**

Zany frequently denotes one who amuses by making ludicrous and crude attempts to mimic the antics and tricks of a professional clown; when used to-day the word often implies merely a silly fellow. *Merry-andrew*, a word little used now, describes one who entertains by comic antics, gestures, postures, or the like. *Buffoon* suggests the employment of rude, low, or coarse means of amusing.

zeal. Syn.: fervor, warmth, enthusiasm, earnestness, passion, devotion. See **ardor.**

zealot. Syn.: enthusiast, devotee, fanatic, bigot, partizan.

Zealot is usually disparagingly used of one who is overzealous or immoderately partizan. *Fanatic* is applied to one who goes to unreasonable, sometimes violent extremes, in maintaining his beliefs (often religious) and carrying out the practices which they dictate. An *enthusiast* is one whose thoughts and energies are given up, sometimes completely, to a doctrine or activity. A *bigot* is so under the tyranny of his own belief that he is hostile to all others.

zealous. Syn.: ardent, fervid, fervent, enthusiastic, earnest, eager, passionate, impassioned, devoted. **Ant.:** indifferent, apathetic, cool, neutral, impartial.

zenith. Syn.: apex, summit, acme, culmination. See **top.**

zero. Syn.: cipher, naught, nothing.

zest. Syn.: flavor, relish, taste, enjoyment, enthusiasm, gusto. See **relish.**

zone. Syn.: girdle, belt, clime, region.

Zone is applied to a (usually imaginary) band or girdle encircling something, as in anatomy or geography, or to a defined region of land or sea marked off for certain purposes: as, the torrid *zone*; a parcel-post or submarine *zone*. **Belt** may also be an encircling band, but the word is often used of a broad and loosely defined strip marked by certain characteristics which distinguish it from the surrounding area: as, the corn or wheat *belt*.

ABBREVIATIONS

IN COMMON USE

(For Abbreviations of the U. S. Federal Agencies see page 2420.)

Many of the abbreviations listed below occur in two or more forms varying slightly, especially with respect to the use of capital or small letters, points of punctuation, and hyphens; in most cases of this kind a single common form has been selected for entry here.

Some abbreviations are used to represent both the singular and the plural of the respective words, but the plural is also often indicated by adding s (before the period) to the abbreviation of the singular. A number of plural forms in very common use or of unusual formation have been noted.

The Roman numerals, I, V, X, etc., are used either without or with a period following; when used after names, as of kings, they are commonly written and printed with a period following, although sometimes without. The Arabic ordinal forms, 1st, 2d (or 2nd), 3d (or 3rd), 4th, etc., are not properly abbreviations, and take no period following.

For other abbreviations used in this book, see the lists at the beginning of the book and at the head of the various supplements.

The principal abbreviations used in the explanations in this list are as follows:—

Brit. . . . British	F. . . . . French	It. . . . Italian	pl. . . . plural
E. . . . . English	G. . . . German	L. . . . . Latin	Sp. . . . Spanish.
	Gr. . . . Greek	Pg. . . . Portuguese	

A

a (no period) *ante* (L.), before.
A (no period) argon.
a. about; accepted; acre; active; adjective; afternoon; aged; alto; *annus* (L.), year; answer; *ante* (L.), before; are (*metric system*); assists (*baseball*); at.
A. Academician; Academy; Alberta (Canada); America; American; Artillery.
A. A. Associate in, or of, Arts.
A. A. A. Agricultural Adjustment Administration; Amateur Athletic Association; American Automobile Association.
A. A. A. L. American Academy of Arts and Letters.
A. A. A. S. American Association for the Advancement of Science.
A. A. C. *anno ante Christum* (L.), in the year before Christ. [General.
A. A. G. Assistant Adjutant-
A. A. P. S. S. American Academy of Political and Social Science.
a. a. r. against all risks.
A. A. S. Fellow [L. *Socius*] of the American Academy of Arts and Sciences.
A. A. S. S. Fellow [L. *Socius*] of the American Antiquarian Society. [Union.
A. A. U. Amateur Athletic
ab. about; [times] at bat (*baseball*).
A. B. able-bodied seaman; *Artium Baccalaureus* (L.), Bachelor of Arts.
abbr. or **abbrev.** abbreviated; abbreviation.
A. B. C. Argentina, Brazil, and Chile.
A. B. C. F. M. American Board of Commissioners for Foreign Missions.

abd. abdicated.
Aber. or **Aberd.** Aberdeen.
A. B. F. M. American Board of Foreign Missions.
ab init. *ab initio* (L.), from the beginning.
abl. ablative.
Abp. Archbishop.
abr. abridged; abridgment.
abs. abstract.
A. B. S. American Bible Society.
absol. absolute; absolutely.
abs. re. *absente reo* (L.), the defendant being absent.
abst. abstract.
abt. about.
Abys. Abyssinia.
ac. account. [nating current.
a. c. account current; alter-
A. C. Alpine Club; *ante Christum* (L.), before Christ; Army-Corps; Athletic Club; Automobile Club.
A. C. A. Associate of the Institute of Chartered Accountants (Brit.).
acad. academy.
acc. acceptance; account; accusative.
accel. *accelerando* (It.), increasing in speed (*music*).
acct. account.
act. active.
actg. acting.
ad. (pl. *ads.*) advertisement.
a. d. after date; *ante diem* (L.), before the day.
A. D. *anno Domini* (L.), in the year of our Lord.
A. D. C. Aide-de-Camp.
Adel. Adelaide (Australia).
ad eund. *ad eundem* [*gradum*] (L.), to the same degree or rank.
ad fin. *ad finem* (L.), to or at the end.
ad inf. *ad infinitum* (L.), to infinity.
ad init. *ad initium* (L.), to or at the beginning.

ad int. *ad interim* (L.), in the meantime.
adj. adjective.
Adj. or **Adjt.** Adjutant.
Adj.-Gen. or **Adjt.-Gen.** Adjutant-General.
ad lib. *ad libitum* (L.), at pleasure, as one wishes, to the amount desired.
ad loc. *ad locum* (L.), to or at the place.
adm. admission.
Adm. Admiral; Admiralty.
admix. administratrix.
admr. administrator.
admrx. or **admx.** administratrix.
adv. ad valorem; adverb; adverbial; adverbially; *adversus* (L.), against; advertisement; advertising; advocate.
Adv. Advent.
ad val. ad valorem.
advt. advertisement.
æ. *ætatis* (L.), of age, aged.
A. E. & P. Ambassador Extraordinary and Plenipotentiary.
A. E. F. American Expeditionary Forces.
A. E. I. O. U. *Austriæ est imperare orbi universo* (L.), it is given to Austria to rule the whole earth.
æt. or **ætat.** *ætatis* (L.), of age, aged.
AF. or **A. F.** Anglo-French.
A. F. A. M. or **A. F. & A. M.** Ancient Free and Accepted Masons.
A. F. C. Air Force Cross (Brit.).
aff. affectionate; affirmative; affirmatively.
afft. affidavit.
Afgh. or **Afghan.** Afghanistan.
A. F. L. or **A. F. of L.** American Federation of Labor.

A. F. M. Air Force Medal (Brit.).
A. F. of L. See *A. F. L.*
Afr. Africa; African.
aft. afternoon.
Ag (no period) *argentum* (L.), silver.
A. G. Adjutant-General; Agent-General; *Aktiengesellschaft* (G.), stock company (*business*); Attorney-General.
a. g. b. any good brand.
agcy. agency.
agric. agricultural; agriculture.
agt. agent.
A. H. *anno Hejiræ* (L.), in the year of or from the Hejira [A.D. 622].
a. h. l. *ad hunc locum* (L.), to or at this place.
A. H. S. *anno humanæ salutis* (L.), in the year of human salvation.
a. h. v. *ad hanc vocem* (L.), at this word.
A. I. American Institute.
A. I. A. American Institute of Architects.
A. I. G. Adjutant-Inspector-General; Assistant Inspector-General.
A. I. N. A. Associate of the Institution of Naval Architects (Brit.).
Al (no period) aluminium.
AL. or **A. L.** Anglo-Latin.
Ala. Alabama.
A. L. A. American Library Association; Authors' League of America.
Alas. Alaska.
Alb. Albania; Albert.
ald. alderman.
Alex. Alexander.
Alf. Alfred.
alg. algebra.
Alg. Algeria; Algernon; Algiers.
alt. alternate; altitude; alto.
Alta. Alberta (Canada).

Am. America; American.

A. M. Albert Medal (Brit.); *anno mundi* (L.), in the year of the world; *ante meridiem* (L.), before noon; *Artium Magister* (L.), Master of Arts; *Ave Maria* (L.), Hail, Mary.

A. M. A. American Medical Association.

Amb. Ambassador.

A. M. D. G. *ad majorem Dei gloriam* (L.), for the greater glory of God.

A. M. E. African Methodist Episcopal.

Amer. America; American.

A. M. I. C. E. Associate Member of the Institution of Civil Engineers (Brit.).

A. M. I. E. E. Associate Member of the Institution of Electrical Engineers (Brit.).

amp. amperage; ampere.

Amst. Amsterdam.

amt. amount.

an. *anno* (L.), in the year.

A. N. A. Associate of the National Academy.

anal. analogous; analogy; analysis; analytic; analytical.

anat. anatomical; anatomy.

anc. ancient.

And. Andrew.

Ang. Anglicè.

Angl. Anglican; Anglicè.

ann. *anni* (L.), years; annual; annuity.

annot. annotated.

anon. anonymous.

ans. answer.

ant. antiquary; antonym.

Ant. Anthony; Antigua.

anth. anthology.

Anth. Anthony.

anthrop. or anthropol. anthropological; anthropology.

antiq. antiquary; antiquities; antiquity.

Antw. Antwerp.

a. o. account of.

A. O. F. Ancient Order of Foresters.

A. O. H. Ancient Order of Hibernians.

aor. aorist.

A. O. S. S. Fellow [L. *Socius*] of the American Oriental Society.

a. p. assessment paid.

A. P. Associated Press.

A. P. A. American Pharmaceutical Association; American Philological Association; American Protective Association.

Apoc. Apocalypse; Apocrypha.

Apocr. Apocrypha.

app. apparent; apparently; appendix; appointed.

appar. apparent; apparently.

approx. approximately.

appx. appendix.

Apr. April.

A. P. R. C. *anno post Romam conditam* (L.), in the year after the founding of Rome [in 753 B.C.].

A. P. S. American Peace Society; American Philosophical Society.

apt. (pl. *apts.*) apartment.

apx. appendix.

aq. *aqua* (L.), water.

aq. dest. *aqua destillata* (L.), distilled water.

A. Q. M. G. Assistant Quartermaster-General.

Ar (no period) argon.

ar. arrival; arrived; arrives.

Ar. Arabic.

a. r. all risks.

A. R. *anno regni* (L.), in the year of the reign.

A. R. A. Associate of the Royal Academy.

Arab. Arabia; Arabic.

Aram. Aramaic.

A. R. A. M. Associate of the Royal Academy of Music.

A. R. C. American Red Cross.

arch. archaic; archaism; archipelago; architect; architectural; architecture.

Arch. Archibald.

archæol. archæological; archæology.

Archd. Archdeacon; Archduke.

A. R. C. M. Associate of the Royal College of Music.

A. R. C. O. Associate of the Royal College of Organists.

A. R. C. S. Associate of the Royal College of Surgeons.

A. R. E. Associate of the Royal Society of Painter-Etchers.

Arg. Argentina.

A. R. I. B. A. Associate of the Royal Institute of British Architects.

arith. arithmetic; arithmetical.

Ariz. Arizona.

Ark. Arkansas.

Arm. Armenian; Armoric.

Armor. Armoric.

arr. arranged; arrival; arrived; arrives.

A. R. R. *anno regni Regis*, or *Reginæ* (L.), in the year of the reign of the King, or the Queen.

A. R. S. A. Associate of the Royal Scottish Academy.

art. article; artillery; artist.

A. R. W. S. Associate of the Royal Water-Colour Society.

As (no period) arsenic.

As. Asia; Asiatic.

AS. or A. S. Anglo-Saxon.

a. s. at sight.

A. S. *anno salutis* (L.), in the year of salvation.

A. S. A. American Statistical Association.

A. S. A. A. Associate of the Society of Accountants and Auditors (London).

A. S. C. E. American Society of Civil Engineers.

A. S. G. B. Aëronautical Society of Great Britain.

A. S. M. E. American Society of Mechanical Engineers.

assd. assigned.

assn. association.

assoc. associate; associated; association.

asst. assistant.

A. S. S. U. American Sunday-School Union.

astr. astronomer; astronomical; astronomy.

astrol. astrologer; astrological; astrology.

astron. astronomer; astronomical; astronomy.

Atl. Atlantic.

ats. at suit of.

A. T. S. American Tract Society.

att. attorney.

attrib. attribute; attributive; attributively.

atty. attorney.

at. wt. atomic weight.

Au (no period) *aurum* (L.), gold.

A. U. C. *ab urbe condita* or *anno urbis conditæ* (L.), in the year since the founding of the city [of Rome, in 753 B.C.].

aud. auditor.

Aud.-Gen. Auditor-General.

Aufl. *Auflage* (G.), edition.

aug. augmentative.

Aug. August; Augustus.

Aus. Austria; Austrian.

Ausg. *Ausgabe* (G.), edition.

Aust. Austria; Austrian.

Aust.-Hung. Austria-Hungary.

Austral. Australasia; Australasian; Australia; Australian.

Auth. Ver. Authorized Version.

aux. or auxil. auxiliary.

av. avenue; average; avoirdupois.

a. v. ad valorem; *annos vixit* (L.), he, or she, lived [so many] years.

A. V. Artillery Volunteers; Authorized Version.

A. V. C. Army Veterinary Corps.

avdp. avoirdupois.

ave. avenue.

avoir. avoirdupois.

A. W. L. absent with leave.

A. W. O. L. absent without leave.

ax. axiom.

Azer. Azerbaijan.

B

B (no period) boron.

b. base; base, or baseman (*baseball*); bass; book; born; brother; by.

B. *Band* (G.), volume; Baron; Bay.

Ba (no period) barium.

B. A. Bachelor of Arts; British Academy; British America; British Association.

Bac. Mus. Bachelor of Music.

bact. bacteriology.

B. Agr. Bachelor of Agriculture.

Bah. Bahamas.

bal. balance.

Bal. Baluchistan.

Balt. or Balto. Baltimore.

Baluch. Baluchistan.

bap. baptized.

Bapt. Baptist.

bar. barometer; barometric; barrel.

Bar. Baruch (Apocrypha).

B. Ar. Bachelor of Architecture.

Barb. Barbados.

B. Arch. Bachelor of Architecture.

barr. barrister.

Bart. Baronet.

B. A. S. Bachelor of Applied Science.

batt. battalion; battery.

batty. battery.

Bav. Bavaria; Bavarian.

BB. *Bände* (G.), volumes.

b. b. bill-book.

bbl. (pl. *bbls.*) barrel.

B. C. Bachelor of Chemistry; Battery Commander; before Christ; British Columbia.

B. Ch. *Baccalaureus Chirurgiæ* (L.), Bachelor of Surgery.

B. C. L. Bachelor of Civil Law.

B. C. S. Bachelor of Commercial Science.

bd. board; bond; bound.

Bd. *Band* (G.), volume.

B. D. Bachelor of Divinity.

Bde. *Bände* (G.), volumes.

bdl. (pl. *bdls.*) bundle.

bds. [bound in] boards.

Be (no period) beryllium (glucinum).

b. e. bill of exchange.

Bech. Bechuanaland.

Beds. Bedfordshire.

bef. before.

B. E. F. British Expeditionary Forces.

Belg. Belgian; Belgium.

Beng. Bengal; Bengali.

Benj. Benjamin.

Berks. Berkshire.

B. ès L. *Bachelier ès Lettres* (F.), Bachelor of Letters.

B. ès S. *Bachelier ès Sciences* (F.), Bachelor of Sciences.

bet. between.

b. f. brought forward.

B. F. A. Bachelor of Fine Arts.

bg. (pl. *bgs.*) bag.

bh. base-hits (*baseball*).

B. Hy. Bachelor of Hygiene.

Bi (no period) bismuth.

B. I. British India.

Bib. Bible; Biblical.

bibliog. bibliographer; bibliographical; bibliography.

biog. biographer; biographical; biography.

biol. biological; biologist; biology.

bis. bissextile.

bk. bank; bark; book (pl. *bks.*).

bkg. banking.

Bklyn. Brooklyn.

bkt. (pl. *bkts.*) basket.

bl. (pl. *bls.*) bale; barrel.

b. l. bill of lading.

B. L. Bachelor of Laws.

bldg. (pl. *bldgs.*) building.

bldr. builder.

B. L. E. Brotherhood of Locomotive Engineers.

B. Lit. or **B. Litt.** *Baccalaureus Lit(t)erarum* (L.), Bachelor of Letters, Bachelor of Literature.

blk. block.

B. LL. *Baccalaureus Legum* (L.), Bachelor of Laws.

B. L. S. Bachelor of Library Science.

blvd. boulevard.

B. M. Bachelor of Medicine; British Museum.

B. M. A. British Medical Association.

B. M. E. Bachelor of Mechanical Engineering; Bachelor of Mining Engineering.

B. Met. Bachelor of Metallurgy.

B. Mus. Bachelor of Music.

bnk. bank.

b. o. branch office; buyer's option.

B. O. Bachelor of Oratory.

Boh. or **Bohem.** Bohemia; Bohemian.

Bol. Bolivia.

Bom. Bombay.

Bon. *Baron* (F.).

Bonne. *Baronne* (F.), Baroness.

bor. borough.

Bost. Boston.

bot. botanical; botanist; botany; bought.

B. O. T. Board of Trade.

boul. boulevard.

bp. baptized.

Bp. Bishop.

b. p. bills payable; *bonum publicum* (L.), the public good.

B. P. British Pharmacopœia.

B. P. H. Bachelor of Public Health.

B. Phil. Bachelor of Philosophy.

bpl. birthplace.

B. P. O. E. Benevolent and Protective Order of Elks.

Br (no period) bromine.

br. branch; brig; brother.

Br. British.

b. r. bills receivable.

Br. Am. British America.

Braz. Brazil; Brazilian.

b. rec. bills receivable.

Bret. Breton.

brev. brevet; brevetted.

brig. brigade.

Brig. Brigadier.

Brig.-Gen. Brigadier-General.

Brisb. Brisbane (Australia).

Brit. Britain; British.

Brit. Mus. British Museum.

bro. (pl. *bros.*) brother.

bryol. bryology.

b. s. balance-sheet; bill of sale.

B. S. Bachelor of Science; Bachelor of Surgery.

B. S. A. Bachelor of Scientific Agriculture.

B. Sc. Bachelor of Science.

Bss. Baroness.

bt. bought.

Bt. Baronet.

B. Th. Bachelor of Theology.

B. th. u. or **B. t. u.** British thermal unit.

bu. bushel; bushels.

Bucks. Buckinghamshire.

bul. bulletin.

Bulg. Bulgaria; Bulgarian.

bull. bulletin.

bus. or **bush.** bushel; bushels.

b. v. book value.

B. V. *Beata Virgo* (L.), Blessed Virgin; *bene vale* (L.), farewell.

B. V. M. *Beata Virgo Maria* (L.), Blessed Virgin Mary.

bvt. brevet.

bx. (pl. *bxs.*) box.

C

c (no period) *circa, circiter,* or *circum* (L.), about.

C (no period) carbon.

C Roman numeral for 100.

c. case; catcher (*baseball*); cent; center (*football*); centesimo; centime; centimeter; century; chapter; child; *circa, circiter,* or *circum* (L.), about; copyright; corner; cost; coupon; cubic; current.

C. Cape; Catholic; centigrade (thermometer); Chairman; Chancellor; Chancery; Church; Code; Commission; Congress; Conservative; Consul; Court.

Ca (no period) calcium.

ca. case; centiare.

C. A. Central America; Chartered Accountant; Chief Accountant; Commercial Agent; Confederate Army; Consular Agent; Controller of Accounts; Court of Appeal.

C. A. C. Coast Artillery Corps.

c.-à-d. *c'est-à-dire* (F.), that is to say, that is.

cal. calendar; calends; calory, calorie.

Cal. California.

Calc. Calcutta.

Calif. California.

Camb. Cambridge.

Cambs. Cambridgeshire.

can. canal; canto.

Can. Canada; Canadian.

c. & f. cost and freight.

Cant. Canterbury; Canticles.

Cantab. *Cantabrigiensis* (L.), of Cambridge.

Cantuar. *Cantuaria* (L.), Canterbury; *Cantuariensis* (L.), of Canterbury.

cap. capital, capital letter (pl. *caps.*); capitalize; *capitulum* or *caput* (L.), chapter, section.

Capt. Captain.

car. carat.

Card. Cardinal.

carp. carpenter; carpentry.

cash. cashier.

cat. catalogue; catechism.

Cat. Catalan.

cath. cathedral.

Cath. Catharine, Catherine; Catholic.

caus. causation; causative.

cav. cavalry.

Cb (no period) columbium.

c. b. cash-book; county borough (Brit.).

C. B. Cape Breton; *Chirurgiæ Baccalaureus* (L.), Bachelor of Surgery; Common Bench; Companion of the Bath (Brit.).

C. B. E. Commander of the Order of the British Empire.

cc. cubic centimeter.

c. c. *compte courant* (F.), account current; cubic centimeter.

C. C. Circuit Court; City Councilor; Civil Code; Civil Court; Common Councilman; Consular Clerk; Country Club; County Clerk; County Commissioner; County Court; Cricket Club.

C. C. A. Circuit Court of Appeals.

C. C. P. Code of Civil Procedure; Court of Common Pleas.

C. Cr. P. Code of Criminal Procedure.

Cd (no period) cadmium.

cd. (pl. *cds.*) cord.

C. D. S. O. Companion of the Distinguished Service Order (Brit.).

Ce (no period) cerium.

C. E. Chief Engineer; Church of England; Civil Engineer; Corps of Engineers.

C. E. F. Canadian Expeditionary Forces.

Celt. Celtic.

cen. central.

cent. centigrade (thermometer); central; century.

ceram. ceramic; ceramics.

cert. certificate.

certfd. certified.

certif. certificate; certificated.

cet. par. *ceteris paribus* (L.), other things being equal.

cf. center fielder (*baseball*); *confer* (L.), compare.

c. f. carried forward; cost and freight.

C. F. Chaplain to the Forces.

c. f. i. cost, freight, and insurance.

cg. centigram.

C. G. Captain-General; Captain of the Guard; Coast-Guard; Consul-General.

cge. carriage.

cge. pd. carriage paid.

C. G. H. Cape of Good Hope.

C. G. M. Conspicuous Gallantry Medal (Brit.).

c. g. s. or **C. G. S.** centimeter-gram-second (system of units).

C. G. S. Commissary-General of Subsistence.

ch. chain; chapter; chief; child; church.

Ch. Chancery; Chinese.

C. H. Captain of the Horse; Clearing-House; Court-House; Custom-House; Order of the Companions of Honour (Brit.).

Chal. or **Chald.** Chaldaic; Chaldee.

Chamb. Chamberlain.

Chanc. Chancellor; Chancery.

chap. chapel; chapter.

Chap. Chaplain.

Chas. Charles.

Ch. B. *Chirurgiæ Baccalaureus* (L.), Bachelor of Surgery.

ch. d'aff. chargé d'affaires.

Ch. E. Chemical Engineer.

chem. chemical; chemist; chemistry.

chem. sym. chemical symbol.

Ches. or **Chesh.** Cheshire.

Chev. Chevalier.

chf. chief.

chgd. charged.

Chi. or **Chic.** Chicago.

Chin. Chinese.

Chir. Doct. *Chirurgiæ Doctor* (L.), Doctor of Surgery.

Ch. J. Chief Justice.

Ch. M. *Chirurgiæ Magister* (L.), Master of Surgery.

Chmn. or **Chn.** Chairman.

Chr. Christian; Christopher.

chron. chronological; chronology.

Chron. Chronicles.

C. I. Channel Islands; Imperial Order of the Crown of India (Brit.).

C. I. D. Criminal Investigation Department (Brit.).

Cie. *Compagnie* (F.), Company.

C. I. E. Companion of the Order of the Indian Empire (Brit.). [freight.

c. i. f. cost, insurance, and

c. i. f. & c. cost, insurance, freight, and commission.

c. i. f. c. & i. cost, insurance, freight, commission, and interest.

c. i. f. i. & e. cost, insurance, freight, interest, and exchange.

Cin. Cincinnati. [Chief.

C. in C. Commander-in-

C. I. O. Congress of Industrial Organizations.

cir. *circa, circiter,* or *circum* (L.), about; circle.

circ. *circa, circiter,* or *circum* (L.), about; circulation.

cit. citation; cited; citizen.

Civ. Serv. Civil Service.

C. J. Chief Justice.

ck. cask; check.

Cl (no period) chlorine.

cl. centiliter; class; clause; clergyman; cloth.

class. classic; classical; classification; classified.

cld. cleared; colored.

Clem. Clement.

clk. clerk.

C. L. S. C. Chautauqua Literary and Scientific Circle.

cm. centimeter.

C. M. Certificated Master; Certificate of Merit; *Chirurgiæ Magister* (L.), Master of Surgery; Church Missionary; Corresponding Member.

C. M. G. Companion of St. Michael and St. George (Brit.).

cml. commercial.

C. M. S. Church Missionary Society (Brit.).

C. M. T. C. Citizens' Military Training Camps.

Co (no period) cobalt.

co. county.

Co. Company.

c. o. care of; carried over.

C. O. Colonial Office; Commanding Officer; conscientious objector (colloq.); Criminal Office; Crown Office.

Coad. or **Coadj.** Coadjutor.

coch. or **cochl.** *cochlear* or *cochleare* (L.), spoonful.

C. O. D. cash, or collect, on delivery.

cog. or **cogn.** cognate.

col. college; collegiate; colonial; colony; color; column.

Col. Colonel; Colorado; Colossians.

coll. collated; collateral; collaterally; colleague; collected; collection; collector; college; collegiate.

collat. collateral; collaterally.

collect. collective; collectively.

colloq. colloquial; colloquialism; colloquially.

Colo. Colorado.

Col.-Sergt. Color-Sergeant.

com. comedy; commentary; commerce; common; commonly; communication.

Com. Commander; Commission; Commissioner; Committee; Commodore.

comb. combination; combined.

comdg. commanding.

Comdr. Commander.

Comdt. Commandant.

Com.-in-Chf. Commander-in-Chief.

comm. commentary.

Comm. Commander; Commodore.

Commr. Commissioner.

Com. Off. Commissioned Officer.

comp. comparative; compiler; complement; composer; composition; compositor; compound.

compar. comparative.

Compy. Company.

Comr. Commissioner.

Com.-Sergt. Commissary-Sergeant.

Com. Ver. Common Version.

con. consolidated; *contra* (L.), against.

conch. conchology.

concr. concrete; concretely.

cong. *congius* (L.), gallon; congregation.

Cong. Congregational; Congress; Congressional.

Cong. Rec. Congressional Record.

conj. conjugation; conjunction; conjunctive.

Conn. Connecticut.

con. sec. or **con. sect.** conic section.

consgt. consignment.

consol. consolidated.

const. constable; constitution; constitutional.

Const. Constantinople.

constr. construction; construed.

cont. containing; contents; continent; continental; continued.

cont. bon. mor. *contra bonos mores* (L.), contrary to good manners.

contemp. contemporary.

contr. contracted; contraction; contractor.

conv. convent; convertible.

coöp. coöperation; coöperative.

Cop. or **Copt.** Coptic.

cor. corner; corrected; correction; correlative; correspondent; corresponding.

Cor. Corinthians; Coroner.

Corn. Cornish; Cornwall.

Cornw. Cornwall.

coroll. corollary.

corp. corporation.

Corp. or **Corpl.** Corporal.

corr. corrected; correction; correlative; correspondent; corresponding.

corrupt. corrupted; corruption.

Cors. Corsica.

cor. sec. corresponding secretary.

cos (no period) cosine.

cosec (no period) cosecant.

cot (no period) cotangent.

coup. coupon.

covers (no period) co-versed sine.

cox. coxswain.

cp. compare; coupon.

c. p. candle-power; charter-party; chemically pure.

C. P. Clerk of the Peace; Common Pleas; Common Prayer; Court of Probate.

C. P. A. Certified Public Accountant.

C. P. H. Certificate in Public Health.

Cpl. Corporal.

C. P. S. *Custos Privati Sigilli* (L.), Keeper of the Privy Seal.

C Q D (no period). See Dictionary.

Cr (no period) chromium.

cr. created; credit; creditor; creek; crown; crowned.

C. R. *Custos Rotulorum* (L.), Keeper of the Rolls.

craniol. craniology.

craniom. craniometry.

cres. or **cresc.** *crescendo* (It.), increasing in sound (*music*).

crim. con. criminal conversation.

crit. critical; criticism.

cryst. or **crystal.** crystallography.

Cs (no period) cæsium.

C. S. Certified Sanitarian; Christian Science; Christian Science practitioner; Civil

Service; Clerk of Session; Clerk to the Signet; *Custos Sigilli* (L.), Keeper of the Seal.

C. S. A. Confederate States Army; Confederate States of America.

C. S. B. Bachelor of Christian Science.

csc (no period) cosecant.

C. S. C. Conspicuous Service Cross (Brit.).

C. S. D. Doctor of Christian Science.

C. S. I. Companion of the Star of India (Brit.).

csk. cask.

C. S. N. Confederate States Navy.

C. S. O. Chief Signal-Officer; Chief Staff-Officer.

C. S. P. *Congregatio Sancti Pauli* (L.), Congregation of St. Paul (Paulist).

ct. cent (pl. *cts.*); certificate; court.

Ct. Connecticut; Count.

c. t. cable transfer.

C. T. A. U. Catholic Total Abstinence Union.

Cte. *Comte* (F.), Count.

Ctesse. *Comtesse* (F.), Countess.

ctf. certificate.

ctge. cartage.

ctl. cental.

cts. centimes; cents.

Ctss. Countess.

Cu (no period) *cuprum* (L.), copper.

cu. or **cub.** cubic.

Cumb. Cumberland.

cum cp. cum (with) coupon.

cum d. or **cum div.** cum (with) dividend.

cum int. cum (with) interest.

cum. pref. cumulative preference, or preferred.

cur. currency; current (the current month). [month].

curt. current (the current

C. V. Common Version.

C. V. O. Commander of the Royal Victorian Order (Brit.). [istration.

C. W. A. Civil Works Admin-

c. w. o. cash with order.

cwt. hundredweight [for L. *centum*, hundred, and E. *weight*].

cyc. cyclopedia; cyclopedic.

C. Z. Canal Zone.

Czechosl. Czechoslovakia.

D

D Roman numeral for 500.

d. date; daughter; day; dead; degree; *denarius*, or *denarii* (L.), penny, or pence; deputy; died; dime; dividend; dollar; dose.

D. Deacon; Democrat; *Deus* (L.), God; *Dom* (Pg.); *Dominus* (L.), Lord; *Don* (Sp.); Dowager; Duchess; duodecimo; Duke; Dutch.

Da. Danish.

d. a. days after acceptance; deposit account.

Dan. Daniel; Danish.

Danl. Daniel.

D. A. R. Daughters of the American Revolution.

dat. dative.

dau. daughter.

Dav. David.

d. b. day-book.

D. B. E. Dame Commander of the Order of the British Empire.

dbk. drawback.

dble. double.

dbt. debit.

d. c. direct current.

D. C. *da capo* (It.), [repeat] from the beginning (*music*); Dental Corps; Deputy Consul; District Court; District of Columbia.

D. C. L. Doctor of Civil Law.

D. C. M. Distinguished Conduct Medal (Brit.). [Law.

D. Cn. L. Doctor of Canon

dd. delivered.

d. d. days after date; days after delivery; demand draft.

D. D. Doctor of Divinity.

D. D. S. Doctor of Dental Surgery.

D. E. Dynamical Engineer.

Dea. Deacon.

deb. debenture.

dec. deceased; declension; decrease.

Dec. December.

decd. deceased.

decl. declension.

decres. or **decresc.** *decrescendo* (It.), decreasing in sound (*music*).

ded. dedicated; dedication; dedicatory.

def. defective; defendant; deferred; definite; definition.

defect. defective.

deft. defendant.

deg. degree.

del. delegate; *delineavit* (L.), he, or she, drew (it).

Del. Delaware.

Dem. Democrat; Democratic.

demonst. demonstrative.

Den. Denmark.

D. Eng. Doctor of Engineering. [tistry.

dent. dental; dentist; den-

dep. departed; department; departs; deponent; deputy.

dept. department. [derived.

der. derivation; derivative;

deriv. derivation; derivative.

D. ès L. *Docteur ès Lettres* (F.), Doctor of Letters.

D. ès S. *Docteur ès Sciences* (F.), Doctor of Sciences.

det. detachment.

Deut. Deuteronomy.

Dev. Devonshire.

D. F. Dean of Faculty; *Defensor Fidei* (L.), Defender of the Faith; *Distrito Federal* (Sp.), Federal District (Mexico).

D. F. C. Distinguished Flying Cross (Brit.).

D. F. M. Distinguished Flying Medal (Brit.).

dft. defendant; draft.

dg. decigram.

D. G. *Dei gratia* (L.), by the grace of God; *Deo gratias* (L.), thanks to God; Director-General; Dragoon Guards.

d. h. *das heisst* (G.), that is to say.

D. H. deadhead (colloq.).

D. Hy. Doctor of Hygiene.

d. i. *das ist* (G.), that is.

dial. dialect; dialectal.

diam. diameter.

dict. dictionary.

dif. difference; differential.

diff. difference; different.

dig. digest.

dim. *diminuendo* (It.), decreasing in sound (*music*); diminutive.

dioc. diocese.

diplom. diplomatic.

Dir. Director.

dis. discount.

disb. disbursement.

disc. discount; discovered.

disct. discount.

disj. disjunctive.

disp. dispensatory.

dissyll. dissyllabic; dissyllable.

dist. district.

Dist. Atty. District Attorney.

distrib. distributive.

div. divide; divided; dividend; divine; divinity; division; divisor; divorced.

D. J. District Judge; *Doctor Juris* (L.), Doctor of Law.

dl. deciliter.

D. L. Deputy Lieutenant.

D. Lit. or **D. Litt.** *Doctor Lit(t)erarum* (L.), Doctor of Letters, Doctor of Literature.

D. L. O. Dead-Letter Office.

D. L. S. Doctor of Library Science.

dm. decimeter.

D. M. Doctor of Mathematics; Doctor of Medicine.

D. M. D. Doctor of Dental Medicine.

D. M. S. Doctor of Medical Science(s).

D. Mus. Doctor of Music.

D. N. B. Dictionary of National Biography.

do. ditto.

d. o. delivery order.

D. O. Doctor of Oratory; Doctor of Osteopathy.

doc. (pl. *docs.*) document.

dol. (pl. *dols.*) dollar.

dom. domestic; dominion.

D. O. M. *Deo Optimo Maximo* (L.), to God, the Best, the Greatest.

dom. econ. domestic economy.

D. O. R. A. Defense of the Realm Act (Brit.).

Dow. Dowager.

doz. dozen; dozens.

D. Ph. Doctor of Philosophy.

D. P. H. Diploma in Public Health; Doctor of Public Health.

D. P. O. Distributing Post-Office.

dpt. department; deponent.

D. P. W. Department of Public Works.

dr. debtor; dram; drawer.

Dr. Doctor.

d. r. dead-reckoning; deposit receipt.

Ed. D. Doctor of Education.

dram. pers. *dramatis personæ* (L.), the persons of the drama, the characters in a play.

Dr.-Ing. *Doktor-Ingenieur* (G.), Doctor of Engineering.

Dr. P. H. Doctor of Public Health; Doctor of Public Hygiene.

Dr. Univ. Par. Doctor of the University of Paris.

d. s. days after sight.

D. S. *dal segno* (It.), [repeat] from the sign (*music*); Doctor of Science.

D. Sc. Doctor of Science.

D. S. C. Distinguished Service Cross.

D. S. M. Distinguished Service Medal.

D. S. O. Distinguished Service Order (Brit.).

d. s. p. *decessit sine prole* (L.), died without issue.

Dss. Duchess.

D. S. Scr. Doctor of Sacred Scripture. [time.

D. S. T. daylight-saving

d. t. delirium tremens (colloq.). [Theology.

D. T. or **D. Th.** Doctor of

D. T. M. Diploma in Tropical Medicine.

Du. Duke; Dutch.

Dub. or **Dubl.** Dublin.

Dur. or **Durh.** Durham.

D. V. *Deo volente* (L.), God willing.

D. V. M. Doctor of Veterinary Medicine.

D. V. M. S. Doctor of Veterinary Medicine and Surgery.

d. v. p. *decessit vita patris* (L.), died in his, or her, father's lifetime.

dwt. pennyweight [for L. *denarius*, penny, and E. *weight*].

Dy (no period) dysprosium.

dyn. or **dynam.** dynamics.

E

e. eldest; errors (*baseball*).

E. Earl; east; eastern; English.

ea. each.

e. & o. e. errors and omissions excepted.

E. B. Encyclopædia Britannica.

Ebor. *Eboracensis* (L.), of York; *Eboracum* (L.), York.

E. C. East Central (postal district, London).

eccl. ecclesiastical.

Eccl. Ecclesiastes.

eccles. ecclesiastical.

Eccles. Ecclesiastes.

Ecclus. Ecclesiasticus (Apocrypha).

econ. economic; economics; economy.

E. C. U. English Church Union.

Ecua. Ecuador.

ed. edited; edition; editor (pl. *eds.*); educated.

Ed. D. Doctor of Education.

Edin. Edinburgh.

edit. edited; edition; editor.

Edm. Edmund.

Ed. M. Master of Education.

eds. editors.

E. D. S. English Dialect Society.

educ. educated; educational.

Edw. Edward.

e. e. errors excepted.

E. E. Electrical Engineer.

E. E. & M. P. Envoy Extraordinary and Minister Plenipotentiary.

E. E. T. S. Early English Text Society.

Eg. Egypt.

e. g. *exempli gratia* (L.), for example.

Egy. Egypt; Egyptian.

Egypt. Egyptian.

E. I. East India; East Indies.

E. L. east longitude.

elec. or **elect.** electric; electrical; electricity.

elem. elementary; elements.

Eliz. Elizabeth; Elizabethan.

E. long. east longitude.

E. M. Earl Marshal; Engineer of Mines; *Equitum Magister* (L.), Master of the Horse.

embryol. embryology.

e. m. f. electromotive force.

Emp. Emperor; Empress.

ency. or **encyc.** encyclopedia.

Encyc. Brit. Encyclopædia Britannica.

E. N. E. east-northeast.

eng. engineer; engineering; engraver; engraving.

Eng. England; English.

Eng. D. Doctor of Engineering.

engin. engineering.

engr. engineer; engraver.

enl. enlarged.

Ens. Ensign.

ent. or **entom.** entomology.

e. o. m. end of the month.

ep. epistle.

Eph. Ephesians.

epi. or **epil.** epilogue.

Epiph. Epiphany.

Epis. or **Episc.** Episcopal.

eq. equal; equivalent.

equiv. equivalent.

Er (no period) erbium.

E. R. East Riding (Yorkshire); East River (New York City); *Eduardus Rex* (L.), King Edward.

erron. erroneous; erroneously.

Esd. Esdras (Apocrypha).

E. S. E. east-southeast.

esp. especially.

espec. especially.

Esq. or **Esqr.** Esquire.

est. established; estate.

Est. Est(h)onia.

estab. established.

Esth. Esther; Esthonia.

E. T. English translation.

et al. *et alibi* (L.), and elsewhere; *et alii* (L.), and others.

etc. *et cetera* (L.), and others, and so forth.

Eth. Ethiopic.

ethnog. ethnography.

ethnol. ethnological; ethnology.

et seq. (pl. *et seqq.* or *et sqq.*) *et sequens* (L.), and the following.

etym. or **etymol.** etymological; etymology.

Eu (no period) europium.

E. U. Evangelical Union.

Eur. Europe; European.

Evang. Evangelical.

evg. evening.

ex. examination; examined; example; except; exception; exchange; excursion; executed; executive; *exit* (L.), he, or she, goes out, or *exeunt* (L.), they go out; export; extract.

Ex. Exodus.

exam. examination; examined.

exc. except; exception; *excudit* (L.), he, or she, struck out, fashioned, or engraved (it); excursion.

Exc. Excellency.

exch. exchange.

exclam. exclamation; exclamatory.

ex cp. ex (without) coupon.

ex d. or **ex div.** ex (without) dividend.

exec. executive.

ex. gr. *exempli gratia* (L.), for example.

ex int. ex (without) interest.

ex lib. *ex libris* (L.), from the books (of).

Exod. Exodus.

ex off. *ex officio* (L.), by virtue of his office, officially.

exp. expired; export; exporter; express.

exr. executor.

exrx. executrix.

ext. extended; extension; exterior; external; extra; extract.

Ezek. Ezekiel.

F

F (no period) fluorine.

f. farthing; fathom; *fecit* (L.), he, or she, made (it); feminine; florin; folio (pl. *ff.*); foot; *forte* (It.), loud (*music*); franc.

F. Fahrenheit (thermometer); folio; French; Friday.

F. A. Field-Artillery.

f. a. a. free of all average.

Fab. Soc. Fabian Society (Brit.).

fac. facsimile; factor; factory.

facsim. or **facsm.** facsimile.

F. A. G. S. Fellow of the American Geographical Society.

Fahr. Fahrenheit (thermometer).

F. A. I. A. Fellow of the American Institute of Architects.

fam. familiar; family.

F. A. M. or **F. & A. M.** Free and Accepted Masons.

far. farad; farthing.

Far. Ind. Farther India.

f. a. s. free alongside ship.

fasc. fascicle.

fath. fathom.

f. b. full-back (*football*).

F. B. Fenian Brotherhood; Free Baptist.

F. B. A. Fellow of the British Academy.

F. B. S. Fellow of the Botanical Society (Brit.).

F. C. Free Church (of Scotland).

F. C. A. Fellow of the Institute of Chartered Accountants (Brit.).

fcap. foolscap.

F. C. C. first-class certificate.

fco. *franco* (It.), franked, postage free.

fcp. foolscap.

F. C. P. Fellow of the College of Preceptors (London).

F. C. S. Fellow of the Chemical Society (Brit.).

fd. fiord; fund.

F. D. *Fidei Defensor* (L.), Defender of the Faith.

Fe (no period) *ferrum* (L.), iron.

Feb. February.

fec. *fecit* (L.), he, or she, made (it).

Fed. Res. Bd. Federal Reserve Board.

Fed. Res. Bk. Federal Reserve Bank.

F. E. I. S. Fellow of the Educational Institute of Scotland.

fem. feminine.

Ferd. Ferdinand.

ff. *fecerunt* (L.), they made (it); folios; following (pages, verses, etc.); *fortissimo* (It.), very loud (*music*).

f. f. a. free foreign agency; free from alongside.

fff. *fortissimo* (It.), very loud (*music*).

F. F. V. first families of Virginia.

F. G. Foot-Guards.

f. g. a. free of general average.

F. G. S. Fellow of the Geological Society (Brit.).

F. I. A. *Fédération Internationale Aéronautique* (F.); Fellow of the Institute of Actuaries (Brit.).

f. i. b. free in bunker.

F. I. C. Fellow of the Institute of Chemistry (Brit.).

fict. fiction.

F. I. D. A. C. *Fédération Interalliée des Anciens Combattants* (F.), Interallied Federation of Former Combatants [veterans of the Allies of the World War].

fig. figurative; figuratively; figure.

Fin. Finland; Finnish.

Finn. Finnish.

fin. sec. financial secretary.

fir. firkin.

fl. florin; *floruit* (L.), flourished; fluid.

Fl. Flanders; Flemish.

Fla. Florida.

Flem. Flemish.

flor. *floruit* (L.), flourished.

F. L. S. Fellow of the Linnean Society (London).

fm. fathom.

F. M. Field-Marshal.

fo. folio.

F. O. Field-Officer.

f. o. b. free on board.

fol. folio; following.

foll. following.

for. foreign.

f. o. r. free on rails.

fort. fortification; fortified.

f. p. foot-pound; full pay; fully paid.

f. p. a. free of particular average.

F. P. S. Fellow of the Philological Society (Brit.); Fellow of the Philosophical Society (Brit.).

fr. fragment; franc (pl. *fr.* or *frs.*); from.

Fr. Father; France; *Frau* (G.); French; Friar; Friday.

F. R. A. M. Fellow of the Royal Academy of Music.

F. R. A. S. Fellow of the Royal Astronomical Society.

F. R. C. I. Fellow of the Royal Colonial Institute.

F. R. C. M. Fellow of the Royal College of Music.

F. R. C. O. Fellow of the Royal College of Organists.

F. R. C. P. Fellow of the Royal College of Physicians.

F. R. C. S. Fellow of the Royal College of Surgeons.

F. R. C. V. S. Fellow of the Royal College of Veterinary Surgeons.

Fred. Frederic(k).

Fredk. Frederick.

freq. frequent; frequentative; frequently.

F. R. G. S. Fellow of the Royal Geographical Society.

F. R. Hist. S. Fellow of the Royal Historical Society.

F. R. Hort. S. Fellow of the Royal Horticultural Society.

Fri. Friday.

F. R. I. B. A. Fellow of the Royal Institute of British Architects.

Fries. Friesic.

Frl. *Fräulein* (G.).

F. R. Met. S. Fellow of the Royal Meteorological Society.

front. frontispiece.

frs. francs.

F. R. S. Fellow of the Royal Society.

F. R. S. A. Fellow of the Royal Society of Arts.

F. R. S. L. Fellow of the Royal Society of Literature.

F. R. S. S. Fellow of the Royal Statistical Society.

frt. freight.

f. s. foot-second.

F. S. A. Fellow of the Society of Antiquaries (Brit.); Fellow of the Society of Arts (Brit.).

F. S. S. Fellow of the Royal Statistical Society.

ft. feet; foot; fort.

fth. or **fthm.** fathom.

fur. furlong.

furl. furlough.

fut. future.

f. v. *folio verso⁻* (L.), on the back of the page.

fwd. forward.

F. Z. S. Fellow of the Zoölogical Society (London).

G

g. gage; gender; genitive; gram; guide; guinea.

G. German; Gulf.

Ga (no period) gallium.

Ga. Georgia.

g. a. general average.

G. A. General Assembly.

Gael. Gaelic.

gal. (pl. *gals.*) gallon.

Gal. Galatians.

G. A. R. Grand Army of the Republic.

gaz. gazette; gazetteer.

g. b. grand bounce (discharge, as from employment: slang).

G. B. Great Britain.

G. B. & I. Great Britain and Ireland.

G. B. E. Knight, or Dame, Grand Cross of the Order of the British Empire.

G. C. Grand Chancellor; Grand Chaplain; Grand Chapter; Grand Commander; Grand Council.

G. C. B. Knight Grand Cross of the Bath (Brit.).

g. c. d. greatest common divisor.

g. c. f. greatest common factor.

G. C. I. E. Knight Grand Commander of the Order of the Indian Empire (Brit.).

g. c. m. greatest common measure.

G. C. M. G. Knight Grand Cross of St. Michael and St. George (Brit.).

G. C. S. I. Knight Grand Commander of the Star of India (Brit.).

G. C. V. O. Knight Grand Cross of the Royal Victorian Order (Brit.).

Gd (no period) gadolinium.

g. d. granddaughter.

G. D. Grand Duchess; Grand Duchy; Grand Duke.

gdn. garden.

gds. goods.

Ge (no period) germanium.

geb. *geboren* (G.), born.

gen. gender; general; genitive; genus.

Gen. General; Genesis; Geneva.

geneal. genealogical; genealogy.

Genl. General.

gent. gentleman.

Geo. George.

geod. geodesy; geodetic.

Geof. or **Geoff.** Geoffrey.

geog. geographer; geographical; geography.

geol. geological; geologist; geology.

geom. geometrical; geometry.

ger. gerund.

Ger. or **Germ.** German; Germany.

gest. *gestorben* (G.), died, deceased.

G. F. A. General Freight-Agent.

g. gr. great gross (144 dozen).

G. H. Q. General Headquarters.

gi. gill; gills.

Gib. Gibraltar.

Gl (no period) glucinum.

G. L. Grand Lodge.

Glasg. Glasgow.

Glos. Gloucestershire.

gloss. glossary.

G. M. Grand Marshal; Grand Master.

g. m. b. good merchantable brand.

G. m. b. H. *Gesellschaft* (or *Genossenschaft*) *mit beschränkter Haftpflicht* (G.), company with limited liability.

G. M. T. Greenwich mean time.

gn. guinea.

G. O. general order.

g. o. b. good ordinary brand.

G. O. P. 'Grand Old Party' (Republican Party).

Goth. Gothic.

gov. government.

Gov. Governor.

Gov.-Gen. Governor-General.

govt. government.

G. P. *Gloria Patri* (L.), Glory to the Father; Graduate in Pharmacy.

G. P. A. General Passenger-Agent.

G. P. M. Grand Past Master.

G. P. O. General Post-Office.

gr. grain; grand; great; gross.

Gr. Grecian; Greece; Greek.

G. R. *Georgius Rex* (L.), King George.

grad. graduate; graduated.

Grad. Arch. Graduate in Architecture.

gram. grammar; grammatical.

grat. gratis.

Gr. Br. or **Gr. Brit.** Great Britain.

Greg. Gregory.

gs. guineas.

g. s. grandson.

G. S. Grand Scribe; Grand Secretary.

gt. gilt; great; *gutta* (L.), a drop (pl. *gtt.*).

G. T. Good Templars.

Gt. Br. or **Gt. Brit.** Great Britain.

g. t. c. good till canceled, or countermanded.
gtd. guaranteed.
gtt. *guttæ* (L.), drops.
Guat. Guatemala.
Gui. Guiana.
Guin. Guinea.
gun. gunnery.

H

H (no period) hydrogen.
h. harbor; height; heir; heller; high; hits (*baseball*); hour; husband.
ha. hectare.
H. A. Horse-Artillery.
Hab. Habakkuk.
Hag. Haggai.
Hamb. Hamburg.
Hants. Hampshire.
har. or **harb.** harbor.
Harv. Harvard.
H. B. C. Hudson's Bay Company.
H. B. M. His, or Her, Britannic Majesty.
h. c. *honoris causa* (L.), for the sake of honor, as a mark of honor.
H. C. Heralds' College; House of Commons.
h. c. f. highest common factor.
H. C. J. High Court of Justice.
h. c. l. high cost of living (colloq.).
H. C. M. His, or Her, Catholic Majesty.
hd. hand.
hdkf. handkerchief.
hdqrs. headquarters.
He (no period) helium.
H. E. His Eminence; His Excellency.
Heb. Hebrew; Hebrews.
hectol. hectoliter.
hectom. hectometer.
Hen. Henry.
her. heraldic; heraldry.
Heref. Herefordshire.
herp. or **herpet.** herpetology.
Herts. Hertfordshire.
Herz. Herzegovina.
hf. half.
Hg (no period) *hydrargyrum* (L.), mercury.
hg. hectogram.
HG. or **H. G.** High German.
H. G. His, or Her, Grace; Horse-Guards.
H. G. D. H. His, or Her, Grand Ducal Highness.
H. H. His, or Her, Highness; His Holiness.
hhd. hogshead.
H. I. Hawaiian Islands.
H. I. H. His, or Her, Imperial Highness.
H. I. M. His, or Her, Imperial Majesty.
Hind. Hindustan; Hindustani.
hist. historian; historical; history.
H. J. *hic jacet* (L.), here lies.
H. J. S. *hic jacet sepultus* (L.), here lies buried.
hl. hectoliter.

H. L. House of Lords.
hm. hectometer.
h. m. *hoc mense* (L.), this month; *hujus mensis* (L.), of this month.
H. M. His, or Her, Majesty.
H. M. S. His, or Her, Majesty's Service; His, or Her, Majesty's Ship.
H. M. S. O. His, or Her, Majesty's Stationery Office.
Ho (no period) holmium.
ho. house.
Holl. Holland.
Hon. Honorable; Honorary.
Honble. Honorable.
Hond. Honduras.
hor. horizon; horology.
horol. horology.
hort. horticultural; horticulture.
Hos. Hosea.
hosp. hospital.
h. p. half pay; horse-power.
h. q. headquarters; *hoc quære* (L.), seek this, see this.
hr. (pl. *hrs.*) hour.
Hr. *Herr* (G.).
H. R. Home Rule; House of Representatives.
H. R. E. Holy Roman Emperor; Holy Roman Empire.
H. R. H. His, or Her, Royal Highness.
H. R. I. P. *hic requiescit in pace* (L.), here rests in peace.
H. R. S. A. Honorary Member of the Royal Scottish Academy.
h. s. *hoc sensu* (L.), in this sense.
H. S. *hic sepultus* (L.), here is buried; *hic situs* (L.), here lies; High School; House-Surgeon.
H. S. H. His, or Her, Serene Highness.
H. S. M. His, or Her, Serene Majesty.
H. S. S. Fellow [L. *Socius*] of the Royal Historical Society.
ht. height.
h. t. *hoc tempore* (L.), at this time; *hoc titulo* (L.), by this title.
H. T. Hawaii Territory.
Hun. or **Hung.** Hungarian; Hungary.
Hunts. Huntingdonshire.
h. w. m. high-water mark.
Hy. Henry.
hyd. or **hydr.** hydraulics; hydrostatics.
hydraul. hydraulics.
hydros. hydrostatics.
H. Y. M. A. Hebrew Young Men's Association.
hyp. hypothesis; hypothetical.
hypot. hypotenuse.

I

I (no period) iodine.
I Roman numeral for 1.
i. interest; intransitive.
I. *Imperator* (L.), Emperor; *Imperatrix* (L.), Empress; Independent; Island; Isle.
Ia. Iowa.

I. A. F. International Aëronautical Federation.
I. & R. See *R. & I.*
i. b. invoice-book.
ib. or **ibid.** *ibidem* (L.), in the same place.
I. C. *Iesus Christus* (L.), Jesus Christ.
I. C. A. A. A. A. Intercollegiate Association of Amateur Athletes of America.
I. C. C. Interstate Commerce Commission.
Ice. or **Icel.** Iceland; Icelandic.
ich. or **ichth.** ichthyology.
I.CH.TH.U.S. or **ICHTHUS** representing the initial letters of Gr. Ἰησοῦς Χριστός Θεοῦ Ὑἱός Σωτήρ, Jesus Christ, Son of God, the Saviour: the Gr. word ἰχθύς (*ichthus*, or *ichthys*) meaning 'fish,' and the fish having been used among the early Christians as a symbol for Christ.
I. C. N. *in Christi nomine* (L.), in Christ's name.
I. C. Z. Isthmian Canal Zone.
id. *idem* (L.), the same.
Id. Idaho.
I. D. Intelligence Department.
Ida. Idaho.
I. D. B. illicit diamond buyer, or buying (South Africa).
i. e. *id est* (L.), that is.
I. G. Inspector-General.
ign. *ignotus* (L.), unknown.
I. H. N. in His name.
i. h. p. indicated horse-power.
I. H. S. ΙΗ(ΣΟΥ)Σ (IESOUS) (Gr.), Jesus; also taken to represent *Iesus Hominum Salvator* (L.), Jesus, Saviour of Men; *In Hoc Signo* (*vinces*) (L.), in this sign [the cross] (shalt thou conquer); *In Hac Salus* (L.), in this [cross] is salvation; and *I* [Christ] *Have Suffered.*
ill. illustrated; illustration.
Ill. or **Ills.** Illinois.
illus. or **illust.** illustrated; illustration.
I. L. P. Independent Labour Party (Brit.).
I. M. Isle of Man.
imit. imitative.
imp. imperative; imperfect; imperial; impersonal; import; imported; importer; *imprimatur* (L.), let it be printed; imprint.
Imp. *Imperator* (L.), Emperor; *Imperatrix* (L.), Empress.
imperf. imperfect.
impers. impersonal.
impf. imperfect.
impr. *imprimerie* (F.), printing-house, press.
improp. improperly.
impv. imperative.
Impx. *Imperatrix* (L.), Empress.
In (no period) indium.
in. (pl. *in.* or *ins.*) inch.

inc. incorporated; increase.
incl. including; inclusive.
incog. incognito.
incor. incorporated; incorrect; incorrectly.
ind. independent; index; indicative.
Ind. Independent; India; Indian; Indiana.
I. N. D. *in nomine Dei* (L.), in the name of God.
indecl. indeclinable.
indef. indefinite.
indic. indicative.
Indo-Eur. Indo-European.
inf. infantry; infinitive; *infra* (L.), below, after.
infin. infinitive.
infra dig. *infra dignitatem* (L.), beneath one's dignity (colloq.).
in init. *in initio* (L.), in or at the beginning.
in lim. *in limine* (L.), on the threshold, at the outset.
in loc. cit. *in loco citato* (L.), in the place cited.
in mem. *in memoriam* (L.), in memory (of).
in pr. *in principio* (L.), in or at the beginning.
I. N. R. I. *Iesus Nazarenus, Rex Iudæorum* (L.), Jesus of Nazareth, King of the Jews.
ins. inches; inspector; insurance.
inscr. inscribed; inscription.
insp. inspector.
Insp.-Gen. Inspector-General.
inst. instant (the present month); institute; institution.
instr. instructor; instrumental.
int. interest; interior; interjection; internal; international; interpreter; intransitive.
intens. intensive.
interj. interjection.
internat. international.
interrog. interrogation; interrogative; interrogatively.
intr. or **intrans.** intransitive.
in trans. *in transitu* (L.), in transit, on the way.
intro. or **introd.** introduction; introductory.
inv. *invenit* (L.), he, or she, designed (it); inventor; invoice.
invt. or **invty.** inventory.
Io. Iowa.
I. O. F. Independent Order of Foresters.
I. O. O. F. Independent Order of Odd Fellows.
I. O. R. Independent Order of Rechabites.
I. O. R. M. Improved Order of Red Men.
I O U I owe you (in an acknowledgment of indebtedness).
i. q. *idem quod* (L.), the same as.
I. Q. intelligence quotient (*psychol.*).
I. Q. E. D. *id quod erat de-*

monstrandum (L.), that which was to be demonstrated.

Ir (no period) iridium.

Ir. Ireland; Irish.

I. R. Inland Revenue; Internal Revenue.

I. R. See *R. & I.*

Ire. Ireland.

I. R. O. Internal Revenue Office; Internal Revenue Officer.

irreg. irregular; irregularly.

is. island; isle.

Is. or **Isa.** Isaiah.

I. S. C. interstate commerce.

isl. (pl. *isls.*) island; isle.

I. S. M. *Iesus Salvator Mundi* (L.), Jesus, Saviour of the World.

I. S. O. Imperial Service Order (Brit.).

isos. isosceles.

iss. issue.

isth. isthmus.

It. Italian; Italy.

ital. italic.

Ital. Italian.

itin. itinerary.

I. W. Isle of Wight.

I. W. S. A. International Women's Suffrage Alliance.

I. W. W. Industrial Workers of the World.

J

j. joule.

J. (pl. *JJ.*) Judge; Justice.

j. a. joint account.

J. A. Judge-Advocate.

J. A. G. Judge-Advocate-General.

Jam. Jamaica.

J. A. M. A. Journal of the American Medical Association.

Jan. January.

Jap. Japan; Japanese.

Jas. James.

Jav. Javanese.

Jc. Junction.

J. C. Jesus Christ; Julius Cæsar; *juris consultus* (L.), jurisconsult.

J. C. B. *Juris Civilis Baccalaureus* (L.), Bachelor of Civil Law.

J. C. D. *Juris Civilis Doctor* (L.), Doctor of Civil Law.

J. C. L. *Juris Canonici Licentiatus* (L.), Licentiate in Canon Law.

J. D. *Juris Doctor* (L.), Doctor of Jurisprudence, Doctor of Law; *Jurum Doctor* (L.), Doctor of Laws.

Jer. Jeremiah; Jersey; Jerusalem.

j. g. junior grade.

JJ. Judges; Justices.

Jn. Junction.

Jno. John.

jnt. joint.

Jo. Joel.

Jon. or **Jona.** Jonathan.

Jos. Joseph.

Josh. Joshua.

jour. or **journ.** journal.

J. P. Justice of the Peace.

Jr. Junior.

jr. g. junior grade.

jt. joint.

Jud. Judges; Judith (Apocrypha).

J. U. D. *Juris Utriusque Doctor* (L.), Doctor of Both Laws [canon and civil].

Judg. Judges.

Jun. Junior.

Junc. Junction.

K

K (no period) *kalium* (L.), potassium.

k. karat, carat; knot.

K. Kaiser; King; Kings; Knight; krone; kronen.

K. A. Knight of St. Andrew (Russia).

kal. kalends, calends.

Kan. or **Kans.** Kansas.

Kath. Katharine, Katherine.

K. B. King's Bench; Knight Bachelor.

K. B. E. Knight Commander of the Order of the British Empire.

K. C. King's Counsel; Knights of Columbus.

K. C. B. Knight Commander of the Bath (Brit.).

K. C. I. E. Knight Commander of the Order of the Indian Empire (Brit.).

K. C. M. G. Knight Commander of St. Michael and St. George (Brit.).

K. C. S. I. Knight Commander of the Star of India (Brit.).

K. C. V. O. Knight Commander of the Royal Victorian Order (Brit.).

Ken. Kentucky.

kg. keg; kilogram.

K. G. Knight of the Garter (Brit.).

K. G. F. Knight of the Golden Fleece (Austria and Spain).

K. H. C. Honorary Chaplain to the King.

K. H. P. Honorary Physician to the King.

K. H. S. Honorary Surgeon to the King.

Ki. Kings.

kilo. or **kilog.** kilogram.

kilom. kilometer.

k. k. *kaiserlich-königlich* (G.), imperial-royal.

K. K. K. Ku Klux Klan.

kl. kiloliter.

km. kilometer; kingdom.

K. M. or **K. Mess.** King's Messenger.

Knt. Knight.

K. O. knock-out (*pugilism*).

K. of C. Knights of Columbus.

K. of P. Knights of Pythias.

K. P. kitchen police; Knight of the Order of St. Patrick (Brit.); Knights of Pythias.

Kr (no period) krypton.

kr. kreutzer; krona; krone; kronen; kroner; kronor.

kt. karat, carat; knot.

Kt. Knight.

K. T. Knight of the Thistle (Brit.); Knights Templars.

kw. kilowatt.

Ky. Kentucky.

L

L elevated railroad, or railway; Roman numeral for 50.

l. leaf; league; left; length; *liber* (L.), book; *libra*, or *libræ* (L.), pound, or pounds (British money); line (pl. *ll.*); link; lira; liter; long; lost.

L. Lady; Lake; Late; Latin; Liberal; London; Lord.

La (no period) lanthanum.

La. Louisiana.

L. A. Law Agent.

lab. laboratory.

Lab. Labrador.

Lam. Lamentations.

Lancs. Lancashire.

lang. language.

Lap. Lapland.

L. A. S. Lord Advocate of Scotland.

lat. latitude.

Lat. Latin.

Latv. Latvia.

lb. (pl. *lbs.*) *libra* (L.), pound (weight).

l. c. letter of credit; *loco citato* (L.), in the place cited; lower-case.

L. C. Library of Congress; Lord Chamberlain; Lord Chancellor.

L. C. B. Lord Chief Baron.

L. C. C. London County Council.

l. c. d. lowest common denominator.

L. C. J. Lord Chief Justice.

l. c. m. least common multiple.

ld. land; limited.

Ld. Lord.

L. D. Light Dragoons.

ldg. landing.

Ldp. Ladyship; Lordship.

L. D. S. Latter-Day Saints; Licentiate of Dental Surgery.

l. e. left end (*football*).

lea. league.

leath. leather.

lect. lecture; lecturer.

leg. legal; *legato* (It.), connected, smooth (*music*); legislative; legislature.

legg. *leggiero* (It.), light, light and rapid (*music*).

Leic. or **Leics.** Leicestershire.

Leip. Leipsic.

Lev. Leviticus.

lex. lexicon.

lexicog. lexicographer; lexicographical; lexicography.

lf. left fielder (*baseball*).

Lfg. *Lieferung* (G.), instalment, part.

l. g. left guard (*football*).

LG. or **L. G.** Low German.

L. G. Life-Guards.

LGr. or **L. Gr.** Late Greek.

l. h. left hand.

L. H. lighthouse.

L. H. A. Lord High Admiral.

l. h. b. left half-back (*football*).

L. H. C. Lord High Chancellor.

L. H. D. *Litterarum Humaniorum Doctor* (L.), 'Doctor of the More Humane Letters,' Doctor of the Humanities.

L. H. T. Lord High Treasurer.

Li (no period) lithium.

L. I. Long Island.

lib. *liber* (L.), book; librarian; library.

Lib. Liberal.

libr. *librairie* (F.), bookseller's shop, publishing-house; librarian; library.

Lieut. Lieutenant.

lin. lineal; linear.

Linc. or **Lincs.** Lincolnshire.

l. i. p. life-insurance policy.

liq. liquid; liquor.

lit. liter; literal; literally; literary; literature.

Lit. B. or **Litt. B.** *Lit(t)erarum Baccalaureus* (L.), Bachelor of Letters, Bachelor of Literature.

Lit. D. or **Litt. D.** *Lit(t)erarum Doctor* (L.), Doctor of Letters, Doctor of Literature.

lith. lithograph; lithography.

Lith. Lithuania; Lithuanian.

lithog. lithograph; lithography.

Litt. B. See *Lit. B.*

Litt. D. See *Lit. D.*

liturg. liturgical; liturgics.

liv. *livraison* (F.), instalment, part; *livre* (F.), book.

Liv. Liverpool.

L. J. Lord Justice.

ll. lines.

LL. or **L. L.** Late Latin.

l. l. *loco laudato* (L.), in the place cited.

L. L. Lord Lieutenant.

L. L. A. Lady Literate in Arts.

LL. B. *Legum Baccalaureus* (L.), Bachelor of Laws.

LL. D. *Legum Doctor* (L.), Doctor of Laws.

LL. L. *Legum Licentiatus* (L.), Licentiate of Laws.

LL. M. *Legum Magister* (L.), Master of Laws.

L. M. Licentiate in Medicine; Licentiate in Midwifery.

loc. cit. *loco citato* (L.), in the place cited.

loc. laud. *loco laudato* (L.), in the place cited.

log. logarithm.

lon. longitude.

Lond. London.

long. longitude.

loq. *loquitur* (L.), he, or she, speaks.

L. P. Lord Provost.

L. P. S. Lord Privy Seal.

lr. lower.

L. R. C. P. Licentiate of the Royal College of Physicians.

L. R. C. S. Licentiate of the Royal College of Surgeons.

l. s. left side.

L. S. Linnean Society (London); *locus sigilli* (L.), the place of the seal.

L. S. A. Licentiate of the Society of Apothecaries (Brit.).

l. s. c. *loco supra citato* (L.), in the place cited above or before.

l. s. d. *libræ, solidi, denarii* (L.), pounds, shillings, pence.

Lt. Lieutenant.

l. t. left tackle (*football*); long ton.

Lt.-Col. Lieutenant-Colonel.

ltd. limited.

Lt.-Gen. Lieutenant-General.

Lt.-Gov. Lieutenant-Governor.

L. Th. Licentiate in Theology.

Lt. Inf. Light Infantry.

Lu (no period) lutecium.

L. U. Liberal-Unionist.

Luth. Lutheran.

lv. leave, or leaves; livre.

lve. leave, or leaves.

l. w. m. low-water mark.

LXX Septuagint.

M

M Roman numeral for 1,000.

m. male; married; masculine; medium; meter; mile; minim; minute; month; moon; morning.

M. Majesty; Manitoba; mark (German money); Marquis, Marquess; Marshal; Master; Member; *meridies* (L.), noon; Middle; Militia; Monday; *Monsieur* (F.) (pl. *MM*.).

M. A. Master of Arts; Military Academy.

Mac. Maccabees (Apocrypha).

Maced. Macedonia.

mach. machinery; machinist.

Mad. Madam; Madrid.

Madag. Madagascar.

mag. magazine.

M. Agr. Master of Agriculture.

Maj. Major.

Maj.-Gen. Major-General.

Mal. Malachi.

man. manual.

Man. Manila; Manitoba.

Manit. Manitoba.

manuf. manufacturing.

mar. maritime; married.

Mar. March.

M. Ar. or **M. Arch.** Master of Architecture.

March. Marchioness.

Marg. Margaret; Margery.

Marq. Marquis, Marquess.

mas. masculine.

M. A. S. Master of Applied Science.

masc. masculine.

Mass. Massachusetts.

mat. matured.

Mat. Matthew.

math. mathematical; mathematician; mathematics.

Matt. Matthew.

Mau. Mauritius.

max. maximum.

Max. Maximilian.

M. B. *Medicinæ Baccalaureus* (L.), Bachelor of Medicine.

M. B. A. Master of Business Administration.

M. B. E. Member of the Order of the British Empire.

M. B. S. or **M. B. Sc.** Master of Business Science.

M. C. Marine Corps; Master Commandant; Master of Ceremonies; Medical Corps; Member of Congress; Military Cross (Brit.).

M. C. E. Master of Civil Engineering.

M. Ch. *Magister Chirurgiæ* (L.), Master of Surgery.

mcht. merchant.

Md. Maryland.

MD. or **M. D.** Middle Dutch.

m. d. *mano destra* (It.), right hand (*music*); memorandum of deposit; months after date.

M. D. *Medicinæ Doctor* (L.), Doctor of Medicine.

Mdlle. *Mademoiselle* (F.).

Mdme. *Madame* (F.).

mdse. merchandise.

Mdx. Middlesex.

Me. Maine.

ME. or **M. E.** Middle English.

M. E. Mechanical Engineer; Methodist Episcopal; Military Engineer; Mining Engineer; Most Excellent.

meas. measure.

mech. mechanical; mechanics.

med. medical; medicine; medieval; medium.

Medit. Mediterranean.

Melan. Melanesia.

Melb. Melbourne.

mem. member; memoir; memorandum; memorial.

memo. memorandum.

mensur. mensuration.

merid. meridian.

Mesop. Mesopotamia.

Messrs. Messieurs.

Met. Metropolitan.

metal. metallurgical; metallurgy.

metaph. metaphysical; metaphysics.

Met. E. Metallurgical Engineer.

meteor. or **meteorol.** meteorological; meteorology.

Meth. Methodist.

metrol. metrology.

Metrop. Metropolitan.

Mex. Mexican; Mexico.

mf. *mezzo forte* (It.), moderately loud (*music*).

M. F. Master of Forestry.

M. F. A. Master of Fine Arts.

mfg. manufacturing.

M. F. H. Master of Foxhounds.

mfr. (pl. *mfrs.*) manufacturer.

Mg (no period) magnesium.

mg. milligram.

mgr. manager.

Mgr. *Monseigneur* (F.); Monsignor (*eccles.*).

MGr. or **M. Gr.** Middle Greek.

M. H. Master of Horticulture; Medal of Honor.

MHG. or **M. H. G.** Middle High German.

M. Hort. Master of Horticulture.

M. H. R. Member of the House of Representatives.

mi. mile; miles; mill; mills.

Mic. Micah.

M. I. C. E. Member of the Institution of Civil Engineers (Brit.).

Mich. Michaelmas; Michigan.

micros. microscopy.

mid. middle.

Mid. Midshipman.

M. I. D. Military Intelligence Division.

Middlx. or **Midx.** Middlesex.

M. I. E. E. Member of the Institution of Electrical Engineers (Brit.).

mil. military; militia.

M. I. M. E. Member of the Institution of Mining Engineers (Brit.).

M. I. Mech. E. Member of the Institution of Mechanical Engineers (Brit.).

min. mineralogical; mineralogy; minim; minimum; mining; minister; minute.

M. I. N. A. Member of the Institution of Naval Architects (Brit.).

mineral. mineralogical; mineralogy.

Minn. Minnesota.

Min. Plen. Minister Plenipotentiary.

Min. Res. Minister Resident.

m. i. p. marine insurance policy.

Mis. *Marquis* (F.).

misc. miscellaneous; miscellany.

Mise. *Marquise* (F.).

Miss. Mississippi.

M. I. T. Massachusetts Institute of Technology.

mkt. market.

ml. milliliter.

ML. or **M. L.** Middle Latin.

M. L. A. Master of Landscape Architecture; Modern Language Association.

MLG. or **M. L. G.** Middle Low German.

Mlle. (pl. *Mlles.*) *Mademoiselle* (F.).

Mlles. *Mesdemoiselles* (F.).

M. L. S. Master of Library Science.

mm. millimeter.

MM. *Messieurs* (F.).

m. m. *mutatis mutandis* (L.), the necessary changes being made.

M. M. Maelzel's metronome (*music*); Military Medal (Brit.).

Mme. (pl. *Mmes.*) *Madame* (F.).

M. M. E. Master of Mechanical Engineering.

Mmes. *Mesdames* (F.).

M. Mus. Master of Music.

Mn (no period) manganese.

M. N. A. S. Member of the National Academy of Sciences.

mng. managing.

Mngr. Monsignor.

Mo (no period) molybdenum.

mo. (pl. *mos.*) month.

Mo. Missouri.

M. O. money-order.

mod. moderate; *moderato* (It.), in moderate time (*music*); modern.

Moham. Mohammedan.

mol. wt. molecular weight.

mon. monastery.

Mon. Monday; Monmouthshire.

Mongol. Mongolian.

Monsig. Monsignor.

Mont. Montana.

Montr. Montreal.

mor. morocco.

Mor. Morocco.

morn. morning.

morph. morphology.

mos. months.

M. P. Member of Parliament; Methodist Protestant; Military Police.

M. P. C. Member of Parliament, Canada.

M. Ph. Master of Philosophy.

m. p. h. miles per hour.

M. P. H. Master of Public Health.

M. P. P. Member of the Provincial Parliament.

Mr. (with pl. *Messrs.*) Mister.

M. R. Master of the Rolls; Missionary Rector.

M. R. A. S. Member of the Royal Asiatic Society.

M. R. C. Medical Reserve Corps.

M. R. C. P. Member of the Royal College of Physicians.

M. R. C. S. Member of the Royal College of Surgeons.

Mrs. (with pl. *Mmes.*) Mistress, 'Missis.' See Dictionary.

MS. or **ms.** (pl. *MSS.* or *mss.*) manuscript.

m. s. *mano sinistra* (It.), left hand (*music*); months after sight.

M. S. Master of Science; Master of Surgery; *memoriæ sacrum* (L.), sacred to the memory (of).

M. S. A. E. Member of the Society of Automotive Engineers.

M. Sc. Master of Science.

M. S. H. Master of Staghounds.

m. s. l. mean sea-level.

MSS. or **mss.** manuscripts.

mt. (pl. *mts.*) mount; mountain.

mtg. meeting; mortgage.

mtgd. mortgaged.

mtge. mortgage.

Mt. Rev. Most Reverend.

mun. municipal.

mus. museum; music; musical; musician.

Mus. B. Bachelor of Music.
Mus. D. Doctor of Music.
Mus. M. Master of Music.
m. v. *mezza voce* (It.), with half the power of the voice, softly (*music*).
M. V. O. Member of the Royal Victorian Order (Brit.).
M. W. Most Worshipful; Most Worthy.
myg. myriagram.
myl. myrialiter.
mym. myriameter.
myth. or **mythol.** mythological; mythology.

N

N (no period) nitrogen.
n. *natus* (L.), born; nephew; net; neuter; new; nominative; note; noun; number.
N. Nationalist; New; noon; Norse; north; northern.
Na (no period) *natrium* (L.), sodium.
N. A. National Academician; National Academy; National Army; North America; North American.
N. A. D. National Academy of Design.
Nah. Nahum.
Nap. Napoleon.
N. A. S. National Academy of Sciences.
nat. national; native; natural.
Nat. Natal.
Nath. Nathaniel.
natl. national.
Nat. Sc. D. Doctor of Natural Science.
naut. nautical.
nav. naval; navigation.
navig. navigation.
Nb (no period) niobium (columbium).
n. b. or **N. B.** *nota bene* (L.), note well, take notice.
N. B. New Brunswick; North Britain (Scotland); North British.
N. C. North Carolina.
N. C. A. A. National Collegiate Athletic Association.
N. C. O. Non-Commissioned Officer.
Nd (no period) neodymium.
n. d. no date.
N. D. North Dakota; *Notre Dame* (F.), Our Lady.
N. Dak. North Dakota.
Ne (no period) neon.
N. E. New England; northeast; northeastern.
N. E. A. National Education Association.
Neb. or **Nebr.** Nebraska.
N. E. D. New English Dictionary (Oxford English Dictionary).
neg. negative; negatively.
Neh. Nehemiah.
nem. con. *nemine contradicente* (L.), no one contradicting, unanimously.
nem. diss. *nemine dissentiente* (L.), no one dissenting, unanimously.

N. Eng. New England.
Neth. Netherlands.
neut. neuter.
Nev. Nevada. [French.
NF. or **N. F.** Norman
n. f. no funds.
N. F. National Formulary; Newfoundland.
Nfld. Newfoundland.
n. g. no good (colloq.).
N. G. National Guard.
NGr. or **N. Gr.** New Greek.
N. H. New Hampshire.
NHG. or **N. H. G.** New High German.
Ni (no period) nickel.
N. I. A. L. National Institute of Arts and Letters.
Nicar. Nicaragua.
Nich. Nicholas.
N. I. R. A. National Industrial Recovery Act.
N. J. New Jersey.
NL. or **N. L.** New Latin.
n. l. *non licet* (L.), it is not permitted; *non liquet* (L.), it is not clear or evident.
N. L. or **N. lat.** north latitude. [Mexico.
N. M. or **N. Mex.** New
N. N. E. north-northeast.
N. N. W. north-northwest.
no. north; northern; *numero* (L.), (by) number (pl. *nos.*). [New Orleans.
N. O. natural order (*bot.*).
nol. pros. *nolle prosequi* (L.), to be unwilling to prosecute.
nom. nominative.
non cul. *non culpabilis* (L.), not guilty.
non obst. *non obstante* (L.), notwithstanding.
non pros. *non prosequitur* (L.), he does not prosecute.
non seq. *non sequitur* (L.), it does not follow.
n. o. p. not otherwise provided for.
nor. north; northern.
Nor. Norman; Norway; Norwegian.
Norf. Norfolk.
Northants. Northamptonshire. [land.
Northumb. Northumber-
Norw. Norway; Norwegian.
nos. numbers.
Notts. Nottinghamshire.
Nov. November.
N. P. Notary Public.
nr. near.
Nr. *Nummer* (G.), number.
N. R. North Riding (Yorkshire); North River (New York City).
N. R. A. National Recovery Act; National Recovery Administration.
N. R. F. Naval Reserve Force. [ficient funds.
n. s. not specified; not suf-
N. S. New Series; New Style (in reckoning time); *Notre Seigneur* (F.), Our Lord; Nova Scotia.
n. s. f. not sufficient funds.
N. S. W. New South Wales.
Nt (no period) niton.
N. T. New Testament;

Northern Territory (Australia).
n. u. name unknown.
Num. Numbers.
numis. numismatic; numismatics.
N. W. North Wales; northwest; northwestern.
N. W. T. Northwest Territories (Canada).
N. Y. New York.
N. Y. C. New York City.
N. Z. New Zealand.

O

O (no period) oxygen.
o. *octarius* (L.), pint; old; only.
o. or **po.** outs or put-outs (*baseball*).
O. Ocean; octavo; Ohio; Old; Ontario; Order.
o. a. on account.
ob. *obiit* (L.), he, or she, died.
Obad. Obadiah.
obdt. obedient.
O. B. E. Officer of the Order of the British Empire.
obj. object; objection; objective.
obl. oblique; oblong.
obs. observation; observatory; obsolete.
ob. s. p. *obiit sine prole* (L.), he, or she, died without issue.
obstet. obstetrical; obstetrics.
oc. ocean.
occas. occasional; occasionally.
Oct. October.
OD. or **O. D.** Old Dutch.
o. d. on demand.
O. D. Officer of the Day; olive drab (of military uniform).
OE. or **O. E.** Old English.
o. e. omissions excepted.
O. E. D. Oxford English Dictionary.
OF. or **O. F.** Old French.
off. office; officer; official.
offg. officiating.
O. F. M. *Ordo Fratrum Minorum* (L.), Order of Friars Minor (Franciscan).
O. F. S. Orange Free State.
OHG. or **O. H. G.** Old High German.
O. H. M. S. On His, or Her, Majesty's Service.
O. K. all right, correct (colloq.). See Dictionary.
Okla. Oklahoma.
ol. *oleum* (L.), oil.
OL. or **O. L.** Old Latin.
OLG. or **O. L. G.** Old Low German.
O. M. old measurement; Order of Merit (Brit.).
ON. or **O. N.** Old Norse.
Ont. Ontario.
op. opposite; opus (work).
o. p. out of print.
O. P. *Ordo Prædicatorum* (L.), Order of Preachers (Dominican).
op. cit. *opere citato* (L.), in the work cited.
opp. opposed; opposite.

opt. optative; optical; optician; optics.
Or. Oregon; Oriental.
o. r. owner's risk.
O. R. C. Officers' Reserve Corps.
ord. ordained; order; ordinance; ordinary; ordnance.
ordn. ordnance.
Ore. or **Oreg.** Oregon.
Or. F. S. Orange Free State.
org. organized.
orig. original; originally.
ornith. ornithological; ornithology.
Os (no period) osmium.
OS. or **O. S.** Old Saxon.
o. s. out of stock.
O. S. Old Series; Old Style (in reckoning time); ordinary seaman.
O. S. A. Order of St. Augustine (Augustinian).
O. S. B. Order of St. Benedict (Benedictine).
O. S. D. Order of St. Dominic (Dominican).
O. S. F. Order of St. Francis (Franciscan).
O. T. Old Testament.
Ott. Ottawa.
Oxf. Oxford; Oxfordshire.
Oxon. *Oxonia* (L.), Oxford, Oxfordshire; *Oxoniensis* (L.), of Oxford.
oz. (pl. *oz.* or *ozs.*) ounce.

P

P (no period) phosphorus.
p. page (pl. *pp.*); part; participle; *partim* (L.), in part; past; perch; *piano* (It.), soft (*music*); pint; pipe; pitcher (*baseball*); pole; population; *post* (L.), after.
P. *Papa* (L.), Pope; *Pater* (L.), Father; *Père* (F.), Father; President; Prince; Progressive; Province.
Pa. Pennsylvania.
p. a. participial adjective; particular average; *per annum* (L.), by the year; private account.
P. A. power of attorney; Purchasing Agent.
Pac. Pacific.
Pal. Palestine.
paleog. paleography.
paleon. or **paleont.** paleontology.
Pales. Palestine.
pam. or **pamph.** pamphlet.
Pan. Panama.
p. & l. profit and loss.
pap. paper.
par. paragraph; parallel; parenthesis; parish.
Para. Paraguay.
paren. parenthesis.
Parl. Parliament; Parliamentary.
part. participle; particle.
pass. *passim* (L.), here and there; passive.
pat. patent; patented.
path. or **pathol.** pathological; pathology.
Pat. Off. Patent Office.
P. A. U. Pan American Union.

payt. payment.

Pb (no period) *plumbum* (L.), lead.

P. B. *Pharmacopœia Britannica* (L.), British Pharmacopœia; Prayer-Book.

pc. (pl. *pcs.*) piece.

p. c. per cent; petty cash; postal card; post-card; price current.

P. C. Penal Code; Perpetual Curate; Police Constable; Privy Council; Privy Councilor.

p. c. b. petty-cash book.

P. C. M. O. Principal Colonial Medical Officer.

Pd (no period) palladium.

pd. paid.

Pd. B. Bachelor of Pedagogy.

Pd. D. Doctor of Pedagogy.

Pd. M. Master of Pedagogy.

p. d. q. pretty damned quick (slang).

P. E. Presiding Elder; Protestant Episcopal.

ped. pedal (*music*).

P. E. I. Prince Edward Island.

pen. peninsula.

P. E. N. International Association of Poets, Playwrights, Editors, Essayists, and Novelists.

Penn. or **Penna.** Pennsylvania.

Pent. Pentecost.

per an. *per annum* (L.), by the year.

per ct. per cent.

perf. perfect.

perh. perhaps.

per pro. or **per proc.** *per procurationem* (L.), by procuration, by the agency of another.

pers. person.

Pers. Persia; Persian.

pert. pertaining.

pes. peseta.

Pet. Peter.

petrog. petrography.

petrol. petrology.

pf. pfennig; preferred.

p. f. *più forte* (It.), louder (*music*).

pfd. preferred.

pfg. pfennig.

pg. page.

Pg. Portugal; Portuguese.

P. G. M. Past Grand Master.

P. H. Public Health.

phar. or **pharm.** pharmaceutical; pharmacopœia; pharmacy.

Phar. D. or **Pharm. D.** Doctor of Pharmacy.

Phar. M. or **Pharm. M.** Master of Pharmacy.

pharmacol. pharmacology.

Ph. B. *Philosophiæ Baccalaureus* (L.), Bachelor of Philosophy.

Ph. C. Pharmaceutical Chemist.

Ph. D. *Philosophiæ Doctor* (L.), Doctor of Philosophy.

Ph. G. Graduate in Pharmacy.

phil. philosophical; philosophy.

Phil. Philadelphia; Philemon; Philip; Philippians; Philippine.

Phila. or **Philada.** Philadelphia.

Phile. or **Philem.** Philemon.

philol. philological; philology.

philos. philosopher; philosophical; philosophy.

Phil. Soc. Philological Society (Brit.).

phon. phonetics.

phonog. phonography.

phonol. phonology.

phot. or **photog.** photographic; photography.

photom. photometry.

phr. phrase.

phren. or **phrenol.** phrenological; phrenology.

phys. physical; physician; physics; physiological; physiology.

physiol. physiological; physiologist; physiology.

phytogeog. phytogeography.

P. I. Philippine Islands.

pinx. *pinxit* (L.), he, or she, painted (it).

Pitts. Pittsburgh.

pizz. *pizzicato* (It.), pinched, played by plucking with the finger (*music*).

P. J. Police Justice; Presiding Judge; Probate Judge.

pk. park; peak; peck (pl. *pks.*).

P. K. piqué.

pkg. (pl. *pkgs.*) package.

pkt. (pl. *pkts.*) packet.

pl. place; plate; plural.

p. l. partial loss.

P. L. Poet Laureate; Primrose League (Brit.).

plat. plateau.

plf. or **plff.** plaintiff.

plup. or **plupf.** pluperfect.

plur. plural.

pm. premium.

P. M. Past Master; Paymaster; Police Magistrate; Postmaster; *post meridiem* (L.), after noon; post-mortem; Provost Marshal.

P. M. G. Paymaster-General; Postmaster-General.

p. n. promissory note.

pneum. pneumatic; pneumatics.

pnxt. *pinxit* (L.), he, or she, painted (it).

po. put-outs (baseball).

P. O. Petty Officer; postal order; post-office; Province of Ontario.

P. O. B. post-office box.

P. O. D. pay on delivery; Post-Office Department.

poet. poetical; poetry.

pol. political; politics.

Pol. Poland; Polish.

pol. econ. political economy.

polit. political; politics.

poly. polytechnic.

P. O. O. post-office order.

pop. popular; population.

port. portrait.

Port. Portugal; Portuguese.

pos. positive.

poss. possessive.

pot. potential.

pp. pages; past participle; *pianissimo* (It.), very soft (*music*).

p. p. partly paid; past participle; *per procurationem* (L.), by procuration, by the agency of another; post-paid, or prepaid.

P. P. parcel post; Parish Priest; *præmissis præmittendis* (L.), the proper forms of prefix or address being observed (a polite formula employed in business circulars, etc., esp. in German use).

P. P. C. *pour prendre congé* (F.), to take leave; President of the Privy Council.

pph. pamphlet.

p. p. i. policy proof of interest.

ppp. *pianissimo* (It.), very soft (*music*).

ppr. or **p. pr.** participle present.

P. P. S. *post postscriptum* (L.), a second postscript.

P. Q. previous question; Province of Quebec.

Pr (no period) praseodymium.

pr. pair (pl. *prs.*); preference; preferred; present; price; priest; printer.

Pr. Prince; Provençal.

P. R. Parliamentary Reports; Porto Rico.

P. R. B. Pre-Raphaelite Brotherhood.

prec. preceding.

pred. predicate.

pref. preface; preference; preferred; prefix.

prelim. preliminary.

prem. premium.

Prem. Premier.

prep. preparatory; preposition.

pres. present; pressure; presumptive.

Pres. President.

Presb. Presbyterian.

Prest. President.

pret. preterit.

prin. principal.

priv. privative.

p. r. n. *pro re nata* (L.), as the occasion may require.

prob. probable; probably; problem.

proc. proceedings.

prod. produced.

Prof. Professor.

Prog. Progressive.

prol. prologue.

prom. promontory; promoted.

pron. pronominal; pronoun; pronounced; pronunciation.

pronom. pronominal.

pronunc. pronunciation.

prop. proper; properly; property; proposition; proprietor.

propr. proprietor.

pros. prosody.

Pros. Atty. Prosecuting Attorney.

Prot. Protestant.

pro tem. *pro tempore* (L.), for the time, temporarily.

prov. provident; province; provincial; provisional.

Prov. Provençal; Proverbs; Provost.

prox. *proximo* [*mense*] (L.), of the next or coming month.

prs. pairs.

Prus. Prussia; Prussian.

Ps. Psalms.

P. S. *postscriptum* (L.), postscript; Privy Seal; Public School; Public Service.

P. S. A. L. Public Schools Athletic League.

pseud. pseudonym.

psych. or **psychol.** psychological; psychologist; psychology.

Pt (no period) platinum.

pt. (pl. *pts.*) part; payment; pint; point; port.

p. t. *pro tempore* (L.), for the time, temporarily.

p. t. o. please turn over.

pub. public; publication; published; publisher; publishing.

pur. purchasing.

pvt. private. [istration.

P. W. A. Public Works Admin-

P. W. D. Public Works Department.

pwt. pennyweight.

pxt. *pinxit* (L.), he, or she, painted (it).

pyrotech. pyrotechnics.

Q

q. *quadrans* (L.), farthing; quart; query; question; quintal; quire.

Q. quarto; Quebec; Queen; Queensland; query; question.

qa. *quadrans* (L.), farthing.

q. b. quarter-back (*football*).

Q. B. Queen's Bench.

Q. C. Queen's Counsel.

q. d. *quasi dicat* (L.), as if one should say; *quasi dictum* (L.), as if said.

Q. E. D. *quod erat demonstrandum* (L.), which was to be demonstrated.

Q. E. F. *quod erat faciendum* (L.), which was to be done.

Q. E. I. *quod erat inveniendum* (L.), which was to be found out.

ql. quintal.

q. l. or **q. lib.** *quantum libet* (L.), as much as you please.

Q. M. Quartermaster.

Q. M. C. Quartermaster Corps.

Q. M. G. Quartermaster-General.

q. p. or **q. pl.** *quantum placet* (L.), as much as you please.

qq. v. *quæ vide* (L.), which (words, etc.) see.

qr. *quadrans* (L.), farthing; quarter; quire (pl. *qrs.*).

q. s. *quantum sufficit* (L.), as much as suffices; quartersection.

qt. (pl. *qts.*) quart.

q. t. quiet (slang).

qu. query; question.
quad. quadrangle.
quar. or **quart.** quarter; quarterly.
Que. Quebec.
Queensl. Queensland.
ques. question.
quot. quotation.
q. v. *quantum vis* (L.), as much as you wish; *quod vide* (L.), which see.
qy. query.

R

R (no period) radical (*chem.*).
r. radius; railroad; railway; rare; received; recto; residence; resides; retired; right; rises; rod; rood; ruble; runs (*baseball*); rupee.
R. Radical; Réaumur (thermometer); *Regina* (L.), Queen; Republican; response; *Rex* (L.), King; River.
Ra (no period) radium.
R. A. Rear-Admiral; Royal Academician; Royal Academy; Royal Artillery.
rad. radical; radix.
Rad. Radical.
R. A. F. Royal Air Force.
rall. *rallentando* (It.), slackening, becoming slower (*music*).
R. A. M. Royal Academy of Music; Royal Arch Mason.
R. A. M. C. Royal Army Medical Corps.
R. & I. *Regina et Imperatrix* (L.), Queen and Empress; *Rex et Imperator* (L.), King and Emperor.
Rb (no period) rubidium.
R. B. A. Royal Society of British Artists.
R. B. S. Royal Society of British Sculptors.
R. C. Red Cross; Roman Catholic.
R. C. M. Royal College of Music.
R. C. O. Royal College of Organists.
R. C. P. Royal College of Physicians.
R. C. S. Royal College of Surgeons.
R. C. V. S. Royal College of Veterinary Surgeons.
Rd (no period) radium.
rd. rendered; road.
r. d. refer to drawer [of check].
R. D. Royal Dragoons; Royal Naval Reserve Decoration (Brit.); Rural Dean; rural delivery.
re. rupee.
r. e. right end (*football*).
R. E. Reformed Episcopal; Royal Engineers; Royal Society of Painter-Etchers.
Réaum. Réaumur (thermometer).
rec. receipt; recipe; record; recorded; recorder.
recd. received.
rec. sec. recording secretary.
rect. receipt; rectory.

redupl. reduplicated; reduplication.
ref. referee; reference; referred; reformation; reformed.
Ref. Ch. Reformed Church.
refl. reflexive; reflexively.
reg. register; registered; registrar; registry; regular; regularly.
Reg. Regent; *Regina* (L.), Queen.
regd. registered.
Reg. Prof. Regius Professor.
regt. regiment.
rel. relative; relatively; religion; religious.
rep. repeat; repeated; report; reported; reporter; representative; republic.
Rep. Republican.
repr. represented; representing; reprint; reprinted.
Repub. Republican.
res. reserve; residence; resides.
ret. retired.
retd. retained; returned.
rev. revenue; reverse; review; revised; revision; revolution.
Rev. Revelation; Reverend.
Rev. Stat. or **Rev. Stats.** Revised Statutes.
Rev. Ver. Revised Version.
rf. right fielder (*baseball*).
R. F. *République Française* (F.). [tillery.
R. F. A. Royal Field-Artillery.
R. F. C. Reconstruction Finance Corporation; Royal Flying Corps.
R. F. D. rural free delivery.
r. g. right guard (*football*).
R. G. S. Royal Geographical Society.
Rh (no period) rhodium.
r. h. right hand.
R. H. Royal Highlanders; Royal Highness. [tillery.
R. H. A. Royal Horse-Artillery.
r. h. b. right half-back (*football*).
rhet. rhetoric; rhetorical.
R. H. G. Royal Horse-Guards.
R. H. S. Royal Historical Society; Royal Horticultural Society; Royal Humane Society.
R. I. Rhode Island; Royal Institute of Painters in Water-Colours; Royal Institution of Great Britain.
R. I. See *R. & I.*
R. I. B. A. Royal Institute of British Architects.
Rich. Richard.
R. I. P. *requiescat* (or *requiescant*) *in pace* (L.), may he or she (or they) rest in peace.
rit. or **ritard.** *ritardando* (It.), retarding (*music*).
riv. river.
rm. (pl. *rms.*) ream.
R. M. Resident Magistrate; Royal Mail; Royal Marines.
R. M. A. Royal Marine Artillery; Royal Military Academy.

R. M. C. Royal Military College.
R. M. S. Railway Mail Service; Royal Mail Steamer.
R. N. Registered Nurse; Royal Navy.
R. N. A. S. Royal Naval Air Service.
R. N. R. Royal Naval Reserve.
ro. recto; rood.
Robt. Robert.
Rom. Roman; Romance; Romans.
Rom. Cath. Roman Catholic.
R. O. T. C. Reserve Officers' Training Corps.
R. P. Reformed Presbyterian; Regius Professor.
R. P. D. *Rerum Politicarum Doctor* (L.), Doctor of Political Science.
R. P. E. Reformed Protestant Episcopal.
r. p. m. revolutions per minute.
R. P. O. Railway Post-Office.
rpt. report.
R. R. Railroad.
R. R. C. Lady of the Royal Red Cross (Brit.).
rs. rupees.
r. s. right side.
R. S. Revised Statutes.
R. S. A. Royal Scottish Academician; Royal Scottish Academy.
R. S. F. S. R. Russian Socialist Federal Soviet Republic.
R. S. P. C. A. Royal Society for the Prevention of Cruelty to Animals.
R. S. V. P. *répondez, s'il vous plaît* (F.), reply, if you please.
rt. right.
r. t. right tackle (*football*).
Rt. Hon. Right Honorable.
Rt. Rev. Right Reverend.
R. T. S. Religious Tract Society (Brit.).
Ru (no period) ruthenium.
Rum. Rumania; Rumanian.
Russ. Russia; Russian.
Rutd. or **Rutl.** Rutlandshire.
R. V. Revised Version.
R. V. O. Royal Victorian Order (Brit.).
R. W. Right Worshipful; Right Worthy.
R. W. S. Royal Water-Colour Society.
Ry. Railway.
R. Y. S. Royal Yacht Squadron.

S

S (no period) sulphur.
s. second; section (pl. *ss.*); series; sets; *siècle* (F.), century; *siehe* (G.), see; singular; *solĭdus*, or *solidi* (L.), shilling, or shillings; son; soprano; substantive; succeeded; sun.
S. Sabbath; Saint (pl. *SS.*);

Saskatchewan; Saturday; Saxon; School; Sea; *Seite* (G.), page; Senate; September; sextodecimo; *signa* (L.), mark, label (*phar.*); *Signor* (It.); Socialist; Society; *Socius* (L.), Fellow; south; southern; Sunday; surplus.
Sa (no period) samarium.
s. a. *sine anno* (L.), without year or date; subject to approval.
S. A. Salvation Army; *Son Altesse* (F.), His, or Her, Highness; South Africa; South African; South America; South American; South Australia.
Sab. Sabbath.
S. A. E. Society of Automotive Engineers.
S. Afr. South Africa; South African.
Salv. Salvador.
Sam. or **Saml.** Samuel.
Sans. Sanskrit.
Sar. Sardinia.
S. A. R. Sons of the American Revolution.
S. A. S. Fellow [L. *Socius*] of the Society of Antiquaries (Brit.).
Sask. Saskatchewan.
Sat. Saturday.
Sax. Saxon; Saxony.
Sb (no period) *stibium* (L.), antimony.
sb. substantive.
S. B. *Scientiæ Baccalaureus* (L.), Bachelor of Science; South Britain (England and Wales).
Sc (no period) scandium.
sc. scene; science; scientific; *scilicet* (L.), to wit, namely, that is to say; scruple; *sculpsit* (L.), he, or she, carved (it).
Sc. Scotch; Scotland; Scots; Scottish.
s. c. small capitals.
S. C. Signal Corps; South Carolina; Staff Corps; Supreme Court.
Scand. Scandinavia; Scandinavian.
s. caps. small capitals.
Sc. B. *Scientiæ Baccalaureus* (L.), Bachelor of Science.
Sc. D. *Scientiæ Doctor* (L.), Doctor of Science.
sch. school; schooner.
sched. schedule.
schr. schooner.
sci. science; scientific.
scil. *scilicet* (L.), to wit, namely.
Sc. M. *Scientiæ Magister* (L.), Master of Science.
Scot. Scotch; Scotland; Scottish.
scr. scruple.
Script. Scriptural; Scripture.
sculp. sculptor; sculpture.
sculps. *sculpsit* (L.), he, or she, carved (it).
sd. sound.
s. d. sight draft; *sine die* (L.), without day, without day fixed for meeting again.

S. D. *Scientiæ Doctor* (L.), Doctor of Science; South Dakota.

S. Dak. South Dakota.

Se (no period) selenium.

S. E. southeast; southeastern.

sec (no period) secant.

sec. second; secretary; section; *secundum* (L.), according to.

sec. art. *secundum artem* (L.), according to art or rule.

sec. leg. *secundum legem* (L.), according to law.

Sec. Leg. Secretary of Legation.

sec. reg. *secundum regulam* (L.), according to rule.

sect. section.

secy. secretary.

seg. segment.

sem. seminary.

Sem. Semitic.

Sen. Senate; Senator; Senior.

Sep. September; Septuagint.

Sept. September; Septuagint.

seq. sequel; *sequens* (L.), the following (pl. *seqq.*).

ser. series; sermon.

Serb. Serbian.

Serg. or **Sergt.** Sergeant.

serv. servant.

Serv. Servian.

servt. servant.

s. f. sinking-fund.

S. F. San Francisco.

sfz. *sforzando* (It.), with force or emphasis (*music*).

s. g. specific gravity.

S. G. Solicitor-General.

sgd. signed.

Sgt. Sergeant.

sh. share; shilling; shillings; shoal; short.

Shak. Shakspere.

shpg. shipping.

shpt. shipment.

S. H. S. Fellow [L. *Socius*] of the Historical Society (Brit.).

s. h. v. *sub hac voce* or *sub hoc verbo* (L.), under this word.

Si (no period) silicon.

S. I. Staten Island.

Sib. Siberia; Siberian.

Sic. Sicilian; Sicily.

sig. *signa* (L.), mark, label (*phar.*); signature.

Sig. *Signor* (It.).

Siga. *Signora* (It.).

Sil. Silesia.

sin (no period) sine.

sing. singular.

Sing. Singapore.

sist. sister.

S. J. Society of Jesus (Jesuit).

S. J. C. Supreme Judicial Court.

S. J. D. *Scientiæ Juridicæ Doctor* (L.), Doctor of Juridical Science.

Skr. or **Skt.** Sanskrit.

S. L. serjeant at law; solicitor at law; south latitude.

S. lat. south latitude.

Slav. Slavic; Slavonic.

sld. sailed; sold.

Sm (no period) samarium.

S. M. *Sa Majesté* (F.), His, or Her, Majesty; *Santa Maria* (It.), Saint (or Holy) Mary; *Scientiæ Magister* (L.), Master of Science; Sergeant-Major; Staff-Major; State Militia.

sm. c. or **sm. caps.** small capitals.

S. M. E. *Sancta Mater Ecclesia* (L.), Holy Mother Church.

S. M. I. *Sa Majesté Impériale* (F.), His, or Her, Imperial Majesty.

s. m. p. *sine mascula prole* (L.), without male issue.

Sn (no period) *stannum* (L.), tin.

s. n. *secundum naturam* (L.), according to nature; *sine nomine* (L.), without name.

Snr. *Senhor* (Pg.).

Snra. *Senhora* (Pg.).

so. south; southern.

s. o. seller's option.

soc. society.

sociol. sociological; sociology.

Soc. Isl. Society Islands.

S. of Sol. Song of Solomon.

S. of T. Sons of Temperance.

sol. solicitor; solution.

Som. Somersetshire.

Somal. Somaliland.

sop. soprano.

S O S (no period). See Dictionary.

sou. south; southern.

sov. sovereign.

sp. special; species; specimen; spelling.

Sp. Spain; Spanish.

s. p. *sine prole* (L.), without issue; supra protest.

S. P. C. A. Society for the Prevention of Cruelty to Animals.

S. P. C. C. Society for the Prevention of Cruelty to Children.

S. P. C. K. Society for Promoting Christian Knowledge (Brit.).

spec. special; specially; specific; specifically.

specif. specific; specifically.

S. P. G. Society for the Propagation of the Gospel.

sp. gr. specific gravity.

Spgs. Springs.

spl. special.

S. P. Q. R. *Senatus Populusque Romanus* (L.), the Senate and People of Rome.

S. P. R. Society for Psychical Research (Brit.).

s. p. s. *sine prole superstite* (L.), without surviving issue.

spt. seaport.

sq. *sequens* (L.), the following (pl. *sqq.*); squadron; square.

Sr (no period) strontium.

Sr. Senior; *Señor* (Sp.).

Sra. *Señora* (Sp.).

S. R. O. standing-room only.

S. R. S. Fellow [L. *Socius*] of the Royal Society.

Srta. *Señorita* (Sp.).

ss. *scilicet* (L.), to wit, namely; sections; shortstop (*baseball*).

SS. Saints; *Seiten* (G.), pages.

S. S. Secret Service; steamship; Sunday-School.

S. S. B. *Sacræ Scripturæ Baccalaureus* (L.), Bachelor of Sacred Scripture.

S. S. C. Solicitor before the Supreme Courts (Scotland).

SS. D. *Sanctissimus Dominus* (L.), Most Holy Lord (a title of the Pope).

S. S. D. *Sacræ Scripturæ Doctor* (L.), Doctor of Sacred Scripture.

S. S. E. south-southeast.

S. S. L. *Sacræ Scripturæ Licentiatus* (L.), Licentiate of Sacred Scripture.

S. S. W. south-southwest.

st. stanza; *stet* (L.), let it stand or remain (*printing*); stone (weight: pl. *st.*); strait (pl. *sts.*); street (pl. *sts.*).

St. Saint.

s. t. short ton.

sta. station.

Sta. *Santa* (It.), Saint (female).

stacc. *staccato* (It.), detached, disconnected(*music*).

Staff. or **Staffs.** Staffordshire.

stat. statute.

S. T. B. *Sacræ Theologiæ Baccalaureus* (L.), Bachelor of Sacred Theology; *Scientiæ Theologicæ Baccalaureus* (L.), Bachelor of Theology.

S. T. D. *Sacræ Theologiæ Doctor* (L.), Doctor of Sacred Theology.

Ste. *Sainte* (F.), Saint (female).

Steph. Stephen.

ster. sterling.

St.-Ex. Stock-Exchange.

stg. sterling.

stk. stock.

S. T. L. *Sacræ Theologiæ Lector* (L.), Reader in Sacred Theology; *Sacræ Theologiæ Licentiatus* (L.), Licentiate of Sacred Theology.

S. T. M. *Sacræ Theologiæ Magister* (L.), Master of Sacred Theology; *Scientiæ Theologicæ Magister* (L.), Master of Theology.

stn. station.

S. T. P. *Sacræ Theologiæ Professor* (L.), Professor of Sacred Theology.

str. steamer; strait.

Str. Setts. Straits Settlements.

sub. subaltern; subscription; substitute; suburb; suburban.

subj. subject; subjunctive.

subst. substantive; substantively; substitute.

suff. suffix.

Suff. Suffolk; Suffragan.

Suffr. Suffragan.

Sun. or **Sund.** Sunday.

sup. superior; superlative;

supine; supplement; *supra* (L.), above, before.

Sup. C. Superior Court; Supreme Court.

superl. superlative.

supp. supplement.

supt. superintendent.

sur. surplus.

Sur. Surrey.

surg. surgeon; surgery; surgical.

surv. surveying; surveyor; surviving.

Sus. Sussex.

sus. per coll. *suspendatur* (or *suspensio*, or *suspensus*) *per collum* (L.), let him be hanged (or hanging, or hanged) by the neck.

s. v. *sub verbo* or *sub voce* (L.), under the word or heading.

S. V. *Sancta Virgo* (L.), Holy Virgin; Sons of Veterans.

S. V. P. *s'il vous plaît* (F.), if you please.

Sw. Sweden; Swedish.

S. W. South Wales; southwest; southwestern.

Swed. Sweden; Swedish.

Switz. Switzerland.

Syd. Sydney (Australia).

syll. syllable; syllabus.

syn. synonym; synonymous.

synop. synopsis.

Syr. Syria; Syriac.

syst. system.

T

t. temperature; *tempore* (L.), in the time of; tenor; tense; *tome* (F.), volume; *tomus* (L.), volume; ton; tonneau (*metric system*); town; transitive; tun.

T. Territory; Testament; *T*(*h*)*eil* (G.), part, volume; Tuesday.

Ta (no period) tantalum.

T. A. Territorial Army (Brit.).

tan (no period) tangent.

Tasm. Tasmania.

Tb (no period) terbium.

t. b. trial balance; tuberculosis (colloq.).

t. b. m. tired business man (colloq.).

t. c. *tre corde* (It.), 'three strings,' release the soft pedal (*music*).

T. D. Territorial Decoration (Brit.).

Te (no period) tellurium.

T. E. Topographical Engineer.

tech. technical; technology.

technol. technology.

tel. telegram; telegraph; telephone.

teleg. telegraphy.

teleph. telephony.

temp. temperature; temporary; *tempore* (L.), in the time of.

ten. tenor; *tenuto* (It.), held, sustained (*music*).

Tenn. Tennessee.

ter. terrace; territory.

term. terminal; termination.

Test. Testament.

Teut. Teutonic.

Tex. Texas.

t. f. till forbidden.

t. g. type genus.

Th (no period) thorium.

Th. *T(h)eil* (G.), part, volume; Thursday.

T. H. Territory of Hawaii.

Th. D. *Theologiæ Doctor* (L.), Doctor of Theology.

theat. theatrical.

Theo. Theodore.

theol. theologian; theological; theology.

theor. theorem.

theos. theosophical; theosophy.

therap. therapeutic; therapeutics.

Thes. or **Thess.** Thessalonians.

thlr. thaler.

Thos. Thomas.

Thurs. Thursday.

Ti (no period) titanium.

Tim. Timothy.

tinct. tincture.

tit. title.

Tit. Titus.

Tl (no period) thallium.

t. l. o. total loss only.

Tm (no period) thulium.

TNT or **T. N. T.** trinitrotoluene; trinitrotoluol.

t. o. telegraph office; turn over.

Tob. Tobit (Apocrypha).

tonn. tonnage.

topog. topographical; topography.

Tor. Toronto.

tox. or **toxicol.** toxicology.

tp. township.

t. p. title-page.

Tr (no period) terbium.

tr. transitive; translated; translation; translator; transpose; treasurer; *trillo* (It.), trill (*music*); trustee.

t. r. tons registered; trust receipts.

traf. traffic.

trag. tragedy.

trans. transactions; transitive; translated; translation; translator; transportation.

transf. transferred.

Transv. Transvaal.

trav. traveler; traveling.

treas. treasurer; treasury.

T. R. H. Their Royal Highnesses.

trig. or **trigon.** trigonometric; trigonometry.

Trin. Trinity.

trop. tropic; tropical.

T. S. twin-screw (steamer).

t. t. telegraphic transfer.

T. T. L. to take leave.

Tu (no period) tungsten.

Tu. Tuesday.

T. U. Trade-Union.

Tues. Tuesday.

Turk. Turkey; Turkish.

twp. township.

ty. territory.

typ. or **typog.** typographer; typographical; typography.

U

U (no period) uranium.

u. uncle; *und* (G.), and.

U. Unionist; University.

U. B. United Brethren.

u. c. *una corda* (It.), 'one string,' soft pedal (*music*); upper-case.

U. C. V. United Confederate Veterans.

U. D. C. United Daughters of the Confederacy.

U. F. C. United Free Church (of Scotland).

U. J. D. *Utriusque Juris Doctor* (L.), Doctor of Both Laws [canon and civil].

U. K. United Kingdom.

Ukr. Ukraine.

ult. ultimate; ultimately; *ultimo [mense]* (L.), of last month.

Unit. Unitarian.

univ. universal; universally; university.

Univ. Universalist.

U. of S. Afr. Union of South Africa.

up. upper.

U. P. United Presbyterian.

Uru. Uruguay.

u. s. *ubi supra* (L.), in the place above (mentioned); *ut supra* (L.), as above.

U. S. United States.

U. S. A. United States Army; United States of America.

U. S. D. United States Dispensatory.

u. s. f. *und so ferner* (G.), and so forth.

U. S. L. United States Legation.

U. S. M. United States Mail; United States Marine(s); United States Mint.

U. S. M. A. United States Military Academy.

U. S. M. C. United States Marine Corps.

U. S. M. H. S. United States Marine Hospital Service.

U. S. N. United States Navy.

U. S. N. A. United States National Army; United States Naval Academy.

U. S. N. G. United States National Guard.

U. S. P. or **U. S. Pharm.** United States Pharmacopœia.

U. S. P. H. S. United States Public Health Service.

U. S. R. C. S. United States Revenue-Cutter Service.

U. S. S. United States Scouts; United States Senate; United States Service; United States Ship.

U. S. S. B. United States Shipping Board.

U. S. Sig. Serv. United States Signal Service.

U. S. S. R. Union of Socialist Soviet Republics.

U. S. S. S. United States Steamship.

usu. usual; usually.

U. S. V. United States Volunteers.

u. s. w. *und so weiter* (G.), and so forth.

Ut. Utah.

ut dict. *ut dictum* (L.), as directed.

ut sup. *ut supra* (L.), as above.

ux. *uxor* (L.), wife.

V

V (no period) vanadium.

V Roman numeral for 5.

v. vector; verb; verse (pl. *vv.*); version; verso; *versus* (L.), against; *verte* (L.), turn over; vice-; *vide* (L.), see; village; vocative; volt; volume; *von* (G.), of.

V. Venerable; Viscount; Volunteers.

Va. Virginia.

v. a. verb active.

V. A. Royal Order of Victoria and Albert (Brit.); Vicar Apostolic; Vice-Admiral.

val. valley.

var. variant; variation; variety; various.

var. lect. *varia lectio* (L.), variant reading.

Vat. Vatican.

v. aux. verb auxiliary.

vb. verb.

vb. n. verbal noun.

V. C. Veterinary Corps; Vice-Chairman; Vice-Chamberlain; Vice-Chancellor; Vice-Consul; Victoria Cross (Brit.).

v. d. various dates.

V. D. Volunteer Officers' Decoration (Brit.).

v. def. verb defective.

v. dep. verb deponent.

Ven. Venerable; Venice.

Venez. Venezuela.

ver. version.

verb. sap., or **verb. sat,** or **verbum sap.** *verbum sapienti sat est* (L.), a word to the wise is sufficient.

verh. *verheiratet* (G.), married.

vers (no period) versed sine.

vers. version.

Ver. St. *Vereinigte Staaten* (G.), United States.

vet. veterinarian; veterinary.

V. F. Vicar Forane.

v. g. *verbi gratia* (L.), for example.

V. G. Vicar-General.

v. i. verb intransitive; *vide infra* (L.), see below.

V. I. Vancouver Island.

Vic. or **Vict.** Victoria.

vil. village.

Visc. Viscount.

viz. *videlicet* (L.), to wit, namely.

v. l. (pl. *vv. ll.*) *varia lectio* (L.), variant reading.

V. M. D. Doctor of Veterinary Medicine.

v. n. verb neuter.

vo. verso.

voc. vocative.

vocab. vocabulary.

vocat. vocative.

vol. volcanic; volcano; volume (pl. *vols.*); volunteer.

volc. volcanic; volcano.

v. p. verb passive.

V. P. or **V. Pres.** Vice-President.

v. r. verb reflexive.

V. R. *Victoria Regina* (L.), Queen Victoria.

V. Rev. Very Reverend.

vs. *versus* (L.), against.

v. s. *vide supra* (L.), see above.

V. S. Veterinary Surgeon.

Vt. Vermont.

v. t. verb transitive.

Vte. *Vicomte* (F.), Viscount.

Vtesse. *Vicomtesse* (F.), Viscountess.

Vul. or **Vulg.** Vulgate.

vulg. vulgar; vulgarly.

vv. verses.

v. v. *vice versa* (L.), the order being changed.

vv. ll. *variæ lectiones* (L.), variant readings.

v. y. various years.

W

W (no period) *wolframium* (L.), tungsten.

w. wanting; watt; week; wide; width; wife; with; won.

W. Wales; Warden; Wednesday; Welsh; west; western.

W. A. West Africa; Western Australia.

W. A. A. C. Women's Army Auxiliary Corps (Brit.).

Wal. or **Wall.** Wallachian; Walloon.

War. or **Warw.** Warwickshire.

Wash. Washington.

w. b. warehouse book; water-ballast; way-bill.

w. c. water-closet; without charge.

W. C. West Central (postal district, London).

W. C. T. U. Woman's Christian Temperance Union.

wd. ward; word.

W. D. War Department.

Wed. Wednesday.

Westm. Westminster.

Westmd. Westmorland.

w. f. wrong font.

whf. wharf.

w. i. when issued.

W. I. West Indian; West Indies.

Wilts. Wiltshire.

W. Ind. West Indian; West Indies.

Wis. or **Wisc.** Wisconsin.

Wisd. Wisdom of Solomon (Apocrypha).

wk. (pl. *wks.*) week.

wkly. weekly.

wks. weeks; works.

W. L. or **W. long.** west longitude.

Wm. William.

W. N. W. west-northwest.

W. O. War Office (Brit.).

Worc. or **Worcs.** Worcestershire.
wp. worship.
W. R. West Riding (Yorkshire).
W. S. Writer to the Signet.
W. S. W. west-southwest.
wt. weight.
W. Va. West Virginia.
w. w. warehouse warrant.
Wy. or **Wyo.** Wyoming.

X

x (no period) ex (without); ex coupon; ex dividend; ex interest.
X (no period) xenon.
X Roman numeral for 10.
X. Χριστός (Christos) (Gr.), Christ.

x-c. or **x-cp.** ex (without) coupon.
x-d. or **x-div.** ex (without) dividend.
Xe (no period) xenon.
x-i. or **x-int.** ex (without) interest.
Xmas. Christmas.
Xn. Christian.
Xnty. Christianity.
XP ΧΡ(ΙΣΤΟΣ) (CHRISTOS) (Gr.), Christ.
Xt. Christ.
Xtian. Christian.
Xty. Christianity.

Y

Y (no period) yttrium.
y. yard; yards; year; years; youngest.

Y. Young Men's Christian Association.
Yb (no period) ytterbium.
Y.B. Year-Book.
yd. (pl. *yds.*) yard.
yeo. yeomanry.
Y. M. C. A. Young Men's Christian Association.
Y. M. H. A. Young Men's Hebrew Association.
Yorks. Yorkshire.
Y. P. S. C. E. Young People's Society of Christian Endeavor.
yr. year (pl. *yrs.*); younger; your.
yrs. years; yours.
Yt (no period) yttrium.
Y. T. Yukon Territory.
Y. W. C. A. Young Women's Christian Association.

Z

Zach. Zachary.
Zan. or **Zanz.** Zanzibar.
z. B. *zum Beispiel* (G.), for example.
Zech. Zechariah.
Zeph. Zephaniah.
Z. G. Zoölogical Garden(s).
Zn (no period) zinc.
zod. zodiac.
zoöchem. zoöchemical; zoöchemistry.
zoögeog. zoögeographical; zoögeography.
zoöl. zoölogical; zoölogist; zoölogy.
Zr (no period) zirconium.
Z. S. Zoölogical Society (London).
Zulu. Zululand.

U. S. Federal Agencies, etc.

AAA	Agricultural Adjustment Agency
AMA	Agricultural Marketing Administration
ARA	Agricultural Research Administration
BAE	Bureau of Agricultural Economics
BLS	Bureau of Labor Statistics
BWC	Board of War Communications
CAA	Civil Aeronautics Administration
CAB	Civil Aeronautics Board
CCC	Commodity Credit Corporation
CFEP	Committee on Fair Employment Practice
CPRB	Combined Production and Resources Board
DPC	Defense Plant Corporation
DSC	Defense Supplies Corporation
FBI	Federal Bureau of Investigation
FCA	Farm Credit Administration
FCC	Federal Communications Commission
FCIC	Federal Crop Insurance Corporation
FDA	Food and Drug Administration, or Food Distribution Administration
FDIC	Federal Deposit Insurance Corporation
FEA	Foreign Economic Administration
FHA	Federal Housing Administration
FHLBA	Federal Home Loan Bank Administration
FPA	Food Production Administration
FPC	Federal Power Commission
FPHA	Federal Public Housing Authority
FRC	Filipino Rehabilitation Commission
FSA	Federal Security Agency
FTC	Federal Trade Commission
FWA	Federal Works Agency
GAO	General Accounting Office
GPO	Government Printing Office
HOLC	Home Owners' Loan Corporation
ICC	Interstate Commerce Commission
MC	Maritime Commission
MRC	Metals Reserve Company
NACA	National Advisory Committee for Aeronautics
NDAC	National Defense Advisory Commission
NHA	National Housing Agency
NLRB	National Labor Relations Board
NRPB	National Resources Planning Board
NWLB	National War Labor Board
NYA	National Youth Administration
OAPC	Office of Alien Property Custodian
OAWR	Office for Agricultural War Relations
OCD	Office of Civilian Defense
OCIAA	Office of Coordinator of Inter-American Affairs
OCS	Office of Contract Settlement
ODT	Office of Defense Transportation

OEM	Office of Emergency Management
OES	Office of Economic Stabilization
OEW	Office of Economic Warfare
OFEA	Office of Foreign Economic Administration
OFEC	Office of Foreign Economic Coordination
OFRRO	Office of Foreign Relief and Rehabilitation Operations
OLLA	Office of Lend-Lease Administration
OPA	Office of Price Administration
OSRD	Office of Scientific Research and Development
OSS	Office of Strategic Services
OWI	Office of War Information
OWM	Office of War Mobilization
OWMR	Office of War Mobilization and Reconversion
PAW	Petroleum Administration for War
PBA	Public Buildings Administration
PHS	Public Health Service
PRA	Public Roads Administration
PWA	Public Works Administration
RDC	Rubber Development Corporation
REA	Rural Electrification Administration
RFC	Reconstruction Finance Corporation
RRA	Retraining and Reemployment Administration
RRB	Railroad Retirement Board
RRC	Rubber Reserve Company
SCS	Soil Conservation Service
SEC	Securities and Exchange Commission
SFAW	Solid Fuels Administration for War
SPB	Surplus Property Board
SSB	Social Security Board
SWPA	Surplus War Property Administration
SWPC	Smaller War Plants Corporation
TVA	Tennessee Valley Authority
UNRRA	United Nations Relief and Rehabilitation Administration
USECC	United States Employees' Compensation Commission
USES	United States Employment Service
USHA	United States Housing Authority
WDC	War Damage Corporation
WFA	War Food Administration
WLB	War Labor Board
WMC	War Manpower Commission
WPA	Work Projects Administration
WPB	War Production Board
WRA	War Relocation Authority
WRB	War Refugee Board
WSA	War Shipping Administration

BUSINESS TERMS

WORDS, PHRASES, AND ABBREVIATIONS COMMONLY USED IN BUSINESS

Edited by EDWARD JONES KILDUFF, M.A.

CHAIRMAN, DEPARTMENT OF BUSINESS ENGLISH, NEW YORK UNIVERSITY
SCHOOL OF COMMERCE, ACCOUNTS, AND FINANCE

A

@ — At; to.

A1 — A designation of first-class grade or quality.

Abst. — Abstract.

Abstract of title — An outline history of the original grant of, subsequent conveyances of, and encumbrances on, a parcel of real estate.

a/c — Account.

Acceptance, trade — See **Trade acceptance.**

Accommodation paper — Negotiable paper, such as checks, notes, etc., indorsed without consideration by one person or party to enable another to obtain cash or credit.

Account — In bookkeeping, a formal record of the debits and credits relating to the person named (or caption placed) at the head of the account.

Account, open — See **Open account.**

Account current — A running or continuous account usually between interrelated companies, between partners, or between partnerships, etc., and not necessarily settled every month.

Account payable — A trade account (one not represented by notes, drafts, etc.) for which payment has not yet been made.

Account receivable — A trade account (one not represented by notes, drafts, etc.) for which payment has not yet been received.

Account rendered — An account presented by creditor to debtor and showing amounts due and payable.

Accrued expense — Expense incurred but not yet paid.

Accrued income — Income earned but not yet received.

Accrued interest — The amount of interest accumulated at a given time but not yet paid (or received).

Accumulative stock (cumulative stock) — Usually preferred stock upon which the dividends, if not paid, accrue and must be paid before a dividend on common stock can be paid.

Ad (*pl.* **ads**) — Advertisement.

Addressograph — A machine that prints addresses upon envelopes, etc., from stencils. [Proprietary name.]

Adjustment — A settlement of a disputed account or claim.

Adv. — Advertisement.

Ad valorem (*Latin*) — According to value.

Advt. — Advertisement.

Agate line — A measure of advertising space. It is $\frac{1}{14}$ of an inch deep and one column wide.

Agt. — Agent.

Amortize — To liquidate or extinguish an indebtedness or other charge usually by periodic payments (or by charges) made to a sinking-fund, to a creditor, or to an account.

Amt. — Amount.

And interest — A term used to indicate that the interest that has accumulated on a bond up to date of transaction is not included in the quoted price.

Appraisal — The act of placing an estimated value on an asset or assets.

Appreciation — The increase in value of property.

Appropriation — Money set apart for a designated purpose.

Arbitrage — The operation of buying a security, commodity, etc., in one market and selling it in another at practically the same time to take advantage of a difference that exists in the quoted prices; also, a somewhat similar operation conducted in the same market.

Arrears — Debts not paid on the date due.

Asked price — See **Bid and asked.**

Assessed valuation — The valuation of property determined by an official for purposes of taxation.

Assets — Resources of a person or business consisting of such items as real property, machinery, raw material, notes, securities, etc.

Assign in blank — To make over a stock certificate or bond without inserting the name of the new owner in the space provided.

At a premium — A security is said to sell *at a premium* if it sells at a price higher than its par value; also, see **Loan at a premium.**

At par — At face value (which see).

At sight — Drafts or demand notes are said to be payable *at sight* if they are to be accepted and paid on presentation.

At the market — An order is said to be given *at the market* if the broker is instructed to buy or sell immediately a specified security or commodity at the best obtainable price in the open market.

Audit — In bookkeeping, an examination of accounts for the purpose of verifying them.

Average (down) — A speculator or investor is said *to average down* if, after having bought a security (or commodity), he later purchases more of the same security (or commodity) at a lower price in order to reduce the average cost of his holdings.

Average (up) — A speculator or investor is said *to average up* if, after having bought a security (or commodity), he later purchases more of the same security (or commodity) at a higher price in order to take advantage of a contemplated further rise in prices.

B

Back order — An order the shipment of which has been delayed because goods were out of stock.

Bad debt — A debt that is considered not to be collectible.

Bal. — Balance.

Balance — Difference between the credit total and the debit total of an account.

Balance due — Unpaid difference represented by the excess of debits over credits.

Balance-sheet — A statement of the financial position of a business on a specified date.

Bbl. — Barrel.

Bdls. — Bundles.

B/E — Bill of exchange.

Bear — In general business, one who believes that conditions are or will be unfavorable; in stock-markets, a bear operator is one who sells short with the expectation of covering at a lower price. See **Covering.**

Bearish — See **Bear.**

Bear market — A more or less prolonged declining market.

Bid and asked — The bid price is the price offered for a security; the asked price is the price at which a holder of a security is willing to sell.

Bid in — The owner or someone especially interested is said *to bid in* property at an auction sale if he makes the successful bid.

Bill-head — Printed form used by merchants for making out itemized statements.

Billing terms — Terms on which goods are sold.

Bill of exchange — See **Draft**.

Bill of lading — An acknowledgment by a common carrier of receipt of goods for transportation.

Bill of sale — A document transferring title in personal property from seller to buyer.

Bill receivable — A bill of exchange (draft) for which payment is outstanding.

Bill rendered — A term used to refer a debtor to an invoice previously submitted.

B/L — Bill of lading (which see).

Blank indorsement — Indorsement of a negotiable instrument consisting of only the name of the indorser.

Blue-sky law — A law to protect the public against unsound investing.

Bona fide (*Latin*) — In good faith; genuine.

Bonded goods — Goods stored in a government warehouse by an importer, who pays storage but does not pay the duty until the goods are removed for sale.

Book value — The value of a security or other asset as shown by the books of account of an individual or organization as distinguished from the actual or market price; as in "the *book value* of the stock of our company is $115 a share, although it is selling at only $95 in the market." Also, the value at which a security or other asset is carried on the books of an individual or organization that owns it as distinguished from the actual or market price; as in "the *book value* of our merchandise inventory is $10,000, whereas its present market price is only $8,500."

Boom — A rapid increase in price, development, numbers, etc.; as a *boom* in real estate, a *boom* in population.

Bradstreet's — One of the commercial agencies which publish financial directories. See **Commercial agency**.

Brand — A trade-mark or trade-name to identify a product, a distributor, or a manufacturer.

Breakage — An allowance or compensation made for the loss resulting from articles broken in transit.

Broker — An agent who deals in securities or commodities on a commission basis.

Brokerage — The commission charged by the agent for transacting business.

Bucket-shop — An office conducted nominally for the transaction of a stock-exchange business. It differs from a legitimate stock-exchange broker's office in that the proprietors do not actually execute the customers' buying or selling orders in the market.

Budget — A careful estimate of expected income and expense, or operating results, for a given period in the future.

Bull — In general business, one who believes that conditions are or will be favorable; in stock-markets, a bull operator is one who buys with the expectation of selling later at a higher price.

Bullish — See **Bull**.

Bull market — A more or less prolonged rising market.

Business cycle — A complete revolution of business activity; *e.g.*, a movement from a period of prosperity through one of depression and gradual improvement back to a period of prosperity.

Buy at the market — See **At the market**.

C

Calendar year — January 1 to December 31, inclusive.

Call — A demand for payment of a note, a subscription, or any other obligation; as a *call* for more margin. Also, in the stock-market, an agreement by which the maker, for value received, gives the holder the privilege of calling upon him for specified stock or commodity within a stated time and at a stated price.

Call loan — Loan of money payable on demand.

Call money — Money borrowed that is subject to return on demand of the lender.

c. & f. — Cost and freight (which see).

Cash discount — A term of sale meaning that the purchaser of merchandise is permitted to deduct a specified percentage from the face of the bill provided he pays the bill within a stipulated period.

Caveat emptor (*Latin*) — Let the buyer beware.

Certified check — A check across which the bank cashier or teller has written his signature to indicate that the bank itself has set aside from the drawer's account sufficient funds to meet the check.

Chain store — One of a group of retail stores in the same kind of business under the same ownership.

Checking account — Bank deposit subject to withdrawal by check at any time by the depositor.

Chgd. — Charged.

Chgs. — Charges.

c. i. f. — A term of sale meaning that cost, insurance, and freight are included in the price quoted.

Circular letter — See **Form letter**.

C/L — Car-load lot.

Clearing-house — A membership organization formed to adjust daily transactions among the members.

Close corporation — An incorporated business the stock of which a few persons control.

Closed shop — A shop employing only workers who are members of a union.

c/o — Care of.

C. O. D. — Cash on delivery.

Collateral — Security pledged for the payment of a loan.

Com. — Commission.

Commercial agency — A concern which investigates for the benefit of its subscribers the financial standing, reputation, and credit rating of individuals, firms, corporations, and others engaged in business.

Commercial paper — Drafts, promissory notes, or other negotiable instruments issued in business and calling for the payment of money.

Commission-merchant — A merchant who sells goods for the owner, who pays him a commission for the service.

Common carrier — An individual or company, such as a railroad or steamship line, which transports the public or goods for hire.

Common stock — Stock which has no preference in the matter of dividends, assets, etc.

Consignee — The person or party to whom merchandise is consigned.

Consignment — A shipment of goods. See **On consignment**.

Consignor — One who sends merchandise to another on consignment.

Consolidation — A combination of two or more businesses into one new and different business organization.

Controlling interest — This term indicates that one person or a small group has obtained by ownership or proxies enough shares to control the policies of the corporation.

Corner — A condition which exists when an individual or group owns or controls a sufficient amount of a stock or of a commodity to be in a position to dictate the price.

Cost and freight — A term of sale meaning that the charge for freight to destination is included in the price of the merchandise.

Coupon — A small certificate attached to a bond and designed to be cut off and presented for payment of interest due; also, a small section of an advertisement designed to be cut off and returned to the advertiser.

Covering — The operation of buying securities that one has sold short, in order to return them to the person from whom they were borrowed; a somewhat similar operation is employed in other markets in completing short selling. See **Selling short**.

C. P. A. — Certified Public Accountant; an accountant who has received a certificate from a State testifying that he has met the requirements for professional practice in that State.

Cr. — Credit.

Credit — Confidence placed in the ability and intention of purchaser of goods or borrower of money to make payment within a limited time; in bookkeeping, an entry representing a value received from the party or category indicated in the title of the account.

Credit memorandum — An informal record that the customer is entitled to an allowance or deduction.

Credit risk — See **Risk**.

Credit standing — Reputation for meeting financial obligations.

c/s — cases.

Ctge. — Cartage.

Cumulative pfd. stock — See **Accumulative stock**.

Current assets — Assets readily convertible into cash without serious sacrifice.

Current expenses — Regularly continuing expenditures for the maintenance and the carrying on of business.

Current liabilities — Indebtedness maturing within one year.

Cutting a melon — The declaring of an extra-large dividend in money or stock to the shareholders of a company.

c. w. o. — Cash with order. A term of sale meaning that payment for the merchandise must accompany the order.

cwt. — Hundredweight.

D

Dating — A term of sale meaning that the time (30 days, 60 days, etc.) allowed for the payment of the merchandise does not begin to run until a specified date in the future.

Dead beat — One who has a reputation for not paying his bills.

Deadhead — One who is given a free privilege, such as a pass to the theater.

Debenture bond — A term used to designate bonds unsecured except by the general assets and credit of the debtor who has issued the bonds.

Debenture stock — A term used to designate stock that has a prior preference over other issues of stock.

Debit — In bookkeeping, an entry representing a value charged to the party or category indicated in the title of the account.

Deficit — Financial shortage arising from an excess of expenses over income; also, an overdraft.

Demurrage — A compensation charged by common carriers (*e.g.*, a railroad) for detention of car or other type of conveyance beyond the specified period permitted.

Deposit slip — The form upon which the depositor lists the money and checks he is depositing at his bank.

Depreciation — Decrease in value due to wear and tear, decay, decline in price, etc.

Dictaphone — A kind of phonograph used in business for recording dictation. [Proprietary name.]

Disbursements, cash — Sums of money paid out.

Discount — Amount deducted for prompt payment or other special reason; also, a payment of interest in advance upon a loan of money.

Discount rate — Rate of interest charged in discounting commercial paper.

Dishonoring a draft — Refusal to pay or to accept a draft on presentation.

Display advertisement — An advertisement that seeks to accomplish its purpose by such means as striking typographical arrangement, color, illustration, etc.

Ditto — The same thing repeated.

Dividend — A pro rata share in an amount to be distributed; commonly, a sum of money paid to shareholders of a corporation out of earnings.

Do. — Ditto.

Dr. — Debtor.

Draft — A written order drawn by one party (the drawer) upon another (the drawee) directing the payment of money to a third party (the payee); also, sometimes the drawer and payee are the same party, in which case the draft is made payable to "ourselves."

Drawee — Person or party on whom a draft is drawn.

Drawer — Person or party who draws a draft.

Drawing account — An account that is charged with advances of money for expenses, on salaries, against earnings, etc.

Drop shipment — An order shipped direct from the factory to the retailer but billed by the wholesaler or jobber.

Dun — To demand payment.

Dun's — One of the commercial agencies which publish financial directories. See **Commercial agency.**

E

ea. — Each.

e. and o.e. — Errors and omissions excepted.

Earnest money — Part of the purchase price paid to bind the bargain; also called hand money.

e.e. — Errors excepted.

e.g. (*Latin*) — Exempli gratia; for example.

e.o.m. — End of month.

etc. (*Latin*) — Et cetera; and others, and so forth.

Even date — The same day.

Ex dividend — A stock is said to sell *ex dividend* if the buyer is not to receive the dividend last declared.

Ex rights — A stock is said to sell *ex rights* if the time has expired during which the owner of the stock possessed a privilege, such as that relating to subscribing to additional stock.

F

Face of bill — Front of bill. See **Face value.**

Face value — Par value; the value printed on the face of a financial instrument or document.

F. A. S. — Free alongside ship (which see).

Fig. — Figure.

Firm style — See **Style.**

Fiscal year — Any yearly period at the end of which a firm determines its financial condition without regard to the calendar year. February 1 to January 31 is an example of a fiscal year. A calendar year must be from January 1 to December 31 inclusive.

Fixed charges — Such charges as depreciation, rent, interest, etc., arising out of the maintenance of fixed assets.

Fixed liabilities — Indebtedness that does not fall due for more than one year.

Flat — See **Sells flat.**

Floating debt — Unfunded indebtedness; see **Funded debt.**

Floating stock — Stock not held for permanent investment and hence available for speculation; stock in the hands of brokers and speculators as distinguished from investors.

F.O.B. — Free on board (which see).

Form letter — A letter, printed, processed, or individually typed, copies of which are sent to a number of readers.

Free alongside ship (F. A. S.) — A term of sale meaning that the seller agrees to deliver the merchandise alongside ship without extra charge to buyer.

Free and clear — The title to real property is said to be *free and clear* if there is no legal claim, such as a mortgage, against it.

Free on board (F. O. B.) — A term of sale meaning that the seller agrees to deliver the merchandise aboard the carrier without extra charge to buyer.

Front foot — A foot of real property abutting on road or other thoroughfare, or water-front.

Funded debt — A debt that exists in the form of long-term obligations.

G

Gilt-edge — Highest quality or grade; highly recommended.

Gold brick — A swindle; a worthless article sold at a price the purchaser supposes a bargain.

Goods — Merchandise or commodities.

Good till cancelled — A provision of an order given to a broker or other agent empowering him to buy or sell a security or commodity at a stipulated price without limitation as to time. In other words, whereas the usual order is good only for the current day, a *G. T. C.* order stands until the principal cancels the order.

Good-will — An intangible asset arising from the favorable reputation a business has acquired through satisfactory service.

Gr. Gro. — Great gross; 1,728 articles.

Gro. — Gross; 144 articles.

Gross income — Total income from all sources before deductions have been made.

Gross profit — The total profit before the expenses of doing business have been deducted; the difference between the cost of goods and the selling price.

Gross receipts — Receipts before any deductions for expenses have been made.

Gross ton — 2,240 lbs.

Gross weight — Total weight without deduction for tare, tret, or waste.

G. T. C. — Good till cancelled (which see).

Guaranty (also spelled **Guarantee**) — An agreement to meet the obligations of another in case he defaults; a promise which secures or insures another against unsatisfactory merchandise or service.

H

Hand money — See **Earnest money.**

Hedging — Buying or selling to protect against a possible loss in another transaction.

hhd. —Hogshead.

Holding company — A company controlling other companies from which it derives its principal income.

Honor a draft — To accept and pay a draft according to the terms.

Hoovenizing — The process of typewriting individually each of a large number of copies of a business letter by means of the automatic, electrically operated typewriter known as the Hooven machine. It is possible to stop this machine, write in a name or other personal matter, and then have the machine resume the typing of the form letter.

Hypothecated accounts — Accounts receivable pledged by the original creditor to another person to secure a loan.

I

Inc. — Incorporated.

Index numbers — A series of numbers which shows relative changes in prices, immigration, etc.

Index prices — See **Index numbers.**

Indorse — The act of a holder in signing his name on the back of a draft, promissory note, check, etc.

Inflation — A condition that exists when there is a rise of prices due to an expansion in paper money or of bank credit.

In re (*Latin*) — With regard to; concerning.

Insolvent — Unable to meet financial obligations; bankrupt.

Instant — The present or current month; *e.g.*, your letter of the 10th *instant*.

In toto (*Latin*) — Entirely.

In transit — On the way from one place to another.

Inv. — Invoice; inventory; invalid.

Invoice — A written list of merchandise, with prices, delivered or sent to a buyer; also, an itemized bill containing the costs which comprise the total charge.

I O U (**I owe you**) — A written acknowledgment of a debt, containing the expression *I O U.*

Item — A separate article or particular.

Itemized bill — An invoice containing a detailed list of purchases or costs.

J

Jobber — A dealer who sells merchandise in quantity to retailers or other jobbers.

Joint account — Usually, a bank account kept in the names of two or more persons or parties and subject to check by any one of them.

Joint and several note — A note signed by two or more persons or parties who " jointly and severally promise to pay." Each person thus becomes individually liable for the full amount of the note.

Journal — In bookkeeping, a book of account in which are recorded in chronological order the original entries of business transactions.

Journal entry — A written entry in an accounting record known as a journal.

K

Kiting checks — In banking, a term usually employed to designate an unethical method used by depositors of drawing against uncollected checks which do not represent bona-fide business transactions. An example of one common method of kiting checks is as follows: An individual living in New York City has an account in a New York bank and another account in a bank in Hartford, Conn. His balance in each bank is $1,000. He is forced to meet immediately a pressing obligation for $2,500. To meet this obligation he draws a check for $2,500 on his New York bank. Before giving this check to his creditor he deposits in his New York bank a check for $1,800 drawn by him on his Hartford bank. This makes his balance in the New York bank $2,800. At the same time he mails to his Hartford bank for deposit a check for $1,800 drawn by him on his New York bank. When this check reaches his Hartford bank, his balance at the Hartford bank will be increased to $2,800. Basing his plan on the fact that it takes several days for his checks to pass through the Clearing House and to be returned to the banks, he continues this process of drawing against one bank and depositing in his other bank until either his operations are detected by the banks or he is able to cover the difference by depositing actual funds.

L

Lamb — An inexperienced speculator.

L. C. L. — Less than car-load lot.

Ledger — In bookkeeping, an account-book of final entry.

Letter-head — The printed heading at the top of a sheet of business stationery; also, the whole sheet.

Letter of credit. — An order issued by one banker upon another in a different place and authorizing the latter to pay to a specified person or party a certain sum to be charged to the account of the writer.

Letter-press copy — A copy of a letter or other business document obtained by moistening the inked surface of the original letter, placing a sheet of paper upon it, and pressing.

Liabilities — Debts or financial obligations.

Lien — A legal claim by which a creditor has a right to seize or hold property for the settlement of a debt.

Limited company — Under English law, a company in which as in a corporation in the United States the liability of each shareholder is limited.

Line of credit — The amount of credit granted to a customer.

Liquid assets — See **Current assets.**

Liquidation — The process of realizing upon assets and of discharging liabilities in winding up the affairs of a business, estate, etc.; in finance, the process of converting securities or commodities into cash for the purpose of taking profits or preventing losses.

List price — Price given in the catalogue; usually, price to ultimate consumer or user.

Loan at a premium (*In the Stock-market*) — When a security is loaned to a borrower who is required to pay a charge or premium, the security is said *to loan at a premium.*

Loan flat (*In the Stock-market*) — When a security is loaned without the loaner's being required to pay interest on the money deposited with him, the security is said *to loan flat.*

Lockout — The closing of a business by the employer because the employees are not willing to accept the terms of the employer.

Long — A speculator who has bought stocks for a rise in prices is said to be *long of stocks* or *long of the market.*

Long pull — Securities are said to be bought for a *long pull* if the purchaser expects that he may have to wait for some time before he can realize the full value on their sale.

Long-term bond — A bond not maturing for a long time.

Long ton — 2,240 pounds.

Loss leader — A popular article which is sold at a loss for the purpose of attracting trade to a retail store.

Ltd. — Limited. See **Limited company.**

Lump sum — An amount of money which is the aggregate or sum of several items.

M

Mailing list — A list of customers or prospective customers to whom letters, advertising matter, etc., are mailed.

Margin — The money or other collateral an investor or speculator in securities deposits with his broker to insure the broker against loss.

Margin of profit — The difference between cost and selling price.

Mark-up — The amount or percentage which a merchant adds to the cost of the article in fixing the selling price.

Maturity — The date set for the payment of a financial obligation.

Mdse. — Merchandise.

Melon — See **Cutting a melon.**

Memo. — Memorandum.

Mercantile agency — A concern which obtains information concerning the financial standing, business reputation, and credit ratings of individuals, firms, and corporations for the benefit of its subscribers.

Mercantile paper — See **Commercial paper.**

Merger — A combination of two or more businesses by the transfer of property to the corporation which continues in existence under the name of one of the businesses.

Messrs. — The abbreviation of the French title of address, *Messieurs* (Sirs).

Mfd. — Manufactured.

Mfg. — Manufacturing.

Mfr. — Manufacturer.

Mgr. — Manager.

Middleman — Usually, an intermediary who operates for his own account and risk in the distribution of goods from producer to consumer.

Milline rate — A rate charged per agate line of advertising space per million circulation.

Mimeograph — An apparatus for making copies of written or typed matter by means of stencils. [Proprietary name.]

Mixed loan — A loan secured by different types of collateral.

M. O. — Money-order.

Money-order — (*Postal*) An order drawn by one post-office on another for a sum deposited by the purchaser, and payable at the second office to the person designated; (*Express*) a similar order issued by an express company.

Mortgage bond — A bond secured by a mortgage on property.

Mtge. — Mortgage.

Multigraph — Combined rotary type-setting and printing machine, commonly used to reproduce typewritten matter. [Proprietary name.]

N

N. B. (*Latin*) — Nota bene; note carefully.

Negotiable — Capable of having full title transferred by indorsement or delivery from the transferor to the transferee.

Net cash — A term of sale meaning that the invoice is not subject to discount.

Net earnings — The amount of earnings after all expenses have been deducted.

Net income — The amount of profit or income remaining after deduction of all charges and expenses.

Net invoice — The total of the invoice after the deduction of discounts.

Net profit — The balance remaining after all charges, discounts, interest, etc., have been deducted from the gross profit.

Net selling price — The price after deduction of trade and cash discounts, rebates, allowances, etc.

Net surplus — The amount of profits remaining after payment of expenses of operation, taxes, insurance, interest on debts, appropriation to sinking-fund, dividends, etc.

Net thirty — A sales term meaning that the invoice is to be paid within 30 days without discount.

Net weight — The weight of goods after deduction for weight of container.

Net worth — The excess of assets over liabilities.

N. G. — No good.

No. — Number.

No protest — This term written on a draft or promissory note indicates that it is not to be protested if not paid.

N. P. — Notary Public.

O

Odd lot — On the New York Stock Exchange, less than 100 shares of stock, or less than $10,000 worth of bonds.

o. e. — Omissions excepted.

O. K. — All correct.

On consignment — Goods are said to be *on consignment* if the consignor retains title to the merchandise until a sale is completed by the consignee.

One-name paper — Unindorsed commercial paper.

On margin — See **Margin.**

On memorandum — See **On consignment.**

On order — Subject to the order of buyer.

Open account — An account to which the credit privilege has been granted; also, an account not in balance.

Opening price — The price at which the first sale of a security or commodity was made after the opening of the market.

Open shop — A factory or shop which employs union and non-union workers.

Option — The right obtained, for a consideration, to exercise a power of choice; *e.g.*, if a prospective purchaser has obtained the right to buy a piece of real estate at a specified price within a stipulated period of time, he is said *to hold an option* on it.

Overdraft — See **Overdraw.**

Overdraw — To draw a check for a larger amount than the drawer has on deposit with the bank.

Overhead — The general cost of running a business; also, the general cost which cannot be assigned to particular production orders.

P

Packaged goods — Goods that are put into convenient containers usually for consumer trade.

Paid-up shares — Securities for which the subscribers have paid in full.

Paid-up value — The amount of life insurance that the insured or beneficiary will receive under the terms of his life insurance policy should the insured discontinue paying his premiums.

P & L — Profit and loss [account]; in bookkeeping, a summary account to which are transferred the balances of accounts showing either a profit or a loss.

Panic — A sudden widespread fear concerning financial affairs.

Paper profits — Profits which are estimated on business or financial dealings not yet closed; unrealized profits.

Par value — The face value. If the face value of a share of stock is $50, its par value is also $50.

Pass-book — The book in which a bank enters the deposits, or deposits and withdrawals, of the depositor for the purpose of providing him with a record of them.

Passing a dividend — The failure by the board of directors to declare a dividend at the regular time.

Past-due account — An account which has matured but which has not been paid.

Payee — The person in whose favor a draft, note, or check is drawn.

Payment stopped — See **Stop payment.**

Pd. — Paid.

Per (*Latin*) — Through; by; for each.

Per annum (*Latin*) — By the year.

Per capita (*Latin*) — By the heads; by individuals.

Per cent (*Latin*) — By the hundred.

Percentage — The rate per hundred.

Per contra (*Latin*) — To the opposite side of an account.

Per diem (*Latin*) — By the day.

Perishable goods — Articles subject to speedy deterioration.

Petitioning creditor — A creditor who requests that a debtor be declared bankrupt and his property liquidated and the proceeds divided among the creditors.

Petty cash — A small cash fund set aside to meet incidental expenditures for office supplies and other small requirements.

Pfd. — Preferred.

Piece rate — The rate of compensation paid per piece.

Pit — A section of the Chicago Board of Trade where trading is done exclusively in one commodity, such as wheat.

Pit traders — Grain brokers who speculate on their own account.

Pkge. — Package.

Pledge — To place personal property in the possession of another as security for a loan.

Plum — In finance, an extra dividend, generally large.

Plunger — One who speculates heavily.

Pm. — Premium.

P. O. — Post-office.

Point — One dollar in the stock-market; one hundredth of a cent in the cotton and coffee markets.

Policy — The general rules by which a business is conducted.

Policy-holder — One who has an insurance policy in his possession or under his control.

Pool — An association of competitors who agree to control the production, market, and price of a commodity for mutual benefit, although they appear to be rivals; (*Stock-market*) a combination of persons to manipulate one or several securities in the stock-market.

Post — A place in the New York Stock Exchange where a particular stock is traded in. In bookkeeping, *to post* means to make entries in a ledger from other books of account.

Postdate — To date an instrument such as a check or invoice with a date later than the current date.

Power of attorney — A written document given by one person or party to another authorizing the latter to act for the former.

p.p. or **per pro.** (*Latin: per procurationem*) — An abbreviation usually placed before or above a signature to indicate limited agency of the person signing.

Pref. — Preferred.

Preferred creditor — A creditor who is legally entitled to a preference in the payment of his claim.

Preferred stock — Stock which has a preference, usually with respect to assets and dividends.

Prem. — Premium.

Premium — (*Stock-market*) The amount paid by the borrower of a stock to the lender of it for the use of the stock. See also **At a premium** and **Loan at a premium.** (*Ins.*) A sum of money paid to underwriters for insurance.

Prepaid — Paid in advance.

Price cutting — The act of selling an article at a price under the usual or advertised price.

Price list — A list of articles for sale, with prices.

Price maintenance — The exercise of control over the resale price of trade-marked merchandise sold for distribution.

Price mark — A code letter, word, or cipher used by a merchant to show the cost of an article.

Proceeds — Net amount obtained from a sale; amount remaining after the deduction of costs (as in discounting notes) or expenses (as in selling through a commission-merchant).

Processing — The act of reproducing letters in facsimile, as by the multigraph, etc.

Produce — Agricultural products.

Promissory note — A written agreement by one person or party to pay to the order of another or to bearer a specified sum on or before a stipulated time in the future.

Promoter — One who initiates the organization of a company, the development of a project, etc.

Pro rata (*Latin*) — In proportion; according to a certain rate.

Pro-rate — To divide or distribute proportionately.

Prospect — A prospective or possible purchaser.

Prospectus — An outline of a proposed business venture used for the purpose of soliciting subscriptions or offering an issue of securities.

Pro tem. (*Latin*) — For the time being.

Protest — A formal notarial certificate attesting the fact that a check, note, or bill of exchange has been presented for acceptance or payment and that it has been refused.

Proximo or **Prox.** (*Latin*) — In or of the next month after the present; as, on the 10th *proximo.*

Proxy — A written authorization empowering another to act for the signer; also the person so empowered.

P.S. — Postscript.

Put — An agreement by which a person acquires for a certain payment the option of selling to another a security or commodity at a stipulated price within a specified time.

Q

Qualified indorsement — An indorsement with the words *without recourse* added. See **Without recourse.**

Quick assets — See **Current assets.**

Quorum — The number of members of a body required to be present to transact business legally.

Quota — A proportional part or share of a fixed total amount, number, or quantity.

Quotation — The statement of the current or market price of a commodity or security.

R

Rally — A rise in prices in the stock-market after a sudden drop.

Rate of exchange — The ratio at which the unit of currency of one country can be exchanged on a given date for the unit of currency of another country.

Rating book — A book published by a commercial agency and containing in code the financial standing of individuals, firms, and corporations engaged in business.

Re (*Latin*) — See **In re.**

Reaction — A drop in the market after a continued advance in prices.

Realtor — A real estate broker who is a member of the National Association of Real Estate Boards.

Rebate — A return of part of an original amount paid for some service or merchandise.

Recd. — Received.

Receipt — A written acknowledgment of payment of an obligation or of the receiving of an article.

Receiver — A person appointed by the court to take charge of a business pending judicial action.

Rediscount — To discount commercial paper a second time; usually, applied to the act of the Federal Reserve Bank in discounting commercial paper for a member bank.

Reference — A person or party to whom one is referred for information concerning reputation, credit standing, etc.

Reg. — Registered.

Registered bond — A bond registered in the owner's name by the issuer as to principal, or principal and interest.

Remit — In business, to send money or its equivalent.

Remittance — Money or its equivalent sent from one place to another.

Rent — Compensation paid for the use of property.

Reserve fund — A fund set aside from the profits to meet contemplated losses or unforeseen contingencies.

Resources — Assets.

Ret. — Returned.

Retailer — A dealer who sells in small quantities to consumers.

Retainer — Usually, a fee given to a lawyer on engaging his services.

Return — The report or statement of financial condition; the yield of a security.

Revenue — Income.

Right — In finance, the privilege which accrues to the owners of the stock of a corporation to subscribe at an advantageous price to additional shares of stock to be issued.

Risk — In business, the degree of hazard in any uncertain undertaking. "Good risk," "fair risk," and "poor risk" are commonly used to indicate the credit standing of customers.

Rolling-stock — Mobile property of a railroad, such as locomotives, cars, etc.

R.R. — Railroad.

Runner — A messenger of a bank or brokerage house.

Running account — An unsettled account to which new items are added from time to time.

Run on a bank — The sudden drawing out of money by a large number of depositors who have lost confidence in the bank.

S

Sag — A slight decline in prices.

Sample — A small quantity to show the quality of the whole.

Saturation point — The market for an article is said to have reached its *saturation point* when additional sales of the article are limited to replacements and to the demand resulting from the growth of population.

Scrip — In finance, usually a certificate representing a fraction of a share of stock; also, a certificate to represent a dividend not paid in cash but deferred to a later date.

S/D — Sight draft.

Seasoned securities — Securities which have gained a favorable investment reputation because of a long record of successful business.

Sec. or **Secy.** — Secretary.

Secured creditor — A creditor who is assured payment by a pledge of property.

Securities — Usually, stocks and bonds.

Securities company — A company which derives its principal income from the securities which it owns of other companies.

Sell at the market — See **At the market.**

Seller's market — A market in which the seller is at an advantage because of scarcity of supply; a rising market.

Selling short — The operation of selling securities that one does not own and of making delivery to the purchaser by borrowing them, in the expectation of a decline in the price of the securities; a somewhat similar operation is employed in other markets, such as wheat, cotton, foreign exchange, etc. In the wheat market, for example, the operation is performed by selling wheat for delivery by a specified date in the future in the expectation of being able to buy that wheat at a lower price before delivery date. Shares of stock may also be sold for future delivery.

Sell out — (*Stock-exchange*) A broker is said *to sell out* a customer if he sells the securities he has been holding for the customer on margin because of the latter's failure to provide necessary additional margin.

Sells flat — Without the addition of interest to the market price.

Settlement — Full payment of a bill or claim.

Sh. — Share.

Shade — To make a small concession in price.

Share — One of the equal parts of the capital stock of a company.

Share certificate — Written evidence that the person or party named therein owns a specified number of shares of a company.

Shipping order — Form giving directions for shipping.

Shipt. — Shipment.

Short — One who is short of the market. See **Selling short.**

Shortage — A discrepancy between quantity of goods received and quantity called for by the invoice or bill of lading, usually due to error in packing or theft in transit; a deficit.

Short shipment — See **Shortage.**

Short ton — 2,000 pounds.

Sight draft — A draft payable upon presentation.

Silent partner — A partner who does not have an active voice in the management of a firm.

Sine die (*Latin*) — Without day; without naming a day.

Single-name paper — Unindorsed commercial paper.

Sinking-fund — A fund established to meet anticipated losses or to extinguish an indebtedness.

Sky-rocketing — Term used to describe the rapid soaring of the price of a security to unnaturally high levels.

Slow assets — Assets which can not readily be converted into cash.

Slump — A decline in prices.

Sold out — See **Sell out.**

Solvent — Financially sound.

Specie — Coined money.

Speculation — Buying or selling with the expectation of profiting by an advance or decline in prices.

Splitting commissions — Sharing commissions with a customer or other person for assistance in completing a business transaction.

Spot cash — Immediate payment of cash.

Spot delivery — Immediate delivery.

Spot goods — Goods ready for immediate delivery.

Spot quotation — Price for immediate delivery.

S. S. — Steamship.

Staple — A principal commodity in a mercantile field.

Statement of account — A transcription of an account since it was last in balance.

Stock — The capital of a company represented by shares; also, the merchandise used in trade.

Stock dividend — A dividend paid in stock.

Stock-taking — The act of inventorying the merchandise used in trade.

Stop order — An order given to a broker to sell out the stock, etc., if and when a designated lower price is reached.

Stop payment — An order by the drawer of a check to his bank not to pay a specified check.

Str. — Steamer.

Striking a balance — Determining the difference between debits and credits in an account.

Stringent money-market — A condition of the market when loans are difficult to obtain and command high rates of interest.

Stub — A small portion of a leaf of a check-book or receipt-book which remains as a memorandum concerning the contents of the detached part.

Style — The name under which one or more persons do business; *e.g.*, firm *style*.

Subject to check — A bank account against which the depositor has the right to draw by check without notice is said *to be subject to check.*

Subsidiary company — A company the controlling interest of which is owned by another company.

Surplus — The amount of undistributed profits.

T

Taking stock — Making an inventory of merchandise on hand.

Talking point — A special feature of a product that differentiates it from competing articles and makes it more desirable to prospective customers.

Tangible assets — Resources in the form of real estate or chattels.

Tape — The ribbon of white paper on which a ticker prints quotations or news. See **Ticker.**

Tare — The allowance for the weight of the container or vehicle.

Tariff — Schedule of prices or rates.

Tel. — Telegraph.

Tender — A bid or offer.

Terms of sale — Conditions on which a sale is made.

Thin margin — A narrow margin. See **Margin.**

Ticker — In finance, the popular name for the electrically operated instrument that prints on a narrow ribbon of paper known as tape market quotations transmitted by telegraph from the board room of an exchange. The stock ticker reports stock quotations; the cotton ticker reports sales of cotton; the news ticker prints general financial news that relates to the markets; etc.

Tickler system — A method which, by means of such a device as a card file, a series of dated folders, etc., assures that a matter held in abeyance will be brought up for attention at a desired time in the future.

Tight money — A condition that exists when it is difficult to borrow money except at a high rate.

Time card — A card upon which are recorded by days the times at which an employee arrived and departed.

Time deposit — A deposit that can be withdrawn by the depositor only after he has given the required advance notice.

Time discount — The discount allowed for payment before the invoice or bill is due.

Time loan — A loan usually for not less than 30 days and not more than six months.

Tip — Private information about the stock-market.

To account rendered — This phrase refers the customer to an itemized bill or statement that was previously sent to him.

Top price — The highest price.

Tracer — An inquiry to ascertain the whereabouts of undelivered merchandise, etc.

Trade acceptance — A time draft or bill of exchange arising from a current sale of merchandise, bearing on its face the written or stamped acceptance of the purchaser of the merchandise.

Trade discount — A deduction granted a customer from list prices.

Trade-mark — A symbol or name attached to merchandise to identify it as the product of a particular maker, and to distinguish it from similar products of other makers.

Trade reference — An individual or company in business to which one is referred for information concerning an applicant's credit standing.

Transaction — An operation in business.

Travelers' checks — Checks issued by a banker, express company, etc., to travelers, who may cash them at corresponding banks or branches of the issuer by indorsing them in sight of the payer.

Trust fund — A fund placed in the hands of a person, persons, or a corporation, in trust for a beneficiary.

Turnover — The number of times that capital is invested and reinvested in a line of merchandise during a specified period of time.

U

Ultimo or **Ult.** (*Latin*) — In or of the month preceding the present; as, your letter of the 5th *ultimo.*

Underwrite — To assume an insurance risk; also, to assume a financial responsibility for an undertaking.

Unfunded debt — See **Funded debt.**

Unlisted securities — Securities which have not been admitted to the regular list of an organized exchange.

Upkeep — Expenditures to keep property in suitable or working condition.

Upset-price — The lowest price at which a person is willing that his property shall be sold at auction.

V

Verbatim (*Latin*) — Word for word,

Via (*Latin*) — By way of,

Vol. — Volume,

Voucher — A receipt or document to establish the authenticity of a business transaction.

W

Watered stock — Stock not fully covered by actual values in the company.

Wholesaler — A dealer who sells merchandise in quantity to retailers or to other wholesalers.

w. i. — When issued.

Wide margin of profit — A large margin of profit. See **Margin of profit.**

Wire — To communicate by telegraph.

Without recourse — The term "without recourse" appearing before an indorsement on the back of a check, promissory note, or bill of exchange frees the indorser of responsibility in case payment is not made at maturity.

Working capital — The amount of capital needed to carry on a business.

Wt. — Weight.

Y

Yield — The return from an investment in interest or dividends, usually figured in percentage.

FOREIGN WORDS, PHRASES, ETC.,
OCCURRING IN ENGLISH USE

For other foreign words and phrases, see main body of Dictionary.

ABBREVIATIONS. — AF., Anglo-French; F., French; G., German; Gr., Greek; It., Italian; L., Latin; OF., Old French; Pg., Portuguese; Sp., Spanish. For other abbreviations, see list at beginning of Dictionary.

A

ab absurdo (L.), from absurdity.

ab æterno (L.), from eternity.

ab ante (L.), from before; in advance.

ab antiquo (L.), from olden time.

à bas (F.), down; down with . . . !

à bâtons rompus (F.), with broken sticks (drumsticks); intermittently; by fits and starts.

ab auctoritate (L.), from authority: see *argumentum ab auctoritate*.

à beau jeu beau retour (F.), for a good turn a good return; tit for tat.

abends wird der Faule fleissig (G.), at evening the lazy man becomes industrious.

a beneplacito (It.), at pleasure.

Aberglaube (G.): see *der Aberglaube ist die Poesie des Lebens*.

abeunt studia in mores (L.), studies develop into habits; pursuits have their effect in conduct or character (*Ovid*, Heroides, xv. 83: cf. *Bacon*, Essays, Of Studies).

ab extra (L.), from without.

ab hoc et ab hac et ab illa (L.), from this man and from this woman and from that woman; from this, that, and the other one; indiscriminately.

ab identitate rationis (L.), from identity of reason; for the same reason.

à bientôt (F.), until soon; until our meeting again soon: said at parting.

ab igne ignem (L.), from fire, fire.

abi in pace (L.), depart in peace.

abiit, excessit, evasit, erupit (L.), he has gone, made off, escaped, broken away (*Cicero*, 2 Catiline, 1).

ab imo pectore (L.), from the bottom of the heart.

ab inconvenienti (L.), from inconvenience: see *argumentum ab inconvenienti*.

ab incunabulis (L.), from the cradle.

ab initio (L.), from the beginning.

ab integro (L.), anew; afresh.

ab intestato (L.), from an intestate person.

ab intra (L.), from within.

ab irato (L.), from an angry person; in anger.

ab officio (L.), from office.

ab officio et beneficio (L.), from office and benefice.

à bon chat bon rat (F.), for good cat good rat (a case of meeting one's match).

à bon droit (F.), with good right; with justice.

à bon marché (F.), at a good bargain; cheap.

abonnement (F.), subscription.

ab origine (L.), from the origin or beginning.

ab ovo (L.), from the egg; from the beginning.

ab ovo usque ad mala (L.), from the egg even to the apples (at a Roman meal); from first to last (*Horace*, Satires, i. 3).

à bras ouverts (F.), with open arms.

abrégé (F.), an abridgment.

absence d'esprit (F.), absence of mind.

absens heres non erit (L.), the absent one will not be the heir (will not be remembered).

absente reo (L.), the defendant being absent.

absit invidia (L.), let no offense be taken.

absit invidia verbo (L.), let no offense be taken at the saying; may it be said without giving offense.

absit omen (L.), may there be no ill omen.

absolvi meam animam (L.), I have relieved my mind.

absque hoc (L.), without this.

absque ulla conditione (L.), without any condition; unconditionally.

abundans cautela non nocet (L.), excessive precaution does no harm.

abundant dulcibus vitiis (L.), they abound with pleasing faults.

ab uno disce omnes (L.), from one learn of all.

ab urbe condita (L.), from the founding of the city (Rome, in 753 B.C.).

abusus non tollit usum (L.), abuse does not do away with use.

a capite ad calcem (L.), from head to heel.

acceptissima semper munera sunt auctor quæ pretiosa facit (L.), most acceptable always are the gifts which the giver makes precious (*Ovid*, Heroides, xvii. 71).

accusare nemo se debet, nisi coram Deo (L.), no one is bound to accuse himself, unless before God.

acerrima proximorum odia (L.), the bitterest enmities are those of persons most nearly related: see *ferme acerrima proximorum odia sunt*.

à chaque saint sa chandelle (F.), to each saint his candle; seek the favor of every possible patron.

Acheruntis pabulum (L.), food for Acheron; ripe for the gallows (*Plautus*, Casina, ii. 1).

à cheval (F.), on horseback; astride.

à cœur ouvert (F.), with open heart; with perfect candor.

à compte (F.), on account; in part payment.

à contre-cœur (F.), against one's will; reluctantly; grudgingly.

à corps perdu (F.), with body lost; headlong; with desperate energy; with might and main.

à coups de bâton (F.), with blows of a stick.

à coups de dictionnaire (F.), with strokes of the dictionary; with continual reference to the dictionary.

à coup sûr (F.), with sure stroke; with certainty.

à couvert (F.), under cover; sheltered; protected.

acta est fabula (L.), the play is done; the performance is over.

acti labores jucundi (L.), labors accomplished are pleasant.

actio ex delicto (L.), an action (at law) arising out of a wrong.

actio personalis moritur cum persona (L.), a personal action (at law) dies with the person.

actum est de republica (L.), it is all over with the republic.

actum et tractatum (L.), done and transacted.

actum ne agas (L.), do not do a thing that is already done.

actus Dei (or **legis**) **nemini facit injuriam** (L.), the act of God (or of the law) does wrong to none.

actus me invito factus non est meus actus (L.), an act done against my will is not my act.

acu rem tetigisti (L.), you have touched the thing with a needle; you have hit the nail on the head.

a cuspide corona (L.), from the spear a crown; from martial achievements glory.

ad absurdum (L.), to an absurdity: see *reductio ad absurdum*.

ad aperturam libri (L.), at the opening of the book; at sight (as reading or translation).

ad arbitrium (L.), at discretion; at will.

ad astra (L.), to the stars.

ad astra per aspera (L.), to the stars through difficulties (motto of Kansas).

a dato (L.), from date.

ad augusta per angusta (L.), to august ends by narrow ways.

ad baculum (L.), to the rod or club; to force.

ad calendas Græcas (L.): see *ad kalendas Græcas*.

ad captandum (L.), for the purpose of catching, captivating, or pleasing.

ad captandum vulgus (L.), for the purpose of catching the crowd; to gain popular favor.

ad clerum (L.), to the clergy.

ad crumenam (L.), to the purse: see *argumentum ad crumenam.*

ad damnum (L.), to the damage or loss (of a plaintiff at law).

à demi (F.), half; by halves.

a Deo et rege (L.), from God and the king.

à dessein (F.), by design; on purpose.

ad eundem (L.), to the same (degree or standing), as in a university.

à deux (F.), of or for two; two at a time.

à deux fins (F.), for two purposes or uses, as a horse suitable for both riding and driving.

à deux mains (F.), with or for two hands; with both hands.

ad extra (L.), in an outward direction.

ad extremum (L.), to the extreme; at last; finally.

ad finem (L.), to, toward, or at the end.

ad gloriam (L.), for glory; without pay.

ad gustum (L.), to the taste; to one's liking.

ad hoc (L.), for this; with respect to this.

ad hominem (L.), to the man: see *argumentum ad hominem.*

ad honorem (L.), for honor; honorary.

adhuc sub judice lis est (L.), the case is still under judicial consideration (*Horace*, Ars Poetica, 78).

ad hunc locum (L.), to or at this place.

ad idem (L.), to the same thing or effect; in agreement.

a die (L.), from that day.

adieu jusqu'au revoir (F.), farewell until we meet again.

adieu, paniers, vendanges sont faites (F.), farewell, baskets, the vintage is over; there is nothing more to be hoped for.

adieu pour toujours (F.), farewell forever.

ad ignorantiam (L.), to ignorance: see *argumentum ad ignorantiam.*

ad inferos (L.), to the lower or nether world; to the infernal regions.

ad infinitum (L.), to infinity; endlessly.

ad initium (L.), to or at the beginning.

ad inquirendum (L.), for making inquiry.

ad instar (L.), after the fashion of; like.

ad interim (L.), in the meantime.

ad internecionem (L.), to extermination.

ad intra (L.), in an inward direction.

ad invidiam (L.), to envy: see *argumentum ad invidiam.*

à discrétion (F.), at discretion; at will.

ad judicium (L.), to the judgment: see *argumentum ad judicium.*

ad kalendas Græcas (L.), at the Greek calends; never (since there were no Greek calends).

ad libitum (L.), at pleasure.

ad limina (L.), to the thresholds: see *ad limina apostolorum.*

ad limina apostolorum (L.), to the thresholds of the apostles; to the basilicas (or sepulchers) of St. Peter and St. Paul at Rome (as in pilgrimage); to the Holy See at Rome (as in official visits of bishops).

ad litem (L.), for the suit or action at law.

ad litteram (L.), to the letter; exactly.

ad longum (L.), at length.

ad majorem Dei gloriam (L.), for the greater glory of God (motto of the order of the Jesuits).

ad manum (L.), at hand; in readiness.

ad misericordiam (L.), to mercy or pity: see *argumentum ad misericordiam.*

ad modum (L.), after the manner of.

admonitus locorum (L.), reminders given by places; local associations.

ad multos annos! (L.), for many years! long life or rule!

ad nauseam (L.), to the point of causing nausea.

ad ostentationem (L.), for show or display.

ad patres (L.), with his fathers; dead.

ad perpetuam rei memoriam (L.), for the perpetual remembrance of the thing.

ad populum (L.), to the people: see *argumentum ad populum.*

ad quem (L.), to which or whom.

ad quod damnum (L.), to what damage.

ad referendum (L.), for referring (said of the acceptance by a diplomatic representative of proposals to be referred to his principal); for further consideration.

ad rem (L.), to the point or purpose.

à droite (F.), to the right.

à droite et à gauche (F.), to right and to left.

adscriptus glebæ (L.), attached to the soil, as a serf.

adsum (L.), I am here; present (as answer to a roll-call).

ad summam (L.), on the whole; to sum up the matter.

ad summum (L.), to the highest point or amount.

ad unguem (L.), to the nail (as work brought to the final touch or test with the finger-nail); to a nicety; perfectly.

ad unum omnes (L.), all, to the last one; all, to a man.

ad usum (L.), according to custom.

ad utrumque paratus (L.), prepared for either alternative.

ad valorem (L.), according to value, as duties levied on goods.

ad verbum (L.), to a word; word for word; verbatim.

ad verecundiam (L.), to reverence: see *argumentum ad verecundiam.*

ad vitam æternam (L.), for eternal life; forever.

ad vitam aut culpam (L.), for life or until fault (said of tenure of office).

ad vivum (L.), to the living part; to the quick; to the life.

advocatus diaboli (L.), the devil's advocate (appointed to argue against a proposed canonization); an adverse critic, esp. of what is deemed good; a detractor.

Advokaten und Soldaten sind des Teufels Spielkameraden (G.), lawyers and soldiers are the devil's playmates.

ægrescitque medendo (L.), and it grows worse with the treatment (*Virgil*, Æneid, xii. 46).

ægri somnia vana (L.), a sick man's empty dreams.

æquabiliter et diligenter (L.), equably and diligently.

æquam memento rebus in arduis servare mentem (L.), remember to keep an even mind in adverse circumstances (*Horace*, Odes, ii. 3).

æquam servare mentem (L.), to keep an even mind: see *æquam memento* (etc.).

æquanimiter (L.), with equanimity.

æquitas sequitur legem (L.), equity follows the law.

æquo animo (L.), with an even mind; with equanimity.

ære perennius (L.), more enduring than bronze: see *exegi monumentum ære perennius.*

æs alienum (L.), another's money; borrowed money; debt.

æs suum (L.), one's own money.

æs triplex (L.), triple bronze (or brass); strong armor (*Horace*, Odes, i. 3).

ætatis (L.), of the age of; aged.

ætatis suæ (L.), of his (or her) age.

æternum vale (L.), farewell forever.

Æthiopem dealbare (L.), to make an Ethiopian white.

affaire d'amour (F.), a love-affair.

affaire de cœur (F.), an affair of the heart.

affaire d'honneur (F.), an affair of honor; a duel.

affiche (F.), a posted notice; a placard; a poster.

affiché (F.), posted up; advertised; paraded.

afflavit Deus et dissipantur (L.), God breathed upon them and they are dispersed: cf. *flavit Jehovah* (etc.).

à fond (F.), to the bottom; thoroughly.

a fonte puro pura defluit aqua (L.), from a pure fountain pure water flows.

à forfait (F.), by contract; by the job.

a fortiori (L.), with stronger reason; all the more.

a fronte præcipitium, a tergo lupus (L.), a precipice in front, a wolf behind.

agaçant, fem. **agaçante** (F.), provoking; alluring; coquettishly enticing.

agacerie (F.), allurement; enticement.

à gauche (F.), to the left.

à genoux (F.), on the knees; kneeling.

agent provocateur (F.), provocatory agent. See Dictionary.

age quod agis (L.), do what you do; attend to, or do thoroughly, what you have in hand.

Agnus Dei (L.), Lamb of God.

à grands frais (F.), at great expense.

agréments (F.), agreeable features or accessories; ornaments; charms.

à haute voix (F.), aloud.

à huis clos (F.), with closed doors; in private.

aide-toi, le ciel t'aidera (F.), help thyself, and Heaven will help thee (*La Fontaine*, Fables, vi. 18).

aïeux (F.), ancestors: see *qui sert bien son pays* (etc.).

aîné, fem. **aînée** (F.), elder; senior.

air noble (F.), noble air; air of distinction.

à jamais (F.), forever.

Aktiengesellschaft (G.), a stock company.

à la (F.), to the; according to the; at or in the; in the (specified) mode, manner, style, or fashion.

à l'abandon (F.), in abandonment; in negligent disorder; at sixes and sevens.

à la belle étoile (F.), at the beautiful star (as if at an inn or lodging-place so called); out under the stars; in the open air at night.

à la bonne heure (F.), at the good hour or right moment; just right; excellent; very well.

à l'abri (F.), under shelter; under cover.

à la campagne (F.), in the country.

à la carte (F.), according to the card, or bill of fare; with a stated price for each dish.

à la chinoise (F.), in the Chinese style.

à la dérobée (F.), by stealth; furtively.

à la fin (F.), in the end; at last; finally.

à la française (F.), in the French style.

à la grecque (F.), in the Greek style.

à la guerre comme à la guerre (F.), in war as in war.

à la lanterne (F.), to the lantern, or street-lamp (on which the mob during the French Revolution hanged their victims).

à la lettre (F.), to the letter; exactly; literally.

à la main (F.), in hand; at hand; by hand.

à l'américaine (F.), in the American style.

à la militaire (F.), in the military style.

à la mode (F.), in the fashion.

à la mort (F.), to the death.

à l'anglaise (F.), in the English style.

à l'antique (F.), in the antique style.

à la parisienne (F.), in the Parisian style.

à la portée de tout le monde (F.), within reach of all the world.

à la russe (F.), in the Russian style.

à la Tartuffe (or **Tartufe**) (F.), in the manner of Tartuffe, or Tartufe (in Molière's play of that name); hypocritically.

a latere (L.), from the side; from beside the Pope, as a legate; collaterally or collateral, as succession to property.

à la volée (F.), on the fly; with prompt seizure of the occasion; without stopping to think.

alea belli incerta (L.), the hazard of war is uncertain.

alea jacta est (L.), the die is cast: see *jacta alea est.*

à l'envi (F.), in emulation; emulously.

alere flammam (L.), to feed the flame; kindle fresh zeal, ardor, etc.

à l'espagnole (F.), in the Spanish style.

à l'extérieur (F.), on the outside; abroad.

à l'extrémité (F.), to or at the extremity or end, as of life or of one's resources.

al fresco (It.), in the open air.

aliam excute quercum (L.), shake some other oak; 'work' some one else.

alias (L.), at another time or place; otherwise; otherwise called.

alia tentanda via est (L.), another way must be tried.

alibi (L.), elsewhere; in another place.

aliena optimum frui insania (L.), it is a very good thing to profit by the madness of others.

alieni appetens, sui profusus (L.), eager for others' property, prodigal of his own (*Sallust*, Catiline, v.).

alieni juris (L.), under the authority of another: cf. *sui juris.*

alieni temporis flores (L.), flowers of another or bygone time.

à l'improviste (F.), unexpectedly; suddenly.

à l'intérieur (F.), in the inside; within; at home.

alio sub sole (L.), under another sun; in another clime.

aliquando bonus dormitat Homerus (L.), sometimes good Homer nods: see *indignor quandoque bonus dormitat Homerus.*

aliquid hæret (L.), something sticks: see *audacter calumniare, semper aliquid hæret.*

aliquis non debet esse judex in propria causa (L.), one should not be judge in his own cause.

alis volat propriis (L.), she flies with her own wings (motto of Oregon).

à l'italienne (F.), in the Italian style.

aliter (L.), otherwise.

aliud est celare, aliud tacere (L.), it is one thing to conceal, another to be silent.

aliud et idem (L.), another thing and yet the same.

aliunde (L.), from another place or source.

alla carta (It.), same as *à la carte.*

alla vostra salute (It.), to your health.

allegans contraria non est audiendus (L.), he who alleges contradictory things is not to be heard.

allez-vous-en! (F.), go away! off with you! begone!

allons (L.), let us go; come on; come.

allzu klug ist dumm (G.), too wise is stupid.

alma mater (L.), fostering mother. See Dictionary.

à l'ordinaire (F.), in the ordinary manner; as usual.

à l'outrance (F.), erron. for *à outrance.*

al più (It.), at most.

alter Christus (L.), another (or a second) Christ (a phrase used to describe the ideal minister of God).

alter ego (L.), another I or self; a second self; an inseparable friend.

alter idem (L.), another self.

alter ipse amicus (L.), a friend is another self.

alternis vicibus (L.), in alternate turns.

alterum tantum (L.), as much more.

altesse (F.), **alteza** (Sp.), **altezza** (It.), highness (used esp. as a title).

altum mare (L.), the deep sea; the high seas.

altum silentium (L.), deep silence.

amabilis insania (L.), a pleasing madness (*Horace*, Odes, iii. 4).

à main armée (F.), with armed hand; by force of arms.

a majori ad minus (L.), from the greater to the less.

amans iratus multa mentitur sibi (L.), an angry lover tells himself many lies (*Publilius Syrus*).

amant, fem. **amante** (F.), a lover.

amantes, amentes (L.), lovers, lunatics.

amantium iræ amoris integratio est (L.), lovers' quarrels are the renewing of love (*Terence*, Andria, iii. 3).

à ma puissance (F.), according to my power; to my utmost.

amare et sapere vix deo conceditur (L.), to love and to be wise is scarcely granted even to a god (*Publilius Syrus*).

amare simul et sapere ipsi Jovi non datur (L.), to love and to be wise at the same time is not given to Jove himself.

amari aliquid (L.), something bitter.

amata bene (L., fem.), well loved.

a maximis ad minima (L.), from the greatest to the least.

à méchant chien court lien (F.), for a vicious dog a short chain.

âme damnée (F.), a damned soul; a blindly devoted adherent or tool.

âme de boue (F.), a soul of mud; a base creature.

amende honorable (F.), honorable amend. See Dictionary.

a mensa et thoro (or **toro**) (L.), from table and bed; from bed and board.

âme perdue (F.), a lost soul; one morally ruined; a desperate character.

à merveille (F.), to a marvel; marvelously.

ami (F.), a friend.

amici fures temporis (L.), friends are thieves of time.

amico d' ognuno, amico di nessuno (It.), everybody's friend, nobody's friend.

amicus curiæ (L.), a friend of the court; a disinterested person who gives advice or suggestions in aid of the court.

amicus humani generis (L.), a friend of the human race.

amicus Plato, amicus Socrates, sed magis amica veritas (L.), Plato is a friend, Socrates is a friend, but truth is more a friend.

amicus usque ad aras (L.), a friend as far as to the altars, or up to the point where religion intervenes; also, a friend even to the altars, or to the final sacrifice.

ami de cour (F.), a court friend; one who makes a polite but meaningless show of friendship.

ami de la famille (F.), a friend of the family.

ami de la maison (F.), a friend of the house.

ami de mouvement (F.), a friend of progress.

ami du peuple (F.), friend of the people (used as the title of a paper published 1789–92 by Marat, the French revolutionary leader, also of Marat himself).

amie (F., fem.), a woman friend; a mistress.

a minori ad majus (L.), from the less to the greater.

à moitié (F.), half; by halves.

à mon avis (F.), in my opinion.

amor nummi (L.), love of money.

amor omnia vincit (or **vincit omnia**) (L.), love conquers all things.

amor patriæ (L.), love of country; patriotism.

amor sceleratus habendi (L.), the accursed love of possessing (*Ovid*, Metamorphoses, i. 131).

amor tussisque non celantur (L.), love and a cough are not hidden.

amour fait beaucoup, mais argent fait tout (F.), love does much, but money does all.

amour-propre (F.), self-love; self-esteem: see *l'amour-propre est* (etc.).

Amphitryon (F.): see *le véritable Amphitryon* (etc.).

a multo fortiori (L.), with much stronger reason.

anathema sit (L.), let him be accursed (*Vulgate*, Gal. i. 8).

a natura rei (L.), from the nature of the case.

ancienne noblesse (F.), the old nobility; the nobility of France before the Revolution of 1789.

ancien régime (F.), the old system of government or order of things; the political and social system of France before the Revolution of 1789.

ancipitis usus (L.), of twofold use.

ancora imparo (It.), still I am learning (said to have been a favorite saying of Michelangelo).

anéantissement (F.), annihilation.

Anglicè (L.), in English.

anguillam cauda tenes (L.), you hold an eel by the tail.

anguis in herba (L.), a snake in the grass: see *latet anguis in herba.*

angulus ridet (L.), that corner of the earth smiles: see *ille terrarum mihi* (etc.).

aniles fabulæ (L.), old wives' tales.

animal implume bipes (L.), a featherless two-footed animal (man).

animal rationale (L.), a rational animal.

animal risibile (L.), an animal that can laugh.

anima mundi (L.), the soul of the world; a spirit supposed to pervade the universe.

animis opibusque parati (L.), prepared in mind and resources (a motto of South Carolina: *Virgil*, Æneid, ii. 799).

animo et corpore (L.), by mind and body; with intention and act.

animo et fide (L.), by courage and faith.

animo, non astutia (L.), by courage, not by craft.

animula vagula, blandula (L.), little soul, evanescent, pleasant (first words of the dying Roman emperor Hadrian's verses addressed to his soul).

animum pictura pascit inani (L.), he feeds his mind on an empty picture (*Virgil*, Æneid, i. 464).

animus furandi (L.), the intention of stealing.

animus meminisse horret (L.), my mind is filled with horror at the recollection (*Virgil*, Æneid, ii. 12).

animus testandi (L.), the intention of making a will.

anno ætatis suæ (L.), in the . . . year of his (or her) age.

anno ante Christum (L.), in the year . . . before Christ.

anno Christi (L.), in the year . . . of Christ.

anno Domini (L.), in the year . . . of our Lord.

anno Hejiræ (L.), in the year . . . of (dating from) the Hejira, or flight of Mohammed from Mecca (A.D. 622).

anno mundi (L.), in the year . . . of the world (that is, counting from a supposed date of the creation of the world).

anno post Romam conditam (L.), in the year . . . after the founding of Rome (753 B.C.).

anno salutis (L.), in the year . . . of salvation.

annosam arborem transplantare (L.), to transplant an old tree.

annos vixit (L.), he (or she) lived . . . years.

anno urbis conditæ (L.), in the year . . . after the founding of the city (Rome, in 753 B.C.).

annuit cœptis (L.), he (God) has favored our undertakings (motto for the uncut reverse of the great seal of the U. S.: cf. *Virgil*, Æneid, ix. 625).

annus mirabilis (L.), wonderful year; year of wonders.

a novo (L.), anew.

ante (L.), before.

ante bellum (L.), before the war.

ante Christum (L.), before Christ.

ante diluvium (L.), before the Flood.

ante litem motam (L.), before the controversy was begun.

ante lucem (L.), before light; before daylight.

ante meridiem (L.), before noon.

ante mortem (L.), before death.

ante tubam trepidat (L.), before the trumpet sounds he is trembling.

ante victoriam ne canas triumphum (L.), before the victory do not sing the triumph.

antiqua homo virtute ac fide (L.), a man of the old-time virtue and good faith (*Terence*, Adelphi, iii. 3).

à outrance (F.), to excess; to the uttermost, or the bitter end; to the death.

apage, Satana! (L.), begone, Satan!

a paribus (L.), from equals.

a parte ante (L.), from the part (of time) before; antecedently.

a parte post (L.), from the part (of time) after; subsequently.

à pas de géant (F.), with a giant's stride.

à peindre (F.), for painting; worth painting: see *fait à peindre.*

aperçu (F.), a glance; a rapid survey; an outline or summary.

à perte de vue (F.), until loss of view; out of sight.

à peu près (F.), nearly; about.

a piacere (It.), at pleasure.

à pied (F.), on foot.

à plaisir (F.), at pleasure.

à plomb (F.), to the plumb; perpendicularly; directly.

a poco a poco (It.), little by little.

à point (F.), to (the right) point; to a nicety; just right; at just the right moment.

apologia (L.), an apology; a formal defense or justification.

Apologia pro Vita Sua (L.), "Apologia for His Life" (title of Cardinal Newman's autobiography).

à portée (F.), within reach.

a posse ad esse (L.), from possibility to actuality.

a posteriori (L.), from the latter or subsequent; from effect to cause; from experience to general laws.

apparatus belli (L.), apparatus of war (instruments, appliances, munitions, stores, etc.).

apparatus criticus (L.), critical apparatus; reference-books, etc., for critical or general literary work.

appel au peuple (F.), an appeal to the people.

appel nominal (F.), a call of names; a roll-call.

appui (F.), support; a point or base of support; a prop.

après (F.), after; afterward; next.

après coup (F.), after the stroke; too late.

après la mort le médecin (F.), after death the doctor.

après moi le déluge (F.), after me the deluge (attributed to Louis XV., also to Mme. de Pompadour).

a prezzo fisso (It.), at a fixed price.

a prima vista (It.), at first sight.

a priori (L.), from the former or antecedent; from cause to effect; from general laws to particular instances.

à prix fixe (F.), at a fixed price.

à propos (F.), to the purpose; pertinently; opportunely; also, as to that subject; speaking of that; by the way.

à propos de bottes (F.), with reference to boots, or speaking of boots (used to introduce a quite irrelevant topic); irrelevantly; without reason.

à propos de rien (F.), with reference or relevance to nothing; without special pertinence, connection, or reason.

apud (L.), with; in; in the writings of.

aqua (L.), water. See Dictionary.

aqua et igni interdictus (L.), forbidden the use of water and fire (in ancient Rome, in token of loss of civic rights, or banishment).

à quatre (F.), of or for four; four at a time.

à quatre épingles (F.): see *tiré à quatre épingles.*

à quatre mains (F.), for four hands.

a quattr' occhi (It.), for four eyes; tête-à-tête.

aquilæ senectus (L.), the old age of an eagle.

aquilam volare doces (L.), you teach an eagle to fly.

aquila non capit muscas (L.), the eagle does not catch flies.

aquí se habla español (Sp.), Spanish is spoken here.

a quo (L.), from which or whom.

à quoi bon? (F.), for what (is it) good? of what use? to what purpose?

ara cœli (or **cœli**) (L.), altar of heaven.

à ravir (F.), ravishingly; delightfully.

arbiter bibendi (L.), arbiter of drinking; a presider over a drinking-party.

arbiter elegantiarum (L.), arbiter of elegances; an authority in matters of taste.

arbre de la liberté (F.): see *l'arbre de la liberté* (etc.).

Arcades ambo (L.), Arcadians, or shepherds, both (*Virgil*, Eclogues, vii. 4); birds of a feather.

Arcadia (L.): see *et in Arcadia ego.*

arcana cælestia (L.), celestial mysteries.

arcana imperii (L.), mysteries of empire; state secrets.

arcana sacra (L.), sacred mysteries.

arc de triomphe (F.), a triumphal arch.

arc-en-ciel (F.), bow in the sky; a rainbow.

ardentia verba (L.), burning words; glowing language.

à rebours (F.), against the nap or grain; the wrong way; backward.

à reculons (F.), backward; retrogradely.

arenæ mandas semina (L.), you commit seeds to the sand.

arena sine calce (L.), sand without lime; loose matter with nothing to bind it together (from a saying of Caligula about the writings of Seneca: see *Suetonius*, Caligula, 53).

argent comptant (F.), ready money.

argumenti causa (L.), for the sake of argument.

argumentum ab auctoritate (L.), an argument derived from authority.

argumentum ab inconvenienti (L.), an argument drawn from the inconvenience or hardship involved.

argumentum ad crumenam (L.), an argument directed to the purse or pecuniary interest.

argumentum ad hominem (L.), an argument addressed to the man, or having a direct personal bearing; an argument deriving its force from the practice, principles, prejudices, etc., of the person addressed or immediately concerned.

argumentum ad ignorantiam (L.), an argument addressed to ignorance, or based on an adversary's ignorance of facts.

argumentum ad invidiam (L.), an argument appealing to envy or ill-will.

argumentum ad judicium (L.), an argument addressed to the judgment or common sense.

argumentum ad misericordiam (L.), an argument appealing to feelings of mercy or pity.

argumentum ad populum (L.), an argument appealing to the people, or to popular sympathies, prejudices, etc.

argumentum ad verecundiam (L.), an argument appealing to reverence or respect, as for an accepted authority.

argumentum baculinum (L.), the argument of the stick or club; the use of force for the purpose of convincing.

argumentum ex concesso (L.), an argument derived from what has been conceded.

ariston metron (Gr. ἄριστον μέτρον), due measure, or moderation, is best.

a rivederci (It.), until our seeing each other again; good-by for the present: cf. *au revoir.*

a rivederla (It.), until seeing you again; good-by for the present: cf. *a rivederci.*

arma in armatos sumere jura sinunt (L.), the laws permit the taking up of arms against those armed.

arma pacis fulcra (L.), arms are the props of peace.

arma virumque cano (L.), arms and the man I sing (*Virgil*, Æneid, i. 1).

armes blanches (F.), white arms; the sword, saber, bayonet, etc., as distinguished from firearms.

arrectis auribus (L.), with ears pricked up (*Virgil*, Æneid, ii. 303).

arrière-garde (F.), the rear-guard.

arrière-pensée (F.), a thought kept back; a mental reservation.

ars artium omnium conservatrix (L.), the art that is the preserver of all arts (printing).

ars est celare artem (L.), art is the concealing of art.

ars longa, vita brevis (L.), art is long, life short (from the Greek of Hippocrates, Aphorism i.).

ars poetica (L.), the art of poetry.

artium baccalaureus (L.), bachelor of arts.

artium magister (L.), master of arts.

art nouveau (F.), new art; the new style of art.

a salti (It.), in leaps; by fits and starts.

asinus ad lyram (L.), an ass at the lyre.

asinus inter simias (L.), an ass among apes.

assez bien (F.), well enough; pretty well.

assumpsit (L.), he undertook (as alleged of the defendant in an action at law for non-fulfilment of contract or agreement: cf. *non assumpsit*).

astra castra, numen lumen (L.), the stars my camp, the Deity my lamp.

Astræa Redux (L.), "Astræa (goddess of justice) Returned" (title of a poem by Dryden on the restoration of Charles II. in 1660).

à tâtons (F.), by feeling one's way; gropingly.

atavis edite regibus (L.), sprung from ancestral kings (*Horace*, Odes, i. 1).

a teneris annis (L.), from tender years.

a tergo (L.), from the back or rear; from behind.

Athanasius contra mundum (L.), Athanasius against the world: cf. *Cato contra mundum.*

à tort (F.), wrongly; wrong.

à tort et à droit (F.), wrong and right; regardless of right and wrong.

à tort et à travers (F.), wrong and athwart; regardless of circumstances or results; without discrimination; at random.

à tort ou à droit (F.), wrong or right; right or wrong.

à toute force (F.), with all force; by all means; in spite of all.

à toutes jambes (F.), with all one's legs; as fast as one's legs can carry one.

à tout hasard (F.), at all hazards; whatever happens.

à tout prix (F.), at any price; whatever the cost.

à tout propos (F.), on every occasion; at every turn; continually.

atra Cura (L.), black Care: see *post equitem sedet atra Cura.*

at spes non fracta (L.), yet hope is not crushed.

attelage (F.), a team of horses, etc.

attendez! (F.), wait! stay!

attendrissement (F.), softened feeling; emotion.

au bout de son latin (F.), at the end of his Latin; at his wits' end.

au cinquième, or **au cinquième étage** (F.), on the fifth floor; in the attic. See *au premier.*

au contraire (F.), on the contrary.

au couchant (F.), to the west: cf. *au levant.*

au courant (F.), in the current (of events); conversant with what is passing or occurring; well informed as to the circumstances, facts, etc., of a case.

auctor pretiosa facit (L.), (gifts which) the giver makes precious: see *acceptissima semper munera* (etc.).

audace (F.), boldness; daring; audacity: see *de l'audace* (etc.).

audaces (or **audentes**) **fortuna juvat** (L.), fortune aids the bold (or the daring).

audacter calumniare, semper aliquid hæret (L.), calumniate boldly, something always sticks.

audacter et sincere (L.), boldly and sincerely.

audacter te vendita, semper aliquid hæret (L.), praise thyself boldly, something always sticks.

audax et cautus (L.), bold and cautious.

aude sapere (L.), dare to be wise.

au désespoir (F.), in despair.

au deuxième, or **au deuxième étage** (F.), on the second floor. See *au premier.*

audi alteram partem (L.), hear the other side (before judging).

audiatur et altera pars (L.), let the other side also be heard.

audio sed taceo (L.), I hear but am silent.

auditque vocatus Apollo (L.), and Apollo hears when invoked (*Virgil*, Georgics, iv. 7).

audi, vide, tace, si vis vivere in pace (L.), hear, see, be silent, if you wish to live in peace.

au fait (F.), in fact; indeed; also, having experience or practical knowledge of a thing; expert; versed.

Aufklärung (G.), enlightenment. See Dictionary.

au fond (F.), at bottom; fundamentally.

auf Wiedersehen (G.), until seeing you again; until we meet again; good-by for the present: cf. *au revoir.*

au grand sérieux (F.), in great seriousness.

aujourd'hui marié, demain marri (F.), to-day married, to-morrow sorry.

aujourd'hui roi, demain rien (F.), to-day king, to-morrow nothing.

au jour le jour (F.), from day to day; from hand to mouth.

au levant (F.), to the east: cf. *au couchant.*

au mieux (F.), at the best; as well as possible.

au naturel (F.), in the natural state; as in nature; simply; plainly; to the life.

au pied de la lettre (F.), to the foot of the letter; to the very letter; quite literally.

au pis aller (F.), in the event of the worst; at worst.

au plaisir de vous revoir (F.), until I have the pleasure of seeing you again: cf. *au revoir.*

au poids de l'or (F.), at the weight of gold; very dear.

au premier, or **au premier étage** (F.), on the first floor or story, that is, the first above the ground floor (F. *rez-de-chaussée*).

au quatrième, or **au quatrième étage** (F.), on the fourth floor. See *au premier.*

aura favoris popularis (L.), the breeze of popular favor.

aura popularis (L.), the popular breeze; popular favor.

aurea mediocritas (L.), the golden mean; the happy medium between extremes.

aureo piscari hamo (L.), to fish with a golden hook; risk more than the game is worth.

au reste (F.), for the rest; besides.

au revoir (F.), until seeing you again; until we meet again; good-by for the present.

au rez-de-chaussée (F.), on the ground floor. See *au premier.*

auribus teneo lupum (L.), I am holding a wolf by the ears (*Terence*, Phormio, iii. 2).

auri sacra fames (L.), accursed hunger for gold (*Virgil*, Æneid, iii. 57).

au royaume des aveugles les borgnes sont rois (F.), in the kingdom of the blind the one-eyed are kings.

aurum potabile (L.), drinkable gold; a cordial containing gold.

au second, or **au second étage** (F.), on the second floor. See *au premier*.

au secret (F.), in close confinement.

au sérieux (F.), in seriousness; seriously.

auspicium melioris ævi (L.), an omen of a better age (motto of the British Order of St. Michael and St. George).

aussitôt dit, aussitôt fait (F.), so soon said, so soon done; no sooner said than done.

Austria (L.): see *bella gerant alii: tu, felix Austria, nube.*

aut amat aut odit mulier, nihil est tertium (L.), a woman either loves or hates, there is no third course (*Publilius Syrus*).

autant de têtes (or **d'hommes**), **autant d'avis** (F.), so many heads (or men), so many opinions; so many men, so many minds.

aut Cæsar aut nihil (L.), either Cæsar or nothing (motto of Cæsar Borgia).

aut Cæsar aut nullus (L.), either Cæsar or nobody.

aut insanit homo aut versus facit (L.), either the man is mad or he is making verses (*Horace*, Satires, ii. 7).

aut inveniam viam aut faciam (L.), I will either find a way or make one.

aut non tentaris aut perfice (L.), either do not attempt or else finish: cf. *aut numquam temptes aut perfice.*

aut numquam temptes aut perfice (L.), either never attempt or else finish.

aut prodesse volunt aut delectare poetæ (L.), poets wish either to profit or to please (*Horace*, Ars Poetica, 333).

autrefois acquit (AF.), formerly acquitted.

autrefois convict (AF.), formerly convicted.

autres temps, autres mœurs (F.), other times, other manners (or ways).

au troisième, or **au troisième étage** (F.), on the third floor. See *au premier.*

aut vincere aut mori (L.), either to conquer or to die.

aux absents les os (F.), for the absent the bones: cf. *sero venientibus ossa.*

aux armes! (F.), to arms!

aux grands maux les grands remèdes (F.), for extraordinary evils extraordinary remedies.

auxilium ab alto (L.), help from on high.

aux soins de (F.), to the care of.

avant-coureur (F.), a forerunner; a harbinger.

avant-garde (F.), the vanguard.

avant-goût (F.), a foretaste.

avant-poste (F.), an outpost.

avant-propos (F.), a preface.

ave atque vale! (L.), hail and farewell!

avec permission (F.), with permission.

avec plaisir (F.), with pleasure.

ave, imperator! (or **ave, Cæsar!**) **morituri te salutant** (or **salutamus**) (L.), hail, emperor (or Cæsar)! those (or we) who are about to die salute thee (salutation of Roman gladiators before a combat).

avenir (F.), time to come; future; prospects.

a verbis ad verbera (L.), from words to blows.

à vieux comptes nouvelles disputes (F.), on old accounts new disputes.

a vinculo matrimonii (L.), from the bond of matrimony.

avise la fin (F.), consider the end.

avito viret honore (L.), he flourishes on ancestral honor.

a viva voce (It.), with the living voice; orally: cf. *viva voce.*

avoir la langue déliée (F.), to have the tongue untied; talk glibly.

à volonté (F.), at will; at pleasure.

a vostro beneplacito (It.), at your pleasure.

à votre santé (F.), to your health.

á vuestra salud (Sp.), to your health.

B

badaud (F.), a gaping idler; a foolishly curious and credulous person.

Bahnhof (G.), a railroad station.

bal abonné (F.), a subscription ball.

bal champêtre (F.), a ball held out of doors.

bal costumé (F.), a costume ball; a fancy dress ball.

ballet d'action (F.), a ballet combining acting with dancing.

ballet divertissement (F.), a ballet entertainment.

ballon d'essai (F.), a balloon of trial; a small balloon sent up before an ascension, to test the wind; something tentative; a 'feeler.'

ballon perdu (F.), a balloon without passengers sent up to drift with the wind.

bal masqué (F.), a masked ball.

bal paré (F.), a dress ball.

baptême du feu (F.), baptism of fire; a first experience under fire, as in battle.

barba tenus sapientes (L.), sages as far as the beard (or bearded appearance).

bas-bleu (F.), a blue-stocking; a woman who affects literary or intellectual tastes.

basis virtutum constantia (L.), constancy the foundation of virtues.

basta! (It.), enough! no more! stop!

bataillons (F.), battalions: see *Dieu est toujours pour les gros bataillons.*

bâton ferré (F.), a staff shod with iron; an alpenstock.

batterie de cuisine (F.), a set of metal kitchen-utensils.

battre la campagne (F.), to beat or scour the country; beat about the bush.

battre le pavé (F.), to beat the pavement; promenade the streets.

bavard, fem. **bavarde** (F.), chattering; prating; garrulous; also, a chatterer or prater.

bavardage (F.), idle talk; chatter; prate.

beatæ memoriæ (L.), of blessed memory.

Beata Virgo Maria (L.), the Blessed Virgin Mary.

beati possidentes (L.), blessed are those who possess.

beau désordre (F.), beautiful or fine disorder.

beau garçon (F.), a handsome fellow; a fine fellow; (ironically) a pretty fellow.

beau geste (F.), a fine gesture (see *gesture, n.*, in Dictionary).

beau jour, pl. *beaux jours* (F.), a fine day; a happy time.

beau monde (F.), the fashionable world.

beau sabreur (F.), a fine saber-man; a dashing cavalryman or soldier.

beauté du diable (F.), beauty of the devil; the mere freshness or bloom of youth (which even the devil once had: see *le diable était beau quand il était jeune*); also, less correctly, beauty or attractiveness suggestive of the devil.

beaux-arts (F.), the fine arts.

beaux esprits (F.), pl.: see *bel esprit.*

beaux yeux (F.), beautiful eyes.

bel air (F.), fine air; the air or bearing of good society.

bel canto (It.), fine singing; the smooth, cantabile style of singing.

bel esprit, pl. *beaux esprits* (F.), a fine or brilliant mind; wit; a person of wit or intellectual pretensions.

Belgæ (L.): see *horum omnium fortissimi sunt Belgæ.*

bella gerant alii: tu, felix Austria, nube (L.), let others wage wars: do thou, happy Austria, marry (attributed to Matthias Corvinus, king of Hungary).

bella, horrida bella (L.), wars, horrid wars (*Virgil*, Æneid, vi. 86).

bellaque matribus detestata (L.), and wars detested by mothers (*Horace*, Odes, i. 1).

belle amie (F., fem.), fair friend; a mistress.

belle assemblée (F.), a fashionable assembly.

belle dame (F.), fair lady.

belle narras (L.), you tell it excellently.

belle passion (F.), ardent affection; tender passion; love.

belle vue (F.), fine view or prospect.

bellum internecinum (L.), internecine war; a war of extermination.

bellum lethale (L.), deadly war.

bellum nec timendum nec provocandum (L.), war is neither to be feared nor to be provoked.

bellum omnium in omnes (L.), a war of all against all.

bel sangue (It.), good or gentle blood.

belua multorum capitum (L.), the monster of many heads; the multitude (see *Horace*, Epistles, i. 1).

bene decessit (L.), he has departed well, or under honorable circumstances.

bene exeat (L.), let him depart well, or with a good character.

beneficium accipere libertatem est vendere (L.), to accept a favor is to sell one's liberty (*Publilius Syrus*).

beneficium invito non datur (L.), a benefit cannot be bestowed on an unwilling person.

bene merentibus (L.), to the well-deserving.

bene nati, bene vestiti, et mediocriter docti (L.), well born, well dressed, and moderately learned.

bene orasse est bene studuisse (L.), to have prayed well is to have endeavored well.

beneplacito (L.), at your good pleasure; by your leave.

bene qui latuit bene vixit (L.), he who has kept well in obscurity has lived well (*Ovid*, Tristia, iii. 4).

bene vale (L.), farewell.

bene vobis! (L.), health to you!

benigno numine (L.), with a favoring providence.

ben trovato (It.), well invented: see *se non è vero* (etc.).

ben venuto (It.), welcome.

besoin (F.), need; necessity; want.

beso las manos (Sp.), I kiss your hands.

besser Rat kommt über Nacht (G.), better counsel comes overnight.

bête (F.), a beast; a stupid person.

bête noire (F.), a black beast; a bugbear; an object of aversion.

bêtise (F.), stupidity; a stupid act or speech; an absurdity; a trifle.

bibere venenum in auro (L.), to drink poison in (out of) gold: see *venenum in auro bibitur.*

biblioteca (Sp. and It.), **bibliotheca** (L.), **Bibliothek** (G.), **bibliothèque** (F.), a library.

bien (F.), well.

bien-aimé, fem. **bien-aimée** (F.), well-beloved.

bien chaussé, fem. **bien chaussée** (F.), well shod, or equipped as to shoes.

bien entendu (F.), well understood; agreed; of course; assuredly.

bien ganté, fem. **bien gantée** (F.), well gloved.

bien perdu, bien connu (F.), blessing flown, blessing known.

bienséance (F.), propriety; decorum.

bienvenu, fem. **bienvenue** (F.), welcome.

bienvenue (F.), a welcome; admission into an association or body, or a feast or treat given in acknowledgment by the person admitted.

bijou (F.), a jewel; a 'gem'; something small and choice.

bijouterie (F.), jewelry.

billet d'amour, or **billet doux** (F.), a love-letter.

bis (L.), twice; a second time.

bis dat qui cito dat (L.), he gives twice who gives quickly.

bis peccare in bello non licet (L.), to blunder twice in war is not allowable.

bis pueri senes (L.), old men are boys twice.

bis vincit qui se vincit in victoria (L.), he conquers twice who conquers (controls) himself in the hour of victory (*Publilius Syrus*).

bitte (G.), (I) beg; pray; please.

blague (F.), empty, extravagant talk; pretentious lying; humbug.

blagueur (F.), one given to blague.

blanchisseuse de fin (F., fem.), a laundress of fine linen.

blandæ mendacia linguæ (L.), falsehoods of a smooth tongue.

blessé, fem. **blessée** (F.), wounded.

blödsinnig (G.), weak-minded; silly; idiotic.

Blut und Eisen (G.), blood and iron: see *Eisen und Blut.*

bodega (Sp.), a wine-cellar or wine-shop.

bois tortu fait feu droit (F.), crooked wood makes a straight fire.

bon accord (F.), good accord; agreement.

bon accueil (F.), a good reception; a welcome.

bona fide (L.), in good faith; in all sincerity; without fraud.

bona fides (L.), good faith.

bon ami (F.), good friend; a lover.

bon an, mal an (F.), good year, bad year; taking the good with the bad.

bona opinio hominum tutior pecunia est (L.), the good opinion of men is safer than money (*Publilius Syrus*).

bona pars bene dicendi est scite mentiri (L.), a good part of speaking well consists in lying skilfully (*Erasmus*).

bona peritura (L.), perishable goods.

bona vacantia (L.), ownerless or unclaimed goods.

bon avocat, mauvais voisin (F.), good lawyer, bad neighbor.

bon camarade (F.), a good comrade; a pleasant and reliable companion in one's experiences.

bon diable (F.), a good devil; a good-natured fellow.

bon enfant (F.), a good child; a good fellow.

bon goût (F.), good taste.

bon gré, mal gré (F.), good will, bad will; willing or unwilling.

bonheur (F.), happiness; good fortune; good luck; a fortunate event or thing.

bonhomie (F.), good nature; unaffected affability.

bonhomme (F.), good man; a good, simple fellow.

boni judicis est ampliare jurisdictionem (L.), it is the part of a good judge to enlarge his jurisdiction (to interpret it liberally, in order to prevent a failure of justice).

boni pastoris est tondere pecus, non deglubere (L.), it is the part of a good shepherd to shear the flock, not to skin it (adapted from words of Tiberius Cæsar, in *Suetonius*, Tiberius, 32).

boni principii finis bonus (L.), from a good beginning a good ending.

bonis avibus (L.), with good birds (as omens); under favorable auspices.

bonjour (F.), good day (used in salutation).

bon jour, bonne œuvre (F.), good day, good work; the better the day, the better the deed.

bon marché (F.), a good bargain.

bon mot, pl. *bons mots* (F.), a good word or expression; a clever saying; a witticism.

bonne (F.), a maid-servant; a child's nurse.

bonne amie (F., fem.), good friend; a sweetheart or mistress.

bonne à tout faire (F.), a maid of all work.

bonne bouche (F.), good mouth; an agreeable taste in the mouth, as from a choice morsel; hence (in English use), a choice morsel; a titbit.

bonne compagnie (F.), good company; good society.

bonne et belle (F., fem.), good and fair.

bonne foi (F.), good faith.

bonne fortune (F.), good fortune; good luck; success.

bonne grâce, pl. *bonnes grâces* (F.), good grace; gracefulness; pl., good graces; favor.

bonne mine (F.), good appearance; pleasant looks.

bonne nuit (F.), good night.

bonnes gens (F.), good people.

bonnes nouvelles adoucissent le sang (F.), good news sweetens the blood.

bonnet (F.): see *jeter son bonnet par-dessus les moulins.*

bonnet de nuit (F.), a nightcap.

bonnet rouge (F.), a red cap, as that adopted by the French revolutionists as a symbol of liberty.

bon sang ne peut mentir (F.), good blood cannot lie; blood will tell.

bons mots (F.), pl.: see *bon mot.*

bonsoir (F.), good evening (used in salutation).

bon ton (F.), good tone; good form or style; good breeding.

bonus dux bonum reddit militem (L.), a good leader makes a good soldier.

bonus vir semper tiro (L.), a good man is always a learner.

bon vivant (F.), a good, luxurious, or high liver; a jovial companion.

bon viveur (F.), one who leads a life of pleasure; a fast liver.

bon voyage (F.), a good journey or voyage (said as a farewell wish to one departing).

bordereau (F.), a memorandum or note; a detailed list, as of documents.

Borgen macht Sorgen (G.), borrowing makes sorrowing.

borné (F.), bounded; limited; contracted; narrow.

bos lassus fortius figit pedem (L.), the weary ox puts down his foot the more firmly.

bottega (It.), a shop.

bouderie (F.), pouting; sulking.

bouleversé (F.), turned upside down; upset; thrown into complete disorder; thoroughly discomposed.

bouleversement (F.), an overturning or upsetting; complete disorder.

bouquetière (F.), a flower-girl.

bourgeois, fem. **bourgeoise** (F.), a member of the middle, esp. the mercantile, class of the people; middle-class; common. See *Le Bourgeois Gentilhomme.*

bourgeoisie (F.), the bourgeois class.

boutez en avant (F.), push forward.

boutique (F.), a shop.

brachium civile (or **seculare**) (L.), the civil (or secular) arm or power.

brevet d'invention (F.), a patent.

breveté (F.), patented.

brevi manu (L.), with a brief or prompt hand; immediately.

brevis esse laboro, obscurus fio (L.), I strive to be brief, I become obscure (*Horace*, Ars Poetica, 25).

brevis oratio penetrat cælum (L.), a short prayer reaches heaven.

briller par son absence (F.), to be conspicuous by one's absence.

brio (It.), animation; vivacity; spirit.

Britannos (L.): see *penitus toto divisos orbe Britannos.*

brûler la chandelle par les deux bouts (F.), to burn the candle at both ends; use up money, strength, etc., twice as fast as is necessary.

brutum fulmen (L.), a thunderbolt that strikes blindly or without effect; an ineffectual show of force.

buonamano (It.), a gratuity; a tip.

Burschenschaft (G.), an association of German university students. See Dictionary.

C

cachot (F.), a dungeon cell, usually subterranean.

cacoëthes carpendi (L.), a mania or morbid passion for finding fault.

cacoëthes loquendi (L.), a mania for talking.

cacoëthes scribendi (L.), a mania for writing or authorship: see *scribendi cacoëthes.*

cadeau (F.), a gift; a present.

cadit quæstio (L.), the question drops; the case is closed.

cæca invidia est (L.), envy is blind.

cæcus amor sui (L.), blind love of self (*Horace*, Odes, i. 18).

cælebs quid agam (L.), what I, a bachelor, am doing (*Horace*, Odes, iii. 8).

cælitus mihi vires (L.), my strength is from heaven.

cælum non animum mutant qui trans mare currunt (L.), they change their sky, not their hearts, who speed across the sea (*Horace*, Epistles, i. 11).

cælum undique, et undique pontus (L.), sky on all sides, and on all sides sea (*Virgil*, Æneid, iii. 193).

Cæsar non supra grammaticos (L.), Cæsar is not above the grammarians. See Dictionary.

café (F.), coffee. See Dictionary.

café chantant, or **café-concert** (F.), a café or restaurant in which musical entertainment is provided.

ça ira (F.), that will go, or go on (a phrase recurring throughout a famous popular song of the French Revolution).

camelot (F.), a street vender, as of small wares or newspapers.

campo santo (It.), holy field; a cemetery.

canaille (F.), riffraff; the rabble.

canam mihi et Musis (L.), I will sing to myself and to the Muses.

candida pax (L.), fair peace (*Ovid*, Ars Amatoria, iii. 502).

canis in præsæpi (L.), the dog in the manger.

cantabit vacuus coram latrone viator (L.), the traveler with empty purse will sing (care-free) in the presence of the robber (*Juvenal*, Satires, x. 22).

cantinière (F.), a canteen-woman.

capiat qui capere possit (L.), let him take who can take.

capistrum maritale (L.), the matrimonial halter (see *Juvenal*, Satires, vi. 43).

capitis deminutio (L.), loss of civil qualification.

capitis nives (L.), the snows of the head (*Horace*, Odes, iv. 13).

capitulum (L.), chapter; section.

captatio benevolentiæ (L.), a currying of favor.

captum te nidore suæ putat ille culinæ (L.), he thinks that thou art taken with the odor from his kitchen (*Juvenal*, Satires, v. 162).

caput (L.), head; chapter; section.

caput inter nubila condit (L.), she (Fame, or Rumor) hides her head among the clouds (*Virgil*, Æneid, iv. 177).

caput lupinum (L.), wolf's head; an outlaw (who by law might be killed like a wolf or any wild beast).

caput mortuum (L.), dead head; residuum. See Dictionary.

cara sposa (It.), dear wife.

carême (F.), Lent.

carent quia vate sacro (L.), because they lack an inspired bard (*Horace*, Odes, iv. 9).

caret initio et fine (L.), it lacks beginning and end.

carmen triumphale (L.), a triumphal song.

carmina morte carent (L.), songs are exempt from death (*Ovid*, Amores, i. 15).

carpe diem, quam minimum credula postero (L.), enjoy the present day, trusting as little as possible to the morrow (*Horace*, Odes, i. 11).

carpere et colligere (L.), to pluck and gather.

carte (F.), a card; a bill of fare; a map or chart.

carte blanche (F.), a blank card; a signed paper left blank to be filled out at the discretion of the receiver; full discretionary power.

carte de visite (F.), a visiting-card.

carte du jour (F.), the bill of fare for the day.

carte du pays (F.), a map of the country.

caserne (F.), a barrack.

cassette (F.): see *les beaux yeux de ma cassette.*

cassis tutissima virtus (L.), virtue is the safest helmet.

castigat ridendo mores (L.), it castigates manners in laughing at them (said of comedy).

castigo te non quod odio habeam, sed quod amem (L.), I chastise thee not because I hate but because I love.

casus (L.), a case; an occurrence, matter, or occasion.

casus belli (L.), an occasion or ground for war.

casus conscientiæ (L.), a case of conscience.

casus fœderis (L.), a case stipulated for in a treaty or compact.

casus fortuitus (L.), a fortuitous occurrence; an inevitable accident.

casus major (L.), a major occurrence; an extraordinary accident, as shipwreck, fire, etc.

casus necessitatis (L.), a case of necessity.

casus omissus (L.), a case not provided for, as by statute.

catalogue raisonné (F.). See Dictionary.

Cato contra mundum (L.), Cato against the world: cf. *Athanasius contra mundum.*

causa causans (L.), a causing cause; a primary cause.

causa causata (L.), a caused cause; an effect which has in turn become a cause.

causa sine qua non (L.), an indispensable cause: see *sine qua non.*

cause célèbre (F.), a celebrated case (in law).

causerie (F.), a talk or chat. See Dictionary.

caute, non astute (L.), cautiously, not craftily.

caveat actor (L.), let the doer beware.

caveat emptor (L.), let the buyer beware.

cave canem (L.), beware of the dog (a frequent inscription at Roman doors).

cavendo tutus (L.), safe through taking care.

cave ne cadas (L.), beware lest thou fall.

cave quid dicis, quando, et cui (L.), beware what thou sayest, when, and to whom.

cave tibi a cane muto et aqua silenti (L.), beware thou of a silent dog and still water.

cedant arma togæ (L.), let arms yield to the gown; let war give way to peace (*Cicero*, De Officiis, i. 22).

cede deo (L.), yield to the god (*Virgil*, Æneid, v. 467).

ce jeune homme ira loin (F.), this young man will go far (achieve success, fame, etc.).

cela m'est égal (F.), that is all the same to me.

cela ne fait rien (F.), that does not matter.

cela va sans dire (F.), that goes without saying; that is understood, or is a matter of course.

cela viendra (F.), that will come.

celsæ graviore casu decidunt turres (L.), lofty towers sink with heavier fall (*Horace*, Odes, ii. 10).

celui qui veut, celui-là peut (F.), who has the will, he has the skill (ability).

ce monde est plein de fous (F.), this world is full of fools.

Cena Domini (L.), the Lord's Supper.

c'en est fait de lui (F.), it is all over with him.

censor morum (L.), censor of manners or morals.

certum est quia impossibile est (L.), it is certain because it is impossible (*Tertullian*).

certum est quod certo reddi potest (L.), that is certain which can be rendered certain.

certum voto pete finem (L.), seek a definite end in your desire; set bounds to your wishes (*Horace*, Epistles, i. 2).

c'est-à-dire (F.), that is to say; that is.

c'est autre chose (F.), that is (quite) another thing.

c'est ça (F.), it is that; it is so.

c'est égal (F.), it is all the same; it makes no difference.

c'est entendu (F.), it is understood; it is agreed.

c'est la guerre (F.), it is war.

c'est le commencement de la fin (F.), it is the beginning of the end (attributed to Talleyrand, speaking of the Hundred Days).

c'est magnifique, mais ce n'est pas la guerre (F.), it is magnificent, but it is not war (said by the French general Bosquet on viewing the charge of the Light Brigade at Balaklava).

c'est plus (or **pire**) **qu'un crime, c'est une faute** (F.), it is more (or worse) than a crime, it is a blunder (variously attributed to Fouché, Talleyrand, and others, on the execution of the Duc d'Enghien by Napoleon).

c'est selon (F.), that is according (to circumstances); that depends.

cestui (OF.), etc. See Dictionary.

c'est une autre affaire (F.), that is another matter.

cetera desiderantur (L.), the rest are missing.

cetera desunt (L.), the rest are wanting.

cetera quis nescit? (L.), who does not know the rest? (*Ovid*, Amores, i. 5).

ceteris paribus (L.), other things being equal.

ceterum censeo (L.), but I think (as a persistent objector would say).

chacun à son goût (F.), every one to his taste.

chacun pour soi (F.), every one for himself.

chacun pour soi, et Dieu pour tous (F.), every one for himself, and God for all.

chambre à coucher (F.), a bedroom.

chambre séparée (F.), a separate or private room.

chanson de geste (F.), an epic poem narrating heroic exploits.

chapeau bas (F.), with the hat off; hat in hand.

chapeaux bas! (F.), hats off!

charcuterie (F.), a pork-butcher's meats, etc., or shop.

charmant, fem. **charmante** (F.), charming.

château en Espagne (F.), a castle in Spain; an air-castle.

chef (F.), a head or chief; a head cook.

chef de cuisine (F.), the (male) head of a kitchen or culinary department; a head cook.

chef-d'œuvre (F.), a masterpiece.

chemin de fer (F.), road of iron; a railroad.

cher ami, fem. **chère amie** (F.), dear friend.

cherchez la femme (F.), look for the woman (since there must be a woman at the bottom of the matter).

chéri, fem. **chérie** (F.), beloved; darling.

cher maître (F.), dear master.

che sarà sarà (It.), what will be will be.

cheval de bataille (F.), a war-horse; a hobby, esp. one 'ridden' in arguing; a mainstay or chief reliance.

chevalier d'industrie (F.), a knight of skill or ingenuity; one who lives unscrupulously by his wits; a sharper.

chez (F.), at the house of; with; among.

chiesa libera in libero stato (It.), a free church in a free state (advocated by Cavour for Italy).

chi lo sa? (It.), who knows it? who knows?

chi sa? (It.), who knows?

chi tace acconsente (or **confessa**) (It.), who remains silent consents (or confesses).

Christe eleïson (L., for Gr. Χριστέ ἐλέησον), Christ, have mercy (in ecclesiastical use).

Christo et ecclesiæ (L.), for Christ and the church (a motto of Harvard University).

chronique scandaleuse (F.), a chronicle of scandal.

ci-devant (F.), heretofore; former; late; ex-.

ciel (F.), the sky; heaven; a canopy.

ci-gît, pl. **ci-gisent** (F.), here lies.

cineri gloria sera venit (L.), to one's ashes glory comes late (*Martial*, Epigrams, i. 25).

circa, or **circiter** (L.), around; about.

circuitus verborum (L.), a roundabout form of words; a circumlocution.

circulus in definiendo (L.), a circle in defining; a faulty form of definition in which the very word or conception to be defined is used to explain the meaning.

circulus in probando (L.), a circle in proving; a faulty form of reasoning in which the conclusion itself is assumed as one of the premises.

circum (L.), around; about.

cito (L.), quickly; soon.

cito maturum, cito putridum (L.), soon ripe, soon rotten.

citoyen, fem. **citoyenne** (F.), a citizen.

civilitas successit barbarum (L.), civilization has succeeded barbarism.

civiliter mortuus (L.), civilly dead; deprived of all civil rights.

civis Romanus sum (L.), I am a Roman citizen (a declaration of political rights not to be denied with impunity: see *Cicero*, 2 Verres, v. 57).

clair de lune (F.), moonlight.

clare constat (L.), it is clearly established; it clearly appears.

clarior e tenebris (L.), brighter from the darkness.

clarum et venerabile nomen (L.), an illustrious and venerable name (*Lucan*, Pharsalia, ix. 202).

classes aisées (F.), the well-to-do classes.

clavam extorquere Herculi (L.), to wrest the club from Hercules.

clef des champs (F.), the key of the fields; liberty or opportunity to depart.

cocher (F.), a coachman; a driver.

cœur de lion (F.), lion-heart; one who has the heart or courage of a lion (applied esp. to Richard I. of England).

cogito, ergo sum (L.), I think, therefore I am (philosophical principle of Descartes).

cognatio movit invidiam (L.), kinship promotes ill feeling.

collectanea (L.), collected passages from various authors or sources.

colloquio jam tempus adest (L.), now the time for conversation is at hand (*Ovid*, Ars Amatoria, i. 607).

colubrem in sinu fovere (L.), to cherish a serpent in one's bosom.

combat (F.): see *et le combat cessa faute de combattants*.

Comédie Humaine (F.): see *La Comédie Humaine*.

comédie larmoyante (F.), tearful comedy; a form of comedy, originating in France in the 18th century, of a pathetic or highly sentimental character.

comes facundus (or **jucundus**) **in via pro vehiculo est** (L.), an entertaining (or pleasant) companion on the way is as good as a carriage (*Publilius Syrus*).

comitas gentium (or **inter gentes**) (L.), the comity of nations (or between nations).

commedia dell' arte (It.), comedy of the craft; an old form of comedy, originating in Italy, performed by a company of professional actors representing stock personages but improvising their speeches.

comme il faut (F.), as it should be; as required by approved usage; properly; proper.

comment vous portez-vous? (F.), how do you do?

comme une âme en peine (F.), like a soul in torment.

commodum ex injuria sua nemo habere debet (L.), no one should have profit from his own wrong-doing.

commune bonum (L.), the (or a) common good.

communibus annis (L.), in common or average years.

communi consensu (L.), by common consent.

compagnon de voyage (F.), a traveling companion.

componere lites (L.), to settle disputes.

compos mentis (L.), of sound mind. See Dictionary.

compos sui (L.), having control of one's self; master of one's self.

compte courant (F.), account current; a running account.

compte rendu (F.), account rendered; a report.

comptoir (F.), a counter; a counting-house; a banking or commercial agency.

con affetto (It.), with feeling.

con amore (It.), with love; with a will; enthusiastically; heartily.

con brio (It.), with spirit.

concedo (L.), I concede; I grant or admit.

concio ad clerum (L.), a discourse to the clergy.

concordia discors (L.), discordant harmony.

concours (F.), concourse; meeting; competition; a competitive contest.

con diligenza (It.), with diligence.

conditio sine qua non (L.), an indispensable condition: see *sine qua non*.

con dolore (It.), with sorrow.

confer (L.), compare.

confiance (F.), confidence: see *la confiance fournit plus* (etc.).

confiserie (F.), confectionery.

conjunctis viribus (L.), with united powers.

conquiescat in pace (L.), may he (or she) rest in peace.

conscia mens recti (L.), a mind conscious of rectitude (*Ovid*, Fasti, iv. 311).

conseil de famille (F.), family council.

conseil des prud'hommes (F.), council of good or discreet men; a council composed of masters and workmen charged with settling labor disputes.

conseil d'état (F.), council of state.

consensus facit legem (L.), agreement, or consent, makes law.

consensus gentium (L.), agreement of peoples; common or general consent.

consensus omnium (L.), agreement of all; universal consent.

consensus tollit errorem (L.), consent removes error.

consilio et animis (L.), by wisdom and courage.

consilio et prudentia (L.), by wisdom and prudence.

con spirito (It.), with spirit.

constantia et virtute (L.), by constancy and virtue.

constat (L.), it is established; it appears; it is manifest or evident.

consuetudo curiæ (L.), the custom of the court.

consuetudo est altera lex (L.), custom is another law.

consuetudo est optima interpres legum (L.), custom is the best interpreter of laws.

consuetudo loci observanda est (L.), the custom of the place is to be observed.

consuetudo pro lege servatur (L.), custom is observed as law.

consule Planco (L.), when Plancus was consul; in the time of one's youth (*Horace*, Odes, iii. 14).

consummatum est (L.), it is finished (*Vulgate*, John, xix. 30).

continuetur remedium (L.), let the remedy be continued.

contra bonos mores (L.), against good manners or morals.

contra felicem vix deus vires habet (L.), against a lucky man a god scarcely has power (*Publilius Syrus*).

contra malum mortis non est medicamen in hortis (L.), against the evil of death there is no remedy in the gardens.

contra negantem principia non est disputandum (L.), there is no arguing with one who denies first principles.

contra pacem (L.), against the peace.

contra quoscumque (L.), against all persons whatsoever.

contraria contrariis curantur (L.), contraries are cured by contraries.

copia verborum (L.), abundance of words.

cor ad cor loquitur (L.), heart speaketh to heart (motto of Cardinal Newman).

coram domino rege (L.), before our lord the king.

coram ipso rege (L.), before the king himself.

coram judice (L.), before the (proper) judge (one having due jurisdiction).

coram non judice (L.), before one not the (proper) judge (not having due jurisdiction).

coram paribus (L.), before equals; before one's peers.

coram populo (L.), before the people; in public.

cordon bleu (F.), blue ribbon. See Dictionary.

cordon sanitaire (F.), a sanitary cordon; a line of guards about an infected district to control communication.

cordons de la bourse (F.), strings of the purse; means of controlling expenditure.

cor inquietum donec requiescat in te (L.), the heart is restless until it rests in thee (*St. Augustine*).

cor ne edito (L.), eat not thy heart.

corpo di Bacco! (It.), body of Bacchus!

corps (F.), body; mass; the main mass; an aggregate; a collective whole.

corps à corps (F.), body to body (as in a struggle); hand to hand.

corps d'armée (F.), an army-corps.

corps de ballet (F.), a company of ballet-dancers.

corps de bataille (F.), the main body of an army drawn up for battle, as distinguished from the wings.

corps de garde (F.), a body of soldiers for guard duty; a guard-room or guard-house.

corps d'élite (F.), a corps or body of picked troops.

corps de logis (F.), the main portion of a building, apart from wings, etc.; a main building; a detached building.

corps de réserve (F.), a body of troops held as a reserve.

corps diplomatique (F.), a diplomatic corps; the entire body of diplomatists accredited to a government.

corps législatif (F.), a legislative body.

corpus (L.), body; mass; substance; a collective whole.

corpus delicti (L.), the body or substance of the offense; the substantial

or essential fact of the offense or crime charged.

corpus juris (L.), a body of law; a collection of laws.

corpus juris canonici (L.), the body of canon law.

corpus juris civilis (L.), the body of civil (or Roman) law.

corpus sine pectore (L.), a body without a soul (see *Horace*, Epistles, i. 4).

corpus valet sed aegrotat crumena (L.), the body is well but the purse is sick (*Erasmus*).

corrigendum (L.), an error to be corrected. See Dictionary.

corruptio optimi pessima (L.), corruption of the best is the worst (corruption).

cor unum, via una (L.), one heart, one way.

cosa ben fatta è fatta due volte (It.), a thing well done is twice done.

così fan tutte (It.), so do they (women) all; they all do it.

cos ingeniorum (L.), a whetstone for the wits.

cottage orné (F.), an ornamented or elegant cottage (as distinguished from the cottage of a laborer).

couleur de rose (F.), rose-color; rose-colored; under a pleasing aspect; in a favorable light.

coup (F.), a stroke. See Dictionary.

coup d'autorité (F.), a stroke of authority; a sudden, decisive move or proceeding.

coup de bonheur (F.), a stroke of good luck.

coup de chapeau (F.), a touching of the hat.

coup de courage (F.), a stroke of courage; a bold stroke.

coup de foudre (F.), a thunderbolt.

coup de grâce (F.), a stroke of grace or mercy. See Dictionary.

coup de hasard (F.), a stroke of chance or luck.

coup de langue (F.), a stroke of the tongue; a spiteful or slanderous remark.

coup de main (F.), a stroke of the hand; a sudden, vigorous attack. See Dictionary.

coup de maître (F.), a master-stroke.

coup de pied (F.), a stroke of the foot; a kick.

coup de poing (F.), a stroke of the fist; a fisticuff.

coup de soleil (F.), a sunstroke.

coup d'essai (F.), a trial stroke; a first attempt.

coup d'état (F.), a stroke of state; a sudden political stroke. See Dictionary.

coup de théâtre (F.), a theatrical stroke. See Dictionary.

coup de tonnerre (F.), a clap of thunder; also, a thunderbolt.

coup de vent (F.), a gust of wind; a gale.

coup d'œil (F.), a glance; a view or prospect. See Dictionary.

coup manqué (F.), a stroke that failed; an abortive attempt.

courage sans peur (F.), courage without fear.

coûte que coûte (F.), cost what it may.

craignez honte (F.), fear disgrace.

crambe repetita (L.), cabbage served up again; an old story (*Juvenal*, Satires, vii. 154).

cras credo, hodie nihil (L.), to-morrow I believe, to-day not at all (*Varro*).

cras ingens iterabimus æquor (L.), to-morrow we shall embark again upon the great sea (*Horace*, Odes, i. 7).

credat Judæus Apella, non ego (L.), let the Jew Apella believe it, not myself (*Horace*, Satires, i. 5).

crede quod habes, et habes (L.), believe that you have (a thing), and you have.

crede ut intelligas (L.), believe in order that you may understand.

credite, posteri! (L.), believe, posterity! (*Horace*, Odes, ii. 19).

credo quia absurdum (L.), I believe it because it is absurd.

credo quia impossibile est (L.), I believe it because it is impossible: cf. *certum est quia impossibile est*.

credula res amor est (L.), love is a credulous thing (*Ovid*, Metamorphoses, vii. 826).

crème de la crème (F.), cream of the cream; the very best.

crescite et multiplicamini (L.), increase and multiply (a motto of Maryland: *Vulgate*, Gen. i. 22).

crescit eundo (L.), it increases as it goes (motto of New Mexico: cf. *Lucretius*, vi. 341).

crescit sub pondere virtus (L.), virtue grows beneath a burden.

crève-cœur (F.), heartbreak; acute grief; vexation; mortification.

cribro aquam haurire (L.), to draw water in a sieve; spend time in vain labor.

crimen falsi (L.), the crime of falsehood or falsifying; forgery.

crimen læsæ majestatis (L.), the crime of lese-majesty; high treason.

croquis (F.), a sketch; a slight drawing; a rough draft.

cruda viridisque senectus (L.), a vigorous and green old age (see *Virgil*, Æneid, vi. 304).

crux criticorum (L.), a crux or puzzle for critics.

crux mathematicorum (L.), a puzzle for mathematicians.

crux medicorum (L.), a puzzle for physicians.

cucullus non facit monachum (L.), the cowl does not make the monk.

cui bono? (L.), for whose benefit? also, for what use? of what good?

cui Fortuna ipsa cedit (L.), to whom Fortune herself yields.

cuilibet in sua arte perito credendum est (L.), any one skilled in his art is to be trusted (in evidence).

cuique suum (L.), to each his own.

cujus est divisio, alterius est electio (L.), whichever (of two parties) makes the division, the other makes the choice.

cujus est solum, ejus est usque ad cælum et ad inferos (L.), who owns the land owns all even to the heavens and to the nether world (all above and below the surface of his land).

cujus regio, ejus religio (L.), whose the region, his the religion; the sovereign determines the religion of his country.

culpæ pœna par esto (L.), let the punishment be proportioned to the crime.

culpa levis (L.), a light or trifling fault.

culpam pœna premit comes (L.), punishment presses close in attendance on crime (*Horace*, Odes, iv. 5).

cum bona venia (L.), with your kind indulgence.

cum grano salis (L.), with a grain of salt; with some allowance.

cum laude (L.), with praise (a phrase of commendation in diplomas): see *magna cum laude* and *summa cum laude*.

cum multis aliis (L.), with many other things.

cum notis variorum (L.), with notes of various commentators.

cum permissu superiorum (L.), with the permission of the superiors or heads.

cum privilegio (L.), with privilege.

cum tacent clamant (L.), when they are silent they cry out (*Cicero*, 1 Catiline, 8).

cum testamento annexo (L.), with the will annexed (used with reference to administration of an estate where there is a will but no executor).

cuneus cuneum trudit (L.), wedge drives wedge.

curiosa felicitas (L.), studied or nice felicity, as of expression (said of Horace: *Petronius*, Satiricon, 118).

currente calamo (L.), with a running pen; fluently; offhand.

custos morum (L.), guardian of manners or morals.

custos regni (L.), guardian of the realm; regent.

custos rotulorum (L.), keeper of the rolls (or records).

custos sigilli (L.), keeper of the seal.

cy pres (AF.), so near; as nearly as possible or practicable (used with reference to a mode of execution employed in the case of a will or trust that cannot be executed literally).

D

dabit deus his quoque finem (L.), the god will grant an end to these also (*Virgil*, Æneid, i. 199).

d'accord (F.), in accord; agreed; in harmony.

da dextram misero (L.), give the right hand to the unfortunate (*Virgil*, Æneid, vi. 370).

da locum melioribus (L.), give place to your betters (*Terence*, Phormio, iii. 2).

dame de compagnie (F.), a lady employed as companion.

dame d'honneur (F.), a maid of honor.

dames de la halle (F.), ladies of the market; market-women.

damnant quod non intelligunt (L.), they condemn what they do not understand (*Quintilian*).

damnatus in metallum (L.), condemned to the mine.

damnosa hereditas (L.), a hurtful or disadvantageous inheritance.

damnosa quid non imminuit dies? (L.), what does not destructive time impair? (*Horace*, Odes, iii. 6).

damnum absque injuria (L.), damage without wrong (affording no ground for legal action).

damnum fatale (L.), damage due to fate or inevitable accident.

danse macabre (F.), the allegorical dance of the skeleton Death dancing with all conditions of men, as represented in medieval art.

dans les petites boîtes les bons onguents (F.), in the little boxes the good ointments (used with complimentary allusion to persons of small size).

dapes inemptæ (L.), feasts unbought (of home production).

dare fatis vela (L.), to give the sails to the fates; sail where fate directs (*Virgil*, Æneid, iii. 9).

dare pondus idonea fumo (L.), (a page) fit to give weight to smoke (*Persius*, Satires, v. 20).

das Ewig-Weibliche zieht uns hinan (G.), the eternal feminine draws us upward; "the Woman-Soul leadeth us upward and on" (*Goethe*, Faust, ii. 5: the second translation being that of Bayard Taylor).

das heisst (G.), that is to say; that is.

das ist (G.), that is.

data et accepta (L.), things given and received; expenditures and receipts.

data fata secutus (L.), following the appointed fates (*Virgil*, Æneid, i. 382).

date obolum Belisario (L.), give a penny to Belisarius (a once great general of the Byzantine Empire, fabled to have become a blind beggar).

Davus sum, non Œdipus (L.), I am Davus, not Œdipus (a slave, not a solver of riddles: *Terence*, Andria, i. 2).

de (L., F., Sp., and Pg., It. *di*), from; of; also, in idiomatic uses, by, with, in, concerning, etc. See Dictionary.

dea certe (L.), a goddess assuredly (*Virgil*, Æneid, i. 328).

de alieno corio liberalis (L.), liberal with another's leather.

de auctoritate mihi commissa (L.), by the authority committed to me.

de auditu (L.), by hearing or hearsay.

debellare superbos (L.), to put down the proud: see *parcere subjectis et debellare superbos*.

debemur morti nos nostraque (L.), we are due to death, we and our works (*Horace*, Ars Poetica, 63).

de bene esse (L.), as being good; of legal sufficiency or validity for the time; provisionally.

debito justitiæ (L.), by debt of justice.

debitum naturæ (L.), the debt to nature; death.

de bon augure (F.), of good augury or omen.

de bon goût (F.), in good taste.

de bonis non administratis (L.), of the goods not administered (in an estate partly settled).

de bonis propriis (L.), from his own goods; out of his own pocket.

de bonne grâce (F.), with a good grace; willingly.

deceptio visus (L.), a deception of vision; an optical illusion.

decet imperatorem stantem mori (L.), it befits an emperor to die standing (reputed dying words of the Roman emperor Vespasian).

decies repetita placebit (L.), though ten times repeated it will please (*Horace*, Ars Poetica, 365).

decipimur specie recti (L.), we are deceived by a semblance of right (*Horace*, Ars Poetica, 25).

de commodo et incommodo (L.), concerning advantage and disadvantage.

decori decus addit avito (L.), he adds honor to ancestral honor.

decumanus fluctus (L.), the tenth wave (traditionally always a large one); a recurring surge or movement of extraordinary extent or force.

decus et tutamen (L.), an ornament and a protection (*Virgil*, Æneid, v. 262).

de die in diem (L.), from day to day.

de dolo malo (L.), from evil intent; from fraud.

de facto (L.), from the fact; in fact; in reality.

défaut (F.), defect; fault: see *il a les défauts* (etc.).

de fide (L.), of the faith (or accepted doctrine); authoritative.

de fond en comble (F.), from foundation to roof; from top to bottom; entirely; thoroughly; utterly.

de fumo in flammam (L.), from the smoke into the flame; out of the frying-pan into the fire.

de gaieté de cœur (F.), from gaiety of heart; for sport; gladly or willingly.

dégoût (F.), distaste; disgust.

de gratia (L.), from or by favor.

de gustibus non est disputandum (L.), about tastes there is no disputing.

de haute lutte (F.), by main strength; by force; with authority.

de (or du) haut en bas (F.), from top to bottom; from head to foot; superciliously; disdainfully.

de haut goût (F.), of high or strong flavor; highly seasoned.

dehors (F.), outside; outside of; foreign to.

Dei gratia (L.), by the grace of God.

Dei judicium (L.), the judgment of God.

de integro (L.), anew; afresh.

Dei sub numine viget (L.), it flourishes under the will of God (motto of Princeton University).

dejecta arbore quivis ligna colligit (L.), when the tree is fallen, any one gathers the wood.

déjeuner (F.), breakfast. See Dictionary.

déjeuner à la fourchette (F.), breakfast with the fork; a breakfast, or luncheon, with meat, fish, etc.

de jure (L.), from right or law; by right; according to law.

délassement (F.), relaxation; recreation.

de l'audace, encore de l'audace, et toujours de l'audace (F.), boldness, again boldness, and always boldness (*Danton*, addressing the French Legislative Assembly, Sept. 2, 1792).

delectando pariterque monendo (L.), by amusing and instructing as well (*Horace*, Ars Poetica, 344).

delegatus non potest delegare (L.), a delegate cannot delegate (his powers).

delenda est Carthago (L.), Carthage must be destroyed (a course urged by Cato the Elder when speaking publicly on any subject whatever).

delineavit (L.), (the person specified) drew it.

délire de grandeur (F.), delirium of grandeur; an insane delusion of one's own greatness, power, wealth, etc.

déluge (F.): see *après moi le déluge*.

de lunatico inquirendo (L.), for inquiring as to a lunatic (used in law of a writ or commission issued by a court in an alleged case of lunacy).

de luxe (F.), of luxury; of especial elegance or fineness.

de mal en pis (F.), from bad to worse.

de mauvaise grâce (F.), with a bad grace; unwillingly.

de mauvais goût (F.), in bad taste.

d'emblée (F.), at the first stroke; in a trice.

demi-jour (F.), half-light; twilight.

de minimis non curat lex (L.), the law does not concern itself with trifles.

démodé (F.), no longer in fashion.

de mortuis nil nisi bonum (L.), of the dead (say) nothing but good.

de nihilo nihil fit (L.), from nothing nothing is made.

de nihilo nihilum (L.), from nothing nothing: see *gigni de nihilo nihilum* (etc.).

de nouveau (F.), anew; afresh; again.

de novo (L.), anew; afresh.

Deo adjuvante non timendum (L.), God helping, there is no need to fear.

Deo duce, ferro comitante (L.), God my guide, my sword my companion.

Deo favente (L.), God favoring.

Deo gratias (L.), thanks to God.

Deo juvante (L.), God helping.

de omnibus rebus et quibusdam aliis (L.), concerning all things and some other things also: cf. *de omni re scibili et quibusdam aliis.*

De Omni Re Scibili (L.), "Concerning Everything Knowable" (title of theses of Pico della Mirandola: see next entry).

de omni re scibili et quibusdam aliis (L.), concerning everything knowable and some other things also (a humorous extension of the title in preceding entry).

Deo monente (L.), God warning.

Deo, non fortuna (L.), from God, not fortune (or chance).

Deo Optimo Maximo (L.), to God, the Best, the Greatest (used as an inscription).

Deo volente (L.), God willing; if God wills.

dépêche (F.), a despatch; a letter, telegram, or message.

dépendance (F.), an outbuilding; an annex to a main building.

de pis en pis (F.), from worse to worse.

de plano (L.), from a level (rather than from the judicial bench); without argument; summarily; also, by manifest right; plainly.

de profundis (L.), out of the depths (*Vulgate*, Ps. cxxix. 1).

de propaganda fide (L.), for propagating the faith.

de proprio motu (L.), of one's (or its) own motion; spontaneously.

der Aberglaube ist die Poesie des Lebens (G.), superstition is the poetry of life (*Goethe*).

de retour (F.), of return; having returned; back again.

der grosse Heide (G.), the great heathen, or pagan (applied by Heine to Goethe).

de rigueur (F.), strictly required, as by etiquette or usage; obligatory; indispensable; imperative.

der Mensch ist was er isst (G.), man is what he eats.

dernier cri (F.), the last cry; the latest thing in fashionable vogue.

dernier ressort (F.), a last resort; a final resource.

déroute (F.), rout, as of a defeated army; complete overthrow; ruin.

der Tag (G.), the day; the day of battle between the navies of Germany and Great Britain, as looked forward to by the Germans before the World War.

descriptio personæ (L.), description of the person (as in a legal document).

designatio personæ (L.), designation of the person (as in a legal document).

desipere in loco (L.), to trifle (unbend playfully) on occasion: see *dulce est desipere in loco.*

désœuvré, fem. **désœuvrée** (F.), unemployed; without occupation; idle.

désœuvrement (F.), lack of occupation; idleness.

de son tort (AF.), of or by his own wrong (used in law of one who without legal right assumes the task of an executor).

désorienté (F.), having lost one's bearings.

dessous des cartes (F.), the under side of the cards; the inside facts of a case; something not generally disclosed.

destitutis ventis remos adhibe (L.), when the winds fail, take to the oars.

desunt cetera (L.), the rest are wanting.

de te fabula narratur (L.), of thyself is the story told: see *mutato nomine de te fabula narratur.*

détenu, fem. **détenue** (F.), one detained in custody; a prisoner.

deterrima belli causa (L.): see *tæterrima belli causa.*

de trop (F.), too much; too many; in the way.

detur digniori (or **dignissimo**) (L.), let it be given to the more worthy (or the most worthy).

detur pulchriori (L.), let it be given to the more beautiful.

Deus avertat! (L.), God forbid!

Deus det! (L.), God grant it!

deus ex machina (L.), a god out of a machine (as an ancient theatrical expedient); a mechanical or unnatural device used to aid a plot; an extraordinary agency for solving a difficulty.

Deus misereatur nostri (L.), God be merciful unto us (*Vulgate*, Ps. lxvi. 1).

deus nobis hæc otia fecit (L.), a god has given us this ease (*Virgil*, Eclogues, i. 6).

Deus vobiscum (L.), God be with you.

Deus vult! (L.), God wills it! (cry of the Crusaders).

deutsche Apotheke (G.), German apothecary's shop or drug-store.

Deutsch gesprochen (G.), German spoken.

Deutschland, Deutschland über alles (G.), Germany, Germany above all (first line, and title, of a patriotic song composed in 1841 by Hoffmann von Fallersleben).

devastavit (L.), he wasted (used in law with reference to one charged with waste while serving in a trust capacity).

de visu (L.), from or by sight.

de vive voix (F.), with the living voice; orally: cf. *viva voce.*

dextro tempore (L.), at a favorable or lucky moment.

di (It.), from; of; also, by, with, etc.: see *de.*

Diable Boiteux (F.): see *Le Diable Boiteux.*

dialectica (L.): see *non in dialectica complacuit Deo* (etc.).

dicamus bona verba (L.), let us speak words of good omen.

Dichtung und Wahrheit (G.), "Poetry and Truth": part of the title of Goethe's autobiography, called in full *Aus meinem Leben: Dichtung und Wahrheit* ("From My Life: Poetry and Truth").

dicta docta pro datis (L.), clever (or fine) speeches in place of gifts (*Plautus,* Asinaria, iii. 1).

dicta tibi est lex (L.), the law has been declared to you (*Horace*, Epistles, ii. 2).

dictum de dicto (L.), a saying from a saying; a hearsay report.

dictum sapienti sat est (L.), a word to the wise is sufficient.

diem perdidi (L.), I have lost a day (attributed to the Roman emperor Titus, on having passed a day without bestowing a gift).

dies datus (L.), a day given or appointed.

dies diem docet (L.), day teaches day.

dies dominicus non est juridicus (L.), the Lord's Day (Sunday) is not a court-day.

dies fasti (L.), in ancient Rome, days lawful for holding courts: cf. *dies nefasti.*

dies faustus (L.), an auspicious or lucky day.

dies infaustus (L.), an inauspicious or unlucky day.

dies iræ (L.), day of wrath. See Dictionary.

dies juridicus (L.), a court-day.

dies nefasti (L.), in ancient Rome, days unlawful for holding courts; inauspicious or unlucky days: cf. *dies fasti.*

dies non, or **dies non juridicus** (L.), a day not a court-day; a day on which courts do not sit.

Dieu aide à trois sortes de personnes: aux fous, aux enfants, et aux ivrognes (F.), God helps three sorts of persons: fools, children, and drunkards.

Dieu avec nous (F.), God with us.

Dieu défende le droit (F.), God defend the right.

Dieu est toujours pour les gros bataillons (F.), God is always for the big battalions (saying quoted by Voltaire).

Dieu et mon droit (F.), God and my right (motto on the royal arms of England).

Dieu vous garde (F.), God guard you.

Die Wacht am Rhein (G.), "The Watch on the Rhine" (title of German national song).

die Zeit ist hin wo Berta spann (G.), the time is past when (Queen) Bertha spun.

difficiles nugæ (L.), laborious trifles (*Martial*, Epigrams, ii. 86).

digito monstrari (L.), to be pointed out with the finger: see *pulchrum est digito monstrari* (etc.).

dignus vindice nodus (L.), a difficulty worthy of the deliverer: see *nec deus intersit* (etc.).

di grado in grado (It.), by degrees.

dilexi justitiam et odivi iniquitatem, propterea morior in exilio (L.), I have loved justice and hated iniquity, therefore I die in exile (*Pope Gregory VII.*).

di majores et minores (L.), gods greater and less.

dimidium facti, qui cœpit, habet (L.), he who has begun has half done (*Horace*, Epistles, i. 2).

Dios y federación (Sp.), God and federation (motto of Venezuela).

dira necessitas (L.), dire necessity (*Horace*, Odes, iii. 24).

dirigo (L.), I direct (motto of Maine).

dis aliter visum (L.), to the gods it has seemed best otherwise (*Virgil*, Æneid, ii. 428).

di salto (It.), at a leap or bound.

discrepant facta ejus cum dictis (L.), his facts differ from his statements (*Cicero*, De Finibus, ii. 30).

diseur, fem. **diseuse** (F.), a sayer, teller, or talker; a professional public entertainer by talking, recitation, etc.

diseur de bons mots (F.), a sayer of clever things; a wit: see *bon mot*.

disjecta membra (L.), scattered limbs, parts, or remains: cf. *disjecti membra poetæ*.

disjecti membra poetæ (L.), limbs of the dismembered poet; scattered fragments or traces of the original (*Horace*, Satires, i. 4).

dissimulare (L.): see *qui nescit dissimulare nescit regnare*.

dit (F.), called; termed.

ditat Deus (L.), God enriches (motto of Arizona).

diu intersit populo (L.), long may he live among the people: see *diuque lætus intersis populo Quirini*.

diuque lætus intersis populo Quirini (L.), and long mayest thou live in happiness among the people of Quirinus (*Horace*, Odes, i. 2).

diverso intuitu (L.), with diverse view or purpose.

divide et impera (L.), divide and rule; create division among subjects in order to maintain control over them (a principle of statecraft advocated by Machiavelli and others).

divide ut regnes (L.), divide that thou mayest rule: cf. *divide et impera*.

Divina Commedia (It.), "Divine Comedy" (title of Dante's great epic, in three parts: "Inferno," or Hell, "Purgatorio," or Purgatory, and "Paradiso," or Paradise).

divisim (L.), separately.

divisum sic breve fiet opus (L.), the work divided will thus be made short (*Martial*, Epigrams, iv. 82).

dixi (L.), I have spoken.

docendo discimus (L.), we learn by teaching.

doctus cum libro (L.), learned with the book; having book-learning.

dolce far niente (It.), sweet doing nothing; pleasant idleness.

doli capax (L.), capable (legally) of wrong-doing (as one able to distinguish between right and wrong).

doli incapax (L.), not capable (legally) of wrong-doing.

dolore (It.), pain; anguish: see *nessun maggior dolore* (etc.).

domat omnia virtus (L.), virtue overcomes all things.

domestiques (F.): see *peu d'hommes ont été admirés* (etc.).

domi manere convenit felicibus (L.),

it is best for the happy to remain at home.

Domine, dirige nos (L.), Lord, direct us (motto of the City of London).

Domine, quo vadis? (L.): see *quo vadis, Domine?*

Dominus illuminatio mea (L.), the Lord is my light (motto of Oxford University: *Vulgate*, Ps. xxvi. 1).

Dominus vobiscum (L.), the Lord be with you (a form of salutation used in liturgical services: see *et cum spiritu tuo*).

domus et placens uxor (L.), home and pleasing wife (*Horace*, Odes, ii. 14).

Domus Procerum (L.), the (British) House of Lords.

domus sua cuique est tutissimum refugium (L.), every man's house is his safest refuge (his castle).

donatio causa mortis (L.), a gift because of death (in prospect of the donor's dying soon, and valid in law only in that event).

donatio inter vivos (L.), a gift between the living.

donatio propter (or **ante**) **nuptias** (L.), a gift on account of (or before) marriage.

donator nunquam desinit possidere antequam donatarius incipiat possidere (L.), the giver never ceases to possess until the receiver begins to possess (legal maxim).

donec corrigatur (L.), until it shall be corrected.

donna è mobile (It.), woman is changeable, or fickle.

donnée (F.), a gift; a datum; the fundamental idea of a literary or dramatic composition.

Donnerwetter! (G.), thunder-weather! thunder!

dono molto aspettato è venduto, non donato (It.), a gift long waited for is sold, not given.

dorer la pilule (F.), to gild the pill.

dormitat Homerus (L.), Homer nods: see *indignor quandoque* (etc.).

double entendre (F., obs.), double meaning (in F. now *double entente*); hence, a word or expression with two meanings, one often indelicate.

double entente (F.), double meaning; equivocal sense.

do ut des (L.), I give that you may give.

d'outre-mer (F.), from beyond the sea.

doux yeux (F.), sweet eyes; sheep's eyes; tender or amorous glances.

dramatis personæ (L.), the persons or characters of a drama.

Drang nach Osten (G.), pressure or impulse toward the East (the Orient), esp. as a direction of political or national development.

droit au travail (F.), the right to labor or employment.

droit d'aubaine (F.), right of succession to the goods of a resident alien at his death (formerly exercised by sovereigns of France).

droit des gens (F.), the law of nations; international law.

droit et avant (F.), right and forward.

droit et loyal (F.), upright and loyal.

drôle (F.), a rogue; an amusing rascal.

ducit amor patriæ (L.), love of country guides.

ducunt volentem fata, nolentem trahunt (L.), the fates lead the

willing man, but drag the unwilling (*Seneca*, Epistles, 107).

du fort au faible (F.), from the strong to the weak; on an average.

du haut en bas (F.): see *de haut en bas*.

dulce bellum inexperto (L.), sweet is war to him who has not tried it.

dulce est desipere in loco (L.), it is pleasant to trifle (unbend playfully) on occasion (*Horace*, Odes, iv. 12).

dulce et decorum est pro patria mori (L.), it is sweet and fitting to die for one's country (*Horace*, Odes, iii. 2).

dum fervet opus (L.), while the work glows; in the heat of action.

dummodo sit dives, barbarus ipse placet (L.), so long as he is rich, even a barbarian is pleasing (*Ovid*, Ars Amatoria, ii. 276).

dum spiro, spero (L.), while I breathe, I hope (a motto of South Carolina).

dum vita est, spes est (L.), while there is life, there is hope.

dum vivimus, vivamus (L.), while we live, let us live.

d'un seul jet (F.), at one cast, stroke, or effort.

dura lex, sed lex (L.), the law is hard, but it is the law.

durante absentia (L.), during absence.

durante beneplacito (L.), during good pleasure, as of a sovereign.

durante minore ætate (L.), during minority, or legal infancy.

durante viduitate (L.), during widowhood.

durante vita (L.), during life.

dux femina facti (L.), a woman was leader in the deed (*Virgil*, Æneid, i. 364).

E

ea fama vagatur (L.), that report is spread abroad (*Virgil*, Æneid, ii. 17).

eau (F.), water. See Dictionary.

eau bénite (F.), holy water.

eau bénite de cour (F.), holy water of the court; smooth, insincere words; empty promises.

eau douce (F.), fresh (not salt) water.

eau gazeuse (F.), gaseous or carbonated water.

eau salée (F.), salt water.

eau sucrée (F.), sugared or sweetened water.

ébauche (F.), a first rough form of a work of art, etc.; an outline; a sketch.

éboulement (F.), a falling down of walls, heavy masses, etc.; a landslide.

ébranlement (F.), a violent shaking; shock.

ebrii gignunt ebrios (L.), drunkards beget drunkards.

ecce! (L.), behold!

ecce homo! (L.), behold the man (Christ)! (*Vulgate*, John, xix. 5).

ecce in justitia regnabit rex (L.), behold, a king shall reign in righteousness (*Vulgate*, Isa. xxxii. 1).

ecce iterum Crispinus adest (L.), behold, here is Crispinus again; here comes that fellow again (*Juvenal*, Satires, iv. 1).

ecce signum! (L.), behold the sign (or proof)!

ecco! (It.), behold! lo! here (am, is, or are) . . . !

éclaircissement (F.), a clearing up; an explanation.

éclat (F.), a burst; a loud clap or peal; a blaze of light; splendor; brilliance.

éclat de rire (F.), a burst of laughter.

école (F.), a school.

école de droit (F.), a law-school.

école de médecine (F.), a school of medicine.

école d'équitation (F.), a riding-school.

école des beaux-arts (F.), a school of the fine arts.

école maternelle (F.), an infant-school.

école militaire (F.), a military school.

école normale (F.), a normal school.

école polytechnique (F.), a polytechnic school.

e contrario (L.), on the contrary.

e converso (L.), conversely.

écrasez (or **écrasons**) **l'infâme** (F.), crush (or let us crush) the infamous thing (favorite expression of Voltaire, with reference to a fanatically intolerant religious system).

écroulement (F.), a falling in pieces or ruins; collapse; a landslide.

edax rerum (L.), the devourer of things: see *tempus edax rerum*.

éditeur (F.), an editor; also, a publisher.

édition de luxe (F.), an especially handsome or sumptuous edition, as of a book.

editiones expurgatæ (L.), expurgated editions.

editio princeps (L.), the first printed edition of a book; a copy of this edition.

edo, ergo sum (L.), I eat, therefore I am.

égalité (F.), equality.

égaré, fem. **égarée** (F.), astray; lost; wandering; bewildered; deranged.

égarement (F.), a going astray; wandering; bewilderment; derangement.

ego et rex meus (or **meus rex**) (L.), I and my king (*Cardinal Wolsey*: often quoted as the expression of a correct Latinist but a poor courtier).

ego hoc feci (L.), I did, or made, this.

eheu fugaces labuntur anni (L.), alas, the flying years glide by (see *Horace*, Odes, ii. 14).

eile mit Weile (G.), make haste slowly.

ein' feste Burg ist unser Gott (G.), a mighty fortress is our God (first line of a hymn by Luther).

einmal, keinmal (G.), one time, no time; once does not count.

Eisenbahn (G.), a railroad.

Eisen und Blut (G.), iron and blood (*Bismarck*).

ejusdem farinæ (L.), of the same flour; of the same nature or kind; birds of a feather.

ejusdem generis (L.), of the same kind.

élan (F.), dash; impetuous ardor. See Dictionary.

elapso tempore (L.), the time having elapsed.

élégant, fem. **élégante** (F.), a person of fashion.

elephantus non capit murem (L.), an elephant does not catch a mouse.

élève (F.), a pupil.

élite (F.), the choice part. See Dictionary.

elixir vitæ (L.), the elixir of life.

éloge (F.), a eulogy; a funeral oration.

éloignement (F.), removal; remoteness; estrangement.

embarras de richesses (F.), embarrassment of riches; an embarrassing amount of wealth or good things.

embarras du choix (F.), embarrassment of choice; a superabundance to choose from.

émeute (F.), a riot.

émeutier (F.), a rioter.

émigré, fem. **émigrée** (F.), an emigrant. See Dictionary.

emitte spiritum tuum (L.), send forth thy spirit (see *Vulgate*, Ps. ciii. 30).

empire des lettres (F.), the empire or domain of letters.

emporté, fem. **emportée** (F.), passionate; hot-headed; hasty.

emportement (F.), transport; passion; rage.

empressé, fem. **empressée** (F.), eager; assiduous; zealously attentive or polite.

empressement (F.), eagerness; alacrity; zealous politeness; display of cordiality.

empta dolore docet experientia (L.), when bought with sorrow experience teaches.

e multis paleis paulum fructus collegi (L.), from much chaff I have gathered a little grain.

emunctæ naris (L.), of cleared nostril; of keen or nice perception (*Horace*, Satires, i. 4).

en ami (F.), as a friend.

en arrière (F.), in or to the rear; backward; behindhand; in arrears.

en attendant (F.), while waiting; in the meantime.

en avant (F.), forward; onward.

en badinant (F.), in jest; in sport.

en beau (F.), in a favorable light.

en bloc (F.), in a block or lump.

en bon chrétien (F.), as or like a good Christian.

en bon train (F.), in good train; going well.

en cabochon (F.), in the cabochon style, as a gem; in rounded, convex form, without facets.

en cachette (F.), in hiding; in secret; secretly.

en cœur (F.), in the shape of a heart.

en croupe (F.), on the croup; on a pillion.

en cueros (Sp.), in the skin; naked.

en cuerpo (Sp.), in the body; without cloak, outer garment, or covering.

en cuerpo y en alma (Sp.), in body and in soul; wholly.

en déshabillé (F.), in dishabille or undress.

en Dieu est ma fiance (F.), in God is my trust.

en échelon (F.), in echelon; like a flight of steps.

en effet (F.), in effect; in fact.

en évidence (F.), in evidence; in plain sight; before the public view.

en face (F.), in the face; to one's face; openly; boldly; in front; opposite.

en famille (F.), in the family; in the family circle.

enfant gâté (F.), a spoiled child.

enfants (F.), children: see *Dieu aide à trois sortes de personnes* (etc.), also *il n'y a plus d'enfants*.

enfants de France (F.), children of France; the children of the king of France.

enfants perdus (F.), lost children; soldiers sent out on especially dangerous duty; a forlorn hope.

enfant terrible (F.), a terrible child; a child given to making embarrassing remarks or disclosures.

enfant trouvé (F.), a foundling.

en fête (F.), in festivity; engaged in a festival; in festal array.

enfin (F.), in fine; to conclude; finally.

en foule (F.), in a crowd.

en garçon (F.), as a bachelor; in bachelor's style.

engoué, fem. **engouée** (F.), infatuated.

engouement, or **engoûment** (F.), infatuation; unreasoning fondness.

en grand (F.), on a large or grand scale; at full size; in gross; as a whole.

en grande tenue (F.), in full dress.

en grande toilette (F.), in full dress.

en grand seigneur (F.), as a great lord; in lordly style.

en haut (F.), on high; above; aloft; upstairs.

en l'air (F.), in the air; without firm basis; unsupported or unduly exposed, as the flank of an army; in commotion or disorder.

en masse (F.), in a mass or body; all together.

en mauvaise odeur (F.), in bad odor; in ill repute.

ennemis (F.): see *nos amis les ennemis*.

ennui (F.), etc. See Dictionary.

en papillotes (F.), in curl-papers.

en passant (F.), in passing; by the way.

en pension (F.), in a boarding-house or a boarding-school.

en plein (F.), in full; fully; entirely.

en plein air (F.), in the open air.

en pleine rue (F.), in the middle of the street.

en plein jour (F.), in broad daylight.

en prince (F.), as a prince; in princely style.

en pure perte (F.), in pure loss or waste; without result; in vain.

en queue (F.), like a tail; in a line or file; in the rear; at one's heels.

en rapport (F.), in relation; in sympathy or accord.

en règle (F.), according to rule; in due form.

en résumé (F.), to sum up; on the whole.

en retraite (F.), in retreat; retreating; in retirement; on the retired list.

en revanche (F.), in revenge; in return.

en route (F.), on the road; on one's way.

ense et aratro (L.), with sword and with plow; with service both in war and in peace.

ense petit placidam sub libertate quietem (L.), with the sword she seeks peaceful quiet under liberty (motto of Massachusetts).

ens legis (L.), a being or thing created by the law, as a corporation.

ens rationis (L.), a thing created by the reason; a product of mental action.

Ens Supremum (L.), the Supreme Being.

en suite (F.), in succession; in a series or set.

en suivant la vérité (F.), in following the truth.

entbehren sollst du! sollst entbehren! (G.), thou shalt do without! shalt do without! (*Goethe*, Faust, i.).

entente (F.), understanding. See Dictionary.

entêté, fem. **entêtée** (F.), completely

possessed by a notion or opinion; obstinately bent; infatuated.

entêtement (F.), obstinacy in opinion; infatuation.

en tout (F.), in all; wholly.

en tout cas (F.), in any case.

en train (F.), in train; in progress; in a fair way; in good spirits.

entrain (F.), spirit; animation; go.

entre chien et loup (F.), between dog and wolf; at twilight: cf. *inter canem et lupum*.

entre-deux (F.), insertion or band-like trimming, as of lace or embroidery.

entre deux feux (F.), between two fires.

entre deux vins (F.), between two wines; half drunk.

entre nous (F.), between ourselves.

entreprenant (F.), enterprising; pushing; bold.

entrepreneur (F.), undertaker; contractor; employer. See Dictionary.

entrez (F.), enter; come in.

en vérité (F.), in truth; verily.

en vigueur (F.), in force, as a law.

en ville (F.), in town; away from home; out.

eo instante (L.), at that instant.

eo nomine (L.), by or under that name.

épatant, fem. **épatante** (F.), amazing; startling.

épicerie (F.), spices; groceries; a grocer's shop.

Epicuri de grege porcum (L.), a pig of Epicurus's drove (*Horace*, Epistles, i. 4).

epistola non erubescit (L.), a letter does not blush (*Cicero*, Epistolæ ad Familiares, v. 12).

e pluribus unum (L.), one out of many (motto of the United States).

épris, fem. **éprise** (F.), enamoured; in love.

epulis accumbere divum (L.), to recline at the feasts of the gods (*Virgil*, Æneid, i. 79).

e pur si muove! (It.), and yet it does move! (attributed to Galileo, just after his recantation of the doctrine of the earth's movement round the sun).

equi et poetæ alendi, non saginandi (L.), horses and poets are to be fed, not fattened (attributed to Charles IX. of France).

equi frenato est auris in ore (L.), the ear of a horse is in his bridled mouth (*Horace*, Epistles, i. 15).

e (or **ex**) **re nata** (L.), from a circumstance or emergency arising; according to the exigencies of the case.

ergo bibamus! (L.), therefore let us drink!

eripuit cælo fulmen sceptrumque tyrannis (L.), he snatched the thunderbolt from heaven and the scepter from tyrants (inscription for a bust of Benjamin Franklin).

eritis sicut dii, scientes bonum et malum (L.), ye shall be as gods, knowing good and evil (*Vulgate*, Gen. iii. 5).

errare est humanum (L.), to err is human.

erst wägen, dann wagen (G.), first weigh, then dare.

escalier (F.), staircase; stairs: see *esprit d'escalier.*

escalier dérobé (F.), a private staircase.

escargot (F.), a snail, esp. of an edible kind.

esclandre (F.), scandal; a scandalous occurrence; a scene.

escrime (F.), fencing.

espérance en Dieu (F.), hope in God.

espiègle (F.), roguish; frolicsome; playful.

espièglerie (F.), roguishness; a roguish or playful trick.

esprit (F.), spirit; mind; intelligence; wit.

esprit borné (F.), a narrow mind.

esprit de corps (F.). See Dictionary.

esprit d'escalier (F.), staircase wit; a reply or remark that occurs to one too late, as it were when descending the stairs instead of in the salon.

Esprit des Lois (F.): see *L'Esprit des Lois.*

esprit follet (F.), a mischievous spirit or sprite.

esprit fort (F.), a strong mind; a free-thinker.

esse quam videri (L.), to be rather than to seem (motto of North Carolina).

est modus in rebus (L.), there is a due measure in things (*Horace*, Satires, i. 1).

esto perpetua (L.), may she be perpetual, or endure forever (motto of Idaho).

esto quod esse videris (L.), be what you seem to be.

est quædam flere voluptas (L.), there is a certain pleasure in weeping (*Ovid*, Tristia, iv. 3).

esurienti ne occurras (L.), oppose not a hungry man.

étage (F.), a story or floor of a house.

et alibi (L.), and elsewhere.

et alii, fem. **et aliæ** (L.), and others.

état, pl. *états* (F.), state; condition; position, rank, or calling; an estate or social order; a government; a commonwealth or nation; pl., the representatives of the three estates (nobility, clergy, and commons) of France before the Revolution, as constituting a political assembly (whether provincial or general).

état-major (F.), the staff of an army, regiment, etc.

États Généraux (F.), the States-General, or general (national) assembly of representatives of the three estates of France before the Revolution.

États Unis d'Amérique (F.), the United States of America.

et cetera (L.), and others; and so forth.

et cum spiritu tuo (L.), and with thy spirit (the response to the salutation *Dominus vobiscum*).

et hoc (or **id**) **genus omne** (L.), and all this (or that) sort of thing.

etiam capillus unus habet umbram suam (L.), even a single hair has its shadow (*Publilius Syrus*).

etiam periere ruinæ (L.), even the ruins have perished (*Lucan*, Pharsalia, ix. 969).

etiam sanato vulnere cicatrix manet (L.), even when the wound is healed the scar remains.

etiam si Cato dicat (L.), even if Cato were to say it.

etiam stultis acuit ingenium fames (L.), hunger sharpens the wits, even of fools.

et id genus omne (L.): see *et hoc genus omne.*

et in Arcadia ego (L.), I too (have lived) in Arcadia (inscription on a tomb in Poussin's picture, "The Shepherds of Arcadia").

et le combat cessa faute de combattants (F.), and the combat ceased for want of combatants (*Corneille*, Le Cid, iv. 3).

et modo quæ fuerat semita facta via est (L.), and what had been only a foot-path became a highway (*Martial*, Epigrams, vii. 61).

étoile (F.), a star.

étoile des braves (F.), the star of the brave; the cross of the French Legion of Honor.

étoile du berger (F.), the shepherd's star; Venus.

étourderie (F.), giddiness; thoughtlessness; a thoughtless act or blunder.

étourdi, fem. **étourdie** (F.), giddy; thoughtless; heedless.

et pourtant j'avais quelque chose là (F.), and yet I had something there (words of the French poet André Chénier, tapping his forehead, as he left prison for the scaffold).

et qui nolunt occidere quemquam posse volunt (L.), even those who do not wish to kill any one would like to be able (*Juvenal*, Satires, x. 96).

étranger, fem. **étrangère** (F.), strange; foreign; a stranger, foreigner, or alien.

étrenne (F.), a New Year's gift; a present.

et semel emissum volat irrevocabile verbum (L.), and the word once uttered flies away never to be recalled (*Horace*, Epistles, i. 18).

et sequentes (L., masc. and fem.), and the following (persons, etc.).

et sequentia (L., neut.), and the following (things or parts).

et sic de ceteris (L.), and so concerning the rest.

et sic de similibus (L.), and so concerning the like.

et surtout, pas de zèle! (F.), and above all, no zeal! (injunction of Talleyrand to his subordinates).

et tu, Brute! (L.), and thou, Brutus! (reproachful exclamation said to have been uttered by Cæsar on seeing Brutus among his assassins).

étude (F.), a study; an exercise.

et voilà justement comme on écrit l'histoire (F.), and that is exactly how one writes history (*Voltaire*, Charlot, i. 7).

euge (L.), well done! bravo!

euge, poeta! (L.), bravo, poet! (*Persius*, Satires, i. 75).

eureka! (properly *heureka*, Gr. εὕρηκα), I have found it! (exclamation attributed to Archimedes on making a discovery: used as the motto of California). See Dictionary.

eventus stultorum magister (L.), the result is the teacher of fools (adapted from *Livy*, xxii. 39).

e vestigio (L.), on the instant; instantly; at once.

Ewigkeit (G.), eternity.

Ewig-Weibliche (G.), the eternal feminine: see *das Ewig-Weibliche zieht uns hinan.*

ex abrupto (L.), abruptly; without preliminaries.

ex abundanti (L.), abundantly; superabundantly.

ex abundantia (L.), out of abundance.

ex abundanti cautela (L.), from abundant or excessive caution.

ex abusu non arguitur ad usum (L.), from abuse there is no argument against use.

ex accidenti (L.), accidentally; as an accident.

ex adverso (L.), from or on the opposite side.

ex æquo (L.), from or on an equality; equally; equitably.

ex æquo et bono (L.), according to what is just and good.

ex Africa semper aliquid novi (L.), from Africa always something new (*Pliny*, Natural History, viii. 6).

ex animo (L.), from the heart; heartily.

ex arena funiculum nectis (L.), you are weaving a rope of sand.

ex auctoritate mihi commissa (L.), by the authority committed to me.

ex auribus cognoscitur asinus (L.), an ass is known by his ears.

ex cathedra (L.), from the chair, or seat of authority; with authority.

excelsior (L.), higher (motto of New York State).

exceptio probat (or **confirmat**) **regulam** (L.), the exception proves (or confirms) the rule.

exceptis excipiendis (L.), the necessary exceptions being made.

excerpta (L.), excerpts; selections; extracts.

ex comitate (L.), out of courtesy.

ex commodo (L.), at one's convenience.

ex concessis (L.), from the things or points conceded.

ex concesso (L.), from what has been conceded: see *argumentum ex concesso*.

ex confesso (L.), confessedly; admittedly.

ex consequenti (L.), by way of consequence.

ex contractu (L.), from contract.

excudit (L.), (the person specified) struck out, fashioned, or engraved it.

ex curia (L.), out of court.

ex debito justitiæ (L.), from obligation of justice.

ex debito naturali (L.), from natural obligation.

ex delicto (L.), from an offense or wrong: see *actio ex delicto*.

ex desuetudine amittuntur privilegia (L.), by disuse privileges are lost.

ex dolo malo (L.), from evil intent; from fraud.

ex dono (L.), by gift; as a present.

ex dono Dei (L.), by the gift of God.

exeat (L.), let him go out, or depart.

exegi monumentum ære perennius (L.), I have completed a monument more enduring than bronze (*Horace*, Odes, iii. 30).

exempla sunt odiosa (L.), examples are odious.

exempli gratia (L.), for the sake of example; for instance.

exemplo plus quam ratione vivimus (L.), we live more by example than by reason.

ex eodem ore calidum et frigidum efflare (L.), from the same mouth to blow hot and cold.

exeunt (L.), they go out.

exeunt omnes (L.), all go out.

ex facie (L.), from or on the face (of a document, etc.).

ex facto jus oritur (L.), from the fact the law arises.

ex fide fortis (L.), strong by faith.

ex fumo dare lucem (L.), from smoke to give light (*Horace*, Ars Poetica, 143).

ex gratia (L.), from grace or favor (rather than from legal right).

ex hypothesi (L.), from or by hypothesis; hypothetically.

exigeant, fem. **exigeante** (F.), exacting; requiring much, or too much.

exiguum natura desiderat (L.), nature wants little (*Seneca*, Epistles, 16).

exilium patitur patriæ qui se denegat (L.), he suffers exile who denies himself to his country (*Publilius Syrus*).

ex improviso (L.), unexpectedly; suddenly.

ex integro (L.), anew; afresh.

exit (L.), he (or she) goes out.

exitus acta probat (L.), the outcome justifies the acts (Washington's motto: *Ovid*, Heroides, ii. 85).

ex lege (L.), from, or arising from, law.

ex libris (L.), from the books or library of.

ex mera gratia (L.), from mere grace or favor.

ex mero motu (L.), from one's mere motion or impulse; of one's own accord.

ex more (L.), from custom; according to custom.

ex natura rei (L.), from the nature of the case.

ex natura rerum (L.), from the nature of things.

ex necessitate (L.), from necessity; necessarily.

ex necessitate rei (L.), from the necessity of the case.

ex nihilo nihil fit (L.), out of nothing nothing is made.

ex nudo pacto non oritur actio (L.), from a bare (or mere) agreement no action arises (in law).

ex officio (L.), by virtue of office; officially.

ex ore parvulorum veritas (L.), out of the mouth of babes (comes) truth.

ex oriente lux, ex occidente lex (L.), from the east (comes) light, from the west law.

ex parte (L.), from or on one side only, as in a controversy; in the interest of one party.

ex parte materna (L.), from or on the mother's side.

ex parte paterna (L.), from or on the father's side.

ex pede Herculem (L.), from the foot (one may know) Hercules.

experientia docet (L.), experience teaches.

experientia docet stultos (L.), experience teaches fools.

experimentum crucis (L.), a crucial experiment or test.

experto crede (or **credite**) (L.), trust one who knows by experience.

expertus metuit (L.), the experienced man fears (*Horace*, Epistles, i. 18).

explicite (L.), explicitly; expressly.

ex post facto, or **ex postfacto** (L.). See Dictionary.

expressio unius est exclusio alterius (L.), express mention of the one is exclusion of the other.

expressis verbis (L.), in express words or terms.

ex professo (L.), professedly; avowedly.

ex propriis (L.), from one's own resources.

ex proprio motu (L.), of one's own motion or accord.

ex proprio vigore (L.), from or by its own force.

ex quocunque capite (L.), from whatever reason.

ex relatione (L.), from or on the information of.

ex re nata (L.): see *e re nata*.

ex scintilla incendium (L.), from a spark a fire.

exstinctus (or **extinctus**) **amabitur idem** (L.), when dead the same man will be loved (*Horace*, Epistles, ii. 1).

ex tacito (L.), tacitly; silently.

ex tempore (L.), on the spur of the moment; offhand.

ex testamento (L.), by testament or will.

extra judicium (L.), beyond the judicial field or scope.

extra modum (L.), beyond measure; to excess.

extra muros (L.), beyond the walls, as of a city.

extra ordinem (L.), beyond the usual order; in an extraordinary manner, measure, degree, etc.

ex turpi causa non oritur actio (L.), from an immoral cause, or consideration, no action arises (in law).

ex umbra in solem (L.), from shadow into sunlight.

ex umbris et imaginibus in veritatem (L.), from shadows and semblances to truth (epitaph of Cardinal Newman).

ex ungue leonem (L.), from the claw (one may know) the lion.

ex uno disce omnes (L.), from one learn of all.

ex usu (L.), of use, service, or benefit.

ex utraque parte (L.), from or on either side.

ex vano (L.), from vain or empty reasons.

ex vita ita discedo tanquam ex hospitio, non tanquam e domo (L.), I depart from life as from an inn, not as from my home (*Cicero*, De Senectute, xxiii.).

ex vi termini (L.), by the force, or meaning, of the term.

ex vitio alterius sapiens emendat suum (L.), from the fault of another a wise man corrects his own (*Publilius Syrus*).

ex vitulo bos fit (L.), from a calf comes an ox.

ex voto (L.), from, or in pursuance of, a vow.

F

fabas indulcat fames (L.), hunger sweetens beans.

faber est quisque fortunæ suæ (L.), every one is the architect of his own fortune.

faber suæ fortunæ (L.), the architect of his own fortune.

fable convenue (F.), a fable agreed upon (Voltaire's definition of history).

fac et excusa (L.), do it and make excuses.

fâcheux, fem. **fâcheuse** (F.), troublesome; annoying; vexatious; also, discontented; peevish.

faciam ut hujus loci dieique meique semper memineris (L.), I will give you cause to remember forever this place, this day, and me (*Terence*, Eunuchus, iv. 7).

facies non omnibus una, nec diversa tamen; qualem decet esse sororum (L.), the face was not the same for all, nor yet wholly different; such as is natural for sisters (*Ovid*, Metamorphoses, ii. 13).

facies tua computat annos (L.), thy face reckons up thy years (*Juvenal*, Satires, vi. 199).

facile est inventis addere (L.), it is easy to add to things already invented.

facile largiri de alieno (L.), it is easy to be generous with others' property.

facile palmam habes (L.), you win the palm easily (*Plautus*, Trinummus, iii.2).

facile princeps (L.), easily the first, foremost, or chief.

facili feminarum credulitate (L.), with the easy credulity of women (*Tacitus*, Annales, xiv. 4).

facilis descensus Averno (L.), easy is the descent to Avernus (*Virgil*, Æneid, vi. 126); the downhill path is an easy one.

facillime princeps (L.), most easily the first or foremost.

facinus quos inquinat æquat (L.), crime reduces to a level those whom it defiles (*Lucan*, Pharsalia, v. 290).

facit indignatio versum (L.), indignation inspires verse (*Juvenal*, Satires, i. 79).

facito aliquid operis ut semper te diabolus inveniat occupatum (L.), keep busy at something so that the devil may always find thee employed (*St. Jerome*).

façon de parler (F.), a way of speaking; a mode or turn of expression (not necessarily to be taken literally).

façonné, fem. **façonnée** (F.), fashioned or wrought; cultivated; finished; elaborately made or ornamented; of fabrics, woven with a figure.

facta, non verba (L.), deeds, not words.

facta sunt potentiora verbis (L.), deeds are more powerful than words.

factum est (L.), it is done.

fadaise (F.), a flat, stupid remark; twaddle; nonsense.

fade (F.), insipid; flat; colorless; dull.

fadeur (F.), insipidity; dullness.

fænum habet in cornu (L.), he has hay on his horn (as an ox, to prevent goring); he is dangerous (*Horace*, Satires, i. 4).

fæx populi (L.), the dregs of the people.

fagot (F.): see *il sent le fagot*.

fainéant, fem. **fainéante** (F.), do-nothing; idle; lazy; an idler.

faire bonne mine (F.), to assume a gracious or friendly expression.

faire de la prose sans le savoir (F.), to make prose without knowing it (which M. Jourdain, in Molière's "Bourgeois Gentilhomme," ii. 6, was surprised and delighted to learn he had been doing all his life).

faire de l'esprit (F.), to be witty.

faire la belle (F.), to put on the airs of a beauty.

faire l'homme d'importance (F.), to play the man of importance; put on airs of importance.

faire mon (or **son**) **devoir** (F.), to do my (or one's) duty.

faire sans dire (F.), to act without talking.

faire suivre (F.), to be forwarded (inscribed on a letter, etc.).

fais ce que vouldras (OF.), do what thou wilt (the rule of Rabelais's imaginary Abbey of Thélème).

fait accompli (F.), an accomplished fact; a thing already done.

fait à peindre (F.), made to be painted; worth painting; strikingly good-looking or beautiful.

fallacia alia aliam trudit (L.), one deceit presses hard upon another (*Terence*, Andria, iv. 4).

fallaci nimium ne crede lucernæ (L.), trust not too much to deceitful (too flattering) lamplight (*Ovid*, Ars Amatoria, i. 245).

falsa demonstratio non nocet (L.), an erroneous description does not invalidate.

falsi crimen (L.): see *crimen falsi*.

falsus in uno, falsus in omnibus (L.), false in one thing, false in all.

fama clamosa (L.), a noisy rumor; a far-reaching scandalous report.

famam extendere factis (L.), to extend fame by deeds.

fama nihil est celerius (L.), nothing is swifter than rumor.

fama semper vivat! (L.), may his (or her) fame live forever!

fama volat (L.), the rumor flies, or spreads swiftly (*Virgil*, Æneid, iii. 121).

fames optimum condimentum (L.), hunger is the best sauce.

famille de robe (F.), a family of the robe, or the magistracy.

farceur (F.), a player of farces; a droll person; a joker; a wag.

fare, fac (L.), say, do.

fari quæ sentiat (L.), to say what one thinks (see *Horace*, Epistles, i. 4).

far niente (It.), doing nothing: cf. *dolce far niente*.

farouche (F.), savage; wild; unsociable; sullen; shy.

farrago libelli (L.), a medley of things for a book (*Juvenal*, Satires, i. 86).

fas est et ab hoste doceri (L.), it is right to be taught even by an enemy (*Ovid*, Metamorphoses, iv. 428).

Fata obstant (L.), the Fates oppose (*Virgil*, Æneid, iv. 440).

Fata viam invenient (L.), the Fates will find a way (*Virgil*, Æneid, x. 113).

fatigatis humus cubile est (L.), to the wearied the ground is a bed.

fatras (F.), a confused medley; a jumble.

fatti maschii, parole femine (It.), deeds are men, words women (a motto of Maryland).

faute (F.): see *c'est plus qu'un crime, c'est une faute*.

faute de mieux (F.), for want of better.

fauteuil (F.), an arm-chair; an official chair; a seat or membership in the French Academy.

faux pas (F.), a false step; a breach of etiquette or propriety.

favete linguis (L.), be favorable, or propitious, with your tongues (as at religious rites); keep a religious silence; be silent (*Horace*, Odes, iii. 1).

fax mentis incendium gloriæ (L.), the fire of glory is a torch to the mind.

fecit (L.), (the person specified) made it (a work of art, etc.).

fecundi calices quem non fecere disertum? (L.), whom have not abundant cups made eloquent? (*Horace*, Epistles, i. 5).

felicitas multos habet amicos (L.), prosperity has many friends.

felicitas nutrix est iracundiæ (L.), prosperity is the nurse of ill temper.

felix culpa! (L.), happy fault! — see *O felix culpa* (etc.).

felix, heu nimium felix (L.), happy, alas, too happy (*Virgil*, Æneid, iv. 657).

felix qui nihil debet (L.), happy is he who owes nothing.

felo de se (L.), a suicide. See Dictionary.

feme (AF.), etc. See Dictionary.

femme (F.), woman; wife.

femme de chambre (F.), a lady's maid; a chambermaid.

femme de charge (F.), a housekeeper.

femme de lettres (F.), a woman of letters; a literary woman.

femme incomprise (F.), a woman who is not understood or appreciated.

femme publique (F.), a prostitute.

femme savante (F.), a learned woman: see *Les Femmes Savantes*.

fendre un cheveu en quatre (F.), to split a hair in quarters; make overfine distinctions.

feræ naturæ (L.), of a wild or untamed nature.

feriis caret necessitas (L.), necessity has no holidays.

feriunt summos fulgura montes (L.), lightnings strike the highest peaks (*Horace*, Odes, ii. 10).

ferme acerrima proximorum odia sunt (L.), about the bitterest enmities are those of persons most nearly related (*Tacitus*, Historiæ, iv. 70).

ferto, fereris (L.), bear, and you shall be borne with.

fervet opus (L.), the work glows, or goes briskly forward (*Virgil*, Georgics, iv. 169).

Fest (G.), a feast or festival; a festivity; a holiday.

festa (It.), a feast, festival, or festivity; a holiday.

festina lente (L.), hasten slowly.

festinatio tarda est (L.), haste is tardy; the more haste the less speed.

fête (F.), a feast or festival; a festive celebration or entertainment; a festal day; a holiday.

fête champêtre (F.), an outdoor festival; a garden-party.

Fête des Morts (F.), the Feast of the Dead, observed on Nov. 2 (All Souls' Day).

Fête-Dieu (F.), the Feast of God; Corpus Christi.

feu, fem. **feue** (F.), lately deceased; late.

feu d'artifice, pl. *feux d'artifice* (F.), a firework; a brilliant display of wit, fancy, etc.

feu de joie (F.), fire of joy; a bonfire kindled in rejoicing or celebration; also, a firing of guns in rejoicing.

feu follet (F.), an ignis fatuus, or will-o'-the-wisp.

feu sacré (F.), sacred fire; the divine fire of genius; divinely inspired ardor or enthusiasm.

fiat confirmatio (L.), let confirmation be made.

fiat experimentum in corpore vili (L.), let experiment be made on a worthless body (or object).

fiat justitia, ruat cælum (L.), let justice be done, though the heavens fall.

fiat lux (L.), let there be light (*Vulgate*, Gen. i. 3).

fiat voluntas tua (L.), thy will be done (*Vulgate*, Mat. vi. 10).

fictio juris (L.), a fiction of law.

fictio legis neminem lædit (L.), a fiction of law injures no one.

fide et amore (L.), by faith and love.

fide et fiducia (L.), by faith and trust.

fide et fortitudine (L.), by faith and fortitude.

fidei coticula crux (L.), the cross is the touchstone of faith.

fidei defensor (L.), defender of the faith (a title of the sovereigns of England, first conferred by Pope Leo X. on Henry VIII. for his book against Luther).

fideli certa merces (L.), for the faithful a sure reward.

fidelis ad urnam (L.), faithful to the urn (to death).

fideliter (L.), faithfully.

fidem qui perdit nihil ultra perdere potest (L.), he who loses credit can lose nothing further (*Publilius Syrus*).

fide, non armis (L.), by faith, not arms.

fide, sed cui vide (L.), trust, but take care whom (you trust).

fides et justitia (L.), faith and justice.

fides probata coronat (L.), proved faith crowns.

fides Punica (L.), Punic faith; treachery: see *Punica fides*.

fides servanda est (L.), faith must be kept.

fi donc! (F.), fie! for shame!

fidus Achates (L.), faithful Achates (*Virgil*, Æneid, vi. 158); a faithful comrade.

fidus et audax (L.), faithful and bold.

fieri curavit (L.), (the person specified) caused this to be made (words used in inscriptions on monuments, etc.).

fiesta (Sp.), a feast, festival, or festivity; a festal day; a holiday.

filius istarum lacrimarum (L.), the son of those tears (said of St. Augustine, during a lapse from the faith, as the object of his mother's anxiety).

filius nullius (L.), a son of nobody; a bastard.

filius populi (L.), a son of the people; a bastard.

filius terræ (L.): see *terræ filius*.

fille (F.), daughter; girl; unmarried woman; maid; female servant.

fille de boutique (F.), a shop-girl.

fille de joie (F.), a prostitute.

fille de service (F.), a maid-servant.

fille d'honneur (F.), a maid of honor.

filleul (F.), a godson; the soldier befriended by a marraine: see *marraine*.

fils (F.), son.

fils de ses œuvres (F.), the son of his own works; a self-made man.

fin (F.), end: see *c'est le commencement de la fin*.

fin de siècle (F.), end of the century. See Dictionary.

finem respice (L.), look to the end.

finis (L.), the end.

finis coronat opus (L.), the end crowns the work.

finis ecce laborum! (L.), behold the end of our labors!

finis litium (L.), the end of litigation.

finis Poloniæ (L.), the end of Poland.

fit fabricando faber (L.), the workman is made by working; practice makes perfect.

flagrante bello (L.), while the war is burning, or raging; during actual hostilities.

flagrante delicto (L.), while the offense is burning, or being actually committed; in the very act.

flânerie (F.), strolling; lounging; idling.

flâneur (F.), a stroller or lounger; an idler.

flavit Jehovah et dissipati sunt (L.), Jehovah sent forth a blast and they were dispersed (inscription on a medal commemorating the destruction of the Spanish Armada in 1588).

flebile ludibrium (L.), a lamentable jest; a tragic subject of laughter.

flectere si nequeo superos, Acheronta movebo (L.), if I cannot bend the powers above, I will move Acheron (the lower world) (*Virgil*, Æneid, vii. 312).

flecti, non frangi (L.), to be bent, not broken.

fleurettes (F.), little flowers; pretty or gallant speeches.

floreat (L.), may it (or he or she) flourish.

floruit (L.), he (or she) flourished (at a time specified).

flosculi sententiarum (L.), flowerets of thought.

flos juventutis (L.), the flower of youth.

fluctuat nec mergitur (L.), it is tossed by the waves but is not overwhelmed (motto of the city of Paris).

flux de bouche (F.), a flux of the mouth; an excessive flow of saliva, or, fig., of words.

flux de paroles (F.), an excessive flow of words.

foi de gentilhomme (F.), (on the) faith of a gentleman.

folio recto (L.), on the right or front side of the leaf (of a book, etc.).

folio verso (L.), on the back of the leaf (of a book, etc.).

fonda (Sp.), an inn or hotel.

fonds (F.), ground; land; capital; stock; fund.

fons et origo (L.), the fount and origin; the originating source.

fons lacrimarum (L.), a fount or source of tears.

fons omnium viventium (L.), the fount or source of all living things (the Deity).

forçat (F.), a criminal condemned to hard labor; a convict.

force majeure (F.), superior force; irresistible compulsion: cf. *vis major*.

forensis strepitus (L.), the din of the forum or market-place.

formaliter (L.), formally; with respect to form.

forsan et hæc olim meminisse juvabit (L.), perhaps it will be pleasant some day to recall even these things (*Virgil*, Æneid, i. 203).

Fors Clavigera (L.), "Chance (or Fate) the Club-bearer" (title used by Ruskin for his series of letters to British working-men).

fortem facit vicina libertas senem (L.), liberty close at hand makes an old man strong (*Seneca*, Hippolytus, i. 139).

fortes fortuna adjuvat (L.), fortune

aids the brave (*Terence*, Phormio, i. 4).

forti et fideli nihil difficile (L.), to the brave and faithful nothing is difficult.

fortis cadere, cedere non potest (L.), the brave man may fall, but cannot yield.

fortiter et recte (L.), bravely and uprightly.

fortiter, fideliter, feliciter (L.), bravely, faithfully, successfully.

fortiter in re, suaviter in modo (L.), vigorously in deed, gently in manner.

fortuito quodam concursu atomorum (L.), by some fortuitous concourse of atoms.

fortunæ filius (L.), a son of fortune (*Horace*, Satires, ii. 6).

fortunæ veniam damus (L.), we grant indulgence to prosperity (*Juvenal*, Satires, xi. 176).

fortuna favet fatuis (L.), fortune favors fools.

fortuna favet fortibus (L.), fortune favors the brave.

fortuna fortes adjuvat (L.), fortune aids the brave.

fortunate senex! (L.), fortunate old man! (*Virgil*, Eclogues, i. 47).

fortune des armes (F.), the fortune of arms or war.

forum conscientiæ (L.), the court of conscience.

fourchette d'Adam (F.), Adam's fork; the fingers.

fous (F.), fools: see *Dieu aide à trois sortes de personnes* (etc.).

fra (It.), brother (title of a friar).

frais (F.), expenses; charges; cost.

Fra Modesto non fu mai priore (It.), Friar Modest never was prior.

franco (It.), franked; postage free.

frangas, non flectes (L.), you may break, but you shall not bend.

frate, pl. *frati* (It.), a (religious) brother; a friar.

fraus est celare fraudem (L.), it is fraud to conceal fraud.

fraus pia (L.), a pious fraud.

fredaine (F.), a prank; an escapade.

frères d'armes (F.), brothers in arms.

fripon (F.), a rogue; a knave; a rascal; a cheat.

friponnerie (F.), roguery; knavery.

froides mains, chaudes amours (F.), cold hands, warm affections.

froideur (F.), coldness; cold indifference; unfriendliness.

front à front (F.), face to face; front to front.

fronti nulla fides (L.), there is no trusting to appearances (*Juvenal*, Satires, ii. 8).

fructu non foliis arborem æstima (L.), judge a tree by its fruit, not by its leaves.

fruges consumere nati (L.), born to consume the fruits of the earth (*Horace*, Epistles, i. 2).

frustra Herculi (L.), in vain against Hercules.

fugere est triumphus (L.), to flee is a triumph.

fugit hora (L.), the hour flies.

fugit velociter hora; vigila, ora, labora (L.), the hour flies swiftly; watch, pray, labor (inscription on a sun-dial).

fuimus Troës (L.), we Trojans have been, or have had our day (*Virgil*, Æneid, ii. 325).

fuit Ilium (L.), Ilium has been; Troy's day is over (*Virgil*, Æneid, ii. 325).

fulmen brutum (L.): see *brutum fulmen*.

fumoir (F.), a smoking-room.

functus officio (L.), having fulfilled one's office; out of office.

fundamentum divisionis (L.), the ground or basis of (logical) division.

fundamentum relationis (L.), the ground of (logical) relation.

funèbre (F.), funeral; funereal; mournful.

funiculaire (F.), a funicular (cable) railway.

fuori le mura (It.), outside the walls (used in the names of certain churches of Rome).

furari litoris arenas (L.), to steal the sands of the seashore.

furiosus furore suo punitur (L.), a madman is punished by his own madness.

furor arma ministrat (L.), rage supplies arms (*Virgil*, Æneid, i. 150).

furor fit læsa sæpius patientia (L.), patience abused too often becomes fury (*Publilius Syrus*).

furor loquendi (L.), a rage for speaking.

furor poeticus (L.), the poetic rage or frenzy.

furor scribendi (L.), a rage for writing.

furor Teutonicus (L.), the Teutonic fury or frenzy.

G

gage d'amour (F.), a pledge or token of love.

gaieté de cœur (F.), gaiety of heart.

galant homme (F.), a man of honor: cf. *homme galant*.

galantuomo (It.), a man of honor.

galère (F.): see *que diable allait-il faire* (etc.).

Gallia est omnis divisa in partes tres (L.), all Gaul is divided into three parts (*Cæsar*, De Bello Gallico, i. 1).

Gallicè (L.), in French.

gamin, fem. **gamine** (F.), a boy or girl of the streets; a shrewd, roguish child.

gaminerie (F.), the spirit, action, or language of a gamin.

garçon (F.), boy; lad; fellow; bachelor; male employee or servant; waiter.

garçon d'honneur (F.), a groomsman at a wedding.

garde (F.), guard, watch, or keeping; care or heed; also, a body of troops, etc., charged with guarding; also, a guard, custodian, or keeper; a guardsman.

garde à cheval (F.), a mounted guard.

garde champêtre (F.), a rural guard; an officer charged with guarding rural property.

garde-chasse (F.), a gamekeeper.

garde du corps (F.), a body-guard.

garde forestier (F.), a forest guard or keeper.

garde mobile (F.), a body of militia liable to general service.

garde nationale (F.), a national guard (militia).

garde royale (F.), a royal guard.

gardez bien (F.), take good care.

gardez la foi (F.), keep the faith.

gare (F.), a railroad station.

garni (F.), garnished; furnished, as lodgings.

gauche (F.), etc. See Dictionary.

gaudeamus igitur (L.), let us then be merry (first words of a famous song, probably of medieval origin, sung by university students in Germany and elsewhere).

gaudet tentamine virtus (L.), virtue (or valor) rejoices in trial.

gaudium certaminis (L.), the joy of battle.

gemitus columbæ (L.), the murmuring of a dove.

gêne (F.), constraint; embarrassment; discomfort; want of ease; pecuniary embarrassment.

gêné, fem. **gênée** (F.), constrained; embarrassed; ill at ease; short of cash.

generale dictum generaliter est interpretandum (L.), a general expression is to be interpreted generally.

genius loci (L.), the genius or tutelary deity of a place; also, the peculiar character of a place with reference to the impression it makes on the mind.

genre (F.), genus; kind; sort; style. See Dictionary.

gens (F.), people; persons; men.

gens d'affaires (F.), business people.

gens de bien (F.), good people.

gens de condition (F.), people of quality or rank.

gens d'église (F.), churchmen; ecclesiastics; the clergy.

gens de guerre (F.), men of war; soldiers.

gens de lettres (F.), people of letters; authors; writers.

gens de loi (F.), men of the law; lawyers.

gens de même farine (F.), people (made) of the same flour; birds of a feather.

gens de mer (F.), men of the sea; seamen.

gens d'épée (F.), men of the sword, or of the military profession; soldiers.

gens de peu (F.), people of humble condition; the lower classes.

gens de plume (F.), people of the pen; writers.

gens de robe (F.), men of the robe; magistrates; lawyers.

gens du monde (F.), people of the world, or of society or fashion.

gens togata (L.), the people wearing the toga; the citizens of ancient Rome.

genus irritabile vatum (L.), the irritable tribe of poets (*Horace*, Epistles, ii. 2).

Germanicè (L.), in German.

Gesundheit! (G.), (your) health!

gibier (F.), game; animals of the chase.

gibier de potence (F.), game for the gibbet; a gallows-bird.

gigni de nihilo nihilum, in nihilum nil posse reverti (L.), from nothing nothing can arise, into nothing nothing can return (*Persius*, Satires, iii. 83).

giovine santo, diavolo vecchio (It.), young saint, old devil.

gloria in excelsis Deo (L.), glory be to God on high (first words of an ancient Christian hymn sometimes called the great, or greater, doxology).

gloria Patri (L.), glory be to the Father (first words of the lesser doxology).

gloria tibi, Domine (L.), glory be to thee, Lord (words used as a liturgical response).

gloria vana florece, y no grana (Sp.), vain glory bears flowers, and not seed.

gloria victis! (L.), glory to the conquered!

gloria virtutis umbra (L.), glory is the shadow of virtue.

glückliche Reise (G.), a prosperous journey (said as a farewell wish to one departing).

Glück macht Mut (G.), luck makes courage.

Glyptothek (G.), a museum of sculpture.

gnädige Frau (G.), gracious madam.

gnädiger Herr (G.), gracious sir.

gnothi seauton (Gr. γνῶθι σεαυτόν), know thyself.

gobe-mouches (F.), a flycatcher (bird); also, a person who swallows or believes everything he hears; a credulous simpleton.

Gott mit uns (G.), God with us (motto of the Prussian Order of the Crown, used also on the German imperial standard).

Gott sei Dank (G.), thank God.

goutte à goutte (F.), drop by drop.

gouvernante (F.), a governor's wife; a female governor; a governess; a housekeeper.

grâce (F.), grace; favor; mercy; pardon; thanks.

grâce à Dieu (F.), thanks to God.

gradatim (L.), step by step; by degrees; gradually.

gradu diverso via una (L.), with different step but on one way.

Gradus ad Parnassum (L.), "Steps to Parnassus" (title of a dictionary of prosody, for aid in writing Latin or Greek verses).

grand, fem. **grande** (F.), great; large; high; grand.

grand bien vous fasse! (F.), great good may it do you!

grande armée (F.), great or grand army (applied esp. to the army organized by Napoleon in 1804, and to that assembled for his campaign of 1812).

grande chère et beau feu (F.), ample cheer and a fine fire.

grande dame (F.), a great lady.

grande fortune, grande servitude (F.), great fortune, great slavery: cf. *magna servitus est magna fortuna*.

grande passion (F.), a great passion; a passionate or violent love for one of the opposite sex.

grandes maisons se font par petite cuisine (F.), great houses are made by a small kitchen (by domestic thrift).

grande tenue (F.), full dress.

grande toilette (F.), full dress.

grand homme (F.), a great man.

grand merci (F.), many thanks.

grand monarque (F.), great or grand monarch (applied esp. to Louis XIV. of France).

grand monde (F.), the great or fashionable world.

grand œuvre (F.), the great work (of the alchemists); the work of transmuting other metals into gold.

grand prix (F.), a great or extraordinary prize.

grand seigneur (F.), a great lord.

gratia gratiam parit (L.), favor begets favor.

gratia placendi (L.), for the sake of pleasing.

gratis dictum (L.), a gratuitous statement; a mere assertion.

gratis pænitet esse probum (L.), one regrets being honest for nothing (*Ovid*, Ex Ponto, ii. 3).

gratis pro Deo (L.), free of cost, for God's sake.

grave delictum (L.), a grave offense.

graviora manent (L.), more grievous things remain (*Virgil*, Æneid, vi. 84).

graviora quædam sunt remedia periculis (L.), some remedies are worse than the dangers (of disease).

gravior remediis quam delicta erant (L.), more grievous in his remedies than the evils were (*Tacitus*, Annales, iii. 28).

gravis ira regum est semper (L.), the wrath of kings is always heavy (*Seneca*, Medea, iii. 494).

greffier (F.), a registrar; a recorder.

gregatim (L.), in flocks or herds.

grex venalium (L.), a herd of hirelings.

grognard (F.), a grumbler; an old soldier (applied esp. to veterans of the Imperial Guard of Napoleon).

grosse tête, peu de sens (F.), big head, little wit.

grossièreté (F.), coarseness; rudeness; grossness; something coarse or gross.

guerra al cuchillo (Sp.), war to the knife.

guerre à mort (F.), war to the death.

guerre à outrance (F.), war to the uttermost.

guerre de course (F.), a war of roving, as by corsairs; privateering.

guerre de plume (F.), a war of the pen (carried on in writing).

gutta cavat lapidem (L.), the drop hollows out the stone.

H

habeas corpus (L.), have the body, or bring the person (before a judge or court). See Dictionary.

habeas corpus ad respondendum (L.), bring the person to make answer.

habeas corpus ad subjiciendum (L.), bring the person to undergo (the action of a court).

habeas corpus ad testificandum (L.), bring the person to testify.

habemus confitentem reum (L.), we have the accused confessing.

habent sua fata libelli (L.), books have their fates.

habet et musca splenem (L.), even a fly has its spleen.

habet salem (L.), he has wit.

habitarunt di quoque silvas (L.), the gods too have dwelt in the woods (*Virgil*, Eclogues, ii. 60).

hac lege (L.), with this law; under this condition.

hac urget lupus, hac canis (L.), on this side a wolf presses, on that a dog (*Horace*, Satires, ii. 2).

hæc olim meminisse juvabit (L.), it will be pleasant some day to recall these things: see *forsan et hæc olim meminisse juvabit*.

hæreticus in grammatica (L.), a heretic in grammar (*Erasmus*).

hanc veniam petimusque damusque vicissim (L.), this indulgence we both ask and grant in return (*Horace*, Ars Poetica, 11).

Hannibal ad portas (L.), Hannibal (the enemy) at the gates (*Cicero*, De Finibus, iv. 9).

hapax legomenon (Gr. ἅπαξ λεγόμενον), a thing said only once; a word or phrase found but once in a text.

Hassgesang (G.), a song of hate.

hasta luego (Sp.), until soon; until our meeting again soon: cf. *à bientôt*.

haud longis intervallis (L.), at no long intervals.

haud passibus æquis (L.), with steps by no means equal.

Hausfrau (G.), a housewife.

haut, fem. **haute** (F.), high; lofty; upper; superior; great; loud.

haut à la main (F.), high-handed; arrogant.

haute nouveauté (F.), high or superior novelty.

haut et bon (F.), great and good.

haut goût (F.), high or strong flavor.

haut ton (F.), high tone or style; the usage or manners of high society.

Heide (G.): see *der grosse Heide*.

hei mihi! (L.), ah me! alas!

Heimweh (G.), homesickness.

helluo librorum (L.), a devourer of books; a bookworm.

heredem Deus facit, non homo (L.), God makes the heir, not man.

heu pietas! heu prisca fides! (L.), alas for piety! alas for the ancient faith! (*Virgil*, Æneid, vi. 878).

heureusement (F.), happily; fortunately; luckily.

heureux, fem. **heureuse** (F.), happy; fortunate; lucky.

heureux au jeu, malheureux en amour (F.), lucky at play (gaming), unlucky in love.

heureux hasard (F.), a lucky chance.

hiatus valde deflendus (L.), a hiatus (or gap) greatly to be deplored.

Hibernicis ipsis Hibernior (L.), more Irish than the Irish themselves.

hic et nunc (L.), here and now.

hic et ubique (L.), here and everywhere.

hic finis fandi (L.), here was an end of the speaking (*Virgil*, Æneid, x. 116).

hic funis nihil attraxit (L.), this line has drawn nothing in.

hic jacet (L.), here lies (used in epitaphs).

hic jacet lepus (L.), here lies the hare; here is the difficulty.

hic labor, hoc opus est (L.), this is labor, this is work: see *hoc opus, hic labor est*.

hic requiescit in pace (L.), here rests in peace (used in epitaphs).

hic sepultus (L.), here is buried (used in epitaphs).

hier stehe ich; ich kann nicht anders; Gott helfe mir! amen! (G.), here I stand; I cannot do otherwise; God help me! amen! (*Luther*, at the Diet of Worms in 1521).

hier wird Deutsch gesprochen (G.), German is spoken here.

hinc illæ lacrimæ (L.), hence those tears (*Terence*, Andria, i. 1).

hinc lucem et pocula sacra (L.), hence light and the sacred drafts (motto of Cambridge University, England).

histoire (F.): see *et voilà justement comme on écrit l'histoire*, also *il a inventé l'histoire*.

historia vero testis temporum, lux veritatis (L.), history is indeed the witness of the times, the light of truth (*Cicero*, De Oratore, ii. 36).

hoc age (L.), this do; do this.

hoc anno (L.), in this year.

hoc erat in more majorum (L.), this was in the manner of our forefathers.

hoc erat in votis (L.), this was among my prayers (*Horace*, Satires, ii. 6).

hoc genus omne (L.), all this sort (*Horace*, Satires, i. 2).

hoch! (G.), hail! health or success (to one)!

hoc loco (L.), in this place.

hoc monumentum posuit (L.), (the person specified) erected this monument.

hoc opus, hic labor est (L.), this is work, this is labor (*Virgil*, Æneid, vi. 129).

hoc quære (L.), seek this; see this.

hoc saxum posuit (L.), (the person specified) placed this stone.

hoc sensu (L.), in this sense.

hoc tempore (L.), at this time.

hoc titulo (L.), by this title.

hoc volo, sic jubeo; sit pro ratione voluntas (L.), this I will, thus I command; let my will serve for reason (*Juvenal*, Satires, vi. 223).

hodie mihi, cras tibi (L.), to-day for me, to-morrow for thee.

hoi polloi (Gr. οἱ πολλοί), the many; the multitude. See Dictionary.

hominibus plenum, amicis vacuum (L.), full of men, empty of friends (*Seneca*, De Beneficiis, vi. 34).

homini ne fidas nisi cum quo modium salis absumpseris (L.), trust no man unless you have consumed a peck of salt with him.

hominis est errare, insipientis perseverare (L.), it is for man to err, for a fool to persist (in error).

homme (F.), man; husband.

homme d'affaires (F.), a man of affairs; a business man; an agent.

homme de bien (F.), a man of worth; a good man.

homme de cour (F.), a courtier.

homme de fortune (F.), a man of fortune; a man who has amassed a fortune.

homme de guerre (F.), a man of war; a soldier.

homme de lettres (F.), a man of letters; a literary man.

homme de paille (F.), a man of straw; a fictitious person.

homme d'épée (F.), a man of the sword; a soldier; a swordsman; a fencer.

homme de plume (F.), a man of the pen; a writer.

homme de robe (F.), a man of the robe; a magistrate; a lawyer.

homme d'esprit (F.), a man of wit.

homme d'état (F.), a statesman.

homme du monde (F.), a man of the world.

homme galant (F.), a ladies' man: cf. *galant homme*.

homo (L.), man; human being.

homo alieni juris (L.), a man who is under the authority of another: cf. *homo sui juris*.

homo homini aut deus aut lupus (L.), man is to man either a god or a wolf.

homo homini lupus (L.), man is a wolf to man: see *lupus est homo homini*.

homo Latinissimus (L.), a most excellent Latinist.

homo multarum litterarum (L.), a man of much learning.

homo nullius coloris (L.), a man of no (recognizable) color; an uncertain quantity (see *Plautus*, Pseudolus, iv. 7).

homo sine religione sicut equus sine freno (L.), a man without religion is like a horse without a bridle.

homo sui juris (L.), a man who is his own master: cf. *homo alieni juris* and *sui juris*.

homo sum: humani nihil a me alienum (L.), I am a man: I consider nothing human as foreign to me (*Terence*, Heauton-timorumenos, i. 1).

homo unius libri (L.), a man of one book: cf. *timeo hominem unius libri*.

honi soit qui mal y pense (F.), shamed be he who thinks evil of it (motto of the British Order of the Garter).

honneur et patrie (F.), honor and country (motto of the French Legion of Honor).

honores mutant mores (L.), honors change manners.

honoris causa (or **gratia**) (L.), for the sake of honor; as a mark of honor.

honos alit artes (L.), honor nourishes the arts (*Cicero*, Tusculan Disputations, i. 2).

honos habet onus (L.), honor has its burden.

horæ canonicæ (L.), canonical hours (prescribed for prayer).

horæ subsicivæ (or **subsecivæ**) (L.), leisure hours.

hora fugit (L.), the hour flies.

horas non numero nisi serenas (L.), I number none but bright hours (inscription for a sun-dial).

horresco referens (L.), I shudder to relate (*Virgil*, Æneid, ii. 204).

horribile dictu (L.), horrible to relate.

hors concours (F.), out of competition; not competing.

hors de combat (F.), out of the fight; disabled.

hors de propos (F.), aside from the purpose; irrelevant.

hors de saison (F.), out of season.

hors d'œuvre (F.), outside the (main) work, building, subject, etc.

hors-d'œuvre (F.), something outside of or additional to a work; a light supplementary dish, as a relish, served at table.

hors la loi (F.), outside the pale of the law; outlawed.

hortus siccus (L.), a dry garden; a collection of dried plants; a herbarium.

horum omnium fortissimi sunt Belgæ (L.), of all these the bravest are the Belgæ (*Cæsar*, De Bello Gallico, i. 1).

hospes, hostis (L.), a stranger, an enemy.

hostis humani generis (L.), an enemy of the human race.

hôtel de ville (F.), a city hall or town hall.

hôtel-Dieu (F.), hotel (or hostel) of God; a hospital.

huissier (F.), an usher; a doorkeeper; a bailiff.

humani nihil alienum (L.), nothing human is foreign (to me): cf. *homo sum: humani nihil* (etc.).

humanum est errare (L.), to err is human.

humilis nec alte cadere nec graviter

potest (L.), the lowly man cannot fall either far or heavily (*Publilius Syrus*).

hunc tu caveto (L.), of him do thou beware (see *Horace*, Satires, i. 4).

hurtar para dar por Dios (Sp.), to steal in order to give for God's sake (to give alms).

hypotheses non fingo (L.), I do not frame hypotheses (*Sir Isaac Newton*).

I

ibidem (L.), in the same place.

ibi semper est victoria ubi concordia est (L.), victory is always where there is concord (*Publilius Syrus*).

ibit eo quo vis qui zonam perdidit (L.), he who has lost his money-belt will go wherever you wish (*Horace*, Epistles, ii. 2).

ich bin der Geist der stets verneint (G.), I am the spirit that ever denies (*Goethe*, Faust, i.).

ich dien (G.), I serve (motto of the Prince of Wales).

ich habe gelebt und geliebet (G.), I have lived and loved (*Schiller*, Die Piccolomini, iii. 7).

ich weiss nicht (G.), I do not know.

ici on parle français (F.), here French is spoken.

idée fixe (F.), a fixed idea; an idea obsessing the mind, as in monomania.

idem (L.), the same.

idem quod (L.), the same as.

idem sonans (L.), sounding the same; alike in sound.

idem velle et idem nolle (L.), to wish the same thing and object to the same thing; have the same likes and dislikes (*Sallust*, Catiline, 20).

id est (L.), that is.

id genus omne (L.), all that sort.

idoneus homo (L.), a suitable or fit man.

id quod erat demonstrandum (L.), that which was to be demonstrated.

id usitatissimum (L.), that most familiar (thing, saying, etc.).

Iesus Hominum Salvator (L.), Jesus, Saviour of Men.

Iesus Nazarenus, Rex Iudæorum (L.), Jesus of Nazareth, King of the Jews.

Iesus Salvator Mundi (L.), Jesus, Saviour of the World.

ignavis semper feriæ sunt (L.), for the lazy it is always holiday.

ignem ne gladio fodito (L.), stir not a fire with a sword.

ignobile vulgus (L.), the ignoble multitude; the mob.

ignorantia excusatur, non juris sed facti (L.), ignorance, not of law but of fact, is excused.

ignorantia (or **ignoratio**) **legis neminem excusat** (L.), ignorance of the law excuses no one.

ignorantia non excusat (L.), ignorance does not excuse.

ignoratio elenchi (L.), ignorance of the refutation; the logical fallacy of arguing to the wrong point.

ignosce sæpe alteri, nunquam tibi (L.), pardon another often, thyself never.

ignoti nulla cupido (L.), for a thing unknown there is no desire (*Ovid*, Ars Amatoria, iii. 397).

ignoto Deo (L.), to the unknown God (*Vulgate*, Acts, xvii. 23).

ignotum per ignotius (L.), the unknown by the more unknown; explanation of the obscure by what is still more obscure.

il a inventé l'histoire (F.), he (Voltaire) has invented history (*Mme. du Deffand*).

il a la mer à boire (F.), he has the sea to drink up (an endless or hopeless task).

il a le diable au corps (F.), he has the devil in his body (in him).

il a les défauts de ses qualités (F.), he has the defects of his qualities (the faults that go with his very virtues).

il faut de l'argent (F.), money is necessary.

il faut laver son linge sale en famille (F.), one should wash one's dirty linen at home (attributed to Voltaire, but made famous by Napoleon).

il faut manger pour vivre, et non pas vivre pour manger (F.), one must eat to live, and not live to eat (*Molière*, L'Avare, iii. 5).

il gran rifiuto (It.), the great refusal (*Dante*, Inferno, iii. 60).

Ilias malorum (L.), an Iliad of woes; a long series of calamities.

ille crucem sceleris pretium tulit, hic diadema (L.), that man got the cross (crucifixion) as the reward of crime, this man a crown (*Juvenal*, Satires, xiii. 105).

ille terrarum mihi præter omnes angulus ridet (L.), that corner of the earth to me smiles more sweetly than all (*Horace*, Odes, ii. 6).

illotis manibus (L.), with unwashed hands; without due preparation.

il n'a ni bouche ni éperon (F.), he has neither mouth nor spur; he feels neither bit nor spur (curb nor stimulus).

il n'a pas inventé la poudre (F.), he did not invent gunpowder; he is no genius.

il ne faut pas défier un fou de faire des folies (F.), one should not defy a fool to commit follies.

il n'est sauce que l'appétit (F.), there is no sauce like appetite.

il n'y a pas à dire (F.), there is nothing to be said.

il n'y a pas de quoi (F.), there is no occasion; it is nothing; don't mention it.

il n'y a plus d'enfants (F.), there are no longer any children (*Molière*, Le Malade Imaginaire, ii. 11).

il n'y a plus de Pyrénées (F.), there are no longer any Pyrenees (attributed to Louis XIV., at his grandson's departure in 1700 to ascend the throne of Spain as Philip V.).

il n'y a point de héros pour son valet de chambre (F.), no man is a hero to his valet.

il n'y a que le premier pas qui coûte (F.), it is only the first step that costs (requires resolution or effort) (*Mme. du Deffand*).

il n'y a que les morts qui ne reviennent pas (F.), it is only the dead that never return (*Barère*).

Il Penseroso (17th century It.), "The Pensive Man" (title of a poem by Milton: a companion to *L'Allegro*).

il sangue del soldato fa grande il capitano (It.), the blood of the soldier makes the captain great.

il sent le fagot (F.), he savors of the

fagot, or of heresy; there is doubt of his piety, or of his sincerity or reliability.

il se recule pour mieux sauter (F.), he draws back in order to leap the better.

ils n'ont rien appris, rien oublié (F.), they have learned nothing and forgotten nothing (said of the French émigrés who returned to France after the Revolution: commonly attributed to Talleyrand).

il va du blanc au noir (F.), he goes from the white to the black (from one extreme to the other).

imitatores, servum pecus (L.), imitators, a servile herd (*Horace*, Epistles, i. 19).

immedicabile vulnus (L.), an incurable wound.

imo pectore (L.), from the bottom of the heart.

impar congressus Achilli (L.), unequally matched in combat against Achilles (*Virgil*, Æneid, i. 475).

impavidum ferient ruinæ (L.), the falling ruins will strike him undismayed (*Horace*, Odes, iii. 3).

impera parendo (L.), govern by complying.

imperium et libertas (L.), empire and liberty.

imperium in imperio (L.), an empire within an empire; a sovereignty within a sovereignty.

implicite (L.), by implication; impliedly.

impos animi (L.), not having control of the mind; feeble-minded.

impossible n'est pas français (F.), impossible is not a French word (adapted from words of Napoleon).

impotentia excusat legem (L.), inability excuses from legal duties.

imprimatur (L.), let it be printed (a formula signed by an official licenser authorizing the printing of a book, etc.).

imprimerie (F.), a printing-house.

imprimis (L.), among the first; in the first place.

in absentia (L.), in or during absence.

in abstracto (L.), in the abstract.

in actu (L.), in the act; in reality.

in æquilibrio (or **equilibrio**) (L.), in equilibrium.

in aëre piscari, in mare venari (L.), to fish in the air, to hunt in the sea.

in æternum (L.), forever.

in ambiguo (L.), in uncertainty; in doubt.

in anima vili (L.), on a worthless living creature (used of scientific experiments, as on the lower animals).

in aqua scribis (L.), you are writing in water.

in arena ædificas (L.), you are building on sand.

in armis (L.), in or under arms.

in articulo mortis (L.), at the moment or point of death.

in banco (L.), in banc or full court; with all or a quorum of the judges present.

in beato omnia beata (L.), in prosperity all things are prosperous.

in bianco (It.), in white; in blank.

in bonam partem (L.), in good part; favorably.

in caducum parietem inclinare (L.), to lean against a falling wall.

in cælo quies (L.), in heaven is rest.

in cælum jacularis (L.), you are shooting into the air.

in camera (L.), in a chamber; in private, or within closed doors (said of a judicial hearing, etc.).

in capite (L.), in chief; of a feudal tenant, holding immediately from the lord or the king.

in cauda venenum (L.), in the tail is the poison.

incendium ignibus extinguitur (L.), fire is extinguished by flames.

incerta pro nullis habentur (L.), things uncertain are counted as nothing.

in Christi nomine (L.), in the name of Christ.

incidis in Scyllam cupiens vitare Charybdim (L.), you fall on Scylla in seeking to avoid Charybdis.

in commendam (L.), in trust, as an ecclesiastical benefice committed to one to hold until it is supplied with a regular incumbent.

in contumaciam (L.), in contumacy.

incredibile dictu (L.), incredible to relate.

incredulus odi (L.), being incredulous, I dislike it (*Horace*, Ars Poetica, 188).

in cumulo (L.), in a heap or mass.

in curia (L.), in court.

incurvat genu senectus (L.), old age bends the knee.

in custodia legis (L.), in the custody of the law.

in Dei nomine (L.), in the name of God.

inde iræ et lacrimæ (L.), thence angers and tears (*Juvenal*, Satires, i. 168).

in Deo speramus (L.), in God we hope (motto of Brown University).

Index Expurgatorius (L.), "Expurgatory Index" (a catalogue of books to be expurgated before being read by Roman Catholics).

Index Librorum Prohibitorum (L.), "Index of Prohibited Books" (a catalogue of books that Roman Catholics are forbidden to read).

index locorum (L.), an index of places.

index nominum (L.), an index of names.

index rerum (L.), an index of subjects.

index verborum (L.), an index of words.

indictum sit (L.), let it be unsaid.

in diem vivere (L.), to live for the day, or from day to day (regardless of the future).

indignor quandoque bonus dormitat Homerus (L.), I am indignant when at times good Homer nods (grows dull or careless) (*Horace*, Ars Poetica, 359).

in divinis (L.), in divine or sacred things.

in Domino (L.), in the Lord.

in dubiis (L.), in doubtful matters.

in dubio (L.), in doubt; in question; undetermined.

industria floremus (L.), we flourish by industry.

in equilibrio (L.): see *in æquilibrio*.

iners malorum remedium ignorantia est (L.), ignorance is a feeble remedy for ills (*Seneca*, Œdipus, iii. 515).

in esse (L.), in being; in actual existence: cf. *in posse*.

inest clementia forti (L.), clemency belongs to the brave.

in excelsis (L.), on high; in the highest; in the highest degree: see *gloria in excelsis Deo*.

in extenso (L.), at full length; in full.

in extremis (L.), in the last stages (of life); at the point of death.

in facie curiæ (L.), in the face, or presence, of the court.

infandum, regina, jubes renovare dolorem (L.), thou biddest me, queen, to revive unutterable grief (*Virgil*, Æneid, ii. 3).

in fieri (L.), in the making; in course of procedure.

infima species (L.), the lowest species.

in fine (L.), in the end.

in flagrante delicto (or **crimine**) (L.), in the very act of committing the offense (or crime).

in flammam ne manum injicito (L.), thrust not thy hand into the flame.

in forma pauperis (L.), in the form or character of a pauper; as a pauper.

in foro conscientiæ (L.), in the court of conscience.

in foro divino (L.), in the divine court; before the divine tribunal.

in foro domestico (L.), in a domestic (not foreign) court.

in foro humano (L.), in a human court; before a human tribunal.

in foro seculari (L.), in a secular court.

infra dignitatem (L.), beneath one's dignity.

in fraudem legis (L.), in fraud, or evasion, of the law.

in futuro (L.), in the future.

in genere (L.), in kind; in like articles.

ingens telum necessitas (L.), necessity is a powerful weapon.

ingrata patria, ne ossa quidem habebis (L.), ungrateful country, thou shalt not have even my bones (attributed to Scipio Africanus the Elder).

in gremio (L.), in the bosom.

in gremio legis (L.), in the bosom, or under the protection, of the law.

in hac parte (L.), on this part or side.

in hac salus (L.), in this (cross) is salvation.

in hoc (L.), in this; as to this.

in hoc signo spes mea (L.), in this sign is my hope.

in hoc signo vinces (L.), in this sign shalt thou conquer (motto said to have been adopted by the Roman emperor Constantine the Great from a vision of a cross, with these words, seen by him before going forth to battle).

in hoc statu (L.), in this state or condition.

in horas (L.), every hour; hourly.

in infinitum (L.), to infinity; endlessly.

in initio (L.), in the beginning.

in invitum (L.), against an unwilling party.

in ipso actu (L.), in the very act.

initium sapientiæ timor Domini (L.), the fear of the Lord is the beginning of wisdom (*Vulgate*, Ps. cx. 10).

in jure (L.), in law; in court.

in jure non remota causa sed proxima spectatur (L.), in law not the remote cause but the immediate is considered.

injuria absque damno (L.), wrong without damage.

injuriarum remedium est oblivio (L.), oblivion is the remedy for injuries.

in jus vocare (L.), to call or summon to court.

in limine (L.), on the threshold; at the outset.

in litteris humanioribus (L.), in the more humane letters, or the humanities.

in loco (L.), in place; in the proper place.

in loco parentis (L.), in the place of a parent.

in loco remoto (L.), in a distant place.

in lumine tuo videbimus lucem (L.), in thy light shall we see light (motto of Columbia University: *Vulgate*, Ps. xxxv. 10).

in magnis et voluisse sat est (L.), in great things even to have had the will is sufficient (*Propertius*, ii. 10).

in malam partem (L.), in bad part; unfavorably.

in manus tuas (L.), into thy hands (*Vulgate*, Luke, xxiii. 46).

in mari aquam quærit (L.), he seeks for water in the sea.

in medias res (L.), into the midst of things.

in medio tutissimus ibis (L.): see *medio tutissimus ibis.*

in meditatione fugæ (L.), in meditation or contemplation of flight.

in memoriam (L.), to the memory (of); in memory.

in mortua manu (L.), in a dead hand; in mortmain.

in naturalibus (L.), in a state of nature; naked.

in nomine (L.), in the name of.

in nomine Dei (L.), in the name of God.

in nomine Domini (L.), in the name of the Lord.

in nubibus (L.), in the clouds; undecided; unrealized; in abeyance (legally).

in nuce (L.), in a nutshell; in small compass.

in nuce Ilias (L.), an Iliad in a nutshell.

in obscuro (L.), in obscurity.

in oculis civium (L.), in the eyes of the citizens; in the public eye.

in omnia paratus (L.), prepared for all things.

inopem me copia fecit (L.), abundance has made me poor (*Ovid*, Metamorphoses, iii. 466).

inopiæ desunt multa, avaritiæ omnia (L.), many things are wanting to poverty, all things to avarice (*Publilius Syrus*).

inops consilii (L.), destitute of counsel (*Livy*, xxvi. 18).

in ovo (L.), in the egg; in the germ.

in pace (L.), in peace.

in pace leones, in proelio cervi (L.), in peace lions, in battle deer.

in partibus (L.): same as *in partibus infidelium.*

in partibus infidelium (L.), in the lands of the infidels (in the Roman Catholic Church, used of bishops bearing honorary titles derived from sees formerly existing in lands now held by the infidels).

in parvo (L.), in little; in miniature.

in pectore (L.), in the breast; in secret: cf. *in petto.*

in perpetuam rei memoriam (L.), in perpetual memory of the thing.

in perpetuum (L.), in perpetuity; forever.

in persona (L.), in person.

in personam (L.), against a person (as a legal proceeding).

in petto (It.), in the breast; in secret; not disclosed (in the Roman Catholic Church, used of cardinals privately appointed by the Pope but not to be announced until a later date).

in pleno (L.), in full.

in poculis (L.), in or during cups; while drinking.

in pontificalibus (L.), in pontificals; in pontifical robes.

in posse (L.), in possibility (rather than in actual existence): cf. *in esse.*

in potentia (L.), in possibility; potentially.

in potestate parentis (L.), in the power of a parent.

in præsenti (L.), at the present time.

in principio (L.), in the beginning.

in propria causa (L.), in one's own suit (at law).

in propria persona (L.), in one's own person; in person.

in prospectu (L.), in prospect; in view.

in puris naturalibus (L.), in a state of pure nature; stark naked.

in re (L.), in the matter of.

in rem (L.), against a thing (as a legal proceeding for its recovery).

in rerum natura (L.), in the nature of things.

in sacris (L.), in sacred things.

in sæcula sæculorum (L.), for ages of ages; forever (*Vulgate*, Gal. i. 5).

insalutato hospite (L.), without saluting one's host; without saying farewell; in all haste.

insculpsit (L.), (the person specified) engraved it.

in se (L.), in itself (or themselves).

in situ (L.), in its original situation or place.

in solido (L.), as a whole; for the whole.

in solo Deo salus (L.), in God alone is salvation.

in spiritualibus (L.), in spiritual things.

instar omnium (L.), like all of them; also, worth them all.

in statu pupillari (L.), in a state of pupilage.

in statu quo (L.), in the state in which (anything was or is); in the same state.

in statu quo ante (or **prius**) (L.), in the same state as before.

in statu quo ante bellum (L.), in the same state as before the war.

in statu quo nunc (L.), in the same state as now.

instaurare omnia in Christo (L.), to establish all things in Christ (motto of Pope Pius X.).

in suo proprio loco (L.), in its own place.

in suspenso (L.), in suspense; in uncertainty.

in te, Domine, speravi (L.), in thee, Lord, have I hoped (*Vulgate*, Ps. xxx. 1).

integer vitæ scelerisque purus (L.), blameless in life and free from crime (*Horace*, Odes, i. 22).

integritate et merito (L.), by integrity and merit.

integros haurire fontes (L.), to draw from pure fountains.

intelligenti pauca (L.), to the intelligent few words; a word to the wise.

intellige ut credas (L.), understand in order that you may believe.

in temporalibus (L.), in temporal things.

in tempore opportuno (L.), in or at an opportune time.

inter alia (or **alios**) (L.), among other things (or other persons).

inter arma caritas (L.), in the midst of arms, or war, charity.

inter arma silent leges (L.): see *silent leges inter arma.*

inter canem et lupum (L.), between dog and wolf; between daylight and dark; at twilight: cf. *hac urget lupus, hac canis.*

inter folia fructus (L.), among the leaves fruit.

intérieur (F.), the interior; the home; home life.

in terminis (L.), in express terms.

inter nos (L.), between or among ourselves.

inter pocula (L.), between cups; while drinking.

in terrorem (L.), for terror; to inspire fear; as a warning.

inter se (L.), between or among themselves.

inter silvas Academi quærere verum (L.), to seek for truth amid the woods of Academus (*Horace*, Epistles, ii. 2).

inter spem et metum (L.), between hope and fear.

inter vivos (L.), between living persons.

in testimonium (L.), in testimony or witness.

in thesi (L.), as a thesis or proposition.

intima præcordia (L.), the inmost breast or heart.

in totidem verbis (L.), in so many words.

in toto (L.), in the whole; entirely.

intra muros (L.), within the walls, as of a city.

in transitu (L.), in transit; on the way.

intra parietes (L.), within the walls, as of a house.

intra vires (L.), within the (legal) powers.

in tuo regno es (L.), you are in your own kingdom (on your own ground).

intuta quæ indecora (L.), things that are unseemly are unsafe (*Tacitus*, Historiæ, i. 33).

in usu (L.), in use.

in usum delphini (L.), for the use of the dauphin (as certain editions of the Latin classics, prepared for the use of the son of Louis XIV. of France); adapted for the use of the young; expurgated.

in usum vulgi (L.), for the use of the multitude.

in utramque fortunam paratus (L.), prepared for either fortune.

in utroque fidelis (L.), faithful in both.

in utroque jure (L.), in both laws (canon and civil).

in utrumque paratus (L.), prepared for either alternative (*Virgil*, Æneid, ii. 61).

in vacuo (L.), in a vacuum.

invenit (L.), (the person specified) designed it.

inverso ordine (L.), in inverse order; inversely.

invidia gloriæ comes (L.), envy is the companion of glory.

in vino veritas (L.), in wine truth; wine prompts to truth.

invita Minerva (L.), Minerva being unwilling; against one's natural bent or genius (see *Horace*, Ars Poetica, 385).

invito domino (L.), the master or owner being unwilling.

in vitro (L.), in glass; in a test-tube: cf. *in vivo*.

in vivo (L.), in or on the living body (used of physiological processes, experiments, etc.): cf. *in vitro*.

io triumphe! (L.), ho, hurrah! (shout of exultation during a Roman triumphal procession).

ipsa sibi obstat magnitudo (L.), his very greatness stands in his way.

ipse agmen (L.), himself an army; a host in himself.

ipse dixit (L.), he himself has said it.

ipsissima verba (L.), the very words.

ipso facto (L.), by the act or fact itself; by or from the very fact.

ipso jure (L.), by the law itself.

ira furor brevis est (L.), anger is a brief madness (*Horace*, Epistles, i. 2).

irremeabilis unda (L.), the wave over which there is no return (the river Styx: see *Virgil*, Æneid, vi. 425).

irrevocabile verbum (L.), a word or utterance that cannot be recalled: see *et semel emissum volat irrevocabile verbum*.

is fecit cui prodest (L.), he did the deed to whose interest it is; the guilty one is he who has something to gain by the crime.

ita dis placuit (L.), thus it has pleased the gods.

ita est (L.), thus it is.

ita lex scripta est (L.), thus the law is written.

Italia farà da sè (It.), Italy will do it by herself (motto in 1848 and later in patriotic struggles for the freedom of Italy).

Italia irredenta (It.), unredeemed Italy; regions near Italy inhabited largely by Italians but subject to other nations.

Italicè (L.), in Italian.

ita vertere seria ludo (L.), thus to turn serious things to sport (*Horace*, Ars Poetica, 226).

ita voluerunt, ita factum est (L.), thus they willed, thus it was done.

item (L.), likewise; also (used in enumerating).

ite, missa est (L.), go, dismissal is given (in the Roman Catholic Church, words pronounced at the close of the mass, just before the final benediction).

iterum (L.), again; once more.

ivresse (F.), drunkenness; intoxication.

ivrognes (F.), drunkards: see *Dieu aide à trois sortes de personnes* (etc.).

J

ja (G.), yes.

j'accuse (F.), I accuse (used by Zola at the head of an open letter denouncing the persecutors of Dreyfus).

jacta alea est (L.), the die is cast (words of Julius Cæsar at crossing the Rubicon, to begin a civil war: *Suetonius*, Julius Cæsar, 32).

jacta est alea (L.), the die is cast: see *jacta alea est*.

Jahre lehren mehr als Bücher (G.), years teach more than books.

jamais arrière (F.), never behind.

jam proximus ardet Ucalegon (L.), already Ucalegon's house next door is on fire (*Virgil*, Æneid, ii. 311).

januæ mentis (L.), the doors of the mind.

januis clausis (L.), with closed doors.

jardin des plantes (F.), a garden of plants; a botanical garden.

Ja und Nein ist ein langer Streit (G.), yes and no is a long dispute.

ja wohl (G.), yes, indeed; certainly.

jefe político (Sp.), a political chief or head; a prefect.

jejunus raro stomachus vulgaria temnit (L.), the hungry stomach seldom scorns common food (*Horace*, Satires, ii. 2).

jejunus venter non audit libenter (L.), a hungry stomach does not willingly listen.

je maintiendrai (F.), I will maintain (motto of the Netherlands).

je maintiendrai le droit (F.), I will maintain the right.

je me fie en Dieu (F.), I trust in God.

je m'en vais chercher un grand peut-être (F.), I go to seek a great perhaps (reputed dying words of Rabelais).

je ne cherche qu'un (F.), I seek but one.

je ne m'en souviens pas (F.), I do not remember.

je n'en vois pas la nécessité (F.), I do not see the necessity for it (reply attributed to a French aristocrat before the Revolution, on being reminded that the people must live).

je ne sais pas (F.), I do not know.

je ne sais quoi (F.), I know not what; an indefinable something.

je n'oublierai jamais (F.), I will never forget.

je prends mon bien partout où je le trouve (F.), I take my property wherever I find it (reply of Molière to the charge of plagiarism).

je suis prêt (F.), I am ready.

jet d'eau (F.), a jet of water, as from a fountain.

jeter son bonnet par-dessus les moulins (F.), to throw one's cap over the mills (to act in defiance of public opinion or the proprieties: said of women).

jeu (F.), play; sport; game; gambling.

jeu de main (F.), hand-play (with blows); rough play; horse-play.

jeu de main, jeu de vilain (F.), rough play, clown's play.

jeu de mots (F.), a play on words; a pun.

jeu d'esprit (F.), a play of wit; a witticism.

jeu de théâtre (F.), stage business, or incidental action.

jeune personne (F.), a young girl.

jeune premier, fem. **jeune première** (F.), an actor or actress who takes youthful leading parts.

jeunesse dorée (F.), gilded youth; rich and fashionable young people.

jeux de prince (F.), prince's sports; diversions of the great at the expense of the lowly (*La Fontaine*, Fables, iv. 4).

je vis en espoir (F.), I live in hope.

je vous (en) prie (F.), I pray you; pray.

Joannes est nomen ejus (L.), his name is John (motto of Porto Rico, which was orig. named San Juan Bautista, 'St. John Baptist,' by Columbus: *Vulgate*, Luke, i. 63).

joci causa (L.), for the sake of the joke.

joie de vivre (F.), the joy of living.

joies de mariage (F.), joys of marriage; pleasures of short duration.

joli, fem. **jolie** (F.), pretty; nice; fine.

jour (F.), day; daylight; daytime.

jour de fête (F.), a fête-day; a festival day; a holiday.

jour de l'an (F.), New Year's Day.

jour gras (F.), a fat day; a day when meat may be eaten: cf. *jour maigre*.

jour maigre (F.), a lean day; a day of abstinence from meat, as prescribed by church discipline: cf. *jour gras*.

journal, pl. *journaux* (F.), a journal; a diary; a newspaper.

journal intime (F.), a private journal, or diary.

jubilate Deo (L.), rejoice in God (*Vulgate*, Ps. xcvii. 4).

jucunda rerum vicissitudo (L.), a pleasant change of circumstances.

jucundi acti labores (L.), pleasant are labors accomplished (*Cicero*, De Finibus, ii. 32).

Judenhetze (G.), persecution of the Jews; anti-Semitic agitation.

judex damnatur cum nocens absolvitur (L.), the judge is condemned when a guilty person is acquitted (*Publilius Syrus*).

judex est lex loquens (L.), the judge is the law speaking.

judicium capitale (L.), capital judgment; the sentence of death.

judicium Dei (L.), the judgment of God.

judicium parium (L.), the judgment of one's peers.

jugulare mortuos (L.), to slaughter the dead; carry bloodshed to the last extreme.

juniores ad labores (L.), the younger men for labors.

Jupiter pluvius (L.), Jupiter the rain-giver.

Jupiter tonans (L.), Jupiter the thunderer.

jurare in verba magistri (L.), to swear to the words of a master: see *nullius addictus jurare in verba magistri*.

jure coronæ (L.), by or in right of the crown.

jure divino (L.), by divine right or law.

jure et facto (L.), by right and by fact.

jure gentium (L.), by the law of nations.

jure humano (L.), by human right or law.

jure mariti (L.), by the right of a husband.

jure matrimonii (L.), by right of marriage.

jure sanguinis (L.), by right of blood.

juris peritus (L.), versed in the law.

juris positivi (L.), of positive or prescribed law.

juris præcepta sunt hæc, honeste vivere, alterum non lædere, suum cuique tribuere (L.), these are the precepts of the law, to live honestly, to harm no one, to render to each his due.

juris utriusque doctor (L.), doctor of both laws (canon and civil).

jus ad rem (L.), a right to a thing.

jus canonicum (L.), canon law.

jus civile (L.), civil law.

jus commune (L.), common law.

jus divinum (L.), divine right or law.

jus et norma loquendi (L.), the law and rule of speech (*Horace*, Ars Poetica, 72).

jus gentium (L.), the law of nations; international law.

jus gladii (L.), the right of the sword.

jus in personam (L.), a right against a person.

jus in re (L.), a right in a thing.

jus inter gentes (L.), the law among nations; international law.

jus mariti (L.), the right of a husband.

jus naturale (L.), natural law.

jus possessionis (L.), right of possession.

jus privatum (L.), private law.

jus proprietatis (L.), right of property.

jus respicit æquitatem (L.), law has regard to equity.

jus scriptum (L.), written law.

justa bella quibus necessaria (L.), wars are just for those to whom they are necessary: see *justum est bellum, Samnites, quibus necessarium.*

justa causa (L.), just cause.

juste milieu (F.), the just mean; the happy medium.

justitiæ propositique tenax (L.), tenacious of justice and of purpose: cf. *justum et tenacem propositi virum.*

justitia omnibus (L.), justice for all (motto of the District of Columbia).

justum est bellum, Samnites, quibus necessarium (L.), war is just, Samnites, for those to whom it is necessary (*Livy*, ix. 1).

justum et tenacem propositi virum (L.), the man who is just, and tenacious of purpose (*Horace*, Odes, iii. 3).

juxta fluvium puteum fodit (L.), he is digging a well near a river.

j'y suis, j'y reste (F.), here I am, here I stay (attributed to the French general MacMahon, at the taking of the Malakoff fortification, in 1855, in the Crimean War).

K

kai ta loipa (Gr. καὶ τὰ λοιπά), and the rest; and so forth; et cetera.

Kamerad (G.), comrade; friend.

Kanonenfutter (G.), cannon-fodder. See Dictionary.

kaputt (G.), smashed; ruined; done for.

Katzenjammer (G.), indisposition following intoxication.

Kellner (G.), a waiter.

Kirche, Küche, und Kinder (G.), church, kitchen, and children (the proper objects of woman's attention, as recommended by William II. of Germany).

kolossal (G.), colossal; gigantic; immense; huge; vast.

Kultur (G.), **Kulturkampf** (G.). See Dictionary.

Kyrie eleïson (L., for Gr. Κύριε ἐλέησον), Lord, have mercy (in ecclesiastical use).

L

l' or **le**, fem. **l'** or **la**, pl. **les** (F.), the: for many phrases beginning thus see second word of phrase.

la belle dame sans merci (F.), the fair lady without mercy.

la belle France (F.), the beautiful France; fair France.

laborare est orare (L.), to labor is to pray.

labor callum obducit dolori (L.), labor hardens one to suffering (*Cicero*, Tusculan Disputations, ii. 15).

labore et honore (L.), with labor and honor.

labor ipse voluptas (L.), labor itself is pleasure.

labor omnia vincit (L.), labor conquers all things (motto of Oklahoma).

labor omnia vincit improbus (L.), persistent labor conquers all things (*Virgil*, Georgics, i. 145).

laborum dulce lenimen (L.), sweet solace of labors (*Horace*, Odes, i. 32).

la bride sur le cou (F.), the bridle on the neck; with free rein; without restraint.

La Comédie Humaine (F.), "The Human Comedy" (Balzac's title for the assemblage of novels in which he undertook to depict the various sides of human life).

la confiance fournit plus à la conversation que l'esprit (F.), confidence does more to make conversation than wit (*La Rochefoucauld*).

lacrimæ rerum (L.), tears for things: see *sunt lacrimæ rerum.*

l'adversité fait les hommes, et le bonheur les monstres (F.), adversity makes men, and prosperity monsters.

læsa majestas (L.), **lèse-majesté** (F.), injured majesty; lese-majesty; high treason.

la fame non ha leggi (It.), hunger has no laws.

l'affaire marche (F.), the affair progresses.

l'affaire s'achemine (F.), the affair is going forward.

la fleur des pois (F.), the flower of the peas; the very flower of elegance, fashion, etc.

la fortune passe partout (F.), fortune passes everywhere.

la garde meurt et ne se rend pas (F.), the guard dies, and does not surrender (attributed to General Cambronne, at Waterloo).

la grande nation (F.), the great nation (France).

laisser-aller (F.), a letting go; unrestraint; laxity; abandon.

laisser-faire (F.), a letting do (as one pleases); a letting alone; non-interference.

laissez dire les sots, le savoir a son prix (F.), let fools talk, knowledge has its value (*La Fontaine*, Fables, viii. 19).

laissez faire (F.), let (them) do (as they please) (a counsel of non-interference or indifference).

laissez faire, laissez passer (F.), let do, let pass (maxim of the 18th century economists, enjoining non-interference with production and with trade).

laissez-passer (F.), a license to pass; a pass.

L'Allegro (It.), "The Cheerful Man" (title of a poem by Milton: a companion to *Il Penseroso*).

la maladie sans maladie (F.), the disease without disease; hypochondria.

la mentira tiene las piernas cortas (Sp.), a lie has short legs (is soon overtaken).

la mort (or **le mort**) **a toujours tort** (F.), death (or the dead man) is always at fault (not the doctor).

l'amour-propre est le plus grand de tous les flatteurs (F.), self-love is the greatest of all flatterers (*La Rochefoucauld*).

langage des dieux (F.), language of the gods; poetry.

langage des halles (F.), language of the markets; billingsgate.

la nuit porte conseil (F.), night brings counsel.

la nuit tous les chats sont gris (F.), at night all cats are gray.

lanx satura (L.), a dish of various fruits; a mixture of ingredients; a medley.

la patience est amère, mais son fruit est doux (F.), patience is bitter, but its fruit is sweet.

la peur a bon pas (F.), fear has a good pace.

lapis philosophorum (L.), the philosophers' stone.

la povertà è la madre di tutte le arti (It.), poverty is the mother of all the arts.

l'appétit vient en mangeant (F.), appetite comes in eating.

la propriété, c'est le vol (F.), property is robbery (*Proudhon*).

lapsus calami (L.), a slip of the pen.

lapsus linguæ (L.), a slip of the tongue.

lapsus memoriæ (L.), a slip of the memory.

l'arbre de la liberté ne croît qu'arrosé par le sang des tyrans (F.), the tree of liberty grows only when sprinkled with the blood of tyrants (*Barère*).

la république des lettres (F.), the republic of letters (*Molière*, Le Mariage Forcé, vi.).

Lares et Penates (L.), Lares and Penates; household gods.

l'argent est un bon passe-partout (F.), money is a good master-key (for unlocking all doors).

larmoyant, fem. **larmoyante** (F.), tearful; lacrymose.

lasciate ogni speranza, voi ch' entrate (It.), all hope abandon, ye who enter here (*Dante*, Inferno, iii. 9).

la speranza è il pan de' miseri (It.), hope is the bread of the miserable.

lateat scintillula forsan (L.), a small spark (of life) may perchance lie hid (motto of the Royal Humane Society of England, devoted to rescuing the drowning and resuscitating those apparently drowned).

latet anguis in herba (L.), a snake lurks in the grass (*Virgil*, Eclogues, iii. 93).

latrante uno, latrat statim et alter canis (L.), when one dog barks, forthwith another dog barks too.

laudant illa sed ista legunt (L.), they praise those (writings) but read these (*Martial*, Epigrams, iv. 49).

laudari a laudato viro (L.), to be praised by a man who is himself praised (see *Cicero*, Epistolæ ad Familiares, xv. 6).

laudator temporis acti (L.), a praiser of time past (*Horace*, Ars Poetica, 173).

laudum immensa cupido (L.), boundless desire for praise (*Virgil*, Æneid, vi. 823).

laus Deo (L.), praise to God.

laus propria sordet (L.), praise of self is debasing.

l'avenir (F.), the future.

la verità è figlia del tempo (It.), truth is the daughter of time.

la vertu n'irait pas si loin si la vanité ne lui tenait compagnie (F.), virtue would not go so far if vanity did not keep her company (*La Rochefoucauld*).

le (F.), the: see *l'*.

lebe hoch (G.), long live; health or success to; hurrah for.

lebe (or leb') wohl (G.), farewell.

le bon temps viendra (F.), the good time will come.

Le Bourgeois Gentilhomme (F.), "The Bourgeois Gentleman" (title of a play by Molière).

le brave des braves (F.), the brave (or bravest) of the brave (applied by Napoleon to Marshal Ney).

le coût fait perdre le goût (F.), the cost makes one lose the taste (for a thing).

lector benevole (L.), kind reader.

Le Diable Boiteux (F.), "The Lame Devil" (title of a satirical romance by Le Sage, of which the devil Asmodeus is the principal character).

le diable était beau quand il était jeune (F.), the devil was beautiful when he was young: see *beauté du diable*.

legant prius et postea despiciant (L.), let them read first and despise afterward.

legatus a latere (L.), a papal legate: see *a latere*.

le génie est une longue patience (F.), genius is an enduring patience (adapted from Buffon).

léger, fem. **légère** (F.), light; nimble; volatile; frivolous; trifling.

légèreté (F.), lightness; levity.

lege totum si vis scire totum (L.), read the whole if you wish to know the whole.

legiones (L.): see *Vare, legiones redde.*

Leitmotiv (G.). See Dictionary.

le jeu ne vaut pas la chandelle (F.), the game is not worth the candle.

le jour viendra (F.), the day will come.

Le Malade Imaginaire (F.), "The Imaginary (or Fancied) Invalid" (title of a play by Molière).

le mieux est l'ennemi du bien (F.), better is the enemy of well; let well enough alone.

le monde est le livre des femmes (F.), the world is women's book.

l'empire, c'est la paix (F.), the empire is peace (*Louis Napoleon*, in 1852).

lene tormentum (L.), mild torment (*Horace*, Odes, iii. 21).

leonina societas (L.), a lion's partnership (in which one partner has all the profits and none of the losses).

le papier souffre tout (F.), the paper suffers everything (submits to everything, good or bad, true or false, that is written upon it).

le pas (F.), the step; the precedence.

le petit gain remplit la bourse (F.), little gains fill the purse.

Le Roi d'Yvetot (F.), "The King of Yvetot" (title of a song by Béranger, about a "good little king" who lived contentedly without glory).

le roi est mort, vive le roi! (F.), the king is dead, long live the king!

le roi et l'état (F.), the king and the state.

le roi le veut (F.), the king wills it.

le roi ne meurt pas (F.), the king does not die.

le roi règne et ne gouverne pas (F.), the king reigns and does not govern (*Thiers*, in 1830).

Le Roi s'Amuse (F.), "The King Amuses Himself" (title of a play by Victor Hugo).

le roi s'avisera (F.), the king will consider.

les (F., pl.), the: see *l'*.

les absents ont toujours tort (F.), the absent are always wrong.

les affaires font les hommes (F.), affairs make men; experience of affairs is the making of men.

le sage entend à demi mot (F.), the wise man understands at half a word.

le savoir a son prix (F.), knowledge has its value: see *laissez dire les sots, le savoir a son prix*.

les beaux yeux de ma cassette (F.), the beautiful eyes of my cash-box (*Molière*, L'Avare, v. 3).

les bras croisés (F.), the arms crossed; with folded arms.

les convenances (F.), the proprieties.

lèse-majesté (F.): see *læsa majestas*.

le sens commun n'est pas si commun (F.), common sense is not so common (*Voltaire*).

les extrêmes se touchent (F.), extremes meet.

Les Femmes Savantes (F.), "The Learned Women" (title of a play by Molière).

les larmes aux yeux (F.), tears in the eyes.

Les Misérables (F.), "The Unfortunates" (title of a novel by Victor Hugo).

les murs ont des oreilles (F.), walls have ears.

les plus sages ne le sont pas toujours (F.), the most wise are not always that.

Les Précieuses Ridicules (F.), "The Ridiculous Précieuses" (title of a play by Molière): see *précieux*.

L'Esprit des Lois (F.), "The Spirit of the Laws" (title of a political work by Montesquieu).

le style, c'est l'homme (F.), the style is the man: cf. *le style est l'homme même*.

le style est l'homme même (F.), the style is the man himself (*Buffon*).

l'état, c'est moi (F.), the state, that is myself; I am the state (saying attributed to Louis XIV.).

l'étoile du nord (F.), the star of the north (motto of Minnesota); the north star.

le tout ensemble (F.), the whole considered together.

lettre chargée (F.), a registered letter.

lettre d'avis (F.), a letter of advice (information).

lettre de cachet (F.). See Dictionary.

lettre de change (F.), a bill of exchange.

lettre de créance (F.), a letter of credence; a credential letter.

lettre de crédit (F.), a letter of credit.

lettre de marque (F.), a letter of marque.

lever de rideau (F.), a curtain-raiser (short play).

le véritable Amphitryon est l'Amphitryon où l'on dine (F.), the true Amphitryon is the Amphitryon with whom one dines (*Molière*, Amphitryon, iii. 5).

l'exactitude est la politesse des rois (F.), punctuality is the courtesy of kings (attributed to Louis XVIII.).

lex appetit perfectum (L.), the law aims at perfection.

lex dubia non obligat (L.), a doubtful law does not bind.

lex loci (L.), the law of the place.

lex loci rei sitæ (L.), the law of the place where the thing is situated.

lex mercatoria (L.), mercantile or commercial law.

lex non cogit ad impossibilia (L.), the law does not compel one to do impossibilities.

lex non scripta (L.), the unwritten law; the common law.

lex regit, arma tuentur (L.), law rules, arms protect (motto on the badge of the U. S. Military Order of the Loyal Legion).

lex scripta (L.), the written law; statute law.

lex semper dabit remedium (L.), the law will always give a remedy.

lex succurrit ignoranti (L.), the law aids the ignorant.

lex talionis (L.), the law of retaliation.

lex terræ (L.), the law of the land.

lex uno ore omnes alloquitur (L.), the law speaks with one mouth to all.

l'homme propose et Dieu dispose (F.), man proposes and God disposes.

liaisons dangereuses (F.), dangerous connections.

liberavi animam meam (L.), I have delivered my soul, or freed my mind (cf. *Vulgate*, Ezek. iii. 19, 21).

libertad y orden (Sp.), liberty and order (motto of Colombia).

libertas et potestas faciendi id quod jure licet (L.), liberty is the power of doing what is permitted by law.

libertas et natale solum (L.), liberty and native land.

liberté, égalité, fraternité (F.), liberty, equality, fraternity (motto of the French Republic).

liberum arbitrium (L.), free will.

libraire (F.), a bookseller.

librairie (F.), a bookseller's shop; a publishing-house.

licentia vatum (L.), license of poets; poetic license.

Licht, Liebe, Leben (G.), light, love, life (motto of Herder).

Lied, pl. *Lieder* (G.), a song, lyric, or ballad.

Liederkranz (G.), a garland or collection of songs; a German male singing society.

Liedertafel (G.), table of songs; a German male singing society; a meeting or entertainment of such a society.

limæ labor (L.), the labor of the file: see *limæ labor et mora*.

limæ labor et mora (L.), the labor and delay of the file; the slow, laborious polishing of literary work (*Horace*, Ars Poetica, 291).

limbus (L. , limbo; a supposed region on the border of hell.

limbus fatuorum (L.), the limbo of fools; the fools' paradise.

limbus infantium (L.), the limbo of infants; the place for the souls of unbaptized infants after death.

limbus patrum (L.), the limbo of the fathers, or patriarchs; the place for the souls of the just who died before the coming of Christ.

l'inconnu (F.), the unknown.

linge sale (F.), dirty linen: see *il faut laver* (etc.).

lingua toscana in bocca romana (It.), the Tuscan tongue in the Roman mouth (the best spoken Italian).

lis litem generat (L.), strife begets strife.

lis pendens (L.), a suit pending, or in progress (used esp. with reference to the effect on property involved in the suit).

lis sub judice (L.), a suit before the judge (or not yet decided).

lit de justice (F.), the bed of justice, or throne used by the king of France when holding sessions of the parliament; also, such a session.

litem lite resolvere (L.), to settle dispute by dispute: see *nil agit exemplum litem quod lite resolvit.*

lite pendente (L.), while the suit is pending.

literæ sine moribus vanæ (L.), learning without morals is vain (motto of the University of Pennsylvania).

litteræ divinæ (L.), divine letters or learning; theology.

litteræ humaniores (L.), the more humane letters or learning; the humanities.

littera scripta manet (L.), the written letter remains.

loci communes (L.), commonplaces.

loco citato (L.), in the place cited.

loco laudato (L.), in the place cited.

loco supra citato (L.), in the place cited above.

locum tenens (L.), one holding the place; a deputy or substitute.

locus classicus (L.), a classical or standard passage, such as is commonly cited to illustrate or explain a subject.

locus criminis (or **delicti**) (L.), the place of the crime (or offense).

locus in quo (L.), the place in which.

locus pænitentiæ (L.), place or opportunity for repentance (cf. *Vulgate,* Heb. xii. 17).

locus sigilli (L.), the place of the seal (on a document, etc.).

locus standi (L.), place of standing; right of place in court; right to appear and be heard before a tribunal.

loin des yeux, loin du cœur (F.), far from the eyes, far from the heart; out of sight, out of mind.

longe aberrat scopo (L.), he is very wide of the mark.

longe absit (L.), far be it.

longo intervallo (L.), with a long interval.

loquitur (L.), he (or she) speaks.

l'ordre règne à Varsovie (F.), order reigns at Warsaw (words of Sébastiani, French minister of foreign affairs, in 1831, in announcing the crushing of the Polish insurrection).

los niños y los locos dicen las ver-

dades (Sp.), children and fools tell the truth.

loyal en tout (F.), loyal in all.

loyauté m'oblige (F.), loyalty binds me.

loyauté n'a honte (F.), loyalty has no shame.

lucidus ordo (L.), lucid order; clear arrangement (*Horace,* Ars Poetica, 41).

lucri bonus est odor (L.), sweet is the odor of money (*Juvenal,* Satires, xiv. 204).

lucri causa (L.), for the sake of gain.

lucus a non lucendo (L.), a grove (so called) from not being light (a phrase used as a type of illogical or absurd derivation or reasoning).

ludere cum sacris (L.), to trifle with sacred things.

lumen naturale (L.), natural enlightenment or intelligence.

lumen soli mutuum das (L.), you are lending light to the sun.

l'union fait la force (F.), union makes strength (motto of Belgium).

lupus est homo homini (L.), man is a wolf to man (*Plautus,* Asinaria, ii. 4).

lupus in fabula (L.), the wolf in the fable (which appeared when spoken of) (*Cicero,* To Atticus, xiii. 33).

lusus naturæ (L.), a sport or freak of nature.

lux et veritas (L.), light and truth (motto of Yale University).

lux in tenebris lucet (L.), the light shineth in darkness (*Vulgate,* John, i. 5).

Lydius lapis (L.), Lydian stone; a touchstone.

M

ma chère (F., fem.), my dear: see *mon cher.*

macte animo (L.), go on in courage; fresh courage to you!

macte nova virtute (L.), go on in new virtue (*Virgil,* Æneid, ix. 641).

ma foi! (F.), my faith! upon my word! indeed!

magister cæremoniarum (L.), master of ceremonies.

magister dixit (L.), the master has spoken.

magna civitas, magna solitudo (L.), a great city, a great solitude.

magna cum laude (L.), with great praise (used in diplomas): see *cum laude.*

magnæ fortunæ pericula (L.), the dangers of great fortune (*Tacitus,* Annales, iv. 13).

magnæ spes altera Romæ (L.), another hope of great Rome (*Virgil,* Æneid, xii. 168).

magna est veritas, et prævalet (L.), great is truth, and it prevails (*Vulgate,* 3 Esdras, iv. 41).

magna est vis consuetudinis (L.), great is the power of habit.

magna servitus est magna fortuna (L.), a great fortune is a great slavery (*Seneca,* Ad Polybium de Consolatione, 26).

magnas inter opes inops (L.), poor amid great riches (*Horace,* Odes, iii. 16).

magna vis est conscientiæ (L.), great is the power of conscience.

magni Dei datum (L.), a gift of the great God.

magnifique (F.), magnificent: see *c'est magnifique* (etc.).

magni nominis umbra (L.), the shadow of a great name: see *stat magni nominis umbra.*

magnopere curandum est ut id teneatur quod ubique, quod semper, quod ab omnibus creditum est (L.), particularly must care be taken to maintain that which everywhere, always, and by all has been believed (principle of faith enunciated by St. Vincent of Lérins).

magnum bonum (L.), a great good.

magnum opus (L.), a great work; one's chief work.

magnum vectigal est parsimonia (L.), economy is a great revenue.

magnus ab integro sæclorum nascitur ordo (L.), the great cycle of ages begins anew (*Virgil,* Eclogues, iv. 5).

magnus Alexander corpore parvus erat (L.), great Alexander was small of body.

magnus Apollo (L.), great Apollo.

main de justice (F.), the hand of justice.

mains froides, cœur chaud (F.), cold hands, warm heart.

maintiens le droit (F.), maintain the right.

maison (F.), house; building; household; family; business house or firm.

maison d'arrêt (F.), house of arrest; a jail.

maison de campagne (F.), a country house or residence.

maison de jeu (F.), house of play; a gambling-house.

maison de retraite (F.), house of retreat; a home for the aged or infirm.

maison de santé (F.), house of health; a private hospital for the sick or insane.

maison de tolérance (F.), a licensed house of prostitution.

maison de ville (F.), a town house or residence; a town hall.

maison garnie (or **meublée**) (F.), a furnished house; a house having furnished rooms or apartments for rent.

maître (F.), master; head or chief; teacher.

maître d'armes (F.), a fencing-master.

maître d'école (F.), a schoolmaster.

maître des hautes œuvres (F.), master of the high works; an executioner.

maître d'hôtel (F.), house master (or manager); a steward; a butler; a hotel landlord.

maître d'œuvre (F.), master of work; a foreman.

maître Jacques (F.), a man (servant) of all work (from Master Jacques, a character in Molière's comedy "L'Avare," who was both coachman and cook).

maîtresse (F., fem.), mistress; female head; female teacher; lady-love; female paramour: cf. *maître.*

maîtresse d'école (F.), a schoolmistress.

maîtresse femme (F.), a capable or superior woman.

major e longinquo reverentia (L.), greater reverence from afar.

majores pinnas nido extendisse (L.), to have spread wings greater than the nest (or aspired above the paternal condition) (*Horace*, Epistles, i. 20).

majori cedo (L.), I yield to a superior.

mal (F.), bad; badly or ill; an ill or evil; pain; sickness; disease.

malade (F.), sick; a sick person.

malade imaginaire (F.), an imaginary (or fancied) invalid: see *Le Malade Imaginaire*.

maladresse (F.), awkwardness; clumsiness; an awkward performance.

mala fide (L.), in bad faith; with or by fraud.

mala fides (L.), bad faith.

mala mens, malus animus (L.), bad mind, bad heart (*Terence*, Andria, i. 1).

malam rem cum velis honestare, improbes (L.), when you wish to dignify a bad thing, censure it (*Publilius Syrus*).

mal à propos (F.), inappropriately; inopportunely.

mal aux (or **de**) **dents** (F.), toothache.

mal de mer (F.), seasickness.

mal de tête (F.), headache.

mal du pays (F.), homesickness.

male narrando fabula depravatur (L.), by bad narrating a story is spoiled.

mal entendu (F.), ill-advised; mistaken.

malentendu (F.), a misunderstanding; a misapprehension.

male parta male dilabuntur (L.), things ill gained are ill lost; ill come, ill go.

malesuada Fames (L.), ill-counseling Hunger (*Virgil*, Æneid, vi. 276).

malgré lui et ses dents (F.), in spite of him and his teeth; despite his opposition.

malgré nous (F.), in spite of us.

malgré soi (F.), in spite of himself.

malgré tout (F.), in spite of all.

malheur (F.), ill fortune; bad luck; a misfortune.

malheureusement (F.), unfortunately; unluckily.

malheureux, fem. **malheureuse** (F.), unfortunate; unlucky; unhappy; miserable.

mali principii malus finis (L.), from a bad beginning a bad ending.

malis avibus (L.), with bad birds or omens; under unfavorable auspices.

malo modo (L.), in a bad manner.

malum in se (L.), a thing bad or wrong in itself.

malum prohibitum (L.), a thing prohibited as wrong.

malum quia prohibitum (L.), a thing wrong because prohibited.

malum vas non frangitur (L.), a worthless vessel is not broken.

malus animus (L.), evil intent.

malus pudor (L.), false shame; false modesty.

malus usus est abolendus (L.), a bad custom should be abolished.

m'amie (F., fem.), my friend; my dear; my love: see *mon ami*.

mañana (Sp.), to-morrow. See Dictionary.

mandamus (L.), we command. See Dictionary.

mania a potu (L.), madness from drinking; delirium tremens.

manibus pedibusque (L.), with hands and feet; with all one's might.

maniéré, fem. **maniérée** (F.), having mannerisms; affected.

manière de parler (F.), manner of speaking; mode or turn of expression.

manière d'être (F.), manner of being; condition; state.

manière de voir (F.), manner of seeing; view; opinion.

man spricht Deutsch (G.), German is spoken (here).

manu forti (L.), with a strong hand.

manu militari (L.), by the military hand; by armed force.

manu propria (L.), with one's own hand.

manus e nubibus (L.), a hand from the clouds.

marchandise qui plaît est à demi vendue (F.), merchandise which pleases is half sold.

marche funèbre (F.), a funeral march; a dead-march.

Märchen (G.), a folk-tale; a legend or fairy story.

mardi gras (F.), Shrove Tuesday, the last day of carnival.

mare altum (L.), the deep sea; the high seas.

mare apertum (L.), the open sea; the high seas.

mare clausum (L.), a closed sea (within the jurisdiction of a particular nation).

mare liberum (L.), the free or open sea.

mare magnum (L.), the great sea; the ocean.

mare nostrum (L.), our sea (to the Romans, the Mediterranean: cf. *Cæsar*, De Bello Gallico, v. 1).

margaritas ante porcos (L.), pearls before swine (see *Vulgate*, Mat. vii. 6).

mariage de convenance (F.), a marriage of convenience or expediency.

mariage de la main gauche (F.), a left-handed or morganatic marriage.

marmite (F.), a pot (for cooking, etc.); a large explosive shell or bomb.

marraine (F.), a godmother; a woman who befriends a particular soldier at the front by letters, presents, etc.: see *filleul*.

mater (L.), mother.

Mater dolorosa (L.), the sorrowful Mother; the mother of Christ sorrowing for her son (often as represented in art).

materfamilias (L.), mother of a family.

materia medica (L.), medical material; substances used as medicine; the branch of medical science concerned with these substances.

matériel (F.), material; the material apparatus or appliances of any work or undertaking: cf. *personnel*.

materiem superabat opus (L.), the workmanship surpassed the material (*Ovid*, Metamorphoses, ii. 5).

matre pulchra filia pulchrior (L.), daughter more beautiful than a beautiful mother: see *O matre pulchra filia pulchrior*.

maudit, fem. **maudite** (F.), cursed; detestable.

mauvais, fem. **mauvaise** (F.), bad; evil; wrong; unpleasant.

mauvaise honte (F.), undue shame or modesty; bashfulness.

mauvaise langue (F.), an evil tongue; a malicious or slanderous talker.

mauvaise tête (F.), a wrong head; a wrong-headed person.

mauvais goût (F.), bad taste.

mauvais pas (F.), bad walking; dangerous ground; a bad situation.

mauvais quart d'heure (F.), a bad quarter of an hour; a brief but unpleasant time or experience.

mauvais sang (F.), bad blood; ill feeling.

mauvais sujet (F.), a bad subject; a worthless fellow.

mauvais ton (F.), bad tone; bad form, style, or breeding.

maxima debetur puero reverentia (L.), the greatest reverence is due to a boy; the greatest regard should be shown for boyish innocence (*Juvenal*, Satires, xiv. 47).

maximum remedium iræ mora est (L.), the greatest remedy for anger is delay (*Seneca*, De Ira, ii. 29).

maximus in minimis (L.), very great in very small things.

maximus novator tempus (L.), time is the greatest innovator.

mea culpa (L.), by my fault.

mea maxima culpa (L.), by my very great fault.

mea virtute me involvo (L.), I wrap myself in my virtue (*Horace*, Odes, iii. 29).

méchant, fem. **méchante** (F.), malicious; mischievous; naughty; bad.

mecum facile redeo in gratiam (L.), I easily become reconciled with myself (*Phædrus*, Fables, v. 3).

medice, cura teipsum (L.), physician, heal thyself (*Vulgate*, Luke, iv. 23).

medicus curat, natura sanat (L.), the physician heals, nature makes well.

mediocria firma (L.), mediocre things are sure.

medio tutissimus ibis (L.), in the middle course thou shalt go safest (*Ovid*, Metamorphoses, ii. 137).

medium tenuere beati (L.), the happy have kept a middle course.

mega biblion, mega kakon (Gr. μέγα βιβλίον, μέγα κακόν), a great (big) book, a great evil.

mehr Licht (G.), more light (from Goethe's last words, asking for more light in the room).

me judice (L.), I being judge; in my opinion.

mélange (F.), a mixture; a medley.

melioribus annis (L.), in happier years (*Virgil*, Æneid, vi. 649).

memento mori (L.), remember to die (that thou must die); a reminder of death. See Dictionary.

mémoire (F.), memory; a memoir; a record; an account.

memorabile nomen (L.), a memorable name.

memorabilia (L.), things worthy to be remembered.

memor et fidelis (L.), mindful and faithful.

memoriæ sacrum (L.), sacred to the memory of.

memoria in æterna (L.), in eternal remembrance.

ménage (F.), housekeeping; a household; a domestic establishment.

ménage de garçon (F.), a bachelor's establishment.

mendacem memorem esse oportet (L.), it behooves a liar to have a good memory.

mens æqua in arduis (L.), an even

mind in adverse circumstances: cf. *æquam memento* (etc.).

mens agitat molem (L.), a mind moves (or animates) the mass (*Virgil*, Æneid, vi. 727).

mens divinior (L.), the more divine mind; the mind exalted by inspiration (*Horace*, Satires, i. 4).

mens et manus (L.), mind and hand (motto of Massachusetts Institute of Technology).

mens legis (L.), the mind, or intent, of the law.

mens, qua nihil est celerius (L.), the mind, than which nothing is swifter (*Cicero*, Orator, lix. 200).

mens regnum bona possidet (L.), a good mind possesses a kingdom (*Seneca*, Thyestes, ii. 380).

mens sana in corpore sano (L.), a sound mind in a sound body (*Juvenal*, Satires, x. 356).

mens sibi conscia recti (L.), a mind conscious within itself of rectitude (*Virgil*, Æneid, i. 604).

mentiri splendide (L.), to lie magnificently: cf. *splendide mendax.*

menus plaisirs (F.), little pleasures; incidental expenditures for personal pleasure.

meo periculo (L.), at my own risk.

meo voto (L.), by my wish.

merci (F.), mercy; favor; will or discretion; thanks.

mer de glace (F.), sea of ice; a glacier with a surface rough as with waves.

mère (F.), mother.

mère de famille (F.), mother of a family.

merum sal (L.), pure salt; genuine wit.

metri gratia (L.), for the sake of the meter or verse.

metron ariston (Gr.): see *ariston metron.*

meum et tuum (L.), mine and thine.

mi-carême (F.), Mid-Lent.

mignon, fem. **mignonne** (F.), small and pretty; delicately pretty; dearly loved; a darling or favorite.

miles gloriosus (L.), boastful soldier (used by Plautus as the title of a comedy).

milieu (F.), the middle; a mean or medium; environment.

minauderie (F.), affected expression of face; simper.

minima de malis (L.), of evils (choose) the least.

mirabile dictu (L.), wonderful to relate.

mirabile visu (L.), wonderful to see.

mirabilia (L.), wonderful things; wonders; miracles.

mirum in modum (L.), in a wonderful manner; astonishingly.

mise en scène (F.), stage setting, as of a play; the surroundings amid which anything is seen.

miserabile vulgus (L.), wretched crowd; rabble.

Misérables (F.): see *Les Misérables.*

miseris succurrere disco (L.), I learn to help the wretched (*Virgil*, Æneid, i. 630).

mitis sapientia (L.), ripe wisdom.

mitte hanc de pectore curam (L.), dismiss this care from thy breast (*Virgil*, Æneid, vi. 85).

mobile perpetuum (L.), something perpetually in motion.

mobile vulgus (L.), the movable or easily moved common people; the excitable or changeable multitude.

mobilia sequuntur personam (L.), movables follow the person (are governed by the law of his domicile).

modo et forma (L.), in manner and form.

modo præscripto (L.), in the manner prescribed.

modus (L.), measure; due measure; manner; mode.

modus faciendi (L.), manner of doing.

modus omnibus in rebus (L.), due measure, or moderation, in all things.

modus operandi (L.), manner or mode of operation.

modus vivendi (L.), mode of living, or getting along; a temporary arrangement between persons or parties pending a settlement of differences.

mole ruit sua (L.), it falls by its own weight: see *vis consili expers mole ruit sua.*

mollissima fandi tempora (L.), times most favorable for speaking (*Virgil*, Æneid, iv. 293).

molliter ossa cubent (L.), may his bones rest undisturbed (*Ovid*, Heroides, vii. 162).

mon ami, fem. **mon amie** or **m'amie** (F.), my friend: see *m'amie.*

mon cher, fem. **ma chère** (F.), my dear.

monde (F.), world; mankind; people; society.

monde savant (F.), the learned world.

mon Dieu (F.), my God (much used by the French as a mild interjection).

monstrum horrendum, informe, ingens (L.), a monster horrible, misshapen, huge (*Virgil*, Æneid, iii. 658).

mont (F.), mount; mountain.

montani semper liberi (L.), mountaineers are always freemen (motto of West Virginia).

mont-de-piété (F.), **monte de piedad** (Sp.), **monte di pietà** (It.), a public pawnbroking establishment.

montes auri pollicens (L.), promising mountains of gold (*Terence*, Phormio, i. 2).

monumentum ære perennius (L.), a monument more enduring than bronze: see *exegi monumentum* (etc.).

mon vieux (F.), my old one; old fellow (used in familiar address).

morceau (F.), bit; piece; morsel; a piece of music, literature, sculpture, etc.

morceau de roi (F.), king's morsel; a dainty bit.

morceau honteux (F.), shameful morsel; the last piece on a dish at table, which is left for good manners.

more Hibernico (L.), in the Irish manner.

more majorum (L.), in the manner of one's ancestors.

more philosophico (L.), in the philosophic manner.

more probato (L.), in the approved manner.

more suo (L.), in one's own manner or way.

morituri te salutamus (L.), we who are about to die salute thee: see *ave, imperator! morituri te salutant.*

mors janua vitæ (L.), death is the gate of life.

mors omnia solvit (L.), death dissolves all things.

mors omnibus communis (L.), death is common to all.

mors ultima ratio (L.), death is the final argument.

mortis causa (L.), because of, or in prospect of, death.

morts (F.), (the) dead: see *il n'y a que les morts* (etc.).

mortuo leoni et lepores insultant (L.), even hares insult a dead lion.

mos pro lege (L.), custom for law.

mot (F.), word; expression; saying; motto; witticism.

mot à mot (F.), word by word.

mot de l'énigme (F.), the word of the enigma; the key to a puzzle or mystery.

mot d'ordre (F.), a watchword.

motos præstat componere fluctus (L.), it is better to quiet the troubled waters (*Virgil*, Æneid, i. 135).

mot pour mot (F.), word for word.

motu proprio (L.), of one's own motion or accord.

moyen âge (F.), the middle ages.

mucho en el suelo, poco en el cielo (Sp.), much on earth, little in heaven.

muet comme un poisson (F.), mute as a fish.

multa docet fames (L.), hunger teaches many things.

multa fidem promissa levant (L.), many promises lessen confidence (*Horace*, Epistles, ii. 2).

multa gemens (L.), groaning much (*Virgil*, Æneid, i. 465).

multa paucis (L.), much in few words.

multis ictibus dejicitur quercus (L.), by many blows the oak is felled.

multum in parvo (L.), much in little.

multum non multa (L.), much, not many things.

mundus vult decipi (L.), the world wishes to be deceived.

munus Apolline dignum (L.), a gift worthy of Apollo (*Horace*, Epistles, ii. 1).

mus non uni fidit antro (L.), a mouse does not trust to one hole.

mutatis mutandis (L.), the necessary changes being made.

mutato nomine (L.), with the name changed.

mutato nomine de te fabula narratur (L.), with the name changed, of thyself is the story told (*Horace*, Satires, i. 1).

mutum est pictura poema (L.), a picture is a silent poem.

mutuus consensus (L.), mutual consent.

N

Napoli (It.): see *vedi Napoli, e poi muori.*

nasci miserum, vivere pœna, angustia mori (L.), to be born is misery, to live suffering, to die anguish (*St. Bernard*).

nascimur poetæ, fimus oratores (L.), we are born poets, we are made orators.

natale solum (L.), natal soil; one's native country.

nati natorum, et qui nascentur ab illis (L.), children's children, and those descended from them (*Virgil*, Æneid, iii. 98).

natura abhorret a vacuo (L.), nature abhors a vacuum.

naturam expellas furca, tamen us-

que recurret (L.), you may drive out nature with a pitchfork, yet will she always return (*Horace*, Epistles, i. 10).

natura non facit saltum (L.), nature makes no leap (or break in procedure).

naufragium in portu facere (L.), to make shipwreck in port; fail on the verge of success.

naufragium sibi quisque facit (L.), each man makes his own shipwreck (*Lucan*, Pharsalia, i. 499).

ne Æsopum quidem trivit (L.), he has not even thumbed the pages of Æsop.

nec bella nec puella (L.), neither beautiful nor a girl.

nec cupias nec metuas (L.), have neither desire nor fear.

nec deus intersit nisi dignus vindice nodus inciderit (L.), nor let a god intervene unless a difficulty shall occur that is worthy of the deliverer (*Horace*, Ars Poetica, 191).

ne cede malis (L.), yield not to misfortunes: see *tu ne cede malis*.

necesse est ut multos timeat quem multi timent (L.), he whom many fear must needs fear many (*Publilius Syrus*).

necessitas non habet legem (L.), necessity has no law.

necessitas publica major est quam privata (L.), public necessity is greater than private (necessity).

nec habeo, nec careo, nec curo (L.), I have not, I want not, I care not.

nec mora nec requies (L.), neither delay nor rest (*Virgil*, Georgics, iii. 110).

nec pluribus impar (L.), not unequal to many (motto of Louis XIV.).

nec prece nec pretio (L.), neither by entreaty nor by bribe.

nec quærere nec spernere honorem (L.), neither to seek nor to spurn honor.

ne credas laudatoribus tuis (L.), believe not those who praise thee.

nec scire fas est omnia (L.), nor is it permitted to know all things (*Horace*, Odes, iv. 4).

nec tecum possum vivere nec sine te (L.), I can neither live with thee nor without thee (*Martial*, Epigrams, xii. 47).

nec temere nec timide (L.), neither rashly nor timidly.

ne exeat (L.), let him not depart (applied in law to a writ forbidding a person to leave the country or the jurisdiction of a court).

ne exeat regno (L.), let him not leave the country.

nefasti dies (L.): see *dies nefasti*.

ne fronti crede (L.), trust not to the appearance.

nein (G.), no.

ne Jupiter quidem omnibus placet (L.), not even Jupiter pleases all.

nemine contradicente (L.), no one contradicting; unanimously.

nemine dissentiente (L.), no one dissenting; unanimously.

nemo bis punitur pro eodem delicto (L.), no one is punished twice for the same offense.

nemo dat quod non habet (L.), no one gives what he does not have.

nemo est heres viventis (L.), no one is heir of a living person.

nemo me impune lacessit (L.), no one attacks me with impunity (motto of Scotland).

nemo repente fuit turpissimus (L.), no one ever became thoroughly base all at once (*Juvenal*, Satires, ii. 83).

nemo solus satis sapit (L.), no one is wise enough alone (*Plautus*, Miles Gloriosus, iii. 3).

nemo tenetur se ipsum accusare (L.), no one is bound to accuse himself.

ne nimium (L.), not too much.

ne plus ultra (L.), no more beyond; no further (used in prohibiting); the uttermost or highest point; the acme.

ne prius antidotum quam venenum (L.), (take) not the antidote before the poison.

ne puero gladium (L.), (give) not a sword to a boy.

ne quid detrimenti respublica capiat (L.), that the republic sustain no injury.

ne quid nimis (L.), nothing to excess.

nervos belli, pecuniam infinitam (L.), the sinews of war, unlimited money (*Cicero*, 5 Philippic, ii. 5).

nervus probandi (L.), the sinew of proof; the chief argument.

nescis, mi fili, quantilla prudentia homines regantur (L.), you do not know, my son, with how little wisdom men are governed (*Oxenstjerna*).

nescis quid serus vesper ferat (L.), you know not what the night may bring.

nescit plebs jejuna timere (L.), a hungry populace knows no fear.

nessun maggior dolore che ricordarsi del tempo felice nella miseria (It.), there is no greater anguish than in misery to remember the happy time (*Dante*, Inferno, v. 121).

n'est-ce pas? (F.), isn't that so?

ne sutor ultra crepidam (L.), let not the cobbler go beyond his last: cf. *sutor ne supra crepidam judicaret*.

ne tentes, aut perfice (L.), attempt not, or finish.

nez retroussé (F.), a turned-up nose.

nicht wahr? (G.), not true? isn't it so?

nihil ad rem (L.), nothing to the point or purpose.

nihil innovetur nisi quod traditum est (L.), let nothing be introduced (as an innovation) except what has been handed down.

nihil præferendum honestati (L.), nothing is to be put before honor (*St. Ambrose*).

nihil quod tetigit non ornavit (L.): see *nullum quod tetigit non ornavit*.

nihil sub sole novum (L.), nothing new under the sun (*Vulgate*, Eccl. i. 10).

nil admirari (L.), to wonder at, or be moved by, nothing (*Horace*, Epistles, i. 6).

nil agit exemplum litem quod lite resolvit (L.), an example accomplishes nothing which settles dispute by dispute (disposes of one difficulty by bringing in another: *Horace*, Satires, ii. 3).

nil conscire sibi (L.), to be conscious of nothing wrong (*Horace*, Epistles, i. 1).

nil debet (L.), he owes nothing.

nil desperandum (L.), nothing is to be despaired of; never despair.

nil dicit (L.), he says nothing; he makes no reply.

nil nisi bonum (L.), nothing but good: see *de mortuis nil nisi bonum*.

nil nisi cruce (L.), nothing except by the cross.

nil sine numine (L.), nothing without the divine will (motto of Colorado).

nil sole et sale utilius (L.), nothing is more useful than sun and salt.

nil temere uxori de servis crede querenti (L.), do not rashly believe a wife complaining of her servants.

nil ultra (L.), nothing beyond.

ni l'un ni l'autre (F.), neither the one nor the other.

nimis poeta (L.), too much a poet.

nimium ne crede colori (L.), trust not too much to fairness of complexion (or face: *Virgil*, Eclogues, ii. 17).

n'importe (F.), it does not matter; no matter.

nisi (L.), if not; unless.

nisi Dominus frustra (L.), except the Lord (keep the city, the watchman waketh but) in vain (motto of Edinburgh: *Vulgate*, Ps. cxxvi. 1).

nisi prius (L.), unless before (in law, now applied to trials of fact by a jury and one judge).

nitor in adversum (L.), I strive against opposition (*Ovid*, Metamorphoses, ii. 72).

nobis judicibus (L.), ourselves being judges; in our opinion.

noblesse oblige (F.), nobility obliges; rank imposes obligations, as of honorable conduct, magnanimity, courtesy, etc.

Noël (F.), Christmas; [*l. c.*] a Christmas carol.

nolens volens (L.), unwilling or willing.

noli irritare leones (L.), do not irritate lions.

noli me tangere (L.), touch me not (*Vulgate*, John, xx. 17).

nolle prosequi (L.), to be unwilling, or not to wish, to prosecute (in law). See Dictionary.

nolo contendere (L.), I do not wish to contend (in law, a defendant's plea accepting conviction but not admitting guilt).

nolo episcopari (L.), I do not wish to be made a bishop.

nom (F.), etc. See Dictionary.

nom de théâtre (F.), a theater name or stage name (as of an actor or actress).

nomen atque omen (L.), a name and also an omen (*Plautus*, Persa, iv. 4).

nomina stultorum parietibus hærent (L.), fools' names stick to the walls (of buildings).

nominatim (L.), by name; expressly.

nominis umbra (L.), the shadow of a name: see *stat magni nominis umbra*.

nom social (F.), the name of a business firm.

non (F.), no; not.

non Angli sed angeli (L.), not Angles but angels (reputed words of Gregory the Great on seeing some English captives in Rome).

non assumpsit (L.), he did not undertake (as pleaded by the defendant in a form of action at law: see *assumpsit*).

non auriga piger (L.), no lazy charioteer.

non compos mentis (L.), not of sound mind. See Dictionary.

non constat (L.), it does not appear; it is not evident.

non cuivis homini contingit adire Corinthum (L.), it does not fall to every man's lot to go to Corinth (*Horace*, Epistles, i. 17).

non culpabilis (L.), not guilty.

non datur tertium (L.), no third (choice) is given.

non decet (L.), it is not fitting.

non deficiente crumena (L.), while the purse does not fail.

nondum omnium dierum sol occidit (L.), not yet has the sun of all days set.

non equidem invideo; miror magis (L.), truly I do not envy; I rather wonder (*Virgil*, Eclogues, i. 11).

non est (L.), he (or it) is not (there): cf. *non est inventus*.

non est fumus absque igne (L.), there is no smoke without fire.

non est inventus (L.), he has not been found.

non est tanti (L.), it is not of such great importance.

non est vivere sed valere vita est (L.), life is not being alive but being well (*Martial*, Epigrams, vi. 70).

non ex quovis ligno Mercurius fit (L.), not out of every kind of wood is a Mercury made.

non in dialectica complacuit Deo salvum facere populum suum (L.), not in dialectic has it pleased God to place his people's salvation (*St. Ambrose*).

non libet (L.), it does not please.

non licet (L.), it is not permitted.

non licet omnibus adire Corinthum (L.), it is not permitted to all to go to Corinth: cf. *non cuivis homini contingit adire Corinthum*.

non liquet (L.), it is not clear; it does not appear (in Roman law, a judicial formula expressing uncertainty as to the guilt or innocence of the accused).

non ministrari, sed ministrare (L.), not to be ministered unto, but to minister (motto of Wellesley College: *Vulgate*, Mat. xx. 28).

non mi ricordo (It.), I do not remember.

non multa sed multum (L.), not many things but much.

non nobis, Domine (L.), not unto us, Lord (*Vulgate*, Ps. cxiii.).

non nobis solum (L.), not for ourselves only.

non nova sed nove (L.), not new things but in a new way.

non obstante (L.), notwithstanding.

non olet pecunia (L.), money has no smell, or bad odor (no matter whence it comes).

non omnia possumus omnes (L.), we cannot all do all things (*Virgil*, Eclogues, viii. 63).

non omnis moriar (L.), I shall not wholly die (*Horace*, Odes, iii. 30).

non passibus æquis (L.), with steps not equal (*Virgil*, Æneid, ii. 724).

non placet (L.), it does not please (used as an expression or vote of dissent: cf. *placet*).

non possumus (L.), we cannot.

non progredi est regredi (L.), not to go forward is to go backward.

non prosequitur (L.), he does not prosecute (in law).

non quis sed quid (L.), not who but what.

non quo sed quomodo (L.), not by whom but how.

non sans droict (OF.), not without

right (motto on Shakspere's coat of arms).

non scribit cujus carmina nemo legit (L.), he is no writer whose verses no one reads (*Martial*, Epigrams, iii. 9).

non semper Saturnalia erunt (L.), the Saturnalia will not last forever; every day cannot be a holiday (*Seneca*, Apocolocyntosis, 12).

non sequitur (L.), it does not follow.

non sibi sed omnibus (L.), not for self but for all.

non sibi sed patriæ (L.), not for self but for country.

non sum qualis eram (L.), I am not what I was (*Horace*, Odes, iv. 1).

non tali auxilio nec defensoribus istis tempus eget (L.), not for such aid or for those defenders does the occasion call (*Virgil*, Æneid, ii. 521).

nonumque prematur in annum (L.), and let it (a writing) be kept back until the ninth year (*Horace*, Ars Poetica, 388).

non vult contendere (L.), he does not wish to contend: see *nolo contendere*.

nos amis les ennemis (F.), our friends the enemy (applied ironically by the French to the allied powers that invaded France 1814–15 and restored the Bourbons to the throne).

nosce te ipsum (L.), know thyself.

nosce tempus (L.), know thy time.

noscitur a (or **ex**) **sociis** (L.), he is known by his companions; it (a word or expression) is understood from the context.

nos poma natamus (L.), (how) we apples swim!

nostro periculo (L.), at our own risk.

nota bene (L.), note well; take notice.

notabilia (L.), things worthy of note.

notanda (L.), things to be noted.

notatu dignum (L.), worthy of note.

Not kennt kein Gebot (G.), necessity knows no law.

Notre-Dame (F.), Our Lady, the Virgin Mary (used in the names of many churches, religious institutions and orders, towns, etc.).

Notre-Seigneur (F.), Our Lord; Jesus Christ.

n'oubliez pas (F.), do not forget.

nous avons changé tout cela (F.), we have changed all that (*Molière*, Le Médecin malgré Lui, ii. 6).

nous dansons sur un volcan (F.), we are dancing on a volcano (said at a ball in Paris just before the revolution of 1830).

nous verrons (F.), we shall see.

nous verrons ce que nous verrons (F.), we shall see what we shall see.

nouveau, fem. **nouvelle** (F.), new.

nouveau riche, pl. *nouveaux riches* (F.), one newly rich; a wealthy parvenu.

nouveauté (F.), novelty; newness; a novelty.

nouveaux mariés (F.), newly married persons.

nouvelle, pl. *nouvelles* (F.), news; a tale; a novelette.

novissima verba (L.), last words.

novus homo (L.), a new man; an upstart or parvenu.

nudis oculis (L.), with the naked eyes; without a telescope.

nudis verbis (L.), in plain words.

nudum pactum (L.), a nude pact; a

contract made without a consideration (in law).

nugæ canoræ (L.), melodious trifles; mere jingles (*Horace*, Ars Poetica, 322).

nuit blanche (F.), a sleepless night.

nulla dies sine linea (L.), no day without a line (orig. referring to the example of the painter Apelles, who let no day pass without practising).

nulla nuova, buona nuova (It.), no news, good news.

nulla regula sine exceptione (L.), no rule without an exception.

nulla vestigia retrorsum (L.): see *vestigia nulla retrorsum*.

nulli secundus (L.), second to none.

nullius addictus jurare in verba magistri (L.), not bound to swear to the words of any master (*Horace*, Epistles, i. 1).

nullius filius (L.): see *filius nullius*.

nullum magnum malum quod extremum est (L.), no evil is great which is the last.

nullum quod tetigit non ornavit (L.), there is nothing that he touched that he did not adorn (from Dr. Johnson's epitaph on Goldsmith).

nunc aut nunquam (L.), now or never.

nunc dimittis servum tuum, Domine, in pace (L.), Lord, now lettest thou thy servant depart in peace (*Vulgate*, Luke, ii. 29).

nunc est bibendum (L.), now is it time to drink (*Horace*, Odes, i. 37).

nunc pro tunc (L.), now for (instead of) then.

nunc vino pellite curas (L.), now banish cares with wine (*Horace*, Odes, i. 7).

nunquam non paratus (L.), never unprepared.

nymphe du pavé (F.), a nymph of the pavement; a girl or woman of the streets.

O

obiit (L.), he (or she) died (as at a time specified).

obiit sine prole (L.), he (or she) died without issue.

obiter dictum, pl. *obiter dicta* (L.), something said by the way, or in passing; an incidental opinion given by a judge, in distinction from his judicial decision on the essential point.

objet d'art (F.), an object of art.

obscurum per obscurius (L.), the obscure by the more obscure: cf. *ignotum per ignotius*.

observanda (L.), things to be observed.

obsta principiis (L.): see *principiis obsta*.

obstupui, steteruntque comæ (L.), I was stupefied, and my hair stood on end (*Virgil*, Æneid, ii. 774).

ob turpem causam (L.), for a base, immoral, or illegal cause.

ob vitæ solatium (L.), for the solace of life; for comfort or pleasure.

oderint dum metuant (L.), let them hate, so long as they fear.

odi memorem compotorem (L.), I hate a drinking companion with a memory.

odi profanum vulgus (L.), I hate the profane (uninitiated, or Philistine) multitude (*Horace*, Odes, iii. 1).

odium medicum (L.), medical hatred; mutual hatred among physicians.

odium theologicum (L.), theological

hatred; mutual hatred among theologians.

œil-de-bœuf (F.), a bull's-eye; a round or oval window.

œuvre, pl. *œuvres* (F.), work.

O felix culpa, quæ talem ac tantum meruit habere Redemptorem! (L.), O happy fault, that was worthy to have so great a Redeemer! (words of St. Augustine, incorporated in an ancient hymn).

officina gentium (L.), the workshop of nations (in which the nations or peoples of the world are made).

ohe! jam satis est (L.), ho there! there is enough now (*Horace*, Satires, i. 5).

ohne Hast, ohne Rast (G.), without haste, without rest (motto of Goethe).

ohne Kaiser kein Reich (G.), without emperor no state (*Bismarck*).

oleo tranquillior (L.), smoother than oil.

olet lucernam (L.), it smells of the lamp: see *redolet lucernam*.

ollæ amicitia (L.), friendship of the pot; cupboard love.

olla male fervet (L.), the pot boils badly; the affair goes ill.

O matre pulchra filia pulchrior (L.), O daughter more beautiful than a beautiful mother (*Horace*, Odes, i. 16).

omen faustum (L.), a favorable omen.

omne bonum desuper (L.), every good thing is from above.

omne ignotum pro magnifico est (L.), everything unknown is thought magnificent (*Tacitus*, Agricola, 30).

omne majus continet in se minus (L.), everything greater contains in itself the less.

omnem movere lapidem (L.), to move every stone, or leave no stone unturned.

omnes honores bonis! (L.), all honors to the good!

omne solum forti patria est (L.), every land to a brave man is his country (*Ovid*, Fasti, i. 493).

omne tulit punctum qui miscuit utile dulci (L.), he has won universal approval who has combined the useful with the agreeable (*Horace*, Ars Poetica, 343).

omne vivum ex ovo (L.), every living thing comes from an egg (adapted from William Harvey).

omnia ad Dei gloriam (L.), all things to the glory of God.

omnia bona bonis (L.), to the good all things are good.

omnia mutantur, nos et mutamur in illis (L.), all things change, and we change with them (attributed to the emperor Lothair I).

omnia reliquit servare rempublicam (L.), he left all to serve the republic (motto on the badge of the U. S. Society of the Cincinnati).

omnia vincit amor (L.), love conquers all things: see next entry.

omnia vincit amor, et nos cedamus amori (L.), love conquers all things, and let us too yield to love (*Virgil*, Eclogues, x. 69).

omnia vincit labor (L.), labor conquers all things.

omnibus hoc vitium est (L.), this fault exists in all (see *Horace*, Satires, i. 3).

omnis ratihabitio retrotrahitur et

mandato priori æquiparatur (L.), every ratification retroacts and is equivalent to a prior command.

on connaît le véritable ami dans le besoin (F.), one knows the true friend in time of need.

on dit (F.), one says; they say; a rumor or report.

on ne fait rien pour rien (F.), one does nothing for nothing.

on ne peut pas sonner et aller à procession (F.), one cannot both ring the bells and go in the procession.

on parle français (F.), French is spoken (here).

on revient toujours à ses premières amours (F.), one returns always to his first loves.

onus probandi (L.), the burden of proving.

ope et consilio (L.), with assistance and counsel.

operæ pretium est (L.), there is recompense for the work; it is worth while.

opera omnia (L.), all the works.

opere citato (L.), in the work cited.

opere in medio (L.), in the midst of work.

opes regum corda subditorum (L.), the riches of kings are the hearts of their subjects.

opposuit natura Alpemque nivemque (L.), nature opposed (to Hannibal) both Alp and snow (*Juvenal*, Satires, x. 152).

opprobrium medicorum (L.), the reproach of physicians (applied to a disease for which physicians have failed to find a remedy).

optima interpres legum consuetudo (L.), custom is the best interpreter of laws.

optimum obsonium labor (L.), labor is the best relish.

optimus interpres rerum usus (L.), usage is the best interpreter of things.

opum furiosa cupido (L.), mad desire for wealth (*Ovid*, Fasti, i. 211).

opus (L.), a work; a production or composition.

opus opificem probat (L.), the work proves the workman.

ora e sempre (It.), now and always.

ora et labora (L.), pray and labor.

ora pro nobis (L.), pray for us (used in litanies).

orator fit, poeta nascitur (L.), the orator is made, the poet is born.

orbis scientiarum (L.), the circle of the sciences.

orbis terrarum (L.), the circle of the earth; the earth or world.

ordem e progresso (Pg.), order and progress (motto of Brazil).

ore rotundo (L.), with well-rounded speech (*Horace*, Ars Poetica, 323).

ore tenus (L.), so far as the mouth; in talking only; by word of mouth.

origo mali (L.), the origin or source of evil.

oro y plata (Sp.), gold and silver (motto of Montana).

O sancta simplicitas! (L.), O sacred (or pious) simplicity! (reputed words of John Huss at the stake, on seeing an old woman bring a stick to cast into the flames).

os à ronger (F.), a bone to pick; something to keep one alive, or busy.

os durum (L.), a hard or brazen face.

O si sic omnia! (L.), oh, if all things were thus!

O tempora! O mores! (L.), oh the times! oh the manners! (*Cicero*, 1 Catiline, 1).

O terque quaterque beati! (L.), O thrice and four times happy! (*Virgil*, Æneid, i. 94).

otia dant vitia (L.), leisure gives vices.

otiosa sedulitas (L.), leisurely diligence.

otium cum dignitate (L.), leisure with dignity; dignified ease.

otium sine dignitate (L.), leisure without dignity; inglorious ease.

otium sine litteris mors est (L.), leisure without books is death (*Seneca*, Epistles, 82).

otium umbratile (L.), ease in retirement.

oublier je ne puis (F.), forget I cannot.

oui (F.), yes.

oui-dire (F.), hearsay.

où sont les neiges d'antan? (F.), "where are the snows of yester-year?" (*Villon*: so translated by D. G. Rossetti).

outre-mer (F.), beyond the sea.

ouvrage de longue haleine (F.), a work of long breath; a long-winded or lengthy performance.

ouvrier, fem. *ouvrière* (F.), a worker; a workman or workwoman; an operative.

oyer et terminer (AF.), to hear and determine; judicial hearing and determining.

P

pace (L.), by or with the leave of. See Dictionary.

pace tanti viri (L.), by the leave (or indulgence) of so great a man.

pace tua (L.), by your leave; with your indulgence.

pacte de famille (F.), a family compact or agreement.

pactum illicitum (L.), an unlawful agreement.

padrone (It.), patron; master. See Dictionary.

paix et peu (F.), peace and little; a peaceful life on a modest income.

pallida Mors (L.), pale Death (*Horace*, Odes, i. 4).

palmam qui meruit ferat (L.), let him bear away the palm who has deserved it.

palma non sine pulvere (L.), the palm not without dust; no prize or success without effort.

panem et circenses (L.), bread and circus-games; food and amusements (*Juvenal*, Satires, x. 81).

papillons noirs (F.), black butterflies; gloomy thoughts.

par accès (F.), by fits; by fits and starts.

par accident (F.), by accident.

par accord (F.), by agreement.

par avance (F.), in advance; by anticipation.

par bene comparatum (L.), a well-matched pair.

parcere subjectis et debellare superbos (L.), to spare the vanquished and put down the proud (*Virgil*, Æneid, vi. 853).

par-ci par-là (F.), here and there; now and then.

par complaisance (F.), out of complaisance.

par conséquent (F.), in consequence; consequently.

par dépit (F.), out of spite.

par éminence (F.), by eminence; preëminently.

parem non fert (L.), he brooks no equal.

par excellence (F.), by excellence or superiority; above all others; preëminently.

par exemple (F.), for example.

par force (F.), by force; perforce.

par hasard (F.), by chance.

pari passu (L.), at an equal pace or rate; in equal proportion.

pari ratione (L.), for a like reason; by like reasoning.

Paris vaut bien une messe (F.), Paris is well worth a mass (attributed to Henry IV. of France, on his conversion to Catholicism).

par le droit du plus fort (F.), by the right of the strongest.

parlez-vous français? (F.), do you speak French?

par manière d'acquit (F.), by way of acquitting one's self or getting rid of a task; in a perfunctory manner.

par negotiis, neque supra (L.), equal to his business, and not above it (*Tacitus*, Annales, vi. 39).

par nobile fratrum (L.), a noble pair of brothers (*Horace*, Satires, ii. 3).

parole d'honneur (F.), word of honor.

par oneri (L.), equal to the burden.

par parenthèse (F.), by way of parenthesis; incidentally.

par pari refero (L.), I return like for like.

pars adversa (L.), the opposite party.

pars magna (L.), a great part: see *quorum pars* (etc.).

pars pro toto (L.), a part for the whole.

parti (F.), part; party; match. See Dictionary.

particeps criminis (L.), a participant in the crime; an accomplice.

particulier (F.), a private person.

partie (F.), part; portion; party; a game or match.

partie carrée (F.), a square party; a party of four persons, usually two men and two women.

partim (L.), in part; partly.

parti pris (F.), a part taken; a decision or opinion formed in advance.

parturiunt montes, nascetur ridiculus mus (L.), the mountains are in labor, a ridiculous mouse will be born (*Horace*, Ars Poetica, 139).

parva componere magnis (L.), to compare small things with great: cf. *parvis componere magna*.

parva leves capiunt animas (L.), small things occupy light minds (*Ovid*, Ars Amatoria, i. 159).

parvis componere magna (L.), to compare great things with small (*Virgil*, Eclogues, i. 24).

pas (F.), step; pace; precedence. See Dictionary.

pas à pas (F.), step by step.

pas à pas on va bien loin (F.), step by step one goes very far.

pas de ballet (F.), a ballet step, figure, or dance.

pas de charge (F.), the charging pace (for troops in battle).

pas de clerc (F.), a clerk's (or novice's) step; a blunder.

pas de deux (or **trois**, or **quatre**) (F.), a dance for two (or three, or four) performers.

pas mal (F.), not bad or badly; good or well enough; a fair amount; a good deal.

pas seul (F.), a dance movement or dance for one performer.

passim (L.), here and there; in various places.

pater (L.), father.

paterfamilias (L.), father of a family.

pater noster (L.), our father (the first two words of the Lord's Prayer in Latin).

pater patriæ (L.), father of his country.

patience passe science (F.), patience surpasses science (the French phrase exhibiting a kind of word-play in the repetition of sounds).

patiens quia æternus (L.), patient because eternal (said of God: *St. Augustine*).

pâtisserie (F.), pastry; a pastry shop.

patres conscripti (L.), the conscript fathers; the senators of ancient Rome.

patria cara, carior libertas (L.), country is dear, but dearer is liberty.

patriis virtutibus (L.), by ancestral virtues.

patris est filius (L.), he is the son of his father (a chip of the old block).

pauca sed bona (L.), few things, but good.

pauca verba (L.), few words.

paucis verbis (L.), in few words.

paupertas omnium artium repertrix (L.), poverty is the inventor of all the arts.

pax Britannica (L.), the peace of Britain; the public peace of the realm of Britain.

pax ecclesiæ (or **Dei**) (L.), the peace of the church (or of God); peace as decreed by the medieval church, in 990 and later, for the protection of consecrated persons and places and of non-combatants generally.

pax in bello (L.), peace in war.

pax regis (L.), the king's peace.

pax Romana (L.), the Roman peace; the public peace throughout the domains of Rome.

pax vobiscum (L.), peace be with you.

pays (F.), country; region; district; native country.

paysage (F.), a landscape.

paysagiste (F.), a landscape-painter.

paysan, fem. **paysanne** (F.), a peasant.

pays latin (F.), the Latin Quarter of Paris.

peccavi (L.), I have sinned.

péché mignon (F.), a darling sin; a favorite peccadillo.

pede Pœna claudo (L.), Vengeance with halting foot: see *raro antecedentem scelestum* (etc.).

peine forte et dure (F.). See *peine*, in Dictionary.

pendente lite (L.), while the suit is pending.

Penelopæ telam retexens (L.), unraveling the web of Penelope.

penitus toto divisos orbe Britannos (L.), the Britons entirely separated from the whole world (*Virgil*, Eclogues, i. 67).

pensée (F.), thought; reflection; remembrance.

pensez à moi (F.), think of me.

pension (F.), a boarding-house; a boarding-school.

per accidens (L.), by accident or chance; as an accidental circumstance.

per ætatem (L.), by reason of one's age.

per ævum (L.), forever.

per ambages (L.), by roundabout ways; with circumlocution; indirectly.

per angusta ad augusta (L.), by narrow ways to august ends.

per annum (L.), by the year; yearly; annually.

per aspera ad astra (L.), through difficulties to the stars: cf. *ad astra per aspera*.

per capita (L.), by heads; for each individual.

per centum (L.), by the hundred; on each hundred.

per contra (It.), on the contrary; on the other hand; on the opposite side of the account; as a set-off.

per curiam (L.), by the court.

per diem (L.), by the day; daily.

père (F.), father.

père de famille (F.), father of a family.

pereunt et imputantur (L.), they (days) pass away and are scored up (against us): see *soles qui nobis pereunt et imputantur*.

per fas et nefas (L.), through right and wrong.

perfervidum ingenium Scotorum (L.), the very ardent temperament of the Scots.

perfide Albion (F.), perfidious Albion (England).

per gradus (L.), by steps; step by step.

periculum in mora (L.), danger in delay.

per incuriam (L.), through carelessness.

per interim (L.), in the meantime.

per jocum (L.), by way of a joke; in jest.

per legem terræ (L.), by the law of the land.

per mare, per terram (L.), by sea, by land (motto of the British Marines).

per mensem (L.), by the month; monthly.

per minas (L.), by threats.

permitte divis cetera (L.), leave the rest to the gods (*Horace*, Odes, i. 9).

pernicibus alis (L.), with swift wings (*Virgil*, Æneid, iv. 180).

per pares (L.), by one's peers.

perpetuum mobile (L.), something perpetually in motion.

perpetuum silentium (L.), perpetual silence.

per procurationem (L.), by procuration; by the agency of another.

per saltum (L.), by a leap; without intermediate steps; skipping over intermediate stages or grades.

per se (L.), by itself; in itself; intrinsically.

Persicos odi, puer, apparatus (L.), the Persian pomp, boy, I hate (*Horace*, Odes, i. 38).

persona grata (L.), an acceptable person; esp., a diplomatic representative who is personally acceptable to the government to which he is accredited.

persona non grata (L.), a person, esp. a diplomatic representative, who is not acceptable: see *persona grata*.

persona standi in judicio (L.), character or capacity of standing in court (as to sue or be sued).

personnel (F.), the body of persons employed in any service or undertaking: cf. *matériel*.

per stirpes (L.), by stocks or families (in law, used of succession to property in which the descendants of one heir share the portion which would have come to that heir if living).

per totam curiam (L.), by the whole court.

per tot discrimina rerum (L.), through so many crises of affairs (*Virgil*, Æneid, i. 204).

pessimi exempli (L.), of the worst example.

petit, fem. **petite** (F.), little; small; petty; insignificant.

petit à petit (F.), little by little.

petit bleu (F.), little blue (paper); a telegram.

petit caporal (F.), the Little Corporal (Napoleon).

petitio principii (L.), a begging of the question.

petit-maître, fem. **petite-maîtresse** (F.), little master or mistress; a young man or woman who affects great elegance of dress, manners, etc.; an exquisite.

petit monde (F.), the little world; common people.

petit souper (F.), little supper; a little supper-party of intimates.

petits soins (F.), little attentions; delicate assiduities.

petit verre (F.), a little glass; a small glass of brandy or liqueur.

peu à peu (F.), little by little.

peu de bien, peu de soin (F.), little wealth, little care.

peu de chose (F.), a small matter; a trifle.

peu de gens savent être vieux (F.), few people know how to be old (*La Rochefoucauld*).

peu d'hommes ont été admirés par leurs domestiques (F.), few men have been admired by their servants (*Montaigne*).

peut-être (F.), maybe; perhaps: see *je m'en vais chercher un grand peut-être*.

pharmacie française (F.), French apothecary's shop or drug-store.

pia desideria (L.), pious regrets.

pia fraus (L.), a pious fraud.

pictor ignotus (L.), an unknown painter.

pièce de résistance (F.), piece of resistance; the most substantial dish, as of meat, at a meal; the main feature or strong point of anything.

pied à pied (F.), foot by foot; step by step.

pied bot (F.), clubfoot.

Pinakothek (G.), a picture-gallery.

pinxit (L.), (the person specified) painted it.

pis aller (F.), a going worst; the worst possibility; a last resource; a makeshift.

piscem natare doces (L.), you are teaching a fish to swim.

place aux dames (F.), place (give place or make way) for the ladies.

placet (L.), it pleases (used as an expression or vote of assent: cf. *non placet*).

plaît-il? (F.), what is your pleasure? what do you wish? what did you say?

planté là, fem. **plantée là** (F.), planted there; unceremoniously abandoned or forsaken; left in the lurch.

plaudite, cives (L.), applaud, citizens (words addressed to the audience at the close of a Roman play).

pleins pouvoirs (F.), full powers.

pleno jure (L.), with full right or authority.

ploratur lacrimis amissa pecunia veris (L.), money lost is mourned with genuine tears (*Juvenal*, Satires, xiii. 134).

plus in posse quam in actu (L.), more in possibility than in fact.

plus minusve (L.), more or less.

plus ou moins (F.), more or less.

plus sage que les sages (F.), more wise than the wise.

poca roba, poco pensiero (It.), little wealth, little care.

pocas palabras (Sp.), few words.

poco a poco (It.), little by little.

poeta nascitur, non fit (L.), the poet is born, not made.

poilu (F.). See Dictionary.

point d'appui (F.), a point of support; a fulcrum; a base of operations.

point du jour (F.), daybreak.

poisson d'avril (F.), fish of April; an April fool trick.

pollice verso (L.), with thumb turned, or turned downward (the sign made by spectators calling for the death of a defeated gladiator).

pondere, non numero (L.), by weight, not by number.

pons asinorum (L.), the bridge of asses (applied to a certain proposition in geometry).

popularis aura (L.), the popular breeze; popular favor.

posada (Sp.), an inn.

posse (L.), etc. See Dictionary.

posse videor (L.), I seem to be able.

possible (F.): see *si c'est possible* (etc.).

possunt quia posse videntur (L.), they can because they think they can (*Virgil*, Æneid, v. 231).

post bellum (L.), after the war.

post bellum auxilium (L.), help after the war; belated aid.

post diluvium (L.), after the Flood.

post equitem sedet atra Cura (L.), behind the horseman sits black Care (*Horace*, Odes, iii. 1).

poste restante (F.). See Dictionary.

post hoc (L.), after this.

post hoc, ergo propter hoc (L.), after this, therefore in consequence of this (exemplifying the logical fallacy of the false cause).

post litem motam (L.), after the controversy was begun.

post meridiem (L.), after noon.

post mortem (L.), after death.

post nubila Phœbus (L.), after the clouds Phœbus (the sun).

post obitum (L.), after death.

post prandium (L.), after dinner.

post prœlia prœmia (L.), after battles rewards.

post tenebras lux (L.), after darkness light.

post tot naufragia portum (L.), after so many shipwrecks the harbor.

potior tempore, potior jure (L.), better (prior) in time, better in right.

potius mori quam fœdari (L.), rather to die than to be dishonored.

potus non frangit jejunium (L.), drinking does not break a fast.

poudre aux yeux (F.), dust in the eyes; something that blinds one to facts.

pour acquit (F.), for quittance (formula of receipt written on paid bills, etc.).

pour ainsi dire (F.), so to speak; as it were.

pour dire adieu (F.), to say farewell.

pour encourager les autres (F.), to encourage others.

pour faire de l'esprit (F.), to show off one's wit.

pour faire rire (F.), to excite laughter.

pour faire visite (F.), to pay a visit.

pour le mérite (F.), for merit.

pour passer le temps (F.), to pass away the time.

pour prendre congé (F.), to take leave.

pour toujours (F.), for always; forever.

pour y parvenir (F.), to arrive there; so as to attain one's end.

pou sto (Gr. ποῦ στῶ), (a place) where I may stand (Archimedes's requisite for moving the earth). See Dictionary.

præmia virtutis (L.), the rewards of virtue.

præmissis præmittendis (L.), the proper forms of prefix or address being observed (a polite formula employed in business circulars, etc., esp. in German use).

præmonitus, præmunitus (L.), forewarned, forearmed.

præstat cautela quam medela (L.), precaution is better than cure.

Præterita (L.), "Things Past" (title of Ruskin's autobiography).

précieux, fem. **précieuse** (F.), precious; exquisite; finically exquisite or refined; a person, esp. a woman (*précieuse*), affecting excessive refinement of taste, language, etc. (applied esp. to women of 17th century French salons): see *Les Précieuses Ridicules*.

précis (F.), an abstract; a summary.

préfet (F.), a prefect; a superior magistrate or administrative official.

premier, fem. **première** (F.), first; leading; a leader; a leading man or woman on the stage; also (*première*), a first public performance of a play, etc.

premier danseur, fem. **première danseuse** (F.), a leading or principal dancer, as in a ballet.

premier pas (F.), the first step; the beginning.

prendre la lune avec les dents (F.), to seize the moon with the teeth (to do the impossible).

prendre un billet de parterre (F.), to take a parterre ticket (to fall down).

près de (F.), near to; in the vicinity of.

presto maturo, presto marcio (It.), soon ripe, soon rotten.

pretium laborum non vile (L.), no mean reward for labors (motto of the Order of the Golden Fleece).

preux chevalier (F.), a valiant knight.

prévenance (F.), thoughtful kindness or attention; obligingness.

prévenant, fem. **prévenante** (F.), anticipating the wishes of others; thoughtfully attentive; obliging; also, prepossessing.

prima caritas incipit a se ipso (L.), charity begins first with one's self.

prima facie (L.), at first view or appearance.

prima inter pares (L.), first among her peers.

primo (L.), in the first place; in the beginning.

primo jefe (Sp.), first chief.

primo mihi (L.), for myself first.

primo occupanti (L.), to the first occupant (as having the best right to property).

primum mobile (L.), the first mover or moving agency.

primus in orbe deos fecit timor (L.), fear first made gods in the world (*Statius*, Thebais, iii. 661).

primus inter pares (L.), first among his peers.

principia, non homines (L.), principles, not men.

principiis obsta (L.), resist the beginnings (*Ovid*, Remedia Amoris, 91).

prior tempore, prior jure (L.), first in time, first in right.

Prisciani caput frangere (L.), to break Priscian's head; violate the rules of grammar.

privatum commodum publico cedit (L.), private advantage yields to public.

pro aris et focis (L.), for altars and firesides.

probatum est (L.), it has been tried or proved.

probitas laudatur et alget (L.), integrity is praised, and freezes (*Juvenal*, Satires, i. 74).

pro bono publico (L.), for the public good.

pro Christo et patria (L.), for Christ and country.

pro confesso (L.), for, or as if, confessed or admitted.

procul a Jove, procul a fulmine (L.), far from Jove, far from his thunderbolt.

procul, O procul este, profani! (L.), keep far off, O far off, ye profane! (*Virgil*, Æneid, vi. 258).

pro Deo et ecclesia (L.), for God and the church.

pro Deo et rege (L.), for God and the king.

pro domo (L.), for the house; for a party, body, etc.

pro ecclesia et pontifice (L.), for the church and the pope.

pro et contra (L.), for and against.

profanum vulgus (L.), the profane multitude: see *odi profanum vulgus*.

pro forma (L.), for form; as a matter of form.

pro forma tantum (L.), for form only.

pro hac vice (L.), for this turn, or occasion.

proh (or **pro**) **pudor!** (L.), oh, shame!

projet (F.), project; plan; design; draft.

projet de loi (F.), a legislative bill.

projet en l'air (F.), project in the air; a chimerical scheme.

pro libertate patriæ (L.), for the liberty of one's country.

pro memoria (L.), for remembrance; for a memorial.

prononcé, fem. **prononcée** (F.), pro-

nounced; decided; marked; prominent.

pro nunc (L.), for now; for the present.

pro patria (L.), for one's country or native land.

prope ad summum, prope ad exitum (L.), near to the top, near to the finish.

propos de table (F.), table-talk.

propria quæ maribus (L.), things which are proper to males, or to husbands (from the 16th century Latin grammar of William Lily).

proprio jure (L.), in one's own right.

proprio motu (L.), of one's own motion or accord.

proprio vigore (L.), by its own force.

propter hoc (L.), on account of this.

propter quod (L.), on account of which.

pro rata (L.), in proportion; proportionally.

pro rege et patria (L.), for king and country.

pro rege, lege, et grege (L.), for king, law, and people.

pro rege sæpe, pro patria semper (L.), for king often, for country always (motto of Colbert, the French statesman).

pro re nata (L.), for a circumstance or emergency arising; as the occasion may require.

pro salute animæ (L.), for the welfare of the soul.

prose (F.): see *faire de la prose sans le savoir*.

pro tanto (L.), for so much; to that extent.

pro tempore (L.), for the time; temporarily.

pro virili parte (L.), according to a man's part, share, or ability.

pro virtute felix temeritas (L.), in place of courage a lucky rashness.

proxime accessit (L.), he came nearest (as second in a contest).

proximo (**mense**) (L.), of the next (month).

prudens futuri (L.), provident of the future.

publicè (L.), before the public; publicly.

pugnis et calcibus (L.), with fists and heels.

pulchrum est digito monstrari et dicier hic est! (L.), it is a fine thing to be pointed out with the finger and have people say, "It is he!" (*Persius*, Satires, i. 28).

pulvis et umbra sumus (L.), we are dust and shadow (*Horace*, Odes, iv. 7).

punctatim (L.), point for point.

punctum comparationis (L.), a point of comparison.

punctum saliens (L.), a salient point; a starting-point.

Punica fides (L.), Punic (Carthaginian) faith; perfidy; treachery.

pur autre vie (AF.), for, or during, the life of another.

pur et simple (F.), pure and simple; unqualified.

purpureus pannus (L.), a purple patch. See *purple patch*, under *purple, a.*, in Dictionary.

pur sang (F.), pure blood; thoroughbred; true-born.

Pyrénées (F.): see *il n'y a plus de Pyrénées*.

Q

quæ e longinquo magis placent (L.), things from afar please the more.

quæ fuerunt vitia mores sunt (L.), things that were vices are now customs.

quæ nocent docent (L.), things that hurt teach.

quæ non valeant singula juncta juvant (L.), things that do not avail singly are effective when united.

quære (L.), ask, or inquire (used to introduce a question).

quære verum (L.), seek the truth.

quæritur (L.), it is asked.

qualche cosa per carità (It.), something for charity.

qualis ab incepto (L.), such as from the beginning (*Horace*, Ars Poetica, 127).

qualis artifex pereo! (L.), what an artist I perish! (reputed words of Nero, commiserating the world's loss by his suicide: *Suetonius*, Nero, 49).

qualis pater, talis filius (L.), as the father, so the son; like father, like son.

qualis rex, talis grex (L.), as the king, so the people.

qualis vir, talis oratio (L.), as the man, so the speech.

qualis vita, finis ita (L.), as the life, so its end.

qualité (F.), quality: see *il a les défauts* (etc.).

quamdiu se bene gesserit (L.), so long as he shall have behaved himself well; during good behavior.

quam proxime (L.), as nearly as possible.

quand même (F.), even though; notwithstanding; come what may.

quandoque bonus dormitat Homerus (L.): see *indignor quandoque bonus dormitat Homerus.*

quantum libet (L.), as much as one pleases.

quantum meruit (L.), as much as one has deserved.

quantum mutatus ab illo (L.), how changed from what he was (see *Virgil*, Æneid, ii. 274).

quantum placeat (L.), as much as pleases, or seems good.

quantum satis (L.), as much as is sufficient.

quantum sufficit (L.), as much as suffices.

quantum valeat (L.), as much as it may be worth.

quantum valebat (L.), as much as it was worth.

quantum vis (L.), as much as you wish.

quare clausum fregit (L.), wherefore he broke the close (committed trespass: used in law).

Quartier Latin (F.), the Latin Quarter of Paris.

quasi (L.), as if; as it were.

quasi dicat (L.), as if one should say.

quasi dictum (L.), as if said.

que diable allait-il faire dans cette galère? (F.), what the devil was he doing in that galley? (*Molière*, Les Fourberies de Scapin, ii. 11).

quelle mouche le pique? (F.), what fly is stinging him? what is irritating him?

quelque chose (F.), something; a trifle.

quem (or **quos**) **Deus** (or **Jupiter**) **perdere vult prius dementat** (L.), him (or those) whom God (or Jupiter) wishes to destroy he first makes mad.

quem di diligunt adolescens moritur (L.), he whom the gods love dies young (*Plautus*, Bacchides, iv. 7).

qu'en dira-t-on? (F.), what will people say?

querelle d'Allemand (F.), German's quarrel (without cause).

querido, fem. **querida** (Sp.), beloved; dear; darling; a lover or mistress.

que sais-je? (F.), what know I? (motto of Montaigne).

qu'est-ce que c'est? (F.), what is it?

que voulez-vous? (F.), what will you? what would you have?

qui a compagnon a maître (F.), who has a companion has a master.

qui bene amat bene castigat (L.), he who loves well chastises well.

qui capit facit (L.), who takes makes; he who takes an accusation to himself makes the accusation.

quid cæco cum speculo? (L.), what has a blind man to do with a mirror?

quid faciendum? (L.), what is to be done?

quid hoc sibi vult? (L.), what does this mean?

quid novi? (L.), what new?

quid nunc? (L.), what now?

qui docet discit (L.), he who teaches learns.

quid prodest? (L.), what good does it do? what profits it?

quid pro quo (L.), something for something; one thing for another.

quidquid delirant reges, plectuntur Achivi (L.), whatever folly their rulers commit, the Greeks suffer the penalty (*Horace*, Epistles, i. 2).

quidquid dignum sapiente bonoque est (L.), whatever is worthy of a wise and good man (*Horace*, Epistles, i. 4).

quid rides? (L.), why do you laugh?

quid times? (L.), what do you fear?

quién sabe? (Sp.), who knows?

quieta non movere (L.), not to disturb quiet things.

qui facit per alium facit per se (L.), he who does a thing through the agency of another does it himself.

qui garde son dîner il a mieux à souper (F.), he who saves his dinner will have more for supper.

qui invidet minor est (L.), he who envies is inferior.

qui jacet in terra non habet unde cadat (L.), he who lies on the ground has no chance to fall.

qui jure suo utitur neminem lædit (L.), he who exercises his own right injures no one.

qui m'aime aime mon chien (F.), who loves me loves my dog.

qui n'a santé, il n'a rien; qui a santé, il a tout (F.), he who has not health has nothing; he who has health has everything.

qui nescit dissimulare nescit regnare (L.), he who knows not how to dissemble knows not how to reign (favorite maxim of Louis XI. of France).

qui nimium probat nihil probat (L.), he who proves too much proves nothing.

qui non proficit deficit (L.), he who does not progress falls back.

qui parcit nocentibus innocentes punit (L.), he who spares the guilty punishes the innocent.

qui scribit bis legit (L.), he who writes reads twice; as an aid to memory, writing a thing once is the equivalent of reading it twice.

quis custodiet ipsos custodes? (L.), who shall keep guard over the guards themselves? (*Juvenal*, Satires, vi. 347).

quis desiderio sit pudor aut modus? (L.), what shame or limit can there be to our grief? (*Horace*, Odes, i. 24).

qui sentit commodum sentire debet et onus (L.), he who feels the benefit should feel the burden also.

qui sert bien son pays n'a pas besoin d'aïeux (F.), who serves his country well has no need of ancestors (*Voltaire*, Mérope, i. 3).

qui s'excuse s'accuse (F.), who excuses himself accuses himself.

qui si parla italiano (It.), here Italian is spoken.

quisque sibi proximus (L.), every one is nearest to himself.

quis, quid, ubi, quibus auxiliis, cur, quomodo, quando? (L.), who, what, where, by what aids, why, how, when? (questions for ascertaining all the circumstances of a case) (*Quintilian*).

quis separabit? (L.), who shall separate? (motto of the Order of St. Patrick).

qui tacet consentit (L.), he who remains silent consents.

qui transtulit sustinet (L.), he who transplanted sustains (motto of Connecticut).

qui va là? (F.), who goes there?

qui vivra verra (F.), who lives will see.

quoad (L.), as to; as far as; as regards.

quoad hoc (L.), as far as this; to this extent; as regards this.

quoad omnia (L.), as regards all things.

quoad sacra (L.), as regards sacred things.

quoad valorem (L.), as regards the value.

quo animo? (L.), with what intention?

quocunque modo (L.), in whatever way.

quocunque nomine (L.), by or under whatever name.

quod avertat Deus! (L.), which may God avert!

quod bene notandum (L.), which is to be well noted.

quod bonum, felix, faustumque sit! (L.), and may it be good, fortunate, and prosperous!

quod di omen avertant! (L.), which omen may the gods avert!

quod erat demonstrandum (L.), which was to be demonstrated.

quod erat faciendum (L.), which was to be done.

quod erat inveniendum (L.), which was to be found out.

quod est absurdum (L.), which is absurd.

quod licet Jovi non licet bovi (L.), what is permitted to Jove is not permitted to the ox.

quod minime reris (L.), what you least suppose.

quod ubique, quod semper, quod ab omnibus creditum est (L.), what everywhere, always, and by all has been believed: see *magnopere curandum est ut id* (etc.).

quod vide (L.), which see.

quo Fata vocant (L.), whither the Fates call.

quo jure? (L.), by what right?

quomodo (L.), in what manner; how.

quomodo vales? (L.), how do you do?

quo non ascendam? (L.), whither shall I not ascend? (ambitious motto of Fouquet, Louis XIV.'s superintendent of finances, who died in prison).

quorum pars magna fui (L.), of which I was (or in which I had) a great part (*Virgil*, Æneid, ii. 6).

quos Deus (or Jupiter) perdere vult prius dementat (L.): see *quem Deus perdere vult prius dementat*.

quos ego— (L.), whom I— (an unfinished threat: *Virgil*, Æneid, i. 135).

quot homines, tot sententiæ (L.), so many men, so many opinions.

quot servi, tot hostes (L.), so many servants, so many enemies.

quousque tandem abutere, Catilina, patientia nostra? (L.), how far, pray, Catiline, will you abuse our patience? (*Cicero*, 1 Catiline, 1).

quo vadis, Domine? (L.), whither goest thou, Lord? (question traditionally said to have been addressed by Peter, fleeing from martyrdom at Rome, to a vision of Christ seen on the Appian Way; with the reply, "I come to be crucified again," leading the apostle to return to Rome).

quo warranto (L.), by what warrant or authority.

R

rabido ore (L.), with rabid mouth; raving.

raison d'état (F.), reason of state.

raison d'être (F.), reason for being, or existence.

ranz des vaches (F.), a Swiss herdsmen's melody.

rappelez-moi à son souvenir (F.), remember me to him.

rara avis (L.), a rare bird; a prodigy (*Persius*, Satires, i. 46).

rara avis in terris (L.), a rare bird on this earth (*Juvenal*, Satires, vi. 165).

rari nantes in gurgite vasto (L.), here and there some swimming in the vast gulf (*Virgil*, Æneid, i. 118).

raro antecedentem scelestum deseruit pede Pœna claudo (L.), rarely has Vengeance, with halting foot, abandoned the wretch fleeing before her (*Horace*, Odes, iii. 2).

rastaquouère (F.), a pretentious adventurer.

rast' ich, so rost' ich (G.), if I rest, I rust.

Rathaus (G.), a council house; a town hall or city hall.

ratio decidendi (L.), reason for deciding; the logic of a decision.

ratione personæ (L.), by reason of, or from the character of, the person.

ravissant, fem. **ravissante** (F.), ravishing; enchanting.

re (L.), in the matter of.

Realpolitik (G.), **Realschule** (G.). See Dictionary.

Recht (G.), right; justice; law.

recipe (L.), take (used in physicians' prescriptions).

rectus in curia (L.), right (blameless) in or before a court.

reçu (F.), received; a receipt.

recueil (F.), a collection, as of writings.

reculer pour mieux sauter (F.), to draw back in order to leap the better.

reddite quæ sunt Cæsaris Cæsari; et quæ sunt Dei Deo (L.), render unto Cæsar the things that are Cæsar's; and unto God the things that are God's (*Vulgate*, Mat. xxii. 21).

redivivus (L.), that lives again; returned to life.

redolet lucernam (or **lucerna**) (L.), it smells of the lamp (savors of nocturnal or laborious study).

reductio ad absurdum (L.), reduction to an absurdity.

reductio ad impossibile (L.), reduction to an impossibility.

re galantuomo (It.), the honest king (applied to Victor Emmanuel, first king of Italy).

regina (L.), queen.

regina cæli (L.), queen of heaven.

regis ad exemplum (L.), after the example of the king.

regium donum (L.), a royal grant.

regnant populi (L.), the people rule (motto of Arkansas).

re infecta (L.), the matter being unfinished.

relata refero (L.), I tell what was told to me.

Religio Laici (L.), "A Layman's Religion" (title of a polemic poem by Dryden).

religio loci (L.), the sacred or awe-inspiring character of the place.

Religio Medici (L.), "A Physician's Religion" (title of a religious treatise by Sir Thomas Browne).

rem acu tetigisti (L.): see *acu rem tetigisti*.

remèdes (F.): see *aux grands maux les grands remèdes*.

remis velisque (L.), with oars and sails; with all one's might.

remittitur (L.), it is remitted; it is sent back.

remittitur damnum (L.), the damages are remitted.

répondez, s'il vous plaît (F.), answer, if you please (usually with reference to an invitation).

répondre en Normand (F.), to answer like a Norman (evasively).

réponse sans réplique (F.), an answer not admitting of a reply.

requiem æternam dona eis (L.), grant them eternal rest (first words of introit of Latin mass for the dead).

requiescat (pl. **requiescant**) **in pace** (L.), may he or she (or they) rest in peace.

res adversæ (L.), adverse things; adversity.

res angusta domi (L.), straitened circumstances at home (*Juvenal*, Satires, iii. 165).

res gestæ (L.), things done; deeds; facts.

res in cardine est (L.), the affair is at a turning-point, or crisis.

res incognitæ (L.), things or matters unknown.

res inter alios (L.), a matter between others.

res ipsa loquitur (L.), the thing itself speaks; the case speaks for itself.

rcs judicata (L.), a thing adjudicated; a case that has been decided.

res judicata pro veritate accipitur (or **habetur**) (L.), a thing adjudicated is received (or held) for truth.

res nullius (L.), a thing belonging to no one.

respice, adspice, prospice (L.), look back, look on, look forward; look to the past, the present, the future (motto of the College of the City of New York).

respice finem (L.), look to the end.

respondeat superior (L.), let the superior answer (for a subordinate or agent).

res publica, or **respublica** (L.), the commonwealth; the state; the republic.

res secundæ (L.), favorable things; prosperity.

resurgam (L.), I shall rise again.

revenons à nos moutons (F.), let us return to our sheep (our subject) (from the 15th century farce of "Patelin").

re vera (L.), in very fact; in truth.

revocate animos (L.), call back your courage (*Virgil*, Æneid, i. 202).

rex (L.), king.

rex convivii (L.), king or master of the feast.

rex datur propter regnum, non regnum propter regem (L.), the king is given for the sake of the kingdom, not the kingdom for the king.

rex non potest peccare (L.), the king can do no wrong.

rex nunquam moritur (L.), the king never dies.

rex regum (L.), king of kings.

rex vini (L.), king of the wine; master of the feast.

rez-de-chaussée (F.), the ground floor, as of a house.

rideau de fer (F.), curtain of iron; a barrier formed along a given line by a heavy, continuous artillery fire.

ride, si sapis (L.), laugh, if thou art wise (*Martial*, Epigrams, ii. 41).

rien ne pèse tant qu'un secret (F.), nothing weighs so heavily as a secret (*La Fontaine*, Fables, viii. 6).

rira bien qui rira le dernier (F.), he will laugh well who laughs last.

rire entre cuir et chair (F.), to laugh between skin and flesh (to one's self, or secretly).

risum teneatis? (L.), can you restrain your laughter? (*Horace*, Ars Poetica, 5).

rive droite (F.), the right bank (of a river, as one faces down stream).

rive gauche (F.), the left bank (of a river: often with reference to the part of Paris south of the Seine).

robe de chambre (F.), a chamber robe; a dressing-gown.

robe de nuit (F.), a night robe; a nightgown or nightshirt.

robur et corporis et animi (L.), strength both of body and of mind.

rois fainéants (F.), do-nothing kings (applied to the later Merovingian kings, whose governing powers had passed into the hands of their mayors of the palace).

rôle d'équipage (F.), the list of a ship's company.

Roma locuta est, causa finita est (L.), Rome has spoken, the case is ended.

ruat cælum (L.), though the heavens fall: see *fiat justitia, ruat cælum*.

rudis indigestaque moles (L.), an unformed and unordered mass (*Ovid*, Metamorphoses, i. 7).

rue (F.), a street.

ruin señor cria ruin servidor (Sp.), a bad master makes a bad servant.

ruit mole sua (L.): see *mole ruit sua*.

rusé, fem. **rusée** (F.), artful; cunning; sly.

ruse contre ruse (F.), trick against trick.

ruse de guerre (F.), a stratagem of war.

rus in urbe (L.), the country in the city (*Martial*, Epigrams, xii. 57).

rusticus abnormis sapiens (L.), a rustic wise though not by academic rule (*Horace*, Satires, ii. 2).

S

sac de nuit (F.), night bag; a bag with conveniences for use at night; a traveling-bag.

sacer vates (L.), an inspired bard: cf. *carent quia vate sacro*.

sacramentum fidelitatis (L.), the oath of fealty.

sacré, fem. **sacrée** (F.), sacred; also, damned; cursed.

Sacré-Cœur (de Jésus) (F.), the Sacred Heart (of Jesus) (the object of a special devotion in the Roman Catholic Church: used in the names of churches, religious societies and institutions, etc.).

sæva indignatio (L.), fierce indignation.

sævas tranquilla per undas (L.), calm amid the raging waves (inscription on a medal commemorating the destruction of the Spanish Armada in 1588).

sævis tranquillus in undis (L.), calm amid the raging waves (motto of William I. of Orange).

sain et sauf (F.), sound and safe; safe and sound.

saint, fem. **sainte** (F.), sacred; holy; saint.

saint de bois (F.), saint of wood; a person who is no true saint; a hypocrite.

saint du jour (F.), saint of the day; a person in present favor or esteem.

sainte nitouche (F., fem.), saintly touch-not (or Saint Touch-not); a feminine goody-goody or demure hypocrite.

sal Atticus (or **Atticum**) (L.), Attic salt; wit.

salle (F.), a hall; a room.

salle à manger (F.), a dining-room.

salle d'armes (F.), hall of arms; an armory; a fencing hall.

salle d'attente (F.), a waiting-room.

salle des pas perdus (F.), hall of lost (or wasted) steps; the great outer hall of a court of justice; a large waiting-room in a public building.

salus mundi (L.), the welfare of the world.

salus populi suprema lex esto (L.), let the welfare of the people be the supreme law (motto of Missouri).

salus ubi multi consiliarii (L.), where there are many counselors there is safety.

salva conscientia (L.), with a safe conscience.

salva dignitate (L.), with uninjured dignity.

salve! (L.), hail!

salvo jure (L.), the right being unimpaired; without prejudice to right.

salvo pudore (L.), without offense to modesty.

salvo sensu (L.), without violation of the sense.

Sancta Mater Ecclesia (L.), Holy Mother Church.

sancta simplicitas (L.), sacred simplicity: see *O sancta simplicitas!*

Sanctitas vestra (L.), your Holiness.

sanctum sanctorum (L.), the holy of holies.

Sand in die Augen (G.), sand (dust) in the eyes: see *poudre aux yeux.*

sang des tyrans (F.), blood of tyrants: see *l'arbre de la liberté ne croît* (etc.).

sangre azul (Sp.), blue blood.

sans cérémonie (F.), without ceremony.

sans changer (F.), without change.

sans compliments (F.), without compliments.

sans Dieu rien (F.), without God, nothing.

sans doute (F.), without doubt; undoubtedly.

sans façon (F.), without ceremony; informally; unceremoniously.

sans gêne (F.), without constraint or embarrassment; without ceremony; free and easy.

sans nombre (F.), without number.

sans pareil (F.), without equal.

sans peine (F.), without trouble; easily; willingly.

sans peur et sans reproche (F.), without fear and without reproach (used esp. of the French Seigneur de Bayard).

sans phrase (F.), without (formal) phrase; in plain language; bluntly.

sans rime et sans raison (F.), without rime and without reason.

sans souci (F.), without care; free from care.

sans tache (F.), without spot; without stain or blemish.

sapere aude (L.), dare to be wise (*Horace*, Epistles, i. 2).

sapiens, in se ipso totus, teres atque rotundus (L.), the wise man, complete in himself, polished and well rounded (see *Horace*, Satires, ii. 7).

sapiens qui prospicit (L.), he is wise who looks ahead.

sapientem pascere barbam (L.), to grow the beard of wisdom (*Horace*, Satires, ii. 3).

sapientum octavus (L.), the eighth of the wise men, or another as wise as the famous seven sages (*Horace*, Satires, ii. 3).

Sartor Resartus (L.), "The Tailor Retailored" (title of a satirical work by Thomas Carlyle).

sat cito si sat bene (L.), quickly enough if well enough.

sat cito si sat tuto (L.), quickly enough if safely enough.

satis eloquentiæ, sapientiæ parum (L.), plenty of eloquence, too little of wisdom (*Sallust*, Catiline, 5).

satis superque (L.), enough and over; enough and to spare.

satis verborum (L.), enough of words.

sat pulchra si sat bona (L.), beautiful enough if good enough.

sauve qui peut (F.), save who can; let each save himself as best he may.

sauve-qui-peut (F.), a general flight or rout in which each seeks to save himself.

savant, fem. **savante** (F.), learned; a learned person.

scala cæli (L.), ladder or staircase to heaven.

scandalum magnatum (L.), slander or defamation of great personages.

schola cantorum (L.), school of singers.

Schrecklichkeit (G.), frightfulness. See Dictionary.

Schwärmerei (G.), rambling fancy; a visionary tendency or habit of mind of a strongly emotional or sentimental character.

scienter (L.), knowingly; wittingly; wilfully.

scribendi cacoëthes (L.), a mania for writing or authorship (*Juvenal*, Satires, vii. 52).

scripsit (L.), (the person specified) wrote it.

sculpsit (L.), (the person specified) carved or engraved it.

scuto bonæ voluntatis tuæ coronasti nos (L.), with the shield of thy good will (or favor) thou hast encompassed us (a motto of Maryland: *Vulgate*, Ps. v. 13).

secours (F.), help; aid; relief; succor.

secret (F.): see *rien ne pèse tant qu'un secret.*

secret de la comédie (F.), secret of the comedy; an open secret.

secret de Polichinelle (F.), secret of Polichinelle (buffoon in the French puppet-show and comedy); an open secret.

secundum artem (L.), according to art or rule.

secundum formam statuti (L.), according to the form of the statute.

secundum legem (L.), according to law.

secundum majus et minus (L.), according to more and less; quantitatively.

secundum naturam (L.), according to nature; naturally.

secundum ordinem (L.), according to order; in order.

secundum regulam (L.), according to rule.

secundum usum (L.), according to usage.

secundum veritatem (L.), according to truth.

se defendendo (L.), in self-defense.

sede vacante (L.), the seat, or the see, being vacant.

sed hæc hactenus (L.), but so much for this.

séduisant, fem. **séduisante** (F.), seductive; alluring.

se habla español (Sp.), Spanish is spoken (here).

Sehnsucht (G.), longing; yearning.

selon le bras la saignée (F.), according to the arm the bleeding; charges in proportion to the purse.

selon le saint l'encens (F.), according to the saint the incense; homage in proportion to importance.

selon les règles (F.), according to the rules.

semble (F.), it seems (in law, used to preface an opinion on a point unsettled).

semel abbas, semper abbas (L.), once an abbot, always an abbot.

semel et simul (L.), once and together.

semel in anno (L.), once in the year.

semel insanivimus omnes (L.), we have all been mad once.

semel pro semper (L.), once for all.

semita (L.), a foot-path: see *et modo quæ fuerat semita facta via est.*

semper avarus eget (L.), the avaricious man is always in want (*Horace*, Epistles, i. 2).

semper eadem (L.), always the same (motto of Queen Elizabeth).

semper felix (L.), always fortunate.

semper fidelis (L.), always faithful (motto of the U. S. Marine Corps).

semper idem (L.), always the same.

semper paratus (L.), always prepared, or ready.

senatus consultum (L.), decree of the senate. See Dictionary.

senatus populusque Romanus (L.), the senate and people of Rome.

senex bis puer (L.), an old man is twice a boy.

seniores priores (L.), elders first.

se non è vero, è ben trovato (It.), if it is not true, it is well invented.

sens commun (F.), common sense: see *le sens commun* (etc.).

sensu bono (L.), in a good sense.

sensu malo (L.), in a bad sense.

sequitur (L.), it follows (as a consequence).

sero (or **tarde**) **venientibus ossa** (L.), for late comers the bones.

serrurerie (F.), locksmiths' work; ornamental work in wrought metal; work in wrought-iron, etc.

serus in cælum redeas (L.), late mayest thou return to heaven; may you live long (*Horace*, Odes, i. 2).

servabo fidem (L.), I will keep faith.

servare modum (L.), to observe moderation.

servum pecus (L.), a servile herd: see *imitatores, servum pecus.*

servus servorum Dei (L.), servant of the servants of God (a title adopted by the popes).

se soumettre ou se démettre (F.), submit or resign (alternative indicated by Gambetta for MacMahon in 1877).

sesquipedalia verba (L.), words a foot and a half long (*Horace*, Ars Poetica, 97).

si c'est possible, c'est fait; si c'est impossible, cela se fera (F.), if it is possible, it is done; if it is impossible, it shall be done (reply of Calonne, French finance minister, to Marie Antoinette's request for money).

sic eunt fata hominum (L.), thus go the fates of men.

sic itur ad astra (L.), thus one goes to the stars (*Virgil*, Æneid, ix. 641).

sic passim (L.), thus here and there, or in various places.

sic semper tyrannis (L.), thus ever to tyrants (motto of Virginia).

sic transit gloria mundi (L.), so passes away the glory of the world (a phrase used in the coronation service of the popes, after the burning of bundles of tow).

sicut ante (L.), as before.

sic utere tuo ut alienum non lædas (L.), so use your own property as not to injure another's.

sicut patribus, sit Deus nobis (L.), as with our fathers, so may God be with us (motto of Boston: cf. *Vulgate*, 3 Kings, viii. 57).

sic volo, sic jubeo (L.), thus I will, thus

I command: cf. *hoc volo, sic jubeo; sit pro ratione voluntas.*

sic volumus (L.), thus we will; such is our will.

si Deus pro nobis, quis contra nos? (L.), if God be for us, who shall be against us? (*Vulgate*, Rom. viii. 31).

si dis placet (L.), if it pleases the gods.

siècle (F.), a century; an age.

siècle d'or (F.), age of gold; the golden age.

siècles des ténèbres (F.), ages of darkness; the dark ages.

si fecisti, nega (L.), if you did it, deny it.

signalement (F.), a description of a person, as for purposes of identification.

si hic esses, aliter sentires (L.), if you were here (in this situation), you would think otherwise.

si jeunesse savait, si vieillesse pouvait! (F.), if youth but knew, if age were able!

silent leges inter arma (L.), the laws are silent in the midst of arms, or war (*Cicero*, Milo, iv. 10).

s'il m'en souvient bien (F.), if I remember aright.

s'il vous plaît (F.), if it pleases you; if you please.

simile simili gaudet (L.), like delights in like.

similia similibus curantur (L.), like things are cured by like (the doctrine of homeopathy).

si monumentum requiris, circumspice (L.), if thou seekest his monument, look around (epitaph of Sir Christopher Wren, the architect, in St. Paul's, London).

simplex munditiis (L.), "plain in thy neatness" (*Horace*, Odes, i. 5: so translated by Milton).

simplicitas (L.): see *O sancta simplicitas!*

simpliciter (L.), simply; by itself; absolutely.

sine anno (L.), without year, or date.

sine cura (L.), without cure (of souls: used with reference to an ecclesiastical benefice).

sine die (L.), without a day (fixed, as for meeting again).

sine dolo malo (L.), without evil intent; without fraud.

sine dubio (L.), without doubt.

sine invidia (L.), without envy or ill-will.

sine ira et studio (L.), without anger and prejudice (*Tacitus*, Annales, i. 1).

sine loco et anno (L.), without place and date (as a book or a title-page).

sine mascula prole (L.), without male issue.

sine mora (L.), without delay.

sine nomine vulgus (L.), the multitude without a name; the nameless herd.

sine odio (L.), without hatred.

sine præjudicio (L.), without prejudice.

sine prole (L.), without issue or children.

sine qua non (L.), without which not; indispensable; absolutely necessary; an indispensable condition.

si parla italiano (It.), Italian is spoken (here).

si parva licet componere magnis (L.), if it is permissible to compare small things with great (*Virgil*, Georgics, iv. 176).

si post fata venit gloria, non propero (L.), if glory comes after death, I am in no haste (*Martial*, Epigrams, v. 10).

si quæris peninsulam amœnam, circumspice (L.), if thou seekest a pleasant peninsula, look around (motto of Michigan).

si quieres hembra, escoge la el sábado y no el domingo (Sp.), if thou desirest a wife, choose her on Saturday and not on Sunday.

si sic omnia! (L.), if all (everything) had been thus!

siste, viator (L.), stop, traveler.

sit non doctissima conjux (L.), may my wife not be very learned (*Martial*, Epigrams, ii. 90).

sit tibi terra levis (L.), may the earth be light upon thee (inscription on ancient Roman tombstones).

sit venia verbo (L.), pardon the expression.

si vis pacem, para bellum (L.), if you wish peace, prepare for war.

société anonyme (F.), a business company which does not bear the names of its members, they being liable only to the amount of their stock.

socius (L.), fellow; associate; member.

socius criminis (L.), partner or accomplice in crime.

soi-disant, fem. **soi-disante** (F.), calling one's self; self-styled; would-be; pretended.

soigné, fem. **soignée** (F.), well cared for; carefully dressed, arranged, or prepared; highly finished; elaborate.

solamen curarum (L.), a solace of cares.

sola nobilitas virtus (L.), virtue is the only nobility.

soles qui nobis pereunt et imputantur (L.), days that pass away and are scored up against us (*Martial*, Epigrams, v. 20).

soli Deo gloria (L.), glory to God alone.

solitude à deux (F.), solitude for two (together).

solitudo (L.), solitude: see *ubi solitudinem faciunt* (etc.).

sol lucet omnibus (L.), the sun shines for all.

solo cedit quod solo implantatur (L.), to the soil accrues what is planted in the soil.

solutus est ambulando (L.), it has been solved by walking, or by practical experiment: see *solvitur ambulando*.

solventur risu tabulæ (L.), the bills (of complaint) will be dismissed with laughter (*Horace*, Satires, ii. 1).

solvitur ambulando (L.), it is solved by walking (by practical experiment: as Diogenes solved the problems raised by Zeno the Eleatic, who argued against the reality of motion).

sortes Virgilianæ (or **Homericæ** or **Biblicæ**) (L.), Virgilian (or Homeric or Biblical) lots; passages from Virgil (or Homer or the Bible) drawn or taken at random as indications of the future.

sot, fem. **sotte** (F.), stupid; foolish; a stupid person; a fool.

sot à triple étage (F.), a three-story (monumental, or egregious) fool.

sottise (F.), stupidity; foolishness; something stupid or foolish.

sotto voce (It.), in an undertone; aside.

sous tous les rapports (F.), in all respects.

soyez ferme (F.), be firm.

spectemur agendo (L.), let us be judged by our actions.

speranza (It.): see *lasciate ogni speranza, voi ch' entrate.*

sperate miseri, cavete felices (L.), hope, ye wretched, beware, ye happy.

spero meliora (L.), I hope for better things.

spes mea Christus (L.), Christ my hope.

spes sibi quisque (L.), let each be his own hope (*Virgil*, Æneid, xi. 309).

splendide mendax (L.), splendidly untruthful (*Horace*, Odes, iii. 11).

spolia opima (L.), rich spoils; in ancient Rome, arms taken in battle by a victorious general from a vanquished leader.

sponte sua (L.), of one's own accord.

sprechen Sie Deutsch? (G.), do you speak German?

spretæ injuria formæ (L.), the insult of slighted beauty (*Virgil*, Æneid, i. 27).

spurlos versenkt (G.), sunk without leaving a trace (a fate recommended in 1917 for ships of Argentina by Count Luxburg, German minister to Argentina, in a despatch to the German Foreign Office).

stans pede in uno (L.), standing on one foot (*Horace*, Satires, i. 4).

stant belli causæ (L.), the causes of war remain (*Virgil*, Æneid, vii. 553).

stare decisis, et non quieta movere (L.), to abide by things decided, and not to disturb settled points.

stare super vias antiquas (L.), to stand upon the ancient ways; be conservative.

stat magni nominis umbra (L.), there remains the shadow of a great name (*Lucan*, Pharsalia, i. 135).

stat pro ratione voluntas (L.), will stands for reason (or justification): cf. *hoc volo, sic jubeo* (etc.).

status quo (L.), the state in which (anything was or is).

status quo ante bellum (L.), the state in which (it was) before the war.

stemmata quid faciunt? (L.), what do pedigrees avail? (*Juvenal*, Satires, viii. 1).

stet fortuna domus! (L.), may the fortune of the house endure!

stilo (or **stylo**) **inverso** (L.), with stylus inverted (in order to erase what has been written).

stilo novo (L.), in the New Style (of reckoning time); according to the Gregorian calendar.

stilo vetere (L.), in the Old Style (of reckoning time); according to the Julian calendar.

stilus virum arguit (L.), the style shows the man.

Strasse (G.), a street.

stratum super stratum (L.), layer upon layer.

studium immane loquendi (L.), a prodigious fondness for talking.

Sturm und Drang (G.), storm and stress (title of a tragedy of Klinger, adopted as descriptive of a phase or period of German literature during the latter half of the 18th century).

stylo inverso (L.): see *stilo inverso.*

sua cuique sunt vitia (L.), each has his own vices.

sua cuique voluptas (L.), each has his own form of pleasure.

sua si bona norint (L.), if only they knew their own blessings (*Virgil*, Georgics, ii. 458).

suaviter in modo, fortiter in re (L.), gently in manner, vigorously in deed.

sub colore juris (L.), under color of law or right.

sub conditione (L.), under the condition.

sub Jove (L.), under Jove, or the sky; in the open air.

sub Jove frigido (L.), under the cold sky (*Horace*, Odes, i. 1).

sub judice (L.), under judicial consideration.

sublata causa tollitur effectus (L.), the cause being removed, the effect is done away with.

sub lege libertas (L.), liberty under law.

sub pœna (L.), under penalty.

sub prætexta juris (L.), under pretext of law.

sub quocunque titulo (L.), under whatever title.

sub rosa (L.), under the rose (as an emblem of secrecy); privately; confidentially.

sub silentio (L.), in silence.

sub specie (L.), under the appearance or form of.

sub verbo (L.), under the word, or heading.

sub voce (L.), under the word, or heading.

succès de scandale (F.), a success of scandal; a success due to scandal or notoriety attaching to something involved.

succès d'estime (F.), a success of esteem (rather than of popularity or profit).

succès fou (F.), a mad (or wildly extravagant) success.

sufficit (L.), it is sufficient.

suggestio falsi (L.), suggestion of the false: see *suppressio veri, suggestio falsi*.

sui generis (L.), of his, her, its, or their own kind; unique.

sui juris (L.), under one's own authority; legally capable of managing one's own affairs: cf. *alieni juris*.

sume superbiam quæsitam meritis (L.), assume the pride earned by thy merits (*Horace*, Odes, iii. 30).

summa cum laude (L.), with the highest praise (used in diplomas): see *cum laude*.

summum bonum (L.), the highest good.

summum jus (L.), highest or extreme law; strict law, as distinguished from equity.

summum jus, summa injuria (L.), extreme law, extreme injustice.

sumptibus publicis (L.), at the public expense.

sunt lacrimæ rerum (L.), there are tears for things (that have happened) (*Virgil*, Æneid, i. 462).

suo jure (L.), in one's own right.

suo loco (L.), in its own place.

suo Marte (L.), by one's own prowess or efforts.

suo tempore (L.), at its own time.

supellex (L.): see *tecum habita* (etc.).

super visum corporis (L.), upon a view of the body.

suppressio veri, suggestio falsi (L.), suppression of the true is suggestion of the false.

supremum vale (L.), farewell for the last time.

sur-le-champ (F.), on the field; on the spot; immediately.

sur le tapis (F.), on the table-cloth (or table); under consideration.

sursum corda (L.), lift up your hearts (words pronounced in the Latin mass just before the preface).

surtout (F.), above all; especially.

suscipere et finire (L.), to undertake and finish.

suspendatur per collum (L.), let him be hanged by the neck.

sutor ne supra crepidam judicaret (L.), let not the cobbler judge beyond his last.

suum cuique (L.), to each his own.

suus cuique mos (L.), each has his own custom.

syllabatim (L.), syllable by syllable.

T

table d'hôte (F.). See Dictionary.

tabula in naufragio (L.), a plank in shipwreck.

tabula rasa (L.), a tablet rubbed clean; a blank tablet (a phrase used to describe Locke's notion of the mind before ideas are present to it).

tace (L.), be silent.

tacent: satis laudant (L.), they are silent: they praise sufficiently (*Terence*, Eunuchus, iii. 2).

tâche sans tache (F.), a work without a fault.

tædium vitæ (L.), weariness of life; ennui.

tæterrima (or **deterrima**) **belli causa** (L.), the most shameful (or the worst) cause of war (woman: *Horace*, Satires, i. 3).

tam facti quam animi (L.), as much in act as in intention.

tam Marte quam Minerva (L.), as much by Mars as by Minerva; as much by fighting, or effort, as by wisdom.

tam Marti quam Mercurio (L.), as much for Mars as for Mercury; as much for war as for business.

tangere ulcus (or **vulnus**) (L.), to touch a sore spot (or wound).

tanquam in speculum (L.), as in a mirror.

tantæ molis erat Romanam condere gentem (L.), so great a task was it to found the Roman race (*Virgil*, Æneid, i. 33).

tantæne animis cælestibus iræ? (L.), are there angers so great in celestial minds? (*Virgil*, Æneid, i. 11).

tant bien que mal (F.), as much well as ill; passably; indifferently.

tant mieux (F.), so much the better.

tanto uberior (L.), so much the richer.

tant pis (F.), so much the worse.

tant s'en faut (F.), so much is lacking; far from it.

tant soit peu (F.), ever so little.

tarde venientibus ossa (L.): see *sero venientibus ossa*.

tecum habita: noris quam sit tibi curta supellex (L.), retire within thyself: thou shalt know how scanty is thy mental equipment (*Persius*, Satires, iv. 52).

Te Deum laudamus (L.), thee, God, we praise (the first words of an ancient Christian hymn).

te judice (L.), thou being judge; in thy judgment.

tel est notre (**bon**) **plaisir** (F.), such is our (good) pleasure.

tel maître, tel valet (F.), like master, like man.

tel père, tel fils (F.), like father, like son.

tempora mutantur, nos et mutamur in illis (L.), times change, and we change with them: cf. *omnia mutantur, nos et mutamur in illis*.

tempori parendum (L.), one must yield to the times.

temptanda via est (L.), a way must be tried (*Virgil*, Georgics, iii. 8).

tempus edax rerum (L.), time the devourer of things (*Ovid*, Metamorphoses, xv. 234).

tempus fugit (L.), time flies.

tempus ludendi (L.), time for playing.

tempus omnia revelat (L.), time reveals all things.

tenax propositi (L.), tenacious of purpose: cf. *justum et tenacem propositi virum*.

te nosce (L.), know thyself.

teres atque rotundus (L.), polished and well rounded: cf. *sapiens, in se ipso totus* (etc.).

terminus ad quem (L.), the limit, end, or point toward which.

terminus a quo (L.), the limit from which; the starting-point.

terræ filius (L.), a son of the earth; a man of humble origin.

terra firma (L.), the firm earth, or land (as opposed to the water).

terra incognita (L.), an unknown land.

terra nova (L.), a new land.

terras irradient (L.), may they illumine the earth (motto of Amherst College).

tertium quid (L.), a third something. See Dictionary.

tertius e cælo cecidit Cato (L.), a third Cato has dropped from heaven (*Juvenal*, Satires, ii. 40).

testis unus, testis nullus (L.), one witness, no witness.

tête de fou ne blanchit pas (F.), a fool's head does not grow white (from care).

textus receptus (L.), a received or accepted text, as of the Greek Testament.

thalatta! thalatta! (Gr. θάλαττα! θάλαττα!), the sea! the sea! (cry of the Greek soldiers on reaching the Euxine Sea after their perilous retreat as described in Xenophon's "Anabasis").

thé (F.), tea.

thé dansant (F.), an afternoon tea (entertainment) at which dancing is a feature.

tibi gratias (L.), thanks to thee.

tibi seris, tibi metis (L.), thou sowest for thyself, thou reapest for thyself.

tiens ta foi (F.), keep thy faith.

tiers état (F.), the third estate (of the French nation as divided before the Revolution); the commons, as distinguished from the nobility and clergy.

timeo Danaos et dona ferentes (L.), I fear the Greeks even when they bring gifts (*Virgil*, Æneid, ii. 49).

timeo hominem unius libri (L.), I fear the man of one book (who knows but one book, and that thoroughly) (*Thomas Aquinas*).

timidi mater non flet (L.), the mother of the timid man does not weep.

timidi nunquam statuerunt tropæum (L.), timid men never set up a trophy.

timor belli (L.), fear of war.

timor fecit deos (L.), fear made the gods: cf. *primus in orbe* (etc.).

tiré à quatre épingles (F.), drawn out with four pins; carefully adjusted; dressed with extreme care.

toga virilis (L.), the manly toga; the garment of manhood.

toison d'or (F.), the golden fleece.

to kalon (Gr. τὸ καλόν), the beautiful; the good.

to pan (Gr. τὸ πᾶν), the all; the universe.

to prepon (Gr. τὸ πρέπον), the becoming; propriety.

totidem verbis (L.), in so many words.

toties quoties (L.), as often (as one), so often (the other); as occasion may require.

totis viribus (L.), with all one's powers.

toto cælo errare (L.), to err by the whole heaven; be greatly mistaken.

totum (L.), the whole; all.

touché (F.), touched; hit, as by the weapon of an adversary in fencing.

toujours perdrix (F.), always partridge; too much of a good thing.

toujours prêt (F.), always ready.

tour de force (F.), a feat of strength, power, or skill.

tour d'expression (F.), a turn of expression.

tour d'ivoire (F.), tower of ivory. See *tower of ivory*, under *tower*², *n.*, in Dictionary.

tourner casaque (F.), to turn one's coat (as a soldier deserting to the enemy); change one's party or principles.

tous frais faits (F.), all expenses paid.

tous songes sont mensonges (F.), all dreams are lies.

tout à coup (F.), all at a stroke; suddenly.

tout à fait (F.), entirely; wholly; quite.

tout à l'heure (F.), just now; a moment ago; in a moment.

tout au contraire (F.), quite to the contrary.

tout à vous (F.), wholly yours; sincerely yours.

tout bien ou rien (F.), everything well or nothing.

tout comme chez nous (F.), just as with us.

tout comprendre, c'est tout pardonner (F.), to understand all is to pardon all.

tout court (F.), quite short; briefly; simply.

tout de même (F.), all the same; nevertheless.

tout de suite (F.), immediately; at once.

tout ensemble (F.), all together. See Dictionary.

tout est perdu fors l'honneur (F.), all is lost save honor (attributed to Francis I. of France after the battle of Pavia).

tout est pour le mieux dans le meilleur des mondes possibles (F.), all is for the best in the best of possible worlds (optimistic doctrine of Leibnitz, derided by Voltaire in "Candide").

tout lasse, tout casse, tout passe (F.), everything wearies, everything breaks, everything passes.

tout le monde (F.), all the world; everybody.

tout le monde est sage après coup (F.), everybody is wise after the event.

tout lui rit (F.), everything smiles upon him.

tout mon possible (F.), all in my power; my utmost.

tout Paris (F.), all Paris.

tout simplement (F.), quite simply.

tout soldat français porte dans sa giberne le bâton de maréchal de France (F.), every French soldier carries in his cartridge-box the baton of a marshal of France (attributed to Napoleon).

tout vient à point à (or **tout vient à temps pour**) **qui sait attendre** (F.), everything comes right to (or everything comes in time for) him who knows how to wait.

tracasserie (F.), worry; bother; vexation; fuss.

traduttori traditori (It.), translators are betrayers.

traînant, fem. **traînante** (F.), dragging; trailing; drawling; languid.

tranchant, fem. **tranchante** (F.), trenchant; sharp; decisive.

transeat in exemplum (L.), let it pass into (or become) an example, or precedent.

Träumerei (G.), dreaming; reverie.

très (F.), very; very much.

très bien (F.), very well.

tres faciunt collegium (L.), three make a corporation.

tria juncta in uno (L.), three joined in one (motto of the British Order of the Bath).

trinoda necessitas (L.), the threefold necessity (the obligation of landowners in Anglo-Saxon times to render military service, to repair bridges, and to repair fortresses).

tripotage (F.), a mess; intriguing; underhand dealing.

triste (F.), sad; sorrowful; melancholy; gloomy; sorry; poor.

tristesse (F.), sadness; melancholy; gloom.

trium litterarum homo (L.), a man of three letters (L. *fur*, 'thief') (*Plautus*, Aulularia, ii. 4).

Troja fuit (L.), Troy has been (its day is over).

truditur dies die (L.), day is pushed on by day; day follows close on another (*Horace*, Odes, ii. 18).

tu ne cede malis (L.), yield thou not to misfortunes (*Virgil*, Æneid, vi. 95).

tu quoque (L.), thou too; you too (a retort casting back a charge upon the accuser).

tu quoque, Brute! (L.), thou too, Brutus! — see *et tu, Brute!*

tutor et ultor (L.), protector and avenger.

tuum est (L.), it is thine.

U

ua mau ke ea o ka aina i ka pono (Hawaiian), the life of the land is established in righteousness (motto of Hawaii).

Übermensch (G.), a superman.

uberrima fides (L.), the fullest faith.

ubi bene, ibi patria (L.), where one is well off, there is one's country.

ubi jus, ibi remedium (L.), where there is a right, there is a remedy.

ubi jus incertum, ibi jus nullum (L.), where the law is uncertain, there is no law.

ubi libertas, ibi patria (L.), where there is liberty, there is my country.

ubi mel, ibi apes (L.), where the honey is, there are the bees.

ubique patriam reminisci (L.), everywhere to remember one's country.

ubi solitudinem faciunt, pacem appellant (L.), where they make a solitude, they call it peace (*Tacitus*, Agricola, 30).

ubi supra (L.), where above; in the place above mentioned.

ultima ratio (L.), the final argument.

ultima ratio regum (L.), the final argument of kings (war).

ultima Thule (L.), farthest Thule. See *Thule*, in Dictionary.

ultima voluntas (L.), the last will (of a testator).

ultimo (mense) (L.), of last (month).

ultimum vale (L.), farewell for the last time.

ultimus regum (L.), the last of the kings.

ultimus Romanorum (L.), the last of the Romans.

ultra licitum (L.), beyond what is permitted.

ultra valorem (L.), beyond the value.

ultra vires (L.), beyond the (legal) powers.

un, fem. **une** (F.), one; a or an: for many phrases beginning thus see second word of phrase.

una voce (L.), with one voice; unanimously.

un bienfait n'est jamais perdu (F.), a kindness is never lost.

und so ferner (G.), and so forth.

und so weiter (G.), and so forth.

une (F., fem.), one; a or an: see *un*.

une fois n'est pas coutume (F.), once is not a habit.

unguibus et rostro (L.), with claws and beak; tooth and nail.

un homme averti en vaut deux (F.), one man warned is worth two.

uni navi ne committas omnia (L.), commit not your all to one ship.

un malheur amène son frère (F.), one misfortune brings its brother.

un malheur ne vient jamais seul (F.), one misfortune never comes alone.

uno animo (L.), with one mind; unanimously.

uno ictu (L.), with or at one stroke.

uno impetu (L.), with one onset; at one effort.

un peu (F.), a little; somewhat.

un poco (It.), a little; somewhat.

unum est necessarium (L.), one thing is needful (*Vulgate*, Luke, x. 42).

unum et idem (L.), one and the same.

unus vir, nullus vir (L.), one man, no man.

urbi et orbi (L.), to the city (Rome) and the world (applied to papal documents so addressed and to the general blessing pronounced by the Pope on certain occasions).

urbis et orbis (L.), of the city (Rome) and the world.

usque ad aras (L.), even to the altars: see *amicus usque ad aras*.

usque ad cælum (L.), even to the heavens: see *cujus est solum* (etc.).

usque ad nauseam (L.), even to nausea.

usque ad satietatem (L.), even to satiety.

usus est tyrannus (L.), custom is a tyrant.

usus loquendi (L.), usage in speaking.

usus te plura docebit (L.), experience will teach thee many things.

utcumque placuerit Deo (L.), howsoever it shall please God.

utile dulci (L.), the useful with the agreeable: see *omne tulit punctum* (etc.).

utinam noster esset (L.), would that he were ours, or one of us.

ut infra (L.), as below.

uti, non abuti (L.), to use, not to abuse.

uti possidetis (L.), as you possess; according to what you now possess; possession of (used with reference to retention by belligerents of what has been acquired in war).

ut lupus ovem amat (L.), as the wolf loves the sheep.

ut mos est (L.), as is the custom (*Juvenal*, Satires, vi. 392).

ut pignus amicitiæ (L.), as a pledge of friendship.

ut supra (L.), as above.

V

vade in pace (L.), go in peace.

vade retro me, Satana (L.), get thee behind me, Satan (*Vulgate*, Mark, viii. 33).

vade, Satana (L.), get thee hence, Satan (*Vulgate*, Mat. iv. 10).

væ victis (L.), woe to the vanquished.

vale (L.), farewell.

valeat quantum valere potest (L.), let it pass for what it is worth.

valet de chambre (F.), a man-servant who attends on his master's person; a valet.

valet de pied (F.), a footman.

valet de place (F.), a man-servant hired for temporary service, as by travelers stopping in a place.

valete ac plaudite (L.), farewell and applaud (words addressed to the audience at the close of a Roman play).

vanitas vanitatum, et omnia vanitas (L.), vanity of vanities, and all is vanity (*Vulgate*, Eccl. i. 2).

vanité (F.), vanity: see *la vertu n'irait pas si loin* (etc.).

Vare, legiones redde! (L.), Varus, give me back my legions! (cry of the Roman emperor Augustus after the defeat of Varus and the destruction of his legions by the Germans: *Suetonius*, Augustus, 23).

varia lectio, pl. *variæ lectiones* (L.), a variant reading.

variorum notæ (L.), notes of various commentators.

varium et mutabile semper femina (L.), woman is ever fickle and changeable (*Virgil*, Æneid, iv. 569).

Vaterland (G.), fatherland; native land.

vaurien (F.), a worthless fellow; a scamp.

vedi Napoli, e poi muori (It.), see Naples, and then die.

vel cæco appareat (L.), it would be apparent even to a blind man.

velis et remis (L.), with sails and oars: cf. *remis velisque*.

vel prece vel pretio (L.), either by entreaty or by bribe; for love or money.

veluti in speculum (L.), just as in a mirror.

vendidit hic auro patriam (L.), this man sold his country for gold (*Virgil*, Æneid, vi. 621).

venenum in auro bibitur (L.), poison is drunk in (out of) gold (*Seneca*, Thyestes, iii. 453).

veniam pro laude peto (L.), I seek indulgence rather than praise (*Ovid*, Tristia, i. 7).

venia necessitati datur (L.), indulgence is granted to necessity.

venienti occurrite morbo (L.), counteract the disease as it approaches (*Persius*, Satires, iii. 64).

veni, vidi, vici (L.), I came, I saw, I conquered (words in which Julius Cæsar is said to have reported his victory over Pharnaces, king of Pontus, in 47 B.C.).

venter non habet aures (L.), the belly has no ears.

ventis secundis (L.), with favorable winds.

ventre affamé n'a point d'oreilles (F.), a hungry belly has no ears.

ventre à terre (F.), belly to ground; at full gallop or speed.

vera incessu patuit dea (L.), the true goddess was revealed by her gait (*Virgil*, Æneid, i. 405).

verbatim et litteratim (L.), word for word and letter for letter.

verbatim, litteratim, et punctatim (L.), word for word, letter for letter, and point for point.

verba volant, scripta manent (L.), spoken words fly away, written ones remain.

verboten (G.), forbidden, as by law; prohibited.

verbum sapienti sat (est), or **verbum sat sapienti** (L.), a word to the wise is sufficient.

Vereinigte Staaten (G.), the United States.

Vergilium vidi tantum (L.), Virgil I merely saw (*Ovid*, Tristia, iv. 10).

veritas (L.), truth (a motto of Harvard University).

veritas nihil veretur nisi abscondi (L.), truth fears nothing but concealment.

veritas odium parit (L.), truth begets hatred.

veritas prævalebit (L.), truth will prevail: cf. *magna est veritas, et prævalet*.

veritas temporis filia (L.), truth is the daughter of time.

veritas vincit (L.), truth conquers.

veritas vos liberabit (L.), the truth shall make you free (motto of Johns Hopkins University: see *Vulgate*, John, viii. 32).

veritatis simplex oratio est (L.), the language of truth is simple.

vérité sans peur (F.), truth without fear.

vers de société (F.), society verse; light, graceful, entertaining poetry, such as to appeal to polite society.

vers libre (F.), free verse. See Dictionary.

versus (L.), against.

vertu (F.), virtue: see *la vertu n'irait pas si loin* (etc.).

vesica piscis (L.). See under *vesica*, in Dictionary.

vestigia nulla retrorsum (L.), no footsteps backward; ever forward: cf. *vestigia terrent* (etc.).

vestigia rerum (L.), traces of things.

vestigia terrent, omnia te adversum spectantia, nulla retrorsum (L.), the footprints frighten (me), all directed toward you, but none back (so the fox in the fable said to the lion: *Horace*, Epistles, i. 1).

veuve (F.), widow.

vexata quæstio, pl. *vexatæ quæstiones* (L.), a vexed or disputed question.

via (L.), way; highway; road; path; course; manner; mode; also, by way of. See *et modo quæ fuerat semita facta via est*.

via amicabili (L.), in a friendly way.

via crucis, via lucis (L.), the way of the cross, the way of light.

via media (L.), a middle course.

via trita, via tuta (L.), the beaten path, the safe path.

vice (L.), in the place of.

vice versa (L.), the order being changed; conversely.

vicisti, Galilæe! (L.), thou hast conquered, Galilean! (reputed dying words of the Roman emperor Julian the Apostate).

victis honor (or **honos**) (L.), honor to the vanquished.

victrix causa diis placuit, sed victa Catoni (L.), the conquering cause was pleasing to the gods, but the conquered to Cato (*Lucan*, Pharsalia, i. 128).

vide (L.), see.

vide ante (L.), see before; see the foregoing.

vide et crede (L.), see and believe.

vide infra (L.), see below.

video meliora proboque: deteriora sequor (L.), I see the better things and approve them: I follow the worse (*Ovid*, Metamorphoses, vii. 20).

vide post (L.), see after; see the following.

vide supra (L.), see above.

videtur (L.), it appears; it seems.

vide ut supra (L.), see as (given) above.

vieille moustache (F.), old mustache; an old soldier.

vie intime (F.), intimate life; the intimately personal or familiar private life.

vi et armis (L.), by force and arms; by main force.

vieux (F.), old: see *peu de gens savent être vieux*.

vieux comme les rues (F.), old as the streets; very old.

vieux routier (F.), an old stager.

vif, fem. **vive** (F.), living; lively; animated; vivid.

vigilantibus, non dormientibus, jura subveniunt (L.), the laws aid the vigilant, not the sleeping.

vigilate et orate (L.), watch and pray.

vigor in arduis (L.), strength in difficulties.

vigueur de dessus (F.), strength from above.

vile donum, vilis gratia (L.), poor gift, poor thanks.

ville qui parlemente est près de se rendre (F.), a city that parleys is near surrendering.

vincet amor patriæ (L.), love of

country will conquer (*Virgil*, Æneid, vi. 823).

vincit omnia veritas (L.), truth conquers all things.

vincit qui patitur (L.), he conquers who endures.

vincit qui se vincit (L.), he conquers who conquers himself.

vinculum matrimonii (L.), the bond of matrimony.

vindex injuriæ (L.), a protector from wrong.

vin ordinaire (F.), ordinary wine. See Dictionary.

vires acquirit eundo (L.), she (Rumor) gains strength as she goes (*Virgil*, Æneid, iv. 175).

virginibus puerisque (L.), for maidens and boys (*Horace*, Odes, iii. 1: used by R. L. Stevenson as the title of an essay).

viribus unitis (L.), with united powers.

virtus in arduis (L.), virtue amid difficulties.

virtus incendit vires (L.), virtue kindles strength.

virtus post nummos (L.), virtue after money; money first, then virtue (*Horace*, Epistles, i. 1).

virtus semper viridis (L.), virtue ever green, or flourishing.

virtus sola nobilitat (L.), virtue alone ennobles.

virtute et fide (L.), by virtue and faith.

virtute et labore (L.), by virtue and labor.

virtute, non verbis (L.), by virtue, not by words.

virtute officii (L.), by virtue of office.

virtute quies (L.), tranquillity through virtue.

virtute securus (L.), secure through virtue.

virtuti, non armis, fido (L.), I trust to virtue, not to arms.

vis a fronte (L.), a force from in front.

vis a tergo (L.), a force from behind; a pushing force.

vis comica (L.), comic power; talent for comedy.

vis conservatrix naturæ (L.), the preserving power of nature.

vis consili expers mole ruit sua (L.), force devoid of judgment falls by its own weight (*Horace*, Odes, iii. 4).

vis formativa (L.), plastic force.

vis inertiæ (L.), the force of inertia.

visite de digestion (F.), visit of digestion; a visit of acknowledgment paid to a person who has entertained one at dinner.

vis major (L.), greater or superior force; a compelling force that nullifies personal responsibility.

vis medicatrix naturæ (L.), the healing power of nature.

vis mortua (L.), dead force; energy not producing motion.

vis motiva, or **vis motrix** (L.), moving force.

vis preservatrix (L.), preserving power.

vis unita fortior (L.), strength united is the more powerful.

vis vitæ (L.), vital force.

vis viva (L.), living or active force.

vita (L.), life: see *ex vita ita discedo* (etc.).

vita brevis, ars longa (L.), life is short, art long: see *ars longa, vita brevis*.

vitæ præcepta beatæ (L.), directions for a happy life (*Horace*, Satires, ii. 4).

vitam impendere vero (L.), to devote one's life to truth (motto of Rousseau: *Juvenal*, Satires, iv. 91).

Vita Nuova (It.), "New Life," or "Early Life" (title of a work by Dante, containing the story of his love for Beatrice).

vita patris (L.), in the father's lifetime.

vita sine litteris mors est (L.), life without books is death.

vitiis nemo sine nascitur (L.), no one is born without faults (*Horace*, Satires, i. 3).

vivat regina! (L.), long live the queen!

vivat respublica! (L.), long live the republic!

vivat rex! (L.), long live the king!

viva voce (L.), with the living voice; by word of mouth; orally.

vive la bagatelle! (F.), long live frivolity!

vive la France! (F.), long live France!

vive la reine! (F.), long live the queen!

vive la république! (F.), long live the republic!

vive l'empereur! (F.), long live the emperor!

vive le roi! (F.), long live the king!

vive l'impératrice! (F.), long live the empress!

vivere parvo (L.), to live on little.

vive ut vivas (L.), live that you may live.

vive, vale! (L.), live and be well! life and health to you! farewell! (*Horace*, Epistles, i. 6).

vivida vis animi (L.), the living force of mind (*Lucretius*, i. 72).

vivimus in posteris (L.), we live in our posterity.

vixere fortes ante Agamemnona (L.), brave men lived before Agamemnon (*Horace*, Odes, iv. 9).

vixit (L.), he has lived; his life is over.

vixit annos (L.), he (or she) lived . . . years.

vogue la galère! (F.), on with the galley! forward, come what may!

voici (F.), see here; behold; here is (are, etc.).

voilà (F.), see there; behold; there is (are, etc.).

voilà tout (F.), that is all.

voiture de place (F.), a carriage for hire at a public stand.

volcan (F.), volcano: see *nous dansons sur un volcan*.

volens et potens (L.), willing and able.

volente Deo (L.), God willing: see *Deo volente*.

volenti non fit injuria (L.), to a willing person no injury is done.

Volkslied, pl. *Volkslieder* (G.), a folk-song.

Volksmärchen (G.), a folk-tale.

volo, non valeo (L.), I am willing, but not able.

volti subito (It.), turn (the leaf or page) quickly (a direction in music).

volventibus annis (L.), with revolving years; after the lapse of years (*Virgil*, Æneid, i. 234).

von (G.), from; of. See Dictionary.

vous l'avez voulu, George Dandin, vous l'avez voulu! (F.), you would have it so, George Dandin, you would

have it so! (*Molière*, George Dandin, i. 9).

vous y perdrez vos pas (F.), you will waste your steps there; you will have your trouble for nothing.

vox barbara (L.), a barbarous word or expression.

vox et præterea nihil (L.), a voice and nothing more.

vox faucibus hæsit (L.), my voice stuck in my throat (*Virgil*, Æneid, ii. 774).

vox populi (L.), the voice of the people.

vox populi vox Dei (L.), the voice of the people is the voice of God.

vox stellarum (L.), the voice of the stars.

voyons (F.), let us see.

vulgo (L.), among the multitude; commonly.

vulnus immedicabile (L.), an incurable wound.

vultus est index animi (L.), the face is the index of the mind.

W

wagon-lit (F.), a sleeping-car.

Wahrheit und Dichtung (G.): see *Dichtung und Wahrheit*.

Wanderjahr (G.), year of wandering. See Dictionary.

Wanderlust (G.), desire to wander. See Dictionary.

Weihnachten (G.), Christmas.

Weltgeist (G.), the world-spirit: see *anima mundi*.

Weltmacht (G.), world-power; power as of one of the dominating nations (powers) of the world.

Weltmacht oder Niedergang (G.), world-power or decline.

Weltpolitik (G.), world-politics. See Dictionary.

Weltschmerz (G.), world-pain. See Dictionary.

wer A sagt muss auch B sagen (G.), who says A must also say B.

wer nicht liebt Wein, Weib, und Gesang, der bleibt ein Narr sein Leben lang (G.), he who loves not wine, woman, and song, remains a fool his whole life long.

wer wagt gewinnt (G.), who ventures wins.

wie befinden Sie sich? (G.), how do you find yourself? how do you do?

wie geht es mit Ihnen? (G.), how goes it with you?

Z

Zeitgeist (G.), the spirit of the time. See Dictionary.

Zollverein (G.), a customs-union of states. See Dictionary.

zonam perdidit (L.), he has lost his money-belt: cf. *ibit eo quo vis qui zonam perdidit*.

zonam solvere (L.), to loose the virgin girdle (as of a Roman bride at the wedding ceremony).

zu Befehl (G.), at command; at your service.

Zukunft (G.), the future.

zum Beispiel (G.), for example.

zwischen uns sei Wahrheit (G.), let there be truth between us.

PROPER NAMES

EXCLUSIVE OF BIOGRAPHY AND GEOGRAPHY

IMPORTANT NAMES RELATING TO HUMAN CULTURE, INCLUDING LITERATURE, THE
ARTS, INTERNATIONAL RELATIONS, RACES AND TRIBES, AND BIBLICAL HISTORY

COMPILED UNDER THE DIRECTION OF JAMES ABBOTT, B.A.

A

Aaron (ar′ọn). 1. See Dictionary, **Aaronic.** 2. The villainous Moor in Shakspere's "Titus Andronicus."

Abaddon. See Dictionary.

Abana (ab′ạ-nä), or **Amana** (am′ạ-nä). A river of Damascus. 2 Kings, v. 12.

Abaris (ab′ạ-ris). In Greek mythology, a Hyperborean sage and healer, who traveled on a golden arrow given him by Apollo.

Abbadides (ab′ạ-didz or -dīdz). A Moslem dynasty of Seville, in Spain, which reigned 1023–91, when it was superseded by the Almoravides.

Abbassides (ạ-bas′idz or ab′ạ-sīdz). A dynasty (750–1258) of califs of Bagdad. The most famous was Harun al-Rashid.

Abbé Constantin, L' (lȧ-bā kôṅ-stäṅ-taṅ). A quiet romance (1882) about a generous parish priest, by Halévy.

Abbey Theatre. A theater in Dublin associated with the Irish National Theatre Society (founded 1901) and the dramas of Synge, Yeats, and Lady Gregory.

Abbot, The. See **Monastery, The.**

Abbotsford (ab′ọts-fọrd). The residence of Sir Walter Scott after 1811, on the Tweed 3 miles above Melrose.

A. B. C. Powers. See Dictionary.

Abdemon (ab′dē-mọn). A Tyrian who is said to have answered all Solomon's riddles and in turn proposed insoluble ones.

Abdiel (ab′di-el). In Milton's "Paradise Lost," the seraph who refused to join Satan in his revolt. He is mentioned by the Jewish cabalists.

Abecedarians (ā′bē-sē-dā′ri-ạnz). A German Anabaptist sect of the 16th century, which rejected all learning (even "A-B-C") as a hindrance to religious inspiration.

Abednego (ạ-bed′nē-gō). See **Shadrach.**

Abel (ā′bel). See Dictionary, **Cain.**

Abelites (ā′bẹl-īts). An African sect, mentioned by St. Augustine, which married without procreating, in order not to hand down inherited sin.

Abencerrages (ạ-ben′sẹ-rā-jez, Sp. ä-ᴃen-thä-rä′Hȧs). A Moorish family of Granada, famous in Spanish romance through their struggle with the family of the Zegris.

Aberdeen (ab-ẹr-dēn′), **The University of.** An institution of learning at Aberdeen, Scotland, incorporated 1860.

Abhidharmapitaka (a-bhi-dhär′mạ-pit′ạ-kä). The section of the Buddhist scriptures which treats of Abhidharma or the supreme truth, philosophy or metaphysics.

Abhimanyu (a-bhi-man′yö). In Hindu legend, the son of Arjuna, slain on the 13th day of the great battle of the Mahabharata.

Abiathar (ạ-bī′ạ-thär). A high priest of Israel, and a companion of David in his exile. 1 Sam. xxii. 20, etc.

Abigail (ab′i-gạl). 1. One of the wives of David, formerly Nabal's wife. 1 Sam. xxv. 42. 2. The daughter of Barabas, in Marlowe's "Jew of Malta." 3. A waiting-maid in Beaumont and Fletcher's play, "The Scornful Lady."

Abigor (ab′i-gôr). In medieval demonology, a demon of high degree, grand duke in the infernal regions.

Abihu (ạ-bī′hū). The second son of Aaron, slain with his brother Nadab for using common fire to burn incense. Lev. x.

Abijah (ạ-bī′jä). The name of several persons in the Old Testament, of whom the most important are: (1) The 2d son of Samuel, one of the unjust judges preceding the King-

dom. 1 Sam. viii. 2. (2) The 2d king of Judah, son of Rehoboam. 2 Chron. xii. 16.

Abimelech (ạ-bim′ẹ-lek). 1. Two kings of Gerar, the first (Gen. xx.) in Abraham's time, the second (Gen. xxvi.) in Isaac's. 2. A son of Gideon. Judges, viii. 31.

Abipones (ä-bē-pō′nāz). A tribe of Indians who occupied, in the 16th century, both sides of the river Paraguay 600 miles above the Paraná.

Abishag (ab′i-shag). A Shunammite woman taken by David to comfort him in his old age. 1 Kings, i. 1–4.

Able McLaughlins, The. A novel (1923) by Margaret Wilson. Pulitzer Prize novel, 1924.

Abnaki (ab-nä′kē). A confederacy of North American Indians, formerly occupying all of Maine and the valley of the St. John River.

Abner (ab′nẹr). Saul's cousin, and commander-in-chief of his army. 1 Sam. xxvi. 5–16.

Abo (ä′bō or ô′bō), **The Peace of.** A treaty (1743) between Russia and Sweden, by which Russia secured southern Finland.

Abou ben Adhem (ä′bö ben ä′dem). A short narrative poem (1838) by Leigh Hunt.

Abraham (ā′brạ-ham). The first of the patriarchs, father of Isaac, and founder of the Hebrew race. Gen. xi.–xxv.

Abrahamites (ā′brạ-ham-īts). 1. A branch of the Paulicians, adherents of Abraham of Antioch. 2. A sect of Bohemian deists which professed to hold the religion of Abraham before his circumcision.

Abraham Lincoln. A play (1918) by John Drinkwater.

Abraham-man. Originally, a mendicant lunatic from Bethlehem Hospital, London; later, any beggar who pretended lunacy.

Abraham's Oak. An ancient tree which stood on the plain of Mamre, near Hebron, Syria, and was believed to be that under which Abraham pitched his tent.

Absalom (ab′sạ-lọm). The third son of David, who rebelled and was slain in the forest of Ephraim. 2 Sam. xiii.–xix.

Absalom, The Tomb of. A tomb in Jerusalem.

Absalom and Achitophel (ạ-kit′ọ-fel). A satire in verse by Dryden, published 1681, directed against the political faction of the Earl of Shaftesbury.

Absaroka (ab-sä′rọ-kä). A tribe of the Hidatsa division of North American Indians, on the Crow reservation, Montana.

Absentee, The. One of the "Tales from Fashionable Life" (1812), by Maria Edgeworth.

Absolute, Captain Jack. A spirited and humorous young officer, the hero of Sheridan's "Rivals."

Absolute, Sir Anthony. A dogmatic and crusty old gentleman, father of the hero of Sheridan's "Rivals."

Absyrtus (ab-sẹr′tus). In Greek legend, the brother of Medea, who cut him into pieces and cast the fragments into the sea to delay her father's pursuit as she fled with Jason.

Abt Vogler (äpt fō′glẹr). A poem (1864) by Robert Browning.

Abu-Hassan (ä′bö-has′ạn). In the "Arabian Nights' Entertainments," a citizen of Bagdad who is granted permission to be calif for one day.

Abul-Hassan Ali ebn Bekar (ä′bȯl-has′ạn ä′lē eb′n be′kär). In the "Arabian Nights' Entertainments," the lover of the calif's favorite.

Abydos (ạ-bī′dos), **The Tablet of.** An inscription in the temple of Seti I. at Abydos, giving a succession of 65 kings

---

fāt, fāte, fär, fȧll, ȧsk, fāre; net, mē, hẹr; pin, pīne; not, nōte, mȯve, nôr; up, lūte, pull; oi, oil; ou, out; (lightened) aviȧry,
ẹlect, agọny, intọ, ụnite; (obscured) errạnt, operạ, ardẹnt, actọr, natụre; ch, chip; g, go; th, thin; ᴛʜ, then; y, you;

of Egypt beginning with Menes and covering about 2,200 years.

Academies. Among the academies of arts and sciences of various nations, the following societies may be mentioned: The Royal Spanish Academy (1713), for the cultivation of the national language; The American Academy of Arts and Sciences (1780), Boston; l'Académie des beaux arts (1648), Paris, a branch of the Institute; l'Académie des inscriptions et belles-lettres (1701), Paris; l'Académie de médecine (1820), Paris; l'Académie des sciences morales et politiques (1795), a branch of the Institute; The Academy of Natural Sciences of Philadelphia (1812); and the Academies of Sciences at Berlin, Copenhagen, Leningrad, and Stockholm.

Academy, The. 1. See Dictionary. 2. The Platonic school of philosophy to the time of Cicero.

Academy, The French. See Dictionary, **academy.**

Acastus (a̯-kas′tus), or **Akastos** (-tos). In Greek legend, one of the Argonauts, the father of Laodamia.

Accademia della Crusca. See Dictionary, **Della-Cruscan.**

Acca Larentia (ak′ä la̯-ren′shi-ä). In Roman legend, a shepherd's wife, nurse of Romulus and Remus; according to some, an earth-goddess, mother of the Lares.

Accolon (ak′ō-lon). In Arthurian romance, a knight who gained possession of the enchanted sword of Arthur through the magic of Morgana (Morgan le Fay).

Aceldama. See Dictionary.

Achæan (a̯-kē′an) **League.** 1. A religious confederation of twelve, later ten, Achæan cities, dissolved about 288 B.C. 2. A political confederation of Achæan and other Greek cities, 281–146 B.C.

Achæi (a̯-kē′i). The Achæans, one of the four principal races of the Greeks. Their chief abodes were southern Thessaly and eastern Peloponnesus.

Achæmenidæ. See Dictionary, **Achæmenian.**

Achamoth (ak′a̯-moth). The name given by the Gnostic Valentinus (2d cent. A.D.) to a lower or imperfect wisdom: the form under which spirit surrenders itself to matter.

Achan (ā′kan). An Israelite of the tribe of Judah, stoned to death for plundering in the sack of Jericho. Josh. vii.

Acharnians (a̯-kär′ni-a̯nz), **The.** A comedy of Aristophanes, produced at the country Dionysia in Athens, 425 B.C.

Achates. See Dictionary.

Achelous (ak-e-lō′us). In Greek mythology, a river god, defeated by Heracles in a struggle over Deianira.

Achernar (a-kér′när). A star of the first magnitude at the southern extremity of the constellation Eridanus.

Acheron. See Dictionary.

Acherusia Palus (ak-e̯-rö′si-ä pā′lus). In ancient geography, the name of several small lakes supposed to be connected with the lower world; notably, the modern Lago del Fusaro, west of Naples.

Achilleis (ak-i-lē′is), or **Achilleid** (-id). 1. An unfinished epic by P. Papinius Statius. 2. Books I., VIII., and XI.–XXII. of the Iliad, regarded by some as being originally a separate epic of which the theme is Achilles' wrath.

Achilles (a̯-kil′ēz). See Dictionary, **Achillean.**

Achilleum (ak-i-lē′um). A place on the promontory of Sigeum, in the Troad, containing according to tradition the tomb of Achilles.

Achish (ā′kish). 1. A Philistine king with whom David sought refuge from Saul. 1 Sam. xxi. 10–15. 2. A Philistine king in the time of Solomon. 1 Kings, ii. 39–40.

Acis (ā′sis). In classical mythology, a beautiful Sicilian shepherd, beloved by Galatea and slain by his rival Polyphemus.

Acis and Galatea (gal-a̯-tē′ä). A pastoral opera (composed about 1722 and played 1732) by Handel, the words being by John Gay.

Accometæ (as-ē̯-mē′tē). A monastic order founded about 430 by Alexander, a Syrian monk.

Acolastus (ak-ō-las′tus). A Latin comedy composed by Willem de Volder, schoolmaster at The Hague (1528), and based on the story of the Prodigal Son.

Acolhuas (ä-kō-lö′ä̯z). A branch of the Nahuatl tribe of central Mexico, traditionally the predecessors of the Aztecas in the valley of Mexico.

Acoma (ä′kō̯-mä). A tribe of North American Indians inhabiting the pueblo of the same name, in western New Mexico.

Acontius (a̯-kon′shi-us). In classical legend, a youth who won the hand of the maiden Cydippe by an ingenious stratagem. The story occurs in Ovid and in Morris's "Earthly Paradise."

Acordad (ä-kôr-däŦн′). A court (suppressed 1813) at Querétaro, Mexico, for the summary trial of brigands and other criminals.

Acrasia (a̯-krā′zi-ä). A Circe-like enchantress in Spenser's "Faerie Queene."

Acres, Bob (bob ā′kèrz). A boor and braggart whose cowardice furnishes part of the low comedy in Sheridan's "Rivals."

Acrisius (a̯-kris′i-us). In Greek mythology, a king of Argos, and father of Danaë.

Actæon (ak-tē′on). In Greek mythology, a hunter who, having seen Artemis bathing, was changed by her into a stag.

Adam Bede (bēd). A novel (1859) by George Eliot.

Adams, Parson Abraham. In Fielding's "Joseph Andrews," a learned but unworldly curate, memorable for his credulity.

Admetus (ad-mē′tus). In Greek mythology, a Thessalian king, one of the Argonauts and husband of Alcestis.

Adonais (ad-ō̯-nā′is). An elegy (1821) by Shelley on the death of Keats.

Adonijah (ad-ō̯-nī′ja̯). A son of David. 1 Kings, i. 5–25.

Adonis. See Dictionary.

Adrastus (a̯-dras′tus). In Greek mythology, a king of Argos, father-in-law of Polynices, and leader of the Seven against Thebes.

Adrienne Toner. A novel (1922) by Anne Douglas Sedgwick.

Æacides (ē̯-as′i-dēz). In Greek mythology, any descendant of Æacus, especially Achilles.

Æacus (ē′a̯-kus). In Greek mythology, the son of Zeus and Ægina, the grandfather of Achilles, and a judge in the lower world.

Aëdon (ā-ē′dọn). In Greek mythology, the wife of Zethus. She killed her son, Itylus, mistaking him for a son of her hated sister-in-law, Niobe.

Æetes (ē̯-ē′tēz). In Greek mythology, a king of Colchis, father of Medea, and custodian of the golden fleece.

Ægæon (ē̯-jē′on). In Greek mythology, the name by which men called Briareus.

Ægeus (ē′jūs). In Greek mythology, a king of Athens, and father of Theseus. He threw himself into the Ægean Sea, which is said to have derived its name from him.

Ægisthus (ē̯-jis′thus). In Greek mythology, the cousin of Agamemnon. He seduced Clytemnestra in Agamemnon's absence, and was later slain by her son Orestes.

Ægle (ē′glē). In Greek mythology: (1) A naiad, mother of the Graces. (2) One of the Hesperides.

Ægyptus (ē̯-jip′tus). In Greek mythology, a king of Egypt and twin brother of Danaus.

Ælia (ē′li-ä) **gens.** A plebeian house of Rome, to which belonged Hadrian and the Antonines.

Aëllo (ā-el′ō). In Greek mythology, one of the Harpies.

Æmilia (ē̯-mil′i-ä). 1. In Spenser's "Faerie Queene," a fair captive of the cannibal giant. 2. In Shakspere's "Comedy of Errors," Ægeon's wife, acting as the abbess of Ephesus.

Æmilia gens. One of the earliest patrician houses of Rome: probably of Sabine origin.

Æmilian (ē̯-mil′i-an) **Way.** An ancient Roman highway built 187 B.C. by the consul Marcus Æmilius Lepidus from Ariminum (Rimini) to Placentia (Piacenza).

Æneas (ē̯-nē′a̯s). In classical mythology, the son of Anchises and Aphrodite: a Trojan hero, later the founder of Lavinium. He is the hero of Virgil's Æneid.

Æneid (ē̯-nē′id), **The.** A Latin epic poem by Virgil, reciting the adventures of Æneas after the fall of Troy. It is a glorification of Rome and of Augustus.

Æolus (ē′ō̯-lus). In Greek mythology: (1) The father and ruler of the winds. (2) A son of Hellen and father of Sisyphus: the mythical progenitor of the Æolian race.

Æpytus (ē′pi-tus). A son of Merope, the slayer of her husband Polyphontes.

Æqui (ē′kwī). A bellicose people of ancient Latium, often allied with the Volscians in war against Rome.

Aërians (ā-ē′ri-ạnz), **The**. A reforming Arian sect of the 4th century, in some respects anticipating modern Presbyterianism.

Æschines (es′ki-nēz) **the Orator**. A Greek statue from Herculaneum, in the Museo Nazionale, Naples.

Æsculapius. Son of Apollo and Coronis. See Dictionary.

Aeshma Daeva (ā-esh′mạ dä-ā′vạ). In Avestan mythology, the demon of anger: the Asmodeus of the Book of Tobit.

Æsir. See Dictionary.

Æson (ē′sọn). In Greek mythology, a king of Iolchus: father of Jason.

Æstii (es′ti-ī). A Prusso-Lettish tribe mentioned by Tacitus.

Æther (ē′thėr). In Greek mythology, the son of Chaos and Darkness, and the brother of Night, Day, and Erebus; in the Orphic hymns, the soul of the world and source of life; later, the expanse of heaven or abode of the gods.

Æthiopis (ē-thī′ọ-pis), or **Lay of Æthiopia, The**. A Greek epic of the Trojan cycle, by Arctinus of Miletus (about 776 B.C.). It continues the Iliad, "from the death of Hector to that of Achilles."

Æthra (ē′thrạ). In Greek mythology, the mother of Theseus: an attendant of Helen at Troy.

Ætna (et′nạ). A Latin didactic poem on the true causes of volcanic action.

Ætolian (ē-tō′li-ạn) **League**. An anti-Macedonian confederation of Greek towns, 338–167 B.C.

Ætolus (ē-tō′lus). In Greek mythology, a son of Endymion and founder of the kingdom of Ætolia.

Afrasiab (ä-frä-si-äb′). In the Shahnamah, a descendant of Tur the son of Faridun, and a Turaman warrior against Iran.

Africaine, L' (lä-frē-kän′). An opera (1865) by Meyerbeer.

African War, The. The war (48–46 B.C.) between Julius Cæsar and the followers of Pompey. The latter were overthrown at Thapsus 46 B.C.

Afridis (a-frē′dēz). A warlike tribe of Afghans south of Peshawar.

Afrikander Bond (äf-ri-kän′dėr bont). A South African association formed (1882) to promote the independence of South Africa.

Agag (ā′gag). An Amalekite king, spared by Saul and slain by Samuel. 1 Sam. xv.

Agamemnon (ag-ạ-mem′non). 1. In Greek mythology, a king of Mycenæ: son of Atreus, brother of Menelaus, and father of Iphigenia. He led the Greeks against Troy. Later he was slain by his faithless wife, Clytemnestra. 2. The greatest of the tragedies of Æschylus.

Aganippe. See Dictionary.

Agao or **Agau** (ä-gou′). A people of the Hamitic family in Abyssinia, or a member of this people; also, its language or dialect.

Agape (ag′ạ-pē). In Spenser's "Faerie Queene," the fairy mother of three knights born at one birth. If one were killed, his power was to pass into the others.

Agasti (a-gas′ti). A Rishi prominent in the Ramayana: the reputed author of a number of Vedic hymns.

Agathon (ag′ạ-thon). A philosophic, partly autobiographical novel (1766) by Wieland.

Agave (ạ-gā′vē). In Greek legend, daughter of Cadmus and mother of Pentheus.

Agelaus (aj-e-lā′us). In Greek mythology: (1) A son of Heracles, and ancestor of Crœsus. (2) A servant of Priam. He exposed Paris on Mount Ida. (3) The bravest of Penelope's suitors, and the last to be slain by Ulysses.

Agenor (ạ-jē′nôr). In Greek legend: (1) A king of Phenicia, father of Cadmus and Europa. (2) One of the slayers of Alcmæon. (3) The Trojan son of Antenor. He wounded Achilles in combat, and rescued Hector from Ajax.

Age of Innocence, The. 1. A noted painting by Sir Joshua Reynolds, of a little girl in a sylvan landscape. 2. A novel (1920) by Edith Wharton, dealing with New York life in the seventies. Pulitzer Prize novel, 1921.

Agger of Servius Tullius, The. A stretch of the Servian Wall of Rome, from the Colline Gate to the Esquiline Gate.

Agib (ā′gib). In the "Arabian Nights' Entertainments": (1) The 3d Calender in "The Three Calenders." (2) A son of Bedreddin Hassan and the Queen of Beauty.

Aglabites (ag′lạ-bīts), **The**. The Arab dynasty preceding the Fatimites. It ruled northern Africa from the beginning of the 9th century to 909.

Aglaia (ạ-glā′yạ). In Greek mythology, one of the Graces.

Aglauros (ạ-glâ′ros). In Greek mythology: (1) The wife of Cecrops. (2) The daughter of Cecrops, noted in Attic legend.

Agnes Grey. A novel (1847) by Anne Brontë ("Acton Bell").

Agni (ag′ni). In Hindu mythology, the god of fire, one of the three chief divinities of the Vedas.

Agnipurana (ag″ni-pö-rä′nạ). A modern, quasi-spurious purana (sacred poem), devoted to the glorification of Siva: supposedly communicated by Agni to Vasishtha.

Agnoëtæ (ag-nọ-ē′tē). 1. A Christian sect of the 4th century, which denied God's omniscience. 2. A sect of the 6th century, which held that Christ, as man, had no knowledge of the time of the judgment day.

Agnus Dei. See Dictionary, and cut.

Agora (ag′ọ-rạ), **The**. A large irregular area near the Acropolis in ancient Athens, used as forum and market-place.

Agræ (ag′rē). A suburb of ancient Athens, extending eastward from opposite the temple of Olympian Zeus, and containing the great stadium in which the Panathenaic games were held.

Agramante (ä-grä-män′tā). A young king of Africa, in the epics of Boiardo and Ariosto.

Agrapha. See Dictionary.

Agravaine (ag′rạ-vān), **Sir**. In medieval romance, a knight of the Round Table, surnamed 'the Proud' (L'Orgueilleux).

Agricane (ä-grē-kä′nā). In Boiardo's "Orlando Innamorato," a Tatar king slain by Orlando in single combat.

Aguecheek (ā′gū-chēk), **Sir Andrew**. A timid, silly, and amusing country squire in Shakspere's "Twelfth Night."

Ahab (ā′hab). A king of Israel, husband of Jezebel. He robbed Naboth of his vineyard, and permitted the worship of Baal. 1 Kings, xvi.–xxii.

Ahalya (ạ-hal′yạ). In Hindu legend, the beautiful wife of the Rishi Gautama; in the Ramayana, the first woman made by Brahma, and by him given to Gautama.

Ahasuerus (ạ-haz-ū-ē′rus). 1. A king of Persia, husband of Esther (Book of Esther; Ezra, iv. 6). 2. A name given to the legendary "Wandering Jew."

Ahava (ạ-hā′vạ). A river or canal in Babylon, by which assembled the second expedition which returned to Jerusalem. Ezra, viii. 15, etc.

Ahaz (ā′haz). A king of Judah, contemporary with Isaiah. He paid tribute to Assyria. 2 Kings, xvi.

Ahaziah (ā-hạ-zī′ạ). 1. A king of Israel, son of Ahab. 1 Kings, xxii. 40. 2. A king of Judah, son of Jehoram. 2 Kings, xxiii. 25.

Ahenobarbus (ạ-hē-nọ-bär′bus). A plebeian family of Rome, to which Nero belonged.

Ahiah (ạ-hī′ạ). A high priest in the reign of Saul. 1 Sam. xiv. 3, 18.

Ahimaaz (ạ-him′ạ-az). 1. The father of Ahinoam, wife of Saul. 1 Sam. xiv. 50. 2. A high priest who supported David during the revolt of Absalom. 2 Sam. xv., xviii.

Ahimelech (ạ-him′ẹ-lek). 1. The father of Abiathar, slain by Saul for helping David. 1 Sam. xxi. 1–9. 2. Son of Abiathar, and a priest in David's reign. 1 Chron. xviii. 16.

Ahithophel (ạ-hith′ọ-fel). A counselor of David who later helped Absalom in his revolt. 2 Sam. xv.–xvii.

Ahnen, Die (dē ä′nẹn). A series (1870–80) of six historical romances by Gustav Freytag.

Aholibamah (ạ-hol-i-bā′mạ). A wife of Esau. Gen. xxxvi. 2.

Ahome (ä-hō′mā). A largely Mexicanized Indian tribe of Piman stock, in Sinaloa.

Ahriman. See Dictionary.

Aht (ät). A division of the Wakashan stock of North American Indians, dwelling chiefly on the west coast of Vancouver Island.

Ahtena (ä′te-nä). A tribe of the northern division of the Athapascan stock of North American Indians: sometimes called Copper Indians, from their habitat on the Copper River, Alaska.

Ahuramazda (ä′hö-rạ-maz′dạ). The Good Spirit in the dual system of Zoroaster. He is in perpetual conflict with Ahriman, or Angra Mainyu, the 'spiritual enemy.'

Ai (ä'ī). A Canaanite city 10 miles north of Jerusalem. It was conquered by Joshua. Josh. vii. 1–5.

Aïda (ä-ē'dä). An opera (1871) by Verdi.

Aienai (ī-ẹ-nī'). A tribe of the Caddo Confederacy.

Aiglon, L' (lä-glôň). 1. A poetic drama (1900) by Rostand. 2. A name, the Eaglet, applied to the son of Napoleon in Rostand's drama of that name.

Aimon. See Aymon.

Aimwell. The young hero of Farquhar's "Beaux' Stratagem," who personates a wealthy nobleman in order to put himself in the way of a rich marriage.

Ainus (ī'nŏz). A non-Japanese tribe dwelling in parts of Yezo, Saghalin, the Kuriles, and the adjacent coast. They represent the primitive population of Japan.

Airavata (ī-rä'vạ-tạ). In Hindu mythology, the prototype of the elephant: the world-elephant of the East, and Indra's beast of burden.

Aitkenites (āt'ken-īts). A party in the Church of England, led by Robert Aitken (d. 1873). Its object was to introduce certain Methodist ideas and practices.

Aix-la-Chapelle (es-lä-shä-pel), **The Congress of.** A congress (1818) of sovereigns and national representatives, which withdrew the army of occupation from France and took France into the European concert.

Aix-la-Chapelle, The Peace of. 1. A treaty (1668) of England, Sweden, and the Netherlands with France (Spain acceding), involving an exchange of territory between France and Spain. 2. A treaty (1748) which ended the War of the Austrian Succession. Austria ceded territory to Spain and confirmed Prussia in the possession of Silesia.

Aja (aj'ạ). In Hindu mythology, a prince of the solar race, son of Raghu (or of Dilipa, son of Raghu).

Ajax (ā'jaks). In Greek legend: (1) A mighty warrior of the Greeks before Troy: son of Telamon and half-brother of Teucer. He killed himself in chagrin when Achilles' armor was awarded to Odysseus. (2) A Locrian king, one of the heroes in the Trojan War: called "the Lesser Ajax."

Akeman (āk'mạn) **Street.** An ancient Roman road in Britain, from Bath to London.

Akerman (ä'ker-män), **The Convention of.** A treaty (1826) between Russia and Turkey, by which Russia secured the navigation of the Black Sea and other rights. Its non-fulfilment by Turkey led to the war of 1828–29.

Akka (äk'kä). A tribe of pygmies discovered in central Africa, between the Nepoko and Aruwimi rivers, by Miani and Schweinfurth.

Akkad (äk'käd or ak'ad), or **Accad.** One of the 4 cities of Nimrod's empire. Gen. x. 10. In the cuneiform inscriptions it evidently includes most of northern Babylonia.

Akra (äk-rä'). A Nigritic tribe of the Gold Coast, West Africa.

Akrura (ạ-krö'rạ). In Hindu mythology, an uncle of Krishna: the holder of the Syamantaka.

Akupara (ak-ö-pä'rạ). In Hindu mythology, the tortoise which upholds the world.

Alabama, The. A famous Confederate cruiser of the American Civil War, sunk by the Kearsarge off Cherbourg, France, June 19, 1864.

Alabama Claims, The. Claims of the United States against Great Britain for damages caused in the Civil War by vessels supplied or fitted out for the Confederacy in British ports. The claims were arbitrated at Geneva (1871–72), and $15,500,000 was awarded.

Alabama Claims Commission, The. The commission of ten members, representing the United States and Great Britain, which concluded (1871) the treaty of Washington, prescribing a modus operandi for the settlement of the Alabama claims.

Aladdin (ạ-lad'in). In the "Arabian Nights' Entertainments," the son of a poor widow in China. He becomes the possessor of a lamp and a ring, both magic; and these command the services of two jinns who gratify all his wishes.

Alais (ȧ-lā), **The Peace of.** A peace (1629) which ended the last of the religious wars in France and disbanded the Huguenots as a political party.

Alamanni (al-ạ-man'ī). A German race of Suevic origin. It occupied the region from the Main to the Danube in the early 3d century.

Alamannic (al-ạ-man'ik) **Federation, The.** A federation of German tribes, chiefly Suevi, in the 3d century.

Alamo (ä'lä-mō), **The.** A mission building in San Antonio, Texas, which withstood a terrible siege by Mexicans in February, 1836. It was taken by assault on March 6, and its entire garrison of American rebels killed, including David Crockett and James Bowie.

Alani (ạ-lā'nī). A people of Scythian origin, dwelling in the Caucasus in the 4th and 5th centuries.

Al Araf (al ä'räf). In Mohammedan theology, a partition between heaven and hell on which are those who desire to enter heaven; a limbo. Poe's poem, "Al Aaraaf" (1829), refers to a star.

Alarodians (al-ạ-rō'di-ạnz). A race which once held the highlands of the present Armenia. Its chief descendants are the modern Georgians.

Alascans (ạ-las'kạnz), **The.** The foreign Protestants in London in the reign of Edward VI. (from John Laski, a Polish follower of Zwingli).

Alasnam (ạ-las'nam). In the "Arabian Nights' Entertainments," the possessor of eight golden statues, a seeker for a ninth which is still more precious. He finds it in the person of a beautiful woman, whom he marries.

Alastor (ạ-las'tor). 1. In Greek mythology, a surname of Zeus in his capacity of avenger. 2. In medieval demonology, the executor of the sentences of the king of hell.

Alastor, or The Spirit of Solitude. A philosophical poem (1816) by Shelley.

Albanenses (al-bạ-nen'sēz). A small medieval sect professing Manichean doctrines: named from Alba (Piedmont).

Albania. See Dictionary.

Albanian (al-bā'ni-ạn) **Gates, The.** The defile of Derbent, between the Caucasus and the Caspian Sea.

Albany, The Duke of. In Shakspere's "King Lear," the husband of Goneril, Lear's eldest daughter.

Albany Regency, The. A clique of New York politicians who controlled (about 1820–1854) the machinery of the Democratic party in the State of New York.

Albemarle (al'bẹ-märl), **The.** A Confederate ironclad ram, built 1863, which did damage to Union steamers early in 1864. She was torpedoed (Oct. 27, 1864) by Lieut. W. B. Cushing from a small launch.

Albert Hall. A covered amphitheater in London, finished 1871.

Albertine (al'bér-tin) **Line, The.** The younger and royal branch of the Saxon house which descended from Albert, duke of Saxony (d. 1500).

Albert Memorial, The. A monument to the memory of the Prince Consort, Albert of Saxe-Gotha (d. 1861), on the south side of Kensington Gardens, London: designed by Sir Gilbert Scott.

Albigenses. See Dictionary.

Albingians (al-bin'ji-ạnz). A Saxon tribe which, in the 8th century, lived north of the Elbe, in the present Holstein.

Albion (al'bi-ọn). In classical mythology, a son of Poseidon and brother of Dercynus or Bergion. He and his brother died in an attack on Heracles as he passed through Liguria with the oxen of Geryon.

Albion's England. A rimed chronicle (1586) of English history, by William Warner.

Albireo (al-bir'ẹ-ō). A double star, of the third magnitude, in the beak of the swan pictured in the constellation Cygnus: remarkable for the contrast of color between its two components.

Albizzi (äl-bēt'sē). A noted Italian family, important in Florentine history in the 14th and 15th centuries.

Al Borak (al bọ-rak'). The legendary winged animal on which Mohammed made his journey to the seventh heaven.

Albrechtsburg (äl'brechts-burch). A huge castle at Meissen, Saxony, founded 1471 by the princes Ernst and Albert. It was later (1710–1860) a porcelain manufactory.

Alcæus (al-sē'us). In Greek legend, a son of Perseus and Andromeda, and an ancestor of Heracles.

Alcántara (äl-kän'tä-rä), **The Knights of.** A Spanish military order (formerly religious as well), created about 1156 to combat the Moors.

Alcázar (äl-kä'thär). 1. The palace of the Moorish kings (later, of Spanish royalty) at Seville. 2. A Moorish palace in Segovia, Spain, occupied by Castilian rulers from the 14th century.

Alceste (al-sest′). 1. The wife of the God of Love in Chaucer's "Prologue to the Legend of Good Women." 2. The title character in Molière's "Misanthrope" (1666). 3. A tragic opera (1767) by Gluck.

Alcestis (al-ses′tis), or **Alceste** (-tē). 1. In Greek mythology, the wife of Admetus. She gave her life for his, and was rescued from the lower world by Heracles. 2. A play by Euripides.

Alchemist, The. A comedy (1610) by Jonson: a satire on the search for the philosophers' stone.

Alcides (al-sī′dēz). A descendant of Alcæus, especially Heracles.

Alcina (äl-chē′nä). In the epics of Boiardo and Ariosto, a fairy who embodies carnal delights: the sister of Logistilla (reason) and Morgana (lasciviousness).

Alcinous (al-sin′ō-us). In the Odyssey, the father of Nausicaa: a king of the Phæacians.

Alciphron (al′si-fron), or **The Minute Philosopher.** A philosophical dialogue (1732) by Berkeley, on the weakness of infidelity.

Alcmæon (alk-mē′on). In Greek legend, a warrior pursued by the Furies for having killed his mother, Eriphyle: eventually slain for having stolen the necklace and robe of Harmonia for his wife Callirrhoe.

Alcmæonidæ (alk-mē-on′i-dē). A noble family of ancient Athens, to which belonged Cleisthenes, Pericles, Alcibiades, and other notable Athenians.

Alcmene (alk-mē′nē). In Greek mythology, the mother, by Zeus, of Heracles: the wife of Amphitryon.

Alcor (al′kôr). A small star of the fifth magnitude, very near to Mizar in the constellation Ursa Major, discernible by a keen eye without the aid of a telescope, and hence sometimes used as a test of vision.

Alcoran. See Dictionary, **Koran.**

Alcyone (al-sī′ō-nē). 1. In classical mythology: (1) The daughter of Æolus and wife of Ceyx, after whose death she was changed into a kingfisher. (2) A Pleiad, daughter of Atlas and Pleione. 2. A star of the third magnitude, greenish in color, in the constellation Taurus: the brightest star in the group known as the Pleiades.

Aldabella (äl-dä-bel′lä). In Ariosto's "Orlando Furioso," the sister of Oliviero and Brandimarte, and wife of Orlando.

Aldebaran (al-deb′a-ran). A star of the first magnitude, red in color, in the constellation Taurus: the eye of the bull which represents the constellation, and the brightest star of the group known as the Hyades.

Aldersgate (äl′dėrz-gāt). A gate in the old city wall of London, at the present junction of Aldersgate Street and St. Martin's-le-Grand.

Aldgate (äld′gāt). The eastern gate of the old London wall, near the junction of Leadenhall Street, Houndsditch, Whitehall, and the Minories.

Aldiborontephoscophornio (al″di-bō-ron″tē-fos″kō-fôr′-ni-ō). A solemnly pompous character in Carey's "Chrononhotonthologos" (1734).

Aldine Press, The. See Dictionary, **Aldine.**

Aldobrandini (äl″dō-brän-dē′nē). A versatile Florentine family, several members of which, especially in the 16th century, gained high rank in literature, law, and the church.

Alecto (a-lek′tō). In Greek mythology, one of the Furies.

Alessandria (ä-les-sän′drē-ä), **The Armistice of.** The disastrous armistice which Napoleon forced upon the Austrians after Marengo (1800).

Alexander (al-eg-zan′dėr). In Greek legend, another name for Paris.

Alexander, The Romance of. One of the most famous romances of the middle ages, from a fabulous account of the Asiatic expedition of Alexander, supposed to have been written in Alexandria early in the 3d century.

Alexander and the Family of Darius. An important painting by Paolo Veronese, in the National Gallery, London.

Alexander Column, The. A column of red polished granite erected (1834) at St. Petersburg (Leningrad) in honor of Alexander I.

Alexander Nevski (nef′skē), **The Cloister of.** A monastery at St. Petersburg (Leningrad), founded by Peter the Great.

Alexander's Feast. An ode (1697) by Dryden, written in honor of St. Cecilia's Day.

Alexandra. In Ariosto's "Orlando Furioso," the Amazon queen.

Alexandre le Grand (à-lek-sän̊dr lė grän̊). A tragedy (1665) by Racine.

Alexandrian Codex, The. An important, nearly complete early manuscript of the Scriptures, written in Greek uncials on parchment: now in the British Museum.

Alexandrine War, The. A war (48–47 B.C.) between Julius Cæsar and the guardians of Ptolemy, Cleopatra's elder brother. It placed Cleopatra and her younger brother on the throne of Egypt.

Alfheim (älf′hām). In Old Norse mythology, the abode of the light Elves, near the sacred well of the Norns.

Alfuros (al-fö′rōz). A descriptive name ('wild,' 'uncivilized') given to native tribes of the north of Celebes and neighboring islands.

Algol (al′gol). A star of the second magnitude, in the head of Medusa in the constellation Perseus: remarkable for its variability, which is presumably due to periodic eclipse by a large satellite.

Algonquian. See Dictionary.

Algonquin (al-gon′kin). A group of tribes of North American Indians of the valleys of the Ottawa River and of the northern tributaries of the St. Lawrence. They were early allies of the French against the Iroquois.

Alhamarides (ä-lä-mär′idz). The last Moorish dynasty in Spain. It ruled in Granada from the middle of the 13th century to 1492.

Alhambra (al-ham′brä), **The.** See Dictionary, **Alhambraic,** and cut.

Ali (ä′lē). The prince's brother who weds the Princess Nourounnihar, in the "Arabian Nights' Entertainments."

Ali Baba. See **Forty Thieves, The.**

Alibamu (ä-lē-bä′mö). A tribe of the Creek confederacy of North American Indians. There are survivors in Louisiana, Texas, and Oklahoma.

Alice. 1. In Shakspere's "Henry V.," an attendant of the Princess Katharine. 2. The little girl who dreams the fantastic adventures of Lewis Carroll's "Alice's Adventures in Wonderland" and "Through the Looking-Glass."

Alice Adams. A novel (1921) by Booth Tarkington: the story of a girl who faced reality sensibly after a foolish attempt at pretense. Pulitzer Prize novel, 1922.

Alice-for-Short. A novel (1907) by William De Morgan, the story of a child rescued from the slums.

Alice's Adventures in Wonderland. A fantasy (1865) for young readers, by Lewis Carroll (C. L. Dodgson): followed (1871) by a continuation, "Through the Looking-Glass."

Alides (al′idz). Descendants of Ali, the fourth calif.

Aliena (ā-li-ē′nä). The name assumed by Celia in Shakspere's "As You Like It."

Alinda (a-lin′dä). A character in Lodge's "Rosalynde," the source of Shakspere's "As You Like It." She corresponds to Celia.

Aliscans (à-lēs-kän̊). A chanson de geste of the 12th century, dealing with the contest between William of Orange (the Christian hero of southern France) and the Saracens.

Alkaid (al-kād′). The star Benetnasch.

Alkoran. See Dictionary, **Koran.**

Allah. See Dictionary.

Allée Verte (à-lā värt). A double avenue of limes in Brussels, along the bank of the Willebroeck Canal.

Allegro, L' (läl-lā′grō), and **Il Penseroso** (ēl pen-se-rō′sō). Companion poems by Milton, written about 1632, on the contrasting pleasures of gaiety and pensiveness.

Allenites (al′en-īts). A short-lived religious sect founded in Nova Scotia by Henry Allen (d. 1784), who held that the creation of the world was a consequence of the fall.

All for Love, or The World Well Lost. A blank-verse tragedy (1678) by Dryden, based on Shakspere's "Antony and Cleopatra."

All Is True. A play, perhaps by Shakspere, important as an earlier form of "Henry VIII." The manuscript was destroyed (1613) when the Globe Theatre burned down.

Allobroges (a-lob′rō-jēz). An ancient Celtic people of southeastern Gaul, subjected to Rome 121 B.C.

---

fat, fāte, fär, fåll, åsk, fāre; net, mē, hėr; pin, pīne; not, nōte, mȯve, nȯr; up, lūte, pùll; oi, oil; ou, out; (lightened) aviảry, ẹlect, agȯny, intȯ, ụnite; (obscured) errạnt, operạ, ardẹnt, actọr, natụre; ch, chip; g, go; th, thin; ᵺ, then; y, you;

Alloway (al'ō-wā) **Kirk.** A ruined church in Ayr, Scotland, near the Doon. Burns rendered it famous in "Tam o' Shanter."

All Sorts and Conditions of Men. A novel (1882) by Walter Besant.

All Souls College. A college of Oxford University, founded 1437 to provide masses for the souls of those killed in the Hundred Years' War.

All's Well That Ends Well. A comedy by Shakspere, played 1601.

All-the-Talents Administration, The. An ironic name for Grenville's (English) administration, 1806–07.

Allworthy, Thomas. In Fielding's "Tom Jones," Tom's foster-father, a man of modest integrity.

Almack's (al'maks). 1. A gaming-club established before 1763 in Pall Mall, London, by William Almack. Later, it became Brooks's, a political club. 2. Fashionable assembly-rooms built by Almack in King Street, St. James (opened 1765).

Almagest, The. See Dictionary.

Almanzor (al-man'zor). 1. A warrior and egotist in Dryden's "Conquest of Granada." See **Drawcansir.** 2. The calif in Chapman's "Revenge for Honor."

Almaviva (äl-mä-vē'vä), **Count.** The successful lover of Rosine in Beaumarchais's "Barbier de Séville."

Almayer's Folly. A novel (1895) by Joseph Conrad. Almayer's previous history is told in "The Outcast of the Islands."

Almeria (al-mē'ri-ä). The supposedly widowed bride in Congreve's "Mourning Bride."

Almohades (al'mō-hādz). A Mohammedan dynasty of northern Africa and Spain, which superseded the Almoravides about the middle of the 12th century.

Almoravides (al-mō'rä-vīdz). A Moslem dynasty of north-western Africa and Spain, founded by Abdallah ben Yasim (d. 1058) and overthrown by the Almohades, 1146–47.

Alnaschar (al-nash'är or -nas'kär). In the "Arabian Nights' Entertainments," the fifth brother of the barber. He incautiously upsets his inheritance (in the form of glassware in a basket) while day-dreaming.

Aloeus (ą-lō'ūs). The son of Poseidon and husband of Iphimedia, the mother of the Aloidæ.

Alogians (ą-lō'ji-ąnz). A heretical sect of Asia Minor in the 2d century. They rejected the gospel of John and the Apocalypse.

Aloidæ (al-ō-i'dē), or **Aloadæ** (ą-lō'ą-dē), or **Aloiadæ** (al-ō-ī'ą-dē). The two giant sons of Poseidon, slain by Apollo for attempting to scale the heavens by piling Ossa on Olympus and Pelion on Ossa. See **Aloeus.**

Alonzo (ą-lon'zō). 1. The King of Naples in Shakspere's "Tempest." 2. The hero of the ballad, "Alonzo the Brave and the Fair Imogene" (1795), by Monk Lewis.

Alpheus (al-fē'us). In Greek mythology, a river-god, son of Oceanus and Tethys: originally a hunter who fell in love with Arethusa.

Alpine Club, The. A London club established 1857, for persons interested in the subject of mountains.

Al Rakim (al ra-kēm'). The fabulous dog which accompanied and guarded the Seven Sleepers.

Alsatia. See Dictionary.

Alsea (al-sē'ä). A tribe of North American Indians of the northwest: now on the Siletz reservation, Oregon.

Al Sirat (al si-rät'). The bridge, fine as a razor's edge, over which must pass all who enter the Mohammedan paradise.

Altahmo (al-tä'mō). A tribe of North American Indians which formerly lived on San Francisco Bay, California.

Altair (al-tār'). A star of the first magnitude in the constellation Aquila.

Altamont (al'tą-mont), **Colonel Jack.** In Thackeray's "Pendennis," the assumed name of J. Amory, an escaped convict, first husband of Lady Clavering and father of Blanche Amory.

Altar of the Dead, The. A story (1895) by Henry James.

Altenstein (äl'ten-shtīn). A summer castle of the dukes of Saxe-Meiningen, south of Eisenach. It is famous in connection with St. Boniface and Luther.

Alterati (äl-tä-rä'tē), **The.** A private musical academy founded 1568 at Florence by seven noblemen. Under its auspices was produced (1596) the first Italian opera, "Daphne."

Althæa (al-thē'ą). In Greek legend, the wife of Œneus and mother of Tydeus, Meleager, and Deianira. It was prophesied that the infant Meleager would not outlive a brand then burning. She quenched the brand, and Meleager survived to become the murderer of her brothers; whereupon she thrust the brand back into the flames.

Alton Locke, Tailor and Poet. A novel (1850) by Charles Kingsley, dealing with industrial conditions in English cities of the 1840's.

Alzire (äl-zēr'). A tragedy (1736) by Voltaire, in which the virtues of the noble Peruvian captive Zamore, its hero, are contrasted with the qualities of civilized man.

Amadis (am'ą-dis) **of Gaul.** A cycle of late medieval romances of chivalry. It is probably of Portuguese or Spanish origin, but has long been best known in Herberay's French version (about 1540).

Amadis of Greece. A Spanish continuation of part of "Amadis of Gaul," said to be by Feliciano de Silva. Its hero is the son of Lisuarte, grandson of Amadis of Gaul.

Amaimon or **Amaymon** (ą-mā'mon). In medieval demonology, one of the four kings of hell, of which he ruled the east part.

Amalek (am'ą-lek). A grandson of Esau and ancestor of the Amalekites. Gen. xxxvi. 12.

Amalings (am'ą-lingz). A royal family said to have ruled the Goths and, later, the Ostrogoths. The male line became extinct (526) with Theodoric the Great.

Amalricians (am-al-rish'iąnz). The pantheist followers of Amalric of Bène (d. about 1206). Ten of them were burned as heretics.

Amalthæa (am-al-thē'ą). 1. In Greek mythology, the nurse of the infant Zeus: variously, a goat which suckled him and a nymph who fed him on goat's milk. 2. In Roman legend, the Sibyl who sold the Sibylline books to Tarquin.

Amana. See Abana.

Amarakosha (am″ą-rą-kō'shä). A celebrated vocabulary of the classical Sanskrit, ascribed to Amarasinha.

Amarant (am'ą-rant). In medieval romance, a giant killed in Palestine by Guy of Warwick.

Amaravati (am-ą-rä'vą-tē). In Hindu mythology, the capital of Indra's heaven, near Meru.

Amaryllis (am-ą-ril'is). 1. A shepherdess or country maiden in the Idyls of Theocritus and in Virgil's Eclogues. 2. In Spenser's "Colin Clout's Come Home Again," a character intended to flatter Alice Spencer, Countess of Derby. 3. In Fletcher's "Faithful Shepherdess," a shepherdess in love with Perigot: the rival of Amoret. 4. In Buckingham's "Rehearsal," a female character intended to cast ridicule upon Dryden.

Amasa (am'ą-sä). A son of David's sister Abigail. He commanded the rebel forces of Absalom. Later, he was slain by Joab. 2 Sam. xvii. 25.

Amati. See Dictionary.

Amazing Marriage, The. A novel (1895) by George Meredith.

Amazons, The. 1. See Dictionary. 2. A fabled tribe of female warriors in South America, about whom an Indian myth existed from the West Indies to Paraguay.

Ambassadors, The. 1. A painting by Holbein the younger, in the National Gallery, London: believed to represent Dinteville and the poet Nicolas Bourbon. 2. A novel (1903) by Henry James, with characteristic treatment of Americans in a European setting.

Ambois (dän-bwä), **Bussy d'.** The partly arrogant, partly noble hero of Chapman's "Bussy d'Ambois."

Amboise (än-bwäz'), **The Conspiracy of.** An unsuccessful Huguenot conspiracy (1560) to seize Francis II. and remove him from the influence of the Guises.

Amboise, The Edict of. An edict of pacification (1563) between the French Catholics and the Huguenots, authorizing the Reformed worship with certain restrictions.

Ambree (am'brē), **Mary.** The heroine of an old English ballad, who, to avenge her lover's death, fights against the Spaniards at the siege of Ghent.

Ambrones (am-brō'nēz). A German tribe mentioned by Livy and Strabo as neighbors of the Teutones on the North Sea.

(variable) ḍ as d or j, ş as s or sh, ţ as t or ch, ẓ as z or zh; o, F. cloche; ü, F. menu; ċh, Sc. loch; ṅ, F. bonbon; ', primary accent; ″, secondary accent; †, obsolete; <, from; +, and; =, equals. See also lists at beginning of book.

Ambrose and the Emperor Theodosius. A painting by Rubens, in the Imperial Gallery, Vienna.

Ambrose's Tavern. A former Edinburgh tavern, the scene of Wilson's "Noctes Ambrosianæ."

Ambrosian (am-brō'ziạn) **Library, The.** A library at Milan, founded (1609) by Cardinal Borromeo.

Ambrosio, or the Monk. A melodramatic and sensational romance (1795) by Matthew Gregory ("Monk") Lewis.

Amelia (ạ-mē'liạ). A novel (1751) by Fielding. Its heroine is the virtuous and devoted wife of a profligate and weakling, Captain Booth.

Amenities of Literature, The. Three volumes (1841) of a projected history of literature, by Isaac D'Israeli.

Amenti (ạ-men'tē). In Egyptian mythology, the lower world; the abode of the dead.

America, The. A wooden keel schooner-yacht designed by George Steers and built (1851) for Commodore J. C. Stevens of the New York Yacht Club. She won the international cup in a race around the Isle of Wight.

American, The. A novel (1877) by Henry James.

American Colonization Society, The. A society organized at Washington in 1817 for the purpose of colonizing free American negroes. It purchased (1821) the land on which was founded the colony of Liberia.

American Legion, The. See Dictionary, **American.**

American Party, The. See Dictionary, **know-nothing.**

American Philosophical Society, The. A scientific body founded (1743) at Philadelphia by Benjamin Franklin (united 1769 with his Junto).

American Scholar, The. An address (1837) by Ralph Waldo Emerson before the Phi Beta Kappa Society at Cambridge, Mass.

American Tragedy, An. A novel (1925) by Theodore Dreiser.

American Volunteers, The. See **Volunteers.**

Amerinds. See Dictionary, **Amerind.**

Amesha Spentas (am'e-shä spen'täz). The seven supreme spirits of Avestan theology, headed by their creator, Ahuramazda. The others are moral or physical abstractions.

Ameto (ä-mā'tō). A prose idyl, with poetical interludes, by Boccaccio. Seven nymphs recite successively the story of their loves.

Amiens (am'i-enz). In Shakspere's "As You Like It," a gentleman in attendance on the duke.

Amiens, The Mise of. The award pronounced (1264) by Louis IX. of France, annulling the Provisions of Oxford, referred to him at the Council of Amiens (1263).

Amiens, The Treaty of. A peace (1802) made by England with France, Spain, and the Batavian Republic. England retained Ceylon and Trinidad, the French abandoned Rome and Naples, and Malta was restored to the Knights of St. John.

Amin (ä-mēn'). In "The Three Ladies of Bagdad" in the "Arabian Nights' Entertainments," the eldest son of Harun al-Rashid. He marries Amine.

Amina (ä-mē'nä). The principal character in Bellini's "La Sonnambula."

Amine (ä-mēn'). In the "Arabian Nights' Entertainments": (1) The wife of Sidi Nouman in "Sidi Nouman." She eats little at table, and he discovers her feasting at night with a ghoul. (2) In "The Three Ladies of Bagdad," Zobeide's sister, who marries Amin without knowing his rank.

Aminta (ạ-min'tạ). 1. A pastoral drama (1573) by Tasso. 2. Heroine of Meredith's "Lord Ormont and His Aminta" (1894).

Amis et Amiles (à-mē-zä à-mēl). A chanson de geste of the late 12th century. Its theme is the adventures of two noble and devoted friends.

Amistad (ä-mēs-tätɦ') **Case, The.** The case of the United States against a Spanish vessel seized (1839) off Cuba by its cargo of kidnapped negroes and taken by them to Connecticut. The Supreme Court held on appeal that the negroes were free and had not committed piracy.

Amis (ä'mis) **the Parson.** A comic poem (about 1230) in Middle High German.

Ammon (am'ọn). The eponymic ancestor of the Ammonites, or "children of Ammon." According to Gen. xix. 38, their ancestor was Ben-ammi, Lot's son by his younger daughter.

Amon (ā'mọn). Son of Manasseh, and a king of Judah. 2 Kings, xxi.

Amoraim (ä-mō'rä-ēm). The rabbis who, commenting upon the Mishnah, evolved (A.D. 200–500) the Gemara (the two constituting the Talmud).

Amoret (am'ọ-ret). 1. In Spenser's "Faerie Queene," the twin sister of Belphœbe: a personification of beauty and, later, as wife of Sir Scudamour, of wifely devotion. 2. In Fletcher's "Faithful Shepherdess," a shepherdess in love with Perigot.

Amorites (am'ọ-rīts). A name for one of the chief races of Canaan; also, the Canaanites in general. Those east of the Jordan were defeated by Moses, and those west of the Jordan by Joshua. Deut. xx. 17; Josh. xxiv. 8–12.

Amorphus (ạ-môr'fus). In Jonson's "Cynthia's Revels," an affected braggart who arbitrates others' quarrels but is himself no fighter.

Amory (ā'mọ-ri), **Blanche.** In Thackeray's "Newcomes," a worthless coquette. See **Pendennis, Arthur,** and **Altamont, Colonel Jack.**

Amory, J. See **Altamont, Colonel Jack.**

Amos (ā'mọs). A Hebrew minor prophet, contemporary with Isaiah: author of the Old Testament book bearing his name.

Amos Barton. One of George Eliot's "Scenes of Clerical Life."

Amour Médecin, L' (là-mör med-san). A comedy (1665) by Molière, satirizing pedantry and charlatanism in medicine.

Amphialus (am-fī'ạ-lus). See **Argalus.**

Amphiaraus (am‴fi-ạ-rā'us). In Greek mythology, brother-in-law of Adrastus: a seer who foresaw the disastrous outcome of the expedition of the Seven against Thebes. See **Eriphyle.**

Amphiareion (am‴fi-ạ-rī'ọn). A sanctuary and oracle of Amphiaraus, near Oropus, in Bœotia, Greece.

Amphictyonic (am-fik-ti-on'ik) **League, The.** A powerful federation of Greek peoples which assumed charge of the temple of Apollo at Delphi and of the Pythian games. Formed near the beginnings of Grecian history, it outlasted Greek independence.

Amphilochus (am-fil'ọ-kus). In Greek legend, a seer, son of Amphiaraus and brother of Alcmæon: one of the Epigoni. He was slain in combat with Mopsus.

Amphion (am-fī'ọn). In Greek mythology, twin brother of Zethus and husband of Niobe: so potent a musician that his lyre charmed the stones of the wall of Thebes into place.

Amphitrite (am-fi-trī'tē). In Greek mythology, the goddess of the sea: daughter of Nereus and wife of Poseidon.

Amphitryon (am-fit'ri-ọn). 1. In Greek legend, son of Alcæus and husband of Alcmene. 2. One of the best comedies of Plautus. 3. (an-fē-trē-ôn) A comedy (1668) by Molière, based on Plautus. See Dictionary.

Ampsivarii (amp-si-vā'ri-ī). A Germanic tribe dislodged from the Rhine by the Romans about A.D. 58. They reappeared in the 4th century.

Amraphel (am'rạ-fel). A king of Shinar, who did battle against the five kings in the Vale of Siddim. Gen. xiv.

Amrita (am-rē'tạ). In Hindu mythology, the beverage of immortality.

Amun (ä'mön). An Egyptian deity whose oracle and chief temple were near Memphis, in the Libyan desert.

Amymone (am-i-mō'nē). In Greek legend, a daughter of Danaus.

Anabaptists. See Dictionary, **Anabaptist.**

Anabasis, The. See Dictionary, **anabasis.**

Anabasis (a-nab'ạ-sis) **of Alexander the Great, The.** An important historical work by Arrian, nearly all of which is extant. It describes Alexander's campaigns and triumphs.

Anadyomene (an‴ạ-di-om'e-nē). In Greek mythology, an epithet ('rising from the sea') of the sea-born Aphrodite.

Anaitis (an-ạ-ī'tis). An ancient Persian goddess of water, vegetation, and all fertility: by the Greeks variously identified with Cybele, Artemis, and Aphrodite.

Anak (ā'nak). Either an individual giant, progenitor of the Anakim, or a collective name for this race of giants. Num. xiii. 33.

Analogy of Religion. A famous treatise by Joseph Butler

(1736), called in full "The Analogy of Religion, Natural and Revealed, to the Constitution and Course of Nature."

Anammelech (a̯-nam′e̯-lek). The Babylonian Anu (*Anu-malik*, 'Anu the counselor'), whose worship was imported into Samaria. 2 Kings, xvii. 31.

Ananias (an-a̯-nī′a̯s). 1. See Dictionary. 2. A Jewish Christian of Damascus, a friend of Paul. Acts, ix. 10–18. 3. The Jewish high priest before whom Paul was tried. Acts, xxiii. 2–5. 4. In Jonson's "Alchemist," a hypocritical Puritan deacon.

Ananias Club. An imaginary organization to which President Roosevelt often referred. See Dictionary, **Ananias.**

Ananus (an′a̯-nus). A high priest of the Jews, son of Seth: apparently the Annas of the gospels (Luke, iii. 2, etc.).

Anargha Raghava (a̯-när′gha̯ rä′gha̯-va̯). A drama of the 13th or 14th century, of which Rama, or Raghava, is hero. It is ascribed to Murari Misra.

Anasitch (ä-nä-sich′). A tribe of the Kusan stock of North American Indians. The survivors are on the Siletz reservation, Oregon.

Anastasian (an-a̯s-tā′shia̯n) **Law, The.** A law (506) of the emperor Anastasius I., directed against usurers.

Anasuya (an-a̯-sö′ya̯). In Hindu lore: (1) The wonder-working wife of the Rishi Atri. She gave Sita an ointment with which to keep herself beautiful forever. (2) A friend of Shakuntala.

Anathema (a-nath′e̯-ma̯). A drama (1909) by Leonid Andreev.

Anathoth (an′a̯-thoth). A city of Benjamin in Palestine: the birthplace of Jeremiah. Jer. xi. 21–23.

Anatol (an′a̯-tōl). A drama (1893) by Arthur Schnitzler.

Anatomy of Abuses, The. A curious account (1583) of the social customs of the period, by Philip Stubbes.

Anatomy of Melancholy, The. An eccentric study (1621) of various types of melancholy, by Robert Burton.

Anaxarete (an-ak-sar′e̯-tē). In Greek legend, a maiden of Cyprus whose desperate lover hanged himself at her door. For her coldness she was changed by Venus into a statue.

Ancæus (an-sē′us). In Greek legend: (1) A son of Poseidon. He was killed in his vineyard by a wild boar just as he was about to drink wine of his own grapes, a seer having predicted when he planted the vineyard that he would not live to enjoy the wine from it. (2) A son of the Arcadian Lycurgus, and one of the Argonauts, killed in the Calydonian hunt.

Anchises (an-kī′sēz). In classical legend, a prince of Troy, father, by Aphrodite, of Æneas, whose wanderings he shared in his old age.

Ancient Mariner, The. A fantastic narrative poem by Coleridge, published 1798 in the "Lyrical Ballads."

Ancren Riwle (angk′ren röl). The 'Rule of Anchoresses,' a Middle English prose treatise on the duties of the monastic life.

Ancyrene Inscription, The. See Dictionary, **Ancyrene.**

Anderida (an-der′i-da̯). A Roman camp in England, usually identified with Pevensey. The South Saxons destroyed it in 491.

Andhaka (an′dha̯-ka̯). In Hindu mythology, a demon with a thousand arms and heads and two thousand eyes and feet. Siva slew him when he tried to carry off the tree of paradise.

Andrássy (on′drä-shē) **Note, The.** A demand (1876) by Austria, Russia, and Germany (England and France approving) that Turkey inaugurate certain political and religious reforms in Bosnia and Herzegovina.

André (äṅ-drä). A novel (1834) by George Sand.

Andrea Chénier (än-drā′ä shā′nyā). An opera (1896) by Umberto Giordano.

Andrea Ferrara. See Dictionary.

Andrews, Joseph. In Fielding's "Joseph Andrews," a handsome footman, represented as the brother of Richardson's Pamela, whose trials Fielding burlesques by subjecting the virtue of Joseph to parallel temptations by his employer, Lady Booby.

Androclus (an′drŏ-klus), or **Androcles** (-klēz). 1. In Roman legend, a slave spared by a lion from whose foot he had, years before, extracted a thorn. 2. The hero of Shaw's drama "Androcles and the Lion" (1912), satirizing the early Christians.

Andromache (an-drom′a̯-kē). 1. In Greek legend, the noble wife of Hector and mother of Astyanax. 2. A drama (about 419 B.C.) of Euripides.

Andromaque (äṅ-dro-mȧk). 1. A tragedy (1667) by Racine. 2. An opera (1780) by Grétry.

Andromeda (an-drom′e̯-da̯). 1. In Greek mythology, the daughter of Cepheus and Cassiopeia, and the wife of Perseus, who rescued her from a sea-monster. 2. A northern constellation near Perseus: represented as a woman chained.

Andromède (äṅ-dro-med). A play (1650) by Corneille.

Andronicus (an-dron′i-kus), **Titus.** The hero of Shakspere's play of that name.

Andvaranaut (änd′vä-rä-nȧt″). The last ring of Andvari's treasure, bearing the curse of destruction to each of its owners: ultimately, the ring of the Nibelungs.

Andvari (änd′vä-rē). In Old Norse mythology, a dwarf in the form of a fish: the possessor of a treasure (the hoard of the Nibelungs) wrested from him by Loki.

Angelica (an-jel′i-ka̯). 1. In the epics of Boiardo and Ariosto, a coquettish princess whom Orlando loved to madness. 2. The witty and piquant heroine of Congreve's "Love for Love."

Angelic Brothers, The. A body of 17th-century Dutch sectaries who believed that they had attained to the state of angelic purity.

Angélique (äṅ-zhā-lēk). 1. The daughter of Argan in Molière's "Malade Imaginaire." 2. The wife of the hero in Molière's "George Dandin."

Angelo (an′je-lō). 1. The duke's deputy in Shakspere's "Measure for Measure." 2. A goldsmith in Shakspere's "Comedy of Errors." 3. A drama (1835) of the 16th century, by Victor Hugo.

Angelo, The Castle of Sant'. The remodeled mausoleum of Hadrian, in Rome.

Angels of Mons, The. A war legend (1915) by Arthur Machen.

Angelus (an′je-lus), **The.** A celebrated painting (1859) by J. F. Millet.

Angevin Line, The. See Dictionary, **Angevin.**

Angiras (an′gi-ras). In Vedic mythology, the ancestor of the Angirases or sons of the gods, beings between gods and men.

Angola (ang-gō′lä). 1. The Ngola tribe. 2. The nation of which the Ngola tribe was the nucleus.

Aniruddha (an-i-röd′dha̯). In Hindu mythology, a warrior hero, grandson of Krishna.

Anna (an′a̯). 1. In apocryphal gospels, the mother of the Virgin Mary. 2. A prophetess of Jerusalem. Luke, ii. 36.

Anna (än′nä), **Donna.** A principal character in Mozart's "Don Giovanni."

Annabel Lee (an′a̯-bel lē). A poem (1849) by Edgar Allan Poe.

Anna Christie (an′ä kris′ti). A drama (1921) by Eugene O'Neill. Pulitzer Prize play, 1922.

Anna Karenina (än′nä kä-re′nye̯-nä). A novel (1878) by Lev Tolstoy, ranked by many as his greatest.

Annals of a Quiet Neighbourhood. A novel (1866) by George Macdonald.

Annals of the Parish, The. A novel (1821) by John Galt.

Anna of the Five Towns. A novel (1902) by Arnold Bennett.

Annapolis Convention, The. A commercial convention (1786) of delegates from five States. It recommended the calling of the Constitutional Convention (1787).

Annas (an′a̯s). A high priest of the Jews. Luke, iii. 2, etc.

Anne of Geierstein (gi′er-stin). A romance (1829) of Switzerland in the 15th century, by Scott.

Annie Laurie (an′i lå′ri). An immensely popular song by William Douglas of Kirkcudbright.

Annunciation, The. The subject of important paintings by Fra Angelico (Florence); Andrea del Sarto (Florence); Signorelli (Volterra); Titian (Venice); and D. G. Rossetti (London).

Annus Mirabilis (an′us mi-rab′i-lis). A poem (1666) by Dryden, on the Dutch war and the London fire of that 'year of wonders.'

Ann Veronica. A novel (1909) by H. G. Wells.

Anomæans (an-ō-mē′a̯nz). A 4th-century sect of extreme Arians.

Ansarii (an-sä′ri-ī). An Arabian people of Syria, in the mountains between the Orontes and Tripolis.

Antæus (an-tē'us). See Dictionary, **Antæan**.

Antares (an-tā'rēz). A star of the first magnitude, red in color: the middle one of three bright stars set closely together in the body of the animal pictured in the constellation Scorpio.

Antenor (an-tē'nọr). In Greek legend, the wisest of the Trojan elders. He advised the return of Helen to Menelaus.

Anteros (an'tē-ros). In Greek mythology, a brother of Eros: god of mutual love and avenger of love unrequited.

Anthology, The. A collection of several thousand short Greek poems by many authors, compiled by Meleager of Gadara in the 1st century B.C., and later added to by other anthologists.

Antiburghers (an-ti-bèr'gèrz), **The.** In the Scotch Secession Church split of 1747, one of the factions, the other being the Burghers.

Anticleia (an-ti-klē'yä). In Greek legend, the mother of Odysseus. She died of grief at his prolonged absence.

Anti-Corn-Law League, The. An association formed 1839 to secure the repeal of the British Corn Laws. Cobden and Bright were leading members.

Anti-Federal Party, The. The party which, before 1789, opposed the adoption of the proposed Constitution of the United States, and, after that, favored its strict construction: later called the Republican or Democratic-Republican, and still later the Democratic party.

Antigone (an-tig'ọ-nē). 1. In Greek legend, a daughter of Œdipus by his mother, Jocaste. She attended him faithfully in exile. For performing forbidden funeral rites over her brother Polynices, she was condemned to be buried alive, but hanged herself. See **Hæmon**. 2. One of the great tragedies of Sophocles. 3. A tragedy (1783) by Alfieri.

Anti-Jacobin, or Weekly Examiner, The. An English paper (1797–98) attacking the French Revolution and its English sympathizers, edited by William Gifford.

Anti-Jacobin Review, The. A monthly (1798–1821) started by John Gifford.

Antilochus (an-til'ọ-kus). In Greek legend, a son of Nestor and friend of Achilles, slain before Troy by Memnon.

Anti-Machiavel (an-ti-mak'i-a-vel). An essay (1740) by Frederick the Great on the duties of sovereigns, intended to confute Machiavelli's "Principe."

Anti-Masonic Party, The. In American politics, a party, most prominent 1826–31, which opposed the alleged influence of freemasonry in civil affairs.

Antiope (an-tī'ọ-pē). In Greek legend: (1) The mother, by Zeus, of Amphion and Zethus. (2) An Amazon, sister of Hippolyte (in some accounts, the mother of Hippolytus by Theseus).

Antipholus (an-tif'ọ-lus) **of Ephesus** and **Antipholus of Syracuse.** In Shakspere's "Comedy of Errors," twin brothers of different temperaments.

Antiquary, The. A romance (1816) by Scott.

Antirent Party, The. See Dictionary, **antirent**.

Antis (än'tēz). The ancient Indian inhabitants of Anti, Peru. Their descendants wander in the forests about the head-waters of the Ucayale.

Antonio (an-tō'ni-ō). 1. The title character of Shakspere's "Merchant of Venice." 2. The usurping duke in Shakspere's "Tempest." 3. The father of Proteus in Shakspere's "Two Gentlemen of Verona." 4. The brother of Leonato in Shakspere's "Much Ado about Nothing."

Antonio and Mellida (mel'i-dä). A tragedy (1602) in two parts by Marston. The second part is also known as "Antonio's Revenge."

Antony. A tragedy (1831) by Alexandre Dumas.

Antony and Cleopatra. A tragedy (1607) by Shakspere.

Anu (ä'nö). 1. In Hindu mythology, a son who, refusing to bear a curse pronounced upon his father, was himself put under a curse, to the effect that his posterity should not possess dominion. 2. The supreme god of the Assyro-Babylonian pantheon: husband of Antu, the mother of the gods.

Anubis (a-nū'bis). In Egyptian mythology, a son of Osiris, identified by the Greeks with Hermes.

Anukis (ä-nö'kis). In Egyptian mythology, a goddess associated with the fertilizing waters of the Nile.

Anunaki (ä-nö-nä'ki). In Assyro-Babylonian mythology, the spirits of the earth, subordinate to the higher gods.

Anwar-i-Suhail (än-wär'ē-sü-hīl'). The Persian version (about 1494) of the "Fables of Bidpai," made by Husain Waiz al-Kashifi.

Anyika. See **Nyika**.

Anzac. See Dictionary.

Apaches. See Dictionary.

Apalachi (ä-pa-lä'chē). A tribe of North American Indians, known since 1526. They dwelt from Florida north to the Appalachians. They are now extinct or absorbed.

Apaturia (ap-a-tū'ri-ä). In Greek antiquity, the solemn annual meeting of the phratries for registering the free-born children born during the preceding year.

Apava (ä'pa-vä). In the Brahmapurana, the being who performed the office of the creator Brahma. He divided himself into two parts, male and female; these produced Vishnu; Vishnu created Viraj; and Viraj brought into the world the first man.

Apemantus (ap-ē-man'tus). In Shakspere's "Timon of Athens," a cynical and churlish philosopher.

Apepi (ä'pe-pē). In Egyptian mythology, the great serpent that led the forces of darkness against the sun-god Ra.

Aphrodite (af-rọ-dī'tē). In Greek mythology, the goddess of love and wedlock, daughter of Zeus and Dione (or, in another legend, risen from the foam of the sea at Cyprus). She is probably of Asiatic origin, and connected with Astarte and Anaitis. See Dictionary, cut.

Apicius (a-pish'ius). A Roman epicure who, having spent a huge sum on choice and rare dishes, committed suicide rather than starve on the moderate fortune remaining to him.

Apocalypse, The. See Dictionary, **apocalypse**.

Apocrypha, The. See Dictionary, **apocrypha**.

Apollinare in Classe (ä-pol-lē-nä'rā ēn kläs'sä), **San.** A church at Ravenna, begun 534, the most important existing early-Christian basilica in Italy.

Apollinare Nuovo (nwô'vō), **San.** A church at Ravenna, built by Theodoric in the 6th century.

Apollinarians (a-pol-i-nä'ri-anz). A religious sect of the 4th century, named from Apollinaris the Younger. It denied the veritable humanity of Christ, asserting that in him the Divine Reason, or Logos, took the place of the ordinary human intellect.

Apollinaris (a-pol-i-nä'ris), **Saint.** The mythical founder and first bishop of the Church of Ravenna.

Apollino (ä-pol-lē'nō). An antique copy of a Greek original statue of the youthful Apollo, in the Tribuna of the Uffizi, Florence.

Apollo. See Dictionary.

Apollo Belvedere. See Dictionary, cut.

Apollo Citharœdus (sith-a-rē'dus). 1. A statue in the Vatican, Rome. 2. A notable antique statue in the Glyptothek, Munich.

Apollo Club, The. A 17th-century club meeting at the Devil Tavern, near Temple Bar, London. Jonson and Herrick were members.

Apollonius of Tyre, The History of. A Greek romance, of which the earliest known version is in Latin prose. It was much translated in the middle ages, and is the source of one of the tales in Gower's "Confessio Amantis" and in part of Shakspere's "Pericles."

Apollo of Tenea (ten'ē-ä), **The.** A primitive Greek statue in the Glyptothek, Munich.

Apollo of Thera (thē'rä), **The.** A Greek archaic statue in the National Museum, Athens.

Apollo Sauroktonos (sâ-rok'tọ-nos). A reproduction in bronze of a statue by Praxiteles, in the Vatican, Rome.

Apollo Slaying the Python. A painting by Turner, in the National Gallery, London.

Apollyon. See Dictionary. (Apollyon also appears in Bunyan's "Pilgrim's Progress," in combat with Christian.)

Apologia pro Vita Sua. An autobiographical treatise (1864) by Cardinal Newman.

Apologie for Poetrie. A plea (1595; written about 1580) for the poet's art, by Sir Philip Sidney.

Apology of Socrates, The. 1. Plato's version of Socrates's defense before his judges. 2. A spurious work on the same subject, wrongly attributed to Xenophon.

Apostles' Creed, The. See Dictionary, **apostle.**

Apostle to the Gentiles, The. St. Paul.

Apostolic Canons. Ordinances and regulations dating from the early centuries of the Christian Church : usually reckoned as 85 in number.

Apostolic Constitutions, The. A collection of different instructions on the duties of clergy and laity, etc., divided into eight books, of which the earliest belong to the late 3d century.

Apostolic Council, The. The first council or synod of the Christian Church, held at Jerusalem about A.D. 50. Acts, xv.

Apostolic Fathers, The. The fathers of the church whose lives overlapped those of any of the apostles.

Apostolics. In Spanish history, a political party which supported the Catholic Church and absolute government after the restoration of the Bourbons: absorbed (1833) by the Carlists.

Apotheosis of Augustus, The. The largest existing cameo, in the Cabinet des Médailles, Paris. It is of Roman workmanship. There are 26 figures, including Julius Cæsar, Tiberius, and Caligula.

Apotheosis of Venice, The. A fresco by Veronese, in the middle of the ceiling of the Sala del Maggior Consiglio of the ducal palace, Venice.

Apoxyomenos (a-pok-si-om′e-nos). An athlete with the strigil, an antique copy of a bronze of Lysippus: found 1849, and now in the Vatican, Rome.

Appiano (äp-pē-ä′nō). An Italian family which ruled Piombino from the 14th century to the 17th.

Appian (ap′i-an) **Way, The.** The most famous of the ancient Roman highways, begun 312 B.C. by Appius Claudius Cæcus. It ran from Rome to Brundisium (Brindisi).

Appius (ap′i-us) **and Virginia.** 1. A tragedy (1654) by Webster, based on a story which occurs in Livy, Chaucer, Gower, and others. 2. A play by R. Bower (c. 1563). 3. One of Macaulay's "Lays of Ancient Rome" (1842).

April Fool, All Fools' Day. See Dictionary, **all.**

Apsaras (ap′sa-ras), pl. **Apsarases.** In Hindu mythology, one of a class of female spirits residing in the breezes. They are wives of the Gandharvas, and are Indra's handmaidens.

Apsley House. The residence of the Duke of Wellington at Hyde Park Corner, London: built (1785) for Lord Bathurst.

Aquila (ak′wi-lä). An early Christian of Ephesus. Acts, xviii. 2.

Aquilin (ak′wi-lin). In Tasso's "Gerusalemme Liberata," the horse of Raimondo.

Aquillia (a-kwil′i-ä) **gens.** In ancient Rome, a patrician and plebeian house of great antiquity.

Aquilo (ak′wi-lō). A Latin personification of the north wind.

Aquitani (ak-wi-tā′nī). An Iberian people of southern Gaul who in Cæsar's time occupied the region between the Garonne and the Pyrenees.

Arabia Deserta (a-rā′bi-ä dē-zèr′tä), **Travels in.** A work (1888) by C. M. Doughty.

Arabian Nights' Entertainments, The, or **A Thousand and One Nights.** A collection of Oriental tales, of Persian, Indian, and Arabian origin. The oldest known manuscript is of the 16th century, but the collection and title certainly existed in the 10th.

Arachne (a-rak′nē). In Greek mythology, a Lydian maiden who challenged Athene to compete with her in weaving, and was turned into a spider.

Araf, Al. See **Al Araf.**

Araminta (ar-a-min′tä). The heroine of Congreve's "Old Bachelor."

Aramis (ȧ-rȧ-mēs). The name (really an assumed one) of the mildest of the trio of heroes in Dumas's "Trois Mousquetaires."

Aranjuez (ä-rän-hwäth′), **The Peace of.** A treaty of alliance against England, concluded (1772) by France and Spain.

Arapaho (a-rap′a-hō). A tribe of North American Indians, once dwelling chiefly on the head-waters of the Platte and Arkansas rivers: now in Oklahoma and Wyoming.

Araucanians (ar-â-kä′ni-anz). A tribe of Indians in southern Chile. They were formidable warriors in the 16th century, but are now mainly agricultural.

Arawaks (ä′rä-wäks). A numerous Indian stock of northern and northeastern South America, distributed in and between other tribes and linguistic stocks.

Arber's English Garner. 8 volumes of modernized selections of English prose and poetry (1402–1715) edited by Edward Arber, 1877–1896.

Arber's English Reprints. 30 volumes of textually exact reprints of English prose and poetry (1516–1712) issued by Edward Arber, 1868–1880.

Arbor Day. See Dictionary.

Arcades (är′ka-dēz). A masque (1634) by Milton.

Arcadia (är-kā′di-ä). 1. A description (late 15th century) of shepherd life, in mingled prose and verse, by Sannazaro. 2. A pastoral romance (1590; written 1580–81) by Sir Philip Sidney. 3. A romance (1589) by Robert Greene. 4. A pastoral romance (1598; written much earlier) by Lope de Vega.

Arc de Triomphe de l'Étoile, L' (lärk dė trē-ônf dė lä-twäl). The largest existing triumphal arch, at the head of the Champs Élysées, Paris: built 1806–36.

Arc de Triomphe du Carrousel, L' (dü kȧ-rö-zel). A triumphal arch built by Napoleon in Paris, to commemorate his victories of 1805–06. It is in the square inclosed by the Louvre and the Tuileries Gardens.

Archelaus (är-ke-lā′us). One of the Heraclidæ, and the traditional founder of the Macedonian royal house.

Arches, Roman. There are surviving triumphal arches built by Constantine (A.D. 312), Caracalla, Hadrian (?), Septimius Severus (A.D. 203), Titus, and Trajan (A.D. 112 and A.D. 114); also, the Arch of Janus Quadrifrons, used in antiquity as a financial center, and the Arch of Augustus or Porta Romana (27 B.C.) at Rimini.

Archimago (är-ki-mä′gō), or **Archimage** (är′ki-māj). A magician in Spenser's "Faerie Queene," typifying hypocrisy and deceit.

Arcite. See **Palamon.**

Arco dei Leoni (är′kō dä′ē lā-ō′nē). A Roman double-arched gateway in Verona, probably of the 3d century.

Arctic, The. A passenger steamship of the Collins Line (the earliest American line of steamships), sunk by collision in the Atlantic, 1854.

Arcturus. See Dictionary.

Arda Viraf Namak (är′dä vē′räf na-mäk′). A Pahlavi religious book in favor among the Parsees. It belongs to Sassanian times.

Arden (är′den). A former English forest of Warwickshire and other parts of the English midland: probably the "forest of Arden" meant by Shakspere in "As You Like It."

Arecunas (ä-rä-kö′näz). A savage race of South American Indians, in the region between the Amazon, Orinoco, and Rio Negro.

Arena Chapel, The. A chapel in Padua, famous for the frescoes begun by Giotto in 1303.

Areopagitica (ar″ē-ō-pa-jit′i-kä), or **Speech for the Liberty of Unlicensed Printing.** A pamphlet (1644) by Milton, advocating freedom of the press.

Areopagus. See Dictionary.

Ares. See Dictionary, and cut.

Arethusa (ar-e-thū′sä). In Greek mythology, a nymph metamorphosed into the spring Arethusa, on the island of Ortygia, to save her from the pursuing river-god Alpheus.

Argalia (är-ga-lē′ä). The brother of Angelica in Boiardo's "Orlando Innamorato." His ghost appears in Ariosto's "Orlando Furioso."

Argalus (är′ga-lus). The husband of Parthenia in Sidney's "Arcadia." He was killed by Amphialus in single combat.

Argan (är-gän). The title character, a hypochondriac, in Molière's "Malade Imaginaire."

Argante. 1. (är-gan′tē) In Spenser's "Faerie Queene," a giantess personifying licentiousness. 2. (är-gänt) A character in Molière's "Fourberies de Scapin."

Argantes (är-gan′tēz). In Tasso's "Gerusalemme Liberata," the bravest of the infidel knights.

Argo, Argonauts. See Dictionary, **Argonaut.**

Argus. See Dictionary.

Ariadne (ar-i-ad′nē). In Greek mythology, a daughter of Minos and Pasiphaë, and wife of Dionysus. She gave Theseus the clue whereby he escaped from the labyrinth.

(variable) ḏ as d or j, ş as s or sh, ṭ as t or ch, ẕ as z or zh; o, F. cloche; ü, F. menu; ch, Sc. loch; n̄, F. bonbon; ′, primary accent; ″, secondary accent; †, obsolete; <, from; +, and; =, equals. See also lists at beginning of book.

Ariane (á-rē-ân). A tragedy (1672) by Corneille.

Ariel (ā′ri-el). 1. One of the chief men sent by Ezra to procure ministers for the sanctuary. Ezra, viii. 16. 2. A name for Jerusalem. Isa. xxix. 3. In cabalistic angelology, one of the seven spirits who preside over the waters, under Michael. 4. A spirit of air in Shakspere's "Tempest." 5. A rebel angel in Milton's "Paradise Lost." 6. Belinda's guardian sylph in Pope's "The Rape of the Lock." 7. A biography of Shelley (1924) by André Maurois.

Aries. See Dictionary.

Arimaspians (ar-i-mas′pi-anz). In classical mythology, a one-eyed people of Scythia.

Arioch (ar′i-ok). 1. One of the kings who attacked the cities in the Vale of Siddim, in Abraham's time. Gen. xiv. 2. Captain of Nebuchadnezzar's guard. Dan. ii. 14. 3. In Milton's "Paradise Lost," one of the rebellious angels overthrown by Abdiel.

Arion (a-rī′on). 1. A legendary Greek poet of Lesbos. Thrown into the sea by sailors, he was rescued by dolphins which he had charmed with his lyre. 2. In Greek legend, a fabulous horse, offspring of Poseidon by Demeter: owned by Heracles and, later, Adrastus.

Aristæus (ar-is-tē′us). In Greek mythology, a son of Apollo and patron deity of husbandmen and shepherds.

Aristarchus (ar-is-tär′kus). An associate of Paul, and his companion in prison in Rome. Acts, xix., xx., xxvii.

Aristophanes' Apology. See **Balaustion's Adventure.**

Arizona (ar-i-zō′nä). A drama (1914) by Augustus Thomas.

Arjuna (är′jö-nä). In Hindu mythology: (1) A chief hero of the Mahabharata, the third reputed son of Pandu, son of Indra and Kunti. He married a sister of Krishna. (2) The same as **Kartavirya.**

Arlberg (ärl′berċh) **Tunnel, The.** A tunnel, 6½ miles long, under the Arlberg, forming part of the railway from Bludenz to Innsbruck: opened 1884.

Arline (är′lēn). The title character in Balfe's "Bohemian Girl."

Arlington House. A mansion on the Virginia heights opposite Washington, D. C., in the national cemetery. It once belonged to George Washington, and later to Robert E. Lee.

Armada, The Invincible or **The Spanish.** See Dictionary, **armada.**

Armadale (är′ma-dāl). A novel (1866) by Wilkie Collins.

Armado (är-mä′dō), **Don Adriano de.** In Shakspere's "Love's Labour's Lost," a verbose and fantastic Spanish braggart.

Armageddon (är-ma-ged′on). In Rev. xvi. 16, the place where is fought "the battle of that great day of God Almighty." See Dictionary.

Armagnacs (är-mä-nyáks), **The.** 1. In the reign of Charles VI. of France, the Orleanists, or opponents of the house of Burgundy: named from Bernard of Armagnac. 2. Bands of lawless mercenaries, chiefly natives of Armagnac, trained in the civil wars between the Armagnacs and Burgundians.

Armande (är-mänd). One of the learned ladies of Molière's "Femmes Savantes." She loves Clitandre, but he prefers her sister Henriette, who is not a femme savante.

Armatoles (är′ma-tōlz). A body of irregular Greek Christian militia in the employ of the Turks from the 15th century to 1821. Many of them joined with Greece in the fight for independence.

Armida (är-mē′dä). 1. An enchantress in Tasso's "Gerusalemme Liberata." 2. Title of operas by Jommelli (1770), Cherubini (1782), and Rossini (1817).

Armide (är-mēd). Title of operas by Lully (1686) and Gluck (1777).

Arminians. See Dictionary, **Arminian.**

Armistice Day. See Dictionary, **armistice.**

Arms and the Man. A drama (1898) by G. B. Shaw, attacking the Victorian conception of a girl in love and, still more, the romantic conception of war: title from the first line of the Æneid.

Army and Navy Club, The. 1. A club in London, established 1838, for commissioned officers. 2. A similar club, established 1871, in New York.

Arne. A story of Norwegian peasant life (1858) by Björnstjerne Björnson.

Arnolphe (är-nolf). In Molière's "École des Femmes," a cynic who tries to bring up a young girl, Agnes, in virtuous innocence and only succeeds in teaching her to deceive him.

Arod (ā′rod). A son of Gad. Num. xxvi. 17.

Arondight (ā′ron-dīt). The sword of Sir Lancelot of the Lake.

Árpád (är′päd) **Dynasty, The.** A dynasty of Hungarian rulers, 1000–1301.

Arquebusiers of St. Andrew. A painting (1633) by Frans Hals, in the town hall at Haarlem, Holland.

Arras (á-räs), **The Lines of.** Fortifications from Arras to Bouchain: crossed by Marlborough 1711.

Arras, The Treaty of. 1. A treaty between Armagnacs and Burgundians, 1414. 2. A treaty between Charles VII. of France and Philip the Good of Burgundy, 1435. 3. A treaty (1482) between Louis XI. of France and Maximilian I., by which France was to receive Artois, Franche-Comté, and other territory.

Arrow Maker, The. A play (1911) by Mary Austin.

Arrow of Gold, The. A novel (1919) by Joseph Conrad.

Arrowsmith, Martin. The title character in Sinclair Lewis's novel "Arrowsmith" (1925): an idealist in science, beset with difficulties in a practical world.

Arsacidæ (är-sas′i-dē). 1. A dynasty of Parthian kings established by Arsaces I. about 250 B.C. 2. A dynasty of Armenian kings, probably founded by a brother of Arsaces III., king of Parthia, in 149 B.C.

Artagnan, D' (där-tä-nyán). One of the chief characters in Dumas's "Trois Mousquetaires," a young Gascon associate of Athos, Porthos, and Aramis.

Artamène (är-tä-män), **or the Grand Cyrus.** A romance in 10 volumes (1650) by Mademoiselle Scudéry.

Artaxaminous (är-tak-sam′i-nus). The King of Utopia in Rhodes's "Bombastes Furioso."

Artaxerxes (är-tak-sêrk′sēz). The king of Persia who sent Ezra and Nehemiah to Jerusalem and consented to the restoration of its defenses: identified with Artaxerxes I. of secular history. Ezra, iv. 7, 8, etc.

Artegal (är′tē-gal). In Spenser's "Faerie Queene," a knight personifying justice. He marries Britomart.

Artemis. See Dictionary, and cut.

Artful Dodger, The. See **Dawkins, John.**

Arthur, King. See Dictionary, **Arthurian.**

Arthurian Cycle of Romances, The. A series of medieval romances, considered by many scholars to be of Celtic origin, but given form largely by French writers. The first extensive treatment of Arthur is to be found in Geoffrey of Monmouth. See **Historia Regum Britanniæ.**

Arthur's. A London club, established 1765.

Arthur's Seat. A hill, 822 feet in height, overlooking Edinburgh from the east.

Artotyrites (är-tō-tī′rīts). An early sect which used bread and cheese in the eucharist and admitted women to the priesthood.

Artsmilsh (ärts′milsh). A collective name for several North American Indian tribes living on Shoalwater Bay and Willapa River, Washington.

Arundel (ar′un-del). The horse of Sir Bevis in medieval romance.

Arundel House. 1. A house which formerly stood near Highgate, London. Lord Bacon died there (1626). 2. A former noted mansion on the Strand, London. In its gardens were the Arundelian Marbles.

Arundelian (ar-un-dē′lyan) **Marbles, The.** Part of a collection of ancient sculptures formed by Thomas Howard, earl of Arundel. It includes the Parian Chronicle, a marble slab picturing events in Greek antiquity. The collection was presented (1667) to Oxford University.

Arundel Society, The. An English society, founded 1849, for the promotion of art.

Arval Brethren, The. See Dictionary.

Aryans (är′yanz or ar′i-anz). See Dictionary, **Aryan.**

As (äs), pl. **Æsir** (ē′sèr or ā′sir). In Old Norse mythology, a member of one of the principal races of gods, the inhabitants of Asgard.

Asa (ā′sä). A king of Judah. 1 Kings, xv. 18–24.

Asakasa (ä-sä′ka-sä) **Pagoda, The.** A picturesque Buddhist tower in Tokyo.

Asaph (ā′sạf). See Dictionary, **Asaphic.**

Ascalaphus (as-kal′ạ-fus). In Greek legend, a son of Acheron, changed into an owl.

Ascalon (as′kạ-lon). 1. See **Askelon.** 2. The sword of St. George, in the tale of the Seven Champions.

Ascanius (as-kā′ni-us), or **Iulus** (ī-ū′lus). In classical legend, the son of Æneas and an ancestor of the Julii.

Ascapart (as′kạ-pärt). A giant conquered by Bevis, in the medieval romance "Bevis of Hampton."

Asclepius (as-klē′pi-us). In early Greek legend, a Thessalian prince and physician; later, the god of medicine and a son of Apollo, slain by jealous Zeus. Æsculapius is his Roman counterpart.

Ascot. See Dictionary.

Asgard. See Dictionary.

Ashango (ä-shän′gō). A Bantu tribe of Gabun, on a plateau between the coast and Franceville.

Ashanti (ä-shän′tē) **War, The.** A campaign of Great Britain against Ashanti (1873–74), in which Wolseley took and burned Kumassi.

Ashbel (ash′bel). A son of Benjamin. Gen. xlvi. 21.

Ashburton Treaty, The. A treaty (1842) between Great Britain and the United States, establishing the present boundary between Maine and Canada, and providing for suppression of the African slave-trade.

Ashdod (ash′dod). One of the chief cities of the Philistines, and a seat of the worship of Dagon. 1 Sam. v. 5.

Asher (ash′ėr). Son of Jacob and Zilpah, and ancestor of the tribe of Asher. Gen. xxx. 13; Num. i. 40.

Ashestiel (ash′es-tēl). A house on the Tweed, near Selkirk, occupied by Sir Walter Scott 1804–11. His autobiography to 1792 ("The Ashestiel Memoir") was written there.

Ashkenaz (ash′kẹ-naz). See Dictionary, **Ashkenazim.**

Ashmolean (ash-mō′lẹ-ạn) **Museum, The.** A museum at Oxford, founded 1679 by Elias Ashmole. The building was erected (1682) by Sir Christopher Wren.

Ashtaroth (ash′tạ-roth). A city of Bashan, east of the Sea of Galilee.

Ashtavakra (ash-tạ-vak′rạ). The hero of a story in the Mahabharata. He was born crooked, but became straight by bathing in the Samanga River.

Ashteroth. See Dictionary, **Ashtoreth, Astarte.**

Ashton, Lady, and **Ashton, Sir William.** The parents of Lucy Ashton in Scott's "Bride of Lammermoor."

Ashton, Lucy. In Scott's "Bride of Lammermoor," the betrothed of Edgar Ravenswood, who, forced by her mother to marry the Laird of Bucklaw (Frank Hayston), goes mad on her bridal night.

Ashtoreth. See Dictionary.

Ash Wednesday. See Dictionary.

Ask (äsk) and **Embla** (em′blä). In Old Norse mythology, the first man and woman, created in Midgard by Odin and other gods out of trees found on the seashore.

Askelon (as′kẹ-lon), or **Ashkelon** (ash′-), or **Ascalon** (as′kạ-lon). One of the chief cities of Philistia, 39 miles southwest of Jerusalem, on the Mediterranean. Zeph. ii. 4.

Aslauga's Knight (ä-slou′gäz nīt). A romance (1814) by Baron de La Motte-Fouqué. Its subject is the love of the knight Froda for a spirit whom he prefers to a woman of flesh and blood.

Asmodeus (as-mọ-dē′us or as-mō′dẹ-us). In Jewish demonology, a destructive spirit of whom many stories are told. Le Sage used him in "Le Diable Boiteux," whence Foote's play (1768) "The Devil on Two Sticks."

Asnapper (as-nap′ėr). A "great and noble" ruler who transplanted certain tribes to the cities of Samaria. Ezra, iv. 10.

Asolando (as-ọ-lan′dō): **Facts and Fancies.** A volume of poems by Browning, published (Dec. 12, 1889) on the day of the author's death.

Asopus (ạ-sō′pus). In Greek mythology, the god of the river Asopus in Sicyonia. He was slain by a thunderbolt of Zeus.

Aspandiyar. See **Isfendiyar.**

Asparagus Gardens, The. A former place of public entertainment in London: celebrated by Brome in his comedy (1635) "Sparagus Garden."

Aspasia. See Dictionary.

Asper (as′pėr). A character in Jonson's "Every Man Out of His Humour," designed as a portrait of Jonson himself.

Aspramonte (äs-prä-mōn′tä). An Italian epic poem (1516) on the defeat of the Saracens by the French under Charlemagne. The authorship is unknown.

Assassination Plot, The. A conspiracy (1696) against the life of William III. of England.

Assassins, The. See Dictionary, **assassin.**

Assembly, The National. In French history, the first of the Revolutionary assemblies, in session 1789–91.

Assiniboin (a-sin′i-boin). A tribe of North American Indians, living in Montana and to the northward in Alberta and Saskatchewan.

Assize of Northampton, The. An English ordinance (1176) supplementing the Assize of Clarendon. It contains instructions to the judges on tenure, reliefs, dower, etc.

Assizes of Jerusalem, The. Two codes of law, one for the nobility and one for the common people, in force under the Christian sovereignty in Jerusalem and Cyprus: formerly attributed to Godfrey of Bouillon.

Associated Counties, The. The English counties which combined on the Parliamentary side in the civil war of 1642–46: Norfolk, Suffolk, Essex, Hertford, Cambridge, Huntingdon, and Lincoln.

Assommoir, L' (lä-so-mwor′). A novel (1877) by Zola.

Assumption of the Virgin, The. There are noteworthy paintings on this subject by Titian (Venice and Verona); Rubens (Antwerp); Perugino (Florence); Guido Reni (London); Murillo (Leningrad); and Guercino (Leningrad). To these may be added the frescoes by Correggio (Parma) and Gaudenzio Ferrari (Vercelli).

Assur. The same as **Asur.**

Astarte (as-tär′tē). 1. See Dictionary. 2. In Byron's "Manfred," the woman guiltily loved by Manfred, for whom he suffers undying remorse.

Astolat (as′tọ-lat). A place in the Arthurian romances sometimes identified with Guildford, in Surrey. It is the home of Elaine in Tennyson's "Lancelot and Elaine" (1859): the same as Shalott in "The Lady of Shalott."

Astolfo (as-tol′fō). 1. In the Charlemagne romances, an English knight. In Ariosto's "Orlando Furioso" he penetrates the Valley of Lost Things in the moon, and there finds (among other things) the lost wits of Orlando. 2. A king of Lombardy in Ariosto's "Orlando Furioso."

Aston Hall. An old mansion (1618–35) near Birmingham, England, said to be the original of Irving's "Bracebridge Hall." It is now a museum belonging to Birmingham.

Astor Library, The. A library founded in New York City 1854 by John Jacob Astor: merged 1895 with the New York Public Library.

Astor Place Riot, The. A riot in New York City, May 10, 1849, between the partizans of the actors Forrest and Macready. It was suppressed by the militia.

Astræa (as-trē′ạ). In classical mythology, the goddess of justice, daughter of Zeus and Themis: the last of the immortals to leave mankind.

Astræa Redux (rē′duks). A poem (1660) by Dryden, celebrating the restoration of Charles II.

Astrée (ás-trā). A pastoral romance by D'Urfé, published between about 1610 and 1627.

Astrolabe (as′trọ-lāb), **The.** An unfinished prose treatise by Chaucer, written about 1391 for the instruction of his "young son" Lewis.

Astrophel (as′trọ-fel). An elegy (1586) by Spenser on Sidney.

Astrophel and Stella. The sonnets (published 1591) in which Sir Philip Sidney (Astrophel) chronicles his love for Penelope Devereux, afterward Lady Rich (Stella).

Asturias (äs-tö′rē-äs), **The Prince of.** A title of the Spanish heir apparent, first assumed 1388.

Astyanax (as-tī′ạ-naks). The young son of Hector and Andromache, thrown from the walls of Troy by the victorious Greeks.

Asur (as′ėr). The supreme national god of Assyria: the "king above all gods."

Asvamedha (as-vä′me-dhä). An ancient Vedic ceremony. A king desirous of offspring let loose for a year a horse of a particular color, tried to subdue all the countries through which it passed, and then, if successful, returned in triumph and sacrificed the horse.

As You Like It. A comedy (about 1599) by Shakspere.

Atala (ȧ-tȧ-lä). A romance by Chateaubriand, published 1801.

Atalanta (at-ȧ-lan′tä). In Greek mythology, a swift-footed maiden who refused all suitors whom she could outstrip. She was vanquished by Hippomenes, who as he ran dropped three golden apples given him by Aphrodite, which the maiden stopped to pick up.

Atalanta in Calydon (kal′i-don). A classical tragedy (1864) by Swinburne.

Atargatis (ȧ-tär′gȧ-tis). A Syrian goddess. At Askelon she was worshiped under the name Derceto, in the form of a mermaid.

Ate (ā′tē). 1. See Dictionary, **Ate²**. 2. In Spenser's "Faerie Queene," a lying and slanderous hag, a friend of Duessa.

Atellan (ȧ-tel′ȧn) **plays.** Early Roman farces and burlesques, originally coarse.

Aten (ä′ten). In Egyptian mythology, the sun's disk, an object of worship.

Athalia (ath-ȧ-li′ȧ). An opera (1733) by Handel.

Athaliah (ath-ȧ-li′ȧ). The daughter of Ahab and Jezebel, wife of Jehoram, and usurper of the throne of Judah. 2 Kings, xi. 1.

Athalie (ȧ-tȧ-lē). 1. A tragedy (1690) by Racine. The title rôle was one of Rachel's greatest parts. Incidental music has been made by various composers. 2. An opera (1844) by Mendelssohn.

Athamas (ath′ȧ-mas). In Greek legend, a son of Æolus, king of Thessaly, and father, by Nephele, of Phrixus and Helle.

Athanasian Creed, The. See Dictionary, **Athanasian.**

Athapascan. See Dictionary.

Atharvan (ȧt-här′vȧn). In Vedic mythology, the priest of fire (Agni) and of soma.

Atharva-Veda (ȧt-här′vȧ-vā′dä). The fourth of the Vedas.

Athelstan (ath′el-stan). The grandson of King Alfred, and hero of the Anglo-Saxon poem "The Battle of Brunanburh" (937). See **Brunanburh, The Battle of.**

Athelstane (ath′el-stān). In Scott's "Ivanhoe," the Thane of Coningsburgh, a slow-witted Saxon of royal descent, suitor of Rowena.

Athenæum (ath-ē-nē′um). 1. See Dictionary. 2. A famous school or university at Rome, founded by Hadrian. 3. A London club, established 1824, primarily for men of scientific or literary attainments.

Athene. See Dictionary, and cut.

Athene Parthenos (ȧ-thē′nē pär′the-nos). A Roman reduced copy, in the National Museum, Athens, of the chryselephantine statue by Phidias in the Parthenon.

Athene Polias (pol′i-as). An original Greek statue, in the Villa Albani, Rome.

Athlete, The. A Greek statue, thought to be a copy of the famous Doryphorus (spear-bearer), the canon of Polyclitus. See Dictionary, **Polyclitan,** and cut.

Athos (ȧ-tos). One of the trio of companions in Dumas's "Trois Mousquetaires."

Atlantes (at-lan′tēz). 1. See Dictionary. 2. In the epics of Boiardo and Ariosto, a magician who lived on Mount Carena in a castle with a wall of glass, where he educated the young Rogero.

Atlantides (at-lan′ti-dēz). In classical mythology, the Pleiades; also, the Hesperides.

Atlantis. See Dictionary.

Atlas. See Dictionary.

Atm (ätm), or **Atmu** (ät′mö), or **Tmu** (tmö). In Egyptian mythology, the setting sun, represented in human form and worshiped at Heliopolis.

Atrebates (ȧ-treb′ȧ-tēz). A tribe of Belgic Gaul, dwelling chiefly in the modern Artois. It joined the confederation against Julius Cæsar.

Atreus (ā′trös). In Greek legend, a king of Mycenæ, and a son of Pelops. He was slain by Ægisthus.

Atri (ä′trē). In early Vedic mythology, one of the seven rishis (in the sky, the seven stars of the Great Bear).

Atridæ (ȧ-tri′dē). Agamemnon and Menelaus, the sons of Atreus.

Atrides (ȧ-tri′dēz). A son of Atreus: usually Agamemnon, occasionally Menelaus.

Atropos (at′rọ-pos). In Greek mythology, one of the Fates.

Attacapan (a-tak′ȧ-pan). A practically extinct linguistic stock of North American Indians, named from its principal tribe, the Attacapa, of Louisiana.

Attila (at′i-lä). 1. A tragedy (1667) by Corneille. 2. An opera (1846) by Verdi. (In the Nibelungenlied the historical Attila is represented under the name of Etzel. In Norse heroic stories, he is called Atli.)

Attis or **Atys** (at′is). A Phrygian deity beloved of Cybele and worshiped in conjunction with her.

Auburn (â′bėrn). The hamlet described by Goldsmith in "The Deserted Village": supposed to be Lissoy, Ireland.

Aucassin et Nicolette (ō-kȧ-san ā nē-ko-let). A French romance of about the 13th century. It narrates the love of Aucassin, son of the Count of Beaucaire, for Nicolette, a captive Saracen maiden.

Audefroi le Bâtard (ōd-frwo lē bȧ-tär). A French trouvère born at Arras in the 12th century.

Audhumla (ou-тнum′lä). In the Old Norse cosmogony, the cow from whose udders flowed the milk which nourished the first created being, the giant Ymir, and his race. She licked out of the ice a being, Buri, whose son, Börr, was the father of Odin.

Audians (â′di-ȧnz). A monastic sect, supposedly heretical, founded by Audius, a Syrian, in the 4th century.

Audience, The. Originally, a superior court of Spain; later, in the American colonies, an administrative body and tribunal of almost viceregal functions.

Audrey (â′dri). 1. An awkward country girl in Shakspere's "As You Like It." 2. A bride in Jonson's "Tale of a Tub."

Auerbach's Keller (ou′ėr-bächs kel′ėr). A wine-cellar in Leipsic, famous from its connection with the Faust legends and with Goethe.

Augarten (ou′gär″tẹn), **The.** A public garden in Vienna, in the Leopoldstadt suburb between the Danube and the Donau Canal. Mozart gave morning concerts in its music-hall in 1782.

Auge (â′jē), or **Augeia** (â-jē′ȧ). In Greek mythology, a priestess of Athene, mother by Heracles of Telephus.

Augeas (â′jē-as or ȧ-jē′as). See Dictionary, **Augean.**

Augsburg (âgz′bẻrg, G. ouks′bùrch), **The Diet of.** A diet summoned (1530) by Charles V., partly to settle the religious dispute in Germany.

Augsburg Confession, The. A Protestant statement of faith drawn up by Melanchthon and approved by Luther. It was read before the Diet of Augsburg, June 25, 1530.

Augsburg Interim, The. A provisional arrangement for settlement of the religious differences in Germany, proclaimed (1548) by Charles V.

Augusta (â-gus′tä). 1. A title of honor conferred upon the women of the Roman imperial house. 2. The name of some seventy Roman towns, one of which was on the site of modern London.

Augustan Age, The. See Dictionary, **Augustan.**

Augustine, The Life of St. A series of 17 frescoes by Benozzo Gozzoli (1465), in the choir of San Agostino, in San Gimignano, Italy.

Augustinian Friars. See Dictionary, **Augustinian.**

Augustus and Livia, The Temple of. A Roman Corinthian temple in Vienne, France. It was remodeled as a church in the middle ages.

Auk (âk). A tribe of North American Indians living on Stephens Passage and on Admiralty and Douglas islands, Alaska.

Auld Lang Syne (âld lang sīn). A song (about 1789) by Burns.

Auld Licht Idylls (âld licht). Stories (1888) by Sir James M. Barrie, of Scottish village life.

Auld Robin Gray. A ballad (1772) by Lady Anne Barnard.

Aulic Council, The. See Dictionary, **aulic.**

Aulintac (ȧ-lin′tak). A tribe of North American Indians, formerly inhabitants of a village near Santa Cruz Mission, California.

Aurelian (â-rē′liȧn) **Way, The.** A principal ancient Roman highway, built toward the close of the republic. It extended from Rome to Pisa, and was later extended into Gaul.

Aurora. 1. See Dictionary. 2. A fresco by Guido Reni, in the Palazzo Rospigliosi, Rome. 3. A fresco by Guercino, on the ceiling of a casino of the Villa Ludovisi, Rome.

Ausci (â′sī). An Aquitanian tribe conquered by Crassus 56 B.C.

Aus dem Leben eines Taugenichts (ous däm lä′ben ī′nes tou′ge-nichts). A romance (1826) by Eichendorff.

Aus Meinem Leben, Dichtung und Wahrheit. See **Dichtung und Wahrheit.**

Auster. See Dictionary.

Austerlitz (ous′tér-lits), **The Sun of.** The dispersal of clouds and mist by a bright sun on the morning of the battle of Austerlitz.

Austin Friars. The monastery of the Friars Eremite of the order of St. Augustine, on the north side of Broad Street, Old London: founded 1253 by Humphrey Bohun.

Australasian Federation, The. The federal union of the British Australian colonies, united 1901 as the Commonwealth of Australia.

Austrian Succession, The War of the. A war (1740–48) of England and Austria against France, Prussia, Spain, and other powers. It broke out when Maria Theresa, daughter of Charles VI., succeeded to the Austrian lands, and was ended by the Peace of Aix-la-Chapelle.

Austro-Prussian War, The. See **Seven Weeks' War, The.**

Austro-Sardinian War, The. See **Italian War of 1859.**

Author's Farce, The. A play (1730) by Fielding. It contains some fun at the expense of the Cibbers.

Autire (ou-ti-rä′). A division of North American Indians which lived in the valley of the Shasta River, California.

Autocrat of the Breakfast-Table, The. See **Breakfast-Table, The Autocrat of the.**

Autodidactus (ä″tō̠-di-dak′tus), **or the Natural Man, The.** A philosophical romance by the Arab philosopher Ibn Tufail (d. 1185).

Autolycus (â-tol′i-kus). 1. In Greek mythology, the thieving son of Hermes. He could make his booty invisible or transform it. 2. A witty, thieving peddler in Shakspere's "The Winter's Tale": a "snapper-up of unconsidered trifles."

Automedon (â-tom′e-don). In Greek legend, the son of Diores: according to Homer, the comrade and charioteer of Achilles.

Autonoë (â-ton′ō̠-ē). In Greek mythology, the daughter of Cadmus, wife of Aristæus, and mother of Actæon.

Avalokiteshvara (av″a̠-lō-ki-tesh′va̠-rä). One of the two Bodhisattvas (Manjushri being the other), an object of worship among the followers of the Great Vehicle as early as A.D. 400.

Avalon. See Dictionary.

Avare, L' (lȧ-vär). A comedy (1668) by Molière, using a plot borrowed from Plautus.

Avars (ä′värz). 1. A people of Ural-Altaic stock, allied to the Huns, who settled in Dacia after A.D. 555. 2. A people of Daghestan, probably allied to the Lesghians.

Ave Maria. See Dictionary, **ave.**

Avernus (a̠-vér′nus), **Lake.** See Dictionary, **Avernus.**

Avesta (a̠-ves′tä), **The.** See Dictionary, **Avesta.**

Avilion (a-vil′yon). The same as **Avalon.**

Aviz (ä-vēsh′), **The Order of St. Benedict of.** A Portuguese order of knighthood, which received the papal confirmation 1162. It has been honorary since 1789.

Avon's Harvest. A poem (1921) by Edwin Arlington Robinson.

Awkward Age, The. A novel (1899) by Henry James.

Axenstrasse (äk′sen-shträ″se). A road from Brunnen to Flüelen, Switzerland, along the eastern side of the Bay of Uri.

Aymarás (ī-mä-räz′). An Indian race which, in very early times, occupied the region about Lake Titicaca and the neighboring valleys of the Andes. It now forms a large part of the population of Bolivia.

Aymon or **Aimon** (ā′mon). A legendary character in old French romances: a prince of Ardennes, duke of Dordogne. He was the father of knights (see **Quatre Fils Aymon**) who are important in Tasso, Pulci, Boiardo, Ariosto, and other romance-writers.

Azazel (a̠-zā′zel). 1. The goat of dismissal, or scapegoat, in the Mosaic ritual of atonement. Lev. xvi. 8, 10–26. 2. In Arabic writers, one of the jinns taken prisoners by the angels for their transgressions. 3. The standard-bearer of the infernal hosts in Milton's "Paradise Lost."

Azaziel (a̠-zā′zi-el). 1. In Faust's "Miraculous Art and Book of Marvels," one of the princes of the infernal kingdom, under Lucifer. 2. A seraph in Byron's "Heaven and Earth," who loves a mortal.

Azhi Dahaka (ä′zhi da̠-hä′kä). Originally, the cloud-serpent of Aryan mythology, the destroying serpent of the Avesta; later, in Iranian myth, a king of Iran who makes a league with Ahriman.

Azor (ä′zôr). The monster, really a transformed prince, in "Beauty and the Beast."

Azrael (az′rā-el). In Jewish and Mohammedan angelology, the angel who separates the soul from the body at the moment of death.

Aztecas (az-tā′käz). See Dictionary, **Aztec.**

Aztec Calendar Stone, The. See **Stone of the Sun, The.**

Aztlan (äzt-län′). A mythical site where the Aztecas are said to have dwelt, or whence they started their journey southward.

Azucena (äd-zö-chä′nä). The old gipsy who stole Manrico, in Verdi's "Il Trovatore."

B

Baal. See Dictionary.

Baalath (bā′a̠l-ath). A town of Dan, probably on the site of the modern Bel'ain.

Baal-Peor (-pē′ôr). A localized aspect of Baal, named from a mountain in Moab. Num. xxv. 3.

Baba Abdalla (bä′bä äb-däl′lä). In the "Arabian Nights' Entertainments," a man who, not satisfied with being made rich by a dervish, demands also a box of magic ointment, by a misuse of which he loses both his riches and his sight.

Bab Ballads. A collection (1869) of humorous verses by W. S. Gilbert.

Babbie. The heroine of Barrie's "The Little Minister."

Babbitt, George. The title character in Sinclair Lewis's novel "Babbitt" (1923).

Babel, Tower of. See Dictionary, **Babel.**

Babenberg (bä′ben-berch). A princely family of Franconia, important in the 9th and 10th centuries. Their castle was on the site of the modern Bamberg.

Babes in the Wood, The. An old English ballad (16th century) of two children left to perish in a wood, through the cruelty of a wicked uncle who desired their death in order to secure their inheritance.

Babists (bäb′ists). See Dictionary, **Babism.**

Babley (bab′li), **Richard.** See **Mr. Dick.**

Babylon (bab′i-lon), **The Modern.** A name often applied to London and other great modern cities.

Babylonica (bab-i-lon′i-ka̠). A romance in 39 books, by Iamblichus, a Syrian rhetorician of the time of Trajan.

Baca (bā′kä), **The Valley of.** A locality probably identical with El-Bakei'a, between Jerusalem and Bethlehem. Ps. lxxxiv. 6.

Bacairis (bä-kä-ē-rēz′). An Indian tribe of central Brazil.

Bacapa (bä-kä′pä), **Saint Ludovicus.** An abandoned mission in southeastern Arizona, founded in the 17th century.

Bacchæ. See Dictionary.

Bacchiadæ (ba-kī′a̠-dē). A ruling family of Corinth, 926–c. 657 B.C.

Bacchus. See Dictionary.

Bacchus and Ariadne. A painting (1523) by Titian, in the National Gallery, London.

Bacis (bā′sis), or **Bakis** (bā′kis). In Greek legend, a Bœotian seer whose oracles were delivered at Heleon.

Back Bay, The. An expansion of the Charles River, now filled in and forming an important section of Boston, Mass.

Backbite, Sir Benjamin. A slanderer in Sheridan's "School for Scandal."

Back to Methuselah. A drama (1920) in five parts, by George Bernard Shaw.

Baconian Theory, The. See Dictionary, **Baconian.**

Bacon's Rebellion. An uprising in Virginia (1676) under Nathaniel Bacon, declared a rebel by Governor Berkeley for heading an unauthorized expedition against the Indians.

Bactrian (bak′tri-an) **Sage, The.** Zoroaster.

Badebec (bȧd-bek). The wife of Gargantua in Rabelais's "Pantagruel." She was the mother of Pantagruel.

(variable) d̠ as d or j, s̠ as s or sh, t̠ as t or ch, z̠ as z or zh; o, F. cloche; ü, F. menu; ch, Sc. loch; ṅ, F. bonbon; ′, primary accent; ″, secondary accent; †, obsolete; <, from; +, and; =, equals. See also lists at beginning of book.

Baden (bä′dẹn), **The Treaty of.** A Franco-German treaty (1714) which, with the treaties of Utrecht and Rastadt, ended the war of the Spanish Succession.

Bad Lands, The. Certain regions of the northwestern United States, especially in South Dakota, characterized by barrenness and fantastic forms of erosion.

Badman, The Life and Death of Mr. An allegory (1680) by John Bunyan, in which the general plan of "Pilgrim's Progress" is inverted.

Badminton (bad′min-tọn), **The.** A London sporting club, founded 1876.

Badoura (ba-dö′rä). The princess of a love-story in the "Arabian Nights' Entertainments."

Badroulboudour (ba-dröl′bö-dör′). The wife of Aladdin in the "Arabian Nights' Entertainments."

Bæbia (bē′bi-ä) **gens.** A plebeian house of ancient Rome. It first achieved the consulship in 182 B.C.

Bagaudæ (ba-gâ′dē). A body of Gallic peasants who rebelled against the Romans at intervals after about 270.

Baggara (bäg-gä′rä). A Hamitic, Arab-speaking nomadic tribe of the upper Nile valley.

Bagimont's (baj′i-monts) **Roll.** A list of the benefices of Scotland, with their valuation, in the late middle ages.

Bagnigge (bag′nij) **Wells.** A popular place of amusement in 18th-century London. It was on the east of Gray's Inn Road, nearly opposite what is now Mecklenburg Square.

Bagratidæ (ba-grat′i-dē). A dynasty of Armenian monarchs which lasted from the 9th to the 11th century.

Bagstock, Major. In Dickens's "Dombey and Son," a "blue-faced," apoplectic officer who turns out to be only a fair-weather friend of Dombey.

Bahaists. See Dictionary, **Bahaism.**

Baharites (bä′hạ-rīts), or **Baharides** (bä′hạ-rīdz). A Mameluke dynasty which ruled Egypt from the middle of the 13th century to the end of the 14th.

Bahman (bä′mạn), **Prince.** Son of the Sultan in a story of the "Arabian Nights' Entertainments."

Bailiff's Daughter of Islington, The. An old ballad of a squire's son and a bailiff's daughter. It is preserved in Percy's "Reliques."

Baillie, or **Bailly, Harry.** The host of the Tabard Inn in Chaucer's "Canterbury Tales."

Bairam, or **Beiram.** See Dictionary.

Bajazet (bȧ-zhȧ-zā′). A tragedy (1672) by Racine.

Bajazet (baj-ạ-zet′), **The Mosque of.** A preëminent example of Moslem architecture, finished 1505, in Constantinople.

Bajura (ba-jö′rä). The standard of Mohammed.

Bakele. See **Kele.**

Bakhtiyari (bäch-tē-yä′rē). A nomadic people of Luristan and Khuzistan, western Persia, allied to the Kurds.

Balaam (bā′lạm). A prophet of Mesopotamia. Num. xxii., xxiii.

Baladan (bal′ạ-dan). The father of Berodach-baladan. 2 Kings, xx. 12.

Balak (bā′lak). A Moabite king who sent for the prophet Balaam to come and curse the Israelites. Num. xxii., xxiii.

Balan. 1. (bā′lan) In Arthurian legend, a brother of Balin. 2. (bȧ-län′) An early French version of "Fierabras," Balan being the father of the hero.

Balarama (bal-ạ-rä′mä). In Hindu mythology, the elder brother of Krishna: according to the Vaishnavas, an incarnation of Vishnu.

Balaustion's (ba-lâs′ti-ọnz) **Adventure.** A poem (1871) by Browning, about a Greek girl of Rhodes. "Aristophanes' Apology" (1875) is a sequel.

Balawat (bä-lä-wät′). An archæologically important mound of ruins about 15 miles east of Mosul. Hormuzd Rassam excavated there (1877) bronze plates from the palace gates of Shalmaneser II., now in the British Museum.

Balder (bâl′dẹr), or **Baldur** (bâl′dẹr). In Old Norse mythology, a son of Odin, and one of the chief deities. He is essentially a sun-god.

Balder Dead. A poem (1855) by Matthew Arnold.

Balderstone, Caleb. In Scott's "Bride of Lammermoor," Ravenswood's servant, who resorts to fantastic expedients to conceal his master's poverty.

Balfour of Burley. In Scott's "Old Mortality," a fanatic leader of the Covenanters.

Balgownie (bal-gou′ni), **The Brig o'.** A high, wide-pointed arch spanning the Don, at Aberdeen, Scotland: built about 1320.

Bali (bal′ē or bul′ē). In Hindu mythology, a Daitya who lost his sovereignty over the three worlds when he promised Vishnu (then in his dwarf incarnation) all the land he could measure with three strides.

Balin (bä′lēn). In Hindu mythology, a monkey king who was slain by Rama.

Balin (bä′lin) and **Balan** (bä′lan). In Arthurian legend, two Northumbrian brothers renowned for valor.

Balin and Balan. One of Tennyson's "Idylls of the King."

Balisarda (bä-lē-sär′dä). In Ariosto's "Orlando Furioso," the enchanted sword stolen from Orlando by Brunello and given to Rogero.

Balkis (bal′kis). The Arabian name of the Queen of Sheba.

Balliol (bal′yọl) **College.** A college of Oxford University, reputed to have been founded by John de Baliol and his wife Devorguila before 1268.

Ballo in Maschera, Un (ön bäl′lö ēn mäs′kä-rä). An opera (1859) by Verdi.

Balmawhapple (bal-mạ-hwap′l), **Falconer of.** A mulish Jacobite in Scott's "Waverley."

Balmoral (bal-mor′ạl) **Castle.** A favorite residence of Queen Victoria, on the Dee about 45 miles west of Aberdeen, Scotland.

Balmung (bäl′mung). In the "Nibelungenlied," the sword of Siegfried.

Balnibarbi (bal-ni-bär′bi). A land "occupied by projectors," visited by Gulliver in Swift's "Gulliver's Travels."

Balthazar or **Balthasar** (bal-thä′zạr). 1. See Dictionary, **Magus.** 2. A merchant in Shakspere's "Comedy of Errors." 3. The name assumed by Portia in Shakspere's "Merchant of Venice."

Baltia (bal′shi-ä). In ancient writers, an island off the coast of Scythia. From it was named the Baltic Sea.

Baltic, The Battle of the. The naval battle of Copenhagen (1801). Campbell has a poem "Battle of the Baltic" (1805).

Bambara (bäm-bä′rä). A Nigritic tribe settled about the head-waters of the Niger.

Bamberg (bäm′berch) **Conference, The.** A conference (1854) of the middle German states, to determine their policy on the Eastern Question, in relation to that of Prussia and Austria.

Ban (ban). In Arthurian romance, a king of Brittany, father of Lancelot of the Lake.

Bana (bä′nä). In Hindu mythology, a thousand-armed Daitya, a friend of Siva and an enemy of Vishnu.

Ba-Nano (bä-nä′nō). A generic name for the native 'Highlanders' of the plateau east of Benguella, West Africa.

Banbury (ban′bẹ-ri) **Cross.** A cross famous in nursery rime, at Banbury, Oxfordshire. It was destroyed in the reign of Elizabeth.

Banbury Man. A Puritan: from Banbury, Oxfordshire, in the 17th century a Puritan community.

Bande Noire (bänd nwor). 1. Any of various infantry companies in the French service in the 16th century. 2. In the French Revolution, speculators in confiscated church property, ancient buildings, etc.

Bangorian (bang-gō′ri-ạn) **Controversy, The.** A controversy stirred up (1717) by Dr. Hoadley, bishop of Bangor, who argued that Christ had not delegated judicial and disciplinary powers to the ministry.

Bankside, The. The south bank of the Thames between the Blackfriars and Waterloo bridges, London, the site of Shakspere's Globe Theatre, and others.

Banks's Horse. A celebrated trick-horse named Morocco, exhibited in London about 1590–1600.

Bannatyne (ban′ạ-tīn) **Club, The.** A Scottish literary club (1823–59), devoted to publication of works on Scottish history and literature. Sir Walter Scott was its first president.

Bannock (ban′ọk). A tribe of North American Indians: the "Robber" Indians. The survivors are mainly on reservations in Idaho.

Banquo (bang′kwō). In Shakspere's "Macbeth," a murdered thane whose ghost appears to Macbeth at a royal banquet.

---

fat, fāte, fär, fåll, åsk, fāre; net, mē, hėr; pin, pīne; not, nōte, mȯve, nôr; up, lūte, pull; oi, oil; ou, out; (lightened) aviạry, ẹlect, agọny, intọ, ụnite; (obscured) errạnt, operä, ardẹnt, actọr, natụre; ch, chip; g, go; th, thin; ᴛн, then; y, you;

Bantu. See Dictionary.

Banyoro. See **Nyoro.**

Banz (bänts). A Benedictine abbey, founded about 1058, near Lichtenfels, Bavaria: now a castle.

Baphomet (baf'ō-met). The imaginary idol which the Templars were accused of worshiping in the middle ages.

Bar, The Confederation of. A union of Polish patriots formed at Bar in 1768 for the purpose of maintaining Polish independence of Russia.

Barabas (bar'ạ-bạs). The title character of Marlowe's "Jew of Malta."

Barabbas (bạ-rab'ạs). A condemned robber whose release was demanded of Pilate by the Jews when they had an opportunity to free Jesus. Mat. xxvii. 16–21.

Barabra (bä-rä'brä). The Nubians of the Nile valley from Assuan to Wadi Halfa.

Barataria (bä-rạ-tä'rẹ-ạ). In Cervantes's "Don Quixote," the island city over which Sancho Panza was made governor.

Barathron (bar'ạ-thron). A steep ravine on the Hill of the Nymphs, Athens, into which the bodies of criminals were anciently thrown.

Barbara Allen's Cruelty. A ballad, given in Percy's "Reliques," relating the fatal cruelty of a lady to her lover.

Barbara Frietchie (frē'chi). A poem (1863) by Whittier, telling the story of an old woman who waves a Union flag from her window in the face of Stonewall Jackson and his victorious army, during the occupation of Frederick, Maryland.

Barbary, Roan. The favorite horse of Richard II.

Barbe-Bleue (bärb-blē). See **Bluebeard.**

Barberini (bär-bā-rē'nē). An Italian noble family dating from the 11th century. One of its members was Pope Urban VIII. See **Barberini Palace.**

Barberini Faun, The. An ancient statue, now in the Glyptothek, Munich.

Barberini Palace. A palace near the Quirinal, Rome, noted for its art treasures. It was begun by Pope Urban VIII. and finished in 1640.

Barberini Vase, The. See **Portland Vase, The.**

Barber of Seville, The. See **Barbier** and **Barbiere.**

Barbican (bär'bi-kạn), **The.** A locality in London, so named from its former watch-tower. Milton lived here 1646–47.

Barbier de Séville, Le (lẹ bär-byā dẹ sā-vēl). A comedy (1775) by Beaumarchais: the first appearance of Figaro in literature.

Barbiere di Siviglia, Il (ēl bär-bē-ā'rä dē sē-vē'lyä). An opéra bouffe (1816) by Rossini, based on Beaumarchais's "Barbier de Séville."

Barchester Novels, The. See **Cathedral Novels, The.**

Barchester Towers. One of the "Cathedral" novels by Trollope, published 1857.

Bar-Cocheba (bär-kok'e-bä). The heroic leader of the Jewish insurrection against the Romans, A.D. 132–35: also called Bar Coziba, from the town Coziba, and Bar Kokba.

Bard, The. A poem (1758) by Gray, opening with the famous apostrophe "Ruin seize thee, ruthless King."

Bardell (bär-del'), **Mrs. Martha.** In Dickens's "Pickwick Papers," Mr. Pickwick's landlady, who construed some remarks of his as a proposal of marriage and sued him for breach of promise.

Bardolph (bär'dolf). One of the bibulous companions of Falstaff in Shakspere's "Henry IV.," "Henry V.," and "The Merry Wives of Windsor."

Barea (bä'rạ-ä). A tribe of the border between Egypt and Abyssinia, speaking a mixed Hamitic language.

Barés or **Barrés** (bä-räz'). A tribe of agricultural Indians on the upper Rio Negro, in northern Brazil and Venezuela.

Bari (bä'rē). A pastoral and agricultural Nigritic tribe of the eastern Sudan, on the White Nile.

Barkal (bär'käl). A hill with noted inscriptions, on the Nile below the fourth cataract, near the ancient Meroë.

Barkis (bär'kis). In Dickens's "David Copperfield," a bashful carrier who proposes marriage to Peggotty by sending her the message "Barkis is willin'."

Barlaam (bär'lā-ạm) **and Josaphat** (jos'ạ-fat). A Syrian romance of the 8th century (Latinized before the 13th). Barlaam is a monk who converts Josaphat, a prince of India, to ascetic Christianity. One incident is the ultimate source of the episode of the caskets in Shakspere's "Merchant of Venice."

Barleycorn, John. See Dictionary, **barleycorn.**

Barmecides, Barmecide's Feast. See Dictionary.

Barnabas (bär'nạ-bạs), **Saint.** The surname of the Cyprian Levite Joses, or Joseph, an apostle. Acts, iv. 36, 37.

Barnabas, The Epistle of. An anonymous epistle dating from the early period of the Christian Church. It emphasizes the separation of Christianity from Judaism.

Barnaby Rudge (bär'nạ-bi ruj). A novel (1841) by Dickens, based on the Gordon Riots.

Barnacle, Lord Decimus Tite. In Dickens's "Little Dorrit," the most exalted of a family conspicuously attached to the Circumlocution Office.

Barnard's Inn. One of the Inns of Chancery, in Holborn, London.

Barnwell, George. The apprentice hero of Lillo's "George Barnwell."

Barons, The War of the. An insurrection of English barons under Simon of Montfort against Henry III., 1263–65.

Barrack-Room Ballads. Poems (1892) by Rudyard Kipling, including "Gunga Din," "Fuzzy Wuzzy," "Danny Deever," and "The Road to Mandalay."

Barren Ground. A novel (1925) by Ellen Glasgow: the theme is character development through suffering.

Barricades, Days of the. The name given to several insurrections in Paris (May 12, 1588; Aug. 26–27, 1648; 1830; 1848; etc.).

Barrier Treaty, The. A treaty signed 1715 at Antwerp by Austria, Great Britain, and the Netherlands, defining Austro-Dutch relations in the strategic towns of the Low Countries.

Barry. A famed St. Bernard dog which saved 40 lives on Mount St. Bernard. His stuffed skin is in the museum at Bern.

Barry Lyndon (lin'dọn), **The Memoirs of.** A picaresque novel (1844) by Thackeray, modeled on Fielding's "Jonathan Wild the Great."

Barsad (bär'sad), **John.** See **Pross, Solomon.**

Bartholo (bär-to-lō). In Beaumarchais's "Barbier de Séville," an old doctor, the jealous guardian of Rosine.

Bartholomew (bär-thol'ō-mū), **Saint.** One of the 12 apostles, probably identical with Nathaniel. Mat. x. 3. His day, in the Roman and Anglican churches, is Aug. 24. See Dictionary, **St. Bartholomew's Day,** under **saint.**

Bartholomew Fair. 1. A fair formerly (1133–1855) held at Smithfield, London, beginning Aug. 24 (O. S.). 2. A comedy (1614) by Ben Jonson, satirizing Puritanism.

Bartholomew the Great, Saint. A Normanesque church in London, founded 1123.

Baruch (bā'ruk). 1. A Jew who repaired a part of the wall of Jerusalem. Neh. iii. 20. 2. The amanuensis and friend of Jeremiah (Jer. xxxii. 13), and nominal author of the Book of Baruch in the Apocrypha.

Barzillai (bär-zil'ạ-ī or bär-zil'ī). A rich Gileadite who helped David escape from Absalom. 2 Sam. xvii. 27.

Barzu-Namah (bär'zö-nä'mä). A Persian epic modeled on the Shahnamah. Its author is unknown.

Basel (bä'zel), **The Confession of.** A Reformed confession (1534) drafted by Œcolampadius and revised by Myconius.

Basel, The Council of. The last (1431–1449) of the 3 great reforming councils of the 15th century.

Basel, The Treaty of. 1. A Franco-Prussian treaty (1795), whereby Prussia withdrew from the coalition against France. 2. A treaty (1795) by which Spain ceded Santo Domingo to France.

Baserac (bä-se-räk'). A village containing the ruins of a Jesuit mission founded about 1642, on the upper Yaqui River in eastern Sonora, Mexico.

Bashan (bā'shạn). A district of Palestine east of the Jordan, reaching from Mount Hermon to the Arnon. It was allotted to the tribe of Manasseh. Num. xxxii. 33. It was famous for its sheep and oxen.

Bashi-Bazouk. See Dictionary, **bashi-bazouk.**

Bashkirs (bȧsh-kērz'). A tribe of mixed Finnish and Tatar race, inhabiting Orenburg, Perm, Samara, Ufa, and Vyatka, Russia.

Basile (bä-zēl). A slanderer in Beaumarchais's "Barbier de

(variable) ḍ as d or j, ṣ as s or sh, ṭ as t or ch, ẓ as z or zh; o, F. cloche; ü, F. menu; ċh, Sc. loch; ṅ, F. bonbon; ', primary accent; ″, secondary accent; †, obsolete; <, from; +, and; =, equals. See also lists at beginning of book.

Séville" and "Mariage de Figaro." His name has become proverbial.

Basilicon Doron (ba-sil′i-kon dō′ron). A work on the divine right of kings, by James I. of England.

Basilisco (bas-i-lis′kō). A braggart in the old play "Soliman and Perseda." His name has become proverbial.

Basing (bā′zing) **House.** A former residence of the Marquis of Winchester, east of Basingstoke. It was destroyed (1645) by Cromwell, after a long defense by the Royalists.

Basket Woman, The. American Indian tales (1904) for children, by Mary Austin.

Bassa or **Basa** (bä′sä). A Nigritic tribe of Liberia, dwelling on the Sess River and the coast.

Bassanio (ba-sä′ni-ō). The successful suitor of Portia in Shakspere's "Merchant of Venice."

Bassarab (bas′a̱-rab). The dynasty which ruled Wallachia almost continuously from about 1300 to 1658.

Bast (bȧst). A lioness-headed or cat-headed goddess of Egyptian mythology. Her special city was Bubastis.

Bastarnæ (bas-tär′nē). An early Germanic tribe of the region about the Black Sea north of the Danube.

Bastille, The. See Dictionary, **bastile.**

Basumbe. See **Sumbe.**

Batavi (ba̱-tā′vī). A German tribe, a branch of the Chatti. In Roman times they dwelt in the Insula Batavorum.

Batavian Republic, The. A republic (1795–1806) formed out of the Netherlands by France.

Bates, Miss. An important character in Jane Austen's "Emma."

Bath, Colonel. In Fielding's "Amelia," a punctilious gentleman, Amelia's benefactor.

Bathsheba (bath-shē′ba̱ or bath′she-ba̱). The wife of Uriah the Hittite, loved by David: later, David's wife and the mother of Solomon. 2 Sam. xi., xii.

Baths of Caracalla (kar-a̱-kal′a̱), **The.** Ancient Roman baths begun A.D. 206 by Severus. Their remains are among the most imposing ruins of the city.

Baths of Diocletian (dī-ō-klē′shia̱n), **The.** Roman baths situated near the Viminal, begun by Diocletian.

Baths of Titus (tī′tus), **The.** Roman baths northeast of the Colosseum, constructed by Titus.

Batonapa (bä-tō-nä′pä). A hill south of Banamichi on the Sonora River, bearing the remains of an ancient fortification of the Opata Indians.

Batrachomyomachia (bat″ra̱-kō-mī″ō-mā′ki-a̱). An ancient Greek mock epic. 316 lines are extant. Homer is parodied in terms of frogs, mice, crabs, and a cat, with Zeus and Athena gravely deliberating above the mêlée.

Battersea (bat′ẽr-sē) **Park.** A modern London park, facing Chelsea Hospital. It is on the Surrey side of the Thames.

Battery, The. A park of 20 acres at the southern extremity of New York City, near the site of an old Dutch fort.

Battiadæ (ba-tī′a̱-dē). A dynasty (631–c. 431 B.C.) of rulers in Cyrene.

Battle, Mrs. Sarah. A whist-playing old lady in Lamb's "Essays of Elia."

Battle above the Clouds, The. A popular name for the battle of Lookout Mountain (1863).

Battle at Sea, The. A painting of Christian ships and Moslem corsairs, by Tintoretto: in the Museum at Madrid.

Battle Bridge (King's Cross). In old London, a locality marked by a bridge across the upper Fleet or Holborn: the supposed scene of a battle between Suetonius and Boadicea.

Battle-Ground, The. A novel (1902) by Ellen Glasgow.

Battle Hymn of the Republic. A patriotic song (1862) by Julia Ward Howe.

Battle Monument, The. A memorial structure in Baltimore, built 1815 to commemorate the defense of the city against the British in 1814.

Battle of Amazons, The. A painting by Rubens, in the old Pinakothek, Munich.

Battle of Blenheim, The. A poem (1798) by Robert Southey.

Battle of Issus, The. A celebrated ancient mosaic from the House of the Faun at Pompeii, now in the Museo Nazionale, Naples.

Battle of Prague, The. A piece of old-fashioned program music (before 1789) by Kotzwara.

Battle of the Books, The. A satire (1697) by Swift, on the famous Bentley-Boyle controversy over the "Epistles of Phalaris."

Battle of the Giants, The. The battle of Marignano or Melegnano (1515).

Battle of the Nations, The. The battle of Leipsic (1813).

Battle of the Spurs, The. 1. The battle of Courtrai (1302). 2. The battle of Guinegate (1513).

Battle of the Standard, The. The battle of Northallerton (1138).

Battle of the Thirty, The. A fight (1351), famous in song and story, beween 30 picked Bretons and 30 Englishmen, near the castles of Ploermel and Josselin, France.

Baubo (bä′bō). In Greek mythology, a minor goddess connected with the Eleusinian myth of Demeter. Goethe used her in the second part of "Faust" to symbolize gross sensuality.

Baucis (bä′sis). See **Philemon.**

Baumgarten (boum′gär″ten), **Konrad.** An Unterwalden patriot, famous in the William Tell legend.

Baurés (bou-rās′). A tribe of agricultural Indians in northern Bolivia, in the forested region about the rivers Mamoré and Baurés.

Bavaria (ba̱-vā′ri-a̱). A bronze statue 67 feet high, standing before the Ruhmeshalle, Munich. It was built (1850) by order of Ludwig I. of Bavaria.

Bavarian Succession, The War of the. A war (1778–79) of Austria against Prussia, Saxony, and Mecklenburg, caused by the extinction of the Bavarian electoral house. It was ended bloodlessly by the Peace of Teschen.

Baviad (bā′vi-ad), **The.** A satire (1794) on the "Della-Cruscan" poets, by William Gifford: followed (1795) by the Mæviad, which added attacks on minor dramatists of the day.

Bavieca (bä-vē-ā′kä). The favorite steed of the Cid.

Bayard (bā′a̱rd, F. bä-yär). The magical legendary horse given by Charlemagne to the four sons of Aymon.

Bayes. A dramatic coxcomb in Buckingham's "Rehearsal," probably intended to represent Dryden.

Bayes's Troops. The soldiers and hobby-horses who fight a stage battle in Buckingham's "Rehearsal," and, when killed, have to get up and walk off stage: a frequent allusion.

Bayeux (bä-yė) **Tapestry.** A strip of linen 231 feet long and 20 inches wide, preserved in the library of Bayeux, France. Its colored embroidery pictures events leading to the Norman conquest of England, and it probably dates from the 11th century. It is ascribed to Matilda, the wife of the Conqueror.

Baynard's (bā′na̱rdz) **Castle.** A fortification on the Thames below Blackfriars, founded by Baynard under the Conqueror: burned 1666.

Bayonne (ba-yon), **The Treaty of.** A Franco-Spanish treaty (1808) by which Charles IV. renounced his right to the Spanish throne.

Bayonne Decree, The. An order (1808) issued by Napoleon, for the seizure of all American vessels then in French ports.

Bay Psalm Book, The. The earliest New England version (1640) of the Psalms, by Richard Mather, Thomas Welde, and John Eliot.

Bayreuth (bī′roit) **Festival, The.** A musical festival held in the Richard Wagner Theater, Bayreuth, for the presentation of Wagner's works: instituted 1876.

Bayswater. A part of London north of Kensington Gardens.

Bazarof (bä-zä′rof). See **Fathers and Sons.**

Bazigars (bä-zē-gärz′). A widely diffused nomadic race of Hindustan: possibly akin to the Gipsies of Europe.

Bazin (bä-zan̊). The lackey of Aramis in Dumas's "Trois Mousquetaires."

Beacon Hill. A hill north of the Common, Boston, on which fires were lighted to warn of Indian attacks: the summit is now occupied by the State House.

Beacon Street. In Boston, Mass., a street extending westward from Tremont Street, along the north side of the Common.

Beagle, The. The brig in which Darwin made his voyage (1831–36) round the world.

Bealbv. A novel (1915) by H. G. Wells.

Bear Flag Battalion, The. An American corps in the early history of California, active in expelling the Mexicans.

Beata Beatrix (bḗ-ā′tȧ bē′ȧ-triks). A painting by Rossetti, in the National Gallery, London.

Beatrice. 1. (bä-ä-trē′chä) In Dante's "Vita Nuova" and "Divina Commedia," a symbolic figure developed from the lady of Dante's love on earth, usually identified with Beatrice Portinari. 2. (bē′ȧ-tris) The gay and wayward niece of Leonato in Shakspere's "Much Ado about Nothing." 3. The sinister heroine of Hawthorne's "Rappaccini's Daughter."

Beatrice Cenci (bä-ä-trē′chä chen′chē). A famous portrait by Guido Reni. The identity of its subject has been disputed.

Beatrix. A novel (1844) by Balzac.

Beauchamp's (bē′chȧmz) **Career.** A novel (1874–75) of British political life, by Meredith.

Beau Nash. A comedy (1825) by Douglas Jerrold, based on the career of Richard Nash (1674–1762), known as the "King of Bath."

Beaurepaire (bō′rė-pār). In Arthurian legend, the castle where Blanchefleur, imprisoned, is delivered by Sir Perceval.

Beauty and the Beast. An old story in which Zémire, to save her father's life, becomes the guest of Azor, a monster. Winning her love by his innate qualities, he regains his natural form, that of a prince.

Beaux' Stratagem, The. A comedy by Farquhar (1707).

Bec (bek). A ruined abbey near Brionne, Eure, France: in the 11th century, a famous seat of learning.

Bede (bēd), **Adam.** The hero of George Eliot's "Adam Bede," a young carpenter of character and intelligence.

Bedford Coffee House. A noted house formerly standing in Covent Garden, London: the resort of Garrick, Fielding, and others.

Bedford House. A mansion formerly standing in Belgrave Square, London: the residence of the Duke of Bedford.

Bedivere (bed′i-vēr), **Sir.** In Arthurian romance, the knight who brought the dying King Arthur to the barge in which the three queens bore him to the Vale of Avalon.

Bedlam. See Dictionary, **bedlam.**

Bedreddin Hassan (bed-red-dēn′ has′an). The son of Noureddin Ali in the "Arabian Nights' Entertainments." His identity is discovered by the superiority of the cheese-cakes which he makes.

Bee, The. A London weekly, written largely by Goldsmith, of which 8 numbers appeared: the first, Oct. 6, 1759.

Beef-Eaters, The. See Dictionary, **beef-eater.**

Beefsteak Club, The. 1. A club of London wits and other notables in the reign of Queen Anne. 2. A similar club established by Sheridan (about 1749) at the Theatre Royal, Dublin, of which Peg Woffington was president. 3. A London club founded (1876) by J. L. Toole.

Beelzebub. See Dictionary.

Beersheba (bē′ėr-shē′bȧ or bē-ėr′she-bȧ). A town at the southern extremity of Palestine. Neh. xi. 27. See **Dan.**

Befana (bä-fä′nä), **The.** In Italian folklore, an old woman who is a sort of Santa Claus and Wandering Jew combined.

Before Dawn. A drama (1889) by Gerhart Hauptmann.

Beggar's Bush, The. A comedy (1622) by Fletcher and others.

Beggar's Opera, The. An opera (1728) by John Gay: still popular.

Beguines. See Dictionary, **Beguine.**

Beguins. See Dictionary, **Beghard.**

Behistun (bā-his-tön′), or **Bisutun** (bē-sö-tön′). A rock near Kirmanshah, western Persia, bearing inscriptions in Persian, Assyrian, and the language of Susiana. The decipherment of these by Sir Henry Rawlinson (1835–37) put Assyriology on a scientific basis.

Bel. See Dictionary.

Bel and the Dragon. A book of the Apocrypha.

Belarius (be-lā′ri-us). In Shakspere's "Cymbeline," the vengeful banished lord who steals Cymbeline's sons.

Belch, Sir Toby. The bibulous and jolly uncle of Olivia in Shakspere's "Twelfth Night."

Belem (bä-laṅ′), **The Monastery of.** A monastery near Lisbon, Portugal, founded 1500 to commemorate the voyage of Vasco da Gama: now an orphan asylum.

Belfegor (bel′fä-gȯr), **Novella di.** A satirical tale (1549) by Machiavelli, of a devil who gladly flees to hell to rid himself of a scold.

Belgæ (bel′jē). 1. See Dictionary, **Belgic.** 2. A personification of Holland in Spenser's "Faerie Queene."

Belgrade (bel-grād′), **Sieges of.** The city has been besieged by the Turks (1442?, 1456, 1521, 1690); by the Elector of Bavaria (1688); by Prince Eugene (1717); and by the Austrians, under Laudon (1789), and again in 1914.

Belgrade, The Treaty of. A treaty (1739) made by Turkey, Austria, and Russia. Russia restored parts of Moldavia and Bessarabia; Austria ceded territory in Wallachia, Bosnia, and Serbia, including Belgrade.

Belgrave Square. A square in Belgravia, London.

Belgravia (bel-grā′vi-ȧ). A fashionable district in the West End of London, adjoining Hyde Park.

Belial. See Dictionary.

Belianis (bel-i-ā′nis) **of Greece.** A continuation (1547) of "Amadis of Gaul," by Jerónimo Fernández.

Bel Inconnu, Le (lė bel aṅ-ko-nü). A secondary romance of the Round Table (13th century), by Renauld de Beaujeu.

Belinda (be-lin′dä). 1. A principal character in Etherege's "Man of Mode." 2. A gay, witty, and level-headed girl in Vanbrugh's "Provoked Wife." 3. An affected lady, in love with Bellmour, in Congreve's "Old Bachelor." 4. The heroine of Pope's "Rape of the Lock." 5. A novel (1801) by Maria Edgeworth.

Bélise (bā-lēz). In Molière's "Femmes Savantes," a self-appreciative lady who thinks all men are in love with her.

Belit (be-lit′). In Assyro-Babylonian mythology, a female deity, wife of Bel; also, an honorary title for any goddess.

Bell, Adam. A legendary English outlaw and skilled archer of the generation before Robin Hood.

Bell, The. 1. A noted old inn in Warwick Lane, London. 2. An inn at Edmonton, near London: remembered in connection with Cowper's ballad of "John Gilpin."

Bellaria (be-lā′ri-ȧ). Pandosto's wife in Greene's "Pandosto." She is the original of Shakspere's Hermione.

Bellarmine (bel′är-min). A drinking-jug with the face of Cardinal Bellarmine on it: originated by the Dutch Protestants in order to ridicule him.

Bellaston (bel′ȧs-tŏn), **Lady.** In Fielding's "Tom Jones," a fashionable sensualist, one of Tom's mistresses.

Belle Dame Sans Merci, La (lä bel däm säṅ mer-sē). 1. A French poem by Alain Chartier (d. about 1440). 2. A ballad by Keats.

Bellegarde (bel-gärd′). A fortress on the Spanish frontier of France, south of Perpignan.

Belle Hélène, La (lä bel ā-len). An opéra bouffe (1864) by Offenbach, with words by Meilhac and Halévy.

Belle Jardinière, La (lä bel zhär-dē-nyār). A Madonna and Child with St. John (1507), by Raphael, in the Louvre, Paris.

Belle Laitière (le-tyär), **La.** A painting by Wouwerman, in the National Gallery, London.

Belle Mignonne (mē-nyon), **La.** A French 18th-century name for a skull illuminated with tapers, often to be seen in the boudoirs of the devout.

Bellerophon, (be-ler′ō-fon), or **Bellerophontes** (be-ler-ō-fon′tēz). In Greek legend, a son of Glaucus, king of Corinth. Mounted on the winged horse Pegasus, from the air he slew the monster Chimæra. Later he tried to ascend to heaven on Pegasus, but Zeus maddened the steed, and Bellerophon was hurled to earth.

Bellerophon, The. 1. A British line-of-battle ship which fought in the Battle of the Nile and at Trafalgar. 2. One of the earliest British armored war-ships, launched 1866.

Bellerus (be-lē′rus). A Cornish giant of legend, supposed to live at Land's End (Bellerium).

Belle Savage, The. [F. La Belle Sauvage.] A former London tavern on Ludgate Hill. Its inn-yard was used in the 16th century for bear-baiting, etc.

Belle's Stratagem, The. A comedy (1780) by Mrs. Cowley.

Bellevue (bel-vü). 1. A noted castle at Cassel, Germany. 2. A former royal castle, southwest of Paris, near Sèvres, destroyed in the French Revolution.

Bellevue (bel′vü) **Hospital.** A large public hospital at the foot of East 26th Street, New York City.

Bellicent (bel′i-sent). In Arthurian romance, Arthur's half-sister.

Bellisant (bel′i-sant). The mother of Valentine and Orson, in the romance named for them.

(variable) ḑ as d or j, ş as s or sh, ţ as t or ch, ʐ as z or zh; o, F. cloche; ü, F. menu; ċh, Sc. loch; ṅ, F. bonbon; ′, primary accent; ″, secondary accent; †, obsolete; <, from; +, and; =, equals. See also lists at beginning of book.

Bellius (bel′i-us), **Martinus.** The name signed to "De hæreticis . . . ," a plea for religious toleration (1554). It was partly the work of Castellio.

Bellona (be-lō′nä). In Roman mythology, the goddess of war: variously the sister, wife, and daughter of Mars.

Bellovaci (be-lov′ạ-sī). A tribe of the Belgian Gauls, whose capital was on the site of the modern Beauvais.

Bells, The. 1. A poem by Edgar Allan Poe. 2. A familiar dramatization (1871) of Erckmann-Chatrian's "Juif Polonais," by Leopold Lewis.

Beloved Disciple, The. The apostle John.

Beloved Physician, The. Saint Luke.

Beloved Vagabond, The. A novel (1906) by W. J. Locke.

Belphœbe (bel-fē′bē). A virgin huntress in Spenser's "Faerie Queene." She represents Queen Elizabeth the woman. See **Gloriana.**

Belshazzar (bel-shaz′ạr). The son of Nebuchadnezzar, and last king of Babylonia. Dan. v. Byron has a poem on the "Vision of Belshazzar" (1815).

Beltane. See Dictionary.

Belteshazzar (bel-tẹ-shaz′ạr). The Babylonian name for Daniel. Dan. i. 7, etc.

Belvedere (bel′vẹ-dēr, It. bel-vā-dā′rā). 1. A portion of the Vatican Palace, Rome. 2. A palace in Vienna, which formerly housed the Imperial Picture Gallery.

Belzoni's (bel-tsō′nēz) **Tomb.** The tomb of Seti I., opened (1817) by Belzoni.

Benaiah (be-nā′yạ). A valiant warrior of David. 2 Sam. xxiii. 20.

Ben Block. A nickname for a sailor.

Bendis (ben′dis). A Thracian lunar goddess.

Benedick. A bachelor in Shakspere's "Much Ado about Nothing." See Dictionary, **benedick.**

Benedictine. See Dictionary.

Benet College. See **Corpus Christi College,** 1.

Benetnasch (be-net′nash). A star of the second magnitude at the extremity of the tail of the bear pictured in the constellation Ursa Major, and the outermost star in the handle of the Dipper.

Benga (beng′gä). A Bantu tribe of Gabun, West Africa, on Corisco and the mainland opposite.

Bengali. See Dictionary.

Ben-hadad (ben-hā′dad). The name of three kings of Syria: (1) A contemporary of Asa, king of Judah. 1 Kings, xv. 18, etc. (2) An ally of Ahab, king of Israel. 1 Kings, xx. 34. (3) A contemporary of Jehoahaz. 2 Kings, xiii. 3.

Ben-Hur (ben-hér′), **a Tale of the Christ.** A historical romance (1880) by Lew Wallace.

Beni-Amer (bā′nē-ä′mėr). A pastoral nomadic Mohammedan tribe in eastern Africa, dwelling in Barca, north of Abyssinia, and also near the Red Sea coast.

Beni-Israel (bā′nē-iz′rạ-el). A colony of Jewish descent at Kolaba, in Bombay. Their language is Mahratti.

Benjamin. See Dictionary.

Bennet, Elizabeth. The admirably sincere, audacious, and original heroine of Jane Austen's "Pride and Prejudice."

Bennett Law, The. A Wisconsin school law (1889–91) requiring that all instruction be given in the English language.

Benoîton (bẹ-nwo-tôn′), **Madame.** A character who never appears, though constantly mentioned, in Sardou's comedy "La Famille Benoîton" (1865). She is proverbial in the expression "to play the part of Madam Benoîton." See **Gamp, Mrs. Sarah.**

Bentinck's Act. An English statute (1845) restricting gambling.

Benton, The. A Federal ironclad gunboat (rebuilt 1861) which took part in the siege of Vicksburg (1863).

Bent Twig, The. A novel (1915) by Dorothy Canfield Fisher.

Benvenuto Cellini (ben-vā-nö′tō chel-lē′nē). An opera (1838) by Berlioz.

Benvolio (ben-vō′li-ō). A cousin and friend of Romeo in Shakspere's "Romeo and Juliet."

Beowulf (bā′ọ-wülf). An Anglo-Saxon epic poem in alliterative verse, probably composed in England in the early 8th century. The setting of the story is Scandinavian.

Beppo (bep′pō). A poem (1818) by Lord Byron.

Berabra (be-rä′brä). See **Barabra.**

Berbers. See Dictionary, **Berber.**

Berchta (berch′tä). In South German lore, a fairy used to frighten children.

Bérénice (bā-rā-nēs). 1. A tragedy (1657) by Thomas Corneille. 2. A historical tragedy (1670) by Racine.

Bergerac (berzh-rȧk), **The Treaty of.** A Roman Catholic and Huguenot treaty of 1577: also called Treaty of Poitiers.

Bergeret, Monsieur (m′syė ber-zhė-rä). The provincial professor in Anatole France's "Contemporary History," a series of four novels: "The Elm Tree on the Mall" (1897); "The Wicker Dummy" (1897); "The Amethyst Ring" (1899); "M. Bergeret in Paris" (1901).

Berkeley (bėrk′li or bärk′li) **Castle.** A Norman castle between Bristol and Gloucester, England, founded soon after the Conquest: the scene of the murder (1327) of Edward II.

Berlin, The Congress of. A European congress (1878) for settlement of Balkan problems.

Berlin, The Royal Library of. A library founded (1661) by the Great Elector, Frederick William.

Berlin, The Treaty of. A treaty (1878) representing the outcome of the Congress of Berlin. It regulated the interrelations of Bulgaria, Turkey, Montenegro, Serbia, Rumania, and Greece.

Berlin, The University of. One of the great European universities, founded 1810.

Berlin Conference. 1. A conference of the powers (1880) to settle the boundary dispute between Greece and Turkey. 2. An international congress (1884–85) to settle African territorial problems. The United States participated.

Berlin Decrees, The. Decrees of Napoleon (1806), declaring Great Britain to be in a state of blockade, forbidding commerce with her, and confiscating English property.

Berlin Memorandum, The. An ultimatum (1876) drawn up by the governments of Austria, Russia, and Germany, for the purpose of ending the Russo-Turkish war.

Bermoothes (bėr-mö′Ŧнez). An old name for the Bermuda Islands.

Bermudas (bėr-mū′dạz), **The.** Slang for a group of alleys and courts near the bottom of St. Martin's Lane, London, formerly a resort of the underworld.

Bernard (bėr′nạrd). The sheep in "Reynard the Fox."

Bernardo (bėr-när′dō). In Shakspere's "Hamlet," an officer who, with Marcellus, first sees the ghost of Hamlet's father.

Bernardo del Carpio (ber-när′dō del kär′pē-ō). A legendary Spanish hero of the 9th century, a nephew of Alfonso the Chaste. He fought against the Moors.

Berta (bär′tä). An African tribe of the lowland west of the Abyssinian plateau.

Bertha, Big. See Dictionary, **Bertha².**

Bertillon System. See Dictionary.

Bertram (bėr′trạm). 1. See **Helena,** 2. 2. A tragedy (1816) by Maturin. The title part was played by Kean.

Bertuccio (ber-töt′chō). A deformed court jester in Tom Taylor's tragedy "The Fool's Revenge."

Bessemer Process. See Dictionary.

Betelgeuse (bet-ẹl-gėz′). A star of the first magnitude, reddish in color, in the right shoulder of the man pictured in the constellation Orion.

Bethany (beth′ạ-ni). A place southeast of the Mount of Olives, near Jerusalem: the dwelling-place of Lazarus. Mat. xxi. 17, etc.

Beth-arbel (beth-är′bel). The scene of a massacre by Shalman: probably the modern Irbid. Hos. x. 14.

Bethel (beth′el). A town 12 miles north of Jerusalem: the resting-place of the ark of the covenant. 1 Sam. vii. 16.

Bethesda. See Dictionary.

Beth-horon (beth-hō′ron), **Nether** and **Upper.** Two villages about 12 miles west of Jerusalem. Between them Joshua smote the Amorites. Josh. x. 10.

Bethlehem (beth′lẹ-ẹm). The birthplace of David and of Jesus, 6 miles south of Jerusalem. Mat. ii. 1.

Bethlehemites (beth′lẹ-ẹm-īts). An Augustinian order founded 1653 in Guatemala.

Bethnal (beth′nạl) **Green.** A borough of London, on the left bank of the Thames east of Spitalfields.

Bethphage (beth′fạ-jē or beth′fāj). A village near Bethany, on the Mount of Olives. Mark, xi. 1.

---

fat, fāte, fär, fȧll, ȧsk, fāre; net, mē, hėr; pin, pīne; not, nōte, mȯve, nôr; up, lūte, pull; oi, oil; ou, out; (lightened) aviạry, ẹlect, agọny, intọ, ụnite; (obscured) errạnt, operạ, ardẹnt, actọr, natụre; ch, chip; g, go; th, thin; Ŧн, then; y, you;

Bethsaida (beth-sā′i-dä). A place on the shore of the Sea of Galilee, probably between Capernaum and Magdala. John, i. 44.

Betrothed, The. 1. A romance by Scott, published 1825. **2.** The English title of Manzoni's "I Promessi Sposi" (1825).

Bett, Miss Lulu. A novel (1920) by Zona Gale, dealing with the second blooming of a spinster who had missed the first. Also, the play (1921) based on the novel. Pulitzer Prize play, 1921.

Beulah (bū′lä). **1.** In Isa. lxii. 4, the name of the land Israel when it shall be "married." **2.** A land of rest and perpetual light in Bunyan's "Pilgrim's Progress."

Beverley, Constance de. The perjured nun in Scott's "Marmion." She is walled in alive in a convent dungeon.

Bevis (bē′vis) **of Hampton, Sir.** A heroic knight in the Arthurian legends and in Drayton's "Polyolbion."

Beyond Life. Essays (1919) by James Branch Cabell which explain his theory of romance.

Beyond Our Power. A drama (1883) by Björnstjerne Björnson.

Beyond the Horizon. A drama (1920) by Eugene O'Neill: the experience of a dreamer. Pulitzer Prize play, 1920.

Bezaleel (be-zal′ē-el). The artificer who executed the works of art on the Hebrew tabernacle. Ex. xxxi. 2–6.

Bhagavadgita (bhä″ga-vad-gē′tä). A Sanskrit dramatic poem of the 1st or 2d century, in which Krishna (Bhagavat) is identified with the Supreme Being.

Bhagavatapurana (bhä″ga-va-ta-pö-rä′nä). The most popular of the puranas. Its best-known book, the 10th, is the history of Krishna. It is ascribed to the grammarian Vopadeva, of about the 10th century.

Bhairava (bhī′ra-vä), **Bhairavi** (-vē). Names of Siva and Devi.

Bharata (bha′ra-tä). In Hindu lore: (1) A hero-king from whom are descended the "Bharatas" of the Rig-Veda. (2) Son of Dasharatha by Kaikeyi, and half-brother of Ramachandra. (3) A prince of the Puru branch of the lunar race, son of Dushyanta and Shakuntala.

Bhavishyapurana (bha-vish′ya-pö-rä′nä). The 'purana of the future,' supposedly a revelation of future events by Brahma to Satanika, a Pandu king.

Bhima (bhē′mä). In Hindu mythology, the reputed second son of Pandu: really the son of his wife Pritha by Vayu, the god of the wind.

Bhrigu (bhri′gö). In Vedic mythology, the class of fire-discoverers and fire-bringers.

Bianca (bi-ang′kä). **1.** The winsome sister of Katharine in Shakspere's "Taming of the Shrew." **2.** A mistress of Cassio in Shakspere's "Othello." **3.** The title character in "The Fair Maid of the Inn," by Massinger, Fletcher, and Rowley.

Bianchi (bē-äng′kē). A Ghibelline political faction ('Whites') in Florence about 1300, opposed to the Neri, or 'Blacks,' who were Guelph. Many, among them Dante, were banished.

Bible of Forty-two Lines, The. A Gutenberg Bible (1450–55), with 42 lines to the column.

Bible of Thirty-six Lines, The. Perhaps the oldest printed edition of the Latin Bible. A copy was given by Gutenberg to a monastery near Mainz. The two-column pages have 36 lines to the column.

Biblia Pauperum (bib′li-ä pâ′pe-rum), or **Bible of the Poor.** A popular manuscript Bible of the middle ages, which existed in many copies. It is supposed to have consisted first of pictures entirely.

Bibliothèque de Ste. Geneviève (bē-blē-o-tek dē sant zhēn-vyäv). Originally, the library (founded 1624) of the Abbey of Ste. Geneviève. The present library (1850) has many fine Aldines, Elzevirs, and incunabula.

Bibliothèque Mazarine (má-zá-rēn). A Paris library founded by Cardinal Mazarin. It is especially rich in bibliographic rarities.

Bibliothèque Nationale (ná-syo-nál). A vast library in the Rue de Richelieu, Paris. Its history goes back farther than that of printing. Henry II. made obligatory the deposit of a copy of each book published in the kingdom.

Biblis. See **Byblis.**

Bidpai (bid′pī), or **Pilpay** (pil′pī), **The Fables of.** An early collection of fables from the Sanskrit, translated into the Persian (Pahlavi), thence into the Syriac (6th century) and the Arabic (8th century), and later (through the Arabic version, the "Kalilah and Dimnah") introduced into European literature. See **Panchatantra.**

Bifröst (bē′frest). In Old Norse mythology, the rainbow bridge of the gods from heaven to earth.

Big Ben. The bell in the clock-tower of the Houses of Parliament, London: cast 1858.

Big-endians, The. See Dictionary, **Big-endian.**

Biglow Papers, The. Two groups (1848, 1867) of satirical political poems by J. R. Lowell.

Bildad (bil′dad). A "Shuhite," one of Job's friends and advisers, in the Book of Job.

Bill of Divorcement, A. A drama (1921) by Clemence Dane (Winifred Ashton).

Biloxi (bi-lok′si). A southern division of North American Indians. The survivors are in Louisiana.

Bimini (bē-mē-nē′). The West Indian name for the region of the mythical Fountain of Youth: variously identified with Florida, Mexico, and the Bahamas.

Binnenhof (bin′en-hof). A group of buildings, partly medieval, at The Hague, in which are the quarters of the States-General and various archives.

Birch, Harvey. See **Spy, The.**

Birdcage Walk. A walk in St. James's Park, London.

Birds, The. A sparkling comedy (414 B.C.) by Aristophanes.

Birds' Christmas Carol, The. A story for children (1888) by Kate Douglas Wiggin.

Birkenhead, The. An English troop steamer wrecked off the Cape of Good Hope, Feb. 26, 1852, with a loss of 400.

Birmingham (bėr′ming-am) **Festival.** A triennial musical festival, established 1768, at Birmingham, England.

Biron (bē-rôn). An attendant of the King of Navarre in Shakspere's comedy "Love's Labour's Lost." He is gay and eloquent, and holds nothing sacred.

Birs Nimrud (bērs nēm-röd′). A mound of ruins northeast of Babylon: the site of the famous temple of Nebo Ezida, probably the original of the Tower of Babel, traditionally built by Nimrod.

Bisa (bē′sä), or **Wa-Bisa** (wä-). A Bantu tribe of northeast Rhodesia, between the Zambezi River and Lake Bangweolo.

Biserta (bē-zer′tä). In Ariosto's "Orlando Furioso," the capital of Agramante, taken by Orlando, Astolfo, and Brandimart.

Bishop Blougram's Apology. A poem (1855) by Robert Browning.

Bishops' Bible, The. The second edition (1540) of the Great Bible (1539), to which Archbishop Cranmer contributed a preface.

Bishopsgate. Once the principal entrance through the northern wall of London. Bishopsgate Street now goes over the spot.

Bisutun. See **Behistun.**

Bit Humri (bēt höm′ri). The Assyrian name of the land of Israel: after Omri, founder of the 4th Israelitish dynasty.

Biton (bī′ton) and **Cleobis** (klē′ō-bis). In Greek legend, sons of Cydippe, a priestess of Hera, who drew their mother's chariot to the temple at Argos. Hera, asked to reward them, caused them to die in their sleep.

Black Act, The. An English statute (1722) designed to suppress the "blacks," associations of lawless persons.

Black Assize, The. The Oxford assize of 1577, in which year Oxford was ravaged by jail-fever.

Black Bess. The famous mare of Dick Turpin.

Black Book, The. 1. See Dictionary, **black book,** under black. **2.** A prose satire (1604) by Middleton, directed against follies and vices of the time.

Black Brunswickers, or **Death's-Head Corps, The.** A corps of 2,000 horsemen equipped by the Duke of Brunswick to operate (1809) against Napoleon in Germany.

Black Country, The. The mining and manufacturing region about Birmingham, England.

Black Crom. An ancient heathen idol of Irish legend.

Black Dwarf, The. A romance (1816) by Scott. The "black dwarf" is Sir Edward Mauley.

Blackfeet, The. See Dictionary, **Blackfoot.**

Black Flags, The. Irregular soldiers in the upper valley

(variable) ḏ as d or j, ṣ as s or sh, ṭ as t or ch, ẕ as z or zh; o, F. cloche; ü, F. menu; c̣h, Sc. loch; n̄, F. bonbon; ′, primary accent; ″, secondary accent; †, obsolete; <, from; +, and; =, equals. See also lists at beginning of book.

of the Red River in Tonquin. They fought against the French in their wars with Annam.

Blackfriars. A locality in the center of London, southwest of St. Paul's, where a monastery of the black friars once stood.

Blackfriars Bridge. One of the great stone bridges of London, the third from the Tower: originally, Pitt Bridge.

Blackfriars Theatre. A playhouse within the City of London, usually given over to plays by the children's companies, but occupied for a time as a winter theater by Shakspere's company. Shakspere was himself a shareholder in Blackfriars.

Black Friday. 1. Good Friday. 2. Any Friday marked by calamity: as Dec. 6, 1745, when news came to London that the Pretender had reached Derby, or May 11, 1866, when a commercial panic began. See also Dictionary, **black.**

Black Hambleton, The. A historic race-course in England.

Black Hand, The. See Dictionary, **black.**

Blackheath. A common in Kent, England: the scene of a Danish defeat (1011), of the risings of Wat Tyler (1381) and Jack Cade (1450), and of the defeat of the Cornish rebels (1497).

Black Hole of Calcutta, The. See Dictionary, **black.**

Black Knight, The. 1. In early romances, the son of Oriana and Amadis of Gaul. 2. A disguise of Richard I. in Scott's "Ivanhoe."

Black Maria. See Dictionary, **black.**

Black Monday. Easter Monday: so called from the terrible storm on that day in 1360, when the English army besieging Paris suffered severely.

Black Mountain Tribes, The. The formerly belligerent tribes on the northwestern frontier of India, west of the upper Indus.

Blackpool, Stephen. In Dickens's "Hard Times," an honest weaver with a drunken wife.

Black Republic, The. Haiti.

Black Rod, The. See Dictionary, **black.**

Blacks, The. See **Bianchi.**

Black Saturday, The. In Scotch history, Aug. 4, 1621, when the (Edinburgh) Parliament passed acts favoring Episcopacy.

Black Valley. A novel (1925) by Raymond Weaver, presenting the futile and depressing life of a missionary colony in Japan.

Black Watch, The. A body of Scotch Highlanders organized 1725 to maintain order in the Highlands: so called from their somber uniform. Later the name was applied to a territorial regiment, the Royal Highlanders.

Bladud (blā′dud). A mythical British king, reputed founder of Bath.

Blanchefleur. See **Flore et Blanchefleur.**

Blanche of Devan. A crazed bride in Scott's "Lady of the Lake."

Blancos (bläng′kōz), or **Blanquillos** (bläng-kēl′yōz). One of the two great political parties (the other being the Colorados) of Uruguay.

Blandamour (blan′da̲-mör), **Sir.** A fickle and vainglorious knight in Spenser's "Faerie Queene," defeated by Britomart.

Bland Silver Bill, The. A United States statute (1878) reëstablishing as a legal tender the silver dollar of 412½ grains troy.

Blanketeers. The half-starved Manchester operatives who met at St. Peter's Field, March 10, 1817, to march to London with a petition of grievances.

Blarney Stone, The. See Dictionary, **blarney.**

Blatant Beast, The. See Dictionary, **blatant.**

Bleak House. A novel (1853) by Dickens. It is based upon a historic and interminable case in chancery.

Bleeding-Heart Yard. A part of London formerly the property of the Hatton family. Dickens uses it in "Little Dorrit."

Blefuscu (ble-fus′kū). An island opposite Lilliput, in Swift's "Gulliver's Travels." It was intended to satirize France.

Blemyes or **Blemmyes** (blem′i-ēz). A nomadic Ethiopian tribe which anciently infested Nubia and Upper Egypt.

Blenheim (blen′em) **Palace.** A palace at Woodstock, Oxfordshire, built by Vanbrugh (1705–16), at the national expense, for the first Duke of Marlborough.

Blessed Damozel, The. A poem by D. G. Rossetti, published 1850: one of the earliest productions of the Pre-Raphaelite movement reflected in literature.

Blessing of Jacob, The. A fine painting (1656) of Rembrandt, in the museum at Cassel, Germany.

Blifil (bli′fil), **Captain John.** In Fielding's "Tom Jones," a vain hypocrite, Tom's enemy.

Blimber (blim′ber), **Dr.** In Dickens's "Dombey and Son," a schoolmaster who crams his pupils with undigested facts. His daughter Cornelia is a short-haired, spectacled pedant, "dry and sandy with working in the graves of deceased languages."

Blind Alley. A novel (1919) by W. L. George.

Blind Beggar's Daughter of Bethnal Green, The. A ballad, preserved in Percy's "Reliques." The heroine's knightly wooer marries her, despite her father's station; and the father then reveals himself as a nobleman, disguised to escape the king's spies.

Bliss. Short stories (1920) by Katherine Mansfield (Mrs. J. Middleton Murry).

Blithedale Romance, The. A novel (1852) by Hawthorne, based on the Brook Farm experiment.

Block, Ben. See **Ben Block.**

Blond Beast, The. See Dictionary, **blond.**

Blood, The Council of. A tribunal organized, 1567, in the Netherlands by the Duke of Alva, to punish enemies of Spanish rule and of the Roman Catholic religion.

Bloody Angle, The. A salient at Spotsylvania Court House, Virginia, a scene of carnage in the battle of May 12, 1864.

Bloody Assizes. A series of trials for treasonable participation in Monmouth's Rebellion (1685). They were conducted by Judge George Jeffreys. Over 300 persons were executed and nearly 1,000 transported.

Bloody Brook. A brook near Deerfield, Mass., the scene of an Indian massacre of settlers in 1675.

Bloomsbury Gang, The. A political clique under the Duke of Bedford, influential about 1790.

Bloomsbury Square. A square north of New Oxford Street, London.

Blore (blōr) **Heath.** A heath near Market Drayton, Shropshire: the scene of the Yorkist victory over the Lancastrians, Sept. 23, 1459.

Blot in the 'Scutcheon, A. A tragedy (1843) by Browning.

Bluebeard. A nickname of the chevalier Raoul, an imaginary person celebrated for his cruelty. He gives his seventh wife, Fatima, the keys of the castle; and she finds in the forbidden room the bodies of the other six. The story goes back at least as far as the 14th century.

Blue Bird, The. The symbol of happiness in the drama of the same name (1908), by Maurice Maeterlinck.

Blue Boy, The. A painting (1779) by Gainsborough, formerly in Grosvenor House, London, now in the U. S.

Blue Coat School, The. See **Christ's Hospital.**

Blue-Gowns. Certain uniformed bedesmen who received alms from the kings of Scotland.

Blue-Grass Region, The. That part of central Kentucky which abounds in blue-grass (*Poa pratensis*).

Blue Grotto, The. A cavern on the shore of Capri, Italy.

Blue Knight, The. In medieval romance, Sir Persaunt of India, overthrown by Sir Gareth.

Blue-Mantle, The. The English pursuivant-at-arms.

Blues, The. In Canadian politics, the conservatives of Quebec.

Blue-Stockings, The. See Dictionary, **blue-stocking.**

Blunderbore. A giant whose boat is scuttled by Jack in "Jack the Giant-Killer."

Boanerges. See Dictionary.

Boar's Head, The. A tavern in Eastcheap, London, celebrated by Shakspere as the scene of Falstaff's carousals.

Boaz (bō′az). 1. A Bethlehemite who, marrying Ruth the Moabitess, became an ancestor of David. Ruth, ii., iii., iv. 2. See **Jachin,** 2.

Bobadil (bob′a̲-dil). A coward and braggart in Jonson's "Every Man in His Humour."

Boboli (bō′bō-lē) **Gardens, The.** Gardens in the rear of the Pitti Palace, Florence. They are filled with fountains, grottoes, and statues.

Bocardo (bō-kär′dō). An old north gate of Oxford, over which was a room used as a prison: destroyed 1771.

Bochica (bō′chē-kä). The name given by the Chibcha Indians to their conception of the Supreme Being, the creator.

Bodhisattva (bō-dhē-sat′vä). In Hindu belief, one who is in the way of attaining perfect knowledge; a Buddha-elect.

Bodleian (bod′lē-an or bod-lē′an) **Library.** A library of Oxford University, reëstablished (1597-1602) by Sir Thomas Bodley. It is notably rich in manuscripts.

Bœotian (bē-ō′shian) **League, The.** A league of independent cities of Bœotia, headed by Thebes: dissolved 171 B.C. or 146 B.C.

Boer War, The. See Dictionary, **Boer.**

Boëthius (bō-ē′thi-us). An early Provençal poem, made up largely of moral reflections from the "De Consolatione" of Boëthius. It probably dates from the 11th century.

Boffin (bof′in), **Nicodemus.** In "Our Mutual Friend," by Dickens, a simple-hearted, illiterate old man who has inherited the estate ("Boffin's Bower") of his late employer, a miserly dustman.

Bohemian Brethren. A Hussite sect in Bohemia, from the 15th century to the 17th.

Bohemian Girl, The. A very popular opera (1843) by Balfe.

Boii (bō′i-ī). 1. A Celtic people of Cisalpine Gaul, important in Roman annals from the 4th to the 2d century B.C. 2. A Celtic tribe which joined the Helvetii in their invasion of Gaul in 58 B.C.

Bois de Boulogne (bwo dė bö-lon-y′). A park in Paris, reached by the Champs Élysées. It is celebrated for its turf, trees, and ornamental ponds. It contains the Longchamp race-course.

Bois de Vincennes (vań-sen). A public park of Paris.

Bois-Guilbert (bwo-gėl-bär), **Brian de.** In Scott's "Ivanhoe," a Norman knight, preceptor of the Knights Templars. He has a violent passion for the Jewess Rebecca.

Bokerly (bō′kėr-li) **Dyke.** Ruins of Roman intrenchments near Farnham, England.

Bold Stroke for a Husband, A. A comedy (1783) by Mrs. Cowley.

Bollandists, The. See Dictionary, **Bollandist.**

Bolotoo (bol-ō-tö′). In Tongan superstition, the land of shades, to which nobles go after death.

Bolsheviks, The. See Dictionary, **Bolshevik.**

Bolt Court. A London street leading from Fleet Street. In it, at No. 84, Samuel Johnson passed his last years.

Bolton Castle. A castle in the West Riding of Yorkshire: the scene of Mary Stuart's imprisonment, 1568-69.

Bolus, Dr. The rime-writing Newcastle apothecary in a humorous poem, "Dr. Bolus," by Colman the Younger.

Bombardinian (bom-bär-din′i-an or bum-), **General.** The bombastic general of the king's forces in Carey's "Chrononhotonthologos."

Bombastes Furioso (bom-bas′tēz fū-ri-ō′sō). A burlesque opera (1790) by William Barnes Rhodes. It burlesques the "Orlando Furioso." See **Fusbos.**

Bona Dea (bō′nä dē′ä). In Roman mythology, a goddess of fecundity, worshiped by women.

Bondei (bon-dā′i), or **Wa-Bondei** (wä-). A Bantu tribe of East Africa, between the Usambara hills and the coast.

Bond Street. The main thoroughfare between Oxford Street and Piccadilly, London. It contains the Grosvenor and Doré galleries and many fashionable shops.

Bongo (bóng′gō). A mixed negro tribe in the basin of the Bahr-el-Ghazal, eastern Sudan: neighbors of the Nyam-Nyam.

Bonhomme, Jacques. See **Jacques Bonhomme.**

Bonhomme Richard (bo-nom rē-shär). The flag-ship of John Paul Jones in his engagement with the Serapis off the Yorkshire coast, Sept. 23, 1779.

Boniface. See Dictionary.

Booby, Lady. See **Andrews, Joseph.**

Book of Common Order, The. The liturgy of the Church of Scotland, taken from the liturgy of the English church at Geneva. It was introduced in 1562.

Book of Common Prayer, The. See Dictionary, **book.**

Book of Martyrs, The. A history (Latin, 1559; English, 1563) of the persecution of Reformers in England, by John Foxe. It was at first known as "Actes and Monuments."

Book of Mormon, The. See **Mormon, The Book of.**

Book of St. Albans, The. A rimed treatise on hawking, hunting, etc. (1486): attributed with partial correctness to Juliana Berners. The 2d edition (1496) has the famous "Treatyse on Fysshynge with an Angle."

Book of Sentences, The. A 12th-century book of theological questions, with answers given on the authority of Scripture and of the Fathers of the Church: by Peter Lombard.

Book of Snobs, The. A collection (1848) of sketches by Thackeray.

Book of the Dead, The. See Dictionary, **book.**

Book of the Duchess, The. A poem (about 1369) by Chaucer. Its subject is the death of the wife of John of Gaunt. Also called "The Death of Blanche the Duchess."

Boötes. See Dictionary.

Booth, Amelia and **Captain.** See **Amelia.**

Bo-Peep (bō-pēp′), **Little.** In a popular nursery rime, a small shepherdess who lost her sheep and "didn't know where to find them."

Borachio (bō-rä′chiō). A villainous follower of Don John, in Shakspere's "Much Ado about Nothing." (*Borachio* is probably from the Spanish name for a leathern wine-bottle, and hence applied to a drunkard.)

Border States, The. Formerly, Delaware, Maryland, Virginia, Kentucky, and Missouri — slave States near free territory. North Carolina, Tennessee, and Arkansas were sometimes included.

Boreas. See Dictionary.

Borghese (bor-gā′zā). A noble family of Siena and Rome. One member became Pope Paul V. in 1605; another married a sister of Napoleon I.

Borghese Gladiator, The. A notable statue by Agasias of Ephesus, in the Louvre, Paris. The subject is probably an athlete or a warrior.

Borghese Mars, The. An antique statue of Mars, in the Louvre, Paris.

Borghese Palace, The. The palace of the Borghese family in Rome, noted for its art collections. It dates from the late 16th century.

Borgia (bôr′jä). A noble family of Spanish origin, which acquired eminence in Italy after 1455, when one of its members became Pope Calixtus III.

Boris Godunov (bo-rēs′ go-dö-nof′). 1. A tragedy (1825) by Pushkin. 2. An opera (1874) by Musorgski, based on Pushkin's drama.

Bororós (bō-rō-rōz′). An Indian tribe of western Brazil, about the head-waters of the Paraguay.

Bors (bôrs). In Arthurian legend: (1) A natural son of King Arthur: also Borre. (2) A knight of the Round Table, nephew of Lancelot: called Sir Bors de Ganis. (3) King of Gaul, brother of King Ban of Benwick or Benoic.

Borsippa (bôr-sip′ä). An ancient city of Babylonia, probably a suburb of Babylon, and perhaps identical with Birs Nimrud.

Bosinney, Philip. A prominent character in Galsworthy's "Man of Property": one who typifies anti-Forsyte ideas. See **Forsyte Saga, The.**

Boston Massacre, The. A clash in Boston, March 5, 1770, between British soldiers and a crowd of citizens, of whom three were killed and several wounded.

Boston Port Bill, The. A bill passed 1774 by Parliament, closing the port of Boston, Mass., after June 1, 1774.

Boston Tea-Party, The. An occasion (Dec. 16, 1773) on which citizens and merchants of Boston boarded English vessels and threw chests of tea into Boston harbor, as a protest against the importation of taxed tea.

Bothwell (both′wel). A tragedy (1874) by Swinburne, on the subject of Mary Queen of Scots.

Botocudos (bō-tō-kö′dōz). An apparently very ancient Indian tribe of eastern Brazil. They are degraded savages.

Bottom, Nick. An ignorant and clownish weaver in Shakspere's "Midsummer Night's Dream." Puck causes him to wear an ass's head, and Titania is made by enchantment to love him.

Bounderby, Joseph. A coarse bully and ostentatiously self-made man in Dickens's "Hard Times."

Bountiful, Lady. A generous-hearted country gentlewoman in Farquhar's "Beaux' Stratagem," whose name has become a synonym for any charitable woman.

Bounty, The. An English ship whose mutineering crew settled on Pitcairn Island, in the South Pacific, and formed (with the natives) a civilized community.

Bourbons, The. See Dictionary, **Bourbon.**

Bourgeois Gentilhomme, Le (lè bör-zhwo zhon̄-tē-yom). A comedy (1670) by Molière, with music by Lully. See **Jourdain, Monsieur.**

Bourignonists (bö-rin'yon-ists). A Quietist sect founded in the 17th century by Antoinette Bourignon.

Bourse, La (lä börs). A novel (1832) by Balzac.

Bovary (bō-vä-rē), **Emma.** The title character of Flaubert's "Madame Bovary" (1857). She is a provincial apothecary's wife who, weary of her dull life, seeks distraction with lovers, falls in debt, and finally poisons herself.

Bow Bells. See **St. Mary de Arcubus.**

Bower of Bliss, The. 1. The garden of the enchantress Armida in Tasso's "Gerusalemme Liberata." 2. The enchanted home of Acrasia in Spenser's "Faerie Queene."

Bowery (bou'ėr-i), **The.** A New York street parallel to Broadway, running from Chatham Square to 7th Street. It was formerly a notorious haunt of ruffians ("Bowery Boys").

Bowling (bō'ling), **Tom.** 1. A sailor in Smollett's "Roderick Random." 2. The hero of a famous song by Dibdin.

Bowling Green. A small open space in New York City, at the foot of Broadway, in the former aristocratic center of the city.

Bow Street. A London street near Covent Garden, in which is located the principal police court, established 1749.

Boxers, The. See Dictionary, **boxer².**

Boyd's. The old White Horse Inn, in Boyd's Close, Canongate, Edinburgh, associated with the Scottish pilgrimage of Johnson and Boswell.

Boyle Lectures. A course of 8 lectures in defense of Christianity, delivered annually at St.-Mary-le-Bow, London: instituted 1692 by Robert Boyle.

Boythorn, Lawrence. In Dickens's "Bleak House," a handsome old man whose bark is worse than his bite.

Bozrah (boz'rä). A city of Bashan, Syria: the modern Busra. Isa. lxiii. 1.

Brabançonne, La (lä brä-bän-son). The Belgian national song, composed 1830 by Jenneval and Van Campenhout.

Brabantio (brạ-ban'shiō). In Shakspere's "Othello," a Venetian senator, father of Desdemona.

Brachylogus (bra-kil'ō-gus). A name given in the 16th century to a manual of Roman law, "Corpus legum," of about the 12th century.

Bradamant (brad'ạ-mant). The sister of Rinaldo in the epics of Boiardo and Ariosto. She is a warrior who wields an enchanted spear. She loves and weds Rogero.

Bragança (brä-gän'sä), or **Braganza** (brä-gän'zạ), **The House of.** The reigning family of Portugal, 1640–1910, and of Brazil from 1822 to 1889.

Braggadocchio (brag-ạ-dō'chiō). See Dictionary, **braggadocio.**

Bragi (brä'gē). In Old Norse mythology, a son of Odin, and god of poetry: Odin's principal scald in Valhalla. His wife is Idun.

Brahma, Brahmana. See Dictionary, **Brahma².**

Brahmandapurana (bräh-män″dạ-pō-rä'nạ). A purana revealed by Brahma, and containing an account of the future Kalpas or "days" of Brahma.

Brahmapurana (bräh″mạ-pō-rä'nạ). One of the more important puranas. It is supposedly a revelation of Brahma to Daksha. Its evident purpose is to promote the worship of Krishna.

Brahmasabha (bräh″mạ-sa'bhä) and **Brahmasamaj** (-sạ-mäj'). An earlier and a later name for the "society of believers in God," founded (1830) by the Hindu reformer Ram Mohan Roy.

Brahmins. See Dictionary, **Brahman.**

Bramble, Tabitha. In Smollett's "Humphry Clinker," the virtuous sister of Matthew Bramble: a ridiculous old maid. She captures the affections of Captain Lismahago, an argumentative Scottish officer who has had romantic adventures among Indians.

Brand. A drama (1885) by Henrik Ibsen.

Brandimart (bran'di-märt). In the epics of Boiardo and Ariosto, the husband of Flordelis, and King of the Distant Islands.

Brangäne (brän-gä'nė). In Wagner's "Tristan und Isolde," Brangwayne or Branwen.

Brangwayne (brang'wän), or **Branwen** (bran'wen). The confidante of Iseult in the romance of "Tristram and Iseult."

Brasenose (bräz'nōz) **College.** A college of Oxford University, founded about 1509 on the site of a former Brasenose Hall.

Brass, Sampson. In Dickens's "Old Curiosity Shop," a shyster lawyer, the tool of Quilp. He is in partnership with his sister Sally.

Brauronia (brâ-rō'ni-ạ). In Greek antiquity, a quadrennial festival at the shrine of Artemis at Brauron, in Attica.

Bravo, The. A romance (1831) of Venice, by J. F. Cooper.

Brazil (brạ-zil'). A mythical island which appeared on old maps of the northern Atlantic Ocean as early as the 14th century.

Bread and Cheese Folk, The. The insurgent party in Haarlem (Netherlands), who took possession of the city in 1492.

Breakfast-Table, The Autocrat of the. A volume of witty informal discourses (1857–58), bound together with a thin thread of story, by Oliver Wendell Holmes: followed (1859) by "The Professor at the Breakfast-Table," and (1872) "The Poet at the Breakfast-Table."

Breck, Alan. A dashing Highland Jacobite in Stevenson's "Kidnapped" and "David Balfour."

Breda (brä-dä'), **The Compromise of.** A Protestant-Catholic league (1566) organized in the Netherlands by the lesser nobility to oppose the Inquisition and protect civil and political liberty.

Breda, The Declaration of. A proclamation of general amnesty (1660) issued from Breda by Charles II. of England.

Breda, The Treaty of. A treaty (1667) of England with Holland, France, and Denmark. New York and New Jersey were confirmed to England, Acadia to France, and Surinam to Holland.

Breitmann (brīt'män), **Hans.** A pen-name of Charles Godfrey Leland. See **Hans Breitmann's Party.**

Brennus (bren'us). The legendary leader of the Senonian Gauls when (about 390 B.C.) they overran Italy and captured Rome. When the gold of the Roman ransom was being weighed, he is said to have cast his sword into the scale, with the famous exclamation "Væ victis!" ("Woe to the conquered!").

Brentford, The Two Kings of. Two burlesque characters who always appear together and act identically in Buckingham's "Rehearsal."

Brera (brā'rä). The Palace of Sciences and Arts at Milan, containing an art gallery and the important Brera Library, founded 1770.

Brer Fox. See **Uncle Remus** and **Brer Rabbit.**

Brer (brur) **Rabbit.** A figure in Harris's "Uncle Remus." Brer Fox has the advantage in every way, but Brer Rabbit usually wins.

Bretigny (brė-tē-nyē), **The Treaty of.** A treaty (1360) between England and France, whereby England renounced claims to the French crown and gave up conquered provinces, but retained the Channel ports and received an indemnity.

Briareus (brī-ā'rē-us). A hundred-armed, fifty-headed giant who helped Zeus against the Titans.

Briary Bush, The. A novel (1921) by Floyd Dell. See **Moon-Calf.**

Brick, Jefferson. In Dickens's "Martin Chuzzlewit," an American journalist, personally mild but politically bloodthirsty.

Bridal of Triermain (trī-ėr-mān'), **The.** A romance in verse (1813) by Scott.

Bride of Abydos (ạ-bī'dos), **The.** A narrative poem (1813) by Byron.

Bride of Lammermoor (lam-ėr-mōr'), **The.** A historical romance (1819) by Scott. See **Ashton, Lucy;** also **Lucia di Lammermoor.**

Bridewell. See Dictionary, **bridewell.**

Bridge of Sighs, The. 1. A bridge in Venice, built 1597. Through a passage of it, prisoners were led for trial from the

Carceri (prisons) to the ducal palace. 2. A bridge leading to the Tombs prison, New York City. 3. A famous poem (1844) by Thomas Hood.

Bridget (brij′et), or **Brigit** (brij′it). A patron saint of Ireland.

Bridgewater House. The town residence of the Earl of Ellesmere, built in London 1847–49, on the site of Cleveland House.

Bridgewater Madonna, The. A small painting (1512) by Raphael, in Bridgewater House, London.

Bridgewater Treatises, The. Eight dissertations (1833–36) in which scientific facts are adduced to illustrate "the power, wisdom, and goodness of God as manifested in the creation." They were the result of a bequest by the Earl of Bridgewater (d. 1829).

Bridoie (brē-dwo′). In Rabelais's "Gargantua and Pantagruel," the ignorant judge who decides causes by means of dice.

Brid′oison (brē-dwo-zôn′). A judge in Beaumarchais's "Mariage de Figaro," derived from Rabelais's Bridoie.

Brigadore (brig′a-dōr). The horse of Sir Guyon in Spenser's "Faerie Queene": derived from Boiardo's Brigliadoro.

Brigantes (bri-gan′tēz). A tribe in Britain which, in the 1st century, occupied the region north of the Humber.

Brigliadoro (brēl-yä-dô′rō). Orlando's horse in Boiardo's "Orlando Innamorato."

Brig o' Balgownie, The. See **Balgownie, The Brig o'.**

Brihaddevata (bri-had-dā′va-tä). An ancient Sanskrit work ascribed to Shaunaka, designed to specify the deity for each verse of the Rig-Veda.

Brihaspati (bri-has-pa′ti). In Vedic mythology, a god personifying the activity of the pious man toward the gods: an intercessor for men with the gods.

Brihatkatha (bri-hat′kat-hä). The 'Great Narration,' a collection of Sanskrit tales by Gunadhya. Somadeva calls it the source of his Kathasaritsagara.

Brihatkathamanjari (bri-hat′kat-hä-man′ja-rē). The 'Great Blossom-Cluster of Tales,' a Sanskrit collection by Kshemendra Vyasadasa, based on the Brihatkatha.

Brihatsamhita (bri-hat-sam′hi-tä). The 'Great Collection,' a Sanskrit astrological work by Varaha Mihira.

Brimming Cup, The. A novel (1921) by Dorothy Canfield Fisher.

Briseis (brī-sē′is). In the Iliad, a beautiful maiden captured by Achilles: indirectly the cause of his quarrel with Agamemnon.

Britain (brit′an). 1. Great Britain; the island comprising England, Scotland, and Wales. 2. In Arthurian romance, Little Britain, or Brittany, in France.

Britanni (bri-tan′ī). A Celtic people of northwest Gaul (modern Bretagne, or Brittany). They are supposed to have been driven out of southwestern Britain by the Anglo-Saxons.

Britannia Tubular Bridge, The. A railway bridge across Menai Strait, Wales, built (1846–50) by Robert Stephenson.

British East Africa Company, The Imperial. A British commercial company, chartered 1888 for development of the territory northeast of Victoria Nyanza. In 1895 its charter was surrendered to the British government.

British Legion, The. A body of British troops which fought (1836) against the Carlists for Queen Isabella of Spain.

British Museum, The. A celebrated museum on Great Russell Street, Bloomsbury, London, founded 1753. Its collections of antiquities are vast, and its library is one of the greatest in the world.

British South Africa Company, The. A British company chartered 1889 for exploitation of Matabeleland and neighboring regions, under Cecil Rhodes. Its territory was later extended to include much of British Central Africa.

Britomartis (brit-ō-mär′tis). In Greek mythology, a Cretan goddess of hunters, fishermen, and sailors: a woman deified by Artemis when she threw herself into the sea to escape the pursuit of Minos.

Britomartis (brit-ō-mär′tis), or **Britomart** (brit′ō-märt). A female knight personifying chastity in Spenser's "Faerie Queene."

Broad Bottom Administration, The. An epithet applied to the Pelham administration (1744–54), because it was based on a coalition of British parties.

Broadway (brôd′wā). A principal business street of New York, extending from Bowling Green northward to 263d Street, and crossing Fifth Avenue diagonally at 23d Street. On and near it between 42d Street and 59th Street are many theaters. See Dictionary, **Great White Way**, under **great.**

Bromide. See Dictionary, **bromide.**

Brompton (bromp′ton). A district of London, S. W., between Kensington and Pimlico, south of Hyde Park.

Brontes (bron′tēz). One of the Cyclopes.

Brooke (brůk), **Dorothea.** In George Eliot's "Middlemarch," a young woman of vague spiritual aspirations, thwarted by her marriage with the Rev. Edward Casaubon, a self-absorbed pedant. After his death she remarries for love.

Brook Farm. The scene of a famous, but unsuccessful, communistic experiment at West Roxbury, Massachusetts, 1841–47, participated in by George Ripley, George W. Curtis, C. A. Dana, Hawthorne, and others.

Brook Kerith, The. A reconstruction of the life of Christ (1916) by George Moore.

Brooklyn (brůk′lin) **Bridge.** A large suspension-bridge over the East River, uniting the boroughs of Manhattan and Brooklyn, New York City. It was built 1867–84. The total length is 5,989 feet.

Brooks of Sheffield. In Dickens's "David Copperfield," the name by which Mr. Murdstone, David's vindictive stepfather, refers to David in order to avoid speaking the child's name in his presence.

Brooks's. A London Conservative club established 1764. See **Almack's.**

Brothers, The. A political club of statesmen and wits established in London in 1713: later merged in the Scriblerus Club. Swift was its treasurer.

Brother Sam. A comedy (1874) by John Oxenford, based on a German play by Gorner. Brother Sam is the brother of Lord Dundreary, and the part was first played by E. A. Sothern. The play is a sequel to "Our American Cousin."

Brothers Karamazov (kä-rä-mä′zof), **The.** A novel (1879–80) by Fedor Dostoevski.

Brown, Tom. The typical healthy British schoolboy and youth in "Tom Brown's School Days" and "Tom Brown at Oxford," by Thomas Hughes.

Brown Bess. The English regulation flintlock musket of the late 18th century.

Brownists, The. See Dictionary, **Brownism.**

Brown, Jones, and Robinson, The Adventures of. Illustrated satirical articles (1854) by Richard Doyle on the manners of the middle-class Englishman abroad.

Brown, Jones, and Robinson, The Struggles of. Articles (1862) by Trollope, with pictures by Millais.

Brownlow (broun′lō), **Mr.** A benevolent old gentleman who befriends the hero of Dickens's "Oliver Twist."

Brownrigg Papers, The. A collection (1860) of essays by Douglas Jerrold.

Broykarre (broi-kär′). The horse of Malagigi, inferior to none in the world but Bayard.

Bructeri (bruk′te-rī). A Germanic tribe of the territory about the upper Ems, which fought against the Romans: ultimately merged in the Franks.

Bruin. See Dictionary.

Brumaire (brü-mār), **The 18th.** Nov. 9, 1799, the beginning of the coup d'état which overthrew the Directory.

Brunanburh (brö′nan-bůrch), **The Battle of.** A battle poem inserted in the Anglo-Saxon Chronicle. It celebrates Athelstan's victory over Anlaf of Ireland and Constantine of Scotland, in 937.

Brunello (brö-nel′lō). A thief in the epics of Boiardo and Ariosto. He rose to kingship, but was eventually hanged.

Brunhild (brön′hilt). In the Nibelungenlied, a legendary queen of Island (Isala-land), the wife of King Gunther, for whom she is won by Siegfried. In the Old Norse Siegfried legend, she is a Valkyr, won by Sigurd for Gunnar.

Brunswick-Lüneburg (brunz′wik-lü′ne-bůrch). A branch of the house of Brunswick from which the reigning house of Great Britain is descended.

Brussels Conference, The. A European convention (1876, 1877), which decided to establish an International African Association to explore and civilize Central Africa.

(variable) ḍ as d or j, ş as s or sh, ṭ as t or ch, ẓ as z or zh; o, F. cloche; ü, F. menu; ch, Sc. loch; n̊, F. bonbon; ′, primary accent; ″, secondary accent; †, obsolete; <, from; +, and; =, equals. See also lists at beginning of book.

Brut (brŏt). A poetical version of the legendary history of Britain, by Layamon (c. 1200): a paraphrase of the "Roman de Brut" of Wace.

Brutus (brö'tus). 1. In "Julius Cæsar," as in history, the assassin of Cæsar: represented by Shakspere as his victim's former friend. 2. A tragedy (1730) by Voltaire.

Brutus the Trojan. A mythical personage who, according to Geoffrey of Monmouth, was the grandson of Æneas and the founder of New Troy (London).

Bryanites (brī'ạn-īts). 1. A Methodist body, the "Bible Christians," founded about 1815 by the Cornish preacher William Bryan. 2. A recent name for the Fundamentalists: from William Jennings Bryan, considered as their spokesman.

Brython (brith'ọn). The Celts of southern Britain who withstood the Teutonic invaders in the mountains of the western coast. Their language (Brythoneg) long survived in Wales, Cumbria, Devon, and Cornwall.

Bubona (bụ-bō'nạ). In Roman mythology, the protectress of cattle.

Bucentaur (bụ-sen'tȧr). The ceremonial ship of the Venetian Republic, used in the former annual rite of wedding the city to the Adriatic. The last Bucentaur (there have been three) was destroyed in 1798 by the French.

Bucephalus. See Dictionary.

Buchanites (buch'ạn-īts), **The.** A Scottish religious sect, the adherents (1784–1848) of Elspeth Buchan, who believed and taught that she was the woman foretold in Rev. xii.

Bucharest (bö-kạ-rest'), **The Treaty of.** A treaty (1812) which ended the Russo-Turkish war and established the Pruth and the lower Danube as the boundary between the two countries.

Buckingham (buk'ing-ạm) **Palace.** The London residence of the British sovereign, at the western end of St. James's Park.

Bucklaw, Laird of (Frank Hayston). See **Ashton, Lucy.**

Bucktails. Originally, members of the Tammany Society, New York; later (1817–26), the Democratic-Republican opponents of De Witt Clinton.

Bucolic Mouth of the Nile, The. An ancient mouth of the Nile, in the middle of the Delta.

Bucolics. See Dictionary, **bucolic.**

Buddha. See Dictionary.

Buddha-Gaya (bŭd'ạ-gī'ạ). An ancient center of Buddhism, in the Gaya district, Bengal. The temple is now in ruins.

Bug Jargal (bŭg zhär-gäl). A novel (1826) by Victor Hugo. Its subject is the revolt of the Santo Domingo negroes. Bug Jargal is a negro of innate nobility, in love with a white woman.

Bugres (bö'gräz). A Brazilian name for the Botocudos and other savage Indians: also applied to howling monkeys.

Bull, A Young. A famous pastoral painting by Paul Potter, in the Royal Gallery at The Hague.

Bull, John. See Dictionary, **John.**

Bull Moose. See Dictionary, **bull¹.**

Bulwer-Clayton Treaty, The. A treaty (1850) whereby Great Britain and the United States pledged themselves to respect the neutrality of the proposed canal across Central America: replaced (1901) by the Hay-Pauncefote Treaty.

Bumble, Mr. A fat, pompous beadle in Dickens's "Oliver Twist."

Bumppo, Nathaniel, or Natty. See **Leatherstocking Tales, The.**

Bundahish (bön'dä-hēsh). A Pahlavi theological work, containing the cosmogony and eschatology of the Mazdayasnians.

Bundesrat. See Dictionary.

Bungay (bung'gạ), **Friar.** A famous conjurer of Edward IV.'s time, introduced into the play of "Friar Bacon and Friar Bungay," by Robert Greene (1592).

Bungen (bŭng'ẹn). The street in Hamelin (Hameln) down which the Pied Piper enticed the children with his music.

Bunhill Fields. A burial-ground for dissenters (1665–1852) near Finsbury Square, London.

Bunker Hill Monument. A monument at Charlestown, Mass., dedicated (1843) on the 68th anniversary of the battle of Bunker (or Breed's) Hill.

Bunsby (bunz'bi), **Captain Jack.** In Dickens's "Dombey and Son," a worthy friend of Captain Cuttle, and the reluctant bridegroom of the widow MacStinger, whose nature is as her name.

Bunthorne (bun'thôrn). A lackadaisical, extravagantly esthetic burlesque figure in Gilbert and Sullivan's "Patience."

Bunting (bun'ting). The name of the legendary Pied Piper of Hamelin.

Burghers, The. A body of Presbyterians in Scotland, constituting (after 1747) one of the divisions of the early Secession Church.

Burgos (bör'gōs), **The Laws of.** A system of Spanish laws (1512) for the better regulation of Indian labor in America.

Burgundian Dynasty, The. A reigning house of Portugal, 1095–1383. It traced its ancestry from Henri, grandson of Robert, the first Duke of Burgundy.

Burial of Sir John Moore, The. A famous poem (1825) by Charles Wolfe.

Buriats (bö'ri-ats). A Buddhist Mongolian people living chiefly in Irkutsk and the Trans-Baikal territory, Siberia.

Buried Alive. A novel (1908) of the extravaganza type by Arnold Bennett. See also **Great Adventure, The.**

Burleigh (bêr'li), **Lord.** A character in Mr. Puff's tragedy "The Spanish Armada," the interpolated burlesque in Sheridan's "Critic." He nods, but speaks no word.

Burley, John. See **Balfour of Burley.**

Burlington Arcade, The. A covered pathway between Piccadilly and Burlington Gardens, with small shops on each side.

Burlington House, Old. A house, originally built about 1665 for the first Earl of Burlington, between Bond Street and Sackville Street, London: in 1868 handed over to the Royal Academy.

Burmese (ber-mēs' or -mēz') **Wars, The.** The wars (1824–26, 1852) which the British waged against Burma. Their result was the cession of Lower Burma.

Bushmen, The. See Dictionary, **Bushman.**

Busirane (bū'si-rān). In Spenser's "Faerie Queene," an enchanter who imprisons Amoretta: named from Busiris.

Busiris (bụ-sī'ris). In Greek mythology, an Egyptian king who, to avert famine, annually sacrificed one stranger. He was slain by Heracles.

Bussy d'Ambois (bü-sē dän-bwä). A tragedy (1607) by Chapman.

Bustan (bös-tän'). The name of several Persian works; most notably, the "Bustan" ('Tree-Garden') of Sadi.

Busybody, The. A comedy by Mrs. Centlivre, produced 1709: followed (1710) by "Marplot." These comedies introduce Marplot, a silly and cowardly bungler who is the prototype of Paul Pry.

Butler's Analogy. See **Analogy of Religion.**

Butterfly, Madame. See **Madame Butterfly.**

Buyides (bū'yidz). A Persian dynasty of the 10th and 11th centuries, overthrown about 1055.

Buzfuz (buz'fuz), **Serjeant.** In Dickens's "Pickwick Papers," Mrs. Bardell's counsel in her suit against Mr. Pickwick.

Byblis (bib'lis), or **Biblis.** In classical mythology, the daughter of Miletus who loved her brother Caunus and was changed into the fountain of Byblis. Ovid tells the story in his "Metamorphoses."

Bye Plot, The. The less important of two conspiracies (1603) to seize the person of James I. of England and thereby to extort certain religious concessions. See **Main Plot, The.**

Byerly (bī'êr-li) **Turk, The.** One of the three Oriental horses (Byerly Turk, Darley Arabian, Godolphin Barb) from which all names in the stud-book trace their descent.

Byron, Harriet. In Richardson's "Sir Charles Grandison," the paragon of young womanhood whom Grandison finally marries.

Byrsa (bêr'sạ), **The.** The citadel of Carthage.

Byzantine (biz'ạn-tin or bi-zan'tin, or -tīn) **Historians, The.** The Greek historians of the Eastern Empire; notably, Zosimus, Procopius, Agathias, Constantine Porphyrogenitus, Anna Comnena, Joannes Cinnamus, and Nicetas.

C

Caaba. See Dictionary, **Kaaba.**

Caaguás (kä-ä-gwäz'), or **Caás** (kä-äz'). A horde of wild South American Indians living on the river Paraná.

---

fat, fāte, fär, fåll, ȧsk, fãre; net, mē, hèr; pin, pīne; not, nōte, mŏve, nôr; up, lūte, pŭll; oi, oil; ou, out; (lightened) aviạry, ẹlect, agọny, intọ, ụnite; (obscured) errạnt, operạ, ardẹnt, actọr, nȧtụre; ch, chip; g, go; th, thin; ᴛн, then; y, you;

Cabal (ką-bal′), **The.** An unpopular group of ministers of Charles II. of England, Clifford, Arlington, Buckingham, Ashley, and Lauderdale, who in 1672 signed a treaty with France for war against Holland: the initials of their names happening to form the word *cabal.*

Cabbages and Kings. 1. See Dictionary, **cabbage²**. 2. Stories (1905) by O. Henry (Sidney Porter).

Cabiri or **Kabeiri** (ką-bī′rī). 1. The seven planets worshiped by the Phenicians. 2. In Greek mythology, deities worshiped with mysteries in Samothrace and elsewhere.

Cacus (kā′kus). In Roman mythology, a fire-spitting giant, son of Vulcan, slain by Hercules for stealing from him some of the cattle of Geryon.

Caddoan (kad′ō-ąn). A linguistic stock of North American Indians, named after its leading division, Caddo.

Caddo (kä′dō) **Confederacy, The.** A confederacy of the Caddoan stock of North American Indians, formerly dwelling in northwestern Louisiana and eastern Texas.

Cadmeia (kad-mē′yä). The citadel or acropolis of Thebes in Bœotia, named from Cadmus, its mythical founder.

Cadmus (kad′mus). In Greek mythology, a son of Agenor, king of Phenicia, and brother of Europa. See Dictionary, **Cadmean.**

Cæcilia (sē-sil′i-ä) **gens.** A plebeian clan in ancient Rome.

Cælia (sē′li-ä) **gens.** A plebeian clan in ancient Rome.

Cælian (sē′li-ąn), **The.** The southeastern hill of the group of Seven Hills of ancient Rome.

Caerleon (kär-lē′ǫn). A town in Monmouthshire, England, the traditional seat of King Arthur's court.

Cæsarea (sez-ą-rē′ä). In ancient geography: (1) a seaport of Palestine. Acts, viii. 40. (2) A city in Cappadocia, Asia Minor.

Cæsarea Philippi (fi-lip′ī). In ancient geography, a town in northern Palestine. Mat. xvi. 13.

Café Procope (kȧ-fā pro-kop). A coffee-house opposite the Comédie Française, frequented by 18th-century wits.

Cahita (kä-hē′tä). A division of the Piman stock of North American Indians, inhabiting the southwestern coast of Sonora and the northwestern coast of Sinaloa, Mexico.

Caiaphas (kā′yą-fąs). The surname of Joseph, Jewish high priest A.D. 27(18?)–36: son-in-law of Annas. John, xi. 49.

Cain (kān). The elder son of Adam and Eve, and the murderer of Abel. Gen. iv.

Cain, a Mystery. A dramatic poem (1821) by Byron.

Cainites (kān′īts). A Gnostic sect of the 2d century, which reverenced Cain, Esau, Korah, and Judas Iscariot.

Ça ira (sä ē-rä). The first popular song (probably 1789) to spring from the French Revolution.

Caités or **Cahetés** (kä-e-tāz′). A powerful, warlike cannibal tribe of Brazilian Indians.

Caius (kā′yus), **Dr.** A French doctor in Shakspere's "The Merry Wives of Windsor."

Caius Cestius (kā′yus ses′ti-us), **The Pyramid of.** A massive sepulchral monument of the time of Augustus, at Rome.

Caius (kēz) **College.** In full, Gonville and Caius College: a college of the University of Cambridge, England, established 1348, refounded 1558.

Cajuns (kā′junz). A name given, in Louisiana, to the descendants of the exiles from Acadia.

Cakes, The Land of. Scotland, famous for its oatmeal cakes.

Calantha (ką-lan′thä). The principal character in Ford's tragedy "The Broken Heart."

Calchaquis (käl-chä-kēz′). A tribe of South American Indians which formerly occupied a part of the modern Argentina.

Calchas (kal′kąs). In Greek legend, a soothsayer who advised the sacrifice of Iphigenia. According to prophecy, he died when he met, in Mopsus, his superior in divination.

Caleb (kā′leb). A Hebrew leader, sent as spy into the land of Canaan. Num. xiii. 6, etc.

Caleb Williams. A novel (1794) by William Godwin. See **Falkland**, 2.

Caledonia. See Dictionary.

Calenders (kal′ęn-dėrz), **The Three.** Three princes disguised as Calenders (begging dervishes) in the "Arabian Nights' Entertainments."

Caleti (ką-lē′tī). An ancient Belgic tribe dwelling in the vicinity of Rouen. They opposed Cæsar (52–51 B.C.).

Caliban (kal′i-ban). 1. See Dictionary. 2. A philosophical drama (1878) by Renan, ostensibly a sequel to Shakspere's "Tempest."

Caliban upon Setebos (set′ę-bos). A poem (1864) by Robert Browning.

Calidore (kal′i-dōr). A knight representing courtesy in Spenser's "Faerie Queene": modeled after Sir Philip Sidney.

Calife de Bagdad, Le (lė kȧ-lēf dė bȧg-dȧd′). An opera (1800) by Boieldieu, words by St. Just.

Calixtines (ką-liks′tinz). A sect of Hussites in Bohemia.

Callias (kal′i-as), **The Peace of.** A peace (371 B.C.) between Athens and Sparta, including their allies except Thebes.

Callimachus (ką-lim′ą-kus). An artist of antiquity (before 396 B.C.), the traditional inventor of the Corinthian column.

Callinicus (kal-i-nī′kus) **of Heliopolis.** An Egyptian architect commonly held to be the inventor of the Greek fire, and to have destroyed by it (about A.D. 670) a Saracen fleet which attacked Constantinople.

Calliope. See Dictionary.

Callirrhoe (ką-lir′ǫ-ē). See **Alcmæon.**

Callisto (ką-lis′tō). In Greek mythology, a nymph attendant on Artemis, punished for an amour with Zeus by being changed into a bear, in which form she was slain by Artemis.

Call of the Wild, The. A tale (1903) by Jack London, in which a dog reverts to the type of his wolfish ancestors.

Calmucks. See Dictionary, **Kalmuck.**

Calpe (kal′pē). The ancient name of the rock of Gibraltar.

Calpurnia (kal-pėr′ni-ä). Cæsar's wife in Shakspere's "Julius Cæsar," historically the daughter of L. Calpurnius Piso Cæsoninus.

Calpurnia (kal-pėr′ni-ä) **gens.** In ancient Rome, a plebeian clan or house.

Calvary. See Dictionary.

Calves' Head Club. An English club said to have been instituted in ridicule of the memory of Charles I., and to have met in secret after the Restoration till 1734.

Calydon (kal′i-don). 1. See Dictionary, **Calydonian**. 2. A great forest, supposed to be in the north of England, celebrated in Arthurian romance.

Calydonian Hunt, The. See Dictionary, **Calydonian.**

Calypso (ką-lip′sō). In Greek legend, a sea-nymph who for seven years detained Odysseus on the island of Ogygia.

Cambray (kam-brā′), **The League of.** An alliance (1508) between Louis XII. of France, the emperor Maximilian I., Ferdinand "the Catholic," and Pope Julius II., for the partition of the Venetian territories.

Cambray, The Peace of. A peace (1529) between Francis I. of France and Charles V.: called "La paix des dames" ('Ladies' Peace'), because the preliminaries were conducted by Louise, mother of Francis I., and Margaret, aunt of Charles V.

Cambridge (kām′brij), **The University of.** A celebrated university at Cambridge, England: a center of learning as early as the 12th century. Its library is notably large and rich in manuscripts.

Cambuscan (kam-bus-kan′ or kam-bus′kąn). A Tatar king in Chaucer's "Squire's Tale," who had wonderful magical possessions: the father of Canace, Camballo, and Algarsife.

Camden (kam′dęn) **Society, The.** An English historical society (formed 1838) for the publication of documents relating to English history.

Camelot (kam′e-lot). The legendary site in England of King Arthur's palace and court.

Camenæ. See Dictionary.

Cameronians. See Dictionary, **Cameronian.**

Cameronites (kam′ę-rǫn-īts). A group of French Protestants, professing a modified Calvinism.

Cames (kä-māz′). A wild tribe of Indians in the southwestern part of the state of São Paulo, Brazil.

Camilla (ką-mil′ä). In Roman legend, a virgin warrior queen of the Volsci. In the Æneid she leads her forces against Æneas.

Camille (kȧ-mēl). The name, and heroine, of the English version of "La dame aux camélias," a play by Dumas *fils.*

Camisards (kam′i-zärdz). French Protestants of the Cévennes who defended their liberties early in the 18th century.

Camorra. See Dictionary.

Campagna di Roma (käm-pä′nyä dē rō′mä), **The.** A large plain of volcanic formation, surrounding Rome: for centuries noted for its malarial climate, but in antiquity covered with villas and towns.

Campaign, The. A poem (1704) by Addison celebrating the battle of Blenheim.

Campanile of Giotto (jot′tō), **The.** A famous tower at Florence, begun (1334) by Giotto. See Dictionary, **campanile**, cut.

Campanile of St. Mark's, The. A high square tower in Venice, begun about 900, finished in the 16th century. It collapsed in 1902, but was rebuilt, being completed in 1912.

Campaspe (kam-pas′pē). The favorite concubine of Alexander, said to have been the model of the famous Venus Anadyomene of Apelles. There is a play "Alexander and Campaspe," by John Lyly (1584).

Campbellite. See Dictionary.

Campeador (käm-pä-ä-ᴛʜôr′), **El.** See Dictionary, **Cid.**

Camperdown. See **Victoria, The.**

Campus Martius (kam′pus mär′shi-us). A plain by the Tiber in ancient Rome, used for military training, sports, and the like.

Cana (kā′nä). A village of Galilee, the scene of two of Christ's miracles. John, ii.; iv. 46, etc.

Canaan. See Dictionary.

Canace (kan′ä-sē). 1. In Greek legend, a daughter of Æolus and Enarete, put to death for her illicit love. 2. In Chaucer's "Squire's Tale," the daughter of Cambuscan.

Cañaris (kän-yä′rēz). A powerful race of Indians who, for several centuries before the conquest, occupied part of what is now western Ecuador.

Candida (kan′di-dä). A drama (1897) by G. B. Shaw, showing a woman who chooses the husband who needs her rather than the poet who loves her.

Candide, ou L'Optimisme (kän-dēd ö lop-tē-mēsm). A philosophical and satirical novel (1759) by Voltaire, advocating a refined Stoicism and self-absorption in one's work.

Candour (kan′dor), **Mrs.** A slanderous woman with an affectation of frank amiability, in Sheridan's "School for Scandal." Her name has become a byword.

Can Grande's Castle. Poems (1918) by Amy Lowell.

Canidia (kä-nid′i-ä). A Neapolitan hetæra beloved by Horace. Her real name was Gratidia.

Caninefates (ka-nin-e-fā′tēz). A German tribe, mentioned by Tacitus as dwelling on the North Sea: closely related to the Batavi, their neighbors on the south.

Canoeiros (kä-nö-ā′röz). The name given by Brazilians to a horde of savage Indians on the Upper Tocantins.

Canongate (kan′on-gāt). The principal street in the Old Town of Edinburgh, originally connecting the suburb of the Canongate with the town proper.

Canon's Yeoman's Tale, The. One of Chaucer's "Canterbury Tales," exposing the tricks of alchemists.

Canopus (kä-nō′pus). A star of the first magnitude in the constellation Argo: the second in order of brightness of the fixed stars.

Canossa (kä-nos′sä). A ruined castle southwest of Reggio nell' Emilia, Italy, celebrated as the scene of the penance (1077) of the emperor Henry IV.

Canterbury College. An ancient college of Oxford University: founded 1361 or 1362, disbanded in the reign of Henry VIII.

Canterbury Tales, The. An uncompleted sequence of tales by Chaucer, for the most part written after 1387. See **Tabard Inn, The.**

Canticles. See Dictionary, **canticle.**

Canuck. See Dictionary.

Capaneus (kap′ä-nūs or kä-pā′nē-us). In Greek mythology, one of the Seven against Thebes, destroyed by Zeus for blasphemy. His wife Evadne threw herself on his funeral pyre.

Capa y Espada (kä′pä ē es-pä′ᴛʜä), **Comedias de.** A class of plays of gallantry and intrigue by Calderón and Lope de Vega: named from the national dress of the chief personages.

Capella (kä-pel′ä). A brilliant star of the first magnitude in the left shoulder of the charioteer pictured in the constellation Auriga.

Capernaum (kä-pėr′nä-um). In the time of Christ, an important place on the western shore of the Sea of Galilee. Mat. iv. 13.

Capet (kā′pet, F. kä-pā). A surname of the kings of France, beginning (987) with Hugh Capet.

Capetians (kä-pē′shianz). A royal family reigning over France (987–1328) as the 3d dynasty.

Capitaine Fracasse (kä-pē-tān frä-käs). A novel (1863) by Gautier. Its title is the stage name adopted by the hero, who joins a company of strolling players.

Capitan (kä-pē-tän). A conventional character of ridiculous bravado in early Italian comedy: introduced in French comedy prior to Molière.

Capitol, The. See Dictionary, **Capitol.**

Capitoline Hill, The. One of the seven hills of ancient Rome, northwest of the Palatine, on the left bank of the Tiber.

Capitoline Museum, The. One of the chief museums of antiquities of Rome, founded 1471.

Caponsacchi, Giuseppe (jö-sep′pä kä-pon-säk′kē). In Browning's "The Ring and the Book," the priest who helps Pompilia to escape from Guido.

Cappella Annunziata dell' Arena, La (lä käp-pel′lä än-nön-tsē-ä′tä del-lä-rä′nä). See **Arena Chapel, The.**

Capricorn. See Dictionary.

Captain, The. 1. An English line-of-battle ship of 72 guns, Commodore Nelson's flag-ship in 1796. 2. One of the earliest English armored turret-ships, launched 1869: foundered off Cape Finisterre with 500 men, 1870.

Captain Macedoine's Daughter. A novel (1920) by William McFee.

Captains Courageous. A story of the Gloucester fishermen (1897) by Rudyard Kipling.

Captives, The. A novel (1920) by Hugh Walpole.

Capua (kap′ū-ä). A city in Italy, famous for its wealth and luxury, in which Hannibal had his winter quarters: figuratively applied to any ruinous self-indulgence.

Capuchins. See Dictionary, **Capuchin.**

Capulet (kap′ū-let). The coarse, jovial, and irascible father of Juliet in Shakspere's "Romeo and Juliet." See **Montague.**

Caracarás (kä-rä-kä-räz′). A horde of South American Indians, of the Tupi-Guarani race. In the 16th century they lived on the western side of the river Paraná.

Caracas (kä-rä′käs). An Indian tribe of Venezuela, which formerly occupied the valleys about the present city of Caracas.

Caradoc (kar′ä-dok), or **Cradock** (krad′ok), **Sir.** In Arthurian romance, the only knight of the Round Table whose wife was chaste.

Carajás (kä-rä-zhäz′). A tribe of uncivilized Indians dwelling in the vicinity of the river Araguaya in Brazil.

Caramurú (kä-rä-mö-rö′). The nickname of a political party in Brazil which sought to secure the restoration of Pedro I. after his abdication in 1831.

Caravan. A collection of short stories (1925) by John Galsworthy.

Carbonari. See Dictionary, **Carbonaro.**

Card, The. A novel (1911) by Arnold Bennett: American title, "Denry the Audacious."

Cardinal College. See **Christ Church.**

Careless Husband, The. A comedy (1704) by Colley Cibber.

Caribs. See Dictionary, **Carib.**

Caripunas (kä-rē-pö′näz). A horde of exceptionally light-colored Brazilian Indians on the river Madeira.

Carisbrooke (kar′iz-bruk) **Castle.** An ancient castle in the Isle of Wight, England, the place of captivity (1647–48) of Charles I.

Carker (kär′kėr), **James.** In Dickens's "Dombey and Son," Dombey's confidential manager, a treacherous rascal.

Carlists, The. See Dictionary, **Carlist.**

Carlovingian (kär-lō-vin′ji-an) **Cycle.** See **Charlemagne Cycle of Romances, The.**

Carlowitz (kär′lō-vits), **The Peace of.** A peace (1699) for 25 years between Austria, Poland, Russia, Venice, and Turkey: memorable for the magnitude of the territorial change ratified, and for the first participation by Turkey and Russia in a general European congress.

Carlton (kärl′tọn), **The.** A London political club, strictly Conservative: founded 1832 by the Duke of Wellington.

Carlton House. A house (built 1709) formerly standing in what is now Carlton House Terrace, London: occupied 1732 by the Prince of Wales, and afterward by the prince regent (George IV.).

Carmagnole, La. See Dictionary, **Carmagnole.**

Carmel (kär′mel). 1. A mountain-ridge in Palestine. 1 Kings, xviii. 19, etc. 2. A city in the mountains of Judah. Josh. xv. 55.

Carmen (kär′men). 1. A story by Mérimée (1847), about a passionate and wild Spanish gipsy girl who is stabbed by her lover, José. 2. An opera (1875) founded on the preceding, by Bizet (words by Meilhac and Halévy).

Carmen Seculare (kär′men sek-ū-lā′rē). A 'secular hymn' composed by Horace on the occasion of the "Secular Games," 17 B.C.

Carnaval de Venise (kär-nȧ-vȧl dė vė-nēz). 1. A popular air heard by Paganini in Venice, on which he wrote a series of burlesque variations. 2. An opera (1853) by Ambroise Thomas.

Carneia (kär-nē′yạ). A Spartan festival, lasting 9 days, in August.

Carnutes (kär-nū′tēz), or **Carnuti** (-tī). An ancient tribe of central Gaul, living in the vicinity of Orléans and Chartres: at war with Cæsar 52–51 B.C.

Carolingians. See Dictionary, **Carolingian.**

Carpet-Baggers. See Dictionary, **carpet-bagger.**

Carrasco (kär-räs′kō), **Samson.** A bachelor or licentiate and practical joker in Cervantes's "Don Quixote."

Carrousel, Place du (plȧs dü kȧ-rö-zel). The space extending along the eastern court of the Tuileries, inclosed by the buildings of the Old and New Louvre, Paris: the site of a great carrousel or tilt in 1662. At the west side stands an arch commemorating the victories of Napoleon I.

Cartel (kär-tel′) **Combination.** In German politics, the temporary union (about 1887) in the Reichstag of the members of the Conservative, National Liberal, and Imperialist parties.

Carton (kär′tọn), **Sydney.** In Dickens's "Tale of Two Cities," a dissipated lawyer who dies by the guillotine to save Charles Darnay, the husband of Lucie Manette, whom Carton unselfishly loves.

Cartoons of Raphael, The. Seven drawings executed 1515–16 for Pope Leo X., to be reproduced in Flemish tapestry: now in the South Kensington Museum, London.

Casa de Contratación de las Indias (kä′sä dē kọn-trä-tä-thē-ōn′ dā läs ēn′dē-äs), or **Council of Seville.** An office established 1503 for the regulation of Spanish commerce with the Indies and the maintenance of a strict Spanish monopoly of American commerce.

Casa d'Oro (dō′rō). A 14th-century Venetian palace with a notably beautiful façade.

Casa Grande (grän′dā). The principal structure of a ruined pueblo on the south bank of the Gila River, Arizona.

Casa Guidi (gwē′dē) **Windows.** A poem (1851) by Mrs. Browning, named from the Casa Guidi, a house in Florence, where it was written.

Casas Grandes (kä′säs grän′dās). Extensive ruins, of unknown origin, in northwestern Sonora, Mexico.

Casaubon (kạ-sâ′bọn), **Rev. Edward.** See **Brooke, Dorothea.**

Case of Rebellious Susan, The. A social drama (1894) by Henry Arthur Jones.

Cassandra. See Dictionary.

Cassia (kash′iạ) **gens.** In ancient Rome, a clan, originally patrician, afterward plebeian.

Cassian (kash′ian) **Way, The.** An ancient Roman highway from Rome to Arretium (Arezzo) and thence to Florence and Lucca.

Cassio (kash′iō), **Michael.** Othello's confidential friend, later the object of his jealousy, in Shakspere's "Othello."

Cassiopeia. See Dictionary, **Cassiopeia's Chair.**

Cassius (kash′ius). In Shakspere's "Julius Cæsar," as in history, the ringleader of the conspirators against Cæsar.

Castalia. See Dictionary.

Castalides (kas-tal′i-dēz). A poetical name for the Muses.

Caste. A social comedy (1867) by T. W. Robertson.

Castle, The. Specifically, Dublin Castle, especially as the seat of government.

Castle Dangerous. A romance (1831) by Scott.

Castle Garden. A circular building (built 1807–11) on the Battery, New York. It now contains an aquarium.

Castle of Indolence, The. A poem (1748) by James Thomson.

Castle of Otranto (ō-trän′tō), **The.** A romance (1764) by Horace Walpole. It anticipated the "Gothic" school.

Castle Rackrent. A short novel (1800) dealing with absentee landlordism in Ireland, by Maria Edgeworth.

Castlewood, Beatrix. See **Esmond, Henry.**

Castlewood, Lady. In Thackeray's "Henry Esmond," the mother of Beatrix Esmond. She secretly loves Henry Esmond (who is captivated by Beatrix), and eventually marries him.

Castor (kas′tọr) and **Pollux** (pol′uks). In Greek mythology, twin sons of Leda, famous for their brotherly affection. Pollux, an immortal, spent alternately one day among the gods, the next in Hades with his dead brother.

Casuals of the Sea. A novel (1916) by William McFee.

Catacombs of Rome. Catacombs in Rome, of which the length of the galleries is estimated at about 600 miles: formed probably for the burial of Christians, chiefly between the 2d century and the 6th.

Cataract of Lodore, The. A poem (1823) by Robert Southey.

Catharine, Saint. 1. According to tradition, a martyr of the primitive church, tortured on the wheel and beheaded (307) at Alexandria. 2. A Dominican nun (1347–80) of Siena, of great fame for sanctity, and reputed to have received the stigmata.

Cathay. See Dictionary.

Cathedral, The. A novel (1923) by Hugh Walpole, analyzing the personality and the family relations of a church official.

Cathedral Novels, The. Novels (1855–67) by Trollope, dealing with the society of a cathedral town in the north of England: "The Warden," "Barchester Towers," "Doctor Thorne," "Framley Parsonage," "The Small House at Allington," and "The Last Chronicle of Barset."

Cathleen ni Hoolihan. A drama (1902) by William Butler Yeats.

Catholic Majesty. A title of the kings of Spain, assumed at times after the Council of Toledo, and permanently since the reign of Ferdinand "the Catholic" (1474–1516).

Cato (kā′tō). A tragedy (1713) by Addison.

Cato Street Conspiracy, or **Thistlewood Conspiracy.** In British history, a plot (discovered 1820), under the lead of Arthur Thistlewood, to assassinate Castlereagh and other ministers.

Catuvellauni (kat′ū-ve-lâ′nī). An ancient British people who lived in the region of Hereford and Bedford.

Caudle, Mrs. The lecturing wife in "Mrs. Caudle's Curtain Lectures," by Douglas Jerrold.

Causeries du Lundi (kōz-rē dü luṅ-dē). A collection of critical articles (1851–62) by Sainte-Beuve.

Cautionary Towns, The. A name given to four towns in the Netherlands (Briel, Flushing, Walcheren, Rammekens) held 1585–1616 by England as security for payment due.

Cavall (ka-val′). King Arthur's dog.

Cavalleria Rusticana (kä-väl-lā-rē′ä rös-tē-kä′nä). An opera (1890) by Mascagni.

Cavendish (kav′ẹn-dish) **College.** A college of Cambridge University, founded 1873.

Cave of the Winds, The. A recess behind the falls of Niagara, between them and the wall of rock.

Cayapós (kä-yä-pōz′). A tribe of Indians of central Brazil.

Cayuga (kạ-yö′gä). A tribe of North American Indians, the smallest tribe of the Iroquois Confederacy.

Cecilia (sẹ-sil′iạ), **Saint.** 1. A Christian martyr at Rome, 230: generally considered the patron saint of music. 2. There are celebrated paintings on this subject by Raphael (in the Accademia at Bologna, Italy) and by Rubens (in the Old Museum, Berlin).

Cecilia, The Story of Saint. Five celebrated frescoes by Domenichino, in San Luigi dei Francesi, Rome.

Cecrops (sē′krops). In Athenian legend, the first king of

Attica and founder of its civilization: commonly represented as half dragon.

Celæno (se-lē'nō). In classical mythology, one of the Harpies; also, one of the Pleiades, a daughter of Atlas.

Celestial City, The. In Bunyan's "Pilgrim's Progress," the goal of the journey, the heavenly Jerusalem.

Celestial Empire. See Dictionary, celestial.

Celestial Omnibus, The. A story (1911) by E. M. Forster.

Celestina (thä-les-tē'nä). A Spanish prose drama (about 1480) in 21 acts or parts, originally called "The Tragicomedy of Calisto and Melibœa."

Celia (sē'li-ą). 1. In Spenser's "Faerie Queene," the mother of Faith, Hope, and Charity. 2. The cousin and friend of Rosalind in Shakspere's "As You Like It." 3. The wife of Corvino in Jonson's "Volpone."

Célimène (sā-lē-mān). An artificial, coquettish, but charming and sparkling fine lady in Molière's "Misanthrope." Her name has become proverbial.

Celtæ (sel'tē). A people of Celtic origin who, according to Cæsar's division of Gaul, occupied what is now central France.

Cenci (chen'chē), **The.** A tragedy in blank verse (1819) by Shelley, on the story of Beatrice Cenci.

Cenomani (sen-ọ-mā'nī). A Celtic people who, according to Livy, crossed the Alps and settled north of the Po about Brescia and Verona.

Cenotaph, The. A national memorial in Whitehall, London, commemorating "The Glorious Dead" of the World War.

Centaur. See Dictionary, centaur.

Centaur (sen'târ), **The.** A novel (1911) by Algernon Blackwood.

Cent Nouvelles Nouvelles (soṅ nö-vel nö-vel). An old French collection of 100 prose tales, from a manuscript of 1456.

Centoatl (sen-tọ-ä'tl). In Mexican mythology, the goddess (or god) of maize and of agriculture.

Cento Novelle Antiche (chen'tō nō-vel'lä än-tē'kä). A collection of 100 tales from ancient and medieval history, the romances of chivalry, and the fabliaux of the trouvères, made in Italy about the end of the 13th century.

Centralists. A political party in Mexico after 1823, favoring a single centralized republican government.

Central Park. The principal park in New York, extending from 59th to 110th Street, and from Fifth to Eighth Avenue.

Central Powers, The. See Dictionary, central.

Cephalus (sef'ą-lus). In Greek legend, a hunter wooed by Eos, but faithful to his wife Procris, whom he accidentally killed while she was spying on him.

Cephas (sē'fąs). A surname given by Christ to Simon: the Aramaic counterpart of the English *Peter*. John, i. 42.

Cepheus (sē'fūs). 1. In Greek legend: (1) A king of Ethiopia, husband of Cassiopeia and father of Andromeda. (2) One of the Argonauts. 2. A northern constellation between Cassiopeia and the pole, represented as an Ethiopian king standing with arms extended.

Cerberus. See Dictionary.

Cerdonians (sẽr-dō'ni-ąnz). A Gnostic sect of the 2d century, which held that there were two first causes, one good and one evil: named from its founder Cerdo.

Cerealia. See Dictionary.

Ceres (sē'rēz). 1. See Dictionary. 2. An antique statue in black-and-white marble, in the Glyptothek at Munich.

Certosa (cher-tō'sä). A former Carthusian monastery near Pavia, Italy, one of the largest and most splendid in the world: now maintained as a national monument.

César Birotteau (sā-zär bē-ro-tō). A novel (1837) by Balzac, about a newly-rich merchant who thirsts for fame.

Ceyx. See Alcyone.

Chadband (chad'band), **Rev. Mr.** In Dickens's "Bleak House," a fat, hypocritical minister, given to platitudes.

Chæreas (kē'rẹ-as) **and Callirrhoe** (ką-lir'ọ-ē). An old Greek romance by Chariton Aphrodisiensis.

Chaimas or **Chaymas** (chī'mäz). An Indian tribe of eastern Venezuela, of Carib stock, formerly numerous and powerful.

Challenger Expedition, The. A British scientific expedition under the direction of Prof. Wyville Thomson, for the exploration of the deep sea, undertaken on board H.M.S. Challenger, 1872–76.

Chalone (chä-lō'nä). A tribe of North American Indians,

formerly residing at and near San Antonio and San Miguel missions, California.

Chalybes (kal'i-bēz). In ancient history: (1) A people in Pontus, near the Black Sea, noted as workers in iron. (2) A people living near the head-waters of the Euphrates.

Chamavi (ką-mā'vī). According to Tacitus, a Germanic tribe originally in the Rhine region north of the Lippe: later, farther eastward.

Champ-de-Mars (shän-dė-märs). A historically important open space in Paris on the left bank of the Seine, now used for military exercises.

Champion, The. A journal ridiculing the Jacobite party, edited by Fielding and a man named Ralph: first issued in 1739.

Champs-Élysées (shän-zā-lē-zā). An avenue, and the gardens surrounding it, in Paris, extending from the Place de la Concorde to the Place de l'Étoile.

Chamunda (chä-mön'dä). In Hindu mythology, an emanation of the goddess Durga.

Chancas (chäng'käz). An ancient Indian tribe of Peru, probably of Quichua stock, who occupied valleys of the Andes.

Chance. A novel (1914) by Joseph Conrad.

Chancery (chän'sẹ-ri) **Lane.** A street in London leading from Fleet Street to Holborn.

Chances, The. A comedy (before 1625) by John Fletcher.

Chanda (chan'dä). In Hindu mythology, a name of the goddess Durga, applied especially to her incarnation for the purpose of destroying the demon Mahisha.

Chandipatha (chan-dē-pät'hą). A poem of 700 verses, forming an episode of the Markandeyapurana, and read daily in the temple of Durga.

Chandra (chan'drą). In Sanskrit, the moon, either as planet or as a deity; hence, any eminent or illustrious person.

Change Alley. An alley in Cornhill, London: the chief center of money transactions in the 18th century.

Chanson de Geste. See Dictionary, chanson de geste.

Chanson de Roland (shän-sȯṅ dė ro-läṅ). A French epic poem of the 11th century, narrating the death of Roland at Roncesvalles and Charlemagne's vengeance on the Saracens.

Chant du Départ (shäṅ dü dä-pär). A popular French military 'song of departure,' by M. J. Chénier.

Chantecler (shäṅt-klär). A romantic drama (1910) by Edmond Rostand, in which the characters are barnyard fowls and animals, which have, however, decidedly human characteristics.

Chanticleer. See Dictionary.

Chapeau de Paille (shä-pō dė pä-y'). A noted painting by Rubens, in the National Gallery, London.

Chapter Coffee House, The. A London coffee-house, noted in the 18th century as the resort of men of letters.

Charge of the Light Brigade, The. A famous poem (1854) by Tennyson, commemorating a charge by English cavalry at Balaklava.

Charing (chär'ing) **Cross.** 1. A cross in memory of Queen Eleanor, erected by Edward I., 1¼ miles west-southwest of St. Paul's, London. 2. The locality where this cross stood.

Charis (kā'ris). In Greek mythology, the personification of grace and beauty: also regarded as a triad, the three Charities.

Charlatan, Le (lė shär-lä-täṅ). A novel (1830) by Balzac.

Charlemagne (shär'lẹ-mān) **Cycle of Romances, The.** A series of medieval romances, of war and adventure, grouped around the venerable figure of Charlemagne.

Charles O'Malley. A novel of adventure (1840) by Charles Lever.

Charlies. A nickname (about 1640) of the night-watchmen of London: from Charles I., who improved the police system.

Charmides (kär'mi-dēz). A dialogue of Plato, on temperance.

Charon. See Dictionary.

Charruas (chä-rö'äz). The usual name of a numerous race of savage and treacherous Indians who occupied, in the 16th century, the region on both sides of the river Uruguay.

Charterhouse (chär'tẽr-hous). A Carthusian monastery (founded 1371) in London: later a hospital, and a school for boys.

Charter Oak, The. A tree which formerly stood in Hartford, Connecticut, in a hollow of which the colonial charter is thought to have been hidden in 1687, when it was revoked by James II.

Chartists. See Dictionary, **Chartist.**

Chartreuse de Parme, La (lä shär-trèz dė pärm). A novel (1839) by Stendhal (Beyle).

Charybdis. See Dictionary, **Scylla.**

Chasidim (chä′si-dĭm), or **Assideans** (as-i-dē′anz). A party which arose among the Jews during the period of the Maccabean struggles, for the defense and maintenance of the Jewish law in all its particulars.

Chasta Costa (chäs′tạ kōs′tạ). A tribe of the Pacific division of the Athapascan stock of North American Indians.

Chastelard (shas′tẹ-lärd). A tragedy (1865) in blank verse, by Swinburne, the first of a trilogy, the other dramas being "Bothwell" (1874) and "Mary Stuart" (1881).

Château de Meillant (shä-tō dė me-yäṅ). A castle of very ancient foundation at St. Amand Montrond, France.

Château Gaillard (gä-yär). A celebrated ruin of a castle built 1197 by Richard Cœur de Lion, near Les Andelys, Eure, France.

Châtelet, Le Grand (lė gräṅ shät-lä). An ancient fortress in Paris, used for a prison and for courts of justice until 1802, when it was destroyed.

Chatsworth (chats′wèrth). An imposing Renaissance palace (begun 1688) on the Derwent, northeast of Bakewell, Derbyshire, England: seat of the Duke of Devonshire.

Chatti or **Catti** (kat′ī). A German tribe, a branch of the Suevi, first mentioned by Strabo.

Chaucer Society, The. A society founded 1868 in England to furnish scholars with material relating to Chaucer.

Chauci (kâ′sī). A German tribe, first mentioned by Strabo, in the region along the North Sea: ultimately merged in the Saxons.

Chauffeurs. See **Garrotteurs.**

Chaumont (shō-môṅ), **The Treaty of.** An offensive and defensive alliance (1814) against Napoleon, by Austria, Great Britain, Prussia, and Russia.

Chautauqua. See Dictionary.

Cheapside (chēp′sīd). The central east-and-west thoroughfare of London, originally a large open common where markets and public assemblies were held.

Chebar (kē′bär). A river in the "land of the Chaldeans," on the banks of which the Jewish exiles lived. Ezek. i. 1, 3.

Cheddar (ched′är) **Cliffs.** A picturesque group of limestone cliffs in the Mendip Hills, Somersetshire, England.

Chedorlaomer (kē″dôr-lạ-ō′mėr). A king of Elam about 2000 B.C., who, according to Gen. xiv., invaded Palestine.

Cheeryble (chēr′i-bl) **Brothers, The.** Charles and Edwin Cheeryble, twin brothers who befriend the hero of Dickens's "Nicholas Nickleby."

Chehalis (chẹ-hā′lis), or **Tsihalis.** A collective name of several tribes of the Salishan stock of North American Indians, living on the Chehalis River and Shoalwater Bay, Washington.

Cheka (chek′ạ). A Central Commission in the Soviet organization for protection against counter-revolution; also, the corresponding local units. Since 1921, the Central Commission has been known as the Department of State.

Chemehuevi (chem-ẹ-hwā′vē). The southernmost of the Paiute tribes of North American Indians.

Chemosh (kē′mosh). The principal deity, or Baal, of the Moabites. 1 Kings, xi. 7, etc.

Cherasco (kā-räs′kō), **The Armistice of.** An armistice concluded 1796 by Napoleon and Victor Amadeus III. of Sardinia.

Cherasco, The Treaty of. A treaty of peace (1631) confirming the treaty of Ratisbon, and ending the war of the Mantuan Succession.

Cherentes or **Xerentes** (shä-ren′tāz). A savage and warlike Indian tribe of Brazil.

Cherokee (cher-ọ-kē′). An important tribe of North American Indians, whose first known center was in the southern Alleghanies.

Cherry Orchard, The. A drama (1904) by Anton Chekhov: an English adaptation is to be found in G. B. Shaw's "Heartbreak House."

Cherusci (kẹ-rus′ī). A German tribe, in the time of Cæsar dwelling about the middle Weser and as far east as the Elbe.

Chesapeake (ches′ạ-pēk), **The.** An American frigate of 38 guns, built 1799. She was defeated off Boston by the British frigate Shannon, June 1, 1813.

Chester (ches′tèr) **Plays, The.** A collection of 24 "mysteries" founded upon scriptural subjects, formerly represented by the gilds of Chester, England, at Whitsuntide.

Chevalier de Saint George (shė-vȧ-lyä dė saṅ zhòrzh). A title assumed by James Stuart, the Old Pretender.

Chevy (chev′i) **Chase.** A famous old English ballad, recounting the incidents of the battle of Otterburn.

Cheyenne (shī-en′). A tribe of North American Indians, divided between Montana and Oklahoma.

Chiaja, La (lä kyä′yä). A fashionable drive in modern Naples.

Chiapanecs (chē-ä-pä-neks′), or **Chapanecs** (chä-pä-neks′), or **Chapas** (chä′päz). A race of Indians formerly powerful in southern Mexico.

Chibchas (chēb′chäz), or **Muyscas** (mö-ēs′käz). A tribe of South American Indians which, before the conquest, occupied the highlands east of the Magdalena.

Chicasa or **Chickasaw** (chik′ạ-sâ). A large tribe or subdivision of North American Indians, chiefly of Mississippi.

Chichevache (chē′chẹ-väch, F. shēsh-vȧsh). In medieval lore, a beast which devoured patient and submissive wives.

Chicomecoatl (chē-kō-me-kō-ä′tl). In Mexican mythology, the goddess of abundance and provisions.

Chilcat (chil′kät). A tribe of North American Indians in Alaska.

Childe Harold's Pilgrimage. A narrative poem (1812–18) by Byron.

Childe Roland to the Dark Tower Came. A poem (1855) by Robert Browning, the title being taken from a line in "King Lear."

Childe Waters. The hero of a popular ballad.

Children of Earth. A drama (1915) by Alice Brown.

Children of the Ghetto. A novel (1892) of Jewish life, by Israel Zangwill.

Children of the Mist. 1. A band of Highland outlaws in Scott's "Legend of Montrose." 2. A famous picture by Landseer. 3. A novel (1898) by Eden Phillpotts.

Children of the Sea. See **Nigger of the Narcissus, The.**

Children of the Soil. A novel (1894) by Henryk Sienkiewicz.

Children's Crusade, The. A disastrous expedition to recover the Holy Sepulcher, undertaken in 1212 by large bodies of French and German children. Thousands perished on the journey, others were enslaved in Egypt, and only a few returned.

Chillingworth, Roger. The injured and vengeful husband in Hawthorne's "Scarlet Letter."

Chillon (shi-lon′, F. shē-yôṅ). A castle in Vaud, Switzerland, on Lake Geneva: famous in literature, especially as the prison of Bonnivard (1530–36).

Chilon (kī′lon), or **Chilo** (kī′lō). A Spartan of the early 6th century B.C., one of the "Seven Sages" of Greece.

Chiltern (chil′tèrn) **Hundreds.** The three hundreds of Stoke, Desborough, and Bodenham, in Buckinghamshire.

Chimæra. See Dictionary, **chimera.**

Chimakuan (chim-ạ-kö′ạn). A linguistic stock of North American Indians in Washington, which once occupied the entire coast region from Puget Sound westward to the Pacific Ocean.

Chimarikan (chim-ạ-rē′kạn). A linguistic stock of North American Indians, formerly living on Trinity and New rivers, California.

Chimu (chē′mö). A once numerous Indian tribe which inhabited the place called "Chan-Chan," near Trujillo, Peru.

Chinantecs (chē-nän-teks′), or **Chinantlas** (chē-nänt′läz). An ancient tribe of Mexican Indians who at the time of the conquest occupied the Sierra Madre Mountains.

Chinchas (chēn′chäz). An ancient people of Peru who occupied the coast valleys south of the Chimu and of the present site of Lima.

Chinese Nightingale, The. A poem (1917) by Vachel Lindsay.

Chingachgook (chin-gach′gük). See **Uncas.**

Chinook. See Dictionary.

Chintamani (chin-tä′mạ-ni). In Sanskrit folklore, a "thought jewel"; the philosophers' stone.

Chippewa. See **Ojibwa.**

Chiquitos (chē-kē'tōz). A numerous race of Indians in northeastern Bolivia.

Chiriguanos (chē-rē-gwä'nōz), or **Chirihuanos** (chē-rē-wä'nōz). A Tupi Indian tribe of Bolivia.

Chiron (kī'ron). In Greek mythology, a wise and beneficent centaur. Accidentally wounded by the poisoned arrow of Heracles, he resigned his immortality to Prometheus.

Chitimachan (shit-i-mash'ạn). A linguistic stock of North American Indians, in Louisiana.

Chittim (kit'im), or **Kittim.** An Old Testament name supposed to designate Cyprus; also, in a wider use, the inhabitants of the western Mediterranean islands and coasts. Isa. xxiii. 1–12.

Chivery (chiv'ẹ-ri), **John.** In Dickens's "Little Dorrit," the sentimental son of a turnkey. He spends his time composing epitaphs.

Chloe (klō'ē). 1. In the Greek romance "Daphnis and Chloe," a country maiden. 2. In Sidney's "Arcadia," a shepherdess. 3. In Jonson's "Poetaster," the ambitious wife of an honest, commonplace citizen. 4. In Fletcher's "Faithful Shepherdess," a wanton shepherdess.

Chloris (klō'ris). 1. In Greek mythology, the goddess of flowers, wife of Zephyrus. 2. In Greek legend, a daughter of Amphion and Niobe.

Chocolatière, La Belle (lä bel sho-ko-lä-tyär'). A portrait of Annette Beldauf, a servant in a Vienna café, by Liotard: in the Dresden gallery.

Chocos (chō'kōz). A race of South American Indians in western Colombia.

Choctaw (chok'tâ). A large tribe or division of North American Indians, living chiefly, in historic times, in Mississippi: called "Flatheads" by early writers, from their custom of compressing the heads of male infants (not to be confounded with the Flatheads of the Salishan stock, for which see Dictionary, **Flathead**).

Choëphori (kọ-ef'ọ-rī), **The.** A tragedy of Æschylus, on the murder of Clytemnestra.

Choir Invisible, The. A novel (1897) by James Lane Allen, dealing with life in Kentucky. The title is taken from George Eliot's poem, "O May I Join the Choir Invisible."

Choles (chō'lāz). A tribe of American Indians of the Maya stock, formerly very numerous in southeastern Guatemala.

Chopunnish (chō-pun'ish), or **Nimapu** (nim'ạ-pö), or **Shahaptan** (shä-hap'tạn). The leading tribe of the Shahaptian stock of North American Indians, living chiefly in Idaho.

Chorazin (kọ-rā'zin). In New Testament geography, a city of Palestine: the modern Kerazeh.

Chorizontes (kō-ri-zon'tēz). The 'separators,' a party among the older critics who maintained that the Iliad and Odyssey were by different authors and of different ages.

Chouans (shö'ạnz, F. shö-äṅ). The royalist insurgents of Brittany during the French Revolution.

Chouans, Les. A novel (1829) by Balzac: more strictly, "Le dernier Chouan."

Chowanoc (chọ-won'ọk). A tribe of North American Indians formerly on the Chowan River in northeastern North Carolina.

Christ, The Entombment of. A noted painting by Titian, in the Louvre, Paris.

Christabel (kris'tạ-bel). 1. The lady-love of Sir Cauline in a famous old ballad. 2. An unfinished poetic fantasy (1816) by Coleridge.

Christ à la Paille. A painting by Rubens, in the Museum of Antwerp, Belgium.

Christ among the Doctors. A painting by Ingres, in the Musée Municipal at Montauban, France.

Christ Bearing the Cross. A celebrated statue by Michelangelo, in Santa Maria sopra Minerva, Rome.

Christ Church. One of the largest and most fashionable colleges of Oxford University, founded 1525 by Cardinal Wolsey as Cardinal College.

Christ Crucified between the Two Thieves. A famous fresco by Fra Angelico, in the Convent of San Marco, Florence.

Christian. See **Pilgrim's Progress.**

Christiana (kris-ṭi-an'ạ). See **Pilgrim's Progress.**

Christian de Neuvillette. See **Cyrano de Bergerac.**

Christian Year, The. A volume (1827) of devotional verse by John Keble.

Christie Johnstone. A novel (1853) by Charles Reade.

Christina Alberta's Father. A novel (1925) by H. G. Wells: the fantastic story of a laundryman who imagines himself the reincarnation of Sargon, King of Kings.

Christmas Carol, The. A Christmas tale (1843) by Dickens.

Christmas Garland, A. A collection of burlesques on contemporary authors (1912) by Max Beerbohm.

Christopher, Saint. A martyr of the 3d century, said to have lived in Syria.

Christopher Robin. The boy for whom the book of children's verse, "When We Were Very Young" (1924), was written: the son of the author, A. A. Milne.

Christ's College. A college of the University of Cambridge, founded 1505 by Margaret, countess of Richmond.

Christ's Hospital. A celebrated school, formerly in London, founded by Edward VI.: moved in 1902 to Horsham, Sussex. It is known as the Blue Coat School.

Chronicle of Paros, The. See **Arundelian Marbles, The.**

Chronicles. See Dictionary, **chronicle.**

Chrononhotonthologos (krō-non″hō-ton-thol'ọ-gos). A stage burlesque (1734) by Henry Carey. The title character is king of Queerummania.

Chrysaor (krī-sā'ôr or kris'ạ-ôr). In classical mythology, a son of Poseidon and Medusa, and father by Callirrhoe of the three-headed Geryon and Echidna.

Chryseis (krī-sē'is). In the Iliad, the beautiful daughter of Chryses, a priest of Apollo. She was captured by Agamemnon, who refused ransom until Apollo had sent a plague upon the Greek camp.

Chryses (krī'sēz). In Homeric legend, a priest of Apollo at Chrysa.

Chuana (chwä'nä). A Bantu nation of South Africa, embracing many tribes, and occupying British Bechuanaland and part of the Transvaal.

Chumashan (chö'mash-ạn). A linguistic stock of North American Indians, embracing a number of coast tribes in California.

Chunchos (chön'chōz). 1. A tribe of Indians in eastern Peru and northern Bolivia. 2. The name given by Tschudi to one of the three great aboriginal races which he supposed to have inhabited Peru from very ancient times.

Chyavana (chyạ-vä'nä). In Sanskrit mythology, a Rishi whom, when old, the Asvins made again a youth.

Cid, The. See Dictionary, **Cid.**

Cid (sid, Sp. thēᴛʜ), **Romances of the.** 1. The Spanish "Poema del Cid," composed about 1200. 2. A later poetic chronicle, "Cronica Rimada de las Cosas de España," probably based on early ballads. 3. The "Chronicle of the Cid," of unknown date. 4. A Spanish tragedy, "Las mocedades del Cid Campeador," by Guillen de Castro (1618). 5. "Le Cid," a tragedy by Corneille, first performed 1636.

Cihuacohuatl (sē-wä″kō-wä'tl). 1. In Mexican mythology, Tonantzin, the first mother of mankind. 2. The title of the Mexican civil head chief.

Cimarrones (sē-mär-rō'nāz). In the Spanish colonies of America, fugitive slaves; particularly, the bands of fugitive negroes who collected on the Isthmus of Panama.

Cimbri (sim'brī). A tribe, probably Teutonic, which invaded Noricum about 113 B.C. and later overran Gaul.

Cimmeria (si-mē'ri-ạ). The country of the Cimmerians. See Dictionary, **Cimmerian.**

Cincinnati (sin-si-nä'ti), **The Society of the.** A hereditary patriotic society founded 1783 by American and foreign officers of the Continental army.

Cinderella. See Dictionary.

Cinna (sin'ạ). A tragedy (1640) by Corneille.

Cinque Ports. See Dictionary.

Cintra (sēn'trä), **The Convention of.** A convention concluded (1808) between the French and the English: by its provisions the French evacuated Portugal.

Cipango (si-pang'gō), or **Zumpango** (zum-pang'gō). The name given by Marco Polo to an island or islands east of Asia. Columbus imagined the West Indies to be outlying portions of it.

---

fat, fāte, fär, fåll, åsk, fāre; net, mē, hėr; pin, pīne; not, nōte, möve, nôr; up, lūte, půll; oi, oil; ou, out; (lightened) aviạry, ẹlect, agọny, intọ, ụnite; (obscured) errạnt, operä, ardẹnt, actọr, natụre; ch, chip; g, go; ᴛʜ, thin; ᴛʜ, then; y, you;

Circe. See Dictionary.

Circumcellions (sėr-kum-sel′iǫnz). A party of Donatists in northern Africa, chiefly peasants, in the 4th and 5th centuries.

Circumlocution Office. In Dickens's "Little Dorrit," the name by which Dickens satirizes the red tape of the English public-office system. The expression has become almost proverbial.

Circus Maximus (sėr′kus mak′si-mus). The great Roman circus in the hollow between the Palatine and the Aventine.

Circus of Romulus (rom′ū-lus) or **Maxentius** (mak-sen′-shius), **The.** A Roman circus (built A.D. 311), the most perfect ancient circus surviving.

Cistercian Friars. See Dictionary, **Cistercian.**

Cithæron (si-thē′ron). In ancient geography, a range of mountains separating Bœotia from Megaris and Attica: celebrated in legend, and sacred to Zeus and to Dionysus.

City Madam, The. A comedy (1632) by Massinger.

City of Destruction, The. In Bunyan's "Pilgrim's Progress," the city from which Christian flees to begin his pilgrimage. It typifies worldliness.

City of Dreadful Night, The. 1. A gloomily imaginative poem (1874) by James Thomson. 2. A tale (1891) by Rudyard Kipling.

City of God, Of the. See **De Civitate Dei.**

Civil War, The. See Dictionary, **civil.**

Clackama (klak′ạ-mä). A large tribe of the Upper Chinook division of North American Indians, in Oregon.

Clärchen (klär′chęn). In Goethe's "Egmont," a simple cottage girl, in love with Egmont.

Clare (klâr) **College.** A college of the University of Cambridge, founded 1326 as University Hall.

Clarendon (klar′ęn-dǫn), **The Assize of.** An English ordinance (1166) modifying the administration of justice.

Clarendon, The Constitutions of. Ordinances adopted 1164 at the Council of Clarendon, fixing the jurisdiction of the civil and ecclesiastical courts.

Clarendon, The Council of. A council (1164) occasioned by the opposition of Thomas à Becket to Henry II.

Clarendon Press, The. A printing establishment in Oxford, England, largely controlled by the university.

Clarissa Harlowe. A novel (1747–48) by Richardson.

Clarisses, Les (lā klä-rēs). A religious sisterhood of the order of Sainte-Claire, founded in 1212.

Clark's Field. A novel (1914) by Robert Herrick.

Claudia (klâ′di-ạ) **gens.** In ancient Rome, a plebeian and patrician clan or house.

Claudio (klâ′di-ō). 1. A young Florentine in love with Hero, in Shakspere's "Much Ado about Nothing." 2. The lover of Juliet in Shakspere's "Measure for Measure."

Claudius. 1. The usurping king, Hamlet's uncle, in Shakspere's "Hamlet." 2. A servant of Brutus in Shakspere's "Julius Cæsar."

Clavering (klav′ėr-ing), **Sir Francis.** In Thackeray's "Pendennis," a baronet who marries the vulgar Mrs. Amory to recoup his losses, and is blackmailed by her first husband, Altamont.

Clavigo (klä-vē′gō). A tragedy (1774) by Goethe.

Clavileño (klä-vē-lā′nyō), **El Alígero.** The wooden horse used by Don Quixote, managed by a wooden pin in its forehead.

Clayhanger. A novel (1910) by Arnold Bennett, portraying the secret ambitions and ideals of an apparently phlegmatic printer. It is the first of a trilogy, the other novels being "Hilda Lessways" (1911) and "These Twain" (1916).

Cleaver, Fanny. In "Our Mutual Friend," by Dickens, a deformed little dolls' dressmaker, "the person of the house": often referred to as "Jenny Wren."

Clélie (klā-lē). A romance (1656) by Mlle. de Scudéry.

Cleobis. See **Biton.**

Cléomadès (klā-o-mȧ-des), **The Adventures of.** An early French poem (about the end of the 13th century), by Adenès le Roi.

Cleopatra's Needles. A pair of Egyptian obelisks of pink granite, transported by Augustus from Heliopolis to Alexandria. One of them is now in London; the other in Central Park, New York.

Clerkenwell (klär′kęn-wel). A district in London, north of the city proper. At one of its several wells the parish clerks of London formerly presented miracle-plays.

Clerk's Tale, The. One of Chaucer's "Canterbury Tales," founded upon Boccaccio's story of Griselda.

Clermont (kler′mont), **The.** The steamship used by Robert Fulton on his first trip from New York to Albany in 1807, in the early days of steam navigation.

Clermont (kler-môn), **The Council of.** A council (1095) convened by Pope Urban II. It proclaimed the first Crusade, and excommunicated Philip I. of France.

Clim or **Clym** (klim) **of the Clough.** In the Robin Hood legends, a celebrated archer.

Clink (klingk), **The.** Before 1780, a prison at one end of Bankside, London. It was for the delinquents of the "Liberty of the Clink," a part of Southwark.

Clio. See Dictionary.

Clitandre (klē-tändr). In Molière's plays: (1) A man of sense and spirit in "Les Femmes savantes." (2) The lover of Angélique in "George Dandin." (3) A delightful marquis in "Le Misanthrope." (4) The lover of Lucinde, who pretends to be a doctor, in "L'Amour médecin."

Cloaca Maxima (klō-ā′kạ mak′si-mä). The chief drain of ancient Rome, built about 600 B.C., and still used.

Clockmaker, The. See **Sayings and Doings of Samuel Slick of Slickville, The.**

Clœlia (klē′li-ạ). In Roman legend, a maiden delivered as a hostage to Porsena. She escaped by swimming the Tiber.

Clœlia (klē′li-ạ) or **Cluilia** (klö-il′i-ạ) **gens.** In ancient Rome, a patrician clan of Alban origin.

Cloister and the Hearth, The. A historical romance (1861) by Charles Reade. Its chief character is the father of Erasmus.

Clotho (klō′thō). In Greek mythology, one of the Fates.

Clotilde (klo-tēld), **Sainte.** A church in Paris, begun 1846.

Cloud (klö), **Saint.** 1. Clodvald, a monk, youngest son of Clodomir, the son of Clovis. 2. A former palace one and one-half miles west of Paris, rebuilt by Louis XIV.: a summer residence of Napoleon III.

Clouds, The. A famous satirical comedy of Aristophanes.

Clout, Colin. A pastoral name assumed by the poet Skelton and later by Spenser.

Club, The. A body of malcontents in the Scottish Parliament, 1689–90.

Cluny. See Dictionary, **Cluniac.**

Clymene (klim′e-nē). In Greek mythology, daughter of Oceanus and Tethys, wife of Iapetus, and mother of Atlas and Prometheus.

Clytemnestra (klī-tem-nes′trạ). In Greek legend, the daughter of Tyndareus and Leda, and wife of Agamemnon. See **Ægisthus.**

Clytie (klī′tę), or **Clytia** (klish′i-ạ). In classical mythology, an ocean nymph who, pining at Apollo's desertion, was metamorphosed into the heliotrope.

Coahuiltecan (kō-ạ-wēl′te-kạn), or **Tejano** (tā-нä′nō). A linguistic stock of North American Indians, in Texas and Mexico.

Coatlicue (kō-ät-lē′kwä). In Mexican mythology, the mother of Huitzilopochtli, the war-god.

Cocadrille (kok′ạ-dril). A fabulous monster in Mandeville's Travels.

Cocamas (kō-kä′mäz). An Indian tribe of eastern Peru.

Cockaigne or **Cocagne** (ko-kān′). A fabled land of luxury and idleness, perhaps in part intended to ridicule the stories of the mythical Avalon: called Lubberland by English 16th-century poets.

Cock Lane Ghost, The. A noted imposture perpetrated 1762 in Cock Lane, Smithfield, London, by a man named Parsons and his daughter.

Cockney School, The. A name derisively given by English Tory critics to a set of writers including Leigh Hunt, Hazlitt, Shelley, and Keats.

Cockpit, The. A London theater (1615–17) which stood on the site of the Drury Lane Theatre.

Cocles, Horatius. See **Horatius Cocles.**

Cocoa-Tree Club. A noted London club, the Tory Cocoa-Tree Chocolate-House of Queen Anne's reign.

Cocytus (kō-sī′tus). 1. A river in Epirus, a tributary of the

Acheron: the modern Vuvos. 2. In classical mythology, a river of Hades, a tributary of the Acheron.

Code Frédéric (kod frā-dā-rēk). A codification of the laws of Prussia made 1751 by Frederick the Great.

Code Napoléon. See Dictionary, **code.**

Code Noir (nwor). An edict (1685) of Louis XIV. of France, regulating the West Indian colonies and the treatment and condition of negroes.

Code of Hammurabi, The. See Dictionary, **code.**

Code of Justinian, The. See Dictionary, **code.**

Code of 1650, The. A code of laws compiled for the colony of Connecticut by Roger Ludlow: sometimes called *Ludlow's Code.*

Cœlebs (sē′lebz). Any bachelor desirous of marrying: from the hero of Hannah More's novel "Cœlebs in Search of a Wife" (1809).

Coffin, Long Tom. A sailor in Cooper's "Pilot."

Cogia Hassan Alhabbal (kō′gyä häs′sän äl-häb′bäl). A story, in the "Arabian Nights' Entertainments," of a poor rope-maker who finds a diamond in a fish, and becomes rich.

Cogia Houssam (hŏs′säm). The captain of the thieves in "Ali Baba and the Forty Thieves," in the "Arabian Nights' Entertainments."

Coignard, Abbé (á-bā kwä-nyär). The central figure in Anatole France's novels of the early eighteenth century, "At the Sign of the Queen Pedauque" (1893) and "The Opinions of M. Jerome Coignard" (1893).

Cokes (kōks), **Bartholomew.** A foolish young squire in Jonson's "Bartholomew Fair."

Colbrand (kŏl′brand), or **Coldbrand** (kōld′brand). A Danish giant, slain by Guy of Warwick.

Colchis (kol′kis). The legendary land of Medea and the Golden Fleece.

Coldbath Fields Prison. A prison in Coldbath Fields, Middlesex, England: originally built in the reign of James I. It was closed in 1886.

Cold Harbour. A very ancient building in London, once a sanctuary for debtors and gamesters.

Coldstream Guards, The. A regiment of British footguards, first enrolled by General Monk at Coldstream 1659–60.

Colimas (kō-lē′mäz). An Indian tribe of New Granada, which resisted the Spaniards fiercely, and was soon destroyed.

Colin Clout (kol′in klout). A poem (c. 1520) by Skelton, satirizing the clergy of his time.

Colin Clout's Come Home Again. A poem (1595) by Spenser.

Colleen Bawn (kol′ēn bân), **The.** A melodrama (1860) by Dion Boucicault, based on Griffin's novel "The Collegians."

Collège de France (ko-läzh dè fräns), or **Collège Royal** (rwo-yàl). An institution of learning in Paris, founded 1529 by Francis I. to counteract the scholasticism of the university.

Collège Mazarin (mâ-zà-rȧn). A college in Paris, founded 1661 by Mazarin.

College Widow, The. A play (1904) by George Ade.

Colline (kol′in) **Gate.** A gate at the northeastern extremity of ancient Rome.

Collins, Rev. Mr. A self-conceited toady in Jane Austen's "Pride and Prejudice."

Cologne (kō-lōn′), **The Three Kings of.** In medieval legend, the three Magi. (See Dictionary, **Magus.**) It is affirmed that their bones are deposited in Cologne Cathedral.

Colomba (ko-lôn-bä). A story (1840) by Mérimée, about a young Corsican girl who incites her brother to play his part in a vendetta.

Colonel Carter of Cartersville. A novel (1891) by F. Hopkinson Smith.

Colonel Jack, The History of. A novel (1722) by Defoe, about the career and repentance of a pickpocket.

Colonna (kō-lon′nä). A famous family of Italian patricians, prominent in the history of Rome from the 12th century to the 16th. Many of its members reached eminence as prelates, soldiers, or statesmen.

Colonus (kō-lō′nus), **The White Hill of,** or **Kolonos Hippios** (kō-lō′nos hip′i-os). A site about 1½ miles northwest of Athens: the birthplace of Sophocles, immortalized by his description in the "Œdipus at Colonus."

Colosseum. See Dictionary.

Colossians. See Dictionary, **Colossian.**

Colossus of Rhodes. See Dictionary, **colossus.**

Columbia. See Dictionary.

Columbiad. See Dictionary.

Columbine. See Dictionary, **Columbine**[3].

Columbus Day. See Dictionary, **Columbus.**

Column of July, or **Colonne de Juillet** (ko-lon dè zhü-yä). A monument in Paris, erected 1840 on the site of the Bastille, in honor of the citizens killed in attacks on the royal government in 1830.

Column of Marcus Aurelius, or **Antonine Column.** A monument in the Piazza Colonna, Rome, erected A.D. 174 in honor of the campaigns against the Marcomanni.

Column of the Congress, or **Colonne du Congrès** (ko-lon dü kôṅ-grä). A monument in Brussels, in commemoration of the Belgian constitutional congress of 1831.

Column of Trajan (trā′jan), **The.** A monument in Rome, dedicated A.D. 114 in honor of the emperor.

Columns of St. Mark and St. Theodore. Two columns in Venice, one bearing a figure of St. Theodore with his crocodile, the other the lion of St. Mark.

Comanche (kō-man′chė). A formerly bellicose tribe of North American Indians, ranging from Wyoming to Texas.

Comédie Française, La (lä ko-mä-dē fräṅ-säz). The official name of the Théâtre Français, formed 1680 by amalgamation of the company of the Marais and that of Molière, but practically having its beginning in the Théâtre de l'Hôtel Bourgogne (established 1552).

Comédie Humaine, La (lä ko-mä-dē ü-män). 'The Human Comedy': Balzac's title (1842) for the assemblage of his novels, duly classified and arranged, in which he proposed, with the addition of further volumes, to depict the various sides of human life.

Comedy of Errors, The. An early comedy by Shakspere, acted 1594.

Come Hither. An anthology of children's verse (1925) by Walter de la Mare.

Comitium (kō-mish′ium). A space near the Roman Forum in which important legal cases were anciently tried.

Commander of the Faithful. A title of the califs, first assumed by Omar, 634–644.

Common, Dol. A prostitute in league with Subtle, in Jonson's "Alchemist."

Common Lot, The. A novel (1904) by Robert Herrick.

Common Sense. An influential pamphlet (1776) by Thomas Paine, advocating entire separation of the American colonies from England.

Comneni (kom-nē′nī). An illustrious and versatile Byzantine family, probably of Italian origin, important from the 10th century to the 15th.

Compagnia della Calza (kom-pä-nyē′ä del′lä käl′tsä). A society existing in Italy during the 15th and 16th centuries, for the production of public and private entertainments.

Complaint of Venus, The. A poem by Chaucer, translated by him late in life from the French of Graunson. A "Complaint of Mars" is appended to it.

Compleat Angler, The. A celebrated work (1653) on the technicalities and the delights of fishing, by Izaak Walton.

Compromise of 1850, The. See **Omnibus Bill, The.**

Comte de Monte-Cristo, Le. See **Monte-Cristo, Le Comte de.**

Comus (kō′mus). 1. In later classical mythology, a young god of revelry, represented by Milton as the son of Bacchus and Circe. 2. A masque by Milton, written for presentation at Ludlow Castle in 1634: published 1637.

Conaire (ko′ne-ri). The hero of a famous epic story in Irish literature.

Conchobar (kon-chō′bär). In Celtic legend, a famous king of Ulster.

Conchos (kon′chōz). A roving Indian tribe of Mexico.

Conciergerie, La (lä kôṅ-syerzh-rē). The old prison of the Palais de Justice in Paris.

Concord, The Temple of. A temple at Girgenti, Sicily: one of the most perfect surviving examples of Hellenic antiquity.

Concordat of 1801, The. An agreement between Napoleon and Pius VII., reëstablishing the Roman Catholic Church in France.

Concordat of 1855, The. An agreement between Francis Joseph of Austria and Pius IX., giving the clergy control of public instruction.

Concordat of Francis I., The. A convention (1516) between Francis I. of France and Leo X., replacing the pragmatic sanction of Bourges.

Concordat of Worms (vôrms), **The.** A convention (1122) between the emperor Henry V. and Calixtus II., ending a contest over investiture.

Concordia (kon-kôr′di-ạ). In Roman mythology, the goddess of harmony, personifying amity.

Conestoga (kon-es-tō′gä). A tribe of North American Indians, formerly living in Pennsylvania and Maryland.

Coney (kō′ni) **Island.** A popular seaside resort at the southwestern extremity of Long Island, 10 miles south of New York.

Confederação do Equador (kon-fe-de-rä-souñ′ dō ā-kwä-dōr′). A political league formed 1824 at Pernambuco, Brazil, to throw off allegiance to the emperor and establish a republic.

Confederación Centro-Americana (kon-fā-ᴛʜe-rä-sē-ōn′ sen′trō-ä-mä-rē-kä′nä). A political league formed 1842 by Nicaragua, Honduras, and Salvador, in an attempt to reunite the states of the Central American Republic. It was soon discontinued.

Confederacy, The. A comedy of intrigue (1705) by Vanbrugh.

Confederation, Articles of. In United States history, the compact or constitution adopted 1777 by the Continental Congress.

Confessio Amantis (con-fes′i-ō a-man′tis). 'The Lover's Confession,' a long poem by Gower, probably written 1383–93.

Confessions, Les (lä kôñ-fe-syôñ). An autobiographical work (written 1766–70) by Rousseau.

Confessions of an English Opium-Eater. An autobiographical work (1821) by De Quincey.

Confessions of Saint Augustine, The. The memoirs of St. Augustine (397), written by himself.

Confines, The Audience of the. The supreme Spanish court of Central America, established 1542.

Conflans (kôñ-fläñ), **The Treaty of.** A treaty (1465) between Louis XI. of France and the dukes of Burgundy, Bourbon, and Brittany, ending the "War of the Public Good."

Congo, The. A poem (1914) by Vachel Lindsay, which gives its name to a volume of poems.

Congo Nation, The. See **Kongo Nation.**

Coningsby (kon′ingz-bi). A political novel (1844) by Disraeli.

Connecticut Yankee at King Arthur's Court, A. A satire on Arthurian romances (1889) by Mark Twain.

Conqueror, The. 1. See Dictionary. 2. A novel (1902) by Gertrude Atherton, based on the life of Alexander Hamilton.

Conquest of Granada, The, or **Almanzor and Almahyde.** A heroic tragedy (1670) by Dryden.

Conrad in Quest of His Youth. A novel (1903) by Leonard Merrick.

Conscious Lovers, The. A sentimental comedy (1722) by Steele.

Consensus Genevensis (kon-sen′sus jen-ḝ-ven′sis). A confession of faith (1552) drawn up by Calvin, designed to unite the Swiss churches on the subject of predestination.

Consensus Tigurinus (tig-ū̠-rī′nus). A confession of faith (1551) drawn up by Calvin and others, designed to unite the Swiss churches on the doctrine of the Lord's Supper.

Conservative Club, The. A London political club, established in 1840.

Consolato del Mare (kon-sō-lä′tō del mä′rä). A code of maritime law (before the 14th century), supposed to be a compilation of the law and trading customs of various Italian cities: the basis of most subsequent compilations of maritime law.

Constance (kon′stạns). 1. In Chaucer's "Man of Law's Tale," the unjustly accused daughter of the Roman emperor. 2. In Shakspere's "King John," the mother of Arthur.

Constance, The Council of. An important council (1414–18) of the Roman Catholic Church, which condemned to death Huss and Jerome of Prague.

Constance, The Treaty of. A treaty of peace (1183) between Frederick Barbarossa and the Lombard League.

Constans (kon′stanz). In Arthurian romance, the grandfather of Arthur.

Constant Couple, The. A comedy by Farquhar, published 1699: followed (1701) by a sequel, "Sir Harry Wildair."

Constantinople, Councils of. Ecumenical councils of this name include: (1) The second (A.D. 381), designed to settle the Arian difficulties. (2) The fifth (553), designed to condemn the Three Chapters. (3) The sixth (680–81), designed to condemn the Monothelites. (4) The eighth (869), designed to condemn Photius.

Constantinople, The Conference of. A conference (1876–77) of the six great powers and Turkey, intended to prevent war between Turkey and Russia.

Constant Nymph, The. A novel (1924) by Margaret Kennedy, presenting a contrast between Bohemianism and conventional respectability: dramatized 1926.

Constitution, The. An American 44-gun frigate, famous for its exploits in the War of 1812: popularly called "Old Ironsides."

Constitution of the United States, The. The fundamental or organic law of the United States, framed 1787 by the Constitutional Convention. It went into effect March 4, 1789.

Consuelo (kôñ-sü-ā-lō). A novel by George Sand (1842), named from its heroine, a Spanish singer.

Consus (kon′sus). An ancient Italian god of the earth and harvest whose festival was celebrated with equestrian sports.

Contes Drolatiques (kôñt drō-lä-tēk). A collection of Rabelaisian tales (1832, 1833, 1837) in the manner and orthography of the 16th century, by Balzac.

Continental Congress, The. A legislative body (1774–81) representing the colonies of North America. It declared independence, carried on the war, and in many respects governed the country.

Contrat Social (kôñ-trä so-syàl). A political work (1762) of remarkable influence, by Rousseau.

Cook's Tale, The. One of Chaucer's "Canterbury Tales," the story (unfinished) of an idle, riotous London apprentice.

Cooper's Hill. A famous poem (1642, revised 1665) by Sir John Denham.

Cooper (kö′per) **Union.** An institution in New York City, founded 1859 by Peter Cooper for the instruction of the working classes.

Cootenay. See **Kitunahan.**

Copehan (kọ̄-pā′hạn). A linguistic stock of North American Indians, in California.

Cophetua (kọ̄-feṯ′ū̠-ạ). In balladry, an African king who marries a beggar maid, Penelophon.

Copmanhurst, The Clerk of. In the Robin Hood stories, Friar Tuck.

Copperfield, David. The central character of Dickens's "David Copperfield." His story, told in the first person, is the most nearly autobiographical of Dickens's novels.

Copperhead. See Dictionary, **copperhead.**

Copt, Coptic. See Dictionary.

Corbenic (kôr′be-nik). In the "Romance of the Grail," the castle built as a shrine for the Holy Grail.

Corcoran (kôr′kọ̄-rạn) **Art Gallery, The.** An art gallery at Washington, D. C.

Cordelia. The youngest daughter of Lear, in Shakspere's "King Lear." See **Lear, King.**

Corinne, ou l'Italie (ko-rēn ö lē-tä-lē). A novel (1807) by Mme. de Staël.

Corinthians, The First and Second Epistles to the. See Dictionary, **Corinthian.**

Coriolanus (kọ̄″ri-ọ̄-lā′nus). A tragedy (about 1608) by Shakspere.

Cornaro (kor-nä′rō) **at Venice, Caterina.** A sumptuous painting by Hans Makart, in the National Gallery, Berlin.

Cornelia. A Roman matron, daughter of the elder Scipio Africanus, mother of the Gracchi. "Cornelia's jewels," in Roman legend her name for her sons, has become proverbial.

Cornelia gens. A celebrated patrician and plebeian clan in ancient Rome.

Cornelian Laws. The body of Roman laws introduced

about 80 B.C. by the dictator L. Cornelius Sulla, to restore the aristocratic form of government.

Cornelius. A Roman centurion stationed at Cæsarea: the first Gentile convert. Acts, x.

Cornhill. One of the principal London streets, once a corn-market.

Cornhuskers. Poems (1918) by Carl Sandburg.

Corniche, La (lä kôr-nēsh'), or **Cornice** (kor-nē'chā). A celebrated coast-road along the Riviera from Nice to Genoa.

Corn-Laws, The. See Dictionary, **corn-law.**

Coroados (kō-rō-ä'dōz). The name given to several different Indian hordes in Brazil.

Corona, De (dē kọ-rō'nạ). The most celebrated oration (330 B.C.) of Demosthenes, defending his own acts and character.

Coronation Stone, The. See **Stone of Scone, The.**

Corpus Christi. See Dictionary.

Corpus Christi (kôr'pus kris'ti) **College.** 1. A college of Cambridge University, founded 1352 by the gilds of Corpus Christi and the Blessed Virgin Mary: called also Benet College. 2. A college of Oxford University, founded 1516 by Richard Fox, bishop of Winchester.

Corpus Juris (kôr'pus jö'ris). A digest of Roman laws, made in the 6th century by order of Justinian: the foundation of all further development of Roman law.

Corsini (kor-sē'nē). A noble Florentine family dating from the 12th century, one member of which became in 1730 Pope Clement XII.

Corso (kôr'sō). One of the principal streets of Rome, the chief scene of the annual carnival.

Cortes. See Dictionary.

Corvei or **Corvey** (kôr'vī). An old and celebrated German Benedictine abbey (founded 813), near Höxter on the Weser.

Corybantes. See Dictionary, **Corybant.**

Corydon (kor'i-dọn). A shepherd in Virgil's seventh eclogue, and in Theocritus; hence, a conventional name in pastoral poetry for a shepherd or a rustic swain.

Cosette (kō-zet'). In Victor Hugo's "Les Misérables," the daughter of Fantine, adopted by Jean Valjean. Her name is given to the second part of the story.

Cosmati (kos-mä'tē). A 12th-century family or school of sculptors in Rome, who originated the scheme of decorated architecture called "Cosmatesque."

Cosmos Club, The. A club (organized 1878) in Washington, D. C., composed chiefly of scientific men.

Cossacks, The. A novel (1852) by Lev Tolstoy.

Cosseans (ko-sē'ạnz). A wild and warlike people formerly inhabiting the Zagros Mountains northeast of Babylon.

Costanoan (kos-tä'nō-ạn). A linguistic stock of North American Indians, in California.

Cotter's Saturday Night, The. A poem (1786) by Burns.

Cottonian (ko-tō'ni-ạn) **Library.** A famous library, especially rich in manuscripts, founded by Sir Robert Bruce Cotton (1571–1631): now in the British Museum.

Cottus (kot'us). A brother of Briareus.

Cotys (kō'tis), or **Cotytto** (kọ-tit'ō). In Greek mythology, a Thracian goddess whose festival, the Cotyttia, was celebrated with licentious revelry.

Council of Ancients, The. In French history, the upper chamber of the French legislature under the constitution of 1795.

Council of Blood, The. In the history of the Netherlands, a court established 1567 by the Duke of Alva to suppress the popular agitation against the tyranny of Philip II. It put to death 1,800 persons in less than three months.

Council of Five Hundred, The. In French history, during the government of the Directory (1795–99), an assembly of 500 members, forming the second branch of the legislative body.

Council of State, The. In France, an advisory body existing since early times, chiefly to give advice upon administrative and legislative matters.

Council of Ten, The. In the old republic of Venice, a secret tribunal (1310–1797), exercising unlimited power.

Council of the Indies, The. A body created 1511 by King Ferdinand, for the regulation of Spanish colonial affairs.

Council of Trent, The. See **Trent, The Council of.**

Counter, The. The name anciently given to two prisons under the rule of the sheriffs of London.

Countess Julie. A drama (1888) by August Strindberg.

Countess Kathleen, The. A drama (1899) by W. B. Yeats.

Count of Monte-Cristo, The. See **Monte-Cristo, Le Comte de.**

Count Robert of Paris. A romance (1831) of 11th-century Crusaders, by Scott.

Country House, The. A novel (1907) by John Galsworthy.

Country Party, The. An English political party in the reign of Charles II., which opposed the court and sympathized with the nonconformists. It developed into the Whig party.

Country Wife, The. See **Pinchwife.**

Court of Lions, The. A celebrated court in the Alhambra.

Court Party, The. An English political party in the reign of Charles II., which supported the policy of the court. It developed into the Tory party.

Courtship of Miles Standish, The. A narrative poem (1858) of early colonial life, by Longfellow. The doughty captain woos by deputy, and the Puritan maiden, Priscilla, prefers the deputy, John Alden.

Cousine Bette, La (lä kö-zēn bet). One of the greatest of Balzac's novels (1846).

Cousin Pons, Le (lẹ kö-zaṅ pôṅs). A novel (1847) by Balzac.

Covent (kuv'ẹnt) **Garden.** 1. A former open space north of the Strand, London. As early as 1222 it was the convent garden of the monks of St. Peter, Westminster. 2. A theater in Bow Street, Covent Garden, London, first built in 1731: important in English theatrical history.

Coventry Plays, The. A series of 42 religious plays acted at Coventry from an early date till about 1591.

Coverley (kuv'ẹr-li), **Sir Roger de.** An amiable country squire belonging to the imaginary club in Addison's "Spectator" papers.

Coviello (kō-vē-el'lō). The conventional clown in old Italian comedy.

Cowgate, The. A once fashionable street in Edinburgh Old Town.

Cowichan (kou'i-chạn). A name given collectively to those Salishan tribes formerly occupying Vancouver Island and its vicinity.

Coxcox. In Mexican mythology, the counterpart of Noah.

Crab. See **Launce.**

Crabtree. A mischief-maker in Sheridan's "School for Scandal."

Cradle of Liberty, The. See **Faneuil Hall.**

Cradock, Sir. See **Caradoc, Sir.**

Craftsman, The. A political periodical, originated 1726 by Nicholas Amhurst: a powerful organ of the opposition to Sir Robert Walpole.

Craigenputtock (krā-gẹn-put'ọk). A farm about 15 miles from Dumfries, Scotland: for some years the home of Thomas Carlyle.

Crane, Ichabod. An awkward and superstitious school-master in Irving's "Legend of Sleepy Hollow."

Cranford. A novel (1851–53) of English village life, by Mrs. Gaskell.

Crapaud, Johnny. See Dictionary, **Johnny.**

Cratchit (krach'it), **Bob.** In Dickens's "Christmas Carol," Scrooge's poor clerk. He and his crippled son, Tiny Tim, are the beneficiaries of Scrooge's change of heart.

Crawley, Rawdon. In Thackeray's "Vanity Fair," the younger son of Sir Pitt Crawley: a dragoon, not too clever or scrupulous, who genuinely loves his wife, Becky Sharp.

Crawley, Rev. Bute. In Thackeray's "Vanity Fair," the brother of the elder Sir Pitt: a horse-racing parson whose wife writes his sermons.

Crawley, Sir Pitt. A coarse, sordid, and picturesque country squire in Thackeray's "Vanity Fair." He has a priggish son of the same name.

Creakle (krē'kl), **Mr.** A bullying schoolmaster in Dickens's "David Copperfield."

Cream of the Jest, The. A novel (1917) by James Branch Cabell, combining the here and now with a dream-romance.

Creation, The. An oratorio (1798) by Haydn.

Crédit Mobilier (kred'it mọ-bē'liẻr, F. krä-dē mo-bē-lyä). 1. In French history, a banking corporation (1852–67) extensively engaged in making loans, promoting enterprises, handling stocks of other companies, and transacting a general banking business. 2. In United States history, a similar corporation, chartered 1863.

Cree (krē). An important tribe of North American Indians in Manitoba, Saskatchewan, etc.

Creek or **Kreek** (krēk). A powerful confederacy of North American Indians which in historic times occupied the greater part of Alabama and Georgia.

Cremorne (krē-môrn′) **Gardens.** A former place of amusement in London, closed 1877.

Crens (kränz), or **Guerens** (gwā-ränz′). The name given by Von Martius to the extensive group of Brazilian Indians to which the Botocudos belong.

Creon (krē′ọn). In Greek legend: (1) A king of Corinth, father-in-law of Jason. (2) A king of Thebes, contemporary with Œdipus.

Crescent Moon, The. A story of Africa (1919) by Francis Brett Young.

Cresphontes (kres-fon′tēz). In Greek mythology, a descendant of Heracles, conqueror of the Peloponnesus, king of Messenia, and husband of Merope.

Cressida (kres′i-dą). The mythical daughter of a Trojan priest, Calchas, beloved of Troilus, in legend a son of Priam. Her name has become a byword for faithlessness. See **Troilus and Cressida.**

Creusa (krē-ū′są). 1. In Greek legend, the bride of Jason, slain by the magic of jealous Medea. 2. In later classical legend, a daughter of Priam and wife of Æneas, lost in the flight from Troy.

Crèvecœur (krev-kėr). A former fort near Herzogenbusch, in the Netherlands.

Crichton (krī′tọn), **The.** A London artistic, scientific, and literary club, established 1872.

Crichton, The Admirable. 1. A name for James Crichton (d. 1582?); hence, a nickname for any person of varied accomplishments. 2. A play (1903) by Sir J. M. Barrie.

Cricket on the Hearth, The. A Christmas tale (1845) by Dickens.

Crime and Punishment. A powerful psychological novel (1866) by Fedor Dostoevski.

Crimean (kri-mē′ąn) **War, The.** A war (1853–56) between Russia and the allied forces of Turkey, France, Great Britain, and Sardinia. It arose through the demand of Russia for a protectorate over the Greek subjects of the sultan. It was closed by the treaty of Paris.

Crime of Sylvestre Bonnard (sēl-vestr bo-när′), **The.** A story (1881) by Anatole France.

Cripplegate. An old gate in the London wall, probably built (886) by King Alfred: pulled down in 1760.

Crispin (kris′pin, F. krēs-paṅ). An impudent, boasting, and witty valet, a conventional character in Italian and French comedy.

Crispin (kris′pin), **Saint.** A Christian martyr (d. about 287), the patron saint of shoemakers.

Cristinos (krēs-tē′nōz). In Spanish history, the partizans of Donna Maria Christina against the Carlists.

Cristóbal Colón (krēs-tō′bäl kō-lōn′). A Spanish armored cruiser, the last ship to surrender in the battle of Santiago (July 3, 1898).

Critias (krit′i-ąs). A dialogue of Plato.

Critic, The. A farce, with interpolated burlesque (1779), by Sheridan.

Critique de L'École des femmes (krē-tēk dė lā-kol dä fäm). A brilliant short play (1663) by Molière.

Critique of Pure Reason. See **Kritik der Reinen Vernunft.**

Crito (krī′tō). A dialogue by Plato.

Crittenden (krit′n-dẹn) **Compromise, The.** A measure urged (1860–61) in the United States Senate by J. J. Crittenden, providing for the reëstablishment of the slave line of 36° 30′ N., and the enforcing of the fugitive-slave laws.

Crockford's (krok′fọrdz). A famous gaming club-house in London.

Crock of Gold, The. A story (1912) by James Stephens.

Crœsus. See Dictionary.

Cromwell (krom′wel, F. krom-wel). A drama (1827) by Hugo.

Cronus (krō′nus), or **Cronos** (krō′nos). In Greek mythology, a Titan, son of Uranus and Gæa and husband of Rhea. He dethroned his father, and was dethroned by Zeus. Saturn is his Roman counterpart.

Croquemitaine (krok-mē-tän). A French legendary monster with which nurses frighten children.

Crosby (kroz′bi) **Hall** or **Place.** An ancient house in Bishopsgate Street, one of the very few medieval dwelling-houses still existing in London.

Crotchet (kroch′et) **Castle.** A novel (1831) by Thomas Love Peacock.

Crown, Oration on the. See **Corona, De.**

Crows, The. A drama (1882) by Henry Becque.

Crucifixion, The. There are notable paintings on this subject by Lucas Cranach (Weimar); Dürer (Dresden); Mantegna (Paris); Van Dyck (Ghent); Rubens (Antwerp); Perugino (Florence); and Tintoretto (Venice).

Crudor (krö′dôr), **Sir.** A knight in Spenser's "Faerie Queene."

Crummles (krum′lz), **Vincent.** The eccentric star and manager of a cheap theatrical troupe in Dickens's "Nicholas Nickleby."

Cruncher, Jerry. In Dickens's "Tale of Two Cities," an employee of Tellson's Bank by day and a body-snatcher ("resurrection man") by night.

Crystal Palace. A huge building of iron and glass, erected in Hyde Park, London, for the exhibition of 1851, and later rebuilt at Sydenham. It was used for popular concerts and entertainments. Destroyed by fire in 1936.

Culdee. See Dictionary.

Cumanas (kö-mä-näz′), or **Cumanagotos** (kö-mä-nä-gō′tōz). An Indian tribe, prominent in the earlier history of Venezuela for its resistance to the efforts of missionaries and slave-hunters.

Cumberland (kum′bėr-lạnd), **Prince of.** The title formerly bestowed on the successor to the crown of Scotland when declared in the king's lifetime.

Cumberland, The. A United States sloop of 30 guns, sunk 1862 by the Confederate ironclad ram, Merrimac.

Cumberland, The Army of the. A Union army in the American Civil War: originally organized 1861 by Buell as the Army of the Ohio.

Cumnor (kum′nọr) **Hall.** An old manor-house in the environs of Oxford, now destroyed: prominent in Scott's "Kenilworth" as the residence of Amy Robsart.

Cup, The. A poetical drama (1881) by Tennyson.

Cupid. See Dictionary.

Cupid and Psyche (sī′kē). 1. An episode in the "Golden Ass" of Apuleius. 2. An antique copy in marble, in the Capitol, Rome, of a Greek original of Hellenistic date.

Cure of Souls, A. A novel (1924) by May Sinclair: a study of a self-indulgent clergyman.

Curetes (kū-rē′tēz). In Greek mythology, Cretan attendants of Zeus.

Curiatii (kū-ri-ā′shi-ī). In Roman legend, three brothers from Alba Longa, who fought against the three Horatii.

Curicancha (kö-rē-kän′chä), or **Coricancha** (kö-rē-kän′chä). The great temple called the Temple of the Sun, at Cuzco, Peru.

Curiosities of Literature, The. A work (1791–1824) by Isaac D'Israeli.

Cursor Mundi (kėr′sọr mun′dī). An English religious epic of the 13th century, which recites the history of the world from creation to doomsday.

Curtain, The. A London playhouse established in Shoreditch in 1576.

Curtana (kėr-tā′nạ), or **Courtain** (kör-tän′), or **Curtein** (kėr-tän′). The sword of Roland; also, the pointless sword carried before the kings of England at their coronation.

Curtius, Marcus (mär′kus kėr′shius). A Roman legendary hero of the 4th century B.C.

Cush (kush). In the Old Testament: (1) The eldest son of Ham. (2) A geographical and ethnographical term, probably for Upper Egypt and the neighboring country.

Custom of the Country, The. 1. A play (before 1628) by Fletcher and Massinger. 2. A novel (1913) by Edith Wharton, dealing with divorce in the United States.

Cutpurse, Moll. A nickname of Mary Frith (1584–1659?), a notorious pickpocket: applied to any woman thief.

(variable) ḏ as d or j, ş as s or sh, ṭ as t or ch, ẕ as z or zh; o, F. cloche; ü, F. menu; ċh, Sc. loch; ṅ, F. bonbon; ′, primary accent; ″, secondary accent; †, obsolete; <, from; +, and; =, equals. See also lists at beginning of book.

Cutter of Coleman Street, The. A comedy (1661) by Cowley.

Cuttle, Captain Edward. In Dickens's "Dombey and Son," a retired sailor with a hook in place of his right hand. One of his favorite expressions is "When found, make a note on."

Cybele (sib′e-lē). A great nature-goddess of Phrygia and of Asia Minor generally, whose worship was carried to Greece and Rome: often called "the Great Mother of the Gods." See Dictionary, **Corybant.**

Cyclic Poets, The. The authors of Greek epic poems (800–550 B.C.) on the Trojan War and the war against Thebes.

Cyclops. See Dictionary.

Cydippe (sī-dip′ē). In Greek legend: (1) See **Acontius.** (2) See **Biton.**

Cymbeline (sim′be-lin). A romantic drama (about 1610) by Shakspere.

Cymry. See Dictionary.

Cynosarges (sī-nō-sär′jēz). A gymnasium of very early foundation in ancient Athens, the earliest home of the Cynic school of philosophy.

Cynosura (sī-nō-sū′rä). In Greek mythology, a nymph of Ida, and nurse of Zeus, metamorphosed into the constellation Ursa Minor.

Cynthia. See Dictionary.

Cynthia's Revels. A satiric comedy (1601) by Jonson. It burlesques, among other plays, Marston's "Antonio and Mellida."

Cynthius (sin′thi-us). Apollo. See Dictionary, **Cynthia.**

Cyparissus (sip-a-ris′us). In Greek mythology, the son of Telephus, metamorphosed into a cypress.

Cypris (sī′pris). A name of Aphrodite: from Cyprus, one of the principal seats of worship of this goddess.

Cyrano de Bergerac (sē-rä-nō de berzh-räk). A romantic drama (1897) by Edmond Rostand, based on the life of a writer of the seventeenth century, famous for his large nose. He wins his cousin, Roxane, whom he himself loves, for the stupid but handsome Christian de Neuvillette.

Cyrene (sī-rē′nē). In Greek mythology, a nymph, mother of Aristæus.

Cyropædia (sī″rō-pē-dī′ä), **The.** A work on the education and deeds of Cyrus the Great of Persia, by Xenophon.

Cytherea (sith-e-rē′ä), or **Cythera** (si-thē′rä). Surnames of Aphrodite: from the island of Cythera.

Cytherea. A novel (1922) by Joseph Hergesheimer.

D

Dabbat (dab′bat). In Mohammedan belief, a monster, the third sign of the coming resurrection.

Dactyls (dak′tilz), or **Dactyli** (dak′ti-lī), or **Daktyloi** (-loi). In classical mythology, supernatural beings of Mount Ida, the discoverers of iron and copper and of the art of working them.

Dædalus (dē′da-lus or ded′a-lus). In Greek mythology, an Athenian architect who built the labyrinth for Minos: the father of Icarus.

Daffodil Fields, The. A narrative poem (1913) by John Masefield.

Dagobert, Chanson du Roi (shän-sôn dü rwo dä-go-bär). A popular satirical French song (before 1789).

Dagon (dā′gon). In the Old Testament, the national god of the Philistines. Judges, xvi. 23, etc.

Dagonet (dag′ō-net), or **Daguenet** (dag′e-net), **Sir.** In Arthurian romance, the fool of King Arthur.

Dail Eireann. See Dictionary.

Daily Bread. Poems (1910) by Wilfrid Wilson Gibson.

Daily Courant, The. The first British daily paper: begun March 11, 1702.

Daimio. See Dictionary, **daimio.**

Daisy Miller. A novel (1878) by Henry James.

Daitya (dīt′yä). In Hindu mythology, a race of demons and giants who warred with the gods and interfered with sacrifices.

Dakota (da-kō′tä). A division of the Siouan stock of North American Indians, whose former habitat was in North and South Dakota and neighboring regions.

Dalai-lama, The. See Dictionary, **lama²**.

Dalgetty (dal-get′i), **Captain Dugald.** A courageous soldier of fortune in Scott's "Legend of Montrose."

Damaged Goods. A drama (1902) by Eugène Brieux.

Damara (dä-mä′rä). The name of two tribes of the former German Southwest Africa.

Damayanti (da-ma-yan′tē). The wife of Nala, and heroine of the tale of Nala and Damayanti, in the Mahabharata.

Dame aux Camélias, La (lä däm ō ká-mā-lyä). A novel (1848) and play (1852) by Dumas *fils*: in English, "Camille."

Dame Blanche, La (lä däm blänsh). A comic opera (1825) by Boïeldieu: libretto by Scribe.

Dame Care. A novel (1886) by Hermann Sudermann.

Dame Durden. See **Durden, Dame.**

Damnation de Faust, La (lä da-nä-syôn de fōst). A cantata (1846) by Berlioz.

Damocles (dam′ō-klēz). See Dictionary, **Damoclean.**

Damœtas (da-mē′tas). 1. In Theocritus and Virgil, a herdsman; hence, in pastoral poetry, a rustic. 2. In Sidney's "Arcadia," a foolish country clown.

Damon (dā′mon). A Syracusan of Roman legend, who barely escaped suffering the death penalty as voluntary hostage for his friend Phintias (Pythias).

Damon and **Pythias.** See **Damon.**

Dan (dan). 1. A son of Jacob by Bilhah. Gen. xxx. 6. 2. One of the 12 Hebrew tribes. Josh. xix. 40. 3. A city on the slopes of Mount Hermon, the most northern landmark of Palestine: hence the common formula "from Dan to Beersheba." Judges, xviii. 29.

Danaë (dan′a-ē). In Greek mythology, a maiden imprisoned by her father Acrisius in a brazen tower. Visited by Zeus in the form of a shower of gold, she became the mother of Perseus.

Danai (dan′ā-ī), or **Danaoi** (-oi). In Greek legend, the Argives: from Danaus.

Danaides. See Dictionary, **Danaidean.**

Danakil (dä-nä-kēl′). A Hamitic tribe of the Ethiopian branch, settled between Abyssinia, Massowa, and Obok.

Danaus (dan′a-us). In Greek mythology, the ruler of Argos. He married his daughters, the Danaides, to their fifty cousins, the sons of Ægyptus, but made them slay their husbands on the wedding night.

Dance of Death, Dance of Macabre (ma-kä′ber). See Dictionary, **macabre.**

Danelaw. See Dictionary.

Danewerk (dän′e-verk). A 9th-century wall from the Schlei to the Treene, erected to protect Denmark against invasion from the south.

Dangle (dang′gl). In Sheridan's "Critic," an amateur critic.

Daniel (dan′yel), **The Book of.** In the original Hebrew Bible, a book in the third division of the canon, the Hagiographa: in all translations, the fourth book of the greater prophets.

Daniel Deronda (de-ron′dä). A novel (1877) by George Eliot.

Danish War, The. See **Schleswig-Holstein War, The.**

Danite. See Dictionary.

Dannebrog. See Dictionary.

Dantès (dän-tes), **Edmond.** The Count of Monte-Cristo, in Dumas's novel of that name.

Dan Tucker (dan tuk′er). A negro song: said to refer to Captain Daniel Tucker, second governor of Bermuda.

Danube Navigation Commission, The International. A commission appointed 1856 by the treaty of Paris, to exercise authority over the Danube mouths.

Daphne (daf′nē). 1. In Greek mythology, a nymph who, pursued by Apollo, was saved by metamorphosis into a laurel-tree. 2. In ancient geography, a famous grove and sanctuary of Apollo, situated near Antioch, Syria. 3. The first true Italian opera (1596), by Giulio Caccini and Jacopo Peri: words by Rinuccini.

Daphnis (daf′nis). In Greek mythology, a son of Hermes by a nymph: a minor pastoral deity, taught music by Pan.

Daphnis and Chloe (klō′ē). A Greek pastoral romance (3d century A.D., or later), attributed to Longus.

Dapple (dap′l). Sancho Panza's ass in Cervantes's "Don Quixote."

Darby and Joan. See Dictionary.

Darcy (där′si), **Mr.** The lover of Elizabeth Bennet in Jane Austen's "Pride and Prejudice."

Dardani (där′da-nī). 1. An ancient Illyrian people of the southern highland of Mœsia. 2. In the Iliad, the inhabitants of Dardania.

Dardanus (där'dạ-nus). In Greek mythology, a son of Zeus and Electra, and ancestor of the Trojans.

Dares (dā'rēz). In the Iliad, a priest of Hephæstus in Troy.

Dares Phrygius (frij'i-us). A Latin work of the fifth century, which pretends to be a translation of Dares's contemporary account of the Trojan War. See **Dares.**

Dark and Bloody Ground, The. An alleged translation of the word Kentucky: a name given to Kentucky in allusion to its early Indian warfare.

Dark Continent, The. Africa.

Dark Flower, The. A novel (1913) by John Galsworthy, unlike most of Galsworthy's work in that the interest is in personal passion rather than in the social order.

Dark Forest, The. A novel (1916) by Hugh Walpole, dealing with events in Russia during the first part of the World War. "The Secret City" (1919) is a sequel.

Dark Lady, The. A woman mentioned in Shakspere's later sonnets: often identified with Mary Fitton.

Dark Lady of the Sonnets, The. A drama (1910) by G. B. Shaw.

Dark Laughter. A novel (1925) by Sherwood Anderson.

Dark Tower, The. A novel (1915) by Francis Brett Young.

Darkwater. Essays and sketches (1920) by W. E. B. Du Bois.

Darley (där'li) **Arabian, The.** See **Byerly Turk, The.**

Darnay (där-nā'), **Charles.** See **Manette, Lucie.**

Darshana (där'shạ-nạ). In Hindu philosophy, any of the six philosophical systems or schools.

Dartle (där'tl), **Rosa.** A disfigured woman in Dickens's "David Copperfield." She constantly says: "I want to know."

Dartmouth College, Case of. A case (1817–19) brought by appeal of the college trustees before the Supreme Court of the United States. The decision, holding that charters are unalterable except by consent of the corporations created by them, had important bearings on the law of corporations. Daniel Webster represented the plaintiffs.

Dasharatha (da-shạ-rat'hä). In Hindu mythology, a prince of the solar race.

Dathan (dā'thạn). A Reubenite chieftain who joined the conspiracy of Korah. Num. xvi.

Dauber. A narrative poem (1913) by John Masefield, showing how a sensitive youth won the respect of his rough fellow-sailors.

Daughter of the Middle Border, A. A story (1921) by Hamlin Garland, presenting his mother's life and adding to his own as given in "A Son of the Middle Border." Pulitzer Prize for the best American biography, 1922.

Daughter of the Regiment, The. See **Fille du Régiment.**

Daughters of the American Revolution, The. A patriotic society organized 1890 in Washington, D. C.

Daughters of the Revolution, The. A patriotic society organized 1891 in New York City.

Daulis (dâ'lis). In ancient geography, a city of Phocis, Greece: the scene of the myth of Tereus, Philomela, and Procne.

David (dā'vid). 1. In Old Testament history, the second king of Israel, succeeding Saul: he became the ideal king of Israel. 1 Sam. xvi., etc. 2. A statue of David by Michelangelo (in the Accademia, Florence); also, a statue of David by Donatello (in the Bargello, Florence).

David, or **Dewi, Saint.** The patron saint of Wales (d. 601).

David Balfour. See **Kidnapped.**

David Copperfield (cop'ėr-fēld). A novel (1850), in part autobiographical, by Dickens.

Davideis (dā-vid'ē-is). An epic poem (1656) on the subject of King David, by Cowley.

David Garrick (gar'ik). A play (1864) adapted by T. W. Robertson from a French play, "Sullivan."

David Grieve, The History of. A novel (1892) by Mrs. Humphry Ward.

David Harum. A novel (1898) by E. N. Westcott, about a shrewd horse-trader and country banker.

Davus (dā'vus). A conventional name for a slave in Latin comedies.

Davy Jones. See Dictionary.

Dawes Plan, The. A plan for balancing the budget and stabilizing the currency of Germany, drawn up by an international committee, of which Charles G. Dawes (Vice-Pres. of U. S., March, 1925) was chairman; the other American member was Owen D. Young. The plan was reported to the Reparations Commission April 19, 1924, and was declared in operation Sept. 1, 1924. It was the outstanding feature of the European situation for 1924.

Dawkins (dâ'kinz), **John** (the "Artful Dodger"). An expert young pickpocket in Dickens's "Oliver Twist."

Day of Doom, The. A poem (1662) by Michael Wigglesworth, which was popular in colonial New England.

Deacon's Masterpiece, The. See **One-Hoss Shay.**

Deadeye, Dick. A humpbacked pirate, a foil to the hero, Ralph Rackstraw, in "H. M. S. Pinafore," by Gilbert and Sullivan.

Dead Heart, The. A play (1859) by Watts Phillips: revised (1889) by W. H. Pollock for Sir Henry Irving.

Deadlock. A psychological novel (1921) by Dorothy Richardson.

Dead Souls. An unfinished novel (1842) by Gogol.

Deæ Matres (dē'ē mā'trēz). Three Teutonic goddesses of plenty.

De Amicitia (dē am-i-sish'i-ạ), or **Lælius** (lē'li-us). A treatise, in dialogue form, devoted to the praise of friendship, by Cicero.

Deans (dēnz), **Jeanie.** The heroine of Scott's "The Heart of Midlothian." She saves, by extraordinary efforts, the life of her wayward half-sister Effie.

Dear Brutus. A drama (1917) by Sir James M. Barrie.

Death and the Fool. A drama (1898) by Hugo von Hofmannsthal.

Death of Blanche the Duchess, The. See **Book of the Duchess, The.**

Death of Cæsar, The. A painting (1867) by Gérôme, of the murdered Cæsar lying at the foot of Pompey's statue.

Death of General Wolfe, The. A painting (1771) by West, in Grosvenor House, London.

Death of Marlowe, The. A tragedy (1837) by R. H. Horne.

Death's-Head Corps, The. See **Black Brunswickers.**

Death's Jest Book. A tragedy (1850) by T. L. Beddoes.

Débâcle, La (lä dä-bäkl). A novel (1892) of the Franco-Prussian War, by Émile Zola. See **Rougon-Macquart.**

Deborah (deb'ọ-rä). 1. A prophetess and judge of Israel. Judges, iv., v. 2. A German drama (1849) by S. H. von Mosenthal, the original of "Leah, the Forsaken."

Decameron (de-kam'ẹ-ron), **The.** A famous collection of 100 tales (1353), by Boccaccio.

Deceleian (des-e-lē'yạn) **War, The.** A name given to the third or final stage of the Peloponnesian War.

Decemvirate. See Dictionary, **decemvir.**

De Civitate Dei (dē siv-i-tā'tē dē'ī). A treatise by St. Augustine, written 413–426, on the permanence of the Christian church.

Declaration of Independence, The. See Dictionary, **declaration.**

Declaration of Independence, The Mecklenburg. See **Mecklenburg Declaration of Independence, The.**

Declaration of Right, The. An affirmation (1689) of the ancient constitutional rights of the English nation: confirmed by Parliament as the Bill of Rights.

Decline and Fall of the Roman Empire, The. A celebrated history by Edward Gibbon, published 1776–88.

De Consolatione Philosophiæ (dē kon-sọ-lā-shi-ō'nē fil-ọ-sō'fi-ē). A celebrated Latin work 'on the consolation of philosophy,' in prose and verse (about A.D. 525), by Boëthius.

Dedan (dē'dan). In Old Testament history: (1) a son of Raamah. Gen. x. 7. (2) A son of Jokshan. Gen. xxv. 3.

Dedlock (ded'lok), **Lady.** In Dickens's "Bleak House," a fashionable and ambitious woman who, before her marriage to Sir Leicester, has had an illegitimate child, Esther Summerson.

Dedlock, Sir Leicester (les'tėr). In Dickens's "Bleak House," a ceremonious but kind baronet, filled with unreasonable prejudices and family pride.

Deerslayer, The. See **Leatherstocking Tales, The.**

Defarge (dẹ-färzh'), **Thérèse** (tā-rāz'). In Dickens's "Tale of Two Cities," the wife of a wine-seller in Paris. She embodies the implacable blood-thirst of the Terror.

Defence of Poesie, The. See **Apologie for Poetrie.**

De Finibus (dē fin'i-bus). A treatise in five books, in dialogue form, on good and evil, by Cicero.

Deformed Transformed, The. A drama (1824), partly founded on Goethe's "Faust," by Byron.

Deianira (dē-yạ-nī'rạ), or **Dejanira** (dej-ạ-nī'rạ). A sister of Meleager and wife of Heracles, whom she unwittingly killed by giving him the blood-stained shirt of Nessus.

De Imitatione Christi (dē im-i-tā-shi-ō'nē kris'tī). A famous medieval religious treatise, of disputed authorship, but commonly ascribed to Thomas a Kempis.

Deïphobus (dē-if'ọ-bus). In Greek legend, a son of Priam and Hecuba, who married Helen after the death of Paris: slain by Menelaus.

Deipnosophists. See Dictionary, **deipnosophist.**

Deirdre. A drama (1907) by W. B. Yeats.

Deirdre of the Sorrows. A drama (1910) by J. M. Synge.

Dejanira. See **Deianira.**

Delaware (del'ạ-wär). A division of the North American Indians, formerly occupying the valley of the Delaware River in Pennsylvania, and the greater part of New Jersey and Delaware.

Delectable Mountains, The. In Bunyan's "Pilgrim's Progress," a range of hills from which the Celestial City is visible.

Delia (dē'li-ạ). A surname of Artemis: from Delos.

Delilah. See Dictionary.

Delius (dē'li-us). A surname of Apollo: from Delos.

Deliverance, The. A novel (1904) by Ellen Glasgow.

Della Crusca, Accademia. See Dictionary, **Della-Cruscan.**

Della-Cruscan School, The. See Dictionary, **Della-Cruscan.**

Delos (dē'los). The smallest island of the Cyclades: in Greek legend, the birthplace of Apollo and Artemis. It was the seat of a great sanctuary in honor of Apollo.

Delos, The Confederacy of. A Hellenic league, formed probably about 477 B.C., which developed into an Athenian empire.

Delphic Amphictyony, The. See **Amphictyonic League.**

Deluge, The. See **With Fire and Sword.**

Demas (dē'mạs). A companion of St. Paul. 2 Tim. iv. 10.

Demeter. See Dictionary.

Demeter (dē-mē'tèr) **of Cnidus** (nī'dus). A Greek statue of the school of Scopas, in the British Museum, London.

Demetrius (dē-mē'tri-us). The name assumed by several pretenders to the Russian throne, 1603–13.

Demodocus (dē-mod'ọ-kus). In the Odyssey, a famous bard at the court of Alcinous.

Demogorgon. See Dictionary.

De Natura Deorum (dē na-tū'rạ dē-ō'rum). Dialogues 'on the nature of the gods,' in three books, by Cicero.

Dendin, Perrin (pe-raṅ doṅ-daṅ). In Rabelais's "Pantagruel," an ignorant peasant, applied to as a judge: a satire on lawyers who prefer the ruin of their clients to the slightest concession.

Deneb (den'eb). A star of the first magnitude toward the tail of the swan pictured in the constellation Cygnus.

Denis or **Denys** (den'is, F. dė-nē), **Saint.** Apostle to the Gauls, patron saint of France: according to legend, beheaded (A.D. 272) at Paris.

Denry the Audacious. See **Card, The.**

De Officiis (dē o-fish'i-is). A treatise (about 44 B.C.) by Cicero, 'on duties.'

De Oratore (dē or-ạ-tō'rē). A rhetorical work (55 B.C.) by Cicero, in dialogue form.

Dépit Amoureux, Le (lė dā-pē-tȧ-mö-rė). A comedy (1654) by Molière.

Deposition from the Cross, The. The subject of paintings by Perugino and other masters.

Derby, The. See Dictionary, **Derby.**

Derceto (dėr'se-tō). See **Atargatis.**

De Republica (dē rẹ-pū'bli-kạ). A philosophical political treatise (54–51 B.C.) in dialogue form, by Cicero, on the best form of government and the duty of the citizen. It exists only in fragments.

De Rerum Natura (dē rē'rum na-tū'rạ). A philosophical and didactic poem, 'on the nature of things,' by Lucretius.

Dernier Chouan, Le (lė der-nyä shö-äṅ). See **Chouans, Les.**

Deronda (dẹ-ron'dạ), **Daniel.** In George Eliot's "Daniel Deronda," a Jew who devotes his life to an effort to restore the Jewish people to its former political prestige.

Descent from the Cross, The. There are noteworthy paintings on this subject by Sodoma (1504), in the Accademia, Siena; David, in the Chapelle du Saint Sang, Bruges; Cavazzola, in the Pinacoteca, Verona; Correggio, in the Pinacoteca, Parma; Titian, in the Accademia, Venice; and Rubens (1614), in the Antwerp cathedral.

Descent of Man, The. A work (1871) by Darwin, developing the biological theories set forth in "The Origin of Species."

Desdemona (dez-dẹ-mō'nạ). See **Othello.**

Desdén con el Desdén, El (el des-dän' cōn el des-dän'). A play by Moreto (1618–69): one of the four classical pieces of the older Spanish drama.

De Senectute (dē sen-ek-tū'tē), or **Cato Major** (kā'tō mā'jôr). A short treatise (45 or 44 B.C.) by Cicero, devoted to the praise of old age.

Deserted Village, The. A poem (1770) by Goldsmith describing 18th-century conditions in the Irish country-side.

Desire Under the Elms. A drama (1924) by Eugene O'Neill, showing the desire for beauty and the power of greed in narrow lives.

Despair, Giant. A giant in Bunyan's "Pilgrim's Progress."

Deucalion (dụ-kā'li-ọn). In Greek legend, a son of Prometheus who, surviving the deluge with his wife Pyrrha, became the ancestor of the renewed human race.

Deuteronomy. See Dictionary.

Deva. See Dictionary, **deva.**

Devarshis (dā-vär'shēz). In Hindu religion, sages who have attained perfection on earth, and have been exalted as demigods to heaven.

Devi (dā'vē). In Hindu mythology, "the goddess," wife of Siva, possessing various forms and names.

Devil, The. An old-time tavern in Fleet Street, London, frequented by Jonson, Shakspere, and other celebrities.

Devil Is an Ass, The. A comedy (1616) by Jonson.

Devil's Bridge. 1. A stone bridge over the Reuss, in the canton of Uri, Switzerland. 2. A bridge (called also Pont-y-Mynach) over the gorge of the Mynach, near Aberystwith, Wales.

Devil's Disciple, The. A drama (1897) by G. B. Shaw.

Devil's Dyke, The. A prehistoric earthwork for defense, in Cambridgeshire, England.

Devil's Parliament, The. A nickname given to the English Parliament (1459) which attainted the leading Yorkists.

Devonshire (dev'ọn-shèr) **Club.** A London Liberal club, established 1875.

Devonshire House. The residence of the Dukes of Devonshire, in Piccadilly, London: razed in 1925.

Dexileos (dek-sil'ẹ-os), **The Monument of.** A beautiful stele on the Sacred Way, Athens. See Dictionary, **stele.**

Dhammapada (dham-mạ-pa'dạ). A portion of the Buddhist Scriptures, the second division of the Khuddakanikaya.

Dhanvantari (dhan-van'tạ-ri). In Hindu lore: (1) A Vedic deity. (2) The physician of the gods. (3) A celebrated physician, one of "the nine gems" of the court of Vikrama.

Dharmashastra (dhär-mạ-shäs'trạ). The whole body of Hindu law; more especially, the laws ascribed to Manu, Yajnavalkya, and other inspired sages.

Dhegiha (dhā'gē-hä). A division of the Siouan stock of North American Indians.

Dhritarashtra (dhri-tạ-räsh'trạ). In Hindu mythology, eldest son of Vichitravirya or Vyasa, and brother of Pandu.

Dhyani Buddha (dhyä'ni bùd'ạ). In the earlier Buddhism, the pure and glorious counterpart in the mystic world of each of the five human Buddhas.

Diable Boiteux, Le (lė dyäbl bwo-tė). A satirical romance (1707) by Le Sage.

Diadochi (dī-ad'ọ-kī). **The.** The six Macedonian generals of Alexander the Great, who partitioned his empire after his death in 323 B.C.

Diadumenos (dī-ạ-dö'me-nos). A Roman reproduction of a famous statue by Polyclitus, in the British Museum.

---

fat, fāte, fär, fȧll, ȧsk, fāre; net, mē, hėr; pin, pīne; not, nōte, mõve, nôr; up, lūte, pùll; oi, oil; ou, out; (lightened) aviạry, ẹlect, agọny, intọ, ụnite; (obscured) errạnt, operạ, ardẹnt, actọr, natụre; ch, chip; g, go; th, thin; ᴛʜ, then; y, you;

Dial, The. An American literary quarterly and organ of the transcendentalists, edited (1840–42) by Margaret Fuller, and (1842–44) by Emerson.

Diamond Necklace, The Affair of the. A celebrated episode involving the French royal family in 1784. Cardinal Rohan, induced by an adventuress to purchase a magnificent necklace for Marie Antoinette, whose favor he hoped to gain, was unable to meet the payments, and the scandal became public.

Diana (dī-an'ä). See Dictionary.

Diana and Actæon. A painting (1559) by Titian, in Bridgewater House, London.

Diana and Callisto. A painting by Titian, in Bridgewater House, London.

Diana Enamorada (dē-ä'nä ā-nä-mō-rä'ᴛʜä). An important pastoral romance (1542), the chief work of Jorge de Montemayor.

Diana of the Crossways. A novel (1884–85) by Meredith. See Warwick, Diana.

Diana of Versailles. A celebrated Greek statue in the Louvre, Paris.

Diana with Her Nymphs. A painting by Domenichino, in the Palazzo Borghese, Rome.

Diavolo, Fra. See Fra Diavolo.

Dice (dī'sē), or **Dike** (dī'kē). In Greek mythology, the daughter of Zeus and Themis: the personification of justice.

Dichtung und Wahrheit aus Meinem Leben (dich'tŭng ŭnt vär'hīt ous mī'nem lä'ben). A work, primarily autobiographical, by Goethe, in 4 vols. (1811, 1812, 1814; 4th vol. posthumous).

Dick, Mr. See Mr. Dick.

Dick's Coffee House. An old coffee-house, originally "Richard's," in Fleet Street, London.

Dictum of Kenilworth, The. An award made 1266 between King Henry III. and the Commons during the siege of Kenilworth.

Didache. See Dictionary.

Diddler, Jeremy. A penniless swindler and sponge in Kenney's "Raising the Wind."

Dido (dī'dō). 1. A surname of the Phenician goddess Astarte, protectress of the citadel of Carthage. 2. A surname of the Tyrian Elissa, founder of Carthage, popularly confused with the preceding. In the "Æneid," she kills herself when abandoned by Æneas.

Dido Building Carthage. A large painting by Turner, in the National Gallery, London.

Didone Abbandonata (dē-dō'nä äb-bän-dō-nä'tä). A tragedy (1724) by Metastasio. It has been set to music by more than forty composers.

Dido, Queen of Carthage, The Tragedy of. A tragedy (1594) by Marlowe.

Dies Iræ. See Dictionary, dies.

Diet of Augsburg, The. See Augsburg, The Diet of.

Diet of Worms, The. See Worms, The Diet of.

Dietrich von Bern (dē'trich fon bern). In German legend, Theodoric the Great.

Digest of Justinian, The. See Corpus Juris.

Diggers. See Dictionary, digger.

Dignity and Impudence. A painting by Landseer, in the National Gallery, London.

Dike. See Dice.

Dilettanti Society, The. A London society (founded 1734) for the encouragement of a taste for the fine arts.

Dimitri Roudine (dē-mē'trē rö-dēn'). A novel (1855) by Turgenev.

Dimmesdale (dimz'dāl), **Arthur.** In Hawthorne's "Scarlet Letter," a Puritan clergyman tortured for years by the burden of guilt which he is unable to confess.

Dimoch or **Dymoke** (dim'ọk). The name of a Lincolnshire family holding since 1377 the feudal office of "champion of England."

Dinah (dī'nä). The daughter of Jacob by Leah. Gen. xxx., xxxiv.

Dinarzade (dī-när-zäd'). The sister of Scheherazade in the "Arabian Nights' Entertainments."

Dindymene (din-di-mē'nē). Cybele.

Dinkard (dēn-kärd'). The largest and most important Pahlavi work, containing a vast amount of information regarding the Zoroastrian religion.

Dinmont (din'mont), **Dandie** (**Andrew**). In Scott's "Guy Mannering," a Scottish farmer of eccentric but manly character.

Dinorah (dē-nō'rä). An opera (1859) by Meyerbeer.

Diocletian (dī-ọ-klē'shian), **The Baths of.** Baths in ancient Rome founded (A.D. 305–306) by Maximian.

Diomedes (dī-ọ-mē'dēz). In Greek legend: (1) The son of Tydeus: of the Greeks before Troy, the next in prowess to Achilles. (2) A Thracian king, son of Ares.

Dione (dī-ō'nē). In Greek mythology, a female Titan, daughter of Oceanus and Tethys, and mother by Zeus of Aphrodite.

Dionysia. See Dictionary.

Dionysus. See Dictionary.

Dioscuri (dī-os-kū'rī). Castor and Pollux, by one account the sons of Leda and Zeus.

Diplomacy. See Dora, 2.

Dipsodes (dip'sōdz), **The.** A people in Rabelais's "Gargantua and Pantagruel," subdued by Pantagruel.

Dipylon (dip'i-lon) **Gate, The.** The chief gateway of ancient Athens.

Diræ (dī'rē). The Furies.

Dirce (dėr'sē). In Greek mythology, a queen of Thebes, punished for her cruelty to Antiope by being bound to the horns of a wild bull.

Directory, The. See Dictionary, directory.

Dis (dis). In Roman mythology, the god of the lower world, Pluto.

Discobolus. See Dictionary, discobolus.

Discordia (dis-kôr'di-ä). The Roman counterpart of Eris, the goddess of dissension.

Discovery, The. 1. A small English ship which (1602–16) made five important voyages of discovery and exploration to North America, including that on which Hudson discovered (1610) Hudson Bay. 2. One of the two steam-vessels (Discovery, Alert) of the British polar expedition (under Captain Sir George Nares) of 1875–76.

Dismas (dis'mas), or **Desmas** (des'mas). The legendary name of the penitent thief crucified with Christ.

Distinguished Service Cross, Distinguished Service Medal. See Dictionary, distinguished.

Distressed Mother, The. A tragedy (1712) by Ambrose Philips, adapted from Racine's "Andromaque."

Dive Bouteille, La (lä dēv bö-tā-y'). An oracle to which Panurge makes a long journey. The Order of the Dive Bouteille was instituted in France in the 16th century in honor of Rabelais.

Dives (dī'vēz). The name given to the "rich man" in the parable of Jesus about Lazarus. Luke, xvi. 19, etc.

Divina Commedia (dē-vē'nä kom-mä'dē-ä). The "Divine Comedy," a celebrated poem (1300–18) by Dante, in 3 parts — Inferno, Purgatorio, Paradiso.

Divine Fire, The. A novel (1904) by May Sinclair.

Divine Tragedy, The. A poem (1871) by Longfellow.

Dixie, Dixie's Land. See Dictionary, Dixie[1].

Djinnestan or **Jinnestan** (jin-nes-tän'). In Persian and Oriental fairy lore, the land of the Jinns.

Dobbin (dob'in), **Major William.** In Thackeray's "Vanity Fair," the devoted friend of George Osborne, the weak husband of Amelia Sedley. He marries Amelia after Osborne's death.

Doctor, The. A romance (1834), in 7 volumes, by Southey.

Doctor Dodipoll (dod'i-pōl). A comedy (1600) by an unknown author: named from a foolish, doddering character.

Dr. Jekyll and Mr. Hyde. A tale (1886) by R. L. Stevenson about a strange case of dual personality.

Dr. Lavendar. An important character in several novels and stories by Margaretta Wade [Margaret] Deland, especially in "Old Chester Tales" (1898) and "Dr. Lavendar's People" (1903).

Dr. Primrose. See Vicar of Wakefield, The.

Doctor's Dilemma, The. A drama (1906) by G. B. Shaw.

Dr. Syntax in Search of the Picturesque, The Tour of. A descriptive and didactic poem (1809–11) by William Combe. Similar Tours "in Search of Consolation" and "in Search of a Wife" followed.

Dodo. A novel (1893) by E. F. Benson, the heroine of which is supposed to be a portrait of Margot Tennant (Lady Asquith).

Dodona (dō-dō′nạ). See Dictionary, **Dodonæan.**

Dods (dodz), **Meg.** The crabbed old mistress of the inn in "St. Ronan's Well," by Scott.

Dodson (dod′sọn) **and Fogg.** The legal advisers of Mrs. Bardell in her breach-of-promise suit, in Dickens's "Pickwick Papers."

Doe, John. See Dictionary, **John.**

Doeg (dō′eg). In the Old Testament, the chief of the herdsmen of Saul. 1 Sam. xxi. 7.

Dogberry. An absurdly pompous and loquacious constable in Shakspere's "Much Ado about Nothing."

Doge's Palace, The. The palace of the doges of Venice, begun (1354) by Marino Falieri.

Dollallolla (dol-ạ-lol′ạ), **Queen.** In Fielding's "Tom Thumb the Great," the wife of King Arthur.

Doll's House, A. The English title of Ibsen's play "Et Dukkehjem" (1879).

Dolly's (dol′iz). A well-known tavern in Paternoster Row, London, dating from the time of Queen Anne.

Dolly Varden. See Dictionary.

Dolores, Grito de (grē′tō dā dō-lō′räs). The first signal of revolt (1810) against Spanish rule in Mexico. The revolt was proclaimed by the parish priest of Dolores, in Guanajuato.

Dolorous Garde (dol′ọ-rus gärd). An earlier name of Joyeuse Garde, in Arthurian legend.

Dombey (dom′bi) **and Son.** A novel (1848) by Dickens: the story of a stern, cold man whose interest and hopes are centered in his boy child, who dies young.

Dome of Many-Colored Glass, A. Poems (1912) by Amy Lowell.

Domesday Book. See Dictionary, **domesday.**

Dominican Friars, The. See Dictionary, **Dominican.**

Domino Noir, Le (lẹ do-mē-nō nwor). A comic opera (1837) by Auber: words by Scribe.

Donatello (don-ä-tel′lō). In Hawthorne's "Marble Faun," a young Tuscan count whose likeness to the statue of the faun by Praxiteles gives the story its name.

Donation of Constantine, The. A medieval forgery, of unknown date and origin. It pretends to be an imperial edict issued (324) by Constantine the Great, conferring the sovereignty of Italy and the West on the papal see.

Donatists, The. See Dictionary, **Donatist.**

Don Carlos (don kär′los). 1. A tragedy (1676) by Otway. 2. A play (1787) by Schiller. 3. An opera (1844) by Costa, words by Tarantini. 4. An opera (1867) by Verdi, words by Méry and Du Locle.

Don César de Bazan (dôn sā-zär dẹ bȧ-zän). 1. A French comedy (1844) by Dumanoir and Dennery, from an episode in Hugo's "Ruy Blas." 2. A comic opera (1872) by Massenet.

Donelson, Fort. See **Fort Donelson.**

Dongan (dong′gạn) **Charter, The.** A charter for the city of New York, granted (1686) by Thomas Dongan: in force till 1730. An early charter of the city of Albany, by the same authority, has the same name.

Don Giovanni (don jō-vän′nē). An opera (1787) by Mozart.

Don Juan (don jū′ạn). 1. An incomplete romantic satirical poem (1819–24) by Byron. 2. A drama (published in 1925) by J. E. Flecker. 3. See Dictionary, **don².**

Don Juan, ou Le Festin de Pierre (dôn zhüän ö lẹ fes-tań dẹ pyär). A comedy (1665) by Molière.

Donna del Lago, La (lä don′nä del lä′gō). An opera (1819) by Rossini, based on Scott's "Lady of the Lake."

Donnithorne (don′i-thôrn), **Arthur.** The young squire who seduces Hetty Sorrel in George Eliot's "Adam Bede."

Donnybrook (don′i-brŭk) **Fair.** A famous fair held in August at Donnybrook, County Dublin, Ireland: established under King John, and suppressed 1855.

Don Pasquale (don päs-kwä′lā). An opera (1843) by Donizetti.

Don Quixote (don kē-HŌ′tā or don kwik′sọt). See Dictionary, **quixotic.**

Don Quixote in England. A comedy (1734) by Fielding.

Don Saltero's (don sȧl-tā′rōz) **Coffee House.** A noted house (founded 1690) formerly in Cheyne Walk, Chelsea, London, containing an eating-house and a museum of natural curiosities.

Don Sanche d'Aragon (dôn sänsh dȧ-rȧ-gôn). A comedy (1650) by Corneille.

Don Sebastian (don se-bas′chạn). One of the later tragedies by Dryden.

Don Sebastiano (don sä-bäs-tē-ä′nō). An opera (1843) by Donizetti.

Dooley, Mr. A humorous character in several volumes (1898–1910) by F. P. Dunne.

Doomsday Book. See Dictionary, **domesday.**

Doon (dōn), or **Doolin** (dō′lin), **of Mayence.** A hero of old French romance.

Dora (dō′rạ). 1. See **Spenlow.** 2. A play (1877) by Sardou: in English, "Diplomacy." 3. A narrative poem (1842) by Tennyson. 4. A name given to "The Defense of the Realm Act" in Great Britain during the World War.

Dorado, El. See Dictionary, **El Dorado.**

Dorante (do-ränt). The name of a courtly and witty gallant in each of Molière's comedies, "Le bourgeois gentilhomme," "L'École des femmes," and "Les fâcheux."

Dorcas. See Dictionary, **Dorcas society.**

Doria Palace. See **Palazzo Doria.**

Doricha (dō′ri-kạ). See **Rhodopis.**

Dorinda (dō-rin′dạ). 1. In Guarini's "Pastor Fido," an impulsive, passionate girl. 2. In Dryden and Davenant's version of "The Tempest," the sister of Miranda. 3. In Farquhar's "Beaux' Stratagem," the daughter of Lady Bountiful.

Dorine (do-rēn). In the old French theatrical nomenclature, the name of the intriguing soubrette, as in Molière's "Tartufe."

Doris (dō′ris). In Greek mythology, the daughter of Oceanus and Tethys, and mother of the Nereids by her brother Nereus.

Dorotea (dō-rō-tā′ä). A dramatic prose romance (1632) by Lope de Vega.

Dorothea (dor-ọ-thē′ạ). 1. A virgin martyr in the persecution of Diocletian: introduced as a character in Massinger and Dekker's "Virgin Martyr." 2. A beautiful unfortunate woman in an episode of Cervantes's "Don Quixote." 3. (G. dō-rō-tā′ä) The principal female character in Goethe's "Hermann und Dorothea." 4. The "peerless Queen of Scots" in Greene's "James the Fourth."

Dorothea, The. A vessel sent (1818) under command of Captain Buchan, with the Trent, on an Arctic expedition.

Dorrit (dor′it), **Amy.** The unselfish daughter of an imprisoned debtor in Dickens's "Little Dorrit."

Dorr's Rebellion. A revolutionary movement in 1842 in Rhode Island, having for its object the introduction of a new State constitution. It was led by T. W. Dorr.

Dort (dôrt), **The Synod of.** An assembly of the Reformed Church of the Netherlands, with delegates from other countries, convened 1618–19 by the States-General to decide the Arminian controversy.

Dorus (dō′rus). In Greek mythology, the ancestor of the Dorians, and usually regarded as the son of Hellen by the nymph Orseis.

Dothan (dō′thạn). In Scripture geography, a place in Samaria, 10 miles north of Shechem. Gen. xxxvii. 17.

Dotheboys (dō′ᴛʜẹ-boiz) **Hall.** In Dickens's "Nicholas Nickleby," a school conducted by Mr. Wackford Squeers, a brutal master who starves and beats his pupils and teaches them little.

Douay Version. See Dictionary, **version.**

Double Dealer, The. A comedy (1693) by Congreve.

Doubting Castle. In Bunyan's "Pilgrim's Progress," the abode of the Giant Despair, in which he locked up Christian and Hopeful.

Doubting Thomas. A name given to any one who is notably skeptical. It refers to the attitude of the apostle Thomas toward Christ after the Resurrection. See John, xx. 24–29.

Douglas (dug′lạs). A tragedy (1756) by John Home.

Dousabel (dō′sạ-bel), or **Dowsabel** (dou′sạ-bel). In old pastoral poems, a common name for a rustic sweetheart.

Dousterswivel (dōs′tẹr-swiv-ẹl), **Herman.** A German swindler in Scott's "Antiquary."

---

fat, fāte, fär, fȧll, ȧsk, fãre; net, mē, hẽr; pin, pīne; not, nōte, mȯve, nȯr; up, lūte, pŭll; oi, oil; ou, out; **(lightened) aviȧry,** ẹlect, agǫny, intǫ, ụnite; (obscured) errạnt, operä, ardẹnt, actǫr, natụre; ch, chip; g, go; ᴛʜ, thin; ᴛʜ, then; y, you;

Dove, The. A pinnace of about 50 tons, one of the two vessels (the other being the Ark) in which Lord Baltimore sent out a colony (1633) to Maryland.

Dover (dō'vẽr), **The Treaty of.** A secret treaty (1670) between Charles II. of England and Louis XIV., arranging the terms of their coöperation against Holland.

Dove's Nest, The. A collection of short stories (1923) by Katherine Mansfield (Mrs. J. Middleton Murry).

Dowgate (dou'gāt). The original water-gate of London.

Downing (dou'ning) **College.** A college in Cambridge University, England, founded 1717 by the will of Sir George Downing.

Downing Street. A short street in the west of London, leading from Whitehall. On it are the Foreign Office and other government offices.

Downs, The Battle of the. An indecisive battle (1666) between the English and the Dutch fleets, off the eastern coast of Kent.

Draft Riot, The. A riot (July 13–16, 1863) in New York City, against the enforcement of the draft for the Federal army.

Dragonnades. See Dictionary, **dragonnade.**

Dragon of Wantley (wont'li), **The.** 1. An old ballad of the victory over a dragon by More of More Hall. 2. A burlesque opera (1737) by Henry Carey and J. F. Lampe.

Dragontea, La (lä drä-gon-tā'ä). A poem by Lope de Vega on the subject of Sir Francis Drake's last expedition and death.

Drake. An epic poem (1908) by Alfred Noyes.

Dramatic Poesy, Essay of. A work (1667) in dialogue form, by Dryden.

Drapier's Letters. A series of letters by Swift against the debasement of the Irish coinage: published (1724) under the pseudonym M. B. Drapier.

Draupadi (drou'pạ-dē). In the Mahabharata, the daughter of Drupada and wife of the five Pandu princes.

Drawcansir. A burlesque character in Buckingham's "Rehearsal," aimed at Dryden's Almanzor.

Dred (dred). A novel (1856) by Harriet Beecher Stowe, named from a runaway negro living in the Dismal Swamp.

Dred Scott Decision, The. A decision (1857) by the U. S. Supreme Court, upholding the right of a master in his slave as property and denying the constitutionality of the Missouri Compromise.

Dresden (drez'dẹn), **The Treaty of.** A treaty (1745) between Prussia, Austria, and Saxony, ending the second Silesian war, and confirming Frederick the Great in the possession of Silesia.

Dreyfus (drā-füs') **Case, The.** The notorious case (1894–1906) of a Jewish captain in the French army, falsely accused of having divulged state secrets to a foreign power.

Drogheda (droch'ẹ-dä), **The Statute of.** A statute (1494–1782) prohibiting the holding of any Irish parliament without the consent of the King of England.

Dromio (drō'mi-ō) **of Ephesus** and **Dromio of Syracuse.** Twin brothers, respectively a stupid servant and a witty one, in Shakspere's "Comedy of Errors."

Druids, The. See Dictionary, **druid.**

Drummer, or The Haunted House, The. A play (1716) by Addison.

Drums. A novel (1925) by James Boyd, about the American Revolution.

Drunken Parliament, The. A nickname of the Scottish Parliament of 1661.

Drupada (drö'pạ-dä). In Hindu lore, the King of Panchala, father of Draupadi.

Drury (drö'ri) **Lane.** A street in London, near the Strand. Near it stands Drury Lane Theatre, one of the principal theaters of London, first opened 1663.

Druses, The. See Dictionary, **Druse**[1].

Dryasdust, The Rev. Dr. Scott's pretended collaborator in the composition of the Waverley Novels: a prosy and pedantic antiquarian.

Dryburgh (drī'bur-ọ) **Abbey.** A highly picturesque ruin near Melrose, Scotland, containing the tomb of Sir Walter Scott.

Dryope (drī'ọ-pē). In Greek mythology, a Thessalian princess beloved by Apollo. The Hamadryads changed her into a poplar.

Dual Alliance, The. See Dictionary, **dual.**

Dualla (dö-äl'ä). The principal tribe, of Bantu stock, of the former German Kamerun, West Africa.

Dual Monarchy, The. See Dictionary, **dual.**

Dublin, The University of. See **Trinity College.**

Dublin Castle. An ancient fortification in the city of Dublin, begun in the 13th century, but mostly of 16th-century and later construction.

Duchess of Malfi (mal'fi), **The.** A tragedy (about 1612) by Webster.

Duchess of Wrexe, The. A novel (1914) by Hugh Walpole.

Duel after the Masquerade, The. A painting by Gérôme, in the Walters collection at Baltimore.

Duenna, The. A musico-dramatic mélange (1775) by Sheridan and Linley.

Duessa (dụ-es'ä). In Spenser's "Faerie Queene," a hag who, disguised as a young and lovely woman, Fidessa, tries to marry the Red Cross Knight. She typifies the Church of Rome and Mary Queen of Scots.

Duke of Exeter's Daughter, The. The rack, introduced 1447 as an instrument of torture in the Tower of London by the Duke of Exeter.

Duke of Guise (gēz), **The.** A tragedy (1682) by Dryden.

Duke of Milan (mi-lan'), **The.** A tragedy (1623) by Massinger.

Duke's Mistress, The. A play (1636) by Shirley.

Duke's Theatre, The. A London theater, first built in 1660.

Dukhobors, The. See Dictionary, **Dukhobors.**

Dulcinea. See Dictionary, **dulcinea.**

Dulcy. A drama (1921) by George S. Kaufman and Marc Connelly.

Dumbarton (dum-bär'tọn) **Castle.** A celebrated fortress overhanging the river Clyde in Scotland.

Dumbiedikes (dum'bi-dīks). A comic swain in Scott's "Heart of Midlothian." Rejected by Jeanie Deans, he forthwith marries another.

Dunciad (dun'si-ad), **The.** A poem in four books (1728–42) by Pope, satirizing various contemporary writers.

Dundreary (dun-drēr'i), **Lord.** A fatuous, indolent Englishman in "Our American Cousin," by Tom Taylor.

Dundrennan (dun-dren'ạn) **Abbey.** A ruined monastery (built 1140) near Kirkcudbright, Scotland.

Dunes, The Battle of the. A victory (1658) by the allied French and English under Turenne over the Spaniards, on the sands near Dunkirk.

Dunmow (dun'mō) **Flitch, The.** A flitch of bacon awarded to any married pair who could take oath after a year and a day of married life that they had not quarreled or ever wished the knot untied. The custom is said to have originated at Little Dunmow, England, in 1244.

Dunnottar (du-not'ạr) **Castle.** A ruined castle, dating from 1392, in Kincardineshire, Scotland.

Dunrobin (dun-rob'in) **Castle.** The seat of the Duke of Sutherland, near Golspie, Scotland, incorporating remains of an 11th-century stronghold.

Dupin, Monsieur (m'syẽ dü-pań). A detective in Poe's story "The Purloined Letter": also in "The Murders in the Rue Morgue" and "The Mystery of Marie Roget."

Duquesne, Fort. See **Fort Duquesne.**

Durandal (dü'rạn-däl) or **Durindana** (dü-rin-dä'nạ). See **Roland.**

Durandarte (dö-rän-där'tä). A legendary Spanish hero of old Spanish ballads, introduced in Cervantes's "Don Quixote."

Durden (dẽr'dẹn), **Dame.** 1. An old song about a careful housewife. 2. In Dickens's "Bleak House," Mr. Jarndyce's pet name for his conscientious ward, Esther Summerson.

Durga (dör'gä). In Hindu mythology, the wife of Siva. Also called Kali.

Dushyanta (dösh-yan'tạ). A king of the lunar race, the husband of Shakuntala.

Dutch Courtezan, The. A comedy (1605) by Marston.

Dutch East India Company, The. See **East India Company,** 2.

Dutch West India Company, The. A commercial association (1621–75) formed in the Netherlands to trade with America and Africa, plant colonies, and attack the colonies and commerce of Spain and Portugal.

(variable) ḍ as d or j, ş as s or sh, ṭ as t or ch, ẓ as z or zh; o, F. cloche; ü, F. menu; ċh, Sc. loch; ṅ, F. bonbon; ', primary accent; ', secondary accent; †, obsolete; <, from; +, and; =, equals. See also lists at beginning of book.

Dwamish (dwä′mish). A small tribe of North American Indians near Seattle, Washington.

Dyak. See Dictionary.

Dying Alexander, The. A remarkable sculptured head, held to be a Greek original of Hellenistic date.

Dying Gaul, The. A celebrated antique statue of the Pergamene school, in the Capitoline Museum, Rome: formerly called "The Dying Gladiator."

Dynasts, The. A drama in three parts (Part I., 1904; Part II., 1906; Part III., 1908) by Thomas Hardy, based on the career of Napoleor.

E

Ea (ā′ä). In Assyro-Babylonian mythology, the god of the ocean and subterranean springs, and of wisdom.

Ea-bani (ā-ä-bä′nē). One of the heroes in the Babylonian Nimrod epic.

Eagle's Nest, The. A celebrated rock, about 1,200 feet high, among the Killarney lakes in Ireland.

Earthly Paradise, The. A collection of narrative poems (1868–70) by William Morris.

Easiest Way, The. A drama (1908) by Eugene Walter.

East Africa Company, The German. See **German East Africa Company, The.**

East Africa Company, The Imperial British. See **British East Africa Company, The Imperial.**

Eastcheap (ēst′chēp). Originally, the eastern marketplace of London: now a small street near the northern end of London Bridge.

East End, The. A large, thickly settled, and impoverished part of London, lying east of the Bank.

Eastern Question, The. The several problems or complications in the international politics of Europe growing out of the presence of the Turkish power.

East India Company, The. 1. A British joint-stock company chartered in 1600 to trade with the East Indies. In the 18th century its conquests led to the organization of British India, and for a time it exercised sovereignty jointly with the crown. Its extra-commercial functions were relinquished in 1858. 2. The name of similar companies chartered in Denmark, Sweden, France, and Holland.

East Lynne. A novel (1861) by Mrs. Henry Wood. Also, the play based on the novel.

Eastward Ho! A comedy (1604–05) by Chapman, Marston, and Jonson: the authors were imprisoned for satirizing the Scots in this play.

Easy, Midshipman. The hero of "Mr. Midshipman Easy" (1836), a sea-story by Marryat.

Ebal (ē′bạl). The mountain in Palestine from which the curse for disobedience to the law was pronounced. Deut. xxvii. 13.

Ebenezer. See Dictionary, ebenezer.

Eblis (eb′lis), or **Iblis** (ib′lis). In Arabian mythology, the chief of the evil spirits: introduced in Beckford's "Vathek."

Ecce Homo. See Dictionary, ecce homo.

Ecce Homo (ek′sē hō′mō): **A Survey of the Life and Work of Jesus Christ.** The chief work (1865) of John Robert Seeley, which created much excitement among various Protestant denominations.

Eccles (ek′lz). The sponging loafer and drunkard in T. W. Robertson's "Caste."

Ecclesiastes. See Dictionary.

Ecclesiazusæ (e-klē″zi-ạ-zū′sē). A comedy of Aristophanes, exhibited in 392 B.C.

Echidna (ē-kid′nạ). In Greek mythology, a female monster, mother of Cerberus, the Chimæra, and the Sphinx.

Echo. See Dictionary, echo.

Eckhardt (ek′härt), or **Eckart, The Trusty.** In the German legend of Frau Holle, an old man, sometimes represented as the companion of Tannhäuser.

École des Femmes, L' (lā-kol dā fám). A comedy (1662) by Molière.

École des Maris, L' (dā mȧ-rē). A comedy (1661) by Molière.

École Polytechnique (po-lē-tek-nēk). A French school of technology, founded 1794 by decree of the Convention.

Écorcheurs, Les (lā-zā-kôr-shèr). Bands of armed adventurers who ravaged France and Belgium in the 15th century.

Ector (ek′tor), or **Hector, Sir.** In Arthurian romance: (1) A faithful knight who brought up the infant Arthur: father of Sir Kay. (2) The brother of Sir Lancelot: called "de Maris" to distinguish him from (1).

Edda. See Dictionary.

Eden. See Dictionary.

Edict of Nantes, The. See Dictionary, edict.

Edinburgh (ed′n-bur-ọ), **The University of.** A famous seat of learning, founded 1582 by James VI. of Scotland.

Edinburgh Review, The. A literary and political (Whig) review, founded 1802 at Edinburgh by Jeffrey, Sydney Smith, and others.

Editha's Burglar. A children's story (1888) by Frances Hodgson Burnett.

Ediya (e-dē′yä). The black tribes which inhabit the island Fernando Po, West Africa.

Edohwe (ed′ọ-hwä). A tribe or division of North American Indians, formerly living in California.

Edom (ē′dom), or **Idumæa** (id-ū-mē′ạ̈). The region in the lowland south of the Dead Sea. The Edomites were descendants of Esau. Num. xx. 14–21.

Edrei (ed′rē-ī). In Old Testament history, the capital of the giant king Og. His kingdom was in Bashan. Josh. xiii. 31.

Edward I. A play (1593) by Peele.

Edward II. A tragedy (about 1590) by Marlowe.

Edward III. A tragedy (1590) sometimes attributed to Marlowe.

Edward IV. A play (1600) by Thomas Heywood.

Edwin Drood (dröd), **The Mystery of.** An unfinished novel (1870) by Dickens.

Efik (ef′ik). An African tribe dwelling around the estuary of the Cross and Old Kalabar rivers in West Africa.

Egdon Heath. The scene of Hardy's "The Return of the Native," which dominates the story.

Egeria (ē-jē′ri-ạ). In Roman legend, one of the Camenæ. She gave Numa Pompilius the forms of worship which he founded.

Eglamore (eg′lạ-mōr), or **Eglamour, Sir.** In Arthurian romance, a valiant knight and heroic champion of the Round Table.

Eglantine, Madame. The prioress of Chaucer's "Canterbury Tales."

Eglon (eg′lon). In Old Testament history, a king of the Moabites. Judges, iii. 14, etc.

Egmont (eg′mont). A tragedy (1788) by Goethe.

Egoist, The. A novel (1879) by Meredith.

Egyptian Expedition, The. An expedition (1798–1801) undertaken by the French against Egypt, with the ultimate object of attacking the British empire in India.

Egyptian Princess, An. A novel (1864) by Ebers.

Eiffel (ī′fẹl, F. e-fel) **Tower, The.** A tower, 984 feet high, of iron framework, in the Champ-de-Mars, Paris, built for the exhibition of 1889.

Eighteen Hundred and Seven, or **Friedland** (frēt′länt). A large painting (1876) by Meissonier, in the Metropolitan Museum of Art, New York.

Eikon Basilike (ī′kon bạ-sil′i-kē). A book describing the tribulations of Charles I. of England, published 1649: attributed to John Gauden.

Eikonoclastes (ī-kon-ọ-klas′tēz). A pamphlet by Milton, written in answer to "Eikon Basilike."

Ein Feste Burg (īn fes′tẹ bůrch). A hymn (probably 1527) by Martin Luther: a version of Psalm xlvi.

Einstein Theory, The. See Dictionary, relativity.

Eisteddfod (ās-teтн′vọd). An annual musical and literary festival and competition in Wales, originating in the ancient triennial assembly of Welsh bards.

Elah (ē′lạh), **The Valley of.** The scene of the duel between David and Goliath. 1 Sam. xvii. 2.

Elaine (ē-lān′). The name of several characters in Arthurian legends, notably: (1) The half-sister of Arthur and mother of his son Mordred. (2) The daughter of King Pelles and mother of Sir Galahad. (3) The "lily maid of Astolat" who pined and died for Lancelot. She appears in Tennyson's "Lancelot and Elaine."

Elath (ē′lath). In scriptural geography, a town of Idumæa, taken by David: the headquarters of Solomon's fleet.

Elder Sister, The. A novel (1925) by Frank Swinnerton, presenting two very different sisters and a negligible man.

Eldest Son, The. A drama (1909) by John Galsworthy.

El Dorado. See Dictionary.

Eleatics (el-ē-at′iks). See Dictionary. The main Eleatic doctrines are developments of the conception of the universal unity of being.

Eleazar (el-ē-ā′zạr). The third son of Aaron, his successor as high priest. Ex. vi. 23, etc.

Electoral Commission, The. In United States history, a board of commissioners created 1877 by act of Congress to decide disputed cases in the election of 1876. Its decisions resulted in the seating of President Hayes.

Electra (ē-lek′trạ). 1. In Greek legend: (1) The daughter of Agamemnon and Clytemnestra. She incited her brother Orestes to avenge the murder of his father. (2) A daughter of Oceanus, and mother by Zeus of Dardanus. (3) One of the Pleiades. 2. A drama by Sophocles. 3. A drama by Euripides. 4. A drama (1903) by Hugo von Hofmannsthal. From this Richard Strauss took the libretto for his opera.

Electrides (ē-lek′tri-dēz). In Greek legend, the Amber Islands, situated at the mouth of the fabulous Eridanus.

Elegy Written in a Country Churchyard. An elegiac poem (1751) by Gray.

Eleusis. See Dictionary, **Eleusinian.**

Eleusis (e-lū′sis), **The Bas-relief of.** A work (early 5th century B.C.) of high artistic importance, in the National Museum, Athens.

Eleutheria. See Dictionary.

Elevation of the Cross, The. The subject of famous paintings by Rubens (Antwerp cathedral) and Van Dyck (Notre Dame at Courtrai, Belgium).

Elgin (el′gin) **Marbles, The.** A collection of Greek sculptures surviving from the Parthenon: the finest existing productions of sculpture. The marbles, now in the British Museum, were brought (1801–1803) from Athens by the Earl of Elgin.

Elhanan (el-hā′nạn). A valiant Hebrew fighter against the Philistines. 2 Sam. xxi. 19.

Eli (ē′lī). A Hebrew judge and high priest. 1 Sam. i. 12, etc.

Elia (ē′li-ạ), **Essays of.** A collection (1823) of characteristic essays by Lamb.

Eliab (ē-lī′ab). The name of several persons in the Old Testament, notably David's eldest brother. 1 Sam. xvi. 6.

Eliakim (ē-lī′ạ-kim). In the Old Testament, the name of several persons; notably the son of Hilkiah and master of Hezekiah's household. 2 Kings, xviii. 18, etc.

Elias (ē-lī′as). In the New Testament, the name of Elijah. Mat. xvi. 14, etc.

Elidure (el′i-dūr). A mythical king of Britain, brother of Artegal.

Eliezer (el-i-ē′zėr). In the Old Testament, the name of several persons, notably: (1) The chief servant of Abraham. Gen. xv. 2. (2) The second son of Moses and Zipporah. Ex. xviii. 4.

Elihu (ē-lī′hū or el′i-hū). The name of several persons in the Old Testament, most notably one of the friends of Job. Job, xxxii.–xxxvii.

Elijah (ē-lī′jạ). A great Hebrew prophet. 1 Kings, xvii.–xxi.

Elimelech (ē-lim′ē-lek). The husband of Naomi. Ruth, i. 1–3.

Eliphalet (ē-lif′ạ-let), or **Eliphelet.** The name of several persons in the Old Testament, most notably two sons of David.

Eliphaz (el′i-faz). Surnamed "the Temanite," the chief of the three friends of Job. Job, ii. 11, etc.

Elisa (ā-lē-zä). An opera (1794) by Cherubini and Saint-Cyr.

Elisena (el-i-se′nạ). In the Spanish cycle of romances, a princess of Brittany, the mother of Amadis of Gaul.

Elisha (ē-lī′shạ). A Hebrew prophet, the attendant and successor of Elijah. 1 Kings, xix. 15–21.

Elisire d'Amore, L' (lä-lē-zē′rä dä-mō′rä). An opera (1832) by Donizetti.

Elissa (ē-lis′ạ). See **Dido,** 2.

Elizabeth (ē-liz′ạ-beth). 1. In the Old Testament, the wife of Aaron. 2. In the New Testament, the wife of Zacharias and mother of John the Baptist. Luke, i. 5–25. 3. The heroine of Wagner's opera "Tannhäuser" (1845).

Ellen's Isle. An island in Loch Katrine, Scotland, famous in early romance, and the favorite haunt of Scott's Lady of the Lake.

Elmo (el′mō), **The Castle of Saint.** A great fortress at Naples, built in the 16th century on a very much earlier structure. There is a fort of the same name at Malta.

Elmoran. See **Masai.**

Elohim. See Dictionary.

Else (el′se). A novel (1881) by Alexander Lange Kielland.

Elsie Venner. See **Venner, Elsie.**

Elsmere, Robert. See **Robert Elsmere.**

Elspeth (el′speth). In Scott's "Antiquary," an apathetic old woman burdened with the guilt of a crime in which she had assisted her mistress.

Elvira (el-vī′rạ or el-vē′rä). The name of important female characters in Dryden's "Spanish Friar," Kotzebue's "Pizarro," Auber's "Masaniello," Bellini's "Puritani," Verdi's "Ernani," and Molière's "Don Juan."

Ely (ē′li) **Chapel.** The chapel of the former palace of the bishops of Ely, in London: a fine example of Decorated architecture.

Ely Place. A place on Holborn Hill, London, the site of the former town house of the bishops of Ely.

Élysée (ā-lē-zā), **The Palace of the.** A palace in Paris, built 1718: now the official residence of the presidents of the republic.

Elysian Fields, Elysium. See Dictionary, **Elysium.**

Elzevir. See Dictionary.

Emanuel. See Dictionary, **Immanuel.**

Embla. See **Ask.**

Emigrants, The. A novel (1925) by Johan Bojer, dealing with the life of Norwegian settlers in North Dakota.

Émile (ā-mēl), **ou De l'Éducation** (dė lä-dü-ká-syóṅ). A treatise (1762) on education, ostensibly a romance, by Rousseau.

Emilia Galotti (ā-mē′lē-ä gä-lot′tē). A tragedy (1772) by Lessing.

Emily (em′i-li). 1. The heroine of Mrs. Radcliffe's "Mysteries of Udolpho." 2. In Dickens's "David Copperfield," the niece of the fisherman Dan Peggotty. She is betrothed to her cousin Ham Peggotty, but is seduced by Steerforth.

Éminence Grise, L' (lä-mē-noṅs grēz). A painting by Gérôme, in the Museum of Fine Arts, Boston, Mass.

Emma. A novel (1816) by Jane Austen.

Emmanuel (e-man′ū-el). See Dictionary, **Immanuel.**

Emmanuel Burden. A novel (1904) by Hilaire Belloc.

Emmanuel College. A college (founded 1584) of Cambridge University, England.

Emmanuel's Land. In Bunyan's "Pilgrim's Progress," the Delectable Mountains.

Emmaus (em′ā-us or e-mā′us). In scriptural geography, a village of Palestine, not far from Jerusalem. Its exact position is unknown. Luke, xxiv. 13.

Emmy Lou. A story (1902) by George Madden Martin, telling a timid child's experiences, especially at school.

Empedocles (em-ped′ō-klēz) **on Etna.** A classical drama (1853; revised 1867) by Matthew Arnold.

Emperor Jones, The. A drama (1920) by Eugene O'Neill, presenting an American negro's unsuccessful attempt at escape from his "subjects."

Empire Day. See Dictionary, **empire.**

Empire State, The. See Dictionary, **empire.**

Empusa (em-pū′sạ). In Greek legend, a cannibal monster sent under various forms by Hecate to frighten travelers.

Enceladus (en-sel′ạ-dus). In Greek mythology, a hundred-armed giant, son of Tartarus and Gæa, fabled as lying beneath the volcano of Mt. Ætna, in Sicily.

Enchanted Horse, The. A fabulous horse in the "Arabian Nights' Entertainments."

Encratites (en′krạ-tīts). In the early history of the church, those ascetics who refrained from marriage and from the use of flesh-meat and wine.

Encyclopædia Britannica (en-sī-klọ-pē′di-ạ bri-tan′i-kạ). A great English "dictionary of arts, sciences, literature, and general information," first published (1768–71) at Edinburgh: 13th edition, 1926.

Encyclopédie (oṅ-sē-klo-pā-dē). A great French encyclopedia. See Dictionary, **encyclopedia.**

Encyclopedists. See Dictionary, **encyclopedist.**

Endeavor, The. A British ship sent to the Pacific by the Royal Society to observe the transit of Venus in 1768.

Endor (en′dôr). In scriptural geography, a village in Palestine, near Tabor, where Saul consulted the "witch of Endor." 1 Sam. xxviii. 7–25.

Endymion (en-dim′i-on). 1. In Greek mythology, a beautiful youth whom Selene, the moon-goddess, caressed as he slept. 2. A poem (1818) by Keats. 3. A novel (1880) by Disraeli.

Endymion, The Sleeping. A classical statue in Parian marble, in the National Museum, Stockholm.

Enemy of Society, An. A drama (1883) by Henrik Ibsen.

Enfant Prodigue, L' (loñ-fäñ pro-dēg′). 1. An opera (1850) by Auber and Scribe. 2. A cantata (1884) by Debussy.

Engagement, The. In English history, an agreement (1647) between Charles I. and the Scottish commissioners, by which the Scottish army was to restore Charles, who consented to an establishment of Presbyterianism in England.

Engedi (en-gē′dī or en′gē-dī). A place abounding in caverns, on the western shore of the Dead Sea, where David hid from Saul. 1 Sam. xxiii. 29.

England's Helicon. A poetical anthology (1600).

English Bards and Scotch Reviewers. A satirical poem (1809) by Byron.

English Pale, The. See Dictionary, **pale**[1].

Enid (ē′nid). In Arthurian romance, a beautiful maiden rescued from neglect and married by Sir Erec. See **Erec and Enid** and **Geraint and Enid**.

Enim (ē′nim), or **Enin** (ē′nin). A fabulous country of great wealth, supposed in the 16th and 17th centuries to exist somewhere on the tributaries of the upper Amazon.

Enoch (ē′nok). In the Old Testament: (1) One of the patriarchs, the father of Methuselah. Gen. v. 18–24. (2) The eldest son of Cain. Gen. iv. 17, 18.

Enoch Arden. 1. A narrative poem (1864) by Tennyson. 2. Incidental music to Tennyson's poem, by Richard Strauss.

Enos (ē′nos). Son of Seth, and grandson of Adam. Gen. v. 6.

Entombment, The. A painting (1507) by Raphael, in the Palazzo Borghese, Rome.

Enyo (e-nī′ō). In Greek mythology, a goddess of war, associated with Ares.

Eos. See Dictionary.

Eostre. See Dictionary, **Easter**.

Eothen (ē-ō′then). A book of travels in the East (1844), by A. W. Kinglake.

Ephesians. See Dictionary, **Ephesian**.

Ephesus (ef′e-sus), **The Council of.** 1. The third ecumenical council, called (A.D. 431) by Theodosius II. in connection with Valentinian III. It included for the first time papal delegates from Rome, and condemned the heresy of Nestorius. 2. The so-called Robber Council, convoked (449) by Theodosius II. It deposed Flavian, patriarch of Constantinople.

Ephialtes (ef-i-al′tēz). One of the Aloidæ.

Ephraim (ē′frā-im). In Old Testament history, the younger son of Joseph; also, the tribe of Israel founded by him. Gen. xlviii. 1, etc.

Epicœne (ep′i-sēn), **or The Silent Woman.** A comedy (1609) by Ben Jonson.

Epigoni (e-pig′ō-nī). In Greek legend, the seven sons of the seven Argive chiefs who unsuccessfully attacked Thebes. They avenged their fathers just before the Trojan War.

Epimetheus (ep-i-mē′thūs). In Greek mythology, the brother of Prometheus and husband of Pandora, whom he accepted as a gift of Zeus, though warned by Prometheus.

Epipsychidion (ep″i-psi-kid′i-on). A poem (1821) by Shelley.

Epithalamium (ep″i-tha-lā′mi-um). A marriage song for his bride (1595) by Spenser.

Epping (ep′ing) **Forest.** A royal forest in southwestern Essex, England: opened to the public as a pleasure-ground in 1882.

Epsom (ep′som) **Wells.** A comedy (1675) by Shadwell.

Equador, Confederação do. See **Confederação do Equador.**

Éraste (ā-rást). The name given to the lover in each of Molière's comedies "Les fâcheux," "M. de Pourceaugnac," and "Le dépit amoureux."

Erastians. See Dictionary, **Erastian.**

Erato. See Dictionary.

Erebus. See Dictionary.

Erebus (er′e-bus), **The.** See **Terror, The,** 2.

Erec (ē′rek) **and Enid** (ē′nid). A metrical romance by Chrétien de Troyes.

Erechtheum (er-ek-thē′um). An Ionic temple in Athens, of the 5th century B.C., remarkable for its architectural variety.

Erechtheus (e-rek′thūs). In Greek legend, a king and tutelary divinity of Athens.

Erewhon (ē′rē-hwon). An account of a Utopian state (1872) by Samuel Butler. Erewhon is for "nowhere" written backward. "Erewhon Revisited" (1901) is a sequel. Note that the name of the heroine, Yram, is Mary written backward.

Erichthonius (er-ik-thō′ni-us). In Greek legend, a king of Athens: son of Hephæstus and grandfather of Erechtheus.

Eridanus (ē-rid′a-nus). In Greek legend, a large river in northern Europe, connected with the myth of Phaëthon.

Eridu (ā′ri-dö). An ancient city in Babylonia, the principal seat of Ea.

Erie (ē′ri). A tribe of North American Indians formerly living in western New York and along the southern shore of Lake Erie. The Senecas conquered (1653) and absorbed them.

Erin. See Dictionary.

Erinyes. See Dictionary, **Erinys.**

Eriphyle (er-i-fī′lē). The sister of Adrastus, slain by her son Alcmæon for inciting her husband Amphiaraus to join the fatal expedition against Thebes.

Eris (ē′ris or er′is). In Greek mythology, the goddess of discord, sister of Ares. See Dictionary, **apple.**

Erl-King, The. See Dictionary, **erl-king.**

Ermine or **Ermyn** (èr′min) **Street.** A Roman road from London northward to Lincoln and York.

Ernani (er-nä′nē). An opera (1844) by Verdi, on the subject of Hugo's "Hernani."

Ernestine (èr′nes-tin) **Line.** The older of the two lines (Ernestine, Albertine) of the house of Saxony.

Eroica (ā-rō′ē-kä) **Symphony, The.** The third (E flat major) symphony of Beethoven: written 1804 in honor of Napoleon.

Eros. See Dictionary.

Ertang (er′tang). The gospel composed and illustrated by Mani, in which he avowed himself to be the Paraclete foretold by Christ.

Erycina (er-i-sī′nä). A surname of Aphrodite.

Erymanthus. See Dictionary, **Erymanthian.**

Erysichthon (er-i-sik′thon). In Greek mythology, a prince who cut down trees in a sacred grove and was punished by a hunger which caused him to devour his own flesh.

Esau (ē′sâ). The son of Isaac and Rebekah, and ancestor of the Edomites. Gen. xxv. 21–34, etc.

Escoceses (es-kō-sā′sāz). A centralist party in Mexican politics, prominent 1826–29.

Escorial (es-kō′ri-al). A celebrated building in Spain (erected 1563–84), 27 miles northwest of Madrid, containing a monastery, palace, church, and mausoleum of the Spanish sovereigns.

Esdraelon (es-drā-ē′lon or es-drā′ē-lon). A valley in Palestine, the scene of Gideon's victory over the Midianites. Judges, vii.

Esdras (ez′dras), **The Books of.** The first two books of the Apocrypha.

Eseldorf (ā′zel-dôrf). A village in Austria, the scene of Mark Twain's "Mysterious Stranger."

Eshcol (esh′kol). A valley near Hebron, in Palestine, from which the spies sent by Moses brought back fine fruit. Num. xiii.

Eskimaux, Eskimos. See Dictionary, **Eskimo.**

Esmeralda (ez-me-ral′dä, F. es-mā-räl-dä). 1. In Victor Hugo's "Notre Dame de Paris," a dancing-girl beloved by Quasimodo, and put to death as a witch. 2. An opera (1883) by A. Goring Thomas.

Esmond, Beatrix. See **Esmond, Henry.**

Esmond, Henry. In Thackeray's "Henry Esmond," a brave and chivalrous youth, in love with his cousin Beatrix, a heartless, ambitious beauty. See **Castlewood, Lady.**

---

fat, fāte, fär, fâll, àsk, fãre; net, mē, hèr; pin, pīne; not, nōte, mŏve, nôr; up, lūte, pùll; oi, oil; ou, out; (lightened) aviary, elect, agony, into, ūnite; (obscured) errant, operä, ardent, actor, natūre; ch, chip; g, go; th, thin; ᴛʜ, then; y, you;

Esplandian (es-plän-dē-än'). In medieval romance, the son of Amadis of Gaul and Oriana: called the Black Knight.

Esprit des Lois (es-prē dā lwo). A celebrated philosophical work (1748) by Montesquieu.

Esquiline (es'kwi-līn) **Hill.** The central hill of the three which form the eastern side of the group of Seven Hills of ancient Rome.

Esquimaux. See Dictionary, **Eskimo.**

Essay of Dramatic Poesy. See **Dramatic Poesy, Essay of.**

Essay on Criticism, An. A treatise in verse (1711) by Pope.

Essay on Man, An. A didactic poem (1732–34) by Pope.

Esselenian (es-ẹ-lē'ni-ạn). A linguistic stock of North American Indians, formerly inhabiting a narrow strip of coast in California.

Essenes. See Dictionary, **Essene.**

Essex (es'eks), **The.** A United States frigate which did noteworthy service in the War of 1812 until captured in the Pacific in March, 1814.

Essex Junto. In United States history, a name first (about 1781) applied to a group of extreme Federalist leaders, mostly of Essex County, Mass., and later to the Federalists generally.

Este (es'tā), **The House of.** One of the most celebrated of the princely houses of Italy. It furnished the leaders of the Guelph party in the 13th and 14th centuries, and included many patrons of the arts.

Esther (es'tèr). 1. One of the books of the Old Testament, named from its principal character. 2. (es-tär) A play by Racine, with music by Moreau, written for the pupils of St. Cyr and performed by them before Louis XIV. 3. An oratorio (1720) by Handel, to words by S. Humphreys from Racine's "Esther."

Esther Waters. A novel (1894) by George Moore: the story of a servant-girl.

Estrildis (es-tril'dis), or **Estrild** (es'trild). The mythical daughter of a German king, loved by Locrine and the mother by him of Sabrina.

Etchmiadzin (ech-myȧd-zēn'). A monastery in Vaghar-shapad, Russian Armenia, the residence of the primate of the Armenian Church.

Eteocles (ẹ-tē'ọ-klēz). In Greek mythology, a brother of Polynices, by whom he was slain. His breach of an agreement made with his brother led to the expedition of the Seven against Thebes.

Eteoclus (ẹ-tē'ọ-klus). In Greek legend, according to some accounts, one of the Seven against Thebes.

Eternal City, The. 1. An epithet of Rome. 2. A novel (1901) by Hall Caine.

Ethan Frome. A novel (1911) by Edith Wharton.

Ethbaal (eth-bā'ạl). A king of Tyre, the father of Jezebel. 1 Kings, xvi. 31.

Étienne du Mont, St. (sań-tā-tyen dü môn). A noted florid-Pointed church in Paris, founded 1517. It contains the rich 13th-century shrine of Ste. Geneviève.

Étoile du Nord, L' (lā-twäl dü nôr). An opera (1854) by Meyerbeer.

Eton (ē'tọn) **College.** One of the most famed of English public schools, founded (1440) by Henry VI.: situated at Eton, in Buckinghamshire.

Étourdi, L' (lā-tör-dē). A comedy (1653) by Molière.

Etrurians, Etruscans. See Dictionary, **Etruscan.**

Ettarre (e-tär'). 1. A character in "The Idylls of the King" by Tennyson. 2. A character in "The Cream of the Jest" by Cabell.

Etzel (et'sẹl). In German heroic legend, the name of Attila.

Euchites (ū'kīts). A 4th-century eastern sect which attached supreme importance to prayer and the presence of the Holy Spirit.

Eugene Aram. A novel (1832) by Bulwer-Lytton.

Eugene Marchbanks. A poet in "Candida," by G. B. Shaw.

Eugene Witla. The hero of Dreiser's novel "The Genius."

Eugénie Grandet (e-zhā-nē grän-dā). A novel (1833) by Balzac.

Eugenius (ū-jē'ni-us). In Sterne's "Tristram Shandy," the friend and mentor of Yorick.

Eugubine (ū'gu̇-bin) **Tables, The.** Seven brazen tablets containing inscriptions, discovered 1444 near Gubbio, Italy: the chief monument of the ancient Umbrian language.

Eulalia (ū-lā'li-ạ), **Saint.** A Spanish virgin martyr, tortured to death (304) during the persecution of Diocletian.

Eulenspiegel, Till or **Tyll** (til oi'lẹn-shpē''gẹl). A German of the 14th century, about whose name have been grouped popular tales of the mischievous pranks of a vagabond peasant.

Eumæus (ū-mē'us). In Homeric legend, the faithful swine-herd of Odysseus, who helped his master slay the suitors of Penelope.

Eumenides. See Dictionary.

Eumenides (ū-men'i-dēz), **The.** A tragedy of Æschylus, exhibited at Athens 458 B.C.: the third of the great trilogy "Agamemnon," "Choëphori," "Eumenides."

Eumolpus (ū-mol'pus). In Greek mythology, a priestly bard, reputed founder of the Eleusinian mysteries.

Eunice (ū'nis). The mother of Timothy. 2 Tim. i. 5.

Eunomia (ū-nō'mi-ạ). In Greek mythology, one of the Horæ.

Eunuchus (ū-nö'kus). A comedy by Terence, founded in great part upon a play of the same name by Menander.

Eupatridæ, The. See Dictionary, **eupatridæ.**

Euphorbus (ū-fôr'bus). In Greek mythology, a brave Trojan, slain by Menelaus. Pythagoras professed to be animated by his soul.

Euphrosyne (ū-fros'i-nē). In Greek mythology, one of the Graces.

Euphues and His England. See Dictionary, **euphuism.**

Euphues, the Anatomy of Wit. See Dictionary, **euphuism.**

Europa (ū-rō'pä). A sister of Cadmus, borne to Crete by Zeus in the form of a white bull: the mother by him of Rhadamanthus, Minos, and Sarpedon.

Europa and the Bull. A painting (1562) by Titian, in Cobham Hall, near Rochester, England.

Eurus (ū'rus). In classical mythology, the east wind personified.

Euryalus (ū-rī'ạ-lus). See **Nisus, 1.**

Euryanthe (ū-ri-an'thē). An opera (1823) by Weber.

Euryclea (ū-ri-klē'ạ). In Homeric legend, the nurse of Odysseus, who after twenty years identified him by a scar.

Eurydice (ū-rid'i-sē). 1. In Greek mythology, the wife of Orpheus, permitted by Pluto to follow her husband out of Hades, but lost to him because he disobediently looked back at her. 2. An opera (1600) by Caccini and Peri, words by Rinuccini. This, with "Daphne," was the beginning of modern opera.

Eurynome (ū-rin'ọ-mē). In Greek mythology, a daughter of Oceanus and mother by Zeus of the Graces.

Eurystheus (ū-ris'thūs). In Greek mythology, a king of Mycenæ, who imposed upon Heracles the twelve labors.

Eusebians (ū-sē'bi-ạnz). The followers of Eusebius of Nicomedia, an Arian bishop of Constantinople in the 4th century of the Christian era.

Eustache, St. (sań-tès-täsh). A large church in Paris, of unique architecture, begun 1532 upon the principles of the late-Pointed style, but with exterior forms and decoration of the Renaissance.

Eustathians (ū-stā'thi-ạnz). 1. The orthodox faction in Antioch in the 4th century, who objected to the replacing of Eustathius, bishop of Antioch, by an Arian. 2. An extreme ascetic sect of the 4th century.

Euterpe. See Dictionary.

Euthydemus (ū-thi-dē'mus). A dialogue of Plato on virtue and instruction in virtue, satirizing the sophists and the older philosophy.

Eutychians (ū-tik'i-ạnz). The followers or adherents of Eutyches, who held that Christ had but one nature, the divine.

Eva, Little. See **Little Eva.**

Evadne (ẹ-vad'nē). 1. See **Capaneus.** 2. A prominent character in Beaumont and Fletcher's "Maid's Tragedy."

Evander (ẹ-van'dèr). In classical legend, a son of Hermes, and founder of an Arcadian colony on the Palatine before the Trojan War.

Evangelical Alliance, The. An association of Christians belonging to the Evangelical denominations, to promote

---

more effective coöperation in Christian work: organized 1846 in London.

Evangeline (ẹ-van′jẹ-lēn). An idyllic poem (1847) by Longfellow, based on the deportation of the Acadians by the British in 1755.

Evan Harrington. A novel (1861) by Meredith.

Eve (ēv). According to the account of the creation in Genesis, the first woman. Gen. iii. 20.

Evelina (ev-ẹ-lī′nạ). A novel (1778) by Frances Burney.

Evelyn Innes. A novel (1896) by George Moore: the detailed life of a successful singer. "Sister Teresa" is a sequel.

Evening's Love, or The Mock Astrologer, An. A comedy (1668) by Dryden.

Everlasting Mercy, The. A dramatic poem (1911) by John Masefield, telling of the conversion of the drunkard Saul Kane.

Everyman. An English morality translated from the Dutch "Elkerlijk": produced about 1529.

Every Man in His Humour. A comedy (1598) by Jonson.

Every Man Out of His Humour. A comedy (1599) by Jonson.

Ewe (ā′wā). An important African nation which occupies the region between the Volta River and Yoruba, in western Africa.

Excalibur (eks-kal′i-bèr), or **Excalibar**, or **Escalibor.** The magic sword of King Arthur.

Excelsior Geyser, The. One of the largest geysers in the world, in the Yellowstone National Park, Wyoming.

Excursion, The. A didactic poem (1814) by Wordsworth.

Exeter (ek′sẹ-tèr) **Book, The.** A manuscript collection of Anglo-Saxon poems given by Bishop Leofric to the library of the cathedral of Exeter, England, between 1046 and 1072.

Exeter College. One of the colleges of Oxford University, England: founded 1314 by Walter de Stapeldon.

Exeter Hall. A building on the Strand, London, used for charitable, religious, and musical assemblies.

Exodus. See Dictionary, **exodus.**

Expunging Resolution. A resolution passed 1837 by the U. S. Senate, to erase from the journal the censure passed by the Senate on President Jackson.

Eyre (âr), **Jane.** The poor and plain, but ardent, governess in Charlotte Brontë's "Jane Eyre." She marries Rochester, her employer. See **Rochester, Edward Fairfax.**

Ezekiel (ẹ-zē′ki-ẹl). One of the major books of prophecy in the Old Testament.

Ezida (ā′zi-dạ). The chief sanctuary of Nebo, the Assyro-Babylonian god of wisdom and literature, in Borsippa, near Babylon.

Ezra (ez′rạ). A short book of chronicles in the Old Testament.

F

Fabel (fā′bẹl), **Peter.** A person supposed to have sold his soul to the devil and then cheated him out of it. He died in the reign of Henry VII. of England. The legend is the subject of a play, "The Merry Devil of Edmonton."

Fabia (fā′bi-ạ) **gens.** A Roman patrician house, probably of Sabine origin. It traced its descent from Hercules and the Arcadian Evander.

Fabian Society, The. See Dictionary, **Fabian.**

Fabian Tactics. See Dictionary, **Fabian.**

Fable for Critics, A. A versified review (1848), by J. R. Lowell, of the writers and critics of America.

Fables in Slang. Humorous fables (1900) by George Ade: several similar volumes by him have followed.

Fabricius (fạ-brish′ius). In Le Sage's "Gil Blas," a verbose writer whose delight was to reduce the obvious to unintelligibility.

Faces in the Dawn. A novel (1914) by Hermann Hagedorn, Jr.

Fadladeen (fad-lạ-dēn′). In Moore's "Lalla Rookh," the grand chamberlain of the harem, who pronounces weighty judgments on both trifles and the weightiest affairs.

Faerie Queene (fā′ėr-i kwēn), **The.** A chivalric romance in verse (1590–1611) by Edmund Spenser, containing an intricate double allegory.

Fafnir (fäf′nir). In the Old Norse version of the Siegfried story, the guardian dragon of the Nibelungs' hoard. He was slain by Sigurd.

Fag. A lying and ingenious servant in Sheridan's "Rivals."

Fagin (fā′gin). In Dickens's "Oliver Twist," a villainous old Jew who employs young boys as thieves. He abducts Oliver.

Fagotin (fạ-go-taṅ). A clever and renowned monkey in Paris, in the time of Molière.

Fairford, Alan. In Scott's "Redgauntlet," a young barrister, the devoted friend of Redgauntlet.

Fair Helen of Kirkconnell. A ballad of a Scottish lady who died in trying to save her lover from being shot by his rejected rival.

Fair Maid of Perth, The. A historical romance (1828) by Scott. Its heroine is Catherine Glover.

Fair Maid of the Inn, The. A comedy by Fletcher, completed by Massinger and perhaps Rowley: printed 1647.

Fairmount Park. A park in Philadelphia. The Centennial Exhibition of 1876 was held in it.

Fair Penitent, The. A tragedy (1703) by Rowe.

Fairservice, Andrew. In Scott's "Rob Roy," a pious, shrewd, rather meddlesome, and cowardly gardener.

Faithful. In Bunyan's "Pilgrim's Progress," a companion of part of Christian's journey. He is put to death at Vanity Fair.

Faithful Shepherdess, The. A pastoral drama (1609?) by Fletcher.

Faith Healer, The. A drama (1909) by William Vaughn Moody.

Falashas (fä-lä′shạz). An Abyssinian tribe which professes the Jewish religion and claims descent from Hebrew immigrants who followed the Queen of Sheba.

Falcon, The. 1. A ship commanded by Raleigh in Sir Humphrey Gilbert's expedition of 1578. 2. A famous London tavern on the Bankside, possibly a haunt of Shakspere.

Falconer of Balmawhapple. See **Balmawhapple.**

Falk. A story (1903) by Joseph Conrad.

Falkland (fâk′lạnd). 1. A romance (1827) by Bulwer-Lytton. 2. The hero-villain of Godwin's "Caleb Williams." He stabs his enemy in a moment of passion, allows innocent persons to hang for the murder, and is thenceforth dominated by a desire for concealment. 3. **Falkland,** or **Faulkland.** In Sheridan's "Rivals," the accepted suitor of Julia.

False Demetrius, The. See **Demetrius.**

Falstaff (fâl′stȧf). 1. A comic opera (1838) by Balfe. 2. An opera (1864) by Nicolai. 3. A popular opera (1893) by Verdi.

Falstaff, Sir John. See Dictionary, **Falstaffian.**

Family Compact, The. A name for three 18th-century treaties, and especially the last (1761), between the French and Spanish Bourbon dynasties. Their effect was to ally Spain with France against England.

Fan (fäng). A powerful African nation of French Equatorial Africa. They are hunters and traders, and retain some traces of cannibalism.

Fanariots or **Phanariots** (fạ-nar′i-ots). The Greek inhabitants of Fanar, Constantinople; more narrowly, the Greek official aristocracy, once politically influential in Constantinople.

Fanciful, Lady. A vain and malicious fine lady in Vanbrugh's comedy "The Provoked Wife."

Faneuil (fan′l, fun′l, or fan′ū-ẹl) **Hall.** A market-house and hall in Boston, Massachusetts, built 1740–42: called "the Cradle of Liberty," because used as a meeting-place by American patriots in the Revolutionary period.

Fang, Mr. A brutal police magistrate in Dickens's "Oliver Twist."

Fanny's First Play. A drama (1911) by George Bernard Shaw, attacking certain conventions of current dramatic criticism.

Fanshawe (fan′shȧ). A romance (1826) by Hawthorne.

Fantine (fäṅ-tēn). In Victor Hugo's "Les Misérables," the ill-fated mother of Cosette.

Far Away and Long Ago. An autobiographical account of childhood in South America (1918) by W. H. Hudson.

Far-Away Princess, The. 1. A romantic drama (produced 1895) by Edmond Rostand. 2. A one-act play by Hermann Sudermann.

Far from the Madding Crowd. One of the Wessex novels by Thomas Hardy: published 1874.

Faridun (fä-ri-dön′). In Persian legend, an Iranian king, one of the chief figures in the Shahnamah. He was son of Abtin and Firanak, and father of Salm, Tur, and Iraj.

Farnese (fär-nā′zā). An illustrious Italian family which ruled the duchy of Parma for two centuries. Pope Paul III., elected in 1534, was one of its members.

Farnese Bacchus, The. A celebrated Greek torso of the 4th century B.C., in the Museo Nazionale, Naples.

Farnese Bull, The. A group of Greek sculpture (3d century B.C.) in the Museo Nazionale, Naples, representing the punishment of Dirce.

Farnese Flora, The. A celebrated antique statue, 11½ feet high, in the Museo Nazionale, Naples.

Farnese Hercules, The. A Greek statue of the early empire, in the Museo Nazionale, Naples.

Farnese Homer, The. A fine antique bust in the Museo Nazionale, Naples.

Farnese Juno, The. A colossal antique bust, a copy of the type of Polyclitus, in the Museo Nazionale, Naples.

Farnese Minerva, The. A Greek statue of Athene Parthenos, found at Velletri: now in the Museo Nazionale, Naples.

Farnese Palace, The. A palace of the Farnese family in Rome, begun in the reign of Leo X. It is adorned with frescoes by Annibale Caracci.

Fascism, Fascisti. See Dictionary.

Fashoda (fä-shō′dä) **Affair, The.** The culminating incident (July–Dec., 1898) in an attempt of France to gain control of the upper Nile. For a time there was danger of a military clash between a French military mission and the Anglo-Egyptian forces under Kitchener.

Fasti (fas′tī). 1. In ancient Rome, semi-official (later, official) lists of court-days, religious festivals, and the like. 2. A poetical Roman calendar by Ovid.

Fasti Capitolini (kap″i-tọ-lī′nī). Marble tablets bearing a register of Roman consuls and other magistrates, excavated at Rome about 1546: now in the Capitol.

Fatal Marriage, or The Innocent Adultery, The. A tragedy (1694) by Southerne.

Fata Morgana (fä′tä môr-gä′nä). 1. The same as **Morgana.** 2. See Dictionary.

Fat Boy, The. See **Joe.**

Fates, The. In Greek mythology, the three goddesses of destiny. Clotho spins the thread of life, Lachesis measures it, and Atropos severs it.

Father, The. A drama (1887) by August Strindberg.

Father Brown. A character in many stories by G. K. Chesterton.

Father of Lies, The. Satan.

Father of the Faithful, The. Abraham.

Father of the People. A title assumed by the absolutist kings of Denmark.

Fathers and Sons. A novel (1862) by Turgenev, in which theoretic nihilism is analyzed in the person of the student Bazarof.

Fathom (fa⊤н′ọm), **Ferdinand, Count.** See **Ferdinand, Count Fathom.**

Fatima (fä′tẹ-mä). 1. The enchantress in "Aladdin, or the Wonderful Lamp," in the "Arabian Nights' Entertainments." 2. The seventh and last wife of Bluebeard, popularly a synonym of feminine curiosity.

Fatimites (fat′i-mīts), or **Fatimides** (fat′i-mīdz). An Arabian dynasty of califs of northern Africa and Syria, 909–1171.

Faubourg St.-Antoine. See **Rue St.-Antoine.**

Faultless Painter, The. A name sometimes given to Andrea del Sarto, as in the poem (1855) by Robert Browning.

Fauna (fâ′nä) and **Faunus** (fâ′nus). See Dictionary, **fauna, faun.**

Faun of Praxiteles, The. The finest surviving copy of a famous original: in the Capitoline Museum, Rome.

Faust (foust). 1. A legend which had its inception in the life of the actual Doctor Johann Faustus, a necromancer of Württemberg in the early 16th century. Its essence is the sale of a human soul to the devil for power or knowledge. It has been made the subject of innumerable works of the imagination. 2. A supreme tragedy by Goethe (Part 1, 1808; Part 2, 1833). 3. An opera (1818) by Spohr. 4. An epic (1836) by Lenau. 5. An opera (1859) by Gounod, still a popular favorite.

Favonius (fạ-vō′ni-us). See Dictionary, **favonian.**

Favorita, La (lä fä-vō-rē′tä). An opera (1840) by Donizetti, one of his finest.

Fawnia (fâ′ni-ạ). The lady loved by Dorastus in Greene's "Dorastus and Fawnia" (renamed "Pandosto"), and the original of Shakspere's Perdita.

Feast of Rose Garlands, The. A painting (1506) by Dürer, in the museum at Prague.

Feathertop. A story (1846) by Nathaniel Hawthorne.

February Revolution, The. The revolution of Feb. 23–24, 1848, in Paris. It led to the abdication of Louis Philippe and the proclamation of a republic.

Federal Constitution, The. See **Constitution of the United States The.**

Federalist, The. A series of 85 essays by Hamilton, Madison, and Jay, issued 1787–88 in advocacy of the proposed Constitution of the United States.

Federalists, The. A political party formed in the United States in 1787, to support the proposed Constitution. Its leaders were Hamilton and John Adams.

Félibre, Félibrige. See Dictionary.

Felix Holt, the Radical. A novel (1866) by George Eliot.

Fellatahs (fe-lä′täz), or **Fellani** (fe-lä′nē). An African people: see **Fula.**

Female Quixote, The. A novel (1752) by Mrs. Lennox, satirizing the "heroic romances" of the French school.

Femme de Trente Ans, La (lä fàm dẹ tront äṅ). A novel (1831) by Balzac.

Femmes Savantes, Les (lā fàm sȧ-väṅt). A comedy (1672) by Molière, adapted from "Les précieuses ridicules."

Fenella (fe-nel′ạ). In Scott's "Peveril of the Peak," an elf-like creature, attendant on the Countess of Derby. She pretends to be a deaf-mute.

Fenians. See Dictionary, **Fenian.**

Fenrir (fen′rir), or **Fenris** (fen′ris). In Old Norse mythology, a gigantic wolf-like water-demon, son of Loki and the giantess Angurboda: slayer of Odin, and slain by Vidar.

Fenton (fen′tọn). The lover of Anne Page in Shakspere's "Merry Wives of Windsor."

Ferdinand (fèr′di-nand). 1. The lover of Miranda in Shakspere's "Tempest." 2. The King of Navarre in Shakspere's "Love's Labour's Lost." 3. A villain and murderer in Webster's "Duchess of Malfi."

Ferdinand, Count Fathom (fa⊤н′ọm). A picaresque novel (1753) by Smollett. Its title character and hero is a repulsive scoundrel, intended to satirize the brutality characteristic of 18th-century careers.

Feridun (fer-i-dön′). The same as **Faridun.**

Fernando Nash. The title character in E. A. Robinson's poem "The Man Who Died Twice."

Feronia (fẹ-rō′ni-ạ). An Etrurian goddess of Sabine origin: patroness of freedmen. Her chief shrine is at the foot of Mount Soracte.

Ferracute (fer′ạ-kūt), or **Ferragus** (fer′ạ-gus). A giant in medieval romance, famous for his possession of a bronze head which answers every question put to it.

Ferragus. A beggar, captain of the mysterious "Treize," in Balzac's novel "Ferragus" (1833).

Fescennine Songs. See Dictionary, **Fescennine.**

Fetter Lane. A London street running from Fleet Street to Holborn Viaduct. Dryden and Otway once lived in it.

Feuillants, Les. See Dictionary, **Feuillant.**

Feuilles d'Automne (fė-y′ dō-ton). A volume of poems (1831) by Victor Hugo.

Feverel, Richard. The hero of Meredith's "Ordeal of Richard Feverel" (1859). He is the victim of a dogmatic father's attempt to rear him by a "system."

Few Figs from Thistles, A. Poems (1920) by Edna St. Vincent Millay.

Fiacre (fyȧkr), **Saint.** An Irish monk who lived for years in France, and died about 670: the patron saint of gardeners.

Fiammetta (fyäm-met′tä). In the works of Boccaccio, a name for Maria (daughter of the King of Naples), whom he loved.

Ficoroni (fē-kō-rō′nē) **Cist**. A cylindrical bronze box bearing one of the finest surviving productions of Greek graphic art: in the Museo Kircheriano, Rome.

Fidele (fi-dē′lē). The name assumed by Imogen, disguised as a boy, in Shakspere's "Cymbeline."

Fidelia (fi-dē′li-ä). A young girl disguised as a boy in Wycherley's "Plain Dealer."

Fidelio (fē-dā′lyō). An opera (1805) by Beethoven. Leonora, the wife of a prisoner, Fernando Florestan, assumes the disguise of a boy (Fidelio) to save her husband's life. The Leonora overtures were written for this opera.

Fidessa (fi-des′ä). See **Duessa**.

Fiebres (fyä′brāz). A nickname for the liberal political parties in Central American countries, especially Guatemala.

Field of Blood, The. The ancient battle-field of Cannæ.

Field of the Cloth of Gold. A plain near Ardres, France, the scene of the meeting in 1520 between Francis I. of France and Henry VIII. of England: so called from the splendor of that occasion.

Field of the Forty Footsteps, The. A place (now built over) behind Montagu House, London, where, according to tradition, grass would not grow on the spots trodden by two brothers who killed each other in a duel.

Field of Waterloo, The. A romance in verse (1815) by Scott.

Fierabras (fē-ā-ra-brä′). 1. One of the most famous paladins of Charlemagne, hero of the French romance bearing his name. 2. An opera (composed 1823) by Schubert.

Fiesco (fē-es′kō). A tragedy (1783) by Schiller.

Fifine (fi-fēn′) **at the Fair**. A poem (1872) by Browning.

Fifth Avenue. An important street of New York City, extending from Washington Square northward to Harlem River.

Fifth Monarchy Men. See Dictionary, **fifth**.

Figaro (fē-gȧ-rō). An original and witty liar, and a recurrent figure in drama and opera. He first appears in "Le barbier de Séville," "Le mariage de Figaro," and "La mère coupable," by Beaumarchais.

Figaro, Le. A satirical Parisian journal, first started 1826.

Figaro, Le Nozze di. See **Nozze di Figaro, Le**.

Figlia di Jorio, La (lä fēl′yä dē yȯ′rē-ō). A tragedy (1904) by Gabriele d'Annunzio.

Figures of Earth. A romance (1921) by James Branch Cabell.

Filida (fē′lē-dä). An extremely popular Spanish romance published 1582 by Luis Gálvez de Montalvo.

Fille du Régiment, La (lä fē-y′ dü rā-zhē-moṅ). An opera (1840) by Donizetti.

Filocopo, Il (ēl fē-lô′kō-pō), or **Filocolo** (fē-lô′kō-lō). A prose version by Boccaccio of "Flore et Blanchefleur."

Filostrato, Il (ēl fē-lô′strä-tō). A narrative poem (1344) by Boccaccio, the original of Chaucer's "Troilus and Cressida."

Filumena (fil-ū-mē′nä), or **Filomena**, or **Philomena, Saint**. A saint accepted by the Roman Catholic Church from an inscription found (1802) on a tomb in the Roman catacombs and construed as "Pax tecum, Filumena."

Financier, The. A realistic novel (1912; revised edition, 1927) by Theodore Dreiser: the adventures of Frank Cowperwood, the hero, are continued in "The Titan" (1914).

Fine-Ear. In the fairy tale of Fortunio, an attendant with so acute an ear that he could hear the grass grow.

Finetta (fi-net′ä). A version (1710) of the Cinderella story by the Comtesse d'Aulnoy.

Fingal (fing′gȧl). An epic poem (1762) by Macpherson, who claimed it was written by Ossian the son of Fingal, and translated by himself from the original Gaelic.

Fingal's Cave. A famous basaltic grotto in the island of Staffa, 7 miles west of Mull, Scotland.

Fingalshöhle (fing′gäls-hė″lė). An overture (1830) by Mendelssohn.

Finn, Huckleberry. See **Tom Sawyer**.

Finsbury (finz′bẹ-ri). A borough of London north of the Thames. It consists of 3 constituencies: Central, Holborn, and East.

Finsbury Park. A London park of 120 acres, on the old grounds of Hornsey Wood House.

Fionn, or **Finn**, or **Find**. The chief figure in the Fenian legends: the Fingal of Macpherson.

Fiote (fyō′te). The Kongo language.

Firbolgs (fėr′bōlchs). A legendary aboriginal race of Ireland, akin to the Silures.

Firm Island. An enchanted island in the romance "Amadis of Gaul."

Firouz Schah (fē′röz shä). In the "Arabian Nights' Entertainments," the Persian prince who wins his bride by means of an enchanted horse.

First Hundred Thousand, The. Sketches of the early days of the Great War (1915) by Ian Hay (Major John Hay Beith).

Fitzwilliam Museum, The. A museum of illuminated manuscripts, engravings, ancient prints, etc., at Cambridge University. The collection, bequeathed 1816, was that of the 7th Viscount Fitzwilliam, who also provided for the building (begun 1837).

Five Hundred, The Council of the. See **Council of Five Hundred, The**.

Five Nations, The. See Dictionary, **five**. The addition of the Tuscaroras completed the "Six Nations."

Five Towns, The. In several novels and stories by Arnold Bennett, a group of towns in the pottery-manufacturing district of northern Staffordshire, England.

Flagellum Dei (flȧ-jel′um dē′ī). Attila, the 'scourge of God.'

Flaminian (flȧ-min′i-ạn) **Way**. One of the oldest and most famous of the Roman roads, built by the censor Caius Flaminius in 220 B.C., northward from Rome to Ariminum (Rimini).

Flammock's (flam′ọks) **Rebellion**. A defeated rebellion (1497) in Cornwall, under Thomas Flammock, occasioned by imposition of a tax to defray the cost of a Scottish war.

Flateyjarbok (flät′ā-yär′bōk). An Icelandic manuscript containing sagas, also annals to 1394: an important source of information about early Norse voyages to America.

Flatheads. 1. See **Choctaw**. 2. See Dictionary, **Flathead**.

Fleance (flē′ạns). In Shakspere's "Macbeth," the young son of Banquo.

Fleet Prison, The. See Dictionary, **fleet**[3].

Fleet Street. A London street running from Ludgate Circus to the Strand and the West End: in the Elizabethan period, a favorite place for puppet-shows, etc.

Flestrin (fles′trin), **Quinbus**. The Lilliputians' name for Gulliver, the Man-Mountain.

Fleta (flē′tä). A Latin book (about 1290) on English law.

Flibbertigibbet. See **Sludge, Dickon**.

Fliegende Holländer, Der (der flē′gẹn-dė hȯl′en-dėr). An opera (1843) by Wagner, based on the well-known legend of the Flying Dutchman.

Flimnap (flim′nap). The Lilliputian premier in Swift's "Voyage to Lilliput," designed as a satire on Sir Robert Walpole.

Floberge (flō-berzh). The sword of Renaud de Montauban.

Flora. 1. See Dictionary, **flora**. 2. A portrait by Titian, in the Uffizi, Florence.

Florac (flō-rȧk), **Vicomte de**. In Thackeray's "Newcomes," a vivacious Frenchman whose mother was Colonel Newcome's first love.

Flora de Barral. The heroine of Conrad's novel "Chance."

Flordelise or **Flordelis** (flôr′dẹ-lis). The wife of Brandimart, in the epics of Boiardo and Ariosto.

Flordespina (flôr-des-pē′nä). A princess who loves Bradamant (who is disguised by her armor), in the epics of Boiardo and Ariosto.

Flore et Blanchefleur (flôr ā bläṅsh-flėr). An early French metrical romance. Its theme is the love of a Christian prince for a Saracen slave-girl, Blanchefleur. See **Filocopo, Il**.

Florestan (flō′res-tän), **Fernando**. See **Fidelio**.

Florian's. A celebrated café in Venice, of late the resort mainly of tourists.

Florida, The. A commerce-destroyer built in England for the Confederate States of America: launched 1862, and captured two years later by the Federal corvette Wachusett.

Florimel (flor′i-mel). 1. A chaste and "goodly" lady in Spenser's "Faerie Queene": a personification of womanly delicacy and sweetness. 2. The heroine of Fletcher and Rowley's "Maid in the Mill." 3. A flirtatious maid of honor in Dryden's "Maiden Queen": one of Nell Gwyn's famous rôles.

Florinda. See **Julian, Count.**

Florismart (flor′is-märt). One of Charlemagne's peers, and a friend of Roland.

Florizel (flor′i-zel). The Prince of Bohemia, in love with Perdita, in Shakspere's "Winter's Tale."

Flos Regum Arthurus (flos rē′gum är-thū′rus), or **Flower of Kings.** A name applied to King Arthur by Joseph of Exeter (c. 1200).

Flower of Old Japan, The. A whimsical poem (1903) by Alfred Noyes.

Fluellen (flö-el′ęn). A pedantic but brave Welsh captain in Shakspere's "Henry V."

Flume (flöm), **The.** A picturesque narrow gorge in the Franconia Mountains, in Lincoln, Grafton County, New Hampshire.

Flute. A bellows-mender in Shakspere's "Midsummer Night's Dream." He acts Thisbe in the interpolated play.

Flute and Violin. A story (1891) by James Lane Allen, which gives its name to a volume.

Flutter, Sir Fopling. An affected man of fashion in Etherege's comedy "The Man of Mode."

Flying Dutchman, The. See Dictionary, **flying.** Also, see **Fliegende Holländer, Der.**

Flying Fish, The, or **Piscis Volans.** See Dictionary.

Foker (fō′kèr), **Harry.** In Thackeray's "Pendennis," a somewhat loud youth, infatuated with Blanche Amory.

Fomalhaut (fō′mạl-ō). A star of the first magnitude in the mouth of the fish in the constellation Piscis Australis.

Fondlewife. An uxorious old man, deceived by his demure young wife, in Congreve's "Old Bachelor."

Fonthill Abbey. A pretentious residence built on Lansdowne Hill, near Bath, England, by Beckford, the author of "Vathek." It had a tower 280 feet high.

Fool of Quality, The. A novel (1766) by Henry Brooke.

Foote's Resolution. A resolution introduced into the U. S. Senate by Samuel A. Foote of Connecticut: the direct occasion of the famous debate (Jan., 1830) between Webster and Hayne.

Foppington, Lord. An empty-headed man of mode in Vanbrugh's "Relapse."

Force Bill, The. 1. A bill to enforce the tariff, passed by Congress in 1833. 2. A bill (1870) to protect civil and political rights in the South. 3. A bill (1871) similar to the preceding. 4. The Lodge bill (defeated in the Senate, 1891), designed to improve the machinery of national elections.

Ford, Master. In Shakspere's "Merry Wives of Windsor," a gentleman who traps Falstaff (who does not know his identity) into a confession of his passion for Mistress Ford.

Ford's Theatre. A former theater in Washington. In it Lincoln was assassinated. It was later used for the record division of the War Department. It collapsed in 1893.

Forest Lovers, The. A romance (1898) by Maurice Hewlett.

Forest of Wild Thyme, The. A poem (1905) by Alfred Noyes.

Formorians (fôr-mō′ri-ạnz). A savage and primitive race which early inhabited Ireland.

Formula of Concord, The. A formula issued 1580 by the Lutheran Church, in an effort to effect an adjustment between extreme Lutheranism and extreme Calvinism.

Fornarina, La (lä for-nä-rē′nä). A picture (about 1509) by Raphael, in the Barberini Palace, Rome: commonly called "Raphael's Mistress."

Forsaken Merman, The. A poem (1849) by Matthew Arnold.

Forseti (for-set′ē). In Norse mythology, the god of justice, son of Balder.

Forsyte, Fleur. Daughter of Soames Forsyte and his second wife: the chief character in Galsworthy's "White Monkey."

Forsyte, Soames. The title character in Galsworthy's "The Man of Property," and an important character in all parts of "The Forsyte Saga" and in "The White Monkey" and "The Silver Spoon" and "Swan Song."

Forsyte Saga, The. A series of three novels and two linking stories (1922), by John Galsworthy, dealing with the effects on many lives of a strong sense of property. The novels are: "The Man of Property" (1906), "In Chancery" (1920), and "To Let" (1921). "The White Monkey" (1924), "The Silver Spoon" (1926), and "Swan Song" (1928) are sequels.

Fort Clinton. In the Revolutionary War, a fort in the highlands of the Hudson, south of West Point.

Fort Dearborn. A United States fort, established 1804, which became the nucleus of Chicago.

Fort Donelson. A Confederate fort on the Cumberland River in northwestern Tennessee. It was captured (1862) by Federal forces under General Grant and Commodore Foote.

Fort Duquesne (dū-kān′). The name given by the French to a fort on the site of the present city of Pittsburgh. They captured it from the English in 1754.

Forth Bridge, The. A cantilever bridge, 8,295 feet long, across the Firth of Forth at Queensferry: built (1882–89) by the North British Railway, at a cost of $16,000,000.

Fort Henry. A Confederate fortification on the Tennessee River, 11 miles west of Fort Donelson (which see). Its fall (Feb. 6, 1862) preceded that of Fort Donelson by ten days.

Fort Independence. One of the defenses of Boston harbor, located on Castle Island.

Fortitude. A novel (1913) by Hugh Walpole.

Fort McHenry. A fort at the entrance of Baltimore harbor, unsuccessfully bombarded by the British in 1814. It was during this bombardment that F. S. Key wrote "The Star-Spangled Banner."

Fort Monroe (mun-rō′), or **Fortress Monroe.** A large fort on Old Point Comfort, at the mouth of the James River, Virginia.

Fort Moultrie (mōl′tri). A fort erected in the War of 1812 on Sullivan's Island, in the main entrance to Charleston harbor. It participated in the bombardment (1861) of Fort Sumter.

Fort Sumter (sum′tèr). A fort in Charleston harbor, South Carolina. Against it was fired the first gun of the Civil War. See **Fort Moultrie.**

Fortuna (fôr-tū′nä). In Roman mythology, the counterpart of Tyche.

Fortunate Islands, The. See Dictionary, **island.**

Fortunatus (fôr-ṭū-nā′tus). The hero of a popular European chap-book of about 1509. He possesses a self-filling purse and a magic hat which takes him wherever he wishes.

Fortune. A painting by Guido Reni, in the Accademia di San Luca, Rome.

Fortune, The. A ship which, in 1621, reached Plymouth, Mass., from London, bringing 35 colonists and letters patent covering grants of land and empowering the grantees to make laws and set up a government.

Fortunes of Nigel (nī′jęl), **The.** A romance (1822) of London in the early 17th century, by Scott.

Fortunio (fôr-tū′ni-ō). An old fairy tale. Fortunio, the daughter of an aged nobleman, serves the king in disguise, aided by a magic horse and 7 accomplished servants. See **Fine-Ear.**

Fort William Henry. A fort at the head of Lake George, New York, captured 1757 by French and Indians under Montcalm.

Forty, The. The 40 members of the French Academy.

Forty-Niners, The. A name given to those who migrated to California after the discovery of gold in 1849.

Forty Thieves, The. One of the tales of the "Arabian Nights' Entertainments": often called "Ali Baba and the Forty Thieves."

Forum Boarium (fō′rum bō-ā′ri-um). The cattle-market of very ancient Rome, west of the Palatine.

Forum Julium (jö′li-um). The earliest of the imperial forums, immediately northeast of the Forum Romanum.

Forum of Augustus, The. The second of the imperial forums, adjoining the northeast side of the Forum Julium.

Forum of Nerva (nèr′vä), **The.** The fourth of the imperial forums, a long, narrow area between the Forum of Vespasian and that of Augustus.

Forum of Trajan (trā′jạn), **The.** The largest and northernmost of the imperial forums, adjoining the Forum of Augustus on the northwest.

Forum of Vespasian (ves-pā′zhiạn), **The,** or **Forum Pacis**

(variable) ḍ as d or j, ş as s or sh, ṭ as t or ch, ẕ as z or zh; o, F. cloche; ü, F. menu; ċh, Sc. loch; ṅ, F. bonbon; ′, primary accent; ″, secondary accent; †, obsolete; <, from; +, and; =, equals. See also lists at beginning of book.

(pā'sis). The third of the imperial forums, and the southernmost. It was built to inclose the temple of Peace dedicated A.D. 75 by Vespasian after the capture of Jerusalem.
Forum Olitorium (ō-li-tō'ri-um). The vegetable-market of ancient Rome, at the southern end of the Campus Martius.
Forum Romanum (rō-mā'num). The forum which, from the time of the earliest kings, was the political center of Rome. It was east of the Capitoline and north of the Palatine.
Forza del Destino, La (lä fôr'tsä del des-tē'nō). An opera (1862) by Verdi.
Fosco (fos'kō), **Count.** The villain in Wilkie Collins's "Woman in White."
Fosse-way (fos'wā), or **The Fosse** (fos). An ancient Roman road in Britain, running from Bath to Lincoln.
Foul Play. A novel (1869) by Charles Reade.
Fountain of Arethusa, The. See **Arethusa.**
Fountain of Castalia, The. See Dictionary, **Castalia.**
Fountain of Youth, The. A mythical spring, sought in the Bahamas and Florida by Ponce de León, Narváez, De Soto, and others. Indians of Central America believed that it was to the northward, and that its waters would cure ills and renew youth.
Fountains Abbey. A Cistercian monastery of the 14th century, near Ripon, England: the most picturesque of ecclesiastical ruins in England.
Fourberies de Scapin, Les (lā förb-rē dė skä-pañ). A comedy (1671) by Molière, based on the "Phormio" of Terence.
Four Horsemen of the Apocalypse, The. A novel (1918) by Vicente Blasco Ibáñez.
Four Million, The. Short stories (1906) by O. Henry (Sidney Porter), dealing with life in New York, especially among clerks and shop-girls.
Four P's, The. An early interlude (printed before 1547) by John Heywood. The P's were a Palmer, a Pardoner, a Poticary, and a Pedlar.
Fourteen Points, The. A statement of the war aims of the Allies, made by President Wilson on January 8, 1918.
Fourteenth of July, The. See Dictionary, **fourteenth** and **bastile.**
Fourth Estate, The. See Dictionary, **estate.**
Fourth of July, The. See Dictionary, **fourth.**
Fourth Party, The. A knot of English Conservatives led by Lord Randolph Churchill, about 1880.
Fox. A tribe of North American Indians, formerly in Wisconsin near Lake Superior: later absorbed into the Sac tribe.
Fra Diavolo (frä dē-ä'vō-lō). A comic opera (1830) by Auber and Scribe, based on the life of the bandit Michele Pezza.
Fragmenta Vaticana (frag-men'tạ vat-i-kā'nạ). A collection of legal documents, dating perhaps from Constantine, preserved (in part) in a palimpsest in the Vatican Library.
Frail, Mrs. In Congreve's "Love for Love," a woman whose nature is as her name: one of Mrs. Bracegirdle's rôles.
Fram (främ). A specially constructed steam-schooner in which (1893–96) Fridtjof Nansen attempted to reach the North Pole.
Framley Parsonage. A novel (1861) by Anthony Trollope, one of the Barchester series.
France Antarctique (fräṅs äṅ-tärk-tēk). The short-lived French Huguenot colony on the bay of Rio de Janeiro, 1555–67.
Francesca da Rimini (frän-ches'kä dä rē'mē-nē). An Italian lady of the 13th century, daughter of Guido da Polenta, lord of Rimini. The tragic story of her love for Paolo, the young brother of her husband, is told by Dante in a famous episode of the "Inferno." It is also the subject of numerous poems, plays, and pictures.
Franciscans. See Dictionary, **Franciscan.**
Franconian (frang-kō'ni-ạn). The German dialect of old Franconian territory along the Rhine, from the confluence of the Murg to its mouth.
Franconian Emperors, The. The line of German emperors from 1024 (Conrad II.) to 1125 (Henry V.).
Franco-Prussian War, The. See Dictionary, **Franco-Prussian;** also **Frankfort, The Peace of.**
Frangipani (frän-jē-pä'nē). A noble Roman family, many members of which were Ghibelline leaders in and after the 11th century.
Frank Cowperwood. See **Financier, The.**
Frankenstein. See Dictionary.
Frankfort, The Council of. An ecclesiastical council (794) at Frankfort-on-the-Main, called for the purpose of considering the acts of the second Council of Nicæa (787).
Frankfort, The Peace of. The treaty signed by the German Empire and France at Frankfort-on-the-Main, May 10, 1871. France ceded Alsace and Lorraine, and agreed to pay in 3 years a war indemnity of $1,000,000,000.
Frankfurter Attentat (fränk'fụr-tėr ä-ten-tät'). A revolutionary outbreak by students and peasants in Frankfort-on-the-Main, April 3, 1833, caused by the hostile attitude of the Bundestag toward the press.
Franklin's Tale, The. One of Chaucer's "Canterbury Tales," purporting to be a lay of Britain, but in part probably derived from Boccaccio's "Filocopo."
Fraternity. A novel (1908) by John Galsworthy.
Fraticelli (frä-tē-chel'lē). From the 13th century to the 15th, a sect of reformed Franciscans.
Fräulein Else (froi'līn el'zė). A novel (1924) by Arthur Schnitzler: the life of a Viennese flapper.
Frea (frā'ä). In Teutonic mythology, a goddess, the same as **Frigg.**
Fredegarius (fred-ẹ-gā'ri-us). The name assigned to the unknown compiler (there were actually three) of an important work on general and early French history to 642.
Frederick. In Shakspere's "As You Like It," the usurping brother of the exiled duke.
Frederiksborg (fred'ėr-iks-bôrg). A royal palace on the island of Zealand, Denmark, built (1602–20) by Christian IV.
Frederiksborg, The Peace of. A peace concluded (1720) at Frederiksborg between Sweden and Denmark.
Freeport, Andrew. The British merchant of the "Spectator" papers of Addison and Steele.
Free-Soil Party, The. See Dictionary, **free-soil.**
Freischütz, Der (der frī'shüts). 1. In German folklore, a marksman who made a compact with the devil whereby he received seven bullets, six of which always hit the mark, the seventh going wherever the devil willed. 2. A romantic opera (1821) by Weber.
French and Indian War, The. See Dictionary, **French.**
French Fury, The. A sudden and secret, but unsuccessful, attack on Antwerp made by French troops under the Duke of Anjou, Jan. 17, 1583.
French Revolution, The. See Dictionary, **revolution.**
Frey (frā). In Norse mythology, the god of earth's fruitfulness and dispenser of wealth: son of Njörd.
Freya (frā'ạ). In Old Norse mythology, the daughter of Njörd and sister of Frey; in later mythology, wife of Odin. She was goddess of fruitfulness and sexual love.
Friar Bacon, The Famous History of. A popular legend concerning Roger Bacon, published (1627) in a tract at London. See **Bungay, Friar.**
Friar Rush. In medieval folklore, a devil disguised as a friar and sent to corrupt men, especially monks. Originally he was probably a mischievous elf like Robin Goodfellow.
Friar's Tale, The. One of Chaucer's "Canterbury Tales."
Friar Tuck. The jolly priest of Robin Hood's band.
Friday. The native companion of Defoe's Robinson Crusoe on his island: so named because Crusoe saved his life on that day.
Friday Club, The. A club instituted 1803 at Edinburgh by Sir Walter Scott.
Friedrichsruh (frēd'richs-rö). The residence of Prince Bismarck, about 15 miles southeast of Hamburg.
Friendship Village. The scene of a series of stories (1908) by Zona Gale: also in "Friendship Village Love Stories" (1909).
Friesian, Friesic. See Dictionary.
Frietchie, Barbara. See **Barbara Frietchie.**
Frigg (frig). In Norse mythology, wife of Odin and queen of the gods, often confounded with Freya.
Frisian. See Dictionary, **Friesian.**
Frithjof's (friᴛʜ'yofs) **Saga.** An Icelandic saga, probably of the 14th century, relating the adventures of the Norwegian hero Frithjof, or Frithiof.
Frog, Nicholas or **Nic.** See **Nicholas Frog.**
Frogmore Lodge. A mansion near Windsor Castle: once

the residence of Queen Victoria's mother, the Duchess of Kent.

Frogs, The. A comedy (405 B.C.) by Aristophanes.

Frolic, The. A British sloop of war captured in 1812 by Captain Jacob Jones in the American sloop of war Wasp.

Frollo (frol'ō), **Claude.** An archdeacon, one of the chief characters in Victor Hugo's "Notre Dame de Paris."

Fronde (frônd), **The.** A parliamentary and aristocratic rebellion against the court party, in the minority of Louis XIV. of France.

Front de Bœuf (frôn dė bėf), **Sir Reginald.** In Scott's "Ivanhoe," a predatory Norman baron, master of the stronghold of Torquilstone.

Frontino (fron-tē'nō). The horse on which Rogero overthrew all his opponents: given him by Brunello, who stole it from Sacripant.

Froth. A foolish gentleman in Shakspere's "Measure for Measure."

Froth, Lord. A solemn fop with a coquettish wife, in Congreve's comedy "The Double Dealer."

Fructidor (frük-tē-dôr), **The 18th.** Sept. 4, 1797, when the majority of the Directory executed a coup d'état against the royalist reaction.

Fruit of the Tree, The. A novel (1907) by Edith Wharton, raising the question of a nurse's right to end the suffering of a patient.

Fudge Family in Paris, The. A satire (1818) by Thomas Moore: followed by a sequel, "The Fudge Family in England."

Fuegians (fū-ē'ji-anz). The Indians of Tierra del Fuego.

Fugger (fug'ér). A Swabian family of Augsburg, famous as merchants and bankers in the 15th and 16th centuries.

Fugitive, The. A drama (1913) by John Galsworthy, dealing with the problem of an unhappy marriage.

Fugitive-Slave Law, The. An act included in the "Omnibus Bill" passed by Congress in 1850. It gave slaveholders increased legal facilities for recovering runaway slaves.

Fula or **Fulah** (fö'lä). A great African people, probably of mixed Berber and negro origin, scattered through the Sudan from Senegal eastward.

Fuller's Field, The. A field near Jerusalem, the location of which has not been identified.

Fulton, The. An American war-ship, the first to be propelled by steam, designed by Robert Fulton and built (1815) at New York.

Fundamentalists, The. In recent usage, those persons who believe that the whole Bible was directly inspired and that its literal interpretation throughout is the ultimate basis of all true knowledge, scientific as well as religious.

Funeral of Atahualpa (ä-tä-wäl'pä), **The.** A painting by the Peruvian artist Luis Montero, representing the obsequies of the Inca sovereign.

Funeral, or Grief à-la-Mode, The. A comedy (1701) by Steele.

Fung-hwang or **Fêng-hwang** (fung'hwäng'). In Chinese lore, a bird of good omen, which appears just before fortunate happenings of great public moment.

Funji (fön'jē). An African tribe occupying the wooded and mountainous region south of Sennar, between the White Nile and the Blue Nile.

Furiæ (fū'ri-ē), or **Furies.** See Dictionary, **fury.**

Furia (fū'ri-ä) **gens.** In ancient Rome, a patrician clan, supposed to have come from Tusculum.

Furies of the Revolution, The. See **Tricoteuses, Les.**

Furor (fū'rôr). In Spenser's "Faerie Queene," a madman, typifying wrath. He is the son of a wretched hag, Occasion. To tame the son the mother must be subdued.

Fürstenberg (für'sten-berċh). A German noble family in Westphalia and Rhineland.

Fürstenbund (für'sten-bunt). A league formed 1785 at the instance of Frederick the Great, by Prussia, Hannover, and Saxony, against the emperor Joseph II. Other states subsequently joined it.

Fury, The. See **Hecla, The.**

Fusberta (föz-ber'tä). Rinaldo's sword in "Orlando Furioso."

Fusbos (fus'bos). In Rhodes's burlesque opera "Bombastes Furioso" (1790), the minister of state. He kills Bombastes, who has killed all the other characters.

G

Gabinian (ga-bin'i-an) **Law, The.** 1. A Roman law (67 B.C.) investing Cn. Pompeius with unlimited command over the Mediterranean, its coasts, and the public treasuries of the provinces. 2. A Roman law (58 B.C.) forbidding loans of money at Rome to foreign legations, with the object of preventing bribery.

Gabriel (gā'bri-el). One of the archangels, appearing usually as a divine messenger. Dan. viii. 16, ix. 21, Luke, i. 19, 26. He so appears in the Koran and in Milton's "Paradise Lost."

Gad (gad). 1. A son of Jacob by Zilpah. Gen. xxx. 11, etc. 2. One of the twelve tribes of Israel. 3. A Hebrew prophet and chronicler at the court of David. 2 Sam. xxiv. 11–19.

Gadsden Purchase, The. A tract of 45,535 square miles, now contained in New Mexico and Arizona, purchased from Mexico for $10,000,000 in 1853, the treaty being negotiated by James Gadsden.

Gadshill (gadz'hil). A hill northwest of Rochester, England, noted as the place where Shakspere's Falstaff encountered the "men in buckram," also as the site of the residence of Charles Dickens.

Gæa (jē'ä). In Greek mythology, the earth-goddess, of whom were born Oceanus, Cronus, and the Titans.

Galahad (gal'a-had), **Sir.** In Arthurian romance, the noblest and purest knight of the Round Table, the son of Lancelot and Elaine.

Galatea (gal-a-tē'ä). 1. In Greek mythology: (1) A Nereid who loved Acis. (2) An ivory statue of a maiden which was brought to life by Aphrodite in response to the prayers of the sculptor, Pygmalion, who had fallen in love with his work, and who later married the maiden. 2. A coquette in Virgil's third eclogue.

Galatea, The Triumph of. A famous fresco (1514) by Raphael, in the Villa Farnesina, Rome.

Galatians (ga-lā'shanz), **The Epistle to the.** An epistle (about A.D. 56) of the apostle Paul to the Galatian churches, vindicating his authority and pleading for the principle of justification by faith.

Galla (gal'ä). An African people living between the Somali on the east and the Berta and Dinka on the west, and from Shoa to the Sabaki River.

Galli (gal'ī). The Gauls; a Celtic-speaking people of ancient Gaul.

Gamaliel (ga-mā'li-el). 1. The name, mentioned in the Talmud, of several descendants of Hillel, who were presidents of the Sanhedrim and patriarchs of the Jewish community in Palestine after the fall of Jerusalem. 2. The preceptor of St. Paul. Acts, xxii. 3.

Gambrinus (gam-brī'nus). A mythical Flemish king, the reputed inventor of beer.

Gamester, The. 1. A play (1633) by Shirley. 2. A comedy (1705) by Mrs. Centlivre. 3. A tragedy (1753) by Edward Moore.

Gammer Gurton's Needle. An early English comedy (performed 1566, printed 1575) in which a housewife loses her needle while mending her husband's breeches.

Gamp (gamp), **Mrs. Sarah** or "Sairey." A tippling old nurse in Dickens's "Martin Chuzzlewit," memorable for her constant references to her mythical friend Mrs. Harris.

Gandharvas (gan-dhär'väz). In Hindu mythology, the heavenly singers at the banquets of the gods. See **Apsaras.**

Ganelon (gan'e-lon), or **Gan** (gän), or **Gano** (gä'nō). In Charlemagne romances, a treacherous paladin causing the death of Roland and the loss of the battle of Roncesvalles.

Ganesha (ga-nā'shä). In Hindu mythology, the lord of the Ganas, or troops of inferior deities, and the god of wisdom.

Ganymede. See Dictionary.

Gaol Gate, The. A drama (1906) by Lady Augusta Gregory.

Gard, Pont du (pôn dü gär). The modern name of a bridge forming part of a celebrated Roman aqueduct, situated northeast of Nîmes, France. See Dictionary, **viaduct,** cut.

Garden of Allah, The. A novel (1905) by Robert Hichens. Also, the play based on the novel.

Garden of the Gods, The. A region near Colorado Springs, Colorado, covered with extraordinary rock-formations.

(variable) ḍ as d or j, ş as s or sh, ṭ as t or ch, z̧ as z or zh; o, F. cloche; ü, F. menu; ċh, Sc. loch; ṅ, F. bonbon; ', primary accent; ", secondary accent; †, obsolete; <, from; +, and; =, equals. See also lists at beginning of book.

Gareth (gā′reth). In Arthurian romance, the nephew of King Arthur.

Gareth and Lynette (li-net′). One of Tennyson's "Idylls of the King."

Gargantua (gär-gan′ṭū-ȧ) and **Pantagruel** (pan-tag′rŏ-el), **The Life of.** A satirical work in prose and verse (1532–1553), by Rabelais. See Dictionary, **Gargantuan.**

Gargery (gär′jer-i), **Joe.** A good-natured, illiterate blacksmith in Dickens's "Great Expectations." He is Pip's brother-in-law. His wife is a shrew.

Garm (gärm). In Old Norse mythology, the demon watchdog of Hel, the goddess of the realm of the dead.

Garrick (gar′ik) **Club, The.** A London club (instituted 1831) for the patronage of the drama.

Garrotteurs (gȧ-ro-tēr), or **Chauffeurs** (shō-fėr′). A band of French brigands which during the Reign of Terror infested the forests of Argères, near Chartres.

Garuda (gar′ö-dȧ). In Hindu mythology, a being, half bird, half man, on which Vishnu rides.

Gath (gath). One of the five confederate cities of the Philistines. 1 Sam. v. 8, 9.

Gauntlet, A. A drama (1883) by Björnstjerne Björnson.

Gautier (gō-tyā), **Marguerite.** A courtezan, the central character of "La dame aux camélias," by Dumas *fils.*

Gavin Dishart (dish′ärt). The title character of Barrie's novel "The Little Minister."

Gavroche (gȧ-vrosh). A street Arab in Victor Hugo's "Les Misérables." He has become a type.

Gawain or **Gawayne** (gä′wän), **Sir.** In Arthurian romance, one of the principal knights of the Round Table.

Gayatri (gä′yȧ-trē). An ancient Sanskrit meter of 24 syllables, generally arranged as a triplet of 3 divisions of 8 syllables each.

Gay Lord Quex, The. A drama (1899) by A. W. Pinero.

Gay Saber (gī or gä sä-bär′). A gild formed (1323) by the magistrates of Toulouse, to restore the Provençal language and culture.

Ge (jē). See **Gæa.**

Gebir (gä′bēr). A long narrative poem (1798) by Walter Savage Landor.

Geez (gēz). The ancient language of Abyssinia.

Gehenna. See Dictionary.

Gellert (gel′ėrt). In Welsh tradition, the faithful hound of Llewelyn.

Gemara. See Dictionary.

Genesis (jen′e-sis). The first book of the Old Testament.

Genetyllis (jen-e-til′is). In Greek mythology, a goddess, protectress of births.

Geneva Bible, The. See Dictionary, **Bible.**

Geneva Convention, The. An international convention (1864) of European states, designed to lessen the needless suffering of soldiers in war.

Génie du Christianisme (zhā-nē dü krēs-tyȧ-nēsm). A work (1802) in defense of Christianity, by Chateaubriand.

Genius, The. A novel written in the documentary style (1915) by Theodore Dreiser.

Gentleman with a Duster, A. See **Mirrors of Downing Street, The.**

George (jôrj), **Saint.** A Christian martyr, native of Cappadocia, and military tribune under Diocletian: the patron saint of England.

George and the Crown, The. A novel (1925) by Sheila Kaye-Smith.

George Barnwell. A domestic tragedy in prose (1731) by George Lillo.

George Dandin (zhôrzh dän-dan), **ou Le Mari Confondu.** A comedy (1660) by Molière.

Georgics (jôr′jiks). A poem on agriculture by Virgil.

Geraint (ge-rānt′). One of the knights of the Round Table.

Geraint and Enid (ē′nid). One of the "Idylls of the King," by Tennyson.

Geraldine (jer′ȧl-dēn) **the Fair.** A child, Lady Elizabeth Fitzgerald, to whom Henry Howard, Earl of Surrey, paid playful court in his sonnets. In Nash's "Jack Wilton, or The Unfortunate Traveller," she appears as Surrey's lady-love.

German Confederation, The. The confederation of German states constituted 1815 by the Congress of Vienna, replacing the ancient empire, each state remaining independent in internal affairs.

German East Africa Company, The. A German company founded 1885 for the exploitation of the German sphere of influence.

Germania (jer-mā′ni-ȧ). A celebrated work by Tacitus, relating to the Germans.

Géronte (zhä-rônt). In French comedy, a common name for a credulous, ridiculous old man.

Gerridge. The plumber in T. W. Robertson's "Caste": a type of the humorous cockney workman.

Gertrude (gėr′trōd). 1. Hamlet's mother, the queen, and wife of Claudius, in Shakspere's "Hamlet." 2. Heroine of Campbell's poem "Gertrude of Wyoming" (1809).

Gerusalemme Liberata (jä-rö-sä-lem′mä lē-bä-rä′tä). An epic poem (1581) by Tasso, on the deliverance of Jerusalem by the Crusaders.

Geryon (jē′ri-on), or **Geryones** (jē-rī′ọ-nēz). In classical mythology, a monster of the extreme west, the possessor of a herd of red cattle which Hercules carried off as one of his 12 labors.

Gês (zhäz), or **Crans** (kränz). A race of Brazilian Indians in northern Goyaz and western Maranhão.

Gesta Romanorum (jes′tä rō-mȧ-nō′rum). A popular collection of stories in Latin, compiled late in the 13th century.

Getæ (jē′tē). In ancient history, a Thracian people dwelling in the modern Bulgaria, and later in the modern Bessarabia.

Gethsemane (geth-sem′ȧ-nē). A garden east of Jerusalem, near the brook Kedron: the scene of Christ's agony and betrayal. Mat. xxvi. 36, etc.

Get-Rich-Quick Wallingford. A character in many stories by George Randolph Chester: a genial, amusing rogue, ever ready with schemes for making money.

Getting Married. A drama (1908) by G. B. Shaw.

Ghent (gent), **The Pacification of.** A union formed 1576 by the Low Countries against Spanish supremacy.

Ghent, The Treaty of. A treaty (1814) between the United States and Great Britain, terminating the War of 1812.

Ghibellines. See Dictionary, **Ghibelline.**

Ghika (gē′kä), or **Ghica.** A family of Albanian origin which furnished rulers of Wallachia and Moldavia in the 17th, 18th, and 19th centuries.

Ghosts. A drama (1881) by Henrik Ibsen.

Giant Despair, The. See **Doubting Castle.**

Giant's Causeway, The. A group of basaltic columns on the coast of Antrim, northern Ireland.

Giaour (jour), **The.** A narrative poem (1813) by Byron.

Gibeah (gib′ē-ȧ). A town in Palestine, probably about 4 miles north of Jerusalem. Judges, xx.

Gibeon (gib′ē-on). A town in Palestine, 6 miles northwest of Jerusalem. Josh. ix. 3, etc. See Dictionary, **Gibeonite.**

Gibil (gē′bil). The Assyro-Babylonian fire-god.

Gibraltar. See Dictionary.

Gideon (gid′ē-on), surnamed **Jerubbaal** (je-rub′ā-ȧl or jer-u-bā′ȧl). A Hebrew liberator and religious reformer, conqueror of the Midianites, and judge in Israel for forty years. Judges, vi. 11, etc.

Gigadibs. A poet in Browning's "Bishop Blougram's Apology."

Gihon (gī′hon). One of the four rivers in Eden. Gen. ii. 13.

Gilbertines (gil′bėr-tins). A religious order founded in England in the first half of the 12th century by St. Gilbert of Sempringham in Lincolnshire.

Gil Blas (zhēl bläs). A picaresque romance (1715-35) by Le Sage.

Gilded Age, The. A humorous novel (1873) by Mark Twain and C. D. Warner.

Gilead (gil′ē-ȧd). A part of Palestine east of the Jordan. Jer. viii. 22, etc.

Giles (jīlz), **Saint.** An anchorite of the 7th century, believed to have been a Greek who emigrated to France: the patron saint of cripples.

Gilgal (gil′gal). The name of various places in Palestine, notably one in the plain of Jordan 3 miles east of the ancient Jericho. Josh. iv. 19–24.

---

fat, fāte, fär, fȧll, ȧsk, fãre; net, mē, hėr; pin, pīne; not, nōte, mŏve, nôr; up, lūte, půll; oi, oil; ou, out; (lightened) aviȧry, ẹlect, agǒny, intǒ, ūnite; (obscured) errȧnt, operȧ, ardẹnt, actǒr, natūre; ch, chip; g, go; th, thin; ᴛʜ, then; y, you;

Ginnungagap (gin′nŏng-ă-gäp). In the Old Norse cosmogony, the "gaping abyss" which originally existed everywhere.

Gioconda, La (lä jō-kōn′dä). 1. See **Mona Lisa.** 2. An opera (1876) by Ponchielli. 3. A drama (1898) by Gabriele d'Annunzio, showing an artist's conflict between art and duty.

Giralda (Hē-räl′dä). The bell-tower of the cathedral at Seville, Spain: so called from the weather-vane, in the form of a statue of Faith.

Girgashites (gẽr′gȧ-shīts). In Old Testament history, a tribe of the Canaanites. Gen. x. 15, 16.

Girl of the Golden West, The. An opera (1910) by Puccini, based on a play by David Belasco.

Girondists. See Dictionary, **Girondist.**

Girouettes (zhē-rö-et). **Les.** A name given (1815) in Paris to those who had deserted the tricolor for the Bourbons, or vice versa, after the fall of Napoleon.

Girton (gẽr′tọn) **College.** A college at Girton, England, founded 1869 for the education of women.

Gitanjali (gi-tän′jȧ-lē). Poems by Rabindranath Tagore (translated from the Bengali, 1912). Nobel Prize, 1913.

Gittites (git′īts). The natives or inhabitants of Gath.

Gjallarhorn (yäl′lär-hôrn). In Scandinavian mythology, the horn of Heimdal.

Glamorgan (glȧ-môr′gạn) **Treaty, The.** A treaty made 1645 with the Roman Catholics of Ireland by the Earl of Glamorgan, containing important concessions to the Catholics in return for military aid.

Glassites (glăs′īts). A religious sect in Scotland, founded by John Glas (1695–1773).

Glaucus (glâ′kus). 1. In Greek legend: (1) The steersman of the Argo: surnamed Pontius. (2) A son of Sisyphus and father of Bellerophon: surnamed Potnieus. He was torn in pieces by his own mares. (3) A son of Minos and Pasiphaë. He was smothered in a jar of honey. (4) A Lycian prince, friend of Diomedes before the Trojan war. 2. The hero of Bulwer-Lytton's "Last Days of Pompeii," an aristocrat who struggles against his love for the blind flower-girl, Nydia.

Glenvarloch (glen-vär′lọch), **Lord.** See **Olifaunt.**

Glimpses of the Moon. A novel (1922) by Edith Wharton.

Glittering Gate, The. A short play (1914) by Lord Dunsany.

Globe, The. A celebrated London theater, built 1599, in which Shakspere was a shareholder, and in which many of his most famous plays were performed.

Gloria. See Dictionary.

Gloriana (glō-ri-an′ȧ). The queen in Spenser's "Faerie Queene." She represents Queen Elizabeth in her royal aspect. See **Belphœbe.**

Glorious Apollo, The. A biography of Byron (1925) by E. Barrington (L. Adams Beck).

Glove, The. An old French story told by Ronsard and retold in many forms by Schiller, Leigh Hunt, Browning, and others.

Glover, Catherine. The heroine of Scott's "Fair Maid of Perth." She is the daughter of Simon the glover.

Gnostic. See Dictionary, **gnostic.**

Goajiros (gō-ä-Hē′rōz). A tribe of Indians in northern South America, occupying the Goajira peninsula northwest of Lake Maracaibo.

Gobbo (gob′ō), **Launcelot.** A whimsical, conceited servant in Shakspere's "Merchant of Venice." He is one of Shakspere's best clowns.

Goblins and Pagodas. A collection of poems (1916) by J. G. Fletcher.

Gobseck (gob-sek). A novel (1830) by Balzac. Gobseck is an avaricious money-lender.

Godiva (gō-dī′vȧ). The wife of Leofric, earl of Mercia (11th century). According to legend, she rode naked through the streets of Coventry, England, to win relief for the people from a burdensome tax.

Godolphin Barb, The. See **Byerly Turk, The.**

Gods and Mr. Perrin, The. A novel (1911) by Hugh Walpole, showing the effect of school atmosphere upon the masters. Published in England as "Mr. Perrin and Mr. Traill."

God Save the King (or **Queen**). The English national anthem: words and music probably composed 1740 by Henry Carey.

God's Fool. A novel (1892) by Maarten Maartens (Joost M. W. van der Poorten-Schwartz).

Gods of the Mountain, The. A romantic drama (1911) by Lord Dunsany.

Gog (gog). A ruler in the land of Magog. Ezek. xxxviii. 2, etc.

Gogmagog (gog′mȧ-gog), or **Goemot,** or **Goemagot.** A giant who held the western part of England in subjection, according to Geoffrey of Monmouth.

Golconda. See Dictionary.

Gold Bug, The. A short story (1843) by Edgar Allan Poe.

Golden Age, The. 1. The perfect age, when every one was happy and there was no evil or sorrow or sickness in the world: in classical mythology, the age of Saturn. 2. A story of children (1895) by Kenneth Grahame.

Golden Ass, The. A fantastic and satirical romance (2d century) by Apuleius.

Golden Bough, The. A monumental study of primitive religious systems (1890–1915), in 12 volumes, by Sir James G. Frazer.

Golden Bowl, The. A novel (1904) by Henry James.

Golden Bull, The. A bull published 1356 at the Diet of Nuremberg by the emperor Charles IV., concerning the election of the King of the Romans.

Golden Doom, The. A drama (1914) by Lord Dunsany.

Golden Fleece, The. See Dictionary, **golden.**

Golden Journey to Samarkand. A poem (1913) by James Elroy Flecker.

Golden Legend, The. 1. A collection of biographies of saints, compiled by Jacobus de Voragine in the 13th century: printed by Caxton, 1483. 2. A dramatic poem (1851) by Longfellow. 3. A cantata (1886) by Sir Arthur Sullivan, who used Longfellow's words.

Golden Rule. See Dictionary, **golden.**

Golgotha. See Dictionary.

Goliath. See Dictionary.

Gomorrah. See Dictionary.

Gondibert (gon′di-bẽrt). An epic poem (1651) by Sir William Davenant.

Goneril (gon′ẽr-il). The eldest of Lear's three daughters, in Shakspere's "King Lear."

Good Friday. 1. See Dictionary, **good.** 2. A dramatic poem (1916) by John Masefield.

Good-Natured Man, The. A comedy (1768) by Goldsmith.

Goody Two Shoes. A nursery tale of a poor child who, having previously owned but one shoe, is so excited by having a pair of shoes that she exhibits them to every one: published 1765, and ascribed to Goldsmith.

Goose, Mother. See **Mother Goose.**

Gopher Prairie. The scene of Sinclair Lewis's "Main Street."

Gorboduc (gôr′bọ-duk). 1. A mythical king of Britain. 2. The first regular English tragedy (1561), written by Norton and Sackville.

Gordius. See Dictionary, **Gordian.**

Gordon Riots, or **No-Popery Riots.** An uprising against the Roman Catholics by a London mob in 1780. It was led by Lord George Gordon.

Gorgon. See Dictionary.

Goshen (gō′shẹn). A pastoral region in Lower Egypt, colonized by the Israelites before the Exodus. Gen. xlv. 10, etc.

Gösta Berling (gẽs′tä bär′ling), **The Story of.** Traditional Swedish stories woven into a tale by Selma Lagerlöf. Nobel Prize, 1909.

Gotha (gō′tä), **Almanach de.** An annual register published (since 1764) in French and German, of the genealogy of the principal royal and aristocratic families of Europe.

Gotham. See Dictionary.

Götterdämmerung (gẽt′ẽr-dem′ẽr-ûng). The fourth part (1876) of Wagner's "Ring des Nibelungen."

Götz von Berlichingen (gẽts fon bẽr′lich-ing-ẹn). A romantic drama (1773; revised 1804) by Goethe.

Govardhana (gō-vär-dhä′nȧ). In Hindu mythology, a mountain in Vrindavana which Krishna induced the cowherds to worship instead of Indra.

Gow (gou), **Henry.** In Scott's "Fair Maid of Perth," an armorer who marries Catherine Glover.

Gowrie (gou′ri) **Conspiracy, The.** An alleged conspiracy

(1600) against James VI. of Scotland, ascribed to the Earl of Gowrie and others.

Goyanás (gō-yä-näz'). A race of Indians formerly occupying the Brazilian coast between Angra dos Reis and Cananea, and, inland, the country about São Paulo.

Goyatacás (gō-yä-tä-käz'). A tribe of Brazilian Indians which, at the time of the conquest, occupied the region near the coast of the modern state of Rio de Janeiro.

Grace Abounding to the Chief of Sinners. An autobiographical work (1666) by Bunyan.

Graces, The. See Dictionary, **grace.**

Gracioso (grä-thē-ō'sō). A comic type added to the stock characters of Spanish comedy by Lope de Vega.

Gradgrind (grad'grīnd), **Thomas.** An excessively practical retired merchant in Dickens's "Hard Times." His daughter Louisa marries Bounderby.

Gradus ad Parnassum. See Dictionary, **gradus.**

Grail, The Holy. See Dictionary, **Grail.**

Grammarian's Funeral, A. A poem (1855) by Robert Browning.

Grand Army of the Republic, The. See Dictionary, **grand.**

Grand Canal, The. The principal canal of Venice.

Grand Cyrus, The. See **Artamène.**

Grande Armée, La (lä gränd är-mā). The French army which Napoleon led against Russia (1812).

Grandet, Père (pâr grän-dā). In Balzac's "Eugénie Grandet," the father of Eugénie: a cold-blooded miser.

Grandison (gran'di-sọn), **Sir Charles.** The central figure of Richardson's "Sir Charles Grandison," supposed to be the ideal embodiment of masculine character and sentiment, as Clarissa Harlowe is of feminine.

Grandissimes (gran'di-sēmz), **The.** A creole story (1880) by G. W. Cable.

Grand Prix, Le (lê grän prē). The great horse-race for three-year-olds at Longchamp, established by Napoleon III.

Grand Prix de Rome, Le (dê rom). A prize given annually by the Academy of Fine Arts in Paris to the most successful competitor in painting, sculpture, engraving, architecture, or music.

Grangousier (grän-gö-zyä). The father of Gargantua in Rabelais's "Gargantua."

Gran Reunión Americana (grän rä-ö-nē-ōn' ä-mä-rē-kä'nä). A secret society of Spanish conspirators, formed in London at the end of the 18th century. Its object was to foment insurrection in the American colonies of Spain.

Grantly, Archdeacon. A prominent character in Trollope's Cathedral Novels. He represents the opposition to Mrs. Proudie.

Gratiano (grä-shi-ä'nō). In Shakspere's "Merchant of Venice," a friend of Bassanio. He marries Nerissa.

Grave Creek Mound, The. A relic of the so-called mound-builders, near Moundsville, W. Va.

Gray Friars. See Dictionary, **friar.**

Gray's Elegy. See **Elegy Written in a Country Church-yard.**

Great Adventure, The. A drama (1913) by Arnold Bennett, based on his novel "Buried Alive."

Great Catherine. A drama (1913) by G. B. Shaw.

Great Divide, The. A drama (1906) by William Vaughn Moody.

Great Eastern, The. The largest steamship prior to 1899 (launched 1858). She was frequently employed in cable-laying.

Great Expectations. A novel (1861) by Dickens.

Great Galeoto, The. A drama (1881) by José Echegaray.

Great Harry, The. The first war-ship (1488) of the British navy.

Greatheart. In Bunyan's "Pilgrim's Progress," the guide and valiant protector of Christiana and her children on their pilgrimage.

Great Russians. See Dictionary, **Russian.**

Great Synagogue, The. A body of men mistakenly conjectured (from the 16th century) to have fixed the Canon and wielded supreme authority in the Jewish nation. Neh. viii.–x.

Great Vehicle, The. See **Mahayana.**

Great War, The. See Dictionary, **great.**

Grecian Coffee-House. A noted London coffee-house where the wits of the 18th century congregated.

Greek Independence, The War of. The series of Greek revolts against the Turks which broke out in 1821.

Greenback Party, The. In American politics, a political party (formed 1874) which urged the suppression of banks of issue and the payment of the United States debt in greenbacks.

Green Mansions. A South American romance (1904) by W. H. Hudson.

Green Mirror, The. A novel (1918) by Hugh Walpole: a sequel is "The Secret City."

Green Mountain Boys, The. The soldiers from Vermont in the American Revolution, first organized by Ethan Allen in 1775.

Greensleeves (grēn'slēvz). An English ballad sung to a tune of the same name.

Green Vault, The. A series of 8 rooms in the royal palace at Dresden, containing an unrivaled collection of precious stones, works of art, etc.

Greenwich (gren'ich) **Village.** The Bohemian quarter of New York City, in and around Washington Square.

Gregorian Calendar. See Dictionary, **Gregorian.**

Gregorian Music. See Dictionary, **Gregorian.**

Grendel. A monster slain by the hero of "Beowulf."

Gresham (gresh'ạm) **College.** An educational foundation (1597) in London.

Gretchen (grech'ẹn). A simple girl of the lower ranks of life, the principal female character of Goethe's "Faust."

Gretna (gret'nạ) **Green.** A farmstead near Springfield, Dumfriesshire, Scotland, notorious for the celebration of irregular marriages contracted by runaway parties from England.

Grève (grāv), **Place de la.** The place of execution of ancient Paris.

Grihastha (gri-hast'hạ). A Brahman in the second stage of his religious life.

Grimm's Law. A phonetic law covering the consonant changes from Indo-European to the Germanic languages and from Low German to High German, formulated by Jakob Grimm (1820–22) and in outline independently by Rask (1819).

Grimwig (grim'wig), **Mr.** In Dickens's "Oliver Twist," a kindly but opinionated old gentleman.

Grip. A talking raven, Barnaby's constant companion, in Dickens's "Barnaby Rudge."

Griselda. In medieval romance, a patient wife whose husband subjects her to cruel and humiliating ordeals as a test of her obedience and devotion. Her story occurs in Boccaccio, Petrarch, and Chaucer.

Grolier (grō'lyä) **Club, The.** A New York club (founded 1884) for the encouragement of book-making as an art.

Grosvenor (grōv'nọr) **Gallery, The.** 1. A private picture-gallery in Grosvenor House, London. 2. A London gallery for the exhibition of paintings of the modern esthetic school, established 1876 by Lord Grosvenor.

Grosvenor Square. A fashionable square in London, east of Hyde Park.

Ground-Hog Day. See Dictionary, **ground-hog.**

Growth of the Soil. A novel (1919) by Knut Hamsun, a story of simple Norwegian life. Nobel Prize, 1920.

Grub Street. See Dictionary.

Grumbletonians (grum-bl-tō'ni-ạnz). In Great Britain in the late 17th century, a nickname for members of the Country party.

Grundy, Mrs. See Dictionary, **Grundy.**

Grütli. See **Rütli.**

Gryphon. See Dictionary, **griffin**[1].

Guaharibos (gwä-ä-rē'bōz). A tribe of Indians of the Carib stock, in southern Venezuela, formerly numerous and formidable.

Guahibos (gwä-ē'bōz). A formerly powerful nomadic Indian tribe of the upper Orinoco valley.

Guanahani (gwä-nä-ä'nē). The native name of the first island discovered (1492) by Columbus, the identity of which is variously conjectured.

Guanas (gwä-näz'). A tribe of South American Indians at present established in the southern part of the state of Matto Grosso, Brazil.

Guanches (gwän′chez). The aboriginal inhabitants of the Canary Islands.

Guaranis (gwä-rä′nēz). A powerful race of South American Indians who, at the time of the conquest, occupied most of the region now included in Paraguay, with parts of Uruguay and of the Brazilian coast.

Guatos (gwä-tōz′). A South American Indian tribe, formerly numerous and warlike, in the swampy regions of the upper Paraguay River.

Guaycurus (gwī-kö-röz′). A tribe of South American Indians on the river Paraguay, in Brazil, formerly nomadic and very numerous.

Gudrun (gö′drön), or **Kudrun** (kö′drön). The heroine of the important Middle High German epic poem called by her name.

Guelphs. See Dictionary, **Guelph.**

Guerrière (ge-ryär), **The.** A British frigate captured by the U.S.S. Constitution, Aug. 19, 1812.

Gueux, Les (lä ge̤). A name assumed by a league of patriots of the Netherlands, formed 1566 to oppose the Inquisition. The epithet was first applied to them in contempt, when they addressed a petition of grievances to Margaret of Parma.

Guido Franceschini (gwē′dō frän-ches-kē′nē). In Browning's "The Ring and the Book," the husband and murderer of Pompilia.

Guildhall (gild′hâl). The council hall of the City of London (rebuilt 1411).

Guinevere (gwin′e̤-vēr). 1. In Arthurian romance, the wife of King Arthur; also **Guenever** (gwen′e̤-vẽr) and **Ganor** (gä-nōr′). 2. One of Tennyson's "Idylls of the King": published 1859.

Gula (gö′lä). In Assyro-Babylonian mythology, a goddess presiding over life and death.

Gulistan (gö-lis-tän′). The most celebrated work (in verse and prose) of the Persian poet Sadi.

Gulliver's Travels. A social and political satire (1726) by Swift, narrating the voyages of Lemuel Gulliver to four imaginary regions — Lilliput, Brobdingnag, Laputa, and the country of the Houyhnhnms.

Gummidge (gum′ij), **Mrs.** In Dickens's "David Copperfield," a "lone, lorn creetur" who keeps house for Mr. Peggotty.

Gunga Din (gung′gä dēn). A poem by Rudyard Kipling about the heroic native water-carrier of a British regiment in India. See **Barrack-Room Ballads.**

Gunpowder Plot, The. See Dictionary, **gunpowder.**

Gunther (gůn′tẽr). In the Nibelungen epic, a Burgundian king, brother of Kriemhild and husband of Brunhild.

Gurth (gẽrth). In Scott's "Ivanhoe," a Saxon swineherd and thrall of Cedric.

Gutnic (göt′nik), or **Gutnish.** The Swedish dialect of the island of Gotland.

Guy and Pauline. A novel (1915) by Compton Mackenzie: American title, "Plasher's Mead."

Guy Fawkes Day. The anniversary of the day, Nov. 5, 1605, on which the Gunpowder Plot was discovered and Fawkes, the agent of the conspirators, seized.

Guy Mannering (man′ẽr-ing). A romance (1815) by Scott.

Guy of Warwick (wor′ik). An English hero of romance who, returning from the Holy Land, lives on his wife's alms without revealing his identity, which she learns only at his death-bed.

Guyon (gī′on), **Sir.** A knight personifying temperance in Spenser's "Faerie Queene." He overcomes Acrasia.

Guzmán de Alfarache (göth-män′ dä äl-fä-rä′chä). A Spanish picaresque romance (1599, 1605) by Alemán, named from its hero.

Gwamba (gwäm′bä). A Bantu tribe occupying the vast tract between Zululand and the Sabi River.

Gyges (jī′jēz). In Greek mythology, a brother of Briareus.

Gymnopædiæ (jim-nō̤-pē′di-ē). A yearly festival in ancient Sparta, with dancing and gymnastics by naked youths.

Gymnosophist. See Dictionary.

H

Habab (hä-bäb′). A nomadic African tribe of the pasturelands northwest of Massawa.

Habakkuk (ha̤-bak′uk or hab′a̤-kuk). A Hebrew prophet and poet, whose book of prophecies is eighth among those of the minor prophets of the Old Testament.

Haddon (had′on) **Hall.** A mansion of the Dukes of Rutland, near Bakewell, Derbyshire, England.

Hades. See Dictionary.

Hadrian's (hā′dri-anz) **Villa.** An assemblage of ancient ruins, near Tivoli, Italy.

Hadrian's Wall. A wall of defense for the Roman province of Britain, constructed by Hadrian between the Solway Firth and the mouth of the Tyne.

Haeltzuk (hä′el-tsůk). 1. A division of the Wakashan stock of North American Indians, comprising 23 tribes. 2. A collective name for a body of North American Indians whose habitat is Millbank Sound and Rivers Inlet, British Columbia.

Hæmon (hē′mon). In Greek mythology, son of Creon and lover of Antigone, after whose death he killed himself.

Hagar (hā′gär). An Egyptian concubine of Abraham, mother of Ishmael. Gen. xvi.

Hagen (hä′gen). In the Nibelungenlied and in Wagner's "Götterdämmerung," the slayer of Siegfried.

Haggai (hag′a̤-ī). The tenth in order of the minor prophets of Israel, whose book of prophecy (520 B.C.) is included in the Old Testament.

Hagiographa. See Dictionary.

Hague (hāg) **Tribunal, The.** The permanent court of arbitration for the peaceful settlement of international disputes, established at The Hague by the International Peace Conference of 1899, and recognized by the Treaty of Versailles (1919).

Hail and Farewell. An autobiography in three parts (Ave, 1911; Salve, 1912; Vale, 1914) by George Moore.

Hail, Columbia. 1. A patriotic American song (1798) by Joseph Hopkinson. 2. Sketches of America (1921) by W. L. George.

Hakluyt (hak′löt) **Society.** A society established (1846) in London to print annotated English editions of rare works on early geography, travels, and history.

Hal (hal), **Prince.** In Shakspere's "Henry IV.," the Prince of Wales, afterward Henry V.

Halakah, Halachah. See Dictionary, **halakah.**

Halcyone. An incorrect variant of **Alcyone.**

Half Moon, The. The vessel in which, in 1609, Henry Hudson crossed the Atlantic and entered the river that bears his name.

Hall of Fame, The. A colonnade, completed in 1900, at New York University, containing tablets and busts in honor of famous Americans.

Hallowe'en. See Dictionary.

Ham. See Dictionary, **Hamite.**

Hamadryad (ham-a̤-drī′ad), **The.** A poem (1846) by Walter Savage Landor.

Hamburgische Dramaturgie (häm′bůr″gish-ĕ drä-mä-tůr-gē′). An important series (1767–69) of dramatic criticisms, by Lessing.

Hameln (hä′meln), or **Hamelin** (ham′e̤-lin), **The Pied Piper of.** In medieval legend, a magician who in 1284 freed the town of Hameln from a plague of rats by playing on his pipe, and who, when refused his reward, led away the children of the town: the subject of a popular poem by Browning.

Hamlet (ham′let). 1. A tragedy (1602; revised, 1604) by Shakspere. 2. An opera (1868) by Ambroise Thomas.

Hampdenshire Wonder, The. A novel (1911) by J. D. Beresford.

Hampton (hamp′ton) **Court.** A royal palace on the Thames, built by Cardinal Wolsey.

Hampton Court Conference, The. A conference appointed 1604 by James I., to settle the disputes between the Puritan and High Church parties in the Church of England.

Handel (han′del) **and Haydn** (hä′dn) **Society.** A musical society founded 1815 at Boston.

Handel Society. An English society (1843–48) for the publication of Handel's works. A similar German society (Händel-Gesellschaft) was formed 1856.

Handy Andy. A novel (1842) by Samuel Lover.

Han dynasty. A celebrated Chinese dynasty (206 B.C.–A.D. 220), founded by Kao-ti.

(variable) d̩ as d or j, s̩ as s or sh, t̩ as t or ch, z̩ as z or zh; o, F. cloche; ü, F. menu; ch, Sc. loch; ṅ, F. bonbon; ′, primary accent; ″, secondary accent; †, obsolete; <, from; +, and; =, equals. See also lists at beginning of book.

Hanging Gardens of Babylon, The. See Dictionary, **seven wonders of the world,** under **wonder.**

Hannah (hǎn′ȧ). The mother of the prophet Samuel. 1 Sam. i., ii.

Hannele (hän′ĕ-lĕ). A poetic drama (1893) by Gerhart Hauptmann.

Hanno (hǎn′ō). A Carthaginian navigator (probably 5th century B.C.) who led a colonizing expedition to the western coast of Africa.

Hanover (hǎn′ō-vẽr) **Square.** A famous square in the West End of London.

Hans Breitmann's Party and Other Ballads. A collection (1868) of burlesque dialect poems by C. G. Leland.

Hanseatic League, The. See Dictionary, **Hanseatic.**

Hansel and Gretel. An opera (1893) by Humperdinck, based on the familiar fairy story.

Hanswurst (häns′vûrst). A conventional buffoon in old German comedy.

Hanuman (hän′ō-mǎn). In Hindu mythology, a monkey chief who is a conspicuous figure in the Ramayana.

Hapi (hä′pē). In Egyptian mythology, the Nile as a deity; the god Nilus.

Happy Boy, A. A story (1860) by Björnstjerne Björnson.

Happy Valley, The. In Johnson's "Rasselas," a garden of peace where lived the Prince of Abyssinia.

Hapsburg (hǎps′bẽrg), or **Habsburg** (häps′bûrch), **The House of.** A German princely family, prominent since the 11th century, which has furnished sovereigns to the Holy Roman Empire, Austria, Spain, etc.

Hapsburg Castle. A castle (built about 1020) on the bank of the Aar, in Aargau, Switzerland: the first seat of the Hapsburgs.

Harbor, The. A novel (1915) by Ernest Poole.

Hard Cash, or **Very Hard Cash.** A novel (1863) by Charles Reade.

Hardcastle, Kate. The lively heroine of "She Stoops to Conquer," by Goldsmith.

Hardcastle, Squire. A gentleman of the old school in "She Stoops to Conquer," by Goldsmith.

Hard Times. A novel (1854) about the "hungry '40's," by Dickens.

Harishchandra (har-ish-chan′drȧ). In Hindu mythology, the 28th king of the solar race, noted for piety and justice.

Harit (har′it), or **Harita** (har′i-tȧ). In Hindu mythology, the mares of Indra, typical of the sun's rays.

Harlequin. See Dictionary, **harlequin.**

Harlot's Progress, The. A series of 6 satirical pictures (completed 1733) by Hogarth.

Harlowe, Clarissa. The heroine of "Clarissa Harlowe," and Richardson's ideal embodiment of feminine character and sentiment. See **Lovelace.**

Harmodius (här-mō′di-us) and **Aristogiton** (a-ris-tọ-jī′ton). Two Athenian youths (killed 514 B.C.) who killed Hipparchus, tyrant of Athens. They are subjects of a famous group in the Museo Nazionale, Naples.

Harmonia (här-mō′ni-ȧ). In Greek mythology, the daughter of Ares and Aphrodite, who was presented, on wedding Cadmus, with a robe and a necklace fatal to all their successive possessors.

Harmonious Blacksmith, The. An air upon which Handel wrote variations.

Harmonists (här′mō-nists). A communistic religious body organized by George Rapp in Württemberg, and conducted by him to Pennsylvania in 1803.

Harold the Dauntless. A romance in verse (1817) by Scott.

Harpagon (är-pȧ-gôṅ). A miserly character in Molière's "L'Avare."

Harpies. See Dictionary, **harpy.**

Harris, Mrs. See **Gamp, Mrs. Sarah.**

Harrison, Dr. In Fielding's "Amelia," a generous clergyman who endeavors to protect Booth against his own weakness.

Harry Lorrequer. A novel (1837) by Charles Lever.

Hartford Convention, The. A convention of delegates from New England states, which met 1814 to voice Federalist opposition in relation to the war against England.

Hartford Wits, The. A group of American poets of the late eighteenth century, of whom the leaders were Barlow, Trumbull, and Dwight.

Harvest. A drama (1910) by Lennox Robinson.

Hasan (hä′sạn), or **Hassan,** and **Husain** (hŏ-sän′). Sons of Ali by Fatima, the daughter of Mohammed. Their fate forms the subject of a drama acted during the Muharram.

Hasis-Adra (hä′sis-ä′drä). In the Babylonian Nimrod epic, a hero, ancestor of Izdubar: the Babylonian counterpart of Noah.

Hassler (has′lẽr) **Expedition, The.** A scientific expedition (1871–72) made under the direction of Louis Agassiz, in the United States Coast Survey steamer Hassler.

Hatchway, Lieutenant Jack. See **Peregrine Pickle.**

Hatchways. A novel (1916) by Ethel Sidgwick.

Hathor. See Dictionary, **Hathoric.**

Hatteraick (hat′ẽr-āk), **Dirk.** A Dutch smuggler in Scott's "Guy Mannering."

Hatun Raymi (ä′tön rī′mē), or **Raymi.** The great feast of the ancient Peruvian Indians.

Hautecombe (ōt-kôṅb). A Cistercian abbey near Chambéry, France, founded 1125.

Havelok (hav′lok) **the Dane, The Lay of.** An English romance (before 1300), named from its hero, a Danish prince rescued by Grim, a fisherman, who built Grimsby with the money given him as reward.

Havilah (hav′i-lȧ). A rich land mentioned in the Biblical description of Eden. Gen. ii. 11, 12.

Hawkeye. In Cooper's "The Last of the Mohicans," the name given to Leatherstocking.

Haymarket, The. A famous London market (1644–1830), the site of the Haymarket Theatre (first erected 1720).

Haymarket Square Riot, The. A riot in Chicago, May 4, 1886, in which seven policemen were killed and many injured by a bomb thrown by an anarchist.

Hay-Pauncefote (hā-pȧns′fút) **Treaty, The.** A treaty (1901) between Great Britain and the United States, modifying the Clayton-Bulwer Treaty, to enable the United States to build the Panama Canal, but preserving the principle of neutrality.

Hayston, Frank (Laird of Bucklaw). See **Ashton, Lucy.**

Hazard of New Fortunes, A. A novel (1889) by W. D. Howells.

Headlong Hall. A burlesque novel (1816) by T. L. Peacock.

Headstone, Bradley. In "Our Mutual Friend," by Dickens, an ungainly schoolmaster in love with Lizzie Hexam. He tries to murder his rival, Wrayburn.

Heartbreak House. A drama (1917) by G. B. Shaw, adapted from Anton Chekhov's "The Cherry Orchard."

Heart of Midlothian (mid-lō′ŦHi-ạn), **The.** A romance (1818) by Scott. See **Deans, Jeanie,** and **Tolbooth.**

Heathcliff. An important character in Emily Brontë's "Wuthering Heights."

Heathen Chinee, The. A humorous poem (1870) by Bret Harte: first known as "Plain Language from Truthful James."

Heavenfield, The Battle of. A battle (634?) near the wall of Antoninus in the north of England, in which Oswald of Northumbria defeated (according to legend, by a miraculous intervention of heaven) the Britons under Cadwallon.

Heavenly Twins, The. A story (1893) by Sarah Grand.

Hebe. See Dictionary.

Hebrews, The Epistle to the. See Dictionary, **Hebrew.**

Hecate. See Dictionary.

Hecla (hek′lȧ), **The.** One of the two ships of Parry's arctic expedition (1821–23), the other being the Fury.

Hector. See Dictionary, **hector.**

Hector, Sir. See **Ector.**

Hecuba (hek′ū-bȧ). 1. In Greek legend, the second wife of Priam. 2. A tragedy (425 B.C.) of Euripides.

Hedda Gabler (hed′ȧ gä′blẽr). A drama (1890) by Henrik Ibsen.

Heep (hēp), **Uriah.** In Dickens's "David Copperfield," an ostentatiously humble hypocrite.

Hegeso (hē-jē′sō), **The Monument of.** A monument (4th century B.C.) in Athens, remarkable for the beauty of its relief-stele.

Hehe (hä′he), or **Wahehe** (wä-hä′he). A strong, warlike Bantu tribe of the region northeast of Lake Nyasa.

---

fat, fāte, fär, fȧll, ȧsk, fãre; net, mē, hẽr; pin, pīne; not, nōte, mŏve, nôr; up, lūte, pùll; oi, oïl; ou, out; (lightened) aviȧry, ęlect, agọny, intọ, ụnite; (obscured) errȧnt, operȧ, ardẹnt, actọr, natūre; ch, chip; g, go; th, thin; ŦH, then; y, you;

Heidenturm (hī′dẹn-tûrm). The same as **Igel Monument, The.**

Heilbronn (hīl′bron), **The Union of.** An alliance (1633) between the Swedes and the German Protestants, to prosecute the war against the Imperialists.

Heil dir im Siegerkranz (hīl dēr im zē′gẹr-kränts). A patriotic Prussian hymn (1790).

Heimat, Die (dē hī′mät). A drama (1893) by Hermann Sudermann, presenting the revolt of a daughter who is also an artist against the traditional restrictions of home. The English version is called "Magda," after the daughter.

Heimdal (hām′däl). In Old Norse mythology, a god of light, the guardian against the giants of the bridge of the gods: the slayer of Loki.

Heimskringla (hāms′kring-lä). The history of the Norse kings, from the earliest mythical times to the battle of Re (1177), by Snorri Sturluson (1179–1241).

Heir-at-Law, The. A comedy (1797) by Colman the younger.

Heir of Redclyffe, The. A romance (1853) by Charlotte M. Yonge.

Hejira. See Dictionary.

Hel (hel). In Old Norse mythology, the goddess of Niflheim, the realm of the dead: the daughter of Loki and the giantess Angurboda.

Helen (hel′en). In Greek legend, the wife of Menelaus, and, according to tradition, the daughter of Zeus and Leda. Her abduction by Paris caused the Trojan War. Her story is told by many writers. She appears in Goethe's "Faust" (1808–1833), in Marlowe's "Doctor Faustus" (1588), in Cabell's "Jurgen" (1919), and in Erskine's "The Private Life of Helen of Troy" (1925).

Helena (hel′ẹ-nä). 1. A tragedy (exhibited in 412 B.C.) of Euripides. 2. In Shakspere's "All's Well That Ends Well," the young wife of the reluctant Count Bertram.

Helen's Babies. A humorous novel (1876) by John Habberton.

Helenus (hel′ẹ-nus). In Greek legend, a son of Priam, celebrated as a prophet.

Heliand (hä′lē-änd). An Old Saxon epic poem (between 822 and 840) in alliterative verse, on the Saviour.

Helias (hē′li-as). The Brabantine counterpart of Lohengrin, the Knight of the Swan.

Helicon. See Dictionary.

Helios (hē′li-os). In Greek mythology, the sun-god, son of the Titan Hyperion and the Titaness Theia.

Hell-Bent fer Heaven. A drama (1923) by Hatcher Hughes: a study of religious ecstasy among the Southern mountaineers. Pulitzer Prize play, 1924.

Helle (hel′ē). In Greek legend, the daughter of Athamas and Nephele, drowned in the Hellespont (whence its name).

Hellen (hel′en). In Greek legend, a king in Phthia (in Thessaly), eponymous ancestor of the Hellenes.

Helmer (hel′mėr), **Nora.** The principal character in Ibsen's drama "A Doll's House." She is treated like a child by her husband, until, awakening to a knowledge of realities, she leaves him.

Helvetii (hel-vē′shi-ī). See Dictionary, **Helvetian.**

Hemicycle of Paul Delaroche (pol dẹ-lä-rosh), **The.** An encaustic mural painting of 75 representative artists and figures typifying the art of all periods, in the amphitheater of the École des Beaux Arts, Paris.

Henriade (oṅ-ryåd). An epic poem by Voltaire, picturing war undertaken in the name of religion.

Henriette (hen-ri-et′, F. oṅ-ryet). A young, simple, natural girl in Molière's "Femmes Savantes."

Henry IV. A historical play, in two parts, by Shakspere.

Henry V. A historical play (1599) by Shakspere.

Henry VI. A play in three parts, thought to have been revised by Shakspere from earlier versions by several collaborating dramatists.

Henry VIII. A historical play (1613) ascribed to Shakspere, Fletcher, and Massinger.

Henry Adams, The Education of. An autobiography (1918) intended as a "study of twentieth-century multiplicity" to balance the author's "Mont Saint Michel and Chartres" (1904), which is a "study of thirteenth-century unity": printed for private circulation, 1906. It received the Pulitzer Prize, 1919.

Henry Esmond (ez′mond). A historical novel (1852) of the time of Queen Anne, by Thackeray. It was followed (1858–59) by a sequel, "The Virginians."

Henry Ryecroft. The leading character in George Gissing's autobiographical novel (1903) "The Private Papers of Henry Ryecroft."

Hephæstus. See Dictionary.

Hephzibah (hef′zi-bạ). The wife of Hezekiah. 2 Kings, xxi. 1. Also, a name to be given to the restored Jerusalem. Isa. lxii. 4.

Heptameron (hep-tam′ẹ-ron). A collection (1558) of 72 stories modeled on the "Decameron," sometimes ascribed solely to Margaret of Navarre, though probably of composite authorship.

Heptateuch. See Dictionary.

Hera. See Dictionary.

Heracles. See Dictionary.

Heraclidæ (her-ạ-klī′dē), **The.** 1. The descendants of Heracles. 2. A tragedy (about 420 B.C.) of Euripides.

Heralds' College. See Dictionary, **herald.**

Hercules. See Dictionary.

Hercules Strangling the Serpents. A painting (1788) by Sir Joshua Reynolds, in the Hermitage Museum, Leningrad.

Here Are Ladies. Stories (1913) by James Stephens.

Herero (hạ-rā′rō), or **Ovaherero** (ō″vä-hạ-rā′rō). A Bantu tribe and language of southwestern Africa, in what is called Damaraland or Hereroland.

Hereward (her′ẹ-wärd) **the Wake.** A historical novel (1866) by Charles Kingsley.

Hermandad (er-män-däтн′). In Spain, originally a voluntary body for the maintenance of public order, later reorganized as a regular national police.

Hermannsschlacht (her′mäns-shlächt). The battle in the Teutoburger Wald in which, in A.D. 9, the Germans under Arminius (Hermann) defeated the Romans under Varus.

Hermann und Dorothea (her′män ụnt dō-rō-tā′ä). An idyllic poem in hexameters (1797), by Goethe.

Hermaphroditus. See Dictionary, **hermaphrodite.**

Hermes (hėr′mēz). See Dictionary.

Hermes Carrying the Infant Bacchus. An original statue by Praxiteles, in the museum at Olympia, Greece.

Hermes of Andros. A statue so named, in the National Museum, Athens: really a sepulchral statue of the 4th century B.C.

Hermes Trismegistus. See Dictionary.

Hermione (her-mī′ọ-nē). 1. In Greek mythology, the daughter of Menelaus and Helen: wife of Neoptolemus, and later of Orestes. 2. The wife of the jealous Leontes in Shakspere's "Winter's Tale." 3. A would-be thinker satirized by Don Marquis in sketches called "Hermione and Her Little Group of Serious Thinkers" (1916). 4. (er-myon) A character in Racine's "Andromaque."

Hermitage, The. 1. A palace at Leningrad, founded by Catharine II. 2. A fashionable resort at Moscow. 3. A chalet built in the valley of Montmorency, France, by Mme. d'Épinay as a retreat for Rousseau. 4. The home of Andrew Jackson, near Nashville.

Hernani (er-nä-nē). A romantic tragedy in verse (1830) by Victor Hugo. See **Ernani.**

Herne's Oak. An aged tree in Windsor Park (blown down 1863), long supposed to have been haunted by a legendary huntsman, Herne.

Hernici (hėr′ni-sī). In ancient history, an Italian people, allied to the Sabines, dwelling in the Apennines.

Hero (hē′rō). 1. In Greek legend, a priestess of Aphrodite at Sestos on the Hellespont: beloved by Leander. See **Hero and Leander.** 2. In Shakspere's "Much Ado about Nothing," the daughter of Leonato, and cousin and friend of Beatrice.

Hero and Leander (lē-an′dėr). 1. A poem (about A.D. 500) by Musæus, of which 340 lines survive. 2. A poem (1598) by Marlowe and Chapman. Leander, a youth of Abydos, swims the Hellespont nightly to visit Hero. One stormy night the lamp in her tower is extinguished and he is drowned. Hero, finding his body washed ashore at the base of her tower, hurls herself to the rocks beside it.

Herodians (hẹ-rō′di-ạnz). A party among the Jews in the time of Christ, adherents of the family of Herod.

(variable) ḍ as d or j, ş as s or sh, ţ as t or ch, ẓ as z or zh; o, F. cloche; ü, F. menu; ċh, Sc. loch; ṅ, F. bonbon; ′, primary accent; ′, secondary accent; †, obsolete; <, from; +, and; =, equals. See also lists at beginning of book.

Herostratus (hĕ-ros′trạ-tus). An Ephesian who set fire (356 B.C.) to the temple of Artemis at Ephesus in order to immortalize himself.

Herrenhausen (her′ẹn-hou″zẹn). A royal palace in Hannover.

Herrings, The Battle of the. The engagement (1429) between the French under Clermont and the English under Fastolf, near Rouvray.

Hertford (här′fọrd or härt′fọrd) **College.** A college of Oxford University, founded about 1282 by Elias de Hertford.

Hertha (hĕr′thạ). 1. A Germanic goddess of fertility. 2. A poem (1871) by Swinburne.

Hervé Riel (er-vä rē-el). A poem (1871) by Robert Browning.

Heshbon (hesh′bon). A city in Palestine, about 36 miles east of Jerusalem. Num. xxi. 26.

Hesione (hĕ-sī′ọ-nē). In Greek legend, a daughter of Laomedon, king of Troy, and Leucippe, rescued from a sea-monster by Heracles.

Hesperia. See Dictionary.

Hesperides (hes-per′i-dēz). 1. See Dictionary. 2. A collection (1648) of lyrical poems by Herrick.

Hesperus (hes′pẹ-rus). In Greek mythology, the evening star: identified by the ancients with Phosphorus, the morning star.

Hester Prynne. The central character in Hawthorne's "The Scarlet Letter."

Hestia. See **Vesta.**

Hesychasts. See Dictionary, **Hesychast.**

Heth (heth). A descendant of Canaan.

Hexam (hek′sạm), **Lizzie.** The object of the rivalry between Wrayburn and Headstone in "Our Mutual Friend," by Dickens.

Hexapla. See Dictionary.

Hexateuch. See Dictionary.

Heyst, Axel. The hero of Joseph Conrad's "Victory."

Hezekiah (hez-ẹ-kī′ạ). A king of Judah. He restored the service of Jehovah and was victorious over the Philistines. 2 Kings, xviii., etc.

Hiawatha (hī-ạ-wâ′thạ). The central figure of "The Song of Hiawatha" (1855), a poem by Longfellow, based on North American Indian legends about a miraculous personage who came to teach the arts of peace.

Hibbert (hib′ẽrt) **Lectures, The.** Lectures on unsettled problems in theology, maintained by a foundation instituted by the trustees of Robert Hibbert (d. 1849).

Hickathrift (hik′ạ-thrift), **Tom.** A mythical English strong man.

Hidatsa (hĕ-dät′sä). A tribe of North American Indians, on the Fort Berthold reservation, North Dakota.

Hidimba (hi-dim′bạ), fem. **Hidimbā** (-bä). In Hindu mythology, a powerful cannibal demon and his sister.

High Bridge. A long, high bridge (built 1842–49) at 175th Street, New York, to carry the Croton aqueduct across the Harlem River into the city.

Highgate, Lord (**Jack Belsize**). See **Newcome, Barnes.**

Highland Mary. The name given by Burns, in a poem (1792), to his dead sweetheart Mary Campbell.

High Life below Stairs. A popular farce (1759) by the Rev. James Townley.

Hilda Lessways. See **Clayhanger.**

Hildebrand (hil′dẹ-brand). An old man who appears in several German legendary romances.

Hildebrandslied (hil′dẹ-bränts-lēt). An Old High German poem in alliterative verse, of unknown authorship: the only extant example of old German heroic poetry.

Hilkiah (hil-kī′ạ). The high priest in the time of Josiah, who discovered the book of the law in the temple. 2 Kings, xxii. 8.

Hinayana (hē-nạ-yä′nạ). The Little Vehicle, the primitive form of Buddhism. See **Mahayana.**

Hind and the Panther, The. A satirical poem (1687) defending Roman Catholicism, by Dryden.

Hindle Wakes. A drama (1912) of the younger generation, by Stanley Houghton.

Hippocrates. See Dictionary, **Hippocratic.**

Hippocrene. See Dictionary.

Hippodamia (hip″ọ-dạ-mī′ạ). In Greek legend: (1) The daughter of Œnomaus, and wife of Pelops. (2) A daughter of Atrax, one of the Lapithæ: wife of Pirithous.

Hippolyta (hi-pol′i-tạ). The betrothed of Theseus in Shakspere's "Midsummer Night's Dream."

Hippolyte (hi-pol′i-tē). In Greek legend, a queen of the Amazons, slain by Heracles.

Hippolytus (hi-pol′i-tus). 1. In Greek legend, the son of Theseus by Hippolyte or Antiope. He was killed as the result of a false accusation by his stepmother Phædra, who was enamoured of him. 2. A tragedy (exhibited 428 B.C.) by Euripides. 3. A tragedy (also "Phædra") by Seneca.

Hiranyagarbha (hi-ran-yạ-gär′bhạ). In the Rig-Veda, a deity who arose in the beginning, the one lord of all beings: identified by Manu with Brahma.

His Family. A novel (1917) by Ernest Poole: Pulitzer Prize novel, 1918.

His House in Order. A drama (1906) by A. W. Pinero.

Historia Regum Britanniæ (his-tō′ri-ạ rē′gum bri-tan′i-ē). A work (in Latin) of mingled history and legend (finished 1147), by Geoffrey of Monmouth. It is the chief ultimate source of Arthurian and Round Table romances in England, France, Germany, and Italy.

History of the Worthies of England, The. See **Worthies of England, The History of the.**

Histriomastix (his″tri-ọ-mas′tiks). 1. A play (before 1599) by Marston. 2. A treatise (1632) designed to promote the total suppression of stage-plays, by Prynne.

Hitchiti (hich′i-tē). A division of North American Indians, whose language was spoken in Georgia and Florida.

Hitopadesha (hi-tō-pạ-dā′shạ). In Sanskrit literature, the book of "Good Counsel," an excellent compilation of ancient ethico-didactic material.

Hivites (hī′vīts). An ancient Canaanite people in northern Palestine. Ex. xxxiv. 11.

Hobson's Choice. See Dictionary.

Hochelaga (hō-shẹ-lä′gạ). An Iroquoian tribe or village of North American Indians, on the site of Montreal when it was discovered (1535). It had disappeared in 1603.

Hodge. See Dictionary.

Hœnir (hẹ′nir). In Old Norse mythology, one of the three gods who created the first man and woman: the giver of sense.

Hogarth (hō′gärth) **Club, The.** A London club (established 1870) for artists.

Hohenschwangau (hō″ẹn-shväng′ou). A medieval stronghold in Swabia, Bavaria, said to have been raised on Roman foundations: entirely rebuilt by Maximilian II.

Hohenstaufen (hō″ẹn-shtou′fẹn). A German princely family, founded in the 11th century, which ruled Germany 1138–1208 and 1215–1254, and Sicily 1194–1266.

Hohenzollern (hō″ẹn-tsol′ẽrn). A German princely family, founded about the 11th century, which ruled Brandenburg from 1415, Prussia from 1701, and the German Empire from 1871 to 1918.

Holda (hol′dä). The same as **Berchta.**

Holger Danske (hol′gẽr dän′skẹ). See **Ogier the Dane.**

Holland House. A mansion (built 1607) in Kensington, London, noted as a social center during the life of the third Lord Holland.

Holmes, Sherlock. A remarkable detective whose powers of ratiocination solve the most baffling mysteries, in many stories by Sir Arthur Conan Doyle.

Holo (hō′lō). A Bantu tribe of Angola, West Africa.

Holofernes (hol-ọ-fẽr′nēz). 1. A general of Nebuchadnezzar: killed by Judith. 2. A schoolmaster in Shakspere's "Love's Labour's Lost."

Holy Alliance, The. See Dictionary, **holy.**

Holy Grail, The. One of Tennyson's "Idylls of the King" (1869). Also, see Dictionary, **Grail.**

Holy Living and **Holy Dying.** Two tractates (1650, 1651) by Jeremy Taylor.

Holy Roman Empire. See Dictionary, **holy.**

Holyrood (hol′i-röd) **Palace.** A large ancient royal palace of Scotland, situated at Edinburgh.

Holy See. See Dictionary, **holy.**

Holy Sepulcher, The Church of the. See Dictionary, **Holy Sepulcher,** under **holy.**

Holy Week. See Dictionary, **holy.**

Holywell Street. A former London street parallel to the Strand: once a street of small book-shops.

Home Counties, The. Middlesex, Surrey, Kent, Essex, and Hertford, in England.

Homeric (hō-mer′ik) **Hymns.** A group of 34 Greek hexameter poems, anciently ascribed to Homer.

Home, Sweet Home. A favorite song, words by John Howard Payne, music probably by Sir Henry Bishop.

Homme Armé, L' (lom är-mā). A famous old French chanson.

Honest Man's Fortune, The. A play (1613) by Fletcher, Massinger, and others.

Honeycomb, Will. An elderly beau in the "Spectator" papers of Addison and Steele.

Honorable Peter Stirling, The. A novel (1894) by Paul Leicester Ford, based on the career of Grover Cleveland.

Hood, Robin. A traditional English outlaw of the 12th century, a popular hero in many ballads. He robbed the rich to give to the poor. One version identifies him with the outlawed Earl of Huntingdon. See also **Sheriff of Nottingham.**

Hoosac (hö′sạk) **Tunnel.** A railroad tunnel (opened 1875), 4¾ miles long, through the Hoosac Mountain, in western Massachusetts.

Hoosier Schoolmaster, The. A story (1871) by Edward Eggleston, about pioneer days in Indiana.

Hop o' My Thumb. A fairy-tale from the French of Perrault, about a diminutive hero who steals the seven-league boots of an ogre.

Horace (o-räs). A tragedy (1640) by Corneille.

Horæ. See Dictionary.

Horatia (hō-rā′shi-ạ) **gens.** A Roman patrician clan.

Horatii (hō-rā′shi-ī), **The Three.** In Roman legend, three brothers celebrated in the reign of Tullus Hostilius for their combat with the three Curiatii of Alba Longa.

Horatio. In Shakspere's "Hamlet," the loyal and sensible friend of Hamlet.

Horatius Cocles (hō-rā′shius kō′klēz). A Roman legendary hero, celebrated for the defense of the bridge over the Tiber against the Etruscans under Lars Porsena.

Horeb (hō′reb). See **Sinai.**

Hormakhu (hôr-mä′khö). In Egyptian mythology, the rising sun: one of the forms of Ra.

Hornberg (hôrn′berċh). The old castle of Götz von Berlichingen, on the Neckar.

Horse-Fair, The. A large painting (1853) by Rosa Bonheur, in the Metropolitan Museum of Art, New York.

Hortensia (hôr-ten′shi-ạ) **gens.** A Roman plebeian clan.

Hortensian (hôr-ten′shiạn) **Law, The.** In ancient Roman history, a law (about 286 B.C.) that the decrees of the Comitia Tributa should bind patricians as well as plebeians.

Horus (hō′rus), or **Hor** (hôr). In Egyptian mythology, a solar deity, the son of Osiris and Isis.

Horvendile. A character in James Branch Cabell's romances, especially prominent in "The Cream of the Jest."

Hosea (hō-zē′ạ). The first of the "minor prophets," author of the Old Testament book of prophecies bearing his name.

Hospitalers of St. John of Jerusalem, The Order of the. See Dictionary, **hospitaler.**

Hôtel de Cluny (ō-tel dė klü-nē). The mansion, in Paris, of the abbots of Cluny in Burgundy: built in the 15th and 16th centuries. It is now a museum of medieval and Renaissance objects of art.

Hôtel de Rambouillet (rän-bö-yā). A famous house in Paris, noted as the center of an exclusive literary circle in the 17th century.

Hôtel de Ville (vēl). A large building (begun 1533, burned 1871, and since rebuilt) in Paris, the headquarters of the municipal government.

Hottentots. See Dictionary, **Hottentot.**

Hougoumont (ö-gö-môṅ), or **Hougomont** (ö-go-môṅ). A tactically important château on the field of Waterloo, held by the right wing of the allies.

Hound of Heaven, The. A mystical poem (1893) by Francis Thompson.

Hounslow (hounz′lō) **Heath.** A heath formerly situated west of Hounslow: long notorious as a resort of highwaymen.

Hour Glass, The. A drama (1904) by W. B. Yeats.

House Boat on the Styx, A. A story (1895) by John Kendrick Bangs, giving a humorous account of the doings of great men and women in their life after death.

House in Demetrius Road, The. A novel (1914) by J. D. Beresford.

House-Mates. A novel (1917) by J. D. Beresford.

House of Fame, The. A poem by Chaucer.

House of Life, The. A series of sonnets (1881) by D. G. Rossetti.

House of Mirth, The. A novel (1905) by Edith Wharton, dealing with the difficulties of a parasite in society.

House of the Seven Gables, The. A romance (1851) of colonial days in Salem, by Hawthorne.

House of the Wolfings, The. A prose romance (1889) by William Morris.

House That Jack Built, The. An accumulative tale given in "Mother Goose's Nursery Rhymes."

Houyhnhnms. See Dictionary, **Houyhnhnm.**

Howard's End. A novel (1911) by E. M. Forster.

How He Lied to Her Husband. A farce (1904) by G. B. Shaw.

Hoxton (hoks′tọn). A district, noted for the number of its charitable institutions, in Shoreditch and Hackney, London.

Huancas (wän′käz). An ancient tribe of Peruvian Indians who inhabited a portion of the present department of Junín.

Huancavillcas (wän-kä-vēl′käz). A powerful tribe of Indians who formerly inhabited the lowlands of eastern Ecuador.

Huastecs (wäs′teks). A tribe of Indians near the coast of eastern Mexico.

Hudibras (hū′di-bras). A mock-heroic poem (1663–78) by Samuel Butler, satirizing the Puritans: named from its hero, a Presbyterian country justice.

Hudson's Bay Company, The. A British joint-stock company chartered 1670 to carry on the fur trade with the Indians of British North America. It still retains trading-posts.

Hugh of Lincoln. An English boy alleged to have been killed by Jews at Lincoln in 1255, whose body the earth miraculously refused to hide.

Hugh Wynne (win). A novel (1897) by S. Weir Mitchell.

Huguenots. See Dictionary, **Huguenot.**

Huguenots, Les (lä üg-nō). An opera (1836) by Meyerbeer.

Huitzilopochtli (wēt-zēl-ō-pōch′tlē). The war-god and principal deity of the Aztecs.

Hull House. A settlement-house at Chicago.

Humahuacas (ö-mä-wä′käz). A tribe of Indians who inhabited the eastern Andes.

Humphrey's (hum′friz) **Walk, Duke.** The middle aisle of old St. Paul's, London, where the tomb of Duke Humphrey was said to be.

Humphry Clinker, The Expedition of. A novel (1771) by Smollett.

Huncamunca (hung′kạ-mung′kạ). The sweet, gentle, amorous daughter of King Arthur, in Fielding's "Tom Thumb the Great."

Hundred Days, The. See Dictionary, **hundred.**

Hundred Years' War, The. See Dictionary, **hundred.**

Hungarian Insurrection, The. A rising (1848–49) in Hungary, under Kossuth, against the tyranny of Austria.

Hunkers. See Dictionary, **Hunker**[1].

Hunter, Mrs. Leo. In Dickens's "Pickwick Papers," a poetess, author of the immortal "Ode to an Expiring Frog."

Hunter's Moon, The. A novel (1925) by Ernest Poole: the story of an unhappy childhood.

Huntingdonians (hun-ting-dō′ni-ạnz). A denomination of Calvinistic Methodists in England and Wales.

Huon de Bordeaux (ü-ôṅ dė bôr-dō). An Old French chanson de geste of the thirteenth century. It contains the famous figure of Auberon, who appears in Spenser and Shakspere as Oberon.

Hupa or **Hoopah** (hö′pä). A tribe of the Pacific division of the Athapascan stock of North American Indians.

Husain. See **Hasan.**

Hutchinsonians (huch-in-sō′ni-ạnz). 1. Those who held, in theology and natural philosophy, the mystic views of

---

(variable) d̩ as d or j, s̩ as s or sh, t̩ as t or ch, z̩ as z or zh; o, F. cloche; ü, F. menu; ċh, Sc. loch; ṅ, F. bonbon; ′, primary accent; ″, secondary accent; †, obsolete; <, from; +, and; =, equals. See also lists at beginning of book.

John Hutchinson (1674–1737). 2. In American history, the followers of Mrs. Anne Hutchinson (d. 1643).

Hyacinthus (hī-a̯-sin′thus). In Greek mythology, a beautiful youth, typifying the vegetation of spring: killed through jealousy by Apollo.

Hyades (hī′a̯-dēz). In Greek mythology, a group of nymphs, sisters of the Pleiades. See also Dictionary.

Hybla (hī′blä). See Dictionary, **Hyblæan.**

Hydaspes (hī-das′pēz). The ancient name of the river Jhelum.

Hyde, Mr. See **Jekyll, Dr.**

Hyde Park. A park in Westminster, London, in which are fashionable drives and promenades. Large popular meetings are held in it.

Hydra. See Dictionary, **hydra.**

Hydriotaphia (hī″dri-ō̯-taf′i-a̯), or **Urn-Burial.** A work (1658) on the vanity of human life, by Sir Thomas Browne.

Hygeia. See Dictionary.

Hyksos (hik′sōs), or **Shepherd Kings.** A succession of foreign rulers of Egypt between the 13th and 18th dynasties, about 2000 B.C.

Hylas (hī′las). In classical mythology, a boy who was a favorite of Heracles. He was carried off by the Naiads.

Hymen. See Dictionary, **Hymen².**

Hymir (hē′mir). In Old Norse mythology, a water-demon, the giant of the winter sea.

Hypatia (hī-pā′shia̯). A historical novel (1853) by Charles Kingsley, based on the life and tragic death of Hypatia, the celebrated female philosopher of Alexandria.

Hyperboreans. See Dictionary, **Hyperborean.**

Hyperion (hī-pē′ri-on or hī-pēr-ī′on). 1. In Greek mythology, a Titan, a son of Uranus and Gæa: the father of Helios, Selene, and Eos. 2. An unfinished poem (1820) by Keats. 3. A romance (1839) by Longfellow.

Hypnos (hip′nos). In Greek mythology, the personification and god of sleep, a brother of Death (Thanatos) and son of Night.

Hyrcania. See Dictionary, **Hyrcanian.**

I

Iacchus (ī-ak′us). In Greek mythology, an Athenian divinity connected with the Eleusinian mysteries: son of Demeter and Zeus.

Iachimo (ī-ak′i-mō or yä′kē-mō). In Shakspere's "Cymbeline," an unscrupulous Roman courtier who slanders Imogen to win a wager.

Iago (ē-ä′gō). See **Othello.**

Iapetus (ī-ap′e-tus). In Greek mythology, a Titan, son of Uranus and Gæa, and father of Prometheus.

Ibo (ē′bō), or **Igbo** (ēg′bō). An important African tribe dwelling at the apex of the Niger delta.

Icaria (ī-kā′ri-a̯). An American coöperative community established (1848) in Texas: removed (1850) to Illinois, and thence (1857) to Iowa.

Icarus (ik′a̯-rus). See Dictionary, **Icarian.**

Icebound. A drama (1923) by Owen Davis, about a selfish New England family. Pulitzer Prize play, 1923.

Iceland Fisherman, An. A novel (1886) by Pierre Loti (Louis Marie Julien Viaud).

Iceni (ī-sē′nī). An ancient British tribe of eastern England, whose queen, Boadicea, headed the insurrection of A.D. 62 against the Romans.

Ichabod (ik′a̯-bod). 1. See Dictionary. 2. A poem (1850) by Whittier.

Iddhi (id′dhi). In Buddhist theology, the ascendancy over matter attained by the Buddhist in the fourth stage of moral perfection.

Ideal Husband, An. A social drama (1895) by Oscar Wilde.

Idiot, The. A novel (1868) by Fedor Dostoevski.

Idler, The. A series of essays (1758–60) by Samuel Johnson.

Idle Thoughts of an Idle Fellow. Sketches (1889) by Jerome K. Jerome.

Idomeneus (ī-dom′e-nūs). In Greek legend, a Cretan king and important chief of the Greek army in the Trojan War.

Idrisites (id′ri-sīts). An Arab dynasty founded in northwestern Africa about 785 by Idris, who claimed descent from Ali. It lasted until about 940.

Idun (ē′dön). In Old Norse mythology, the goddess who had in her custody, in Asgard, the apples eaten by the gods to preserve their youth.

Idylls of the King. A series of 12 poems (1859–85) by Tennyson, based on the Arthurian romances.

If Winter Comes. A novel (1922) by A. S. M. Hutchinson.

Igel (ē′gel) **Monument, The.** A Roman funeral tower of the late 3d century, near Treves, Prussia.

Igerna (i-gér′nä), or **Yguerne** (i-gérn′). In Arthurian legend, the wife of Gorlois, and the mother (by Uther) of Arthur.

Ignoramus (ig-nō̯-rā′mus). A famous academic comedy (1615) by George Ruggle.

Igor (ē′gor), **The Song of the Band of.** A Russian medieval epic, describing the struggle of Prince Igor and his army against pagan hordes from the southwest.

Igorot. See Dictionary.

I Have a Rendezvous with Death. War poem (1916) by Alan Seeger.

Île de la Cité (ēl dè lä sē-tā). An island in the Seine, the most ancient part of Paris, and the site of Notre Dame and of the Palais de Justice.

Île Saint-Louis (ēl sañ-lö-ē). An island in the Seine, at Paris, to the east of the Île de la Cité.

Ilia (il′i-a̯). See **Rhea Silvia.**

Iliad. See Dictionary.

Ilithyia (il-i-thī′yä). In Greek mythology, the goddess who presides over childbirth.

Illinois (il-i-noi′ or -noiz′). A confederacy of North American Indians which formerly occupied Illinois and adjoining regions westward. It was powerful before 1765.

Illyria (i-lir′i-a̯). See Dictionary, **Illyrian.**

Il Penseroso. See **Allegro, L'.**

Ilse (il′ze). In German lore, a princess who was changed into the river Ilse.

Ilus (ī′lus). In Greek legend, the son of Tros and mythical founder of Ilium.

Imaginary Conversations. Five volumes of conversations (1824–1829) between people of note, by Walter Savage Landor.

Imagists. A group of twentieth century poets, among whom Hilda Doolittle ("H. D."), F. S. Flint, and J. G. Fletcher are prominent.

Imhotep (ĕm-hō′tep). In Egyptian mythology, the god of knowledge, first-born of Ptah and Sekhmet.

Imitation of Christ, The. See **De Imitatione Christi.**

Imogen (im′ō̯-jen). In Shakspere's "Cymbeline," the daughter of Cymbeline and wife of Posthumus.

Imogene (im′ō̯-jen). See **Alonzo, 2.**

Imperial Guard, The. See **Old Guard, The, 1.**

Importance of Being Earnest, The. A drama (1899) by Oscar Wilde, with an extravagant plot and clever dialogue.

In a German Pension. Stories (1911) by Katherine Mansfield (Mrs. J. Middleton Murry).

Inca of Perusalem, The. A drama (1915) by G. B. Shaw.

Indian Emperor, or The Conquest of Mexico by the Spaniards, The. A play (1665) by Dryden: a sequel to "The Indian Queen."

Indian Mutiny. See Dictionary, **sepoy.**

Indian Summer. 1. See Dictionary, **Indian.** 2. A novel (1885) by W. D. Howells.

Indra (in′drä). The Vedic god who presides over the deities of the middle realm (the air).

Indulgence, Declarations of. In English history, royal proclamations (1671 or 1672, 1687) of greater liberty to nonconformists.

Infanta Maria Teresa, The. The flagship of Admiral Cervera in the Spanish-American war, sunk in the battle of Santiago, July 3, 1898.

Inferno, The. See Dictionary, **inferno.**

Inghamites (ing′am-īts). An 18th-century English denomination combining elements of Methodism and Moravianism: founded by Benjamin Ingham.

Ingoldsby (ing′goldz-bi) **Legends, The.** A series of humorous tales in verse and prose (1840–47) by Thomas Ingoldsby (Richard Harris Barham). The best known is probably "The Jackdaw of Rheims."

In Memoriam (in mē-mō′ri-am). A long elegiac poem

---

fat, fāte, fär, fåll, ȧsk, fãre; net, mē, hér; pin, pīne; not, nōte, möve, nôr; up, lūte, pull; oi, oil; ou, out; (lightened) aviȧry, ēlect, agȯny, intȯ, ūnite; (obscured) errȧnt, operä, ardent, actȯr, natūre; ch, chip; g, go; th, thin; ᴛʜ, then; y, you;

(1850) by Tennyson, on his friend Arthur Henry Hallam.

In Mizzoura. A drama (1916) by Augustus Thomas.

Inner Temple, The. See Dictionary, **inn.**

Innocent Adultery, The. See **Fatal Marriage, The.**

Innocents Abroad. A book of travels (1869) by Mark Twain (S. L. Clemens).

Inns of Chancery, The. In London, inns subordinate to the Inns of Court.

Inns of Court, The. See Dictionary, **inn.**

In Ole Virginia. A collection of short stories (1887) by Thomas Nelson Page, in negro dialect: "Marse Chan" is perhaps the best known.

Insatiate Countess, The. A tragedy (1610) attributed to Marston.

Inside of the Cup, The. A novel (1913) by Winston Churchill.

Instauratio Magna (in-stå-rā′shi-ō mag′nä). The comprehensive philosophical work partly completed by Bacon, of which his "Novum Organum" is the nucleus.

Institute of France, The. An association of the members of the five French academies, for the advancement of science, the publication of discoveries, etc.

Institutes of Justinian, The. See Dictionary, **institute.**

International, The. See Dictionary, **international.**

International African Association, The. An international commission for the exploration and civilization of central Africa, provided for at the Brussels conference of 1876.

In the Days of the Comet. A romance (1906) by H. G. Wells.

In the Shadow of the Glen. A drama (1903) by J. M. Synge.

Invalides, Hôtel des (ō-tel dā-zań-vȧ-lēd). A great establishment founded at Paris in 1670 for disabled and infirm soldiers.

Invictus (in-vik′tus). A poem (1888) by W. E. Henley: written 1875.

Invincible Armada, The. See Dictionary, **armada.**

Invisible Empire, The. See Dictionary, **invisible.**

Io (ī′ō). In Greek mythology, the daughter of Inachus of Argos, changed by jealous Hera into a white heifer.

Iolaus (ī-ō-lā′us). In Greek legend, the companion and charioteer of Heracles.

Iolcus (ī-ol′kus). The point of embarkation of the Argonauts, in Thessaly, on the site of the modern Volo.

Ion (ī′on). 1. In Greek mythology, the son, by Apollo, of Erechtheus's daughter Creusa: the eponymous ancestor of the Ionians. 2. A drama (about 424 B.C.) of Euripides.

Iowa (ī′ō-wä). A Tciwere tribe of North American Indians, some of whom survive in Kansas and Oklahoma.

Iphigenia (if″i-jē-nī′ȧ). In Greek legend, the daughter of Agamemnon and Clytemnestra. At Tauris, where she was a priestess of Artemis, she saved the life of her brother Orestes, and helped him to escape with the celebrated image of the goddess.

Iphigenia among the Tauri. A late play of Euripides.

Iphigenia at Aulis. A posthumous play of Euripides.

Iphigénie (ē-fē-zhā-nē). A tragedy (1674) by Racine.

Iphigenie auf Tauris (if-ē-gä′nē-ė ouf tou′ris). A psychological drama (1787) by Goethe.

Iphigénie en Aulide (ē-fē-zhā-nē oǹ ō-lēd). An opera (1774) by Gluck.

Iphigénie en Tauride (tō-rēd). An opera (1779) by Gluck.

Iquitos (ē-kē′tōz). An Indian tribe dwelling north of the upper Amazon, near the boundary between Peru and Ecuador.

Iraj (i-räj′). In the Shahnamah, son of Faridun by Arnivaz. He was slain by his half-brother Tur.

Irene (ī-rē′nē). A tragedy (1749) by Samuel Johnson.

Irène (ē-rän). A tragedy (1778) by Voltaire.

Irene Heron. An important character in "The Forsyte Saga," first married to Soames Forsyte and later to his cousin, Young Jolyon.

Iris (ī′ris). In Greek mythology, a messenger of the gods, regarded as the goddess of the rainbow.

Irminsul (ėr′min-söl). A Saxon idol cast down by Charlemagne near Eresburg (the modern Stadtberg) about 772.

Iron Cross, The. See Dictionary, **iron.**

Iron Gates, The. A celebrated defile in the Danube, at the confines of Serbia, Rumania, and the former Hungary.

Ironsides, Old. See **Constitution, The.**

Ironsides, The. The regiment led by Cromwell; later, his entire army.

Iron Woman, The. A novel (1911) by Margaret Deland.

Iroquoian (ir-ō-kwoi′an), **Iroquois** (-kwoi′). See Dictionary.

Irredentists. See Dictionary, **irredentist.**

Irus (ī′rus). In Homeric legend, a gigantic, voracious beggar who kept watch over Penelope's suitors.

Irvingites. See Dictionary, **Irvingite.**

Isaac (ī′zak). A patriarch, son of Abraham and Sarah. Gen. xvii. 19.

Isaac, The Sacrifice of. A painting by Rembrandt, in the Hermitage Museum, Leningrad.

Isaac the Jew, or **Isaac of York.** See **Rebecca.**

Isabel Archer. The heroine of Henry James's novel "The Portrait of a Lady."

Isabella. 1. A character in Ariosto's "Orlando Furioso." 2. The object of the base passion of Angelo in Shakspere's "Measure for Measure."

Isabella, or The Pot of Basil. A poem (1820) by John Keats.

Isabelle (ē-zȧ-bel). The young ward of Sganarelle in Molière's "École des maris."

Isaiah (ī-zā′yä or ī-zī′yä). See Dictionary, **Isaian.**

Isenbras (ī′zen-bras), or **Isumbras** (ī′zum-bras), **Sir.** A knight in medieval romance.

Isengrim (ī′zen-grim), **Sir.** The wolf in "Reynard the Fox."

Iseult (i-sölt′ or is′ölt). In Arthurian romance: (1) Daughter of Anguish, king of Ireland, and wife of Mark, king of Cornwall, loved by Tristram (Tristan). (2) Daughter of Hoel (Howell), king of Brittany, and wife of Tristram.

Isfendiyar (is-fen-di-yär′), or **Asfandiyar** (as-fan-di-yär′). A hero of the Shahnamah, son of King Gushtasp.

Ishbosheth (ish-bō′sheth). A son and successor of Saul. 2 Sam. ii. 8–32.

Ishmael, Ishmaelite. See Dictionary.

Ishtar. See Dictionary.

Isidorian Decretals (iz-i-dō′ri-an dē-krē′talz), **The.** A code of canons, foreign and native, promulgated in Spain in the 6th century, and later accepted throughout the Roman Catholic Church.

Isis. See Dictionary.

Islam. See Dictionary.

Island of the Great Mother, The. A satire on feminism (1925) by Gerhart Hauptmann.

Island Pharisees, The. A novel (1904) by John Galsworthy.

Islands of the Blessed or **Blest.** See Dictionary, **island.**

Isles, Lord of the. A title assumed at times from the 12th century to the 16th by Scottish chiefs in the islands west of Scotland. See also **Lord of the Isles, The.**

Israel. See Dictionary.

Israel in Egypt. An oratorio (1739) by Handel.

Israfil (iz′ra̤-fil or -fēl). In the Koran, the angel of music. Poe has a poem, "Israfel" (1831).

Issachar (is′a̤-kär). A patriarch, son of Jacob and Leah. Gen. xxx. 18. Also, one of the 12 tribes. Deut. xxvii. 12.

Isthmian Games. See Dictionary, **isthmian.**

Isthmian Sanctuary, The. A sanctuary on the Isthmus of Corinth, the seat of the Isthmian Games.

Italian, The. A mystery novel (1797) by Ann Radcliffe.

Italian War of 1859, The. A partly successful war of France and Sardinia against Austria, for the liberation and unification of Italy.

Ithamar (ith′a̤-mär). The youngest son of Aaron. Num. iii. 2.

Ithuriel (i-thö′ri-el). An angel in Milton's "Paradise Lost," sent by Gabriel to find out Satan.

Itineraries of Antoninus, The. Two official lists of the roads of the Roman Empire, with distances by land and sea.

It Is Never Too Late to Mend. A novel (1856) by Charles Reade.

It Never Can Happen Again. A novel (1909) by William De Morgan, commenting on the English Church ban on marriage with a deceased wife's sister.

Itys (ī′tis). In Greek legend, the son of Tereus and Procne.

Iulus. See **Ascanius.**

(variable) ḏ as d or j, s̩ as s or sh, t̩ as t or ch, z̩ as z or zh; o, F. cloche; ü, F. menu; ċh, Sc. loch; ń, F. bonbon; ′, primary accent; ″, secondary accent; †, obsolete; <, from; +, and; =, equals. See also lists at beginning of book.

Ivanhoe (ī'van-hō). A romance (1820) of the time of Richard I., by Scott. Its hero is Wilfred, Knight of Ivanhoe.

Ivan Ilyitch, The Death of. A story (1886) by Count Lev Tolstoy.

Ivan Ivanovitch. See Dictionary.

Ivory Gate, The. In classical mythology, the gate of Sleep through which false dreams come forth.

Ivory Tower, The. A novel (1917) by Henry James.

I. W. W. See Dictionary, **industrial.**

Ixion (ik-sī'on). In Greek legend, a king of the Lapithæ, father of Pirithous, and father (by a cloud which Zeus caused to take the form of Hera) of the Centaurs.

Izdubar (iz-dö-bär'). The principal hero of ancient Babylonian legends: a prototype of Nimrod.

J

Jabesh-Gilead (jā'besh-gil'ē-ad). An important town in Gilead, Palestine. Judges, xxi. 9.

Jabez (jā'bez). In 1 Chron. iv. 9, a man more honorable than his brethren.

J'accuse (zhä-küz). The first words of an open letter by Zola (1898), denouncing the persecutors of Dreyfus.

Jachin (jā'kin). 1. The fourth son of Simeon. Gen. xlvi. 10. 2. One of two columns (Jachin, Boaz) in the court of Solomon's temple. 1 Kings, vii. 21.

Jack and Jill. A nursery song of the mishap of two children sent for a pail of water.

Jack and the Bean-Stalk. A familiar nursery tale.

Jackdaw of Rheims (rēmz), **The.** See **Ingoldsby Legends, The.**

Jack Frost. See Dictionary.

Jack Horner. An old nursery rime of a hero who pulls a plum out of his Christmas pie.

Jack-in-the-Green. A puppet character of the English May Day games.

Jack Sheppard. 1. Defoe's account (1724) of the notorious criminal of that name. 2. A novel (1839) by Ainsworth on the same subject.

Jack Sprat. See Dictionary.

Jack the Giant-Killer. A nursery legend of the 12th century, translated into Latin by Geoffrey of Monmouth.

Jacob (jā'kob). The twin brother of Esau, and father of the 12 patriarchs. Gen. xxv. 24–34.

Jacob Faithful. A novel (1834) of seafaring life by Frederick Marryat.

Jacobins, Jacobites. See Dictionary, **Jacobin, Jacobite.**

Jacob's Staff. The group of three bright stars in a straight line in the Belt of Orion.

Jacob Stahl, The History of. A novel (1911) by J. D. Beresford, the first of a trilogy, the other novels being "A Candidate for Truth" (1912) and "The Invisible Event" (1915).

Jacob's Well. A well near Shechem, the scene of Jesus's conversation with a woman of Samaria. John, iv. 5–30.

Jacquerie. See Dictionary.

Jacques Bonhomme (zhäk bo-nom). A general name for the French peasant.

Jael (jā'el). The wife of Heber the Kenite, and slayer of Sisera. Judges, iv. 17–22.

Jagellons (yä-gel'onz). A dynasty which reigned in Poland 1386–1572. It was founded in 1386 by Jagello, grand duke of Lithuania, who reigned as Wladyslaw II. of Poland.

Jagersfontein (yä'gers-fon-tān) **Excelsior, The.** A diamond of 971 carats, found at Jagersfontein, South Africa, in 1893.

Jains, or **Jainas.** See Dictionary, **Jain, Jaina.**

James. In the New Testament: (1) An apostle, son of Zebedee and brother of the apostle John. Mat. iv. 21. (2) "James the Lord's brother," author of the Epistle of James. Gal. i. 19; Mark, iv. 3. (3) An apostle, "James the son of Alphæus." Mat. x. 3.

James IV. A historical play (about 1591) by Robert Greene.

James, The Army of the. A Federal army in the American Civil War. It operated (1864) in conjunction with the Army of the Potomac.

James, The General Epistle of. In the New Testament, an epistle by "James the Lord's brother," addressed from Jerusalem to the twelve tribes of the Dispersion.

James Morell. The husband of Candida in G. B. Shaw's play. See **Candida.**

Jameson Raid, The. An unsuccessful raid into the Transvaal in Dec., 1895, by about 600 men headed by Dr. Leander Starr Jameson. Its object was to obtain redress for alleged grievances of the Uitlanders.

James Wait. The negro in Conrad's "Nigger of the Narcissus."

Jamrud (jäm-röd'). A ruined fort at the entrance to the Khyber Pass, west of Peshawar.

Jamshid (jam-shēd'). In Firdausi, the wonder-working fourth king of the earliest (Pishdadian) dynasty.

Janaka (jan'a-kä). In Hindu legend: (1) A king of Mithila, of the solar race, "born without a progenitor." (2) King of Videha and father of Sita.

Jane Clegg. A drama (1911) by St. John Ervine.

Jane Eyre (âr). A novel (1847) by Charlotte Brontë, remarkable for its portrayal of romantic passion.

Janet's Repentance. One of George Eliot's "Scenes of Clerical Life."

Janice Meredith. A novel (1899) by Paul Leicester Ford.

Janiculum (ja-nik'ū-lum). A ridge on the right bank of the Tiber, in Rome, opposite the Capitoline and the Aventine.

Janitor's Boy, The. A poem (1924) which gives its name to a collection of poems by Nathalia Crane, written when the author was twelve.

Janizaries. See Dictionary, **janizary.**

Jannes (jan'ēz) and **Jambres** (jam'brēz). St. Paul's names for the magicians who withstood Moses at Pharaoh's court. 2 Tim. iii. 8.

Jansenists. See Dictionary, **Jansenist.**

Janus. See Dictionary.

Japhet (jā'fet), or **Japheth** (-feth). See Dictionary, **Japhetic.**

Jaques (jā'kwēz, or, as F., zhäk). A disillusioned and satiric observer of life, in Shakspere's "As You Like It." He is usually called "the melancholy Jaques."

Jarley (jär'li), **Mrs.** In Dickens's "Old Curiosity Shop," the proprietress of Jarley's waxworks. She befriends Little Nell.

Jarndyce (järn'dis), **John.** In Dickens's "Bleak House," the owner of Bleak House, and the benevolent guardian of Esther Summerson. He always explains his fits of ill temper by saying: "The wind is in the east."

Jarnsida (yärn'sē-dä). The first Norwegian law code promulgated in Iceland (1271).

Jarvie (jär'vi), **Bailie Nicol.** A Glasgow magistrate in Scott's "Rob Roy."

Jasher (jā'shėr), **The Book of.** A lost book of Hebrew national songs, quoted in Josh. x. 13 and 2 Sam. i. 18.

Jason (jā'son). In Greek legend, the leader of the Argonautic expedition. He was the son of Æson and Polymede, and the husband of Medea.

Jataka (jä'ta-kä). In Buddhist lore, a former birth of Sakyamuni; also, a narrative regarding it. The Jataka narratives include many fables and parables of wide popular diffusion.

Jats (jäts). A people of northwestern India, now mainly agriculturists. In early times they offered vigorous resistance to the Moslem invaders of India.

Java Head. A novel (1919) by Joseph Hergesheimer.

Javan (jā'van). A son of Japhet and ancestor of Elisha. Gen. x. 2.

Javert (zhá-vär'). In Victor Hugo's "Les Misérables," a crafty and inexorable police officer.

Jayadratha (ja-yad'rat-hä). In Hindu mythology, a prince of the lunar race, king of Sindhu.

Jay's Treaty. A treaty (1794) between Great Britain and the United States. It provided for British surrender of the northwestern military posts, settled the eastern boundary, and arranged for the payment of American claims, etc.

Jean-Christophe (zhän-krès-tof). The title character of Romain Rolland's novel in three parts (1904–1912).

Jeanne d'Arc (zhän därk). 1. An opera (1873) by Gounod. 2. A drama (1906) by Percy Mackaye.

Jebusites (jeb'ū-zīts). A Canaanitish nation from which David captured Mount Zion. 2 Sam. v. 6–9.

---

fat, fāte, fär, fȧll, àsk, fâre; net, mē, hėr; pin, pīne; not, nōte, mŏve, nôr; up, lūte, pull; oi, oil; ou, out; (lightened) aviąry, ęlect, agǫny, intǫ, ūnite; (obscured) errant, operą, ardent, actǫr, natūre; ch, chip; g, go; th, thin; ᴛʜ, then; y, you;

Jehoahaz (jē-hō′a̱-haz). A king of Israel, son of Jehu. 2 Kings, xiii. 1–9.

Jehoiachin (jē-hoi′a̱-kin). A king of Judah, carried into captivity by Nebuchadnezzar. 2 Chron. xxxvi. 8–10.

Jehoiada (jē-hoi′a̱-dạ). A high priest of Judah, who brought up the prince Joash in the temple. 2 Kings, xi. 4, etc.

Jehoiakim (jē-hoi′a̱-kim). A king of Judah, son of Josiah. 2 Kings, xxiii. 34–37.

Jehoram (jē-hō′ram). 1. A king of Israel, son of Ahab: also **Joram** (jō′ram). 2 Kings, iii, 1. 2. A king of Judah, son of Jehoshaphat. 2 Kings, viii. 16.

Jehoshaphat (jē-hosh′a̱-fat). A king of Judah, son of Asa. 2 Chron. xvii., etc.

Jehu (jē′hū). 1. Son of Hanani: a prophet of Judah under Jehoshaphat. 2 Chron. xix. 2. 2. The first of a new dynasty in Israel. 2 Kings, ix., x. 3. See Dictionary.

Jekyll (jē′kil), **Dr.** A physician who, by a miraculous drug, can transform himself into a vicious being known as Mr. Hyde, in R. L. Stevenson's "Dr. Jekyll and Mr. Hyde."

Jellyby (jel′i-bi), **Mrs.** In Dickens's "Bleak House," a woman so absorbed in missionary enterprises that she has no time for her household.

Jemez (hā′māz). A linguistic stock of North American Indians, occupying a tract on the Jemez River, New Mexico.

Jenkinson, Ephraim. A venerable-looking swindler in Goldsmith's "Vicar of Wakefield."

Jenkinson, Mrs. Mountstuart. In Meredith's "Egoist," an epigrammatic lady who says always "the remembered if not the right thing."

Jenkins's Ear, The War of. A popular name for the war begun in 1739 between Great Britain and Spain. Its immediate cause was the alleged torture by the Spaniards of a British sailor, Robert Jenkins.

Jennie Gerhardt. A realistic novel (1911) by Theodore Dreiser.

Jenny Wren. See **Cleaver, Fanny.**

Jephthah (jef′thä). 1. A judge of Israel. Judges, xi.–xiv. 2. An oratorio (1751) by Handel.

Jeremiah (jer-ē-mī′ạ). The second of the major prophets of Israel. His history is given in the Old Testament book which bears his name.

Jeremy. The story (1919) of a small boy, from the boy's point of view, by Hugh Walpole. "Jeremy and Hamlet" (1923) is a sequel.

Jericho (jer′i-kō). A city of the Canaanites, taken by the Israelites under Joshua. Josh. v., vi. See Dictionary.

Jeroboam (jer-ọ-bō′am). 1. A king of Israel, and leader of the northern tribes against Rehoboam. 1 Kings, xi.–xiv. 2. The most prosperous of the kings of Israel: son of Joash. 2 Kings, xiv.

Jerome in the Wilderness. A painting by Titian, in the Brera, Milan.

Jerusalem (jē-rö′sa̱-lem), **The Council of.** A council of the apostles, elders, and brethren, which dealt with the recognition, etc., of Gentile Christians. Acts, xv. 23, etc.

Jerusalem, The Kingdom of. A Christian kingdom in Syria, 1100–87, largely under French influence.

Jerusalem Chamber, The. A room in Westminster Abbey in which hung tapestries bearing scenes of the history of Jerusalem.

Jerusalem Delivered. See **Gerusalemme Liberata.**

Jessamy Bride, The. 1. A name given by Oliver Goldsmith to Mary Horneck. 2. A novel (1897) by F. Frankfort Moore.

Jesse (jes′ẹ). The father of David of Israel. 1 Sam. xvi.

Jessica (jes′i-ka̱). Shylock's daughter in Shakspere's "Merchant of Venice." She elopes with Lorenzo, taking her father's jewels and money.

Jesuits. See Dictionary, **Jesuit.**

Jesus College. 1. A college of Cambridge University, founded 1496 on the site of a Benedictine monastery. 2. A college of Oxford University, founded 1571 by Queen Elizabeth.

Jesus Disputing with the Doctors. A painting by Paolo Veronese, in the Royal Museum, Madrid.

Jethro (jeth′rō). The Midianite father of Zipporah. Ex. xviii.

Jeu de Paume (zhė dė pōm), **The Hall of the.** A building

at Versailles, in which the representatives of the Third Estate met June 20, 1789.

Jeunesse Dorée (zhė-nes dọ-rā). A band of young Frenchmen who formed an anti-Jacobite faction in 1794.

Jewels of the Madonna. An opera (1911) by Wolf-Ferrari.

Jew of Malta, The. A tragedy (written about 1588) by Marlowe. The title character, Barabas, represents the Jew's reciprocal hatred of his persecutors.

Jezebel. See Dictionary.

Jicarilla (hē-kä-rēl′yä). An Athapascan tribe of North American Indians, skilled in basketry. Their present abode is in northern New Mexico.

Jim Bludso. Hero of the poem "Jim Bludso of the Prairie Belle" (1871) by John Hay: one of the "Pike County Ballads."

Jim Crow. See Dictionary.

Jingle, Alfred, or **Charles Fitz Marshall.** In Dickens's "Pickwick Papers," an itinerant swindler and glib sponge. He speaks in head-lines, with the verbs left mostly to the imagination.

Jo. A little London waif in Dickens's "Bleak House."

Joab (jō′ab). The commander of King David's army, and slayer of Abner and of Absalom. 2 Sam. ii., iii., etc.

Joachimites (jō′a̱-kim-īts). The adherents of an Italian mystic, Joachim (d. about 1200), who divided history into the reigns of the Father (to the birth of Christ), the Son (to 1260), and the Holy Spirit (from 1260 onward).

Joan (jōn). A mythical female pope of about 855–58.

Joan and Peter. A novel (1918) by H. G. Wells, dealing with the faults of the English educational system.

Joannites (jō-an′īts). The adherents of John Chrysostom after his deposition (404) from the patriarchate of Constantinople.

Joan of Arc. A painting by Bastien-Lepage, in the Metropolitan Museum, New York.

Joash (jō′ash). 1. A king of Israel, who plundered the temple. 2 Kings, xiii. 9–25. 2. A king of Judah, son of Ahaziah. 2 Kings, xi., xii.

Job (jōb). The much-afflicted hero of the Old Testament book of poetry and philosophy bearing his name.

Job's Coffin. A group of stars in the constellation Delphinus.

Job's Comforter. See Dictionary.

Jocaste (jō-kas′tē), or **Epicaste** (ep-i-kas′tē). In Greek legend, the wife of Laius, and the mother, and later the wife, of Œdipus.

Joe. In Dickens's "Pickwick Papers," a plump youth who divides his energy impartially between eating and sleeping.

Joel (jō′el). The second of the minor prophets of Israel, and author of the Old Testament book bearing his name.

Joe Miller. See Dictionary.

John, Don. In Shakspere's "Much Ado about Nothing," the bastard brother of Don Pedro of Arragon.

John, The Gospel of. The fourth gospel, attributed to John, "the disciple whom Jesus loved."

John Barleycorn. See Dictionary, **barleycorn.**

John Bull. See Dictionary, **John.**

John Bull, The History of. A satire (1712) by Arbuthnot: originally entitled "Law Is a Bottomless Pit."

John Bull's Other Island. A drama (1904) by G. B. Shaw.

John Company. See Dictionary, **John.**

John Dory. A ballad frequently referred to in the 16th and 17th centuries.

John Ferguson. A drama (1915) by St. John Ervine.

John Gabriel Björkman (byėrk′män). A drama (1897) by Henrik Ibsen.

John Gilpin (gil′pin). A humorous ballad (1782, 1785) by Cowper, about a staid citizen whose horse runs away with him.

John Halifax, Gentleman. A novel (1857) by Dinah Maria Mulock.

John Inglesant. A romance (1881) by J. H. Shorthouse.

John (the Baptist) **in the Desert, St.** 1. A painting by Titian, in the Accademia, Venice. 2. A painting by Raphael, in the Uffizi, Florence.

John the Baptist. 1. The forerunner of Jesus. Mat. iii. 2. A drama (1898) by Hermann Sudermann.

John the Baptist, The Life of. 7 frescoes (1490) by Ghirlandaio, in Santa Maria Novella, Florence.

Jolyon. A name borne by three members of the Forsyte family: the grandfather, Old Jolyon; the father, Young Jolyon or Jo (the artist); and the son, called Jon. See **Forsyte Saga, The.**

Jonah. See Dictionary.

Jonathan (jon′a-than). A son of Saul, and bosom friend of David. 1 Sam. xiii., etc.

Jonathan, Brother. See Dictionary, **brother.**

Jonathan Wild the Great, The History of. A story (1743) by Fielding. It is at once a picaresque novel and a satire on the means by which human "greatness" may be achieved.

Jones, Tom. In Fielding's "Tom Jones," an impulsive and manly but easy-going youth. It transpires that he is the (illegitimate) nephew of his foster-father, Allworthy, whose heir he becomes. He marries Sophia Western.

Jongleur de Notre Dame. An opera (1902) by Massenet.

Jörd (yérd). In Old Norse mythology, the goddess Earth, wife of Odin and mother of Thor.

Jörn Uhl (yérn öl). A novel (1901) by Gustav Frenssen.

Joseph (jō′zẹf). 1. A son of Jacob and Rachel, sold by his brethren into Egypt. Gen. xxx. 22–24, xxxvii. 1. 2. The husband of Mary, the mother of Jesus. Mat. i. 16–25.

Joseph Andrews. A novel (1742) by Fielding, started as a burlesque of Richardson's "Pamela."

Joseph of Arimathea (ar″i-ma-thē′ạ). A rich Israelite who secretly believed in Jesus Christ. Mat. xxvii. 57–60.

Joseph Vance. A novel (1906) by William De Morgan.

Joshua (josh′ū-ạ). The successor of Moses as leader of the Israelites. Ex. xvii. 9–14; Book of Joshua.

Josiah (jō-sī′ạ). A king of Judah, son of Amon: slain at the battle of Megiddo. 2 Kings, xxii., etc.

Jotapata (jō-ta-pā′tạ). An ancient fortress in Galilee, on what is now Tel Jefât. Starved into surrender in the Judeo-Roman war, its garrison committed suicide.

Jotham (jō′tham). A king of Judah. 2 Kings, xv. 32–38.

Jötunheim (yé′tön-hām). In Old Norse mythology, the outer world, or realm of giants; Utgard.

Jourdain (zhör-daṅ), **Monsieur.** In Molière's "Bourgeois Gentilhomme," a plain citizen eager for self-cultivation, and astounded to discover that he has talked in prose all his life.

Journal of a Voyage to Lisbon, A. A record kept by Henry Fielding on a voyage which he took in a vain effort to recover his health: published 1755.

Journal to Stella. A private personal record kept by Swift for Esther Johnson (Stella), 1710–13.

Jove. See Dictionary.

Joyeuse (zhwo-yéz). The sword of Charlemagne.

Joyeuse Garde (gärd), or **Garde Joyeuse.** In medieval romance, the castle of Lancelot of the Lake.

Joy of Living, The. A drama (1902) by Hermann Sudermann.

Jubal (jō′bạl). Son of Lamech by Adah, and the inventor of musical instruments. Gen. iv. 21.

Judah (jō′dạ). The fourth son of Jacob and Leah. Gen. xxix. 35, etc. Also, the powerful tribe of his descendants. Num. i. 26.

Judas Iscariot. See Dictionary, **Judas.**

Judas Maccabæus (jō′das mak-a-bē′us). An oratorio (1747) by Handel.

Jude (jöd) or **Judas, Saint.** One of the 12 apostles, probably identical with Thaddæus and Lebbæus. Mat. x. 3.

Jude, The Epistle of. A short book of the New Testament, written by a "brother of James" (and possibly of Jesus).

Jude the Obscure. A tragic novel (1896) by Thomas Hardy.

Judge, The. A novel (1922) by Rebecca West (Cecily Fairfield).

Judges, The Book of. A book of the Old Testament, containing the history of Israel under the leaders ("judges") from Deborah and Barak to Samuel.

Judging of Jurgen, The. See **Jurgen.**

Judgment of Paris, The. 1. A painting by Rubens, in the museum at Dresden. 2. A painting by Rubens, in the National Gallery, London.

Judith (jö′dith). An Old English poem, probably of the 10th century, based on the Bible story of Judith.

Judith, The Book of. An apocryphal book of the Old Testament. Judith, a native of Bethulia, delivers her people by entering the camp of Holofernes and slaying him in his sleep.

Judy (jö′di). See Dictionary, **Punch**[2].

Juggernaut. See Dictionary.

Juif Errant, Le (lè zhwēf e-räṅ). 1. A romance (1844–45) by Eugène Sue. 2. An opera (1852) by Halévy.

Julia (jöl′yạ). 1. A girl loved by Proteus in Shakspere's "Two Gentlemen of Verona." 2. The object of Falkland's unreasoning jealousy in Sheridan's "Rivals."

Julia gens. A celebrated patrician house of ancient Rome, whose eponymous ancestor was Iulus, the son or grandson of Æneas.

Julian, Count. In Spanish legend, a governor of Andalusia in the 8th century. His daughter Florinda being seduced by Roderic, he betrayed Ceuta to the Moors in revenge.

Julianists (jöl′yạn-ists). Adherents of Julian, bishop of Halicarnassus in the early 6th century. They were Monophysites who held the body of Christ to be incorruptible.

Juliet (jö′li-et). The heroine of Shakspere's "Romeo and Juliet." She is a daughter of Capulet, and loves Romeo, of the implacably hostile house of Montagu.

Julius Cæsar (jöl′yus sē′zạr). A historical tragedy (about 1600) by Shakspere.

Julius Le Vallon. A novel (1916) by Algernon Blackwood, dealing with reincarnation.

July Revolution, The. A revolution which overthrew the (French) government of Charles X. and established that of Louis Philippe, in July, 1830.

Jumala (yö′mä-lä). In Finnish mythology, the highest god: a divinity of the air, and protector of flocks. The word also means godhead in general.

Jumanas (zhö-mä-näz′). A race of Indians in northwestern Brazil.

Jumping Frog of Calaveras County, The. A story (1865) by Mark Twain.

Jungle, The. A novel (1906) by Upton Sinclair, presenting the life of workers in the Chicago packing industry.

Jungle Book, The. A collection (1894) of stories by Rudyard Kipling, dealing with animal life in the jungles of India: followed (1895) by "The Second Jungle Book."

Junius (jö′nyus). The pen-name of the unknown author of letters (1768–72) against the British ministry, printed in the London "Public Advertiser": possibly Sir Philip Francis.

Junkers. See Dictionary, **junker.**

Juno. See Dictionary.

Junto (jun′tō). A group of English Whigs, influential under William III. and Anne.

Jupiter. See Dictionary.

Jupiter Ammon (am′ọn) or **Amun** (ä′mön). Jupiter as identified with the Egyptian Amun.

Jupiter of Otricoli (ō-trē′kō-lē), **The.** A marble mask restored as a bust: the finest surviving antique head of Zeus.

Jupiter Stator (stā′tôr). Jupiter the stayer-of-flight, or giver of victory.

Jurgen (jér′gen). A romance (1919) by James Branch Cabell: followed by "The Judging of Jurgen" (1920).

Juris (zhö-rēz′). A formerly powerful Indian tribe of the Brazilian state of Amazonas.

Justice. A drama (1910) by John Galsworthy, attacking the English system of criminal law.

Justinian Code. See Dictionary, **code.**

Just So Stories. Stories (1902) by Rudyard Kipling, dealing with animal life.

Jutes. See Dictionary, **Jute**[2].

Juventas (jö-ven′tas). In Roman mythology, the goddess of youth; Hebe.

Jyotisha (jyō′ti-shạ). The Vedic calendar, a short tract containing the knowledge required for fixing the days and hours of the Vedic sacrifices.

K

Ka (kä). In Hindu theology, the inexplicable, the unknown. It is applied as a name to any chief god or object of worship.

Kaaba. See Dictionary.

Kabandha (ka-band′hạ). In the Ramayana, a monstrous Rakshasa slain by Rama.

Kabbala, or **Cabala.** See Dictionary, **cabala.**

Kabirpanthis (ka̤-bĕr-punt'hēz). The influential sect which adheres to the doctrines of Kabir, the Hindu religious reformer.

Kabyles. See Dictionary, **Kabyle.**

Kaddish. See Dictionary.

Kadesh Barnea (kā'desh bär'nē̤-ā̤). 1. The headquarters of the Israelites in their desert wanderings, on the southern boundary of the East Jordan territory. Num. xiii. 26. 2. The capital of the Hittites, on the Orontes near Tel Nebi Mende.

Kado Hadacho (kä'dō hä-dä'chō), or **Caddoques.** The leading tribe of the Caddo Confederacy of North American Indians.

Kaf (käf). In Oriental legend, a range of hills girdling the earth: the abode of the jinns.

Kafir, or **Kaffir.** See Dictionary.

Kahoda (ka̤-hō'dä̤). A learned Brahman, father of Ashtavakra.

Kai (kī), pl. **Kayan** (ka̤-yän'). A Persian word meaning 'king,' prefixed to the names of the old Iranian kings Kawus, Khusrau, Qubad, and Luhrasp (also, by some, to Gayumart or Kayumarth).

Kaiyuh-khotana (kī'yö-chō-tä'na̤). A northern Athapascan tribe of North American Indians, dwelling in the interior of Alaska. They are fishermen and traders.

Kaku (kä-kö'), or **Kakui** (kä-kö-ē'). In the Shahnamah, a grandson of Zohak, who fought with Salm and Tur against Faridun, and was slain by Minuchihr in single combat.

Kalah Shergat (kä'lä sher-gät'). The ruins of ancient Assur, 50 miles south of Mosul.

Kalanemi (kä-la̤-nä'mē). In Hindu mythology, in the Ramayana, a Rakshasa, uncle of Ravana.

Kalanos (kal'a̤-nos), or **Calanus** (cal'a̤-nus). A Brahman prophet, said to have burned himself alive before the death of Alexander the Great, which he had predicted.

Kalapooian (kal-a̤-pö'ya̤n). A linguistic stock of North American Indians, formerly numerous in Oregon.

Kalayavana (kä-la̤-ya'va̤-na̤). In Hindu mythology, a foreign king who led a force of barbarians against Krishna. The god lured him into the cave of Muchukunda, by whose glance he was consumed.

Kalevala (kä'lä-vä''lä). The national epic of Finland. Longfellow used its form and meter in "Hiawatha."

Kali (kä'lē). In Hindu mythology, the bloody consort of Siva: formerly worshiped with human sacrifices. She is also known as Durga.

Kalikapurana (kä''lē̤-kä-pö-rä'na̤). A secondary purana of 9,000 stanzas, urging the worship of Kali.

Kalilag (ka-lē''lag) **and Damnag** (dam'nag). The Syriac version of "The Fables of Bidpai" (see **Bidpai**). It is named from the two jackals that figure in the introduction.

Kalilah (ka-lē'lä) **and Dimnah** (dim'nä). The Arabic version of "The Fables of Bidpai" (see **Bidpai**). Cf. **Kalilag and Damnag.**

Kaliya (kä'li-yä). In Hindu mythology, a five-headed serpent-king dwelling in the Yamuna (Jumna).

Kaliyuga (ka-li-yö'gä). The Sanskrit name of the last and worst of the four yugas or ages: the iron age, conceived as lasting 432,000 years (from 3102 B.C.).

Kalki (kal'kē). In Hindu mythology, the name of the 10th and last incarnation of Vishnu, at the end of the Kaliyuga.

Kalmashapada (kal-mä-sha̤-pä'dä̤). In Hindu mythology, a king of the solar race, son of Sudasa. In the Mahabharata he is a cannibal for 12 years.

Kalmucks. See Dictionary, **Kalmuck.**

Kalpa (kal'pä). In Hindu mythology, a day of Brahma: 1,000 yugas, or 432,000,000 years.

Kalpasutras (kal-pa̤-sö'träz). The Vedic works descriptive of the ceremonial prescribed for Vedic sacrifices, expressed in brief rules (sutras).

Kama (kä'mä). The Hindu god of love: husband of Rati ('pleasure') or Priti ('affection'), and father of Trisha ('desire') and Aniruddha ('the unrestrained').

Kamadhenu (kä-ma̤-dhä'nö). In Hindu mythology, the fabulous cow that gratifies all wishes.

Kamba (käm'bä), or **Wakamba** (wä-). An African tribe of British East Africa, dwelling north of Mount Kilimanjaro.

Kanakas. See Dictionary, **Kanaka.**

Kandu (kan'dö). In Hindu mythology, a sage beguiled by the nymph Pramlocha, sent by Indra. He lived with her for several hundred years, and was the father by her of Marisha.

Kansa. 1. (kan'sä) In Hindu mythology, a second cousin of Krishna: king of Mathura. 2. (kan'sä), or **Kaw.** A Siouan tribe of North American Indians, which gave its name to Kansas. A few survive in Oklahoma.

Kansas-Nebraska Bill, The. An act of Congress (1854) providing for organization of the Territories of Kansas and Nebraska.

Kanuri (kä'nṳ-ri). A Nigritic nation of the central Sudan, west of Lake Chad.

Kapila (kap'i-lä). The reputed founder of the Sankhya system of Hindu philosophy.

Karageorgevich (kä-ra̤-jôr'je̤-vich). The Serbian dynasty founded by Karageorge ("Black George"), b. about 1766.

Karaites (kä'rä̤-īts). A Jewish sect which rejects the traditional law fixed by the Talmud, and recognizes only the Pentateuch as binding.

Karen (kä-ren'). A partly Christianized native race of Burma and Siam.

Karlings (kär'lingz). The Carolingians.

Karlstein (kärl'shtīn). A castle southwest of Prague, built 1348-57 by Charles IV. for safe-keeping of the Bohemian crown jewels.

Karmathians (kär-mä'thi-a̤nz). A Mohammedan sect which arose in Turkey late in the 9th century, led by Karmat, a poor laborer. They were communistic, and rejected all revelation.

Karna (kär'na̤). In Hindu mythology, son of Pritha or Kunti by Surya ('the sun') before her marriage to Pandu: the unknown half-brother of the Pandavas.

Karshvan (kärsh'vän). In the Avesta, each of the seven divisions of the world.

Kartavirya (kär-ta̤-vēr'yä). A hero of Hindu mythology, in the Vishnupurana.

Karttikeya (kär-ti-kā'yä). In Hindu mythology, the god of war: also called Skanda.

Kashyapa (kash'ya̤-pä). A sage to whom are ascribed some Vedic hymns; in later mythology, husband of Aditi and of 12 other daughters of Daksha, and father by them of gods, demons, men, and all animals.

Kataba (ka̤-tä'bä), or **Catawba** (ka̤-tâ'bä). A division of North American Indians, which once included 28 federated tribes, mainly in South Carolina.

Katakana (kä-ta̤-kä'na̤). One of the two styles of writing the Japanese syllabary of 48 letters (the other being Hiragana).

Katha (kat'hä). 1. A Hindu sage, founder of a school of the Yajur-Veda. 2. The best known of the Upanishads.

Katharine, or **Katharina.** The shrew in Shakspere's "Taming of the Shrew." She is eventually tamed by the rough treatment of her husband, Petruchio.

Katharnava (kat-här'na̤-vä). A collection, in Sanskrit, of about 35 comparatively modern stories, attributed to Shivadasa.

Kathasaritsagara (kat-hä''sa̤-rit-sä'ga̤-rä). An 11th-century collection of stories in Sanskrit, made by Somadeva of Kashmir from a larger work, the Brihatkatha.

Katipunan (kä''tē̤-pö-nän'). A Filipino secret society, headed by Andres Bonifacio, leader of the rebellion against Spain in 1896. The banner of this organization is now the Filipino flag.

Kaumodaki (kou-mō'da̤-kē). The bludgeon used by Krishna against Indra. It was given him by Varuna.

Kautsa (kout'sä). A rationalistic Hindu philosopher who rejected the Veda and the Brahmanas. Yaska, the author of the Nirukta, replied to him.

Kavi (kä'vē). The ancient sacred language of Java.

Kaviraja (ka-vi-rä'jä). The author of the important Sanskrit poem Raghavapandaviya, a 10th-century blending of the material of both the Ramayana and the Mahabharata.

Kavyani (kä-vyä-nē'). In Persian mythology, the standard of Kawah, a leathern apron reared on a spear.

Kaw. See **Kansa,** 2.

Kawah (kä-wä'). In Persian mythology, the blacksmith

(variable) d̤ as d or j, s̤ as s or sh, t̤ as t or ch, z̤ as z or zh; o, F. cloche; ü, F. menu; c̱h, Sc. loch; ṅ, F. bonbon; ', primary accent; '', secondary accent; †, obsolete; <, from; +, and; =, equals. See also lists at beginning of book.

who, when his sons were slain to feed the serpents of Dahak, summoned Faridun to make war on Dahak.

Kay, Sir. In Arthurian romance, the foster-brother and seneschal of Arthur: called "the Rude" and "the Boastful."

Kayanian (ka̤-yä′ni-a̤n). The collective name of several Iranian kings to whose names "Kai" is prefixed.

Kayanush (kä-yä-nush′). In the Shahnamah, a brother of Faridun. With another brother, Purmayah, he enviously tries to destroy Faridun.

Kearsarge (kēr′särj), **The.** A corvette which, commanded by Captain John A. Winslow, defeated the Confederate cruiser Alabama off Cherbourg in 1864. She was wrecked in the Caribbean in 1894.

Keble (kē′bl) **College.** A college of Oxford University, founded as a memorial to John Keble: incorporated 1870.

Kedar (kē′där). A son of Ishmael, and ancestor of the Kedarenes, one of the most important tribes of the ancient Arabs. Gen. xxv. 13.

Kedron (kē′dron), or **Kidron** (kid′ron). A brook to the north and east of Jerusalem, emptying into the Dead Sea. 2 Sam. xv. 23.

Kelati Nadiri (ke-lä′tē nä-dē′rē). A strong fortress in Khorasan, Persia, near the Russian frontier.

Kele (ke-lā′), or **Bakele** (bä-). An African tribe of French Equatorial Africa.

Kenai. See **K'naia-khotana.**

Kenilworth. A historical romance (1821) of the reign of Elizabeth, by Scott. See **Robsart, Amy.**

Kenites (kē′nīts). In Bible history, a nomadic Midianitish people dwelling in the Sinaitic peninsula: later probably absorbed in the Israelites.

Kennicott, Carol. The heroine of Sinclair Lewis's "Main Street."

Kensal (ken′sa̤l) **Green.** A cemetery in the northwest of London.

Kensington (ken′zing-ton). A borough of London, west-southwest of St. Paul's, containing Kensington Gardens and Palace, and also Holland House.

Kentons, The. A novel (1907) by W. D. Howells.

Kent's Cavern. A cave near Torquay, Devonshire, noted for its paleolithic flint tools and animal remains.

Kentucky Cardinal, A. A story (1895) by James Lane Allen.

Kentucky Resolutions, The. Nine resolutions, prepared by Thomas Jefferson and passed 1798 by the Kentucky legislature, nullifying the "alien and sedition laws."

Keresan (ke-rē′sa̤n). A linguistic stock of North American Indians, occupying parts of New Mexico in the Rio Grande and tributary valleys.

Keresaspa (ke-re-säs′pä). In the Avesta, a hero of the race of Sama, slayer of the dragon Srvara.

Kern-baby (kèrn′bā-bi), or **Kernababy** (kèr′na̤-bā-bi). A harvest folk-festival of northern England and Scotland. The last gleanings of the fields were made into an image of the harvest goddess and burned.

Kew Observatory. The central meteorological observatory of Great Britain, built 1769 by George III.

Khafra (kaf′ra̤). An Egyptian king of the 4th dynasty, builder of the second of the great pyramids of Gizeh.

Khem (kem). In Egyptian mythology, one of the eight great gods, embodying the generative principle.

Khoikhoin (koi-koin′). The native name of the Hottentots.

Khufu (kö′fö). An Egyptian king of the 4th dynasty, builder of the great pyramid at Gizeh.

Khumbaba (kûm-bä′bä), or **Chumbaba,** or **Humbaba.** In the Nimrod epic, the last Elamitic ruler of Babylonia in Erech: slain by Izdubar and Ea-bani.

Khuns (köns), or **Khonsu** (kon′sö). In Egyptian mythology, the son of Amun-Ra and Mut, with whom he forms the Theban triad.

Kickapoo (kik′a̤-pö). An Algonquian tribe of North American Indians, prominent in the history of the Ohio valley to the end of the War of 1812.

Kidnapped. A historical romance (1886) by R. L. Stevenson: followed (1893) by a sequel, "David Balfour" (first entitled "Catriona").

Kim. A long story (1901) of native and Anglo-Indian life in India, by Rudyard Kipling.

King Argimenes (är-ji-mē′nēz) **and the Unknown Warrior.** A drama (1914) by Lord Dunsany.

King Arthur, or the British Worthy. A dramatic opera (1691) by Dryden and Purcell.

King Cole. See **Old King Cole.**

King George's War. In American history, the war of Great Britain and its American colonies against the French and Indians: the American phase of the War of the Austrian Succession, 1741–48.

King Horn. An English heroic poem of the 13th century.

King Hunger. A drama (1907) by Leonid Andreev.

Kingis Quair (kwīr or kwär). An allegorical love poem by James I. of Scotland, written in honor of Lady Jane Beaufort.

King James Version. See Dictionary, **king.**

King John. A historical play (before 1598) by Shakspere. It is based on "The Troublesome Reign of King John," a play acted about 1588, and ascribed to Peele and others.

King Lear. A tragedy (written 1605) by Shakspere, ranking as one of his greatest.

King Lear of the Steppe, A. A short story (1870) by Turgenev.

King of Men, The. Zeus (Jupiter); also, Agamemnon.

King Philip's War. The war (1675–76) between the New England colonists and the confederated Indians under Philip, their chief. He was killed at Mount Hope, R. I.

King's College. A college of Cambridge University, founded 1441 by Henry VI.

King William's War. In American history, the war of Great Britain and its colonies against the French and Indians: the American phase of the struggle between Louis XIV. and various European powers, 1689–97.

Kioko (kyō′kō), or **Makioko** (mä-). A Bantu tribe of the upper Kasai valley.

Kiowan (kī′ō-wa̤n). A linguistic stock of North American Indians, now represented by one tribe (in Oklahoma), the Kiowa.

Kipps. A novel (1905) by H. G. Wells.

Kirghiz. See Dictionary.

Kirjath-jearim (kèr′jath-jē′a̤-rim). A town of the Gibeonites, 7 miles west-northwest of Jerusalem. Josh. ix. 17.

Kirkdale Cave. A cavern in the West Riding of Yorkshire, England, famous for its remains of mammals.

Kirke's Lambs. An ironic name for the English regiment commanded by Colonel Percy Kirke, notorious for its cruelty during the insurrection of Monmouth, 1685.

Kishon (kī′shon). The scene of Barak's victory over Sisera: a small river flowing into the Bay of Acre. Judges, iv. 7.

Kit-Cat Club, The. See Dictionary, **kit-cat.**

Kitchen Cabinet, The. A few adherents of President Andrew Jackson who were thought to have more influence with him than his official cabinet.

Kit's Coty House. A noted dolmen near Aylesford, Kent.

Kittim. See **Chittim.**

Kitunahan (ki-tö-nä′han), or **Kootenay,** or **Cootenai.** A linguistic stock of North American Indians, occupying parts of British Columbia and Montana.

Klamath (klä′mat). A tribe of North American Indians, inhabiting mainly the shores of Upper Klamath Lake and Sprague River, Oregon.

Klikitat (klik′i-tat). A tribe of North American Indians, now on the Yakima reservation, Washington.

Klingsor. An enchanter in Wagner's opera "Parsifal."

K'naia-khotana (kni′a̤-chō-tä′na̤), or **Kenai** (ke-nī′). A northern Athapascan tribe of North American Indians, living along Cook Inlet and the Kenai Peninsula, Alaska.

Knecht Ruprecht (knecht rö′precht). The German genius of Christmas, precursor to St. Nicholas (Santa Claus).

Knickerbocker's History of New York. A burlesque history (1809) of New York by Washington Irving. It was written under the name of Diedrich Knickerbocker. See Dictionary, **Knickerbocker.**

Knight of La Mancha (lä män′chä), **The.** Cervantes's Don Quixote.

Knight of the Burning Pestle, The. A mock-heroic play (1613) by Beaumont and Fletcher.

Knight of the Rueful or **Sorrowful Countenance, The.** Cervantes's Don Quixote.

Knight of the Swan, The. Lohengrin.

---

fat, fāte, fär, fȧll, ȧsk, fāre; net, mē, hèr; pin, pīne; not, nōte, mōve, nôr; up, lūte, pùll; oi, oil; ou, out; (lightened) avia̤ry, ēlect, ago̤ny, into̤, ṳnite; (obscured) erra̤nt, opera̤, ardent, acto̤r, natṳre; ch, chip; g, go; th, thin; ᴛʜ, then; y, you;

Knights, The. A comedy (424 B.C.) of Aristophanes.

Knightsbridge. 1. Formerly, the bridge across the Tyburn, London, by which the old Reading road passed. 2. The street which forms the southern boundary of Hyde Park, London.

Knights of the Round Table, The. See Dictionary, **Round Table,** under round².

Knight's Tale of Palamon and Arcite, The. One of Chaucer's "Canterbury Tales," derived from Boccaccio's "Teseide."

Knight's Vision, The. An allegorical painting by Raphael, in the National Gallery, London.

Know-nothing Party, The. See Dictionary.

Kochab (kō′kab). A star of the second magnitude in the constellation Ursa Minor, formerly (at the time of Ptolemy) the pole-star, being then considerably nearer the pole than Polaris.

Kohath (kō′hath). The second son of Levi, and ancestor of the Kohathites, the family of the Levites which had charge of the ark in the wilderness. Gen. xlvi. 11.

Koh-i-noor, Koh-i-nur. See Dictionary, **kohinoor.**

Kolis (kō′lĕz). An aboriginal tribe in the hills of central India. They have preserved their original language and customs.

Kolokol (kol′o-kol). A Russian revolutionary journal founded (1857) in London by Alexander Hertzen. Copies were smuggled into Russia.

Kolokol, Czar. The great bell in the Kremlin, Moscow.

Koluschan (kō-lush′an). A linguistic stock of North American Indians, inhabiting the northwest coast from Portland Canal to the Copper River, Alaska.

Konde (kon′dā), or **Makonde** (mä-). A Bantu tribe of Portuguese East Africa, on the Rovuma River.

Kongo (kong′gō) **Nation.** A vast Bantu tribe of West Africa, occupying both banks of the Lower Congo River.

König Rother (kē′nich rō′tèr). A Middle High German epic of the 12th century. Rother, a legendary hero, wins the daughter of King Constantine of Constantinople.

Königsstuhl (kē′nichs-shtöl). A stone structure on the left bank of the Rhine, 6 miles south of Coblenz, where the Rhenish electors met in the 14th and 15th centuries.

Kootenay. See **Kitunahan.**

Koppenberg (kop′en-berch). The mountain into which disappeared the legendary Pied Piper of Hameln and the bewitched children.

Korah (kō′rä). A leader in a rebellion against Moses and Aaron. Num. xvi. His supposed descendants constituted a gild of temple musicians.

Koran, The. See Dictionary.

Koreish (kō-rīsh′). A powerful Arab tribe of which Mohammed was a member. It acquired the guardianship of the Kaaba as early as the 5th century.

Krakatit (krä′kä-tēt). A novel (1925) by Karel Čapek, about the discovery of an explosive that could annihilate civilization.

Kremlin, The. See Dictionary, **kremlin.**

Kreutzer (kroit′sèr) **Sonata, The.** 1. The most famous of the violin sonatas of Beethoven, dedicated to Rodolphe Kreutzer. 2. A major novel (1890) of Lev Tolstoy.

Kriemhild (krēm′hilt). The legendary heroine of the "Nibelungenlied," wife of Siegfried and avenger of his death. She is the counterpart of the Old Norse Gudrun.

Krishna (krish′nä). A chief Hindu deity: an avatar of Vishnu.

Kritik der Reinen Vernunft (krē-tēk′ der rī′nen fer-nûnft′). A famous philosophical work (1781; revised 1787), by Kant.

Krook (krūk), **Mr.** In Dickens's "Bleak House," a toper who dies by spontaneous combustion.

Kubla Khan. A poetic fragment (1816) by Coleridge, supposed to have been composed in a dream.

Ku Klux Klan. See Dictionary, **Ku Klux.**

Kumara (kö-mä′rä). 'The Youth': an epithet of the eternally youthful Hindu god of war, Skanda.

Kumarila (kö-mä′ri-lä). A celebrated Hindu philosopher and opponent of the Buddhists.

Kundry (kûn′dri). A character in Wagner's opera, "Parsifal": by Klingsor's order she tempts Amfortas and Parsifal.

Kunti (kŏn′tē). In Hindu mythology, daughter of the Yadava prince Shura, and mother of Karna by the Sun.

Kural (kö-räl′). An important collection of gnomic stanzas in the Tamil language, made about the 3d century by Tiruvalluvar.

Kurds, The. See Dictionary, **Kurd.**

Kurma (kör′mä) **Avatar, The.** The second or 'tortoise' incarnation of Vishnu, in which the back of the god served as a pivot for the mountain Mandara.

Kuru (kö′rö). In Hindu mythology, a prince of the lunar race, ancestor of Dhritarashtra and Pandu.

Kusan (kö′zan). A linguistic stock of North American Indians who lived on Coos Bay and at the mouth of Coquille River, Oregon. The survivors are on the Siletz reservation.

Kutab Minar (kö′täb mē-när′). A lofty column near Delhi, begun about 1200 to commemorate the Mohammedan conquest of the Panjab.

Kutchin (ku-chin′). A general name for many tribes of the northern division of the Athapascan stock of North American Indians, dwelling west of the Mackenzie River in British North America and in the Yukon valley, Alaska.

Kuvera (kö-vā′rä). In Hindu mythology, the chief of the evil beings dwelling in darkness, corresponding to Pluto; later, the god of riches.

Kworatem (kwō′rä-tem). A division of the Quoratean stock of North American Indians, dwelling on Salmon River, California.

L

Labadists (lab′a-dists). Up to the 18th century, a sect of Christian communists, followers of Jean de Labadie.

Laban (lā′ban). The Syrian father-in-law of Jacob. Gen. xxiv. 29-60.

La Bella (lä bel′lä). A portrait by Titian, in the Pitti gallery, Florence.

Labyrinth (lab′i-rinth), **The.** 1. See Dictionary, **labyrinth.** 2. A drama (1903) by Paul Hervieu.

Laches (lā′kēz). A dialogue of Plato, on courage.

Lachesis (lak′e-sis). In Greek mythology, one of the Fates.

Lachish (lā′kish). A frontier fortress of the Canaanites between Gaza and Eleutheropolis, captured by Joshua. 2 Kings, xiv. 19.

Ladies' Mile, The. A drive in Hyde Park, London, on the north side of the Serpentine.

Ladislaw (lad′is-lä), **Will.** In George Eliot's "Middlemarch," the clever but mediocre artist who eventually makes Dorothea Brooke happy.

Lady Baltimore. A novel (1906) by Owen Wister.

Lady Day. See Dictionary, **lady.**

Lady from the Sea, The. A drama (1889) by Henrik Ibsen.

Lady Macbeth (mak-beth′). See **Macbeth.**

Lady of Lyons, The. A play (1838) by Bulwer-Lytton.

Lady of Quality, A. A novel (1896) by Frances Hodgson Burnett.

Lady of Shalott (sha-lot′), **The.** A poem (1832) by Tennyson.

Lady of the Aroostook, The. A novel (1879) by W. D. Howells: the story of a New England girl, the only woman passenger on the Aroostook to Venice.

Lady of the Lake, The. 1. A name given, in Arthurian romance, to Vivian, the mistress of Merlin. 2. A romance in verse (1810) by Scott. The "lady of the lake" is Ellen Douglas.

Lady or the Tiger, The. A story (1884) by Frank R. Stockton, which is famous for leaving its riddle unanswered.

Lady Windermere's Fan. A clever society drama (1892) by Oscar Wilde.

Laertes (lā-ėr′tēz). 1. In Greek legend, the father of Odysseus. 2. The fiery brother of Ophelia in Shakspere's "Hamlet."

Læstrygones. See Dictionary, **Læstrygonian.**

La Force (lä fôrs). An ancient Parisian prison, built 1265.

La Gloire (lä glwär). The first fully equipped ironclad ship, launched 1858.

Lagthing (läg′ting). The upper house of the Norwegian Storthing.

L'Aiglon. See **Aiglon, L'.**

Laius (lā′yus). In Greek legend, a king of Thebes.

Lake Poets, The. See Dictionary, **lake³**.

Lakmé. An opera (1886) by Delibes.

Lakshmi (laksh′mē). In Hindu mythology, the goddess of fortune.

Lalla Rookh. A long narrative poem (1817) about an East Indian princess, by Thomas Moore.

L'Allegro. See Allegro, L', and Il Penseroso.

Lambeth (lam′beth) **Articles, The.** Nine articles (1595) intended to embody Calvinistic doctrine.

Lambeth Palace. The London residence of the Archbishop of Canterbury.

Lamech (lā′mek). In Old Testament history: (1) The son of Methusael. Gen. iv. 18–24. (2) The son of Methuselah. Gen. v. 25–31.

Lamentations. A book of the Old Testament, ascribed by tradition to Jeremiah.

Lamia (lā′mi-ä). 1. In classical mythology: (1) A daughter of Poseidon. (2) The daughter of Belus. 2. A celebrated Athenian courtezan of the fourth century B.C. 3. A narrative poem (1820) by Keats.

Lammas. See Dictionary.

Lammle (lam′l), **Alfred.** In "Our Mutual Friend," by Dickens, a fortune-hunting swindler. He and Sophronia Akershem marry, each mistakenly believing the other to be wealthy.

Lancelot. 1. A hero of Arthurian romance, the greatest of Arthur's knights and the lover of Queen Guinevere. 2. A poem (1919) by Edwin Arlington Robinson.

Land League, The Irish. A league formed 1879 by the Irish Nationalist Party, for organized resistance to the payment of rent.

Land of Heart's Desire, The. A romantic drama (1894) by W. B. Yeats.

Land o' the Leal, The. A famous poem (1798) by Lady Nairne.

Landsthing (läns′ting). The upper house of the Danish Rigsdag.

Languish, Lydia. The sentimentally romantic heroine of Sheridan's "Rivals."

Laocoön (lā-ok′ō-on). 1. In Greek legend, a priest of Apollo at Troy. 2. A famous antique group in the Vatican, Rome. 3. A critical treatise (1766) by Lessing on the boundaries between literature and the plastic arts.

Laodamas (lā-od′a-mas). In Greek legend, a son of Eteocles, and king of Thebes.

Laodamia (lā-od-a-mī′ä). 1. In Greek legend, the wife of Protesilaus, with whom she voluntarily died. 2. A poem (1815) by Wordsworth.

Laodiceans. See Dictionary, **Laodicean.**

Laodogant (lā-ō′dō-gant). In Arthurian romance, the father of Guinevere.

Laomedon (lā-om′e-don). In Greek legend, the son of Ilus and Eurydice, father of Priam, and founder and king of Troy.

Laos (lä′ōz). A race northeast of Siam proper, allied to the Siamese.

Lapithæ. See Dictionary.

Laputa. See Dictionary, **Laputan.**

Lara (lä′rä). A narrative poem (1814) by Byron.

La Rochelle (lä rō-shel), **The Peace of.** A peace (1573) whereby Charles IX. granted the Protestants partial toleration.

Lars Porsena (pôr′se-nä). In Macaulay's "Horatius" ("Lays of Ancient Rome," 1842), the Etruscan king against whose forces Horatius defended the bridge, the story being based on Livy.

Last Days of Pompeii, The. A historical romance (1834) by Bulwer-Lytton.

Last Judgment, The. The subject of noted paintings by Fra Angelico (Berlin, Florence), Michelangelo (Rome), Rubens (Munich), and others.

Last Leaf, The. A poem (1833) by O. W. Holmes, describing an old man.

Last of the Mohicans, The. See **Leatherstocking Tales.**

Last Supper, The. The subject of several paintings, of which the most famous is by Leonardo da Vinci (Milan).

Last Token, The. A painting by Gabriel Max, in the Metropolitan Museum, New York.

Last Tournament, The. One of the "Idylls of the King," by Tennyson.

Lateran, Lateran Council. See Dictionary, **Lateran.**

Latimer, Darsie. In Scott's "Redgauntlet," a youth who proves to be Sir Arthur Darsie Redgauntlet, nephew of the titular Redgauntlet.

Latini (lä-tī′nī). In early Roman history, the people inhabiting Latium.

Latin League, The. A confederation of the cities of Latium, in Italy, existing from the earliest historic times till 338 B.C.

Latin Quarter, The. The quarter of Paris on the south side of the Seine, frequented for centuries by students.

Latinus (lä-tī′nus). In Roman legend, a king of Latium, father of Lavinia.

Latin War, The Great. A war between Rome and Latium, 340–338 B.C.

Latona (lä-tō′nä). The Roman counterpart of Leto.

Latter-Day Saints. The Mormons.

Laughing Water. See **Minnehaha.**

Launce (läns). A punning clown in Shakspere's "Two Gentlemen of Verona." He addresses amusing reproaches to Crab, his dog.

Launfal (lân′fal), **Sir.** In Arthurian romance, a knight of the Round Table. Lowell's "Vision of Sir Launfal" uses the name in a story of his own invention.

Laurentian Library. See Dictionary, **Laurentian.**

Lautaro (lou-tä′rō) **Society, The.** A secret political society, originally established in Spain early in the 19th century, with the aim of emancipating Spanish South America.

Lava Lane. A collection of poems (1925) by Nathalia Crane. See **Janitor's Boy, The.**

Lavengro (lav′en-grō). An autobiographical work (1851) by George Borrow, telling of Gipsy life and language.

Lavinia (lä-vin′i-ä). In Roman legend, the daughter of Latinus, and wife of Æneas.

Lawrence (lâ′rens), **Saint.** 1. A Christian martyr of the 3d century. 2. A prelate of the early English church, successor to St. Augustine as archbishop of Canterbury.

Lay of the Last Minstrel, The. A romance in verse (1805) by Scott. It tells a heroic tale of the Scottish border in the 16th century.

Lays of Ancient Rome. A volume of ballads (1842) by Macaulay.

Lazarillo de Tormes (lä-thä-rēl′yō dä tôr′mäs). The first picaresque novel (Spanish), formerly attributed to Diego Hurtado de Mendoza (first known edition 1553).

Lazarus (laz′a-rus). 1. The brother of Mary and Martha, and friend of Jesus, who raised him from the dead. John, xi. 1–44; xii. 1–18. 2. A character in one of the parables of Jesus. Luke, xvi. 19.

League, The. In French history, the Holy League formed in the Catholic interest in 1576.

League of Nations, The. The organization of states to promote world peace which was created by the Treaty of Versailles (1919).

League of the German Princes, The. See **Fürstenbund.**

League of the Public Weal. A union of powerful French nobles against Louis XI., formed about 1465 under the leadership of Charles the Bold of Burgundy.

Leah (lē′ä). Elder daughter of Laban, and first wife of Jacob. Gen. xxix.

Leander (lē-an′dėr). See **Hero and Leander.**

Leaning Tower of Pisa, The. A cylindrical campanile at Pisa, begun 1174. It is 181 feet high, and inclines 13 feet 8 inches from the perpendicular.

Lear (lēr), **King.** 1. A mythical king of Britain. 2. In Shakspere's "King Lear," an aged king who divides his kingdom between Goneril and Regan, his elder daughters, disinheriting the youngest, Cordelia. When Goneril and Regan have turned against him, Cordelia comes to his rescue with armed forces. She is captured and put to death; and Lear dies of a broken heart.

Learoyd. See **Mulvaney, Terence.**

Leatherstocking Tales, The. A series of novels by Cooper about a frontiersman and pioneer, Nathaniel Bumppo (the Leatherstocking). In order of the action, the volumes are: "The Deerslayer," 1841; "The Last of the Mohicans," 1826; "The Pathfinder," 1840; "The Pioneers," 1823; "The Prairie," 1827.

Leatherwood God, The. A novel (1916) by W. D. Howells.

---

fat, fāte, fär, fåll, åsk, fāre; net, mē, hėr; pin, pīne; not, nōte, mȯve, nôr; up, lūte, pull; oi, oil; ou, out; (lightened) avi̯ary; ḝlect, agȯny, intȯ, ṳnite; (obscured) erra̯nt, opera̱, arde̱nt, acto̱r, natṳre; ch, chip; g, go; th, thin; ᴛʜ, then; y, you;

Leaves of Grass. A collection of poems by Whitman, enlarged repeatedly after the first edition (1855).

Lecoq (lĕ-kok'). A celebrated detective in' the stories of Gaboriau, especially in "File Number 113" (1861) and "Monsieur Lecoq" (1869).

Le Coq d'Or. An opera (1910) by Rimski-Korsakov.

Leda (lē'dä). In Greek mythology, the wife of Tyndareus, and mother by Zeus of Helen, Clytemnestra, Castor, and Pollux.

Legend of Good Women, The. An unfinished poem by Chaucer, based on stories from Ovid, Livy, etc.

Legend of Montrose, A. A historical romance (1819) of Scotland in the 17th century, by Scott.

Legend of Sleepy Hollow, The. A tale in Irving's "Sketch-Book."

Legion of Honor, The. See Dictionary, **legion**.

Legree (lĕ-grē'), **Simon.** The brutal slave-dealer in "Uncle Tom's Cabin," by Harriet Beecher Stowe.

Leiden des Jungen Werthers, Die (dē li'dẹn des yůng'ẹn vär'tèrs). A sentimental novel (1774), in the form of letters, by Goethe: known in English as "The Sorrows of Werther."

Leigh (lē), **Sir Amyas.** A powerful, chivalrous sailor, the hero of Charles Kingsley's "Westward Ho!"

Le Moyne (lĕ mwän). A French family which, in the 17th and 18th centuries, played an important part in the French colonization of North America.

Lemuel (lem'ū-ẹl). An unknown king, identified with Solomon by rabbinical commentators. Prov. xxxi. 1, 4.

Lenæa (lẹ-nē'ä). The "feast of vats," an ancient Greek festival in honor of Dionysus.

Lenguas or **Lengoas** (leng'gwäz). A tribe of South American Indians, formerly numerous and formidable in the Gran Chaco region.

Lenore. 1. (lä-nō'rẹ) A ballad (1774) by Bürger. 2. (lẹ-nôr') A poem (1831) by Poe.

Lenox (len'ọks) **Library, The.** A public reference library founded in New York in 1870 by James Lenox: merged (1895) in the New York Public Library.

Lent. See Dictionary, **Lent**[1].

Leonarda. A drama (1879) by Björnstjerne Björnson.

Leonora (lā-ō-nō'rä). 1. See **Fidelio**. 2. The heroine of Verdi's opera "Il Trovatore."

Leontes (lẹ-on'tēz). The jealous king in Shakspere's "Winter's Tale."

Leporello (lā-pō-rel'lō). A cowardly valet in Mozart's opera "Don Giovanni."

Lesbia (lez'bi-ä). The name by which Clodia, the favorite of Catullus, is referred to in his poems.

Lesghians (lez'gi-ạnz). A collection of tribes living in Dagestan, in the Caucasus.

Les Misérables. See **Misérables, Les**.

Lesson in Anatomy, The. A painting (1632) by Rembrandt, in the museum at The Hague, Holland.

Lethe (lē'thē). 1. In Greek mythology, the personification of oblivion, a daughter of Eris. 2. See Dictionary.

Leto (lē'tō). In Greek mythology, the daughter of the Titan Cœus and Phœbe, and mother by Zeus of Apollo and Artemis.

Levana (le-vā'nä). In Roman mythology, a goddess, the protectress of children.

Levi (lē'vī). A son of Jacob and Leah, and ancestor of the Levites. Gen. xxix. 34, etc.

Leviathan (lẹ-vī'ạ-thạn), **or The Matter, Form, and Power of a Commonwealth, Ecclesiastical and Civil.** A philosophical treatise (1651) on the idea of absolutism in government, by Hobbes.

Leviticus (lẹ-vit'i-kus). A canonical book of the Old Testament, the third book of the Pentateuch.

Lewes (lū'es), **The Mise of.** An agreement (1264) between the English defeated party under Henry III. and the barons under Simon of Montfort, providing for native councilors and the reorganization of Parliament.

Libby (lib'i) **Prison, The.** A notorious Confederate military prison in Richmond, Virginia, during the Civil War.

Liberal Party, The. The name by which the British Whig party has been known since about 1832.

Liberal Unionists. In British politics, a party formed in 1886 by the secession from the Liberal party of those who objected to Gladstone's Home Rule proposals.

Liberation, The War of. A name given by the Germans to the war of the Allies against the French, 1813–14.

Liberator, The. An antislavery paper published at Boston 1831–65, edited by W. L. Garrison.

Liberty Bell, The. A famous bell in Independence Hall, Philadelphia, popularly believed to have been the first bell to announce the adoption of the Declaration of Independence.

Liberty Bond. See Dictionary, **liberty**.

Liberty Enlightening the World. A colossal figure (1886) by Bartholdi, on Bedloe's Island in New York Bay, given by the French people to America.

Liberty Tree, The. An elm-tree formerly standing on Washington Street, Boston, upon which effigies of objectionable persons were hung during the Stamp Act excitement.

Libitina (lib-i-tī'nä). An ancient Italian goddess of gardens, vineyards, and voluptuous pleasures, and also of death.

Libro d'Oro (lē'brō dō'rō). A roll or register of the noble families of an Italian state or province of the middle ages, with a list of their estates; hence, any list of titles of honor or the like.

Licinia (lī-sin'i-ä) **gens.** A celebrated plebeian house, of uncertain origin, in ancient Rome.

Lick (lik) **Observatory.** An observatory founded and endowed by James Lick and transferred to the University of California in 1888. It is situated on the summit of Mt. Hamilton, Santa Clara County, California.

Lieder ohne Worte (lē'dèr ô'nẹ vor'tẹ). A series of pianoforte pieces by Mendelssohn.

Life and Death of Jason, The. A poem (1867) by William Morris.

Life and Opinions of Tristram Shandy, The. See **Tristram Shandy, The Life and Opinions of**.

Life of Christ, The. A remarkable series of six paintings (about 1640) by Rembrandt, in the Old Pinakothek, Munich.

Life of Man, The. A symbolic drama (1906) by Leonid Andreev.

Ligeia (lī-jē'ä). A story (1838) by E. A. Poe.

Light Brigade, The Charge of the. A celebrated charge made by the Light Brigade of 670 men, under Lord Cardigan, on a Russian battery at Balaklava, Oct. 25, 1854: the subject of a well-known poem by Tennyson.

Light of Asia, The. A poem (1878) by Sir Edwin Arnold.

Light of the World, The. A noted picture by Holman Hunt, at Keble College, Oxford.

Light That Failed, The. A novel (1891) by Rudyard Kipling.

Lilith (lil'ith). 1. According to the Talmudists, Adam's first wife. 2. A demon that dwells in deserted places. Isa. xxxiv. 14.

Lillibullero (lil''i-bu-lē'rō), or **Lilliburlero** (-bèr-lē'rō). A political song (about 1686) by Lord Wharton, satirizing James II. of England for an unwelcome nomination to the lord-lieutenancy of Ireland.

Lilliputians. See Dictionary, **Lilliputian**.

Lily Bart. The heroine of Edith Wharton's "The House of Mirth."

Lily Dale. A typical Victorian heroine, the leading character in Trollope's "The Small House at Allington," appearing also in "The Last Chronicle of Barset."

Limerick (lim'ẹ-rik), **The Treaty of,** or **Pacification of.** A treaty (1691) between the English commander Ginkel and the Irish commander Sarsfield, granting privileges to the Irish Catholics.

Limitation of Armaments, The Conference for. An international conference at Washington, Nov. 12, 1921, to Feb. 6, 1922, at which a Four Power Treaty on Pacific Affairs was signed, and also a Five Power Naval Treaty, setting limits to the naval programs of Great Britain, United States, Japan, France, and Italy, in the ratio 5–5–3–1.75–1.75.

Lincei (lēn-chā'ē), **The.** An Italian academy, founded in 1603, with the special object of studying physical science. Galileo and Colonna were among the members.

Lincoln (ling'kọn) **College.** A college of the University of Oxford, founded 1427, refounded 1478.

Lincoln Memorial, The. The national monument in Washington, dedicated on Memorial Day, 1922: it balances the Washington Monument as seen from the White House.

Lincoln's Inn Fields. The largest square in London, near the junction of High Holborn and Chancery Lane. It was laid out by Inigo Jones.

Lindabrides (lin-dab′ri-dēz). A character in the "Mirror of Knighthood"; whence, a common name for a mistress or courtezan.

Linda Condon. A novel (1919) by Joseph Hergesheimer.

Linga Purana (ling′gä pŏ-rä′nä). A Hindu sacred poem of 11,000 stanzas on the objects of life.

Lingard, Captain. A character in some of Joseph Conrad's novels, "Almayer's Folly," "The Rescue," etc.

Lingoa Geral (lēng′gwä zhä-räl′). The Indian language formerly universal in the settlements of the interior of Brazil, and still spoken on the upper Amazon.

Lion Hunt, The. A large painting by Rubens, in the Old Pinakothek at Munich.

Lion of Chæronea (ker-ō-nē′ä), **The.** The monument on the common tomb of the Greeks who fell in the battle (338 B.C.) against Philip of Macedon.

Lion of St. Mark, The. A symbolical winged lion, the characteristic device of Venice.

Lion's Mouth, The. A famous hole or opening in the wall of the antechamber of the Great Council in the Doge's palace, Venice, through which anonymous accusations were passed in.

Lipan (lē-pän′). A tribe of the Apache group of North American Indians. It moved from central Texas into Mexico early in the 19th century.

Lismahago (lis-mą-hā′gō), **Captain.** See **Bramble, Tabitha.**

Lisuarte (lis′ū-ärt). In the "Amadis" romances: (1) The King of England, and father of Oriana. (2) The grandson of Amadis.

Literary Club, The. A London club founded 1764 by Sir Joshua Reynolds, Samuel Johnson, and others.

Literary Lapses. A collection of humorous sketches (1910) by Stephen Leacock.

Little Breeches. A poem (1871) by John Hay: in "Pike County Ballads."

Little Corporal. See Dictionary, **little.**

Little Dorrit (dor′it). A novel (1857) by Dickens.

Little Dream, The. A drama (1911) by John Galsworthy.

Little Emily, or **Em'ly.** See **Emily,** 2.

Little-endian. See Dictionary.

Little Englander. See Dictionary, **little.**

Little Entente. See Dictionary, **little.**

Little Eva. A frail child who dies prematurely, in Mrs. Stowe's "Uncle Tom's Cabin." She is the daughter of the owner of Tom.

Little Eyolf (ā′olf). A drama (1895) by Henrik Ibsen.

Little French Girl, The. A novel (1924) by Anne Douglas Sedgwick: the experiences of Alix, who is transplanted from an unconventional French atmosphere to an ordinary, middle-class English home.

Little John. See **Nailor, John.**

Little Lord Fauntleroy (fânt′lẹ-roi). A popular story for children (1885) by Frances Hodgson Burnett.

Little Minister, The. A novel (1891) by Sir J. M. Barrie, about a strictly trained Scotch minister who falls in love with a gipsy; the play (1897) based on the novel.

Little Nell. In Dickens's "Old Curiosity Shop," a pathetic child who, wandering with her aged grandfather in search of a refuge from vicious surroundings, dies in a country cottage.

Little Orphant Annie. The subject of a poem (1885) by James Whitcomb Riley.

Little Parliament, The. The Parliament convened 1653 by Cromwell. It had only 140 members.

Little Russians. See Dictionary, **Russian.**

Little Vehicle, The. See **Hinayana.**

Little Women. A popular story for girls (1868-69) by Louisa M. Alcott. It is followed by "Little Men" (1871) and by "Jo's Boys" (1886).

Livelihood. Poems (1917) by W. W. Gibson.

Lloyd's (loidz). An association at the Royal Exchange, London, comprising underwriters, merchants, ship-owners, and brokers, for the furtherance of commerce, especially marine insurance. It has published since 1716 Lloyd's List, a periodical containing shipping intelligence.

Locarno Security Treaties. Compacts agreed upon at Locarno, Switzerland, October 5-16, 1925, by representatives of Germany, France, Belgium, Great Britain, Italy, Poland, and Czechoslovakia.

Lochinvar (loch-in-vär′). A ballad by Scott, in "Marmion," about a youth who boldly carries off his lady on the verge of her forced marriage to another.

Locked Chest, The. A drama (1916) by John Masefield.

Locksley (loks′li). The reputed birthplace of Robin Hood.

Locksley Hall. A poem (1842) by Tennyson, followed by "Locksley Hall Sixty Years After" (1886).

Locofocos (lō-kọ-fō′kōz). The equal-rights or radical section of the Democratic party in the United States about 1835.

Locrine (lō′krīn). A mythical king of England, the eldest son of Brut, and the father of Sabrina.

Log, King. In Æsop's Fables, a worthless, heavy log sent by Jove to the frogs who prayed for a king.

Logone (lō-gō′nā). A tribe of the central Sudan, southeast of Lake Chad.

Logris (lō′gris), or **Logria** (-gri-ą). In Arthurian romance, England.

Lohengrin (lō′ẹn-grin). 1. In German legend, the mythical knight of the swan, the son of Parzival, and a knight of the Holy Grail. 2. A romantic music-drama (1847) by Wagner.

Loka (lō′kạ). In Hindu works, a world.

Lokapalas (lō-kạ-pä′lạz). In Hindu mythology: (1) The deities who preside over the eight points of the compass. (2) Elephants which help to protect these eight regions.

Loki (lō′kẹ). In Old Norse mythology, the god of destruction, the son of Laufey or Nal by the giant Farbauti, and the father of the Midgard-serpent, the Fenris-wolf, and Hel.

Lollards. See Dictionary, **Lollard.**

Lolo (lō′lō), or **Balolo** (bä-lō′lō). A great Bantu nation of Belgian Congo, occupying the basins of the Lulongo, Tshuapa, and Lomami rivers.

Lombard (lom′bärd) **League, The.** An association between several cities of northern Italy, founded 1167 for protection against Frederick Barbarossa.

Lombards. See Dictionary, **Lombard.**

Lombard Street. See Dictionary, **Lombard.**

London, The Treaty of. The name of each of several treaties concluded at London: (a) by England, France, and Russia (1827); (b) by England, France, Austria, Prussia, and Russia (1831); (c) by England, France, Russia, and Bavaria (1832); (d) by the signatory powers of the treaty of Paris of 1856 (1871).

London, The University of. An educational institution founded 1836 in London.

London Company, The. A company of merchants and others, formed to plant colonies in America. It founded (1607) a colony at Jamestown, Va.

London Protocol, The. 1. The protocol (1852) by which the great powers recognized Prince Christian of Glücksburg as heir to Denmark. 2. The protocol (1877) by which the great powers called upon Turkey to make peace with Montenegro and to carry out certain reforms.

London Wall. A Roman wall built (350-369) around London.

Long Acre. A street in London near Covent Garden, running into Drury Lane. It was long the headquarters of carriage-builders.

Long Bridge. A bridge about a mile long, across the Potomac at Washington, D.C. It was the main avenue of communication with the Army of the Potomac during the Civil War.

Longchamp (lôn-shän′). A race-course at the end of the Bois de Boulogne, west of Paris.

Longinus (lon-jī′nus), also **Longis** (lon′jis), or **Longius** (lon′ji-us). The name given in the middle ages to the soldier who pierced the side of Jesus.

Long Parliament, The. The Parliament which assembled Nov. 3, 1640, was expelled by Cromwell in 1653, reconvened in 1659, and was dissolved in 1660.

Long Tom. A 42-pound gun, captured 1798 from the French

by the English, sold to the Americans, and used in the War of 1812.

Long Tom Coffin. See **Coffin, Long Tom.**

Looking Backward: 2000–1887. A socialistic utopian story (1888) by Edward Bellamy.

Lord Jim. A novel (1900) by Joseph Conrad, dealing with the efforts of an Englishman in the Malay country to atone for a single failure in courage.

Lord of Misrule. See Dictionary, **lord.**

Lord of the Isles, The. A romance in verse (1815) by Scott.

Lorelei (lō′rẹ-lī). A ballad (1823) by Heinrich Heine. The first form of this legend is in a ballad (1802) by Klemens Brentano.

Lorenzo (lọ-ren′zō). A gentleman who elopes with Jessica, in Shakspere's "Merchant of Venice."

Lorna Doone (dōn), **a Romance of Exmoor.** A novel (1869) by R. D. Blackmore.

Lorraine, or **Hapsburg-Lorraine** (haps′bẻrg-lo-rān′), **The House of.** A royal house descended from Francis of Lorraine. After the middle of the 18th century it furnished Holy Roman emperors, Austrian sovereigns, and rulers of Tuscany.

Lorrequer (lor′ẹ-kẻr), **Harry.** A novel of adventure (1837) by Charles Lever.

Lost Silk Hat, The. A short play (1914) of sophisticated humor, by Lord Dunsany.

Lot (lot). 1. In Old Testament history, the son of Haran and nephew of Abraham. Gen. xiii. 1–12, etc. 2. In Arthurian legend, a king of Norway, according to Geoffrey of Monmouth, or of Orkney, according to Malory.

Lothair. A novel of fashionable life (1870) by Disraeli.

Lothario (lọ-thā′ri-ō). 1. An unscrupulous libertine in Rowe's "Fair Penitent." His name has become a synonym for any individual of his type. 2. An aristocratic gentleman in "Wilhelm Meisters Lehrjahre," by Goethe.

Lotophagi (lọ-tof′ạ-jī). In Greek legend, the lotus-eaters; in historical times, a people living on the northern coast of Africa in Tripoli and Tunis.

Louisburg (lö′is-bẻrg or lö′ẹ-bẻrg). A ruined fortress on the coast of Cape Breton, Nova Scotia, taken 1745 from the French by a New England force under Pepperell, restored 1748, and retaken 1758 by the British under Amherst.

Louise. An opera (1900) by Charpentier.

Louisiana Purchase, The. The huge territory which the United States purchased from France in 1803. It extended from the Mississippi to the Rocky Mountains and from the Gulf of Mexico to British America.

Louvre (lövr). A royal palace (begun 1541) in Paris, largely occupied since 1793 by a famous museum.

Love for Love. A comedy (1695) by Congreve.

Lovelace. In Richardson's "Clarissa Harlowe," the Lothario who, to overcome Clarissa's resistance to his advances, drugs her. He makes a belated offer of marriage, but Clarissa dies of mortification and grief.

Lover's Complaint, A. A poem (1609) by Shakspere.

Lovers' Progress, The. A play by Fletcher and Massinger, printed 1647.

Love's Labour's Lost. A comedy (1589) by Shakspere.

Love's Labour's Won. A play ascribed to Shakspere by Francis Meres (1598), perhaps the original of "Much Ado about Nothing."

Luba (lö′bä), or **Baluba** (bä-lö′bä). A great Bantu nation of the Belgian Congo.

Lucayans (lö-kī′ạnz). The aboriginal inhabitants of the Bahama Islands, the first Americans encountered by Columbus.

Lucerne (lụ-sẻrn′), **The Lion of.** A famous piece of sculpture by Thorwaldsen at Lucerne, commemorating the heroism of the Swiss guards in the attack (1792) on the Tuileries.

Luchaze (lö-chä′zä), or **Baluchaze** (bä-lö-chä′zä). A Bantu tribe of Angola, West Africa.

Lucia (lö′shiä), **Saint.** A martyr of the primitive church in Syracuse, who perished during the persecution of Diocletian: the patroness especially of those who suffer from distemper of the eyes.

Lucia di Lammermoor (lö-chē′ä dē läm-mer-mör′). An opera (1835) by Donizetti, based on Scott's "Bride of Lammermoor."

Lucifer. See Dictionary.

Lucile. A romantic novel in verse (1860) by the Earl of Lytton (Owen Meredith).

Lucina (lụ-sī′nä). In Roman mythology, the goddess who presided over childbirth.

Luck of Eden Hall, The. A drinking-cup long preserved at Eden Hall in Cumberland: according to legend, associated with the luck of the Musgrave family.

Luck of Roaring Camp, The. A story (1870) by Bret Harte, about a mining camp. The Luck is the name given to a baby.

Lucretia (lụ-krē′shiä). In Roman legend, the wife of Tarquinius Collatinus, whose rape by Sextus Tarquinius led to the overthrow of the Tarquins.

Lucy Desborough. The heroine of Meredith's "The Ordeal of Richard Feverel."

Lud (lud). A mythical king of Britain.

Luddites (lud′īts). The rioters who attempted to destroy machinery in England, 1811–16.

Ludgate (lud′gāt). A gate in the western part of the old city wall of London. It was destroyed in 1760. Near it stood a debtors' prison of the same name.

Ludovisi Ares (lö-dō-vē′zē ā′rēz), **The.** A colossal antique marble statue in the Museo delle Terme, Rome.

Ludovisi Juno, The. A colossal head, probably by an Attic artist of the early 4th century B.C., in the Museo delle Terme, Rome.

Luke (lök), **The Gospel of.** The third gospel, attributed by tradition to Luke, the companion of St. Paul.

Lumpkin, Tony. A clownish boor and practical joker in Goldsmith's "She Stoops to Conquer."

Luna (lü′nä). The Italian goddess of the moon.

Lunda (lön′dä). A Bantu people in the Belgian Congo and Angola.

Lundy's (lun′diz) **Lane.** A road leading westward from Niagara River, near Niagara Falls, where a battle was fought (1814) between the Americans and the British.

Lunéville (lü-nā-vēl′), **The Peace of.** A treaty (1801) between the Holy Roman emperor and France. It was the beginning of the end of the Holy Roman Empire.

Lupercalia (lö-pẻr-kā′li-ä). One of the most ancient Roman festivals, celebrated every year in February.

Lupercus (lụ-pẻr′kus). A Roman rural deity, the protector of flocks: identified with Faunus and Pan.

Luray (lụ-rā′) **Cave.** A large cave in Page County, Va., near Luray. It is especially remarkable for enormous stalactites.

Lusiad (lü′si-ad), **The.** The national epic (1572) of Portugal, by Camoëns.

Lusitania (lü-si-tā′ni-ä), **The.** A Cunard liner, torpedoed without warning by a German submarine off the south coast of Ireland, May 7, 1915, and sunk with a loss of nearly 1,200 lives.

Luxembourg (lük-soṅ-bör), **The Palace of the.** A palace in Paris, built (1615–20) by Debrosse for Maria de' Medici.

Lyæus (lī-ē′us). A surname of Bacchus.

Lyceum. See Dictionary, **lyceum.**

Lycidas (lis′i-dạs). An elegy (1637) by Milton in memory of his friend Edward King. The name is borrowed from a shepherd in Virgil's Eclogues.

Lydgate, Dr. In George Eliot's "Middlemarch," a young physician whose ambition is thwarted by the selfish narrowness of a beautiful wife, Rosamond Vincy.

Lyonnesse (lī-ọ-nes′), or **Leonnoys.** In Arthurian romance, a mythical region near Cornwall, supposed to have been submerged by the sea.

Lyrical Ballads. A collection (1798) of poems by Wordsworth and Coleridge. It gave a considerable impulse to the Romantic movement in England.

Lysicrates (lī-sik′rạ-tēz), **The Choragic Monument of.** A small shrine of the Corinthian order, in Athens, erected by Lysicrates to celebrate the victory (335 B.C.) of the chorus which he had been chosen to furnish. It is regarded as the finest example of this type of monument.

Lysis (lī′sis). A dialogue of Plato on friendship.

Lysistrata (lī-sis′trạ-tä). A comedy of Aristophanes, exhibited 411 B.C.

(variable) ḓ as d or j, ṣ as s or sh, ṯ as t or ch, ẓ as z or zh; o, F. cloche; ü, F. menu; ċh, Sc. loch; ṅ, F. bonbon; ′, primary accent; ″, secondary accent; †, obsolete; <, from; +, and; =, equals. See also lists at beginning of book.

M

Maat (mạ-ät′). In Egyptian mythology, the goddess of truth, offspring of the sun.

Mab (mab), **Queen.** A mischievous, tantalizing fairy in English folklore, often mentioned by Shakspere, Jonson, Drayton, and Milton. Shelley, in "Queen Mab," makes her control human thoughts.

Maba (mä′bä). The Negritic ruling tribe of Wadai, in the north central Sudan.

Mabinogion (mab-i-nō′gi-on), **The.** A name loosely given to the collection of medieval Welsh romances which was translated (1838–49) by Lady Charlotte Guest (Schreiber).

Macaire (mạ-kär′). A Franco-Italian chanson de geste, containing the original version of the story of the dog of Montargis.

Macarians (mạ-kā′ri-ạnz). A severely ascetic 4th-century sect.

Macbeth (mạk-beth′). 1. A tragedy by Shakspere. 2. In Shakspere's "Macbeth," a thane and general of Scotland, who, at the instigation of his wife, Lady Macbeth, kills the lawful king and becomes king himself. 3. An opera (1847) by Verdi.

Maccabees (mak′ạ-bēz). A family of heroes, deliverers of Judea during the Syrian persecutions of 175–164 B.C. They founded a dynasty of priest-kings which lasted until 40 B.C.

Maccabees, The Books of the. The last two books of the Apocrypha, recording the struggles of the Maccabees, 168–135 B.C.

Macduff (mạk-duf′). In Shakspere's "Macbeth," the Thane of Fife, whose family is butchered by Macbeth's order.

Macedonian (mas-ẹ-dō′ni-ạn) **Wars, The.** Wars between Rome and Macedonia, intermittently from 214 to 148 B.C.

MacFlecknoe (mạk-flek′nō), **or a Satire on the True Blue Protestant Poet T. S.** A satirical poem (1682) by Dryden, directed against Shadwell (who is depicted as the literary heir of Richard Flecknoe, a poet notorious for his bad verses). It served Pope as model for his "Dunciad."

McFlimsey, Miss Flora. In W. A. Butler's poem "Nothing to Wear" (1857), the woman who shopped continually and yet had nothing to wear.

Machpelah (mak-pē′lạ). A cave in Hebron, the burial-place of the patriarchs. Gen. xxiii. 9.

MacIvor (mạk-ē′vọr), **Flora.** The heroine of Scott's "Waverley," a sister of the Highland chief Fergus MacIvor.

McKinley Act, The. A revision of the tariff schedule, principally upward, in force in the United States 1890–94.

MacLeod (mạ-kloud′) **Case, The.** The trial and acquittal (1841) of a British subject implicated in the burning of the "Caroline" (1837) in Niagara River.

MacStinger, Mrs. See **Bunsby, Captain Jack.**

McTeague. A novel (1899) by Frank Norris, about early days in California.

Madame Bovary. See **Bovary, Emma.**

Madame Butterfly. An opera (1904) by Puccini, based on a drama by David Belasco and John Luther Long: libretto by Giuseppe Giacosa.

Madame de Treymes (trām). A story (1907) by Edith Wharton, showing the conflict between the French and the American social systems.

Madeleine (mȧd-lān), **The Church of the.** A great Roman-Corinthian church in Paris, begun under Louis XV. and completed 1842.

Madelon (mȧd-loṅ). One of the characters satirized in Molière's "Précieuses ridicules." See **Polixène.**

Mad Heracles, The. A tragedy (c. 420 B.C.) by Euripides.

Madi (mä′dē). An African tribe dwelling on the Nile north of Lake Albert Nyanza.

Madison Square. A public park in New York City, east of Fifth Avenue between 23d Street and 26th Street.

Madoc (mad′ok). 1. A legendary Welsh prince, said to have discovered America about 1170. 2. A poem (1805) by Robert Southey.

Madonna (mạ-don′ä). See Dictionary. There are famous paintings of this subject by Andrea del Sarto, Bellini, Botticelli, Cimabue, Correggio, Fra Angelico, Fra Bartolommeo, Holbein, Mantegna, Murillo, Raphael, Titian, Van Dyck, Leonardo da Vinci, and others.

Madonna of the Future, The. A story (1879) by Henry James.

Mador (mā′dọr), **Sir.** In Arthurian romance, a knight slain by Lancelot for defaming Guinevere.

Madras House, The. A drama (1910) by Granville-Barker.

Madrid, The Treaty of. A treaty (1526) between France and the Holy Roman Empire, whereby Francis I. was released and France ceded Burgundy.

Mad World, My Masters, A. 1. A dialogue (1603) by Nicholas Breton. 2. A play (about 1606) by Middleton.

Mæonides (mē-on′i-dēz). A surname of Homer, by one account a native of Mæonia.

Mæviad (mē′vi-ad), **The.** See **Baviad, The.**

Maffia. See Dictionary, **maffia.**

Magda. See **Heimat, Die.**

Magdalen (mag′dạ-len). There are celebrated paintings of this subject by Correggio (Dresden), Rubens (Lille), Tintoretto (Venice), Titian (Florence and Leningrad), and Veronese (Turin).

Magdalen, Mary. See Dictionary, **magdalen.**

Magdalen (môd′lin) **College.** A college of Oxford University, founded 1457 by Bishop Waynflete.

Magdalene (môd′lin) **College.** A college of Cambridge University, founded 1519.

Magdeburg (mäg′dẹ-búrċh), **The Centuries of.** An ecclesiastical history of the first 13 Christian centuries, published at Basel 1560–74.

Magi. See Dictionary, **Magus.**

Magic Flute, The. See **Zauberflöte, Die.**

Magna Charta or **Magna Carta** (mag′nạ cär′tạ). The 'great charter' of English liberties, forced from King John by the English barons at Runnymede, June 15, 1215.

Magnalia Christi Americana (mag-nā′li-ạ kris′tī ạ-mer-i-kā′nạ). An ecclesiastical history of New England (1702) by Cotton Mather.

Magnificent Ambersons, The. A novel (1918) by Booth Tarkington, the story of a Middle West family. Pulitzer Prize novel, 1919.

Magog (mā′gog). In the Old Testament, the land ruled by Gog (Ezek. xxxviii. 2): thought to be identical with Lydia.

Magwitch (mag′wich), **Abel.** An escaped convict in Dickens's "Great Expectations."

Mahabharata (mạ-hä-bhä′rạ-tạ). One of the two chief epics of ancient India (the other being the Ramayana). Its central subject is the war between the Kauravas and the Pandavas.

Mahadeva (mạ-hä-dā′vạ). 1. A name of Siva. 2. A Buddhist schismatic teacher thought to have lived about 200 years after the Buddha.

Mahadevi (mạ-hä-dā′vē). A name of Devi, the wife of Siva.

Mahanaim (mä-hạ-nā′im). In the Old Testament, an unidentified place east of the Jordan. Gen. xxxii. 2.

Mahapralaya (mạ-hä-pra′lạ-yạ). In Hindu belief, the destruction of all things at the end of the present cycle or kalpa.

Mahapuranas (mạ-hä-pọ-rä′nạz). The Vishnupurana and the Bhagavatapurana.

Mahayana (mạ-hä-yä′nạ). The Great Vehicle, the later and popular form of Buddhism. See **Hinayana.**

Mahdi. See Dictionary.

Mahican (mä-hē′kạn). A tribe or confederacy of North American Indians, centralized formerly in the upper Hudson valley.

Mahound. See Dictionary.

Mahratti. See Dictionary.

Maia (mā′yạ). 1. In Greek mythology, the eldest of the Pleiades, mother by Zeus of Hermes. 2. In Roman mythology, the Bona Dea.

Maiden Lane. 1. A London street between Covent Garden and the Strand. 2. A New York street running southeast from Broadway opposite Cortlandt Street.

Maid Marian. In the Robin Hood ballads, Robin's sweetheart, who follows him to the greenwood as a page and lives with his band as a virgin huntress.

Maid of Sker, The. A novel (1872) by R. D. Blackmore.

Maid's Tragedy, The. A play (about 1611) by Beaumont and Fletcher.

Maine, The. A United States battle-ship, sunk by an explosion in the harbor of Havana, Feb. 15, 1898, with a loss of 266 lives.

Main Plot, The. The principal one of two plots (1603) in favor of Arabella Stuart against James I. of England. See **Bye Plot, The.**

Main Street. A novel (1920) by Sinclair Lewis, exposing the sordid life of an American small town.

Maison Carrée (mā-zôn kȧ-rā). A Roman temple at Nîmes, France, assigned to the beginning of the 1st century.

Maison Dorée (do-rā), **La.** A former famous restaurant on the Boulevard des Italiens, Paris, built 1839.

Major Barbara. A drama (1905) by G. B. Shaw.

Making of an Englishman, The. A novel (1914) by W. L. George.

Makioko. See **Kioko.**

Malachi (mal′ȧ-kī). The last of the Hebrew minor prophets. The book bearing his name closes the Old Testament.

Malade Imaginaire, Le (lė mȧ-lȧd ē-mȧ-zhē-nār). A comedy (1673) by Molière: one of his most brilliant.

Malagigi (mal-ȧ-jē′jē). In the Charlemagne romances, an enchanter and magician, cousin of Rinaldo.

Malagrowther (mal-ȧ-grou′ᴛʜėr), **Malachi.** A pen-name used by Scott in 1826.

Malagrowther, Sir Mungo. An elderly and embittered courtier in Scott's "Fortunes of Nigel."

Malakoff (mal′ȧ-kof). One of the principal fortifications of Sebastopol, carried by the French in 1855.

Malaprop (mal′ȧ-prop), **Mrs.** The "old weather-beaten she-dragon" of Sheridan's "Rivals," noted for her misapplication of words.

Malatesta (mä-lä-tes′tä). An Italian family, members of which ruled Rimini from the 13th century to the 15th.

Malays. See Dictionary, **Malay.**

Malbrouck (mäl-brŏk). A famous French song of the early 18th century ("Malbrouck s'en va-t-en guerre").

Malebolge (mä-lā-bōl′jä). The 8th circle of hell in Dante's "Inferno."

Malintzin (mä-lēn′tzēn). The Indian name of Marina, the Indian mistress of Cortes and guide of the Spanish army in Mexico.

Mall (mâl), **The.** A promenade in St. James's Park, London; also, a promenade in Central Park, New York.

Malta, The Knights of. See Dictionary, **Maltese.**

Malvolio (mal-vō′li-ō). In Shakspere's "Twelfth Night," the self-important steward of Olivia, who imagines that his mistress is in love with him.

Mambrino (mäm-brē′nō). In the Charlemagne romances, a pagan king, possessor of a wondrous golden helmet.

Mamelucos (mä-mä-lö′kōs). The Jesuit name for Brazilian slave-hunters in the 17th century.

Mamelukes. See Dictionary, **Mameluke.**

Mamertines (mam′ėr-tīnz). A band of Campanian mercenaries whose seizure of Messana (Sicily) about 282 B.C. led indirectly to the first Punic War.

Mammon, Sir Epicure. A worldling and sensualist in Jonson's "Alchemist."

Man against the Sky, The. A poem (1916) by Edwin Arlington Robinson, which gives its name to a volume of poems.

Man and Superman. A drama (1903) by G. B. Shaw, attacking the conventional idea of woman's passive rôle in courtship and marriage.

Manasseh (mȧ-nas′ė). In the Old Testament: (1) A son of the patriarch Joseph. Gen. xli. 51. (2) One of the 10 Hebrew tribes. Num. i. 10. (3) A king of Judah, son of Hezekiah. 2 Kings, xxi.

Manchester New College. A college at Oxford, originally a Unitarian institution in London.

Manchu Dynasty. See Dictionary, **Manchu.**

Manciple's Tale, The. One of Chaucer's "Canterbury Tales," based on one of the "Metamorphoses" of Ovid.

Manco Capac (män′kō kä-päk′). The traditional founder of the Inca monarchy of Peru.

Mandæans. See Dictionary, **Mandæan.**

Mandan (man′dan). A western tribe of North American Indians. A few survive in North Dakota.

Mandingo. See Dictionary.

Manette (mȧ-net′), **Lucie.** In Dickens's "Tale of Two Cities," the gentle daughter of Dr. Manette whose mind has crumbled during his long imprisonment in the Bastille: later the wife of Charles Darnay, a French émigré.

Manfred (man′fred). 1. A dramatic poem (1817) by Byron. 2. An opera (1852) by Schumann, who used Byron's words. 3. A character in Walpole's "Castle of Otranto."

Manhattan Transfer. A novel (1925) by John Dos Passos.

Mania (mā′ni-ȧ). An old Italian goddess of the dead (Manes), mother by Mercury of the Lares.

Manicheans. See Dictionary, **Manichean.**

Manilian (mȧ-nil′i-ȧn) **Law, The.** A law proposed 66 B.C. by Caius Manilius, granting Pompey supreme command in the East: defended by Cicero in "Pro Lege Manilia."

Man in the Iron Mask, The. 1. A mysterious Bastille prisoner who died in 1703. 2. See **Trois Mousquetaires, Les.**

Manito, or **Manitou.** See Dictionary, **manito.**

Manoa (mä-nō′ä). A fabled city of extraordinary wealth, supposed to exist on an island in Lake Parima.

Manoah (mȧ-nō′ä). The father of Samson. Judges, xiii. 2, etc.

Man of Destiny, The. A drama (1897) by G. B. Shaw, satirizing the conception of Napoleon as a figure of heroic proportions.

Man of Feeling, The. A famous novel of "sensibility" (1771) by Henry Mackenzie.

Man of Law's Tale, The. One of Chaucer's "Canterbury Tales."

Man of Mode, or Sir Fopling Flutter, The. A comedy (1676) by Etherege.

Manon (mȧ-nôn). An opera (1884) by Massenet, based on Abbé Prévost's "Manon Lescaut."

Manon Lescaut (les-kō). 1. A romance (1733) by Abbé Prévost. Its heroine, Manon, is a girl of strong desires, rendered physically inconstant to her lover by an overpowering desire for luxury. 2. An opera (1893) by Puccini.

Mansfield College. A college founded at Oxford in 1886, primarily for dissenters.

Mansfield Park. A novel (1814) by Jane Austen.

Mansion House, The. The official residence of the lord mayor of London.

Mansos (män′sōz). A wandering tribe of aborigines, first met in southern New Mexico in the 17th century. The survivors inhabit northern Chihuahua, Mexico.

Mantalini (man-tȧ-lē′nē). In Dickens's "Nicholas Nickleby," a foppish parasite who bankrupts his industrious wife.

Man That Corrupted Hadleyburg, The. A story (1900) by Mark Twain (S. L. Clemens).

Manu (mä′nö). In Sanskrit lore, mankind; also, any one of a class of demiurgic beings, each of whom presides over a cycle of time.

Manuel. The principal character in Cabell's "Figures of Earth."

Man Who Died Twice, The. A poem (1924) by Edwin Arlington Robinson. Pulitzer Prize poem, 1925.

Man Who Married a Dumb Wife, The. A drama (produced 1912) by Anatole France.

Man Who Understood Women, The. A story which gives its name to a collection (1908) by Leonard Merrick.

Man Who Was Thursday, The. A novel (1908) by Gilbert K. Chesterton.

Man without a Country, The. A story (1863) by Edward Everett Hale, about a self-expatriated officer of the United States army.

Man with the Hoe, The. A poem (1899) by Edwin Markham, suggested by a painting by Millet.

Maradick at Forty. A novel (1910) by Hugh Walpole. The character Maradick reappears in "Portrait of a Man with Red Hair" (1925).

Marah (mā′rä). 1. See Dictionary. 2. Naomi, the mother-in-law of Ruth. Ruth, i. 20.

Marais, Le (lė mä-rā). In the French Revolution, the members of the assembly who sat in the lower part of the chamber ('the marsh').

Marandaise (mar′ȧn-dāz). The sword of Ryance.

Marañones (mä-rä-nyō′näz). The followers of Aguirre, 16th-century Spanish adventurer in South America.

Marble Faun, The. A romance (1860) by Hawthorne.

Marcella. A novel (1894) by Mrs. Humphry Ward: a sequel is "Sir George Tressady" (1896).

Marcellians (mär-sel′i-ạnz). The followers of Marcellus, bishop of Ancyra in the 4th century. Their doctrine is akin to that of the Sabellians.

Marcellinists (mär-se-lin′ists). The adherents of Marcellina, a female Gnostic of Rome in the 2d century.

Marcellus (mär-sel′us). An illustrious Roman plebeian family of the Claudia gens.

Marchioness, The. A little half-starved servant of Sampson Brass in Dickens's "Old Curiosity Shop": so named by Dick Swiveller, the devil-may-care fellow who eventually marries her.

Marcian (mär′shian) **Codex, The.** A codex of the Iliad, discovered at Venice in the 18th century. Its publication (1778) revolutionized Homeric studies.

Marcionites (mär′shion-īts). The followers of Marcion of Sinope, a Gnostic teacher of the 2d century.

Marco Bozzaris. A poem (1827) by Fitz-Greene Halleck.

Marcomanni (mär-kō-man′ī). A Germanic tribe, a branch of the Suevi, first mentioned by Cæsar.

Mardi gras. See Dictionary.

Mare au Diable, La (lä mär ō dyäbl). An idyllic story (1846) by George Sand.

Marforio (mär-fō′ri-ō). An ancient statue, perhaps of Mars, now in the Capitoline Museum, Rome. On it, in Rome, in the 16th century, were posted retorts to the lampoons of Pasquin. See Dictionary, **Pasquin.**

Margites (mär-jī′tēz). An ancient Greek comic poem, held by Aristotle to contain the germ of stage comedy.

Maria (mạ-rī′ä). 1. Olivia's witty attendant in Shakspere's "Twelfth Night." 2. The second wife of Petruchio in Fletcher's "Woman's Prize, or the Tamer Tamed" (before 1633), a sequel to Shakspere's "Taming of the Shrew." 3. The witty young bride of Charles Surface in Sheridan's "School for Scandal." 4. (mä-rē′ä) A princess, said to be an illegitimate daughter of King Robert of Naples, loved by Boccaccio and portrayed by him under the name Fiammetta.

Mariage de Figaro, Le. See **Figaro.**

Mariamne (mä-ri-am′nē). 1. The wife of Herod I. of Judea, whom he put to death in a fit of jealous rage. 2. The title of various tragedies: notably, by Alexandre Hardy (1610), Tristan L'Hermite (1636), and Voltaire (1724).

Marian, Maid. See **Maid Marian.**

Mariana (mä-ri-an′ä). 1. A Florentine girl in Shakspere's "All's Well That Ends Well." 2. A lady betrothed to Angelo in Shakspere's "Measure for Measure."

Marianne (mȧ-ryän). 1. See Dictionary. 2. A French republican secret society of 1851 and the years following.

Marianne, ou les Aventures de la Comtesse de . . . . A long novel (1731–41) by Marivaux, important in the history of modern realism.

Maria Stuart. A tragedy (1801) by Schiller.

Maricopa (mä-rẹ-kō′pä). An Indian tribe of Arizona.

Marie Antoinette and Her Children. A portrait by Mme. Lebrun, in the palace of Versailles.

Marie de Médicis, The Life of. A series of 21 paintings by Rubens, in the Louvre, Paris.

Marina (mạ-rī′nä). The daughter of Pericles, in Shakspere's "Pericles."

Marino Faliero (mä-rē′nō fäl-yä′rō). A tragedy (1820) by Byron.

Marion Delorme (mȧ-ryôn dė-lôrm). A historical play (1831) by Victor Hugo.

Mariposa (mar-i-pō′sä) **Grove.** A grove of gigantic sequoias in Mariposa County, California.

Maritana (mar-i-tä′nä). An opera (1845) by Wallace.

Marius (mä-rē-üs). A principal character in "Les Misérables," by Victor Hugo.

Marius (mä′ri-us) **the Epicurean.** A philosophical novel (1885) by Walter Pater.

Marjory Daw. A story (1873) by T. B. Aldrich.

Mark, Basilica of St. A superb basilica founded 830 in Venice, and given its definitive form in 1052.

Mark, King. In Arthurian romance, a treacherous ruler of Cornwall.

Mark, The Gospel of. The second gospel in the New Testament.

Marlborough House. A London residence built 1710 by Wren. It now belongs to the British government.

Marley (mär′li), **Jacob.** In Dickens's "Christmas Carol," the former partner of Scrooge, whose ghost appears on Christmas Eve.

Marlow (mär′lō). A character in several of Joseph Conrad's novels, "Chance," "Lord Jim," etc.

Marlow, Young. The hero of Goldsmith's "She Stoops to Conquer," a youth diffident with women of his own class, but at his ease with domestics. Kate Hardcastle "stoops to conquer" him by posing as a barmaid.

Marmion (mär′mi-ọn). A romance in verse (1808) by Scott. Its hero, Lord Marmion, is slain at Flodden Field.

Marner (mär′nėr), **Silas.** The title character of George Eliot's "Silas Marner," a poor weaver whose life has been wrecked by a false accusation.

Maronites. See Dictionary, **Maronite.**

Marprelate (mär′prel″āt), **Martin.** The name signed to various pamphlets directed by the Puritans against the defenders of the English Church discipline, about 1589.

Marriage. A novel (1912) by H. G. Wells.

Marriage à la Mode. 1. A play (1673) by Dryden. 2. A series of six paintings (1745) by Hogarth, in the National Gallery, London. 3. A comedy (1707) by Cibber.

Marriage at Cana, The. 1. A painting by Veronese, in the museum at Dresden. 2. A painting by Veronese, in the Louvre, Paris. 3. A painting by Tintoretto, in Santa Maria della Salute, Venice.

Marriage of St. Catharine of Siena, The. The subject of several famous pictures: notably, two by Correggio (Paris, Naples); a triptych by Memling (Bruges); and paintings by Murillo (Cadiz), Rubens (Antwerp), and Veronese (Venice).

Marriage of the Virgin, The. 1. A painting by Perugino, in the musée at Caen, France. 2. A painting by Raphael, in the Brera, Milan.

Marrow Men, The. Adherents of the evangelical side of a doctrinal controversy in the Church of Scotland, about 1719–22. Their position was based on "The Marrow of Modern Divinity" (1644), by Edward Fisher.

Marrucini (mar-ö-sī′nī). An ancient Italian people allied to the Marsi. They dwelt north of Samnium.

Mars (märz). The ancient Roman god of war, identified with the Greek Ares.

Mars, The Hill of. See Dictionary, **Areopagus.**

Marse Chan. See **In Ole Virginia.**

Marseillaise. See Dictionary.

Marshall, Charles Fitz. See **Jingle, Alfred.**

Marshalsea (mär′shạl-sē) **Prison, The.** A prison in Southwark, London, famous latterly as a debtors' prison: abolished 1849.

Marshes of Glynn, The. A poem (1878) by Sidney Lanier.

Marsi (mär′sī). A Germanic tribe first mentioned by Strabo: probably a part of the Sygambri.

Marsic War, The. See **Social War, The,** 2.

Marsiglio (mär-sēl′yō). A Saracen king in the Charlemagne romances.

Mars in Repose. A Greek statue of the school of Lysippus, in the Museo delle Terme, Rome. See Dictionary, **Ares,** cut.

Marsyas (mär′si-ạs). In Greek mythology, a Phrygian musical rival of Apollo, flayed by the god for his presumption.

Martano (mär-tä′nō). A character in Ariosto's "Orlando Furioso," probably the original of Spenser's Braggadocchio.

Martha. 1. (mär′thạ) The sister of Lazarus, whose house in Bethany Jesus often visited. Luke, x. 38–42; John, xi. 1–44. 2. (mär′tä) A character in Goethe's "Faust." 3. An opera (1847) by Flotow.

Martin Chuzzlewit (chuz′l-wit). Novel (1844) by Dickens.

Martin Eden. An autobiographical novel (1909) by Jack London.

Martinists (mär′tin-ists). 1. The controversial supporters of Martin Marprelate. 2. The members of a pietistic sect formed by the Chevalier St.-Martin shortly before the French Revolution.

Martyrdom of St. George, The. A painting by Veronese, in San Giorgio, Verona.

Martyrdom of St. Lawrence, The. A painting by Rubens, in the Old Pinakothek, Munich.

Martyrios (mär-tē'rē-ōs) **Mine, The.** A possibly mythical gold-mine of the interior of Brazil, first reported about 1685.

Martyrs, Les (lā mär-tēr). A prose epic (1809) on the triumph of Christianity over paganism, by Chateaubriand.

Mary (mā'ri). In the New Testament: (1) The virgin mother of Jesus. Mat. i. 18–25. (2) The sister of Lazarus and Martha. Luke, x. 38–42.

Mary Barton. A novel (1848) by Mrs. Gaskell.

Maryland! My Maryland! A song (1861) by J. R. Randall, sung to the tune of "Lauriger Horatius" by the Confederates in the American Civil War.

Marylebone Gardens. A former place of entertainment in London, on High Street, Marylebone: celebrated for about a century after 1650.

Mary Magdalene. 1. See Dictionary, **magdalen.** 2. A drama (1910) by Maurice Maeterlinck.

Mary Olivier. A novel (1919) by May Sinclair.

Masa (mä'sä). An ethnic and linguistic group of the central Sudan.

Masada (mä-sä'dä). In Jewish history, a stronghold west of the Dead Sea, founded by the Maccabees, famous for the self-destruction of its garrison of 1,000 Zealots when besieged by the Romans.

Masai (mä-sī'), or **Elmoran** (el-mō-rän'). An African nation of the great plateau east of Lake Victoria.

Mascarille (más-ká-rēl). In "L'Étourdi," "Le dépit amoureux," and "Les précieuses ridicules," by Molière, a skilfully intriguing valet whose name has become a synonym for lying ingenuity and effrontery.

Masks and Faces. A dramatization (1854) of Charles Reade's "Peg Woffington," by Reade and Tom Taylor.

Maskwell. The sinister hypocrite in Congreve's "Double Dealer."

Mason and Dixon's Line. See Dictionary.

Masongo. See **Songo.**

Masora, Masorete. See Dictionary.

Massachuset (mas-ạ-chö'set). In the early 17th century, a tribe or confederacy of North American Indians dwelling near Massachusetts Bay from Plymouth to Salem.

Massachusetts Bay. A colony founded 1628 at Salem, Mass., under John Endicott. Winthrop, the second governor, founded Boston in 1630.

Massacre of the Innocents, The. 1. A painting by Tintoretto, in the Scuola di San Rocco, Venice. 2. A painting by Rubens, in the Old Pinakothek, Munich.

Massagetæ (ma-saj'e-tē). An ancient nomadic people, allied to the Scythians, dwelling northeast of the Caspian Sea.

Massilians (ma-sil'i-ạnz). The early Semi-Pelagians of Marseilles.

Master Builder, The. A play (1892) by Henrik Ibsen.

Masterman Ready. A juvenile story (1841) of seafaring life, by Frederick Marryat.

Master of Ballantrae, The. A novel (1889) by Robert Louis Stevenson.

Master of the Inn, The. A novel (1908) by Robert Herrick.

Mater Dolorosa (mā'tèr dō-lō-rō'sä). A painting (1554) by Titian, in the royal museum, Madrid.

Maternity. A drama (1903) by Eugène Brieux.

Matrimonio Segreto, Il (ēl mä-trē-mō'nē-ō sā-grā'tō). An opera (1792) by Cimarosa.

Matris (mā'trēz). In Hindu theology, the personified energies of the gods, worshiped by the Shaktas.

Matsya Avatara (mat'syạ a-vạ-tä'rä). The first incarnation of Vishnu, in the form of the fish which saved Manu (primeval mankind) from the deluge.

Matsya Purana (pö-rä'nä). A purana of about 15,000 stanzas, supposed to have been related to Manu by Vishnu in his *matsya* (fish) incarnation.

Mattathias (mat-ạ-thī'ạs) **the Hasmonean.** The father of the Maccabees.

Matthew (math'ū), **Gospel of.** The first gospel in the New Testament.

Matthew's Bible. A folio Bible (1537) compiled by John Rogers (under the name of Thomas Matthew), a friend of Tyndale, based on the versions of Tyndale and Coverdale.

Matthias (mạ-thī'ạs). The apostle chosen to take the place of Judas Iscariot. Acts, i. 26.

Maud. A poem (1855) by Tennyson.

Maud Muller. A poem (1866) by Whittier.

Maui (mou'ē). A tribal hero of New Zealand legend, and later of Hawaiian.

Maumbury (mâm'bẹ-ri) **Rings.** The best-preserved Roman amphitheater in England. It is south of Dorchester.

Maupin (mō-pan), **Mademoiselle de.** The heroine of Gautier's "Mademoiselle de Maupin" (1835), a novel of epicurean sexual adventure.

Maurice (mā'ris), **Saint.** The legendary commander of the "Theban Legion," martyred 286.

Maurya (môr'yä). The central figure in Synge's play "Riders to the Sea."

Mausoleum. See Dictionary, **mausoleum.**

Maximes (måk-sēm). A collection (1665, etc.) of moral maxims by La Rochefoucauld.

Mayapan (mä-yä-pän'). A legendary ancient settlement of Maya Indians in Yucatan. See Dictionary, **Maya²**.

May Day. A comedy (1601) by Chapman; also, a comedy (1775) ascribed to Garrick.

Mayfair. A fashionable locality east of Hyde Park, London.

Mayflower, The. The ship in which the Pilgrim Fathers sailed from Southampton to the New World in 1620.

May Laws, The. A series of Prussian laws (1873–74) curtailing the power of the church in secular affairs.

Mayo (mä'yō). A division of the Cahita branch of the Piman stock of North American Indians, inhabiting parts of Sonora and Sinaloa, Mexico.

Mayor of Casterbridge, The. A novel (1886) by Thomas Hardy.

Maypole Inn. See **Willet, Joe.**

Mazarin (maz'ạ-rin) **Bible, The.** The first printed Bible, printed at Mainz by Gutenberg, 1455–56: a copy of it was discovered in the Mazarin Library, Paris, in the eighteenth century.

Mazeppa (mạ-zep'ä). A narrative poem (1819) by Byron.

Mdewakanton (mdä-wä'kän-tŏn). A Dakota tribe of North American Indians. They fought under Little Crow in the Minnesota outbreak of 1862.

Meal-Tub Plot, The. A pretended anti-Protestant conspiracy (1679), trumped up by Dangerfield.

Measure for Measure. A comedy (1604) by Shakspere.

Mecklenburg Declaration of Independence, The. A declaration of American independence of England, said to have been made at Charlotte, North Carolina, May 20 or 31, 1775, by citizens of Mecklenburg County.

Medea (mẹ-dē'ä). 1. In Greek legend, a sorceress, daughter of Æetes of Colchis, and wife of Jason, whom she assisted in obtaining the Golden Fleece. Later she murdered her rival Creusa, and married Ægeus, by whom she had a son Medus, regarded as the ancestor of the Medes. 2. A play (431 B.C.) by Euripides. 3. A tragedy by Seneca. 4. A tragedy (1761) by Richard Glover. 5. An opera (1812) by Mayr.

Médecin malgré lui, Le (lẹ med-san mál-grä lwē). A comedy (1666) by Molière.

Médée (mā-dā). The title of tragedies by La Péruse (1553), Pierre Corneille (1635), and Legouvé (1855); also, of a lyric tragedy (1693) by Thomas Corneille and Charpentier, and of an opera (1797) by Cherubini.

Median (mē'di-ạn) **Wall, The.** A defensive wall anciently extending from the Tigris to the Euphrates north of Babylon.

Medici (med'ẹ-chē). An illustrious Italian family, notable for its statesmen and patrons of the arts, especially during the Renaissance. It furnished rulers of Florence and Tuscany, as well as two popes, Leo X. and Clement VII.

Meditations. The usual name for the philosophical work by Marcus Aurelius Antoninus.

Medusa. See Dictionary.

Mefistofele (mā-fēs-tō'fä-lä). An opera (1868) by Boito.

Megæra (mẹ-jē'rä). In Greek mythology, one of the Furies.

Megalesian (meg-ạ-lē'shiạn) **Games, The.** A six-day festival of ancient Rome, held in April in honor of Cybele.

Megarics (me-gar'iks). A school of philosophy founded by

(variable) ḍ as d or j, ş as s or sh, ṭ as t or ch, ẓ as z or zh; o, F. cloche; ü, F. menu; çh, Sc. loch; ṅ, F. bonbon; ', primary accent; ", secondary accent; †, obsolete; <, from; +, and; =, equals. See also lists at beginning of book.

Euclid of Megara. It combined the Socratic ethics with the Eleatic metaphysics.

Meghazils (me-ghä-zĕlz'). Two ancient Phenician monuments near Amrit.

Megiddo (me-gid'ō). A city and fortress of the tribe of Manasseh, near Mount Carmel. Josh. xvii. 11, etc.

Meistersinger von Nürnberg, Die (dē mīs'tėr-zing″ėr fon nürn'berċh). An opera (1868) by Wagner.

Mekhitarists (mek-i-tär'ists). An order of Armenian monks founded 1701 at Constantinople by Peter Mekhitar, and confirmed 1712 by the Pope. Their chief seat is the island of San Lazzaro, near Venice.

Melampus (me-lam'pus). In Greek legend, a soothsayer whose ears, cleansed by the tongues of serpents which he had saved from death, understood the voices of birds and beasts.

Melchites. See Dictionary, **Melchite**.

Melchizedek (mel-kiz'ẹ-dek). In the Old Testament, a priest-king of Salem: discussed by the author of the Epistle to the Hebrews (v. 6–10, etc.) as a spiritual prototype of Christ.

Meleager (mel-ẹ-ā'jėr). 1. In Greek legend, the heroic son of Œneus and Althæa. He was an Argonaut, and slayer of the Calydonian boar. See **Althæa**. 2. A statue in the Vatican, of Meleager with his hunting-dog.

Meleager and Atalanta. A painting by Rubens, in the Old Pinakothek, Munich.

Melema (me-lā'mä), **Tito.** See **Romola**.

Melibœus (mel-i-bē'us). A shepherd in Virgil's first eclogue.

Melibœus, The Tale of. One of Chaucer's "Canterbury Tales."

Melicertes (mel-i-sėr'tēz). In Greek mythology, a son of Athamas and Ino. Ino leaped with him into the sea, where he became the sea divinity Palæmon.

Melissa (me-lis'ạ). 1. In Greek legend, wife of Periander of Corinth, who murdered her in a fit of jealousy. 2. An enchantress who befriends Rogero and Bradamant, in Ariosto's "Orlando Furioso."

Melkarth (mel'kärth). The tutelary god of Tyre, identified with the Greek Melicertes.

Melmoth (mel'moth), or **Melmoth the Wanderer.** A "Gothic" romance (1820) by C. R. Maturin.

Melpomene (mel-pom'e-nē). 1. See Dictionary. 2. An antique statue in the Louvre, Paris: one of the largest surviving ancient sculptures.

Melting Pot, The. A play (1908) by Israel Zangwill, suggesting a somewhat idealistic amalgamation of races and cultures in the United States.

Melusina (mel-ụ-sī'nạ). In French legend, a water-fay who married Raymond, son of a Comte de la Forêt. On one day of each week she was half woman and half serpent.

Memnon (mem'non). In Greek legend, an Oriental or Ethiopian hero slain by Achilles in the Trojan War.

Memoirs of a Baby. A humorous story (1904) by Josephine Dodge Bacon.

Memorial Day. See Dictionary, **memorial**.

Menæchmi (me-nek'mī). A comedy of Plautus, based on the confused identities of twin brothers.

Menahem (men'ạ-hem). A king of Israel, who obtained the throne after killing Shallum, the murderer of Zachariah. 2 Kings, xv. 14–21.

Mendel. A novel (1916) by Gilbert Cannan.

Mendel's Law. See Dictionary, **Mendelian** and **Mendelism**.

Mendesian (men-dē'shiạn) **Goat, The.** A sacred animal of Egyptian mythology, held to be a manifestation of Osiris, and symbolizing the productive force in nature.

Mendoza (men-dō'thä) **Codex, The.** A historically important European copy, with Spanish translation, of an Aztec manuscript: published 1625 by Purchas, and now in the Bodleian Library.

Menelaus (men-e-lā'us). In Greek legend, the son of Atreus, brother of Agamemnon, and husband of Helen.

Menelaus with the Corpse of Patroclus. An antique group in marble (a Roman copy of a Greek original) in the Loggia dei Lanzi, Florence.

Menkalinan (men-kal'i-nan). A remarkable binary star of the second magnitude, in the right shoulder of the charioteer pictured in the constellation Auriga.

Mennonites. See Dictionary, **Mennonite**.

Meno (mē'nō), or **Menon** (mē'non). A dialogue of Plato, on the teachableness of virtue.

Menominee (me-nom'i-nē). A tribe of North American Indians, now on a reservation in Wisconsin.

Menschenhass und Reue (men'shẹn-häs ụnt roi'ė). A drama (1790) by Kotzebue: translated into English as "The Stranger," and altered and improved by Sheridan.

Mephibosheth (me-fib'ọ-sheth). The son of Jonathan, and grandson of Saul. 2 Sam. iv. 4.

Mephistopheles. See Dictionary.

Mercadet (mer-kȧ-dā). A play by Balzac (acted posthumously, 1851).

Mercedonius (mėr-sẹ-dō'ni-us). In the old Roman calendar, an intercalary month of 22 or 23 days, inserted every second year between the 23d and 24th of February.

Merchant of Venice, The. A comedy (about 1598) by Shakspere.

Merchant's Tale, The. One of Chaucer's "Canterbury Tales."

Merciless Parliament, The. An English Parliament of 1388, noted for its cruelty to the adherents of Richard II.

Mercury. See Dictionary.

Mercury, The Belvedere. A Greek statue of the best period, in the Vatican.

Mercury Fastening His Sandal. An antique marble statue, in the Glyptothek, Munich.

Mercutio (mėr-kū'shiō). In Shakspere's "Romeo and Juliet," a gay and reckless friend of Romeo, slain in a duel with Tybalt.

Meribah (mer'i-bạ). In the wilderness south of Palestine, the locality where Moses smote the rock and produced water. Ex. xvii. 7.

Merlin (mėr'lin). 1. In Arthurian legend, a magician and seer. 2. A poem (1917) by Edwin Arlington Robinson.

Mermaid Club, The. A club said to have been established (1603) by Sir Walter Raleigh. It met at the Mermaid Tavern, London.

Merodach (mer'ọ-dak). One of the 12 major gods of Assyro-Babylonian mythology: son of Ea.

Merope (mer'ọ-pē). 1. In Greek mythology, one of the Pleiades. 2. A tragedy (1858) by Matthew Arnold.

Mérope (mā-rop). A play (1743) by Voltaire.

Merovingians. See Dictionary, **Merovingian**.

Merrilies (mer'i-lēz), **Meg.** A weird gipsy woman in Scott's "Guy Mannering."

Merrimac, The. 1. A United States frigate sunk on the abandonment of the Norfolk navy-yard in 1861, raised by the Confederates, renamed the Virginia, and rebuilt with iron armor above the water-line. She inaugurated the era of armored war-ships. See **Monitor**. 2. A collier sunk by Richmond Pearson Hobson, June 3, 1898, in the entrance to Santiago Harbor, Cuba, in an attempt to block the channel.

Merry, Merry Cuckoo, The. See **Welsh Honeymoon, The**.

Merry Wives of Windsor, The. A comedy (about 1600) by Shakspere.

Mertetefs (mer-te-täfs'). The wife of Seneferu, the last king of Egypt of the 3d dynasty. She is the subject of a famous portrait-statue.

Meru (mā'rö). In Hindu mythology, the central mountain, abode of the gods.

Merveilleuse (mer-ve-yėz). The sword of Doon, or Doolin, of Mayence.

Mesha (mē'shạ), or **Mesa** (mē'zạ). A king of Moab. See Dictionary, **Moabite stone**.

Meshach (mē'shak). See **Shadrach**.

Messiah, The. 1. A pastoral (1712) by Pope. 2. An oratorio (1742) by Handel.

Messias. An epic poem (1748–73) by Klopstock.

Messidor. See Dictionary.

Metamorphoses (met-ạ-môr'fọ-sēz). A poetical work by Ovid, treating of the principal classical legends.

Metaphysical Poets, The. See Dictionary, **metaphysical**.

Meteora (me-tā'ō-rä). A group of monasteries near Trikkala, Thessaly, built on nearly perpendicular rocks.

Methusael (me-thū'sạ-el). The father of Lamech the father of Jubal. Gen. iv. 18.

Methuselah. See Dictionary.

Metis (mē'tis). In Greek mythology, daughter of Oceanus and Tethys and first wife of Zeus: a personification of prudence.

Metropolitan Museum of Art, The. An institution organized 1870 in New York City for the collection of works of art and the furtherance of artistic culture. Its building is in Central Park opposite East 82d Street.

Mettle of the Pasture, The. A novel (1903) by James Lane Allen.

Mexican War, The. See Dictionary, **Mexican.**

Miami (mī-am'ĭ). A tribe of North American Indians which inhabited southeastern Wisconsin in the 17th century.

Micah (mī'kȧ). 1. An Ephraimite who, after stealing from his mother, repented and made restitution. Judges, xvii. 2. The sixth of the minor prophets, and the third in the Septuagint, author of the Old Testament book bearing his name.

Mi-Carême. See Dictionary.

Micawber (mi-kä'bẽr), **Wilkins.** In Dickens's "David Copperfield," the improvident and impecunious father of a family. His ill luck is chronic, but it is equaled by his faith that "something will turn up."

Michabo (mich'ȧ-bō). In Algonquian legend, the Great Hare.

Michael (mī'kĕl or mī'kȧ-el). 1. A militant archangel. Dan. x. 13, etc. 2. A pastoral poem (1800) by Wordsworth.

Michael, The. A small bark, one of the two ships of Frobisher's first expedition, the other being the Gabriel.

Michael, The Archangel. A painting by Guido Reni, in Santa Maria dei Cappuccini, Rome.

Michael, The Order of Saint. An order of knighthood instituted 1469 by Louis XI. of France.

Michael and His Lost Angel. A drama (1896) by Henry Arthur Jones.

Michaelmas. See Dictionary.

Michel (mĭch'ĕl), **Cousin.** A humorous personification of the German nation.

Michmash (mik'mash). A stronghold of the Philistines near Jerusalem. 1 Sam. xiv. 5.

Micmac (mik'mak). A tribe of North American Indians in Nova Scotia, New Brunswick, and neighboring regions.

Micromégas (mē-kro-mā-gȧs). A philosophical romance (1752) by Voltaire.

Midas (mī'dȧs). In Greek legend, a Phrygian king, son of Gordius and Cybele, who was given by Dionysus the power of turning into gold whatever he touched.

Mid-Channel. A social drama (1909) by Arthur Wing Pinero.

Middle Ages. See Dictionary, **ages in history,** under **age.**

Middlemarch. A novel (1872) by George Eliot. See **Brooke, Dorothea.**

Midgard (mid'gärd). In Old Norse mythology, the abode of humanity, joined to heaven by the rainbow bridge of the gods.

Midgardsorm (mid'gärdz-ôrm). In Old Norse mythology, the great sea-serpent which encircles the earth, offspring of Loki and a giantess. It is slain by Thor.

Midian (mid'ĭ-ạn). The fourth son of Abraham by Keturah. Gen. xxv. 2.

Midrash. See Dictionary, **midrash.**

Midsummer Night's Dream, A. 1. A comedy (1595) by Shakspere. 2. A famous overture (1826) by Mendelssohn.

Miggs (migz), **Miss.** In Dickens's "Barnaby Rudge," a shrewish servant, later a turnkey, who pursues Tappertit with her attentions.

Mignon (mē-nyôn). 1. The pathetic daughter of an aged Italian harper in Goethe's "Wilhelm Meisters Lehrjahre." 2. An opera (1866) by Ambroise Thomas.

Mihrgan (mēr-gän'). The Persian festival of the autumnal equinox, supposed to have been instituted by Faridun.

Mikado (mi-kä'dō), **The.** A comic opera (1885) by W. S. Gilbert and Arthur Sullivan.

Milan, The Edict of. An edict of toleration of the Christians, promulgated 313 by Constantine and Licinius.

Miles Gloriosus (mī'lēz glō-ri-ō'sus). A character in Plautus's comedy of the same name which was imitated in several Elizabethan dramas. See **Parolles** and **Bobadil.**

Milesians (mi-lē'shianz or -zhianz). 1. The inhabitants of Miletus. 2. See Dictionary, **Milesian.**

Milesian Tales or Fables. Witty and obscene short stories of a type popular among the Greeks and Romans.

Miles Standish. The principal character in Longfellow's "The Courtship of Miles Standish" (1858).

Milestones. A drama (1912) by Arnold Bennett and Edward Knoblauch (Knoblock).

Milky Way. See Dictionary, **milky.**

Millamant (mil'ạ-mant). The brilliant and charming heroine of Congreve's "Way of the World."

Miller, Daisy. The heroine of "Daisy Miller" (1878), a story by Henry James about an American girl abroad whose naïve innocence makes her the victim of scandal.

Miller of Old Church, The. A novel (1911) by Ellen Glasgow.

Miller's Tale, The. One of Chaucer's "Canterbury Tales."

Mill on the Floss, The. A novel (1860) by George Eliot. See **Tulliver, Maggie.**

Milo (mī'lō), or **Milon** (mī'lon). A Greek athlete of the 6th century B.C., frequently a victor in the Olympic and the Pythian games.

Mimir (mē'mir). In Old Norse mythology, a gigantic water-demon who dwelt at the root of the tree Yggdrasil.

Minerva (mi-nẽr'vȧ). 1. The Roman counterpart of Athene. 2. An antique statue in marble, in the Glyptothek, Munich.

Minerva Medica, The. A fine antique statue in Parian marble, in the Vatican, Rome.

Minerva Pacifera, The. An antique statue, found at Velletri, now in the Capitoline Museum, Rome.

Minerva Press, The. A printing-house of London, which, in the 18th century, was noted for its publication of trashy novels.

Ming (ming). The Chinese ruling dynasty 1368–1644.

Minims. See Dictionary, **minim.**

Minna von Barnhelm (min'ä fon bärn'helm). A comedy (1767) by Lessing: the first German national drama to deal with contemporary events.

Minnehaha (min-ē-hä'hä), or **Laughing Water.** A Dakota Indian maiden, the bride of Hiawatha in Longfellow's "Song of Hiawatha."

Minnesingers. See Dictionary, **minnesinger.**

Minories (mī'nor-iz), **The.** A section of London, on the left bank of the Thames, near the Tower.

Minors. See Dictionary, **friar.**

Minos (mī'nos). In Greek legend, a king and lawgiver of Crete: after death, a judge in the lower world.

Minotaur (min'ō-târ). In Greek mythology, a man-eating monster confined in the Cretan labyrinth: killed by Theseus.

Minyæ (min'i-ē). In Greek legend, a semi-mythical race descended from Minyas, who founded Orchomenus. They included most of the Argonauts.

Minyas (min'i-ạs). See **Minyæ.**

Mira (mī'rȧ). A variable star in the constellation Cetus, remarkable for the great range and the irregularity of its variation in brightness.

Miracle of St. Anthony of Padua, The. A painting by Van Dyck, in the Palais des Beaux-Arts, Lille, France.

Miracle of St. Mark, The. A painting by Tintoretto, in the Accademia, Venice.

Miracle-Plays. See Dictionary, **miracle-play.**

Miraculous Draught of Fishes, The. A painting by Rubens, in Notre Dame, Malines, Belgium.

Mirañas (mē-rä'nyäz). Indians, said to be cannibalistic, in Colombia and northwestern Brazil.

Miranda (mi-ran'dȧ). In Shakspere's "Tempest," Prospero's daughter, loved by Ferdinand.

Mireille (mē-rā-y'). An opera (1864) by Gounod, based on Mistral's "Mirèio."

Mirèio (mē-rā'yō). A poem (1859) of Provençal life, by Mistral; written in the Provençal dialect, with a French translation.

Miriam (mir'i-ạm). 1. A Hebrew prophetess, sister of Moses and Aaron. Ex. xv. 20. 2. A character in Hawthorne's "The Marble Faun."

Mirror for Magistrates, The. An English compilation of poems illustrating the tragic consequences of ambition

---

(variable) ḏ as d or j, ş as s or sh, ṭ as t or ch, ẕ as z or zh; o, F. cloche; ü, F. menu; ċh, Sc. loch; ṅ, F. bonbon; ', primary accent; ", secondary accent; †, obsolete; <, from; +, and; =, equals. See also lists at beginning of book.

in the lives of men famous in English history: issued in 1559, and frequently thereafter with additions.

Mirrors of Downing Street, The. A study of English statesmen (1921) of the war and post-war periods, by "A Gentleman with a Duster" (Harold Begbie).

Mirrors of Washington, The. A study of American public men (1921) in the manner of "The Mirrors of Downing Street," by Clinton W. Gilbert.

Misalliance. A drama (1910) by G. B. Shaw.

Misanthrope, Le (lĕ mē-zän-trŏp). A comedy (1666) by Molière.

Misenus (mī-sē′nus). In Roman legend, a companion of Æneas.

Misérables, Les (lä mē-zā-räbl). A powerful novel (1862) by Victor Hugo, in 5 parts: "Fantine," "Cosette," "Marius," "L'Idylle rue Plumet," and "Jean Valjean."

Mishnah. See Dictionary, **mishnah.**

Misisaga (mis-i-sä′gä), or **Missisauga** (-sä′gä). A tribe of North American Indians which dwelt mainly north of Lake Huron in the 17th century.

Mississippi Scheme, The. A speculative scheme for paying off the national debt of France, originated by John Law. It culminated in a financial panic in 1720.

Missouri. A North American Indian tribe of Siouan stock, long consolidated with the Oto.

Missouri Compromise, The. An agreement (1820) between the pro- and anti-slavery factions in the United States, providing for the exclusion of slavery from any State that should be formed out of the part of the Louisiana Purchase lying north of the southern boundary of Missouri, with the exception of Missouri itself.

Mr. Britling Sees It Through. A novel (1916) by H. G. Wells, expressing the mental conflicts arising from the Great War.

Mr. Dick. Richard Babley, the mildly insane elderly protégé of Betsey Trotwood, in Dickens's "David Copperfield."

Mr. Gilfil's Love Story. One of George Eliot's "Scenes of Clerical Life."

Mr. Perrin and Mr. Traill. See **Gods and Mr. Perrin, The.**

Mr. Pim Passes By. A drama (1919) by A. A. Milne.

Mr. Polly, History of. A novel (1910) by H. G. Wells, portraying an ineffectual English tradesman.

Mr. Sludge, the Medium. A poem (1864) by Robert Browning.

Mrs. Alving. An important character in Ibsen's "Ghosts."

Mrs. Caudle's Curtain Lectures. A series of humorous monologues (1846) by Douglas Jerrold.

Mrs. Dane's Defence. A drama (1900) by Henry Arthur Jones.

Mrs. Hauksbee. A character in many of Kipling's stories of Anglo-Indian life.

Mrs. Proudie. See **Proudie, Bishop.**

Mrs. Warren's Profession. A drama (1893) by G. B. Shaw, the production of which was forbidden until 1902.

Mrs. Wiggs of the Cabbage Patch. A story (1901) by Alice Hegan Rice.

Mithra (mith′rä), or **Mithras** (mith′ras). In Persian mythology, the god of light, later of the sun.

Mithridate (mē-trē-dàt). A tragedy (1673) by Racine.

Mithridatic (mith-ri-dat′ik) **Wars.** Three wars (88–63 B.C.) between Rome and Mithridates, king of Pontus.

Mitre (mī′tèr), **The.** A former noted tavern in Mitre Court, off Fleet Street, London: a favorite resort of Samuel Johnson.

Mixco (mēs′kō). A formidable stronghold of the ancient Cakchiquel Indians of Guatemala, captured 1525 by the Spaniards.

Mixtecs (miks′teks), or **Mixtecas** (mēs-tä′käz). A numerous Indian stock of southern Mexico, in the mountains of western Oaxaca and vicinity.

Mizar (mī′zär). A binary star of the second magnitude, in the constellation Ursa Major: the middle star in the handle of the Dipper.

Mizpah (miz′pä). 1. The name of more than one place mentioned in the Old Testament; notably, a height 5 miles northwest of Jerusalem. 2. See Dictionary.

Mizraim (miz′rä-im). The ancient Hebrew name of Egypt.

Mjöllnir (myèl′nir). In Old Norse mythology, the hammer used by Thor against the giants.

Mnemosyne (nē-mos′i-nē). In Greek mythology, the goddess of memory, daughter of Uranus and Gæa, and mother (by Zeus) of the Muses.

Mnevis (nē′vis). In Egyptian mythology, the sacred bull of Heliopolis.

Moab, Moabite stone. See Dictionary, **Moabite.**

Mob, The. A drama (1914) by John Galsworthy, dealing with a question of international morality.

Moby-Dick. A sea tale (1851) by Herman Melville, about a white whale.

Mocoas (mō-kō′äz). A tribe of South American Indians, in southern Colombia.

Modern Instance, A. A novel (1882) by William Dean Howells, dealing with the marriage of a selfish, unprincipled man and a high-spirited, undisciplined girl.

Modern Painters. A long treatise on art (1843–60) by Ruskin.

Modoc (mō′dok). A tribe of North American Indians, dwelling principally in Oregon.

Modoc War, The. A war (1872–73) between United States troops and Modoc Indians under Captain Jack.

Modred (mō′dred). In Arthurian romance, the treacherous nephew of Arthur.

Mœræ (mē′rē). The Fates.

Mœris (mē′ris), **Lake.** According to Herodotus, a former artificial lake in Egypt, 50 miles southwest of Cairo.

Mœsogoths (mē′sō-goths). The Christianized agricultural Goths who settled in Mœsia in the 4th century.

Mogollon (mō-gō-lyōn′ or mō-gō-yōn′). A division of the Gileño (Apache) tribe of North American Indians, living in Arizona and New Mexico.

Mogul (mō-gul′), **The Great.** 1. An Indian diamond of 280 carats, said to have been seen (1665) at the court of Aurangzeb. 2. See Dictionary, **Mogul.**

Mohave or **Mojave** (mō-hä′vä). A tribe of North American Indians, dwelling chiefly on the east side of the Colorado River, from the Needles to the Black Cañon.

Mohawk (mō′hâk). A tribe of North American Indians, formerly resident along the Mohawk River, New York.

Mohegan (mō-hē′gạn). A tribe of North American Indians, dwelling chiefly on the Thames River, Connecticut, in the 17th century.

Mohican. See **Mahican.**

Mohocks (mō′hoks). See Dictionary, **Mohock.**

Mojave. See **Mohave.**

Molech (mō′lek). The same as **Moloch.**

Molinists (mō′li-nists). 1. Adherents of the theological doctrines of the Jesuit Luis Molina. 2. The Quietists, followers of the theologian Miguel de Molinos.

Molino del Rey (mō-lē′nō del rā). A place 4 miles west of the city of Mexico, stormed by United States troops Sept. 8, 1847.

Moll Flanders. A novel (1722) by Defoe, about the career and repentance of a harlot.

Molly Maguires (mạ-gwīrz′), **The.** 1. A lawless secret society organized in Ireland about 1843, chiefly for intimidation of the agents of the landlords. The members disguised themselves as women. 2. A similar organization in the mining regions of Pennsylvania, which was suppressed in 1877.

Moloch. See Dictionary.

Molossus (mō-los′us). In Greek legend, the son of Neoptolemus and Andromache.

Mombuttu (mom-but′tö). A great tribe of central Africa, settled in a fertile tract on the river Welle.

Momus (mō′mus). In Greek mythology, a god personifying censure and mockery. Hesiod makes him the son of Night.

Mona. An opera (1912) by Horatio Parker.

Mona Lisa (mō′nä lē′zä). A famous portrait by Leonardo da Vinci, in the Louvre, Paris. Its subject is "La Gioconda," wife of the Florentine Fr. del Giocondo.

Monastery, The. A historical romance (1820) by Scott: followed (1820) by a sequel, "The Abbot."

Mongol Empire, The. An Asiatic empire founded by Jenghis Khan (d. 1227).

Moniplies (mun′i-plīz), **Richie** (Richard). An honest, pedantic servant of Olifaunt in Scott's "Fortunes of Nigel."

Moniteur (mo-nē-tẻr). The official French governmental journal, 1799–1868.

Monitor, The. A vessel built under the direction of John Ericsson for the purpose of engaging the Confederate frigate Merrimac, and launched early in 1862. It consisted of a low hull surmounted by a revolving turret for the guns, and was armored. On March 9, 1862, it engaged and checked the Merrimac in Hampton Roads.

Monk, The. See **Ambrosio.**

Monks, The. A collection of poems (1886) by Émile Verhaeren.

Monmouth's Rebellion. An unsuccessful rebellion (1685) against James II. of England, led by the Duke of Monmouth, who was defeated, captured, and beheaded.

Monna Vanna. The title character in the drama (1902) by Maurice Maeterlinck.

Monroe Doctrine, The. See Dictionary.

Monsieur Beaucaire (m'syẻ bō-kẚr). A story (1900) by Booth Tarkington.

Mons Meg (monz meg). An old cannon in the castle at Edinburgh, made at Mons.

Montagnais (môn-tả-nyä). A collective name for: (1) The group of North American Indian tribes in Quebec north of the St. Lawrence. (2) Four tribes of North American Indians of Athapascan stock, occupying the interior of British North America.

Montagnards (môn-tả-nyär). 1. A collective name for six North American Indian tribes of Athapascan stock, dwelling in the interior of British North America. 2. In French history, the members of the Mountain.

Montague (mon'tạ-gū). The father of Romeo in Shakspere's "Romeo and Juliet." He is head of the house of Montague, whose ancient feud with the house of Capulet separates the lovers and leads to the tragedy.

Montanists (mon'tạ-nists). A sect of Christian adventists founded in the 2d century by Montanus of Phrygia.

Montauk (mon-tȧk'). A tribe of North American Indians which occupied eastern Long Island, New York, before 1788.

Monte Cassino (mōn'tä käs-sē'nō). A monastery on a high hill 45 miles northwest of Naples. Founded 529 by St. Benedict, it is the cradle of the Benedictine order.

Monte-Cristo, Le Comte de (lẻ kôn̄t dẻ môn-tä-krẽs-tō). An enormously popular romance (1844–45) by Dumas *père*.

Montesinos (mōn-tä-sē'nōs). A character in medieval romance. Don Quixote visits his cave, in Cervantes's great satire.

Monte Testaccio (mōn'tä tes-tät'chō). A hill southwest of the Aventine, Rome, composed of fragments of pottery of ancient times.

Montgomery Charter, The. A charter granted to the city of New York by John Montgomery, and in force 1730–1830.

Monticello (mon-tẹ-sel'ō). An estate, formerly the residence of Thomas Jefferson, near Charlottesville, Virginia.

Montmartre (môn-märtr). A quarter in the northern part of Paris: formerly a separate commune.

Montoni. The villain in Mrs. Radcliffe's "The Mysteries of Udolpho."

Mont Saint Michel (môn̄ san̄ mē-shel) **and Chartres** (shärtr). See **Henry Adams, The Education of.**

Monument, The. A column 202 feet in height, north of the Thames near London Bridge. It was designed by Wren to commemorate the great fire of 1666.

Moon, The Mountains of the. A range placed by Ptolemy in the interior of Africa, and supposed to contain the sources of the Nile.

Moon and Sixpence, The. A novel (1919) by Somerset Maugham, supposed to be based on the life of the artist Gauguin.

Moon-Calf. A novel (1920) by Floyd Dell. A sequel is "The Briary Bush" (1921).

Moonlight Sonata, The. A name given without warrant to the sonata in C sharp minor of Beethoven's Opus 27.

Moonstone, The. A novel of mystery (1868) by Wilkie Collins.

Moorfields. A former recreation ground outside the wall of old London, in the region of the present Finsbury Square.

Mopsus (mop'sus). In Greek legend, a seer, the son of Apollo and Manto.

Moquelumnan (mō-kel-um'nạn). A linguistic stock of North American Indians, formerly dwelling in the region about the present San Francisco, California.

Morals of Marcus Ordeyne, The. A novel (1905) by W. J. Locke.

Moravians. See Dictionary, **Moravian.**

Mordecai (môr'dẹ-kī). In the book of Esther, a Jew of the tribe of Benjamin. The feast of Purim commemorates his deliverance of Esther and the Jews from Haman.

Mordure (môr-dūr'). The same as **Excalibur.**

Mordvinians (môrd-vin'i-ạnz). A Russianized Finnic people dwelling chiefly in central European Russia.

Morey Letter, The. A letter forged (1880) in the name of J. A. Garfield, favoring Chinese cheap labor. It was addressed to a fictitious H. L. Morey.

Morgana (môr-gä'nạ), or **Morgaine** (môr'gān), or **Morgan le Fay** (môr'gạn lẻ fā). In Celtic and Arthurian lore, the fairy sister of King Arthur.

Morgante Maggiore, Il (ēl mor-gän'tä mäd-jō'rä). A heroic romance in verse (1485), partly burlesque, by Luigi Pulci. Its central figure is the giant Morgante.

Morgiana (môr-gi-an'ạ). A slave of Cassim and Ali Baba, in the "Arabian Nights' Entertainments."

Morglay (môr'glā). The sword of Sir Bevis of Hampton.

Morini (mor'i-nī). A Celtic people who dwelt in the region of the modern Boulogne.

Morlaks (môr'laks). A Slavic people, related to the Serbs, dwelling in Istria, Croatia, and Dalmatia.

Mormon, The Book of. An alleged abridgment by the prophet Mormon of a record of certain ancient peoples in America, written on golden plates, and discovered and translated (1827–30) by Joseph Smith. It is accepted as authoritative by the Mormon Church.

Mormons. See Dictionary, **Mormon.**

Moro. See Dictionary.

Morocco. See **Banks's Horse.**

Morosini (mo-rō-sē'nē). A Venetian family which became prominent in the 10th century. It included eminent prelates, statesmen, and soldiers, as well as a number of doges.

Morpheus (môr'fūs or môr'fẹ-us). See Dictionary.

Morris, Dinah. The preacher and heroine in "Adam Bede."

Morro, El (el mor'rō). A rock and plateau in western New Mexico, important for the numerous inscriptions on its vertical walls, many of them dating from the Spanish conquest.

Morro Castle. 1. A fort and political prison at the entrance to Havana harbor, Cuba. 2. A similar castle at Santiago de Cuba.

Morse alphabet. See Dictionary.

Morte d'Arthur (môrt där'thẻr). 1. A compilation and translation of French Arthurian romances made by Sir Thomas Malory and printed by Caxton in 1485. 2. One of Tennyson's "Idylls of the King," later expanded and named "The Passing of Arthur."

Morven (môr'ven). A mythical Scottish kingdom in the poems of Ossian.

Mosè in Egitto (mō-zä' ēn ä-jēt'tō). An opera (1818) by Rossini.

Moses (mō'zez). 1. The organizer of the Israelitish nation, and its first great lawgiver. Ex. ii.–Deut. xxxiv. 2. A statue by Michelangelo, in San Pietro in Vincoli, Rome.

Moses Striking the Rock. A painting (1649) by Poussin, in the Hermitage Museum, Leningrad.

Mosquitos (mos-kē'tōs). The Spanish name for a race of mixed African and Indian blood, in eastern Nicaragua and Honduras.

Mother. 1. A story (1906) by Maksim Gorki. 2. A novel (1911) by Kathleen Norris.

Mother, The. A drama (1891) by Hermann Bahr.

Mother Goose. The semi-legendary author of the familiar nursery jingles called "Mother Goose's Melodies." Apparently she is akin to the French Queen Goosefoot (Reine Pédauque).

Mother of the Gods, The. Cybele.

Mother's Day. See Dictionary, **mother**[2].

Mother Shipton. A mythical prophetess, formerly believed to have foretold (in the reign of Henry VIII.) most modern inventions and the end of the world, which her verses claimed would occur in 1881.

Mother's Recompense, The. A novel (1925) by Edith Wharton: what happens to a mother and daughter as a result of the mother's early disregard of convention.

Mountain, The. See Dictionary, **mountain.**

Mountain Meadows Massacre, The. A massacre of about 120 non-Mormon emigrants in southern Utah, Sept. 11, 1857. It was believed to have been instigated by Mormons.

Mount of Olives, The. An oratorio by Beethoven.

Mount Vernon. The former residence and the burial-place of George Washington, in Fairfax County, Virginia, on the Potomac.

Mourning Bride, The. A tragedy (1697) by Congreve.

Mouse Tower, The. A medieval watch-tower on a rock in the Rhine, near Bingen.

Mowgli (mou′gli). A native boy suckled by wolves and reared among animals of the jungle, in Rudyard Kipling's "Jungle Books."

Moyen de Parvenir (mwo-yan̄ dĕ pär-vĕ-nēr). An eccentric Rabelaisian work (1610) by Béroalde de Verville.

Mozarabs. See Dictionary, **Mozarab.**

Mpongwe (mpŏng′gwe). A Bantu tribe of French Equatorial Africa, dwelling about the Gabun estuary.

Mrichchhakatika (mrich-ch-hạ-ka-ti-kä′). A Sanskrit drama of unknown authorship, the "Little Clay Cart," dating perhaps from the 6th century or even earlier.

Muata-Yamvo (mwä′tä-yäm′vō). The title of the king of the Lunda people in southwestern Africa, once the greatest of African potentates.

Much Ado about Nothing. A comedy (about 1598) by Shakspere.

Mucklewrath (muk′l-räth), **Habakkuk.** In Scott's "Old Mortality," a fanatical preacher in the Covenanters' army.

Muggletonians (mug-l-tō′ni-ạnz). A former sect founded in England about 1651 by Lodowick Muggleton and John Reeve, who claimed to be the "two witnesses" in Rev. xi. 3.

Muharram. See Dictionary.

Mulciber (mul′si-bẽr). A surname of Vulcan.

Mullens, Priscilla. See **Priscilla Mullens.**

Mulligan Letters, The. A series of business letters written by J. G. Blaine. Falling into the hands of a bookkeeper, Mulligan, they were used in 1876 and 1884 in an attempt to prove the writer guilty of corruption.

Mulvaney (mul-vā′ni), **Terence.** The gigantic and witty Irishman of Rudyard Kipling's "Soldiers Three," and the companion of Ortheris, the sharp little cockney, and Learoyd, a saturnine Yorkshireman.

Mumbo Jumbo. See Dictionary, **mumbo-jumbo.**

Mummer's Wife, A. A novel (1884) by George Moore.

Muras (mö′räz). A formerly powerful horde of Brazilian Indians on the middle Amazon.

Muratorian (mū-rạ-tō′ri-ạn) **Fragment** or **Canon, The.** A summary of the canonical books of the New Testament, in popular and illiterate language of about the time of Marcus Aurelius.

Murdstone (mẽrd′stōn), **Edward.** See **Brooks of Sheffield.**

Murray Hill. An elevated district of New York City between 34th Street and 40th Street, named from a Quaker family who owned an estate on it.

Musagetes (mū-saj′e-tēz). Apollo, 'leader of the Muses.'

Musée des Antiquités Nationales (mü-zā dā-zän̄-tē-kē-tä nȧ-syo-nȧl). A museum in the château of St.-Germain-en-Laye, containing prehistoric objects and relics of early civilization.

Muses. See Dictionary, **Muse**[1].

Museum, The. 1. A hill south of the Acropolis, Athens. 2. An institution of learning in ancient Alexandria, founded by Ptolemy I.

Muskhogean. See Dictionary.

Muski (mös′kē). A people dwelling north of Cappadocia, mentioned in the cuneiform inscriptions: possibly the Moschi of Greek writers.

Muspellsheim (mös′pels-hām). In the Old Norse cosmogony, the realm of fire in the south, ruled by Surtr.

Mut (möt). In Egyptian mythology, 'the mother,' consort of Amun-Ra, and a personification of the female principle.

Mutiny Act, The. An act passed annually by the British Parliament, 1689–1879, providing for the punishment of mutiny and desertion and for the maintenance of a standing army.

My Ántonia (än′tō-nẹ-ạ). A novel (1918) by Willa Sibert Cather, presenting pioneer life in Nebraska.

Myrmidon (mẽr′mi-dọn). In Greek mythology: (1) A son of Zeus, reputed ancestor of the Myrmidons. (2) See Dictionary.

Myrrha (mir′ạ). In Greek legend, the mother of Adonis.

Myrtilus (mẽr′ti-lus). In Greek legend, a charioteer whose curses, when he was thrown into the sea by Pelops, brought innumerable woes upon the descendants of Pelops.

Mysteries of Udolpho, The. A romance (1794) of mysterious horrors, by Mrs. Radcliffe.

Mysterious Stranger, The. A satire (1916) by Mark Twain, written 1898.

Mytyl (mit′il). A child in Maeterlinck's drama "The Blue Bird." See **Tyltyl.**

N

Naaman (nā′ạ-man). A Syrian captain cured of leprosy by bathing in the Jordan. 2 Kings, v.

Nabal (nā′bạl). See **Abigail,** 1.

Naboth's Vineyard. A piece of property which a superior desires and takes away from one not in a position to prevent the wrong: from Ahab's treatment of Naboth, 1 Kings, xxi.

Nachen, The. An English ship which explored parts of the New England coast, beginning in 1615.

Nachi (nä′chē), or **Nadchés.** A nearly extinct tribe or confederacy of North American Indians which dwelt near the present Natchez, Mississippi.

Nachiketas (na-chi-kā′tas). In Hindu legend, the son of Vajashravasa.

Nadab (nā′dab). 1. See **Abihu.** 2. Son and successor of Jeroboam of Israel. 1 Kings, xiv.–xv.

Naglfar (nä′gl-fär). In Scandinavian mythology, the ship of the giants in Ragnarök.

Nahuas (nä′wäz), or **Nahuatlecas** (nä-wä-tlä′kạz). The Indian tribes, collectively, which dominated the Mexican plateau at the time of the Spanish conquest.

Nahum (nā′hum). The 7th minor prophet of the Old Testament.

Nailor (nā′lọr), **John.** A follower of Robin Hood, known as "Little John" because of his gigantic stature.

Nala (nä′lạ). 1. In the Mahabharata, the husband of Damayanti. 2. In the Ramayana, a monkey chief of supernatural powers.

Nan, The Tragedy of. A drama (1909) by John Masefield.

Nana (nä-nä). A novel (1880) by Zola.

Nanaa (nä′nạ-ä). In Assyro-Babylonian mythology, a goddess whose shrine was at Erech.

Nancy. In Dickens's "Oliver Twist," the mistress of Bill Sikes, by whom she is brutally murdered.

Nanda (nan′dạ). In Sanskrit mythology, a cowherd, the foster-father of Krishna.

Nanine (nȧ-nēn). A comedy (1749) by Voltaire, based on Richardson's "Pamela."

Nanking, The Treaty of. See **Opium War, The.**

Nantes, The Edict of. See Dictionary, **edict.**

Nanticoke (nan′ti-kōk). A large tribe of North American Indians which inhabited the eastern shore of Maryland in the 17th century.

Naomi (nā′ọ-mī or nạ-ō′mī). In the Bible, the mother-in-law of Ruth. Ruth, i. 2, etc.

Naphtali (naf′tạ-lī). In the Old Testament: (1) A son of Jacob and Bilhah. Gen. xxx. 8. (2) A tribe of Israel. Num. i. 15, 43.

Napoléon le Petit (nȧ-po-lā-ón̄ lĕ pė-tē). A satire (1852) by Victor Hugo, directed against Napoleon III.

Narasinha (na-rạ-sin′hạ). In Hindu legend, the fourth incarnation of Vishnu, in form half man, half lion.

Narcissus (när-sis′us). 1. In Greek mythology, a beautiful youth who fell in love with his own image in water, pined away, and was metamorphosed into the narcissus. 2. A Greek statuette, found at Pompeii: now in the Museo Nazionale, Naples.

Nariman (na-rē-män′). In the Shahnamah, a warrior killed in attacking Sipand, and avenged by Rustam.

Narraganset (nar-a-gan′set). An important former North American Indian tribe of Rhode Island, west of Narragansett Bay.

Nassau (nas′â or nä′sou), **The House of.** A European princely family, founded in the 12th century, which has furnished stadholders of the Netherlands and rulers since 1815.

Nassau (nas′â) **Hall.** The original name of the college which became Princeton University.

Naströnd (nä′strend). In Scandinavian mythology, the place of punishment for the wicked.

Nathan (nā′than). In the Old Testament: (1) A prophet, adviser and admonisher of David. 2 Sam. vii. 1–17. (2) A son of David. 2 Sam. v. 14.

Nathanael (na-than′a-el). One of the disciples of Jesus: possibly to be identified with Bartholomew. John, i. 45–51.

Nathan der Weise (nä′tän der vī′ze). A drama (1779) by Lessing. The title character is an idealized Jewish sage.

Nathan Hale. A drama (1898) by Clyde Fitch.

National Academy of Design, The. An organization founded in New York City in 1826 for the cultivation of the fine arts.

National Assembly, The. In French history, the first Revolutionary assembly, 1789–91.

National Cemetery, The. A cemetery at Arlington, Virginia, in which many Union soldiers of the Civil War, and soldiers of later wars, are buried.

National Convention, The. In French history, the sovereign assembly (1792–95) which abolished the monarchy.

National Gallery, The. An important picture-gallery on Trafalgar Square, London. The present building was opened 1838.

Nations, The Battle of the. The battle of Leipsic, Oct. 16, 18, and 19, 1813, in which the Prussians, Russians, Austrians, and Swedes defeated the French.

Natural Bridge, The. A limestone arch, 215 feet high, near Lexington, Virginia; also, any of similar arches elsewhere.

Nausicaa (nâ-sik′ā-a). In Homeric legend, the daughter of Alcinous, king of the Phæacians.

Navajo (nav′a-hō). The principal tribe of the southern division of the Athapascan stock of North American Indians.

Naval Academy, The United States. An institution for the training of naval officers, situated at Annapolis, Maryland: founded 1845.

Nazarene. See Dictionary.

Nazarites. See Dictionary, **Nazarite.**

Neæra (ne-ē′rä). A name for a maiden in Latin pastoral poetry: used by Milton in "Lycidas."

Nebo (nē′bō). In Assyro-Babylonian mythology, one of the principal gods, son of Merodach and husband of Tashmet.

Nebuchadnezzar (neb″u-kad-nez′ar). A king of Babylonia. Dan. i.-iv.

Negrito. See Dictionary.

Nehemiah (nē-he-mī′a), **The Book of.** A book of the Old Testament, probably in part by Nehemiah, a Hebrew cupbearer of Artaxerxes I. of Persia.

Neith (nē′ith), or **Net** (net). In Egyptian mythology, the unbegotten mother of the sun.

Neleus (nē′lūs). In Greek mythology, son of Poseidon and Tyro, founder of Pylus in Messenia, and father of Nestor.

Nelson Monument, The. A column and statue in Trafalgar Square, London, commemorative of Lord Nelson's naval exploits.

Nemean (ne-mē′an or nē′me-an) **Games.** One of the four national festivals of the ancient Greeks. (See **Olympic, Pythian,** and **Isthmian Games.**) It was celebrated at Nemea in the 2d and 4th year of each Olympiad.

Nemesis (nem′e-sis). In Greek mythology, a goddess presiding over the allotment of due good and evil to man: hence associated with retribution.

Neoptolemus. See **Pyrrhus.**

Nephele (nef′e-lē). In Greek legend, the wife of Athamas, and mother of Phrixus and Helle.

Neptune. See Dictionary.

Nereids. See Dictionary, **Nereid.**

Nereus (nē′rūs). See Dictionary, **Nereid.**

Neri (nā′rē). See **Bianchi.**

Nerissa (ne-ris′a). In Shakspere's "Merchant of Venice," the waiting-maid of Portia.

Nervii (nėr′vi-ī). An ancient Belgic people, defeated by Cæsar 57 B.C.

Nessus (nes′us). In Greek legend, a centaur shot by Heracles with a poisoned arrow. Heracles was himself fatally poisoned by a garment stained with the blood of Nessus, sent to him by Deianira, who thought that it would preserve his love for her.

Nestor. See Dictionary.

Neutral Ground, The. That part of Westchester County, New York, which lay between the British and the American lines during the Revolutionary War. Cooper's "Spy" (1821) is a tale of this region.

Neveu de Rameau, Le (lė nė-vė dė rä-mō). A satirical and philosophical work of fiction (about 1760) by Diderot.

Nevil Beauchamp (bē′cham). The hero of George Meredith's "Beauchamp's Career."

Neville's (nev′ilz) **Cross.** A place near Durham, England: the scene of an English victory over the Scots in 1346.

Nevski Prospekt (nef′ske pros-pekt′). The principal street of the former St. Petersburg (Leningrad).

New Atalantis, The. A famous *chronique scandaleuse* (1709) by Mary de la Rivière Manley.

New Atlantis, The. An allegorical romance (before 1617) by Francis Bacon. See Dictionary, **Atlantis.**

Newburg Addresses, The. Two anonymous letters (1783) written by John Armstrong, setting forth the grievances of the American Revolutionary soldiers.

New College, or College of St. Mary Winton. A college of Oxford University, founded 1379.

Newcome (nū′kum), **Barnes.** In Thackeray's "Newcomes," the brother of Ethel, and Clive Newcome's cousin. He ill-treats his wife, who flees for refuge to her former lover, Lord Highgate.

Newcome, Clive. In Thackeray's "Newcomes," Colonel Newcome's son, a young artist who eventually marries his cousin Ethel.

Newcome, Colonel. In Thackeray's "Newcomes," a simple, gallant, and unworldly retired officer, the father of Clive Newcome and the uncle of Ethel and Barnes. He loses his fortune and dies a pensioner in the Charterhouse.

Newcome, Ethel. In Thackeray's "Newcomes," Colonel Newcome's niece, destined by her grandmother for a brilliant match. In the end she marries her cousin Clive.

Newcomes, The. A novel (1855) by Thackeray.

Newdigate (nū′di-gat) **Prize, The.** An annual prize for verse at Oxford University: founded by Sir Roger Newdigate (1719–1806).

New England Confederation, The. A union of the New England colonies (1643–84) for defense against the Indians and the Dutch.

New England Nun, A. A short story (1891) by Mary E. Wilkins Freeman.

New England Primer, The. A famous elementary book of instruction (2d ed., Boston, about 1691).

New Forest, The. A forest region in southwestern Hampshire, England, covering 144 square miles. The tract was forcibly afforested by William the Conqueror for use as a hunting demesne.

Newgate (nū′gat). 1. The western gate by which the Watling Street left London. 2. A prison located at Newgate, destroyed 1902.

Newgate Calendar, The. A biographical record of notorious prisoners confined in Newgate.

New Grub Street. A novel (1891) by George Gissing. See Dictionary, **Grub Street.**

New Hampshire. Poems (1923) by Robert Frost.

Newly-Married Couple, The. A drama (1865) by Björnstjerne Björnson.

New Machiavelli, The. A novel (1910) by H. G. Wells.

New Men, The. A drama (1888) by Hermann Bahr.

Newnham (nūn′am) **College.** A college of Cambridge University, founded 1875 for the higher education of women.

(variable) ḏ as d or j, ş as s or sh, ṯ as t or ch, ẕ as z or zh; o, F. cloche; ü, F. menu; ċh, Sc. loch; ṅ, F. bonbon; ′, primary accent; ″, secondary accent; †, obsolete; <, from; +, and; =, equals. See also lists at beginning of book.

New Place. The house of Shakspere's residence and death at Stratford-on-Avon.

New Testament, The. See Dictionary, **testament.**

New Way to Pay Old Debts, A. A comedy by Massinger, printed 1632, and still famous for the character of Sir Giles Overreach.

New York Public Library, The. A library founded 1895 in New York City by consolidation of the Astor, Lenox, and Tilden libraries. The present building was opened 1911.

Nez Percés (nā per-sāz'). The 'pierced nose' Indians: a French name applied esp. to the principal Shahaptian tribe, the Chopunnish.

Ngola (ngō'lä). A Bantu tribe of the Kambu and Hamba valleys, West Africa.

Nibelungenlied (nē'bẹ-lùng-ẹn-lēt''). A Middle High German epic, given its present form by an unknown author in South Germany during the first half of the 13th century. See **Ring des Nibelungen, Der.**

Nibelungs (nē'bẹ-lùngz), **The.** In German legend: (1) A race of Northern dwarfs, named from their king, Nibelung. (2) The followers of Siegfried, who captured the Nibelungs' hoard. (3) Later, the Burgundians.

Nicene Councils, The. See Dictionary, **Nicene.**

Nicene Creed, The. See Dictionary, **Nicene.**

Nicholas (nik'ọ-lạs), **Saint.** A bishop in Asia Minor (4th century). He owes his position as Santa Claus (Saint Nicolaus) to the legendary incident of his providing dowries for the three daughters of a poor man by throwing purses of gold into their window on three successive nights.

Nicholas Frog. A nickname for the Dutch, in Arbuthnot's "History of John Bull."

Nicholas Nickleby (nik'l-bi). A novel (1838–39) by Dickens.

Nicias (nish'i-ạs), **The Peace of.** A truce negotiated by Nicias between Athens and Sparta, 421 B.C.

Nickleby (nik'l-bi), **Mrs.** The weak and characterless mother of the hero of Dickens's "Nicholas Nickleby."

Nicodemus (nik-ọ-dē'mus). A Pharisee and "ruler of the Jews" who visited Jesus by night. John, iii. 1–21.

Nicolette. See **Aucassin et Nicolette.**

Nicomachean (ni-kom-ạ-kē'ạn) **Ethics.** An ethical treatise by Aristotle.

Niflheim (nif'l-hām). In the Old Norse cosmogony, the world of fog in the north.

Niflhel (nif'l-hel). In Old Norse mythology, the realm of the goddess Hel; the abode of the dead.

Nigger of the Narcissus, The. A novel (1899) by Joseph Conrad, showing the power of superstitious fear among sailors. In America, called "The Children of the Sea."

Night at an Inn, A. A drama of retribution (1917), by Lord Dunsany.

Nightmare Abbey. An eccentric novel (1818) by T. L. Peacock.

Night's Lodging, A. A drama (1902) by Maksim Gorki.

Nights with Uncle Remus. See **Uncle Remus.**

Night Thoughts. A religious and moralistic poem (1742–45) by Edward Young.

Night-Watch, The. A painting (1642) by Rembrandt, in the Rijks Museum, Amsterdam. It represents a daylight assembly of the civic guard.

Nike (nī'kē). 1. In Greek mythology, the goddess of victory. 2. A statue by Pæonius, dedicated about 420 B.C., and now in the museum at Olympia.

Nike Apteros (ap'tẹ-ros), or **Wingless Victory, The Temple of.** An Ionic temple, 18 by 27 feet, by the Propylæa, Athens: excavated 1835.

Nile, The Battle of the. The British naval victory of Aug. 1–2, 1798, in which Nelson shattered the French fleet under Brueys.

Nils, The Wonderful Adventures of. Stories for children (1906) by Selma Lagerlöf.

Niña (nē'nyä), **The.** See **Santa Maria.**

Ninety-Three. See **Quatre-Vingt-Treize.**

Nine Worthies, The. Nine heroes of medieval story: Joshua, David, Judas Maccabæus; Hector, Alexander, Julius Cæsar; Arthur, Charlemagne, Godfrey of Bouillon (sometimes Bertrand du Guesclin and Guy of Warwick).

Ninus (nī'nus). The legendary founder of Nineveh and of the Assyrian empire: husband of Semiramis.

Niobe (nī'ọ-bē). In Greek mythology, the daughter of Tantalus and wife of Amphion of Thebes. She provoked Apollo and Artemis to vengeance by taunting their mother Leto with the number and beauty of her own children.

Niobe Group, The. A collection of 18 antique statues, now in the Uffizi, Florence. They show Niobe in the midst of her children, who are being struck down by the shafts of Apollo and Artemis.

Nipmuc (nip'muk). A general name for the North American Indian tribes which inhabited central Massachusetts and adjacent regions.

Nipper, Susan. In Dickens's "Dombey and Son," a sharp-tongued maid.

Nirvana. See Dictionary, **nirvana.**

Nisroch (nis'rok). An Assyrian god in whose temple Sennacherib was murdered. 2 Kings, xix. 37.

Nisus (nī'sus). 1. In classical legend, a follower of Æneas and bosom friend of Euryalus, whom he would not abandon to save his own life. 2. In Greek legend, a king of Megara. See **Scylla, 2.**

Njörd (nyèrd). In Old Norse mythology, the father of Frey and Freya: the dispenser of riches.

Noah (nō'ạ). A patriarch, the son of Lamech. With his family and animals of every species, he survived the deluge. Gen. v.–ix.

Nobel Prizes. Prizes awarded annually from the bequest of Alfred B. Nobel, a Swedish scientist. They are given for achievement during the preceding year in physics, chemistry, medicine, literature, and the promotion of peace.

Noche Triste (nō'chä trēs'tä). June 30, 1520, the night on which the forces of Cortes were nearly annihilated during their attempted withdrawal from Tenochtitlan (Mexico City).

Noctes Ambrosianæ (nok'tēz am-brō-ẓi-a'nē). A series of essays (1822–35) in dialogue, chiefly by John Wilson.

Nocturne. A novel (1917) by Frank Swinnerton.

Nod (nod). The land to which Cain fled, eastward from Eden. Gen. iv. 16.

Noli Me Tangere (nō'lī mē tan'jẹ-rē). 1. The title of two famous paintings on the subject of John, xx. 17: (1) By Rembrandt, in Buckingham Palace. (2) By Titian, in the National Gallery, London. 2. See **Social Cancer, The.**

No More Parades. A novel (1925) by Ford Madox Ford: a continuation of "Some Do Not" (1924).

No-Popery Riots. See **Gordon Riots.**

Norma (nôr'mạ). An opera (1831) by Bellini.

Norman Conquest, The. See Dictionary, **Norman.**

Norman's Woe. A reef outside Gloucester harbor, mentioned in Longfellow's "Wreck of the Hesperus."

Norn. See Dictionary.

Northanger (nôr-thang'gèr) **Abbey.** A novel by Jane Austen, satirizing the "Gothic" romances, or "school of terror." It was written 1798; published 1818.

North of Boston. Poems (1914) by Robert Frost.

Northumberland House. A historic house formerly on the Strand, London: removed 1873–74.

Norval (nôr'vạl), **Young.** A youth in Home's "Douglas," really the son of Lady Randolph by a former marriage. Lord Randolph kills him before discovering the relationship.

Norwich (nor'ij) **Festival, The.** A triennial musical festival at Norwich, England: established 1824.

Nostoi (nos'toi). A Greek epic of about 740 B.C., by Agias of Trœzen, relating the return of the Achæan heroes from Troy.

Nostromo (nos-trō'mō). A novel (1904) by Joseph Conrad, about the South American seaboard.

Notre Dame (nōtr däm). A famous and imposing cathedral in Paris, begun 1163.

Notre Dame de Paris (dẹ pȧ-rē). A historical romance (1831) by Victor Hugo.

Nouvelle Héloïse, Julie ou la (zhü-lē ö lä nö-vel ā-lō-ēz). A sentimental novel of passion (1761) by Rousseau.

Novum Organum (nō'vum ôr'gạ-num). The chief philosophico-scientific work of Francis Bacon, published (in Latin) 1620.

Noyades (nwo-yäd). In the Reign of Terror, executions by drowning practised by Carrier at Nantes, 1793–94.

Nozze di Figaro, Le (lä not'sä dē fē'gä-rō). An opera (1786) by Mozart, based on "Le Mariage de Figaro," by Beaumarchais.

Nubas (nōō′băz). A mixed Negritic and Hamitic people inhabiting the Nile valley between the first and second cataracts.

Nuits, Les (lā nwē). Four poems (1835–37) by Alfred de Musset: "Nuit de Mai," "Nuit de Décembre," "Nuit d'Août," and "Nuit d'Octobre."

Numa Pompilius (nū′mȧ pom-pil′i-us). The legendary second king of Rome, 715–672 B.C. He was the reputed introducer of many religious and political institutions. See **Egeria.**

Numbers. The fourth book of the Old Testament: so called because it relates the numbering of the Israelites after the exodus from Egypt.

Numitor (nū′mi-tôr). In Roman legend, the grandfather of Romulus and Remus.

Nun's Priest's Tale, The. One of Chaucer's "Canterbury Tales": the story of Chanticleer's escape from the fox.

Nu-pieds (nü-pyā). The Norman peasants who, revolting at Avranches against unjust taxation, were ruthlessly quelled by Richelieu.

Nut-Brown Maid, The. A famous ballad of the late 15th century.

Nyam-Nyam (nyäm-nyäm′), or **Sandeh** (sän′de). An African people, formerly cannibals, dwelling in the basins of the Welle and Shari rivers.

Nyamwezi (nyäm-wā′zē), or **Wanyamwezi** (wä-). A Bantu nation inhabiting a region south of Lake Victoria.

Nyaya (nyä′yȧ). One of the six systems of Hindu philosophy: a method of philosophical inquiry into all branches of knowledge, especially dialectic.

Nydia (nid′i-ȧ). See **Glaucus,** 2.

Nyika (nyē′kä), or **Anyika** (ä-nyē′kä). A Bantu tribe of the region of Mombasa.

Nym (nim). In Shakspere's "Merry Wives of Windsor" and "Henry V.," a thieving companion of Falstaff.

Nymphæum (nim-fē′um). The hill northwest of the Pnyx, southwest of Athens. It abounds in remains of prehistoric Athens.

Nyoro (nyō′rō), or **Banyoro** (bä-nyō′rō). A Bantu tribe, dwelling on the plateau between Lakes Albert and Victoria.

O

Oaks, The. A race for three-year-old fillies run annually at Epsom, England, on the Friday after the Derby. It was established in 1779.

Oannes (ō-an′nēz). In Babylonian mythology, a sea-born monster which taught the Babylonians letters and science.

Obadiah (ō-bȧ-dī′ȧ). A minor Hebrew prophet, author of the Old Testament book which bears his name.

Obed (ō′bed). The son of Ruth and grandfather of David. Ruth, iv. 17.

Oberlé, Les (lā-zō-ber-lā). A novel (1901) by René Bazin.

Obermann (ō-ber-män). A novel (1804) by Étienne de Sénancour: a study, in a series of letters, of disillusionment.

Oberon (ō′bẹ-rọn). 1. A romantic poem (1780) by Wieland. 2. An opera (1826) by Weber. 3. In Shakspere's "Midsummer Night's Dream," the king of the fairies and husband of their queen, Titania. See **Huon de Bordeaux.**

Oblivion, The Act of. An English act of amnesty (1660) for all political offenses committed during the Commonwealth.

Obongo (ō-bong′gō), or **Abongo** (ȧ-bong′gō). A tribe of pygmies in French Equatorial Africa.

Obrenovich (ō-bren′ō-vich). The family which ruled Serbia 1817–42 and 1858–1903.

Observations of Bel. A Babylonian astronomical work dating from the time of Sargon I.

Oceanus (ō-sē′ȧ-nus). 1. See Dictionary, **ocean.** 2. In classical mythology, the ocean personified: husband of Tethys.

Ochiltree (ōch′l-trē), **Edie.** In Scott's "Antiquary," a licensed beggar, called "Blue Gown" from the color of his professional costume.

O'Connell's Tail. A nickname for the parliamentary following of Daniel O'Connell after 1830.

Octavian (ok-tā′vi-ạn) **Library, The.** The earliest Roman library open to the public, founded by Augustus in honor of his sister Octavia, and destroyed by fire about A.D. 80.

October Club, The. A former club of English Tories, very influential in the reign of Anne.

Octopus, The. A novel (1901) by Frank Norris, the first of a trilogy (left incomplete at author's death), "The Epic of the Wheat": it presents the growth of the wheat in the fields. The second member of the trilogy is "The Pit," which presents the wheat as the source of the nation's wealth.

Odelsthing (ō′dels-ting). The lower house of the Norwegian Storthing or parliament.

Odéon (o-dā-ôṅ). A historic theater of Paris, subsidized by the state as an offshoot of the Comédie Française.

Odeum of Herodes or **of Regilla.** See Dictionary, **odeum,** and cut.

Odin. See Dictionary.

Odysseus (ō-dis′ūs). In Greek mythology, the son of Laertes, husband of Penelope, and father of Telemachus. See Dictionary, **Odyssey.**

Odyssey, The. See Dictionary.

Œdipe (ā-dēp). 1. A tragedy (1659) by Corneille. 2. A tragedy (1718) by Voltaire.

Œdipus (ed′i-pus or ē′di-). In Greek legend, a king of Thebes, son of Laius and Jocaste, and slayer of the Sphinx. His involuntary patricide and marriage to his mother, and his subsequent misery, made him a frequent subject of tragedy.

Œdipus Coloneus (kō-lō-nē′us). A tragedy of Sophocles, posthumously exhibited about 402 B.C.

Œdipus Tyrannus (ti-ran′us). A tragedy of Sophocles, considered by many his masterpiece.

Œneus (ē′nūs). In Greek legend, king of Calydon, husband of Althæa, and father of Meleager and Tydeus.

Œnomaus (en-ō-mā′us or ē-nō-). In Greek mythology, a son of Ares and father of Hippodamia, whose suitors he killed until Pelops overcame him by strategy and won her.

Œnone (ē-nō′nē). In classic myth, a nymph on Mount Ida, the wife of Paris. Tennyson has a poem "Œnone."

Offa's (of′ȧz) **Dyke.** An intrenchment between the Wye and the Dee, near the Welsh-English border, built in the 8th century by Offa for defense against the Welsh.

Of Human Bondage. A novel (1915) by W. Somerset Maugham.

O'Flaherty, V. C. A drama (1915) by G. B. Shaw.

Og (og). An Amorite king of Bashan, defeated by the Hebrews. He was a giant. Deut. iii. 11.

Ogier (ō′ji-èr) **the Dane.** In medieval legend, one of the mightiest of Charlemagne's paladins: as Holger Danske, a Danish national hero.

Oglala (og-lä′lä). A division of the Sioux Indians. Also, **Ogallala.**

Ohio Company, The. A company of Southern colonists who received (1749) a grant of 500,000 acres in the Ohio valley.

Ojibwa (ō-jib′wä), or **Chippewa** (chip′ẹ-wä). A large tribe of North American Indians, divided between the United States and Canada in the Great Lakes region.

Old Bachelor, The. A comedy (1693) by Congreve.

Old Bailey Court, The. The principal criminal court in London.

Oldbuck, Jonathan. An eccentric and irritable, but benevolent, collector of coins and medals in Scott's "Antiquary."

Old Chester. The scene of many short stories by Margaret Deland. See **Dr. Lavendar.**

Old Colony, The. The part of eastern Massachusetts occupied by the Plymouth Colony.

Old Creole Days. Stories (1879) by George W. Cable.

Old Curiosity Shop, The. A novel (1840–41) by Dickens.

Old Delabole. A novel (1915) by Eden Phillpotts.

Oldenburg (ōl′dẹn-bèrg, G. ol′dẹn-bûrch). A noble German family which gained prestige in the 15th century. One of its branches is the Danish royal family.

Old English. A drama (1924) by John Galsworthy.

Old English Baron, The. A romantic novel (1777) by Clara Reeve.

Old Guard, The. 1. The imperial guard created 1804 by Napoleon. It made the last French charge at Waterloo. 2. In American politics, the ultraconservative element of the Republican party.

Old Ironsides. See **Constitution, The.**

Old King Cole. A nursery rime, probably connected with

the King Cole who, according to the old chroniclers, reigned in Britain in the 3d century.

Old Ladies, The. A novel (1924) by Hugh Walpole: an analysis of three old women living together who have no understanding of one another.

Old Man of the Mountain, The. 1. The chief of the order of Assassins. 2. A frequent name for the Profile in Franconia Notch, New Hampshire.

Old Man of the Sea, The. In the "Arabian Nights' Entertainments," a monster who clung tenaciously to the back of Sindbad.

Old Mole. A novel (1914) by Gilbert Cannan.

Old Mortality. A romance (1816) of the Covenanter uprising of 1679, by Scott. Robert Paterson, who passed his life restoring the gravestones of Covenanters, was known as "Old Mortality."

Old Oaken Bucket, The. A familiar song (1817) by Samuel Woodworth.

Old Testament, The. See Dictionary, **testament**.

Oldtown Folks. A novel (1869) of old-time New England, by Harriet Beecher Stowe.

Old Wives' Tale, The. 1. A comedy (1595) by Peele. 2. A novel (1908) by Arnold Bennett.

Oléron (ō-lā-rôṅ), **The Judgments of.** The oldest collection of modern maritime laws, promulgated about the middle of the 12th century.

Olifaunt (ol′i-fạnt), **Nigel** (**Lord Glenvarloch**). The hero of Scott's "Fortunes of Nigel."

Olivant (ol′i-vant). See **Roland.**

Oliver (ol′i-vėr). 1. One of the 12 peers of Charlemagne. See Dictionary, **Roland.** 2. The brother of Orlando, and Celia's lover, in Shakspere's "As You Like It."

Oliver le Dain (ol′i-vėr lė daṅ). The barber and favorite adviser of Louis XI. of France, introduced by Scott in "Quentin Durward."

Oliver Twist. A novel (1838) by Dickens.

Olivia (ō-liv′i-ạ). 1. See **Viola.** 2. A treacherous woman in Wycherley's "Plain Dealer." 3. A principal character in Goldsmith's "Good-Natured Man." 4. One of the vicar's daughters in Goldsmith's "Vicar of Wakefield."

Olney (ol′ni) **Hymns, The.** A collection of hymns (1779) by William Cowper and John Newton.

Olympic Games, The. See Dictionary, **Olympic.**

Olympieum (ō-lim-pi-ē′um), **The.** A ruined temple of Zeus at Athens, founded by Pisistratus and completed in the reign of Hadrian.

Olynthiac (ō-lin′thi-ak) **Orations, The.** Three orations (349–348 B.C.) by Demosthenes, begging Athenian support of Olynthus against Philip II. of Macedon.

Om (ōm). A mystic devotional word of frequent occurrence in Hindu worship and religious literature.

Ommiads (o-mī′adz), or **Omayyads** (o-mī′yadz). A dynasty of califs, A.D. 661–750, which claimed descent from Omayya.

Omnibus Bill, The. A series of compromise measures passed 1850 by Congress, largely through Clay's influence. They included a fugitive-slave law, abolition of slavery in the District of Columbia, and provisions for admission of California as a free state.

Omphale (om′fạ-lē). In Greek legend, a Lydian paramour of Heracles.

Omri (om′rī). A king of Israel. 1 Kings, xvi. 16–28.

Onca (on′kạ). In Phenician mythology, the goddess of wisdom.

One-Hoss Shay, The Wonderful. A poem (1858) by O. W. Holmes: the main title is "The Deacon's Masterpiece."

Oneida (ō-nī′dạ). A tribe of North American Indians, former inhabitants of the region east of Oneida Lake, New York.

Oneida Community, The. A religious communistic brotherhood established 1847 on Oneida Creek, New York.

One of Ours. A novel of the World War (1922) by Willa Sibert Cather: Pulitzer Prize novel, 1923.

Onesimus (ō-nes′i-mus). A converted slave and disciple of Paul. Col. iv. 9.

One Woman's Life. A novel (1913) by Robert Herrick.

Onias Menelaus (ō-nī′ạs men-e-lā′us). A corrupt high priest of the Jews (172–162 B.C.) whose abuses led to the revolt of the Maccabees.

Onondaga (on-ọn-dä′gä). A tribe of North American Indians which formerly inhabited the region about Onondaga Lake, New York.

On the Staircase. A novel (1914) by Frank Swinnerton.

Ophelia (ọ-fē′liạ). The daughter of Polonius, in Shakspere's "Hamlet." She is driven to madness and suicide by Hamlet's capricious treatment.

Ophites (of′īts). An early Gnostic body, prominent in the 2d century.

O Pioneers! A novel (1913) by Willa Sibert Cather, presenting pioneer life in Nebraska.

Opium War, The. A war (1840–42) between Great Britain and China, caused by the Chinese government's attempt to prevent the importation of opium. It was ended by the Treaty of Nanking.

Ops (ops). In Roman mythology, wife of Saturn and goddess of plenty.

Orange (or′ạnj, F. o-räṅzh), **The House of.** A European princely family, the former rulers of the principality of Orange (which fell to the House of Nassau in 1530 and later to France, the House of Nassau retaining the title Prince of Orange). William III. of England was of this house, as is the present royal family of the Netherlands.

Orangemen. A secret politico-religious (anti-Romanist) organization formed 1795 in Ireland, now widespread and influential.

Orc (ôrk), **The.** 1. In the epics of Boiardo and Ariosto, a man-eating giant who spares women. 2. In Ariosto's "Orlando Furioso," a sea-monster killed by Orlando.

Orcus (ôr′kus). A Latin name for Hades.

Orders of Knighthood. See Dictionary, **bath**[1], **garter**, and **thistle**.

Ordinance of 1787, The. An act of Congress which secured to the Northwest Territory freedom from slavery and provided for its future division.

Ordovices (ôr-dọ-vī′sēz). See Dictionary, **Ordovician.**

Oregon, The. A United States battle-ship which made a famous run of 14,516 nautical miles to join the Atlantic fleet on the outbreak of the Spanish-American War in 1898.

Oresteia (ō-res-tē′yä). A trilogy by Æschylus, founded on the history of the family of Agamemnon. See **Agamemnon, Choëphori, The,** and **Eumenides, The.**

Orestes (ō-res′tēz). 1. In Greek legend, son of Agamemnon and Clytemnestra, and brother of Electra. 2. A play of Euripides, exhibited 409 B.C.

Orestes and Electra. 1. A group in marble, probably a late Greek original, in the Museo delle Terme, Rome. 2. A group of antique sculpture in the Museo Nazionale, Naples.

Orfeo (or-fā′ō). A dramatic pastoral (1483) by Politian.

Orfeo ed Euridice (ed ä-ö-rē′dē-chä). An opera (1762) by Gluck.

Orgon (ôr-gôṅ). In Molière's "Tartufe," a credulous dupe.

Oriana (ō-ri-an′ạ). An English princess beloved by Amadis in "Amadis of Gaul."

Origenists (or′i-jen-ists). The followers of the theologian Origen (d. about 254).

Origines (ō-rij′i-nēz). A historical work in seven books, partly extant, by Cato the Censor.

Origin of Species, The. A work (1859) by Darwin, in which he first elaborated his theory of biological evolution.

Orion (ō-rī′ọn). In Greek mythology, a giant and hunter, eventually slain by Artemis.

Orlando. 1. (or-län′dō) The Italian form of **Roland.** 2. (ôr-lan′dō) In Shakspere's "As You Like It," the younger brother of Oliver, and Rosalind's suitor.

Orlando Furioso (or-län′dō fö-rē-ō′sō). A romantic epic by Ariosto, published 1515 and later added to. It continues the "Orlando Innamorato" of Boiardo.

Orlando Innamorato (ēn-nä-mō-rä′tō). A metrical romance by Boiardo, left unfinished 1494.

Orloff (ôr′lof) **Diamond, The.** A gem of 193 carats, formerly the chief ornament of the Russian imperial scepter.

Ormulum (ôr′mụ-lum), **The.** A series of metrical homilies on the New Testament, with paraphrases, by Orm or Ormin: composed early in the 13th century.

Oroonoko (ō-rö-nō′kō), **or the Royal Slave.** A melodramatic novel (about 1658) by Aphra Behn: dramatized (1696) by Southerne.

---

fat, fāte, fär, fȧll, ȧsk, fāre; net, mē, hėr; pin, pīne; not, nōte, mŏve, nôr; up, lūte, pṳll; oi, oil; ou, out; (lightened) avïary, ẹlect, agōny, intọ, ụnite; (obscured) errạnt, operä, ardẹnt, actọr, natṳre; ch, chip; g, go; th, thin; ᴛʜ, then; y, you;

Orphan Island. A novel (1925) by Rose Macaulay.

Orphée aux Enfers (ôr-fā ō-zoṅ-fär'). An opéra bouffe (1858) by Offenbach.

Orpheus (ôr'fūs). In Greek mythology, a son of Apollo, and a marvelous player of the lyre. See **Eurydice.**

Orpheus and Eurydice. See **Orfeo ed Euridice.**

Orsini (or-sē'nē). An Italian noble family of Rome, celebrated for its feud with the Colonna family. Among its famous members were the Popes Celestine III., Nicholas III., and Benedict XIII.

Orsino (ôr-sē'nō). The Duke of Illyria in Shakspere's "Twelfth Night," at first in love with Olivia, later with Viola.

Orson. See **Valentine and Orson.**

Ortheris (ôr'thẹ-ris). See **Mulvaney.**

Osage (ō'sāj). A North American Indian tribe of Siouan stock, surviving in Oklahoma.

Osbaldistone (oz-bạl-dis'tọn), **Francis.** Ostensibly the hero of Scott's "Rob Roy," and a cousin of the villainous Rashleigh Osbaldistone.

Osborne (oz'bọrn), **George.** See **Dobbin, Major William.**

Osborne, Mr. In Thackeray's "Vanity Fair," a hard-fisted merchant who disinherits his son George for marrying Amelia Sedley, the daughter of a bankrupt.

Oscans (os'kạnz). See Dictionary, **Oscan.**

Osiris (ọ-sī'ris). In Egyptian mythology, a chief god, the principle of good and of creativeness, identified with the Nile.

Ossian (osh'ịan). See Dictionary, **Ossianic.**

Otello (ō-tel'lō). 1. An opera (1816) by Rossini. 2. An opera (1887) by Verdi.

Othello (ọ-thel'ō). 1. A tragedy by Shakspere, acted 1604. 2. The hero of Shakspere's "Othello," a Moor of Venice. Driven to insane jealousy and suspicion by the machinations of the subtle villain Iago, he strangles his wife Desdemona, whose innocence and fidelity he does not realize until too late.

Otomacs (ō-tō-mäks'). A degraded tribe of Indian clay-eaters which dwelt along the middle Orinoco in the 18th century.

Otomis (ō-tō-mēz'). An Indian tribe of the Mexican plateau, perhaps resident there before the Toltec invasion.

O'Trigger, Sir Lucius. A fortune-hunting Irishman in Sheridan's "Rivals," memorable because of his passion for dueling.

Ottawa (ot'ạ-wạ). A tribe of North American Indians which dwelt north and west of the Huron territory. They were allies of the French in the 18th century.

Ottilie (o-tē'lē-ẹ). The central figure of Goethe's "Wahlverwandtschaften." She is modeled upon Minna Herzlieb.

Otus (ō'tus). One of the Aloidæ.

Our American Cousin. A comedy (1858) by Tom Taylor. (Lincoln was attending a performance of this play when he was assassinated.)

Our Mutual Friend. A novel (1865) by Dickens.

Our Village. Sketches (1819–32) of village life by Mary Russell Mitford.

Outcast of the Islands, The. A novel (1896) by Joseph Conrad: the outcast's later life is told in "Almayer's Folly."

Ouvidor (ō-vē-dôr'). A principal business street of Rio de Janeiro.

Overland Route, The. 1. The route from England to India through France, Italy, and the Suez Canal. 2. The former principal land route from the eastern United States to California via Utah.

Overreach, Sir Giles. An extortioner finally outwitted by his victims, in "A New Way to Pay Old Debts," by Massinger.

Overruled. A drama (1912) by G. B. Shaw.

Over the Hill to the Poorhouse. A poem (1871) by Will Carleton.

Oxford, The Provisions of. A set of articles passed (1258) by the "Mad Parliament," curtailing the arbitrary power of the king and providing for redress of grievances in political, ecclesiastical, and fiscal affairs. See **Amiens, The Mise of.**

Oxford, The University of. The older of the two great English universities, founded in the 12th century.

Oxford Movement, The. See Dictionary.

Oxford School, The. The Tractarians.

Oxford Street. The principal commercial road between the northwest of London and the City: formerly Tyburn Road.

Oxford Tracts, The. See **Tracts for the Times.**

P

Pacific, The War of the. The war (1879–83) in which Chile defeated Bolivia and Peru.

Pacolet (pak'ọ-let). A dwarf in "Valentine and Orson," the owner of an enchanted wooden steed.

Pacte de Famine (pȧkt dẹ fȧ-mēn'). A French monopoly, during the reign of Louis XV., organized to cause a factitious scarcity of grain.

Padma Purana (pad'mạ pọ-rä'nạ). In Sanskrit literature, a Vishnuite purana in five books, dating from the 12th century.

Padua, The University of. One of the celebrated universities of Europe, founded in the 13th century.

Page, Anne. In Shakspere's "Merry Wives of Windsor," a girl who rejects both Slender and Dr. Caius, her parents' choices, for Fenton.

Page, Master. In Shakspere's "Merry Wives of Windsor," the father of Anne Page.

Pagliacci, I (ē pä-lyä'chē). An opera (1892) by Leoncavallo.

Paiute or **Piute** (pī'ūt). A group of North American Indians of Shoshonean stock, dwelling in Nevada, Utah, and Arizona.

Paix des Dames (pā dā däm). A name for the treaty of Cambray (1529).

Pakht (pächt). In Egyptian mythology, a lioness-headed goddess, nearly indistinguishable from Bast.

Palace of Pleasure, The. A collection (1566–67) of 100 tales translated into English from Greek, Latin, Italian, and French by William Painter. Elizabethan dramatists, including Shakspere, drew numerous plots from it.

Palaces of the Cæsars, The. A large group of structures on the Palatine in Rome, begun by Augustus.

Pala d'Oro (pä'lä dō'rō). The Byzantine retable of the high altar of St. Mark's in Venice.

Palæmon (pa-lē'mọn). In Greek mythology, the sea divinity into which Melicertes was metamorphosed.

Palæologus (pā-lẹ-ol'ọ-gus). A Byzantine family from which came the rulers of the Eastern Empire from 1261 to the death of Constantine in 1453.

Palais Bourbon (pȧ-lā bör-bôṅ). A palace in Paris, begun 1722: now the Chamber of Deputies.

Palais de Justice (dẹ zhüs-tēs). A congeries of ancient and modern buildings in Paris, on L'Île de la Cité. Its nucleus is the palace of the earlier Merovingian kings.

Palais du Trocadéro (dü trō-kä-dā-rō). A building on the Seine in Paris, containing museums and a concert-hall: built 1878.

Palais Royal (rwo-yȧl). A palace in Paris, built by Richelieu 1619–36, and by him left to Louis XIII.

Palamedes (pal-ạ-mē'dēz). In Greek legend, son of Nauplius and Clymene, and one of the expedition against Troy.

Palamites (pal'ạ-mīts). A sect of Christian mystics in the 14th century. Their doctrine was formulated by Gregorius Palamas.

Palamon (pal'ạ-mon) **and Arcite** (är'sīt). Two noble youths whose friendly rivalry for the love of the noble Emilia, Emily, or Emelye, has been told by Boccaccio in "Teseide," Chaucer in the "Knight's Tale," Dryden in "Palamon and Arcite," Fletcher and a collaborator (possibly Shakspere) in "The Two Noble Kinsmen," and others.

Palatine (pal'ạ-tīn) **Hill, The.** One of the seven hills of Rome, southeast of the Capitoline.

Palazzo Doria (pä-lät'sō dō'rē-ä). 1. A large palace in Rome, containing art-galleries: formerly known as the Pamphili Doria. 2. A palace in Genoa, containing noteworthy frescoes.

Palazzo Pitti (pēt'tē). A massive palace in Florence, designed by Brunelleschi, and begun about 1435.

Palazzo Vecchio (vek'kē-ō). A historically and artistically interesting palace in Florence, begun 1298.

Pales (pā'lēz). In Roman mythology, a guardian deity of shepherds and flocks.

Palinurus (pal-i-nū'rus). In Greek legend, the helmsman of Æneas.

(variable) ḍ as d or j, ş as s or sh, ṭ as t or ch, ẕ as z or zh; o, F. cloche; ü, F. menu; ċh, Sc. loch; ṅ, F. bonbon; ', primary accent; ", secondary accent; †, obsolete; <, from; +, and; =, equals. See also lists at beginning of book.

Pallas. See Dictionary.

Pallas (pal′as), **The Albani.** A Greek bust in Pentelic marble, of colossal size, in the Glyptothek, Munich.

Pallas of Velletri (vel-lā′trē), **The.** A Roman copy of a Greek original, of colossal size, in the Louvre, Paris.

Pall Mall (pel mel or pal mal). A street in London, leading from Trafalgar Square to the Green Park.

Palmerin (pal′me-rin) **Romances, The.** A series of 8 Spanish romances of chivalry, in imitation of the Amadis romances.

Pamela. 1. (pa-mē′lä) A character in Sidney's "Arcadia," whose name (but not its pronunciation) Richardson borrowed for his first novel. 2. (pam′ẹ-lä) A novel (1740) by Richardson. Its heroine, Pamela Andrews, is a servant who inspires her master, "Mr. B.," with a base passion, which she resists so pertinaciously that he marries her.

Pamphili (päm-fē′lē) **Doria.** See **Palazzo Doria.**

Pan. See Dictionary, **Pan**[2].

Pan, Peter. See **Peter Pan.**

Panagia (pa-nä′gi-ạ). In the Greek church, a title, 'all-holy,' of the Virgin Mary.

Panama, The Audience of. A Spanish court and governing body formerly located at Panama: established 1538.

Pan-American Exposition, The. An exposition of the work of the peoples of North and South America, at Buffalo, N. Y., in 1901.

Panchatantra (pan-chạ-tan′trä). A celebrated Sanskrit book of fables: the source of the tales known in Europe as the Fables of Bidpai.

Pandareos (pan-dā′rē-os). In Greek legend, a Milesian who stole and gave to Tantalus the golden dog made by Hephæstus.

Pandarus (pan′dạ-rus). In Greek legend, a leader of the Lycians and an ally of the Trojans in the siege of Troy. See Dictionary, **pander.**

Pandavas (pän′dạ-väz). In the Mahabharata, the descendants of Pandu.

Pandemos (pan-dē′mos). A surname of Aphrodite.

Pandion (pan-dī′ọn). In Greek legend, a king of Athens, father of Procne and Philomela.

Pandora. See Dictionary, **Pandora**[1].

Pandosto (pan-dos′tō), **or the Triumph of Time.** A romance (1588) by Robert Greene, on which Shakspere based his "Winter's Tale."

Pandrosos (pan′drọ-sos). In Greek mythology, a daughter of Cecrops.

Pandu (pän′dö). In the Mahabharata, brother of Dhritarashtra and father of the Pandavas or Pandu princes.

Pangloss (pan′glos), **Doctor.** 1. In Voltaire's "Candide," the optimistic tutor of Candide. 2. In Colman the younger's "Heir-at-Law," a satirical portrait of the mercenary tutor of the period.

Panhellenius (pan-he-lē′ni-us). In Greek mythology, a surname of Zeus.

Pan Michael. A prominent character in Sienkiewicz's historical trilogy. See **With Fire and Sword.**

Pantagruel (pan-tag′rọ-el, F. pän-tȧ-grü-el). See Dictionary, **Pantagruelian.**

Panthays (pan′thāz). The Mohammedans of Yunnan, China.

Pantheon. See Dictionary, **pantheon.**

Panthéon (pän-tā-ôṅ). The Church of Ste. Geneviève, Paris, begun under Louis XV.: now a mausoleum for famous Frenchmen.

Pantibibla (pan-ti-bib′lä). A legendary antediluvian city of Babylonia, used as a storehouse for books.

Panurge (pa-nèrj′, F. pȧ-nürzh). In Rabelais's "Gargantua and Pantagruel," an irresistible rascal, companion of Pantagruel.

Panza (pan′zạ, Sp. pän′thä), **Sancho.** The credulous and amusing esquire of Don Quixote in Cervantes's romance.

Paolo and Francesca (pä′ọ-lō, frän-ches′kạ). A poetic drama (1899) by Stephen Phillips. See also **Francesca da Rimini.**

Papago (pä′pä-gō). An agricultural tribe of North American Indians, inhabiting part of southern Arizona.

Papirian (pạ-pir′i-ạn) **Law.** A supposed collection of ancient Roman laws, made by a Caius or Sextus Papirius.

Paracelsus. A poem (1835–36) by Browning.

Paradise. A notable fresco by Orcagna, in Santa Maria Novella, Florence.

Paradise Lost. An epic poem (1667) in 12 books by Milton. Its subject is the fall of man.

Paradise Regained. A minor epic in 4 books (1671) by Milton. Its subject is the temptation of Christ in the wilderness.

Paradiso (pä-rä-dē′zō). The third part of Dante's "Divina Commedia."

Paragot (pȧ-rȧ-gō). The title character in W. J. Locke's "The Beloved Vagabond."

Paraguayan War, The. The same as **Triple Alliance, The War of the.**

Parallel Lives. See **Plutarch's Lives.**

Paran (pā′rạn). In the Old Testament, a wilderness south of Palestine, where the Israelites wandered before entering Canaan.

Parashurama (pa-rạ-shö-rä′mạ). In Hindu legend, the first of the three Ramas, and the sixth incarnation of Vishnu.

Parc-aux-Cerfs (pärk′ō-sär). A house in Versailles, famous as a harem of Louis XV.

Pardoner's Tale, The. One of Chaucer's "Canterbury Tales."

Pardoner's Wallet, The. Essays (1905) by Samuel McChord Crothers.

Parian (pā′ri-ạn) **Chronicle, The.** See **Arundelian Marbles, The.**

Parima (pä-rē′mä or pä-rē-mä′). A mythical lake, once supposed to exist in northern South America. See **Manoa.**

Paris (par′is). In Greek legend, a Trojan youth, son of King Priam and Hecuba. His abduction of Menelaus's queen, Helen, led to the Trojan War, at the end of which he was killed by Philoctetes.

Paris, The First Peace of. See **Paris, Treaties of,** 3.

Paris, The Second Peace of. See **Paris, Treaties of,** 4.

Paris, The Siege of. The successful siege of the French capital by the Germans, 1870–71.

Paris, The University of. The oldest European university, organized in 1200 by the union of schools founded under the successors of Charlemagne.

Paris, Treaties of. 1. Great Britain with France, Spain, and Portugal, 1763. 2. Great Britain with France, Spain, and the United States, 1783. 3. France with Great Britain, Russia, Austria, and Prussia, 1814. 4. Between the same parties, 1815. 5. Russia with Turkey, Great Britain, France, and Sardinia, 1856. 6. The United States with Spain, 1898.

Paris Garden. A circus for bull-baiting and bear-baiting, near the Globe Theatre, London. It antedated the reign of Henry VIII.

Parjanya (pär-jan′yạ). In Vedic mythology, the god of rain.

Parliament, The Mad. A great council held at Oxford in 1258 to deal with evasions by Henry III. of the obligations imposed by Magna Charta.

Parliament of Fowls, The. A poem by Chaucer, thought to celebrate the betrothal of Richard II. and Anne of Bohemia.

Parliament of Paris, The. The principal tribunal of justice of the French monarchy from before 1300 to the Revolution.

Parnassian. See Dictionary.

Parnassus (pär-nas′us). The subject of frescoes by: (1) Raphael Mengs (1760), in the Villa Albani, Rome. (2) Raphael, in the Vatican.

Parnassus, Mount. A painting by Mantegna, in the Louvre.

Parnellite (pär′nel-īt) **Party, The.** The Irish Nationalist party after 1879, when it came under the leadership of Parnell.

Parolles (pạ-rol′es). A braggart in Shakspere's "All's Well That Ends Well" (1602).

Parsifal (pär′si-fäl). A music-drama by Wagner, who composed the poem 1877, the music 1879. The first performance was at Bayreuth in 1882. See **Parzival** and **Perceval.**

Parson Adams. See **Adams, Parson Abraham.**

Parson Manders. An important character in Ibsen's "Ghosts."

Parson's Tale, The. One of Chaucer's "Canterbury Tales."

---

fat, fāte, fär, fȧll, ȧsk, fāre; net, mē, hėr; pin, pīne; not, nōte, möve, nôr; up, lūte, pủll; oi, oil; ou, out; (lightened) aviạry, ẹlect, agǫny, intǫ, ụnite; (obscured) errạnt, operạ, ardẹnt, actǫr, natụre; ch, chip; g, go; th, thin; ᴛʜ, then; y, you;

Parthenia (pär-thē′ni-ạ). In Sidney's "Arcadia," the wife of Argalus, who assumes the armor of a knight to avenge his death at the hands of Amphialus.

Parthenon (pär′the-non). The temple of Athene Parthenos on the Acropolis at Athens. See also **Elgin Marbles, The.** There is a reproduction of the Parthenon in Centennial Park, Nashville, Tennessee, completed 1925.

Parthenope (pär-then′ọ-pē). In Greek mythology, a Siren said to have been drowned and cast up at Naples, which was anciently called by her name.

Partington, Mrs. 1. The dame of Sydney Smith's anecdote about the housewife who tried to mop a high tide out of her house at Sidmouth. ("The Atlantic beat Mrs. Partington.") 2. A humorous character, noted for her misuse of words, invented by B. P. Shillaber, whose "Life and Sayings of Mrs. Partington" appeared 1854.

Partridge. In Fielding's "Tom Jones," Tom's faithful attendant, formerly a schoolmaster, later a barber. He is remembered best for his naïve excitement on seeing Garrick as Hamlet.

Parzival (pärt′sē-väl). The title and legendary hero of an epic poem (1205–15) by Wolfram von Eschenbach. Its theme is the search for the Holy Grail. Parzival is the German counterpart of Perceval.

Pasiphaë (pạ-sif′ạ-ē). In Greek legend, the daughter of Helios, wife of Minos, and mother of Ariadne and, by the white bull given to Minos by Poseidon, of the Minotaur.

Passage to India, A. A novel (1924) by E. M. Forster, showing sympathetic understanding of both sides in Anglo-Indian conflicts.

Passepartout (päs-pär-tö). In Jules Verne's "Around the World in Eighty Days" (1872), the valet of the hero.

Passing of the Third Floor Back, The. A symbolical play (1907) by Jerome K. Jerome, based on his own short story of the same name.

Passionate Elopement, The. A novel (1911) by Compton Mackenzie.

Passionate Friends, The. A novel (1913) by H. G. Wells.

Passionate Pilgrim, A. A story (1875) by Henry James.

Passion-Play, The. A dramatic representation of Christ's passion, given at Oberammergau, Bavaria, at regular intervals: performed in fulfilment of a vow made in 1633, when the inhabitants of the village were saved from a plague.

Paston (pas′tọn) **Letters, The.** A series of letters of historical interest (1424–1509), written or received by members of the Paston family of Norfolk, England.

Pastoral Symphony, The. 1. A short interlude in Handel's "Messiah." 2. The sixth symphony of Beethoven.

Pastor Fido (päs-tōr′ fē′dō). A pastoral drama (1585) by Guarini.

Patala (pä-tä′lạ). In Hindu mythology, a division of the infernal region, inhabited by supernatural beings.

Patelin (pȧt-laṅ). A cheat, a character in the French comedy (15th century) "La Farce de Maître Patelin" (or "L'Avocat Pathelin"), in which occurs the line "Revenons à nos moutons."

Paternoster (pat′ĕr-nos-tėr) **Row.** A London street, north of St. Paul's, long famous as a center of book-publishing.

Pathfinder, The. See **Leatherstocking Tales, The.**

Patience. A comic opera (1881) by W. S. Gilbert and Arthur Sullivan.

Patrician, The. A novel (1911) by John Galsworthy.

Patriot, The (Piccolo mondo antico). A novel (1896) by Antonio Fogazzaro, the first of a trilogy, the others being "The Sinner" (Piccolo mondo moderno, 1901) and "The Saint" (Il Santo, 1901).

Patroclus (pạ-trō′klus). In Homeric legend, the friend of Achilles, slain by Hector.

Patterne (pat′ėrn), **Sir Willoughby** (wil′ọ-bi). The title character of Meredith's "Egoist," a refined embodiment of masculine self-appreciation.

Paul Bunyan. A marvelous imaginary hero of Northwestern lumber camps.

Paul et Virginie (pol ā vēr-zhē-nē). A pastoral novel (1788) by Bernardin de Saint-Pierre.

Paulians (pâ′li-ạnz). A Unitarian body of the 3d century, founded in Syria by Paul of Samosata.

Paulicians (pâ-lish′ạnz). A dualistic sect of Christians founded in the 7th century, probably by Constantine of Syria.

Paul's Cross. A wooden cross near St. Paul's, London, at which the folkmoot assembled: replaced in the 15th century by a stone cross.

Paul's Walk. The nave of old St. Paul's, London, which was a common rendezvous for the transaction of business, and a haunt of idle and disreputable persons.

Pavement of Martyrs, The. The place of the battle of Tours (732): so called by the Moors.

Paviotso (pä-vē-ō′tsō). A western confederacy of 28 small tribes of North American Indians of Shoshonean stock in western Nevada and southern Oregon.

Pawnee or **Pani** (pȧ-nē′). A western confederacy of North American Indians of Caddoan stock, of which a remnant is on a reservation in Oklahoma.

Pax Vobis (paks vō′bis). A small picture of Christ crowned with thorns, by Raphael, in the Palazzo Tosio, Brescia, Italy.

Paytiti, or **Gran Paytiti** (grän pä-ē-tē′tē). A fabled empire established by Incas fleeing from Peru after the conquest.

Pazzi (pät′sē). A powerful Florentine family, noted for an unsuccessful conspiracy (1478) against the Medici.

Peabody (pē′bod-i) **Institute, The.** An institution founded at Baltimore by George Peabody in 1857. It contains a library, an art-gallery, etc.

Peace, The. A comedy by Aristophanes, exhibited 419 B.C.

Peace of God, The. A name sometimes given to the figure (1891) by Augustus Saint-Gaudens on the grave of Mrs. Henry B. Adams, in Rock Creek Cemetery, Washington, D. C. It is also called "Grief" and "Death."

Peachum (pēch′um). In Gay's "Beggar's Opera," a receiver of stolen goods, the father of Polly Peachum.

Peachum, Polly. The heroine of Gay's "Beggar's Opera." She is the bride of Macheath, the leader of a band of highwaymen, and remains constant to him in his troubles, even though learning of his affairs with other charmers.

Peacock Pie. Poems (1913) for children, by Walter de la Mare.

Pearl, The. A Middle English poem of religious symbolism (c. 1475).

Pearl Fishers, The. An opera (1863) by Bizet.

Peasants, The. A novel on the epic scale by Wladyslaw Reymont, dealing with life on the soil in Poland. In four volumes (English translation 1924–25): "Autumn"; "Winter"; "Spring"; and "Summer." Nobel Prize, 1924.

Peasants' Rebellion, The. See **Wat Tyler's Rebellion.**

Peck's Bad Boy and His Pa. A story (1882) by George W. Peck.

Pecksniff. See Dictionary.

Peebles (pē′blz), **Peter.** A litigious drunkard and ne'er-do-well in Scott's "Redgauntlet."

Peele Castle. A castle in the Isle of Man, celebrated in a famous poem by Wordsworth.

Peelites (pēl′īts). A British party of adherents of Sir Robert Peel, formed after the repeal of the corn-laws (1846).

Peeping Tom of Coventry. See Dictionary, **peeping.**

Peer Gynt (pār günt). A drama (1876) by Henrik Ibsen.

Pegasus. See Dictionary.

Peggotty (peg′ọ-ti), **Clara.** In Dickens's "David Copperfield," David's homely, devoted nurse, who marries Barkis. She is the sister of Dan Peggotty, the retired boatman, and the aunt of Ham Peggotty and of Little Em'ly.

Peg Woffington. A novel (1852) by Charles Reade, based on the life of the actress of that name.

Pekah (pē′kä). A king of Israel. 2 Kings, xv. 25–31.

Pekahiah (pek-ạ-hī′ạ). A king of Israel, son of Menahem. 2 Kings, xv. 22–26.

Peking, The Peace of. A treaty (1860) by which Great Britain and France won concessions from China.

Pelasgi (pe-las′jī). See Dictionary, **Pelasgian.**

Peleg (pē′leg). In the Old Testament, the son of Eber. Gen. x. 25.

Peleus (pē′lūs). In Greek legend, a king of the Myrmidons, son of Æacus, and father of Achilles.

Pelham. A novel (1828) of fashionable life and politics by Bulwer-Lytton.

Pelias (pē′li-ạs). In Greek legend, a son of Poseidon. He appears in the legends of Jason.

(variable) ḍ as d or j, ș as s or sh, ṭ as t or ch, ẓ as z or zh; o, F. cloche; ü, F. menu; ch, Sc. loch; ṅ, F. bonbon; ′, primary accent; ′, secondary accent; †, obsolete; <, from; +, and; =, equals. See also lists at beginning of book.

Pelican, The. The ship in which Drake sailed around the world, 1577–80.

Pelides (pē-lī'dēz). A son of Peleus, especially Achilles.

Pelleas (pel'ē-as). In Arthurian romance, a knight of the Round Table.

Pelleas and Ettarre (e-tär'). One of Tennyson's "Idylls of the King."

Pelléas et Mélisande (pe-lā-ás ā mā-lē-sänd). 1. A drama (1892) by Maurice Maeterlinck. 2. An opera based on Maeterlinck's drama by Claude Debussy (1902).

Pelles (pel'ēz), **Sir.** In Arthurian romance, the father of Elaine, the mother of Galahad.

Pelle the Conqueror. A novel in four parts (1906–1916) by Martinus Andersen Nexö, dealing with the labor movement in Denmark.

Pellinore (pel'i-nōr), **Sir.** In Arthurian romance, a knight of the Round Table.

Pelops (pē'lops). In Greek legend, a son of Tantalus, and father of Atreus and Thyestes.

Pembroke College. 1. A college of Cambridge University, founded by the Countess of Pembroke, 1347. 2. A college of Oxford University, founded 1624.

Pendennis (pen-den'is). A novel (1850) by Thackeray.

Pendennis, Arthur. A successful young writer, the central figure of Thackeray's "Pendennis" and the professed "author" of "The Newcomes." After some imprudent love affairs, including that with Blanche Amory, he settles down to marriage with his foster-sister Laura.

Pendennis, Laura. See **Pendennis, Arthur.**

Pendennis, Major. In Thackeray's "Pendennis," Arthur Pendennis's uncle, a worldly old dandy: a finished portrait of the gentlemanly tuft-hunter.

Penelope. See Dictionary.

Penelophon (pē-nel'ō-fon). See **Cophetua.**

Penguin Island. A satire (1908) by Anatole France.

Peninsular Campaign, The. The campaign of the Federal army (1862) for the capture of Richmond, Virginia, by way of the peninsula between the James and York rivers.

Peninsular War, The. The operations of 1808–14, by British, Spanish, and Portuguese forces, against the French in Spain and southern France.

Pennacook (pen'ā-kúk), or **Pawtucket** (pâ-tuk'et). A confederacy of North American Indians which dwelt in the Merrimac valley, New Hampshire, in the 17th century.

Pennsylvania Avenue. The principal avenue of Washington, D. C. Its principal section extends from the Capitol to the Treasury.

Pennsylvania Dutch, The. See Dictionary, **Dutch.**

Penobscot (pe-nob'skot). A North American Indian tribe of Maine.

Penrod. The story of a small boy (1914) by Booth Tarkington.

Penruddock's (pen-rud'oks) **Rebellion.** An unsuccessful uprising (1655) in behalf of Charles II. of England.

Pensacola (pen-sā-kō'lä). An extinct tribe of North American Indians, formerly resident near Pensacola Bay.

Pensées sur la Religion (poñ-sā sür lä rē-lē-zhyôñ). A philosophical and theological work (1670) by Pascal.

Penseroso, Il. See **Allegro, L'.**

Pentameron (pen-tam'ē-ron), **The.** A work (1837) by Landor on Roman and Italian literature, in the form of a dialogue.

Pentamerone (pen-tä-mä-rō'nä), **Il.** A collection (1672) by Basile of stories in the Neapolitan dialect.

Pentapolis (pen-tap'ō-lis). In ancient and medieval history, a state consisting of five cities, as: (*a*) Cyrene, Apollonia, Barca, Arsinoë, Berenice; (*b*) Sodom, Gomorrah, Admah, Zeboim, Segor; (*c*) Ascalon, Gaza, Gath, Ekron, Ashdod; (*d*) Rimini, Ancona, Fano, Pesaro, Sinigaglia.

Pentarchy (pen'tär-ki). See Dictionary, **pentarchy.** Specifically, 1815–1865, Austria, France, Great Britain, Prussia, and Russia.

Pentecost of Calamity, The. A war book (1915) by Owen Wister, giving the author's impressions of Germany in 1914.

Penthesilea (pen″the-si-lē'ä). In Greek legend, an Amazon queen who fought with the Trojans against the Greeks, and was slain by Achilles.

Pentheus (pen'thūs). In Greek legend, a Theban king, torn to pieces by his mother Agave and other mænads for interfering with a Bacchic festival.

People's Palace, The. An institution in East London for the entertainment and instruction of the working population.

Pepysian (pēp'si-an or pep'si-an) **Library, The.** The library of Samuel Pepys, now in a separate building at Magdalene College, Cambridge.

Pequot (pē'kwot). A former tribe of North American Indians, the most ferocious in southern New England in the early 17th century.

Pequot War, The. A war of extermination, 1636–38, waged by the settlers of Connecticut against the Pequot Indians.

Perceforêt (pers-fo-rā). A medieval French romance dealing with the history of Britain before the reign of Arthur.

Perceval (pėr'se-val). A medieval legend of the search of Perceval for the Holy Grail. Its first poetic form was a 12th-century epic by Chrétien de Troyes.

Percy's Reliques. See **Reliques of Ancient English Poetry.**

Perdita (pėr'di-tä). The daughter of Leontes and Hermione in Shakspere's "Winter's Tale." She is reared as a shepherdess.

Peregrine Pickle (per'ē-grin pik'l), **The Adventures of.** A novel (1751) by Smollett. Peregrine is a handsome and brutal young reprobate sowing his wild oats. The novel is chiefly notable for the characters of Hawser Trunnion, a retired sea-dog, and Lieutenant Jack Hatchway, his boon companion.

Père Lachaise (pär lä-shāz), **The Cemetery of.** A celebrated cemetery in the eastern part of Paris.

Perennial Bachelor, The. A novel (1925) by Anne Parrish, in which the lives of three adoring sisters are ruined by the selfishness of their brother.

Perfect Tribute, The. A story (1906) by Mary Raymond Shipman Andrews, about Lincoln.

Pergamus (pėr'gā-mus), or **Pergamum** (-mum). The citadel of Troy.

Pericles (per'i-klēz), **Prince of Tyre** (tīr). A play (1609) ascribed in part to Shakspere.

Perion (pē'ri-on). In the romance of Amadis of Gaul, a king, the father of Amadis.

Perizzites (per'i-zīts). A Canaanitish people which dwelt west of the Jordan. 2 Chron. viii. 7.

Perla (per'lä), **La.** A painting of the Holy Family by Raphael, in the Royal Museum at Madrid.

Permians (pėr'mi-anz), or **Permyaks** (pėrm'yaks). A Finnic people of Perm, Russia.

Pernelle (per-nel), **Madame.** The mother of Orgon in Molière's "Tartufe."

Perpetual Peace, The. A name given to the treaty of 1516 between France and the Swiss Confederation.

Persæ (pėr'sē). A tragedy (472 B.C.) of Æschylus, celebrating the victory of Salamis.

Persecutions, The Ten. The persecutions of Christians under Roman emperors from Nero to Diocletian.

Persephone (pėr-sef'ō-nē). In Greek mythology, the daughter of Zeus and Demeter, wife of Hades, and queen of the lower world: a personification of the changes in the seasons. See **Proserpina.**

Perseus (pėr'sūs). 1. See Dictionary. 2. A statue (1553) by Cellini in the Loggia dei Lanzi, Florence. 3. A statue (1800) by Canova in the Vatican.

Perseus and Andromeda. 1. A painting by Rubens, in the Hermitage Museum, Leningrad. 2. A painting by Tintoretto, in the Hermitage Museum, Leningrad.

Perseus and Medusa. See Dictionary, **Perseus,** and cut.

Persian Fighting, A. A statuette in the Vatican: one of the Pergamenian copies from the four groups presented to Athens about 200 B.C. by Attalus I. of Pergamum.

Persians, The. One of the extant dramas of Æschylus.

Persian Wars, The. The intermittent struggle between Persia and Greece, 500–449 B.C.

Persuasion. A novel (1818) by Jane Austen.

Perth, The Convention of. An assembly (1305) summoned by Edward I. of England to send Scottish representatives to Parliament.

Peter, originally **Simon.** One of the 12 apostles, a fisherman, the reputed author of the two New Testament epistles bearing his name.

Peter Funk. A bogus bidder at auctions, employed merely to raise the price against intending purchasers.

Peterhouse. See **St. Peter's College.**

Peter Ibbetson. A novel (1892) by George Du Maurier.

Peterloo (pē'tẽr-lö) **Massacre, The.** A riot, Aug. 16, 1819, at St. Peter's Field, Manchester, England. An assembly, mainly of the working class, was charged by the military.

Peter Pan. A play (1904) and story (1906) by Sir J. M. Barrie, about an elfish boy who, never growing up, lives perennially in the "Never-never Land" of childhood.

Peter Schlemihl (pā'tẽr shlā-mēl'). "The Story of a Man without a Shadow" (1814), by Chamisso.

Peter Simple. A novel (1834) of seafaring adventure, by Frederick Marryat.

Peter Wilkins. A tale of fantastic adventures (1750?) by Robert Paltock.

Petit André (pė-tē-tän-drä). An executioner of Louis XI.'s time: introduced in Scott's "Quentin Durward."

Petition of Right, The. An act of Parliament (1628) securing the citizenry against taxation save by act of Parliament, and against imprisonment without due process.

Petruchio (pē-trö'chi-ō or -ki-ō). See **Katharine.**

Petulengro (peṭ-ū-leng'grō), **Jasper.** A young gipsy chief in "Lavengro" and "The Romany Rye," by George Borrow.

Peveril (pev'ẽr-il) **of the Peak.** A romance (1823) of the reign of Charles II., by Scott.

Pfahlgraben (pfäl'grä″bẹn). A line of fortifications built by the Romans about A.D. 70, from Ratisbon northwestward, for protection against the Germans.

Phæacia (fē-ā'shi-ạ). In Homeric legend, a land visited by Odysseus after the fall of Troy: possibly Corcyra.

Phædra (fē'drä). In Greek legend, the daughter of Minos and Pasiphaë, sister of Ariadne, and wife of Theseus. See **Hippolytus.**

Phædrus (fē'drus). A dialogue of Plato, named from one of his Athenian friends.

Phaëthon (fā'ẹ-thọn). In Greek mythology: (1) The sungod, Helios. (2) The son of Helios and Prote. See Dictionary, **phaëton.**

Phantom Rickshaw, The. A story of Anglo-Indian life (1888) by Rudyard Kipling.

Phaon (fā'ọn). In Greek legend, a boatman of Mytilene, the favorite of Sappho.

Pharamond (far'ạ-mọnd). The legendary first king of France. He is also a character in the Arthurian cycle of romances.

Pharsalia (fär-sā'li-ạ). An epic poem in 10 books, by Lucan. It deals with the civil war between Cæsar and Pompey.

Phebo (fā'bō), **Donzel del.** The Knight of the Sun, a famous character in old Spanish romance, reproduced in "The Mirror of Knighthood."

Phèdre (fādr). A classical tragedy (1677) by Racine.

Phi Beta Kappa (fī bē'tạ, or bā'tạ, kap'ạ) **Society, The.** In American colleges, a nominally secret fraternity, founded 1776, to which undergraduates of high scholastic rank are admitted.

Philander. See Dictionary.

Philanderer, The. A drama (1893) by G. B. Shaw, satirizing the New Woman.

Philaster (fi-las'tẽr), **or Love Lies a-Bleeding.** A play (1609) by Beaumont and Fletcher.

Philemon (fi-lē'mọn). In Greek legend, a poor Phrygian who, with his wife Baucis, offered hospitality to Zeus and Hermes in disguise, and was rewarded.

Philemon, The Epistle of Paul to. A New Testament epistle, written by Paul during his first captivity at Rome.

Philinte (fē-laṅt'). The friend of Alceste in Molière's "Misanthrope."

Philip (fil'ip). 1. One of the twelve apostles. 2. "The Evangelist," a deacon and preacher in the Christian church of the 1st century.

Philip IV. 1. An equestrian portrait by Velasquez, in the Royal Museum, Madrid. 2. A portrait by Velasquez, in the Louvre.

Philip, The Adventures of. A minor novel (1862) by Thackeray.

Philip Nolan. The title character in Edward Everett Hale's story "The Man without a Country" (1863).

Philippians (fi-lip'i-ạnz), **The Epistle to the.** An epistle written by Paul (probably about A.D. 63) to the church in Philippi.

Philip the King. A drama (1914) by John Masefield.

Phillips Academy. A preparatory school for boys at Andover, Mass., founded 1778 by John and Samuel Phillips.

Phillips Exeter Academy. A school for boys at Exeter, N. H., founded 1781 by John Phillips.

Philobiblon (fī-lọ-bib'lọn). A treatise on books by Richard de Bury (Richard Aungerville), finished 1345.

Philoctetes (fil-ọk-tē'tēz). In Greek legend, a famous archer, the friend and armor-bearer of Heracles.

Philomela (fil-ọ-mē'lä). 1. A novel (1592) by Robert Greene. 2. See Dictionary, **Philomel.** 3. A poem (1853) by Matthew Arnold.

Philtre, Le (lė fēltr). A popular opera (1831) by Auber and Scribe.

Phinehas (fin'ē-hạs). A high priest of Israel, son of Eleazar. Ex. vi. 25.

Phineus (fī'nūs or fin'ē-us). In Greek mythology, a suitor of Andromeda, who, at her wedding with Perseus, was turned to stone at sight of the Gorgon's head.

Phintias. See **Damon.**

Phlegethon. See Dictionary.

Phœbe (fē'bẹ). In classical mythology: (1) See Dictionary, **Phœbe**[1]. (2) A Titaness, daughter of Uranus and Gæa.

Phœnix (fē'niks). 1. In Greek legend: (a) A brother or father of Europa, and reputed ancestor of the Phenicians. (b) Son of Amyntor and Hippodamia, and teacher and attendant of Achilles. 2. See Dictionary, **phenix.**

Phœnix, The. A theater in St. Giles-in-the-Fields, London, destroyed 1649.

Phœnix and the Turtle, The. A poem (1601) by Shakspere.

Phœnix Park. A public park in Dublin, Ireland: the scene of the assassination (1882) of Lord Frederick Cavendish and Thomas H. Burke.

Phorbas (fôr'bạs). In Greek legend, son of Lapithes. He freed Rhodes from a plague of serpents. Eventually he was slain by Apollo in a boxing contest.

Phorcydes (fôr'si-dēz). In Greek mythology, three daughters of Phorcys and Ceto, named Dino, Pephredo, and Enyo. They possessed one eye and one tooth in common.

Phormio (fôr'mi-ō). The title and chief character of a comedy by Terence.

Phosphorus (fos'fọ-rus). 1. In Greek mythology, the morning star, son of Astræus and Eos. See **Hesperus.** 2. In Arthurian legend, a name for Sir Persaunt of India.

Phrixus (frik'sus). In Greek mythology, the brother of Helle. He sacrificed to Zeus the ram bearing the golden fleece, which he gave to Æetes.

Phryne (frī'nē). A famous Athenian courtezan of the 4th century B.C.: possibly the model of the "Aphrodite Anadyomene" of Apelles.

Phryne before the Areopagus. A painting (1861) by Gérôme.

Phut (fut). A son of Ham, supposed by some commentators to have been the ancestor of the Libyans. Gen. x. 6.

Phyllis (fil'is). 1. In Greek legend, the betrothed of Demophon, metamorphosed into an almond-tree. 2. See Dictionary.

Physiologus (fiz-i-ol'ọ-gus). A bestiary, or collection of allegories based on the supposed natural history of animals, popular in the middle ages.

Piasts (pyästs). The earliest dynasty of Polish rulers: so called from Piast, the supposed founder. It ended in Poland in 1370.

Piazza, The. An arcade of Covent Garden Market, London.

Piazza della Signoria (pyät'sä del'lä sē-nyō-rē'ä), **or del Gran Duca** (del grän dö'kä). The chief public square of Florence, Italy.

Piazza del Popolo (del pô'pō-lō). A square in Rome, at the beginning of the Corso.

Piazza di Spagna (dē spä'nyä). A square in Rome: so called from the residence of the Spanish ambassador.

(variable) ḏ as d or j, ş as s or sh, ṭ as t or ch, ẓ as z or zh; o, F. cloche; ü, F. menu; ċh, Sc. loch; ṅ, F. bonbon; ′, primary accent; ″, secondary accent; †, obsolete; <, from; +, and; =, equals. See also lists at beginning of book.

Picards (pik'ärdz). An Adamite sect in Bohemia early in the 15th century.

Piccadilly (pik'a-dil-i). The great London thoroughfare between Hyde Park Corner and the Haymarket.

Piccolomini (pēk-kō-lō'mē-nē). An Italian noble family, prominent in Siena from the 13th century to the 18th. It furnished two Popes, Pius II. and Pius III.

Piccolomini, Die (dē pik-ō-lō'mē-nē). A tragedy (1799) by Schiller, the second part of the "Wallenstein" trilogy.

Pickwick, Samuel. In Dickens's "Pickwick Papers," the founder of the Pickwick Club. He is a benevolent, simple-minded gentleman, and becomes the center of a series of farcical adventures. Words are said to be used "in a Pickwickian sense" when they do not have the usual implications.

Pickwick Club, The. The imaginary club created by Dickens in "The Pickwick Papers."

Pickwick Papers, The, or **Posthumous Papers of the Pickwick Club.** A novel (1837) consisting of loosely connected humorous episodes, by Dickens.

Pictured Rocks, The. See Dictionary, **pictured.**

Pictures of the Floating World. Poems (1919) by Amy Lowell.

Picus (pī'kus). In Italian mythology, a god of agriculture, regarded as a son of Saturn.

Pied Piper, The. See **Hameln, The Pied Piper of.**

Pieria, Pierian Spring, Pierides. See Dictionary, **Pierian.**

Piers Plowman (pērs plou'man, or pērz), **The Vision of.** An allegorical and satirical, intensely religious poem of the second half of the 14th century, attributed to William Langland.

Pietà (pyā-tä'). See Dictionary, **pietà.** Among well-known examples are those by Van Dyck (Munich), Andrea del Sarto (Vienna), Quentin Massys (Antwerp), and Michelangelo (Rome).

Pigeon, The. A drama (1912) by John Galsworthy, presenting the difference between real kindliness and cold "charity."

Pigott (pig'ot) **Diamond, The.** A famous diamond weighing 49 carats, brought to England by Earl Pigott.

Pilate, The Arch of. An arch spanning the Via Dolorosa in Jerusalem: supposed to belong to the time of Hadrian.

Pilate's Staircase. See **Scala Santa.**

Pilgrimage of Grace, The. An insurrectionary occupation (1536–37) of York, England, by 30,000 rebels under Robert Aske. It was a protest against the policies of Henry VIII.

Pilgrim of Eternity, The. A biography of Byron (1925) by John Drinkwater.

Pilgrim's Progress, The. A famous allegory (1678) by John Bunyan composed in prison between 1660 and 1672. It narrates the adventures of the hero, Christian, on his pilgrimage to the heavenly Jerusalem from the City of Destruction, in which he was born. A second part (1684) recounts the similar adventures of Christiana, Christian's wife, and her children.

Pillars of Society. A drama (1878) by Henrik Ibsen.

Pilpay. See **Bidpai.**

Piman (pē'man). A linguistic stock of North American Indians, now resident in southern Arizona and northwestern Mexico.

Pinafore, H. M. S. A comic opera (1878) by W. S. Gilbert and Arthur Sullivan.

Pinch, Tom. An ungainly, kind-hearted employee of Pecksniff in Dickens's "Martin Chuzzlewit."

Pinchwife. In Wycherley's comedy "The Country Wife" (1673), the foolish husband who tries to keep his wife in a state of ignorance.

Pincian (pin'shi-an) **Hill, The.** A hill in northern Rome, near the Quirinal.

Pindaris (pin-dä'rēz). A horde of mounted robbers in India in the 17th and 18th centuries, dispersed 1818.

Pinerolo (pē-nā-rō'lō), **The Pacification of.** A treaty (1655) between France and the English Commonwealth, providing for the cessation of the Waldensian persecution.

Pioneers, The. See **Leatherstocking Tales, The.**

Pip. See **Pirrip, Philip.**

Piper, The. A drama (1909) by Josephine Preston Peabody, for children.

Piper, Tom. A character in the English morris-dance.

Pippa Dances, And. A drama (1906) by Gerhart Hauptmann.

Pippa Passes. A dramatic idyl (1841) by Browning. Pippa, a poor working-girl, passes with a song at crucial moments in the lives of the other personæ.

Piran (pir'an) **Round.** An ancient open-air theater in Cornwall.

Pirate, The. A romance (1822) by Scott. The action takes place among the Shetland and Orkney Islands in the 17th century.

Pirates of Penzance (pen-zans'), **The.** A comic opera (1879) by W. S. Gilbert and Arthur Sullivan.

Pirithous (pī-rith'ō-us). See Dictionary, **Lapithæ.**

Pirrip (pir'ip), **Philip.** The hero of Dickens's "Great Expectations." He is usually called "Pip," a childish corruption of his real name.

Piscis Volans. See Dictionary, **Flying Fish.**

Pishacha (pi-shä'chä). In Hindu mythology, a class of demons, perhaps originally personifications of the ignis fatuus.

Pison (pī'son). A river mentioned in Gen. ii. 11.

Pistol. A blustering boon companion of Falstaff in Shakspere's "Henry IV.," Part ii., "Henry V.," and "The Merry Wives of Windsor."

Pit, The. A novel (1903) by Frank Norris. See also **Octopus, The.**

Pitcher, Molly. The wife of a Revolutionary soldier, who, at the battle of Monmouth, June 28, 1778, served the cannon at which her husband had just fallen.

Pitris (pi'triz). In Hindu belief, the shades or spirits of the departed.

Pitt Diamond, The. A famous diamond of 137 carats, sold by Thomas Pitt (1717) to the Regent of Orléans for about $675,000.

Pitti Palace, The. See **Palazzo Pitti.**

Piute. See **Paiute.**

Pizarro. An English version (1799) of Kotzebue's "Spaniards in Peru."

Place de la Bastille (plås dè lä bås-tē-y'). The historically important site of the Bastille, at the end of the Rue St.-Antoine, Paris.

Place de la Concorde (kôn-kôrd). A famous square in Paris, west of the Tuileries Gardens.

Place du Carrousel (dü kȧ-rö-zel). A square west of the Louvre, Paris.

Place Vendôme (voñ-dōm). A square in Paris, north of the Seine, laid out under Louis XIV.

Plagiary (plā'ji-a-ri), **Sir Fretful.** A satirical portrait of Cumberland in Sheridan's "Critic."

Plague of Serpents, The. A ceiling painting by Tintoretto, in the Scuola di San Rocco, Venice.

Plain Dealer, The. A comedy (1674) by Wycherley, based on Molière's "Misanthrope."

Plain Tales from the Hills. A collection of short stories (1888) by Rudyard Kipling.

Plantagenet. See Dictionary.

Platine (plä'tin) **Colonies, The.** The Spanish colonies which bordered on the Rio de la Plata and its tributaries.

Platine States, The. The countries of Uruguay, Paraguay, and Argentina.

Plato. A Greek bust in bronze, of the 4th century B.C., now in the Museo Nazionale, Naples.

Plausible, Lord. An insinuating fop in Wycherley's "Plain Dealer."

Playboy of the Western World, The. A drama (1907) by John Millington Synge.

Players, The. A New York club founded by Edwin Booth and incorporated 1888. Its house is at 16 Gramercy Park.

Pléiade, La (lä plā-yäd). See Dictionary, **Pleiad.**

Pleiades. See Dictionary.

Plessis-les-Tours (ple-sē-lä-tör). A ruined castle near Tours, France, once the residence of Louis XI.

Pliable. In Bunyan's "Pilgrim's Progress," a character who deserts Christian at the first difficulty.

Pliant, Dame. In Jonson's "Alchemist," a foolish widow who marries Lovewit.

Pliant, Sir Paul and **Lady.** In Congreve's "Double Dealer," an uxorious old husband and his wanton wife.

---

fat, fāte, fär, fȧll, ȧsk, fāre; net, mē, hėr; pin, pīne; not, nōte, mȯve, nôr; up, lūte, pull; oi, oil; ou, out; (lightened) avĭary, ḙlect, agŏny, intŏ, ụnite; (obscured) errạnt, operạ, ardẹnt, actọr, natụre; ch, chip; g, go; th, thin; ᴛʜ, then; y, you;

Plumed Serpent, The. A novel (1926) by D. H. Lawrence: a story of modern Mexico.

Plutarch's Lives. A collection of 46 biographies of famous Greeks and Romans by Plutarch (b. A.D. 46).

Pluto. 1. See Dictionary. 2. A nymph, mother of Tantalus.

Plutus (plō'tus). In classical mythology, a personification of wealth. He is a son of Demeter, and is associated with Eirene, or Peace.

Plymouth (plim'uth) **Colony.** The colony established in southeastern Massachusetts by the English Pilgrims in 1620: united with Massachusetts Bay Colony in 1691.

Plymouth Rock. A rock at Plymouth, Mass., on which the Pilgrim Fathers are said to have landed in 1620.

Pnyx (niks). A place of assembly in ancient Athens, named from the hill on which it was situated.

Podsnap (pod'snap), **Mr.** A pompous gentleman in "Our Mutual Friend," by Dickens. He is distinguished for his intimate knowledge of the exact designs of Providence.

Poetaster, The. A satirical comedy (1602) by Jonson, supposed to be an attack on Dekker and Marston.

Poet at the Breakfast-Table, The. See **Breakfast-Table, The Autocrat of the.**

Poets' Corner, The. A space in Westminster Abbey, London, containing busts and other memorials of illustrious English writers.

Poictesme (pwo-tām). The land of romance in the stories of James Branch Cabell.

Poins (poinz). A dissolute companion of Falstaff and of Prince Hal in Shakspere's "Henry IV."

Pointed Roofs. A psychological novel (1916) by Dorothy Richardson.

Polabians (pō-lā'bi-anz). A branch of the Polish Slavs, formerly resident in the Lower Elbe valley.

Poland, The Partition of. Any one of three partitions of Poland, as follows: (1) Between Russia, Prussia, and Austria, 1772–73. (2) Between Russia and Prussia, 1793. (3) Between Russia, Prussia, and Austria, 1795.

Polaris (pō-lā'ris). The pole-star or north star, a star of the second magnitude situated close to the north pole of the heavens, being at the extremity of the tail of the bear pictured in the constellation Ursa Minor, and being the outermost star in the handle of the Little Dipper.

Polexandre (po-lek-sändr). A heroic romance (1632) by Gomberville.

Polish Corridor, The. The strip of land running through German territory which was given to Poland by the Treaty of Versailles as an outlet to the sea.

Polish Succession, The War of the. A war (1733–38) of France, Spain, and Sardinia against Austria and Russia, occasioned by a disputed election to the throne of Poland.

Politics. A treatise on the state by Aristotle.

Polixène (po-lek-sän). The name assumed by Madelon in Molière's "Précieuses ridicules."

Pollux. See **Castor.**

Polly. A ballad-opera (1728) by Gay: a sequel to "The Beggar's Opera."

Polonius (pō-lō'ni-us). The sententious father of Ophelia in Shakspere's "Hamlet."

Polychronicon (pol-i-kron'i-kon). A chronicle of universal history to 1342, by Ranulf Higden.

Polydore (pol'i-dōr). 1. A name assumed by Guiderius in Shakspere's "Cymbeline." 2. The brother of Castalio in Otway's "Orphan," who impersonates Castalio on the latter's wedding night.

Polydorus (pol-i-dō'rus). In Greek legend, the youngest son of Priam, killed by Achilles or Polymestor.

Polyeucte (pol-yėkt). 1. A tragedy (1640) by Corneille. 2. An opera (1878) by Gounod.

Polyhymnia. See Dictionary.

Polynices (pol-i-ni'sēz). In Greek legend, brother of Eteocles. The expedition of the Seven against Thebes was organized to restore him to the throne of Thebes.

Polyolbion (pol-i-ol'bi-on), **or a Chorographical Description . . . of Great Britain.** A poem (1613–22) by Drayton: it is filled with antiquarian knowledge.

Polyphemus (pol-i-fē'mus). In Greek legend, a giant having one large eye in the center of his forehead: chief among the Cyclopes, and blinded by Odysseus.

Polyphonic prose. A style of writing adopted by several poets: its most conspicuous exponent was Amy Lowell.

Polyxena (po-lik'se-na). In Greek legend, daughter of Priam and Hecuba and bride of Achilles. At her wedding Achilles was slain by Paris, and Polyxena was later sacrificed by the Greeks.

Pomœrium (pō-mē'ri-um). A sacred area in ancient Rome, outside Roma Quadrata. Its boundary was traced by a plow drawn by a cow and a bull.

Pomona (pō-mō'na). In Roman mythology, the goddess of fruit-trees.

Pompeii (pom-pā'yē), **The Last Day of.** A modern painting by Brülow, in the Hermitage Museum, Leningrad.

Pompeii, The Last Days of. See **Last Days of Pompeii, The.**

Pompey's Pillar. A Corinthian column of red granite at Alexandria, erected A.D. 302 in honor of Diocletian.

Pompey the Great, The Tragedy of. A drama (1901) by John Masefield.

Pompilia. The heroine of Robert Browning's "The Ring and the Book."

Pons Milvius (ponz mil'vi-us). A bridge that anciently crossed the Tiber about 2 miles from Rome: the scene of the rout of Maxentius by Constantine, A.D. 312.

Ponte Vecchio (pōn'tā vek'kē-ō). A bridge over the Arno in Florence: rebuilt 1345.

Pontiac's War. An Indian war (1763) between the settlers of the western frontier and an Indian confederacy under Pontiac.

Pontifex, Ernest. The hero of Samuel Butler's "The Way of All Flesh."

Pont Neuf (pôn nėf). A bridge in Paris, crossing the Seine near the Louvre: built by Henry IV.

Pooh-Bah (pö'bä'). A versatile office-holder in "The Mikado," by Gilbert and Sullivan.

Poor Relations. A novel (1919) by Compton Mackenzie.

Poor Richard's Almanac. An almanac (1732–57) published by Benjamin Franklin, rich in proverbial wisdom.

Poor White. A novel (1920) by Sherwood Anderson.

Popish Plot, The. An alleged plot (1678) to murder Charles II. and to establish the Roman Catholic religion in England by force. It was chiefly contrived by the impostor Titus Oates.

Popul Vuh (pō-pöl' vö). A collection of quasi-primitive legends of the Quiché Indians of Guatemala, set down by Fray Francisco Ximenes in the 18th century.

Porcupine, The. A drama (1915) by Edwin Arlington Robinson.

Porsena (pôr'se-na), **Lars.** In early Roman legend, a king of Clusium in Etruria.

Porta Maggiore (pôr'tä mäd-jō'rā). The most imposing of the ancient gates in the walls of Rome.

Porte, or Sublime Porte, The. See Dictionary, **Porte.**

Porteous (pôr'tyus) **Riots, The.** Riots in Edinburgh, Scotland, in 1736, after troops under Captain John Porteous had fired on a crowd at an execution. Scott uses the incident in "The Heart of Midlothian."

Porte St.-Antoine (pôrt sañ-tän-twän). A former triumphal arch in Paris, over the Rue St.-Antoine near the Bastille.

Porte St.-Denis (sañ-dė-nē). A triumphal arch on the Boulevard St.-Denis, Paris, built 1672.

Porte St.-Martin (sañ-mär-tañ). A triumphal arch on the Boulevard St.-Martin, Paris, built 1674.

Porthos (pôr-tos). See **Trois Mousquetaires, Les.**

Portia (pôr'shia). In Shakspere's "Merchant of Venice," an heiress in love with Bassanio. Disguised, she conducts the defense of Antonio in the court scene. See **Shylock.**

Portland Vase, The. A famous urn, 10 inches high, discovered 1630 in a sarcophagus near Rome, and now in the British Museum. See Dictionary, **vase,** and cut.

Portrait of a Lady, The. A novel (1881) by Henry James: the story of an American woman abroad.

Portrait of a Man with Red Hair. A novel (1925) by Hugh Walpole. See **Maradick at Forty.**

Port-Royal. A Cistercian abbey which stood about 17 miles southwest of Paris: founded 1204. In the 17th century it became a famous center of Jansenism.

(variable) ḍ as d or j, ş as s or sh, ṭ as t or ch, ẓ as z or zh; o, F. cloche; ü, F. menu; ċh, Sc. loch; ṅ, F. bonbon; ′, primary accent; ′, secondary accent; †, obsolete; <, from; +, and; =, equals. See also lists at beginning of book.

Portunus (pôr-tū′nus), or **Portumnus** (pôr-tum′nus). In Roman mythology, the protecting god of harbors.

Poseidon. See Dictionary.

Posthumous Papers of the Pickwick Club. See **Pickwick Papers, The.**

Potash and Perlmutter. Amusing Jewish characters in stories and plays by Montague Glass.

Potiphar (pot′i-fär). An officer of Pharaoh and owner of Joseph. Potiphar's wife tried to seduce Joseph. Gen. xxxix.

Potiphar Papers, The. Satirical articles (1853) by G. W. Curtis.

Pot of Broth, A. A drama (1902) by William Butler Yeats.

Pottawattomi (pot-a-wot′o-mi). A once powerful tribe of Indians, western allies of England in the wars of 1775 and 1812.

Potterism. A novel (1920) by Rose Macaulay.

Poultry-Yard, The. A painting (1660) by Jan Steen, in the royal gallery at The Hague.

Power of Darkness, The. A drama (1888) by Count Lev Tolstoy.

Powhatan (pou-ha-tan′). A confederacy of North American Indians which occupied parts of Virginia and Maryland in the 17th century.

Poyning's Law. Two acts of the Irish Parliament, passed 1494, curtailing the political liberties of Ireland.

Poyser (poi′zèr), **Mrs.** A farmer's wife, amusingly shrewd and ready of tongue, in George Eliot's "Adam Bede."

Prabodhachandrodaya (pra-bō′dha-chan-drō′da-yä). An allegorical drama in Sanskrit, of about the 12th century, by Krishna Mishra.

Præstigiar (prē-stij′i-är). A canine embodiment of the devil in early versions of the Faust legend.

Prairial Insurrection, The. An unsuccessful revolt of the Paris populace against the Convention, 1st Prairial, year 3 (May 20, 1795).

Prairie, The. See **Leatherstocking Tales, The.**

Praise of Folly. A satirical work (1511) by Erasmus in praise of folly.

Prajapati (pra-jä′pa-tē). In Vedic lore, a special genius presiding over procreation; also, an epithet of Surya, Indra, and others.

Prajna Paramita (praj′nä pä′ra-mi-tä). The principal sutra of the Great Vehicle, or Mahayana school of Buddhists. It means 'Transcendental Wisdom.'

Prakrit. See Dictionary.

Prater (prä′tèr). A public park of Vienna, on an island in the Danube.

Pratishakhya (pra-ti-shä′khyä). The name of any one of a group of phonetico-grammatical Vedic commentaries. Four are extant.

Précieuses Ridicules, Les (lä prä-syèz rē-dē-kül). A comedy (1659) by Molière, satirizing the fashionable literary coteries of the period.

Prelude, The. A long philosophical poem (1850) by Wordsworth.

Prelude to Adventure, The. A novel (1912) by Hugh Walpole.

Pre-Raphaelites. See Dictionary, **Pre-Raphaelite.**

Presburg (pres′bûrch), **The Peace of.** A treaty (1805) between France and Austria.

President, The. 1. An American frigate, built 1794, captured 1815 by the British. 2. An American steamer lost (1841) with all on board, on a voyage from New York to Liverpool.

Prester John. See Dictionary, **prester.**

Pretorian (prē-tō′ri-an) **Camp, The.** A camp outside the walls of ancient Rome, established by Tiberius.

Pretty Lady, The. A novel (1918) by Arnold Bennett.

Priam (prī′am). In Greek legend, son of Laomedon, husband of Hecuba, and father of Hector and Paris. He was the last king of Troy, at the capture of which he was slain by Neoptolemus.

Priapus. See Dictionary, **Priapic.**

Price, Fanny. The meek heroine of Jane Austen's "Mansfield Park."

Pride and Prejudice. A novel (1813) by Jane Austen, written 1796–97.

Pride's Purge. The exclusion from the House of Commons,

Dec., 1648, of about 100 members who favored compromise with the royal party. It was carried out by a force under Colonel Thomas Pride.

Prig, Betsey. A nurse, and friend of Mrs. Gamp, in Dickens's "Martin Chuzzlewit."

Primrose League, The. A league founded 1883 in London in support of the Conservative principles advocated by Disraeli: so named from his favorite flower.

Princess, The. An anti-feminist narrative poem (1847) by Tennyson.

Princess Casamassima, The. A novel (1886) by Henry James.

Princesse de Clèves, La (lä pran-ses dé kläv). A novel (1677) by Mme. de La Fayette, in which contemporary personages are presented under a historic disguise.

Princess Ida, or Castle Adamant. An opera (1884) by W. S. Gilbert and Arthur Sullivan, burlesquing Tennyson's "Princess."

Princess Maleine (mà-län), **The.** A drama (1889) by Maurice Maeterlinck.

Princes Street. The principal street of Edinburgh, Scotland.

Principe, Il (èl prēn′chē-pä). A political treatise by Machiavelli, completed 1513, defining the function of a benevolent despot.

Principia (prin-sip′i-ä). A famous treatise (1686) by Sir Isaac Newton, on the mathematical principles of physics.

Prioress's Tale, The. One of Chaucer's "Canterbury Tales": the story of a miracle of the Virgin, performed in behalf of a little school-boy.

Priscilla. The wife of Aquila. Acts, xviii. 2.

Priscilla Mullens (pri-sil′ä mul′enz). A Puritan maiden, the heroine of Longfellow's "Courtship of Miles Standish."

Prisoner of Chillon, The. A famous poem (1816) by Byron, on the imprisonment of Bonnivard.

Prisoner of Zenda, The. A romance (1894) by Anthony Hope (Sir A. H. Hawkins), telling the adventures of a young Englishman at an imaginary European court: a sequel is "Rupert of Hentzau."

Private Papers of Henry Ryecroft, The. See **Henry Ryecroft.**

Procne (prok′nē). See Dictionary, **procnias.**

Procris (prō′kris). See **Cephalus.**

Procrustes (prō-krus′tēz). See Dictionary, **Procrustean.**

Procyon (prō′si-on). A star of the first magnitude in the constellation Canis Minor.

Prodigal Son, The. An oratorio (1869) by Arthur Sullivan.

Professor, The. A novel (1855) by Charlotte Brontë.

Professor at the Breakfast-Table, The. See **Breakfast-Table, The Autocrat of the.**

Professor's House, The. A novel (1925) by Willa Sibert Cather.

Profeta, Il (èl prō-fä′tä). An opera (1849) by Meyerbeer.

Profile, The. A group of rocks resembling a human profile, on the side of Profile Mountain, Franconia, New Hampshire.

Promessi Sposi, I (ē prō-mes′sē spō′zē). The principal novel (1825–27) of Manzoni.

Prometheus (prō-mē′thūs). 1. See Dictionary, **Promethean.** 2. A drama by Goethe, begun 1773. 3. A ballet (1802) by Beethoven.

Prometheus Bound. A tragedy of Æschylus.

Prometheus Unbound. A lyrical drama (1820) by Shelley.

Promised Land, The. 1. See Dictionary, **promised.** 2. An autobiographical account (1912) of an immigrant girl's experiences in the United States, by Mary Antin.

Propylæa (prop-i-lē′ä). The monumental gateway to the Acropolis, begun 437 B.C. by Mnesicles.

Proscritto, Il (èl prō-skrēt′tō). 1. An opera (1840) by Nicolai. 2. The title of the French production (1846) of Verdi's "Ernani."

Proserpina (prō-sèr′pi-nä), or **Proserpine** (pros′èr-pin). The Roman counterpart of Persephone.

Prospero (pros′pe-rō). The father of Miranda and rightful duke of Milan, in Shakspere's "Tempest."

Pross (pros), **Solomon,** alias **John Barsad.** A spy and thorough villain in Dickens's "Tale of Two Cities." He robs his sister, the worthy Miss Pross. Later he becomes a turnkey in a Paris prison.

Protagoras (prō-tag'ō-ras). A dialogue of Plato on the nature of virtue.

Protesilaus (prō-tes-i-lā'us). In Greek legend, the first Greek slain in the Trojan War.

Protestantenverein (prō-tes-tän'ten-fer-īn''). An association of liberal German Protestants formed 1863 at Frankfort-on-the-Main.

Proteus (prō'tūs or prō'tē-us). 1. In classical mythology, a sea-god, son of Oceanus and Tethys. 2. The fickle and treacherous friend of Valentine in Shakspere's "Two Gentlemen of Verona."

Prothalamion. See Dictionary, **prothalamion.**

Proudie, Bishop. In Trollope's Cathedral Novels, the Bishop of Barchester, married to an active and socially troublesome wife.

Proverbial Philosophy. A didactic work (1838–76) in verse, by Martin Farquhar Tupper.

Proverbs. One of the books of the Old Testament, made up of sayings of the wise men of Israel, including Solomon.

Provincial Letters. A series of 18 letters (1656–57) by Pascal, defending Jansenism against the Jesuits.

Provisions of Oxford, The. See **Oxford, The Provisions of.**

Provoked Husband, The. A comedy (1728) begun by Vanbrugh and finished by Cibber.

Provoked Wife, The. A comedy (1697) by Vanbrugh.

Pry, Paul. The title character of a comedy (1825) by John Poole. His name has become a synonym for an officious meddler.

Prynne (prin), **Hester.** The adulteress in Hawthorne's "Scarlet Letter," condemned to wear a scarlet A on her breast as penance for her sin.

Psalms (sämz). A book of the Old Testament, containing 150 psalms and hymns, many of which are ascribed to David.

Pseudo-Demetrius. See **Demetrius.**

Pseudodoxia Epidemica (sū-dō-dok'si-a ep-i-dem'i-ka), **or an Enquiry into Vulgar Errors.** The best-known treatise (1646) of Sir Thomas Browne.

Psyche. See Dictionary.

Psyche (sī'kē) **of Capua, The.** A Greek torso of the school of Praxiteles, in the Museo Nazionale, Naples.

Ptah (ptä). In Egyptian mythology, a deity representing the creative force.

Publilian (pub-lil'i-an) **Law, The.** A Roman law passed about 471 B.C. through the efforts of Publilius Volero, which in effect entitled the plebeians to initiate legislation.

Publilian Laws, The. Laws proposed by Publilius Philo about 339 B.C., increasing the political power of the plebeians.

Pucelle (pū-sel) **La.** 1. An epic (1656) on Joan of Arc, by Chapelain. 2. A burlesque epic (1755) by Voltaire.

Puck. See Dictionary, **puck.**

Puck of Pook's Hill. Stories for children (1906) by Rudyard Kipling.

Pudding, Jack. A clown in English folklore.

Pudd'nhead Wilson. The title character in a novel (1894) by Mark Twain (S. L. Clemens).

Puelches (pō-el'chäz). Indians of Araucanian stock, in the western part of Argentina.

Puff. A literary humbug, author of the play rehearsed in Sheridan's "Critic."

Pul (pul). In the Old Testament, an Assyrian king. 2 Kings, xv. 19, 20.

Pulitzer Prizes. Prizes awarded annually for the best American drama, the best American novel, the best American biography, the best American history, the best American book of verse, the best American editorial, the best American cartoon. First awarded in 1917. Named for Joseph Pulitzer.

Pumblechook (pum'bl-chuk), **Mr.** In Dickens's "Great Expectations," a pompous old man who bullies Pip.

Punch. A humorous illustrated London weekly, founded 1841.

Punch, Punchinello. See Dictionary, **Punch².**

Purana. See Dictionary, **purana.**

Pure, Simon. See Dictionary, **simon-pure.**

Purgatorio, Il (ēl pōr-gä-tō'rē-ō). The second part of Dante's "Divina Commedia."

Purgon (pür-gôn). A comic physician in Molière's "Malade imaginaire."

Purim (pū'rim). An annual Jewish festival, on the 14th and 15th of Adar. Esther, ix. 20–32.

Puritani di Scozia, I (ē pö-rē-tä'nē dē skôt'sē-ä). An opera (1835) by Bellini: usually called "I Puritani."

Purmayah (pōr-mä-yä'). In the Shahnamah: (1) The peacock-colored cow that nourished the infant Faridun. (2) See **Kayanush.**

Purple Land, The. An account of life in South America (1885) by W. H. Hudson.

Puseyites. See **Tractarians, The.**

Pushan (pö'shan). In the Vedic hymns, a god who protects and multiplies cattle and other human possessions.

Puss-in-Boots. The hero of a nursery tale from the French (1697) of Perrault. The clever cat makes the fortune of his master, a miller's son.

Put Yourself in His Place. A melodramatic novel (1870) by Charles Reade.

Pygmalion (pig-mā'li-on). 1. In Greek legend: (1) The brother of Dido. (2) A sculptor and king of Cyprus, who fell in love with an ivory statue which he had made. See **Galatea.** 2. A drama (1912) by G. B. Shaw.

Pygmalion and Galatea. A fairy comedy (1871) by W. S. Gilbert.

Pylades (pil'a-dēz). In Greek legend, a nephew of Agamemnon, friend of Orestes, and husband of Electra.

Pyramids, The. See Dictionary, **pyramid.**

Pyramids, The Battle of the. A French victory (July 21, 1798) over the Mamelukes, near the Pyramids of Gizeh.

Pyramus (pir'a-mus). In classical legend, a youth of Babylon, the lover of Thisbe.

Pyrenees, The Peace of the. A treaty (1659) between France and Spain, signed on an island of the Bidassoa.

Pyrrha (pir'a). See **Deucalion.**

Pyrrhus (pir'us), or **Neoptolemus** (nē-op-tol'e-mus). In Greek legend, a son of Achilles and one of the heroes of the Trojan War. He slew Priam, and married Andromache and, later, Hermione.

Pythian Games. See Dictionary, **Pythian.**

Pythias. The common form of the name **Phintias.**

Pythius (pith'i-us). In Greek mythology, Apollo, slayer of the Python.

Python. See Dictionary.

Q

Quadruple Alliance, The. A league against Spain, formed 1718 by Great Britain, France, Austria, and the Netherlands.

Quadruple Treaty, The. A league formed 1834 by Great Britain, France, Spain, and Portugal against the usurpers Don Carlos of Spain and Dom Miguel of Portugal.

Quai d'Orsay (kä dôr-sā). The quay along the south bank of the Seine in Paris, on which are the department of foreign affairs and other government offices; hence, the French foreign office, or the government in general.

Quality of Mercy, The. A novel (1892) by W. D. Howells.

Quality Street. A drama (1901) by Sir James M. Barrie.

Quasimodo (kwas-i-mō'dō). A misshapen dwarf in Victor Hugo's "Notre Dame de Paris."

Quatre Fils Aymon, Les (lä kätr fēs ā-môn). 1. A medieval French romance about Renaud, Guiscard, Adelard, and Richard, the four sons of Aymon de Dordogne. 2. An opera (1844) by Balfe.

Quatre Vents de l'Esprit (kätr von dė les-prē). A volume (1881) containing poems and a drama by Victor Hugo.

Quatre-Vingt-Treize (kätr-van-trāz). A historical novel (1874) by Victor Hugo. Its scene is northwestern France during the Revolution (1793).

Quauhtemoc. The last Aztec sovereign of Mexico.

Queed. A novel (1911) by Henry Sydnor Harrison.

Queen Anne's War. The name given in America to the American portion (1702–13) of the War of the Spanish Succession, fought against the French and Indians.

Queen Mab. A poem (1813) by Shelley.

Queen Mary. A poetic drama (1875) by Tennyson.

Queen of Corinth, The. A play (printed 1647) by Fletcher, Massinger, and others: produced before 1618.

(variable) ḍ as d or j, ş as s or sh, ṭ as t or ch, ẓ as z or zh; o, F. cloche; ü, F. menu; ċh, Sc. loch; ṅ, F. bonbon; ', primary accent; ', secondary accent; †, obsolete; <, from; +, and; =, equals. See also lists at beginning of book.

Queen's College. A college of Oxford University, founded 1340 in honor of the consort of Edward III.

Queens' College. A college of Cambridge University, founded 1448 by Margaret of Anjou and refounded 1465 by Elizabeth Woodville.

Queen's Marie, The. An old Scottish ballad relating the death of Mary Hamilton.

Queen's Quair, The. A romantic novel (1904) by Maurice Hewlett, based on the life of Mary Queen of Scots.

Queerummania (kwẽr-um-mā′ni-ạ). See **Chrononhoton-thologos.**

Quemada, La (lä kā-mä′dä or -ᴛʜä). A group of massive ruins of unknown origin, 35 miles from Zacatecas, Mexico.

Quentin Durward (dẽr′wạrd). A romance (1823) by Scott. The hero, an archer of the Scottish guard, seeks his fortune in France in the reign of Louis XI.

Querecho (kā-rā′chō). A hunting tribe of Apache stock, first encountered 1541 in New Mexico by Coronado.

Querendis (kā-ren-dēz′). A powerful Indian race which, in the 16th century, occupied what is now the province of Buenos Aires.

Querer por Solo Querer (kā-rãr′ pōr sō′lō kā-rãr′). A play (1649) by Mendoza.

Quetzalcohuatl (ket-säl-kọ-wä′tl). A hero-god of the ancient Mexicans.

Quichés (kē-chāz′). A powerful Indian tribe of Guatemala in the time of the conquest. They were of Maya stock.

Quichuas (kē-chō′ạz). The dominant Indian race of Peru at the time of the conquest.

Quickly, Mistress. A servant in Shakspere's "Merry Wives of Windsor"; a hostess in his "Henry IV." and "Henry V."

Quilp (kwilp). A malignant dwarf in Dickens's "Old Curiosity Shop."

Quinames (kē-nä′māz), or **Quinametin** (kē-nä-mä-tēn′). In Nahuatl tradition, a gigantic race, the first inhabitants of the Anahuac plateau.

Quirinal, The. See Dictionary, **Quirinal.**

Quirinalia (kwir-i-nā′li-ạ). An ancient Roman festival in honor of Quirinus, celebrated Feb. 17, the anniversary of Romulus's supposed apotheosis.

Quirinus (kwi-rī′nus). See Dictionary, **Quirinal.**

Quirk, Gammon, and Snap. A firm of solicitors in Samuel Warren's "Ten Thousand a Year."

Quiteria (kē-tā′rē-ä). In Cervantes's "Don Quixote," the lost bride of Camacho.

Quito (kē′tō), **The Audience of.** The chief governing body of Quito (Ecuador) in the colonial period.

Quito, The Kingdom of. The ancient domain of the Quitu Indians, in the highlands of Ecuador.

Quitus (kē′tōz). An ancient Indian tribe, once regnant in the highlands of Ecuador: subdued by the Incas 1460–87.

Quivas (kē′väz). A savage Indian tribe of Venezuela, resident near the confluence of the Orinoco and the Meta.

Quivira, La Gran (lä grän kē-vē′rä). See **Tabirá.**

Quixote (kwik′sọt, Sp. kē-ᴀ̄ō′tä), **Don.** See Dictionary, **quixotic.**

Quomodo (kwō-mō′dō). An ambitious woolen-draper in Middleton's "Michaelmas Term."

Quoratean (kwō-rä-tē′ạn), or **Quoratem** (kwō′rä-tem). A linguistic stock of North American Indians, formerly numerous on the Klamath, Trinity, and Salmon rivers.

Quo Vadis? A historical romance (1895) of the time of Nero, by Henryk Sienkiewicz.

Quran. See Dictionary, **Koran.**

Qwinctunnetun (chwin″shtun-nä′tun). A subdivision of the Pacific branch of the Athapascan stock of North American Indians. The survivors are on the Siletz reservation, Oregon.

R

Ra (rä). In Egyptian mythology, the sun-god and supreme deity.

Rab and His Friends. A story (1859) by John Brown (1810–82) about a Scotch carrier, his wife, and their mastiff, Rab. Rab, the real hero, so grieves after the death of his master and mistress that he has to be shot.

Rab-mag (rab-mag′). The title of a Babylonian officer. Jer. xxxix. 3.

Rabshakeh (rab-shak′ẹ). The title of a Babylonian officer, probably general or commander. 2 Kings, xviii. 17.

Rachel (rā′chẹl). The daughter of Laban, sister of Leah, wife of Jacob, and mother of Joseph and Benjamin. Gen. xxix.–xxxv.

Radcliffe Library. A library, originally medical, connected with Oxford University: founded by John Radcliffe (d. 1714).

Radha (rä′dhä). In Sanskrit mythology: (1) The foster-mother of Karna. (2) A cowherd, the favorite mistress of Krishna among the cowherds.

Ra-en-ka (rä-en-kä′). The statue of an overseer of public works in the time of the 4th Egyptian dynasty: now in the Museum at Cairo.

Raffles. See Dictionary.

Raft of the Medusa, The. A powerful romantic painting (1819) by Géricault, in the Louvre, Paris.

Raghava (rä′ghạ-vạ). In Sanskrit mythology, 'descendant of Raghu,' a name of Ramachandra.

Raghu (ra′ghö). In Hindu mythology, an ancient king, ancestor of Ramachandra or Raghava.

Raghuvansha (ra-ghö-van′shạ). A Sanskrit poem of about the 4th century, on the history of Ramachandra, ascribed to Kalidasa.

Ragman Roll. 1. A collection of parchments recording the fealty of Scottish nobles, clergy, and gentry to Edward I. of England in 1296. 2. A poem printed by Wynkyn de Worde, containing, in alternate stanzas, lists of good and of evil women.

Ragnar Lodbrok (räg′när lōd′brōk). A Norse viking, supposed to have invaded England near the end of the 8th century.

Ragnarök (räg′nä-rẹk). In Old Norse mythology, the destruction of the gods and of all things in a great battle with the evil powers.

Rahab (rā′hab). A woman of Canaan who protected two Israelitish spies sent out by Joshua. Josh. ii.

Rahu (rä′hö). In Sanskrit mythology, the demon who devours sun and moon at times of eclipse.

Raising the Wind. A farce by James Kenney (1780–1849).

Rajput. See Dictionary.

Rake's Progress, The. A series of eight pictures (1735) by Hogarth, in the Soane Museum, London.

Rákos (rä′kosh), **The Field of.** A large plain near Budapest, the scene of combats in 1849, and a former meeting-place of Hungarian diets.

Rakshasa (rak′shạ-sä). In Hindu belief, any one of numerous evil demons.

Ralph Roister Doister. The earliest extant English comedy, written by Nicholas Udall some years before 1566, when it was printed.

Rama (rä′mạ). The name of each of three heroes of Hindu mythology — Balarama, Parashurama, and Ramachandra: especially the last-named.

Ramachandra (rä-mạ-chan′drạ). The hero of the Ramayana, and a character in the Mahabharata.

Ramadan. See Dictionary.

Ramah (rā′mä). In the Old Testament, the name of several places in Palestine. Josh. xviii. 25, 1 Sam. i. 19, etc.

Ramatapaniyopanishad (rä″mạ-tä-pạ-nē″yō-pa-ni-shad′). A upanishad of about the 11th century, in which Rama is worshiped as the supreme god.

Ramayana (rä-mä′yạ-nạ). One of the two great epics of India (the other being the Mahabharata). It is ascribed to the poet Valmiki, and was probably composed early in the Christian era. See **Ramachandra.**

Rambler, The. A periodical (1750–52) published in London by Samuel Johnson, in imitation of the "Spectator."

Rambouillet (rän-bö-yä) **Decree, The.** A decree of Napoleon (1810), providing for the seizure and sale of American ships.

Ramesseum (ram-e-sē′um). A monumental temple built by Rameses II. at Thebes in Egypt.

Ramman (räm′män). The Assyro-Babylonian god of storms.

Ramnes (ram′nēz). One of the three tribal divisions of the ancient Romans: supposed to constitute the Latin element.

Ramona (rạ-mō′nạ). A novel (1884) by Helen Hunt Jackson, dealing with the wrongs suffered by the North American Indians.

Ramoth-gilead (rā'mọth-gil'ẹ-ạd). A city of Gilead frequently mentioned in the Old Testament: it has been variously identified.

Ran (rän). In Old Norse mythology, the sea-goddess, who caught drowning men in her net.

Random, Roderick. In Smollett's "Roderick Random," a good-humored but unprincipled young Scottish adventurer.

Ranelagh (ran'ẹ-lä) **Gardens.** Before 1805, gardens in Chelsea, London, the scene of many wild entertainments and orgies.

Ranz des Vaches (räṅs dä våsh). A Swiss call, sung or blown on the Alpine horn, to lead cattle to the higher pastures.

Rape of Lucrece (lū-krēs'), **The.** 1. A narrative poem (1594) by Shakspere. 2. A tragedy (1608) by Heywood.

Rape of the Lock, The. A mock-heroic poem (1712, 1714) by Pope.

Rape of the Sabines, The. 1. A painting by Rubens, in the National Gallery, London. 2. A group in marble by Giovanni da Bologna, in the Loggia dei Lanzi, Florence. 3. A painting by Luca Giordano, in the museum at Dresden.

Rappaccini's (räp-pät-chē'nēz) **Daughter.** A fanciful and symbolistic tale by Hawthorne, in "Mosses from an Old Manse" (1846).

Rappists (rap'ists), or **Rappites** (-īts). See **Harmonists.**

Rarahu. A novel of Tahiti (1880) by Pierre Loti (Louis Marie Julien Viaud): later known as "The Marriage of Loti."

Raskolnikov (ras-kol'ni-kof). The leading character in Dostoevski's "Crime and Punishment."

Rasselas (ras'ẹ-las). A philosophical romance (1759) by Samuel Johnson. It shows the vanity of human happiness.

Rastatt (rä'shtät), **The Convention of.** A secret agreement (1797) between France and Austria, providing for the delivery to France of the left bank of the Rhine.

Rastatt, The Peace of. A treaty (1714) between France and Austria, preliminary to the treaty of Baden.

Ratisbon (rat'is-bon) **Interim, The.** A provisional arrangement (1541) between Catholics and Protestants, devised by Charles V. of the Holy Roman Empire.

Ratnavali (rat-nä'vạ-lē). "The Pearl Necklace," a Sanskrit drama of the 7th century.

Ratsey's Ghost. A rare tract, probably printed before 1606, reciting the exploits of Gamaliel Ratsey, a notorious robber.

Rattlin (rat'lin), **Jack.** A sailor in Smollett's "Roderick Random."

Räuber, Die (dē roi'bẹr). A play (1781) by Schiller.

Raurici (râ'ri-sī), or **Rauraci** (râ'rạ-sī). A Germanic tribe of the upper Rhine, mentioned by Cæsar.

Raven, The. A poem (1845) by Poe.

Ravenshoe. A novel (1862) by Henry Kingsley.

Ravenswood, Edgar. See **Ashton, Lucy.**

Razor. An intriguing valet in Vanbrugh's "Provoked Wife."

Reading Gaol (red'ing jāl), **The Ballad of.** A poem (1898) by Oscar Wilde, written in prison.

Reading the Will. A famous painting (1820) by Wilkie, in the New Pinakothek, Munich.

Rebecca. In Scott's "Ivanhoe," the beautiful daughter of Isaac the Jew, a money-lender. She secretly loves Ivanhoe.

Rebecca of Sunnybrook Farm. A children's story (1903) by Kate Douglas Wiggin.

Rebecca West. 1. A character in Ibsen's "Rosmersholm." 2. The pen name of Cecily Fairfield.

Rebekah (rẹ-bek'ạ). The sister of Laban, wife of Isaac, and mother of Esau and Jacob. Gen. xxii., xxiv., etc.

Rebellion, The Great. In English history, the period 1642–1660, including the Parliamentary war against the crown, the execution of Charles I., the Commonwealth, and the Protectorate.

Recruiting Officer, The. A comedy (1706) by Farquhar.

Recuyell of the Historyes of Troye. A French collection translated by Caxton about 1470, and supposed to have been the first book printed in English.

Red Badge of Courage, The. A novel (1895) by Stephen Crane, giving a realistic picture of the Civil War.

Red Book of Hergest, The. A Welsh manuscript of the 14th century, at Jesus College, Oxford, containing the tales known in English as the Mabinogion.

Red Cross Knight, The. A knight personifying holiness in Spenser's "Faerie Queene." He also represents St. George of England.

Red Cross Society, The. See Dictionary, **red**[1].

Redemption, The. An oratorio (1882) by Gounod.

Redgauntlet (red'gånt'let). A romance (1824) by Scott. Its title character is a fanatical Jacobite of the 18th century.

Red Lily, The. A novel (1894) by Anatole France.

Red Lions, The. An exclusive English club, originating 1839 in a dinner of members of the British Association at the Red Lion, Birmingham.

Red Riding-Hood, Little. The heroine of a familiar nursery tale.

Red River Expedition, The. 1. In the American Civil War, an unsuccessful expedition up the Red River valley, undertaken to recover western Louisiana. 2. The Canadian expedition (1870) under Wolseley which quelled the insurrection under Riel, in the valley of the Red River of the North.

Red Robe, The. A drama (1900) by Eugène Brieux.

Red Rose, The. The emblem of the House of Lancaster in the Wars of the Roses.

Red Rover, The. A sea novel (1827) by J. F. Cooper.

Red Sticks, The. The irreconcilable Creek Indians who remained hostile to the United States after the War of 1812. They erected red poles in their villages as a symbol of war.

Reef, The. A novel (1912) by Edith Wharton.

Reeve's Tale, The. One of Chaucer's "Canterbury Tales."

Reformation Symphony, The. Mendelssohn's symphony in D minor, written 1830 for the tercentenary of the Augsburg Confession.

Reform Bill, The. A bill (1832) for the purpose of increasing the number of voters in elections to the British House of Commons.

Reform War, The. A Mexican civil war (1857–61), occasioned by the adoption of a modern constitution which restricted the power of the clergy.

Regan (rē'gạn). See **Lear, King.**

Regent Diamond, The. Same as **Pitt Diamond, The.**

Regent's Park. A large park in northwestern London, containing the Zoölogical Gardens.

Regent Street. A principal street of the West End, London. It extends from Portland Place to Waterloo Place.

Règne Animal, Le (lẹ rän-y' å-nē-mål). A zoölogical treatise in 4 vols. (1817) by Georges Cuvier: the basis of pre-Darwinian classification.

Rehearsal, The. A farce (1671) by George Villiers, duke of Buckingham, and others. It ridicules the bombastic rimed plays of Dryden and other contemporaries.

Rehoboam (rē-họ-bō'ạm). The first king of Judah. 1 Kings, xi., xii., xiv., etc.

Rehoboth (rẹ-hō'bọth). The name of three places mentioned in the Old Testament: (1) A city near Nineveh. (2) A city near the Euphrates (Rahabeh?). (3) A well south of Beersheba.

Reichsland (rīchs'länt). From 1871 to 1918, a German designation of Alsace-Lorraine.

Reichsrat, Reichstag. See Dictionary.

Reign of Terror, The. See Dictionary, **reign.**

Reine de Saba, La (lä rän dẹ sä-bä). An opera (1862) by Gounod.

Reine Margot (mär-gō), **La.** A romance (1845) by Dumas *père.*

Rejected Addresses. A collection of parodies on major living poets of England (1812), by James and Horace Smith.

Relief of Lucknow, The. A play (1862) by Dion Boucicault. It contains the famous incident, probably apocryphal, of Jessie Brown and the approach of the relief playing "The Campbells are coming."

Religio Laici (rẹ-lij'i-ō lā'i-sī). A polemic poem (1682) by Dryden.

Religio Medici (med'i-sī). A treatise (1642) by Sir Thomas Browne: one of the important milestones in the progress of English prose style.

Reliques of Ancient English Poetry. A collection of

English popular ballads (1765) gathered and edited by Bishop Thomas Percy.

Remi (rē'mī). A Belgic people whose capital was Rheims. They were allies of Cæsar.

Remonstrance, The Grand. A protest (1641) by the English House of Commons against the abuses in the reign of Charles I.

Remonstrants, The. See Dictionary, **remonstrant.**

Remus (rē'mus). In Roman legend, the brother of Romulus.

Remus, Uncle. See **Uncle Remus.**

Renaissance. See Dictionary, **renaissance.**

Renaud (rē-nō). The French name of Rinaldo.

René (rē-nā). A romance (1802) by Chateaubriand.

Re Pastore, Il (ēl rä päs-tō'rā). A dramatic cantata (1775) by Mozart.

Repose in Egypt, The. Paintings by Murillo and Van Dyck, both in the Hermitage Museum, Leningrad.

Republic, The. A description of an ideal commonwealth, by Plato.

Rescue, The. A novel (1920) by Joseph Conrad.

Research Magnificent, The. A novel (1915) by H. G. Wells.

Resen (rē'sen). An ancient city of Assyria. Its site has not been identified.

Reservoir of the 1,001 Columns, The. A reservoir in Constantinople, built by Constantine.

Resolute, The. An arctic exploring ship which was abandoned off Melville Island (1854) by Belcher during his search for Franklin, and found by an American whaler (1855) near Cape Mercy.

Resolution, The. A ship in which, with the Discovery, Sir Thomas Button explored Hudson Bay, 1612–13.

Restoration, The. 1. See Dictionary, **restoration.** 2. The return of the Jews to Palestine about 537 B.C. 3. The return of the Bourbons to power in 1814, and again in 1815.

Resurrection. A novel (1900) by Count Lev Tolstoy, giving a picture of exile in Siberia.

Return of the Native, The. One (1878) of the major Wessex novels of Thomas Hardy.

Return of the Prodigal, The. A drama (1905) by St. John Hankin.

Return of the Soldier, The. A novel (1918) by Rebecca West (Cecily Fairfield).

Reuben (rö'ben). 1. The eldest son of Jacob and Leah. Gen. xxix., xxx., etc. 2. One of the 12 tribes, consisting of descendants of Reuben. Num. xxxii.

Reunion, The Chambers of. Special courts of annexation established 1680 by Louis XIV. at Metz, Besançon, Tournai, and Breisach. Their action led to the Wars of Reunion between France and the allied powers.

Revelation of St. John the Divine, The. See Dictionary, **revelation.**

Revenge for Honor. A tragedy (published 1654) ascribed to Chapman.

Revenge of Hamish, The. A ballad (1887) by Sidney Lanier.

Reveries of a Bachelor. Sketches (1850) by Ik Marvel (Donald G. Mitchell). "Dream Life" (1851) is a sequel.

Revival of Learning. See Dictionary, **revival.**

Revolt of Islam, The. A narrative poem (1818) by Shelley.

Revolt of Mother, The. A short story (1891) by Mary E. Wilkins Freeman.

Revolt of the Angels, The. A religious satire (1914) by Anatole France.

Revolutionary Tribunal, The. In French history, a special court (1793–95) established by the Convention to deal with attacks on the Revolution.

Revolutionary War, The. See Dictionary, **revolution.**

Revolution of 1848, The. The French revolution which overthrew the government of Louis Philippe.

Revolution of July, The. The French revolution (1830) which overthrew Charles X.

Reynard (rā'nạrd or ren'ạrd) **the Fox.** 1. A satirical epic poem in which the characters are animals. There are many versions, from the 10th century to the 16th. 2. A narrative poem (1920) by John Masefield.

Rhadamanthus (rad-ạ-man'thus). In Greek mythology, a son of Zeus and Europa, associated with his brother Minos and with Æacus as a judge in the lower world.

Rhea (rē'ạ). In Greek mythology, a daughter of Uranus and Gæa, wife of Cronus, and mother of Zeus and other major deities.

Rhea Silvia, or Ilia. In Roman legend, a vestal virgin, mother by Mars of Romulus and Remus.

Rheineck (rī'nek). A noted castle on the left bank of the Rhine, 22 miles northwest of Coblenz.

Rheinfels (rīn'fels). A castle of the 13th century in the Rhine Province, near St. Goar: considered the most imposing ruin on the Rhine.

Rheingold (rīn'golt), **Das.** See **Ring des Nibelungen, Der.**

Rhesus (rē'sus). In Greek legend, a Thracian ally of the Trojans, slain by Odysseus and Diomedes.

Rhine, The Confederation of the. A confederation (1806–13) of German states under the protectorate of Napoleon.

Rhine Cities, The League of. A union formed 1254 by Mainz, Worms, and other German cities for the purpose of maintaining peace.

Rhipæi Montes (ri-pē'ī mon'tēz). A range of mountains supposed by the ancient Greeks to be at the extreme north of the world.

Rhoda Fleming. A novel (1865) by George Meredith.

Rhodes Scholarships. A number of scholarships at Oxford University established by the will of Cecil John Rhodes (d. 1902), providing for the support of selected students from the British colonies, Germany, and the States and Territories of the United States.

Rhodopis (rō-dō'pis). A name (lit. 'rosy-faced') of Doricha, a celebrated Greek courtezan mentioned by Sappho.

Rialto, The. See Dictionary, **Rialto.**

Ribbon Society, The. A secret association formed about 1808 in Ireland in opposition to the Orangemen. Its badge was a green ribbon.

Riceyman Steps. A novel (1924) by Arnold Bennett.

Richard II. A historical play (about 1595) by Shakspere.

Richard III. A historical play thought to have been revised by Shakspere about 1594 from an original left unfinished by Marlowe.

Richard Feverel, The Ordeal of. See **Feverel, Richard.**

Richard Roe. See Dictionary.

Richard Yea-and-Nay. A romance (1900) by Maurice Hewlett.

Richelieu. A historical play (1839) by Bulwer-Lytton.

Riches. A stage version, still used, of Massinger's "City Madam" (licensed 1632).

Ridd, John. The hero of the novel "Lorna Doone."

Rideau (rē'dō) **Hall.** The official residence of the governor-general of Canada, at Ottawa.

Riders to the Sea. A drama (1904) by John M. Synge, suggesting an effect of destiny in the life of old Maurya, whose husband and sons are all drowned.

Rienzi (rē-en'zē). 1. A historical romance (1835) by Bulwer-Lytton. 2. An opera (1842) by Wagner.

Riffis (rif'ēz), or **Riffians** (rif'i-ạnz). The inhabitants of the Rif Mountains in northern Morocco.

Rigel (rī'jel). A brilliant star of the first magnitude in the left foot of the man pictured in the constellation Orion.

Rightful Heir, The. A play (1869) by Bulwer-Lytton.

Rights, The Bill of. 1. A confirmation (1689) by William and Mary of the Declaration of Right prepared by the English Parliament. 2. A statement of the personal rights of citizens, incorporated in the Constitution of the United States as Amendments I.–X.

Rights of Man, The. A reply (1791) by Thomas Paine to Burke's "Reflections on the Revolution in France."

Rigoletto (rē-gō-let'tō). An opera (1851) by Verdi.

Rigsdag. See Dictionary.

Rig-Veda. See Dictionary, **Veda.**

Rima (rē'mä). An important character, the "bird-girl," in W. H. Hudson's "Green Mansions." The figure of Rima in Jacob Epstein's memorial to Hudson, in London, roused violent controversy in 1925.

Rime of the Ancient Mariner, The. See **Ancient Mariner, The.**

Rimini, Francesca da. See **Francesca da Rimini.**

Rimmon (rim′ọn). A Scriptural variant of Ramman. 2 Kings, v. 18.

Rinaldo (ri-nal′dō). One of the bravest of the paladins of Charlemagne: cousin of Orlando (Roland), and owner of the famous steed Bayard.

Rind (rind). In Norse mythology, one of Odin's wives: the earth's crust personified.

Ring and the Book, The. A poem (1868–69) by Browning, based on a celebrated criminal case of the Italian Renaissance, in which the same events are rehearsed in monologue from a succession of points of view.

Ring des Nibelungen, Der (der ring des nē′bẹ-lúng-ẹn). A sequence of four music-dramas by Wagner: "Das Rhein-gold" (1869); "Die Walküre" (1870); "Siegfried" (1876); and "Götterdämmerung" (1876). It is based on Icelandic sagas.

Riot Act. See Dictionary, **riot.**

Rip Van Winkle. A story by Washington Irving about a ne'er-do-well who sleeps 20 years and wakes to find every-thing changed: published in the "Sketch-Book" (1819). Also, the play by Dion Boucicault, based on the story.

Rise of Silas Lapham (lap′ạm), **The.** A novel (1885) by W. D. Howells: the story of the rise and decline of a self-made American business-man.

Rishi (rish′i). In Vedic literature, a poet, or 'singer of sacred songs.'

Rising of the Moon, The. A drama (1907) by Lady Augusta Gregory.

Ritusanhara (ri-tö-sạn-hä′rä). A Sanskrit poem on the six seasons of India, by Kalidasa. It was the first book ever printed in Sanskrit (Calcutta, 1792).

Rival Queens, or The Death of Alexander the Great, The. The best-known tragedy (1677) of Nathaniel Lee.

Rivals, The. A brilliant comedy (1775) by Sheridan.

Riverside Drive. A boulevard bordering the Hudson, ex-tending from 72d Street to Dyckman Street, New York.

Roaring Forties, The. See Dictionary, **roaring.**

Robber Council, The. See **Ephesus, The Council of.**

Robbers, The. See **Räuber, Die.**

Robert Elsmere. A novel (1888) by Mrs. Humphry Ward about an English clergyman whose intellectual doubts force him to abandon strict orthodoxy.

Robert le Diable (ro-bär lẹ dyäbl). An opera (1831) by Meyerbeer.

Robin Adair (ạ-dâr′). A song which became popular in England in the 18th century. It is sung to the Irish air "Eileen Aroon."

Robinetta (rob-i-net′ä). A half-length portrait by Reynolds, in the National Gallery, London. The subject was Miss Lewis, later the Hon. Mrs. Tollemache.

Robin Goodfellow. See Dictionary.

Robinson Crusoe. A romance (1719) by Defoe about a mariner of York who, shipwrecked, lives adventurously for years upon a small island, until rescued by ạ passing vessel.

Robot. A machine-made man, in Karel Čapek's fantastic melodrama, "R. U. R." (1923).

Rob Roy. A romance (1818) by Scott. The title character is Robert Macgregor, a famous Scottish outlaw.

Robsart (rob′särt), **Amy.** In Scott's "Kenilworth," the unacknowledged wife of Lord Robert Dudley, whom he denies before Queen Elizabeth.

Rochester, Edward Fairfax. The passionate, self-willed employer of the governess heroine of Charlotte Brontë's "Jane Eyre."

Rocky Road to Dublin, The. Poems (1915) by James Stephens.

Roderick Dhu (rod′ĕr-ik dö). A Highland chieftain in Scott's "Lady of the Lake."

Roderick Hudson. A novel (1876) by Henry James: the story of an American abroad.

Roderick Random. A novel (1748) by Smollett.

Rodilardus (rō-di-lär′dus). In Rabelais's "Pantagruel," a huge cat which attacks Panurge.

Rodomont (rod′ọ-mont). See Dictionary, **rodomontade.**

Rogero (rō-jā′rō). In the epics of Boiardo and Ariosto, a Saracen knight who accepts Christianity for the sake of Bradamant.

Roi des Montagnes, Le (lẹ rwo dä môn-tän-y′). A novel of Greece (1856) by Edmond About.

Roi d'Yvetot, Le (lẹ rwo dēv-tō). An enormously popular song (1813) by Béranger.

Roi s'Amuse (sạ-müz), **Le.** A historical drama (1832) by Victor Hugo, set in the reign of Francis I.

Rois Fainéants, Les (lā rwo fā-nā-äṅ). The Merovingian successors of Dagobert I., who were little more than figure-heads.

Rokeby (rōk′bi). A romance in verse (1813) by Scott.

Roland (rō′lạnd). A famous paladin of Charlemagne. (See Dictionary.) He had a wonderful horn, Olivant, and a no less wonderful sword, Durandal, or Durindana.

Roll-Call, The. A painting (1874) of the Grenadier Guards after a winter battle in the Crimea, by Lady Butler (Eliza-beth Thompson): in Windsor Castle.

Roll-Call of the Last Victims of the Terror, The. A painting (1850) by Müller, in the palace of Versailles.

Romance. 1. A novel (1903) by Joseph Conrad and Ford Madox Hueffer (Ford). 2. A drama (1913) by E. B. Sheldon.

Romance of the Forest, The. A romance (1791) by Mrs. Radcliffe.

Roman Comique (ro-män ko-mēk). The unfinished history (1651) of a troupe of strolling players, written in the pica-resque manner, by Scarron.

Roman de la Rose (dẹ lä rōz). An elaborate allegory in verse, begun (13th century) by Guillaume de Lorris and completed by Jean de Meun.

Roman de Troie (trwo). A verse romance (c. 1160) based on the story of Troy, by Benoît de Sainte-Maure. It was translated into Latin by Guido delle Colonne (c. 1287), and contains the earliest known form of the story of Troilus and Cressida.

Roman d'un Jeune Homme Pauvre, Le (duṅ zhẹ-nom pōvr). A novel (1857) by Octave Feuillet.

Romanov or **Romanoff** (ro-mä′nof). The imperial dynasty which ruled Russia from 1613 to the abdication of Nicholas II. in 1917.

Romans, The Epistle to the. In the New Testament, one of the more important doctrinal epistles of Paul, written about A.D. 58 to the Christian community at Rome.

Romans of the Decadence. A painting (1847) by Couture, in the Luxembourg Museum, Paris.

Romany (rom′ạ-ni) **Rye, The.** An autobiographical work (1857) by George Borrow: a sequel to "Lavengro."

Roma Quadrata (rō′mä kwod-rä′tä). Earliest fortified Rome, situated on the Palatine and surrounded by a quad-rangular wall.

Romaunt of the Rose. A fragmentary English trans-lation of the "Roman de la Rose," by late tradition ascribed to Chaucer, and possibly a corrupted version of his work.

Romeo (rō′mẹ-ō) **and Juliet** (jö′li-et). 1. A tragedy by Shakspere, produced between 1591 and 1596. 2. A dramatic symphony, the fifth, by Berlioz (1839). 3. An opera by Zingarelli (1796). 4. An opera by Bellini, entitled in Italian "I Capuletti ed i Montecchi" (1830). 5. An opera by Gounod (1867).

Romola (rom′ọ-lạ). A historical novel (1863) by George Eliot. The title character is a young Florentine woman who, after a marriage with the hedonistic Tito Melema, comes under the influence of Savonarola and through faith and service finds peace.

Romulus (rom′ụ-lus). In Roman legend, the founder of the city (753 B.C.) and its first king. He was the son of Mars by Rhea Silvia. He and his brother Remus (whom he even-tually killed) were suckled by a wolf. The Romans deified him as Quirinus.

Roncesvalles (ron′sẹ-valz), F. **Roncevaux** (rôṅs-vō). The scene of the defeat of the rear-guard of Charlemagne's army in 778, and of the death of Roland. It is in the Pyrenees, 20 miles northeast of Pamplona.

Rood (röd), **The Black.** A cross of gold, supposed to contain a fragment of the true cross, taken to Scotland by the wife of Malcolm III. All trace of it is lost.

Roodee (rö′dē). A meadow near Chester, England, partly surrounded by a Roman wall, and used from early times as a race-course.

Rookery, The. A former slum, part of St. Giles's, London.

Rori (rō′rē), or **Warori** (wä-rō′rē). A dog-eating Bantu tribe, dwelling north of Lake Nyasa.

Rory O'More (rō'ri ō̞-mōr'). A romantic novel (1837) by Samuel Lover.

Rosalind (roz'ạ-lind or -līnd). 1. The lady to whom Colin Clout (Spenser) pays unsuccessful court in the "Shepherd's Calendar." Her identity has not been established. 2. The vivacious daughter of the exiled duke in Shakspere's "As You Like It." She loves Orlando.

Rosalynde, or Euphues' Golden Legacy. A euphuistic pastoral romance (1590) by Thomas Lodge: the source of the plot of Shakspere's "As You Like It."

Rosamond (roz'ạ-mọnd). An opera (1707) by Addison.

Rosamond's Bower. A subterranean labyrinth in Blenheim Park, Woodstock, England, said to have been built by Henry II. for Rosamond Clifford.

Rosamond's Pond. Before 1770, a pond in St. James's Park, London, "consecrated to love and elegiac poetry."

Rose, The. 1. A London playhouse on the Bankside, Southwark, opened about 1592 by Henslowe. 2. An ordinary in Russell Street, Covent Garden, London, near the theaters, and much frequented about 1667.

Rosencrantz (rō'zẹn-krants) and **Guildenstern** (gil'dẹn-stẹrn). Sycophants and spies in Shakspere's "Hamlet."

Rosenkavalier. An opera (1911) by Richard Strauss.

Rosetta (rō-zet'ạ) **Stone, The.** A slab of black basalt found 1799 near the Rosetta mouth of the Nile. Its inscriptions of pre-Christian origin provided the first key to the interpretation of Egyptian hieroglyphics.

Rosicrucians. See Dictionary, **Rosicrucian.**

Rosinante. See Dictionary.

Rosmersholm. A drama (1887) by Henrik Ibsen.

Rosmunda (roz-mun'dä). A tragedy (1783) by Alfieri.

Rotary Club. See Dictionary, **rotary.**

Rothschild (roths'child, G. rōt'shilt). A Jewish family of financiers which established a banking house at Frankfort-on-the-Main in the 18th century, and, later, branches at Vienna, London, and Paris.

Rotten Row. In Hyde Park, London, a fashionable thoroughfare for equestrians.

Rough Riders, The. See Dictionary, **rough-rider.**

Rougon-Macquart (rö-gôṅ-mà-kär'). The name of a family in a long series of novels (1871–1893) by Émile Zola.

Roundheads. See Dictionary, **Roundhead.**

Round Table, The. See Dictionary, **round²**.

Round the Corner. A novel (1913) by Gilbert Cannan.

Rowena (rō-wē'nạ). 1. The legendary daughter of Hengist, and wife of Vortigern. 2. In Scott's "Ivanhoe," the ward of Cedric, an heiress of royal Saxon descent. She marries Ivanhoe.

Rowley (rou'li) **Poems, The.** Poems (1769) which Chatterton, the real author, attributed to a mythical priest of the 15th century.

Rowton (rou'tọn) **Heath.** The scene, near Chester, England, of a Royalist defeat (1645) by the Parliamentary army.

Roxane. See **Cyrano de Bergerac.**

Royal Academy of Arts, The. A London society, founded 1768, for the encouragement of contemporary art.

Royal George, The. An English man-of-war which sank at Spithead, Aug. 29, 1782, while being refitted, with a loss of 800 lives. There is a poem, "On the Loss of the Royal George" (1803), by Cowper (written 1782).

Royal Society, The. A London association, incorporated 1662, for the advancement of the physical and other sciences.

Royal Society Club, The. A London club, formed about 1709, consisting largely of fellows of the Royal Society.

Royal Sovereign, The. 1. The flag-ship of Collingwood at Trafalgar. 2. A British battle-ship rebuilt with armor in 1864.

Ruanda (rö-än'dä), or **Waruanda** (wä-rö-än'dä). A fierce and powerful Bantu tribe dwelling to the north of Lake Tanganyika, Africa.

Rubáiyát (rö-bäi'yät), **The.** 'Quatrains,' the best-known work of the Persian Omar Khayyam (fl. 1100), familiar in English through the version by FitzGerald.

Rübezahl (rü'bẹ-tsäl). In German folklore, a mountain spirit of the Riesengebirge.

Rubicon. See Dictionary.

Rudabah (rö-dä-bä'). In the Shahnamah, the daughter of Mihrab, wife of Zal, and mother of Rustam.

Rudder Grange. A novel (1879) by Frank R. Stockton.

Ruddigore, or the Witches' Curse. A comic opera (1887) by W. S. Gilbert and Arthur Sullivan.

Rudelsburg (rö'dẹls-búrċh). A ruined castle near Kösen, on the Saale, Prussian Saxony.

Rudge, Barnaby. In Dickens's "Barnaby Rudge," a simple-minded lad who becomes accidentally involved in the No-Popery Riots. See **Grip.**

Rüdiger (rü'di-gẹr). A principal character in the "Nibelungenlied."

Rudra (rö'drä). In the Rig-Veda, the lord of the Maruts: the storm-god.

Rue de la Paix (rü dẹ lä pā). A street of fine shops in Paris, running from the Place de l'Opéra southward.

Rue de Rivoli (rē-vo-lē). An important street of Paris, leading from the Place de la Concorde to the Rue St.-Antoine.

Rue St.-Antoine (sañ-täṅ-twän). An ancient street in Paris. It leads from the Rue de Rivoli to the Place de la Bastille, whence it continues as the Rue du Faubourg St.-Antoine.

Rue St.-Honoré (sañ-to-no-rā). A street in Paris, running from the Rue du Pont Neuf past the Place du Théâtre Français.

Ruetli. See **Rütli.**

Ruggiero (röd-jä'rō). A variant of **Rogero.**

Rugii (rö'ji-ī). A Germanic tribe, originally from the Baltic, which fought under Attila and took part in the conquest of Britain.

Ruhmeshalle (rö'mes-häl″ẹ). A Doric Hall of Fame in Munich: completed 1853.

Rule a Wife and Have a Wife. An extremely popular comedy (1624) by Fletcher.

Rule Britannia. An English national anthem: words by Thomson and Mallet, music by Arne. This was composed for the mask "Alfred" (1740).

Rump Parliament, The. The remnant of the Long Parliament after Pride's Purge (which see).

Rum Row. That part of the Atlantic just off the New England, New York, and New Jersey coasts, the scene of rum-running operations.

Runaway. A novel (1925) by Floyd Dell.

Runnymede or **Runnimede** (run'i-mēd), or **Runnemede.** A meadow on the south bank of the Thames in Surrey, 21 miles from London. See **Magna Charta.**

Rush, Friar. See **Friar Rush.**

Rustam (rus'tạm), or **Rustum.** A hero in the Shahnamah. As narrated in Matthew Arnold's "Sohrab and Rustum," he slays in single combat his son Sohrab (Suhrab), of whose relation to him he is ignorant.

Ruteni (rö-tē'nī). An ancient people of southern Gaul.

Ruth (röth). A Moabitess whose story is told in the Old Testament Book of Ruth. She married Boaz in Bethlehem, and was an ancestress of David.

Rutherford and Son. A drama (1912) by Githa Sowerby.

Ruthven (röth'vẹn or riv'ẹn), **The Raid of.** A conspiracy in 1582, at Castle Ruthven, near Perth, Scotland, involving the seizure of James VI.

Ruthwell Cross. An obelisk at Ruthwell, on the Scottish border, thrown down by the Presbyterians in 1642. It contained Northumbrian runes of about the 8th century.

Rütli (rüt'lē), or **Grütli** (grüt'lē). A mountain meadow near Lucerne, Switzerland, famous as the legendary scene of the formation of the Swiss League against Austria in 1307.

Rutuli (rö'tụ-lī). In Roman legend, a people of Latium. Their capital was Ardea. Turnus, their king, appears in the stories of Æneas.

Ruy Blas (rüẹ bläs). 1. A tragedy (1838) by Victor Hugo. 2. An opera (1869) by Marchetti.

Ryance (rī'ạns), or **Ryence** (rī'ẹns). In Arthurian lore, a king of Ireland and Wales, and possessor of the sword Marandaise.

Rye House Plot, The. A plot to assassinate Charles II. and James, Duke of York, in 1683: named from the isolated house in Hertfordshire in which the conspirators supposedly met.

S

Sabazius (sạ-bā'zhi-us). A Phrygian god of nature, partially identified by the Greeks with Zeus and with Dionysus.

Sabbatarians. See Dictionary, **Sabbatarian.**

Sabeans. See Dictionary, **Sabean**[1].

Sabellians (sạ-bel'i-ạnz). 1. A primitive Italian people which included the Sabines, Samnites, etc. 2. Followers of Sabellius, who attempted to explain the doctrine of the Trinity on philosophical principles.

Sabians. See Dictionary, **Sabian.**

Sabines (sā'bīnz). See Dictionary, **Sabine.**

Sabines, The Rape of the. See Dictionary, **Sabine.**

Sabinum (sạ-bī'num). The country villa of Horace, not far from Tivoli: celebrated in his poetry as the "Sabine farm."

Sabra (sā'brä). In the ancient ballads of "St. George and the Dragon," the maiden rescued from the dragon, and afterward married to the knight.

Sabrina (sạ-brī'nä). The legendary daughter of Locrine, drowned in the river Severn, of which the Roman name was Sabrina.

Sac, Sauk (såk). A tribe of North American Indians whose earliest known habitat was in the eastern peninsula of Michigan, and who settled in northern Wisconsin.

Sacharissa (sak-ạ-ris'ạ). A lady (Lady Dorothy Sydney) celebrated by Waller in his poems.

Sachsenspiegel (zäk'sẹn-shpē"gẹl). A widely influential book summarizing the laws of northern Germany, composed in Latin (about 1230) by Eike von Repgow.

Sacred and Profane Love. A painting by Titian, in the Palazzo Borghese, Rome.

Sacred Band, The. 1. A band of 300 Thebans formed to take part in the wars of the 4th century B.C. against Sparta: destroyed 338 B.C. at Chæronea. 2. A company of Greeks formed 1821 by Alexandros Ypsilanti for service against the Turks: destroyed in the battle of Dragasani.

Sacred Nine, The. The Muses.

Sacred Wars, The. In Greek history, four wars undertaken by members of the Amphictyonic League in defense of the shrine of Delphi: (1) 600–590 B.C. (596–586?). (2) About 448 B.C. (3) 357–346 B.C. (4) 339–338 B.C.

Sacred Way, The. 1. The ancient road from Athens to Eleusis, starting at the Dipylon Gate and traversing the Pass of Daphne. 2. The first street of ancient Rome to be established on the low ground beneath the hills.

Sacrificial Stone, The. The stone on which human victims were sacrificed before the war-god Huitzilopochtli, in the principal Aztec temple at Mexico: now in the Mexican national museum.

Sacripant (sak'ri-pant). 1. A character in the epics of Boiardo and Ariosto. 2. A character in Alessandro Tassoni's "Secchia Rapita" (1622).

Sadducees. See Dictionary, **Sadducee.**

Sad Shepherd, The. An unfinished pastoral drama by Jonson (published posthumously in 1641), on the subject of Robin Hood.

Sagittarius. See Dictionary.

Sagittary (saj'i-tā-ri). See Dictionary, **sagittary.**

Saho (sä'hō), or **Shoho** (shō'hō). A large tribe of poor pastoral nomads, dwelling between Abyssinia and Annesley Bay (Red Sea).

St. Agnes, The Eve of. A narrative poem (1818) by Keats.

St.-Antoine, Faubourg. See **Rue St.-Antoine.**

St. Bartholomew, The Massacre of. See Dictionary, **St. Bartholomew's Day,** under saint.

Saint Cecilia's Day, Ode for. See **Alexander's Feast.**

St.-Denis (sań-dė-nē), **Rue.** A street in Paris, leading north from the Rue de Rivoli to the Boulevard St.-Denis.

Sainte-Anne (sańt-än). A pilgrim resort in the department of Morbihan, France.

Sainte-Chapelle (sańt-shä-pel). A chapel in Paris, the most perfect example of Pointed architecture: built 1248 by St. Louis as the chapel of his palace, to receive and enshrine the crown of thorns.

St. Elian's (ē'liạnz) **Well.** A celebrated well in Denbighshire, known as "the head of the cursing-wells," and associated with ancient superstition.

St. Elmo. See **Elmo, The Castle of Saint.**

Saint George and the Dragon. The subject of many paintings, notably one (1506) by Raphael, in the Hermitage Museum, Leningrad.

St.-Germain-l'Auxerrois (sań-zher-mań-lōk-se-rwo). The parish church of the kings of France, in Paris, dating from the 12th century to the 16th.

St. Gotthard (sänt goth'ärd, F. sań go-tär), **The Tunnel of the.** The railway tunnel through the St. Gotthard group, extending 9 miles, from Göschenen to Airolo: opened 1882.

St. James's (jämz'ez) **Palace.** A palace in London, adapted as a royal residence by Henry VIII. It gives to the British court its official title.

St. James's Park. A public park of 87 acres, in London, especially associated with the private life of Charles II.

Saint Joan. A drama (1922) by G. B. Shaw, based on the career of Joan of Arc.

St. John Lateran (lat'e-rạn). A famous church in Rome, "the mother and head of all churches": originally erected by Constantine.

St. John's College. 1. A college of Cambridge University, founded 1511 by Lady Margaret Beaufort. 2. A college of Oxford University, founded 1555.

St. John's Fire. A drama (1900) by Hermann Sudermann.

St. John's Wood. A quarter in the northwestern part of London, now a large colony of villas.

St. Margaret's. A historic church in Westminster, London, founded by Edward I. Caxton and Raleigh were buried in it.

St. Mark's (Venice). See **Mark, Basilica of St.**

St. Mark's Square. The principal square in Venice, containing St. Mark's Church and the Campanile.

St. Martin's le Grand. A very ancient former monastery and church in London.

St. Mary de Arcubus (dē är'kụ-bus), or **le Bow** (lė bō), or **Bow Church.** A church in London, on Cheapside, within the sound of whose celebrated bells all cockneys are born. It was designed by Wren, and begun 1671.

St. Mary's College. See **Winchester School.**

St. Mary's the Great. The official university church at Cambridge, England, built between 1487 and 1519.

St. Mary the Virgin, The Church of. The official university church at Oxford, England. The existing choir dates from 1460.

St. Michael Overcoming Satan. A painting (1518) by Raphael, in the Louvre, Paris.

St.-Ouen (sań-tö-oń), **The Declaration of.** A proclamation (1814) to the French nation by Louis XVIII., promising a constitution.

Saint Patrick's Day. A farce (1775) by Sheridan.

St. Paul, or **Paulus.** Mendelssohn's first oratorio (1836).

St. Paul's. A cathedral in London, begun 1675, after the designs of Wren, in place of the old cathedral (11th century to the 13th). Its magnificent dome is one of the most imposing in existence.

St. Paul's Churchyard. The open space surrounding St. Paul's Cathedral, London.

St. Paul without the Walls. A famous 4th-century basilica at Rome, unfortunately burned 1823, but as far as possible reproduced.

St. Peter's. The great metropolitan church of the See of Rome, of pseudo-Roman architecture. The pedimented dome is one of the most magnificent achievements of architecture.

St. Peter's College, or **Peterhouse.** The oldest college of Cambridge University, founded as a hospital in 1257 and as a college 1280–86 by Hugh de Balsham, bishop of Ely.

Saint-Preux (sań-prė). An important character, the lover of Julie, in Rousseau's novel "La nouvelle Héloïse."

St. Ronan's Well. A romance (1824) by Sir Walter Scott.

St. Sepulchre. A Norman church dating from 1101, in Cambridge, England.

Saints' Everlasting Rest, The. A devotional work (1650) by Richard Baxter.

St.-Sulpice (sań-sül-pēs). A large church at Paris, built by Louis XIV.

Salamanca (sal-ạ-mang'kä), **The Council** or **Junta of.** A meeting (apparently 1486–87) of scholars to consider the projects of Columbus. The majority were against them.

Salammbô (sä-läm-bō). A novel (1862) by Flaubert: the history of Hannibal's sister Salammbô.

Salarian (sạ-lā′ri-ạn) **Way, The.** A celebrated ancient Roman highway, from Rome up the Tiber valley to Reate (Rieti), across the Apennines, and down the valley of the Tronto to the Adriatic, where branches led to Ancona and Adria.

Salathiel (sạ-lā′thi-el). A romance (1827) by George Croly, on the subject of the Wandering Jew.

Salem (sā′lem). 1. The place, of uncertain identity, of which Melchizedek was king. Heb. vii. 1, 2. 2. An ancient name of Jerusalem.

Salian (sā′li-ạn) **Emperors, The.** The same as **Franconian Emperors, The.**

Salic Law. See Dictionary, **Salic.**

Salisbury (sâlz′be-ri) **Cathedral.** The most beautiful of English churches, built 1220–60, in a uniform and dignified early-Pointed style.

Salish (sā′lish). The leading tribe of the Salishan stock of North American Indians, formerly living in Montana: wrongly called Flatheads by surrounding tribes.

Salishan (sā′lish-ạn). A linguistic stock of North American Indians, living in British Columbia, Montana, Washington, and Oregon.

Sallust (sal′ust), **The Gardens of.** A noted imperial pleasure-ground in ancient Rome, built originally by Sallust.

Sally in Our Alley. 1. A popular song with an original melody by Henry Carey, composed about the middle of the 18th century. 2. A comedy (1826) by Douglas Jerrold.

Salm (salm). In the Shahnamah, the eldest of the three sons (Salm, Tur, Iraj) of Faridun.

Salmacis (sal′mạ-sis). In Greek mythology, the nymph of a fountain in Caria, united with Hermaphroditus into one person.

Salmagundi (sal-mạ-gun′di). A humorous periodical (1807) published by Washington Irving, J. K. Paulding, and William Irving. A second series, by Paulding alone, was published 1819.

Salome (sạ-lō′me). 1. The daughter of Herodias, whose dancing so pleased Herod that he gave her the head of John the Baptist at her request: wife of Philip and later of Aristobulus. 2. A drama (1891) by Oscar Wilde. 3. An opera (1905) by Richard Strauss, based on Wilde's play.

Salon, Le (lě sạ-lôṅ). 1. The gallery at the Louvre in which exhibitions of art were held. 2. See Dictionary, **salon.**

Salpêtrière, La (lä sȧl-pe-trē-är′). A large hospital or almshouse for infirm, insane, and otherwise helpless women in Paris. The general hospital was founded 1656 by royal edict.

Salt River. See Dictionary, **salt².**

Saltwater Ballads. A collection of poems (1902) by John Masefield.

Salus (sā′lus). The Roman goddess of health and prosperity: in part identified with the Greek Hygeia.

Salvation Army, The. See Dictionary, **salvation.**

Salvation Nell. A drama (1908) by E. B. Sheldon.

Salve Regina. See Dictionary, **salve³.**

Sam (sam). One of the great heroes of the Shahnamah, son of Nariman, father of Zal, and grandfather of Rustam.

Samaritans. See Dictionary, **Samaritan.**

Samnites (sam′nīts). See Dictionary, **Samnite.**

Samnite (sam′nīt) **Wars, The.** In Roman history, the wars between Rome and the Samnites, 343–290 B.C.

Sampson, Dominie. A homely and awkward schoolmaster in Scott's "Guy Mannering."

Sam Slick. See **Sayings and Doings of Samuel Slick.**

Samson (sam′son). The fifteenth in order of the "judges" of Israel, a performer of Herculean exploits. Judges, xiii.–xvi.

Samson Agonistes (ag-ọ-nis′tēz). An English drama (1671) in the Greek form by Milton. Its subject is the Biblical Samson.

Samson and Delilah. An opera (1877) by Saint-Saëns.

Samuel (sam′ū-el), **The Books of.** In the Old Testament, two books comprising the history of Israel from the birth of the prophet Samuel to the end of the reign of David.

Sanballat (san-bal′ạt). The chief opponent of Nehemiah in his endeavors to restore the city of Jerusalem. Neh. iv.

San Carlo (sän kär′lō). The largest and most famous theater of Naples: originally built 1737.

Sancho Panza (sang′kō pan′zạ, Sp. sän′chō pän′thä). See **Panza, Sancho.**

Sandeh. See **Nyam-Nyam.**

Sandemanians (san-dẹ-mā′ni-ạnz). The followers of Robert Sandeman, son-in-law and disciple of John Glas. See **Glassites.**

Sandford and Merton, The History of. A didactic story (1783–89) for juvenile readers, by Thomas Day.

Sangraal, or **Sangreal.** See Dictionary.

Sangrado (säng-grä′dō), **Doctor.** In Le Sage's "Gil Blas," a physician whose treatment consists in profuse bloodletting and the drinking of hot water.

Sanhedrim. See Dictionary, **sanhedrim.**

Sanine. A novel (1908) by Mikhail Artsybashev.

San Juan (sän hwän) **Hill.** A hill southeast of Santiago, Cuba, captured by United States troops July 1, 1898.

Sankhya (sän′khyạ). The third of the six systems of Hindu philosophy, ascribed to the sage Kapila. It repudiates the notion that matter can originate from spirit, and that anything can be produced from nothing.

Sankhyakarika (sän-khyạ-kä′ri-kä). In Sanskrit literature, a collection of memorial verses by Ishvarakrishna, in which the Sankhya philosophy is summarized.

Sansculotte. See Dictionary, **sansculotte.**

Sans Souci (säṅ sö-sē). A palace at Potsdam, Prussia, built by Frederick the Great 1745–47, and enlarged and adorned by Frederick William IV.

San Stefano (sän stef′ä-nō), **The Treaty of.** A treaty (1878) between Russia and Turkey, which ended the Russo-Turkish war.

Santa Ana (sän′tä ä′nä). A tribe of North American Indians which inhabit a pueblo of the same name in north-central New Mexico.

Santa Claus (san′tạ klâz). The patron saint of children, dispenser of gifts on Christmas Eve. See **Nicholas, Saint.**

Santal (san-täl′) **Insurrection, The.** An unsuccessful revolt (1855) by the Santals of the Rajmahal Hills, Bengal.

Santa Maria (sän′tä mä-rē′ä). The flag-ship of Columbus in his voyage of 1492. It and two smaller vessels, the Pinta and the Niña, made up his fleet.

Santa Maria degli Angeli (sän′tä mä-rē′ä dā′lyē än′jä-lē). A church on the site of the Baths of Diocletian, Rome: constructed by Michelangelo.

Santa Maria del Popolo (del pô′pō-lō). A church at Rome, founded (1099?), according to tradition, to quiet the phantom of Nero, whose burial-place was beneath it.

Santa Maria del Sole (del sō′lä). A circular temple (now a church) at Rome, dating from the beginning of the empire: now held to be the temple of Hercules, but familiarly known as that of Vesta.

Santa Maria in Ara Cœli (ā′rạ sē′lī). An old and interesting church at Rome, possessing the miracle-working image of the Santissimo Bambino. See Dictionary, **bambino.**

Santa Maria in Cosmedin (kos′me-din). A very early church at Rome.

Santa Maria Maggiore (mäd-jō′rā). A church at Rome, built A.D. 352.

Santa Maria Novella (nō-vel′lä). A church in Florence, built 1278–1349, of Tuscan Gothic architecture.

Santa Maria sopra Minerva (sō′prä mē-ner′vä). The only medieval church in Rome which retains its Pointed forms and decoration. It was built over a temple of Minerva. It contains notable paintings and sculptures.

Sant' Angelo, The Castle of. See **Angelo, The Castle of Sant'.**

Santa Sophia. See **Sophia, St.**

Sant' Elmo Castle. See **Elmo, The Castle of Saint.**

Sapphira (sa-fī′rạ). A woman who, with her husband Ananias, was struck dead for lying. Acts, v.

Saracens. See Dictionary, **Saracen.**

Sarah (sā′rạ). The wife of Abraham and mother of Isaac: earlier Sarai. Gen. xvii. 15–22, etc.

Sarama (sạ-ra′mä). In the Rig-Veda, a dog, a messenger of Indra and the Angirases, who finds the stolen cows of Indra.

Sarasvati (sạ′rạs-wạ-tē). 1. In the Rig-Veda, a mighty river and its genius, who protects and blesses the dwellers upon its banks. 2. A little sacred river, personified as Brahma's wife, the patron goddess of sacrifice.

Sardanapalus (sär″dạ-nạ-pā′lus). A tragedy (1821) by Byron.

---

fat, fāte, fär, fȧll, ȧsk, fãre; net, mē, hèr; pin, pīne; not, nōte, mōve, nôr; up, lūte, púll; oi, oil; ou, out; (lightened) aviạry, ẹlect, agọny, intọ, ụnite; (obscured) errạnt, operạ, ardẹnt, actọr, natụre; ch, chip; g, go; th, thin; ᴛʜ, then; y, you;

Sard Harker. A novel (1924) by John Masefield, combining mystery, exotic adventure, and picturesque description.

Sardinian Convention, The. A convention (1855) between Sardinia, France, and Great Britain, by which Sardinia agreed to furnish a military contingent against Russia in the Crimean War.

Sarpedon (sär-pē′don). In Greek legend: (1) A son of Zeus and Europa, and king of the Lydians: often confounded with (2) a Lycian prince, son of Zeus and Laodamia, killed by Patroclus in the Trojan War.

Sartor Resartus (sär′tor rē-sär′tus). An eccentric satirical and philosophical work (1833–34) by Carlyle.

Sarv (särv). In the Shahnamah, a king of Yemen whose three daughters were wedded to the three sons of Faridun.

Sassanidæ (sa-san′i-dē), or **Sassanids** (sas′a-nidz), or **Sassanians** (sa-sā′ni-anz). The Persian dynasty which ruled about 226–641.

Sassenach. See Dictionary.

Sastean (sas′tē-an), or **Shastan** (shas′tan). A linguistic stock of North American Indians, formerly living mainly in California.

Satan. See Dictionary.

Satanic School, The. In 19th-century English literary history, a name first given by Southey to a class of writers supposed to oppose the received principles of morality. Among them were Byron, Moore, Shelley, Bulwer-Lytton, and Victor Hugo.

Satiræ (sa-tī′rē). One of the earliest novels of character and manners, surviving only in somewhat disconnected episodes. It was written by Petronius Arbiter, possibly that Petronius whom Nero compelled to commit suicide.

Satire Ménippée (sa-tēr mä-nē-pā). A French political satire (1594) in prose and verse, directed against the League: written by 7 men, most of them lawyers.

Satiromastix (sat′i-rō-mas′tiks). A satirical play (1601) by Dekker.

Saturn. See Dictionary.

Saturnalia. See Dictionary.

Satyrane (sat′i-rān). The son of a satyr in Spenser's "Faerie Queene." Bred in the woods, he shows the might and bravery of man in his natural state.

Saul (sâl). 1. The first king of Israel. 1 Sam. ix. 2. The original name of the apostle Paul. Acts, ix. 1–31, etc. 3. An oratorio (1739) by Handel. 4. A tragedy (1783) by Alfieri. 5. A poem (1845) by Browning.

Saul Kane. See **Everlasting Mercy, The.**

Savitri (sä′vi-trē). 1. The verse of the Rig-Veda (III. lxii. 10) repeated by every Brahman at his morning and evening devotions: also called Gayatri. 2. The heroine of an episode of the Mahabharata.

Savoy (sa-voi′), **The.** A former London palace, now a chapel royal (dedicated 1511), of the Perpendicular style.

Savoy, The House of. A royal house of Europe, members of which have been dukes of Savoy since 1416, kings of Sardinia since 1720, and kings of Italy since 1861.

Savoy Conference, The. A futile conference (1661) in London between 21 Episcopalians and 21 Presbyterians, to secure ecclesiastical unity.

Savoy Operas, The. A name for the succession of comic operas by W. S. Gilbert and Arthur Sullivan, produced at the Savoy Theatre, London. Among these were " Patience," "Iolanthe," " The Mikado," " Ruddigore," " The Yeomen of the Guard," and " The Gondoliers."

Sawyer, Bob. A rollicking, though impecunious, young medical student in Dickens's "Pickwick Papers."

Saxnot (säks′nōt). In Germanic mythology, a name of the god of war, appearing in Anglo-Saxon as a son of Woden (Odin).

Saxon Dynasty, The. A line of German kings and emperors of the Holy Roman Empire, 919–1024.

Saxons. See Dictionary, **Saxon.**

Saxon Shore, The. That portion of the eastern and southern British coast which was exposed to forays of Saxon pirates at the time of the Roman occupation.

Sayings and Doings of Samuel Slick of Slickville, The. (Also called "The Clockmaker.") A series of sketches (1837–40) by T. C. Haliburton, about a shrewd and humorous Yankee clockmaker and peddler.

Scævola (sev′ō-la), **C. Mucius.** A Roman hero who, according to legend, burned his right hand rather than reveal the details of a conspiracy against Porsena.

Scala, La (lä skä′lä). A theater in Milan, one of the largest in the world: inaugurated 1778.

Scala Santa (skä′lä sän′tä), or **Pilate's Staircase.** A stairway of St. John Lateran, Rome, consisting of 28 marble steps, said to have come from the house of Pilate in Jerusalem. It may be ascended only by penitents on their knees.

Scandinavians. See Dictionary, **Scandinavian.**

Scapin (skå-pań). A wily, intriguing valet in Molière's comedy "Les fourberies de Scapin."

Scaramouche, or **Scaramuccia.** See Dictionary, **Scaramouch.**

Scarecrow, The. A drama (1908) by Percy Mackaye.

Scarlet, Will. One of the companions of Robin Hood: also known as Scadlock and Scathelock.

Scarlet Letter, The. A romance (1850) of adultery and retribution in colonial New England, by Hawthorne.

Scenes of Clerical Life. A group (1858) of stories by George Eliot: "Amos Barton," "Mr. Gilfil's Love Story," and "Janet's Repentance."

Schamir (shä′mēr). A mysterious worm which, according to Persian and other traditions woven by the Jews around the legends of Solomon, was able to cut the hardest stone.

Scheherazade or **Sheherazade** (she-hē-ra-zäd′), or **Shahrazad** (shä-ra-zäd′). A character in the "Arabian Nights' Entertainments," wife of Schariar, sultan of India, to whom she nightly relates tales so interesting that he spares her life.

Schism, The Great. 1. The division between the Latin and Greek churches, which began in the 9th century. 2. The division (1378–1417) between parties in the Roman Catholic Church, which adhered to different popes.

Schleissheim (shlīs′hīm). A royal Bavarian castle, 8 miles north of Munich, containing a noted picture-gallery.

Schleswig-Holstein (shlās′vich-hol′shtīn) **War, The.** 1. A war (1848–50) between Schleswig-Holstein and Denmark, resulting in the restoration of Danish rule. 2. A war of Austria and Prussia against Denmark in 1864 to prevent the incorporation of Schleswig with Denmark.

Schmalkaldic (shmäl-käl′dik). See **Smalkaldic.**

Schönbrunn (shēn′brun). A historically important imperial castle 3 miles southwest of Vienna, noted for its gardens and works of art.

Schönbrunn, The Proclamation of. A proclamation (1805) by Napoleon I., declaring that the Bourbon dynasty in Naples had ceased to reign.

Schönbrunn, The Treaty of. 1. A treaty (1805) between Napoleon I. and Haugwitz (acting for Prussia), in which mutual cessions of territory were made. 2. A treaty (1809) between Napoleon I. and Francis I. of Austria, called also the treaty of Vienna.

School for Scandal, The. A comedy (1777) by Sheridan.

Schoolmaster, The. A treatise on education (1570) by Roger Ascham.

School of Athens, The. A fresco by Raphael, in the Vatican, Rome. A full-size cartoon for the picture is in the Ambrosian Library at Milan.

Schwabach (shvä′bäch) **Articles, The.** 1. Articles of religion established 1528 by the Margrave of Brandenburg-Ansbach as the basis of the Reformation in his territories. 2. Seventeen articles drawn up by Luther and submitted to the convention of Schwabach, subsequently forming the basis of the Augsburg Confession.

Scipios (sip′i-ōz), **The Tombs of the.** A group of ancient Roman tombs on the Appian Way, near Rome.

Sciron (sī′ron). In Greek legend, a robber who frequented the region near Megara, and forced strangers over the rocks into the sea. He was slain by Theseus.

Scone, The Stone of. See **Stone of Scone, The.**

Scotichronicon (skō-ti-kron′i-kon), **The.** A Scottish chronicle written by John of Fordun (to 1153), and by Walter Bower (to 1436).

Scotists (skō′tists). The followers of Duns Scotus. His fundamental doctrine is that distinctions which the mind inevitably draws, though non-existent apart from their relations to mind, are to be considered as real.

Scotland Yard. A short street in London, near Trafalgar

Square, formerly the site of the London police headquarters, now removed to New Scotland Yard, on the Thames Embankment; hence, a name for the London police.

Scots Greys. A regiment of British dragoons, first organized about 1683 under Claverhouse.

Scots Wha Hae wi' Wallace Bled. A patriotic song by Burns: also called " Bannockburn."

Scottish Chiefs. A romance (1810) based on Scottish history, by Jane Porter.

Scourge of God, The. See **Flagellum Dei.**

Scrap of Paper, A. A popular play adapted by Palgrave Simpson from "Les pattes de mouche" (1861), by Sardou.

Scribe, The. A celebrated early Egyptian statue (5th dynasty), in the Louvre Museum, Paris.

Scriblerus (skrib-lē'rus) **Club, The.** A club of writers in London, founded 1714 by Swift to satirize literary incompetence, and including as members Pope, Bolingbroke, Gay, and others.

Scrooge (skrōj), **Ebenezer.** A miserly curmudgeon in Dickens's "Christmas Carol."

Scudamour (skū'da-mōr), **Sir.** The knightly lover of Amoret in Spenser's "Faerie Queene."

Scylla (sil'ä). 1. See Dictionary. 2. In Greek mythology, the daughter of Nisus of Megara, who cut from her father's head the lock of hair on which his life depended.

Scythians. See Dictionary, **Scythian.**

Sea Garden. A collection of poems (1916) by H. D. (Mrs. Richard Aldington).

Sea Gull, The. A drama (1896) by Anton Chekhov.

Sea Horses. A romance (1925) by Francis Brett Young.

Seasons, The. 1. A poem in four parts (1726–30), by James Thomson. 2. An oratorio (1801) by Haydn.

Sea-Wolf, The. A novel (1904) by Jack London.

Seb (seb). In Egyptian mythology, the father of Osiris, and god of the earth.

Sebastian (se-bas'chan). See **Viola.**

Sebek (seb'ek). In Egyptian mythology, the crocodile-headed god, seemingly a double of Set, the god of evil.

Secession, The Ordinances of. Ordinances passed 1860–61 by 11 southern States, declaring their withdrawal from the Union.

Secession, The War of. See Dictionary, **secession.**

Second Blooming, The. A novel (1914) by W. L. George.

Second Jungle Book, The. See **Jungle Book, The.**

Second Mrs. Tanqueray, The. A play (1893) by Pinero.

Second Nun's Tale, The. One of Chaucer's "Canterbury Tales." Its subject is the life and passion of St. Cecilia.

Secret Agent, The. A novel (1907) by Joseph Conrad.

Secret City, The. A novel (1919) by Hugh Walpole. See also **Green Mirror, The.**

Secret Places of the Heart, The. A novel (1922) by H. G. Wells.

Sedley (sed'li), **Amelia.** See **Osborne, Mr.,** and **Dobbin, Major William.**

Sedley, Joseph (Jos). In Thackeray's "Vanity Fair," the brother of Amelia Sedley. He is a fat, sensual, timid dandy, who becomes one of Becky Sharp's victims.

See! the Conquering Hero Comes! An air in Handel's "Joshua" (1748), used again in his "Judas Maccabæus."

Segusiani (se-gū-si-ā'ni). In the time of Julius Cæsar, a Gallic people living in the valley of the Rhone, near Lyons.

Sejanus (sē-jā'nus) **His Fall.** A tragedy (1603) by Jonson.

Selene (se-lē'nē). In Greek mythology, the goddess of the moon, daughter of Hyperion and Thea.

Seleucians (se-lū'si-anz). A 3d-century sect, adherents to the doctrines of Seleucus of Galatia and of Hermogenes, that baptism by water is not to be used, and that there is no resurrection of the body and no visible paradise.

Seleucidæ (se-lū'si-dē), or **Seleucids** (se-lū'sidz). A dynasty founded in Asia about 312 B.C. by Seleucus, one of the generals of Alexander the Great. It lasted until about 64 B.C.

Self-Denying Ordinance, The. An ordinance (1645) requiring members of the English Parliament holding military or civil office to vacate such positions in 40 days.

Seljuks (sel-jöks'). See Dictionary, **Seljuk.**

Sellers, Colonel Mulberry. A visionary Southern speculator of buoyant optimism in "The Gilded Age," by Mark Twain and C. D. Warner.

Selwyn (sel'win) **College.** A college of Cambridge University, founded 1882 to meet the wants of students of the Church of England unable to attend the more expensive colleges.

Semele (sem'e-lē). 1. In Greek mythology, the daughter of Cadmus and Harmonia, and mother by Zeus of Dionysus. 2. An oratorio-like musical drama (1744) by Handel.

Seminole (sem'i-nōl). A tribe of North American Indians who left the main body of the Creek Confederacy and settled in Florida.

Semiramide (sä-mē-rä'mē-dā). The title of various Italian operas, notably those by Rossini (1823) and Gluck ("Semiramide Riconosciuta," 1748).

Semiramis (se-mir'a-mis). In Greek legends, an Assyrian queen of surpassing greatness: the founder of Babylon. See **Ninus.**

Semites. See Dictionary, **Semite.**

Semnones (sem-nō'nēz or sem'no-nēz). A German tribe, a principal branch of the Suevi, situated about the middle Elbe eastward to the Oder.

Sempronia (sem-prō'ni-ä) **gens.** A Roman clan containing several noted families in the time of the republic: notably that of the Gracchi.

Seneca (sen'e-ka). The largest tribe of the Iroquois Confederacy of North American Indians, conspicuous in the wars west of Lake Erie. When first known it was located in western New York, later moving south along the Allegheny.

Senones (sen'o-nēz). In ancient history: (1) A people of the Cisalpine Gauls, conquered by the Romans about 283 B.C. (2) A tribe in central Gaul, which revolted against Cæsar 54–52 B.C.

Sense and Sensibility. A novel (1811) by Jane Austen: written 1797–98.

Sentimental Journey through France and Italy, A. A loosely connected series (1768) of travel sketches by Sterne.

Sentimental Tommy. A novel (1896) by Sir J. M. Barrie: a sequel is "Tommy and Grizel" (1900).

Sepoy Mutiny, The. See Dictionary, **sepoy.**

September Convention, The. A treaty (1864) between France and Italy, by which France was to withdraw troops from Rome in two years, and Italy was to guarantee the retention of Rome by the Pope.

September Laws, The. Laws (1835) restricting the freedom of the French press.

September Massacres, The. See Dictionary, **Septembrist.**

Septembrists, The. See Dictionary, **Septembrist.**

Septennial Act, The. An act (1716) which prolonged the possible life of English Parliaments from three to seven years.

Septuagint, The. See Dictionary, **Septuagint.**

Sepulcher, Knights of the Holy. A military order established 1099 by Godfrey of Bouillon to watch the sepulcher of Christ.

Sepulcher, The Holy. See Dictionary, **holy.**

Sequani (sek'wa-nī). In ancient history, a people of eastern Gaul.

Seraglio (se-ral'yō). The chief or official palace of the former Sultan of Turkey at Constantinople, which contained government buildings, mosques, etc., as well as the Sultan's harem.

Serapeum (ser-a-pē'um), or **Serapion.** 1. The great Egyptian sanctuary near Memphis, where the Apis bulls were buried. 2. A famous temple of Serapis in ancient Alexandria, destroyed by Theodosius.

Serapis (se-rā'pis). A deity of Egyptian origin whose worship was introduced into Greece and Rome.

Serapis, The. A British man-of-war captured by John Paul Jones after a desperate engagement, Sept. 23, 1779. See **Bonhomme Richard.**

Serbs. See Dictionary, **Serb.**

Sere (sā'rā). A once powerful tribe of the eastern Sudan.

Serer (se-rār'). A negro tribe of Senegal, Africa.

Sergius (sèr'ji-us), **Saint.** A martyr (d. about 300) whose cult is celebrated particularly by the Eastern Church.

Serpent Column, The. A bronze column 18 feet high in Constantinople: the base of the golden tripod set up in the sanctuary at Delphi from the spoils of the Persians at Platæa, 479 B.C.

Serpentine (sẽr'pẹn-tīn), **The.** An artificial pond in Hyde Park, London, made by order of Queen Caroline.

Servant in the House, The. A symbolical drama (1908) by Charles Rann Kennedy.

Servile Wars, The. Three wars (134–71 B.C.) conducted by the Romans against insurgent slaves. The third was also called "the war of the gladiators."

Sesostris (se-sos'tris). In ancient Greek legend, a king of Egypt, said to have conquered the world.

Set (set). In Egyptian mythology, the god of evil, brother or son and deadly opponent of Osiris: called by the Greeks Typhon.

Setebos (set'ẹ-bos). A Patagonian god, mentioned by Caliban in Shakspere's "Tempest," and by Browning in "Caliban upon Setebos."

Seth (seth). The third son of Adam. Gen. iv. 25.

Setibos (sā-tē'bōz). Indians of northern Peru, of the Pano linguistic stock.

Settlement, The Act of, or **Succession Act.** An act of the British Parliament (1701) regulating the succession to the throne.

Seven against Thebes, The. 1. See Dictionary, **seven.** 2. A tragedy by Æschylus, exhibited 468 B.C.

Seven Bishops, The Case of the. A famous English trial (1688), of Archbishop Sancroft and 6 bishops, who were acquitted of the charge of libel in protesting against the order of James II. that his "declarations for liberty of conscience" be read in the churches.

Seven Champions of Christendom, The. See Dictionary, **seven.**

Seven Cities, The Island of the. A fabled island supposed in the 14th and 15th centuries to exist in the Atlantic, west of Europe: frequently called by the geographers of the time Antilla or Antillia.

Seven Dials. A locality in London, long notorious as a center of poverty and crime.

Seven Hills of Rome, The. See Dictionary, **seven.**

Seven Keys to Baldpate. A farce (1913) by George M. Cohan, based upon a novel by E. D. Biggers.

Seven Lamps of Architecture, The. A treatise on architecture (1849) by Ruskin.

Seven Sages, The. See Dictionary, **sage**[1].

Seven Sleepers of Ephesus, The. See Dictionary, **seven.**

Seventeen. A story (1915) by Booth Tarkington, about Willie Baxter, who wanted to be called William.

Seventy, The. 1. The Jewish Sanhedrim. 2. The body of disciples mentioned in Luke, x. 3. The body of scholars who were the traditional authors of the Septuagint. 4. Certain missionary officials in the Mormon Church.

Seven Weeks' War, The. The war of 1866 (sometimes called the Austro-Prussian war), caused immediately by the Schleswig-Holstein question and indirectly by the long rivalry between Austria and Prussia. It resulted in Prussia's becoming the leading power in Germany, and in Italy's acquiring Venetia.

Seven Who Were Hanged, The. A realistic story (1908) by Leonid Andreev.

Seven Wise Masters, The. An old collection of tales of Eastern origin.

Seven Wise Men of Greece, The. See Dictionary, **sage**[1].

Seven Wonders of the World, The. See Dictionary, **wonder.**

Seven Years' War, The. See Dictionary, **seven.**

Severus (se-vē'rus), **The Wall of.** A wall built about 208, by the emperor Septimius Severus, between the Tyne and the Solway in Britain, as a defense against northern inroads.

Seville (sev'il or sẹ-vil'), **The Archives of.** A great collection of documents relating to colonial (particularly American) affairs, at Seville, Spain.

Seville, The Council of. See **Casa de Contratación de las Indias.**

Seville, The Treaty of. A treaty between Great Britain, Spain, and France (1729), ending the war between England and Spain, leaving England in possession of Gibraltar, and establishing a close alliance of the three powers.

Sextus Tarquinius (seks'tus tär-kwin'i-us). In Roman legend, the son of Tarquinius Superbus, whose rape of Lucretia led to the fall of the Tarquins.

Sforza (sfôr'tsä). An Italian family founded by Muzio Attendolo Sforza, a peasant who achieved military eminence about 1400. His descendants became dukes of Milan.

Sganarelle (sgä-nà-rel). A comic character in ancient comedy, introduced by Molière (with appropriately different traits) in "Sganarelle, ou le cocu imaginaire," "Don Juan," "L'Amour médecin," "Le médecin malgré lui," etc.

Shadow-Line, The. A novel (1917) by Joseph Conrad.

Shadrach (shā'drak). A companion of Daniel: one of the three (Shadrach, Meshach, Abednego) thrown into the fiery furnace of Nebuchadnezzar. Dan. iii. 12–30.

Shafiites (shaf'i-īts). The members of one of the four divisions or sects of orthodox Mohammedans, or Sunnites.

Shahaptian (shä-hap'ti-ạn). A linguistic stock of North American Indians which inhabited a large territory along the Columbia River and its tributaries.

Shahnamah (shä'nä'mä). 1. The great Persian epic of Firdausi. 2. A Turkish epic by Firdausi al Thauil.

Shahrazad. See **Scheherazade.**

Shakas (shä'käz). A people, probably Turks or Tatars, who anciently spread along the west of India to the mouths of the Indus. They were routed in a great battle about A.D. 78.

Shaktas (shäk'täz). In India, the worshipers of the divine power under its female representation.

Shakti (shak'ti). In Hindu religion, the energy or active power of a deity personified as his wife, and worshiped under various names.

Shakuntala (shạ-kún'tạ-lä). A great drama by Kalidasa, named from its heroine.

Shallow. A country justice in Shakspere's "Henry IV." Part ii., and in "The Merry Wives of Windsor": traditionally said to be a caricature of Sir Thomas Lucy.

Shamash (shä'mäsh). The Assyro-Babylonian sun-god.

Shamrock, The. The name of each of four sloop yachts, unsuccessful challengers for the America's cup, built for Sir Thomas Lipton since 1899.

Shandy (shan'di), **Captain.** See **Uncle Toby.**

Shandy, Tristram. See **Tristram Shandy.**

Shandy, Walter. In Sterne's "Tristram Shandy," the father of Tristram. His innumerable theories and whimsies fill the considerable part of the novel which precedes the birth of the nominal hero.

Shannon, The. See **Chesapeake, The.**

Sharon (shär'ọn), **The Plain of.** A plain, celebrated for its fertility, in western Palestine. 1 Chron. v. 16.

Sharp, Becky (Rebecca). In Thackeray's "Vanity Fair," an unscrupulous little adventuress who by her cleverness and audacity makes her way into society, but afterward loses her reputable standing.

Shaw Memorial, The. The relief of Robert Gould Shaw with his troops (begun 1884, erected 1897), on Beacon Hill, Boston, by Augustus Saint-Gaudens. Shaw was commander of the first negro regiment enlisted in the North in the Civil War, the Fifty-Fourth Massachusetts. He was killed in Charleston Harbor in 1863.

Shawnee (shà-nē'). An Algonquian tribe formerly in the east-central U. S., now in Oklahoma.

Shays's Rebellion. A post-Revolutionary insurrection (1786–87) in western Massachusetts against the State government: led by Daniel Shays.

Sheba (shē'bä), **The Queen of.** 1. A queen of the Sabeans who came to Jerusalem to test the wisdom of Solomon. 1 Kings, x. In Arabic legends her name is Balkis. 2. An opera (1875) by Goldmark.

Sheherazade. See **Scheherazade.**

Shelburne Essays. Eleven volumes of literary criticism (1904–21) by Paul Elmer More.

Sheldonian (shel-dō'ni-ạn) **Theatre, The.** A theater at Oxford University, built 1664–69 by Archbishop Sheldon. Sir Christopher Wren designed it.

Shem (shem). One of the three sons of Noah, represented as the ancestor of the Semitic races. Gen. x. 21.

Shenandoah (shen-ạn-dō'ạ), **The.** 1. A vessel built 1863 at Glasgow, and sold to the Confederates 1864. As a privateer she captured 38 United States vessels during the Civil War. 2. The U. S. dirigible which was destroyed in a squall near Ava, Ohio, on September 3, 1925.

Sheol. See Dictionary.

Shepherd's Calendar, The. A pastoral poem (1579) in 12 eclogues, by Spenser.

Sheridan's Ride. A famous incident of the battle of Cedar Creek, Virginia, Oct. 19, 1864. Sheridan, hearing the battle from Winchester, rode 20 miles to his soldiers and turned defeat into victory. The occurrence is the subject of a poem by T. B. Read.

Sheriff of Nottingham. The officer who represents Norman law in the Robin Hood stories, and who is usually outwitted by Robin and his men. Also, a character in the opera "Robin Hood," by Reginald De Koven.

Sherman Bill, The. An act of Congress (1890) directing the purchase of silver bullion to the amount of 4,500,000 ounces per month, and the issue of treasury notes in payment: repealed 1893.

Sherwood Forest. A forest in Nottinghamshire, England: the scene of the legendary exploits of Robin Hood.

Shesha (shā′shä). In Hindu mythology, a thousand-headed serpent, regarded as the symbol of eternity.

She Stoops to Conquer. A comedy (1773) by Goldsmith, one of the best of its period.

She Would If She Could. A very successful comedy (1668) by Etherege.

Sheyenne. See **Cheyenne.**

Shiahs. See Dictionary, **Shiah.**

Shilluk (shil′ŏk). A large negro tribe of the eastern Sudan.

Shiloah. The same as **Siloam.**

Shiloh (shī′lō). A town in Ephraim, Palestine, which contained the sanctuary of the ark of the covenant. Josh. xviii. 1.

Shimonoseki (shē″mō-nō-sā′kē), **The Treaty of.** A treaty of peace (1895) between China and Japan, by which China recognized the independence of Korea, ceded territory to Japan, agreed to pay a war indemnity, and granted important commercial privileges.

Shinar (shī′när). In Bible geography, the tract of land between the Euphrates and Tigris down to the Persian Gulf.

Shipman's Tale, The. One of Chaucer's "Canterbury Tales."

Ship of Fools, The. A translation (1508) by Alexander Barclay, through the Latin and French, of Brant's "Narrenschiff." It is the first English book in which the New World is mentioned.

Shirley (shėr′li). A novel (1849) by Charlotte Brontë. The heroine, Shirley Keeldar, an impulsive girl who inherits and administers her father's estate, is an idealized portrait of Emily Brontë.

Shiva. See Dictionary, **Siva.**

Shoemaker's Holiday, The. A comedy (1599) by Dekker.

Shoes of Happiness, The. A poem (1915) by Edwin Markham.

Shoho. See **Saho.**

Shooting of Dan McGrew, The. A poem (1907) by Robert W. Service, in "The Spell of the Yukon."

Shoreditch (shŏr′dich). A metropolitan borough of London, situated north of the Thames.

Short Parliament, The. The Parliament which sat Apr. 13–May 5, 1640.

Shoshonean. See Dictionary.

Shoshoni (shǒ-shō′nē). The most northerly division of the Shoshonean stock of North American Indians, formerly of the Snake River region of Idaho.

Shottery (shot′ėr-i). A village in Warwickshire, noted as the residence of Anne Hathaway, Shakspere's wife.

Showing-up of Blanco Posnet, The. A drama (1909) by G. B. Shaw.

Shri (shrē). The Hindu goddess of beauty and fortune, Lakshmi.

Shrimp-Girl, The. A painting by Hogarth, in the National Gallery, London.

Shropshire Lad, A. Poems (1896) by A. E. Housman.

Shylock (shī′lok). A Jewish money-lender in Shakspere's "Merchant of Venice." He lends 3,000 ducats to Bassanio on the condition that, if they be not repaid by the promised date, he shall be allowed to cut a pound of flesh from the body of Antonio, Bassanio's surety. His attempt to consummate this hard bargain is balked by the wit of Portia.

Sia (sē′ä). A tribe of North American Indians inhabiting a pueblo of the same name on the Rio Jemez, in New Mexico.

Siberian Railway, The. A railway constructed 1891–99 by the Russian government, traversing Siberia and Manchuria, from Cheliabinsk to Vladivostok, over 4,000 miles.

Sibylline Books, Sibylline Oracles. See Dictionary, **sibylline.**

Sibyls. See Dictionary, **sibyl.**

Sibyls, The. Paintings by Michelangelo, alternating with his figures of the prophets, on the vaulting of the Sistine Chapel, Rome.

Sicambri (si-kam′brī). See **Sugambri.**

Sicilian Vespers. See Dictionary, **Sicilian.**

Sick Man of the East, The. See Dictionary, **sick**[2].

Siculi (sik′ū-lī). One of the early peoples of Sicily and southern Italy, probably allied to the Latins.

Siddhartha (si-där′thä). The personal name of the founder of Buddhism.

Siddons, Mrs. A portrait (1784) by Gainsborough, in the National Gallery, London.

Siddons as the Tragic Muse, Mrs. A painting (1783) by Reynolds, in the Huntington Collection, San Marino, Cal.

Sidney Sussex College. A college of Cambridge University, founded 1595 by the Countess of Sussex.

Siege of Corinth, The. A narrative poem (1816) by Byron.

Siege of Rhodes, The. A play by Davenant, produced 1656 as a musical spectacle: practically the first opera presented in England.

Siege of the Legations, The. The siege (1900) of the foreign legations in Peking by Boxers and Chinese troops.

Siege of Troy, The. See **Recuyell of the Historyes of Troye.**

Siege (sēj) **Perilous, The.** In Arthurian romance, a vacant seat at the Round Table, which could be filled only by the predestined finder of the Holy Grail.

Siegfried (sēg′frēd, G. zēch′frēt), or **Sigfrid.** A mythical prince of Niderland on the lower Rhine: the hero of the Nibelungenlied, and the Sigurd of the Old Norse version.

Siegfried. One of the four parts of Wagner's musical tetralogy "Der Ring des Nibelungen."

Sif (sēf). In Old Norse mythology, the wife of Thor.

Sigambri. See **Sugambri.**

Sigeum (si-jē′um). In ancient geography, a promontory and town in the Troad, Asia Minor: the legendary station of the Greek fleet in the Trojan War.

Sightless, The. A drama (1891) by Maurice Maeterlinck.

Sigurd (sē′gėrd). In the northern Volsunga Saga, the Siegfried of the Nibelungenlied.

Sigurd the Volsung. An epic poem (1876) by William Morris.

Sigyn (sē′gün). In Norse mythology, the wife of Loki.

Sihasapa (sē-hä′sạ-pä). A tribe of Sioux Indians, often mistakenly called Blackfoot or Blackfeet.

Sikes (sīks), **Bill.** In Dickens's "Oliver Twist," a brutal thief, housebreaker, and murderer. He persecutes Oliver, and kills Nancy, who has befriended Oliver.

Sikhs. See Dictionary, **Sikh.**

Sikh (sēk) **Wars.** Two wars (1845–49) between the British under Sir Hugh Gough and the Sikhs, in which the power of the Sikhs was completely broken.

Siksika (sik′si-kä). A northwestern confederacy of North American Indians, in northern Montana and the adjacent part of Canada.

Silas Marner (mär′nėr), **the Weaver of Raveloe.** A novel (1861) by George Eliot.

Silenus. See Dictionary.

Silenus (sī-lē′nus) **and Bacchus.** A Greco-Roman group in marble, in the Glyptothek, Munich.

Silenus and Satyrs. A painting by Rubens, in the Old Pinakothek, Munich.

Silesian Wars, The. Three wars waged (1740–63) by Frederick the Great against Austria for the possession of Silesia. The third was the Seven Years' War.

Siloam (si-lō′ạm), or **Siloah** (si-lō′ä). A pool in Jerusalem. Neh. iii. 15.

Silures (sil′ū-rēz). An ancient British people chiefly in what is now southeastern Wales, at the time of the Roman conquest of Britain.

---

fat, fāte, fär, fȧll, ȧsk, fāre; net, mē, hėr; pin, pīne; not, nōte, mōve, nôr; up, lūte, pùll; oi, oil; ou, out; (lightened) aviạry, ēlect, agǒny, intǒ, ūnite; (obscured) errạnt, operạ, ardẹnt, actǒr, natūre; ch, chip; g, go; th, thin; ᴛʜ, then; y, you;

Silvanus or **Sylvanus** (sil-vā'nus). In Italian mythology, a god, protector of woods, fields, herds, etc.

Silver, John. A one-legged pirate in R. L. Stevenson's "Treasure Island."

Silver Box, The. A drama (1909) by John Galsworthy.

Silvia or **Sylvia** (sil'vi-ä). 1. The spirited daughter of the duke of Milan in Shakspere's "Two Gentlemen of Verona." She is loved by Valentine. 2. The heroine of Farquhar's "Recruiting Officer." 3. The forsaken mistress of Vainlove in Congreve's "Old Bachelor."

Simancas (sē-mäng'käs), **The Archives of.** A collection of documents relating to Spain and its colonies, formed 1543 by order of Charles V.: kept in the old castle of Simancas.

Simeon (sim'ē-on). 1. One of the patriarchs, a son of Jacob and Leah. Gen. xxix. 33. 2. One of the tribes of the Israelites, descended from the patriarch Simeon.

Simon (sī'mon). In the New Testament: (1) The original name of Peter. (2) A brother or relative of Jesus, often identified with Simon the Canaanite (or Simon Zelotes): one of the apostles. (3) A tanner of Joppa at whose house St. Peter resided. (4) Simon, surnamed Magus, a sorcerer of Samaria. Acts, viii. 5-24.

Simon Pure. See Dictionary, **simon-pure.**

Simoom. A drama (1891) by August Strindberg.

Simple Simon. In a popular nursery rime, a character who asks for a sample without intending to purchase.

Simplon (san-plôn) **Railway, The.** A railway, constructed (1898–1905) from Brieg, Switzerland, to Iselle, Italy, running through a tunnel about 12¼ miles long in the Simplon Mountain.

Simurgh (si-mörg'). In the Shahnamah, the huge bird that reared the infant Zal.

Sin (sin). The Assyro-Babylonian moon-god.

Sinai (sī'nī or sī'nā-ī). In the Bible, the mountain (also called Horeb), of uncertain identity, from which the law was given to Moses. Ex. xix.

Sinai, The Convent of. A convent on Mount Sinai, with a great Byzantine church built in the reign of Justinian: also called **The Convent of St. Catharine.**

Sindbad (sind'bad), or **Sinbad, the Sailor.** A story in the "Arabian Nights' Entertainments." Sindbad is a wealthy citizen of Bagdad, who relates the adventures of his seven wonderful voyages.

Sing Sing. The New York State prison at Ossining.

Sinister Street. A novel in two parts (Part i., 1913; Part ii., 1914) by Compton Mackenzie. Part i. was first entitled "Youth's Encounter." The two-part novel is followed by "The Early History of Sylvia Scarlett" (1918) and by "Sylvia and Michael" (1919).

Sinn Fein. See Dictionary.

Sin of David, The. A drama (1904) by Stephen Phillips.

Sinon. See Dictionary.

Sion. See Zion.

Sion College. A London college, founded 1623 as a college and almshouse. It contains the most valuable theological library in London.

Siouan. See Dictionary.

Sioux (sö). The Dakota proper, as distinguished from the Assiniboin tribe of the Dakota division of North American Indians.

Sipand (si-pand'). In the Shahnamah, the fortress taken and burned by Rustam to avenge Nariman's death.

Sir Charles Grandison (gran'di-son). A novel (1753) by Richardson.

Sir Courtly Nice. A comedy (1685) by John Crowne, named from the principal character, an insignificant but self-important fop.

Sirens. See Dictionary, **siren.**

Sir Fopling Flutter. See **Man of Mode, The.**

Sir Gawayne (gä'wān) **and the Green Knight.** An early English romance (about 1360).

Sir George Tressady. See **Marcella.**

Sir Harry Wildair. See **Constant Couple, The.**

Siris (sī'ris). An extraordinary series of philosophical reflections (1744) concerning tar-water as a panacea, by Bishop Berkeley.

Sir John Oldcastle. A play (1600) by Drayton, Munday, Hathaway, and Wilson: written to vindicate Oldcastle from

the aspersions supposed to be implied in Shakspere's Falstaff.

Sir Launcelot Greaves, The Adventures of. A burlesque romance (1760–61) by Smollett, in the mode of Cervantes's "Don Quixote."

Sir Martin Mar-all, or the Feigned Innocence. A comedy (1668) by Dryden, named from the principal character, a foolish, blundering knight.

Sir Patrick Spens (spens). A Scottish popular ballad about a knight sent by the king on a mission to Norway and lost with all his crew on the voyage home.

Sir Roger de Coverley. See **Coverley, Sir Roger de.**

Sisera (sis'ē-rä). The commander-in-chief of the army of Jabin, treacherously slain by Jael. Judges, iv.

Sister Beatrice. A drama (1910) by Maurice Maeterlinck.

Sister Carrie. A novel (1900) by Theodore Dreiser, the frankness of which has had an important influence on later American writers.

Sister Helen. A ballad (1851) by Dante Gabriel Rossetti, based on sympathetic magic.

Sistine Chapel, The. See Dictionary, **Sistine.**

Sistine Madonna, The. See Dictionary, **Sistine.**

Sistova (sis'tō-vä), **The Peace of.** A treaty (1791) between Turkey and Austria, fixing as boundaries practically those established by the peace of Belgrade (1739).

Sisyphus. See Dictionary, **Sisyphean.**

Sita (sē'tä). The heroine of the Ramayana.

Siva. See Dictionary.

Six Articles, The Act of. In English history, an act (1539) asserting (1) transubstantiation, (2) the sufficiency of communion in one kind, (3) celibacy of the clergy, (4) the maintenance of vows of chastity, (5) the continuation of private masses, and (6) auricular confession.

Six Cities, The. In German history, the cities Bautzen, Zittau, Löbau, Kamenz, Görlitz, and Lauban, which formed (1346) a league against plundering knights, and received privileges.

Six Months' War. The Franco-German war, July, 1870–Jan., 1871.

Six Nations, The. See **Five Nations, The.**

Sixtine Chapel, Sixtine Madonna. See Dictionary, **Sistine.**

Skadi (skä'dē). In Old Norse mythology, a giantess, wife of Njörd.

Skanda (skan'dä). In Hindu mythology, the younger of the sons (Ganesha, Skanda) of Siva: the god of war.

Skandapurana (skan″da-pö-rä'nä). In Sanskrit literature, a purana of 81,800 stanzas, in which Skanda is the narrator.

Skeggs (skegz), **Carolina Wilhelmina Amelia.** One of the town ladies who imposed upon the innocent family of the Vicar, in Goldsmith's "Vicar of Wakefield."

Sketch-Book, The. A collection (1819–20) of tales and sketches by Irving.

Skidbladnir (skid'blad″nir). In Norse mythology, the ship of Frey.

Skimpole (skim'pōl), **Harold.** In Dickens's "Bleak House," an esthetic sponge and amateur artist, supposed by some to be a caricature of Leigh Hunt.

Skiold (skyōld), or **Skjöld** (skyëld). In Norse mythology, the son of Odin, and a mythical king of Denmark.

Skirnir (skir'nir). In Old Norse mythology, the messenger of the gods, especially of Frey.

Skirophoria (skir-ō-fō'ri-ä). An ancient Attic festival in honor of Athene.

Skittagetan (skit-a-gē'tan). A linguistic stock of North American Indians, inhabiting islands off the west coast of British America.

Slabs of the Sunburnt West. Poems (1922) by Carl Sandburg.

Slave-Ship, The. A painting by J. M. W. Turner, in the Lothrop collection, Boston.

Slave States, The. Those of the United States in which slavery flourished before the Civil War: Virginia, North Carolina, South Carolina, Georgia, Florida, Alabama, Mississippi, Louisiana, Texas, Arkansas, and Tennessee (all of which seceded), and Missouri, Kentucky, Maryland, and Delaware.

Slavonians. See Dictionary, **Slavonian.**

(variable) ḍ as d or j, ş as s or sh, ṭ as t or ch, ẓ as z or zh; o, F. cloche; ʼ ü, F. menu; ċh, Sc. loch; ṅ, F. bonbon; ʹ, primary accent; ″, secondary accent; †, obsolete; <, from; +, and; =, equals. See also lists at beginning of book.

Sleep and Death. A group of Greek sculpture, dating from about the beginning of the Roman Empire, in the royal museum at Madrid.

Sleeping Ariadne (ar-i-ad'nē), **The.** A fine antique copy of a Greek statue, probably of the Pergamene school: in the Vatican, Rome.

Sleeping Beauty, The. In Perrault's fairy-tales, a princess who falls into a magic sleep. The story is common in French, German, and English.

Sleepy Hollow. The scene of Ichabod Crane's adventures in Irving's "Legend of Sleepy Hollow."

Sleipnir (slāp'nir). In Old Norse mythology, the eight-footed steed of Odin.

Slender, Abraham. A silly provincial gentleman, cousin to Shallow, in Shakspere's "Merry Wives of Windsor."

Slick, Sam. See **Sayings and Doings of Samuel Slick.**

Slipslop, Mrs. In Fielding's "Joseph Andrews," a woman of easy virtue.

Sloane (slōn) **Museum, The.** The library and collections of Sir Hans Sloane (d. 1753), bequeathed to the English nation. They formed a nucleus of the British Museum.

Slop, Dr. In Sterne's "Tristram Shandy," the choleric and bigoted accoucheur who breaks Tristram's nose.

Slope, Obadiah. An unctuous clergyman in Trollope's "Barchester Towers." See **Cathedral Novels, The.**

Slough of Despond, The. See Dictionary, **slough**[1].

Slovaks. See Dictionary, **Slovak.**

Slovenes. See Dictionary, **Slovene.**

Sludge, Dickon (or **Flibbertigibbet**). In Scott's "Kenilworth," a mischievous urchin.

Sly, Christopher. The drunken tinker in the prologue to Shakspere's "Taming of the Shrew."

Smalkaldic (smäl-käl'dik) **Articles, The.** The articles of Protestant faith formulated by Luther and submitted in 1537 to an assembly at Smalkald (Schmalkalden).

Smalkaldic League, The. A league formed at Smalkald in 1531 by Protestant princes and free cities, for defense against the emperor Charles V.

Smalkaldic War, The. The unsuccessful war (1546–47) waged by the Smalkaldic League against Charles V.

Smartas (smär'täz), or **Smarta Brahmans.** One of the three principal religious classes (Shaivas, Smartas, Vaishnavas) of the Hindus proper of the present day. They believe that man's spirit is identical with the one Spirit.

Smectymnuus (smek-tim'nū-us). The professed author of a controversial tract against episcopacy, written in the middle of the 17th century. The word is made up from the initials of the names of the authors.

Smintheus (smin'thūs). In Greek mythology, a surname of Apollo.

Smith, Wayland. See **Wayland the Smith.**

Smithfield. A locality in London, north of St. Paul's, long famous for its cattle-market and as the scene of Bartholomew Fair. It was the scene of Wat Tyler's death (1381), and the place where many Protestants suffered death at the stake in the reign of Mary.

Smithsonian Institution. See Dictionary, **Smithsonian.**

Snakes. A name given to the Shoshoni.

Snark, The. An imaginary beast in Lewis Carroll's poem "The Hunting of the Snark" (1876).

Sneer. A disagreeable critic in Sheridan's "Critic."

Sneerwell, Lady. A beautiful widow, a scandalmonger, in Sheridan's "School for Scandal."

Snodgrass (snod'gräs), **Augustus.** In Dickens's "Pickwick Papers," the Pickwick Club's poetic member.

Snow-Bound. A poem, a winter idyl of New England life (1866), by Whittier.

So Big. A novel (1924) by Edna Ferber. Pulitzer Prize novel, 1925.

Social Cancer, The. A novel (1886) by José Rizal, describing the condition of the Philippine Islands under the rule of the Spanish friars. "Noli Me Tangere" is the title of the Spanish edition. A sequel is "The Filibusters."

Social War, The. 1. In Greek history: (1) A war (357?–355 B.C.) in which Athens was defeated by her former allies Byzantium, Chios, Cos, and Rhodes. (2) A war (220–217 B.C.) between the Achæan and Ætolian leagues. 2. A rebellion (90–88 B.C.) against Rome by most of her allies in

central and southern Italy, including the Marsi, Samnites, etc., caused by the refusal of the Romans to extend the privileges of Roman citizenship. Rome made many concessions and suppressed the rebellion.

Society of Arcadians, The. A society founded 1690 in Italy for the purpose of establishing in literature the simplicity of the pastoral age.

Society of Friends, The. See Dictionary, **friend.**

Society of Jesus, The. See Dictionary, **Jesuit.**

Socinians. See Dictionary, **Socinian.**

Sodom. See Dictionary.

Sofonisba (sō-fō-nēs'bä). There are tragedies of this title by: (1) Galeotto del Carretto (1502): the first Italian tragedy. (2) Trissino (1515): the first Italian tragedy of note. (3) Alfieri (1783).

Soga (sō'gä), or **Wasoga** (wä-sō'gä). A large Bantu tribe of the northern shore of Lake Victoria.

Soho (sō-hō') **Square.** A square in London, south of Oxford Street, made in the reign of Charles II., and once called King's Square.

Sohrab and Rustum. See **Rustam.**

Soldiers Three. A collection (1889) of stories by Rudyard Kipling, dealing with types of the common British soldier in India. See **Mulvaney, Terence.**

Solemn League and Covenant, The. See Dictionary, **covenant.**

Solness (sol'nes). The superstitious, egotistical, cowardly "master builder" in Ibsen's "Master Builder."

Solomon. 1. See Dictionary. 2. An epic poem (1718) by Matthew Prior. 3. An oratorio (1749) by Handel.

Soma. See Dictionary, **soma**[2].

Somali. See Dictionary.

Somanatha (sō-ma̤-nät'hä̤). A celebrated Linga, or emblem of Siva, or the temple where it was set up at Somanathapattana in Gujarat.

Some Chinese Ghosts. A collection of stories (1887) by Lafcadio Hearn.

Somehow Good. A novel (1908) by William De Morgan: the title is from the familiar lines from "In Memoriam," liv.

Somerset (sum'ėr-set) **House.** A palace in the Strand, London, originally built 1549: now used for government offices.

Somnus (som'nus). The Roman counterpart of the Greek Hypnos.

Sompnour's Tale, The. See **Summoner's Tale, The.**

Sonderbund (zon'dėr-bunt). A reactionary league of most of the Roman Catholic cantons of Switzerland, formed 1843. It was overthrown (1848) in a war upon it by the Swiss Confederation.

Songhoi. See **Surhai.**

Songo (song'gō), or **Masongo** (mä-song'gō). A Bantu tribe of Angola, Africa.

Song of Myself. A poem (1855) by Walt Whitman.

Song of Solomon, The. See Dictionary, **song.**

Song of the Chattahoochee, The. A poem (1877) by Sidney Lanier.

Song of the Lark, The. A novel (1915) by Willa Sibert Cather: title taken from the familiar painting of Jules Breton.

Song of the Shirt, The. A poem (1843) by Hood.

Song of the Three Holy Children, The. An addition to the Book of Daniel, found in the Septuagint and in the Apocrypha, purporting to be the prayer and song of the three Hebrews in the fiery furnace.

Songs without Words. The English title of Mendelssohn's "Lieder ohne Worte."

Sonnambula, La (lä son-näm'bö-lä). An opera (1831) by Bellini.

Sonnets from the Portuguese. A sonnet-sequence (1850) by Elizabeth Barrett Browning.

Son of Don Juan, The. A drama (1892) by José Echegaray.

Son of the Middle Border, A. An autobiographical story (1917) by Hamlin Garland.

Sons and Lovers. A novel (1913) by D. H. Lawrence.

Sopherim (sō'fe̤-rim). Hebrew scribes whose task it was to explain the law and adapt it to conditions, and to multiply copies of the Torah.

Sophia (sō-fī'ä̤), **St.** The venerable metropolitan church of the Greeks at Constantinople, built by Justinian: since 1453 a mosque.

---

fat, fāte, fär, fȧll, ȧsk, fāre; net, mē, hėr; pin, pīne; not, nōte, mȯve, nôr; up, lūte, pull; oi, oil; ou, out; (lightened) aviȧry, ĕlect, agȯny, intȯ, ūnite; (obscured) errȧnt, operȧ, ardȧnt, actȯr, natūre; ch, chip; g, go; th, thin; ғн, then; y, you;

Sophia, The Little St. The church of Sts. Sergius and Bacchus at Constantinople, finished A.D. 565 by Justinian, and now a mosque.

Sophocles (sof'ō-klēz). A famous Greek portrait-statue, of about 300 B.C., in the Lateran Museum, Rome.

Sorbonne, La (lä sôr-bon). See Dictionary, **Sorbonist.**

Sorbs (sôrbz). See **Wends**, 2.

Sordello (sor-del'lō). A poem (1840) by Browning. Its action takes place in northern Italy in the 13th century.

Sorosis (sō-rō'sis). The first women's club in the United States, founded 1868 in New York.

Sorrel (sor'el), **Hetty.** The first love of Adam Bede.

Sorrows of Werther, The. See **Leiden des Jungen Werthers, Die.**

Soter (sō'tèr). A Greek surname meaning savior or preserver, applied to various gods and men—Zeus, Ptolemy I. of Egypt, etc.

Soul of a Bishop, The. A novel (1917) by H. G. Wells.

Source, La (lä sōrs). A painting (1856) by Ingres, in the Louvre, Paris.

Souriquois. The same as **Micmac.**

South Africa Company, The British. See **British South Africa Company, The.**

South American Revolution, The. The political movement and war (1810–26) by which the Spanish South American colonies became independent. The immediate cause was the chaotic condition of Spanish affairs produced by Napoleon's invasion of Spain.

Southcottians (south-kot'i-anz). A religious sect of the 19th century, founded by Joanna Southcott in England. Its members looked forward to her giving birth to another Messiah.

South Kensington Museum, The. A museum, now the Victoria and Albert Museum, at Brompton, London, opened 1857. It contains several museums, the National Gallery of British Art, the Royal College of Science, the National Art Training Schools, libraries, etc.

South Sea Bubble, The. A financial scheme whereby the South Sea Company (incorporated 1711) assumed a large part of the British national debt in return for an annual fixed sum and a monopoly of British trade with the Pacific islands and South America. It collapsed in 1720.

Sovereign of the Seas, The. The largest of the early English war-ships (100 guns), launched 1637 at Woolwich.

Spain, The Era of. An era, long used in Spain, beginning with the first day of the year 38 B.C.

Spanish-American War, The. See Dictionary, **Spanish-American.**

Spanish Armada, The. See Dictionary, **armada.**

Spanish Fury, The. The three days' sack of Antwerp by mutinous Spanish troops in Nov., 1576.

Spanish Gold. An adventure story (1908), with an Irish setting, by George A. Birmingham (Canon J. O. Hannay).

Spanish Gypsy, The. 1. A play (1623) by Middleton and Rowley. 2. A poem (1868) by George Eliot.

Spanish Main, The. See Dictionary, **Spanish.**

Spanish Succession, The War of the. A war arising out of disputes about the succession in Spain on the death of Charles II. It was fought 1701–14 by the emperor and the naval powers against France and her allies. It ended with the recognition of Philip of Anjou (Philip V.) as king of Spain.

Spanish Tragedy, The. A "tragedy of blood" (about 1590) by Kyd.

Sparagus Garden. See **Asparagus Gardens.**

Spasmodic School, The. A name given collectively to various 19th-century writers, on account of their supposedly unnatural style. Among them were Massey, Dobell, Bailey, and Alexander Smith.

Specie Circular, The. In United States history, an order (1836) by the Secretary of the Treasury directing payment for public lands to be made to government agents in gold and silver, in order to check speculative purchases.

Spectator, The. An English daily, written chiefly by Addison and Steele, published March 1, 1711–Dec. 6, 1712.

Spectra. Verse (1916) by Witter Bynner and Arthur Davison Ficke, satirizing some tendencies in contemporary poetry. It was taken seriously when first published, under the pseudonyms of Emanuel Morgan and Anne Knish.

Speed. The servant of Valentine in Shakspere's "Two Gentlemen of Verona."

Speed the Plough. See Dictionary, **Grundy.**

Speedwell, The. A ship of about 60 tons burden which sailed (1620) from Southampton with the Mayflower for New England: sent back from Plymouth, England, owing to mishaps.

Spenlow (spen'lō), **Dora.** David's frail "child-wife" in Dickens's "David Copperfield."

Spens, Sir Patrick. See **Sir Patrick Spens.**

Sphinx, The. See Dictionary, **sphinx.**

Sphinx, The Temple of the. The family mausoleum of Khafra (incorrectly called a temple), lying a short distance southeast of the Sphinx at Gizeh: built of blocks of red granite and alabaster.

Spica (spī'kä). A star of the first magnitude in the spike of grain held by the left hand of the woman pictured in the constellation Virgo.

Spielberg (shpēl'berċh). A former fortress and state prison near Brünn, Moravia.

Spitalfields (spit'al-fēldz). A quarter of London, north of the Tower, formerly noted as a seat of silk-manufacture.

Spoils of Poynton, The. A novel (1879) by Henry James.

Spoon River Anthology, The. A collection of free-verse autobiographies (1915) by Edgar Lee Masters.

Spreading the News. A drama (1904) by Lady Augusta Gregory.

Spring Garden. A place of refreshment in St. James's Park, London, fashionable in the 17th century.

Spring's Awakening. A drama (1896) by Frank Wedekind: a tragedy of youth.

Spurs, The Battle of the. 1. The victory (1302) of the Flemings over the French at Courtrai: so called from the number of gilt spurs captured. 2. The victory of the English over the French at Guinegate, 1513: so called from precipitate flight of the French.

Spy, The. A historical novel (1821) by J. F. Cooper. The activities of the spy, Harvey Birch, are carried on in southeastern New York (the "Neutral Ground") during the American Revolution.

Square. See **Thwackum.**

Squeers (skwērz). See **Dotheboys Hall.**

Squire of Dames, The. In Spenser's "Faerie Queene," a knight pledged to the service of ladies in distress.

Squire's Tale, The. One of Chaucer's "Canterbury Tales," left unfinished. Spenser continues it in the fourth book of "The Faerie Queene."

Sraosha (sra-ō'shä). In the Avesta, a Yazata, or sacred being, who first taught the law and is the especial foe of Aeshma.

Stabat Mater (stā'bat mā'tèr). In the Roman Catholic liturgy, a sequence on the Virgin Mary at the crucifixion, written about 1300 by Jacobus de Benedictis. Music for it has been written by Palestrina, Pergolesi, Rossini, Dvořák, and others.

Stadium. See Dictionary, **stadium.**

Stagirite, The. See Dictionary, **Stagirite.**

Stalky and Company. A story (1899) by Rudyard Kipling, about life in an English school.

Stamp Act, The. See Dictionary, **stamp.**

Standard, The Battle of the. A victory gained 1138 by the English, led by Archbishop Thurston, over the Scots under King David, near Northallerton, Yorkshire: so called from the English banner.

Stanley Falls. A series of falls in the upper Congo, situated near the equator: named from Henry M. Stanley.

Staple of News, The. A comedy (1625) by Jonson.

Star and Garter, The. A famous tavern formerly standing in Pall Mall, London.

Star Chamber, The. A former court of civil and criminal jurisdiction in England, which sat without a jury, and was noted for its summary methods: abolished 1641.

Star-Spangled Banner, The. The American national anthem, composed 1814 by Francis Scott Key, at the bombardment of Fort McHenry by the British. It is set to the music of "Anacreon in Heaven."

States-General, The. The legislative assemblies of France before the revolution of 1789; also, those of the Netherlands.

(variable) d̦ as d or j, ş as s or sh, ț as t or ch, z̧ as z or zh; o, F. cloche; ū, F. menu; ċh, Sc. loch; ṅ, F. bonbon; ', primary accent; ″, secondary accent; †, obsolete; <, from; +, and; =, equals. See also lists at beginning of book.

State Street. A street in Boston, Mass., noted as a financial center.

Stator. See **Jupiter Stator.**

Staubbach (shtoup'bäch). A waterfall in the Bernese Oberland, Switzerland, near Lauterbrunnen: height, 980 feet.

Steele Glas, The. A satire in blank verse (1576), by Gascoigne.

Steenie (stē'ni). A name given by James I. of England to the Duke of Buckingham, on account of a fancied resemblance to St. Stephen.

Steerforth, James. In Dickens's "David Copperfield," a schoolmate who befriends David, but later is the seducer of Little Emily.

Stella (stel'ä). 1. See **Astrophel and Stella.** 2. Swift's name for Esther Johnson, to whom he is thought to have been secretly married in 1716.

Stella del Nord, La (lä stel'lä del nôrd). See **Étoile du Nord, L'.**

Stenterello (sten-tä-rel'lō). In Florentine comedy, a farcical personage who assumes various parts.

Stentor (sten'tor). In Greek legend, a Greek herald before Troy.

Stephen (stē'ven), **Saint.** A deacon of the church at Jerusalem, stoned to death by the people: the first Christian martyr. Acts, vi., vii.

Stevenson Road. A road constructed by the British between Lakes Nyasa and Tanganyika.

Stewart Diamond, The. A large diamond of a light-yellow tinge, found 1872 in South Africa: weight, about 288 carats uncut.

Steyne (stīn), **The Marquis of.** In Thackeray's "Vanity Fair," a cynical old nobleman who is soundly thrashed by Rawdon Crawley for his attentions to Becky Sharp, Rawdon's wife.

Stirling Bridge, The Battle of. A victory over the English gained 1297 at Stirling by the Scots under Wallace.

Stockholm, The Treaties of. Treaties by which Sweden, in return for money, ceded Bremen and Verden to Hannover (1719) and Stettin and other territory to Prussia (1720).

Stoke Poges (stōk pō'jis). A village in Buckinghamshire, England, the burial-place of Thomas Gray. He composed there his "Elegy Written in a Country Churchyard."

Stolzenfels (shtolt'sen-fels). A picturesque castle, founded in the 13th century, situated on a height above the Rhine, near Coblenz: restored as a royal residence by Frederick William IV.

Stonehenge (stōn'henj'). A celebrated prehistoric monument consisting of huge upright stones, on Salisbury Plain, Wiltshire, England.

Stone Mountain. The mountain near Atlanta on the side of which is to be sculptured a memorial to the soldiers of the Confederacy, begun by Gutzon Borglum.

Stone of Scone, The. A famous stone, formerly at Scone, Scotland, upon which the Scottish kings sat at coronation: now beneath the coronation chair in Westminster Abbey.

Stone of the Sun, The. An Aztec monument, carved (about 1512) with characters representing divisions of time, and supposed to serve as a calendar: in the National Museum of Mexico.

Stones of Venice. A treatise on art (1851) by Ruskin.

Stork, King. In Æsop's Fables, a stork sent by Jupiter to eat up the frogs who complained of King Log.

Storm and Stress. See **Sturm und Drang.**

Storthing (stôr'ting). The national parliament of Norway, composed of two houses, the Lagthing and the Odelsthing.

Story of an African Farm, The. A novel (1883) by Olive Schreiner.

Story Teller's Story, A. An autobiographical narrative (1925) by Sherwood Anderson.

Stradella (strä-del'lä). 1. An opera (1837) by Flotow: rewritten as "Alessandro Stradella" (1844). 2. An opera (1837) by Niedermeyer.

Strafford (straf'ord). A tragedy (1837) by Browning.

Strafford Going to Execution. A painting (1835) by Delaroche, in Stafford House, London.

Strand. One of the chief thoroughfares of London, extending southeast from Fleet Street to Charing Cross.

Strange Case of Dr. Jekyll and Mr. Hyde, The. See **Dr. Jekyll and Mr. Hyde.**

Stranger, The. See **Menschenhass und Reue.**

Strap, Hugh. In Smollett's "Roderick Random," a faithful follower of the hero, who treats him shabbily.

Strasburg (stras'berg), **The Oath of.** A mutual contract of protection, sworn to by Kings Louis the German and Charles the Bald and their armies (A.D. 842): the first document in the vulgar tongue in the history of France and Germany.

Strawberry Hill. Horace Walpole's country house, near Twickenham, Surrey, England.

Street, The. A popular name for the part of New York in and near Wall Street, famous as a financial center.

Strelna (strel'nä). A Russian royal palace, situated on the Gulf of Finland near Leningrad.

Strephon (stref'on). A shepherd in Sidney's "Arcadia." In English poetry, a conventional name of a lover.

Strife. A drama (1909) by John Galsworthy, dealing with the conflict between capital and labor.

Strozzi (strot'sē). A Florentine family, rivals of the Medici. After the overthrow of the Republic in 1530 they settled in Venice and elsewhere.

Strudel, Der (der shtrö'del). A formerly dangerous whirlpool in the Danube, near Grein in Upper Austria.

Struldbrugs (struld'brugz). In Swift's "Gulliver's Travels," an immortal race, inhabitants of Luggnagg.

Stuart, or Stewart, or Steuart (stū'ärt). A royal family reigning in Scotland 1371–1603, and in England and Scotland jointly 1603–1714 (except for the period of the Commonwealth).

Stubaithal (shtö'bī-täl). An Alpine valley in Tyrol, famous for its sublime scenery.

Stundists (shtun'dists). A Russian sect, mainly evangelical and Protestant in tenets and practices, originating about 1860.

Sturdza (stûr'dzä), or **Sturza** (stûr'tsä). A Rumanian family whose members, especially in the 19th century, were associated with the government of Moldavia and of Rumania.

Sturm und Drang (shtûrm ûnt dräng). A period in German literature (about 1770–90) noted for the impetuosity of thought and style of the younger writers.

Stutly (stut'li), **Will.** A character in the Robin Hood cycle of English legend.

Stymphalides (stim-fal'i-dēz). In Greek legend, a flock of fierce birds near Lake Stymphalus. Heracles killed them as one of his twelve labors.

Styx (stiks). In Greek mythology: (1) a daughter of Oceanus, the goddess of the river Styx, by whom the most solemn oaths were sworn. (2) A mighty river, the tenth part of the water of Oceanus, which flows in the lower world.

Suben (sö'ben). In Egyptian mythology, the counterpart of the Roman Lucina.

Sublime Porte, The. See Dictionary, **Porte.**

Subtle (sut'l). The title character, a knavish cheat, in Jonson's "Alchemist."

Succoth (suk'oth). 1. A place in Palestine, destroyed by Gideon. Judges, viii. 5–16. 2. The place of the first encampment of the Israelites in the Exodus. Ex. xii. 37.

Such Is Life. A drama (1902) by Frank Wedekind.

Suessiones (swes-i-ō'nēz). An ancient people of Gallia Belgica in the vicinity of Soissons: subjugated 57 B.C. by Cæsar.

Suevi (swē'vī). According to Cæsar, the largest and most warlike of the Germanic tribes.

Sufis (su'fēz), or **Safis**, or **Safawis**. A dynasty of Persian monarchs who reigned from about 1501 to 1736.

Sugambri (sū-gam'brī), or **Sigambri** (si-gam'brī), or **Sicambri** (si-kam'brī). A German tribe situated, in the time of Cæsar, on the right bank of the lower Rhine.

Suhrab (sö-hräb'). See **Rustam.**

Suiones (sū-ī'ō-nēz). According to Tacitus, the collective name of the Germanic inhabitants of Scandinavia.

Suivante, La (lä swē-vänt). A comedy (1634) by Corneille, in which the character of the soubrette makes its first appearance.

Suleiman (sö-lä-män'), **The Mosque of.** A mosque in Constantinople, begun 1550.

Sulpicians (sul-pish′ạnz). A Roman Catholic order of priests, established about 1645 at Paris by the Abbé Olier, to train young men for the clerical office.

Sumbe (sȯm′bä), or **Basumbe** (bä-sȯm′bä). A Bantu nation of Angola, Africa.

Sumeria (sụ-mē′ri-ạ). In the Assyrian inscriptions, southern or lower Babylonia, identified with Shinar.

Sumer Is Icumen In. An English folk-song of the thirteenth century set to a round or canon.

Summa Theologiæ (sum′ạ thē-ọ-lō′ji-ē). 1. A theological work by Thomas Aquinas. 2. A theological work by Alexander of Hales.

Summer in Arcady, A. A story (1895) by James Lane Allen.

Summerson (sum′ėr-sọn), **Esther.** The lovable heroine of Dickens's "Bleak House." She proves to be Lady Dedlock's illegitimate daughter.

Summoner's or **Sompnour's Tale, The.** One of Chaucer's "Canterbury Tales."

Sumter, Fort. See **Fort Sumter.**

Sune. See **Zuñi.**

Sunken Bell, The. A poetic drama (1896) by Gerhart Hauptmann.

Sunnites (sun′īts). A Mohammedan sect comprising the greater part of the Moslem world, differing from the Shiites in recognizing the first three califs as legitimate successors of Mohammed, and in accepting six books which purport to contain oral utterances of Mohammed.

Sunnyside. The house in which Washington Irving resided at Irvington, New York: originally called "Wolfert's Roost."

Supper at Emmaus, The. The subject of noted paintings in the Louvre, Paris, by Rembrandt and by Titian.

Suppliants, The. A tragedy by Æschylus, first exhibited in 462 B.C.

Supplicants, The. In Scottish history, those who protested, about 1637–38, against Laud's policy in Scotland: known later as Covenanters.

Supremacy, The Act of. 1. An English statute (1534) which proclaimed Henry VIII. the supreme head of the English church. 2. An English statute (1558–59) vesting spiritual authority in the crown, to the exclusion of all foreign jurisdiction.

Surface, Charles. A gay and amiable rake in Sheridan's "School for Scandal."

Surface, Joseph. A malicious hypocrite in Sheridan's "School for Scandal": called "the Tartufe of sentiment."

Surhai (sö-rī′), or **Songhoi** (son-goi′). A great negro nation of the west-central Sudan.

Surprise Plot, The. The same as **Bye Plot, The.**

Surtr (sėrtr). In Scandinavian mythology, a fire-giant of Ragnarök.

Surya (sör′yạ). In the Rig-Veda, one of the two most common designations (Savitar, Surya) of the Sun.

Suryasiddhanta (sör″yạ-sid-dhän′tạ). A celebrated astronomical work in Sanskrit, said to be a direct revelation from the Sun.

Susanna (sọ-zan′ạ). An oratorio (1749) by Handel.

Susanna, The History of. One of the books of the Apocrypha: an addition to the Book of Daniel.

Susanna and the Elders. A painting (1637) by Rembrandt, in the Royal Gallery at The Hague.

Suspense. A novel (1925) by Joseph Conrad, left unfinished at the author's death.

Suspicious Husband, The. A comedy (1747) by Dr. Hoadley.

Sussex Gorse. A novel (1916) by Sheila Kaye-Smith, depicting the struggle with the soil.

Sutherland (suᴛʜ′ėr-lạnd) **Falls.** A noted cascade, 1,900 feet in height, near Milford Sound, New Zealand.

Sutra (sö′trạ). In Sanskrit, a brief rule, or a book of such rules.

Sveaborg (svā′ä-bȯr-y′). A fortress in the harbor of Helsingfors, Finland: constructed 1749.

Svengali. See **Trilby.**

Swabian (swä′bi-ạn) **Emperors, The.** The German-Roman emperors who reigned from 1138 to 1254: the Hohenstaufen line.

Swabian League, or **Swabian Cities' League, The.** A league of various Swabian cities, formed 1376 and later extended, as a defense against the extortions and depredations of the counts of Württemberg. It decayed after 1388.

Swabian League, The Great. A league of Swabian cities and governments formed 1488 for the maintenance of the public peace: dissolved in 1533.

Swabian Poets, The. In German literature: (1) A former collective name of.the Minnesingers. (2) A group of modern poets of Württemberg, the chief of whom were Uhland, Kerner, and Schwab.

Swamp Angel, The. A name given by Federal soldiers to an 8-inch Parrott gun placed in a swamp outside Charleston, and used during the siege. It burst in 1863.

Swan, The. A playhouse built about 1594–95 on the Bankside, Southwark, London.

Swan, The Knight of the. A famous myth, perhaps of Brabantine origin, the subject of numerous romances in English, French, and German. The Knight of the Swan is Lohengrin in the Round Table cycle; elsewhere Helias, Salvius, Gerhard the Swan, and others.

Swan of Avon (ā′vọn). A name often given to Shakspere, whose home was on the river Avon.

Swanwhite. A drama (1901) by August Strindberg.

Swaraj (swạ-räj′). The rallying cry of the Nationalist Party in India. The term, which means self-rule, is associated especially with the followers of Mahatma Gandhi.

Swarga (swär′gä). In Hindu mythology, the heaven of Indra, on Mount Meru.

Swedenborgians (swē-dn-bȯr′ji-ạnz). The believers in the theology and religious doctrines of Swedenborg; the New-Churchmen.

Swiss Family Robinson, The. A romance (1813) by J. R. Wyss.

Swiss Guards, The. A corps of Swiss mercenaries in the French service, 1616–1830. They are celebrated for their valor in the defense of the Tuileries (1792), commemorated in Thorvaldsen's "Lion of Lucerne."

Swithin (swith′in), or **Swithun** (swith′un), **Saint.** A 9th-century bishop of Winchester who, according to fable, performed many miraculous cures after his death. Rain on this saint's day, July 15, is popularly reputed to portend rain for 40 days following.

Swiveller (swiv′l-ėr), **Dick.** A character in Dickens's "Old Curiosity Shop."

Sword Blades and Poppy Seed. Poems (1914) by Amy Lowell.

Syamantaka (syạ-man′tạ-kạ). In Hindu mythology, a celebrated jewel of which the story is told in the Vishnupurana.

Sycorax (sik′ọ-raks). A witch, the mother of Caliban in Shakspere's "Tempest"; in Dryden and Davenant's version, his sister.

Sylphide, La (lä sēl-fēd). A ballet (1832) by Schneitzhöffer and Nourrit. La Sylphide was one of Taglioni's greatest parts.

Sylvia. See **Silvia.**

Sylvia Scarlett. See **Sinister Street.**

Symphony, The. A poem (1875) by Sidney Lanier.

Symplegades (sim-pleg′ạ-dēz). In the legend of the Argonauts, two rocky islets at the entrance of the Bosporus into the Black Sea, which strike together at intervals.

Symposium (sim-pō′zi-um), **The.** 1. A celebrated work by Plato, on love. 2. A work by Xenophon, describing the character of Socrates.

Syndics of the Arquebusiers. A painting (1657) by Van der Helst, in the Rijks Museum, Amsterdam.

Syndics of the Gild of the Clothmakers. A painting (1661) by Rembrandt, in the Rijks Museum, Amsterdam.

Synod, The Holy Governing. The highest ecclesiastical authority in the Russian Church: instituted 1721 by Peter the Great.

Synod, The Robber. See **Ephesus, The Council of,** 2.

Synod of Dort, The. See **Dort, The Synod of.**

Syntax, Dr. A pious and amiable clergyman in Combe's "Tour of Dr. Syntax in Search of the Picturesque."

Syrinx (sir′ingks). In Greek mythology, a nymph who was changed by Pan into a reed.

(variable) ḍ as d or j, ṣ as s or sh, ṭ as t or ch, ẓ as z or zh; o, F. cloche; ü, F. menu; ċh, Sc. loch; ń, F. bonbon; ′, primary accent; ″, secondary accent; †, obsolete; <, from; +, and; =, equals. See also lists at beginning of book.

T

Tabard (tab'ärd) **Inn, The.** An ancient hostelry of Southwark, London, the assembling-place of Chaucer's Canterbury pilgrims: condemned 1866.

Tabernacle, The. 1. A portable sanctuary of the Hebrews before the temple was built. Ex. xxv.–xxvii., xxxvi.–xxxviii. 2. A place of assembly of the Mormons, Salt Lake City, Utah: built 1864–67.

Tabirá (tä-bē-rä'). The ruined pueblo on the mesa of Jumanos, New Mexico: often called "la gran Quivira."

Tabitha (tab'i-thạ), or **Dorcas** (dôr'kạs). A Christian woman at Joppa, miraculously restored to life by the apostle Peter. Acts, ix. 36–41.

Tables, The. A group of members of the privy council and others, which opposed the introduction of episcopacy into Scotland, 1638–39. They sat at the tables in the Parliament House.

Table-Talk. 1. A poetical dialogue (1782) by Cowper. 2. Essays (1821–57) by Hazlitt. 3. Essays (1835) by Coleridge.

Tabor (tā'bọr), **Mount.** A wooded mountain east of Nazareth: the traditional scene of the Transfiguration. Mention of it in the Old Testament is frequent.

Tacanas (tä-kä'näz). Indians of northern Bolivia forming a distinct linguistic family.

Tackers, The. The English Tories who, in 1704, tried to carry their point by tacking a rider to a revenue bill.

Tacna-Arica (täk'nä-ä-rē'kä) **Award.** The decision of the boundary dispute between Chile and Peru made by President Coolidge as arbitrator on March 9, 1925.

Taensa (tä-en'sä). A confederacy of North American Indians, formerly of Louisiana, near St. Joseph on the west bank of the Mississippi.

Taffy. A nickname for any Welshman.

Tahmurath (tä-mö-rät'). In the Avesta and in Firdausi, a hero who vanquishes demons and subdues Ahriman.

Tai or **Thai** (tī). The principal race of the Indo-Chinese peninsula, including the Siamese.

Tainos (tī'nōz). The ancient Indian inhabitants of Haiti.

Tai-ping (tī'ping') **Rebellion, The.** The great Chinese rebellion of 1850 against the Manchu dynasty, led by Hung Siu-tsuan.

Tajak (tä-zhäk'). All persons of Iranian descent in central and western Asia.

Taj Mahal (täj mạ-häl'), **The.** The famous and exquisite mausoleum erected by Shah Jehan for his favorite wife, at Agra, India. See Dictionary, **taj,** and cut.

Takilman (tä-kil'mạn). A former linguistic stock of North American Indians, on the upper part of Rogue River, Oregon: now reduced to one small tribe, the Takelma.

Taku (tä'kö') **Forts, The.** Forts at the mouth of the river Peiho, China, taken by English and French forces (1858, 1860) and by the allies (1900).

Talamancas (tä-lä-mäng'käz). Indians of the district of Talamanca, Costa Rica.

Tale of a Tub, A. 1. A comedy (1634) by Jonson. 2. A satire by Swift, written about 1696.

Tale of Two Cities, A. A historical novel (1859) by Dickens. Much of the action takes place in Paris during the French Revolution.

Tales of a Grandfather. Four series of historical stories (1827–30) by Scott.

Tales of a Wayside Inn. A series (1863) of narrative poems by Longfellow.

Tales of Hoffmann. An opera (1881) by Offenbach.

Tales of My Landlord. A collective name for seven of the Waverley Novels: "Old Mortality," "The Black Dwarf," "The Heart of Midlothian," "The Bride of Lammermoor," "A Legend of Montrose," "Count Robert of Paris," and "Castle Dangerous."

Taliesin (tal-i-es'in). A legendary, perhaps mythical, Celtic bard of the 6th century. The poems ascribed to him are of considerably later date.

Talisman, The. A romance of the Crusades (1825) by Scott.

Talmud. See Dictionary, **Gemara, mishnah, Talmud.**

Talos (tā'los). 1. In Greek legend, the inventive nephew of Dædalus, by whom he was slain. 2. A man of brass made by Hephæstus for Minos, to guard Crete.

Talus (tā'lus). The iron executor of Justice in Spenser's "Faerie Queene," Bk. V.

Tamanacs (tä-mä-näks'). Indians of Bolivar, Venezuela, south of the lower Orinoco.

Tamarisk Town. A novel (1919) by Sheila Kaye-Smith.

Tamburlaine the Great. A tragedy in two parts (1587) by Marlowe.

Tamils (tam'ilz). See Dictionary, **Tamil.**

Taming of the Shrew, The. A comedy (1603) by Shakspere.

Tammany (tam'ạ-ni) **Hall.** 1. A powerful political organization in New York City, which usually controls the local Democratic party. 2. The building in which the Tammany organization has its headquarters.

Tammuz (tam'uz). A Babylonian god of the springtime and of vernal vegetation.

Tam o' Shanter. A famous poem (1791) by Burns, telling of Tam's wild ride homeward by night, pursued by witches, after his market-day potations.

Tamoyos (tä-mō'yoz). A powerful Indian tribe which at the time of the conquest dominated the Brazilian coast from Cape Frio to Rio de Janeiro.

Tanaim (tä-nä'im). The Jewish rabbis in the Mishnic period, A.D. 10–220: the authors of the Mishnah.

Tanaquil (tan'ạ-kwil). In Roman legend, the wife of the first Tarquin, king of Rome.

Tancrède (tän-kred). A play (1760) by Voltaire.

Tancredi (tän-krä'dē). An opera (1813) by Rossini.

Tanglewood Tales. A series of tales (1853) by Hawthorne, for children.

Tanit (tä'nit). A Phenician goddess. Her symbol was the solar disk with a crescent.

Tannhäuser (tän'hoi-zèr). A Middle High German lyric poet of the 13th century. A well-known legend tells of his stay with Venus in the Venusberg, and his repentance.

Tannhäuser und der Sängerkrieg auf Wartburg (únt der zeng'èr-krēch ouf värt'búrch). An opera (1845) by Wagner.

Tanoan (tä'nọ-ạn). A linguistic stock of North American Indians, inhabiting communal pueblos in the main and tributary valleys of the Rio Grande.

Tanqueray (tang'kẹ-rä), **Paula.** The title character in Pinero's "Second Mrs. Tanqueray."

Tantalus (tan'tạ-lus). In Greek mythology, a son of Zeus and the nymph Pluto: father of Pelops and Niobe. For revealing secrets of the gods, he was condemned to stand, hungry and thirsty, in water up to his chin, under a tree laden with fruit.

Tante. A novel (1911) by Anne Douglas Sedgwick.

Tantra (tan'trạ). In Sanskrit literature, a religious treatise teaching magical formulas for worship of the gods or the attainment of superhuman power.

Taos (tä'ōs). The northernmost of the Pueblo tribes of North American Indians, 50 miles northeast of Santa Fé, New Mexico.

Tapajos (tä-pä-zhōsh'). An Indian tribe, probably of Tupi race, which occupied the territory about the mouth of the river Tapajos in the 16th and 17th centuries.

Tapes (tä-päz'). Indians of the Guarani race who formerly occupied territory between the rivers Paraná and Uruguay. The Jesuits had many missions among them.

Tapley (tap'li), **Mark.** Martin's optimistic servant and fellow adventurer in Dickens's "Martin Chuzzlewit."

Tappertit (tap'èr-tit), **Simon.** A conceited apprentice in Dickens's "Barnaby Rudge." He aspires to the hand of Dolly Varden.

Taprobane (ta-prob'ạ-nē). 1. The ancient name of Ceylon. 2. A fabulous island in the dominion of Prester John. Mandeville recounts various of its marvels.

Tarahumar (tä-rä-hö-mär'). A large division of the Piman stock of North American Indians, dwelling in the higher parts of Sonora and Chihuahua, Mexico.

Taras Bulba (tä-räs' böl'bä). A historical novel (1835; later rewritten and enlarged) by Nikolay Gogol. It is a story of a Cossack warrior of the 16th century.

Tarascos (tä-räs'kōz). A formerly powerful Indian nation of Mexico, in territory now included in Michoacan.

Tarasque (tȧ-räsk). A legendary monster that anciently ravaged the neighborhood of Tarascon, France.

---

fat, fāte, fär, fåll, åsk, fåre; net, mē, hèr; pin, pīne; not, nōte, mōve, nôr; up, lūte, pùll; oi, oil; ou, out; (lightened) avīạry, ẹlect, agọny, intọ, ụnite; (obscured) errạnt, operä, ardẹnt, actọr, natüre; ch, chip; g, go; th, thin; ғн, then; y, you;

Tar Baby, The. One of the best-known stories in Harris's "Uncle Remus."

Tarpeian (tär-pē'ạn) **Rock, The.** A peak of the Capitoline, Rome, from which condemned criminals were hurled: named in allusion to the maid Tarpeia, slain there by Sabine soldiers after she had betrayed the citadel to them.

Tarquins (tär'kwinz). A famous family to which belonged the fifth and seventh kings of early Rome.

Tarshish (tär'shish). In the Old Testament: (1) A son of Javan. Gen. x. 4. (2) A place, variously identified, with which trade was carried on by sea. 2 Chron. ix. 21.

Tartarin (tär-tȧ-raṅ). A gasconading humbug in several stories by Daudet, as in "Tartarin de Tarascon."

Tartarus (tär'tạ-rus). In Greek mythology, a sunless abyss below Hades. In it Zeus imprisoned the Titans. Later, it is a place of punishment for the wicked.

Tartufe or **Tartuffe** (tär-tüf). A famous comedy (1667) by Molière. The title character is the arch-hypocrite of modern drama.

Tashmet (tash'met). In Assyro-Babylonian mythology, the wife of Nebo. Her shrine was in Erech.

Task, The. A descriptive poem (1785) by Cowper.

Tasker Jevons. A novel (1916) of the Great War, by May Sinclair: in America, "The Belfry."

Tatler, The. An English triweekly conducted by Steele and Addison, Apr. 12, 1709–Jan. 2, 1711.

Tattersall's (tat'ẽr-sâlz). A sporting establishment and auction mart for horses, opened in London about 1770 by Richard Tattersall.

Taurian (tâ'ri-ạn) **Games, The.** In ancient Rome, games held in honor of the infernal gods.

Tchishi (chē'shē). The Warm Springs (Aguas Calientes) Apache Indians of New Mexico. Their chief, Victorio, was killed in 1880.

Tchuvashes (chö-väsh'ez). A mixed Finnic and Tatar people of eastern Russia, near the Volga.

Tciwere (chē-wä'rä). A division of the Siouan stock of North American Indians, chiefly in Oklahoma.

Teague (tāg or tēg). A nickname for any Irishman.

Teapot Dome. A Wyoming oil-field in connection with which there was a government investigation of graft in 1923–24. Men prominent in official circles were involved.

Tearless Battle, The. The battle of the Arcadians and Argives against the Spartans, 367 B.C., in which the Spartans suffered no losses.

Tea Water Spring, The. Formerly, a famous spring toward the lower end of Manhattan Island, whose water was prized for making tea. The spring was a popular resort before the Revolution.

Teazle (tē'zl), **Lady.** The imprudent, though innocent, young wife of Sir Peter in Sheridan's "School for Scandal."

Tecumseh (tē-kum'sè), **The.** An ironclad, single-turreted monitor of the U. S. Navy. It was one of Farragut's fleet in the attack on Mobile, and was torpedoed in Mobile Bay Aug. 5, 1864.

Tegnum (teg'num). The medieval students' name for Galen's treatise on the art of medicine.

Tekke-Turcomans (tek'kä-tẽr'kọ-mạnz). A race of Tatar nomads in central Asia, on the frontiers of Persia, Afghanistan, and Asiatic Russia.

Telamon (tel'ạ-mon). In Greek legend, son of Æacus, brother of Peleus, and father of Ajax.

Telegonus (tē-leg'ọ-nus). In Greek legend: (1) A son of Proteus, slain by Hercules. (2) A son of Odysseus and Circe. He killed Odysseus and married Penelope.

Tel-el-Amarna (tel'el-ạ-mär'nä). The ruins of a residence of Amenophis IV., where were discovered (1887–88) 300 tablets bearing diplomatic correspondence of Egyptian kings with Babylonia, Assyria, etc.

Telemachus (tē-lem'ạ-kus). In Greek legend, the son of Odysseus and Penelope. With his father, he slew the suitors of Penelope.

Télémaque, Les Aventures de (lā-zȧ-voṅ-tür dè tā-lā-mȧk). A romance (1699) by Fénelon: one of the famous classics of French literature.

Telephus (tel'e-fus). In Greek legend, the son of Heracles and Auge: king of Mysia at the time of the expedition against Troy.

Tellus (tel'us). In Roman mythology, a goddess personifying the earth.

Téméraire (tā-mā-rär), **The.** A line-of-battle ship captured from the French at the battle of the Nile. She was Captain Harvey's ship at Trafalgar, where she fought next the Victory. It is the subject of a painting by Turner (1839), "The Fighting Téméraire."

Tempest, The. 1. A romantic and idyllic play by Shakspere, produced 1611. 2. A distorted revision of the preceding by Dryden and Davenant, produced 1667. 3. An opera by Shadwell, based on Shakspere (1673). 4. An opera by Garrick, based on Shakspere and Dryden (1756). 5. Incidental music by Arthur Sullivan, first performed 1862.

Templars (tem'plärz), **The.** A military order founded at Jerusalem about 1118 among the Crusaders: suppressed 1312.

Temple, Le (lè toṅ-pl). A fortified lodge of the Knights Templars in Paris, built soon after 1128. Its chapel stood until 1650, and a square tower until 1810. (In the latter Louis XVI. was imprisoned 1792–93.)

Temple, The. 1. The religious edifice of the Jews in Jerusalem, first reared by Solomon. 1 Kings, vi., vii. 2. In the middle ages, the lodge of the Knights Templars in London, of which only the Temple Church (finished 1185) remains. The Inns of Court (Middle Temple and Inner Temple) now occupy the site. 3. In Salt Lake City, Utah, the chief religious building of the Mormons, built 1853–92.

Temple Bar. A famous gateway before the Temple in London. It formerly divided Fleet Street from the Strand.

Temple Bar Memorial, The. A monument which replaced the old Temple Bar, removed 1878.

Temple Gardens. Gardens of the Temple, London, separated from the Thames by the Victoria Embankment.

Temple of Fame, The. A poem (1715) by Pope, based on Chaucer's "House of Fame."

Temple of the Cross, The. One of the ruined edifices at Palenque, Mexico, important for the sculptures found in it.

Temple of the Great Dragon, or of Heaven, The. A splendid Chinese temple at Peking, constructed about 1420.

Temple of the Sun, The. See **Curicancha.**

Temptation of St. Anthony, The. 1. A painting (1604) by Pieter Breughel the younger, in the museum at Dresden. 2. A painting by Tintoretto, in San Trovaso, Venice.

Ten, The Council of. A powerful and arbitrary secret tribunal (1310–1797) in the republic of Venice, at first of 10 members, later 17.

Tenant of Wildfell Hall, The. A novel (1848) by Anne Brontë.

Tencteri (tengk'tē-rī). A Germanic tribe defeated by Julius Cæsar near the confluence of the Maas with the Rhine.

Tennessee, The Army of the. A Federal army in the Civil War, commanded successively by Halleck, Grant, Sherman, McPherson, Howard, and Logan.

Tenth Legion, The. A Roman legion celebrated for its valor in the time of Julius Cæsar.

Ten Thousand a Year. A novel (1839–41) by Samuel Warren, about a conceited shopman, Tittlebat Titmouse, who inherits a large estate.

Teocalli (tā-ọ-käl'ē). The great temple in Tenochtitlán (the modern Mexico City), finished about 1486. The name is also applied to any pyramidal temple in Mexico.

Teoyaomiqui (tā"ọ-you-mē'kē). A stone idol dug up near the Teocalli at Mexico City: now in the Mexican National Museum. It probably represents the Nahuatl war-god, Huitzilopochtli.

Tepanecs (tep'ạ-neks). A Nahuatl tribe of the Mexican valley: originally a branch of the Tezcucans who settled on Lake Tezcuco about 1168.

Tepehuan (tā-pā-wän'). A tribe of North American Indians on the eastern slope of the Sierra Madre in the state of Durango, Mexico.

Terah (tē'rä). Abraham's father. Gen. xi. 26.

Termagant (tẽr'mạ-gạnt). A name given to the god of the Saracens in medieval romances, where he is linked with Mahound.

Terminalia (tẽr-mi-nä'li-ạ). An annual festival in honor of Terminus, the Roman god of boundaries. It was held Feb. 23.

Terminus (tẽr'mi-nus).   See **Terminalia.**

Terpsichore (tẽrp-sik'ō-rē).   The Muse of the choral dance and of the dramatic chorus which developed from it.   She is a companion of Melpomene.

Terra (tẽr'ạ).   In Roman mythology, a goddess personifying the earth.

Terre, La (lä tär).   A realistic novel (1887) by Zola.

Terrible Meek, The.   A drama (1911) by Charles Rann Kennedy.

Terror, The.   1. See Dictionary, **Reign of Terror**, under **reign.**   2. One of the arctic exploring vessels of Sir John Franklin, 1845–47, the other being the Erebus.

Terry Alts (tẽr'i alts), **The.**   A body of rebels in County Clare, Ireland, about the beginning of the 19th century.

Tertullianists (tẽr-tul'iạn-ists).   In the 3d and 4th centuries, those African Montanists who followed the views of Tertullian.

Tess of the D'Urbervilles.   A tragic novel (1891) by Thomas Hardy: the story of a village girl who kills her betrayer after having been repudiated by her husband.

Tethys (tē'this).   In Greek mythology, a sea-goddess.

Tetrapolis (te-trap'ō-lis), **The Chaldean.**   The four cities, Babylon, Akkad, Erech, and Calneh.

Tetrapolitan (tet-rạ-pol'i-tạn) **Confession, The.**   A confession of faith submitted at the Diet of Augsburg (1530) by representatives of Constance, Lindau, Memmingen, and Strasburg.

Teucer (tū'sẽr).   In Greek legend: (1) A son of Scamander, and the first king of Troy.   (2) A noted archer, son of Telamon and step-brother of Ajax.   He was said to have founded Salamis in Cyprus.

Teufelsdröckh (toi'fẹls-drẽk).   The pretended author of "Sartor Resartus."   He is an eccentric Professor of Things in General at the University of Weissnichtwo.

Teutones (tū'tō-nēz).   A Germanic people who were formidable antagonists of the Roman armies before 102 B.C., when they were nearly destroyed by Marius at Aquæ Sextiæ.

Teutonic Order, The.   A religious and military order founded by German knights at Acre in 1190.   It was powerful from the 13th century to the 15th.

Tewkesbury Chronicle, The.   A chronicle of ecclesiastical history kept (1066–1263) at the Abbey of Tewkesbury.

Tezcatlipoca (tās-kät-lē-pō'kä).   In Aztec mythology, a principal deified shaman.   Human sacrifices were made to him.

Tezcucans (tās-kö'kạnz).   An ancient Nahuatl tribe of the valley of Mexico.   In 1520 they assisted Cortes in his siege of Mexico City.

Thaddæus (tha-dē'us).   See **Jude, Saint.**

Thaddeus of Warsaw.   A historical romance of Poland (1803), by Jane Porter.

Thaïs.   1. (thā'is) An Athenian courtezan, mistress of Alexander the Great and, after his death, of Ptolemy Soter.   2. (tä-ēs) A novel (1890) by Anatole France.   3. An opera (1894) by Massenet.

Thalia (thạ-lī'ạ).   The Muse of comedy and idyllic poetry.

Thallo (thal'ō).   In Greek mythology, one of the Hours.

Thames (temz) **Embankment, The.**   A broad drive with sidewalks, constructed 1864–70 in London along the north bank of the Thames from Blackfriars Bridge to Westminster.

Thamyris (tham'i-ris).   In Greek legend, a Thracian singer deprived of sight and voice for boasting that he could surpass the Muses.

Thanatopsis (than-ạ-top'sis).   An early poem (1817) by Bryant.

Thanatos (than'ạ-tos).   In Greek mythology, the personification of Death, brother of Sleep.

Thargelia (thär-jē'li-ạ).   A festival celebrated in ancient Athens on the 6th and 7th of the month Thargelion, in honor of the Delian Apollo and of Artemis.

Theagenes (thē-aj'e-nēz) **and Chariclea** (kar-i-klē'ạ).   A Greek romance of the 4th century, by one Heliodorus.

Theatins (thē'ạ-tinz).   An Italian monastic order, founded 1524 to combat the Reformation.

Theatre, The.   The first London theater, built 1576 by James Burbage, the father of Richard Burbage.

Théâtre de la Foire (tā-ätr dẹ lä fwär).   A puppet-theater set up by provincial comedians at the fairs of St.-Germain and St.-Laurent, outside Paris, as far back as 1595.

Théâtre Français, Le (lẹ tā-ätr frän-sā).   The most noted theater in France, situated on the Rue St.-Honoré, Paris.   It is subsidized by the government, and is the chief home of the regular drama.

Théâtre Italien, Le (lẹ tā-ätr ē-tä-lyan).   The old opera-house in the Rue Le Peletier, Paris.

Theatre Royal, The.   The Drury Lane Theatre, London.

Thebaid (thē'bā-id), **The.**   An epic poem by Statius.   Its theme is the expedition of the Seven against Thebes.   It was composed about A.D. 80–92.

Thébaide, La (lä tā-bä-ēd).   A play (1664) by Racine.

Theban Legion, The.   A legion in the army of Maximian which, according to legend, refused to assist in the persecution of Christians, was twice decimated, and was finally exterminated.

Theia (thē'yạ).   One of the Titanesses.

Their Wedding Journey.   A novel (1871) by W. D. Howells.

Themis (thē'mis).   A Greek goddess personifying law, order, and abstract justice.

Theodosian (thē-ō-dō'shi-ạn) **Code, The.**   A collection of Roman laws from Constantine to Theodosius II., published 438 in 16 books.

Theogony (thē-og'ō-ni), **The.**   An ancient Greek poem attributed to Hesiod.   It treats of the origin of the order of nature from chaos, and of the origin of the gods.

Theophrastus Such (thē-ō-fras'tus such), **The Impressions of.**   A series of essays (1879) by George Eliot.

Thermidorians (thẽr-mi-dō'ri-ạnz), **The.**   The moderate party in the French Revolution, who approved the overthrow of Robespierre on the 9th Thermidor, year 2 (July 27, 1794).

Thersites (thẽr-sī'tēz).   In Greek legend, the most vindictive and impudent of the Greeks before Troy.   (He appears in Shakspere's "Troilus and Cressida.")

Thervings (thẽr'vingz).   One of the great branches into which the Goths divided about the year 200 (the other being the Greutungs or Ostrogoths): also called Visigoths or West Goths.

These Lynnekers.   A novel (1916) by J. D. Beresford, dealing with family life and revolt against its restraints.

Theseum (thē-sē'um), **The.**   A temple, probably of Hephæstus, at Athens: one of the most perfect surviving Greek temples.   See Dictionary, and cut.

Theseus (thē'sūs or thē'sẹ-us).   1. In Greek legend, the chief hero of Attica, son of Ægeus and Æthra.   He captured the Marathonian bull, slew the Minotaur, found his way through the Cretan labyrinth, fought the Amazons, was one of the Argonauts, and took part in the Calydonian hunt.   He loved, but deserted, Ariadne.   Lycomedes slew him in Scyros.   2. The Duke of Athens in Shakspere's "Midsummer Night's Dream."

Thespian (thes'pi-ạn) **Maids, The.**   The Muses.

Thessalonians (thes-ạ-lō'ni-ạnz), **The Epistles to the.**   Two of the Pauline epistles in the New Testament.   Their main theme is the second advent of Christ.

Thetis (thē'tis).   In Greek mythology, the chief of the Nereids, and mother by Peleus of Achilles.

They Knew What They Wanted.   A drama (1924) by Sidney Howard.   Pulitzer Prize play, 1925.

Thing (ting).   In the Scandinavian countries, an assembly, parliament, or court of law.

Thinker, The.   One of the best-known figures by Auguste Rodin, originally designed as part of a monumental gateway, "La Porte de l'Enfer," now in the Musée Rodin, Paris.   Also used on Rodin's tomb at Meudon.

Thirteenth District, The.   A novel (1902) by Brand Whitlock.

Thirty Tyrants, The.   1. A body which usurped the government of Athens 404–403 B.C.   The most important of them was Critias.   2. The body of pretenders to the Roman Empire in the reigns of Valerian, Gallienus, etc.

Thirty Years' War, The.   A religious and political war (1618–48) in central Europe, caused by friction between the Catholics and the Protestants of the Empire.   France

---

fat, fāte, fär, fåll, ȧsk, fãre; net, mē, hẽr; pin, pīne; not, nōte, mõve, nôr; up, lūte, pull; oi, oil; ou, out; (lightened) aviạry, ẹlect, agọny, intọ, ụnite; (obscured) errạnt, oper̤ä, ardẹnt, actọr, natụre; ch, chip; g, go; th, thin; ᴛʜ, then; y, you;

and Sweden were the gainers, Germany the heaviest loser. The treaty of Westphalia ended the struggle.

Thisbe (thiz′bē). In classical legend, a maiden of Babylon, loved by Pyramus. The two made love secretly through a hole in the wall between their houses, their parents being opposed. Pyramus killed himself when he saw blood which he mistakenly believed to be Thisbe's.

Thomas (tom′ạs), **Saint,** or **Didymus** (did′i-mus). One of the 12 apostles. John, xx. 24–29.

Thomas the Rhymer, or **True Thomas.** Thomas of Erceldoune (1220?–97?), a Scottish poet and seer noted in folklore. According to popular legend, he was led away by the Queen of Faery, and lived with her three years.

Thomists (tō′mists). The followers of Thomas Aquinas in his attempt to reconcile Aristotelian philosophy with the Christian faith.

Thor (thôr). The god of thunder, second principal deity of the ancient Scandinavians. He was the son of Odin and of Jörd (the earth).

Thorvaldsen (tôr′väl-sẹn) **Museum, The.** A museum at Copenhagen, completed 1848: the mausoleum of the sculptor Thorvaldsen and a repository of many of his works.

Those Barren Leaves. A novel (1925) by Aldous Huxley: satire on a literary house-party.

Thoth (thoth or tōt). An Egyptian divinity whom the Greeks identified with Hermes: the god of speech and of letters.

Thousand and One Days, The. A series of Persian tales, modeled on the "A Thousand and One Nights."

Thousand and One Nights, A. See **Arabian Nights' Entertainments, The.**

Thraetaona (thrä-ā-tạ-ō′nạ̈). In the Avesta, a hero who fetters the serpent Dahaka.

Threadneedle Street. A commercial street leading from the Bank of England, London.

Three Black Pennys, The. A novel (1917) by Joseph Hergesheimer.

Three Chapters, The. An edict (about A.D. 545) of Justinian, condemning the writings of Theodore of Mopsuestia, those of Theodoret in defense of Nestorius and against Cyril, and the letter of Ibas to Maris; also, the writings so condemned.

Three Daughters of Monsieur Dupont, The. A problem play (1897) by Eugène Brieux.

Three Kings of Cologne, The. The three wise men of the East, Kaspar, Melchior, and Balthasar.

Three Men in a Boat. A humorous account of a holiday excursion (1889) by Jerome K. Jerome.

Three Musketeers, The. See **Trois Mousquetaires, Les.**

Three Pretty Men. A novel (1916) by Gilbert Cannan: in America, "Three Sons and a Mother."

Three Sisters, The. A novel (1914) by May Sinclair: a study of feminine psychology.

Three Soldiers. A realistic story (1921) of the Great War by John Dos Passos.

Three Sons and a Mother. See **Three Pretty Men.**

Through the Looking-Glass. See **Alice's Adventures in Wonderland.**

Thrums. The scene of many of Sir James Barrie's stories, especially "A Window in Thrums," and "The Little Minister": it represents Kirriemuir, Barrie's birthplace.

Thrym (thrim). In Old Norse mythology, the giant who stole Mjöllnir, the hammer of Thor.

Thuban (thö-bän′). A star of the fourth magnitude (though formerly estimated as of the second) in the constellation Draco: about 2750 B.C. it occupied the position of the pole-star. See **Kochab.**

Thule (thū′lē). A region or island north of Britain, the location of which has been a matter of controversy for some two thousand years.

Thunderer, The. 1. Zeus (Jove). 2. The London "Times."

Thunder on the Left. A novel (1925) by Christopher Morley, presenting a man in middle life faced by the boy-he-used-to-be.

Thwackum (thwak′um) and **Square.** In Fielding's "Tom Jones," a pair of tutors in whom Fielding satirizes the theological pedantry of education. Square holds by the natural virtue of man; Thwackum deduces everything from original sin.

Thyestes (thī-es′tēz). In Greek legend, son of Pelops, brother of Atreus, and father of Ægisthus. He seduced his brother's wife, and in revenge Atreus slew Thyestes's sons.

Thyrsis (thêr′sis). 1. A herdsman in the Idyls of Theocritus. 2. A shepherd in the Eclogues of Virgil. 3. In Renaissance and Elizabethan literature, a shepherd or rustic. 4. An elegy (1867) by Matthew Arnold on his friend A. H. Clough.

Ti (tē). A nobleman of Egypt of the time of the 5th dynasty, of whom many statues were found in the walls of his tomb.

Tiahuanacu (tē-ä-wä-nä′kö). A group of ancient ruins in western Bolivia, near the southern end of Lake Titicaca.

Tiamat (tē-ä′mät). In Assyro-Babylonian mythology, the personification of primeval chaos, depicted as a dragon.

Tiber (tī′bêr). A colossal recumbent statue of the early Roman Empire, in the Louvre, Paris.

Ticket-of-Leave Man, The. A play (1863) by Tom Taylor.

Tiers État (tyär-zä-tä). That portion of the French nation which belonged neither to the privileged classes (nobility and clergy) nor to the peasantry; the burghers.

Tiglath-Pileser (tig′lath-pi-lē′zêr). A king of Assyria, who reduced Pekah of Israel to vassalage. 2 Kings, xv. 29.

Tigurini (tig-ū-rī′nī). One branch of the Helvetii. It was cut to pieces by Cæsar, 58 B.C.

Tihua (tē′wä). A division of the Tanoan stock of North American Indians, occupying pueblos in Chihuahua, Mexico, also Taos, northern New Mexico, and elsewhere.

Tilburina (til-bū-rī′nạ̈). The daughter of the governor of Tilbury Fort, in the interpolated burlesque in Sheridan's "Critic": a character in whom the sorrows of tragic heroines are burlesqued.

Times, The. A leading London newspaper, founded 1785 as "The London Daily Universal Register."

Timon (tī′mọn) **of Athens.** A tragedy (about 1607) partly by Shakspere.

Timothy (tim′ọ-thi), or **Timotheus** (ti-mō′thẹ-us). A disciple and companion of the apostle Paul, to whom Paul wrote the two New Testament epistles bearing his name.

Timuquanan (tim-ọ-kwä′nạn). A linguistic stock of North American Indians, formerly occupying the peninsula of Florida.

Tinker's Wedding, The. A drama (1903) by J. M. Synge.

Tintern (tin′têrn) **Abbey.** A ruined medieval abbey, of the 13th century, in Monmouthshire, 17 miles from Bristol.

Tiny Tim. See **Cratchit, Bob.**

Tiresias (tī-rē′si-ạs). In Greek legend, a Theban seer, blinded by Athene, whom he saw bathing. She relented, and gave him prophetic vision.

Tisiphone (ti-sif′ọ-nē). One of the Furies.

Titan. 1. (tī′tạn) A classical name for the sun personified. 2. (tē-tän′) A romance (1803) by Jean Paul Richter.

Titan, The. A novel (1914) by Theodore Dreiser. See also **Financier, The.**

Titania (ti-tā′ni-ạ̈). See **Oberon, 3.**

Titanic, The. A passenger steamship of the White Star line, which, Apr. 14–15, 1912, was sunk by collision with an iceberg on her maiden voyage from Southampton to New York, with a loss of over 1,500 lives.

Titans (tī′tạnz). In Greek mythology, a race of primordial deities, children of Uranus and Gæa (Heaven and Earth). In the oldest accounts, there were six male and six female Titans. See **Tartarus.**

Tithonus (ti-thō′nus). In Greek mythology, a son or brother of Laomedon, beloved by Eos. He was metamorphosed into a grasshopper.

Tittlebat Titmouse. See **Ten Thousand a Year.**

Titurel (tit′ū-rel). A hero of the legend of the Holy Grail: the grandfather of Parzival. He appears in poems of Wolfram von Eschenbach.

Titus (tī′tus). A convert and companion of the apostle Paul, to whom Paul wrote the short New Testament epistle bearing Titus's name.

Titus Andronicus (an-dron′i-kus). A tragedy, probably in part by Shakspere, produced 1594.

Tityus (tit′i-us). In Greek mythology, the son of Zeus or of Gæa: a giant, and father of Europa.

Tlaloc (tlä-lōk'). In Aztec mythology, the god of rain.

Tlaxcalans (tläs-kä'lạnz). A tribe of Indians of Nahuat-lecan stock, who occupied the present Tlaxcala, east of the valley of Mexico. They first resisted, then aided, Cortes (1519).

Tmu. See **Atm.**

Tobias (tō-bī'ạs). The son of Tobit, in the Book of Tobit.

Tobias and the Angel, The Family of. A painting by Rembrandt, in the Louvre, Paris.

Tobikhar (tō-bik-här'). A division of North American Indians, now chiefly under the Mission agency, California.

Tobit (tō'bit), **The Book of.** A romance, one of the apocryphal books of the Old Testament.

Toby, Uncle, or **Captain Shandy.** See **Uncle Toby.**

Todgers (toj'ẽrz), **Mrs.** In Dickens's "Martin Chuzzlewit," a boarding-house mistress who has a "soft heart" for Mr. Pecksniff.

Together. A novel (1908) by Robert Herrick.

To Have and to Hold. A novel (1900) by Mary Johnston, describing the early days of the Virginia colony.

Toilers of the Sea, The. See **Travailleurs de la Mer, Les.**

Tolbooth (tōl'bōᴛн). The Edinburgh city jail, demolished 1817. It was popularly called "the heart of Midlothian"; whence the title of one of Scott's romances.

Told by an Idiot. A novel (1923) by Rose Macaulay.

Toledo (tō-lē'dō) **War, The.** A bloodless dispute (1835) between Ohio and Michigan, both States claiming the city of Toledo.

Tolentino (tō-len-tē'nō), **The Peace of.** A treaty (1797) between Napoleon and Pope Pius VI. The latter ceded Avignon, Bologna, and other territory.

Toleration, The Act of. A statute (1689) conditionally removing the oppressive restrictions upon English dissenters.

Toltecs (tol'teks). A traditional, possibly mythical, Indian stock which occupied the Mexican plateau for several centuries before the arrival of the Aztecas.

Tom and Jerry, or Life in London. A novel (1821–22) by Pierce Egan, containing the adventures of Jerry Hawthorn, Corinthian Tom, and Bob Logic: illustrated by Cruikshank.

Tom Brown's School Days. A story (1857) of life at Rugby, by Thomas Hughes: followed (1861) by "Tom Brown at Oxford."

Tombs, The. A prison in New York City, built 1838 and remodeled 1897–99. It occupies the block bounded by Centre, Leonard, Lafayette, and Franklin streets.

Tom Gate, The. A gate of Christ Church College, Oxford, completed (1682) by Wren.

Tom Jones. A novel (1749) by Fielding, regarded as his masterpiece. Tom, the foundling foster-son of Squire Allworthy, is the typical 18th-century young blade. After numerous racy adventures he settles down and marries an heiress, Sophia Western.

Tommy and Grizel. See **Sentimental Tommy.**

Tommy Atkins. Any private of the British army; also, the rank and file collectively.

Tommy Sandys. The title character in Barrie's "Sentimental Tommy."

Tom o' Bedlam. An incurable lunatic.

Tom Quad (kwod). The quadrangle of Christ Church College, Oxford.

Tom's. A former London coffee-house frequented in the 18th century by many famous personages.

Tom Sawyer, The Adventures of. A novel (1876) by Mark Twain, made up of the escapades of an irrepressible and sharp-witted lad in a small Missouri town about the middle of the 19th century. In a sequel, "The Adventures of Huckleberry Finn" (1884), the son of the town drunkard makes a wild journey down the Mississippi on a raft with a runaway slave.

Tom Thumb. A diminutive hero of folk-tales. See also **Hop o' My Thumb.**

Tom Thumb the Great. A satirical burlesque (1730) by Fielding.

Tongas (tong-gäs'). A tribe of North American Indians on an island at the mouth of Portland Canal and on Prince of Wales Island, Alaska.

Tonikan (ton'i-kạn). A linguistic stock of North American

Indians which lived (1700) in Mississippi, on the lower Yazoo. The few survivors are in Louisiana.

Tonkawan (tong'kạ-wạn). A linguistic family of North American Indians which occupied several parts of Texas about 1719. Only one tribe remains.

Tonnante, La (lä to-näṅt). The first ironclad: one of five floating batteries built by Napoleon III. in the Crimean War. It was launched 1855 at Brest.

Tono-Bungay. A novel (1909) by H. G. Wells.

Toodle (tö'dl), **Mr.** In Dickens's "Dombey and Son," a stoker, husband of Polly Toodle, Paul Dombey's nurse, and sire of Robin Toodle, known as "The Biler."

Toots (töts), **Mr.** In Dickens's "Dombey and Son," a swain hopelessly in love with Florence Dombey.

Tophet (tō'fet). A place at the southeastern extremity of Gehenna, south of Jerusalem. There the idolatrous Jews worshiped the fire-gods. Jer. vii. 31, 32.

Topsy (top'si). A mischievous little negress in "Uncle Tom's Cabin," by Harriet Beecher Stowe.

Torah (tō'rä). A Jewish name for the Pentateuch.

Torgau (tôr'gou) **Articles, The.** A document (1530) which was the basis of the Augsburg Confession.

Torgau Book, The. A document (1576) which was the basis of the Formula of Concord.

Tories (tō'riz). 1. In English history, the more conservative of the two great political parties which arose late in the 17th century. 2. The loyalist or British party in America in the Revolutionary period.

Torquato Tasso (tôr-kwä'tō täs'sō). A drama (1790) by Goethe.

Torquilstone (tôr'kwil-stōn). In Scott's "Ivanhoe," the castle of Front de Bœuf.

Torso Belvedere. A celebrated sitting figure (Hercules), signed by Apollonius of Athens: in the Vatican, Rome.

Tosca, La. An opera (1900) by Puccini, based on Sardou's drama (1887): libretto by Illica and Giacosa.

Tottel's (tot'lz) **Miscellany.** The first poetical miscellany in English, issued 1557 by Richard Tottel. The principal authors represented were Wyatt, Surrey, and Nicholas Grimald.

Touchstone. A philosophical clown in Shakspere's "As You Like It."

Tower Hill. A hill northwest of the Tower of London, formerly the place of execution of those sentenced for treason.

Tower of London, The. The ancient palace-citadel of London, on the Thames at the southeast angle of the old walled city. The present building goes back to William the Conqueror. It has been palace, prison, mint, and arsenal.

Tower of the Winds, The. The water-clock erected by the Syrian Andronicus Cyrrhestes at Athens in the 1st century B.C.: surmounted by a weather-vane of a bronze Triton.

Toxophilus (tok-sof'i-lus): **The Schools and Partitions of Shooting.** A treatise (1545) on archery, by Roger Ascham.

Toynbee (toin'bē) **Hall.** A club-like college in Whitechapel, London, founded 1885 to provide education and recreation for the poor districts of London.

Trachiniæ (tra-kin'i-ē). A play by Sophocles. Its theme is the death of Heracles at Trachis.

Tractarians (trak-tā'ri-ạnz), or **Puseyites** (pū'zi-īts), **The.** The adherents of the doctrines of the Oxford School, as set forth in the Tracts for the Times.

Tract No. 90. The last of the "Tracts for the Times," written by Newman. It attempts to reconcile the Thirty-nine Articles of the Church of England with the doctrines of the Council of Trent. It resulted in Newman's entering the Roman Catholic Church.

Tracts for the Times, or **Oxford Tracts.** Ninety pamphlets (Oxford, 1833–41) setting forth the doctrinal basis of the Tractarian movement toward primitive, patristic Christianity and sacramentalism, and away from liberalism and rationalism.

Traddles (trad'lz), **Thomas.** A simple and honest friend of David in Dickens's "David Copperfield." His talent for the cultivation of difficulties leads him to marry one of the "ten daughters of a poor curate."

Trafalgar (trạ-fal'gär) **Square.** A square in London, containing the monument commemorating Nelson's victory over the French (1805).

---

fat, fāte, fär, fåll, åsk, fāre; net, mē, hėr; pin, pīne; not, nōte, mŏve, nôr; up, lūte, pùll; oi, oil; ou, out; (lightened) avīạry, ẹlect, agǫny, intǫ, ụnite; (obscured) errạnt, operä, ardẹnt, actǫr, natụre; ch, chip; g, go; ᴛh, thin; ᴛʜ, then; y, you;

Tragic Comedians, The. A novel (1881) by George Meredith.

Traitors' Gate. The Southwark end of London Bridge, where after 1577 were exhibited the heads of persons put to death for treason.

Trajan's Wall. 1. Remnants of a Roman fortification in Bessarabia, between the Pruth and the Black Sea. 2. Similar remnants in the Dobrudja, between the Danube and the Black Sea.

Tramping Methodist, The. A novel (1908) by Sheila Kaye-Smith.

Transcendentalists, The. See Dictionary, **transcendentalist.**

Transfiguration, The. A famous painting by Raphael, in the Vatican, Rome.

Trans-Siberian Railway, The. See **Siberian Railway.**

Transvaal War, The. See Dictionary, **Boer.**

Trappists (trap′ists). A Cistercian monastic order, founded 1140 in the village of Soligny-la-Trappe, Orne, France.

Trastevere (träs-tā′vä-rā). A working-men's quarter of Rome, on the right bank of the Tiber about the Janiculum.

Travailleurs de la Mer, Les (lä trȧ-vȧ-yèr dè lä mär). A novel (1866) of the Channel Islands, by Victor Hugo.

Travel Diary of a Philosopher, The. A book of travels (1925) by Count Hermann Keyserling, in search not of adventure but of truth.

Traveling Man, The. A drama (1910) by Lady Augusta Gregory.

Traveller, The. A famous poem (1765) by Goldsmith.

Traviata, La (lä trä-vē-ä′tä). An opera (1853) by Verdi.

Treasure Island. A tale (1883) of pirates and treasure, by R. L. Stevenson.

Treasury of Atreus, The. A subterranean structure at Mycenæ, in Argolis, of Cyclopean or Pelasgic origin.

Treaty Elm, The. The elm beneath which William Penn negotiated his treaty (1682) with the Indians. Its supposed site is occupied by a small park in Philadelphia.

Trebizond (treb′i-zond), **The Empire of.** A Byzantine realm (1204–1461) on the southern coast of the Black Sea.

Trent, The. A British steamer on which were seized (1861), by Captain Wilkes of the U. S. Navy, the Confederate commissioners to Europe, Mason and Slidell. The U. S. government disavowed the act.

Trent, The Council of. A famous council held at Trent, in Tyrol, intermittently from 1545 to 1563. It condemned the Reformation and formulated many of the present doctrines of the Roman Catholic Church.

Treveri (trev′e̯-rī). A Celtic or Germanic people of eastern Gaul, near the Moselle, in and after the time of Cæsar.

Trevi (trā′vē), **The Fountain of.** A celebrated fountain in Rome, just east of the Corso.

Trial of Jesus, The. A passion-play (1925) by John Masefield.

Triangulum Australe (trī-ang′gū-lum âs-trā′lē). A southern constellation having the form of a triangle.

Trianon, Le Grand (lè grän trē-ȧ-nôń). A long, low palace at Versailles, built by Louis XIV. for Mme. de Maintenon, and later used as a royal residence.

Trianon, Le Petit (pè-tē). The favorite abode of Marie Antoinette, a neo-classical villa in the park at Versailles.

Triboci (trib′ō-sī). A Germanic tribe mentioned by Cæsar, on the middle Rhine east of the Vosges.

Tribuna, La (lä trē-bö′nä). A room in the Uffizi Gallery, Florence, containing many noted works of art, among them the Medicean Venus.

Tribute-Money, The. 1. A fresco by Masaccio, in the Brancacci Chapel of the Carmine, Florence. 2. A painting (about 1514) by Titian, in the museum at Dresden.

Tricoteuses, Les (lä trē-ko-tèz). The women who, in the French Revolution, frequented tribunals and places of execution and sat calmly knitting.

Tridentine Council, The. Same as **Trent, The Council of.**

Triennial Act, The. An act of Parliament (1694) which limited the duration of Parliaments, and also the interval between them, to three years. See **Septennial Act, The.**

Trifels (trē′fels), **The.** A ruined imperial fortress near Annweiler, in the Rhine Palatinate. Richard the Lion-Hearted was imprisoned there in 1193.

Triglaw (trē′gläf). The chief divinity of the Pomeranian Slavs.

Trilby. A novel (1894) by Du Maurier, in which a hypnotist, Svengali, develops in Trilby, an artists' model, a wonderful singing voice.

Trim, Corporal. In Sterne's "Tristram Shandy," Uncle Toby's military servant.

Trimalchio (tri-mal′ki-ō). In the "Satiræ" of Petronius Arbiter, a rich and ignorant parvenu who gives an elaborate banquet.

Trimmers, The. An English group which (1680–90) followed the Marquis of Halifax in trimming between the Whigs and the Tories.

Trimurti (tri-mör′ti). The Hindu triad, Brahma, Vishnu, and Siva, associated in a triune impersonation of the Supreme Spirit.

Trinculo (tring′kṳ-lō). A jester in Shakspere's "Tempest."

Trinity Church. 1. A notable Episcopalian church in Boston, Mass., designed by H. H. Richardson and consecrated 1877. 2. One of the oldest religious foundations in New York City. The present building was erected 1846.

Trinity College. 1. The largest college of Cambridge University, founded 1546 by Henry VIII. 2. A college of Oxford University, founded 1554.

Trinity College, or **The University of Dublin.** The leading educational institution of Ireland, founded 1591 by Queen Elizabeth.

Trinity Hall. A college of Cambridge University, occupied chiefly by students of law: founded 1350.

Trinobantes (trin-ō-ban′tēz). A people which, in the early history of Britain, occupied the unforested parts of the present Essex and Middlesex.

Tripitaka (tri-pit′ạ-kạ̈). A collective name for the 3 classes into which fall the sacred writings of the southern Buddhists: Sutrapitaka, Vinayapitaka, Abhidharmapitaka.

Triple Alliance, The. 1. A league (1668) of England, Sweden, and the Netherlands against France. 2. A league (1717) of France, Great Britain, and the Netherlands against Spain. 3. A league (1883) of Germany, Austria-Hungary, and Italy, originally against Russia. It became inoperative on the outbreak of the World War of 1914–18.

Triple Alliance, The War of the. A war (1865–70) of Paraguay against Brazil, Uruguay, and Argentina, resulting disastrously to Paraguay.

Triple Entente, The. See Dictionary, **triple.**

Tripolitan War, The. A Mediterranean war (1801–05) between the United States and Tripoli, caused by the depredations of the Tripolitan corsairs.

Triptolemus (trip-tol′e̯-mus). In Greek mythology, a favorite of Demeter: the inventor of the plow and patron of agriculture.

Trismegistus. See Dictionary, **Hermes Trismegistus.**

Tristan (tris′tạn). See **Tristram of Lyonnesse, Sir.**

Tristan und Isolde (tris′tän únt ē-zol′dè). 1. An epic poem of the latter half of the 12th century, by Eilhard von Oberge. 2. A famous epic poem of the late 12th century, by Gottfried von Strassburg. 3. An opera (1865) by Wagner.

Tristram (tris′trạm) **of Lyonnesse, Sir.** One of the most famous knights of the Round Table. His love for Iseult (Yseult, Isolde), wife of King Mark, is the subject of innumerable romances. Also, **Tristan.**

Tristram Shandy (shan′di), **The Life and Opinions of.** An eccentric novel (1759–67) by Sterne, more famous for the characters of Walter Shandy, his wife, his brother Uncle Toby, and the Widow Wadman than for that of the title character, who is not even born until late in the narrative.

Trita (tri-tä′). A Vedic god who appears principally in combat with demons and dragons.

Triton (trī′ton). In classical mythology, a son of Poseidon and Amphitrite, with whom he dwelt in a golden submarine palace. In later myth, there are many Tritons, companions of the Nereids.

Triumph of Cæsar, The. A series of 9 paintings in tempera on linen, each 9 feet square, by Mantegna, in Hampton Court Palace, England.

Triumph of Death, The. A fresco in the Campo Santo, Pisa, formerly ascribed to Orcagna, but now to the Lorenzetti (before 1350).

(variable) ḍ as d or j, ş as s or sh, ṭ as t or ch, ẓ as z or zh; o, F. cloche; ü, F. menu; ċh, Sc. loch; ń, F. bonbon; ′, primary accent; ″, secondary accent; †, obsolete; <, from; +, and; =, equals. See also lists at beginning of book.

Triumph of Silenus, The. A painting by Rubens, in the Old Museum, Berlin.

Triumph of the Egg, The. A book of impressions of American life (1921) by Sherwood Anderson.

Triumvirate (trī-um′vi-rāt), **The First.** An alliance, with division of power (60 B.C.), of Julius Cæsar, Pompey, and Crassus.

Triumvirate, The Second. An alliance, with division of power (43 B.C.), of Octavius, Mark Antony, and Lepidus.

Trivia (triv′i-ȧ), **or the Art of Walking the Streets of London.** A delightful burlesque poem (1716) by Gay.

Trocadéro (trō-kä-dā-rō). A square in Paris on the right bank of the Seine, opposite the Champ-de-Mars.

Troilus (trō′i-lus). See **Cressida.**

Troilus and Cressida (kres′i-dȧ). 1. A poem by Chaucer, based on Boccaccio's "Filostrato": written about 1382. 2. A tragedy by Shakspere, thought to be a revision of an older play: produced about 1600. 3. A rewritten version of Shakspere's play by Dryden, published 1678.

Trois Couleurs, Les (lā trwo kö-lėr). A popular French song, written by Adolphe Vogel to celebrate the return of the tricolor (1830).

Trois Mousquetaires, Les (lā trwo mös-kė-târ). A romance of adventure (1844) in the time of Richelieu, by Dumas *père*. The three guardsmen are Athos, Porthos, and Aramis. The chief character is D'Artagnan. This romance is the first of a trilogy, the other volumes being "Twenty Years After" (1845) and "The Vicomte de Bragelonne" (1847), which is in two parts, "Louise de La Vallière" and "The Man in the Iron Mask."

Trojan Cycle, The. A group of legends or poems relating to the Trojan War.

Trojan War, The. In Greek legend, a ten years' war waged by the Greeks under Agamemnon, king of Mycenæ and Argolis, against the Trojans and their allies, for the recovery of Helen, wife of Menelaus, king of Sparta (and brother of Agamemnon), who had been carried off by Paris, son of Priam, king of Troy.

Trotter, Job. In Dickens's "Pickwick Papers," the servant of Alfred Jingle.

Trotwood, Betsey. In Dickens's "David Copperfield," David's eccentric but kind-hearted great-aunt.

Troublesome Reign of King John, The. See **King John.**

Trovatore, Il (ēl trō-vä-tō′rä). A very popular opera (1853) by Verdi.

Troy (troi). An ancient city of the Troad, famed as the object of the Greek siege in the Trojan War: held by Schliemann and others to have been on the site of the Greek Ilium (the modern Hissarlik).

Truce of God, The. A suspension of hostilities or feuds on holy days, etc., observed at various times in the 11th and 12th centuries by countries of Europe.

True Thomas. See **Thomas the Rhymer.**

Trulliber (trul′i-bėr), **Parson.** In Fielding's "Joseph Andrews," a coarse curate, the antithesis of Parson Adams.

Trunnion (trun′yon), **Commodore Hawser.** See **Peregrine Pickle, The Adventures of.**

Truth, The. A drama (1906) by Clyde Fitch.

Tsimshian (tsim-shē-än′). The chief division of the Chimmesyan stock of North American Indians, living mainly on Skeena River, western British Columbia.

Tubal (tū′bȧl). One of the sons of Japheth. Gen. x. 2.

Tubal-cain (tū′bȧl-kān′). Son of Lamech and Zillah: a pioneer in brass and iron work. Gen. iv. 22.

Tübingen (tü′bing-en) **School, The.** A modern rationalistic school of interpretation of the New Testament. It had its rise (1825–60) at the University of Tübingen, Germany, under F. C. Baur.

Tuck, Friar. See **Friar Tuck.**

Tucunas (tö-kö′näz). Indians of the upper Amazon and its Peruvian and Brazilian branches. They are harmless savages, among whom the Jesuits labored 1683–1727.

Tudor (tū′dor). An English dynasty descended on the male side from Owen Tudor, on the female side from John of Gaunt through the Beauforts. Henry VII., Henry VIII., Edward VI., Mary, and Elizabeth were Tudors.

Tugendbund (tö′gent-bunt). A German association formed at Königsberg, 1808, with the secret aim of throwing off the French yoke. It was nominally dissolved in 1809, but actually continued influential for some years.

Tuileries (twē′le-riz, F. twēl-rē), **The Palace of the.** A former royal residence in Paris, connected with the Louvre. It was begun by Catharine de' Medici. In 1792 it was the seat of the Convention. It was burned by the Commune in 1871.

Tulkinghorn (tul′king-hôrn), **Mr.** A character in Dickens's "Bleak House," the family solicitor of Sir Leicester Dedlock.

Tullia (tul′i-ȧ). In Roman legend, a daughter of Servius Tullius. As wife of Lucius Tarquinius, she rode to the senate-house to greet her husband as king, and on her return drove over the dead body of her father, whom Tarquinius had murdered.

Tulliver (tul′i-vėr), **Maggie.** In George Eliot's "Mill on the Floss," the miller's daughter. Her generous impulsiveness exposes her to the condemnation of the unsympathetic. With her brother Tom, whose character is the opposite of hers, she is drowned in a flood.

Tunguses (tŏng-gö′zez). A nomadic Mongolian people of eastern and central Siberia, east of the Yenisei and in the Amur basin.

Tupi (tö′pē). One of the most important of the South American Indian linguistic stocks, extending over much of Brazil, Paraguay, and Uruguay.

Tupis (tö′pēz). A general name for Brazilian Indians of the Tupi stock, especially near the coast.

Tupman (tup′man), **Tracy.** In Dickens's "Pickwick Papers," a member of the Pickwick Club who is particularly susceptible to the tender passion.

Tur (tör). In the Shahnamah, the second of the three sons (Salm, Tur, Iraj) of Faridun.

Turin (tū′rin), **The Treaty of.** 1. A peace (1696) between France and Savoy. 2. An armistice (1796) between Napoleon and Sardinia.

Turveydrop (tėr′vi-drop), **Mr.** A fatuous "model of deportment" in Dickens's "Bleak House."

Tusayan (tö-sä-yän′). A confederacy of North American Indian tribes inhabiting pueblos on the summits of mesas in northeastern Arizona. Also, **Tuçayan.**

Tuscarora (tus-kȧ-rō′rä). A tribe of North American Indians, now in New York and Ontario. In colonial days they inhabited North Carolina.

Tusculan (tus′kū-lȧn) **Disputations, The.** A work in 5 books by Cicero, consisting of conversations represented as taking place at Cicero's estate at Tusculum.

Tuskegee Institute (tus-kē′gē). A school at Tuskegee, Alabama, for the education and training of negroes: founded 1880, and organized by Booker T. Washington.

Tussaud's (tu-sōz′) **Waxworks, Madame.** A collection of waxworks representing notable persons and various curiosities, on the Marylebone Road, London. The original collection was made by Madame Tussaud, a Swiss, and brought to London 1802.

Tuxedo (tuk-sē′dō) **Club, The.** A fashionable club whose house is at Tuxedo, New York.

Tvashtri (twash′tri). In Hindu mythology, the artisan of the gods: the Hephæstus (Vulcan) of the Indian pantheon.

Tweedledum and **Tweedledee.** In Lewis Carroll's "Alice's Adventures in Wonderland," two identical characters who fight about nothing. The phrase comes from a couplet written by Byrom (d. 1763) about the contention between adherents of Handel and of Buononcini:

"Strange all this difference should be
'Twixt Tweedledum and Tweedledee."

Tweed Ring, The. A group of Tammany Hall politicians who, under the leadership of William M. Tweed, got control of the financial affairs of New York City about 1870 and misappropriated millions of dollars.

Twelfth Night, or What You Will. A comedy (1602) by Shakspere.

Twelve Tables, The. The tables on which were promulgated, in Rome (451–450 B.C.), the rules of law which were most important in daily affairs.

Twenty-one Demands, The. Demands made upon China by Japan in 1915, which secured for Japan predominance in Shantung.

---

fat, fāte, fär, fȧll, ȧsk, fâre; net, mē, hėr; pin, pīne; not, nōte, möve, nôr; up, lūte, pull; oi, oil; ou, out; (lightened) aviȧry, ēlect, agŏny, intŏ, ūnite; (obscured) errȧnt, operä, ardent, actor, natũre; ch, chip; g, go; th, thin; ŦH, then; y, you;

Twenty Years After. See **Vingt Ans Après.**

Twice-Told Tales. Two series (1837, 1842) of fanciful tales by Hawthorne.

Two Drovers, The. A tale (1827) by Scott.

Two Foscari (fos'kä-rē), **The.** A tragedy (1821) by Byron.

Two Gentlemen of Verona, The. A comedy (before 1595) by Shakspere.

Two Lives. A poem (1925) by William Ellery Leonard: a tragedy of love and insanity.

Two Noble Kinsmen, The. A play based on the tale of Palamon and Arcite, by Fletcher and another (perhaps Shakspere): printed 1634.

Two Sicilies (sis'i-liz), **The Kingdom of the.** The united kingdom of Sicily and southern Italy, at various periods from the 12th century to the 19th.

Two Years before the Mast. A narrative (1840) of life at sea, by Richard Henry Dana.

Tybalt (tib'alt). Juliet's cousin in Shakspere's "Romeo and Juliet." He forces a quarrel in which he kills Mercutio, and is in turn killed by Romeo.

Tyburn (tī'bėrn). A former place of public execution in London: named from a former small tributary of the Thames.

Tyburnia (tī-bėr'ni-ä). A fashionable quarter of London, north of Hyde Park: named from the former Tyburn.

Tyburn Road. See **Oxford Street.**

Tyburn Tree. Before 1783, the public gallows in London.

Tyche (tī'kē). In Greek mythology, the goddess of fortune: corresponding to the Roman Fortuna.

Tydides (ti-dī'dēz). Diomedes, son of Tydeus.

Tyltyl (til'til). A child in Maeterlinck's drama "The Blue Bird." See **Mytyl.**

Tyndaridæ (tin-dar'i-dē). Castor and Pollux, by one account the sons of Leda and Tyndareus.

Tynewald (tin'wold), **The.** The independent bicameral parliament of the Isle of Man.

Typee. An account of adventures in the South Sea Islands (1846) by Herman Melville.

Typhon. See **Set.**

Typhoon. A story (1903) by Joseph Conrad.

Tyr (tēr). In Norse mythology, the god of war and victory, son of Odin. He is represented with one hand, the other having been bitten off by the wolf Fenrir.

Tzigane, La (lä tsē-gän). An opera (1877) by Strauss.

Tzumé (tzö-mā'). A traditional or perhaps mythical hero of the Tupi Indians of Brazil.

U

Ubii (ū'bi-ī). A Germanic people dwelling, in Cæsar's time, on the right bank of the Rhine, north of the Taunus region.

Uchean (ū-chē'an), or **Yuchi** (yö'chē). A linguistic stock of North American Indians, formerly of the coastal part of South Carolina. A few survive in Oklahoma.

Uffizi (öf-fēt'sē). One of the world's chief art galleries, situated in Florence near the Arno, and connected with the Pitti galleries by a covered gallery over the Ponte Vecchio: founded in the 15th century.

Uigurs (ö-ē'görz). A Turkish people dwelling chiefly in the Tian-shan region of Central Asia.

Uiracocha (wē-rä-kō'chä). The supreme deity of the ancient Peruvians.

Ulm (ŭlm), **The Capitulation of.** The surrender (1805) of Mack's Austrian army to Napoleon.

Ulm, The Truce of. A truce (1647) between the Franco-Swedish forces and the Bavarians.

Ulster, The Settlement or **Plantation of.** The colonization (1609-11) of large parts of Ulster with English and Scottish settlers.

Ulster Rebellion, The. An outbreak (1641) of the Irish in Ulster against the English colonists.

Ultramontane Party, The. In German politics before the World War, the Center party, which opposed legislation supposed to be anti-Catholic.

Ulysses (ū-lis'ēz). 1. The Latin name for Odysseus. 2. A poem (1842) by Alfred Tennyson. 3. A drama (1902) by Stephen Phillips. 4. A psychological novel (1922) by James Joyce.

Uma (ö'mä). A name of the goddess Devi.

Umatilla (ū-ma-til'ä). A tribe of Shahaptian Indians on the Umatilla reservation, Oregon.

Umbriel (um'bri-el). A dusky sprite in Pope's "Rape of the Lock."

Umbundu (öm-bön'dö). A native language of West African tribes which are settled between Benguella and the Kuangu River.

Una (ū'na). "A lovely ladie," the personification of truth, in Spenser's "Faerie Queene." She marries the Red Cross Knight.

Uncas (ung'kas). Son of Chingachgook, a Mohican chief: the title character of Cooper's "Last of the Mohicans."

Uncle Remus (rē'mus): **His Songs and His Sayings.** A collection (1880) of plantation tales and folklore, by J. C. Harris: followed (1883) by "Nights with Uncle Remus." The stories are presented as if told by an old plantation negro.

Uncle Toby. In Sterne's "Tristram Shandy," the brother of Walter Shandy: a retired captain, famous for his military pedantries, sentimentality, modesty, and gallantry. See **Wadman, Widow.**

Uncle Tom's Cabin. A novel about slavery (1852) by Harriet Beecher Stowe. It was enormously popular in the northern States, and had been translated into 9 languages before the end of 1852.

Uncommercial Traveller, The. A collection of sketches (1860) by Dickens.

Under the Greenwood Tree. A rural idyl in prose (1872) by Thomas Hardy.

Under Western Eyes. A novel (1911) by Joseph Conrad.

Undine (un'dēn, G. ün-dē'nė). A tale (1811) by Baron de La Motte-Fouqué. Undine is a water-sprite endowed with a soul by marriage with a mortal.

Undiscovered Country, The. A story (1880) by W. D. Howells.

Undying Fire, The. A novel (1919) by H. G. Wells.

Uniformity, The Act of. 1. An act of the English Parliament (1549) providing for uniformity of religious service. 2. An act of the English Parliament (1662) requiring clergymen to make oath of canonical obedience and to declare the unlawfulness of bearing arms against the sovereign.

Unigenitus Dei Filius (ū-ni-jen'i-tus dē'ī fil'i-us). A papal bull (1713) of Clement XI., condemning the Jansenists.

Union, The Act of. 1. A statute (1535-36) enacting the political union of Wales to England. 2. A statute (1706) uniting the kingdoms of England and Scotland from May 1, 1707.

Union Jack. See Dictionary, under **union.**

Union League Club, The. A social and political (Republican) club of New York City, organized 1863. Its house is at Park Avenue and 37th Street.

Union Square. A public park in New York City, bounded by Broadway, 14th Street, Fourth Avenue, and 17th Street.

United African Company, The. A British mercantile company formed for operation on the Niger: chartered (1886) as the Royal Niger Company.

United Brethren, The. See Dictionary, **Moravian.**

United Irishmen, The. An Irish society formed 1791 by Wolfe Tone for the purpose of procuring parliamentary reform and the repeal of the penal laws: later, a revolutionary secret society.

United Provinces, The. The 7 provinces of the Low Countries which formed (1579) the Union of Utrecht, thus laying the basis for the republic of the Netherlands. They were Holland, Zealand, Utrecht, Friesland, Gelderland, Groningen, and Overyssel.

United States, The. The American frigate in which (1812) Decatur captured the British frigate Macedonian.

University College. 1. The oldest college of Oxford University, established 1280. (There is a legend that it was founded 872 by King Alfred.) 2. A non-sectarian London college founded 1828. It is now part of the University of London.

Unknown Soldier, or **Unknown Warrior, The.** See Dictionary, under **unknown.**

Unlearned Parliament, The. A parliament convened (1404) at Coventry by Henry IV.: so named because

---

lawyers were excluded from it. Also called **Parliament of Dunces.**

Unleavened Bread. A novel (1900) by Robert Grant.

Unnatural Combat, The. A play (1619) by Massinger.

Unsocial Socialist, An. A novel (1883) by George Bernard Shaw.

Unter den Linden (ün'tér den lin'dẹn). A famous, very broad street of Berlin, on which are the university, the former imperial palace, the academy, etc.

Upanishads (ọ-pan'i-shadz). Very ancient speculative treatises of the Hindus: the basis of the philosophy of Hinduism, and the Veda of all educated Hindus.

Upper Chinook (chi-nök'). One of the divisions of the Chinookan stock of North American Indians, embracing 6 tribes.

Upper Rhine Circle, The. One of the 10 circles of the ancient German Empire, mainly west of the Rhine.

Upper Saxon Circle, The. One of the 10 circles of the ancient German Empire, in which the electorate of Saxony was included.

Ur (ér). The place from which Abraham set out for Canaan: probably Uru, identified with the ruins of Mughair on the Euphrates. Gen. xv. 7.

Urania (ū-rā'ni-ạ). In Greek mythology, the Muse of astronomy and celestial forces.

Uranus (ū'rạ-nus). In classical mythology, the son of Gæa (Earth) and by her the father of the Titans and the Cyclopes. Cronus (Time), the youngest of the Titans, overthrew him. Also, the outermost but one of the major planets.

Uriah (ū-rī'ạ). A Hittite officer, husband of Bathsheba. David contrived his death in battle. 2 Sam. xi.

Urian (ū'ri-ạn, G. ö'rẹ-än), **Sir.** A name formerly used to designate an unknown or unmentionable person.

Uriel (ū'ri-ẹl). 1. One of the seven archangels, mentioned in 2 Esdras as the good angel. 2. An archangel in Milton's "Paradise Lost." 3. An archangel in Longfellow's "Golden Legend."

Urim (ū'rim) and **Thummim** (thum'im). Mystical objects (or parts of one object) in a pouch upon the breastplate worn by the high priests of Israel: evidently connected with a mode of divination. Their exact nature is not known. Ex. xxviii. 30.

Urner Loch (ür'nér loch), **The.** A tunnel between the Devil's Bridge and Andermatt in the St. Gotthard Pass, Switzerland.

Ursula (ér'sụ-lạ), **Saint.** In Christian legend, a British saint and martyr, said to have been put to death, with 11,000 virgins, by an army of Huns at Cologne.

Urugal (ö-rö-gäl'). The 'great city': the Hades of the Babylonians.

Urvashi (ör'vạ-shē). In the Rig-Veda, 'longing,' 'desire,' personified as a woman loved by Pururavas.

Usbegs (us'begz). A Turkish people of various central Asian cities, where they form the influential class.

Ushas (ö-shas'). In the Vedas, the Dawn, daughter of the Sky and sister of Night.

Usipetes (ū-sip'ẹ-tēz). A Germanic tribe defeated by Cæsar on the left bank of the Rhine near the confluence of the Maas.

Uskoks (ús'koks). Fugitives from Bosnia and Serbia who went to Venetian and Hungarian lands in the 16th century to escape Turkish tyranny.

Utatlán (ö-tät-län'). The ancient seat of the Quiché Indians of Guatemala, near the modern Santa Cruz del Quiché.

Ute (ūt). An important division, embracing 15 tribes, of the Shoshonean stock of North American Indians, now on reservations in Colorado and Utah.

Utgard (öt'gärd). See **Jötunheim.**

Utgard-Loki (öt'gärd-lö'kẹ). In Norse mythology, the chief of the giants. His dwelling-place was Utgard.

Utopia (ū-tō'pi-ạ). A political romance (in Latin, 1516) treating of an imaginary ideal commonwealth, by Sir Thomas More.

Utrecht (ū'trekt), **The Peace of.** The peace (1713) which, by means of several different treaties, ended the War of the Spanish Succession. It involved extensive transfers of territory among Great Britain, Austria, Spain, Prussia, and Portugal, in both Europe and the New World.

Utrecht, The Union of. See **United Provinces, The.**

Uxmal (öz-mäl'). A ruin covering several square miles in Yucatan, Mexico, 70 miles south of Merida, probably representing the culture of a Maya people.

Uz (uz). The home of Job, possibly in Hauran, Syria. Job, i. 1.

Uzziah (u-zī'ạ). A name of Azariah, king of Judah and son of Amaziah. 2 Chron. xxvi. 1.

Uzziel (u-zī'el or uz'i-el). In Milton's "Paradise Lost," an angel next in power to Gabriel.

V

Vach (väch). In the Rig-Veda, a feminine personification of speech; the Word (Logos): later identified with the goddess Sarasvati.

Vai (vī). A negro tribe of Liberia, north of Monrovia.

Vaikuntha (vī-kön'thạ). In later Hindu mythology, Vishnu's heaven, either in the northern ocean or on the eastern peak of the mythical Mount Meru.

Vainlove. A capricious character in Congreve's "Old Bachelor."

Vain Oblations. Stories (1914) by Katharine Fullerton Gerould.

Valentine. 1. Silvia's lover and Proteus's friend in Shakspere's "Two Gentlemen of Verona." 2. A gentleman attending the duke in Shakspere's "Twelfth Night." 3. The principal character in Congreve's "Love for Love." 4. In Goethe's "Faust," the brother of Gretchen. He is killed by Faust in a street affray.

Valentine and Orson (ôr'sọn). A romance of the Charlemagne cycle, about twins born in a forest. One, carried off by a bear, became uncouth; the other, Valentine, was found by King Pepin and became a courtier.

Vale of Content, The. A drama (1895) by Hermann Sudermann.

Valhalla (val-hal'ạ). In Old Norse mythology, the abode of Odin in Asgard; the paradise for heroic warriors slain in battle. See **Valkyrs.**

Valjean (väl-zhäṅ), **Jean.** The principal character of Victor Hugo's "Les Misérables."

Valkyrs (val'kirz). In Norse mythology, the company of handmaidens of Odin. They ride through the air to battle, and with their spears designate for Valhalla the heroes who shall fall.

Valley of Decision, The. A novel (1902) by Edith Wharton.

Valley of Humiliation, The. The place where Christian fights Apollyon in Bunyan's "Pilgrim's Progress."

Valley of the Shadow of Death, The. A valley which Christian must traverse on his way to the Celestial City, in Bunyan's "Pilgrim's Progress." See Ps. xxiii. 4.

Vallombrosa (väl-lom-brō'sä). A famous abbey east of Florence, founded about 1038 by Gualbert.

Valois (väl-wo), **The House of.** A French dynasty, 1328–1589: a branch of the Capetian family.

Vamana (vä'mạ-nạ). The fifth, or dwarf, incarnation of Vishnu: the subject of the Vamanapurana.

Vandals (van'dạlz). A Germanic race which in the 5th century ravaged Gaul and Spain, and, in 455, Rome.

Vanderdecken (van'dėr-dek-ẹn). The captain of the Flying Dutchman in the English form of that legend. He was condemned to sail round the Cape of Good Hope forever.

Vangiones (van-jī'ọ-nēz). In the time of Cæsar, a Germanic tribe on the left side of the middle Rhine.

Vanguard, The. The flagship of Nelson at the battle of the Nile.

Vanir (vä'nir). In Old Norse mythology, a race of gods originally at war with the Æsir (see **As**), but later received into Asgard. Frey and Freya were of the Vanir.

Vanity Fair. 1. In Bunyan's "Pilgrim's Progress," a fair which goes on perpetually in the town of Vanity. It symbolizes worldly ostentation and frivolity. 2. A novel by Thackeray (1847–48), regarded by many as his masterpiece. Its title is taken from Bunyan's "Pilgrim's Progress."

Varaha (vạ-rä'hạ). The third, or boar, incarnation of Vishnu.

Varangians (vạ-ran'ji-ạnz). Norse warriors who ravaged the coast of the Baltic about the 9th century. They formed the Varangian Guard of the Byzantine emperors about the 11th century.

Varden (vär′dẹn), **Dolly.** In Dickens's "Barnaby Rudge," the coquettish daughter of a prosperous locksmith.

Varennes (và-ren), **The Flight to.** An unsuccessful attempt of the French royal family to escape, June 20–22, 1791.

Varney (vär′ni), **Richard.** The villainous master of horse to the Earl of Leicester, in Scott's "Kenilworth."

Varuna (va′rö-nạ). In Vedic mythology, a supreme god of the heavens, ruling over the waters, the night, and the West, and judging and punishing wrong-doers.

Vashti (vash′tī). The queen of Ahasuerus. Esther, i. 9–22.

Vathek (vath′ek). A pseudo-Oriental romance by William Beckford: originally written in French (1782).

Vatican (vat′i-kạn), **The.** A hill in Rome, on the right bank of the Tiber, opposite the Pincian. On it are St. Peter's and the Vatican Palace.

Vatican Council, The. The 20th ecumenical council (1869–70). It affirmed the infallibility of the Pope when speaking *ex cathedra.*

Vatican Fragments, The. Parts of a summary of rules of law derived from the writings of jurisconsults and from imperial constitutions, 163–372: discovered in the Vatican Library, and published 1823.

Vatican Palace, The. The chief residence of the Popes since 1377. It is supposed to contain some 11,000 rooms, halls, chapels, etc.

Vauxhall (väks′hâl) **Gardens.** A former popular pleasure resort in London, on the Thames above Lambeth.

Veda (vā′dạ). The Hindu sacred scripture. See Dictionary.

Vedanta (vạ-dän′tạ). A Hindu system of philosophy and theology, founded on the Vedas.

Veddahs (ved′ạz). An ancient people of Ceylon, possibly aboriginal.

Vega (vē′gạ). A brilliant star of the first magnitude, white in color, in the constellation Lyra.

Vehmgerichte (fām′gẹ-rich″tė). Medieval tribunals in Germany, chiefly in Westphalia, in the 14th and 15th centuries.

Vendée (lä von̈-dā), **The War of La.** The royalist war (1793–96) against the French Revolution, carried on chiefly in Vendée and Brittany.

Vendôme, Place (plàs von̈-dōm). A public square in Paris, north of the Seine.

Vendôme Column, The. A column erected (1806–10) by Napoleon in the Place Vendôme in honor of the Grand Army. It was destroyed 1871 by the Commune, but replaced 1875.

Veneti (ven′ẹ-tī). 1. An ancient people which dwelt near the head of the Adriatic. 2. An ancient Celtic people of Brittany, near the Bay of Biscay: subdued by Cæsar 56 B.C.

Venice as Queen of the Sea. An allegorical painting by Tintoretto, on the ceiling of the Sala del Collegio in the ducal palace, Venice.

Venice Preserved. 1. A historical tragedy (1682) by Otway. 2. A drama (1904) by Hugo von Hofmannsthal.

Venner (ven′ėr), **Elsie.** The heroine of O. W. Holmes's "Elsie Venner" (1861), a girl who owes abnormal peculiarities to a snake-bite received by her mother.

Venus (vē′nus). The Roman counterpart of Aphrodite.

Venus and Adonis (ạ-dō′nis). 1. A narrative poem (1593) by Shakspere. 2. A painting (1647) by Guercino, in the museum at Dresden. 3. A painting by Rubens, in the Hermitage Museum, Leningrad. 4. A painting by Veronese, in the Royal Museum, Madrid.

Venusberg (vā′nus-berċh). The Hörselberg, between Eisenach and Gotha. According to medieval legend, Venus held her pagan court in the caverns of this mountain.

Venus Genetrix (vē′nus jen′ẹ-triks). 1. A Roman copy of a Greek original held to represent a celebrated work by Alcamenes: in the Louvre, Paris. 2. An antique marble statue, held to be a copy of a bronze statue by Arcesilaus: in the Vatican Museum.

Venus of Cnidus, The. The best antique reproduction of the type of the famous statue by Praxiteles, in the Vatican, Rome.

Venus of Medici, The. An antique Greek original statue of marble, in the Tribuna of the Uffizi, Florence.

Venus of Melos, The. The most famous extant Greek statue of antiquity, found 1820 in the island of Melos, and now in the Louvre, Paris.

Venus of Milo, The. The same as **Venus of Melos, The.**

Venus of the Hermitage, The. An antique statue of Parian marble, found 1859 in Rome, and now in the Hermitage Museum, Leningrad.

Venus of the Shell, The. A painting (1520) by Titian, in Bridgewater House, London.

Venus of Urbino, The. A masterpiece by Titian, in the Tribuna of the Uffizi, Florence. It is the portrait of Eleonora Gonzaga, duchess of Urbino.

Vêpres Siciliennes, Les (lä vặpr sē-sē-lyen). An opera (1855) by Verdi.

Veragua (vā-rä′gwä), **The Dukes of.** The successors to the honors of Christopher Columbus. The original dukedom was awarded Luis Columbus on his abandonment (1536) of his claim to the viceroyalty of the Indies.

Vercelli (ver-chel′lē) **Book, The.** A manuscript collection of Anglo-Saxon verse and prose, discovered (1822) at Vercelli, Italy.

Verdun (ver-dun̈), **The Treaty of.** A treaty made 843 by the sons of Louis le Débonnaire, whereby the boundaries of the later France, Germany, and Italy were partly fixed.

Vere de Vere, Lady Clara. A poem (1842) by Tennyson, praising simple goodness and condemning aristocratic pride.

Verlorene Handschrift, Die (dē fer-lō′rẹ-nė hänt′shrift). 'The Lost Manuscript,' one of the chief novels (1864) of Freytag.

Vernon (ver′non), **Di (Diana).** In Scott's "Rob Roy," a high-spirited royalist beauty.

Verona, The Congress of. A European congress (1822) which resulted in the intervention (1823) of France in Spain.

Veronica (vẹ-ron′i-kạ), **Saint.** In Christian legend, a woman who gave to Jesus on his way to Calvary a cloth to wipe his brow. Upon the cloth was miraculously left a likeness of his face.

Versailles (ver-sälz′, F. ver-sä-y′), **The Preliminaries of.** The preliminaries of peace between France and Germany (Feb., 1871): ratified by the treaty of Frankfort.

Versailles, The Treaty of. The treaty (1919) made by the Entente allies with Germany at the close of the World War of 1914–18. Its terms left Germany at the mercy of the allies economically, stripped her of her colonial empire, and made provision for the League of Nations.

Vertumnus (ver-tum′nus). The Roman divinity of gardens and orchards, worshiped as the god of spring.

Vesta (ves′tạ). The ancient Roman goddess of the hearth and hearth-fire: corresponding to the Greek Hestia.

Vestini (ves-tī′nī). An ancient people of central Italy, probably akin to the Sabines, their western neighbors.

Veta Madre (vā′tä mä′drä). A silver lode about 8 miles long, near Guanajuato, Mexico: discovered 1558.

Via (vī′ạ) **Æmilia, Via Appia,** etc. See **Æmilian Way, Appian Way,** etc.

Via Dolorosa (dol-ọ-rō′sä). A name given to the road from the Mount of Olives to Golgotha.

Via Egnatia (eg-nā′shi-ạ). A Roman military road 534 Roman miles long, from Dyrrachium (Durazzo) on the Adriatic to Cypsela (Ipsala). It traversed Illyria, Macedonia, and Thrace.

Via Latina (lạ-tī′nạ). The great Roman highway from Rome to Casilinum (near Capua). Its course was followed by the invasions of Pyrrhus and Hannibal.

Via Mala (vē′ä mä′lä). A picturesque road south of Tusi, canton of Grisons, Switzerland, traversing a deep and narrow chasm.

Vicar of Bray, The. A well-known song, long attributed to a soldier of George I. A version dating from Queen Anne's time has been found.

Vicar of Wakefield, The. A sentimental and humorous novel (1766) by Goldsmith. Dr. Primrose, the vicar, is a simple-minded country clergyman who preserves his modesty and nobility through good and ill fortune.

Vicinal (vis′i-nạl) **Way, The.** An old Roman road in Britain, by which produce was brought from Essex farms to London.

Victoria. In Roman mythology, victory personified.

Victoria, La. One of the vessels of Magalhães (Magellan).

1519–21. She was the only one to return around the Cape of Good Hope, and was thus the first vessel known to have circumnavigated the globe.

Victoria, The. A British armored battle-ship sunk off Tripoli, Syria, June 22, 1893, by collision with a companion vessel, the Camperdown. Nearly 340 lives were lost.

Victoria Bridge. A tubular iron bridge across the St. Lawrence at Montreal, built by Robert Stephenson 1854–59: replaced (1898) by the Victoria Jubilee Bridge.

Victoria Tower. The tall tower on the Houses of Parliament, London.

Victory. 1. A Greco-Roman statue in bronze, in the Museo Antico at Brescia. 2. A novel (1915) by Joseph Conrad.

Victory, The. The flag-ship of Lord Nelson at Trafalgar.

Victory, The Wingless. See **Nike Apteros.**

Victory Loosing Her Sandal. A famous relief from the balustrade of the Temple of Nike Apteros, now in the Acropolis Museum, Athens. It is of the early 4th century B.C.

Victory of Lepanto, The. A memorial picture by Veronese, in the Sala del Collegio of the ducal palace at Venice.

Victory of Samothrace, The. A colossal statue of a winged figure, of Hellenistic date, found in Samothrace 1863, and now in the Louvre, Paris.

Vidar (vē′där). In Norse mythology, a powerful god, son of Odin and the giantess Grid.

Vienna, Sieges of. Vienna has been besieged twice, unsuccessfully, by the Turks: in 1529, by Sultan Solyman; and in 1683, by Kara Mustapha, when it was relieved by Sobieski and Charles, duke of Lorraine.

Vienna, The Congress of. A European congress (1814–15) for settling the affairs of Europe. It resulted in wholesale restorations and annexations of territory, the restoration of the Bourbons in France, the formation of the German Confederation, the creation of a new kingdom of Poland, etc.

Vienna, The Treaty of. 1. A treaty (1738) ending the War of the Polish Succession. 2. A treaty (1864) ending the Schleswig-Holstein war, Denmark renouncing all rights to the territory involved. 3. A treaty (1866) by which Austria ceded Venetia to Italy.

Vienna, The University of. A university founded 1365, especially notable for its medical faculty.

Vigilantes (vij-i-lǎn′tāz). In the California of the early 1850's, and in other western regions under frontier conditions, bodies of unofficial police organized among the citizens to preserve order and administer summary justice.

Vigiles (vij′i-lēz). In ancient Rome, a corps of police and firemen under military discipline.

Vikramorvashi (vi-krạ-mōr′vạ-shē). A celebrated drama by Kalidasa, second in merit, among Sanskrit plays, only to the Shakuntala.

Vili (vē′lē). In Norse mythology, a brother of Odin.

Villa Albani (vēl′lä äl-bä′nē). A Roman villa on the Salarian way, founded 1760 by Cardinal Alessandro Albani.

Villa Aldobrandini (äl″dō-brän-dē′nē). A villa at Frascati, near Rome, built for Cardinal Aldobrandini in the late 16th century.

Villa Borghese (bor-gā′zā). A villa just outside the Porta del Popolo, Rome. It was founded by Cardinal Scipio Borghese. It contains fine sculptures.

Villa Ludovisi (lö-dō-vē′zē). A villa within the walls of Rome, erected in the early 17th century by Cardinal Ludovisi. Its grounds were divided in 1885.

Villa Medici (med′ẹ-chē). A Roman villa south of the Pincio, built 1540. The Medicis acquired it about 1600. In it Galileo was confined 1630–33. In 1801 the French Academy of Art was transferred to it.

Villa Nazionale (nä″tsē-ō-nä′lä). The principal public park and promenade of Naples: formerly the Villa Reale. Its aquarium, belonging to the zoölogical station, was opened 1874.

Villa Pallavicini (päl″lä-vē-chē′nē). A villa at Pegli, Italy, famous for its elaborate decoration and its extensive gardens.

Villa Rica (vēl′yä rē′kä). The first town founded (1519) in Mexico by Cortes. It was in the vicinity of the present Vera Cruz.

Villette (vi-let′). A novel (1853) by Charlotte Brontë.

Viminal (vim′i-nạl), **The.** The northeasternmost of the seven hills of ancient Rome, north of the Esquiline.

Vinayapitaka (vin″ạ-yạ-pit′ạ-kä). That class of the sacred Buddhist writings which treats of the discipline of the order.

Vincy (vin′si), **Rosamond.** See **Lydgate, Dr.**

Vineam Domini (vin′ẹ-am dom′i-nī). An anti-Jansenist bull issued by Pope Clement XI. in 1705.

Vinegar Bible, The. An edition printed 1717 at the Clarendon Press, Oxford, with "Parable of the Vinegar" instead of ". . . Vineyard" as the heading of Luke, xx.

Vingt Ans Après (vaṅ-tän-zȧ-prā). A sequel (1845) to "Les Trois Mousquetaires," by Dumas père: followed (1848–50) by "Dix ans plus tard, ou le vicomte de Bragelonne."

Viola (vī′ọ-lạ). The heroine of Shakspere's "Twelfth Night." Disguised as a page, she wins the heart of the duke whose service she enters. She is embarrassed by the attentions of the Countess Olivia, who falls in love with her, but who eventually marries Viola's twin brother Sebastian.

Virgilia (vẹr-jil′i-ạ). The wife of Coriolanus, in Shakspere's "Coriolanus."

Virginia. In Roman legend, the daughter of Virginius, slain by him (449 B.C.) to save her from the decemvir Appius Claudius.

Virginia, The Army of. A Federal army which, under Pope, fought in the second battle of Bull Run (1862), after which it was discontinued.

Virginian, The. A novel (1902) of the American West, by Owen Wister.

Virginians, The. See **Henry Esmond.**

Virginia Plan, The. A sketch of a plan for a constitution, presented to the Constitutional Convention (1787) by Edmund Randolph of Virginia.

Virginia Resolutions, The. Resolutions declaring the Alien and Sedition Acts unconstitutional, prepared by Madison and passed (1798) by the Virginia legislature.

Virginius. See **Virginia.**

Virgin of the Rosary, The. A painting by Murillo, in the Royal Museum, Madrid.

Virgin Soil. A novel (1876) by Ivan Turgenev.

Visconti (vēs-kōn′tē). A famous Lombard family, which became prominent in the 11th century and long ruled Milan.

Vishnu (vish′nö). The second member of the Hindu triad (Brahma, Vishnu, Siva): regarded as the preserver, Brahma being the creator and Siva the destroyer. He is incarnated in ten principal avatars.

Vishnupurana (vish″nö-pö-rä′nạ). One of the most important of the puranas: the history of Vishnu.

Vision of Don Roderick, The. A narrative poem (1811) by Scott.

Vision of Ezekiel (ẹ-zē′ki-ẹl), **The.** A painting by Raphael, in the Pitti Gallery, Florence.

Vision of Judgment, A. A poem (1821) by Southey.

Vision of Judgment, The. A burlesque (1822) of Southey's poem, by Byron.

Vision of Mirza (mèr′zạ), **The.** An allegory of human life by Addison, in No. 159 of the "Spectator."

Vision of Piers Plowman, The. See **Piers Plowman.**

Vision of Sir Launfal (lȧn′fạl), **The.** A poem (1845) by James Russell Lowell, in which Sir Launfal, about to set out in quest of the Grail, learns in a vision that it is to be found at home in charitable and kindly deeds.

Vitalians (vi-tā′li-ạnz). A band of pirates of the Baltic and North seas about 1400.

Vita Nuova (vē′tä nwô′vä). A work of mingled prose and verse by Dante, finished about 1307.

Viti (vē′tē), or **Maviti** (mä-). A tribe of Zulu marauders in East Africa, who ravaged the region between the Rovuma and Rufiji rivers about 1850.

Vittoria Corombona (vi-tō′ri-ạ kor-ọm-bō′nạ), or **The White Devil.** A tragedy (1607) by Webster.

Vivian (viv′i-ạn). In Arthurian legend, an enchantress, the mistress of Merlin. Also, **Vivien.**

Vivian Grey. A brilliant early novel (1826–27) by Disraeli.

Vizcaya (vēth-kä′yä). A Spanish armored cruiser, taken by the U. S. S. Iowa off Santiago de Cuba, July 3, 1898.

Volpone (vol-pō′nẹ), **or the Fox.** A comedy (1605) by Jonson.

Volscians (vol′siạnz). An ancient Italian people in southern Latium, subdued by Rome late in the 4th century B.C.

Volsunga Saga (vol′sùng-gä sä′gä). In Old Norse literature, the mythical history of the Volsungs and Nibelungs. Its central hero is Sigurd (the Siegfried of the Nibelungenlied). It is the principal source of Wagner's "Ring des Nibelungen."

Volumnia (vō-lum′ni-ä). The mother of Coriolanus in Shakspere's "Coriolanus."

Völund. See **Wayland the Smith.**

Volunteers of America, The. A religious organization founded 1896 by Mr. and Mrs. Ballington Booth at the time of their separation from the Salvation Army.

Vorparlament (fōr′pär-lä-ment″). A provisional assembly at Frankfort-on-the-Main, 1848, which met to prepare the way for a German parliament.

Votan (vō-tän′). A hero-god of Indians of the Maya stock in southern Mexico and Guatemala.

Voyage autour de ma Chambre, Un (uṅ vwo-yäzh ō-tör de mä shäṅbr). A work (1794) by Xavier de Maistre. It is a whimsical account of what goes on in the mind of a soldier confined to barracks.

Voyage Out, The. A novel (1915) by Virginia Woolf.

Voysey Inheritance, The. A drama (1905) by Granville-Barker.

Vulcan (vul′kạn). The Roman counterpart of Hephæstus.

Vulcanalia (vul-kạ-nā′li-ạ). An ancient Roman festival in honor of Vulcan, celebrated August 23 with games and with sacrifice of fishes.

Vulgar Errors. See **Pseudodoxia Epidemica.**

Vulgate (vul′gāt). A Latin version of the Scriptures, accepted as the authorized version of the Roman Catholic Church. It was prepared by Jerome near the end of the 4th century. It was the first book printed (about 1455).

V. V.'s Eyes. A novel (1913) by Henry Sydnor Harrison.

Vye (vī), **Eustacia.** A beautiful, ill-fated woman in Hardy's "Return of the Native."

W

Wa-Bisa. See **Bisa.**

Wa-Bondei. See **Bondei.**

Wacht am Rhein, Die (dē vächt äm rīn). A German popular song, words (1840) by Schneckenburger, music (1854) by Karl Wilhelm. It was first extensively used 1870–71.

Wadham (wod′ạm) **College.** A college of Oxford University, founded 1612 by Nicholas Wadham.

Wadman (wod′mạn), **Widow.** In Sterne's "Tristram Shandy," a designing widow who seeks to captivate Uncle Toby.

Wagner (väg′nėr). Faust's pedantic famulus and interlocutor, in Goethe's "Faust."

Wahabis (wạ-hä′bēz). The followers of Abd al-Wahhab (1691?–1787?), a Mohammedan reformer. His successors formed a dominion in central Arabia, temporarily overthrown (1818) by Ibrahim Pasha.

Wahlverwandtschaften, Die (dē väl′fer-vänt″shäf-tẹn). "Elective Affinities," a psychological novel (1809) by Goethe.

Wahnfried (vän′frēt). The villa at Bayreuth in which Richard Wagner spent the closing years of his life.

Wakashan (wä′kash-ạn). A linguistic stock of North American Indians, on Vancouver Island and the opposite mainland, and also the region of Cape Flattery, Washington.

Wakefield Mystery Plays, The. A cycle of 32 naïve plays on Scriptural subjects, perhaps earlier than the 14th century. They were played at the fairs of Woodkirk or Widkirk, near Wakefield, England.

Wake Robin. Nature sketches (1871) by John Burroughs.

Walapai (wäl′ạ-pī). A tribe of North American Indians in Arizona, between the great bend of the Colorado and the Cerbat and Aquarius Mountains.

Walcheren (väl′chêr-ẹn) **Expedition, The.** An unsuccessful British expedition (1809) against the French on the island of Walcheren.

Walden, or Life in the Woods. An account (1854) by Thoreau of his life as a recluse at Walden Pond, Concord.

Waldenses (wol-den′sēz), or **Waldensians** (-siạnz). The members of a reforming body of Christians, followers of Pierre Waldo of Lyons, formed about 1170. They later joined the Reformation movement.

Walhalla. The same as **Valhalla.**

Walhalla (väl-häl′ä), or **Temple of Fame, The.** A building founded 1830 near Regensburg, Bavaria, by Ludwig I. It contains sculptured reliefs of scenes from German history, and busts of famous Germans.

Walküre, Die (dē väl-kü′rė). See **Ring des Nibelungen.**

Walla Walla (wol′ạ wol′ạ). A tribe of North American Indians of the northwest, now on the Umatilla reservation, Oregon.

Wallenstein (väl′ẹn-shtīn). A historical trilogy by Schiller: (1) "Wallensteins Lager," 1798; (2) "Die Piccolomini," 1799; (3) "Wallensteins Tod," 1799.

Wall of Antoninus, The. A rampart erected from the Firth of Forth to the Firth of Clyde, early in the reign of Antoninus Pius, to check the northern barbarians of Britain.

Wall of Aurelian, The. A fortified inclosure of part of Rome, including the Pincian, Monte Testaccio, the Vatican, and the Janiculum: begun A.D. 271.

Wall of China, The Great. A wall for defense against northern tribes, about 1,500 miles long, from Shanhaikwan along the northern frontiers of Chihli, Shansi, Shensi, and Kansu: begun by the emperor Tsin Chi-hwangti 214 B.C.

Walloon (wo-lön′) **Guard, The.** A Spanish body-guard (1703–1822) of Walloon troops.

Walloons. 1. A people found chiefly in southern Belgium, descended from the Belgæ with an admixture of Germanic and other elements. 2. In America, the Huguenots from Artois, many of whom came to colonial New York.

Walpurgis (väl-pur′gis) **Night.** 1. The night before May 1, when, according to German popular superstition, the witches hold revels on the Brocken in the Harz Mountains, in company with their master the devil. 2. A choral symphony (1833; revised 1844) by Mendelssohn, to words by Goethe.

Waltham Abbey. A restored abbey church in the town of Waltham Abbey, Essex. The original abbey was founded by King Harold.

Wamba (wom′bạ). In Scott's "Ivanhoe," a jester who risks his life to save his master, Cedric the Saxon.

Wampanoag (wom-pạ-nō′ag). A tribe of North American Indians which once occupied the eastern shore of Narragansett Bay. Massasoit and his son King Philip were of this tribe.

Wanda (won′dạ). A legendary Polish queen, said to have reigned about A.D. 700.

Wandering Jew, The. A legendary character condemned to roam without rest because he struck Christ on the day of crucifixion. "Thou shalt wander on the earth till I return," was the sentence pronounced upon him.

Wandering Willie. A blind fiddler in Scott's "Redgauntlet."

Wanyamwezi. See **Nyamwezi.**

Wapping (wop′ing). A quarter of London, along the north bank of the Thames below the Tower.

Wappinger (wop′in-jėr). A tribe or confederacy of North American Indians which occupied the east bank of the Hudson from Poughkeepsie to Manhattan Island: merged after 1640 with the Delawares.

War and Peace. A historical novel (1864–69) on the grand scale, by Tolstoy. It is a picture of Russian society during the Napoleonic wars.

Wardle (wär′dl), **Mr.** A genial country gentleman in Dickens's "Pickwick Papers," host and friend of the Pickwick Club and master of Joe, the fat boy.

War of 1812, The. A war (1812–15), largely naval, between the United States and Great Britain. It was occasioned by British interference with American shipping. The Treaty of Ghent was signed in December, 1814, but the news did not reach all the forces until well into the following year.

War of Liberation, The. The war undertaken by Germany (1813), with the aid of Russia, Great Britain, and other allies, to shake off the influence of Napoleon.

War of Secession, The. The American Civil War (1861–65).

War of the American Revolution, The. See Dictionary, revolution.

War of the Rebellion, The. The American Civil War (1861–65).

War of the Worlds, The. A romance (1898) by H. G. Wells.

Warori. See **Rori.**

(variable) ḍ as d or j, ṣ as s or sh, ṭ as t or ch, ẓ as z or zh; o, F. cloche; ü, F. menu; ch, Sc. loch; ṅ, F. bonbon; ′, primary accent; ″, secondary accent; †, obsolete; <, from; +, and; =, equals. See also lists at beginning of book.

Warrington, George. In Thackeray's "Pendennis," a clever, cynical, melancholy man, who is a true friend to Pendennis. His family appear in "The Virginians."

Warrior, The. The first English ironclad to be constructed entirely of metal: launched 1860.

Wars of the Roses, The. The prolonged struggle (1455–85) for the English throne between the rival houses of Lancaster (red rose) and York (white rose): so called from the badges of the two houses.

Wartburg (värt′bûrċh). A princely residence at Eisenach, Germany. In one of its buildings Luther found asylum, 1521–22.

Wartburg, The Contest of. A semi-legendary contest of minnesingers about 1206. It gave rise to an epic, "Der Krieg von Wartburg" (about 1300); and Wagner uses the idea in his "Meistersinger."

Wartburg, The Festival of. A commemorative festival of German students, arranged to celebrate the tercentenary of the Reformation: held on the 4th anniversary (Oct. 18, 1817) of the battle of Leipsic.

Waruanda. See **Ruanda.**

Warwick, Diana. The heroine of Meredith's "Diana of the Crossways," an Irish beauty and wit supposed to have been modeled to some extent upon Mrs. Caroline Norton.

Wasco (wäs′kō). A Chinook tribe of North American Indians, dwelling on the Warm Spring reservation, Oregon.

Washaki (wäsh′a̱-kē). The easternmost of the Shoshoni tribes of North American Indians: now on the Shoshoni reservation in western Wyoming.

Washington, The Treaty of. A treaty (1871) between the United States and Great Britain, providing for the settlement of the Alabama claims, the fisheries dispute, and the San Juan boundary.

Washington Arms Conference, The. See **Limitation of Armaments, The Conference for.**

Washington Centennial Arch, The. An arch, erected 1890–92, over the Fifth Avenue entrance to Washington Square, New York City.

Washington Elm, The. A venerable elm in Cambridge, Massachusetts, under which Washington assumed command of the Continental forces in 1775: cut down in 1924.

Washington Monument, The. An obelisk-shaped tower of white marble, 555 feet high, built (1848–84) in the city of Washington in honor of George Washington.

Wasoga. See **Soga.**

Wasps, The. A comedy (422 B.C.) by Aristophanes.

Waste. A drama (1907) by Granville-Barker.

Waterloo Bridge. A bridge over the Thames at London, designed and built (1811–17) by John Rennie. It was opened on the 2d anniversary of the battle of Waterloo.

Waterloo Place. A square in London, between Carlton House Terrace and Regent Street. In its center is the Crimean monument.

Water Music, The. A series of 21 movements by Handel, played by an orchestra on a boat in which the composer followed the barge of George I. as he proceeded to Whitehall in 1715.

Watling (wot′ling) **Street.** One of the principal Roman roads in Britain. It ran from Dover through Canterbury and London to Chester. Also, a name given to the Milky Way.

Watson, Doctor. The friend and confidant of Sherlock Holmes, in many of the detective stories of A. Conan Doyle.

Wat (wot) **Tyler's Rebellion.** A revolt (1381) of peasants of Essex and Kent, who marched on London and took possession of the city under the leadership of Wat Tyler.

Waverley. A romance (1814) by Scott: the first of the Waverley novels. Its hero, Waverley, is a young Englishman involved in the Scottish Jacobite insurrection of 1745.

Waverley Dramas, The. A series of eight plays (1818–24) based on romances of Scott.

Waverley Novels, The. The romances of Scott, so called from "Waverley," the first of the series.

Wayland the Smith. In English folklore, an invisible, marvelously skilled smith: a counterpart of the Scandinavian Völund and the German Wieland.

Wayland Wood. A wood near Watton, England, the legendary scene of the murder of the "Babes in the Wood."

Way of All Flesh, The. A novel by Samuel Butler, published posthumously (1903). It expresses with pungent effect the author's impatience of family restraints and conventional requirements.

Way of the World, The. A comedy (1700) by Congreve.

Wealth of Nations, The. The chief work (1776) of Adam Smith, and the foundation of the science of political economy.

Weavers, The. A drama (1893) by Gerhart Hauptmann.

Weddahs. The same as **Veddahs.**

Wegg (weg), **Silas.** In Dickens's novel "Our Mutual Friend," a wooden-legged rascal employed by the ignorant Boffin to read to him. Wegg tries to blackmail his benefactor.

Weird Sisters, The. The three witches in Shakspere's "Macbeth," corresponding to the Norns of Scandinavian mythology.

Weissnichtwo (vīs′niċht-vō). An imaginary city in Carlyle's "Sartor Resartus."

Weitspekan (wīt′spek-a̱n). A linguistic stock of North American Indians, of the lower Klamath valley and the adjacent coast of northwestern California. It comprises the Yurok Indians.

Welfs (velfs). A German princely house, from which descended the Brunswick and Hanover lines. (**Guelph** is the Italianized form of the same name.)

Weller (wel′ēr), **Samuel.** In Dickens's "Pickwick Papers," the witty cockney servant of Mr. Pickwick.

Weller, Tony. In Dickens's "Pickwick Papers," the father of Sam Weller: a ruddy stage-coachman, memorable for his well-founded distrust of widows.

Well of the Saints, The. A drama (1905) by J. M. Synge.

Welsh Honeymoon, The. A one-act drama (1917) by Jeannette Marks which, together with "The Merry, Merry Cuckoo," won the prize in the Welsh National Theatre Competition.

Wemmick (wem′ik), **John.** In Dickens's "Great Expectations," a law clerk who is sentimental outside of business.

Wends (wendz). 1. An early name given by the Germans to their Slavic neighbors. 2. The Sorbs, a branch of the Slavic race living in Lusatia.

Wendy. The young girl in Barrie's "Peter Pan."

Werner (ver′nēr). A tragedy by Byron. The title-rôle was considered (1830) one of Macready's most effective parts.

Werther. An opera (1894) by Massenet.

Wessex (wes′eks). One of the Saxon kingdoms in Britain. Under Alfred's successors it developed into the kingdom of England. In the 10th and 11th centuries it was an earldom comprising the territory south of the Thames.

Wessex Novels, The. The novels by Thomas Hardy about the region in southwestern England which he calls Wessex, the name of the kingdom of the West Saxons.

West End, The. The aristocratic residential section of London.

Western, Sophia. In Fielding's "Tom Jones," the lovely and amiable daughter of Squire Western, a boisterous and irascible type of the fond father.

Western Empire, The. The western portion of the Roman realm after its division in A.D. 395.

Western Reserve, The. A tract of about 3,500,000 acres, now part of Ohio, reserved by Connecticut when that State ceded its western claims to the Government in 1786.

Westminster (west′min-stēr). A borough of London containing the abbey, Houses of Parliament, and government buildings.

Westminster, The Provisions of. Ordinances passed (1259) through the influence of the English barons in Parliament, for redress of grievances: supplementary to the Provisions of Oxford (1258).

Westminster Abbey. The most famous of London churches, rebuilt in the 13th century by Henry III. and Edward I. It is the burial-place of many of England's distinguished men.

Westminster Assembly, The. A convocation (1643–49) summoned by the Long Parliament to advise on the settling of the liturgy and other ecclesiastical affairs of England. Most of its members were Presbyterians. It evolved the Directory of Public Worship, the Confession of Faith, and the Larger and Shorter Catechisms.

Westminster Hall. A structure adjoining, on the west, the Houses of Parliament, to which it serves as a vestibule. It was formerly part of the ancient Palace of Westminster.

Westminster Palace. 1. The London Houses of Parliament. 2. A former royal residence in Westminster, supposed to have existed as early as the reign of Canute. It was burned in 1834.

Westminster School. A noted preparatory school at Westminster, England, first established by Henry VIII.

West-Östlicher Divan, Der (der vest′ĕst′lĭċh-ẽr dē-vän′). A collection (1819) of lyric poems by Goethe, partly on Oriental subjects.

Westphalia (west-fā′li-ạ), **The Peace of.** The treaties signed at Münster and Osnabrück (1648) which ended the Thirty Years' War. One of its principal results was to establish the autonomy of the German states. Switzerland and Holland achieved their independence.

Westphalian Circle, The. One of the former 10 circles of the German Empire. Cologne and Aix-la-Chapelle were the principal cities included.

Westward Ho! 1. A comedy (1607) by Dekker and Webster. 2. A historical romance (1855) by Kingsley, dealing with English seamen's adventures on the Spanish Main in the time of Drake.

What Every Woman Knows. A drama (1908) by Sir J. M. Barrie.

What Maisie Knew. A novel (1897) by Henry James.

What Price Glory. A drama (1924) by Laurence Stallings and Maxwell Anderson, combining a realistic and a romantic treatment of the World War.

What's O'Clock. A collection of poems (1925) by Amy Lowell.

When We Dead Awaken. A drama (1900) by Henrik Ibsen.

Where the Blue Begins. A fantasy (1922) by Christopher Morley.

Whigs (hwigz), **The.** 1. The more liberal of the two great English parties which arose late in the 17th century. 2. The patriotic or American party during the American Revolutionary period. 3. An American political party (1834–53) which favored a loose construction of the Constitution and a high protective tariff. It split on the question of slavery.

While Paris Laughed. A collection of stories (1918) by Leonard Merrick.

Whiskerandos (hwis-kẽr-an′dōz). A burlesque tragedy character in the interpolated play rehearsed in Sheridan's "Critic."

Whisky Rebellion, The. An outbreak (1794) in western Pennsylvania against an excise duty on spirits and on stills.

Whisky Ring, The. A conspiracy (1872–75) of distillers and government officials to defraud the U. S. government of excise taxes.

Whitby, The Synod of. An ecclesiastical council (664) at Whitby, England, to decide the Easter and tonsure questions. It resulted in the triumph of the Roman over the Celtic party.

Whiteboys. Members of an illegal agrarian association in Ireland, formed about 1761. It tried to secure justice by intimidation and terrorization.

Whitechapel. A quarter of eastern London inhabited by the poorer classes and by criminals.

Whitechapel Murders, The. A series of atrocious murders committed in Whitechapel about 1889 by a mysterious "Jack the Ripper." The victims were prostitutes.

White Company, The. 1. A band of freebooters led by Bertrand du Guesclin from France into Spain in 1366. 2. A band of English adventurers who ravaged northern Italy in the 14th century, under the leadership of Sir John Hawkwood. 3. A band of assassins organized in Toulouse in the 13th century by "the ferocious Folquet," bishop of Toulouse. 4. A historical romance (1891) by A. Conan Doyle, based on the career of Du Guesclin's band.

White Devil, The. See **Vittoria Corombona.**

Whitefriars. A London district, named from an order of Carmelites established there in 1241.

Whitehall. The main London thoroughfare between Trafalgar Square and the Houses of Parliament.

Whitehall Palace. A palace in London, originally built in the reign of Henry III.: partly destroyed by fire in 1615.

White Hart, The. A noted tavern in Southwark, London.

Whiteheaded Boy, The. An Irish drama (1920) by Lennox Robinson.

White Horse of Berkshire, The. A rude figure made by cutting away turf on the Chalk Downs near Wantage, Berkshire: traditionally ascribed to Alfred the Great.

White Huns, The. An ancient people, probably Turkish, of Central Asia: regarded as ancestors of the Turkomans.

White Indians, The. A name given to blond Indians living in Darien (eastern Panama). It has been suggested that they are descendants of Norwegians who came to America before Columbus; it is claimed by others that they are biological mutations from brown Indians.

White Lady, The. In German folklore, the ancient goddess Holda or Berchta.

White Lady of Avenel, The. In Scott's "The Monastery," the tutelary spirit of the house of Avenel.

White Monkey, The. A novel (1924) by John Galsworthy, portraying the restlessness of a certain class of young English people after the Great War. See **Forsyte Saga, The.**

White Peacock, The. A novel (1911) by D. H. Lawrence.

White People, The. A story of the supernatural (1917) by Frances Hodgson Burnett.

White Russians. See Dictionary, **Russian.**

White's. A noted club in St. James's Street, London, established 1698 as a chocolate-house.

White Sheep, The. The Turkoman conquerors of Persia, about 1468.

White Stone, The. A religious satire (1905) by Anatole France.

White Surrey. The favorite horse of Richard III. of England.

White Tower, The. The oldest part of the Tower of London.

Why Marry? A drama (1917) by Jesse Lynch Williams. Pulitzer Prize play, 1918.

Wichita (wich′i-tả). A confederacy of the Caddoan stock of North American Indians, formerly dwelling from Kansas southward to the Brazos River, Texas.

Wickfield, Agnes. In Dickens's "David Copperfield," a young woman of admirable character who becomes David's second wife.

Wide, Wide World, The. A novel (1850) by Susan Warner.

Widowers' Houses. A drama (1892) by G. B. Shaw.

Widow in the Bye Street, The. A narrative poem (1912) by John Masefield.

Wieland (vē′länt). See **Wayland the Smith.**

Wife of Bath, The. A pilgrim in Chaucer's "Canterbury Tales," a free-spoken, much-married woman of the middle class.

Wife of Sir Isaac Harman, The. A novel (1914) by H. G. Wells.

Wildair, Sir Harry. A gay and reckless man of fashion in Farquhar's "Constant Couple" and "Sir Harry Wildair."

Wild Duck, The. A drama (1885) by Henrik Ibsen.

Wildfire, Madge. In Scott's "Heart of Midlothian," a giddy young woman crazed by betrayal and desertion.

Wild Huntsman, The. A spectral hunter in folklore, especially in Germany: the subject of a ballad, "Der wilde Jäger" (1786), by Bürger.

Wilhelm Meisters Lehrjahre (vil′helm mīs′tẽrs lär′yä″rė). An enormously influential novel (1795–96) by Goethe: followed (1821–29) by "Wilhelm Meisters Wanderjahre" (vän′-dẽr-yä″rė).

Wilhelmshöhe (vil′helms-hė″ė). A castle near Cassel, Germany, in which Napoleon III. was imprisoned after Sedan.

Wilhelm Tell (vil′helm tel). A drama by Schiller, produced in 1804.

Willet (wil′et), **Joe.** In Dickens's "Barnaby Rudge," the son of the pig-headed landlord of the Maypole Inn. After a succession of mishaps, he marries Dolly Varden.

William and Mary, The War of. The American part of the war (1689–97) between England and France. It was fought against the French of Canada and their Indian allies.

William of Cloudeslie (kloudz′li). An archer, the subject of an English popular ballad.

Willis's Rooms. A later name of Almack's assembly-rooms, London.

Will's Coffee-House. A famous coffee-house in Russell Street, London, in the time of Dryden.

Wilmot Proviso, The. An antislavery amendment to a bill (1846) for the purchase of territory from Mexico. The bill never came to a vote in the U. S. Senate, although it passed the House.

Wimble, Will. A good-natured idler in Addison's "Spectator" papers.

Winchester School, or **St. Mary's College.** An important English public school, founded in Winchester (1393) by William of Wykeham.

Windsor Beauties, The. A series of 11 portraits of beauties of Charles II.'s court, by Sir Peter Lely. Ten are in Hampton Court Palace; the eleventh is lost.

Windsor Castle. An English royal residence at Windsor: founded by William the Conqueror, and enlarged by various later sovereigns.

Windy McPherson's Son. A novel (1916) by Sherwood Anderson.

Winesburg, Ohio. Short stories (1919) by Sherwood Anderson, presenting small-town American life from a somewhat depressing point of view.

Wingless Victory, The Temple of. See **Nike Apteros.**

Wings of the Dove, The. A novel (1902) by Henry James.

Winkelried, Arnold von (är'nolt fon ving'kel-rēt). A Swiss patriot who, according to legend, purchased a Swiss victory at Sempach (1386) by grasping all the Austrian pikes he could reach and burying them in his own breast.

Winkle, Nathaniel. In Dickens's "Pickwick Papers," a member of the Pickwick Club who excels in sports—until given a chance to exhibit his skill.

Winkle, Rip Van. See **Rip Van Winkle.**

Winnebago (win-ē-bā'gō). An important tribe of North American Indians, of the Siouan stock. They live in Wisconsin and Nebraska.

Winter Palace, The. The imperial residence in the former St. Petersburg, Russia.

Winter's Tale, The. A romantic play (about 1611) by Shakspere.

Wisby (wiz'bi), **The Laws of.** An old code of sea laws named from the town of Wisby (Visby) on the island of Gotland, Sweden: based partly on the Judgments of Oléron.

Wisdom of Solomon, The Book of the. One of the deuterocanonical books of the Old Testament. Protestant critics ascribe it to the 2d or 1st century B.C.

Wise Men of the East, The. See **Three Kings of Cologne.**

Wishfort, Lady. A decayed belle in Congreve's "Way of the World": one of his most effective characters.

Wishoskan (wish'os-kan). A linguistic stock of North American Indians of the coastal region about Humboldt Bay, Cal.: also known as "Diggers."

Witches' Sabbath, The. The same as **Walpurgis Night.**

Witching Hour, The. A drama (1908) by Augustus Thomas.

Witch of Endor, The. See **Endor.**

Witenagemot (wit'ē-na-gē-mōt'). The great national parliament or council, in the Anglo-Saxon period of English history.

With Fire and Sword. The first (1884) of a trilogy of Polish historical romances by Henryk Sienkiewicz. The other volumes are "The Deluge" (1886) and "Pan Michael" (1887).

Without Dogma. A psychological novel (1891) by Henryk Sienkiewicz.

Wittelsbach (vit'els-bäch). An ancient German princely family which furnished rulers to Bavaria, the Palatinate, Brandenburg, Germany, and Sweden.

Wittenberg (vit'en-berch), **The Concord of.** An agreement (1536) between Saxon and Swiss Reformers.

Witwou'd (wit'wůd). In Congreve's "Way of the World," a character whose repartee always falls flat.

Wolf of Gubbio, The. A drama (1913) by Josephine Preston Peabody, based on the well-known story of St. Francis and the wolf.

Woman in White, The. A long and involved mystery story (1860) by Wilkie Collins.

Woman of No Importance, A. A society drama (1893) by Oscar Wilde.

Woman's Prize, or the Tamer Tamed, The. See **Maria,** 2.

Woman's Victory, The. A novel (1906) by Maarten Maartens (Joost M. W. van der Poorten-Schwartz).

Women. A novel (1925) by Booth Tarkington.

Women in Love. A novel (1921) by D. H. Lawrence.

Wonder-Book, The. A collection (1851) of tales from mythological sources, by Hawthorne.

Wooden Horse, The. A novel (1909) by Hugh Walpole.

Woodman, Spare That Tree. A well-known short poem by G. P. Morris (d. 1864).

Woodstock. A romance (1826) of the 17th century, by Scott.

Woodstock, The Assize of. A code (1184) proclaimed by Henry II. of England for regulation of the forests.

Woolwich (wůl'ich). A borough of London, south of the Thames, containing a great arsenal.

Worcester (wůs'tẽr) **College.** A college of Oxford University, incorporated 1714.

Workhouse Ward, The. A drama (1908) by Lady Augusta Gregory.

Works and Days. The chief poem of Hesiod, treating of the labors of the farmer and of days lucky and unlucky for performing them.

World Court, The. See Dictionary, **world.**

Worldly Wiseman, Mr. In Bunyan's "Pilgrim's Progress," a man of worldly knowledge but devoid of spiritual insight.

World's Fairs. Of international expositions of industrial and artistic products, the following are among the most important: London, 1851, 1862; Paris, 1855, 1867, 1878, 1889, 1900, 1931, 1937; Vienna, 1873; Philadelphia, 1876, 1926; Chicago, 1893, 1933—34; Buffalo, 1901; St. Louis, 1904; San Francisco, 1915, 1939—40; New York, 1939—40.

World War, The. See Dictionary, **world.**

Worms (wẽrmz, G. vôrms), **The Diet of.** A famous diet held at Worms in 1521 for the purpose of checking the Reformation. Before it Luther defended his doctrines.

Worthies of England, The History of the. A collection of short biographies (1662, posthumous) by Thomas Fuller: considered his masterpiece.

Wotan, Woden. Respectively, the Old High German and the Anglo-Saxon forms of the name **Odin.**

Wrayburn (rā'bẽrn), **Eugene.** In "Our Mutual Friend," by Dickens, a flippant and indolent young attorney, the rival of Bradley Headstone.

Wrestlers, The. A Greek original antique group in marble, in the Tribuna of the Uffizi, Florence.

Wuthering (wuŦH'ẽr-ing) **Heights.** A novel (1846) of extraordinary power and atmosphere, by Emily Brontë.

Wyandotte (wī'an-dot). A tribe of North American Indians, formerly dwelling in Ontario. They were allies of the French until Pontiac's war. Survivors are chiefly in Oklahoma.

Wyandotte Constitution, The. The constitution (1859) under which Kansas was admitted to the Union.

Wyatt's Rebellion. The unsuccessful revolt (1553–54) against Queen Mary, in favor of Lady Jane Grey, led by the Duke of Suffolk and Sir Thomas Wyatt the younger.

Wych (wich) **Street.** A London street near Clement's Inn. It was a haunt of the notorious Jack Sheppard.

Wycliffites. See Dictionary, **Lollard.**

X

Xanthippe (zan-thip'ē or zan-tip'ē). The wife of Socrates, proverbial as a scold.

Xanthus (zan'thus). An ancient city of Lycia, Asia Minor, near the mouth of the Xanthus River. Important antiquities have been discovered there.

Xenien (ksā'ni-en). A series of epigrams by Goethe and Schiller, chiefly on writers of the time.

Ximanas. The same as **Jumanas.**

Ximena (ʜē-mä'nä). In Spanish history and legend, the wife of the Cid.

Xincas (ʜēng'käz). An extinct Indian tribe of southern Guatemala, near the Pacific: found by Alvarado in 1524.

Xingu (zing'gū). A story (1916) by Edith Wharton, in which a clever woman exposes the pseudo-information of a group of clubwomen.

Xiquitos. The same as **Chiquitos.**

Xisuthrus (zi-sö′thrus). According to Berosus, the historiographer of Chaldea, the last of the first decade of mythical kings of Babylonia. He corresponds to the Biblical Noah and to the Hasis-Adra or Hasisatra of the cuneiform account of the deluge.

Xosa (ksō′sä), or **Amaxosa** (ä-mä-). A Bantu tribe of British South Africa, closely related to the Zulus.

Xury (zū′ri). A servant of Crusoe in Defoe's "Robinson Crusoe."

X. Y. Z. Mission, The. An American embassy to France in 1797, consisting of C. C. Pinckney, Marshall, and Gerry. An attempt was made by three French agents (disguised as X., Y., and Z.) to bribe them.

Y

Yaguas (yä-gwäz′), or **Yahuas** (yä-wäz′). Wild Indians of northern Peru, on the upper Amazon between Nauta and Pebas.

Yahoos (yä-höz′). See Dictionary, **Yahoo.**

Yahweh. See Dictionary.

Yakala (yä-kä′lä), or **Mayakala** (mä-). A Bantu tribe of the lower Kwangu (Quango) valley, in the Belgian Congo and in Angola.

Yakima (yak′i-mä). A tribe of North American Indians of the northwest, now on Yakima reservation, Washington.

Yakonan (yak′ọ-nạn). A linguistic stock of North American Indians, composed of four tribes on the Siletz reservation, Oregon.

Yakuts (yä-köts′). A people of Turkish or mixed Turkish origin, dwelling near the Lena in Siberia.

Yale Bowl. An athletic field at Yale University surrounded by a great elliptical structure for spectators.

Yama (yam′ä). In the Rig-Veda, the god who rules in heaven over the blessed (Manes, Fathers, or Pitris). In later interpretation, Yama and his twin sister Yami are the first human pair, who have preceded all to the realm beyond.

Yankee Doodle (yang′kẹ dö′dl). An American national air, probably of English 18th-century origin. The traditional author is a Dr. Schuckburgh, a surgeon in the French and Indian War.

Yankton (yangk′tọn). A tribe of the Siouan stock of North American Indians, in South Dakota.

Yao (you), or **Wayao** (wä-you′). A large Bantu tribe of East Africa, between the upper Rovuma, the Lujenda, and the mountains east of Lake Nyasa.

Yaqui (yä′kẹ). An important division of the Cahita (Piman) Indians, in the state of Sonora, Mexico: notable for their warlike spirit.

Yaquina (yạ-kwin′ä). The chief tribe of the Yakonan stock.

Yeast: a Problem. A novel (1851) by Charles Kingsley, dealing with English agricultural conditions in the "hungry '40's."

Yellow Jacket, The. A drama (1912) by G. C. Hazelton and J. H. Benrimo, to some degree imitating Chinese drama.

Yellowplush Papers, The. A collection (1841) of sketches by Thackeray.

Yeomen of the Guard, The. A comic opera (1888) by W. S. Gilbert and Arthur Sullivan.

Yeye (yä′yạ). A savage Bantu tribe of South Africa, north of Lake Ngami.

Yezidis (yez′i-dēz). A people or sect of Mesopotamia, akin to the Kurds: commonly called "devil-worshipers."

Ygerne (i-gèrn′). In Arthurian romance, mother of King Arthur.

Yggdrasil (ig′drạ-sil). In Scandinavian mythology, the ash-tree which binds together earth, heaven, and hell.

Ymir (ē′mir). See **Audhumla.**

Yoga (yō′gä). See Dictionary.

Yokut (yō′kut). The southern division of the Mariposan stock of North American Indians. Its remnants are now under the Mission agency, California.

Yorick (yor′ik). 1. The king's jester whose skull is apostrophized in the graveyard scene of Shakspere's "Hamlet." 2. A humorous parson in Sterne's "Tristram Shandy." He claims descent from Shakspere's Yorick.

York, The House of. A branch of the English royal line of Plantagenet, descended from the third and fifth sons of Edward III. (the dukes of Clarence and of York). Kings of this branch (1461–85) were Edward IV., Edward V., and Richard III. See **Wars of the Roses, The.**

York and Lancaster, The Wars of. See **Wars of the Roses, The.**

York House. A former palace in London, on the Strand west of Salisbury House: a town residence of the archbishops of York.

York Place. A name formerly applied to Whitehall Palace, London.

York Plays or **Mysteries, The.** A cycle of 48 plays performed by the Crafts of York on Corpus Christi Day, in the 14th, 15th, and 16th centuries.

Yoruba (yō′rọ-bä). A formerly powerful negro kingdom of Africa, occupying the eastern half of the Slave Coast, between Dahomey and Benin, and extending northeast to the Niger.

Young Earnest. A novel (1915) by Gilbert Cannan.

Young England. A Tory and aristocratic group which, about 1844, opposed free trade and radicalism and advocated restoring the former order of things. Disraeli was one of its leaders, and his "Sybil" was part of its propaganda.

Young Germany. A literary and political school, characterized by innovation and experimentation, in the Germany of Heine's period.

Young Ireland. An Irish political group which, about 1840–50, broke with O'Connell and advocated physical force. It participated in the uprising of 1848.

Young Italy. An association of republican agitators, active about 1834 under the leadership of Mazzini.

Youth and the Bright Medusa. Stories (1920) by Willa Sibert Cather.

Youth, and Two Other Stories. Stories (1902) of the sea, by Joseph Conrad.

Yram. See **Erewhon.**

Ysengrimus. See **Isengrim, Sir.**

Yseult. See **Iseult.**

Ysopet (ē-zo-pā′). A collection of about 100 fables in verse by Marie de France.

Yucatecs (yö-kạ-teks′). A name often given to the Mayas of Yucatan.

Yuchi. See **Uchean.**

Yukian (ū′ki-ạn). A linguistic stock of North American Indians (including the Yuki tribe), chiefly on the Round Valley reservation, California.

Yukonikhotana (yö-kon″i-chō-tä′nạ). A tribe of the northern Athapascan stock of North American Indians, living along the Yukon River between the Koyukuk and the Tanana.

Yuman (yö′mạn). A linguistic stock of North American Indians in the extreme southwestern part of the United States and northern Lower California.

Yurok (yö′rok). A division of North American Indians in California, along the Klamath River and on the coast.

Yurucares (yö-rö-kä-räz′). Indians of Bolivia, northeast of La Paz, at the foot of the mountains and in the forested plains between the Mamoré and the Beni.

Yuste (yös′tä). A convent in Spain, east of Plasencia: the place of retirement of Charles V. after his abdication.

Yvetot, Le Roi d'. See **Roi d'Yvetot, Le.**

Z

Zaccheus (za-kē′us). A tax-collector who, because "little of stature," climbed a sycamore-tree to see Jesus. Luke, xix. 1–10.

Zachariah (zak-ạ-rī′ạ). A king of Israel, son of Jeroboam. 2 Kings, xv. 8–11.

Zacharias (zak-ạ-rī′ạs). A priest of the Jews, slain "between the temple and the altar." 2 Chron. xxiv. 20, 21; Mat. xxiii. 35.

Zadkiel (zad′ki-ẹl). In rabbinical lore, the angel of the planet Jupiter.

Zadok (zā′dok). A chief priest in the time of David. 2 Sam. xv. 24–29.

Zagloba. A prominent character in the historical trilogy of Sienkiewicz: has been called the Polish Falstaff. See **With Fire and Sword.**

Zaide (zä-ē′dè). An opera (about 1780) by Mozart.

(variable) ḏ as d or j, ş as s or sh, ṭ as t or ch, ẓ as z or zh; o, F. cloche; ü, F. menu; ċh, Sc. loch; ṅ, F. bonbon; ′, primary accent; ″, secondary accent; †, obsolete; <, from; +, and; =, equals. See also lists at beginning of book.

Zaïre (zä-ēr). A tragedy (1733) by Voltaire, based partly on Shakspere's "Othello."

Zamore (zà-môr). See **Alzire**.

Zanga (zang′gà). The principal character in Young's "Revenge": a favorite rôle of Macready and J. P. Kemble.

Zanoni (za-nō′ni). A romantic novel (1842) by Bulwer-Lytton.

Zápolya (zä′pọl-yo). A Hungarian ruling family, 1526–71.

Zaporozhians (zap-ọ-rō′zhi-ạnz). A warlike division of the Cossacks, compelled to remove from the lower Dnieper to the Crimea in the 18th century.

Zapotec-Mixtec (zä-pọ-tek′miks′tek). A linguistic stock of Mexican Indians, principally in Oaxaca.

Zapotecs (zä-pọ-teks′). Indians of Mexico, occupying most of Oaxaca: before the conquest, a powerful nation.

Zara (zä′rà). A character in Congreve's "Mourning Bride."

Zaramo (zä-rä′mō). A Bantu tribe of East Africa, between the Kingani and Rufiji rivers.

Zarathustra (zä-rạ-thös′trạ), or **Zoroaster**. The founder of the Perso-Iranian national religion of the period from the Achæmenidæ to the end of the Sassanian dynasty. He interpreted the preëxisting mythology in terms of spiritual and moralized conceptions.

Zarpanit (zär′pạ-nit). In Assyro-Babylonian mythology, the wife of Merodach (Marduk).

Zauberflöte, Die (dē tsou′bėr-flė″tė). "The Magic Flute": an opera (1791) by Mozart.

Zealots (zel′ọts). A politico-religious party in Judea. After the Roman conquest, which they resisted, the survivors formed a community in northern Arabia, near Medina.

Zebedee (zeb′ẹ-dē). The father of the apostles James and John. Mat. iv. 21.

Zebulun (zeb′ū-lun). The 10th son of Jacob, and ancestor of one of the 12 tribes of Israel. Gen. xxx. 20.

Zechariah (zek-ạ-rī′ạ). A prophet of Israel, author of the Old Testament book of prophecy bearing his name.

Zedekiah (zed-ẹ-kī′ạ). The last king of Judah before the Babylonian captivity. 2 Kings, xxiv. 17–20.

Zémire (zā-mēr). "Beauty," in "Beauty and the Beast."

Zenaga (ze-nä′gä). A Berber dialect of southern Morocco, spoken chiefly by the negro population.

Zend (zend). The language of the Avesta: an ancient form of Iranian or Persian, deciphered in the 19th century.

Zenelophon (zẹ-nel′ọ-fọn). Penelophon. Shakspere's "Love's Labour's Lost," iv. 1. 67. See **Cophetua**.

Zenith. A bustling American city, the scene of Sinclair Lewis's "Babbitt."

Zenobia (ze-nō′bi-ạ). In Hawthorne's "Blithedale Romance," an impulsive, passionate woman who drowns herself.

Zephaniah (zef-ạ-nī′ạ). The author of the Old Testament book of prophecy bearing his name.

Zephyrus (zef′i-rus). In classical mythology, the west wind personified: a benignant deity.

Zerlina (dzer-lē′nä). A female character in Mozart's opera "Don Giovanni."

Zerubbabel (ze-rub′ạ-bel). One of the leaders of the first expedition to return to Judea from Babylonian captivity. Ezra, ii. 1, 2.

Zetes (zē′tēz). In classical mythology, a son of Boreas.

Zethos (zē′thos). In Greek mythology, the brother of Amphion.

Zeus (zūs). In Greek mythology, the all-powerful master of the gods: son of Cronus and Rhea. He dethroned his father. Hera was his consort. His most renowned sanctuaries were at Olympia and Dodona.

Zeus, The Olympian. A colossal chryselephantine statue of Zeus by Phidias, placed in the temple at Olympia, re-moved in the 5th century to Constantinople, and burned in 476. The face and hands of this statue were of ivory.

Zeus, The Temple of. See **Olympieum, The**.

Zeus Nicephorus (nī-sef′ọ-rus). A colossal antique statue found at the Villa Barberini, Rome, and now in the Hermitage Museum, Leningrad.

Zimbabwe (zim-bäb′wä). A ruined city in Mashonaland, discovered 1871.

Zimri (zim′rī). A king of Israel, overthrown by Omri. 1 Kings, xvi. 10–18.

Zingarella, La (lä tsēng-gä-rel′lä). A famous painting by Correggio, in the Museo Nazionale, Naples.

Zion (zī′ọn), or **Sion** (sī′ọn), **Mount**. A hill on which was situated the old city of Jerusalem. The name is sometimes applied to the city as a whole; also, symbolically, to (1) the Christian Church and (2) the Christian heaven.

Zipas (tsē′päz). The chiefs of the ancient Chibcha Indians of Colombia.

Zipporah (zi-pō′rä). The wife of Moses: a daughter of the Midianite priest Jethro.

Znaim (znīm), **The Armistice of**. The Franco-Austrian truce (1809) which preceded the peace of Vienna.

Zoan (zō′an). A place in Egypt, 20 miles north of Tel-el-Kebir: probably the residence of Joseph. Num. xiii. 22.

Zobeide (zọ-bä′de). In the "Arabian Nights' Entertainments," the wife of the calif Harun al-Rashid.

Zohar (zō′här). A cabalistic work, of disputed date and authorship, in the form of a commentary on the Pentateuch.

Zollverein (tsol′fer-īn″). A union of German states for maintenance of a common tariff. It began (1828) with an agreement between Prussia and Hesse, and eventually spread through the entire former German Empire.

Zongora (zong-gō′rä). The principal tribe of the kingdom of Karagwe in East Africa, on the southwest shore of Lake Victoria.

Zophiel (zō′fi-el). A cherub in Milton's "Paradise Lost."

Zoroaster (zō-rọ-as′tėr). The same as **Zarathustra**.

Zoroastrians (zō-rọ-as′tri-ạnz). The followers of Zoroaster or Zarathustra; at present, the Guebers and Parsees of Persia and India.

Zouaves (zọ-ävz′). 1. Soldiers of a corps of light infantry in the French army, conspicuous because of their showy Oriental uniform. They were organized in 1831 in Algeria. 2. Soldiers of volunteer regiments (1861–65) in the U. S. army whose dress resembled the French Zouave uniform.

Zouaves, The Papal. A corps of French soldiers organized (1860) at Rome for the defense of the temporal sovereignty of the Pope. They served in France (1870–71) against the Germans and the Commune.

Zuleika (zọ-lē′kạ) **Dobson, or An Oxford Love Story.** A fictional extravaganza (1911) by Max Beerbohm.

Zulu (zö′lö). A great Bantu nation of South Africa, occupying the coastal region between Natal and Lourenço Marques.

Zuñi (zö′nyē). A tribe of North American Indians which inhabits the largest of the Indian pueblos, in western New Mexico.

Zurich (zö′rik), **The Peace of**. A treaty (1859) made by Austria with France and Sardinia. Austria ceded a large part of Lombardy.

Zwillingsbrüder, Die (dē tsvil′ings-brü″dėr). "The Twin Brothers": a musical farce (1820) by Schubert and Hofmann.

Zwinger (tsving′ėr). A famous museum in Dresden, containing, among its 2,500 paintings, works by Correggio, Titian, Veronese, Rembrandt, Holbein, and others, and Raphael's Sistine Madonna.

---

fat, fāte, fär, fȧll, ȧsk, fāre; net, mē, hèr; pin, pīne; not, nōte, möve, nôr; up, lūte, pull; oi, oil; ou, out; (lightened) aviạry, ẹlect, agọny, intọ, ūnite; (obscured) errạnt, operạ, ardẹnt, actọr, natụre; ch, chip; g, go; th, thin; ᴛʜ, then; y, you;

BIOGRAPHICAL NAMES

The principal abbreviations used in this list are as follows:—

A.D.	anno Domini (in the year of our Lord; after Christ)	Can.	Canadian	Gr.	Greek	Pol.	Polish
		Cath.	Catholic	Hung.	Hungarian	pron.	pronounced; pronunciation
Am.	American (when used alone, meaning of the U. S.)	cent.	century	Ir.	Irish		
		Chin.	Chinese	It.	Italian	Rom.	Roman
		d.	died	Jap.	Japanese	Russ.	Russian
b.	born	Dan.	Danish	Mex.	Mexican	Sc.	Scotch; Scottish
B.C.	before Christ	Eng.	English	misc.	miscellaneous	Scand.	Scandinavian
Bohem.	Bohemian	esp.	especially	Norw.	Norwegian	Sp.	Spanish
Br.	British	fl.	flourished	orig.	originally	Swed.	Swedish
c.	circa (about)	Fr.	French	Pers.	Persian	Turk.	Turkish
		Ger.	German	Pg.	Portuguese	U.S.	United States

For other abbreviations, see list at beginning of Dictionary.

A

Aali Pasha. See *Ali Pasha* (1815—71).

Aasen (ä′sen), Ivar Andreas (1813—96), Norw. philologist and lexicographer.

Abarbanel (ä-bär-bä-nel′), Isaac. See *Abrabanel.*

Abbadie (ȧ-bȧ-dē), Jacques (also called James, or Jakob, Abbadie) (1654?—1727), Fr. Protestant clergyman and theologian, in England and Ireland.

Abbas I. (äb′bäs) ("the Great") (1557—1628), shah of Persia (1586—1628).

Abbas II. (Abbas Hilmi) (1874—1944), khedive of Egypt (1892—1914) (son of Tewfik Pasha).

Abbas Mirza (mēr′zä) (1783?—1833), Pers. prince, and military commander in wars against Russia.

Abbe (ab′ē), Cleveland (1838—1916), Am. meteorologist.

Abbey (ab′i), Edwin Austin (1852—1911), Am. painter, in England.

Abbott (ab′ǫt), Jacob (1803—79), Am. author, writer of books for the young.

Abbott, Lyman (1835—1922), Am. clergyman and writer (son of Jacob).

Abd Allah ibn Yasin (äbd äl′lä ibn yä-sēn′) (d. c1059), Moslem missionary to Berbers in southwestern Sahara, and founder of sect known as Almoravides and its empire and dynasty in northern Africa and Spain.

Abd al-Rahman I. (äl-rä′män) (731—788), emir of Cordova (756—788).

Abd al-Rahman III. (891—961), calif of Cordova (912—961).

Abd-el-Kader (äbd′el-kä′dėr) (1807?—83), Arab chief, leader against the French in Algeria.

Abd-el-Krim (-krim′) (real name Mohammed ben Abd-el-Krim) (c1883—   ), Riff (Berber) leader of revolt against the Spanish and the French in northern Morocco (1921—26).

Abd-er-Rahman (-ėr-rä′män). See *Abd al-Rahman.*

Abdul-Aziz (äb′dül-ä-zēz′) (also Abd al-Aziz) (1830—76), sultan of Turkey (1861—76) (brother of Abdul-Medjid).

Abdul-Aziz (also Abd al-Aziz) (1881—   ), sultan of Morocco (1894—1908).

Abdul-Hamid I. (-hä-mēd′) (also Abd al-Hamid) (1725—89), sultan of Turkey (1774—89) (son of Ahmed III.).

Abdul-Hamid II. (1842—1918), sultan of Turkey (1876—1909) (son of Abdul-Medjid).

Abdul-Medjid (-mẹ-jēd′) (also Abd al-Madjid) (1823—61), sultan of Turkey (1839—61) (son of Mahmud II.).

Abdur-Rahman Khan (äb′dûr-rä′män kän) (1844—1901), amir of Afghanistan (1880—1901) (grandson of Dost Mohammed Khan).

Abel (ā′bel), Sir Frederick Augustus (1827—1902), Eng. chemist.

Abélard (ab′ẹ-lärd, Fr. ȧ-bā-lär), Pierre (1079—1142), Fr. scholastic philosopher.

Abercrombie (ab′ėr-krum-bi), James (1706—81), Br. general.

Abercromby (ab′ėr-krum-bi), Sir Ralph (1734—1801), Br. general.

Aberdeen (ab-ėr-dēn′), George Hamilton Gordon, 4th Earl of (1784—1860), Br. statesman.

Abernethy (ab′ėr-nẹ-thi), John (1764—1831), Eng. surgeon.

Abney (ab′ni), Sir William de Wiveleslie (1843—1920), Eng. physicist.

About (ȧ-bö), Edmond François Valentin (1828—85), Fr. novelist and misc. writer.

Abrabanel (ä-brä-bä-nel′) or **Abravanel** (ä-brä-vä-nel′), Isaac (also called Abarbanel) (1437—1508), Pg. Jewish Biblical scholar, and statesman in Portugal and Castile.

Abruzzi (ä-bröt′sē), Duke of the (Prince Luigi Amedeo of Savoy-Aosta) (1873—1933), It. naval officer, mountain-climber, and arctic explorer (son of Amadeus, Duke of Aosta).

Absalon (äb′sä-lon) or **Axel** (äk′sel) (1128—1201), Dan. archbishop, warrior, and statesman.

Abt (äpt), Franz (1819—85), Ger. musical composer.

Abu-Bekr (ä′bö-bek′r) (573—634), (first) Arabian calif (632—634) (father-in-law of Mohammed).

Ache (dȧsh), Caran d'. Pseudonym of Emmanuel Poiré.

Achenbach (ä′chen-bäch), Andreas (1815—1910), Ger. landscape-painter.

Achenbach, Oswald (1827—1905), Ger. landscape-painter (brother of Andreas).

Achmet. See *Ahmed.*

Acosta (dä ä-kos′tä), José de (1539?—1600), Sp. Jesuit missionary in Peru, and author.

Acton (ak′tǫn), John Emerich Edward Dalberg-Acton, 1st Baron (1834—1902), Eng. historical scholar (grandson of Sir John F. E.).

Acton, Sir John Francis Edward (1736—1811), Eng. officer in Italian naval service, and prime minister of Naples under Ferdinand IV., born in France.

Acuña (dä ä-kö′nyä), Cristóbal de (1597—1676?), Sp. Jesuit missionary, and explorer of the Amazon.

Adam (ȧ-dän), Adolphe Charles (1803—56), Fr. composer of comic opera.

Adam, Mme. (Juliette Lamber) (1836—1936), Fr. writer.

Adam (ad′ạm), Robert (1728—92), Br. architect.

Adam de la Halle (ȧ-dän dè lä äl) (c1240—c1288), Fr. poet and dramatist.

Adams (ad′ạmz), Charles Francis (1807—86), Am. statesman and diplomatist (son of John Q.).

Adams, Henry (1838—1918), Am. historical writer (son of Charles F.).

(variable) ḍ as d or j, ṣ as s or sh, ṭ as t or ch, ẓ as z or zh; o, F. cloche; ü, F. menu; ch, Sc. loch; ṅ, F. bonbon; ′, primary accent; ″, secondary accent; †, obsolete; <, from; +, and; =, equals. See also lists at beginning of book.

2599

Adams, John (1735—1826), 2d president of U. S. (1797—1801).

Adams, John Couch (1819—92), Eng. astronomer.

Adams, John Quincy (1767—1848), 6th president of U. S. (1825—29) (son of John).

Adams, Maude (professional name of Maude Kiskadden) (1872—   ), Am. actress.

Adams, Samuel (1722—1803), Am. patriot and statesman.

Adams, Thomas (d. after 1653), Eng. Puritan divine and preacher.

Adams, William Taylor ("Oliver Optic") (1822—97), Am. writer, esp. of books for the young.

Addams (ad′ạmz), Jane (1860—1935), Am. settlement-worker and writer.

Addington (ad′ing-tọn), Henry. See *Sidmouth, 1st Viscount.*

Addison (ad′i-sọn), Joseph (1672—1719), Eng. essayist.

Ade (ād), George (1866—   ), Am. humorist and playwright.

Adler (äd′lẽr), Felix (1851—1933), Ger.-Am. educator, lecturer, and writer, founder of N. Y. Society for Ethical Culture.

Adolf or **Adolph** (a-dolf′), or **Adolphus** (a-dol′fus) (of Nassau) (c1255—98), king of Germany (1292—98).

Adrian I. (ā′dri-ạn) (d. 795), It. ecclesiastic, pope (772—795).

Adrian IV. (Nicholas Breakspear) (c1100—59), Eng. ecclesiastic, pope (1154—59).

A. E. Literary signature used by G. W. Russell.

Ælfred. See *Alfred.*

Ælfric (al′frik) (surnamed Grammaticus) (c955—c1020), Eng. abbot and author.

Æneas Sylvius (ẹ-nē′ạs sil′vi-us). See *Pius II.*

Æschines (es′ki-nēz) (fl. c400 B.C.), Gr. philosopher.

Æschines (389—314 B.C.), Athenian orator.

Æschylus (es′ki-lus) (525—456 B.C.), Gr. tragic poet.

Æsop (ē′sop) (fl. c560 B.C.), supposed Gr. fabulist.

Æthelbald, etc. See *Ethelbald,* etc.

Æthelstan. See *Athelstan.*

Aëtius (ā-ē′shius) (396?—454), Rom. general, victor over Attila at Châlons-sur-Marne.

Affonso I. (äf-fôň′sọ) (c1110—85), count of Portugal (1112—39), and first king of Portugal (1139—85).

Agassiz (ag′ạ-si, Fr. ȧ-gȧ-sē), Jean Louis Rodolphe (1807—73), Swiss-Am. naturalist.

Agatha (ag′ạ-thạ), Saint (d. 251?), Sicilian virgin martyr.

Agathocles (a-gath′ọ-klēz) (361?—289 B.C.), tyrant of Syracuse.

Agesilaus II. (a-jes-i-lā′us) (c444—360? B.C.), Gr. general, king of Sparta (c401—360? B.C.).

Agnes (ag′nes), Saint (d. c304, or earlier), Rom. virgin martyr.

Agnesi (ä-nyā′zē), Maria Gaetana (1718—99), It. (female) mathematician.

Agnew (ag′nū), David Hayes (1818—92), Am. surgeon.

Agostino di Duccio (ä-gos-tē′nō dē döt′chō) (c1418—c1498), It. sculptor and architect.

Agricola (a-grik′ọ-lạ), Cnæus Julius (A.D. 37—93), Rom. general and administrator, governor of Britain (father-in-law of Tacitus).

Agricola, Georg (real name Bauer) (1490—1555), Ger. scholar and mineralogist.

Agricola, Johann (orig. Johann Schnitter) (1492 or 1494—1566), Ger. Protestant reformer.

Agricola, Rodolphus (orig. Roelof Huysmann) (1443—85), Dutch scholar.

Agrippa (a-grip′ạ), Marcus Vipsanius (63—12 B.C.), Rom. naval and military commander, and statesman.

Agrippina (ag-ri-pī′nạ) ("the younger") (A.D. 16?—59?), daughter of Germanicus Cæsar, and niece and fourth wife of the Rom. emperor Claudius I., and mother of Nero: a woman notorious for intrigue and crime.

Aguesseau (dȧ-ge-sō), Henri François d' (1668—1751), Fr. jurist.

Aguinaldo (ä-gē-näl′dō), Emilio (1870—   ), Filipino insurrectionist.

Ahmad (ä′mạd) (1898—1930), shah of Persia (1909—25).

Ahmed I. (ä′med) or **Achmet I.** (äch′met) (1589—1617), sultan of Turkey (1603—17) (grandson of Amurath III.).

Ahmed III. (1673—1736), sultan of Turkey (1703—30) (son of Mohammed IV.).

Ahmed Vefik Pasha (vef′ik pȧ-shä′) (1819?—90?), Turk. statesman and scholar.

Aicard (ä-kär), Jean (1848—1921), Fr. poet, dramatist, and misc. writer.

Aidan (ā′dạn), Saint (d. 651), Ir. monk and bishop, in England.

Ailly (dä-yē), Pierre d' (1350—1420), Fr. cardinal and theologian.

Ainsworth (ānz′wẽrth), William Harrison (1805—82), Eng. novelist.

Airy (ār′i), Sir George Biddell (1801—92), Eng. astronomer.

Aisha (ä′ẹ-shä) or **Ayesha** (ä′yẹ-shä) (613?—678), favorite wife of Mohammed (daughter of Abu-Bekr).

Akbar (äk′bär) (1542—1605), Mogul emperor of Hindustan (1556—1605) (son of Humayun).

Akenside (ā′kẹn-sīd), Mark (1721—70), Eng. poet.

Ala-ed-Din (ä-lä′ed-dēn′) (also called Aladdin) (fl. c1330), Turk. statesman (son of Osman I.).

Alain de Lille (ȧ-laň dẻ lēl) (Alanus ab, or de, Insulis, "the Universal Doctor") (c1114—1203?), Fr. theologian and Latin poet.

Alarcón (dä ä-lär-kōn′), Hernando de (fl. 1540), Sp. navigator, explorer of California coast.

Alarcón, Pedro Antonio de (1833—91), Sp. writer and politician.

Alarcón y Mendoza (ē men-dō′thä), Juan Ruiz de (c1588—1639), Sp. dramatist, born in Mexico.

Alaric (al′ạ-rik) (376?—410), king of the Visigoths, and conqueror of Rome (410).

A Lasco (ä läs′kō), Johannes. See *Laski, Jan.*

Alba, Duke of. See *Alva.*

Alban (âl′bạn or al′bạn), Saint (d. 303?), first Christian martyr of Britain.

Albany (âl′bạ-ni), Countess of (Luise von Stolberg-Gedern) (1753—1824), Ger. princess (wife of Charles Edward Stuart, later mistress of Vittorio Alfieri).

Albategnius (al-bạ-teg′ni-us) (Muhammad ben Djabir ben Sinan al-Battani) (c850—929), Arab astronomer.

Alberoni (äl-bä-rō′nē), Giulio (1664—1752), It. cardinal, and prime minister of Spain (1714?—19).

Albert I. (al′bẽrt) (1875—1934), king of the Belgians (1909—34) (nephew of Leopold II., king of the Belgians).

Albert I. (in German, Albrecht, pron. äl′brecht, called "the Bear") (c1100—70), margrave of Brandenburg (1150—70).

Albert III. (surnamed Achilles) (1414—86), elector of Brandenburg (1470—86).

Albert I. (in German, Albrecht) (c1250—1308), king of Germany (1298—1308) (son of Rudolf I.).

Albert (in German, Albrecht) (1490—1568), grand master of the Teutonic Knights, and first duke of Prussia (grandson of Albert III. of Brandenburg).

Albert (Albert Francis Charles Augustus Emmanuel, Prince of Saxe-Coburg-Gotha) (1819—61), prince consort of England (cousin and husband of Queen Victoria).

Albert (Albrecht Friedrich Rudolf) (1817—95), archduke of Austria, and field-marshal (son of Archduke Charles).

Albert (dàl-bär′), Eugen d' (1864—1932), pianist and composer in Germany, born in Scotland of Fr.-Br. parentage.

Alberti (äl-bär′tē), Leon Battista (1404—72), It. architect, sculptor, painter, poet, musician, and scholar.

Albertus Magnus (al-bẽr′tus mag′nus) (Albert von Bollstädt) (1206?—80), Ger. scholastic philosopher.

Alboin (al′boin) (d. 573?), king of the Lombards (c561—573?), founder of the Lombard kingdom in Italy.

Alboni (äl-bō′nē), Marietta (Countess Pepoli, Mme. Ziéger) (1823—94), It. operatic contralto singer.

Albornoz (dä äl-bor-nōth′), Gil Álvarez Carillo de (c1300—67), Sp. cardinal, and papal general and statesman.

Albret (dàl-brä), Jeanne d' (1528—72), queen of Navarre (1555—72) (mother of Henry IV. of France).

Albright (âl′brīt), Jacob (name orig. Albrecht) (1759—1808), Am. clergyman, founder of religious denomination called Evangelical Association.

Albumazar (äl-bö-mä′zạr) (Abu Mashar) (805?—885), Arab astronomer.

Albuquerque (dä äl-bö-kär′kè), Affonso de (1453–1515), Pg. navigator and conqueror in the East.

Alcæus (al-sē′us) (fl. c600 B.C.), Gr. lyric poet.

Alcamenes (al-kam′ę-nēz) (fl. c440–c402 B.C.), Gr. sculptor.

Alcibiades (al-si-bī′ą-dēz) (c450–404 B.C.), Athenian politician and general.

Alcman (alk′mąn) (fl. c650 B.C.), Gr. lyric poet, of Sparta.

Alcott (âl′kǫt), Amos Bronson (1799–1888), Am. educationist and writer.

Alcott, Louisa May (1832–88), Am. author (daughter of Amos B.).

Alcuin (al′kwin) (735–804), Eng. ecclesiastic and scholar.

Alden (âl′dęn), John (1599–1687), Eng. settler at Plymouth, Mass. (1620).

Aldred (al′dred) (d. 1069), Eng. ecclesiastic, archbishop of York.

Aldrich (âl′drich), Thomas Bailey (1836–1907), Am. poet and misc. writer.

Aldus Manutius (al′dus mą-nū′shius). See *Manutius*.

Aleksyeev (ä-leks-yä′yef), Evgeni Ivanovich (1843–), Russ. admiral, and viceroy in the Far East (1903–04).

Aleksyeev, Mikhail Vasilevich (1857–1918), Russ. general, opponent of the Bolsheviki.

Alemán (ä-lä-män′), Mateo (1547–c1609), Sp. novelist.

Alembert (dȧ-lon-bâr), Jean le Rond d′ (1717–83), Fr. mathematician and philosopher.

Alessi (ä-les′sē), Galeazzo (1500 or 1512–72), It. architect.

Alexander I. (al-eg-zan′dėr) (Prince of Battenberg) (1857–93), prince of Bulgaria (1879–86).

Alexander III. ("Alexander the Great") (356–323 B.C.), king of Macedonia (336–323 B.C.) and conqueror (son of Philip II. of Macedonia).

Alexander III. (Orlando Bandinelli) (d. 1181), It. ecclesiastic, pope (1159–81).

Alexander VI. (Rodrigo Borgia) (1431–1503), Sp. ecclesiastic, pope (1492–1503).

Alexander I. (in Russian, Aleksandr Pavlovich) (1777–1825), czar of Russia (1801–25) (son of Czar Paul I.).

Alexander II. (in Russian, Aleksandr Nikolaevich) (1818–81), czar of Russia (1855–81) (son of Czar Nicholas I.).

Alexander III. (in Russian, Aleksandr Aleksandrovich) (1845–94), czar of Russia (1881–94) (son of Alexander II.).

Alexander I. (1078?–1124), king of Scotland (1107–24) (son of Malcolm III.).

Alexander II. (1198–1249), king of Scotland (1214–49) (son of William the Lion).

Alexander III. (1241–85), king of Scotland (1249–85) (son of Alexander II.).

Alexander I. (Alexander Obrenovich) (1876–1903), king of Serbia (1889–1903) (son of Milan I.).

Alexander I. (Alexander Karageorgevich) (1888–1934), king of the Serbs, Croats, and Slovenes (Yugoslavia) (1921–34) (son of Peter I.).

Alexander, Sir George (orig. George Alexander Gibb Samson) (1858–1918), Eng. actor and theatrical manager.

Alexander, Sir Harold R. L. G. (1891–), Brit. general.

Alexander, John White (1856–1915), Am. painter.

Alexander, William ("Lord Stirling") (1726–83), Am. gen.

Alexander John I. (in full, Alexander John Cuza) (1820–73), prince of Rumania (1861–66).

Alexander Karageorgevich (kä-rą-jôr′ję-vich) (1806–85), prince of Serbia (1842–58) (son of Karageorge).

Alexander Nevski (nef′skē), Saint (1220?–63), Russ. prince, warrior, and statesman.

Alexander of Hales (hālz) ("the Irrefragable Doctor") (d. 1245), Eng. scholastic theologian.

Alexander Severus (se-vē′rus), Marcus Aurelius (name orig. Bassianus) (208–235), Rom. emperor (222–235) (cousin and successor of Elagabalus).

Alexandra (al-eg-zan′drä) (Alexandra Caroline Marie Charlotte Louisa Julia) (1844–1925), queen of Edward VII. of Great Britain (daughter of Christian IX. of Denmark).

Alexeieff (ä-leks-yä′yef). See *Aleksyeev*.

Alexis (a-lek′sis) or **Alexius** (a-lek′si-us) (in Russian, Aleksyey Mikhaylovich) (1629–76), czar of Russia (1645–76) (son of Czar Michael).

Alexis or **Alexius** (in Russian, Aleksyey Petrovich) (1690–

1718), Russ. czarevitch, condemned for high treason and imprisoned (son of Peter the Great).

Alexis, Willibald. Pseudonym of G. W. H. Häring.

Alexius I. (Alexius Comnenus) (1048–1118), Byzantine emperor (1081–1118).

Alfieri (äl-fyä′rē), Count Vittorio (1749–1803), It. dramatic poet.

Alfonso I. or **Alphonso I.** (al-fon′sō) (of Portugal). See *Affonso I.*

Alfonso V. ("Alfonso the Magnanimous") (1385–1458), king of Aragon, Sicily, and Sardinia (1416–58), and of Naples (1443–58).

Alfonso I. ("the Catholic") (d. 757), king of Asturias (739–757).

Alfonso III. ("the Great") (d. 912?), king of Asturias and León (866–910?).

Alfonso VI. ("the Brave") (c1030–1109), king of León (1065–1109), and (as Alfonso I.) king of Castile (1072–1109) (son of Ferdinand the Great).

Alfonso IX. (or **VIII.** or **III.**) ("the Noble") (1155–1214), king of Castile (1158–1214).

Alfonso X. ("the Wise") (1221–84), king of Castile and León (1252–82) (son of Ferdinand III. of Castile).

Alfonso XII. (1857–85), king of Spain (1874–85) (son of Isabella II.).

Alfonso XIII. (1886–1941), king of Spain (1886–1931) (son of Alfonso XII.).

Alford (âl′fǫrd), Henry (1810–71), Eng. divine, scholar, and writer.

Alfred (al′fred) (or Ælfred) ("Alfred the Great") (849–901), king of the West Saxons in England (871–901) (brother of Ethelred I.).

Alger (al′jėr), Horatio (1834–99), Am. writer, esp. of books for the young.

Ali (ä′lē) (in full Ali ibn Abu Talib, called "the Lion of God") (c600–661), Arabian calif (656–661) (cousin and son-in-law of Mohammed).

Ali Bey (bā) (1728?–73), Mameluke chief, ruler of Egypt in revolt against Turkey.

Alighieri. See *Dante Alighieri.*

Ali Pasha (ä′lē pȧ-shä′) (called Ali Arslan, or ′Ali the Lion,′ and "the Lion of Janina") (1741–1822), pasha of Janina (1788–1822).

Ali Pasha (Muhammed Emin Ali Pasha) (1815–71), Turk. statesman.

Allegri (äl-lā′grē), Antonio. See *Correggio.*

Allen (al′ęn), Ethan (1737–89), Am. Revolutionary officer.

Allen, Ira (1751–1814), Am. soldier and politician (brother of Ethan).

Allen, James Lane (1849–1925), Am. novelist.

Allen, Richard (1760–1831), Am. negro Methodist bishop.

Allenby (al′ęn-bi), Edmund Henry Hynman Allenby, 1st Viscount (1861–1936), Eng. field-marshal.

Alleyn (al′ęn), Edward (1566–1626), Eng. actor and philanthropist.

Allibone (al′i-bōn), Samuel Austin (1816–89), Am. bibliographer.

Allingham (al′ing-ąm), William (1824–89), Ir. poet.

Allston (âl′stǫn), Washington (1779–1843), Am. painter.

Almagro (dä äl-mä′grō), Diego de (1475?–1538), Sp. adventurer, associate of Pizarro in Peru.

Al-Mansur (äl-män-sör′) (Abu Djafar Abdallah) (712?–775), Eastern calif (754?–775), founder of Bagdad.

Al-Mansur (commonly called Almanzor) (939–1002), regent of Cordova.

Alma-Tadema (al′mä-tad′ę-mä), Sir Lawrence, orig. Laurens (1836–1912), Dutch-Eng. painter.

Almeida (dä äl-mä′ę-dä), Francisco de (c1450–1510), Pg. military and naval commander, first viceroy of Portuguese India.

Almqvist (älm′kvist), Karl Jonas Ludvig (1793–1866), Swed. novelist and misc. writer.

Alp Arslan (älp är-slän′) (Mohammed ben Daud) (1029?–72), Seljuk sultan of Persia (1059?–72).

Alphonso. See *Alfonso.*

Althorp (âl′thôrp), Viscount. See *Spencer, 3d Earl.*

Alva (al′vä, Sp. äl′vä) or **Alba** (al′bä, Sp. äl′bä), Fernando

---

(variable) ḍ as d or j; ş as s or sh; ṭ as t or ch; ẓ as z or zh; o, F. cloche; ü, F. menu; ċh, Sc. loch; ṅ, F. bonbon; ′, primary accent; ″, secondary accent; †, obsolete; <, from; +, and; =, equals. See also lists at beginning of book.

Álvarez de Toledo, Duke of (1508—82), Sp. general, and military administrator of Netherlands (1567—73).

Alvarado (dä äl-vä-rä′ᵭꜱꜰ), Alonso de (d. c1553), Sp. soldier in conquests of Mexico and Peru.

Alvarado, Pedro de (1495?—1541), Sp. conqueror in Mexico and Guatemala.

Alvarez (äl′vä-resh), Francisco (d. after 1540), Pg. priest and traveler in Abyssinia.

Álvarez (äl′vä-räs), Juan (1780?—1867?), Mex. general and politician.

Alvensleben (fon äl′vᵉns-lä″bᵉn), Konstantin von (1809—92), Prussian general.

Alverstone (al′vᵉr-stᵒn), Richard Everard Webster, Viscount (1842—1915), Eng. jurist, lord chief justice (1900—13).

Alvinczy or **Alvinzi** (äl′vin-tsē), Joseph (Freiherr von Barberek) (1735—1810), Austrian field-marshal, born in Hungary.

Amadeus (am-ạ-dē′us) (in Spanish, Amadeo, in Italian, Amedeo) (1845—90), It. prince (Duke of Aosta), and king of Spain (1870—73) (brother of Humbert I.).

Amalric I. See *Amaury I.*

Amati (ä-mä′tē), Niccolò (1596—1684), It. violin-maker, of Cremona.

Amato (ä-mä′tō), Pasquale (1878—1942), It. operatic barytone singer.

Amaury I. (ạ-mâ′ri, Fr. à-mō-rē) or **Amalric I.** (ạ-mal′rik) (1135?—73), king of Jerusalem (1162—73).

Amboise (däⁿ-bwäz), Georges d' (1460—1510), Fr. cardinal and statesman.

Ambrose (am′brōz), Saint (340?—397), bishop of Milan.

Amenhotep III. See *Amenophis III.*

Amenophis III. (am-e-nō′fis) or **Amenhotep III.** (am-en-hō′tep) (fl. c1400 B.C.), king of Egypt, of 18th dynasty.

Ames (āmz), Fisher (1758—1808), Am. orator and statesman.

Ames, Oakes (1804—73), Am. manufacturer, capitalist, and politician.

Amherst (am′ᵉrst), Jeffrey Amherst, Baron (1717—97), Eng. field-marshal.

Amicis (dä ä-mē′chēs), Edmondo de (1846—1908), It. writer.

Amiel (à-myel), Henri Frédéric (1821—81), Swiss diarist, critic, and poet.

Ammanati (äm-mä-nä′tē), Bartolommeo (1511—92), Florentine architect and sculptor.

Ammianus Marcellinus (am-i-ā′nus mär-sᵉ-lī′nus) (c330—c395), Rom. historian, born at Antioch.

Ammonius Saccas (a-mō′ni-us sak′ạs) (c175—c242), Gr. philosopher, of Alexandria, regarded as founder of Neoplatonic school.

Amory (ā′mᵒ-ri), Thomas (1691?—1788), Eng. writer.

Ampère (äⁿ-pâr), André Marie (1775—1836), Fr. physicist.

Amsdorf (fon äms′dôrf), Nikolaus von (1483—1565), Ger. Protestant reformer.

Amundsen (ä′mund-sᵉn), Roald (1872—1928), Norw. explorer, discoverer of south pole (1911), crossed north pole by airship (1926).

Amurath I. (ä-mö-rät′) or **Murad I.** (mö′räd) (1319—89), sultan of Turkey (1359—89) (grandson of Osman I.).

Amurath II. or **Murad II.** (1403?—51), sultan of Turkey (1421—51) (grandson of Bajazet I.).

Amurath III. or **Murad III.** (1546—95), sultan of Turkey (1574—95) (grandson of Solyman I.).

Amurath IV. or **Murad IV.** (1611—40), sultan of Turkey (1623—40) (son of Ahmed I.).

Amyot (à-myō), Jacques (1513—93), Fr. bishop and translator.

Amyraut (à-mē-rō), Moïse, or Moses (as Latinized, Amyraldus) (1596—1664), Fr. Protestant theologian.

Anacreon (a-nak′rē-ᵒn) (c563—c478 B.C.), Gr. lyric poet.

Anaxagoras (an-ak-sag′ō-rạs) (c500—c428 B.C.), Gr. philosopher.

Anaximander (a-nak-si-man′dᵉr) (c611—c547 B.C.), Gr. philosopher.

Anaximenes (an-ak-sim′ᵉ-nēz) (d. c500 B.C.), Gr. philosopher.

Anaya (ä-nä′yä), Pedro María (1795—1854), Mex. general.

Ancona (däng-kō′nä), Alessandro d' (1835—1914), It. literary historian and critic.

Ancre (däⁿ-kr), Marquis d'. See *Concini, Concino.*

Ancus Marcius (ang′kus mär′shius) (d. 616 B.C.), 4th (legendary) king of Rome (640—616 B.C.) (reputed grandson of Numa Pompilius).

Andalò, Brancaleone d'. See *Brancaleone d'Andalò.*

Andersen (än′dᵉr-sᵉn), Hans Christian (1805—75), Dan. author, esp. of fairy-tales.

Anderson (an′dᵉr-sᵒn), Mary Antoinette (Mrs. de Navarro) (1859—1940), Am. actress.

Anderson, Richard Henry (1821—79), Am. Confederate general.

Anderson, Robert (1805—71), Am. general.

Anderson, Sherwood (1876—1941), Am. author.

Andrada e Silva (dä än-drä′dä ā sēl′vä), José Bonifacio de (1765—1838), Brazilian statesman and scientist.

Andrássy (on′drä-shē), Gyula, or Julius, Count (1823—90), Hung. statesman.

Andrássy, Gyula, or Julius, Count (1860—1929), Hung. statesman (son of Count Andrássy, 1823—90).

André (än′drā or an′dri), John (1751—80), Eng. soldier in America, hanged as a British spy during Revolutionary War.

Andreä (än-drä′e), Jakob (1528—90), Ger. Protestant theologian.

Andrea del Sarto (än-drä′ä del sär′tō). See *Sarto, Andrea del.*

Andrée (än′drā), Salomon August (1854—97?), Swed. engineer and aëronautic arctic explorer.

Andreev (än-drä′yef), Leonid Nikolaevich (1871—1919), Russ. author.

Andrew (an′drō), John Albion (1818—67), Am. statesman, governor of Massachusetts (1861—66).

Andrewes (an′drōz), Lancelot (1555—1626), Eng. bishop and writer.

Andrews (an′drōz), Roy Chapman (1884—   ), Am. naturalist and explorer.

Andronicus I. (an-drō-nī′kus) (Andronicus Comnenus) (c1110—85), Byzantine emperor (1183—85) (grandson of Alexius I., and cousin of Manuel I.).

Andronicus, Livius (c284—204 B.C.), Rom. epic and dramatic poet.

Andros (an′dros), Sir Edmund (1637—1714), Eng. colonial governor in America.

Angelico (än-jel′ē-kō), Fra (also known as Fra Giovanni da Fiesole, orig. Guido, or Guidolino, di Pietro) (1387—1455), It. painter.

Angell (än′jel), James Burrill (1829—1916), Am. educator.

Angell, James Rowland (1869—   ), Am. psychologist and educator (son of James B.).

Angoulême (däⁿ-gö-lãm), Marie Thérèse Charlotte, Duchesse d' (1778—1851), daughter of Louis XVI. of France.

Ångström (ông′strēm), Anders Jöns (1814—74), Swed. physicist.

Angus (ang′gus), Archibald Douglas, 5th Earl of (called "the Great Earl" and "Bell the Cat") (1449?—1514), Sc. politician.

Anna (an′ạ) (1693—1740), empress of Russia (1730—40) (niece of Peter the Great).

Anna Comnena (kom-nē′nạ) (1083—1148), Byzantine princess and historian (daughter of Emperor Alexius I.).

Anne (an) (1665—1714), queen of Great Britain and Ireland (1702—14) (successor of William III., and sister of Mary II.).

Anne Boleyn or **Bullen.** See *Boleyn, Anne.*

Anne de Beaujeu (dᵉ bō-zhᵉ) or **Anne of France** (1460—1522), regent of France (1483—91) (daughter of Louis XI.).

Anne of Austria (1601—66), queen of Louis XIII. of France, and regent during minority of her son Louis XIV.

Anne of Brittany (1476?—1514), queen of Charles VIII. and of Louis XII. of France.

Anne of Cleves (klēvz) (1515—57), fourth wife of Henry VIII. of England.

Anne of Denmark (1574—1619), queen of James I. of England.

Anne of France. See *Anne de Beaujeu.*

Annunzio (dän-nön′tsē-ō), Gabriele d' (Prince of Montenevoso) (1863-1938), It. poet, dramatist, novelist, and soldier.

Anselm (an′selm), Saint (1033—1109), archbishop of Canterbury, and scholastic theologian and philosopher, born in Piedmont.

---

fat, fāte, fär, fȧll, ȧsk, fâre; net, mē, hėr; pin, pīne; not, nōte, mȯve, nôr; up, lūte, p˙ull; oi, oil; ou, out; (lightened) aviȧry, ᵉlect, agȯny, intᵒ, ᵾnite; (obscured) errᵃnt, operᵃ, ardᵉnt, actᵒr, natᵾre; ch, chip; g, go; th, thin; ꜰн, then; y, you;

Anselm of Laon (d. 1117), Fr. scholastic theologian.

Ansgar (ans'gär), or **Anschar** or **Anskar** (ans'kär), Saint (in Latin, Ansgarius or Anscharius, called "the Apostle of the North") (801—865), Frankish missionary to Denmark, Sweden, and northern Germany.

Anson (an'son), George Anson, Baron (1697—1762), Eng. admiral.

Anson, Sir William Reynell (1843—1914), Eng. legal writer.

Antenor (an-tē'nor) (fl. c509 B.C.), Gr. sculptor.

Anthemius (an-thē'mi-us) (fl. c532), Byzantine Gr. mathematician and architect, born at Tralles, in Asia Minor.

Anthony (an'tō-ni or an'thō-ni) or **Antony** (an'tō-ni), Saint (c251—c356), Egyptian hermit, founder of eremitical Christian monasticism. According to legend, the hermit was subjected by demons to fleshly temptation and to torment, but by prayer was enabled to resist and prevail against sin.

Anthony (an'thō-ni), Susan Brownell (1820—1906), Am. social reformer, advocate of woman's rights.

Anthony (an'tō-ni or an'thō-ni) (or **Antony**) **of Padua**, Saint (1195—1231), Franciscan monk and preacher in Italy and France, born in Portugal.

Antigonus (an-tig'ō-nus) (surnamed Cyclops) (382?—301 B.C.), general of Alexander the Great, and king of Macedonia (306—301 B.C.).

Antiochus III. (an-tī'ō-kus) ("the Great") (238?—187 B.C.), king of Syria (223—187 B.C.).

Antipater (an-tip'a-tėr) (398?—319 B.C.), Macedonian general and regent.

Antisthenes (an-tis'thē-nēz) (c444—c365 B.C.), Gr. philosopher, founder of Cynic school.

Antoine (än-twän'), André (1857—1943), Fr. actor and theatrical manager.

Antonelli (än-tō-nel'lē), Giacomo (1806—76), It. cardinal and papal statesman.

Antoninus (an-tō-nī'nus), Marcus Aurelius (orig. Marcus Annius Verus) (121—180), Rom. emperor (161—180) and philosopher (adopted son of Emperor Antoninus Pius).

Antoninus Pius (pī'us) (Titus Aurelius Fulvus Boionius Arrius Antoninus) (A.D. 86—161), Rom. emperor (138—161) (adopted son of Emperor Hadrian).

Antonius (an-tō'ni-us), Marcus (commonly known as Mark Antony) (c83—30 B.C.), Rom. general, member of Second Triumvirate.

Antony. See *Anthony.*

Anzengruber (än'tsen-grö''bėr), Ludwig (1839—89), Austrian dramatist and novelist.

Apelles (a-pel'ēz) (fl. c335 B.C.), Gr. painter.

Apicius (a-pish'ius), Marcus Gabius (fl. A.D. c14), Rom. epicure.

Apollodorus (a-pol-ō-dō'rus) (fl. c420 B.C.), Gr. painter.

Apollonius of Perga (ap-o-lō'ni-us, pėr'gä) (b. c262 B.C.), Gr. geometrician.

Apollonius of Rhodes (fl. c200 B.C.), Gr. epic poet.

Apollonius of Tyana (tī'a-nä) (fl. 1st cent.), Gr. philosopher.

Apponyi (op'pōn-yē), Albert, Count (1846—1933), Hung. statesman.

Appuleius. See *Apuleius.*

Apraksin (a-präk'sen), Fedor Matvyeevich (1671—1728), Russ. admiral, founder of Russian navy.

Apuleius or **Appuleius** (ap-ū-lē'yus), Lucius (b. c125), Rom. romance-writer and philosopher, of northern Africa.

Aquinas (a-kwī'nas), Thomas (Thomas of Aquino, "the Angelic Doctor") (1225?—74), It. scholastic theologian, and saint.

Arabi Pasha (ä-rä'bē pa-shä') (Ahmed el-Arabi) (1841?—1911), Egyptian soldier and revolutionary leader.

Arago (a-ra-gō), Dominique François (1786—1853), Fr. astronomer and physicist.

Aram (ā'ram), Eugene (1704—59), Eng. schoolmaster and philologist, executed for murder.

Aranda (ä-rän'dä), Pedro Pablo Abarca de Bolea, Count of (1718—99?), Sp. statesman and diplomatist.

Arany (or'on-y'), János (1817—82), Hung. poet.

Arblay (där'blā), Mme. d' (Frances Burney) (1752—1840), Eng. novelist (daughter of Charles Burney).

Arbogast (är'bō-gast) (d. 394), general in Roman service, probably of Frankish parentage.

Arbuthnot (är-buth'not or är'buth-not), John (1667—1735), Br. physician and writer.

Arc, Jeanne d'. See *Joan of Arc.*

Arcadius (är-kā'di-us) (377?—408), Eastern Rom. emperor (395—408) (son of Theodosius I., and brother of Emperor Honorius).

Arcesilaus (är-ses-i-lā'us) (c316—c241 B.C.), Gr. Skeptic philosopher.

Archer (är'chėr), William (1856—1924), Br. dramatic critic, playwright, and translator.

Archilochus (är-kil'ō-kus) (fl. c650 B.C.), Gr. lyric poet.

Archimedes (är-ki-mē'dēz) (c287—212 B.C.), Gr. mathematician and inventor, of Syracuse.

Ardashir I. (är-da-shēr') or **Ardshir I.** (ärd-shēr') (also called Artaxerxes I.) (d. 241?), king of Persia (212?—241?).

Arditi (är-dē'tē), Luigi (1822—1903), It. musical composer and conductor.

Aretino (ä-rä-tē'nō), Pietro (1492—1556), It. satirist and dramatist.

Argall (är'gal), Sir Samuel (1572?—1626), Eng. adventurer, deputy governor of Virginia.

Argyll (är-gīl'), Archibald Campbell, 5th Earl of (1530—73), Sc. politician.

Argyll, Archibald Campbell, 8th Earl of (Marquis of Argyll) (1598 or 1607—1661), Sc. politician and soldier, beheaded on charge of treason.

Argyll, Archibald Campbell, 9th Earl of (1629?—85), Sc. politician and soldier, beheaded on charge of treason (son of 8th Earl).

Argyll, George John Douglas Campbell, 8th Duke of (1823—1900), Br. statesman and writer.

Argyll, John Douglas Sutherland Campbell, 9th Duke of (Marquis of Lorne) (1845—1914), Br. statesman and writer, governor-general of Canada (1878—83) (son of 8th Duke, and son-in-law of Queen Victoria).

Ariosto (ä-rē-ôs'tō), Lodovico, or Ludovico (1474—1533), It. poet, author of "Orlando Furioso."

Ariovistus (ä''ri-ō-vis'tus) (fl. 58 B.C.), Ger. chief, who invaded Gaul and was defeated by Julius Cæsar.

Arista (ä-rēs'tä), Mariano (1802—55), Mex. general.

Aristarchus (ar-is-tär'kus) (fl. c280—c264 B.C.), Gr. astronomer.

Aristarchus (c220—c145 B.C.), Gr. grammarian and critic, at Alexandria.

Aristides (ar-is-tī'dēz) ("the Just") (d. 468? B.C.), Athenian statesman and general.

Aristippus (ar-is-tip'us) (c435—c356 B.C.), Gr. philosopher, founder of Cyrenaic school.

Aristogiton. See *Harmodius.*

Aristophanes (ar-is-tof'a-nēz) (c450—c385 B.C.), Gr. writer of comedy.

Aristotle (ar'is-tot-l) ("the Stagirite") (384—322 B.C.), Gr. philosopher, founder of Peripatetic school.

Arius (a-rī'us or ā'ri-us) (c256—336), presbyter and heretic at Alexandria, founder of Arianism.

Arkwright (ärk'rīt), Sir Richard (1732—92), Eng. inventor (of spinning machinery).

Arlington (är'ling-ton), Henry Bennet, Earl of (1618—85), Eng. politician and diplomatist.

Armagnac (där-mä-nyàk), Bernard VII., Comte d' (d. 1418), Fr. partizan leader.

Arminius (är-min'i-us) (Latinized from Armin, or Hermann) (17 B.C.—A.D. 21), Ger. chieftain, liberator of western Germany from Roman dominion.

Arminius, Jacobus (orig. Jacob Harmensen) (1560—1609), Dutch Protestant theologian, author of Arminian doctrines.

Armstrong (ärm'strong), John, or Johnnie (d. 1528?), Sc. freebooter.

Armstrong, John (1709—79), Br. physician, poet, and misc. writer.

Armstrong, John (1758—1843), Am. soldier and diplomatist.

Arnaldus Villanovanus (är-nal'dus vil''a-nō-vā'nus). See *Arnold of Villanova.*

Arnaud (är-nō), Henri (1641—1721), pastor and leader of the Waldenses of Piedmont.

Arnaud de Villeneuve (dė vēl-nėv'). See *Arnold of Villanova.*

Arnauld (är-nō), Antoine ("tne Great Arnauld") (1612—94), Fr. Jansenist theologian and polemical writer.

Arndt (ärnt), Ernst Moritz (1769—1860), Ger. poet and patriot.

Arne (ärn), Thomas Augustine (1710—78), Eng. musical composer.

Arnim (fon är'nim), Elisabeth, or Bettina, von (Elisabeth Brentano) (1785—1859), Ger. writer (wife of L. A. von Arnim, sister of Klemens Brentano).

Arnim, Harry Karl Kurt Eduard, Graf von (1824—81), Ger. diplomatist.

Arnim, Ludwig Achim von (1781—1831), Ger. poet and novelist.

Arnim or **Arnheim** (fon ärn'him), Hans (or Johann) Georg von (1581—1641), Ger. general in Thirty Years' War.

Arnobius (är-nō'bi-us) (called Arnobius Afer) (fl. c300), Christian apologist, of northern Africa.

Arnold (är'nold), Benedict (1741—1801), Am. Revolutionary general and traitor.

Arnold, Sir Edwin (1832—1904), Eng. poet.

Arnold, Henry H. (1886—   ), Am. general.

Arnold, Matthew (1822—88), Eng. poet (son of Thomas).

Arnold, Thomas (1795—1842), Eng. clergyman and educator, head-master of Rugby.

Arnold of Brescia (c1100—55), It. religious reformer.

Arnold of Villanova (vil-a-nō'vä) (in French, Arnaud de Villeneuve; as Latinized, Arnaldus Villanovanus) (c1240—1313?), physician, alchemist, and astrologer, said to have been born in Spain.

Arnolfo di Cambio (är-nōl'fō dē käm'bē-ō) (also called Arnolfo di Lapo) (c1232—c1300), It. architect and sculptor.

Arnould (är-nō), Sophie (1744—1803), Fr. operatic soprano singer.

Arnulf (är'nulf) (c850—899), king of Germany (887—899), and Rom. emperor (896—899).

Árpád (är'päd) (d. 907), first ruler of the Magyars in Hungary.

Arrhenius (är-rā'nē-us), Svante August (1859—1927), Swed. physicist and chemist.

Arrian (ar'i-an) (Flavius Arrianus) (A.D. c95—c175), Gr. historian and philosopher.

Arsaces I. (är'sa-sēz) (fl. c250 B.C.), reputed founder of kingdom of Parthia.

Artaxerxes I. (är-tak-sėrk'sēz) (d. 425? B.C.), king of Persia (465—425? B.C.) (son of Xerxes I.).

Artaxerxes II. (surnamed Mnemon) (d. c359 B.C.), king of Persia (404?—c359 B.C.) (grandson of Artaxerxes I.).

Artaxerxes I. (d. 241?). See *Ardashir I.*

Artedi (är-tā'dē), Peter (1705—35), Swed. naturalist.

Artemisia (är-tē-mish'i-a) (d. 350 B.C.), ruler of Caria (353—350 B.C.) (wife of Mausolus).

Artevelde (vän är'tė-vel-dė), Jacob van (c1290—1345), Flemish popular leader.

Artevelde, Philip van (c1340—82), Flemish popular leader (son of Jacob).

Arthur (är'thėr) (fl. c500?), Br. king, hero of the Arthurian legends.

Arthur (1187—1203), duke (or count) of Brittany (nephew of King John of England).

Arthur, Chester Alan (1830—86), 21st president of U. S. (1881—85).

Arthur, Timothy Shay (1809—85), Am. writer, author of "Ten Nights in a Bar-Room."

Artigas (är-tē'gäs), José (1755—1851), South Am. soldier and politician, dictator of Uruguay.

Artsybashev (är-tsi-bä'shef), Mikhail Petrovich (1878—1927), Russ. author.

Arundel (ar'un-del), Henry Fitzalan, 12th Earl of (c1511—80), Eng. soldier and statesman.

Arundel, Thomas (1353—1414), Eng. prelate, archbishop of Canterbury.

Asbjörnsen (äs-byėrn'sen), Peter Christen (1812—85), Norw. folklorist and naturalist.

Asbury (az'be-ri), Francis (1745—1816), Am. Methodist bishop (the first ordained in U. S.), born in England.

Ascham (as'kam), Roger (1515—68), Eng. scholar and author.

Asclepiades (as-klē-pī'a-dēz) (fl. c100 B.C.), Gr. physician, at Rome.

Asdrubal (az'drö-bal). See *Hasdrubal.*

Aselli (ä-sel'lē) or **Asellio** (ä-sel'lē-ō), Gaspare (1581?—1626), It. anatomist.

Ashburton (ash'bėr-ton), Alexander Baring, 1st Baron (1774—1848), Eng. financier and statesman (son of Sir Francis Baring).

Ashmole (ash'mōl), Elias (1617—92), Eng. antiquary.

Ashurbanipal. See *Asurbanipal.*

Askew (as'kū), Anne (Mrs. Kyme) (1521?—46), Eng. Protestant martyr.

Asoka (a-sō'ka) (d. 226? B.C.), Buddhist king of India (264?—226? B.C.) (grandson of Chandragupta).

Aspasia (as-pā'shia) (fl. c445 B.C.), Athenian courtezan (born at Miletus), mistress of Pericles.

Asquith, Herbert Henry. See *Oxford and Asquith, 1st Earl of.*

Assurbanipal. See *Asurbanipal.*

Aston (as'ton), Francis William (1877—1945), Eng. physicist and chemist.

Astor (as'tor), John Jacob (1763—1848), Ger.-Am. merchant.

Astor, Viscountess (Nancy Witcher Langhorne, Mrs. Shaw) (1879—   ), first woman to sit in the British House of Commons, born in U. S.

Asurbanipal or **Assurbanipal** (ä-sör-bä'nę-päl), or **Ashurbanipal** (ä-shör-bä'nę-päl) (in Greek, Sardanapalus) (d. 626? B.C.), king of Assyria (668—626? B.C.) (son of Esarhaddon).

Atahualpa or **Atahuallpa** (ä-tä-wäl'pä) (d. 1533), last Inca king of Peru (half-brother of Huascar).

Athanasius (ath-a-nā'shius), Saint ("the Father of Orthodoxy") (296 or 293—373), bishop of Alexandria, and theologian.

Athelstan (ath'el-stan) (or Æthelstan) (895?—940), king of the English (925—940) (son of Edward the Elder).

Atossa (a-tos'a) (fl. c529—c519 B.C.), daughter of Cyrus the Great, and wife successively of Cambyses, Smerdis, and Darius I., and mother by the last of Xerxes I.

Atterbom (ät'tėr-bom), Per Daniel Amadeus (1790—1855), Swed. poet.

Atterbury (at'ėr-ber"i), Francis (1662—1732), Eng. bishop, controversialist, and politician.

Attila (at'i-la) ("the Scourge of God") (d. 453), king of the Huns (433—453), and conqueror.

Aubé (ō-bā), Jean Paul (1837—1916), Fr. sculptor.

Auber (ō-bār), Daniel François Esprit (1782—1871), Fr. operatic composer.

Aubigné (dō-bē-nyä), Jean Henri Merle d'. See *Merle d'Aubigné.*

Aubigné, Théodore Agrippa d' (1552—1630), Fr. Huguenot soldier, historian, and poet.

Aubrey (à'bri), John (1626—97), Eng. antiquary.

Aubusson (dō-bü-sôn), Pierre d' (1423—1503), Fr. military leader, esp. against the Turks.

Auchinleck (ô-kin-lek'), Sir Claude J. E. (1884—   ), Brit. general.

Auckland (âk'land), George Eden, Earl of (1784—1849), Eng. statesman (son of 1st Baron Auckland).

Auckland, William Eden, 1st Baron (1744—1814), Eng. statesman and diplomatist.

Audley (âd'li), Thomas Audley, Baron (c1488—1544), Eng. politician, lord chancellor (1533—44).

Audran (ō-drän), Edmond (1842—1901), Fr. composer.

Audubon (â'dū-bon), John James (1785—1851), Am. ornithologist.

Auenbrugger von Auenbrug (ou'en-brüg"ėr fon ou'en-brüch), Leopold (1722—1809), Austrian physician.

Auerbach (ou'er-bäch), Berthold (1812—82), Ger. novelist.

Auersperg (ou'ėrs-perch), Adolf Wilhelm Daniel, Prince (1821—85), Austrian statesman.

Auersperg, Anton Alexander, Graf von ("Anastasius Grün") (1806—76), Austrian poet.

Auer von Welsbach (ou'ėr fon vels'bäch), Karl. See *Welsbach.*

Augereau (ozh-rō), Pierre François Charles (Duc de Castiglione) (1757—1816), marshal of France.

Augier (ō-zhyā), Guillaume Victor Émile (1820—89), Fr. dramatist.

Augustine (â-gus'tin or â'gus-tin), Saint (354—430), bishop and theologian, of northern Africa.

Augustine or **Austin** (âs'tin), Saint (d. 604), Rom. monk and missionary, first archbishop of Canterbury.

Augustus (â-gus'tus) (the title of Caius Julius Cæsar Octavianus, orig. Caius Octavius) (63 B.C.—A.D. 14), first Rom. emperor (27 B.C.—A.D. 14) (grandnephew and heir of Caius Julius Cæsar).

Augustus II. ("the Strong") (1670—1733), king of Poland (1697—1704, 1709—33), and (as Frederick Augustus I.) elector of Saxony (1694—1733).

Augustus III. (1696—1763), king of Poland and (as Frederick Augustus II.) elector of Saxony (1733—63) (son of Augustus II.).

Aulard (ō-lär), François Victor Alphonse (1849—1928), Fr. historian.

Aumale (dō-mȧl), Henri Eugène Philippe Louis d'Orléans, Duc d' (1822—97), Fr. general (son of Louis Philippe, king of the French).

Aumont (dō-môṅ), Jean d' (1522—95), marshal of France.

Aungerville (än'jėr-vil), Richard. See *Bury, Richard de.*

Aurangzeb or **Aurungzeb** (â'rung-zeb') (1618—1707), Mogul emperor of Hindustan (1658—1707).

Aurelian (â-rē'liạn) (Lucius Domitius Aurelianus) (c212—275), Rom. emperor (270—275).

Aurelianus (â-rē-li-ā'nus), Cælius (fl. 5th cent.), Latin medical writer, of northern Africa.

Aurungzeb. See *Aurangzeb.*

Ausonius (â-sō'ni-us), Decimus Magnus (c310—c395), Rom. poet.

Austen (âs'tẹn), Jane (1775—1817), Eng. novelist.

Austin (âs'tin), Alfred (1835—1913), Eng. poet laureate.

Austin, John (1790—1859), Eng. writer on jurisprudence.

Austin, Stephen Fuller (1793—1836), Am. pioneer in Texas.

Austin, Saint. See *Augustine, Saint* (d. 604).

Avalos (dä-vä'lōs), Ferdinando Francesco d'. See *Pescara.*

Avebury (āv'bẹ-ri), John Lubbock, 1st Baron (1834—1913), Eng. naturalist and writer.

Avellaneda (ä-vel-yä-nä'тнä), Nicolás (1836—85), Argentine statesman, president of Argentina (1874—80).

Avempace (ä-vem-pä'thä) (Ibn Bajja) (d. 1138), Arab philosopher, in Spain.

Avenarius (ä-vẹ-nä'rẹ-us), Richard Heinrich Ludwig (1843—96), Ger. philosopher, born in Paris.

Avenzoar (av-ẹn-zō'är) (Ibn Zuhr) (c1075—1162), Arab physician, of Seville.

Averroës (a-ver'ō-ēz) (Ibn Rushd) (c1126—98), Arab physician and philosopher, of Cordova.

Avicebron (ä-vē-thä-brōn') (Solomon ben Judah ibn Gabirol) (c1021—58?), Sp. Jewish philosopher and poet.

Avicenna (av-i-sen'ä) (Ibn Sina) (980—1037), Arab physician and philosopher.

Ávila (dä ä'vē-lä), Gil González de (c1577—1658), Sp. Jesuit, biographer, and antiquary.

Avogadro (ä-vō-gä'drō), Amedeo (Count of Quaregna) (1776—1856), It. physicist and chemist.

Axel. See *Absalon.*

Ayesha. See *Aisha.*

Ayllón (dä ī-lyōn'), Lucas Vázquez de (c1475—1526), Sp. adventurer and colonizer in America.

Aymer de Valence (ā'mėr dẹ val'ẹns) (Earl of Pembroke) (d. 1324), Eng. soldier and politician.

Ayrton (är'tọn), William Edward (1847—1908), Eng. electrical engineer and inventor.

Ayscue (ās'kū), Sir George (d. 1671?), Eng. admiral.

Aytoun (ā'tọn), William Edmonstoune (1813—65), Sc. poet and misc. writer.

Ayub Khan (ä-yöb' kän) (1855—1914), Afghan prince (son of Shere Ali Khan), and military leader against his cousin Abdur-Rahman Khan.

Azeglio (däd-zäl'yō), Massimo Taparelli, Marchese d' (1798—1866), It. statesman and author.

B

Babar. See *Baber.*

Babbage (bab'āj), Charles (1792—1871), Eng. mathematician and inventor.

Babbitt (bab'it), Irving (1865—1933), Am. educator and critic.

Baber (bä'bėr) or **Babar** (bä'bär) (real name Zahir al-Din Muhammad) (1483—1530), conqueror in India and founder of the Mogul empire.

Babeuf (bȧ-bėf'), François Noël (1760—97), Fr. political agitator and revolutionist.

Babington (bab'ing-tọn), Anthony (1561—86), Eng. Rom. Cath. conspirator.

Bacchylides (ba-kil'i-dēz) (fl. c470 B.C.), Gr. lyric poet.

Baccio della Porta (bät'chō del'lä pôr'tä). See *Bartolommeo, Fra.*

Bach (fon bäch), Alexander, Freiherr von (1813—93), Austrian statesman.

Bach, Johann Sebastian (1685—1750), Ger. musical composer.

Bach, Karl Philipp Emanuel (1714—88), Ger. musical composer (son of Johann S.).

Bache (bāch), Alexander Dallas (1806—67), Am. physicist.

Bacon (bā'kọn), Francis (Baron Verulam, Viscount St. Albans) (1561—1626), Eng. philosopher and statesman.

Bacon, Leonard (1802—81), Am. Congregational clergyman, historian, and editor.

Bacon, Nathaniel (1642?—76), Virginia patriot, born in England.

Bacon, Sir Nicholas (1509—79), Eng. statesman (father of Francis).

Bacon, Roger ("the Admirable Doctor") (c1214—c1294), Eng. philosopher.

Baden-Powell (bā'dn-pou'el) **of Gilwell,** Robert Stephenson Smyth Baden-Powell, 1st Baron (1857—1941), Eng. general and writer, founder (1908) of organization of Boy Scouts.

Badius (bä'dẹ-us), Jodocus (called Badius Ascensius, properly Josse Bade) (1462—1535), Flemish printer and writer, in Paris.

Badoglio (bä-dô'lyō), Pietro (1871—   ), It. marshal.

Bæda. See *Bede.*

Baedeker (bā'dė-kėr, Ger. bä'dė-kėr), Karl (1801—59), Ger. publisher of guide-books for travelers.

Baekeland (bā'kẹ-lạnd), Leo Hendrik (1863—1944), Belgian-Am. chemist.

Baer (fon bär), Karl Ernst von (1792—1876), Russ. biologist.

Baeyer (fon bä'yėr), Johann Friedrich Wilhelm Adolf von (1835—1917), Ger. chemist.

Baffin (baf'in), William (d. 1622), Eng. navigator, explorer of Baffin Bay.

Bagehot (baj'ọt), Walter (1826—77), Eng. economist.

Baggesen (bäg'gẹ-sẹn), Jens Immanuel (1764—1826), Dan. poet, writing in Danish and German.

Bagration (bȧ-grȧ-tẹ-ôn'), Prince Petr Ivanovich (1765—1812), Russ. general.

Bailey (bā'li), Liberty Hyde (1858—   ), Am. botanist, horticulturist, and educator.

Bailey, Nathan, or Nathaniel (d. 1742), Eng. lexicographer.

Bailey, Philip James (1816—1902), Eng. poet, author of "Festus."

Baillie (bā'li), Joanna (1762—1851), Br. poet.

Bailly (bä-yē'), Jean Sylvain (1736—93), Fr. astronomer and politician.

Bain (bān), Alexander (1818—1903), Sc. psychologist, logician, and educationist.

Bainbridge (bān'brij), William (1774—1833), Am. commodore.

Baird (bärd), Sir David (1757—1829), Br. general.

Baius (bä'yus), Michael (name orig. Michel de Bay) (1513—89), Belgian theologian.

Bajazet I. (baj-ạ-zet') or **Bayazid I.** (bä-yä-zēd') (1347—1403), sultan of Turkey (1389—1403) and conqueror (son of Amurath I.), overcome by Timur.

Bajazet II. (1447?—1512), sultan of Turkey (1481—1512) (son of Mohammed II.).

Baker (bā'kėr), George Fisher (1840—1931), Am. financier.

Baker, George Pierce (1866—1935), Am. educator, teacher of dramatic composition at Harvard and Yale.

Baker, Newton Diehl (1871—1937), Am. lawyer, Secretary of War (1916—21).

Baker, Sir Samuel White (1821—93), Eng. explorer and hunter in Africa.

Bakst (bäkst), Léon (1866—1924), Russ. painter and designer.

(variable) ḏ as d or j, ṣ as s or sh, ṭ as t or ch, ẓ as z or zh; o, F. cloche; ü, F. menu; ċh, Sc. loch; ṅ, F. bonbon; ', primary accent; ", secondary accent; †, obsolete; <, from; +, and; =, equals. See also lists at beginning of book.

Bakunin (bå-kö′nyẹn), Mikhail Aleksandrovich (1814—76), Russ. anarchist and writer.

Balakirev (bå-lå-kē′ref), Mili Aleksyeevich (1837—1910), Russ. musical composer.

Balboa (dä bäl-bō′ä), Vasco Núñez de (c1475—1517), Sp. adventurer and colonial administrator, discoverer of the Pacific.

Baldensperger (bål-dań-sper-zhä), Philippe Jules Fernand (1871—), Fr. educator and author.

Baldwin I. (båld′win) (1058—1118), king of Jerusalem (1100—18) (brother of Godfrey of Bouillon).

Baldwin I. (Baldwin IX., Count of Flanders) (1171—1205), a leader of the fourth crusade, and first of the emperors of the Latin Empire at Constantinople (1204—05).

Baldwin, James Mark (1861—1934), Am. psychologist.

Baldwin, Robert (1804—58), Can. statesman.

Baldwin of Bewdley (būd′li), Stanley Baldwin, 1st Earl (1867—), Eng. statesman.

Bale (bāl), John (1495—1563), Eng. Protestant bishop, dramatist, and misc. writer. [poser.

Balfe (balf), Michael William (1808—70), Ir. operatic composer.

Balfour (bal′för), Arthur James Balfour, 1st Earl of (1848—1930), Br. statesman and philosophical writer.

Balfour, Francis Maitland (1851—82), Br. biologist (brother of Arthur J.).

Balfour, Sir James (d. 1583), Sc. judge and political intriguer.

Baliol or **Balliol** (bāl′yọl), Edward de (d. 1363), claimant to the throne of Scotland (son of John de Baliol, 1249—1315).

Baliol or **Balliol,** John de (d. 1269), Eng. baron, founder of Balliol College, Oxford.

Baliol or **Balliol,** John de (1249—1315), king of Scotland (1292—96) (successor of Queen Margaret, and son of John de Baliol, d. 1269).

Ball (bål), John (d. 1381), Eng. priest, a leader in the peasants' (Wat Tyler's) revolt.

Ball, Sir Robert Stawell (1840—1913), Br. astronomer.

Ball, Thomas (1819—1911), Am. sculptor.

Ballantyne (bal′ạn-tīn), Robert Michael (1825—94), Br. writer of tales for boys.

Balliol. See *Baliol.*

Ballou (ba-lö′), Hosea (1771—1852), Am. Universalist clergyman and theologian.

Balmaceda (bäl-mä-sä′ŦHä), José Manuel (1838?—91), Chilean statesman, president of Chile (1886—91).

Baltimore (bål′ti-mōr), Cecilius (or Cecil) Calvert, 2d Baron (1605?—75), Eng. nobleman, first proprietor of colony of Maryland (son of 1st Baron).

Baltimore, George Calvert, 1st Baron (c1580—1632), Eng. statesman, projector of colony of Maryland.

Balue (dè lä bá-lü), Jean, or Jean de la (1421?—91), Fr. cardinal and politician.

Balzac (dè bál-zàk), Honoré de (1799—1850), Fr. novelist.

Bancroft (bang′krôft or ban′krôft), George (1800—91), Am. historian.

Bancroft, Hubert Howe (1832—1918), Am. historian.

Bancroft, Sir Squire Bancroft (1841—1926), Eng. actor and theatrical manager.

Bandello (bän-del′lō), Matteo (1480—1562), It. novelist.

Banér (bä-när′), Johan (1596—1641), Swed. field-marshal in Thirty Years' War.

Banks (bangks), Sir Joseph (1743—1820), Eng. naturalist.

Banks, Nathaniel Prentiss (1816—94), Am. legislator and general.

Banting (ban′ting), Sir Frederick Grant (1891—1941), Can. research physician.

Bantock (ban′tọk), Sir Granville (1868—1946), Eng. musical composer.

Banville (dè bäṅ-vēl), Théodore Faullain de (1823—91), Fr. poet and misc. writer.

Baraguay d'Hilliers (bå-rà-gä dē-lyä), Achille, Comte (1795—1878), Fr. marshal.

Barbacena (dä bär-bä-sä′nä), Felisberto Caldeira Brant Pontes, Marquis de (1772—1841), Brazilian soldier and statesman.

Barbara (bär′bạ-rạ), Saint (d. 235? or 306?), Christian virgin martyr.

Barbarelli (bär-bä-rel′lē), Giorgio. See *Giorgione.*

Barbarossa (bär-bạ-ros′ä). See *Frederick I.* (emperor).

Barbarossa, Arudj, or Horuk (d. 1518), Turk. corsair, conqueror and ruler of Algiers (1516—18) (brother of Khair-ed-Din Barbarossa).

Barbarossa, Khair-ed-Din, or Khair al-Din (d. 1546), ruler of Algiers (1518—46), founder with his brother Arudj Barbarossa of Turkish rule in northern Africa.

Barbaroux (bär-bä-rö), Charles Jean Marie (1767—94), Fr. revolutionist.

Barbauld (bär′båld), Mrs. (Anna Letitia Aikin) (1743—1825), Eng. poet and misc. writer.

Barbazan (dè bär-bä-zäṅ), Arnaud Guillaume, Sire de (c1360—1431), Fr. general.

Barbey d'Aurevilly (bär-bā dō-rè-vē-yē), Jules Amédée (1808—89), Fr. author.

Barbiano (bär-bē-ä′nō), Count Alberico (d. 1409), It. condottiere.

Barbon (bär′bọn), **Barebone** (bär′bōn), or **Barebones** (bär′bōnz), Praise-God (1596?—1679), Eng. Baptist preacher, and member of the parliament of July—Dec., 1653 ("Barebone's Parliament").

Barbosa du Bocage (dä bär-bō′zä dü bo-käzh′), Manoel Maria de (1765?—1805), Pg. poet.

Barbour (bär′bèr), John (1316?—95), Sc. poet.

Barbusse (bär-büs), Henri (1875—1935), Fr. author.

Barclay (bär′kli), Alexander (c1476—1552), Br. poet.

Barclay, John (1582—1621), Sc. poet and romance-writer, writing in Latin.

Barclay, Robert (1648—90), Sc. Quaker theological writer.

Barclay de Tolly (bär′klä dè tol′ē), Prince Michael Andreas (called in Russia Prince Mikhail Bogdanovich) (1761—1818), Russ. field-marshal.

Barebone or **Barebones.** See *Barbon.*

Barents (bä′rents), Willem (c1550—97), Dutch navigator in Arctic Ocean.

Barère de Vieuzac (bà-rär dè vyè-zàk), Bertrand (1755—1841), Fr. revolutionist and politician.

Baret or **Barret** (bar′et), John (d. c1580), Eng. lexicographer.

Barham (bär′ạm), Richard Harris ("Thomas Ingoldsby") (1788—1845), Eng. divine and humorist.

Baring (bär′ing). See *Ashburton* and *Cromer.*

Baring, Sir Francis (1740—1810), Eng. merchant and financier.

Baring-Gould (-göld′), Sabine (1834—1924), Eng. clergyman, novelist, and misc. writer.

Barker, H. G. Granville-. See *Granville-Barker.*

Barlow (bär′lō), Joel (1754—1812), Am. poet.

Barnard (bär′nạrd), Frederick Augustus Porter (1809—89), Am. educator.

Barnard, George Grey (1863—1938), Am. sculptor.

Barnave (bär-näv), Antoine Pierre Joseph Marie (1761—93), Fr. revolutionist and orator.

Barnby (bärn′bi), Sir Joseph (1838—96), Eng. musical composer and conductor.

Barnes (bärnz), Robert (1495—1540), Eng. Protestant reformer and martyr.

Barneveldt or **Barneveld** (bär′nè-velt), Jan van Olden (real name Johan van Oldenbarneveldt) (1547—1619), Dutch statesman.

Barnfield (bärn′fēld), Richard (1574—1627), Eng. poet.

Barnum (bär′num), Phineas Taylor (1810—91), Am. showman.

Barocchio (bä-rok′kē-ō) or **Barozzi** (bä-rot′sē), Giacomo, or Jacopo (called Da Vignola) (1507—73), It. architect.

Baroche (bà-rosh), Pierre Jules (1802—70), Fr. statesman.

Baroja y Nessi (bä-rō′Hä ē nes′sē), Pío (1872—), Sp. physician and novelist.

Baronius (ba-rō′ni-us) or **Baronio** (bä-rō′nē-ō), Cesare (1538—1607), It. cardinal and ecclesiastical historian.

Barozzi, Giacomo, or Jacopo. See *Barocchio.*

Barras (dè bà-räs), Paul Jean François Nicolas, Comte de (1755—1829), Fr. revolutionist, a member of the Directory.

Barrès (bà-res), Maurice (1862—1923), Fr. novelist, misc. writer, and politician.

Barrett (bar′et), Lawrence (1838—91), Am. actor.

Barrett, Wilson (orig. William Henry Barrett) (1846—1904), Eng. actor and playwright.

Barrie (bar′i), Sir James Matthew (1860—1937), Sc. novelist and dramatist.

Barron (bar'ọn), James (1769–1851), Am. commodore.

Barrot (bȧ-rō), Camille Hyacinthe Odilon (1791–1873), Fr. statesman.

Barrow (bar'ō), Isaac (1630–77), Eng. divine and mathematician.

Barry (bar'i), Sir Charles (1795–1860), Eng. architect.

Barry, John (1745–1803), Am. commodore, born in Ireland.

Barry, Comtesse du. See *Du Barry.*

Barrymore (bar'i-mōr), Ethel (professional name of Ethel Blythe, Mrs. Colt) (1879–   ), Am. actress (niece of John Drew, b. 1853).

Barrymore, John (professional name of John Blythe) (1882–1942), Am. actor (brother of Ethel).

Bart (bär), Jean (1651–1702), Fr. naval commander.

Bartas (dü bär-täs), Guillaume de Salluste, Seigneur du (1544–90), Fr. poet.

Bartels (fon bär'tels), Hans von (1856–1913), Ger. painter.

Barth (bärt), Heinrich (1821–65), Ger. explorer and geographer in Africa.

Barthélemy Saint-Hilaire (bär-tāl-mē sȧṅ-tē-lär), Jules (1805–95), Fr. scholar and statesman.

Bartholdi (bär-tol-dē), Frédéric Auguste (1834–1904), Fr. sculptor.

Barthou (bär-tō), Louis (1862–1934), Fr. statesman and author.

Bartlett (bärt'let), John (1820–1905), Am. publisher and compiler.

Bartlett, John Russell (1805–86), Am. bibliographer, lexicographer, and historical writer.

Bartlett, Paul Wayland (1865–1925), Am. sculptor.

Bartolini (bär-tō-lē'nē), Lorenzo (1777–1850), It. sculptor.

Bartolommeo (bär-tō-lom-mā'ō), Fra (also known as Baccio della Porta, orig. Bartolommeo di Pagholo del Fattorino) (1475–1517), It. painter.

Bartolozzi (bär-tō-lot'sē), Francesco (1727–1815), It. engraver.

Barton (bär'tọn), Clara (1821–1912), Am. philanthropist, organizer of American Red Cross Society.

Barton, Elizabeth ("the Maid of Kent") (1506?–34), Eng. nun and religious impostor.

Bartram (bär'trạm), John (1699–1777), Am. botanist.

Bary, H. A. de. See *De Bary.*

Barye (bȧ-rē), Antoine Louis (1795–1875), Fr. sculptor, esp. of animals.

Basedow (bä'zĕ-dō), Johann Bernhard (orig. Johann Berend Bassedau) (1723–90), Ger. educational reformer.

Bashkirtseff (bȧsh-kĕrt'sef), Marie (in Russian, Mariya Konstantinovna Bashkirtseva) (1860–84), Russ. painter and diarist.

Basil (baz'il or bā'zil), Saint ("Basil the Great") (329–379), bishop and theologian, of Asia Minor.

Baskerville (bas'kẽr-vil), John (1706–75), Eng. type-founder and printer.

Bass (bȧs), George (d. 1812?), Eng. surgeon, and circumnavigator of Tasmania.

Bassi (bäs'sē), Ugo (1800?–49), It. preacher and patriot.

Bassompierre (dè bȧ-sôṅ-pyär), François de (1579–1646), Fr. soldier and diplomatist, marshal of France.

Bastian (bäs'tẹ-än), Adolf (1826–1905), Ger. traveler and ethnologist.

Bastian (bas'tyạn), Henry Charlton (1837–1915), Eng. physician, physiologist, and biologist.

Bastiat (bȧs-tyä), Claude Frédéric (1801–50), Fr. political economist.

Bastien-Lepage (bȧs-tyaṅ-lè-päzh), Jules (1848–84), Fr. painter.

Bataille (bȧ-tä-y'), Henry (1872–1922), Fr. dramatist and poet.

Bateson (bāt'sọn), William (1861–1926), Eng. biologist.

Bath (bȧth), William Pulteney, Earl of (1684–1764), Eng. politician.

Báthori (bä'tō-rẹ), István, or Stephen (c1533–86), Hung. noble, prince of Transylvania (1571–76), and king of Poland (1575–86).

Batthyányi or **Batthyány** (bot'yän-yẹ), Lajos, or Louis, Count (1806 or 1809–49), Hung. statesman and patriot.

Baudelaire (bōd-lär), Pierre Charles (1821–67), Fr. poet and critic.

Bauer (bou'ẽr), Bruno (1809–82), Ger. Biblical critic, and historian.

Baumé (bō-mā), Antoine (1728–1804), Fr. chemist.

Baumgarten (boum'gär"tẹn), Alexander Gottlieb (1714–62), Ger. philosopher.

Baur (bour), Ferdinand Christian (1792–1860), Ger. Protestant Biblical critic and theologian.

Baxter (bak'stẽr), Richard (1615–91), Eng. nonconformist divine, and writer.

Bayard (bā'ạrd, Fr. de bä-yär), Pierre Terrail, Seigneur de (c1473–1524), Fr. soldier, renowned for his chivalric virtues and called "the knight without fear and without reproach."

Bayard (bī'ạrd), Thomas Francis (1828–98), Am. statesman and diplomatist.

Bayazid. See *Bajazet.*

Bäyer (bā'yẽr). See *Baeyer.*

Bayle (bäl), Pierre (1647–1706), Fr. philosopher and critic.

Bayly (bā'li), Thomas Haynes (1797–1839), Eng. poet.

Bazaine (bȧ-zän), François Achille (1811–88), Fr. marshal, tried and imprisoned for the surrender of Metz to the Germans.

Bazin (bȧ-zaṅ), René François Nicolas Marie (1853–1932), Fr. novelist and misc. writer.

Bazzi (bät'sē), Giovanni Antonio. See *Sodoma.*

Beaconsfield (bē'kọnz-fēld or bek'ọnz-fēld), Benjamin Disraeli, Earl of (1804–81), Eng. statesman and novelist.

Beardsley (bērdz'li), Aubrey Vincent (1872–98), Eng. artist in black and white.

Beaton or **Bethune** (bē'tọn), David (1494–1546), Sc. cardinal and statesman.

Beattie (bā'ti or bē'ti), James (1735–1803), Sc. poet and philosophical writer.

Beatty (bē'ti), David Beatty, 1st Earl (1871–1936), Br. admiral.

Beauchamp (dè bē'chạm), Richard de. See *Warwick, Earl of* (1382–1439).

Beaufort (bō'fọrt or bū'fọrt), Edmund. See *Somerset, 2d Duke of.*

Beaufort (dè bō-fôr), François de Vendôme, Duc de (1616–69), Fr. politician and naval officer (grandson of Henry IV. of France).

Beaufort (bō'fọrt or bū'fọrt), Henry (d. 1447), Eng. cardinal and statesman (son of John of Gaunt, and half-brother of Henry IV. of England).

Beauharnais (dè bō-är-nā), Alexandre, Vicomte de (1760–94), Fr. general, born in Martinique (first husband of Joséphine, who later became the wife of Napoleon I.).

Beauharnais, Eugène de (1781–1824), Fr. general and statesman, viceroy of Italy (son of Alexandre and Joséphine de Beauharnais, and stepson of Napoleon I.).

Beauharnais, Eugénie Hortense de. See *Hortense* (wife of Louis Bonaparte).

Beauharnais, Joséphine de. See *Josephine* (first wife of Napoleon I.).

Beaumanoir (dè bō-mȧ-nwor), Jean, Sire de (fl. c1350), Fr. soldier.

Beaumarchais (dè bō-mär-shā), Pierre Augustin Caron de (1732–99), Fr. dramatist.

Beaumont (bō'mont), Francis (1584–1616), Eng. dramatic poet.

Beauregard (bō'rẹ-gärd), Pierre Gustave Toutant (1818–93), Am. Confederate general.

Beaux (bō), Cecilia (1863?–1942), Am. painter.

Bebel (bā'bẹl), Ferdinand August (1840–1913), Ger. socialist leader and writer.

Beccaria (dè bek-kä-rē'ä), Cesare Bonesana, Marchese di (1735–94), It. economist and publicist.

Becket (bek'et), Thomas (called Thomas à Becket and Thomas of London) (1118?–70), Eng. prelate, archbishop of Canterbury.

Beckford (bek'fọrd), William (1759–1844), Eng. writer, author of "Vathek."

Beckwith (bek'with), James Carroll (1852–1917), Am. painter.

Becquerel (bek-rel), Alexandre Edmond (1820–91), Fr. physicist (son of Antoine C.).

Becquerel, Antoine César (1788–1878), Fr. physicist.

Becquerel, Antoine Henri (1852—1908), Fr. physicist (son of Alexandre E.).

Bede (bēd) or **Bæda** (bē'dạ) ("the Venerable Bede") (673?—735), Eng. monk and ecclesiastical historian.

Bede, Cuthbert. Pseudonym of Edward Bradley.

Bedford (bed'fọrd), Duke of. See *John of Lancaster*.

Bédier (bā-dyā), Charles Marie Joseph (1864—1938), Fr. scholar.

Beebe (bē'bẹ), William (1877—   ), Am. naturalist.

Beecher (bē'chẽr), Henry Ward (1813—87), Am. preacher and reformer (son of Lyman).

Beecher, Lyman (1775—1863), Am. clergyman.

Beechey (bē'chi), Sir William (1753—1839), Eng. portrait-painter.

Beerbohm (bēr'bōm), Sir Max (1872—   ), Eng. author and caricaturist (half-brother of Sir Herbert Beerbohm Tree).

Beethoven (vän bā'tō-vẹn), Ludwig van (1770—1827), Ger. musical composer.

Begas (bā'gäs), Karl (1794—1854), Ger. painter.

Begas, Reinhold (1831—1911), Ger. sculptor (son of Karl).

Bégin (bā-zhaṅ), Louis Nazaire (1840—1925), Can. cardinal.

Behaim (bā'hīm) or **Behem** (bā'hem), Martin (1459? or 1436?—1506?), Ger. cosmographer.

Behmen, Jakob. See *Böhme*.

Behn (bān), Mrs. (Aphra, or Afra, Johnson) (1640—89), Eng. dramatist and novelist.

Behring. See *Bering*.

Behring (fon bā'ring), Emil von (1854—1917), Ger. physician.

Beissel (bī'sẹl), Johann Conrad (1690—1768), Ger.-Am. mystic, founder of religious sect called Seventh-Day Dunkers.

Belasco (be-las'kō), David (1854—1931), Am. playwright and theatrical manager.

Belcher (bel'chẽr), Jonathan (1681—1757), Am. politician, colonial governor of Massachusetts and New Jersey.

Belinski (bye-lyēn'skẹ). See *Byelinski*.

Belisarius (bel-i-sā'ri-us) (c505—565), Byzantine general.

Bell (bel), Acton. Pseudonym of Anne Brontë.

Bell, Alexander Graham (1847—1922), Sc.-Am. scientist, inventor of telephone.

Bell, Sir Charles (1774—1842), Br. physician and anatomist.

Bell, Currer. Pseudonym of Charlotte Brontë.

Bell, Ellis. Pseudonym of Emily Brontë.

Bell, John (1797—1869), Am. political leader.

Bellamy (bel'ạ-mi), Edward (1850—98), Am. writer.

Bellarmino (bel-lär-mē'nō), in English **Bellarmine** (bel'-ạr-min), Roberto Francesco Romolo (1542—1621), It. cardinal and theologian.

Bellay (dü be-lā), Joachim du (c1522—60), Fr. poet and critic.

Belle-Isle (dẹ bel-ēl'), Charles Louis Auguste Fouquet, Duc de (1684—1761), Fr. marshal and statesman (grandson of Nicolas Fouquet).

Bellenden (bel'ẹn-dẹn), John (also called Ballenden and Ballentyne) (fl. 1530—87), Sc. translator.

Bellenden, William (d. 1633?), Sc. classical scholar.

Bellingham (bel'ing-ạm), Richard (1592—1672), colonial governor of Massachusetts, born in England.

Bellini (bel-lē'nē), Gentile (c1427—1507), Venetian painter (son of Jacopo).

Bellini, Giovanni (c1428—1516), Venetian painter (brother of Gentile).

Bellini, Jacopo (c1400—c1470), Venetian painter.

Bellini, Vincenzo (1801—35), It. operatic composer.

Belloc (be-lok'), Hilaire (1870—   ), Eng. author.

Bellows (bel'ōz), George Wesley (1882—1925), Am. painter.

Boltraffio (bol-träf'fē-ō) or **Boltraffio** (bol-träf'fē-ō), Giovanni Antonio (1467—1516), It. painter.

Belzoni (bel-tsō'nē), Giovanni Battista (1778—1823), It. archæological explorer of Egypt.

Bem (bem), Józef (1795—1850), Pol. general.

Bembo (bem'bō), Pietro (1470—1547), It. cardinal and scholar.

Benavente y Martínez (bā-nä-ven'tā ē mär-tē'näth), Jacinto (1866—   ), Sp. dramatist.

Benbow (ben'bō), John (1653—1702), Eng. admiral.

Benedek (fon bā'nẹ-dek), Ludwig von (1804—81), Austrian general, born in Hungary.

Benedetti (ben-e-det'tē), Vincent, Comte (1817—1900), Fr. diplomatist.

Benedetto da Majano (bā-nä-det'tō dä mä-yä'nō) (1442—97), Florentine sculptor and architect.

Benedict XIV. (ben'ẹ-dikt) (Prospero Lorenzo Lambertini) (1675—1758), It. ecclesiastic, pope (1740—58).

Benedict XV. (Giacomo della Chiesa) (1854—1922), It. ecclesiastic, pope (1914—22).

Benedict of Nursia (nẽr'shiạ), Saint (c480—543), It. monk, founder of Benedictine order.

Benelli (bā-nel'lē), Sem (1877—   ), It. poet and dramatist.

Beneš (ben'esh), Edvard (1884—   ), Bohem. patriot and writer, and statesman of Czechoslovakia.

Benjamin (ben'jạ-min), Judah Philip (1811—84), Am. Jewish lawyer and Confederate statesman, later lawyer and legal writer in England, born in West Indies.

Bennet (ben'et), Henry. See *Arlington, Earl of*.

Bennett (ben'et), Enoch Arnold (1867—1931), Eng. novelist and misc. writer.

Bennett, James Gordon (1795—1872), Sc.-Am. journalist.

Bennett, James Gordon (1841—1918), Am. newspaper publisher (son of J. G. Bennett, 1795—1872).

Bennigsen (ben'ig-sẹn), Count Levin August Theophil (1745—1826), Russ. general, born in Germany.

Bennigsen (fon ben'ich-sẹn), Rudolf von (1824—1902), Ger. statesman.

Benson (ben'sọn), Arthur Christopher (1862—1925), Eng. educator, essayist, and misc. writer (son of Edward W.).

Benson, Edward Frederic (1867—1940), Eng. novelist (brother of Arthur C.).

Benson, Edward White (1829—96), Eng. divine, archbishop of Canterbury.

Benson, Sir Frank Robert (1858—1939), Eng. actor and theatrical manager (brother of 1st Baron Charnwood).

Benson, Frank Weston (1862—   ), Am. painter.

Benson, Robert Hugh (1871—1914), Eng. Rom. Cath. priest, and writer (brother of Edward F.).

Benson, William Shepherd (1855—1932), Am. admiral.

Bentham (ben'tạm or ben'thạm), Jeremy (1748—1832), Eng. philosopher and jurist.

Bentinck (ben'tingk), William. See *Portland, 1st Earl of*.

Bentinck, William George Frederick Cavendish (known as Lord George Bentinck) (1802—48), Eng. politician.

Bentley (bent'li), Richard (1662—1742), Eng. scholar and critic.

Benton (ben'tọn), Thomas Hart (1782—1858), Am. statesman.

Béranger (dẹ bā-räṅ-zhā), Pierre Jean de (1780—1857), Fr. poet.

Berchtold (fon berch'tolt), Leopold, Graf von (1863—   ), Austrian diplomatist and statesman.

Berengar I. (ber'en-gär) (also called Berengario, Berengarius, and Bérenger) (d. 924), king of Italy (888—924) (grandson of Louis I. of France).

Berengar II. (d. 966), king of Italy (950—961) (grandson of Berengar I.).

Berengarius (ber-en-gā'ri-us) (Bérenger de Tours) (c998—1088), Fr. theologian.

Berenson (ber'ẹn-sọn), Bernhard (1865—   ), Russ.-Am. writer on art, in Florence.

Beresford (ber'ez-fọrd), Charles William de la Poer Beresford, Baron (1846—1919), Br. admiral.

Beresford, John (1738—1805), Ir. statesman.

Beresford, John Davys (1873—1947), Eng. novelist.

Beresford, William Carr Beresford, Viscount (1768—1854), Br. general.

Bergerac (dẹ berzh-rȧk), Savinien Cyrano de (1620?—55), Fr. dramatist and romance-writer.

Bergh (bèrg), Henry (1813—88), Am. philanthropist, founder of the American Society for the Prevention of Cruelty to Animals.

Bergson (berg-sôṅ), Henri Louis (1859—1941), Fr. philosopher.

Bering or **Behring** (bē'ring, Dan. bā'ring), Vitus (1680—1741), Dan. navigator in Russian service.

Berkeley (bẽrk'li or bärk'li), George (1685—1753), Ir. bishop and philosopher.

Berkeley, Sir William (1610?—77), colonial governor of Virginia, born in England.

Berlichingen (fon ber'lich-ing-ẹn), Götz (or Gottfried) von ("Götz with the Iron Hand") (1480—1562), Ger. robberknight.

Berliner (bẻr'lin-ẻr), Emile (1851—1929), Ger.-Am. inventor.

Berlioz (ber-lẻ-ōz'), Hector (1803—69), Fr. musical composer.

Bernadotte (bẻr-nạ-dot', Fr. ber-nȧ-dot), Jean Baptiste Jules. See *Charles XIV.* (of Sweden).

Bernard (ber-när), Claude (1813—78), Fr. physiologist.

Bernard, Simon (1779—1839), Fr. soldier and engineer, for some years in the service of the U. S.

Bernard, Tristan (orig. Paul Bernard) (1866—), Fr. dramatist and novelist.

Bernardin de Saint-Pierre (ber-när-dȧṅ dè saṅ-pyär), Jacques Henri (1737—1814), Fr. naturalist and writer, author of "Paul et Virginie."

Bernard of Clairvaux (bẻr'nạrd or bẻr-närd', Fr. ber-när, klär-vō), Saint ("the Mellifluous Doctor") (1090—1153), Fr. abbot, preacher, and theologian.

Bernard of Cluny (klü-nē) or **of Morlaix** (môr-lā) (fl. c1140), Fr. monk and Latin poet.

Bernard of Menthon (moṅ-tôṅ), Saint (923—1008), priest and archdeacon of Aosta, founder of Alpine hospices.

Berners (bẻr'nẻrz), John Bourchier, 2d Baron (1467—1533), Eng. statesman and translator.

Bernhard (bern'härt) (Duke of Saxe-Weimar) (1604—39), Ger. Protestant general in Thirty Years' War.

Bernhardi (fon bern-här'dē), Friedrich von (1849—1930), Ger. general and military writer.

Bernhardt (bẻrn'härt, Fr. ber-när), Sarah (professional name of Rosine Bernard, Mme. Damala) (1845—1923), Fr. actress.

Bernini (ber-nē'nē), Giovanni Lorenzo (1598—1680), It. architect, sculptor, and painter.

Bernoulli or **Bernouilli** (ber-nö-yē'), Daniel (1700—82), Swiss mathematician and physicist (son of Jean).

Bernoulli or **Bernouilli**, Jacques (1654—1705), Swiss mathematician.

Bernoulli or **Bernouilli**, Jean (1667—1748), Swiss mathematician (brother of Jacques).

Bernstein (bern-staṅ), Henry (1876—), Fr. dramatist.

Bernstorff (fon bern'shtôrf), Andreas Peter, Graf von (1735—97), Dan. statesman, born in Germany (nephew of Johann H. E.).

Bernstorff, Johann Hartwig Ernst, Graf von (1712—72), Dan. statesman, born in Germany.

Bernstorff, Johann Heinrich, Graf von (1862—1939), Ger. diplomatist, ambassador to U. S. (1908—17).

Berosus (bẹ-rō'sus) or **Berossus** (bẹ-ros'us) (fl. c260 B.C.), Babylonian historian, astronomer, and astrologer, writing in Greek.

Berry or **Berri** (ber'i, Fr. dè be-rē), Charles Ferdinand, Duc de (1778—1820), Fr. prince and soldier (son of Charles X. of France).

Berry or **Berri**, Duchesse de (Marie Caroline Ferdinande Louise) (1798—1870), It. Bourbon princess (wife of Charles Ferdinand, Duc de Berry, and mother of Comte de Chambord).

Berthelot (bert-lō), Henri Mathias (1861—1931), Fr. general.

Berthelot, Pierre Eugène Marcelin (1827—1907), Fr. chemist.

Berthier (ber-tyä), Louis Alexandre (Prince de Neufchâtel, Prince de Wagram) (1753—1815), Fr. marshal, and chief of staff under Napoleon I.

Berthollet (ber-to-lā), Claude Louis, Comte (1748—1822), Fr. chemist.

Bertillon (ber-tē-yôṅ), Alphonse (1853—1914), Fr. anthropometrist.

Bertrand (ber-träṅ), Henri Gratien, Comte (1773—1844), Fr. general, who accompanied Napoleon to St. Helena.

Bertrand, Louis Marie Émile (1866—), Fr. author.

Bertran de Born (ber-träṅ dè bôrn). See *Born.*

Berwick (ber'ik), James Fitzjames, Duke of (1670—1734), marshal of France (illegitimate son of James II. of England).

Berzelius (ber-sā'lẹ-ùs), Jöns Jakob, Baron (1779—1848), Swed. chemist.

Besant (bez'ạnt), Mrs. (Annie Wood) (1847—1933), Eng. theosophist and writer.

Besant (bẹ-zant'), Sir Walter (1836—1901), Eng. novelist and misc. writer.

Besnard (bā-när), Paul Albert (1849—1934), Fr. painter.

Bessarion (be-sā'ri-on), Johannes, or Basilius (c1395—1472), Gr. scholar and Roman Catholic cardinal, born at Trebizond.

Bessemer (bes'ẹ-mér), Sir Henry (1813—98), Eng. engineer, inventor of Bessemer process of steel-making.

Bessières (be-syär), Jean Baptiste (Duc d'Istrie) (1768—1813), Fr. marshal.

Bestuzhev-Ryumin (bes-tö'zhef-ryö'mẹn), Count Aleksyey Petrovich (1693—1766), Russ. diplomatist and statesman.

Bethmann-Hollweg (fon bāt'män-hol'väch), Theobald von (1856—1921), Ger. statesman, imperial chancellor (1909—17).

Bethune, David. See *Beaton, David.*

Betterton (bet'ẻr-tọn), Thomas (1635?—1710), Eng. actor.

Betti (dē bet'tē), Bernardino di. See *Pinturicchio.*

Beust (fon boist), Friedrich Ferdinand, Graf von (1809—86), Ger. statesman, in the service of Saxony and Austria.

Beveridge (bev'ẹ-rij), Albert Jeremiah (1862—1927), Am. lawyer, senator, and author.

Bewick (bū'ik), Thomas (1753—1828), Eng. wood-engraver.

Beyerlein (bī'ẻr-līn), Franz Adam (1871—), Ger. novelist and dramatist.

Beyle (bāl), Marie Henri ("Stendhal") (1783—1842), Fr. novelist and critic.

Beza (bē'zä), Théodore (Théodore de Bèze) (1519—1605), Fr. Calvinist reformer and theologian.

Bias (bī'as) (fl. c570 B.C.), one of the seven sages of ancient Greece.

Bibulus (bib'ū-lus), Marcus (or Lucius) Calpurnius (d. 48 B.C.), Rom. politician, opponent of Julius Cæsar.

Bichat (bē-shä), Marie François Xavier (1771—1802), Fr. physiologist and anatomist.

Biddle (bid'l), John (1615—62), Eng. Unitarian theologian.

Biddle, Nicholas (1786—1844), Am. financier.

Bielinski (bye-lyẹn'skẹ). See *Byelinski.*

Bienville (dè byaṅ-vēl), Jean Baptiste Le Moyne, Sieur de (1680—1767?), Fr. colonial governor of Louisiana, born in Canada (brother of Sieur d'Iberville).

Bierbaum (bẻr'boum), Otto Julius (1865—1910), Ger. poet, novelist, and misc. writer.

Bierstadt (bẻr'stät), Albert (1830—1902), Am. landscape-painter, born in Germany.

Bigelow (big'ẹ-lō), John (1817—1911), Am. writer, editor, and diplomatist.

Bigordi (bē-gôr'dē), Domenico. See *Ghirlandajo.*

Billaud-Varenne (bē-yō-vä-ren), Jean Nicolas (1756—1819), Fr. revolutionist.

Billings (bil'ingz), Josh. Pseudonym of H. W. Shaw.

Binet (bē-nā), Alfred (1857—1911), Fr. psychologist.

Binger (baṅ-zhär), Louis Gustave (1856—), Fr. army officer, explorer in Africa, and administrator.

Binney (bin'i), Horace (1780—1875), Am. lawyer and legal writer.

Bion (bī'ọn) (fl. c100 B.C.), Gr. bucolic poet.

Biot (bē-ō), Jean Baptiste (1774—1862), Fr. physicist.

Bird (bẻrd), Robert Montgomery (1806?—54), Am. novelist and dramatist.

Birdwood (bẻrd'wùd), William Riddell Birdwood, 1st Baron (1865—), Br. field-marshal.

Birgitta (bẻr-jit'ạ) or **Brigitta** (bri-jit'ạ) or **Bridget** (brij'et), Saint (c1302—73), Swed. nun and mystic.

Birkenhead (bẻr'kẹn-hed), Frederick Edwin Smith, 1st Earl of (1872—1930), Eng. lawyer, statesman, and writer.

Birney (bẻr'ni), James Gillespie (1792—1857), Am. abolitionist.

Biron (dè bē-rôṅ), Armand de Gontaut, Baron de (1524—92), Fr. marshal.

Biron, Armand Louis de Gontaut, Duc de (Duc de Lauzun) (1747—93), Fr. military commander.

Biron, Charles de Gontaut, Duc de (1562—1602), Fr. admiral and marshal, executed for treason (son of Baron de Biron).

Birrell (bir'el), Augustine (1850—1933), Eng. statesman and essayist.

Bismarck (biz'märk, Ger. fon bis'märk), Otto Eduard Leopold, Prince von (1815—98), Prussian statesman, first imperial chancellor of modern Germany (1871—90).

Bispham (bis'fạm), David Scull (1857—1921), Am. barytone singer.

Bissing (fon bis'ing), Moritz Ferdinand, Freiherr von (1844—1917), Ger. general, military administrator in Belgium.

Bisson (bē-sôn), Alexandre Charles Auguste (1848—1912), Fr. dramatist.

Bitter (bit'ėr), Karl Theodore Francis (1867—1915), Austrian-Am. sculptor.

Bivar (dä bē-vär'), Rodrigo (or Ruy) Díaz de. See *Cid.*

Bizet (bē-zā), Alexandre César Léopold (called Georges Bizet) (1838—75), Fr. musical composer.

Björnson (byėrn'son), Björnstjerne (1832—1910), Norw. poet, novelist, and dramatist.

Black (blak), Jeremiah Sullivan (1810—83), Am. jurist and statesman.

Black, Joseph (1728—99), Sc. chemist, born in France.

Black, William (1841—98), Br. novelist.

Black Hawk (1767—1838), Am. Indian chief.

Blackie (blak'i), John Stuart (1809—95), Sc. scholar, translator, and misc. writer.

Blackmore (blak'mōr), Sir Richard (c1650—1729), Eng. physician and poet.

Blackmore, Richard Doddridge (1825—1900), Eng. novelist.

Black Prince, The. See *Edward* (Prince of Wales, son of Edward III.).

Blackstone (blak'stōn), Sir William (1723—80), Eng. legal writer and judge.

Blaine (blān), James Gillespie (1830—93), Am. statesman.

Blaise, Saint. See *Blasius.*

Blake (blāk), Robert (1599—1657), Eng. admiral.

Blake, William (1757—1827), Eng. poet and artist.

Blakelock (blāk'lok), Ralph Albert (1847—1919), Am. painter.

Blanc (blän), Jean Joseph Charles Louis (1811—82), Fr. socialist, politician, and historian.

Blanche of Castile (blänch) (1188?—1252), queen of Louis VIII. of France (daughter of Alfonso IX. of Castile).

Bland (bland), Richard Parks (1835—99), Am. legislator.

Biasco Ibáñez (bläs'kō ē-Bä'nyäth), Vicente (1867—1928), Sp. novelist and politician.

Blashfield (blash'fēld), Edwin Howland (1848—1936), Am. painter.

Blasius (blā'zi-us) or **Blaise** (blāz), Saint (d. 316), bishop and martyr of Armenia, patron saint of wool-combers. It is said that in the course of his martyrdom his flesh was torn with iron wool-combs.

Blavatsky (blä-vät'skẹ), Mme. (Elena Petrovna Hahn) (1831—91), Russ. theosophist and traveler.

Blennerhasset (blen-ėr-has'et), Harman (1764 or 1765—1831), Br. lawyer in America, implicated in schemes of Aaron Burr.

Blériot (blā-rē-ō), Louis (1872—1936), Fr. inventor and aviator.

Blessington (bles'ing-ton), Countess of (Marguerite Power, Mrs. Farmer) (1789—1849), Br. novelist and misc. writer.

Bliss (blis), Tasker Howard (1853—1930), Am. general.

Blondel (blôn-del), Jacques François (1705—74), Fr. architect.

Bloomfield (blööm'fēld), Robert (1766—1823), Eng. poet.

Blount (blunt), Thomas (1618—79), Eng. lexicographer and misc. writer.

Blowitz (dė blō-vēts), Henri Georges Stephane Adolphe Opper de (1825—1903), Fr. journalist, born in Bohemia.

Blücher (fon blüch'ėr), Gebhard Leberecht von (1742—1819), Prussian field-marshal.

Bluecher (blüch'ėr). See *Blücher.*

Blumenbach (blö'men-bäch), Johann Friedrich (1752—1840), Ger. physiologist and anthropologist.

Blumenthal (blö'men-täl), Oskar (1852—1917), Ger. playwright.

Blunt (blunt), Wilfrid Scawen (1840—1922), Eng. poet and publicist.

Bluntschli (blúnch'lē), Johann Kaspar (1808—81), Swiss-Ger. jurist.

Boabdil (bō-äb-dēl') (Abu Abdallah) (d. after 1492), last Moorish king of Granada (1482—92).

Boadicea (bō''ạ-di-sē'ä) (d. A.D. 62), Br. queen, leader of an unsuccessful revolt against Roman rule in Britain.

Bobadilla (dä bō-Bä-ᴛHēl'yä), Francisco de (d. 1502), Sp. official, as governor of colony of Hispaniola the successor of

Columbus, whom he sent back to Spain in chains on charges of maladministration (1500).

Bocage or **Boccage.** See *Barbosa du Bocage.*

Boccaccio (bok-kät'chō), Giovanni (1313—75), It. poet and novelist, author of "Decameron."

Böckh (bėk), Philipp August (1785—1867), Ger. classical scholar.

Böcklin (bėk'lēn), Arnold (1827—1901), Swiss painter.

Bodel (bo-del), Jean (d. c1205), Fr. dramatist and poet.

Bodin (bo-dañ), Jean (1530—96), Fr. political philosopher.

Bodley (bod'li), Sir Thomas (1545—1613), Eng. diplomatist and scholar, founder of Bodleian Library at Oxford.

Bodmer (bōd'mėr), Johann Jakob (1698—1783), Swiss scholar, critic, and poet, writing in German.

Bodoni (bō-dō'nē), Giambattista (1740—1813), It. printer.

Boece (bō-ēs'), Hector (also called Boyce and, as Latinized, Boëthius) (c1465—1536), Sc. historian.

Boeckh (bėk). See *Böckh.*

Boecklin (bėk'lēn). See *Böcklin.*

Boehm (bėm), Sir Joseph Edgar (1834—90), Austrian-Eng. sculptor.

Boehme (bė'mė). See *Böhme.*

Boehm von Bawerk (bėm fon bä'verk). See *Böhm von Bawerk.*

Boerhaave (bör'hä-vė), Hermann (1668—1738), Dutch physician.

Boëthius (bō-ē'thi-us) or **Boëtius** (bō-ē'shius), Anicius Manlius Severinus (c475—c525), Rom. philosopher and statesman.

Boëthius, Hector. See *Boece.*

Boétie, Étienne de La. See *La Boétie.*

Bohemond I. (bō'hẹ-mond) or **Bohemund I.** (bō'hẹ-mund) (Marc Bohemond, or Bohemund) (Prince of Tarentum and of Antioch) (1056?—1111), Norman adventurer and crusader, born in Italy (son of Robert Guiscard).

Böhme (bė'mė) or **Behmen** (bā'men), Jakob (1575—1624), Ger. mystic.

Böhm von Bawerk (bėm fon bä'verk), Eugen (1851—1914), Austrian economist and statesman.

Bohn (bōn), Henry George (1796—1884), Eng. publisher.

Bohr (bōr), Niels Henrik David (1885—   ), Dan. physicist.

Boiardo or **Bojardo** (bo-yär'dō), Matteo Maria (Count of Scandiano) (1434?—94), It. poet.

Boïeldieu (bo-yel-dyė), François Adrien (1775—1834), Fr. composer of comic opera.

Boileau-Despréaux (bwo-lō-dä-prä-ō), Nicolas (1636—1711), Fr. critic, poet, and satirist.

Boissy d'Anglas (dė bwo-sē dän-gläs), François Antoine, Comte de (1756—1826), Fr. statesman.

Boito (bō'ē-tō), Arrigo (1842—1918), It. musical composer and poet.

Bojer (boi'ėr), Johan (1872—   ), Norw. novelist and playwright.

Bok (bok), Edward William (1863—1930), Dutch-Am. editor and writer.

Boker (bō'kėr), George Henry (1823—90), Am. poet and dramatist.

Boldrewood (bōl'dėr-wůd), Rolf. Pseudonym of T. A. Browne.

Boleyn (bůl'in) or **Bullen** (bůl'en), Anne (1507?—36), second wife of Henry VIII. of England, and mother of Queen Elizabeth.

Bolingbroke (bol'ing-brůk), Henry of. See *Henry IV.* (of England).

Bolingbroke, Henry St. John, 1st Viscount (1678—1751), Eng. statesman and writer.

Bolívar (bol'i-vär), Simon (in Spanish, Simón Bolívar, pron. bō-lē'vär) (1783—1830), Venezuelan general and statesman, leader in revolt against Spanish rule in South America.

Bolland (bol'ạnd), Jean (1596—1665), Belgian Jesuit hagiologist.

Bologna (dä bō-lō'nyä), Giovanni da (real name Jean Bologne) (c1524—1608), Flemish sculptor, in Italy.

Boltraffio. See *Beltraffio.*

Bomba (bom'bä), or **King Bomba.** Sobriquet of Ferdinand II. of the Two Sicilies.

Bonaparte (bō'nạ-pärt), Charles Louis Napoléon. See *Napoleon III.*

Bonaparte, Charles Lucien Jules Laurent (Prince of Canino) (1803—57), Fr. naturalist (son of Lucien).

Bonaparte, François Charles Joseph. See *Napoleon II.*

Bonaparte, Jérôme (1784—1860), Fr. marshal, king of Westphalia (1807—13) (brother of Napoleon I.).

Bonaparte, Joseph (1768—1844), king of Naples and of Spain (brother of Napoleon I.).

Bonaparte, Louis (1778—1846), king of Holland (1806—10) (brother of Napoleon I.).

Bonaparte, Lucien (Prince of Canino) (1775—1840), Fr. revolutionist and diplomatist (brother of Napoleon I.).

Bonaparte, Marie Anne Elisa (Mme. Bacciochi) (1777—1820), grand duchess of Tuscany (sister of Napoleon I.).

Bonaparte, Marie Annonciade Caroline (Mme. Murat) (1782—1839), sister of Napoleon I., and wife of Joachim Murat.

Bonaparte, Marie Pauline (Mme. Leclerc, Princess Borghese) (1780—1825), sister of Napoleon I.

Bonaparte, Napoléon. See *Napoleon I.*

Bonaparte, Napoléon Eugène Louis Jean Joseph (called Prince Imperial) (1856—79), Fr. prince (son of Napoleon III.).

Bonaparte, Napoléon Joseph Charles Paul (called Prince Napoleon, also "Plon-Plon") (1822—91), Fr. general and politician (son of Jérôme).

Bonar (bon′ẽr), Horatius (1808—89), Sc. clergyman and hymn-writer.

Bonaventura (bō″nä-ven-tö′rä), Saint (Giovanni di Fidanza, "the Seraphic Doctor") (1221—74), It. scholastic theologian.

Bonchamp (dẽ bôn-shän), Charles Melchior Artus, Marquis de (1760—93), Fr. soldier and Vendean leader. [painter.

Bone (bōn), Sir Muirhead (1876—), Br. etcher and

Bonheur (bo-nẽr), Marie Rosalie (called Rosa Bonheur) (1822—99), Fr. painter of animal life.

Boniface VIII. (bon′i-fās) (Benedetto Gaetani) (c1235—1303), It. ecclesiastic, pope (1294—1303).

Boniface, Saint (name orig. Winfrid or Wynfrith, called "the Apostle of Germany") (680?—755?), Eng. monk, missionary, and archbishop, in Germany.

Bonington (bon′ing-tọn), Richard Parkes (1801—28), Eng. painter.

Bonivard or **Bonnivard** (dẽ bo-nē-vär), François de (1493—1570), Swiss ecclesiastic and patriot.

Bonnat (bo-nä), Léon Joseph Florentin (1833—1922), Fr. painter.

Bonner (bon′ẽr), Edmund (1500?—69), Eng. Rom. Cath. bishop.

Bonneville (bon′vil), Benjamin L. E. (1793—1878), Am. soldier, and explorer of Rocky Mountains, born in France.

Bonnivard, François de. See *Bonivard.*

Boole (böl), George (1815—64), Eng. mathematician and logician.

Boone (bōn), Daniel (1735—1820), Am. backwoodsman and pioneer.

Booth (böth), Edwin Thomas (1833—93), Am. actor (son of Junius B.).

Booth, John Wilkes (1839?—65), Am. actor, assassin of Abraham Lincoln (brother of Edwin T.).

Booth, Junius Brutus (1796—1852), Eng.-Am. actor.

Booth, William ("General Booth") (1829—1912), Eng. revivalist, founder of the Salvation Army.

Bopp (bop), Franz (1791—1867), Ger. philologist.

Borah (bōr′ạ), William Edgar (1865—1940), Am. senator (from Idaho).

Borchgrevink (bôrch′grẹ-vingk), Carsten Egeberg (1864—), Norw. antarctic explorer.

Bordeaux (bôr-dō), Henry (1870—), Fr. novelist and misc. writer.

Borden (bôr′dẹn), Sir Robert Laird (1854—1937), Can. statesman, premier of Canada (1911—20).

Bordone (bor-dō′nä), Paris (c1500—71), Venetian painter.

Borghese (bor-gä′zä), Princess. See *Bonaparte, Marie Pauline.*

Borgia (bôr′jä), Cesare (Duke of Valentinois and Romagna) (1476?—1507), It. cardinal, politician, and military leader (son of Pope Alexander VI.).

Borgia, Lucrezia (1480—1519), duchess of Ferrara (sister of Cesare).

Borgia, Rodrigo. See *Alexander VI.* (pope).

Borglum (bôr′glum), John Gutzon de la Mothe (1867—1941), Am. sculptor and painter.

Borglum, Solon Hannibal (1868—1922), Am. sculptor (brother of John G. de la M.).

Boris III. (bō′ris) (1894—), king (or czar) of the Bulgarians (1918—) (son of Ferdinand I. of Bulgaria).

Boris Godunov. See *Godunov.*

Born (dẽ bôrn), Bertran (or Bertrand) de (c1140—c1210), Fr. troubadour and soldier.

Borodin (bo-ro-dēn′), Aleksandr Porfirevich (1834—87), Russ. chemist and musical composer.

Borromeo (bor-rō-mā′ō), Carlo (1538—84), It. cardinal, ecclesiastical reformer, and saint.

Borrow (bor′ō), George Henry (1803—81), Eng. author.

Bosanquet (bō′zạn-ket), Bernard (1848—1923), Eng. philosophical writer.

Boscán Almogaver (bos-kän′ äl-mō-gä-vär′), Juan (c1495—1542), Sp. poet.

Boscawen (bos′kạ-wen), Edward (1711—61), Eng. admiral.

Boscovich (bos′kọ-vich), Ruggiero Giuseppe (1711—87), It. mathematician, astronomer, and physicist, born in Dalmatia.

Bose (bōz), Sir Jagadis Chandra (1858—1937), East Indian scientist.

Bossuet (bo-süä), Jacques Bénigne (1627—1704), Fr. bishop, pulpit orator, and writer.

Boswell (boz′wẹl), James (1740—95), Br. writer, biographer of Dr. Johnson.

Botha (bō′tä), Louis (1863—1919), South African general and statesman.

Bothwell (both′wel), James Hepburn, 4th Earl of (c1536—78), Sc. nobleman, third husband of Mary Queen of Scots.

Botticelli (bot-tē-chel′lē), Sandro (properly Alessandro di Mariano Filipepi) (1444?—1510), Florentine painter.

Botzaris. See *Bozzaris.*

Boucher (bö-shä), Alfred (1850—), Fr. sculptor.

Boucher, François (1703—70), Fr. painter.

Bouchor (bö-shôr), Joseph Félix (1853—), Fr. painter.

Boucicault (bö′sẹ-kō), Dion (1822—90), Ir. dramatist and actor.

Bougainville (dẽ bö-gaṅ-vēl), Louis Antoine de (1729—1811), Fr. soldier and navigator.

Bouguereau (bö-gẹ-rō), Adolphe William (1825—1905), Fr. painter.

Bouillé (dẽ bö-yä), François Claude Amour, Marquis de (1739—1800), Fr. general.

Bouillon (dẽ bö-yôṅ), Henri de La Tour d'Auvergne, Duc de (1555—1623), Fr. marshal (son-in-law of William I. of Orange).

Boulanger (bö-läṅ-zhä), Georges Ernest Jean Marie (1837—91), Fr. general and politician.

Boulle or **Boule** (böl), André Charles (1642—1732), Fr. cabinet-maker.

Bourbaki (bör-bȧ-kē), Charles Denis Sauter (1816—97), Fr. general.

Bourbon (bör′bọn, Fr. dẽ bör-bôṅ), Charles, Duc de (Constable Bourbon) (1490—1527), Fr. general, constable of France.

Bourdaloue (bör-dȧ-lö), Louis (1632—1704), Fr. Jesuit and pulpit orator.

Bourgeois (bör-zhwo), Léon Victor Auguste (1851—1925), Fr. statesman and author.

Bourget (bör-zhä), Paul Charles Joseph (1852—1935), Fr. novelist, critic, and poet.

Bourinot (bö′ri-nō), Sir John George (1837—1902), Can. historian.

Bourne (börn), Francis (1861—1935), Eng. cardinal.

Bourne, Hugh (1772—1852), Eng. preacher, founder of sect known as Primitive Methodists.

Bourrienne (dẽ bö-rē-en), Louis Antoine Fauvelet de (1769—1834), Fr. diplomatist, and writer of memoirs.

Boussingault (bö-saṅ-gō), Jean Baptiste Joseph Dieudonné (1802—87), Fr. chemist.

Boutet de Monvel (bö-tä dẽ môṅ-vel), Louis Maurice (1850—1913), Fr. painter and illustrator.

Boutroux (bö-trö), Étienne Émile Marie (1845—1921), Fr. philosopher.

Bouts (bouts), Dirk, or Dierick (c1410—75), Dutch painter.

(variable) ḏ as d or j, ş as s or sh, ṯ as t or ch, ẕ as z or zh; o, F. cloche; ü, F. menu; ch, Sc. loch; ṅ, F. bonbon; ′, primary accent; ″, secondary accent; †, obsolete; <, from; +, and; =, equals. See also lists at beginning of book.

Boutwell (bout′wel), George Sewall (1818–1905), Am. politician.

Bouvier (bö-vēr′, Fr. bö-vyä), John (1787–1851), Fr.-Am. jurist.

Bowdich (bou′dich), Thomas Edward (1791–1824), Eng. traveler in Africa, and scientific writer.

Bowditch (bou′dich), Nathaniel (1773–1838), Am. mathematician.

Bowdoin (bō′dn), James (1727–90), Am. statesman.

Bowles (bōlz), Samuel (1826–78), Am. journalist.

Bowring (bou′ring), Sir John (1792–1872), Eng. statesman, linguist, and writer.

Boydell (boi′del), John (1719–1804), Eng. engraver and print-publisher.

Boyer (bwo-yä), Jean Pierre (1776–1850), Haitian general, president of Haiti (1818–43).

Boyle (boil), Robert (1627–91), Br. chemist and physicist (brother of 1st Earl of Orrery).

Boyle, Roger. See *Orrery, 1st Earl of*.

Boz (boz). Pseudonym of Charles Dickens.

Bozzaris or **Botzaris** (bo-zar′is, Gr. bot′sä-rēs), Markos (c1788–1823), Gr. patriot.

Bracegirdle (brās′gèr′dl), Anne (called Mrs. Bracegirdle) (c1663–1748), Eng. actress.

Bracton (dè brak′ton), Henry de (also called Bratton and Bretton) (d. 1268), Eng. ecclesiastic and jurist.

Braddock (brad′ok), Edward (1695–1755), Br. general, in America.

Braddon (brad′on), Mary Elizabeth (Mrs. Maxwell) (1837–1915), Eng. novelist.

Bradford (brad′ford), John (1510?–55), Eng. Protestant preacher and martyr.

Bradford, William (1590–1657), Eng. settler at Plymouth, Mass. (1620), governor of the colony, and historian.

Bradford, William (1663–1752), early Am. printer, born in England.

Bradlaugh (brad′lä), Charles (1833–91), Eng. freethinker and radical politician.

Bradley (brad′li), Edward ("Cuthbert Bede") (1827–89), Eng. clergyman and writer.

Bradley, Francis Herbert (1846–1924), Eng. philosophical writer.

Bradley, Henry (1845–1923), Eng. philologist and lexicographer.

Bradley, James (1693–1762), Eng. astronomer.

Bradshaw (brad′shâ), George (1801–53), Eng. publisher, esp. of railway guides.

Bradshaw, John (1602–59), Eng. judge, one of the regicides.

Bradstreet (brad′strēt), Simon (1603–97), colonial governor of Massachusetts, born in England.

Bradstreet, Mrs. (Anne Dudley) (1612?–72), Am. poet, born in England (wife of Simon).

Bradwardine (brad′wár-dēn), Thomas ("the Profound Doctor") (c1290–1349), Eng. archbishop, theologian, and mathematician.

Braga (brä′gä), Theophilo (1843–1924), Pg. scholar, author, and statesman.

Bragg (brag), Braxton (1817–76), Am. Confederate general.

Bragg, Sir William Henry (1862–1942), Eng. physicist.

Bragg, William Lawrence (1890–), Eng. physicist, born in Australia (son of Sir W. H.).

Brahe (brä or brä′e), Tycho (1546–1601), Dan. astronomer.

Brahms (bräms), Johannes (1833–97), Ger. musical composer.

Braid (brād), James (c1795–1860), Br. physician, and writer on hypnotism.

Brainerd (brā′nèrd), David (1718–47), Am. missionary to the Indians.

Bramah (bram′ä), Joseph (1748–1814), Eng. inventor.

Bramante (brä-män′tä), Donato d'Agnolo (c1444–1514), It. architect and painter.

Brancaleone d'Andalò (bräng″kä-lä-ō′nä dän-dä-lō′) (d. 1258), It. statesman, of Bologna, elected dictator of Rome.

Brand (brand), John (1744–1806), Eng. antiquary.

Brandan (bran′dan), Saint. See *Brendan*.

Brandeis (bran′dīs), Louis Dembitz (1856–1941), Am. lawyer, associate justice of U. S. Supreme Court.

Brandes (brän′des), Georg Morris Cohen (1842–1927), Dan. critic and literary historian.

Brandl (brän′dl), Alois (1855–1940), Austrian-Ger. English philologist and literary historian.

Brandon (bran′don), Charles. See *Suffolk, Charles Brandon, 1st Duke of*.

Brangwyn (brang′win), Sir Frank (1867–), Br. painter, etcher, and designer.

Brant (brant), Joseph (native name Thayendanegea) (1742–1807), Am. Indian chief.

Brant (bränt), Sebastian (1457–1521), Ger. satiric poet.

Branting (brän′ting), Hjalmar (1860–1925), Swed. socialist leader and statesman.

Brantôme (dè brän-tōm), Pierre de Bourdeille, Seigneur de (c1540–1614), Fr. writer of memoirs.

Bratianu (brä-tē-ä′nö), Ion (1821–91), Rumanian statesman.

Brauchitsch (fon brou′chich), Heinrich Alfred Hermann Walther von (1881–), Ger. general.

Brauwer, Adriaen. See *Brouwer*.

Bravo (brä′vō), Nicolás (1790?–1854), Mex. general.

Brazza (dä brät′sä), Pierre Paul François Camille Savorgnan de (1852–1905), Fr. explorer and colonial administrator in Africa, of Italian parentage.

Breckinridge (brek′in-rij), John Cabell (1821–75), Am. politician and Confederate general, vice-president of U. S. (1857–61).

Brederode (brä′dè-rō-dè), Hendrik, Count (1531–68), Flemish leader, opponent of Spanish rule in the Netherlands.

Breitinger (brī′ting-èr), Johann Jakob (1701–76), Swiss scholar and critic, writing in German.

Bremer (brä′mèr), Fredrika (1801–65), Swed. novelist.

Brendan (bren′dan), Saint (of Ardfert and Clonfert) (also called Brenainn and Brandan) (484–577), Ir. monk, hero of legendary voyage to island in the Atlantic ("St. Brendan's Island").

Brennus (bren′us) (fl. 390 B.C.), Gallic chief, said to have invaded Italy and to have besieged the Capitol at Rome. Cf. *Manlius, Marcus*.

Brentano (bren-tä′nō), Klemens (1778–1842), Ger. author.

Breton (brè-tôn), Jules Adolphe Aimé Louis (1827–1906), Fr. painter.

Breton (brit′on), Nicholas (1545?–1626?), Eng. poet and prose-writer.

Bretón de los Herreros (brä-tōn′ dä lōs er-rä′rōs), Manuel (1796–1873), Sp. poet and dramatist.

Brewer (brö′èr), David Josiah (1837–1910), Am. jurist, associate justice of U. S. Supreme Court (1889–1910).

Brewster (brö′stèr), Sir David (1781–1868), Sc. physicist.

Brewster, William ("Elder Brewster") (1560?–1644), Eng. settler at Plymouth, Mass. (1620), one of the leaders of the Pilgrims.

Brialmont (brē-ál-môn), Henri Alexis (1821–1903), Belgian general, and military engineer and writer.

Brian (brī′an) (known as Brian Boru, Boroimhe, or Boroma) (926–1014), king of Ireland (1002–14).

Briand (brē-än), Aristide (1862–1932), Fr. statesman.

Bride, Saint. See *Bridget* (452?–523).

Bridges (brij′ez), Robert (1844–1930), Eng. poet laureate.

Bridget (brij′et) or **Brigid** (brij′id) or **Bride** (brīd), Saint (452?–523), Ir. abbess, a patron saint of Ireland.

Bridget, Saint (of Sweden). See *Birgitta*.

Bridgewater (brij′wâ″tèr), Francis Henry Egerton, 8th Earl of (1756–1829), Eng. clergyman, who bequeathed money to provide for the series of treatises bearing his name ("Bridgewater Treatises").

Bridgman (brij′man), Frederic Arthur (1847–1928), Am. painter, in Paris.

Brieux (brē-è), Eugène (1858–1932), Fr. dramatist.

Briggs (brigz), Charles Augustus (1841–1913), Am. clergyman, theologian, and Biblical scholar.

Briggs, Henry (1561–1631), Eng. mathematician.

Bright (brīt), John (1811–89), Eng. orator and statesman.

Bright, Richard (1789–1858), Eng. physician.

Brigid, Saint. See *Bridget* (452?–523).

Brigitta, Saint. See *Birgitta*.

Brindley (brind′li), James (1716–72), Eng. engineer.

Brinton (brin′ton), Daniel Garrison (1837–99), Am. archæologist and ethnologist.

Brinvilliers (dĕ braṅ-vē-lyā), Marquise de (Marie Madeleine d'Aubray) (1630?—76), Fr. poisoner.

Brissot (brē-sō), Jacques Pierre (called Brissot de Warville) (1754—93), Fr. politician and writer, a leader of the Girondists.

Britannicus (bri-tan'i-kus) (orig. Claudius Tiberius Germanicus) (A.D. 41?—55), son of Emperor Claudius I. and Messalina, poisoned by Nero.

Broca (brō-kä), Paul (1824—80), Fr. surgeon and anthropologist.

Brock (brok), Sir Isaac ("the Hero of Upper Canada") (1769—1812), Eng. general and administrator in Canada.

Broglie (dĕ bro-y'), Achille Charles Léonce Victor, Duc de (1785—1870), Fr. statesman.

Broglie, Jacques Victor Albert, Duc de (1821—1901), Fr. statesman and historian (son of Achille C. L. V., Duc de Broglie).

Broke (brŭk), Sir Philip Bowes Vere (1776—1841), Eng. admiral.

Brome (brōm), Richard (d. 1652?), Eng. dramatist.

Brongniart (brôṅ-nyär), Adolphe Théodore (1801—76), Fr. botanist (son of Alexandre).

Brongniart, Alexandre (1770—1847), Fr. mineralogist and geologist.

Brontë (bron'tä), Anne ("Acton Bell") (1820—49), Eng. novelist (sister of Charlotte).

Brontë, Charlotte (Mrs. Nicholls, "Currer Bell") (1816—55), Eng. novelist.

Brontë, Emily Jane ("Ellis Bell") (1818—48), Eng. novelist (sister of Charlotte).

Brooke (brŭk), Fulke Greville, 1st Baron (1554—1628), Eng. poet and statesman.

Brooke, Henry (1703?—83), Ir. novelist and misc. writer.

Brooke, Sir James (1803—68), Eng. soldier and traveler, raja of Sarawak (in Borneo).

Brooke, Rupert (1887—1915), Eng. poet.

Brooks (brŭks), Phillips (1835—93), Am. Protestant Episcopal bishop, and pulpit orator.

Brougham and Vaux (brōm, vȧks), Henry Peter Brougham, 1st Baron (1778—1868), Br. statesman, jurist, orator, and writer.

Brouwer or **Brauwer** (brou'ėr), Adriaen (c1605—38), Flemish painter.

Brown (broun), Charles Brockden (1771—1810), Am. novelist.

Brown, Ford Madox (1821—93), Eng. painter (grandson of John Brown, 1735—88).

Brown, Goold (1791—1857), Am. grammarian.

Brown, Jacob (1775—1828), Am. general.

Brown, John (1735—88), Sc. physician.

Brown, John ("of Osawatomie") (1800—59), Am. abolitionist.

Brown, John (1810—82), Sc. physician and author.

Brown, Robert (1773—1858), Br. botanist.

Browne (broun), Charles Farrar ("Artemus Ward") (1834—67), Am. humorist.

Browne, Hablot Knight ("Phiz") (1815—82), Eng. artist, noted as illustrator.

Browne, Maximilian Ulysses, Graf von (1705—57), Austrian field-marshal, born in Switzerland.

Browne, Robert (c1550—c1633), Eng. Puritan theologian, advocate of Brownism.

Browne, Sir Thomas (1605—82), Eng. physician and author.

Browne, Thomas Alexander ("Rolf Boldrewood") (1826—1915), Australian novelist.

Browne, William (1591—1643?), Eng. pastoral poet.

Brownell (brou-nel'), William Crary (1851—1928), Am. critic.

Browning (brou'ning), Robert (1812—89), Eng. poet.

Browning, Mrs. (Elizabeth Barrett) (1806—61), Eng. poet (wife of Robert).

Brown-Séquard (broun-sā-kär), Charles Édouard (1817—94), Fr.-Am. physiologist, born in Mauritius.

Bruce (brös), Sir David (1855—1931), Br. physician and bacteriologist, specialist in tropical diseases.

Bruce, James (1730—94), Sc. traveler in Africa.

Bruce, Robert de, or Robert. See *Robert I.* (of Scotland).

Bruch (brŭċh), Max (1838—1920), Ger. musical composer and conductor.

Bruckner (brŭk'nėr), Anton (1824—96), Austrian organist and composer.

Bruehl (brül). See *Brühl*.

Brugmann (brŭċh'män), Karl (1849—1919), Ger. comparative philologist.

Brugsch (brŭċhsh), Heinrich Karl (1827—94), Ger. Egyptologist.

Brühl (fon brül), Heinrich, Graf von (1700—63), favorite and prime minister at the court of Saxony.

Brummell (brum'el), George Bryan (called Beau Brummell) (1778—1840), Eng. leader of fashion.

Brune (brün), Guillaume Marie Anne (1763—1815), Fr. marshal.

Bruneau (brü-nō), Alfred (1857—1934), Fr. composer and critic of music.

Brunehaut. See *Brunhilda*. ˥

Brunelleschi (brö-nel-les'kē) or **Brunellesco** (brö-nel-les'kō), Filippo (1377—1446), Florentine architect and sculptor.

Brunetière (brün-tyär), Ferdinand (1849—1906), Fr. literary critic.

Brunhilda (brön-hil'dä) or **Brunehaut** (Fr. brün-hō) (d. 613), queen of the eastern Franks (sister-in-law of Chilperic I.).

Bruno (brö'nō), Saint (c1030—1101), monk, born at Cologne, founder of Carthusian order.

Bruno, Giordano (c1548—1600), It. philosopher.

Brunswick (brunz'wik), Karl Wilhelm Ferdinand, Duke of (1735—1806), Ger. general.

Brush (brush), Charles Francis (1849—1929), Am. electrician and inventor.

Brusilov (brö-sē''of), Aleksyey Aleksyeevich (1853—1926), Russ. general.

Brutus (brö'tus), Lucius Junius (fl. 509 B.C.), Rom. patriot. According to legend, he was a nephew of Tarquinius Superbus, the last of the kings of Rome; he led the revolution that expelled the Tarquins and established the republic, becoming one of the first two consuls; and he caused his two sons to be put to death in his sight, for connection with a conspiracy to restore Tarquinius Superbus to power.

Brutus, Marcus Junius (85 or 79 or 78—42 B.C.), Rom. general and provincial administrator, one of the assassins of Julius Cæsar.

Bryan (brī'ạn), William Jennings (1860—1925), Am. political leader.

Bryant (brī'ạnt), William Cullen (1794—1878), Am. poet.

Bryce (brīs), James Bryce, Viscount (1838—1922), Br. historical and political writer, statesman, and diplomatist.

Bucer (bū'sėr) or **Butzer** (böt'sėr), Martin (name orig. Kuhhorn) (1491—1551), Ger. Protestant reformer.

Buchan (buk'ạn), John. See *Tweedsmuir, 1st Baron*.

Buchanan (bu-kan'ạn or bū-kan'ạn), George (1506—82), Sc. historian and scholar.

Buchanan, James (1791—1868), 15th president of U. S. (1857—61).

Büchner (büċh'nėr), Friedrich Karl Christian Ludwig (1824—99), Ger. physician and philosopher.

Buck (buk), Dudley (1839—1909), Am. organist and composer.

Buckingham (buk'ing-ạm), Henry Stafford, 2d Duke of (in Stafford line) (1454?—83), Eng. politician, who supported and later revolted against Richard III., and was captured and executed.

Buckingham, George Villiers, 1st Duke of (1592—1628), Eng. courtier and politician.

Buckingham, George Villiers, 2d Duke of (1628—87), Eng. politician and author (son of 1st Duke).

Buckland (buk'lạnd), William (1784—1856), Eng. divine and geologist.

Buckle (buk'l), Henry Thomas (1821—62), Eng. historian.

Buckner (buk'nėr), Simon Bolivar (1823—1914), Am. Confederate general.

Buddha (bŭd'ä) (meaning 'the Enlightened,' a title of Siddhartha, also known as Gautama or Gotama, and Sakyamuni) (c568?—c488? B.C.), philosopher and religious teacher of India, founder of Buddhism.

Budé (bü-dā), Guillaume (also called Budæus) (1467—1540), Fr. scholar.

Budge (buj), Sir Ernest Alfred Thompson Wallis (1857–1934), Eng. Orientalist.

Budgell (buj'el), Eustace (1686–1737), Eng. essayist and misc. writer.

Buechner (büch'nèr). See *Büchner*.

Buell (bū'el), Don Carlos (1818–98), Am. general.

Buelow (bü'lō). See *Bülow*.

Buffalo Bill. Sobriquet of W. F. Cody.

Buffon (dè bü-fôn), Georges Louis Leclerc, Comte de (1707–88), Fr. naturalist.

Buhl (böl). See *Boulle*.

Bull (búl), Ole Bornemann (1810–80), Norw. violinist.

Bullant (bü-län), Jean (c1515–78), Fr. architect.

Bullard (búl'ärd), Robert Lee (1861–   ), Am. general.

Bullen, Anne. See *Boleyn, Anne*.

Buller (búl'èr), Sir Redvers Henry (1839–1908), Eng. general.

Bullinger (búl'ing-èr), Heinrich (1504–75), Swiss Protestant reformer.

Bülow (fon bü'lō), Bernhard Heinrich Martin Karl, Prince von (1849–1929), Ger. statesman and diplomatist, imperial chancellor (1900–09).

Bülow, Dietrich Heinrich, Freiherr von (1757–1807), Ger. military writer (brother of Friedrich W.).

Bülow, Friedrich Wilhelm, Freiherr von (Graf von Dennewitz) (1755–1816), Prussian general.

Bülow, Hans Guido von (1830–94), Ger. pianist and conductor.

Bülow, Karl von (1846–1921), Ger. field-marshal.

Bulwer (búl'wèr), Sir Henry. See *Dalling and Bulwer*.

Bulwer-Lytton. See *Lytton*.

Bunau-Varilla (bü-nō-vȧ-rē-yä), Philippe Jean (1859–1940), Fr. engineer, and diplomatist in service of Republic of Panama.

Bunce (buns), William Gedney (1840–1916), Am. painter.

Bunin (bö'nyęn), Ivan Aleksyeevich (1870–   ), Russ. author.

Bunner (bun'èr), Henry Cuyler (1855–96), Am. writer, esp. of short stories.

Bunsen (fon bún'zęn), Christian Karl Josias, Freiherr von (1791–1860), Prussian scholar and diplomatist.

Bunsen, Robert Wilhelm (1811–99), Ger. chemist.

Bunyan (bun'yȧn), John (1628–88), Eng. religious writer, author of "Pilgrim's Progress."

Buonaparte (It. bwô-nä-pär'tä). See *Bonaparte*.

Buonarroti (bwô-när-rô'tē), Michelangelo. See *Michelangelo*.

Buoninsegna, Duccio di. See *Duccio di Buoninsegna*.

Burbage (bèr'bäj), James (d. 1597), Eng. actor and theatrical manager.

Burbage, Richard (c1567–1619), Eng. actor, friend of Shakspere (son of James).

Burbank (bèr'bangk), Luther (1849–1926), Am. horticulturist, originator of new fruits, flowers, etc.

Burchell (bèr'chel), William John (1782?–1863), Eng. explorer and naturalist.

Burckhardt (búrk'härt), Jakob (1818–97), Swiss writer on art.

Burckhardt, John Lewis (1784–1817), Swiss-Eng. traveler and Orientalist.

Burdach (búr'däch), Karl Friedrich (1776–1847), Ger. physiologist.

Burdett (bèr-det'), Sir Francis (1770–1844), Eng. politician.

Bürger (bür'gèr), Gottfried August (1748–94), Ger. poet.

Burgersdyk (bür'chèrs-dīk), Francis (Franciscus Burgersdicius) (1590–1629), Dutch logician.

Burgh (dè bèrg), Hubert de (d. 1243), Eng. statesman and chief justiciary.

Burghley (bèr'li), William Cecil, 1st Baron (1520–98), Eng. statesman.

Burgoyne (bèr-goin'), John (1722–92), Eng. general and dramatist.

Burián von Rajecz (bö'ṛę-än fon rä'yets), István, or Stephen, Count (1851–1922), Hung. diplomatist and statesman.

Buridan (bü-rē-dän), Jean (c1300–c1358), Fr. scholastic philosopher.

Burke (bèrk), Edmund (1729–97), Br. statesman, orator, and writer.

Burke, Robert O'Hara (1820–61), Australian explorer, born in Ireland.

Burlingame (bèr'ling-gām), Anson (1820–70), Am. legislator and diplomatist.

Burnand (bèr-nand'), Sir Francis Cowley (1836–1917), Eng. playwright, humorist, and editor.

Burne-Jones (bèrn'jōnz'), Sir Edward Coley Burne (1833–98), Eng. painter and designer.

Burnet (bèr'net), Gilbert (1643–1715), Br. bishop and historian.

Burnett (bèr-net'), Mrs. Frances Hodgson (Frances Eliza Hodgson, Mrs. Burnett, later Mrs. Townesend) (1849–1924), Eng.-Am. author.

Burney (bèr'ni), Charles (1726–1814), Eng. composer and historian of music.

Burney, Frances. See *Arblay*.

Burnouf (bür-nöf), Eugène (1801–52), Fr. Orientalist.

Burns (bèrnz), John (1858–   ), Eng. labor leader and cabinet minister.

Burns, Robert (1759–96), Sc. poet.

Burns, William John (1861–1932), Am. detective.

Burnside (bèrn'sīd), Ambrose Everett (1824–81), Am. general.

Burr (bèr), Aaron (1756–1836), Am. politician, vice-president of U. S. (1801–05).

Burritt (bur'it), Elihu ("the Learned Blacksmith") (1810–79), Am. peace advocate and linguist.

Burroughs (bur'ōz), John (1837–1921), Am. writer on natural history.

Burton (bèr'tọn), Sir Richard Francis (1821–90), Eng. traveler and author.

Burton, Robert (1577–1640), Eng. author.

Bury (ber'i), John Bagnell (1861–1927), Br. historian and classical scholar.

Bury, Richard de (real name Richard Aungerville) (1281?–1345), Eng. bishop, diplomatist, and bibliophile.

Busch (bush), Julius Hermann Moritz (1821–99), Ger. political and misc. writer.

Busch, Wilhelm (1832–1908), Ger. humorous draftsman and verse-writer.

Bushnell (bush'nel), Horace (1802–76), Am. Congregational clergyman and theologian.

Busoni (bö-zō'nē), Ferruccio Benvenuto (1866–1924), It. pianist and composer.

Bustamante (bös-tä-män'tä), Anastasio (1780–1853), Mex. soldier and politician.

Bute (būt), John Stuart, 3d Earl of (1713–92), Br. statesman, favorite of George III. of England.

Butler (but'lèr), Benjamin Franklin (1818–93), Am. general and political leader.

Butler, Lady Elizabeth (Elizabeth Southerden Thompson) (1844–1933), Br. artist, chiefly noted as a painter of military subjects, born in Switzerland.

Butler, James. See *Ormonde, Duke of*.

Butler, Joseph (1692–1752), Eng. bishop and theologian.

Butler, Nicholas Murray (1862–   ), Am. educator.

Butler, Samuel (1612–80), Eng. satiric poet.

Butler, Samuel (1835–1902), Eng. philosophical writer, novelist, and misc. writer, author of "The Way of All Flesh."

Butler, William Allen (1825–1902), Am. lawyer and poet.

Butzer, Martin. See *Bucer*.

Buxtorf (búks'tôrf), Johann ("the elder") (1564–1629), Ger.-Swiss Hebraist and rabbinical scholar.

Buxtorf, Johann ("the younger") (1599–1664), Swiss Hebraist (son of "the elder").

B. V. Initials of "Bysshe Vanolis," used as a signature by James Thomson (1834–82).

Byelinski (bye-lyēn'skę), Vissarion Grigorevich (1811–48), Russ. critic.

Byng (bing), John (1704–57), Eng. admiral, executed for neglect of duty.

Byng of Vimy (vē'mē), Julian Hedworth George Byng, Viscount (1862–1935), Eng. general, governor-general of Canada (1921–26).

Byrd (bèrd), Richard Evelyn (1888–   ), Am. naval officer (made non-stop flight by aëroplane from Spitzbergen to north pole and back, 1926; and from N. Y. to France, 1927).

Byrd, William (1543?–1623), Eng. musical composer.

Byron (bī′ron), George Noel Gordon Byron, 6th Baron (1788—1824), Eng. poet.

Byron, Henry James (1834—84), Eng. playwright and actor.

C

Cabanel (ká-bá-nel), Alexandre (1823—89), Fr. painter.

Cabanis (ká-bá-nēs), Pierre Jean Georges (1757—1808), Fr. physician and philosopher.

Cabell (kab′el), James Branch (1879—   ), Am. author.

Cabet (ká-bā), Étienne (1788—1856), Fr. communist and writer.

Cabeza de Vaca (kä-bā′thä dä vä′kä), Álvar Núñez (c1490—c1564), Sp. adventurer in America.

Cable (kā′bl), George Washington (1844—1925), Am. novelist.

Cabot (kab′ot), John (Giovanni Caboto) (c1450—98?), It. navigator in English service, who made voyage to North America in 1497.

Cabot, Sebastian (1474?—1557), Eng. navigator and cosmographer (son of John).

Cabral (kä-bräl′), Pedro Alvarez (1460?—1526?), Pg. navigator.

Cabrera (kä-brä′rä), Ramón (Count of Morella) (1810—77), Sp. Carlist general.

Cáceres (kä′sä-räs), Andrés Avelino (1836—1923), Peruvian general and statesman.

Cada Mosto (dä kä′dä mōs′tō), Alvise (or Luigi) da (1432?—80?), It. navigator in Portuguese service, explorer of west coast of Africa.

Cade (kād), John (called Jack Cade) (d. 1450), Br. rebel leader.

Cadillac (ká-dē-yàk), Antoine de La Mothe (1657?—1730), Fr. soldier and administrator in America, founder of Detroit.

Cadman (kad′man), Charles Wakefield (1881—1946), Am. musical composer.

Cadogan (ka-dug′an), William Cadogan, 1st Earl (1675—1726), Br. general.

Cadorna (kä-dôr′nä), Count Luigi (1850—1928), It. general.

Cadoudal (ká-dö-däl′), Georges (1771—1804), Fr. royalist conspirator.

Cædmon (kad′mon) (fl. 670), Anglo-Saxon poet.

Cælius Aurelianus (sē′li-us â-rē-li-ā′nus). See *Aurelianus, Cælius.*

Cæsalpinus (ses-al-pī′nus). See *Cesalpini.*

Cæsar (sē′zär), Caius Julius (102 or 100—44 B.C.), Rom. general, statesman, and historian.

Cagliari. See *Caliari.*

Cagliostro (käl-yōs′trō), Count Alessandro (assumed name of Giuseppe Balsamo) (1743—95), It. adventurer.

Caillaux (kä-yō), Joseph (1863—1944), Fr. politician, minister of finance, and premier.

Caillié or **Caillé** (kä-yā), René (1799—1838), Fr. traveler in Africa.

Caine (kān), Sir Thomas Henry Hall (1853—1931), Eng. novelist.

Caird (kärd), Edward (1835—1908), Br. philosopher.

Cajal, Santiago Ramón y. See *Ramón y Cajal.*

Cajetan (kaj′e-tan) (real name Tommaso de Vio) (1469—1534), It. cardinal and theologian.

Calamy (kal′a-mi), Edmund (1600—66), Eng. Presbyterian divine.

Calamy, Edmund (1671—1732), Eng. nonconformist divine and biographer (grandson of Edmund Calamy, 1600—66).

Caldara (käl-dä′rä), Polidoro (often called Polidoro da Caravaggio) (c1492—1543), It. painter.

Calder (kál′dèr), Alexander Milne (1846—1923), Sc.-Am. sculptor.

Calder, Alexander Stirling (1870—1945), Am. sculptor (son of Alexander M.).

Calderón de la Barca (käl-dä-rōn′ dä lä bär′kä), Pedro (1600—81), Sp. dramatist and poet.

Calderwood (kál′dèr-wud), David (1575—1650), Sc. clergyman and church historian.

Calderwood, Henry (1830—97), Sc. clergyman and philosopher.

Calepino (kä-lä-pē′nō), Ambrogio (1435—1511), It. lexicographer.

Calhoun (kal-hōn′), John Caldwell (1782—1850), Am. statesman, vice-president of U. S. (1825—32).

Caliari or **Cagliari** (käl′yä-rē), Paolo (commonly called Paul Veronese) (1528—88), It. painter, of Venetian school.

Caligula (ka-lig′ū-la) (Caius Cæsar Augustus Germanicus) (A.D. 12—41), Rom. emperor (A.D. 37—41) (son of Germanicus Cæsar, and grandnephew and successor of Tiberius).

Calixtus (kä-liks′tús), Georg (1586—1656), Ger. Lutheran theologian.

Calleja del Rey (käl-yä′нä del rä′ẹ), Félix María (1750—1820?), Sp. general, in Mexico.

Calles (käl′yäs or kä′yäs), Plutarco Elías (1877—1945), Mex. politician and general, president of Mexico (1924—28).

Callimachus (ka-lim′a-kus) (c310—c240 B.C.), Gr. poet and scholar, at Alexandria.

Calmet (kál-mā), Augustin (1672—1757), Fr. monk, Biblical scholar, and historian.

Calonne (dè ká-lon), Charles Alexandre de (1734—1802), Fr. finance minister.

Calvé (kál-vā), Mme. (professional name of Emma de Roquer, Mme. Gaspari) (1866?—1942), Fr. operatic soprano singer.

Calverley (kal′vèr-li), Charles Stuart (1831—84), Eng. poet and translator.

Calvert (kal′vèrt). See *Baltimore.*

Calvert, Leonard (1606?—47), first Eng. colonial governor of Maryland (brother of 2d Baron Baltimore).

Calvin (kal′vin), John (orig. Jean Chauvin, or Cauvin) (1509—64), Fr. Protestant reformer and theologian, at Geneva.

Cambacérès (dè kän-bá-sā-res), Jean Jacques Régis de (Duc de Parme) (1753—1824), Fr. jurist and statesman.

Cambio, Arnolfo di. See *Arnolfo di Cambio.*

Cambon (kän-bôn), Jules Martin (1845—1935), Fr. administrator and diplomatist (brother of Pierre P.).

Cambon, Pierre Paul (1843—1924), Fr. diplomatist.

Cambronne (kän-bron), Pierre Jacques Étienne, Comte (1770—1842), Fr. general.

Cambyses (kam-bī′sēz) (d. 521 B.C.), king of Persia (529—522 B.C.) (son of Cyrus the Great). See *Smerdis.*

Camden (kam′den), Charles Pratt, 1st Earl (1714—94), Eng. jurist and statesman.

Camden, William (1551—1623), Eng. antiquary and historian.

Cameron (kam′e-ron), Richard (d. 1680), Sc. Presbyterian minister, a leader of the Covenanters.

Cameron, Simon (1799—1889), Am. political leader.

Cameron, Verney Lovett (1844—94), Eng. explorer in Africa.

Camillus (ka-mil′us), Marcus Furius (d. 365 B.C.), Rom. general and statesman.

Camoëns (dä kam′ō-ens), Luis de (in Portuguese, Luis de Camões) (1524?—80), Pg. poet.

Campanella (käm-pä-nel′lä), Tommaso (1568—1639), It. philosopher.

Campbell (kam′bel or kam′el), Alexander (1788—1866), Ir.-Am. clergyman, founder of Disciples of Christ.

Campbell, Archibald. See *Argyll, Earl of.*

Campbell, Colin. See *Clyde, Baron.*

Campbell, John Campbell, 1st Baron (1779—1861), Br. jurist and writer.

Campbell, Robert. See *Macgregor, Robert.*

Campbell, Thomas (1777—1844), Br. poet and misc. writer.

Campbell-Bannerman (-ban′èr-man), Sir Henry (orig. Henry Campbell) (1836—1908), Br. statesman.

Campeggio (käm-ped′jō), Lorenzo (1472?—1539), It. cardinal and ecclesiastical diplomatist.

Camper (käm′pèr), Pieter (1722—89), Dutch anatomist and naturalist.

Camphausen (kämp′hou″zen), Wilhelm (1818—85), Ger. painter.

Campion (kam′pi-on), Edmund (1540—81), Eng. Jesuit.

Campion, Thomas (1567—1620), Eng. poet and musician.

Campoamor y Campoosorio (dä käm″pō-ä-mōr′ ē käm″pō-ō-sō″rē-ō), Ramón de (1817—1901), Sp. poet, philosophical writer, and politician.

Campomanes (dä käm-pō-mä′näs), Pedro Rodríguez, Count de (1723—1802), Sp. statesman and economist.

Canaletto (kä-nä-let′tō) (real name Antonio Canal, or Canale) (1697—1768), Venetian painter.

Canaris (kä-nä'rēs). See *Kanaris.*

Canby (kan'bi), Edward Richard Sprigg (1819–73), Am. general.

Candolle (dè kän-dol), Augustin Pyramus de (1778–1841), Swiss botanist.

Canfield (kan'fēld), Dorothy. See *Fisher, Dorothy Canfield.*

Can Grande (kän grän'dä). See *Scala, Can Grande della.*

Canisius (kä-nē'sḝ-ùs), Petrus (name orig. De Hondt) (1521 or 1524–97), Dutch Jesuit and theologian, in Germany.

Canning (kan'ing), Charles John Canning, Earl (1812–62), Eng. statesman (son of George Canning).

Canning, George (1770–1827), Eng. statesman.

Canning, Sir Stratford. See *Stratford de Redcliffe, Viscount.*

Cannizzaro (kän-nē-tsä'rō), Stanislao (1826–1910), It. chemist.

Cannon (kan'ọn), Joseph Gurney (1836–1926), Am. political leader.

Cano (del kä'nō), Juan Sebastián del (c1460–1526), Sp. navigator under command of Magellan, and first circumnavigator of the globe.

Canova (kä-nō'vä), Antonio (1757–1822), It. sculptor.

Cánovas del Castillo (kä'nō-väs del käs-tēl'yō), Antonio (1828–97), Sp. statesman and author.

Canrobert (kän-ro-bär), François Certain (1809–95), Fr. marshal.

Cantemir (kän-tye-mēr'), Demetrius (1673–1723), prince of Moldavia (1710–11), and scholar and historian.

Cantù (kän-tö'), Cesare (1807–95), It. historian.

Canute (kạ-nūt'), or **Cnut** or **Knut** (knöt) ("the Great") (994?–1035), king of England (1017–35), of Denmark (1018?–35), and of Norway (1028?–35) (son of Sweyn).

Capel (kap'el), Arthur. See *Essex, 1st Earl of.*

Capella (ka-pel'ä), Martianus Minneus Felix (5th cent.), Latin encyclopedist, of northern Africa.

Capello (kä-pel'lō) or **Cappello**, Bianca (1548?–87), Venetian adventuress, later (as wife of Francesco de' Medici) grand duchess of Tuscany.

Capet (kä'pet, Fr. kȧ-pā). See *Hugh Capet.*

Capistrano (dē kä-pēs-trä'nō), Giovanni di (1386–1456), It. friar, preacher, inquisitor, and saint.

Capito (kä'pē-tō), Wolfgang Fabricius (name orig. Köpfel) (1478–1541), Ger. Protestant reformer.

Capo d'Istria (kä'pō dēs'trē-ä), Count Giovanni Antonio (Joannes Capodistrias) (1776–1831), diplomatist in Russian service (born in Corfu), president of Greece (1828–31).

Cappello (käp-pel'lō). See *Capello.*

Capponi (käp-pō'nē), Marquis Gino (1792–1876), It. statesman and historian.

Capponi, Piero (1447?–96), Florentine soldier and statesman.

Caprivi de Caprara de Montecuccoli (fon kä-prē've dä kä-prä'rä dä mōn-tä-kök'kō-lē), Georg Leo, Graf von (1831–99), Ger. soldier and statesman, imperial chancellor (1890–94).

Capus (kȧ-pü), Vincent Marie Alfred (1858–1922), Fr. dramatist and misc. writer.

Caracalla (kar-ạ-kal'ạ), Marcus Aurelius Antoninus (name orig. Bassianus) (188–217), Rom. emperor (211–217) (son of Emperor Lucius Septimius Severus).

Caracci. See *Carracci.*

Caracciolo (kä-rät'chō-lō) or **Caraccioli** (kä-rät'chō-lē), Prince Francesco (1748 or 1732–99), Neapolitan admiral, hanged as republican revolutionist.

Caractacus (kạ-rak'tạ-kus) or **Caradoc** (kar'ạ-dok) (fl. A.D. c50), Br. king, leader against Roman invaders of Britain.

Caran d'Ache (kȧ-rän dȧsh). Pseudonym of Emmanuel Poiré.

Caravaggio (dä kä-rä-väd'jō), Michelangelo da (properly Michelangelo Morigi, Merigi, or Amerigi) (1569–1609), It. painter.

Caravaggio, Polidoro da. See *Caldara, Polidoro.*

Cardano (kär-dä'nō), Girolamo (also known as Jerome Cardan and Hieronymus Cardanus) (1501–76), It. physician, mathematician, and philosopher.

Cardigan (kär'di-gạn), James Thomas Brudenell, 7th Earl of (1797–1868), Eng. general, commander of Light Brigade in famous charge at Balaklava (1854).

Carducci (kär-döt'chē), Giosuè (1836–1907), It. poet.

Carew (kạ-rö' or kā'ri), Thomas (c1595–c1645), Eng. poet.

Carey (kā'ri), Henry (d. 1743), Eng. poet and musical composer.

Carey, Henry Charles (1793–1879), Am. political economist.

Carey, William (1761–1834), Eng. missionary and Orientalist in India.

Carleton (kärl'tọn), Sir Guy. See *Dorchester, 1st Baron.*

Carlisle (kär-līl'), George William Frederick Howard, 7th Earl of (1802–64), Eng. statesman and writer.

Carlisle, John Griffin (1835–1910), Am. statesman.

Carloman (kär'lọ-mạn) (d. 884), king of the Franks (879–884) (brother of Louis III.).

Carlos I. (kär'lōs) (1863–1908), king of Portugal (1889–1908).

Carlos, Don (1545–68), heir to the Spanish throne, who died in prison (son of Philip II.).

Carlos, Don (Carlos María Isidro, later known as Count of Molina) (1788–1855), Sp. prince, and pretender to the throne (brother of Ferdinand VII.).

Carlos, Don (Count of Montemolín) (1818–61), pretender to the Spanish throne (son of Don Carlos, 1788–1855).

Carlos, Don (Duke of Madrid) (1848–1909), pretender to the Spanish throne (nephew of Don Carlos, 1818–61).

Carlstadt. See *Karlstadt.*

Carlyle (kär-līl'), Thomas (1795–1881), Br. essayist and historian.

Carmagnola (kär-mä-nyō'lä), Francesco Bussone, Count of (1390?–1432), It. military leader, in service of Milan and Venice.

Carman (kär'mạn), William Bliss (1861–1929), Can. poet in U. S.

Carmen Sylva (kär'men sil'vạ). Pseudonym of Elizabeth, queen of Rumania.

Carnegie (kär-neg'i), Andrew (1835–1919), Sc.-Am. capitalist and philanthropist.

Carnot (kär-nō), Lazare Hippolyte (1801–88), Fr. politician and writer (brother of Nicolas L. S.).

Carnot, Lazare Nicolas Marguerite (1753–1823), Fr. general and statesman.

Carnot, Marie François Sadi (1837–94), Fr. statesman, president of France (1887–94) (son of Lazare H.).

Carnot, Nicolas Léonard Sadi (1796–1832), Fr. physicist (son of Lazare N. M.).

Carol (kä'rol). See *Charles I., Charles II.,* of Rumania.

Caroline (kar'ọ-līn) (Wilhelmina Caroline) (1683–1737), queen of George II. of England.   [IV. of England.

Caroline Amelia Elizabeth (1768–1821), queen of George

Caroline Matilda (1751–75), queen of Christian VII. of Denmark and Norway (sister of George III. of England).

Carolus Duran (kȧ-ro-lüs dü-rän). See *Duran, Carolus.*

Caron (kȧ-rôn), René Édouard (1800–76), Can. statesman and jurist.

Carpaccio (kär-pät'chō), Vittore (c1450–c1522), It. painter, of Venetian school.

Carpeaux (kär-pō), Jean Baptiste (1827–75), Fr. sculptor.

Carr (kär), Robert. See *Somerset, Earl of.*

Carracci (kär-rät'chē) or **Caracci** (kä-rät'chē), Agostino (1557–1602), It. painter and engraver (cousin or nephew of Lodovico).

Carracci or **Caracci**, Annibale (1560–1609), It. painter (brother of Agostino).

Carracci or **Caracci**, Lodovico (1555–1619), It. painter, of Bologna, founder of Bolognese school.

Carranza (kär-rän'sä), Venustiano (1859–1920), Mex. politician and general, president of Mexico (1915–20).

Carrara (dä kär-rä'rä), Jacopo da (d. 1324), It. soldier, lord of Padua (1318–24).

Carrel (kȧ-rel), Alexis (1873–1944), Fr. surgeon, in America.

Carreño (kär-rā'nyō), Teresa (Mme. Sauret, Mme. G. Tagliapietra, Mme. Eugen d'Albert, Mme. A. Tagliapietra) (1853–1917), Venezuelan pianist.

Carrier (kȧ-ryā), Jean Baptiste (1756–94), Fr. revolutionist.

Carrière (kȧ-ryär), Eugène Anatole (1849–1906), Fr. painter.

Carroll (kar'ọl), Charles ("of Carrollton") (1737–1832), Am. patriot and legislator.

Carroll, John (1735–1815), Am. Rom. Cath. archbishop.

Carroll, Lewis. Pseudonym of C. L. Dodgson.

Carson (kär′sọn), Christopher ("Kit Carson") (1809—68), Am. frontiersman and scout.

Carson, Sir Edward Henry (Baron Carson) (1854—1935), Ir. lawyer and politician, and cabinet minister and jurist in England.

Carstares or **Carstairs** (kär′stárz), William (1649—1715), Sc. divine and statesman.

Carter (kär′tẻr), Howard (1873—1939), Eng. archæologist in Egypt, discoverer of tomb of Tutankhamen (1922).

Carteret (kär′tẻr-et), Sir George (c1610—80), Eng. royalist politician.

Carteret, John. See *Granville, Earl*.

Carteret, Philip (d. 1796), Eng. naval officer and navigator.

Cartier (kär-tyä), Sir George Étienne (1814—73), Can. statesman.

Cartier, Jacques (1491—1557), Fr. navigator, discoverer of St. Lawrence River.

Carton de Wiart (kär-tôṅ dẻ vẻ-är), Henry, Comte (1869—), Belgian statesman.

Cartouche (kär-tösh), Louis Dominique (1693—1721), Fr. robber.

Cartwright (kärt′rīt), Edmund (1743—1823), Eng. clergyman, inventor of weaving and wool-combing machinery (brother of John).

Cartwright, John (1740—1824), Eng. political reformer.

Cartwright, Peter (1785—1872), Am. Methodist preacher.

Cartwright, Thomas (c1535—1603), Eng. Puritan divine and controversialist.

Carus (kä′rủs), Paul (1852—1919), Ger.-Am. philosophical writer and editor.

Caruso (kä-rö′zō), Enrico (1873—1921), It. operatic tenor singer.

Carver (kär′vẻr), John (1575?—1621), Eng. settler at Plymouth, Mass. (1620), and first governor of the colony.

Carver, Jonathan (c1725—80), Am. traveler.

Cary (kā′ri), Alice (1820—71), Am. poet and misc. writer.

Cary, Henry Francis (1772—1844), Eng. writer and translator.

Cary, Phœbe (1824—71), Am. poet (sister of Alice).

Casabianca (dẻ kä-zä-byäṅg′kä), Louis de (1752?—98), Fr. naval officer.

Casanova de Seingalt (kä-sä-nō′vä dẻ saṅ-gàl), Giovanni Jacopo (1725—98), It. adventurer.

Casas, Bartolomé de las. See *Las Casas*.

Casaubon (kạ-sâ′bọn, Fr. kȧ-zō-bôṅ), Isaac (1559—1614), Fr. classical scholar.

Casement (kās′mẹnt), (Sir) Roger David (1864—1916), Ir. official in British consular service, hanged for treason.

Casimir I. (kas′i-mẻr) (1015—58), king of Poland (1040—58).

Casimir III. ("the Great") (1310?—70), king of Poland (1333—70).

Casimir IV. (1427—92), king of Poland (1447—92) (son of Jagello).

Casimir-Périer (kȧ-zē-mēr-pā-ryä), Auguste Casimir Victor Laurent (1811—76), Fr. statesman (son of Casimir Pierre Périer).

Casimir-Périer, Jean Paul Pierre (1847—1907), Fr. statesman, president of France (1894—95) (son of Auguste C. V. L.).

Caslon (kaz′lọn), William (1692—1766), Eng. type-founder.

Cass (kas), Lewis (1782—1866), Am. statesman.

Cassagnac (dẻ kȧ-sȧ-nyȧk), Bernard Adolphe Granier de (1806—80), Fr. journalist and politician.

Cassagnac, Paul Adolphe Marie Prosper Granier de (1843—1904), Fr. journalist and politician (son of Bernard A. G.).

Cassatt (kạ-sat′), Mary (1845?—1926), Am. painter, in Paris.

Cassini (kȧ-sē-nē) César François (called Cassini de Thury) (1714—84), Fr. astronomer and topographer (son of Jacques).

Cassini, Giovanni Domenico (1625—1712), It.-Fr. astronomer.

Cassini, Jacques (1677—1756), Fr. astronomer (son of Giovanni D.).

Cassini, Jacques Dominique, Comte de (1748—1845), Fr. astronomer (son of César F.).

Cassiodorus Senator (kas″i-ọ-dō′rus se-nā′tọr), Flavius Magnus Aurelius (c480—c575), Latin historical and theological writer.

Cassius Dio. See *Dio Cassius*.

Cassius Longinus (kash′ius lon-jī′nus), Caius (d. 42 B.C.), Rom. politician and general, leader of conspiracy against Julius Cæsar.

Cassivellaunus (kas″i-ve-lȧ′nus) (fl. 54 B.C.), Br. prince, leader of native tribes against Julius Cæsar.

Castagno (del käs-tä′nyō), Andrea del (1390—1457), Florentine painter.

Castelar (käs-tä-lär′), Emilio (1832—99), Sp. statesman, orator, and author.

Castelnau (dẻ kȧs-tel-nō), Michel de (Sieur de Mauvissière) (c1520—92), Fr. soldier and diplomatist.

Castelnau, Noël Marie Joseph Édouard, Vicomte de Curières de (1851—), Fr. general.

Castiglione (käs-tēl-yō′nä), Count Baldassarre (1478—1529), It. diplomatist and author.

Castilla (käs-tēl′yä), Ramón (1797—1867), Peruvian generȧ and statesman, president of Peru (1845—51, 1855—62).

Castle (kȧs′l), Egerton (1858⸺1920), Eng. novelist.

Castlemaine (kȧs′l-mān), Countess of. See *Cleveland, Duchess of*.

Castlereagh (kȧs-l-rā′), Robert Stewart, Viscount. See *Londonderry, 2d Marquis of*.

Castro (käs′trō), Cipriano (1860—1924), Venezuelan soldier and politician, president of Venezuela (1901—09).

Castro, Inés de (d. 1355), Sp. noblewoman, mistress (and later perhaps wife) of Dom Pedro, crown-prince of Portugal.

Castro, João de (1500—48), Pg. commander, viceroy of Portuguese India.

Castro, Vaca de (d. 1558), Sp. magistrate, governor of Peru.

Castruccio Castracani (käs-tröt′chō käs-trä-kä′nē) (1281?—1328), It. soldier, Ghibelline leader, and duke of Lucca.

Catesby (kāts′bi), Mark (1679?—1749), Eng. naturalist.

Catesby, Robert (1573—1605), Eng. conspirator, one of the leaders in the Gunpowder Plot.

Catharine I. (kath′ạ-rin) (c1683—1727), consort of Peter the Great, and empress of Russia (1725—27).

Catharine II. ("the Great," born Sophia Augusta Frederica of Anhalt-Zerbst) (1729—96), consort of Czar Peter III., and empress of Russia (1762—96).

Catharine de' Medici (dä med′ẹ-chē) (in French, Catherine de Médicis) (1519—89), queen of Henry II. of France, and mother of Francis II., Charles IX., and Henry III.

Catharine of Alexandria, Saint (d. 307), virgin martyr. According to legend, she was condemned to torture or death on a wheel (or wheels), which by a miracle was destroyed, the saint later being beheaded.

Catharine of Aragon (1485—1536), first wife of Henry VIII. of England, and mother of Mary I. of England.

Catharine of Siena, Saint (1347—80), It. ascetic and mystic (Dominican tertiary).

Cathelineau (kȧt-lẻ-nō), Jacques (1759—93), Fr. Vendean leader.

Cather (kaŦH′ẻr), Willa Sibert (1876—), Am. novelist.

Catherine (kath′ẹ-rin). See *Catharine*.

Catiline (kat′i-līn) (Lucius Sergius Catilina) (c108—62 B.C.), Rom. politician and conspirator.

Catlin (kat′lin), George (1796—1872), Am. painter, traveler, and writer.

Cato (kā′tō), Marcus Porcius ("the elder," called Cato the Censor) (234—149 B.C.), Rom. statesman, general, and author.

Cato, Marcus Porcius ("the younger," called Cato Uticensis) (95—46 B.C.), Rom. soldier, statesman, and Stoic philosopher (great-grandson of "the elder").

Cats (käts), Jacob (1577—1660), Dutch poet.

Catullus (kạ-tul′us), Caius Valerius (c87—c54 B.C.), Rom. lyric poet.

Catulus (kat′ụ-lus), Caius Lutatius (fl. 242 B.C.), Rom. naval commander.

Caulaincourt (dẻ kō-laṅ-kör), Armand Augustin Louis, Marquis de (Duc de Vicence) (1772—1827), Fr. general and diplomatist.

Cavaignac (kȧ-va-nyȧk), Éléonore Louis Godefroy (1801—45), Fr. journalist and politician (son of Jean B.).

Cavaignac, Jacques Marie Eugène Godefroy (1853—1905), Fr. politician (son of Louis E.).

Cavaignac, Jean Baptiste (1762—1829), Fr. revolutionist.

Cavaignac, Louis Eugène (1802—57), Fr. general (brother of Éléonore L. G.).

Cavalcanti (kä-väl-kän′tē), Guido (d. 1300), It. poet, friend of Dante.

Cavallotti (kä-väl-lot′tē), Felice Carlo Emanuele (1842—98), It. dramatist and politician.

Cavell (kav′l), Edith (1865—1915), Eng. nurse, executed by the Germans in Belgium.

Cavendish (kav′en-dish). See *Devonshire* and *Newcastle.*

Cavendish. Pseudonym of Henry Jones.

Cavendish, Henry (1731—1810), Eng. chemist and physicist.

Cavendish, Thomas (1555?—92), Eng. freebooter, and circumnavigator of the globe.

Cavour (dē kä-vŏr′), Camillo Benso, Conte di (1810—61), It. statesman.

Caxias (kä′shē-äsh), Duke of. See *Lima e Silva, Luis Alves de.*

Caxton (kak′stọn), William (c1422—91), Eng. printer (earliest), and translator and writer.

Cayley (kā′li), Arthur (1821—95), Eng. mathematician.

Cecchi (chek′kē), Giammaria (1518—87), It. writer of comedies.

Cecil (ses′il). See *Burghley* and *Salisbury.*

Cecilia (sē-sil′iạ), Saint (d. c230?), Rom. virgin martyr, patroness of music, esp. church music.

Cecil of Chelwood (ses′il, chel′wŭd), Edgar Algernon Robert Cecil, Viscount (Lord Robert Cecil) (1864—   ), Eng. statesman (son of 3d Marquis of Salisbury).

Celestine V. (sel′es-tīn), Saint (Pietro di Morrone) (c1215—96), It. hermit and monk, pope (1294).

Cellini (chĕl-lē′nē), Benvenuto (1500—71), It. sculptor, artist in metal, and autobiographer.

Celsius (sel′sẹ-ŭs), Anders (1701—44), Swed. astronomer.

Celsus (sel′sus) (fl. c178), Platonist philosopher and antichristian writer.

Celsus, Aulus (or Aurelius) Cornelius (fl. A.D. c50), Rom. writer, esp. on medicine.

Cenci (chen′chē), Beatrice (1577—99), It. girl, executed for parricide.

Centlivre (sent-liv′ẽr or sent-lē′vẽr), Mrs. Susannah (c1667—1723), Eng. actress and dramatist.

Cervantes Saavedra (sẽr-van′tēz, Sp. dä ther-vän′täs sä-ä-vä′drä), Miguel de (1547—1616), Sp. novelist, dramatist, and poet, author of "Don Quixote."

Cervera y Topete (ther-vā′rä ē tō-pā′tä), Pascual (Count de Jerez and Marquis de Santa Ana) (1839—1909), Sp. admiral.

Cesalpini (chä-zäl-pē′nē) or **Cesalpino** (chä-zäl-pē′nō), Andrea (also called Cæsalpinus) (1519—1603), It. physician, physiologist, and botanist.

Cesnola (dē ches′nō-lä), Count Luigi Palma di (1832—1904), It.-Am. archæologist.

Céspedes (dä säs′pā-тнäs), Carlos Manuel de (1819—74), Cuban patriot, president of the revolutionary republic of Cuba (1869—73).

Cetewayo or **Cetywayo** (set-i-wä′yō) or **Ketchwayo** (kech-wä′yō) (d. 1884), Zulu chief.

Cézanne (sā-zàn), Paul (1839—1906), Fr. painter.

Chabot (shá-bō), François (1759?—94), Fr. revolutionist.

Chabot, Philippe de (Seigneur de Brion, Comte de Charny) (1480?—1543), Fr. admiral.

Chabrier (shá-brē-ā), Alexis Emmanuel (1841—94), Fr. musical composer.

Chadwick (chad′wik), George Whitefield (1854—1931), Am. musical composer.

Chaffee (chaf′ē), Adna Romanza (1842—1914), Am. general.

Chaliapin or **Chaliapine.** See *Shaliapin.*

Chalmers (chä′mẽrz), Thomas (1780—1847), Sc. divine.

Chaloner (chal′ọn-ẽr), Sir Thomas (1521—65), Eng. diplomatist and writer.

Chamberlain (chām′bẽr-lạn), Arthur Neville (1869—1940), Eng. statesman (half-brother of Sir J. A.).

Chamberlain, Joseph (1836—1914), Eng. statesman.

Chamberlain, Sir Joseph Austen (1863—1937), Eng. statesman (son of Joseph).

Chamberlin (chām′bẽr-lin), Clarence Duncan (1893—   ), Am. aviator (made non-stop flight N. Y. to Germany, 1927).

Chambers (chām′bẽrz), Ephraim (c1680—1740), Eng. encyclopedist.

Chambers, Robert William (1865—1933), Am. novelist.

Chambers, Sir William (1726—96), Br. architect.

Chambord (dè shän-bôr), Henri Charles Ferdinand Marie Dieudonné d'Artois, Comte de (Duc de Bordeaux) (1820—83), Fr. Bourbon prince, claimant to throne of France (son of Duc and Duchesse de Berry, and grandson of Charles X.).

Chamfort (shän-fôr), Sébastien Roch Nicolas (1741—94), Fr. epigrammatist and misc. writer.

Chaminade (shá-mē-näd), Cécile Louise Stéphanie (Mme. Carbonel) (1861—1944), Fr. pianist and composer.

Chamisso (fon shä-mis′ō), Adelbert von (1781—1838), Ger. poet and misc. writer.

Champeaux, William of. See *William of Champeaux.*

Champlain (sham-plān′, Fr. dè shän-plaṅ), Samuel de (1567—1635), Fr. explorer, colonizer, and governor of Canada.

Champollion (shän-pol-yôṅ), Jean François (1790—1832), Fr. Egyptologist.

Chancellor (chàn′sẹ-lọr), Richard (d. 1556), Eng. navigator in White Sea, establisher of trade with Russia.

Chandos (chan′dos), Sir John (d. 1370), Eng. soldier.

Chandragupta (chan-drạ-gup′tạ) (in Greek, Sandrocottus) (fl. c300 B.C.), king of northern India (c315—c296 or c291 B.C.).

Channing (chan′ing), Edward (1856—1931), Am. educator and historian.

Channing, William Ellery (1780—1842), Am. clergyman and writer.

Chantrey (chàn′tri), Sir Francis Legatt (1781—1841), Eng. sculptor.

Chanute (sha-nūt′), Octave (1832—1910), Fr.-Am. engineer and aëronautic inventor.

Chapelain (shàp-laṅ), Jean (1595—1674), Fr. poet and critic.

Chaplin (chap′lin), Charles Spencer (1889—   ), Eng.-Am. comic actor in moving pictures.

Chapman (chap′mạn), George (1559?—1634), Eng. poet and dramatist.

Chaptal (shàp-tàl), Jean Antoine (Comte de Chanteloup) (1756—1832), Fr. chemist and statesman.

Charcot (shär-kō), Jean Baptiste Étienne Auguste (1867—1936), Fr. physician and polar explorer (son of Jean M.).

Charcot, Jean Martin (1825—93), Fr. physician.

Chardin (shär-daṅ), Jean Baptiste Siméon (1699—1779), Fr. painter.

Chares (kā′rēz) (fl. c280 B.C.), Gr. sculptor, of Rhodes, designer of Colossus of Rhodes.

Charette de La Contrie (shä-ret dè lä kôṅ-trē), François Athanase (1763—96), Fr. Vendean leader.

Charlemagne (shär′lẹ-mān, Fr. shär-lè-män-y′) ("Charles the Great") (c742—814), king of the Franks (768—814), and (as Charles I.) Rom. emperor (800—814) (son of Pepin the Short).

Charles I. (chärlz) (in German, Karl, pron. kärl) (1887—1922), emperor of Austria and (as Charles IV.) king of Hungary (1916—18) (grandnephew of Francis Joseph I.).

Charles (Karl Ludwig Johann) (1771—1847), archduke of Austria, and general (son of Emperor Leopold II.).

Charles ("Charles the Bold") (1433—77), duke of Burgundy (1467—77) (son of Philip the Good).

Charles I. ("Charles the Bald") (823—877), king of the Franks (843—877) (as Charles II., Rom. emperor, 875—877) (son of Louis the Pious, and half-brother of Lothair I. and Louis the German).

Charles II. ("Charles the Fat") (839—888), king of the Franks (885—887) (as Charles III., Rom. emperor, 881—887) (successor of Carloman, and son of Louis the German).

Charles III. ("Charles the Simple") (879—929), king of the Franks (893—922 or 929) (successor of Eudes, and son of Louis II.).

Charles IV. ("Charles the Fair") (1294—1328), king of France (1322—28) (brother of Philip V.).

Charles V. ("Charles the Wise") (1337—80), king of France (1364—80) (son of John II.).

Charles VI. ("Charles the Well-Beloved") (1368—1422), king of France (1380—1422) (son of Charles V.).

Charles VII. ("Charles the Victorious") (1403—61), king of France (1422—61) (son of Charles VI.).

Charles VIII. (1470—98), king of France (1483—98) (son of Louis XI.).

Charles IX. (1550—74), king of France (1560—74) (brother of Francis II.).

Charles X. (1757—1836), king of France (1824—30) (brother of Louis XVIII.).

Charles I. (1600—49), king of Great Britain and Ireland from 1625, executed in 1649 (son of James I.).

Charles II. (1630—85), king of Great Britain and Ireland (1660—85) (son of Charles I.).

Charles I. (of Anjou) (1220 or 1226—85), king of Naples (1266—85) and Sicily (1266—82) (brother of Louis IX. of France).

Charles III. (of Durazzo) (1345—86), king of Naples (1382—86) (as Charles II., king of Hungary, 1385—86).

Charles III., Rom. emperor. See *Charles II.*, king of the Franks.

Charles IV. (1316—78), emperor of the Holy Roman Empire (1347—78) and king of Bohemia (1346—78) (son of John of Luxemburg).

Charles V. (1500—58), emperor of the Holy Roman Empire (1519—58), and (as Charles I.) king of Spain (1516—56) (grandson of Emperor Maximilian I., and son of Philip I. of Castile).

Charles VI. (1685—1740), emperor of the Holy Roman Empire (1711—40) (brother of Joseph I.).

Charles VII. (Charles Albert of Bavaria) (1697—1745), emperor of the Holy Roman Empire (1742—45).

Charles I. (in Rumanian, Carol, orig. Prince Karl of Hohenzollern) (1839—1914), prince regnant of Rumania (1866—81), and king of Rumania (1881—1914).

Charles II. (in Rumanian, Carol) (1893—), king of Rumania (1930—40) (son of Ferdinand I. of Rumania).

Charles I., king of Spain. See *Charles V.* (emperor).

Charles II. (1661—1700), king of Spain (1665—1700) (son of Philip IV.). [brother of Ferdinand VI.].

Charles III. (1716—88), king of Spain (1759—88) (half-

Charles IV. (1748—1819), king of Spain (1788—1808) (son of Charles III.). [of Gustavus Vasa].

Charles IX. (1550—1611), king of Sweden (1604—11) (son

Charles X. (Charles Gustavus) (1622—60), king of Sweden (1654—60) (cousin of Christina of Sweden).

Charles XI. (1655—97), king of Sweden (1660—97) (son of Charles X. of Sweden).

Charles XII. (1682—1718), king of Sweden (1697—1718) (son of Charles XI. of Sweden).

Charles XIV. (1763—1844), king of Sweden and Norway (1818—44), in 1810 (as Charles John) elected crown-prince of Sweden (orig. Jean Baptiste Jules Bernadotte, a French marshal under Napoleon).

Charles XV. (1826—72), king of Sweden and Norway (1859—72) (son of Oscar I.).

Charles Albert (in Italian, Carlo Alberto) (1798—1849), king of Sardinia (1831—49).

Charles Edward Stuart (Charles Edward Louis Philip Casimir Stuart, "the Young Pretender") (1720—88), son of James Francis Edward Stuart and grandson of James II. of England, and pretender to the crown of England.

Charles Emmanuel I. (e-man′ū-el) ("the Great," also called, in Italian, Carlo Emanuele) (1562—1630), duke of Savoy (1580—1630).

Charles Martel (mär-tel′) ('Charles the Hammer') (c690—741), Frankish ruler, victor over Saracens (732) (son of Pepin of Heristal).

Charlevoix (dė shär-lė-vwo), Pierre François Xavier de (1682—1761), Fr. Jesuit traveler in America, and historian.

Charnwood (chärn′wüd), Godfrey Rathbone Benson, 1st Baron (1864—), Eng. author (brother of Sir F. R. Benson).

Charpentier (shär-poṅ-tyā), Gustave (1860—), Fr. musical composer.

Chartier (shär-tyā), Alain (c1390—c1440), Fr. poet and political writer.

Chase (chās), Salmon Portland (1808—73), Am. statesman and jurist, chief justice of U. S. Supreme Court (1864—73).

Chase, William Merritt (1849—1916), Am. painter.

Chastelard (dė shät-lär), Pierre de Boscosel de (c1540—63), Fr. poet, at the court of Mary Queen of Scots.

Chastellux (dė shät-lü), François Jean, Marquis de (1734—88), Fr. general and writer.

Chateaubriand (dė shȧ-tō-brē-äṅ), François René, Vicomte de (1768—1848), Fr. author and statesman.

Chatham (chat′ạm), William Pitt, 1st Earl of (1708—78), Eng. statesman and orator.

Chatrian, Alexandre. See *Erckmann-Chatrian*.

Chatterton (chat′ėr-tọn), Thomas (1752—70), Eng. poet.

Chaucer (châ′sėr), Geoffrey (c1340—1400), Eng. poet.

Chaykovski (chī-kof′skẹ), Petr Ilich (1840—93), Russ. musical composer.

Cheke (chēk), Sir John (1514—57), Eng. Greek scholar.

Chekhov (che′chof), Anton Pavlovich (1860—1904), Russ. dramatist and story-writer.

Chelmsford (chelmz′fọrd), Frederic Thesiger, 1st Baron (1794—1878), Eng. jurist.

Chelmsford, Frederic Augustus Thesiger, 2d Baron (1827—1905), Eng. general (son of 1st Baron).

Chemnitz or **Kemnitz** (kem′nits), Martin (1522—86), Ger. Lutheran theologian.

Chénier (dė shā-nyā), André Marie de (1762—94), Fr. poet.

Cheops (kē′ops) or **Khufu** (kö′fö) (fl. c3900 or c3700 or c2700 B.C.), king of Egypt, of 4th dynasty, builder of great pyramid at Gizeh.

Cherbuliez (shär-bü-lyä), Charles Victor (1829—99), Swiss-Fr. novelist and misc. writer.

Chernyshevski (cher-ni-shef′skẹ), Nikolay Gavrilovich (1828—89), Russ. novelist and misc. writer.

Cherubini (kā-rö-bē′nē), Maria Luigi Carlo Zenobio Salvatore (1760—1842), It. musical composer.

Chesterfield (ches′tėr-fēld), Philip Dormer Stanhope, 4th Earl of (1694—1773), Eng. statesman, wit, and letter-writer.

Chesterton (ches′tėr-tọn), Gilbert Keith (1874—1936), Eng. author.

Chevalier (shė-vȧ-lyā), Sulpice Guillaume. See *Gavarni, Paul.*

Cheyne (chā′ni), Thomas Kelly (1841—1915), Eng. clergyman and Biblical critic.

Chiang Kai-shek (chẹ-äng′ kī′shek′), (1886—), Chin. gen.

Chicherin (chẹ-cher′ẹn), Georgi Vasilevich (1872—), Russ. soviet minister of foreign affairs.

Child (chīld), Francis James (1825—96), Am. scholar.

Child, Mrs. (Lydia Maria Francis) (1802—80), Am. writer.

Childebert I. (chil′dẹ-bėrt, Fr. shēl-dė-bār) (c495—558), king of the Franks (511—558) (son of Clovis I.).

Childeric I. (chil′dẹ-rik) (in French, Childéric, pron. shēl-dä-rēk) (c437—481), king of the Salian Franks (458?—481).

Childs (chīldz), George William (1829—94), Am. newspaper publisher and philanthropist.

Chillingworth (chil′ing-wėrth), William (1602—44), Eng. divine and theologian.

Chilon (kī′lon) or **Chilo** (kī′lō) (fl. c560 B.C.), one of the seven sages of ancient Greece.

Chilperic I. (chil′pẹ-rik) (in French, Chilpéric, pron. shēl-pä-rēk) (539—584), king of the western Franks (561—584) (son of Clotaire I.).

Chippendale (chip′ẹn-dāl), Thomas (d. 1779), Eng. cabinet-maker and furniture-designer.

Chlopicki (chlo-pits′kẹ), Józef (1771—1854), Pol. general.

Chmielnicki (chmyel-nits′kẹ), Bogdan (1593?—1657), Cossack chief, leader in wars against the Poles.

Choate (chōt), Joseph Hodges (1832—1917), Am. lawyer and diplomatist.

Choate, Rufus (1799—1859), Am. lawyer, orator, and statesman.

Chodowiecki (chō-dō-vyets′kẹ), Daniel Nikolaus (1726—1801), Pol.-Ger. painter and engraver.

Choiseul (dė shwo-zėl), César, Duc de (Comte du Plessis-Praslin) (1598—1675), Fr. marshal.

Choiseul, Étienne François, Duc de (1719—85), Fr. statesman.

Chopin (sho-paṅ), Frédéric François (1810—49), Pol.-Fr. composer and pianist.

Chosroes. See *Khusrau.*

Chouan (shö-äṅ), Jean. See *Cottereau, Jean.*

Chrétien de Troyes (krā-tyaṅ dė trwo) (fl. 1150—82), Fr. poet.

Christ (krīst). See *Jesus.*

(variable) d̦ as d or j, ș as s or sh, ț as t or ch, z̦ as z or zh; o, F. cloche; ü, F. menu; c̥h, Sc. loch; ṅ, F. bonbon; ′, primary accent; ″, secondary accent; †, obsolete; <, from; +, and; =, equals. See also lists at beginning of book.

Christian I. (kris'chạn) (1426—81), king of Denmark and Norway (1448—81), and of Sweden (1457—71).

Christian II. (1481—1559), king of Denmark and Norway (1513—23), and of Sweden (1520—21) (grandson of Christian I.).

Christian III. (1503—59), king of Denmark and Norway (1534—59) (grandson of Christian I.).

Christian IV. (1577—1648), king of Denmark and Norway (1588—1648) (grandson of Christian III.).

Christian VII. (1749—1808), king of Denmark and Norway (1766—1808).

Christian VIII. (1786—1848), king of Denmark (1839—48).

Christian IX. (1818—1906), king of Denmark (1863—1906).

Christian X. (1870—1947), king of Denmark (1912—1947) (son of Frederick VIII. of Denmark).

Christina (kris-tē'nạ) (1626—89), queen of Sweden (1632—54) (daughter of Gustavus Adolphus, 1594—1632).

Christine de Pisan (krēs-tēn dẹ pē-zän) (c1363—c1431), It.-Fr. writer in verse and prose.

Christophe (krēs-tof), Henri (1767—1820), negro general, king of Haiti (1811—20).

Christopher (kris'tọ-fẹr), Saint (d. c250?), Christian martyr, probably of Syria. According to legend, Christopher, who was of great height and strength, piously devoted himself to carrying pilgrims across a river. One day a child sought his assistance; but during the passage the child's weight became so oppressive that Christopher was scarcely able to reach the opposite shore. There the child revealed himself as Christ, his bearer thereafter being known as Christopher, 'the Christ-bearer.'

Chrysippus (krī-sip'us) (c280—c207 B.C.), Gr. Stoic philosopher.

Chrysoloras (kris-ọ-lō'rạs), Manuel (c1355—1415), Byzantine Gr. scholar, teacher of Greek in Italy.

Chrysostom, Saint John. See *John Chrysostom.*

Church (chẹrch), Sir Richard (1784—1873), Br. military officer, and general in Greek service.

Church, Richard William (1815—90), Eng. divine and writer (nephew of Sir Richard).

Churchill (chẹrch'il), Charles (1731—64), Eng. poet and satirist.

Churchill, John. See *Marlborough, 1st Duke of.*

Churchill, Randolph Henry Spencer (known as Lord Randolph Churchill) (1849—95), Eng. statesman.

Churchill, Winston (1871—1947), Am. novelist.

Churchill, Winston Leonard Spencer (1874—   ), Eng. politician and writer (son of Randolph H. S.).

Churchyard (chẹrch'yärd), Thomas (c1520—1604), Eng. soldier, poet, and misc. writer.

Churriguera (chör-rē-gä'rä), José (d. 1725), Sp. architect and sculptor.

Cibber (sib'ẹr), Colley (1671—1757), Eng. actor and dramatist.

Cicero (sis'ẹ-rō), Marcus Tullius (106—43 B.C.), Rom. orator, statesman, and author.

Cid (sid, Sp. thēŦH) (meaning 'Lord' or 'Chief,' a title of Rodrigo, or Ruy, Díaz de Bivar, also called El Campeador, 'the Champion') (c1040—99), Castilian warrior, soldier of fortune in wars between Christians and Moors in Spain.

Cimabue (chē-mä-bō'ä), Giovanni (1240?—c1302), Florentine painter.

Cima da Conegliano (chē'mä dä kō-nāl-yä'nō), Giovanni Battista (c1460—1517?), It. painter, of Venetian school.

Cimon (sī'mọn) (c507—449 B.C.), Athenian military and naval commander, and statesman (son of Miltiades).

Cincinnatus (sin-si-nā'tus), Lucius Quinctius (c519—after 439 B.C.), Rom. dictator. According to the story, Cincinnatus, who lived on his farm, left the plow to obey his country's summons to the dictatorship at a time when the Roman army was in a perilous position. He promptly defeated the enemy, and at the end of 16 days resigned his office, returning to his farm as a simple citizen.

Cinna (sin'ạ), Lucius Cornelius (d. 84 B.C.), Rom. politician and military leader, adherent of Marius and opponent of Sulla.

Cinq-Mars (dẹ san-mär), Henri Coiffier de Ruzé, Marquis de (1620—42), Fr. conspirator, favorite of Louis XIII. of France.

Cione (dē chō'nä), Andrea di. See *Orcagna.*

Cisneros, Francisco Jiménez de. See *Jiménez de Cisneros.*

Civilis (si-vī'lis), Claudius (or Julius) (fl. A.D. c70), leader of Batavian revolt against Rome.

Claiborne or **Clayborne** (klā'bôrn), William (1589?—1676?), Virginia colonist and politician, born in England.

Clapperton (klap'ẹr-tọn), Hugh (1788—1827), Br. naval officer, and explorer in Africa.

Clare (klār) or **Clara** (klar'ạ), Saint (1194—1253), It. abbess, founder of order of Franciscan nuns (Poor Clares).

Clare, John (1793—1864), Eng. poet.

Clare, Richard de. See *Pembroke, 2d Earl of.*

Clarendon (klar'ẹn-dọn), Edward Hyde, 1st Earl of (1609—74), Eng. statesman and historian.

Clarendon, George William Frederick Villiers, 4th Earl of (in Villiers line) (1800—70), Eng. diplomatist and statesman.

Claretie (klär-tē), Jules Arsène Arnaud (1840—1913), Fr. novelist and misc. writer.

Clark (klärk), Champ (1850—1921), Am. political leader.

Clark, Francis Edward (name orig. Symmes) (1851—1927), Am. clergyman, founder of Society of Christian Endeavor.

Clark, George Rogers (1752—1818), Am. soldier and pioneer.

Clark, Mark W. (1896—   ), Am. lieut. gen.

Clark, William (1770—1838), Am. soldier and explorer, joint commander with Meriwether Lewis of expedition to Oregon (brother of George R.).

Clarke (klärk), Charles Cowden (1787—1877), Eng. writer, editor, and lecturer.

Clarke, James Freeman (1810—88), Am. Unitarian clergyman, and author.

Clarke, Mrs. Mary Cowden (Mary Victoria Novello) (1809—98), Eng. writer and editor, compiler of a concordance to Shakspere (wife of Charles C.).

Clarke, Samuel (1675—1729), Eng. divine and philosopher.

Clarkson (klärk'sọn), Thomas (1760—1846), Eng. anti-slavery agitator.

Claude Lorrain (klâd lọ-rän', Fr. klōd lo-rań) (real name Claudẹ Gelée, or Gellée) (1600—82), Fr. landscape-painter, in Italy.

Claudian (klâ'di-ạn) (Claudius Claudianus) (c365—408?), Latin epic poet and panegyrist, born probably at Alexandria.

Claudius I. (klâ'di-us) (Tiberius Claudius Drusus Nero Germanicus) (10 B.C.—A.D. 54), Rom. emperor (A.D. 41—54) (son of N. C. Drusus, and uncle and successor of Caligula).

Claudius II. (Marcus Aurelius Claudius, surnamed Gothicus) (214—270), Rom. emperor (268—270).

Claudius, Appius (surnamed Cæcus) (d. after 280 B.C.), Rom. statesman.

Claudius, Appius. See *Virginia.*

Clausewitz (fon klou'zẹ-vits), Karl von (1780—1831), Prussian general and military writer.

Clausius (klou'zẹ-ùs), Rudolf Julius Emanuel (1822—88), Ger. physicist.

Claverhouse (klav'ẹrz), John Graham of. See *Dundee, Viscount.*

Clay (klā), Henry (1777—1852), Am. statesman and orator.

Clayborne. See *Claiborne.*

Clayton (klā'tọn), John Middleton (1796—1856), Am. statesman.

Cleanthes (klẹ-an'thēz) (fl. c250 B.C.), Gr. Stoic philosopher.

Clearchus (klẹ-är'kus) (d. 401 B.C.), Spartan general.

Cleasby (klēz'bi), Richard (1797—1847), Eng. Icelandic philologist.

Cleisthenes (klīs'thẹ-nēz) (fl. 508 B.C.), Athenian statesman and reformer.

Clemenceau (klẹ-mon-sō), Georges Eugène Benjamin (1841—1929), Fr. physician, journalist, author, and statesman.

Clemens (klem'ẹnz), Samuel Langhorne ("Mark Twain") (1835—1910), Am. humorist and misc. writer.

Clement I. (klem'ẹnt), Saint (also called Clemens Romanus) (d. c100), bishop of Rome.

Clement V. (Bertrand de Got) (1264?—1314), Fr. ecclesiastic, pope (1305—14).

Clement VII. (Giulio de' Medici) (1478?—1534), It. ecclesiastic, pope (1523—34) (nephew of Lorenzo de' Medici).

Clement XIV. (Lorenzo Ganganelli, orig. Giovanni Vincenzo

Antonio Ganganelli) (1705—74), It. ecclesiastic, pope (1769—74).

Clément (klā-moṅ), Jacques (c1567—89), Fr. Dominican friar, who assassinated Henry III. of France.

Clement of Alexandria (c150—c215), Gr. Christian theologian.

Cleobulus (klē-ọ-bū′lus) (fl. c580 B.C.), one of the seven sages of ancient Greece.

Cleomenes III. (klē-om′ẹ-nēz) (d. 220? B.C.), king of Sparta (236?—220? B.C.), general, and reformer.

Cleon (klē′on) (d. 422 B.C.), Athenian politician and general.

Cleopatra (klē-ọ-pā′trạ or klē-ọ-pat′rạ) (69—30 B.C.), last queen of Egypt, mistress of Julius Cæsar, and later mistress and ally of Marcus Antonius.

Cleveland (klēv′lạnd), Duchess of (Barbara Villiers, Countess of Castlemaine) (1641—1709), mistress of Charles II. of England.

Cleveland, John (1613—58), Eng. poet and satirist.

Cleveland, (Stephen) Grover (1837—1908), 22d and 24th president of U. S. (1885—89, 1893—97).

Clifford (klif′ọrd), Rosamond ("Fair Rosamond") (d. c1176), mistress of Henry II. of England.

Clifford, William Kingdon (1845—79), Eng. mathematician and philosophical writer.

Clinton (klin′tọn), De Witt (1769—1828), Am. statesman (son of James).

Clinton, George (1739—1812), Am. statesman, vice-president of U. S. (1805—12).

Clinton, Sir Henry (c1738—95), Eng. general, in America.

Clinton, James (1736—1812), Am. general (brother of George).

Clisson (dẹ klē-sóṅ), Olivier de (1336—1407), Fr. military leader.

Clisthenes (klis′thẹ-nēz). See *Cleisthenes.*

Clive (klīv), Mrs. Catherine, or Kitty (Catherine Raftor) (1711—85), Eng. actress.

Clive of Plassey (pläs′ẹ), Robert Clive, Baron (1725—74), Eng. general and statesman, in India.

Clodd (klod), Edward (1840—1930), Eng. scientific and misc. writer.

Clodius (klō′di-us), Publius (surnamed Pulcher) (d. 52 B.C.), Rom. politician.

Cloots or **Clootz** (dẹ klōts), Jean Baptiste du Val-de-Grâce, Baron de (called Anacharsis Cloots) (1755—94), Fr. revolutionist, born in Prussia.

Clotaire I. (klọ-târ′) (497—561), king of the Franks (558—561) (son of Clovis I.).

Clotilda (klọ-til′dạ) or **Clotilde** (klo-tēld), Saint (c475—545), wife of Clovis I., king of the Franks, whose conversion to Christianity is attributed to her influence.

Clouet (klö-ā), François (often called Janet) (d. c1572), Fr. painter.

Clough (kluf), Arthur Hugh (1819—61), Eng. poet.

Clovis I. (klō′vis) (c465—511), king of the Franks (481—511) (son of Childeric I., and first king of Merovingian line).

Clyde (klīd), Colin Campbell, Baron (orig. Colin Macliver) (1792—1863), Br. field-marshal.

Clymer (klī′mẹr), George (1739—1813), Am. patriot.

Clynes (klīnz), John Robert (1869—   ), Eng. labor leader and cabinet minister.

Cnut. See *Canute.*

Cobbett (kob′et), William (1766—1835), Eng. writer and politician.

Cobden (kob′dẹn), Richard ("the Apostle of Free Trade") (1804—65), Eng. statesman and political economist.

Cobham (kob′ạm), Lord. See *Oldcastle, Sir John.*

Coccejus (kok-tsā′yus), Johannes (name orig. Koch) (1603—69), Dutch Biblical scholar and theologian.

Cochrane (kok′rạn), Thomas. See *Dundonald, 10th Earl of.*

Cockburn (kō′bẹrn), Sir Alexander James Edmund (1802—80), Br. jurist, lord chief justice of England (1859—80).

Codrington (kod′ring-tọn), Sir Edward (1770—1851), Eng. admiral.

Cody (kō′di), William Frederick ("Buffalo Bill") (1846—1917), Am. scout and showman.

Coehoorn (vän kö′hörn), Menno, Baron van (1641—1704), Dutch soldier and military engineer.

Cœur (kẹr), Jacques (c1395—1456), Fr. merchant and financier.

Cohn (kōn), Ferdinand Julius (1828—98), Ger. botanist.

Coke (kōk or kúk), Sir Edward (1552—1634), Eng. judge and writer on law.

Colbert (kol-bār), Jean Baptiste (1619—83), Fr. statesman and financier.

Cole (kōl), Timothy (1852—1931), Am. wood-engraver, born in England.

Colenso (kọ-len′sō), John William (1814—83), Eng. divine and Biblical critic, bishop of Natal.

Coleoni, Bartolommeo. See *Colleoni.*

Coleridge (kōl′rij), John Duke Coleridge, 1st Baron (1820—94), Eng. judge, lord chief justice (1880—94).

Coleridge, Samuel Taylor (1772—1834), Eng. poet, philosopher, and critic.

Colet (kol′et), John (1467?—1519), Eng. theologian and educationist.

Colfax (kol′faks), Schuyler (1823—85), Am. statesman, vice-president of U. S. (1869—73).

Coligny or **Coligni** (dẹ ko-lē-nyē), Gaspard de (1519—72), Fr. admiral and Huguenot leader.

Colleoni (kol-lā-ō′nē) or **Coleoni** (ko-lā-ō′nē), Bartolommeo (1400—75), It. military leader, esp. in service of Venice.

Collier (kol′yẹr), Jeremy (1650—1726), Eng. nonjuring divine and controversialist.

Collier, John Payne (1789—1883), Eng. editor and Shaksperian critic.

Collins (kol′inz), Anthony (1676—1729), Eng. deistic writer.

Collins, Michael (1890—1922), Ir. Sinn Fein leader.

Collins, William (1721—59), Eng. poet.

Collins, William Wilkie (1824—89), Eng. novelist.

Collot d'Herbois (ko-lō der-bwo), Jean Marie (1750—96), Fr. revolutionist.

Collyer (kol′yẹr), Robert (1823—1912), Am. Unitarian clergyman, born in England.

Colman (kōl′mạn), George ("the elder") (1732—94), Eng. dramatist.

Colman, George ("the younger") (1762—1836), Eng. dramatist (son of "the elder").

Colomb or **Colombe** (ko-lóṅ), Michel (1431?—1512), Fr. sculptor.

Colonna (kō-lon′nä), Vittoria (c1490—c1547), It. poet (wife of Marchese di Pescara).

Colt (kōlt), Samuel (1814—62), Am. inventor (of revolver).

Columba (kọ-lum′bä), Saint (521—597), Ir. monk and missionary in Scotland.

Columbanus (kol-um-bā′nus) or **Columban** (kọ-lum′bạn), Saint (543—615), Ir. monk and missionary in France and Italy.

Columbus (kọ-lum′bus), Christopher (in Italian, Cristoforo Colombo, in Spanish, Cristóbal Colón) (c1446—1506), It. navigator in Spanish service, discoverer of America (1492).

Columella (kol-ū-mel′ạ), Lucius Junius Moderatus (fl. A.D. c50), Rom. writer on agriculture.

Colvin (kol′vin), Sir Sidney (1845—1927), Eng. literary and art critic.

Combe (kōm), Andrew (1797—1847), Sc. physician and phrenologist (brother of George).

Combe, George (1788—1858), Sc. phrenologist.

Combe (köm or kōm), William (1741—1823), Eng. writer, creator of Dr. Syntax.

Combes (kóṅb), Justin Louis Émile (1835—1921), Fr. statesman.

Comenius (kọ-mē′ni-us), Johann Amos (Johann Amos Komensky) (1592—1670), Moravian bishop and educational reformer.

Comines or **Commines** (dẹ ko-mēn), Philippe de (c1445—c1511), Fr. historian.

Commodus (kom′ọ-dus), Lucius Ælius Aurelius (also called Marcus Antoninus) (161—192), Rom. emperor (180—192) (son of Emperor Marcus Aurelius Antoninus).

Comnena, Anna. See *Anna Comnena.*

Comnenus (kom-nē′nus). See *Alexius I., Andronicus I.,* and *Manuel I.* (Byzantine emperors).

Comonfort (kō-mon-fôrt′), Ignacio (1812—63), Mex. general and politician.

Comte (kóṅt), Isidore Auguste Marie François Xavier (1798—1857), Fr. philosopher, founder of positivism.

Concini (kon-chē'nē), Concino (Marquis d'Ancre) (d. 1617), It. adventurer, marshal of France and minister of Louis XIII.

Condé (dė kôṅ-dā), Henri I. de Bourbon, Prince de (1552–88), Fr. Huguenot leader (son of Louis I. de Bourbon, Prince de Condé).

Condé, Henri II. de Bourbon, Prince de (1588–1646), Fr. courtier (son of Henri I. de Bourbon, Prince de Condé).

Condé, Louis I. de Bourbon, Prince de (1530–69), Fr. general and Huguenot leader.

Condé, Louis II. de Bourbon, Prince de (Duc d'Enghien, "the Great Condé") (1621–86), Fr. general (son of Henri II. de Bourbon, Prince de Condé).

Condell (kun'del), Henry (d. 1627), Eng. actor, friend of Shakspere.

Condillac (dė kôṅ-dē-yȧk), Étienne Bonnot de (1715–80), Fr. philosopher.

Condorcet (dė kôṅ-dȯr-sā), Marie Jean Antoine Nicolas Caritat, Marquis de (1743–94), Fr. mathematician and philosopher.

Conegliano, Cima da. See *Cima da Conegliano*.

Confalonieri (kōn″fä-lō-nyä'rē), Count Federico (1785–1846), It. revolutionist.

Confucius (kǫn-fū'shius) (551 or 550–478 B.C.), Chin. sage and moral teacher.

Congreve (kong'grēv), William (1670–1729), Eng. dramatist.

Congreve, Sir William (1772–1828), Eng. inventor.

Conington (kō'ning-tǫn), John (1825–69), Eng. classical scholar.

Conkling (kongk'ling), Roscoe (1829–88), Am. politician.

Connaught and Strathearn (kon'ȧt, strath-ẽrn'), Prince Arthur William Patrick Albert, Duke of (1850–1942), Eng. field-marshal, governor-general of Canada (1911–16) (3d son of Queen Victoria).

Conrad I. (kon'rad) (in German, Konrad, pron. kon'rät) (d. 918), king of Germany (911–918).

Conrad II. (c990–1039), emperor of the Holy Roman Empire (1024–39).

Conrad III. (1093–1152), king of Germany (1138–52) (nephew of Emperor Henry V.).

Conrad IV. (1228–54), king of Germany (1250–54) (son of Emperor Frederick II.).

Conrad, Joseph (orig. Teodor Jozef Konrad Korzeniowski) (1857–1924), Eng. novelist, of Polish birth.

Conradin (kon'rä-dēn) ("Conrad the Younger") (1252–68), duke of Swabia (son of Conrad IV. of Germany), and claimant to throne of Sicily, executed by Charles of Anjou.

Conrad of Marburg (d. 1233), Ger. papal inquisitor.

Consalvi (kon-säl'vē), Ercole (1757–1824), It. cardinal and papal statesman.

Conscience (kôṅ-syóṅs), Hendrik (1812–83), Flemish novelist.

Constable (kun'stȧ-bl), John (1776–1837), Eng. landscape-painter.

Constans I. (kon'stanz) (Flavius Julius Constans) (c320–350), Rom. emperor (337–350) (brother of Constantine II.).

Constant (kôṅ-stäṅ), Jean Joseph Benjamin (1845–1902), Fr. painter.

Constant de Rebecque (dė rė-bek), Henri Benjamin (1767–1830), Fr. author and politician.

Constantine I. (kon'stan-tīn or kon'stan-tēn) ("Constantine the Great," Flavius Valerius Aurelius Constantinus) (272 or 274 or 288–337), Rom. emperor (306–337, alone 323–337), establisher of Christianity as the official religion of the empire (son of Constantius I., and son-in-law of Emperor Maximian).

Constantine II. (Flavius Claudius Constantinus) (316?–340), Rom. emperor (337–340) (son of Constantine the Great).

Constantine I. (1868–1923), king of the Hellenes (1913–17, 1920–22) (son of George I., king of the Hellenes).

Constantius I. (kon-stan'shius) (Flavius Valerius Constantius, surnamed Chlorus) (250?–306), Rom. emperor (305–306) (son-in-law of Emperor Maximian).

Constantius II. (Flavius Julius Constantius) (317–361), Rom. emperor (337–361) (brother of Constantine II.).

Conti (kōn'tē), Niccolò (fl. 1419–44), It. merchant and traveler in the East.

Conway (kon'wā), Thomas (1733–c1800), Ir. soldier in France, general in American service in Revolutionary War.

Conway of Allington, William Martin Conway, Baron (1856–1937), Eng. art critic, mountain-climber, and geographer.

Cook (kŭk), Eliza (1818–89), Eng. poet.

Cook, James (1728–79), Eng. navigator.

Cook, Thomas (1808–92), Eng. tourist agent, originator of travel systems.

Cooke (kŭk), Jay (1821–1905), Am. banker and financier.

Coolidge (kō'lij), Calvin (1872–1933), 30th president of U. S. (1923–29).

Cooper (kö'pẽr), Anthony Ashley. See *Shaftesbury*.

Cooper (kö'pẽr or kúp'ẽr), James Fenimore (1789–1851), Am. novelist.

Cooper, Peter (1791–1883), Am. inventor, manufacturer, and philanthropist.

Coote (köt), Sir Eyre (1726–83), Br. general, in India.

Cope (kōp), Edward Drinker (1840–97), Am. paleontologist and biologist.

Copeland (kōp'lȧnd), William Taylor (1797–1868), Eng. manufacturer of porcelain.

Copernicus (kǭ-pẽr'ni-kus), Nicolaus (Niklas Koppernigk) (1473–1543), Pol. astronomer.

Copley (kop'li). See *Lyndhurst*.

Copley, John Singleton (1737–1815), Am.-Eng. painter.

Coppée (ko-pā), François Édouard Joachim (1842–1908), Fr. poet, dramatist, and writer of tales.

Coquelin (kok-laṅ), Benoît Constant (Coquelin aîné) (1841–1909), Fr. actor.

Coquelin, Ernest Alexandre Honoré (Coquelin cadet) (1848–1909), Fr. actor (brother of Benoît C.).

Coquerel (kok-rel), Athanase Laurent Charles (1795–1868), Fr. Protestant clergyman and theological writer.

Coray, Adamantios. See *Koraïs*.

Corday d'Armont (kôr-dā där-môṅ), Marie Anne Charlotte (1768–93), Fr. revolutionary heroine, who assassinated Marat.

Córdoba (dā kôr'dō-Bä) or **Córdova** (dā kôr'dō-vä), Francisco Hernández (or Fernández) de (d. 1518?), Sp. adventurer, discoverer of Yucatan.

Córdoba or **Córdova**, Francisco Hernández de (c1475–1526), Sp. soldier, explorer in Nicaragua.

Córdoba or **Córdova**, Gonzalo Hernández de (commonly known as Gonsalvo de Córdoba, also called "the Great Captain") (1453–1515), Sp. general.

Corelli (kǭ-rel'i), Marie (1864–1924), Eng. novelist.

Coriolanus (kō″ri-ǭ-lā'nus), Caius (or Cnæus) Marcius. A legendary Rom. general and patrician leader of the 5th century B.C., who, in revenge for being exiled, led an army against Rome, but was turned from his purpose by the appeals of his mother, his wife, and the matrons of Rome, and withdrew his army.

Cornaro (kor-nä'rō), Caterina (1454–1510), queen of Cyprus (1473–89), born in Venice.

Corneille (kôr-nä-y'), Pierre (1606–84), Fr. dramatic poet.

Cornelia (kôr-nē'liȧ) (d. after 121 B.C.), Rom. matron, daughter of Scipio the Elder, and mother of T. S. and C. S. Gracchus. To a lady who asked to see her jewels, she is said to have displayed, as the only jewels of which she was proud, her two sons.

Cornelius (fon kôr-nā'lẹ-ús), Peter von (1783–1867), Ger. painter.

Cornelius, Peter (1824–74), Ger. writer and musical composer.

Cornell (kôr-nel'), Ezra (1807–74), Am. capitalist and philanthropist, founder of Cornell University.

Cornwall (kôrn'wȧl), Barry. Pseudonym of B. W. Procter.

Cornwallis (kôrn-wol'is), Charles Cornwallis, 1st Marquis (1738–1805), Eng. general and statesman.

Coronado (dā kō-rō-nä'ᵵHō), Francisco Vásquez de (c1500–after 1542), Sp. soldier, explorer of southwestern part of U. S.

Corot (ko-rō), Jean Baptiste Camille (1796–1875), Fr. landscape-painter.

Correggio (kor-red'jō) (real name Antonio Allegri) (1494–1534), It. painter.

Cortereal (kôr-tä-rä-äl'), Gaspar (c1450–1501?), Pg. navigator along coast of North America.

Cortes or **Cortez** (kôr′tez), Hernando, or Hernan (in Spanish, Hernán Cortés) (1485–1547), Sp. soldier, conqueror of Mexico.

Cortot (kôr-tō), Alfred Denis (1877–   ), Swiss-Fr. pianist.

Coryate or **Coryat** (kor′i-ạt), Thomas (1577?–1617), Eng. traveler and writer.

Cosgrave (koz′grāv), William Thomas (1880–   ), Ir. political leader, president of executive council of the Irish Free State.

Cosimo, Piero di.   See *Piero di Cosimo.*

Cosmas (koz′mạs) and **Damian** (dā′mi-ạn), Saints (d. 287?), brothers, physicians, and Christian martyrs in Asia Minor, patron saints of physicians and apothecaries.

Costa Cabral (dä kos′tä kä-bräl′), Antonio Bernardo da (Count de Thomar) (1803–89), Pg. statesman.

Coster or **Koster** (kos′tėr), Lourens Janszoon (fl. c1440), reputed Dutch inventor of printing with movable types.

Coster or **Koster**, Samuel (1579–1662?), Dutch dramatist.

Cotgrave (kot′grāv), Randle (d. c1634), Eng. lexicographer.

Cotman (kot′mạn), John Sell (1782–1842), Eng. landscape-painter and etcher.

Cottereau (kot-rō), Jean (called Jean Chouan) (1757–94), Fr. royalist insurgent leader.

Cotton (kot′n), Charles (1630–87), Eng. poet and translator.

Cotton, John (1585–1652), Puritan divine in Massachusetts, born in England.

Coucy (dė kö-sē), Robert de (d. 1311), Fr. architect.

Coué (kö-ā), Émile (1857–1926), Fr. pharmacist, advocate of healing by optimistic autosuggestion.

Coues (kouz), Elliott (1842–99), Am. naturalist.

Coulomb (dė kö-lôn), Charles Augustin de (1736–1806), Fr. physicist.

Coulter (kōl′tėr), John Merle (1851–1928), Am. botanist.

Couperin (köp-raṅ), François (1668–1733), Fr. harpsichord player and composer.

Couperus (kö-pär′ús), Louis (1863–1923), Dutch poet and novelist.

Courbet (kör-bā), Gustave (1819–77), Fr. painter.

Cousin (kö-zaṅ), Jean (c1500–90?), Fr. painter, engraver, and sculptor.

Cousin, Victor (1792–1867), Fr. philosopher, educationalist, and critic.

Couthon (kö-tôṅ), Georges (1756?–94), Fr. revolutionary leader.

Couture (kö-tür), Thomas (1815–79), Fr. painter.

Coverdale (kuv′ẽr-dāl), Miles (1488–1568), Eng. divine, and translator of the Bible.

Cowell (kou′el), John (1554–1611), Eng. jurist.

Cowley (kou′li), Abraham (1618–67), Eng. poet.

Cowper (kö′pẽr or kou′pẽr), William Cowper, 1st Earl (c1665–1723), Eng. jurist and statesman.

Cowper, William (1731–1800), Eng. poet (grandnephew of 1st Earl Cowper).

Cox (koks), David (1783–1859), Eng. painter, esp. in water-color.

Cox, James Middleton (1870–   ), Am. politician.

Cox, Kenyon (1856–1919), Am. painter, and writer on art.

Cox, Palmer (1840–1924), Am. writer and illustrator, born in Canada.

Cox, Samuel Sullivan ("Sunset Cox") (1824–89), Am. politician and writer.

Crabb (krab), George (1778–1851), Eng. philologist, compiler, and legal writer.

Crabbe (krab), George (1754–1832), Eng. poet.

Craddock (krad′ọk), Charles Egbert.   Pseudonym of Mary N. Murfree.

Cradock (krad′ọk), Sir Christopher George Francis Maurice (1862–1914), Eng. admiral.

Craig (krāg), Sir James.   See *Craigavon, 1st Viscount.*

Craigavon (krāg-ā′vọn), James Craig, 1st Viscount (1871–1940), Ir. politician, 1st prime minister of Northern Ireland.

Craigie (krā′gi), Mrs. (Pearl Mary Teresa Richards, "John Oliver Hobbes") (1867–1906), Am.-Eng. novelist and dramatist.

Craik (krāk), Mrs. (Dinah Maria Mulock) (1826–87), Eng. novelist.

Cram (kram), Ralph Adams (1863–1942), Am. architect and writer.

Cramp (kramp), Charles Henry (1828–1913), Am. ship-builder.

Cranach or **Kranach** (krä′näċh), Lukas ("the elder") (1472–1553), Ger. painter and engraver.

Cranach, Lukas ("the younger") (1515–86), Ger. painter (son of "the elder").

Crane (krān), Stephen (1871–1900), Am. author.

Crane, Walter (1845–1915), Eng. painter, illustrator, decorator, designer, and writer.

Cranmer (kran′mẽr), Thomas (1489–1556), Eng. Protestant reformer and martyr, first Protestant archbishop of Canterbury.

Crashaw (krash′â), Richard (1613?–49?), Eng. poet.

Crassus (kras′us), Marcus Licinius (surnamed Dives, 'the Rich') (c114–53 B.C.), Rom. general, member of First Triumvirate.

Cratinus (kra-tī′nus) (c520–c423 B.C.), Gr. writer of comedy.

Crawford (krâ′fọrd), Francis Marion (1854–1909), Am. novelist, in Italy (son of Thomas).

Crawford, Thomas (1814–57), Am. sculptor.

Crawford, William Harris (1772–1834), Am. statesman.

Creasy (krē′si), Sir Edward Shepherd (1812–78), Eng. historian.

Crébillon (dė krā-bē-yôṅ), Prosper Jolyot de (1674–1762), Fr. dramatic poet.

Credi (dē krā′dē), Lorenzo di (1459–1537), Florentine painter.

Crescentius (kre-sen′shius) (d. 998), Rom. noble, leader of national party against German emperor and pope.

Cresilas (kres′i-lạs) (fl. c450 B.C.), Gr. sculptor, born in Crete.

Crèvecœur (dė krev-kẽr), Hector Saint-John de (1731–1813), Fr. agriculturist and writer, in America.

Crichton (krī′tọn), James ("the Admirable Crichton") (1560–82?), Sc. scholar and adventurer.

Crile (krīl), George Washington (1864–1943), Am. surgeon.

Crillon (dė krē-yôṅ), Louis des Balbes de Berton de (1541–1615), Fr. general.

Crispi (krēs′pē), Francesco (1819–1901), It. statesman.

Crispin (kris′pin), Saint (d. 287?), Rom. missionary, shoe-maker, and martyr in France, patron saint of shoemakers.

Critias (krit′i-ạs) (d. 403 B.C.), Athenian politician, orator, and author.

Crittenden (krit′n-dẹn), John Jordan (1787–1863), Am. statesman.

Crivelli (krē-vel′lē), Carlo (fl. 1468–93), It. painter, of Venetian school.

Croce (krō′chā), Benedetto (1866–   ), It. critic and philosophical writer.

Crockett (krok′et), David (1786–1836), Am. pioneer and politician.

Crockett, Samuel Rutherford (1860–1914), Sc. novelist.

Crœsus (krē′sus) (d. after 546 B.C.), king of Lydia (560–546 B.C.), famed for his wealth, who was conquered by Cyrus the Great.

Croll (krōl), James (1821–90), Sc. geologist and scientific writer.

Croly (krō′li), George (1780–1860), Br. divine and writer.

Crome (krōm), John (1768–1821), Eng. landscape-painter.

Cromer (krō′mẽr), Evelyn Baring, 1st Earl of (1841–1917), Eng. statesman and diplomatist (grandson of Sir Francis Baring).

Cromwell (krom′wel), Oliver (1599–1658), Eng. general and statesman, Lord Protector of the Commonwealth (1653–58).

Cromwell, Richard (1626–1712), Eng. soldier and politician, Lord Protector of the Commonwealth (1658–59) (son of Oliver).

Cromwell, Thomas (Earl of Essex) (1485?–1540), Eng. statesman.

Cronaca (kron′ä-kä), Simone.   See *Pollajuolo, Simone.*

Cronje (kron′yė), Piet Arnoldus (c1835–1911), Boer general.

Crook (krúk), George (1828–90), Am. general.

Crookes (krúks), Sir William (1832–1919), Eng. chemist and physicist.

Cropsey (krop′si), Jasper Francis (1823–1900), Am. landscape-painter.

Crosby (kroz′bi), Howard (1826–91), Am. clergyman.

Cross (krôs), Mrs. (Mary Ann Evans, "George Eliot") (1819–80), Eng. novelist.

Crowne (kroun), John (d. 1703?), Br. dramatist.

Cruden (krö′dn), Alexander (1701–70), Br. maker of Bible concordance.

Cruikshank (krúk′shangk), George (1792–1878), Eng. caricaturist, illustrator, and painter.

Cruveilhier (krü-ve-yā), Jean (1791–1874), Fr. physician and anatomist.

Ctesias (tē′si-as) (fl. c400 B.C.), Gr. physician and historian.

Cudworth (kud′werth), Ralph (1617–88), Eng. clergyman and philosopher.

Cui (kū-ē′), César Antonovich (1835–1918), Russ. military engineer and musical composer.

Cujas (kü-zhäs), Jacques (also known as Cujacius, real name Cujaus) (1522–90), Fr. jurist.

Cumberland (kum′bēr-land), Richard (1631?–1718), Eng. bishop and moral philosopher.

Cumberland, William Augustus, Duke of (1721–65), Eng. military commander (son of George II. of England).

Cunningham (kun′ing-ham or -am), Alan Gordon (1887–), Br. lieutenant-general.

Cunningham, Sir Andrew B. (1883–), Br. admiral.

Cunningham, Sir John H. D. (1885–), Br. admiral.

Curie (kü-rē), Pierre (1859–1906), Fr. physicist and chemist.

Curie, Mme. (Marie Sklodowska) (1867–1934), Pol. physicist and chemist in France (wife of Pierre Curie).

Curran (kur′an), John Philpot (1750–1817), Ir. politician.

Curtin (kēr′tin), Andrew Gregg (1817–94), Am. statesman.

Curtin, Jeremiah (1840–1906), Am. linguist.

Curtis (kēr′tis), Charles (1860–1936), Am. statesman, vice-president of U. S. (1929–33).

Curtis, Cyrus Hermann Kotzschmar (1850–1933), Am. publisher.

Curtis, George Ticknor (1812–94), Am. lawyer, legal writer, and historian.

Curtis, George William (1824–92), Am. author and publicist.

Curtiss (kēr′tis), Glenn Hammond (1878–1930), Am. aëronautic inventor.

Curtius (kúr′tsē-ús), Ernst (1814–96), Ger. archæologist and historian.

Curtius (kēr′shius), Marcus (d. 362 B.C.), legendary Rom. patriot. A deep chasm is said to have opened in the forum, which, it was prophesied, could be closed only by throwing into it Rome's greatest treasure. Thereupon Curtius, declaring that Rome had no treasure more precious than a brave citizen, leaped into the chasm, which closed after him.

Curzon of Kedleston (kēr′zon, ked′l-ston or kel′son), George Nathaniel Curzon, Marquis (1859–1925), Eng. statesman and writer.

Cusanus (kū-zā′nus), Nicolaus (Nicholas of Cusa, real name Chrypffs or Krebs) (1401–64), Ger. cardinal, theologian, and philosopher.

Cushing (kúsh′ing), Caleb (1800–79), Am. statesman and diplomatist.

Cushman (kúsh′man), Charlotte Saunders (1816–76), Am. actress.

Cushman, Robert (c1580–1625), one of the Eng. founders of the colony at Plymouth, Mass.

Custer (kus′tēr), George Armstrong (1839–76), Am. general.

Custine (dè küs-tēn), Adam Philippe, Comte de (1740–93), Fr. general.

Cuthbert (kuth′bērt), Saint (d. 687), Eng. monk and bishop.

Cuvier (kü-vyā), Georges Léopold Chrétien Frédéric Dagobert, Baron (1769–1832), Fr. naturalist.

Cuyp or **Kuyp** (koip), Aelbert (1620–91), Dutch painter (son of Jacob G.).

Cuyp, Jacob Gerritszoon (1575 or 1594–after 1649), Dutch painter.

Cuza (kö′zä), Alexander John. See *Alexander John I.*

Cynewulf (kin′e-wúlf) (fl. c800), Anglo-Saxon poet.

Cyprian (sip′ri-an), Saint (Thascius Cæcilius Cyprianus) (c200–258), Christian bishop, writer, and martyr, of Carthage.

Cyril (sir′il), Saint (c315–386), bishop and theologian, of Jerusalem.

Cyril, Saint (d. 444), bishop and theologian, of Alexandria.

Cyril, Saint (also known as Constantine, called "the Apostle of the Slavs") (827–869), Gr. missionary, scholar, and bishop (brother of Saint Methodius).

Cyrus (si′rus) ("the Great" or "the Elder") (d. 529 B.C.), Pers. conqueror, founder of Persian empire.

Cyrus ("the Younger") (d. 401 B.C.), Pers. satrap, leader of an unsuccessful expedition of troops (including about 10,000 Greek mercenaries) against his brother Artaxerxes II.

Czartoryski (chär-to-ris′kē), Prince Adam Jerzy (1770–1861), Pol. statesman.

Czernin (cher′nin), Ottokar, Graf (1872–1932), Austrian diplomatist and statesman.

Czerny (cher′nē), Karl (1791–1857), Austrian pianoforte teacher and composer.

Czerny George (cher′nē). See *Karageorge.*

D

Dagnan-Bouveret (dä-nyäṅ-bö-vrä), Pascal Adolphe Jean (1852–1929), Fr. painter.

Dagobert I. (dag′ō-bért, Fr. dà-go-bär) (c600–638), king of the Franks (628–638) (grandson of Chilperic I.).

Daguerre (dà-gär), Louis Jacques Mandé (1789–1851), Fr. inventor (of daguerreotype process).

Dahlgren (dal′gren), John Adolf (1809–70), Am. admiral.

Dakin (dā′kin), Henry Drysdale (1880–), Eng.-Am. research chemist.

Daladier (dà-là-dyā), Édouard (1884–), Fr. statesman.

Dalberg (fon däl′berch), Karl Theodor Anton Maria, Freiherr von (1744–1817), Ger. prelate, statesman, and writer.

Dalcroze (dàl-krōz), Émile Jaques- (1865–), Swiss musical composer, exponent of eurhythmics. [Virginia.

Dale (dāl), Sir Thomas (d. 1619), Eng. colonial governor of

Dalhousie (dal-hö′zi or dal-hou′zi), James Andrew Broun Ramsay, Marquis of (1812–60), Br. statesman, and administrator in India.

Dallas (dal′as), George Mifflin (1792–1864), Am. statesman and diplomatist, vice-president of U. S. (1845–49).

Dalling and Bulwer (dál′ing, búl′wėr), William Henry Lytton Earle Bulwer, Baron (Sir Henry Bulwer) (1801–72), Eng. diplomatist and author (brother of 1st Baron Lytton).

Dalou (dà-lö), Jules (1838–1902), Fr. sculptor.

Dalrymple (dal-rim′pl), Sir David (Lord Hailes) (1726–92), Sc. judge and historian (great-grandson of 1st Viscount Stair).

Dalrymple, Sir James. See *Stair, 1st Viscount.*

Dalrymple, John. See *Stair, Earl of.*

Dalton (dál′ton), John (1766–1844), Eng. chemist and physicist.

Daly (dā′li), John Augustin (1838–99), Am. playwright and theatrical manager.

Damasus I. (dam′a-sus), Saint (c304–384), Rom. cleric, pope (366–384).

Damian, Saint. See *Cosmas.*

Damiani (dä-mē-ä′nē), Pietro (1007–72), It. cardinal, clerical and monastic reformer, and saint.

Damien (dà-myaṅ), Father (Joseph de Veuster) (1840–89), Belgian Rom. Cath. missionary to lepers of Molokai.

Damiens (dà-myaṅ), Robert François (1715–57), Fr. fanatic, who made an unsuccessful attempt upon the life of Louis XV.

Dampier (dam′pēr), William (1652–1715), Eng. buccaneer, navigator, and writer.

Damrosch (dam′rosh), Leopold (1832–85), Ger.-Am. musical conductor.

Damrosch, Walter Johannes (1862–), Ger.-Am. musical conductor and composer (son of Leopold).

Dana (dā′na), Charles Anderson (1819–97), Am. journalist.

Dana, James Dwight (1813–95), Am. geologist and mineralogist.

Dana, Richard Henry (1787–1879), Am. poet and essayist.

Dana, Richard Henry (1815–82), Am. writer and jurist (son of R. H. Dana, 1787–1879).

Danby (dan′bi), Earl of. See *Leeds, 1st Duke of.*

Dandolo (dän′dō-lō), Andrea (1307 or 1310–54), doge of Venice (1343–54), and historian.

Dandolo, Brancaleone. See *Brancaleone d'Andalò.*

Dandolo, Enrico (c1108–1205), doge of Venice (1192–1205).

Daniel (dan′yel), Samuel (1562–1619), Eng. poet and historian.

Daniell (dan′yĕl), John Frederic (1790—1845), Eng. physicist and chemist.

Daniels (dan′yĕlz), Josephus (1862—   ), Am. journalist, Secretary of the Navy (1913—21).

Danilo (dä-nē′lō) (Danilo Petrovich Niegosh) (d. 1735), prince-bishop of Montenegro (1696—1735).

Danilo I. (Danilo Petrovich Niegosh) (1826—60), prince of Montenegro (1851—60).

Dannat (dan′ạt), William T. (1853—1929), Am. painter, in Paris.

Dannecker (fon dän′ek-ẽr), Johann Heinrich von (1758—1841), Ger. sculptor.

Dantan (däṅ-täṅ), Antoine Laurent (1798—1878), Fr. sculptor.

Dantan, Jean Pierre ("Dantan the Younger") (1800—69), Fr. sculptor, noted for caricature statuettes (brother of Antoine L.).

Dantan, Joseph Édouard (1848—97), Fr. painter (son of Jean P.).

Dante Alighieri (dan′tẽ, It. dän′tä ä-lē-gyä′rē) (orig. Durante Alighieri) (1265—1321), It. poet, author of "Divina Commedia."

Danton (däṅ-tôṅ), Georges Jacques (1759—94), Fr. revolutionary leader.

Darboy (där-bwo), Georges (1813—71), Fr. archbishop, executed by order of Commune of 1871.

Dargomyzhski (där-go-mish′skẽ), Aleksandr Sergyeevich (1813—69), Russ. musical composer.

Darío (dä-rē′ō), Rubén (otherwise Félix Rubén García Sarmiento) (1867—1916), Nicaraguan poet and prose-writer.

Darius I. (dạ-rī′us) (Darius Hystaspes) (558?—486? B.C.), king of Persia (521—486? B.C.).

Darling (där′ling), Sir Ralph (1775—1858), Eng. general, governor of New South Wales (1825—31).

Darmesteter (där-me-stĕ-tär), Arsène (1846—88), Fr. philologist and lexicographer.

Darmesteter, James (1849—94), Fr. Orientalist (brother of Arsène).

Darnley (därn′li), Henry Stuart (or Stewart), Lord (1545—67), second husband of Mary Queen of Scots, and father of James I. of England (son of Matthew Stuart, Earl of Lennox).

Dartmouth (därt′muth), William Legge, 2d Earl of (1731—1801), Eng. politician.

Darwin (där′win), Charles Robert (1809—82), Eng. naturalist (grandson of Erasmus Darwin and of Josiah Wedgwood).

Darwin, Erasmus (1731—1802), Eng. naturalist and poet.

Das (däs), Chitta Ranjan (1870—1925), East Indian politician, leader of the Swaraj party.

Dasent (dā′sẹnt), Sir George Webbe (1817—96), Eng. scholar.

Daubenton (dō-boṅ-tôṅ), Louis Jean Marie (1716—1799 or 1800), Fr. naturalist.

Daubeny (då′bẹ-ni), Charles Giles Bridle (1795—1867), Eng. chemist, geologist, and botanist.

Daubigny (dō-bē-nyē), Charles François (1817—78), Fr. landscape-painter.

Daudet (dō-dā), Alphonse (1840—97), Fr. author.

Daumier (dō-myā), Honoré (1808—79), Fr. caricaturist and painter.

Daun (fon doun), Leopold Joseph Maria, Graf von (1705—66), Austrian field-marshal.

Davenant (dav′ẹ-nạnt), Sir William (1606—68), Eng. poet and dramatist.

Davenport (dav′ẹn-pōrt), John (1597—1670), Eng. Puritan divine in America, one of the founders of colony at New Haven, Conn. (1638).

David (dā′vid), Saint (also called Dewi) (d. 601), Welsh bishop, patron saint of Wales.

David I. (1084—1153), king of Scotland (1124—53) (successor and brother of Alexander I., and son of Malcolm III.).

David II. (1324—71), king of Scotland (1329—71) (son of Robert I.).

David (dä-vēd), Félicien César (1810—76), Fr. musical composer.

David, Jacques Louis (1748—1825), Fr. painter.

David, Pierre Jean (known as David d'Angers) (1788 or 1789—1856), Fr. sculptor.

Davidson (dā′vid-sọn), John (1857—1909), Br. poet and dramatist.

Davidson, Randall Thomas Davidson, Baron (1848—1930), Br. prelate, archbishop of Canterbury.

Davies (dā′vẹz), William Henry (1871—1940), Br. poet.

Davis (dā′vis), Jefferson (1808—89), Am. statesman, president of the Confederacy.

Davis or **Davys** (dā′vis), John (c1550—1605), Eng. navigator, esp. in arctic regions.

Davis, John William (1873—   ), Am. lawyer and diplomatist.

Davis, Richard Harding (1864—1916), Am. writer.

Davis, William Morris (1850—1934), Am. geologist.

Davitt (dav′it), Michael (1846—1906), Ir. political leader.

Davout (dä-vo), Louis Nicolas (Duc d'Auerstädt and Prince d'Eckmühl) (1770—1823), Fr. marshal.

Davy (dā′vi), Sir Humphry (1778—1829), Eng. chemist.

Dawes (dåz), Charles Gates (1865—   ), Am. financier, vice-president of U. S. (1925—29).

Dawson (då′sọn), Sir John William (1820—99), Can. geologist.

Day (dā), Thomas (1748—89), Eng. writer, author of "Sandford and Merton."

Deák (dā′äk), Ferencz, or Francis (1803—76), Hung. statesman.

Dean (dēn), Bashford (1867—1928), Am. zoölogist.

Deane (dēn), Silas (1737—89), Am. diplomatist.

Dearborn (dēr′born), Henry (1751—1829), Am. general.

De Bary (dẹ bä′rē), Heinrich Anton (1831—88), Ger. botanist.

Debs (debz), Eugene Victor (1855—1926), Am. labor and socialist leader.

Debussy (dẹ-bü-sē), Claude Achille (1862—1918), Fr. musical composer.

Decamps (dẹ-käṅ), Alexandre Gabriel (1803—60), Fr. painter.

Decatur (dẹ-kā′tẽr), Stephen (1779—1820), Am. commodore.

Decius (dē′shius), Caius Messius Quintus Trajanus (201—251), Rom. emperor (249—251).

Dee (dē), John (1527—1608), Eng. mathematician and astrologer.

Deffand (dü de-fäṅ), Marquise du (Marie de Vichy-Chamrond) (1697—1780), Fr. woman of wit and friend of men of letters.

Defoe (dẹ-fō′), Daniel (1661?—1731), Eng. novelist and misc. writer.

De Forest (dẹ for′est), Lee (1873—   ), Am. inventor.

Defregger (fon dā′freg-ẽr), Franz von (1835—1921), Austrian-Ger. painter.

Degas (dẹ-gä), Hilaire Germain Edgard (1834—1917), Fr. painter.

Dehmel (dā′mẹl), Richard (1863—1920), Ger. poet.

De Kalb (dẹ kalb), Baron. See *Kalb, Johann.*

Dekker (dek′ẽr), Eduard Douwes ("Multatuli") (1820—87), Dutch author.

Dekker, Thomas (1570?—1641?), Eng. dramatist.

De Koven (dẹ kō′vẹn), Henry Louis Reginald (1861—1920), Am. musical composer.

Delacroix (dẹ-lä-krwo), Ferdinand Victor Eugène (1799—1863), Fr. painter.

Delambre (dẹ-läṅbr), Jean Baptiste Joseph (1749—1822), Fr. astronomer.

Deland (dẹ-land′), Mrs. Margaret (Margaretta Wade Campbell) (1857—1945), Am. novelist.

Delane (dẹ-lān′), John Thadeus (1817—79), Eng. journalist.

Delany (dẹ-lā′ni), Mrs. (Mary Granville) (1700—88), Eng. letter-writer and autobiographer.

De la Ramée (dẹ lä rä-mā′), Marie Louise (orig. Marie Louise Ramé, "Ouida") (1839—1908), Eng. novelist.

De la Rey (dẹ lä rā′ẹ), Jacobus Hercules (1847—1914), Boer general.

Delaroche (dẹ-lä-rosh), Hippolyte Paul (1797—1856), Fr. painter.

Delavigne (dẹ-lä-vēn-y′), Jean François Casimir (1793—1843), Fr. poet and dramatist.

De La Warr (del′ạ-wär) or **Delaware** (del′ạ-wär), Thomas West, 3d (or 12th) Baron (1577—1618), Eng. colonial governor of Virginia.

Delbrück (del'brük), Berthold (1846—1922), Ger. philologist.

Delbrück, Hans (1848—1929), Ger. historian.

Delbrück, Martin Friedrich Rudolf von (1817—1903), Prussian statesman.

Delcassé (del-kȧ-sā), Théophile (1852—1923), Fr. statesman.

Delescluze (dĕ-lä-klüz), Louis Charles (1809—71), Fr. journalist and political agitator.

Delibes (dė-lēb), Clément Philibert Léo (1836—91), Fr. musical composer.

Delitzsch (dā'lich), Franz (1813—90), Ger. theologian and Hebraist.

Delitzsch, Friedrich (1850—1922), Ger. Assyriologist (son of Franz).

Delius (dā'lẹ-ús), Frederick (1862—1934), musical composer in France, born in England of Ger. parentage.

Della Quercia, Jacopo. See *Quercia*.

Della Robbia. See *Robbia*.

De Long (dẹ lông), George Washington (1844—81), Am. naval officer and arctic explorer.

Delorme or **de Lorme** (dė-lôrm), Marion (1613?—50), Fr. courtezan.

Delorme or **de L'Orme,** Philibert (c1510—70), Fr. architect.

Deluc (dė-lük), Jean André (1727—1817), Swiss-Eng. geologist and physicist.

Delyannis (del-yän'is), Theodoros (1826—1905), Gr. statesman.

Dembinski (dem-bin'skẹ), Henryk (1791—1864), Pol. general.

Democritus (dẹ-mok'ri-tus) ("the Laughing Philosopher") (c460—c370 B.C.), Gr. philosopher.

De Morgan (dẹ môr'gạn), Augustus (1806—71), Eng. mathematician and logician.

De Morgan, William Frend (1839—1917), Eng. artist in stained glass and ceramics, and novelist (son of Augustus).

Demosthenes (dẹ-mos'thẹ-nēz) (384?—322 B.C.), Athenian orator and statesman.

Denham (den'ạm), Dixon (1786—1828), Eng. army officer, and explorer in Africa.

Denham, Sir John (1615—69), Br. poet.

Denikin (dye-nyē'kẹn), Anton Ivanovich (1872—), Russ. general, opponent of the Bolsheviki.

Denis (den'is) (of Portugal). See *Diniz*.

Denis or **Denys** (den'is, Fr. dė-nē), Saint (d. c275), missionary bishop of Paris, and martyr, patron saint of France.

Dennie (den'ĭ), Joseph (1768—1812), Am. journalist.

Dennis (den'is), John (1657—1734), Eng. critic and dramatist.

Dent (dent), Joseph Mallaby (1849—1926), Eng. publisher, publisher of Everyman's Library.

Depew (dẹ-pū'), Chauncey Mitchell (1834—1928), Am. lawyer and politician.

Deprés (dė-prā), Josquin. See *Des Prés*.

Depretis (dā-prā'tēs), Agostino (1813—87), It. statesman.

De Quincey (dẹ kwin'si), Thomas (1785—1859), Eng. author.

Derby (där'bi or dėr'bi), Edward George Geoffrey Smith Stanley, 14th Earl of (1799—1869), Eng. statesman.

Derby, Edward George Villiers Stanley, 17th Earl of (1865—), Eng. statesman and diplomatist (grandson of 14th Earl).

Dernburg (dern'bůrch), Bernhard (1865—1937), Ger. official, agent of German government in U. S. (1914—15).

De Robeck (dė rō'bek), Sir John Michael (1862—1928), Br. admiral.

Déroulède (dā-rö-led), Paul (1846—1914), Fr. author and politician.

Derzhavin (dyer-zhä'vẹn), Gavriil Romanovich (1743—1816), Russ. poet.

Desaix de Veygoux (dė-sā dė vȧ-gö), Louis Charles Antoine (1768—1800), Fr. general.

Descartes (dā-kärt), René (1596—1650), Fr. philosopher and mathematician.

Deschanel (dā-shȧ-nel), Paul Eugène Louis (1856—1922), Fr. statesman and author, president of France (1920).

Desiderio da Settignano (dā-sē-dā'rē-ō dä set-tē-nyä'nō) (1428—64), It. sculptor.

Desiderius (des-i-dē'ri-us) (d. after 774), last king of the Lombards (756—774), overthrown by Charlemagne.

Desmoulins (dā-mö-laṅ), Lucie Simplice Camille Benoist (1760—94), Fr. revolutionist and political writer.

De Soto. See *Soto*.

Despenser (lė de-spen'sėr), Hugh le ("the elder") (1262?—1326), Eng. court favorite.

Despenser, Hugh le ("the younger") (d. 1326), Eng. court favorite (son of "the elder").

Des Prés (dā prā), Josquin (also called Josquin, or Josse, Deprés or Deprez) (c1450—1521), Fr. musical composer.

Dessalines (dā-sȧ-lēn), Jean Jacques (1758—1806), negro emperor of Haiti (1804—06).

Destinn (des'tin), Emmy (real name Kittl) (1878—1930), Bohem. operatic soprano singer.

Destouches (dā-tösh), Philippe Néricault (orig. Philippe Néricault) (1680—1754), Fr. dramatist.

Detaille (dė-tä-y'), Jean Baptiste Édouard (1848—1912), Fr. painter, esp. of military subjects.

De Valera (dā vȧ-lär'ä), Eamonn (1882—), Ir. educator and republican (Sinn Fein) leader, born in New York of Spanish and Irish parentage.

Devereux (dev'ẹ-rö). See *Essex, Earl of*.

De Vinne (dẹ vin'ẹ), Theodore Low (1828—1914), Am. printer.

Devlin (dev'lin), Joseph (1872—1934), Ir. political leader.

Devonshire (dev'ọn-shėr), Georgiana Cavendish, Duchess of (Georgiana Spencer) (1757—1806), Eng. beauty and social leader.

Devonshire, Spencer Compton Cavendish, 8th Duke of (Marquis of Hartington) (1833—1908), Eng. statesman.

Devonshire, Victor Christian William Cavendish, 9th Duke of (1868—1938), Eng. governor-general of Canada (1916—21) (nephew of 8th Duke).

Dewar (dū'ạr), Sir James (1842—1923), Br. chemist and physicist.

De Wet (dė vet), Christiaan Rudolf (1854—1922), Boer general.

Dewey (dū'i), George (1837—1917), Am. admiral.

Dewey, John (1859—), Am. philosopher.

Dewey, Melvil (1851—1931), Am. librarian.

De Winter (dė vin'tėr), Jan Willem (1750—1812), Dutch admiral.

De Witt (dė vit), Cornelius (1623—72), Dutch political leader and naval officer (brother of Jan).

De Witt, Jan (1625—72), Dutch statesman.

Dexter (deks'tėr), Henry Martyn (1821—90), Am. Congregational clergyman, and historian.

Diane de Poitiers (dē-ȧn dė pwo-tyā) (Mme. de Brézé, later created Duchesse de Valentinois) (1499—1566), mistress of Henry II. of France.

Dias (dē'äsh), Bartholomeu (c1450—1500), Pg. navigator, discoverer of Cape of Good Hope.

Diaz (dē'äts), Armando (Duca della Vittoria) (1861—1928), It. general, marshal of Italy.

Diaz (dē'äs), Porfirio (1830—1915), Mex. general and statesman, president of Mexico (1877—80, 1884—1911).

Diaz de la Peña (dē-äz dė lä pā-nyä), Narcisse Virgile (1807—76), Fr. painter.

Dibdin (dib'din), Charles (1745—1814), Eng. song-writer, musical composer, and dramatist.

Dibdin, Thomas Frognall (1776—1847), Eng. bibliographer (nephew of Charles).

Dickens (dik'enz), Charles (1812—70), Eng. novelist.

Dickinson (dik'in-sọn), Emily (1830—86), Am. poet.

Dickinson, John (1732—1808), Am. statesman and publicist.

Dicksee (dik'sẹ), Sir Francis Bernard (1853—1928), Eng. painter.

Diderot (dēd-rō), Denis (1713—84), Fr. philosopher, dramatist, and misc. writer.

Didot (dē-dō), Ambroise Firmin (1790—1876), Fr. printer, publisher, and writer (son of Firmin).

Didot, Firmin (1764—1836), Fr. printer, type-founder, publisher, and writer.

Diebitsch (dē'bich), Count Hans Karl Friedrich Anton (known in Russia as Count Ivan Ivanovich Dibich-Zabalkanski) (1785—1831), Russ. field-marshal, born in Germany.

Diemen (vän dē'men), Anthony van (1593—1645), Dutch admiral, and administrator in the East Indies.

Diesel (dē'zẹl), Rudolf (1858—1913), Ger. engineer, inventor of the Diesel engine.

Dieskau (dēs'kou), Ludwig August (1701—67), Ger. general in French service, in America.

Diez (dēts), Friedrich Christian (1794—1876), Ger. philologist.

Digby (dig'bi), Sir Everard (1578—1606), Eng. conspirator, one of the leaders in the Gunpowder Plot.

Digby, Sir Kenelm (1603—65), Eng. naval commander, diplomatist, and author (son of Sir Everard).

Dilke (dilk), Sir Charles Wentworth (1843—1911), Eng. politician and writer.

Dillenius (di-lā'nẹ-ŭs) or **Dillen** (dil'ẹn), Johann Jakob (1687—1747), Ger.-Eng. botanist.

Dillon (dil'ọn), John (1851—1927), Ir. political leader.

Dingley (ding'li), Nelson (1832—99), Am. statesman.

Diniz (dē-nēsh') (also called, in English, Denis or Dionysius) (1261—1325), king of Portugal (1279—1325).

Dinwiddie (din-wid'i or din'wid-i), Robert (1693?—1770), Br. official, lieutenant-governor of Virginia.

Dio Cassius (dī'ō kash'ius) (Dion Cassius Cocceianus) (c150—c235), Rom. historian, writing in Greek.

Diocletian (dī-ọ-klē'shian) (Caius Aurelius Valerius Diocletianus, surnamed Jovius) (245—313), Rom. emperor (284—305).

Diodati (dē-ō-dä'tē), Giovanni (1576—1649), Swiss Protestant clergyman and theologian.

Diodorus Siculus (dī-ọ-dō'rus sik'ụ-lus) (d. after 21 B.C.), Gr. historian, born in Sicily.

Diogenes (dī-oj'ẹ-nēz) (c412—c323 B.C.), Gr. Cynic philosopher.

Diogenes Laërtius (lạ-ẽr'shius) (fl. 3d? cent.), Gr. biographer.

Dionysius (dī-ọ-nish'ius) ("the elder") (430?—367 B.C.), tyrant of Syracuse.

Dionysius (of Portugal). See *Diniz*.

Dionysius Exiguus (ek-sig'ụ-us) (fl. c500—c540), Rom. monk and scholar, reputed introducer of reckoning by the Christian era.

Dionysius of Halicarnassus (fl. c8 B.C.), Gr. historian and rhetorician, in Rome.

Diophantus (dī-ọ-fan'tus) (fl. 3d or 4th cent.), Gr. mathematician, of Alexandria.

Dioscorides (dī-os-kor'i-dēz) (fl. 1st? cent.), Gr. medical writer.

Disraeli (diz-rā'li), Benjamin. See *Beaconsfield*.

D'Israeli (diz-rā'li), Isaac (1766—1848), Eng. writer (father of Benjamin Disraeli).

Dix (diks), John Adams (1798—1879), Am. statesman and general.

Dobell (dọ-bel'), Sydney Thompson (1824—74), Eng. poet and critic.

Dobson (dob'sọn), Henry Austin (1840—1921), Eng. poet, essayist, and biographer.

Doddridge (dod'rij), Philip (1702—51), Eng. nonconformist divine, and writer.

Dodge (doj), Mary Abigail ("Gail Hamilton") (1830?—96), Am. writer.

Dodge, Mrs. (Mary Elizabeth Mapes) (1831—1905), Am. writer, esp. of books for the young.

Dodgson (doj'sọn), Charles Lutwidge ("Lewis Carroll") (1832—98), Eng. mathematician and writer of books for children.

Dodsley (dodz'li), Robert (1703—64), Eng. bookseller, editor, and misc. writer.

Doellinger (dẽl'ing-ẽr). See *Döllinger*.

Dolci (dōl'chē) or **Dolce** (dōl'chä), Carlo, or Carlino (1616—86), Florentine painter.

Dolet (do-lā), Étienne (1509—46), Fr. scholar and printer, executed on charge of atheism.

Döllinger (fon dẽl'ing-ẽr), Johann Joseph Ignaz von (1799—1890), Ger. Rom. Cath. theologian and church historian, excommunicated in 1871.

Dollond (dol'ọnd), John (1706—61), Eng. optician, inventor of achromatic telescope.

Dolomieu (dẹ do-lo-myẹ), Déodat Guy Silvain Tancrède Gratet de (1750—1801), Fr. geologist and mineralogist.

Dombrowski (dom-brof'skẹ), Jan Henryk (1755—1818), Pol. general.

Domenichino (dō-mä-nē-kē'nō) (real name Domenico Zampieri) (1581—1641), It. painter.

Domett (dom'et), Alfred (1811—87), Br. colonial statesman, and poet.

Dominic (dom'i-nik), Saint (1170—1221), Sp. preacher, founder of Dominican order.

Domitian (dọ-mish'ian) (Titus Flavius Domitianus) (A.D. 51—96), Rom. emperor (A.D. 81—96) (brother of Emperor Titus).

Donatello (don-ä-tel'lō) (properly Donato di Niccolò di Betto Bardi) (c1386—1466), Florentine sculptor.

Donati (dō-nä'tē), Giovanni Battista (1826—73), It. astronomer.

Donatus (dọ-nā'tus) (called Donatus the Great) (fl. c315), schismatic bishop of Carthage.

Donatus, Ælius (fl. c350), Rom. grammarian and commentator.

Donizetti (dō-nē-dzet'tē), Gaetano (1797—1848), It. operatic composer.

Donnay (do-nā), Maurice Charles (1859—   ), Fr. dramatist.

Donne (don or dun), John (1573—1631), Eng. divine.

Donoso Cortés (dō-nō'sō kor-tās'), Juan Francisco María de la Salud (Marquis of Valdegamas) (1809—53), Sp. diplomatist and author.

Doolittle (dö'lit'l), James H. (1896—   ), Am. maj. gen.

Dorchester (dôr'ches-tẽr), Guy Carleton, 1st Baron (1724—1808), Br. general and administrator in Canada.

Doré (do-rā), Paul Gustave (1832—83), Fr. illustrator, painter, and sculptor.

Doria (dō'rē-ä), Andrea (1468?—1560), Genoese admiral.

Dorr (dôr), Thomas Wilson (1805—54), Am. politician.

D'Orsay, Comte. See *Orsay*.

Dorset (dôr'set), Charles Sackville, 6th Earl of (1638—1706), Eng. courtier and poet.

Dorset, Thomas Sackville, 1st Earl of (1536—1608), Eng. statesman and poet.

Dost Mohammed Khan (dōst mọ-häm'ed kän) (1788?—1863), amir of Afghanistan (1826—39, 1842—63).

Dostoevski (dos-to-yef'skẹ), Fedor Mikhaylovich (1821—81), Russ. novelist.

Dou, Douw, or **Dow** (dou), Gerard (1613—75), Dutch painter.

Dougherty (dō'ẽr-ti), Denis J. (1865—   ), Am. cardinal.

Doughty (dou'ti) Charles Montagu (1843—1926), Eng. traveler and author.

Douglas (dug'lạs), Archibald. See *Angus, 5th Earl of*.

Douglas, Gawin, or Gavin (c1474—1522), Sc. bishop and poet (son of 5th Earl of Angus).

Douglas, Sir James (called "the Good Sir James" and "the Black Douglas") (c1286—1330), Sc. military leader.

Douglas, James Douglas, 2d Earl of (c1358—88), Sc. military leader.

Douglas, James. See *Morton, 4th Earl of*.

Douglas, Stephen Arnold (1813—61), Am. political leader.

Douglass (dug'lạs), Frederick (1817—95), Am. negro orator and journalist.

Doulton (dōl'tọn), Sir Henry (1820—97), Eng. manufacturer of pottery.

Doumergue (dö-mãrg), Gaston (1863—1937), Fr. statesman, president of France (1924—31).

Doumic (dö-mēk), René (1860—1937), Fr. critic.

Douw or **Dow**, Gerard. See *Dou*.

Dow (dou), Lorenzo (1777—1834), Am. itinerant preacher.

Dow, Neal (1804—97), Am. prohibitionist.

Dowden (dou'dn), Edward (1843—1913), Ir. critic and poet.

Dowie (dou'i), John Alexander (1848—1907), Sc.-Am. "divine healer," founder of religious community (Zion City, Ill.).

Dowson (dou'sọn), Ernest Christopher (1867—1900), Eng. poet.

Doyle (doil), Sir Arthur Conan (1859—1930), Br. physician, novelist, and misc. writer (nephew of Richard).

Doyle, Richard (1824—83), Eng. caricaturist, illustrator, and water-color artist.

Drachmann (dräch'män), Holger Henrik Herholdt (1846—1908), Dan. poet, dramatist, and misc. writer.

Draco (drā'kō) (fl. c621 B.C.), Athenian legislator.

Dragomirov (drạ-go-mē'rof), Mikhail Ivanovich (1830—1905), Russ. general.

Drake (drāk), Sir Francis (c1540–96), Eng. buccaneer, circumnavigator of the globe, and admiral.

Drake, Joseph Rodman (1795–1820), Am. poet.

Draper (drā'pẽr), John William (1811–82), Eng.-Am. physiologist, chemist, and philosophical writer.

Drayton (drā'ton), Michael (1563–1631), Eng. poet.

Dreiser (dri'zẽr), Theodore (1871–   ), Am. novelist and misc. writer.

Drew (drö), John (1825–62), Ir.-Am. comedian.

Drew, John (1853–1927), Am. actor (son of John and Louisa Lane Drew).

Drew, Mrs. (Louisa Lane) (1820–97), Eng.-Am. actress (wife of John Drew, 1825–62).

Drexel (drek'sel), Anthony Joseph (1826–93), Am. banker and philanthropist.

Dreyfus (drā-füs), Alfred (1859–1935), Fr. artillery officer (Jewish), convicted of treason on forged evidence (1894, 1899), but finally declared innocent (1906).

Drinkwater (dringk'wâ-tẽr), John (1882–1937), Eng. poet, dramatist, and critic.

Driver (dri'vẽr), Samuel Rolles (1846–1914), Eng. divine and Biblical scholar.

Droysen (droi'zen), Johann Gustav (1808–84), Ger. historian.

Drummond (drum'ond), Henry (1851–97), Sc. clergyman and writer.

Drummond, Thomas (1797–1840), Br. engineer and administrator, inventor of Drummond light.

Drummond, William Henry (1854–1907), Ir.-Can. physician and poet.

Drummond of Hawthornden (hâ'thôrn-den), William (1585–1649), Sc. poet.

Drusus (drö'sus), Nero Claudius (surnamed Germanicus) (39–9 B.C.), Rom. general (brother of Emperor Tiberius).

Dryden (dri'den), John (1631–1700), Eng. poet, dramatist, and misc. writer.

Drygalski (fon dri-gäl'skē), Erich von (1865–   ), Ger. arctic and antarctic explorer.

Duane (dū-ān'), William (1760–1835), Am. journalist and politician.

Du Barry (dü bà-rē), Comtesse (born Marie Jeanne Bécu) (1746?–93), mistress of Louis XV. of France.

Du Bartas, Seigneur. See *Bartas.*

Du Bellay, Joachim. See *Bellay.*

Dubois (dü-bwo), Guillaume (1656–1723), Fr. cardinal and statesman.

Dubois, Paul (1829–1905), Fr. sculptor and painter.

Du Bois-Reymond (-rā-môn), Emil (1818–96), Ger. physiologist.

Du Cange (dü känzh), Charles du Fresne, Sieur (1610–88), Fr. philologist and historian.

Duccio, Agostino di. See *Agostino di Duccio.*

Duccio di Buoninsegna (döt'chō dē bwô-nēn-sā'nyä) (c1260–c1320?), It. painter, of Sienese school.

Du Chaillu (dü shä-yü), Paul Belloni (1835 or 1838–1903), Am. explorer and traveler, esp. in Africa.

Duché (dū-shā'), Jacob (1737–98), Am. clergyman and writer.

Duchesne (dü-shān), Père. See *Hébert, J. R.*

Duckworth (duk'wẽrth), Sir John Thomas (1748–1817), Eng. admiral.

Ducos (dü-kō), Pierre Roger (1754–1816), Fr. politician.

Dudevant (düd-vän), Mme. (Amandine Lucile Aurore Dupin, "George Sand") (1804–76), Fr. novelist.

Dudley (dud'li), Edmund (c1462–1510), Eng. lawyer and politician.

Dudley, Lord Guildford (d. 1554), son of Duke of Northumberland, and husband of Lady Jane Grey with whom he was executed.

Dudley, John. See *Northumberland, Duke of.*

Dudley, Joseph (1647–1720), Am. politician, colonial governor of Massachusetts and New Hampshire.

Dudley, Robert. See *Leicester, Earl of.*

Duerer (dü'rẽr). See *Dürer.*

Dufaure (dü-fōr), Jules Armand Stanislas (1798–1881), Fr. statesman.

Dufferin and Ava (duf'ẽr-in, ä'vä), Frederick Temple Hamilton-Temple-Blackwood, 1st Marquis of (1826–1902),

Br. administrator and diplomatist, governor-general of Canada (1872–78).

Duffy (duf'i), Sir Charles Gavan (1816–1903), Ir. politician in Ireland and Australia, and author.

Dufour (dü-för), Guillaume Henri (1787–1875), Swiss general, cartographer, and military writer.

Dufrénoy (dü-frā-nwo), Ours Pierre Armand Petit (1792–1857), Fr. geologist and mineralogist.

Dugdale (dug'dāl), Sir William (1605–86), Eng. antiquary.

Dughet (dü-gā), Gaspard (also called Gaspard Poussin) (1613–75), It. landscape-painter, of French parentage (brother-in-law of Nicolas Poussin).

Du Guesclin (dü gä-klañ), Bertrand (c1320–80), Fr. military leader, constable of France.

Duilius (dū-il'i-us), Caius (fl. 260 B.C.), Rom. consul, commander in first Roman naval victory.

Dukas (dü-kä), Paul (1865–1935), Fr. musical composer.

Dulac (dü-läk), Edmund (1882–   ), Fr.-Eng. painter and illustrator.

Dulong (dü-lôn), Pierre Louis (1785–1838), Fr. physicist and chemist.

Dumas (dü-mä), Alexandre Davy de La Pailleterie (Dumas père) (1802–70), Fr. novelist and dramatist.

Dumas, Alexandre (Dumas fils) (1824–95), Fr. dramatist and novelist (son of Alexandre D. de La P.).

Du Maurier (dü mä'ri-ā), George Louis Palmella Busson (1834–96), Fr.-Eng. artist and novelist.

Du Maurier, Sir Gerald (1873–1934), Eng. actor and theatrical manager (son of George L. P. B.).

Dumba (dùm'bä), Constantin Theodor (1856–   ), Austrian diplomatist, ambassador to U. S. (1913–15).

Dumont d'Urville (dü-môn dür-vēl), Jules Sébastien César (1790–1842), Fr. naval officer and navigator.

Dumouriez (dü-mö-ryä), Charles François (1739–1823), Fr. general.

Dunant (dü-nän), Jean Henri (1828–1910), Swiss philanthropist, originator of movement resulting in foundation of International Red Cross Society.

Dunbar (dun-bär'), William (c1460–c1525), Sc. poet.

Duncan I. (dung'kan) (d. 1040), king of Scotland (1034–40), murdered by Macbeth.

Duncan, Adam Duncan, 1st Viscount (1731–1804), Br. admiral.

Dundas (dun-das'), Henry. See *Melville, 1st Viscount.*

Dundee (dun-dē'), John Graham of Claverhouse, Viscount ("Bonnie Dundee") (1649?–89), Sc. soldier, persecutor of the Covenanters.

Dundonald (dun-don'ald), Thomas Cochrane, 10th Earl of (Lord Cochrane) (1775–1860), Br. admiral.

Dunne (dun), Finley Peter (1867–1936), Am. humorist, creator of Mr. Dooley.

Dunois (dü-nwo), Jean, Comte de ("the Bastard of Orléans") (c1403–68), Fr. military leader (illegitimate son of Duc d'Orléans, 1372–1407).

Dunsany (dun-sā'ni), Edward John Moreton Drax Plunkett, 18th Baron (1878–   ), Ir. author.

Duns Scotus (dunz skō'tus), Joannes ("the Subtle Doctor") (c1265–c1308), Sc. (or Ir. or Eng.) scholastic theologian.

Dunstan (dun'stan), Saint (910? or 925?–988), Eng. monk, archbishop of Canterbury, and statesman.

Dupanloup (dü-pän-lö), Félix Antoine Philibert (1802–78), Fr. bishop.

Dupleix (dü-pleks), Joseph François (1697–1763), Fr. administrator, governor-general of the French establishments in India (1742–54).

Du Plessis-Praslin (dü ple-sē-prä-lan), Comte. See *Choiseul, César, Duc de.*

Du Pont (dü pont), Samuel Francis (1803–65), Am. admiral (grandson of P. S. Du Pont de Nemours).

Dupont de l'Eure (dü-pôn dè lẽr), Jacques Charles (1767–1855), Fr. lawyer and statesman.

Du Pont de Nemours (dü pôn dè nė-mör), Pierre Samuel (1739–1817), Fr. political economist, and statesman.

Dupré (dü-prā), Jules (1812–89), Fr. landscape-painter.

Dupuy de Lôme (dü-pwē dè lôm), Stanislas Charles Henri Laurent (1816–85), Fr. naval architect.

Dupuytren (dü-pwē-tran), Guillaume, Baron (1777–1835), Fr. surgeon and anatomist.

---

fat, fāte, fär, fâll, àsk, fāre; net, mē, hẽr; pin, pīne; not, nōte, mȯve, nȯr; up, lūte, pùll; oi, oil; ou, out; (lightened) aviȧry, elect, agȯny, intȯ, ūnite; (obscured) errȧnt, operȧ, ardent, actȯr, natūre; ch, chip; g, go; th, thin; ᴛн, then; y, you;

Duquesne (dü-kān), Abraham, Marquis (1610—88), Fr. naval commander.

Duquesnoy (dü-kā-nwo), François (also called François Flamand and Il Fiammingo) (1594—1646?), Flemish sculptor, in Italy.

Duran (dü-rän), Carolus (real name Charles Auguste Émile Durand) (1837—1917), Fr. painter.

Dürer (dü′rẽr), Albrecht (1471—1528), Ger. painter and engraver.

D'Urfey (dẽr′fĭ), Thomas (1653—1723), Eng. dramatist and poet.

Durham (dur′ạm), John George Lambton, 1st Earl of (1792—1840), Eng. statesman and diplomatist.

Duroc (dü-rok), Géraud Christophe Michel (Duc de Frioul) (1772—1813), Fr. general and diplomatist.

Duruy (dü-rüē), Jean Victor (1811—94), Fr. historian.

Duse (dō′zā), Eleonora (Signora Checchi) (1859—1924), It. actress.

Duval (dṳ-vȧl′), Claude (1643—70), Fr.-Eng. highwayman.

Duvergier de Hauranne (dü-ver-zhyā dė ō-rän), Jean (commonly known as Abbé de Saint-Cyran) (1581—1643), Fr. abbot and Jansenist theologian.

Dvořák (dvôr′zhäk), Anton (1841—1904), Bohem. musical composer.

Dwight (dwīt), Timothy (1752—1817), Am. theologian, educator, and writer.

Dwight, Timothy (1828—1916), Am. clergyman and educator (grandson of Timothy Dwight, 1752—1817).

Dyck, Anthonis van. See *Van Dyck.*

Dyer (dī′ẽr), John (1700?—58), Br. clergyman and poet.

E

Eads (ēdz), James Buchanan (1820—87), Am. engineer.

Eakins (ā′kĭnz), Thomas (1844—1916), Am. painter and sculptor.

Eames (āmz), Emma (Mrs. Julian Story, Mme. Emilio de Gogorza) (1867—   ), Am. operatic soprano singer.

Earle (ẽrl), John (c1601—65), Eng. bishop and writer.

Early (ẽr′li), Jubal Anderson (1816—94), Am. Confederate general.

Eastlake (ēst′lāk), Sir Charles Lock (1793—1865), Eng. painter, and writer on art.

Eastlake, Charles Lock (1836—1906), Eng. writer on art (nephew of Sir Charles L.).

Eastman (ēst′mạn), George (1854—1932), Am. inventor (in field of photography) and philanthropist.

Ebers (ā′bẽrs), Georg Moritz (1837—98), Ger. Egyptologist and novelist.

Ebert (ā′bẽrt), Friedrich (1871—1925), Ger. political leader (Social Democrat), 1st president of Germany (1919—25).

Eccelino. See *Ezzelino.*

Ecgberht. See *Egbert.*

Echegaray y Eizaguirre (ā″chā-gä-rī′ ē ā″thä-gẽr′rä), José (1833?—1916), Sp. mathematician, statesman, and dramatist.

Echenique (ā-chā-nē′kä), José Rufino (1808—79), Peruvian general and statesman.

Eck (fon ek), Johann Maier von (1486—1543), Ger. theologian, opponent of the Reformation.

Eckhart (ek′härt) or **Eckart** (ek′ärt), Johannes ("Meister Eckhart") (c1260—1327?), Ger. mystic.

Eddington (ed′ing-tọn), Sir Arthur Stanley (1882—1944), Eng. astronomer.

Eddy (ed′ĭ), Mrs. (Mary Baker, Mrs. Glover, Mrs. Patterson) (1821—1910), founder of Christian Science.

Eden (ē′dn). See *Auckland.*

Eden, Anthony (1897—   ), Brit. statesman.

Edgar (ed′gär) (944—975), king of the English (959—975) (brother of Edwy).

Edgeworth (ej′wẽrth), Henry Essex (known as Edgeworth de Firmont) (1745—1807), Ir.-Fr. priest, last confessor of Louis XVI. of France.

Edgeworth, Maria (1767—1849), Eng. novelist.

Edison (ed′ĭ-sọn), Thomas Alva (1847—1931), Am. electrician and inventor.

Edmund I. (ed′mund) (c922—946), king of the English (940—946) (half-brother and successor of Athelstan, and son of Edward the Elder).

Edmund II. (surnamed Ironside) (c989—1016), king of the English (1016) (son of Ethelred II.).

Edmund, Saint (Edmund Rich) (c1170—1240), Eng. ascetic and preacher, archbishop of Canterbury.

Edmund (Earl of Lancaster, called "Edmund Crouchback") (1245—96), Eng. military leader (son of Henry III. of England).

Edmunds (ed′mundz), George Franklin (1828—1919), Am. lawyer and statesman.

Edred (ed′red) (d. 955), king of the English (946—955) (brother of Edmund I.).

Edrisi. See *Idrisi.*

Edward (ed′wạrd) ("Edward the Elder") (d. 924), king of the Angles and Saxons (901—924) (son of Alfred the Great).

Edward ("the Martyr") (963?—978), king of the English (975—978) (son of Edgar).

Edward ("the Confessor") (c1004—66), king of England (1042—66) (son of Ethelred II.).

Edward I. ("Edward Longshanks") (1239—1307), king of England (1272—1307) (son of Henry III.).

Edward II. (1284—1327), king of England (1307—27) (son of Edward I.).

Edward III. (1312—77), king of England (1327—77) (son of Edward II.).

Edward IV. (1442—83), king of England (1461—70, 1471—83) (successor of Henry VI., and son of Richard, Duke of York, 1411—60, and first king of house of York).

Edward V. (1470—83), king of England (1483) (murdered in Tower of London) (son of Edward IV.).

Edward VI. (1537—53), king of England and Ireland (1547—53) (son of Henry VIII. and Jane Seymour).

Edward VII. (Albert Edward) (1841—1910), king of Great Britain and Ireland and of the British dominions beyond the seas, and emperor of India (1901—10) (son of Queen Victoria).

Edward VIII. (Duke of Windsor) (1894—   ), king of Great Britain, Ireland, and the British dominions beyond the seas, and emperor of India (1936) (son of George V.).

Edward (Prince of Wales, called "the Black Prince") (1330—76), Eng. military commander (son of Edward III. of England). [Eng. Egyptologist and writer.

Edwards (ed′wạrdz), Amelia Ann Blandford (1831—92),

Edwards, Jonathan (1703—58), Am. theologian and metaphysician.

Edwards, Jonathan (1745—1801), Am. theologian (son of Jonathan Edwards, 1703—58).

Edwin (ed′win) (585?—633), king of Northumbria (617—633).

Edwy (ed′wi) (c940—959), king of the English (955—959) (nephew and successor of Edred, and son of Edmund I.).

Égalité (ā-gȧ-lē-tā), Philippe. See *Orléans, Duc d'* (1747—93).

Egan (ē′gạn), Pierce (1772?—1849), Eng. writer, esp. on sports.

Egbert (eg′bẽrt) (or Ecgberht) (d. 839), king of the West Saxons (802—839), first overlord of the English (829—839).

Egede (ā′ge-de), Hans (1686—1758), Norw. missionary to Greenland.

Eggleston (eg′l-stọn), Edward (1837—1902), Am. novelist and misc. writer.

Eginhard. See *Einhard.*

Egmont or **Egmond** (eg′mont), Lamoral, Count of (Prince of Gavre) (1522—68), Flemish military leader and patriot.

Ehrlich (ār′lĭch), Paul (1854—1915), Ger. physician.

Eichendorff (fon ī′chẹn-dôrf), Joseph, Freiherr von (1788—1857), Ger. poet, novelist, and dramatist.

Eichhorn (īch′hôrn), Johann Gottfried (1752—1827), Ger. Biblical critic, and historian.

Eiffel (e-fel), Alexandre Gustave (1832—1923), Fr. engineer, constructor of the Eiffel Tower in Paris.

Einhard (īn′härt) or **Eginhard** (ā′gin-härt) (c770—840), Frankish biographer of Charlemagne.

Einstein (īn′stīn, Ger. īn′shtīn), Albert (1879—   ), Ger.-Swiss (Jewish) theoretical physicist, developer of the theory of relativity.

Eisenhower (ī′zn-hou-ẽr), Dwight D. (1890—   ), Am. gen.

Eisner (īs′nẽr), Kurt (1867—1919), Ger. (Bavarian) socialist.

Elagabalus (ē-lạ-gab′ạ-lus) or **Heliogabalus** (hē″li-ọ-gab′ạ-lus) (Marcus Aurelius Antoninus, orig. Varius Avitus Bassianus) (205?—222), Rom. emperor (218—222).

Eldon (el'dọn), John Scott, 1st Earl of (1751—1838), Eng. jurist.

Eleanor (el'ạ-nọr) **of Aquitaine** (1122?—1204), queen of Henry II. of England.

Elgar (el'gär), Sir Edward (1857—1934), Eng. musical composer.

Elgin (el'gin), James Bruce, 8th Earl of (12th Earl of Kincardine) (1811—63), Br. administrator and diplomatist, governor-general of Canada (1846—54) (son of 7th Earl).

Elgin, Thomas Bruce, 7th Earl of (11th Earl of Kincardine) (1766—1841), Br. diplomatist, who removed Elgin Marbles from Athens to England.

Elia (ē'li-ạ). Pseudonym of Charles Lamb.

Élie de Beaumont (ā-lē dẹ bō-môṅ), Jean Baptiste Armand Louis Léonce (1798—1874), Fr. geologist.

Eligius (e-lij'i-us) or **Éloi** (ā-lwo), Saint (c588—659), Fr. goldsmith and bishop, patron saint of goldsmiths.

Eliot (el'i-ọt), Charles William (1834—1926), Am. educator.

Eliot, George. Pseudonym of Mrs. Cross.

Eliot, Sir John (1592—1632), Eng. statesman.

Eliot, John ("the Apostle of the Indians") (1604—90), Am. missionary and translator.

Elizabeth (ẹ-liz'ạ-bẹth) (1533—1603), queen of England and Ireland (1558—1603) (successor of Mary I., and daughter of Henry VIII. and Anne Boleyn).

Elizabeth (Pauline Elisabeth Ottilie Luise, "Carmen Sylva") (1843—1916), queen of Charles I. of Rumania, and author.

Elizabeth (1709—62), empress of Russia (1741—62) (daughter of Peter the Great).

Elizabeth, Madame (Élisabeth Philippine Marie Hélène) (1764—94), Fr. princess, guillotined (sister of Louis XVI.).

Elizabeth Farnese (fär-nā'zā) (of Parma) (1692—1766), queen of Philip V. of Spain.

Elizabeth of Hungary, Saint (1207—31), landgravine of Thuringia, celebrated for charity.

Ellenborough (el'ẹn-bur-ọ̄), Edward Law, 1st Baron (1750—1818), Eng. jurist, lord chief justice (1802—18).

Ellenborough, Edward Law, Earl of (1790—1871), Eng. statesman (son of 1st Baron Ellenborough).

Ellis (el'is), Alexander John (orig. Alexander John Sharpe) (1814—90), Eng. philologist, phonetician, and mathematician.

Ellis, George (1753—1815), Eng. misc. writer.

Ellis, Sir Henry (1777—1869), Eng. antiquary.

Ellis, Henry Havelock (1859—1939), Eng. scientific and misc. writer.

Ellsworth (elz'wèrth), Lincoln W. (1880—   ), Am. explorer, crossed north pole in airship with Amundsen in 1926, crossed antarctic region in aëroplane in 1935.

Ellsworth, Oliver (1745—1807), Am. statesman and jurist, chief justice of U. S. Supreme Court (1796—1800).

Elman (el'män), Mischa (1891—   ), Russ. violinist.

Éloi, Saint. See *Eligius*.

Elphinstone (el'fin-stọn), George Keith. See *Keith, Viscount*.

Elphinstone, Mountstuart (1779—1859), Eng. statesman and historian.

Elssler (els'lèr), Fanny (1810—84), Austrian dancer.

Ely (ē'li), Richard Theodore (1854—1943), Am. political economist.

Elyot (el'i-ọt), Sir Thomas (c1490—1546), Eng. scholar and diplomatist.

Elzevir (el'zẹ-vēr), Abraham (orig. Elsevier or Elzevier) (1592—1652), Dutch printer (nephew of Bonaventure).

Elzevir, Bonaventure (1583—1652), Dutch printer (son of Louis).

Elzevir, Louis (c1540—1617), Dutch printer.

Emanuel (e-man'ụ-el) (of Portugal). See *Manoel*.

Emerson (em'ẻr-sọn), Ralph Waldo (1803—82), Am. essayist and poet.

Emin Pasha (ā'mēn pȧ-shä') (real name Eduard Schnitzer) (1840—92), administrator and explorer in Africa, born in Germany.

Emmet (em'et), Robert (1778—1803), Ir. revolutionist.

Empedocles (em-ped'ọ-klēz) (c490—c430 B.C.), Gr. philosopher and statesman.

Emser (em'zẻr), Hieronymus (1477—1527), Ger. theologian, opponent of Luther.

Encina (del en-thē'nä), Juan del (c1469—c1534), Sp. poet and dramatist.

Endecott or **Endicott** (en'di-kọt), John (1588?—1665), colonial governor of Massachusetts, born in England.

Engels (eng'ẹls), Friedrich (1820—95), Ger. socialist writer, in England.

Enghien (doṅ-gaṅ), Louis Antoine Henri de Bourbon-Condé, Duc d' (1772—1804), Fr. prince, executed by order of Napoleon I.

English (ing'glish), Thomas Dunn (1819—1902), Am. physician and writer, author of the song "Ben Bolt."

Ennius (en'i-us), Quintus (239—169? B.C.), Rom. poet.

Entragues (doṅ-träg), Catherine Henriette de Balzac d' (Marquise de Verneuil) (1579—1633), mistress of Henry IV. of France.

Éon de Beaumont (dā-ôṅ dẹ bō-môṅ), Charles Geneviève Louis Auguste André Timothée d' (called Chevalier d'Éon) (1728—1810), Fr. political agent and adventurer.

Eötvös (ẻt'vẹsh), József, Baron (1813—71), Hung. statesman and author.

Epaminondas (e-pam-i-non'dạs) (c418—362 B.C.), Theban general and statesman.

Epictetus (ep-ik-tē'tus) (fl. c100), Gr. Stoic philosopher.

Epicurus (ep-i-kū'rus) (342?—270 B.C.), Gr. philosopher, founder of Epicurean school.

Epimenides (ep-i-men'i-dēz) (fl. c600 B.C.), Cretan poet and prophet.

Epiphanius (ep-i-fā'ni-us), Saint (c315—402?), bishop and theologian, born in Palestine.

Episcopius (ep-is-kō'pi-us), Simon (orig. Simon Bisschop) (1583—1643), Dutch Arminian theologian.

Epstein (ep'stīn), Jacob (1880—   ), Eng. sculptor, born in New York of Russian-Polish parents.

Erasmus (e-raz'mus), Desiderius (Gerhard Gerhards) (1466?—1536), Dutch classical scholar, theologian, and satirist.

Erastus (e-ras'tus), Thomas (name orig. Lieber or Liebler) (1524—83), Swiss-Ger. physician and theologian.

Eratosthenes (er-ạ-tos'thẹ-nēz) (276?—195? B.C.), Gr. mathematician, astronomer, and geographer, at Alexandria.

Erceldoune, Thomas of. See *Thomas of Erceldoune*.

Erckmann-Chatrian (erk-män-shȧ-trē-äṅ). Signature of Émile Erckmann (1822—99) and Alexandre Chatrian (1826—90), Fr. collaborating novelists and dramatists.

Erdmann (ert'män), Johann Eduard (1805—92), Ger. philosophical writer, born in Russia.

Eric IX. (er'ik), Saint (d. 1160), king of Sweden (1150?—60).

Eric XIV. (1533—77), king of Sweden (1560—68) (son of Gustavus Vasa).

Ericsson (er'ik-sọn), John (1803—89), Swed.-Am. engineer and inventor.

Ericsson, Leif. See *Leif Ericsson*.

Eric the Red (er'ik) (fl. 985), Scand. colonizer of Greenland.

Erigena (e-rij'ẹ-nạ), Joannes Scotus (fl. c850), Ir. philosopher and theologian.

Ernest Augustus (ẻr'nest ȧ-gus'tus) (in German, Ernst August) (1771—1851), duke of Cumberland, and king of Hanover (1837—51) (brother of William IV. of England).

Erskine (ẻr'skin), Ebenezer (1680—1754), Sc. dissenting clergyman and theologian.

Erskine, John (1695—1768), Sc. writer on law.

Erskine, John (1879—   ), Am. educator and author.

Erskine, Thomas Erskine, 1st Baron (1750—1823), Br. lawyer and orator.

Erzberger (erts'ber-gẻr), Matthias (1875—1921), Ger. politician and writer (assassinated).

Esarhaddon (ē-sȧr-had'ọn) (d. 668 B.C.), king of Assyria (680—668 B.C.) (son of Sennacherib).

Escobar y Mendoza (es-kō-bär' ē men-dō'thä), Antonio (1589—1669), Sp. Jesuit and casuist.

Escobedo (es-kō-Bā'ᵀHō), Mariano (1827—1902), Mex. general.

Espartero (es-pär-tā'rō), Baldomero (1792—1879), Sp. general and statesman.

Esprémesnil (dā-prā-mā-nēl), Jean Jacques Duval d' (1746—94), Fr. politician, born in India.

---

fat, fāte, fär, fȧll, ȧsk, fãre; net, mē, hẻr; pin, pīne; not, nōte, mõve, nôr; up, lūte, pu̇ll; oi, oil; ou, out; (lightened) aviạry; ẹlect, agọny, intọ, ụnite; (obscured) errạnt, operạ̈, ardẹnt, actọr, natụre; ch, chip; g, go; th, thin; ᴛʜ, then; y, you;

Espy (es'pi), James Pollard (1785—1860), Am. meteorologist.

Essex (es'eks), Arthur Capel, 1st Earl of (1631—83), Eng. statesman.

Essex, Robert Devereux, 2d Earl of (1567—1601), Eng. soldier, favorite of Queen Elizabeth, executed on charge of treason (son of 1st Earl, 1541?—76).

Essex, Robert Devereux, 3d Earl of (1591—1646), Eng. parliamentary general in civil war (son of 2d Earl).

Essex, Walter Devereux, 1st Earl of (1541?—76), Eng. soldier.

Estaing (des-tan̄), Charles Hector, Comte d' (1729—94), Fr. admiral.

Estienne or **Étienne** (ā-tyen), Henri (c1460—1520), Fr. printer.

Estienne or **Étienne,** Henri (1528—98), Fr. printer and scholar (son of Robert).

Estienne or **Étienne,** Robert (1503—59), Fr. printer and scholar (son of Henri, c1460—1520).

Estournelles de Constant (des-tör-nel dė kôn̄-stän̄), Paul Henri Benjamin, Baron d' (1852—1924), Fr. diplomatist, statesman, and writer.

Estrées (des-trā), Gabrielle d' (Mme. d'Amerval de Liancourt, later created Marquise de Monceaux and Duchesse de Beaufort) (1573—99), mistress of Henry IV. of France.

Ethelbald (eth'el-bȧld) (or Æthelbald) (d. 757), king of Mercia (716—757).

Ethelbald (or Æthelbald) (d. 860), king of the West Saxons in England (855 or 858—860) (son of Ethelwulf).

Ethelbert (eth'el-bėrt) (or Æthelberht) (d. 866), king of the West Saxons in England (860—866) (brother of Ethelbald).

Ethelfleda (eth'el-flē″dȧ) (or Æthelflæd) (d. 918?), ruler of Mercia (sister of Edward the Elder, and daughter of Alfred the Great).

Ethelred I. (eth'el-red) (or Æthelred I.) (d. 871), king of the West Saxons in England (866—871) (brother of Ethelbert).

Ethelred II. (or Æthelred II.) ("the Unready") (968?—1016), king of the English (978—1016) (half-brother and successor of Edward the Martyr, and son of Edgar).

Ethelwulf (eth'el-wulf) (or Æthelwulf) (d. 858), king of the West Saxons in England (839—855 or 858) (son of Egbert).

Etherege (eth'ėr-ej), Sir George (1635?—91), Eng. dramatist.

Étienne. See *Estienne.*

Eucken (oi'ken), Rudolf Christoph (1846—1926), Ger. philosopher.

Euclid (ū'klid) (fl. c300 B.C.), Gr. geometrician, at Alexandria.

Euclid of Megara (b. c450 B.C.), Gr. philosopher.

Eudes (ėd) or **Odo** (ō'dō) (Count of Paris) (d. 898), king of the Franks (887 or 888—898) (successor of Charles II.).

Eudocia (ū-dō'shiȧ) (orig. Athenais) (401? or 393?—c460), wife of the Eastern Rom. emperor Theodosius II.

Eugene (ū-jēn'), Prince (François Eugène de Savoie-Carignan) (1663—1736), Austrian general, born in France.

Eugénie (ė-zhä-nē) (Eugenia María de Montijo) (1826—1920), empress of the French, born in Spain (wife of Napoleon III.).

Euler (oi'lėr), Leonhard (1707—83), Swiss mathematician.

Eupolis (ū'pọ-lis) (fl. 429—c415 B.C.), Gr. writer of comedy.

Euripides (ū-rip'i-dēz) (480?—406? B.C.), Gr. tragic poet.

Eusebius (ū-sē'bi-us) **of Cæsarea** (also called Eusebius Pamphili) (c260—c340), Christian bishop and church historian, of Palestine.

Eustachio (ā-ös-tä'kē-ō), Bartolommeo (as Latinized, Eustachius) (d. 1574), It. anatomist.

Eutropius (ū-trō'pi-us) (d. 399?), minister of the Eastern Rom. emperor Arcadius.

Eutyches (ū'ti-kēz) (378?—454?), Gr. monk and heresiarch, at Constantinople.

Evald, Johannes. See *Ewald.*

Evans (ev'ȧnz), Sir Arthur John (1851—   ), Eng. archæologist.

Evans, Augusta Jane. See *Wilson, Mrs.*

Evans, Robley Dunglison (1846—1912), Am. admiral.

Evarts (ev'ärts), William Maxwell (1818—1901), Am. lawyer and statesman.

Evelyn (ev'ẹ-lin or ēv'lin), John (1620—1706), Eng. diarist and misc. writer.

Everett (ev'ėr-et), Edward (1794—1865), Am. statesman, orator, and writer.

Ewald (ā'vält), Georg Heinrich August (1803—75), Ger. Orientalist and Biblical scholar.

Ewald or **Evald** (ā'väl), Johannes (1743—81), Dan. poet.

Ewell (ū'el), Richard Stoddert (1817—72), Am. Confederate general.

Ewing (ū'ing), Mrs. (Juliana Horatia Gatty) (1841—85), Eng. writer of books for children.

Exmouth (eks'muth), Edward Pellew, 1st Viscount (1757—1833), Eng. admiral.

Eyck (vän īk), Hubert (or Huybrecht) van (c1366—1426), Flemish painter.

Eyck, Jan van (c1385—1440), Flemish painter (brother of Hubert).

Eyre (ār), Edward John (1815—1901), Eng. explorer in Australia, and governor of Jamaica.

Ezekiel (e-zē'ki-ẹl), Moses Jacob (1844—1917), Am. sculptor, in Rome.

Ezzelino (et-se-lē'nō) or **Eccelino** (et-che-lē'nō) (called Ezzelino da Romano) (1194—1259), It. Ghibelline leader.

F

Faber (fā'bėr), Frederick William (1814—63), Eng. Rom. Cath. priest, theologian, and hymn-writer.

Faber, Jacobus (also called Faber Stapulensis, orig. Jacques Lefèvre d'Étaples) (c1455—c1536), Fr. Biblical scholar.

Faber (fā'bėr), Johann (name orig. Heigerlin) (1478—1541), Ger. Rom. Cath. bishop and polemical writer.

Fabius Maximus (fā'bi-us mak'si-mus), Quintus (surnamed Verrucosus, and called Cunctator, 'the Delayer') (d. 203 B.C.), Rom. general, opponent of Hannibal.

Fabius Pictor (pik'tọr), Quintus (b. c254 B.C.), Rom. historian, writing in Greek.

Fabre (fäbr), Jean Henri (1823—1915), Fr. entomologist.

Fabre d'Églantine (dä-glän̄-tēn), Philippe François Nazaire (name orig. Fabre) (1755?—94), Fr. dramatist and revolutionist.

Fabricius (fa-brish'ius), Hieronymus (in Italian, Girolamo Fabrizi or Fabrizio) (1537—1619), It. anatomist and surgeon.

Fabyan (fā'bi-ạn), Robert (d. 1513), Eng. chronicler.

Faguet (fȧ-gā), Émile (1847—1916), Fr. critic and misc. writer.

Fahrenheit (fä'ren-hīt), Gabriel Daniel (1686—1736), Ger. physicist.

Fairbanks (fâr'bangks), Charles Warren (1852—1918), Am. politician, vice-president of U. S. (1905—09).

Fairbanks, Douglas (1883—1939), Am. actor in moving pictures.

Fairfax (fâr'faks), Edward (d. 1635), Eng. poet, translator of Tasso's "Jerusalem Delivered."

Fairfax, Ferdinando Fairfax, 2d Baron (1584—1648), Eng. parliamentary general in civil war (nephew of Edward Fairfax).

Fairfax, Thomas Fairfax, 3d Baron (1612—71), Eng. parliamentary general in civil war (son of 2d Baron).

Fairfax, Thomas Fairfax, 6th Baron (1692—1782), Eng. colonist in Virginia.

Faisal (fā'sạl) (or Feisal, or Feisul) (1885—1933), Arab emir or prince, king of Iraq (Mesopotamia) (1921—33).

Faithorne (fā'thôrn), William (1616?—91), Eng. engraver and painter.

Faivre (fāvr), Jules Abel (1867—   ), Fr. painter and caricaturist.

Falconer (fâ'kn-ėr or fâk'nėr), William (1732—69), Sc. poet and lexicographer.

Falconio (fäl-kō'nē-ō), Diomede (1842—1917), It.-Am. cardinal.

Falguière (fäl-gyär), Jean Alexandre Joseph (1831—1900), Fr. sculptor and painter.

Falieri (fäl-yā'rē), Marino (also called Falier or Faliero) (c1278—1355), doge of Venice (1354—55).

Falk (fälk), Paul Ludwig Adalbert (1827—1900), Ger. statesman.

Falkenhayn (fon fäl'ken-hīn), Erich von (1861—1922), Ger. general.

Falkland (fâk'land), Lucius Cary, 2d Viscount (1610?—43), Eng. politician and writer.

(variable) ḍ as d or j, ş as s or sh, ṭ as t or ch, z̧ as z or zh; o, F. cloche; ü, F. menu; ċh, Sc. loch; n̄, F. bonbon; ', primary accent; ″, secondary accent; †, obsolete; <, from; +, and; =, equals. See also lists at beginning of book.

Fallières (fȧl-yȧr), Clément Armand (1841–1931), Fr. statesman, president of France (1906–13).

Fallopio (fäl-lō′pē-ō), Gabriello (as Latinized, Fallopius) (1523–62), It. anatomist.

Faneuil (fan′l, fun′l, or fan′ū-ẹl), Peter (1700–43), Am. merchant, founder of Faneuil Hall, in Boston.

Fanshawe (fan′shâ), Sir Richard (1608–66), Eng. diplomatist, translator, and poet.

Fantin-Latour (fän-tän-lä-tör), Ignace Henri Jean Théodore (1836–1904), Fr. painter, and designer of lithographs.

Farabee (far′ạ-bē), William Curtis (1865–1925), Am. anthropologist and explorer.

Faraday (far′ạ-dā), Michael (1791–1867), Eng. physicist and chemist.

Farel (fȧ-rel), Guillaume (1489–1565), Fr. Calvinist reformer, in Switzerland.

Farinelli (fä-rē-nel′lē) (professional name of Carlo Broschi) (1705–82), It. male soprano.

Farini (fä-rē′nē), Luigi Carlo (1812–66), It. physician, statesman, and historian.

Farley (fär′li), John Murphy (1842–1918), Am. cardinal, born in Ireland.

Farman (fär-män), Henry (1875–), Fr. aëronautic inventor.

Farnese (fär-nā′zā), Alessandro (1545–92), duke of Piacenza and Parma, and general in service of Spain (son of Margaret of Parma).

Farnese, Elizabeth. See *Elizabeth Farnese.*

Farquhar (fär′kwạr or fär′kạr), George (1678–1707), Ir. dramatist.

Farragut (far′ạ-gut), David Glasgow (1801–70), Am. admiral.

Farrar (far′ạr), Frederic William (1831–1903), Eng. divine, and theological and misc. writer.

Farrar, Geraldine (Mrs. Lou Tellegen) (1882–), Am. operatic soprano singer.

Fastolf (fas′tolf), Sir John (1378?–1459), Eng. soldier and landowner, in some part the prototype of Shakspere's Sir John Falstaff. Cf. *Oldcastle, Sir John.*

Fatima (fä′tẹ-mä) (c606–632?), daughter of Mohammed, and wife of Ali.

Faucit (fâ′sit), Helen (Helena Saville Faucit, Lady Martin) (1817–98), Eng. actress.

Faure (fōr), François Félix (1841–99), Fr. statesman, president of France (1895–99).

Fauré (fō-rā), Gabriel Urbain (1845–1924), Fr. musical composer.

Faust, Johann (printer). See *Fust.*

Favre (fävr), Gabriel Claude Jules (1809–80), Fr. lawyer, orator, and statesman.

Fawcett (fâ′set), Henry (1833–84), Eng. statesman and political economist.

Fawkes (fâks), Guy (1570–1606), Eng. conspirator, one of the leaders in the Gunpowder Plot.

Fayolle (fȧ-yol), Émile (1852–1928), Fr. general, marshal of France.

Febronius (fȧ-brō′nẹ-ús), Justinus. Pseudonym of J. N. von Hontheim.

Fechner (fech′nẹr), Gustav Theodor (1801–87), Ger. physicist, psychologist, and philosopher.

Fedor I. (fyô′dor) or **Feodor I.** (fạ-ô′dor) (in Russian, Fedor Ivanovich) (1557–98), czar of Russia (1584–98) (son of Ivan IV.).

Feisal or **Feisul.** See *Faisal.*

Fell (fel), John (1625–86), Eng. divine and educator, bishop of Oxford.

Fellenberg (fon fel′ẹn-berᴄʜ), Philipp Emanuel von (1771–1844), Swiss educator.

Felltham or **Feltham** (fel′thạm), Owen (1602?–68), Eng. author.

Felton (fel′tọn), Cornelius Conway (1807–62), Am. classical scholar.

Fénelon (fān-lôṅ), François de Salignac de La Mothe- (1651–1715), Fr. archbishop and author.

Fenton (fen′tọn), Edward (d. 1603), Eng. navigator.

Feodor I. See *Fedor I.*

Ferber (fẽr′bẽr), Edna (1887–), Am. short-story writer and novelist.

Ferdinand I. (fẽr′di-nand) (1793–1875), emperor of Austria (1835–48) (son of Emperor Francis II.).

Ferdinand I. (Prince of Saxe-Coburg-Gotha) (1861–), prince regnant of Bulgaria (1887–1908), and king (or czar) of the Bulgarians (1908–18).

Ferdinand I. (in Spanish, Fernando, called "the Great") (d. 1065), king of Castile (1035?–65) and León (1037–65).

Ferdinand III. ("the Saint") (1199–1252), king of Castile (1217–52) and León (1230–52) (grandson of Alfonso IX.).

Ferdinand V. ("the Catholic") (1452–1516), king of Spain (as Ferdinand II., king of Aragon, 1479–1516, and king of Sicily, 1468–1516; as Ferdinand III., king of Naples, 1502–16; as Ferdinand V., joint ruler of Castile with his wife Isabella I., 1474–1504, and sole ruler of united Spain, 1506–16).

Ferdinand VI. (1712–59), king of Spain (1746–59) (son of Philip V.).

Ferdinand VII. (1784–1833), king of Spain (1808, and 1814–33) (son of Charles IV.).

Ferdinand I. (1503–64), emperor of the Holy Roman Empire (1558–64), and king of Bohemia and of Hungary (1526–64) (brother of Emperor Charles V.).

Ferdinand II. (1578–1637), emperor of the Holy Roman Empire (1619–37), and king of Hungary (1618–37) and of Bohemia (1617–37) (cousin of Emperor Matthias, and grandson of Emperor Ferdinand I.).

Ferdinand III. (1608–57), emperor of the Holy Roman Empire (1637–57) (son of Emperor Ferdinand II.).

Ferdinand I. (Prince Ferdinand of Hohenzollern) (1865–1927), king of Rumania (1914–27) (nephew of Charles I. of Rumania).

Ferdinand I. (1751–1825), king of the Two Sicilies (1816–25) (from 1759, as Ferdinand IV., king of Naples, and as Ferdinand III., king of Sicily) (son of Charles III. of Spain).

Ferdinand II. ("King Bomba") (1810–59), king of the Two Sicilies (1830–59) (grandson of Ferdinand I., 1751–1825).

Fergusson (fẽr′gu-sọn), James (1808–86), Sc. writer on architecture.

Fermat (dè fer-mä), Pierre de (1601–65), Fr. mathematician.

Fernández (fer-nän′däth), Juan (fl. c1570), Sp. navigator.

Fernel (fer-nel), Jean (1497–1558), Fr. physician.

Ferrar (fer′ạr), Robert (d. 1555), Eng. Protestant bishop and martyr.

Ferrari (fer-rä′rē), Giuseppe (1812–76), It. philosophical and historical writer.

Ferrari, Paolo (1822–89), It. dramatist.

Ferrer, Saint Vincent. See *Vincent Ferrer.*

Ferrer Guardia (fer-rär′ gwär′dyä), Francisco (1859–1909), Sp. educator and agitator, executed for complicity in a rising at Barcelona.

Ferrero (fẽr-rä′rō), Guglielmo (1872–1942), It. historian and sociologist.

Ferri (fer′rē), Enrico (1856–), It. socialist leader, and criminologist.

Ferrier (fer′i-ẽr), James Frederick (1808–64), Sc. metaphysician.

Ferrier, Susan Edmonstone (1782–1854), Sc. novelist.

Ferry (fe-rē), Jules François Camille (1832–93), Fr. statesman.

Fersen (fon fer′sẹn), Hans Axel, Count von (1755–1810), Swed. statesman.

Fessenden (fes′ẹn-dẹn), William Pitt (1806–69), Am. statesman.

Festus (fes′tus), Sextus Pompeius (2d? cent.), Latin grammarian.

Feuerbach (foi′ẽr-bäᴄʜ), Anselm (1829–80), Ger. painter (nephew of Ludwig A.).

Feuerbach, Ludwig Andreas (1804–72), Ger. philosopher (son of P. J. A. von Feuerbach).

Feuerbach, Paul Johann Anselm von (1775–1833), Ger. jurist and writer on criminal law.

Feuillet (fẽ-yā), Octave (1821–90), Fr. novelist and dramatist.

Fiacre (fyȧkr), Saint (d. c670), Ir. monk in France, patron saint of gardeners.

Fichte (fiᴄʜ′tè), Johann Gottlieb (1762–1814), Ger. philosopher.

Ficino (fē-chē'nō), Marsilio (1433—99), It. philosophical writer.

Field (fēld), Cyrus West (1819—92), Am. capitalist, projector of first Atlantic cable.

Field, David Dudley (1805—94), Am. lawyer (brother of Cyrus W.).

Field, Eugene (1850—95), Am. journalist and poet.

Field, Stephen Johnson (1816—99), Am. jurist, associate justice of U. S. Supreme Court (1863—97) (brother of Cyrus W.).

Fielding (fēl'ding), Henry (1707—54), Eng. novelist.

Fields (fēldz), James Thomas (1817—81), Am. publisher and author.

Fiennes (fīnz), William. See *Saye and Sele, 1st Viscount.*

Fieschi (fyes'kē), Giuseppe (1790—1836), Corsican conspirator, who made an attempt on the life of Louis Philippe.

Fiesole (dä fyä'zō-lā), Fra Giovanni da. See *Angelico, Fra.*

Fiesole, Mino da. See *Mino da Fiesole.*

Filangieri (fē-län-jā'rē), Carlo (1784—1867), It. general and statesman (son of Gaetano).

Filangieri, Gaetano (1752—88), It. jurist.

Filelfo (fē-lel'fō), Francesco (1398—1481?), It. humanist, scholar, and poet.

Fillmore (fil'mōr), Millard (1800—74), 13th president of U. S. (1850—53).

Filmer (fil'mẽr), Sir Robert (d. 1653), Eng. political writer.

Finch (finch), Heneage. See *Nottingham, 1st Earl of* (1621—82).

Fini (fē'nē), Tommaso. See *Masolino da Panicale.*

Finlay (fin'lā), George (1799—1875), Br. historian, in Greece.

Finsen (fin'sen), Niels Ryberg (1860—1904), Dan. physician.

Firdausi (fēr-dou'sē) or **Firdusi** (fēr-dö'sē) (pseudonym of Abul Kasim Mansur) (c940—1020), Pers. epic poet.

Fischer (fish'ẽr), Emil (1852—1919), Ger. chemist.

Fischer, Ernst Kuno Berthold (1824—1907), Ger. philosopher.

Fish (fish), Hamilton (1808—93), Am. statesman.

Fisher (fish'ẽr), Dorothy Canfield (Dorothea Frances Canfield, Mrs. Fisher) (1879—   ), Am. author.

Fisher, George Park (1827—1909), Am. theologian and historian.

Fisher, Irving (1867—   ), Am. political economist.

Fisher, John (1459 or 1469—1535), Eng. bishop and cardinal.

Fisher of Kilverstone (kil'vẽr-ston), John Arbuthnot Fisher, 1st Baron (1841—1920), Br. admiral.

Fiske (fisk), Bradley Allen (1854—1942), Am. admiral and inventor.

Fiske, John (orig. Edmund Fiske Green) (1842—1901), Am. philosophical writer and historian.

Fiske, Mrs. (Minnie Davey, known as Minnie Maddern) (1865—1932), Am. actress.

Fitch (fich), Ralph (fl. 1583—1606), Eng. traveler and trader in the East.

Fitch, William Clyde (1865—1909), Am. playwright.

Fitzgerald (fits-jer'ald), Lord Edward (1763—98), Ir. politician and revolutionist.

FitzGerald, Edward (1809—83), Eng. poet and translator.

Fitzherbert (fits-hẽr'bẽrt), Mrs. (Maria Anne Smythe, Mrs. Weld) (1756—1837), wife of George IV. of England.

Fitzjames (fits-jāmz'), James. See *Berwick, Duke of.*

Fitzroy (fits-roi'), Robert (1805—65), Eng. naval officer, hydrographer, and meteorologist.

Flacius Illyricus (flā'shius i-lir'i-kus), Matthias (orig. Matthias Vlacich) (1520—75), Lutheran theologian and scholar, born in Istria.

Flamininus (flam-i-nī'nus), Titus Quinctius (c230—174? B.C.), Rom. general and statesman.

Flaminius (fla-min'i-us), Caius (d. 217 B.C.), Rom. statesman and general, defeated by Hannibal.

Flammarion (flä-mȧ-rē-ôn), Camille (1842—1925), Fr. astronomer.

Flamsteed (flam'stēd), John (1646—1719), Eng. astronomer.

Flaubert (flō-bār), Gustave (1821—80), Fr. novelist.

Flaxman (flaks'man), John (1755—1826), Eng. sculptor and draftsman.

Fléchier (flā-shyā), Valentin Esprit (1632—1710), Fr. bishop and pulpit orator.

Flecker (flek'ẽr), James Elroy (1884—1915), Eng. poet and dramatist.

Fleming (flem'ing), Sir John Ambrose (1849—1945), Eng. electrician.

Fletcher (flech'ẽr), Andrew ("of Saltoun") (1655—1716), Sc. politician and political writer.

Fletcher, Giles (c1549—1611), Eng. diplomatist, poet, and misc. writer.

Fletcher, Giles (1588?—1623), Eng. poet (brother of Phineas).

Fletcher, John (1579—1625), Eng. dramatic poet.

Fletcher, Joseph Smith (1863—1935), Eng. writer, esp. of mystery stories.

Fletcher, Phineas (1582—1650), Eng. poet (son of Giles Fletcher, c1549—1611).

Fleuranges (dė flė-ränzh), Robert de La Marck, Seigneur de (1491—1537), Fr. marshal and historian.

Fleury (dė flė-rē), André Hercule de (1653—1743), Fr. cardinal and statesman.

Fleury, Claude (1640—1723), Fr. ecclesiastical historian.

Flexner (fleks'nẽr), Simon (1863—1946), Am. physician and pathologist.

Flinders (flin'dẽrz), Matthew (1774—1814), Eng. navigator, explorer of coast of Australia.

Flint (flint), Austin (1812—86), Am. physician.

Flint, Austin (1836—1915), Am. physician and physiologist (son of Austin Flint, 1812—86).

Flood (flud), Henry (1732—91), Ir. statesman and orator.

Flor (dė flōr), Roger di (d. 1306?), military adventurer, of Ger.-It. parentage, in service of Byzantine Empire.

Florida-Blanca or **Floridablanca** (flō-rē'r̄Hä-bläng'kä), José Moñino, Count of (1728—1808), Sp. statesman.

Florio (flō'ri-ō), John (1553?—1625), Eng. lexicographer and translator.

Flotow (fon flō'tō), Friedrich von (1812—83), Ger. operatic composer.

Flower (flou'ẽr), Sir William Henry (1831—99), Eng. zoölogist.

Foch (fosh), Ferdinand (1851—1929), Fr. general, marshal of France (and British field-marshal).

Fogazzaro (fō-gät-sä'rō), Antonio (1842—1911), It. novelist and poet.

Foix (dė fwo), Gaston de (Duc de Nemours) (1489—1512), Fr. general in Italy.

Fonseca (dä fon-sā'kä), Juan Rodríguez de (1451—1524), Sp. ecclesiastic and administrator, opponent of Columbus.

Fonseca (dä foṅ-sā'kä), Manoel Deodoro da (1827—92), Brazilian general and politician, first president of Brazil (1891).

Fontaine (fôṅ-tän), Pierre François Léonard (1762—1853), Fr. architect.

Fontana (fōn-tä'nä), Felice (1730—1805), It. physiologist and naturalist.

Fontenelle (dė fôṅt-nel), Bernard Le Bovier de (1657—1757), Fr. author.

Fonvizin (fon-vē'zẹn), Denis Ivanovich (1744—92), Russ. writer of comedy.

Foote (fút), Andrew Hull (1806—63), Am. admiral.

Foote, Samuel (1720—77), Eng. actor and playwright.

Forain (fo-raṅ), Jean Louis (1852—1931), Fr. painter and caricaturist.

Forbes (fôrbz), Archibald (1838—1900), Br. war correspondent.

Forbes, Duncan (1685—1747), Sc. judge and statesman.

Forbes, James David (1809—68), Sc. physicist.

Forbes-Robertson (-rob'ẽrt-son), Sir Johnston (1853—1937), Eng. actor and theatrical manager.

Ford (fōrd), Ford Madox (orig. Ford Madox Hueffer) (1873—1939), Eng. novelist and misc. writer (grandson of Ford Madox Brown).

Ford, Henry (1863—1947), Am. automobile manufacturer.

Ford, John (1586—after 1639), Eng. dramatist.

Ford, Paul Leicester (1865—1902), Am. biographer and novelist.

Foresti (fo-res'tē), Eleutario Felice (c1793—1858), It. patriot, and scholar in U. S.

Forrest (for'est), Edwin (1806—72), Am. tragedian.

Forrest, John Forrest, Baron (1847—1918), Australian explorer and statesman.

Forster (fôr'stèr), Edward Morgan (1879—), Eng. novelist.

Forster, John (1812—76), Eng. biographer and critic.

Forster, William Edward (1818—86), Eng. statesman.

Fort (fôr), Paul (1872—), Fr. poet and dramatist.

Fortescue (fôr'tes-kū), Sir John (c1394—c1476), Eng. jurist.

Fortescue, Sir John (c1531—1607), Eng. statesman.

Fortunatus (fôr-tū-nā'tus), Venantius Honorius Clementianus (c535—c600), It. bishop of Poitiers and Latin poet.

Fortuny (for-tö'nē), Mariano José María Bernardo (1838—74), Sp. painter.

Foscari (fos'kä-rē), Francesco (1372?—1457), doge of Venice (1423—57).

Foscolo (fos'kō-lō), Ugo (orig. Niccolò Foscolo) (1778—1827), It. author and patriot, born in the Ionian Islands.

Fosdick (foz'dik), Harry Emerson (1878—), Am. clergyman.

Foster (fos'tèr), John Watson (1836—1917), Am. lawyer and diplomatist.

Foster, Stephen Collins (1826—64), Am. song-writer and composer.

Foucault (fö-kō), Jean Bernard Léon (1819—68), Fr. physicist.

Fouché (fö-shā), Joseph (Duc d'Otrante) (1763—1820), Fr. statesman, minister of police under Napoleon I.

Foucquet. See *Fouquet.*

Fouqué (fö-kā), Friedrich Heinrich Karl, Freiherr de La Motte- (1777—1843), Ger. poet and novelist.

Fouquet or **Foucquet** (fö-kā), Jean (c1415—c1485), Fr. painter.

Fouquet or **Foucquet,** Nicolas (Marquis de Belle-Isle) (1615—80), superintendent of finance in France under Louis XIV.

Fouquier-Tinville (fö-kyä-tań-vēl), Antoine Quentin (1747?—95), Fr. revolutionist.

Fourcroy (dè för-krwo), Antoine François, Comte de (1755—1809), Fr. chemist.

Fourdrinier (för-dri-nēr'), Henry (1766—1854), Eng. inventor of paper-making machinery).

Fourier (fö-ryā), François Marie Charles (1772—1837), Fr. socialist.

Fourier, Jean Baptiste Joseph, Baron (1768—1830), Fr. mathematician and physicist.

Fournier (för-nyā), Pierre Simon (1712—68), Fr. type-founder and writer.

Fox (foks), Charles James (1749—1806), Eng. statesman and orator.

Fox, George (1624—91), Eng. preacher and writer, founder of the Society of Friends.

Foxe (foks), John (1516—87), Eng. martyrologist.

Foy (fwo), Maximilien Sébastien (1775—1825), Fr. general and orator.

Fracastoro (frä-käs-tō'rō), Girolamo (1483—1553), It. physician and poet.

Fra Diavolo (frä dē-ä'vō-lō) (popular name of Michele Pezza) (1771?—1806), It. bandit, and military leader in Bourbon service in Italy.

Fragonard (frà-go-när), Jean Honoré (1732—1806), Fr. painter.

Frampton (framp'tọn), Sir George James (1860—1928), Eng. sculptor.

France (fräńs), Anatole. Pseudonym of J. A. Thibault.

Francesca (del'lä frän-ches'kä), Piero della (properly Piero de' Franceschi, also called Piero da San Sepolcro) (c1420—92), It. painter.

Franceschi (dä frän-ches'kē), Piero de'. See *Francesca, Piero della.*

Franchet d'Espérey (fräń-shä des-pā-rā), Louis Félix Marie François (1856—), Fr. general (born in Algeria), marshal of France.

Francia (frän'chä) (real name Francesco Raibolini) (1450?—1517), It. painter, engraver, and goldsmith.

Francia (frän'sē-ä), José Gaspar Rodríguez (called Dr. Francia) (c1757—1840), dictator of Paraguay (1814—40).

Francis I. (fran'sis), emperor of Austria. See *Francis II.* (emperor).

Francis I. (in French, François, pron. fräń-swo) (1494—1547), king of France (1515—47) (successor of Louis XII.).

Francis II. (1544—60), king of France (1559—60) (son of Henry II., and first husband of Mary Queen of Scots).

Francis I. (in German, Franz, pron. fränts) (1708—65), emperor of the Holy Roman Empire (1745—65) (husband of Maria Theresa of Austria).

Francis II. (1768—1835), last emperor of the Holy Roman Empire (1792—1806), and (as Francis I.) first emperor of Austria (1804—35) (son of Leopold II.).

Francis II. (1836—94), king of the Two Sicilies (1859—61) (son of Ferdinand II., 1810—59).

Francis, Sir Philip (1740—1818), Br. politician and writer (reputed author of "Junius's Letters" — see *Junius*).

Francis Ferdinand (Franz Ferdinand) (1863—1914), archduke of Austria, heir apparent to thrones of Austria and Hungary, assassinated at Sarajevo, Bosnia, June 28, 1914 (nephew of Francis Joseph I.).

Francis Joseph I. (1830—1916), emperor of Austria (1848—1916), and king of Hungary (1867—1916) (nephew of Emperor Ferdinand I. of Austria).

Francis of Assisi (äs-sē'zē), Saint (Francesco Bernardone) (1181 or 1182—1226), It. preacher and mystic, founder of Franciscan order.

Francis of Paula (pou'lä), Saint (1416—1507), It. monk, founder of order of Minims.

Francis of Sales (sälz, Fr. säl), Saint (1567—1622), Rom. Cath. bishop of Geneva, born in Savoy.

Francis Xavier, Saint. See *Xavier, Francis.*

Franck (fräńk), César Auguste (1822—90), Belgian-Fr. musical composer.

Franck (frangk), Harry Alverson (1881—), Am. traveler and author. [writer and mystic.

Franck or **Frank** (frängk), Sebastian (1499?—1542), Ger.

Francke (fräng'kè), August Hermann (1663—1727), Ger. Pietist clergyman, educator, and philanthropist.

Franco (fräng'kō), Francisco (1892—), Sp. general and statesman. [chemist.

Frankland (frangk'lånd), Sir Edward (1825—99), Eng.

Franklin (frangk'lin), Benjamin (1706—90), Am. statesman, diplomatist, scientist, and author.

Franklin, Sir John (1786—1847), Eng. arctic explorer.

Franz (fränts), Robert (orig. Robert Franz Knauth) (1815—92), Ger. musical composer, esp. of songs.

Fraser (frā'zèr), Simon. See *Lovat.*

Frater Georgius (frā'tèr jôr'jius). See *Martinuzzi, George.*

Fraunhofer (fon froun'hō''fèr), Joseph von (1787—1826), Ger. optician.

Frazer (frā'zèr), Sir James George (1854—1941), Br. anthropologist, folklorist, and misc. writer.

Fréchette (frā-shet), Louis Honoré (1839—1908), Can. poet, writing in French.

Fredegond (fred'ē̦-gond) (c545—597), mistress, later wife, of Chilperic I.

Frederick V. (fred'ē̦-rik) (1596—1632), elector of the Palatinate (1610—23), and king of Bohemia (1619—20).

Frederick III. (1609—70), king of Denmark and Norway (1648—70) (son of Christian IV.).

Frederick IV. (1671—1730), king of Denmark and Norway (1699—1730) (grandson of Frederick III. of Denmark).

Frederick VI. (1768—1839), king of Denmark (1808—39) and of Norway (1808—14) (son of Christian VII.).

Frederick VIII. (1843—1912), king of Denmark (1906—12) (son of Christian IX.).

Frederick I. (in German, Friedrich, pron. frēd'rich) (1657—1713), first king of Prussia (1701—13) (as Frederick III., elector of Brandenburg, from 1688) (son of Frederick William of Brandenburg).

Frederick II. ("Frederick the Great") (1712—86), king of Prussia (1740—86) (son of Frederick William I.).

Frederick III. (1831—88), king of Prussia and Ger. emperor (1888) (son of Emperor William I.).

Frederick I. (surnamed Barbarossa) (c1123—90), emperor of Holy Roman Empire (1152—90) (nephew of Conrad III.).

Frederick II. (1194—1250), emperor of Holy Roman Empire (1218—50), and (as Frederick I.) king of Sicily (1198—1250) (son of Emperor Henry VI.).

Frederick III. ("the Wise") (1463—1525), elector of Saxony (1486—1525), noted as protector of Martin Luther.

---

fat, fāte, fär, fåll, ásk, fāre; net, mē, hèr; pin, pīne; not, nōte, mŏve, nôr; up, lūte, půll; oi, oil; ou, out; (lightened) aviạry, ẹlect, agǫny, intọ, ụnite; (obscured) errạnt, operạ, ardẹnt, actọr, natụre; ch, chip; g, go; th, thin; ᴛH, then; y, you;

Frederick II. (or **I.** or **III.**) (of Aragon) (1272—1337), king of Sicily (1296—1337).

Frederick Augustus I. (in German, Friedrich August) (1750—1827), king of Saxony (1806—27).

Frederick Augustus III. (1865—1932), king of Saxony (1904—18).

Frederick Charles, Prince (in German, Friedrich Karl) (1828—85), Prussian general (nephew of William I. of Prussia).

Frederick William (in German, Friedrich Wilhelm, called "the Great Elector") (1620—88), elector of Brandenburg (1640—88).

Frederick William I. (1688—1740), king of Prussia (1713—40) (son of Frederick I. of Prussia).

Frederick William II. (1744—97), king of Prussia (1786—97) (nephew of Frederick the Great).

Frederick William III. (1770—1840), king of Prussia (1797—1840) (son of Frederick William II.).

Frederick William IV. (1795—1861), king of Prussia (1840—61) (son of Frederick William III.).

Frederick William (1882—   ), crown-prince of Germany (1888—1918), and Ger. general (son of Emperor William II.).

Freeman (frē'man), Edward Augustus (1823—92), Eng. historian.

Freeman, Mrs. (Mary Eleanor Wilkins) (1862—1930), Am. novelist and writer of short stories.

Freiligrath (frī'lich-rät), Ferdinand (1810—76), Ger. poet.

Frelinghuysen (frē'ling-hī″zen), Frederick (1753—1804), Am. soldier and politician.

Frelinghuysen, Frederick Theodore (1817—85), Am. lawyer and statesman (nephew of Theodore).

Frelinghuysen, Theodore (1787—1862), Am. legislator and educator (son of Frederick).

Frémiet (frā-myā), Emmanuel (1824—1910), Fr. sculptor.

Frémont (frē-mont′), John Charles (1813—90), Am. explorer, general, and political leader.

Fremstad (frem′städ), Olive (Mrs. Sutphen, Mrs. Brainard) (c1870—   ), Swed.-Am. operatic soprano singer.

French (french), Daniel Chester (1850—1931), Am. sculptor.

French, Sir John Denton Pinkstone. See *Ypres, 1st Earl of.*

Freneau (fre-nō′), Philip (1752—1832), Am. poet.

Frenssen (fren′sen), Gustav (1863—   ), Ger. clergyman and novelist.

Frere (frēr), Sir Henry Bartle Edward (1815—84), Br. administrator (nephew of John H.).

Frere, John Hookham (1769—1846), Eng. diplomatist and author.

Fresenius (frā-zā′nē-us), Karl Remigius (1818—97), Ger. chemist.

Fresnel (frā-nel), Augustin Jean (1788—1827), Fr. physicist.

Freud (froit), Sigmund (1856—1939), Austrian physician and psychologist.

Freund (froint), Wilhelm (1806—94), Ger. philologist and lexicographer.

Freycinet (dė frā-sē-nā), Charles Louis de Saulces de (1828—1923), Fr. statesman.

Freytag (frī′täch), Gustav (1816—95), Ger. novelist and dramatist.

Frick (frik), Henry Clay (1849—1919), Am. manufacturer and capitalist.

Frimont (fon frē-môṅ), Johann Maria Philipp, Graf von (1759—1831), Austrian general.

Frith or **Fryth** (frith), John (1503—33), Eng. Protestant writer and martyr.

Fröbel (frė′bel), Friedrich (1782—1852), Ger. educational reformer, founder of the kindergarten system.

Froben (frō′ben), Johannes (as Latinized, Frobenius) (1460—1527), Ger. printer and scholar.

Frobisher (frō′bi-shėr), Sir Martin (1535?—94), Eng. navigator.

Froebel (frė′bel). See *Fröbel.*

Frohman (frō′man), Charles (1860—1915), Am. theatrical manager.

Froissart (froi′särt, Fr. frwo-sär), Jean (c1337—c1410), Fr. chronicler.

Fromentin (fro-moṅ-taṅ), Eugène (1820—76), Fr. painter and writer.

Frontenac (dė frôṅt-nȧk), Louis de Buade, Comte de (c1620—98), Fr. governor of Canada.

Frontinus (fron-tī′nus), Sextus Julius (A.D. c40—c103), Rom. military officer, engineer, and tactician.

Fronto (fron′tō), Marcus Cornelius (c100—c175), Rom. orator and rhetorician, born in northern Africa.

Frost (frôst), Robert (1875—   ), Am. poet.

Froude (frōd), James Anthony (1818—94), Eng. historian.

Fry (frī), Mrs. (Elizabeth Gurney) (1780—1845), Eng. prison reformer.

Fryatt (frī′at), Charles Algernon (1872—1916), Eng. sea-captain, executed by the Germans.

Fuad I. (fö′äd) (Ahmed Fuad) (1868—1936), sultan of Egypt (1917—22), king of Egypt (1922—36) (son of Ismail Pasha).

Fulda (fùl′dä), Ludwig (1862—1939), Ger. dramatist, poet, and misc. writer.

Fulk or **Fulc** (fùlk) (Count of Anjou) (1092?—1143), king of Jerusalem (1131—43).

Fuller (fùl′ėr), George (1822—84), Am. painter.

Fuller, Melville Weston (1833—1910), Am. jurist, chief justice of U. S. Supreme Court (1888—1910).

Fuller, Sarah Margaret. See *Ossoli.*

Fuller, Thomas (1608—61), Eng. divine and historian.

Fulton (fùl′ton), Robert (1765—1815), Am. engineer and inventor.

Funck-Brentano (fùṅk-braṅ-tȧ-nō), Frantz (1862—   ), Fr. historian, born in Luxemburg.

Funston (fun′ston), Frederick (1865—1917), Am. general.

Furetière (für-tyär), Antoine (1619—88), Fr. lexicographer and misc. writer.

Furness (fėr′nes), Horace Howard (1833—1912), Am. Shaksperian scholar.

Furnivall (fėr′ni-val), Frederick James (1825—1910), Eng. philologist and editor.

Fürst (fürst), Walter (fl. c1307), legendary hero in Swiss struggle for independence against Austria.

Fuseli (fū′ze-li), John Henry (orig. Johann Heinrich Füssli) (1741—1825), Swiss-Eng. painter, and writer on art.

Fust (föst) or **Faust** (foust), Johann (d. 1466?), Ger. printer, associated with Gutenberg and Schöffer.

Fyt (fīt), Jan (1611?—61), Flemish painter, esp. of animals.

G

Gabirol (gä-bē-rōl′). See *Avicebron.*

Gaboriau (gä-bo-ryō), Émile (1833 or 1835—73), Fr. novelist.

Gaddi (gäd′dē), Agnolo (1333?—96), Florentine painter (son of Taddeo).

Gaddi, Gaddo (c1260—1333?), Florentine painter and mosaic-worker.

Gaddi, Taddeo (c1300—66?), Florentine painter and architect (son of Gaddo).

Gade (gä′dė), Niels Wilhelm (1817—90), Dan. musical composer.

Gadsden (gadz′den), Christopher (1724—1805), Am. patriot and legislator.

Gadsden, James (1788—1858), Am. soldier and diplomatist (grandson of Christopher).

Gadski (gät′skē), Johanna (Frau Tauscher) (1872—1932), Ger. operatic soprano singer.

Gage (gāj), Thomas (1721—87), Br. general, in America.

Gaines (gānz), Edmund Pendleton (1777—1849), Am. general.

Gainsborough (gānz′bur-ọ), Thomas (1727—88), Eng. painter.

Gairdner (gärd′nėr), James (1828—1912), Br. historian.

Gaiseric. See *Genseric.*

Gaius (gā′yus) (c110—c180), Rom. jurist.

Galba (gal′bä), Servius Sulpicius (5 B.C.—A.D. 69), Rom. emperor (A.D. 68—69).

Galdós, Benito Pérez. See *Pérez Galdós.*

Gale (gāl), Zona (Mrs. Breese) (1874—1938), Am. writer.

Galen (gā′len) (Claudius Galenus) (c130—c200), Gr. physician and medical writer.

Galerius (ga-lē′ri-us) (Galerius Valerius Maximianus) (d. 311), Rom. emperor (305—311) (son-in-law of Emperor Diocletian).

Galilei (gä-lē-lā′ē), Galileo (commonly known as Galileo, pron. gal-i-lē′ō, It. gä-lē-lä′ō) (1564—1642), It. physicist and astronomer.

Gall (gàl, Ger. gäl), Franz Joseph (1758—1828), Ger. physician and phrenologist.

Gallatin (gal′a̤-tin), Albert (1761—1849), Am. statesman and financier, born in Switzerland.

Gallaudet (gal-ȧ-det′), Thomas Hopkins (1787—1851), Am. clergyman, and educator of deaf-mutes.

Galle (gäl′ė), Johann Gottfried (1812—1910), Ger. astronomer.

Galli-Curci (gäl′lē-kör′chē), Mme. (Amelita Galli, Marchesa Curci, Mrs. Samuels) (1889—   ), It. operatic soprano singer in America.

Gallieni (gȧ-lyä-nē), Joseph Simon (1849—1916), Fr. general, explorer, and colonial administrator (made marshal of France in 1921, after his death).

Gallienus (gal-i-ē′nus), Publius Licinius Valerianus Egnatius (d. 268), Rom. emperor (253—268) (son and colleague of Emperor Valerian).

Galliffet (dė gȧ-lē-fä), Gaston Alexandre Auguste, Marquis de (1830—1909), Fr. general.

Gallitzin (ga-lit′sin), Demetrius Augustine (also known as Augustine Smith) (1770—1840), Russ.-Am. Rom. Cath. priest and missionary.

Galsworthy (gälz′wėr″тHi), John (1867—1933), Eng. novelist and dramatist.

Galt (gàlt), John (1779—1839), Sc. novelist.

Galton (gàl′tǫn), Sir Francis (1822—1911), Eng. scientist and writer on heredity (grandson of Erasmus Darwin).

Galuppi (gä-löp′pē), Baldassare (1706—85), It. musical composer.   [coverer of galvanism.

Galvani (gäl-vä′nē), Luigi (1737—98), It. physician, dis-

Gama (dä gä′mä), Vasco da (c1469—1524), Pg. navigator, discoverer of sea route to India.

Gambarelli (gäm-bä-rel′lē). See *Rossellino.*

Gambetta (gam-bet′a̤, Fr. gäṅ-be-tä), Léon (1838—82), Fr. statesman.   [general.

Gamelin (gȧm-laṅ), Maurice Gustave (1872—   ), Fr.

Gandhi (gänd′hē), Mohandas Karamchand (1869—   ), East Indian political reformer, advocate of non-coöperation.

Garay (dä gä-rī′), Juan de (1541—1582 or 1592), Sp. soldier, founder of Buenos Aires.

Garber (gär′bér), Daniel (1880—   ), Am. painter.

García (gär-thē′ä), Manuel (1805—1906), Sp. teacher of singing, in London (son of Manuel del P. V. García).

García, Manuel del Popolo Vicente (1775—1832), Sp. singer, teacher of singing, and composer.

García Iñiguez (gär-sē′ä ē′nyē-gäs), Calixto (1836—98), Cuban patriot and general.

Garcilaso de la Vega (gär-thē-lä′sō dä lä vä′gä) (1503—36), Sp. soldier and poet.

Garcilaso de la Vega ("the Inca") (c1535—1616), Peruvian historian, in Spain.

Garden (gär′dn), Mary (1877—   ), Sc.-Am. operatic soprano singer.

Gardiner (gärd′nėr), Samuel Rawson (1829—1902), Eng. historian.

Gardiner, Stephen (between 1483 and 1490—1555), Eng. bishop and lord chancellor.   [of U. S. (1881).

Garfield (gär′fēld), James Abram (1831—81), 20th president

Garibaldi (gar-i-bàl′di, It. gä-rē-bäl′dē), Giuseppe (1807—82), It. patriot and general.   [misc. writer.

Garland (gär′la̤nd), Hamlin (1860—1940), Am. novelist and

Garner (gär′nėr), John Nance (1869—   ), Am. legislator, vice-president of U. S. (1933—41).

Garnet or **Garnett** (gär′net), Henry (1555—1606), Eng. Jesuit, put to death on charge of complicity in the Gunpowder Plot.

Garnett, Richard (1835—1906), Eng. librarian and author.

Garnier (gär-nyä), Jean Louis Charles (1825—98), Fr. architect.

Garnier, Marie Joseph François (called Francis Garnier) (1839—73), Fr. naval officer, and explorer in eastern Asia.

Garrick (gar′ik), David (1717—79), Eng. actor and theatrical manager.

Garrison (gar′i-sǫn), William Lloyd (1805—79), Am. abolitionist and writer.

Garshin (gär-shēn′), Vsevolod Mikhaylovich (1855—88), Russ. story-writer.

Garth (gärth), Sir Samuel (1661—1719), Eng. physician and poet.

Gary (gā′ri), Elbert Henry (1846—1927), Am. lawyer and steel manufacturer.

Gascoigne (gas-koin′), George (c1525—77), Eng. poet.

Gaskell (gas′kel), Mrs. (Elizabeth Cleghorn Stevenson) (1810—65), Eng. novelist.

Gasquet (gas-kā′), Francis Aidan (1846—1929), Eng. cardinal and scholar.

Gassendi (gȧ-saṅ-dē) or **Gassend** (gȧ-soṅ), Pierre (1592—1655), Fr. philosopher and scientist.

Gates (gāts), Horatio (1728—1806), Am. Revolutionary general, born in England.

Gates, Sir Thomas (fl. 1596—1621), Eng. colonial governor of Virginia.

Gatling (gat′ling), Richard Jordan (1818—1903), Am. inventor (of Gatling gun).

Gauden (gà′dęn), John (1605—62), Eng. bishop and writer.

Gauguin (gō-gaṅ), Paul (1848—1903), Fr. painter.

Gaulle (dė gōl), Charles A. J. M. de (1890—   ), Fr. gen.

Gaunt, John of. See *John of Gaunt.*

Gauss (gous), Karl Friedrich (1777—1855), Ger. mathematician.

Gautama (gà′ta̤-mä). See *Buddha.*

Gautier (gō-tyä), Théophile (1811—72), Fr. poet, novelist.

Gavarni (gȧ-vär-nē), Paul (real name Sulpice Guillaume Chevalier) (1801 or 1804—66), Fr. caricaturist and illustrator.

Gaveston (gav′es-tǫn), Piers (Earl of Cornwall) (d. 1312), favorite of Edward II. of England.

Gay (gā), John (1685—1732), Eng. poet and dramatist.

Gay-Lussac (gä-lü-sàk), Joseph Louis (1778—1850), Fr. chemist and physicist.

Geary (gär′i or gēr′i), John White (1819—73), Am. general and politician.

Gebhardt (fon gep′härt), Eduard von (1838—1925), Ger. painter, born in Russia.

Geddes (ged′es), Sir Auckland Campbell (1879—   ), Br. anatomist, administrator, and diplomatist (brother of Sir E. C.).

Geddes, Sir Eric Campbell (1875—1937), Br. administrator and cabinet minister.

Gegenbaur (gā′gęn-bour), Karl (1826—1903), Ger. anatomist.

Geikie (gē′ki), Sir Archibald (1835—1924), Sc. geologist.

Geikie, James (1839—1915), Sc. geologist (brother of Sir Archibald).

Geiler von Kaysersberg (gī′lėr fon kī′zėrs-berċh), Johann (1445—1510), Ger. pulpit orator.

Geissler (gīs′lėr), Heinrich (1814—79), Ger. mechanician and inventor.

Gellert (gel′ėrt), Christian Fürchtegott (1715—69), Ger. poet and misc. writer.

Gellius (jel′i-us), Aulus (c130—c175), Rom. author.

Gelon (jē′lǫn) (d. 478 B.C.), Sicilian ruler, tyrant of Syracuse.

Gemistus (je-mis′tus), Georgius (known as Plethon, and Gemistus Plethon) (c1355—1450), Byzantine Gr. Platonic philosopher and scholar.

Genêt or **Genest** (zhė-nä), Edmond Charles (1765—1834), Fr. diplomatist, later citizen of U. S.

Genevieve (jen′ę-vēv), Saint (in French, Geneviève, pron. zhėn-vyäv) (c422—512), Fr. nun, patron saint of Paris.

Genghis Khan. See *Jenghis Khan.*

Genlis (dė zhoṅ-lēs), Comtesse de (Stéphanie Félicité Ducrest de Saint-Aubin) (1746—1830), Fr. writer and educator.

Gennaro (jen-nä′rō), Santo, or San. See *Januarius.*

Genseric (jen′sę-rik) or **Gaiseric** (gī′zę-rik) (c390—477), king of the Vandals, conquerer in northern Africa and Italy.

Geoffrey (jef′ri) (surnamed Plantagenet) (1113—51), count of Anjou (husband of Matilda, daughter of Henry I. of England, and father of Henry II. of England).

Geoffrey of Monmouth (1100?—54), Eng. chronicler.

Geoffroy (zho-frwo), Étienne François (1672—1731), Fr. chemist.

Geoffroy Saint-Hilaire (saṅ-tē-lär), Étienne (1772—1844), Fr. zoölogist.

Geoffroy Saint-Hilaire, Isidore (1805—61), Fr. zoölogist (son of Étienne).

George (jôrj), Saint (d. 303?), Christian martyr, supposed to have been born in Asia Minor and put to death in Asia Minor or Palestine, patron saint of England. According to legend, he saved the daughter of a king in Libya from a dragon which had ravaged the region, afterward slaying the dragon and winning the king's people to Christianity.

George I. (Elector of Hanover) (1660—1727), king of Great Britain and Ireland (1714—27) (successor of Queen Anne, and great-grandson of James I., and first king of house of Hanover).

George II. (1683—1760), king of Great Britain and Ireland (1727—60) (son of George I.).

George III. (1738—1820), king of Great Britain and Ireland (1760—1820) (successor and grandson of George II.).

George IV. (1762—1830), king of Great Britain and Ireland (1820—30) (son of George III.).

George V. (1865—1936), king of Great Britain, Ireland, and the British dominions beyond the seas, and emperor of India (1910—36) (son of Edward VII.).

George VI. (1895—), king of Great Britain, Ireland, and the British dominions beyond the seas, and emperor of India (1936—) (brother of Edward VIII.).

George I. (1845—1913), king of the Hellenes (1863—1913) (son of Christian IX. of Denmark).

George II. (1890—1947), king of the Hellenes (1922—23, 1935—47) (son of Constantine I., king of the Hellenes).

George (called "the Bearded") (1471—1539), duke of Saxony (1500—39).

George, David Lloyd. See *Lloyd George.* [of single tax.

George, Henry (1839—97), Am. political economist, advocate

George, Walter Lionel (1882—1926), Eng. novelist and misc. writer, born in France. [painter, born in Rome.

Gérard (zhā-rär), François Pascal, Baron (1770—1837), Fr.

Gerard (je-rärd'), John (1545—1612), Eng. botanist.

Gerhardt (ger'härt), Paul (1607?—76), Ger. clergyman and religious poet. [1824], Fr. painter.

Géricault (zhā-rē-kō), Jean Louis André Théodore (1791—

Germain (jėr-mān'), Lord George. See *Sackville, 1st Viscount.*

Germanicus Cæsar (jėr-man'i-kus sē'zär) (15 B.C.—A.D. 19), Rom. general and provincial administrator (son of N. C. Drusus, and brother of Emperor Claudius I.).

Gérôme (zhā-rōm), Jean Léon (1824—1904), Fr. painter and sculptor.

Geronimo (je-ron'i-mō) (c1834—1909), Am. Indian chief.

Gerry (ger'i), Elbridge (1744—1814), Am. statesman, vice-president of U. S. (1813—14).

Gerson (dė zher-sôn), Jean Charlier de (1363—1429), Fr. theologian.

Gertsen (gert'sen), Aleksandr Ivanovich. See *Hertzen.*

Gervinus (ger-vē'nús), Georg Gottfried (1805—71), Ger. historian and critic.

Gesenius (gä-zā'nē-ús), Friedrich Heinrich Wilhelm (1786—1842), Ger. Orientalist and Biblical critic.

Gesner (fon ges'nėr), Konrad von (1516—65), Swiss naturalist and writer.

Gessler (ges'lėr), Hermann (d. c1307), legendary Austrian magistrate in Switzerland during Swiss struggle for independence, killed by William Tell.

Ghazali (ga-zä'lē), Abu Hamid Muhammad ibn Muhammad al- (1058—1111), Arab theologian and philosopher.

Gherardesca (del'lä gä-rär-des'kä), Ugolino della (d. 1289?), party leader at Pisa, imprisoned and starved to death with his sons and grandsons (or nephews).

Ghiberti (gē-bär'tē), Lorenzo (1378?—1455), Florentine sculptor.

Ghirlandajo (gēr-län-dä'yō) (Domenico di Tommaso Curradi di Doffo Bigordi, called Il Ghirlandajo, 'the Garland-Maker') (1449—94), Florentine painter.

Giacosa (jä-kō'sä), Giuseppe (1847—1906), It. dramatist.

Giambelli (jäm-bel'lē) or **Gianibelli** (jä-nē-bel'lē), Federigo (fl. c1585), It. military engineer, for a time in the service of England.

Gibbon (gib'on), Edward (1737—94), Eng. historian.

Gibbons (gib'onz), Grinling (1648—1720), Eng. wood-carver and sculptor.

Gibbons, James (1834—1921), Am. cardinal.

Gibbs (gibz), Sir Philip (1877—), Eng. journalist, novelist, and misc. writer.

Gibson (gib'son), Charles Dana (1867—1944), Am. illustrator.

Gibson, John (1790—1866), Eng. sculptor.

Giddings (gid'ingz), Joshua Reed (1795—1864), Am. legislator and antislavery leader.

Gide (zhēd), André Paul Guillaume (1869—), Fr. author.

Gieseler (gē'zė-lėr), Johann Karl Ludwig (1792—1854), Ger. church historian.

Gifford (gif'ord), William (1756—1826), Eng. critic, editor, and misc. writer.

Gigli (jēl'yē), Beniamino (1890—), It. operatic tenor singer.

Gilbart (gil'bärt), James William (1794—1863), Eng. writer on banking.

Gilbert (gil'bėrt), Sir Alfred (1854—1934), Eng. sculptor.

Gilbert, Cass (1859—1934), Am. architect.

Gilbert, Sir Humphrey (1539?—83), Eng. soldier and navigator, and colonizer in America (half-brother of Sir Walter Raleigh, 1552?—1618).

Gilbert, Sir William Schwenck (1836—1911), Eng. dramatist and humorist.

Gilbert (gil'bėrt) or **Gilberd** (gil'bėrd), William (1540—1603), Eng. physician and scientist.

Gilbert of Sempringham (sem'pring-am), Saint (c1083—1189), Eng. priest, founder of religious order called the Gilbertines.

Gildas (gil'das) (516?—570?), Br. historian.

Gilder (gil'dėr), Richard Watson (1844—1909), Am. editor and poet.

Gildersleeve (gil'dėr-slēv), Basil Lanneau (1831—1924), Am. classical scholar.

Giles (jīlz), Saint (fl. 7th? cent.), hermit and monk in France, born at Athens, patron saint of cripples.

Gilfillan (gil-fil'an), George (1813—78), Sc. clergyman and misc. writer.

Gilfillan, Robert (1798—1850), Sc. poet.

Gill (gil), Sir David (1843—1914), Sc. astronomer, at Cape of Good Hope (1879—1907).

Gill, Theodore Nicholas (1837—1914), Am. zoölogist.

Gillett (ji-let'), Frederick Huntington (1851—1935), Am. legislator.

Gillette (ji-let'), William (1855—1937), Am. actor and playwright.

Gillmore (gil'mōr), Quincy Adams (1825—88), Am. general and military engineer.

Gillray (gil'rā), James (1757—1815), Eng. caricaturist.

Gilman (gil'man), Daniel Coit (1831—1908), Am. educator.

Ginkel (van ging'kel), Godart van (1st Earl of Athlone) (1630—1703), Dutch general, in English service.

Gioberti (jō-bär'tē), Vincenzo (1801—52), It. philosopher and politician.

Giolitti (jō-lēt'tē), Giovanni (1842—1928), It. statesman.

Giordano (jor-dä'nō), Luca (1632—1705), It. painter.

Giordano, Umberto (1867?—), It. operatic composer.

Giorgione (jor-jō'nā) (Giorgio Barbarelli, or Zorzo da Castelfranco) (1477?—1511), It. painter, of Venetian school.

Giotto (jot'tō) or **Giotto di Bondone** (dē bon-dō'nā) (c1266—1337), Florentine painter and architect.

Giovanni (dē jō-vän'nē), Mino di. See *Mino da Fiesole.*

Giovanni da Bologna. See *Bologna, Giovanni da.*

Giraldus Cambrensis (ji-ral'dus kam-bren'sis) (Gerald, or Giraldus, de Barri) (1146?—1220?), Welsh ecclesiastic and historical writer.

Girard (dė zhē-rär), Philippe Henri de (1775–1845), Fr. mechanician, inventor of flax-spinning machine.

Girard (ji-rärd'), Stephen (1750—1831), Fr.-Am. merchant, banker, and philanthropist.

Girardin (dė zhē-rär-dań), Émile de (1802 or 1806—81), Fr. journalist and politician.

Girodet-Trioson (zhē-ro-dā-trē-o-zôn), Anne Louis (orig. Girodet de Roussy) (1767—1824), Fr. painter.

Gissing (gis'ing), George Robert (1857—1903), Eng. novelist.

Giulio Romano (jōl'yō rō-mä'nō) (also known as Giulio Pippi, real name Giulio di Pietro di Filippo de' Giannuzzi) (1492?—1546), It. painter and architect.

Giusti (jös'tē), Giuseppe (1809—50), It. satirical poet.

Glackens (glak'ĕnz), William J. (1870—1938), Am. painter and illustrator.

Gladden (glad'n), Washington (1836—1918), Am. clergyman and writer.

Gladstone (glad'stọn), William Ewart (1809—98), Eng. statesman and writer.

Glanvill or **Glanvil** (glan'vil), Joseph (1636—80), Eng. clergyman and philosophical writer.

Glanville or **Glanvill** (dĕ glan'vil), Ranulf de (d. 1190), chief justiciary of England, reputed author of an early treatise on English law.

Glasgow (glas'gō), Ellen Anderson Gholson (1874—1945), Am. novelist.

Glauber (glou'bĕr), Johann Rudolf (1604—68), Ger. chemist.

Glazebrook (glāz'brůk), Sir Richard Tetley (1854—   ), Eng. physicist.

Glazunov (glä-zö-nof'), Aleksandr Konstantinovich (1865—1936), Russ. musical composer.

Gleim (glīm), Johann Wilhelm Ludwig (1719—1803), Ger. poet.

Glendower (glen'dör or glen'dou''ĕr), Owen (Owain ab Gruffydd) (1359?—1416?), Welsh rebel.

Gleyre (glâr), Charles Gabriel (1806—74), Swiss-Fr. painter.

Glinka (gling'kä), Mikhail Ivanovich (1803?—57), Russ. musical composer.

Gluck (glůk), Alma (professional name of Reba Fiersohn, Mme. Efrem Zimbalist) (1884—1938), Rumanian-Am. soprano singer.

Gluck, Christoph Willibald (1714—87), Ger. operatic composer.

Godefroy (god-frwo), Frédéric Eugène (1826—97), Fr. lexicographer and literary historian.

Godfrey (god'fri), Thomas (1736—63), Am. poet and dramatist.

Godfrey of Bouillon (bö-yôn) (c1060—1100), one of the leaders in the first Crusade.

Godiva (gọ-dī'vä) ("Lady Godiva") (fl. c1050), benefactress of monasteries (wife of Leofric, earl of Mercia). According to legend, the earl promised his wife to remit a heavy toll imposed upon the people of Coventry if she would ride naked through the streets of the place. This she did, covered only by her long hair, and thus won relief for the people. According to a later story, the people were commanded to keep within doors and not look out at her. A tailor, afterward called Peeping Tom, who bored a hole through his shutter and peeped, was stricken blind.

Godkin (god'kin), Edwin Lawrence (1831—1902), Ir.-Am. journalist.

Godolphin (gọ-dol'fĭn), Sidney Godolphin, 1st Earl of (1645—1712), Eng. statesman and financier.

Godowski (go-dof'skẹ), Leopold (1870—1938), Russ. pianist and composer.

Godoy (dä gọ-ᴛᴛᴛᴛᴛᴛᴛᴛ), Manuel de (Duke of Alcudia) (1767—1851), Sp. statesman, favorite of Charles IV. and Queen Maria Luisa.

Godunov (go-dö-nof'), Boris Fedorovich (1552—1605), Russ. regent, and czar (1598—1605) (brother-in-law of Fedor I.).

Godwin (god'win) (or Godwine) (d. 1053), earl of the West Saxons in England.   [writer (wife of William).

Godwin, Mrs. (Mary Wollstonecraft) (1759—97), Eng.

Godwin, Parke (1816—1904), Am. journalist.   [writer.

Godwin, William (1756—1836), Eng. novelist and misc.

Goebbels (gĕb'ĕls), Paul Joseph (1897—1945), Ger. (Nazi) minister for enlightenment of the people and propaganda.

Goeben (fon gĕ'bẹn), August Karl von (1816—80), Prussian general.

Goering (gĕ'ring). See *Göring.*

Goerres (gĕr'es), **Goertz** (gĕrts). See *Görres, Görtz.*

Goes (vän dĕr gös), Hugo van der (d. 1482), Flemish painter.

Goethals (gō'thạlz), George Washington (1858—1928), Am. general and engineer.

Goethe (fon gĕ'tẹ), Johann Wolfgang von (1749—1832), Ger. poet, dramatist, and misc. writer.

Goetz (gĕts). See *Götz.*

Goffe or **Gough** (gof), William (c1605—79?), Eng. Puritan and regicide, who died in exile in America.

Gogh (vän goch), Vincent van (1853—90), Dutch painter.

Gogol (gọ'gol), Nikolay Vasilevich (1809—52), Russ. novelist and dramatist.

Goldmark (golt'märk), Karl (1830—1915), Austrian musical composer.

Goldoni (gol-dō'nẹ), Carlo (1707—93), It. dramatist.

Goldsborough (gōldz'bur-ọ), Louis Malesherbes (1805—77), Am. admiral.

Goldsmith (gōld'smith), Oliver (1728—74), Br. poet, novelist, and dramatist.

Golgi (gōl'jē), Camillo (1843—1926), It. pathologist and histologist.

Goltz (fon der golts), Kolmar, Freiherr von der (1843—1916), Ger. general and military writer.

Gomarus (gọ'mạ-rus), Franz (1563—1641), Flemish-Dutch Calvinistic theologian.

Gómez (gọ'mäs), Juan Vicente (1857?—1935), Venezuelan general, pres. of Venezuela (1910—14, 1915—29, 1931—35).

Gómez y Báez (ē bä'äs), Máximo (c1836—1905), Cuban patriot and general.

Gompers (gom'pĕrz), Samuel (1850—1924), Am. labor leader, born in England.

Goncharov (gon-chá-rof'), Ivan Aleksandrovich (1812—91), Russ. novelist.

Goncourt (dĕ gôṅ-kör), Edmond Louis Antoine Huot de (1822—96), Fr. novelist and misc. writer.

Goncourt, Jules Alfred Huot de (1830—70), Fr. novelist and misc. writer (brother of Edmond).

Góngora y Argote (dä gōn'gō-rä ē är-gō'tä), Luis de (1561—1627), Sp. poet.

Gonsalvo de Córdoba (gon-säl'vō dä kôr'dō-bä). See *Córdoba, Gonzalo Hernández de.*

Gooch (gōch), Sir Daniel (1816—89), Eng. engineer.

Goode (gůd), George Brown (1851—96), Am. ichthyologist.

Goodrich (gůd'rich), Samuel Griswold ("Peter Parley") (1793—1860), Am. writer.

Goodwin (gůd'win), Nathaniel Carl (1857—1919), Am. actor.

Goodwin, William Watson (1831—1912), Am. classical scholar.

Goodyear (gůd'yĕr), Charles (1800—60), Am. inventor (of vulcanized rubber).

Gorchakov (gor-chá-kof'), Prince Aleksandr Mikhaylovich (1798—1883), Russ. diplomatist and statesman.

Gordon (gôr'dọn), Adam Lindsay (1833—70), Australian poet, born in the Azores.

Gordon, Charles George ("Chinese Gordon") (1833—85), Eng. soldier and administrator.

Gordon, Lord George (1751—93), Eng. agitator.

Goremykin (go-re-mē'kẹn), Ivan Longinovich (1840—1917), Russ. statesman.

Gorgas (gôr'gạs), William Crawford (1854—1920), Am. sanitarian, surgeon-general in U. S. Army.   [general.

Görgei or **Görgey** (gĕr'gä-ẹ), Arthur (1818—1916), Hung.

Gorges (gôr'jez), Sir Ferdinando (c1566—1647), Eng. military and naval commander, proprietor of colony of Maine.

Gorgias (gôr'ji-ạs) (c485—c380 B.C.), Gr. sophist and rhetorician.

Göring (gĕ'ring), Hermann Wilhelm (1893—1946), Ger. (Nazi) field-marshal and statesman.   [vich Pyeshkov.

Gorki (gôr'kẹ), Maksim.   Pseudonym of Aleksyey Maksimo-

Gorm (gôrm) ("the Old") (d. c940), king of Denmark.

Görres (fon gĕr'es), Johann Joseph von (1776—1848), Ger. political and historical writer.

Gorst (gôrst), Sir Eldon (1861—1911), Br. statesman and administrator (son of Sir John E.).

Gorst, Sir John Eldon (1835—1916), Eng. statesman.

Gort (gôrt), John Standish Surtees Prendergast Vereker, 6th Viscount (1886—   ), Br. general.

Gortchakoff (gor-chá-kof'). See *Gorchakov.*

Gorton (gôr'tọn), Samuel (c1600—77), Eng. mystic, preacher, and writer, in America.   [statesman in Swedish service.

Görtz (fon gĕrts), Georg Heinrich von (1668—1719), Holstein

Goschen (gō'shẹn), George Joachim Goschen, 1st Viscount (1831—1907), Eng. statesman and financier.

Gosnold (gos'nọld), Bartholomew (d. 1607), Eng. navigator, a founder of Jamestown settlement in Virginia.

Gossaert or **Gossart** (gos'ärt), Jan. See *Mabuse, Jan.*

Gosse (gos), Sir Edmund William (1849—1928), Eng. critic and poet (son of Philip H.).

---

fat, fāte, fär, fȧll, ȧsk, fāre; net, mē, hėr; pin, pīne; not, nōte, mȯve, nôr; up, lūte, půll; oi, oil; ou, out; (lightened) avĭạry; ẹlect, agọny, intọ, ūnite; (obscured) errạnt, operạ, ardẹnt, actọr, natụre; ch, chip; g, go; th, thin; ᴛн, then; y, you;

Gosse, Philip Henry (1810—88), Eng. zoölogist.
Gotama (gō'ta̧-mä). See *Buddha*.
Göthe (gė'tė). See *Goethe*.
Gottfried von Strassburg (got'frēt fon shträs'bûrċh) (fl. 1210), Ger. epic poet, author of "Tristan und Isolde."
Gottschalk (got'shälk) (c805—868?), Ger. theologian.
Gottschalk (got'shälk), Louis Moreau (1829—69), Am. pianist and composer.
Gottsched (got'shet), Johann Christoph (1700—66), Ger. critic and misc. writer.
Götz (gėts), Hermann (1840—76), Ger. musical composer.
Gough (gof), Sir Hubert de la Poer (1870—   ), Br. general.
Gough, Hugh Gough, 1st Viscount (1779—1869), Br. field-marshal.
Gough, John Bartholomew (1817—86), Am. temperance lecturer, born in England.
Gough, William. See *Goffe*.
Goujon (gö-zhoṅ), Jean (c1510—c1566), Fr. sculptor.
Gould (gōld), Benjamin Apthorp (1824—96), Am. astronomer.
Gould, Jay (1836—92), Am. capitalist.
Gounod (gö-nō), Charles François (1818—93), Fr. musical composer.
Gouraud (gö-rō), Henri Joseph Étienne (1867—1946), Fr. general.
Gourko (gör'kō). See *Gurko*.
Gourmont (dė gör-môṅ), Rémy de (1858—1915), Fr. author.
Gouvion Saint-Cyr (dė gö-vyôṅ saṅ-sēr), Laurent, Marquis de (1764—1830), Fr. marshal.
Gower (gou'ėr or gōr), John (c1325—1408), Eng. poet.
Gowrie (gou'ri), John Ruthven, 3d Earl of (1578?—1600), Sc. nobleman, killed with his brother by followers of James VI. of Scotland (later James I. of England), according to James during an attempt of the two brothers, in an alleged conspiracy, to murder or kidnap him.
Goya y Lucientes (dä gō'yä ē lö-thȩ̇-en'täs), Francisco José de (1746—1828), Sp. painter and etcher.
Goyen (van goi'ȩn), Jan van (1596—1656), Dutch painter.
Gozzi (got'sē), Count Carlo (1720?—1806), It. dramatist.
Gozzoli (got'sō-lē), Benozzo (real name Benozzo di Lese) (1420?—98?), Florentine painter.
Graaf (dė gräf), Regnier de (1641—73), Dutch physician and anatomist.
Gracchus (grak'us), Caius Sempronius (153?—121 B.C.), Rom. political reformer (brother of T. S. Gracchus).
Gracchus, Tiberius Sempronius (163?—133 B.C.), Rom. political reformer (son of Cornelia).
Graefe (grä'fė). See *Gräfe*.
Gräfe (fon grä'fė), Albrecht von (1828—70), Ger. oculist (son of Karl F.).
Gräfe, Karl Ferdinand von (1787—1840), Ger. surgeon.
Grafly (grä'fli), Charles (1862—1929), Am. sculptor.
Grafton (gráf'to̧n), Richard (d. c1572), Eng. printer and chronicler.
Graham (grā'a̧m), James. See *Montrose, 1st Marquis of*.
Graham, Thomas (1805—69), Br. chemist.
Graham of Claverhouse (klav'ėrz), John. See *Dundee, Viscount*.
Gramont (dė grä-môṅ), Antoine Agénor Alfred, Duc de (Prince de Bidache) (1819—80), Fr. diplomatist and statesman.
Gramont, Philibert, Comte de (1621—1707), Fr. courtier and adventurer.
Granados y Campiña (grä-nä'ᴛHōs ē käm-pē'nyä), Enrique (1867—1916), Sp. composer and pianist.
Granby (gran'bi), John Manners, Marquis of (1721—70), Eng. general.
Granier de Cassagnac (grä-nyä dė ká-sà-nyàk). See *Cassagnac*.
Grant (grant), Mrs. (Anne Macvicar, known as Mrs. Grant of Laggan) (1755—1838), Sc. writer.
Grant, James Augustus (1827—92), Br. army officer, and explorer in Africa.
Grant, Robert (1852—1940), Am. novelist.
Grant, Ulysses Simpson (orig. Hiram Ulysses Grant) (1822—85), Am. general, and 18th president of U. S. (1869—77).
Granvelle (Fr. dė gräṅ-vel) or **Granvella** (Sp. dä gräṅ-vel'yä),

Antoine Perrenot de (1517—86), Sp. cardinal and statesman, born at Besançon.
Granville (gran'vil), John Carteret, Earl (1690—1763), Eng. statesman.
Granville-Barker (-bär'kėr), Harley Granville (1877—1946), Eng. dramatist and producer of plays.
Gras (grä), Félix (1844—1901), Provençal poet and novelist.
Grasse (dė gräs), François Joseph Paul, Comte de (Marquis de Grasse-Tilly) (1722—88), Fr. admiral.
Gratian (grā'shia̧n) (Flavius Gratianus) (359—383), Rom. emperor (375—383) (son of Valentinian I.).
Gratianus (grā-shi-ā'nus) or **Gratian** (fl. c1145), It. compiler of canon law.
Grattan (grat'a̧n), Henry (1746—1820), Ir. statesman and orator.
Graves (grāvz), Richard (1715—1804), Eng. novelist and poet.
Gray (grā), Asa (1810—88), Am. botanist.
Gray, Elisha (1835—1901), Am. electrician and inventor.
Gray, Thomas (1716—71), Eng. poet.
Greathead (grāt'hed), Henry (1757—1816), Eng. life-boat inventor.
Greco, El. See *Theotocopuli*.
Greeley (grē'li), Horace (1811—72), Am. journalist and politician.
Greely (grē'li), Adolphus Washington (1844—1935), Am. general, arctic explorer, and meteorologist.
Green (grēn), John Richard (1837—83), Eng. historian.
Green, Matthew (1696—1737), Eng. poet.
Green, Thomas Hill (1836—82), Eng. philosopher.
Greenaway (grēn'a̧-wā), Kate (1846—1901), Eng. painter and illustrator.
Greene (grēn), Nathanael (1742—86), Am. Revolutionary general.
Greene, Robert (c1560—92), Eng. dramatic poet and misc. writer.
Greenough (grēn'ō), Horatio (1805—52), Am. sculptor.
Greenough, James Bradstreet (1833—1901), Am. Latin scholar.
Grégoire (grā-gwor), Henri (1750—1831), Fr. ecclesiastic, revolutionist, and writer.
Gregory I. (greg'ō-ri), Saint ("Gregory the Great") (c540—604), It. cleric, pope (590—604).
Gregory VII., Saint (Hildebrand) (c1020—85), It. ecclesiastic, pope (1073—85).
Gregory XIII. (Ugo Buoncompagni) (1502—85), It. ecclesiastic, pope (1572—85).
Gregory XVI. (Bartolommeo Alberto Cappellari) (1765—1846), It. ecclesiastic, pope (1831—46).
Gregory, Lady (Augusta Persse) (1852—1932), Ir. dramatist and misc. writer.
Gregory of Nazianzus (nā-zi-an'zus), Saint (c329—390?), bishop and theologian, of Asia Minor.
Gregory of Neocæsarea (nē″ō-sez-a̧-rē'ä), Saint (name orig. Theodorus, often called Gregory Thaumaturgus) (c213—c270), bishop and theologian, of Asia Minor.
Gregory of Nyssa (nis'ä), Saint (c335—c395), bishop and theologian, of Asia Minor (brother of Saint Basil).
Gregory of Tours, Saint (538?—594), Frankish bishop and historian.
Grenfell (gren'fel), Sir Wilfred Thomason (1865—1940), Eng. physician and missionary to fishermen, in Labrador and Newfoundland.
Grenville (gren'vil), George (1712—70), Eng. statesman (brother of Earl Temple).
Grenville or **Greynvile,** Sir Richard (c1541—91), Eng. naval commander.
Grenville, Richard Temple. See *Temple, Earl*.
Grenville, William Wyndham Grenville, Baron (1759—1834), Eng. statesman (son of George).
Gresham (gresh'a̧m), Sir Thomas (1519?—79), Eng. merchant and financier.
Gresham, Walter Quinton (1832—95), Am. general, jurist, and statesman.
Grétry (grā-trē), André Ernest Modeste (1741—1813), Fr. operatic composer.
Greuze (grėz), Jean Baptiste (1725—1805), Fr. painter.
Greville (grev'il), Fulke. See *Brooke, 1st Baron*.

Grévy (grā-vē), François Paul Jules (1807–91), Fr. statesman, president of France (1879–87).

Grew (grö), Nehemiah (1641–1712), Eng. physician and botanist.

Grey (grā), Charles Grey, 2d Earl (1764–1845), Eng. statesman.

Grey, Sir George (1812–98), Eng. colonial governor, and writer.

Grey, Henry George, 3d Earl (1802–94), Eng. statesman (son of 2d Earl).

Grey, Lady Jane (Lady Jane Dudley) (1537–54), Eng. noblewoman executed as usurper to crown of England (great-granddaughter of Henry VII. of England, and wife of Lord Guildford Dudley).

Grey of Fallodon, Edward Grey, Viscount (Sir Edward Grey) (1862–1933), Eng. statesman.

Griboyedov (grē-bo-ye'dof), Aleksandr Sergyeevich (1795–1829), Russ. dramatist and diplomatist.

Grieg (grēg), Edvard Hagerup (1843–1907), Norw. musical composer.

Griffenfeldt or **Griffenfeld** (grif'ẹn-felt), Peder Schumacher, Count (1635–99), Dan. statesman.

Griffin (grif'in), Gerald (1803–40), Ir. novelist and dramatist.

Griffith (grif'ith), Arthur (1872–1922), Ir. Sinn Fein leader.

Grijalva (dä grē-Häl'vä), Juan de (c1489–1527), Sp. explorer of Mexico.

Grillparzer (gril'pär''tsẹr), Franz (1791–1872), Austrian poet and dramatist.

Grimaldi (gri-mäl'di), Joseph (1779–1837), Eng. pantomimist and actor.

Grimm (fon grim), Friedrich Melchior, Baron von (1723–1807), Fr. writer, born in Germany.

Grimm, Jakob Ludwig Karl (1785–1863), Ger. philologist, scholar, and collector of fairy-tales.

Grimm, Wilhelm Karl (1786–1859), Ger. philologist, scholar, and collector of fairy-tales (brother of Jakob L. K.).

Grimmelshausen (fon grim'ẹls-hou''zẹn), Hans Jakob Christoffel von (c1625–76), Ger. author.

Grindal (grin'dạl), Edmund (1519?–83), Eng. Protestant prelate, archbishop of Canterbury.

Grisi (grē'sē), Giulia (Comtesse de Melcy, Contessa di Candia) (1811–69), It. operatic soprano singer.

Griswold (griz'wọld), Rufus Wilmot (1815–57), Am. editor and critic.

Grocyn (grō'sin), William (c1446–1519), Eng. Greek scholar.

Grolier de Servières (grō-lyā dẹ ser-vyär), Jean (Vicomte d'Aguisy) (1479–1565), Fr. bibliophile.

Groot (grōt), Gerhard, or Geert (as Latinized, Gerhardus Magnus) (1340–84), Dutch mystic, founder of the religious society called Brethren of the Common Life.

Gros (grō), Antoine Jean, Baron (1771–1835), Fr. painter.

Grose (grōs), Francis (c1731–91), Eng. antiquary.

Gross (grōs), Hans (1847–1915), Austrian criminologist.

Grosseteste (grōs'test), Robert (c1175–1253), Eng. bishop and scholar.

Grote (grōt), George (1794–1871), Eng. historian.

Grotius (grō'shius), Hugo (Hugo de Groot) (1583–1645), Dutch jurist, statesman, and theological and misc. writer.

Grouchy (dẹ grö-shē), Emmanuel, Marquis de (1766–1847), Fr. marshal.

Grousset (grö-sā), Paschal (1844–1909), Fr. journalist and politician, member of Commune of 1871.

Grove (grōv), Sir George (1820–1900), Eng. editor, and writer on music.

Gruen (grün). See *Grün.*

Gruenewald (grü'nẹ-vält). See *Grünewald.*

Grün (grün), Anastasius. Pseudonym of Graf von Auersperg.

Grundtvig (grúnt'vig), Nikolai Frederik Severin (1783–1872), Dan. theologian, poet, and misc. writer.

Grünewald (grü'nẹ-vält), Matthias (d. c1530), Ger. painter.

Guardi (gwär'dē), Francesco (1712–93), Venetian painter.

Guarini (gwä-rē'nē), Giovanni Battista (1537–1612), It. poet.

Guarneri (gwär-nā'rē), Giuseppe Antonio (Joseph Guarnerius) (1683–1745), It. violin-maker, of Cremona.

Guericke (fon gä'ri-kẹ), Otto von (1602–86), Ger. physicist.

Guérin (dẹ gä-raṅ), Eugénie de (1805–48), Fr. writer (sister of Georges M.).

Guérin, Georges Maurice de (1810–39), Fr. author.

Guérin, Jules (1866–   ), Am. painter and illustrator.

Guerrero (ger-rä'rō), Vicente (1782?–1831), Mex. revolutionary leader.

Guesde (ged), Jules Basile (1845–1922), Fr. socialist leader.

Guest (gest), Lady Charlotte. See *Schreiber.*

Guevara (dä gä-vä'rä), Antonio de (c1490–1545), Sp. bishop, chronicler, and misc. writer.

Guicciardini (gwēt-chär-dē'nē), Francesco (1483–1540), It. statesman and historian.

Guidi (gwē'dē), Tommaso. See *Masaccio.*

Guido d'Arezzo (gwē'dō dä-ret'sō) (c990–c1050), It. or Fr. monk, reformer of musical notation.

Guido Reni. See *Reni, Guido.*

Guilbert (gēl-bār), Yvette (Mme. Schiller) (1868–   ), Fr. singer and entertainer.

Guilford (gil'fọrd), Francis North, 1st Baron (1637–85), Eng. lawyer and statesman.

Guilford, Frederick North, 2d Earl of (Lord North) (1732–92), Eng. statesman (great-grandson of 1st Baron Guilford).

Guillaume de Lorris (gē-yōm dẹ lo-rēs) (fl. c1230), Fr. poet, author of first part of "Roman de la Rose."

Guilmant (gēl-män), Félix Alexandre (1837–1911), Fr. organist and composer.

Guimerá (gē-mä-rä'), Ángel (1849–1924), Catalan poet and dramatist.

Guiney (gī'ni), Louise Imogen (1861–1920), Am. poet and essayist, in England.

Guiscard, Robert. See *Robert Guiscard.*

Guise (dẹ güēz), Charles de Lorraine, Cardinal de. See *Lorraine, Cardinal de.*

Guise, François de Lorraine, 2d Duc de (1519–63), Fr. general and statesman.

Guise, Henri I. de Lorraine, 3d Duc de (1550–88), Fr. general and politician (son of 2d Duc de Guise).

Guise, Henri II. de Lorraine, 5th Duc de (1614–64), Fr. soldier and adventurer (grandson of 3d Duc de Guise).

Guitry (gē-trē), Lucien (1860–1925), Fr. actor.

Guitry, Sacha (1885–   ), Fr. actor and dramatist, born in Russia (son of Lucien).

Guizot (gē-zō), François Pierre Guillaume (1787–1874), Fr. historian and statesman.

Gundobad (gun'dọ-bad) or **Gundobald** (gun'dọ-bȧld) (d. 516), king of the Burgundians.

Gunter (gun'tẹr), Edmund (1581–1626), Eng. mathematician.

Gurko (gör'kō), Osip Vladimirovich (1828–1901), Russ. general.

Gurney (gẹr'ni), Edmund (1847–88), Eng. philosophical writer and investigator of psychical phenomena.

Gustavus I. (gus-tā'vus) (in Swedish, Gustaf, commonly known as Gustavus Vasa) (1496–1560), king of Sweden (1523–60).

Gustavus II. (Gustavus Adolphus) (1594–1632), king of Sweden (1611–32) (son of Charles IX. of Sweden).

Gustavus III. (1746–92), king of Sweden (1771–92).

Gustavus IV. (Gustavus Adolphus) (1778–1837), king of Sweden (1792–1809) (son of Gustavus III.).

Gustavus V. (1858–   ), king of Sweden (1907–   ) (son of Oscar II.).

Gutenberg (gö'tẹn-berch), Johann (real name Johann Gensfleisch) (c1398–1468), Ger. printer, reputed inventor of printing with movable types.

Gutzkow (gúts'kō), Karl Ferdinand (1811–78), Ger. novelist, dramatist, and misc. writer.

Guy of Lusignan (gī, Fr. gē, lü-zē-nyäṅ) (d. 1194), king of Jerusalem (1186–92), and king of Cyprus (1192–94).

Guyon (gī'ọn, Fr. gē-yôṅ), Mme. (Jeanne Marie Bouvier, Mme. de La Motte-Guyon) (1648–1717), Fr. mystic and writer.

Guyot (gē-yō), Yves (1843–1928), Fr. politician, economist, and publicist.

Guzmán Blanco (gös-män' bläng'kō), Antonio (1830–99), Venezuelan political leader.

---

fat, fāte, fär, fȧll, ȧsk, färe; net, mē, hẹr; pin, pīne; not, nōte, mȯve, nȯr; up, lūte, pủll; oi, oil; ou, out; (lightened) avīạry, ẹlect, agọny, intọ, ụnite; (obscured) errạnt, operạ, ardẹnt, actọr, natụre; ch, chip; g, go; th, thin; ŦH, then; y, you;

Gwyn or **Gwinn** (gwin), Eleanor, or Nell (1650—87), Eng. actress, mistress of Charles II.

Gyp (zhēp). Pseudonym of Comtesse de Martel de Janville.

H

Haakon I. or **Hakon I.** (hâ′kon) ("the Good") (d. 961), king of Norway (934?—961) (son of Harald I. of Norway).

Haakon VII. (before election to throne of Norway, Prince Charles of Denmark) (1872—   ), king of Norway (1905—   ) (son of Frederick VIII. of Denmark).

Häckel (hek′el). See *Haeckel*.

Hacket (hak′et), John (1592—1670), Eng. bishop and writer.

Hackett (hak′et), Horatio Balch (1808—75), Am. Biblical scholar.

Haden (hā′dn), Sir Francis Seymour (1818—1910), Eng. surgeon and etcher.

Hading (à-dan), Jane (professional name of Jeanne Alfrédine Tréfouret, Mme. Koning) (1859—1941), Fr. actress.

Hadley (had′li), Arthur Twining (1856—1930), Am. educator and political economist (son of James).

Hadley, James (1821—72), Am. philologist and Greek scholar.

Hadrian (hā′dri-an) (Publius Ælius Hadrianus) (A.D. 76—138), Rom. emperor (117—138).

Hadrian (popes). See *Adrian*.

Haeckel (hek′el), Ernst Heinrich (1834—1919), Ger. biologist and philosophical writer.

Haendel (hen′del). See *Handel* (*Händel*).

Haering (hā′ring). See *Häring*.

Hafiz (hä′fiz) (pseudonym of Shams-ed-Din Muhammad) (d. c1389), Pers. lyric poet.

Hagenbach (hä′gen-bäch), Karl Rudolf (1801—74), Swiss theologian and church historian.

Haggard (hag′ärd), Sir Henry Rider (1856—1925), Eng. novelist.

Hahnemann (hä′ne-män), Samuel Christian Friedrich (1755—1843), Ger. physician, founder of homeopathy.

Haidar Ali. See *Hyder Ali*.

Haig (hāg), Douglas Haig, 1st Earl (1861—1928), Br. field-marshal.

Hailes (hālz), Lord. See *Dalrymple, Sir David*.

Hainisch (hī′nish), Michael (1858—1940), Austrian writer, president of Austria (1920—28).

Hakluyt (hak′lŏt), Richard (1552?—1616), Eng. geographer and compiler.

Hakon. See *Haakon*.

Halbe (häl′be), Max (1865—   ), Ger. dramatist.

Haldane (hâl′dān), John Scott (1860—1936), Br. physiologist and scientist (brother of Viscount Haldane).

Haldane, Richard Burdon Haldane, Viscount (1856—1928), Br. statesman, jurist, and philosophical writer.

Haldimand (hâl′di-mand), Sir Frederick (1718—91), Swiss general in service of Great Britain in America, governor in Canada (1778—84).

Hale (hāl), Edward Everett (1822—1909), Am. clergyman and author.

Hale, George Ellery (1868—1938), Am. astronomer.

Hale, John Parker (1806—73), Am. statesman.

Hale, Sir Matthew (1609—76), Eng. jurist, lord chief justice (1671—76).

Hale, Nathan (1755—76), Am. patriot, executed by British as a spy.

Hales (hālz), John ("the Ever-Memorable") (1584—1656), Eng. divine and scholar.

Halévy (à-lā-vē), Jacques François Fromental Élie (1799—1862), Fr. musical composer.

Halévy, Ludovic (1834—1908), Fr. dramatist and novelist.

Haliburton (hal′i-bėr-ton), Thomas Chandler (1796—1865), Nova Scotia judge and humorist, creator of Sam Slick.

Halifax (hal′i-faks), Charles Montagu, Earl of (1661—1715), Eng. statesman, financier, and poet.

Halifax, George Savile, 1st Marquis of (1633—95), Eng. statesman, orator, and writer.

Hall (hâl), Charles Francis (1821—71), Am. arctic explorer.

Hall, Edward (c1499—1547), Eng. chronicler.

Hall, Fitzedward (1825—1901), Am. philologist in England.

Hall, Granville Stanley (1846—1924), Am. educator and psychologist.

Hall, Joseph (1574—1656), Eng. bishop and satirist.

Hall, Marshall (1790—1857), Eng. physician.

Hallam (hal′am), Henry (1777—1859), Eng. historian.

Halleck (hal′ek), Fitz-Greene (1790—1867), Am. poet.

Halleck, Henry Wager (1815—72), Am. general.

Haller (fon häl′ėr), Albrecht von (1708—77), Swiss anatomist.

Halley (hal′i), Edmund (1656—1742), Eng. astronomer.

Hals (häls), Frans (1580?—1666), Dutch painter.

Halsey (hâl′si), Jr., William F. (1882—   ), Am. admiral.

Hamerton (ham′ėr-ton), Philip Gilbert (1834—94), Eng. artist and writer.

Hamilcar (ha-mil′kär) (surnamed Barca or Barcas) (d. 229? B.C.), Carthaginian general.

Hamilton (ham′il-ton), Alexander (1757—1804), Am. statesman and political writer.

Hamilton, Anthony, Count (1646?—1720), Fr. courtier and writer (born in Ireland), chiefly notable as author of the memoirs of his brother-in-law Comte de Gramont.

Hamilton, Lady Emma (born Amy, or Emily, Lyon) (1765?—1815), mistress of Viscount Nelson.

Hamilton, Gail. Pseudonym of Mary A. Dodge.

Hamilton, Sir Ian Standish Monteith (1853—   ), Br. general.

Hamilton, John McLure (1853—1936), Am.-Eng. portrait-painter.

Hamilton, Sir William (1788—1856), Sc. philosopher.

Hamilton, Sir William Rowan (1805—65), Br. mathematician.

Hamlin (ham′lin), Hannibal (1809—91), Am. statesman, vice-president of U. S. (1861—65).

Hammond (ham′ond), Henry (1605—60), Eng. divine and scholar.

Hammond, John Hays (1855—1936), Am. mining engineer.

Hammond, John Hays (1888—   ), Am. inventor (son of J. H. Hammond, 1855—1936).

Hammurabi (ham-ö-rä′bē) or **Khammurabi** (kam-ö-rä′bē) (fl. c2250 or c2100 or c1950 B.C.), king of Babylonia.

Hampden (hamp′den), John (1594—1643), Eng. parliamentary leader.

Hampden, Walter (professional name of Walter Hampden Dougherty) (1879—   ), Am. actor.

Hampton (hamp′ton), Wade (1754—1835), Am. general.

Hampton, Wade (1818—1902), Am. politician and Confederate general (grandson of Wade Hampton, 1754—1835).

Hamsun (häm′sun), Knut (1859—   ), Norw. novelist.

Hancock (han′kok), John (1737—93), Am. statesman, first signer of Declaration of Independence.

Hancock, Winfield Scott (1824—86), Am. general.

Handel (han′del), George Frederick (in German, Georg Friedrich Händel, pron. hen′del) (1685—1759), Ger.-Eng. musical composer.

Hanna (han′a), Marcus Alonzo (1837—1904), Am. business man and politician.

Hannibal (han′i-bal) (247—183? B.C.), Carthaginian general, enemy of Rome (son of Hamilcar Barca).

Hanno (han′ō) ("Hanno the Great") (c275—c195 B.C.), Carthaginian general and statesman, opponent of Hamilcar Barca and Hannibal.

Hanotaux (à-no-tō), Albert Auguste Gabriel (1853—1944), Fr. statesman and historian.

Harald (har′ald) or **Harold** (har′old) ("Harold Bluetooth") (d. 986?), king of Denmark (c940—986?) (son of Gorm the Old).

Harald I. or **Harold I.** (surnamed Haarfager or Harfagr) (d. 933), king of Norway (860—930?).

Harald III. or **Harold III.** (surnamed Haardraade or Hardrade) (1015—66), king of Norway (1046—66).

Harbord (här′bord), James Guthrie (1866—   ), Am. general.

Harcourt (här′kort), Simon Harcourt, 1st Viscount (c1661—1727), Eng. statesman.

Harcourt, Sir William George Granville Venables Vernon (1827—1904), Eng. statesman.

Hardecanute (här″de-ka-nūt′), **Hardicanute** (här″di-ka-nūt′), or **Hardacnut** (här-da-knöt′) (c1019—42), king of England (1040—42), and of Denmark (1035—42) (half-brother and successor of Harold I., and son of Canute).

Hardee (här′dẹ), William Joseph (1815—73), Am. Confederate general.

Harden (här′dẹn), Maximilian (orig. Witkowski) (1861—1927), Ger. journalist and author.

Hardenberg (fon här′dẹn-berċh), Friedrich von ("Novalis") (1772—1801), Ger. author.

Hardenberg, Karl August, Prince von (1750—1822), Prussian statesman.

Hardie (här′di), James Keir (1856—1915), Br. labor leader.

Harding (här′ding), Warren Gamaliel (1865—1923), 29th president of U. S. (1921—23).

Hardinge (här′ding), Henry Hardinge, 1st Viscount (1785—1856), Eng. field-marshal.

Hardinge of Penshurst (penz′hèrst), Charles Hardinge, 1st Baron (1858—   ), Eng. diplomatist and statesman (grandson of 1st Viscount Hardinge).

Hardouin (är-dwaṅ), Jean (1646—1729), Fr. Jesuit and classical scholar.

Hardouin-Mansart, Jules. See *Mansart*.

Hardy (är-dē), Alexandre (c1570—c1631), Fr. dramatist.

Hardy (här′di), Thomas (1840—1928), Eng. novelist and poet.

Hare (hâr), Augustus John Cuthbert (1834—1903), Eng. writer.

Hare, Sir John (1844—1921), Eng. actor and theatrical manager.

Hargraves (här′grāvz), Edmund Hammond (1816—91), Eng. colonist, pioneer in gold-mining in Australia.

Hargreaves (här′grēvz), James (d. 1778), Eng. inventor (of spinning machinery).

Häring (hâ′ring), Georg Wilhelm Heinrich ("Willibald Alexis") (1798—1871), Ger. novelist.

Harington (har′ing-tọn), Sir John (1561—1612), Eng. poet, translator, and misc. writer.

Harkness (härk′nes), Albert (1822—1907), Am. Latin scholar.

Harlan (här′lạn), John Marshall (1833—1911), Am. jurist, associate justice of U. S. Supreme Court (1877—1911).

Harland (här′lạnd), Henry ("Sidney Luska") (1861—1905), Am.-Eng. novelist.

Harland, Marion. Pseudonym of Mrs. Terhune.

Harley (här′li), Robert. See *Oxford, 1st Earl of*.

Harmensen (här′men-sen), Jacob. See *Arminius*.

Harmodius (här-mō′di-us) and **Aristogiton** (a-ris-tọ-jī′ton) (d. 514 B.C.), Athenian tyrannicides, slayers of Hipparchus.

Harmsworth (härmz′wèrth). See *Northcliffe* and *Rothermere*.

Harnack (fon här′näk), Adolf von (1851—1930), Ger. theologian and church historian, born in Russia.

Harney (här′ni), William Selby (1800—89), Am. general.

Haro (dä ä′rō), Don Luis de (1598—1661), Sp. statesman, favorite of Philip IV. (nephew of Count of Olivares).

Harold I. (har′ọld) (surnamed Harefoot) (d. 1040), king of England (1035—40) (son of Canute).

Harold II. (c1022—66), king of England (1066) (successor of Edward the Confessor, and son of Earl Godwin).

Harold (of Norway). See *Harald*.

Harold Bluetooth. See *Harald*.

Harpignies (är-pē-nyē), Henri Joseph (1819—1916), Fr. landscape-painter.

Harriman (har′i-mạn), Edward Henry (1848—1909), Am. railroad financier.

Harrington (har′ing-tọn), James (1611—77), Eng. political writer.

Harris (har′is), James. See *Malmesbury, 1st Earl of*.

Harris, Joel Chandler (1848—1908), Am. writer, creator of Uncle Remus.

Harrison (har′i-sọn), Benjamin (c1740—91), Am. patriot.

Harrison, Benjamin (1833—1901), 23d president of U. S. (1889—93) (grandson of William H.).

Harrison, Frederic (1831—1923), Eng. philosophical and misc. writer.

Harrison, Henry Sydnor (1880—1930), Am. novelist.

Harrison, Lovell Birge (1854—1929), Am. painter (brother of T. Alexander).

Harrison, Thomas Alexander (1853—1930), Am. painter.

Harrison, William Henry (1773—1841), Am. general, and 9th president of U. S. (1841) (son of Benjamin Harrison, c1740—91).

Hart (härt), Albert Bushnell (1854—1943), Am. historian and educator.

Hart, Sir Robert (1835—1911), Br. official, administrator in Chinese service.

Harte (härt), Francis Bret (1839—1902), Am. writer, esp. of short stories.

Hartington (här′ting-tọn), Marquis of. See *Devonshire, 8th Duke of*.

Hartley (härt′li), David (1705—57), Eng. physician and philosopher.

Hartmann (fon härt′män), Felix von (1851—1919), Ger. cardinal.

Hartmann, Karl Robert Eduard von (1842—1906), Ger. philosopher.

Hartmann von Aue (fon ou′ė) (c1170—after 1210), Ger. poet.

Hartzenbusch (här′tsẹn-búsh), Juan Eugenio (1806—80), Sp. dramatist.

Harun al-Rashid (hä-rön′ äl-rä-shēd′) (763 or 766—809), calif of Bagdad (786—809).

Harvard (här′vặrd), John (1607—38), Eng. clergyman in America, first benefactor of Harvard College.

Harvey (här′vi), Gabriel (c1545—1630), Eng. writer.

Harvey, George Brinton McClellan (1864—1928), Am. editor and diplomatist.

Harvey, Sir John Martin- (1863—   ), Eng. actor and theatrical manager.

Harvey, William (1578—1657), Eng. physician, discoverer of circulation of blood.

Hasdrubal (haz′drö-bạl) (d. 221 B.C.), Carthaginian general (son-in-law of Hamilcar Barca).

Hasdrubal (d. 207 B.C.), Carthaginian general (brother of Hannibal).

Hasdrubal (fl. c150 B.C.), Carthaginian general, conquered by Scipio the Younger.

Hase (fon hä′zė), Karl August von (1800—90), Ger. theologian and church historian.

Hassam (has′ạm), Childe (1859—1935), Am. painter.

Hasting (hãs′ting) or **Hastings** (hãs′tingz) (9th cent.), Scand. viking.

Hastings, Francis Rawdon-Hastings, 1st Marquis of (orig. Francis Rawdon) (1754—1826), Br. military commander, governor-general of India.

Hastings, Warren (1732—1818), Eng. statesman, first governor-general of India.

Hastings, William Hastings, Baron (c1430—83), Eng. soldier and ambassador, accused of treason by Duke of Gloucester (later Richard III.) and beheaded.

Hatasu (hä′tä-sö), or **Hatshepsut** (hät-shep′süt), or **Hatchepset** (hät-chep′set) (fl. c1500 B.C.), queen of Egypt, of 18th dynasty.

Hatto I. (hät′ō) (c850—913), archbishop of Mainz, and regent of Germany.

Hatton (hat′n), Sir Christopher (1540—91), lord chancellor of England, and favorite of Queen Elizabeth.

Hatzfeld (häts-feld), Adolphe (1824—1900), Fr. lexicographer and critic.

Hauff (houf), Wilhelm (1802—27), Ger. novelist and poet.

Haugwitz (fon houk′vits), Christian August Heinrich Kurt, Graf von (1752—1831), Prussian statesman.

Haupt (houpt), Paul (1858—1926), Ger.-Am. Assyriologist and Biblical scholar.

Hauptmann (houpt′män), Gerhart (1862—1946), Ger. dramatist and poet.

Haussmann (ōs-män), Georges Eugène, Baron (1809—91), Fr. administrator and politician.

Haüy (ä-üē), René Just (known as Abbé Haüy) (1743—1822), Fr. mineralogist.

Havelock (hav′lok), Sir Henry (1795—1857), Eng. general, in India.

Hawke (hâk), Edward Hawke, 1st Baron (1705—81), Eng. admiral.

Hawker (hâ′kèr), Robert Stephen (1803—75), Eng. poet.

Hawkins (hâ′kinz), Sir Anthony Hope ("Anthony Hope") (1863—1933), Eng. novelist.

Hawkins or **Hawkyns** (hâ′kinz), Sir John (1532—95), Eng. slave-trader and admiral.

---

fat, fāte, fär, fȧll, ȧsk, fâre; net, mē, hẽr; pin, pīne; not, nōte, mōve, nôr; up, lūte, pull; oi, oil; ou, out; (lightened) aviȧry, ẹlect, agọny, intọ, ūnite; (obscured) errạnt, operạ, ardẹnt, actọr, natūre; ch, chip; g, go; th, thin; ŦH, then; y, you;

Hawkins or **Hawkyns,** Sir Richard (1562?—1622), Eng. buccaneer and naval commander (son of Sir John).

Hawkwood (dẻ hȧk'wụd), Sir John de (d. 1394), Eng. condottiere, esp. in service of Florence.

Hawthorne (hȧ'thȯrn), Nathaniel (1804—64), Am. writer of romances and tales.

Hawtrey (hȧ'tri), Sir Charles (1858—1923), Eng. actor and theatrical manager.

Hay (hā), John (1838—1905), Am. statesman and author.

Haydn (hā'dn, Ger. hī'dn), Franz Joseph (1732—1809), Austrian musical composer.

Haydon (hā'dọn), Benjamin Robert (1786—1846), Eng. historical painter.

Hayes (hāz), Patrick Joseph (1867—1938), Am. cardinal.

Hayes, Rutherford Birchard (1822—93), 19th president of U. S. (1877—81).

Haynau (fon hī'nou), Julius Jakob, Freiherr von (1786—1853), Austrian general.

Hayne (hān), Isaac (1745—81), Am. patriot.

Hayne, Paul Hamilton (1831—86), Am. poet (nephew of Robert Y.).

Hayne, Robert Young (1791—1839), Am. political leader.

Haywood (hā'wụd), Mrs. (Eliza Fowler) (1693?—1756), Eng. novelist and misc. writer.

Hazlitt (haz'lit), William (1778—1830), Eng. critic and essayist.

Head (hed), Sir Francis Bond (1793—1875), Eng. soldier, traveler, and author, and colonial governor in Canada.

Healy (hē'li), Timothy Michael (1855—1931), Ir. political leader, governor-general of the Irish Free State (1922—28).

Hearn (hẻrn), Lafcadio (1850—1904), writer in English in America and Japan, born of Ir.-Gr. parentage in Leucadia, Ionian Islands, and a naturalized citizen of Japan.

Hearne (hẻrn), Thomas (1678—1735), Eng. antiquary.

Hearst (hẻrst), William Randolph (1863—   ), Am. publisher.

Heath (hēth), William (1737—1814), Am. Revolutionary general.

Hebbel (heb'ẹl), Friedrich (1813—63), Ger. poet and dramatist.

Heber (hē'bẻr), Reginald (1783—1826), Eng. bishop and hymn-writer.

Hébert (ā-bãr), Jacques René ("Père Duchesne") (1757—94), Fr. journalist and revolutionist.

Hecker (hek'ẻr), Isaac Thomas (1819—88), Am. Rom. Cath. priest, founder of the Paulists.

Hedin (hā-dēn'), Sven Anders (1865—   ), Swed. explorer in Asia.

Heem (dẻ hām), Jan Davidsz de (c1600—83?), Dutch painter.

Heemskerk (vän hāms'kerk), Jacob van (1567—1607), Dutch admiral.

Hegel (hā'gẹl), Georg Wilhelm Friedrich (1770—1831), Ger. philosopher.

Hegesippus (hej-ẹ-sip'us) (fl. c150—c180), Christian writer at Rome, born (apparently) in Palestine.

Heiberg (hī'berch), Johan Ludvig (1791—1860), Dan. poet, dramatist, and critic.

Heidenstam (fon hī'dẹn-stäm), Karl Gustaf Verner von (1859—1940), Swed. poet, novelist, and misc. writer.

Heifetz (hī'fets), Jascha (1901—   ), Russ. violinist in America.

Heilprin (hīl'prin), Angelo (1853—1907), Am. naturalist, born in Hungary.

Heine (hī'nẻ), Heinrich (1797—1856), Ger. poet and misc. writer.

Heinsius (hīn'sẹ-ụs), Daniel (1580—1655), Dutch classical scholar and poet.

Heinsius, Nikolaas (1620—81), Dutch classical scholar and Latin poet (son of Daniel).

Helena (hel'ẹ-nä), Saint (c248—c330), mother of Constantine the Great, celebrated for her piety.

Heliodorus (hē"li-ọ-dō'rus) (fl. c400), Gr. romance-writer.

Heliogabalus. See *Elagabalus.*

Helleu (e-lẻ), Paul César (1859—1927), Fr. artist, esp. in dry-point.

Helmholtz (fon helm'holts), Hermann Ludwig Ferdinand von (1821—94), Ger. physiologist and physicist.

Helmont (vän hel'mont), Jan Baptista van (1577—1644), Flemish physician and chemist.

Héloïse (ā-lō-ēz) (c1101—64), pupil, mistress, and wife of Abélard, later abbess.

Helper (hel'pẻr), Hinton Rowan (1829—1909), Am. writer.

Helps (helps), Sir Arthur (1813—75), Eng. author.

Helst (vän dẻr helst), Bartholomeus van der (1613?—70), Dutch painter.

Helvétius (hel-vē'shius, Fr. el-vā-sē-üs), Claude Adrien (1715—71), Fr. philosopher.

Hemans (hē'mạnz), Mrs. (Felicia Dorothea Browne) (1793—1835), Eng. poet.

Heming or **Hemminge** (hem'ing), John (d. 1630), Eng. actor, friend of Shakspere.

Hémon (ā-môṅ), Louis (1880—1913), Fr. novelist, in Canada.

Hempel (hem'pẹl), Frieda (Mrs. Kahn) (1885—   ), Ger.-Am. operatic soprano singer.

Henderson (hen'dẻr-sọn), Alexander (c1583—1646), Sc. Presbyterian divine and diplomatist.

Henderson, Arthur (1863—1935), Br. labor leader and cabinet minister.

Hendricks (hen'driks), Thomas Andrews (1819—85), Am. statesman, vice-president of U. S. (1885).

Hengist (heng'gist) or **Hengest** (heng'gest) (d. 488), a chief of the Jutes, joint founder with his brother Horsa of the English kingdom of Kent.

Henle (hen'lẻ), Friedrich Gustav Jakob (1809—85), Ger. physiologist and anatomist.

Henley (hen'li), William Ernest (1849—1903), Eng. poet and critic.

Hennepin (hen'ẹ-pin, Fr. en-paṅ), Louis (c1640—after 1701), Belgian Rom. Cath. missionary and explorer in America.

Henner (en-ãr), Jean Jacques (1829—1905), Fr. painter.

Henri (hen'rī), Robert (1865—1929), Am. painter.

Henrietta Maria (hen-ri-et'ä mạ-rē'ä) (1609—69), queen of Charles I. of England (daughter of Henry IV. of France).

Henry I. (hen'ri) (called Henry Beauclerc, or 'Henry Fine-Scholar') (1068—1135), king of England (1100—35) (brother of William II.).

Henry II. (of Anjou) (1133—89), king of England (1154—89) (successor of King Stephen, and grandson of Henry I., and son of Geoffrey of Anjou, and first king of Plantagenet line).

Henry III. (of Winchester) (1207—72), king of England (1216—72) (son of King John).

Henry IV. (of Bolingbroke) (1367—1413), king of England (1399—1413) (successor of Richard II., and son of John of Gaunt, and first king of house of Lancaster).

Henry V. (of Monmouth) (1387—1422), king of England (1413—22) (son of Henry IV.).

Henry VI. (of Windsor) (1421—71), king of England (1422—61, 1470—71) (son of Henry V.).

Henry VII. (1457—1509), king of England (1485—1509) (successor of Richard III., and first king of house of Tudor).

Henry VIII. (1491—1547), king of England (1509—47) and of Ireland (1541—47) (son of Henry VII.).

Henry I. (in French, Henri, pron. oṅ-rē) (1008?—60), king of France (1031—60) (son of Robert II.).

Henry II. (1519—59), king of France (1547—59) (son of Francis I.).

Henry III. (1551—89), king of France (1574—89) (brother of Charles IX.).

Henry IV. (of Navarre) (1553—1610), king of France (1589—1610) (successor of Henry III., and first king of house of Bourbon).

Henry I. (in German, Heinrich, pron. hīn'rich, called "the Fowler") (c876—936), king of Germany (919—936).

Henry II., Saint (972 or 973—1024), emperor of the Holy Roman Empire (1002—24) (great-grandson of Henry the Fowler).

Henry III. ("the Black") (1017—56), emperor of the Holy Roman Empire (1039—56) (son of Conrad II.).

Henry IV. (1050—1106), emperor of the Holy Roman Empire (1056—1106) (son of Henry the Black).

Henry V. (1081—1125), emperor of the Holy Roman Empire (1106—25) (son of Emperor Henry IV.).

Henry VI. (1165—97), emperor of the Holy Roman Empire (1190—97) (son of Frederick Barbarossa).

(variable) ḍ as d or j, ş as s or sh, ţ as t or ch, ẓ as z or zh; o, F. cloche; ü, F. menu; ċh, Sc. loch; ṅ, F. bonbon; ', primary accent; ", secondary accent; †, obsolete; <, from; +, and; =, equals. See also lists at beginning of book.

Henry VII. (1269—1313), emperor of the Holy Roman Empire (1308—13).

Henry ("the Lion") (1129—95), duke of Saxony and Bavaria.

Henry, Joseph (1797—1878), Am. physicist.

Henry, O. Pseudonym of W. S. Porter.

Henry, Patrick (1736—99), Am. orator and statesman.

Henry of Portugal (called "Henry the Navigator") (1394—1460), Pg. prince and soldier, promoter of geographical study and exploration (son of King John I.).

Henryson (hen′ri-son), Robert (c1430—c1500), Sc. poet.

Henslowe (henz′lō), Philip (d. 1616), Eng. theatrical manager.

Henty (hen′ti), George Alfred (1832—1902), Eng. writer of books for boys.

Hepplewhite (hep′l-hwīt), George (d. 1786), Eng. cabinet-maker and furniture-designer.

Heraclitus (her-a-klī′tus) ("the Weeping Philosopher") (c535—c475 B.C.), Gr. philosopher.

Heraclius (her-a-klī′us) (c575—641), Byzantine emperor (610—641).

Hérault de Séchelles (ā-rō dè sā-shel), Marie Jean (1760—94), Fr. revolutionist.

Herbart (her′bärt), Johann Friedrich (1776—1841), Ger. philosopher.

Herbert (her′bèrt), George (1593—1633), Eng. poet.

Herbert, Sir Thomas (1606—82), Eng. traveler in Persia, and writer.

Herbert, Victor (1859—1924), Ir.-Am. musical composer and conductor.

Herbert of Cherbury, Edward Herbert, 1st Baron (1583—1648), Eng. philosopher and historian.

Herder (fon her′dèr), Johann Gottfried von (1744—1803), Ger. critical, philosophical, and misc. writer.

Heredia (dè ā-rä-dē-ä), José Maria de (1842—1905), Fr. poet, born in Cuba.

Hereward (her′e-wàrd) ("Hereward the Wake") (fl. c1070), Eng. outlaw and patriot, famous for resistance to Norman rule.

Hergesheimer (her′ges-hī″mèr), Joseph (1880—   ), Am. novelist.

Hering (hā′ring), Ewald (1834—1918), Ger. physiologist and psychologist.

Herkimer (her′ki-mèr), Nicholas (1715?—77), Am. Revolutionary general.

Herkomer (her′kō-mèr, Ger. fon her′kō″mèr), Sir Hubert von (1849—1914), Eng. painter, born in Bavaria.

Hermant (er-män), Abel (1862—   ), Fr. author.

Hermes (her′mes), Georg (1775—1831), Ger. Rom. Cath. theologian.

Hero. See *Heron.*

Herodas (hē-rō′das) or **Herondas** (hē-ron′das) (fl. 3d cent. B.C.), Gr. poet.

Herodotus (he-rod′ō-tus) (484?—425? B.C.), Gr. historian.

Hérold (ā-rold), Louis Joseph Ferdinand (1791—1833), Fr. operatic composer.

Heron (hē′ron) or **Hero** (hē′rō) (fl. 1st cent., or earlier), Gr. mathematician and mechanician, of Alexandria.

Herondas. See *Herodas.*

Herrera (dā er-rā′rä), Fernando de (1534?—97), Sp. poet.

Herrera, Francisco (1576—1656), Sp. painter.

Herrera, Francisco (1622—85), Sp. painter (son of Francisco Herrera, 1576—1656).

Herrera, José Joaquín de (1792—1854), Mex. general and statesman, president of Mexico (1844—45, 1848—51).

Herreros, Manuel Bretón de los. See *Bretón de los Herreros.*

Herrick (her′ik), Myron T. (1854—1929), Am. diplomatist.

Herrick, Robert (1591—1674), Eng. poet.

Herrick, Robert (1868—1938), Am. novelist.

Herriot (e-rē-ō), Édouard (1872—   ), Fr. author, political leader, and statesman.

Herschel (her′shel), Caroline Lucretia (1750—1848), Ger.-Eng. astronomer (sister of Sir William).

Herschel, Sir John Frederick William (1792—1871), Eng. astronomer (son of Sir William).

Herschel, Sir William (orig. Friedrich Wilhelm Herschel) (1738—1822), Ger.-Eng. astronomer.

Hertling (fon hert′ling), Georg, Graf von (1843—1919), Ger. statesman, imperial chancellor (1917—18).

Hertz (herts), Heinrich (1857—94), Ger. physicist.

Hertz, Henrik (1798—1870), Dan. poet and dramatist.

Hertzen or **Herzen** (hert′sen), Alexander (in Russian, Aleksandr Ivanovich Gertsen) (1812—70), Russ. novelist and political writer.

Hertzog (hert′sŏch), James Barry Munnik (1866—   ), South African general, political leader, and statesman.

Hervey (her′vi), James (1714—58), Eng. divine and devotional writer.

Hervieu (er-vyė), Paul Ernest (1857—1915), Fr. dramatist and novelist.

Herzen. See *Hertzen.*

Herzl (herts′l), Theodor (1860—1904), Austrian Jewish journalist and writer, founder of Zionism.

Herzog (her′tsŏch), Johann Jakob (1805—82), Swiss-Ger. theologian and encyclopedist.

Hesiod (hē′si-od) (fl. 8th? cent. B.C.), Gr. poet.

Hesychius (hē-sik′i-us) (fl. 5th? cent.), Gr. grammarian, of Alexandria.

Heuglin (fon hoi′glin), Theodor von (1824—76), Ger. traveler and ornithologist, esp. in Africa.

Hewlett (hū′let), Maurice Henry (1861—1923), Eng. novelist.

Heylyn or **Heylin** (hā′lin), Peter (1600—62), Eng. divine, controversialist, and historian.

Heyse (fon hī′zė), Paul Johann Ludwig von (1830—1914), Ger. novelist, dramatist, and poet.

Heywood (hā′wůd), John (1497?—1580?), Eng. dramatist and epigrammatist.

Heywood, Thomas (d. c1650), Eng. dramatist and misc. writer.

H. H. Literary signature of Mrs. Helen Hunt Jackson.

Hibben (hib′en), John Grier (1861—1933), Am. educator and philosophical writer.

Hichens (hich′enz), Robert Smythe (1864—   ), Eng. novelist.

Hicks (hiks), Elias (1748—1830), Am. Quaker preacher, founder of branch of Friends called Hicksites.

Hidalgo y Costilla (ē-däl′gō ē kos-tēl′yä), Miguel (1753—1811), Mex. priest and revolutionary leader.

Hiero I. (hī′e-rō) or **Hieron I.** (hī′e-ron) (d. 467 B.C.), tyrant of Syracuse (brother of Gelon).

Hiero II. or **Hieron II.** (d. 216 B.C.), king of Syracuse.

Hieronymus (hī-e-ron′i-mus). See *Jerome, Saint.*

Higginson (hig′in-son), Thomas Wentworth (1823—1911), Am. author.

Hilary (or **Hilarius**) **of Arles** (hil′a-ri, hi-lā′ri-us), Saint (c401—449), Fr. archbishop.

Hilary (or **Hilarius**) **of Poitiers,** Saint (c300—368), Fr. bishop and theologian.

Hildebrand (hil′de-brand). See *Gregory VII.*

Hildebrandt (hil′dė-bränt), Ferdinand Theodor (1804—74), Ger. painter.

Hill (hil), Ambrose Powell (1825—65), Am. Confederate general.

Hill, David Bennett (1843—1910), Am. politician.

Hill, David Jayne (1850—1932), Am. educator, diplomatist, and author.   [born in Canada.

Hill, James Jerome (1838—1916), Am. railroad promoter,

Hill, Octavia (1838—1912), Eng. social reformer.

Hill, Sir Rowland (1795—1879), Eng. educator and administrator, originator of penny postage.

Hillel (hil′el) (fl. c30 B.C.—A.D. c10), Jewish scholar and sage at Jerusalem, born in Babylonia.   [composer.

Hiller (hil′èr), Ferdinand (1811—85), Ger. pianist and musical

Himmler (him′lėr), Heinrich (1900—45), Ger. (Nazi) official, chief of political police.

Hincks (hingks), Sir Francis (1807—85), Can. statesman and Br. colonial governor, born in Ireland.

Hincmar (hingk′mär) (c806—882), Fr. archbishop.

Hindenburg (fon hin′den-bůrch), Paul von Beneckendorff und von (1847—1934), Ger. field-marshal, 2d president of Germany (1925—34).

Hipparchus (hi-pär′kus) (d. 514 B.C.), tyrant of Athens (brother of Hippias).

Hipparchus (fl. 146—126 B.C.), Gr. astronomer and mathematician.

Hippias (hip′i-as) (d. c490 B.C.), tyrant of Athens (son of Pisistratus).

---

fat, fāte, fär, fȧll, ȧsk, fāre; net, mē, her; pin, pīne; not, nōte, mȯve, nôr; up, lūte, půll; oi, oil; ou, out; (lightened) avĭary, ėlect, agȯny, intȯ, ūnite; (obscured) errant, operä, ardent, actor, natūre; ch, chip; g, go; th, thin; ᴛʜ, then; y, you:

Hippocrates (hi-pok'ra̱-tēz) (460?–c357 B.C.), Gr. physician.

Hippolytus (hi-pol'i-tus) (d. c236), Christian theologian and schismatic bishop, in Rome.

Hirohito (hē-rō-hē'tō) (1901–), emperor of Japan (1926–) (son of Emperor Yoshihito).

Hirsch (dė hirsh), Maurice, Baron de (Moritz Hirsch, Freiherr auf Gereuth) (1831–96), Ger. Jewish philanthropist.

Hitler (hit'lėr), Adolf (1889–1945), "leader" (G. *führer* or *fuehrer*) and chancellor of Germany (born in Austria).

Hittorf (hit'ȯrf), Johann Wilhelm (1824–1914), Ger. physicist.

Hittorff (hit'ȯrf, Fr. ē-tȯrf), Jacques Ignace (1792–1867), Fr. architect, born at Cologne.

Hoar (hōr), George Frisbie (1826–1904), Am. legislator.

Hobart (hō'ba̱rt), Garret Augustus (1844–99), Am. politician, vice-president of U. S. (1897–99).

Hobbema (hob'e-mä), Meyndert (c1638–1709), Dutch landscape-painter.

Hobbes (hobz), John Oliver. Pseudonym of Mrs. Craigie.

Hobbes, Thomas (1588–1679), Eng. philosopher.

Hobson (hob'son), Richmond Pearson (1870–1937), Am. naval officer, politician, and prohibitionist.

Hoccleve (hok'lēv) or **Occleve** (ok'lėv), Thomas (1370?–1450?), Eng. poet.

Hoche (osh), Lazare (1768–97), Fr. general.

Hodler (hōd'lėr), Ferdinand (1853–1918), Swiss painter.

Hoe (hō), Richard March (1812–86), Am. manufacturer and improver of printing-presses.

Hoeffding (hėf'ding). See *Höffding*.

Hoelderlin (hėl'dėr-lēn). See *Hölderlin*.

Hoelty (hėl'tē). See *Hölty*.

Hofer (hō'fėr), Andreas (1767–1810), Tyrolese patriot.

Hoff (vänt hof), Jacobus Hendricus van't (1852–1911), Dutch chemist.

Höffding (hėf'ding), Harald (1843–1931), Dan. philosopher.

Hoffman (hof'man), Charles Fenno (1806–84), Am. author.

Hoffmann (hof'män), August Heinrich (Hoffmann von Fallersleben) (1798–1874), Ger. poet and scholar.

Hoffmann, Ernst Theodor Amadeus (1776–1822), Ger. romance-writer.

Hofmann (fon hof'män), August Wilhelm von (1818–92), Ger. chemist.

Hofmann, Heinrich (1824–1911), Ger. painter.

Hofmann, Josef (1876–), Pol.-Am. pianist and composer.

Hofmann, Ludwig von (1861–), Ger. painter (nephew of Heinrich Hofmann).

Hofmann or **Hoffmann,** Melchior (c1498–1543?), Ger. Anabaptist preacher.

Hofmannsthal (fon hof'mäns-täl), Hugo von (1874–1929), Austrian poet and dramatist.

Hogarth (hō'gärth), William (1697–1764), Eng. painter and engraver.

Hogg (hog), James ("the Ettrick Shepherd") (1770–1835), Sc. poet.

Hohenlohe-Schillingsfürst (fon hō'en-lō"e̱-shil'ings-fürst), Chlodwig Karl Viktor, Prince von (1819–1901), Ger. statesman, imperial chancellor (1894–1900).

Hojeda, Alonso de. See *Ojeda*.

Hokusai (hō'kö-sä-ė̱) (1760–1849), Jap. painter and illustrator.

Holbein (hol'bīn), Hans ("the elder") (c1460–1524), Ger. painter.

Holbein, Hans ("the younger") (1497?–1543), Ger. painter (son of "the elder").

Holberg (hol'berċh), Ludvig, Baron (1684–1754), Dan. dramatist and misc. writer, born in Norway.

Holcroft (hol'krȯft), Thomas (1745–1809), Eng. dramatist and misc. writer.

Hölderlin (hėl'dėr-lēn), Johann Christian Friedrich (1770–1843), Ger. poet.

Holinshed (hol'inz-hed), Raphael (d. c1580), Eng. chronicler.

Holland (hol'and), John Philip (1842–1914), Ir.-Am. inventor (of submarine boat).

Holland, Josiah Gilbert ("Timothy Titcomb") (1819–81), Am. author and editor.

Hollar (hol'är), Wenceslaus (in Bohemian, Vaclav Holar) (1607–77), Bohem. engraver and etcher, in England.

Holles (hol'es), Denzil Holles, 1st Baron (1599–1680), Eng. statesman.

Holmes (hōmz), Mrs. (Mary Jane Hawes) (c1839–1907), Am. novelist.

Holmes, Oliver Wendell (1809–94), Am. physician and author.

Holmes, Oliver Wendell (1841–1935), Am. jurist, associate justice of U. S. Supreme Court (1902–32) (son of O. W. Holmes, 1809–94).

Holroyd (hol'roid), Sir Charles (1861–1917), Eng. painter and etcher.

Holst (fon holst), Hermann Eduard von (1841–1904), Russ.-Ger.-Am. historian.

Holt (hōlt), Henry (1840–1926), Am. publisher and author.

Hölty (hėl'tē), Ludwig Heinrich Christoph (1748–76), Ger. poet.

Home (hōm), Daniel Dunglas (1833–86), Sc. spiritualist medium.

Home, Henry. See *Kames, Lord*.

Home, John (1722–1808), Sc. dramatist.

Homer (hō'mėr) (c10th cent. B.C.), supposed Gr. epic poet, reputed author of "Iliad" and "Odyssey."

Homer, Mrs. (Louise Dilworth Beatty) (c1872–), Am. operatic contralto singer.

Homer, Winslow (1836–1910), Am. painter.

Hondecoeter or **Hondekoeter** (hon'dė-kö-tėr), Melchior (1636?–95), Dutch painter, esp. of birds.

Hone (hōn), William (1780–1842), Eng. political satirist and misc. writer.

Honorius I. (ho̱-nō'ri-us) (d. 638), It. ecclesiastic, pope (625–638).

Honorius, Flavius (384–423), Western Rom. emperor (395–423) (brother of Emperor Arcadius, and son-in-law of Stilicho).

Hontheim (fon hont'hīm), Johann Nikolaus von ("Justinus Febronius") (1701–90), Ger. Rom. Cath. prelate and theologian.

Hooch or **Hoogh** (dė hōċh), Pieter de (c1630–78?), Dutch painter.

Hood (hud), John Bell (1831–79), Am. Confederate general.

Hood, Samuel Hood, 1st Viscount (1724–1816), Eng. admiral.

Hood, Thomas (1799–1845), Eng. poet and humorist.

Hooft (hȯft), Pieter Corneliszoon (1581–1647), Dutch poet and historian.

Hooker (huk'ėr), Joseph (1814–79), Am. general.

Hooker, Sir Joseph Dalton (1817–1911), Eng. botanist and traveler (son of Sir William J.).

Hooker, Richard (1554?–1600), Eng. theological writer.

Hooker, Thomas (1586?–1647), Eng. Puritan divine, one of the founders of the colony of Connecticut.

Hooker, Sir William Jackson (1785–1865), Eng. botanist.

Hooper (hö'pėr), John (c1495–1555), Eng. Protestant bishop and martyr.

Hoorn (hōrn) or **Hoorne** (hōr'nė). See *Horn, Count of* (1518–68).

Hoover (hö'vėr), Herbert Clark (1874–), Am. mining engineer, administrator of war relief in Belgium and food administrator in U. S., 31st president of U. S. (1929–33).

Hope (hōp), Anthony. Pseudonym of Sir A. H. Hawkins.

Hopkins (hop'kinz), Esek (1718–1802), Am. commodore.

Hopkins, Johns (1795–1873), Am. financier and philanthropist, founder of Johns Hopkins University.

Hopkins, Mark (1802–87), Am. clergyman and educator.

Hopkins, Samuel (1721–1803), Am. divine and theologian.

Hopkins, Stephen (1707–85), Am. patriot.

Hopkinson (hop'kin-son), Francis (1737–91), Am. patriot and writer.

Hoppner (hop'nėr), John (1758–1810), Eng. portrait-painter.

Horace (hor'a̱s) (Quintus Horatius Flaccus) (65–8 B.C.), Rom. poet.

Horatius Cocles (ho̱-rā'shius kō'klēz). A legendary hero of ancient Rome, said to have defended a bridge leading to the city against the whole Etruscan army under Porsena, while the Romans broke down the bridge behind him, and finally to have escaped by swimming across the river.

Horn (hȯrn), Arvid Bernhard, Count (1664–1742), Swed. statesman.

Horn (hȯrn), Philip of Montmorency-Nevele, Count of (also

Hoorn, Hoorne, or Hornes) (1518—68), Flemish soldier and patriot.

Hornaday (hôr'nạ-dā), William Temple (1854—1937), Am. zoölogist.

Horne (hôrn), Henry Sinclair Horne, Baron (1861—1929), Br. general.

Horne, Robert Stevenson Horne, Viscount (1871—1940), Br. administrator and statesman.

Hornung (hôr'nung), Ernest William (1866—1921), Eng. novelist.

Horrocks (hor'ọks), Jeremiah (1617?—41), Eng. astronomer.

Horsa (hôr'sạ) (d. 455), a chief of the Jutes, joint founder with his brother Hengist of the English kingdom of Kent.

Hortense (or-toṅs) (Eugénie Hortense de Beauharnais) (1783—1837), wife of Louis Bonaparte, king of Holland (daughter of Alexandre and Joséphine de Beauharnais, and mother of Napoleon III.).

Horthy (hôr'tẹ) **de Nagybánya,** Nikolaus (1868—), Hung. admiral, regent of Hungary (1920—).

Hosmer (hoz'mèr), Harriet Goodhue (1830—1908), Am. sculptor.

Hotspur (hot'spèr). See *Percy, Sir Henry.*

Houdin, Robert. See *Robert-Houdin.*

Houdini (hŏ'dẹ-nẹ), Harry (name orig. Erich Weiss) (1874—1926), Am. magician and writer.

Houdon (ö-dôṅ), Jean Antoine (1741—1828), Fr. sculptor.

Houghton (hō'tọn), Alanson Bigelow (1863—1941), Am. diplomatist.

Houghton (hou'tọn), Richard Monckton Milnes, 1st Baron (1809—85), Eng. statesman, poet, and misc. writer.

House (hous), Edward Mandell (1858—1938), Am. political agent.

Housman (hous'mạn), Alfred Edward (1859—1936), Eng. classical scholar and poet.

Houssaye (ŏ-sā), Arsène (name orig. Housset) (1815—96), Fr. author.

Houston (hūs'tọn), David Franklin (1866—1940), Am. educator and cabinet officer.

Houston, Samuel, or Sam (1793—1863), Am. soldier and political leader, and president of Texas.

Hovenden (hō'vẹn-dẹn), Thomas (1840—95), Ir.-Am. painter.

Howard (hou'ạrd), Bronson (1842—1908), Am. playwright.

Howard, Catharine (d. 1542), fifth wife of Henry VIII. of England.

Howard, Charles. See *Nottingham, 1st Earl of.*

Howard, George William Frederick. See *Carlisle, 7th Earl of.*

Howard, Henry. See *Surrey, Earl of.*

Howard, John (1726—90), Eng. philanthropist and prison reformer.

Howard, Oliver Otis (1830—1909), Am. general.

Howard, Sir Robert (1626—98), Eng. dramatist (brother-in-law of John Dryden).

Howard, Thomas. See *Norfolk, Duke of.*

Howard, William. See *Stafford, Viscount.*

Howe (hou), Elias (1819—67), Am. inventor (of sewing-machine).

Howe, John (1630—1705), Eng. Puritan theologian.

Howe, Joseph (1804—73), Can. statesman.

Howe, Mrs. (Julia Ward) (1819—1910), Am. poet, misc. writer, and reformer.

Howe, Richard Howe, Earl (1726—99), Eng. admiral.

Howe, William Howe, 5th Viscount (1729—1814), Eng. general, in America (brother of Richard, Earl Howe).

Howell (hou'el), James (1594?—1666), Br. author.

Howells (hou'elz), William Dean (1837—1920), Am. novelist.

Howitt (hou'it), William (1792—1879), Eng. writer.

Howitt, Mrs. (Mary Botham) (1799—1888), Eng. writer (wife of William).

Hoyle (hoil), Edmund, or Edmond (1672—1769), Eng. writer on card-games.

Hrabanus Maurus (hrä-bä'nús mou'rús). See *Rabanus Maurus.*

Hrdlička (hrd'lich-kạ), Aleš (1869—1943), Bohem.-Am. anthropologist.

Hrolf. See *Rollo.*

Hroswitha or **Hrosvitha** (hros'vē''tạ) (also called Hrots-

witha and Roswitha) (c935—c1000), Ger. nun, chronicler, and dramatist, writing in Latin.

Huascar (wäs'kär) (c1495—1533), Inca king of Peru, overthrown by his half-brother Atahualpa.

Huber (hŏ'bèr), Johannes (1830—79), Ger. philosophical and theological writer, a leader of the religious body called Old Catholics.

Hubert (hū'bèrt, Fr. ü-bär), Saint (d. 727?), Fr. bishop, patron saint of hunters.

Huc (ük), Évariste Régis (1813—60), Fr. Rom. Cath. missionary and traveler in China and Tibet.

Hudson (hud'sọn), Henry (d. 1611?), Eng. navigator and explorer.

Hudson, William Henry (1841—1922), Eng. naturalist and author, born in Argentina of parents from the U. S.

Huerta (wär'tä), Victoriano (1854—1916), Mex. general, and provisional president of Mexico (1913—14).

Huggins (hug'inz), Sir William (1824—1910), Eng. astronomer.

Hugh Capet (hū kā'pet) (in French, Hugues Capet, pron. üg kȧ-pā') (c938—996), king of France (987—996) (successor of Louis V., and first king of Capet line).

Hughes (hūz), Charles Evans (1862—), Am. statesman and jurist, chief justice of U. S. Supreme Court (1930—).

Hughes, Sir Sam (1853—1921), Can. soldier, and minister of militia and defense.

Hughes, Thomas (1822—96), Eng. author.

Hughes, William Morris (1864—), Australian statesman, born in Wales.   [dramatist, and novelist.

Hugo (hū'gō, Fr. ü-gō), Victor Marie (1802—85), Fr. poet,

Hull (hul), Cordell (1871—), Am. statesman.

Hull, Isaac (1773—1843), Am. commodore.

Hull, William (1753—1825), Am. general.

Humayun (hö-mä-yön') (1508—56), Mogul emperor of Hindustan (son of Baber).

Humbert I. (hum'bèrt) (in Italian, Umberto, pron. öm-bär'tō) (1844—1900), king of Italy (1878—1900) (son of Victor Emmanuel II.).

Humboldt (hum'bōlt, Ger. fon hùm'bolt), Friedrich Heinrich Alexander, Freiherr von (1769—1859), Ger. naturalist and traveler.

Humboldt, Karl Wilhelm, Freiherr von (1767—1835), Ger. philologist, misc. writer, and statesman (brother of Friedrich H. A.).

Hume (hūm), David (1711—76), Sc. philosopher and historian.

Humperdinck (hùm'pèr-dingk), Engelbert (1854—1921), Ger. musical composer.

Humphrey (hum'fri) (Duke of Gloucester, called "Good Duke Humphrey") (1391—1447), Eng. soldier and statesman (youngest son of Henry IV. of England).

Hunt (hunt), James Henry Leigh (1784—1859), Eng. essayist, poet, and misc. writer.

Hunt, Richard Morris (1828—95), Am. architect (brother of William M.).

Hunt, William Henry (1790—1864), Eng. water-color painter.

Hunt, William Holman (1827—1910), Eng. painter.

Hunt, William Morris (1824—79), Am. painter.

Hunter (hun'tèr), John (1728—93), Br. surgeon, anatomist, and physiologist (brother of William).

Hunter, Robert Mercer Taliaferro (1809—87), Am. political leader.

Hunter, William (1718—83), Br. physician, anatomist, and physiologist.

Huntington (hun'ting-tọn), Ellsworth (1876—), Am. explorer in Asia.

Hunyadi or **Hunyady** (hún'yod-ẹ), János, or John (also called Johannes Corvinus Huniades) (c1387—1456), Hung. patriot and statesman, general against the Turks.

Hurst (hèrst), Fannie (Mrs. Danielson) (1889—), Am. novelist and playwright.

Huskisson (hus'ki-sọn), William (1770—1830), Eng. statesman and financier.

Huss or **Hus** (hus, Ger. hùs), John (1369?—1415), Bohem. religious reformer and martyr.

Hutcheson (huch'ẹ-sọn), Francis (1694—1746), Ir.-Sc. philosopher.

Hutchinson (hŭch′in-sọn), Mrs. (Anne Marbury) (1590?— 1643), Eng. religious enthusiast in New England.

Hutchinson, Arthur Stuart Menteth (1880—   ), Br. novelist, born in India.

Hutchinson, Thomas (1711—80), Am. magistrate and historical writer, governor of Massachusetts (1769—74).

Hutten (fọn hút′ẹn), Ulrich von (1488—1523), Ger. humanist, poet, and satirist.

Hutton (hŭt′n), James (1726—97), Sc. geologist.

Huxley (hŭks′li), Aldous Leonard (1894—   ), Eng. writer (grandson of Thomas H.).

Huxley, Thomas. Henry (1825—95), Eng. biologist and writer.

Huygens or **Huyghens** (hī′genz, Dutch hoi′chens), Christiaan (1629—95), Dutch mathematician, astronomer, and physicist (son of Constantijn).

Huygens or **Huyghens,** Constantijn (1596—1687), Dutch poet and diplomatist.

Huysmans (ü-ēs-män), Joris Karl (1848—1907), Fr. novelist.

Hyacinthe (yä-sȧnt), Père. See *Loyson.*

Hyde (hīd), Douglas (1860?—   ), Ir. author and Celtic scholar.

Hyder Ali (hī′dẽr ä′lē) or **Haidar Ali** (hī′dȧr ä′lē) (d. 1782), Mohammedan military leader in India, ruler of Mysore.

Hyndman (hīnd′mạn), Henry Mayers (1842—1921), Eng. socialist leader and writer.

Hypatia (hī-pā′shiạ) (d. 415), female mathematician and Neoplatonic philosopher, of Alexandria.

Hyslop (his′lọp), James Hervey (1854—1920), Am. psychologist.

I

Iamblichus (ī-ăm′bli-kus) (d. c333), Neoplatonic philosopher, born in Syria.

Ibáñez, Vicente Blasco. See *Blasco Ibáñez.*

Iberville (dē-ber-vēl), Pierre Le Moyne, Sieur d' (1661—1706), Fr. naval officer, and colonizer in America, born in Canada (brother of Sieur de Bienville).

Ibn Batuta (ibn bä-tö′tä) (1304—78), Arab traveler.

Ibn Gabirol (ibn gä-bē-rōl′). See *Avicebron.*

Ibn Khaldun (ibn käl-dön′) (1332—1406), Arab historian.

Ibn Rushd (ibn rùshd). See *Averroës.*

Ibn Sina (ibn sē′nä). See *Avicenna.*

Ibn Zuhr (ibn zör). See *Avenzoar.*

Ibrahim Pasha (ib-rä-hēm′ pä-shä′) (1789—1848), Egyptian general, and governor of Syria (son, or adopted son, of Mehemet Ali).

Ibsen (ib′sẹn, Norw. ip′sẹn), Henrik (1828—1906), Norw. dramatist and poet.

Ibycus (ib′i-kus) (fl. c530 B.C.), Gr. lyric poet.

Ictinus (ik-tī′nus) (fl. 450—438 B.C.), Gr. architect, chief designer of the Parthenon at Athens.

Ida (ī′dạ) (d. 559), king of the Angles in northern Northumbria (547—559).

Iddesleigh (idz′lĭ), Stafford Henry Northcote, 1st Earl of (1818—87), Eng. statesman.

Idrisi (id-rē′sē) or **Edrisi** (ed-rē′sē) (c1099—after 1154), Arab geographer.

Ieyasu. See *Iyeyasu.*

Iglesias (ē-glä′sē-äs), José María (1823—91), Mex. judge, politician, and historian.

Ignatius (ig-nā′shius), Saint (called Ignatius Theophorus) (d. c107?), bishop of Antioch, theologian, and martyr.

Ignatius Loyola, Saint. See *Loyola, Ignatius.*

Igor (ē′gor), Prince (1151—1202), Russ. warrior against the heathen.

Immermann (im′ẽr-män), Karl Leberecht (1796—1840), Ger. dramatist and novelist.

Inchbald (inch′bȧld), Mrs. (Elizabeth Simpson) (1753—1821), Eng. novelist, playwright, and actress.

Indy (dȧn-dē), Paul Marie Théodore Vincent d' (1851—1931), Fr. musical composer.

Inge (ing), William Ralph (1860—   ), Eng. clergyman and author, dean of St. Paul's Cathedral, London.

Ingelow (in′jẹ-lō), Jean (1820—97), Eng. poet and novelist.

Ingersoll (ing′gẽr-sọl), Robert Green (1833—99), Am. lawyer, orator, and antichristian writer and lecturer.

Ingoldsby (ing′gọldz-bi), Thomas. Pseudonym of R. H. Barham.

Ingres (ȧngr), Jean Auguste Dominique (1780—1867), Fr. painter.

Inness (in′es), George (1825—94), Am. landscape-painter.

Inness, George (1854—1926), Am. painter (son of George Inness, 1825—94).

Innocent II. (in′ọ-sẹnt) (Gregorio Papareschi) (d. 1143), It. ecclesiastic, pope (1130—43).

Innocent III. (Giovanni Lotario de' Conti) (1161?—1216), It. ecclesiastic, pope (1198—1216).

Innocent IV. (Sinibaldo de' Fieschi) (d. 1254), It. ecclesiastic, pope (1243—54).

Innocent XI. (Benedetto Odescalchi) (1611—89), It. ecclesiastic, pope (1676—89).

Irenæus (ī-rẹ-nē′us), Saint (c130—c202), bishop of Lyons and theologian, born in Asia Minor. [(780—802).

Irene (ī-rē′nē or ī-rēn′) (c752—803), Byzantine empress

Ireton (īr′tọn), Henry (1611—51), Eng. general and regicide (son-in-law of Oliver Cromwell).

Ironside (ī′ẽrn-sīd), Sir William Edmund (1880—   ), Br. general. [theologian.

Irving (ẽr′ving), Edward (1792—1834), Sc. preacher and

Irving, Sir Henry (orig. John Henry Brodribb) (1838—1905), Eng. actor and theatrical manager.

Irving, Washington (1783—1859), Am. author.

Isaacs (ē′säks), Jorge (1837—95), Colombian novelist and poet, author of "María."

Isaacs (ī′zạks), Sir Rufus Daniel. See *Reading, 1st Marquis of.*

Isabella I. (iz-ạ-bel′ạ) ("the Catholic") (1451—1504), joint ruler (1474—1504) of Castile and León, with her husband Ferdinand V., and patron of Columbus.

Isabella II. (María Isabel Luisa) (1830—1904), queen of Spain (1833—68) (daughter of Ferdinand VII.).

Isabella of France (1292—1358), queen of Edward II. of England.

Isabey (ē-zȧ-bā), Eugène Louis Gabriel (1804—86), Fr. painter (son of Jean B.).

Isabey, Jean Baptiste (1767—1855), Fr. miniature-painter.

Isæus (ī-sē′us) (c420—c350 B.C.), Athenian orator.

Isidore (iz′i-dōr), Saint (c1070—1130), Sp. day-laborer (plowman) noted for his piety, patron saint of peasants and day-laborers.

Isidore of Seville (Isidorus Hispalensis) (c560—636), Sp. archbishop and Latin encyclopedist.

Isla (dä ēs′lä), José Francisco de (1703—81), Sp. Jesuit preacher and satirist.

Ismail Pasha (is-mä-ēl′ pä-shä′) (1830—95), viceroy and khedive of Egypt (1863—79) (son of Ibrahim Pasha).

Isocrates (ī-sok′rạ-tēz) (436—338 B.C.), Athenian orator.

Israels (ēs-rä-els′), Joseph (1824—1911), Dutch painter.

Ito (ē′tō), Prince Hirobumi (1841—1909), Jap. statesman.

Iturbide (dä ē-tör-bē′τнä), Agustín de (1783—1824), Mex. revolutionist, and emperor of Mexico (1822—23).

Ivan III. (ī′vạn, Russ. ē-vän′) (in Russian, Ivan Vasilevich, called "Ivan the Great") (1440—1505), grand duke of Moscow (1462—1505).

Ivan IV. (in Russian, Ivan Vasilevich, called "Ivan the Terrible") (1530—84), first czar of Russia (1547—84) (grand duke of Moscow from 1533) (grandson of Ivan III.).

Iyeyasu (ē″yä-yä′sö) or **Ieyasu** (ē″ä-yä′sö) (1542—1616), Jap. general and statesman, first shogun of the Tokugawa family.

J

Jablochkoff (yä′bloch-kof), Paul (in Russian, Pavel Nikolaevich Yablochkov) (1847—94), Russ. electrical engineer and inventor.

Jacks (jaks), Lawrence Pearsall (1860—   ), Eng. clergyman, educator, and author.

Jackson (jak′sọn), Andrew (1767—1845), Am. general, and 7th president of U. S. (1829—37).

Jackson, Frederick George (1860—1938), Eng. army officer and arctic explorer.

Jackson, Mrs. Helen Hunt (Helen Maria Fiske, Mrs. Hunt, "H. H.") (1831—85), Am. poet and novelist.

(variable) ḍ as d or j, ş as s or sh, ṭ as t or ch, z̧ as z or zh; o, F. cloche; ü, F. menu; ch, Sc. loch; ṅ, F. bonbon; ′, primary accent; ″, secondary accent; †, obsolete; <, from; +, and; =, equals. **See also lists at beginning of book.**

Jackson, Thomas Jonathan ("Stonewall Jackson") (1824—63), Am. Confederate general.

Jacobi (jạ-kō′bi), Abraham (1830—1919), Ger.-Am. physician and pediatrist.

Jacobi (yä-kō′bē), Friedrich Heinrich (1743—1819), Ger. philosopher.

Jacobi, Moritz Hermann von (1801—74), Ger. physicist, in Russia.

Jacobsen (yä′kọp-sẹn), Jens Peter (1847—85), Dan. novelist.

Jacobus de Voragine (jạ-kō′bus dē vō-raj′i-nē) (c1230—c1298), It. archbishop, compiler of "Golden Legend."

Jacquard (zhȧ-kär), Joseph Marie (1752—1834), Fr. inventor (of loom attachment).

Jagello (yä-gel′lō) or **Jagiello** (yä-gyel′lō) (1350?—1434), grand duke of Lithuania (1377—86), and (as Ladislaus, or Wladyslaw, II.) king of Poland (1386—1434).

Jagow (fon yä′gō), Gottlieb von (1863—1935), Ger. statesman.

Jahn (yän), Friedrich Ludwig (1778—1852), Ger. educator and patriot, originator of the turnverein movement.

Jaime (Hī′mä), Don (Duke of Madrid) (1870—1931), pretender to the Spanish throne (son of Don Carlos, 1848—1909).

James I. (jāmz) (1566—1625), king of Great Britain and Ireland (1603—25) (as James VI., king of Scotland from 1567) (successor of Queen Elizabeth, and son of Mary Queen of Scots, and first king in England of house of Stuart).

James II. (1633—1701), king of Great Britain and Ireland (1685—88) (brother of Charles II.).

James I. (1394—1437), king of Scotland (1406—37) (son of Robert III.).

James II. (1430—60), king of Scotland (1437—60) (son of James I.).

James III. (1451—88), king of Scotland (1460—88) (son of James II.).

James IV. (1473—1513), king of Scotland (1488—1513) (son of James III.).

James V. (1512—42), king of Scotland (1513—42) (son of James IV.).

James VI., king of Scotland. See *James I.,* king of Great Britain and Ireland.

James, George Payne Rainsford (1799—1860), Eng. novelist.

James, Henry (1843—1916), Am.-Eng. novelist (brother of William).

James, Jesse W. (1847—82), Am. outlaw.

James, William (1842—1910), Am. psychologist and philosopher.

James Francis Edward Stuart (Prince of Wales, known as Chevalier de St. George, also as "the Old Pretender") (1688—1766), son of James II. of England, and pretender to the crown of England.

Jameson (jām′sọn), Mrs. (Anna Brownell Murphy) (1794—1860), Br. writer.

Jameson, Sir Leander Starr (1853—1917), Br. physician, and administrator and statesman in South Africa.

Jamieson (jā′mi-sọn), John (1759—1838), Sc. clergyman and lexicographer.

Jammes (zhȧm), Francis (1868—1938), Fr. poet and prose-writer.

Janauschek (yä′nou-shek), Fanny, or Franziska (1830—1904), Bohem.-Am. actress.

Janet (zhȧ-nā), Paul (1823—99), Fr. philosophical writer.

Janet, Pierre (1859—   ), Fr. psychologist (nephew of Paul).

Janin (zhȧ-naṅ), Jules Gabriel (1804—74), Fr. novelist and critic.

Jansen (jan′sẹn, Dutch yän′sẹn), Cornelis (as Latinized, Cornelius Jansenius) (1585—1638), Dutch-Belgian Rom. Cath. bishop and theologian, founder of Jansenism.

Janson, Nicolas. See *Jenson.*

Januarius (jan-ụ-ā′ri-us), Saint (in Italian, Gennaro) (d. c305), It. bishop and martyr, patron saint of Naples.

Jasmin (zhȧs-maṅ), Jacques (name orig. Boé) (1798—1864), Provençal poet.

Jastrow (jas′trō), Morris (1861—1921), Am. Semitic scholar, born in Poland.

Jaurès (zhō-res), Jean Léon (1859—1914), Fr. socialist leader and writer.

Jay (jā), John (1745—1829), Am. statesman and jurist, chief justice of U. S. Supreme Court (1789—95).

Jean de Meun (zhäṅ dẹ muṅ) or **Meung** (muṅ) (born Jean Clopinel) (c1250—c1305), Fr. poet, continuer of "Roman de la Rose."

Jeanne d'Albret (zhän dȧl-brä). See *Albret.*

Jeanne d'Arc. See *Joan of Arc.*

Jean Paul (zhäṅ poul). Pseudonym of J. P. F. Richter.

Jebb (jeb), Sir Richard Claverhouse (1841—1905), Br. classical scholar.

Jefferies (jef′riz), Richard (1848—87), Eng. naturalist and writer.

Jefferson (jef′ẹr-sọn), Joseph (1829—1905), Am. comedian.

Jefferson, Thomas (1743—1826), 3d president of U. S. (1801—09).

Jeffrey (jef′ri), Francis (Lord Jeffrey) (1773—1850), Sc. critic, editor, and jurist.

Jeffreys (jef′riz), George Jeffreys, 1st Baron (1648—89), Br. judge, infamous for conduct of "bloody assizes."

Jellachich (yel′ä-chich), Joseph, Count (1801—59), Croatian general and statesman.

Jellicoe (jel′i-kō), John Rushworth Jellicoe, 1st Earl (1859—1935), Eng. admiral.

Jenatsch (yä′näch), Georg (1596—1639), Swiss military and political leader.

Jenghis (or **Genghis**) **Khan** (jen′gis kän) (name orig. Temuchin) (1162—1227), Mongol conqueror in Asia.

Jenkin (jeng′kin), Henry Charles Fleeming (1833—85), Eng. engineer and electrician.

Jenkinson (jeng′kin-sọn). See *Liverpool, Earl of.*

Jenner (jen′ẹr), Edward (1749—1823), Eng. physician, discoverer of vaccination.

Jenner, Sir William (1815—98), Eng. physician.

Jenson (jen′sọn, Fr. zhoṅ-sôṅ) or **Janson** (zhäṅ-sôṅ), Nicolas (d. c1481), Fr. printer at Venice, improver and introducer of roman type.

Jeritza (ye′rit-sä), Maria (Baroness Popper, Mrs. Sheehan) (1887—   ), Austrian operatic soprano, born in Moravia.

Jerome (jẹ-rōm′ or jer′ọm), Saint (in Latin, Hieronymus, or, in full, Eusebius Sophronius Hieronymus) (c340—420), monk and scholar of Latin Church, maker of Latin version of Bible known as Vulgate.

Jerome (jẹ-rōm′), Jerome Klapka (1859—1927), Eng. humorist and playwright.

Jerome of Prague (d. 1416), Bohem. religious reformer and martyr.

Jerrold (jer′ọld), Douglas William (1803—57), Eng. dramatist and humorist.

Jervis (jär′vis or jẹr′vis), John. See *St. Vincent, Earl of.*

Jessopp (jes′ọp), Augustus (1824—1914), Eng. clergyman and writer.

Jesus (jē′zus) (Jesus of Nazareth, Jesus Christ, Christ Jesus, or Christ) (7? B.C.—A.D. 29), the founder of the Christian religion (a Jew by race, born at Bethlehem, Judea, lived at Nazareth, Galilee, crucified at Jerusalem, Judea, all in Palestine, Syria).

Jevons (jev′ọnz), William Stanley (1835—82), Eng. economist and logician.

Jewel (jō′el), John (1522—71), Eng. Anglican bishop and theologian.

Jewett (jō′et), Sarah Orne (1849—1909), Am. writer.

Jiménez de Cisneros (Hē-mä′nāth dā thēs-nā′rōs), Francisco (known as Cardinal Ximenes, Eng. pron. zi-mē′nēz) (1436—1517), Sp. cardinal and statesman.

Jiménez de Quesada (kā-sä′THä), Gonzalo (c1495—1546 or 1579), Sp. soldier and adventurer in America.

Joachim (yō′ä-ċhim), Joseph (1831—1907), Hung.-Ger. violinist and composer.

Joan (jōn) ("the Fair Maid of Kent") (1328—85), wife of Edward, Prince of Wales (the Black Prince), and mother of Richard II. of England.

Joanna I. (jō-an′ä) (1326—82), queen of Naples (1343—82).

Joan of Arc (jōn or jō-an′, ärk) (in French, Jeanne d'Arc, pron. zhän därk, born Jeanneton Darc, called "the Maid of Orléans") (1412—31), Fr. heroine.

João I. See *John I.* (of Portugal).

Joffre (zhofr), Joseph Jacques Césaire (1852—1931), Fr. general, marshal of France.

---

fat, fāte, fär, fȧll, ȧsk, fāre; net, mē, hẹr; pin, pīne; not, nōte, mŏve, nôr; up, lūte, pṳll; oi, oil; ou, out; (lightened) aviạry, ẹlect, agọny, intọ, ụnite; (obscured) errạnt, operạ, ardẹnt, actọr, natụre; ch, chip; g, go; th, thin; ᴛʜ, then; y, you;

Jogues (zhōg), Isaac (1607—46), Fr. Jesuit missionary to North American Indians.

Johann Parricida (yō-hän′ pä-rē-tsē′dä). See *John* ("the Parricide").

John (jon) ("John the Fearless") (1371—1419), duke of Burgundy (1404—19) (son of Philip the Bold).

John ("John Lackland") (1167?—1216), king of England (1199—1216) (brother of Richard I.).

John I. (in French, Jean, pron. zhäṅ) (b. and d. 1316), king of France (1316) (son of Louis X.).

John II. ("John the Good") (1319—64), king of France (1350—64) (son of Philip VI.).

John II. (John Casimir) (1609—72), king of Poland (1648—68) (son of Sigismund III.).

John III. (John Sobieski) (1624—96), king of Poland (1674—96).

John I. (in Portuguese, João, pron. zhŏ-ouṅ′, called "the Great") (1357—1433), king of Portugal (1385—1433).

John I., Saint (d. 526), It. ecclesiastic and martyr, pope (523—526).

John XXII. (Jacques d'Euse) (1249—1334), Fr. ecclesiastic, pope (1316—34).

John ("the Parricide," in German Johann Parricida, also known as John of Swabia) (1290—after 1313), Ger. prince, murderer of his uncle, Albert I. of Germany.

John or **Juan** (hwän), Don (of Austria) (1547?—78), Sp. military and naval commander (illegitimate son of the Emperor Charles V., and half-brother of Philip II. of Spain).

John, Augustus Edwyn (1879—   ), Br. painter.

John Chrysostom (kris′ǫs-tǫm or kri-sos′tǫm), Saint (c347—407), bishop of Constantinople, preacher, and theologian, born at Antioch.

John Frederick ("the Magnanimous") (1503—54), elector of Saxony (1532—54).

John of Bologna. See *Bologna, Giovanni da.*

John of Damascus (Johannes Damascenus, called Chrysorrhoas) (d. c754), Christian monk and theologian, of Syria.

John of Gaunt (gänt) (Duke of Lancaster) (1340—99), Eng. soldier and statesman, founder of house of Lancaster (son of Edward III. of England, and father of Henry IV.).

John of Lancaster (John Plantagenet, Duke of Bedford) (1389—1435), Eng. soldier and statesman (son of Henry IV. of England).

John of Leyden (real name Jan Beukelszoon, also called Johann, or Jan, Bockelson or Bockold) (1509?—36), Dutch Anabaptist fanatic.

John of Luxemburg (1296—1346), king of Bohemia (1311—46) (son of Emperor Henry VII.).

John of Nepomuk (nä′pō-múk), Saint (d. 1393), Bohem. ecclesiastic, patron saint of Bohemia.

John of Salisbury (c1115—80), Eng. ecclesiastic, scholar, and writer, bishop of Chartres (1176—80).

Johnson (jon′sǫn), Andrew (1808—75), 17th president of U. S. (1865—69). [California].

Johnson, Hiram Warren (1866—1945), Am. senator (from

Johnson, Hugh Samuel (1882—1942), Am. general, National Recovery Administrator (1933—34).

Johnson, Sir John (1742—1830), Am. Tory leader in Revolutionary War (son of Sir William).

Johnson, Reverdy (1796—1876), Am. lawyer and legislator.

Johnson, Richard Mentor (1780 or 1781—1850), Am. legislator, vice-president of U. S. (1837—41). [and poet.

Johnson, Robert Underwood (1853—1937), Am. editor

Johnson, Samuel (Dr. Johnson) (1709—84), Eng. author and lexicographer.

Johnson, Sir William (1715—74), Br. colonist and soldier in America.

Johnston (jon′stǫn or jon′sǫn), Albert Sidney (1803—62), Am. Confederate general.

Johnston, Alexander Keith (1804—71), Sc. geographer.

Johnston, Alexander Keith (1844—79), Sc. geographer and explorer (son of A. K. Johnston, 1804—71).

Johnston, Sir Harry Hamilton (1858—1927), Eng. explorer and official in Africa, and author.

Johnston, Joseph Eggleston (1807—91), Am. Confederate general.

Johnston, Mary (1870—1936), Am. novelist.

Joinville (dè zhwaṅ-vēl), François Ferdinand Philippe Louis Marie d'Orléans, Prince de (1818—1900), Fr. naval officer (son of Louis Philippe of France).

Joinville, Jean, Sire de (c1224—c1319), Fr. chronicler.

Jókai (yō′ko-ē̜), Mór, or Maurus (1825—1904), Hung. novelist, dramatist, and misc. writer.

Joliet or **Jolliet** (jō′li-et, Fr. zho-lyā), Louis (1645—1700), Can. explorer of the Mississippi.

Jomini (zhō-mē-nē), Henri, Baron (1779—1869), Swiss military writer, and general in French and Russian service.

Jommelli (yom-mel′lē), Niccolò (1714—74), It. musical composer.

Jones (jōnz), Henry ("Cavendish") (1831—99), Eng. physician, and writer on whist and other games.

Jones, Henry Arthur (1851—1929), Eng. dramatist.

Jones, Inigo (1573—1652), Eng. architect.

Jones, John Paul (orig. John Paul) (1747—92), Am. naval officer, born in Scotland.

Jones, Sir William (1746—94), Eng. Orientalist and jurist.

Jonson (jon′sǫn), Benjamin, usually called Ben (1573?—1637), Eng. dramatist and poet.

Jordaens (yôr′däns), Jacob (1593—1678), Flemish painter.

Jordan (jôr′dạn), David Starr (1851—1931), Am. naturalist and educator.

Joseffy (yǫ-zef′ē̜), Rafael (1852?—1915), Hung.-Am. pianist.

Joseph I. (jō′zẹf) (1678—1711), emperor of Holy Roman Empire (1705—11) (son of Emperor Leopold I.).

Joseph II. (1741—90), emperor of Holy Roman Empire (1765—90) (son of Emperor Francis I. and Maria Theresa of Austria).

Joseph (zhō-zef), Père ("the Gray Eminence," orig. François Leclerc du Tremblay) (1577—1638), Fr. monk, confidant of Cardinal Richelieu.

Josephine (jō′zẹ-fēn) (in French, Joséphine, pron. zhō-zā-fēn) (Vicomtesse de Beauharnais, born Marie Josèphe Rose Tascher de La Pagerie) (1763—1814), first wife of Napoleon I.

Josephus (jō-sē′fus), Flavius (A.D. 37?—c95); Jewish historian, writing in Aramaic and Greek.

Josquin Des Prés (zhos-kaṅ dā prā). See *Des Prés, Josquin.*

Joubert (zhō-bār), Joseph (1754—1824), Fr. moralist and essayist.

Joubert (you′bèrt), Petrus Jacobus (1831—1900), Boer general and statesman.

Jouffroy (zhō-frwo), Théodore Simon (1796—1842), Fr. philosophical writer.

Joule (joul), James Prescott (1818—89), Eng. physicist.

Jourdan (zhōr-däṅ), Jean Baptiste, Comte (1762—1833), Fr. marshal.

Jovian (jō′vi-ạn) (Flavius Claudius Jovianus) (c332—364), Rom. emperor (363—364).

Jowett (jou′et), Benjamin (1817—93), Eng. theologian, educator, and Greek scholar.

Jowett, John Henry (1864—1923), Eng. preacher and author.

Joyce (jois), James (1882—1941), Ir. novelist and misc. writer.

Juan of Austria. See *John, Don.*

Juárez (hwä′räs), Benito Pablo (1806—72), Mex. statesman, president of Mexico (1858—63, 1867—72).

Judah I. (jō′dạ) (called Judah ha-Nasi, 'Judah the Prince,' and also known as Rabbi) (c135—c220), leader of Jews of Palestine, and redactor of the Mishnah.

Judson (jud′sǫn), Adoniram (1788—1850), Am. Baptist missionary in Burma.

Jugurtha (jǫ-gèr′thạ) (d. 104 B.C.), king of Numidia (grandson of Masinissa).

Julian (jōl′yạn) ("Julian the Apostate," Flavius Claudius Julianus) (331—363), Rom. emperor (361—363) (nephew of Constantine the Great, and cousin and brother-in-law of Constantius II.).

Julius II. (jōl′yus) (Giuliano della Rovere) (1443—1513), It. ecclesiastic, pope (1503—13) (nephew of Sixtus IV.).

Jung (yùng), Carl Gustav (1875—   ), Swiss physician, psychologist, and psychoanalyst.

Junípero Serra (hō-nē′pä-rō ser′rä). See *Serra.*

Junius (jō′nyus). Pseudonym of the unknown author of a series of political letters which appeared in London, 1768—72. Cf. *Francis, Sir Philip.*

(variable) ḍ as d or j, ş as s or sh, ṭ as t or ch, ẓ as z or zh; *o*, F. cloche; ü, F. menu; ċh, Sc. loch; ṅ, F. bonbon; ′, primary accent; ″, secondary accent; †, obsolete; <, from; +, and; =, equals. See also lists at beginning of book.

Junker (yŭng'kėr), Wilhelm (1840—92), Russ. explorer in Africa.

Junot (zhü-nō), Andoche (Duc d'Abrantès) (1771—1813), Fr. general.

Junot, Madame (Duchesse d'Abrantès, born Laurette, or Laure, de Saint-Martin Permon) (1784—1838), Fr. writer of memoirs (wife of Andoche).

Jusserand (zhüs-räṅ), Jean Adrien Antoine Jules (1855–1932), Fr. diplomatist and author.

Jussieu (dė zhü-syė), Adrien de (1797—1853), Fr. botanist (son of Antoine L.).

Jussieu, Antoine Laurent de (1748—1836), Fr. botanist (nephew of Bernard).

Jussieu, Bernard de (1699—1776), Fr. botanist.

Justin I. (jus'tin) (c450—527), Byzantine emperor (518—527).

Justin II. (d. 578), Byzantine emperor (565—578) (nephew of Justinian I.).

Justinian I. (jus-tin'i-ạn) ("Justinian the Great," Flavius Anicius Justinianus) (483—565), Byzantine emperor (527—565) (nephew of Justin I.).

Justin Martyr, Saint (c100—c165), Christian apologist and martyr, born in Syria.

Juvenal (jö'vẹ-nạl) (Decimus Junius Juvenalis) (A.D. c60—c140), Rom. satiric poet.

K

Kadelburg (kä'dẹl-börċh), Gustav (1851—1925), Ger. actor and playwright.

Kalakaua (kä-lä-kou'ä) (David Kalakaua) (1836—91), king of Hawaiian Islands (1874—91).

Kalb (kalb, Ger. kälp), Johann (commonly called Baron de Kalb) (1721—80), Ger. soldier in French service, and general in American Revolutionary army.

Kaledin (kȧ-lye'dyẹn), Aleksyey Maksimovich (1861—1918), Russ. general; opponent of the Bolsheviki.

Kalidasa (kä-lẹ-dä'sä) (6th? cent., or earlier), Hindu poet and dramatist.

Kalm (kälm), Peter (1715—79), Swed. botanist, and traveler in America.

Kálnoky (käl'nō-kẹ), Gustav Siegmund, Graf (1832—98), Austrian statesman and diplomatist.

Kames (kāmz), Henry Home, Lord (1696—1782), Sc. judge and philosophical writer.

Kamimura (kä-mẹ-mö'rä), Baron Hikonojo (1850—1916), Jap. admiral.

Kanaris (kä-nä'rēs), Konstantinos (1790—1877), Gr. naval officer, and statesman.

Kane (kān), Elisha Kent (1820—57), Am. physician and arctic explorer.

Kant (känt), Immanuel (1724—1804), Ger. philosopher.

Kapnist (kȧp-nyēst'), Vasili Vasilevich (1757—1824), Russ. poet and dramatist.

Kapp (käp), Wolfgang (1868—1922), Ger. conspirator (leader of revolt against the German Republic, 1920), born in New York.

Kapteyn (käp'tīn), Jacobus Cornelius (1851—1922), Dutch astronomer.

Karageorge (kä'rạ-jȯrj') (Kara George or Czerny George, meaning 'Black George,' name orig. George, or Djordje, Petrovich) (1766?—1817), Serbian leader against the Turks.

Karageorgevich. See *Alexander Karageorgevich* (of Serbia).

Karamzin (kȧ-rȧm-zēn'), Nikolay Mikhaylovich (1766?—1826), Russ. historian and misc. writer.

Karlstadt or **Carlstadt** (kärl'shtät) (real name Andreas Rudolf Bodenstein) (1480?—1541), Ger. Protestant reformer.

Károlyi (kä'rōl-yẹ), Michael, Count (1875—   ), Hung. politician, provisional president of people's republic (1919).

Karr (kär), Jean Baptiste Alphonse (1808—90), Fr. author.

Katharine or **Katherine.** See *Catharine*.

Kato (kä'tō), Viscount Takaaki (1860—1926), Jap. diplomatist and statesman.

Kato, Baron Tomosaburo (1859—1923), Jap. admiral and statesman.

Katsura (kät'sö-ṟä), Prince Taro (1847—1913), Jap. general and statesman.

Kauffmann (kouf'män), Angelica (Maria Anna Angelica Kauffmann, Signora Zucchi) (1741—1807), Swiss painter, in Italy and England.

Kaulbach (fon koul'bäċh), Wilhelm von (1805—74), Ger. painter and illustrator.

Kaulbars (koul'bärs), Baron Aleksandr Vasilevich (1844—   ), Russ. traveler and general.

Kaunitz-Rietberg (fon kou'nits-rēt'berċh), Wenzel Anton, Prince von (1711—94), Austrian statesman and diplomatist.

Kaye-Smith (kā'smith'), Sheila (Mrs. Fry) (1887—   ), Eng. novelist.

Kean (kēn), Charles John (1811?—68), Eng. actor (son of Edmund).

Kean, Edmund (1787—1833), Eng. tragedian.

Kean, Mrs. (Ellen Tree) (1805—80), Eng. actress (wife of Charles J.).

Keane (kēn), Augustus Henry (1833—1912), Br. ethnologist.

Kearny (kär'ni), Philip (1815—62), Am. general.

Keats (kēts), John (1795—1821), Eng. poet.

Keble (kē'bl), John (1792—1866), Eng. clergyman and religious poet.

Keen (kēn), William Williams (1837—1932), Am. surgeon.

Keene (kēn), Charles Samuel (1823—91), Eng. illustrator and caricaturist.

Keene, Laura (Mrs. Taylor, Mrs. Lutz) (1826—73), Eng.-Am. actress.

Keith (kēth), George (10th earl marischal) (1693?—1778), Sc. Jacobite, in Spain and Prussia.

Keith, George Keith Elphinstone, Viscount (1746—1823), Br. admiral.

Keith, James Francis Edward (1696—1758), Sc. general in Russian service, and Prussian field-marshal (brother of George).

Kekulé von Stradonitz (kā'kö-lä fon shträ'dō-nits), Friedrich August (1829—96), Ger. chemist.

Keller (kel'ėr), Gottfried (1819—90), Swiss poet and novelist, writing in German.

Kellermann (kel'ėr-män), Bernhard (1879—   ), Ger. novelist.

Kellermann (ke-ler-män), François Christophe (Duc de Valmy) (1735—1820), Fr. marshal.

Kellermann, François Étienne (Duc de Valmy) (1770—1835), Fr. general (son of François C.).

Kellogg (kel'ọg), Clara Louise (Mrs. Carl Strakosch) (1842—1916), Am. operatic soprano singer.

Kellogg, Frank Billings (1856—1937), Am. lawyer, diplomatist, and statesman.

Kelvin (kel'vin), William Thomson, Baron (1824—1907), Br. mathematician and physicist.

Kemal Pasha (ke-mäl' pȧ-shä') (Ghazi Muṣtafa Kemal Pasha, after 1934 Kemal Ataturk) (1880—1938), Turk. military and political leader, president of Turkey (1923—38).

Kemble (kem'bl), Charles (1775—1854), Eng. actor (brother of John P.).

Kemble, Frances Anne, or Fanny (Mrs. Butler) (1809—93), Eng.-Am. actress and writer (daughter of Charles).

Kemble, John Philip (1757—1823), Eng. tragedian (brother of Mrs. Siddons).

Kemnitz, Martin. See *Chemnitz*.

Kempis, Thomas a. See *Thomas a Kempis*.

Ken (ken), Thomas (1637—1711), Eng. nonjuring bishop, and hymn-writer.

Kendal (ken'dạl), William Hunter (professional name of William Hunter Grimston) (1843—1917), Eng. actor and theatrical manager.

Kendal, Mrs. (professional name of Margaret, or Madge, Robertson, Mrs. Grimston, Dame Madge Grimston) (1849—1935), Eng. actress (wife of W. H. Grimston (W. H. Kendal), and sister of T. W. Robertson).

Kendall (ken'dạl), William Sergeant (1869—1938), Am. painter and sculptor.

Kennan (ken'ạn), George (1845—1924), Am. traveler and writer.

Kennedy (ken'ẹ-di), John Pendleton (1795—1870), Am. politician and novelist.

Kenneth I. (ken'eth) (called MacAlpin) (d. c860), king of Scotland (c850—c860).

Kent (kent), James (1763—1847), Am. jurist.

Kent, Rockwell (1882—   ), Am. painter.

---

fat, fāte, fär, fȧll, ȧsk, fãre; net, mē, hėr; pin, pīne; not, nōte, mȯve, nȯr; up, lūte, pụll; oi, oil; ou, out; (lightened) aviạry, ẹlect, agọny, intọ, ụnite; (obscured) errạnt, operä, ardẹnt, actọr, natụre; ch, chip; g, go; th, thin; ᴛʜ, then; y, you;

Kenton (ken′tọn), Simon (1755—1836), Am. backwoodsman and pioneer.

Keokuk (kē′ọ-kuk) (c1780—1848), Am. Indian chief.

Kepler (kep′lẽr), Johann (1571—1630), Ger. astronomer.

Kerenski (ke-ren′skẹ or ker′en-skẹ), Aleksandr Fedorovich (1881—   ), Russ. revolutionary leader (moderate socialist), premier (1917).

Kerner (ker′nẽr), Andreas Justinus (1786—1862), Ger. poet and misc. writer.

Kéroualle (dẹ kä-rö-ȧl), Louise Renée de (Duchess of Portsmouth) (1649—1734), Fr. mistress of Charles II. of England.

Ketteler (fon ket′ẹl-ẽr), Wilhelm Emanuel von (1811—77), Ger. Rom. Cath. bishop and ultramontane leader.

Key (kā), Ellen (1849—1926), Swed. author, lecturer, and feminist.

Key (kē), Francis Scott (1780—1843), Am. poet, author of "Star-Spangled Banner."

Keyes (kēz), Sir Roger John Brownlow (1872—1945), Br. admiral.

Keynes (kānz), John Maynard (1883—1946), Eng. economist and writer.

Keyserling (kī′zẽr-ling), Hermann Alexander, Graf (1880—1946), Ger. philosophical and misc. writer, born in Russia.

Khammurabi. See *Hammurabi.*

Khufu. See *Cheops.*

Khusrau I. (kus-rou′), **Khosru I.** (kos-rö′), or **Chosroes I.** (kos′rọ-ēz) (d. 579), king of Persia (531—579).

Khusrau II., Khosru II., or **Chosroes II.** (d. 628), king of Persia (590?—628) (grandson of Khusrau I.).

Kidd (kid), Benjamin (1858—1916), Eng. sociologist.

Kidd, William ("Captain Kidd") (c1645—1701), Br. privateer, hanged for piracy.

Kielland (chel′län), Alexander Lange (1849—1906), Norw. novelist.

Kierkegaard (kyer′kẹ-gâr), Sören Aaby (1813—55), Dan. philosophical and theological writer.

Kilham (kil′ạm), Alexander (1762—98), Eng. Methodist preacher and sectarian leader.

Killigrew (kil′i-grö), Thomas (1612—83), Eng. dramatist and theatrical manager.

Kilpatrick (kil-pat′rik), Hugh Judson (1836—81), Am. general.

King (king), Ernest J. (1878—   ), Am. admiral.

King, Rufus (1755—1827), Am. statesman.

King, William Lyon Mackenzie (1874—   ), Can. statesman, premier of Canada (1921—26, 1926—30, 1935—   ) (grandson of W. L. Mackenzie).

King, William Rufus (1786—1853), Am. statesman, vice-president of U. S. (1853).

King Bomba. See *Bomba.*

Kinglake (king′lāk), Alexander William (1809—91), Eng. historian and traveler.

Kingsley (kingz′li), Charles (1819—75), Eng. clergyman, novelist, and poet.

Kingsley, Henry (1830—76), Eng. novelist (brother of Charles).

Kingsley, Mary Henrietta (1862—1900), Eng. traveler and author (niece of Charles and Henry).

Kingston (king′stọn), William Henry Giles (1814—80), Eng. writer, esp. of books for boys.

Kipling (kip′ling), Rudyard (1865—1936), Eng. prose-writer and poet, born in India.

Kirby (kẽr′bi), William (1759—1850), Eng. entomologist.

Kirchhoff (kirch′hof), Gustav Robert (1824—87), Ger. physicist.

Kirk (kẽrk), John Foster (1824—1904), Can.-Am. historian and bibliographer.

Kirkcaldy (kẽr-kâl′di) ("of Grange"), Sir William (d. 1573), Sc. soldier and politician.

Kirkwood (kẽrk′wûd), Samuel Jordan (1813—94), Am. statesman, governor of Iowa (1860—64, 1876—77).

Kitasato (kē-tä-sä′tō), Shibasaburo (1856—1931), Jap. physician and bacteriologist.

Kitchener (kich′ẹn-ẽr) **of Khartoum,** Horatio Herbert Kitchener, 1st Earl ("K. of K.") (1850—1916), Br. field-marshal and war minister.

Kitto (kit′ō), John (1804—54), Eng. religious writer and compiler.

Kittredge (kit′rej), George Lyman (1860—1941), Am. philologist and educator.

Klapka (klop′ko), György, or George (1820—92), Hung. general.

Klaproth (kläp′rōt), Martin Heinrich (1743—1817), Ger. chemist.

Kléber (klā-bār), Jean Baptiste (1753—1800), Fr. general.

Klein (klīn), Felix (1849—1925), Ger. mathematician.

Kleist (fon klīst), Heinrich von (1777—1811), Ger. dramatist and novelist.

Klinger (fon kling′ẽr), Friedrich Maximilian von (1752—1831), Ger. dramatist and novelist.

Klinger, Max (1857—1920), Ger. painter, etcher, and sculptor.

Klopstock (klop′shtok), Friedrich Gottlieb (1724—1803), Ger. poet.

Kluck (fon klúk), Alexander von (1846—1934), Ger. field-marshal.

Kluge (klö′gẹ), Friedrich (1856—   ), Ger. philologist.

Knaus (knous), Ludwig (1829—1910), Ger. painter.

Kneller (nel′ẽr), Sir Godfrey (orig. Gottfried Kniller) (1646—1723), Ger.-Eng. portrait-painter.   [in France.

Knight (nīt), Daniel Ridgway (1845?—1924), Am. painter,

Knobelsdorff (fon knō′bẹls-dôrf), Georg Wenzeslaus von (1699—1753), Ger. architect.

Knowles (nōlz), James Sheridan (1784—1862), Br. dramatist.

Knox (noks), Henry (1750—1806), Am. Revolutionary general.

Knox, John (1505?—72), Sc. religious reformer and historian.

Knox, Philander Chase (1853—1921), Am. statesman.

Knox, (William) Franklin (1874—   ), Am. publisher and political leader.

Knut. See *Canute.*

Koberger (kō′ber-gẽr) or **Koburger** (kō′búr-gẽr), Anthoni (c1440—1513), Ger. printer and publisher.   [bacteriologist.

Koch (koch), Robert (1843—1910), Ger. physician and

Kock (dẹ kok), Charles Paul de (1794—1871), Fr. novelist.

Kodama (kō′dä-mä), Viscount Gentaro (1852—1906), Jap. general.

Koelliker (kèl′i-kẽr). See *Kölliker.*

Koerner (kẽr′nẽr). See *Körner.*

Kolchak (kol-chäk′), Aleksandr Vasilevich (1874—1920), Russ. admiral, leader against the Bolsheviki.

Kölliker (fon kèl′i-kẽr), Albert von (1817—1905), Swiss-Ger. anatomist, physiologist, and histologist.

Komura (kō′mö-rä), Marquis Jutaro (1855—1911), Jap. statesman and diplomatist.

Konrad von Marburg (kon′rät fon mär′búrċh). See *Conrad of Marburg.*

Koraïs (ko-rä′ēs) or **Coray** (ko-rä′), Adamantios (1748—1833), Gr. scholar and patriot, born at Smyrna.

Körner (kẽr′nẽr), Karl Theodor (1791—1813), Ger. poet and patriot.

Korngold (kôrn′golt), Erich Wolfgang (1897—   ), Austrian musical composer.

Kornilov (kor-nyē′lof), Lavr Georgievich (1870—1918), Russ. general, opponent of the Bolsheviki.

Korolenko (ko-ro-lyeng′kō), Vladimir Galaktionovich (1853—1921), Russ. author.

Kosciusko (kos-i-us′kō), Thaddeus (in Polish, Tadeusz Kosciuszko) (1746—1817), Pol. patriot and general, who served as an officer in the American Revolutionary army.

Kossuth (kosh′út), Ferencz, or Francis (1841—1914), Hung. statesman (son of Lajos).

Kossuth, Lajos, or Louis (1802—94), Hung. patriot and orator.

Koster. See *Coster.*

Kotzebue (fon kot′sẹ-bö), August Friedrich Ferdinand von (1761—1819), Ger. dramatist and misc. writer.

Kovalevsky (ko-vȧ-lef′skẹ), Mme. Sonya, or Sophie (in Russian, Sofiya Vasilevna Kovalevskaya, born Korvin-Krukovskaya) (1850—91), Russ. mathematician.

Krafft or **Kraft** (kräft), Adam (c1450—1507), Ger. sculptor.

Krafft-Ebing (fon kräft′ā′bing), Richard, Freiherr von (1840—1902), Ger. psychiatrist.

Kranach. See *Cranach.*

Krapotkin (krȧ-pot′kẹn). See *Kropotkin.*

(variable) ḍ as d or j, ṣ as s or sh, ṭ as t or ch, ẓ as z or zh; o, F. cloche; ü, F. menu; ċh, Sc. loch; ṅ, F. bonbon; ′, primary accent; ″, secondary accent; †, obsolete; <, from; +, and; =, equals. See also lists at beginning of book.

Krasinski (krä-shĕn'skĕ), Count Zygmunt (1812—59), Pol. poet, born in Paris.

Krauskopf (krous'kopf), Joseph (1858—1923), Ger.-Am. rabbi and writer.

Kreisler (krīs'lêr), Fritz (1875—   ), Austrian violinist.

Kreutzer (kroit'sêr, Fr. krĕt-sär), Rodolphe (1766—1831), Fr. violinist and composer.

Kropotkin (kro-pot'kẹn), Prince Petr Alekseyevich (1842—1921), Russ. geographer and anarchist, in England.

Krüdener (fon krü'dẹ-nêr), Baroness von (Barbara Juliane von Vietinghoff) (1764—1824), Russ. Pietist and writer.

Kruger (krü'gẹr), Stephanus Johannes Paulus ("Oom Paul") (1825—1904), Boer statesman, president of the South African Republic.

Krupp (krup), Alfred (1812—87), Ger. manufacturer of cannons, etc.

Kubelik (kö'be-lik), Jan (1880—1940), Bohem. violinist.

Kublai Khan (köb'lī kän) (1216?—94), Mongol emperor (1259—94), founder of the Mongol dynasty in China (grandson of Jenghis Khan).

Kuenen (kü'nẹn), Abraham (1828—91), Dutch Biblical critic.

Kun (kun), Béla (1886—   ), Hung. communist leader.

Kunz (könts), George Frederick (1856—1932), Am. expert in precious stones.

Kuprin (kö-prēn'), Aleksandr Ivanovich (1870—1938), Russ. novelist and short-story writer.

Kuroki (kö'rọ-kē), Count Tamemoto (1844—1923), Jap. general.

Kuropatkin (kö-ro-pät'kẹn), Aleksyey Nikolaevich (1848—1925), Russ. general.

Kutuzov (kö-tö'zof) or **Golenishchev-Kutuzov**, Mikhail Illarionovich (Prince of Smolensk) (1745—1813), Russ. field-marshal.

Kuyp. See *Cuyp.*

Kyd (kid), Thomas (1558—94), Eng. dramatist.

Kynaston (kin'ạ-stọn), Edward (c1640—1706), Eng. actor.

L

Labadie (dẹ lä-bȧ-dē), Jean de (1610—74), Fr. Protestant mystic and separatist.

Labiche (lȧ-bēsh), Eugène Marin (1815—88), Fr. dramatist.

La Boétie (dẹ lä bọ-ȧ-sē), Étienne de (1530—63), Fr. writer.

Labori (lȧ-bo-rē), Fernand Gustave Gaston (1860—1917), Fr. advocate and legal writer.

Labouchere (lab-ọ-shär'), Henry (1798—1869). See *Taunton, Baron.*

Labouchere, Henry (1831—1912), Eng. journalist and politician (nephew of Henry Labouchere, Baron Taunton).

Laboulaye (dẹ lä-bö-lä), Édouard René Lefebvre de (1811—83), Fr. jurist, politician, and historical writer.

La Bourdonnais (dẹ lä bör-do-nä), Bertrand François Mahé de (1699—1753), Fr. naval commander.

La Bruyère (dẹ lä brü-yär), Jean de (1645—96), Fr. moralist, author of "Caractères."

Lacaille (dẹ lȧ-kä-y'), Nicolas Louis de (1713—62), Fr. astronomer.

La Calprenède (dẹ lä kȧl-prẹ-ned), Gauthier de Costes de (c1610—63), Fr. novelist and dramatist.

Lacépède (dẹ lȧ-sȧ-ped), Bernard Germain Étienne de Laville, Comte de (1756—1825), Fr. naturalist.

La Chaise (dẹ lä shäz), François d'Aix de (1624—1709), Fr. Jesuit, confessor to Louis XIV.

La Chaussée (dẹ lä shō-sä), Pierre Claude Nivelle de (1692—1754), Fr. dramatist.

Lachmann (läch'män), Karl (1793—1851), Ger. philologist.

La Condamine (dẹ lä kôn-dȧ-mēn), Charles Marie de (1701—74), Fr. traveler, geographer, and mathematician.

Lacordaire (lȧ-kôr-där), Jean Baptiste Henri (1802—61), Fr. Dominican and pulpit orator.

Lactantius Firmianus (lak-tan'shius fẽr-mi-ā'nus), Lucius Cælius, or Lucius Cæcilius (c260—c325), Latin Christian apologist, born in northern Africa.

Lacy or **Lascy** (fon lä'sē), Franz Moritz, Graf von (1725—1801), Austrian field-marshal, born in Russia (son of Count Peter Lacy).

Lacy (lä'si or lä'sē), Count Peter (1678—1751), Russ. general, born in Ireland.

Ladd (lad), George Trumbull (1842—1921), Am. psychologist, and philosophical and misc. writer.

Ladislaus (lad'is-läs) or **Ladislas** (lad'is-läs), Saint (1040—95), king of Hungary (1077—95).

Ladislaus II. See *Jagello.*

Laënnec (lä-e-nek), René Théophile Hyacinthe (1781—1826), Fr. physician, inventor of stethoscope.

La Farge (lạ färj), John (1835—1910), Am. painter, and artist in stained glass.

Lafayette or **La Fayette** (lä-fạ-yet', Fr. dẹ lä-fȧ-yet), Marie Jean (or Joseph) Paul Roch Yves Gilbert Motier, Marquis de (1757—1834), Fr. general and statesman, who served in the American Revolutionary army.

La Fayette (dẹ lä fȧ-yet), Comtesse de (Marie Madeleine Pioche de La Vergne) (1634—92), Fr. novelist.

Lafitte (lȧ-fēt), Jean (1780?—1826?), Fr. smuggler and pirate in the Gulf of Mexico.

La Follette (lä fol'et), Robert Marion (1855—1925), Am. legislator and political leader.

La Fontaine (dẹ lä fôn-tän), Jean de (1621—95), Fr. poet, fabulist, and misc. writer.

Lafontaine (lä-fon-tän'), Sir Louis Hypolite (1807—64), Can. statesman and judge.

Lagerlöf (lä'gẽr-lẽf), Selma (1858—1940), Swed. author.

Lagrange (lä-gränzh), Joseph Louis, Comte (1736—1813), Fr. mathematician, born in Italy.

La Halle, Adam de. See *Adam de la Halle.*

Laharpe or **La Harpe** (dẹ lä-ärp), Frédéric César de (1754—1838), Swiss political leader.

Laharpe or **La Harpe**, Jean François de (name orig. Delharpe or Delaharpe) (1739—1803), Fr. critic and dramatist.

Laing (läng), Alexander Gordon (1793—1826), Sc. explorer in Africa.

Lake (läk), Gerard Lake, 1st Viscount (1744—1808), Eng. general.

Lake, Kirsopp (1872—   ), Eng.-Am. theologian.

Lake, Simon (1866—   ), Am. engineer and naval architect.

Lalande (dẹ lä-länd), Joseph Jérôme Lefrançais de (1732—1807), Fr. astronomer.

Lally (dẹ lȧ-lē), Thomas Arthur, Comte de (Baron de Tollendal) (1702—66), Fr. general and administrator in India.

Lally-Tollendal (-to-lon-dȧl), Trophime Gérard, Marquis de (1751—1830), Fr. politician and writer (son of Thomas Arthur, Comte de Lally).

Lalo (lȧ-lō), Édouard Victor Antoine (1823—92), Fr. musical composer.

Lamar (lạ-mär'), Lucius Quintus Cincinnatus (1825—93), Am. legislator and jurist, associate justice of U. S. Supreme Court (1888—93).

La Marck (dẹ lä märk), Guillaume (or William) de ("the Wild Boar of the Ardennes") (c1446—85), Belgian outlaw and rebel leader.

Lamarck (dẹ lä-märk), Jean Baptiste Pierre Antoine de Monet de (1744—1829), Fr. naturalist.

La Marck, Robert de. See *Fleuranges, Seigneur de.*

La Marmora (dē lä mär'mō-rä), Alfonso Ferrero, Marchese di (1804—78), It. general and statesman.

Lamartine (dẹ lȧ-mär-tēn), Alphonse Marie Louis de (1790—1869), Fr. poet, historian, and statesman.

Lamb (lam), Charles ("Elia") (1775—1834), Eng. essayist and misc. writer.

Lamb, Mary Ann (1764—1847), Eng. writer (sister of Charles).

Lamb, William. See *Melbourne, 2d Viscount.*

Lamballe (dẹ län-bȧl), Princesse de (Marie Thérèse Louise de Savoie-Carignan) (1749—92), Fr. princess, born in Italy, friend of Marie Antoinette, and murdered by mob.

Lambert (lam'bẽrt), Saint (c635—c700), Frankish bishop and martyr.

Lambert, John (1619—83?), Eng. parliamentary general in civil war.

Lambton (lam'tọn), John George. See *Durham, 1st Earl of.*

Lamennais (dẹ lȧ-me-nä), Hugues Félicité Robert de (1782—1854), Fr. priest, and writer on religion and politics.

La Mettrie (dẹ lä me-trē), Julien Offray de (1709—51), Fr. physician and philosopher.

Lamoricière (dė lá-mo-rē-syār), Christophe **Léon Louis** Juchault de (1806—65), Fr. general.

Lancaster (lang′kas-tėr), Duke of. See *John of Gaunt*.

Lancaster, Earl of. See *Edmund* (1245—96).

Lancaster, Sir James (d. 1618), Eng. sea-captain, and trader with the East Indies.

Lancaster, Joseph (1778—1838), Eng. educationist.

Lanciani (län-chä′nē), Rodolfo Amedeo (1846—1929), It. archæologist.
[in Africa.

Lander (lan′dėr), Richard Lemon (1804—34), Eng. explorer

Landon (lan′dọn), Alfred Mossman (1887—   ), Am. political leader, governor of Kansas.

Landon, Letitia Elizabeth (Mrs. Maclean, "L. E. L.") (1802—38), Eng. poet and novelist.

Landor (lan′dọr), A. Henry Savage (1865?—1924), Eng. artist and explorer (grandson of Walter S.).

Landor, Walter Savage (1775—1864), Eng. author.

Landseer (land′sēr), Sir Edwin Henry (1802—73), Eng. animal-painter.
[and Arabic scholar.

Lane (lān), Edward William (1801—76), Eng. Egyptologist

Lane, Sir Ralph (d. 1603), Eng. adventurer, and colonial governor in America.

Lanfranc (lan′frangk) (c1005—89), archbishop of Canterbury and scholar, born in Lombardy.

Lang (lang), Andrew (1844—1912), Br. poet, critic, and misc. writer.

Langdell (lang′del), Christopher Columbus (1826—1906), Am. legal writer and educator.

Langdon (lang′dọn), John (1741—1819), Am. statesman.

Langland (lang′land), William (c1330—c1400), supposed Eng. poet, reputed author of "Piers Plowman."

Langley (lang′li), Edmund of. See *York, 1st Duke of*.

Langley, Samuel Pierpont (1834—1906), Am. astronomer and aëronautic inventor.

Langmuir (lang′mūr), Irving (1881—   ), Am. chemist.

Langton (lang′tọn), Stephen (d. 1228), Eng. cardinal, and archbishop of Canterbury.

Lanier (lạ-nēr′), Sidney (1842—81), Am. poet.

Lankester (lang′kes-tėr), Sir Edwin Ray (1847—1929), Eng. zoölogist.

Lanman (lan′man), Charles Rockwell (1850—1941), Am. Sanskrit scholar.

Lannes (län), Jean (Duc de Montebello) (1769—1809), Fr. marshal.

La Noue (dė lä nö), François de (called Bras de Fer, 'Arm of Iron') (1531—91), Fr. Huguenot soldier.

Lansdowne (lanz′doun), Henry Charles Keith Petty-Fitzmaurice, 5th Marquis of (1845—1927), Eng. statesman, governor-general of Canada (1883—88) (grandson of 3d Marquis).

Lansdowne, Henry Petty-Fitzmaurice, 3d Marquis of (1780—1863), Eng. statesman (son of 1st Marquis).

Lansdowne, William Petty-Fitzmaurice, 1st Marquis of (Earl of Shelburne) (1737—1805), Br. statesman.

Lansing (lan′sing), Robert (1864—1928), Am. lawyer and statesman.

Lanzi (län′tsē), Luigi (1732—1810), It. archæologist and writer on art.

Lao-tsze (lä′ō-tsė′) (b. c604 B.C.), Chin. philosopher, reputed founder of Taoism.

La Pérouse (dė lä pä-röz), Jean François de Galaup, Comte de (1741—88?), Fr. naval officer and navigator.

Laplace (dė lá-plás), Pierre Simon, Marquis de (1749—1827), Fr. astronomer and mathematician.

Larcom (lär′kọm), Lucy (1826—93), Am. poet.

La Rochefoucauld (dė lä rosh-fö-kō), François, Duc de (Prince de Marcillac) (1613—80), Fr. writer, author of "Maximes."

La Rochejaquelein (dė lä rosh-zhák-lań), Henri du Vergier, Comte de (1772—94), Fr. Vendean leader.

Larousse (lá-rös), Pierre Athanase (1817—75), Fr. grammarian, lexicographer, and encyclopedist.

La Salle (dė lä sál), Jean Baptiste de (1651—1719), Fr. priest, educator, and saint, founder of order of Brothers of the Christian Schools.

La Salle, René Robert Cavelier de (1643—87), Fr. explorer of the Ohio and the Mississippi.

Lascaris (las′kạ-ris), Theodore. See *Theodore I*.

Las Casas (dä läs kä′säs), Bartolomé de (1474—1566), Sp. monk, reformer, and historian.

Las Cases (dė läs käz), Emmanuel Augustin Dieudonné, Marquis de (1766—1842), Fr. historian, for a time with Napoleon I. at St. Helena.

Laski (läs′kē), Jan (as Latinized, Johannes a Lasco) (1499—1560), Pol. Protestant reformer.

Lassalle (lä-sál′), Ferdinand (1825—64), Ger. socialist.

Lassus (las′us), Orlandus (also called Orlando di Lasso, orig. Roland de Lattre) (1520? or 1530?—94), Belgian musical composer.

Latimer (lat′i-mėr), Hugh (c1490—1555), Eng. Protestant bishop, reformer, and martyr.

Latini (lä-tē′nē), Brunetto (c1210—94?), It. statesman, scholar, and poet.

La Tour d'Auvergne (dė lä tör dō-värn-y′), Théophile Malo Corret de (name orig. Corret; called "the first grenadier of France") (1743—1800), Fr. soldier.

Latude (lá-tüd), Jean Henry (also called Danry and Masers de Latude) (1725—1805), Fr. adventurer, a prisoner in the Bastille.

Laud (låd), William (1573—1645), Eng. prelate, archbishop of Canterbury.

Lauder (lä′dėr), Sir Harry MacLennan (1870—   ), Sc. singer and entertainer.

Lauderdale (lä′dėr-dāl), John Maitland, Duke of (1616—82), Sc. politician.

Laudon or **Loudon** (fon lou′don), Gideon Ernst, Freiherr von (1717—90), Austrian field-marshal.

Laudonnière (dė lō-do-nyār), René de (d. after 1586), Fr. Huguenot colonizer in Florida (1564).

Laurens (lō-roṅs), Jean Paul (1838—1921), Fr. painter.

Laurier (lä′ri-ā), Sir Wilfrid (1841—1919), Can. statesman, premier of Canada (1896—1911).

Lauzun (dė lō-zuṅ), Antonin Nompar de Caumont, Duc de (1632—1723), Fr. courtier and soldier.

La Vallière (dė lä vá-lyār), Françoise Louise de La Baume Le Blanc, Duchesse de (1644—1710), mistress of Louis XIV. of France.

Laval-Montmorency (dė lá-vál-môṅ-mo-roṅ-sē), François Xavier de (1623—1708), Fr. prelate in Canada.

Lavater (lä′vä-tėr), Johann Kaspar (1741—1801), Swiss theologian, poet, and physiognomist.

Lavedan (láv-däṅ), Henri (1859—1940), Fr. dramatist.

Laveran (láv-räṅ), Charles Louis Alphonse (1845—1922), Fr. physician.

Lavery (lav′ėr-i), Sir John (1856—1941), Br. painter.

Lavigerie (lá-vēzh-rē), Charles Martial Allemand (1825—92), Fr. archbishop of Algiers, and cardinal.

Lavisse (lá-vēs), Ernest (1842—1922), Fr. historian and educator.

Lavoisier (lá-vwo-zyā), Antoine Laurent (1743—94), Fr. chemist.

La Voisin (lä vwo-zaṅ) (real name Catherine Deshayes, Mme. Monvoisin) (d. 1680), Fr. sorceress and poisoner.

Law (lä), Andrew Bonar (1858—1923), Br. statesman, born in Canada.

Law, Edward. See *Ellenborough*.

Law, John (1671—1729), Sc. financier, promoter of Mississippi Scheme in France.

Law, William (1686—1761), Eng. divine, and religious writer.

Lawrence (lä′rẹns), Saint (d. 258), Rom. Christian martyr. According to legend, he was burned alive on a gridiron.

Lawrence, David Herbert (1885—1930), Eng. novelist and misc. writer.

Lawrence, George Alfred (1827—76), Eng. novelist.

Lawrence, Sir Henry Montgomery (1806—57), Br. general and administrator in India.

Lawrence, James (1781—1813), Am. naval officer.

Lawrence, John Laird Mair Lawrence, 1st Baron (1811—79), Br. statesman and administrator in India (brother of Sir Henry M.).

Lawrence, Stringer (1697—1775), Eng. soldier in India.

Lawrence, Sir Thomas (1769—1830), Eng. painter.

Lawrence (changed to Shaw in 1927), Thomas Edward (1888—1935), Br. archæologist and soldier in western Asia.

Lawton (lä′tọn), Henry Ware (1843—99), Am. general.

Layamon (lä′yạ-mọn or lä′ạ-mọn) (fl. c1200), Eng. chronicler in verse.

Layard (lä′ạrd), Sir Austen Henry (1817—94), Eng. archæologist.

Lea (lē), Henry Charles (1825—1909), Am. historian.

Leake (lēk), William Martin (1777—1860), Eng. military officer, and topographer and antiquary.

Lear (lēr), Edward (1812—88), Eng. artist and humorist.

Lebœuf (lẹ-bẹf), Edmond (1809—88), Fr. marshal.

Le Braz (lẹ brä), Anatole (1859—1926), Fr. author.

Le Brun (lẹ bruṅ) or **Lebrun** (lẹ-bruṅ), Charles (1619—90), Fr. painter.

Lebrun, Charles François (Duc de Plaisance) (1739—1824), Fr. statesman and writer.

Le Brun or **Lebrun**, Mme. (Marie Anne Élisabeth Vigée, often called Mme. Vigée-Lebrun) (1755—1842), Fr. painter.

Lecky (lek′i), William Edward Hartpole (1838—1903), Br. historian.

Lecocq (lẹ-kok), Alexandre Charles (1832—1918), Fr. composer of operettas.

Lecocq or **Le Coq**, Robert (c1310—68?), Fr. bishop and politician.

Le Conte (lẹ kont), Joseph (1823—1901), Am. geologist.

Leconte de Lisle (lẹ-kôṅt dẹ lēl), Charles Marie René (1818—94), Fr. poet.

Lecouvreur (lẹ-kö-vrẹr), Adrienne (1692—1730), Fr. actress.

Ledru-Rollin (lẹ-drü-ro-laṅ), Alexandre Auguste (1807—74), Fr. radical politician.

Ledyard (led′yạrd), John (1751—89), Am. traveler.

Lee (lē), Ann (Mrs. Stanley, "Mother Ann") (1736—84), Eng. religious visionary, founder of Shakers in America.

Lee, Arthur (1740—92), Am. diplomatist (brother of Richard H.).

Lee, Charles (1731—82), Am. general, born in England.

Lee, Fitzhugh (1835—1905), Am. general (nephew of R. E. Lee).

Lee, Francis Lightfoot (1734—97), Am. patriot (brother of Richard H.).

Lee, Henry ("Light-Horse Harry") (1756—1818), Am. general.

Lee, Nathaniel (1653?—92), Eng. dramatist.

Lee, Richard Henry (1732—94), Am. patriot and statesman.

Lee, Robert Edward (1807—70), Am. Confederate general (son of Henry).

Lee, Sir Sidney (1859—1926), Eng. biographer and critic.

Lee, Vernon. Pseudonym of Violet Paget.

Leech (lēch), John (1817—64), Eng. caricaturist and illustrator.

Leeds (lēdz), Thomas Osborne, 1st Duke of (Earl of Danby) (1631—1712), Eng. statesman.

Leeuwenhoek or **Leuwenhoek** (vän lä′vẹn-húk), Antonius van (1632—1723), Dutch microscopist and naturalist.

Lefebvre (lẹ-fävr), François Joseph (Duc de Dantzig) (1755—1820), Fr. marshal.

Lefèvre d'Étaples (lẹ-fävr dä-tápl), Jacques. See *Faber, Jacobus.*

Legendre (lẹ-zhoṅdr), Adrien Marie (1752—1833), Fr. mathematician.

Legge (leg), William. See *Dartmouth, 2d Earl of.*

Legouis (lẹ-gwē), Émile (1861—1937), Fr. scholar.

Legouvé (lẹ-gö-vä), Gabriel Jean Baptiste Ernest Wilfrid (1807—1903), Fr. dramatist.

Legros (lẹ-grō), Alphonse (1837—1911), Fr.-Eng. painter and etcher.

Lehár (le′här), Franz (1870—   ), Hung. composer of operettas.

Lehmann (lä′män), Lilli (Frau Kalisch) (1848—1929), Ger. operatic soprano singer.

Leibl (lī′bl), Wilhelm (1844—1900), Ger. painter.

Leibnitz or **Leibniz** (fon līp′nits), Gottfried Wilhelm, Freiherr von (1646—1716), Ger. philosopher, mathematician, and political writer.

Leicester (les′tẹr), Robert Dudley, Earl of (1532?—88), Eng. courtier, favorite of Queen Elizabeth (son of Duke of Northumberland).

Leichhardt (līch′härt), Friedrich Wilhelm Ludwig (1813—48?), Ger. explorer in Australia.

Leidy (lī′di), Joseph (1823—91), Am. anatomist, biologist, and naturalist.

Leif Ericsson (lēf er′ik-sọn) (fl. 1000), Scand. navigator, discoverer of "Vinland" (Nova Scotia?) (son of Eric the Red).

Leighton (lä′tọn), Frederic Leighton, Baron (1830—96), Eng. painter and sculptor.

Leighton, Robert (1611—84), Sc. archbishop and theological writer.

Leisler (līs′lẹr), Jacob (d. 1691), de facto (insurgent) colonial governor of New York, born in Germany.

L. E. L. Literary signature of Letitia E. Landon.

Leland (lē′lạnd), Charles Godfrey (1824—1903), Am. author.

Leland, John (c1506—52), Eng. antiquary.

Leloir (lẹ-lwor), Alexandre Louis (1843—84), Fr. painter (son of Jean B. A.).

Leloir, Jean Baptiste Auguste (1809—92), Fr. painter.

Lely (lē′li), Sir Peter (orig. Pieter van der Faes) (1618—80), Dutch-Eng. portrait-painter.

Lemaître (lẹ-mätr), Antoine Louis Prosper (called Frédérick Lemaître) (1800—76), Fr. actor.

Lemaître, François Élie Jules (1853—1915), Fr. critic, dramatist, and misc. writer.

Leman (lẹ-män), Gérard Mathieu Joseph Georges (1851—1920), Belgian general, defender of Liége.

Lemercier (lẹ-mer-syä), Jacques (c1585—1654?), Fr. architect.

Lemon (lem′ọn), Mark (1809—70), Eng. editor, playwright, and misc. writer.

Lemonnier (lẹ-mo-nyä), Pierre Charles (1715—99), Fr. astronomer.

Le Moyne (lẹ mwän). See *Bienville* and *Iberville.*

Lemoyne (lẹ-mwän), François (1688—1737), Fr. painter.

Lemprière (lem-prẹr′), John (c1765—1824), Eng. classical scholar.

Lenard (le-närt′), Philipp (1862—   ), Ger. physicist, born in Hungary.

Lenau (lä′nou), Nikolaus. Pseudonym of Nikolaus Niembsch von Strehlenau.

Lenbach (fon len′bäch), Franz von (1836—1904), Ger. portrait-painter.

Lenclos (loṅ-klō), Ninon de (real name Anne Lenclos) (1616?—1706?), Fr. woman notable for her amours and later for social leadership.

L'Enfant (loṅ-fäṅ), Pierre Charles (1755—1825), Fr.-Am. soldier and engineer, who laid out city of Washington.

Lenin (len′in, Russ. lye′nyẹn), Nikolay (real name Vladimir Ilich Ulyanov) (1870—1924), Russ. Bolshevik leader, head of the soviet government.

Lennox (len′ọks), Matthew Stuart (or Stewart), Earl of (1516—71), Sc. politician and soldier, and regent of Scotland.

Lenormant (lẹ-nôr-mäṅ), François (1837—83), Fr. archæologist and historian.

Lenôtre (lẹ-nōtr), André (1613—1700), Fr. architect and landscape-gardener.

Lenthall (lent′âl), William (1591—1662), Eng. politician, speaker of House of Commons.

Lenz (lents), Oskar (1848—1925), Ger.-Austrian explorer in Africa.

Leo I. (lē′ō) ("the Thracian") (c400—474), Eastern Rom. emperor (457—474).

Leo III. ("the Isaurian") (c680—741), Byzantine emperor (717—741).

Leo V. ("the Armenian") (d. 820), Byzantine emperor (813—820).

Leo I., Saint ("Leo the Great") (d. 461), It. cleric, pope (440—461).

Leo III., Saint (d. 816), It. ecclesiastic, pope (795—816).

Leo X. (Giovanni de' Medici) (1475—1521), It. ecclesiastic, pope (1513—21) (son of Lorenzo de' Medici).

Leo XII. (Annibale della Genga) (1760—1829), It. ecclesiastic, pope (1823—29).

Leo XIII. (Gioacchino Pecci) (1810—1903), It. ecclesiastic, pope (1878—1903).

Leochares (lẹ-ok′ạ-rēz) (fl. c350 B.C.), Gr. sculptor.

Leofric (lẹ-of′rik) (d. 1057), earl of Mẹrcia.

León, Juan Ponce de. See *Ponce de León.*

Leonardo da Pisa (lā-ō-när′dō dä pē′zä) (Leonardo Fibonacci) (fl. c1200–c1225), It. mathematician.

Leonardo da Vinci. See *Vinci*.

Leoncavallo (lā″ōn-kä-väl′lō), Ruggiero (1858–1919), It. [operatic composer.

Leonidas I. (lē-on′i-dạs) (d. 480 B.C.), Spartan king and general, killed defending pass of Thermopylæ. [poet.

Leopardi (lā-ō-pär′dē), Count Giacomo (1798–1837), It.

Leopold I. (lē′ọ-pōld) (1676–1747), prince of Anhalt-Dessau (1693–1747), and Prussian field-marshal.

Leopold I. (1790–1865), king of the Belgians (1831–65).

Leopold II. (1835–1909), king of the Belgians (1865–1909) (son of Leopold I., king of the Belgians).

Leopold III. (1901–), king of the Belgians (1934–) (son of Albert I., king of the Belgians).

Leopold I. (1640–1705), emperor of Holy Roman Empire (1658–1705) (son of Emperor Ferdinand III.).

Leopold II. (1747–92), emperor of Holy Roman Empire (1790–92) (brother of Joseph II.).

Leopold II. (1797–1870), grand duke of Tuscany (1824–59).

Lepidus (lep′i-dus), Marcus Æmilius (d. 13 B.C.), Rom. politician, member of Second Triumvirate.

Le Play (lẹ plä), Pierre Guillaume Frédéric (1806–82), Fr. engineer and sociologist.

Lepsius (lep′sẹ-ùs), Karl Richard (1810–84), Ger. Egyptologist and philologist.

Lerdo de Tejada (lãr′dō dä tᾱ-Hä′ʀHä), Sebastián (1825–89), Mex. statesman, president of Mexico (1872–76).

Lerma (lãr′mä), Francisco de Sandoval y Rojas, Duke of (c1555–1625), Sp. statesman.

Lermontov (lyer′mon-tof), Mikhail Yurevich (1814–41), Russ. poet and novelist.

Leroy-Beaulieu (lẹ-rwo-bō-lyẹ), Anatole (1842–1912), Fr. historical and political writer.

Leroy-Beaulieu, Pierre Paul (1843–1916), Fr. political economist (brother of Anatole).

Le Sage (lẹ säzh), Alain René (1668–1747), Fr. novelist and dramatist, author of "Gil Blas."

Leschetizky (lesh-ẹ-tit′skẹ), Theodor (1830–1915), Austrian (Polish) pianist and teacher.

Lescot (les-kō), Pierre (c1510–78), Fr. architect.

Leslie (les′li or lez′li), Alexander. See *Leven, 1st Earl of.*

Lespinasse (dẹ les-pē-nás), Julie Jeanne Éléonore de (1732–76), Fr. letter-writer.

Lesseps (dẹ le-seps), Ferdinand, Vicomte de (1805–94), Fr. diplomatist, promoter of Suez Canal.

Lessing (les′ing), Gotthold Ephraim (1729–81), Ger. critic and dramatist.

L'Estrange (les-trãnj′), Sir Roger (1616–1704), Eng. journalist and pamphleteer.

Leszczynski (lesh-chin′skẹ). See *Stanislaus I.* (of Poland), also *Marie Leszczynska.*

Leuwenhoek. See *Leeuwenhoek.*

Leven (lē′vẹn), Alexander Leslie, 1st Earl of (c1580–1661), Sc. general, long in Swedish service.

Lever (lē′vẹr), Charles James (1806–72), Ir. novelist.

Leverrier (lẹ-ve-ryä), Urbain Jean Joseph (1811–77), Fr. astronomer.

Lewes (lū′es), George Henry (1817–78), Eng. philosophical and misc. writer.

Lewis (lū′is), Matthew Gregory ("Monk Lewis") (1775–1818), Eng. novelist and misc. writer.

Lewis, Meriwether (1774–1809), Am. explorer, joint commander with William Clark of expedition to Oregon.

Lewis, Sinclair (1885–), Am. novelist.

Leyden (lī′dẹn), John (1775–1811), Sc. Orientalist and writer.

Leyden, Lucas van. See *Lucas van Leyden.*

L'Hôpital or **L'Hospital** (dẹ lō-pē-tàl), Michel de (c1505–73), Fr. statesman.

Liddell (lid′ẹl), Henry George (1811–98), Eng. clergyman and classical scholar.

Liddon (lid′on), Henry Parry (1829–90), Eng. divine and pulpit orator.

Lie (lē), Jonas (1880–1940), Norw.-Am. painter (nephew of Jonas L. E. Lie, 1833–1908).

Lie, Jonas Lauritz Edemil (1833–1908), Norw. novelist.

Liebermann (lē′bẹr-män), Max (1847–1935), Ger. painter and etcher.

Liebig (fon lē′biċh), Justus, Freiherr von (1803–73), Ger. chemist.

Liebknecht (lēp′knecht), Karl Paul August Friedrich (1871–1919), Ger. socialist, leader of the Spartacans (son of Wilhelm).

Liebknecht, Wilhelm (1826–1900), Ger. socialist leader.

Liggett (lig′et), Hunter (1857–1935), Am. general.

Lightfoot (līt′fut), John (1602–75), Eng. divine and Hebraist.

Lightfoot, Joseph Barber (1828–89), Eng. bishop, theologian, and Biblical scholar.

Ligne (dẹ lēn-y′), Charles Joseph, Prince de (1735–1814), Austrian general and writer, born in Belgium.

Liguori (dä lē-gwō′rē), Alfonso Maria de' (1696–1787), It. bishop, theologian, and saint, founder of order of Redemptorists.

Li Hung-chang (lē hùng-chäng′) (1823–1901), Chin. statesman.

Liliencron (fon lēl′yẹn-krōn), Detlev, Freiherr von (1844–1909), Ger. poet and novelist.

Lilienthal (lēl′yẹn-täl), Otto (1848–96), Ger. aëronautic inventor.

Liliuokalani (lē″lẹ-ọ-ō-kä-lä′nē) (Lydia Kamekeha Liliuokalani, Mrs. Dominis) (1838–1917), queen (1891–93) and last monarch of Hawaiian Islands (sister and successor of Kalakaua).

Lillo (lil′ō), George (1693–1739), Eng. dramatist.

Lilly (lil′i), William (1602–81), Eng. astrologer.

Lily or **Lilye** (lil′i), William (c1468–1522), Eng. Latin grammarian.

Lima e Silva (dä lē′mä ā sēl′vä), Luis Alves de (Duke of Caxias) (1803–80), Brazilian general and statesman.

Liman von Sanders (lē′män fon zän′dẹrs), Otto (1855–1929), Ger. general.

Limosin (lē-mō-zan) or **Limousin** (lē-mö-zan), Léonard (c1505–c1577), Fr. painter of enamel.

Linacre (lin′ạ-kẹr), Thomas (c1460–1524), Eng. physician and classical scholar.

Lincoln (ling′kọn), Abraham (1809–65), 16th president of U. S. (1861–65).

Lincoln, Benjamin (1733–1810), Am. Revolutionary general.

Lincoln, Joseph Crosby (1870–1944), Am. novelist.

Lind (lind), Jenny (Mrs. Goldschmidt) (1820–87), Swed.-Eng. soprano singer.

Lindau (lin′dou), Paul (1839–1919), Ger. author.

Lindbergh (lind′bẹrg), Charles August (1902–), Am. aviator (made non-stop flight, alone, N. Y. to Paris, 1927).

Lindley (lind′li), John (1799–1865), Eng. botanist.

Lindsay or **Lyndsay** (lin′zi), Sir David (c1490–c1555), Sc. poet.

Lindsay, Nicholas Vachel (1879–1931), Am. poet.

Lindsey (lin′zi), Theophilus (1723–1808), Eng. Unitarian clergyman and theologian.

Linevich (lyẹ-nye′vich), Nikolay Petrovich (1838–1908), Russ. general.

Lingard (ling′gärd), John (1771–1851), Eng. Rom. Cath. priest and historian.

Linnæus (li-nē′us), Carolus (in Swedish, Karl von Linné) (1707–78), Swed. botanist.

Linschoten or **Linschooten** (vän lin′skō-tẹn), Jan Huygen van (1563?–1611), Dutch voyager.

Linton (lin′tọn), William James (1812–97), Eng.-Am. woodengraver, political reformer, and writer.

Lippi (lēp′pē), Filippino, or Lippino (1458?–c1505), Florentine painter (son of Filippo).

Lippi, Fra Filippo (c1406–69), Florentine painter.

Lipsius (lip′sẹ-ùs), Justus (Joest Lips) (1547–1606), Flemish scholar.

Lissauer (lis′ou″ẹr), Ernst (1882–), Ger. poet.

List (list), Friedrich (1789–1846), Ger. political economist.

Lister (lis′tẹr), Joseph Lister, Baron (1827–1912), Eng. surgeon, introducer of antiseptic surgery.

Liszt (list), Franz (1811–86), Hung. pianist and composer.

Littleton (lit′l-tọn), Sir Thomas (c1407–81), Eng. jurist.

Littré (lē-trä), Maximilien Paul Émile (1801–81), Fr. philos.

Litvinov (lit-vē′nôf), Maxim (1876–), Russ. statesman.

Liutprand (lẹ-öt′prand) or **Luitprand** (lö′it-prand) (c922–c972), It. bishop and historian.

(variable) d̦ as d or j, ṣ as s or sh, ț as t or ch, z̦ as z or zh; o, F. cloche; ü, F. menu; ċh, Sc. loch; ṅ, F. bonbon; ′, primary accent; ″, secondary accent; †, obsolete; <, from; +, and; =, equals. See also lists at beginning of book.

Liverpool (liv′ẽr-pöl), Charles Jenkinson, 1st Earl of (1727—1808), Eng. statesman.

Liverpool, Robert Banks Jenkinson, 2d Earl of (1770—1828), Eng. statesman (son of 1st Earl).

Livingston (liv′ing-stọn), Edward (1764—1836), Am. jurist and statesman (brother of Robert R.).

Livingston, Philip (1716—78), Am. patriot.

Livingston, Robert R. (1746—1813), Am. jurist and statesman.

Livingstone (liv′ing-stọn), David (1813—73), Sc. missionary and explorer in Africa.

Livius Andronicus (liv′i-us an-drọ-nī′kus). See *Andronicus, Livius.*

Livy (liv′i) (Titus Livius) (59 B.C.—A.D. 17), Rom. historian.

Llewelyn or **Llewellyn** (lọ-el′in) (Llywelyn ab Gruffydd) (d. 1282), Welsh prince, supporter of English barons in war against Henry III., and killed in revolt against Edward I.

Lloyd George (loid jôrj), David (1863—1945), Br. statesman.

Lochner (loċh′nẽr), Stephan ("Meister Stephan") (d. 1451?), Ger. painter, of Cologne school.

Locke (lok), David Ross ("Petroleum V. Nasby") (1833—88), Am. humorist.

Locke, John (1632—1704), Eng. philosopher.

Locke, William John (1863—1930), Eng. novelist.

Locker-Lampson (lok′ẽr-lamp′sọn), Frederick (orig. Frederick Locker) (1821—95), Eng. poet.

Lockhart (lok′ärt or lok′härt), John Gibson (1794—1854), Sc. writer and editor, biographer of Sir Walter Scott.

Lockyer (lok′yẽr), Sir Joseph Norman (1836—1920), Eng. astronomer.

Lodge (loj), Henry Cabot (1850—1924), Am. senator (from Massachusetts) and author.

Lodge, Sir Oliver Joseph (1851—1940), Eng. physicist and writer.

Lodge, Thomas (c1558—1625), Eng. dramatist, poet, and misc. writer.

Loeb (lōb), Jacques (1859—1924), Ger.-Am. physiologist and experimental biologist.

Loeffler (lẽf′lẽr), Friedrich (1852—1915), Ger. physician and bacteriologist.

Löffler (lẽf′lẽr). See *Loeffler.*

Logan (lō′gạn), John (native name Tah-gah-jute) (c1725—80), Am. Indian chief.

Logan, John Alexander (1826—86), Am. general and legislator.

Logue (lōg), Michael (1840—1924), Ir. cardinal.

Loisy (lwo-zē′), Alfred Firmin (1857—   ), Fr. Rom. Cath. Biblical critic and theologian, excommunicated in 1908.

Lola Montez (lō′lạ mon′tez). See *Montez, Lola.*

Lombard, Peter. See *Peter Lombard.*

Lombardo (lom-bär′dō), Pietro (real name Pietro Solaro) (c1435—c1515), It. architect and sculptor.

Lombroso (lom-brō′zō), Cesare (1836—1909), It. physician and criminologist.

Loménie de Brienne (dẽ lo-mā-nē dẽ brē-en), Étienne Charles de (1727—94), Fr. prelate and politician.

Lomonosov (lo-mo-nọ′sof), Mikhail Vasilevich (1711—65), Russ. poet, philologist, and scientist.

London (lun′dọn), Jack (1876—1916), Am. novelist.

Londonderry (lun′dọn-der″i), Charles William Stewart, later Vane, 3d Marquis of (1778—1854), Br. general and diplomatist (half-brother of 2d Marquis).

Londonderry, Robert Stewart, 2d Marquis of (Viscount Castlereagh) (1769—1822), Br. statesman.

Longchamp (lôn-shän), William of (d. 1197), bishop of Ely, and chancellor and chief justiciary of England.

Longfellow (lông′fel″ō), Henry Wadsworth (1807—82), Am. poet.

Longinus (lon-jī′nus), Cassius (c213—273), Gr. rhetorician and philosophical critic.

Longstreet (lông′strēt), James (1821—1904), Am. Confederate general.

Longueville (dẽ lông-vēl), Duchesse de (Anne Geneviève de Bourbon-Condé) (1619—79), Fr. political leader, and Jansenist (sister of Louis II. de Bourbon, Prince de Condé).

Longus (long′gus) (fl. 3d? cent.), Gr. romance-writer.

Longworth (lông′wẽrth), Nicholas (1782—1863), Am. horticulturist.

Longworth, Nicholas (1869—1931), Am. legislator (great-grandson of N. Longworth, 1782—1863).

Lope de Vega (lō′pä dä vä′gä). See *Vega Carpio.*

López (lō′päs), Carlos Antonio (1790—1862), president of Paraguay (1844—62).

López, Francisco Solano (1827?—70), president of Paraguay (1862—70) (son of Carlos Antonio).

Lorenz (lō′rents), Adolf (1854—1946), Austrian orthopædic surgeon.

Lorenzetti (lo-ren-tset′tē), Ambrogio (d. 1348?), It. painter, of Sienese school (brother of Pietro).

Lorenzetti, Pietro (fl. 1305—48), It. painter, of Sienese school.

Lorenzo (lo-ren′tsō), Don (also called Lorenzo Monaco) (c1370—c1425), It. monk and painter, in Florence.

Lorenzo di Pietro (dē pye′trō) (called Il Vecchietta) (1412?—80), Sienese painter, sculptor, goldsmith, and architect.

Loris-Melikov (lō′rẹs-me′lyẹ-kof), Count Mikhail Tarielovich (1826?—88), Russ. general and statesman.

Lorme, Marion de. See *Delorme, Marion.*

Lorne (lôrn), Marquis of. See *Argyll, 9th Duke of.*

Lorrain, Claude. See *Claude Lorrain.*

Lorraine (dẽ lo-rän), Charles, Cardinal de (also called Cardinal de Guise) (1524—74), Fr. prelate and statesman (brother of 2d Duc de Guise).

Lorraine. See *Guise.*

Lorris, Guillaume de. See *Guillaume de Lorris.*

Lortzing (lôrt′sing), Gustav Albert (1803—51), Ger. operatic composer.

Lossing (los′ing), Benson John (1813—91), Am. historian.

Lothair or **Lothaire** (lọ-thâr′) (941—986), king of the Franks (954—986) (son of Louis IV.).

Lothair I. or **Lothaire I.** (c795—855), Rom. emperor (843—855) (son of Louis the Pious, and half-brother of Charles the Bald).

Lothair II. or **Lothaire II.** (in German, Lothar, pron. lō′tär, called "the Saxon") (c1070—1137), emperor of the Holy Roman Empire (1125—37).

Loti (lo-tē), Pierre. Pseudonym of L. M. J. Viaud.

Lotto (lot′tō), Lorenzo (1480?—1556), It. painter.

Lotze (lot′sẹ), Rudolf Hermann (1817—81), Ger. philosopher, psychologist, and physiologist.

Loubet (lö-bā′), Émile (1838—1929), Fr. statesman, president of France (1899—1906).

Loudon, Gideon Ernst, Freiherr von. See *Laudon.*

Loudon (lou′dọn), John Claudius (1783—1843), Br. landscape-gardener, and writer on horticulture.

Louis I. (lö′i or lö′is, Fr. lö-ē) (called Louis le Débonnaire, also Louis the Pious) (778—840), king of the Franks and Rom. emperor (814—840) (son of Charlemagne).

Louis II. ("Louis the Stammerer") (846—879), king of the Franks (877—879) (son of Charles I.).

Louis III. (c863—882), king (conjointly with Carloman) of the Franks (879—882) (son of Louis II.).

Louis IV. ("Louis d'Outremer") (921—954), king of the Franks (936—954) (successor of Rudolf, and son of Charles III.).

Louis V. ("Louis le Fainéant") (967?—987), king of the Franks (986—987) (son of Lothair).

Louis VI. ("Louis the Fat") (c1080—1137), king of France (1108—37) (son of Philip I.).

Louis VII. ("Louis the Young") (c1120—80), king of France (1137—80) (son of Louis VI.).

Louis VIII. ("Louis the Lion") (1187—1226), king of France (1223—26) (son of Philip II.).

Louis IX. (Saint Louis) (1215—70), king of France (1226—70) (son of Louis VIII.).

Louis X. ("Louis the Quarreler") (1289—1316), king of France (1314—16) (son of Philip IV.).

Louis XI. (1423—83), king of France (1461—83) (son of Charles VII.).

Louis XII. ("the Father of the People") (1462—1515), king of France (1498—1515) (successor of Charles VIII., and son of Duc d'Orléans, 1391—1465, and first king of branch line of Valois-Orléans).

Louis XIII. (1601—43), king of France (1610—43) (son of Henry IV.).

fat, fāte, fär, fåll, ȧsk, fāre; net, mē, hẽr; pin, pīne; not, nōte, mŏve, nôr; up, lūte, pùll; oi, oil; ou, out; (lightened) aviȧry, ẹlect, agŏny, intö, ụnite; (obscured) errạnt, operạ, ardẹnt, actọr, natụre; ch, chip; g, go; th, thin; ᴛн, then; y, you;

Louis XIV. ("Louis the Great") (1638—1715), king of France (1643—1715) (son of Louis XIII.).

Louis XV. (1710—74), king of France (1715—74) (great-grandson of Louis XIV.).

Louis XVI. (1754—93), king of France from 1774, deposed in 1792, guillotined in 1793 (grandson of Louis XV.).

Louis XVII. (1785—95), titular king of France (1793—95) (son of Louis XVI.).

Louis XVIII. (1755—1824), king of France (1814—24) (successor of Napoleon I., and brother of Louis XVI.).

Louis (in German, Ludwig, pron. löt′vich, called "the German") (804—876), king of Germany (843—876) (son of Louis the Pious, and half-brother of Charles the Bald).

Louis II. (825?—875), king of Italy (844—875) and Rom. emperor (855—875) (son of Lothair I.).

Louis IV. ("the Bavarian") (1287?—1347), emperor of the Holy Roman Empire (1314—47) (grandson of Rudolf I. of Germany).

Louis I. (in German, Ludwig) (1786—1868), king of Bavaria (1825—48).

Louis II. (1845—86), king of Bavaria (1864—86) (grandson of Louis I. of Bavaria).

Louise (lö-ēz′) (Auguste Wilhelmine Amalie Luise) (1776—1810), queen of Frederick William III. of Prussia.

Louis Philippe (lö-ē fē-lēp′) (1773—1850), king of the French (1830—48) (successor of Charles X., and son of Duc d'Orléans, 1747—93).

Lounsbury (lounz′bė-ri), Thomas Raynesford (1838—1915), Am. scholar and critic.

L'Ouverture, Toussaint. See *Toussaint L'Ouverture.*

Louvois (dė lö-vwo), François Michel Le Tellier, Marquis de (1641—91), Fr. statesman, minister of war under Louis XIV.

Louÿs (lö-ē), Pierre (1870—1925), Fr. poet and novelist.

Lovat (luv′at), Simon Fraser, 12th Baron (c1667—1747), Sc. Jacobite intriguer.

Lovat, Simon Fraser, Master of (1726—82), Sc. soldier (son of 12th Baron).

Lovejoy (luv′joi), Elijah Parish (1802—37), Am. abolitionist.

Lovelace (luv′lās), Richard (1618—58), Eng. poet.

Lover (luv′ėr), Samuel (1797—1868), Ir. novelist, artist, and musical composer.

Low (lö), Will Hicok (1853—1932), Am. painter, designer, and writer on art.

Lowden (lou′dn), Frank Orren (1861—   ), Am. political leader.

Lowe (lö), Sir Hudson (1769—1844), Br. general, governor of St. Helena (1815—21) during captivity of Napoleon I.

Lowe, Robert. See *Sherbrooke, Viscount.*

Lowell (lö′el), Abbott Lawrence (1856—1943), Am. educator and political writer (brother of Percival).

Lowell, Amy (1874—1925), Am. poet and critic (sister of Abbott L.).

Lowell, James Russell (1819—91), Am. poet, essayist, and diplomatist.

Lowell, Percival (1855—1916), Am. astronomer.

Loyola (lö-yō′lä or loi-ō′lä), Ignatius (Ignatius de Loyola, or Iñigo de Loyola) (1491—1556), Sp. soldier, priest, and saint, founder of Jesuit order (Society of Jesus).

Loyson (lwo-zôn), Charles (known as Père Hyacinthe) (1827—1912), Fr. pulpit orator.

Lubbock (lub′ok), Sir John. See *Avebury.*

Lucan (lū′kan) (Marcus Annæus Lucanus) (A.D. 39—65), Rom. poet.

Lucas (lū′kas), Edward Verrall (1868—1938), Eng. author.

Lucas van Leyden (lö′käs vän lī′dẹn) (real name Lucas Jacobsz) (c1494—1533), Dutch painter and engraver.

Lucia (lū′shia) or **Lucy** (lū′si), Saint (c283—303?), Sicilian virgin martyr.

Lucian (lū′shian) (c120—c180), Gr. satirist.

Lucilius (lū-sil′i-us), Caius (c180—103 B.C.), Rom. satiric poet.

Lucretia (lū-krē′shia) (d. 510 B.C.). In Roman legend, the wife of Tarquinius Collatinus, distinguished for her beauty and virtue. Being raped by Sextus Tarquinius, a son of Tarquinius Superbus, the last of the kings of Rome, she told of her dishonor, enjoined vengeance, and stabbed herself to death. The crime led to the banishment of the Tarquins and the establishment of the republic.

Lucretius (lū-krē′shius) (Titus Lucretius Carus) (c96—c55 B.C.), Rom. philosophical poet.

Lucullus (lū-kul′us), Lucius Licinius (c110—57? B.C.), Rom. general and provincial administrator.

Lucy, Saint. See *Lucia.*

Lucy (lū′si), Sir Thomas (1532—1600), Eng. landowner and magistrate, alleged to have prosecuted Shakspere for deer-stealing, and supposed to be caricatured in Shakspere's Justice Shallow.

Ludendorff (fon lö′dẹn-dôrf), Erich Friedrich Wilhelm von (1865—1937), Ger. general.

Ludlow (lud′lö), Edmund (1617?—92), Eng. military leader, and regicide.

Ludwig (löt′vich). See *Louis.*

Luini (lö-ē′nē), Bernardino (c1475—c1533), It. painter.

Luitprand. See *Liutprand.*

Luks (löks), George Benjamin (1867—1933), Am. painter.

Lully (lü-lē), Jean Baptiste (orig. Giovanni Battista Lulli) (1633?—87), It.-Fr. musical composer.

Lully (lul′i), Raymond (Ramón Lull, "the Enlightened Doctor") (c1235—1315), Sp. missionary and philosopher.

Luna (dä lö′nä), Álvaro de (d. 1453), constable of Castile, and royal favorite.

Lundy (lun′di), Benjamin (1789—1839), Am. abolitionist.

Lusignan, Guy of. See *Guy of Lusignan.*

Luska (lus′kä), Sidney. Pseudonym of Henry Harland.

Luther (lūt′ėr), Hans (1879—   ), Ger. statesman.

Luther (lö′thėr), Martin (1483—1546), Ger. religious reformer, theological writer, and translator of the Bible.

Lutyens (lut′yenz), Sir Edwin Landseer (1869—   ), Eng. architect.

Luxembourg (dė lük-son-bör), François Henri de Mont-morency-Bouteville, Duc de (1628—95), Fr. marshal.

Lyautey (lyō-tā), Hubert (1854—1934), Fr. general, administrator in Morocco, marshal of France.

Lycurgus (lī-kėr′gus) (9th? cent. B.C.), Spartan legislator, reputed founder of Spartan constitution.

Lycurgus (c396—c325 B.C.), Athenian orator and statesman.

Lydekker (li-dek′ėr), Richard (1849—1915), Eng. naturalist.

Lydgate (lid′gāt), John (c1370—c1451), Eng. poet.

Lyell (lī′el), Sir Charles (1797—1875), Br. geologist.

Lyly (lil′i), John (1554?—1606), Eng. dramatist and romance-writer.

Lyndhurst (lind′hėrst), John Singleton Copley, Baron (1772—1863), Eng. jurist and statesman, born in America (son of J. S. Copley, 1737—1815).

Lyndsay, Sir David. See *Lindsay.*

Lyon (lī′on), Mary (1797—1849), Am. educator, founder of Mount Holyoke Seminary.

Lyon, Nathaniel (1818—61), Am. general.

Lyons (lī′onz), Edmund Lyons, 1st Baron (1790—1858), Eng. admiral.

Lysander (lī-san′dėr) (d. 395 B.C.), Spartan naval commander and statesman.

Lysias (lis′i-as) (c450—c380 B.C.), Athenian orator.

Lysimachus (lī-sim′a-kus) (c360—281 B.C.), Macedonian general of Alexander the Great, and king of Thrace (306—281 B.C.).

Lysippus (lī-sip′us) (fl. c360—c316 B.C.), Gr. sculptor.

Lytton (lit′on), Edward George Earle Lytton Bulwer-Lytton, 1st Baron (1803—73), Eng. novelist, dramatist, and politician.

Lytton, Edward Robert Bulwer-Lytton, 1st Earl of ("Owen Meredith") (1831—91), Eng. diplomatist and poet (son of 1st Baron Lytton).

M

Maas. See *Maes.*

Mabillon (mȧ-bē-yôn), Jean (1632—1707), Fr. monk and historical scholar.

Mabuse (mȧ-büz), Jan (real name Jan Gossaert, or Gossart) (c1470—1541?), Flemish painter.

McAdam (mak-ad′am), John Loudon (1756—1836), Sc. highway official, inventor of the process of macadamizing roads.

McAdoo (mak′a-dö), William Gibbs (1863—1941), Am. lawyer, Secretary of the Treasury (1913—18).

MacArthur (mạk-är'thẽr), Arthur (1845—1912), Am. gen.

MacArthur, Douglas (1880—   ), Am. gen.

Macaulay (mạ-kâ'li), Thomas Babington Macaulay, Baron (1800—59), Eng. essayist, historian, poet, and statesman.

Macbeth (mạk-beth') (d. 1057), king of Scotland (1040—57) (successor of Duncan I.).

M'Carthy (mạ-kär'thi), Justin (1830—1912), Ir. politician, historian, and novelist.

M'Carthy, Justin Huntly (1861—1936), Br. novelist, playwright, and historian (son of Justin).

McClellan (mạ-klel'ạn), George Brinton (1826—85), Am. general.

McClintock (mạ-klin'tọk), Sir Francis Leopold (1819—1907), Br. naval officer and arctic explorer.

McCloskey (mạ-klos'ki), John (1810—85), first Am. cardinal.

McClure (mạ-klör'), Sir Robert John Le Mesurier (1807—73), Br. naval officer and arctic explorer.

McCook (mạ-kŭk'), Alexander McDowell (1831—1903), Am. general.

McCormack (mạ-kôr'mạk), John (1884—1945), Ir.-Am. tenor singer.

McCormick (mạ-kôr'mik), Cyrus Hall (1809—84), Am. inventor (of harvesting machinery).

McCosh (mạ-kosh'), James (1811—94), Sc.-Am. educator and philosophical writer.

McCulloch (mạ-kul'ọch), John Ramsay (1789—1864), Br. statistician and economist.

McCullough (mạ-kul'ọ), John Edward (1837—85), Ir.-Am. tragedian.

Macdonald (mȧk-do-nȧl), Étienne Jacques Joseph Alexandre (Duc de Tarente) (1765—1840), Fr. marshal.

Macdonald (mạk-don'ạld), Flora (1722—90), Sc. Jacobite heroine, who helped Charles Edward Stuart to escape after the battle of Culloden (1746).

MacDonald, George (1824—1905), Sc. novelist and poet.

Macdonald, Sir Hector Archibald (1853—1903), Br. general.

MacDonald, James Ramsay (1866—1937), Br. labor leader and statesman.

Macdonald, Sir John Alexander (1815—91), Can. statesman, premier of Canada (1867—73, 1878—91), born in Scotland.

MacDonough (mạk-don'ọ), Thomas (1783—1825), Am. naval officer.

MacDowell (mạk-dou'el), Edward Alexander (1861—1908), Am. musical composer.

McDowell, Irvin (1818—85), Am. general.

Macfarren (mạk-far'ẹn), Sir George Alexander (1813—87), Eng. composer, and writer on music.

MacGahan (mạ-gan'), Januarius Aloysius (1844—78), Am. war correspondent.

McGee (mạ-gē'), Thomas D'Arcy (1825—68), Ir.-Can. journalist and politician.

Macgregor (mạ-greg'ọr) or **Campbell,** Robert (commonly called Rob Roy) (1671—1734), Sc. freebooter.

Mach (mäch), Ernst (1838—1916), Austrian physicist and psychologist.

Machiavelli (mä-kyä-vel'lē), Niccolò (1469—1527), It. statesman, historian, and misc. writer.

Mackail (mạ-kāl'), John William (1859—   ), Br. scholar.

MacKaye (mạ-kī'), James Steele (1842—94), Am. actor and dramatist.

MacKaye, Percy (1875—   ), Am. dramatist and poet (son of J. S.).

M'Kenna (mạ-ken'ä), Reginald (1863—   ), Eng. statesman and financier.

Mackensen (fon mäk'ẹn-zẹn), August von (1849—1945), Ger. field-marshal.

Mackenzie (mạ-ken'zi), Sir Alexander (1755?—1820), Sc. explorer in northwestern Canada.

Mackenzie, Alexander (1822—92), Can. statesman, premier of Canada (1873—78), born in Scotland.

Mackenzie, Compton (1883—   ), Eng. novelist.

Mackenzie, Henry (1745—1831), Sc. novelist.

Mackenzie, Sir Morell (1837—92), Br. physician.

Mackenzie, William Lyon (1795—1861), Can. journalist, politician, and insurgent leader, born in Scotland.

McKim (mạ-kim'), Charles Follen (1847—1909), Am. architect.

McKinley (mạ-kin'li), William (1843—1901), 25th president of U. S. (1897—1901).

Mackintosh (mak'in-tosh), Sir James (1765—1832), Br. statesman, philosopher, and historian.

Macklin (mak'lin), Charles (professional name of Charles McLaughlin) (c1697—1797), Br. actor and dramatist.

Mack von Leiberich (mäk fon lī'bẹ-rich), Karl, Freiherr (1752—1828), Austrian general.

Maclaren (mạ-klar'ẹn), Ian. Pseudonym of John Watson.

McLennan (mạk-len'ạn), John Ferguson (1827—81), Sc. ethnologist.

Macleod (mạ-kloud'), Fiona. Pseudonym of William Sharp.

Macleod, Norman (1812—72), Sc. clergyman and writer.

Maclise (mạ-klēs'), Daniel (1806—70), Br. painter.

MacMahon (dẽ mȧk-mȧ-ón), Marie Edme Patrice Maurice, Comte de (Duc de Magenta) (1808—93), Fr. marshal, president of France (1873—79).

McMaster (mạk-mȧs'tẽr), John Bach (1852—1932), Am. historian.   [arctic explorer.

MacMillan (mạk-mil'ạn), Donald Baxter (1874—   ), Am.

MacMonnies (mạk-mun'iz), Frederick William (1863—1937), Am. sculptor and painter.

McNary (mạk-nā'ri), Charles Linza (1874—1944), Am. senator (from Oregon) and political leader.

MacNeil (mạk-nēl'), Hermon Atkins (1866—   ), Am. sculptor.   [Am. general.

Macomb (mạ-kōm' or mạ-kōm'), Alexander (1782—1841),

Macpherson (mạk-fẽr'sọn), James (1736—96), Sc. translator or author of "Poems of Ossian."

McPherson, James Birdseye (1828—64), Am. general.

Macquarie (mạ-kwor'i), Lachlan (1762?—1824), Br. general, governor of New South Wales (1809—21).

Macready (mạ-krē'di), William Charles (1793—1873), Eng. tragedian.

Macrobius (mạ-krō'bi-us), Ambrosius Theodosius (fl. c400), Latin author.

MacVeagh (mạk-vā'), Wayne (1833—1917), Am. lawyer and diplomatist.

Madden (mad'n), Sir Charles Edward (1862—1935), Br. admiral.

Madero (mä-ᴛHā'rō), Francisco Indalecio (1873—1913), Mex. political leader, president of Mexico (1911—13).

Madison (mad'i-sọn), James (1751—1836), 4th president of U. S. (1809—17).

Madison, Mrs. (known as Dolly Madison, born Dorothy Payne, later Mrs. Todd) (1772—1849), wife of James.

Madvig (mäd'vig), Johan Nikolai (1804—86), Dan. philologist and statesman.

Mæcenas (mē-sē'nạs), Caius Cilnius (between 73 and 63—8 B.C.), Rom. statesman, and patron of literature.

Maes or **Maas** (mäs), Nicolaas (1632—93), Dutch painter.

Maeterlinck (mä'tẽr-lingk, Fr. me-ter-laṅk), Maurice (1862—   ), Belgian-Fr. poet, dramatist, and misc. writer.

Magellan (mạ-jel'ạn), Ferdinand (in Portuguese, Fernão de Magalhães; in Spanish, Fernando de Magallanes) (c1480—1521), Pg. navigator in Spanish service, discoverer of Strait of Magellan and Philippine Islands.

Magendie (mȧ-zhaṅ-dē), François (1783—1855), Fr. physiologist.

Magnusen (mäg'nö-sẹn), Finn (Finnur Magnusson) (1781—1847), Icelandic scholar and archæologist.

Magruder (mạ-grö'dẽr), John Bankhead (1810—71), Am. Confederate general.

Mahaffy (mạ-haf'i), Sir John Pentland (1839—1919), Ir. classical scholar.

Mahan (mạ-han'), Alfred Thayer (1840—1914), Am. naval officer and writer on naval history.

Mahdi (mä'dē), The. See Mohammed Ahmed.

Mahler (mä'lẽr), Gustav (1860—1911), Austrian musical composer and conductor.

Mahmud I. or **Mahmoud I.** (mä-möd') (1696—1754), sultan of Turkey (1730—54) (nephew of Ahmed III.).

Mahmud II. (1785—1839), sultan of Turkey (1808—39) (son of Abdul-Hamid I.).

Mahomet. See Mohammed.

Mahony (mä'ọ-ni), Francis Sylvester ("Father Prout") (1804—66), Ir. priest, humorist, poet, and journalist.

---

fat, fāte, fär, fȧll, ȧsk, fãre; net, mē, hẽr; pin, pīne; not, nōte, mȯve, nȯr; up, lūte, pu̇ll; oi, oil; ou, out; (lightened) aviᶐry, ẹlect, agọny, intọ, ụnite; (obscured) errȧnt, operᶐ, ardẹnt, actọr, natūre; ch, chip; g, go; th, thin; ᴛH, then; y, you;

Maimonides (mī-mon′i-dēz) (Moses ben Maimon, "Rambam") (1135—1204), Jewish scholar and philosopher.

Maine (mān), Sir Henry James Sumner (1822—88), Eng. legal scholar and historian.

Maintenon (dė mańt-nóń), Marquise de (Françoise d'Aubigné, Mme. Paul Scarron) (1635—1719), second wife of Louis XIV. of France (granddaughter of T. A. d'Aubigné).

Maistre (dė mãstr), Joseph Marie, Comte de (1754—1821), Fr.-Sardinian diplomatist, philosopher, and writer.

Maistre, Xavier de (1763—1852), Fr. writer (brother of Joseph M.).

Maitland (māt′lạnd), Frederic William (1850—1906), Eng. legal scholar and historian.

Maitland, John. See *Lauderdale, Duke of.*

Majano, Benedetto da. See *Benedetto da Majano.*

Makarov (mȧ-kä′rof), Stepan Osipovich (1848—1904), Russ. admiral and hydrographer.

Makart (mä′kärt), Hans (1840—84), Austrian painter.

Malcolm III. (mal′kọm) (called Canmore) (d. 1093), king of Scotland (1057—93) (son of Duncan I.).

Malebranche (dė mȧl-bränsh), Nicolas de (1638—1715), Fr. philosopher.

Malesherbes (dė mȧl-zãrb), Chrétien Guillaume de Lamoignon de (1721—94), Fr. statesman (guillotined).

Malherbe (dė mȧl-ãrb), François de (1555—1628), Fr. poet and critic.

Malibran (mȧ-lē-bräń), Mme. (Marie Félicité García, Mme. Malibran, Mme. de Bériot) (1808—36), operatic singer, born in Paris of Sp. parentage (daughter of Manuel del P. V. García).

Mallarmé (mȧ-lär-mā), Stéphane (1842—98), Fr. poet.

Mallet du Pan (mȧ-lä dü pän), Jacques (1749—1800), Swiss-Fr. publicist.

Mallock (mal′ọk), William Hurrell (1849—1923), Eng. novelist, and philosophical and sociological writer.

Malmesbury (mämz′bẹ-ri), James Harris, 1st Earl of (1746—1820), Eng. diplomatist.

Malone (mạ-lōn′), Edmund (1741—1812), Ir. critic and Shaksperian scholar.

Malory (mal′ọ-ri), Sir Thomas (fl. 1470), Eng. translator and compiler of "Morte d'Arthur."

Malot (mȧ-lō), Hector Henri (1830—1907), Fr. novelist.

Malpighi (mäl-pē′gē), Marcello (1628—94), It. anatomist and physiologist.

Malthus (mal′thus), Thomas Robert (1766—1834), Eng. political economist.

Mamiani della Rovere (mä-myä′nē del′lä rō′vä-rä), Count Terenzio (1799?—1885), It. author and statesman.

Manchester (man′ches-tėr), Edward Montagu, 2d Earl of (1602—71), Eng. general and statesman.

Mancini (män-chē′nē), Hortense (Duchesse de Mazarin) (1646—99), favorite at the courts of France and England, born in Italy (niece of Jules Mazarin).

Mancini, Pasquale Stanislao (1817—88), It. jurist and statesman.

Mandeville (man′dẹ-vil), Bernard (1670?—1733), Dutch-Eng. philosophical and satirical writer.

Mandeville, Sir John. The ostensible (English) author of a 14th century book of travels (claimed as his own experiences) to the Holy Land, Egypt, India, China, etc. The work, written originally in French, the oldest known manuscript being dated 1371, was actually compiled, at least in large part, from earlier works. The compiler is supposed to have been Jehan de Bourgogne, also known as Jehan à la Barbe (died 1372), a Liége physician who may have come originally from England.

Manes. See *Mani.*

Manet (mȧ-nā), Édouard (1832—83), Fr. impressionist painter.

Manetho (man′e-thō) (fl. c250 B.C.), Egyptian priest and chronicler, writing in Greek.

Manfred (man′fred) (in Italian, Manfredi) (1232?—66), king of Sicily (1258—66) (illegitimate son of Emperor Frederick II.).

Mangan (mang′gạn), James Clarence (1803—49), Ir. poet.

Mangin (män-zhań), Charles Marie Emmanuel (1866—1925), Fr. general.

Mani (mä′nē), **Manes** (mä′nēz), or **Manichæus** (man-i-kē′us) (216?—276?), Pers. religious teacher, founder of Manicheism.

Manin (mä-nēn′), Daniele (1804—57), Venetian patriot and statesman.

Manley (man′li), Mary de la Rivière (called Mrs. Manley) (1663—1724), Eng. writer.

Manlius (man′li-us), Marcus (surnamed Capitolinus) (d. 384 B.C.), Rom. consul. According to legend, one night when the Gauls under Brennus tried to take the Capitol by surprise, Manlius was awakened by the cackling of geese, quickly rallied a few men, and repelled the attack.

Mann (man), Horace (1796—1859), Am. educational reformer.

Mann (män), Thomas (1875—   ), Ger. author.

Manners (man′ėrz). See *Granby* and *Rutland.*

Manning (man′ing), Henry Edward (1808—92), Eng. cardinal.

Manning, William Thomas (1866—   ), Am. Protestant Episcopal bishop, born in England.

Manoel I. (mä-nọ-āl′) or **Manuel I.** (man′ū-el) (also known as Emanuel, called "the Happy") (1469—1521), king of Portugal (1495—1521).

Manoel II. or **Manuel II.** (also known as Emanuel) (1889—1932), king of Portugal (1908—10) (son of Carlos I.).

Mansart or **Mansard** (män-sär), François (1598—1666), Fr. architect.

Mansart or **Mansard**, Jules Hardouin- (orig. Jules Hardouin) (1645 or 1646—1708), Fr. architect (grandnephew of François).

Mansel (man′sẹl), Henry Longueville (1820—71), Eng. metaphysician.

Mansfeld (fon mäns′felt), Ernst, Graf von (1580—1626), Ger. general in Protestant service in Thirty Years' War.

Mansfield (mans′fēld), Richard (1854—1907), Am. actor, born in Berlin of Eng. and Russ.-Ger. parentage.

Mansfield, William Murray, 1st Earl of (1705—93), Br. jurist, lord chief justice of England (1756—88).

Mansur, Al-. See *Al-Mansur.*

Mantegna (män-tā′nyä), Andrea (1431—1506), It. painter and engraver.

Manteuffel (fon män′toi″fẹl), Edwin Hans Karl, Freiherr von (1809—85), Prussian field-marshal.

Manuel I. (man′ū-el) (Manuel Comnenus) (c1120—80), Byzantine emperor (1143—80) (grandson of Alexius I.).

Manuel II. (Manuel Palæologus) (c1350—1425), Byzantine emperor (1391—1425).

Manuel (of Portugal). See *Manoel.*

Manutius (mạ-nū′shius), Aldus (in Italian, Aldo Manuzio, Manuzzi, or Manucci) (1450—1515), It. printer and classical scholar, originator of italic type.

Manzoni (män-tsō′nē), Alessandro (1785—1873), It. novelist and poet.

Map (map), Walter (d. c1209), Eng. ecclesiastic and author.

Mar (mär), John Erskine, 6th (or 11th) Earl of (1675—1732), Sc. politician and Jacobite leader.

Marat (mȧ-rä), Jean Paul ("the Friend of the People") (1743—93), Fr. revolutionary leader.

Marbot (dė mär-bō), Jean Baptiste Antoine Marcelin, Baron de (1782—1854), Fr. general and writer.

Marceau (mär-sō) (for Marceau-Desgraviers), François Séverin (1769—96), Fr. general.

Marcel (mär-sel), Étienne (d. 1358), Fr. political reformer.

Marcellinus, Ammianus. See *Ammianus Marcellinus.*

Marcellus (mär-sel′us), Marcus Claudius (c268—208 B.C.), Rom. general.

March (märch), Francis Andrew (1825—1911), Am. philologist.

March, Peyton Conway (1864—   ), Am. general (son of Francis A.).

Marchand (mär-shań), Jean Baptiste (1863—1934), Fr. general, and explorer in Africa.

Marcianus (mär-shi-ā′nus) or **Marcian** (mär′shiạn) (c390—457), Eastern Rom. emperor (450—457).

Marcion (mär′shiọn) (fl. c140—c165), Asia Minor heretical Christian leader at Rome.

Marck, Guillaume de La. See *La Marck.*

Marconi (mär-kō′nē), Guglielmo (1874—1937), It. electrician, perfecter of wireless telegraphy.

(variable) ḍ as d or j, ş as s or sh, ṭ as t or ch, ẓ as z or zh; o, F. cloche; ü, F. menu; ch, Sc. loch; ń, F. bonbon; ′, primary accent; ″, secondary accent; †, obsolete; <, from; +, and; =, equals. See also lists at beginning of book.

Marcus Aurelius (mär′kus â-rē′lius). See *Antoninus, Marcus Aurelius.*

Marcy (mär′si), William Learned (1786—1857), Am. statesman.

Mardonius (mär-dō′ni-us) (d. 479? B.C.), Pers. general (son-in-law of Darius I.).

Marées (fon mä′rās), Hans von (1837—87), Ger. painter.

Margaret (mär′gạ-ret), Saint (also known as Saint Marina) (3d? cent.), virgin martyr, of Asia Minor.

Margaret (1353—1412), queen (regent) of Denmark, Norway, and Sweden (daughter of Waldemar IV.).

Margaret, Saint (c1045—93), queen of Malcolm III. of Scotland (granddaughter of Edmund II. of England).

Margaret (1283—90), queen of Scotland (1285—90) (successor and granddaughter of Alexander III.).

Margaret of Anjou (1430—82), queen of Henry VI. of England (daughter of René I. of Anjou).

Margaret of Austria (Duchess of Savoy) (1480—1530), regent of the Netherlands under Emperors Maximilian I. and Charles V. (1507—30) (daughter of Emperor Maximilian I.).

Margaret of Austria (1522—86). See *Margaret of Parma.*

Margaret of Navarre (Margaret of Valois, or of Angoulême) (1492—1549), queen of Navarre, Fr. writer of verse and prose, reputed author of "Heptameron."

Margaret of Parma, or **of Austria** (Duchess of Parma) (1522—86), regent of the Netherlands under Philip II. of Spain (1559—67) (illegitimate daughter of Emperor Charles V.).

Margaret of Valois, or **of France** (1553—1615), first queen of Henry IV. of France, divorced 1599 (daughter of Henry II. of France and Catharine de' Medici).

Margueritte (mär-gė-rēt), Paul (1860—1918), Fr. novelist.

Margueritte, Victor (1866—1942), Fr. novelist (brother of Paul).

Maria II. (mạ-rē′ạ, Pg. mä-rē′ä) (called Maria da Gloria) (1819—53), queen of Portugal (1834—53) (daughter of Pedro I. of Brazil).

Maria Christina (mạ-rē′ạ kris-tē′nạ) (1806—78), queen of Ferdinand VII. of Spain, regent for Isabella II. (1833—40).

Maria Christina (1858—1929), queen of Alfonso XII. of Spain, regent (1885—1902).

Maria de' Medici (mä-rē′ä dā med′ẹ-chē) (in French, Marie de Médicis) (1573—1642), second queen of Henry IV. of France (granddaughter of Cosimo de' Medici the Great, and mother of Louis XIII. of France).

Maria Luisa (lö-ē′zä) (of Parma) (1751—1819), queen of Charles IV. of Spain.

Maria Theresa (mạ-rē′ạ te-rē′sạ) (in German, Maria Theresia) (1717—80), archduchess of Austria, and queen of Hungary and Bohemia (1740—80) (daughter of Emperor Charles VI., and wife of Emperor Francis I., 1708—65).

Marie Antoinette (mar′ẹ an-tọ-net′, Fr. mȧ-rē än-two-net′) (Marie Antoinette Josèphe Jeanne) (1755—93), queen of Louis XVI. of France (daughter of Emperor Francis I., 1708—65, and Maria Theresa of Austria).

Marie de France (mȧ-rē dė fräns) (fl. c1175—c1190), Fr. poet and fabulist.

Marie Leszczynska (lesh-chin′skạ) (1703—68), queen of Louis XV. of France (daughter of Stanislaus I., Leszczynski, of Poland).

Marie Louise (lö-ēz) (1791—1847), second wife of Napoleon I. (daughter of Francis I. of Austria).

Marie Thérèse (tā-rāz) (of Austria) (1638—83), queen of Louis XIV. of France (daughter of Philip IV. of Spain).

Mariette (mȧ-rē-et), Auguste (1821—81), Fr. Egyptologist.

Marinetti (mä-rē-net′tē), Filippo Tommaso (1876—1944), It. futurist poet and misc. writer, born in Alexandria.

Marini (mä-rē′nē) or **Marino** (mä-rē′nō), Giambattista (1569—1625), It. poet.

Marion (mar′i-ọn), Francis (1732—95), Am. Revolutionary general.

Mariotte (mȧ-rē-ot), Edme (c1620—84), Fr. physicist.

Maris (mä′ris), Jacob (1837—99), Dutch painter.

Marius (mä′ri-us), Caius (c155—86 B.C.), Rom. general and politician, opponent of Sulla.

Marivaux (dė mȧ-rē-vō), Pierre Carlet de Chamblain de (1688—1763), Fr. dramatist and novelist.

Markham (märk′ạm), Sir Clements Robert (1830—1916), Eng. traveler, geographer, and writer.

Marlborough (märl′bur-ọ), John Churchill, 1st Duke of (1650—1722), Eng. general.

Marlborough, Sarah Churchill, Duchess of (Sarah Jennings) (1660—1744), wife of 1st Duke of Marlborough, and favorite of Queen Anne of England.

Marlowe (mär′lō), Christopher (1564—93), Eng. poet and dramatist.

Marlowe, Julia (professional name of Sarah Frances Frost, Mrs. Taber, Mrs. E. H. Sothern) (1865—   ), Am. actress, born in England.

Marmont (dė mär-môn), Auguste Frédéric Louis Viesse de (Duc de Raguse) (1774—1852), Fr. marshal.

Marmontel (mär-môn-tel), Jean François (1723—99), Fr. author.

Marnix (vän mär′niks), Philips van. See *Sainte-Aldegonde.*

Marot (mȧ-rō), Clément (1497?—1544), Fr. poet.

Marquette (mär-ket), Jacques (1637—75), Fr. Jesuit missionary, and explorer of the Mississippi.

Marryat (mar′i-ạt), Frederick (1792—1848), Eng. naval officer and novelist.

Mars (märs), Mlle. (professional name of Anne Françoise Hippolyte Boutet) (1779—1847), Fr. actress.

Marsh (märsh), Othniel Charles (1831—99), Am. paleontologist.

Marshal (mär′shạl), William. See *Pembroke, 1st Earl of.*

Marshall (mär′shạl), Alfred (1842—1924), Eng. economist.

Marshall, Archibald (1866—1934), Eng. novelist.

Marshall, George C. (1880—   ), Am. gen.

Marshall, John (1755—1835), Am. statesman and jurist, chief justice of U. S. Supreme Court (1801—35).

Marshall, Thomas Riley (1854—1925), Am. politician, vice-president of U. S. (1913—21).

Marsilius of Padua (mär-sil′i-us) (Marsiglio Mainardino) (c1270—1342?), It. physician, and writer on politics and religion.

Marston (mär′stọn), John (c1575—1634), Eng. dramatist and satirist.

Marston, Philip Bourke (1850—87), Eng. poet.

Martel, Charles. See *Charles Martel.*

Martel de Janville (dė mär-tel dė zhän-vēl), Comtesse de (Sybille Gabrielle Marie Antoinette de Riquetti de Mirabeau, "Gyp") (1850—1932), Fr. novelist.

Martial (mär′shiạl) (Marcus Valerius Martialis) (A.D. c40—c102), Rom. epigrammatist.

Martin (mär′tin), Saint (c316—397 or 400), bishop of Tours. He is said while a young soldier to have divided his cloak with a beggar, and to have had that night a vision of Christ, which led to his baptism.

Martin, Homer Dodge (1836—97), Am. landscape-painter.

Martin, Luther (1748—1826), Am. lawyer.

Martin, Sir Theodore (1816—1909), Br. translator and biographer.

Martineau (mär′ti-nō), Harriet (1802—76), Eng. writer (sister of James).

Martineau, James (1805—1900), Eng. Unitarian clergyman, and writer on philosophy and religion.

Martínez Campos (mär-tē′näth käm′pōs), Arsenio (1834 or 1831—1900), Sp. general and statesman.

Martínez de la Rosa (dä lä rō′sä), Francisco (1789—1862), Sp. statesman and author.

Martini (mär-tē′nē), Simone (also called Simone di Martino, and Simone Memmi) (1283?—1344), It. painter, of Sienese school.

Martinuzzi (mär-tē-nöt′sē), George (real name György Utiešenović, known as Frater Georgius) (1482—1551), Hung. statesman and cardinal.

Martyn (mär′tin), John (1699—1768), Eng. botanist.

Marvel (mär′vel), Ik. Pseudonym of D. G. Mitchell.

Marvell (mär′vel), Andrew (1621—78), Eng. poet and satirist.

Marx (märks), Karl (1818—83), Ger. socialist.

Marx, Wilhelm (1863—   ), Ger. statesman.

Mary I. (mā′ri) ("Bloody Mary") (1516—58), queen of England and Ireland (1553—58) (successor of Edward VI., daughter of Henry VIII. and Catharine of Aragon, and wife of Philip II. of Spain).

Mary II. (1662—94), queen of Great Britain and Ireland,

---

fat, fāte, fär, fȧll, ȧsk, fāre; net, mē, hėr; pin, pīne; not, nōte, mȯve, nôr; up, lūte, pull; oi, oil; ou, out; (lightened) aviạry; ẹlect, agọny, intọ, ụnite; (obscured) errạnt, operạ, ardẹnt, actọr, natụre; ch, chip; g, go; th, thin; ฅH, then; y, you;

joint ruler with her husband, William III. (1689—94) (daughter of James II.).

Mary (Princess Victoria Mary of Teck) (1867—   ), queen of George V. of Great Britain.

Mary (Mary Queen of Scots, or Mary Stuart) (1542—87), queen of Scotland (1542—67) (daughter of James V.).

Mary of Burgundy (1457—82), duchess of Burgundy (daughter of Charles the Bold, and wife of the Austrian archduke who after her death became Emperor Maximilian I.).

Mary of Guise, or **of Lorraine** (1515—60), queen of James V. of Scotland (mother of Mary Queen of Scots).

Mary of Modena (1658—1718), queen of James II. of England.

Mary Stuart. See *Mary*, queen of Scotland.

Masaccio (mä-zät′chō) (real name Tommaso Guidi) (1402?—29?), It. painter, of Florentine school.

Masaniello (mä-zä-nyel′lō) (properly Tommaso Aniello) (1622?—47), It. fisherman, leader of insurrection against Spanish oppression in Naples.

Masaryk (mä′sä-rēk), Thomas Garrigue (1850—1937), Moravian scholar and patriot, 1st president of Czechoslovakia (1918—35).

Mascagni (mäs-kä′nyē), Paolo (1752—1815), It. anatomist.

Mascagni, Pietro (1863—1945), It. operatic composer.

Masefield (māz′fēld), John (1878—   ), Eng. poet, dramatist, and misc. writer.

Masham (mash′ạm), Lady (Abigail Hill) (d. 1734), favorite of Queen Anne of England.

Masinissa or **Massinissa** (mas-i-nis′ä) (c238—149 B.C.), king of Numidia, allied with Scipio the Elder against Carthage.

Maskelyne (mas′kẹ-lin), Nevil (1732—1811), Eng. astronomer.

Masolino da Panicale (mä-zō-lē′nō dä pä-nē-kä′lä) (real name Tommaso Fini) (1383?—c1447), It. painter, of Florentine school.

Mason (mā′sn), Alfred Edward Woodley (1865—   ), Eng. novelist.

Mason, George (1725—92), Am. political leader.

Mason, James Murray (1798—1871), Am. legislator and Confederate commissioner (grandson of George).

Mason, John (1586—1635), Eng. naval commander, founder of colony of New Hampshire.

Mason, John (1600—72), Am. colonial military commander, born in England.

Mason, Lowell (1792—1872), Am. musical composer.

Maspero (mȧs-pė-rō), Gaston Camille Charles (1846—1916), Fr. Egyptologist.

Massasoit (mas′ạ-soit) (c1580—1662), Am. Indian chief.

Masséna (mȧ-sā-nä), André (Prince d'Essling) (1758—1817), Fr. marshal.

Massenet (mȧs-nā), Jules Émile Frédéric (1842—1912), Fr. musical composer.

Massey (mas′ĭ), Gerald (1828—1907), Eng. poet and Egyptologist.

Massillon (mȧ-sē-yôṅ), Jean Baptiste (1663—1742), Fr. bishop and pulpit orator.

Massinger (mas′in-jėr), Philip (1583—1640), Eng. dramatist.

Massinissa. See *Masinissa*.

Masson (mas′ọn), David (1822—1907), Sc. biographer, editor, and essayist.

Masson (mȧ-sôṅ), Louis Claude Frédéric (1847—1923), Fr. historian.

Massys (mä-sīs′), Quentin, or Quintin (also called Matsys, Messys, and Metsys) (c1460—1530), Flemish painter.

Masters (mȧs′tėrz), Edgar Lee (1869—   ), Am. poet.

Mather (maтн′ėr), Cotton (1663—1728), Am. clergyman and author (son of Increase Mather, and grandson of John Cotton).

Mather, Increase (1639—1723), Am. clergyman.

Mathew (math′ū), Theobald ("the Apostle of Temperance") (1790—1856), Ir. Rom. Cath. priest and temperance advocate.

Matilda (mạ-til′dä) or **Maud** (mâd) (1080—1118), first wife of Henry I. of England (daughter of Malcolm III. of Scotland).

Matilda or **Maud** (1102—67), daughter of Henry I. of England, and cousin and opponent of King Stephen, and wife of Geoffrey of Anjou, and mother of Henry II.

Matilda (of Boulogne) (1103?—52), queen of King Stephen of England.

Matilda (1046—1115), countess of Tuscany.

Matisse (mȧ-tēs), Henri (1869—   ), Fr. painter and sculptor.

Matsys (mät-sīs′). See *Massys*.

Matthew (math′ū) **of Paris** (c1200—59), Eng. monk and chronicler.

Matthews (math′ūz), James Brander (1852—1929), Am. educator and author.

Matthias I. (mạ-thī′ạs) (surnamed Corvinus, and called "the Great") (1443—90), king of Hungary (1458—90) (son of János Hunyadi).

Matthias (1557—1619), emperor of the Holy Roman Empire (1612—19), and king of Hungary (1608—18) and of Bohemia (1611—17) (brother of Rudolf II.).

Maturin (mat′ū-rin), Charles Robert (1782—1824), Ir. novelist and dramatist.

Maud. See *Matilda*.

Maude (mâd), Cyril Francis (1862—   ), Eng. actor and theatrical manager.

Maude, Sir Frederick Stanley (1864—1917), Eng. general.

Maudsley (mâdz′li), Henry (1835—1918), Eng. physiologist.

Maugham (mâm), William Somerset (1874—   ), Eng. novelist and playwright.

Maunoury (mō-nö-rē), Michel Joseph (1847—1923), Fr. general (made marshal of France in 1923, after his death).

Maupassant (dė mō-pȧ-säṅ), Henri René Albert Guy de (1850—93), Fr. novelist and writer of short stories.

Maupeou (dė mō-pö), René Nicolas Charles Augustin de (1714—92), Fr. politician.

Maupertuis (dė mō-per-twē), Pierre Louis Moreau de (1698—1759), Fr. mathematician and astronomer.

Maurepas (dė mōr-pä), Jean Frédéric Phélipeaux, Comte de (1701—81), Fr. statesman.

Maurer (fon mou′rėr), Georg Ludwig von (1790—1872), Ger. jurist and statesman.

Maurice (mâ′ris) (Flavius Tiberius Mauricius) (c539—602), Byzantine emperor (582—602).

Maurice (in German, Moritz) (1521—53), duke and (later) elector of Saxony.

Maurice, Sir Frederick Barton (1871—   ), Eng. general.

Maurice, Frederick Denison (1805—72), Eng. divine and writer.

Maurice of Nassau (Prince of Orange) (1567—1625), Dutch general and statesman (son of William I. of Orange).

Maurice of Nassau (1604—79). See *Nassau-Siegen*.

Maurokordatos (mäv″ro-kôr-dä′tos), Prince Alexandros (1791—1865), Gr. statesman, born at Constantinople.

Maurus (mâ′rus) or **Maur** (Fr. mōr), Saint (d. 584), Benedictine abbot in France, born in Italy.

Maury (mâ′ri), Matthew Fontaine (1806—73), Am. naval officer and hydrographer.

Mausolus (mȧ-sō′lus) (d. 353 B.C.), satrap or king of Caria (377—353 B.C.).

Mauve (mōv), Anton (1838—88), Dutch painter.

Mavrocordatos (mäv″ro-kôr-dä′tos). See *Maurokordatos*.

Mawson (mâ′sọn), Sir Douglas (1882—   ), Australian geologist and antarctic explorer.

Max (mäks), Gabriel (1840—1915), Ger. painter, born in Bohemia.

Maxim (mak′sim), Hiram Percy (1869—1936), Am. engineer and inventor (son of Sir Hiram).

Maxim, Sir Hiram Stevens (1840—1916), Am.-Eng. engineer and inventor.

Maxim, Hudson (orig. Isaac Maxim) (1853—1927), Am. engineer and inventor (brother of Sir Hiram).

Maximian (mak-sim′i-ạn) (Marcus Aurelius Valerius Maximianus, surnamed Herculius) (d. 310), Rom. emperor (286—305).

Maximilian I. (mak-si-mil′yạn) (1459—1519), emperor of the Holy Roman Empire (1493—1519).

Maximilian II. (1527—76), emperor of the Holy Roman Empire and king of Bohemia and Hungary (1564—76) (son of Emperor Ferdinand I.).

Maximilian I. (1573—1651), duke and (later) elector of Bavaria.

Maximilian (1832—67), archduke of Austria, and emperor of Mexico (1864—67) (brother of Francis Joseph I.).

Maxwell (maks'wel), James Clerk (1831—79), Br. physicist.

Maxwell, William Babington (1866—1938), Eng. novelist (son of M. E. Braddon).

May (mā), Philip William (called Phil May) (1864—1903), Eng. illustrator and caricaturist.

Mayer (fon mī'ėr), Julius Robert von (1814—78), Ger. physicist.

Mayo (mā'ō), Charles Horace (1865—1939), Am. surgeon (brother of William J.).

Mayo, William James (1861—1939), Am. surgeon.

Mazarin (maz'ą-rin, Fr. mȧ-zȧ-rȧṅ), Jules (in Italian, Giulio Mazarini) (1602—61), Fr. cardinal and statesman, born in Italy.

Mazeppa or **Mazepa** (mą-zep'ą), Ivan Stepanovich (1644?—1709), hetman of the Cossacks.

Mazzini (mät-sē'nē), Giuseppe (1805—72), It. patriot, revolutionist, and author.

Meade (mēd), George Gordon (1815—72), Am. general.

Meagher (mä'hėr), Thomas Francis (1823—67), Ir. revolutionist, and general in America.

Mechnikov (mech'ni-kof), Ilya Ilich. See *Metchnikoff*.

Medici (dä med'ē-chē), Alessandro de' (1510?—37), first duke of Florence (1532—37).

Medici, Cosimo, or Cosmo, de' ("the Elder") (1389—1464), Florentine banker, statesman, and patron of art and letters.

Medici, Cosimo, or Cosmo, de' ("the Great") (1519—74), duke of Florence (1537—74), and first grand duke of Tuscany (1569—74).

Medici, Lorenzo de' ("Lorenzo the Magnificent") (1449?—92), ruler of Florence, poet, and patron of art and letters (grandson of Cosimo de' Medici the Elder).

Medici. See *Catharine de' Medici* and *Maria de' Medici*.

Meer (vän dėr mär), Jan van der ("the elder") (1628—91), Dutch painter.

Meer, Jan van der (often called Jan Vermeer van Delft) (1632—75), Dutch painter.

Meer, Jan van der ("the younger") (1656—1705), Dutch painter (son of "the elder").

Mehemet Ali (mä'hȩ-met ä'lē) or **Mohammed Ali** (1769—1849), viceroy of Egypt.

Méhul (mā-ül), Étienne Henri, or Étienne Nicolas (1763—1817), Fr. musical composer.

Meighen (mē'ȩn), Arthur (1874—   ), Can. statesman, premier of Canada (1920—21, 1926).

Meigs (megz), Montgomery Cunningham (1816—92), Am. engineer and general.

Meilhac (me-yȧk), Henri (1831—97), Fr. dramatist.

Meissonier (me-so-nyā), Jean Louis Ernest (1815—91), Fr. painter.

Meister Stephan (mī'stėr shtef'än). See *Lochner, Stephan*.

Melanchthon (me-langk'thǫn, Ger. mä-länch'ton) or **Melanthon** (me-lan'thǫn), Philipp (orig. Philipp Schwarzerd) (1497—1560), Ger. religious reformer, theological writer, and educator.

Melanthius (me-lan'thi-us) or **Melanthus** (me-lan'thus) (fl. c335 B.C.), Gr. painter.

Melba (mel'bą), Mme. (professional name of Nellie Porter Mitchell, Mrs. Armstrong, Dame Nellie Armstrong) (1861—1931), Australian operatic soprano singer.

Melbourne (mel'bǫrn), William Lamb, 2d Viscount (1779—1848), Eng. statesman.

Melchers (mel'chėrz), Gari (1860—1932), Am. painter.

Melchthal (fon melch'täl), Arnold von (fl. c1307), legendary hero in Swiss struggle for independence against Austria.

Meléndez Valdés (mä-len'däth väl-dās'), Juan (1754—1817), Sp. poet.

Mellon (mel'ǫn), Andrew William (1855—1937), Am. financier, Secretary of the Treasury (1921—32).

Melville (mel'vil), Andrew (1545—1622), Sc. scholar and Presbyterian leader.

Melville, Henry Dundas, 1st Viscount (1742—1811), Br. statesman.

Melville, Herman (1819—91), Am. author.

Memling (mem'ling) or **Memlinc** (mem'lingk), Hans (c1430—94), Flemish painter.

Memmi (mem'mē), Simone. See *Martini, Simone*.

Mena (dä mä'nä), Juan de (1411—56), Sp. poet.

Ménage (mā-näzh), Gilles (1613—92), Fr. scholar.

Menander (me-nan'dėr) (342—291 B.C.), Gr. writer of comedy.

Mencius (men'shius) (385 or 372—289 B.C.), Chin. sage and moral teacher.

Mencken (meng'kȩn), Henry Louis (1880—   ), Am. editor and author.

Mendaña de Neyra (men-dä'nyä dä nā'ȩ-rä), Álvaro (1541—95), Sp. navigator.

Mendel (men'dȩl), Gregor Johann (1822—84), Austrian monk and scientific investigator.

Mendelssohn (men'dȩls-zōn), Moses (1729—86), Ger. Jewish philosopher.

Mendelssohn-Bartholdy (-bär-tol'dē), Jakob Ludwig Felix (1809—47), Ger. musical composer (grandson of Moses Mendelssohn).

Mendelyeev (men-del-yä'yef), Dmitri Ivanovich (1834—1907), Russ. chemist.

Mendès (mań-des), Catulle (1841—1909), Fr. poet, dramatist, and misc. writer.

Mendoza (dä men-dō'thä), Diego Hurtado de (1503—75), Sp. diplomatist, poet, and misc. writer.

Mendoza, Íñigo López de. See *Santillana, Marquis of*.

Mendoza, Pedro González de (1428—95), Sp. cardinal and statesman (son of Marquis of Santillana).

Menelik II. (men'e-lik) (1844—1913), emperor of Abyssinia (1889—1913).

Menéndez de Avilés (mä-nen'däth dä ä-vē-lās'), Pedro (1519—74), Sp. admiral and colonial governor, founder of St. Augustine, Florida (1565).

Menes (mē'nēz) (fl. c4750? B.C.), the traditional first king of Egypt, founder of 1st dynasty.

Mengs (mengs), Anton Raphael (1728—79), Ger. painter.

Menno Simons (men'ō sī'mǫnz) (1492—1559), Dutch religious reformer, leader of Mennonites in Holland.

Menocal (mä-nō-käl'), Mario García (1869—   ), president of Cuba (1913—21).

Menshikov (men'shȩ-kof), Prince Aleksandr Danilovich (1663?—1729), Russ. general and statesman.

Menshikov, Prince Aleksandr Sergyeevich (1787—1869), Russ. general and admiral (great-grandson of Aleksandr D.).

Menzel (fon men'tsȩl), Adolf Friedrich Erdmann von (1815—1905), Ger. painter, illustrator, and lithographer.

Mercator (mėr-kā'tǫr), Gerardus (orig. Gerhard Kremer) (1512—94), Flemish cartographer.

Mercié (mer-syā), Marius Jean Antonin (1845—1916), Fr. sculptor and painter.

Mercier (mer-syā), Désiré (1851—1926), Belgian cardinal and patriot.

Mercier, Louis Sébastien (1740—1814), Fr. dramatist and misc. writer.

Meredith (mer'ȩ-dith), George (1828—1909), Eng. novelist and poet.

Meredith, Owen. Pseudonym of 1st Earl of Lytton.

Merezhkovski (mer-esh-kof'skē), Dmitri Sergyeevich (1865—1941), Russ. novelist and critic.

Mergenthaler (mer'gȩn-tä''lėr), Ottmar (1854—99), Ger.-Am. inventor (of linotype machine).

Mérimée (mā-rē-mā), Prosper (1803—70), Fr. novelist and misc. writer.

Merivale (mer'i-vāl), Charles (1808—93), Eng. divine and historian.

Merle d'Aubigné (merl dō-bē-nyä), Jean Henri (1794—1872), Swiss Protestant clergyman and church historian.

Merlin (mer-lań), Antoine Christophe (called Merlin de Thionville) (1762—1833), Fr. revolutionist.

Merlin, Philippe Antoine, Comte (called Merlin de Douai) (1754—1838), Fr. lawyer and politician.

Merrick (mer'ik), Leonard (name orig. Miller) (1864—1939), Eng. novelist.

Merritt (mer'it), Wesley (1836—1910), Am. general.

Merry del Val (mer'rē del väl), Raphael, or Rafael (1865—1930), Sp. cardinal and papal statesman, born in London.

---

fat, fāte, fär, fȧll, ȧsk, fãre; net, mē, hėr; pin, pīne; not, nōte, mȯve, nôr; up, lūte, pùll; oi, oil; ou, out; (lightened) aviȧry, ȩlect, agǫny, intǫ, ūnite; (obscured) errȧnt, operȧ, ardȩnt, actǫr, natūre; ch, chip; g, go; th, thin; ᴙн, then; y, you;

Merton (de mer'ton), Walter de (d. 1277), Eng. prelate, bishop of Rochester and founder of Merton College, Oxford.

Méryon (mā-ryoṅ), Charles (1821—68), Fr. etcher.

Mesdag (mes'dăch), Hendrik Willem (1831—1915), Dutch marine painter.

Mesmer (mes'mer), Franz (or Friedrich) Anton (1733—1815), Ger. physician, originator of theory of mesmerism.

Messager (me-sà-zhā), André Charles Prosper (1853—1929), Fr. composer of operettas and conductor.

Messalina or **Messallina** (mes-a-lī'na) (d. A.D. 48), third wife of the Rom. emperor Claudius I., notorious for her infamous life.

Metastasio (mä-tä-stä'zē-ō), Pietro (orig. Pietro Trapassi) (1698—1782), It. poet and dramatist.

Metcalf (met'kăf), Willard Leroy (1858—1925), Am. painter.

Metchnikoff (mech'ni-kof), Élie (in Russian, Ilya Ilich Mechnikov) (1845—1916), Russ. physiologist and bacteriologist, in France.

Methodius (me-thō'di-us), Saint ("the Apostle of the Slavs") (826—885), Gr. missionary, scholar, and archbishop (brother of Saint Cyril, 827—869).

Methuen (meth'ū-en), Paul Sanford Methuen, 3d Baron (1845—1932), Eng. field-marshal.

Meton (mē'ton) (fl. c432 B.C.), Gr. astronomer, introducer of the Metonic cycle.

Metsu (met'sü) or **Metzu** (met'zü), Gabriel (1630?—67), Dutch painter.

Metternich (fon met'er-nich), Klemens Lothar Wenzel, Prince von (1773—1859), Austrian diplomatist and statesman.

Meun or **Meung**, Jean de. See *Jean de Meun.*

Meunier (me-nyā), Constantin (1831—1905), Belgian sculptor and painter.

Meyer (mī'er), Konrad Ferdinand (1825—98), Swiss poet and novelist, writing in German.

Meyerbeer (mī'er-bār), Giacomo (Jakob Meyer Beer, orig. Jakob Liebmann Beer) (1791—1864), Ger. operatic composer.

Meynell (men'el), Alice (Alice Christiana Thompson, Mrs. Wilfrid Meynell) (1850—1922), Eng. poet and essayist (sister of Lady Elizabeth Butler).

Miaulis or **Miaoulis** (mē-ou'lēs), Andreas Vokos (orig. Andreas Vokos, or Bokos) (1768?—1835), Gr. admiral.

Michael VIII. (mī'kel) (Michael Palaeologus) (1234—82), Byzantine emperor (1261—82).

Michael (in Russian, Mikhail Fedorovich Romanov) (1596—1645), czar of Russia (1613—45) (first czar of the house of Romanov).

Michael Obrenovich (ō-bren'ō-vich) (Obrenovich III.) (1823?—68), prince of Serbia (1839—42, 1860—68) (son of Milosh Obrenovich).

Michaux (me-shō), André (1746—1802), Fr. botanist and traveler.

Michaux, François André (1770—1855), Fr. botanist (son of André).

Michel (me-shel), Clémence Louise (1830—1905), Fr. anarchist.

Michelangelo (mī-kel-an'je-lō, It. mē-kel-än'je-lō) (Michelangelo Buonarroti) (1475—1564), It. sculptor, painter, architect, and poet.

Michelet (mēsh-lā), Jules (1798—1874), Fr. historian and misc. writer.

Michelozzi (mē-ke-lot'sē), Michelozzo (also called Michelozzo di Bartolommeo) (c1396—1472?), It. architect and sculptor.

Michelson (mī'kel-son), Albert Abraham (1852—1931), Am. physicist, born in Germany.

Mickiewicz (mits-kyā'vich), Adam (1798—1855), Pol. poet.

Middleton (mid'l-ton), Arthur (1742—87), Am. patriot.

Middleton, Conyers (1683—1750), Eng. divine and controversialist.

Middleton, Thomas (c1570—1627), Eng. dramatist.

Midhat Pasha (me-dhät' pà-shä') (1822—84), Turk. statesman.

Mieris (văn mē'ris), Frans van ("the elder") (1635—81), Dutch painter.

Mieris, Frans van ("the younger") (1689—1763), Dutch painter (grandson of "the elder").

Mifflin (mif'lin), Thomas (1744—1800), Am. general and statesman.

Migne (mēn-y'), Jacques Paul (1800—75), Fr. Rom. Cath. priest, and publisher of theological works.

Mignet (mē-nyā), François Auguste Marie (1796—1884), Fr. historian.

Miguel (mē-gäl'), Dom (Maria Evaristo Miguel) (1802—66), Pg. prince, and usurper (1828—34) (brother of Pedro I. of Brazil).

Miklosich (fon mik'lō-shich), Franz von (1813—91), Austrian Slavic scholar and lexicographer.

Milan I. (mē'län) (1854—1901), king of Serbia (1882—89) (as Obrenovich IV., prince regnant of Serbia, 1868—82) (cousin of Michael Obrenovich).

Miles (mīlz), Nelson Appleton (1839—1925), Am. general.

Mill (mil), James (1773—1836), Br. philosopher, historian, and economist.

Mill, John Stuart (1806—73), Eng. philosopher and economist (son of James).

Millais (mil'ā), Sir John Everett (1829—96), Eng. painter.

Millay (mi-lā'), Edna St. Vincent (Mrs. Boissevain) (1892—), Am. poet.

Miller (mil'er), Cincinnatus Heine ("Joaquin Miller") (1841—1913), Am. poet.

Miller, Henry John (1860—1926), Eng.-Am. actor and theatrical manager.

Miller, Hugh (1802—56), Sc. geologist and writer.

Miller, William (1782—1849), Am. preacher and prophet, founder of Adventists.

Millerand (mēl-räṅ), Alexandre (1859—1943), Fr. statesman, president of France (1920—24).

Millet (mil'et), Francis Davis (1846—1912), Am. painter and writer.

Millet (mē-lā), Jean François (1814—75), Fr. painter.

Millikan (mil'i-kan), Robert Andrews (1868—), Am. physicist.

Millöcker (mil'e-ker), Karl (1842—99), Austrian composer of operettas.

Mills (milz), Roger Quarles (1832—1911), Am. legislator.

Milman (mil'man), Henry Hart (1791—1868), Eng. divine and historian.

Milne (miln), Alan Alexander (1882—), Eng. novelist, playwright, and misc. writer.

Milne, John (1850—1913), Eng. geologist and seismologist.

Milne-Edwards (mēl-nà-dwärs), Alphonse (1835—1900), Fr. naturalist (son of Henri).

Milne-Edwards, Henri (1800—85), Fr. naturalist, born in Belgium.

Milner (mil'ner), Alfred Milner, Viscount (1854—1925), Eng. statesman and colonial administrator.

Milnes (milz or milnz), Richard Monckton. See *Houghton, 1st Baron.*

Milosh Obrenovich (mē'losh ō-bren'ō-vich) (Obrenovich I.) (1780—1860), Serbian military leader, and prince of Serbia (1817—39, 1858—60).

Miltiades (mil-tī'a-dēz) (d. c488 B.C.), Athenian general, victor at Marathon.

Milton (mil'ton), John (1608—74), Eng. poet.

Mimnermus (mim-ner'mus) (fl. c630 B.C.), Gr. elegiac poet.

Mina (mē'nä), Francisco Espoz y (1782?—1836), Sp. guerrilla leader.

Mina, Francisco Javier (1789—1817), Sp. soldier in Spain and Mexico (nephew of Francisco Espoz y Mina).

Mind (mint), Gottfried ("the Raphael of Cats") (1768—1814), Swiss painter.

Minghetti (mēn-get'tē), Marco (1818—86), It. statesman and economist.

Mino da Fiesole (mē'nō dä fyä'zō-lä) (properly Mino di Giovanni) (1431?—84), It. sculptor.

Minot (mī'not), Laurence (1300?—52?), Eng. poet.

Minsheu (min'shū), John (fl. c1617), Eng. lexicographer.

Minto (min'tō), Gilbert John Elliot-Murray-Kynynmound, 4th Earl of (1845—1914), Br. soldier and administrator, governor-general of Canada (1898—1904).

Minton (min'ton), Herbert (1793—1858), Eng. manufacturer of pottery and porcelain.

Minucius Felix (mi-nū'shius fē'liks), Marcus (fl. c180), Rom. Christian apologist.

(variable) d as d or j, s as s or sh, t as t or ch, z as z or zh; o, F. cloche; ü, F. menu; ch, Sc. loch; ṅ, F. bonbon; ', primary accent; ', secondary accent; †, obsolete; <, from; +, and; =, equals. See also lists at beginning of book.

Minuit (mĭn'ū-ĭt) or **Minnewit** (mĭn'e̍-wĭt), Peter (c1580–1641), colonial governor in Dutch and Swedish service in America, born in Germany.

Mirabeau (dė mē-rà-bō), Honoré Gabriel Victor Riquetti, Comte de (1749–91), Fr. statesman and orator.

Miramón (mē-rä-mōn'), Miguel (1832–67), Mex. general.

Miranda (mē-rän'dä), Francisco (c1750–1816), Venezuelan adventurer and revolutionist.

Miranda, Sá de. See *Sá de Miranda*.

Mirandola, Pico della. See *Pico della Mirandola*.

Mirbeau (mēr-bō), Octave Henri Marie (1850–1917), Fr. novelist and dramatist.

Mirko (mēr'kō), Prince (Mirko Petrovich Niegosh) (1820–67), Montenegrin military commander (brother of Danilo I.).

Mistral (mēs-tràl), Frédéric (1830–1914), Provençal poet.

Mitchel (mĭch'e̍l), John (1815–75), Ir. journalist and agitator, for many years in U. S.

Mitchell (mĭch'e̍l), Donald Grant ("Ik Marvel") (1822–1908), Am. writer.

Mitchell, John (1870–1919), Am. labor leader.

Mitchell, Maria (1818–89), Am. astronomer.

Mitchell, Silas Weir (1829–1914), Am. physician and novelist.

Mitford (mĭt'fọrd), Mary Russell (1787–1855), Eng. author.

Mitford, William (1744–1827), Eng. historian.

Mithridates VI. (mĭth-rĭ-dā'tēz) or **Mithradates VI.** (mĭth-rȧ-dā'tēz) ("the Great") (c132–63 B.C.), king of Pontus (120?–63 B.C.), enemy of Rome.

Mitre (mē'trā), Bartolomé (1821–1906), Argentine statesman, president of Argentina (1862–68).

Mivart (mī'vạrt), St. George Jackson (1827–1900), Eng. biologist.

Mnemon (nē'mon). See *Artaxerxes II.*

Mnesicles (nes'ĭ-klēz) (fl. c437 B.C.), Gr. architect.

Modjeska (mō-jes'kạ), Helena (professional name of Helena Opid, Mme. Modrzejewska, Mme. Chlapowska) (1840–1909), Pol.-Am. actress.

Modjeski (mō-jes'ki), Ralph (name orig. Modrzejewski) (1861–1940), Pol.-Am. civil engineer (son of Helena Modjeska).

Moe (mö), Jörgen Engebretsen (1813–82), Norw. bishop, folklorist, and poet.

Moehler (mė'lėr). See *Möhler*.

Mohammed (mō-ham'ed), **Mahomet** (mȧ-hom'et), or **Muhammad** (mō-häm'ạd) (570?–632), Arabian prophet, founder of Islam or Mohammedanism.

Mohammed II. ("the Great") (1430–81), sultan of Turkey (1451–81), and capturer of Constantinople (1453) (son of Amurath II.).

Mohammed IV. (1642?–92?), sultan of Turkey (1648–87) (nephew of Amurath IV.).

Mohammed V. (1844–1918), sultan of Turkey (1909–18) (brother of Abdul-Hamid II.).

Mohammed VI. (1861–1926), sultan of Turkey (1918–22) (brother of Mohammed V.).

Mohammed Ahmed (ä'med) ("the Mahdi") (c1848–85), Sudanese Moslem leader, who founded in the Egyptian Sudan the independent government overthrown in 1898.

Mohammed Ali. See *Mehemet Ali*.

Möhler (mė'lėr), Johann Adam (1796–1838), Ger. Rom. Cath. theologian.

Mohun (mō'hun or mön), Charles Mohun, 5th Baron (c1675–1712), Eng. brawler and duelist.

Moir (moir), David Macbeth (1798–1851), Sc. physician, novelist, and poet.

Moissan (mwo-säṅ), Henri (1852–1907), Fr. chemist.

Molay or **Molai** (dė mo-lä), Jacques de (c1243–1314), Fr. Templar, last grand master of the Knights Templars.

Molé (mo-lä), Louis Mathieu, Comte (1781–1855), Fr. statesman.

Molière (mo-lyär), Jean Baptiste Poquelin (born Jean Baptiste Poquelin) (1622–73), Fr. dramatist.

Molina (mō-lē'nä), Luis (1535–1600), Sp. Jesuit theologian.

Molinos (dä mō-lē'nōs), Miguel de (1640–96), Sp. priest and mystic, founder of Quietism.

Mollien (mo-lyaṅ), Nicolas François, Comte (1758–1850), Fr. finance minister.

Molnár (mol'när), Ferencz, or Franz (1878–   ), Hung. dramatist and novelist.

Molotov (mo'lo-tof), Vyacheslav Mikhaylovich (real name Skryabin) (1890–   ), Soviet Russian statesman, minister of foreign affairs.

Moltke (fon molt'kė), Helmuth Johannes Ludwig von (1848–1916), Ger. general (nephew of Helmuth K. B.).

Moltke, Helmuth Karl Bernhard, Graf von (1800–91), Prussian field-marshal.   [and archæologist.

Mommsen (mom'zen), Theodor (1817–1903), Ger. historian

Monaco (mon'ä-kō), Lorenzo. See *Lorenzo, Don.*

Moncey (dė môn-sā), Bon Adrien Jeannot de (Duc de Conegliano) (1754–1842), Fr. marshal.

Monck. See *Monk*.

Monet (mo-nā), Claude (1840–1926), Fr. painter.

Monge (mônzh), Gaspard (1746–1818), Fr. mathematician.

Monier-Williams (mō'ni-ėr-wil'yạmz), Sir Monier (1819–99), Br. Orientalist.   [(1608–70), Eng. general.

Monk or **Monck** (mungk), George (1st Duke of Albemarle)

Monluc. See *Montluc*.

Monmouth (mon'muth), James Scott, Duke of (1649–85), Eng. rebel (son of Lucy Walter, and reputed illegitimate son of Charles II.), leader of insurrection against James II.

Monro (mun-rō'), Sir Charles Carmichael (1860–1929), Br. general.   [U. S. (1817–25).

Monroe (mun-rō'), James (1758–1831), 5th president of

Montagu (mon'tạ-gū), Charles. See *Halifax, Earl of.*

Montagu, Lady Mary Wortley (Mary Pierrepont) (1689–1762), Eng. letter-writer.

Montaigne (mon-tän', Fr. dė môn-tän-y'), Michel Eyquem de (1533–92), Fr. essayist.

Montalembert (dė môn-tä-loṅ-bār), Charles Forbes René, Comte de (1810–70), Fr. publicist and historian.

Montalembert, Marc René, Marquis de (1714–1800), Fr. military engineer and writer.

Montcalm de Saint-Véran (mont-käm', Fr. dė môṅ-kàlm dė saṅ-vä-räṅ), Louis Joseph, Marquis de (1712–59), Fr. general in America.

Montecuccoli (mōn-tä-kök'kō-lē) or **Montecuculi** (mōn-tä-kö'kö-lē), Raimondo, Count of (Duke of Melfi) (1609–80), Austrian general, born near Modena, Italy.

Montefiore (mon″tė-fę̄-ō'rē), Sir Moses Haim (1784–1885), Eng. Jewish philanthropist, born in Italy.

Montemayor (dä mōn″tä-mä-yōr'), Jorge de (c1520–61), Pg. poet and novelist, writing in Spanish.

Montemezzi (mōn-tä-med'zē), Italo (1875–   ), It. musical composer.

Montespan (dė môṅ-tes-päṅ), Marquise de (Françoise Athénaïs de Rochechouart) (1641–1707), mistress of Louis XIV. of France.

Montesquieu (dė môṅ-tes-kyė), Charles Louis de Secondat, Baron de La Brède et de (1689–1755), Fr. philosophical historian and misc. writer.

Montessori (mōn-tes-sō'rē), Maria (1870–   ), It. physician and educationist.

Monteverde (mōn-tä-vär'dä) or **Monteverdi** (mōn-tä-vär'dē), Claudio (1567–1643), It. musical composer.

Montez (mon'tez), Lola (assumed name of Marie Dolores Eliza Rosanna Gilbert, later Mrs. James, Comtesse de Landsfeld, Mrs. Heald, Mrs. Hull) (1818–61), dancer and adventuress (born in Ireland), mistress of Louis I. of Bavaria.

Montezuma II. (mon-tę-zō'mä) (c1477–1520), last Aztec emperor of Mexico (1503–20).

Montfort (mont'fort, Fr. dė môṅ-fôr), Simon de (c1160–1218), Fr. soldier and crusader.

Montfort, Simon of (Earl of Leicester) (c1208–65), Eng. soldier and statesman, born in France (son of Simon de Montfort, c1160–1218).

Montgolfier (môṅ-gol-fyä), Jacques Étienne (1745–99), Fr. aëronautic inventor (brother of Joseph M.).

Montgolfier, Joseph Michel (1740–1810), Fr. aëronautic inventor.

Montgomery, Sir Bernard L. (1887–   ), Br. gen.

Montgomery (mont-gum'e̍-ri), James (1771–1854), Sc. poet.

Montgomery, Richard (1736–75), Am. general.

Monti (mōn'tē), Vincenzo (1754–1828), It. poet.

Montluc or **Monluc** (dė môn-lük), Blaise de Lasseran-Massencome, Seigneur de (c1503–77), Fr. marshal and historian.

Montmorency (dė môṅ-mo-roṅ-sē), Anne, Duc de (1493?–1567), Fr. marshal, and constable of France.

Montmorency, Henri II., Duc de (1595–1632), Fr. marshal (grandson of Anne de Montmorency).

Montpensier (dė môṅ-poṅ-syä), Anne Marie Louise d'Orléans, Duchesse de (called La Grande Mademoiselle) (1627–93), Fr. princess, and writer of memoirs (daughter of Duc d'Orléans, 1608–60, and wife of Duc de Lauzun).

Montpensier, Antoine Marie Philippe Louis d'Orléans, Duc de (1824–90), Fr. prince, unsuccessful candidate for the Spanish throne in 1870 (son of Louis Philippe of France).

Montrose (mon-trōz'), James Graham, 1st Marquis of (1612–50), Sc. royalist leader, hanged at Edinburgh.

Moody (mōʹdi), Dwight Lyman (1837–99), Am. evangelist.

Moody, William Vaughn (1869–1910), Am. poet and dramatist.

Moor, Antonis. See *Mor.*

Moore (mōr or mōr), George (1852–1933), Ir. novelist, dramatist, and critic.

Moore, George Foot (1851–1931), Am. Biblical scholar and historian of religions.

Moore, Sir John (1761–1809), Br. general.

Moore, John Bassett (1860–   ), Am. publicist.

Moore, Thomas (1779–1852), Ir. poet.

Mor or **Moor** (mōr), Antonis (also known as Antonio Moro and Sir Anthony More) (c1512–c1576), Dutch painter.

Moraes (dä mō-rīsh'), Francisco de (c1500–72), Pg. romance-writer.

Moraes Barros (bär'rŏsh), Prudente José de (1841–1902), Brazilian politician, president of Brazil (1894–98).

Moran (mō-ran'), Patrick Francis (1830–1911), Australian cardinal, born in Ireland.

Moratín (dä mō-rä-tēn'), Leandro Fernández de (1760–1828), Sp. dramatist and poet.

Moray (mur'i), Thomas Randolph, 1st Earl of (d. 1332), Sc. warrior and statesman (nephew of Robert I. of Scotland).

Moray or **Murray,** James Stuart (or Stewart), 1st Earl of (in Stuart line) (1531?–70), Sc. statesman, regent of Scotland (half-brother of Mary Queen of Scots).

Mordaunt (môr'dạnt), Charles. See *Peterborough, 3d Earl of.*

More (mōr), Sir Anthony. See *Mor, Antonis.*

More, Hannah (1745–1833), Eng. religious and misc. writer.

More, Henry (1614–87), Eng. philosophical writer.

More, Paul Elmer (1864–1937), Am. editor, essayist, and critic.

More, Sir Thomas (1478–1535), Eng. statesman and author.

Moreau (mo-rō), Gustave (1826–98), Fr. painter.

Moreau, Jean Victor (1763–1813), Fr. general.

Morelli (mo-rel'lē), Giovanni ("Ivan Lermolieff") (1816–91), It. patriot and writer on art, writing in German.

Morelos y Pavón (mō-rā'lōs ē pä-vōn'), José María (1765–1815), Mex. priest and revolutionary leader.

Morgagni (mor-gä'nyē), Giovanni Battista (1682–1771), It. anatomist.

Morgan (môr'gạn), Conwy Lloyd (1852–1936), Eng. zoölogist.

Morgan, Daniel (1736–1802), Am. Revolutionary general.

Morgan, Edwin Dennison (1811–83), Am. political leader, governor of New York (1859–63).

Morgan, Sir Henry (c1635–88), Br. buccaneer, later lieutenant-governor of Jamaica.

Morgan, John Hunt (1826–64), Am. Confederate general.

Morgan, John Pierpont (1837–1913), Am. financier, philanthropist, and art collector.

Morgan, John Pierpont (1867–1943), Am. financier (son of J. P., 1837–1913).

Morgan, Lewis Henry (1818–81), Am. ethnologist.

Morgan, Thomas Hunt (1866–1945), Am. zoölogist.

Morier (mō'ri-ėr), James Justinian (1780?–1849), Eng. traveler and novelist.

Morigi (mo-rē'jē), Michelangelo. See *Caravaggio, Michelangelo da.*

Morison (mor'i-sọn), James (1816–93), Sc. clergyman, founder of sect called Evangelical Union.

Morland (môr'lạnd), George (1763–1804), Eng. painter.

Morley (môr'li), Christopher Darlington (1890–   ), Am. author.

Morley, Edward Williams (1838–1923), Am. chemist and physicist.

Morley, Henry (1822–94), Eng. literary critic and historian.

Morley, Thomas (1557–1603?), Eng. musical composer.

Morley of Blackburn (blak'bėrn), John Morley, Viscount (1838–1923), Eng. statesman, biographer, and essayist.

Mornay (dė môr-nä), Philippe de (Seigneur du Plessis-Marly, called du Plessis-Mornay) (1549–1623), Fr. diplomatist, politician, and Huguenot leader.

Morny (dė môr-nē), Charles Auguste Louis Joseph, Duc de (1811–65), Fr. statesman (half-brother of Napoleon III.).

Moro (mō'rō), Antonio. See *Mor, Antonis.*

Morosini (mo-rō-sē'nē), Francesco (1618–94), Venetian military and naval commander, and doge (1688–94).

Morris (mor'is), Clara (real name Morrison, Mrs. Harriott) (1849–1925), Am. actress and writer, born in Canada.

Morris, George Pope (1802–64), Am. journalist and poet.

Morris, Gouverneur (1752–1816), Am. statesman and diplomatist.

Morris, Sir Lewis (1833–1907), Br. poet.

Morris, Robert (1734–1806), Am. patriot and financier, born in England.

Morris, William (1834–96), Eng. poet and artist.

Morrison (mor'i-sọn), Richard James ("Zadkiel") (1795–1874), Eng. astrologer.

Morrison, Robert (1782–1834), Eng. Protestant missionary to China, and Chinese scholar.

Morse (môrs), Samuel Finley Breese (1791–1872), Am. inventor (of telegraph apparatus).

Mortier (môr-tyä), Édouard Adolphe Casimir Joseph (Duc de Trévise) (1768–1835), Fr. marshal.

Mortimer (môr'ti-mėr), Roger (1st Earl of March) (1287?–1330), Eng. soldier and politician, favorite of Isabella of France, queen of Edward II. of England.

Morton (môr'tọn), James Douglas, 4th Earl of (c1525–81), Sc. statesman, and regent of Scotland, beheaded on charge of complicity in the murder of Darnley.

Morton, John (c1420–1500), Eng. prelate (archbishop of Canterbury and cardinal) and statesman.

Morton, Levi Parsons (1824–1920), Am. banker, vice-president of U. S. (1889–93).

Morton, Oliver Perry (1823–77), Am. statesman, governor of Indiana (1861–67).

Morton, Thomas (c1590–1646), Eng. adventurer in New England, and writer.

Morton, Thomas (1764?–1838), Eng. dramatist.

Morton, William Thomas Green (1819–68), Am. dentist, introducer of ether as an anesthetic.

Mosby (mōz'bi), John Singleton (1833–1916), Am. Confederate soldier.

Moscheles (mosh'e-les), Ignaz (1794–1870), Bohem. pianist and composer.

Moschus (mos'kus) (fl. c150 B.C.), Gr. bucolic poet.

Moszkowski (mosh-kof'skē), Moritz (1854–1925), Ger. pianist and composer, of Polish parentage.

Motherwell (muᴛн'ėr-wel), William (1797–1835), Sc. poet.

Motley (mot'li), John Lothrop (1814–77), Am. historian.

Mott (mot), Mrs. (Lucretia Coffin) (1793–1880), Am. social reformer, advocate of woman's rights.

Moultrie (mōl'tri), William (1731–1805), Am. gen.

Mounet-Sully (mō-nā-sü-lē) Jean (born Jean Sully Mounet) (1841–1916), Fr. actor.

Mountbatten (mount-bat'n), Lord Louis (1900–   ), Brit. admiral.

Mount Stephen (mount stē'vẹn), George Stephen, Baron (1829–1921), Can. financier and railroad promoter, born in Scotland.

Moussorgski (mō-sôrg'skē). See *Musorgski.*

Mowat (mou'ạt), Sir Oliver (1820–1903), Can. statesman.

Mowbray (mō'brạ), Thomas. See *Norfolk, 1st Duke of.*

Moxon (mok'sọn), Joseph (1627–1700), Eng. mathematician, geographer, and technical writer.

Mozart (mō'zärt, Ger. mō'tsärt), Wolfgang Amadeus (1756–91), Austrian musical composer.

Mudie (mū'di), Charles Edward (1818–90), Eng. bookseller and publisher, founder of Mudie's Lending Library.

Mueller (mül'ėr). See *Müller.*

Muensterberg (mün'stėr-berch). See *Münsterberg.*

Muenzer (mün′tsèr). See *Münzer.*

Muggleton (mug′l-tǫn), Lodowicke (1609—98), Eng. religious fanatic, founder of sect known as Muggletonians.

Muhammad. See *Mohammed.*

Mühlbach (mül′bäch), Luise. Pseudonym of Frau Mundt.

Mühlenberg (mü′lẹn-berch) or **Muhlenberg** (mü′lẹn-bèrg), Heinrich Melchior (1711—87), Ger.-Am. Lutheran clergyman.

Muhlenberg (mü′lẹn-bèrg), John Peter Gabriel (1746—1807), Am. clergyman, Revolutionary general, and politician (son of Heinrich M.).

Muhlenberg, William Augustus (1796—1877), Am. Episcopal clergyman, hymn-writer, and philanthropist (great-grandson of Heinrich M.).

Muir (mūr), John (1838—1914), Am. naturalist and writer, born in Scotland.

Mulcaster (mul′kas-tèr), Richard (c1530—1611), Eng. schoolmaster and educationist.

Müller (mül′èr), Friedrich Max (1823—1900), Ger.-Eng. Orientalist, philologist, and misc. writer (son of Wilhelm).

Müller, Johannes Peter (1801—58), Ger. physiologist and anatomist.

Müller, Wilhelm (1794—1827), Ger. poet.

Mulock (mū′lok), Dinah Maria. See *Craik, Mrs.*

Mulready (mul′red-i), William (1786—1863), Br. painter.

Multatuli (mōl-tä-tö′lē). Pseudonym of E. D. Dekker.

Mun (dė muṅ), Adrien Albert Marie, Comte de (1841—1914), Fr. politician and writer.

Mundelein (mun′dẹ-līn), George William (1872—1939), Am. cardinal.

Mundt (mùnt), Frau (Klara Müller, "Luise Mühlbach") (1814—73), Ger. novelist.

Munkácsy (mùn′kä-chē), Mihály, or Michael (real name Michael Lieb) (1844—1900), Hung. painter.

Munsey (mun′si), Frank Andrew (1854—1925), Am. publisher.

Münsterberg (mün′stèr-berch), Hugo (1863—1916), Ger. psychologist and writer, in America.

Münzer (mün′tsèr), Thomas (c1490—1525), Ger. religious enthusiast.

Murad. See *Amurath.*

Murat (mü-rä), Joachim (1767—1815), Fr. marshal, and (as Joachim Napoleon) king of Naples (1808—15) (brother-in-law of Napoleon I.).

Murat, Mme. See *Bonaparte, Marie Annonciade Caroline.*

Muratori (mö-rä-tö′rē), Lodovico Antonio (1672—1750), It. Rom. Cath. priest, antiquary, and historian.

Murchison (mèr′chi-sǫn), Sir Roderick Impey (1792—1871), Br. geologist.

Murfree (mèr′frē), Mary Noailles ("Charles Egbert Craddock") (1850—1922), Am. novelist.

Murger (mür-zhàr), Henri (1822—61), Fr. writer.

Murillo (mū-ril′ō, Sp. mö-rēl′yō), Bartolomé Esteban (1617—82), Sp. painter.

Murner (mùr′nèr), Thomas (1475—1537), Ger. priest and satirist.

Murray (mur′i), Lord George (1694—1760), Sc. Jacobite general.

Murray, George Gilbert Aimé (1866—   ), Br. classical scholar.

Murray, Sir James Augustus Henry (1837—1915), Br. philologist and lexicographer.

Murray, James Stuart, 1st Earl of. See *Moray.*

Murray, John (1741—1815), Am. Universalist clergyman, born in England.

Murray, Lindley (1745—1826), Am.-Eng. grammarian.

Musa (mö′sä) (Musa ibn Nosair) (640—716?), Arab general and administrator, conqueror in northern Africa and Spain.

Musæus (mū-sē′us) (fl. c500), Gr. poet.

Musorgski (mö-sôrg′skẹ), Modest Petrovich (1839—81), Russ. musical composer.

Musset (dė mü-sä), Louis Charles Alfred de (1810—57), Fr. poet, dramatist, and writer of fiction.

Mussolini (mös-sō-lē′nē), Benito (1883—1945), It. journalist, soldier, and statesman, leader of the Fascisti, premier (1922—45).

Mutsuhito (möt-sǫ-hē′tō) (1852—1912), emperor of Japan (1867—1912).

Myers (mī′èrz), Frederic William Henry (1843—1901), Eng. poet, essayist, and investigator of psychical phenomena.

Myron (mī′rǫn) (fl. c450 B.C.), Gr. sculptor.

N

Nachtigal (näch′tē-gäl), Gustav (1834—85), Ger. physician and explorer in Africa.

Nadir (nä′dèr) (c1688—1747), shah of Persia (1736—47).

Nævius (nē′vi-us), Cnæus (c270—c200 B.C.), Rom. dramatic and epic poet.

Nairne (nãrn), Baroness (Carolina Oliphant) (1766—1845), Sc. poet.

Nana Sahib (nä′nạ sä′ib) (real name Dandhu Panth) (1825?—after 1859), a native leader in the East Indian Sepoy Mutiny of 1857.

Nansen (nän′sẹn), Fridtjof (1861—1930), Norw. arctic explorer, scientist, and diplomatist.

Nanteuil (näṅ-tė-y′), Robert (1623?—78), Fr. engraver.

Napier (nä′pi-èr or nạ-pēr′), Sir Charles (1786—1860), Br. admiral (cousin of Sir Charles J.).

Napier, Sir Charles James (1782—1853), Br. general and administrator.

Napier, John (1550—1617), Sc. mathematician, inventor of logarithms.

Napier, Sir William Francis Patrick (1785—1860), Br. general, and military historian (brother of Sir Charles J.).

Napier of Magdala (mag′dạ-lạ), Robert Cornelis Napier, 1st Baron (1810—90), Br. field-marshal.

Napoleon I. (nạ-pō′lẹ-ǫn) (in French, Napoléon, pron. nả-po-lā-ôṅ) (Napoléon Bonaparte, or Buonaparte) (1769—1821), emperor of the French, 1804—14 and during 1815 (Fr. general, born in Corsica, first consul of France 1799—1804).

Napoleon II. (François Charles Joseph Bonaparte, Duc de Reichstadt) (1811—32), titular emperor of the French (son of Napoleon I. and Marie Louise).

Napoleon III. (Charles Louis Napoléon Bonaparte, known as Louis Napoleon) (1808—73), emperor of the French, 1852—70 (president of France, 1848—52) (son of Louis Bonaparte, and nephew of Napoleon I.).

Nares (nãrz), Sir George Strong (1831—1915), Br. naval officer and explorer.

Narses (när′sēz) (c478—c573), Byzantine general.

Narváez (dä när-vä′äth), Pánfilo de (c1478—1528), Sp. soldier and adventurer in America.

Narváez, Ramón María (Duke of Valencia) (1800—68), Sp. soldier and statesman.

Nasby (naz′bi), Petroleum V. Pseudonym of David Ross Locke.

Nash (nash), Richard (called Beau Nash, and known also as "the King of Bath") (1674—1762), Eng. leader of fashion.

Nash or **Nashe,** Thomas (1567—1601), Eng. poet, dramatist, and misc. writer.

Nasmyth (nä′smith), James (1808—90), Br. inventor.

Nasr-ed-Din (näs′r-ed-dēn′) (1829?—96), shah of Persia (1848—96).

Nassau (nas′â, Dutch nä′sou), Maurice of. See *Maurice of Nassau* and *Nassau-Siegen.*

Nassau-Siegen (nä′sou-zē′gẹn), Joan (or Jaan) Maurits, Count of (called Maurice of Nassau) (1604—79), Dutch general and administrator.

Nast (nåst), Thomas (1840—1902), Am. caricaturist, born in Germany.

Nattier (nả-tyä), Jean Marc (1685—1766), Fr. painter.

Neale (nēl), John Mason (1818—66), Eng. divine and author.

Neander (nē-an′dèr, Ger. nä-än′dèr), Johann August Wilhelm (orig. David Mendel) (1789—1850), Ger. theologian and church historian.

Nebuchadnezzar (neb″ū-kạd-nez′ạr) or **Nebuchadrezzar** (neb″ū-kạd-rez′ạr) (d. 561 B.C.), king of Babylonia (604?—561 B.C.).

Necho (nē′kō) (fl. c600 B.C.), king of Egypt, of 26th dynasty.

Necker (nek′èr, Fr. ne-kàr), Jacques (1732—1804), Fr. financier and statesman, born at Geneva.

Neilson (nēl′sǫn), Lilian Adelaide (professional name of Elizabeth Ann Brown, Mrs. Lee) (1848—80), Eng. actress.

Neisser (nī′sèr), Albert (1855—1916), Ger. physician.

Nekrasov (nye-krä′sof), Nikolay Aleksyeevich (1821—77), Russ. poet.

Nelson (nel′sǫn), Horatio Nelson, Viscount (1758—1805), Eng. admiral.

Nelson, Thomas (1738—89), Am. patriot.

Nemours (dḕ nė-mōr′), Louis Charles Philippe Raphaël d'Orléans, Duc de (1814—96), Fr. prince and soldier (son of Louis Philippe of France).

Nepomuk, Saint John of. See *John of Nepomuk.*

Nepos (nē′pos), Cornelius (c99—c24 B.C.), Rom. historical and biographical writer.

Neri (nā′rē), Philip (Filippo Neri) (1515—95), It. priest and saint, founder of Congregation of the Oratory.

Nernst (nernst), Walter (1864—1941), Ger. physicist and inventor.

Nero (nē′rō) (Nero Claudius Cæsar Drusus Germanicus, orig. Lucius Domitius Ahenobarbus) (A.D. 37—68), Rom. emperor (A.D. 54—68) (son of Agrippina, and adopted son of Claudius I.).

Nerva (nėr′vạ), Marcus Cocceius (A.D. c32—98), Rom. emperor (A.D. 96—98).

Nerval (dḕ ner-väl′), Gérard de (born Gérard Labrunie) (1808—55), Fr. author.

Nesselrode (nes′ẹl-rō″dḕ), Count Karl Robert (1780—1862), Russ. diplomatist and statesman.

Nessler (nes′lėr), Victor (1841—90), Ger. operatic composer.

Nestorius (nes-tō′ri-us) (d. c451), Syrian bishop and heretic.

Nettleship (net′l-ship), Henry (1839—93), Eng. Latin scholar.

Neuville (dḕ nė-vēl′), Alphonse Marie de (1836—85), Fr. painter, esp. of military subjects.

Neville (nev′il), Richard. See *Warwick, Earl of.*

Nevin (nev′in), Ethelbert (1862—1901), Am. musical composer.

Nevin, John Williamson (1803—86), Am. clergyman and theologian.

Newbolt (nū′bōlt), Sir Henry John (1862—1938), Eng. poet and naval historian.

Newcastle (nū′kȧs-l), William Cavendish, Duke of (1592—1676), Eng. royalist soldier, and writer.

Newcastle, Thomas Pelham-Holles, Duke of (1693—1768), Eng. statesman.

Newcomb (nū′kǫm), Simon (1835—1909), Am. astronomer, born in Canada.

Newman (nū′mạn), John Henry (1801—90), Eng. cardinal, theologian, and author.

Newport (nū′pōrt), Christopher (c1565—1617), Eng. navigator, commander of expedition that founded Jamestown, Va. (1607).

Newton (nū′tǫn), Alfred (1829—1907), Eng. zoölogist.

Newton, Sir Isaac (1642—1727), Eng. natural philosopher.

Ney (nā), Michel (Duc d'Elchingen, Prince de La Moskova) (1769—1815), Fr. marshal.

Nicholas (nik′ō-lạs), Saint (fl. 4th cent.), bishop in Asia Minor, patron saint of Russia and protector of children.

Nicholas I., Saint ("Nicholas the Great") (d. 867), It. ecclesiastic, pope (858—867).

Nicholas V. (Tommaso Parentucelli, or Tommaso da Sarzana) (1397?—1455), It. ecclesiastic, pope (1447—55).

Nicholas I. (in Russian, Nikolay Pavlovich) (1796—1855), czar of Russia (1825—55) (brother of Czar Alexander I.).

Nicholas II. (in Russian, Nikolay Aleksandrovich) (1868—1918), czar of Russia (1894—1917) (son of Czar Alexander III.).

Nicholas (in Russian, Nikolay Nikolaevich) (1856—1929), Russ. grand duke, and military commander (nephew of Czar Alexander II.).

Nicholas I. (Nikola Petrovich Niegosh) (1841—1921), prince regnant of Montenegro (1860—1910), and king of Montenegro (1910—18) (nephew of Danilo I., and son of Prince Mirko).

Nicholas of Cusa (kū′zạ). See *Cusanus.*

Nicholson (nik′ǫl-sǫn), William (1753—1815), Eng. scientific writer and inventor.

Nicias (nish′i-ạs) (d. 414 B.C.), Athenian general and statesman.

Nicolai (nē-kō-lī′), Otto (1810—49), Ger. operatic composer.

Nicolls (nik′ǫlz), Richard (1624—72), first Eng. colonial governor of New York.

Nicot (nē-kō), Jean (1530—1600), Fr. diplomatist and scholar, introducer of tobacco into France.

Niebuhr (nē′bŏŏr), Barthold Georg (1776—1831), Ger. historian (son of Karsten).

Niebuhr, Karsten (1733—1815), Ger. traveler in Arabia.

Niel (nē-el), Adolphe (1802—69), Fr. marshal.

Niembsch von Strehlenau (nēmpsh fon shtrā′lẹ-nou), Nikolaus ("Nikolaus Lenau") (1802—50), Austrian poet.

Niepce (nyeps), Joseph Nicéphore (1765—1833), Fr. inventor (associated with Daguerre).

Nietzsche (nē′chė), Friedrich Wilhelm (1844—1900), Ger. philosophical writer.

Nigel (nī′jẹl) (known as Nigel Wireker) (fl. c1190), Eng. monk and satirist.

Nightingale (nī′ting-gāl or nī′tin-gāl), Florence (1820—1910), Eng. philanthropist, reformer of hospital nursing.

Nilsson (nil′sǫn), Christine (Mme. Rouzaud, Countess Casa di Miranda) (1843—1921), Swed. soprano singer.

Nimitz (nim′its), Chester W. (1885—   ), Am. admiral.

Nitti (nēt′tē), Francesco Saverio (1868—   ), It. statesman.

Nivelle (nē-vel), Robert Georges (1856—1924), Fr. general.

Noailles (dḕ nǫ-ä-y′), Adrien Maurice, Duc de (1678—1766), Fr. marshal.

Noailles, Louis Marie, Vicomte de (1756—1804), Fr. general.

Nobel (nō′bẹl, Swed. nō-bel′), Alfred Bernhard (1833—96), Swed. inventor and manufacturer of explosives, establisher of the Nobel Prizes (five prizes, of about $35,000 each, awarded annually, without distinction as to nationality, for eminence in the fields of physics, chemistry, medicine and physiology, and literature, and for the promotion of peace).

Nodier (no-dyā), Charles (1780—1844), Fr. author.

Nogi (nō′gē), Count Maresuke (1849—1912), Jap. general.

Noguchi (nō′gŏŏ-chē), Hideyo (1876—1928), Jap. physician and bacteriologist, in America.

Nollekens (nol′ẹ-kenz), Joseph (1737—1823), Eng. sculptor.

Nordau (nôr′dou), Max Simon (1849—1923), Ger. Jewish physician and writer in Paris, born in Hungary.

Nordenskiöld (nôr′dẹn-shẹld), Nils Adolf Erik, Baron (1832—1901), Swed. geologist and arctic explorer, born in Finland.

Nordenskjöld (nôr′dẹn-shẹld), Nils Otto Gustaf (1869—1928), Swed. arctic and antarctic explorer.

Nordica (nôr′di-kạ), Mme. (professional name of Lillian Norton, Mrs. Gower, Mrs. Döme, Mrs. Young) (1859—1914), Am. operatic soprano singer.

Norfolk (nôr′fǫk), Thomas Mowbray, 1st Duke of (in Mowbray line) (1366?—99), Eng. soldier and statesman.

Norfolk, Thomas Howard, 3d Duke of (1473—1554), Eng. soldier and politician.

Norfolk, Thomas Howard, 4th Duke of (1536—72), Eng. politician (son of Earl of Surrey).

Norris (nor′is), Frank (1870—1902), Am. novelist.

Norris, John (1657—1711), Eng. divine and philosopher.

Norris, William Edward (1847—1925), Eng. novelist.

North (nôrth), Christopher. Pseudonym of John Wilson.

North, Sir Dudley (1641—91), Eng. financier and economist (brother of 1st Baron Guilford).

North, Francis. See *Guilford, 1st Baron.*

North, Lord Frederick. See *Guilford, 2d Earl of.*

North, Roger (1653—1734), Eng. lawyer and historian (brother of 1st Baron Guilford).

North, Sir Thomas (1535?—1601?), Eng. translator.

Northcliffe (nôrth′klif), Alfred Charles William Harmsworth, Viscount (1865—1922), Br. newspaper publisher.

Northcote (nôrth′kǫt), Sir Stafford Henry. See *Iddesleigh, 1st Earl of.*

Northumberland (nôr-thum′bẹr-lạnd), Henry Percy, 1st Earl of (1342—1408), Eng. military leader.

Northumberland, John Dudley, Duke of (1502?—53), Eng. politician and soldier (son of Edmund Dudley).

Norton (nôr′tǫn), Mrs. (Caroline Elizabeth Sarah Sheridan, Mrs. Norton, later Lady Stirling-Maxwell) (1808—77), Eng. poet and novelist (granddaughter of Richard B. B. Sheridan).

Norton, Charles Eliot (1827—1908), Am. scholar and editor.

(variable) ḍ as d or j, ṣ as s or sh, ṭ as t or ch, ẓ as z or zh; o, F. cloche; ü, F. menu; ċh, Sc. loch; ṅ, F. bonbon; ′, primary accent; ″, secondary accent; †, obsolete; <, from; +, and; =, equals. See also lists at beginning of book.

Nostradamus (nos-tra-dā′mus) (Michel de Nostredame) (1503—66), Fr. astrologer.

Nottingham (not′ing-am), Charles Howard, 1st Earl of (also known as 2d Baron Howard of Effingham) (1536—1624), Eng. admiral.

Nottingham, Heneage Finch, 1st Earl of (1621—82), Eng. jurist and statesman.

Novalis (nō-vä′lis). Pseudonym of Friedrich von Hardenberg.

Novatian (nō-vā′shian) (Novatianus) (fl. 251), Rom. schismatic bishop.

Noyes (noiz), Alfred (1880—   ), Eng. poet.

Noyes, John Humphrey (1811—86), Am. communitarian, founder of Oneida Community.

Numa Pompilius (nū′ma pom-pil′i-us) (d. 672 B.C.), 2d (legendary) king of Rome (715—672 B.C.). He is said to have introduced the early Roman religious worship, having received instruction concerning it from the nymph Egeria.

Nunes (nō′nāsh), Pedro (as Latinized, Petrus Nonius) (1492—1577), Pg. writer on mathematics and navigation.

Núñez (nō′nyäs), Rafael (1825—94), Colombian statesman, president of Colombia (1880—82, 1884—94).

Núñez Cabeza de Vaca (nō′nyäth kä-bā′thä dä vä′kä), Álvar. See *Cabeza de Vaca.*

Nye (nī), Edgar Wilson (known as "Bill Nye") (1850—96), Am. humorist.

O

Oates (ōts), Titus (1649—1705), Eng. conspirator, chief contriver of sham Popish Plot against life of Charles II.

Obregón (ō-brā-gōn′), Álvaro (1880—1928), Mex. general, president of Mexico (1920—24).

Obrenovich (ō-bren′ō-vich). See *Milosh Obrenovich, Michael Obrenovich,* and *Milan I.* (of Serbia).

O'Brien (ō-brī′en), William (1852—1928), Ir. journalist and politician.

O'Brien, William Smith (1803—64), Ir. revolutionist.

Occam or **Ockham,** William. See *William of Occam.*

Occleve. See *Hoccleve.*

Ochs (oks), Adolph S. (1858—1935), Am. newspaper publisher.

O'Connell (ō-kon′el), Daniel (1775—1847), Ir. political agitator, and orator.

O'Connell, William Henry (1859—   ), Am. cardinal.

O'Connor (ō-kon′or), Feargus Edward (1794—1855), Ir. politician, and Chartist leader.

O'Connor, Roderick, Roderic, or Rory (1116—98), last king of Ireland.

O'Connor, Thomas Power (1848—1929), Ir. politician and journalist.

Octavia (ok-tā′vi-a) (d. 11 B.C.), sister of the Rom. emperor Augustus, and wife of Marcus Antonius.

Octavius (ok-tā′vi-us), Caius. See *Augustus.*

Odo (ō′dō) (c1036—97), Norman bishop, and earl of Kent (half-brother of William I. of England).

Odo. See *Eudes.*

Odoacer (ō-dō-ā′ser) (434?—493), barbarian ruler of Italy after 476, defeated and slain by Theodoric.

O'Donnell (ō-don′el), Leopold (in Spanish, Leopoldo O'Donnell y Jorris) (Duke of Tetuán) (1809—67), Sp. general and statesman.

O'Donnell, Patrick (1856—1927), Ir. cardinal.

Odoric (ō′do-rik) ("of Pordenone") (c1286—1331), It. Franciscan missionary and traveler in Asia.

Œcolampadius (ek′ō-lam-pā′di-us), Johannes (real name Heussgen or Hussgen) (1482—1531), Ger. Protestant reformer.

Oehlenschläger (ė′len-shlä″ger). See *Öhlenschläger.*

Oersted (ėr′sted). See *Örsted.*

Offenbach (of′en-bäk, Fr. of-an-bäk), Jacques (1819—80), Ger.-Fr. composer of operettas.

Ogilvie (ō′gl-vi), John (1797—1867), Sc. lexicographer.

Oglethorpe (ō′gl-thôrp), James Edward (1696—1785), Eng. general, founder of the colony of Georgia (1733).

O'Higgins (ō-hig′inz, Sp. ō-ē′gēns), Bernardo (c1776—1842), Chilean general and statesman.

Öhlenschläger (ė′len-shlä″ger), Adam Gottlob (1779—1850), Dan. poet and dramatist.

Ohm (ōm), Georg Simon (1787—1854), Ger. physicist.

Ohnet (ō-nā), Georges (1848—1918), Fr. novelist and dramatist.

Ojeda or **Hojeda** (dä ō-hä′тнä), Alonso de (c1468—1515), Sp. navigator and adventurer.

O'Keefe or **O'Keeffe** (ō-kēf′), John (1747—1833), Ir. dramatist.

Oku (ō′kö), Count Yasukata (1845—1930), Jap. field-marshal.

Okuma (ō′kö-mä), Marquis Shigenobu (1838—1922), Jap. statesman.

Olaf I. (ō′läf) (Olaf Trygvesson, or Trygvasson) (d. 1000), king of Norway (995?—1000).

Olaf II., Saint (Olaf Haraldsson) (995—1030), king of Norway (1015—28).

Olbers (ol′bers), Heinrich Wilhelm Matthias (1758—1840), Ger. astronomer.

Oldcastle (ōld′kas-l), Sir John (Lord Cobham) (d. 1417), Eng. soldier, and Lollard leader and martyr. A character of this name appeared in a play from which Shakspere adapted his "Henry IV."; from this character Shakspere developed one at first called Oldcastle, but subsequently Falstaff. Cf. *Fastolf, Sir John.*

Oldenbarneveldt (ōl′den-bär′ne-velt). See *Barneveldt.*

Oldfield (ōld′fēld), Anne (called Mrs. Oldfield) (1683—1730), Eng. actress.

Oldham (ōld′am), John (1653—83), Eng. satirical poet.

Olevianus (ō-lä-vē-ä′nus), Kaspar (1536—87), Ger. Protestant reformer and theologian.

Oliphant (ol′i-fant), Laurence (1829—88), Br. traveler and writer.

Oliphant, Mrs. (Margaret Oliphant Wilson) (1828—97), Br. novelist and misc. writer.

Olivares (ō-lē-vä′räs), Gaspar de Guzmán, Count of (Duke of San Lúcar de Barrameda) (1587—1645), Sp. statesman, favorite of Philip IV.

Oliver (ol′i-ver), Andrew (1706—74), Am. politician, stamp-distributor at Boston (1765) and lieutenant-governor of Massachusetts (1770—74).

Ollivier (o-lē-vyä), Olivier Émile (1825—1913), Fr. statesman and historian.

Olmsted (om′sted or um′sted), Frederick Law (1822—1903), Am. landscape-architect and writer.

Olmsted, Frederick Law (1870—   ), Am. landscape-architect (son of F. L. Olmsted, 1822—1903).

Olney (ol′ni), Richard (1835—1917), Am. lawyer and statesman.

Oman (ō′man), Sir Charles William Chadwick (1860—1946), Br. historian.

Omar I. (ō′mär) (Omar ibn al-Khattab) (582?—644), Arabian calif (634—644).

Omar Khayyam (kī-yäm′) (d. 1123?), Pers. poet, mathematician, and astronomer.

Omer Pasha (ō′mer pa-shä′) (orig. Michael Lattas) (1806—71), Turk. general, born in Croatia.

O'Neill (ō-nēl′), Eugene Gladstone (1888—   ), Am. dramatist.

O'Neill, Hugh (2d Earl of Tyrone) (1540?—1616), Ir. rebel.

Opie (ō′pi), John (1761—1807), Eng. painter.

Opie, Mrs. (Amelia Alderson) (1769—1853), Eng. author (wife of John).

Opitz (ō′pits), Martin (ennobled as Opitz von Boberfeld) (1597—1639), Ger. poet and critic.

Oppenheim (op′en-hīm), Edward Phillips (1866—1946), Eng. novelist.

Optic (op′tik), Oliver. Pseudonym of W. T. Adams.

Orange (or′anj), Prince of. See *Maurice of Nassau, William I.* (of Orange), and *William III.* (of Great Britain).

Orcagna (or-kä′nyä) (also called Arcagnuolo or Arcagnolo, real name Andrea di Cione) (1308?—68?), Florentine painter, sculptor, and architect.

Orchardson (ôr′chard-son), Sir William Quiller (1835—1910), Br. painter.

Orellana (dä ō-re-lyä′nä), Francisco de (c1500—c1545), Sp. explorer of the Amazon.

Orford (ôr′ford), Horatio (or Horace) Walpole, 4th Earl of (1717—97), Eng. author and letter-writer (son of 1st Earl).

Orford, Robert Walpole, 1st Earl of (Sir Robert Walpole) (1676—1745), Eng. statesman.

Orgetorix (ôr-jet′ō̱-riks) (fl. c60 B.C.), Helvetian chieftain.

Origen (or′i-jen) (c185–c254), Christian theologian and teacher, of Alexandria.

Orlando (or-län′dō), Vittorio Emanuele (1860–   ), It. statesman.

Orléans (dôr-lā-äṅ), Charles, Duc d' (1391–1465), Fr. poet (son of Duc d'Orléans, 1372–1407, and nephew of Charles VI. of France).

Orléans, Jean Baptiste Gaston, Duc d' (1608–60), Fr. political intriguer and soldier (son of Henry IV. of France).

Orléans, Louis, Duc d' (1372–1407), Fr. politician and soldier, regent of France (brother of Charles VI. of France).

Orléans, Louis Philippe Joseph, Duc d' ("Philippe Égalité") (1747–93), Fr. political leader (great-grandson of Duc d'Orléans, 1674–1723).

Orléans, Philippe, Duc d' (1640–1701), Fr. military leader (son of Louis XIII. of France, and brother of Louis XIV.).

Orléans, Philippe, Duc d' (1674–1723), Fr. general, regent of France (1715–23) (son of Duc d'Orléans, 1640–1701).

Ormonde (ôr′mond), James Butler, 1st Duke of (1610–88), Ir. statesman and soldier.

Ormonde, James Butler, 2d Duke of (1665–1745), Ir. politician and soldier (grandson of 1st Duke).

Orosius (ō̱-rō′s̱ius), Paulus (fl. 415), Christian theologian and historian, born in Spain.

Orpen (ôr′pen), Sir William (1878–1931), Br. painter.

Orrery (or′ē̱-ri), Roger Boyle, 1st Earl of (1621–79), Br. soldier, statesman, and dramatist.

Orsay (dôr-sā), Alfred Guillaume Gabriel, Comte d' (1801–52), Fr. leader of fashion in London.

Orsini (or-sē′nē), Felice (1819–58), It. revolutionist, who made an attempt on the life of Napoleon III.

Örsted (ĕr′sted), Hans Christian (1777–1851), Dan. physicist.

Ortelius (ôr-tē′li-us) (Abraham Oertel, or Ortel) (1527–98), Flemish geographer and cartographer.

Osborn (oz′bọrn), Henry Fairfield (1857–1935), Am. paleontologist.

Oscar I. (os′kär) (1799–1859), king of Sweden and Norway (1844–59) (son of Charles XIV. of Sweden).

Oscar II. (1829–1907), king of Sweden (1872–1907) and Norway (1872–1905) (brother of Charles XV. of Sweden).

Osceola (os-ē̱-ō′lả) (c1804–38), Am. Indian chief.

O'Shaughnessy (ō̱-shâ′nē̱-si), Arthur William Edgar (1844–81), Eng. poet.

Osiander (ō̱-zē̱-än′dèr), Andreas (name orig. Hosemann) (1498–1552), Ger. Lutheran reformer.

Osler (ōz′lèr), Sir William (1849–1919), Can. physician, in U. S. and England.

Osman I. (os-män′) or **Othman I.** (oth-män′) (1259–1326), Turk. chieftain, founder of Ottoman empire.

Osman Digna (dig′nä) (c1836–1926), soldier in the Sudan, general in service of Mohammed Ahmed ("the Mahdi").

Osmeña (os-mā′nyả), Sergio (18..–   ), Filipino political leader, 1st vice-president of Philippine Commonwealth (1935–   ).   [general.

Osorio (ō̱-zō′rē̱-ō), Manoel Luis (1808–79), Brazilian

Ossoli (os′sō̱-lē), Marchesa (Sarah Margaret Fuller) (1810–50), Am. writer.

Ostade (vän os-tä′dè), Adriaan van (1610–85), Dutch painter.

Ostade, Isaak van (1621–49), Dutch painter (brother of Adriaan).

Osterman (os′tèr-män), Count Andrey Ivanovich (orig. Heinrich Johann Friedrich Ostermann) (1686–1747), Russ. statesman, born in Germany.

Ostrovski (os-trof′skē̱), Aleksandr Nikolaevich (1823–86), Russ. dramatist.

Ostwald (ost′vält), Wilhelm (1853–1932), Ger. chemist, born in Russia.

Oswald (oz′wạld), Saint (605?–642), king of Northumbria (634–642), defeated and slain by Penda.

Othman (oth-män′) (Othman ibn Affan) (c574–656), Arabian calif (644–656) (son-in-law of Mohammed).

Othman I. See *Osman I.*

Otho (ō′thō). See *Otto*.

Otis (ō′tis), James (1725–83), Am. patriot and orator.

Otterbein (ot′èr-bīn), Philip William (1726–1813), Ger.-

Am. clergyman, founder of religious denomination called United Brethren in Christ.

Otto I. (ot′ō) ("the Great") (912–973), king of Germany (936–973), and emperor of Holy Roman Empire (962–973) (son of Henry the Fowler).

Otto IV. (c1182–1218), emperor of Holy Roman Empire (1208–18) (son of Henry the Lion).

Otto I. (1815–67), king of Greece (1832–62) (son of Louis I. of Bavaria).

Ottocar II. or **Ottokar II.** (ot′ō̱-kär) (c1230–78), king of Bohemia (1253–78).

Otway (ot′wā), Thomas (1652–85), Eng. dramatist.

Oudinot (ö-dē-nō), Nicolas Charles (Duc de Reggio) (1767–1847), Fr. marshal.

Ouida (wē′dả).   Pseudonym of M. L. de la Ramée (see *De la Ramée*).

Outram (ö′trạm), Sir James (1803–63), Eng. general in India.

Overbeck (ō′vèr-bek), Johann Friedrich (1789–1869), Ger. painter, in Rome.

Overbury (ō′vèr-ber″i), Sir Thomas (1581–1613), Eng. writer.

Ovid (ov′id) (Publius Ovidius Naso) (43 B.C.–A.D. 17?), Rom. poet.

Oviedo y Valdés (dä ō-vē̱-ä′ᴙнō ē väl-däs′), Gonzalo Fernández de (1478–1557), Sp. historian.

Owen (ō′en), John (1616–83), Eng. nonconformist divine and theologian.

Owen, Sir Richard (1804–92), Eng. anatomist and zoölogist.

Owen, Robert (1771–1858), Br. social reformer.

Owen, Robert Dale (1801–77), Am. social reformer, politician, spiritualist, and author, born in Scotland (son of Robert).

Oxenstjerna or **Oxenstierna** (ok′sẹn-shär-nä), or **Oxenstiern** (ok′sẹn-stērn), Axel Gustafsson, Count (1583–1654), Swed. statesman.

Oxford (oks′fọrd), Robert Harley, 1st Earl of (1661–1724), Eng. statesman.

Oxford and Asquith (as′kwith), Herbert Henry Asquith, 1st Earl of (1852–1928), Eng. statesman.

Oxley (oks′li), John (1781–1828), Australian explorer, born in England.

Oyama (ō′yä-mä), Prince Iwao (1842–1916), Jap. field-marshal.

Ozanam (o-zȧ-nȧm), Antoine Frédéric (1813–53), Fr. historian and critic.

P

Pachmann (dẹ päch′män), Vladimir de (1848–1933), Russ. pianist.

Pachomius (pa-kō′mi-us), Saint (c292–c346), Egyptian hermit, founder of first Christian monastery.

Packard (pak′ạrd), Alpheus Spring (1839–1905), Am. naturalist.

Paderewski (pä-dẹ-ref′skẹ), Ignace Jan (1860–1941), Pol. pianist, composer, patriot, and statesman.

Padilla (dä ᴙнēl′yä), Juan López de (d. 1521), Sp. patriot and insurrectionary leader.

Páez (pä′äs), José Antonio (1790–1873), Venezuelan general and politician.

Paganini (pä-gä-nē′nē), Niccolò (1784–1840), It. violinist.

Page (pāj), Thomas Nelson (1853–1922), Am. novelist and diplomatist.

Page, Walter Hines (1855–1918), Am. editor, publisher, and diplomatist.

Paget (paj′et), Violet ("Vernon Lee") (1856–1935), Eng. essayist, in Italy.

Paine (pān), Robert Treat (1731–1814), Am. patriot and jurist.

Paine, Thomas (1737–1809), Eng.-Am. political and deistic writer.

Painlevé (paṅ-lẹ-vä), Paul (1863–1933), Fr. scientist and statesman.

Palacio Valdés (pä-lä′thyō väl-däs′), Armando (1853–1938), Sp. novelist and critic.

Palacký (pä′läts-kē̱), František (1798–1876), Bohem. historian and politician.

Palæologus (pā-lē-ol′ō-gus). See *Manuel II.* and *Michael VIII.* (Byzantine emperors).

Palestrina (dä pä-les-trē′nä), Giovanni Pierluigi da (1526?—94), It. musical composer.

Paley (pā′li), William (1743—1805), Eng. divine and philosopher.

Palfrey (pâl′fri), John Gorham (1796—1881), Am. divine and historian.

Palgrave (pâl′grāv), Francis Turner (1824—97), Eng. critic and poet.

Palissy (pȧ-lē-sē), Bernard (c1510—89?), Fr. potter, enameler, and writer.

Palladio (päl-lä′dē-ō), Andrea (1518—80), It. architect.

Palladius (pạ-lā′di-us), Rutilius Taurus Æmilianus (fl. 4th cent.), Rom. writer on agriculture.

Pallavicino (päl″lä-vē-chē′nō) or **Pallavicini** (päl″lä-vē-chē′nē), Pietro Sforza (1607—67), It. cardinal and historian.

Palma (päl′mä), Jacopo (called Palma Vecchio, 'Palma the Elder') (c1480—1528), It. painter, of Venetian school.

Palma, Jacopo (called Palma Giovane, 'Palma the Younger') (1544?—1628), Venetian painter (grandnephew of Palma Vecchio).

Palma, Tomás Estrada (1835?—1908), Cuban statesman, first president of Cuba (1902—06).

Palmer (pä′mẽr), Ray (1808—87), Am. clergyman and hymn-writer.

Palmerston (pä′mẽr-stọn), Henry John Temple, 3d Viscount (1784—1865), Eng. statesman.

Palsgrave (pâlz′grāv), John (c1480—1554), Eng. French grammarian.

Paltock (pâl′tok), Robert (1697—1767), Eng. novelist, author of "The Life and Adventures of Peter Wilkins."

Paludan-Müller (pä′lö-dän-mül′ẽr), Frederik (1809—76), Dan. poet.

Pamphilus (pam′fi-lus) (fl. c390—c350 B.C.), Gr. painter.

Pamphilus, Saint (d. 309), Christian scholar and martyr, of Syria.

Pancras (pang′kras) or **Pancratius** (pan-krā′shius), Saint (d. c304, or earlier), Rom. Christian martyr.

Panin (pä′nyẹn), Count Nikita Ivanovich (1718—83), Russ. statesman.

Paoli (pä′ō-lē), Pasquale (1725—1807), Corsican patriot and general.

Paparrhegopoulos (pä″pä-rē-gop′ō-los), Konstantinos (1815—91), Gr. historian.

Papias (pā′pi-ạs) (fl. c130), Christian writer, of Phrygia.

Papin (pȧ-paṅ), Denis (1647—1714?), Fr. physicist.

Papineau (pȧ-pē-nō), Louis Joseph (1786—1871), Can. political leader and rebel.

Papini (pä-pē′nē), Giovanni (1881—   ), It. author.

Papinian (pạ-pin′i-ạn) (Æmilius Papinianus) (c140—212), Rom. jurist.

Pappenheim (fon päp′ẹn-hīm), Gottfried Heinrich, Graf von (1594—1632), Ger. general in imperial service in Thirty Years' War.

Paracelsus (par-ạ-sel′sus) (assumed name of Theophrastus Bombast von Hohenheim) (1493?—1541), Swiss-Ger. physician and alchemist.

Pardo (pär′dō), Manuel (1834—78), Peruvian statesman, president of Peru (1872—76).

Pardo Bazán (bä-thän′), Emilia (Señora Quiroga) (1852?—1921), Sp. novelist and critic.

Paré (pȧ-rā), Ambroise (1517—90), Fr. surgeon.

Parini (pä-rē′nē), Giuseppe (1729—99), It. poet.

Paris (pä-rēs), Bruno Paulin Gaston (1839—1903), Fr. philologist and critic.

Paris (dẽ pȧ-rē), Louis Philippe Albert d'Orléans, Comte de (1838—94), Fr. prince, claimant to the throne of France (grandson of Louis Philippe of France).

Paris (par′is), Matthew. See *Matthew of Paris.*

Park (pärk), Mungo (1771—1806?), Sc. explorer in Africa.

Parker (pär′kẽr), Alton Brooks (1852—1926), Am. jurist and political leader.

Parker, Sir Gilbert (1862—1932), Can.-Eng. novelist.

Parker, Horatio William (1863—1919), Am. musical composer.

Parker, Louis Napoleon (1852—1944), Eng. musical composer and playwright.

Parker, Matthew (1504—75), Eng. Protestant divine, archbishop of Canterbury.

Parker, Theodore (1810—60), Am. preacher and reformer.

Parkhurst (pärk′hẽrst), Charles Henry (1842—1933), Am. clergyman and reformer.

Parkman (pärk′mạn), Francis (1823—93), Am. historian.

Parley (pär′li), Peter. Pseudonym of S. G. Goodrich.

Parmenides (pär-men′i-dēz) (fl. c475 B.C.), Gr. Eleatic philosopher.

Parnell (pär-nel′), Charles Stewart (1846—91), Ir. political leader.

Parnell, Thomas (1679—1718), Br. poet.

Parr (pär), Catharine (1512—48), sixth wife of Henry VIII. of England.

Parrhasius (pa-rā′shius) (fl. c400 B.C.), Gr. painter.

Parrish (par′ish), Maxfield (1870—   ), Am. painter and illustrator.

Parry (par′i), Sir Charles Hubert Hastings (1848—1918), Eng. musical composer and writer on music.

Parry, Sir William Edward (1790—1855), Eng. naval officer and arctic explorer.

Parsons (pär′sọnz) or **Persons** (pẽr′sọnz), Robert (1546—1610), Eng. Jesuit and controversialist.

Parsons, Theophilus (1750—1813), Am. jurist.

Parsons, Theophilus (1797—1882), Am. legal and religious writer (son of Theophilus Parsons, 1750—1813).

Parsons, Thomas William (1819—92), Am. poet and translator.

Parsons, William Barclay (1859—1932), Am. civil engineer.

Partridge (pär′trij), William Ordway (1861—1930), Am. sculptor and writer.

Pascal (pas′kạl, Fr. pȧs-kȧl), Blaise (1623—62), Fr. philosopher, mathematician, and physicist.

Paskevich (pȧs-kye′vich), Ivan Fedorovich (Prince of Warsaw) (1782—1856), Russ. field-marshal.

Pasquier (pȧs-kyā), Étienne (1529—1615), Fr. jurist, historian, and misc. writer. [man.

Pasquier, Étienne Denis, Duc de (1767—1862), Fr. states-

Passfield (pȧs′fēld), Sidney James Webb, 1st Baron (1859—   ), Eng. writer on sociology and economics, and cabinet minister. [peace advocate.

Passy (pȧ-sē), Frédéric (1822—1912), Fr. economist and

Passy, Paul Édouard (1859—   ), Fr. phonetician.

Pasteur (pȧs-tẽr), Louis (1822—95), Fr. chemist.

Pastorius (pas-tō′ri-us), Francis Daniel (1651—1719?), Ger. settler in Pennsylvania. [painter.

Pater (pȧ-tā), Jean Bȧptiste Joseph (1695—1736), Fr.

Pater (pā′tẽr), Walter Horatio (1839—94), Eng. critic and essayist.

Paterson (pat′ẽr-sọn), William (1658—1719), Sc. promoter and financier, founder of the Bank of England.

Patiño (pä-tē′nyō), José (1666?—1736), Sp. statesman.

Patkul (fon pät′kul), Johann Reinhold von (1660—1707), politician and agitator of Livonia (now in Latvia, etc.).

Patmore (pat′mōr), Coventry Kersey Dighton (1823—96), Eng. poet.

Patrick (pat′rik), Saint (name orig. Sucat) (c389—c461), Br. missionary and bishop in Ireland, patron saint of Ireland.

Patti (pat′ē), Adelina (Marquise de Caux, Signora Nicolini, Baroness Cederström) (1843—1919), operatic soprano singer, born at Madrid of It. parentage.

Pattison (pat′i-sọn), Mark (1813—84), Eng. author.

Patton (pat′n), Francis Landey (1843—1932), Am. Presbyterian clergyman and educator.

Pau (pō), Paul Mary César Gérald (1848—1932), Fr. general.

Paul III. (pâl) (Alessandro Farnese) (1468—1549), It. ecclesiastic, pope (1534—49).

Paul V. (Camillo Borghese) (1552—1621), It. ecclesiastic, pope (1605—21).

Paul I. (in Russian, Pavel Petrovich) (1754—1801), czar of Russia (1796—1801) (son of Peter III. and Catharine II.).

Paul I. (1901—   ), king of the Hellenes (1947—   ) (brother of George II., deceased king of the Hellenes).

Paul (poul), Jean. Pseudonym of J. P. F. Richter.

Paulding (pâl′ding), Hiram (1797—1878), Am. admiral.

Paulding, James Kirke (1779—1860), Am. writer.

Paul of the Cross, Saint (Paolo Francesco Danei) (1694—1775), It. priest, founder of the order of Passionists.

Paulsen (poul'zẹn), Friedrich (1846–1908), Ger. philosopher and educationist.

Paulus (på'lus), Julius (fl. c220), Rom. jurist.

Paulus, Lucius Æmilius (surnamed Macedonicus) (c229–160 B.C.), Rom. general.

Paulus Diaconus (dī-ak'ọ̄-nus) (c720–c800), Lombard monk and historian.

Paul Veronese (vā-rō-nā'zā). See *Caliari*.

Pauncefote (pâns'fút), Julian Pauncefote, Baron (1828–1902), Eng. diplomatist.

Pausanias (på-sā'ni-ạs) (d. 470? B.C.), regent of Sparta, and military and naval commander (nephew of Leonidas I.).

Pausanias (fl. c175), Gr. traveler and topographer.

Pausias (på'ṣi-ạs) (fl. c360–c330 B.C.), Gr. painter.

Paxton (paks'tọn), Sir Joseph (1801–65), Eng. landscape-gardener, botanical writer, and architect.

Payn (pān), James (1830–98), Eng. novelist.

Payne (pān), John Howard (1791–1852), Am. writer, author of "Home, Sweet Home."

Peabody (pē'bod-i), Andrew Preston (1811–93), Am. clergyman, educator, and writer.

Peabody, George (1795–1869), Am. merchant, banker, and philanthropist, in London.

Peacock (pē'kok), Reginald. See *Pecock*.

Peacock, Thomas Love (1785–1866), Eng. novelist and poet.

Peale (pēl), Charles Willson (1741–1827), Am. portrait-painter.

Peale, Rembrandt (1778–1860), Am. painter, esp. of portraits (son of Charles W.).

Pearse (pērs), Padraic H. (1879–1916), Ir. teacher, writer, and republican leader.

Pearson (pēr'sọn), John (1613–86), Eng. bishop and theologian.

Pearson, Karl (1857–1936), Eng. mathematician and scientist.

Peary (pēr'i), Robert Edwin (1856–1920), Am. naval officer and arctic explorer, discoverer of north pole (1909).

Pecock or **Peacock** (pē'kok), Reginald (c1395–c1460), Br. bishop and theologian.

Pedro I. (pē'drō, Pg. pā'drō) (1798–1834), first emperor of Brazil (1822–31) (as Pedro IV., king of Portugal, 1826).

Pedro II. (Dom Pedro de Alcantara) (1825–91), emperor of Brazil (1831–89) (son of Pedro I.).

Pedro (pē'drō, Sp. pā'drō) ("the Cruel") (1334?–69), king of Castile and León (1350–69).

Peel (pēl), Sir Robert (1788–1850), Eng. statesman.

Peele (pēl), George (1558?–97?), Eng. dramatist.

Peirce (pērs), Benjamin (1809–80), Am. mathematician and astronomer.

Peirce, Charles Sanders (1839–1914), Am. logician, mathematician, and physicist (son of Benjamin).

Peisistratus (pī-sis'trạ-tus). See *Pisistratus*.

Peixoto (pā-shō'tọ), Floriano (1842–95), Brazilian general and politician, president of Brazil (1891–94).

Pelagius (pe-lā'ji-us) (fl. c400–418), Br. monk and heretic, founder of Pelagianism.

Pelham (pel'ạm), Sir Henry (1695?–1754), Eng. statesman (brother of Duke of Newcastle, 1693–1768).

Pellew (pe-lö'), Sir Edward. See *Exmouth, 1st Viscount*.

Pellico (pel'lē-kō), Silvio (1788–1854), It. dramatist and misc. writer, long imprisoned by the Austrians.

Pellissier (pe-lē-syā), Georges (1852–1918), Fr. critic.

Pelopidas (pe-lop'i-dạs) (d. 364 B.C.), Theban general and statesman.

Pemberton (pem'bėr-tọn), John Clifford (1814–81), Am. Confederate general.

Pembroke (pem'brúk), Richard de Clare, 2d Earl of (also called Richard Strongbow) (d. 1176), Eng. statesman, and soldier in Ireland.

Pembroke, William Marshal, 1st Earl of (in Marshal line) (c1146–1219), Eng. soldier and statesman, regent of England (1216–19).

Penda (pen'dä) (d. 655), king of Mercia (626?–655).

Penn (pen), Sir William (1621–70), Eng. admiral.

Penn, William (1644–1718), Eng. Quaker, founder of Pennsylvania (son of Sir William).

Pennant (pen'ạnt), Thomas (1726–98), Br. naturalist and antiquary.

Pennell (pen'el), Joseph (1860–1926), Am. etcher, illustrator, and writer.

Penrose (pen'rōz), Boies (1860–1921), Am. senator (from Pennsylvania).

Pepe (pā'pā), Guglielmo (1783–1855), It. general and patriot.

Pepin (pep'in) (in French, Pépin, pron. pā-pȧṅ; known as Pepin of Heristal) (d. 714), Frankish ruler.

Pepin ("the Short") (714?–768), king of the Franks (751–768) (son of Charles Martel, and first king of Carolingian line).

Pepperell or **Pepperrell** (pep'ėr-el), Sir William (1696–1759), Am. colonial military commander.

Pepys (pēps or peps), Samuel (1633–1703), Eng. diarist.

Percier (per-syā), Charles (1764–1838), Fr. architect.

Percy (pėr'si), Henry. See *Northumberland, 1st Earl of*.

Percy, Sir Henry (called "Hotspur") (1364–1403), Eng. military leader (son of 1st Earl of Northumberland).

Percy, Thomas (1729–1811), Eng. bishop and antiquary, editor of "Reliques of Ancient English Poetry."

Perdiccas (pėr-dik'ạs) (d. 321 B.C.), Macedonian general of Alexander the Great.

Perdita (pėr'di-tạ). See *Robinson, Mrs.*

Pereda (dā pā-rā'ᴛʜä), José María de (1834–1906), Sp. novelist.

Père Duchesne (pär dü-shän). See *Hébert, J. R.*

Père Hyacinthe (pär yä-saṅt). See *Loyson*.

Pérez (pā'rāth), Antonio (c1540–1611), Sp. courtier and politician.

Pérez Galdós (gäl-dōs'), Benito (1845–1920), Sp. novelist and dramatist.

Pergolesi (per-gō-lā'zē) or **Pergolese** (per-gō-lā'zā), Giovanni Battista (1710–36), It. musical composer.

Peri (pā'rē), Jacopo (1561–1633), It. operatic composer.

Periander (per-i-an'dėr) (fl. 625–585 B.C.), tyrant of Corinth, one of the seven sages of ancient Greece.

Pericles (per'i-klēz) (c490–429 B.C.), Athenian statesman.

Périer (pā-ryā), Casimir Pierre (1777–1832), Fr. statesman.

Périer, Casimir-. See *Casimir-Périer*.

Perkin (pėr'kin), Sir William Henry (1838–1907), Eng. chemist.

Pérochon (pā-ro-shȯṅ), Ernest (1885–   ), Fr. author.

Perrault (pe-rō), Charles (1628–1703), Fr. critic, and writer of fairy-tales.

Perrault, Claude (1613–88), Fr. physician and architect (brother of Charles).

Perrers (per'ėrz), Alice (also known as Alice de Windsor) (d. 1400), mistress of Edward III. of England.

Perry (per'i), Bliss (1860–   ), Am. educator, editor, and author.

Perry, Matthew Calbraith (1794–1858), Am. commodore (brother of Oliver H.).

Perry, Oliver Hazard (1785–1819), Am. commodore.

Perseus (pėr'sūs) (c212–after 167 B.C.), last king of Macedonia (179–168 B.C.).

Pershing (pėr'shing), John Joseph (1860–   ), Am. general.

Persigny (dė per-sē-nyē), Jean Gilbert Victor Fialin, Duc de (1808–72), Fr. politician.

Persius (pėr'shius) (Aulus Persius Flaccus) (A.D. 34–62), Rom. satiric poet.

Persons, Robert. See *Parsons*.

Perugino (pā-rö-jē'nō) (real name Pietro Vannucci) (1446–1524), It. painter, of Umbrian school.

Peruzzi (pā-röt'sē), Baldassare (1481–1536?), It. architect and painter.

Pescara (pes-kä'rä), Ferdinando Francesco d'Avalos, Marchese di (1490?–1525), It. general in service of Emperor Charles V. (husband of Vittoria Colonna).

Pestalozzi (pes-tä-lot'sē), Johann Heinrich (1746–1827), Swiss educational reformer, writing in German.

Pétain (pā-taṅ), Henri Philippe Benoni Omer Joseph (1856–   ), Fr. general, marshal of France.

Peter I. (pē'tėr) (in Russian, Petr Alekseevich, called "Peter the Great") (1672–1725), czar of Russia (1682–1725) (son of Czar Alexis).

Peter III. (in Russian, Petr Fedorovich; orig. Karl Peter Ulrich of Holstein-Gottorp) (1728–62), czar of Russia

---

(variable) ḏ as d or j, ṣ as s or sh, ṭ as t or ch, ẓ as z or zh; o, F. cloche; ü, F. menu; ċh, Sc. loch; ṅ, F. bonbon; ', primary accent; ', secondary accent; †, obsolete; <, from; +, and; =, equals. See also lists at beginning of book.

(1762) (grandson of Peter the Great, and nephew of Empress Elizabeth).

Peter I. (Peter Karageorgevich) (1844—1921), king of Serbia (1903—18), and of the Serbs, Croats, and Slovenes (1918—21) (son of Alexander Karageorgevich).

Peter II. (Peter Karageorgevich) (1923—   ), king of Yugoslavia (1934—   ) (son of Alexander I., 1888–1934).

Peterborough (pē'tẽr-bur-ọ), Charles Mordaunt, 3d Earl of (1658—1735), Eng. general, admiral, and diplomatist.

Peter Lombard (pē'tẽr lom'bärd) ("Master of Sentences") (c1100—1160 or 1164), It. theologian, bishop of Paris.

Peters (pē'tẽrz) or **Peter** (pē'tẽr), Hugh (1598—1660), Eng. preacher and politician, executed as regicide.

Peters (pā'tẽrs), Karl (1856—1918), Ger. explorer and colonial organizer in Africa.   [preacher of the first Crusade.

Peter the Hermit (c1050—1115), Fr. hermit and monk, a

Pétion (pā-tyôṅ), Alexandre (1770—1818), Haitian military and political leader, president of Haiti (1807—18).

Pétion de Villeneuve (dẽ vēl-nẽv), Jérôme (1753?—94), Fr. revolutionist.   [(1823—49), Hung. poet.

Petöfi (pet'ė-fẹ), Sándor, or Alexander (name orig. Petrovics)

Petrarch (pē'trärk) (in Italian, Francesco Petrarca) (1304—74), It. poet.

Petrie (pē'tri), Sir William Matthew Flinders (1853—1942), Eng. Egyptologist (grandson of Matthew Flinders).

Petronius Arbiter (pē-trō'ni-us är'bi-tẽr) (d. A.D. c66), Rom. novelist.

Petty (pet'i), Sir William (1623—87), Eng. statistician and economist.

Petty-Fitzmaurice (-fits-mâ'ris). See *Lansdowne, Marquis of.*

Pfleiderer (pflī'dẽr-ẽr), Otto (1839—1908), Ger. Protestant theologian.

Phædo (fē'dō) or **Phædon** (fē'don) (fl. c400 B.C.), Gr. philosopher.

Phædrus (fē'drus) (fl. A.D. c40), Rom. fabulist.

Phalaris (fal'ạ-ris) (d. 554 or 549 B.C.), tyrant in Sicily.

Pheidias (fī'di-ạs). See *Phidias.*

Phelps (felps), Austin (1820—90), Am. clergyman, educator, and writer.

Phelps, Elizabeth Stuart. See *Ward, Mrs.*

Phelps, William Lyon (1865—1943), Am. educator, essayist, and critic.

Phidias (fid'i-ạs) (c500—c432 B.C.), Gr. sculptor.

Philip II. (fil'ip) (382—336 B.C.), king of Macedonia (359—336 B.C.) and general.

Philip I. (fil'ip) (in French, Philippe, pron. fē-lēp) (1052—1108), king of France (1060—1108) (son of Henry I.).

Philip II. (Philip Augustus) (1165—1223), king of France (1180—1223) (son of Louis VII.).

Philip III. ("Philip the Bold") (1245—85), king of France (1270—85) (son of Louis IX.).

Philip IV. ("Philip the Fair") (1268—1314), king of France (1285—1314) (son of Philip III.).

Philip V. ("Philip the Tall") (1293?—1322), king of France (1316—22) (successor and uncle of John I.).

Philip VI. (of Valois) (1293—1350), king of France (1328—50) (successor and cousin of Charles IV., and nephew of Philip IV., and first king of house of Valois).

Philip I. ("the Handsome") (1478—1506), king of Castile (1504—06) (son-in-law and successor of Isabella I., and son of Emperor Maximilian I., and founder of Hapsburg line in Spain).

Philip II. (1527—98), king of Spain (1556—98) (son of Emperor Charles V.).

Philip III. (1578—1621), king of Spain (1598—1621) (son of Philip II.).

Philip IV. (1605—65), king of Spain (1621—65) (son of Philip III.).

Philip V. (Duke of Anjou) (1683—1746), king of Spain (1700—46) (successor of Charles II., and grandson of Louis XIV. of France, and first king in Spain of house of Bourbon).

Philip ("Philip the Bold") (1342—1404), duke of Burgundy (1363—1404) (son of John II. of France).

Philip ("Philip the Good") (1396—1467), duke of Burgundy (1419—67) (son of John the Fearless).

Philip, King (native name Metacom or Metacomet) (d. 1676), Am. Indian chief (son of Massasoit).

Philip Neri, Saint. See *Neri, Philip.*

Philippa (fi-lip'ạ) **of Hainault** (c1314—69), queen of Edward III. of England, and patroness of Froissart.

Philippe Égalité (fē-lēp ā-gȧ-lē-tā). See *Orléans, Duc d'* (1747—93).

Philips (fil'ips), Ambrose (1675?—1749), Eng. poet and dramatist.

Phillips (fil'ips), David Graham (1867—1911), Am. novelist.

Phillips, Edward (1630—c1696), Eng. lexicographer and misc. writer (nephew of John Milton).

Phillips, Stephen (1868—1915), Eng. poet and dramatist.

Phillips, Wendell (1811—84), Am. orator and reformer.

Phillpotts (fil'pots), Eden (1862—   ), Eng. novelist, playwright, and poet, born in India.

Philo (fī'lō) or **Philo Judæus** (jọ-dē'us) (c20 B.C.—A.D. c50), Hellenistic Jewish philosopher, of Alexandria.

Philolaus (fil-ọ-lā'us) (b. c480 B.C.), Gr. Pythagorean philosopher, born in Italy.

Philopœmen (fil-ọ-pē'men) (252?—183 B.C.), Gr. general.

Phipps (fips), Henry (1839—1930), Am. manufacturer, capitalist, and philanthropist.

Phipps or **Phips**, Sir William (1651—95), Am. sea-captain, and colonial governor of Massachusetts.

Phiz (fiz). Pseudonym of H. K. Browne.

Phocion (fō'shiọn) (c402—317 B.C.), Athenian statesman and general.

Photius (fō'shius) (c820—c891), Byzantine Gr. scholar, and patriarch of Constantinople.

Phryne (frī'nē) (fl. c336 B.C.), Gr. courtezan.

Phrynichus (frin'i-kus) (fl. 511—476 B.C.), Gr. tragic poet.

Picabia (pē-kä-bē-ä), Francis (1878—   ), Fr. painter.

Picard (pē-kär), Charles Émile (1856—1941), Fr. mathematician.

Picasso (pē-käs'sō), Pablo (1881—   ), Sp.-Fr. painter and sculptor.

Piccinni (pēt-chēn'nē), Niccolò (1728—1800), It. operatic composer.

Piccolomini (pēk-kō-lō'mē-nē), Octavio (Duke of Amalfi) (1599—1656), It. general, esp. in imperial service in Thirty Years' War.

Pichegru (pēsh-grü), Charles (1761—1804), Fr. general.

Pickens (pik'ẹnz), Andrew (1739—1817), Am. Revolutionary general.

Pickering (pik'ẽr-ing), Edward Charles (1846—1919), Am. astronomer.

Pickering, Timothy (1745—1829), Am. patriot and statesman.

Pickett (pik'et), George Edward (1825—75), Am. Confederate general.

Pickford (pik'fọrd), Mary (family name Smith, Mrs. Moore, Mrs. Douglas Fairbanks, Mrs. Rogers) (1893—   ), Am. actress in moving pictures, born in Canada.

Pico della Mirandola (pē'kō del'lä mē-rän'dō-lä), Count Giovanni (1463—94), It. humanist, philosopher, and theologian.

Pierce (pērs), Franklin (1804—69), 14th president of U. S. (1853—57).

Piero di Cosimo (pyä'rō dē koz'ē-mō) (real name Pietro di Lorenzo) (1462?—1521?), Florentine painter.

Pierola (dä pē-ā-rō'lä), Nicolás de (1839—1913), Peruvian politician, president of Peru (1895—99).

Pietro, Lorenzo di. See *Lorenzo di Pietro.*

Pigalle (pē-gȧl), Jean Baptiste (1714—85), Fr. sculptor.

Pike (pīk), Zebulon Montgomery (1779—1813), Am. soldier and explorer.

Pillow (pil'ō), Gideon Johnson (1806—78), Am. Confederate general.

Pilon (pē-lôṅ), Germaiṅ (c1535—90), Fr. sculptor.

Piloty (fon pē-lō'tē), Karl von (1826—86), Ger. painter.

Pilsudski (pil-sùt'skẹ), Józef (1867—1935), Pol. general, 1st president of Poland (1918—22).

Pinchot (pin'shō), Gifford (1865—1946), Am. forester and politician.

Pinckney (pingk'ni), Charles (1758—1824), Am. statesman.

Pinckney, Charles Cotesworth (1746—1825), Am. soldier and statesman.

Pinckney, Thomas (1750—1828), Am. soldier and statesman (brother of Charles C.).

---

fat, fāte, fär, fȧll, ȧsk, fãre; net, mē, hẽr; pin, pīne; not, nōte, mŏve, nôr; up, lūte, pùll; oi, oil; ou, out; (lightened) aviạry, ẽlect, agọny, intọ, ụnite; (obscured) errạnt, operạ, ardẹnt, actọr, natụre; ch, chip; g, go; th, thin; ᴛʜ, then; y, you;

Pindar (pin′där) (c522—c443 B.C.), Gr. lyric poet.

Pindar, Peter. Pseudonym of John Wolcot.

Pinero (pi-när′ō), Sir Arthur Wing (1855—1934), Eng. dramatist.

Pinkerton (ping′kĕr-tọn), Allan (1819—84), Am. detective, born in Scotland.

Pinto (pēn′tọ), Fernão Mendes (1509?—83), Pg. traveler in the East and writer.

Pinturicchio (pēn-tö-rēk′kē-ō) (real name Bernardino di Betti) (1454—1513), It. painter, of Umbrian school.

Pinzón (pēn-thōn′), Martín Alonso (c1440—93?), Sp. navigator with Columbus.

Pinzón, Vicente Yáñez (c1460—c1524), Sp. navigator with Columbus, and discoverer of Brazil (brother of Martín A.).

Piombo (del pyom′bō), Sebastiano del (real name Sebastiano Luciani) (1485—1547), It. painter.

Piozzi (pi-oz′ĭ, It. pē-ot′sē), Mrs. (Hester Lynch Salusbury, Mrs. Thrale) (1741—1821), Eng. writer, friend of Dr. Johnson.

Pippi (pēp′pē), Giulio. See *Giulio Romano.*

Pippin (pip′in). See *Pepin.*

Pirandello (pē-rän-del′lō), Luigi (1867—1936), It. novelist, dramatist, and poet.

Pisan, Christine de. See *Christine de Pisan.*

Pisanello (pē-zä-nel′lō). See *Pisano, Vittore.*

Pisani (pē-zä′nē), Vettor (d. 1380), Venetian admiral.

Pisano (pē-zä′nō), Andrea (also called Andrea da Pontedera) (c1270—c1349), It. sculptor and architect.

Pisano, Giovanni (c1240—c1320), It. sculptor and architect (son of Niccolò).

Pisano, Niccolò (c1206—78), It. sculptor and architect.

Pisano, Vittore (called Pisanello) (c1380—1456?), It. painter and medalist.

Pisistratus (pi-sis′trạ-tus) (c605—527 B.C.), tyrant of Athens.

Pissarro (pē-sȧ-rō), Camille (1830?—1903), Fr. impressionist painter, born in West Indies.

Pitman (pit′mạn), Sir Isaac (1813—97), Eng. schoolmaster, inventor of phonography.

Pitt (pit), William (1708—78). See *Chatham, 1st Earl of.*

Pitt, William (1759—1806), Eng. statesman (son of 1st Earl of Chatham).

Pittacus (pit′ạ-kus) (c650—c570 B.C.), one of the seven sages of ancient Greece.

Pius II. (pī′us) (Enea Silvio Piccolomini, also known as Æneas Sylvius) (1405—64), It. ecclesiastic and writer, pope (1458—64).

Pius IV. (Giovanni Angelo Medici) (1499—1565), It. ecclesiastic, pope (1559—65).

Pius V., Saint (Michele Ghisleri) (1504—72), It. ecclesiastic, pope (1566—72).

Pius VI. (Giovanni Angelo Braschi) (1717—99), It. ecclesiastic, pope (1775—99).

Pius VII. (Luigi Barnaba Chiaramonti) (1740—1823), It. ecclesiastic, pope (1800—23).

Pius VIII. (Francesco Saverio Castiglioni) (1761—1830), It. ecclesiastic, pope (1829—30).

Pius IX. (Giovanni Maria Mastai-Ferretti) (1792—1878), It. ecclesiastic, pope (1846—78).

Pius X. (Giuseppe Sarto) (1835—1914), It. ecclesiastic, pope (1903—14).

Pius XI. (Achille Ambrogio Damiano Ratti) (1857—1939), It. ecclesiastic, pope (1922—39).

Pius XII. (Eugenio Pacelli) (1876—   ), It. ecclesiastic, pope (1939—   ).

Pizarro (pi-zä′rō, Sp. pē-thär′rō), Francisco (1471 or 1475—1541), Sp. soldier, conqueror of Peru.

Planché (plän-shā′), James Robinson (1796—1880), Eng. dramatist and antiquary.   [of operettas.

Planquette (plän-ket), Robert (1850?—1903), Fr. composer

Plantagenet (plan-taj′ẹ-net), Geoffrey. See *Geoffrey.*

Plantagenet, John. See *John of Lancaster.*   [Antwerp.

Plantin (plän-tȧn), Christophe (1514—89), Fr. printer, at

Platen-Hallermund (fon plä′tẹn-häl′ĕr-mṳnt), August, Graf von (1796—1835), Ger. poet and dramatist.

Plato (plā′tō) (427?—347 B.C.), Gr. philosopher, founder of Academic school.

Platt (plat), Thomas Collier (1833—1910), Am. politician.

Plautus (plâ′tus), Titus Maccius (c254—c184 B.C.), Rom. dramatist.

Plehve (plā′vė), V. K. See *Pleve.*

Plethon (plē′thon). See *Gemistus.*

Pleve (plā′vė), Vyacheslav Konstantinovich (1846—1904), Russ. administrator.

Plimsoll (plim′sọl), Samuel ("the Sailors' Friend") (1824—98), Eng. politician, inaugurator of shipping reform.

Pliny (plin′i) (Caius Plinius Secundus, "Pliny the Elder") (A.D. 23—79), Rom. naturalist, encyclopedist, and misc. writer.

Pliny (Caius Plinius Cæcilius Secundus, "Pliny the Younger") (A.D. 62?—c113), Rom. author and orator (nephew of Pliny the Elder).

Plon-Plon (plôn-plôn). See *Bonaparte, Napoléon Joseph Charles Paul.*

Plotinus (plọ-tī′nus) (205?—270?), Neoplatonic philosopher in Rome, born in Egypt.

Plücker (plük′ĕr), Julius (1801—68), Ger. mathematician and physicist.

Pluecker (plük′ĕr). See *Plücker.*

Plumer (plö′mĕr), Herbert Charles Onslow Plumer, 1st Viscount (1857—1932), Eng. field-marshal.

Plutarch (plö′tärk) (A.D. c46—c120), Gr. biographer and misc. writer.

Pobyedonostsev (pob-ye-do-nos′tsef), Konstantin Petrovich (1827—1907), Russ. jurist and administrator.

Pocahontas (pō-kạ-hon′tạs) (Rebecca Rolfe) (1595?—1617), Am. Indian woman (daughter of Powhatan, and wife of John Rolfe).

Pococke (pō′kok), Edward (1604—91), Eng. Arabic and Biblical scholar.

Poděbrad (pod′ye-bräd), George of (1420—71), king of Bohemia (1458—71).

Poe (pō), Edgar Allan (1809—49), Am. poet and writer of tales.

Poerio (pō-ā′rē-ō), Carlo (1803—67), Neapolitan patriot.

Pogge (pog′ė), Paul (1839—84), Ger. explorer in Africa.

Poggendorff (pog′ẹn-dôrf), Johann Christian (1796—1877), Ger. physicist.

Poincaré (pwaṅ-kȧ-rä), Jules Henri (1854—1912), Fr. mathematician.

Poincaré, Raymond (1860—1934), Fr. statesman, president of France (1913—20).

Poiré (pwo-rä), Emmanuel ("Caran d'Ache") (1858—1909), Fr. illustrator and caricaturist, born in Russia.

Pole (pōl), Reginald (1500—58), Eng. cardinal, and last Rom. Cath. archbishop of Canterbury.

Pole (dė lä pōl), Richard de la (d. 1525), pretender to the crown of England (nephew of Edward IV. and Richard III.).

Pole, William de la. See *Suffolk, William de la Pole, 1st Duke of.*

Polignac (dė pọ-lē-nyȧk), Jules Auguste Armand Marie, Prince de (1780—1847), Fr. statesman and diplomatist.

Politian (pọ-lish′ịan) (in Italian, Angelo Poliziano, orig. Angelo Ambrogini) (1454—94), It. classical scholar and poet.

Polk (pōk), James Knox (1795—1849), 11th president of U. S. (1845—49).

Polk, Leonidas (1806—64), Am. Protestant Episcopal bishop and Confederate general.

Pollajuolo (pol′′lä-yö-ō′lō), Antonio (real name Antonio di Jacopo Benci) (1429?—98), It. painter and sculptor.

Pollajuolo, Pietro (real name Pietro di Jacopo Benci) (1443—96?), It. painter (brother of Antonio).

Pollajuolo, Simone (also called Simone Cronaca, real name Simone di Tommaso d'Antonio) (1457—1508), It. architect.

Pollock (pol′ọk), Sir Frederick (1845—1937), Eng. legal scholar and misc. writer.

Pollok (pol′ọk), Robert (1798—1827), Sc. poet.

Polo (pō′lō), Marco (c1254—c1324), It. traveler in Asia.

Polybius (po-lib′i-us) (c205—c123 B.C.), Gr. historian.

Polycarp (pol′i-kärp) (A.D. 69?—155), bishop of Smyrna and Christian martyr.

Polyclitus (pol-i-klī′tus) or **Polycletus** (pol-i-klē′tus) (fl. c450—c420 B.C.), Gr. sculptor.

Polycrates (po-lik′rạ-tēz) (d. 522? B.C.), tyrant of Samos (c535—522? B.C.).

Polygnotus (pol-ig-nō′tus) (fl. c450 B.C.), Gr. painter.

(variable) ḍ as d or j, ş as s or sh, ṭ as t or ch, ẓ as z or zh; o, F. cloche; ü, F. menu; ċh, Sc. loch; ṅ, F. bonbon; ′, primary accent; ″, secondary accent; †, obsolete; <, from; +, and; =, equals. See also lists at beginning of book.

Pombal (dä pom-bäl′), Sebastião José de Carvalho e Mello, Marquis de (1699—1782), Pg. statesman.

Pompadour (dė pôṅ-pȧ-dör), Marquise de (Jeanne Antoinette Poisson, Mme. Lenormand d′Étioles) (1721—64), mistress of Louis XV. of France.

Pompey (pom′pi) ("Pompey the Great," properly Cnæus Pompeius Magnus) (106—48 B.C.), Rom. general, member of First Triumvirate.

Ponce de León (pŏn′thä dä lā-ōn′), Juan (c1460—1521), Sp. soldier, discoverer of Florida.

Ponchielli (pon-kyel′lē), Amilcare (1834—86), It. operatic composer.

Pond (pond), John (1767—1836), Eng. astronomer.

Poniatowski (pō-nyä-tof′skẹ), Józef Anton (1762—1813), Pol. prince, and marshal of France (nephew of Stanislaus II.).

Poniatowski. See *Stanislaus II.* (of Poland).

Pontiac (pon′ti-ak) (c1720—69), Am. Indian chief.

Pope (pōp), Alexander (1688—1744), Eng. poet.

Pope, John (1822—92), Am. general.

Poppæa Sabina (po-pē′ạ sa-bī′nä) (d. A.D. 65), a wife of the Rom. emperor Nero.

Porphyry (pôr′fi-ri) (orig. Malchus) (233?—c304), Gr. scholar and Neoplatonic philosopher in Rome, born in Syria.

Porsena (pôr′sẹ-nạ) or **Porsenna** (pôr-sen′ạ), Lars. A legendary Etruscan king, said to have attacked Rome in order to restore the banished Tarquinius Superbus to the throne. Cf. *Horatius Cocles*, and *Scævola*.

Porson (pôr′sọn), Richard (1759—1808), Eng. Greek scholar.

Portales (pôr-tä′läs), Diego José Victor (1793—1837), Chilean politician.

Portalis (pôr-tȧ-lēs), Jean Étienne Marie (1745—1807), Fr. jurist and statesman.

Porter (pōr′tėr), David (1780—1843), Am. naval officer.

Porter, David Dixon (1813—91), Am. admiral (son of David).

Porter, Fitz-John (1822—1901), Am. general (nephew of David).

Porter, Horace (1837—1921), Am. soldier and diplomatist.

Porter, Jane (1776—1850), Eng. novelist.

Porter, Noah (1811—92), Am. educator.

Porter, William Sydney ("O. Henry") (1867—1910), Am. writer of short stories.

Portland (pōrt′lạnd), William Bentinck, 1st Earl of (1649?—1709), Dutch-Eng. statesman, friend and confidential adviser of William III. of England.

Porto-Riche (dė pôr-tō-rēsh), Georges de (1849—1930), Fr. dramatist.

Portsmouth (pōrts′muth), Duchess of. See *Kéroualle.*

Porus (pō′rus) (d. 321? B.C.), a prince of India, conquered by Alexander the Great.

Potemkin (pọ-tem′kin, Russ. po-tyom′kẹn), Prince Grigori Aleksandrovich (1739—91), Russ. statesman, and favorite of Catharine II.

Potocki (po-tots′kẹ), Count Stanislaw Kostka (1752—1821), Pol. statesman.

Potter (dė po-tär), Louis Joseph Antoine de (1786—1859), Belgian political leader, and writer.

Potter (pot′ėr), Paul (1625—54), Dutch painter.

Pound (pound), Ezra Loomis (1885—   ), Am. poet and misc. writer, in Europe.

Pound, Roscoe (1870—   ), Am. legal writer and educator.

Poussin (pö-saṅ), Gaspard. See *Dughet.*

Poussin, Nicolas (1594—1665), Fr. painter.

Powers (pou′ėrz), Hiram (1805—73), Am. sculptor, in Florence.

Powhatan (pou-hạ-tan′) (c1550—1618), Am. Indian chief.

Poynings (poi′ningz), Sir Edward (1459—1521), Eng. soldier and diplomatist, lord deputy of Ireland.

Poynter (poin′tėr), Sir Edward John (1836—1919), Eng. painter and designer.

Pozzo di Borgo (pot′sō dē bôr′gō), Count Carlo Andrea (1764—1842), Corsican politician, and (later) diplomatist in Russian service.

Pradier (prȧ-dyä), James (1792—1852), Swiss-Fr. sculptor.

Pradilla (prä-ᴛнēl′yä), Francisco (1847—1921), Sp. painter.

Prado (prä′ᴛнō), Mariano Ignacio (1826—1901), Peruvian soldier and politician, president of Peru (1876—79).

Praed (prād), Winthrop Mackworth (1802—39), Eng. poet.

Pratt (prat), Charles. See *Camden, 1st Earl.*

Praxiteles (prak-sit′ẹ-lēz) (fl. c350 B.C.), Gr. sculptor.

Préault (prā-ō), Antoine Auguste (1809—79), Fr. sculptor.

Preble (preb′l), Edward (1761—1807), Am. naval officer.

Preller (prel′ėr), Friedrich (1804—78), Ger. landscape-painter.

Preller, Friedrich (1838—1901), Ger. landscape-painter (son of Friedrich Preller, 1804—78).

Prescott (pres′kọt), William (1726—95), Am. Revolutionary officer.

Prescott, William Hickling (1796—1859), Am. historian.

Pretorius (prā-tō′rẹ-ús), Andries Wilhelmus Jacobus (1799—1853), Boer leader and military commander.

Pretorius, Marthinus Wessels (1818?—1901), Boer soldier and statesman, president of the South African Republic and of the Orange Free State (son of Andries W. J.).

Prévost (prā-vō), Eugène Marcel (1862—1941), Fr. novelist and dramatist.

Prévost d′Exiles (deg-zēl), Antoine François (Abbé Prévost) (1697—1763), Fr. novelist, author of "Manon Lescaut."

Price (prīs), Richard (1723—91), Br. nonconformist minister, and writer on finance, politics, and morals.

Price, Sterling (1809—67), Am. Confederate general.

Prichard (prich′ạrd), James Cowles (1786—1848), Eng. physician and ethnologist.

Pride (prīd), Thomas (d. 1658), Eng. soldier and regicide.

Prideaux (prid′ō), Humphrey (1648—1724), Eng. divine and historical writer.

Priestley (prēst′li), Joseph (1733—1804), Eng. nonconformist divine, chemist, and misc. writer.

Prim (prēm), Juan (Marquis de los Castillejos) (1814—70), Sp. general and statesman.

Primaticcio (prē-mä-tēt′chō), Francesco (1504—70), It. painter, in France.

Primo de Rivera (prē′mō dä rē-vä′rä) **y Orbaneja,** Miguel (Marqués de Estella) (1870—1930), Sp. general, military ruler, and premier.

Pringle-Pattison (pring′gl-pat′i-sọn). See *Seth.*

Pringsheim (prings′hīm), Nathanael (1823—94), Ger. botanist.

Prinsep (prin′sep), Valentine Cameron (called Val Prinsep) (1838—1904), Eng. painter, born in India.

Prior (prī′ọr), Matthew (1664—1721), Eng. poet.

Priscian (prish′iạn) (Priscianus Cæsariensis) (fl. c500), Latin grammarian.

Pritchard (prich′ạrd), Mrs. (Hannah Vaughan) (1711—68), Eng. actress.

Prjevalsky (przhe-väl′skẹ). See *Przhevalski.*

Proclus (prō′klus) (410?—485), Gr. Neoplatonic philosopher.

Procopius (prọ-kō′pi-us) (c490—c562), Byzantine Gr. historian.

Procter (prok′tėr), Adelaide Ann (1825—64), Eng. poet (daughter of Bryan W.).

Procter, Bryan Waller ("Barry Cornwall") (1787—1874), Eng. poet.

Proctor (prok′tọr), Richard Anthony (1837—88), Eng. astronomer.

Propertius (prọ-pėr′shius), Sextus (c50—c15 B.C.), Rom. elegiac poet.

Protagoras (prọ-tag′ọ-ras) (c481—411? B.C.), Gr. sophist and philosopher.

Protogenes (prọ-toj′ẹ-nēz) (fl. 330—300 B.C.), Gr. painter.

Proudhon (prö-dôṅ), Pierre Joseph (1809—65), Fr. socialist and political writer.

Proust (pröst), Marcel (1871—1922), Fr. novelist.

Prout (prout), Father. Pseudonym of Francis Sylvester Mahony.

Prudentius (prọ-den′shius), Aurelius Clemens (348—after 405), Latin Christian poet, of Spain.

Prud′hon (prü-dôṅ), Pierre Paul (1758—1823), Fr. painter.

Prynne (prin), William (1600—69), Eng. Puritan politician and polemical writer.

Przhevalski (przhe-väl′skẹ), Nikolay Mikhaylovich (1839—88), Russ. general, and explorer in Asia.

Przybyszewski (przhi-bi-shef′skẹ), Stanislaw (1868—   ), Pol. novelist and dramatist, writing in German and Polish.

Ptolemy I. (tol′ẹ-mi) (surnamed Soter) (367?—283 B.C.), king of Egypt (306—285 B.C.), born in Macedonia, founder of Macedonian dynasty in Egypt.

Ptolemy II. (surnamed Philadelphus) (309?—247? B.C.), king of Egypt (285—247? B.C.) (son of Ptolemy I.).

Ptolemy (Claudius Ptolemæus) (fl. 127—151), Gr. mathematician, astronomer, and geographer, at Alexandria.

Publilius Syrus (pub-lil′i-us sī′rus) (fl. c43 B.C.), Rom. writer of mimes and maxims.

Puccini (pōt-chē′nē), Giacomo (1858—1924), It. operatic composer.

Pufendorf (fon pö′fęn-dôrf), Samuel, Freiherr von (1632—94), Ger. jurist and historian.

Pugachev (pö-gà-chef′), Emelyan Ivanovich (d. 1775), Russ. impostor, and pretender to the throne.

Puget (pü-zhā), Pierre (1622—94), Fr. sculptor, painter, and architect.

Pugin (pū′jin), Augustus Welby Northmore (1812—52), Eng. architect.

Pulaski (pū-las′ki), Count Casimir (name in Polish, Pulawski) (1748—79), Pol. patriot, and general in the American Revolutionary army.

Pulci (pōl′chē), Luigi (1432—87?), It. poet.

Pulitzer (pū′lit-sėr), Joseph (1847—1911), Hung.-Am. journalist.

Pullman (pùl′man), George Mortimer (1831—97), Am. inventor (of Pullman cars).

Pulteney (pult′ni), William. See *Bath, Earl of.*

Pupin (pū-pēn′), Michael Idvorsky (1858—1935), Am. physicist and inventor, born in Hungary.

Purcell (pėr′sęl), Henry (1658?—95), Eng. musical composer.

Purchas (pėr′chàs), Samuel (1575?—1626), Eng. compiler of books of travel.

Pusey (pū′zi), Edward Bouverie (1800—82), Eng. divine and theologian.

Pushkin (pùsh′kin, Russ. pōsh′kęn), Aleksandr Sergyeevich (1799—1837), Russ. poet and story-writer.

Putnam (put′nam), George Haven (1844—1930), Am. publisher and author.

Putnam, Herbert (1861—   ), Am. librarian (brother of George H.).

Putnam, Israel (1718—90), Am. Revolutionary general.

Putnam, Rufus (1738—1824), Am. general and pioneer.

Puttkamer (fon pùt′kä″mėr), Robert Viktor von (1828—1900), Prussian statesman.

Puvis de Chavannes (pü-vē dė shá-vàn), Pierre (1824—98), Fr. painter.

Pyeshkov (pyesh-kof′), Aleksyey Maksimovich ("Maksim Gorki") (1868—1936), Russ. author.

Pyle (pīl), Howard (1853—1911), Am. painter, illustrator, and writer.

Pym (pim), John (1584—1643), Eng. parliamentary leader.

Pynson (pin′sǫn), Richard (d. 1530), Eng. printer, born in Normandy.

Pyrrho (pir′ō) (c365—c275 B.C.), Gr. Skeptic philosopher, founder of Pyrrhonism.

Pyrrhus (pir′us) (c318—272 B.C.), king of Epirus, and general.

Pythagoras (pi-thag′ǫ-ràs) (c582—c500 B.C.), Gr. philosopher, religious teacher, and mathematician.

Q

Q (no period). Literary signature of Sir A. T. Quiller-Couch.

Quarles (kwärlz), Francis (1592—1644), Eng. poet.

Quatrefages de Bréau (dė kàtr-fäzh dė brä-ō), Jean Louis Armand de (1810—92), Fr. naturalist and ethnologist.

Quay (kwā), Matthew Stanley (1833—1904), Am. politician, senator from Pennsylvania.

Quercia (del′lä kwär′chä), Jacopo della (c1374—1438), It. sculptor.

Quesada, Gonzalo Jiménez de. See *Jiménez de Quesada.*

Quesnay (kā-nā), François (1694—1774), Fr. physician and economist, founder of school of physiocrats.

Quesnel (kā-nel), Pasquier (1634—1719), Fr. Jansenist theologian.

Quevedo y Villegas (dā kā-vā′ᴛʜō ē vē-lyā′gäs), Francisco Gómez de (1580—1645), Sp. satirist, poet, and novelist.

Quezon (kā′zon), Manuel L. (1878—1944), Filipino political leader, 1st president Philippine Commonwealth (1935—   ).

Quiller-Couch (kwil′ėr-kōch′), Sir Arthur Thomas ("Q") (1863—   ), Eng. novelist and critic.

Quin (kwin), James (1693—1766), Eng. actor.

Quincy (kwin′zi), Josiah (1744—75), Am. patriot.

Quincy, Josiah (1772—1864), Am. statesman and scholar (son of Josiah Quincy, 1744—75).

Quinet (kē-nā), Edgar (1803—75), Fr. historian, poet, and misc. writer.

Quintana (kēn-tä′nä), Manuel José (1772—1857), Sp. poet and patriot.

Quintilian (kwin-til′iạn) (Marcus Fabius Quintilianus) (A.D. c35—c95), Rom. rhetorician.

R

Raabe (rä′bė), Wilhelm (1831—1910), Ger. novelist.

Rabanus Maurus (rä-bä′nús mou′rús) (Hrabanus Maurus) (c776—856), Ger. archbishop, teacher, and writer.

Rabelais (rab-ę-lā′, Fr. ráb-lä), François (c1490—1553), Fr. satirist and humorist.

Rachel (rà-shel), Mlle. (professional name of Élisa, or Élisabeth, Félix) (1821?—58), Fr. tragédienne.

Rachmaninoff (ràch-mä′nyę-nof). See *Rakhmaninov.*

Racine (rà-sēn), Jean Baptiste (1639—99), Fr. tragic dramatist.

Rackham (rak′ạm), Arthur (1867—1939), Eng. painter and illustrator.

Radcliffe (rad′klif), Mrs. (Ann Ward) (1764—1823), Eng. novelist.

Radetzky (rä-det′skę), Johann Joseph Wenzel, Graf (1766—1858), Austrian field-marshal.

Raeburn (rä′bėrn), Sir Henry (1756—1823), Sc. portrait-painter.

Raemaekers (rä′mä-kėrs), Louis (1869—   ), Dutch artist, noted for cartoons.

Raff (räf), Joseph Joachim (1822—82), Ger. musical composer.

Raffaëlli (rà-fà-e-lē), Jean François (1850—1924), Fr. painter, sculptor, and etcher.

Raffles (raf′lz), Sir Thomas Stamford (1781—1826), Eng. colonial administrator.

Rafinesque (rà-fę-nesk′), Constantine Samuel (1784—1842), Fr.-Am. botanist, born in Turkey.

Raglan (rag′lạn), Fitzroy James Henry Somerset, 1st Baron (1788—1855), Eng. field-marshal.

Raibolini (rä-ę-bō-lē′nē), Francesco. See *Francia.*

Raikes (rāks), Robert (1735—1811), Eng. philanthropist, promoter of Sunday-schools.

Raimondi (rä-ę-mōn′dē), Marcantonio (c1480—c1534), It. engraver.

Rais (dė räs or rā), Gilles de. See *Retz, Gilles de.*

Rakhmaninov (ràch-mä′nyę-nof), Sergyey Vasilevich (1873—1943), Russ. composer and pianist.

Rákóczy (rä′kō-tsę), Ferencz, or Francis, II. (1676—1735), Hung. patriot, prince of Transylvania (1704—11).

Raleigh or **Ralegh** (rà′li), Sir Walter (1552?—1618), Eng. statesman, explorer, and author.

Raleigh, Sir Walter (1861—1922), Eng. educator and literary critic.

Rambaud (räṅ-bō), Alfred Nicolas (1842—1905), Fr. historian.

Rambouillet (dė räṅ-bö-yā), Marquise de (Catherine de Vivonne) (1588—1665), Fr. social patron of literature and learning.

Rameau (rà-mō), Jean Philippe (1683—1764), Fr. musical theorist and composer.

Rameses II. (ram′ę-sēz) or **Ramses II.** (ram′sēz) (fl. 13th cent. B.C.), king of Egypt, of 19th dynasty.

Rameses III. or **Ramses III.** (fl. c1200 B.C.), king of Egypt, of 20th dynasty.

Ramón y Cajal (rä-mōn′ ē kä-ᴴäl′), Santiago (1852—1934), Sp. histologist and pathologist.

Rampolla del Tindaro (räm-pol′lä del tēn′dä-rō), Mariano (1843—1913), It. cardinal and papal statesman.

Ramsay (ram′zi), Allan (1686—1758), Sc. poet.

Ramsay, Sir Andrew Crombie (1814—91), Br. geologist.

Ramsay, Sir William (1852—1916), Br. chemist.

Ramses. See *Rameses.*

Randolph (ran′dolf), Edmund Jennings (1753—1813), Am. statesman (nephew of Peyton).

Randolph, John ("of Roanoke") (1773–1833), Am. statesman.

Randolph, Peyton (1723–75), Am. patriot.

Randolph, Thomas (1605–35), Eng. poet and dramatist.

Randolph, Thomas. See *Moray, 1st Earl of* (d. 1332).

Ranger (rān'jėr), Henry Ward (1858–1916), Am. landscape-painter.

Ranjit Singh or **Runjeet Singh** (run-jēt' sing) (1780–1839), maharaja of the Punjab.

Ranke (fon räng'kė), Leopold von (1795–1886), Ger. historian.

Raphael (raf'ā-el or rā'fā-el) (Raffaele Santi, or Sanzio) (1483–1520), It. painter.

Rapin (dė rá-pań), Paul de (Sieur de Thoyras) (1661–1725), Fr. historian.

Rapin, René (1621–87), Fr. Jesuit, critic, and writer of Latin verse.

Rapp (räp), George (1757 or 1770–1847), Ger.-Am. religious and social reformer.

Rashi (rä'shē) (Solomon ben Isaac) (1040–1105), Fr. Jewish scholar and commentator.

Rask (räsk), Rasmus Christian (1787–1832), Dan. philologist.

Rasmussen (räs'mö-sẹn), Knud (1879–1933), Dan. arctic explorer, born in Greenland.

Raspail (räs-pä-y'), François Vincent (1794–1878), Fr. chemist and radical politician.

Rasputin (räs-pö'tẹn), Grigori Efimovich (1871–1916), Russ. monk, favorite of the Russian imperial family (assassinated).

Rathenau (rä'tẹ-nou), Walther (1867–1922), Ger. industrialist, writer, and statesman (assassinated).

Rauch (rouch), Christian Daniel (1777–1857), Ger. sculptor.

Ravaillac (rá-vá-yák), François (1578–1610), Fr. fanatic, who assassinated Henry IV. of France.

Ravel (rá-vel), Maurice (1875–1937), Fr. musical composer.

Rawlinson (rå'lin-sọn), George (1812–1902), Eng. historian (brother of Sir H. C.).

Rawlinson, Sir Henry Creswicke (1810–95), Eng. diplomatist and Orientalist.

Rawlinson, Henry Seymour Rawlinson, Baron (1864–1925), Eng. general (son of Sir H. C.).

Ray or **Wray** (rā), John (1627–1705), Eng. naturalist.

Rayleigh (rā'li), John William Strutt, 3d Baron (1842–1919), Eng. physicist.

Raymond IV. (rā'mọnd) (Raymond de Saint-Gilles) (d. 1105), count of Toulouse (1088–1105), a leader in the first Crusade.

Raymond VI. (1156–1222), count of Toulouse (1195–1222), a supporter of the Albigenses (great-grandson of Raymond IV.).

Read (rēd), Thomas Buchanan (1822–72), Am. poet and painter.

Reade (rēd), Charles (1814–84), Eng. novelist and dramatist.

Reading (red'ing), Rufus Daniel Isaacs, 1st Marquis of (1860–1935), Eng. jurist, diplomatist, and statesman, lord chief justice (1913–21).

Rea Silvia. See *Rhea Silvia.*

Réaumur (dė rā-ō-mür), René Antoine Ferchault de (1683–1757), Fr. physicist and naturalist.

Récamier (rā-ká-myā), Mme. (Jeanne Françoise Julie Adélaïde Bernard) (1777–1849), Fr. leader in literary and political circles.

Reclus (rė-klü), Jean Jacques Élisée (1830–1905), Fr. geographer.

Redfield (red'fēld), Edward Willis (1869–   ), Am. painter.

Redmond (red'mọnd), John Edward (1851–1918), Ir. political leader.

Redon (rė-dóń), Odilon (1840–1916), Fr. painter, etcher, and lithographer.

Reed (rēd), Thomas Brackett (1839–1902), Am. political leader.

Reger (rā'gėr), Max (1873–1916), Ger. musical composer.

Regiomontanus (rē″ji-ọ-mon-tā'nus) (real name Johann Müller) (1436–76), Ger. mathematician and astronomer.

Regnard (rė-när or rė-nyär), Jean François (1655–1709), Fr. dramatist.

Regnault (rė-nō or rė-nyō), Alexandre Georges Henri (1843–71), Fr. painter (son of H. V. Regnault).

Regnault, Henri Victor (1810–78), Fr. chemist and physicist.

Régnier (dė rā-nyā), Henri François Joseph de (1864–1936), Fr. poet and novelist.

Regulus (reg'ū-lus), Marcus Atilius (d. 250? B.C.), Rom. general.

Rehan (rē'ạn), Ada (real name Crehan) (1860–1916), Ir.-Am. actress.

Reichstadt (dė rīch'shtät), Duc de. See *Napoleon II.*

Reid (rēd), Thomas (1710–96), Sc. philosopher.

Reid, Thomas Mayne (1818–83), Br. novelist.

Reid, Whitelaw (1837–1912), Am. journalist and diplomatist.

Reil (rīl), Johann Christian (1759–1813), Ger. physician and anatomist.

Reinach (re-näk), Joseph (1856–1921), Fr. publicist.

Reinach, Salomon (1858–1932), Fr. archæologist and author (brother of Joseph).

Reinhardt (rīn'härt), Max (1873–1943), Austrian-Ger. actor and producer of plays.

Réjane (rā-zhän), Mme. (professional name of Gabrielle Charlotte Réju, Mme. Porel) (1857–1920), Fr. actress.

Relly (rel'i), James (1722?–78), Br. Universalist preacher.

Rembrandt (rem'brant, Dutch rem'bränt) (Rembrandt Harmens van Rijn, or van Ryn) (1606–69), Dutch painter and etcher.

Remigius (re-mij'i-us) or **Remi** (rė-mē), Saint ("the Apostle of the Franks") (c437–c533), Fr. archbishop.

Remington (rem'ing-tọn), Frederic (1861–1909), Am. illustrator, painter, sculptor, and author.

Remsen (rem'zẹn), Ira (1846–1927), Am. chemist and educator.

Remus (rē'mus). See *Romulus.*

Renan (rė-näń), Joseph Ernest (1823–92), Fr. Orientalist, historian, and misc. writer.

René I. (rė-nā) ("René the Good") (1409–80), duke of Anjou, and titular king of Naples.

Reni (rā'nē), Guido (1575–1642), It. painter.

Rennie (ren'i), John (1761–1821), Br. engineer.

Renoir (rė-nwor), Pierre Auguste (1841–1919), Fr. painter.

Renouf (rė-nöf), Émile (1845–94), Fr. painter.

Repplier (rep'li-ėr), Agnes (1858–   ), Am. essayist.

Requeséns (rā-kā-sens'), Luis de Zúñiga y (d. 1576), Sp. military commander, and administrator of Netherlands (1573–76).

Reshid Pasha (re-shēd' pá-shä') (1802–58), Turk. statesman.

Reszke (dė resh'ke), Édouard de (1856–1917), Pol. operatic bass singer (brother of Jean).

Reszke, Jean de (1853–1925), Pol. operatic tenor singer.

Rethel (rā'tẹl), Alfred (1816–59), Ger. historical painter.

Retz (rets, Fr. dė räs) or **Rais** (dė räs or rä), Gilles de (born Laval) (1404–40), Fr. marshal (executed for murder), whose name is associated with the story of "Bluebeard."

Retz, Jean François Paul de Gondi, Cardinal de (1614–79), Fr. ecclesiastic, politician, and writer of memoirs.

Retzius (ret'sẹ-ùs), Anders (1796–1860), Swed. anatomist.

Retzius, Magnus Gustaf (1842–1919), Swed. anatomist and anthropologist (son of Anders).

Reuchlin (roich'lēn), Johann (1455–1522), Ger. humanist and Hebraist.

Reuter (roi'tėr), Fritz (1810–74), Ger. dialect poet and novelist.

Reuter, Paul Julius Reuter, 1st Baron de (1821–99), Ger.-Eng. founder of a well-known news agency.

Revere (rẹ-vēr'), Paul (1735–1818), Am. engraver and patriot.

Reymont (rā'mont), Wladyslaw Stanislaw (1868–1925), Pol. novelist and poet.

Reynolds (ren'ọldz), John Fulton (1820–63), Am. general.

Reynolds, Sir Joshua (1723–92), Eng. portrait-painter.

Reza Shah Pahlavi. See *Riza Shah Pahlavi.*

Rhea (or **Rea**) **Silvia** (rē'ạ sil'vi-ạ). See *Romulus.*

Rhodes (rōdz), Cecil John (1853–1902), Eng. administrator and statesman in South Africa.

Rhodes, James Ford (1848–1927), Am. historian.

Rhodopis (rọ-dō'pis) or **Rhodope** (rọ-dō'pē) (real name Doricha) (fl. c600 B.C.), Gr. courtezan, born in Thrace.

---

fat, fāte, fär, fåll, åsk, fāre; net, mē, hėr; pin, pīne; not, nōte, mȯve, nȯr; up, lūte, pull; oi, oil; ou, out; (lightened) aviạry, ẹlect, agọny, intọ, ụnite; (obscured) errạnt, operạ, ardẹnt, actọr, natụre; ch, chip; g, go; th, thin; ᴛʜ, then; y, you;

Ribault or **Ribaut** (rē-bō), Jean (c1520—65), Fr. Huguenot colonizer in South Carolina and Florida.

Ribbentrop (fon rib'ẹn-trop), Joachim von (1893—1946), Ger. (Nazi) diplomatist and minister for foreign affairs.

Ribera (dä rē-bä'rä), Jusepe de (called Lo Spagnoletto, pronounced lō spä-nyō-let'tō, and meaning 'the Little Spaniard') (1588—1656), Sp. painter, at Naples. [statesman.

Ribot (rē-bō), Alexandre Félix Joseph (1842—1923), Fr.

Ribot, Augustin Théodule (1823—91), Fr. painter.

Ribot, Théodule Armand (1839—1916), Fr. psychologist.

Ricardo (ri-kär'dō), David (1772—1823), Eng. political economist. [man.

Ricasoli (rē-kä'sō-lē), Baron Bettino (1809—80), It. states-

Ricci (rēt'chē), Matteo (1552—1610), It. Jesuit missionary in China.

Riccio, David. See *Rizzio, David.*

Rice (rīs), Alexander Hamilton (1875—   ), Am. physician, geographer, and explorer.

Richard I. (rich'ärd) (called Richard Cœur de Lion, or 'Richard Lion-Heart') (1157—99), king of England (1189—99) (son of Henry II.).

Richard II. (1367—1400), king of England (1377—99) (successor and grandson of Edward III., and son of Black Prince).

Richard III. (Duke of Gloucester) (1452—85), king of England (1483—85) (successor and uncle of Edward V.).

Richards (rich'ärdz), Theodore William (1868—1928), Am. chemist.

Richardson (rich'ärd-sọn), Charles (1775—1865), Eng. lexicographer.

Richardson, Henry Hobson (1838—86), Am. architect.

Richardson, Samuel (1689—1761), Eng. novelist.

Richelieu (rish'ẹ-lö, Fr. dè rē-shẹ-lyẹ̀), Armand Jean du Plessis, Duc de (1585—1642), Fr. cardinal and statesman.

Richepin (rēsh-paṅ), Jean (1849—1926), Fr. poet, dramatist, and novelist.

Richmond (rich'mọnd), Charles Lennox, 3d Duke of (1735—1806), Eng. statesman and diplomatist.

Richter (rich'tèr), Adrian Ludwig (1803—84), Ger. painter and illustrator.

Richter, Gustav Karl Ludwig (1823—84), Ger. painter.

Richter, Jean Paul Friedrich ("Jean Paul") (1763—1825), Ger. humorist and misc. writer.

Richthofen (fon richt'hō'fẹn), Ferdinand, Freiherr von (1833—1905), Ger. traveler, geologist, and geographer.

Ricimer (ris'i-mèr) (d. 472), Rom. general, of barbarian parentage, master of Western Empire (456—472).

Ridley (rid'li), Nicholas (c1500—55), Eng. Protestant bishop and martyr.

Riedesel (fon rē'dè-zel), Friedrich Adolf, Freiherr von (1738—1800), Ger. general in British service in America.

Riego y Núñez (del rē-ä'gō ē nö'nyäth), Rafael del (1784?—1823), Sp. soldier and revolutionist.

Riehl (rēl), Wilhelm Heinrich (1823—97), Ger. novelist and historical writer.

Riel (rē-el), Louis (1844—85), Can. insurgent leader.

Riemann (rē'män), Georg Friedrich Bernhard (1826—66), Ger. mathematician.

Rienzi (rẹ-en'zẹ) or **Rienzo** (rẹ-en'zō), Cola di (1313?—54), Rom. orator, and tribune of the people.

Riesener (rē'zè-nèr), Jean Henri (1734—1806), Fr. cabinet-maker, born in Germany.

Rietschel (rē'chẹl), Ernst (1804—61), Ger. sculptor.

Rigaud (rē-gō), Hyacinthe (1659—1743), Fr. painter.

Riis (rēs), Jacob August (1849—1914), Dan.-Am. civic reformer and writer.

Riley (rī'li), James Whitcomb (1853?—1916), Am. poet.

Rimbaud (raṅ-bō), Arthur (1854—91), Fr. poet.

Rimmer (rim'èr), William (1816—79), Am. sculptor, born in England.

Rimski-Korsakov (rēm'skẹ-kȯr-sä-kof'), Nikolay Andreevich (1844—1908), Russ. musical composer.

Rinehart (rīn'härt), Mrs. (Mary Roberts) (1876—   ), Am. novelist and playwright.

Ripley (rip'li), George (1802—80), Am. editor and critic.

Ripley, William Zebina (1867—1941), Am. economist and ethnologist.

Ripon (rip'ọn), Frederick John Robinson, 1st Earl of (1782—1859), Eng. statesman.

Ripon, George Frederick Samuel Robinson, 1st Marquis of (1827—1909), Eng. statesman (son of 1st Earl).

Ristich (ris'tich), Jovan (1831—99), Serbian statesman.

Ristori (rēs-tō'rē), Adelaide (Marchesa del Grillo) (1822—1906), It. tragédienne.

Rita (rē'tạ), Saint (of Cascia) (1386—1456), It. nun and ascetic.

Ritschl (rich'l), Albrecht (1822—89), Ger. Protestant theologian.

Ritschl, Friedrich Wilhelm (1806—76), Ger. classical philologist.

Ritschl, Otto (1860—   ), Ger. Protestant theologian (son of Albrecht).

Ritter (rit'èr), Karl (1779—1859), Ger. geographer.

Riviere (rē-vyär'), Briton (1840—1920), Eng. painter.

Rizal (rē-säl'), José (1861—96), Filipino patriot, physician, and novelist, writing in Spanish.

Riza Shah Pahlavi (rē'zạ shä päh'lạ-vē) (c1875—1944), Pers. soldier and statesman, shah of Persia (1925—   ).

Rizzio (rēt'sē-ō) or **Riccio** (rēt'chō), David (c1533—66), It. secretary and favorite of Mary Queen of Scots.

Robbia (del'lä rob'bē-ä), Andrea della (1435?—1525?), It. sculptor, working esp. in enameled terra-cotta (nephew of Luca).

Robbia, Giovanni della (1469—1529?), It. sculptor (enameled terra-cotta) (son of Andrea).

Robbia, Girolamo della (1488—1566), It. sculptor and architect, in France (brother of Giovanni).

Robbia, Luca della (1399 or 1400—1482), It. sculptor, noted for work in enameled terra-cotta.

Robert I. (rob'èrt, Fr. ro-bär') (c865—923), king of the Franks (922—923) (rival of Charles III., and brother of Eudes).

Robert II. ("Robert the Pious") (971?—1031), king of France (996—1031) (son of Hugh Capet).

Robert I. (rob'èrt) (Robert de Bruce or Robert Bruce, often called "Robert the Bruce" or "the Bruce") (1274—1329), king of Scotland (1306—29).

Robert II. (called "the Steward") (1316—90), king of Scotland (1371—90) (successor and nephew of David II., and grandson of Robert I., and first king in Scotland of the house of Stuart).

Robert III. (c1340—1406), king of Scotland (1390—1406) (son of Robert II.).

Robert de Coucy. See *Coucy.*

Robert Guiscard (gēs-kär') (real name Robert de Hauteville) (c1015—85), Norman adventurer and conqueror in Italy, duke of Apulia and Calabria (1059—85).

Robert-Houdin (ro-bär-ö-daṅ), Jean Eugène (1805—71), Fr. conjurer and mechanician.

Robert of Gloucester (fl. 1260—1300), Eng. chronicler in verse.

Roberts (rob'èrts), Frederick Sleigh Roberts, Earl (1832—1914), Br. field-marshal.

Robertson (rob'èrt-sọn), Frederick William ("Robertson of Brighton") (1816—53), Eng. divine and preacher.

Robertson, Thomas William (1829—71), Eng. dramatist.

Robertson, William (1721—93), Sc. historian.

Robertson, Sir William Robert (1860—1933), Eng. field-marshal.

Robespierre (dè ro-bes-pyär), Maximilien Marie Isidore de (1758—94), Fr. revolutionary leader.

Robinson (rob'in-sọn), Edward (1794—1863), Am. Biblical scholar.

Robinson, Edwin Arlington (1869—1935), Am. poet.

Robinson, James Harvey (1863—1936), Am. educator and historical writer.

Robinson, John (1576?—1625), Eng. Puritan divine, at Leyden.

Robinson, Mrs. (Mary Darby, known as "Perdita") (1758—1800), Eng. actress and writer.

Robinson. See *Ripon.*

Rob Roy (rob roi). See *Macgregor, Robert.*

Robusti (rō-bös'tē), Jacopo. See *Tintoretto.*

Roca (rō'kä), Julio Argentino (1843—1914), Argentine general and statesman, president of Argentina (1880—86, 1898—1904).

Rocafuerte (rō-kä-fwär'tä), Vicente (1783—1847), Ecuadorian statesman.

Roch (rok), Saint (in Italian, Rocco) (c1295—1327), Fr. ministrant to the plague-stricken, and protector against pestilence and sickness.

Rochambeau (dĕ ro-shän-bō), Donatien Marie Joseph de Vimeur, Vicomte de (1750—1813), Fr. general (son of Comte de Rochambeau).

Rochambeau, Jean Baptiste Donatien de Vimeur, Comte de (1725—1807), Fr. general in American Revolutionary War, later marshal of France.

Rochefort (rosh-fôr), Henri (Victor Henri, Marquis de Rochefort-Luçay) (1830—1913), Fr. journalist, playwright, and politician.

Rochefoucauld, François, Duc de La. See *La Rochefoucauld.*

Rochejaquelein, Henri du Vergier, Comte de La. See *La Rochejaquelein.*

Rochester (roch′es-tẽr), John Wilmot, 2d Earl of (1647—80), Eng. courtier and poet.

Rockefeller (rok′ẹ-fel″ẽr), John Davison (1839—1937), Am. capitalist and philanthropist.

Rockefeller, John Davison (1874—   ), Am. capitalist and philanthropist (son of John D., born 1839).

Rockingham (rok′ing-ạm), Charles Watson-Wentworth, 2d Marquis of (1730—82), Eng. statesman.

Rod (rod), Louis Édouard (1857—1910), Swiss-Fr. novelist and critic.

Rodbertus (rod-ber′tus), Johann Karl (1805—75), Ger. economist and socialist.

Rodenbach (ro-den-bàk), Georges (1855—98), Belgian poet and novelist.

Roderick or **Roderic** (rod′ẹ-rik) (d. 711), last king of Visigoths of Spain, defeated by Arabs under Tarik.

Roderick. See *O'Connor, Roderick.*

Rodgers (roj′ẽrz), John (1771—1838), Am. naval officer.

Rodgers, John (1812—82), Am. admiral (son of John Rodgers, 1771—1838).

Rodin (ro-dań), Auguste (1840—1917), Fr. sculptor.

Rodman (rod′mạn), Hugh (1859—1940), Am. admiral.

Rodney (rod′ni), Cæsar (1728—84), Am. patriot.

Rodney, George Brydges Rodney, 1st Baron (1718—92), Eng. admiral.

Roe (rō), Edward Payson (1838—88), Am. clergyman and novelist.

Roebling (rōb′ling), John Augustus (1806—69), Ger.-Am. civil engineer and bridge-builder.

Roebling, Washington Augustus (1837—1926), Am. civil engineer and bridge-builder (son of John A.).

Roemer (rẽ′mẽr). See *Römer.*

Roentgen (rent′gen). See *Röntgen.*

Roger I. (roj′ẽr) (Roger de Hauteville) (1031—1101), Norman adventurer and conqueror in Italy, count of Sicily (1072—1101) (brother of Robert Guiscard).

Roger II. (1093?—1154), king of Sicily (1130?—54) (son of Roger I.).

Rogers (roj′ẽrz), James Edwin Thorold (1823—90), Eng. political economist.

Rogers, John (c1500—55), Eng. Protestant divine and martyr.

Rogers, John (1829—1904), Am. sculptor, esp. of statuette groups.

Rogers, Randolph (1825—92), Am. sculptor in Italy.

Rogers, Robert (1727—1784 or 1800), Am. soldier, Tory leader in Revolutionary War.

Rogers, Samuel (1763—1855), Eng. poet.

Roget (rō-zhā′), Peter Mark (1779—1869), Eng. physician and author.

Rogier (ro-zhyā), Charles (1800—85), Belgian statesman.

Rohan (dĕ rō-äṅ), Henri, Duc de (1579—1638), Fr. general, writer, and Huguenot leader.

Rohan, Louis René Édouard, Prince de (1734—1803), Fr. cardinal and politician.

Rohlfs (rōlfs), Friedrich Gerhard (1831—96), Ger. explorer in Africa.

Rokitansky (fon rō-ki-tän′skẹ), Karl, Freiherr von (1804—78), Austrian anatomist and pathologist.

Roland de La Platière (ro-läṅ dĕ lä plà-tyär), Jean Marie (1734—93), Fr. statesman and writer.

Roland de La Platière, Mme. (Manon Jeanne Phlipon) (1754—93), Fr. leader in political circles, and writer of memoirs (wife of Jean M.).

Rolando (rō-län′dō), Luigi (1773—1831), It. anatomist.

Rolf. See *Rollo.*

Rolfe (rolf), John (1585—1622?), Eng. colonist in Virginia (husband of Pocahontas).

Rolland (ro-läṅ), Romain (1866—1945), Fr. novelist and misc. writer.

Rolle of Hampole (rōl, ham′pōl), Richard (c1290—1349), Eng. hermit and religious writer.

Rollo (rol′ō), **Rolf** (rolf), or **Hrolf** (hrolf) (d. 932?), Scand. viking, who became ruler of Normandy.

Romanes (rō-mä′nez), George John (1848—94), Can.-Eng. biologist and psychologist.

Romano, Giulio. See *Giulio Romano.*

Römer (rẽ′mẽr), Ole, or Olaus (1644—1710), Dan. astronomer.

Romilly (rom′i-li), Sir Samuel (1757—1818), Eng. legal reformer.

Romney (rom′ni or rum′ni), George (1734—1802), Eng. painter.

Romulus (rom′ū-lus). According to legend, the first king of Rome, said to have founded the city in 753 B.C., and to have reigned until 716 B.C. As the story runs, he was one of the twin sons of the god Mars and the vestal virgin Rhea Silvia. The mother was buried alive for violation of her vows; the children were thrown into the Tiber, but drifted ashore and were suckled by a she-wolf. In a quarrel about the newly founded Rome, Romulus slew his brother Remus for mocking him by leaping over the unfinished city wall. Finally Romulus was translated to heaven by his father Mars, and was worshiped by the Romans as a divinity.

Ronge (rong′ẹ), Johannes (1813—87), Ger. religious reformer, founder of sect called German Catholics.

Ronsard (dĕ rôṅ-sär), Pierre de (1524—85), Fr. poet.

Röntgen (rent′gen), Wilhelm Konrad (1845—1923), Ger. physicist, discoverer of Röntgen rays.

Roon (fon rōn), Albrecht Theodor Emil, Graf von (1803—79), Prussian field-marshal.

Roosevelt (rō′zẹ-velt, commonly rōz′velt), Franklin Delano (1882—1945), 32d president of U. S. (1933—45).

Roosevelt, Theodore (1858—1919), 26th president of U. S. (1901—09).

Root (rōt), Elihu (1845—1937), Am. lawyer and statesman.

Ropes (rōps), John Codman (1836—99), Am. lawyer and military historian.   [lithographer.

Rops (rō), Félicien (1833—98), Belgian etcher, painter, and

Rosa (rō′zä), Salvator (1615—73), It. painter, of Neapolitan school.   [dictator.

Rosas (dä rō′säs), Juan Manuel de (1793—1877), Argentine

Roscellinus (ros-e-li′nus) (also called Roscelin and Rucelin) (b. c1050), Fr. scholastic philosopher.

Roscius (rosh′ius), Quintus (d. c62 B.C.), Rom. actor, esp. in comedy.

Roscoe (ros′kō), Sir Henry Enfield (1833—1915), Eng. chemist.

Roscommon (ros-kom′ọn), Wentworth Dillon, 4th Earl of (1633?—85), Br. poet (nephew of 1st Earl of Strafford).

Rosebery (rōz′bẹ-ri), Archibald Philip Primrose, 5th Earl of (1847—1929), Eng. statesman and author.

Rosecrans (rō′zẹ-kranz), William Starke (1819—98), Am. general.

Rosegger (rō′zeg-ẽr), Peter (1843—1918), Austrian novelist.

Rosellini (rō-zel-lē′nē), Ippolito (1800—43), It. Egyptologist.

Rosenkranz (rō′zẹn-kränts), Johann Karl Friedrich (1805—79), Ger. philosopher.

Rose of Lima (rōz), Saint (1586—1617), Peruvian ascetic, first American saint.

Rosmini-Serbati (ros-mē′nē-ser-bä′tē), Antonio (1797—1855), It. philosopher.

Rosny (rō-nē), J. H. Pseudonym of the brothers Joseph Henri Honoré Boëx ("J. H. Rosny, aîné") (1856—1940) and Séraphin Justin François Boëx ("J. H. Rosny, jeune") (1859—   ), Fr. collaborating novelists, born in Belgium.

Ross (rôs or ros), Mrs. Betsy (Elizabeth Griscom, Mrs. Ross, Mrs. Ashburn, Mrs. Claypoole) (1752—1836), Am. woman (upholsterer in Philadelphia), maker of first U. S. flag.

Ross, Edward Alsworth (1866—   ), Am. sociologist.

Ross, Sir James Clark (1800—62), Eng. naval officer, and arctic and antarctic explorer (nephew of Sir John).

Ross, Sir John (1777—1856), Br. naval officer and arctic explorer.

Ross, Robert (1766—1814), Eng. general, who captured Washington, D. C., in 1814.

Ross, Sir Ronald (1857—1932), Br. physician and bacteriologist, specialist in tropical diseases.

Rosselli (ros-sel′lē), Cosimo (1439—1507), Florentine painter.

Rossellino (ros-sel-lē′nō), Antonio (real name Antonio di Matteo di Domenico Gambarelli) (1427—78?), It. sculptor and architect (brother of Bernardo).

Rossellino, Bernardo (real name Bernardo di Matteo di Domenico Gambarelli) (1409—64), It. sculptor and architect.

Rossetti (rō-set′ē), Christina Georgina (1830—94), Eng. poet (sister of Dante G.).

Rossetti, Dante Gabriel (1828—82), Eng. poet and painter.

Rossetti, William Michael (1829—1919), Eng. critic and editor (brother of Dante G.).

Rossi (ros′sē), Count Pellegrino (1787—1848), It. economist and statesman.

Rossini (ros-sē′nē), Gioacchino Antonio (1792—1868), It. operatic composer.

Rostand (ros-tän′), Edmond (1868—1918), Fr. dramatist.

Rostopchin (ros-top′chēn), Count Fedor Vasilevich (1763—1826), Russ. general, military governor of Moscow in 1812.

Roswitha (ros′vē″tä). See *Hroswitha.*

Rotch (rōch), Abbott Lawrence (1861—1912), Am. meteorologist.

Rothenstein (rō′tẹn-stīn), Sir William (1872—1945), Eng. painter and draftsman.

Rothermere (roₜH′ẽr-mēr), Harold Sidney Harmsworth, 1st Viscount (1868—1940), Eng. newspaper publisher (brother of Viscount Northcliffe).

Rothschild (roths′child, Ger. rōt′shilt), Mayer Amschel (c1743—1812), Ger. Jewish banker, of Frankfort-on-the-Main, founder of the European banking-house of Rothschild.

Rotrou (dẽ rō-trō), Jean de (1609—50), Fr. dramatist.

Roubillac or **Roubiliac** (rö-bē-yåk′), Louis François (1695—1762), Fr. sculptor, in England.

Rouget de Lisle (rö-zhä dẽ lēl), Claude Joseph (1760—1836), Fr. military engineer, writer of the "Marseillaise."

Rousseau (rö-sō), Jean Jacques (1712—78), Swiss-Fr. philosopher and author.

Rousseau, Pierre Étienne Théodore (1812—67), Fr. landscape-painter.

Roux (rö), Pierre Paul Émile (1853—1933), Fr. physician and bacteriologist.

Rovigo (dẽ rō-vē-gō), Duc de. See *Savary, A. J. M. R.*

Rowan (rō′an), Stephen Clegg (1808—90), Am. admiral, born in Ireland.

Rowe (rō), Nicholas (1674—1718), Eng. dramatist and poet.

Rowland (rō′lạnd), Henry Augustus (1848—1901), Am. physicist.

Rowlandson (rō′lạnd-sọn), Thomas (1756—1827), Eng. artist, noted as illustrator and caricaturist.

Rowley (rou′li), William (1585?—1642?), Eng. dramatist.

Roy (roi), Rob. See *Macgregor, Robert.*

Royce (rois), Josiah (1855—1916), Am. philosopher and educator.

Royer-Collard (rwo-yä-ko-lär), Pierre Paul (1763—1845), Fr. statesman and philosopher.

Rozhdestvenski (rozh-dest-ven′skẹ), Zinivi Petrovich (1848—1909), Russ. admiral.

Rubens (rö′benz), Peter Paul (1577—1640), Flemish painter.

Rubinstein (rö′bin-stīn), Anton (1829—94), Russ. pianist and composer.

Rückert (rük′ẽrt), Friedrich (1788—1866), Ger. poet and translator.

Rudagi (rö′dä-gē) (d. c950), Pers. poet.

Rude (rüd), François (1784—1855), Fr. sculptor.

Rudini (rö-dē-nē′), Antonio Starabba, Marchese di (1839—1908), It. statesman.

Rudolf or **Rudolph** (rö′dolf) (Duke of Burgundy) (d. 936), king of the Franks (923—936) (successor and son-in-law of Robert I.).

Rudolf I. or **Rudolph I.** (of Hapsburg) (1218—91), king of Germany (1273—91).

Rudolf II. or **Rudolph II.** (1552—1612), emperor of Holy Roman Empire (1576—1612), and king of Bohemia (1576—1611) and of Hungary (1576—1608) (son of Emperor Maximilian II.).

Rueda (dä rọ-ā′ₜHä), Lope de (d. c1565), Sp. actor and dramatist.

Ruffo (röf′fō), Fabrizio (1744—1827), It. cardinal and politician.

Ruhmkorff (röm′kôrf) or **Rühmkorff** (rüm′kôrf), Heinrich Daniel (1803—77), Ger.-Fr. mechanician, inventor of Ruhmkorff coil.

Ruisdael or **Ruisdaal.** See *Ruysdael.*

Ruiz (rö-ēth′), Juan (fl. c1350), Sp. priest and poet.

Rumford (rum′fọrd), Count. See *Thompson, Sir Benjamin.*

Runeberg (rö′nẹ-ber-y′), Johan Ludvig (1804—77), Finnish poet, writing in Swedish.

Runjeet Singh. See *Ranjit Singh.*

Rupert (rö′pẽrt) (Count Palatine of the Rhine, later Duke of Cumberland, called Prince Rupert) (1619—82), cavalry leader in royalist service in English civil war, and admiral under Charles II. of England, born at Prague (son of Elector Frederick V. of the Palatinate, and nephew of Charles I. of England).

Rupert (in German, Rupprecht, pron. rö′precht) (1869—   ), crown-prince of Bavaria (1913—18), and Ger. field-marshal.

Rurik (rö′rik) (d. 879), Scand. prince, founder of the Russian monarchy.

Rush (rush), Benjamin (1745—1813), Am. physician and patriot.

Rush, James (1786—1869), Am. physician and writer (son of Benjamin).

Rush, Richard (1780—1859), Am. statesman and diplomatist (son of Benjamin).

Ruskin (rus′kin), John (1819—1900), Eng. author, art critic, and social reformer.

Russell (rus′el), Bertrand Arthur William Russell, 3d Earl (1872—   ), Eng. philosophical and mathematical writer (grandson of 1st Earl Russell).

Russell, Charles Edward (1860—1941), Am. writer.

Russell, George William ("A. E.") (1867—1935), Ir. poet, misc. writer, and painter.

Russell, Henry Norris (1877—   ), Am. astronomer.

Russell, John Russell, 1st Earl (Lord John Russell) (1792—1878), Eng. statesman and author.

Russell, William (Lord Russell) (1639—83), Eng. statesman, beheaded on charge of complicity in the Rye House Plot.

Russell, William Clark (1844—1911), Eng. writer, esp. of sea tales.

Russell, Sir William Howard (1820—1907), Br. war correspondent.

Russell of Killowen (kil-ō′en), Charles Russell, Baron (1832—1900), Ir. jurist, lord chief justice of England (1894—1900).

Rutebeuf (rüt-bêf) (fl. 1245—85), Fr. poet.

Rutherford (ruₜH′ẽr-fọrd), Mark. Pseudonym of W. H. White.

Rutherford of Nelson, Ernest Rutherford, Baron (1871—1937), Eng. physicist, born in New Zealand.

Ruthven (röth′vẹn or riv′ẹn), John. See *Gowrie, 3d Earl of.*

Rutland (rut′lạnd), John James Robert Manners, 7th Duke of (Lord John Manners) (1818—1906), Eng. politician.

Rutledge (rut′lej), Edward (1749—1800), Am. patriot (brother of John).

Rutledge, John (1739—1800), Am. statesman and jurist, associate justice of U. S. Supreme Court (1789—91).

Ruysbroek (vän rois′brük), Jan van (1293—1381), Dutch mystic.

Ruysdael, Ruisdael, or **Ruisdaal** (vän rois′däl), Jacob van (1628?—82), Dutch landscape-painter.

Ruyter (dẽ roi′tẽr), Michel Adriaanszoon de (1607—76), Dutch admiral.

Ryder (rī′dẽr), Albert Pinkham (1847—1917), Am. painter.

Rymer (rī′mẽr), Thomas (1641—1713), Eng. antiquary, critic, and misc. writer.

(variable) d̦ as d or j, ş as s or sh, ț as t or ch, z̧ as z or zh; o, F. cloche; ü, F. menu; c̆h, Sc. loch; ṅ, F. bonbon; ′, primary accent; ″, secondary accent; †, obsolete; <, from; +, and; =, equals. See also lists at beginning of book.

S

Saadi. See *Sadi.*

Sabatier (sȧ-bȧ-tyä), Paul (1854–1941), Fr. chemist.

Sabatier, Paul (1858–1928), Fr. theologian and historian.

Sabatini (sab-ȧ-tē′nē), Rafael (1875–   ), It.-Eng. historical novelist and misc. writer.

Sabellius (sȧ-bel′i-us) (fl. c220), presbyter and heresiarch, of northern Africa.

Sacheverell (sȧ-shev′ẹ-rẹl), Henry (1674?–1724), Eng. preacher and politician.

Sacheverell, William (1638–91), Eng. statesman.

Sachs (zäks), Hans (1494–1576), Ger. poet and misc. writer.

Sachs, Julius von (1832–97), Ger. botanist.

Sackville (sak′vil), George Sackville, later George Germain, 1st Viscount (1716–85), Eng. general and statesman.

Sackville. See *Dorset, Earl of.*

Sá de Miranda (dä sä dä mē-rän′dä), Francisco de (c1485–1558), Pg. poet, writing in Portuguese and Spanish.

Sadi or **Saadi** (sä′dē) (c1184–1291?), Pers. poet, writing in Persian and Arabic.

Sadler (sad′lẽr), Sir Ralph (1507–87), Eng. statesman.

Sagasta (sä-gäs′tä), Praxedes Mateo (1827–1903), Sp. statesman.

Sage (sāj), Russell (1816–1906), Am. financier.

Saint-Arnaud (dẽ sȧṅ-tär-nō), Armand Jacques Leroy de (1801–54), Fr. marshal.

St. Clair (sānt klâr), Arthur (1734–1818), Am. general, born in Scotland.

Saint-Cyr, Gouvion. See *Gouvion Saint-Cyr.*

Saint-Cyran (dẽ saṅ-sē-räṅ), Abbé de. See *Duvergier de Hauranne.*

Sainte-Aldegonde (dẽ saṅ-tȧl-dẽ-gôṅd), Philips van Marnix, Baron de (1538–98), Flemish writer and statesman.

Sainte-Beuve (saṅt-bẽv), Charles Augustin (1804–69), Fr. critic.

Saint-Évremond (dẽ saṅ-tävr-môṅ), Charles de Marguetel de Saint-Denis, Seigneur de (1613?–1703), Fr. author.

Saint-Gaudens (sānt-gȧ′dẹnz), Augustus (1848–1907), Am. sculptor, born in Ireland.

Saint-Hilaire (dẽ saṅ-tē-lâr), Augustin François César Prouvençal de (called Auguste de Saint-Hilaire) (1799–1853), Fr. botanist and traveler.

St. John (sānt jon), Henry. See *Bolingbroke, 1st Viscount.*

Saint-Just (dẽ saṅ-zhüst), Louis Antoine Léon de (1767–94), Fr. revolutionary leader.

Saint-Pierre, Bernardin de. See *Bernardin de Saint-Pierre.*

Saint-Saëns (saṅ-säṅs), Charles Camille (1835–1921), Fr. composer and pianist.

Saintsbury (sānts′bẹ-ri), George Edward Bateman (1845–1933), Eng. literary critic and historian.

Saint-Simon (sānt-sī′mọn, Fr. dẽ saṅ-sē-môṅ), Claude Henri de Rouvroy, Comte de (1760–1825), Fr. socialist and writer.

Saint-Simon, Louis de Rouvroy, Duc de (1675–1755), Fr. soldier, diplomatist, and writer of memoirs.

St. Vincent (sānt vin′sẹnt), John Jervis, Earl of (1735–1823), Eng. admiral.

Sakyamuni (sä-kyȧ-mö′nē). See *Buddha.*

Sala (sä′lȧ), George Augustus Henry (1828–95), Eng. journalist and misc. writer.

Saladin (sal′ȧ-din) (Salah-ed-Din Yusuf ibn Ayub) (1137–93), sultan of Egypt and Syria (1175?–93), capturer of Jerusalem and opponent of the crusaders.

Salandra (sä-län′drä), Antonio (1853–1931), It. statesman.

Saldanha (säl-dän′yä), João Carlos de Oliveira e Daun, Duke of (1791–1876), Pg. statesman and general (grandson of Marquis of Pombal).

Sale (sāl), George (c1697–1736), Eng. Orientalist.

Salisbury (sâlz′bẹ-ri), Robert Cecil, 1st Earl of (1563?–1612), Eng. statesman (son of 1st Baron Burghley).

Salisbury, Robert Arthur Talbot Gascoyne Cecil, 3d Marquis of (1830–1903), Eng. statesman.

Sallust (sal′ust) (Caius Sallustius Crispus) (86–34 B.C.), Rom. historian.

Salviati (säl-vyä′tē), Antonio (1816–90), It. specialist in mosaic work and glass-making, reviver of Venetian glass industry.

Salvini (säl-vē′nē), Tommaso (1829–1916), It. tragedian.

Samain (sȧ-maṅ), Albert Victor (1858–1900), Fr. poet.

Samoset (sam′ọ-set, also sȧ-mos′et) (fl. 1621–53), Am. Indian, friend of Plymouth colonists.

Sampson (samp′sọn), William Thomas (1840–1902), Am. admiral.

Sancroft (sang′krôft), William (1617–93), Eng. divine, nonjuring archbishop of Canterbury.

Sand (sand, Fr. sänd), George. Pseudonym of Mme. Dudevant.

Sandburg (sand′bẽrg), Carl (1878–   ), Am. poet.

Sandeau (sän-dō), Léonard Sylvain Jules (1811–83), Fr. novelist.

Sandrocottus (san-drọ-kot′us). See *Chandragupta.*

Sandys (sandz), Edwin (1516?–88), Eng. archbishop.

Sandys, George (1578–1644), Eng. traveler and poet (son of Edwin).

Sangallo (dä säng-gäl′lō), Antonio da ("the elder," real name Antonio Giamberti) (1455?–1534), It. architect and military engineer (brother of Giuliano).

Sangallo, Antonio da ("the younger," real name Antonio Cordiani) (1485?–1546), It. architect (nephew of Giuliano, and of Antonio, 1455?–1534).

Sangallo, Francesco da (real name Francesco Giamberti) (1493?–1570?), It. sculptor (son of Giuliano).

Sangallo, Giuliano da (real name Giuliano Giamberti) (1445–1516), It. architect, sculptor, and military engineer.

Sankey (sang′ki), Ira David (1840–1908), Am. singer and hymn-writer, associated in evangelistic work with D. L. Moody.

San Martín (dä sän mär-tēn′), José de (1778–1850), Argentine general and statesman, liberator of Chile and Peru from Spanish rule.

Sannazaro (sän-nä-dzä′rō), Jacopo (1458–1530), It. poet.

San Sepolcro (dä sän sä-pōl′krō), Piero da. See *Francesca, Piero della.*

Sanson (sän-sôṅ), Charles Henri (b. 1739 or 1740), public executioner of Paris, executed Louis XVI. (1793) (the office of executioner was hereditary in the Sanson family).

Sansovino (sän-sō-vē′nō), Andrea (real name Andrea Contucci) (1460–1529), It. sculptor and architect.

Sansovino, Jacopo (real name Jacopo Tatti) (1477?–1570), It. sculptor and architect.

Santa Anna or **Santa Ana** (dä sän′tä ä′nä), Antonio López de (1795–1876), Mex. general and politician.

Santa Cruz (sän′tä krôth), Álvaro de Bazán, Marquis of (1526–88), Sp. admiral.

Santa Cruz (sän′tä krös), Andrés (c1794–1865), Bolivian general and politician.

Santander (sän-tän-där′), Francisco de Paula (1792–1840), Colombian general and statesman.

Santayana (san-tȧ-yä′nȧ), George (1863–   ), Am. poet, essayist, and philosophical writer, born in Spain.

Santerre (sän-târ), Antoine Joseph (1752–1809), Fr. revolutionist and general.

Santi (sän′tē). See *Raphael.*

Santillana (sän-tē-lyä′nä), Íñigo López de Mendoza, Marquis of (1398–1458), Sp. poet.

Santos-Dumont (sän-tos-dü-môṅ), Alberto (1873–1932), Brazilian aëronautic inventor in France.

Sanzio (sän′tsē-ō). See *Raphael.*

Sapor II. (sā′pọr) or **Shapur II.** (shä-pör′) ("the Great") (310?–379?), king of Persia (310?–379?).

Sappho (saf′ō) (fl. c600 B.C.), Gr. lyric poetess, of Lesbos.

Sarasate y Navascués (dä sä-rä-sä′tä ē nä-väs-kō-ās′), Pablo Martín Melitón de (1844–1908), Sp. violinist.

Sarazin. See *Sarrazin.*

Sarcey (sär-sā), Francisque (1828–99), Fr. dramatic critic.

Sardanapalus (sär″dȧ-nȧ-pā′lus). See *Asurbanipal.*

Sardou (sär-dö), Victorien (1831–1908), Fr. dramatist.

Sargent (sär′jẹnt), Charles Sprague (1841–1927), Am. arboriculturist.

Sargent, John Singer (1856–1925), Am. painter (esp. of portraits) in England, born in Italy.

Sargon I. (sär′gon) (fl. c3800 or c2800 or c2500 B.C.), king of Babylonia.

Sargon II. (d. 705 B.C.), king of Assyria (722–705 B.C.).

Sarmiento (sär-myen′tō), Domingo Faustino (1811–88),

Argentine educator and statesman, president of Argentina (1868—74).

Sarpi (sär′pē), Pietro, known as Paolo (Fra Paolo) (1552—1623), Venetian patriot, scholar, and historian.

Sarrail (sà-rä-y′), Maurice Paul Emmanuel (1856—1929), Fr. general.

Sarrazin or **Sarazin** (sà-rà-zaṅ), Jacques (1588?—1660), Fr. sculptor.

Sarsfield (särs′fēld), Patrick (Earl of Lucan) (d. 1693), Ir. Jacobite general.

Sartain (sär-tān′), John (1808—97), Eng.-Am. engraver.

Sarto (del sär′tō), Andrea del (properly Andrea d'Agnolo) (1486—1531), Florentine painter.

Saturninus (sat-ėr-nī′nus), Lucius Apuleius (d. 100 B.C.), Rom. politician.

Saur, Christopher. See *Sower*.

Saussure (dė sō-sür), Horace Bénédict de (1740—99), Swiss naturalist and physicist.

Savage (sav′áj), Richard (d. 1743), Eng. poet.

Savary (sà-và-rē), Anne Jean Marie René (Duc de Rovigo) (1774—1833), Fr. general and politician.

Savigny (fon sä′vin-yē), Friedrich Karl von (1779—1861), Ger. jurist.

Savile (sav′il), George. See *Halifax, 1st Marquis of*.

Savonarola (sä″vō-nä-rō′lä), Girolamo (1452—98), It. monk, reformer, and martyr.

Saxe (saks), John Godfrey (1816—87), Am. humorous poet.

Saxe (dė säks), Maurice, Comte de (orig. Moritz, Graf von Sachsen) (1696—1750), Fr. marshal, born in Germany.

Saxo Grammaticus (sak′sō gra-mat′i-kus) (c1150—c1206), Dan. chronicler.

Sayce (sās), Archibald Henry (1846—1933), Eng. clergyman and Orientalist.

Saye and Sele (sā, sēl), William Fiennes, 1st Viscount (1582—1662), Eng. statesman.

Scævola (sev′ō-lä), Caius Mucius. A legendary hero of ancient Rome who, when Porsena was besieging Rome, entered that king's camp to kill him, but slew by mistake the royal secretary. Threatened with death by fire, Scævola thrust his right hand into the fire, and held it there without flinching. This so impressed Porsena that he ordered Scævola released; and when told by Scævola that there were 300 other Roman youths sworn to kill him, he made peace with the Romans and withdrew his army.

Scala (del′lä skä′lä), Can Grande della (1291—1329), lord of Verona (1311—29) and Ghibelline leader, patron of Dante.

Scaliger (skal′i-jėr), Joseph Justus (1540—1609), Fr. scholar (son of Julius C.).

Scaliger, Julius Cæsar (1484—1558), It. scholar, critic, philosopher, and scientist.

Scanderbeg or **Skanderbeg** (skan′dėr-beg) (in Turkish, Iskander Bey, 'Prince Alexander,' real name George, or Giorgio, Castriota) (1403?—67?), Albanian patriot and leader against the Turks, lord of Albania and Epirus (1461—67?).

Scarlatti (skär-lät′tē), Alessandro (1659—1725), It. musical composer.

Scarpa (skär′pä), Antonio (1747—1832), It. anatomist and surgeon.

Scarron (skà-rôṅ), Paul (1610—60), Fr. novelist, dramatist, and burlesque poet.

Schadow (shä′dō), Johann Gottfried (1764—1850), Ger. sculptor.

Schaff (shäf), Philip (1819—93), Am. theologian and church historian, born in Switzerland.

Schamyl. See *Shamyl*.

Scharnhorst (fon shärn′hôrst), Gerhard Johann David von (1755—1813), Prussian general.

Scharwenka (shär-veng′kä), Franz Xaver (1850—1924), Ger. pianist and composer.

Schaudinn (shou′din), Fritz (1871—1906), Ger. zoölogist and biologist.

Scheele (shä′le), Karl Wilhelm (1742—86), Swed. chemist.

Scheffel (fon shef′ęl), Joseph Viktor von (1826—86), Ger. poet and novelist.

Scheffer (shef′ėr, Fr. she-fär), Ary (1795—1858), Fr. painter, born in Holland.

Scheidemann (shī′dė-män), Philipp (1865—1939), Ger. political leader (Social Democrat), premier (1919).

Schelling (shel′ing), Ernest Henry (1876—1939), Am. pianist and composer.

Schelling, Friedrich Wilhelm Joseph von (1775—1854), Ger. philosopher.

Schenkel (sheng′kęl), Daniel (1813—85), Swiss-Ger. Protestant theologian.

Schiaparelli (skyä-pä-rel′lē), Giovanni Virginio (1835—1910), It. astronomer.

Schiff (shif), Jacob Henry (1847—1920), Ger.-Am. financier and philanthropist.

Schiller (fon shil′ėr), Johann Christoph Friedrich von (1759—1805), Ger. poet, dramatist, and misc. writer.

Schillings (fon shil′ings), Max von (1868—1933), Ger. musical composer.

Schinkel (shing′kęl), Karl Friedrich (1781—1841), Ger. architect and painter.

Schlegel (fon shlä′gel), August Wilhelm von (1767—1845), Ger. poet, translator, and critic.

Schlegel, Karl Wilhelm Friedrich von (1772—1829), Ger. critic and scholar (brother of August W.).

Schleiden (shlī′dęn), Matthias Jakob (1804—81), Ger. botanist.

Schleiermacher (shlī′ėr-mä″chėr), Friedrich Ernst Daniel (1768—1834), Ger. theologian and philosopher.

Schley (slī), Winfield Scott (1839—1911), Am. admiral.

Schliemann (shlē′män), Heinrich (1822—90), Ger. archæologist.

Schmidt (shmit), Kaspar ("Max Stirner") (1806—56), Ger. philosophical writer.

Schnitzler (shnits′lėr), Arthur (1862—1931), Austrian physician, dramatist, and novelist.

Schoeffer (shėf′ėr). See *Schöffer*.

Schoenberg (shėn′berċh). See *Schönberg*.

Schoenlein (shėn′līn). See *Schönlein*.

Schöffer (shėf′ėr), Peter (c1425—1502?), Ger. printer, associated with Fust.

Schofield (skō′fēld), John McAllister (1831—1906), Am. general.

Schomberg (shom′bėrg, Ger. fon shom′berċh), Friedrich Hermann von (name orig. Schönberg, known in France as Frédéric Armand de Schomberg, and in England as Frederick Herman, Duke of Schomberg) (1615—90), Ger. soldier in various foreign services (marshal of France, and general under William III. of England).

Schomburgk (shom′bėrk, Ger. shom′börk), Sir Robert Hermann (1804—65), Ger.-Eng. explorer in British Guiana.

Schönberg (shėn′berċh), Arnold (1874—   ), Austrian musical composer.

Schongauer (shon′gou″ėr), Martin (also called Hipsch Martin, and Martin Schön) (c1446—c1488), Ger. painter and engraver.

Schönlein (shėn′līn), Johann Lukas (1793—1864), Ger. physician.

Schopenhauer (shō′pęn-hou″ėr), Arthur (1788—1860), Ger. philosopher.

Schouler (skō′lėr), James (1839—1920), Am. lawyer and historian.

Schreiber (shrī′bėr), Lady (Charlotte Elizabeth Bertie, Lady Guest) (1812—95), Eng. Welsh scholar.

Schreyer (shrī′ėr), Adolf (1828—99), Ger. painter.

Schubert (shō′bėrt), Franz Peter (1797—1828), Austrian musical composer.

Schumann (shō′män), Robert Alexander (1810—56), Ger. musical composer.

Schumann, Frau (Klara Josephine Wieck) (1819—96), Ger. pianist (wife of Robert A.).

Schumann-Heink (-hīngk′), Mme. (Ernestine Rössler, Frau Heink, Frau Schumann, Mrs. Rapp) (1861—1936). Austrian-Am. operatic contralto singer.

Schurman (shùr′mạn), Jacob Gould (1854—1942), Am. educator and diplomatist, born in Canada.

Schurz (shùrts), Carl (1829—1906), Ger.-Am. general, statesman, and publicist.

Schuyler (skī′lėr), Philip John (1733—1804), Am. general and statesman.

Schwab (shwäb), Charles M. (1862—1939), Am. steel manufacturer and capitalist.

Schwab (shväp), Gustav (1792—1850), Ger. poet.

Schwann (shvän), Theodor (1810—82), Ger. physiologist, in Belgium.

Schwarz (shvärts), Berthold (orig. Konstantin Anklitzen) (fl. 14th cent.), Ger. monk and alchemist, reputed inventor of gunpowder and firearms.

Schwarzenberg (fon shvär′tsen-berċh), Karl Philipp, Prince von (1771—1820), Austrian field-marshal.

Schwatka (shwot′kạ), Frederick (1849—92), Am. explorer.

Schweinfurth (shvīn′fûrt), Georg August (1836—1925), Ger. explorer in Africa, born in Russia.

Schwenkfeld or **Schwenckfeld** (fon shvengk′felt), Kaspar von (1490—1561), Ger. Protestant reformer and mystic.

Schwerin (fon shvä-rēn′), Kurt Christoph, Graf von (1684—1757), Prussian field-marshal.

Schwind (fon shvint), Moritz von (1804—71), Austrian-Ger. painter and illustrator.

Scipio (sip′i-ō) (Publius Cornelius Scipio Africanus Major, "Scipio the Elder") (237 or 234—183 B.C.), Rom. general, victor over Hannibal.

Scipio (Publius Cornelius Scipio Æmilianus Africanus Minor, "Scipio the Younger") (c185—129 B.C.), Rom. general, besieger and destroyer of Carthage (son of L. Æ. Paulus, and adopted son of a son of Scipio the Elder).

Scopas (skō′pạs) (fl. c395—c350 B.C.), Gr. sculptor and architect.

Scoresby (skōrz′bi), William (1760—1829), Eng. sea-captain in arctic whale-fishery.

Scoresby, William (1789—1857), Eng. arctic explorer, scientific writer, and divine (son of William Scoresby, 1760—1829).

Scot (skot), Michael (c1175—c1235), Sc. mathematician, scholar, and astrologer.

Scott (skot), Sir George Gilbert (1811—78), Eng. architect.

Scott, Hugh Lenox (1853—1934), Am. general.

Scott, John. See *Eldon, 1st Earl of.*

Scott, Michael (1789—1835), Br. novelist.

Scott, Robert Falcon (1868—1912), Eng. naval officer and antarctic explorer.

Scott, Sir Walter (1771—1832), Sc. novelist and poet.

Scott, Winfield (1786—1866), Am. general.

Scotus (skō′tus). See *Duns Scotus* and *Erigena.*

Scriabin (skrya′ben). See *Skryabin.*

Scribe (skrēb), Augustin Eugène (1791—1861), Fr. dramatist.

Scudéry (dė skü-dā-rē), Madeleine de (1607—1701), Fr. novelist.

Seaman (sē′mạn), Sir Owen (1861—1936), Eng. humorist and editor.

Search (sėrch), Edward. Pseudonym of Abraham Tucker.

Sebastian (se-bas′chạn), Saint (d. c288?), Rom. soldier and Christian martyr, protector against pestilence. According to legend, he was bound to a stake and shot with arrows, but surviving was beaten to death.

Sebastian (in Portuguese, Sebastião, pron. sā-bäs-tẹ-ouṅ′) (1554—78), king of Portugal (1557—78).

Seddon (sed′ọn), Richard John (1845—1906), New Zealand statesman (born in England), premier of New Zealand (1893—1906).

Sedgwick (sej′wik), John (1813—64), Am. general.

Seeley (sē′li), Sir John Robert (1834—95), Eng. historian.

Segantini (sā-gän-tē′nē), Giovanni (1858—99), It. painter, born in Tyrol.

Ségur (dė sā-gür), Louis Philippe, Comte de (1753—1830), Fr. diplomatist and historian.

Ségur, Philippe Paul, Comte de (1780—1873), Fr. general and historian (son of Louis P.).

Seidl (zī′dl), Anton (1850—98), musical conductor, born in Hungary.

Sejanus (sẹ-jā′nus), Lucius Ælius (d. A.D. 31), Rom. soldier, favorite of Emperor Tiberius.

Selden (sel′dẹn), John (1584—1654), Eng. jurist and scholar.

Seleucus I. (se-lū′kus) (surnamed Nicator) (c358—281? B.C.), Macedonian general of Alexander the Great, and ruler and conqueror in Babylonia, Syria, etc.

Selim I. (sē′lim or se-lēm′) (c1465—1520), sultan of Turkey (1512—20) (son of Bajazet II.).

Selim III. (1761—1808), sultan of Turkey (1789—1807) (nephew of Abdul-Hamid I.).

Selkirk (sel′kėrk), Alexander (orig. Alexander Selcraig) (1676—1721), marooned Sc. sailor, supposed prototype of Robinson Crusoe.

Sella (sel′lä), Quintino (1827—84), It. statesman and financier.

Selous (sẹ-lös′), Frederick Courteney (1851—1917), Eng. traveler, hunter, and soldier, in Africa.

Sembrich (zem′briċh), Marcella (professional name of Praxede Marcelline Kochanska, Frau Stengel) (1858—1935), Austrian (Polish) operatic soprano singer.

Semler (zem′lėr), Johann Salomo (1725—91), Ger. Biblical critic and church historian.

Semmelweis (zem′ẹl-vīs), Ignaz Philipp (1818—65), Hung. physician.

Semmes (semz), Raphael (1809—77), Am. Confederate naval officer.

Semonides (sẹ-mon′i-dēz) **of Amorgos.** See *Simonides of Amorgos.*

Sénancour (dė sā-nän-kör), Étienne Pivert de (1770—1846), Fr. author.

Seneca (sen′ẹ-kạ), Lucius (or Marcus) Annæus (c54 B.C.—A.D. c39), Rom. rhetorician.

Seneca, Lucius Annæus (c4 B.C.—A.D. 65), Rom. philosopher and tragedy-writer (son of L. A. Seneca, c54 B.C.—A.D. c39).

Senior (sē′nyọr), Nassau William (1790—1864), Eng. political economist and misc. writer.

Sennacherib (se-nak′ẹ-rib) (d. 681 B.C.), king of Assyria (705—681 B.C.) (son of Sargon II.).

Serao (sā-rä′ō), Matilde (Signora Scarfoglio) (1856—1927), It. novelist, born in Greece.

Serapion (se-rä′pi-ọn), Saint (fl. c350), bishop, of northern Egypt.

Serlio (sär′lē-ō), Sebastiano (1475—1554), It. architect, and writer on architecture.

Serpa Pinto (sär′pä pēň′tọ), Alexandre Alberto da Rocha (1846—1900), Pg. army officer, and explorer in Africa.

Serra (ser′rä), Miguel José (commonly known as Junípero Serra) (1713—84), Sp. Franciscan missionary to Indians of California.

Serrano y Domínguez (ser-rä′nō ē dō-mēn′gäth), Francisco (Duke de la Torre) (1810—85), Sp. general and statesman.

Sertorius (sėr-tō′ri-us), Quintus (d. 72 B.C.), Rom. general, and opponent of Rome in Spain.

Servandoni (ser-vän-dō′nē), Gian Gerolamo Niccolò, or Jean Jérôme Nicolas (1695—1766), It. designer, painter, and architect, in France.

Servetus (sėr-vē′tus), Michael (real name Miguel Serveto) (1511—53), Sp. physician and theologian, burned as heretic at Geneva.

Servius Tullius (sėr′vi-us tul′i-us) (d. 534 B.C.), 6th (legendary) king of Rome (578—534 B.C.) (son-in-law of Tarquinius Priscus).

Seth (seth), Andrew (full name Andrew Seth Pringle-Pattison) (1856—1931), Sc. philosophical writer.

Seton (sē′tọn), Ernest Thompson (orig. Ernest Evan Seton Thompson) (1860—1946), Eng. writer and illustrator, in America.

Settignano, Desiderio da. See *Desiderio da Settignano.*

Settle (set′l), Elkanah (1648—1724), Eng. poet and playwright.

Seurat (sė-rä), Georges Pierre (1859—91), Fr. painter.

Severus (se-vē′rus), Alexander. See *Alexander Severus.*

Severus, Lucius Septimius (146—211), Rom. emperor (193—211).

Severus, Sulpicius. See *Sulpicius Severus.*

Sevier (se-vēr′), John (1745—1815), Am. pioneer, soldier, and politician.

Sévigné (dė sā-vē-nyä), Marquise de (Marie de Rabutin-Chantal) (1626—96), Fr. letter-writer.

Sewall (sū′ạl), Samuel (1652—1730), Am. jurist, born in England.

Seward (sū′ạrd), William Henry (1801—72), Am. statesman.

Sextus Empiricus (seks′tus em-pir′i-kus) (fl. c200), Gr. physician and Skeptic philosopher.

Sextus Tarquinius (tär-kwin′i-us). See *Lucretia.*

---

fat, fāte, fär, fȧll, ȧsk, fāre; net, mē, hėr; pin, pīne; not, nōte, mȯve, nȯr; up, lūte, pu̇ll; oi, oil; ou, out; (lightened) aviạry, ẹlect, agọny, intọ, ụnite; (obscured) errạnt, operạ, ardẹnt, actọr, natụre; ch, chip; g, go; th, thin; ᴛʜ, then; y, you;

Seydlitz (fon zīt′lits), Friedrich Wilhelm von (1721—73), Prussian cavalry general.

Seymour (sē′mŏr), Edward. See *Somerset, 1st Duke of.*

Seymour, Sir Edward Hobart (1840—1929), Eng. admiral.

Seymour, Horatio (1810—86), Am. political leader.

Seymour, Jane (c1510—37), third wife of Henry VIII. of England, and mother of Edward VI.

Sforza (sfôr′tsä), Francesco (1401—66), It. condottiere, and duke of Milan (1450—66) (son of Giacomuzzo A.).

Sforza, Giacomuzzo (or Muzio) Attendolo (1369—1424), It. condottiere.

Sforza, Lodovico (called "the Moor") (1451—1508), duke of Milan (1494—1500) (son of Francesco).

Shackleton (shak′l-ton), Sir Ernest Henry (1874—1922), Br. antarctic explorer.

Shadwell (shad′wel), Thomas (1642?—92), Eng. dramatist.

Shafter (shaf′tẽr), William Rufus (1835—1906), Am. general.

Shaftesbury (shâfts′bẹ-ri), Anthony Ashley Cooper, 1st Earl of (1621—83), Eng. statesman.

Shaftesbury, Anthony Ashley Cooper, 3d Earl of (1671—1713), Eng. moral philosopher (grandson of 1st Earl).

Shaftesbury, Anthony Ashley Cooper, 7th Earl of (1801—85), Eng. philanthropist.

Shakspere or **Shakespeare** (shāk′spẽr), William (1564—1616), Eng. poet and dramatist.

Shaler (shā′lẽr), Nathaniel Southgate (1841—1906), Am. geologist.

Shaliapin (shȧ-lyä′pẹn), Fedor Ivanovich (1873—1938), Russ. operatic bass singer.

Shalmaneser II. (shal-mȧ-nē′zẽr) (d. 825? B.C.), king of Assyria (860—825? B.C.).

Shamyl or **Schamyl** (shä′mil) (1797—1871), Caucasian military and religious leader against Russia.

Shannon (shan′on), Sir James Jebusa (1862—1923), Eng. portrait-painter, born in U. S.

Shapur II. See *Sapor II.*

Sharp (shärp), James (1618—79), Sc. prelate, archbishop of St. Andrews.

Sharp, William ("Fiona Macleod") (1855—1905), Sc. poet, critic, and writer of tales.

Shaughnessy (shȧ′nẹ-si), Thomas George Shaughnessy, 1st Baron (1853—1923), Can. railroad manager, born in U. S.

Shaw (shâ), George Bernard (1856—   ), Ir. dramatist, critic, and novelist. [humorist.

Shaw, Henry Wheeler ("Josh Billings") (1818—85), Am.

Shaw, Thomas Edward. See *Lawrence, Thomas Edward.*

Shays (shāz), Daniel (1747—1825), Am. insurgent.

Shearer (shēr′ẽr), Thomas (fl. c1788), Eng. furniture-designer.

Shedd (shed), William Greenough Thayer (1820—94), Am. Presbyterian theologian.

Sheil (shēl), Richard Lalor (1791—1851), Ir. politician, orator, and dramatist.

Shelburne (shel′bẽrn), Earl of. See *Lansdowne, 1st Marquis of.*

Shelley (shel′i), Percy Bysshe (1792—1822), Eng. poet.

Shelley, Mrs. (Mary Wollstonecraft Godwin) (1797—1851), Eng. author (wife of Percy B. Shelley, and daughter of William and Mary Godwin).

Shenstone (shen′ston), William (1714—63), Eng. poet.

Sheppard (shep′ärd), John, or Jack (1702—24), Eng. robber.

Shepstone (shep′ston), Sir Theophilus (1817—93), South African statesman, born in England.

Sheraton (sher′ȧ-ton), Thomas (1751—1806), Eng. cabinet-maker, furniture-designer, and writer.

Sherbrooke (shẽr′bruk), Robert Lowe, Viscount (1811—92), Eng. statesman.

Shere Ali Khan (shēr ä′lē kän) (1825—79), amir of Afghanistan (1863—79) (son of Dost Mohammed Khan).

Sheridan (sher′i-dan), Philip Henry (1831—88), Am. general.

Sheridan, Richard Brinsley Butler (1751—1816), Br. dramatist, orator, and politician.

Sherman (shẽr′man), James Schoolcraft (1855—1912), Am. politician, vice-president of U. S. (1909—12).

Sherman, John (1823—1900), Am. statesman (brother of William T.).

Sherman, Roger (1721—93), Am. patriot.

Sherman, Stuart Pratt (1881—1926), Am. educator and critic.

Sherman, William Tecumseh (1820—91), Am. general.

Shevchenko (shef-cheng′kŏ), Taras Grigorevich (1814—61), Russ. poet, of the Ukraine (Little Russia).

Shirlaw (shẽr′lâ), Walter (1838—1909), Am. painter, born in Scotland.

Shirley (shẽr′li), James (1596—1666), Eng. dramatist.

Shirley, William (1694—1771), Eng. general, and colonial governor of Massachusetts.

Shore (shōr), Jane (d. 1527), mistress of Edward IV. of England.

Shorthouse (shôrt′hous), Joseph Henry (1834—1903), Eng. novelist.

Shovel (shuv′l), Sir Cloudesley (also written Sir Clowdisley Shovell) (c1650—1707), Eng. admiral.

Shrewsbury (shrōz′bẹ-ri or shrōz′bẹ-ri), Charles Talbot, Duke of (1660—1718), Eng. statesman.

Shrewsbury, John Talbot, 1st Earl of (c1388—1453), Eng. military leader.

Shuster (shŏ′stẽr), William Morgan (1877—   ), Am. government official and publisher, treasurer-general of Persia (1911—12).

Shuvalov (shŏ-vä′lof), Count Petr Andreevich (1827—89), Russ. diplomatist.

Sibelius (si-bā′lẹ-ŭs), Jean Julius Christian (1865—   ), Finnish musical composer.

Sibert (sī′bẽrt), William Luther (1860—1935), Am. general and engineer.

Sickert (zik′ẽrt), Walter Richard (1860—1942), Ger.-Eng. painter and etcher.

Sickingen (fon zik′ing-ẹn), Franz von (1481—1523), Ger. knight, supporter of the Reformation.

Sickles (sik′lz), Daniel Edgar (1825—1914), Am. general.

Siddhartha (si-där′thä). See *Buddha.*

Siddons (sid′onz), Mrs. (Sarah Kemble) (1755—1831), Eng. actress (sister of John P. and Charles Kemble).

Sidgwick (sij′wik), Henry (1838—1900), Eng. philosopher and economist.

Sidmouth (sid′muth), Henry Addington, 1st Viscount (1757—1844), Eng. statesman.

Sidney or **Sydney** (sid′ni), Algernon (1622—83), Eng. politician and writer, beheaded on charge of treason.

Sidney, Sir Philip (1554—86), Eng. poet, romance-writer, and soldier.

Siebold (fon zē′bolt), Philipp Franz von (1796—1866), Ger. naturalist and explorer in Japan.

Siemens (fon zē′mẹns), Ernst Werner von (1816—92), Ger. electrical engineer and inventor.

Siemens (sē′mẹnz, Ger. zē′mẹns), Sir William (orig. Karl Wilhelm Siemens) (1823—83), Ger.-Eng. physicist, electrical engineer, and inventor (brother of E. W. von Siemens).

Siemering (zē′mẽr-ing), Rudolf (1835—1905), Ger. sculptor.

Sienkiewicz (syen-kyä′vich), Henryk (1846—1916), Pol. novelist.

Sievers (zē′fẽrs), Eduard (1850—1932), Ger. philologist.

Sieyès (syä-yes), Emmanuel Joseph, Comte (Abbé Sieyès) (1748—1836), Fr. ecclesiastic, statesman, and writer.

Sigel (sē′gel), Franz (1824—1902), Ger.-Am. general.

Sigismund (sij′is-mund, Ger. zē′gis-mŭnt) (1368—1437), emperor of the Holy Roman Empire (1411—37), and king of Hungary (1387—1437) and of Bohemia (1419—37) (brother of Emperor Wenceslaus).

Sigismund I. (sij′is-mund) (1467—1548), king of Poland (1506—48) (son of Casimir IV.).

Sigismund II. (Sigismund Augustus) (1520—72), king of Poland (1548—72) (son of Sigismund I.).

Sigismund III. (Sigismund Vasa) (1566—1632), king of Poland (1587—1632), and king of Sweden (1594—1604) (nephew of Sigismund II.).

Signorelli (sē-nyo-rel′lē), Luca (1441?—1523?), It. painter.

Sigourney (sig′ẽr-ni), Mrs. (Lydia Huntley) (1791—1865), Am. poet and misc. writer.

Sigsbee (sigz′bẹ), Charles Dwight (1845—1923), Am. admiral.

(variable) ḍ as d or j, ş as s or sh, ţ as t or ch, ҙ as z or zh; o, F. cloche; ü, F. menu; c̓h, Sc. loch; ṅ, F. bonbon; ′, primary accent; ″, secondary accent; †, obsolete; <, from; +, and; =, equals. See also lists at beginning of book.

Sill (sil), Edward Rowland (1841—87), Am. poet.

Silliman (sil'i-man), Benjamin (1779—1864), Am. scientist.

Silliman, Benjamin (1816—85), Am. chemist (son of Benjamin Silliman, 1779—1864).

Silverman (sil'vẽr-man), Joseph (1860—1930), Am. rabbi.

Simeon (sim'ẽ-on) (d. c927), Bulgarian emperor.

Simeon Stylites (stī-lī'tēz), Saint (c390—459), Syrian ascetic, first of the stylites, or pillar-hermits.

Simms (simz), William Gilmore (1806—70), Am. writer.

Simnel (sim'nel), Lambert (c1475—after 1534), Eng. impostor, personator of Earl of Warwick (nephew of Edward IV. and Richard III.) and pretender to the crown of England.

Simon (sē-môṅ), Jules (real name Jules François Simon Suisse) (1814—96), Fr. statesman, philosopher, and author.

Simon, Richard (1638—1712), Fr. priest and Biblical critic.

Simonides of Amorgos (sī-mon'i-dēz, a-môr'gos) (also called Semonides) (fl. c650 B.C.), Gr. poet.

Simonides of Ceos (sē'os) (556?—468? B.C.), Gr. lyric poet.

Simpson (simp'son), Sir James Young (1811—70), Sc. physician.

Sims (simz), James Marion (1813—83), Am. surgeon and gynecologist.

Sims, William Sowden (1858—1936), Am. admiral, born in Canada.

Sinclair (sing'klãr), May (18. . —1946), Eng. novelist.

Sinding (sin'ding), Christian (1856—1941), Norw. musical composer.

Sisley (sēs-lā), Alfred (1839—99), Fr. painter, of Eng. parentage.

Sismondi (dẽ sēs-môṅ-dē), Jean Charles Léonard Simonde de (1773—1842), Swiss historian and economist, writing in French.

Sitting Bull (1834?—90), Am. Indian chief.

Sixtus IV. (siks'tus) (Francesco della Rovere) (1414—84), It. ecclesiastic, pope (1471—84).

Sixtus V. (Felice Peretti) (1521—90), It. ecclesiastic, pope (1585—90).

Skanderbeg. See *Scanderbeg.*

Skeat (skēt), Walter William (1835—1912), Eng. clergyman and philologist.

Skelton (skel'ton), John (c1460—1529), Eng. poet.

Skinner (skin'ẽr), Otis (1858—1942), Am. actor.

Skobelev (skô'be-lyef), Mikhail Dmitrievich (1843—82), Russ. general.

Skryabin (skryä'bẽn), Aleksandr Nikolaevich (1872—1915), Russ. composer and pianist.

Slade (slād), Felix (1790—1868), Eng. art-collector, and patron of fine arts.

Slatin (fon slä'tēn), Rudolf Carl, Freiherr von (known as Slatin Pasha) (1857—1932), Austrian soldier and administrator in the British service in the Sudan.

Slidell (slī-del'), John (1793—1871), Am. legislator and Confederate commissioner.

Sloan (slōn), John (1871—   ), Am. painter and etcher.

Sloane (slōn), Sir Hans (1660—1753), Br. physician and naturalist.

Slocum (slō'kum), Henry Warner (1827—94), Am. general.

Sluter (slö'tẽr), Claus (d. 1406?), Flemish sculptor.

Smart (smärt), Benjamin Humphrey (c1786—1872), Eng. grammarian, lexicographer, and philosophical writer.

Smart, Christopher (1722—71), Eng. poet.

Smeaton (smē'ton), John (1724—92), Eng. civil engineer.

Smedley (smed'li), Francis Edward (called Frank Smedley) (1818—64), Eng. novelist.

Smerdis (smẽr'dis) (assumed name of Gaumata) (d. 521 B.C.), Magian usurper of Persian throne (522—521 B.C.), who pretended to be the brother, Smerdis (actually murdered by Cambyses), of King Cambyses. In despair of regaining the throne, Cambyses committed suicide; but the false Smerdis was surprised and killed by Darius Hystaspes and others, Darius succeeding to the throne.

Smetana (smet'a-nä), Friedrich (1824—84), Bohem. musical composer.

Smiles (smīlz), Samuel (1812—1904), Br. biographer and misc. writer.

Smith (smith), Adam (1723—90), Sc. political economist.

Smith, Albert Richard (1816—60), Eng. writer and public entertainer.

Smith, Alexander (1865—1922), Sc.-Am. chemist.

Smith, Alfred Emanuel (1873—1944), Am. political leader, governor of New York.

Smith, Arthur Donaldson (1864—1939), Am. explorer in Africa.

Smith, Edmund Kirby (1824—93), Am. Confederate general.

Smith, Francis Hopkinson (1838—1915), Am. civil engineer, artist, and novelist.

Smith, George (1840—76), Eng. Assyriologist.

Smith, Gerrit (1797—1874), Am. philanthropist and abolitionist.

Smith, Goldwin (1823—1910), Br. historian, essayist, and writer on politics.

Smith, Horace (properly Horatio Smith) (1779—1849), Eng. poet and misc. writer (brother of James).

Smith, James (1775—1839), Eng. poet and misc. writer.

Smith, John ("Captain John Smith") (1580—1631), Eng. adventurer, colonist in Virginia (1607), and explorer.

Smith, Joseph (1805—44), Am. 'prophet,' founder of Mormonism.

Smith, Sydney (1771—1845), Eng. divine, misc. writer, and wit.

Smith, William (1769—1839), Eng. geologist.

Smith, Sir William (1813—93), Eng. classical scholar and lexicographer.

Smith, William Robertson (1846—94), Br. Orientalist and Biblical scholar.

Smith, Sir William Sidney (1764—1840), Eng. admiral.

Smith-Dorrien (-dor'i-en), Sir Horace Lockwood (1858—1930), Eng. general.

Smithson (smith'son), James (in early life known as James Lewis Macie) (1765—1829), Eng. scientist, founder of the Smithsonian Institution in Washington, D. C.

Smollett (smol'et), Tobias George (1721—71), Br. novelist.

Smuts (smuts), Jan Christiaan (1870—   ), South African general and statesman.

Smyth (smīth), Dame Ethel Mary (1858—1944), Eng. musical composer.

Snaith (snāth), John Collis (1876—1936), Eng. novelist.

Snorri Sturluson (snor'rē stör'lö-son) (Snorre, or Snorro, Sturleson or Sturlason) (1179—1241), Icelandic historian and poet.

Snowden (snō'den), Philip Snowden, Viscount (1864—1937), Eng. journalist, labor leader, and cabinet minister.

Snyders (snī'dẽrs), Frans (1579—1657), Flemish painter.

Sobieski (sō-byes'kē). See *John III.* (of Poland).

Socinus (sō-sī'nus), Faustus (Fausto Sozzini) (1539—1604), It. Protestant theologian, in Poland (nephew of Lælius).

Socinus, Lælius (Lelio Sozzini) (1525—62), It. Protestant theologian.

Socrates (sok'ra-tēz) (469?—399 B.C.), Athenian philosopher.

Socrates (c380—after 439), Byzantine Gr. church historian.

Soddy (sod'i), Frederick (1877—   ), Eng. chemist.

Sodoma (sô'dō-mä) (real name Giovanni Antonio Bazzi) (1477—1549), It. painter.

Solís (dä sō-lēs'), Juan Díaz de (d. 1516), Sp. navigator.

Sologub (so-lo-göb'), Fedor (real name Fedor Kuzmich Teternikov) (1864—1927), Russ. author.

Solon (sō'lon) (c638—c558 B.C.), Athenian lawgiver, one of the seven sages of ancient Greece.

Solovev (so-lo-vyof'), Sergyey Mikhaylovich (1820—79), Russ. historian.

Solovev, Vladimir Sergyeevich (1853—1900), Russ. philosopher and sociologist (son of Sergyey M.).

Solyman I. (sol'i-man) or **Suleiman I.** (sö-lā-män') ("the Magnificent," also called Solyman II.) (1495?—1566), sultan of Turkey (1520—66) (son of Selim I.).

Somers (sum'ẽrz), John Somers (or Sommers), Baron (1651—1716), Eng. statesman and jurist.

Somerset (sum'ẽr-set), Edmund Beaufort, 2d Duke of (in Beaufort line) (d. 1455), Eng. soldier and statesman (grandson of John of Gaunt).

Somerset, Edward Seymour, 1st Duke of (1506?—52), Eng. statesman (brother of Jane Seymour).

Somerset, Fitzroy James Henry. See *Raglan, 1st Baron.*

Somerset, Robert Carr (or Ker), Earl of (d. 1645), Br. politician, favorite of James I.

Somerville (sum'ẽr-vil), Mrs. (Mary Fairfax, Mrs. Greig) (1780–1872), Br. scientific writer.

Somerville or **Somervile** (sum'ẽr-vil), William (1675–1742), Eng. poet.

Sonnino (son-nē'nō), Baron Sidney (1847–1922), It. statesman.

Sontag (zon'täch), Henriette (Countess Rossi) (1806–54), Ger. operatic soprano singer.

Sophie Charlotte (sō'fĭ shär'lǫt) (1668–1705), queen of Frederick I. of Prussia.

Sophocles (sof'ǫ-klēz) (495?–406? B.C.), Gr. tragic poet.

Sophocles, Evangelinus Apostolides (1807–83), Gr.-Am. scholar and lexicographer.

Sophonisba (sō-fǫ-niz'bä) (d. 204? B.C.), the Carthaginian wife of Syphax, king of western Numidia, at whose overthrow the conqueror Masinissa, to whom she had early been betrothed, married her. When commanded by his ally, Scipio the Elder, to surrender her as a former enemy to Rome, Masinissa sent her poison, with which she killed herself.

Sordello (sor-del'lō) (c1200–after 1269), It.-Provençal poet.

Sorel (so-rel), Agnes (c1422–50), mistress of Charles VII. of France.

Sorel, Albert (1842–1906), Fr. historian.

Sorolla y Bastida (so-rōl'yä ē bäs-tē'ᴛʜä), Joaquín (1863–1923), Sp. painter.

Sothern (suᴛʜ'ẽrn), Edward Askew (1826–81), Eng. comedian.

Sothern, Edward Hugh (1859–1933), Am. actor (son of Edward A.).

Soto (dä sō'tō), Hernando (or Fernando) de (c1500–42), Sp. soldier and explorer in America, who reached the Mississippi in 1541.

Soubise (dẽ sö-bēz), Charles de Rohan, Prince de (1715–87), Fr. marshal.

Soufflot (sö-flō), Jacques Germain (1713?–80?), Fr. architect.

Soulé (sö-lā'), Pierre (1802–70), Am. politician, born in France.

Soulouque (sö-lök), Faustin Élie (1785?–1867), negro general and politician, president of Haiti (1847–49), and emperor (1849–59).

Soult (sölt), Nicolas Jean de Dieu (Duc de Dalmatie) (1769–1851), Fr. marshal and politician.

Sousa (sö'zǎ), John Philip (1854–1932), Am. musical conductor and composer.

South (south), Robert (1634–1716), Eng. divine.

Southampton (south-amp'tǫn), Henry Wriothesley, 3d Earl of (1573–1624), Eng. soldier and statesman, one of Shakspere's patrons.

Southcott (south'kǫt), Joanna (1750–1814), Eng. religious fanatic.

Southey (souᴛʜ'ĭ or suᴛʜ'ĭ), Robert (1774–1843), Eng. poet and misc. writer.

Southworth (south'wẽrth), Mrs. (Emma Dorothy Eliza Nevitte) (1819–99), Am. novelist.

Sower or **Saur** (sour), Christopher (1693–1758), Ger.-Am. printer.

Sozomen (soz'ǫ-men) (c400–c450), Gr. church historian, born in Palestine.

Spagnoletto, Lo. See *Ribera.*

Spargo (spär'gō), John (1876–   ), Eng.-Am. writer on socialism and other subjects.

Sparks (spärks), Jared (1789–1866), Am. historian and biographer.

Spartacus (spär'tǎ-kus) (d. 71 B.C.), a Thracian who became a slave and gladiator in Italy, and leader of an insurrection of slaves.

Spee (fon shpā), Maximilian, Graf von (1861–1914), Ger. admiral, born in Copenhagen.

Speke (spēk), John Hanning (1827–64), Eng. explorer, discoverer of source of the Nile.

Spelman (spel'mǎn), Sir Henry (c1564–1641), Eng. historian and antiquary.

Spencer (spen'sẽr), Herbert (1820–1903), Eng. philosopher.

Spencer, John Charles Spencer, 3d Earl (Viscount Althorp) (1782–1845), Eng. statesman.

Spener (shpā'nẽr), Philipp Jakob (1635–1705), Ger. clergyman and theologian, originator of Pietism.

Spengler (shpeng'lẽr), Oswald (1880–1936), Ger. philosophical writer.

Spenser (spen'sẽr), Edmund (c1552–99), Eng. poet.

Spielhagen (shpēl'hä″gǝn), Friedrich (1829–1911), Ger. novelist.

Spinello (spē-nel'lō) or **Spinello Aretino** (ä-rä-tē'nō) (c1330–c1410), It. painter, of Florentine school.

Spinola (spē'nō-lä), Ambrogio (Ambrosio Spínola, Marqués de los Balbases) (1569?–1630), It. general in Spanish service.

Spinoza (spi-nō'zǎ), Baruch (also called Benedict de Spinoza) (1632–77), Dutch Jewish philosopher.

Spitteler (shpit'ẽl-ẽr), Carl (1845–1924), Swiss poet and misc. writer, writing in German.

Spode (spōd), Josiah (1754–1827), Eng. potter.

Spohr (shpōr), Louis (1784–1859), Ger. violinist and composer.

Spontini (spon-tē'nē), Gasparo Luigi Pacifico (1774–1851), It. musical composer.

Spottiswoode (spot'is-wŭd), John (also Spottiswood and Spotswood) (1565–1639), Sc. prelate and historian, archbishop of St. Andrews.

Sprague (sprāg), William (1831–1915), Am. soldier and senator, governor of Rhode Island (1860–63).

Spurgeon (spẽr'jǫn), Charles Haddon (1834–92), Eng. Baptist preacher.

Spurzheim (shpörts'hīm), Johann Kaspar (1776–1832), Ger. phrenologist.

Squarcione (skwär-chō'nä), Francesco (1394–1474), It. painter, of Padua, founder of Paduan school.

Staël-Holstein (stä'el-hōl'stīn, Fr. dẽ stäl-ol-staṅ), Baronne de (Anne Louise Germaine Necker, known as Madame de Staël) (1766–1817), Fr. author (daughter of Jacques Necker).

Stafford (staf'ǫrd), Henry. See *Buckingham, 2d Duke of.*

Stafford, William Howard, Viscount (1614–80), Eng. nobleman, beheaded for alleged complicity in the Popish Plot.

Stahl (shtäl), Georg Ernst (1660–1734), Ger. physician and chemist.

Stainer (stā'nẽr), Sir John (1840–1901), Eng. composer and organist.

Stair (stār), James Dalrymple, 1st Viscount (1619–95), Sc. jurist and statesman.

Stair, John Dalrymple, 1st Earl of (1648–1707), Sc. lawyer and statesman (son of 1st Viscount).

Stair, John Dalrymple, 2d Earl of (1673–1747), Sc. general and diplomatist (son of 1st Earl).

Stalin (stä'lyĕn), Iosif Vissarionovich, or Joseph (real name Dzhugashvili) (1879–   ), Russ. Bolshevik leader, head of the soviet government.

Stambulov (stäm-bö'lof), Stefan (1854–95), Bulgarian statesman (assassinated).

Standish (stan'dish), Miles, or Myles (c1584–1656), Eng. settler at Plymouth, Mass. (1620), military captain of the colony.

Stanford (stan'fǫrd), Sir Charles Villiers (1852–1924), Br. musical composer.

Stanhope (stan'ǫp), Charles Stanhope, 3d Earl (1753–1816), Eng. statesman, scientist, and inventor (grandson of 1st Earl).

Stanhope, Lady Hester Lucy (1776–1839), Eng. eccentric, for a time private secretary to her uncle, the younger William Pitt (daughter of 3d Earl).

Stanhope, James Stanhope, 1st Earl (1673–1721), Eng. general and statesman.

Stanislaus I. (stan'is-lâs) (Stanislaus Leszczynski) (1677–1766), king of Poland (1705–09, 1733–35).

Stanislaus II. (Stanislaus Augustus Poniatowski) (1732–98), king of Poland (1764–95).

Stanley (stan'li), Arthur Penrhyn (1815–81), Eng. divine, theologian, and historian.

Stanley, Sir Henry Morton (orig. John Rowlands) (1841–1904), Br. explorer in Africa.

Stanley. See *Derby, Earl of.*

Stanton (stan'tǫn), Edwin McMasters (1814–69), Am. statesman.

(variable) ḍ as d or j, ꜱ as s or sh, ṭ as t or ch, ᴢ as z or zh; o, F. cloche; ü, F. menu; ċh, Sc. loch; ṅ, F. bonbon; ′, primary accent; ″, secondary accent; †, obsolete; <, from; +, and; =, equals. See also lists at beginning of book.

Stanton, Mrs. (Elizabeth Cady) (1815—1902), Am. social reformer, advocate of woman's rights.

Stark (stärk), Harold R. (1880—   ), Am. admiral.

Stark (stärk), John (1728—1822), Am. general.

Statius (stā'shius), Publius Papinius (A.D. c45—c96), Rom. poet.

Stauffacher (shtou'fä"chêr), Werner (fl. c1307), legendary hero in Swiss struggle for independence against Austria.

Stead (sted), William Thomas (1849—1912), Eng. journalist.

Stedman (sted'man), Edmund Clarence (1833—1908), Am. poet and critic.

Steel (stēl), Mrs. (Flora Annie Webster) (1847—1929), Eng. novelist.

Steele (stēl), Sir Richard (1672—1729), Br. essayist and dramatist.

Steen (stān), Jan (1626—79), Dutch painter.

Stefánsson (stef'än-son), Vilhjálmur (1879—   ), Am. arctic explorer, born in Canada.

Stein (fom ûnt tsúm shtīn), Heinrich Friedrich Karl, Freiherr vom und zum (1757—1831), Prussian statesman.

Steinach (shtī'näch), Eugen (1861—1944), Austrian physiologist and research biologist, originator of rejuvenation methods.

Steinlen (stań-loń), Théophile Alexandre (1859—1923), Swiss-Fr. painter and illustrator.

Steinmetz (stīn'mets), Charles Proteus (1865—1923), Ger.-Am. electrician.

Steinmetz (fon shtīn'mets), Karl Friedrich von (1796—1877), Prussian field-marshal.

Stendhal (stoń-dàl). Pseudonym of M. H. Beyle.

Steno (stā'nō), Nicolaus (1638—86), Dan. Rom. Cath. bishop, and anatomist and naturalist.

Stephan (fon shtef'än), Heinrich von (1831—97), Ger. statesman, organizer of the imperial postal administration.

Stephen (stē'ven) (1097?—1154), king of England (1135—54) (successor and nephew of Henry I.).

Stephen I., Saint (c975—1038), first king of Hungary (997—1038).

Stephen, Sir James Fitzjames (1829—94), Eng. jurist.

Stephen, Sir Leslie (1832—1904), Eng. biographer and critic (brother of Sir James F.).

Stephen Báthori. See *Báthori.*

Stephens (stē'venz), Alexander Hamilton (1812—83), Am. statesman, vice-president of the Confederacy.

Stephens, James (1882—   ), Ir. novelist, poet, and misc. writer.

Stephenson (stē'ven-son), George (1781—1848), Eng. engineer, improver of the steam locomotive.

Stephenson, Robert (1803—59), Eng. engineer (son of George).

Stepniak (step-nyäk'), Sergius (real name Sergyey Mikhaylovich Kravchinski) (1852—95), Russ. revolutionist and writer, exile in England.

Sterne (stêrn), Laurence (1713—68), Eng. clergyman and novelist.

Stesichorus (stē-sik'ō-rus) (c640—c555 B.C.), Gr. lyric poet, of Sicily.

Steuben (stū'ben, Ger. fon shtoi'ben), Frederick William Augustus Henry Ferdinand von (called Baron Steuben) (1730—94), Prussian-Am. general in Revolutionary War.

Stevens (stē'venz), Alfred (1818—75), Eng. sculptor and designer.

Stevens (ste-vańs), Alfred (1828—1906), Belgian painter, in Paris.

Stevens (stē'venz), Thaddeus (1792—1868), Am. abolitionist and statesman.

Stevenson (stē'ven-son), Adlai Ewing (1835—1914), Am. politician, vice-president of U. S. (1893—97).

Stevenson, Robert (1772—1850), Sc. civil engineer.

Stevenson, Robert Louis Balfour (1850—94), Sc. novelist, essayist, and poet (grandson of Robert).

Stewart (stū'ärt), Balfour (1828—87), Br. physicist.

Stewart, Charles (1778—1869), Am. admiral.

Stewart, Dugald (1753—1828), Sc. philosopher.

Stewart. See *Londonderry.*

Stewart. See *Stuart.*

Steyn (stīn), Martinus Theunis (1857—1916), Boer statesman, last president of Orange Free State.

Stigand (stig'and) (d. 1072), Eng. ecclesiastic, archbishop of Canterbury.

Stilicho (stil'i-kō), Flavius (d. 408), Rom. general and statesman.

Stillingfleet (stil'ing-flēt), Edward (1635—99), Eng. bishop and theologian.

Stimson (stim'son), Henry Lewis (1867—   ), Am. lawyer and statesman.

Stirling (stêr'ling), James Hutchison (1820—1909), Sc. philosopher.

Stirner (shtir'nêr), Max. Pseudonym of Kaspar Schmidt.

Stockton (stok'ton), Francis Richard (1834—1902), Am. writer of humorous tales.

Stockton, Richard (1730—81), Am. patriot.

Stockton, Robert Field (1795—1866), Am. naval officer (grandson of Richard).

Stoddard (stod'ärd), Richard Henry (1825—1903), Am. author.

Stoessel (shtès'el). See *Stössel.*

Stokes (stōks), Sir George Gabriel (1819—1903), Br. mathematician and physicist.

Stolypin (sto-lē'pēn), Petr Arkadevich (1863—1911), Russ. statesman.

Storm (shtôrm), Theodor (1817—88), Ger. poet and novelist.

Stormonth (stôr'munth), James (1824—82), Sc. lexicographer.

Storrs (stôrz), Richard Salter (1821—1900), Am. Congregational clergyman.

Story (stō'ri), Joseph (1779—1845), Am. jurist, associate justice of U. S. Supreme Court (1811—45).

Story, William Wetmore (1819—95), Am. sculptor, poet, and misc. writer (son of Joseph).

Stoss (shtōs), Veit (c1440—1533), Ger. sculptor and woodcarver.

Stössel (shtès'el), Anatole Mikhaylovich (1848—1915), Russ. general.

Stothard (stoᴛʜ'ärd), Thomas (1755—1834), Eng. painter and illustrator.

Stow (stō), John (c1525—1605), Eng. chronicler and antiquary.

Stowe (stō), Mrs. (Harriet Elizabeth Beecher) (1811—96), Am. writer, author of "Uncle Tom's Cabin" (sister of H. W. Beecher).

Strabo (strā'bō) (c63 B.C.—after A.D. 21), Gr. geographer and historian.

Strachey (strā'chi), Giles Lytton (1880—1932), Eng. author.

Stradivari (strä-dē-vä'rē), Antonio (as Latinized, Antonius Stradivarius) (c1644—1737), It. violin-maker, of Cremona.

Strafford (straf'ord), Thomas Wentworth, 1st Earl of (1593—1641), Eng. statesman (chief adviser of Charles I.), impeached and executed.

Strang (strang), William (1859—1921), Br. painter, etcher, and engraver.

Stratford de Redcliffe (strat'ford dè red'klif), Stratford Canning, Viscount (1786—1880), Eng. diplomatist (cousin of George Canning).

Strathcona and Mount Royal (strath-kō'nä, mount roi'al), Donald Alexander Smith, 1st Baron (1820—1914), Can. financier, railroad promoter, and statesman, born in Scotland.

Straus (strous), Oscar Solomon (1850—1926), Am. diplomatist, cabinet officer, and writer, born in Germany.

Strauss (shtrous), David Friedrich (1808—74), Ger. theological and misc. writer.

Strauss, Johann (1804—49), Austrian composer of dance-music.

Strauss, Johann (1825—99), Austrian composer of dance-music and operettas (son of Johann Strauss, 1804—49).

Strauss, Richard (1864—   ), Ger. musical composer and conductor.

Stravinski (strä-vēn'skē), Igor Fedorovich (1882—   ), Russ. musical composer.

Stresemann (shtrā'zè-män), Gustav (1878—1929), Ger. statesman and writer.

Strickland (strik'land), Agnes (1796—1874), Eng. historical writer.

Strindberg (strind'ber-y'), Johan August (1849—1912), Swed. novelist, dramatist, and essayist.

Strongbow (strŏng′bō), Richard. See *Pembroke, 2d Earl of.*

Struensee (fon strö′ęn-zā), Johann Friedrich, Count von (1737—72), Dan. politician (born in Germany), and favorite of Caroline Matilda of Denmark.

Strutt (strut), Joseph (1749—1802), Eng. engraver and antiquary.

Strype (strīp), John (1643—1737), Eng. ecclesiastical historian and biographer.

Stuart (stū′ạrt), Arabella (1575—1615), cousin of James I. of England.

Stuart, Gilbert (1755—1828), Am. portrait-painter.

Stuart, James. See *Moray.*

Stuart, James Ewell Brown (1833—64), Am. Confederate general.

Stuart, John McDouall (1815—66), Australian explorer, born in Scotland.

Stuart, Mary. See *Mary,* queen of Scotland.

Stuart, Moses (1780—1852), Am. Biblical scholar.

Stuart. See *Charles Edward Stuart* and *James Francis Edward Stuart.*

Stubbs (stubz), William (1825—1901), Eng. bishop and historian.

Stuck (fon shtŭk), Franz von (1863—1928), Ger. painter and sculptor.

Stucley or **Stukely** (stūk′li), Thomas (c1525—78), Eng. adventurer.

Stukeley (stūk′li), William (1687—1765), Eng. antiquary.

Sturdee (stêr′dę), Sir Frederick Charles Doveton (1859—1925), Eng. admiral.

Sturgis (stêr′jis), Russell (1836—1909), Am. architect, and writer on art.

Sturluson. See *Snorri Sturluson.*

Sturm (shtŭrm), Johannes (1507—89), Ger. educational reformer.

Sturt (stêrt), Charles (1795—1869), Br. explorer in Australia.

Stuyvesant (stī′vę-sạnt), Peter (1592—1672), Dutch colonial governor of New Netherland (New York).

Suárez (swä′räth), Francisco (1548—1617), Sp. Jesuit theologian.

Suchet (sü-shā′), Louis Gabriel (Duc d'Albufera) (1770—1826), Fr. marshal.

Suckling (suk′ling), Sir John (1609—42), Eng. poet.

Sucre (dā sö′krā), Antonio José de (1793—1830), South Am. general and liberator, born in Venezuela.

Sudermann (zö′dėr-män), Hermann (1857—1928), Ger. dramatist and novelist.

Sue (sü), Marie Joseph ("Eugène Sue") (1804—57), Fr. novelist.

Suess (züs), Eduard (1831—1914), Austrian geologist.

Suetonius (swē-tō′ni-us) (Caius Suetonius Tranquillus) (A.D. c75—c160), Rom. historian.

Suffolk (suf′ǫk), Charles Brandon, 1st Duke of (d. 1545), Eng. nobleman, favorite of Henry VIII.

Suffolk, William de la Pole, 1st Duke of (1396—1450), Eng. soldier and statesman.

Suffren de Saint-Tropez (dė sü-frän dė san-tro-pes), Pierre André de (1726—88), Fr. admiral.

Suger (sü-zhär) (c1081—1151), Fr. ecclesiastic, statesman, and historian.

Suidas (sū′i-das) (fl. c970), Gr. lexicographer.

Suleiman I. See *Solyman I.*

Sulla (sul′ạ), Lucius Cornelius (surnamed Felix) (138—78 B.C.), Rom. general and dictator.

Sullivan (sul′i-vạn), Sir Arthur Seymour (1842—1900), Eng. musical composer.

Sullivan, John (1740—95), Am. Revolutionary general.

Sullivan, Mark (1874—), Am. journalist and historian.

Sully (sul′i), James (1842—1923), Eng. psychologist.

Sully (sul′i, Fr. dė sü-lē), Maximilien de Béthune, Duc de (Baron de Rosny) (1560—1641), Fr. statesman, minister of Henry IV.

Sully-Prudhomme (sü-lē-prü-dom), René François Armand (1839—1907), Fr. poet.

Sulpicius Severus (sul-pish′ius se-vē′rus) (c363—c425), Latin Christian writer, of southern France.

Sumarokov (sö-mả-rô′kof), Aleksandr Petrovich (1718—77), Russ. dramatist and misc. writer.

Sumner (sum′nėr), Charles (1811—74), Am. statesman.

Sumner, Edwin Vose (1797—1863), Am. general.

Sumner, William Graham (1840—1910), Am. political economist.

Sumter (sum′tėr), Thomas (1734—1832), Am. Revolutionary general.

Sunday (sun′dạ), William Ashley ("Billy Sunday") (1863—1935), Am. evangelist.

Sunderland (sun′dėr-lạnd), Charles Spencer, 3d Earl of (1674—1722), Eng. politician (son of 2d Earl).

Sunderland, Robert Spencer, 2d Earl of (1640—1702), Eng. politician.

Sun Yat-sen (sùn yät-sen′) (1867—1925), Chin. political leader.

Suppé (fon zú-pā′), Franz von (1820—95), Austrian composer of operettas.

Surrey (sur′i), Henry Howard, Earl of (1517?—47), Eng. poet (son of 3d Duke of Norfolk).

Surtees (sėr′tēz), Robert Smith (1803—64), Eng. writer of sporting novels.

Suso (zō′zō), Heinrich (also called Seuse) (c1300—66), Ger. monk and mystic.

Suttner (fon zùt′nėr), Baroness von (Bertha von Kinsky) (1843—1914), Austrian novelist and peace advocate.

Suvarov (sö-vär′of) or **Suvorov** (sö-vor′of), Count Aleksandr Vasilevich (Prince Italiski) (1729—1800), Russ. field-marshal.

Sverdrup (sver′drŭp), Otto (1854—1930), Norw. arctic explorer.

Swammerdam (swä′mėr-däm), Jan (1637—80), Dutch naturalist.

Swedenborg (swē′dęn-bôrg), Emanuel (orig. Emanuel Swedberg) (1688—1772), Swed. scientist, philosopher, and mystic.

Sweet (swēt), Henry (1845—1912), Eng. philologist and phonetician.

Swetchine (sve-chēn′), Mme. (in Russian, Sofiya Petrovna Svyechina, born Soymonova) (1782—1857), Russ. mystic and author, in Paris.

Sweyn (swān) (d. 1014), king of Denmark (986?—1014) (son of Harald Bluetooth).

Swift (swift), Jonathan (1667—1745), Br. satirist, dean of St. Patrick's, Dublin.

Swinburne (swin′bėrn), Algernon Charles (1837—1909), Eng. poet and critic.

Swinnerton (swin′ėr-tǫn), Frank Arthur (1884—), Eng. novelist and critic.

Swithin (swith′in or swiᵺ′in) or **Swithun** (swith′un or swiᵺ′un), Saint (d. 862), Eng. bishop.

Sybel (fon zē′bęl), Heinrich von (1817—95), Ger. historian.

Sydenham (sid′ęn-ạm), Thomas (1624—89), Eng. physician.

Sydney. See *Sidney.*

Sylva (sil′vạ), Carmen. Pseudonym of Elizabeth, queen of Rumania.

Sylvester (sil-ves′tėr), James Joseph (1814—97), Eng. mathematician.

Sylvius (sil′vi-us) (real name Jacques Dubois) (1478—1555), Fr. anatomist.

Sylvius, Æneas. See *Pius II.*

Syme (sīm), James (1799—1870), Sc. surgeon.

Symonds (sim′ǫndz), John Addington (1840—93), Eng. author.

Symons (sī′mǫnz), Arthur (1865—), Br. poet and critic.

Synesius (si-nē′shius) (c370—c415), Christian bishop and Neoplatonist, of northern Africa.

Synge (sing), John Millington (1871—1909), Ir. dramatist.

Syphax (sī′faks) (d. c203 B.C.), king of western Numidia, conquered by Masinissa.

T

Taaffe (fon tä′fė), Eduard, Graf von (1833—95), Austrian statesman.

Tabarin (tả-bả-raṅ) (assumed name of Jean Salomon) (c1584—1633), Parisian street mountebank and buffoon.

Tabb (tab), John Bannister (1845—1909), Am. Roman Catholic priest, educator, and poet.

Tacitus (tas′i-tus), Cornelius (A.D. c55—c120), Rom. historian.

Taft (taft), Lorado (1860—1936), Am. sculptor.

Taft, William Howard (1857—1930), 27th president of U. S. (1909—13), and chief justice of U. S. Supreme Court (1921—30).

Taglioni (täl-yō'nē), Maria (Comtesse des Voisins) (1804?—84), ballet-dancer, born in Sweden of It.-Swed. parentage.

Tagore (tạ-gōr'), (Sir) Rabindranath (1861—1941), Bengalese poet and misc. writer in Bengali and English.

Taillefer (tä-y'-fär) (d. 1066), Norman bard and soldier, who fell in the battle of Hastings.

Taine (tān), Hippolyte Adolphe (1828—93), Fr. historian, philosopher, and critic.

Tait (tāt), Archibald Campbell (1811—82), Br. prelate, archbishop of Canterbury.

Tait, Peter Guthrie (1831—1901), Sc. mathematician and physicist.

Takahira (tä-kä-hē'rä), Baron Kogoro (1854—   ), Jap. diplomatist.

Takamine (tä-kä-mē'ne), Jokichi (1854—1922), Jap. chemist, in U. S.

Talbot (tål'bọt), William Henry Fox (1800—77), Eng. archæologist and scientist, one of the inventors of photography.

Talbot.   See *Shrewsbury*.

Talfourd (tål'fọrd), Sir Thomas Noon (1795—1854), Eng. jurist, dramatist, and misc. writer.

Talleyrand-Périgord (tal'i-rand, Fr. dè tä-le-räṅ-pä-rē-gôr), Charles Maurice de (Prince de Bénévent) (1754—1838), Fr. statesman and diplomatist.

Tallien (tå-lyaṅ), Jean Lambert (1767—1820), Fr. revolutionist.

Talma (tål-mä), François Joseph (1763—1826), Fr. tragedian.

Talmage (tal'mạj), Thomas De Witt (1832—1902), Am. Presbyterian preacher.

Tamayo y Baus (tä-mä'yō ē bä'ös), Manuel (1829—98), Sp. dramatist.

Tamerlane (tam-ẽr-län').   See *Timur*.

Tancred (tang'kred) (d. 1112), Norman adventurer, one of the leaders of the first Crusade.

Tandy (tan'di), James Napper (1740—1803), Ir. rebel.

Taney (tå'ni), Roger Brooke (1777—1864), Am. jurist, chief justice of U. S. Supreme Court (1836—64).

Tarbell (tär'bel), Edmund Charles (1862—1938), Am. painter.

Tardieu (tär-dyè), André Pierre Gabriel Amédée (1876—1945), Fr. writer, politician, and diplomatist.

Tarik or **Tariq** (tä'rik) (fl. c711), Arab general under Musa ibn Nosair, conqueror in Spain.

Tarkington (tär'king-tọn), Newton Booth (1869—1946), Am. novelist and playwright.

Tarleton (tärl'tọn), Sir Banastre (1754—1833), Eng. officer in American Revolutionary War.

Tarpeia (tär-pē'yạ).   In Roman legend, a Roman maiden who agreed to betray the Capitoline citadel to the Sabines for the gift of what they wore on their left arms. As they entered, instead of rewarding her with the golden bracelets she had meant, they threw their shields on her and crushed her to death.

Tarquinius (tär-kwin'i-us), Sextus. See *Lucretia*.

Tarquinius Priscus (pris'kus), Lucius ("Tarquin the Elder") (d. 578 B.C.), 5th (legendary) king of Rome (616—578 B.C.).

Tarquinius Superbus (sụ-pẽr'bus), Lucius ("Tarquin the Proud") (d. after 510 B.C.), 7th and last (legendary) king of Rome (534—510 B.C.) (son of Tarquinius Priscus).

Tarr (tär), Ralph Stockman (1864—1912), Am. geologist.

Tasman (täs'män), Abel Janszoon (1602?—59), Dutch navigator, discoverer of Tasmania and New Zealand.

Tasso (tas'ō, It. täs'sō), Torquato (1544—95), It. poet, author of "Jerusalem Delivered."

Tate (tāt), Nahum (1652—1715), Br. poet and dramatist.

Tatian (tä'shiạn) (fl. c150), Christian apologist, born in Mesopotamia.

Tauchnitz (fon touċh'nits), Christian Bernhard, Freiherr von (1816—95), Ger. publisher, esp. of works of British and American authors.

Tauler (tou'lẽr), Johann (c1300—61), Ger. mystic.

Taunton (tân'tọn), Henry Labouchere, Baron (1798—1869), Eng. statesman.

Taussig (tou'sig), Frank William (1859—1940), Am. political economist.

Tautphœus (fon tout-fä'ủs), Baroness von (Jemima Montgomery) (1807—93), Br. novelist in Germany.

Taylor (tā'lọr), Bayard (1825—78), Am. poet, translator, and misc. writer.

Taylor, Frederick Winslow (1856—1915), Am. engineer, specialist in scientific management.

Taylor, Sir Henry (1800—86), Eng. poet and dramatist.

Taylor, Isaac (1787—1865), Eng. religious and misc. writer.

Taylor, Isaac (1829—1901), Eng. divine and philologist (son of Isaac Taylor, 1787—1865).

Taylor, Jeremy (1613—67), Eng. bishop, and theological and devotional writer.

Taylor, John ("the Water Poet") (1580—1653), Eng. writer of prose and verse.

Taylor, Tom (1817—80), Eng. dramatist and misc. writer.

Taylor, Zachary (1784—1850), Am. general, and 12th president of U. S. (1849—50).

Tchaikovsky (chī-kof'skē). See *Chaykovski*.

Tchekhoff (che'chof). See *Chekhov*.

Tchernyshevski (cher-ni-shef'skē). See *Chernyshevski*.

Tchitcherin (chę-cher'ẹn). See *Chicherin*.

Tecumseh (tẹ-kum'sẹ) (1768?—1813), Am. Indian chief.

Tegakwitha (teg-ạ-kwith'ä). See *Tekakwitha*.

Tegetthoff (fon tä'get-hof), Wilhelm, Freiherr von (1827—71), Austrian admiral.

Tegnér (teng-när'), Esaias (1782—1846), Swed. poet.

Tekakwitha (tek-ạ-kwith'ä), Catherine (1656—80), Am. Indian convert to Rom. Cath. faith, venerated for her pious life.

Telesio (tā-lā'zē-ō), Bernardino (1509—88), It. philosopher.

Telford (tel'fọrd), Thomas (1757—1834), Sc. civil engineer.

Tell (tel), William (Wilhelm Tell) (fl. c1307), legendary hero in Swiss struggle for independence against Austria. The story goes that Tell, a skilful bowman, refused to salute the cap of Austria set up by Gessler, the Austrian governor, in the market-place at Altdorf, and was hence condemned to death unless he should shoot an apple from the head of his little son. His shot succeeded in doing this, and he then revealed another arrow with which he had intended to kill Gessler if the shot had failed. He was ordered to prison, escaped, killed Gessler, and freed his country.

Téllez (tel'yäth), Gabriel ("Tirso de Molina") (1571?—1648), Sp. dramatist.

Temple (tem'pl), Frederick (1821—1902), Eng. prelate, archbishop of Canterbury.

Temple, Richard Temple Grenville, later Richard Grenville-Temple, Earl (1711—79), Eng. statesman (brother of George Grenville).

Temple, Sir William (1628—99), Eng. statesman, diplomatist, and author.

Teniers (ten'yẽrz, Flemish te-nẽrs'), David ("the elder") (1582—1649), Flemish painter.

Teniers, David ("the younger") (1610—90), Flemish painter (son of "the elder").

Tenniel (ten'yẹl), Sir John (1820—1914), Eng. cartoonist and illustrator.

Tennyson (ten'i-sọn), Alfred Tennyson, 1st Baron (1809—92), Eng. poet.

Ter Borch (ter bôrċh) or **Terburg** (ter'bôrċh), Gerard (1617—81), Dutch painter.

Terence (ter'ẹns) (Publius Terentius Afer) (c190—c159 B.C.), Rom. dramatist.

Teresa, Saint. See *Theresa*.

Terhune (tẽr-hūn'), Mrs. (Mary Virginia Hawes, "Marion Harland") (1830—1922), Am. novelist and misc. writer.

Terpander (tẽr-pan'dẽr) (fl. c676 B.C.), Gr. musician and poet.

Terry (ter'i), Alfred Howe (1827—90), Am. general.

Terry, Ellen Alicia (Mrs. George Frederick Watts, Mrs. Wardell, Mrs. Carew, Dame Ellen Carew) (1848—1928), Eng. actress.

Tertullian (tẽr-tul'iạn) (Quintus Septimius Florens Tertullianus) (c150—after 220), Christian theologian, of northern Africa.

---

fat, fāte, fär, fåll, ȧsk, fãre; net, mē, hẽr; pin, pīne; not, nōte, mȯve, nôr; up, lūte, pull; oi, oil; ou, out; (lightened) aviạry, ẹlect, agọny, intọ, ụnite; (obscured) errạnt, operạ, ardẹnt, actọr, natụre; ch, chip; g, go; th, thin; ᴛʜ, then; y, you;

Tesla (tes'lä), Nikola (1857—1943), Am. electrician and inventor, born in Austria-Hungary.

Tethmosis III. See *Thothmes III*.

Tetrazzini (tā-trät-sē′nē), Luisa (Signora Bazelli, Signora Vernati) (1874—1940), It. operatic soprano singer.

Tetzel (tet′sel), Johann (1465?—1519), Ger. Dominican monk, and preacher of indulgences.

Tewfik Pasha (tū′fik pà-shä′), Mohammed (1852—92), khedive of Egypt (1879—92) (son of Ismail Pasha).

Thackeray (thak′e-ri), William Makepeace (1811—63), Eng. novelist, born in India.

Thaïs (thā′is) (fl. c330 B.C.), Gr. courtezan, mistress of Alexander the Great.

Thales (thā′lēz) (c640—c546 B.C.), Gr. philosopher, one of the seven sages of ancient Greece.

Thaulow (tou′lō), Fritz (1847—1906), Norw. painter.

Thaxter (thak′ster), Mrs. (Celia Laighton) (1836—94), Am. poet.

Thayer (thār), Abbott Handerson (1849—1921), Am. painter.

Themistocles (the-mis′tō-klēz) (c527—c460 B.C.), Athenian statesman and naval commander.

Theobald (thē′ō-bàld), Lewis (1688—1744), Eng. Shaksperian commentator and editor.

Theocritus (thē-ok′ri-tus) (fl. 3d cent. B.C.), Gr. bucolic poet.

Theodora (thē-ō-dō′rä) (d. 547?), Byzantine empress (wife of Justinian I.).

Theodore I. (thē′ō-dōr) (Theodore Lascaris) (d. 1222), emperor of Nicæa in Asia Minor (1204—22).

Theodore of Mopsuestia (mop-sū-es′ti-ä) (c350—428), Gr. Biblical scholar and theologian, born at Antioch.

Theodoret (thē-od′ō-ret) (c390—c457), bishop, theologian, and church historian, of Syria.

Theodoric (thē-od′ō-rik) ("the Great") (c454—526), king of the Ostrogoths, ruler of Italy after 493.

Theodosius I. (thē-ō-dō′shius) ("Theodosius the Great") (c346—395), Eastern Rom. emperor (379—395).

Theodosius II. (401—450), Eastern Rom. emperor (408—450) (son of Emperor Arcadius).

Theognis (thē-og′nis) (fl. 6th cent. B.C.), Gr. elegiac poet.

Theophrastus (thē-ō-fras′tus) (c372—287 B.C.), Gr. philosopher.

Theotocopuli (tā-ō″tō-kō-pö′lē), Dominico (called El Greco, pronounced el grä′kō, and meaning 'the Greek') (1548?—1614), Sp. painter, architect, and sculptor, born in Crete.

Theramenes (thē-ram′e-nēz) (d. 404? B.C.), Athenian statesman.

Theresa or **Teresa** (te-rē′sä), Saint (Teresa Sánchez Cepeda Dávila y Ahumada) (1515—82), Sp. Carmelite nun and mystic.

Théroigne de Méricourt (tā-rwän-y′ dè mä-rē-kör) (real name Anne Josèphe Terwagne) (1762—1817), Fr. revolutionary heroine.

Thesiger (thes′i-jer). See *Chelmsford*.

Thespis (thes′pis) (fl. 6th cent. B.C.), Gr. tragic poet.

Theuriet (tè-ryä), Claude Adhémar André (1833—1907), Fr. novelist and poet.

Thibaudeau (tē-bō-dō), Antoine Clair, Comte (1765—1854), Fr. politician and historian.

Thibault (tē-bō), Jacques Anatole ("Anatole France") (1844—1924), Fr. author.

Thierry (tye-rē), Amédée Simon Dominique (1797—1873), Fr. historian (brother of J. N. A.).

Thierry, Jacques Nicolas Augustin (1795—1856), Fr. historian.

Thiers (tyâr), Louis Adolphe (1797—1877), Fr. statesman and historian, president of France (1871–73).

Thirlwall (thèrl′wal), Connop (1797—1875), Eng. bishop and historian.

Thoma (tō′mä), Hans (1839—1924), Ger. painter.

Thoma, Ludwig (1867—1921), Ger. author.

Thomas (tom′as), Augustus (1857—1934), Am. playwright.

Thomas (to-mä), Charles Louis Ambroise (1811—96), Fr. musical composer.

Thomas (tom′as), George Henry (1816—70), Am. general.

Thomas, James Henry (1875—   ), Eng. labor leader, politician, and cabinet minister.

Thomas, Theodore (1835—1905), Ger.-Am. musical conductor.

Thomas à Becket (à bek′et). See *Becket, Thomas*.

Thomas a Kempis (à kem′pis) (properly Thomas Hamerken, or Hammerken) (1380?—1471), Ger. ecclesiastic and writer, reputed author of "De Imitatione Christi."

Thomas Aquinas. See *Aquinas*.

Thomas of Celano (chä-lä′nō) (c1200—c1255), It. Franciscan friar, biographer of St. Francis of Assisi, and supposed author of the Latin hymn " Dies Iræ."

Thomas of Erceldoune (èr′sel-dön) ("Thomas the Rhymer") (1220?—97?), Sc. poet.

Thomas of Woodstock (wùd′stok) (Duke of Gloucester) (1355—97), Eng. politician (son of Edward III. of England).

Thompson (tomp′son), Sir Benjamin (Count Rumford) (1753—1814), Am.-Eng. physicist, and administrator in Bavaria.

Thompson, Ernest Evan Seton. See *Seton, Ernest Thompson*.

Thompson, Francis (1859—1907), Eng. poet.

Thompson, Silvanus Phillips (1851—1916), Eng. physicist.

Thomson (tom′son), Elihu (1853—1937), Am. electrician and inventor, born in England.

Thomson, James (1700—48), Br. poet, author of "The Seasons."

Thomson, James ("B. V.") (1834—82), Br. poet.

Thomson, Sir John Arthur (1861—1933), Sc. naturalist.

Thomson, Joseph (1858—95), Sc. explorer in Africa.

Thomson, Sir Joseph John (1856—1940), Eng. physicist.

Thomson, Sir William. See *Kelvin*.

Thoreau (thō′rō or thō-rō′), Henry David (1817—62), Am. naturalist and author.

Thorfinn (thôr′fin) (also called Thorfinn Karlsefni, or Karlsefne) (fl. 1002—07), Scand. navigator, explorer of coast of North America.

Thornhill (thôrn′hil), Sir James (1675—1734), Eng. painter.

Thornycroft (thôr′ni-krôft), Sir William Hamo (1850—1925), Eng. sculptor.

Thorvaldsen or **Thorwaldsen** (tôr′väl-sen), Bertel (1770—1844), Dan. sculptor.

Thothmes III. (thoth′mēz) or **Tethmosis III.** (teth-mō′sis) (fl. c1475 B.C.), king of Egypt, of 18th dynasty (nephew and stepson of Queen Hatasu).

Thrale (thrāl), Mrs. See *Piozzi*.

Thrasybulus (thras-i-bū′lus) (d. c389 B.C.), Athenian general and statesman.

Throckmorton (throk′môr-ton) or **Throgmorton** (throg′-môr-ton), Sir Nicholas (1515—71), Eng. diplomatist and politician.

Thucydides (thū-sid′i-dēz) (c460—c400 B.C.), Gr. historian.

Thugut (fon tö′göt), Johann Amadeus Franz de Paula, Freiherr von (1736—1818), Austrian diplomatist and statesman.

Thurlow (thèr′lō), Edward Thurlow, 1st Baron (1731—1806), Eng. jurist and statesman.

Thurman (thèr′man), Allen Granbery (1813—95), Am. jurist and political leader.

Thurn (törn), Heinrich Matthias, Count (1580—1640), Bohem. soldier, leader of Bohemian Protestants at beginning of Thirty Years' War.

Thyssen (tēs′en), August (1840—1926), Ger. industrial magnate.

Tiberius (tī-bē′ri-us) (Tiberius Claudius Nero Cæsar) (42 B.C.—A.D. 37), Rom. emperor (A.D. 14—37) (stepson of Emperor Augustus).

Tibullus (ti-bul′us), Albius (c54—c19 B.C.), Rom. elegiac poet.

Tickell (tik′el), Thomas (1686—1740), Eng. poet and essayist.

Ticknor (tik′nor), George (1791—1871), Am. author.

Tieck (tēk), Johann Ludwig (1773—1853), Ger. poet, critic, and misc. writer.

Tiepolo (tyä′pō-lō), Giovanni Battista (1696—1770), It. painter, of Venetian school.

Tiffany (tif′a-ni), Charles Lewis (1812—1902), Am. jeweler.

Tiffany, Louis Comfort (1848—1933), Am. painter and designer, specialist in ornamental glass (son of Charles L.).

Tiglath-Pileser I. (tig′lath-pi-lē′zer) (fl. c1120 B.C.), king of Assyria.

Tiglath-Pileser III. (name orig. Pulu or Pul) (d. 727 B.C.), king of Assyria (745—727 B.C.).

Tilden (til′dẹn), Samuel Jones (1814—86), Am. lawyer and statesman.

Tillotson (til′ǫt-sọn), John (1630—94), Eng. divine, archbishop of Canterbury.

Tilly (til′i, Fr. tē-yē), Johann Tserclaes, Count of (1559—1632), general, esp. in service of Catholic League in Thirty Years' War, born in Brabant.

Timæus (ti-mē′us) (c345—c250 B.C.), Gr. historian, of Sicily.

Timoleon (ti-mō′lẹ-ǫn) (d. 337 B.C.), Gr. statesman and general, in Sicily.

Timotheus (ti-mō′thẹ-us) (c446—c357 B.C.), Gr. musician and dithyrambic poet.

Timrod (tim′rod), Henry (1829—67), Am. poet.

Timur or **Timour** (tē-mör′) (also called Timur Leng, commonly known as Tamerlane) (1333?—1405), Tatar conqueror, born near Samarkand.

Tinayre (tē-nãr), Mme. (Marguerite Suzanne Marcelle Chasteau) (1872—   ), Fr. novelist.

Tindal (tin′dạl), Matthew (c1653—1733), Eng. deistic writer.

Tindale, William. See *Tyndale*.

Tintoretto (tēn-to-ret′tō) (real name Jacopo Robusti) (1518—94), Venetian painter.

Tippoo Sahib (ti-pö′ sä′ib) (1749?—99), sultan of Mysore, India (son of Hyder Ali).

Tirpitz (fon tir′pits), Alfred von (1849—1930), Ger. admiral and statesman.

Tirso de Molina (tēr′sō dä mō-lē′nä). Pseudonym of Gabriel Téllez.

Tischendorf (fon tish′ẹn-dôrf), Lobegott Friedrich Konstantin von (1815—74), Ger. Biblical critic.

Tissaphernes (tis-ạ-fêr′nēz) (d. 395 B.C.), Pers. statesman and general.

Tissot (tē-sō), James Joseph Jacques (1836—1902), Fr. painter.

Tisza (tē′so), István, or Stephen, Count (1861—1918), Hung. statesman, assassinated (son of Kálmán).

Tisza, Kálmán (1830—1902), Hung. statesman.

Titchener (tich′ẹ-nêr), Edward Bradford (1867—1927), Eng.-Am. psychologist.

Titcomb (tit′kọm), Timothy. Pseudonym of J. G. Holland.

Titian (tish′ạn) (real name Tiziano Vecelli, or Vecellio) (c1477—1576), Venetian painter.

Titus (tī′tus) (Titus Flavius Sabinus Vespasianus) (A.D. 40 or 41—81), Rom. emperor (A.D. 79—81) (son of Emperor Vespasian).

Tocqueville (dẹ tok-vēl′), Alexis Charles Henri Maurice Clérel de (1805—59), Fr. statesman and historian.

Todd (tod), David (1855—   ), Am. astronomer.

Todhunter (tod′hun-têr), Isaac (1820—84), Eng. mathematician.

Todleben or **Totleben** (tŏt′lä″ben), Count Franz Eduard Ivanovich (1818—84), Russ. general and military engineer.

Togo (tō′gō), Count Heihachiro (1847—   ), Jap. admiral.

Tojo (tō′jō), Hideki (1885—   ), Jap. gen. and statesman.

Toland (tō′lạnd), John (orig. Janus Junius Toland) (1670—1722), Br. deistic and misc. writer.

Toledo (dä tō-lä′ᴛнō), Francisco de (c1515—84?), Sp. administrator, viceroy of Peru.

Tolstoi (tol-stoi′), Count Aleksyey Konstantinovich (1818—75), Russ. novelist, dramatist, and poet.

Tolstoy, Count Lev Nikolaevich (1828—1910), Russ. novelist and social reformer, author of "War and Peace" and "Anna Karenina."

Tompkins (tomp′kinz), Daniel D. (1774—1825), Am. statesman, vice-president of U. S. (1817—25).

Tone (tōn), Theobald Wolfe (1763—98), Ir. revolutionist.

Tooke (tŏk or tŭk), John Horne (name orig. John Horne) (1736—1812), Eng. politician and philologist.

Toole (tōl), John Lawrence (1830—1906), Eng. comedian.

Toombs (tömz), Robert (1810—85), Am. Confederate politician and general.

Toplady (top′lạ-di), Augustus Montague (1740—78), Eng. divine, controversialist, and religious poet.

Torquemada (dä tôr-kä-mä′ᴛнä), Tomás de (1420—98), Sp. inquisitor-general.

Torricelli (tor-rē-chel′lē), Evangelista (1608—47), It. physicist and mathematician.

Torrigiano (tor-rē-jä′nō), Pietro (1472—c1522), It. sculptor.

Torstensson or **Torstenson** (tôr′stẹn-son), Lennart (Count of Ortala) (1603—51), Swed. field-marshal in Thirty Years' War.

Tory (tō-rē), Geoffroy (c1480—1533), Fr. printer, engraver, and writer.

Toscanelli (tos-kä-nel′lē), Paolo dal Pozzo (1397—1482), It. physician, astronomer, and geographer.

Toscanini (tos-kä-nē′nē), Arturo (1867—   ), It. musical conductor.

Tosti (tos′tē), Sir Francesco Paolo (1846—1916), It. musical composer in England.

Totila (tot′i-lạ) (real name Badvila) (d. 552), king of Ostrogoths in Italy (541—552).

Totleben. See *Todleben*.

Toulouse-Lautrec (dẹ tö-löz-lō-trek), Henri de (1864—1901), Fr. painter, designer, and lithographer.

Tourgée (tör-zhā′), Albion Winegar (1838—1905), Am. lawyer and novelist.

Tournefort (dẹ törn-fôr), Joseph Pitton de (1656—1708), Fr. botanist.

Tourneur (têr′nêr), Cyril (1575?—1626), Eng. poet and dramatist.

Toussaint L'Ouverture (or **Louverture**) (tö-san lö-vertür) (real name François Dominique Toussaint) (1743—1803), negro military and political leader, one of the liberators of Haiti.

Townshend (toun′zẹnd), Charles Townshend, 2d Viscount (1674—1738), Eng. statesman.

Townshend, Charles (1725—67), Eng. politician (grandson of 2d Viscount Townshend).

Townshend, Sir Charles Vere Ferrers (1861—1924), Eng. general.

Toynbee (toin′bẹ), Arnold (1852—83), Eng. economist and social reformer.

Traherne (trạ-hêrn′), Thomas (1637?—74), Eng. poet and religious writer.

Trajan (trā′jạn) (Nerva Trajanus, orig. Marcus Ulpius Trajanus) (A.D. 52 or 53—117), Rom. emperor (A.D. 98—117) (adopted son of Emperor Nerva).

Trauttmansdorff (fon trout′mäns-dôrf), Maximilian, Graf von (1584—1650), Austrian statesman.

Tree (trē), Ellen. See *Kean, Mrs*.

Tree, Sir Herbert Beerbohm (orig. Herbert Beerbohm) (1853—1917), Eng. actor and theatrical manager.

Treitschke (fon trīch′kẹ), Heinrich von (1834—96), Ger. historian.

Trench (trench), Richard Chevenix (1807—86), Br. archbishop, philologist, and misc. writer.

Trenck (fon der trengk), Franz, Freiherr von der (1711—49), Austrian soldier, commander of pandours.

Trenck, Friedrich, Freiherr von der (1726—94), Ger. soldier and adventurer, guillotined in Paris (cousin of Franz).

Trendelenburg (tren′dẹ-lẹn-börch″), Friedrich Adolf (1802—72), Ger. philosopher.

Trevelyan (trẹ-vel′yạn), Sir George Otto (1838—1928), Eng. biographer, historian, and statesman.

Treviranus (trä-vē-rä′nús), Gottfried Reinhold (1776—1837), Ger. naturalist.

Treviranus, Ludolf Christian (1779—1864), Ger. botanist (brother of Gottfried R.).

Tribonian (tri-bō′ni-ạn) (Tribonianus) (d. c545), Rom. jurist, at Constantinople.

Trikoupis or **Tricoupis** (trẹ-kö′pēs), Charilaos (1832—96), Gr. statesman (son of Spyridon).

Trikoupis or **Tricoupis**, Spyridon (1788—1873), Gr. statesman and author.

Trochu (tro-shü), Louis Jules (1815—96), Fr. general.

Trollope (trol′up), Anthony (1815—82), Eng. novelist.

Trollope, Mrs. (Frances Milton) (1780—1863), Eng. novelist, and writer of books of travel (mother of Anthony).

Tromp (tromp), Cornelis (1629—91), Dutch admiral (son of Martin H.).

Tromp, Martin Harpertzoon (1597—1653), Dutch admiral.

Trotski (trot′skẹ), Lev Davidovich, or Leon (real name Leiba,

---

fat, fāte, fär, fåll, åsk, fãre; net, mē, hẻr; pin, pīne; not, nōte, mȯve, nȯr; up, lūte, pùll; oi, oil; ou, out; (lightened) aviạry, ẹlect, agǫny, intǫ,̓ ūnite; (obscured) errạnt, operạ, ardẹnt, actǫr, natụre; ch, chip; g, go; th, thin; ᴛн, then; y, you;

or Lev Davidovich, Bronstein) (1879–1940), Russ. Bolshevik leader, soviet minister of war and marine.

Trotsky or **Trotzky.** See *Trotski.*

Trowbridge (trō'brij), John Townsend (1827–1916), Am. novelist, poet, and writer of fiction for the young.

Troyon (trwo-yôṅ), Constant (1810–65), Fr. painter.

Trudeau (trö'dō), Edward L. (1848–1915), Am. physician.

Truman (trö'man), Harry S. (1884–), 33rd president of U. S. (1945–).

Trumbull (trum'bùl), John (1750–1831), Am. poet.

Trumbull, John (1756–1843), Am. painter (son of Jonathan Trumbull, 1710–85).

Trumbull, Jonathan (1710–85), Am. patriot.

Trumbull, Jonathan (1740–1809), Am. statesman (son of Jonathan Trumbull, 1710–85).

Truxtun (truks'tun), Thomas (1755–1822), Am. naval officer.

Tryon (trī'on), William (1725?–88), Br. colonial governor.

Tschaikowsky (chī-kof'skē). See *Chaykovski.*

Tschudi (chö'dē), Ægidius, or Gilg (1505–72), Swiss historian.

Tsu Hsi (tsē shē), **Tzu Hsi** (tsē shē), or **Tsze Hsi** (tsē shē) (1834–1908), empress dowager and regent of China.

Tucker (tuk'er), Abraham ("Edward Search") (1705–74), Eng. philosopher and moralist.

Tullus Hostilius (tul'us hos-til'ĭ-us) (d. 640 B.C.), 3d (legendary) king of Rome (672–640 B.C.).

Tupper (tup'er), Sir Charles (1821–1915), Can. statesman, premier of Canada (1896).

Tupper, Sir Charles Hibbert (1855–), Can. statesman (son of Sir Charles).

Tupper, Martin Farquhar (1810–89), Eng. poet.

Turenne (dè tü-ren), Henri de La Tour d'Auvergne, Vicomte de (1611–75), Fr. marshal (son of Duc de Bouillon, and grandson of William I. of Orange).

Turgenev (tör-gen'yef), Ivan Sergyeevich (1818–83), Russ. novelist.

Turgot (tür-gō), Anne Robert Jacques (Baron de l'Aulne) (1727–81), Fr. statesman, financier, and economist.

Turner (tèr'nèr), Joseph Mallord William (1775–1851), Eng. painter.

Turner, Sharon (1768–1847), Eng. historian.

Turner, William (d. 1568), Eng. divine, physician, and botanist.

Turpin (tèr'pin), Richard, or Dick (1706–39), Eng. highwayman. [on agriculture.

Tusser (tus'èr), Thomas (1524?–80), Eng. writer (in verse)

Tutankhamen or **Tut-ankh-amen** (töt-ängk-ä'men) (fl. 14th cent. B.C.), king of Egypt, of 18th dynasty (tomb discovered in 1922). [Am. painter.

Twachtman (twächt'man), John Henry (1853–1902),

Twain (twān), Mark. Pseudonym of S. L. Clemens.

Tweed (twēd), William Marcy (1823–78), Am. politician, convicted of robbing New York City and imprisoned.

Tweedsmuir (twēdz'mūr), John Buchan, 1st Baron (1875–1940), Br. novelist, historian, and misc. writer, governor-general of Canada (1935–40).

Tyler (tī'lèr), John (1790–1862), 10th president of U. S. (1841–45). [revolt.

Tyler, Wat, or Walter (d. 1381), Eng. rebel, leader in peasants'

Tylor (tī'lor), Sir Edward Burnett (1832–1917), Eng. anthropologist.

Tyndale or **Tindale** (tin'dal), William (c1492–1536), Eng. religious reformer, translator of the Bible, and martyr.

Tyndall (tin'dal), John (1820–93), Br. physicist.

Tyrone (ti-rōn'), 2d Earl of. See *O'Neill, Hugh.*

Tyrrell (tir'el), George (1861–1909), Ir. Jesuit and theologian, expelled from the order for sympathy with modernism.

Tyrtæus (tèr-tē'us) (fl. 7th cent. B.C.), Gr. elegiac poet.

Tyrwhitt (tir'it), Sir Reginald Yorke (1870–), Br. admiral.

Tzu Hsi. See *Tsu Hsi.*

U

Überweg (ü'bèr-vāch), Friedrich (1826–71), Ger. philosophical writer.

Uccello (öt-chel'lō), Paolo (real name Paolo di Dono) (1396 or 1397–1475), Florentine painter.

Udall or **Udal** (ü'dal), Nicholas (1505–56), Eng. schoolmaster, dramatist, and scholar.

Ueberweg (ü'bèr-vāch). See *Überweg.*

Ugolino della Gherardesca (ö-gō-lē'nō del'lä gä-rär-des'kä). See *Gherardesca.*

Uhde (fon ö'dè), Fritz Karl Hermann von (1848–1911), Ger. painter.

Uhland (ö'länt), Johann Ludwig (1787–1862), Ger. poet and misc. writer.

Ulfilas (ul'fi-las) or **Wulfila** (wùl'fi-lä) (c311–c382), Gothic bishop, translator of the Bible into Gothic.

Ulpian (ul'pi-an) (Domitius Ulpianus) (c170–228?), Rom. jurist, born at Tyre.

Unamuno y Jugo (dā ö-nä-mö'nō ē Hö'gō), Miguel de (1864–1936), Sp. educator and author.

Underwood (un'dèr-wùd), Oscar Wilder (1862–1929), Am. legislator.

Urban II. (èr'ban) (Odo, or Otho) (c1042–99), Fr. ecclesiastic, pope (1088–99).

Urfé (dür-fā), Honoré d' (1568–1625), Fr. romance-writer, author of "Astrée."

Urquhart (èr'kàrt, Sc. èr'chàrt), Sir Thomas (1611–60), Sc. author and translator.

Urquiza (dā ör-kē'sä), Justo José de (1800–70), Argentine general and politician.

Ursins (dä-zür-saṅ), Princesse des (Marie Anne de la Trémoille, Princesse de Chalais, Mme. degli Orsini) (1642–1722), Fr. lady in waiting at the court of Philip V. of Spain, famous for her political influence.

Ursinus (èr-sī'nus), Zacharias (name orig. Bär) (1534–83), Ger. Protestant theologian.

Ursula (èr'sū-lä), Saint. A legendary British Christian princess said to have been put to death, with 11,000 attendant virgins, by the Huns, at Cologne, in the 3d (or 5th) century.

Ussher or **Usher** (ush'èr), James (1581–1656), Br. archbishop and scholar.

V

Vaca, Cabeza de. See *Cabeza de Vaca.*

Vaca de Castro (vä'kä dā käs'trō). See *Castro, Vaca de.*

Valdemar. See *Waldemar.*

Valdés, Armando Palacio. See *Palacio Valdés.*

Valdés (dā väl-dās'), Juan de (c1500–41?), Sp. theologian, in Italy.

Valdés, Juan Meléndez. See *Meléndez Valdés.*

Valdivia (dā väl-dē'vyä), Pedro de (c1498–1554?), Sp. soldier, conqueror of Chile.

Valdo (väl-dō). See *Waldo.*

Valens (vā'lenz) (c328–378), Eastern Rom. emperor (364–378) (brother of Valentinian I.).

Valentine (val'en-tīn), Saint (d. c270?), Christian martyr at Rome.

Valentinian I. (val-en-tin'ĭ-an) (Valentinianus) (321?–375), Rom. emperor (364–375) (brother of Emperor Valens).

Valentinian II. (Valentinianus) (c371–392), Rom. emperor (375–392) (son of Valentinian I.).

Valentinian III. (Valentinianus) (419?–455), Western Rom. emperor (425–455) (grandson of Theodosius I.).

Valentinus (val-en-tī'nus) (d. c160), Gnostic leader, in Rome.

Valera, Eamonn de. See *De Valera.*

Valera y Alcalá Galiano (vä-lā'rä ē äl-kä-lä' gä-lē-ä'nō), Juan (1824–1905), Sp. diplomatist, novelist, and misc. writer.

Valerian (va-lē'ri-an) (Publius Licinius Valerianus) (d. after 260), Rom. emperor (253–260), captured by Persians.

Valéry (vä-lā-rē), Paul (1871–1945), Fr. poet and misc. writer.

Valla (väl'lä), Laurentius (born Lorenzo della Valle) (c1407–57), It. humanist and critic.

Vallandigham (va-lan'di-gam), Clement Laird (1820–71), Am. politician.

Vámbéry (väm'bā-rē), Ármin, or Arminius (1832–1913), Hung. traveler and Orientalist.

Vanbrugh (van'brö), Sir John (1664–1726), Eng. dramatist and architect.

(variable) ḍ as d or j, ş as s or sh, ṭ as t or ch, ẓ as z or zh; o, F. cloche; ü, F. menu; ċh, Sc. loch; ṅ, F. bonbon; ', primary accent; ", secondary accent; †, obsolete; <, from; +, and; =, equals. See also lists at beginning of book.

Van Buren (van bū'rẹn), Martin (1782—1862), 8th president of U. S. (1837—41).

Vancouver (van-kö'vẻr), George (1758—98), Eng. navigator.

Vanderbilt (van'dẻr-bilt), Cornelius (called "Commodore Vanderbilt") (1794—1877), Am. capitalist.

Van der Meer, Jan. See *Meer, Jan van der.*

Van der Weyden, Rogier. See *Weyden.*

Vandevelde (vän-dẻ-vel'dẻ). See *Velde.*

Van Diemen, Anthony. See *Diemen.*

Van Doren (van dôr'ẹn), Carl (1885—   ), Am. literary critic.

Van Dorn (van dôrn), Earl (1820—63), Am. Confederate general.

Van Dyck (van dīk) or **Vandyke** (van-dīk'), Sir Anthony (orig. Anthonis van Dyck) (1599—1641), Flemish painter, for some years in England.

Van Dyke (van dīk), Henry (1852—1933), Am. clergyman, educator, diplomatist, and author.

Vane (vān), Sir Henry (1589—1654 or 1655), Eng. statesman.

Vane, Sir Henry, or Sir Harry (1613—62), Eng. statesman and author, executed on charge of treason (son of Sir Henry Vane, 1589—1654 or 1655).

Van Gogh, Vincent. See *Gogh.*

Van Hise (van hīs), Charles Richard (1857—1918), Am. geologist and educator.

Van Horne (van hôrn), Sir William Cornelius (1843—1915), Can. railroad manager, and financier, born in U. S.

Vannucci (vän-nöt'chē), Pietro. See *Perugino.*

Van Rensselaer (van ren'sẹ-lẻr), Stephen ("the Patroon") (1765—1839), Am. general and political leader.

Van Sweringen (van swer'in-jẹn), Mantis James (1881—1935), Am. railroad financier (brother of O. P.).

Van Sweringen, Oris Paxton (1879—1936), Am. railroad financier.

Van't Hoff (vänt hof), J. H. See *Hoff.*

Vargas (vär'gäs), José María (1786—1854), Venezuelan physician and politician.

Varoli (vä-rō'lē), Costanzo (1543?—75), It. anatomist.

Varro (var'ō), Marcus Terentius (c116—27? B.C.), Rom. scholar and author.

Varus (vā'rus), Publius Quintilius (d. A.D. 9), Rom. general, defeated by Arminius.

Vasari (vä-zä'rē), Giorgio (1511—74), It. painter, architect, and art historian.

Vasco da Gama (väs'kō dä gä'mä). See *Gama.*

Vassar (vas'ạr), Matthew (1792—1868), Am. brewer and philanthropist (born in England), founder of Vassar College.

Vattel (dẻ vȧ-tel), Emerich de (1714—67), Swiss jurist and publicist.

Vauban (dẻ vō-bän), Sébastien Le Prestre de (1633—1707), Fr. military engineer and marshal.

Vaudreuil (dẻ vō-drẻ-y'), Philippe de Rigaud, Marquis de (1640?—1725), Fr. administrator in Canada.

Vaudreuil-Cavagnal (-kȧ-vȧ-nyȧl), Pierre François de Rigaud, Marquis de (1698—1765), Fr. colonial governor in America, born in Canada (son of Marquis de Vaudreuil).

Vaughan (vân), Bernard (1847—1922), Eng. Jesuit preacher (brother of Herbert).

Vaughan, Henry ("the Silurist") (1622—95), Br. poet (of Wales).

Vaughan, Herbert (1832—1903), Eng. cardinal.

Vautier (vō-tyä), Benjamin (1829—98), Swiss-Ger. painter.

Vecchietta (vek-kē-et'tä). See *Lorenzo di Pietro.*

Vedder (ved'ẻr), Elihu (1836—1923), Am. painter and illustrator, in Italy.

Vega, Garcilaso de la. See *Garcilaso de la Vega.*

Vega Carpio (dä vā'gä kär'pyō), Lope Félix de (called Lope de Vega) (1562—1635), Sp. dramatist and poet.

Vegetius Renatus (ve-jē'shius re-nä'tus), Flavius (fl. c400), Rom. military writer.

Veit (fīt), Philipp (1793—1877), Ger. painter (grandson of Moses Mendelssohn).

Velásquez (vä-läs'kȧth) or **Velázquez** (vä-läth'kȧth), Diego Rodríguez de Silva y (1599—1660), Sp. painter.

Velde (vän dẻ vel'dẻ), Adriaan van de (1636?—72), Dutch painter (brother of Willem van de Velde, 1633—1707).

Velde, Willem van de ("the elder") (1611?—93), Dutch marine painter, for some years in England.

Velde, Willem van de ("the younger") (1633—1707), Dutch marine painter, in England (son of Willem van de Velde, 1611?—93).

Venantius Fortunatus (ve-nan'shius fôr-tū-nä'tus). See *Fortunatus.*

Vendôme (dẻ voñ-dōm), François de. See *Beaufort, Duc de.*

Vendôme, Louis Joseph, Duc de (Duc de Penthièvre) (1654—1712), Fr. general (great-grandson of Henry IV. of France).

Venizelos (ve-nẹ-ze'los), Eleutherios (1864—1936), Gr. statesman, born in Crete.

Vercingetorix (vẻr-sin-jet'ọ-riks) (d. 45? B.C.), Gallic chieftain, conquered by Caesar.

Verdi (vâr'dē), Giuseppe (1813—1901), It. musical composer.

Vereshchagin (ver-esh-chä'gẹn), Vasili Vasilevich (1842—1904), Russ. painter of military and other subjects.

Verga (vâr'gä), Giovanni (1840—1922), It. novelist.

Vergennes (dẻ ver-zhen), Charles Gravier, Comte de (1717—87), Fr. statesman and diplomatist.

Vergil. See *Virgil.*

Vergniaud (dẻ ver-nyō), Pierre Victurnien (1753—93), Fr. orator and revolutionist.

Verhaeren (ver-hä'rẹn), Émile (1855—1916), Belgian poet.

Verlaine (ver-lān), Paul (1844—96), Fr. poet.

Vermeer van Delft (ver-mär' vän delft), Jan. See *Meer, Jan van der* (1632—75).

Verne (vârn), Jules (1828—1905), Fr. novelist.

Vernet (ver-nā), Antoine Charles Horace (called Carle Vernet) (1758—1835), Fr. painter (son of Claude J.).

Vernet, Claude Joseph (1714—89), Fr. painter.

Vernet, Émile Jean Horace (1789—1863), Fr. painter, esp. of military subjects (son of Antoine C. H.).

Verneuil (dẻ ver-nẻ-y'), Marquise de. See *Entragues.*

Vernier (ver-nyā), Pierre (1580—1637), Fr. mathematician.

Vernon (vẻr'nọn), Edward ("Old Grog") (1684—1757), Eng. admiral.

Veronese (vā-rō-nā'zä), Paul. See *Caliari.*

Veronica (vẹ-ron'i-kạ), Saint. According to legend, a pious woman of Jerusalem who, having pity for Christ as he carried his cross to Calvary, offered him a cloth to wipe his brow, and received it back miraculously marked with the imprint of his face.

Verplanck (vẻr-plangk'), Gulian Crommelin (1786—1870), Am. scholar and writer.

Verrazano (dä ver-rä-tsä'nō), Giovanni da (c1480—1527?), It. navigator.

Verres (ver'ēz), Caius (d. 43 B.C.), Rom. politician, governor of Sicily, prosecuted by Cicero for extortion.

Verrocchio (del ver-rok'kē-ō), Andrea del (real name Andrea di Michele di Francesco de' Cioni) (1435—88), It. goldsmith, sculptor, and painter.

Vesalius (ve-sā'li-us), Andreas (1514—64), Belgian anatomist.

Vespasian (ves-pā'zhiạn) (Titus Flavius Sabinus Vespasianus) (A.D. 9—79), Rom. emperor (A.D. 70—79).

Vespucci (ves-pöt'chē), Amerigo (as Latinized, Americus Vespucius) (1451—1512), It. merchant and adventurer, from whom America is named.

Viardot-Garcia (vyär-dō-gär-thē'ä), Pauline (Michelle Ferdinande Pauline García, Mme. Viardot) (1821—1910), Fr. operatic singer, born in Paris of Sp. parentage (daughter of Manuel del P. V. García, and sister of Mme. Malibran).

Viaud (vyō), Louis Marie Julien ("Pierre Loti") (1850—1923), Fr. naval officer and author.

Vicente (vē-sen'tạ), Gil (c1470—c1536), Pg. dramatist, writing in Portuguese and Spanish.

Vico (vē'kō), Giovanni Battista (1668—1744), It. philosopher and jurist.

Victor I. (vik'tọr), Saint (d. 198?), bishop of Rome (189?—198?).

Victor Amadeus II. (am-ạ-dē'us) (in Italian, Vittorio Amedeo) (1666—1732), duke of Savoy (1675—1730), and king of Sicily (1713—20) and of Sardinia (1720—30).

Victor Emmanuel I. (e-man'ū-el) (in Italian, Vittorio Emanuele) (1759—1824), king of Sardinia (1802—21).

Victor Emmanuel II. (1820—78), king of Sardinia (from 1849), and first king of Italy (1861—78) (son of Charles Albert of Sardinia).

Victor Emmanuel III. (1869—   ), king of Italy (1900—   ) (son of Humbert I.).

Victoria (vik-tō′ri-ą) (1819–1901), queen of Great Britain and Ireland (1837–1901), and empress of India (1876–1901) (successor and niece of William IV.).

Victoria (vēk-tō′rē-ä), Guadalupe (orig. Manuel Félix Fernández) (1789–1843), Mex. general, and first president of Mexico (1824–29).

Victor-Perrin (vēk-tôr-pe-raṅ), Claude (Duc de Bellune, real name Victor Claude Perrin) (1764–1841), Fr. marshal.

Vidocq (vē-dok), François Eugène (1775–1857), Fr. adventurer, convict, and (later) detective.

Viète (vyāt), François (Franciscus Vieta) (1540–1603), Fr. mathematician.

Vieuxtemps (vyė-toṅ), Henri (1820–81), Belgian violinist and composer.

Vigée-Lebrun (vē-zhā-lė-bruṅ), Mme. See *Le Brun, Mme.*

Vignola (dä vē-nyō′lä), Giacomo Barocchio da. See *Barocchio.*

Vigny (dė vē-nyē), Alfred Victor, Comte de (1797–1863), Fr. poet, novelist, and dramatist.

Villa (vē′yä), Francisco ("Pancho Villa," real name said to be Doroteo Arango) (1872?–1923), Mex. bandit and revolutionist.

Villani (vēl-lä′nē), Giovanni (c1275–1348), It. chronicler.

Villanovanus (vil″ą-nǫ-vā′nus), Arnaldus. See *Arnold of Villanova.*

Villari (vēl′lä-rē), Pasquale (1827–1917), It. historian and misc. writer.

Villars (dė vē-lär), Claude Louis Hector, Duc de (1653–1734), Fr. marshal.

Villehardouin (dė vēl-är-dwaṅ), Geoffroi de (c1160–c1213), Fr. chronicler.

Villemain (vēl-maṅ), Abel François (1790–1870), Fr. historian and critic.

Villeneuve (dė vēl-nėv), Pierre Charles Jean Baptiste Silvestre de (1763–1806), Fr. admiral.

Villeroi (dė vēl-rwo), François de Neufville, Duc de (1644–1730), Fr. marshal.

Villiers (vil′ėrz or vil′yėrz), Barbara. See *Cleveland, Duchess of.*

Villiers, Charles Pelham (1802–98), Eng. statesman (brother of 4th Earl of Clarendon).

Villiers, George. See *Buckingham, Duke of.*

Villiers, George William Frederick. See *Clarendon, 4th Earl of.*

Villiers de l'Isle-Adam (dė vē-yä dė lēl-à-däṅ), Philippe Auguste Mathias, Comte de (1838–89), Fr. poet, novelist, and dramatist.

Villon (vē-lóṅ or vē-yóṅ), François (1431–after 1463), Fr. poet.

Vincent (vin′sęnt) or **Vincentius** (vin-sen′shius), Saint (d. 304?), Sp. deacon and martyr.

Vincent de Paul (vin′sęnt dę pâl, Fr. vaṅ-soṅ dė pōl), Saint (1576–1660), Fr. priest, founder of Congregation of Priests of the Mission, and of Sisters of Charity.

Vincent Ferrer (fer′ėr), Saint (in Spanish, San Vicente Ferrer, pron. fer-rär′) (1350 or 1355–1419), Sp. Dominican preacher.

Vincent of Beauvais (c1190–c1264), Fr. monk and Latin encyclopedist.

Vincent of Lérins (lā-raṅs), Saint (d. c450), Fr. theologian.

Vinci (dä vēn′chē), Leonardo da (1452–1519), It. painter, sculptor, architect, engineer, and scholar.

Vinogradoff (vē-nǫ-grä′dof), Sir Paul (1854–1925), Russ.-Eng. jurist and historian.

Viollet-le-Duc (vyo-lā-lė-dük), Eugène Emmanuel (1814–79), Fr. architect, archæologist, and writer on art.

Virchow (vėr′chou, Ger. fēr′chō), Rudolf (1821–1902), Ger. pathologist, anthropologist, and politician.

Virgil or **Vergil** (vėr′jil) (Publius Vergilius Maro) (70–19 B.C.), Rom. poet, author of "Æneid."

Virgil or **Vergil,** Polydore (c1470–1555?), It.-Eng. ecclesiastic and historian.

Virginia (vėr-jin′i-ą). In Roman legend, a beautiful maiden who in 449 B.C. was slain by her father, Lucius Virginius, a centurion, to keep her from falling a prey to the lust of the decemvir Appius Claudius, an act which led to the overthrow of the decemvirs.

Virginius (vėr-jin′i-us), Lucius. See *Virginia.*

Vischer (fish′ėr), Peter (c1455–1529), Ger. sculptor.

Visconti (vēs-kōn′tē), Ennio Quirino (1751–1818), It. archæologist.

Visconti, Gian Galeazzo (1347–1402), first duke of Milan (1395–1402).

Visconti, Matteo (1250–1322), lord of Milan (1295–1322).

Visconti-Venosta (-vä-nôs′tä), Marquis Emilio (1829–1914), It. statesman.

Visin (fon fē′zin), Denis von. See *Fonvizin.*

Vitruvius (vi-trö′vi-us) (Marcus Vitruvius Pollio) (fl. c14 B.C.), Rom. architect and engineer.

Vittorino da Feltre (vēt-to-rē′nō dä fel′trä) (real name Vittorino Ramboldini) (1378–1446), It. humanist and educator.

Vitus (vī′tus), Saint (d. c303?), Christian martyr, in Rome.

Vivarini (vē-vä-rē′nē), Antonio (Antonio da Murano) (d. c1470), It. painter.

Vivarini, Bartolommeo (Bartolommeo da Murano) (fl. 1450–99), It. painter (brother of Antonio).

Viviani (vē-vyä-nē), René (1863–1925), Fr. statesman.

Vladimir (vlad′i-mēr, Russ. vlä-dyē′mēr), Saint ("the Great") (c956–1015), grand prince of Russia (980–1015).

Vogler (fō′glėr), Georg Joseph (known as Abt, or Abbé, Vogler) (1749–1814), Ger. organist and composer.

Vogt (fōkt), Karl (1817–95), Ger.-Swiss naturalist.

Voisin. See *La Voisin.*

Volstead (vol′sted), Andrew J. (1860–), Am. Congressman, author of Volstead Act (1919) for enforcing 18th Amendment to Constitution of U. S. (national prohibition).

Volta (vol′tä), Alessandro, Count (1745–1827), It. physicist.

Voltaire (dė vol-tär), François Marie Arouet de (orig. François Marie Arouet) (1694–1778), Fr. philosopher and author.

Vondel (vän den von′del), Joost van den (1587–1679), Dutch poet and dramatist.

Voronoff (vor′ǫ-nof), Serge (1866–), Russ. surgeon in Paris, experimentalist in the grafting of organs and parts.

Vortigern (vôr′ti-gėrn) (fl. c450), a king of southeastern Britain who is said to have invited the Jutes to Britain to aid him against the northern tribes.

Voss (fos), Johann Heinrich (1751–1826), Ger. poet and translator.

Vossius (vosh′ius) or **Voss** (vos), Gerard Jan (1577–1649), Dutch scholar and theologian.

Vries (dė vrēs), Hugo de (1848–1935), Dutch botanist.

W

Wace (wäs) (fl. 1170), Anglo-Norman chronicler in verse.

Wackenroder (väk′ęn-rō″dėr), Wilhelm Heinrich (1773–98), Ger. author.

Waddington (wod′ing-tǫn, Fr. vä-daṅg-tôṅ), William Henry (1826–94), Fr. archæologist, statesman, and diplomatist, of English parentage.

Wade (wād), Benjamin Franklin (1800–78), Am. statesman.

Wagner (wag′nėr, Fr. våg-när), Charles (1851–1918), Fr. Protestant clergyman and writer.

Wagner (Ger. väg′nėr), Wilhelm Richard (1813–83), Ger. composer and author, originator of the music drama.

Wainewright (wān′rīt), Thomas Griffiths (1794–1852), Eng. artist and critic, and poisoner.

Waite (wāt), Morrison Remick (1816–88), Am. jurist, chief justice of U. S. Supreme Court (1874–88).

Wakefield (wāk′fēld), Edward Gibbon (1796–1862), Eng. colonial organizer and statesman.

Walburga (wäl-bur′gä), Saint. See *Walpurgis.*

Waldeck-Rousseau (vål-dek-rö-sō), Pierre Marie René (1846–1904), Fr. statesman.

Waldemar I. (wol′dę-mär or väl′dę-mär) (or Valdemar I.) ("the Great") (1131–82), king of Denmark (1157–82).

Waldemar II. (or Valdemar II.) ("the Victorious") (1169?–1241), king of Denmark (1202–41) (son of Waldemar I.).

Waldemar IV. (or **III.**) (or Valdemar IV., or III.) (c1317–75), king of Denmark (1340–75).

Waldersee (fon väl′dėr-zā), Alfred, Graf von (1832–1904), Prussian general.

Waldo (väl-dō), Pierre, or Peter (also called Valdo, Waldes, or

Valdez) (fl. c1170), merchant of Lyons, founder of sect of Waldenses.

Waldseemüller (vält′zā-mül′ĕr), Martin (also called Hylacomylus) (c1470–c1521), Ger. geographer.

Waldteufel (vält′toi′fĕl, Fr. väl-tĕ-fel), Émile Charles (1837–1915), Fr. composer of dance-music.

Walker (wâ′kĕr), Amasa (1799–1875), Am. political economist.

Walker, Francis Amasa (1840–97), Am. economist and educator (son of Amasa).

Walker, Frederick (1840–75), Eng. painter and illustrator.

Walker, John (1732–1807), Eng. actor and lexicographer.

Walker, Robert James (1801–69), Am. statesman.

Walker, William (1824–60), Am. filibuster. [and traveler.

Wallace (wol′as), Alfred Russel (1823–1913), Eng. naturalist

Wallace, Henry Agard (1888–   ), Am. agriculturist and cabinet member, vice-president of U. S. (1941–   ).

Wallace, Lewis, or Lew (1827–1905), Am. general and novelist.

Wallace, Sir William (c1272–1305), Sc. military leader against the English, and national hero.

Wallace, William Vincent (1813?–65), Ir. musical composer.

Wallack (wol′ak), James William (c1794–1864), Eng.-Am. actor and theatrical manager.

Wallack, Lester (born John Johnstone Wallack) (1820–88), Am. actor and theatrical manager (son of James W.).

Wallenstein (wol′ĕn-stīn, Ger. fon väl′ĕn-shtīn) or **Waldstein** (fon vält′shtīn), Albrecht Wenzel Eusebius von (Duke of Friedland) (1583–1634), imperial general in Thirty Years' War, born in Bohemia.

Waller (wol′ĕr), Edmund (1606–87), Eng. poet.

Waller, Sir William (c1597–1668), Eng. general.

Wallis (wol′is), John (1616–1703), Eng. mathematician.

Wallon (vå-lôn), Henri Alexandre (1812–1904), Fr. historian and politician.

Walpole (wâl′pōl or wol′pōl), Horace, and Sir Robert. See *Orford, Earl of.*

Walpole, Sir Hugh Seymour (1884–1941), Eng. novelist, born in New Zealand.

Walpurgis (väl-pûr′gis), Saint (also called Walpurga and Walburga) (d. c780), Eng. missionary and abbess in Germany.

Walsingham (wâl′sing-am), Sir Francis (1530?–90), Eng. statesman.

Walter (wâl′tĕr), Hubert (d. 1205), Eng. prelate and statesman, archbishop of Canterbury.

Walter, John (1739–1812), Eng. newspaper proprietor.

Walter, John (1776–1847), Eng. journalist and newspaper proprietor (son of John Walter, 1739–1812).

Walter, Lucy (c1630–58), mistress of Charles II. of England, and mother of the Duke of Monmouth.

Walther von der Vogelweide (väl′tĕr fon der fō′gĕl-vī″dĕ) (fl. 1198–1228), Ger. minnesinger.

Walton (wâl′ton), George (1740–1804), Am. lawyer and patriot.

Walton, Izaak (1593–1683), Eng. writer, author of "Compleat Angler."

Wanamaker (won′a-mā″kĕr), John (1838–1922), Am. merchant.

Wappers (väp′ĕrs), Gustave, Baron (1803–74), Belgian painter.

Warbeck (wâr′bek), Perkin (1474?–99), impostor (born in Flanders), personator of Richard, Duke of York (son of Edward IV.), and pretender to the crown of England.

Warburton (wâr′bĕr-ton), William (1698–1779), Eng. bishop, controversialist, and critic.

Ward (wârd), Sir Adolphus William (1837–1924), Eng. historian and literary critic.

Ward, Artemas (1727–1800), Am. Revolutionary general.

Ward, Artemus. Pseudonym of C. F. Browne.

Ward, Mrs. (Elizabeth Stuart Phelps) (1844–1911), Am. novelist.

Ward, Mrs. Humphry (Mary Augusta Arnold) (1851–1920), Eng. novelist, born in Tasmania (granddaughter of Thomas Arnold, and niece of Matthew Arnold).

Ward, James (1843–1925), Eng. psychologist and philosophical writer.

Ward, John Quincy Adams (1830–1910), Am. sculptor.

Ward, Lester Frank (1841–1913), Am. geologist and sociologist.

Ward, Wilfrid Philip (1856–1916), Eng. biographer and essayist (son of William G.).

Ward, William George (1812–82), Eng. Rom. Cath. theologian.

Warfield (wâr′fēld), David (1866–   ), Am. actor.

Warham (wâr′am), William (c1450–1532), Eng. prelate and statesman, archbishop of Canterbury.

Warner (wâr′nĕr), Charles Dudley (1829–1900), Am. author.

Warner, Seth (1743–84), Am. Revolutionary officer.

Warner, Susan ("Elizabeth Wetherell") (1819–85), Am. novelist and religious writer, author of "The Wide, Wide World."

Warner, William (1558?–1609), Eng. poet.

Warren (wor′en), Joseph (1741–75), Am. physician and patriot.

Warren, Samuel (1807–77), Br. novelist, lawyer, and legal writer.

Warton (wâr′ton), Joseph (1722–1800), Eng. critic and poet.

Warton, Thomas (1728–90), Eng. critic, literary historian, and poet (brother of Joseph).

Warwick (wor′ik), Richard de Beauchamp, Earl of (1382–1439), Eng. soldier and statesman.

Warwick, Richard Neville, Earl of ("the Kingmaker") (1428–71), Eng. warrior and statesman.

Washburn (wosh′bĕrn), Cadwallader Colden (1818–82), Am. general and political leader (brother of E. B. Washburne).

Washburne (wosh′bĕrn), Elihu Benjamin (1816–87), Am. statesman and diplomatist.

Washington (wosh′ing-ton), Booker Taliaferro (1859?–1915), Am. negro writer and educator.

Washington, George (1732–99), Am. general, and 1st president of U. S. (1789–97).

Washington, Mrs. (Martha Dandridge, Mrs. Custis) (1732–1802), wife of George.

Wassermann (fon väs′ĕr-män), August von (1866–1925), Ger. physician and bacteriologist.

Wassermann, Jakob (1873–1934), Ger.-Austrian novelist.

Waterton (wâ′tĕr-ton), Charles (1782–1865), Eng. naturalist and traveler.

Watson (wot′son), Henry Brereton Marriott (1863–1921), Br. novelist, born in Australia.

Watson, John ("Ian Maclaren") (1850–1907), Sc. clergyman and novelist.

Watson, Richard (1737–1816), Eng. bishop, writer, and chemist.

Watson, Thomas (1557?–92), Eng. poet.

Watson, Sir William (1858–1935), Eng. poet.

Watt (wot), James (1736–1819), Br. engineer and inventor, perfecter of steam-engine.

Watteau (wä-tō′, Fr. vä-tō), Jean Antoine (1684–1721), Fr. painter.

Watterson (wot′ĕr-son), Henry (1840–1921), Am. journalist.

Watts (wots), George Frederick (1817–1904), Eng. painter and sculptor.

Watts, Isaac (1674–1748), Eng. theologian and hymn-writer.

Watts-Dunton (-dun′ton), Walter Theodore (1832–1914), Eng. poet, critic, and novelist.

Wauters (vō-tärs), Émile (1846–1933), Belgian painter.

Wayland (wā′land), Francis (1796–1865), Am. Baptist clergyman, educator, and author.

Wayne (wān), Anthony ("Mad Anthony") (1745–96), Am. general.

Webb (web), Alexander Stewart (1835–1911), Am. general and educator.

Webb, Sidney James. See *Passfield, 1st Baron.*

Weber (vā′bĕr), Ernst Heinrich (1795–1878), Ger. physiologist and anatomist.

Weber, Georg (1808–88), Ger. historian.

Weber, Karl Maria Friedrich Ernst, Freiherr von (1786–1826), Ger. musical composer.

Weber, Wilhelm Eduard (1804–91), Ger. physicist (brother of Ernst H.).

---

fat, fāte, fär, fȧll, ȧsk, fãre; net, mē, hėr; pin, pīne; not, nōte, mõve, nôr; up, lūte, pull; oi, oil; ou, out; (lightened) aviȧry, ėlect, agŏny, intŏ, ụnite; (obscured) errȧnt, operᾱ, ardȩnt, actǫr, natụre; ch, chip; g, go; th, thin; ᴛʜ, then; y, you;

Webster (web'stèr), Daniel (1782—1852), Am. statesman and orator.

Webster, John (fl. 1602—24), Eng. dramatist.

Webster, Noah (1758—1843), Am. lexicographer and misc. writer.

Webster, Sir Richard Everard. See *Alverstone, Viscount.*

Wedekind (vä'dè-kint), Frank (1864—1918), Ger. dramatist.

Wedgwood (wej'wùd), Josiah (1730—95), Eng. potter.

Weed (wēd), Thurlow (1797—1882), Am. journalist and politician.

Weenix (vä'niks), Jan (1640—1719), Dutch painter (son of Jan B.).

Weenix, Jan Baptist (1621—60), Dutch painter.

Weingartner (vīn'gärt″nèr), Paul Felix (1863—1942), Austrian musical composer and conductor.

Weir (wēr), Julian Alden (1852—1919), Am. painter (son of Robert W.).

Weir, Robert Walter (1803—89), Am. painter.

Weismann (vīs'män), August (1834—1914), Ger. biologist.

Welch (welch), William Henry (1850—1934), Am. pathologist.

Welhaven (vel'hä-ven), Johan Sebastian Cammermeyer (1807—73), Norw. poet and critic.

Welles (welz), Gideon (1802—78), Am. statesman.

Wellesley (welz'li), Arthur. See *Wellington, 1st Duke of.*

Wellesley, Richard Colley Wellesley, Marquis (1760—1842), Br. statesman and administrator (brother of 1st Duke of Wellington).

Wellington (wel'ing-ton), Arthur Wellesley, 1st Duke of (1769—1852), Br. general and statesman.

Wells (welz), David Ames (1828—98), Am. economist.

Wells, Herbert George (1866—1946), Eng. novelist and misc. writer.

Welsbach (fon vels'bäch), Karl Auer, Freiherr von (1858—1929), Austrian chemist and inventor.

Wemyss. See *Wester Wemyss.*

Wenceslaus (wen'ses-lâs) or **Wenzel** (ven'tsel) (1361—1419), emperor of the Holy Roman Empire (1378—1400), and king of Bohemia (1378—1419) (son of Emperor Charles IV.).

Wentworth (went'wèrth), Benning (1696—1770), Am. colonial governor of New Hampshire.

Wentworth, Thomas. See *Strafford, 1st Earl of.*

Werfel (ver'fel), Franz V. (1890—1945), Austrian poet, dramatist, and misc. writer.

Wergeland (ver'ge-län), Henrik Arnold (1808—45), Norw. poet.

Werner (ver'nèr), Abraham Gottlob (1750—1817), Ger. geologist.

Werner, Anton Alexander von (1843—1915), Ger. painter.

Werner, Friedrich Ludwig Zacharias (1768—1823), Ger. poet and dramatist.

Wesley (wes'li or wez'li), Charles (1707—88), Eng. Methodist preacher and hymn-writer (brother of John).

Wesley, John (1703—91), Eng. preacher, founder of Methodism.

West (west), Benjamin (1738—1820), Am.-Eng. painter.

Westcott (west'kot), Brooke Foss (1825—1901), Eng. bishop, Biblical scholar, and theologian.

Westermann (ves-ter-män), François Joseph (1751—94), Fr. general.

Wester Wemyss (wes'tèr wēmz), Rosslyn Erskine Wemyss, Baron (1864—1933), Br. admiral.

Westinghouse (wes'ting-hous), George (1846—1914), Am. inventor.

Westmacott (west'ma-kot), Sir Richard (1775—1856), Eng. sculptor.

Wetherell (weᴛн'èr-el), Elizabeth. Pseudonym of Susan Warner.

Weyden (vän dèr vī'den), Rogier van der (orig. Roger de la Pasture) (c1400—64), Flemish painter.

Weyler y Nicolau (wä-ē-lär' ē nē-kō-lä'ö), Valeriano (Marquis of Teneriffe, Duke of Rubí) (1838—1930), Sp. general, esp. in Cuba, and politician.

Weyman (wā'man), Stanley John (1855—1928), Eng. novelist.

Whalley (hwol'i), Edward (d. c1675), Eng. general and regicide, who died in exile in America (cousin of Oliver Cromwell).

Wharton (hwâr'ton), Mrs. (Edith Newbold Jones) (1862—1937), Am. novelist.

Wharton, Francis (1820—89), Am. legal and theological writer.

Wharton, Thomas Wharton, 1st Marquis of (1648—1715), Eng. statesman.

Whately (hwāt'li), Richard (1787—1863), Eng. archbishop, theologian, and misc. writer.

Wheaton (hwē'ton), Henry (1785—1848), Am. lawyer and diplomatist.

Wheatstone (hwēt'ston), Sir Charles (1802—75), Eng. physicist and inventor.

Wheeler (hwē'lèr), Benjamin Ide (1854—1927), Am. educator.

Wheeler, Joseph (1836—1906), Am. general.

Wheeler, William Almon (1819—87), Am. legislator, vice-president of U. S. (1877—81).

Whewell (hū'el), William (1794—1866), Eng. philosopher and scientist.

Whipple (hwip'l), Edwin Percy (1819—86), Am. essayist and critic.

Whistler (hwis'lèr), James Abbott McNeill (1834—1903), Am. painter and etcher, in England.

Whiston (hwis'ton), William (1667—1752), Eng. clergyman, theologian, and mathematician.

White (hwīt), Andrew Dickson (1832—1918), Am. educator, historian, and diplomatist.

White, Edward Douglass (1845—1921), Am. jurist, chief justice of U. S. Supreme Court (1910—21).

White, Sir George Stuart (1835—1912), Br. field-marshal.

White, Gilbert (1720—93), Eng. writer on natural history.

White, Henry Kirke (1785—1806), Eng. poet.

White, Joseph Blanco (orig. José María Blanco) (1775—1841), Eng. clergyman, theological writer, and poet, born in Spain.

White, Richard Grant (1822—85), Am. author and Shaksperian scholar.

White, Stanford (1853—1906), Am. architect (son of Richard G.).

White, William Hale ("Mark Rutherford") (1831—1913), Eng. novelist and misc. writer.

Whitefield (hwit'fēld), George (1714—70), Eng. Methodist preacher.

Whitehead (hwīt'hed), William (1715—85), Eng. poet.

Whitelock (hwit'lok), Bulstrode (1605—75), Eng. statesman.

Whitgift (hwit'gift), John (1530?—1604), Eng. prelate, archbishop of Canterbury.

Whitlock (hwit'lok), Brand (1869—1934), Am. writer and diplomatist.

Whitman (hwit'man), Walt (1819—92), Am. poet.

Whitney (hwit'ni), Mrs. (Adeline Dutton Train) (1824—1906), Am. writer, esp. of books for girls.

Whitney, Eli (1765—1825), Am. inventor (of cotton-gin).

Whitney, Josiah Dwight (1819—96), Am. geologist.

Whitney, William Dwight (1827—94), Am. philologist and lexicographer (brother of Josiah D.).

Whittier (hwit'i-èr), John Greenleaf (1807—92), Am. poet.

Whittingham (hwit'ing-am), Charles (1767—1840), Eng. printer.

Whittingham, Charles (1795—1876), Eng. printer (nephew of Charles Whittingham, 1767—1840).

Whittington (hwit'ing-ton), Richard (d. 1423), lord mayor of London. According to a popular tale, Whittington, being an ill-treated scullion in London, fled from his employment, but turned back at the sound of bells that seemed to say, "Turn again, Whittington, lord mayor of London." After his return it appeared that a cat, his only resource, contributed to the freight of a merchant vessel, had been sold at an enormous price to an African potentate, thus furnishing the foundation of his fortune.

Whymper (hwim'pèr), Edward (1840—1911), Eng. artist, mountain-climber, and explorer.

Whyte-Melville (hwīt'mel'vil), George John (1821—78), Br. soldier and novelist.

Wickliffe or **Wiclif,** John. See *Wyclif.*

Widukind. See *Wittekind.*

(variable) ḍ as d or j, ş as s or sh, ṭ as t or ch, ẕ as z or zh; o, F. cloche; ü, F. menu; ċh, Sc. loch; ṅ, F. bonbon; ′, primary accent; ″, secondary accent; †, obsolete; <, from; +, and; =, equals. See also lists at beginning of book.

Wieland (vē'länt), Christoph Martin (1733—1813), Ger. poet, novelist, and misc. writer.

Wieniawski (vye-nyäf'skḝ), Henryk (1835—80), Pol. violinist.

Wiertz (vērts), Antoine Joseph (1806—65), Belgian painter.

Wiffen (wif'ẹn), Jeremiah Holmes (1792—1836), Eng. poet, translator of Tasso's "Jerusalem Delivered."

Wilamowitz-Möllendorff (fon vē-lä-mō'vits-mèl'ẹn-dôrf), Ulrich von (1848—1931), Ger. classical scholar.

Wilberforce (wil'bẻr-fōrs), Samuel (1805—73), Eng. bishop (son of William).

Wilberforce, William (1759—1833), Eng. statesman, philanthropist, and religious writer.

Wilbrandt (vil'bränt), Adolf (1837—1911), Ger. novelist, dramatist, and poet.

Wilbrord, Saint. See *Willibrord*.

Wilbur (wil'bẻr), John (1774—1856), Am. Quaker preacher, founder of branch of Friends called Wilburites.

Wild (wīld), Jonathan (1682?—1725), Eng. receiver of stolen goods, and informer.

Wilde (wīld), Oscar O'Flahertie Wills (1856—1900), Br. dramatist and poet.

Wildenbruch (fon vil'dẹn-brúch), Ernst von (1845—1909), Ger. dramatist, poet, and novelist.

Wiley (wī'li), Harvey Washington (1844—1930), Am. chemist.

Wilfrid (wil'frid) or **Wilfrith** (wil'frith), Saint (634?—709), Eng. prelate, bishop of York.

Wilhelmina I. (vil-hel-mē'nä) (1880—   ), queen of the Netherlands (1890—   ) (daughter of William III. of the Netherlands).

Wilkes (wilks), Charles (1798—1877), Am. admiral and explorer.

Wilkes, John (1727—97), Eng. politician.

Wilkie (wil'ki), Sir David (1785—1841), Sc. painter.

Wilkins (wil'kinz), Mary Eleanor. See *Freeman, Mrs.*

Wilkinson (wil'kin-sọn), James (1757—1825), Am. general and adventurer.

Wilkinson, Sir John Gardner (1797—1875), Eng. traveler and Egyptologist.

Willard (wil'ạrd), Edward Smith (1853—1915), Eng. actor.

Willard, Mrs. (Emma Hart) (1787—1870), Am. educator.

Willard, Frances Elizabeth (1839—98), Am. educator, writer, and temperance advocate.

Willcocks (wil'koks), Sir William (1852—1932), Br. engineer.

William I. (wil'yạm) ("William the Conqueror") (Duke of Normandy) (1027 or 1028—87), king of England (1066—87) (first king of Norman line).

William II. (called William Rufus, or 'William the Red') (1056?—1100), king of England (1087—1100) (son of William I.).

William III. (Prince of Orange) (1650—1702), king of Great Britain and Ireland (1689—1702) (successor and nephew of James II., and husband of Mary II.).

William IV. (1765—1837), king of Great Britain and Ireland (1830—37) (brother of George IV.).

William I. (in German, Wilhelm, pron. vil'helm) (1797—1888), king of Prussia (1861—88), and Ger. emperor (1871—88) (brother of Frederick William IV.).

William II. (1859—1941), king of Prussia and Ger. emperor (1888—1918) (son of Emperor Frederick III.).

William I. (1772—1843), king of the Netherlands (1815—40).

William II. (1792—1849), king of the Netherlands (1840—49) (son of William I.).

William III. (1817—90), king of the Netherlands (1849—90) (son of William II.).

William I. (Prince of Orange and Count of Nassau, called "William the Silent") (1533—84), Dutch statesman and soldier (born in Germany), leader of the revolt of the Netherlands against Spain.

William ("William the Lion") (1143—1214), king of Scotland (1165—1214) (grandson of David I.).

William of Champeaux (shän-pō) (c1070—1121), Fr. bishop and scholastic philosopher.

William of Malmesbury (mämz'bẹ-ri) (c1090—c1143), Eng. monk and historian.

William of Occam or **Ockham** (ok'ạm) ("the Singular and Invincible Doctor") (d. 1349?), Eng. scholastic philosopher.

William of Wykeham (wik'ạm) (1324—1404), Eng. bishop and lord chancellor.

Williams (wil'yạmz), Eleazar (1787?—1858), Am. missionary to the Indians.

Williams, Sir George (1821—1905), Eng. merchant and philanthropist, founder of Young Men's Christian Association.

Williams, John (1582—1650), Eng. archbishop and politician.

Williams, Roger (c1604—83), Eng. settler in America, pioneer of religious liberty, and founder of the colony of Rhode Island.

Williams, Talcott (1849—1928), Am. journalist and educator.

Willibrord (wil'i-brôrd) or **Wilbrord** (wil'brôrd), Saint ("the Apostle of the Friesians") (c657—738?), Eng. missionary, and archbishop of Utrecht.

Willingdon (wil'ing-dọn), Freeman Freeman-Thomas, 1st Marquis of (1866—1941), Eng. statesman, governor-general of Canada (1926—31).

Willis (wil'is), Nathaniel Parker (1806—67), Am. writer.

Willkie (wil'ki), Wendell Lewis (1892—1944), Am. lawyer, industrialist, and political leader.

Willoughby (wil'ọ-bi), Sir Hugh (d. 1554), Eng. soldier and arctic navigator.

Wills (wilz), William John (1834—61), Australian explorer, born in England.   [jurist.

Wilmot (wil'mot), David (1814—68), Am. legislator and

Wilson (wil'sọn), Alexander (1766—1813), Sc.-Am. ornithologist and poet.   [novelist.

Wilson, Mrs. (Augusta Jane Evans) (1835—1909), Am.

Wilson, Edmund Beecher (1856—1939), Am. zoölogist.

Wilson, Henry (orig. Jeremiah Jones Colbaith) (1812—75), Am. statesman, vice-president of U. S. (1873—75).

Wilson, Sir Henry Hughes (1864—1922), Br. field-marshal (assassinated).

Wilson, James (1742—98), Am. patriot and jurist, associate justice of U. S. Supreme Court (1789—98), born in Scotland.

Wilson, John ("Christopher North") (1785—1854), Sc. author.

Wilson, Richard (1714—82), Br. landscape-painter.

Wilson, (Thomas) Woodrow (1856—1924), 28th president of U. S. (1913—21).

Wilson, William Lyne (1843—1900), Am. educator and legislator.

Wimborne (wim'bọrn), Ivor Churchill Guest, 1st Viscount (1873—1939), Eng. administrator in Ireland (grandson of Lady Schreiber).

Wimpffen (dẻ vaṅ-fen), Emmanuel Félix de (1811—84), Fr. general.

Wimpheling (vim'fẹ-ling) or **Wimpfeling** (vimp'fẹ-ling), Jakob (1450—1528), Ger. humanist and educationist.

Winckelmann (ving'kẹl-män), Johann Joachim (1717—68), Ger. archæologist and writer on classical art.

Windelband (vin'dẹl-bänt), Wilhelm (1848—1915), Ger. philosophical writer.

Windham (wind'ạm), William (1750—1810), Eng. statesman.

Windisch-Grätz (tsö vin'dish-gräts'), Alfred Candidus Ferdinand, Prince zu (1787—1862), Austrian field-marshal.

Windthorst (vint'hôrst), Ludwig (1812—91), Ger. statesman.

Winebrenner (wīn'bren''ẻr), John (1797—1860), Am. clergyman, founder of religious body called Church of God (Winebrennerians).

Wingate (wing'gạt), Sir Francis Reginald (1861—   ), Br. general and administrator in the Sudan.

Winkelried (fon ving'kẹl-rēt), Arnold von (d. 1386), Swiss patriot.

Winslow (winz'lō), Edward (1595—1655), Eng. settler at Plymouth, Mass. (1620), and governor of the colony.

Winslow, John Ancrum (1811—73), Am. admiral.

Winsor (win'zọr), Justin (1831—97), Am. librarian and historian.

Winthrop (win'thrọp), John (1588—1649), colonial governor of Massachusetts, born in England.

Winthrop, John (1606—76), colonial governor of Connecticut, born in England (son of John Winthrop, 1588—1649).

Winthrop, Robert Charles (1809—94), Am. statesman and orator.

Winthrop, Theodore (1828—61), Am. author and soldier.

Wireker, Nigel. See *Nigel*.

Wirth (virt), Karl Joseph (1879—   ), Ger. statesman.

Wise (wīz), Isaac Mayer (1819—1900), Am. rabbi, editor, and writer, born in Bohemia.

Wise, Stephen Samuel (1872—   ), Am. rabbi, born in Hungary.

Wiseman (wīz'man), Nicholas Patrick Stephen (1802—65), Br. cardinal and writer.

Wishart (wish'ärt), George (c1513—46), Sc. Protestant reformer and martyr.

Wislicenus (vis-lē-tsā'nús), Johannes (1835—1902), Ger. chemist.

Wissmann (fon vis'män), Hermann von (1853—1905), Ger. explorer and administrator in Africa.

Wister (wis'tèr), Owen (1860—1938), Am. novelist and misc. writer (grandson of Frances Anne Kemble).

Wither (wiŧH'èr), George (1588—1667), Eng. poet.

Witherspoon (wiŧH'èr-spŏn), John (1723—94), Sc.-Am. Presbyterian divine, educator, and statesman.

Witte (vit'è), Count Sergius (in Russian, Sergyey Yulevich Vitte) (1849—1915), Russ. statesman.

Wittekind (wit'ẹ-kind) or **Widukind** (wid'ŏ-kind) (d. c807), Saxon warrior, opponent of Charlemagne.

Wittgenstein (vit'gẹn-shtīn), Count Ludwig Adolf Peter (Prince of Sayn-Wittgenstein-Ludwigsburg) (1769—1843), Russ. field-marshal.

Wladyslaw II. (vlä'dis-läf). See *Jagello*.

Woehler (vè'lèr). See *Wöhler*.

Woffington (wof'ing-tọn), Margaret (called Peg Woffington) (c1714—60), Ir. actress.

Wöhler (vè'lèr), Friedrich (1800—82), Ger. chemist.

Wolcot (wŭl'kọt), John ("Peter Pindar") (1738—1819), Eng. satiric poet.

Wolcott (wŭl'kọt), Oliver (1726—97), Am. patriot.

Wolcott, Oliver (1760—1833), Am. statesman (son of Oliver Wolcott, 1726—97).

Wolf (volf), Friedrich August (1759—1824), Ger. classical scholar.

Wolf, Hugo (1860—1903), Austrian musical composer, esp. of songs.

Wolfe (wŭlf), Charles (1791—1823), Ir. poet, author of "The Burial of Sir John Moore."

Wolfe, James (1727—59), Eng. general, killed at the battle of Quebec.

Wolff or **Wolf** (fon volf), Christian, Freiherr von (1679—1754), Ger. philosopher and mathematician.

Wolff, Kaspar Friedrich (1733—94), Ger. anatomist and physiologist, in Russia.

Wolf-Ferrari (volf'fer-rä'rē), Ermanno (1876—   ), It. musical composer.

Wolfram von Eschenbach (vol'främ fon esh'ẹn-bäch) (fl. c1210), Ger. epic poet, author of "Parzival."

Wollaston (wŭl'a-stọn), William (1660—1724), Eng. philosophical writer.

Wollaston, William Hyde (1766—1828), Eng. chemist and physicist.

Wollstonecraft (wŭl'stọn-kräft), Mary. See *Godwin, Mrs.*

Wolseley (wŭlz'li), Garnet Joseph Wolseley, Viscount (1833—1913), Br. field-marshal.

Wolsey (wŭl'zi), Thomas (1475?—1530), Eng. cardinal and statesman.

Wolzogen (fon vol'tsō'gẹn), Ernst, Freiherr von (1855—1934), Ger. dramatist and novelist.

Wood (wŭd), Anthony (Anthony à Wood) (1632—95), Eng. antiquary and historian.

Wood, Mrs. Henry (Ellen Price) (1814—87), Eng. novelist, author of "East Lynne."

Wood, Sir Henry Evelyn (1838—1919), Eng. field-marshal.

Wood, Sir Henry Joseph (1869—   ), Eng. musical conductor.

Wood, Leonard (1860—1927), Am. general and territorial administrator.

Woodberry (wŭd'ber-i), George Edward (1855—1930), Am. poet and critic.

Woodward (wŭd'wärd), Sir Arthur Smith (1864—   ), Eng. geologist and paleontologist.

Woodward, John (1665—1728), Eng. geologist and naturalist.

Woodworth (wŭd'wèrth), Samuel (1785—1842), Am. poet, author of "The Old Oaken Bucket."

Woolman (wŭl'man), John (1720—72), Am. Quaker preacher and writer.

Woolner (wŭl'nèr), Thomas (1825—92), Eng. sculptor and poet.

Woolsey (wŭl'si), Theodore Dwight (1801—89), Am. educator and author.

Worcester (wûs'tèr), Elwood (1862—1940), Am. clergyman and writer.

Worcester, Joseph Emerson (1784—1865), Am. lexicographer.

Worde, Wynkyn de. See *Wynkyn de Worde*.

Wordsworth (wèrdz'wèrth), Christopher (1774—1846), Eng. divine, educator, and scholar (brother of William).

Wordsworth, Christopher (1807—85), Eng. bishop, scholar, and author (son of Christopher Wordsworth, 1774—1846).

Wordsworth, William (1770—1850), Eng. poet.

Worth (wèrth), William Jenkins (1794—1849), Am. general.

Wotton (wot'ọn), Sir Henry (1568—1639), Eng. diplomatist and author.

Wouwerman (vou'vèr-män) or **Wouwermans** (vou'vèr-mäns), Philips (1619—68), Dutch painter.

Wrangel or **Wrangell** (fon vrän'gel), Baron Ferdinand Petrovich von (1796—1870), Russ. admiral and explorer.

Wrangel, Baron Petr Nikolaevich (1878—1928), Russ. general, opponent of the Bolsheviki.

Wray, John. See *Ray*.

Wrede (vrā'dè), Karl Philipp, Prince (1767—1838), Bavarian field-marshal.

Wren (ren), Sir Christopher (1632—1723), Eng. architect.

Wright (rīt), Sir Almroth Edward (1861—   ), Br. physician.

Wright, Joseph (1855—1930), Eng. philologist and lexicographer.

Wright, Orville (1871—   ), Am. aëronautic inventor (brother of Wilbur).

Wright, Thomas (1810—77), Eng. antiquary.

Wright, Wilbur (1867—1912), Am. aëronautic inventor.

Wriothesley (rots'li), Henry. See *Southampton, 3d Earl of.*

Wulfila. See *Ulfilas*.

Wundt (vùnt), Wilhelm Max (1832—1920), Ger. physiologist, psychologist, and philosopher.

Wurmser (fon vùrm'zèr), Dagobert Siegmund, Graf von (1724—97), Austrian field-marshal, born in Alsace.

Wu Ting-fang (wö ting-fäng') (1842?—1922), Chin. diplomatist and statesman.

Wyant (wī'ạnt), Alexander H. (1836—92), Am. landscape-painter.

Wyatt (wī'ạt), Sir Thomas (1503?—42), Eng. diplomatist and poet.

Wyatt, Sir Thomas (c1521—54), Eng. soldier and conspirator, leader in rebellion against Mary I. (son of Sir Thomas Wyatt, 1503?—42).

Wycherley (wich'èr-li), William (c1640—1716), Eng. dramatist.

Wyclif or **Wycliffe** (wik'lif), John (d. 1384), Eng. religious reformer, and translator of the Bible.

Wykeham, William of. See *William of Wykeham*.

Wyndham (win'dạm), Sir Charles (1837—1919), Eng. actor and theatrical manager.

Wynkyn de Worde (wing'kin dè wôrd) (real name Jan van Wynkyn) (d. 1534?), Eng. printer, born in Alsace.

Wyntoun (win'tọn), Andrew of (fl. c1400), Sc. monk and chronicler.

Wyss (vis), Johann Rudolf (1781—1830), Swiss writer, author of "Swiss Family Robinson."

Wythe (with), George (1726—1806), Am. patriot and jurist.

X

Xavier (zav'i-èr or zā'vi-èr), Francis (Francisco de Xavier, or Javier, called "the Apostle of the Indies") (1506—52), Sp. Jesuit, missionary (esp. in India and Japan), and saint.

Xenocrates (ze-nok'ra-tēz) (396—314 B.C.), Gr. Platonic philosopher.

Xenophanes (ze-nof'a-nēz) (c570—c480 B.C.), Gr. philosopher, reputed founder of Eleatic school.

(variable) ḍ as d or j, ṣ as s or sh, ṭ as t or ch, ẓ as z or zh; o, F. cloche; ü, F. menu; ch, Sc. loch; ń, F. bonbon; ', primary accent; ", secondary accent; †, obsolete; <, from; +, and; =, equals. See also lists at beginning of book.

Xenophon (zen'ọ̄-fọn) (c434–c355 B.C.), Gr. historian and misc. writer.

Xerxes I. (zẽrk'sēz) (c519–465 B.C.), king of Persia (486?–465 B.C.) (son of Darius I. and Atossa).

Ximenes (zi-mē'nēz), Cardinal. See *Jiménez de Cisneros.*

Ximénez (Hē-mä'näth). See *Jiménez.*

Y

Yale (yāl), Elihu (1648–1721), Eng. colonial official, patron of Yale College.

Yamagata (yä-mä-gä'tä), Prince Aritomo (1838–1922), Jap. field-marshal and statesman.

Yancey (yan'si), William Lowndes (1814–63), Am. politician.

Yates (yāts), Edmund Hodgson (1831–94), Eng. journalist and novelist.

Yates, Richard (1818–73), Am. political leader, governor of Illinois (1861–65).

Yeardley (yẽrd'li), Sir George (c1580–1627), Eng. colonial governor of Virginia.

Yeats (yāts), William Butler (1865–1939), Ir. poet, dramatist, and essayist.

Yersin (yer-saṅ), Alexandre Émile John (1863–), Swiss physician and bacteriologist.

Yonge (yung), Charlotte Mary (1823–1901), Eng. novelist and misc. writer.

York (yôrk), Edmund of Langley, 1st Duke of (1341–1402), Eng. military leader, founder of house of York (son of Edward III. of England).

York, Frederick Augustus, Duke of (1763–1827), Eng. military leader (son of George III.).

York, Richard, 3d Duke of (1411–60), Eng. statesman, head of house of York (grandson of 1st Duke of York, Edmund of Langley, and father of Edward IV. and Richard III.).

Yoshihito (yō-shẹ̄-hē'tō) (1879–1926), emperor of Japan (1912–26) (son of Emperor Mutsuhito).

Young (yung), Arthur (1741–1820), Eng. traveler and agricultural writer.

Young, Brigham (1801–77), Am. Mormon leader.

Young, Edward (1683–1765), Eng. poet, author of "Night Thoughts."

Young, Owen D. (1874–), Am. lawyer and financier.

Young, Thomas (1773–1829), Eng. physician, physicist, and Egyptologist.

Younghusband (yung'huz″band), Sir Francis Edward (1863–1942), Br. soldier, explorer, and writer.

Ypres (ē'pr), John Denton Pinkstone French, 1st Earl of (1852–1925), Eng. field-marshal.

Ypsilanti (ip-si-lan'ti) or **Ypsilantis** (ip-si-lan'tis), Alexandros (1792–1828), Gr. patriot.

Ypsilanti or **Ypsilantis**, Demetrios (1793–1832), Gr. patriot (brother of Alexandros).

Ysaÿe (ē-zä'yè), Eugène (1858–1931), Belgian violinist.

Yuan Shi-kai or **Yuan Shih-kai** (yü-än' shē-kī') (1859–1916), Chin. statesman, president of Chinese Republic (1912–16).

Yule (yōl), Sir Henry (1820–89), Br. military engineer and Orientalist.

Z

Zadkiel (zad'ki-ẹl). Pseudonym of R. J. Morrison.

Zaehnsdorf (zänz'dôrf), Joseph (1816–86), Hung.-Eng. bookbinder.

Zaïmis (zä'ẹ̄-mēs), Alexandros (1855–1936), Gr. statesman.

Zamacois (thä-mä-kō'ēs), Eduardo (1842–71), Sp. painter.

Zamojski (zä-moi'skẹ̄), Jan (1541–1605), Pol. statesman and general.

Zangwill (zang'wil), Israel (1864–1926), Eng. Jewish novelist and dramatist.

Zankov (tsäng'kof), Dragan (1827–1911), Bulgarian politician.

Zarathustra. See *Zoroaster.*

Zeller (tsel'ẽr), Eduard (1814–1908), Ger. philosophical writer.

Zeno (zē'nō) (d. 491), Eastern Rom. emperor (474–491) (son-in-law of Emperor Leo I.).

Zenobia (ze-nō'bi-ạ) (d. after 272), queen of Palmyra in Syria (267–272), conquered by Romans.

Zeno of Citium (zē'nō, sish'i-um) (c336–c264 B.C.), Gr. philosopher, founder of Stoic school.

Zeno of Elea (ē'lẹ̄-ạ) (fl. c450 B.C.), Gr. philosopher.

Zeppelin (zep'ẹ-lin, Ger. fon tsep-ẹ-lēn'), Ferdinand, Graf von (1838–1917), Ger. general, and aëronautic inventor.

Zeuxis (zūk'sis) (fl. c430–c400 B.C.), Gr. painter.

Ziem (zyäṅ), Félix François Georges Philibert (1821–1911), Fr. painter.

Zieten or **Ziethen** (fon tsē'tẹn), Hans Joachim von (1699–1786), Prussian general.

Zimbalist (zim'bȧ-list), Efrem (1889–), Russ. violinist.

Zinzendorf (fon tsin'tsẹn-dôrf), Nikolaus Ludwig, Graf von (1700–60), Ger. reformer, reviver of religious body of Moravians.

Ziska (zis'kȧ), John (in Bohemian, Ján Žižka, pron. zhizh'kä) (c1370–1424), Bohem. general and Hussite leader.

Zola (zō'lȧ, Fr. zo-lä), Émile (1840–1902), Fr. novelist.

Zorilla (tho-rēl'yä), Manuel Ruiz (1834–95), Sp. politician.

Zorn (zôrn), Anders Leonhard (1860–1920), Swed. painter, etcher, and sculptor.

Zoroaster (zō-rọ̄-as'tẽr) or **Zarathustra** (zä-rạ-thös'trä) (fl. c1000? B.C.), Pers. religious teacher, founder of Magian religion.

Zorrilla y Moral (thor-rēl'yä ē mo-räl'), José (1817–93), Sp. poet and dramatist.

Zosimus (zō'si-mus) (fl. 5th cent.), Gr. historian.

Zrinyi (zrēn'yẹ̄), Miklós (or Nicholas), Count (1508–66), Hung. warrior against the Turks.

Zrinyi, Miklós (or Nicholas), Count (1616 or 1620–64), Hung. general against the Turks, and epic poet (great-grandson of Miklós Zrinyi, 1508–66).

Zuloaga (thö-lō-ä'gä), Ignacio (1870–1945), Sp. painter.

Zumalacárregui (thö-mä″lä-kär'rä-gē), Tomás (1788–1835), Sp. Carlist general.

Zurbarán (thör-bä-rän'), Francisco (1598–1662), Sp. painter.

Zweig (tsvīch), Stefan (1881–1942), Austrian author.

Zwingli (tsving'lē), Ulrich, or Huldreich (1484–1531), Swiss Protestant reformer.

GEOGRAPHICAL NAMES

GIVING FOR THE PLACES OF ESPECIAL INTEREST THE SPELLING, PRONUN-
CIATION, LOCATION, SIZE, POLITICAL RELATIONS, AND
OTHER SIGNIFICANT FACTS

BY

STEPHEN SARGENT VISHER, Ph.D. (CHICAGO)

MEM. ASSOC. AM. GEOGRS., F. R. G. S., SOC. DE GEOG. (PARIS), GEOL. SOC. AM.,
PROFESSOR OF GEOGRAPHY, INDIANA UNIVERSITY

In the selection of the names for this supplement, great care was taken to choose those of greatest present and prospective interest. All places considered by educators as essential for geography pupils to know are included, as well as those mentioned frequently in representative books of regional geography and travel. In addition, American towns of over 9,500 population are included, and many smaller places of especial interest. In foreign lands a somewhat higher limit is used, ranging from 10,000 population in the English-speaking countries to about 30,000 in China and India, for example, but many smaller places are included if of especial interest. The longer rivers, highest mountains, active volcanoes, chief and strategic islands, notable waterfalls, and other conspicuous or important places of each country are included so far as the limits of space permit. Numerous names and facts of interest not found in most gazetteers are given. The populations are given to the nearest thousand and the areas to the nearest 1,000 square miles.

The inclusion of latitude and longitude permits a prompt location of the place on a map even if the map does not show the place. For rivers, the location given is the mouth, and for regions, the center, except for provinces or departments having the same name as their capital city, in which case the capital is located.

☞ *For the population according to the Census of 1940 of places in the United States having 5,000 or more inhabitants, and of the States and possessions of the United States, see the end of this list.*

TABLE OF ABBREVIATIONS USED

* capital or county seat	*el.* elevation or altitude	*Neth.* Netherlands
# latitude and longitude	*Eng.* England	*oc.* ocean
ab. about	*est.* estimate	*Pa.* Pennsylvania
Agri. Agricultural	*ext.* extreme	*pen.* peninsula
Alb. Alberta	*Fr.* France or French	*pk.* peak
anc. ancient	*ft.* feet	*pop.* population in 1,000's
area (ar.) area in 1,000 square miles	*Ga.* Georgia	*prov.* province
Arch. archipelago	*Ger.* Germany or German	*riv.* river
Ark. Arkansas	*Ill.* Illinois	*S.* south or southern
Aust. Australia	*Ind.* Indiana	*spt.* seaport
bet. between	*isl.* island	*ter., terr.* territory
Br. British	*Ky.* Kentucky	*tn.* town
Br. Col. British Columbia	*La.* Louisiana	*trib.* tributary
C. central	*len.* length	*twp.* township
Car. Carolina	*Mass.* Massachusetts	*univ.* university
comm. commune	*Md.* Maryland	*Va.* Virginia
Cz-S. Czechoslovakia	*mi.* miles	*vil.* village
dept. department	*Mo.* Missouri	*vol.* volcano
dist. district	*mt.* mountain	*W.* west or western
E. east or eastern	*N.* north or northern	*Y-S.* Yugoslavia

For other abbreviations, see supplement of Abbreviations (page 2406).

A

Aachen (ä′chẹn), *Fr.* **Aix-la-Chapelle,** *anc.* Aquisgranum, city, ext. N. W. Rheinland, Prussia, W. Ger., pop. 154; treaties 1668, 1748; woolens; ✗ 50:45 N, 6:2 E.

Aalborg (ȧl′bôrg), city, N. Jutland, Denmark, pop. 58; ✗ 57:1 N, 9:55 E.

Aalesund (ä′le-sönd), see **Alesund.**

Aar (är) or **Aare** (ä′re), riv., C. Switz., to Rhine riv., len. 180 mi.; gorge; ✗ 47:38 N, 8:15 E.

Aarau (är′ou), city, N. C. Switz., on Aar riv.; * of Aargau canton, pop. 11; ✗ 47:25 N, 8:5 E.

Aargau (är′gou) or **Argovie,** canton, N. C. Switz., area 0.5, pop. 241, * Aarau, pop. 11; ✗ 47:25 N, 8:10 E.

Aarhus (âr′hös), spt., E. Jutland, Denmark, pop. 81; ✗ 56:11 N, 10:15 E.

Abaco (ä′bä-kō), isl., N. Bahamas, area ab. 0.2, pop. 4; ✗ 26:15 N, 77:15 W.

Abbeville (àb-vēl′), city, N. Fr., near mouth of Somme riv., pop. 21; ✗ 50:5 N, 1:50 E.

Aberavon (ab-ẽr-ä′vọn), spt. city, Glamorgan, S. Wales, pop. 15; ✗ 51:36 N, 3:49 W.

Aberdare (ab-ẽr-dâr′), city, N. Glamorgan, S. Wales, pop. 55; ✗ 51:43 N, 3:27 W.

Aberdeen (ab-ẽr-dēn′), county, E. C. Scotland, area 1.8, pop. 301, and its *, pop. 160, a spt.; Univ. of Aberdeen; ✗ 57:12 N, 2:10 W. — city, N. E. S. Dak., pop. 17; State Industrial School; ✗ 45:30 N, 98:30 W. — spt. city, S. W. Wash., pop. 19; lumber; ✗ 47 N, 123:50 W.

Abersychan (ab-ẽr-suk′ạn), city, Monmouthshire, Eng., near Newport, pop. 27; iron; ✗ 51:43 N, 3:4 W.

Abertillery (ab-ẽr-til′ẽr-i), city, Monmouthshire, Eng., pop. 38; ✗ 51:44 N, 3:8 W.

Aberystwith (ab-ẽr-ist′with), spt. city, Cardigan, W. C. Wales, pop. 11; Univ. College of Wales; ✗ 52:25 N, 4:3 W.

Abilene (ab′i-lēn), tn., N. C. Texas, pop. 27; Abilene and Simmons Colleges; ✗ 32:30 N, 99:45 W.

Åbo (ä′bō; *Sw.* ô′bö) or **Turku,** spt., S. W. Finland, pop. 58; univ.; ✗ 60:26 N, 22:18 E.

Åbo-Björneborg (ô′bō-byẽr′ne-bôrg), see **Turku-Pori.**

Abruzzi e Molise (ä-bröt′sē ä mō-lē′zä), dept., E. C. Italy, area 6.4, pop. 1,433; ✗ 42:15 N, 13:10 E.

Abyssinia (ab-i-sin′i-ä), empire, N. E. Africa, area 350, pop. ab. 10,000, * Addis Ababa, pop. ab. 65; ✗ 8 N, 40 E.: annexed by Italy in 1936.

Abyssinian Plateau (ab-i-sin′i-ạn), highland, N. E. Africa, mostly 5,000 to 10,000 ft.; ✗ 8 N, 40 E.

Acadia (ạ-kā′di-ä), former name for Nova Scotia.

Acapulco (ä-kä-pöl′kō), Pacific spt., Guerrero, S. Mexico, pop. 7; ✗ 16:59 N, 99:56 W.

Accra (ak′rä) or **Akkra,** spt. city, * of Gold Coast, Br. W. Africa, pop. 73; ✗ 5:40 N, 0:20 W.

Accrington (ak′ring-tọn), city, Lancashire, N. W. Eng., pop. 44; ✗ 53:46 N, 2:21 W.

Achin or **Acheen** (ä-chēn′), Dutch dependency, N. W. Sumatra, E. Indies, area 21, pop. 736; * Kuta Raja; ✗ 4:15 N, 97 E.

Aconcagua (ä-kon-kä′gwä), mt. pk., Andes, C. W. Argentina, el. 23,003 ft., highest peak in W. hemisphere; ✗ 32:30 S, 70:10 W. — prov., C. Chile, nearby, area 5, pop. 117; ✗ 32:20 S, 71 W.

Acre (ä-krä′), ter., ext. W. Brazil, area 57, pop. 93; ✗ 10 S, 70 W. — **Acre** (ä′kẽr), **Accre** or **Akkra,** spt., N. W. Palestine, pop. 6; ✗ 32:56 N, 35:2 E.

Actium (ak′shi-um), cape and anc. tn., N. W. Greece; naval battle, 31 B.C.; ✗ 38:55 N, 20:48 E.

Acton (ak′tọn), a borough of London, Eng., pop. 57; ✗ 51:30 N, 0:17 W.

Ada (ä′dä), tn., W. C. Ohio, pop. 2; Ohio Northern Univ.; ✗ 40:46 N, 83:50 W.

Adabazar (ä″dä-bä-zär′), an Asiatic suburb of Constantinople, pop. 25; ✗ 40:51 N, 30:23 E.

Adalia (ä-dä′lē-ä), prov., S. Turkey, pop. 225; and its *, on Gulf of Adalia, pop. 30; ✗ 36:54 N, 30:41 E.

Adamawa (ä-dä-mä′wä), highlands and dist. N. Cameroon, Fr. Equatorial Africa; ✗ 8 N, 13 E.

Adams (ad′ạmz), bridge between India and Ceylon, over shoals; ✗ 9:15 N, 79:30 E. — tn., N. W. Mass., pop.

twp. 13; ✗ 42:35 N, 73:7 W. — pk., Cascade range S. W. Wash., el. 12,470 ft.; ✗ 46:14 N, 121:30 W.

Adana (ä-dä′nạ), prov., Asiatic Turkey, N. W. of Syria, pop. 138, and its *, pop. 64; ✗ 36:55 N, 35:10 E.

Adda (ä′dä), riv., Alps, N. Italy through Lake Como to Po riv., len. 180 mi.; ✗ 46:10 N, 9:20 E.

Addis Ababa (äd′is ä′bä-bạ, äd′is ä′wạ-wạ), city, * of Abyssinia, pop. 65; ✗ 9 N, 38:30 E.

Adelaide (ad′ẹ-lād), city, S. E. S. Australia, state *, pop. with suburbs, 318; Univ. of Adelaide; ✗ 34:56 S, 138:36 E.

Aden (ä′dẹn or ā′dẹn), Br. protectorate, S. W. Arabia, area 9, pop. 100, and its *, a spt., pop. ab. 50; ✗ 12:45 N, 45:12 E.

Aden, Gulf of, portion of Arabian Sea bet. Arabia and Somaliland, N. E. Africa; ✗ 12 N, 47 E.

Adernò (ä-där-nō′), city, W. slope of Mt. Etna, Sicily, pop. comm. 30; ✗ 37:39 N, 14:50 E.

Adige (ä′dē-jä), *anc.* Athesis, riv., ext. N. Italy to Gulf of Venice, len. 220 mi.; ✗ 45:10 N, 12:20 E.

Adirondack (ad-i-ron′dak), mt. range, N. New York; summit Mt. Marcy, el. 5,344 ft.; ✗ 43:45 N, 74:30 W.

Adis Abeba, see **Addis Ababa.**

Admiralty (ad′mi-rạl-ti), group isls., N. E. of Papua, largest is Manus Isl.; Australian Mandate; ✗ 2:5 S, 147 E.

Adramyti (ad-rạ-mit′i), gulf, W. Asia Minor, behind Mytilene Isl.; ✗ 39:30 N, 26:45 E. — tn., near its head (also called **Edremid**), pop. ab. 5; ✗ 39:36 N, 27:3 E.

Adrian (ā′dri-ạn), tn. S. E. Mich., pop. 14; Adrian College; ✗ 41:54 N, 84:3 W.

Adrianople (ad″ri-ạn-ō′pl) or **Edirne,** city, European Turkey, head of navigation on Maritza riv., pop. 56; ✗ 41:40 N, 26:35 E.

Adriatic (ā-dri-at′ik or ad-ri-at′ik), sea, arm of Mediterranean sea, E. of Italy, len. 500 mi.; ✗ 43 N, 15 E.

Ægades (ẹ-gā′dēz), group small isls., W. tip of Sicily, pop. 12; ✗ 37:58 N, 12:3 E.

Ægean (ẹ-jē′ạn), sea, part of Mediterranean sea bet. Greece and Asia Minor, len. 350 mi., width, 200 mi.; ✗ 39 N, 25 E.

Ægina (ẹ-jī′nạ), gulf, S. of Athens, Greece; ✗ 37:45 N, 23:30 E. — isl. therein, with its spt., pop. 6; ✗ 37:45 N, 23:27 E.

Ætna, see **Etna.**

Afghanistan (af-gän-i-stän′), country between India and Persia, Baluchistan and Russian Turkestan, area ab. 250, pop. ab. 12,000, * Kabul, pop. 100; ✗ 33 N, 65 E.

Afghan Turkestan (af′gạn tör-ke-stän′), region of Afghanistan N. of Hindu Kush Mts.; ✗ 36 N, 67 E.

Afium (ä-fē-öm′) or **Afium Karahissar,** city, S. W. C. Asia Minor, pop. 37; ✗ 38:35 N, 30:30 E.

Africa (af′ri-kä), continent S. of Europe, area 11,600, len. 4,970, width 4,700, pop. ab. 154,000; ✗ 10 N, 2C E.

Agincourt (aj′in-kört; *Fr.* à-zhaṅ-kör), vil. near Calais, N. France; battle, 1415; ✗ 50:28 N, 2:3 E.

Agra (ä′grä), city, United Provinces, N. C. India, pop. 230; ✗ 27:10 N, 78:10 E.

Agram (ä′gräm), *Slav.* **Zágráb** (zäg′räb), city, N. W. Yugoslavia, pop. 108; ✗ 45:48 N, 15:59 E.

Aguascalientes (ä′gwäs-kä-lyen′tās), state, S. W. C. Mex., area 3, pop. 132, and its *, pop. 62; ✗ 21:50 N, 102:30 W.

Agulhas (ä-gö′lyäs), cape, S. tip of Africa; ✗ 34:30 S, 20 E.

Ahlen (äl′ẹn), city, Prussia, C. Ger., pop. 22; ✗ 51:46 N, 7:53 E.

Ahmedabad (ä-med-ä-bäd′), city, N. Bombay prov., W. India, pop. 314; ✗ 23 N, 72:35 E.

Ahmednagar (ä-med-nug′ẽr), city, C. Bombay, Br. India, pop. 42; ✗ 19:5 N, 74:48 E.

Aidin (ī-dēn′), Turkish prov., S. W. Asia Minor, pop. 180, and its *, pop. ab. 30; ✗ 37:50 N, 27:50 E.

Aigun (ī′gön), city on Amur riv., N. Manchuria, pop. ab. 32; ✗ 50 N, 127:30 E.

Ain (aṅ), dept., E. Fr. near Geneva, area 2.2, pop. 316, * Bourg, pop. 20; ✗ 46 N, 5 E.

Aino (ī′nō), region, C. Yezo (Hokkaido) Isl., Japan; home of a primitive tribe; ✗ 43:30 N, 143 E.

Aintab (īn-täb′), prov., S. C. Asiatic Turkey, pop. 174, and its *, pop. 48; ✗ 37:4 N, 37:25 E.

Air (ä-ẽr′, or īr), or **Asben,** important oasis, S. C. Sahara, N. Africa; ✗ 18 N, 8 E.

Airdrie (âr′drē), city 10 mi. E. of Glasgow, Scotland, pop. 25; ✗ 55:52 N, 3:59 W.

Aisne (ān), *anc.* Axona, riv., N. Fr., len. 175 mi. to Oise riv.; # 49:25 N, 2:50 E. — dept., N. E. Fr., touching Belg., area 2.9, pop. 422; * Laon, pop. 19; # 49:35 N, 3:35 E.

Aix (es or eks), *anc.* Aquae Sextiae, city, S. Fr., 15 mi. N. of Marseille, pop. 30; # 43:30 N, 5:30 E.

Aix-la-Chapelle (-lä-shä-pel), see **Aachen.**

Aix-les-Bains (-lä-ban), tn., Savoie, Alps of S. E. Fr.; hot springs; anc. resort; # 45:40 N, 5:58 E.

Ajaccio (ä-yät′chō), spt., * of Corsica, pop. 23; birthplace of Napoleon; # 41:55 N, 8:45 E.

Ajmer (äj-mēr′), city, N. W. India, * of prov. of Ajmer-Merwara, pop. 114; # 26:35 N, 74:40 E.

Ajmer-Merwara (äj-mēr′mer-wä′rä), prov., N. W. India surrounded by Rajputana, area 3, pop. 495, * Ajmer, pop. 114; # 26:27 N, 74:37 E.

Akabah (ä′kä-bä), see **Aqaba.**

Akamagaseki (ä″kä-mä-gä-sä′kē), see **Shimonoseki.**

Akashi (ä′kä-shē), a W. suburb of Kobe, S. W. Honshu Isl., Japan, pop. 37; # 34:39 N, 135 E.

Akershus (ä′kers-hös), flyker (prov.), S. E. Norway, about Oslo, area 2, pop. 180; # 60 N, 10:45 E.

Akita (ä-kē′tä), city, N. Honshu Isl., Japan, pop. 44; # 39:50 N, 140:10 E.

Akkerman (ä′ker-män) or **Cetatea Alba,** spt. city, ext. E. Romania, pop. 34; # 46:11 N, 30:23 E.

Akkra (äk-rä′), see **Accra** and **Acre.**

Akmolinsk (äk-mo-lyēnsk′), Russian prov., Kirghiz steppe, area 225, pop. 1,064, and its *, pop. 10; # 51:30 N, 71:20 E.

Akron (ak′ron), city, N. E. Ohio, pop. 245; Municipal Univ.; Buchtel College; rubber goods; # 41:6 N, 81:30 W.

Aksu (äk-sö′), city, N. Tarim Basin, Chinese Turkestan, pop. 15; # 41:25 N, 80:20 E.

Alabama (al-a-bä′mä), state, S. E. U.S.A., bet. Ga. and Miss., area 52, pop. 2,833, * Montgomery, pop. 78; chief city, Birmingham, pop. 268; # 33 N, 87 W. — riv., N. E. Ala. S. to Mobile Bay, len. 350 mi.; # 30:50 N, 87:55 W.

Ala-dagh (ä′lä-däch′), three short mt. ranges, S. E. and N. E. Asia Minor and Armenia; summits ab. 11,000 ft.; # 40 N, 43 E; 38 N, 35 E; 40:30 N, 32 E.

Alagóas (ä-lä-gō′äsh), state, E. Brazil, area 11, pop. 979, * Maceió, pop. 74; # ab. 10 S, 35 W.

Alagöz (ä-lä-gēz′), vol. pk., Caucasus mts., el. 13,500 ft.; # 40:33 N, 44:10 E.

Alai (ä-li′), mts., W. spur of Tian Shan range, Russian Turkestan and Pamir Plateau, summits, 16,000 to 18,000 ft.; # 40 N, 73 E.

Alameda (al-a-mä′dä), city, suburb of San Francisco, W. C. Calif., pop. 36; # 37:45 N, 122:17 W.

Åland (ô′länd), isls., Baltic sea bet. Sweden and Finland, part of latter; # 60:10 N, 20 E.

Ala Shan (ä-lä′ shän′), prov., W. Inner Mongolia; # 40:30 N, 102 E. — mt. range bet. China proper and Mongolia; summits over 16,000 ft.; # 38:30 N, 105:45 E.

Alashehr (ä-lä-she′hr), *anc.* Philadelphia, city, Smyrna, Turkey, pop. 22; # 38:21 N, 28:30 E.

Alaska (a-las′ka), terr. of U.S.A., N. W. N. Am., area 591, pop. 73, * Juneau, pop. 6; # 65 N, 150 W. — pen., the S. W. extension of mainland of Alaska, len. 400 mi.; # 56 N, 160 W.

Alaska Range (-), E. W. mt. range, S. Alaska, highest, Mt. McKinley, el. 20,300 ft.; # 63 N, 150 W. [# 42:45 N, 2:45 W.

Alava (ä′lä-vä), prov., N. Spain, area 1.2, pop. 106, * Vitoria;

Albacete (äl-bä-thä′tä), prov., S. E. C. Spain, area 5.7, pop. 350, and its *, pop. 47; # 38:58 N, 1:55 W.

Albania (al-bä′ni-a), kingdom, S. W. Balkan pen., area 11, pop. 1,000, * Tirana; # 41 N, 20 E.: annexed by Italy in 1939.

Albany (âl′ba-ni), city E. C. New York, state *, on Hudson riv., pop. 131; # 42:44 N, 73:45 W. — tn., S. W. Ga., pop. 19; # 31:40 N, 84:10 W. — riv., W. Ontario to James Bay, len. 610 mi.; # 52:20 N, 81:45 W.

Albay (äl-bī′), spt. city, S. E. Luzón, Philippine Isls., pop. 53; # 13:8 N, 123:42 E.

Albemarle (al′be-märl), sound, ab. 60 mi. long, N. E. N. Car., # 36 N, 76 W.

Alberta (al-bēr′ta), prov., S. W. Canada, ar. 255, pop. 732, * Edmonton, pop. 86; # 55 N, 115 W.

Albert Edward (al′bert ed′ward), mt. pk., Owen Stanley range, Papua, E. Indies, el. 13,030 ft.; # 8:25 S, 147: 15 E.

Albert Nyanza (al′bert nyan′zä), lake, C. Africa, len. 100 mi., area 7.7; # 2 N, 31 E.

Albertville (al-bär-vēl), tn., * of Katanga prov., Belgian Congo, on Lake Tanganyika; # 6 S, 29:10 E.

Albi or **Alby** (äl-bē), tn., * of Tarn dept., S. Fr., pop. 27; cathedral; # 43:55 N, 2:10 E.

Albion (al′bi-on), tn., S. C. Mich., pop. 8; Albion college; # 42:15 N, 84:50 W. — anc. name of England.

Albula (äl′bu-lä), tunnel, len. 3.6 mi., under Albula pass, (el. 7,595 ft.), Grisons, S. E. Switz.; # 46:35 N, 9:50 E.

Albuquerque (al-bū-kēr′kē), city, C. New Mexico, pop. 35; State Univ.; # 35:5 N, 106:45 W.

Alcamo (äl′kä-mō), city, N. W. Sicily, pop. 48; Saracen and Greek ruins; # 38 N, 12:57 E.

Alcaráz (äl-kä-räth′), tn., S. C. Spain, near Sierra de Alcaráz, pop. 12; # 38:44 N, 2:26 W.

Alcoy (äl-koi′), city, Alicante prov., S. E. Spain, pop. 36; # 38:43 N, 0:27 W.

Alderney (âl′der-ni), Br. isl., Eng. Channel, pop. 2; dairy cattle; # 49:40 N, 2:15 W.

Aldershot (âl′der-shot), tn., N. E. Hampshire, Eng., pop. 30; military camp; # 51:14 N, 0:50 W.

Alemtejo (ä-lan-tä′zhö), prov., S. C. Portugal, area 9.2, pop. 501, * Évora, pop. 11; 38 N, 8 W.

Alençon (á-loṅ-sóṅ), tn., * of Orne dept., N. W. Fr., pop. 15; lace; # 48:25 N, 0:10 E.

Aleppo (a-lep′ō), terr., N. Syria, area 30, pop. 996, and its *, pop. 140; # 36:5 N, 37:20 E.

Alessandria (äl-es-sän′drē-ä), prov., Piedmont, N. W. Italy, area 2, pop. 782, and its *, pop. 78; # 44:54 N, 8:77 E.

Alesund (á′le-sönd), spt., S. W. Norway, pop. 16; fisheries; # 62:27 N, 6:12 E.

Aletsch (ä′lech), pk., Bernese Alps, S. W. Switz., el. 13,721 ft.; 46:28 N, 8 E. — largest Swiss glacier, len. 13 mi.; # 46:25 N, 8:3 E.

Aleutian Islands (a-lū′shian ī′landz), arch. of numerous isls., W. from Alaska pen. for 1,000 mi.; # 52 N, 175 W.

Alexander Archipelago (al-eg-zan′der är-ki-pel′a-gō), numerous isls., S. E. Alaska, chief tn., Sitka; # 56:30 N, 135 W.

Alexandretta (al″eg-zan-dret′a) or **Iskanderun** (is-kän-de-rön′), spt. city, N. W. corner of Syria on Gulf of Alexandretta, pop. ab. 15; # 36:35 N, 36:15 E.

Alexandria (al-eg-zan′dri-a), spt. city, Nile delta, N. Egypt, pop. 445; # 31:10 N, 29:50 E. — city, C. La., pop. 27; # 31:25 N, 92:25 W. — city, N. E. Va., opposite D. C., pop. 34; # 38:49 N, 77:3 W.

Älfsborg or **Älvsborg** (alfs-bôr′y′), prov., S. W. Sweden, area 5, pop. 307, * Vänersborg; # 58:40 N, 12:30 E.

Algarve (äl-gär′vä) or **Faro,** prov., S. Portugal, area 1.9, pop. 268, * Faro, pop. 13; # 37:15 N, 8 W.

Algeciras (äl-hä-thē′räs), spt. city, S. Spain, pop. 19; # 36:8 N, 5:30 W.

Algeria (al-jē′ri-a), Fr. possession, N. Africa, area 222, pop. 5,802, * Algiers, pop. 207; wine; cork; # 37 N, 5 E.

Algiers (al-jērz′), dept. of N. C. Algeria; pop. 1,789, and its *, the spt. city, * of Algeria, pop. 207; # 36:40 N, 3:5 E.

Alicante (ä-lē-kän′tä), prov., S. E. Spain, area 2.2, pop. 514, and its *, a spt., pop. 67; # 38:21 N, 0:29 W.

Aligarh (ä-li-gur′), city near Delhi, N. C. India, pop. 67; # 27:50 N, 78:15 E.

Aling Gungri (ä′ling gun′grē), mt. pk., Tibet, S. C. Asia, el. 24,000 ft.; # 32:48 N, 81:3 E.

Alkmaar (älk-mär′), city, N. Holland, W. C. Neth., pop. 26; # 52:38 N, 4:44 E.

Allahabad (äl-ä-hä-bäd′), city on Ganges riv., N. C. India, pop. 157; univ.; # 25:35 N, 81:55 E.

Allegheny (al′ē-gā-ni), plateau, eroded upland, W. Pa., W. Va., E. Ky. and E. Tenn.; bituminous coal; # 41 N, 79 W. — riv., N. W. Pa., and S. W. New York to Pittsburgh, forming with Monongahela, the Ohio riv., len. 350 mi.; # 40:26 N, 80:1 W. — county, W. C. Pa., area 0.72, pop. 1,412 (1940), * Pittsburgh; # 40:27 N, 80 W.

Allenstein (äl′en-shtīn), city, C. E. Prussia, N. E. Ger., pop. 37; # 53:45 N, 19:28 E.

Allentown (al′en-toun), city, S. E. C. Pa., pop. 97, Muhlenberg College; # 40:38 N, 75:30 W.

Alliance (a-li′ans), city, E. C. Ohio, pop. 22; Mt. Union College; # 40:56 N, 81:7 W.

(variable) ḍ as d or j, ş as s or sh, ţ as t or ch, ẓ as z or zh; o, F. cloche; ü, F. menu; ch, Sc. loch; ṅ, F. bonbon; ′, primary accent; ″, secondary accent; †, obsolete; <, from; +, and; =, equals. See also lists at beginning of book.

Allier (ȧl-yā), riv., S. C. Fr. to Loire riv., len. 190 mi.; ⌗ 46:58 N, 3:5 E. — dept., C. Fr., area 2.8, pop. 371, * Moulins; ⌗ 46:20 N, 3 E.

Alloa (al′ō-ä), spt., head of Firth of Forth, C. Scotland, pop. 12;⌗⌗ 56:6 N, 3:47 W.

Alloway (al′ō-wā), hamlet, S. Ayrshire, S. W. Scotland; birthplace of Robert Burns; ⌗ 55:26 N, 4:39 W.

Almadén (äl-mä-ᴛнän′), tn., S. C. Spain, pop. 10; mercury mines; ⌗ 38:48 N, 4:51 W.

Almansa (äl-män′sä), tn., Murcia, S. E. Spain, pop. 13; ⌗ 38:54 N, 1:7 W.

Almelo (äl-mä-lō′), city, Overyssel, E. C. Neth., pop. 26; ⌗ 52:22 N, 6:40 E.

Almería (äl-mä-rē′ä), prov., ext. S. C. Spain, area 3.4, pop. 343, and its *, a spt., pop. 47; ⌗ 36:50 N, 2:32 W.

Alost (ä′lŏst) or **Aalst** (älst), city, 14 mi. N. W. of Brussels, Belgium, pop. 36; ⌗ 50:57 N, 4:3 E.

Alpena (al-pē′nä), tn., N. E. Mich., pop. 13; fluxing limestone quarries; ⌗ 45:3 N, 83:28 W.

Alpes-Maritimes (ȧlp mȧr-ē-tēm), dept., ext. S. E. Fr., area 1.4, pop. 358, * Nice, pop. 156; ⌗ 43:50 N, 7 E.

Alps (alps), mts., S. C. Europe, Fr. to Austria, summit Mt. Blanc, el., 15,781 ft.; ⌗ 46 N, 10 E.

Alsace (äl-zȧs), dept., W. Ger. 1871 to 1919, now depts. of Bas-Rhin and Haut-Rhin, Fr.; 48:30 N, 7:30 E.

Altai (äl-tī′), lofty E.–W. mt. range, C. Asia, mostly in Outer Mongolia, highest 11,000 to 12,000 ft.; ⌗ 48 N, 90 E.

Altenburg (äl′tĕn-búrch), city, E. Thuringia, S. C. Ger., pop. 42; ⌗ 50:59 N, 12:25 E.

Alton (âl′tǫn), city, S. W. Ill., on Mississippi riv., pop. 31; Shurtleff College; ⌗ 38:55 N, 90:10 W.

Altona (äl′tō-nä), a W. suburb of Hamburg, Ger., but in Prussia; port on Elbe riv., pop. 182; ⌗ 53:33 N, 9:55 E.

Altoona (al-tō′nä), city, S. W. C. Pa., pop. 80; R. R. shops; ⌗ 40:30 N, 78:28 W.

Altyn Tagh (äl-tin′ täg′), prov., N. Tibet, C. Asia; — mt. range therein; ⌗ 37 N, 87 E.

Aluta (o-lū′to), riv., Transylvania, crossing Carpathian mts. in Red Tower Pass, to Danube riv., len. 280 mi.; ⌗ 43:45 N, 24:50 E.

Alwar (ul′wur), a native state of Rajputana, N. W. India, area 3, pop. 709, and its *, pop. 45; ⌗ 27:40 N, 76:40 E.

Amagasaki (ä″mä-gä-sä′kē), suburb of Osaka, Honshu Isl., Japan, pop. 44; ⌗ 34:44 N, 135:25 E.

Amalfi (ä-mäl′fē), spt. on gulf of Salerno, Campania, S. Italy, pop. 8, formerly 50; famous cathedral; ⌗ 40:38 N, 14:36 E.

Amarillo (a-mä-ril′ō), city, N. W. Texas, pop. 52; ⌗ 35:20 N, 101:50 W.

Amazon (am′ȧ-zon), world's largest riv., ab. 3,500 mi. long, Andes mts. to Atlantic oc. across N. Brazil; ⌗ 1:30 S, 52 W.

Amazonas (ä-mä-zō′näs), state, N. Brazil, area 705, pop. 439, * Manáos, pop. 89. — (-sō′näs) dept., N. Peru, area 14, pop. 80, * San Carlos; ⌗ 5:50 S, 78 W.

Ambala (um-bä′lạ), city, E. Punjab, N. W. India, pop. 76; ⌗ 30:25 N, 76:50 E.

Amberg (äm′berċh), city, N. E. C. Bayern (Bavaria), S. W. Ger., pop. 26; ⌗ 49:27 N, 11:50 E.

Amboina (am-boi′nä), administrative div. of Dutch E. Indies, area 17, pop. 400. — important isl. S. of Ceram, area 0.4, pop. 40, and its *, pop. 9; ⌗ 3:45 S, 128:15 E.

Amboise (än-bwäz), historic tn., C. Fr., pop. 5; castle; ⌗ 47:26 N, 1 E.

Ambridge (am′brij), tn., S. W. Pa., pop. 19; ⌗ 40:37 N, 80:15 W.

America, Central (ạ-mer′i-kạ), S. N. Am., from S. Mex. to Panama; ⌗ 12 N, 86 W.

America, Middle, Mex., C. Am., and W. Indies; ⌗ 20 N, 90 W.

America, North. Continent, area ab. 9,456, pop. ab. 145,000. El. ⅓ of continent ranges from sea level to 600 ft.; 1% is above 10,000 ft., average ab. 2,250 ft., highest point, Mt. McKinley, 20,300 ft., lowest, Death Valley, 280 ft. below sea level; ⌗ ab. 47 N, 97 W.

America, South. Continent, S. E. of N. Am., area ab. 7,000, pop. ab. 64,000; ⌗ 10 S, 60 W.

Amersfoort (ä′mers-fōrt), city, 12 mi. N. E. of Utrecht, S. C. Neth., pop. 34; ⌗ 52:10 N, 5:24 E.

Ames (āmz), tn., C. Iowa, pop. 13; State Agricultural College; ⌗ 42:2 N, 93:39 W.

Amherst (am′ẽrst), tn., W. C. Mass., pop. 6; Amherst and State Agricultural Colleges; ⌗ 42:21 N, 72:30 W. — tn. ext. W. Nova Scotia, pop. 10; ⌗ 45:49 N, 64:13 W.

Amiens (am′i-enz; Fr. ȧ-mē-an), city, N. E. Fr., * of Somme dept., pop. 93; battles 1914, 1918; splendid cathedral; ⌗ 49:55 N, 2:20 E.

Amirante (am′i-rant), numerous small Br. isls., 500 mi. N. of Madagascar; ⌗ 0:7 S, 55 E.

Amoy (ä-moi′), spt. city, Formosa Strait, China, pop. est. 300; ⌗ 24:30 N, 118:15 E.

Amritsar (um-rit′sär), city near Lahore, N. W. India, pop. 265; ⌗ 31:50 N, 74:55 E.

Amsterdam (am′stĕr-dam), spt. city on Zuider Zee and ship canal, W. C. Neth., pop. 706; Univ. of Amsterdam; ⌗ 52:23 N, 4:54 E. — city, E. C. New York, pop. 33; ⌗ 42:45 N, 74:10 W.

Amu-Darja (ä-mö′där′yä), anc. Oxus, riv., Pamirs to Aral Sea, S. W. Asia, len. 1,400 mi.; ⌗ 43:40 N, 59:25 E. — prov., Soviet Russia in Asia; area 43, pop. 254; ⌗ 42 N, 62 E.

Amur (ä-mör′), riv., N. Mongolia to Pacific oc., len. 2,700 mi.; ⌗ 51:30 N, 139 E. — prov., E. Siberia, area 155, pop. 230; ⌗ 52 N, 133 E. — prov., Mongolia, see **Heilung-Kiang.**

Anaconda (an-ạ-kon′dạ), tn., S. W. Mont., pop. 11; copper smelters; ⌗ 46:10 N, 112:55 W.

Anáhuac (ä-nä′wäk), plateau, C. Mex., includes Valley of Mexico City; ⌗ 20 N, 100 W.

Anatolia (an-ạ-tō′li-ä), vast plateau in Asia Minor between Black and Mediterranean seas; ⌗ 39 N, 35 E.

Ancachs (än-käċhs′), dept., N. W. C. Peru, area 15, pop. 580, * Huaraz, pop. 15; ⌗ 9:40 S, 78 W.

Anchorage (ang′kŏr-āj), spt. tn., S. C. Alaska, on government R. R., pop. 3; ⌗ 61:12 N, 149:55 W.

Ancohuma (äng-kō-ö′mä), mt. pk., of Mount Sorata, Bolivia, el. 21,700 ft.; ⌗ 15:54 S, 68:27 W.

Ancona (än-kō′nä), prov., Marche, N. E. Italy, area 0.7, pop. 335, and its *, a spt., pop. 66; ⌗ 43:38 N, 13:30 E.

Andalusia (an-dạ-lö′shi-ä), Sp. **Andalucía** (än″dä-lö-thē′ä), region, S. W. Spain, including prov. of Seville, Huelva, Córdoba and Cádiz; ⌗ 36:35 N, 5:15 W.

Andaman (an′dạ-mạn) and **Nicobar** (nik-ō-bär′) **Islands,** two groups isls., E. Bay of Bengal, administered by the Indian Government, area 3, pop. 27; ⌗ 12 N, 93 E.

Anderlecht (än′dĕr-leċht), suburb of Brussels, Belg., pop. 68; ⌗ 50:50 N, 4:15 E.

Anderson (an′dĕr-sǫn), city, E. C. Ind., pop. 42; ⌗ 40:6 N, 85:40 W. — tn., N. W. S. Car., pop. 19; college; ⌗ 34:30 N, 82:40 W.

Andersonville (an′dĕr-sǫn-vil), vil., S. W. Ga.; national cemetery; former military prison; ⌗ 32:10 N, 84 W.

Andes (an′dēz), mt. system, W. S. America extending from ext. S. to N., very continuous and lofty, highest pk., Aconcagua, el., 23,003 ft.; ⌗ 15 S, 70 W.

Andes, Los (Sp. lōs än′dās), ter., N. W. Argentina, area 35, pop. 3, * San Antonio; ⌗ 25 S, 67:30 W.

Andijan (än-di-jän′), city, E. Russian Turkestan, pop. 82; ⌗ 40:50 N, 72:20 E.

Andizhan (än-di-zhän′), see **Andijan.**

Andorra (än-dor′rä), principality, E. Pyrenees, area 0.2, pop. 5; ⌗ 42:30 N, 1:35 E.

Andover (an′dō-vĕr), tn., N. E. Mass., 22 mi. N. of Boston, pop. 11; theol. seminary and school; ⌗ 42:40 N, 71:8 W.

Andria (än′drẹ-ä), city, Apulia, S. E. Italy, pop. 53; cathedral; ⌗ 41:14 N, 16:16 E.

Andros (an′dros), isl. E. of Athens, Gr., len. 25 mi., spt. thereon; ⌗ 37:50 N, 24:55 E. — double isl., W. Bahamas, largest of group, len. 110 mi., pop. 7; ⌗ 24:30 N, 78 W.

Androscoggin (an-dros-kog′in), riv., S. W. Me., 170 mi. to Atlantic oc.; ⌗ 43:55 N, 70 W.

Angers (än-zhā), city, W. C. Fr.; * of Maine-et-Loire, pop. 86; ⌗ 47:30 N, 0:33 W.

Anglesey (ang′gl-sẹ), isl. and county ext. N. W. Wales, area 0.2, pop. 52, * Holyhead, pop. 12; ⌗ 53:15 N, 4:25 W.

Anglia, East (ang′gli-ạ), part of Eng., N. E. of London; ⌗ 52:30 N, 1 E. See **Cambridge, Essex, Norfolk, Suffolk.**

Anglo-Egyptian Sudan (ang′glō), country, N. E. Africa, area 1,014, pop. 3,400, * Khartoum, pop. 31 (with suburbs, pop. 124); ⌗ 15:30 N, 32:30 E.

Angola (ang-gō′lạ), Portuguese colony, S. W. Africa, area 480, pop. 5,000, * São Paulo de Loanda, pop. 50; ⌗ 12 S, 17 E.

Angora (ang-gō′rạ) or **Ankara,** prov., Asiatic Turkey, pop. 534, and its *, pop. 123, * of Turkey; ⌗ 39:50 N, 32:45 E.

---

fat, fāte, fär, fȧll, ȧsk, fāre; net, mē, hẽr; pin, pīne; not, nōte, mŏve, nôr; up, lūte, pu̇ll; oi, oil; ou, out; (lightened) aviạry, ēlect, agǫny, intǫ, ụnite; (obscured) errạnt, operạ, ardẹnt, actǫr, natụre; ch, chip; g, go; th, thin; ᴛн, then; y, you;

Angoulême (än-gö-lãm), *anc.* Inculisma, city, W. C. Fr., * of Charente dept., pop. 38; # 45:40 N, 0:12 E.

Angra (äng'grä), spt., * of Portuguese colony of Azores, mid-Atlantic, pop. 13; # 38:40 N, 27:15 W.

Anhalt (än'hält), a free state of C. Germany, area 0.9, pop. 351, * Dessau, pop. 58; # 51:50 N, 12 E.

Anhui or **Anhwei** (än-hwä'ē), prov., E. C. China, area 55, pop. est. 20,000, * Anking; # 32 N, 117:30 E.

Anjou (an'jö; *Fr.* äň-zhö), *anc.* prov., W. C. Fr., Loire Valley, * Angers, pop. 86; # 47:30 N, 0:30 W.

Ankara (äng'kä-rä), Turkish name for Angora.

Anking (än'king'), city, E. C. China, * of Anhwei prov., pop. est. 110; # 30:33 N, 117:7 E.

Ann, cape, N. E. Mass., N. of Mass. Bay; # 42:40 N, 70:35 W.

Annam (ä-nam' or än-näm'), protectorate, E. C. part of Fr. Indo-China, area 57, pop. 5,989, * Hué; # 16 N, 108 E.

Annapolis (a-nap'ō-lis), tn., on Chesapeake Bay, C. Md., pop. 13, U. S. Naval Academy; # 38:58 N, 76:30 W. — tn., Bay of Fundy, Nova Scotia, pop. 1; apples; formerly Port Royal; # 44:45 N, 65:35 W.

Ann Arbor (an är'bor), city, S. E. Mich., pop. 30; State Univ.; # 42:18 N, 83:45 W.

Anniston (an'is-ton), city, N. E. C. Ala., pop. 26; # 33:30 N, 85:50 W.

Ansbach (äns'bäch), city, * of Mittelfranken, N. W. Bayern, (Bavaria), S. W. Ger., pop. 22; # 49:17 N, 10:32 E.

Ansonia (an-sō'ni-ạ), city, S. W. C. Conn., pop. 19; # 41:25 N, 73:3 W.

Antananarivo (än-tä-nä-nä-rē'vō), *Fr.* **Tananarive,** city, C. Madagascar, its *, pop. 58; # 18:50 S, 47:30 E.

Antarctic (ant-ärk'tik) or **Southern Ocean,** oc. S. of Antarctic Circle; # 66:33 S.

Antarctica (ant-ärk'ti-kạ), land around S. pole, possibly larger than Europe; # 90 S.

Anticosti (an-ti-kos'ti), isl. in estuary of St. Lawrence riv., area 2, len. 130 mi., part of Quebec; # 49 N, 63 W.

Antietam (an-tē'tạm), creek, Pa. and Md. to Potomac riv.; battle, Md., 1862; national military park; # 39:24 N, 77:45 W.

Antigua (än-tē'gwä), isl., Leeward Isl., W. Indies, area 0.1, pop. 29; Br. colony; # 17 N, 61:45 W.

Antilibanus (an-ti-lib'ạ-nus), mts., W. Syria, E. of Lebanon Mts., summit, Mt. Hermon, el. 9,050 ft.; # 34 N, 36:30 E.

Antilles (an-til'lēz or än-tēl), chain of isls., W. Indies, larger W. ones (Cuba, Haiti, Porto Rico, Jamaica, known as Greater Antilles; # 19 N, 75 W.; smaller S. ones, known as Lesser Antilles; # 14 N, 61 W.

Antioch (an'ti-ok), city, N. W. Syria, pop. ab. 30; # 36:5 N, 36:12 E.

Antioquia (än-tē-ō'kē-ä), dept., N. W. Colombia, area 23, pop. 823, * Medellín, pop. 79. — a tn., in same, pop. ab. 10; # 6:20 N, 76:10 W.

Antipodes (an-tip'ō-dēz), group of small isls., 460 mi. S. E. of New Zealand, antipodal to Britain; # 49:30 S, 178:30 E. — loosely applied to Australia and New Zealand.

Antisana (än-tē-sä'nä), volcano, el. 19,335 ft., Andes of Ecuador; # 0:30 S, 78:20 W. — vil. thereon, el. 13,300 ft., one of world's highest.

Anti-Taurus (an'ti-tâ'rus), mt. range, N. of Taurus mts., S. W. C. Asia Minor; # 39 N, 37 E.

Antofagasta (än'tō-fä-gäs'tä), prov., N. Chile, area 46, pop. 172, and its *, pop. 56; chief nitrate port; terminus of R.R. to Bolivia; # 24 S, 70:10 W.

Antofalla (än-tō-fäl'yä), vol. mt. pk., Andes of N. Chile, el. ab. 20,900 ft.; # 25:30 S, 68:5 W.

Antrim (an'trim), county, N. E. N. Ireland State, area 1, pop. 194; # 54:45 N, 6:15 W.

Antung (än'tung'), spt., Yellow Sea, ext. S. E. Manchuria, pop. est. 102; # 39:59 N, 124:30 E.

Antwerp (ant'wẽrp), *Fr.* **Anvers,** prov., N. C. Belgium, area 1, pop. 1,065, and its *, pop. 301 (with suburbs 450); now on a ship canal and a leading spt.; # 51:13 N, 4:25 E.

Anvers (äň-vär), see **Antwerp.**

Aomori (ä-ō'mō-ri), spt. city, ext. N. Honshu Isl., Japan, pop. 59; # 40:55 N, 140:40 E.

Apalachee (äp-ä-läch'ē), bay, ext. N. E. part of Gulf of Mex.; # 29:30 N, 84 W.

Apalachicola (ap"ạ-lach-i-kō'lä), navigable riv., W. Fla., len. 90 mi. to Gulf of Mex.; # 29:50 N, 85 W.

Apeldoorn (ä'pel-dōrn), city, Gelderland, E. C. Neth., pop. 53; # 52:14 N, 5:58 E.

Apennines (ap'e-nīnz), mt. range N. to S., Italy, highest, Gran Sasso, el. 9,583 ft.; # 42:30 N, 13:30 E.

Apia (ä'pē-ä), spt. * of W. Samoa, S. Pacific oc.; # 13:50 S, 171:50 W.

Apo (ä'pō), vol. mt., S. E. Mindanao, highest in Philippines, el. 9,610 ft.; # 6:55 N, 125:15 E.

Apolda (ä-pol'dä), an E. suburb of Weimar, Thuringia, S. C. Ger., pop. 25; # 51:2 N, 11:30 E.

Appalachian (ap-ạ-lach'i-ạn or ap-ạ-lā'chi-ạn), range of low mts., N. E. Ala. to N. Me., highest peak, Mt. Mitchell, W. N. Car., el. 6,711 ft.; # 37 N, 82 W.

Appalachicola, see **Apalachicola.**

Appenzell (äp'pen-tsel), canton, N. E. Switz., area 0.2, pop. 70, and its *, pop. 15; # 47:20 N, 9:24 E.

Appleton (ap'l-ton), city, E. C. Wis., pop. 28; Laurence College; # 44:16 N, 88:27 W.

Appomattox (ap-ō-mat'oks), riv. and vil., C. Va.; Lee's surrender, Apr. 9, 1865; # 37:21 N, 78:50 W.

Apsheron (äp-shä-ron'), pen. and cape, W. Caspian Sea; Baku oil field; # 40:20 N, 50:10 E.

Apulia (ä-pō'lē-ä), dept., S. E. Italy, area 7.4, pop. 2,297; # 41:20 N, 15:10 E.

Apuré (ä-pō-rä'), riv., S. W. Venezuela to Orinoco riv., len. 300 mi.; # 7:45 N, 66:55 W.

Apurímac (ä-pō-rē'mäk), dept., S. C. Peru, area 8.2, pop. 177, * Abancay; # 14 S, 73 W. — riv., Peruvian Andes to Ucayali riv., len. 500 mi.; # 12 S, 74 W.

Aqaba (ä'kä-bä), gulf, N. E. part of Red Sea, and spt. at its tip; # 29 N, 34:40 E.

Aquila (ä'kwē-lä) or **Aquila degli Abruzzi,** prov., C. Italy, area 2.5, pop. 396, and its *, pop. 24; # 42:22 N, 13:22 E.

Aquileia (ä-kwē-lā'yä), tn., N. E. Italy, at head of Adriatic Sea, pop. 1; important Roman city; # 45:48 N, 13:20 E.

Aquitania (ak-wi-tā'ni-ạ), lowland, S. W. Fr., a former prov.; # 45 N, 1 W.

Arabia (ạ-rā'bi-ạ), pen., S. W. Asia, area ab. 1,000, pop. 5,000 to 10,000; # 25 N, 45 E. See **Asir, Hadramaut, Hejaz, Jebel Shammar, Nejd, Oman,** and **Yemen.**

Arabian Sea (ạ-rā'bi-ạn), N. part of Indian oc., bet. India and Arabia; # 18 N, 65 E.

Aracaju (ä-rä-kä-zhö'), city, E. Brazil, * of Sergipe state, pop. 37; # 10:55 S, 37:4 W.

Arad (or'od), city, ext. W. C. Romania, on Maros riv., pop. 63; # 46:11 N, 21:19 E.

Arafura (ä-rä-fö'rä), sea, bet. N. Australia and Papua; # 9:15 S, 133 E.

Aragon (ar'ạ-gon), region, N. E. Spain, a former prov.; # 41:30 N, 1 W.

Araguaya, Rio (ä-rä-gwī'yä), riv., S. C. Brazil, N. to Rio Tocantins, len. ab. 1,000 mi.; # 5:20 S, 48:30 W.

Aral (ar'ạl), lake or inland sea, Russian Turkestan, area 26, el. 160 ft.; # 44 N, 60 E.

Ararat (ar'a-rat), vol. pk., E. Asia Minor, N. W. corner of Persia, el. 16,925 ft.; # 39:50 N, 44:20 E.

Arauco (ä-rou'kō), prov., W. C. Chile, area 2.2, pop. 60, * Lebu; # 37:30 S, 73 W.

Aravalli (ar-a-vä'lē), range of hills, Rajputana, N. W. India, len. 200 mi.; # 25:20 N, 73:40 E.

Araxes (a-rak'sēz), riv., Armenia to Caspian Sea, len. 500 mi.; # ab. 39 N, 49 E.

Arbroath (är-brōTH'), spt., Forfar Co., E. Scotland, pop. 19; # 56:34 N, 2:35 W.

Arcadia (är-kā'di-ạ), wide, shallow gulf, W. Morea pen., S. Greece; # 37:25 N, 21:40 E.

Archangel (ärk'än'jel), spt., White Sea, N. W. Russia, at mouth of Dvina riv.; pop. 45; # 64:35 N, 40:50 E.

Arctic Circle (ärk'tik), parallel of latitude 66:33 N, longest day, June 21, 24 hrs. long.

Arctic Ocean, oc. N. of N. America, Asia, and Arctic circle, area ab. 5,000, greatest known depth, 13,200 ft.

Ardèche (är-desh), dept., S. C. Fr., area 2.1, pop. 294, * Privas; # 44:30 N, 4:30 E.

Ardennes (är-den), dept., ext. N. E. Fr., area 2, pop. 278, * Mézières, pop. 10; # 49:35 N, 4:30 E. — rugged plateau, S. Belg., Luxemburg and N. E. Fr.; # 50:10 N, 5:10 E.

Ardmore (ärd'mōr), tn., S. C. Okla., pop. 17; # 34:10 N, 97:10 W.

Arequipa (ä-rä-kē′pä), dept., S. Peru, area 22, pop. 230, and its *, pop. 60; # 16:20 S, 71:25 W. — mt. pk. therein, el. 18,373 ft.

Arezzo (ä-ret′sō), *anc.* Arrétium, prov., Tuscany, Italy, area 1.3, pop. 299, and its *, pop. 52; # 43:25 N, 11:53 E.

Argæus (är-jē′us) or **Erjias** (ėr-jē′äs), mt., C. Asia Minor, highest in Turkey, el. 12,992 ft.; # 38:31 N, 35:19 E.

Argenteuil (är-zhoṅ-tė-y′), a N. suburb of Paris, Fr., pop. 32; # 48:57 N, 2:15 E.

Argentina (är-jen-tē′nä), federal republic, S. and E. S. America, area 1,153, pop. 12,761, * Buenos Aires, pop. 2,318; wheat, corn, flaxseed, meat, wool, and hides; # 36 S, 64 W.

Argonne (är-gon), region, dept. of Ardennes and Meuse, N. E. Fr.; forest; battles, 1918; # 49 N, 5 E.

Argos (är′gos), tn., head of Gulf of Argos, or Argolis, E. Morea, S. E. Greece, pop. 9; # 37:48 N, 22:42 E.

Argovie (är-go-vē), see **Aargau.**

Argyll (är-gīl′), county, W. C. Scotland, area 3, pop. 76, * Inveraray, pop 1; # 56:18 N, 5:5 W.

Arica (ä-rē′kä), spt., Tarapacá prov., ext. N. Chile, pop. 13; # 18:32 S, 70:22 W.

Ariège (ä-rē-ezh), dept., Pyrenees, S. Fr., area 1.9, pop. 173, * Foix; # 43 N, 1:35 E.

Arizona (ar-i-zō′nä), state, S. W. U.S.A., bet. N. Mex. and Calif., area 114, pop. 499, * Phœnix, pop. 65; second city, Tucson, pop. 37; # 34 N, 112 W.

Arkadelphia (är-kạ-del′fi-ạ), tn., S. W. C. Ark., pop. 5; three colleges; # 34:6 N, 93:4 W.

Arkansas (är′kạn-sâ or är-kan′zas), state, S. C. U.S.A., bet. Mo. and La., area 53, pop. 1,949, * Little Rock, pop. 88; second city, Ft. Smith, pop. 37; # 35 N, 92 W.

Arkansas City, tn., S. E. C. Kan., pop. 13; # 37:3 N, 97:3 W.

Arkansas River, riv., C. Colo., to Mississippi riv., Ark., S. E., len. 2,000 mi.; # 34 N, 91:5 W. — **Royal Gorge** of, C. Colo.; # 38:25 N, 105:15 W.

Arlberg (ärl′berch), pass, el. 5,900 ft., and tunnel 6½ mi., ext. W. Austria; # 47:5 N, 10:10 E.

Arles (ärlz, *Fr.* ärl), *anc.* Arelas, city near mouth of Rhône riv., S. Fr., pop. 31; # 43:40 N, 4:42 E.

Arlington (är′ling-ton), tn., E. C. Mass., pop. 40; # 42:25 N, 71:9 W. — vil., N. E. Va., opp. Washington, D. C.; national cemetery; # 38:53 N, 77:5 W.

Armagh (är-mä′), county, S. C. N. Ireland State, area 0.5, pop. 120, and its *, pop. 7; # 54:21 N, 6:45 W.

Armenia (är-mē′ni-ä), soviet republic, N. W. of Persia, area 15, pop. 1,214, * Erivan, pop. 90; — also neighboring parts of Turkey and Persia, home of Armenians; # 40 N, 42 E.

Armentières (är-moṅ-tē-âr), city, N. Fr., 10 mi. N. W. of Lille, pop. 15; # 50:45 N, 2:50 E.

Armorica (är-mor′i-kạ), upland region W. Fr., esp. Brittany, an anc. province; # ab. 46 N, 3 W.

Arnhem (ärn′hem), city, * of Gelderland, S. C. Neth., pop. 74; # 51:59 N, 5:55 E.

Arno (är′nō), *anc.* Arnus, riv., Tuscany, Italy, to Ligurian Sea, len. 140 mi.; # 43:40 N, 10:15 E.

Arnstadt (ärn′shtät), dist., C. Thuringia, S. C. Ger., area 0.3, pop. 80, and its *, pop. 22; # 50:50 N, 10:55 E.

Aroostook (ạ-rös′tuk), riv. and valley, N. E. Maine; potatoes; # 46:30 N, 68 W.

Arran (ar′ạn), isl., Bute County, Firth of Clyde, S. W. Scotland, len. 20 mi., area 0.2, pop. 5; # 55:35 N, 5:15 W.

Arras (á-räs), city, N. Fr., * of Pas-de-Calais, pop. 25; # 50:20 N, 2:45 E.

Arrowrock (ar′ō-rok), Reclamation Service dam, Boise riv., S. W. Idaho, height 348.5 ft.; highest in world; # ab. 43:37 N, 116 W.

Arta (är′tä), *anc.* Ambracia, tn., S. W. Greece, on Arta riv., near Gulf of Arta, pop. 7; # 39:5 N, 21 E.

Artois (är-two), anc. prov., N. E. Fr.; artesian wells; # 50:20 N, 2:30 E.

Aru (ä-rö′), isl. group, S. of Dutch Papua, area 3, pop. 22; # 6 S, 134:30 E.

Aruba (ä-rö′bä), isl., near Venezuela, part of Dutch W. Indies, area .07, pop. 7; # 7 N. 70 W.

Asahigawa (ä-sä′hē-gä′wä), city, C. Hokkaido (Yezo) isl. Japan, pop. 72; # 43:47 N, 142:20 E.

Asben (äs-ben′), see **Air.**

Asbury Park (az′bė-ri), seacoast resort, E. C. New Jersey, pop. 15; # 40:15 N, 74 W.

Ascension (a-sen′shọn), vol. isl., S. Atlantic oc., Br., area .03, pop. .2; * Georgetown; # 7:55 S, 14:20 W.

Aschaffenburg (ä-shäf′en-bürch), city, N. W. Bayern (Bavaria), S. W. Ger., on Main riv., pop. 33; # 49:58 N, 9:10 E.

Aschersleben (äsh′ėrs-lä-ben), city, Sachsen prov., Prussia, C. Ger., pop. 29; # 51:45 N, 11:28 E.

Ascoli Piceno (äs′kō-lē pē-chä′nō), prov., Marche, E. Italy, area 0.8, pop. 265, and its *, pop. 32; # 42:52 N, 13:35 E.

Ashanti (a-shän′tē), middle dist. of Br. Gold Coast, W. Africa; # 8 N, 2 W.

Asheville (ash′vil) city, W. N. Car., pop. 51; winter resort in mt. valley; college; # 35:30 N, 82:40 W.

Ashfield (ash′fēld), suburb of Sydney, New S. Wales, Australia, pop. 34; # 33:53 S, 151:8 E.

Ashikaga (ä′shi-kä′gä), city, C. Honshu Isl., Japan, pop. 39; # 36:25 N, 139:30 E.

Ashland (ash′lạnd), city, E. Ky., on Ohio riv., pop. 30; college; # 38:28 N, 82:40 W. — tn., on Lake Superior, N. W. Wis., pop. 11; college; # 46:35 N, 90:45 W.

Ashtabula (ash-tạ-bū′lạ), city, N. E. Ohio, pop. 25; a port on Lake Erie; # 41:52 N, 80:50 W.

Ashton-under-Lyne (ash′tọn-un′dėr-līn′), suburb of Manchester, N. W. C. Eng., pop. 44; # 53:29 N, 2:6 W.

Asia (ā′shiạ or ā′zhiạ), the largest continent, area 17,000, pop. ab. 1,124,000; # ab. 42 N, 90 E.

Asia Minor (mī′nọr), see **Anatolia.**

Asir (ä-sēr′), principality, S. W. Arabia, bet. Hejaz and Yemen, pop. ab. 1,000, * Sabiyah or Sabia; # 19 N, 43 E.

Askhabad (äs-kä-bäd′), city, * of Russian Transcaspia, pop. 42; # 37:57 N., 58:23 E.

Askja (äsk′yä), vol., E. C. Iceland, el. 3,376 ft.; # 65 N, 17 W.

Asmara (äs-mä′rä), tn., * of Eritrea, Italian possession on Red Sea, N. E. Africa, pop. 15, el. ab. 7,700 ft.; # 15:20 N, 38:55 E.

Asnières (ä-nē-âr), a N. suburb of Paris, Fr., pop. 50; # 48:54 N, 2:17 E.

Asosan (ä′sọ-sän′), vol. mt., Kyushiu Isl., Japan, crater 12 mi. across; el. 5,630 ft.; # 32:54 N, 131:3 E.

Aspros (äs′prōs), *anc.* Achelous (ak-ē-lō′us), riv., S. W. Greece, len. 120 mi.; # 38:20 N, 21:5 E.

Assam (as-sam′), prov., N. E. India, N. W. of Burma, area 53, pop. 7,606, * Shillong, pop. ab. 7; tea; # 26 N, 93 E.

Assiniboine (a-sin′i-boin), riv., S. Sask. to Red riv., len. 450 mi.; # 50:30 N, 97 W.

Assisi (ä-sē′sē), vil., Perugia (Umbria), C. Italy; pop. 18; birthplace of St. Francis; # 43:5 N, 12:35 E.

Assuan (äs-swän′) or **Aswan,** *anc.* Syene, tn., Egypt, on Nile riv., pop. 11; # 24:5 N, 32:55 E. — dam nearby, 6,400 ft. long. — also prov. of upper Egypt, area 0.2, pop. 253; # 24 N, 33 E.

Assyria (ạ-sir′i-ä), great anc. empire, S. W. Asia, * Nineveh; # ab. 36 N, 43 E.

Asti (äs′tē), *anc.* Hasta, city, Piedmont, N. W. Italy, pop. comm. 40; # 44:54 N, 8:10 E.

Aston Manor (as′tọn), a N. borough of Birmingham, Eng., pop. 75; # 52:30 N, 1:52 W.

Astoria (as-tō′ri-ä), tn., ext. N. W. Oregon, mouth of Columbia riv., pop. 10; # 46:12 N, 123:48 W.

Astrakhan (äs-trä-chän′), prov., S. E. Russia, area 91, pop. 1,300, and its *, at mouth of Volga riv., pop. 144; univ.; # 46:15 N, 48:10 E.

Asturias (äs-tö′rē-äs), former prov., N. W. Spain, present Oviedo; # 43:15 N, 5:45 W.

Asunción (ä-sön-thē-ōn′), city, on Paraguay riv., * of Paraguay, pop. 100; # 25:30 S, 57:30 W.

Asyût or **Assiut** (ä-syöt′), city on Nile riv., N. Egypt, pop. 51; # 27:12 N, 31:11 E.

Atacama (ä-tä-kä′mä), prov., N. Chile, area 31, pop. 48. — desert, N. Chile, chief source of nitrate; # 24 S, 69:10 W.

Atalanti (at-ạ-lan′ti), channel bet. W. Eubœa Isl., E. Greece, and mainland; # 38:45 N, 23:15 E.

Atbara (ät′bä-rä), riv., large N. trib. of Nile, from N. Abyssinia; len. ab. 500 mi.; — tn., at mouth of Atbara riv.; # 17:50 N, 34:2 E.

Atchison (ach′i-sọn), tn., N. E. Kansas, on Missouri riv., pop. 13; college; # 39:35 N, 95:15 W.

---

fat, fāte, fär, fȧll, ȧsk, fâre; net, mē, hėr; pin, pīne; not, nōte, möve, nôr; up, lūte, pull; oi, oil; ou, out; (lightened) aviạry, ẹlect, agọny, intọ, ŭnite; (obscured) errạnt, operạ, ardẹnt, actọr, natụre; ch, chip; g, go; th, thin; ᴛʜ, then; y, you;

Atchison, Topeka, and Santa Fe Railway System, Chicago to Pacific Coast, etc., total mileage 12,210.

Athabaska (ath-ạ-bas′kạ), former dist. N. W. Canada. — lake, N. W. Saskatchewan and N. E. Alberta, area 3; # 59 N, 110 W. — riv., S. Alb. to Athabaska lake, len. 1,000 mi.; # 58:40 N, 111 W.

Athens (ath′enz), city, S. E. Greece, its *, pop. 350; univ.; # 37:59 N, 23:45 E. — city, N. C. Ga., pop. 21; State Univ.; # 33:50 N, 83:20 W. — tn., C. S. Ohio, pop. 8, Ohio Univ.; # 39:20 N, 82:10 W.

Athol (ath′ol), tn., N. C. Mass., pop. 11; # 42:39 N, 72:14 W.

Athos (ath′os), mt., el. 6,350 ft. and N. pen., E. Khalkidike pen., N. E. Greece; # 40:9 N, 24:20 E.

Atlanta (at-lan′tạ), city, N. C. Ga., its *, pop. 302; univ.; # 33:50 N, 84:20 W.

Atlantic City (at-lan′tik), S. E. seacoast resort of New Jersey, pop. 64; # 39:20 N, 74:28 W.

Atlantic Ocean (at-lan′tik), ocean bet. America and Europe-Africa, area 31,530, greatest known depth, 27,360 ft.

Atlas (at′lạs), mt. range in N. W. Africa, Morocco and Algeria, summit, Mt. Tizi, el. 14,764 ft.; # 34 N, 2 E.

Attica (at′i-kạ), region about anc. Athens, S. E. Greece; # ab. 38:10 N, 23 E.

Attleboro (at′l-bur-ọ), city, S. E. Mass., pop. 22; # 41:56 N, 71:15 W.

Aube (ōb), riv., E. C. Fr. to Seine riv., len. 130 mi.; # 48:35 N., 3:45 E. — dept., N. E. Fr., area 2.3, pop. 228, * Troyes, pop. 55; # 48:20 N, 4:5 E.

Aubervilliers (ō-ber-vē-lyä), a N. suburb of Paris, Fr., pop. 40; # 48:55 N, 2:23 E.

Auburn (a′bẽrn), city, W. C. New York, pop. 36; state prison; # 42:55 N; 76:38 W. — city, 11 mi. S. of Sydney, Aust., pop. 15; # ab. 34 S, 151:12 E. — city, S. W. C. Me., pop. 20; # 44:8 N, 70:18 W. — tn., E. C. Ala., pop. 2; Ala. Polytechnic Inst; # 32:38 N, 85:30 W.

Auckland (âk′lạnd), chief spt., New Zealand, N. N. Island, pop. 173; Auckland Univ.; # 36:52 S, 174:46 E. — prov. dist., New Zealand, area 25, pop. 370; # 38 S, 176 E.

Aude (ōd), dept., S. coast of Fr., area 2.4, pop. 287, * Carcassonne, pop. 31; # 43:15 N, 3:15 E.

Aue (ou′ē), city, Sachsen (Saxony), near Zwickau, Ger., pop. 21; # 50:34 N, 12:42 E.

Augsburg (âgz′bẽrg, _Ger._ ouks′bùrch), city on Lech riv., * of Schwaben, Bayern (Bavaria), S. W. Ger., pop. 162; univ.; # 48:20 N, 10:53 E.

Augusta (â-gus′tạ), city, E. C. Ga., on Savannah riv., pop. 66; # 33:30 N, 82 W. — city, S. C. Me., state *, pop. 19; # 44:18 N, 69:50 W.

Aurora (â-rō′rạ), city, N. E. Ill., pop. 47; college; # 41:45 N, 88:25 W. — tn., S. C. New York, pop. 0.4; Wells College; # 42:46 N, 76:23 W.

Ausable (ô-sā′b'l), riv., New York to Lake Champlain through Ausable Chasm; # 44:30 N, 73:30 W.

Aussig (ou′sich), city, on Elbe riv., Bohemia, pop. 37; coal; chemicals; # 50:40 N, 14:2 E.

Austerlitz (ous′tẽr-lits), vil., Moravia, Czechosl., pop. 4; battle 1805; # 49:9 N, 16:55 E.

Austin (âs′tin), city, S. C. Texas, state * and univ., pop. 88; # 30:25 N, 97:35 W. — tn., S. E. Minn., pop. 18; # ab. 43:41 N, 93 W.

Australasia (âs-trạ-lā′shiạ), Australia, New Zealand and isls. of S. Pacific oc.

Australia (âs-trā′liạ), continent, S. hemisphere, S. E. of Asia, area 2,948, pop. 6,867; # 23 S, 134 E. — Commonwealth of, Br. Dominion, Australia and Tasmania, area 2,975, pop. 5,837, * (formerly) Melbourne, pop. 1,024 (with suburbs), * Canberra.

Australian Alps (âs-trā′liạn), highest Aust. range, S. E. Aust., summit, Mt. Kosciusko, el. 7,328 ft.; # 37:15 S, 147:30 E.

Austria (âs′tri-ạ) or **Österreich**, C. Europe, area 32, pop. 6,760, *Vienna, pop. 1,866; # 47:30 N, 14:30 E; former republic absorbed into Germany in 1938.

Austria, Lower, prov., N. E. Austria, area 7.5, pop. 1,509; #48 N, 16 E. [# 48 N, 14 E.

Austria, Upper, prov., N. W. Austria, area 4.6, pop. 902;

Autun (ō-tuṅ), tn., Saône-et-Loire dept., S. E. C. Fr., pop. 14; Roman ruins; # 46:58 N, 4:18 E.

Auvergne (ō-vãrn-y′), plateau, S. C. Fr.; ancient prov.,* Clermont; # 45 N, 3 E.

Avellaneda (ä-vä-lyä-nä′ᴛнä), suburb of Buenos Aires, E. Argentina, pop. 46; # 34:43 S, 58:25 W.

Avellino (ä-vel-lē′nō), prov., Campania, Italy, area 1.2, pop. 403, and its *, pop. 26; # 46:8 N, 12:14 E.

Aveyron (à-ve-rôṅ), riv., S. C. Fr. to Garonne riv., len. 150 mi.; # 44:5 N, 1:2 E. — dept., S. C. Fr., area 3.4, pop. 333, * Rodez; # 44:20 N, 2:40 E.

Avignon (à-vē-nyôṅ), _anc._ Avenio, city, S. Fr., on Rhône riv., * of Vaucluse dept., pop. 49; # 43:55 N, 4:50 E.

Avila (ä′vē-lä), prov., W. C. Spain, area 3, pop. 208, and its *, pop. 12; # ab. 40:38 N, 4:43 W.

Avlona (äv-lō′nä), sp. Albania, pop. 6.5; # 40:27 N, 19:30 E.

Avon (ā′vọn), riv., C. Eng. to Severn riv., past Stratford, len. 80 mi.; # 52 N, 2:10 W. — riv., Wiltshire past Bristol to Severn riv.; # 51:27 N, 2:44 W.

Awaji (ä-wä′jē), isl., Inland Sea, Japan, area 0.2, pop. 211, # 34:25 N, 134:52 E.

Ayacucho (ī-ä-kö′chō), dept., S. W. Peru, area 18, pop. 302, and its *, pop. 14; # 12:50 S, 74:18 W. — tn., Buenos Aires prov., E. Argentina, pop. 20; # 37:8 S, 58:27 W.

Ayr (âr), county, S. W. Scotland, area 1.1, pop. 299, and its *, pop. 36; # 55:20 N, 4:30 W.

Ayuthia (ä-yö′thē-ä), city, S. C. Siam, on Menam riv., pop. 50; former *; # 14:25 N, 100:30 E.

Azerbaijan (äz-er-bī-jän′), soviet republic, E. Transcaucasian Russia; area 34, pop. 2,097, * Baku, pop. 250; # 40 N, 47 E. — prov., N. W. Persia, * Tabriz; # 37 N, 48 E.

Azores (à-zōrz′), group 9 isls. in Mid-Atlantic, area 1, pop. 243, * Angra, pop. 10; Portuguese; # 38:30 N, 28 W.

Azov (ä′zof), Sea of, N. E. extension of Black Sea, len. 230 mi.; # 46 N, 36:30 E.

Aztec Ruin (az′tek), U. S. National Monument, New Mex., prehistoric pueblo of 500 rooms; # 36:50 N, 108 W.

B

Bab-el-Mandeb (bäb-el-män′deb), strait bet. N. E. Africa and S. W. Arabia; outlet of Red Sea; # 12:30 N, 43:30 E.

Babylon (bab′i-lọn), anc. city on Euphrates riv., C. Mesopotamia near Kerbela; # 32:40 N, 44:25 E.

Badajoz (bäd-ä-hōs′), prov., S. W. Spain, area 8.5, pop. 656, and its *, pop. 41; # 38:49 N, 6:56 W.

Baden (bä′dẹn), republic, S. W. Ger., area 5.8, pop. 2,320, * Karlsruhe, pop. 145; # 47:55 N, 7:45 E. — city, C. Baden, pop. 26; # 48:46 N, 8:13 E. — (Oberbaden), city, C. N. Switz., pop. 9; # 47:28 N, 8:15 E.

Bad Lands, rugged, largely barren area of peculiar erosion, S. W. C. S. Dak., N. W. Neb.; fossils; also in S. W. N. Dak., and locally elsewhere in semi-arid regions.

Baffin (baf′in), large isl. bet. Greenland and Hudson Bay, len. 1,000 mi., area 236; # 70 N, 70 W.

Baffin Bay (baf′in bā), part of Arctic oc., W. of N. and C. Greenland, E. of Baffin Isl., # 75 N, 65 W.

Bagdad or **Baghdad** (bäg-däd′; bag′dad), prov. of C. Iraq, area 55, pop. 1,360, and city on Tigris riv., pop. 125, * of Iraq; # 33:15 N; 44:25 E.

Baguio (bä-gē-ō′), mt. tn., N. of Manila, summer residential station, pop. 5; el. 4,961 ft.; # 16:25 N, 120:35 E.

Bahamas (bạ-hä′mạz), group of Br. isls., N. W. Indies, area 4, pop. 67, * Nassau, pop. 8; # 25 N, 75 W.

Bahawalpur (bä-hä-wäl-pör′), native state, N. W. India, area 15, pop. 781, and its *, pop. 19; # 29:20 N, 71:35 E.

Bahia (bä-ē′ä), state, E. Brazil, area 204, pop. 3,334, * San Salvador (sometimes known as Bahia), pop. 283; # 13 S, 38:20 W.

Bahía Blanca (bä-ē′ä bläng′kä), spt. city, S. E. Argentina, pop. 44; # 38:40 S, 62:5 W.

Bahrein (bä-rān′), five isls., W. C. Persian Gulf, area 0.2, pop. 120, * Manama, pop. 35; Br. protectorate; # 26 N, 50:3 E.

Bahr el Abiad (bähr el ä-bē-äd′) and **Azrek** (äz′rek), see **Nile, White** and **Blue.**

Bahr el Ghazal (bähr el ghä-zäl′), upper affluents of the White Nile, N. Africa. — S. prov. of Anglo-Egyptian Sudan, area 114, pop. 1,000; # 9:24 N, 30 E.

(variable) ḍ as d or j, ş as s or sh, ṭ as t or ch, ẓ as z or zh; _o,_ F. cloche; ü, F. menu; ċh, Sc. loch; ṅ, F. bonbon; ′, primary accent; ″, secondary accent; †, obsolete; <, from; +, and; =, equals. See also lists at beginning of book.

Baikal (bī'käl), lake, S. Siberia, len. 400 mi., area 11, depth over 4,700 ft.; # 54 N, 108 E.

Baitarani (bī-tur'ā̆-nē), riv., Orissa, N. E. India to Bay of Bengal, len. 400 mi.; # ab. 20:40 N, 87 E.

Baja California (bä'Hä kä-lē-fôr'nyä), terr., N. W. Mex., pen. of Lower Calif., area 58, pop. 63, * LaPaz, pop. 5; # 28 N, 114 W.

Baker (bā'kèr), mt., Cascades, N. W. Wash., el. 10,750 ft.; # 48:45 N, 121:48 W.

Bakersfield (bāk'èrz-fēld), city, S. E. C. Calif., pop. 29; petroleum; # 35:22 N, 119 W.

Baku (bä-kö'), pen. in Caspian Sea, rich oil field. — city therein, * of Azerbaijan Republic, pop. 250; # 40:25 N, 49:50 E.

Balabac (bä-lä'bäk), strait, bet. Borneo and Balabac Isl., Philippines; # 7:30 N, 117 E.

Balaton (bol'ot-ọn) or **Platten,** lake, W. C. Hungary, len. 50 mi.; # 46:50 N, 17:40 E.

Balboa (bäl-bō'ä), spt., Canal Zone, Pacific end of Panama canal; # 8:56 N, 79:34 W.

Baldwin (bâld'win), tn., E. C. Kansas, pop. 1; Baker Univ.; #38:42 N, 95:18 W.

Bâle (bäl), see **Basel.**

Balearic (bal-ē̆-ar'ik), isls., W. Mediterranean sea, Spanish prov., area 2, pop. 342, * Palma, pop. 82; # 39:30 N, 3 E.

Bali (bä'lē), isl., Dutch E. Indies, just E. of Java, area 2; # 8:30 S, 115 E.

Balkan (bâl'kạn) **Mountains,** E.–W. range, Bulg., highest, 7,840 ft.; # 42:45 N, 25:30 E.

Balkan Peninsula, S. E. Europe, bet. Adriatic and Ægean seas, or Adriatic, Ægean, and Black seas; # 42 N, 22 E.

Balkash (bäl-käsh'), lake, Kirghiz Steppe, W. C. Asia, area 0.7; # 46:30 N, 76 E.

Balkh (bälkh), *anc.* Bactra, prov. N. C. Afghanistan, and its *, pop. 10; "Mother of Cities"; # 36:45 N, 66:50 E.

Ballarat (bal-ā̆-rat'), city, S. W. Victoria, Australia, pop. 40; gold; # 37:35 S, 144 E.

Balmain (bal-mān'), municipal suburb of Sydney, Australia, pop. 32; # 33:53 S, 151:12 E.

Baltic (bâl'tik), sea bet. Sweden and Germany, Finland, etc., len. 1,000 mi., area 160; # 56 N, 17 E.

Baltimore (bâl'ti-mōr), city, N. C. Md., on Chesapeake Bay, pop. 859; Johns Hopkins Univ., Goucher College, Loyola Univ., State College for Women; # 39:18 N, 76:38 W.

Baltimore and Ohio, R.R., Chicago to New York via Washington, D. C., total mileage 5,397.

Baluchistan (bal-ō-chis-tän'), region bet. India and Persia, Br. part, area 9, pop. 421; Agency Territories, area 45; native states, area 81, pop. 415, * Quetta, pop. 49; # 28 N, 65 E.

Bamberg (bäm'berċh), city, N. Bayern (Bavaria), S. C. Ger., pop. 49; cathedral; # 49:52 N, 10:52 E.

Bamian (bä-mē-än'), pass over Hindu Kush mts., N. W. Afghanistan, el. 12,000 ft.; # 34:55 N, 68 E.

Banahao (bä-nä'hou), vol. S. E. of Manila, Luzón, Philippines, el. 7,178 ft.; # 14:5 N, 121:30 E.

Banat (bä-nät'), prov., S. W. Romania, area 11, pop. 1,582; # 45:54 N, 20:39 E. — mt. mass therein; # 45:40 N, 21 E.

Banbury (ban'bē-ri), tn., Oxfordshire, S. C. Eng., pop. 13; # 52:4 N, 1:21 W.

Banda (bän'dä), sea, bet. Celebes and Papua, E. Indies; # 6 S, 128 E.

Bandar Abbas (bän-där' ȧb-bäs'), spt., S. E. C. Persia, on strait of Ormuz, pop. 10; # 27:15 N, 56:20 E.

Bandelier (ban-da-lēr'), national monument, 18 mi. W. of Santa Fé, N. C. New Mex.; cliff dwellings and caves; # 35:50 N, 106:30 W.

Banff (banf), county, N. E. Scotland, area 0.6, pop. 54, and its *, a spt.; # 57:40 N, 2:35 W. — tn., S. C. Alberta, mt. resort. — Canadian National Park near by; # 51:25 N, 115:3 W.

Bangalore (bang-gạ-lōr'), chief city and * of Mysore, S. India, pop. 238; # 12:55 N; 77:30 E.

Banganapalle (bung'gạ-nạ-pul'ē), native state and tn. near Madras, S. E. India, area 0.2, pop. 37; # 15:19 N, 78:17 E.

Bangkok (bang-kok'), spt. city on the Menam riv., * of Siam, Indo-China, pop. 931; # 13:45 N, 100:30 E.

Bangor (ban'gǒr), city, S. C. Maine, pop. 30; # 44:40 N,

68:50 W. — spt. tn., Carnarvon, Wales, pop. 11; # ab. 53:13 N, 4:7 W.

Bangweolo (bang-wē-ō'lō), marsh, former lake, N. E. N. Rhodesia, len. 150 mi.; # 11 S, 30 E.

Banjermasin (bän-yèr-mäs'in), spt., S. coast of Borneo, * of Dutch Borneo, E. Indies, pop. 52; # 3:15 S, 114:35 E.

Banjuwangis (bän-yö-wäng'gis), spt., S. E. Java, E. Indies, pop. 20; # 8:15 S, 114:15 E.

Banka or **Bangha** (bäng'kä), isl. E. of Sumatra, Dutch E. Indies, area 5, pop. 154, * Muntok; tin mines; # 2:15 S, 106 E.

Banks (bangks), isl., Arctic oc., W. of Victoria Isl.; area 25, # 73 N, 120 W. — isl., Torres Strait, ext. N. E. Australia; # 10:10 S, 142:15 E.

Bankstown (bangks'toun), tn., near Sydney, New S. Wales, Australia, pop. 13; # 33:55 S, 151:1 E.

Bannockburn (ban'ọk-bèrn), tn., N. E. Sterling, S. C. Scotland; battle, 1314; # 56:5 N, 3:55 W.

Bantam (bän-täm' or ban'tạm), district, W. Java, area 3, pop. 900; * Serang. — village therein, first Dutch settlement in E. Indies; dwarf fowls; # 6:5 S, 106:8 E.

Bantry (ban'tri), bay, Cork County, S. W. Ireland and spt. on same; # 51:38 N, 9:30 W.

Baranof (bä-rä'nof), isl., Alexander arch., S. Alaska, len. 105 mi.; spt. Sitka; # 57 N, 135 W.

Barbados (bär-bä'dōz), isl., S. E. W. Indies, area 0.2, pop. 158, Br. colony, * Bridgetown, pop. 13; # 13:15 N, 59: 30 W.

Barbary (bär'bạ-ri), loosely applied to Africa, N. of Sahara and W. of Egypt.

Barberton (bär'bèr-tọn), city, N. E. Ohio, pop. 24; now a suburb of Akron; # 41:3 N, 81:35 W.

Barbuda (bär-bö'dä), isl., Br. W. Indies, area 0.06, dependency of Antiqua; # 17:40 N, 61:40 W.

Barca (bär'kạ) or **Bengazi,** region, N. E. Libya, N. Africa, E. of Gulf of Sidra, pop. 500; Italian; # 32:20 N, 21 E.

Barcelona (bär-sẹ-lō'nạ), prov., N. E. Spain, area 3, pop. 1,435, and its *, spt., pop. 977; univ.; # 41:30 N, 2:10 E. — city, N. E. Venezuela, pop. 11; # 10:11 N, 64:45 W.

Bareilly (bar-ā'lē), city, E. of Delhi, N. C. India, pop. 129; # 28:20 N, 79:20 E.

Barents (bä'rents), sea, part of Arctic oc., N. of E. Europe; # 75 N, 40 E.

Barfrush or **Barfurush** (bär-fu-rösh'), city, N. C. Persia, near Caspian Sea, pop. ab. 50; # 36:40 N, 52:55 E.

Bar Harbor (bär här'bǒr), summer resort, Mt. Desert Isle, S. E. Maine, pop. 4; # 44:23 N, 68:12 W.

Bari delle Puglie (bä'rē del-lä pūl-yä), prov., Apulia, E. Italy, area 2, pop. 953, and its *, *anc.* Barium, a spt., pop. 115; univ.; # 41:8 N, 16:51 E.

Bar-le-Duc (bär-lẹ-dük'), city, N. E. C. Fr., * of Meuse dept., pop. 17; # 48:45 N, 5:10 E.

Barlee (bar'lē), lake, S. W. W. Australia, 100 mi. long; # 29 S, 119:3 E.

Barmen (bär'men), city on Wupper riv., adjoining Elberfeld, Ger., pop. 185; textiles; # 51:15 N, 7:5 E.

Barnaul (bär-na-öl'), city, * of Altai prov., C. Siberia, pop. 66; # 53:23 N, 83:40 E.

Barnsley (bärnz'li), city, 15 mi. N. of Sheffield, C. Eng., pop. 70; # 53:33 N, 1:29 W.

Barnstaple (bärn'stạ-pl), spt. on Barnstaple Bay, N. Devon, S. W. Eng.; pop. 14; # 51:5 N, 4:5 W.

Baroda (bä-rō'dä), a native state, W. C. India, area 8, pop. 2,127, and its *, pop. 95; # 22:25 N, 73:20 E.

Barquisimeto (bär-kē-sē'mä-tō), city, N. W. C. Venezuela, * of Lara, pop. 24; # 10:6 N, 69:25 W.

Barranquilla (bär-rän-kēl'yä), city, N. Colombia, pop. 81, the * of Atlantico, on Magdalena riv., 17 mi. from Puerto Colombia; # 11 N, 74:55 W.

Barre (bar'i), tn., C. Vermont, pop. 11; granite and marble; # 44:15 N, 72:30 W.

Barrhead (bär-hed'), a S. suburb of Glasgow, Scotland, pop. 12; # 55:48 N, 4:24 W.

Barrier Reef, Great, coral reef 1,250 mi. long, N. E. Australia; # 19:45 S, 148 E.

Barrow (bar'ō), spt. city, Westmorland, N. W. Eng., pop. 75; # 54:9 N, 3:13 W. — point, most N. point of Alaska; # 71:20 N, 156:25 W. — village near same; # 71:15 N, 156:

---

fat, fāte, fär, fåll, ȧsk, fãre; net, mē, hẽr; pin, pīne; not, nōte, mŏve, nôr; up, lūte, pu̇ll; oi, oil; ou, out; (lightened) aviạry, ẹlect, agǫny, intọ, ūnite; (obscured) errạnt, operạ, ardẹnt, actǒr, natūre; ch, chip; g, go; th, thin; ᴛʜ, then; y, you;

25 W. — riv., S. E. Ireland, S. to Waterford Haven, len. 90 mi.; # 52:15 N, 7 W.

Barry (bar'i), spt. city, 10 mi. W. of Cardiff, S. E. Wales, pop. 40; coal; # 51:24 N, 3:18 W.

Bartlesville (bär'tlz-vil), oil center city, N. E. Okla., pop. 16; # 36:45 N, 95:55 W.

Barwon (bär'wun), riv., N. E. New S. Wales, Australia, trib. of Darling riv., len. 500 mi.; # 29:55 S, 146:30 E.

Basel or **Basle** (bä'zel), canton, N. W. Switz., area 0.2, pop. 82; and an independent city therein, on Rhine riv., pop. 136; univ.; # 47:35 N, 7:32 E.

Bashi (bä-shē') **Channel**, strait bet. Philippines and Formosa; # 21:30 N, 121 E.

Bashkir (bäsh'kēr), soviet republic, E. C. Russia, area 40, pop. 1,268, * Ufa, pop. 103; # 54:50 N, 55:55 E.

Basin, Great, large region of interior drainage, S. W. U.S.A., Nevada; # 39 N, 117 W.

Basle (bä'zel) see **Basel.**

Basque (bâsk), area, N. Spain, near Fr., former prov.; home of Basque race; # 43 N, 2 W.

Basra (bus'rä), prov. of S. Iraq, area 54, pop. 786, and spt. city near head of Persian Gulf, pop. ab. 20; # 30:35 N, 47:4 E.

Bas-Rhin (bä-raň), dept., N. E. Fr., formerly Lower Alsace, area 1.9, pop. 688, * Strasbourg, pop. 181; # 49 N, 7:45 E.

Bass (bâs), strait bet. Australia and Tasmania, least width 80 mi.; # 40 S, 146 E.

Bassein (bäs-sēn'), dist., S. Burma, area 4, pop. 441, and its *, pop. 32; # 16:45 N, 94:45 E.

Basses-Alpes (bäs-zàlp), dept., S. E. Fr., area 2.7, pop. 92, * Digne, pop. 6; # 44 N, 6:10 E.

Basse-Terre (bäs-târ), spt., * of Guadeloupe, Fr. W. Indies, pop. 8; # 16 N, 61:35 W. — (**Basseterre**) spt., * of St. Christopher, Br. W. Indies, pop. 10; # ab. 17:20 N, 62:45 W.

Bastar (bus'tär), a native state in S. E. C. India, area 13, pop. 464, * Jagdalpur; # 19 N, 81:30 E.

Bastia (bäs-tē'ä), spt. city, N. Corsica, pop. comm. 33.

Basutoland (bä-sö'tō-land), a Br. protected native state in S. Africa, included in the Union of S. Africa; a rugged plateau, area 12, pop. 498,* Maseru, pop. 3; # 28 S, 28 E.

Bataan (ba-tan'), prov., Luzón, Philippines.

Batavia (ba̤-tā'vi-ạ), prov., W. Java, area 4.5, pop. 2,200, and its * a spt. city, * of Dutch E. Indies, pop. 437; # 6:15 S, 106:45 E. — tn., N. W. New York, pop. 17; # 43 N, 78:12 W.

Bath (bâth), city near Bristol, Somerset, S. W. Eng., pop. 69; # 51:25 N, 2:24 W. — spt. city, S. W. Me., pop. 10; # ab. 43:52 N, 69:50 W.

Bathurst (bâth'ĕrst), tn., E. C. New S. Wales, Australia, pop. 10; # 33:20 S, 149:50 E. — spt. tn., * of Gambia, W. Africa, pop. 9; # 13:24 S, 16:36 E.

Baton Rouge (bat'ọn rözh), city, S. E. La., state *, pop. 35, State Univ.; # 30:30 N, 91:15 W.

Battambang (bât-tàm-bäng'), important tn., N. W. Cambodia, Fr. Indo-China; # 13 N, 103:15 E.

Battersea (bat'ĕr-sē), a borough of London, Eng., on Thames riv., pop. 168; 51:28 N, 0:10 W.

Battle Creek (bat'l krēk), city, S. W. C. Mich., pop. 43; Sanitarium; college; # 42:20 N, 85:13 W.

Batum (bä-töm'), city, E. shore of Black Sea, free port of Transcaucasia, pop. 46; # 41:40 N, 41:35 E.

Bautzen (bout'sẹn), div. Sachsen (Saxony), S. Ger., area 1, pop. 432, and its *, pop. 39; # 51:12 N, 14:30 E.

Bavaria (ba̤-vā'ri-ạ), see **Bayern.**

Bavarian Alps, portion of Alps mts. along S. border of W. Ger.; # 47:30 N, 11 E.

Bay City, city, E. C. Mich., near Saginaw Bay, pop. 48; # 43:35 N, 83:50 W.

Bayern (bī'ĕrn), *Eng.* **Bavaria**, republic, S. Ger., area 31, pop. 7,399, * München, pop. 672; # 49 N, 11 E.

Bayonne (bä-yön'), city, N. E. New Jersey, pop. 79, near New York City; petroleum refining; # 40:40 N, 74:7 W. — (bà-yon), city S. W. Fr., near W. end of Pyrenees mts., pop. 28; # 43:28 N, 1:28 W.

Bayreuth (bī'roit), city, * of Oberfranken, Bayern (Bavaria), pop. 35; # 49:55 N, 11:32 E.

Beacon (bē'kọn), tn., S. E. New York, pop. 13; # 41:26 N, 73:58 W.

Beatrice (bē'a̤-tris), tn., S. E. Neb., on Blue riv., pop. 11; # 40:18 N, 96:45 W.

Beaumont (bō'mont), city, S. E. Texas, on Neches riv., pop. 59; petroleum; # 30:10 N, 94:5 W.

Beauvais (bō-vä), city, 40 mi. N. of Paris, Fr., * of Oise dept., pop. 20; cathedral; # 49:25 N, 2:3 E.

Beaver Falls (bē'vĕr fâlz), tn., S. W. Penn. on Beaver riv., pop. 17; Geneva College; # 40:47 N, 80:22 W.

Bechuanaland (bech-ö-ä'nạ-land), Br. protectorate, S. Africa, area 275, pop. 153; # 22 S, 25 E. — div. of Cape prov. of Union of S. Africa, area 52, pop. 120; # 27 S, 22 E.

Bedford (bed'fọrd), county, S. E. C. Eng., area 0.5, pop. 206, and its *, pop. 41; # 52:12 N, 0:27 W. — tn., S. W. Ind., pop. 13; cut building limestone; # 38:50 N, 86:30 W.

Beersheba (bē-ẹr-shē'ba̤), tn., ext. S. Palestine; in ruins; # 31:15 N, 34:45 E.

Behring see **Bering.**

Beilan (bā-län'), mt. pass, N. W. of Aleppo, Syria; from Anatolia; # 37 N, 36:30 E.

Beira (bā'rä), prov., N. C. Portugal, area 9.2, pop. 1,598, * Coimbra; # 40:10 N, 8:20 W. — spt., Port. E. Africa, pop. ab. 5; # 19:50 S, 34:50 E.

Beirut (bā-röt', *anc.* Berytus, spt. city, * of Syria, pop. 180; American College; port of Damascus; # 33:53 N, 35:30 E.

Belem (bā-laň'), often called Pará, spt. city, * of Pará, N. E. Brazil, near mouth of Amazon riv., formerly a great rubber port, pop. 293; # 1:30 S, 48:20 W.

Belfast (bel'fâst), spt. city on Belfast Lough, * of N. Ireland, pop. 429; univ.; shipbuilding; # 54:38 N, 5:57 W.

Belfort (bel-fôr), ter., E. Fr., area 0.2, pop. 94, and its *, pop. 32; # 47:40 N, 6:55 E. — pass bet. Jura and Vosges mts. from Rhine valley to Rhône via Doubs valley; important historically; # 47:38 N, 6:52 E.

Belgian Congo, see **Congo.**

Belgique, Royaume de (rwä-yōm dè bel-zhēk), official name of Belgium.

Belgium (bel'ji-um), kingdom, N. W. Europe, bordering Fr., Ger., Neth., area 12, pop. 7,666, * Brussels, pop. 787 (with suburbs); # 51 N, 4:30 E.

Belgrade, *Serbian* **Beograd** (bel-grad', bä-ō-grad'), city, on Danube and Sava rivs., * of Yugoslavia, pop. 112; univ.; # 44:50 N, 20:30 E.

Belitoeng, see **Billiton.**

Belize (be-lēz'), spt. tn., * of Br. Honduras, pop. 17; # 17:20 N, 88:2 W.

Bellaire (bel-âr'), city, S. E. Ohio, pop. 14; a suburb of Wheeling, W. Va.; # 40:3 N, 80:45 W.

Bellary (bel-lä'rē), city, S. C. India, pop. 40; # 15:10 N, 77 E.

Belle-Fourche (bel-försh'), riv., E. C. Wyo., to Cheyenne riv., S. Dak., len. 200 mi.; # ab. 44:30 N, 102:20 W. — irrigation project with one of world's largest earth dams, near Bellefourche, S. Dak.; # ab. 44:45 N, 103:30 W.

Belle-Île (bel-ēl), isl., S. of Brittany, Fr.; resort; # 47:15 N, 3:15 W.

Belle-Isle (bel-īl), strait bet. Newfoundland and Labrador, connecting Gulf of St. Lawrence and Atlantic oc., width 10–15 mi. — tiny isl. therein; # 51:15 N, 56:15 W.

Belleville (bel'vil), tn., N. E. New Jersey, pop. 28; # 40: 48 N, 74:9 W. — city, S. W. Ill., pop. 28; # 38:30 N, 90 W. — tn., S. E. Ontario, pop. 12; colleges; # 44:10 N, 77:25 W.

Bellingham (bel'ing-ạm), city, N. W. Wash., on Puget Sound, pop. 29; lumber; # 48:45 N, 122:30 W.

Bellinzona (bel-lin-zō'nä) or **Bellenz** (bel'lents), city, Ticino Canton, S. E. Switz., pop. 10; # 46:15 N, 9:2 E.

Bello Horizonte (bel'ō ō-rē-zọn'tä), tn., * of Minas Geraes, Brazil, pop. 56; # 19:54 S, 43:30 W.

Belluno (bel-lö'nō), prov., Venetia, N. E. Italy, area 1.3, pop. 235, and its *, on Piave riv., pop. 27; # 46:10 N, 12:13 E.

Beloit (be-loit'), city, S. C. Wis., on Rock riv.; pop. 25; Beloit College; # 42:3 N, 89:1 W.

Belton (bel'tọn), tn., E. C. Texas, pop. 5; Baylor College; # 31:4 N, 97:30 W.

Benares (be-nä'rez), a native state, N. E. C. India, area 0.8, pop. 363, and its *, on Ganges riv., pop. 198; # 25:2 N, 83 E.

Benderabbas (ben-dĕr-äb'bäs), see **Bandar Abbas.**

Bendigo (ben′di-gō), city, N. C. Victoria, Australia, pop. 33; gold mining; # 36:40 S, 144:20 E.

Benevento (ben-e-ven′tō), prov., Campania, S. C. Italy, area 0.8, pop. 267, and its *, pop. 28; Trajan's arch; # 41: 8 N, 14:43 E.

Bengal (ben-gâl′), prov., delta of Ganges-Brahmaputra rivs., N. E. India, area 69, pop. 46,696; also native states, area 5, pop. 897,* Calcutta, pop. 1,328 (with suburbs); # 23:3 N, 90 E.

Bengal, Bay of, N. E. part of Indian oc., bet. India and Burma; # 15 N, 90 E.

Bengazi (ben-gä′zē), *anc.* Berenice, tn., Barca, N. Africa, * of Cyrenaica, Libya; pop. 35; # 32:10 N, 20:2 E.

Benguella (ben-gā′lä), dist., Angola, W. Africa and its spt., pop. 4; # 12:35 S, 13:26 E.

Beni (bā-nē′), riv., trib. of Madeira riv., N. Bolivia, len. ab. 600 mi.; # 10:30 S, 65:20 W.

Benin (be-nēn′), region, S. Nigeria, and its *, on Benin riv., pop. ab. 84; # 6:30 N, 6:5 E.

Benin, Bight of, open bay, N. Gulf of Guinea, W. Africa; # 5 N, 4 E.

Beni Suef (bā′nē swef′), city, N. Egypt, pop. 32; # 29:6 N, 31:5 E.

Benkulen (ben-kū′len), spt., S. W. C. Sumatra, pop. 10; # 3:45 S, 102:15 E.

Ben Lomond (ben lō′mond), mt., E. of Loch Lomond, N. Scotland, el. 3,192 ft.; # ab. 56:8 N, 4:30 W. — mt., E. Tasmania, el. 5,010 ft.; # 41:40 S, 147:40 E.

Ben Macdhui (ben mak-dö′ē), pk., C. Highlands of Scotland, el. 4,296 ft.; # 57:5 N, 3:38 W.

Ben Nevis (ben nev′is), pk., Inverness, Scotland, highest in British Isles, el. 4,406 ft.; # 56:48 N, 4:59 W.

Bennington (ben′ing-tǫn), tn., S. W. Vermont, pop. 8; # 42:52 N, 73:13 W.

Benoni (be-nō′ni), city, Transvaal, U. of S. Africa, pop. 48, white, 14; gold mines ; # 26:10 S, 28:24 E.

Benton Harbor (ben′tǫn), tn., S. W. Mich., on Lake Michigan, pop. 17; # 42:5 N, 86:30 W.

Benue (ben′wē), see **Binue.**

Beograd, see **Belgrade.**

Beppu (bep′pō), spt. city, N. E. Kyushiu Isl., Japan, pop. 38; # 33:17 N, 131:30 E.

Berar (bā-rär′), a former prov. of the Deccan, India, area 18, pop. 3,081. See **Central Provinces.**

Berber (bèr′bèr), prov. on Nile, Anglo-Egyptian Sudan, and its *, pop. ab. 10; # 18 N, 34:15 E.

Berbera (bèr-bā′rä), chief city of Br. Somaliland, N. E. Africa, pop. 30; # 10:20 N, 45:10 E.

Berchem (ber′chem), suburb of Antwerp, Belgium, pop. 34; # 51:12 N, 4:25 E.

Berdichev (ber-dē′chef), city, on Bug riv., Ukraine, S. W. Russia, pop. 77; # 49:40 N, 28:15 E.

Bergamo (ber′gä-mō), prov., C. Lombardy, N. W. Italy, area 1, pop. 556, and its *, *anc.* Bergomum, pop. 62; # 45:41 N, 9:43 E.

Bergen (ber′gen), spt., S. W. Norway, pop. 91; fisheries; # 60:2 N, 5:2 E.

Bering (bā′ring or bē′ring), sea, N. portion of Pacific oc., N. of Aleutian Isls., area 878, greatest known depth 13,422 ft.; # 57 N, 180 W. — strait bet. Alaska and Asia, width 36 mi.; # 65:15 N, 168:45 W.

Berkeley (bèrk′li), city, on San Francisco Bay, W. C. Calif., pop. 86; State Univ.; # 37:52 N, 122:17 W.

Berkshire (bèrk′shir), county, S. C. Eng., area 0.7, pop. 295, * Reading, pop. 93; # 51:26 N, 1 W. — Hills, low mts., W. Mass., highest, 3,535 ft.; resorts; # 49:20 N, 73:10 W.

Berlin (bèr-lin′), city, a prov. of Prussia and * of Prussia and of Germany, pop. 3,931; univ.; # 52:31 N, 13:24 E. — city, N. C. New Hampshire, pop. 19; # 44:30 N, 71:12 W. — see **Kitchener.**

Bermejo (ber-mā′hō), riv., N. Argentina, trib. of Paraguay riv., len. 550 mi.; # 27 S, 58:20 W.

Bermondsey (bèr′mǫnd-zi), a borough of London, Eng., pop. 119; # 51:30 N, 0:4 W.

Bermudas (bèr-mū′däz), isl., N. Atlantic oc., 700 mi. S. E. of New York, area 0.02, pop. 31, * Hamilton, pop. 4; winter resort; Br. naval base; # 32:20 N, 64:45 W.

Bern (bern) or **Berne,** canton, W. C. Switz., area 2.7, pop. 674, its *, the * of Switz., pop. 105; univ.; # 47 N, 7:28 E.

Bernburg (bern′bùrch), city on Mulde riv., Anhalt state, C. Ger., pop. 34; # 51:48 N, 11:45 E.

Bernese Alps (bèrn′ēz), mt. range, S. W. Switz.; summit Finsteraarhorn, el. 14,026 ft.; # 46:30 N, 8 E.

Bernina (ber-nē′nä), mt. pk. 13,295 ft. and pass, 7,640 ft., Rhætian Alps, S. E. Switz.; # 46:24 N, 10 E.

Berry or **Berri** (ber′i; *Fr.* ber-rē), old prov., C. France, now depts. of Cher and Indre; # 46:40 N, 1:50 E.

Berwick (ber′ik; bèr′wik), county, ext. S. E. Scotland, area 0.5, pop. 27, * Duns; # ab. 55:50 N, 2:10 W. — tn., N. E. C. Pa., pop. 13; # 41:5 N, 76:17 W.

Berwyn (ber′win), ridge, N. C. Wales; # 52:50 N, 3:30 W. — suburb of Chicago, Ill., pop. 48; # 41:50 N, 87:49 W.

Besançon (be-zän-sôn), *anc.* Vesontio, city, E. C. Fr., * of Doubs dept., pop. 56; watches; # 47:15 N, 6:2 E.

Bessarabia (bes-ạ-rā′bi-ạ), prov., N. E. Romania, area 17, pop. 2,345, * Chisinau (Kishinev), pop. 114; # 47 N, 29 E.

Bessemer (bes′ę-mèr), suburb of Birmingham, Ala., pop. 23; # 33:25 N, 86:50 W.

Bethany (beth′ạ-ni), vil., in Palestine, 2 mi. E. of Jerusalem; # 31:47 N, 35:14 E.

Bethlehem (beth′lę-ęm), tn., 5½ mi. S. W. of Jerusalem, Palestine, pop. 7; birthplace of Jesus Christ; # 31:43 N, 35:1 E. — city, E. C. Pa., pop. 58; Lehigh Univ.; steel; # 40:4 N, 75:27 W.

Bethnal Green (beth′nạl grēn), a borough, N. E. London, Eng., pop. 117; # 51:31 N, 0:3 W.

Béthune (bā-tün), city, N. E. Fr., near Lille, pop. 17; # 50:3 N, 2:40 E.

Beuthen (boi′tẹn), city, ext. S. E. Ger., pop. 62; # 50:21 N, 18:58 E.

Beverley (bev′èr-li), tn., * of E. Riding, Yorkshire, N. E. Eng., pop. 13; # 53:50 N, 0:25 W. — **Beverly,** city, N. E. Mass., pop. 26; # 42:32 N, 70:57 W.

Béziers (bā-ziā), city, Hérault dept., S. Fr., pop. 56; # 43:2 N, 3:15 E.

Bhagalpur (bhäg-ạl-pör′), city on Ganges riv., Bihar prov., N. E. India, pop. 69; # 25:15 N, 87 E.

Bhatpara (but-pä′rä), city, 22 mi. N. of Calcutta, N. E. India, pop. 50; # 22:54 N, 88:25 E.

Bhaunagar (bou-nug′år), native state near Bombay, area 3, pop. 426, and its * (often called Kathiawar), pop. 59; # ab. 21:46 N, 72:11 E.

Bhopal (bhō-pâl′), native state, C. India, area 7, pop. 692, and its *, pop. 45; # 23:20 N, 77:25 E.

Bhutan (bhö-tän′), Br. protectorate in Himalaya mts., N. of Assam, India, area 20, pop. 250, * Punakha (winter) and Tasichozong (summer); # 27:30 N, 90:30 E.

Bialystok (byä′li-stok), county, N. C. Poland, area 12.6, pop. 1,303, and its *, pop. 77; # 53 N, 23:5 E.

Biarritz (bē-är-rēts), coastal resort ext. S. W. Fr., pop. 18; # 43:28 N, 1:30 W.

Bicêtre (bē-sātr), suburb of Paris, Fr.; famous asylum; # 48:49 N, 2:22 E.

Bida (bē′dä), city, on Niger riv., * of Nupe prov., C. Nigeria, pop. ab. 90; # 9 N, 6:3 E.

Biddeford (bid′e-fǫrd), city, S. W. Me., pop. 20; # 43:28 N, 70:30 W.

Biebrich (bē′brich), a S. suburb of Wiesbaden, W. Ger., pop. 21; # 50:2 N, 8:14 E.

Biel (bēl), or **Bienne** (byen), city, on Bieler Sea, N. W. Switz., pop. 35; # 47:10 N, 7:15 E.

Bielefeld (bē′le-felt), city, Westphalia (Westfalen), W. Prussia, W. C. Ger., pop. 85; # 52:2 N, 8:30 E.

Bienne (byen), see **Biel.**

Bighole, mt. basin, Silver Bow Co., S. W. Mont.; national monument, Indian defeat, 1877; # ab. 46 N, 113 W.

Bighorn, riv., C. Wyo., to Yellowstone riv., len. 400 mi.; # 46:50 N, 107:25 W. — mt., range, N. C. Wyo., summit, Cloud Peak, el. 13,165 ft.; # 44:3 N, 107:30 W.

Bight (bīt), **Great Australian,** wide, open bay, S. Australia; # 33 S, 130 E.

Bihar (bē′hor), mt. mass, W. Romania, within Hungary basin, el. 6,105 ft.; # 46:30 N, 23 E. — city, Patna dist., Bihar and Orissa prov., India, pop. 45; # 25:11 N, 85:32 E.

Bihar and Orissa (be-här′, ō-ris′ạ), prov., N. E. India, area 83, pop. 34,002, surrounding native states, area 46, pop. 3,960, chief city, Patna, pop. 120; # 25 N, 86 E.

Bikaner (bi-ka̱-nēr′ or bē-ka̱-när′), native state in Rajputana, N. W. India, area 28, pop. 661, and its *, pop. 69; # 28:5 N, 73:15 E.

Bilbao (bil-bä′ō), spt., N. Spain, * of Vizcaya prov., pop. 120; iron ore; # 43:15 N, 2:58 W.

Billings (bil′ingz), city, S. E. C. Mont., pop. 23; # 45:43 N, 108:30 W.

Billiton (bil-li-ton′) *Du.* **Blitoeng**, isl., Dutch E. Indies, area 2, pop. 69; tin; # 2:55 S, 108 E.

Biloxi (bi-lok′si), tn., S. E. Miss., on Biloxi Bay, Gulf of Mexico, pop. 17; resort; # 30:30 N, 88:55 W.

Bingen (bing′ęn), tn., on Rhine riv., Hessen, S. W. Ger., pop. 10; tower; # 49:58 N, 7:55 E.

Bingham (bing′a̱m), tn., 16 mi. S. W. of Salt Lake City, Utah, pop. 3; copper mines, $21,000,000 in 1920; # 40:13 N, 112:10 W.

Binghamton (bing′a̱m-to̱n), city, C. S. New York, pop. 78; # 42:5 N, 75:55 W.

Binh-Dinh (bin′y′-din′y′), spt. city, S. E. Annam, Fr. Indo-China, pop. 74; # 13:54 N, 109:7 E.

Binue (bin′wē) or **Benue**, riv., Nigeria, W. Africa, chief E. trib. of Niger riv., len. ab. 800 mi.; # 8:10 N, 6:55 E.

Biobio (bē-ō-bē′ō), prov., C. Chile, area 5.4, pop. 107, * Los Angeles; # 37:30 S, 72 W. — riv., largest in Chile, Andes to Pacific near Concepción; # ab. 36:50 S, 73 W.

Birkenhead (bėr′kęn-hed), city, opp. Liverpool, W. Eng., pop. 151; # 53:23 N, 3:2 W.

Birmingham (bėr′ming-a̱m), city, S. W. C. Eng., pop. 946, with suburbs 1,260; steel; Univ. of Birmingham; # 52:30 N, 1:55 W. — city, N. C. Ala., pop. 268; steel; univ.; # 33:30 N, 86:50 W.

Bisbee (biz′bē), tn., S. C. Ariz., pop. 6; leading copper mines; # 31:30 N, 109:50 W.

Biscay (bis′ka̱), bay, part of Atlantic oc. bet. Spain and Brittany, Fr.; # 45 N, 3 W.

Biskra (bis′krä), oasis and tn., N. Sahara of Algeria, pop. 11; # 34:50 N, 5:40 E.

Bismarck (biz′märk), tn., C. N. Dak., state *, pop. 15; # 46:45 N, 100:45 W. — archipelago, group of 100 isls., E. of Papua, area 16, pop. ab. 176; Australian Mandate; # 5 S, 151 E.

Bitlis (bit-lēs′), prov., E. Turkish Asia Minor, pop. 31, and its *, pop. ab. 25; # 38:15 N, 42:10 E.

Bitolia (bē-tō′li-a̱) or **Monastir**, city, ext. S. Yugoslavia, pop. 28; # 41:2 N, 21:20 E.

Bitter Lakes (bit′ėr lāks), two lakes, Great and Little, passed through by Suez Canal, len. 25 mi.; # 30:20 N, 32:22 E.

Bitterroot (bit′ėr-rōt), mt. range bet. Idaho and Mont.; # 46 N, 114 W. — riv., paralleling the range, a trib. of Clark's Fork of Columbia riv.; apples; # 46 N, 114:20 W.

Biwa (bē′wä), largest lake in Japan, S. W. Honshu Isl.; len. 40 mi.; # 35:15 N, 136 E.

Biysk (bēsk), city, W. Siberia, pop. 18; # 52:40 N, 85:40 E.

Bizerta (bē-ser′tä), spt. city, Tunis, pop. 26; # 37:19 N, 9:50 E.

Björneborg (byėr′ne-bȯrg), see **Turku-Pori.**

Blackburn (blak′bėrn), suburb of Manchester, W. C. Eng., pop. 129; # 53:45 N, 2:32 W. — pk., S. E. Alaska, el. 16,140 ft.; # 61:45 N, 143:15 W.

Black Earth Belt, zone, S. Russia, Chernigov prov., etc., exceptionally fertile; # 50 N, 35 E.

Black Forest (*Ger.* **Schwarzwald**), mts., ext. S. W. Ger., highest 4,950 ft.; # 48:15 N, 8:15 E.

Black Hills, mts., S. W. S. Dak., and N. E. Wyo., highest Harney Pk., el. 7,242 ft.; gold; # 44 N, 104 W.

Blackpool (blak′pōl), spt. city, Lancashire, W. Eng., pop. 75; # 53:50 N, 3 W.

Black Republic, see **Haiti.**

Black Sea (blak sē), *anc.* Euxine, sea bet. S. Russia and Asia Minor, area 165, greatest depth ab. 7,200 ft.; # 44 N, 34 E.

Blackwater (blak′wȧ″tėr), riv., Cork County, S. Ireland, len. 100 mi. to Youghal Bay; # ab. 51:55 N, 7:51 W.

Blagovyeshchensk (blȧ-go-vyesh′chensk), city, on Amur riv., E. Siberia, pop. 64; # 50:25 N, 127:30 E.

Blanc, Mont (blän, mȯn), highest pk. in Alps, el. 15,781 ft., divided bet. Fr. and Italy; # 45:48 N, 6:50 E.

Blanca (blang′ka̱), pk., S. C. Colo., highest in Sangre de Cristo range, el. 14,390 ft.; # 37:30 N, 105:35 W.

Blanco (bläng′kō), cape, N. W. Africa; # 21 N, 17 W. — cape, most N. point of Africa; # 33:14 N, 8:38 W.— cape, N. W. Peru; # 4:16 S, 78:45 W. — (blang′kō), cape, most W. point of Oregon; # 42:52 N, 124:35 W.

Blenheim (blen′im) or **Blindheim** (blint′hīm), vil., Bavaria, S. W. Ger. ; battle 1704; # 48:37 N, 10:47 E.

Blida (blē-dä′), city, N. C. Algeria, pop. 36; # 36:30 N, 2:49 E.

Bloemfontein (blŏm′fon-tān), city, provincial * of Orange Free State, Union of S. Africa, pop. 39, one-half white; # 29:8 S, 26:40 E.

Blois (blwo), city, W. C. Fr., * of Loir-et-Cher dept., pop. 24; # 47:35 N, 1:25 E.

Bloomfield (blŏm′fēld), a N. suburb of Newark, New Jersey, pop. 42; # 40:48 N, 74:12 W.

Bloomington (blŏm′ing-to̱n), city, N. E. C. Ill., pop. 33; Ill. Wesleyan Univ.; # 40:31 N, 89 W. — tn., S. W. C. Ind., pop. 21; Ind. Univ.; # 39:9 N, 86:31 W.

Bluefield (blö′fēld), city, ext. S. West Va., pop. 21; # 37:15 N, 81:14 W.

Bluefields (blö′fēldz), spt. tn., E. Nicaragua; pop. 7; bananas; # 12 N, 83:55 W.

Blue Grotto (blö grot′ō), cave, Capri Isl., Bay of Naples, Italy; # 40:33 N, 14:14 E.

Blue Island (blö i′la̱nd), suburb of Chicago, Ill., pop. 17; # 41:40 N, 87:42 W.

Blue Mountains (blö moun′ta̱nz), range, N. E. Ore. and S. E. Wash.; # 45 N, 119 W. — range, E. New S. Wales, Australia; # 33:30 S, 150 E. — range, E. Jamaica, Br. W. I.; # 18 N, 77 W.

Blue Ridge, S. E. front range of Appalachian system, E. Pa. to N. Ga.; # 38 N, 79 W.

Bocholt (bȯch′olt), city, Westfalen, W. Ger., pop. 30; # 51:50 N, 6:37 E.

Bochum (bȯch′ŭm), city, Ruhr Valley, W. Prussia in Ger., pop. 156; # 51:3 N, 7:10 E.

Bodensee (bō′den-zä), see **Constance.**

Bœotia (bē-ō′shi-a̱), dist. and anc. republic, S. E. Greece, * Thebes; # 38:20 N, 23:40 E.   [# 4:40 N, 74:15 W.

Bogotá (bō-gō-tä′), city, * of Colombia, pop. 331, el. 8,600 ft.;

Bohemia (bọ-hē′mi-a̱), prov., N. W. Czechoslovakia, area 20.1, pop. 7,109, * Praha, pop. 848; # 49:55 N, 13:40 E.: absorbed into Germany in 1938 and 1939.

Bohemian (bọ-hē′mi-a̱n) **Forest** (*Ger.* Böhmerwald), mts. bet. Bavaria and Bohemia, highest ab. 4,800 ft.; # 49:25 N, 12:45 E.

Bohol (bō-hol′), isl., S. C. Philippines, area 1.5, pop. 243; # 9:55 N, 124:15 E.

Boise (boi′zā), city, S. W. C. Idaho, on Boise riv., state *, pop. 26; # 43:37 N, 116:14 W.

Bois-le-Duc (bwo-lė-dük′), *Dutch* 's Hertogenbosch, city, * of N. Brabant, S. Neth., pop. 41; # 51:42 N, 5:19 E.

Bokhara (bō-khä′rä), state, C. Asia, Russian Turkestan, area 79, pop. ab. 3,000, and its *, pop. 75; now part of Uzbek; # 39:48 N, 64:25 E.

Boksburg (boks′bėrg), city, Transvaal, Union of S. Africa, pop. 38, whites, 12; # 26:12 S, 28:13 E.

Bolama (bō-lä′mä), spt., on isl. of Bolama, * of Port. Guinea, pop. 4; # 11:34 N, 15:30 W.

Bolan (bō′län), mt. pass, N. E. Baluchistan, len. 54 mi.; # 29:45 N, 67:35 E.

Bolívar (bō-lē′vär), dept., N. Colombia, area 22, pop. 457, * Cartagena, pop. 51; # ab. 10:25 N, 75:40 W. — state, E. Venezuela, pop. 66, * Ciudad Bolívar; # 6 N, 64 W.

Bolivia (bō-liv′i-a̱), republic, in W. S. America, area 514, pop. 3,226, * LaPaz and Sucre; tin; # 18 S, 64 W.

Bologna (bō-lōn′yä), prov., Emilia, N. E. C. Italy, area 1.5, pop. 643, and its *, pop. 211; univ.; # 44:29 N, 11:20 E.

Bolson di Mapimi (bol′sȯn dē mä-pē′mē), depression, N. E. Mex., area 30; # 27 N, 103 W.

Bolton (bōl′to̱n), suburb of Manchester, W. C. Eng., pop. 182; cotton spinning; # 53:35 N, 2:25 W.

Boma (bō′mä), spt. tn., near mouth of Congo riv., until 1923, * of Belgian Congo; # 5:52 S, 13:9 E.

Bombay (bom-bā′), prov., W. C. India, area 123, pop. 19,348; surrounding native states, area 64, pop. 7,409, and its *, spt. and largest city of India, pop. 1,176; univ.; # 18:55 N, 72:5 E.

Bon (bon) or **Ras Addar** (räs ăd′där), cape, N. Africa, near Sicily; # 37:4 N, 11 E.

Bonaire (bo-när′), isl. near Venezuela, area 0.1, pop. 9, part of Dutch W. Indies; # 12:10 N, 68:15 W.

Bône (bōn) or **Bona**, spt. city, N. E. Algeria, pop. 45; # 36:58 N, 7:47 E.

Boni (bō′nē), gulf, conspicuous S. indentation, Celebes, E. Indies; # 4 S, 121 E.

Bonifacio (bō-nē-fä′chō), strait bet. Sardinia and Corsica; least width 7 mi. — spt. on S. Corsica, pop. 4; # 41:25 N, 9:15 E.

Bonn (bon), city on Rhine riv., S. W. Prussia, S. W. Ger., pop. 90; univ.; # 50:45 N, 7 E.

Boone (bōn), tn., W. C. Iowa, pop. 12; # 42:6 N, 93:50 W.

Boothia (bōō′thi-ȧ), most N. pen. of N. America; N. magnetic pole; # 70 N, 95 W.

Bootle (bōō′tl), suburb of Liverpool, W. C. Eng., pop. 82; # 53:27 N, 3:1 W.

Borås (bō-rōs′), city, S. W. Sweden, pop. 30; # 57:42 N, 12:59 E.

Bordeaux (bôr-dō), spt. city, S. W. Fr., * of Gironde dept., pop. 267; wine; univ.; # 44:50 N, 0:30 W.

Borgerhout (bor′gėr-hout), an E. suburb of Antwerp, Belgium, pop. 53; # 51:13 N, 4:26 E.

Borneo (bôr′nẹ-ō), isl., E. Indies, area 238, pop. 1,883; # 0:30 N, 114 E; Dutch part, area 207, pop. 1,625; Br. part, area 31, pop. 258; # 4 N, 115 E.

Bornholm (born′hōlm), E. isl. of Denmark, S. of Sweden, area 0.2, pop. 44; # 55:10 N, 15 E.

Bornu (bôr-nö′), div. of N. E. Nigeria, W. Africa, * Kuka; # 12 N, 13 E.

Bosnia (boz′ni-ȧ) **and Herzegovina**, prov., N. W. Yugoslavia, area 20, pop. 1,890; * Sarajevo; # 44:46 N, 16:30 E.

Bosporus (bos′pō-rus), narrow strait, bet. Black Sea and Sea of Marmora, past Constantinople, len. 19 mi.; # 41:10 N, 29:2 E.

Boston (bôs′tọn), spt. city, E. C. Mass., state *, pop. 771, with suburbs, 2,351; Boston, N. E. Univ., and Simmons College; Harvard Univ. in suburb; # 42:20 N, 71:7 W. — tn., Lincolnshire, E. C. Eng., pop. 17; # 53 N, 0:1 W. — low mts., N. Ark.; # 35:50 N, 93 W.

Botany Bay (bot′ȧ-ni bā), bay near Sydney, S. E. Australia, former penal colony; # 33:58 S, 151:12 E.

Bothnia (both′ni-ȧ), gulf, N. part of Baltic Sea, bet. Sweden and Finland, len. 400 mi.; # 63 N, 20 E.

Botoşani (bō-tō-shä′nē), city, N. Moldavia, N. C. Romania, pop. 33; # ab. 47:45 N, 26:35 E.

Bottrop (bot′rop), a N. W. suburb of Essen, W. Ger., pop. 77; # 51:31 N, 6:54 E.

Bouches-du-Rhône (bōsh-dü-rōn), dept., S. coast of Fr., area 2, pop. 842, * Marseille, pop. 586; # 43:30 N, 5 E.

Bougainville (bö-gań-vēl′), isl., Solomon Isls., S. Pacific oc., area 3.5, pop. 42; Australian mandate; # 6 S, 155 E.

Boulder (bōl′dėr), tn., N. E. C. Colo., pop. 13; State Univ.; # 40:5 N, 105:20 W.

Boulogne-sur-Mer (bö-lon-y′-sür-mär), spt. 20 mi. S. W. of Calais, N. Fr., pop. 55; # 50:45 N, 1:40 E.

Boulogne-sur-Seine (bö-lon-y′-sür-sān), a S. W. suburb of Paris, Fr., pop. 68; # 48:50 N, 2:14 E.

Boundary Peak (boun′dȧ-ri pēk), mt., W. Nev., state's highest pk., el. 13,145 ft.; # ab. 39:20 N, 119:58 W.

Bourges (börzh), city, C. Fr., * of Cher dept., pop. 46; # 47:5 N, 2:30 E.

Bourgogne (bör-gon-y′), see **Burgundy.**

Bournemouth (bōrn′muth), spt. and resort city, S. C. Eng., pop. 82; # 50:45 N, 1:55 W.

Bow (bō), riv., Canadian Rockies W. of Banff to S. Saskatchewan riv., len. 300 mi.; # 49:55 N, 111:45 W.

Bowling Green (bō′ling grēn), tn., S. W. C. Kentucky, pop. 15; college; # 37 N, 86:20 W.

Boyacá (bō-yä-kä′), dept., N. C. Colombia, area 16, pop. 657, * Tunja, pop. 10; # 5:40 N, 73:40 W. — tn. therein, pop. 7.

Boyne (boin), riv., N. E. Ireland, len. 70 mi.; battle, 1690; # 53:45 N, 6:22 W.

Brabant (brȧ-bänt′; Fr. brȧ-bän), prov., C. Belgium, area 1.3, pop. 1,573, * Brussels, pop. 787; # 50:45 N, 4:30 E.

Brabant, North, prov. of S. Neth., area 1.9, pop. 780, * 's Hertogenbosch, pop. 41; # 51:30 N, 5:15 E.

Brach (bräch) or **Brazza**, isl., C. Dalmatia, Y.-S., len., 30 mi.; pop. 25; # 43:18 N, 16:40 E.

Braddock (brad′ok), suburb of Pittsburgh, Pa., pop. 18; Braddock's defeat, 1765; # 40:24 N, 79:53 W.

Bradford (brad′fọrd), city near Leeds, N. C. Eng., pop. 291; # 53:47 N, 1:45 W. — tn., N. W. C. Pa., pop. 18; # 41:59 N, 78:44 W.

Braga (brä′gä), city, N. W. Portugal, * of Entre-Douro-e-Minho prov., pop. 25; cathedral; # 41:35 N, 8:26 W.

Brahmaputra (brä-mȧ-pö′trȧ), riv., Tibet to Bay of Bengal, len. ab. 1,700 mi.; # 23:50 N, 89:45 E.

Braïla (brä-ē′lä), city on Danube riv., S. E. C. Romania, pop. 66; # 45:20 N, 27:50 E.

Brainerd (brā′nėrd), tn., N. C. Minn., pop. 12; # ab. 46:26 N, 94:21 W.

Branco (bräng′kō), riv., N. Brazil to Rio Negro, len. ab. 500 mi.; # 1:30 S, 61:50 W.

Brandenburg (brän′den-bůrch), prov., Prussia, N. C. Ger., area 15, pop. 2,611, and its *, pop. 59; # 52:25 N, 12:35 E.

Brandon (bran′dọn), pk., ext. S. W. Ireland, el. 3,127 ft.; # 52:15 N, 10:15 W. — city, S. W. Manitoba, pop. 15; # 49:5 N, 99:5 W.

Brantford (brant′fọrd), city, S. Ontario, on Grand riv., pop. 29; # 43:1 N, 80:15 W.

Brasov (brä′shōf) or **Brasso**, city, Transylvanian Alps, C. Romania, pop. 41; # 45:38 N, 25:34 E.

Bratislava (brä-ti-slä′vȧ), Ger. **Pressburg**, city on Danube riv., S. W. Slovakia, S. E. Czechoslovakia, pop. 93; univ.; # 48:12 N, 17:8 E.

Braunschweig (broun′shvīch), Eng. **Brunswick**, free state, C. Ger., area 1.4, pop. 508, and its *, pop. 145; univ.; # 52:18 N, 10:32 E.

Brazil (brȧ-zil′), the largest and most populous S. American republic, area 3,285, pop. 43,247, * Rio de Janeiro, pop. 1,711; coffee; # 12 S, 52 W. — tn., S. W. C. Ind., pop. 8; brick and tile; # 39:30 N, 87:6 W.

Brazilian Current (brȧ-zil′iȧn), warm oc. current, W. S. Atlantic oc., counterpart of Gulf Stream; # 25 S, 40 W.

Brazilian Highland (brȧ-zil′iȧn), plateau, S. E. Brazil, mostly 2,000 to 4,000 ft., chief region of coffee culture; much iron in N.; # 22 S, 45 W.

Brazos (brä′zos), riv., N. Texas to Gulf of Mexico, len. 850 mi.; # 28:55 N, 95:25 W.

Brazza (brät′sä), see **Brach.**

Brazzaville (brä-zà-vēl), city on Congo riv. opp. Leopoldville, * of Fr. Equatorial Africa, pop. ab. 5; # 4:15 S, 15:20 E.

Brecknock (brek′nok), or **Brecknockshire**, county, S. E. Wales, area 0.7, pop. 61, * Brecon, pop. 6; # 52 N, 3:25 W.

Breda (brä-dä′), city, N. Brabant, S. C. Neth., pop. 30; # 51:39 N, 4:51 E.

Bremen (brem′ẹn), free city, N. Ger., on Weser riv., area 0.1, pop. 290, with associated ter., pop. 331; # 53:5 N, 8:50 E.

Bremerhaven (brem′ėr-hä″vn), outer port of Bremen, Ger., at mouth of Weser riv., pop. 23; # 53:36 N, 8:35 E.

Brenner (bren′ėr), pass, Italian-Austrian frontier, el. 4,470 ft.; R. R., Munich to Venice; # 47 N, 11:30 E.

Brentford (brent′fọrd), city, suburb of London, Eng., pop. 17, * of Middlesex Co.; # 51:29 N, 0:19 W.

Brescia (brä′shä), anc. Brixia, prov., Lombardy, N. W. Italy, area 1.8, pop. 652, and its *, pop. 100; # 45:30 N, 10:15 E.

Breslau (bres′lou), city on Oder riv., Silesia, S. E. Ger., pop. 553; univ.; # 51:6 N, 17:2 E.

Brest (brest), spt. city, Brittany, N. W. Fr., pop. 74; # 48:25 N, 4:30 W.

Brest Litovsk (brest lē-tofsk′), city, Grodno prov., E. Poland, pop. 40; # 51:55 N, 23:35 E.

Bretagne (brė-tän-y′), see **Brittany.**

Bridal Veil (brīd′ȧl vāl), cataract, height 620 ft., Yosemite Valley, Calif.; # 37:45 N, 119:30 W.

Bridgeport (brij′pōrt), city, S. W. Conn., on Long Island Sound, pop. 147; # 41:13 N, 73:12 W.

Bridgeton (brij′tọn), tn., S. W. New Jersey, pop. 16; # 39:27 N, 75:15 W.

Bridgetown (brij′toun), spt., * of Barbados, Br. W. Indies, pop. 13; # 13:7 N, 59:38 W.

Brieg (brēch), city on Oder riv., Silesia, S. E. Ger., pop. 28; # 50:52 N, 17:27 E.

Brighton (brī′tọn), spt. city, Sussex, S. Eng., pop. 137;

#50:50 N, 0.9 W. — suburb of Melbourne, Australia, pop. 21; #37:54 S, 145 E.

Brindisi (brēn'dẹ-sē), *anc.* Brundisium, spt. city, Apulia, S. E. Italy, pop. comm. 28; #40:35 N, 17:50 E.

Brisbane (briz'bān), spt. city, * of Queensland, E. C. Australia, pop. 78, pop. within 10 mi. radius, 236; Univ. of Queensland; #27:30 S, 153 E.

Bristol (bris'tọl), city on Avon riv., Gloucester, S. W. Eng., pop. 385; Univ. of Bristol; #51:27 N, 2:36 W. — city, W. C. Conn., pop. 30; #41:44 N, 72:37 W. — city, ext. N. E. Tenn. and adjacent Va., pop. 14; college; #36:33 N, 82:11 W. — tn., S. E. Pa., pop. 12; #40:5 N, 74:55 W.

Bristol Bay (bris'tọl bā), S. E. Bering Sea, S. W. Alaska; #58 N, 159 W.

Bristol Channel (bris'tọl chan'ẹl), arm of Atlantic oc. bet. Wales and S. W. Eng., including estuary of Severn riv.; #51:20 N, 3:30 W.

Britain (brit'ạn), see **Great Britain**.

British America (brit'ish), Canada and Newfoundland, sometimes also Br. Middle America.

British Columbia, prov., S. W. Canada, area 356, pop. 694, * Victoria, pop. 39; #55 N, 125 W.

British Empire, United Kingdom, India, several dominions (Canada, Australia, S. Africa, New Zealand), and numerous colonies, area 13,356, pop. 449,583, * London, Eng.

British Guiana (brit'ish gē-än'ạ), see **Guiana, British**.

British Isles (brit'ish īlz), group isls., Great Britain, Ireland, Isle of Man and others, area 122, pop. 47,500; #54 N, 2 W.

Brittany (brit'ạ-ni), *Fr.* **Bretagne,** pen., N. W. Fr., anc. prov.; #48 N, 3 W.

Brno (bėr'nō), or **Brünn**, city, C. Czechoslovakia, * of Moravia, pop. 222; univ.; #49:12 N, 16:38 E.

Broach (brōch), riv. port, city, N. Bombay prov., W. C. India, pop. 43; #21:41 N, 73:1 E.

Brocken (brok'ẹn), summit of Harz mts., W. C. Ger., el. 3,745 ft.; #51:50 N, 10:40 E.

Brockton (brok'tọn), city, S. E. Mass., pop. 62; shoes; #42:4 N, 71:1 W.

Brody (brō'di), city, S. E. Poland, pop. 17; castle; Jewish center; #50:8 N, 25:9 E.

Broken Hill, city, W. New S. Wales, Australia, pop. 23; gold, lead and zinc; one of world's greatest mining districts; #32 S, 141:35 E.

Bromberg (brom'berch), see **Bydgoszcz**.

Bronx (brongks), county, S. E. New York, area .041, pop. 1,395, a N. borough of New York City; #40:52 N, 73:52 W.

Brookings (brŭk'ingz), tn., E. C. S. Dak., pop. 5; State Agri. College; #44:20 N, 96:47 W.

Brookline (brŭk'līn), suburb of Boston, pop. 50; #42:21 N, 71:7 W.

Brooklyn (brŭk'lin), a borough on W. Long Island, part of New York City, pop. 2,698; #40:40 N, 73:58 W.

Brooks Range (brŭks rānj), mt. range, N. Alaska and N. W. Canada; #68 N, 145 W.

Broussa (brō'sä), see **Brusa**.

Brownsville (brounz'vil), tn. near mouth of Rio Grande riv., S. Texas, pop. 22; #26:10 N, 97:25 W.

Brownwood (broun'wŭd), tn., C. Texas, pop. 13; Howard Payne Univ.; #31:41 N, 99:2 W.

Bruchsal (brŭch'zäl), city, N. Baden, S. W. Ger., pop. 16; #49:7 N, 8:36 E.

Bruges or **Brugge** (brō'jez; *Fr.* brüzh), city, N. W. Belgium, * of W. Flanders, pop. 53; #51:13 N, 3:15 E.

Brunei (brō-nī'), Br. protectorate, N. W. Borneo, area 4, pop. 24, and its spt. and *, pop. 10; #4:3 N, 115 E.

Brünn (brün), see **Brno**.

Brunswick (brunz'wik), a N. suburb of Melbourne, Australia, pop. 44; #37:43 S, 145 E. — tn., S. W. Me., pop. 7; Bowdoin College; #43:57 N, 70 W. — spt. city, S. E. Ga., pop. 15; #31:15 N, 81:25 W. — see **Braunschweig**.

Brusa or **Broussa** (brō'sä), prov., Asiatic Turkey, N. W. Asia Minor, pop. 251, and its *, 50 mi. S. of Constantinople, pop. 65; #40:10 N, 29:3 E.

Brussels (brus'ẹlz), city, C. Belgium, its *, pop. 787 (with suburbs); Univ. of Brussels; #50:50 N, 4:20 E.

Bryce Canyon (brīs kan'yun), national monument, Pink Cliff, S. W. Utah, fantastic erosion and gorgeous coloring; ab. 37:30 N, 111:40 W.

Bryn Mawr (brin mär), suburb of Philadelphia, pop. 3; Bryn Mawr College; #40:3 N, 75:17 W.

Brzesc Litewski (bzheshch lē-tef'skẹ), see **Brest Litovsk**.

Bucaramanga (bō-kä-rä-män'gä), city, N. C. Colombia, pop. 25; #7 N, 73:25 W.

Bucharest (bō-kạ-rest'), see **Bucuresci**.

Buckingham (buk'ing-ạm), county, S. C. Eng., area 0.7, pop. 236, and its *, pop. 5; #52 N, 0:59 W.

Bucuresci (bù-cù-resh'ti), *Eng.* **Bucharest**, city, S. C. Romania, its *, pop. 345; univ.; #44:25 N, 26:10 E.

Bucyrus (bū-sī'rus), tn., N. C. Ohio, pop. 10; #40:52 N, 82:58 W.

Budapest (bō'dạ-pest), city, on Danube riv., * of Hungary, pop. 929; univ.; #47:30 N, 19:5 E.

Budejovice (bù'dyä-yō-vē-tse), **Budejovitsa** or **Budweis**, city, S. Bohemia, pop. 44; with suburbs, 58; beer; #48:59 N, 14:28 E.

Budweis (bŏd'vīs), see **Budejovice**.

Buĕa (bō-ā'ä), spt. tn., former * of German Kamerun, W. Africa; #4:9 N, 9:6 E.

Buena Vista (bwā'nä vēs'tä), battlefield, 1847, Coahuila, Mex; #25:22 N, 101 W.

Buenos Aires (bwā'nōs ī'räs), largest city of S. hemisphere, E. Argentina, spt. and *, pop. 2,318; univ.; #34:40 S, 58:30 W. — the chief prov. of Argentina, area 118, pop. 2,337, * La Plata, pop. 160; #35 S, 60 W.

Buer (bōr), a N. E. suburb of Essen, Ruhr Valley, W. Ger., pop. 98; #51:34 N, 7:3 E.

Buffalo (buf'ạ-lō), city at E. end of Lake Erie, W. New York, pop. 576; Univ. of Buffalo; Canisius College; #42:55 N, 78:51 W.

Bug (bōg), riv., S. E. Poland to Vistula riv. near Warsaw, len. 450 mi.; #ab. 52:20 N, 20:30 E. — riv., C. Russia to estuary of Dnieper, len. 470 mi.; #47 N, 31:55 E.

Buitenzorg (boi'tẹn-zorch), residential city in mts., 36 mi. S. of Batavia, Java, pop. 47; famous botanical garden; #6:45 S, 106:45 E.

Bukhara (bō-kä'rä), see **Bokhara**.

Bukken or **Bukn** (bùk'kẹn), fjord, S. W. Norway, Stavenger; #59:10 N, 5:35 E.

Bukovina (bō-kō-vē'nä), prov., N. C. Romania, area 4, pop. 812, * Czernowitz; #48 N, 25:30 E.

Bulgaria (bul-gä'ri-ạ), kingdom, S. E. Europe, area 39.8, pop. 5,008, * Sofia, pop. 154; #42:30 N, 25:30 E.

Bundi (bồn'dê), native state, Rajputana, N. W. India, area 2, pop. 187, and its *, pop. 16; #25:27 N, 75:41 E.

Bungo (bùng'gō), strait bet. Kyushiu and Shikoku isls., Japan; #33 N, 132:15 E.

Bunker Hill (bung'kẹr hil), hill in Boston, Mass.; fight 1775.

Burg (bùrch), a N. E. suburb of Magdeburg, Prussia, pop. 24; #52:16 N, 11:52 E.

Burgas (bör-gäs'), spt. on Gulf of Burgas, W. Black Sea, C. E. Bulgaria, pop. 22; #42:30 N, 27:30 E.

Burgenland (bör'gẹn-länt), prov., E. Austria, area 1.5, pop. 286; #47:30 N, 16:30 E.

Burgos (bör'gōs), prov., N. C. Spain, area 5.5, pop. 330, and its *, pop. 32; #42:15 N, 3:40 W.

Burgundy (bėr'gun-di), *Fr.* **Bourgogne**, region, C. Fr., former kingdom; #47 N, 4:30 E. — **Gate**, or **Belfort Pass**, important pass bet. Rhine and Rhône valleys, E. Fr.; #47:38 N, 6:52 E.

Burlington (bėr'ling-tọn), city, N. W. Vermont, on Lake Champlain, pop. 28; State Univ.; #44:30 N, 73:15 W. — city, S. E. Iowa, on Miss. riv., pop. 26; #40:50 N, 91:15 W.

Burma (bėr'mä), Br. dependency, S. E. Asia, E. of India, area 262, pop. 14,667; * Rangoon; #22 N, 96 E.

Burma Road, highway, Burma to Chungking, China.

Burnley (bėrn'li), a N. suburb of Manchester, W. C. Eng.

Burton-on-Trent (bėr'tọn-on-trent), city, Stafford, C. Eng., pop. 50; #52:48 N, 1:37 W.

Buru (bō'rō), isl., Moluccas, E. Indies, area 3, pop. 20; #3:30 S, 126:45 E. — cape, ext. S. Asia; Malay Pen.; #1:16 N, 103:31 E.

Bury (ber'i), a N. suburb of Manchester, W. C. Eng., pop. 57; #53:36 N, 2:18 W. — tn., * of W. Suffolk, S. E. Eng., pop. 17; #ab. 52:15 N, 0:44 E.

Bushire (bō-shēr'), spt., S. C. Persia, pop. ab. 25; #28:55 N, 50:45 E.

Busra (bus'rä), see **Basra.**

Bussum (bus'um) or **Bassum,** city, 12 mi. S. E. of Amsterdam, Neth., pop. 21; # 52:17 N, 5:13 E.

Bute (būt), county of isls., S. W. Scotland, area 0.2, pop. 18, * Rothesay, pop. 15; # 55:30 N, 5:30 W.

Butler (but'lẽr), city, W. C. Pa., pop. 24; # 40:52 N, 79:56 W.

Butte (būt), city, S. W. C. Mont., pop. 37; copper mines; State School of Mines; # 46:5 N, 112:30 W.

Buzeu (bö-zyö'), or **Buzău,** dept., S. E. C. Romania, area 2, pop. 278 and its *, pop. 29; # 45:9 N, 26:51 E.

Buzzards Bay (buz'ärdz bä), inlet of Atlantic oc., S. E. Mass., 30 mi. long; # 41:40 N, 70:45 W.

Bydgoszcz (bid'goshch), *Ger.* **Bromberg,** city, N. W. Poland, pop. 88; # 53:9 N, 18 E.

Byelaya (bye'lȧ-yȧ), riv., E. Russia., Ural Mts. to Kama riv., len. 800 mi.; # 56 N, 53 E. — city, N. W. Russia, near Estonia, pop. 60; # 58:15 N, 29:8 E.

Byzantium (bi-zan'ṭium), anc. city on site of modern Constantinople.

C

Cabot (kab'ọt), strait bet. Newfoundland and Cape Breton Isl., N. S.; # 47:30 N, 60 W.

Cáceres (kä'thä-räs), prov., W. C. Spain, area 7.7, pop. 409, and its *, pop. 20; # 39:27 N, 6:24 W.

Cadillac (ka'di-lak), tn., C. Mich., pop. 10; # 44:15 N, 85:25 W.

Cádiz (kā'diz; *Sp.* kä'ᴛнēth), *anc.* Gades, spt., S. W. Spain, pop. 82; # 36:29 N, 6:18 W.

Cádiz and Ceuta, prov., ext. S. Spain and N. W. Africa (Ceuta), area 2.8, pop. 583, * Cádiz, pop. 82.

Caen (käṅ), city, Calvados dept., N. coast of Fr., pop. 54; univ.; abbeys; # 49:12 N, 0:18 W.

Caerleon (kär-lē'on), tn. on Ush riv., Monmouthshire, S. W. Eng., pop. 2; King Arthur's Court; # 51:37 N, 2:57 W.

Caerphilly (kär-fil'i), city, 10 mi. N. of Cardiff, S. E. Wales, pop. 37; # 51:34 N, 3:13 W.

Caesarea (sez-ȧ-rē'ȧ), see **Kaisarieh.**

Cagayan (kä-gä-yän'), riv., C. to N. Luzón, Philippines, len. 220 mi.; # 18:15 N, 121:35 E.

Cagliari (käl-yä'rē), prov., S. Sardinia, area 5, pop. 530, and its *, a spt., pop. 62; univ.; # 39:13 N, 9:7 E.

Cahors (kȧ-ôr'), tn., * of dept. of Lot, S. C. Fr., pop. 12; # 44:28 N, 1:30 E.

Cairo (kī'rō), city, * of Egypt, on Nile riv., at base of delta, pop. 791; # 30:2 N, 31:13 E. — city, ext. S. Ill., pop. 14; # 36:59 N, 89:8 W.

Caithness (kāth'nes), county, ext. N. E. Scotland, area 0.7, pop. 26, * Wick; # 58:30 N, 3:30 W.

Cajamarca (kä-ᴴä-mär'kä), dept., N. W. Peru, area 13, pop. 442, and its *, pop. 12; # 7:5 S, 78:28 W.

Cajon (kä-hōn'), pass bet. Valley of Calif. and Mohave desert, S. Calif.; # 34:20 N, 117:30 W.

Calabar (kal-ȧ-bär'), city, S. E. Nigeria, on Calabar riv., pop. ab. 50; # 5 N, 8:20 E.

Calabria (ka-lā'bri-ȧ), *anc.* Bruttium, dept., S. Italy ("toe"), area 5.8, pop. 1,512; # 39 N, 16:30 E.

Calais (kal'ā; kal'is), spt. on Strait of Dover, ext. N. Fr., pop. 73; # 50:58 N, 1:50 E.

Calamata (kä-lä-mät'tä), city, * of Messina, ext. S. Greece, pop. 21; # ab. 37 N, 22:10 E.

Calcutta (kal-kut'ȧ), port, Ganges delta, N. E. India, * of Bengal, pop. with suburbs, 1,328; former * of Br. India; univ.; # 22:30 N, 88:30 E.

Calgary (kal'ga-ri), city, S. Alberta, pop. 83; Provincial Univ.; # 51:5 N, 114:5 W.

Cali (kä'lē), city, S. W. Colombia, pop. 64, * of dept. of Valle; # 3:40 N, 76:45 W.

Calicut (kal'i-kut), spt. city, Malabar coast, S. W. India, pop. 82; # 11:15 N, 75:45 E.

California (kal-i-fôr'ni-ȧ), state, S. W. U.S.A. bet. Nev. and the Pacific oc., area 158, pop. 6,907, * Sacramento, pop. 106; largest cities, San Francisco, pop. 635, Los Angeles, pop. est. 1,504; # 36 N, 120 W. — **Gulf of,** arm of Pacific oc., E. of Lower Calif., len. 750 mi.; # 27 N, 111 W.

California, Lower, S. W. pen. of N. America, len. 750 mi., a ter. of Mex., area 58, pop. 63; # 27 N, 113 W.

Callao (käl-lä'ō or käl-yä'ō), city, chief spt. of Peru, near Lima, pop. 75; # 12:10 S, 77 W.

Caltanissetta (käl-tä-nē-set'tä), prov., C. Sicily, area 1.3, pop. 386, and its *, pop. 60; # 37:26 N, 14:7 E.

Calvados (kȧl-vȧ-dōs), dept., N. coast of Fr., area 2.2, pop. 385, * Caen, pop. 54; # 49:12 N, 0:18 W.

Camagüey (kä-mä-gwä'), prov., E. C. Cuba, area 10, pop. 237, and its *, pop. 92; # 21:25 N, 78 W.

Cambay (kam-bā'), gulf, W. India, N. of Bombay; # 21 N, 72:30 E. — spt. city thereon, pop. 27; # 22:19 N, 72:38 E.

Camberwell (kam'bẽr-wel), borough of London, Eng., pop. 267; # 51:28 N, 0:4 W. — an E. suburb of Melbourne, Australia, pop. 24; # 37:49 S, 145:4 E.

Cambodia (kam-bō'di-ä), Fr. protectorate, S. W. Indo-China, area 68, pop. 2,450, * Phnom-Penh, pop. 72; # 12 N, 105 E. — point, ext. S. pt. of Indo-China; # 8:45 N, 104:35 E.

Cambrai (kam-brä'; *Fr.* käṅ-brä), city, Nord dept., N. E. Fr., pop. 26; battles 1917, 1918; # 50:12 N, 3:10 E.

Cambrian (kam'bri-ạn), low mt. range of W. Wales; # 52:30 N, 3:40 W.

Cambridge (kām'brij), county, S. E. C. Eng., area 0.5, pop. 130, and its *, pop. 59; Cambridge Univ.; # 52:12 N, 0:10 E. — suburb of Boston, Mass., pop. 111; Harvard Univ.; Mass. Institute of Technology; Radcliffe College; # 42:22 N, 71:7 W. — tn., S. E. C. Ohio, pop. 15; # 40:3 N, 81:35 W. — gulf, N. W. Australia; # 14:45 S, 128:20 E.

Camden (kam'dẹn), city, S. W. New Jersey, on Delaware riv., pop. 118, an E. suburb of Philadelphia, Pa.; # 39:57 N, 75:7 W.

Cameroon (kam-ẹ-rōn'), that part of the former Ger. Kamerun, now under Fr., the Br. portion having been absorbed in Nigeria, area 166, pop. 1,500, * Yaoundé; # 4 N, 12 E.

Campagna (käm-pän'yä), low, malarial plain, N. W. of Rome, Italy; 41:50 N, 12:25 E.

Campania (kam-pā'ni-ạ), dept., S. W. Italy, area 6.3, pop. 3,547, * Naples, pop. 772; # 41 N, 14:30 E.

Campeche (käm-pā'chä), gulf, S. W. part of Gulf of Mexico; # 19 N, 94 W. — state, pen. of Yucatan, S. E. Mex., area 18, pop. 70, and its *, a spt., pop. 17; # 19 N, 90 W.

Campine (käṅ-pēn), coal field, Limburg to Antwerp, E. Belgium; # 51:10 N, 5 E.

Campobasso (käm-pō-bäs'sō), prov., Abruzzi, E. C. Italy, area 1.7, pop. 341, and its *, pop. 16; # 41:32 N, 14:40 E.

Canada (kan'ȧ-dä), Br. dominion, N. N. America, area 3,730, pop. 10,377, * Ottawa, pop. 127; largest city, Montreal, pop. 819; # ab. 56 N, 95 W.

Canada, Lower, former name of Quebec.

Canadian (kạ-nā'di-ạn), riv., N. E. New Mex., across Okla., to Arkansas riv., len. 900 mi.; # 35:45 N, 95:5 W.

Canadian National, R. R., Halifax to Vancouver and Prince Rupert, highest point, 3,700 ft.; mileage, 26,060.

Canadian Pacific System, transcontinental R. R. lines, S. Canada, highest point, 5,344 ft., completed 1885, total mileage 19,101; and trans-Atlantic and trans-Pacific steamship lines.

Canal Zone (kạ-nal' zōn), strip 10 mi. wide across Isthmus of Panama, including canal, area 0.5, pop. 52; part of U.S.A.; # 9:10 N, 79:45 W.

Canary Islands (kạ-nā'ri), group of isls. near N. W. coast of Africa, a province of Spain, area 3, pop. 482, * Santa Cruz, pop. 78; # 29 N, 16 W.

Canberra (kan'bẽr-ȧ), tn., Federal Ter., S. E. New S. Wales, capital of Australia since 1927, pop. 5; # 35:20 S, 149:10 E.

Candia or **Kandia** (kan'di-ä), spt. city, Greek isl. of Crete, pop. 25; # 35:21 N, 25:7 E. — isl., see **Crete.**

Canea or **Kanea** (ka-nē'ȧ), spt. city, * of Crete, pop. 25; # 35:30 N, 24:1 E.

Canelones (kä-nä-lō'näs), dept., S. Uruguay, area 1.8, pop. 127, and its *, pop. 10; # 34:32 S, 56:8 W.

Cannes (kȧn), coastal resort, S. E. Fr., pop. 31; # 43:32 N, 7 E.

Canonsburg (kan'ọnz-bẽrg), suburb of Pittsburgh, Pa., pop. 13; # 40:16 N, 80:15 W.

Canso (kan'sō), cape, N. E. Nova Scotia; # 45:18 N, 61 W.

Cantabrian (kan-tā'bri-ạn), mt. range, N. Spain, extending the Pyrenees mts.; # 43 N, 6 E.

Cantal (käṅ-tȧl), dept., C. Fr., area 2.2, pop. 199, * Aurillac; # 45 N, 2:30 E.

Canterbury (kan'tẽr-ber-i), city, Kent, S. E. Eng., pop. 23;

51:18 N, 1:2 E. — city, suburb of Sydney, Australia, pop. 38; # 33:55 S, 151:7 E. — prov., E. S. Island, New Zealand, area 14, pop. 199; # 43:45 S, 172 E.

Canton (kan-ton'), city, on Kiang riv., S. China, * of Kwangtung prov., pop. est. 1,360, * of revolutionary S. China; # 23:7 N, 113:15 E. — (kan'ton), city, N. E. C. Ohio, pop. 108; # 40:48 N, 81:25 W. — tn., C. Ill., pop. 12; # 40:34 N, 90:2 W. — tn., N. New York, pop. 3; St. Lawrence Univ.; # 44:43 N, 75:9 W.

Cantyre (kan-tīr') or **Kintyre,** pen., W. Scotland, len. 40 mi., to within 20 mi. of N. Ireland; # 55:30 N, 5:35 W.

Cape Ann, see **Ann, Cape.**

Cape Breton Island (brit'on), N. E. part of Nova Scotia; # 46:30 N, 61 W.

Cape Coast Castle (kāp kōst kás'l), spt. city, Gold Coast, W. Africa, pop. 15; # 5:6 N, 1:15 W.

Cape Cod Canal, ship canal across base of Cape Cod, Mass., opened 1914, len. 8 mi., depth 25 ft.; see **Cod, Cape.**

Cape Colony. See **Cape of Good Hope.**

Cape Girardeau (kāp jē-rär-dō'), tn., S. E. Mo., on Mississippi riv., pop. 19; # 37:20 N, 89:40 W.

Cape Haitien (kāp hā'ti-en), Fr. **Cap-Haïtien,** spt. city, Haiti, pop. 20; # 19:50 N, 72:20 W.

Cape of Good Hope, cape, S. Africa; — prov. of Union of S. Africa, comprising colony proper, area 209, pop. 1,694, and six other areas totaling 68, and pop. of 1,100, * Cape Town, pop. 207; # 33 S, 24 E.

Cape Town (kāp toun), spt. city near S. tip of Africa, * of Cape of Good Hope, pop. 207 (113 white); Univ. of Cape Town; # 33:55 S, 18:25 E.

Cape Verde (kāp vėrd), most W. cape of Africa, also Portuguese isls., 300 mi. W. of cape, area 1.5, pop. 150, * Praia, pop. 21; # 14:50 N, 24:30 W.

Cape York Peninsula, part of N. E. Australia bet. Gulf of Carpentaria and Pacific oc.; # 14 S, 143 E.

Capri (kä'prē), anc. Capreæ, tiny isl., Bay of Naples, Italy, pop. 5; Blue Grotto; # 40:33 N, 14:14 E.

Capua (kap'ū-ä), tn., Campania, S. Italy, pop. comm. 13; # 41:7 N, 14:11 E.

Capulin (kȧ-pū'lin), national monument, near Des Moines, N. E. New Mex., a recently active volcano; # 36:48 N, 103:50 W.

Caracas (kä-rä'käs), chief city, * of Venezuela, pop. 203; # 10:30 N, 66:55 W; its port is La Guaira.

Carbondale (kär'bon-dāl), city, N. E. Pa., pop. 19; # 41:33 N, 75:31 W.

Carcassonne (kȧr-kȧ-son'), anc. Carcaso, city, ext. S. Fr., * of Aude dept., pop. 29; castle; # 43:12 N, 2:25 E.

Cárdenas (kär'dā-näs), spt. city, N. W. Cuba, pop. 34; # 23:5 N, 81:15 W.

Cardiff (kär'dif), spt., ext. S. E. Wales, * of Glamorganshire, pop. 226; coal; # 51:30 N, 3:12 W.

Cardigan (kär'di-gan), county on Cardigan Bay, W. C. Wales, area 0.7, pop. 61, and its *, pop. 4; # 52:6 N, 4:36 W.

Caribbean (kar-i-bē'an), sea bet. C. America, the W. Indies and S. America, area 1,770, greatest known depth 20,568 ft.; # 15 N, 73 W.

Caribbees (kar'i-bēz), see **West Indies.**

Carinthia (kȧ-rin'thi-ä), prov., S. Austria, area 3.7, pop. 371, * Klagenfurt, pop. 27; # 46:45 N, 12:40 E.

Carlisle (kär-līl'), city, Cumberland Co., N. W. Eng., pop. 55; # 54:54 N, 3 W. — tn., C. Pa., pop. 14; Gov. Indian and Dickinson colleges; # 40:12 N, 77:10 W.

Carlow (kär'lō), county, Leinster, S. E. Ireland, area 0.3, pop. 36, and its *, pop. 7; # 52:51 N, 6:56 W.

Carlsbad (kärls'bäd), or **Karlovy Vary,** tn., N. W. Bohemia, pop. 17; famous watering place; # 50:15 N, 12:55 E.

Carlsbad Cave (kärls'bad kāv), enormous limestone cavern, near Carlsbad, S. E. New Mex., a U. S. national monument # 32.27 N, 104:12 W.

Carmania (kär-mā'ni-ä), anc. prov. of Persia, see **Kerman.**

Carmarthen (kär-mär'ᴛнen), county on Carmarthen Bay, S. Wales, area 0.9, pop. 175, and its *, pop. 10; # 51:51 N, 4:20 W.

Carmel (kär'mel), mt., N. W. Palestine, el. 1,742 ft.; 32:48 N, 35 E.

Carnac (kȧr-nȧk'), tn., Brittany, N. W. Fr., pop. 3; huge prehistoric stone ruins; # 47:36 N, 3:5 W.

Carnarvon (kär-när'von), county, N. W. Wales on Carnarvon Bay, area 0.6, pop. 131, and its *, pop. 8; # 53:9 N, 4:17 W.

Carnegie (kär-nā'gi or -neg'i), a manufacturing suburb of Pittsburgh, Pa., pop. 13; # 40:24 N, 80:5 W.

Carnic Alps (kär'nik alps), range, N. boundary of Venezia, Italy; # 46:40 N, 12:45 E.

Carniola (kär-ni-ō'lä), former crownland of Austria, now part of **Slovenia,** prov., N. W. Yugoslavia; # 46 N, 14:30 E; see **Slovenia.**

Carnsore (kärn'sôr), cape, ext. S. E. Ireland; # 52:10 N, 6:22 W.

Carolina (kar-ō-lī'nä), see **North Carolina** and **South Carolina.**

Caroline (kar'ō-līn), group of 500 small isls. E. of Philippines, area 1, pop. 36; Japanese Mandate, * Yap and Ponape; # 3 to 6 N, 137 to 163 E.

Carpathian (kär-pā'thi-an), mt. range, S. E. C. Europe, len. 800 mi.; summit, High Tatra, Cz.–S., highest 8,737 ft., and Kuhorn, N. W. Romania, el. 7,506 ft.; # 47 N, 24 E.

Carpentaria (kär-pen-tä'ri-ä), great gulf, N. Australia, len. 350 mi.; # 14 S, 140 E.

Carrara (kär-rä'rä), city, Tuscany, Italy, pop. 49; statuary marble; # 44:10 N, 10:5 E.

Carrick (kar'ik), a S. suburb of Pittsburgh, S. W. Pa., pop. 13; # 40:24 N, 79:59 W.

Carrickfergus (kar-ik-fėr'gus), spt., 9 mi. N. E. of Belfast, N. Ireland, pop. 10; # 54:43 N, 5:49 W.

Carso (kär'sō), region of rugged topography, ext. N. E. Italy; # 45:40 N, 14 E.

Carson City (kär'son), tn., S. W. Nev., state *, pop. 2; # 39:9 N, 119:45 W.

Carstensz (kar'stens), pk., Snow Mts., Papua, highest in the E. Indies, el. 15,969 ft.; # 45 N, 137:10 E.

Cartagena (kär-tạ-jē'nä; Sp. kär-tä-ʜä'nä), spt. city, Murcia, S. E. Spain, pop. 97; # 37:40 N, 1:5 W. — spt. city, N. Colombia, pop. 86;* of dept. of Bolivar; # 10:25 N, 75:40 W.

Cartago (kär-tä'gō), city, C. Costa Rica, C. America, pop. 20; earthquakes 1841, 1910; # 9:55 N, 84 W. — tn., W. C. Colombia, pop. 19; # 4:42 N, 76:13 W.

Carthage (kär'thạj), anc. city, Tunis, N. Africa; # 36:52 N, 10:18 E. — tn., S. W. Mo., pop. 11; # 37:7 N, 94:19 W. — tn., W. C. Ill., pop. 3; college; # 40:25 N, 91:10 W.

Casablanca (kä-sä-bläng'kä), spt. city, N. W. Morocco, pop. 111; # 33:37 N, 7:35 W.

Casa Grande (kä'sä grän'dä), national monument, prehistoric ruins near Florence, Ariz.; # 33 N, 111:22 W.

Cascade (kas-kād'), mt. range, N. W. U.S.A., Mt. Shasta, N. Calif. to Mt. Baker, N. Wash.; # 45 N, 112 W; highest peak, Mt. Tacoma (Rainier), el. 14,408 ft. — tunnel, E. of Seattle, Wash., len. 3 mi.; # 47:40 N, 121 W.

Casco (kas'kō), bay, S. E. Me., near Portland; many islands; # 43:35 N, 70:10 W.

Caserta (kä-zer'tä), prov., Campania, S. Italy, area 2, pop. 823, and its *, pop. 35; cathedral and palace; # 41:3 N, 14:21 E.

Cashmere (kash-mēr'), see **Kashmir.**

Casper (kas'pėr), city, C. Wyo., pop. 18; petroleum refineries; # 42:50 N, 106:15 W.

Caspian (kas'pi-an) **Sea,** anc. Caspium, salt lake bet. S. W. Europe and Asia, len. 760 mi., width 270 mi.; area 169, el. 85 ft. below sea level; # 40 N, 50 E.

Cassel (käs-sel'), see **Kassel.**

Castellammare (käs-tel-läm-mä'rä), spt., Bay of Naples, S. Italy, pop. 26; coral; resort; # 40:41 N, 14:29 E.

Castellón (käs-tel-yōn'), prov., Valencia, E. Spain, area 2.5, pop. 297, and its *, pop. 35; # 39:57 N, 0:5 W.

Castile (kas-tēl'), region, C. and N. Spain, former kingdom and prov. of Old Castile (N. C. Sp.), and New Castile (C. Sp.); # 41 N, 4 W.

Castres (käs-tr), city, Tarn dept., S. Fr., pop. 28; # 43:35 N, 2:15 E.

Catalonia (kat-ạ-lō'ni-ä), autonomous region, N. E. Spain; * Barcelona, pop. 977; # 42 N, 2 E.

Catamarca (kä-tä-mär'kä), prov., N. W. Argentina, area 37, pop. 115 and its *, pop. 13; # 28:27 S, 65:47 W.

Catanduanes (kä-tän-dwä'näs), isl., E. C. Philippines, area 1, pop. 64; # 13:45 N, 124:15 E.

Catania (kä-tä′nē-ä), prov., E. Sicily, area 2, pop. 876, and its *, a spt., pop. 252; univ.; # 37:20 N, 15 E.

Catanzaro (kä-tän-dzä′rō), prov., Calabria, S. Italy, area 2, pop. 514, and its *, a spt., pop. 36; # 38:55 N, 16:39 E.

Cataracts (kat′a-rakts), rapids of Nile riv., one in Egypt and five (2 to 6) in Anglo-Egyptian Sudan; # 18 to 24 N, 30 to 33 E.

Catawba (ka-tå′bå), riv., N. and S. Car., to Santee riv., len. 300 mi.; # ab. 33:45 N, 81:35 W.

Catskill (kats′kil), low mts., S. E. C. New York, highest, Slide mt., el. 4,204 ft.; # 41:50 N, 74:45 W. — aqueduct, New York water supply, len. 110 mi. — tn. near mts., pop. 5.

Cattaro (kät′tä-rō), or **Kotor**, spt. on gulf of same name, Dalmatia, Yugoslavia, pop. 14; # 42:25 N, 18:46 E.

Cattegat (kat′e-gat), see **Kattegat**.

Cauca (kou′kä), riv., W. Colombia, trib. to Magdalena riv., len. 600 mi.; # 9 N, 74:40 W.

Caucasia (kâ-kā′si̯ä), div. of Russia in and near Caucasus Mts.; # 43 N, 44 E.

Caucasus (kâ′ka-sus), mt. range bet. Black and Caspian seas, highest mt. Elbruz, el. 18,463 ft.; # 42 N, 45 E.

Caulfield (kâl′fēld), suburb of Melbourne, Australia, pop. 41; # 37:53 S, 145:2 E.

Cautin (kou-tēn′), prov., S. C. Chile, area 6.4, pop. 194, * Temuco, pop. 29; # 39 S, 72:30 W.

Cauvery (kâ′ve̯-ri), riv., W. Ghats to Bay of Bengal, S. India, len. 400 mi.; # 11:20 N, 79:45 E.

Cavalla or **Kavala** (kä-vä′lä), spt. city, E. Macedonia, N. E. Greece, pop. 23; # 40:58 N, 24:25 E.

Cavan (kav′an), county of Irish Free State, part of Ulster, area 0.7, pop. 91, and its *, pop. 3; # 54 N, 7:22 W.

Cavite (kä-vē′tä), fortified spt. near Manila, Philippine Isls., pop. 22; # 14:30 N, 120:52 E.

Cawnpore (kân-pōr′), city on Ganges riv., N. India, pop. 216; # 26:25 N, 80:20 E.

Cayambé (kä-yäm-bā′), vol. pk., N. Ecuador, el. 19,270 ft.; # 0:0, 78 W.

Cayenne (kä-yen′ or kī-en′), city on Cayenne isl., * of Fr. Guiana, pop. 10; # 5 N, 52:20 W.

Caymans (kī-mänz′), three isls., W. Indies, to Jamaica, pop. 6; # 19:20 N, 81:20 W.

Cayuga (kā-yö′gä), lake, W. C. New York (Ithaca), len. 40 mi.; # 42:45 N, 76:45 W.

Ceará (sā-ä-rä′), state, E. Brazil, area 57, pop. 1,319, * Fortaleza, pop. 79, sometimes called Ceará; # 3:50 S, 38:30 W.

Cebú (sā-bö′), isl., C. Philippines, area 2, and spt. thereon, pop. 66; # 10:25 N, 123:55 E.

Cedar Rapids (sē′dar rap′idz), city, S. E. Ia., pop. 62; Coe College and State Teachers College; # 41:50 N, 91:35 W.

Celaya (sā-lä′yä), city in Guanajuato State, S. C. Mex., pop. 23; # 20:30 N, 100:45 W.

Celebes (sel-ē′bēz), isl., Dutch E. Indies, area 69, pop. 3,008; # 2 S, 121 E. — sea bet. Borneo, Philippines and Celebes; # 3:30 N, 122 E.

Celle (tsel′é), city, 22 mi. N. E. of Hannover, C. Ger., pop. 26; # 52:37 N, 10:5 E.

Cenis (se̯-nē), pk., Alps, E. Fr.; — famous pass, el. 6,835 ft. — oldest tunnel through Alps, 1871, len. 7.5 mi.; # 45:15 N, 6:55 E.

Central America, continental N. America S. of Mexico, 6 republics and Br. Honduras, area 221, pop. ab. 7,880; # 12 N, 86 W.

Central Asia (sen′tral ā′shi̯ä), vaguely defined region N. of Himalaya and Hindu Kush Mts.; Tibet, Turkestan and Mongolia; # 45 N, 85 E.

Central Falls (sen′tral fâlz), city, N. E. Rhode Island, near Pawtucket, pop. 25; # 41:55 N, 71:27 W.

Centralia (sen-trā′li̯-a̯), city, S. C. Ill., pop. 16; # 38:31 N, 89:8 W. — tn., S. W. Wash., pop. 7; # 46:45 N, 123 W.

Central India, official name of a group of native states, C. India, area 52, pop. 5,997, * Indore; # 25 N, 77 E.

Central Park (sen′tral pärk), famous park, New York City, area 850 acres; Metropolitan Museum of Art.

Central Provinces and Berar (bā-rär′), prov., C. India, area 100, pop. 13,913, * Nagpur, pop. 145; # 22 N, 80 E.

Cephalonia (sef-a̯-lō′ni̯-a̯) or **Kefalonia**, isl., W. Greece, len. 32 mi., area 0.4, pop. 81, * Argostoli; # 38:15 N, 20:40 E.

Ceram (se-ram′; Pg. se-räṅ′), isl., Dutch E. Indies, bet. Papua and Celebes, area 7, pop. 83; # 3:10 S, 129:30 E.

Cerigo (cher-ē′gō) or **Kythera**, Greek isl. bet. Crete and pen. of Morea, area 0.1, pop. 13; # 36:15 N, 23 E.

Cernauti (cher-nou′tē), or **Czernowitz**, city, Bukovina, ext. N. C. Romania, pop. 87; univ.; # 48:20 N, 25:50 E.

Cerro del Mercedario (ser′rō del mer-sā-ᴛʜä′rē-ō), mt. pk., Andes of Chile and Argentina, el. 21,884 ft.; # 32 S, 70:10 W.

Cerro de Pasco (ser′rō dā päs′kō), tn., C. Peru, el. 14,280 ft., pop. 7; rich silver and copper mines; # 10:55 S, 76 W.

Cerro Gordo (ser′rō gôr′dō; Sp. ther′rō gōr′dō), mt. and pass, N. W. of Vera Cruz, Mex.; # 24:50 N, 102:5 W.

Cervin (ser-vaṅ), see **Matterhorn**.

Ceskoslovenska Republika (ches″kō-slō-ven′skä), official name of Czechoslovakia.

Cetatea Alba (che-tä-tä′a̯ äl′bä), see **Akkerman**.

Cette (set), spt. city, S. Fr., terminus of Canal du Midi, pop. 32; # 43:25 N, 3:45 E.

Cettinje or **Cetinje** (chet-tēn′yä), * of Montenegro, S. W. Yugoslavia, pop. 5; # 42:24 N, 18:55 E.

Ceuta (sū′ta̯; Sp. thā′ö-tä), Spanish possession in N. Morocco, on Strait of Gibraltar, pop. 48; # 35:54 N, 5:17 W.

Cévennes (sā-ven), mts., S. E. margin Auvergne plateau, S. C. Fr., highest mt., Mezenc, el. 5,753 ft.; # 45 N, 4 E. — old dist., N. E. part of Languedoc, Fr.; ab. 45 N, 4 E.

Ceylon (sē-lon′), isl., E. of S. India, a Br. colony, area 25, pop. 4,504, * Colombo, pop. 244; # 8 N, 80 E.

Chachani (chä-chä′nē), mt., S. Peru, el. ab. 20,000 ft.; meteorological station; # 16:14 S, 71:36 W.

Chaco, El (el chä′kō), ter., N. Argentina, area 53, pop. 58, * Resistencia, pop. 21; # 26:36 S, 60 W. — semi-arid, subtropical region of N. Argentina and adjacent Bolivia and Paraguay; quebracho; petroleum; # 23 S, 58 W.

Chaco Canyon (chä′kō kan′yun), valley, N. W. New Mex.; ancient ruins, a national monument; # 36 N, 108 W.

Chad (chäd), lake in N. C. Africa, area, 10 to 500; # 14 N, 14 E. — Fr. colony, N. C. Africa, area 502, pop. 1,271.

Chagres (chä′gres), riv., Panama, through Gatun Lake to Caribbean Sea; # 9:19 N, 80 W.

Chalcidice (kal-sid′i-sē), or **Khalkidike**, pen., N. E. Greece; # 40:30 N, 23:25 E.

Chalcis (kal′sis), spt., W. Euboea isl., E. Greece, pop. 13; # 38:29 N, 23:38 E.

Châlons-sur-Marne (shä-lôṅ-sür-màrn), city, N. E. Fr., * of Marne dept., pop. 31; # 48:58 N, 4:25 E.

Châlon-sur-Saône (shä-lôṅ-sür-sōn), city, E. C. Fr., pop. 32; # 46:45 N, 4:55 E.

Chamba (chum′bä), native hill state, Punjab, N. W. India, area 3, pop. 142, and its *, pop. 6; # 32:40 N, 76 E.

Chambal (chum-bul′), riv., N. C. India, trib. of Jumna, len. 600 mi.; # 26:30 N, 79:20 E.

Chambersburg (chām′bèrz-bèrg), tn., S. C. Pa., pop. 15; Wilson College; # 39:50 N, 77:40 W.

Chambéry (shäṅ-bä-rē), city, * of Savoie, S. E. Fr., pop. 17; # 45:35 N, 5:55 E.

Chambord (shäṅ-bôr), vil., Loir-et-Cher, Fr., notable château and park; # 47:37 N, 1:32 E.

Chamonix (shà-mō̯-nē), valley and village, N. of Mt. Blanc, E. Fr., resort; # 45:55 N, 6:50 E.

Champagne (sham-pān′; Fr. shäṅ-pàn-y′), region, N. C. Fr., anc. prov., * Troyes; # 48:20 N, 4:5 E.

Champaign (sham-pān′), city, N. E. C. Ill., pop. 23; # 40:8 N, 88:18 W.

Champlain (sham-plān′), lake bet. New York and Ver., len. 125 mi.; # 44:40 N, 73:15 W.

Chandernagore (chun″dèr-na̯-gōr′), Fr. city prov. on a mouth of Ganges riv., India, pop. 25; # 22:55 N, 88:20 E.

Chandi Sevu (chän′dē sā′vö), vil., C. Java, Dutch E. Indies; splendid ancient ruins; # ab. 7:30 N, 111 E.

Changchowfu (chäng′chou-fö′), spt. city, Fukien prov., Formosa strait, S. E. China, pop. est. 500; # 24:30 N, 117:45 E.

Changchun (chäng′chun) or **Kwanchengtze**, city, Kirin prov., C. Manchuria, pop. 80; # ab. 44 N, 126 E.

Changsha (chäng-shä′), city, S. E. C. China, * of Hunan prov., pop. est. 536; # 28:20 N, 113 E.

Chang-Tang (chäng-täng′), vast plateau and prov., C. Tibet, C. Asia; # 34 N, 90 E.

---

fat, fāte, fär, fåll, åsk, fāre; net, mē, hèr; pin, pīne; not, nōte, mǒve, nôr; up, lūte, pùll; oi, oil; ou, out; (lightened) aviạry, ẹlect, agōny, intọ, ụnite; (obscured) errạnt, operä, ardẹnt, actọr, natụre; ch, chip; g, go; th, thin; ᴛʜ, then; y, you;

Changteh (chäng'te'), city, Hunan prov., S. E. China, pop. est. 300; # 29 N, 111:40 E.

Channel Islands, Br. isls. near coast of Fr., area 0.1, pop. 90; * St. Helier; # 49:30 N, 2:30 W. See **Alderney, Guernsey, Jersey.**

Chantilly (shän-tē-yē), tn., Oise dept., N. Fr., pop. 6; laces; races and château; # ab. 49:29 N, 2:22 E.

Chanute (chå-nōt'), tn., S. E. Kan., pop. 10, 37:39 N, 95:29 W.

Chapala (chä-pä'lä), lake, S. W. Mex. Plateau, area 1.3, len. 50 mi., largest in Mex.; # 20:10 N, 103 W.

Chapel Hill (chap'el hil), tn., W. C. N. Car., pop. 1; State Univ.; # ab. 35:5 N, 79:3 W.

Charente (shå-roñt), riv., S. C. Fr. to Atlantic oc., len. 200 mi.; # 46 N, 1 W. — dept., W. C. Fr., area 2.3, pop. 316, * Angoulême, pop. 38; # 45:40 N, 0:0 W.

Charente-Inférieure (shå-roñt añ-fä-rē-ėr), dept., W. C. Fr., area 2.8, pop. 418, * La Rochelle, pop. 40; # 45:40 N, 1 W.

Charleroi (shär-lé-rwä), city, 31 mi. S. of Brussels, Belgium, pop. 27; # 50:25 N, 4:30 E. — tn., S. W. Pa., near Pittsburgh, pop. 11; # 40:8 N, 79:55 W.

Charles (chärlz), cape, ext. S. Md., in Chesapeake Bay; # 37:5 N, 76 W. — riv. through Boston to Atlantic oc., len. 75 mi.; # 42:22 N, 71:5 W. — cape, E. Labrador, ext. E. pt. of mainland of N. America; # 51:20 N, 55:35 W.

Charles Louis, see **Snow Mts., Papua.**

Charleston (chärlz'ton), city, S. W. C. West Va., state *, pop. 68; # 38:20 N, 81:35 W. — spt., S. E. S. Car., pop. 71; 2 colleges; earthquake 1886; # 32:50 N, 79:50 W.

Charlestown (chärlz'toun), part of Boston, Mass.

Charlotte (shär'lot), city, S. W. C. N. Car., pop. 101; Smith Univ.; # 35:20 N, 80:50 W.

Charlotte Amalie (shär-lot' ä-mä'lye), now known as St. Thomas, spt., St. Thomas Isl., * of Am. Virgin isls., W. Indies, pop. 10; # 18:20 N, 64:55 W.

Charlottenburg (shär-lot'ten-búrch), a W. div. of Berlin, Ger., pop. 334; # 52:30 N, 13:20 E.

Charlottesville (shär'lots-vil), tn., N. W. C. Va., pop. 19; State Univ.; # 38:3 N, 78:30 W.

Charlottetown (shär'lot-toun), tn., * of Prince Edward Isl., Canada, pop. 12; Prince of Wales College; # 46:30 N, 63:20 W.

Charters Towers (chär'tėrz tou'ėrz), tn., N. C. Queensland, Australia, pop. dist. 15; # 20:05 S, 145:20 E.

Chartres (shärtr), city, N. C. Fr., * Eure-et-Loir, pop. 23; cathedral; # 48:25 N, 1:30 E.

Château-Thierry (shä-tō-tye-rē), tn., N. E. Fr., on Marne riv., pop. 8; battle 1918; # 49:2 N, 3:25 E.

Chatham (chat'am), city, 25 mi. E. of London, S. E. Eng., pop. 42; military and naval station; # 51:23 N, 0:31 E. — tn., ext. S. W. Ontario, pop. 13; # 42:25 N, 82:12 W. — isl. group, 500 mi. E. of New Zealand, area 0.4, pop. 0.4, to New Zealand; # 43:52 S, 170:42 E.

Chattahoochee (chat-å-hō'chē), riv., N. E. Ga., to Apalachicola riv., len. 500 mi.; # 30:45 N, 84:50 W.

Chattanooga (chat-å-nō'gä), city, S. E. Tenn., pop. 128; univ.; battle Nov. 1863; # 35:10 N, 85:20 W.

Chautauqua (shå-tå'kwä), lake, S. W. New York; tn. and summer educational center; # 42:10 N, 79:30 W.

Chaux-de-Fonds, La (shō-dė-fóñ), city, 10 mi. N. W. of Neuchâtel, N. W. Switz., pop. 38; # 47:6 N, 6:50 E.

Chefoo (chē-fö'), port, Shantung Pen., N. E. China, pop. est. 89; # 37:35 N, 121:24 E.

Chekiang (chē'kyäng'), prov., S. E. C. China, area 37, pop. est. 22,000, * Hangchow, pop. 340; # 29:15 N, 120 E.

Chelan (shē-lan'), lake in glacial gorge, N. C. Wash., len. 55 mi., 1,400 ft. deep; to Columbia riv.; # 48:10 N, 120: 30 W.

Chelmsford (chemz'förd), city, * of Essexshire, Eng., pop. 21; # 51:44 N, 0:25 E.

Chelsea (chel'si), a borough of London, Eng., pop. 64; Carlyle's residence; 51:29 N, 0:11 W. — a N. E. suburb of Boston, Mass., pop. 41; # 42:24 N, 71:2 W.

Cheltenham (chelt'n-am), city, Gloucestershire, S. W. Eng., pop. 48; # 51:57 N, 2:5 W.

Chelyabinsk (chel-yä-bēnsk'), city, E. slope Ural Mts., E. C. Russia, pop. 61; # 55:10 N, 61:10 E.

Chelyuskin (chel-yös'kin), cape, ext. N. Asia; # 76:10 N, 105 E.

Chemnitz (kem'nits), city, C. Sachsen (Saxony), S. Ger., pop. 323; cotton goods; # 50:50 N, 12:55 E.

Chemulpo (shē-mul-pō'), spt. of Seoul, Korea, pop. 30; treaty port; # 37:30 N, 126:45 E.

Chenab (chē-nâb'), riv., trib. of upper Indus riv., N. W. India, len. 500 mi.; # 29:20 N, 71:15 E.

Chengtu (chung-tö'), city, S. W. China Proper, * of Szechwan prov., pop. est. 450; # 30:45 N, 104:15 E.

Cher (shär), riv., S. C. Fr. to Loire riv., len. ab. 200 mi.; # 47:15 N, 0:28 E. — dept., C. Fr., area 2.8, pop. 305, * Bourges, pop. 46; # 47:5 N, 2:30 E.

Cherbourg (sher'börg; *Fr.* sher-bör), spt., N. Normandy, Fr., pop. 44; naval arsenal; # 49:40 N, 1:35 W.

Cheribon or **Tjeribon** (sher'i-bon), spt., N. C. Java, pop. 33; # 6:45 S, 108:30 E.

Cherim (sher'im), prov. of E. Mongolia; # 45:15 N, 121 E.

Chernigov (cher-nyē'göf), prov., N. Ukraine, S. W. Russia, area 13, pop. 1,800, and its *, pop. 33; # 51:25 N, 31:15 E.

Cherso (ker'sō), isl., S. of Fiume, Italy, area 0.2, pop. 10, and its chief spt., pop. 8; # 44:45 N, 14:25 E.

Chesapeake (ches'å-pēk), bay, Md. and Va., 200 mi. long, 4–40 mi. wide; # 38 N, 76 W.

Cheshire (chesh'ir), or **Chester** (ches'tėr), county, W. C. Eng., area 0.9, pop. 1,025, * Chester, pop. 41; # 53:12 N, 2:55 W.

Chester (ches'tėr), city, 15 mi. S. of Liverpool, W. C. Eng., pop. 41; # 53:12 N, 2:55 W. — city, S. E. Pa., pop. 59; college; # 39:50 N, 75:25 W.

Chesterfield (ches'tėr-fēld), city, Derby, C. Eng., pop. 64; # 53:15 N, 1:25 W.

Cheviot (chev'i-ot), hills, boundary bet. Eng. and Scotland, highest 2,676 ft.; sheep; # 55:20 N, 2:30 W.

Cheyenne (shi-en'), city, S. E. Wyo., state *, pop. 22; # 41:10 N, 104:45 W. — riv., E. Wyo. to Missouri riv., C. S. Dak., len. 500 mi.; # 44:50 N, 100:50 W.

Chiapas (chē-ä'päs), state, S. Mex., area 27, pop. 423, * Tuxtla Gutiérrez, pop. 11; # 17 N, 93 W.

Chicago (shi-kä'gō), city on Lake Michigan, N. E. Ill., pop. 3,397, with suburbs, pop. over 4,499; Univ. of Chicago, Northwestern, De Paul and Loyola Univs., Armour and Lewis Insts.; # 41:50 N, 87:40 W.

Chicago Heights (shi-kä'gō hīts), a S. suburb of Chicago, Ill., pop. 22; # 41:30 N, 87:40 W.

Chicago, Milwaukee & St. Paul (shi-kä'gō, mil-wå'kē, sänt pål), R.R., Chicago and midwest to Seattle, Wash., highest point, 6,350 ft., completed 1909, total mileage 11,205.

Chichester (chich'es-tėr), tn., S. W. W. Sussex, Eng., pop. 12; cathedral; # 50:50 N, 0:46 W.

Chickasha (chik'å-shä), tn., S. C. Okla., pop. 14; State College for Women; # 35:1 N, 97:55 W.

Chiclayo (chē-klä'yō), spt. city, N. W. Peru, * of Lambayeque dept., pop. 25; # ab. 6:30 S, 80 W.

Chico (chēk'ō), tn., N. Calif., pop. 9; Teachers College; # 39:42 N, 121:50 W.

Chicopee (chik'ō-pē), city, S. W. C. Mass. on Chicopee riv., pop. 42; # 42:9 N, 72:35 W.

Chiemsee (kem'zā), lake, S. E. Bavaria, S. W. Ger., area .05; castle; # 47:50 N, 12:28 E.

Chiengmai (chi-eng-mi'), see **Kiangmai.**

Chieti (kē-ā'tē), prov., Abruzzi e Molise, Italy, area 1.1, pop. 376, and its *, *anc.* Teate, pop. 31; # 42:22 N, 14:10 E.

Chihli (chē'lē), prov., N. China, area 116, pop. est. 30,000, * Tientsin, pop. est. 800; # 39:40 N, 117 E. — gulf, N. W. part of Yellow Sea; # 38:30 N, 118:30 E.

Chihuahua (chē-wä'wä), state, N. W. Mex., area 90, pop. 402, and its *, pop. 40; # 28:40 N, 106:15 W.

Chile (chil'e; *Sp.* chē'lā) or **Chili** (chi'li), republic, W. S. America, len. 2,600 mi., area 290, pop. 4,597, * Santiago, pop. 696; nitrate; # 40:35 S, 72 W.

Chilkoot (chil'köt), pass near Skagway, Alaska, el. 3,500 ft.; # ab. 59:40 N, 135:40 W.

Chillán (chēl-yän'), city, S. C. Chile, pop. 31, * of Ñuble; # 36:35 S, 72:10 W.

Chillicothe (chil-i-koth'ē), city, S. C. Ohio, pop. 20; # 39:20 N, 82:58 W.

Chillon (shē-yóñ), castle, E. end of Lake Geneva, W. Switz.; # 46:25 N, 6:56 E.

Chiloé (chē-lō-ā′), prov., S. Chile, area 7, pop. 110; chiefly a large island; # 43 S, 74 W.

Chimborazo (chim-bō-rä′zō), vol. mt., el. 20,498 ft., Andes of Ecuador; # 1:70 S, 78:50 W. — prov. surrounding pk., area 3, pop. 122.

China (chī′nạ), republic, E. Asia, area ab. 4,278, pop. est. 485,000, * Nanking, pop. 525; # 30 N, 110 E.

China Proper, part of China E. of Tibet and S. E. of the Great Wall, "the 18 provinces", area 1,534, pop. ab. 300,000; # 32 N, 115 E.

China Sea, South, part of Pacific oc. bet. Asia and Philippines and Borneo; # 12 N, 114 E. — **East**, sea bet. Yellow sea and the Pacific oc.; # 30 N, 126 E.

Chincha (chin′chạ), small isls. near coast of W. Peru, formerly important as source of guano; # 13:40 S, 76:20 W.

Chindwin (chin-dwin′), riv., chief trib. of Irrawaddy riv., C. Burma, len. 500 mi.; # 21:20 N, 95:15 E.

Chinkiang (chin-kyäng′), city near mouth of Yangtse riv., E. China, pop. est. 170; # 32:10 N, 119:33 E.

Chinook (chi-nŏk′), tn., N. C. Montana.

Chios (kī′os), Greek isl., E. Ægean sea, pop. 63, and its *, pop. 14; a dept.; # 38:22 N, 26:10 E.

Chishima (chē′shē-mä), Japanese name for **Kurile Islands.**

Chisinau (kē-shē-nĕ′ọ), see **Kishinef.**

Chiswick (chiz′ik), a W. suburb of London, Eng., pop. 41; # 51:29 N, 0:16 W.

Chita (chē-tä′), Soviet republic, E. Siberia, area 653, pop. 1,812, and its *, pop. 78, E. of Lake Baikal; # 51:55 N, 113:55 E.

Chivilcoy (chē-vēl-koi′), city, 95 mi. W. of Buenos Aires, E. Argentina, pop. 28; # 34:46 S, 60 W.

Choiseul (shwä-zèl′), Br. isl. E. of Papua, len. 90 mi.; # 7:10 S, 157 E.

Cholon (shō-lôn′), city adjacent to Saigon, Fr. Cochin-China, pop. 217; # 10:45 N, 106:30 E.

Chosen (chō′sen), Japanese name for **Korea.**

Chosen Strait, see **Korea Strait.**

Choumen (shọ′men), dist., N. E. Bulgaria, area 2.3, pop. 323, and its *, pop. 24 (also called Shumen, Sumla); # 43:15 N, 26:55 E.

Christchurch (krīst′chèrch), chief city and spt., E. C. S. Island, New Zealand, pop. 115; Canterbury College; # 43:25 S, 172:40 E.

Christiania (kris-tē-ä′nē-ä), see **Oslo.**

Christmas Island (kris′mạs ī′lạnd), Br. isl., Indian oc., 200 mi. S. of Java, area 0.06, pop. 1; # 10:25 S, 105:43 E. — largest atoll in Pacific oc., 30 mi. across, part of Br. colony of Gilbert and Ellice Isls.; # 1:57 N, 157:27 W.

Chubut (chọ-bōt′), ter., S. Argentina, area 93, pop. 33, * Rawson; # 44 S, 69 W. — riv., C. Patagonia, Argentina, len. 450 mi.; # 43:40 S, 64:20 W.

Chudskoye (chùt′skō-ye), see **Peipus.**

Chungking (chung-kēng′), city on Yangtse riv., Szechwan prov., S. W. China, pop. est. 539; # 29:30 N, 106:5 E.

Chuquibamba (chö-kē-bäm′bä), mt. pk., Andes, S. W. Peru, 90 mi. N. W. of Arequipa, el. ab. 21,000 ft.; # ab. 16 S, 77:40 W.

Chuquicamata (chö-kē-kä-mä′tä), tn., N. Chile, pop. 15; world's greatest copper mine; # ab. 22 S, 69 W.

Chur (kör) or **Coire**, city, Grisons, E. Switz., pop. 16; # 46:53 N, 9:33 E.

Churchill (chèrch′il), riv., N. Saskatchewan to Hudson Bay, len. ab. 1,000 mi.; # 58:50 N, 94:5 W.

Chuvash (chọ′vàsh), autonomous soviet area, E. C. Russia, area 6.7, pop. 758, * Cheboksary on Volga riv. (includes former Kazan prov.); # ab. 55:45 N, 49 E.

Cibao (sē-bä′ō), mt. range, S. E. Haiti Isl., highest, Loma Tina, el. 10,300 ft., highest in W. Indies; # 19 N, 70:30 W.

Cicero (sis′ẹ-rō), a W. suburb of Chicago, Ill., pop. 65; # 41:51 N, 87:46 W.

Cienfuegos (syen-fwä′gōs), spt. city, S. C. Cuba, pop. 73; # 22:15 N, 80:30 W.

Cilicia (si-lish′iạ), anc. Roman prov., S. E. Asia Minor; # 36:40 N, 34 E.

Cilician Gates (si-lish′iän) or **Gülek Boghaz**, pass, Taurus Mts., S. E. Asia Minor; # 37:18 N, 34:45 E.

Cimarron (sē-mä-rōn′), riv., N. E. New Mex. to Arkansas riv., Okla., len. 650 mi.; # 36:15 N, 96:5 W.

Cincinnati (sin-si-nä′ti), city, S. W. Ohio, on Ohio riv., pop. 456, with suburbs, 789; Univ. of Cincinnati; # 39:10 N, 84:30 W. [8:55 E.

Cinto (chin′tō), highest pk. in Corsica, el. 8,890 ft.; # 42:25 N,

Ciscaucasia (sis-kô-kā′shiạ), prov. of Russia just N. of Caucasus Mts.; # 43 N, 45 E. [# 35:53 N, 14:24 E.

Città Vecchia (chēt-tä′ vek′kē-ä), city, C. Malta, pop. 9;

Ciudad Bolívar (syö-ᴛᴴäᴛᴴ′ bō-lē′vär), city, E. Venezuela on Orinoco riv., pop. 20, * of Bolívar; # 8 N, 64 W.

Ciudad Juárez (syö-ᴛᴴäᴛᴴ′ hwä′räs), Mexican tn., opposite El Paso, Tex., pop. 40; # ab. 31:40 N, 106:30 W.

Ciudad Real (thē-ö-ᴛᴴäᴛᴴ′ rā-äl′), prov., S. C. Spain, area 7.6, pop. 440, and its *, pop. 19; # 38:58 N, 3:58 W.

Ciudad Trujillo (syö-ᴛᴴäᴛᴴ′ trö-hēl′yō), new name given in 1936 to **Santo Domingo;** see **Santo Domingo.**

Ciudad Victoria (syö-ᴛᴴäᴛᴴ′ vēk-tō′rē-ä) or **Victoria**, city, N. E. Mex., * of Tamaulipas, pop. 18; # 23:45 N, 99:10 W.

Civitavecchia (chē-vē-tä′vek′kē-ä), chief port of Roma, Italy, pop. 19; ruins; # 42:6 N, 11:48 E.

Clackmannan (klak-man′ạn), county, S. C. Scotland, area .05, pop. 32, and its *, pop. 2; # 56:6 N, 3:45 W.

Claremont (klâr′mont), tn., W. New Hampshire, pop. 12; # 43:23 N, 72:20 W. — suburb of Los Angeles, Calif., pop. 3; Pomona College; # ab. 34:10 N, 117:45 W. — a S. suburb of Cape Town, U. of S. Africa, pop. 13; # ab. 34 S, 18:30 E.

Clark's Fork (klärks fôrk), riv., W. Mont. through Pend Oreille Lake to Columbia riv., len. 700 mi.; # 49 N, 117:40 W.

Clarksburg (klärks′bèrg), city, C. West Va., on Monongahela riv., pop. 31; # 39:15 N, 80:25 W.

Clear (klēr), cape, ext. S. Ireland, on Clear Isl.; # 51:25 N, 9:30 W.

Cleburne (klē′bèrn), tn., C. Texas, pop. 11; # 32:25 N, 97:25 W.

Clermont-Ferrand (kler-môn-fe-rän′), city, S. C. Fr., * of Puy-de-Dôme dept., pop. 83; # 45:45 N, 3:2 E.

Cleve (klā′vẹ), suburb of Düsseldorf, Rheinprovinz, W. Ger., pop. 20; # 51:47 N, 6:8 E.

Cleveland (klēv′lạnd), city, N. Ohio, port on Lake Erie, pop. 878, with suburbs, pop. 1,215; steel; Western Reserve Univ.; Case Inst.; # 41:29 N, 81:40 W.

Cleveland Heights (klēv′lạnd hīts), a residential E. suburb of Cleveland, Ohio, pop. 55; # 41:30 N, 81:35 W.

Clichy (klē-shē), a N. W. suburb of Paris, Fr., pop. 50; # 48:54 N, 2:18 E.

Clifton (klif′tọn), city, N. E. New Jersey, near Passaic, pop. 49; # 40:52 N, 74:9 W.

Clinton (klin′tọn), tn., C. Mass., pop. 12; # 42:25 N, 71:40 W. — tn., C. New York, pop. 1; Hamilton College; # ab. 41:45 N, 73:50 W. — city, E. C. Iowa, pop. 26; # 41:47 N, 90:18 W. — tn., W. C. Ind., pop. 7; # 39:38 N, 87:25 W.

Cluj (klözh) or **Kolozsvar**, city, Transylvania, C. Romania, pop. 61; # 46:44 N, 23:33 E.

Clyde (klīd), riv., S. W. Scotland to Firth of Clyde, len. 106 mi.; canalized; ship building; # 55:55 N, 4:30 W.

Clydebank (klīd′bank), a W. suburb of Glasgow, Scotland, pop. 47; # 55:56 N, 4:34 W.

Clydesdale (klīdz′dāl), see **Lanark.**

Coahuila (kō-ä-wē′lä), state, N. Mex., area 64, pop. 394, * Saltillo, pop. 35; # 27 N, 102 W.

Coalville (kōl′vil), city, Leicestershire, Eng., pop. 20; # 52:43 N, 1:21 W.

Coast Range (kōst rānj), low mt. ranges, Lower Calif. to N. W. Wash. or S. Alaska along Pacific coast; highest, San Gorgonis Mt., Calif., el. 11,485 ft.; # 45 N, 123:30 W; sometimes called Coast Mts. in Br. Columbia.

Coatbridge (kōt′brij), an E. suburb of Glasgow, Scotland, pop. 46; # 55:50 N, 4:5 W.

Coatesville (kōts′vil), city, S. E. Pa., pop. 14; # 39:59 N, 75:50 W.

Cobalt (kō′bält), tn., W. Ontario, pop. 6; silver mines; # 47:20 N, 79:50 W.

Cobán (kō-bän′), city, N. C. Guatemala, pop. 27; # 15:40 N, 90:25 W.

Coblenz (kō′blents), city on Rhine and Moselle rivs., W. Ger., pop. 59; # 50:20 N, 7:35 E.

---

fat, fāte, fär, fȧll, ȧsk, fâre; net, mē, hèr; pin, pīne; not, nōte, mōve, nôr; up, lūte, pull; oi, oil; ou, out; (lightened) aviạry, ẹlect, agọny, intọ, ụnite; (obscured) errạnt, operạ, ardẹnt, actọr, natụre; ch, chip; g, go; th, thin; ᴛʜ, then; y, you;

Coburg (kō′bûrċh), a N. div. of Bayern (Bavaria), S. C. Ger., area 0.2, pop. 74, and its *, pop. 24; # 50:18 N, 10:55 E. — suburb of Melbourne, Australia, pop. 18; # 37:44 S, 144:57 E.

Cocanada (kō-ka-nä′dä), spt. city at mouth of Godavari riv., S. E. India, pop. 53; # 16:58 N, 82:15 E.

Cochabamba (kō-chä-bäm′bä), dept., N. W. C. Bolivia, area 25, pop. 535, and its *, pop. 34 (el. 8,394 ft.); # 17:25 S, 66:10 W.

Cochin (kō-chēn′ or kō′chin), native state, Madras prov., S. E. India, area 1, pop. 979, and a city therein, pop. 21; # 9:55 N, 76:10 E.

Cochin-China (kō′chin-chī′nạ), colony, S. part of Fr. Indo-China, area 26, pop. 3,979, * Saigon, pop. 112, with suburbs, pop. 329; # 10 N, 106 E.

Cocos (kō′kōz) or **Keeling** (kē′ling), isls., N. E. Indian oc., part of Straits Settlements, area .01, pop. 1; # ab. 12:5 S, 96:54 E.

Cod (kod), cape, ext. E. Mass., hooked N; # 42:5 N, 70:15 W; — bay, nearly enclosed by hook of Cape Cod; Canal, see **Cape Cod**.

Cœur d'Alene (kėr dä-lān′), tn., N. Idaho, pop. 10; silver mines. — lake nearby; # 47:30 N, 116:50 W.

Coffeyville (kof′i-vil), tn., S. E. Kan., pop. 17; # 37:5 N, 95:45 W.

Cognac (kō-nyȧk), city, Charente, S. W. Fr., pop. 19; brandy; castle; # 45:40 N, 0:20 W.

Cohoes (kō-hōz′), city, E. C. New York, near Troy, pop. 22; # 42:48 N, 73:45 W.

Coimbatore (kō-im-bạ-tōr′), city, S. W. India, pop. 66; # 11 N, 77 E.

Coimbra (kō-ēm′brä), city, N. C. Portugal, pop. 21; univ.; # 40:15 N, 8:20 W.

col or **kol** (kol), pass or depression in the divide bet. drainage systems.

Colchagua (kōl-chä′gwä), prov., C. Chile, area 4, pop. 166, * San Fernando; # 34:30 S, 71 W.

Colchester (kōl′ches-tėr), spt. city, Essex, S. E. Eng., pop. 43; # 51:52 N, 0:50 E.

Cold Spring Harbor, tn., N. W. Long Isl., New York, pop. 2; resort; marine station; biological research; # 40:53 N, 73:28 W.

Colima (kō-lē′mä), state, S. W. Mex., area 2, pop. 92, and its *, pop. 27. — volcano near, el. 12,750 ft.; # 19:35 N, 103:45 W.

Collingwood (kol′ing-wụd), a N. E. part of Melbourne, Australia, pop. 34; # 37:48 S, 145:2 E.

Collinsville (kol′inz-vil), tn., S. W. Ill., near E. St. Louis, pop. 10; # ab. 38:38 N, 90 W.

Colmar (kōl′mär), city, Rhine Valley, E. Fr., pop. 47; # 48:5 N, 7:21 E.

Cöln (kėln), *Eng.* **Cologne,** city on Rhine riv., * of Rheinland, Ger., pop. 693; univ.; # 50:57 N, 6:55 E.

Colne (kōln), city, 26 mi. N. E. of Manchester, N. C. Eng., pop. 25; # 53:52 N, 2:10 W.

Cologne (kō-lōn′), see **Cöln.**

Colombia (kō-lom′bi-ạ), republic, N. W. S. America, area 449, pop. 8,700, * Bogotá, pop. 331; # 4 N, 74 W.

Colombo (kō-lom′bō), spt., W. Ceylon, its *, pop. 244; # 7 N, 79:45 E.

Colón (kō-lōn′), city, Atlantic end of Panama Canal, though not in Canal Zone, pop. 57; # 9:22 N, 79:54 W. — city, Matanzas prov., Cuba, pop. 28; # 22:44 N, 80:55 W.

Colorado (kol-ọ-rä′dō), state, W. C. U.S.A., bet. Kan. and Utah, area 104, pop. 1,123, * Denver, pop. 322; second city, Pueblo, pop. 52; # 39 N, 106 W. — national monument, Mesa Co., W. C. Colo., erosion features. — riv., from Grand Lake, N. C. Colo., to Gulf of Calif., len. 1,360 mi.; Grand Canyon in N. W. Ariz.; # 31:50 N, 114:45 W. — riv., W. Tex. to Gulf of Mex., len. 900 mi.; # 28:45 N, 96 W. — riv., N. Patagonia, Argentina, Andes Mts. to Atlantic oc., len. 900 mi.; # 39:40 S, 62 W. — desert, S. E. Calif., area ab. 2; # 34:30 N, 116 W.

Colorado Springs (kol-ọ-rä′dō springz), city, E. C. Colo., pop. 37; Colo. College; summer resort; # 38:50 N, 104:50 W.

Columbia (kō-lum′bi-ạ), city, C. S. Car., state *; State Univ.; two colleges; pop. 62; # 33:55 N, 81 W. — tn., S. E. C. Pa., pop. 12; # 40:2 N, 76:30 W. — tn., N. C. Mo., pop. 18;

State Univ.; # 38:50 N, 92:15 W. — riv., S. Br. Columbia to Pacific oc., bet. Wash. and Ore., len. 1,400 mi.; # 46:15 N, 124:30 W. — mt. peak, Rockies, E. Br. Columbia, third in S. Canada, el. 12,740 ft.; # 52:10 N, 117:40 W.

Columbus (kō-lum′bus), city, S. W. C. Ohio, state *, pop. 306; State Univ.; Capital Univ.; # 39:57 N, 83 W. — tn., N. E. Miss., pop. 14; State Univ.; # 33:30 N, 88:25 W. — tn., W. C. Ga., pop. 53; # 32:30 N, 84:50 W.

Colwyn Bay (kol′win bā), coastal tn., N. Wales, 30 mi. W. of Liverpool, pop. 19; # 53:17 N, 3:41 W.

Comacchio (kō-mäk′kē-ō), tn., near large salt lake and marsh, S. E. Po valley, N. E. Italy, pop. 12; salt works; # 44:40 N, 12:10 E.

Commander Islands (kọ-màn′dėr ī′lạndz), small isls. bet. Kamchatka and Aleutian Isls., N. Pacific oc.; # 54:50 N, 166:30 W.

Como (kō′mō), prov., Lombardy, N. Italy, area 1.1, pop. 631, and its * on Lake Como, pop. 48; # 45:47 N, 9:5 E.

Como, Lago di (kō′mō, lä′gō dē), lake, Lombardy, N. Italy, len. 35 mi.; resort; # 46 N, 9:15 E.

Comorin (kom′ọ-rin), cape, S. tip of India; # 8:15 N, 77:20 E.

Comoro (kom′ọ-rō), group isls. bet. N. Madagascar and Africa, area 1, pop. 109; to Fr.; # 12 S, 43 E.

Compiègne (kôṅ-pyen-y′), city, N. Fr., on Oise riv., pop. 16; palace; # 49:25 N, 2:50 E.

Comstock (kom′stok), silver lode and mines near Virginia City, Nev., yielded $36,000,000 in 1877; # 39:20 N, 119:38 W.

Concepción (kōn-sep-syōn′), prov., S. C. Chile, area 3, pop. 248, and its *, pop. 64; # 36:50 S, 73 W. — tn., Panay Isl., Philippines, pop. 17; # 11:17 N, 123:14 E.

Conception Point (kọn-sep′shọn), cape, S. W. Calif.; # 34:28 N, 120:30 W.

Concha (kon′chä), highest mt. in Venezuela, Mérida range, el. 15,416 ft.; # 8:5 N, 70:47 W.

Concord (kong′kọrd), city, S. C. New Hampshire, state *, pop. 27; # 43:12 N, 71:32 W. — tn., N. E. Mass., pop. 8; fight, April 19, 1775; # 42:29 N, 72:23 W. — tn., C. N. Car., pop. 16; # 35:25 N, 80:37 W.

Concordia (kon-kôr′di-ạ), city, E. Argentina, on Uruguay riv., pop. 21; # 31:23 S, 58:2 W.

Coney Island (kō′ni ī′lạnd), seaside resort off S. shore of Long Isl., near New York City; # 40:40 N, 74 W.

Congo or **Kongo** (kong′gō), riv., E. Equatorial Africa to Gulf of Guinea, Atlantic oc., 3,000 mi.; great volume and power at falls; # 6 S, 12:30 E.

Congo, Belgian, colonial possession in Equatorial Africa, area 910, pop. 8,500, * Leopoldville, pop. 5; # 5 S, 25 E.

Conjeeveram (kon-jē-vėr-um′), city just S. of Madras, S. E. India, pop. 61; # ab. 13 N, 80:15 E.

Connaught (kon′ât), prov. of N. W. Irish Free State, area 7, pop. 611; # 53:45 N, 9 W; — vil., Ontario near R.R. bridge across St. Lawrence riv., len. 3,500 ft.; # 45 N, 75 W.

Connecticut (kọ-net′i-kut), state, N. E. U.S.A., bet. New York and Mass., area 5, pop. 1,709, * Hartford, pop. 166; next city, New Haven, pop. 161; # 41:30 N, 72:30 W. — riv., N. New Hampshire to Long Isl. Sound, len. 410 mi.; # 41:20 N, 72:25 W.

Connellsville (kon′elz-vil), tn., S. W. Pa., on Youghiogheny riv., pop. 14; coke; # 40:2 N, 79:35 W.

Connersville (kon′ėrz-vil), tn., S. E. C. Ind., pop. 13; # 39:38 N, 85:7 W.

Constance (kon′stạns), lake, N. E. Switz., S. W. Ger., len. 50 mi., area 0.2, el. 1,306 ft., depth 835 ft.; # 47:35 N, 9:25 E. — city thereon, see **Konstanz.**

Constantine (kôṅ-stäṅ-tēn′), dept., N. E. Algeria, area 34, pop. 2,163, and its *, pop. 78; # 36:21 N, 6:35 E.

Constantinople (kon-stan-ti-nō′pl) or **Istanbul,** *anc.* Byzantium, city on Bosporus, ext. S. E. Europe, pop. 881; # 41:1 N, 29 E.

Constantza (kon-stan′zạ), spt. city, S. E. Romania, pop. 28; # 44:10 N, 28:40 E.

Continental Divide, line of summits bet. drainage systems, in U. S. often applied to Front Range of Rockies bet. drainage to Gulf of Calif. and Gulf of Mex.

Cooch Behar (kōch bā-här′), native state in Bengal, N. E. India, area 1, pop. 592, and its *, pop. 11; # 26:15 N, 89:20 E.

Cook (kụk), county, N. E. Ill., area 0.93, pop. 4,063 (1940), * Chicago; # 41:50 N, 87:50 W.

(variable) d̠ as d or j, ş as s or sh, t̠ as t or ch, z̧ as z or zh; o, F. cloche; ü, F. menu; ċh, Sc. loch; ṅ, F. bonbon; ′, primary accent; ′, secondary accent; †, obsolete; <, from; +, and; =, equals. See also lists at beginning of book.

Cook Inlet, gulf, S. coast of Alaska, len. 200 mi.; # 60 N, 152 W.

Cook or **Hervey Islands,** isls. bet. New Zealand and Society Isls., area 0.2, pop. 8; to New Zealand; # 20 S, 160 W.

Cook, Mount, summit S. Alps, S. Isl., New Zealand, el. 12,349 ft.; # 43:20 S, 170:15 E. — S. Alaska, el. 13,758 ft.; # 60:11 N, 140:1 W.

Cook Strait, strait bet. N. and S. Isls., New Zealand; # 41 S, 174:30 E.

Coolgardie (kōl-gär'di), gold mining center, S. W. W. Australia, now part of Kalgoorlie, pop. 8; # 30:55 S,121:20 E.

Coon Butte (kōn bŭt) or **Meteor Crater,** peculiar hill with crater, E. C. Ariz.; # 35:2 N, 111:2 W.

Coorg (kōrg), prov. of S. India, area 2, pop. 164, * Mercara; # 12:30 N, 75:30 E.

Coosa (kōo'sä), riv., junct. of Oostanaula and Etowah riv., Ga., to Alabama riv., len. 350 mi.; # 32:20 N, 86:30 W.

Copán (kō-pän'), tn., W. Honduras, pop. 4; Maya ruins; # 14:50 N, 89 W.

Copenhagen (kō-pĕn-hā'gĕn), officially, **Kjöbenhavn,** spt., Seeland Isl., * of Denmark, pop. 561, pop. with suburbs, 701; univ.; # 55:40 N, 12:35 E.

Cöpenick (kĕ'pe-nik), a S. E. div. of Berlin, Ger., pop. 65; # 52:27 N, 13:36 E.

Copiapó (kō-pē-ä-pō'), active vol. in N. Chile, el. 16,60̈ ft.; # 27:30 S, 70:20 W.

Coppermine (kop'ēr-mīn), riv., N. W. Ter., Canada, to Coronation Gulf, Arctic oc., len. 525 mi.; # 67:50 N, 115:45 W.

Coquimbo (kō-kĕm'bō), prov., N. C. Chile, area 14, pop. 160, * La Serena. — spt. tn. in same, pop. ab. 15; # 29:56 S, 71:21 W.

Coral Sea (kor'ạl sē), part of Pacific oc., N. E. of Australia, area 1,000; # 15 S, 154 E.

Corcyra (kôr-si'rạ), see **Corfu.**

Cordilleras (kôr-dil-yä'räz), mt. system extending from Cape Horn along W. Coast to Alaska, most often applied to Andes.

Córdoba (kôr'dō-Bä) or **Cordova** (kor'dō-vä), prov., S. W. C. Spain, area 5.3, pop. 590, and its *, pop. 75; # 37:52 N, 4:50 W. — prov., W. C. Argentina, area 67, pop. 896, and its *, pop. 289; univ.; # 31:30 S, 64:5 W.

Corea (kō-rē'ạ), see **Korea.**

Corfu (kor-fō', kôr-fō'), anc. Corcyra, isl., N. W. Greece, len. 50 mi., area 0.3, and spt. city thereon, pop. 27; # 39:30 N, 18:50 E.

Corinth (kor'inth), city, S. C. Greece, at head of Gulf of Corinth, pop. 5; # 37:55 N, 22:55 E. — isthmus, width 4 to 8 mi., connecting pen. of Morea with mainland of S. Greece, severed by ship canal; # 37:55 N, 22:55 E.

Cork (kôrk), county, area 3, pop. 391, and spt. city, Munster, S. Irish Free State, pop. 78; Univ. College; # 51:55 N, 8:30 W.

Corning (kôr'ning), city, W. C. New York, pop. 16; # 42:8 N, 77:5 W.

Cornwall (kôrn'wȧl), county, S. W. Eng., area 1.4, pop. 321, * Bodmin; tin mines; # 50:30 N, 4:35 W. — canal, Ontario, len. 11 mi., depth 14 ft.; # 45:5 N, 74:40 W.

Coromandel (kor-ō-man'del), div. of coast, S. E. India near Madras; # 13 N, 80:20 E.

Coronation Gulf (kor-ō-nā'shọn gulf), N. Canada, part of Arctic oc. bet. Victoria Isl. and mainland; # 68 N, 112 W.

Corpus Christi (kôr'pus kris'ti), tn., S. C. Texas, on lagoon of Gulf of Mex., pop. 12; # 27:49 N, 97:21 W.

Corregidor (kor-reg'i-dôr, Sp. kọr-rạ̈-ᴇ̣-dôr'), isl., entrance Manila Bay, Philippines.

Corrèze (kor-rez), dept., C. Fr., area 2.3, pop. 274, * Tulle.

Corrientes (kor-rē-en'tes), prov., N. E. Argentina, area 34, pop. 896, and its *, pop. 29; # 27:30 S, 58:40 W.

Corse (kôrs) or **Corsica,** isl., N. W. Mediterranean sea, a dept. of Fr., area 3.4, pop. 282, * Ajaccio; # 42 N, 9 E. — cape, N. tip of Corsica; # 43 N, 9:22 E.

Corsica (kôr'si-kạ), see **Corse.**

Corsicana (kôr-si-kän'ạ), tn., N. E. C. Texas, pop. 12.

Cortland (kôrt'lạnd), tn., S. C. New York, pop. 16; # 42:35 N, 76:10 W.

Coruña (kō-rōn'yä), prov., ext. N. W. Spain, area 3, pop. 720, and its *, pop. 68, a spt.; # 43:23 N, 8:25 W.

Corvallis (kor-val'is), tn., W. C. Oregon, pop. 8; State Agri. College; # 44:35 N, 123:18 W.

Cosenza (kō-zen'tzä), prov., Calabria, S. Italy, area 2.6, pop. 496, and its *, pop. 30; # 39:19 N, 16:18 E.

Coshocton (kō-shok'tọn), tn., E. C. Ohio, pop. 12; # 40:17 N, 81:52 W.

Cosigüina (kō-sē-gwē'nä), active vol., N. W. Nicaragua, C. America, el. 3,830 ft.; eruption 1835; # 13 N, 87:35 W.

Costa Rica (kos'tä rē'kä), republic, C. America, just N. of Panama, area 23, pop. 592, * San José, pop. 71; # ı0 N, 84 W.

Côte-d'Or (kōt-dôr), dept., E. C. Fr., area 3.4, pop. 321, * Dijon, pop. 79; # 47:10 N, 4:45 E.

Côtes de Moselle (kōt dė mō-zel), escarpment N. of Paris, Fr., steepest towards N.; # 49 N, 6 E.

Côtes-du-Nord (kōt-dü-nôr), dept., Brittany, N. W. Fr., area 2.8, pop. 558, * St. Brieuc; # 48:30 N, 3 W.

Cöthen, see **Köthen.**

Cotopaxi (kō-tō-paks'i; Sp. kō-tō-pä'ᴴē), vol., N. C. Ecuador, el. 19,498 ft.; # 0:30 S, 79:30 W.

Cotrone (kō-trō'nä), spt. tn., Calabria, S. W. Italy, pop. 11; anc. Greek city; # 39:8 N, 17:9 E.

Cotswold (kots'wōld), range of hills, Gloucestershire, S. W. Eng.; Cotswold sheep; # 51:50 N, 2:50 W.

Cottbus (kot'bús) or **Kottbus,** city, 68 mi. S. E. of Berlin, Ger., pop. 50; # 51:46 N, 14:20 E.

Cottian Alps (kot'i-ạn alps), mt. range, France-Italy; # 44:40 N, 7 E.

Council Bluffs (koun'sil blufs), city, S. W. Iowa, across Missouri riv. from Omaha, Neb., pop. 41; # 41:20 N, 95:50 W.

Courland (kōr'lạnd), former prov., N. W. Russia, now most of Latvia; # 56:55 N, 22 E.

Courtrai (kōr-trā), city, S. W. Belgium, pop. 37; center of linen industry; # 50:50 N, 3:15 E.

Coventry (kuv'ẹn-tri), city, 20 mi. E. of Birmingham, C. Eng., pop. 131; # 52:25 N, 1:33 W.

Covington (kuv'ing-tọn), city, N. Ky., pop. 62; suburb of Cincinnati, Ohio; # 39:7 N, 84:31 W.

Cowdenbeath (kou'den-bēth), tn., Fife, S. E. Scotland, pop. 14; # 56:6 N, 3:21 W.

Cowes (kouz), spt. tn., N. Isle of Wight, Eng., pop. 10; regatta; # 50:45 N, 1:38 W.

Cradle (krä'dl), mt., summit of Tasmania, el. 5,069 ft.; # 41:45 S, 146 E.

Craiova (krä-yō'vä), city, Wallachia, S. W. Romania, pop. 52; # 44:18 N, 23:48 E.

Crakow (krä'kō) or **Krakow,** city, S. W. Poland, pop. 182; univ.; # 50:5 N, 19:55 E.

Cranston (kranz'tọn), city, N. E. C. Rhode Island, near Providence, pop. 47; # 41:48 N, 71:28 W.

Crater Lake (krä'tẽr läk), lake, S. W. Ore., 1,996 ft. deep, in engulfed volcano; a national park, area 0.25; # 43 N, 122:8 W.

Crawfordsville (krä'fọrdz-vil), tn., W. C. Indiana, pop. 11; Wabash College; # 40:2 N, 86:55 W.

Crécy or **Cressy** (krä-sē), tn., Somme dept., N. Fr., pop. 2; battle 1346; # 50:15 N, 1:50 E.

Crefeld (krä'felt), see **Krefeld.**

Cremona (krē-mō'nä), prov., Lombardy, N. Italy, area 0.7, pop. 358, and its *, on the Po riv., pop. 59; violins; # 45:18 N, 10:2 E.

Cressy, see **Crécy.**

Crêt de la Neige (krä dė lä näzh), highest pk. in Jura Mts., S. E. Fr., el. 5,654 ft.; # 46:12 N, 6 E.

Crete (krēt) or **Candia,** Greek isl., S. E. of Morea, area 3.1, len. 150 mi., pop. 345, * Canea, pop. 25; # 35:10 N, 25 E.

Creuse (krėz), dept., C. Fr., area 2.2, pop. 228, * Guéret; # 46 N, 2 E.

Creusot, Le (krė-zō), city, S. E. C. Fr., pop. 38; mining and manufacturing; # 46:48 N, 4:28 E.

Crewe (krō), city, W. C. Eng., 15 mi. N. W. of Stoke, pop. 47; # 53:7 N, 2:30 W.

Crillon (kril'ọn), mt., S. Alaska, el. 12,730 ft.; # 58:41 N, 137 W.

Crimea (kri-mē'ạ, krī-mē'ạ) or **Taurida,** pen. in Black Sea, area 15; # 45:20 N, 34 E. — Soviet republic, area 15, pop. 762, * Simferopol, pop. 69; # 45 N, 34 E.

Crimmitschau (krim'mit-shou), city, W. Sachsen (Saxony), S. Ger., near Glauchau, pop. 27; # 50:48 N, 12:30 E.

Crisana (krē-sä'nä), prov., ext. W. Romania, area 8, pop. 1,317; # 46:30 N, 22:30 E.

---

fat, fāte, fär, fȧll, ȧsk, fâre; net, mē, hẽr; pin, pīne; not, nōte, mȯve, nôr; up, lūte, púll; oi, oil; ou, out; (lightened) aviạry, ẹlect, agọny, intọ, ūnite; (obscured) errạnt, operạ̈, ardẹnt, actọr, natūre; ch, chip; g, go; th, thin; ᴛH, then; y, you;

Cristóbal (kris-tō′bäl), spt., adjacent to Colón, Canal Zone, Atlantic end of Panama Canal, pop. 1; # 9:21 N, 79:54 W.

Croatia and Slavonia (krō-ā′shią, sla-vō′ni-ą), prov. of N. W. Yugoslavia, area 17, pop. 2,740, * Zágráb; # 45:15 N, 15:5 E.

Croix (krwä), city, N. E. Fr., suburb of Roubaix, pop. 17; carpets; # ab. 50:42 N, 3:10 E.

Cronstadt or **Kronstadt** (krōn′stät), outer port, on isl. of Leningrad, N. W. Russia, pop. 67; # 59:55 N, 29:35 E. — canal to Leningrad, len. 16 mi., depth 20 ft.

Crown Point (kroun point), vil. on Lake Champlain, N. E. New York; # 43:59 N, 73:28 W.

Croydon (kroi′dọn), suburb of London, S. E. Eng., pop. 193; # 51:23 N, 0.6 W.

Ctesiphon (tes′i-fon), ruins, S. of Bagdad, Irak, C. Mesopotamia; # 33 N, 44:40 E.

Cuba (kū′bą), largest isl. W. Indies, and a republic, area 44, pop. 4,109, * Havana, pop. 560; sugar; # 22 N, 79 W.

Cucuta (kö′kö-tä), city, N. E. Colombia, pop. 29; # 7:47 N, 72:50 W.

Cuddalore (kud-dą-lōr′), spt. city, near Pondichéry, S. E. India, pop. 57; # 11:46 N, 79:46 E.

Cuenca (kwän′kä), prov., E. C. Spain, area 6.6, pop. 284, and its *, pop. 13; # 40:4 N, 2:14 W. — city, S. W. Ecuador, pop. 50, * of Azuay prov.; # 2:50 S, 79:10 W.

Culebra (kö-lā′brä), tn., Canal Zone, near Gaillard (Culebra) Cut, pop. 10; # 9:3 N, 79:39 W.

Culiacán (kö-lē-ä-kän′), tn., * of Sinaloa, Mex., pop. 22; # 24:45 N, 107:30 W.

Culion (kö-lyōn′), isl., W. C. Philippines, area 0.4; leper colony; # 11:45 N, 120 E.

Cumberland (kum′bẽr-lạnd), county, N. W. Eng., area 1.5, pop. 273, * Carlisle, pop. 55; # ab. 54:54 N, 3 W. — city, N. W. Md., pop. 39; # 39:37 N, 78:45 W. — **Gap**, pass, height 1,315 ft., Va.–Ky.–Tenn.; # ab. 36:36 N, 83:40 W. — riv., S. E. Ky. to Ohio riv., len. 650 mi.; # 37:10 N, 88:25 W.

Cumbrian (kum′bri-ạn), hills, "mountains," S. Cumberland, N. W. Eng.; # 54:40 N, 3:20 W.

Cundinamarca (kön″dē-nä-mär′kä), dept., C. Colombia, area 8, pop. 812, * Bogota, pop. 166; # 4:40 N, 74:15 W.

Cuneo (kö-nā′ō), prov., Piedmont, N. W. Italy, area 2.9, pop. 624, and its *, pop. 32; # 44:20 N, 7:20 E.

Curaçao (kū-rą-sō′), isl., Caribbean Sea, near coast of Venezuela, area 0.2, pop. 35; # 12:10 N, 69 W. — Dutch colony consisting of six isls., W. Indies, area 0.4, pop. 56, * Willemstad, pop. 17.

Curicó (kö-rē-kō′), prov., C. Chile, area 3, pop. 108, and its *, pop. 16; # 35 S, 72 W.

Curitiba (kö-rē-tē′bä), city, * of Paraná, Brazil, pop. 79; univ.; # 25:26 S, 49:16 W.

Curzola (kör′dzo-lä) or **Korchula**, isl., S. Dalmatia, Yugoslavia, area 0.2, len. 30 mi., pop. 30; # 42:55 N, 16:50 E.

Cutch or **Kutch** (kuch), native state on Gulf of Cutch, N. W. India, area 8, pop. 485, * Bhuj; # 23 N, 70 E. — **Rann of**, large salt marsh N. and E. of state, area ab. 9; # 24 N, 70 E.

Cuttack (kut-tak′), city, delta of Mahanadi riv., E. C. India, pop. 53; # 20:25 N, 85:45 E.

Cuxhaven (kuks-hä′vn; *Ger.* kúks-hä′fẹn), outer port of Hamburg, Ger., pop. 18; # 53:53 N, 8:40 E.

Cuyabá (kwē-yä-bä′), city, * of Matto Grosso, Brazil, pop. 34; # 15:40 S, 56:10 W.

Cuyahoga (kī-ą-hō′gä), county, N. Ohio, area 0.46, pop. 1,217 (1940), * Cleveland; # 41:20 N, 81:40 W.

Cuyahoga Falls, tn., N. E. Ohio, near Akron, pop. 14; # 41:7 N, 81:29 W.

Cuzco (kös′kō), dept., S. E. Peru, area 56, pop. 439, and its *, pop. 28; ancient Inca ruins; # 13:20 S, 72:20 W.

Cyclades (sik′lą-dēz), ab. 200 isls., S. Ægean sea, a dept. of Greece, area 1, pop. 122, * Hermoupolis; # 37 N, 25:15 E.

Cyprus (sī′prus), Br. isl., E. Mediterranean sea, len. 150 mi., area 3.6, pop. 311, * Nicosia, pop. 18; # 35 N, 33 E.

Cyrenaica (sir-ē-nā′i-ką), prov., N. E. Libya, N. Africa (Barca); # 31 N, 22 E.

Cyrene (sī-rē′nē), anc. city and ter., Cyrenaica; # 32:49 N, 21:50 E.

Cyzicus (siz′i-kus), anc. city on S. shore of Sea of Marmora, Turkey; # 40:20 N, 28:32 E.

Czechoslovakia (chek″ọ-slọ-vak′i-ą), former republic, C. Europe, N. part of earlier Austria-Hungary, area 54, pop. 14,730, * Praha (Prague), pop. 848; # 49 N, 18 E.: absorbed into Germany and Hungary in 1938 and 1939.

Czernowitz (cher′nō-vits) or **Cernauti**, city, N. C. Romania, pop. 111; univ.; # 48:20 N, 25:50 E. [# 50:49 N, 19:5 E.

Czestochowa (chen-stō-kô′vä), city, W. C. Poland, pop. 136;

D

Dacca (dak′ą), city, N. E. Bengal, N. E. India, pop. 119; univ.; # 23:50 N, 90:20 E.

Dagestan (dä-ges-tän′) or **Daghestan**, Soviet republic, S. E. Russia, area 14, pop. 798, * Petrovsk, a spt. on Caspian sea; # 42 N, 47 E.

Dagö (dä′gō), isl., Baltic sea, W. Estonia, len. 40 mi.; # 58:50 N, 22:45 E.

Dahna (däн′nä) or **Roba El Khali**, desert, S. Arabia; # 21 N, 50 E.

Dahomey (dä-hō′mi), colony, Fr. W. Africa, area 42, pop. 842, * Porto Novo; # 9 N, 2 E.

Dairen (dī′ren), formerly **Dalny**, spt., Japanese Manchuria, pop. 175; # 38:55 N, 121:40 E.

Dakar (dä-kär′), spt. city, * of Fr. W. Africa and the Sahara, pop. 25; # 14:40 N, 17:20 E.

Dakota (dą-kō′tą), former ter., N. C. U.S.A., see **North Dakota** and **South Dakota**. — riv., E. C. N. Dak. S. across S. Dak. to Missouri riv., len. 500 mi.; # 42:55 N, 97:25 W.

Dal Elf (däl elf), riv., W. C. Sweden to Gulf of Bothnia at Gable, len. 300 mi.; # 60:35 N, 35:17 E.

Dalhousie (dal-hou′zi), tn. and summer resort, Punjab, N. W. India, pop. 8; # 32:32 N, 76 E.

Dallas (dal′ąs), city, N. E. C. Texas, pop. 295; college; univ.; # 32:45 N, 96:45 W.

Dalles (dalz) of the Columbia, gorge and rapids, where Columbia riv. crosses Cascade range, N. W. Ore. — S. W. Wash.; # 45:40 N, 122 W.

Dalmatia (dal-mā′shi-ą), prov., ext. W. Yugoslavia, area 4.9, pop. 621; # 44:20 N, 15:40 E.

Dalmatian Coast (dal-mā′shi-ạn kōst), E. coast, Adriatic, Montenegro, N. to Istria Pen.; # 43 N, 17 E.

Dalny (däl′ni), see **Dairen.**

Daman (dä-män′), see **Damão.**

Damanhur (dä-män-hör′), city, Nile delta, N. Egypt, pop. 48; # 31 N, 30:28 E.

Damão (dä-moun′), spt., Portuguese colony, W. India, N. of Bombay, area 0.1, pop. ab. 15; # 20:25 N, 72:45 E.

Damaraland (dä-mä′rä-land), N. part of former Ger. S. W. Africa; # 22:10 S, 17 E.

Damascus (dą-mas′kus), ter., of S. Syria, area 20, pop. 706, and its *, the * of the Syrian Federation, pop. 170; very ancient; # 33:30 N, 36:15 E.

Damietta (dam-i-et′tą), city, Nile delta, N. Egypt, pop. 31; # 31:21 N, 31:49 E.

Danbury (dan′bẹ-ri), city, S. W. C. Conn., pop. 22; hats; # 41:25 N, 73:30 W.

Danish West Indies, now Virgin Isls., U.S.A.

Danmark (dän′märk), **Kongeriget**, official name for Denmark.

Danube (dan′ūb), *Ger.* **Donau**, riv., Black Forest, S. W. Ger., E. to the Black Sea, len. 1,725 mi.; internationalized 1919; # 46 N, 29 E.

Danville (dan′vil), city, S. C. Va., pop. 33; # 36:40 N, 79:20 W. — city, E. C. Ill., pop. 37; # 40:10 N, 87:38 W. — tn., C. Ky., pop. 7; Centre College; # 37:40 N, 84:45 W.

Danzig (dant′sik), former free city, spt. on Danzig Gulf, Baltic Sea, near mouth of Vistula riv.; area 0.8, pop. 415; univ.; # 54:20 N, 18:40 E: taken by Germany, 1939.

Dapsang (dup-sung′), **Godwin-Austen**, mt., Kashmir, el. 28,265 ft.; # 35:50 N, 76:30 E.

Darbhanga (dä-bän′gä), city, N. E. India, near Nepal, pop. 63; # 26:10 N, 85:57 E.

Dardanelles (där-dą-nelz′), *anc.* Hellespont, strait bet. Ægean sea and Sea of Marmora, len. 40 mi., width 1 to 5 mi.; # 40:15 N, 26:30 E.

Dar-es-Salaam (där-es-sä-läm′), spt., * of Tanganyika Ter., Br. E. Africa, pop. 25; # 6:40 S, 39:10 E.

Darfur (där′för), region, S. W. Anglo-Egyptian Sudan, area 170, pop. 750, * El Fasher; # 13 N, 24 E.

(variable) ḍ as d or j, ṣ as s or sh, ṭ as t or ch, ẓ as z or zh; *o*, F. cloche; ü, F. menu; ċh, Sc. loch; ṅ, F. bonbon; ′, primary accent; ″, secondary accent; †, obsolete; <, from; +, and; =, equals. See also lists at beginning of book.

Dariel (dä-rē-el′), chief pass across C. Caucasus mts., N. of Tiflis, el. ab. 6,000 ft.; # 42:45 N, 44:45 E.

Darien (dä′ri-en; *Sp.* dä-rē-en′), gulf, ext. S. W. part of Caribbean sea; # 9 N, 77 W. — isthmus of, old name for Isthmus of Panama.

Darjiling or **Darjeeling** (där-jēl′ing), city and sanitarium, N. Bengal, N. E. India, el. 8,000 ft., pop. 25; # 27 N, 88: 25 E.

Darling (där′ling), riv., Dividing range, E. Australia to Murray riv., len. 1,160 mi.; # 34 S, 142:5 E.

Darlington (där′ling-ton), city, Durham, N. E. Eng., pop. 67; # 54:32 N, 1:34 W.

Darmstadt (därm′shtät), city, * of Hessen, S. W. Ger., pop. 89; univ.; # 49:50 N, 8:38 E.

Dartmoor (därt′mör), moor and forest area, S. Devon, S. W. Eng.; # 50:35 N, 4 W.

Darton (där′ton), suburb of Barnsley, C. Eng., pop. 11; # 53:36 N, 1:32 W.

Darwen (där′wen), city, S. C. Lancastershire, N. W. Eng., pop. 39; # 53:42 N, 2:29 W.

Darwin (där′win), spt., * N. Ter., Australia, pop. 1; # 12:20 S, 130:55 E. — mt., C. Tierra del Fuego, S. S. America, el. 7,005 ft.; # 54:15 S, 69:22 W.

Dasht i Kavir (dusht i kav′ir), great desert, E. C. Persia; # 34:30 N, 56 E.

Date Line (dāt līn), line, mostly along meridian of 180°, where day is dropped if going west or added if going east.

Daugavpils (dou′gáf-pēls), city, mouth of Dvina riv., S. Latvia, pop. 45; # 56 N, 26:30 E.

Dauphiné (dō-fē-nā), mt. region, former prov., S. E. Fr., N. of Provence; # 45 N, 5:30 E.

Davao (dä′vou) or **Davado**, bay, S. E. Mindanao and spt. on same, pop. 13; # 7 N, 125:30 E.

Davenport (dav′en-pōrt), city, E. C. Iowa, on Mississippi riv., pop. 66; college; # 41:30 N, 90:35 W.

Davidson (dä′vid-son), tn., W. C. N. Car., pop. 2; Davidson College; # 35:28 N, 80:49 W.

Davis Strait (dā′vis strāt), portion of Atlantic oc., W. of Greenland, width 200–500 mi.; # 65 N, 60 W.

Davos-Platz (dä′vōs-pläts), resort in Davos Valley, E. Switz., pop. 10, el. 5,000 ft.; # 46:48 N, 9:49 E.

Dawson (dâ′son), tn., on Yukon riv., * of Yukon Ter., Canada, pop. 3; # 64:5 N, 139:20 W.

Dayton (dä′ton), city, S. W. Ohio, pop. 211; cash registers; Municipal Univ.; # 39:48 N, 84:15 W.

Daytona (dā-tō′na), tn., N. E. Fla., pop. 23; # 29:14 N, 81:3 W.

Dead Sea (ded sē), salt sea, E. Palestine, area 0.4, len. 46 mi., el. 1,293 ft. below sea level; # 31:30 N, 35:30 E.

Deadwood (ded′wud), mining tn., Black Hills, S. W. S. Dak., pop. 4; # 44:30 N, 103:50 W.

Deal (dēl), spt. tn., ext. E. Kent, S. E. Eng., pop. 13; # 51:13 N, 1:24 E.

Death Valley (deth val′i), depression, S. E. Calif., 276 ft. below sea level; lowest land in W. hemisphere; # 36:15 N, 116:40 W.

Debreczin (de′bret-sin), city, E. C. Hungary, pop. 103; univ.; # 47:30 N, 21:25 E.

Decatur (dę-kā′tėr), city, C. Ill., pop. 59; Millikin Univ.; # 39:52 N, 88:57 W. — tn., an E. suburb of Atlanta, Ga., pop. 17; Scott College; # 33:46 N, 84:15 W.

Deccan (dek′kan), broad pen., S. India; # 16 N, 78 E.

Dedeagach (de-de-ä-gäch′), spt. city, on Gulf of Enos, Thrace, N. E. Greece, pop. ab. 3; # 40:50 N, 25:52 E.

Dee (dē), riv., N. C. Scotland to N. Sea at Aberdeen, len. 75 mi.; # 57:10 N, 2:5 W. — riv., N. C. Wales, past Chester to Irish Sea, len. 90 mi.; # 53:15 N, 3 W.

Dekalb (dē-kälb′), tn., N. E. Ill., pop. 9; State Teachers College; # 41:55 N, 88:45 W.

Dekkan (dek′kan), see **Deccan.**

Delagoa (del-a-gō′a), bay in Portuguese E. Africa, len. 55 mi.; # 27 S, 33 E. — cape near same.

Delaware (del′a-wār), state, M. E. U.S.A., bet. Md. and New Jersey, area 2, pop. 267, * Dover, pop. 6; chief city, Wilmington, pop. 113; # 39 N, 75:30 W. — riv., Catskill Mts. to Delaware Bay, len. 375 mi.; # 39:50 N, 75:15 W. — tn., C. Ohio, pop. 9; Ohio Wesleyan Univ.; # 40:17 N, 83:2 W.

Delaware Bay, estuary, bet. E. Del. and S. New Jersey, len. 70 mi.; # 39 N, 75:15 W.

Delaware Water Gap, gorge cut by Delaware riv. through the E. Appalachian Mts., W. New Jersey and N. E. Pa., 1,400 ft. deep. — tn. near by, summer resort; # ab. 41 N, #75:10 W.

Delft (delft), city, 5 mi. S. of The Hague, Neth., pop. 48; porcelain; # 52:4 N, 4:21 E.

Delgado (del-gä′dō), cape, ext. N. E. Portuguese E. Africa; # 10:30 S, 40:30 E.

Delhi (del′ę), prov. in Punjab, N. India, area 0.6, pop. 488, and its *, pop. 304, the * of Br. India; # 28:35 N, 77:20 E.

Delmenhorst (del′men-hörst), city, Oldenburg, Ger., pop. 25; # 53:3 N, 8:37 E.

Delos (dē′los), tiny Greek isl., Cyclades, S. W. Ægean sea; an oracle of Apollo; # 37:23 N, 25:18 E.

Delphi (del′fī), anc. tn., Phocis Isl., W. Ægean sea; had an oracle of Apollo; # 38:29 N, 22:30 E.

Del Rio (del rē′ō), tn., S. W. C. Texas, on Rio Grande riv., pop. 13; # 29:25 N, 100:50 W.

Demavend (dem-ä-vend′), mt. pk., Elburz Mts., N. Persia, el. 18,606 ft.; # 36:5 N, 52 E.

Demerara (dem-ė-rä′rä), riv., Br. Guiana to Atlantic oc. at Georgetown, len. 200 mi.; # 6:50 N, 58:20 W.

Denain (dė-naň), city, Nord, N. Fr., pop. 22; coal and steel; # 50:19 N, 3:23 E.

Denbigh (den′bi), county, N. Wales, area 0.6, pop. 155, and its *, pop. 7; # 53:11 N, 3:25 W.

Denison (den′i-son), city, N. E. C. Texas, pop. 16; # 33:45 N, 96:32 W.

Denmark (den′märk), kingdom, Jutland pen., N. Europe and adjacent isls., area 16.6, pop. 3,268, * Copenhagen, pop. 561; # 56 N, 9 E.

Dent Blanche (don blänsh), mt. pk., Pennine Alps, S. Switz., near Matterhorn, el. 14,318 ft.; # 46 N, 7:38 E.

Denton (den′ton), tn., N. E. Texas, pop. 11; College of Industrial Arts; # 33:11 N, 97:9 W.

D'Entrecasteaux (don-tr-käs-tō), Br. isls. E. of Papua, area 7; # 9:30 S, 150:45 E. — cape, ext. S. W. Australia; # 34:51 S, 116:1 E.

Denver (den′vėr), city, N. E. C. Colo., * of state, pop. 322; el. 5,300 ft.; Denver Univ.; # 39:40 N, 105 W.

Denver and Rio Grande Western (den′vėr, rē′ō grand′), R.R., Denver to Salt Lake City via Royal Gorge, completed 1871, highest point, 10,239 ft., total mileage, 2,593.

Deptford (det′ford), a S. borough of London, Eng., pop. 113; # 51:29 N, 0:2 W.

Derby (dėr′bi or där′bi), county, S. C. Eng., area 1, pop. 714, and its *, pop. 133; porcelain; racing; # 52:56 N, 1:30 W. — tn., S. W. C. Conn., pop. 10; # 41:21 N, 73:4 W.

Derry (der′i), see **Londonderry.**

Derwent (dėr′went), riv., N. E. York to the Humber, Eng., len. 70 mi. — trib. of Trent riv., in Derby, len. 50 mi. — riv., Cumberlandshire to Irish Sea, len. 33 mi. — riv., Durham, N. E. Eng., # 54:58 N, 1:40 W.

Deschutes (dä-shöt′), riv., Cascade Mts., S. W. Ore. to Columbia riv., len. 200 mi.; over 1,000,000 horse-power; # 45:40 N, 120:52 W.

Deshnef or **East Cape,** cape, ext. E. Asia; # 66 N, 170 E.

Des Moines (dė moin), city, S. W. C. Iowa, state *, pop. 160; Drake and Des Moines Univs.; # 41:35 N, 93:30 W. — riv., S. W. Minn., S. to Mississippi riv., len. 450 mi.; # 40:25 N, 91:25 W.

Despoto Dagh (des′pō-tọ däch′), see **Rhodope Mts.,** Bulgaria.

Dessau (des′sou), city, * of Anhalt Free State, C. Ger., pop. 70; # 51:50 N, 12:15 E.

Detmold (det′mōld), city, * of Lippe, W. C. Ger., pop. 16; # 51:55 N, 8:50 E.

Detroit (dę-troit′), city, S. E. Mich., pop. 1,623, with suburbs, pop. 2,296; automobiles; Detroit Univ.; # 42:23 N, 83:5 W. — riv., bet. Lakes St. Clair and Erie; # 42:18 N, 83:7 W.

Deutsches Reich (doich′es rīch), official name of Germany.

Deux-Sèvres (dė sevr), dept., W. C. Fr., area 2.3, pop. 310, * Niort; # 46:30 N, 0:20 W.

Deventer (de′ven-tėr), city on Yssel riv., Overyssel, Neth., pop. 33; # 52:15 N, 6:8 E.

---

fat, fāte, fär, fâll, ȧsk, fãre; net, mē, hėr; pin, pīne; not, nōte, möve, nôr; up, lūte, pùll; oi, oil; ou, out; (lightened) aviȧry, ęlect, agọny, intọ, ūnite; (obscured) errant, operä, ardent, actọr, natūre; ch, chip; g, go; th, thin; ᴛʜ, then; y, you;

Devils Lake (dev′lz lăk), salt lake, N. E. N. Dak., len. 50 mi.; # 48:10 N, 99 W. — tn. near by, pop. 6; Sullys Hill National Park.

Devils Postpile (dev′lz pōst′pīl), national monument, Sierras, C. Calif., mass of basaltic columns; # 37:45 N, 119:10 W.

Devils Tower, volcanic plug, 1,200 ft. above base, N. Black Hills, Crook Co., N. E. Wyo., national monument; # ab. 44:30 N, 104:30 W.

Devon (dev′on), county, S. W. Eng., area 2.5, pop. 709, * Exeter, pop. 60; # 50:45 N, 3:45 W.

Devonport (dev′on-pōrt), former spt., S. W. Devonshire, now part of Plymouth, pop. 82; # 50:24 N, 4:10 W.

Dewsbury (dūz′ber-i), city, W. Riding, York, N. C. Eng., pop. 55; # 53:42 N, 1:37 W.

Dhaulagiri (dou-lä-gē′rē), pk., Himalayas, W. Nepal, el. 26,826 ft.; # 28:45 N, 83:30 E.

Dholpur (dhol-pōr′), native state, N. C. India, area 1, pop. 230, and its *, pop. 16; # 26:42 N, 77:53 E.

Diarbekir (dē-är-be-kēr′), prov., S. E. Asiatic Turkey, pop. 145, and its *, *anc.* Amida, on Tigris riv., pop. ab. 38; # 37:50 N, 40:10 E.

Dickson (dik′son), city, N. E. Pa., pop. 12; # 41:27 N, 75:40 W.

Dieppe (dē-ep), spt. city, N. Fr., on English Channel, pop. 24; # 49:55 N, 1:10 E.

Dijon (dē-zhôn), city, E. C. Fr., * of Côte-d'Or, pop. 79; cathedral; univ.; Burgundy wine; # 47:20 N, 5:1 E.

Dinaric Alps (di-nar′ik alps), range, along Dalmatian coast, W. Yugoslavia; # 43:45 N, 16:30 E.

Dindings (din-dingz′), isls., part of Br. Straits Settlements, area 0.2, pop. 12; # 4:15 N, 101 E.

Dinosaur (dī′no-sôr), national monument, N. E. Utah, large fossils; # 40:23 N, 109:6 W.

Dinslaken (dins′lä-ken), suburb of Düsseldorf, N. Ger., pop. 25; # 51:33 N, 6:43 E.

Dismal Swamp (diz′mal swomp), in S. E. Va. and N. E. N. Car., len. 30 mi.; # 36:30 N, 76:30 W.

District of Columbia, federal area separated from Md., S. E. U.S.A., entirely occupied by federal *, Washington, pop. 663, area .07; # 38:54 N, 77 W.

Distrito Federal (dēs-trē′tō fä-de-räl′), federal district, C. Mex., area 0.6, pop. 906, * Mexico City, pop. 615; # 19:18 N, 99:10 W.

Dithmarschen (dit′mär-shen), *Eng.* **Ditmarsh**, swampy region, W. Holstein, N. Ger., diked to keep out the sea; # 54:15 N, 9 E.

Diu (dē′ŭ), spt., small isls., a Portuguese colony, W. India, N. W. of Bombay, pop. ab. 15; # 20:40 N, 71 E.

Dividing Range, Great, low mt. range, E. Australia; # 23 S, 146 E.

Dnieper (nē′per), *anc.* Borysthenes, riv., W. C. Russia to Dnieper Bay, Black sea, len. 1,330 mi.; # 46:25 N, 32:30 E.

Dniester (nēs′ter), riv., Galicia to Black sea, len. 800 mi.; # 46:10 N, 30:30 E.

Döbeln (dė′beln), city, C. Sachsen (Saxony), S. Ger., pop. 23; # 51:10 N, 13:10 E.

Dobruja (dō-brŭ′jä), div. ext. S. E. Romania, area 6, pop. 390; # 44:30 N, 28:30 E.

Dodecanese (dō-dek-ȧ-nēs′), group Italian isls., S. E. Ægean sea; area 0.5, pop. 64; # 36:45 N, 26:45 E.

Dogger Bank (dog′er bangk), shallow area in N. sea, 70 mi. E. of N. Eng., depth 60–120 ft.; fishing grounds; # 55 N, 3 E.

Dolomites (dol′ō-mīts), mt. range ext. N. Italy, highest, Marmolada, 11,020 ft.; # 46:20 N, 11:45 E.

Dominica (dom-i-nē′kȧ), isl., Leeward Isls., W. Indies, area 0.3, pop. 39, * Roseau, pop. 7; # 15:30 N, 61:20 W.

Dominican Republic (do-min′i-kan), W. Indian republic, E. Haiti, area 19, pop. 1,545, * Santo Domingo (renamed Ciudad Trujillo in 1936), pop. 71; # 19 N, 70 W.

Domremy-la-Pucelle (dôn-rė-mē-lä-pü-sel′), vil., N. E. Fr., birthplace of Joan of Arc; # 48:26 N, 5:39 E.

Don (don), riv., W. C. Russia to Sea of Azov, len. 1,150 mi.; # 47:10 N, 39:25 E. — prov., S. E. Russia, area 64, pop. 3,600, * Rostov, pop. 121; univ.; # 47:10 N, 39:40 E. — riv., S. Yorkshire, Eng., to the Humber, len. 60 mi.; # 53:43 N, 0:52 W. — riv., Aberdeenshire, Scotland, len. 62 mi.; # 57:11 N, 2:4 W.

Donau (dō′nou), S. E. div. of Württemberg, S. W. Ger., area 2.4, pop. 591, * Ulm, on the Danube. (*Ger.* Donau) riv., pop. 59; # 48:15 N, 9:30 E.

Doncaster (dong′kas-ter), city, Yorkshire, N. C. Eng., pop. 55; # 53:32 N, 1:7 W.

Donegal (don′ē-gâl), bay and county, N. W. Ireland, area 1.8, pop. 169; # 54:41 N, 8:5 W.

Donets or **Donetz** (dō-nets′), riv., S. Russia to Don riv. near Sea of Azov, len. 450 mi.; # 47:35 N, 40:55 E. — coal field near riv.; Russia's chief field since 1919; # 48 N, 39 E.

Dongola (dong′gō-lä), prov., N. Anglo-Egyptian Sudan, area 124, pop. ab. 120, * Meroë; # 18 N, 32 E.

Donora (dō-nôr′ä), tn., S. W. Pa., on the Monongahela riv., pop. 13; # ab. 40:12 N, 79:50 W.

Don Pedro (don pē′drō), dam, near Modesto, Sierra foothills, C. Calif., height 283 ft.; # 37:37 N, 121 W.

Doon (dōn), riv., from Lake Doon to Firth of Clyde at Ayr, Scotland; # 55:25 N, 4:37 W.

Dordogne (dôr-dôn-y′), riv., S. C. Fr., W. to Gironde riv., len. 170 mi., # 45 N, 0:30 W. — dept., S. W. C. Fr., area 3.5, pop. 397, * Périgueux, pop. 28; caves; paintings; # 45:10 N, 0:45 E.

Dordrecht (dôr′dreċht), spt. city on Waal (Rhine) riv., 10 mi. S. E. of Rotterdam, Neth., pop. 55; # 51:50 N, 4:40 E.

Dore (dôr), mt. pk., S. C. Fr., el. 6,188 ft.; # 45:30 N, 2:48 E.

Doris (dō′ris), *anc.* country, E. C. Greece; # 38:40 N, 22:25 E.

Dornoch (dôr′noċh), spt. tn. on Dornoch Firth, N. E. Scotland; # 57:52 N, 4:5 W.

Dorpat (dor′pät), former name of Tartu, city, C. Estonia, pop. 50; univ.; # 58:25 N, 26:45 E.

Dorset (dôr′set) or **Dorsetshire**, county, C. S. Eng., area 1, pop. 228, * Dorchester; # 50:40 N, 2:30 W.

Dort (dôrt), see **Dordrecht**.

Dortmund (dôrt′munt), city, Westphalia, N. W. Ger., pop. 320; iron mines; # 51:31 N, 7:27 E.

Dothan (dō′than), tn., S. E. Ala., pop. 17; # 31:11 N, 85:21 W.

Douai (dö-ā), city, N. Fr., 15 mi. S. of Lille, pop. 36; # 50:25 N, 3:3 E.

Doubs (dö), riv., W. Switz., to Saône riv., len. 220 mi.; # 46:50 N, 5 E. — dept., E. C. Fr., area 2.1, pop. 285, * Besançon, pop. 56; # 46:45 N, 6:15 E.

Douglas (dug′las), spt. city, * of Isle of Man, Britain, pop. |20; # 54:9 N, 4:30 W. — tn., S. E. Ariz., pop. 9; copper; # 31:25 N, 109:30 W.

Douro (dō′rọ̄) or **Duero** (dö-ā′rō), riv., N. C. Spain, across Portugal to Atlantic oc., at Oporto, len. 500 mi.; # 41:5 N, 8:25 W.

Dover (dō′ver), spt. city, Kent, S. E. Eng., pop. 41; # 51:8 N, 1:18 E. — tn., S. E. New Hampshire, pop. 15; # 43:12 N, 70:55 W. — tn., N. C. New Jersey, pop. 10; # 40:55 N, 74:35 W. — tn., C. Del., state *, pop. 6; # 39:10 N, 75:33 W. — strait bet. S. E. Eng. and N. W. Fr., least width, 20 mi.; # 51 N, 1:30 E.

Down (doun), the S. E. County of N. Ireland, area 0.9, pop. 204, * Downpatrick; # 54:20 N, 6 W.

Downs (dounz), low ridges, S. Eng., N. Downs in Kent, S. Downs in Sussex and Hampshire, W. Downs in Dorset and Wiltshire. — roadstead bet. Godwin Sands and Kent, S. E. Eng.; naval battles, 1639, 1666; # 51:15 N, 1:30 E.

Drakensberg (drä′kenz-bérg) or **Kwathlamba** (kwät-läm′bä), mts., Natal and Cape prov., S. E. Africa, length 700 mi., summit, 10,988 ft.; # 26:30 S, 30 E.

Drama (drä′mä), *anc.* Drabescus, tn., N. E. Greece, pop. 15; # 41:8 N, 24:10 E.

Drammen (dräm′men), spt. city, S. E. Norway, 20 mi. S. W. of Oslo, pop. 26; # 59:44 N, 10:12 E.

Drau (drou), see **Drave**.

Drave (drä′ve), riv., E. Trentino prov., Italy, E. to Danube riv., len. 450 mi.; # 45:30 N, 18:55 E.

Drente (dren′te) or **Drenthe**, prov., E. Neth., area 1, pop. 221, * Assen; # 52:50 N, 6:40 E.

Dresden (drez′den), city on Elbe riv., * of Sachsen (Saxony), S. Ger., pop. 608; scientific and musical instruments; # 51:3 N, 13:45 E. — a surrounding div. of E. Sachsen, area 1.7, pop. 1,326.

Driftless Area (drift′les ā′rē-ȧ), region, S. W. Wis. and adjacent parts of Minn., Iowa, and Ill., which were not covered by the glacier; rugged and lacking glacial drift.

(variable) ḍ as d or j, ṣ as s or sh, ṭ as t or ch, ẓ as z or zh; o, F. cloche; ü, F. menu; ċh, Sc. loch; ṅ, F. bonbon; ′, primary accent; ″, secondary accent; †, obsolete; <, from; +, and; =, equals. See also lists at beginning of book.

Drin (drēn), *anc.* Drilo, riv., S. W. Yugoslavia, across Albania to Adriatic sea, len. 180 mi.; # 41:45 N, 19:30 E.

Drina (drē'nä), *anc.* Drinus, riv., Montenegro, N. to Sava riv., len. 160 mi.; # 44:50 N, 19:17 E.

Drogheda (droch'e-dä), spt., Louth County, N. E. C. Ireland, pop. 13; convents; battles 1649, 1690; # 53:45 N, 6:21 W.

Drohobycz (drō'hō-büch), city, Galicia, S. E. Poland, pop. 35; # 49:23 N, 23:28 E.

Drôme (drōm), riv., E. trib. of Rhône riv., len. 60 mi.; # 44:45 N, 4:45 E. — dept., S. E. C. Fr., area 2.5, pop. 264, * Valence, pop. 20; # 44:40 N, 5:10 E.

Dry Tortugas (drī tôr-tö'g̣ạz), ten isls., W. of Key West, Fla.; # 24:40 N, 82:50 W.

Dublin (dub'lin), county and city on Dublin Bay, E. C. Ireland, * of State of Ireland, pop. with suburbs, 450; Univ. College and Trinity College; # 53:20 N, 6:15 W.

Du Bois (dū bois), tn., N. W. C. Pa., pop. 12; # 41:10 N, 78:45 W.

Dubuque (dū-būk'), city, N. E. Iowa, on Mississippi riv., pop. 44; college; # 42:30 N, 90:40 W.

Dudley (dud'li), suburb of Birmingham, S. W. C. Eng., pop. 58; # 52:31 N, 2:10 W.

Duero (dö-ā'rō), see **Douro.**

Duisburg (dö'is-bûrch), city, junction Ruhr and Rhine rivs., W. Ger., pop. 272; greatest river port in Europe; hardware; # 51:28 N, 6:45 E.

Duluth (dū-lôth'), city, N. E. Minn., pop. 101; port at W. end of Lake Superior; # 46:47 N, 92:6 W.

Dumbarton (dum-bär'ton), county, W. C. Scotland, area 0.2, pop. 148, and its *, a spt. 15 mi. W. of Glasgow, pop. 23; # 55:57 N, 4:31 W.

Dumfries (dum-frēs'), county, S. C. Scotland, area 1, pop. 73, and its *, pop. 16; # 55:6 N, 3:36 W.

Düna (dü'nä) or **Western Dvina**, riv., W. Russia to Gulf of Riga, Latvia, len. 600 mi.; # 57 N, 24 E.

Dünaburg (dü'nä-bûrch), see **Dvinsk.**

Duncansbay Head (dung'kạnz-bā hed), N. E. Cape, N. Scotland; # 58:40 N, 3 W.

Dundalk (dun-dâk'), spt. on Dundalk Bay, * of Louth County, N. E. Irish Free State, pop. 13; # 54 N, 6:29 W.

Dundee (dun-dē'), spt. city, C. E. Scotland, pop. 170; # 56:30 N, 2:58 W.

Dunedin (dun-ē'din), spt. city, S. E. S. Island, New Zealand, pop. 76; univ.; # 45:45 S, 170:30 E.

Dunfermline (dun-fèrm'lin), city, Fife, S. E. Scotland, pop. 41; # 56:5 N, 3:28 W.

Dunkirk (dun'kèrk), *Fr.* **Dunkerque**, spt. city, ext. N. Fr., pop. 39; # 51 N, 2:28 E. — city, S. W. New York, pop. 18; # 42:30 N, 79:22 W.

Dunmore (dun-mōr'), a N. E. suburb of Scranton, N. E. Pa., pop. 23; # ab. 41:30 N, 75:30 W.

Dunnet Head (dun'et hed), N. extremity of Great Britain; # 58:40 N, 3:30 W.

Dunoon (dun-ön'), spt. 25 mi. W. of Glasgow, Scotland, pop. 15; # 55:57 N, 4:56 W.

Duquesne (dū-kān'), suburb of Pittsburgh, Pa., pop. 21; # 40:22 N, 79:57 W.

Durango (dö-räng'gō), state, W. C. Mex., area 42, pop. 339, and its *, pop. 32; # 24 N, 104:40 W.

Durazzo (dö-rät'sō), *anc.* Epidamnus or Dyrrhachium, spt. W. C. Albania, pop. 5; # 41:25 N, 19:25 E.

Durban (dèr'ban), spt., Natal, Union of S. Africa, pop. 146, (57 whites); # 29:50 S, 30:55 E.

Düren (dü'ren), city, 23 mi. S. W. of Köln, Rheinland, W. Ger., pop. 37; # 50:48 N, 6:29 E.

Durham (dur'ạm), county, N. E. Eng., area 1, pop. 1,479, and its *, pop. 18; cathedral; Univ. of Durham; dual purpose cattle; # 54:47 N, 1:34 W. — city, N. C. N. Car., pop. 60; Duke Univ.; # 36 N, 78:50 W. — tn., S. E. New Hampshire, pop. 1; State Univ.; # 43:8 N, 70:53 W.

Durlach (dúr'läch), an E. suburb of Karlsruhe, Baden, S. W. Ger., pop. 18; # 49:2 N, 8:28 E.

Düsseldorf (düs'sel-dôrf), city on Rhine riv., * of Westfalen (Westphalia), pop. 429; hardware; # 51:14 N, 6:45 E.

Dutch Borneo (duch bôr'ne-ō), S. E. part of isl. of Borneo, area 207, pop. 1,625, * Banjermasin, pop. 52; # 0:0, 115 E.

Dutch East Indies (duch ēst in'diz), colonies of Netherlands, Malaysia, area 764, pop. 49,351, * Batavia, pop. 437; # 5 N, 120 E.

Dutch New Guinea (duch nū gin'i), W. half of Papua, area 161, pop. 195; # 3 S, 136 E.

Dutch West Indies, six isls. (largest, Curaçao), and Surinam or Dutch Guiana, S. America, area 55, pop. 190; # (isls.) 13 N, 69 W.

Dvina (dvē-nä'), **Dwina** or **Düna**, riv., W. C. Russia across Latvia to Gulf of Riga, len. 600 mi. (often called Düna or W. Dvina; # 57 N, 24 E. — riv., N. C. Russia to White sea, len. 1,000 mi.; # 64:15 N, 41:50 E.

Dvinsk (dvēnsk), former name of **Daugavpils**, city, S. Latvia, pop. 45; # 56 N, 26:30 E.

Dykh-tau (dich-tou'), mt. pk., C. Caucasus range, el. 17,054 ft.; # 43:5 N, 43:15 E.

E

Ealing (ē'ling), a W. suburb of London, S. E. Eng., pop. 68; # 51:30 N, 0:19 W.

Earth, The, or **The World.** Third planet from sun, mean distance 93 mil. mi.; diameter (without atmosphere), polar 7,899.964 mi.; equator 7,926.687 mi.; area, 196,940 (water ab. 139,685; land 57,255); pop. est. 2,127,000.

East Africa, British, see **Kenya, Tanganyika, Uganda.**

East Anglia (ēst ang'gli-ạ), anc. div. S. E. Eng., N. E. of London, modern Norfolk and Suffolk; # 52:30 N, 1 E.

Eastbourne (ēst'bèrn), spt. city, E. Sussex, S. E. Eng., pop. 62; # 50:48 N, 0:15 E.

East Cape (ēst kāp), E. extremity of Asia; # 66 N, 170 W. — E. point of N. Isl., New Zealand; # 37:30 S, 178:30 E.

East Chicago (ēst shi-kä'gō), lakeport city, N. W. Ind., pop. 55; # 41:38 N, 87:29 W.

East China Sea (ēst chī'nạ sē), part of Pacific oc., E. of C. China, bet. it and S. Japan; # 30 N, 126 E.

East Cleveland (ēst klēv'lạnd), an E. suburb of Cleveland, O., pop. 39; # 41:32 N, 81:35 W.

Easter Island (ēs'tèr ī'lạnd), isl. in S. Pacific oc., 2,000 mi. W. of Chile; to Chile; great stone images; # 27:30 S, 109:30 W.

Eastern Ghats (ēs'tèrn gâts), range along E. margin of Deccan plateau; # 17 N, 81 E.

East Flanders (ēst flan'dèrz), prov., N. W. Belgium, area 1.2, pop. 1,108, * Ghent, pop. 164; # 51 N, 3:45 E.

East Ham (ēst ham), suburb of London, Eng., pop. 146; # 51:32 N, 0:3 E.

East Indies (ēst in'diz), several archipelagoes, N. of Australia, and E. of Indo-China; Malaysia; sometimes also loosely to Indo-China; # 5 N, 122 E.

East Liverpool (ēst liv'èr-pöl), city, E. Ohio, on Ohio riv.; pop. 24; pottery; # 40:40 N, 80:38 W.

East London (ēst lun'dọn), spt. city, cape prov., S. E. Africa, pop. 35 (20 white); # 33:2 S, 27:55 E.

East Lothian (ēst lō'thi-ạn) or **Haddington,** county, S. E. Scotland, area 0.2, pop. 47, * Haddington, pop. 4; # 56:55 N, 2:45 W.

Easton (ēs'tọn), city, E. C. Pa., pop. 34; Lafayette College; # 40:42 N, 75:10 W.

East Orange (ēst or'ạnj), city, N. E. New Jersey, pop. 69, a W. suburb of Newark; phonographs; # 40:46 N, 74:13 W.

East Providence (ēst prov'i-dẹns), suburb of Providence, R. I., pop. 32; # 41:51 N, 71:21 W.

East Prussia (ēst prush'ä), *Ger.* **Östpreussen,** prov., Prussia, N. E. Ger., area 14.9, pop. 2,270, * Königsberg, pop. 266; # 54 N, 20:30 E.

East Riding, York (ēst rīd'ing), administrative county, Yorkshire, N. E. Eng., area 1.1, pop. 461, * Beverley and Hull; # 53:55 N, 0:30 W.

East River (ēst riv'èr), W. portion of Long Isl. Sound, New York City; # 40:42 N, 74 W.

East St. Louis (ēst sänt lö'is or lö'i), city, S. W. Ill., pop. 76; across the Mississippi riv. from St. Louis; # 38:37 N, 90:8 W.

East Youngstown (ēst yungz'toun), suburb of Youngstown, N. E. Ohio, pop. 16; # 41:5 N, 80:40 W.

Eau Claire (ō klār), city, N. W. C. Wis., pop. 31; # 44:35 N, 91:25 W.

Eberswalde (ā'bèrz-väl-dè), city, 28 mi. N. E. of Berlin, Ger., pop. 29; # 52:50 N, 13:49 E.

Ebro (a'brō), *anc.* Iberius, riv., C. N. Spain to Mediterranean sea, len. 470 mi.; # 40:40 N, 0:40 E.

Eccles (ek'lz), a W. suburb of Manchester, W. C. Eng., pop. 45; # 53:29 N, 2:20 W.

Ecuador (ek'wạ-dor, *Sp.* ā-kwä-ᵺHŌr'), republic of N. W. S. America, area 118–171, pop. ab. 2,757, * Quito, pop. 118; # 2 S, 76 W.

Edam (ē'dam), spt., E. N. Holland prov., Neth., pop. 7; cheese; # 52:32 N, 5:3 E.

Eddystone (ed'i-stọn), famous light on rock in English Channel, S. E. of Cornwall, Eng., # 50:10 N, 4:15 W.

Ede (ā'dẹ), city, Gelderland, C. Neth., pop. 25; # ab. 52:5 N, 5:40 E.

Eden (ē'dẹn), riv., Westmorland to head of Solway Firth, N. W. Eng., len. 70 mi.; # 54:57 N, 3 W.

Edgecumbe (ej'kum), active volcano and cape near Sitka, Alaska; # 57:3 N, 135:50 W.

Edinburgh (ed'n-bur-ọ), city, S. E. Scotland, its *, pop. 428; castle; Univ. of Edinburgh; # 55:55 N, 3:12 W.

Edmonton (ed'mọn-tọn), a N. suburb of London, Eng., pop. 70; # 51:36 N, 0:4 W. — city, S. C. Alberta, its *, pop. 86; Univ. of Alberta; # 53:40 N, 113:30 W.

Edward (ed'wạrd), lake, C. Africa, len. 50 mi.; # 1 S, 29:40 E.

Edwards (ed'wạrds), plateau, S. W. Texas; goats; #.31 N, 102 W.

Eggischhorn (eg'ish-hôrn), mt. pk., S. C. Switz., el. 9,626 ft.; famous for its view; # 46:26 N, 8:7 E.

Egmont (eg'mont), vol. peak, S. W. N. Isl., New Zealand, el. 8,260 ft.; # 39:3 S, 173:50 E.

Egypt (ē'jipt), independent state, N. E. Africa, area 350, (fertile area 12); pop. 13,400, * Cairo; # 26 N, 29 E.

Eifel (ī'fel), volcanic region, S. Rheinland, S. W. Ger.; # 50:10 N, 6:30 E.

Eindhoven (īnd'hō-vẹn), city, N. Brabant, S. C. Neth., pop. 56; # 51:26 N, 5:28 E.

Eire (ār'ẹ), Irish name for State of Ireland.

Eisenach (ī'zẹn-äċh), city, N. W. Thuringia, S. C. Ger., pop. 43; # 50:58 N, 10:17 E.

Eisleben (īs'lā-bẹn), city, Sachsen prov., 39 mi. W. N. W. of Leipzig, pop. 24; birthplace of Luther; # 51:32 N, 11:33 E.

Ekaterinburg or **Yekaterinburg** (ye-kä″tye-rẹn-búrċh'), prov., area 61, pop. 1,949. — city, its *, E. slope Ural mts., C. E. Russia, pop. 52; univ.; # 57:5 N, 60:30 E.

Ekaterinodar (ye-kä″tye-rē-no-där'), city on Kuban riv., near Sea of Azov, S. E. Russia, pop. 90; univ.; # 45:2 N, 39 E.

Ekaterinoslav (ye-kä″tye-rē-no-släf'), prov., C. Ukraine, area 11, pop. 1,702. — city, its *, on Dnieper riv., pop. 180; # 48:28 N, 35 E.

Elam (ē'lam), *anc.* country, S. Persia, * Susa; # 32 N, 48 E.

Elba (el'bä), isl. bet. Corsica and Italy, area .08, pop. 30; Livorno prov., Tuscany; # 42:46 N, 10:15 E.

Elbe (el'bẹ), riv., Bohemia, N. to North sea near Hamburg, Ger., len. 700 mi.; # 53:50 N, 9 E.

Elberfeld (el'bèr-felt), city, on Wupper riv., N. W. Ger., pop. 165; adjoins Barmen; laces; cottons; # 51:15 N, 7:5 E.

Elbert (el'bèrt), mt., highest peak in Colo., el. 14,420 ft.; 39 N, 106:25 W.

Elbing (el'bing), spt. city, N. Frisches Haff, E. Prussia, N. E. Ger., pop. 67; # 54:13 N, 18:18 E.

Elbrus (el-brös'), mt., W. Caucasus, el. 18,468 ft., highest in Europe; # 43:15 N, 42:25 E.

Elburz (el-börz'), mt. range, N. Persia, S. Coast of Caspian sea, summit, Mt. Demavend, el. 18,606 ft.; # 36 N, 51:30 E.

El Capitán (el käp-i-tän'), pk., ext. W. Texas, el. 9,020 ft.; # ab. 31:50 N, 104:50 W. — pk. with cliff 3,300 ft. high, Yosemite Valley, Calif.; # 37:45 N, 119:30 W.

Eldorado (el-dō-rä'dō), tn., S. E. Kansas, pop. 10; # 37:49 N, 96:51 W.

Elephant Butte (el'ẹ-fạnt būt), butte, S. W. New Mex., dam and irrigation reservoir, latter 40 mi. long, 2,600,000 cu. ft., 2½ times Assuan, Egypt, reservoir; # 31:10 N, 107:3 W.

Elets or **Yelets** (ye-lyets'), city, Orel prov., S. C. Russia, pop. 57; # 52:45 N, 38:37 E.

Elgin (el'jin), city, N. E. Ill., on Fox riv., pop. 38; watches; # 42:3 N, 88:22 W.

Elginshire (el'gin-shèr), see **Moray.**

Elgon (el'gon), active volcano, S. E. Uganda, C. Africa, el. 14,146 ft.; # 1:10 N, 35:10 E.

El Haza or **El Hasa** (el hä'za), region, former kingdom, C. E. Arabia, bordering Persian Gulf; # 26 N, 50 E.

Elisavetgrad (ye-lē'sạ-vyet-grät'), city, C. Ukraine, S. W. Russia, pop. 72; # 48:32 N, 32:18 E.

Elisavetpol (ye-lē'sạ-vyet-pol'y'), city, C. Azerbaijan republic, Transcaucasia, pop. 63; # 40:43 N, 46:20 E.

Elizabeth (ē-liz'ạ-bẹth), city, N. E. New Jersey, near New York City, pop. 110; # 40:40 N, 74:13 W.

Elk (elk), mt. range, W. C. Colo., highest, Castle pk., el. 14,259 ft.; # 39 N, 106:50 W.

Elkhart (elk'härt), city, N. C. Ind., pop. 33; musical instruments; # 41:40 N, 85:58 W.

Ellesmere (elz'mēr), isl., Arctic oc., W. of N. Greenland, area 40, # 80 N, 80 W.

Ellice (el'is), isls., subequatorial C. Pacific oc., area 0.01, pop. 4; part of Br. colony of Gilbert and Ellice isls.; # 9 S, 175 E.

Ellis Island (el'lis ī'lạnd), immigrant examination station, Upper New York harbor; # 40:42 N, 74:3 W.

Elmira (el-mī'rạ), city, C. S. New York, pop. 45; college; reformatory; # 42:5 N, 76:50 W.

El Misti (el mēs'tē), prominent vol. in S. Peru, el. 19,200 ft.; # 16:16 S, 71:30 W.

El Paso (el pä'sō), city, ext. W. Texas, on Rio Grande riv., pop. 97; # 31:50 N, 106:30 W.

Elster (el'stèr), riv., Erzgebirge to Saale riv., past Leipzig and Halle; # 51:32 N, 11:49 E.

Elwood (el'wud), tn., C. Ind., pop. 11; kitchen cabinets; # 40:17 N, 85:52 W.

Ely (ē'li), isl. county, S. E. C. Eng., area 0.4, pop. 74, and its *; old castle; # 52:25 N, 0:15 E. — tn., W. Nev.; smelters; # 39:20 N, 114:50 W.

Elyria (ē-lir'i-ạ), city, N. C. Ohio, pop. 25; # 41:22 N, 82:8 W.

Emden (em'dẹn), spt., Hannover, Prussia, N. W. Ger., pop. 28; # 53:22 N, 7:10 E.

Emerald Isle (em'ẹ-rạld īl), see **Ireland.**

Emilia (ā-mēl'ē-ä), dept., N. Italy, area 8.6, pop. 3,033; * Bologna, pop. 211; # 44:35 N, 10:10 E.

Emmen (em'ẹn), city, Drenthe prov., N. E. Neth., pop. 44; # 52:46 N, 6:53 E.

Emporia (em-pō'ri-ạ), tn., E. C. Kans., pop. 13; college; # 38:30 N, 96:15 W.

Ems (emz), riv., N. W. Ger., Westphalia to estuary on N. sea, len. 200 mi.; # 53:20 N, 7:15 E. — resort tn., near Koblenz, S. W. Ger., pop. 7; # 50:20 N, 7:40 E.

Enderby (en'dèr-bi), isl., Antarctic oc., # 67 S, 50 E.

Endicott (en'di-kọt), tn., S. C. New York, pop. 18; # ab. 42:4 N, 76:5 W. — mt. range, N. Alaska; # 68 N, 149 W.

Enfield (en'fēld), a N. suburb of London, Eng., pop. 61; rifles; # ab. 51:40 N, 0:5 W.

Engadine (en-gä-dēn'), valley of Inn riv., E. Switz.; len. 50 mi.; resorts; # 46:40 N, 10 E.

England (ing'glạnd), *anc.* Albion, div. of British Empire, all of isl. of Great Britain except Scotland and Wales, area 51, pop. 37,794, * London, pop. 4,483, with suburbs, pop. 8,655; # 52:40 N, 1 W.

England and Wales, administrative unit of United Kingdom, area 58, pop. (1924), 38,747.

Englewood (eng'gl-wud), a New Jersey suburb of New York City, pop. 19; # 40:55 N, 74 W; — a ward, former suburb, S. Chicago, Ill.; # 41:47 N, 87:36 W.

English Channel (ing'glish chan'ẹl), part of Atlantic oc., bet. England and France; 20 to 100 mi. wide; # 50 N, 1 W.

English Lake District (lāk dis'trikt), region, Cumberland and Westmorland, N. W. Eng.; # 54:30 N, 3 W.

Enid (ē'nid), city, N. W. Okla., pop. 28; oil refineries; Phillips Univ.; # 36:26 N, 97:52 W.

Enns (ens), riv., W. C. Austria to Danube riv., len. 160 mi.; # 48:15 N, 14:30 E.

Enos (ā'nōs), spt. on Gulf of Enos near mouth of Maritz riv., S. W. European Turkey, pop. 7; # 40:43 N, 26:5 E.

Enschede (en'skạ-dẹ), city, E. Overyssel, E. C. Neth., pop. 44; # 52:15 N, 6:50 E.

Entebbe (en-teb'e), tn. on N. shore of Lake Victoria, * of Uganda, Africa, pop. 6; # 0:5 N, 32:25 E.

Entre Ríos (en'trä rē'ōs), prov., N. E. Argentina, bet. Paraná and Uruguay rivs., area 29, pop. 531; * Paraná, pop. 36; # 33 S, 59 W. — (en'tre rē'ush), tn., Minas Geraes State, Brazil, pop. 29; # 20:47 S, 44:23 W.

Épernay (ā-per-nä), a N. suburb of Paris, Fr., pop. 22; # 49:2 N, 3:55 E.

Ephesus (ef′e-sus), ancient city, 35 mi. S. of Smyrna, Asia Minor; ruins; # 37:58 N, 27:18 E.

Épinal (ā-pē-nàl), city, ext. E. Fr., * of Vosges dept., pop. 30; # 48:10 N, 6:30 E.

Epirus (ē-pī′rus), dept., N. W. Greece, area 3.2, pop. 214, * Yannina; # 39:15 N, 21 E.

Epsom (ep′sọm), tn., 14 mi. S. of London, Eng., pop. 19; races; # 51:20 N, 0:16 W.

Erebus (er′ē-bus), vol. near Antarctica, el. 13,370 ft.; # 77:30 S, 167 E.

Erfurt (er′fûrt), city, S. Prussia, S. C. Ger., pop. 135; # 51 N, 11:2 E.

Erie (ē′ri), one of Great Lakes bet. Ontario and Ohio–New York, len. 239 mi., area 10, el. 573 ft.; # 42 N, 81 W. — city, N. W. Pa., on Lake Erie, pop. 117; # 42:8 N, 80:5 W. — county, W. New York, area 1, pop. 798 (1940), * Buffalo; # 42:50 N, 78:40 W.

Erie Canal (ē′ri kạ-nal′), canal, Hudson riv., at Albany, New York, to Lake Erie at Buffalo, 363 mi., completed 1825; very important for four decades; rebuilt, completed 1916.

Erie System, R.R., New York, Buffalo, Chicago, total mileage, 2,687.

Erin (ē′rin; er′in), see **Ireland.**

Eritrea (ā-rē-trā′ä), an Italian possession in N. E. Africa, on the Red sea, area 46, pop. est. 406, * Asmara; # 15 N, 40 E.

Erivan (er-i-vän′), city, E. Asia Minor, * of Armenian Soviet Republic, pop. 90; # 40:15 N, 44:35 E.

Erjias (ēr-jē′ạs), see **Argæus.**

Erlangen (er′läng-ẹn), city, 10 mi. N. of Nürnberg, Bayern (Bavaria), S. W. Ger., pop. 29; univ.; # 49:33 N, 11 E.

Errigal (er-i-gôl′), pk., Donegal, N. W. Ireland, el. 2,486 ft., # 55 N, 8:10 W.

Erzerum or **Erzeroum** (erz-röm′), prov., E. C. Asiatic Turkey, area 19, pop. 301, and its *, pop. ab. 30; # 39:50 N, 41:10 E.

Erzgebirge (ärts′gẹ-bir″gè), range, S. Saxony and N. W. Czechoslovakia; highest 4,080 ft.; # 50:30 N, 13 E.

Escanaba (es-kạ-nô′bä), tn., N. pen. of Michigan, pop. 15; copper; # 45:45 N., 87:3 W.

Escaut (es-kō), Fr. name of Scheldt riv.

Esch (esh), mining center, N. Duchy of Luxemburg, pop. 21; # 49:56 N, 5:56 E.

Eschweiler (esh′vī-lèr), city, Rhein prov. W. Ger., pop. 26; # 50:48 N, 6:15 E.

Eskilstuna (esk′il-stö-nä), city, S. E. Sweden, pop. 30; # 59:16 N, 16:30 E.

Eskishehr (es′ki-shehr′), anc. Douglæam, city, Brusa, W. Turkey in Asia, pop. 40; meerschaum; # 39:44 N, 30:30 E.

España (es-pän′yä), Spanish name for Spain.

Espirito Santo (es-pē′rē-tọ sän′tọ), state of E. Brazil, area 17, pop. 457, * Victoria, pop. ab. 10; # 20 S, 41 W.

Essen (es′ẹn), city, Ruhr riv., near Rhine, N. W. Ger., pop. 466; steel; # 51:25 N, 6:58 E.

Essendon (es′ẹn-dọn), suburb of Melbourne, Australia, pop. 35; # 37:46 S, 144:54 E.

Essequibo (es-ā-kē′bō), riv., S. Br. Guiana, N. Atlantic oc., len. 550 mi.; # 6:30 N, 58:45 W.

Essex (es′eks), county, S. E. Eng., area 1.5, pop. 1,468, * Chelmsford; # 51:44 N, 0:30 E.—county, N. E. New Jersey, area 0.13, pop. 837 (1940), * Newark; # 40:46 N, 74:20 W.

Esslingen (es′ling-ẹn), city, 10 mi. E. of Stuttgart, S. W. Ger., pop. 40; # 48:45 N, 9:15 E.

Estes Park (es′tiz), summer resort, E. of Rocky Mt. National Park, N. C. Colo.; # ab. 40:25 N, 105:30 W.

Esthonia (es-thō′ni-ä), form of **Estonia.**

Estonia (es-tō′ni-ä), officially **Eesti Wabariik**, republic on Baltic Sea and Gulf of Finland, area 17, pop. 1,111, * Tallinn (Reval), pop. 130; # 58:45 N, 26 E.

Estremadura (es-trä-mä-dōō′rä), region, S. W. Spain, former prov., including provs. of Cáceres and Badajoz; # 39:30 N, 6 W. — (esh-trä-mä-dö′rä) prov., W. C. Portugal, ar. 6.9; pop. 1,505, * Lisbon, pop. 486; # 39 N, 8:40 W.

Etah (ē′tä), vil., N. W. Greenland, most N. tn. in W. hemisphere; # 78:20 N, 72:42 W.

Ethiopia (ē-thi-ō′pi-ä), official English name of Abyssinia.

Etna (et′nạ), active vol., E. Sicily, el. 10,758 ft.; # 37:5 N, 14:55 E.

Eton (ē′tọn), tn., Buckinghamshire, S. C. Eng., pop. 3; Eton College; # 51:30 N, 0:36 W.

Etruria (ē-trö′ri-ạ), anc. country of Italy, now Tuscany.

Ettrick (et′rik), riv., Selkirkshire, S. E. Scotland to Yarrow riv., through famous forest, len. 32 mi.; # 55:40 N, 3 W.

Eubœa (ū-bē′ạ), or **Euripos**, isl., len. 110 mi., E. C. Greece; with C. Greece, a dept., area 1.6, pop. 1,125, * Chalkis; # 38:30 N, 24 E.

Euganean (ū-gä′nẹ-ạn), range of hills, W. Padua prov., Venetia, N. E. Italy, height 1,890 ft.; # 45:20 N, 11:30 E.

Eugene (ū-jēn′), tn., W. C. Ore., pop. 21; State Univ.; # 44:2 N, 123:4 W.

Eupen (oi′pẹn) **and Malmédy** (màl-mä-dē), prov., ext. E. Belgium, German till 1919, area 0.4, pop. 59, * Eupen, pop. 15; # 50:25 N, 6:10 E.

Euphrates (ū-frā′tēz), riv., Armenia, Asia Minor to Persian Gulf, len. 1,700 mi.; # 30 N, 48:20 E.

Eurasia (ū-rā′shiạ), Europe and Asia.

Eure (èr), riv. and dept., N. C. Fr., area 2.3, pop. 303, * Evreux; # 49:15 N, 1:15 E.

Eure-et-Loir (èr-ā-lwor), dept., N. C. Fr., area 2.3, pop. 251, * Chartres, pop. 24; # 48:30 N, 1:30 E.

Eureka (ū-rē′kạ), tn., N. W. Calif., pop. 17; # 40:47 N, 124:10 W.

Europe (ū′rọp), continent, W. part of Eurasia, area 3,754; pop. ab. 455,000; # 52 N, 25 E.

Euxine (ūk′sin), anc. name for Black sea.

Evanston (ev′ạn-stọn), city, N. E. Ill., on lake shore N. of Chicago, pop. 65; Northwestern Univ.; # 42:3 N, 87:41 W.

Evansville (ev′ạnz-vil), city, S. W. Ind., on Ohio riv., pop. 97; Evansville College; # 38 N, 87:35 W.

Everest (ev′ẽr-est), pk., E. Himalayas, el. est. 29,141 ft., highest in world; # 28 N, 87 E.

Everett (ev′ẽr-et), suburb of Boston, Mass., pop. 47; # 42:25 N, 71:3 W. — city, N. W. C. Wash., pop. 30; lumber; # 48 N, 122:12 W.

Everglades (ev′ẽr-glādz), swampy region S. Fla., area ab. 8, surrounding Lake Okechobee; # 27 N, 81 W.

Évora (ev′ọ-rä), dist., Alemtejo prov., S. C. Portugal, and its *, pop. 18; # 38:35 N, 7:52 W.

Exeter (ek′sẹ-tèr), city, S. C. Devon, S. W. Eng., pop. 60; # 50:42 N, 3:32 W.

Exmoor (eks′mör), region, N. Devon, S. W. Eng., " Lorna Doone"; # 51:10 N, 3:45 W.

Eyre (âr), salt lake, S. Australia, el. − 39 ft., len. 125 mi., area 4; # 28:30 S, 137:30 E. — broad pen., S. Australia; # 33 S, 136 E.

Ezel (ē′zel), isl., in Baltic sea, W. Estonia, len. 60 mi.; # 58:25 N, 22:45 E.

F

Fachan (fä-chän′) or **Fatshan** (fät-shän′), city, Kwangtung prov., S. E. China, near Canton, pop. est. 500; # 23:2 N, 113:10 E.

Faenza (fä-en′tsä), city, Emilia, N. E. C. Italy, pop. comm. 40; # 44:47 N, 11:50 E.

Faeroe (fä′rō) see **Faroe.**

Fairbanks (fâr′bangks), tn., C. Alaska on Tanana riv., pop. 3; # 64:45 N, 147:50 W.

Fairmont (fâr′mont), city, N. C. W. Va., pop. 23; # 39:30 N, 80:10 W.

Fairweather (fâr′wẹṯẖ-ẽr), mt. pk., S. E. Alaska, el. 15,292 ft.; # 58:55 N, 137:30 W. — cape, S. E. Alaska, # 58:55 N, 138 W.

Faiyum or **Fayum** (fī-öm′), prov. W. of Nile riv., in Middle Egypt, area 0.7, pop. 508, and a city therein, pop. 44; # 29:15 N, 30:47 E.

Falkirk (fâl′kèrk), city, midway bet. Glasgow and Edinburgh, pop. 34; # 56 N, 3:50 W.

Falkland (fâk′lạnd), group of 200 isls., W. S. Atlantic oc., British colony, area 6, pop. 3, * Stanley; # 52 S, 60 W.

Fall Line (fâl lïn), line bet. coastal plain and harder rocks to the inland in E. and S. E. U.S.A., marked by rapids or falls along streams; site of many cities, Trenton, Philadelphia, Baltimore, Richmond, Augusta, etc.

---

fat, fāte, fär, fàll, àsk, fāre; net, mē, hèr; pin, pīne; not, nōte, mōve, nôr; up, lūte, pùll; oi, oil; ou, out; (lightened) aviạry, ẹlect, agọny, intọ, ūnite; (obscured) errạnt, operä, ardẹnt, actọr, natūre; ch, chip; g, go; th, thin; ᴛʜ, then; y, you;

Fall River (fôl riv′ẽr), spt. city on Narragansett Bay, S. E. Mass., pop. 115; cottons; # 41:40 N, 71:10 W.

Falmouth (fal′muth), tn., a spt., S. W. Cornwall, S. W. Eng., pop. 13; # 50:7 N, 5:5 E.

Falster (fäl′stẽr), isl., S. E. Denmark, S. of Seeland, area 2, pop. 40; # 54:50 N, 12 W.

Farewell (fār-wel′⌒), cape, ext. S. Greenland, # 60 N, 44 W. — cape, New Zealand: # 40:30 S, 172:45 E.

Fargo (fär′gō), city, S. E. N. Dak., pop. 33; State Agri. College; Fargo College; # 46:50 N, 96:55 W.

Faribault (fãr′i-bō), tn., S. E. Minn., pop. 15; # 44:21 N, 93:18 E.

Faro (fä′rō), spt. city ext. S. Portugal, * of Algarve prov., pop. 13; # 37 N, 7:51 W.

Faroe (fä′rō), or **Faeroe**, group of isls., N. Atlantic oc., bet. Shetlands and Iceland, Danish, area 0.5, pop. 21, * Thorshavn, pop. 2; # 62 N, 7 W.

Farrell (far′ẽl), city, N. W. Pa., pop. 14; # 41:14 N, 80:30 W.

Farrukhabad (fur-ruk-ä-bäd′) or **Furruckabad**, city on Ganges riv., N. C. India, pop. 52; # 27:20 N, 79:35 E.

Fars (färs), *anc.* Persis, prov., S. W. Persia, pop. 1,700, * Shiraz, pop. 50; # 29 N, 52 E.

Farther India, E. India or Burma.

Fatshan (fät-shän′), see **Fachan.**

Fayetteville (fā-yet′vil), tn., N. W. Ark., pop. 8; State Univ.; # 36:4 N, 94:10 W.

Fayum, see **Faiyum.**

Fear (fēr), riv., S. E. N. Car., and cape, # 34:20 N, 78 W.

Feather River (feтн′ẽr riv′ẽr), riv., N. E. Calif., to Sacramento riv., len. 150 mi.; # 38:45 N, 121:35 W. — canyon in Sierra Mts., R.R. pass.

Federal Capital Territory, district containing the present capital of Australia, separated from New S. Wales, area 1, pop. 7, * Canberra, pop. 5; # 35:30 S, 149 E.

Fengtien (feng′tyen′), prov., S. E. Manchuria, pop. 10,000, * Mukden; # 41:30 N, 123 E.

Fens (fenz), marshy region about the head of The Wash, E. England; # 52:50 N, 0:10 W.

Ferencz József (fer′ents yō′zhef) or **Gerlsdorfer Spitze** (gerls′dôrf-ẽr shpit′se), summit of Carpathians, E. Czechoslovakia, el. 8,735 ft; # 49:10 N, 20:8 E.

Fergana (fer-gä′nä), former prov. of E. Russian Turkestan, area 55, pop. 2,000, * Tashkent; # 41 N, 69 E.

Fermanagh (fẽr-man′ȧ), the S. W. county of N. Ireland, area 0.7, pop. 62, * Enniskillen; # 54:15 N, 7:40 W.

Ferozepore (fē-rōz-pōr′), city, Punjab, N. W. India, pop. 54; # 31 N, 74:30 E.

Ferrara (fer-rä′rä), prov., Emilia, N. E. C. Italy, area 1, pop. 346, and its *, pop. 108; univ.; # 44:50 N, 11:35 E.

Ferrol, El (fer-rōl′), spt. city, Coruña, Galicia, N. W. Spain, pop. 31; arsenal; # 43:35 N, 8:15 W.

Fez (fez), city, N. E. Morocco, one of the *′s; pop. 125; # 34 N, 4:55 W.

Fezzan (fez-zän′), portion of Libya, including oases in the Sahara, N. Africa; # 27 N, 13 E.

Fife (fīf) or **Fifeshire**, county, S. E. Scotland, area 0.5, pop. 290, * Cupar; # 56:10 N, 3:10 W.

Fife Ness (fīf nes), pen., bet. Firths of Forth and Tay, E. Scotland; # 56:18 N, 2:35 W.

Fiji (fē′jē), Br. colony occupying 250 isls., S. W. Pacific oc., area 7, pop. 157, * Suva, pop. 2; # 17:45 S, 178 E.

Findlay (find′lȧ), city, N. W. Ohio, pop. 20; Findlay College; # 41:5 N, 83:39 W.

Fingal's Cave (fing′gȧlz kāv), see **Staffa.**

Finger Lakes, five long glacial lakes, S. C. New York, esp. Cayuga and Seneca; # 42:40 N, 76:50 W.

Finistère (fin-is-târ), dept., tip of Brittany, N. W. Fr., area 2.7, pop. 763, * Quimper; # 48:10 N, 4 W.

Finisterre (fin-is-târ′), cape, W. tip of N. Spain, # 42:50 N, 9:20 W.

Finland (fin′lȧnd), *Finnish* **Suomen Tasavalta** (swô′men tä′sȧ-väl-tȧ), republic, N. Europe, formerly prov., N. W. Russia, area 133, pop. 3,435, * Helsinki (Helsingfors), pop. 201; # 63 N, 27 E.

Finmarken (fin′mär-ken), the most N. prov. of Norway, area 19, pop. 44, * Hammerfest; # 70 N, 23 E.

Finsbury (finz′bẽ-ri), a borough of London, Eng., pop. 76; # 51:34 N, 0:6 W.

Finsteraarhorn (fin-ster-är′hôrn), mt. pk., S. W. Switz., summit of Bernese Alps, el. 14,026 ft.; # 46:32 N, 8:8 E.

Firenze (fē-ren′tsä), prov., Tuscany, N. C. Italy, area 1.9, pop. 982, and its *, *Eng.* Florence, pop. 254, on Arno riv.; # 43:46 N, 11:15 E.

Firozpur, see **Ferozepore.**

Firth of Clyde (fẽrth ov klīd), see **Clyde.**

Fitchburg (fich′bẽrg), city, N. C. Mass., pop. 42; # 42:35 N, 71:50 W.

Fitzroy (fits-roi′), riv., Queensland, Australia, Dividing range to Pacific oc. at Rockhampton, len. 180 mi.; # 23:30 S, 150:40 E. — riv., N. W. Australia to King Sound, len. 300 mi.; # 17:30 S, 123:30 E. — a N. suburb of Melbourne, Australia, pop. 35; # 37:46 S, 145 E.

Fiume (fē-ō′mā), prov., Venezia, N. E. Italy, pop. 85, and its *, a spt., pop. 45; # 45:21 N, 14:24 E.

Flagstaff, tn., N. C. Ariz., base of San Francisco Mts., pop. 5; el. 6,900 ft.; Lowell (astronomical) Observatory; # 35:10 N, 111:45 W.

Flanders, East (flan′dẽrz), prov., N. W. Belgium, area 1.2, pop. 1,108, * Ghent (Gand), pop. 164; # 51 N, 3:45 E.

Flanders, West, prov., ext. N. W. Belgium, area 1.1, pop. 852, * Bruges, pop. 53; # 51 N, 3 E.

Flathead (flat′hed), lake, N. W. Mont., 30 × 12 mi.; # 47:40 N, 114 W.

Flattery (flat′ẽr-i), cape, N. W. extremity of Wash., and the most W. point of U.S. mainland; # 48:28 N, 124:45 W.

Flensburg (flens′bûrch), spt., E. Jutland, N. Ger., pop. 64; # 54:45 N, 9:30 E.

Flinders (flin′dẽrz), isl., bet. Australia and Tasmania; # 40 N, 148 E. — low mts., S. E. S. Australia; # 31 S, 138:50 E.

Flint (flint), city, E. C. Mich., pop. 152; automobiles; # 43 N, 83:40 W.

Flintshire (flint′shẽr), county, N. E. Wales, area 0.3, pop. 106, * Mold; # 53:10 N, 3:15 W.

Florence (flor′ẽns), *It.* **Firenze,** *anc.* Florentia, city, Tuscany, N. Italy, pop. 254; # 43:46 N, 11:15 E. — tn., N. W. Ala., on Tennessee riv., pop. 15; Muscle Shoals; # 34:50 N, 87:50 W. — tn., E. C. S. Car., pop. 16; # 34:11 N, 79:47 W.

Flores (flō′res), isl., Dutch E. Indies, area 6, pop. 250; # 8:45 S, 121:30 E. — sea bet. Celebes and Flores; # 7 S, 122 E.

Florianopolis (flō″rē-á-nō′pō-lĕs, *Eng.* -nop′ō-lis) or **Desterro**, spt. city, * Santa Catharina, Brazil, pop. 41; 27:40 S, 48:30 W.

Florida (flor′i-dȧ), state, S. E. U.S.A., bet. Atlantic oc. and Gulf of Mexico, area 59, pop. 1,897, * Tallahassee, pop. 16, other cities: Jacksonville and Tampa, pop. 173 and 108, Miami, 172 (1940); # 30 N, 83 W.

Florida Keys (flor′i-dȧ kēz), chain of small isls., S. Fla. and E. of Key West; # 24:40 N, 81 W.

Florida Strait (flor′i-dȧ strāt), strait bet. Fla., and Bahamas and Cuba; # 25 N, 80 W.

Flushing (flush′ing) or **Vlissingen**, spt. city, ext. S. W. Neth., pop. 22; crossing to England; # 51:25 N, 3:32 E.

Fly (flī), riv., largest in Papua, C. to S. E., len. 600 mi.; # 8:15 S, 142 E.

Foggia (fod′jä), prov., Apulia, E. C. Italy, area 2.7, pop. 459, and its *, pop. 67; # 41:27 N, 15:34 E.

Folgefonden (fol′ge-fon-den), large snowfield, S. Norway, el. ab. 5,500 ft., feeds many glaciers; # 60 N, 7 E.

Folkestone (fōk′stǫn), spt. city on Strait of Dover, near Dover, S. E. Eng., pop. 34; # 51:7 N, 1:6 E.

Fond du Lac (fon dö lak), city, N. E. Wis., pop. 27; # 43:45 N, 88:25 W.

Fonseca (fōn-sā′kä), bay, C. America, touching Nicaragua, Honduras, and Salvador; U.S. naval base; # 13 N, 87:45 W.

Fontainebleau (fôn-tän-blō′), tn., 37 mi. S. E. of Paris, Fr., pop. 15; palace; # 48:24 N, 2:42 E.

Foochow (fō-chou′), spt. city, S. E. China, * of Fukien prov., pop. est. 321; # 26:15 N, 119:20 E.

Footscray (fùts′krā), a W. suburb of Melbourne, Australia, pop. 34; # 37:49 S, 144:53 E.

Foraker (fōr′ȧ-kẽr), mt. pk., S. C. Alaska, near Mt. McKinley, el. 17,000 ft.; # 62:45 N, 151:40 W.

Forest Park, a W. suburb of Chicago, Ill., pop. 15; # 41:52 N, 87:49 W.

Forfar (fôr′fär), county, E. C. Scotland, area 0.8, pop. 267, and its *, a spt., pop. 10; castle; # 56:38 N, 2:52 W.

(variable) ḍ as d or j, ş as s or sh, ţ as t or ch, ẓ as z or zh; o, F. cloche; ü, F. menu; ċh, Sc. loch; ṅ, F. bonbon; ′, primary accent; ″, secondary accent; †, obsolete; <, from; +, and; =, equals. See also lists at beginning of book.

Forlì (for-lē'), prov., Emilia, N. E. C. Italy, area 1.1, pop. 391, and its *, pop. 52; #44:13 N, 12:3 E.

Formosa (fôr-mō'sä), *Jap.* **Taiwan,** Japanese isl. near China, area 14, pop. 3,655; * Taihoku; #23:30 N, 121 E. — ter., ext. N. Argentina, area 41, pop. 24 and its *; #26:15 S, 58:6 W.

Forst (fôrst), city, Brandenburg, Prussia, N. Ger., pop. 36; #51:45 N, 14:38 E.

Fortaleza (fôr-tä-lā'zä), spt. city, E. Brazil, * of Ceará, pop. 143; #3:50 S, 38:30 W.

Fort Collins (fôrt kol'inz), tn., N. E. Colo., pop. 12; State Agricultural College; #40:34 N, 105:4 W.

Fort-de-France (fôr-dė-fräns), spt. city, * of Martinique, West Indies, pop. 26; #14:35 N, 61:5 W.

Fort Dodge (fôrt doj), city, N. W. C. Iowa, pop. 23; #42:30 N, 94:15 W.

Forth (fôrth), firth, N. E. Scotland, len. 50 mi.; #56:5 N, 3 W. — R.R. bridge near Edinburgh, Scotland, len. of central span, 1,700 ft., next to Quebec, longest in world.

Fort Madison (fôrt mad'i-sọn), tn., ext. S. E. Iowa, pop. 14; #40:40 N, 91:19 W.

Fort Monroe (fôrt mun-rō'), ft. at entrance to Hampton Roads, Va.; #37 N, 76:20 W.

Fort Scott (fôrt skot), tn., S. E. Kans., pop. 11; #37:50 N, 94:45 W.

Fort Smith (fôrt smith), city, W. C. Ark., pop. 37; #35:25 N, 94:25 W.

Fort Wayne (fôrt wän), city, N. E. Ind., pop. 118; #41:5 N, 85:10 W.

Fort William (fôrt wil'yạm), city, N. W. side of Lake Superior, Ont., pop. 21; wheat port; #48:20 N, 89:20 W.

Fort Worth (fôrt wẽrth), city, N. E. C. Texas, pop. 178; univ.; #32:45 N, 97:20 W.

Fostoria (fos-tō'ri-ạ), tn., N. W. Ohio, pop. 13; #41:10 N, 83:25 W.

Fotheringhay (foтн'ẽr-ing-gā), parish and castle, Northamptonshire, N. Eng.; #52:31 N, 0:26 W.

Foveaux (fō-vō'), strait bet. S. and Steward Isls., New Zealand; #46:30 S, 168 E.

Fowchow (fou-chou'), city, S. E. Szechwan prov., S. W. China, pop. 100; #29:40 N, 107:15 E.

Fox (foks), riv., S. E. Wis. to Green Bay, len. 250 mi.; #44:30 N, 88 W. — riv., S. E. Wis. S. to Illinois riv. at Ottawa, len. 220 mi.; #41:20 N, 88:50 W.

Foyers or **Fyers** (foi'ẽrz), small riv. to Lake Ness, N. Scotland, falls, 205 ft.; #57:16 N, 4:28 W.

Framingham (frā'ming-ham), tn., E. C. Mass., pop., twp. 23; #42:17 N, 71:25 W.

France (frans), republic, W. Europe, area 212.7, pop. 39,210, * Paris, pop. 2,906; second city, Marseille, pop. 586; #47 N, 3 E.

Franconia (frang-kō'ni-ạ), see **Mittelfranken, Oberfranken** and **Unterfranken.**

Frankenthal (fräng'kẹn-täl), city, Palatinate dist., Bavaria, S. W. Ger., pop. 24; #49:32 N, 8:21 E.

Frankfort (frangk'fọrt), tn., N. C. Ky., state *, pop. 11; #38:12 N, 84:55 W. — tn., C. Ind., pop. 14; #40:17 N, 86:35 W. — see **Frankfurt.**

Frankfurt (frängk'fúrt), city on Main riv., S. W. Ger., pop. 458; univ.; #50:8 N, 8:40 E. — city on Oder riv., E. C. Ger., pop. 69; #52:22 N, 14:30 E.

Franklin (frangk'lin), N. dist. of N. W. Territories of Canada, N. Isls. and pen., area 552; #69 N, 100 W. — tn., N. W. Pa., on Allegheny riv., pop. 10; #41:25 N, 79:50 W.

Franz Josef Land (fränts yō'zef länt), group of isls., Arctic oc., N. of E. Europe; #81 N, 60 E.

Fraser (frā'zẽr), riv., S. Br. Columbia to Puget Sound, len. 695 mi.; #49:12 N, 123:10 W.

Frederick (fred'ẽr-ik), tn., N. W. Md., pop. 16; Hood College; #39:25 N, 77:25 W.

Fredericton (fred'ẽr-ik-tọn), tn., S. C. New Brunswick, prov. *, pop. 8; Univ. of New Brunswick; #45:55 N, 66:40 W.

Frederiksberg (fred'ẽr-iks-bẽrg), a S. W. suburb of Copenhagen, Denmark, pop. 97; #55:42 N, 12:35 E.

Frederikshavn (fred'ẽr-iks-hä"vn), spt., N. E. Jutland, Denmark, pop. 9; #57:25 N, 10:30 E.

Fredrikstad (fred'rik-städ), spt., S. E. Norway, pop. 16; #59:12 N, 10:58 E.

Freeport (frē'pōrt), city, N. W. Ill., pop. 22; #42:22 N, 89:37 W. — tn., Nassau Co., New York, pop. 20; #40:38 N, 73:35 W.

Freetown (frē'toun), spt. city, * of Br. Sierra Leone, W. Africa, pop. 44; greatest spt. in W. Africa; coaling station; excellent harbor; #8:30 N, 13:15 W.

Freiberg (frī'berch), city, C. Sachsen (Saxony), S. Ger., pop. 34; #50:55 N, 13:22 E.

Freiburg (frī'bûrch), city, S. Baden, S. W. Ger., pop. 91; univ.; #48 N, 7:50 E. — see **Fribourg.**

Freital (frī'täl), suburb of Dresden, Sachsen (Saxony), S. Ger., pop. 36; #ab. 51 N, 13:45 E.

Fremantle (frē'man-tl), port suburb of Perth, W. Australia, pop. 18; #32:3 S, 115:45 E.

Fremont (frē-mont'), tn. N. W. Ohio, pop. 15; #41:20 N, 83:7 W. — tn., E. C. Neb., pop. 12; #41:30 N, 96:30 W.

French Equatorial Africa, comprises four colonies and a mandate, Gabun, area 122, pop. 1,300; Middle Congo, area 150, pop. 1,390; Ubangi-Shari, area 208, pop. 1,590; Chad Ter., area 502, pop. 2,090; Cameroon Mandate, area 166, pop. 1,500. Total area 1,149; pop. 7,870; #4 S, 17 E.

French India (french in'di-ạ), five small provs., coast of India, area 0.2, pop. 267; see **Chandernagore, Karikal, Mahé, Pondichéry** and **Yanaon.**

French Indo-China (in'dō-chī'nạ), Fr. possessions, S. E. Asia, area 274, pop. 19,983, * Hanoi, pop. 100; #15 N, 107 E.

French Oceania (ō-shẹ-an'i-ạ), numerous scattered isls., E. S. Pacific oc., area 1.5, pop. 32; * Papeete on Tahiti, pop. 5; 17 S, 148 W.

French West Africa and the **Sahara,** group of colonies in W. Africa. See **Dahomey, Guinea, Ivory Coast, Mauritania, Niger, Senegal, Sudan,** and **Volta.** Total area 1,800, total pop. 12,284; #18 N, 1 W.

French West Indies, area 1, pop. 522; see **Guadeloupe, Martinique, St.-Pierre;** #15 N, 62 W.

Fresno (fres'nō), city, S. C. Calif., pop. 61; normal school; raisins; #36:44 N, 119:46 W.

Fribourg (frē-bōr), canton, W. C. Switz., area 0.6, pop. 143, and its *, pop. 21; #46:49 N, 7:10 E.

Friedrichshain (frēd-richs-hīn'), an E. div. of Berlin, Ger., pop. 330; #52:31 N, 13:32 E.

Friendly Islands, see **Tonga.**

Friesland (frēz'lạnd) or **Vriesland,** prov., N. E. Neth., area 1.2, pop. 395, * Leeuwarden, pop. 46; #53:10 N, 5:50 E.

Frio (frē'ō), cape, prominent projection E. of Rio de Janeiro, Brazil; #23:1 S, 42:2 W.

Frisches Haff (frish'es häf), coastal lake, E. Prussia, N. E. Ger., len. 60 mi.; #54:30 N, 19:50 E.

Frisian Islands (friz'iạn i'lạndz), three lines of coastal isls., S. N. sea. —, N., off W. Jutland; #55 N, 8:30 E. —, E., off Germany and E. Neth.; #53:45 N, 7 E. —, W., off Zuider Zee; dairy cattle from the last; #53:20 N, 5 E.

Front Range (frunt rānj), E. range of Rocky Mts., in Colo. and Wyo.; #42 N, 106 W.

Fuchow (fö-chou'), see **Foochow.**

Fuego (fwä'gō), vol. mt., C. Guatemala, el. 12,500 ft.; #ab. 15 N, 90 W.

Fujisan (fö-jē-sän') or **Fujiyama** (fö"jē-yä'mä), vol. cone, near Tokyo, Japan, el. 12,395 ft.; #35:25 N, 138:45 E.

Fukien (fö-kē-en'), prov., S. E. coast of China, area 46, pop. est. 13,000, * Foochow, pop. est. 321; #26 N, 118 E.

Fukui (fö'kö-ē), inland city, W. C. Honshu isl., Japan, pop. 60; #36:3 N, 136:15 E.

Fukuoka (fö-kö-ō'kä), city, N. Kyushiu isl., Japan, pop. 146; #33:32 N, 130:27 E.

Fukushima (fö-kö-shē'mä), inland city, N. E. C. Honshu isl., Japan, pop. 41; #ab. 37:30 N, 140:30 E.

Fukuyama (fö-kö-yä'mä), city, S. W. Honshu, Japan, pop. 34; #34:30 N, 133:25 E.

Fulda (fúl'dä), a very old city on Fulda riv., Hessen-Nassau, Prussia, pop. 26; #50:33 N, 9:40 E.

Fulham (fúl'ạm), a S. W. borough of London, Eng., pop. 158; #ab. 51:29 N, 0:10 W.

Fulton (fúl'tọn), tn., N. W. C. New York, pop. 13; #43:19 N, 76:28 W.

Funchal (fön-shäl'), spt. city, * of Madeira Isls., pop. 60; winter resort; #32:38 N, 16:58 W.

Fundy (fun′di), bay, bet. Nova Scotia and New Brunswick, Canada; notable tides, sometimes 70 ft.; # 45 N, 66 W.

Fünfkirchen (fünf′kirch-ẹn), **Ipek** or **Pécs**, city, S. Hungary, pop. 40; univ.; now known as Pecs; # 46:5 N, 18: 13 E.

Furruckabad (fur-ruk-ä-bäd′), see **Farrukhabad**.

Fürstenwalde (fürs′tẹn-väl-dẹ), city; 30 mi. S. E. of Berlin, Ger., pop. 23; # 52:22 N, 14:4 E.

Fürth (fürt), city on Regnitz riv., near Nürnberg, S. W. Ger., pop. 73; # 49:28 N, 11 E.

Fusan (fö-sän′), spt. city, S. E. Korea, pop. 78 (Japanese pop. 35); # 35:5 N, 129 E.

Fyen (fün), **Fünen** or **Odense**, isl., C. Denmark, area 1.2, pop. 263, chief town, Odense, pop. 49; # 55:20 N, 10:30 E.

Fyne, Loch (fīn), arm of sea, Argyll, W. Scotland, len. 45 mi.; # 56 N, 5:25 W.

Fyzabad (fī-zä-bäd′), city on Ganges riv., C. N. India, pop. 57; # 26:45 N, 82:15 E.

G

Gabes (gä′bes), Mediterranean gulf, Tunis, N. Africa; # 34 N, 12 E.

Gabun (gä-bön′), colony, part of Fr. Congo, area 122, pop. 389, * Libreville, pop. 2; # 2 S, 12 W. — riv. in same.

Gadsden (gadz′dẹn), city, N. E. Ala., pop. 37; # 34 N, 86:5 W. — **Purchase**, strip, S. Ariz. and New Mex., area 29.7; purchased from Mexico, 1853; copper; # 32 N, 110 W.

Gaeta (gä-ā′tä), spt. on Gulf of Gaeta, N. Campania, S. Italy, pop. 5; cathedral; ancient resort; # 41:12 N, 13:35 E.

Gäfle (yev′lẹ), see **Gävle**.

Gainesville (gānz′vil), tn., N. C. Florida, pop. 14; State Univ.; # 29:40 N, 82:20 W. — tn., N. C. Ga.; pop. 10; Brenau College; # 34:18 N, 83:47 W.

Gairdner (gärd′nẹr), lake, S. Australia, len. 130 mi.; # 32 S, 131:40 E.

Galápagos (gä-lä′pä-gōs), group of isls., area 3, pop. 4; 600 mi. W. of coast, part of Ecuador; famous turtles; # 0:20 S, 91 W.

Galashiels (gal-ạ-shēlz′), tn., Selkirk co., S. E. Scotland, pop. 13; # 55:39 N, 2:48 W.

Galati (gä-läts′y′) or **Galatz** (gä′läts), city on lower Danube riv., Romania, pop. 74; # 45:30 N, 28 E.

Galatia (gạ-lā′shiạ), anc. Roman prov., C. Asia Minor; # 39:40 N, 34 E.

Galdhöpiggen (gȧl-hẹ-pē′yẹn), mt. pk., S. W. Norway, highest in N. Europe, el. 8,785 ft.; # 61:35 N, 8:10 E.

Galesburg (gālz′bẽrg), city, N. W. Ill., pop. 29; Knox and Lombard colleges; # 40:55 N, 90:25 W.

Galicia (gạ-lish′i̇ạ), former prov. ext. N. W. Spain, now divided into Coruña, Lugo, Orense and Pontevedra; # 41 N, 8 W. — former crownland, E. Austria, now in Poland and Romania; # 49:40 N, 19:10 E.

Galilee, Sea of, lake, N. E. Palestine, len. 14 mi., el. 682 ft. below sea level; # 32:50 N, 35:30 E.

Galle (gäl), spt. city, S. W. Ceylon, pop. 39; # 6:20 N, 80: 12 E.

Gallinas (gäl-yē′näs), cape, N. Colombia, the most N. point of S. America; # 12:30 N, 71:30 W.

Gallipoli (gäl-lēp′ō-lē), pen., S. E. Thrace, bordering Dardanelles (Hellespont), len. 50 mi.; # 40:28 N, 26:40 E.

Galloway (gal′ō-wā), region, ext. S. W. Scotland; Galloway cattle; # 55 N, 5:2 W.

Galt (gȧlt), tn., S. W. Ontario, pop. 13; # 43:20 N, 80:18 W.

Galveston (gal′ves-tọn), spt. city, S. E. Texas, on isl. bet. Galveston Bay and Gulf of Mexico, pop. 61; hurricane in 1900; # 29:18 N, 94:48 W.

Galway (gȧl′wā), county, W. Ireland, area 2.4, pop. 182, and its *, a spt. on Galway Bay; Univ. College; # 53:13 N, 9:2 W.

Gambia (gam′bi-ạ), Br. crown colony and protectorate of W. Africa, area 4 (colony, .004), pop. 240; * Bathurst; pop. 9. — riv., in same; len. 500 mi.; # 18:30 N, 16 W.

Gand (gäṅ), see **Ghent**.

Gandak (gun-dak′), riv., Himalayas of Nepal to Ganges at Patna, N. India; # 25:45 N, 85:15 E.

Ganges (gan′jēz), riv., Himalayas, N. India to Bay of Bengal, len. 1,500 mi.; # 23:20 N, 90:30 E.

Ganges-Brahmaputra Delta (gan′jēz-bräh-mạ-pö′trạ), delta, head of Bay of Bengal, area ab. 32; # 23 N, 89 E.

Gannett (gan′et), highest pk. in Wyo., Wind River Mts., el. 13,785 ft.; # 43:20 N, 109:40 W.

Gard (gär), dept., S. Fr., area 2.3, pop. 396, * Nîmes, pop. 83; # 4 N, 4:20 E.

Garda (gär′dä), lake, Lombardy, N. Italy, len. 35 mi.; # 45:45 N, 10:40 E.

Garden of the Gods, scenic area, C. Colo, near Manitou and Colorado Springs; # 38:52 N, 105 W.

Gardinas (gär-din′as), formerly **Grodno**, city, S. Lithuania, pop. 62; # 53:40 N, 23:40 E.

Gardner (gard′nẽr), tn., N. C. Mass., pop. twp. 20; # 42:35 N, 71:59 W.

Garfield (gär′fēld), city, N. E. New Jersey, pop. 28; # 40:53 N, 74:7 W.

Gargano (gär-gä′nō), prominent E. cape, C. Italy; "the spur," len. 30 mi.; # 41:50 N, 16 E.

Garhwal (gur-wäl′), native Indian state bordering Tibet, area 4, pop. 485, * Tehri; # 30:30 N, 79 E.

Garonne (gä-rôn), riv., C. Pyrenees, N. E. to Gironde, len. 350 mi.; # 45 N, 0:30 W.

Garonne, Haute, see **Haute-Garonne**.

Gary (gā′ri), lakeport city, N. W. Ind., pop. 112; steel; # 41:36 N, 87:20 W.

Gascony (gas′kọ-ni), region, S. W. Fr., ancient prov., * Auch; # 43:40 N, 0:35 E.

Gaspé (gȧs-pā), pen., bet. St. Lawrence estuary and gulf; S. E. part of Quebec; fishing grounds; # 49 N, 65 W.

Gastein (gäs′tīn), alpine valley, N. Austria; hot springs and alpine resort; # 47:10 N, 30:5 E.

Gastonia (gas-tō′ni-ạ), tn., S. W. C. N. Car., pop. 21; # 35:15 N, 81:12 W.

Gateshead (gāts′hed), a S. suburb of Newcastle, N. E. Eng., pop. 128; # 54:50 N, 1:36 W.

Gatun (gä-tön′), artificial lake, created by Gatun dam, Canal Zone, area 0.2. — tn., near by, pop. 2; # 9:17 N, 79: 55 W.

Gaul (gȧl), Roman name for Belgium, France and Switzerland.

Gavarnie (gȧ-vär-nē), cascade, Hautes-Pyrénées prov., S. Fr., height 1,385 ft.; second in Europe; # 42:43 N, 0:1 W.

Gävle or **Gäfle** (yev′lẹ), prov., S. E. Sweden, area 8, pop. 274, and its *, a spt., pop. 39; # 60:30 N, 16:50 E.   [N, 85 E.

Gaya (gi′ạ), city, N. E. India, S. E. Benares, pop. 68; # 24:45

Gaza (gā′zạ), dist., S. Palestine, and its *, also known as **Ghuzzeh**, a spt., pop. 17; # 31:30 N, 34:25 E. — a minor subdivision of S. Port. E. Africa; # 23:30 S, 33:53 E.

Gdynia (g′dēn′yä), spt. city, N. W. Poland, on Danzig Gulf 12 mi. N. W. of Danzig, pop. 30; # 54:30 N, 18:33 E.

Geelong (gē-lông′), spt. suburb of Melbourne, Australia, pop. 37; # 38:20 S, 144:25 E.   [135:30 E.

Geelvink (gāl′vingk), large bay, N. W. Papua; # 2:30 S,

Geestemünde (gās′tẹ-mün-dẹ), spt., Hannover, N. W. Ger., on Weser riv., pop. 25; # 53:35 N, 8:35 E.

Gelderland (gel′dẽr-länt), see **Guelders**.

Gelligaer (gel-i-gïr′), city, E. Glamorgan, S. E. Wales, pop. 43; # ab. 51:38 N, 3:13 W.

Gelsenkirchen (gel-zen-kirch′ẹn), city, Ruhr valley, N. W. Ger., pop. 206; coke; # 51:30 N, 7:9 E.

Gemmi (gem′mē), R.R. tunnel under pass, el. 7,640 ft., 20 mi. N. of Simplon tunnel, Switz.; # 46:24 N, 7:37 E.

Genesee (jen-ẹ-sē′), riv., N. Pa., N. to Lake Ontario; falls at Rochester; len. 145 mi.; # 43:15 N, 77:40 W.

Geneva (jẹ-nē′vạ), city on W. tip of Lake Geneva, ext. W. Switz., pop. 135, * of League of Nations; univ.; # 46:12 N, 6:10 E. — tn., W. C. New York, pop. 16; Hobart College; # 42:52 N, 77 W. — lake, S. W. Switz. and adj. Fr., len. 45 mi.; area 0.2, el. 1,230 ft.; depth 1,100 ft.; outlet, Rhône riv.; # 46:25 N, 6:20 E.

Genève (zhẹ-nâv′) or **Genf**, canton, ext. W. Switz., area 0.1, pop. 171, * Geneva; # 46:12 N, 6:10 E.

Genf (genf), see **Geneva**.

Genova (jen′ō-vä), *Eng.* **Genoa**, prov., Liguria, N. W. Italy, area 1.3, pop. 976, and its *, a spt. on the Gulf of Genova, pop. 316; univ.; # 44:20 N, 8:58 E.

Gensan (gen′sän′), *Jap.* **Wönsan** (wun′sän′), treaty port, E. Korea, pop. 17; # 39:5 N, 127:30 E.

George (jôrj), lake, N. E. New York, len. 36 mi.; resort; # 43:35 N, 73:35 W.

Georgetown (jôrj′toun), spt. city, the * of Br. Guiana, pop. 56; # 6:50 N, 58:20 W. — tn., C. Texas, pop. 4; S. W. Univ.: # 30:37 N, 97:40 W. — spt. tn., * of Penang, Straits Settlements, Malay; # 5:15 N, 100:15 E. — a part of Washington, D. C.; univ.; # 38:54 N, 77:4 W.

Georgia (jôr′jiä), state, S. E. U.S.A., bet. Fla. and S. Car.; area 59, pop. 3,124, * Atlanta, pop. 302; second city, Savannah, pop. 96. # 33 N, 83 W., — soviet republic, ext. S. E. Russia, E. of Black Sea area 26, pop. 2,493, * Tiflis, pop. 200; # 42 N, 43 E.—, **strait of,** bet. Vancouver Isl. and mainland of Br. Columbia, width ab. 30 mi.; # 50 N, 125 W.

Georgian Bay (jôr′jiạn bā), N. E. part of Lake Huron, Canada, area ab. 6; # 45:30 N, 81 W.

Gera (gā′rä), city, E. Thuringia, S. C. Ger., pop. 81. — dist. adjacent, area 0.3, pop. 92; # 50:52 N, 12:5 E.

German Commune (jėr′mạn) or **German-Volga,** autonomous soviet, S. E. Russia, area 8, pop. 454, * Marxstadt (Pokrovsk); # ab. 51:30 N, 46:5 E.

Germantown (jėr′mạn-toun), N. W. part of Philadelphia, Pa.; # ab. 40:2 N, 75:12 W.

Germany (jėr′mạ-ni), republic, N. C. Europe, area 245, pop. 86,000, * Berlin; #51:30 N, 12:30 E.

Germiston (jėr′mis-tọn), city, near Johannesburg, S. E. Africa, pop. 42, white, 17; # 26:14 S, 28:10 E.

Gerona (ḥā-rō′nä), prov., ext. N. E. Spain, area 2.3, pop. 325, and its *, pop. 18; # 42:2 N, 2:23 E.

Gers (zhâr), dept., S. W. Fr., area 2.4, pop. 194, * Auch; # 43:40 N, 0:25 E.

Gettysburg (get′iz-bėrg), vil., S. E. Pa., pop. 6; battle 1863; national cemetery; Gettysburg College; # 39:51 N, 77:15 W.

Gevelsberg (gā′fẹls-berċh), city, Westfalen, W. Ger., pop. 21; # 51:18 N, 7:19 E.

Ghara (gä′rä), see **Sutlej.**

Ghats (gâts), low mts., S. India, along E. and W. margins of Deccan Plateau; # 17 N, 81 E., 15 N, 74:30 E.

Ghent (gent) or **Gand,** city, W. C. Belgium, * of E. Flanders, pop. 164; State Univ.; # 51:6 N, 3:42 E.

Ghor (gôr), rift or crack through which the Jordan riv. flows to Dead Sea, Palestine; # 31:55 N, 35:33 E.

Ghuzzeh (guz′e), see **Gaza.**

Giant's Causeway, remarkable volcanic rock formation, N. Ireland, visible from trans-Atlantic steamers rounding N. Ireland; # 55:14 N, 6:32 W.

Gibraltar (ji-brâl′tặr), Br. crown colony, pen., S. Spain, E. of Strait of Gibraltar, area .002, pop. 21; strongly fortified rock; height 1,408 ft.; # 36:8 N, 5:25 W.

Gibraltar, Strait of, bet. Africa and Europe, entrance to Mediterranean Sea, least width 8¼ mi.; # 36 N, 5:30 W.

Giessbach (gēs′bäċh), falls, height 1,074 ft., near Brienz, C. Switz.; # 46:44 N, 8:2 E.

Giessen (gēs′ẹn), city, N. W. Hessen, S. W. Ger., pop. 34; univ.; # 50:35 N, 8:40 E.

Gifu (gē′fö), city, C. Honshu isl., Japan, pop. 82; # 35:30 N, 136:45 E.

Gijón (ḥē-ḥōn′), spt., Oviedo, N. Spain, pop. 58; # 43:25 N, 5:45 W.

Gila (hē′lä), riv., W. C. New Mexico to Colorado riv., len. 550 mi.; # 32:44 N, 114:38 W. — national monument, Mogollon Mts., New Mex.; cliff dwellings; # 33:12 N, 108:25 W.

Gilbert and Ellice Islands (gil′bėrt, el′is i′lạndz), Br. colony, many small scattered isls., equatorial C. Pacific oc., area 0.2, pop. 30; # 0:0 N, 175 E.

Gilead (gil′ẹ-ạd), mt., 25 mi. N. N. E. of Dead Sea, el. 3,596 ft.; # 32:3 N, 35:42 E.

Gillingham (gil′ing-ạm), a S. E. suburb of London, Eng., pop. 48; # 51:24 N, 0:34 E.

Gilolo (jē-lō′lō), see **Jilolo.**

Girgenti (jėr-jen′tē), prov., S. W. Sicily, area 1.2, pop. 411, and its *, a spt., pop. 30; # 37:18 N, 13:34 E.

Gironde (ji-rond′, *Fr.* zhē-rônd), estuary of Garonne and Dordogne rivs., S. W. Fr.; # 45:30 N, 0:45 W. — dept., S. W. Fr., area 4.1, pop. 819, * Bordeaux, pop. 267; # 45:30 N, 1:2 W.

Gisborne (giz′bọrn), spt. city, E. N. Island, New Zealand, pop. 15; # 38:40 S, 178 E.

Giza (gē′zä) or **Gizeh** (gē′ze), prov., N. Egypt, area 0.4, pop. 524, and its *, near Cairo and the pyramids, pop. 19; # 30:1 N, 31:10 E.

Glace Bay (glàs bā), suburb of Sydney, Cape Breton Isl., N. S., pop. 17; # 46:10 N, 59:58 W.

Glacier National Park (glā′shiėr), park, est. 1910, N. W. Mont.; fine mt. scenery and glacial lakes; area 1.3; # 48:40 N, 113:30 W.

Gladbach (glät′bäċh), see **München-Gladbach.**

Gladbeck (glät′bek), a N. E. suburb of Köln, W. Ger., pop. 60; # 51:34 N, 7 E.

Glamorgan (glạ-môr′gạn) or **Glamorganshire,** county, S. E. Wales, area 0.8, pop. 1,253, * Cardiff, pop. 226; # 51:30 N, 3:30 W.

Glarus (glä′rụs), canton, E. C. Switz., area 0.3, pop. 34, and its *, pop. 5; # 47:5 N, 9:3 E.

Glasgow (glas′gō), spt. city, S. W. Scotland, pop. 1,051, with suburbs, ab. 1,500; Univ. of Glasgow; shipbuilding; # 55:50 N, 4:15 W.

Glastonbury (glas′tọn-ber-i), tn., C. Somerset, S. W. Eng., pop. 6; abbey; # 51:8 N, 2:43 W.

Glauchau (glou′ċhou), city on Mulde riv., Sachsen, S. Ger., pop. 27; # 50:48 N, 12:32 E.

Gleiwitz (glī′vits), city, ext. S. E. Ger., pop. 81; # 50:17 N, 18:40 E.

Glencoe (glen-kō′), valley in Argyllshire, Scotland; # 56:40 N, 5 W. — a N. suburb of Chicago, Ill., pop. 7; # 42:7 N, 87:47 W.

Glendale (glen′dāl), city, S. W. Calif., pop. 83; # 34:9 N, 118:15 W.

Glen More (glen môr), depression across N. Scotland, Loch Linnhe to Moray Firth, len. 62 mi.; Lochs Ness, Albin and Tochy; # 57:15 N, 4:40 W.

Glens Falls (glenz fâlz), city, E. C. New York, pop. 19; # 43:20 N, 73:37 W.

Globe (glōb), tn., S. E. Ariz., pop. 6; copper mines; # 33:25 N, 110:45 W.

Glockner (glok′nėr), mt. pk., Tyrol, W. Austria, el. 12,461 ft.; # 47:7 N, 12:42 E.

Glogau (glō′gou), city on Oder riv., Silesia, S. E. Ger., pop. 26; # 51:40 N, 16:6 E.

Glommen (glôm′men), riv., C. Norway to Kristian Fjord, len. ab. 350 mi.; # 61:30 N, 10:30 E.

Glossa (glos′ä, or glôs′ä), *anc.* Acroceraunia, cape, S. W. Albania, Strait of Otranto; # 40:25 N, 19:17 E.

Gloucester (glos′tėr), city, on riv. Severn, S. W. Eng., pop. 53; # 51:55 N, 2:15 W. — spt. city, N. E. Mass., pop. 24; fishing port; # 42:37 N, 70:40 W. — a New Jersey suburb of Philadelphia, pop. 14; # 39:54 N, 75:7 W.

Gloucestershire (glos′tėr-shėr) or **Gloucester** (glos′tėr), county, S. W. Eng., area 1.2, pop. 758, * Gloucester, pop. 53; # 51:55 N, 2:15 W.

Gloversville (gluv′ėrz-vil), city, E. C. New York, pop. 23; gloves; # 43:4 N, 74:25 W.

Gmünd (gmünt), city, E. C. Württemberg, S. W. Ger., pop. 21; # 48:48 N, 9:47 E.

Goa (gō′ä), Portuguese colony, S. W. India, area 1, pop. 516, and its *, a spt.; # 15:35 N, 74 E.

Gobi (gō′bē), desert, mostly in Mongolia, E. C. Asia; area ab. 500; # 44 N, 104 E.

Godavari (gō-dä′vạ-rē), riv., W. Ghats, E. to Bay of Bengal, S. India, len. 900 mi.; # 16:50 N, 82:25 E. — dist., Madras, area 2.5; pop. 1,471; # 17:20 N, 82 E.

Godwin-Austen (god′win-âs′ten), mt. pk., Karakoram Range, Tibet, el. 28,265 ft.; # 35:50 N, 76:30 E.

Gogra (gōg′rä), riv., largest N. trib. of Ganges riv., N. India, len. 570 mi.; # 25:45 N, 84:35 E.

Gold Coast (gōld kōst), Br. colony on Gulf of Guinea, W. Africa, area 80, pop. 2,030, * Accra, pop. 38; # 6 N, 1 W.

Golden (gōl′dn), tn., N. C. Colo., pop. 3; State School of Mines; # 39:45 N, 105:11 W.

Golden Gate (gōl′dn gāt), inlet to San Francisco Bay, W. Calif.; # 37:48 N, 122:30 W.

Golden Horn (gōl′dn hôrn), inner harbor of Constantinople, Turkey; # 41 N, 29 E.

Goldfield (gōld′fēld), mining tn., S. W. Nev., pop. 2; # 37:42 N, 117:15 W.

Goldsboro (gōldz′bur-ọ), tn., S. E. C. N. Car., pop. 17; # 35:24 N, 78 W.

Gomal (gō-mul′), important pass bet. Punjab, N. W. India, and Afghanistan, height ab. 7,500 ft.; # 32:3 N, 70:6 E.

---

fat, fāte, fär, fâll, àsk, fāre; net, mē, hėr; pĭn, pīne; not, nōte, mŏve, nôr; up, lūte, pùll; oi, oil; ou, out; (lightened) aviạry, ẹlect, agọny, intọ, ụnite; (obscured) errạnt, operạ, ardẹnt, actọr, natụre; ch, chip; g, go; th, thin; ᴛʜ, then; y, you;

Gomel (gŏ'mĕl), city on Dnieper riv., S. E. Russia, pop. 96; #52:25 N, 30:55 E.

Gonaïves (go-nä-ēv'), bay, isl., and spt. tn., W. Haiti, pop. 8; #19:35 N, 72:40 W.

Good Hope, Cape of, promontory, Cape prov., tip of S. Africa; #34:20 S, 18:30 E.

Goodwin Sands (gŭd'win), sandbar and quicksand flats off E. coast of Kent, S. E. Eng.; many wrecks and engulfings; #51:15 N, 1:35 E.

Göppingen (gĕp'ing-ĕn), city, E. C. Württemberg, S. W. Ger., pop. 22; #48:43 N, 9:40 E.

Gorakhpur (gō-ruk-pōr'), city, N. C. India, pop. 58; #26:45 N, 83:22 E.

Gorizia (gō-rēt'sē-ä) or **Görz** (gĕrts), city, 20 mi. N. of Trieste, N. E. Italy, pop. 31; #45:56 N, 13:40 E.

Görlitz (gĕr'lits), city, W. Silesia, S. E. Ger., pop. 85; #51:10 N, 15 E.

Goshen (gō'shĕn), tn., N. Ind., pop. 11; college; #41:38 N, 85:50 W. — **Hole,** prominent basin, E. Wyo.; irrigated; #41:45 N, 104 W.

Goslar (gos'lär), city in the Harz mts., Hannover, Prussia, pop. 21; #51:55 N, 10:25 E.

Göta (yĕ'tä), or **Götha,** riv., outlet of Väner Lake, S. W. Sweden, len. 50 mi.; great water power; #57:43 N, 11:58 E.

Göteborg (yĕ-tĕ-bôr'y'), prov., S. W. Sweden, area 2, pop. 436, and its *, a spt., pop. 229; univ.; #57:43 N, 11:58 E.

Gotha (gō'tä), city, N. W. Thuringia, S. W. Ger., pop. 46; #50:57 N, 10:40 E. — dist. adjacent, area 0.4, pop. 97.

Gothland (got'länd), region, S. Sweden, area 35.7, pop. 2,950; #58 N, 14 E.

Göttingen (gĕt'ing-ĕn), city, Hannover, N. W. Ger., pop. 41; univ.; #51:35 N, 9:55 E.

Gottland (got'länd), isl., in mid-Baltic, S. E. Sweden, area 1.2, pop. 57; #57:45 N, 18:45 E.

Gouda (gou'dä), city, 11 mi. N. E. of Rotterdam, Neth., pop. 27; cheese; #54:1 N, 4:42 E.

Goulburn (gōl'bĕrn), tn., S. E. New S. Wales, Australia, pop. 12; #34:45 S, 149:40 E.

Govan (guv'ąn), a W. borough, recently a suburb of Glasgow, Scotland, pop. 90; #55:52 N, 4:19 W.

Governors Island, ft. isl., New York Bay; to U. S. govt.; #ab. 40:40 N, 74 W.

Gower (gou'ĕr), pen., S. C. Wales; #51:35 N, 4:15 W.

Goyaz (gō-yäzh'), state, E. C. Brazil, area 255, pop. 512, and its *, pop. 21; #16:30 S, 49:50 W; contains site of the future capital of Brazil.

Graham (grā'ąm), part of W. Antarctica, S. of S. S. America; #64:20 S, 61:50 W.

Grampians (gram'pi-ąnz), E. W. mt. range, N. Scotland, summit, Ben Nevis, el. 4,406 ft.; #57 N, 3:45 W.

Granada (grą-nä'dä, Sp. grä-nä'тнä), prov., S. Spain, area 4.9, pop. 593, and its *, pop. 114; univ.; #37:13 N, 3:41 W. — region S. Spain including Malaga, Granada and Almeria provs.; #37:30 N, 3:10 W. — city on Lake Nicaragua, C. America, pop. 17; #11:58 N, 85:58 W.

Gran Canaria (grän kä-nä'rē-ä), largest of Canary Isls., len. 35 mi., pop. 180; city, Las Palmas; #ab. 28 N, 16 W.

Gran Chaco (grän chä'kō), see **Chaco.**

Grand Bank, shoal water, S. E. of Newfoundland, area ab. 40; fishing; #45 N, 52 W.

Grand Canal, canal, Tientsin S. 600 mi. to Hangchow, N. E. China; #34:30 N, 118 E.

Grand Canyon, gorge of Colorado riv., N. W. Ariz., len. ab. 200 mi., depth 2,000 to 6,000 ft.; a National Park; #36:10 N, 113:10 W.

Grand Coulee (kŏ'lĕ), dry canyon, S. E. Wash., cut by Columbia riv. in glacial period; over 400 ft. deep; #47 N, 119:20 W.

Grande, Rio (rē'ō grän'dä), riv., S. C. Colo., to Gulf of Mexico, len. 1,770 mi., from El Paso, Texas, the boundary bet. U.S.A. and Mexico; #26 N, 97:10 W. — riv., S. E. Brazil to Paraná riv., len. 600 mi.; #21:45 S, 41:58 W.

Grand Falls (grand fâlz), cascade, Hamilton riv., N. E. Quebec, Labrador pen., height 316 ft.; #53:35 N, 64:24 W. — tn., N. E. Newfoundland; enormous paper mill; #48:56 N, 55:41 W.

Grand Forks (grand fôrks), tn., N. E. N. Dak., pop. 20; State Univ.; #47:55 N, 97:5 W.

Grand Haven (grand hā'vĕn), lake port and resort, W. C. Mich., pop. 9; #43:3 N, 86:15 W.

Grand Island (grand i'lạnd), tn., S. C. Neb., pop. 19; college; #40:55 N, 98:25 W.

Grand Rapids (grand rap'idz), city, S. W. Mich., pop. 164; furniture; college; #43 N, 85:45 W.

Grand River, riv., N. W. S. Dak., to Missouri riv., len. 180 mi.; #ab. 45:22 N, 100:30 W. — former name of Colorado riv., from Grand Lake, Colo., to its junction with Green riv., len. 350 mi. — see **Grande, Rio.**

Grand Trunk Pacific, Canadian National, R. R. lines, Montreal to Prince Rupert, Br. Col., total mileage 3,567, highest point 3,712 ft., completed 1914.

Granite City (gran'it), an Ill. suburb of St. Louis, pop. 23; steel; #38:42 N, 90:9 W.

Granite Peak, mt., S. C. Mont., state's highest pk., el. 12,850 ft.; #45:10 N, 109:45 W.

Gran Quivira, national monument near Manzano, C. New Mexico, ruins of Spanish Mission; #ab. 34:25 N, 106:10 W.

Gran Sasso (grän säs'sō), highest pk. of Apennines, 70 mi. E. of Rome, Italy, el. 9,583 ft.; #42:28 N, 13:28 E.

Granville (gran'vil), city, near Sydney, New S. Wales, Australia, pop. 15; #33:50 S, 151:1 E. — tn., C. Ohio, pop. 2; Denison Univ.; #40:3 N, 82:33 W.

Gratz, see **Graz.**

Graubünden (grou-bünd'ĕn) or **Grisons,** canton, ext. E. Switz., area 2.8, pop. 120; * Chur; #46:40 N, 9:40 E.

Gravesend (grāvz'end), city, 15 mi. E. of London, Eng., on Thames riv., pop. 28; #51:27 N, 0:23 E.

Graz or **Gratz** (gräts), city on Mura riv., S. E. Austria, pop. 153; univ.; #47:3 N, 15:28 E.

Great Barrier Reef, coral reef along N. E. Australia, len. 1,250 mi.; #18 S, 148 E.

Great Basin, region of interior drainage, S. W. U.S.A., esp. Nevada; area ab. 210; #40 N, 117 W.

Great Bear, lake, N. W. Canada, area 12, greatest length and width, 200 × 200 mi.; #66 N, 121 W.

Great Britain (grāt brit'n), largest isl. of Europe, area 89, pop. 42,000; #54 N, 2 W.; see **United Kingdom.**

Great Falls (grāt fâlz), city, W. C. Mont., pop. 30; #47:30 N, 111:20 W. — of Missouri riv., five falls nearby, combined height 612 ft.

Great Lakes, see **Erie, Huron, Michigan, Ontario** and **Superior.**

Great Northern Railway, R. R., St. Paul, Glacier Park, Seattle, summit 5,202 ft., completed 1897, total mileage 8,251.

Great Plains (grāt plāns), semi-arid zone, E. of Rocky Mts., U.S.A. and S. W. Canada; #45 N, 105 W.

Great Salt Lake, shallow lake, N. Utah, area 2.3, len. 80 mi., maximum depth 60 ft.; #41 N, 112:30 W.

Great Slave Lake, N. W. Ter., N. W. Canada, area 11, len. 300 mi.; #61:30 N, 114 W.

Great Wall of China, wall, len. 1,300 mi., along N. W. border of China proper; #39 N, 110 E.

Greece (grēs), kingdom, S. Balkan pen., and neighboring isls., area 49, pop. 5,536, * Athens, pop. 350; #39 N, 22 E.

Greeley (grē'li), tn., N. E. Colo., pop. 16; State Teachers College; #40:30 N, 104:50 W.

Green (grēn), riv., W. C. Wyo. to Colo. riv., Utah; #38:15 N, 109:55 W. — riv., S. E. Ky. to Ohio riv., len. 350 mi.; #37:55 N, 87:30 W.

Green Bay (grēn bā), chief inlet of Lake Michigan, N. E. Wis., len. 90 mi.; #45 N, 87:30 W. — city thereon, pop. 46; #44:30 N, 88 W.

Greencastle (grēn'kȧs'l), tn., S. W. C. Ind., pop. 5; DePauw Univ.; #39:35 N, 86:50 W.

Greenfield (grēn'fēld), tn., N. W. Mass., pop. twp. 16; #42:38 N, 72:38 W.

Greenland (grēn'lạnd), world's largest isl., N. E. N. America, area 827, Danish colony, pop. 14, * Sydproven, pop. 1; #70 N, 40 W.

Greenland Sea (grēn'lạnd sē), part of Arctic oc. bet. Greenland and Spitzbergen; #75 N, 10 W.

Green Mountains, mts., N. W. Ver., summit Mt. Mansfield, el. 4,406 ft.; #44 N, 73 W.

Greenock (grēn'ok), city, 20 mi. W. of Glasgow, S. W. Scotland, pop. 82; shipbuilding; #55:56 N, 4:45 W.

(variable) ḍ as d or j, ş as s or sh, ṭ as t or ch, ẓ as z or zh; o, F. cloche; ü, F. menu; ċh, Sc. loch; ń, F. bonbon; ', primary accent; ", secondary accent; †, obsolete; <, from; +, and; =, equals. See also lists at beginning of book.

Greensboro (grēnz′bur-ọ), city, W. C. N. Car., pop. 59; N. Car. and Greensboro colleges; #36:5 N, 79:40 W.

Greensburg (grēnz′bẽrg), city, S. W. Pa., pop. 17; #40:20 N, 79:31 W. — tn., S. E. Ind., pop. 6; #39:18 N, 85:32 W.

Greenville (grēn′vil), city, N. W. S. Car. pop. 35; Furman Univ.; #34:50 N, 82:20 W. — tn., N. W. Miss., on Mississippi riv., pop. 21; #33:25 N, 91:5 W. — tn., N. E. Texas, pop. 14; #ab. 32:40 N, 95:25 W.

Greenwich (grin′ij), a S. E. borough of London, pop. 100, Royal Observatory; prime meridian; #51:28 N.

Greifswald (grīfs′vält), tn., Pomerania, N. E. Ger., near Baltic sea, pop. 27; univ.; #54:10 N, 13:25 E.

Greiz (grīts), dist. ext. E. Thuringia, S. C. Ger., area 0.15, pop. 50, and its *, pop. 37; #50:39 N, 12:12 E.

Grenada (gren-ā′dạ), isl., S. Lesser Antilles, Br. W. Indies, area 0.1, pop. 66; #12:10 N, 61:40 W.

Grenoble (gre-nō-bl), city, S. E. Fr., * of Isère dept., pop. 77; Univ. of Grenoble; #45:12 N, 5:45 E.

Greylock (grā′lok), highest point in Mass., el. 3,505 ft.; #42:40 N, 73:9 W.

Grimsby (grimz′bi), spt. city on the Humber, E. C. Eng., pop. 82; #53:32 N, 0:3 W.

Grindelwald (grin′dẹl-vält), resort near many peaks, C. Switz., pop. 4; #ab. 46:37 N, 8:3 E.

Grinnell (grin-el′), tn., C. Iowa, pop. 5; Grinnell College; #41:45 N, 92:45 W.

Griqualand (grē′kwạ-land) **East,** native ter., prov. of Cape of Good Hope, S. Africa, area 7, pop. 265; #31 S, 29 E.

Grisons (grē-zōń), see **Graubünden.**

Grodno (grod′no), former name of Gardinas, city, S. Lithuania, pop. 62; #53:40 N, 23:40 E.

Groningen (grō′ning-ẹn), prov., ext. N. E. Neth., area 0.9, pop. 379, and its *, pop. 95; Univ. of Groningen; #53:12 N, 6:33 E.

Grosseto (gros-sā′tō), prov., Tuscany, N. W. C. Italy, area 1.7, pop. 165, and its *, pop. 18; #42:45 N, 11:5 E.

Grove City (grōv), tn., N. W. Pa., pop. 6; Grove City College; #ab. 41:10 N, 80:9 W.

Grünberg (grün′berch), city, Silesia, S. E. Ger., pop. 25.

Guadalajara (gwä-ᴛʜä-lä-hä′rä), prov., C. Spain, area 4.7, pop. 199, and its *, pop. 14; #40:38 N, 3:11 W.—city, S. W. Mex., * of Jalisco, pop. 119; #20:45 N, 103:40 W.

Guadalcanal (gwä″dạl-kạ-nal′, Sp. gwä″ᴛʜäl-kä-näl′), isl. in Solomons, S. Pacific.

Guadalquivir (gwä-dạl-kwiv′ẽr, Sp. gwä-ᴛʜäl-kē-vēr′), anc. Bætis, riv., S. Spain, W. to Atlantic oc., len. 374 mi.

Guadeloupe (gwä′dẹ-lōp, Fr. gwäd-lōp), isl., Lesser Antilles, area 0.5, pop. ab. 200; a Fr. colony, W. Indies, area 0.7, pop. 229, * Basse-Terre, pop. 8; #16:20 N, 61:30 W.

Guadiana (gwä-dē-ä′nä, gwä-ᴛʜē-ä′nä), riv., E. C. Spain, and S. E. Portugal to Atlantic oc., len. 515 mi.; #37:20 N, 7:25 W.

Guaira, La (lä gwī′rä), the spt. of Caracas, Venezuela, pop. 12; #10:38 N, 66:54 W.

Guam (gwäm), isl., Ladrone Isls., 600 mi. E. of Philippines, area 0.2, pop. 22, * Agaña; to U.S.A.; #13:30 N, 144:45 E.

Guanajuato (gwä″nä-ʜō-ä′tō), state, C. Mex., area 11, pop. 860, and its *, pop. 36; silver mines, #21 N, 101 W.

Guantánamo (gwän-tä′nä-mō), spt. city, E. Cuba, pop. 53; U. S. Naval Station; #20:20 N, 75:15 W.

Guaporé (gwä-pō-rā′), riv. bet. Bolivia and Brazil to R. Mamoré, len. 900 mi.; #11:50 S, 65:30 W.

Guardafui (gwär-dä-fwē′), cape, ext. E. Africa; #11:55 N, 51:15 E.

Guatemala (gwä-tē-mä′lạ, Sp. gwä-tä-mä′lä), republic across N. C. America, area 42, pop. 3,002; #15 N, 90 W; and its *, pop. 165, el. ab. 4,850 ft.; #14:36 N, 90:27 W.

Guaviare (gwä-vē-ä′rä), riv., E. Colombia, trib. of Orinoco, len. ab. 700 mi.; #3:55 N, 68:20 W.

Guayaquil (gwī-ä-kēl′), gulf, Ecuador, chief indentation of W. tropical America; #3 S, 80 W. — city at the head of gulf, pop. 140, * of prov. of Guayas; #2:10 S, 79:50 W.

Gubbio (gōb′bẹ-ō), anc. Iguvium, tn., Perugia (Umbria), C. Italy, pop. comm. 27; ruins and relics; #43:21 N, 12:35 E.

Güben (gü′bẹn), city, Brandenburg, Prussia, pop. 40; #51:57 N, 14:44 E.

Guelders (gel′dẽrz) or **Gelderland,** prov. E. C. Neth., area 1.9, pop. 767, * Arnhem, pop. 74; #52:10 N, 5:50 E.

Guelph (gwelf), city, S. Ontario, pop. 18; #43:30 N, 80:20 W.

Guernsey (gẽrn′zi), one of Br. Channel isls., area .03, pop. 40; dairy cattle; #49:30 N, 2:30 W.

Guerrero (ger-rä′rō), state, S. W. Mex., area 25, pop. 532, * Chilpancingo, pop. 6; #17:30 N, 100 W.

Guiana (gē-ä′nạ), **British,** a colony, N. S. America, area 89, pop. 337, * Georgetown, pop. 64; #4 N, 58 W. — **Dutch,** colony, N. S. America, area 54, pop. 171, * Paramaribo, pop. 45; #3 N, 56 W. — **French,** colony, N. S. America, area 35, pop. 44, * Cayenne, pop. 10; #4 N, 53 W. — plateau and mt. range in S. Guiana and esp. in S. E. Venezuela; #5 N, 63 W.

Guinea (gin′i), region in S. W. N. Africa, N. of Gulf of Guinea, Fr., Port. and Br. possessions; #12 N, 13 W.

Guinea, Spanish, or **Río Muni,** Sp. possession, equatorial W. Africa, area 10, pop. 150, * Santa Isabel, on isl. of Fernando Po, pop. 8; #1:30 N, 10:20 E.

Guipúzcoa (gē-pōth′kō-ä), prov., N. coast of Spain, area 0.7, pop. 268, * San Sebastian, pop. 8; #43:10 N, 2:10 W.

Gülek Boghaz (gü-lek′ bō-gäz′), see **Cilician Gates.**

Gulf of Bothnia, see **Bothnia.**

Gulf of Mexico (mek′si-kō), portion of Atlantic oc., bet. U.S.A., Mex., Yucatan and Cuba; maximum extent 1,100 mi. E.-W. and 800 N.-S.; greatest depth 12,750 ft.; #25 N, 90 W.

Gulf Stream, warm oc. current flowing N. just E. of Fla.; reaches N. W. Europe as a drift.

Gümüljina (gü-mül-jē′nä), city, Thrace, C. Greece, pop. 21; #41:6 N, 25:25 E.

Gunnison (gun′i-sọn), riv., S. W. Colo. to Colorado riv., len. 200 mi.; diverted through mts. for irrigation (tunnel 6 mi.); #38:33 N, 107 W.

Güstrow (güs′trō), city, C. Mecklenburg-Schwerin, N. Ger., pop. 19; #53:45 N, 12:10 E.

Gütersloh (gü′tẽrs-lō), city, Westfalen, W. Ger., pop. 22; #51:55 N, 8:25 E.

Guthrie (guth′ri), tn., C. Okla., pop. 10; former *; #35:50 N, 97:25 W.

Gwadar (gwä′där), spt. city, S. W. Baluchistan, part of Oman; pop. 4; #25:15 N, 62:25 E.

Gwalior (gwä′lẹ-ôr), native state, C. India, area 25, pop. 3,186, * Lashkar, pop. 80; #26:14 N, 78:10 E.

Györ (dyẽr) or **Raab,** city, N. W. Hungary, pop. 50, junction of Raab and Danube rivs.; #47:41 N, 17:38 E.

H

Haag, Den (häch), see **Hague, The.**

Haarlem (här′lẹm), city, 10 mi. W. of Amsterdam, Neth., pop. 81; #52:23 N, 4:39 E.

Haarlemmermeer (här″le-mẽr-mär′), city, W. C. Neth., pop. 25; #52:20 N, 4:40 E.

Habana (ä-bä′nä), see **Havana.**

Hachi (hä′chē) or **Hachioji,** city, C. Honshu isl., Japan, pop. 45; #35:10 N, 139:5 E.

Hackensack (hak′ẹn-sak), a New Jersey suburb of New York, pop. 26; #40:53 N, 74:3 W.

Hackney (hak′ni), a borough of E. London, Eng., pop. 222; #51:33 N, 0:3 W.

Haddington (had′ing-tọn), tn., Scotland, * of E. Lothian (Haddingtonshire), pop. 4; birthplace of Knox; #55:57 N, 2:46 W.

Hadramaut or **Hadramut** (hä-drä-mât′), coastal region of S. Arabia, area ab. 80, pop. ab. 150; #17 N, 50 E.

Hagen (hä′gen), city, Ruhr valley, W. Prussia, W. Ger., pop. 99; #51:22 N, 7:28 E.

Hagerstown (hä′gẽrz-toun), city, N. W. Md., pop. 32; #39:40 N, 77:45 W.

Hague, Cap de la (ạg), cape, tip of Norman pen., N. Fr.; #49:45 N, 1:58 W.

Hague, The (häg), city, W. C. Neth., its *, pop. 383; World Peace Court; #52:7 N, 4:18 E.

Haifa (hī′fä), dist., N. Palestine, and its *, a spt., pop. 25; #32:50 N, 35 E.

Hail (hä′ẹl), city, N. C. Arabia, * of Jebel Shammar, pop. ab. 20; #27:25 N, 41:45 E.

Hainan (hī-nän′), Chinese isl., S. China sea, area 13, pop. 2,000; * Kiungchau; #19 N, 110 E.

fat, fāte, fär, fåll, åsk, fãre; net, mē, hẽr; pin, pīne; not, nōte, mōve, nôr; up, lūte, pùll; oi, oil; ou, out; (lightened) aviạry, ẹlect, agọny, intọ, ụnite; (obscured) errạnt, operạ, ardẹnt, actọr, natụre; ch, chip; g, go; th, thin; ᴛʜ, then; y, you·

Hainaut (e-nō), prov., S. W. Belgium, area 1.4, pop. 1,243, * Mons, pop. 28; # 50:30 N, 4 E.

Haiphong (hī-fóng′), port of Hanoi and chief port of Tonking, N. E. Fr. Indo-China, pop. 27; # 21 N, 106:35 E.

Haiti (hā′ti, *Fr.* à-ē-tē), isl., W. Indies, area 30, pop. 4,545, also called Santo Domingo; # 19 N, 71 W. — republic, W. part of isl., area 10, pop. 3,000 (est.), * Port-au-Prince, pop. 125.

Hakodate (hä-kō-dä′te), spt. city, S. tip of Yezo isl., Japan, pop. 194; # 41:40 N, 140:35 E.

Halberstadt (häl′bér-shtät), city, 30 mi. S. W. of Magdeburg, C. Ger., pop. 48; # 51:53 N, 11:3 E.

Haleakala (hä″lä-ä″kä-lä′), extinct vol. pk., isl. of Maui, Hawaiian isls., el. 10,032 ft.; # 20:48 N, 156:15 W.

Halicarnassus (hal″i-kär-nas′us), anc. city, W. Asia Minor; modern Budrum; # 37:3 N, 27:28 E.

Halifax (hal′i-faks), city, 25 mi. N. E. of Manchester, C. Eng., pop. 100; # 53:43 N, 1:51 W. — spt. city, * of Nova Scotia, pop. 59; univ.; Br. naval station; # 44:39 N, 63:35 W.

Halle (häl′e), city, S. C. Ger., pop. 192; univ.; # 51:30 N, 12 E.

Hallstatt (häl′shtät), scenic lake and tn., W. C. Austria, pop. 1; Pre-Roman antiquities; # 47:35 N, 13:35 E.

Halmahera (häl-mä-hä′rä) or **Jilolo** (jē-lō′lō), isl., largest of the Moluccas, Dutch E. Indies, area 13, pop. 149; # 0:45 N, 128 E.

Halmstad (hälm-städ′), spt. city, S. W. Sweden, pop. 18; # 56:41 N, 12:50 E.

Hälsingborg (hel-sing-bôr′y′), spt. city, S. W. Sweden, pop. 49, near Denmark; # 56:4 N, 12:45 E.

Hama (hä′mä), city, N. W. C. Syria, pop. ab. 35; # 35:20 N, 36:45 E.

Hamadan (hä-mä-dän′), city, W. C. Persia, pop. ab. 35; also a prov., area 15; # 34:50 N, 48:15 E.

Hamamatsu (hä-mä-mät′sö), city, S. C. Honshu isl., Japan, pop. 92; # 34:40 N, 137:45 E.

Hamborn (häm′bôrn), city, Ruhr Valley, W. Prussia, W. Ger., pop. 126; # 51:25 N, 6:47 E.

Hamburg (ham′bèrg, *Ger.* häm′bùrch), free city and state, N. Ger., area 0.16, pop. 1,134, and its *, leading German port, on Elbe riv., pop. 1,054; univ.; # 53:34 N, 10 E.

Hameln (hä′meln), city, Hannover, N. Ger., pop. 25; # 52:40 N, 9:23 E.

Hamilton (ham′il-ton), S. suburb of Glasgow, Scotland, pop. 41; # 55:46 N, 4:2 W. — city, W. end of Lake Ontario, Canada, pop. 156; # 43:15 N, 79:50 W. — city, S. W. Ohio, pop. 51; # 39:22 N, 84:35 W. — city, N. N. Isl., New Zealand, pop. 16; # 37:43 S, 175:17 E. — tn., S. C. New York, pop. 2; Colgate Univ., # 42:50 N, 75:34 W.

Hamilton or **Grand**, riv., E. Quebec, through Lake Melville, to Hamilton Inlet, Labrador, len. 315 mi.; # 53:35 N, 60 W. — falls, 316 ft. in height; # 53:35 N, 64:24 W.

Hamilton, Mount, pk., Coast Range, W. C. Calif., el. 4,209 ft.; Lick Observatory of Univ. of Calif.; # 37:20 N, 121:40 W.

Hamm (häm), city, Westfalen, W. Ger., pop. 50; locomotives; # 51:40 N, 7:48 E.

Hammerfest (häm′mer-fest), spt. tn. on isl., N. Norway, pop. 3; most N. town in Europe; # 70:25 N, 23:40 E.

Hammersmith (ham′er-smith), a borough of London, Eng., pop. 130; # 51:30 N, 0:14 W.

Hammond (ham′ond), city, N. W. Ind., pop. 70; # 41:37 N, 87:31 W.

Hampshire (hamp′shir), parliamentary county, S. C. Eng., including counties of Southampton and Isle of Wight, area 1.6, pop. 1,005, * Winchester, pop. 23; # 51:5 N, 1:15 W.

Hampstead (hamp′sted), a borough of London, Eng., pop. 86; # 51:34 N, 0:11 W.

Hampton Roads (hamp′ton rōdz), S. extension of Chesapeake Bay, mouth of James riv., Va.; # 37 N, 76:20 W.

Hamtramck (ham-tram′ik), an industrial suburb surrounded by Detroit, Mich., pop. 50; # 42:25 N, 83:4 W.

Hamun-i-Helmand (hä-mön′i-hel′mund), marsh and lake, E. border of Persia, area 20; # 31 N, 61:15 E.

Hanau (hä′nou) an E. suburb of Frankfurt, Ger., pop. 38; # 50:8 N, 8:56 E.

Handegg (hän′deg), falls of Aar riv., C. Switz., height 236 ft.; # 46:36 N, 8:15 E.

Handsworth (hanz′wèrth), a N. borough of Birmingham, Eng., pop. 69; # 52:30 N, 1:55 W.

Hangchow (häng′chou), spt. city on Hangchow Bay, S. E. China, * of Chekiang prov., pop. est. 340; # 30:15 N, 120:7 E.

Han-Kiang (hän-kyäng), trib. of Yangtse-Kiang, W. China, len. 700 mi.; # 30:40 N, 114:15 E.

Hankow (hän-kou′), city on Yangtse-Kiang riv., C. China proper, pop. est. 1,468; # 30:35 N, 114:18 E.

Hannibal (han′i-bal), city, N. E. Mo., on the Mississippi riv., pop. 21; # 39:35 N, 91:25 W.

Hannover (hän-nō′vèr), *Eng.* **Hanover**, prov., Prussia, N. W. Ger., area 15, pop. 3,028, and its *, pop. 414; # 52:20 N, 9:40 E.

Hanoi (hä-nō′i), inland city, * of Tonking and Fr. Indo-China, pop. 74; Univ. of Indo-China; # 21 N, 105:45 E.

Hanover (han′ō-vèr), tn., W. New Hampshire, pop. 2; Dartmouth College; # 43:43 N, 72:18 W. — tn., S. E. Ind., near Madison, pop. 1; Hanover College; # ab. 38:43 N, 85:28 W. — see **Hannover**.

Hanse Towns (hans) or **Hanseatic League** (han″se-at′ik lēg), commercial confederacy (Middle Ages) of N. Ger. and Scandinavian cities.

Hanyang (hän-yäng′), city, Hupeh prov., S. E. C. China, pop. est. 400; adjoins Hankow; # 30:34 N, 114:18 E.

Harar (hä-rär′), walled city of S. E. Abyssinia, pop. ab. 40; # 8:45 N, 42 E.

Harbin (här-bēn′), city, C. Manchuria, pop. est. 165; # 45:40 N, 126:30 E.

Harburg (här′bùrch), a S. suburb of Hamburg, N. C. Ger., pop. 73; # 53:28 N, 9:58 E.

Hardanger (här′däng-èr), fjord, S. W. Norway, len. 110 mi.; # 59:55 N, 5:50 E.

Harlem (här′lem), riv., part of Hudson riv., bet. Bronx and Manhattan, New York City; # 40:48 N, 73:56 W.

Harney (här′ni), peak, summit of Black Hills, S. W. S. Dak., el. 7,242 ft.; # 43:55 N, 103:30 W.

Harper's Ferry (här′perz fer′i), village, E. W. Va.; John Brown's raid, 1859; # 39:20 N, 77:45 W.

Harrisburg (har′is-berg), city, S. E. C. Pa., on Susquehanna riv., state *, pop. 84; # 40:16 N, 76:52 W.

Harrison (har′i-son), a New Jersey suburb of New York, pop. 14; # 40:45 N, 74:9 W.

Harrogate (har′ō-gāt), city, W. C. York, Eng.; mineral springs; resort; pop. 28; # 54 N, 1:33 W.

Harspränget (här-sprong′et), cascade, Stora Luleå riv., N. Sweden, height 245 ft.; # ab. 66 N, 20 E.

Hartford (härt′ford), city, * of Conn., centrally located on Conn. riv., pop. 166; Trinity College; # 41:48 N, 72:40 W.

Hartlepool (här′tl-pöl), spt., Durham, N. E. Eng., adjoining W. Hartlepool, pop. 21; coal; # 54:43 N, 1:10 W.

Harwich (har′ij), spt., Essex, S. E. Eng., pop. 16; transchannel service; # 51:54 N, 1:15 E.

Harz (härts), low mt. mass, S. C. Ger., highest Brocken, el. 3,745 ft.; # 51:45 N, 10:30 E.

Haspe (häs′pè), city, Westfalen, W. Ger., pop. 26; # 51:21 N, 7:26 E.

Hasselt (häs′elt), city, N. E. Belgium, * of Limbourg, pop. 16; # 50:56 N, 5:21 E.

Hastings (häs′tingz), spt., S. E. Sussex, S. E. Eng., pop. 66; battle, 1066; # 50:33 N, 0:26 E. — tn., S. C. Neb., pop. 15; college; # 40:30 N, 98:25 W. — tn., S. E. N. Isl., New Zealand, pop. 14; # 39:39 S, 176:51 E.

Hatteras (hat′er-as), cape, ext. E. N. Car., on low isl., dangerous; # 35:20 N, 75:30 W.

Hattiesburg (hat′iz-berg), tn., S. E. C. Miss., pop. 21; # 31:19 N, 89:18 W.

Haugesund (hou′gē-son), tn., S. W. Norway, pop. 17; # 59:25 N, 5:20 E.

Hauran (hä-ö-rän′), vol. plateau, Syria, N. E. of Sea of Galilee and S. of Damascus; # 33 N, 36:20 E.

Haute-Garonne (ōt-gà-rôn), dept. S. Fr., area 2.5, pop. 425, * Toulouse, pop. 175; # 43:25 N, 1:25 E.

Haute-Loire (ōt-lwor), dept. S. C. Fr., area 1.9, pop. 269, * LePuy; # 45 N, 3:50 E.

Haute-Marne (ōt-märn), dept. E. C. Fr., area 2.4, pop. 199, * Chaumont; # 48:10 N, 5:15 E.

Hautes-Alpes (ōt-zälp), dept. S. E. Fr., area 2.2, pop. 89, * Gap; # 44:40 N, 6:30 E.

Haute-Saône (ōt-sōn), dept. E. C. Fr., area 2.1, pop. 228, * Vesoul; # 47:40 N, 6:20 E.

Haute-Savoie (ōt-sà-vwo), dept. S. E. Fr., area 1.8, pop. 236, * Annecy; # 46 N, 6:20 E.

Hautes-Pyrénées (ōt-pē-rā-nä), dept. S. W. Fr., area 1.7, pop. 186, * Tarbes; # 43 N, 0:10 E.

Haute-Vienne (ōt-vyen), dept. W. C. Fr., area 2.1, pop. 350, * Limoges, pop. 90; # 46 N, 1:15 E.

Haut-Rhin (ō-raṅ), dept. N. E. Fr., formerly Upper Alsace, area 1.4, pop. 517, * Colmar, pop. 47; # 48 N, 7:30 E.

Havana (hạ-van'ạ), *Sp.* **Habana**, prov. of Cuba, area 3, pop. 782, and its *, a spt., pop. 560; Univ. of Havana; # 23:8 N, 82:23 W.

Havel (hä'fel), riv., N. C. Ger. to Elbe riv., len. 225 mi.; # 52:50 N, 12 E.

Haverford (hav'ĕr-fọrd), a N. W. suburb of Philadelphia, Pa.; Haverford College; # ab. 40 N, 75:20 W.

Haverhill (hā'vĕr-il), city, N. E. Mass., pop. 47; # 42:48 N, 71:10 W.

Havre (à-vr), chief port of N. Fr., pop. 163; # 49:30 N, 0:8 E. — (hä'vĕr), tn., N. C. Mont., pop. 6; # 48:35 N, 109:45 W.

Hawaii (hä-wī'ē), largest isl. of Hawaiian group, area 4, chief city, Hilo, pop. 17; # 19:45 N, 155:30 W. — national park, includes volcanoes, esp. lava lake of Kilauea.

Hawaii, Territory of, ter. of U.S.A., the Hawaiian Islands, area 6, pop. 423; * Honolulu, pop. 179.

Hawaiian Islands (hä-wī'yạn ī'lạndz), group isls., Mid. N. Pacific oc., area 6, pop. 423; # 20:30 N, 157 W.

Hawash (hä'wäsh), riv., S. Abyssinia to Lake Assal, len. ab. 500 mi.; # 8:38 N, 39:40 E.

Hawke's Bay (hâks bā), prov. E. N. Island, New Zealand, about Hawke Bay; # 39:15 S, 177:30 E.

Hayti (hā'ti), see **Haiti.**

Haza, El (el hä'zà), district, W. coast Persian Gulf N. of Oman, Arabia; # 26 N, 50 E.

Hazleton (hā'zl-tọn), city, E. C. Pa., pop. 38; # 40:58 N, 75:58 W.

Hebrides (heb'ri-dēz), isls., W. of Scotland, area 3, pop. 100, chief isl., Lewis; # 58 N, 7 W.

Hebron (hē'brọn), city, S. C. Palestine, pop. 17; # 31:30 N, 35:5 E.

Hecla or **Hekla** (hek'lạ), vol., S. C. Iceland, el. 5,105 ft.; # 63:55 N, 19:40 W.

Hedjaz or **Hejaz** (hej-äz'), kingdom, W. Arabia, area ab. 150, pop. ab. 850, * Mecca, pop. ab. 55; # 25 N, 38 E.

Heerlen (hār'lẹn), city, Limburg, S. Neth., pop. 36; # 50:52 N, 5:55 E.

Heidelberg (hī'dẹl-bĕrg), city, S. Baden, S. W. Ger., pop. 72; univ.; # 49:25 N, 8:42 E.

Heijo-pi (hā-jō'pē), city, Korea; see **Pyengyang.**

Heilbronn (hīl-bron'), city, N. Württemberg, S. W. Ger., pop. 45; very old city; # 49:10 N, 9:12 E.

Heilung-Kiang (hā-lung'kyäng'), prov., N. Manchuria, area 203, pop. 1,500, * Tsitsihar, pop. 50; # 48:30 N, 124 E.

Hejaz (hej-äz'), see **Hedjaz.**

Hekla (hek'lạ), see **Hecla.**

Helder (hel'dĕr), spt. city, N. tip of N. Holland, Neth., pop. 30; # 52:58 N, 4:45 E.

Helena (hel'ē-nä), tn., W. C. Mont., state *, gov. 17; college; # 46:35 N, 112 W.

Helgoland (hel'gō-länt), Ger. isl., strongly fortified till 1919, S. E. North Sea, off Elbe estuary; # 54:15 N, 7:55 E.

Helicon (hel'i-kọn), mt., Bœotia, S. E. C. Greece, el. 5,128 ft.; # 38:20 N, 22:53 E.

Heliopolis (hē-li-op'ō-lis), ruins of ancient city near Cairo, Egypt; # 30:5 N, 31:17 E.

Hellenic Republic, official name of Greece.

Helles (hel'es), cape, S. tip of Gallipoli pen.; # 40:3 N, 26:10 E.

Hellespont (hel'es-pont), see **Dardanelles.**

Helmand (hel'mund), riv., N. E. Afghanistan to lake, E. Persia, len. 600 mi.; # 31:20 N, 61:30 E.

Helmond (hel'mont, *Fr.* el-môṅ), city, N. Brabant, S. C. Neth., pop. 21; # 51:29 N, 5:39 E.

Helsingfors (hel'sing-fors), **Helsinki,** spt., S. W. Finland, its *, pop. 201; 2 universities; # 60:10 N, 24:58 E.

Helsingör (hel'sing-gĕr), spt., N. E. Seeland isl., Denmark, pop. 14; # 56:2 N, 12:33 E.

Helsinki (hel'sēn-kē), official name for Helsingfors.

Helvetia (hel-vē'shiạ), see **Switzerland.**

Henderson (hen'dĕr-sọn), tn., N. W. Ky., on Ohio riv., pop. 13; # 37:50 N, 87:35 W.

Hengelo (heng'ē-lō), city, E. Overyssel, E. C. Neth., pop. 28; # ab. 52:16 N, 6:47 E.

Henley (hen'li), tn., on Thames riv., Oxfordshire, 35 mi. W. of London, S. E. Eng., pop. 6; boat races; # 51:33 N, 0:55 W.

Hennepin (hen'ē-pin), county, E. Minn., area 0.56, pop. 569 (1920), * Minneapolis; # 45 N, 93:20 W.

Henry (hen'ri), cape, S. E. Va., mouth of Chesapeake Bay; # 36:52 N, 76 W. — mt. range, S. E. Utah; # 38 N, 110:30 W.

Herat (her-ät'), prov., N. W. Afghanistan, and its *, pop. 121; # 34:35 N, 62:10 E.

Hérault (ā-rō), dept., S. coast of Fr., area 2.4, pop. 488, * Montpellier, pop. 82; # 43:40 N, 3:20 E.

Herculaneum (hĕr-kū-lā'nẹ-um), buried city, side of Mt. Vesuvius, Italy; 40:48 N, 14:15 E.

Hereford (her'ē-fọrd), county, S. W. C. Eng., area 0.8, pop. 113, and its *, pop. 23; cathedral; beef cattle; # 52:5 N, 2:45 W.

Herford (her'fôrt), city, Westfalen, W. Ger., pop. 36; # 52:7 N, 8:40 E.

Herisau (hā'rē-zou), city, Appenzell, N. E. Switz., pop. 15; # 47:23 N, 9:17 E.

Herkimer (her'ki-mĕr), tn., C. New York, pop. 10; # 43:3 N, 75 W.

Hermannstadt (her'män-shtät), see **Sibiu.**

Hermon (her'mun), mt., Antilibanus range, Palestine, el. 9,050 ft.; # 33:28 N, 35:55 E.

Hermosillo (här-mō-sēl'yō), city, N. W. Mexico, * of Sonora, pop. 20; # 29:10 N, 110:55 W.

Herne (her'nè), a N. suburb of Bochum, Ruhr val., W. Ger., pop. 66; # 51:32 N, 7:12 E.

Herrin (her'in), coal mining tn., S. C. Ill., pop. 9; # 37:50 N, 89 W.

Hertford (här'fĕrd), county, S. E. Eng., area 0.6, pop. 333, and its *, pop. 16; 20 mi. N. of London; # 51:48 N, 0:4 W.

Herzegovina (her-tse-gō-vē'nä), see **Bosnia and Herzegovina.**

Hessen (hes'ẹn), republic, S. W. C. Ger., area 3, pop. 1,351, * Darmstadt, pop. 82; # 49:35 N, 8:46 E.

Hessen-Nassau (hes'ẹn-näs'ou), prov., Prussia, S. W. C. Ger., area 6, pop. 2,401, * Kassel, pop. 105; # 50:10 N, 8 E.

Hetch-Hetchy (hech'hech'i), valley N. of Yosemite, Sierras, Calif.; Tuolumne riv. dammed, chief source of San Francisco water supply; # 37:57 N, 119:46 W.

Hibbing (hib'ing), iron mining city, N. E. Minn., pop. 16; # 47:25 N, 92:50 W.

Hidalgo (*Sp.* ē-тнäl'gō), state, C. Mexico, area 9, pop. 628, * Pachuca, pop. 39; # 20:30 N, 99 W.

Highland Park, a suburb of Detroit, S. E. Mich., pop. 51; # 42:26 N, 83:7 W. — a N. suburb of Chicago, Ill., pop. 14; # 42:12 N, 87:43 W.

Highlands (hī'lạndz), Scottish, rugged region, N. Scotland, summit Ben Nevis, el. 4,406 ft.; # 57 N, 4 W.

High Point, tn., W. C. N. Car., pop. 38; furniture; # ab. 35:55 N, 80:2 W.

Hilden (hil'dẹn), an E. S. E. suburb of Düsseldorf, W. Ger., pop. 20; # 51:10 N, 6:57 E.

Hildesheim (hil'des-hīm), city, Hannover, W. C. Ger., pop. 58; # 52:10 N, 9:58 E.

Hilo (hē'lō), E. spt., isl. of Hawaii, second city of Hawaii Ter., pop. 17; # 19:45 N, 155:5 W.

Hilversum (hil'vĕr-sum), city, 16 mi. S. E. of Amsterdam, pop. 43; # 52:14 N, 5:11 E.

Himalaya (hi-mä'lạ-yạ, sometimes pron. him-ạ-lā'yạ), lofty range, N. border of India, len. 1,500 mi., summit, Mt. Everest, el. 29,152 ft.; # 28 N, 84 E.

Himeji (hē'me-jē), city near Kobe, S. Honshu isl., Japan, pop. 46; # 34:50 N, 134:45 E.

Hindenburg (hin'dẹn-bûrch), formerly **Zabrsze,** city, Upper Silesia, S. E. Ger., pop. 73; # 50:19 N, 18:47 E.

---

fat, fāte, fär, fȧll, ȧsk, fāre; net, mē, her; pin, pīne; not, nōte, mȯve, nȯr; up, lūte, pùll; oi, oil; ou, out; (lightened) aviạry, ẹlect, agọny, intọ, ūnite; (obscured) errạnt, operạ, ardẹnt, actọr, natụre; ch, chip; g, go; th, thin; тн, then; y, you;

Hindu Kush (hin′dŏ kŏsh), lofty range, Afghanistan, W. from Himalayas, S. W. Asia, highest, Tirach Mir, el. ab. 25,420 ft.; # 36 N, 70 E.

Hindustan (hin-dŏ-stän′), Persian name for India, esp. N. W. India.

Hirosaki (hē-rō-sä′kē), inland city, N. Honshu isl., Japan, pop. 36; # 40:34 N, 140:27 E.

Hiroshima (hē-rō-she′mä), spt. city, S. Honshu isl., Japan, pop. 196; # 34:28 N, 132:30 E.

Hirschberg (hirsh′bĕrċh), city, Silesia, S. E. Ger., pop. 29; # 50:54 N, 15:43 E.

Hispaniola (his-pan-yō′lä), former name of Haiti isl.

Hoang Hai (hwäng′hī), see **Yellow Sea.**

Hoangho (hwäng′hō), see **Hwangho.**

Hobart (hō′bärt), spt. city, S. Tasmania, state *, pop. with suburbs, 52; # 42:55 S, 147:20 E.

Hoboken (hō′bō-kĕn), city, N. E. New Jersey, a suburb of New York City, pop. 50; Stevens Institute of Technology; # 40:45 N, 74:3 W.

Höchst (hĕċhst), a W. suburb of Frankfurt, S. W. Ger., pop. 31; # 50:6 N, 8:33 E.

Hodeida (hō-dā′dä or hō-dī′dä), spt., Red Sea, chief port of Yemen, S. W. Arabia, pop. ab. 50; # 14:45 N, 43 E.

Hódmezővásárhely (hŏd′me-zĕ-vä′shär-hel-y′), city on Tisza riv., S. E. Hungary, pop. 61; # 46:25 N, 20:16 E.

Hoek van Holland (hŏk vän hol′änt), *Eng.*, **Hook of Holland,** spt., S. W. S. Holland, Neth., port for extensive passenger traffic to Eng.; # 52 N, 4:7 E.

Hof (hōf), city on Saale riv., N. E. Bayern (Bavaria), pop. 40; # 50:18 N, 11:55 E.

Hofuf (hō-fōf′), see **Hufuf.**

Hog Island, isl., Delaware Bay, near Philadelphia; world's greatest shipbuilding center, 1917–20; # 39:52 N, 75:15 W.

Hohenzollern (hō′ĕn-tsol-lern), prov., Prussia, ext. S. W. Ger., area 0.4, pop. 72; # 48:19 N, 9 E.

Hokkaido (hŏk′kī-dō), formerly **Hokushu** or **Yezo,** large N. isl. of Japan, area 30, pop. 1,134; # 43 N, 141 E.

Hokushu (hō-kō-shō′), see **Hokkaido.**

Holborn (hō′bọrn), a borough of London, Eng., pop. 43; # 51:31 N, 0:7 W.

Holland (hol′ạnd), S. part of Lincolnshire, E. C. Eng., area 0.4, pop. 85; # 52:50 N, 0:5 E. — tn. S. W. Mich., pop. 15; lake port; Hope College; # 42:45 N, 86:12 W. — see **Netherlands.**

Holland, North, prov. of C. Neth., area 1.1, pop. 1,362; chief city, Amsterdam, pop. 706; # 52:30 N, 4:45 E.

Holland, South, prov., S. W. C. Neth., area 1.1, pop. 1,761; chief city, Rotterdam, pop. 537; # 51:45 N, 4:30 E.

Hollywood (hol′i-wụd), a W. suburb of Los Angeles, Calif.; moving picture films; # 34:8 N, 118:21 W.

Holstein (hōl′shtīn), prov., S. Denmark, held by Ger., 1866–1919; # 54:15 N, 9:30 E.

Holston (hōl′stọn), riv., N. and S. Forks riv., Tenn., to Tenn. riv., len. 350 mi.; # 36:50 N, 81:50 W.

Holyhead (hol′i-hed), spt., Anglesey, N. W. Wales, pop. 12; # 53:19 N, 4:40 W.

Holyoke (hōl′yōk), city, S. W. C. Mass., pop. 54; writing paper; # 42:12 N, 72:40 W.

Homberg (hom′bĕrċh), suburb of Düsseldorf, Rheinland, W. Ger., pop. 27; # 51:27 N, 6:42 E.

Homestake (hōm′stāk), gold mine, Lead, Black Hills, S. Dak.

Homestead (hōm′sted), suburb of Pittsburgh, Pa., pop. 19; # 40:24 N, 79:55 W.

Homs (hōms), city, W. C. Syria, pop. ab. 60; # 34:45 N, 36:45 E.

Honan (hō-nän′), prov., C. China Proper, area 70, pop. est. 31,000, * Kaifeng; # 34 N, 113 E.

Hondu (hon′dō), see **Honshu.**

Honduras (hon-dō′rạs), republic, N. C. America, area 44, pop. 963, * Tegucigalpa, pop. ab. 40; # 15 N, 87 W.

Honduras, British, crown colony, N. C. America, S. of Yucatan, area 9, pop. 57, * Belize, pop. 17; # 17 N, 88:40 W.

Hongkong (hong′kong′), Br. colony on isl. of Hongkong and mainland, S. China, area 0.4, pop. 625; * Victoria (often called Hongkong); # 22:15 N, 114:10 E.

Honolulu (hon-ọ-lō′lō), spt. city, on Oahu isl., * of Hawaii Ter., pop. 179; territorial univ.; # 21:18 N, 157:52 W.

Honshu (hon′shō), or **Honshiu,** chief isl. of Japan, area 87, pop. ab. 50,000; # 37 N, 138 E.

Hood (hụd), vol. pk., N. W. Ore., highest in state, el. 11,225 ft.; # 45:25 N, 121:45 W. — River Valley, E. of peak; apples; # 45:40 N, 121:31 W.

Hooghly (hōg′lē), riv., the mouth of the Ganges flowing past Calcutta, India; # 22:15 N, 88:5 E.

Hook of Holland, see **Hoek van Holland.**

Hoosac (hō′sạk), low mt. range, N. W. Mass.; R.R. tunnel, len. 4.75 mi.; 1873; # ab. 42:40 N, 73:5 W.

Hopkinsville (hop′kinz-vil), tn., S. W. Ky., pop. 12; college; # 36:50 N, 87:30 W.

Hoquiam (hō′kwi-ạm), spt. tn., W. C. Wash., pop. 11; # 47 N, 123:52 W.

Hörde (hĕr′dĕ), a S. E. suburb of Dortmund, W. Ger., pop. 35; # 51:29 N, 7:30 E.

Horn (hôrn), cape, at the S. extremity of S. America, on one of Tierra del Fuego isls.; # 56 S, 66 W.

Hornell (hôr-nel′), city, S. W. New York, pop. 17; # 42:22 N, 77:40 W.

Hornsey or **Hornsea** (hôrn′zi), spt., 15 mi. N. W. of Hull, E. C. Eng., pop. 87; # 53:54 N, 0:10 W.

Horsens (hor′sẹns), spt. city, E. Jutland, Denmark, pop. 28; # 55:52 N, 9:50 E.

Horseshoe Curve, famous curve on Penna. R.R., Allegheny escarpment near Altoona, Pa.; # ab. 40:30 N, 78:30 W.

Hot Springs (hot springz), tn., S. W. C. Ark., pop. 21; resort; oldest National Park; # 34:30 N, 93:10 W. — tn., resort, S. W. S. Dak., pop. 4; # 43:26 N, 103:32 W.

Housatonic (hō-sạ-ton′ik), riv., N. W. Mass. to Long Island Sound, len. 150 mi.; # 41:12 N, 73:10 W.

Houston (hūs′tọn), city, S. E. Texas, pop. 385; ship canal to Gulf at Galveston; Rice Institute; # 29:45 N, 95:20 W.

Hove (hōv), suburb of Brighton, coastal, S. E. Eng., pop. 44; # 50:50 N, 0:11 W.

Howe (hou), cape, S. E. Australia; # 37:35 S, 150 E.

Howrah (hou′rä), suburb of Calcutta, India, pop. 180; # 22:40 N, 88:20 E.

Huancavelica (wän′kä-vä-lē′kä), dept., S. W. Peru, area 8.3, pop. 224, and its *, pop. 8; # 12:40 S, 75:6 W.

Huánuco (wä′nō-kō), dept., C. Peru, area 15, pop. 145, and its *, pop. 9; # 9:57 S, 76:18 W.

Huascarán (wäs-kä-rän′), prominent pk., W. Peru, el. 22,168 ft.; # 9:20 S, 77 W.

Hubli (hō′bli), city, S. W. India, W. of Goa, pop. 69; # 15:18 N, 75:10 E.

Huddersfield (hud′ĕrz-fēld), city, 20 mi. N. W. of Manchester, N. C. Eng., pop. 112; # 53:40 N, 1:50 W.

Hudson (hud′sọn), riv., New York state, from Adirondacks to New York Harbor, len. 350 mi.; # 40:45 N, 74 W. — tn., S. E. New York, pop. 12; # 42:16 N, 73:46 W.

Hudson Bay (hud′sọn bā), large bay, N. E. Canada, len. 850 mi., area ab. 500; # 59 N, 84 W.

Hudson Strait (hud′sọn strāt), strait bet. Baffin Isl. and Quebec, least width ab. 100 mi., len. 500 mi.; # 62 N, 70 W.

Hué (ü-ā), city, E. C. Fr. Indo-China, * of Annam, pop. 61; # 16:30 N, 107:20 E.

Huelva (wel′vä), prov., ext. S. W. Spain, area 4, pop. 331, and its *, a spt., pop. 36; sardine fisheries; # 37:15 N, 6:57 W.

Hufuf (hō-fōf′), or **Hofuf,** largest city of Nejd, Arabia, pop. 30; # 25:22 N, 49:41 E.

Huila (wē′lä), vol. mt., Andes, S. W. Colombia, el. ab. 18,000 ft.; # 3 N, 76:5 W. — prov. surrounding pk., area 8, pop. 183, * Neiva.

Hukow (hō′kou), city, Yangtse riv., Kiangsi prov., E. C. China, pop. est. 50; # 29:43 N, 116:24 E.

Hull (hul), officially Kingston-on-Hull, spt. city on the Humber, York Co., N. E. C. Eng., pop. 287; # 53:43 N, 0:20 W. — city, S. Quebec, pop. 24; # 45:26 N, 75:44 W.

Humber, The (hum′bĕr), estuary of Oise and Trent rivs., C. E. Eng., len. 40 mi.; past Hull; # 53:39 N, 0:0 E.

Humboldt (hum′bōlt), riv., N. C. Nev. to Humboldt Lake, len. 375 mi.; # 40:10 N, 118:25 W. — or Peruvian, cold S. current, W. coast of S. America, N. almost to Ecuador.

Hunan (hō-nän′), prov., S. E. C. China, area 83, pop. est. 28,000, * Changsha, pop. est. 536; # 27:45 N, 111:30 E.

(variable) ḍ as d or j, ş as s or sh, ţ as t or ch, ẓ as z or zh; *o*, F. cloche; ü, F. menu; ċh, Sc. loch; ṅ, F. bonbon; ′, primary accent; ″, secondary accent; †, obsolete; <, from; +, and; =, equals. See also lists at beginning of book.

Hunchun (hŏn'chŏn'), city on Hunchun riv., S. E. Manchuria, pop. est. 21; # 42:54 N, 130:25 E.

Hungary (hung'gạ-ri), kingdom, S. E. C. Europe, area (with additions from Czechoslovakia in 1938 and 1939) 45, pop. 11,600, * Budapest; # 47 N, 19 E.

Hun Ho (hŏn hō), riv., N. China, Mongolia past Peking to Yellow sea, len. 350 mi.; # 39:10 N, 117 E.|

Hunsrück (hŭns'rŭk), rugged region, W. of Rhine, S. W. Ger.; # 50 N, 7:25 E.

Huntingdon (hŭn'ting-dọn), county, S. E. C. Eng., area 0.4, pop. 55, and its *, pop. 4; birthplace of Cromwell; # 52:20 N, 0:11 W.

Huntington (hŭn'ting-tọn), city, S. W. W. Va., on Ohio riv., pop. 79; # 38:25 N, 82:28 W. — city, N. E. C. Ind., pop. 14; Huntington College; # 40:52 N, 85:32 W.

Hupeh (hö-pä'), prov., S. E. C. China, area 71, pop. est. 27,000, * Wuchang, pop. est. 500; # 31:15 N, 112 E.

Huron (hū'rọn), lake bet. Mich. and Ontario, area 23, el. 581 ft.; # 45 N, 82 W. — tn., E. C. S. Dak. pop. 11; Huron College; # 44:24 N, 98:15 W.

Hurricane Fault Cliff, escarpment, N. Ariz. to N. Utah, E. edge of Great Basin; # ab. 39 N, 112 W.

Hutchinson (huch'in-sọn), city, C. Kansas, pop. 30; # 38:20 N, 97:50 W.

Hwangho (hwäng'hō), **Hoangho** or **Yellow River**, riv., E. Tibet to Gulf of Chihli, Yellow Sea, len. ab. 2,300 mi.; # 37:50 N, 118:35 E.

Hyde Park (hīd pärk), famous park in W. London, Eng.; # 51:30 N, 0:11 W. — a S. ward of Chicago, Ill., formerly a suburb; # 41:44 N, 87:36 W. — a part of Boston, Mass.; # 42:15 N, 71:8 W.

Hyderabad (hī''dĕr-ä-bäd'), a native state in Deccan, S. India, area 0.83, pop. 12,472, and its *, pop. 404; # 17:15 N, 78:30 E. — a city on lower Indus riv., N. W. India, pop. 76; # 25:25 N, 68:30 E.

Hyères (ē-âr'), city, S. E. Fr., 10 mi. E. of Toulon, pop. 21; winter resort; # 43:10 N, 6:10 E.

Hyndman (hīnd'mạn), pk., S. E. C. Idaho, highest in state, el. 12,078 ft.; # 43:40 N, 114 W.

I

Iasi or **Jassy** (yäs'ē), city, Moldavia, N. C. Romania, pop. 76; # 47:10 N, 27:37 E.

Ibadan (ē-bä'dän), city, S. E. Nigeria, W. Africa, pop. est. 150; # 7:40 N, 3:50 E.

Iberia (ī-bē'ri-ạ), pen., S. W. Europe; Spain and Portugal; # 40 N, 5 W.

Iceland (īs'lạnd), isl. kingdom in N. Atlantic oc., bet. Greenland and Europe, area 40, pop. 118, * Reykjavik, pop. 36; # 65 N, 18 W.

Ichang (ē-chäng'), city on Yangtse riv., S. W. C. China Proper, pop. est. 60; # 30:40 N, 111:25 E.

Ichinomiya (ē-chin-ō'mi-yä), a N. suburb of Nagoya, S. Honshu isl., Japan, pop. 35; # 35:17 N, 136:45 E.

Ida (ī'dạ), mt. pk., N. W. Asia Minor, overlooking Troy and the Ægean, el. 5,750 ft.; # 39:42 N, 27 E. — pk. in Crete; # 35:14 N, 24:48 E.

Idaho (ī'dạ-hō), state, N. W. U.S.A., bet. Mont. and Ore., area 84, pop. 525, * Boise, pop. 26; second city, Pocatello, pop. 18; # 44 N, 115 W.

Idria (ēd'rē-ä), tn., ext. N. E. Italy, pop. 6; mercury and copper mines; # 46 N, 14:2 E.

Ifni (ĕf'nẹ), Spanish possession, W. coast of Morocco, area 1, pop. 20; # 29:10 N, 10:20 W.

Igidi (ē-gē'dē), sand desert, N. W. part of Sahara; # 25 N, 7 W.

Iguassú (ē-gwä-sö'), riv., trib. of Paraná riv., S. Brazil; # 25:55 S, 50:18 W. — falls, waterfalls of great volume on boundary between Brazil and Argentina, height 210 ft.; # 25:40 S, 54:33 W. — tn., a N. suburb of Rio de Janeiro, Brazil, pop. 33; # ab. 22:50 S, 43:20 W.

Ijssel or **Yssel** (īs'ẹl), a delta branch of the Rhine riv., Neth., len. 70 mi.; # 52:18 N, 6:7 E.

Île de France (ēl dẹ fräns), ancient prov., N. C. Fr., * Paris; # 49 N, 2:30 E.

Ilford (il'fẽrd), a N. E. suburb of London, Eng., pop. 80; # 51:33 N, 0:3 E.

Ili (ē'lē) or **Kulja**, city, * of Sinkiang prov., W. China, pop. ab. 60; # 43:51 N, 81:10 E. — riv., Tian Shan Mts., len. 800 mi. to Lake Balkash, C. Asia; # 45 N, 74:50 E.

Ilion (il'i-ọn), tn., C. New York, on Erie Canal, pop. 9; typewriters; # 43 N, 75 W.

Illampu (ēl-yäm'pö), see **Sorata**.

Ille-et-Vilaine (ēl-ä-vē-län), dept., N. W. Fr., area 2.7, pop. 559, * Rennes, pop. 82; # 48:10 N, 1:30 W.

Illimani (ēl-yẹ-mä'nē), prominent peak, E. of La Paz, Bolivia, el. 21,188 ft.; # 16:50 S, 67:20 W.

Illinois (il-i-noi' or -noiz'), state, E. C. U.S.A., bet. Ind. and the Mississippi riv., area 57, pop. 7,897, * Springfield, pop. 76; chief city, Chicago, pop. 3,397; # 40 N, 89 W. — riv., N. E. Ill., to Mississippi riv., len. 435 mi.; # 38:55 N, 90:30 W.

Illinois Central, R.R., Chicago to New Orleans, midwest, total mileage, 4,845.

Iloilo (ē-lō-ē'lō), spt. city on isl. of Panay, Philippines, pop. 49; # 10:40 N, 122:35 E.

Ilorin (ē-lō-rēn'), prov., S. W. Nigeria, area 6, pop. 250, and its *, pop. 70; # 8:30 N, 4:20 E.

Imaharu (ē-mä-hä'rö), spt., N. W. Shikoku isl., Japan, pop. 38; # 34:5 N, 133 E.

Imbros (im'bros), Turkish isl., Ægean sea near Dardanelles, area 0.2, pop. 7; # 40:10 N, 25:40 E.

Imperia (im-pē'ri-ä), prov., Liguria, N. W. Italy, area 0.5, pop. 151, * Porto Maurizio, pop. 26; # 43:53 N, 8:1 E.

Imperial Valley (im-pē'ri-ạl), flat region near head of Gulf of Lower Calif., in S. E. Calif. and adjacent Mex.; irrigated and very productive; # 32:45 N, 115:35 W.

Imphal (imp'hul), see **Manipur**.

Independence (in-dẹ-pen'dẹns), tn., S. E. Kansas, pop. 12; # 37:9 N, 95:43 W. — tn., N. W. C. Mo., pop. 16; # 39:4 N, 94:25 W.

India (in'di-ạ), or **Indian Empire**, Br. colony, S. Asia, area 1,803, pop. 352,838, * Delhi, pop. 304; associated Native States, area 710, pop. 72,000; # 20 N, 78 E.

Indiana (in-di-an'ạ), state, E. C. U.S.A., bet. Ill. and Ohio, area 36, pop. 3,428, * Indianapolis, pop. 387; second city, Fort Wayne, pop. 118; # 40 N, 86 W. — tn., W. Pa., pop. 10; State Teachers College; # 40:40 N, 79:10 W.

Indianapolis (in''di-ạ-nap'ọ-lis), city, C. Ind., state *, pop. 387; Butler College; Ind. Univ. Medical and Dental Schools; # 39:44 N, 86:12 W.

Indian Ocean, oc., S. of Asia, E. of Africa, W. of Australia, area 28,350, greatest depth, 22,968 ft.; # 10:15 S, 108:5 E.

Indianola (in-di-ạn-ō'lä), tn., S. C. Iowa, pop. 4; Simpson College; # ab. 41:21 N, 93:27 W.

Indian Territory, former ter., S. C. U.S.A., area 31; now in E. Okla.; # 35 N, 96 W.

Indies, see **East Indies, West Indies**.

Indo-China (in'dō-chī'nạ), Fr. possession, S. E. Asia, area 274, pop. 19,983, consisting of Cochin-China, Annam, Cambodia, Tonking and Laos, * Hanoi, pop. 100; # 20 N, 105 E.

Indonesia (in-dō-nē'shiạ), an occasional name for E. Indies.

Indore (in-dōr'), native state, C. India, area 9, pop. 1,148, and its *, pop. 93; # 22:50 N, 75:55 E.

Indre (aṅdr), riv., C. Fr. to Loire riv.; # 47:15, 0:25 E. — dept., C. Fr., area 2.7, pop. 261, * Châteauroux; # 46:55 N, 1:22 E.

Indre-et-Loire (aṅdr-ā-lwär), dept., W. C. Fr., area 2.4, pop. 328, * Tours, pop. 75; # 47:20 N, 0:30 E.

Indus (in'dus), riv., W. Tibet, across N. W. India to Arabian sea, len. 2,000 mi.; # 24:5 N, 67:15 E.

Ingolstadt (ing'ol-shtät), city on Danube riv., Bayern, S. W. Ger., pop. 27; # 48:45 N, 11:25 E.

Inland Sea of Japan, sea bet. Honshu and Shikoku isls., Japan; len. 240 mi.; # 34 N, 132:45 E.

Inn (in), riv., E. Switz. to Danube riv., N. Austria, len. 320 mi.; # 48:35 N, 12:55 E.

Innsbruck (ins'brŭk), city on Inn riv., Tyrol, W. Austria, pop. 56; univ.; # 47:47 N, 11:24 E.

Insterburg (in'stẽr-bŭrch), city, E. Prussia, N. E. Ger., pop. 39; # 54:38 N, 21:48 E.

Interlaken (in'tẽr-lä-kẹn), tourist center bet. Thuner See and Brienzer See, C. Switz., pop. 4; # 46:42 N, 7:51 E.

Invercargill (in-vẽr-kär'gil), spt. city, S. tip of S. Island, New Zealand, pop. 21; # 46:20 S, 168:30 E.

---

fat, fāte, fär, fȧll, ȧsk, fãre; net, mē, hẽr; pin, pīne; not, nōte, mȯve, nȯr; up, lūte, pu̇ll; oi, ȯil̟, ou, out; (lightened) aviȧry, ẹlect, agȯny, intȯ, u̇nite; (obscured) errạnt, operä, ardẹnt, actọr, naṭu̇re; ch, chip; g, gȯ; th, thin; ᴛн, then; y, you;

Inverness (in-vẽr-nes′), county, W. C. Scotland, area 4, pop. 78, and its *, pop. 21; # 57:30 N, 4:13 W.

Ionian (ī-ō′ni-ạn), isls., dept. W. Greece, area 0.9, pop. 224; # 37:15 N, 21:15 E. — sea bet. S. Italy, E. Sicily and Greece; # 38 N, 18 E.

Ios (ī′os), Greek isl., S. Ægean Sea, area .05; pop. 2; # 36:43 N, 25:18 E.

Iowa (ī′ō-wạ), state, N. C., U.S.A., between Miss. and Missouri rivs., area 56, pop. 2,538, * Des Moines, pop. 160; second city, Sioux City, pop. 82; # 42 N, 93 W.

Iowa City, tn., S. E. C. Iowa, pop. 17; State Univ.; # 41:40 N, 91:30 W.

Ipek (ē-pek′), see **Fünfkirchen.**

Ipoh (ē′pō), chief city, Perak, Federated Malay States, pop. 39; # 4:35 N, 101:4 E.

Ipswich (ips′wich), spt. city, Suffolk Co., S. E. Eng., pop. 82; # 52:5 N, 1:10 E. — city near Brisbane, Queensland, pop. 21; # 27:50 S, 152:40 E.

Iquique (ē-kē′kä), spt. city, N. W. Chile, * of Tarapacá prov., pop. 37; # 20:20 N, 70:5 W.

Iquitos (ē-kē′tōs), city, E. Peru, head of extensive navigation on Amazon riv., pop. 15; # 3:50 S, 73:20 W.

Irak, see **Iraq.**

Iraklion (ē-rak′lẹ-on), see **Candia.**

Iran (ē-rän′), local name for Persia. — **Plateau of,** most of Persia, and W. Afghanistan; # 32 N, 57 E.

Iraq or **Irak** (ē-räk′), kingdom, Mesopotamia, between Persia and Arabia, area 143, pop. 2,849, * Bagdad, pop. 125; # 34 N, 44 E.

Irazú (ē-rä-sö′), vol., Costa Rica, near Cartago, el. 11,325 ft.; # 9:58 N, 84 W.

Ireland (īr′lạnd), large W. isl. of British Isles, area 32, pop. 4,229; # 53 N, 8 W; see **Ireland, Northern,** and **Ireland, State of.**

Ireland, Northern, N. part of Ireland, area 5, a state of United Kingdom, pop. 1,256, * Belfast, pop. 429; # 54:40 N, 6:30 W.

Ireland, State of, or **Eire** (âr′ẹ) (from 1922 until 1937 called **Irish Free State** or **Saorstat Eireann**), state; Ireland, except N. Ireland, area 27, pop. 2,973, * Dublin, with suburbs, pop. 450; # 53 N, 8 W. [# 54 N, 5 W.

Irish Sea (ī′rish), part of Atlantic oc. bet. Ireland and Eng.;

Irkutsk (ir-kõtsk′), gov. near Lake Baikal, N. E. Asia, area 280, pop. 696, and its *, pop. 108; # 52:12 N, 104:35 E.

Iron Gates, gorge cut by Danube riv. through Carpathian mts.; rapids; canal; # 44:40 N, 22:35 E.

Ironton (ī′ẽrn-tọn), tn., S. C. Ohio, on Ohio riv., pop. 16; # 38:31 N, 82:40 W.

Ironwood (ī′ẽrn-wùd), city, N. pen. of Mich., pop. 13; # 46:28 N, 90:12 W.

Irrawaddy (ir-ạ-wod′i), riv., E. Tibet, S. across Burma to Bay of Bengal, len. ab. 1,000 mi.; # 16 N, 95:50 E.

Irtysh (ir′tish), riv., Altai Mts., C. Asia to Ob riv., len. ab. 2,000 mi.; # 58 N, 68 E.

Irvine (ẽr′vin), spt. at mouth of Irvine riv., on Irvine Bay, Ayr, S. W. Scotland, pop. 12; # 55:36 N, 4:39 W.

Irvington (ẽr′ving-tọn), suburb of Newark, New Jersey, pop. 55; # 40:43 N, 74:14 W.

Isar (ē′zär), riv., E. Austria, past Munich to Danube riv., len. 215 mi.; # 48:50 N, 13 E.

Ischia (ēs′kē-ä), small isl., N. W. of Bay of Naples, pop. 27, and spt. thereon, pop. ab. 7; # 40:43 N, 13:55 E.

Ischl (ish′l), tn., W. C. Austria, pop. 10; watering place; # 47:43 N, 13:34 E.

Isère (ē-zâr′), riv., Alps to Rhône riv., len. 150 mi.; # 45 N, 4:50 E. — dept., S. E. Fr., area 3.2, pop. 526, * Grenoble, pop. 77; # 45:10 N, 5:40 E.

Iserlohn (ē-zer-lōn′), city, Westfalen, W. Ger., pop. 31; # 51:22 N, 7:42 E.

Isfahan (is-fạ-hän′), city, S. C. Persia, pop. ab. 80; also a prov.; # 32:45 N, 51:40 E.

Ishim (ish′im), riv., S. W. Siberia to Irtysh-Ob riv., len. ab. 1,000 mi.; # 57:50 N, 71 E.

Ishpeming (ish′pẹ-ming), mining tn., N. Mich., pop. 9; # 46:31 N, 87:41 W.

Isker (is′ker), riv., S. W. Bulgaria, past Sofia to the Danube, len. ab. 250 mi.; # 43:45 N, 24:25 E.

Island, official name of Iceland.

Islay (ī′lä), isl., W. Scotland, N. of Ireland, len. 30 mi.; # 55:45 N, 6:15 W.

Isle of Man, isl., Irish Sea, area 0.2, pop. 60, * Douglas; resort; # 54:15 N, 4:30 W.

Isle of Pines (īl ov pīnz), isl., S. of W. Cuba, terr. of Cuba; # 21:40 N, 82:45 W.

Isle of Wight, see **Wight.**

Isle Royal (īl roi′ạl), isl., Lake Superior, part of Mich.; resort; # 48 N, 89 W.

Islington (iz′ling-tọn), a borough of London, Eng., pop. 330; # 51:32 N, 0:6 W.

Ismail (ēs-mȧ-ēl′) or **Tuchkov,** city, Danube delta, Romania, pop. 86; # 45:21 N, 28:46 E.

Ismid (is-mēd′), prov., N. W. Asia Minor, pop. 243, and its *, (anc. Nicomedia), on gulf of Ismid, 40 mi. S. E. of Constantinople; # 40:53 N, 29:30 E.

Isonzo (ē-zon′tsō), anc. Sontius, riv., len. ab. 75 mi., Alps to Gulf of Trieste, N. E. Italy; # 45:44 N, 13:30 E.

Ispahan (is-pạ-hän′), see **Isfahan.**

Israel (iz′rạ-el), anc. kingdom, N. Palestine; # ab. 32 N, 35:30 E.

Istanbul (ē-stän-bõl′), Turkish name for Constantinople.

Istria (is′tri-ạ), pen., N. Adriatic Sea, N. E. Italy; # 45:15 N, 14 E.

Italy (it′ạ-li), kingdom, S. Europe, area 120, pop. 38,756, * Roma, pop. 692; largest city, Milano, pop. 836; # 43 N, 13 E.

Itasca (ī-tas′kä), small lake, N. Minn., el. 1,460 ft., near the source of the Mississippi riv.; # 47:13 N, 95:11 W.

Itatiaya, Mt. (ē-tä-tē-ä′yä), highest peak in Brazil, near Rio de Janeiro, el. 8,898 ft.; # 22:23 S, 44:46 W.

Ithaca (ith′ạ-kä), city, S. W. C. New York, pop. 20; Cornell Univ.; # 42:25 N, 76:30 W. — isl., W. Greece, and spt. thereon; # 38:22 N, 20:45 E.

Ivanovo-Voznesensk (ē-vä′no-vọ-voz-nye-syensk′), city, Vladinia prov., C. Russia, pop. 108; # 57:5 N, 41:2 E.

Iviza (ē-vē′thä) or **Ibiza,** W. isl., Balearic Isls., W. Mediterranean Sea, area 0.2, pop. 27, and its *, pop. 7; Spanish; # 39 N, 1:30 E.

Ivory Coast, a colony of Fr. W. Africa, area 122, pop. 1,546, * Bingerville; # 8 N, 5 W.

Ixelles (ēk-sel), a S. division of Brussels, Belgium, pop. 92; # 50:48 N, 4:20 E.

Ixtaccihuatl (ēs-täk-sē′hwät-l), vol. near Mexico City, Mex., el. 17,342 ft.; # 19:15 N, 98:40 W.

J

Jabalpur (jub-ạl-pör′), see **Jubbulpore.**

Jablunka (yäb-lön′kä), pass, N. Carpathians, Cz.-S., el. 1,970 ft., R.R., Breslau to Hungary; # 49:30 N, 18:45 E.

Jackson (jak′sọn), city, S. C. Miss., state *, pop. 62; Millsaps College; # 32:20 N, 90:10 W. — city, S. C. Mich., pop. 50; state prison; # 42:16 N, 84:26 W. — city, W. C. Tenn., pop. 24; Union Univ.; # 35:35 N, 88:50 W. — **Port,** bottle harbor of Sydney, Australia; # 33:51 S, 151:16 E. — county, W. Mo., area 0.61, pop. 478 (1940), * Independence; chief city, Kansas City; # 39:10 N, 94:20 W.

Jacksonville (jak′sọn-vil), city, N. E. Florida, on St. Johns riv., pop. 173; # 30:25 N, 81:40 W. — city, W. C. Ill., pop. 20; Ill. and Ill. Woman's colleges; # 39:45 N, 90:20 W.

Jacmel (zhäk-mel′), city, Haiti, pop. est. 15; # 18:14 N, 72:34 W.

Jade (yä′dẹ), bay, N. W. Ger.; # 53:30 N, 8:8 E.

Jaén (Hä-ān′), prov., S. C. Spain, area 5.2, pop. 615, and its *, pop. 35; # 37:46 N, 3:49 W.

Jaffa (jaf′fạ or yäf′fä), anc. Joppa, spt. of Jerusalem, W. Palestine, pop. 48; # 32:2 N, 34:45 E.

Jaffna (jäf′nä), spt. city, N. Ceylon, pop. 42; # 9:45 N, 80:5 E.

Jagst (yägst), N. E. div. of Württemberg, S. W. Ger., area 2, pop. 421, * Ellwangen; # 48:59 N, 9:55 E.

Jaipur or **Jeypore** (jī-pör′), native state, N. W. India, area 16, pop. 2,339, and its *, pop. 120; # 26:57 N, 75:50 E.

Jaisalmer (jī-sạl-mēr′), native state, N. W. India, area 16, pop. 68, and its *, pop. 5; # 26:55 N, 70:57 E.

Jalisco (Hä-lēs′kō), state, S. W. Mexico, area 33, pop. 1,192, * Guadalajara, pop. 119; # 20 N, 104 W.

Jamaica (jạ-mā′kä), isl., S. of Cuba, W. Indies, Br. crown

(variable) ḍ as d or j, ş as s or sh, ţ as t or ch, ẕ as z or zh; o, F. cloche; ü, F. menu; ćh, Sc. loch; ṅ, F. bonbon; ′, primary accent; ″, secondary accent; †, obsolete; <, from; +, and; =, equals. See also lists at beginning of book.

colony, area 4, pop. 1,139, * Kingston, pop. 63; bananas; # 18 N, 77:30 W. — bay, W. Long Isl., bordering Brooklyn; # 40:38 N, 73:52 W.

James (jāmz), riv.,W. C. Va.,to Chesapeake Bay, len. 450 mi.; # 37:20 N, 77:15 W. — riv., also called Dakota riv., E. N. Dak., across S. Dak. to Missouri riv., len. ab. 500 mi.; # 42:55 N, 97:25 W. — **Bay**, S. part of Hudson Bay, Canada, len. 250 mi.; # 53 N, 80 W.

Jamestown (jāmz′toun), city, S. W. New York, pop. 43; # 42:8 N, 79:20 W. — ruined village, E. Va., first Eng. settlement in U.S.A., 1607; # 37:12 N, 76:45 W. — tn., E. N. Dak., pop. 9; college; # 46:55 N, 98:45 W.

Jamnagar (jäm-nug′är), native state, Kathiawar, India.

Janesville (jānz′vil), city, S. C. Wis., pop. 23; # 42:38 N, 89 W.

Japan (ja̤-pan′), monarchy, 412 Japanese isls.,area 149, pop. 59,737, with Korea, Formosa, Pescadores and Karafuto, area 261, pop. ab. 80,000, * Tokyo, pop. 1,995; # 36 N, 139 E.

Japan, Sea of, part of Pacific oc. bet. Japanese isls. and Asia, area 405, greatest known depth, 10,200 ft.; # 40 N, 134 E.

Japan Current, warm current corresponding to Gulf Stream, W. Pacific oc., and as a drift in N. and N. E. Pacific oc.

Jara (jä′rä), mt. peak, E. Tibet Plateau, W. C. China, el. 25,584 ft.; # 30:30 N, 102 E.

Jaroslaw (yä′rō-släv), city on San riv., Galicia, S. Poland, pop. 24; # 50:5 N, 22:25 E. — see **Yaroslavl.**

Jarrow (jar′ō), spt., Tynemouth, Durham, N. E. Eng., pop. 36; Venerable Bede; # 54:59 N, 1:28 W.

Jassy or **Iasi** (yäs′sē), city, Moldavia, N. C. Romania, pop. 76; # 47:10 N, 27:37 E.

Java (jä′vä), isl., Dutch E. Indies, area 51, pop. 41,719, * Batavia, pop. 437; sugar, rubber; # 7:30 S, 111 E. — cape, W. end of Java; # 6:49 S, 105:14 E. — sea bet. Java and Borneo; # 5:15 S, 112 E.

Javary (zhä-vä-rē′), riv. bet. Peru and Brazil to Amazon riv., len. 450 mi.; # 4:30 S, 71 W.

Jaxartes, see **Yaxartes.**

Jeannette (ję-net′), tn., S. W. Pa., near Greensburg, pop. 16; # 40:20 N, 79:33 W.

Jebel Shammar (jeb′el shum′ma̤r), an emirate of Arabia, N. of Nejd, pop. ab. 200, * Hail, pop. ab. 20; # 28:30 N, 42 E.

Jeddah (jed′dä), see **Jiddah.**

Jefferson City (jef′ẽr-sǫn), city, centrally located, * of Mo., pop. 24; # 38:40 N, 92:15 W.

Jeffersonville (jef′ẽr-sǫn-vil), tn., an Indiana suburb of Louisville, Ky., pop. 11; # 38:17 N, 85:45 W.

Jelgava (yel′gä-vä) or **Mitau** (mē′tou), city, S. Latvia, pop. 25; # 56:40 N, 23:30 E.

Jemmapes (zhě-måp′) or **Jemappes,** tn., Hainout, S. Belgium, near Mons, pop. 14; battle, 1792; # 50:27 N, 3:52 E.

Jena (yā′nä), city, on Saale riv., N. E. Thuringia, S. C. Ger., pop. 54; univ.; # 50:56 N, 11:35 E.

Jerez (Hä-rāth′), city, 10 mi. N. of Cádiz, S. Spain, pop. 67; sherry wine; # 36:40 N, 6:10 W.

Jericho (jer′i-kō), tn. and anc. city, N. E. of Jerusalem, Palestine; # 31:50 N, 35:30 E.

Jersey (jẽr′zi), isl., one of Br. Channel isls., area .05, pop. 50; dairy cattle; # 49:15 N, 2:10 W.

Jersey City, city and port, E. New Jersey, opposite New York City, pop. 301; # 40:43 N, 74:3 W.

Jerusalem (ję-rō′sa̤-lem), city, C. Palestine, its *, pop. 63; # 31:46 N, 35:14 E.

Jewel Cave, limestone cavern, S. E. Black Hills, S. Dak.; national monument; # 43:46 N, 103:50 W.

Jeypore (jī-pōr′), see **Jaipur.**

Jhansi (jän′sē), city, N. C. India, pop. 70; # 25:30 N, 78:40 E.

Jhelum (jē′lum), riv., trib. of Chenab riv., Kashmir, N. W. Punjab, N. W. India, len. 450 mi.; # 31:15 N, 72:15 E.

Jiddah (jid′dä) or **Jeddah,** spt. on Red Sea, near Mecca, Arabia, pop. ab. 20; # 21:35 N, 39:10 E.

Jilolo (jē-lō′lō) or **Halmahera,** isl., Dutch E. Indies, area 13, pop. 149; # 0:45 N, 128 E.

Jind (jēnd), native state, Punjab, N. W. India, area 1, pop. 308, and its *, pop. 8; # 29:19 N, 76:23 E.

Jodhpur (jōd-pōr′), native state, N. W. India, area 35, pop. 465, and its *, pop. 73; # 26:15 N, 73 E.

Johannesburg (yō-hän′nes-bu̇rch), city, Transvaal prov.,

Union of S. Africa, largest city in S. Africa, pop. 288 (152 white); rich gold mines; Univ. of Witwatersrand; # 26:12 S, 28:5 E.

John Day (jon dā), riv., Blue Mts., E. Ore. to Columbia riv., len. 250 mi.; fossils; # 44:45 N, 120:35 W.

Johnson City (jon′sǫn), tn., N. E. Tenn., pop. 25; # 36:18 N, 82:21 W. — tn., suburb of Binghamton, S. New York, pop. 18; # ab. 42:5 N, 75:50 W.

Johnstone (jon′stǫn), tn., 10 mi. W. of Glasgow, Scotland, pop. 12; # 55:50 N, 4:31 W.

Johnstown (jonz′toun), city, S. W. C. Pa., pop. 67; flood 1889; # 40:20 N, 78:52 W. — tn., E. C. New York, pop. 11; # 43:1 N, 74:26 W.

Johore (jō-hōr′), Br. protectorate, S. W. Malay Pen., area 8, pop. 282, * Johore Bahru, pop. 15; # 2 N, 103:30 E.

Jokjakarta (jok-yä-kär′tä) *Dutch* **Djokjakarta,** residency, S. Java, area 1, pop. 1,120, and its *, pop. 80; # 7:55 S, 110:15 E.

Joliet (jō′li-et), city, N. E. Ill., pop. 42; state prison; # 41:30 N, 88:5 W.

Jolo (Hō-lō′), isl., Sulu arch., Philippine isls., and its spt., pop. 6; # 6 N, 121:25 E.

Jönköping (yẽn′che̤-ping), prov., S. W. Sweden, area 4.4, pop. 230, and its *, on Lake Wetter, pop. 30; # 57:48 N, 14:13 E.

Joplin (jop′lin), city, S. W. Mo., pop. 37; lead and zinc; # 37:10 N, 94:50 W.

Joppa (jo′pä), see **Jaffa.**

Jordan (jôr′da̤n), riv., S. W. of Galilee, len. ab. 135 mi. to Dead sea, Palestine; # 31:45 N, 35:30 E.

Jostedalsbrae (yō′ste-däls-bra′), snowfield, S. Norway, feeding 24 glaciers, largest in Europe; el. ab. 6,800 ft.; # 61:40 N, 7 E.

Juan de Fuca (jō′an de̤ fū′ka̤), strait bet. Vancouver Isl. and N. W. Wash., len. 100 mi., width 15 to 20 mi.; # 48:25 N, 124:30 W.

Juan Fernandez (Hō-än′ fer-nän′däth), isl. and group, S. Pacific oc., 400 mi. W. of Chile (Alex. Selkirk, original Robinson Crusoe); to Chile; # 33:50 S, 79:30 W.

Juba (jō′bä), riv., S. C. Abyssinia, S. to Indian oc., len. ab. 500 mi.; # 0:10 S, 42:40 E.

Jubbulpore (jub-bul-pōr′), or **Jabalpur,** city, N. C. India, pop. 109; # 23:15 N, 79:50 E.

Judea (jō-dē′ä), anc. kingdom, later Roman prov., S. Palestine; # 31:45 N, 35 E.

Jugoslavia, see **Yugoslavia.**

Jujuy (Hō-Hwē′), prov., N. W. Argentina, area 15, pop. 80, and its *, pop. 8; # 24:10 S, 65:20 W.

Julian Alps (jō′lya̤n alps), range, N. E. boundary of present Italy; highest, 9,400 ft.; # 46 N, 14:15 E.

Julier (zhü-lyā, yōl′yẽr), mt. pass, Grisons, Switz., el. 7,500 ft.; # 46:29 N, 9:44 E.

Jullundur (jul-lun′dẽr), city, Punjab, N. W. India, pop. 71; # 31:19 N, 75:18 E.

Jumet (zhü-mā), a N. suburb of Charleroi, S. Belgium, pop. 29; # ab. 50:30 N, 4:30 E.

Jumna (jum′nä), riv., S. trib. Middle Ganges, N. India, len. 850 mi.; # 26:30 N, 79:20 E.

Junagarh (jō-na̤-gur′), native state, Kathiawar pen., W. India, area 3, pop. 465, and its *, pop. 45; # 21:31 N, 70:36 E.

Juncal (Hōn-käl′), mt. pk., ab. 33 mi. S. of Aconcagua, S. Andes, el. ab. 19,358 ft.; # 33 S, 69:50 W.

Juneau (jō-nō′), spt. tn., * of Ter. of Alaska, pop. 6; # 58:25 N, 134:30 W.

Jungfrau (yu̇ng′frou), pk., Bernese Alps, S. W. Switz., el. 13,668 ft.; # 46:35 N, 7:58 E.

Junín (Hō-nēn′), city, E. C. Argentina, pop. 22; # 34:30 S, 60:58 W. — dept., C. Peru, area 23, pop. 394; * Cerro de Pasco; # 11:5 S, 75:56 W.

Jura (jō′rä), isl., Argyll, W. Scotland; # 56 N, 5:55 W. — Paps of, 3 mt. pks. thereon; highest, 2,571 ft. — (zhü-rà) dept., E. Fr., area 2, pop. 229, * Lons-le-Saunier; # 46:47 N, 5:45 E.

Jura Mountains, range, folded mts., N. W. Switz. and adjacent Fr., summit in Switz., 5,524 ft. (Mt. Tendre), summit in France, 5,654 ft. (Crêt de La Niege); # 47 N, 6:30 E.

Juruá (zhō-rū-ä′), riv., trib. of upper Amazon in W. Brazil, len. ab. 800 mi.; # 2:35 S, 65:50 W.

---

fat, fāte, fär, fåll, åsk, fãre; net, mē, hẽr; pin, pīne; not, nōte, mŏve, nôr; up, lūte, pu̇ll; oi, oil; ou, out; (lightened) avia̤ry, e̤lect, ago̤ny, into̤, ṳnite; (obscured) erra̤nt, opera̤, arde̤nt, acto̤r, natṳre; ch, chip; g, go; th, thin; ᴛʜ, then; y, you;

K

Jutland (jut'lḁnd) or **Jylland,** peninsular part of Denmark, area 11.4, pop. 1,498; ⌗ 56 N, 9 E.

Kabinda (kä-bēn'dä) or **Cabinda,** part of Portuguese W. Africa (Angola) N. of Congo riv., area 3, and its *, a spt., pop. 10; ⌗ 5:34 S, 12 E.

Kabul (kä'bul), prov., N. E. Afghanistan and its * and the national *, pop. ab. 100; ⌗ 34:35 N, 69 E. — riv. E. to Indus riv., len. ab. 360 mi.; ⌗ 34 N, 72 E.

Kafiristan '(kä-fē-ri-stän'), E. prov. of Afghanistan, area ab. 5; ⌗ 35:30 N, 70 E.

Kagoshima (kä-gō'shē-mä), spt. city, S. Kyushiu Isl., Japan, pop. 125; ⌗ 31:35 N, 130:35 E.

Kaietur (kī-e-tör'), falls of Potaro riv., a trib. of Essequibo riv. in Br. Guiana, height 760 ft.; ⌗ 5:5 N, 59:25 W.

Kaifeng (kī-feng'), city, C. China Proper, * of Honan prov., pop. est. 200; ⌗ 34:55 N, 114:20 E.

Kaisarieh or **Caesarea**(kī-sä-rē'ye), prov., C. Asiatic Turkey, pop. 202, and its *, pop. 50; ⌗ 38:40 N, 35:25 E.

Kaiserslautern (kī'zėrs-lou-tėrn), city, Rheinpfalz, S. W. Ger., pop. 59; ⌗ 49:27 N, 7:45 E.

Kaiser Wilhelm Canal (kī'zėr vil'helm), see **Kiel Cánal.**

Kalahari (kä-lä-hä'rē), desert region of S. W. Africa, area ab. 350; ⌗ 21 S, 25 E.

Kalamazoo (kal'ḁ-mḁ-zō'), city, S. W. Mich., pop. 54; College and State Normal; ⌗ 42:20 N, 85:38 W.

Kalat (kȧ-lät'), native state, Baluchistan, S. Asia, area ab. 73, pop. ab. 328, and its chief city, pop. 12; ⌗ 29:10 N, 66:35 E.

Kalgan (käl'gän), city, Chihli prov., N. China, pop. est. 30; ⌗ 40:50 N, 114:55 E.

Kalgoorlie (kal-gör'li), gold mining tn., S. C. W. Australia, pop. 8; ⌗ 30:40 S, 121:30 E.

Kalisz (kä'lyēsh), city, S. C. Poland, pop. 45; ⌗ 51:45 N, 18:5 E.

Kalmar (käl'mär), prov., S. E. Sweden, area 4.5, pop. 231, and its *, a spt., pop. 18; ⌗ 56:40 N, 16:22 E.

Kalmuck (kal'muk), autonomous area, S. E. Soviet Russia, * Astrakhan; ⌗ 46:15 N, 48:10 E.

Kalmyk (kal'mēk), autonomous Soviet area, N. Russia, area 38, pop. 126, * Archangel, spt. on White sea; ⌗ ab. 64:35 N, 40:50 E.

Kama (kä'mḁ), riv., E. Russia to Volga riv., near Kazan, len. ab. 1,100 mi.; ⌗ 55:15 N, 49:15 E.

Kamchatka (käm-chät'kä), pen., N. E. Asia, len. 1,000 mi.; ⌗ 57 N, 158 E. — prov., Siberia, area 502, pop. 37; ⌗ 60 N, 155 E. — riv. in same, len. 310 mi. to Bering sea; ⌗ 55:20 N, 159:20 E.

Kamerun (kä-mė-rön'), former Ger. colony, W. Africa, now in Fr. W. Africa and Br. Nigeria. — mts. bet. Cameroons and Nigeria, highest, Mongo, el. 13,353 ft.; ⌗ 4 N, 13 E.

Kampen (käm'pėn), city on Yssel riv., Overyssel, Neth., pop. 20; ⌗ 52:34 N, 5:55 E.

Kanara (ku'nä-rä), dist., S. W. Coast India, partly in provs. of Bombay and Madras; ⌗ 13 N, 75 E.

Kanawha (kḁ-nô'wḁ), riv., N. W. Va., to Ohio riv., len. 450 mi.; ⌗ 38:20 N, 81:35 W.

Kanazawa (kä-nä-zä'wä), spt. city, N. W. C. Honshu Isl., Japan, pop. 147; ⌗ 35:20 N, 136:37 E.

Kanchanjanga (kän-chun-jun'gä), see **Kinchinjinga.**

Kandahar (kun-dä-här'), prov., C. Afghanistan and its *, pop. with suburbs 60; ⌗ 31:45 N, 65:45 E.

Kandy (kän'dē), city, C. of Ceylon, pop. 32; temples; ⌗ 7:30 N, 80:35 E.

Kanea or **Canea** (ka-nē'ḁ), spt. city, Greek isl., Crete, pop. 25; ⌗ 35:30 N, 24:1 E.

Kanem (kä'nem), dist. N. E. of Lake Chad, Fr. Equatorial Africa, area 22, pop. 100, * Mao; ⌗ 14:30 N, 15 E.

Kangaroo (kang-gḁ-rö'), isl., S. of S. Australia, len. 90 mi.; ⌗ 35:40 S, 137 E.

Kankakee (kang-kḁ-kē'), city, N. E. Ill., pop. 22; ⌗ 41:8 N, 87:50 W.

Kano (kä-nō'), city, N. Nigeria, near Lagos, pop. ab. 100; ⌗ 12:15 N, 8:30 E.

Kansas (kan'zḁs), state, C. U.S.A., bet. Mo. and Colo., area 82, pop. 1,801, * Topeka, pop. 68; chief city, Kansas City, pop. 121; ⌗ 39 N, 98 W.

Kansas City, city, N. W. C. Mo., on Missouri riv., pop. 399; Kansas City Univ.; ⌗ 39:15 N, 94:30 W. — city, N. E. Kansas, contiguous with Kansas City, Mo., pop. 121; ⌗ 39:15 N, 94:35 W.

Kansu (kän-sö'), prov., W. C. China Proper, area 125, pop. est. 5,900, * Lanchowfu; ⌗ 35:30 N, 105 E.

Kapuas (kä'pṳ-äs), largest riv. of Borneo, C. to S. W., len. 450 mi.; ⌗ 0:15 S, 109:5 E. — mt. range bet. Dutch and Br. Borneo; ⌗ 1:30 N, 113:30 E.

Kapurthala (ka-pör'thḁ-lḁ), native state, Punjab, N. W. India, area 0.6, pop. 284, and its *, pop. 19; ⌗ 31:20 N, 75:20 E.

Kara (kä'rä), sea, part of Arctic oc., bet. Novaya Zemlya and Siberia; ⌗ 72 N, 65 E. — riv., Azerbaijan; 40 N, 48:30 E. — mts., Yugoslavia; ⌗ 42:15 N, 21:30 E. — lake, Mongolia; ⌗ 48:15 N, 92:10 E.

Kara Bugaz (kä-rä' bö-gäz'), gulf, almost landlocked, S. Caspian sea; ⌗ 41 N, 54 E.

Karachi (kḁ-rä'chē), spt., ext. W. India, delta of Indus riv., pop. 217; ⌗ 24:55 N, 67 E.

Karafuto (kä-rȧ-fö'tō), Japanese part of isl. of Sakhalin, area 14, pop. 106; ⌗ 48 N, 142:15 E.

Karakoram (kä-rä-kō'räm), lofty E.-W. mt. range,W.Tibet; ⌗ 35:30 N, 78 E. — pass thereon, el. 18,317 ft.; ⌗ 35:33 N, 77:55 E.

Karasu (kä-rä'sö), prov., W. C. Turkish Asia Minor, pop. 372, * Balikesser or Balikesri; ⌗ 38:15 N, 42:24 E.

Karauli (kar-ou-lē'), native state, Rajputana, N. W. India, area 1, pop. 134, and its *, pop. 20; ⌗ 26:30 N, 77:4 E.

Karelia (kär-ä-lē'ä), soviet republic. N. W. Russia, bordering Finland, area 29, pop. 144, * Petrodzavodsk; ⌗ ab. 61:41 N, 34:20 E.

Karikal (kä-ri-käl'), Fr. prov., S. C. India, near Negapatam, area .05, pop. 53, and its *, pop. 16; ⌗ 10:55 N, 79:50 E.

Karimata (kä-rė-mä'tä), strait bet. Borneo and Sumatra; ⌗ 2 S, 108:30 E.

Karlovy Vary (kär'lṑ-vē vä'rē) (Carlsbad), tn., N. W. Bohemia, Cz-S., pop. 17; resort; ⌗ 50:15 N, 12:55 E.

Karlsbad (kärls'bät), see **Karlovy Vary.**

Karlskrona (kärls'krō-nä), spt. city, ext. S. E. Sweden, pop. 28; ⌗ 56:10 N, 15:30 E.

Karlsruhe (kärls'rö-ė), city, * of Baden republic, S. W. Ger., pop. 145; ⌗ 49:2 N, 8:25 E.

Karlstad (kärl'städ), city on Lake Väner, S. W. Sweden, pop. 20; ⌗ 59:25 N, 13:25 E.

Karroo (kä-rö'), plateau, el. 3,000–4,000 ft., S. Cape prov., Union of South Africa; ⌗ 33 S, 22 E.

Kars (kärs), vilayet, N. E. C. Turkish Asia Minor, pop. est. 63; ⌗ 40:40 N, 43:10 E.

Karshi (kär'shē), city, Bokhara, Russian Turkestan, pop. 25; ⌗ 38:52 N, 65:56 E.

Karst (kärst) or **Küstenland,** see **Carso.**

Karun (kä-rön'), riv., W. Persia to head of Persian Gulf, len. ab. 450 mi.; ⌗ 31:57 N, 50 E.

Kasai (kä-sī'), riv., chief S. trib. of Congo riv., equatorial Africa, len. ab. 1,500 mi.; ⌗ 3:10 S, 17:10 E.

Kashan (kä-shän'), city, C. Persia, pop. ab. 35, also a prov.; ⌗ 33:55 N, 51:10 E.

Kashgar (käsh-gär'), prov., riv. (len. 500 mi.) and city (pop. 65), W. Sinkiang prov., W. China; ⌗ 39:30 N, 75:50 E.

Kashmir (kash-mēr'), native state, N. of W. Himalayas, W. India, area 84, pop. 3,321, * Srinagar, pop. 142; ⌗ 34 N, 76 E.

Kassai, see **Kasai.**

Kassel (kä'sel), city, S. C. Ger., pop. 168; ⌗ 51:17 N, 9:30 E.

Kastamuni (käs-tä-mö'nē), prov., N. C. Asiatic Turkey, area 20, pop. 412, and its *, pop. 20; ⌗ 41:20 N, 33:40 E.

Katahdin (kḁ-tä'din), mt., highest peak in Me., el. 5,273 ft.; ⌗ 45:54 N, 68:55 W.

Katanga (kä-täng'gä), prov., E. Belgian Congo, * Albertville, on Lake Tanganyika; radium mines; ⌗ 10 S, 27 E.

Katharina (kä-tä-rē'nä), only ice-free N. Russian port, ext. N. W. Russia; ⌗ 69:10 N, 33:30 E.

Kathiawar (kät''ẹ-ä-wär'), pen., W. India, area 23, bet. Gulfs of Cutch and Cambay, pop. ab. 2,500; ⌗ 22 N, 71 E.

Katmai (kat'mī), active volcano, explosion 1912, S. W. Alaska, and National Monument, including Valley of 10,000 Smokes; ⌗ 58 N, 155 W.

(variable) ḏ as d or j, ṣ as s or sh, ṯ as t or ch, ẕ as z or zh; o, F. cloche; ü, F. menu; ċh, Sc. loch; ṅ, F. bonbon; ', primary accent; ", secondary accent; †, obsolete; <, from; +, and; =, equals. See also lists at beginning of book·

Katmandu (kät-män-dö′), city, C. Nepal, its *, pop. 80; # 27:50 N, 85:20 E.

Katoomba (kȧ-töm′bȧ), tn., S. E. C. New S. Wales, Australia, pop. 10; # 33:42 S, 150:17 E.

Katowice (kä-tō-vē′tse) or **Kattowitz**, city, Poland, N. W. of Crakow; pop. 45; # 50:16 N, 19:1 E.

Katrine, Loch (kat′rin), beautiful lake, 8 mi. long, S. W. Perthshire, Scotland; Scott's "Lady of the Lake"; # 56:15 N, 4:30 W.

Kattegat (kat′ē-gat), strait bet. Jutland and Sweden, width 40 to 70 mi.; # 57 N, 11 E.

Kattowitz (kä′tō-vits), see **Katowice**.

Kauai (kou-ī′), most N. W. large isl. of Hawaii, area 0.5; # 22:5 N, 159:30 W.

Kavala or **Cavalla** (kä-vä′lä), spt., ext. N. E. Greece, pop. 23; # 40:58 N, 24:25 E.

Kaveri (kä′vẹ-ri), see **Cauvery**.

Kawagoe (kä-wȧ-gō′e), a N. suburb, of Tokyo, Japan, pop. 32; # 35:54 N, 139:30 E.

Kawasaki (kä-wȧ-sä′kẹ), a S. suburb of Tokyo, Japan, pop. 55; # 35:32 N, 139:43 E.

Kazan (kä-zän′), former prov., E. C. Russia, area 25, pop. 2,700, and its *, on Volga riv., pop. 195; now in Chuvash Soviet Republic; univ.; # 55:45 N, 49:5 E. — riv., Quebec to Hudson Bay, len. 450 mi.; # 63:28 N, 97 W.

Kazanlik (kä-zän′lik), tn., Tunja valley, S. E. Bulgaria, pop. 10; attar of roses; # 42:38 N, 25:25 E.

Kazbek (käz′bek), *anc.* Prometheus, mt., C. Caucasus, el. 16,546 ft.; # 42:40 N, 44:25 E.

Kazvin (käz-vēn′), city, N. W. C. Persia, pop. ab. 35, also a prov., area ab. 14; # 36:15 N, 50 E.

Kearny (kär′ni), a W. suburb of Newark, New Jersey, pop. 39; # 40:46 N, 74:9 W.

Kebnekaisse (cheb′nẹ-kī′sẹ), mt. pk., N. Sweden, highest in Sweden, el. 7,005 ft.; # 67:55 N, 18:30 E.

Kecskemét (kech′kem-āt), city, S. E. C. Hungary, pop. 73; # 46:54 N, 19:44 E.

Kedah (kä′dä), Br. protected state, W. Malay pen., area 3.8, pop. 339, * Alor Star, pop. 11; # 6:7 N, 100:20 E.

Kedarnath (kä-där′nät) or **Kidarnath**, mt. pk., E. Kashmir, Himalaya Mts., el, 22,853 ft.; # ab. 30:30 N, 79 E.

Keeling (kē′ling), see **Cocos**.

Keelung (kē′lŭng′), chief port of Taiwan (Formosa), N. coast, pop. 38; # 25:5 N, 121:35 E.

Keene (kēn), tn., S. W. New Hampshire, pop. 14; resort; # 42:55 N, 72:15 W.

Keewatin (kē-wä′tin), S. E. dist. of N. W. Territories of Canada, area 229; # 63 N, 90 W.

Keighley (kēth′li), city, West Riding, York, C. Eng., 16 mi. W. N. W. of Leeds, pop. 42; # 53:53 N, 1:55 W.

Keijo-fu (kā′jō-fö), Japanese name for Seoul.

Kelantan (kẹ-län-tän′), a Br. protected state, E. coast Malay pen., area 6, pop. 309, * Kota Bharu, pop. 11; # 6 N, 102: 10 E.

Kelat, see **Kalat**.

Keltsy (kyel′tsi), see **Kielce**.

Kempten, city, Bavaria, S. Ger., pop. 22; # 47:30 N, 10: 18 E.

Kenai (ke-nī′), pen., S. C. Alaska, mts. and tn. on same; # 60:30 N, 150 W.

Kenia (kä′nẹ-ä), see **Kenya**.

Kenilworth (ken′il-wẽrth), tn., Warwick, S. C. Eng., pop. 7; ruined castle; # 52:22 N, 1:35 W.

Kenmore (ken′mōr), tn., N. E. Ohio, suburb of Akron, pop. 18; # ab. 41:6 N, 81:30 W.

Kennebec (ken-ẹ-bek′), riv., N. Me. to Atlantic oc., len. 150 mi.; # 44:40 N, 69:45 W.

Kenosha (ke-nō′shȧ), city, S. E. Wis., pop. 49; # 42:40 N, 87:50 W.

Kensington (ken′zing-tọn), a W. borough of London, Eng., pop. 176; Br. Museum; # 51:30 N, 0:12 W.

Kent (kent), county, ext. S. E. Eng., area 1.5, pop. 1,142, * Maidstone, pop. 39; # 51:15 N, 0:20 E.

Kentucky (ken-tuk′i), state, S. E. C. U.S.A., between Tenn. and the Ohio riv., area 41, pop. 2,846, * Frankfort, pop. 11; chief city, Louisville, pop. 319; # 38 N, 85 W. — riv., E. Ky. to Ohio riv., len. 380 mi.; # 38:45 N, 85:5 W.

Kenya (kä′nẹ-ä), a Br. crown colony, E. Africa, area 212,

---

pop. 2,360, * Nairobi, pop. 24; # 1 N, 38 E. — vol. mt. therein, el. 17,040 ft.; # 1 S, 37:30 E.

Keokuk (kē′ọ-kuk), city, ext. S. E. Iowa, pop. 15; large hydroelectric power dam on Mississippi riv.; # 40:30 N, 91:30 W.

Kerak (ke-räk′), region E. of Palestine (see **Trans-Jordania**) and tn. therein; # 31:13 N, 35:35 E.

Kerbela (kẽr′be-lä), city, S. W. Bagdad, C. Iraq, pop. ab. 50, across Euphrates riv. from anc. Babylon; # 32:45 N, 44 E.

Kerch (kerch), spt., E. end. of Crimea, on Kerch strait, S. Russia, pop. 56; # 45:25 N, 36:29 E.

Kerguelen (kẽrg′ẹ-len), Fr. isl.; desolate; # 49 S, 70 E.

Kerkrade (kerk′rä-dẹ), city, Limburg, S. Neth., pop. 28; # ab. 50:50 N, 6:5 E.

Kerman (ker-män′), city, S. E. C. Persia, pop. ab. 70, also a prov.; area ab. 115; # 30:30 N, 57:5 E.

Kermanshah (ker-män-shä′), city, W. C. Persia, pop. ab. 50; # 34:10 N, 47 E.

Kern (kẽrn), riv., S. Sierra Nevada mts., Calif., to Kern and Tulare lakes, len. 200 mi.; # 35:10 N, 119:10 W.

Kerry (ker′i), county, Munster, S. W. Ireland, area 1.8, pop. 160, * Killarney; Kerry cattle; # 51:55 N, 9:45 W.

Kesteven (kes′tẹ-vẹn), part of Lincolnshire, E. C. Eng., area 0.7, pop. 108; # 53 N, 0:30 W.

Kew (kū), parish, Surrey Co., near London, Eng.; botanical gardens; # 51:28 N, 0:17 W.

Kewanee (kē-wä′nē), city, N. W. C. Ill., pop. 17; # 41:15 N, 89:56 W.

Keweenaw (kē′wẹ-nȧ), pen., N. Mich., in Lake Superior; copper mines; # 47:20 N, 88:10 W.

Key West (kē west), city on isl., off coast of S. Florida, pop. 13; # 24:40 N, 81:50 W.

Khabarovka (khä-bä-rof′kä) or **Khabarovsk**, city on lower Amur riv., E. Siberia, pop. 49; # 48:40 N, 135:10 E.

Khaibar (chī′bẽr), see **Khyber**.

Khairpur (kīr-pör′), native state, Lower Indus Valley, N. W. India, area 6, pop. 193, and its *, pop. 16; # ab. 27 N, 69 E.

Khalkidike or **Chalcidice** (kal-sid′i-sē), tripartite pen., N. E. Greece; # 40:30 N, 23:25 E.

Khalkis or **Chalcis** (kal′sis), spt., W. Eubœa isl., E. Greece, pop. 13; # 38:29 N, 23:38 E.

Kham (käm), prov., S. E. Tibet, C. Asia; # 30:15 N, 97 E.

Khangai (khän-gī′), lofty mt. range, Outer Mongolia, C. Asia; # 48 N, 99 E.

Khan Tengri (khän ten′grē), see **Tengri, Khan**.

Kharbin, see **Harbin**.

Kharga (kär′gȧ), oasis, W. of Nile, Middle Egypt, and town therein; # 25 N, 31 E.

Kharkov (chär′kof), prov., Ukraine, S. W. Russia, area 21, pop. 3,300 and its *, the * of Ukraine, pop. 312; # 50 N, 36:15 E.

Kharput (chär-pöt′), * of Mamuret-el-Aziz prov., Armenia, pop. 20; # 38:40 N, 39:16 E.

Khartoum (chär-töm′), city, at junction of Blue Nile and Nile in Egypt, pop. 31, with suburbs, pop. 124; # 15:30 N, 32:30 E.

Khasi Hills (chä′sẹ), low mts., W. Assam, N. E. India; tea; # 25:45 N, 91:30 E.

Khelat (ke-lät′), see **Kalat**.

Kherson (cher-sŏn′), prov., S. W. Ukraine, S. W. Russia, area 27, pop. 3,500, and its *, a spt. on Gulf of Odessa, pop. 67; # 46:40 N, 32:35 E.

Khingan (chin-gän′), mt. range, W. Manchuria and E. Mongolia; # 48 N, 121 E.

Khiva (chē′vä), soviet, Russian Turkestan, C. Asia, area 24, pop. 519, and its *, pop. 5; now part of Uzbek Republic; # 42 N, 59 E.

Khokand (cho-känt′), see **Kokand**.

Khorasan (chō-rä-sän′), prov., N. E. Persia, * Meshed, pop. 70; # 36 N, 59 E.

Khotan (chō-tän′), city (pop. 30) and riv., S. W. Chinese Turkestan; # 37 N, 79:50 E.

Khyber (chī-bẽr) or **Khaibar**, important pass, N. W. India (near Peshawar), to Afghanistan, el. 6,825 ft.; # 34:10 N, 71:10 E.

Kialing-Ho (kyä-ling′hō), navigable trib. of Yangtse-Kiang riv., Szechwan prov., S. W. China, len. 500 mi.; # 29:30 N, 106:15 E.

---

fat, fāte, fär, fȧll, ȧsk, fāre; net, mē, hẽr; pin, pīne; not, nōte, möve, nôr; up, lūte, pṳll; oi, oil; ou, out; (lightened) aviȧry, ẹlect, agọny, intọ, ụnite; (obscured) errȧnt, operȧ, ardẹnt, actọr, natṳre; ch, chip; g, go; th, thin; ᴛʜ, then; y, you;

Kianfu (kyän′fö′), city, Kiangsi prov., S. E. China, pop. est. 30; # 27:5 N, 114:50 E.

Kiangmai (kyäng′mi′) or **Chiengmai,** city, N. C. Siam, pop. 100; # 18:50 N, 98:58 E.

Kiangsi (kyäng′sē′), prov., S. E. C. China, area 69, pop. est. 24,000, * Nanchang, pop. ab. 300; # 27:30 N, 115:30 E.

Kiangsu (kyäng′sö′), prov., E. C. China, on coast, area 39, pop. est. 28,000, * Nanking, pop. 525; # 33 N, 120 E.

Kiaochow (kyou′chou′), see **Kiauchow.**

Kiauchow (ki-ou′chou′) or **Kiachau,** port and bay, S. Shantung pen., N. E. China, pop. est. 34; formerly leased to Germany; # 36:18 N, 120:20 E.

Kibo (ki′bō), see **Kilimanjaro.**

Kickinghorse, riv. and R.R. pass, S. E. Br. Columbia, Canadian Rockies; two spiral tunnels on Canadian Pacific R.R.; # 51:27 N, 116:18 W.

Kidarnath, see **Kedarnath.**

Kidderminster (kid′ėr-min-stėr), city, N. Worcestershire, S. W. C. Eng., 16 mi. S. W. of Birmingham, pop. 24; carpets; # 52:23 N, 2:14 W.

Kieff (kē′ef), see **Kiev.**

Kiel (kēl), spt. city, N. Baltic end of Kiel Canal, Jutland pen., pop. 212; univ.; # 54:20 N, 10:10 E. — ship canal across base of Danish pen., len. 61 mi., depth 45 ft., completed 1895, deepened 1913–1914; # 54:15 N, 9:30 E.

Kielce or **Kieltse** (kē-elt′se), county, S. W. Poland, area 10, pop. 2,536, and its *, pop. 41; # 50:50 N, 20:40 E.

Kiev (kē′ef), prov., S. W. Russia, area 20, pop. 4,600, and its *, a * of Ukraine, pop. 435; univ.; # 50:20 N, 30:25 E.

Kii Channel (kē′ē), strait bet. E. Shikoku and Honshu isls., Japan; # 33:45 N, 134:55 E.

Kilauea (kē-lou-ā′ä), crater, side of Mauna Loa, isl. of Hawaii, el. 4,040 ft., active; # 19:25 N, 155:15 W.

Kilimanjaro (kil-ē-män-jä′rö), vol. mt. in equatorial Br. E. Africa, el. 19,455 ft., highest in Africa; # 3 S, 37 E.

Kilkenny (kil-ken′i), county, Leinster prov., S. E. Ireland, area 0.8, pop. 75, and its *, pop. 11; castle and cathedral; # 52:40 N, 7:15 W.

Killarney (ki-lär′ni), tn., S. W. Ireland, * of Kerry Co., pop. 6, and lakes nearby; # 52 N, 9:34 W.

Killiecrankie (kil-i-krang′ki), pass, Grampian Mts., N. C. Scotland; battle, 1689; # 56:44 N, 3:46 W.

Kilmarnock (kil-mär′nok), city, 20 mi. S. of Glasgow, Scotland, pop. 37; # 55:38 N, 4:32 W.

Kimberley (kim′bėr-li), city in Cape of Good Hope, Union of S. Africa, pop. 40; diamond mines; # 28:50 S, 24:40 E.

Kincardine (kin-kär′din), county, E. C. Scotland, area 0.4, pop. 42, * Stonehaven; # 56:55 N, 2:30 W.

Kinchinjinga (kin-chin-jing′gä), mt. pk., Himalayas, near Mt. Everest, Nepal, el. 28,146 ft.; # 27:45 N, 88:10 E.

King County, county, N. W. Wash., area 2.1, pop. 505 (1940), * Seattle; # 47:37 N, 122:20 W.

Kings, riv., S. Sierra Nevada Mts., Calif., to Tulare lake and San Joaquin riv., len. 120 mi.; gorge; # 36:10 N, 119:45 W. — county, S. E. New York, area .071, pop. 2,698, a S. borough of New York City; # 40:40 N, 73:58 W.

Kings Norton (kingz nôr′ton), a borough of Birmingham, Eng.; # 52:24 N, 1:56 W.

King Sound (king sound), gulf, N. W. Australia, len. 100 mi.; # 17 S, 123:30 E.

Kingston (king′ston), spt. city, S. E. Jamaica, its *, pop. 63; # 18 N, 76:50 W. — city, S. E. New York, pop. 29; # 41:59 N, 74 W. — city, E. end of Lake Ontario, Ont., pop. 22; Queens Univ. and Royal Military College; naval station; # 44:15 N, 76:30 W. — -on-Hull, spt.city, E. C. Eng., pop. 287; official name of Hull; # 53:43 N, 0:20 W.

Kingtehchin (king′te-chin′), city, Kiangsi prov., S. E. China, pop. est. 500; porcelain; # 29:10 N, 117:30 E.

Kinnaird (ki-närd′), cape, ext. E. Scotland; # 57:40 N, 2 W.

Kinross (kin-ros′), county, S. E. C. Scotland, area .08, pop. 8, and its *, pop. 3; # 56:17 N, 3:25 W.

Kintyre (kin-tīr′) or **Cantyre,** pen., W. Scotland, len. 40 mi.; # 55:30 N, 5:35 W.

Kioto (kē-ō′tō), see **Kyoto.**

Kirghiz (kir-gēz′), soviet republic, Russian Turkestan, area 844, pop. 5,059, * Orenburg; #48 N, 62 E.

Kirin (kē′rēn′), prov., S. C. Manchuria, area 105, pop. ab. 6,000, and its *, pop. est. 100; # 43:55 N, 126:40 E.

Kirkcaldy (kėr-kȧ′di), spt. on Firth of Forth, S. E. Scotland, pop. 40; # 56:7 N, 3:10 W.

Kirkcudbright (kėr-kö′bri), county, ext. S. Scotland, area 0.9, pop. 35, and its *, pop. 2; # 54:50 N, 4:3 W.

Kirkintilloch (kėrk-in-til′oċh), suburb, N. E. of Glasgow, Scotland, pop. 12; # 55:56 N, 4:9 W.

Kirkwall (kėrk′wȧl), spt., * of Orkney Isls., Scotland, on Pomona isl., pop. 4; # 58:58 N, 2:55 W.

Kirman, see **Kerman.**

Kiryu (kē′ri-ö), city, 55 mi. N. of Tokyo, Japan, pop. 43; # 36:24 N, 139:19 E.

Kishewada (kēsh-e-wä-dä′), a S. suburb of Osaka, Japan, pop. 32; # 34:26 N, 135:22 E.

Kishinef (kēsh-ē-nef′), former name of Chisinau, city, Bessarabia, N. E. Romania, pop. 114; #46:55 N, 28:50 E.

Kispest (kish-pesht′), suburb of Budapest, Hungary, pop. 51; # 47:29 N, 19:7 E.

Kistna (kist′nȧ), riv., W. Ghats, E. to Bay of Bengal, S. India, len. ab. 500 mi.; # 15:50 N, 80:55 E.

Kitchener (kich′ę-nėr), formerly **Berlin,** city, S. Ontario, pop. 22; # 43:25 N, 80:35 W.

Kiukiang (kyö′kyäng′), city, on Yangtse riv., S. E. C. China, pop. est. 53; # 29:43 N, 116:5 E.

Kiungchau (kē-öng′chou′), spt., Hainan isl., S. China, pop. est. 59; # 20 N, 110:20 E.

Kiusiu (kyö′syö′), see **Kyushiu.**

Kizil (kiz′il), riv., N. W. Persia to Caspian Sea, len. 450 mi.; # 37:30 N, 50:5 E.

Kizil Irmak (kiz′il ir-mäk′), anc. Halys, riv., N. C. Asia Minor to Black Sea, len. 600 mi.; #41:40 N, 36 E.

Kjöbenhavn (kė-pn-houn′), see **Copenhagen.**

Kjölen (chè′lęn), mt. range bet. Norway and Sweden, summit, Mt. Kebnekaisse, el. 7,005 ft.; # 65 N, 14 E.

Klagenfurt (klä′gen-fúrt), city, S. C. Austria, pop. 27, * of Carinthia; #46:40 N, 14:20 E.

Klaipeda (klī′pe-dä), Lithuanian name for **Memel,** dist. and city; see **Memel.**

Klamath (kla′math), riv., S. W. Ore., through Klamath lake and mts. to Pacific oc., N. W. Calif., len. ab. 250 mi.; #41:30 N, 124:5 W.

Klar (klär), riv., S. Sweden, entering Lake Väner (Wener); # 59:24 N, 13:30 E.

Klausenburg (klou′zen-búrċh), see **Kolozsvar.**

Klondike (klon′dīk), riv., Yukon ter., N. W. Canada to Yukon riv.; gold fields; # 64 N, 139:30 W.

Klyuchev (klyü′chef), or **Kluchevskaya,** vol. pk., S. Kamchatka, el. 16,124 ft., highest in N. E. Asia; # 56 N, 160:30 E.

Knoxville (noks′vil), city, E. C. Tenn., pop. 112; State Univ.; college; # 35:50 N, 84 W.

Kobdo (kob′dō), prov., N. W. Mongolia, and its *, pop. 12. — riv. in same; #48:15 N, 91:35 E.

Kobe (kō′be), spt. city, S. Honshu isl., Japan, pop. 644; # 34:40 N, 135:10 E.

Koblenz (kō′blents), see **Coblenz.**

Kochi (kō′chē), spt. city, S. Shikoku isl., Japan, pop. 66; # 33:32 N, 133:35 E.

Kodiak (kod-yak′), isl., N. Pacific oc., near base of Alaska pen., len. 100 mi.; # 57:40 N, 152:30 W.

Kofu (kō′fö), inland city, C. Honshu isl., Japan, pop. 68; # 35:45 N, 138:40 E.

Kokand (ko-känt′) or **Khokand,** city, Sir-Daria prov., Russian Turkestan, pop. 112; #40:30 N, 71 E.

Kokomo (kō′kō-mō), city, N. C. Ind., pop. 37; # 40:30 N, 86:8 W.

Koko Nor (kō′kō nôr′), prov., N. C. Tibet, C. Asia. — lake therein, len. 65 mi.; # 37 N, 100:15 E.

Kokura (kō′kú-rä), city, ext. N. Kyushiu isl., Japan, pop. 52; # 33:50 N, 130:55 E.

Kola (kō′lä), pen., ext. N. W. Russia, N. W. of White Sea and town thereon; # 67 N, 38 E.

Kolberg (kol′berċh), spt., Baltic Sea, Pomerania, N. E. Ger., pop. 33; # 54:10 N, 15:37 E.

Kolhapur (kō-lä-pör′), native state, N. of Goa, S. W. India, area 3, pop. 834, and its *, pop. 56; # 16:45 N, 74:10 E.

Kolima (kō-lē-mä′), see **Kolyma.**

Kolin (ko-lēn′), tn. on Elbe riv., C. Bohemia, pop. 16; battle, 1757; # 50:2 N, 15:15 E.

Kolmar (kŏl′mär), see **Colmar.**

Köln (kĕln), see **Cöln.**

Kolomea (kō-lō-mä′ä) or **Kolomyja** (-yä), city, Galicia, S. E. Poland, on Prut riv., pop. 41; # 48:32 N, 25:1 E.

Kolozsvar (kŏ′lŏsh-vär), **Klausenburg,** now **Cluj,** city, Transylvania, C. Romania, pop. 61; univ.; # 46:44 N, 23:33 E.

Kolyma (kö-li-mä′), riv., Stanovoi mts., N. E. Siberia to Arctic oc., len. ab. 1,000 mi.; # 67:42 N, 161:50 E.

Konakry (kō-nȧ-krē′), spt. city, * of Fr. Guinea, W. Africa, pop. 7; # 9:29 N, 13:42 W.

Kongmoon (kông′mön′), city, Si-kiang riv., near Hongkong, S. E. China, pop. est. 77; # 22:31 N, 113:5 E.

Kongo (kong′gō), see **Congo.**

Koniah (kō′nē-ä), prov., S. C. Asiatic Turkey, pop. 527, and its *, *anc.* Iconium, city in S. C. Asia Minor, pop. 71; # 37:50 N, 32:25 E.

Konieh (kō′nē-e), see **Koniah.**

Königliche Weinberge (kĕ′nich-li-chĕ vīn′ber″gĕ), suburb of Praha, Bohemia, Cz-S., pop. 77; # ab. 50:5 N, 14:28 E.

Königsberg (kĕ′nichs-berch), city, N. mouth of Pregel riv., E. Prussia, pop. 275; univ.; # 54:45 N, 20:30 E.

Königshütte (kĕ′nichs-hüt-ê), see **Królewska Huta.**

Konin (kō′nyēn), pen., N. Russia, E. of White Sea; # 68 N, 45 E.

Konstanz (kon′shtänts), dist., S. E. Baden, S. W. Ger., area, 1.6, pop. 338, and its *, a city on Lake Constance, pop. 32; # 47:39 N, 9:10 E.

Kootenay (kō′tḗ-nä), riv., S. E. Br. Columbia, N. Mont. and Idaho, to Columbia riv., len. 400 mi.; # 49:10 N, 115:15 W. — lake, S. E. Br. Columbia, len. 75 mi.; # 49:40 N, 116:55 W.

Kordofan (kor-dō-fän′), prov., C. Anglo-Egyptian Sudan, area 114, pop. ab. 500, * El Obeid; # 13:30 N, 30 E.

Korea (kō-rē′ä), *Jap.* **Chosen,** pen., E. Asia, Japanese possession, area 85, pop. 18,313, * Seoul, pop. 271; # 38 N, 128 E.

Korea Strait, strait bet. Korea and Japan; # 34:30 N, 129 E.

Korinchi (kō-rēn′chi), mt., highest of Barisan mts., Sumatra, el. 12,484 ft.; # 0:40 S, 101:15 E.

Koriyama (kŏ-rḗ-yä′mä), a N. suburb of Osaka, S. Honshu isl., Jap., pop. 43; # 34:39 N, 135:46 E.

Körös (kĕ′rĕsh), riv., Bihar mts., W. Romania to Theis riv., Hungary, len. ab. 350 mi.; coal field; # 46:45 N, 20:12 E.

Kos (kos), Greek isl., S. E. Ægean Sea, area 0.1, pop. 10. — spt. thereon; # 36:45 N, 27:20 E.

Kosciusko (kos-i-us′kō), mt., highest in Australia, S. E. New S. Wales, el. 7,328 ft.; # 36:27 S, 148:20 E.

Košice (kŏ′shit-se) or **Kassa,** city, E. Slovakia, E. Czecho-slovakia, pop. 52; # 48:74 N, 21:16 E.

Köslin (kĕz′lin), city, Pomerania, N. E. Ger., pop. 29; # 54:12 N, 16:12 E.

Kosso-gol (kos′sŏ-gol), lake, N. W. Mongolia, len. 90 mi.; # 51 N, 100:30 E.

Kostroma (kos-trō-mä′), prov., C. Russia, area 30, pop. 1,200, and its *, pop. 48, on Volga riv.; # 57:40 N, 40:50 E.

Kotah (kō′tä), native state, N. W. India, area 6, pop. 630, and its *, pop. 32; # 25:11 N, 75:51 E.

Köthen or **Cöthen** (kĕ′tĕn), city, Anhalt state, C. Ger., pop. 27; # 51:45 N, 11:58 E.

Kovno (kov′nō) or **Kaunas,** city, S. C. Lithuania, its *, pop. 92; univ.; # 54:50 N, 23:50 E.

Koweit or **Kuwait** (kō-wät′), sultanate, N. W. coast of Persian Gulf, pop. ab. 50, and its *, pop. 25; Br. protectorate; # 29 N, 48 E.

Kowloon (kō′lön′), spt. city, part of Br. colony of Hongkong, coast of S. China, pop. 140; # 22:20 N, 114:10 E.

Kra (krä), **Isthmus of,** narrowest, lowest section of Malay pen., width 35 mi., el. 100 ft., site of projected ship canal; # 10:30 N, 98:50 E.

Krakatua (krä-kä-tö′ä), isl. and volcano bet. Sumatra and Java; terrific explosion, 1883; # 6:15 S, 105:30 E.

Krakow or **Crakow** (krä′kō), city, S. W. Poland, pop. 182; univ.; # 50:5 N, 19:55 E.

Krasnovodsk (kräs-nō-vodsk′), city, E. shore Caspian Sea, opp. Baku, pop. 10; starting point of Transcaspian R.R.; # 40 N, 53 E.

Krasnoyarsk (kräs-nō-yärsk′), city on Yenisei riv. and Trans-Siberian R.R., pop. 63; # 56:5 N, 92:55 E.

Krefeld (krä′felt), city, Rheinland, W. Prussia, W. Ger., pop. 130; # 51:23 N, 6:30 E.

Kremenchug (krä-men-chōg′), city on Dnieper riv., S. C. Russia, pop. 99; # 49:5 N, 33:25 E.

Kreuzberg (kroits′berch), a S. div. of Berlin, Ger., pop. 368; # 52:29 N, 13:22 E.

Kreuznach (kroits′näch), a watering place, 21 mi. W. S. W. of Mainz, S. W. Ger., pop. 26; # 49:51 N, 7:52 E.

Kristiania (kris-tē-ä′nē-ä), glacial fjord, S. E. Norway to Oslo; # 59:30 N, 10:40 E. — see **Oslo.**

Kristiansand (kris-tyȧn-sän′), spt., ext. S. Norway, pop. 17; # 58:5 N, 8 E.

Kristiansund (kris-tyȧn-sun′), spt. on isl., W. C. Norway, pop. 15; # 63:7 N, 7:45 E.

Krk (kĕrk) or **Veglia,** isl., N. Dalmatia, Yugoslavia, len. 25 mi.; # 45:5 N, 14:35 E.

Królewska Huta (krṵ-lef′skä hö′tä), *Ger.* **Königshütte,** city, S. W. Poland, pop. 75; # 50:18 N, 18:58 E.

Kronstadt (krōn′shtät), outer port on isl. W. of Leningrad, N. W. Russia, pop. 67; # 59:55 N, 29:35 E.

Krugersdorp (krṵ′gêrs-dôrp), city near Johannesburg, U. of S. Africa, pop. 43, white 13; # 26:9 S, 27:53 E.

Kuala Lumpur (kwä′lä lům-pör′), spt. city, * of Selangor, Malaysia, pop. ab. 80; # 3:15 N, 101:45 E.

Kuban (kö-bän′), riv., Mt. Elbruz, Caucasus mts., W. to Sea of Azov and Black Sea, len. ab. 500 mi.; # 45:10 N, 37:10 E. — city on same, also called **Ekaterinodar,** pop. 90; # 45:2 N, 39 E.

Kubanga (kṵ-bän′gä), riv., C. Angola, E. to Kalahari desert, S. C. Africa, len. ab. 800 mi.; # 19 S, 22:30 E.

Kuch Behar (köch bä-här′), see **Cooch Behar.**

Kuching (kö′ching), spt., chief city, Sarawak, Br. Borneo, pop. 30; # 1:50 N, 110:20 E.

Kuenlun (kwen-lön′), lofty E–W mt. range, N. Tibet, len. 1,500 mi., highest over 20,000 ft.; # 35:30 N, 88 E.

Kufara (kö′fä-rä), oasis, Libyan desert, N. E. Africa; # 24 N, 22 E.

Kuka (kö′kä) or **Kukawa,** city, N. E. Nigeria, near Lake Chad, pop. ab. 50, * of Bornu; # 12:55 N, 13:30 E.

Kuldja (köl′jä), see **Kulja.**

Kulja (köl′jä), prov. N. Sinkiang, C. Asia, and its *, also known as **Ili,** pop. ab. 60; # 44 N, 81 E.

Kum (köm), prov., C. Persia and its *, pop. ab. 35; # 34:38 N, 50:56 E.

Kumamoto (kö-mä-mō-tō′), city, W. Kyushiu isl., Japan, pop. 147; # 32:50 N, 130:45 E.

Kumbakonam (köm-bȧ-kō′nȧm), interior city, far S. India, pop. 61; # 10:58 N, 79:25 E.

Kuopio (kö-ō′pē-ō), dept., S. C. Finland, area 14, pop. 362 and its *, pop. 19; # 62:50 N, 27:35 E.

Kurdistan (kör-di-stän′), plateau region, S. E. Asia Minor, area ab. 74; peopled largely by Kurds; # 37 N, 43 E. — prov., N. W. Persia; # 36 N, 46 E. — **Southern,** prov. in N. E. Mesopotamia; # 36 N, 44 E.

Kure (kö′re), spt. on S. W. Honshu isl., Japan, pop. 139; naval station; # 34:20 N, 132:40 E.

Kurg (körg), see **Coorg.**

Kurile (kö′ril), *Jap.* **Chishima,** 31 isls., N. Japan, area 6, pop. 3; # 48 N, 152 E.

Kurisches Haff (kö′rish-es häf), coastal lake, E. Prussia and Lithuania, len. 60 mi.; # 55 N, 21 E.

Kurland (kör′lȧnd), former Russian prov., see **Latvia.**

Kursk (körsk), prov., S. W. C. Russia, area 18, pop. 3,000, and its *, pop. 83; # 51:44 N, 36:15 E.

Kurume (kö′rṵ-me), city near Nagasaki, W. Kyushiu isl., Japan, pop. 72; # 33:20 N, 130:30 E.

Kushiro (kö′shē-rō), inland city on Lake Kushiro, Yezo isl., Japan, pop. 42; # 43:57 N, 144:22 E.

Kustanai (kùs′tȧ-nī′), city, * of Turgai prov., Asiatic Russia, pop. 25; # 53:24 N, 63:40 E.

Küstenland (küs′tĕn-länt), former prov., S. W. Austria, on Adriatic Sea, now in Italy and Y-S.; # 45:30 N, 13:40 E.

Kutais (kö-tīs′), former prov., Transcaucasian Russia, area 8, pop. 1,008, and its *, city, W. C. Georgian Republic, pop. 50; # 42:20 N, 42:35 E.

Kuwait (kṵ-wīt′; kö-wät′), see **Koweit.**

Kwanchengtze (kwän′chĕng-tse′), city, Manchuria; see **Changchun.**

Kwangchowwan (kwäng′chou′wän′), spt. city, S. China, pop. 59; leased to France; # 21:15 N, 110:30 E.

Kwangsi (kwäng-sē′), prov., S. E. China, area 77, pop. est. 12,000, * Kweilin; # 24 N, 109 E.

Kwangtung (kwäng-tōng′), prov., S. E. China, area 100, pop. est. 37,000, * Canton, pop. est. 1,360; # 23:30 N, 114 E. — or **Kwantung**, S. end of Liaotung pen., Manchuria, leased to Japan, area 1, pop. ab. 500, * Dairen; # 39 N, 121:30 E.

Kwantung, see **Kwangtung.**

Kweichow (kwä′chou′), prov., S. W. China Proper, area 67, pop. est. 11,000, * Kweiyang, pop. est. 100; # 27 N, 106: 30 E.

Kweihwating (kwä-hwä-ting′), city, Shansi prov., N. C. China, pop. est. 200; # 40:36 N, 111:43 E.

Kweiyang (kwä′yäng′), city, S. W. China Proper, * of Kweichow prov., pop. est. 100; # 26:30 N, 106:50 E.

Kyoto (kē-ō′tō), interior city, S. C. Honshu isl., Japan, pop. 680, former *; Imperial Univ.; # 35 N, 135:45 E.

Kythera (kith′e-rä) or **Cerigo,** anc. Cythera, Greek isl. bet. Crete and pen. of Morea, area 0.1, pop. 13; # 36:15 N, 23 E.

Kyushiu or **Kiushu** (kē-ō′shō), isl., S. W. Japan, area 14, pop. 7,250; # 32:45 N, 131 E.

L

Laaland (lå′länd), isl., S. E. Denmark, area 0.5, pop. 74; # 54:50 N, 11:30 E.

Labrador (lab-rạ-dôr′), pen., N. E. Br. America, bet. Hudson Bay and Atlantic oc. and Gulf of St. Lawrence, area ab. 500; # 55 N, 70 W. — E. coastal strip of same, area 120, pop. 4; with Newfoundland, a Br. dominion; # 56 N, 61 W.

Lachine (lä-shēn′), city, S. Quebec, pop. 15; # 45:26 N, 73:40 W. — canal, St. Lawrence riv., just above Montreal, len. 8¼ mi., cost $14,000,000; # 45:25 N, 73:40 W.

Lackawanna (lak-ạ-won′ä), city, W. New York, pop. 24; # 42:49 N, 78:51 W.

Laconia (lạ-kō′ni-ạ), gulf and anc. country, S. C. Morea, S. Greece; # 36:45 N, 22:45 E. — tn., S. E. New Hampshire, pop. 13; # 43:22 N, 71:30 W.

La Crosse (lạ krôs), city, W. C. Wis., on Mississippi riv., pop. 43; # 43:50 N, 91:20 W.

Ladoga (lä′dō-gä), lake, S. E. Finland and N. W. Russia, largest in Europe, len. 140 mi.; area 7, depth 800 ft., outlet, Neva riv.; # 61 N, 31 E.

Ladrone (lạ-drōn′) or **Mariana Isls.,** small isls., E. of Philippines, Japanese mandate except Guam (U.S.A.), pop. 5; # 18 N, 146 E.

Lafayette (lä-fä-yet′), city, N. W. C. Ind., pop. 29; Purdue Univ.; # 40:26 N, 86:54 W. — tn., S. C. La., pop. 19; State Institute; # 30:11 N, 92 W. — National Park, Mt. Desert Isl., Me.; # 44:20 N, 68:15 W.

Lago di Garda (lä′gō dē gär′dä), see **Garda.**

Lagos (lä′gos), spt. city, * of Nigeria, on isl. of Lagos, pop. 42; # 6:30 N, 3:20 E.

Lagosta (lä-gōs′tä), Italian isl., Dalmatian coast, E. Adriatic Sea, len. 6 mi., pop. 2; # 42:45 N, 16:50 E.

La Grange (lä-gränj′), city, N. W. Ga., pop. 22; college; # 31:3 N, 85 W.

La Guaira (lä gwī′rä), see **Guaira.**

Laguna de Bay (lä-gö′nä dā bä′ḝ), lake, S. E. of Manila, Luzon, Philippines; # 14:25 N, 121:15 E.

Lahore (lä-hōr′), city, Punjab, N. W. India, pop. 282; # 31:45 N, 74:20 E.

Laibach (lī′bäch), former name of **Ljubljana.**

Lake Charles, tn., S. W. La., pop. 21; # 30:15 N, 93:15 W.

Lake Forest, a N. suburb of Chicago, Ill., pop. 7; Lake Forest College; # 42:14 N, 87:49 W.

Lakeland, tn., C. Fla., E. of Tampa, pop. 22; S. College; # ab. 28:5 N, 81:55 W.

Lakewood (lāk′wûd), a suburb of Cleveland, Ohio, pop. 69; # 41:29 N, 81:46 W.

Lambayeque (läm-bä-yā′kä), dept., N. W. Peru, area 5, pop. 124, * Chiclayo; # 6:31 S, 79:55 W.

Lambeth (lam′beth), a S. borough of London, Eng., pop. 303; # 51:30 N, 0:7 W.

Lamia (lä′mi-ạ), tn., E. C. Greece, near pass of Thermopylæ and head of Gulf of Lamia, pop. 11; # 38:55 N, 22:25 E.

Lanai (lä′nä-ḝ), isl., Hawaiian Isls., area 0.14; # 20:50 N, 156:55 W.

Lanark (lan′ärk) or **Clydesdale,** county, S. W. Scotland, including Glasgow, area 0.9, pop. 1,582, and its *, pop. 6; # 55:40 N, 3:47 W.

Lancaster (lang′kạs-tẽr), county, C. W. Eng., area 1.8, pop. 4,928, and its *, pop. 41; # 54:4 N, 2:50 W. — city, S. E. Pa., pop. 61; Franklin and Marshall College; # 40:5 N, 76:22 W. — city, S. C. Ohio, pop. 22; # 39:40 N, 82:35 W.

Lanchowfu (län′chou′fö′) or **Lanchau,** city, W. C. China Proper, * of Kansu prov., pop. est. 500; # 36:15 N, 103:50 E.

Landes (länd), coastal dept., S. W. Fr., area 3.6, pop. 264, * Mont-de-Marsan; sand marshes; forestry; # 44 N, 1 W.

Landsberg (länts′berch), city, on the Warthe riv., Brandenburg, N. Ger., pop. 45; # 52:44 N, 15:15 E.

Land's End (landz end), S. W. tip of Eng.; # 50:5 N, 5:45 W.

Landshut (länts′höt), city, * of Niederbayern (Lower Bavaria), S. W. Ger., pop. 26; # 48:33 N, 12:10 E.

Landskrona (länds′krō-nä), spt. city, S. Sweden, 20 mi. N. E. of Copenhagen, pop. 20; # 55:51 N, 12:50 E.

Langres (längr), plateau, E. C. Fr.; # 47:45 N, 5:15 E.

Languedoc (läng-dŏk), ancient prov., S. Fr., * Toulouse; # 43:45 N, 1:25 E.

Lansford (langz′fẽrd), tn., E. C. Pa., pop. 9; # ab. 40:50 N, 75:55 W.

Lansing (lan′sing), city, S. C. Mich., state *, pop. 79; State Agri. College; # 42:45 N, 84:35 W.

Laoag (lä-wäg′), spt. city, N. W. Luzón, Philippine Isls., pop. 38; # 18:10 N, 120:35 W.

Laon (loń), city, N. E. Fr., * of dept. of Aisne, pop. 19; battles, 1917–18; # 49:35 N, 3:35 E.

Laos (lä′oz), N. W. part of Fr. Indo-China, area 83, pop. 850, * Vientiane; # 19 N, 104 E.

La Pampa (lä päm′pä), ter., S. W. C. Argentina, area 56, pop. 142, * Santa Rosa; # 37 S, 65 W.

La Paz (lä päth, Eng. lä päz), dept., W. C. Bolivia, area 41, 726, its * and chief city, pop. 200; # 16:40 S, 68 W.

La Pérouse (lä pā-röz), Jap. **Soya,** strait bet. Yezo and Karafuto isls., Japan; # 45:40 N, 142 E.

Lapland (lap′land), region, N. Sweden, Finland and N. W. Russia; Lapps; # 68 N, 25 E.

La Plata (lä plä′tä), spt. city, the * of Buenos Aires prov., E. Argentina, pop. 191; univ.; # 34:54 S, 57:59 W. — **Rio de** (Eng. River Plate), estuary, 185 mi. long, of Paraná and Uruguay rivs., bet. Argentina and Uruguay; # 34:30 S, 58 W.

La Porte (lạ pōrt′), city, N. W. Ind., pop. 16; # 41:35 N, 86:43 W.

Lara (lä′rä), state, N. C. Venezuela, area 7.7, pop. 220, * Barquisimeto, pop. 24; # 10 N, 69:30 W.

Laramie (lar′ạ-mi), tn., S. E. Wyo., pop. 11; State Univ.; # 41:25 N, 105:35 W. — mt. range just E. of city, N. extension of Front Range of Rockies; highest, Laramie Peak, el. 10,000 ft.; # 42:16 N, 105:23 W.

Larderello (lär-de-rel′lō), vil., S. Tuscany, N. W. C. Italy, 23 mi. S. W. of Siena; hot springs and their use in the production of electric power, since 1912; # ab. 43:5 N, 11:2 E.

Laredo (lä-rä′dō), city on Rio Grande, S. Texas, pop. 39; # 27:45 N, 99:30 W.

La Rioja (lä rē-ō′Hä), prov., N. W. Argentina, area 38, pop. 89, and its *, pop. 13; # 29:20 S, 67:2 W.

Larissa (lä-rēs′ä), city, Thessaly, E. C. Greece, pop. 21; # 39:38 N, 22:25 E.

La Rochelle (lä rō-shel′), spt., W. C. Fr., pop. 36; # 46:10 N, 1:5 W.

Larvik (lär′vēk), spt., S. E. Norway, pop. 11; # 59:5 N, 10:2 E.

La Salle (lä sal′), city, N. W. C. Ill., pop. 13; # 41:20 N, 89:8 W. — vil., W. New York, pop. 6; # 43:4 N, 78:58 W.

Las Bela (lus bä′lä), native state, Baluchistan, S. Asia, area 7, pop. 51, * Bela; # 25:40 N, 67 E.

Lashkar (lush-kur′), city, C. India, * of Gwalior State, pop. 80; # 26:15 N, 78:15 E.

Las Palmas (läs päl′mäs), spt. city, Gran Canaria, Canary Isls., Spain, pop. 67; # 28:6 N, 15:30 W.

Lassa (läs′sä), see **Lhasa.**

Lassen Peak (las′ẹn pēk), volcano, N. Calif., active since 1915, only active volcano in continental U.S.A., el. 10,465 ft.; National Park, 1916; # 40:26 N, 121:35 W.

(variable) ḍ as d or j, ṣ as s or sh, ṭ as t or ch, ẓ as z or zh; o, F. cloche; ü, F. menu; ċh, Sc. loch; ṅ, F. bonbon; ′, primary accent; ″, secondary accent; †, obsolete; <, from; +, and; =, equals. See also lists at beginning of book.

Latakia (lä-tä-kē′ä), spt. city, N. W. Syria, pop. ab. 20; #35:32 N, 35:58 E.

Latium (lā′shi-um), anc. country, Italy, S. E. of Rome; #ab. 41:30 N, 13 E.

Latvia (lat′vi-ą), republic on Baltic sea, area 24, pop. 1,909, * Riga, pop. 285; #57 N, 24 E.

Launceston (län′ses-tǫn), city, N. Tasmania, pop. with suburbs, 26; #41:30 S, 147:20 E.

Laurel (lâ′rĕl), tn., S. E. C. Miss., pop. 21; #31:40 N, 89:10 W.

Laurentides (lâ′ren-tēdz), Canadian National Park, Laurentian Highlands, S. Quebec; #47:40 N, 71:20 W.

Lausanne (lō-zän), city on Lake Geneva, W. Switz., pop. 69; univ.; #46:32 N, 6:40 E.

Lauterbrunnen (lou′tẽr-brün-ẹn), tn., S. C. Switz., in grand glacial gorge, with many side waterfalls; resort; pop. 3; #46:36 N, 7:54 E.

Laval (lä-väl′), city, N. W. C. Fr., * of Mayenne, pop. 25; #48:5 N, 0:45 W.

Lawrence (lâ′rẹns), city, N. E. Mass., pop. 84; #42:40 N, 71:12 W. — tn., N. E. C. Kansas, pop. 14; State Univ.; #38:58 N, 95:18 W.

Lead (lēd), tn., Black Hills, S. W. S. Dak., pop. 8; Homestake gold mine; #44:23 N, 103:50 W.

Leadville (led′vil), mining tn., C. Colo., pop. 5; el. 10,200 ft.; #39:17 N, 106:23 W.

Leavenworth (lev′ẹn-wẽrth), city, N. E. Kansas, pop. 19; Federal prison; #39:25 N, 94:55 W.

Lebanon (leb′ą-nǫn), city, S. E. Pa., pop. 27; #40:22 N, 76:25 W. — tn., N. C. Tenn., pop. 6; Cumberland Univ.; #36:15 N, 86:21 W. — **Great**, ter. of S. W. Syria, pop. ab. 629, * Beirut, pop. 80; #ab. 33:35 N, 35:37 E.

Lebanon Mountains, range, near coast, W. Syria, summit 10,049 ft.; #33:35 N, 35:37 E.

Lecce (lech′ā), prov., Apulia, S. E. Italy, area 2.6, pop. 611, and its *, pop. 39; #40:23 N, 18:11 E.

Le Creusot (lĕ krẽ-zō′), see **Creusot, Le**.

Leeds (lēdz), city, York, N. C. Eng., pop. 470; Univ. of Leeds; #53:48 N, 1:35 W.

Leeuwarden (lā′wär-dẹn), city, Friesland, N. E. Neth., pop. 46; #53:11 N, 5:45 E.

Leeuwin (lō′in), cape, S. W. tip of Australia; #34:15 S, 115:5 E.

Leeward (lū′ärd), isls., N. Lesser Antilles, W. Indies; Br. and Fr.; #17 N, 62 W.

Leghorn (leg′hôrn), see **Livorno**.

Legnago (lā-nyä′gō), ft. tn. on Adige riv., N. E. Italy, pop. comm. 15; battle 1917; #45:11 N, 11:19 E.

Lehigh (lē′hī), valley and county, N. E. Pa.; cement; anthracite coal; #40:32 N, 75:35 W.

Leicester (les′tẽr), county, S. C. Eng., area 0.8, pop. 496 and its *, pop. 240; #52:35 N, 1:10 W.

Leiden (lī′dẹn), city, S. W. C. Neth., pop. 68; Univ. of Leiden; #52:10 N, 4:30 E.

Leigh (lē), city, 12 mi. W. of Manchester, W. C. Eng., pop. 47; #53:29 N, 2:31 W.

Leine (lī′nẽ), riv., N. W. Ger., past Hannover to Aller riv., len. 115 mi.; #52:45 N, 9:35 E.

Leinster (len′stẽr or lin-), prov., S. E. Ireland, area 8, pop. 1,162; #52:45 N, 7 W.

Leipzig (līp′sik), city, Sachsen (Saxony), S. Ger., pop. 660; univ.; printing; fur market; a div. of N. Saxony, area 1.4, pop. 1,222; #51:18 N, 12:20 E.

Leith (lēth), the port section of Edinburgh, Scotland, pop. 80; #55:58 N, 3:10 W.

Lek (lek), riv., one of the mouths of the Rhine riv., past Rotterdam, len. 90 mi.; #51:55 N, 4:15 E.

Leman (lē′mąn), **Lake**, Lake of Geneva.

Lemans, Le, see **Mans, Le**.

Lemberg (lem′berch), former name of **Lvóv**.

Lemnos (lem′nos) or **Stalimini**, Greek isl., N. E. Ægean Sea, area 0.2, pop. 27, * Kastro; #39:55 N, 25:15 E.

Lena (lē′nä, *Russ.* lye′nä), riv., Lake Baikal region, Siberia to Arctic oc., len. 2,800 mi.; #71:15 N, 128 E.

Leningrad (len′in-grad), prov., N. W. Russia, area 17, pop. 2,000 and its *, formerly **St. Petersburg** and **Petrograd**, former * of Russia; pop. 1,044; univ.; #59:55 N, 30:15 E.

Lens (lon̊), city, N. E. Fr., 15 mi. S. of Lille, pop. 32; #50:28 N, 2:50 E.

Leominster (lem′in-stẽr), city, N. C. Mass., pop. 22; #42:30 N, 71:46 W.

Leon (lē′on), *Sp.* **León** (lā-ōn′), prov., N. W. Spain, area 5.9, pop. 419, and its *, pop. 18; #42:37 N, 5:34 W. — old prov., including also Zamora and Salamanca. — city, N. W. Nicaragua, former *, pop. 38; #12:30 N, 87 W. — city, Guanajuato, S. C. Mexico, pop. 58; #21:5 N, 101:50 W.

Leopold (lē′ǫ-pōld), lake, W. Belgian Congo, len. 90 mi.; #3 S, 19 E.

Leopoldville (lē′ǫ-pōld-vil), tn. on Congo riv., * of Belgian Congo since 1923, pop. ab. 5; #4:20 S, 15:17 E.

Lepanto (le-pan′tō) or **Naupactus**, spt., S. C. Greece on Gulf of Corinth, pop. 3; naval battle 1571; #38:25 N, 21:50 E.

Lepontine Alps (lẹ-pon′tin alps), range, S. E. C. Switz.; #46:30 N, 8:30 E.

Lérida (lā′rẹ-ₜHä), prov., Catalonia, N. E. Spain, area 4.7, pop. 327, and its *, pop. 21; #41:38 N, 0:38 E.

Lesbos (lez′bos), see **Mytilene**.

Lesina (les′ē-nä) or **Hvar**, isl., S. Dalmatia, Yugoslavia, len. 45 mi.; #43:7 N, 16:45 E.

Lethbridge (leth′brij), tn., S. Alberta, pop. 11; #49:50 N, 112:50 W.

Levallois-Perret (lẽ-väl-wä-pe-re), a N. suburb of Paris, Fr., pop. 74; #48:53 N, 2:17 E.

Levant (lẽ-vant′), lands bordering E. shore of Mediterranean and Ægean Seas, esp. Syria and Palestine; #35 N, 36 E.

Lévis (*Fr.* lā-vē or lev′is), tn., across the St. Lawrence riv. from Quebec, pop. 10; #46:48 N, 71:12 W.

Levkas (lev′käs) or **Santa Maura**, isl., W. C. Greece, and its *, pop. 6; #38:40 N, 20:40 E.

Lewes (lū′es), tn., * of Sussex, Eng., pop. 12; #50:53 N, 0:1 W.

Lewis (lū′is), chief isl., Outer Hebrides, W. Scotland, len. 60 mi., N. tip called Butt of Lewis; #58:30 N, 6:20 W.

Lewis and Clark, National monument, Jefferson Co., W. Mont.; a notable limestone cavern; #ab. 46 N, 111:40 W.

Lewisburg (lū′is-bẽrg), tn., E. C. Pa., pop. 4; Bucknell Univ.; #40:58 N, 76:57 W.

Lewisham (lū′ish-ạm), a borough of London, Eng., pop. 174; #51:27 N, 0:1 W.

Lewiston (lū′is-tǫn), city, S. W. C. Me., pop. 39; Bates College; #44:7 N, 70:14 W.

Lewistown (lū′is-toun), tn., C. Pa., pop. 13; #40:34 N, 77:35 W.

Lexington (lek′sing-tǫn), tn., N. E. Mass., pop. 13; battle April 19, 1775; #42:27 N, 71:14 W. — city, N. E. C. Ky., pop. 49; State and Transylvania univs.; #38:5 N, 84:32 W. — tn., W. C. Va., pop. 4; Washington and Lee Univ.; Va. Military Inst.; #37:46 N, 79:25 W.

Leyden (lī′dẹn), see **Leiden**.

Leyte (lā′ē-tä or lā′tä), isl., C. Philippines, area 3; #10:45 N, 124:50 E.

Leyton (lā′tǫn), a N. E. suburb of London, Eng., pop. 125; #51:34 N, 0:1 W.

Lhasa (lhä′sä), city, S. C. Asia, * of Tibet, pop. 20; el. ab. 12,000 ft.; #29:50 N, 91 E.

Liao (lẹ-ou′), riv., S. Manchuria to Yellow Sea, len. 600 mi.; #40:50 N, 122:15 E.

Liaotung (lē-ou′túng′), pen., S. W. Manchuria; #40 N, 123 E.

Liaoyang (lyou-yäng′), city, S. Manchuria, pop. 40; #41:20 N, 123:15 E.

Liard (lē-är′; -ärd), riv., N. Br. Columbia and S. Yukon ter. to Mackenzie riv., len. 550 mi.; #61:50 N, 121:25 W.

Libau (lē′bou), see **Liepaja**.

Libertad (lē-ber-täₜH′), dept., N. W. Peru, area 10, pop. 251, * Trujillo, pop. 25; #7:50 S, 78:38 W.

Liberec (lē′bẽr-ets) *formerly* **Reichenberg**, city, N. E. Bohemia, pop. 35; textiles; #50:47 N, 15:3 E.

Liberia (lī-bē′ri-ą), a W. African negro republic, area 40, pop. est. 2,000, * Monrovia, pop. 6; #7 N, 10 W.

Libreville (lē-br-vēl′), spt. city, Fr. Equatorial Africa, * of Gabun; #0:30 N, 9:35 E.

Libya (lib′i-ą) or **Libia Italiana**, colony of N. Africa, bet. Tunisia and Egypt, area 406, pop. 1,000, * Tripoli; #28 N, 20 E.

Licata (lē-kä′tä) or **Alicata**, spt., S. Sicily, pop. 25; # 37:6 N, 13:55 E.

Lichfield (lich′fēld), tn., S. E. Staffordshire, W. C. Eng., pop. 8; cathedral; # 52:41 N, 1:49 W.

Lichtenberg (lich′tĕn-berćh), an E. div. of Berlin, Ger., pop. 196; # 52:31 N, 13:27 E.

Lidcombe (lid′kǫm), a S. suburb of Sydney, E. New S. Wales, Australia, pop. 12; # ab. 33:56 S, 151:12 E.

Liechtenstein (lich′tĕn-shtīn), principality bet. Austria and Switz., area .06, pop. 11, * Vaduz, pop. 1; # 47:10 N, 9:32 E.

Liége (lē-āzh′), prov., E. Belgium, area 1.1, pop. 875, and its *, pop. 165; State Univ.; # 50:40 N, 5:33 E.

Liegnitz (lēg′nits), city, Silesia, S. E. Ger., pop. 72; # 51:12 N, 16:12 E.

Lienkiang (lē-en-kyäng′), see **Linkiang.**

Liepaja (lē′ĕ-pä-yä) *formerly* **Libau**, spt. city, S. W. Latvia, pop. 77; # 56:35 N, 21:5 E.

Lierre (lē-ār), city, 8 mi. S. E. of Antwerp, Belgium, pop. 27; # 51:9 N, 4:34 E.

Lietuva (li-at′u-vä), official name of Lithuania.

Liguria (li-gū′ri-ą̇), coastal dept., N. W. Italy, area 2.1, pop. 1,336, * Genova, pop. 316; # 44 N, 7:55 E.

Ligurian Sea (li-gū′ri-ąn sē), part of Mediterranean Sea, N. of Corsica; # 43:30 N, 9 E.

Lille (lēl), city, ext. N. E. Fr., * of Nord dept., pop. 201; univ.; # 50:40 N, 3 E.

Lima (lē′mä), city, the * of Peru, near coast, pop. 370, with suburbs, 220; Univ. of San Marcos; # 12:20 S, 76:20 W. — (lī′mä), city, N. W. Ohio, pop. 45; # 40:38 N, 84:7 W.

Limbourg (laṅ′bör) or **Limburg**, prov., N. E. Belgium, area 1, pop. 317, * Hasselt, pop. 16; # 51 N, 5:25 E.

Limburg (lim′burćh), prov., ext. S. E. Neth., area 0.8, pop. 471, * Maastricht; # 51:20 N, 6 E. — See **Limbourg.**

Limerick (lim′ĕ-rik), county and city, Munster, S. W. Ireland, area 1, pop. 104 and 39; # 52:40 N, 8:36 W.

Limoges (lē-mōzh′), city, S. W. C. Fr., * of Haute-Vienne dept., pop. 90; porcelain; # 45:45 N, 1:15 E.

Limón (lē̇-mōn′), spt. town, Costa Rica, C. America, pop. 12; bananas; # 10 N, 83:10 W.

Limousin (lē-mö-zaṅ′), anc. prov., S. C. Fr.; # 45:35 N, 1:30 E.

Limpopo (lim-pō′pō), riv., N. C. Union of S. Africa, E. to Indian oc., len. ab. 900 mi.; # 25:10 S, 33:30 E.

Linares (lē-nä′räs), city, Jaén, S. C. Spain, pop. 40; mines; # 38:7 N, 3:39 W. — prov., C. Chile, area 4, pop. 119 and its *, pop. 12; # 35:49 S, 71:44 W.

Lincoln (ling′kǫn), county, E. C. Eng., area 2.7, pop. 602, and its *, pop. 67; # 53:15 N, 0:35 W. — city, S. E. Neb., state *, pop. 82; State Univ.; # 40:50 N, 96:50 W. — tn., C. Ill., pop. 13; college; # 40:10 N, 89:20 W. — For the divisions of Lincoln co., see **Holland, Kesteven** and **Lindsey;** # 53:14 N, 0:32 W.

Linden (lin′dĕn), a S. suburb of Hannover, W. C. Ger., pop. 82; # 52:20 N, 9:35 E.

Lindesnäs (lin′es-nes) or **The Naze,** cape, S. tip of Norway; # 58 N, 7:2 E.

Lindsey (lin′zi), part of Lincolnshire, E. C. Eng., area 1.5, pop. 409; # 53:25 N, 0:20 W.

Linkiang (lēn-kyäng′), city, Kiangsi prov., China, pop. est. 220; # 28 N, 115:24 E.

Linköping (lin′chĕ-ping), city, S. Sweden, pop. 28; # 58:25 N, 15:37 E.

Linlithgow (lin-lith′gō), see **West Lothian.**

Linnhe, Loch (lin′e), arm of sea, Argyll, W. Scotland, len. 40 mi.; # 56:35 N, 5:25 W.

Linz (lints), city on Danube riv., N. W. Austria, pop. 102; # 48:18 N, 14:15 E.

Lion, Gulf of the (li′ǫn), wide bay of Mediterranean Sea, S. Fr.; # 43:15 N, 4 E.

Lipari (lē′pä-rē), group of 7 vol. isls., N. of E. Sicily, part of Messina prov., Italy; # 38:30 N, 14:55 E. — largest of these and spt. on same, pop. 16; castle; # 38:28 N, 14:56 E.

Lippe (lip′ĕ), riv., Westphalia, N. W. Ger., W. to Rhine riv., len. 150 mi.; # 51:38 N, 6:33 E. — state, N. W. Ger., area 0.5, pop. 166, * Detmold, pop. 15; # 52 N, 9 E.

Lisboa (lēz-bō′ä), *Eng.* **Lisbon** (liz′bǫn), spt. city at mouth of Tagus riv., S. W. Portugal, its *, pop. 486; univ.; # 38:44 N, 9:15 W.

Lisle (līl), see **Lille.**

Lismore (liz-mōr′), tn., N. E. New S. Wales, Australia, pop. 10; # 28:40 S., 153:15 E.

Lithgow (lith′gō), town, E. C. New S. Wales, Australia, pop. 13; # 33:29 S, 150:9 E.

Lithuania (lith-ū-ā′ni-ą̇), officially **Lietuva**, Baltic republic, area 20, pop. 2,400, * Kaunas (Kovno); # 55:30 N, 24 E.

Little Falls (lit′l fâlz), tn., E. C. New York, pop. 10; # 43:4 N, 74:53 W.

Little Rock (lit′l rok), city, C. Ark., on Arkansas riv., state *, pop. 88; college; bauxite mines; # 34:50 N, 92:20 W.

Liverpool (liv′ẽr-pöl), spt. city, W. C. Eng., pop. 838, with suburbs, pop. 1,300; wheat and cotton markets; Univ. of Liverpool; # 53:25 N, 3 W.

Livingstone (liv′ing-stǫn), tn. at falls of Zambezi, * of N. Rhodesia, S. Africa; # 17:50 S, 25:50 E.

Livorno (lē-vôr′nō), *Eng.* **Leghorn,** prov., Tuscany, N. W. C. Italy, area 0.1, pop. 144, and its *, a spt., pop. 115; # 43:33 N, 10:17 E.

Lizard Head (liz′ård hed), pen., S. Cornwall, S. tip of Eng.; # 49:57 N, 5:12 W.

Ljubljana (lyö′blyä-na), *Ger.* **Laibach** (lī′bäch), city, N. W. Yugoslavia, * of Slovenia, pop. 53; # 46:2 N, 14:30 E.

Llandaff (lan-daf′), tn., a N. suburb of Cardiff, S. E. Wales, pop. 9; cathedral; # 51:30 N, 3:14 W.

Llandudno (lan-düd′nō), coastal resort tn., ext. N. Wales, pop. 19; # 53:19 N, 3:50 W.

Llanelly (la-neth′li), spt. city, Carmarthen, S. Wales, pop. 37; # 51:41 N, 4:10 W.

Llanos (lyä′nōs), vaguely defined plains region of N. S. America, grassy plains or savannah; # ab. 5 N, 70 E.

Llanquihue (lyän-kē′wä), prov., S. Chile, area 35, pop. 137, * Puerto Montt, pop. 10; # 41:15 S, 72:50 W.

Llullaillaco (lyö-lyi-lyä′kō), mt., N. E. Chile, el. 20,243 ft.; # 24:48 S, 68:28 W.

Loanda (lō-än′dä), ter. of Angola, Portuguese W. Africa, and its *, spt., pop. 50; # 8:50 S, 13:30 E.

Loango (lō-äng′gō), spt. city, S. W. Fr. Equatorial Africa, pop. ab. 10; # 4:10 S, 12 E.

Lob Nor (lōb nōr′), see **Lop Nor.**

Locarno (lō-kär′nō), tn., S. E. Switz., pop. 6; pact, 1925; # 46:12 N, 8:46 E.

Lochleven (loćh-lē′vn), lake and castle, Kinross-shire, E. C. Scotland; # 56:12 N, 3:25 W.

Lockport (lok′pört), city, N. W. New York, on Erie Canal; pop. 24; # 43:15 N, 78:40 W.

Lodi (lō′dē), city, Milan prov., N. Italy, pop. comm. 28; battle 1796; # 45:17 N, 9:29 E.

Lódz (lōdz), prov., W. C. Poland, area 7, pop. 2,251 and its *, pop. 452; univ.; # 51:46 N, 19:25 E.

Loetschberg, see **Lötschberg.**

Lofoten (lō-fō′ten), isl. group, N. W. Norway, pop. 43; fisheries; # 68:30 N, 15 E.

Logan (lō′gan), tn., N. Utah, pop. 12; State Agri. College; # 41:40 N, 110:40 W. — mt., vol. pk., ext. S. W. Yukon ter., Canada, el. 19,359 ft.; # 60:50 N, 140:30 W.

Logansport (lō′gąnz-pört), city, on Wabash riv., N. C. Ind., pop. 20; # 40:43 N, 86:28 W.

Logroño (lō-grōn′yō), prov., N. C. Spain, area 2, pop. 195, and its *, pop. 28; # 42:26 N, 2:36 W.

Loire (lwär), riv., C. Fr., to Atlantic oc., len. 593 mi., longest in Fr.; # 47:15 N, 1:30 W. — dept., S. C. Fr., area 1.9, pop. 637, * St.-Étienne, pop. 168; # 45:40 N, 4 E.

Loire, Haute (ōt lwär), see **Haute-Loire.**

Loire-Inférieure (lwä-raṅ-fā-ryėr), dept., W. Fr., area 2.7, pop. 650, * Nantes, pop. 184; # 47:25 N, 1:40 W.

Loiret (lwä-rā), dept., N. C. Fr., area 2.6, pop. 337, * Orleans, pop. 69; # 48 N, 2:15 E.

Loir-et-Cher (lwär-ā-shār), dept., C. Fr., area 2.5, pop. 252, * Blois, pop. 24; # 47:35 N, 0:30 W.

Lomami (lō-mä′mē), riv., S. trib., Upper Congo, C. Africa; len. ab. 800 mi.; # 0:50 N, 24:10 E.

Lomas de Zamora (lō′mäs dä sä-mō′rä), suburb of Buenos Aires, E. Argentina, pop. 27; # 34:43 S, 58:25 W.

Loma Tina (lō′mä tē′nä), mt., S. Dominican Republic, Haiti, el. 10,300 ft., highest in W. Indies; # 18:37 N, 70:36 W.

Lombardy (lom'bär-di), dept., N. Italy, area 9.2, pop. 5,080, * Milano, pop. 836; # 45:35 N, 8:55 E.

Lombok (lom-bok'), isl., Dutch E. Indies, 100 mi. E. of Java, area 2, pop. 618; # 8:45 S, 116:30 E.

Lomond, Loch (lō-mọnd, loch), lake, 20 mi. long, 18 mi. N. W. of Glasgow, Scotland; # 56:8 N, 4:35 W.

London (lun'dọn), city, S. E. Eng., * of Br. Empire, pop. 4,564, with suburbs pop. 8,655; Univ. of London; Br. Museum; cathedral; # 51:3 N, 0:7 W. — city, S. Ontario, pop. 61; W. Univ.; # 43 N, 81:20 W.

Londonderry (lun'dọn-der-i), county, N. C. N. Ireland, area 0.8, pop. 141, and its *, a parliamentary borough, pop. 41; # 55 N, 7:28 W.

Long Beach, seaside resort, S. of Los Angeles, S. Calif., pop. 164; # 33:47 N, 118:12 W.

Long Branch, tn., N. E. New Jersey, seaside summer resort, pop. 17; # 40:20 N, 74 W.

Long Island, isl., Atlantic oc., ext. E. New York, len. 120 mi., area 1.7, pop. 3,000; # 40:40 N, 73:35 W.

Long Island Sound, bet. Conn. and Long Isl., len. 110 mi.; # 41:10 N, 73 W.

Longs Peak (lôngz pēk), conspicuous pk., continental divide, N. C. Colo., el. 14,255 ft.; # 40:20 N, 105:40 W.

Longview, city, ext. S. W. Wash., on Columbia riv., pop. ab. 12; lumber; # ab. 46:10 N, 123:40 W.

Lonneker (lon'e-kèr), city, S. E. Overysell, E. Neth., pop. 22; # 52:16 N, 6:55 E.

Lookout Mountain (lùk'out), range in Ga., Tenn. and Ala.; battle, Chattanooga, Tenn., Nov. 24, 1863; # 35 N, 85:25 W.

Lopatka (lō-pät'kä), cape, S. tip of Kamchatka, N. E. Asia; # 51 N, 157 E.

Lopez (lō'päth), cape, Gulf of Guinea, Fr. Equatorial Africa; # 1:50 S, 9 E.

Lop Nor (lōp nōr'), temporary lake, mouth of Tarim riv., Chinese Turkestan; # 40 N, 90 E.

Lorain (lō-rān'), city, Lorain county, N. C. Ohio, on Lake Erie, pop. 44; # 41:28 N, 82:10 W.

Lorca (lôr'käj), city, Murcia, S. E. Spain, pop. 75; # 37:42 N, 1:40 W.

Loreto (lō-rā'tō), dept., E. Peru, area 163, pop. 101, * Iquitos, pop. 15; # 6:20 S, 74 W. — tn., Marche, N. E. C. Italy, pop. comm. 8; Catholic shrine; pilgrimages; # 42:26 N, 13:58 E.

Lorient (lō-ryon), spt., S. Brittany, N. W. Fr., pop. 39; # 47:45 N, 3:20 W.

Lorne (lôrn), region, Argyll, W. Scotland, bordering Firth of Lorne; # 56:20 N, 5:40 W.

Lörrach (lèr'räch), city, S. W. Baden, S. W. Ger., pop. 16; # 47:40 N, 7:38 E.

Lorraine (lo-rān), former kingdom, then a div. of Fr. and then of Ger., area 2.4, pop. 655; # 49 N, 6:30 E; see **Moselle.**

Los Andes (lōs än'däz), ter., ext. N. W. Argentina, area 35, pop. 3, * San Antonio de Los Cobres; # 25 S, 67:30 W.

Los Angeles (lōs ang'gẹ-les or los an'jẹ-les), city, Los Angeles county, S. Calif., pop. 1,504; resort; petroleum; oranges; branch of Univ. of Calif.; Occidental Univ.; Univ. of S. Calif.; # 34:3 N, 118:15 W.

Lot (lot), riv., S. C. Fr. to Garonne riv., len. 300 mi.; # 44:15 N, 0:20 E. — dept., S. C. Fr., area 2, pop. 177, * Cahors, pop. 12; # 44:28 N, 1 E.

Lot-et-Garonne (lo-tā-gà-ron), dept., S. C. Fr., area 2.1, pop. 240, * Agen; # 44:20 N, 0:30 E.

Lothian (lō'ғHi-ạn), see **East, Mid-** and **West Lothian.**

Lötschberg (lètsh'berch), R.R. tunnel, Oberland, S. Switz., len. 9¼ mi., 1913, el. 4,080 ft., under Lötschberg Pass, el. 8,840 ft.; # ab. 46:26 N, 7:43 E.

Lough Derg (loch derg'; dèrg'), lake, an enlargement of Shannon riv., S. C. Ireland; # 52:55 N, 8:20 W.

Lough Neagh (lok nā, also loch nā), lake, C. N. Ireland State, area 0.2; # 54:35 N, 6:25 W.

Louisburg (lō'is-bèrg), spt., Cape Breton, Nova Scotia, pop. 1; captured though strongly fortified, 1745, 1758; # 45:55 N, 59:58 W.

Louise (lō-ēz'), glacial lake, Canadian Rockies, near Laggan, Alberta, el. 5,670 ft.; resort; # 51:25 N, 116:14 W.

Louisiade (lō-ē-zē-äd'), group of isls., E. of Papua, Malaysia; # 11 S, 153 E.

Louisiana (lō-ē-zi-an'ạ), state, S. C. U.S.A., bet. Miss. and Texas, area 49, pop. 2,364, * Baton Rouge, pop. 35; chief city, New Orleans, pop. 495; # 31 N, 92 W.

Louisville (lō'is-vil or lō'i-vil), city, N. W. Ky., on Ohio riv., pop. 319; Univ. of Louisville; # 38:15 N, 85:45 W.

Louisville and Nashville (lō'is-vil and nash'vil), R.R., Louisville, S. to La., Fla., total mileage 5,043.

Lourenço Marques (lọ-ren'sō mär'kes), spt., * of Portuguese E. Africa, on Delagao Bay, pop. 13; # 25:45 S, 32:30 E.

Louvain (lō-vaň), city, 15 mi. E. of Brussels, Belgium, pop. 41; Univ. of Louvain; # 50:52 N, 4:45 E.

Low Archipelago (lō är-ki-pel'ạ-gō), numerous small coral isls., C. S. Pacific oc., E. of Tahiti, Fr., also known as Tuamotu and Paumotu isls.; # 20 S, 140 W.

Low Countries (lō kun'triz), loosely applied to Netherlands, and sometimes also to Belgium and Denmark.

Lowell (lō'el), city, N. E. Mass., pop. 101; # 42:38 N, 71:22 W.

Lower California (lō'èr kal-i-fōr'ni-ạ), pen., N. W. Mexico, area 63, pop. 52; # 28 N, 114 W.

Lower Franconia (lō'èr frang-kō'ni-ạ), see **Unterfranken.**

Lowestoft (lō'stoft), spt. city, opp. Yarmouth, E. Eng., pop. 45; # 52:32 N, 1:43 E.

Loyalty Islands (loi'ạl-ti i'lạndz), group Fr. isls., 60 mi. E. of New Caledonia, S. Pacific oc., area 0.8, pop. ab. 5; # 21 S, 167:15 E.

Lozère (lō-zār), dept., S. C. Fr., area 2, pop. 109, * Mende; # 44:32 N, 3:45 E.

Lubbock (lub'ọk), tn., N. W. C. Texas, pop. 32; State Technological College; # 33:35 N, 101:45 W.

Lübeck (lü'bek), free city and state, N. E. Ger., area 0.1, pop. 127, and its *, a spt., pop. 120; ship building; # 53:50 N, 10:40 E.

Lublin (lō'blin), city, S. C. Poland, pop. 94; univ.; # 51:15 N, 22:34 E. — county surrounding, area 12, pop. 2,088; # 50:50 N, 22:30 E.

Lucania (lū-kā'ni-ạ), anc. dist., S. W. Italy; # ab. 40 N, 16 E.

Lucca (lök'kä), prov., Tuscany, N. W. C. Italy, area 0.8, pop. 390, and its *, pop. 79; cathedral; # 43:50 N, 10:29 E.

Lucerne (lū-sèrn', Fr. lü-sern), see **Luzern.**

Luchu Islands (lō'chö i'lạndz), see **Riukiu.**

Luckenwalde (lù'kẹn-väl'dè), city, 29 mi. S. W. of Berlin, Ger., pop. 25; # 52:6 N, 13:11 E.

Lucknow (luk'nou), city, N. C. India, pop. 241; # 26:55 N, 80:55 E.

Lüdenscheid (lü'dẹn-shīt), city, Westfalen, W. Ger., pop. 33; # 51:13 N, 7:37 E.

Lüderitz (lü'dèr-its), spt. city, S. W. mandate of S. W. Africa; diamonds; pop. 5; # 26:30 S, 15:30 E.

Ludwigsburg (lōt'vichs-bùrch), city, 10 mi. N. of Stuttgart, Württemberg, S. W. Ger., pop. 28; # 48:55 N, 9:10 E.

Ludwigshafen (lōt'vichs-hä-fẹn), city on Rhine riv., opposite Mannheim, S. W. Ger., pop. 100; aniline dyes; # 49:30 N, 8:25 E.

Lugano (lō-gä'nō) or **Luis**, city on Lago di Lugano, S. E. Switz., pop. 13; # 46:2 N, 8:57 E.

Lugo (lō'gō), prov., N. W. Spain, area 3.8, pop. 462, and its *, pop. 28; # 42:59 N, 7:32 W. — tn., Ravenna prov., N. Italy, pop. 28; # 44:25 N, 11:54 E.

Lukmanier (lök-män'yer), pass, S. Alps, N. of Lake Maggiore, el. 6,288 ft.; # 46:34 N, 8:48 E.

Lund (lönd), city, S. Sweden, 20 mi. E. of Copenhagen, Denmark, pop. 24; univ.; # 55:42 N, 13:10 E.

Lüneburg (lü'nè-bùrch), city, Hannover, N. W. C. Ger., pop. 29, and nearby heath (heide), 50 mi. across; # 53:15 N, 10:25 E.

Lünen (lü'nẹn), a N. suburb of Dortmund, W. Ger., pop. 24; # 51:37 N, 7:31 E.

Lunéville (lü-nā-vēl'), city, N. E. Fr., 15 mi. S. E. of Nancy, pop. 24; # 48:35 N, 6:30 E.

Lunga (lun'gä) or **Dugi** (dö'gè), isl., W. C. Dalmatia, Y-S., len. 30 mi.; # 44:3 N, 15 E.

Lungchow (lùng'chou), port, Kwangsi prov., ext. S. C. China, pop. est. 20; # 22:21 N, 106:45 E.

Luray (lū-rā'), limestone cavern, Shenandoah val., Va., 78 mi. S. W. of Washington, D. C.; # 38:38 N, 78:28 W.

Lusitania (lū-si-tā'ni-ạ), occasional name for Portugal; an anc. kingdom of S. W. Iberia; # 40 N, 7 W.

Luton (lūt′ọn), city, 30 mi. N. N. W. of London, S. E. Eng., pop. 59; # 51:53 N, 0:25 W.

Lüttich (lüt′tich), see **Liége.**

Luxembourg (luk′sẹm-bẽrg, *Fr.* lük-soṅ-bör), prov., S. E. Belgium, area 1.7, pop. 222, * Arlon, pop. 8; # 50 N, 5:30 E.

Luxemburg (luk′sẹm-bẽrg), grand duchy, bet. Ger., Fr. and Belgium, since 1922 in Belgium customs union, area 1, pop. 261 and its *, pop. 48; # 49:35 N, 6:12 E.

Luxor (luk′sôr), tn., on site of ancient Thebes, Nile Valley, Upper Egypt, pop. 15; # 25:40 N, 32:39 E.

Luzern (lù-tsern′), *Fr.* **Lucerne,** canton, Switz., area 0.6, pop. 177, and its *, pop. 44, on Lake Luzern; # 47:5 N, 8:16 E.

Luzón or **Luçón** (lö-zon′, *Sp.* lö-thōn′), chief isl. of Philippines, area 41, pop. 4,000, * Manila, pop. 285; # 15:30 N, 121 E.

Lvóv (lvûf), form of Lwów, city, Galicia, S. Poland, pop. 219; univ.; # 49:50 N, 23:55 E.

Lwów or **Lemberg,** see **Lvóv.**

Lycia (lish′i-ạ), anc. dist., S. Asia Minor; # ab. 36:50 N, 30 E.

Lydia (lid′i-ạ), anc. country, W. Asia Minor; # ab. 38 N, 28 E.

Lynchburg (linch′bẽrg), city, S. W. C. Va., on James riv., pop. 45; Lynchburg and Randolph-Macon Woman's colleges; # 37:30 N, 79:10 W.

Lynn (lin), city, E. C. Mass., pop. 98; # 42:28 N, 70:57 W. — Canal, fjord, S. Alaska, len. 75 mi. or if extension bet. isls. be included, 220 mi.; # 58:50 N, 135 W.

Lyon (lē-ôṅ), *Eng.* **Lyons** (li′ọnz), city, S. E. C. Fr., * of Rhône dept., pop. 562; silks; univ.; # 45:45 N, 4:50 E.

Lyonnais (lē-ọ̄-nā), anc. prov., S. E. Fr.; # ab. 45:45 N, 4:25 E.

Lyons (li′ọns), see **Lyon.**

Lys (lēs), riv., N. W. Fr. to Escaut or Scheldt riv., in Belgium, len. 100 mi.; # 50:58 N, 3:30 E.

Lyublin (lyù′blyẹn), see **Lublin.**

Lyublyana, see **Ljubljana.**

M

Maas (mäs), riv., Dutch part of Meuse riv., to Rhine Delta; # 51:44 N, 4:50 E.

Maastricht (mäs′tricht), city, * of Limburg prov., S. Neth., pop. 57; sandstone; # 50:52 N, 5:35 E.

Macao (mä-kä′ō), Portuguese colony on isl. of Macao, S. E. coast of China, area .004, pop. 75; # 22:10 N, 113:35 E.

Macassar (mä-käs′sạr), strait bet. Borneo and Celebes, E. Indies; # 2 S, 118 E. — spt. city, S. W. Celebes, pop. 20; an important port; # 5:15 S, 119:30 E.

Macau (mo′kō), city, Csanâd County, Hungary, on Mures riv., pop. 37; # 46:13 N, 20:29 E.

MacDonnell (mak-don′nẹl), low mt. range, C. Australia; # 24 S, 132 E.

Macedonia (mas-ẹ-dō′ni-ạ), anc. country, N. of anc. Greece; — N. part of Greece, est. pop. 295, W., pop. 291; chief city, Salonika; # 40:45 N, 22:30 E.

Maceió (mä-sā-yō′), spt. city, ext. E. Brazil, * of Alagôas, pop. 74; # 9:49 S, 35:40 W.

Macerata (mä-chä-rä′tä), prov., Marche, N. E. C. Italy, area 1, pop. 268 and its *, pop. 24; univ.; # 43:46 N, 13:28 E.

Macgillicuddy's Reeks (mạ-gil-i-kud′iz rēks), mts. of Kerry, S. W. Ireland, highest Irish mts., summit, Carrantuohill, el. 3,434 ft.; # 52 N, 9:45 W.

Mackenzie (mạ-ken′zi), riv., N. W. Canada, Great Slave Lake to Arctic oc., len. 900, or with Peace riv., ab. 2,500 mi.; # 69 N, 134 W. — dist., S. W. part of N. W. Ter. of Canada, area 542; # 63 N, 115 W.

Mackinac (mak′i-nà), strait bet. lakes Michigan and Huron; least width, 4 mi.; # 45:48 N, 84:50 W.

Mâcon (mä-kôṅ), city, E. C. Fr., * of Saône-et-Loire, pop. 20; burgundy; # 46:18 N, 4:50 E.

Macon (mā′kọn), city, C. Ga., pop. 58; Wesleyan and Mercer univs.; # 32:45 N, 83:40 W.

Macquarie (mạ-kwor′i), riv., E. New S. Wales, Australia, to Darling riv., len. 750 mi.; # 30:15 S, 147:30 E.

Madagascar (mad-ạ-gas′kär), Fr. isl., Indian oc., 240 mi. E. of Africa, area 225, len. 980 mi., pop. 3,272 (19 whites), * Antananarivo, pop. 58; # 20 S, 47 E.

Madeira (mä-dā′ē̇-rä, mạ-dē′rạ), group of 5 isls., belonging to Portugal, area .315, pop. 170, * Funchal; # 32:40 N, 16:45 W.

— chief isl. of group; # 32:40 N, 17 W. — chief trib. of Amazon riv., len. ab. 3,100 mi.; # 3:35 S, 59 W. — falls, series of rapids on Madeira riv., now circumvented by a costly R.R ; # 9:32 S, 65:15 W.

Madina, see **Medina.**

Madison (mad′i-sọn), city, S. C. Wis., state * and univ., pop. 67; # 43:5 N, 89:25 W. — tn., S. E. Ind., on Ohio riv., pop. 7; State Park; Hanover College near; # 38:45 N, 85:28 W.

Madras (mạ-dràs′), prov., S. E. India, area 142, pop. 43,319, and its *, spt., pop. 527; associated native states, area 10, pop. 5,460; univ.; # 16 N, 81 E.

Madrid (mạ-drid′, *Sp.* mä-drēтн′), prov., C. Spain, area 3, pop. 1,141 and its *, the * of Spain, pop. 814; univ.; # 40:20 N, 3:45 W.

Madura (mad′ù-rä), isl., 5 mi. N. E. C. Java, Dutch E. Indies, administratively a part of Java, area 1.7; # 7:5 S, 113:20 E. — city, ext. S. India, pop. 139; # 9:55 N, 78:15 E.

Maebashi (mä-e-bä′shē), inland city, C. Honshu isl., Japan, pop. 74; # 36:25 N, 139:5 E.

Maesteg (mīs′teg), city, S. Wales, pop. 29; # 51:36 N, 3:39 W.

Maestricht, see **Maastricht.**

Mafeking (maf′e-king), tn., * of Bechuanaland, but just in Cape Province, pop. 2; # 25:50 S, 25:50 E.

Magallanes (mä-gäl-yä′näs), ter., S. Chile, area 65, pop. 29, * Punta Arenas; # 50 S, 74 W.

Magdalena (mäg-dä-lä′nä), chief riv. of Colombia, len. 1,060 mi. to Caribbean sea; # 10 N, 74:40 W. — dept., area 19, pop. 211; # 10:45 N, 74:55 W. — bay, and fine harbor, S. W. Lower Calif.; # 24:30 N, 112 W.

Magdeburg (mäg′dẹ-bùrch), city on Elbe riv., * of Sachsen (Saxony) prov., Prussia, pop. 287; # 52:10 N, 11:40 E.

Magellan (mạ-jel′ạn), strait bet. Tierra del Fuego and the S. extremity of the mainland of S. America, len. 300 mi., discovered 1520; # 53:30 S, 70:45 W.

Maggiore (mäd-jô′rä), *anc.* Verbanus, lake, N. Italy and S. Switz., len. 40 mi.; # 46 N, 8:40 E.

Mahanoy City (mä-hạ-noi′ sit′i), coal mining city, E. C. Pa., pop. 13; # 40:47 N, 76:8 W.

Mahé (mä-ā′), Fr. city and colony, Malabar coast of S. W. India, pop. 11; # 11:50 N, 75:25 E.

Mahón (mä-ōn′), spt., Minorca, Balearic Isls., Spain, pop. 15; # 39:53 N, 4:21 E.

Maidenhead (mād′ẹn-hed), tn. on Thames riv., S. E. C. Eng., pop. 17; # 51:32 N, 0:44 W.

Maidstone (mād′stọn), city, Kent, S. E. Eng., pop. 39; 32 mi. E. S. E. of London; # 51:16 N, 0:31 E.

Maikop (mī′kop), city, Azerbaijan republic, Transcaucasia, pop. 45; # 44:38 N, 40:2 E.

Main (mān, *Ger.* mīn), riv., S. W. Ger., Bohemia Forest W. to Rhine riv. at Mainz, len. 305 mi.; # 50 N, 8:15 E.

Maine (mān), state, N. E. U.S.A., bordering Canada and New Hampshire, area 33, pop. 847, * Augusta, pop. 19; largest city, Portland, pop. 74; # 45 N, 69 W. — anc. prov., N. W. C. Fr., * Le Mans; # ab. 48 N, 0:2 E.

Maine-et-Loire (mān-ä-lwär), dept., W. C. Fr., area 2.8, pop. 475, * Angers, pop. 86; # 47:25 N, 0:30 W.

Mainland (mān′lạnd), chief isl. of Japan; see **Honshu.** — chief isl. of Orkneys; # 59 N, 3:10 W.

Mainz (mīnts), *Fr.* **Mayence** (mä-yoṅs), city on Rhine riv., Hessen, S. W. Ger., pop. 109; # 49:50 N, 8 E.

Maipo (mī′pö), mt., N. W. Argentina, height 17,421 ft.; # 34:5 S, 69:30 W. — riv., Andes to Pacific oc., C. Chile, len. 150 mi.; # 33:35 S, 71:44 W.

Maitland (māt′lạnd), tn., E. New S. Wales, pop. 12; # 32:45 S, 151:35 E.

Majorca (ma-jôr′kạ), *Sp.* **Mallorca** (mäl-yor′kä), largest isl., Balearic Isls., W. Mediterranean Sea, area 1.3, pop. 257, * Palma; # 39:30 N, 3 E.

Makassar, see **Macassar.**

Mako, see **Macau.**

Malabar (mal-ạ-bär′), region, S. W. coast of India, * Calicut; # 11 N, 75:45 E.

Malacca (mạ-lak′ạ), S. W. part of Br. Straits Settlements, area 0.7, pop. 161, and its *, a spt. tn., pop. 21; # 2:20 N, 102:15 E. — strait bet. Sumatra and Malay pen., width 30–200 mi.; # 3 N, 101 E.

Maladetta (mä-lä-det′tä), pk. or lofty group, C. Pyrenees, Spain, el. 11,169 ft., highest in range; # 42:39 N, 0:39 E.

Málaga (mä′lä-gä), prov., S. Spain, area 2.8, pop. 567, and its *, a spt., pop. 160; # 36:45 N, 4:25 W.

Malakka, see Malacca.

Mälar (mä′lär), lake, S. E. Sweden, extends 80 mi. W. from Stockholm, area 0.4; contains over 1,200 islands; # 59:28 N, 17 E.

Malaspina Glacier (mä-läs-pē′nä), piedmont coastal glacier, S. slope of Mount St. Elias, S. E. Alaska, larger than Rhode Island; # 59:50 N, 140:30 W.

Malaya, British (mạ-lä′yą), Br. possessions, Malay pen., S. E. Asia and nearby small isls., area 53, pop. 3,332, * Singapore; # 4 N, 102 E.

Malay Archipelago (mạ-lä′ or mä′lä är-ki-pel′ạ-gō) or **Malaysia** (mạ-lä′shạ), isls., S. E. Asia, E. Indies; # 1 S, 118 E.

Malay States, Federated, Br. protectorate, S. Malay pen., area 28, pop. 1,325, * Kuala Lumpur, pop. 80; # 4 N, 102 E.

Malden (mäl′dẹn), city, E. C. Mass., pop. 58; # 42:26 N, 71:4 W.

Malines (mäl-ēn), see **Mechlin.**

Malin Head (mäl′in hed), N. tip of Ireland; # 55:22 N, 7:25 W.

Malleco (mäl-yä′kō), prov., C. Chile, area 3.3, pop. 121, * Angol; # 38:10 S, 72:35 W.

Mallorca (mäl-yôr′kä), see **Majorca.**

Malmö (mälm′ė), spt., S. Sweden, 20 mi. E. of Copenhagen, Denmark, pop. 116; # 55:35 N, 13 E.

Malta (mäl′tä), isl. bet. Sicily and Africa, area 0.1, pop. 224; chief city and port, Valletta; Br. Naval Station; # 35:55 N, 14:25 E.

Maltese Islands (mäl-tēs′ i′lạndz), Malta, Goza and Comino, Br. possessions, Mediterranean Sea, S. of Sicily; # 36 N, 25 E.

Mamaroneck (mạ-mar′ọ-nek), a N. suburb of New York City, pop. 13; # 40:57 N, 73:44 W.

Mammoth Cave (mam′ọth kāv), limestone cavern, Edmonson Co., W. C. Ky.; # 37:13 N, 86:9 W.

Mammoth Hot Springs (mam′ọth hot springz), administrative headquarters, Yellowstone National Park, N. Wyo.; # 44:59 N, 110:48 W.

Mamoré (mä-mō-rä′), riv., E. Bolivia, N. to Rio Madeira, len. 700 mi.; # 10:32 S, 65:30 W.

Mamuret-el-Aziz (mä-mu-ret′el-ä-zēz′), prov., Armenia, E. Asiatic Turkey, pop. 200, * Kharput; # 38:40 N, 39 E.

Man (man), **Isle of,** isl., Irish Sea, part of Great Britain, area 0.2, pop. 60, * Douglas, pop. 20; # 54:15 N, 4:30 W.

Managua (mä-nä′gwä), city, N. W. Nicaragua, federal *, pop. 115, on Lake Managua; # 12 N, 86:15 W.

Manama (mä-nä′mạ) or **Manameh,** spt. city, * of Bahrein isls., Persian Gulf, pop. 35; pearls; # 26:18 N, 50:39 E.

Manáos (mä-nä′ọs), city, the * of Amazonas state, N. E. Brazil, on Rio Negro riv., near the Amazon riv., pop. 76; # 3 S, 60 W.

Manche (mänsh), dept., Normandy, N. Fr., area 2.5, pop. 426, * St.-Lô; # 49:5 N, 1:30 W.

Manchester (man′ches-tèr), city on ship canal, W. C. Eng., pop. 766, pop. with suburbs 2,200; univ.; # 53:30 N, 2:13 W. — city, S. C. New Hampshire, pop. 78; # 43 N, 71:30 W.

Manchukuo (man′chö-kwō′), independent state (proclaimed under Japanese auspices 1932) including former Manchuria, N. E. Asia, area ab. 500, pop. ab. 33,000, * Hsinking (formerly Changchun), pop. 80; # 45 N, 127 E.

Manchuria (man-chö′ri-ạ), Chinese ter., N. E. Asia, area 364, pop. ab. 27,000, * Mukden, pop. ab. 250; # 45 N, 127 E; see **Manchukuo.**

Mandalay (man′dạ-lā, man-dạ-lā′), city on Irrawaddy riv., C. Burma, pop. 148; # 22 N, 96 E.

Manhattan (man-hat′ạn), borough of New York City, coextensive with Manhattan isl., pop. 1,890; # 40:44 N, 73:59 W. — tn., N. E. Kansas, pop. 12; State Agri. College; # 39:15 N, 96:35 W.

Manila (mạ-nil′ä; *Sp.* mä-nē′lä), spt. city, on Luzón isl., * of Philippines, pop. 390; univ.; # 14:35 N, 120:58 E.

Manila Bay, large bay, W. C. Luzón, Philippines; battle, May 1, 1898; # 14:40 N, 120:45 E.

Manipur (mun′ē̦-pör), native state, N. E. India, area 8, pop. 384, and its *, pop. 75; univ.; # 24:44 N, 93:58 E.

Manissa (mä-nis′ä), *anc.* Magnesia, city, S. W. Asia Minor,

* of Saroukhan, pop. 30; battle, 190 B.C.; # 38:25 N, 27:40 E.

Manistee (man-is-tē′), tn. on Manistee riv., N. W. lower pen. of Mich., pop. 9; # 44:15 N, 86:20 W.

Manitoba (man-i-tō′bä), prov., S. C. Canada, area 252, pop. 700, * Winnipeg, pop. 216; # 55 N, 97 W. — lake therein, area 2, len. 120 mi.; # 50:30 N, 98:30 W.

Manitoulin (man-i-tö′lin), isl., N. Lake Huron to Ontario, len. 80 mi., greatest width 28 mi.; # 45:45 N, 82 W.

Manitowoc (man″i-tō-wok′), city, C. E. Wis., pop. 24; # 44:8 N, 87:40 W.

Manizales (mä-nę̦-sä′läs), city, N. W. Colombia, the * of Caldas, pop. 43; # 5:5 N, 75:35 W.

Mankato (man-kä′tō), tn., S. E. C. Minn., pop. 16; State Teachers College; # 44:20 N, 94 W.

Mannheim (män′hīm), city on the Rhine, N. Baden, S. W. Ger., pop. 242; # 49:30 N, 8:28 E.

Mans, Le (mäṅ), city, N. W. C. Fr., * of Sarthe dept., pop. 72; # 48 N, 0:15 E.

Mansfield (manz′fēld), city, Nottingham, S. C. Eng., pop. 46; # 53:8 N, 1:12 W. — city, N. C. Ohio, pop. 37; # 40:47 N, 82:32 W. — mt., highest in Vt., el. 4,406 ft.; # 44:35 N, 72:45 W.

Mansurah, El (män-sö′rä), city, Nile delta, Egypt, pop. 49; # 31:2 N, 31:22 E.

Mantova (män′tō-vä), see **Mantua.**

Mantua (man′țü-ä), prov., Lombardy, N. Italy, area 0.9, pop. 377 and its *, pop. 37; # 45:9 N, 10:48 E.

Manych (mạ̈-nich′), depression bet. Caspian Sea and Sea of Azov, former outlet of Caspian, len. 350 mi.; # 47 N, 43 E.

Manzanillo (män-thä-nēl′yō), spt. city, S. E. Cuba, pop. 61; # 20:19 N, 77:10 W. — spt. city, Colima, S. W. Mexico; # 19 N, 104:30 W.

Maracaibo (mä-rä-kī′bō), sea level lake in N. W. Venezuela, len. 100 mi.; # 9:20 N, 71:30 W. — gulf bet. Colombia and Venezuela; # 11:30 N, 71 W. — city, N. W. Venezuela, * of Zulia state, pop. 47; # 10:40 N, 71:50 W.

Marajó (mä-rä-zhō′), isl., mouth of the Amazon, N. E. Brazil, len. 165 mi., area ab. 2; # 1 S, 50 W.

Marakesh (mä-rȧ-kesh′), **Marrakesh** or **Morocco,** city, W. C. Morocco, N. W. Africa, pop. 145; # 31:38 N, 7:59 W.

Maramuresh (mä-rä-mö′resh), prov., N. W. Romania, area 6, pop. 767; # 47:30 N, 23:30 E.

Maranhão (mä-rän-youṅ′), state, N. E. Brazil, area 134, pop. 874, * São Luiz, pop. 53; # 4:40 S, 45 W.

Marañón (mä-rä-nyōn′), riv., Peruvian part of the upper Amazon riv., len. 1,000 mi.; # 4:55 S, 73:55 W.

Marathon (mar′ạ-thon), vil. on plain, Attica, 18 mi. N. E. of Athens, Greece; battle, 490 B.C.; # 38:8 N, 24 E.

Marburg (mär′bûrch), city, Hessen-Nassau prov., Prussia, pop. 24; univ.; # 50:49 N, 8:45 E.

March (märch) or **Morava,** riv., N. Moravia, S. to Danube riv., len. 210 mi.; # 48:13 N, 17 E.

Marche (mär′kä), dept., N. C. C. Italy, area 3.7, pop. 1,148, * Ancona, pop. 66; # 43:20 N, 13 E.

Marco Polo (mär′kō pō′lō), mt. range, Tibet, part of Kuenlun range; # 35:38 N, 95 E.

Marcy (mär′si), mt., highest peak of Adirondack Mts., N. E. New York, el. 5,344 ft.; # 44:8 N, 73:55 W.

Mar del Plata (mär del plä′tä), seaside resort, Cape Corrientes, S. E. Argentina, pop. 28; # 38:5 S, 57:30 W.

Mardin (mär-dēn′), prov., S. E. Asiatic Turkey, pop. 175, and its *, pop. 31; # 37:15 N, 40:45 E.

Mare (mär), isl., San Francisco Bay, U. S. Naval Station; # ab. 37:46 N, 122:23 W.

Marengo (mä-reng′gō), vil., Piedmont, N. W. Italy; battle, 1800; # 45:16 N, 10:45 E. — vil. and cave, S. Ind.; # 38:23 N, 86:24 W.

Margate (mär′gāt), spt. city, N. E. Kent, S. E. Eng., pop. 48; # 51:24 N, 1:21 E.

Margelan (mär-ge-län′), city, Russian Turkestan, pop. 49; # 40:25 N, 71:50 E.

Mari (mä′rẹ), autonomous soviet area, S. E. Russia, area 6, pop. 300; # ab. 40 N, 53 E.

Maria di Leuca (mä-rē′ä dē lö′kä), **Santa,** cape, ext. S. E. Italy; # ab. 39:45 N, 18:25 E.

Mariana (mä-rē-ä′nä), see **Ladrone Islands.**

Maribor (mä′rẹ-bor) or **Marburg** (mär′bŭrch), city, Slovenia, on Drave riv., ext. N. Yugoslavia, pop. 31; # 46:35 N, 15:40 E.

Marienbad (mä-rē′ẹn-bät), watering place, N. W. Bohemia, pop. 7; # 49:58 N, 12:42 E.

Marienburg (mä-rē′ẹn-bŭrch), city, 26 mi. S. of Danzig, N. Ger., pop. 21; # 54:2 N, 19:3 E.

Marietta (mä-ri-et′ä), city, S. E. Ohio, on Ohio riv., pop. 15; Marietta College; # 39:25 N, 81:30 W.

Marinduque (mä-rẹn-dö′kä), isl., C. Philippines, area 0.4, pop. 57, * Boac; # 13:20 N, 122 E.

Marinette (mar-i-net′), tn., N. E. Wis., pop. 14; # 45:7 N, 87:35 W.

Marion (mar′i-ọn), city, N. W. C. Ohio, pop. 31; # 40:37 N, 83:7 W. — city, N. E. C. Ind., pop. 27; Marion College; # 40:33 N, 85:44 W. — tn., S. Ill., pop. 9; # 37:45 N, 88:54 W. — county, C. Ind., area 0.4, pop. 461 (1940), * Indianapolis; # 39:44 N, 86:12 W.

Maritime (mar′i-tīm), alpine range, S. E. Fr.; # 44:15 N, 7 E. — former prov., Far E. Republic, Siberia, area 166, pop. 533; since 1923 part of Amur prov.; # 50 N, 137 E. — **Provinces**, Nova Scotia, New Brunswick and Prince Edward Isl.; # 47 N, 65 W.

Maritza (mä-rēt′sä), anc. Hebrus, riv., W. Bulgaria, N. Ægean Sea, len. 300 mi.; # 40:45 N, 26 E.

Marlborough (märl′bur-ọ), city, E. C. Mass., pop. 15; # 42:22 N, 71:35 W. — prov., N. E. S. Isl., New Zealand, area 4, pop. 18; # 41:50 S, 173:30 E.

Marmara (mär′mạ-rä), sea bet. Europe and Asia, Bosporus and Dardanelles; # 40:40 N, 28 E. — isl. therein, area 0.1; — spt. thereon; # 40:42 N, 27:40 E.

Marmolada (mär-mọ-lä′dä), mt., highest of Dolomites, N. Italy, el. 11,020 ft.; # 46:27 N, 11:52 E.

Marmora (mär′mọ-rä), see **Marmara.**

Marne (märn), riv., E. C. Fr. to Seine riv., len. 325 mi.; battle, 1914; # 48:49 N, 2:24 E. — dept., N. E. C. Fr., area 3.2, pop. 367, * Châlons-sur-Marne; # 48:55 N, 4 E.

Marne (Haute), see **Haute-Marne.**

Maros (mor′ōsh), riv., Carpathian Mts. W. to Tisza riv., Romania, len. 500 mi.; # 46:25 N, 23:58 E.

Marquesas (mär-kā′sạs), group of Fr. isls., S. Pacific oc., far S. S. E. of Hawaii, area 0.5, pop. 2; # 9 S, 139 W.

Marquette (mär-ket′), port on Lake Superior, N. Mich., pop. 16; # 46:30 N, 87:20 W.

Marra (mär′rä), mts., S. W. Anglo-Egyptian Sudan, in Dafur; # 13 N, 25 E.

Marrakesh, see **Marakesh.**

Marrickville (mar′ik-vil), suburb of Sydney, New S. Wales, Australia, pop. 42; # 33:55 S, 151:9 E.

Marsala (mär-sä′lä), anc. Lilybæum, spt. city, ext. W. Sicily, pop. comm. 65; # 37:47 N, 12:26 E.

Marseille (mär-sā′y′), Eng. Marseilles (mär-sälz′), anc. Massilia, spt., S. Fr., chief port of S. Europe, pop. 586; tropical oils; # 43:18 N, 5:25 E.

Marshall (mär′shạl), group of 24 isls., S. W. C. Pacific oc., pop. 10, Japanese mandate; chief isl. and * Jaluit; # 10 N, 165 E. — tn., N. E. Texas, pop. 18; # 32:30 N, 94:25 W.

Marshalltown (mär′shạl-toun), city, C. Iowa, pop. 19; # 42:5 N, 92:55 W.

Martaban (mär-tạ-bän′), gulf, S. of Burma Proper and spt. on same; # 16 N, 97 E.

Martha's Vineyard (mär′thạz vin′yạrd), isl., S. E. Mass., len. 23, pop. 5; # 41:20 N, 70:40 W.

Martinique (mär-ti-nēk′), Fr. isl., Lesser Antilles, area 0.4, pop. 244, * Fort-de-France, pop. 26; # 14:30 N, 61 W.

Martinsburg (mär′tinz-bẽrg), tn., ext. N. E. W. Va., pop. 15; # 39:28 N, 77:55 W.

Martins Ferry (mär′tinz fer′i), tn., C. E. Ohio, pop. 15; # 40:7 N, 80:44 W.

Marwar (mär′wär), see **Jodhpur.**

Maryborough (mā′ri-bur-ọ), tn., E. C. Queensland, Australia, pop. 11; # 25:40 S, 152:40 E.

Maryland (mer′i-lạnd), state, S. E. U.S.A., bet. Va. and Pa., area 12, pop. 1,821. * Annapolis, pop. 13; chief city, Baltimore, pop. 859; # 38:50 N, 76:35 W.

Marylebone, St. (mä′ri-lẹ-bōn), borough, N. W. London, Eng., pop. 104; # 51:31 N, 0:10 W.

Marysville (mā′riz-vil), butte, N. C. Calif., el. 2,132 ft., and tn. nearby, pop. 7; college; # 39:5 N, 121:38 W.

Maryville, tn., E. Tenn., pop. 6; Maryville College; # ab. 35:44 N, 83:55 W.

Masampo (mä-säm′pō) or **Masan** (mä-sän′), naval station, S. Korea, pop. 23; # 35:15 N, 128:30 E.

Masbate (mäs-bä′tä), isl., C. Philippines, area 1.2, pop. 29, and its *, pop. 11; # 12:15 N, 123:30 E.

Mascarene (mäs-kạ-rēn′), isls., E. of Madagascar in S. Indian oc.; includes Réunion (Fr.) and Mauritius (Br.); # 20 S. 54 E.

Mashhad (mash-had′), see **Meshed.**

Maskat (mus-kat′), see **Muskat.**

Mason City (mā′sọn si′ti), city, N. E. Iowa, pop. 27; # 43:15 N, 93:15 W.

Massachusetts (mas-ạ-chö′sets), state, N. E. U.S.A., bet. New York and Atlantic oc., area 8, pop. 4,317, * Boston, pop. 771; second city, Worcester, pop. 194; # 42:30 N, 72 W.

Massa e Carrara (mäs′sä ä kär-rä′rä), prov., Tuscany, N. W. C. Italy, area 0.4, pop. 179, and its *, pop. 34; # 43:3 N, 10:54 E.

Massawa (mäs-sä′wä), spt. on Red Sea in Eritrea, pop. 3; # 16:5 N, 39:15 E.

Massillon (mas′il-ọn), city, N. E. Ohio, pop. 27; # 40:48 N, 81:35 W.

Massive, Mount (màs′iv), pk., C. Colo., next to Elbert, highest in state, el. 14,402 ft.; # 39:15 N, 106:30 W.

Masulipatam (mạ-sö′li-pạ-täm′), spt. city, Madras prov., S. E. India, pop. 44; # 16:9 N, 81:12 E.

Matabeleland (ma-tạ-bē′lẹ-land), prov., S. Rhodesia, pop. 180, * Bulawayo; # 19 S, 30 E.

Matamoros (mä-tä-mō′rọs), spt. city, N. E. Mex., opp. Brownsville, Tex. pop. 18; # 25:51 N, 97:29 W.

Matanzas (ma-tan′zạs), prov., N. W. Cuba, area 3, pop. 328, and its *, pop. 63; # 23 N, 81:45 W.

Matapan (mä-tä-pän′), cape, ext. S. Greece; # 36:22 N, 22:30 E.

Matsue (mät′sö-e), spt. city, N. C. Honshu isl., Japan, pop. 41; # 35:30 N, 133 E.

Matsumoto (mät-sù-mō′tọ), inland city, C. Honshu isl., Japan, pop. 63; # 36:15 N, 138 E.

Matsuyama (mät-sù-yä′mä), chief city of Shikoku isl., Japan, pop. 58; # 33:50 N, 132:50 E.

Matsuye (mät′sù-ye), see **Matsue.**

Matterhorn (mät′ẽr-hôrn), Fr. **Mont Cervin**, pk., Pennine Alps, Italian-Switz. line, el. 14,705 ft.; # 45:57 N, 7:48 E.

Matto Grosso (mät′ọ grōs′ọ), state, S. C. Brazil, area 570, pop. 247, * Cuyabá; # 14 S, 56 W; — an indefinite region of S. W. Brazil; # 15 S, 55 W.

Mattoon (ma-tön′), tn., E. C. Ill., pop. 16; # 39:30 N, 88:24 W.

Maubeuge (mō-bėzh′), city, Nord dept., N. Fr., pop. 23; # 50:15 N, 3:55 E.

Maui (mou′ē), second isl., Hawaiian isls., area 0.7; # 20:45 N, 156:15 W.

Maule (mou′lä), prov., W. C. Chile, area 2.8, pop. 113, * Cauquenes; # 36:5 S, 72:40 W.

Maumee (mâ-mē′), riv., N. E. Ind., N. W. Ohio, to Lake Erie near Toledo, len. 175 mi.; # 41:35 N, 83:35 W.

Maumee-Wabash Canal, canal, lake Erie at Toledo to Ohio riv. at Evansville, Ind.; important 1831–1857.

Mauna Kea (mou′nä kä′ä), extinct volcano, isl. of Hawaii, el. 13,825 ft.; # 19:55 N, 155:29 W.

Mauna Loa (mou′nä lō′ä), active volcano, isl. of Hawaii, el. 13,675 ft.; # 19:29 N, 155:38 W.

Mauritania (mâ-rē-tā′ni-ạ), colony, Fr. W. Africa, area 145, pop. 285; # 19 N, 9 W.

Mauritius (mâ-rish′ius), isl. in Indian oc., a Br. colony, area 0.1, pop. 382, * Port Louis, pop. 52; # 20 S, 57:50 E.

May (mā), cape, S. ext. S. New Jersey, in Delaware Bay; # 38:56 N, 74:55 W.

Mayaguez (mä-yä-gwäs′), spt. city, W. Puerto Rico, pop. 50; # 18:10 N, 67:10 W.

Mayence (mả-yäns), see **Mainz.**

Mayenne (mả-yen), dept., N. W. C. Fr., area 2, pop. 262, * Laval, pop. 25; # 48:18 N, 0:30 W.

Mayo (mä′ọ), county, N. W. Connaught, N. W. Ireland, area 2, pop. 192, * Castlebar; # 54:10 N, 9:40 W.

(variable) ḍ as d or j, ṣ as s or sh, ṭ as t or ch, ẓ as z or zh; o, F. cloche; ü, F. menu; ch, Sc. loch; ṅ, F. bonbon; ′, primary accent; ′, secondary accent; †, obsolete; <, from; +, and; =, equals. See also lists at beginning of book

Mayotte (mä-yōt′), isl., S. E. Indian oc., part of Fr. colony of Mayotte and Comoro isls., area 0.1, pop. 14; area of colony 1, pop. 110; # 12:47 S, 45:20 E.

Maywood (mā′wŭd), a W. suburb of Chicago, pop. 27; # 41:58 N, 87:48 W.

Mazar-i-Sharif (mà-zär′ē-shạ-rēf′), prov., N. C. Afghanistan and its *, pop. 46; # 36:45 N, 67:9 E.

Mazatlán (mä-sät-län′), spt. city, Sinaloa, N. W. Mexico, pop. 16; mining; # 23:15 N, 106:30 W.

McAlester (mạk-al′es-tėr), tn., S. E. Okla., pop. 12; # 34:55 N, 95:50 W.

McKeesport (mạ-kēz′pōrt), city, S. W. Pa., near Pittsburgh, pop. 55; # 40:21 N, 79:51 W.

McKees Rocks (mạ-kēz′ roks), an industrial suburb N. W. of Pittsburgh, Pa., pop. 17; # ab. 40:30 N, 80:5 W.

McKinley (mạ-kin′li), mt., S. C. Alaska, el. 20,300 ft., highest peak of North America; # 63 N, 151 W.

Meadville (mēd′vil), city, N. W. Pa., pop. 19; Allegheny College; # 41:42 N, 80:10 W.

Meaux (mō), tn., 27 mi. E. N. E. of Paris, Fr., pop. 14; # 48:58 N, 2:53 E.

Mecca (mek′ạ), city, W. Arabia, * of Hejaz, pop. ab. 55; birthplace of Mohammed; # 21:30 N, 39:45 E.

Mechlin (mek′lin) or **Malines**, city midway bet. Brussels and Antwerp, Belgium, pop. 60; # 51:3 N, 4:27 E.

Mecklenburg-Schwerin (mek′lẹn-bůrch shvä-rēn′), republic, N. Ger., area 5, pop. 685, * Schwerin, pop. 46; # 53:51 N, 11:28 E.

Mecklenburg-Strelitz (strä′lits), republic, N. Ger., area 1.1, pop. 112, * Neu Strelitz, pop. 11; # 53:22 N, 13:4 E.

Medellín (mā-ᴛʜɛl-yēn′), city, N. W. Colombia, pop. 87, * of Antioquia; mining; # 6:15 N, 75:50 W.

Medford (med′fọrd), city, E. C. Mass., pop. 63; Tufts College; # 42:25 N, 71:5 W.

Media (mē′di-ạ), anc. country, now in N. and W. Persia; # ab. 35 N, 50 E.

Medicine Hat (med′i-sin hat), tn., S. E. Alberta, pop. 10; # 50:05 N, 110:45 W.

Medina (mạ-dē′nạ) or **Madina**, city, C. Hejaz, W. Arabia, pop. ab. 15; Mohammed's tomb; pilgrimages; # 24:30 N, 39:45 E.

Mediterranean (med″i-tẹ-rā′nẹ-ạn), sea, bet. Africa, Europe and Asia Minor, area 1,145, greatest known depth, 12,276 ft.; # 35 N, 20 E.

Médoc (mā-dok), dist., N. W. Gironde dept., S. W. Fr.; wines; # 45:10 N, 0:1 W.

Meerane (mā-rä′nė), city, W. Sachsen, S. Ger., pop. 24; # 50:50 N, 12:28 E.

Meerut (mē′rut), city, N. of Delhi, N. C. India, pop. 123; # 28:55 N, 77:50 E.

Megara (meg′a-rä), spt. tn., 21 mi. W. of Athens, Greece, pop. 10; # 38 N, 23:21 E.

Meissen (mī′sẹn), city on Elbe riv., C. Sachsen, S. Ger., pop. 41; Dresden china; # 51:10 N, 13:28 E.

Meknes (mek′nez), city, W. Morocco, N. W. Africa, pop. 38; # 33:54 N, 5:39 W.

Mekong (mā-kong′), riv., Tibet to S. China Sea, len. 2,500 mi.; # 10:10 N, 106:40 E.

Melanesia (mel-ạ-nē′shi-ạ), groups of isls., S. of equator, W. S. Pacific oc.; # 10 S, 160 E.

Melbourne (mel′bọrn), spt. city, Victoria, S. E. Australia, pop. with suburbs, 1,024; Univ. of Melbourne; # 37:48 S, 144:58 E.—, **South**, pop. 47; # 37:50 S, 145 E.— **port**, pop. 13; # 37:50 S, 144:57 E.

Meleda (mel′ä-dä) or **Mljet**, isl., S. Dalmatia, Yugoslavia, len. 25 mi.; # 42:45 N, 17:30 E.

Melos (mē′los) or **Milo**, Greek isl., S. W. Ægean Sea, area .06, pop. 5; Venus of Milo; # 36:40 N, 24:30 E.   [71:4 W

Melrose (mel′rōz), city, E. C. Mass., pop. 23; # 42:28 N,

Melville (mel′vil), lake, 125 mi. long, E. Labrador; # 54 N, 59 W. — pen., N. W. Ter., Canada; # 68 N, 84 W. — sound, part of Arctic oc., bet. Victoria Isl. and Melville Isl.; # 75 N, 105 W. — isl., N. Australia; # 11:30 S, 131 E.

Memel (mā′mel), *Polish* **Niemen**, riv., W. C. Russia to Baltic Sea at Memel, len. 565 mi.; # 55:30 N, 21 E.— dist., N. East Prussia, area 1.1, pop. 153, and its * (spt. city), pop. 39; # 55:30 N, 21 E; under League of Nations 1919–23, taken by Lithuania in 1923, taken by Germany in 1939.

Memphis (mem′fis), city, S. E. Tenn., on Mississippi riv., pop. 293; S. W. College; # 35:15 N, 90 W. — anc. city, * of Anc. Egypt, 12 mi. S. of Cairo; # 29:51 N, 31:14 E.

Memphremagog (mem-frẹ-mā′gog), lake, N. Ver. and S. Quebec, len. 30 mi.; # 45:10 N, 72:15 W.

Menai (men′ī), strait bet. Anglesey isl. and mainland of N. Wales; bridged; # 53:8 N, 4:20 W.

Menam (mā-näm′), riv., N. Siam to Gulf of Siam, len. 700 mi.; # 13:30 N, 100:30 E.

Mendocino (men-dō-sē′nō), cape, ext. W. Calif.; # 40:25 N, 124:25 W.

Mendoza (men-dō′sä), prov., W. C. Argentina, area 57, pop. 333, and its *, pop. 59; # 33 S, 68:40 W.

Mentawi (men-tä′vī), isls. near S. E. coast of Sumatra, E. Indies; # 2 S, 98:30 E.

Mentone (men-tō′nä), coastal resort, ext. S. E. Fr., pop. 18; # 43:45 N, 7:32 E.

Mequinez (mek′i-nez) see **Meknez.**

Meran (mā-rän′), health resort, Trentino, N. Italy, pop. 12; # 46:41 N, 11:9 E.

Merced (mėr-sẹd′), riv., Yosemite Park, C. Calif., to San Joaquin riv., len. 150 mi.; # 37:22 N, 121 W. — or Nevada Fall, in Yosemite Valley, height 700 ft.; # 37:31 N, 120:20 W.

Mercedario (mer-sä-ᴛʜä′rē-ō), pk., Andes Mts., N. W. Argentina, el. 21,884 ft.; # 32 S, 70:10 W.

Mercedes (mer-sä′ᴛʜäs), city, C. Argentina, * of San Luis prov., pop. 26; # 34:35 S, 59:29 W. — city, S. W. Uruguay, pop. 23; # 33:12 S, 58:4 W.

Mercia (mėr′shiä), anc. Anglo-Saxon kingdom, C. Eng.; # ab. 52 N, 1 W.

Mer de Glace (mâr-dė-glås), glacier, best known in Alps, N. slope of Mt. Blanc, Fr.; # 45:50 N, 6:50 E.

Mergui (mer-gē′), archipelago, S. Burma; and a spt. on Malay pen., pop. 12; # 11:30 N, 98:30 W.

Mérida (mā′rē-ᴛʜä), city, * of Yucatan, Mex., pop. 62; # 20:50 N, 89:50 W. — state, N. W. Venezuela, pop. 123, and its *, pop. 14; # 8:40 N, 71:15 W.

Meriden (mer′i-dẹn), city, S. C. Conn., pop. 39; silver ware; # 41:30 N, 72:48 W.

Meridian (mẹ-rid′i-ạn), city, E. C. Miss., pop. 35; college; # 32:30 N, 88:45 W.

Merionethshire (mer-i-on′eth-shir), county, W. C. Wales, area 0.6, pop. 45, * Dolgelly; # 52:52 N, 3:55 W.

Meroë (mer′ọ-ē), area bet. Nile and Atbara rivs., Anglo-Egyptian Sudan; # 16 N, 34:20 E. — tn., in same, sometimes called Assur; # 17 N, 33:42 E.

Merrimac (mer′i-mak), riv., N. New Hampshire to Atlantic oc., len. 150 mi.; # 42:50 N, 70:55 W.

Merseburg (mer′zė-bůrch), a W. suburb of Leipzig, Ger., pop. 25; # 51:21 N, 12 E.

Mersey (mėr′zi), riv., C. Eng., W. past Liverpool to Irish Sea, len. 70 mi.; # 53:20 N, 2:55 W.

Merthyr Tydfil (mėr′thėr tid′vil), city, S. E. Wales, pop. 83; # 51:48 N, 3:28 W.

Merv (merv or merf), old city and oasis, Russian Turkestan, * of district of Merv, pop. 11; # 37:50 N, 61:35 E.

Mesabi (mẹ-sä′bẹ), low range, N. E. Minn., el. 1,920 ft.; yields ab. one-fourth of world's iron ore; # 49:37 N, 92:4 W.

Mesa Verde (mā′sä vär′dä), table land, S. W. Colo.; ruins of cliff dwellers; national park, 1906; area 0.1; # 37:15 N, 108:30 W.

Meshed (mėsh′hed), city, N. E. Persia, pop. ab. 70; # 36:25 N, 59:25 E.

Mesolonghi (mä-sō-long′gē), spt., S. W. Greece, on Gulf of Corinth, pop. 8; # 38:25 N, 21:28 E.

Mesopotamia (mes″ọ-pọ-tä′mi-ạ), lowland bet. Arabia and Persia, esp. land bet. Tigris and Euphrates rivs. therein; also applied to kingdom of Iraq, q.v.; # 32 N, 46 E.

Messenia (me-sē′ni-ạ), *anc.* Messena, gulf, S. Morea pen., S. Greece; # 36:45 N, 22:15 E.

Messina (me-sē′nä), prov., N. E. Sicily, area 1.2, pop. 582, and its *, a spt., pop. 176; earthquake, 1908; # 38:10 N, 15:25 E. — strait bet. Sicily and Italy, 2¼ mi. wide; # 38 N, 15:35 E.

Meta (mā′tä), riv., Bogota, Colombia, N. E. to Orinoco riv., len. 650 mi.; # 6:25 N, 67:50 W.

Methuen (mẹ-thū′ẹn), city, N. E. Mass., 27 mi. N. N. W. of Boston, pop. 22; # 42:43 N, 71:12 W.

Metz (mets), city, Lorraine, N. E. Fr., * of Moselle dept., pop. 62; # 49:5 N, 6:10 E.

Meurthe-et-Moselle (mèrt-ā-mo-zel), dept., ext. E. Fr., area 2, pop. 504, * Nancy, pop. 113; # 48:40 N, 6 E.

Meuse (mūz; mèz), riv., N. W. France, across E. Belgium to Rhine delta, Neth., len. 575 mi.; # 51:44 N, 4:50 E. — (mèz) dept., N. E. Fr., area 2.4, pop. 207, * Bar-le-duc, pop. 17; # 49:10 N, 5:22 E.

Mewar (mā-wär'), see **Udaipur.**

Mexborough (meks'bur-ọ̄), tn., W. Riding, Yorkshire, N. Eng., pop. 15; # 53:30 N, 1:17 W.

Mexico (mek'si-kō), republic, S. N. America, area 767, pop. 16,553, * Mexico City, pop. 961; # 24 N, 103 W. — state, C. Mex., area 9, pop. 880, * Toluca, pop. 31; # 19:30 N, 99 W. — **Gulf of**, part of Atlantic oc., bet. U.S.A., Cuba and Mexico, area 716, greatest depth 12,714 ft.; # 25 N, 90 W.

Mexico City, city, S. C. Mexico, federal *, pop. 615, el. 7,350 ft.; univ.; # 19:30 N, 99:8 W.

Mezen (me-zen'y'), riv., N. Russia to White Sea, len. 550 mi.; # 65:30 N, 44:20 E.

Mézières (mā-zyär'), tn., N. E. Fr., * of Ardennes dept., pop. 10; # 49:46 N, 4:44 E.

Miami (mī-am'i), city, S. E. Florida, pop. 172 (1940); winter coast resort; # 25:40 N, 80:20 W. — riv., W. Ohio S. to Ohio riv., len. 160 mi.; # 39:10 N, 84:18 W.

Michigan (mish'i-gạn), state, N. E. C. U.S.A., bet. Wis. and Lakes Superior and Huron, area 58, pop. 5,256, * Lansing, pop. 79; chief city, Detroit, pop. 1,623; # 44 N, 85 W. — lake, bet. Wis. and Mich., area 22, el. 581 ft.; # 44 N, 87 W.

Michigan City, city, N. W. Ind., pop. 26; lake port; # 41:45 N, 86:54 W.

Michoacán (me-chō-ä-kän'), state, S. W. Mexico, area 23, pop. 936, * Morelia, pop. 40; # 19 N, 102 W.

Micronesia (mī-krọ-nē'shi-ạ), groups of smaller isls., N. of equator, S. W. N. Pacific oc.; # 10 N, 158 E.

Middlebury (mid'l-ber-i), tn., W. C. Vermont, pop. 2; Middlebury College; # 44:2 N, 73:7 W.

Middlesbrough (mid'lz-brọ), spt., Tees mouth, N. E. Eng., pop. 135; steel; # 54:37 N, 1:15 W.

Middlesex (mid'l-seks), county, bordering London, S. E. Eng., area 0.2, pop. 1,253; # 51:33 N, 0:20 W. — county, N. E. Mass., area 0.8, pop. 971, * Lowell and Cambridge; # 42:30 N, 71:15 W.

Middletown (mid'l-toun), tn., C. Conn., pop. 26, Wesleyan Univ.; # 41:36 N, 72:38 W. — city, S. W. Ohio, pop. 31; # 39:30 N, 84:28 E. — city, S. E. New York, pop. 22; # 41:29 N, 74:30 W.

Midlothian (mid-lō'ᴛʜi-ạn) or **Edinburghshire**, county, S. E. Scotland, area 0.4, pop. 511, * Edinburgh, pop. 428; # 55:51 N, 3:15 W.

Milano (mē-lä'nō), *Eng.* **Milan** (mi-lan'), prov., Lombardy, N. Italy, area 1.2, pop. 1,906, and its *, *anc.* Mediolanum, pop. 836; celebrated cathedral; # 45:28 N, 9:10 E.

Miletus (mī-lē'tus), anc. city, E. Ægean coast; # 37:30 N, 27:15 E.

Milford (mil'fọrd) **Haven**, spt. town, S. Pembroke, S. W. Wales; # 51:43 N, 5:2 W. — (**Milford**) twp., C. Mass., pop. 15; # 42:12 N, 71:30 W.

Milledgeville (mil'ej-vil), tn., C. Ga., pop. 7; State Univ.; # 33:6 N, 83:14 W.

Millville (mil'vil), city, in S. C. New Jersey, 40 mi. S. of Philadelphia, pop. 15; # 39:23 N, 75:3 W.

Milo (mē'lō), modern **Melos**, q.v.

Milwaukee (mil-wâ'kē), city, S. E. Wis., on Lake Michigan, pop. 587; Marquette Univ., Downer College; # 43 N, 87:55 W.

Minas de Ríotinto (mē'näs dā rē'ọ̄-tēn'tō), tn., S. W. Spain, pop. 13; copper mines; # 37:42 N, 6:33 W.

Minas Geraes (mē'näsh zhä-rīsh'), state, S. E. Brazil, area 229, pop. 5,889, * Bello Horizonte; # 18 S, 44 W.

Minch, The (minch), channel bet. Scotland and Outer Hebrides; # 58 N, 6 W.

Mindanao (mēn-dä-nä'ō), large S. isl., Philippines, area 37, pop. 500, chief city, Zamboanga, pop. 31; # 7:30 N, 125 E.

Minden (min'dẹn), city, Westfalen, W. Ger., pop. 27; # 52:18 N, 8:55 E.

Mindoro (mēn-dō'rō), isl., C. Philippines, area 4; pop. 72; # 13 N, 121 E.

Minho (mēn'yō), *Sp.* **Miño** (mēn'yō), riv., N. W. Spain to Atlantic oc. along N. boundary of Portugal, len. 171 mi.; # 41:52 N, 8:50 W. — prov. (Entre-Douro-e-Minho), N. W. Portugal, area 2.8, pop. 1,304, * Braga, pop. 22; # 41:30 N, 8:30 W.

Minneapolis (min-ē-ap'ọ-lis), city, S. E. C. Minn., pop. 492, with adjacent St. Paul, pop. 911; flour milling; State Univ.; # 45 N, 93:15 W.

Minnehaha (min-ē-hä'hä), falls of a trib. of Mississippi riv., Minneapolis, E. Minn., height 50 ft.; # 44:55 N, 93:12 W.

Minnesota (min-ē-sō'tạ), state, N. C. U.S.A., bet. Canada and Iowa, area 85, pop. 2,792, * St. Paul, pop. 288; chief city, Minneapolis, pop. 492; # 46 N, 95 W. — riv., N. E. S. Dak. E. to Mississippi riv., len. 475 mi.; # 44:53 N, 93:11 W.

Minorca (mi-nôr'kạ), E. isl. of Balearic Isls., W. Mediterranean Sea, area 0.3, pop. 42, * Mahón; # 40 N, 4 E.

Minot (mī'nọt), tn., N. W. C. N. Dak., pop. 17; # 48:20 N, 101:15 W.

Minsk (minsk), prov., C. W. Russia, area 35, pop. 2,900, and its *, pop. 101; # 53:50 N, 27:35 E.

Minya, El (mēn'yạ), city on Nile riv., N. Egypt, pop. 35; # 29:15 N, 30:44 E.

Miquelon (mēk-lôn), Fr. isl., S. coast of Newfoundland, area .09; # 47 N, 56:20 W.

Mirzapur (mèr'zä-pör), city, N. C. India, on Ganges riv.; pop. 55; # 25:10 N, 82:37 E.

Mishawaka (mish-ạ-wô'kạ), city, N. C. Ind., contiguous with South Bend, pop. 28; # 41:40 N, 86:15 W.

Misiones (mē-sē-ō'näs), ter. ext. N. E. Argentina, area 11.5, pop. 69, * Posadas; # 27 S, 54:30 W.

Miskolcz (mish'kōltz), city, N. E. Hungary, pop. 57; # 48:10 N, 20:50 E.

Mississippi (mis-i-sip'i), state, S. E. C. U.S.A. bet. Ala. and La., area 47, pop. 2,184, * Jackson, pop. 62; second city, Meridian, pop. 35; # 33 N, 90 W. — riv., N. C. Minn., to Gulf of Mexico, len. 3,160, with Missouri riv., len. 4,194 mi.; # 29 N, 89:20 W.

Missolonghi (mis-ō-long'gē), see **Mesolonghi.**

Missoula (mi-zö'lạ), tn., W. C. Mont., pop. 18; State Univ.; # 46:50 N, 113:50 W.

Missouri (mi-zö'ri), state, N. C. U.S.A., bet. Ill. and Kan., area 69, pop. 3,785, * Jefferson City, pop. 24; chief city, St. Louis, pop. 816; # 38 N, 93 W. — riv., W. Mont., to Mississippi riv., N. St. Louis, len. ab. 3,000 mi.; # 38:40 N, 90:20 W.

Misti, El (mēs'tē), vol. pk., S. Peru, see **El Misti.**

Mitau (mē'tou) or **Jelgava** (yel'gä-vä), city, S. Latvia, pop. 25; # 56:40 N, 23:30 E.

Mitchell (mich'ẹl), mt. pk., W. N. Car., highest point in E. U.S.A., el. 6,711 ft.; # 35:40 N, 82:30 W; — tn., S. E. C. S. Dak., pop. 11; Dak. Wesleyan Univ.; # 43:30 N, 98 W.

Mitilini (mit-i-lē'nẹ), see **Mytilene.**

Mito (mē'tō), city, N. E. C. Honshu isl., Japan, pop. 47; # 36:30 N, 140:30 E.

Mittelfranken (mit'ẹl-fräng″kẹn), N. W. C. div. of Bayern (Bavaria), Ger., area 3, pop. 990, * Ansbach, pop. 22; # 49:20 N, 10:40 E.

Miyakonojo (mē″yạ-kō-nō'jō), city S. E. Kyushiu isl., Japan, pop. 30; # 31:44 N, 131:3 E.

Miyazaki (mē″yạ-zä'kē), spt. city, S. E. Kyushiu isl., Japan, pop. 43; # 31:56 N, 131:26 E.

Mizen Head (miz'ẹn hed), S. W. tip of Ireland; # 51:27 N, 9:49 W.

Mljet (m'lyet'), see **Meleda.**

Moab (mō'ab), anc. kingdom E. of Dead Sea; # ab. 31:30 N, 36 E.

Moberly (mō'bèr-li), tn., N. C. Mo., pop. 13; # 39:27 N, 92:28 W.

Mobile (mō-bēl'), spt. city, S. W. Ala., on Mobile Bay of Gulf of Mexico (len. 36 mi.), pop. 79; # 30:40 N, 88:10 W.

Moca (mō'kä), city, N. C. Dominican Republic, Haiti, pop. 38; # 19:24 N, 70:29 W.

Moçambique, see **Mozambique.**

Mocha (mō'kạ), spt., Yemen, S. W. Arabia; coffee; # 13:20 N, 43:15 E.

Modena (mō'dä-nä), prov., Emilia, N. E. C. Italy, area 1, pop. 396, and its *, pop. 84; # 44:40 N, 10:55 E.

(variable) ḍ as d or j, ṣ as s or sh, ṭ as t or ch, ẓ as z or zh; o, F. cloche; ü, F. menu; ċh, Sc. loch; ṅ, F. bonbon; ', primary accent; ″, secondary accent; †, obsolete; <, from; +, and; =, equals. See also lists at beginning of book.

Modica (mŏd'ē-kä), city, S. E. Sicily, pop. comm. 49; castle; # 36:50 N, 14:45 E.

Moffat (mŏf'ạt), R.R. tunnel, C. Colo., el. ab. 10,000 ft., len. 6 mi.; # ab. 39:50 N, 105:30 W.

Mogadishu (mō-gä-dē'shö), spt., * of Italian Somaliland, N. E. Africa, pop. 14; # 2:10 N, 45:20 E.

Mogilev (mo'gē-lyof), city, on Dnieper riv., S. W. Russia, pop. 53; # 53:55 N, 30:10 E. — city, on Dniester riv., Ukraine, pop. 33; # 49:52 N, 34:30 E.

Mohammerah (mō-häm'me-rä), city, ext. S. W. Persia, on Karun riv., pop. ab. 10; # 30:35 N, 48:10 E.

Mohawk (mō'hȧk), riv., C. New York to Hudson riv., len. 160 mi., the chief pass across Appalachian Mts.; # 42:50 N, 73:40 W.

Mojave (mō-hä'vä), desert, S. Calif.; # 35 N, 117:30 W.

Moji (mō'jē), spt. city, ext. N. of Kyushiu isl., Japan, pop. 95; # 33:58 N, 131 E.

Mokpo (mŏk'pō), treaty port, S. W. Korea, pop. 10; # 34:55 N, 126:25 E.

Moldau (mol'dou), or **Vltava** (vl'tȧ-vȧ), riv., S. Bohemia to Elbe riv., len. 270 mi.; # 50:50 N, 14:30 E.

Moldova (mol-dō'vä), div. of N. C. Romania, area 15, pop. 2,145; chief town, Jassy, pop. 76; # 46:45 N, 27 E.

Molenbeek (mo-lon'bāk), a W. suburb of Brussels, Belgium, pop. 78; # 50:50 N, 4:18 E.

Molfetta (mōl-fet'tä), spt. city, Apulia, S. E. Italy, pop. comm. 43; # 41:12 N, 16:37 E.

Moline (mō-lēn'), city, N. W. Ill., on Mississippi riv., pop. 34; agricultural machinery; # 41:30 N, 90:25 W.

Mollendo (mōl-yen'dō), spt. tn., S. Peru, pop. 7; R.R. to Bolivia; # 17 S, 71:50 W.

Molokai (mō-lō-kī'), isl., Hawaiian isls., area 0.3; leper station; # 21:15 N, 157 W.

Moluccas (mō-luk'ạz), isls., Dutch E. Indies, area 30, pop. 428; # 0:30 S, 128 E. — sea, bet. Celebes and Moluccas or Spice isls.; # 1 S, 125 E.

Mombasa (mom-bä'sä), isl. and city, Kenya ter., Br. E. Africa, area .02, pop. 32; # 4:10 S, 39:40 E.

Monaco (mon'ä-kō), principality, Mediterranean coast, S. E. Fr., area .008, pop. 23, and its *, pop. 2; # 43:44 N, 7:24 E.

Monaghan (mon'ạ-chạn or mon'ạ-gạn), county, N. Irish Free State, area 0.5, pop. 71, and its *, pop. 3; # 54:15 N, 6:58 W.

Mona Passage (mō'nạ pas'ạj), strait bet. Haiti and Porto Rico, width 80 mi.; # 18 N, 67:20 W.

Monastir (mon-ȧs-tēr') or **Bitolj** (bē'tōl-y'), city, ext. S. Yugoslavia, pop. 28; # 41:2 N, 21:20 E.

Mönch (mĕnch), pk., bet. Jungfrau and Finsteraarhorn, S. C. Switz., el. 13,465 ft.; # 46:33 N, 8 E.

Moncton (mungk'tọn), city, E. New Brunswick, pop. 17; # 46:5 N, 64:50 W.

Monessen (mo-nes'n), city, near Charleroi, S. W. Pa., pop. 20; # 40:10 N, 79:55 W.

Mongolia (mon-gō'li-ạ), region, N. E. Asia, area about 1,500, pop. ab. 2,000, * Urga, pop. ab. 30; # 45 N, 102 E. — **Inner,** part bordering China, similar to China; # 47 N, 111 E. — **Outer,** more remote part, Chinese protectorate, sparsely settled; # 47 N, 101 E.

Monmouth (mon'muth) or **Monmouthshire,** county, ext. S. W. C. Eng., area 0.5, pop. 451; # 51:49 N, 2:43 W.

Monongahela (mō-non-gạ-hē'lạ), riv., N. C. W. Va., to Ohio riv. at Pittsburgh, len. 300 mi.; # 39:50 N, 79:56 W.

Monreale (mōn-rā-ä'lā), city, N. W. Sicily, pop. comm. 20; cathedral; # 38:4 N, 13:16 E.

Monroe (mun-rō'), tn., N. E. La., pop. 28; # 32:30 N, 92:10 W. — tn., S. E. Mich., pop. 18; # 41:55 N, 83:28 W; — county, W. New York, area 0.64, pop. 438, * Rochester; # 43:15 N, 77:45 W.

Mons (môns), city, S. W. Belgium, * of Hainaut, pop. 27; # 50:30 N, 3:58 E.

Monserrat (mōn-ser-rät'), see **Montserrat.**

Montana (mon-tä'nạ, -tan'ạ), state, N. W. U.S.A., bet. Canada and Wyo., area 147, pop. 559, * Helena, pop. 15; chief city, Butte, pop. 37; # 47 N, 109 W.

Montauban (môn-tō-bän'), city, S. Fr., * of Tarn-et-Garonne, pop. 26; # 44:1 N, 1:28 E.

Montauk (mon-tôk'), point, E. end of Long Isl., New York; # 41:5 N, 71:52 W.

Mont Blanc, see **Blanc, Mont.**

Mont Cenis, see **Cenis.**

Montclair (mont-klâr'), city, N. E. New Jersey, pop. 40; # 40:49 N, 74:13 W.

Monte Carlo (mŏn'tạ kär'lō, *Eng.* mon'tẹ), tn., Monaco principality, S. E. Fr., pop. 10; gambling; # 43:44 N, 7:24 E.

Montenegro (mŏn-tā-nā'grō), former kingdom, now prov., S. W. Yugoslavia, area 3.7, pop. 200, * Cettinje; # 42:45 N, 18:40 E.

Monterey (mon-tẹ-rā'), tn., S. W. C. Calif., pop. 10, former state *; resort; # 36:35 N, 121:56 W. — Bay, shallow indentation, coast of S. Calif.; # 36:45 N, 121:50 W.

Monterrey (mŏn-te-rā'), city, N. E. Mexico, * of Nuevo León, pop. 132; # 25:45 N, 100:20 W.

Montevideo (mon-tẹ-vid'ẹ-ō), spt. city, * of Uruguay, pop. 683; # 34:55 S, 56:12 W.

Montgomery (mont-gum'ẹ-ri), city, S. E. C. Ala., state *, pop. 78; State Women's College; # 32:30 N, 86:20 W.

Montgomeryshire (mont-gum'ẹ-ri-shėr) or **Montgomery,** county, C. Wales, area 0.8, pop. 51, * Montgomery, pop. 1; # 52:34 N, 3:9 W.

Montmorency (mont-mọ-ren'si), waterfall, 8 mi. from Quebec, height 265 ft.; # 46:53 N, 71:10 W.

Montpelier (mont-pē'lyėr), tn., C. Ver., state *, pop. 8; # 44:18 N, 72:35 W.

Montpellier (môn-pe-lyä), city, S. Fr., * of Hérault dept., pop. 82; Univ. of Montpellier; # 43:40 N, 3:55 E.

Montreal (mont-rẹ-âl'), spt. city, on St. Lawrence riv., S. W. Quebec, pop. 819; McGill and Montreal univs.; cathedrals; # 45:35 N, 73:35 W.

Montreuil (môn-trė-y'), an E. suburb of Paris, Fr., pop. 51; # 48:52 N, 2:25 E.

Montreux (môn-trė), tn., Lake of Geneva, W. Switz., pop. 17; resort; # 46:27 N, 6:55 E.

Montserrat (mŏnt-ser-rät', mont-se-rat'), mt., N. E. of Barcelona, E. Spain; el. 4,058 ft.; monastery; # 41:30 N, 1:45 E. — isl., Br. W. Indies, area 0.3, pop. 12; # 16:42 N, 62:13 W.

Monza (mŏn'tsä), city, Milan prov., Lombardy, N. Italy, pop. comm. 53; # 45:35 N, 9:15 E.

Moorhead (mōr'hed), tn., N. W. Minn., adjacent to Fargo, N. Dak., pop. 9; Concordia and State Teachers colleges; # 46:50 N, 96:50 W.

Moosehead (mös'hed), lake, C. Me., len. 36 mi.; # 45:50 N, 69:40 W.

Moosejaw (mös'jä), city, S. C. Sask., pop. 19; # 50:25 N, 105:25 W.

Moquegua (mō-kā'gwä), prov., S. W. Peru, area 6, pop. 43, and its *, pop. 6; # 17:15 S, 70:46 W. [# 28:51 N, 78:49 E.

Moradabad (mō-räd-ä-bäd'), city, N. C. India, pop. 111;

Morava (mō-rä'vä), riv., N. Moravia, S. to Danube riv., len. 210 mi.; # 48:13 N, 17 E. — riv., Y-S., N. to Danube near Belgrade, len. ab. 300 mi.; # 44:45 N, 21:5 E.

Moravia (mọ-rā'vi-ạ), prov., C. Cz-S., area 8.6, pop. 2,825, * Brno or Brünn; # 49:20 N, 17 E.: absorbed into Germany in 1938 and 1939.

Moravská-Ostrava (mo'räf-skä os'trȧ-vä), see **Ostrava.**

Moray (mur'ạ) or **Elgin,** county, N. E. Scotland, area 0.5, pop. 39, * Elgin, a spt. on Moray Firth; # 57:39 N, 3:18 W.

Moray Firth (mur'ạ fėrth), arm of sea, N. E. Scotland, len. 40 mi.; # 57:38 N, 4 W.

Morbihan (môr-bē-äṅ), dept., S. Brittany, N. W. Fr., area 2.7, pop. 546, * Vannes, pop. 16; # 47:55 N, 2:50 W.

Morea (mọ-rē'ä), *anc.* Peloponnesus, S. large pen. of Greece; area 8.7; # 37:30 N, 22:15 E.

Morecambe (mōr'kạm), coastal resort on Morecambe Bay, N. Lancaster, N. W. Eng., pop. 19; 54:10 N, 3 W.

Morelia (mō-rä'lē-ä), city, S. W. Mexico, * of Michoacán, pop. 40; # 19:40 N, 101:10 W.

Morelos (mō-rä'lōs), state, C. Mexico, area 2, pop. 104, * Cuernavaca; # 18:45 N, 99 W.

Morgantown (môr'gạn-toun), tn., ext. N. E. W. Va., pop. 17; State Univ.; # 39:37 N, 79:58 W.

Morioka (mō'rē-ō'kä), inland city, N. Honshu isl., Japan, pop. 50; # 39:42 N, 141:9 E.

Morocco (mọ-rok'ō), a sultanate of N. W. Africa, chiefly under Fr. control, area 231, pop. 6,000, * Fez, pop. 125; # 32 N, 5 W.

---

fat, fāte, fär, fȧll, ȧsk, fãre; net, mē, hėr; pin, pīne; not, nōte, mȯve, nôr; up, lūte, p·ull; oi, oil; ou, out; (lightened) aviạry, ẹlect, agọny, intọ, ụnite; (obscured) errạnt, operạ, ardẹnt, actọr, natụre; ch, chip; g, go; th, thin; ᴛʜ, then; y, you;

Mororan, see **Muroran.**

Morristown (mor′is-toun), tn., in N. C. New Jersey, pop. 15; # 40:46 N, 74:29 W.

Mörs (mĕrs), a N. W. suburb of Duisburg, W. Ger., pop. 26; # 51:27 N, 6:37 E.

Morvan (môr-väṅ), mt. range, C. Fr., highest 2,959 ft.; # 47:10 N, 4:5 E.

Moscow (mos′kou), prov., C. Russia, area 13, pop. 3,300, and its *, the * of Soviet Union, pop. 1,772; univ.; # 55:45 N, 37:35 E. — tn., N. W. Idaho, pop. 6; State Univ.; # 46:45 N, 117 W.

Moselle (mo-zel), riv., Vosges mts., E. C. Fr., to Rhine riv., in W. Ger., len. 320 mi.; # 50:20 N, 7:35 E. — dept., N. E. Fr., area 2.4, pop. 589, * Metz; formerly part of Alsace-Lorraine; # 49:5 N, 6:30 E.

Moskva (mosk-vä′), official name of Moscow, Russia.

Mostar (mos-tär′), chief city and former * of Herzegovina, S. W. Yugoslavia, pop. 17; # 43:20 N, 17:48 E.

Mosul (mō-sōl′), prov., N. Iraq, area 35, pop. 703, and its *, on Tigris riv., opp. Nineveh, pop. 70; oil wells; # 36:5 N, 43 E.

Motherwell (mu′ᴛнĕr-wel), city, 10 mi. S. E. of Glasgow, Scotland, pop. 70; # 55:47 N, 4 W.

Moukden, see **Mukden.**

Moulmein (mōl-mīn′), spt. city, mouth Salween riv., S. C. Burma, pop. 61; # 16:25 N, 97:30 E.

Mound City Group, national monument near Chillicothe, Ohio; prehistoric Indian mounds; # ab. 39:20 N, 83 W.

Moundsville (moundz′vil), tn., ext. N. W. Va., pop. 14; # 39:55 N, 80:48 W.

Mountain Ash (moun′tặn ash), city, S. Wales, near Merthyr Tydfil, pop. 43; # 51:42 N, 3:23 W.

Mountain Republic (moun′tặn rē-pub′lik), soviet republic, S. Russia, N. of Caucasus Mts., area 17, pop. 808, * Vladikavkaz, pop. 76; # 43:3 N, 44:42 E.

Mount Carmel (mount kär′mel), city, S. E. C. Pa., pop. 18; # 40:47 N, 76:29 W. — tn., S. E. Ill., pop. 7; # 38:25 N, 87:45 W.

Mount Desert (mount de-zèrt′), isl., coast of Me., 8 × 14 mi.; summer resort; Lafayette National Park; # 44:20 N, 68:15 W.

Mount McKinley (mount mặ-kin′li), National Park, S. C. Alaska, including highest mt. in N. America; height 20,300 ft.; # 63 N, 151 W.

Mount Olympus (mount ō-lim′pus), National Monument, including Olympic Mts., N. W. Wash.; # 47:50 N, 124 W.

Mount Pleasant, tn., S. E. Iowa, pop. 5; Ia. Wesleyan Univ.; # ab. 40:58 N, 91:35 W.

Mount Rainier (mount rā′nẽr), National Park, W. Wash., including Mount Tacoma; # 46:50 N, 121:45 W.

Mount Vernon (mount vẽr′nọn), a N. suburb of New York City, pop. 67; # 40:51 N, 73:52 W. — home of George Washington, on Potomac riv., 15 mi. below Washington, D. C.; # 38:44 N, 77:2 W. — tn., S. Ill., pop. 15; # 38:22 N, 88:52 W. — tn., E. C. Iowa, pop. 1; Cornell College; # ab. 41:50 N, 91:28 W.

Mozambique (mō-zặm-bēk′), Portuguese E. Africa, area 428, pop. 3,000, * Lourenço Marques, pop. 13; # 18 S, 35 E. — city, spt. on island, pop. 8; # 15:5 S, 40:35 E. — Channel, bet. Madagascar and Africa, least width 280 mi.; # 20 S, 40 E.

Muharrak (mö-här′uk), isl., Bahrein Isls., Persian Gulf, and spt. thereon, pop. 20; # 26:14 N, 50:37 E.

Mühlhausen (mül-hou′zẹn), city, Sachsen (Saxony) prov., Prussia, 21 mi. N. W. of Gotha, pop. 37; # 51:15 N, 10:28 E.

Muir (mūr), glacier to sea, S. E. Alaska, area 0.4; # 59 N, 136 W. — Woods, National Monument, Mt. Tamalpais, Calif., near San Francisco; # ab. 38:50 N, 122:35 W.

Mukden (mök-den′), city, S. W. Manchuria, its *, pop. ab. 250; # 42 N, 123:30 E.

Mulde (mül′dẹ), riv., Erzgebirge to Elbe riv., len. 150 mi.; # 50:45 N, 13:30 E.

Mulhacén (möl-ä-thän′), pk., S. Spain, summit of Sierra Nevada Mts., el. 11,660 ft., highest in W. Europe; # 37:5 N, 3:17 W.

Mülhausen (mül-hou′zẹn), see **Mulhouse.**

Mülheim (mül′hīm), city on Ruhr riv., W. Ger., pop. 126; # 50:58 N, 7:1 E. — city on Rhine riv., opposite old Cologne, now part of Cologne, pop. 50; # 51:25 N, 6:50 E.

Mulhouse (mül-öz), city, Haut-Rhin (Alsace), E. C. Fr., pop. 99; # 47:45 N, 7:25 E.

Mull (mul), isl., Argyll Co., W. Scotland, len. 30 mi., pop. 5; # 56:20 N, 6 W.

Multan (möl-tän′), city on Chenab riv., Punjab, N. W. India, pop. 85; # 30:15 N, 71:35 E.

Multnomah (mult-nō′mặ), waterfall, N. slope of Mt. Hood, N. W. Ore., height 850 ft.; # ab. 45:45 N, 121:45 W.

München (mün′chẹn), *Eng.* **Munich,** city on Isar riv., * of Bayern (Bavaria), Ger., pop. 672; univ.; # 48:9 N, 11:35 E.

München-Gladbach (mün′chẹn-glät′bäch), city, Rheinland, ext. W. C. Ger., pop. 114; # 51:12 N, 6:25 E.

Muncie (mun′si), city, E. C. Ind., pop. 50; glass fruit-jars; State Teachers College; # 40:10 N, 85:28 W.

Munich (mū′nik), see **München.**

Munster (mun′stẽr), prov., S. W. Ireland, area 0.9, pop. 1,035, * Cork; # 52:30 N, 9 W.

Münster (mün′stẽr), city, Westphalia, W. Prussia, W. Ger., pop. 105, univ.; # 51:55 N, 7:35 E.

Mur (mör) or **Mura,** riv., W. Austria, E. to Drave riv., len. 250 mi.; # 46:17 N, 17 W.

Muradabad (mü′rud-ä-bäd′), see **Moradabad.**

Murano (mö-rä′nō), isl. and tn., a N. suburb of Venice, Italy, pop. 8; glass works; cathedral; # 45:27 N, 12:22 E.

Murchison (mẽr′ki-sọn), waterfall on Upper Nile riv., height 120 ft.; # ab. 2 N, 31:30 E.

Murcia (mẽr′shi-ặ), prov., S. E. Spain, area 4.4, pop. 643, and its *, pop. 147; # 37:55 N, 1:10 W. — former prov., including also Albacete; # 38:30 N, 1:45 W.

Mures (mü′resh), see **Maros.**

Müritz (mü′rits), lake, Mecklenburg, N. Ger., len. 17 mi.; # 53:50 N, 12:45 E.

Murman Coast (mör-män′ kōst), Arctic coast of Russia, W. of White Sea; # 69 N, 35 E.

Muroran (mō′rọ-rän), spt. city, S. W. Yezo isl., Japan, pop. 50; # 42:18 N, 140:59 E.

Murphysboro (mẽr′fiz-bur-ọ), tn., S. W. Ill., pop. 9; # 37:45 N, 89:22 W.

Murray (mur′ặ), riv., chief Australian stream, Australian Alps to sea near Adelaide, S. Australia, 1,500 mi., # 35:2 S, 139:25 E.

Murrumbidgee (mur′um-bid-jē), riv., S. W. New S. Wales, Australia, trib. of Murray riv., len. 1,300 mi.; irrigation reservoir; # 34:40 S, 143:15 E.

Muscat, see **Muskat.**

Muscatine (mus-kặ-tēn′), city, S. E. Iowa, pop. 18, on Muscatine riv.; pearl buttons; # 41:25 N, 91:5 W.

Muscle Shoals (mus′l shōlz), rapids of Tennessee riv., W. Ala., dammed at Florence by Wilson Dam; great federal hydro-electric plant; # 34:47 N, 87:40 W.

Muscovy (mus′kọ-vi), an old name of Russia.

Muskat (mus-kat′), spt., S. E. Arabia, * of Oman, pop. with adjacent Matrak, ab. 20; # 23:40 N, 58:40 E.

Muskegon (mus-kē′gọn), city, W. C. Mich., pop. 48, lake port and resort. — **Heights,** a suburb, pop. 16; # 43:20 N, 86:25 W.

Muskogee (mus-kō′gē), city, E. C. Okla., pop. 32; oil refineries; # 35:45 N, 95:25 W.

Musselburgh (mus′l-bur-ọ), port, 10 mi. E. of Edinburgh, Scotland, pop. 17; golfing; # 55:56 N, 3:3 W.

Mustagh (mös′täch), see **Karakoram.**

Mustagh Ata (mös-täch′ ä-tä′), pk., Pamirs, S. W. C. Asia, el. 24,430 ft.; # 38:15 N, 75:10 E.

Muttra (mut′trä), city, United prov., N. C. India, pop. 53; # 27:28 N, 77:41 E.

Muzaffarpur (mụ-zuf′ặr-pör), city, Bihar, N. C. India, pop. 49; # 26:7 N, 85:27 W.

Mweru (mwä′rō), lake bet. Belgian Congo and Rhodesia, len. 90 mi.; # 9 S, 28:50 E.

Mycenæ (mī-sē′nẽ), anc. city, ext. S. E. Greece; # 37:43 N, 22:46 E.

Mysia (mish′i-ặ), anc. country, N. W. Asia Minor; # ab. 40 N, 32 E.

Mysore (mī-sōr′), native state, S. India, area 29, pop. 979, and its *, pop. 84; univ.; # 12:15 N, 76:36 E.

Mytilene (mit-i-lē′nē) or **Lesbos,** Greek isl., N. E. Ægean Sea, area 0.7, pop. 147; — or **Kastro,** its *, pop. 18; # 39:5 N, 26:35 E.

(variable) ḍ as d or j, ṣ as s or sh, ṭ as t or ch, ẓ as z or zh; o, F. cloche; ü, F. menu; ch, Sc. loch; ṅ, F. bonbon; ′, primary accent; ″, secondary accent; †, obsolete; <, from; +, and; =, equals. See also lists at beginning of book.

N

Nabha (nä′bä), native state, Punjab, N. W. India, area 1, pop. 263, and its *, pop. 19; # 30:25 N, 76:9 E.

Nablus (nä-blōs′), *anc.* Shechem, tn., N. Palestine, pop. 16; # 32:15 N, 35:15 E.

Nafud, see **Nefud.**

Naga (nä′gä), inland city, S. E. Luzón, Philippine Isls., pop. 10; # 13:37 N, 123:10 E. — city, Cebú isl., Philippine Isls., pop. 21; # ab. 10:15 N, 123:45 E.

Nagano (nä′gä-nọ), inland city, C. Honshu isl., Japan, pop. 67; # 36:40 N, 138:10 E.

Nagaoka (nä′gä-ō′kä), inland city, N. W. C. Honshu isl., Japan, pop. 53; # 37:27 N, 138:50 E.

Nagasaki (nä-gä-sä′kẹ), spt. city, W. Kyushiu isl., Japan, pop. 189; coal; shipyard; # 32:48 N, 129:55 E.

Nagoya (nä′gō-yä), interior city, S. C. Honshu isl., Japan, pop. 769 (1925), third city in Japan; # 35:15 N, 136:55 E.

Nagpur (näg-pōr′), city, C. India, * of C. Prov., pop. 145; # 21:15 N, 79:10 E.

Nagy-kanizsa (nod″y′-ko′nẹ-zho), city, S. W. Hungary, pop. 30; # 46:27 N, 17:2 E.

Nagy-Szeben (nod″y′-se′ben), *Ger.* **Hermannstadt,** now **Sibiu,** city, W. C. Romania, pop. 33; # 45:48 N, 24:9 E.

Nagy-Várad (nod″y′-vä′rod), *Ger.* **Grosswardein** (now **Oradia Mare**), city, ext. N. W. Romania, pop. 64; 46:55 N, 21:50 E.

Naha (nä′hä) or **Nawa** (nä′wä), spt. city on Riukiu or Luchu isl., Japan, pop. 54; # 26:11 N, 127:41 E.

Nairn (närn), county, N. E. Scotland, area 0.2, pop. 8, and its *, a spt., pop. 5; # 57:35 N, 3:53 W.

Nairobi (nī-rō′bẹ), tn., * of Kenya colony, Br. E. Africa, pop. 24; # 1:25 S, 36:50 E.

Namangan (nä-män-gän′), city, E. Russian Turkestan, pop. 103; # 41 N, 71:35 E.

Namaqualand (nä-mä′kwä-land), region, S. part of S. W. Africa Mandate; # 26 S, 18 E.

Namur (nä′mör, nȧ-mür′), prov., S. C. Belgium, area 1.4, pop. 351, and its *, pop. 31; # 50:30 N, 4:50 E.

Nanchang (nän-chäng′), city, S. E. C. China, * of Kiangsi prov., pop. est. 300; # 28:35 N, 116 E.

Nancy (nan′si, *Fr.* näṅ-sē), city, E. Fr., on Meurthe riv., * of Meurthe-et-Moselle, pop. 113; univ.; # 48:40 N, 6:15 E.

Nanda Devi (nun′dä dā′vē), mt. pk., Himalayas, N. India, el. 25,661 ft.; # 30:23 N, 80:1 E.

Nanga Parbat (nun′gä pur′but), mt. pk., Himalayas, N. W. Kashmir, el. 26,625 ft.; # 35:15 N, 74:20 E.

Nan Hai (nän-hī), see **South China Sea.**

Nanking (nän′king′), city on Yangtse-Kiang, * of Kiangsu prov., China, also of China, pop. 525; # 32 N, 118:55 E.

Nanning (nän′ning′), city, S. China on Si-kiang riv., * of Kwangsi prov., pop. est. 67; # 21:50 N, 108 E.

Nan Shan (nän′shän′), broad mt. range, N. E. part of Tibet, C. Asia; # 38 N, 98 E. — mt. range, China; # 27 N, 110 E.

Nantes (nants or näṅt), spt. city, Loire estuary, W. Fr., * of Loire-Inférieure dept., pop. 184; # 47:15 N, 1:30 W.

Nanticoke (nan′ti-kōk), mining city, E. C. Pa., pop. 24; # 41:15 N, 76 W.

Nantucket (nan-tuk′et), isl., S. E. Mass., len. 15 mi., area 0.1; summer resort; # 41:18 N, 70:5 W.

Naperville (nä′pẽr-vil), tn., N. E. Ill., pop. 5; Northwestern College; # ab. 41:45 N, 88:10 W.

Napier (nä′pi-ẽr), spt. city, S. E. N. Island, New Zealand, pop. 18; # 39:30 S, 177 E.

Naples (nä′plz), see **Napoli.**

Napo (nä′pō), riv., N. Ecuador to Amazon riv., len. ab. 700 mi., along tentative Ecuador-Colombia boundary; # 2 S, 74:34 W.

Napoli (nä′pō-lē), *Eng.* **Naples,** prov., Campania, S. W. C. Italy, area 0.4, pop. 1,469, and its *, *anc.* Neapolis, chief spt. of Italy, pop. 772, on bay, 22 mi. long; univ.; # 40:50 N, 14:15 E.

Nara (nä′rä), city near Osaka, Honshu isl., Japan, pop. 49; # 34:40 N, 135:42 E.

Narba, see **Nabha.**

Narbada (nur-bud′ä), riv., C. India, W. to Gulf of Cambay, Arabian sea, len. 800 mi.; # 21:38 N, 74 E.

Narbonne (när-bọn), city, Aude dept., S. Fr., pop. 29; # 43:12 N, 3 E.

Narenta (nä-ren′tä), *anc.* Naro, riv., C. Yugoslavia to Adriatic Sea, len. 140 mi.; # 43 N, 17:30 E.

Narragansett (nar-ạ-gan′set), bay, S. E. Rhode Isl. to Fall River, Mass.; len. 28 mi.; # 41:25 N, 71:27 W.

Narva (när′vä), city, N. E. Estonia, pop. 27; # 59:22 N, 28:8 E.

Narvik (när′vik), spt. on a Norwegian fjord, pop. 6; port for Swedish iron ores; # 68:25 N, 17:30 E.

Nashua (nash′ū-ạ), city, S. C. New Hampshire, pop. 33; # 42:45 N, 71:32 W.

Nashville (nash′vil), city, N. C. Tenn., state *, pop. 167; Vanderbilt and Fisk Univs.; Peabody College; # 36:10 N, 86:45 W.

Nassau (nas′ȧ), spt., * of Bahama isls., pop. 13; # 25 N, 77:30 W.

Natal (nạ-täl′), prov. of Union of S. Africa, area 35, pop. 1,429, * Pietermaritzburg, pop. 36; # 28 S, 31 E. — spt., * of Rio Grande do Norte, Brazil, pop. 31; # 5:47 S, 35:12 W.

Natchez (nach′ez), tn., S. W. Miss., on Mississippi riv., pop. 13; # 31:35 N, 91:25 W.

National Parks (nash′ọn-ạl pärks), see **Glacier, Yellowstone, Yosemite,** etc.

Natural Bridge (naṭ′ū-rạl brij) of Virginia, famous limestone bridge, near Luray Cave, W. C. Va.; height, 215 ft., span, 90 ft.; # 38:41 N, 78:28 W.

Natural Bridges (naṭ′ū-rạl brij′ez) of Utah, national monument, S. E. Utah, largest Rainbow Arch, height, 309 ft., span 278 ft.; # 37:30 N, 110 W.

Naugatuck (nä′gạ-tuk), city, S. E. Conn., on Naugatuck riv., pop. 15; # 41:31 N, 73:3 W.

Naumburg (noum′bürch), city, 27 mi. S. W. of Leipsic, C. Ger., pop. 29; # 51:9 N, 11:48 E.

Navajo (nav′ạ-hō), Indian reservation and national monument (cliff dwellings), N. Ariz.; # 36:30 N, 109:50 W.

Navanagar (nuv′ạ-nug′ȧr), native state, Kathiawar pen., W. India, area 4, pop. 345, and its *; # 22:25 N, 70:5 E.

Navarra (nä-vär′rä), prov., N. Spain, area 4, pop. 338, * Pamplona, pop. 34; # 42:45 N, 1:40 W.

Navarre (nạ-vär′), former kingdom, S. W. Fr. and N. E. Spain; # ab. 42 N, 2 E.

Nawa (nä′wä), see **Naha.**

Naxos (nak′sos), Greek isl., S. C. Ægean sea, area 0.2, pop. 16, and spt. thereon, pop. 2; # 37:5 N, 25:30 E.

Nayarit (nä-yä-rēt′), ter., W. C. Mexico, area 11, pop. 157, * Tepic, pop. 15; # 22:10 N, 105 W. — Sierra de, mt. range, W. C. Mexico; # 22:30 N, 104:30 W.

Nazareth (naz′ạ-reth), tn., N. Palestine, pop. 7; childhood home of Jesus Christ; # 32:45 N, 35:14 E. — city, Pernambuco, ext. E. Brazil, pop. 87; # 7:43 S, 35:13 W.

Naze (näz), hooked spit, E. Essex, S. E. Eng.; # 51:52 N, 1:18 E. — cape, S. tip of Norway; # 58 N, 7:2 E.

Neanderthal (nä-än′dẽr-täl), valley near Düsseldorf, S. W. Ger.; famous skull of early man; # ab. 51:10 N, 7:34 E.

Near East (nēr ēst), includes Asia Minor, Syria, Palestine; sometimes also Balkans.

Neath (nēth), city, 10 mi. N. E. of Swansea, S. Wales, on Neath riv.; pop. 19; # 51:39 N, 3:49 W.

Nebraska (nẹ-bras′kạ), state, N. C. U.S.A., bet. S. Dak. and Kansas, area 78, pop. 1,316, * Lincoln, pop. 82; chief city, Omaha, pop. 224; # 42 N, 99 W.

Neckar (nek′kär), div. of N. Württemberg, S. W. Ger., area 1.3, pop. 930, * Stuttgart, pop. 324; # 48:59 N, 9:5 E. — riv., Black Forest to Rhine riv., S. W. Ger., len. 210 mi.; # 49:30 N, 8:28 E.

Nederlanden (nä′dẽr-län-dẹn), **Koninkrijk der,** official name of Netherlands.

Nefud (ne-föd′), desert, N. C. Arabia; # 29 N, 41 E.

Negapatam (neg″ạ-pạ-täm′), coastal city, ext. S. E. India, pop. 54; # 10:45 N, 79:50 E.

Negri Sembilan (nä′grẹ sem-bē-län′), one of Federated Malay States, area 3, pop. 179, * Seremban, pop. 17; # 2:45 N, 102:15 E.

Negro, Rio (rē′ō nä′grō), riv., N. Patagonia, Argentina, len. 700 mi.; # 40 S, 64:50 W. — large N. trib. of Amazon riv., N. W. Brazil, len. 1,050 mi.; # 3 S, 60 W. — riv., S. Brazil, Uruguay to Rio de la Plata, len. 350 mi.; # 33:8 S, 58:5 W.

Negros (nä′grōs), isl., C. Philippines, area 5, pop. 500; # 10 N, 123 E.

---

fat, fāte, fär, fȧll, ȧsk, fāre; net, mē, hẽr; pin, pīne; not, nōte, mōve, nȯr; up, lūte, pu̇ll; oi, oil; ou, out; (lightened) aviạry, ẹlect, agọny, intọ, u̇nite; (obscured) errạnt, operạ, ardẹnt, actọr, natūre; ch, chip; g, go; th, thin; ᴛH, then; y, you;

Neisse (nĭs'ĕ), city on Neisse riv., Upper Silesia, Prussia, pop. 32; # 50:29 N, 17:20 E.

Nejd (nejd), sultanate, occupying most of Arabia, area ab. 900, pop. ab. 3,000, * Riyadh, pop. 30; # 24 N, 46 E.

Nellore (nel-lōr'), dist., E. Madras, S. E. India, area 8, pop. 1,386, and its *, pop. 36; # 14:27 N, 80:1 E.

Nelson (nel'son), riv., Manitoba, Lake Winnipeg to Hudson Bay, 500 mi.; # 57 N, 93 W. — prov., N. S. Isl., New Zealand, area 11, pop. 48, and its *, pop. 11; # 41:20 S, 173:25 E.

Nepal (ne-pâl'), kingdom bet. N. C. India and Tibet, area 54, pop. 5,600, * Katmandu, pop. 80; Br. protectorate; # 28 N, 85 E.

Nero (nē'rō), deep, near Guam, W. Pacific oc., depth 31,614 ft., now second; # 12 N, 148 E.

Netherlands (neᴛн'ẽr-landz), kingdom, N. W. Europe, bordering N. Sea, Ger. and Belgium, area 13, pop. 7,213, * The Hague, pop. 383; # 52 N, 5:30 E.

Néthou, Pic de (pēk dĕ nā-tö') or **Maladetta**, pk., C. Pyrenees, el. 11,169 ft., highest of Pyrenees; # 42:39 N, 0:39 E.

Netley (net'li), vil., Hampshire, S. Eng.; abbey; military hospital; # 50:53 N, 1:21 W.

Neuchâtel (nè-shá-tel) or **Neuenburg**, canton, W. Switz., area 0.3, pop. 131, and its *, on Lake of Neuchâtel, pop. 23; # 47 N, 6:58 E.

Neuenburg (noi'en-búrch), see **Neuchâtel**.

Neufchâtel (nè-shâ-tel), tn., N. Fr., 25 mi. N. of Rouen, pop. 4; cheese; # 49:50 N, 1:26 E.

Neuilly-sur-Seine (nè-yē-sür-sãn), a N. W. suburb of Paris, Fr., pop. 52; # 48:53 N, 2:17 E.

Neukölln (noi-kėln'), a S. E. div. of Berlin, Ger., pop. 285; # 52:27 N, 13:27 E.

Neumünster (noi'mün-stėr), city, base of Jutland pen., Prussia. pop. 40; # 54:5 N, 10 E.

Neunkirchen (noin'kirch-en), mining tn., Saar Basin, pop. 35; # 49:21 N, 7:11 E.

Neuquén (nā-ō̄-kān'), ter., S. W. Argentina, area 41, pop. 38, and its *, pop. 1. # 38 S., 69:50 W.

Neusiedler (noi'zēd-lėr), lake, N. W. Hungary and E. Austria, len. 25 mi.; # 47:45 N, 16:45 E.

Neuss (nois), a W. suburb of Düsseldorf, W. Prussia, pop. 45; # 51:12 N, 6:42 E.

Neustadt (noi'shtät), suburb of Ludwigshafen, Ger., pop. 21, # 49:21 N, 8:8 E.

Neustrelitz (noi-strä'lits), tn., * of Mecklenburg-Strelitz, N. Ger., pop. 12; # 53:20 N, 13:5 E.

Neuwied (noi'vēt), a N. suburb of Coblenz, S. W. Ger., pop. 20; # 50:26 N, 7:28 E.

Neva (nē'vä), riv., Lake Ladoga to Gulf of Finland, through Leningrad, len. 60 mi.; canalized for ships; # 59:55 N, 30:15 E.

Nevada (ne-vä'dä), state, W. U.S.A., bet. Calif. and Utah, area 111, pop. 110, * Carson City, pop. 2; chief city, Reno, pop. 21; # 39 N, 117 W.

Nevado de Toluca (nä-vä'ᴛнō dä tō-lö'kä), mt. pk., S. C. Mex., el. 15,020 ft.; # 19:5 N, 99:50 W.

Nevers (nè-vär), city, C. Fr., * of Nièvre dept., pop. 30; cathedral; # 47 N, 3:10 E.

Nevis (nev'is), isl., Br. W. Indies, area .05, pop. 13; # 17:18 N, 62:37 W.

New Albany (nū âl'ba-ni), city, S. E. Ind., on Ohio riv., pop. 25; # 38:16 N, 85:45 W.

New Amsterdam (nū am'stėr-dam), Dutch tn. on Manhattan isl., now part of New York City; # 40:44 N, 73:59 W.

Newark (nū'ẽrk), city, N. E. New Jersey, pop. 430; # 40:43 N, 74:12 W. — city, C. Ohio, pop. 31; # 40:5 N, 82:28 W. — tn., N. Dela., pop. 5; State Univ.; # 39:42 N, 75:43 W. — tn., C. Eng., pop. 17; # 53:4 N, 0:49 W.

New Bedford (nū bed'ford), spt. city, S. E. Mass., pop. 110; formerly a chief whaling port; # 41:38 N, 71 W.

New Bern (nū bêrn), tn., E. C. N. Car., pop. 12; # 35:10 N, 77:10 W.

New Britain (nū brit'n), city, C. Conn., pop. 69; # 41:35 N, 72:50 W. — largest isl., Bismark Arch., E. Indies, area 10, pop. ab. 71, * Rabaul, pop. ab. 5; # 5:30 S, 151 E.

New Brunswick (nū brunz'wik), prov., E. Canada, E. of Me., area 28, pop. 408, * Fredericton, pop. 8; # 47 N, 66 W. — city, N. C. New Jersey, pop. 33; Rutgers College; # 40:30 N, 74:30 W.

Newburgh (nū'bẽrg), city, S. E. New York, on Hudson riv., pop. 32; # 41:30 N, 74:3 W.

Newburyport (nū'bẽr-i-pōrt), city, N. E. Mass., pop. 14; # 42:48 N, 70:53 W.

New Caledonia (nū kal-ē-dō'ni-ä), isl., S. Pacific oc., 800 mi. E. of Australia, area 8, pop. 51, * Noumêa, pop. 10; Fr. penal colony; # 21:20 S, 165:40 E.

Newcastle (nū'kás-l), city on Tyne riv., N. E. Eng., pop. 284, with suburbs, pop. 470; # 55 N, 1:36 W. — city, E. C. Ind., pop. 17; # 39:54 N, 85:27 W. — spt. city, E. C. New S. Wales, Australia, pop. with suburbs, 90; coal; # 33 S, 151:50 E. — tn., Staffordshire, C. Eng., pop. 20.

New Castle, city, W. C. Pa., pop. 48; # 41 N, 80:22 W.

Newchwang (nū'chwäng'), city on Liao riv., S. Manchuria, pop. 82; # 41 N, 122:35 E.

New England (nū ing'gland), six states, N. E. U.S.A., Conn., Mass., R. I., Ver., N. H., and Me.; # 42 N, 71 W. — region N. E. New S. Wales, Australia, with mt. range therein; # 30 S, 152 E.

Newfoundland (nū'fund-land), isl., N. E. of N. America, area 43, pop. 290, forming, with Labrador (area 120, pop. 4), a Br. self-governing colony, * St. John's, pop. 60; # 49 N, 55 W.

New Granada (nū gra-nä'dä), early name for Colombia.

New Guinea (nū gin'i) or **Papua**, isl., N. of Australia, area 330, pop. ab. 625; # 0:6 S, 141 E. — ter., Australian Mandate, former Ger. Papua, Bismarck Arch., Solomon isls., etc., area ab. 70, pop. ab. 150; # 5 S, 145 E.

New Hampshire (nū hamp'shir), state, N. E. U.S.A., bet. Me. and Ver.; area 9, pop. 492, * Concord, pop. 27; chief city, Manchester, pop. 78; # 44 N, 71:30 W.

New Haven (nū hā'vn), city, S. C. Conn., pop. 161; Yale University; # 41:22 N, 72:57 W.

New Hebrides (nū heb'ri-dēz), isls., group 1,000 mi. N. E. Australia, area 5, pop. 60; joint Br. and Fr. rule; # 16 S, 167 E.

New Ireland (nū īr'land), second isl., Bismarck Arch., E. Indies, area 3, pop. ab. 22; # 3:30 S, 152:30 E.

New Jersey (nū jẽr'zi), state, N. E. U.S.A., bet. Pa. and the Atlantic oc., area 8, pop. 4,160, * Trenton, pop. 125; chief city, Newark, pop. 430; # 40:45 N, 74:10 W.

New Kensington (nū ken'sing-ton), tn., S. W. Pa., pop. 24; # 40:38 N, 79:50 W.

New London (nū lun'don), city, S. E. Conn., pop. 30; Conn. College; # 41:20 N, 72:6 W.

Newmarket (nū'mär-ket), tn., Suffolk and Cambridge, Eng., pop. 10; races; # 52:15 N, 0:24 E.

New Mexico (nū mek'si-kō), state, S. W. U.S.A., bordering Mexico and Texas, area 123, pop. 532, * Santa Fé, pop. 20; chief city, Albuquerque, pop. 35; # 35 N, 106 W.

New Orleans (nū ôr'lē-anz), city, S. E. La., on Mississippi riv., pop. 495; Tulane and Loyola univs.; cotton market; # 30 N, 90:3 W.

New Philadelphia (nū fil-a-del'fi-ä), tn., E. C. Ohio, pop. 12; # 40:30 N, 81:30 W.

New Plymouth (nū plim'uth), spt. city, W. N. Island, New Zealand, pop. 14; # 39 S, 174:5 E.

New Pomerania, New Britain (E. Indies).

Newport (nū'pōrt), spt. on Severn estuary, Monmouth, S. W. Eng., pop. 95; coal; # 50:40 N, 1:15 W. — city, N. Ken., pop. 31; suburb of Cincinnati, Ohio; # 39:4 N, 84:28 W — city on isl., S. C. Rhode Isl., pop. 31; resort; # 41:27 N, 71:22 W. — tn., * of Isle of Wight, S. Eng., pop. 11; # 50:42 N, 1:18 W.

Newport News (nū'pōrt nūz), spt. city, S. E. Va., pop. 37; # 37 N, 76:26 W.

New Providence (nū prov'i-dens), isl., Bahamas, area .01, pop. 20; # 25:3 N, 77:25 W.

New Rochelle (nū rō-shel'), a N. suburb of New York City, pop. 58; New Rochelle College; # 40:53 N, 73:47 W.

Newry (nū'ri), tn., S. E. Northern Ireland, pop. 12; # 54:11 N, 6:20 W.

New Siberia (nū sī-bē'ri-ä), four isls., Arctic oc., N. of C. Siberia; # 76 N, 142 E.

New South Wales (nū south wälz), state, E. Australia, area 309, pop. 2,218, * Sydney, pop. 891 (with suburbs); # 32 S, 147 E.

Newton (nū'ton), a W. suburb of Boston, Mass., pop. 70;

(variable) ḏ as d or j, s as s or sh, t as t or ch, z as z or zh; o, F. cloche; ü, F. menu; ċh, Sc. loch; ṅ, F. bonbon; ', primary accent; ", secondary accent; †, obsolete; <, from; +, and; =, equals. See also lists at beginning of book.

Boston College; # 42:23 N, 71:9 W. — tn., E. C. Kansas, pop. 11; # 38:3 N, 98:21 W.

Newtown (nū′toun), a S. W. suburb of Sydney, Australia, pop. 28; # ab. 33:50 S, 151 E.

New Westminster (nū west′min-stėr), suburb of Vancouver, S. W. Br. Columbia, pop. 15; # 49:13 N, 122:52 W.

New Windsor, see **Windsor.**

New York (nū yôrk), state, N. E. U.S.A., bordering Pa. and Canada; #43 N, 76 W; area 49, pop. 13,479, * Albany, pop. 131; chief city, New York, pop. 7,455. — spt. city, S. E. New York, pop. 7,455, with its suburbs in New York and New Jersey, pop. over 11,691; Columbia Univ.; New York Univ.; Fordham Univ.; College of City of New York; Hunter College; Manhattan College; # 40:43 N, 73:58 W.

New York Bay (nū yôrk bā), part of Atlantic oc., bet. New Jersey and Long Isl.; Upper Bay; # 40:40 N, 74:3 W; Lower Bay; # 40:30 N, 74:6 W.

New York Central System (nū yôrk sen′trạl), R.R., Chicago to New York; total mileage 6,928.

New Zealand (nū zē′lạnd), dominion of Br. Empire on isls. of New Zealand, S. W. Pacific oc., area 103, pop. 1,574, * Wellington, pop. 115; # 41:40 S, 174:55 E.

Nganking (ngän′king′), see **Anking.**

Niagara (nī-ag′ạ-rạ), riv. bet. Lakes Erie and Ontario; # 43:15 N, 79:4 W.

Niagara Falls, falls of Niagara riv., height Horseshoe Falls, 158 ft., American Falls, 167 ft. — city, New York side of falls, pop. 78; college; # 43:7N, 79:2 W; — city, Canadian side, pop. 15; # 43:6 N, 79:3 W.

Nias (nē-äs′), isl., W. of C. Sumatra, E. Indies, area 2, pop. 161; # 1 N, 97:30 E.

Nicæa (nī-sē′ä), tn., Anatolia; Council of Nicæa, 325, 787; # 40:26 N, 29:43 E. — see **Nice.**

Nicaragua (nik-ạ-rä′gwä), republic, C. America, area 52, pop. 1,134, * Managua, pop. 115; # 13 N, 85 W. — lake, ext. S. W. Nicaragua, 92 × 34 mi.; # 11:30 N, 85:30 W.

Nice (nēs), anc. Nicæa, coastal resort city, ext. S. E. Fr.; pop. 156; # 43:40 N, 7:20 E.

Nicholas II Land (nik′ọ-lạs), long isl., N. of N. pen. of Asia; # 80 N, 100 E.

Nicobar (nik-ọ-bär′), isl. group, bet. Sumatra and Burma, area 0.6, pop. 10; Br.; # 8 N, 93:30 E.

Nicopolis (ni-kop′ọ-lis) or **Nikopoli,** tn., N. C. Bulgaria on Danube riv.; pop. 6; ruins; # 39:1 N, 20:45 E.

Nictheroy (nik-te-roi′), city, S. E. Brazil, * of state of Rio de Janeiro and suburb of Rio, pop. 86; # 22:55 S, 43:6 W.

Nidwalden (nēd′väl-dẹn), half canton, C. Switz., area 0.1, pop. 14; # 46:57 N, 8:25 E.

Niederbayern (nē′dẽr-bī-ẽrn), Eng. **Lower Bavaria,** E. C. part of Bayern, S. Ger., area 4.3, pop. 756, * Landshut, pop. 21; # 48:40 N, 12:30 E.

Niederschlesien (nē′dẽr-shlā′zẹ-ẹn), Eng. **Lower Silesia,** prov., S. E. Ger., area 10.3, pop. 3,157, * Liegnitz, pop. 67; # 51:12 N, 16:12 E.

Niemen (nē′men), Polish portion of Memel riv.

Nieuport (nyẽ-pōr), spt., W. Flanders, W. Belgium, pop. 4; | # 51:8 N, 2:46 E.

Nièvre (nyevr), dept., C. Fr., area 2.7, pop. 270, * Nevers, pop. 30; # 47:10 N, 3:13 E.

Niger (nī′jẽr), riv., in N. W. Africa, entering Gulf of Guinea, len. 3,000 mi.; # 5:30 N, 6:10 E. — Fr. colony, W. Africa, area 405, pop. 1,150, * Zinder, pop. ab. 3; # 15 N, 5 W.

Nigeria (nī-jē′ri-ạ), a Br. colony and protectorate in W. Africa, area 386, pop. 18,070, * Lagos, on isl. of Lagos, pop. 42; # 10 N, 8 E.

Niigata (nē-ẹ-gä′tä), spt. city, N. W. Honshu isl., Japan, pop. 109; # 37:55 N, 139 E.

Niihau (nē-ẹ-hä′ö), isl., Hawaiian Isls., area 0.1; # 21:50 N, 160:10 W.

Niitaka (nē′tä-kä), mt. range, Taiwan (Formosa); summit, Niitakayama or Mt. Morrison, 14,272 ft.; # 23:30 N, 121:15 E.

Nijmegen (nī′mä-gẹn) or **Nimeguen,** city on Waal riv., Gelderland, Neth., pop. 72; # 51:51 N, 5:52 E.

Nikaria (nī-kä′ri-ạ), anc. Icaria, Greek isl., S. E. Ægean Sea, area 0.1, pop. 10; # 37:35 N, 26:20 E.

Nikko (nēk′kō), tn., C. Honshu isl., Japan; resort; sacred temple; # 36:45 N, 139:40 E.

Nikolaievsk (nē-kō-lī′efsk), city, mouth of Amur riv., E. Siberia, pop. 85; # 53 N, 141:5 E.

Nikolayev (nē-kō-lī′ef) or **Nikolaiev,** city, Bug riv. estuary, S. Russia, pop. 95; # 46:58 N, 32 E.

Nile (nīl), riv., N. E. Africa, Lakes Albert and Victoria to Mediterranean sea, len. 3,600 mi.; # 31:30 N, 31 E. — **Blue** or **Bahr el Azrek,** E. trib. of Nile, Lower Abyssinia; # 13 N, 34 E. — **White,** the Upper Nile riv.; # 15:30 N, 32:30 E.

Niles (nīlz), tn., N. E. Ohio, pop. 16; # 41:13 N, 80:50 W. — tn., S. C. Mich., pop. 11; # 41:48 N, 86:20 W.

Nilgiri (nēl-ger′ē), mts., S. Deccan plateau, S. India; summit, 8,760 ft.; # 11:24 N, 76:47 E.

Nimeguen (nim′ä-gen), see **Nijmegen.**

Nîmes or **Nismes** (nēm), city, S. Fr., * of Gard dept., pop. 83; Roman ruins; # 43:50 N, 4:25 E.

Nineveh (nin′ẹ-ve), anc. city,* of Assyria, Tigris riv., opposite Mosul; # 36:25 N, 42:50 E.

Ningpo (ning′pō′), spt. city, E. C. China, pop. est. 284; # 29:55 N, 121:30 E.

Niobrara (nī-ō-brä′rạ), riv., N. W. Neb. to Missouri riv., len. 450 mi.; # 42:55 N, 98 W.

Niort (nyôr), city, * of Deux-Sèvres, W. C. Fr., pop. 24; # 46:19 N, 0:28 W.

Nipigon (nip′i-gon), lake, just N. of Lake Superior, area 1.7; # 48:55 N, 88:10 W.

Nipissing (nip′i-sing), lake, S. E. Ontario, on proposed Georgian Bay-Ottawa riv. ship canal route; # 46:20 N, 80 W.

Nippon (nip′on′), Japanese name for Japan or for Honshu isl.

Nippur (nip-pör′), anc. city, S. of Babylon; # ab. 32 N, 44:30 E.

Niris (nē′ris), lake, playa and tn. (pop. 9), S. C. Persia; # 29:30 N, 53:30 E.

Nis or **Nish** (nēsh), city, Serbia, S. E. Yugoslavia, pop. 25; # 43:25 N, 21:50 E.

Nismes (nēm), see **Nîmes.**

Nissa (nēs′sạ), see **Nish.**

Nizam's Dominions (nẹ-zämz′ dọ-min′yọnz), see **Hyderabad.**

Nizhni-Novgorod (nēzh′ni-nov′go-rod), prov., E. C. Russia, area 20, pop. 2,000, and its *, on Volga riv., pop. 109; annual fair; univ.; # 56:20 N, 43:55 E.

Nogales (nọ-gä′les), tn., on Ariz.-Mexican boundary, total pop. 11; # 31:21 N, 110:55 W.

Nome (nōm), spt., on Nome Cape, N. W. Alaska, pop. 2; gold placers; # 64:30 N, 165:35 W.

Noordbrabant (nōrd′brä-bänt), prov., S. Neth., area 2, pop. 880, * Bois-le-Duc, pop. 41; # 51:30 N, 5:15 E.

Nord (nôr), dept., ext. N. Fr., area 2.2, pop. 1,788, * Lille, pop. 201; # 50:15 N, 3:40 E.

Nordenskjöld (nôr′dẹn-shẹld), sea, part of Arctic oc., N. of C. Siberia; # 74 N, 130 E.

Nordhausen (nôrt′hou-zẹn), city, Harz mts., Sachsen, Prussia, pop. 35; # 51:30 N, 10:48 E.

Nordkyn (nôr′kün), cape, N. E. Norway, 45 mi. E. of N. cape, N. ext. of Europe mainland; lat. 70:50 N.

Nordland (nôr′län), prov. of N. C. Norway, area 15, pop. 173, * Bodö; # 67 N, 15 E.

Norfolk (nôr′fọk), county, ext. E. Eng., area 1.8, pop. 504, * Norwich, pop. 124; # 52:35 N, 1 E. — spt. city, S. E. Va., pop. 144; # 36:52 N, 76:18 W.

Norge (nôr′gè), Norwegian name for Norway.

Norman (nôr′mạn), tn., C. Okla., near the *, pop. 11; State Univ.; # 35:10 N, 97:25 W.

Normandy (nôr′mạn-di), region, N. W. Fr., ancient prov.; * Rouen; # 49 N, 0:0.

Norristown (nor′is-toun), city, S. E. Pa., pop. 38; # 40:8 N, 75:20 W.

Norrköping (nôr′chẹ-ping), city, spt., S. E. Sweden, pop. 59; # 58:30 N, 16 E.

North Adams (nôrth ad′ạmz), city, N. W. Mass., 33 mi. E. of Albany, N. Y., pop. 22; # 42:43 N, 73:6 W.

North America, see **America, North.**

Northampton (nôrth-amp′tọn), city, S. W. C. Mass., pop. 25; Smith College; # 42:15 N, 72:40 W. — county, S. C. Eng., area 1, pop. 348; includes Peterborough; # 52:15 N, 1 W; and its * pop. 93; # 52:15 N, 0:53 W.

North Borneo (nôrth bôr′nẹ-ō), Br. colony, N. Borneo, E. Indies, area 31, pop. 257, * Sandakan, pop. 12; # 6 N, 117 E.

---

fat, fâte, fär, fåll, ȧsk, fâre; net, mē, hėr; pin, pīne; not, nōte, mȯve, nôr; up, lūte, pûll; oi, oil; ou, out; (lightened) aviȧry, ẹlect, agọny, intọ, ūnite; (obscured) errạnt, operạ, ardẹnt, actọr, nat̠ṵre; ch, chip; g, go; th, thin; ᴛн, then; y, you;

North Brabant (brä-bant′), see **Noordbrabant.**

North Braddock (brad′uk), an E. suburb of Pittsburgh, Pa., pop. 16; # 40:24 N, 79:53 W.

North Cape (kāp), N. tip of Scandinavia, on isl., # 71 N, 25:20 E. — N. end of New Zealand; # 34:30 S, 172:40 E.

North Carolina (kar-ọ-lī′nạ), state, S. E. U.S.A., bordering Va. and the Atlantic oc., area 52, pop. 3,572, * Raleigh, pop. 47; chief city, Charlotte, pop. 101; # 36 N, 80 W.

North Channel (nôrth chan′ẹl), strait bet. N. Ireland and Scotland, least width 14 mi.; # 55:10 N, 5:50 W.

North Dakota (dạ-kō′tä), state, N. C. U.S.A., bet. Minn. and Mont.; area 71, pop. 642, * Bismarck, pop. 15; chief city, Fargo, pop. 33; # 47 N, 100 W.

Northern Ireland, see **Ireland.**

Northern Pacific, R.R., St. Paul, Yellowstone Park, Seattle, highest point, 5,569 ft.; completed 1883; total mileage; 6,701.·

Northern Territory (nôr′ᴛʜẻrn ter′ǐ-tọ-ri), ter. N. C. Australia, area 524, pop. 6, * Darwin, pop. ab. 1; # 20 S, 133 E.

Northfield (-fēld), suburb of Minneapolis, Minn., pop. 4; St. Olaf and Carlson colleges; # 44:29 N, 93:10 W.

Northfleet (-flēt′), an E. suburb of London, Eng., on Thames riv., pop. 16; # 51:27 N, 0:20 E.

North Holland (hol′ạnd), see **Holland, North.**

North Island, N. isl. of New Zealand, area 44, pop. 741; # 38 S, 175 E.

North Little Rock (lit′l rok), a N. suburb of the * of Arkansas, pop. 21; # 34:53 N, 92:20 W.

North Manchester (man′ches-tẻr), tn., N. C. Ind., pop. 3; Manchester College; # 40:58 N, 85:48 W.

North Platte (plat), riv., N. C. Colo. to Platte riv., len. 510 mi.; # 41:15 N, 101:50 W. — tn., S. W. Neb., pop. 12; # 41:15 N, 100:50 W.

North Pole, N. end of axis of earth's rotation, Peary (U.S.A.), April, 1909; # 90 N.

North Riding (rīding), administrative county, Yorkshire, N. Eng., area 2, pop. 456, * York and Northallerton; # 54:20 N, 1:30 W.

North River, Hudson riv., bet. New York City and New Jersey; # 40:45 N, 74 W.

North Sea, part of Atlantic oc., E. of Great Britain, W. of Denmark, area 201, greatest depth, 1,998 ft.; # 56 N, 2 E.

North Sydney (sid′ni), a N. div. of Sydney, New S. Wales, pop. 48; # 33:50 S, 151:13 E.

North Tonawanda (ton-ạ-won′dạ), city, N. W. New York, pop. 20; # 43:2 N, 78:53 W.

North Truchas (trö′chäs), mt. pk., N. C. New Mexico, highest pt. in state, el. 13,306 ft.; # 36 N, 105:40 W.

Northumberland (nôr-thum′bẻr-lạnd), county, ext. N. E. Eng., area 2, pop. 746, * Newcastle; pop. 284; # 55:15 N, 2 W.

Northwest Cape, cape, W. Australia; # 21:45 S, 114:10 E.

North West Frontier Province, prov., N. W. India, area 13, pop. 4,684, * Peshawar, pop. 122; # 34 N, 72 E.

North-West Territories, ter., N. W. Canada, area 1,242, pop. 10, * Ottawa; # 64 N, 105 W.

Northwich (-wich), city, Cheshire, W. C. Eng., pop. 16; salt works; # 53:16 N, 2:31 W.

Norton (nôr′tọn), sound, W. C. Alaska; # 64:30 N, 163 W.

Norwalk (nôr′wȧk), city, S. W. Conn., pop. 40; # 41:9 N, 73:25 W.

Norway (nôr′wä), kingdom, W. Scandinavian pen., N. W. Europe, area 125, pop. 2,650, * Oslo (formerly Christiania), pop. 258; # 64 N, 11 E.

Norwich (nor′ij or nor′ich), city, Norfolk Co., E. Eng., pop. 124; cathedral; # 52:40 N, 1:15 E. — (nôr′wich or -ich), city, S. E. Conn., pop. 24; # 41:31 N, 72:3 W.

Norwood (nôr′wůd), tn., S. E. Mass., pop. 15; # 42:14 N, 71:19 W. — city, S. W. Ohio, pop. 34; # 39:10 N, 84: 23 W.

Noto (nō′tō), pen., prominent projection, N. C. Honshu isl., Japan; # 37:30 N, 136:55 E. — comm. E. Sicily, pop. 32; # 36:53 N, 15:3 E.

Notre Dame (nō′tr dȧm′), a N. suburb of South Bend, N. Ind.; Notre Dame Univ.; # 41:45 N, 86:18 W.

Nottingham (not′ing-ạm), county, E. S. C. Eng., area 0.8, pop. 641, and its *, pop. 269; # 52:58 N, 1:10 W.

Nouméa (nö″mä′ä), spt. tn., * of New Caledonia, S. Pacific oc.; pop. 10; # 22:17 S, 166:28 E.

Novara (nō-vä′rä), prov., Piedmont, N. W. Italy, area 2.5, pop. 725, and its *, pop. 56; # 45:28 N, 8:37 E.

Nova Scotia (nō′vạ skō′shiạ), formerly **Acadia,** pen., prov. S. E. Canada, area 21, pop. 513, * Halifax, pop. 59; # 45 N, 64 W.

Novaya Zemlya (nō′vä-yä zem-lyä′) or **Nova Zembla** (nō′vạ zem′blä), two large islands, Arctic oc., N. E. Russia, len. 700 mi., area 35, pop. 0.1; # 72:77 N, 52:69 E.

Novgorod (nov′go-rod), prov., N. W. Russia, area 20, pop. 906, and its *, pop. 27; # 58:35 N, 31:15 E.

Novi Sad (nō′vē säd), city on Danube riv., N. E. Yugoslavia; pop. 40; # 45:15 N, 19:50 E.

Novocherkask (no′vo-cher-käsk′), city on Don riv., S. Russia, pop. 61; # 47:25 N, 40:5 E.

Novonikolaievsk (no′vo-nē-ko-lä′yefsk), city, * of W. Siberia; pop. 68; # 55:30 N, 82:40 E.

Novorossiisk (no′vo-ro-sēsk′), city, spt. on E. Black Sea, pop. 61; oil; # 44:42 N, 37:45 E.

Nowawes (nō′vä-ves), suburb of Potsdam, Brandenburg, N. Ger., pop. 27; # 52:23 N, 13:7 E.

Nubia (nū′bi-ạ), anc. name for region of Upper Nile; # ab. 21 N, 32 E.

Nubian Desert (nū′bi-an dez′ẻrt), arid region, N. E. Anglo-Egyptian Sudan, E. of Nile; # 21 N, 34 E.

Ñuble (nyö′blä), prov., S. C. Chile, area 3, pop. 241, * Chillán, pop. 31; # 36:30 S, 72:8 W.

Nueve de Julio (nwä′vä dä hö′lyō), city, E. C. Argentina, pop. 40; # 35:21 S, 60:48 W.

Nuevo León (nwä′vō lä-ōn′), state, N. E. Mexico, area 25, pop. 336, * Monterrey, pop. 74; # 25:30 N, 99:30 W.

Numazu (nö′mä-zö), city, Japan, pop. 38; # 35:7 N, 138:51 E.

Nuneaton (nun-ē′tọn), a borough of Birmingham, Eng., pop. 42; # 52:31 N, 1:28 W.

Nuremberg (nū′rẹm-bẻrg), see **Nürnberg.**

Nürnberg (nürn′berch), *Eng.* **Nuremberg,** city, N. C. Bayern, S. W. Ger., pop. 384; univ.; toys; pencils; # 49:27 N, 11:5 E.

Nyasa (nyäs′sä) or **Nyassa,** lake, S. E. Africa, area 9, len. 360 mi.; outlet, Shirwa riv., trib. of Zambezi riv.; # 12 S, 34:30 E.

Nyasaland (nyäs′sä-lạnd), Br. protectorate on W. and S. shores of Lake Nyasa, S. E. Africa, area 39, pop. 1,175, * Zomba, pop. ab. 4; # 14 S, 34 E.

Nyezhin (nye′zhēn), city, Chernigov prov., Ukraine, S. W. Russia, pop. 57; # 51:8 N, 31:53 E.

Nyíregyháza (nyē′red-yhä-zo), city, N. E. Hungary, pop. 43; # 47:58 N, 21:43 E.

Nyland (nü′länd), *Finnish* **Undenmaan,** prov., S. Finland, area 4.4, pop. 457, * Helsinki; # 60:25 N, 25 E.

O

Oahu (ō-ä′hö), third largest isl., Hawaiian Isls., area 0.6, * Honolulu, pop. 179; # 21:45 N, 158 W.

Oakland (ōk′lạnd), city on San Francisco Bay, W. C. Calif., pop. 302; Mills College; # 37:40 N, 122:19 W. — **Oakland City,** tn., S. W. Ind., pop. 3; Oakland City College.

Oak Park (ōk pärk), a W. suburb of Chicago, N. E. Ill., pop. 66; # 41:53 N, 87:48 W.

Oaxaca (wä-нä′kä), state, S. Mexico, area 36, pop. 1,085, and its *, pop. 38; # 17:10 N, 96:50 W.

Ob (ōb), riv., C. Asia to Gulf of Ob, Arctic oc., len. 2,600 mi.; # 66:36 N, 69 E.

Oberammergau (ō″bẻr-äm′ẻr-gou), vil., S. Bavaria, S. W. Ger., pop. 2; Passion Play; # 47:36 N, 11:4 E.

Oberbayern (ō-bẻr-bī′ẻrn), S. E. part of Bavaria, S. Ger., area 6.7, pop. 1,704, * München, pop. 681; # 48:2 N, 11:40 E.

Oberfranken (-fräng′kẹn), N. E. div. of Bayern (Bavaria), S. Ger., area 2.8, pop. 759, * Bayreuth, pop. 33; # ab. 50 N, 11:30 E.

Oberhausen (-hou-zẹn), city, lower Ruhr valley, W. Ger., pop. 104; # 51:28 N, 6:50 E.

Oberland (-länt), lofty region, Bernese Alps, S. W. Switz.; # 46:38 N, 7:45 E.

Oberlin (ō′bẻr-lin), tn., N. C. Ohio, pop. 4; Oberlin College; # 41:15 N, 82:15 W.

(variable) ḍ as d or j, ş as s or sh, ṭ as t or ch, ẓ as z or zh; o, F. cloche; ü, F. menu; ċh, Sc. loch; ṅ, F. bonbon; ′, primary accent; ″, secondary accent; †, obsolete; <, from; +, and; =, equals. See also lists at beginning of book.

Oberpfalz (-pfälts), *Eng.* **Upper Palatinate**, N. E. part of Bayern (Bavaria), Ger., area 3.9, pop. 630, * Regensburg, pop. 74; # 49:25 N, 12 E.

Oberschlesien (-shlä´zē-ęn), *Eng.* **Upper Silesia**, prov., S. E. Ger., area 3.7, pop. 1,371, * Breslau, pop. 538; # 51 N, 17 E.

Obi (ō´bē), see **Ob.**

Obwalden (op´väl-dęn), canton, Switz., area 0.2, pop. 18; # 46:50 N, 8:25 E.

Oceanica (ō-shē-an´i-kä) or **Oceania**, Australia and isls. of S. Pacific.

Ocean Island (ō´shąn i´lạnd), isl., near equator, C. Pacific oc., * of Br. colony of Gilbert and Ellice Isls., pop. 2; phosphate; # 0:45 S, 169:50 E. — isl., S. C. N. Pacific oc., to U.S.A.; # 28:25 N, 178:26 W.

Odaru, see **Otaru.**

Odenkirchen (ō´dęn-kirch´ęn), a N. suburb of Köln, W. Ger., pop. 20; # 51:80 N, 6:27 E.

Odense (ō´dęn-se), city, C. Fyen Isl., Denmark, pop. 49; with suburbs, 62; # 55:25 N, 10:27 E.

Oder (ō´dėr), riv., Carpathian Mts., S. W. Ger., N. E. to Stettiner Haff, Baltic sea, len. 550 mi.; # 53:35 N, 14:35 E.

Odessa (ō-des´ä), port, Black Sea, Ukraine, Russia, pop. 317; grain-port; univ.; # 46:29 N, 30:45 E.

Offenbach (of´ęn-bäch), city on Main riv., Hessen, S. W. Ger., pop. 79, a suburb of Frankfurt; # 50:6 N, 8:45 E.

Offenburg (of´ęn-bůrch), city, C. Baden, S. W. Ger., pop. 17; # 48:28 N, 7:53 E.

Ogaki (ō´gä-kē), city, C. Honshu isl., Japan, pop. 34; # 35:20 N, 136:36 E.

Ogden (og´dęn), city, N. C. Utah, pop. 44; R.R. center; # 41:15 N, 112:1 W.

Ogdensburg (og´dęnz-bėrg), city, N. New York, on St. Lawrence riv., pop. 16; # 44:40 N, 75:30 W.

O'Higgins (ō-hig´inz), prov., C. Chile, area 2.2, pop. 119, * Rancagua; # 34 S, 70:40 W.

Ohio (ō-hī´ō), state, E. C. U.S.A., bet. Lake Erie and Ohio riv., area 41, pop. 6,908, * Columbus, pop. 306, chief city, Cleveland, pop. 878; # 40 N, 83 W. — riv., Pittsburgh, Pa., to Mississippi riv., len. 963 mi.; # 37 N, 89:10 W.

Ohligs (ō´lichs), suburb of Solingen, Rheinland, W. Ger., pop. 30; # 51:10 N, 7:1 E.

Oil City (oil sit´i), city, N. W. Pa., pop. 20; world's first oil well, 1859; # 41:27 N, 79:40 W.

Oise (wäz), riv., N. E. Fr. to Seine near Paris, len. 186 mi.; # 49 N, 2:4 E. — dept., Paris Basin, N. C. Fr., area 2.3, pop. 388, * Beauvais, pop. 20; # 49:35 N, 3:11 E.

Oita (ō´ē-tä), spt. city, N. E. Kyushiu isl., Japan, pop. 53; # 33:15 N, 131:40 E.

Oka (ō-kä´), riv., S. W. C. Russia, N. E. to Volga riv., len. 900 mi.; # 56:10 N, 44 E.

Okanogan (ō-kan´ō-gạn), lake, S. C. Br. Col., len. 70 mi., and riv. from it to Columbia riv., Wash., len. 90 mi.; falls therein; U. S. irrigation project along val.; # 50 N, 119: 30 W.

Okayama (ō-kä-yä´mä), city, S. C. Honshu isl., Japan, pop. 125; # 34:40 N, 133:55 E.

Okazaki (ō-kä-zä´kē), inland city, S. C. Honshu isl., Japan, pop. 45; # 35 N, 137:10 E.

Okeechobee (ō-kē-chō´bē), lake, everglades of S. Fla., len. 40 mi.; # 27 N, 81 W.

Okhotsk (ō-chotsk´), sea, part of Pacific oc. bet. Kamchatka pen. and Siberia; area 582, greatest depth 10,554 ft.; # 54 N, 150 E.

Oklahoma (ō-klạ-hō´mä), state, S. C. U.S.A., bet. Kan. and Texas, area 70, pop. 2,336, * Oklahoma City, pop. ab. 204; second city, Tulsa, pop. 142; # 36 N, 98 W.

Oklahoma City, city, C. Okla., state *, pop. ab. 204; Oklahoma City College; # 35:27 N, 97:30 W.

Okmulgee (ōk-mul´gē), city, E. C. Okla., pop. 16; # 35:35 N, 95:59 W.

Öland (ė´länd), isl., S. E. Sweden, len. 90 mi.; area 0.5, pop. 39; # 57 N, 17 E.

Oldbury (ōld´bėr-i), a S. W. suburb of Birmingham, W. C. Eng. pop. 37; # 52:30 N, 2:1 W.

Oldenburg (ōl´dęn-bėrg; *Ger.* ōl´dęn-bůrch), republic, N. Ger., area 2.5, pop. 552, and its *, pop. 52; # 53:10 N, 8:12 E.

Old Forge (ōld fōrj), tn., near Scranton, N. E. Pa., pop. 12; # 41:22 N, 75:40 W.

Oldham (ōld´ạm), suburb of Manchester, W. C. Eng., pop. 148; cotton spinning; # 53:33 N, 2:7 W.

Olean (ō-lē-an´), city, S. W. New York, pop. 22; # 42:5 N, 78:28 W.

Olenek (o-lye-nyók´), riv., N. Siberia, to Arctic oc., len. ab. 1,000 mi.; # 72 N, 120 E.

Olivet (ol´i-vet), ridge, E. of Jerusalem, Palestine; # 31:47 N, 35:13 E. — tn., S. C. Mich., pop. 1; Olivet College; # 42:28 N, 84:59 W.

Olmütz (ol´müts), see **Olomouc.**

Olomouc (o´lo-mo-ůts) or **Olomouts** (o´lo-möts), city, Moravia, C. Cz-S., pop. 57; # 49:35 N, 17:15 E.

Olonets (ō-lō´nets), prov., N. W. Russia, area 49, pop. 450, and its *, near Lake Lagoda, pop. 2; # 50:50 N, 32:50 E.

Olympia (ō-lim´pi-ä), tn., W. C. Wash., state *, pop. 13; # 47:2 N, 122:54 W. — plain, *anc.* Elis, Greece; Olympic games; # 37:39 N, 21:39 E.

Olympic Mountains (ō-lim´pik), part of coast range, N. W. Wash.; summit, Mt. Olympus; # 47:50 N, 124 W.

Olympus (ō-lim´pus), mt. pk. N. E. C. Greece, el. 9,730 ft.; # 40:5 N, 22:18 E. — pk., Olympic Mts., N. W. Wash., el. 8,150 ft.; # 47:45 N, 123:45 W.

Olyphant (ol´i-fạnt), tn., N. E. Pa., pop. 9; # ab. 41:28 N, 75:33 W.

Omaha (ō´mạ-hâ), city, E. C. Neb., on Missouri riv., pop. 224; meat packing; Creighton and Omaha univs.; # 41:20 N, 95:55 W.

Oman (ō-män´), sultanate of S. E. Arabia, area 82, pop. ab. 500, * Muskat, pop. 10; # 23 N, 57 E. — **Gulf of,** N. W. part of Arabian Sea, entrance to Persian Gulf; # 24:30 N. 59 E.

Omdurman (om-dör´män), city, near Khartoum, Anglo-Egyptian Sudan, pop. 79; # 15:37 N, 32:32 E.

Omsk (omsk), city, on Irtysh and Om rivs., W. C. Siberia, pop. 145; # 55:10 N, 73:50 E.

Omuda (ō´mö-dä), **Omuta** or **Omura**, city near Nagasaki, W. Kyushiu isl., Japan, pop. 68; # 32:55 N, 130 E.

Onega (ō-nā´gä), lake, N. W. Russia, second in Europe, area 3.7, len. 140 mi.; maximum depth, 740 ft.; # 62 N, 35 E.

Oneida (ō-nī´dä), tn., C. New York, pop. 10; # 43:8 N, 75:38 W. — lake, Mohawk valley, W. C. New York, len. 20 mi.; # 43:12 N, 75:55 W.

Oneonta (ō-nē-on´tä), tn., S. E. C. New York, pop. 12; # 42:25 N, 75:6 W.

Onondaga (on-on-dä´gä), saline lake, near Syracuse, C. New York, len. 5 mi.; # 43:5 N, 76:13 W.

Ontake (ōn´tä-ke), mt., C. Honshu isl., Japan, el. 10,449 ft.; # 35:55 N, 137:30 E.

Ontario (on-tā´ri-ō), lake, smallest of the Great Lakes, bet. N. Y. and Ontario; area 7, el. 247 ft.; # 43:37 N, 79:20 W. — prov., S. E. Canada, area 407, pop. 3,432, * Toronto, pop. 631; # 46 N, 80 W.

Opava (ō´pä-vä), *Ger.* **Troppau**, city, * of Silesia prov., N. Cz-S., pop. 33; # 49:58 N, 17:55 E.

Oporto (ō-pōr´tō), spt. city, N. W. Portugal, pop. 203, port wine; # 41:15 N, 8:40 W.

Oppeln (op´ęln), city on Oder riv., S. E. Ger., pop. 41; # 50:41 N, 17:55 E.

Oradia Mare (ō-rä´diä mä´re), *formerly* **Nagy-Várad**, city, ext. N. W. Romania, pop. 64; # 46:55 N, 21:50 E.

Oraefa (ė´re-fä), highest peak in Iceland, S. E. coast, el. 6,429 ft.; # 64 N, 16:30 W.

Oran (ō-rän´), dept., Fr. N. W. Algeria, pop. 1,305, and its *, pop. 141; # 35:40 N, 0:20 W.

Orange (or´ạnj), riv., S. W. Transvaal to Atlantic oc., len. 1,100 mi.; # 28:30 S, 16:55 E. — city, N. E. New Jersey, pop. 36; # 40:46 N, 74:14 W.

Orange Free State, prov., Union of S. Africa, area 50, pop. 629, * Bloemfontein, pop. 39; # 28 S, 28 E.

Örebro (ė´re-brö), prov., S. E. C. Sweden, area 3.6, pop. 223, and its *, pop. 36; 98 mi. W. of Stockholm; # 59:16 N, 15:14 E.

Oregon (or´ē-gọn), state, N. W. U.S.A., bet. Wash. and Calif.; area 97, pop. 1,090, * Salem, pop. 31; chief city, Portland, pop. 305; # 44 N, 120 W.

Orel (ō-rel´), prov., S. C. Russia, area 10, pop. 1,515, and its *, on Oka riv., pop. 64; univ.; # 52:55 N, 36 E.

Ore Mountains (ōr), see **Erzgebirge.**

---

fat, fāte, fär, fåll, åsk, fãre; net, mē. hėr; pin, pīne; not, nōte, möve, nôr; up, lūte, půll; oi, oil; ou, out; (lightened) aviạ̄ry, ęlect, agȯny, intọ, ụnite; (obscured) errạnt, operä, ardẹnt, actọr, natụre; ch, chip; g, go; th, thin; ʈн, then; y, you;

Orenburg (ō′rĕn-bûrċh), former prov., S. E. Russia, and adjacent Asia, area 73, pop. 2,100, and its *, on Ural riv., pop. 109; now * of Kirghiz Republic; # 51:50 N, 55:10 E.

Orense (ō-ren′sä), prov., Galicia, N. W. Spain, area 2.7, pop. 411, and its *, pop. 18; # 42:18 N, 7:50 W.

Orient (ō′ri-ĕnt), **The,** a vague term including Asia, especially E. Asia.

Oriente (ō-rĕ-en′tä), prov., E. Cuba, area 14, pop. 820, * Santiago, pop. 74; # 20:30 N, 75:45 W.

Orihuela (ō-rē-wā′lä), city, 10 mi. N. E. of Murcia, S. Spain, pop. 33; # 38:7 N, 0:54 W.

Orinoco (ō-ri-nō′kō), riv., N. South America, draining most of Venezuela and N. E. Colombia into the Atlantic oc., len. 1,600 mi.; # 8:30 N, 61 W.

Orissa (ō-ris′sä), subprovince, N. W. C. India; # 22 N, 85 E. see **Bihar and Orissa.**

Orizaba (ō-rē-sä′Bä), vol., S. E. Mexico, el. 18,546 ft.; # 19:2 N, 97:13 W. — city near by, pop. 35; cotton manufactures; # 18:50 N, 97:6 W.

Orkney (ôrk′ni), isls. N. of Britain, a county of Scotland, area 0.4, pop. 24, * Kirkwall, pop. 4; # 59 N, 3 W.

Orlando (ôr-lan′dō), city, C. Fla. pop. 37; # 28:35 N, 81:30 W.

Orléans (ôr-lā-äṅ), city, N. C. Fr., * of Loiret dept., pop. 69; # 47:55 N, 1:58 E. — (ôr′lē-ạnz), parish, S. E. La., area 0.18, pop. 495 (1940), * New Orleans; # 30 N, 90 W.

Ormes Head (ôrmz hed), pen., N. Wales; watering places; # 53:20 N, 3:50 W.

Ormuz (ôr′muz), strait bet. Persian Gulf and Gulf of Oman; # 26:30 N, 56:30 E. — anc. spt. on isl. in Persian Gulf; # 27:5 N, 56:28 E.

Orne (ôrn), dept., N. W. C. Fr., area 2.4, pop. 275, * Alençon, pop. 15; # 48:44 N, 0:0.

Orono (ō′rŏ-nō), suburb of Bangor, Me., pop. 4; State Univ.; # 44:54 N, 68:38 W.

Ortegal (ôr′tĕ-gạl), cape, most N. tip of Iberia, W. Spain; # 43:45 N, 7:54 W.

Ortler (ôrt′lêr), pk., highest in Bergamo Alps, N. Italy, el. 12,802 ft.; # 46:31 N, 10:34 E.

Oruro (ō-rō′rō), dept., W. C. Bolivia, area 21, pop. 141, and its *, the former * of Bolivia; pop. 33; # 17:55 S, 67:19 W.

Osage (ō′sāj, ō-sāj′), riv., E. C. Kan. to Missouri riv., Mo., len. 490 mi.; # 38:33 N, 92:3 W.

Osaka (ō-sä′kä), largest city in Japan, S. Honshu isl. on Osaka Bay, pop. 2,115; # 34:41 N, 135:30 E.

Osel or **Ezel** (ē′zel), isl., Baltic sea, W. Estonia, len. 60 mi.; 58:25 N, 22:45 E.

Osh (ôsh), city, E. Russian Turkestan, pop. 48; # 40:30 N, 72:55 E.

Oshkosh (ôsh′kosh), city, E. C. Wis., pop. 39; # 44 N, 88:30 W.

Oskaloosa (os′kạ-lō′sạ), tn., S. E. Iowa, pop. 11; # 41:18 N, 92:40 W.

Oslo (ō′slō) (formerly Christiania), spt., S. E. Norway, * of Norway, pop. 258; univ.; # 59:55 N, 10:45 E.

Osnabrück (os′nä-brük), city, S. Hannover, W. Ger., pop. 88; # 52:18 N, 8:5 E.

Ossa (os′ä), mt., Thessaly, E. Greece, el. 6,405 ft.; # 39:50 N, 22:43 E.

Ossett (os′et), a S. suburb of Leeds, N. C. Eng., pop. 15; # 53:42 N, 1:35 W.

Ossining (os′i-ning), formerly **Sing Sing,** tn. on Hudson riv., S. E. New York, pop. 16; state prison; # 41:12 N, 73:50 W.

Ostend (os-tend′), spt. city, W. Belgium, pop. 44; # 51:13 N, 2:58 E.

Osterfeld (ōs′tĕr-felt), a N. W. suburb of Essen, Westfalen, W. Ger., pop. 32; # 51:29 N, 6:52 E.

Österreich (ĕs′tĕr-rīċh), the German name of Austria; see **Austria.**

Ostia (os′ti-ạ), anc. spt. of Rome, Italy, at S. mouth of Tiber riv.; ruins; # 41:45 N, 12:18 E.

Ostrava (os′trạ-vạ) or **Mahrisch-Ostrau,** or **Moravská-Ostrava,** city, S. E. Cz-S., pop. 42; # 49:51 N, 18:18 E.

Oswego (ōs-wē′gō), city, N. W. C. New York, on Lake Ontario, pop. 22; # 43:25 N, 76:30 W.

Otago (ō-tä′gō), prov., S. S. Island, New Zealand, area 25, pop. 199; # 45 S, 169 E.

Otaru (ō′tä-rō) or **Odaru,** spt. city, S. W. Yezo isl., Japan, pop. 134; # 43:13 N, 141 E.

Othrys (oth′ris), mt. range, E. C. Greece; # 39:2 N, 22:43 E.

Otranto (ō′trän-tō), strait connecting Adriatic and Ionian Seas, Mediterranean Sea, width 44 mi.; # 40 N, 18:45 E. — spt., ext. S. E. Italy, pop. 3; castle and cathedral; # 40:8 N, 18:28 E.

Otsu (ō′tsŭ), city on Biwa Lake, C. Honshu isl., Japan, pop. 34; # 35:1 N, 135:50 E.

Ottawa (ot′ạ-wạ), riv., S. E. Ontario, 685 mi. to St. Lawrence riv. at Montreal; # 45:25 N, 74 W. — city, ext. E. Ontario, * of Canada, pop. 127; Ottawa Univ.; # 45:25 N, 75:42 W. — tn., N. C. Ill., pop. 16; # 41:20 N, 88:50 W.

Ottoman Empire (ot′ō-mạn), former name of Turkey.

Ottumwa (o-tum′wạ), city, S. E. Iowa, pop. 32; # 41 N, 92:25 W.

Ouachita (wosh′i-tâ), riv., W. Ark. to Red riv., len. 550 mi.; # 31:10 N, 91:50 W. — mts., rugged region, S. E. Okla. and S. W. Ark.; # 34:30 N, 95 W.

Oudh (oud), see **United Provinces of Agra and Oudh.**

Oulun (ō′lún), formerly **Uleåborg,** dept., N. Finland, area 65, pop. 382, and its *, a spt., pop. 21; # 65:3 N, 25:35 E.

Ouse (ōz), riv., Norfolk to The Wash, E. Eng., len. 160 mi.; # 52:37 N, 0:22 E. — riv., to head of The Humber, len. 57 mi.; # 53:40 N, 0:45 W; also certain other English rivs.

Outremont (ō-tr-môṅ), tn., a W. suburb of Montreal, S. E. Quebec, pop. 13; # ab. 45:35 N, 73:40 W.

Overijssel, see **Overyssel.**

Overyssel or **Overijssel** (ō′vĕr-ĭs-ẹl), prov., E. C. Neth., area 1.3, pop. 461, * Zwolle, pop. 38; # 52:25 N, 6:30 E.

Oviedo (ō-vē-ā′dō, ō-vyā′ᵺō), prov., N. Spain, area 4.2, pop. 761, and its *, anc. Asturias, a spt., pop. 76; univ.; cathedral; # 43:15 N, 5:45 W.

Owens (ō′enz), riv., E. Calif. S. to Owens Lake, len. 120 mi.; Los Angeles aqueduct intake; # 36:25 N, 118 W.

Owensboro (ō′enz-bur-ọ), city, N. W. Ky., pop. 30; # 37:45 N, 87:5 W.

Owen Sound (ō′en), lake port tn., Georgian Bay, Ontario, pop. 12; # 44:35 N, 80:56 W.

Owen Stanley Range (ō′en stan′li rǎnj), mts., E. Papua, E. Indies, highest 13,030 ft.; # 9 S, 147:30 E.

Owosso (ō-wos′ō), tn., C. Mich., pop. 14; # 43 N, 84:15 W.

Oxford (oks′fọrd), city, S. C. Eng., pop. 57; Oxford Univ.; # 51:45 N, 1:15 W. — tn., N. Miss., pop. 3; State Univ.; # 34:20 N, 89:34 N. — tn., S. W. Ohio, pop. 3; Miami univ.; # 39:31 N, 84:45 W.

Oxfordshire (oks′fọrd-shir), county, S. C. Eng., area 0.7, pop. 190, * Oxford, pop. 57; # 51:45 N, 1:15 W.

Oxus (ok′sus), **Amu-Daria** or **Amu-Darja,** riv., Pamir plateau to Lake Aral, len. 1,400 mi.; # 43:40 N, 59:25 E.

Ozaka, see **Osaka.**

Ozark (ō′zärk), low dissected plateau, S. Mo. and N. Ark.; # 37 N, 93 W.

P

Pachuca (pä-chō′kä), city, C. Mexico, * of Hidalgo, pop. 39; silver mines; # 20:3 N, 98:45 W.

Pacific Ocean (pạ-sif′ik), largest ocean, bet. America and Asia and Australia, area 70,000, greatest depth found (1924), 32,636 ft., 145 mi. S. E. of Tokyo.

Padang (pä-däng′), spt., W. C. Sumatra, E. Indies, pop. 38; # 0:55 S, 100:25 E.

Paddington (pad′ing-tọn), a borough of London, Eng., pop. 144; # 51:31 N, 0:10 W. — city, W. C. New S. Wales, Australia, pop. 26; # 32:10 S, 145:4 E.

Paderborn (pä-dĕr-bôrn′), city, Westfalen, C. Ger., pop. 33; # 51:43 N, 8:45 E.

Padova (pä′dō-vä), *Eng.* **Padua,** prov., Venetia, N. E. Italy, area 0.8, pop. 588, and its *, pop. 112; Univ. of Padua; # 45:23 N, 11:52 E.

Padua (pad′ū-ạ), see **Padova.**

Paducah (pa-dū′kä), city on Ohio riv., W. Ky., pop. 34; # 37:5 N, 88:35 W.

Pag (päg) or **Pago** (pä′gō), isl., Dalmatia, S. W. Yugoslavia, len. 40 mi. and its spt., pop. 4; # 44:30 N, 15 E.

Pagopago (päng′gō-päng′gō), fine harbor, Tutuila, American

Samoa, S. Pacific oc.; naval and coaling station; # 14:19 S, 170:41 W.

Pahang (pä-häng'), one of Federated Malay States, area 14, pop. 146; # 3:30 N, 103 E.

Paisley (pāz'li), city suburb of Glasgow, N. C. Scotland, pop. 87; # 55:50 N, 4:26 W.

Pak-ho (päk'hō'), riv., trib. of Si-kiang, S. China.

Pakhoi (päk'hoi'), spt. city, Gulf of Tonking, S. China, pop. est. 35; # 21:30 N, 109 E.

Palatinate (pạ-lat'i-nạt), see **Rheinpfalz.**

Palawan (pä-lä'wän), isl., W. Philippines, area 4, pop. ab. 40; # 9:30 N, 118:30 E.

Palembang (pä-lem-bäng'), Dutch district, N. E. Sumatra, area 33, pop. 828, and its chief city, pop. 74; many houses raised over water; # 2:55 S, 104:40 E.

Palencia (pä-län'thē-ä), prov., N. C. Spain, area 3, pop. 189, and its *, pop. 20; # 42 N, 4:35 W.

Palermo (pạ-lĕr'mō), prov., N. W. Sicily, area 1.9, pop. 860, and its *, a spt., pop. 394; univ.; # 38:10 N, 13:25 E.

Palestine (pal'es-tīn), Br. mandate, S. W. Asia, area 9, pop. 757, * Jerusalem, pop. 63; # 31:30 N, 35 E. — tn., E. C. Texas, pop. 12; # 31:45 N, 95:40 W.

Palestrina (pä-les-trē'nä), *anc.* Praeneste, tn., 22 mi. S. E. of Rome, Italy, pop. 7; ruins; # 41:49 N, 12:55 E.

Palisades (pal-i-sādz'), W. cliff of Hudson riv., S. E. New York and N. New Jersey; # 40:53 N, 73:57 W.

Palk (påk), strait bet. Ceylon and India; width 40 mi.: bridged; # 10 N, 80 E.

Palma (päl'mä), isl., N. W. Canary Isls., area 0.3, pop. 46; # 28:40 N, 17:50 W. — spt., W. Majorca, * of Balearic Isls., Spain, pop. 82; # 39:34 N, 2:41 E.

Palmas (päl'mäs), cape, S. Liberia, S. W. Africa; # 3:30 N, 7:30 W. — chief city of Gran Canaria, Canary Isls., pop. ab. 50; # 28:5 N, 15:27 W.

Palm Beach (päm bēch), tn., S. E. Florida; winter resort; pop. with W. Palm Beach, ab. 37; # 26:42 N, 80:2 W.

Palm Canyons (päm kan'yọns), national park, Riverside Co., S. Calif.; # ab. 33:45 N, 116:30 W.

Palmerston (pä'mèr-stọn), city, S. W. N. Island, New Zealand, pop. 18; # 40:20 S, 175:40 E.

Palmyra (pal-mī'rạ), ruins of large anc. city, C. Syria; # 34:30 N, 38:15 W.

Palo Alto (pä'lō äl'tō), tn., W. C. Calif., pop. 17; Stanford Univ.; # 37:27 N, 122:10 W.

Palos (pä'lōs), spt. on Rio Tinto, 47 mi. W. S. W. of Seville, S. W. Spain, pop. 2; Columbus sailed, August 3, 1492; # 37:13 N, 6:52 W.

Pamir (pä-mēr'), lofty plateau, S. W. China, where Hindu Kush, Tian Shan and Himalayan ranges converge; summits over 25,000 ft.; # 38 N, 73:30 E.

Pamlico (pam'li-kō), sound, 80 mi. long, bet. N. Car. mainland and coastal isls.; # 35:30 N, 76 W.

Pampa (päm'pä) or **La Pampa**, ter., C. Argentina, area 56, pop. 142, * Santa Rosa; # 37 S, 65 W.

Pampanga (päm-pän'gä), riv., C. Luzón to Manila Bay, len. 120 mi.; # 14:45 N, 120:40 E.

Pampas (päm'päs), highly productive region of Argentina, the E. C. part; area ab. 250; # 36 S, 62 W.

Pamplona (päm-plō'nä), city, N. Spain, * of Navarra prov., pop. 34; # 42:45 N, 1:40 W.

Panama (pan-ạ-mä'), republic of S. C. America, area 32, pop. 467, and its *, pop. 114, on Pacific end of Panama Canal, though not in Canal Zone; # 9 N, 79:35 W. — **Isthmus of,** isthmus bet. N. and S. America, least width ab. 30 mi., formerly isthmus of Darien. — canal, across isthmus of Panama, len. 44 mi., crest 85 ft.; # 9:10 N, 79:56 W. — **Gulf of,** portion of Pacific oc. in bend of Isthmus; # 8 N, 79:20 W.

Panay (pä-nī'), isl., C. Philippines, area 4, pop. 744, chief city, Iloilo, pop. 49; # 11 N, 122:30 E.

Panjab (pun-jäb'), see **Punjab.**

Pankow (päng'kō), a N. div. of Berlin, Ger., pop. 99; # 52:35 N, 13:24 E.

Pantellaria (pän-tel-lä-rē'ä), Italian isl. bet. Sicily and Tunis, area .03, pop. 9, and its port; convict depot; # 36:48 N, 12 E.

Pantin (pän-tan'), a N. E. suburb of Paris, Fr., pop. 39; # 48:53 N, 2:25 E.

Paotingfu (pä-ō-ting'fö), city, Chihli prov., N. China, pop. 150; # 38:25 N, 115:26 E.

Papeete (pä'pä-ä-tä), chief tn., Tahiti, and * of Fr. Oceania, pop. 4; # 17:33 S, 149:34 W.

Paphlagonia (paf-lạ-gō'ni-ạ), anc. country and Roman prov., S. coast of Black Sea; # ab. 42 N, 3 E.

Paphos (pä'fos), anc. tn., S. W. Cyprus; # 34:48 N, 32:25 E.

Paps (paps), see **Jura.**

Papua (pä'pō-ä), or **New Guinea** (gin'i), isl., N. of Australia, area 330, pop. 625, half Dutch, half Australian; # 0:6 S, 141 E. — ter., Australian, S. E. Papua, area 88, pop. 276, * Port Moresby; # 7 S, 143 E.

Pará (pä-rä'), state, N. E. Brazil, area 526, pop. 984, * Belem (often called Pará), pop. 236; # 1:30 S, 48:20 W.

Paraguay (par'ạ-gwä or pä-rä-gwī'), republic, S. South America, bet. Paraná and Paraguay riv., area 67–98, pop. 700–1,000, * Asunción, pop. 100; # 24 S, 56 W. — riv., 1,500 mi. long to Paraná riv.; # 27:20 S, 58:20 W.

Parahyba (pä-rä-ē'bä), state, ext. E. Brazil, area 22, pop. 961, and its *, a spt., pop. 53; # 7:11 S, 34:50 W. — see **Parnahyba.**

Paramaribo (par-ạ-mar'i-bō), spt. city, * of Dutch Guiana or Surinam, pop. 45; # 5:50 N, 55:20 W.

Paraná (pä-rä-nä'), riv., S. South America, to Rio de la Plata, len. 2,000 mi.; # 34 S, 58:30 W. — state S. Brazil, area 77, pop. 686, * Curitiba; # 24:45 S, 51 W. — city, * of Entre Ríos prov., Argentina, pop. 44; # 31:42 S, 60:32 W.

Pariña (pä-rēn'yä), cape, N. W. Peru, ext. W. S. America; # 4:30 S, 81:30 W.

Paris (par'is; *Fr.* på-rē), city, * of Fr., on Seine riv., 107 mi. from Atlantic oc., pop. 2,906; Univ. of Paris; # 48:52 N, 2:20 E. — city, N. E. Texas, pop. 19; # 33:35 N, 95:32 W. — tn., E. C. Ill., pop. 9; # 39:35 N, 87:44 W.

Paris Basin (par'is bä'sin), valley, N. C. Fr., centers at Paris; # 48:52 N, 2:20 E.

Park (pärk), lofty mt. range, C. Colo.; # 40:50 N, 106:50 W. — N, Middle, S., mt. basins, Colo.; # 40:45 N, 106:20 W; # 40:10 N, 106:20 W; # 39 N, 105:50 W.

Parkersburg (pär'kèrz-bèrg), city, N. W. W. Va., on Ohio riv., pop. 30; # 39:16 N, 81:32 W.

Parma (pär'mä), prov., anc. duchy, Emilia, N. E. C. Italy, area 1.3, pop. 362, and its *, pop. 63; # 44:47 N, 10:17 E.

Parnahyba or **Parahyba** (pär-nä-ē'bä), riv. S. E. Brazil, N. E. to Atlantic oc., len. 540 mi.; # 3.1 S, 41 W.

Parnassus (pär-nas'us) or **Liakura** (lyä'kù-rä), mt. pk., S. C. Greece, el. 8,068 ft.; # 38:32 N, 22:35 E.

Pärnu (pär'nö), prov., Gulf of Riga, Estonia, and its *, a spt., pop. 19; # 58:25 N, 24:30 E.

Paros (pä'ros), Greek isl., C. Cyclades, S. Ægean sea, area .06, pop. 12; fine marble; # 37:5 N, 25:22 E.

Parramatta (par-ạ-mat'ä), city, 14 mi. N. W. of Sydney, E. New S. Wales, Aust., pop. 15; # 33:49 S, 151 E.

Parry (par'i), isl. group, most N. W. Arctic isls., N. of N. America; # 75 N, 110 W.

Parsons (pär'sọnz), city, S. E. Kansas, pop. 14; # 37:18 N, 95:16 W.

Parthia (pär'thi-ä), anc. country, N. E. Persia; # 35 N, 57 W.

Partick (pär'tik), a borough, recently a suburb of Glasgow, Scotland; pop. 68; # 55:52 N, 4:18 W.

Pasadena (pas-ạ-dē'nä), suburb of Los Angeles, S. Calif., pop. 82; Calif. Institute of Technology; # 34:10 N, 118:9 W.

Pas-de-Calais (pä-dè-kä-lä), dept., ext. N. Fr., area 2.6, pop. 990, * Arras, pop. 26; # 50:30 N, 2:20 E.

Passaic (pạ-sā'ik), city, N. E. New Jersey; pop. 61; # 40:52 N, 74:8 W.

Passaro (päs'sä-rō), cape, S. E. Sicily; # 36:40 N, 15:5 E.

Passau (päs'sou), city, E. Bavaria, S. Ger., on Inn and Danube rivs., pop. 24; # 48:35 N, 13:24 E.

Pasto (päs'tō), vol. pk., S. W. Colombia, el. 13,990 ft. — city on its side, the * of Nariño, pop. ab. 20; univ.; # 1:11 N, 77:30 W.

Patagonia (pat-ạ-gō'ni-ä), dry region of S. Argentina, from Andes to Atlantic oc.; # 46 S, 68 W.

Paternò (pä-ter-nō'), tn., on S. slope of Mt. Etna, Sicily, pop. comm. 23; hot springs; # 43:33 N, 13:25 E.

Paterson (pat'ér-sọn), city, N. E. New Jersey, pop. 140; silks; # 40:55 N, 74:10 W.

Pathfinder (path'fīnd-èr), dam, N. Platte riv., S. E. C. Wyo., height 218 ft.; irrigation; # ab. 42:25 N, 106:50 W.

---

fat, fāte, fär, fåll, åsk, fãre; net, mē, hèr; pin, pīne; not, nōte, mŏve, nôr; up, lūte, pùll; oi, oil; ou, out; (lightened) aviạry, ẹlect, agọny, intọ, ūnite; (obscured) errạnt, operạ, ardẹnt, actọr, natūre; ch, chip; g, go; th, thin; � then; y, you;

Patiala (put-ē-ä′lä), native state, Punjab, N. W. India, area 5, pop. 1,500, and its *, pop. 47; # 30:20 N, 76:20 E.

Patjitan (pat-ye-tan′), port on S. coast of Java, on bay and river of same name; # 8:15 S, 111:4 E.

Patmos (pat′mos), isl., S. E. Ægean sea, Italian control, area .02, pop. 3, and its *; # 37:20 N, 26:32 E.

Patna (pat′nä), city, Ganges riv., N. E. India, E. of Benares, pop. 120; univ.; # 25:40 N, 85:15 E.

Patras (pä′träs), spt. city, N. Morea, S. Greece, pop. 61; "currants"; # 38:15 N, 21:45 E.

Pau (pō), city, Basses-Pyrénées, S. W. Fr., pop. 37; resort; # 43:15 N, 0:25 W.

Paulo Affonso (pou′lŏ äf-fŏn′sŏ), series of three falls with total height of 275 ft., São Francisco riv., E. Brazil; # 9:18 S, 38:19 W.

Paumotu (pou-mō′tö), a native name for the Low Archipelago, S. E. Pacific, Fr.

Pavia (pä-vē′ä), prov., Lombardy, N. Italy, area 1.1, pop. 469, and its *, anc. Ticinum, pop. 42; univ.; # 45:15 N, 9:10 E.

Pawtucket (pâ-tuk′et), city, N. E. Rhode Island, pop. 76; # 41:50 N, 71:25 W.

Paysandú (pī-sän-dö′), dept., C. W. Uruguay, area 5.1, pop. 83, and its *, pop. 26; # 32:19 S, 58:8 W.

Peabody (pē′bod-i), city, N. E. Mass., pop. 22; # 42:30 N, 71 W.

Peace (pēs), riv., Br. Columbia and W. Alberta to Slave riv., len. ab. 1,000 mi.; # 58:55 N, 111:5 W.

Pearl (pèrl), riv., N. C. Miss., to Gulf of Mex., len. 350 mi.; # 30:1 N, 89:35 W. — harbor, near Honolulu, Hawaiian Isls.; U. S. Naval base; # 21:20 N, 158 W.

Pechili (pä′chē-lē), see **Chihli.**

Pechora (pe-chó′rä), riv., Ural mts., N. E. Russia to Pechora bay, Arctic oc., len. 900 mi.; # 65:30 N, 52 E.

Pecos (pā′kōs), riv., N. C. New Mex., to Rio Grande, len. 800 mi.; # 29:20 N, 101:20 W.

Pécs (päch), city, S. Hungary, pop. 40; univ.; # 46:5 N, 18:13 E.

Peebles (pē′blz), county, S. E. Scotland, area 0.3, pop. 15, and its *, pop. 6; # 55:40 N, 3:12 W.

Peekskill (pēk′skil), tn., S. E. New York, pop. 17; # 41:18 N, 73:57 W.

Pei or **Pai** (pā), riv., N. E. China, through Tientsin to Gulf of Chihli, len. 150 mi.; # 39 N, 117:41 E.

Peiping (pā′ping′) (formerly **Peking**), city, N. China, former * of China; pop. with suburbs 1,400; # 40 N, 116 E.

Peipus (pī′pös), Russian **Chudskoye**, lake, Estonia-Russian boundary, len. 93 mi.; # 58:45 N, 27:30 E.

Pekalongan (pä-kä-lon′gän), dist., N. C. Java, pop. 2,269, and its *, pop. 48; # 6:54 S, 109:42 E.

Pekin (pē′kin), tn., C. Ill., pop. 19; # 40:35 N, 89:35 W.

Peking (pē′king′), see **Peiping.**

Pelée (pe-lā′), vol. mt., N. Martinique, el. 4,428 ft.; eruption 1902, killing 30,000 persons; # 14:45 N, 82:40 W.

Pelew (pē-lö′), isls., small group, E. of Philippines; Japanese mandate; # 7:30 N, 134:30 E.

Peloponnesus (pel′ŏ-po-nē′sus), modern **Morea**, S. pen. of Greece, a dept., pop. 945; # 37:30 N, 22:15 E.

Pelotas (pā-lō′täsh), spt. city, Rio Grande do Sul, S. E. Brazil, pop. 82; # 31:42 S, 52:23 W.

Pelvoux (pel-vö), mt. pk., Alps, S. E. Fr., el. 13,462 ft.; # 44:58 N, 6:25 E.

Pemba (pem′bä), Br. isl., near E. coast of equatorial Africa; area 0.6, pop. 83; # 5 S, 39:50 E.

Pembroke (pem′brŭk), county, ext. S. W. Wales, area 0.6, pop. 82, and its *, a spt., pop. 15; # 51:39 N, 4:57 W.

Penang (pe-nang′), Br. isl., Straits Settlements, area 0.1, pop. 310, chief town, Georgetown; # 5:15 N, 100:15 E.

Penarth (pē′nġrth), a suburb of Cardiff, S. W. Wales, pop. 17; # 51:27 N, 3:11 W.

Pend d′Oreille (pend dō-rēl′), lake, N. Idaho, area 0.3; # 48:15 N, 116:22 W.

Peneius (pe-nē′yus), anc. Peneus, riv., C. Greece to Gulf of Salonika, len. 125 mi.; # 39:55 N, 22:45 E.

Peninsula, The (pē-nin′sū-lä), Iberia; # 40 N, 4 W. — district in S. E. Va. bet. York and James rivs.; Civil War Campaign; # 37 N, 76:30 W.

Pennine Alps (pen′in (-īn) alps), mt. range, N. Italy and adj.

Switz. and Fr., summit, Mt. Blanc, el. 15,780 ft.; # 46 N, 7:30 E.

Pennine Chain, range low mts., C. to N. Eng., highest Cross Fell, el. 2,930 ft.; # 54 N, 2 W.

Pennsylvania (pen-sil-vā′ni-ä), state, N. E. U.S.A., bordering N. Y. and Md., area 45, pop. 9,900, * Harrisburg, pop. 84; chief city, Philadelphia, pop. 1,931; yields one fourth of world's coal output; # 41 N, 78 W.

Pennsylvania Lines, R.R., New York to Chicago, via Philadelphia and Pittsburgh; total mileage 11,561.

Penobscot (pe-nob′skot), riv., N. Maine to Penobscot bay, Atlantic oc., len. 350 mi.; # 44:30 N, 68:50 W.

Pensacola (pen-sa̧-kō′la̧), spt. city, N. W. Florida, pop. 37. — bay, N. W. Fla.; navy aviation station; # 30:30 N, 87:15 W.

Pentelikon (pen-tel′i-kon), mt., 10 mi. N. E. of Athens, Greece, el. 3,640 ft.; fine marble; # ab. 38 N, 24 E.

Penza (pen′za̧), prov., C. Russia, area 15, pop. 1,800 and its *, pop. 80; # 53:10 N, 45:3 E.

Peoria (pē-ō′ri-ä), city, C. Ill., on Illinois riv., pop. 105; Bradley Institute; # 40:42 N, 89:36 W.

Pera (pā′rä), N., foreign part of Constantinople, Turkey; # 41:3 N, 29 E.

Perak (pā-räk′), one of Federated Malay States, area 8, pop. 599, chief city Ipoh, pop. 39; # 4:40 N, 101 E.

Perche (persh), old div. of N. C. France; # 48:10 N, 1 E.

Perdu (per-dü), mt. pk., C. Pyrenees, Spain, el. 11,000 ft.; # 42:40 N, 0:1 E.

Pergamum (pèr′ga̧-mum), mod. Bergama, anc. city, W. Asia Minor, * of Roman Asia; # 39:7 N, 27:13 E.

Périgueux (pā-rē-gè), city, * of Dordogne dept., S. W. C. Fr., pop. 28; # 45:12 N, 0:45 E.

Perim (pa-rēm′), Br. isl. in straits of Aden, bet. Africa and Asia; # 12:38 N, 43:25 E.

Perim-Dagh (pä-rēm′däg), mt., S. W. Bulgaria, highest Yeltepe, el. 8,680 ft.; # 41:45 N, 23:25 E.

Perlis (per′lis), a Br. protected state on W. coast of Malay pen., area 0.3, pop. 40, * Kangar; # 6:30 N, 100:15 E.

Perm (perm), prov., E. C. Russia, area 83, pop. 1,779, and its * on Kama riv., pop. 74; # 58 N, 56:20 E.

Pernambuco (per-näm-bö′kō), state, E. Brazil, area 38, pop. 2,155, * Recife (often called Pernambuco), pop. 239; # 8:9 S, 34:47 W.

Perpignan (per-pēn-yän), city, S. Fr., near S. E. end of Pyrenees, * of Pyrénées-Orientales, pop. 54; # 42:40 N, 2:55 E.

Persepolis (pèr-sep′ō-lis), anc. city, 30 mi. N. E. of Shiraz, S. C. Persia; anc. * of Persia; # 29:55 N, 52:55 E.

Persia (pèr′sha̧), kingdom, S. W. Asia, area 628, pop. 9,000, * Teheran, pop. 220; # 33 N, 55 E.

Persian (pèr′sha̧n), gulf bet. Persia and Arabia, len. 600 mi.; # 27 N, 51 E.

Perth (pèrth), county, C. Scotland, area 2.4, pop. 123, and its *, a port on Firth of Tay, S. E. Scotland, pop. 33; # 56:20 N, 3:30 W. — city, S. W. Australia, * of W. Australia, on Swan riv., pop. 64, with suburbs, 172; # 31:56 S, 115:50 E.

Perth Amboy (pèrth am′boi or am-boi′), spt. city, N. E. C. New Jersey, pop. 41; chemicals and refining; # 40:31 N, 74:16 W.

Peru (pē-rö′; Sp. pā-rö), republic, W. tropical S. America, area ab. 532, pop. ab. 6,500, * Lima, pop. 370; # 10 S, 74 W. — tn., N. C. Ind., pop. 12; # 40:47 N, 86:3 W.

Perugia (pā-rö′jä) or **Umbria** (um′bri-a̧), dept., C. Italy, area 3, pop. 636, * Perugia, pop. 73; univ.; cathedral; # 43:8 N, 12:22 E.

Peruvian Current (pē-rö′vi-a̧n), see **Humboldt.**

Pesaro (pā′zä-rō), prov., Marche, N. E. C. Italy, area 1.1, pop. 281, and its *, a spt., pop. 30; # 43:54 N, 12:54 E.

Pescadores (pes-kä-dō′res), Jap. **Hokoto**, 37 isls., S. of Japan, area .05, pop. 52; # 23:30 N, 119:35 E.

Peshawar (pe-shou′ur), city, near Khyber Pass, N. W. India, * of N. W. Frontier prov., pop. 104; # 34 N, 71:32 E.

Peterborough (pē′tẽr-bur-ọ), city, S. E. Ontario, pop. 19; # 44:25 N, 78:15 W. — **Soke of**, administrative county attached to Northamptonshire, E. C. Eng., area .08, pop. 47; # 52:35 N, 0:14 W.

Peterhead (pē-tẽr-hed′), spt., ext. E. Scotland, pop. 13; # 57:30 N, 1:45 W.

Petermann (pā′tẽr-män), pk., E. Greenland, el. ab. 11,000 ft.; # 72:45 N, 29:35 W.

Petersburg (pē′tẽrz-bẽrg), city, S. E. C. Va., pop. 31; # 37:20 N, 77:20 W.

Petersham (pē′tẽr-shạm), a close suburb of Sydney, S. E. Australia, pop. 26; # 33:53 S, 151:12 E.

Petra (pē′trạ), ruins of anc. city, S. E. Palestine; # 30:16 N, 35:13 E.

Petrified Forest (pet′ri-fīd for′est), national monument, Gila and Apache counties, E. C. Ariz., area .04; # ab. 34:50 N, 109:50 W.

Petrograd (pye-tro-grät′), see **Leningrad**.

Petropavlovsk (pye-tro-päv′lofsk), spt. city, S. E. Kamchatka pen., E. Asia; pop. 42; # 53 N, 159:5 E. — city, Kirghiz Republic, pop. 36; # 55 N, 69 E.

Pforzheim (pôrts′hīm), city, C. Baden, S. W. Ger., pop. 78; celluloid; # 48:53 N, 8:40 E.

Phenicia, see **Phœnicia**.

Philadelphia (fil-ạ-del′fi-ạ), city, S. E. Pa., on Delaware riv., pop. 1,931; Univ. of Pa.; Temple Univ.; # 39:58 N, 75:10 W. — anc. name of **Alashehr**, Anatolia; # 38:21 N, 28:30 E.

Philippeville (fē-lēp-vēl′), city, N. E. Algeria, pop. 34; # 36:54 N, 6:54 E.   [# 41:2 N, 24:18 E.

Philippi (fi-lip′ī), anc. tn., N. E. Greece; St. Paul's church;

Philippine Islands (fil′i-pēn, -pin, -pīn), archipelago of 7,000 isl., S. W. N. Pacific, area 115, pop. 16,356, * Manila, pop. 390; commonwealth (under U. S. sovereignty); # 11 N, 123 E.

Philippopolis (fil-ip-op′ọ-lis), see **Plovdiv**.

Philistia (fi-lis′ti-ạ), anc. country W. of Palestine, on coast; # 31:30 N, 34:35 E.

Phillipsburg (fil′ips-bẽrg), city, N. W. New Jersey, pop. 18; # 40:39 N, 75:12 W.

Phnôm-Penh, see **Pnom-Penh**.

Phœnicia (fẹ-nish′i-ạ), anc. country, W. of Palestine, on Mediterranean (Phœnician) sea; # 32 N, 35 E.

Phœnix (fē′niks), city, S. C. Ariz., its *, pop. 65; # 33:30 N, 112:5 W.

Phœnixville (fē′niks-vil), tn., E. C. Pa., pop. 12; iron; # 40:8 N, 75:30 W.

Phrygia (frij′i-ạ), very anc. country, C. and N. W. Asia Minor; # 40 N, 30 E.

Phyengyang (pyeng′yäng′), see **Pyengyang**.

Piacenza (pē-ä-chen′tsä), prov., Emilia, N. E. C. Italy, area 1, pop. 291, and its *, anc. Placentia, on the Po riv., pop. 58; # 45:1 N, 9:40 E.

Piatigorsk (pyä-tē-gorsk′), city, Georgian Republic, pop. 47; # 44:4 N, 42:8 E.

Piauhy (pē-ou-ē′), state, N. E. Brazil, area 95, pop. 609, * Therezina; # 8 S, 42 W.

Piave (pē-ä′vä), riv., Alps, N. Italy, to Gulf of Venice, len. 137 mi.; # 45:33 N, 12:45 E.

Picardy (pik′ạr-di), anc. prov., N. E. Fr.; # 49:30 N, 3 E.

Pic d'Aneto (pēk d′än-e-tō), highest pk., Pyrenees, N. E. Spain, el. 11,169 ft.; # 42:40 N, 0:45 E.

Pic de Montcalm (môn-kälm), pk., Pyrenees, S. Fr., el. 10,105 ft.; # 42:45 N, 1:30 E.

Pic du midi d'Ossau (pēk dü mē-dē dô-sō), pk., Pyrenees, S. Fr., el. 9,466 ft.; # 42:50 N, 0:25 W.

Picher (pich′ẽr), tn., ext. N. E. Okla., pop. 6; zinc; # 36:57 N, 94:50 W.

Pico Alto (pē′kō äl′tō), vol. pk., Pico isl., Azores, el. 7,619 ft.; # 38:30 N, 28:20 W.

Pico Concha (pē-kō kōn′chä), mt. pk., W. Venezuela, highest in Ven., el. 15,500 ft.; # 8:5 N, 70:47 W.

Piedmont (pēd′mont), dept., N. W. Italy, area 11.3, pop. 3,384, * Turin, pop. 502; # 44:40 N, 7:45 E. — plateau bet. coastal plain and Appalachian mts., Va., N. Car., S. Car., Ga.; # 38 N, 78:20 W.

Pierre (pēr), tn., C. S. Dak., on Missouri riv., state *, pop. 4; # 44:25 N, 100:20 W.

Pietermaritzburg (pē-tẽr-mär′its-bẽrg), city, * of Natal, S. E. Africa, pop. 36, half white; # 29:30 S, 30:30 E.

Pike's (pīks), mt. pk., C. Colo., el. 14,108 ft., ascended by cog-rail and auto road; # 38:50 N, 105:10 W.

Pilcomayo (pēl-kō-mī′ō), riv., Bolivia ab. 1,000 miles to Paraguay riv., opposite Asunción; # 25:25 S, 57:40 W.

Pillars of Hercules (pil′ạrz ov hẽr′kū-lēz), anc. name for Strait of Gibraltar; Gibraltar rock and Atlas Mountains; # 36 N, 5:30 W.

Pilsen (pil′sẹn) or **Plzen**, city, W. C. Bohemia, pop. 88, with suburbs, 111; beer; # 49:45 N, 13:22 E.

Pinar del Río (pē-när′del rē′ō), prov., W. Cuba, area 5.2, pop. 273, and its *, pop. 49; # 22:25 N, 83:45 W.

Pindus (pin′dus), mt. range, C. Greece, highest, Parnassus, el. 8,068 ft.; # 39:15 N, 21:30 E.

Pine Bluff (pīn bluf), city, S. E. C. Ark., pop. 21; # 34:10 N, 92 W.

Pines, Isle of (pīnz), isl., S. of W. Cuba, area 1.2, pop. 3: # 21:40 N, 82:45 W.

Pingyang (ping′yäng′), see **Pyengyang**.

Piotrków (pyôtr-kúf), city 28 mi. S. S. E. of Lódz, Poland, pop. 41; # 51:24 N, 19:41 E.

Piqua (pik′wạ), city, S. W. C. Ohio, pop. 16; # 40:12 N, 84:17 W.

Piræus (pī-rē′us), the port of Athens, S. E. Greece, pop. 177: # 37:57 N, 23:40 E.

Pirmasens (pir′mä-sens), city, Palatinate, Bavaria, S. W. Ger., pop. 43; boots and shoes; # 49:12 N, 7:37 E.

Pirna (pir′nä), city on Elbe riv., S. E. suburb of Dresden, S. Ger., pop. 30; # 50:57 N, 13:57 E.

Pisa (pē′zä), prov., Tuscany, N. W. Italy, area 1.2, pop. 361, and its *, pop. 69; Leaning Tower; univ.; # 43:43 N, 10:23 E.

Pissevache (pēs-väsh), falls, Valais, S. W. Switz., height 215 ft.; # ab. 46:8 N, 7 E.

Pistoia (pēs-tō′yä), anc. Pistoria, city, Tuscany, N. W. C. Italy, pop. comm. 68; # 43:55 N, 10:54 E.

Pitcairn (pit-kärn′ or pit′kärn), tiny remote Br. isl., S. E. S. Pacific oc., pop. .02; mutineers, 1790; # 25 S, 130 W.

Pittsburg (pits′bẽrg), city, S. C. Kansas, pop. 18; coal; # 37:30 N, 94:45 W.

Pittsburgh (pits′bẽrg), city, S. W. Pa., pop. 672, with suburbs, pop. 1,994; steel; Univ. of Pittsburgh; Carnegie Inst.; # 40:27 N, 80 W.

Pittsfield (pits′fēld), city, W. C. Mass., pop. 50; # 42:28 N, 73:15 W.

Pittston (pits′tọn), city, N. E. Pa., pop. 18; coal; # 41:20 N, 75:41 W.

Piura (pyō′rä), dept., N. W. Peru, area 17, pop. 214, and its *, pop. 11; # 5:9 S, 80:40 W.

Plainfield (plān′fēld), city, N. C. New Jersey, pop. 37; # 40:38 N, 74:30 W.

Plainpalais (plan-pä-lā), a S. suburb of Geneva, Switz., pop. 35; # 46:10 N, 6:10 E.

Planitz (plä′nits), a suburb of Zwickau, Sachsen (Saxony), S. Ger., pop. 24; # 50:42 N, 12:28 E.

Plata, Rio de la (plä′tä), Eng. River Plate, estuary, S. E. S. America, len. 185 mi.; # 35 S, 57 W. — **La**, see **La Plata**.

Platt (plat), national park, Murray Co., S. C. Okla.; sulphur springs; # 34:30 N, 96:55 W.

Platte (plat), riv., N. C. Colo. to Missouri riv., len. 1,260 mi.; 315 mi. from junction of N. and S. Platte; # 41 N, 95:50 W.

Platten (plät′tẹn) or **Balaton** (bol′ot-on), lake, W. C. Hungary, len. 50 mi.; # 46:50 N, 17:40 E.

Plattsburg (plats′bẽrg), tn., N. E. New York, on Lake Champlain, pop. 16; # 44:45 N, 73:30 W.

Plauen (plou′ẹn), city, S. W. Sachsen (Saxony), S. Ger. pop. 110; # 50:30 N, 12:8 E.

Plevna (plev′nä) or **Pleven**, city, N. C. Bulgaria, pop. 27; # 43:25 N, 24:38 E.

Ploésti (plô-yesht′y), city, 30 mi. N. of Bucharest, S. E. Romania, pop. 57; # 44:50 N, 25:50 E.

Plomb du Cantal (plôn dü kän-tàl), vol. cone, S. C. Fr., el. 6,096 ft.; # 45:1 N, 2:50 E.

Plovdiv (plôv′dif), Eng. **Philippopolis**; dept., S. C. Bulgaria, area 2.6, pop. 489 and its *, on Maritza riv., pop. 63; # 42:8 N, 24:45 E.

Plymouth (plim′uth), spt. city, Devon, S. W. Eng., pop. 193; # 50:24 N, 4:7 W. — city, N. E. Pa., pop. 16; # 41:16 N, 75:55 W. — tn., S. E. Mass., pop. (twp.) 13; founded 1620; # 41:57 N, 70:40 W.

Plzen, see **Pilsen**.

Pnom-Penh (pnom-pen′), city, * of Cambodia, on Mekong riv., Fr. Indo-China, pop. 88; # 11:30 N, 104:55 E.

Po (pō), anc. Padus, riv., Alps, N. W. Italy to Adriatic sea, len. 418 mi.; # 44:55 N, 12:28 E.

Pocahontas (pō-ka̤-hon'ta̤s), important coal field, W. Va. and Va.; # 38 N, 80:30 W.

Pocatello (pō-ka̤-tel'ō), city, S. E. Idaho, pop. 18; # 42:50 N, 112:25 W.

Podolia (pọ̄-dō'li-ä) or **Podolsk** (po-dôl'ysk), prov., ext. S. W. Ukraine, S. Russia, area 13, pop. 3,000, and its *; # 48:50 N, 28 E.

Point Danger, cape, ext. E. Australia; # 28:10 S, 153:35 E.

Pointe-à-Pitre (pwaṅt-ä-pētr), city, Guadeloupe, Fr. W. Indies, pop. 28; fine harbor; # 16:17 N, 61:31 W.

Poitiers (pwo-tyā), city, * of Vienne dept., W. C. Fr., pop. 41; battles, 732, 1356; univ.; # 46:32 N, 0:20 E.

Poitou (pwo-tö), old prov., W. Fr., * Poitiers; # 46:36 N, 0:20 E. — **Gate of,** wide pass near Poitiers connecting Aquitaine and the Paris Basin; # ab. 46:36 N, 0:20 E.

Pola (pō'lä), prov., Istria pen., N. E. Italy, pop. 299, and its *, a spt., pop. 49; # 44:50 N, 13:50 E.

Poland (pō'la̤nd), former republic bet. Germany and Russia, area 150, pop. 35,000, *Warsaw; #52 N, 21 E: conquered by Germany and divided bet. Germany and Russia, 1939.

Polar (pō'la̤r), regions within Arctic and Antarctic circles (66½ N and S); N. Pole reached April 6, 1909, by Peary; S. Pole, Dec. 14, 1911, by Amundsen and Jan. 18, 1912, by Scott; #90 N and 90 S.

Poltava or **Pultava** (pol-tä'vä), prov., N. Ukraine, S. C. Russia, area 15, pop. 2,400, and its *, pop. 72; # 49:45 N, 34:15 E.

Polynesia (pol-i-nē'shi̤ä), groups of isls., S. Pacific oc. E. of Fiji; including Hawaiian isls.; # ab. 170 W, 10 S.

Pommern (pom'mern), *Eng.* **Pomerania**, prov. of Prussia, N. E. Ger., area 11.7, pop. 1,918, * Stettin, pop. 233; # 53:40 N, 14:20 E.

Pomona (pọ̄-mō'na̤), suburb of Los Angeles, Calif., pop. 24; # 34:5 N, 117:42 W; — largest of Orkney isls., area 0.2, pop. 14; # 59 N, 3 W.

Pompeii (pom-pā'yē), anc. city, on slopes of Vesuvius, S. Italy; covered 79 A.D.; # 40:45 N, 14:29 E.

Ponce (pōn'sā), city, S. W. C. Puerto Rico, pop. 65 ; # 18 N, 66:40 W.

Pondichéry (pôṅ-dē-shä-rē), Fr. prov., S. E. India, S. of Madras, area 0.1. pop. 171, and its *, a spt., pop. 47; # 12 N, 79:45 E.

Ponta Delgada (pōn'tä del-gä'dä), spt., largest city, Azores isls., pop. 18; # 37:42 N, 25:40 W.

Pontchartrain, Lake (pon'chär-trān), portion of Gulf of Mexico, N. of New Orleans; # 30:10 N, 90 W.

Pontefract (pon'tē-frakt), a S. E. suburb of Leeds, N. C. Eng., pop. 17; # 53:42 N, 1:18 W.

Pontevedra (pōn-tā-vā'drä), prov., N. W. Spain, area 1.7, pop. 545, and its *, a spt., pop. 25; # 42:27 N, 8:35 W.

Pontiac (pon'ti-ak), city, S. E. Mich., pop. 67; # 42:40 N, 83:20 W.

Pontine (pon'tin or -tīn), malarial marshy plain, S. E. of Rome, Italy; # 41:20 N, 13:10 E.

Pontus (pon'tus), anc. country just S. of Black Sea (Pontus Euxinus); # 40:30 N, 37 E.

Pontypridd (pont-ē-priᴛʜ'), city, E. Glamorgan, S. E. Wales, pop. 47; # 51:37 N, 3:21 W.

Poole (pöl), spt. city on Poole Harbor, Dorset, S. Eng., pop. 44; # 50:43 N, 2 W.

Poona (pö'na̤), city, 75 mi. S. E. of Bombay, W. India, pop. 215; # 18:30 N, 73:45 E.

Poopó (pō-ō-pō'), lake, S. W. Bolivia, len. 80 mi., alt. ab. 12,000 ft.; # 19 S, 67 W.

Poplar (pop'la̤r), an E. borough of London, Eng., pop. 162; # 51:31 N, 0:1 W.

Popocatapetl (pō-pō-kä-ta̤-pet'l), vol., near Mexico City, Mex., el. 17,843 ft.; # 19 N, 98:7 W.

Port Adelaide (pōrt ad'ē-lād), suburb of Adelaide, S. Aust., pop. 30; # 34:50 S, 138:30 E.

Port Antonio (pōrt an-tō'ni-ō), spt. town, N. E. Jamaica, Br. West Indies, winter resort; pop. 6; # 18:10 N, 76: 28 W.

Port Arthur (pōrt är'thėr), city, N. W. side of Lake Superior, pop. 15; wheat lake port; # 48:30 N, 89:10 W. — spt., ext. S. E. Texas, pop. 46; # 29:55 N, 93:55 W. — spt., Kwangtung pen., Yellow Sea, Manchuria, pop. 18; Japanese since 1904; # 38:45 N, 121:14 E.

Port-au-Prince (pôr-tō-praṅs, pōrt'ō-prins'), spt. city, * of Haiti, pop. 125; # 18:35 N, 72:25 W.

Port Chester (pōrt ches'tėr), tn., S. E. New York, 22 mi. N. E. of New York City, pop. 23; # 41 N, 73:39 W.

Port Darwin (pōrt där'win), spt. tn., * of N. Ter. of Aust., pop. 5; # 12 S, 131 E.

Port Elizabeth (pōrt ē-liz'a̤-beth), spt. city, Cape of Good Hope, U.S. Africa, pop. 46; # 33:58 S, 25:30 E.

Port Glasgow (pōrt glas'gō), city, 15 mi. W. of Glasgow, Scotland, pop. 21; # 55:56 N, 4:41 W.

Port Huron (pōrt hū'ron), city, S. E. C. Mich., on St. Claire riv., pop. 33; # 42:58 N, 82:30 W.

Port Jackson (pōrt jak'son), bottle bay on which Sydney is located, S. E. Aust.; # 33:50 S, 151:10 E.

Port Jervis (pōrt jėr'vis), tn., S. E. New York, on Delaware riv., pop. 10; # 41:22 N, 74:42 W.

Portland (pōrt'la̤nd), spt. city, N. W. Ore., on Willamette riv., near Columbia riv., pop. 305; Reed College; # 45:32 N, 122:40 W. — spt. city, S. Maine, pop. 74; # 43:35 N, 70: 15 W.

Portland, Isle of, pen., S. Dorset, Eng.; # 50:32 N, 2:30 W.

Port Louis (pōrt lö'is), spt. city, * of Mauritius, S. Indian oc., pop. 52; # 20:10 S, 57:30 E.

Port Melbourne (pōrt mel'bŏrn), the port of Melbourne, Vic., S. E. Aust., pop. 13; # 37:51 S, 144:56 E.

Port Moresby (pōrt mōrz-bi), spt., S. E. Papua, * of Australian Papua; pop. 2; # 9:30 S, 147:15 E.

Porto Alegre (por'tọ̄ ä-lā'gre), spt. city, S. Brazil, * of Rio Grande do Sul, pop. 322; # 30:15 S, 51 W.

Port of Spain (pōrt ov spān), spt. city, * of Trinidad, Br. W. Indies, pop. 64; # 10:39 N, 61:31 W.

Porto Maurizio (por'tō mou-rēt'sē-ō), spt., Imperia prov., Liguria, N. W. Italy, pop. 26; # 43:53 N, 8:1 E.

Porto Montt (pōr-tō mōnt), see **Puerto Montt.**

Porto Novo (por'tō nō'vo), spt. city, * of Dahomey, Fr. W. Africa, pop. ab. 30; # 6:28 N, 2:42 E.

Porto Rico (pōr'tō rē'kō), isl., W. Indies, area 3.4, pop. 1,869; ter. of the U.S.A.; name officially changed in 1932 to **Puerto Rico;** see **Puerto Rico.**

Port Philip (pōrt fil'ip), bay, S. E. Aust., Melbourne at its head; len. 31 mi.; # 37:55 S, 144:54 E.

Port Royal (pōrt roi'a̤l), see **Annapolis,** Nova Scotia.

Port Saïd (pōrt sä-ēd'), spt. city, Egypt, at Mediterranean end of Suez Canal, pop. 91; # 31:16 N, 32:19 E.

Portsmouth (pōrts'muth), spt. city, Hampshire, S. Eng., pop. 231; chief Br. Naval Station; # 50:46 N, 1:5 W. — spt. city, S. E. Va., pop. 51; U. S. navy yard; # 36:50 N, 76:19 W. — spt. city, S. E. New Hampshire, pop. 15; # 43:5 N, 70:50 W. — city, S. C. Ohio, on Ohio riv. and Ohio canal; pop. 40; # 38:45 N, 83 W.

Port Sudan (pōrt sō-dän'), port, Anglo-Egyptian Sudan, on Red Sea; # 19:35 N, 37:10 E.

Portugal (pōr'ṭụ-ga̤l, *Port.* pōr'tù-gäl'), republic, S. W. Iberia, area 35.5, pop. 6,033, * Lisbon, pop. 486; # 40 N, 8 W.

Portuguese Colonies (pōr'ṭụ-gēz kol'ọ̄-niz), see **Angola, Damão, Diu, Goa, Guinea, Macao, Mozambique.**

Portuguesa (pōr-tù-gā'sä), **Republica,** Portuguese name for Portugal.

Posen (pō'zen), officially **Poznan,** county, W. Poland, area 10, pop. 1,974, and its *, pop. 170; univ.; # 52:25 N, 16:58 E. — a prov. of Prussia, N. Ger., bordering Poland, pop. 337; # 52:30 N, 15:45 E.

Potenza (pō-ten'tsä), prov., Calabria, S. W. Italy, area 3.9, pop. 469, and its *, pop. 18; destructive earthquake, 1857; # 40:38 N, 15:48 E.

Potomac (pọ̄-tō'ma̤k), riv., N. W. Va., past Washington, D. C., to Chesapeake Bay, len. 450 mi.; # 38 N, 76:30 W.

Potosi (pō-tō-sē'), dept., S. W. Bolivia, area 45, pop. 531, and its *, altitude 13,022 ft., pop. 30; silver; # 19:30 S, 65:40 W.

Potsdam (pots'däm), city, 17 mi. S. W. of Berlin, Ger., pop. 62; former royal palaces; # 52:24 N, 13:4 E.

Pottstown (pots'toun), city, S. E. Pa., pop. 20; # 40:15 N, 75:38 W.

Pottsville (pots'vil), city, S. E. C. Pa., pop. 25; # 40:41 N, 76:12 W.

Poughkeepsie (pọ̄-kip'si), city, S. E. New York, on Hudson riv., pop. 40; Vassar College; # 41:47 N, 73:56 W.

Powder (pou'dẽr), riv., C. Wyo. to Yellowstone riv., len. 400 mi.; # 46:35 N, 105:25 W.

Poznan (poz'nän), see **Posen.**

Pozsony (pō'zhŏn-y'), see **Pressburg.**

Pozzuoli (pŏt-sö-ō'lē), *anc.* Puteoli, a S. W. suburb of Naples, Italy, pop. comm. 28; # 40:49 N, 14:7 E.

Prague (präg), see **Praha.**

Praha (prä'hä), *Ger.* **Prague,** city, C. Bohemia, * of Cz-S. until 1939, pop. 848; univ.; # 50:5 N, 14:28 E.

Prahran (prä-ran'), a S. E. suburb of Melbourne, Victoria, Australia, pop. 50; # 37:51 S, 145:3 E.

Praia (prī'ä), spt. city, * of Cape Verde Isls., W. Africa, pop. 21; # 14:53 N, 23:30 W.

Prairie Plains (prā'rĭ plänz), region, C. and N. C. U.S.A. bet. Great Plains and forested region of Ind. and S. Ill.; # 42 N, 91 W.

Prairie Provinces, Manitoba, Saskatchewan and Alberta; # 52 N, 110 W.

Prato (prä'tō), a N. W. suburb of Firenze (Florence), N. C. Italy, pop. 53; cathedral; # 43:53 N, 11:7 E.

Pregel (prä'gel), riv., N. Poland, to Frisches Haff, past Königsberg, len. 180 mi.; # 54:30 N, 20:25 E.

Prenzlau (prents'lou), city, Brandenburg, N. C. Ger., pop. 21; # 53:19 N, 13:25 E.

Pressburg (pres'bůrch) or **Bratislava,** city, S. E. Cz-S., pop. 93; # 48:12 N, 17:8 E.

Preston (pres'tọn), city, Lancastershire, W. C. Eng., pop. 128; # 53:46 N, 2:43 W.

Prestwich (prest'wich), a N. W. suburb of Manchester, W. C. Eng., pop. 19; # 53:32 N, 2:17 W.

Pretoria (prē-tō'ri-ä), city, * of Transvaal and seat of executive government of Union of S. Africa, pop. 74 (45 white); Transvaal Univ.; # 25:45 S, 28:10 E.

Preussen (proi'sẹn), see **Prussia.**

Pribilof (prē-bē-lof'), isls., E. Bering Sea, Alaska, to U.S.A.; fur seal grounds; # 56:30 N, 170 W.

Přibram (przhě'bräm), city, S. W. C. Bohemia, pop. 19; silver mines; pilgrimages; # 49:40 N, 14:2 E.

Prince Edward Island (prins ed'wẽrd ī'lạnd), isl. and prov. thereon, Gulf of St. Lawrence, E. Canada, area 2, pop. 89, * Charlottetown, pop. 12; fox farms; # 46:30 N, 63 W.

Prince of Wales (prins ov wālz), cape, N. W. Alaska, most W. part of N. American mainland, Bering Strait; # 65:30 N, 168 W. — isl., ext. S. Alaska, area 15; copper mines; marble; # 55:30 N, 133 W.

Prince Rupert (prins rö'pẽrt), spt., N. W. Br. Columbia, pop. 6; terminus of Grand Trunk Pacific R.R.; # 54:19 N, 130:20 W.

Princeton (prins'tọn), tn., C. New Jersey, pop. 8; Princeton Univ.; # 40:22 N, 74:40 W. — tn., S. W. Ind., pop. 8; # 38:22 N, 87:35 W.

Pripet (prēp'et), riv., C. Poland to Dnieper riv., len. 350 mi.; wide marshes; # 51:10 N, 30:30 E.

Prishtina (prēsh'ti-nä), tn., C. Serbia, pop. 18; # 42:40 N, 21:8 E.

Prizren (prē'zren), tn., S. C. Serbia, pop. 21; # 42:15 N, 20:45 E.

Progreso (prō-grā'sō), spt., Yucatan, Mex., pop. 6; sisal port; # 21:15 N, 89:45 W.

Prostějov (pros'tye-yof), city, Moravia, C. Cz-S., pop. 31; # 49:29 N, 17:8 E.

Provence (pro-voňs), anc. prov., S. E. Fr.; # 44 N, 6 E.

Providence (prov'i-dẹns), city, N. E. Rhode Island, state *, pop. 254; with suburbs, 712; jewelry; Brown Univ.; State College; # 41:48 N, 71:28 W.

Provo (prō'vō), tn., N. C. Utah, pop. 18; Brigham Young Univ.; # 40:10 N, 111:41 W.

Prussia (prush'ä), *Ger.* **Preussen,** free state, N. Ger., area 113, pop. 38,138, * Berlin, pop. 3,931; # 51 N, 10 E.

Prut (prŏt) or **Pruth** (prŏth), riv., S. Poland, S. to Danube riv., len. 380 mi.; # 45:30 N, 28:10 E.

Przemysl (pzhem'isl), city, S. Poland, pop. 48; # 49:45 N, 22:30 E.

Pskov (pskof), prov., N. W. Russia, area 17, pop. 1,400, and its *, pop. 35; # 57:50 N, 28:20 E.

Pudsey (pud'zi), a W. suburb of Leeds, N. C. Eng., pop. 14; # 53:47 N, 1:41 W.

Pudukotai (pö-dö-kot'ī), native state, Madras prov., S. E.

India, area 1, pop. 427, and its *, pop. 26; # 10:33 N, 78:52 E.

Puebla (pwäb'lä), state, S. E. C. Mexico, area 13, pop. 1,023, and its *, pop. 115; # 19:3 N, 98:10 W.

Pueblo (pweb'lō), city, S. E. C. Colo., pop. 52; smelters; # 38:25 N, 104:40 W.

Puerto México (pwer'tō mä'нē-kō), spt., N. end of R.R. crossing Isthmus of Tehuantepec; # 18 N, 94:30 W.

Puerto Montt (pwer'tō mōnt), spt. tn., S. C. Chile, S. end of R.R., pop. 10; # 41:40 S, 73:20 W.

Puerto Rico (pwer'tō rē'kō), isl., W. Indies, area 3.4, pop. 1,869, * San Juan, pop. 169; ter. of the U.S.A.; # 18:15 N, 66:30 W; formerly also called **Porto Rico.**

Puget (pū'jet), sound, an estuary-fjord, N. W. Wash., and bet. Vancouver isl. and Wash.; # 47:20 N, 122:28 W.

Pullman (půl'mạn), tn., E. Wash., pop. 4; State College of Agri.; # 46:44 N, 117:12 W. — a S. W. industrial dist. of Chicago, Ill.; # 41:42 N, 87:37 W.

Punjab (pun-jäb'), prov., N. W. India, area 99, pop. 20,685, * Lahore, pop. 282, surrounds several native states, area 37, pop. 4,416; # 30 N, 74 E.

Puno (pö'nō), dept., S. E. Peru, area 26, pop. 700, and its *, pop. 12; # 15:53 S, 70:3 W.

Punta Arenas (pŏn'tä ä-rā'näs), most S. city in the world, * of Magallanes ter., Chile, pop. 20; # 53:8 S, 70:56 W.

Punxsutawney (pungk-sö-tô'ni), tn., S. W. C. Pa., pop. 9; # 41 N, 79 W.

Purús (pö-rös'), riv., E. Peru to Amazon riv., len. ab. 1,500 mi.; # 3:50 S, 61:30 W.

Putumayo (pö-tö-mä'yō), riv., Peru and S. E. Colombia, trib. of upper Amazon, len. ab. 750 mi.; # 3 S, 68 W.

Puy-de-Dôme (püē-dē-dōm), vol. cone, S. C. Fr., el. 4,807 ft.; # 45:46 N, 2:57 E. — dept., S. C. Fr., area 3.1, pop. 491, * Clermont-Ferrand, pop. 83; # 45:40 N, 3:15 E.

Pyatigorsk (pyä-tye-gôrsk'), see **Piatigorsk.**

Pyengyang (pyeng'yäng'), **Heijo-Phyengyang** or **Pingyang,** city, N. W. Korea, pop. 87; # 39 N, 126:5 E.

Pyramid (pir'ạ-mid), lake, N. W. Nevada, len. 35 mi.; # 40 N, 119:30 W.

Pyrenees (pir'ẹ-nēz), mt. range bet. Spain and Fr., highest, Pic d'Aneto, el. 11,169 ft.; # 43 N, 1 E.

Pyrénées, Hautes (pē-rä-nä, ōt), see **Hautes-Pyrénées.**

Pyrénées-Orientales (pē-rä-nä-zō-rē-oň-tál), dept., ext. S. Fr., area 1.6, pop. 218, * Perpignan, pop. 54; # 42:35 N, 2:20 E.

Pyrgos (pir'gōs), tn., W. Morea pen., S. W. Greece, pop. 13; # 37:40 N, 21:25 E.

Q

Qirghiz (kir-gēz'), see **Kirghiz.**

Quarnero (kwär-nä'rō), gulf, N. E. Adriatic to Fiume, Italy; len. 60 mi.; # 44:45 N, 14:15 E.

Quebec (kwẹ-bek'), prov., E. Canada, area 707, pop. 2,874, and its *, a spt., pop. 131; Laval Univ.; # 46:48 N, 71:15 W. — **Bridge,** R.R. Cantilever bridge across St. Lawrence riv., len. C. span, 1,800 ft., longest in world; # 46:46 N, 71:15 W.

Quedlinburg (kväd'lin-bůrch), city, Harz mts., C. Ger., pop. 27; # 51:47 N, 11:8 E.

Queen Charlotte (kwēn shär'lọt), group of isls., Pacific oc., N. W. Br. Columbia, area ab. 6; # 53 N, 132 W. — sound bet. N. Vancouver Isl. and the mainland; # 51 N, 127 W.

Queens (kwēnz), county, S. E. New York, area 0.11, pop. 1,298; a Brooklyn borough of New York; # 40:42 N, 73:50 W.

Queensland (kwēnz'lạnd), state, N. E. Australia, area 671, pop. 816, * Brisbane, pop. 78; pop. within 10 mi. radius, 236; # 23 S, 145 E.

Queenstown (kwēnz'tọn), spt. in Cork Harbor, S. E. Ireland, a port of call, pop. 8; official Irish name now Cobh; # 51:53 N, 8:15 W. — tn., lower end of Niagara Gorge, S. Ontario; # 43:10 N, 79:4 W.

Quelpart (kwel'pärt), isl., W. end Korea Strait, area 0.7, pop. 134; to Japan; chief tn., Saishu, pop. 50; # 33:25 N, 126:30 E.

Querétaro (kä-rä'tä-rō), state, C. Mexico, area 4, pop. 220, and its *, pop. 33; # 20:45 N, 100:30 W.

Quetta (kwet'tä), city, N. E. Baluchistan, and its *, pop. 49; # 30:15 N, 67:5 E.

---

fat, fāte, fär, fåll, åsk, fāre; net, mē, hẽr; pin, pīne; not, nōte, mŏve, nôr; up, lūte, půll; oi, oil; ou, out; (lightened) avĭạry, ẹlect, agọny, intọ, ụnite; (obscured) errạnt, operạ, ardẹnt, actọr, natụre; ch, chip; g, go; th, thin; ᴛн, then; y, you;

Quezaltenango (kä-säl-tä-näng′gō), city, S. W. Guatemala, pop. 30; # 14:50 N, 91:50 W.

Quincy (kwin′zi), city, E. C. Mass., pop. 76; # 42:16 N, 71:1 W.—city, W. C. Ill., on Mississippi riv., pop. 40; # 39:50 N, 91:20 W.

Quingur (kwin′gur′), lofty mt. region, Pamirs, C. Asia;— (1) pk., el. ab. 25,146 ft.;—(2) pk., el. 25,200 ft.; # 38:40 N, 75:15 E.

Quintana Roo (kēn-tä′nä rō′ō), ter., E. Yucatan, Mexico, area 19, pop. 11, * Santa Cruz de Bravo, pop. 2; # 19 N, 88 W.

Quito (kē′tō), city, * of Ecuador, pop. 118, el. 9,348 ft.; # 0:10 S, 78:30 W.

Quoddy Head (kwod′i hed), cape, N. E. Me., most E. point of U.S.A.; # 44:45 N, 66:55 W.

R

Raab (räp), riv., S. E. Austria to Danube in Hungary, len. 160 mi.; navigable; # 47:41 N, 17:38 E. — city, now officially **Györ**, at its mouth, pop. 50; # 47:41 N, 17:38 E.

Rabât (rä-bät′), spt. city, * of Fr. Zone, Morocco, pop. 31; # 34:2 N, 6:50 W.

Rabaul (rä′boul), spt., New Britain Isl., Bismarck Arch., * of Ter. of New Guinea, pop. ab. 5; # 4:10 S, 152:20 E.

Race (rās), cape, ext. S. E. Newfoundland; # 46:30 N, 53 W.

Racine (ra̤-sēn′), city, S. E. Wis., on Lake Michigan, pop. 67; # 42:45 N, 87:50 W.

Radcliffe (rad′klif), a N. W. suburb of Manchester, W. C. Eng., pop. 25; # 53:34 N, 2:20 W.

Radnor (rad′nor), county, E. C. Wales, area 0.5, pop. 24, and its *; # 52:13 N, 3:6 W.

Radom (rä′dōm), city, C. Poland, pop. 62; # 51:25 N, 21:9 E.

Ragusa (rä-gö′sä), tn., S. E. Sicily, pop. comm. 38. — (Dubrovnik), spt., S. Dalmatia, Yugoslavia, pop. 13; # 42:38 N, 18:9 E.

Rahway (rä′wā), tn., N. E. New Jersey, pop. 17; # 40:37 N, 74:17 W.

Rainbow Bridge (rān′bō bridj), natural bridge, S. E. Utah; greatest known, span 278 ft., height 309 ft.; Natural Bridges (national monument); # ab. 37:10 N, 110:50 W.

Rainier (rä-nēr′) or **Tacoma**, vol. pk., S. W. Wash., el. 14,408 ft. in Mt. Rainier National Park; # 46:52 N, 121:45 W.

Rajputana (räj-pö-tä′nä), block of 20 native states, N. W. India, area 129, pop. 9,844; # 27:30 N, 74 E.

Raleigh (rä′li), city, C. N. Car., state *, pop. 47; State Agri. College; Shaw Univ.; # 35:45 N, 78:40 W.

Rambouillet (räṅ-bö-yā), vil., 28 mi. S. W. of Paris, pop. 6; castle and famous park; # 48:40 N, 1:50 E.

Rampur (räm-pör′), native state, N. C. India, area 0.9, pop. 454, and its *, pop. 73; # 28:45 N, 79:10 E.

Ramsbottom (ramz′bot″om), a N. suburb of Manchester, W. C. Eng., pop. 15; # 53:39 N, 2:19 W.

Ramsgate (ramz′gāt), spt. city, ext. E. Kent, Eng., pop. 37; seaside resort of London; # 51:22 N, 1:25 E.

Rand (rand), **The** or **Witwatersrand**, rocky ridge near Johannesburg, S. Africa; gold fields; # 26 S, 27:30 E.

Randers (rän′ers), city, N. E. C. Jutland, Denmark, pop. 26, with suburbs, 31; # 56:28 N, 10:2 E.

Randwick (rand′wik), a S. E. suburb of Sydney, New S. Wales, Australia, pop. 51; # 33:56 S, 151:15 E.

Ranger (rān′jėr), city, N. C. Texas, pop. 5; # 32:35 N, 98:45 W.

Rangoon (räng-gön′), spt. city, mouth of Irrawaddy riv., S. Burma, pop. 342; # 16:45 N, 96:5 E.

Rann (run) **of Cutch**, great salt marsh in native state of Cṳtch, W. India; area ab. 9; # 24 N, 70 E.

Rappahannock (rap-a̤-han′ok), riv., W. Va., to Chesapeake Bay, len. 155 mi.; # 38 N, 76:55 W.

Ras Dashan (räs dä-shän′), highest mt. in Abyssinia, N. E. Africa, el. 15,158 ft.; # 13 N, 38:20 E.

Ratibor (rä′tē-bor), city, ext. S. E. Ger., pop. 41; # 50:6 N, 18:13 E.

Ratisbon (rat′is-bon), see **Regensburg**.

Ravenna (ra̤-ven′ä), prov., Emilia, N. E. C. Italy, area 0.7, pop. 258, and its *, pop. 72; # 44:23 N, 12: 20 E.

Rawalpindi (rä-ul-pin′dē), city, ext. N. W. India, pop. 101; # 33:50 N, 73:5 E.

Rawtenstall (rô′ten-stôl′), city, 15 mi. N. of Manchester, Eng., pop. 28; # 53:42 N, 2:18 W.

Reading (red′ing), city, 35 mi. W. of London, S. Eng., pop. 93; # 51:26 N, 1 W. —city, S. E. Pa., pop. 111; # 40:20 N, 75:55 W.

Recife (rä-sē′fä), often called **Pernambuco**, spt. city, * of Pernambuco, N. E. Brazil, pop. 473; # 8 S, 35 W.

Recklinghausen (rek′ling-hou″zen), mining city, S. W. Westphalia, W. Ger., pop. 60; # 51:36 N, 7:11 E.

Redditch (red′ich), a S. suburb of Birmingham, N. C. Eng., pop. 16; # 52:18 N, 1:56 W.

Reden (rä′den), see **Rheden**.

Redfern (red′fėrn), a suburb of Sydney, S. E. Australia, pop. 24; # 33:53 S, 151:12 W.

Redlands (red′landz), tn., S. W. Calif., pop. 14; Univ. of Redlands; 34:5 N, 117:8 W.

Red River of the North, riv., Lake Traverse, S. Dak., to Lake Winnipeg, len. 700 mi.; # 50:25 N, 96:55 W.

Red River of the South, riv., N. Texas to Mississippi riv. near mouth, len. 1,200 mi.; # 31:10 N, 92 W.

Red Sea, narrow sea bet. Arabia and N. E. Africa, len. 1,450 mi., area 178, greatest depth, 7,254 ft.; # 21 N, 38 E.

Reelfoot (rēl′fut), lake, N. W. Tenn., len. 35 mi.; made by earthquake of 1811; # 36:25 N, 89:20 W.

Regensburg (rä′gens-bùrch), city on Danube riv., * Oberpfalz, Bayern, S. Ger., pop. 74; castle; # 49:2 N, 12:5 E.

Regent's Park (rē′jents pärk), park, N. W. London, Eng.; # 51:32 N, 0:9 W.

Reggio di Calabria (red′jo dē kä-lä′brē-ä), prov., Calabria, S. W. Italy, area 1.2, pop. 502, and its *, anc. Rhegium, a spt. on Strait of Messina, pop. 59; # 38:6 N, 15:39 E.

Reggio nell' Emilia (red′jō nel lä-mē′lē-ä), prov., Emilia, N. E. C. Italy, area 0.9, pop. 347, and its *, pop. comm. 83; # 44:43 N, 10:36 E.

Regina (rē-jī′nä), city, S. C. Saskatchewan, prov. *, pop. 53; # 50:30 N, 104:40 W.

Reichenbach (rī-ċhen-bäċh), city, W. Sachsen (Saxony), S. W. C. Ger., pop. 31; # 50:35 N, 12:18 E. — riv., C. Switz., and falls, height 295 ft.; # 46:43 N, 8:11 E.

Reichenberg (rī′ċhen-berċh) or **Liberec**, city, N. E. Bohemia, pop. 35; textiles; # 50:47 N, 15:3 E.

Reims or **Rheims** (rēmz; Fr. raṅs), city, Marne dept., N. E. C. Fr., pop. 77; cathedral; # 49:15 N, 4 E.

Reindeer (rān′dēr), lake, N. E. Saskatchewan, area 2; # 57 N, 102:30 W.

Reinickendorf (rī′ni-ken-dôrf), a N. div. of Berlin, Ger., pop. 104; # 52:34 N, 13:28 E.

Remscheid (rem′shīt), city, 20 mi. N. E. of Köln, W. Ger., pop. 76; cutlery; # 51:13 N, 7:10 E.

Rendina (ren-dē′nä) or **Rendino**, gulf, N. Ægean Sea, N. of Khalkidike pen., N. E. Greece; # 40:45 N, 23:45 E.

Renfrew (ren′frö), county, S. W. Scotland, area 0.2, pop. 300, and its *, a W. suburb of Glasgow, pop. 14; # 55:52 N, 4:28 W.

Rennes (ren), city, N. W. Fr., * of Ille-et-Vilaine, pop. 82; univ.; # 48:5 N, 1:40 W.

Reno (rē′nō), tn., W. Nevada, pop. 21; State Univ.; # 39:32 N, 119:48 W. — (rä′no), riv., Apennines past Bologna to Adriatic Sea, len. 100 mi.; # 44:30 N, 12:14 E.

Rensselaer (ren′se-lėr), tn., E. C. New York, near Albany, pop. 11; # 42:44 N, 73:45 W.

Republican (rē-pub′li-ka̤n), riv., E. C. Colo. to Kansas riv., len. 500 mi.; # 39:5 N, 96:55 W.

Resht (resht), spt. city, Caspian Sea, N. W. Persia, pop. ab. 35; # 37:25 N, 49:45 E.

Resistencia (rä-sēs-ten′syä), city, * of Chaco ter., N. Argentina, pop. 21; # 27:20 S, 58:58 W.

Réunion (rä-ü-nyòṅ), Fr. isl. colony, 420 mi. E. of Madagascar, area 0.1, pop. 172, * St.-Denis, pop. 21; # 21 S, 55:30 E.

Reutlingen (roit′ling-en), city, C. Württemberg, S. W. Ger., pop. 30; # 48:29 N, 9:10 E.

Reval (rä′väl), former name of **Tallinn**.

Revere (re̤-vēr′), a N. suburb of Boston, Mass., pop. 34; # 42:25 N, 71:2 W.

Rewa (rä′wä), native state, C. India, area 13, pop. 1,402, and its *, pop. 21; # 24:35 N, 81:20 E.

Reykjavik (rāk′yä-vik), spt. city, S. W. Iceland, its *, pop. 36; # 64 N, 22 W.

Rhætia (rē'shi-ạ), Roman prov., now Tyrol and E. Switz.; # 47 N, 10 E.

Rhætian Alps (rē'shiạn alps), range, E. Switz., W. Austria; # 46:50 N, 10 E.

Rheden or **Reden** (rā'dẹn), city, S. C. Gelderland, E. C. Neth., pop. 22; # 52 N, 6:6 E.

Rheims (rēmz), see **Reims.**

Rheinland (rīn'länt), same as **Rheinprovinz.**

Rheinpfalz (rīn'pfälts), *Eng.* **Palatinate**, part of Bayern (Bavaria), W. of Rhine riv., S. W. Ger., area 2.4, pop. 926, * Speyer, pop. 25; # 49:19 N, 7:50 E.

Rheinprovinz (rīn'pro-vints), prov., W. Ger., area 9.5, pop. 7,235, * Köln, pop. 690; # 51:30 N, 6:30 E.

Rhenish Bavaria (ren'ish bạ-vā'ri-ạ), see **Rheinpfalz.**

Rheydt (rīt), a S. suburb of Gladbach, Rheinland, W. Ger., pop. 45; # 51:10 N, 6:26 E.

Rhin (Bas-) (rȧṅ, bä), see **Bas-Rhin.**

Rhine (rīn), riv., S. Switz. to N. Sea, Neth., len. 810 mi.

Rhinefall (rīn'fȧl), see **Schaffhausen.**

Rhode Island (rōd ī'lạnd), state, N. E. U.S.A., bet. Mass. and Conn., area 1.2, pop. 713, * Providence, pop. 254; second city, Pawtucket, pop. 76; # 41:30 N, 71:30 W.

Rhodes (rōdz), isl., ext. S. E. Ægean Sea, area 0.6, pop. 30, and its *, a spt., pop. 14; Italian control; # 36 N, 28 E.

Rhodesia (rọ-dē'zhi-ạ), ter. of Br. S. Africa; N. Rhodesia, area 291, pop. 932, (3 white), * Livingstone; 14 S, 29 E. — S. Rhodesia, area 149, pop. 804 (34 white), * Salisbury; # 19 S, 30 E.

Rhodope (rod'ọ-pē), mt. range, S. Bulgaria, highest 9,610 ft.; # 41:40 N, 24 E.

Rhondda (hron'ғнä), city, C. Glamorgan, S. E. Wales, pop. 163; coal; # 51:39 N, 3:29 W.

Rhône (rōn), riv., S. Switz., through Lake Geneva and Fr., to Mediterranean Sea, len. 504 mi.; # 43:20 N, 4:55 E. — dept., S. E. C. Fr., area 1.1, pop. 957, * Lyon, pop. 562; # 45:55 N, 4:30 E.

Rhyl (hril), coastal tn., N. Wales, pop. 13; 20 mi. W. of Liverpool; # 53:19 N, 3:29 W.

Riad (rē-äd'), see **Riyadh.**

Richmond (rich'mọnd), city, E. C. Va., state *, on James riv.; univ.; pop. 193; # 37:30 N, 77:29 W. — a S. W. borough of New York City, pop. 174; # 40:3ᶠ N, 74:9 W. — a W. suburb of London, Eng., pop. 32; # 51:28 N, 0:18 W. — an E. suburb of Melbourne, Aust., pop. 43; # 37:50 S, 145:5 E. — a N. E. suburb of San Francisco, Calif., pop. 24; # 37:56 N, 122:22 W. — city, E. C. Ind., pop. 35; Earlham College; # 39:50 N, 84:55 W.

Riesa (rē'zä), city on Elbe riv., N. C. Sachsen (Saxony), S. Ger., pop. 24; # 51:18 N, 13:18 E.

Riesengebirge (rē'zẹn-gȩ-bėr'gȩ), range bet. Silesia and Bohemia, one of the Sudeten range, highest 5,258 ft.; # 50:45 N, 15:40 E.

Riff (rif), **Er,** hilly coast region of Morocco; # 35 N, 4: 30 W.

Riga (rē'gä), spt. on Gulf of Riga, Baltic Sea, * of Latvia, pop. 285; univ.; # 56:55 N, 24:15 E.

Rilo-Dagh (rē-lō-däg'), mt., W. Bulgaria, el. 9,636 ft.; # 42:2 N, 23:30 E.

Rimini (rē'mẹ-nē), *anc.* Ariminum, spt. Emilia, N. E. C. Italy, pop. comm. 51; # 44:2 N, 12:32 E.

Rio de Janeiro (rē'ō dä zhạ-nā'rō; *Port.* rē'ọ dä zhä-ne'ē̤-rọ), the * and chief city of Brazil, pop. 1,711; beautiful surroundings; fine harbor; univ.; # 23 S, 43:20 W. — state, S. E. Brazil, area 16, pop. 1,559, * Nictheroy, pop. 86; # 22:30 S, 43 W.

Rio de Oro (rē'ō dä ō'rō), Sp. N. W. Africa, area 109, pop. 0.5, * Villa Cisneros; # 24 N, 14 W.

Rio Grande (rē'ō grän'dä), riv., see **Grande, Rio.**

Rio Grande do Norte (rē'ọ grän'de dọ nôr'te), state, N. E. Brazil, area 20, pop. 537, * Natal, pop. 10; # 6 S, 37 W.

Rio Grande do Sul (rē'ọ grän'de dọ sȯl'), state, S. Brazil, area 110, pop. 2,183, * Porto Alegre, pop. 179; # 30:10 S, 52:5 W.

Rioja, La (rȩ-ō'ʜä), prov., N. W. Argentina; see **La Rioja.**

Río Muni (rē'ō mö'nē), see **Guinea, Spanish.**

Rio Negro (rē'ō nā'grō), ter., C. Argentina, area 80, pop. 52; # 39 S, 67:30 W. — riv., see **Negro, Rio.**

Rio Teodora (rē'ō tä-ō-dō'rä), see **Roosevelt,** riv., Brazil.

Ripon (rip'ọn), tn., C. York, Eng., pop. 8; cathedral; # 54:8 N, 1:31 W. — tn., S. E. Wis.; pop. 5; college; # 43:52 N, 88:50 W.

Riukiu or **Ryukyu Islands** (rȩ-ō'kyō'), 55 isls. bet. Japan and Formosa, area 1; # 26:30 N, 128 E.

River Rouge (riv'ẽr rözh), a S. suburb of Detroit, Mich.; pop. 17; # 42:15 N, 83:7 W.

Riverside (riv'ẽr-sīd), suburb of Los Angeles, Calif., pop. 35; # 34 N, 117:22 W.

Riviera (rē-vyä'rä), ext. S. E. Fr. and W. Italy, along Mediterranean Sea; resorts; # 44 N, 9 E.

Rivoli (rē'vō-lē), tn., N. Turin, N. Italy, pop. 8; palace; # 45:3 N, 7:31 E.—vil., near Verona, N. Italy; battle, 1795; # 45:36 N, 10:49 E.

Riyadh (rē-äd'), * of Nejd, C. Arabia, pop. ab. 35; # 24:50 N, 46: 40 E.

Rjukanfos (ryö'kän-fōs), cascade on Maan riv., S. Norway, height 793 ft.; # 59:52 N, 8:31 E.

Roanne (ro-ȧn), city, E. C. Fr., Loire dept., pop. 38; # 46:2 N, 4:5 E.

Roanoke (rō'ạ-nōk), riv., S. W. Va., to Albemarle Sound, 340 mi.; # 36:20 N, 76:30 W. — city, S. W. C. Va., pop. 69; # 37:20 N, 79:55 W.

Robson (rob'sọn), mt. peak, Cariboo range, Canadian Rockies, S. E. Br. Columbia, el. 13,068 ft.; National Park; # 53:5 N, 119:20 W.

Roca (rō'kä), cape, W. extremity of continental Europe, near Lisbon, Portugal; # 38:40 N, 9:31 W.

Rochdale (roch'dāl), a N. E. suburb of Manchester, N. W. C. Eng., pop. 93; # 53:37 N, 2:9 W.

Rochefort (rosh-fôr), city, Charente dept., near coast, W. Fr., pop. 29; # 45:55 N, 1 W.

Rochelle, La (ro-shel), see **La Rochelle.**

Rochester (roch'es-tẽr), city, W. C. New York, pop. 325; photographic and optical equipment and materials; Univ. of Rochester; # 43:15 N, 77:38 W. — city, N. C. Kent, S. E. Eng., pop. 31; cathedral; # 51:24 N, 0:31 E. — tn., S. E. Minn., pop. 26; Mayo hospital; # 44:6 N, 92:30 W. — tn., S. E. New Hampshire, pop. 12; # 43:21 N, 71 W.

Rock (rok), riv., S. E. C. Wis., to Mississippi riv., 330 mi.; # 41:30 N, 90:30 W.

Rockford (rok'fọrd), city, N. C. Ill., on Rock Riv., pop. 85; furniture; Rockford College; # 42:20 N, 89:3 W.

Rockhampton (rok-hamp'tọn), spt. city, E. C. Queensland, Australia, pop. 24; # 23:20 S, 150:30 E.

Rock Hill (rok'hil), tn., N. W. C. S. Car., pop. 15; Winthrop College; # 34:50 N, 81:10 W.

Rock Island (rok ī'lạnd), city, N. W. Ill., on Mississippi riv., pop. 43; Gov. arsenal; Augustana College; # 41:25 N, 90:35 W.

Rockville Center (rok'vil), tn., S. E. New York, pop. 19; # 40:37 N, 73:38 W.

Rocky Mount (rok'i mount), tn., E. C. N. Car., pop. 26; # 35:56 N, 77:47 W.

Rocky Mountains, group of ranges, N. Mex., to N. W. Canada, bet. Great Plains and Great Basin. Individual ranges have distinctive names; # 46 N, 110 W. — National Park, S. Alberta; # 51:10 N, 115:50 W.

Rocky Mountain National Park, N. C. Colo., created 1915; area 0.4; # 40:20 N, 105:42 W.

Rodosto (rō-dos'tō), *anc.* Bisanthe, spt., Sea of Marmora, pop. 19; # 41 N, 27:30 E.

Rogers (roj'ẽrz), mt., highest pk. in Va., el. 5,719 ft.; # 36:37 N, 81:33 W.

Rogue (rōg), riv., Cascade mts., near Crater Lake, W. Ore. to Pacific oc., len. 150 mi.; water power; apples; # 42:25 N, 124:30 W.

Roma (rō'mä), *Eng.* **Rome** (rōm), city, S. W. Italy, pop. 692, * of Italy and of the Roman Catholic Church; univ.; # 41:54 N, 12:25 E.

Romania (rọ-mä'ni-ạ), kingdom, S. E. Europe, area 122, pop. 17,393; * Bucuresci (Bucharest), pop. 345; # 46 N, 26 E.

Rome (rōm), city, W. C. New York, pop. 34; # 43:15 N, 75:30 W. — tn., N. W. Ga., pop. 26; # 34:15 N, 85:10 W. — see **Roma.**

Romney (rom'ni), marsh, Kent, S. E. Eng.; Romney sheep; # 51:3 N, 0:55 E.

Roosevelt (rō'zẹ-velt), dam and reservoir lake, Salt riv. irrigation project, S. W. C. Ariz.; dam, height, 284 ft.,

---

fat, fāte, fär, fȧll, ȧsk, fâre; net, mē, hẽr; pin, pīne; not, nōte, mŏve, nôr; up, lūte, pǔll; oi, oil; ou, out; (lightened) aviᶻry, ē̤lect, agǒny, intọ, ūnite; (obscured) errạnt, operä, ärdẹnt, actọr, natūre; ch, chip; g, go; th, thin; ᴛн, then; y, you;

len. 1,080 ft.; # 33:40 N, 111:10 W. — tn., N. E. C. New Jersey, pop. 11; # ab. 40:20 N, 74:20 W. — riv. (Rio Teodora), large S. trib. of Rio Madeira, C. Brazil, len. 550 mi.; # 5:20 S, 60:25 W.

Roquefort (rŏk-fôr), see **Rochefort.**

Rosa, Monte (rō'sä), pk., Pennine Alps, Italy-Switz., el. 15,217 ft.; second Alpine pk.; # 46 N, 7:53 E.

Rosario (rō-sä'rē-ō), city and port on Paraná riv., N. E. C. Argentina, pop. 511; # 32:55 S, 60:35 W.

Rosetta (rō-zet'ä), spt. tn., near the Rosetta mouth of the Nile riv., Egypt; Rosetta linguistic stone; # 31:22 N, 30:20 E.

Ross and Cromarty (rôs, krom'är-ti), county, N. Scotland, area 3, pop. 67, * Dingwall; # 57:40 N, 4:50 W.

Ross Sea (rôs), gulf of Antarctic oc., S. of New Zealand, len. 1,000 mi.; # 75:30 S, 175 W.

Rostock (ros'tok), spt. on Baltic, Mecklenburg-Schwerin, N. Ger., pop. 78; univ.; ship building; # 54:10 N, 12:10 E.

Rostoff (ros-tof'), city, mouth of the Don riv., S. C. Russia, pop. 121; # 47:10 N, 39:40 E.

Rotherham (roʈн'ẽr-ạm), suburb of Sheffield, C. Eng., pop. 70; # 53:26 N, 1:21 W.

Rothesay (roth'sä), spt., isl. of Bute, S. W. Scotland, pop. 15; # 55:50 N, 5:4 W.

Rotterdam (rot'ẽr-dam), spt., Maas riv., on one of the Rhine mouths, S. W. Neth., pop. 537; # 51:56 N, 4:29 E.

Roubaix (rö-bā'), city, ext. N. E. Fr., 10 mi. N. E. of Lille, pop. 113; # 50:42 N, 3:10 E.

Rouen (rwoñ), city on Seine riv., N. Fr., pop. 124; cathedral; # 49:28 N, 1:5 E.

Roulers (rö-lā'), city, W. Flanders, W. Belgium, pop. 25; # 50:55 N, 3:5 E.

Roumania, see **Romania.**

Rovigo (rō-vē'gō), prov., Venetia, N. E. Italy, area 0.7, pop. 287, and its *, pop. 15; # 45:6 N, 13:37 E.

Roxburgh (roks'bur-ọ), county, ext. S. E. Scotland, area 0.4, pop. 43, * Jedburgh; # 55:25 N, 2:30 W.

Royal Gorge (roi'ạl gôrj), canyon of the Arkansas riv., Rocky Mountains, Canyon City, Colo.; # 38:28 N, 105: 14 W.

Rozendaal (rō'zẹn-däl), city, W. N. Brabant, S. W. Neth., pop. 20; # 51:32 N, 4:29 E.

Ruapehu (rö-ä-pā'hö), vol. pk., N. Isl., New Zealand, el. 9,008 ft.; # 39:15 S, 175:45 E.

Rubicon (rö'bi-kọn), small riv., N. E. C. Italy to the Adriatic sea; # 44:10 N, 12:26 E.

Rudolf (rö'dolf), lake, C. Africa, len. 180 mi.; area 3.5; # 4 N, 36 E.

Rudolstadt (rö'dol-shtät), dist., C. Thuringia, S. C. Ger., area 0.2, pop. 62, and its *, pop. 15; # 50:43 N, 11:22 E.

Rugby (rug'bi), tn., Warwickshire, S. C. Eng.; pop. 25; boys' school; # 52:22 N, 1:16 W.

Rügen (rü'gen), isl., Baltic Sea, part of Pomerania, Ger., area 0.4, pop. 51; # 54:20 N, 13:3 E.

Ruhr (rör), riv., Westphalia, N. Ger., to Rhine riv., len. 150 mi.; # 51:17 N, 6:32 E. — valley, chief coal mining and industrial area of Ger.; # 51:30 N, 6:42 E.

Rumania (rö-mā'ni-ạ), officially **Romania,** q. v.

Rumelia (rö-mē'li-ạ), old name for European Turkey or other Balkan regions. — **E. Rumelia,** southern Bulgaria.

Ruschuk (rös-chök'') or **Russe,** city on Danube riv., N. E. Bulgaria, pop. 42; # 43:50 N, 26 E.

Russenia (rö-sēn'i-ạ), see **Ruthenia.**

Russia (rush'ạ). **1. Russian Socialist Federal Soviet Republic** (**R. S. F. S. R.**), or **Soviet Russia,** republic, more or less the territory of former Russia, E. Europe and W. and N. Asia. **2. Union of Socialist Soviet Republics** (**U. S. S. R.**), union of Russian Socialist Federal Soviet Republic and other soviet republics, area 8,170, pop. 139,760, * Moscow.

Russia, White, soviet republic, S. C. Russia, * Minsk.

Rüstringen (rüs'tring-ẹn), city, N. Oldenburg, N. Ger., adjoining Wilhelmshaven, pop. 47; # 53:35 N, 8:2 E.

Ruthenia (rö-thē'ni-ạ), prov., N. E. Cz.-S., area 4.9, pop. 725; # 48:25 N, 23 E.: absorbed into Hungary in 1938—39.

Rutherglen (ruʈн'ẽr-glen), a S. E. suburb of Glasgow, Scotland, pop. 25; # 55:49 N, 4:13 W.

Rutland (rut'lạnd), county, E. C. Eng., area 0.15, pop. 18,

* **Oakham;** # 52:38 N, 0:40 W. — city, S. W. Ver., pop. **17;** marble; # 43:38 N, 72:58 W.

Ruwenzori (rö-wen-zō'rē), mt. range, boundary Uganda and Belgian Congo, Africa, summit 16,790 ft.; # 1 N, 31 E.

Ryazan (rē-ä-zän'), prov., N. C. Russia, area 16, pop. 2,158, and its *, pop. 41; # 54:42 N, 39:50 E.

Ryukyu, see **Riukiu.** [32; # 56:20 N, 34:19 E.

Rzhev (rzhef), city on Volga riv., Tver, W. C. Russia, pop.

S

Saale (zä'lẽ), riv., S. C. Ger., Bavaria to Elbe riv., len. 250 mi.; # 51:57 N, 11:55 E.

Saalfeld (zäl'felt), dist., S. Thuringia, S. C. Ger., area 0.2, pop. 74, and its *, on Saale riv., pop. 18; # 50:40 N, 11:22 E.

Saane (zä'nẹ), riv., Fribourg, W. Switz., len. 80 mi. to Aar riv.; important valley; # 46:54 N, 7:14 E.

Saar (zär), riv., Vosges mts., Fr., N. to Moselle riv. near Trier, Ger., len. 150 mi.; coal field; # 49:17 N, 6:46 E. — basin, coal; area 0.8; French control 1919—1935, returned to Germany 1935; # 49:20 N, 7 E.

Saarbrücken (zär'brük-ẹn), city on Saar riv., S. Rheinland, S. W. Ger., pop. 125; # 49:15 N, 7 E.

Sabine (sa-bēn'), riv., N. E. Texas to Gulf of Mex. bet. Texas and La., len. 460 mi.; # 29:45 N, 93:50 W.

Sabiyah (sä-bē'yạ), * of Asir, S. W. Arabia; # 17:10 N, 43 E.

Sable (sä'bl), cape, ext. S. W. Florida; # 25:10 N, 81:10 W. — cape, ext. S. Nova Scotia; # 43:30 N, 65:40 W.

Sachsen (zäk'sẹn), Eng. **Saxony,** state, S. Ger., area 5.8, pop. 4,970, * Dresden, pop. 608; # 51 N, 13 E. — prov., Prussia, S. C. Ger., area 9.7, pop. 3,279, * Magdeburg, pop. 288; # 52 N, 11:30 E.

Sacramento (sak-rạ-men'tọ), city, C. Calif., state *, on Sacramento riv., pop. 106; # 38:37 N, 121:30 W. — riv., N. W. Calif. to San Francisco Bay, len. 600 mi.; # 38:5 N, 121:52 W.

Sado (sä'dō), isl., N. W. of C. Honshu isl., Japan, area 0.3, pop. 107; # 38 N, 138:15 E.

Safad or **Safed** (sä'fed), tn., N. W. Palestine, pop. 9; # 32:58 N, 35:28 E.

Safid Rud (sä-fēd' röd'), spt. at mouth of Kizil or Safid riv. (len. 450 mi.), Caspian Sea, N. W. Persia; # 37 N, 49:40 E.

Saga (sä'gä), city, N. W. Kyushiu isl., Japan, pop. 42; # 33:18 N, 130:18 E.

Sagami (sä'gä-mē), bay near Yokohama, S. Honshu isl., Japan; earthquake, Sept. 1, 1923; # 35:15 N, 139:10 E.

Saghalien (sä-gä-lēn'), see **Sakhalin.**

Saginaw (sag'i-nâ), city, N. E. C. Mich., pop. 83; # 43:25 N, 83:55 W. — bay, Lake Huron, N. E. Mich., len. 55 mi.; # 43:45 N, 83:45 W.

Saguenay (sag-ẹ-nā'), riv., S. C. Quebec, to St. Lawrence riv., len. 400 mi.; # 48:20 N, 69:30 W.

Sahama (sä-hä'mä), see **Sajama.**

Sahara (sä-hä'rä), the great desert, N. Africa; # 23 N, 8 E.

Saharanpur (sạ-här-ạn-pör'), city, N. C. India, pop. 62; # 29:55 N, 77:40 E.

Saida (sī'dä), anc. Sidon, spt., S. W. Syria, pop. 15; # 33:35 N, 35:20 E.

Saigon (sī-gōn'), spt., * of Cochin-China, S. Fr. Indo-China, pop. 112; # 10:45 N, 106:33 E.

Saima (sī'mä), largest lake of Finland, area 0.6; # 61:10 N, 28:40 E.

Saint Albans (sänt ȧl'bạnz), tn., Hertfordshire, S. E. Eng., pop. 26; cathedral; # 51:45 N, 0:18 W.

St. Andrews (ȧn'drŏz), tn. on St. Andrews Bay, Fifeshire, E. Scotland, pop. 9; Univ. of St. Andrews; # 56:21 N, 2:48 W.

St. Anthony (ȧn'thọ-ni), falls of Mississippi riv. at Minneapolis; height 18 ft.; flour mills; # 44:56 N, 93:15 W.

St. Augustine (â'gus-tēn), sea coast tn., N. E. Florida, pop. 12; oldest town in United States, 1565; # 29:50 N, 81:25 W.

St. Bernard (bẽr-närd'), mt. pass, Alps; Great, in Pennine Alps, bet. Switz. and Italy, el. 8,108 ft.; # 45:50 N, 7:5 E. — Little, Maritime Alps, bet. Fr. and Italy, el. 7,177 ft.; # 45:40 N, 6:50 E.

St. Boniface (bon'i-fās), suburb of Winnipeg, Manitoba, pop. 13; # 49:54 N, 97:3 W.

St. Catharines (kath'ạ-rinz), city, S. Ontario, pop. 20; # 43:10 N, 79:13 W.

St. Christopher (kris'tọ-fẽr), see **St. Kitts.**

St. Clair (klâr), riv., outlet of Lake Huron, entering Lake St. Clair, len. 30 mi.; # 42:30 N, 82:45 W.

St. Cloud (kloud), city, C. Minn., pop. 24; State Teachers College; granite; # 45:30 N, 94:15 W. — **St.-Cloud** (saṅ klō), a W. suburb of Paris, Fr.; # 48:50 N, 2:15 E.

St. Croix (kroi), riv. bet. Me. and New Brunswick; # 45:25 N, 67:28 W. — riv. bet. Wis. and Minn., len. 200 mi.; 46 N, 92:25 W. — isl., one of three American Virgin Isls., E. of Porto Rico, area .08, pop. 13; # 17:44 N, 64:50 W.

St.-Denis (saṅ dė-nē), a N. suburb of Paris, Fr., pop. 76; burial place of Fr. kings; abbey and church; # 48:56 N, 2:22 E. — city, Réunion isl., S. Indian oc., pop. 22; # 20:55 S, 55:30 E.

St.-Dié (saṅ-dyā), city, N. E. Fr., Vosges dept., ext. E. Fr., pop. 23; # 48:18 N, 6:58 E.

St.-Dizier (saṅ-dē-zyā), city, N. E. Fr., on Marne riv., pop. 18; # 48:35 N, 4:58 E.

St. Elias (sānt ē-lī′as), mt. pk., ext. S. W. Yukon ter., Canada, el. 18,024 ft.; # 60:20 N, 141 W.

St.-Étienne (saṅ tā-tyen), city, S. C. Fr., * of Loire dept., pop. 168; steel; # 45:25 N, 4:25 E.

St. Francis (sānt fran′sis), riv., S. Mo. and N. E. Ark., len. 450 mi.; land survey system of W. C. states commencing from junction of this riv. and the Mississippi; # 34:15 N, 90:30 W.

St. Gallen (sānt gäl′en), canton, N. E. Switz., area 0.8, pop. 296, and its *, pop. 70; cotton, lace; # 47:27 N, 9:24 E.

St. George (sānt jôrj), bay and cape, Newfoundland; # 48:20 N, 59 W. — shallow gulf, S. E. Argentina; # 46 S, 66 W. — tn., * of Grenada, Br. W. Indies, pop. 5; # 12:3 N, 61:45 W.

St. George's (jôr′jez), channel bet. S. W. Wales and S. E. Ireland, width 43 mi.; # 52 N, 6 W.

St.-Germain-en-Laye (saṅ zher-maṅ-oṅ-lā), a W. suburb of Paris, Fr., pop. 20; château; forest; treaties 1570, 1632, 1679, 1919; # 48:54 N, 2:5 E.

St.-Gilles (saṅ zhēl), a S. suburb of Brussels, Belgium, pop. 70; # 50:46 N, 4:20 E.

St. Gotthard (sānt goth′ärd; *Fr.* saṅ go-tär), R.R. tunnel through LePontine Alps, S. C. Switz., len. 9¾ mi.; el. 3,785 ft.; # 46:40 N, 8:40 E.

St. Helena (he-lē′na), Br. isl., S. Atlantic oc., area .05, pop. 3, * Port Jamestown; Napoleon's exile, 1815–1821; # 16 S, 5:40 W.

St. Helens (hel′enz), city, bet. Liverpool and Manchester, W. C. Eng., pop. 107; # 53:27 N, 2:44 W. — vol. mt. pk., S. W. Wash., el. 10,000 ft.; slight eruption, 1867; # 46:12 N, 122:12 W.

St. Helier (hel′yėr), spt. town, C. Jersey, * of Channel Isls., English Channel, pop. 30; # 49:10 N, 2:7 W.

St. Hyacinthe (hī′a-sinth), tn., S. Quebec, pop. 11; # 45:40 N, 72:55 W.

St. John (jon), spt. city, Bay of Fundy, New Brunswick, pop. 47; # 45:16 N, 66:10 W. — riv., N. New Brunswick to Bay of Fundy, at St. John, len. ab. 500 mi.; # 45:50 N, 66:10 W. — isl., American Virgin Isls., W. Indies, area .02, pop. 1; # 18:20 N, 64:42 W. — spt. tn., * of Antigua, Br. W. Indies, pop. 7; # 17:9 N, 61:51 W.

St. John's (jonz), spt. city, S. E. Newfoundland, its *, pop. 38; # 47:40 N, 52:40 W. — riv., C. Florida to Atlantic oc., len. 400 mi.; # 30:40 N, 81:25 W.

St. Joseph (jō′zef), city, N. W. Mo., on Missouri riv., pop. 76; # 39:45 N, 94:50 W. — riv., S. W. Mich. and N. Ind. to Lake Michigan at St. Joseph, Mich. (pop. 7); len. 260 mi.; # 42:3 N, 86:32 W.

St. Kilda (kil′da), a S. suburb of Melbourne, Australia, pop. 39; # 37:52 S, 144:59 E.

St. Kitts (kits), isl., Br. W. Indies, area .06, pop. 37; * Basseterre; # 17:20 N, 62:45 W.

St. Lawrence (lâ′rens), riv., N. E. N. America, Lake Superior to Atlantic oc., len. 760, or if Great Lakes are included, 2,000 mi.; # 49:30 N, 65:30 W. — **Gulf of**, portion of Atlantic oc. W. of Newfoundland and N. of Nova Scotia, area ab. 90; # 48 N, 61 W.

St. Louis (sānt lŏ′is, -lŏ′i), city, E. C. Mo. on Missouri riv., pop. 816, with suburbs ab. 1,368; Washington and St. Louis univs.; # 38:38 N, 90:15 W. — (saṅ lŏ-ē), spt. city, * of Senegal, Fr. W. Africa, pop. 23; # 16:10 N, 16:30 W.

St. Lucia (lŏ′shia, lŏ-sē′a), isl., Windward Isls., Br. W. Indies, area 0.2, pop. 54; * Castries; # 13:50 N, 61 W.

St.-Malo (saṅ-ma-lō), spt., Brittany, N. W. Fr., pop. 12; resort; fishing fleet; # 48:40 N, 2 W.

St. Marylebone (sānt mâr′i-le-bōn), a N. W. borough of London, Eng., pop. 104; # 51:31 N, 0:10 W.

St. Marys (mā′riz), riv., Lake Superior to Lake Huron, with falls, len. 40 mi.; Soo Canal; # 46:31 N, 84:21 W.

St.-Maurice (saṅ-mō-rēs), town, upper Rhône Valley, S. W. Switz., pop. 2.5; # 46:13 N, 7 E.

St.-Mihiel (saṅ-mē-yel), tn., N. E. Fr., on Meuse riv., pop. 5; battle, 1918; # 48:50 N, 5:30 E.

St. Moritz (sānt mō′rits), resort center, Engadine, S. E. Switz., pop. 3; el. 6,037 ft.; # 46:30 N, 9:46 E.

St.-Nazaire (saṅ na-zār), spt. city, Loire estuary, W. Fr., pop. 42; # 47:18 N, 2:15 W.

St.-Nicolas (saṅ nē-ko-lä′), city, 10 mi. W. of Antwerp, Belgium, pop. 35; # 51:10 N, 4:8 E.

St.-Omer (saṅ to-mâr), city, N. Fr., 25 mi. S. E. of Calais, pop. 19; # 50:45 N, 2:15 E.

St.-Ouen (saṅ tö-oṅ), a N. suburb of Paris, Fr., pop. 51; # 48:37 N, 4:24 E.

St. Pancras (sānt pang′kras), a N. W. borough of London, Eng., pop. 211; # 51:32 N, 0:7 W.

St. Paul (pâl), city, S. E. C. Minn., state *, pop. 288; Hamline, Macalester and State Agri. colleges; # 44:58 N, 93:5 W. — (saṅ pol), city, Réunion isl., pop. 20; # 21 S, 55:30 E.

St. Petersburg (pē′tėrz-bėrg), city on Tampa Bay, W. C. Florida, pop. 61; # 27:40 N, 82:45 W. — see **Leningrad.**

St.-Pierre (saṅ pyâr), spt. city, Martinique, destroyed 1902 by eruption of Mt. Pelée; # 14:42 N, 61:10 W. — city, Réunion isl., pop. 28; # 21:20 S, 55:32 E. — tiny Fr. isl., just S. of Newfoundland; pop. 4; # 46:45 N, 56:15 W.

St. Pölten (sānt′ pėl′ten), city, 30 mi. W. of Vienna, Austria, pop. 32; # 48 N, 15:38 E.

St.-Quentin (saṅ-koṅ-taṅ), city, N. Fr., midway bet. Paris and Lille, pop. 37; battles, 1557, 1918; # 49:50 N, 3:15 E.

St. Roque (sānt rōk; rō-kā′), see **São Roque.**

St. Thomas (tom′as), city, S. W. Ontario, pop. 16; # 42:45 N, 81:15 W. — isl., U. S. Virgin Isls., W. Indies, area .03, pop. 11; # 18:20 N, 64:55 W. — (**São Thomé**), isl., Gulf of Guinea, W. Africa, area 0.3, pop. 59, * S. Thomé; a chief source of cocoa; Portuguese; # 20 N, 6:50 E.

St. Vincent (vin′sent), isl., S. Lesser Antilles, Br. W. Indies, area 0.15, pop. 47, * Kingstown, pop. 4; # 13:15 N, 61 W. — cape, S. W. tip of Portugal; # 37:5 N, 8:55 W. — gulf, S. E. S. Australia, to Adelaide; # 35 S, 138 E.

Saïs (sā′is), anc. * of Lower Egypt, on Nile delta; # 30:58 N, 30:45 E.

Sajama (sä-Hä-mä), mt. pk., W. C. Bolivia, el. 21,045 ft.; # 17:59 S, 68:55 W.

Sakai (sä′kī′), city near Kobe, S. Honshu isl., Japan, pop. 105; # 34:35 N, 135:28 E.

Sakhalin (sä-chä-lyēn′), isl., E. of S. Siberia; N. part, Russian, area 15, pop. 14; S. part, Japanese, area 13, pop. 106; # 52 N, 143 E.

Salado (sä-lä′FHō), trib. of Paraná riv., N. Argentina, len. ab. 1,000 mi.; # 31:40 S, 60:30 W. — riv., E. Argentina to Plata estuary, len. 400 mi.; # 36 S, 57 W.

Salamanca (sä-lä-män′kä; *Eng.* sal-a-mang′ka), prov., W. C. Spain, area 4.8, pop. 313, and its *, pop. 33; univ.; # 40:55 N, 5:30 W. — tn., S. W. New York, pop. 9; # 42:8 N, 78:45 W.

Salambria (sä-läm-brē′a), see **Peneius.**

Salamis (sal′a-mis), anc. city, E. Cyprus; # ab. 35 N, 34 E. — isl., Gulf of Ægina, S. of Athens, Greece; naval battle, 480 B.C.; # 37:58 N, 23:30 E.

Salem (sā′lem), spt. city, N. E. Mass., pop. 41; # 42:30 N, 70:58 W. — city, N. W. Ore., state *, pop. 31; Willamette Univ.; # 44:58 N, 123:1 W. — city, S. India, pop. 53; # 11:40 N, 78:20 E. — tn., E. C. Ohio, pop. 12; # 40:55 N, 80:51 W.

Salerno (sä-ler′nō), prov., Campania, S. W. C. Italy, area 1.9, pop. 584, and its *, a spt., pop. 52; # 40:41 N, 14:47 E.

Salford (sâl′ford), a close W. suburb of Manchester, W. C. Eng., pop. 242; # 53:29 N, 2:16 W.

Salina (sa-lī′na), city, C. Kansas, pop. 21; Kan. Wesleyan Univ.; # 38:50 N, 97:40 W.

---

fat, fāte, fär, fâll, ȧsk, fāre; net, mē, hėr; pin, pīne; not, nōte, mŏve, nôr; up, lūte, pull; oi, oil; ou, out; (lightened) aviȧry, ḝlect, agǫny, intǫ, ūnite; (obscured) errȧnt, operȧ, ardḝnt, actǫr, natūre; ch, chip; g, go; th, thin; ᴛʜ, then; y, you;

Salina Cruz (sä-lē′nä krös), spt., Gulf of Tehuantepec, S. Mex., pop. 6; # 16:10 N, 95:20 W.

Salisbury (sålz′ber-i), city on Salisbury Plain, Wiltshire, Eng., pop. 21; cathedral; # 51:3 N, 1:50 W. — tn., W. C. N. Car., pop. 19; # 35:37 N, 80:28 W. — tn., * of S. Rhodesia, pop. 5; # 17:50 S, 31:10 E.

Saloniki (sä-lọ-nē′kẹ) or **Salonica**, *anc.* Thessalonica, spt. city on Gulf of Saloniki, E. Greece, pop. 248; # 40:40 N, 23 E. — dept., E. Greece, pop. 505; # 40:50 N, 22:40 E.

Salop (sal′up), see **Shropshire.**

Salta (säl′tä), prov., N. Argentina, area 48, pop. 154, its *, pop. 31; # 24:40 S, 65:20 W.

Saltcoats (sålt′kōts), spt., Ayr Co., S. W. Scotland, pop. 13; # 55:38 N, 4:47 W.

Saltillo (säl-tēl′yō), city, N. Mexico, * of Coahuila, pop. 35; # 25:25 N, 101:4 W.

Salt Lake, Great (sålt lāk), lake, N. Utah, len. 80 mi., el. 4,218 ft., greatest depth 48 ft.; # 41 N, 112:30 W.

Salt Lake City (sålt lāk sit′i), city, N. C. Utah, pop. 150, state *; State Univ.; # 40:44 N, 111:50 W.

Salto (säl′tō), dept., W. Uruguay, area 4.9, pop. 84, and its *, pop. 30, a riv. port; meat packing; # 31:20 S, 57:40 W.

Salton (sål′tọn), sink, lowest portion of Imperial Valley, S. E. Calif., submerged by Colorado riv., 1906, forming Salton Sea; el. 287 ft. below sea-level; # 33:20 N, 115:45 W.

Salt Range, mt. range, ext. N. W. India; # 32:30 N, 72 E.

Salt River (sålt riv′ẽr), riv., E. Ariz. to Gila riv., len. 200 mi., irrigation project; Roosevelt dam; # 33:20 N, 112:20 W.

Salvador (säl-vä-ᴛʜōr′, sal′vạ-dȯr), republic, Pacific side of C. America, area 13, pop. 1,665, * San Salvador, pop. 102; # 13:30 N, 89 W.

Salween (sal-wēn′), riv., E. Tibet, S. across Burma to Bay of Bengal, len. 1,700 mi.; # 16:30 N, 97:50 E.

Salwin, see **Salween.**

Salzach (zält′säch), riv., Tyrol, Austria, Salzburg to Inn riv., len. 130 mi.; # 48:12 N, 12:55 E.

Salzburg (zälts′bŭrch), prov., W. C. Austria, area 2.8, pop. 223 and its *, pop. 38; # 47:47 N, 13 E.

Samaná (sä-mä-nä′), bay, E. Santo Domingo, len. 40 mi.; splendid harbor; spt. thereon, pop. 9; # 19:20 N, 69:15 W.

Samar (sä′mär), isl., C. Philippines, area 5, pop. 380; # 12:30 N, 124:25 E.

Samara (sȧ-mä′rȧ), prov., S. E. C. Russia, area 40, pop. 2,800, and its *, on Volga riv., pop. 171; univ.; # 53:20 N, 50:20 E.

Samarang (sä-mä-räng′), see **Semarang.**

Samarcand (säm-är-känd′), prov., Russian Turkestan, area 27, pop. 1,184, and its *, pop. 98; # 39:45 N, 66:50 E.

Samaria (sạ-mä′ri-ạ), anc. kingdom and modern prov. bet. Jordan riv. and Mediterranean Sea, and its *; # 32:17 N, 35:12 E.

Samarkand, see **Samarcand.**

Sambre (sän-br), riv., Fr. and Belgium, 100 mi. to Meuse riv.; # 50:27 N, 4:54 E.

Samnium (sam′ni-um), anc. country, C. Italy, E. of Rome; * Bovianum; # 41:30 N, 14:30 E.

Samoa (sạ-mō′ạ), group of isls., N. W. S. Pacific oc., area 1.3, pop. 50; # 13:50 S, 172 W. — **American**, isl. of Tutuila, etc., E. Samoa, area 0.1, pop. 13. — **Territory of W.**, several isls., area 1, pop. 37; New Zealand mandate.

Samos (sä′mos), Greek isl., E. C. Ægean Sea, area 0.2, pop. 69, a dept.; # 37:42 N, 26:45 E.

Samothraki (sä-mō-thrä′kẹ) or **Phengari**, Greek isl., N. E. Ægean Sea, area .07, pop. 5; # 40:25 N, 25:35 E.

Samoyede (sȧ-mo-yed′ye) or **Yalmal**, pen., N. W. Siberia, bet. Gulf of Ob and Kara Sea; len. 380 mi.; # 70 N, 69 E.

Samsun (säm-sȯn′), spt. city, N. Asia Minor, pop. 25; # 41:15 N, 36:20 E.

San (sän), riv., Carpathian Mts. N. to Vistula riv., len. 280 mi.; # 46:20 N, 15 E.

Sana (sä-nä′), city, S. W. Arabia, * of Yemen, pop. ab. 42; # 15:45 N, 44:5 E.

San Angelo (san an′jẹ-lō), tn., W. C. Texas, pop. 26; oil; # 31:25 N, 100:21 W.

San Antonio (san an-tō′ni-ō), city, S. C. Texas, pop. 254; college; # 29:25 N, 98:25 W. — cape, ext. W. Cuba; # 21:50 N, 84:55 W.

San Bernardino (san bẽr-när-dē′nō), city, near Los Angeles, Calif., pop. 44; # 34:7 N, 117:20 W. — mt. range and chief

pk., S. Calif., el. 10,630 ft.; # 34:8 N, 117 W. — pass, Alps of S. Switz., el. 6,766 ft.; # 46:29 N, 9:11 E. — county, S. E. Calif., area 20.2, largest in U.S.A., larger than 4 smallest states; half the size of Va., Ky. or Ohio; pop. 161 (1940); # 35 N, 116 W.

San Cristóbal (sän krēs-tō′bäl), city, ext. W. Venezuela, * of Tachira, pop. 21; # 7:40 N, 72:30 W.

Sancti Spiritus (sängk′tē spē′rẹ-tös), city, C. Cuba, pop. 86; # 22 N, 79:30 W.

Sandhurst (sand′hẽrst), vil., Berkshire, Eng., pop. 3; military college; # 51:21 N, 0:49 W.

San Diego (san dē-ā′gō), spt. city, ext. S. W. Calif., on San Diego Bay, pop. 203; # 32:45 N, 117:10 W.

San Domingo, see **Santo Domingo.**

Sandur (sun-dȯr′), native state, Madras prov., S. W. India, area 0.2, pop. 12; # 15 N, 76:36 E.

Sandusky (san-dus′ki), city, N. C. Ohio, on Sandusky Bay, Lake Erie, pop. 25; # 41:27 N, 82:44 W.

Sandwich Islands (sand′wich), see **Hawaiian Islands.**

Sandy Hook (san′di hủk), cape, near New York City, bet. Lower Bay and Atlantic oc.; # 40:28 N, 74 W.

San Francisco (san fran-sis′kō), spt. city, W. C. Calif., pop. 635, with suburbs ab. 1,429; earthquake and fire, 1906; # 37:45 N, 122:28 W. — **Bay**, estuary, W. C. Calif., len. 50 mi.; entrance is Golden Gate; # 37:50 N, 122:20 W. — mt. mass, N. C. Ariz., highest in state, el. 12,611 ft.; # 35:30 N, 112 W.

Sangay (säng-gī′), active vol., C. Ecuador, el. 19,220 ft.; # 2 S, 78:20 W.

Sangli (säng′glẹ), native state, W. India, area 1.1, pop. 221 and its *, pop. 21; # 16:52 N, 74:36 E.

Sangre de Cristo (säng′grä dä krēs′tō), lofty mt. range, S. C. Colo., to N. C. New Mex.; highest, Blanca pk., el. 14,390 ft.; # 37 N, 105:30 W.

San Joaquin (san wä-kēn′), riv., S. E. Calif. to Sacramento riv., near San Francisco Bay, len. 350 mi.; # 38:3 N, 121:52 W.

San José (sän ʜō-sā′), Costa Rica, pop. 151, and its *, pop. 71, the federal *; # 9:55 N, 84:10 W. — (san họ-zā′), city, S. E. C. Calif., pop. 68; prunes; St. Joseph College; # 37:21 N, 121:54 W.

San Juan (sän (*Eng.* san) ʜō-än′), spt. city, N. E. Puerto Rico, its *, pop. 169; # 18:30 N, 66:10 W. — prov., W. C. Argentina, area 38, pop. 141, and its *, pop. 17; # 31:30 S, 68:34 W. — mt. range, S. W. Colo. and N. New Mexico, several peaks above 14,000 ft.; # 37:30 N, 107 W. — isls., Puget Sound, N. W. Wash.; # 48:30 N, 123:2 W.

Sankt Moritz (zängkt mō′rits), see **St. Moritz.**

San Luis (sän lö-ēs′), prov., C. Argentina, area 29, pop. 138, and its *, sometimes called Mercedes, pop. 26; # 33:18 S, 66:21 W. — (*Port* São Luiz), often called **Maranhão**, spt. city, N. E. Brazil, * of Maranhão, pop. 53; # 2:30 S, 44:30 W. — **Park**, mt. basin, S. C. Colo.; # 37:45 N, 106 W.

San Luis Potosi (sän lö-ēs′ pō-tō-sē′), state, N. C. Mexico, area 24, pop. 446, and its *, pop. 74; # 22:10 N, 101 W.

San Marino (sän mä-rē′nō), republic, N. E. C. Italy, oldest state in Europe, area .04, pop. 12; # 43:56 N, 12:25 E.

San Matias (sän mä-tē′äs), gulf in N. E. Patagonia, Argentina; # 42 S, 64 W.

San Miguel (sän mē-gel′), city, E. San Salvador, C. America, pop. 34. — vol. near city, el. 6,000 ft.; # 14:30 N, 88:15 W.

San Pablo (san pä′blō), bay, the N. portion of San Francisco bay, Calif.; # 38:5 N, 122:25 W.

San Pedro (san pē′drō), spt. portion of Los Angeles, Calif., on San Pedro bay and channel; # 33:45 N, 118:12 W. — port on Paraná riv., Argentina, pop. 25; # 33:38 S, 59:40 W.

San Pier d'Arena (sän pyär′ da-rä′nä), a W. suburb of Genoa, Italy, pop. 42; # 44:24 N, 8:56 E.

San Remo (sän rä′mō), spt., Riviera, Liguria, N. W. Italy, pop. comm. 23; resort; # 43:48 N, 7:47 E.

San Roque (sän rō′kä), see **São Roque.**

San Salvador (sän säl-vä-ᴛʜōr′), isl., E. Bahamas, pop. 4; first land seen by Columbus; # 24 N, 74:30 W. — city, * of Salvador, pop. 102; # 13:40 N, 89:15 W.

San Sebastian (sän sä-bäs-tē-än′), spt. city, N. Spain, W. end of Pyrenees; resort; summer residence of the court; pop. 66; # 43:18 N, 2 W.

Santa Ana (san′tä an′ạ; *Sp.* sän′tä ä′nä), city, N. W. Salvador, C. America, pop. 71; # 14 N, 89:35 W. — city, S. of Los Angeles, Calif., pop. 32; # 33:46 N, 117:52 W.

Santa Barbara (san'tạ bär'bạ-rạ), city, coast of S. Calif., pop. 35; Spanish mission; earthquake, 1925; # 34:25 N, 119:45 W. — three isls. 25 mi. off this coast, and the Channel bet.; # 33:29 N, 119:4 W.

Santa Catalina (san'tạ ka-tạ-lē'nạ), isl. 20 mi. long, off the coast of S. Calif.; tourist resort; # 33:20 N, 118:30 W.

Santa Catharina (sän'tä kä-tä-rē'nä), Brazilian state, area 37, pop. 669, * Florianopolis; # 27 S, 51 W.

Santa Clara (san'tạ klär'ạ; Sp. sän'tä klä'rä), prov., C. Cuba, area 8, pop. 701, and its *, pop. 69; # 22:22 N, 80:2 W. — valley, N. Calif.; prunes; # 37:22 N, 122 W.

Santa Cruz (san'tạ kröz), spt. city, Tenerife isl., * of Canarias (Canary Isls.), Spain, pop. 78; # 28:27 N, 16:15 W. — dept. E. Bolivia, area 145, pop. 382, and its *, pop. 18; # 17:30 S, 62 W. — ter., S. Argentina, area 109, pop. 13; # 48 S, 70 W. — tn. on Monterey Bay, W. C. Calif., pop. 17; # 37 N, 122:2 W. — largest of Santa Barbara isls., S. Calif., len. 25 mi.; # 34 N, 119:45 W.

Santa Fé (san'tạ fā; Sp. sän'tä fā'), tn., N. C. New Mexico, state *, pop. 20; founded ab. 1605; # 35:45 N, 105:55 W. — prov., N. E. C. Argentina, area 51, pop. 1,123, and its *, pop. 60; # 31:40 S, 60:20 W.

Santa Fe Lines, the Atchison, Topeka, and Santa Fe Railway System; Chicago southwest to Pacific Coast, etc., total mileage 12,210.

Santa Isabel (sän'tä ē-sä-bel') or **Mitre**, mt. pk., near * of Spanish Guinea, Africa, el. 9,185 ft.; # 1:21 N, 9:55 E.

Santa Maria (sän'tä mä-rē'ä), vol. pk., W. Guatemala, el. ab. 12,500 ft.; # 14:47 N, 91:34 W.

Santa Monica (san'tä mon'i-kạ), seaside resort near Los Angeles, Calif., on Santa Monica Bay, pop. 54; # 34:1 N, 118:29 W.

Santander (sän-tän-dãr'), prov., N. Spain, area 2.1, pop. 335, and its *, a spt., pop. 74; # 43:25 N, 3:55 W. — **Sur** and **Norte**, depts., N. E. Colombia, combined area 24, pop. 680; # 6:50 N, 73:30 W; 7:50 N, 73 W.

Santee (san-tē'), riv., junction of Wateree and Congaree riv., S. Car., to Atlantic oc., len. 200 mi.; # 33:10 N, 79:10 W.

Santiago (sän-tē-ä'gō), prov., C. Chile, area 6, pop. 685, and its *, pop. 696, the * of Chile; univ.; # 33:25 S, 70:45 W.

Santiago de Cuba (sän-tē-ä'gō dä kö'bä), spt. city, S. E. Cuba, pop. 74; battles, 1898; # 20 N, 75:45 W.

Santiago del Estero (sän-tē-ä'gō del es-tā'rō), prov., N. C. Argentina, area 55, pop. 322, and its *, pop. 23; # 27:50 S, 64:17 W.

Santiago de los Caballeros (sän-tē-ä'gō dä lōs kä-bäl-yä'-rōs), city, N. Dominican Republic, Haiti; pop. 17; # 19:30 N, 70:45 W.

Santo Domingo (sän'tō dō-mēng'gō), city, * of Dominican Republic, Haiti, pop. 71; founded 1496; # 18:30 N, 70 W; in 1936 renamed **Ciudad Trujillo.** See also **Haiti.**

Santorin (sän-tō-rēn'), Greek isl., Ægean Sea, area .03, pop. 16; spt. Thera; # 36:25 N, 25:28 E.   [# 23:55 S, 46:20 W.

Santos (sän'tŏsh), city, São Paulo, S. E. Brazil, pop. 160;

San Vicente (sän vē-sen'tä), city, Salvador, C. America, pop. 31; # 13:39 N, 88:46 W.

São Francisco (souň fräň-sēsh'kö), riv., E. Brazil, Minas Geraes, 1,800 mi. to Atlantic oc.; with falls, height 276 ft., in lower part; # 10:30 S, 36:25 W.

Saône (sōn), riv., Vosges mts., E. Fr., to Rhône riv. at Lyon, len. 300 mi.; # 45:45 N, 4:55 E.

Saône (Haute), see **Haute-Saône.**

Saône-et-Loire (sōn-ā-lwär), dept., S. E. C. Fr., area 3.3, pop. 555, * Mâcon, pop. 20; # 46:35 N, 4:30 E.

São Paulo (souň pou'lö), state, S. E. Brazil, chief source of world's coffee, area 95, pop. 4,592, and its *, the third largest city in S. America, pop. 1,120; # 23:35 S, 46:37 W.

São Paulo de Loando, see **Loanda.**

São Roque (souň rō'kạ), cape, N. E. Brazil, # 5:26 S, 35:15 W.

São Salvador (souň säl-vä-dōr'), see **Bahía.**

São Thomé (souň tō-mä'), see **Saint Thomas.**

Sapporo (säp'pō-rō), inland city, S. W. Yezo isl., Japan, pop. 145; univ.; # 43:5 N, 141:15 E.

Sapulpa (sạ-pul'pạ), tn., N. E. Okla., pop. 12; # 36 N, 96:9 W.

Saragossa (sar-ạ-gos'ạ), see **Zaragoza.**

Sarajevo or **Sarayevo** (sä-rä'yạ-vō), city, Bosnia, E. C. Yugoslavia, pop. 66; # ab. 43:50 N, 18:25 E.

Saranac (sar'ạ-nak), three lakes, Adirondack mts., New York; resorts; # 44:16 N, 74:8 W.

Saratoga Springs (sar-ạ-tō'gä), tn., E. C. New York, pop. 14; resort; Skidmore College; # 43:7 N, 73:45 W.

Saratov (sä-rä'tof), prov., S. E. Russia, area 37, pop. 3,100, and its *, on the Volga riv., pop. 206; # 51:35 N, 46 E.

Sarawak (sä-rä'wäk), a Br. protectorate, N. W. Borneo, area 42, pop. 600, * Kuching, pop. 30; # 2:30 N, 113 E.

Sardinia (sär-din'i-ạ), Italian isl., W. of Italy, S. of Corsica, area 9.3, pop. 864; # 40 N, 9 E.

Sardis (sär'dis), anc. * of Lydia, W. Asia Minor; ruins; # ab. 39 N, 27 W.

Sargasso Sea (sär-gas'ō sē), part of N. Atlantic oc. E. of W. Indies; occasionally containing much floating seaweed; # 30 N, 60 W.

Sarine (sä-rēn), see **Saane.**

Sarmatia (sär-mä'shi-ạ), anc. name of W. Russia and Poland.

Sarnia (sär'ni-ạ), city, S. E. of Lake Huron, Ontario, opp. Port Huron, Mich., pop. 15; # 42:58 N, 82:28 W.

Saros (sä'ros), gulf, N. E. Ægean Sea, N. of Gallipoli pen.; # 40:35 N, 26:30 E.

Sarre, see **Saar.**

Sarthe (sårt), dept., N. W. C. Fr., area 2.4, pop. 389, * Le Mans, pop. 72; # 48 N, 0:10 E.

Sasebo (sä'se-bō), spt. city, N. W. Kyushiu isl., Japan, pop. 96; naval base; # 33:15 N, 129:45 E.

Saskatchewan (sas-kach'ē-wạn), prov., W. C. Canada, area 252, pop. 922, * Regina, pop. 53; # 54 N, 106 W. — riv., S. Alberta to Lake Winnipeg, len. 1,205 mi.; # 53:30 N, 100:20 W.

Saskatoon (sas-kạ-tōn'), city, S. C. Saskatchewan, pop. 26; provincial univ.; # 52:9 N, 106:45 W.

Sassari (säs'sä-rē), prov., N. Sardinia, area 4.1, pop. 334, and its *, pop. 43; # 40:44 N, 8:34 E.

Satsuma (sät-sö'mä), prov., S. W. Kyushiu isl., Japan; porcelain; Satsuma oranges; # 31:50 N, 130:20 E.

Satul Mare (sät'öl mä're) or **Satmar**, city, N. W. Romania, pop. 35; # 47:48 N, 22:53 E.

Sault Ste. Marie (sö sänt mä'ri), city, E. end of Lake Superior, Ontario, pop. 21; # 46:31 N, 84:20 W. — tn., N. Mich., pop. 16, opposite; # 46:30 N, 84:21 W.

Sault Ste. Marie Canal, three parallel canals on St. Marys riv., bet. Lakes Superior and Huron, len. 1.6 mi.; first constructed 1855, extended 1895; traffic heaviest in the world; # 46:30 N, 84:21 W.

Saumur (sō-mür), tn., Maine-et-Loire, N. E. Fr., pop. 16; castle; cavalry school; # 47:15 N, 0:15 W.

Sava (sä'vä) or **Save**, riv., N. W. Yugoslavia, E. to Danube riv. at Belgrade, len. 600 mi.; # 44:50 N, 20:30 E.

Savaii (sä-vi'ē), largest isl. of Samoa, area 0.6; New Zealand mandate; # 13:40 S, 172:35 W.

Savannah (sạ-van'ä), spt. city, S. E. Ga., pop. 96; cotton port; naval stores; # 32:4 N, 81:6 W. — riv., N. W. S. Car., bet. Ga. and S. Car., to Atlantic oc., len. 450 mi.; # 32:3 N, 80:55 W.

Save (säv), see **Sava.**

Savoie (sä-vwä), dept., Alps, S. E. Fr., area 2.4, pop. 225, * Chambéry, pop. 17; # 45:30 N, 6:20 E.

Savoie (Haute), see **Haute-Savoie.**

Savona (sä-vō'nä), coastal city, N. Genoa, N. Italy, pop. comm. 50; resort; # 44:17 N, 8:30 E.

Sawatch (sạ-wach'), or **Saguache**, mt. range, C. Colo., highest, Mt. Elbert, 14,420 ft.; # 38:30 N, 106:30 W.

Saxe (saks), divs. of Thuringia, S. C. Ger., includes Saxe-Altenburg, pop. 41; Saxe-Meiningen, pop. 270; and Saxe-Weimar, pop. 433; # 51 N, 12 E.

Saxony (sak'sọ-ni), see **Sachsen.**

Sayan (sä-yàn'), mt. range, C. Asia, W. border of Mongolia; highest 11,447 ft.; 53 N, 93 E.

Scafell (skä-fel'), mt. pk., Cumberland, N. W. Eng., highest in Eng., el. 3,210 ft.; # 54:27 N, 3:13 W.

Scandinavia (skan-di-nā'vi-ạ), Norway, Sweden and Denmark.

Scania (skā'ni-ạ) or **Skåne**, region, S. Sweden; # 56 N, 13 E.

Scarborough (skär'bu-rō), spt. resort city, Yorkshire, N. E. Eng., pop. 46; # 54:17 N, 0:26 W.

---

fat, fāte, fär, fåll, åsk, fãre; net, mē, hėr; pin, pīne; not, nōte, mōve, nôr; up, lūte, půll; oi, oil; ou, out; (lightened) aviȧry, ėlect, agŏny, intọ, ūnịte; (obscured) errạnt, operạ, ardẹnt, actọr, natụre; ch, chip; g, go; th, thin; ᴛʜ, then; y, you;

Schaerbeek (skär'bāk), an E. suburb of Brussels, Belg., pop. 109; #50:50 N, 4:22 E.

Schaffhausen (shäf'hou-zẹn), canton, ext. N. Switz., area 0.1, pop. 50, and its *, on Rhine riv., pop. 20; #47:41 N, 8:38 E. — falls of Rhine nearby, height 62 ft.; #47:43 N, 8:34 E.

Schaumburg-Lippe (shoum'bůrch-lip'ė), state, C. Ger., area 0.1, pop. 49, * Bückeburg, pop. 6; #52:22 N, 9:10 E.

Schelde (skel-de'), see **Scheldt.**

Scheldt (skelt), E. and W. arms of the sea, Zeeland, S. Neth., len. 30 and 50 mi.; #51:40 N, 3:45 E. — riv., see **Escaut.**

Schemnitz (shem'nits), city, S. C. Cz.-S., pop. 16; mines; #48:27 N, 18:54 E.

Schenectady (skẹ-nek'tạ-di), city, E. C. New York, pop. 88; electrical and R.R. equipment; Union College; #42:48 N, 73:55 W.

Schiedam (skē-däm'), a W. suburb of Rotterdam, Neth., pop. 43; #51:54 N, 4:23 E.

Schleswig (shläs'vich), spt. on Baltic, * of Schleswig-Holstein state, N. Ger., pop. 20; #54:32 N, 9:35 E.

Schleswig-Holstein (shläs'vich hōl'shtīn), prov., Prussia, base of Danish pen., area 5.8, pop. 1,535; * Schleswig, pop. 20; #54:30 N, 9:30 E.

Schmalkalden (shmäl'käl-dẹn), tn., Hessen-Nassau, S. W. Prussia, pop. 10; Protestant League, 1531; #50:43 N, 10:28 E.

Schönebeck (shẹ'nė-bek), tn., Saxony, S. C. Ger., pop. 23; salt works; chemicals; #52 N, 11:45 E.

Schöneberg (shẹ'nė-berch), a S. div. of Berlin, Ger., pop. 222; #52:29 N, 13:18 E.

Schouwen (skou'ẹn), isl., Zeeland, S. Neth., len. 20 mi.; #51:40 N, 3:45 E.

Schuylkill (skōl'kil), riv., S. E. Pa., entering Delaware riv. in Philadelphia, len. 120 mi.; #39:53 N, 75:12 W.

Schwaben (shvä'bẹn), *Eng.* **Swabia,** S. W. div. of Bayern (Bavaria), S. W. Ger., area 3.9, pop. 865, * Augsburg, pop. 166; #48:10 N, 10:30 E.

Schwarzwald (shvärts'vält), *Eng.* **Black Forest,** low mts., ext. S. W. Ger., highest Feldberg, el. 4,950 ft.; #48 N, 8 E; — div., Württemberg, S. W. Ger., area 1.8, pop. 584; #48:30 N, 8:50 E.

Schweidnitz (shvīt'nits), city, S. E. Ger., pop. 30; #50:51 N, 16:28 E.

Schweinfurt (shvīn'fůrt), city on Main riv., N. W. Bayern (Bavaria), S. W. Ger., pop. 36; #50:4 N, 10:14 E.

Schweiz (shvīts), **Suisse,** or **Svizzera,** Ger., Fr. and It. official names for Switzerland.

Schwelm (shvelm), an E. suburb of Barmen, Westfalen, W. Ger., pop. 22; #51:17 N, 7:17 E.

Schwerin (shvä-rēn'), city, * of Mecklenburg-Schwerin, N. Ger., pop. 46; #53:37 N, 11:25 E.

Schwyz (shvēts), canton, C. Switz., area 0.4, pop. 60, and its *, pop. 8; #47:3 N, 8:40 E.

Scilla (shēl'lä), headland, Italian side of Strait of Messina; #38:14 N, 15:43 E.

Scilly (sil'i), group of 141 small isls., 30 mi. S. W. of Land's End, Eng., part of Cornwall, pop. 2; #49:55 N, 6:20 W.

Scio (sī'ō or shē'ō), see **Chios.**

Scioto (sī-ō'tō), riv., N. C. Ohio to Ohio riv., 225 mi.; #38:35 N, 83 W.

Scotia (skō'shi-ạ), anc. name of Scotland. — suburb of Schenectady, N. Y., pop. 8; #ab. 42:48 N, 73:55 W.

Scotland (skot'lạnd), div. of Great Britain, N. Britain, area 30, pop. 4,882, * Edinburgh, pop. 428; #56 N, 4 W.

Scottish Highlands (skot'ish hī'lạndz), rugged region, N. Scotland, summit Ben Nevis, el. 4,406 ft.; #57 N, 4 W.

Scottish Lowlands (lō'lạndz), lowland across S. C. Scotland, Glasgow to Edinburgh; #56 N, 4 W.

Scott's Bluff (skots bluf), national monument, highest point in Neb. on old Oregon Trail and N. Platte riv. — tn., nearby, pop. 12; #41:53 N, 103:41 W.

Scranton (skran'tọn), city, N. E. C. Pa., pop. 140; anthracite; silk; #41:25 N, 75:40 W.

Scutari (skö'tạ-rẹ), lake, Montenegro-Albania, len. 30 mi. — Albanian city, thereon; pop. 32; #42:5 N, 19:30 E. — see **Skutari.**

Scylla, see **Scilla.**

Scyros, see **Skyros.**

Scythia (sith'i-ạ), anc. name of region N. and E. of Caspian Sea; #41 N, 70 E.

Seattle (sẹ-at'l), city, W. C. Wash., on Puget Sound, pop. 368 (1940); State Univ.; #47:37 N, 122:20 W.

Sebastopol (sẹ-bas'tọ-pōl), spt. city, S. Crimea, S. Russia, pop. 71; #44:35 N, 33:30 E.

Sechwan (sä-chō-än'), see **Szechwan.**

Secunderabad (sẹ-kun″dė-rä-bäd'), see **Sikandarabad.**

Sedalia (sẹ-dā'li-ạ), city, W. C. Mo., pop. 20; #38:44 N, 93:12 W.

Sedan (sẹ-däň), city, N. E. Fr., on Meuse riv., pop. 18; battles, 1870; #49:40 N, 5 E.

Seeland (sē'lạnd) or **Sjaelland,** isl., E. Denmark, area 2.9, pop. 1,004, * Copenhagen, pop. 561; #55:30 N, 11:45 E.

Segovia (sä-gō'vi-ä), prov., N. C. Spain, area 2.6, pop. 165, and its *, pop. 15; #40:54 N, 4:10 W.

Seine (sān), riv., C. Fr., through Paris to English Channel, len. 480 mi.; #49:30 N, 0:30 E. — dept., N. C. Fr., area 0.2, pop. 4,412, * Paris, pop. 2,906 ; #48:52 N, 2:20 E.

Seine-et-Marne (sān-ā-màrn), dept., N. Fr., area 2.3, pop. 349, * Melun; #48:40 N, 3 E.

Seine-et-Oise (sān-ā-wäz), dept., N. Fr., area 2.2, pop. 922, * Versailles, pop. 65; #48:40 N, 2 E.

Seine-Inférieure (sān-aň-fā-ryēr), dept., N. Fr., area 2.4, pop. 881, * Rouen, pop. 124; #49:40 N, 1 E.

Seistan (sä-ēs-tän'), lowland, lake and marsh, E. Persia, and dist., W. Afghanistan; #30:50 N, 61:10 E.

Selangor (se-läng-gōr'), one of Federated Malay States, area 3, pop. 401, * Kuala Lumpur, pop. ab. 80; #3 N, 101:30 E.

Selenga (sä-leng'gä), riv., Khangai Mts., Mongolia to Lake Baikal, len. 700 mi.; #52:15 N, 106:30 E.

Seleucia (sel-ū'ṣi-ạ), anc. coast city, Syria; #ab. 35 N, 36 E. — anc. city of Babylonia; #33 N, 44:25 E.

Selkirk (sel'kẻrk), county, S. E. Scotland, area 0.2, pop. 21, and its *, pop. 6; #55:32 N, 2:50 W. — mt. range, S. E. Br. Columbia, highest Sir Donald, el. 10,808 ft.; #51 N, 117 W.

Selma (sel'mä), city, S. C. Ala., on Alabama riv., pop. 20; #32:30 N, 87:5 W.

Semarang (sem-ä-räng') or **Samarang,** spt., N. C. Java, pop. 158, * of Semarang residency, pop. ab. 2,700; #7 S, 110:30 E.

Semeru (sem'ẻr-ö), vol., E. Java, el. 12,044 ft.; #8:5 S, 112:55 E.

Semipalatinsk (se-mẹ-pä-lä-tyẹnsk'), prov., steppe region, S. W. Asia, area 178; pop. 1,225, and its *, pop. 44; #50:28 N, 80:13 E.

Semmering (zem'ẻr-ing), pass, ext. W. Austria, el. 2,940 ft., and tunnel; R.R. bet. Vienna and Trieste; #ab. 47:36 N, 15:50 E.

Sendai (sen-dī') or **Sensai,** city, N. E. Honshu isl., Japan, pop. 143; univ.; #38:15 N, 141 E.

Seneca (sen'ẹ-kạ), lake, falls, and tn. (pop. 6), S. C. New York; #42:50 N, 76:50 W.

Senegal (sen-ẹ-gâl'), *Fr.* **Sénégal** (sä-nä-gàl), riv., Fr. W. Africa, to Atlantic oc. at St. Louis, len. 900 mi.; #16:10 N, 16:30 W. — Fr. colony, a div. of Fr. W. Africa, area 74, pop. 1,266, * St. Louis, pop. 23; #15 N, 14 W.

Senegambia (sen-ẹ-gam'bi-ạ), region bet. Senegal and Gambia rivs., Fr. W. Africa; #15 N, 15 W.

Sennar (se-när'), dist. bet. White and Blue Nile rivs.; #11:50 N. 33:40 E. — prov. therein, and its *, pop. 8; #13:35 N, 33:34 E.

Senta (sen'tä), city on Tisza riv., N. E. Yugoslavia, pop. 31; #45:53 N, 20:4 E.

Seoul (sẹ-öl'), *Jap.* **Keijo-fu** (kā'jō-fö), city, W. C. Korea, * Chosen, pop. 271 (73 Japanese); #37:45 N, 127 E.

Sequoia National Park (sẹ-kwoi'ạ), S. C. Calif., area 0.2; "Big Trees"; #36:30 N, 118:45 W.

Seraing (se-raň), a W. suburb of Liége, E. C. Belgium, pop. 37; #50:37 N, 5:32 E.

Serang (sä-räng'), see **Ceram.**

Serb-Croat-Slovene (sẻrb-krō'at-slō-vēn'), state, see **Yugoslavia.**

Serbia (sẻr'bi-ạ), div. of S. E. Yugoslavia, area 37, pop. 4,250, * Beograd, pop. 112; #43:10 N, 22 E.

Seres, see **Serres.**

Sereth (se-ret'), riv., N. Romania S. to Danube riv., len. 270 mi.; #45:30 N, 27:40 E.

Sergipe (ser-zhē'pe), state, N. E. Brazil, area 8, pop. 477, * Aracajú, pop. 37; # 10:40 S, 37 W.

Seriphos (se-rē'fos), Greek isl., Cyclades, S. W. Ægean sea; pop. 4; iron ore; # 37:8 N, 24:30 E.

Serra da Estrella (ser'rä dä esh-trel'lä), mt. range, C. Portugal, summit 6,540 ft.; # 40:25 N, 7:30 W.

Serres or **Seres** (se'res), nome, E. Macedonia, N. E. Greece, area 1.5, pop. 119, and its *, pop. 14; # 41:5 N, 23:35 E.

Servia (sěr'vi-ä), see **Serbia**.

Sétif (sā-tēf), city, Algeria, pop. 31; # 36:11 N, 5:25 E.

Setúbal (sā-tö'bäl), spt. on Setúbal Bay, 20 mi. S. E. of Lisbon, Portugal, pop. 37; # 38:31 N, 8:53 W.

Sevanga (sye-väng'gä), lake, S. W. Azerbaijan, S. W. Asia, len. 60 mi.; # 40:20 N, 45:20 E.

Sevastopol, see **Sebastopol**.

Seven Falls, series of cascades S. W. of Colorado Springs, C. Colo., total height 266 ft.; # ab. 38:47 N, 104:55 W.

Severn (sev'ĕrn), riv., S. Wales and S. W. Eng., to Bristol Channel, len. 210 mi.; # 51:30 N, 2:40 W.

Sevilla (sā-vēl'yä), *Eng.* **Seville** (sev'il or sẹ-vil'), prov., S. W. Spain, area 5.4, pop. 748, and its *, pop. 227; univ.; # 37:20 N, 5:50 W.

Sèvres, Deux, see **Deux-Sèvres**.

Sewanee (sẹ-wä'nē), village, S. Tenn., pop. 1; Univ. of the South; # 35:11 N, 85:56 W.

Seward (sū'ạrd), pen. bet. Norton and Kotzebue Sounds, W. Alaska; # 65:30 N, 164 W.

Seychelles (sā-shel'), Br. isls. in Indian oc., 600 mi. N. E. of Madagascar, area 0.2, pop. 25; # 4 S, 55 E.

Sfax (sfäks), spt. city, Tunis, N. Africa; pop. ab. 50; # 34:43 N, 10:41 E.

Shahjahanpur (shä-jạ-hän'pör), city, N. C. India, pop. 73; # 27:45 N, 79:50 E.

Shahpur (shäh-pör'), anc. city, S. W. Persia; # ab. 32 N, 50 E.

Shamo (shä'mō'), a Chinese name for the Desert of Gobi.

Shamokin (shạ-mō'kin), city, S. E. C. Pa., pop. 19; # 40:47 N, 76:35 W.

Shanghai (shang-hī'), treaty port, N. mouth of Yangtse-Kiang, E. C. China, pop. est. 1,500; # 31:15 N, 121:30 E.

Shanhaikwan (shän-hī-kwän'), city, Chihli prov., N. China, pop. est. 80; # 40 N, 119:48 E.

Shannon (shan'ọn), chief riv. of Ireland, len. 200 mi., S. W. to Atlantic oc.; # 52:40 N, 9:30 W.

Shansi (shän'sē'), prov., N. C. China Proper, area 82, pop. 11,655, * Taiyuan, pop. 230; # 38:15 N, 112:30 E.

Shan States (shan), div., E. C. Burma, India; # 22 N, 98 E.

Shantung (shän-túng'), pen. in Yellow Sea and a prov. of China, area 56, pop. est. 31,000, * Tsinan; # 36:30 N, 119 E.

Shaohingfu (shou-hing-fö'), city, Chekiang prov., S. E. C. China, pop. est. 200; # 30 N, 120:39 E.

Shar Dagh (shär däg), Balkan mt. range, S. E. Yugoslavia, highest, Idubotrn, el. 10,065 ft.; # 42 N, 21 E.

Shari (shä'rē), riv., Fr. Equatorial Africa to Lake Chad, len. ab. 1,400 mi.; # 13 N, 14:30 E.

Shark (shärk), bay, W. Australia, len. 150 mi.; # 25:20 S, 113:30 E.

Sharon (shär'ọn), city, W. C. Pa., pop. 26; # 41:15 N, 80:30 W. —coast plain, anc. W. Palestine; # 32 N, 34:54 E.

Shasi or **Shashi** (shä'sē'), treaty port on lower Yangtse riv., China; pop. est. 161; # 30:16 N, 112:18 E.

Shasta (shas'tạ), vol. pk., N. C. Calif., el. 14,162 ft.; # 41:22 N, 122:10 W.

Shatt-el-Arab (shät-el-ä'räb), riv., formed by junction of Tigris and Euphrates, len. 100 mi., to Persian Gulf; # 29:55 N, 48:30 E.

Shawinigan Falls (shô'in-i-gạn), tn., S. C. Quebec, pop. 11; # 46:31 N, 72:46 W.

Shawnee (shạ-nē'), city, C. Okla., pop. 22; # 35:21 N, 96:59 W.

Sheba (shē'bạ), tn., near Beersheba, S. anc. Palestine; # 31:15 N, 34:51 E.

Sheboygan (shẹ-boi'gạn), city, E. C. Wis., pop. 41; # 43:48 N, 87:45 W.

Shechem (shē'kem), see **Nablus**.

Sheerness (shēr-nes'), spt. tn. at mouth of Thames, Kent, Eng., pop. 19; gov. dockyards; # 51:27 N, 0:44 E.

Sheffield (shef'ēld), city, C. Eng., pop. 524; cutlery; Sheffield Univ.; # 53:22 N, 1:30 W.

Shelbyville (shel'bi-vil), tn., S. E. Ind., pop. 11; # 39:31 N, 85:46 W.

Shenandoah (shen-ạn-dō'ạ), city, E. C. Pa., in Shenandoah Valley, pop. 20; # 40:47 N, 76:12 W. —riv., N. Va., to Potomac riv., len. 200 mi.; # 39:20 N, 77:45 W.

Shengking (sheng'king') or **Fengtien,** prov., Manchuria, area 56, pop. 10,000, * Mukden; pop. 250; # 41:30 N, 123 E.

Shensi (shen-sē'), prov., W. C. China Proper, area 75, pop. est. 9,000, * Sianfu, pop. est. 700; # 35 N, 109 E.

Sherbrooke (shĕr'brúk), city, S. E. Quebec, pop. 25; # 45:27 N, 71:55 W.

Sheridan (sher'i-dạn), tn., N. C. Wyo., pop. 11; irrigation; # 44:45 N, 106:55 W.

Sherman (shĕr'mạn), city, N. E. Texas, pop. 17; Austin College; # 33:35 N, 96:35 W.

's Hertogenbosch ('s her-tō'gẹn-bos), city, N. Brabant prov., S. Neth., pop. 41; # 51:42 N, 5:19 E.

Sherwood Forest, anc. royal forest, chiefly in Nottinghamshire, C. Eng.; # 53:8 N, 1:5 W.

Shetland (shet'lạnd), isls., N. of Britain, a county of Scotland, area 0.5, pop. 24, * Lerwick; ponies; # 60:30 N, 1:15 W.

Shields, South (shēlds), see **South Shields**.

Shikarpur (shi-kär'pör), city, N. W. India, near Indus riv., pop. 54; # 28 N, 68:40 E.

Shikoku (shē-kō'kö), isl., Japan, S. of Honshu isl., area 7, pop. 3,500; # 33:45 N, 133:30 E.

Shillong (shēl-lōng'), tn., N. E. India, * of Assam prov., pop. 17; tea; # 25:45 N, 91:55 E.

Shiloh (shī'lō), national park, S. W. Tenn.; battle, 1862; # 35:2 N, 88:23 W.

Shimizu (shē'mẹ-zö), city, Japan, pop. 46; # 35:1 N, 138:27 E.

Shimonoseki (shē-mō-nō-sä'kē), spt. city, ext. S. W. of Honshu isl., Japan, pop. 92; # 33:58 N, 130:58 E. —narrow strait bet. Honshu and Kyushiu isls., Japan; # 33:58 N, 130:58 E.

Shinar (shī'när), a biblical name for Babylonia.

Shipka (ship'kä), pass (R.R.), across C. Balkan mts., N. C. Bulgaria, alt. 4,376 ft.; # 42 45 N, 25:25 E.

Shiraz (shē'räz), city, S. C. Persia, pop. ab. 50, * of Fars prov.; # 29:40 N, 52:25 E.

Shitomir (zhẹ-to-mēr') or **Zhitomir,** city, Ukraine, S. W. Russia, pop. 87; # 50:19 N, 28:40 E.

Shizuoka (shē-zú-ō'kä), coastal city, S. C. Honshu isl., Japan, pop. 85; # 35 N, 138:28 E.

Shoa (shō'ä), a part of Ethiopia or Abyssinia, pop. ab. 1,500, * Addis Abeba; # 9:30 N, 38:30 E.

Sholapur (shō-lä-pör'), city, E. S. E. of Bombay, S. C. India, pop. 120; # 17:45 N, 76 E.

Shoreditch (shōr'dich), a N. borough of London, Eng., pop. 104; # 51:32 N, 0:5 W.

Shoshone (shọ-shō'nē), riv., Yellowstone Park, N. W. Wyo. to Bighorn riv., len. 120 mi.; dam, near Cody, height 328 ft., next to Arrowrock Dam, highest in world; # 44:50 N, 108:10 W. —falls, cataracts of Snake riv., S. C. Idaho, height 210 ft.; imposing; # 42:35 N, 114:24 W. —cavern, near Cody, Wyo., a national monument; # 44:39 N, 109:6 W.

Shreveport (shrĕv'pōrt), city, N. W. La., on Red riv., pop. 98; Centenary College; # 32:30 N, 93:45 W.

Shrewsbury (shröz'ber-i), city, * of Shropshire, W. C. Eng., pop. 31; # 52:42 N, 2:45 W.

Shropshire (shrop'shir), county, W. C. Eng., area 1.4, pop. 243, * Shrewsbury, pop. 31; Shropshire sheep; # 52:36 N, 2:45 W.

Shumla (shöm'lä), **Choumen** or **Sumla,** city, N. E. Bulgaria, pop. 24; # 43:15 N, 26:55 E.

Shusha (shö-shä'), city, Azerbaijan, S. W. Asia, pop. 43; # 39:44 N, 46:45 E.

Si (sē), see **Si-kiang**.

Sialkot (sē-äl-kōt'), city, Punjab, N. W. India, pop. 71; # 32:30 N, 74:25 E.

Siam (sī-am'), kingdom, bet. Burma and Fr. Indo-China, area 200, pop. 9,618, * Bangkok, pop. 931; # 16 N, 102 E. — **Gulf of,** gulf bet. Malay pen. and Fr. Indo-China; # 10 N, 101:30 E.

Sianfu (sē'än-fö'), city, W. C. China Proper, * of Shensi prov., pop. est. 700; # 34:25 N, 108:55 E.

Siangtan (sẹ-äng'tän'), city, Hunan prov., S. C. China, pop. est. 500; # 28 N, 112:55 E.

---

fat, fāte, fär, fåll, ȧsk, fãre; net, mē, hėr; pin, pīne; not, nōte, möve, nôr; up, lūte, púll; oi, oil; ou, out; (lightened) aviạry; ẹlect, agọny, intọ, ụnite; (obscured) errạnt, oper̤ä, ardẹnt, actọr, natụre; ch, chip; g, go; th, thin; ᴛʜ, then; y, you;

Siberia (sī-bē′ri-ạ), N. Asia, part of Soviet Russia, area 3,406, pop. 8,497; # 62 N, 100 E.

Sibiu (sē-byö′) *formerly* **Hermannstadt**, city, Transylvania, W. C. Romania; pop. 33; # 45:48 N, 24:9 E.

Sicilies, The Two (sis′i-liz), former kingdom, Sicily and S. Italy.

Sicily (sis′i-li), Italian isl., S. of Italy, area 9.9, pop. 4,061, * Palermo, pop. 394; # 37:30 N, 14 E.

Sicyon (sish′i-on), anc. city, 9 mi. N. W. of Corinth, Greece; # ab. 38 N, 22:50 E.

Sidi-bel-Abbès (sē-dē-bel-à-bes′), city, N. W. Algeria, pop. 38; # 35:11 N, 0:42 W.

Sidon (sī′dọn), see **Saida.**

Sidra (sid′rạ), gulf, Libya, C. N. Africa; # 32 N, 19 E.

Siedlce (sye′dl-tse), prov., N. C. Poland, area 5.5, pop. 1,003, and its *, pop. 23; # 52:11 N, 22:17 E.

Siegen (zē′gẹn), city, S. W. Ger., pop. 31; # 50:52 N, 8:2 E.

Siena (sē-ā′nä), prov., Tuscany, N. W. C. Italy, area 1.5, pop. 248, and its *, pop. 44; cathedral; univ.; # 43:18 N, 11:18 E.

Sierra Leone (si-er′ạ lẹ-ō′nẹ, lẹ-ōn′), a Br. colony and protectorate of W. Africa; colony, area 4, pop. 85; protectorate, area 27, pop. 1,328, * Freetown, pop. 44; # 8 N, 12 W.

Sierra Madre (si-er′ạ mä′drä), mt. ranges, part of the Cordilleras in E. and W. Mexico; # 25 N, 100 W; 27 N, 107 W.

Sierra Maestra (syer′rä mä-es′trä), mt. range, E. Cuba, summit, Turquino, el. 8,397 ft.; # 20:15 N, 76 W.

Sierra Nevada (si-er′ạ nẹ-vä′dạ), steep, lofty mt. range, E. Calif., highest pk., Mt. Whitney, el. 14,501 ft.; # 38 N, 119:30 W. — mt. range, S. Spain, summit Mulhacén, el. 11,660 ft.; # 37 N, 3 W.

Sikandarabad or **Secunderabad** (sẹ-kun″dặr-ä-bäd′), borough, formerly a suburb of Hyderabad, S. India, pop. 84; # 28:27 N, 77:45 E.

Sikhota Alin (sē-chô′tä ä-lēn′), low plateau, S. E. Siberia, bet. Amur riv. and Pacific oc.; # 47 N, 137 E.

Si-kiang (sē-kē-äng′), riv., Yunnan, S. W. China to S. China sea near Hongkong, len. 1000 mi.; # 22:20 N, 113:15 E.

Sikkim (sik′im), native state, N. E. India, bet. Nepal and Bhutan, area 3, pop. 88, * Gangtok; # 27:30 N, 88:30 E.

Silesia (si-lē′shi-ạ), S. E. part of Prussia, see **Nieder-** and **Oberschlesien.** — prov., N. C. Cz.-S., area 1.7, pop. 672, * Opava; # 50 N, 17:30 E.: absorbed into Germany in 1938.

Silistria (si-lis′tri-ạ), region, S. E. Romania, area 3, pop. 274; # 44:5 N, 27:15 E.

Simbirsk (sẹm-bērsk′), prov., S. E. C. Russia, area 16, pop. 1,657 and its *, on Karna riv., pop. 77; univ.; # 54:15 N, 48:15 E.

Simferopol, see **Simpheropol.**

Simla (sim′lạ), hill station, N. E. Punjab, N. W. India, summer * of India, pop. 38; el. 7,000 ft.; # 31:12 N, 77:10 E.

Simpheropol (sim-fer-ō′pol-y′) or **Simferopol**, city, C. Crimea, * of soviet Crimea, pop. 84; # 44:58 N, 34:5 E.

Simplon (saṅ-plôṅ), pass, Lepontine Alps, Switz.-Italy, el. 6,582 ft., and R.R. tunnel, len. 12¼ mi., opened 1906, el. 2,312 ft.; much used; # 46:15 N, 8:10 E.

Sinai (sī′nī; sī′nä), pen., N. end of Red Sea, and mt. therein, el. 8,530 ft.; # 29 N, 34 E.

Sinaloa (sē-nä-lō′ä), state, N. W. Mexico, area 28, pop. 341, * Culiacán, pop. 14; # 25 N, 107 W.

Sind (sind), region about delta of Indus riv., N. W. India; # 26 N, 69 E.

Singanfu (sē-ngän′fö), see **Sianfu.**

Singapore (sing-gạ-pōr′), spt. city on isl. of Singapore, S. end of Malay pen.; pop. of isl. 458, of city 350; rubber; pineapples; # 1:18 N, 103:55 E.

Sing Sing (sing sing), former name of **Ossining**, New York.

Sinkiang (sin-kyäng′), Chinese prov. bet. Tibet and Mongolia, C. Asia, area 550, pop. 2, 200, * Ili; # 40:30 N, 86 E.

Sinope (si-nō′pẹ), pen. of Asia Minor in Black Sea and spt. thereon, pop. 10; # 42 N, 35 E.

Sioux City (sö sit′i), city, N. W. Iowa, on Missouri riv., pop. 82; Morningside College; # 42:30 N, 96:20 W.

Sioux Falls (sö fâlz), city, S. E. S. Dak., on Sioux riv., pop. 41; # 43:32 N, 96:48 W.

Siracusa (sē-rä-kö′zä), *Eng.* **Syracuse**, prov., S. E. Sicily, area 1.4, pop. 537, and its *, a spt., pop. 50; # 37:3 N, 15:18 E.

Sir-Daria (sēr-där′yä), prov., S. Turkestan repub., W. Asia, area 151, pop. 1,840, * Tashkent, pop. 201; # 45:40 N, 63 E. — riv., see **Yaxartes.**

Sirmur (sēr-mör′), a hill state in Punjab, N. W. India, area 1, pop. 140; # 30:40 N, 77:20 E.

Sistan, see **Seistan.**

Sistova (sis′tō-vä) or **Svichtov**, tn., Danube port, N. C. Bulgaria, pop. 13; Peace of Sistova, 1791; # 43:36 N, 25:21 E.

Sitka (sit′kạ), village, S. E. Alaska, former *, pop. 2; contains a national monument; # 57:10 N, 135:20 W.

Siut (sē-öt′), see **Asyût.**

Sivas (sē-väs′), prov., E. C. Turkish Asia Minor, area 24, pop. 1,058, and its *, pop. 65; # 39:50 N, 37:12 E.

Siwalik (sẹ-wä′lik), hills, N. W. frontier, India; fossils; # 30:10 N, 78 E.

Sjaelland (shal′lân) or **Seeland**, isl., E. Denmark, area 2.9, pop. 1,004, * Copenhagen, pop. 561; # 55:30 N, 11:45 E.

Skagen (skä′gẹn), spt. on the Skaw, N. E. tip of Jutland, Denmark; # 57:45 N, 10:35 E.

Skagerrak (skag′ẹr-rak), strait bet. Jutland, Denmark and Norway, average width 75 mi.; # 57:30 N, 8 E.

Skagway (skag′wä), village, S. E. Alaska, terminus of R.R. to Upper Yukon, pop. 1; # 59:25 N, 135:15 W.

Skaw, The (skâ), cape, N. E. Jutland, Denmark; # 57:45 N, 10:35 E.

Skien (shēn), inland city, S. E. Norway, pop. 17; Ibsen's birthplace; # 59:12 N, 9:38 E.

Skjäggedal Fos (shyeg′ge-däl′ fôs), cascades near Hardanger Fjord, W. Norway, height 530 ft.; # 60:7 N, 6:45 E.

Skoplje (skôp′lye), **Usküb** or **Uskup**, city, S. E. Yugoslavia, pop. 41; # 42 N, 21:29 E.

Skutari or **Scutari** (skö′tạ-rẹ), Turkish prov., E. of Bosporus, pop. 212, and its *, a suburb of Constantinople, pop. 100; # 41:1 N, 29:2 E.

Skye (skī), isl., Inner Hebrides, W. Scotland, len. 48 mi., pop. 12; # 57:20 N, 6:20 W.

Skyros (skē′rọs), anc. Scyros, Greek isl., N. Sporades, W. C. Ægean sea, len. 20 mi.; pop. 4; # 38:50 N, 24:35 E.

Slave (slāv), coast of W. Equatorial Africa, esp. N. coast of Gulf of Guinea; # 6:20 N, 3 E. — see **Great Slave Lake.**

Slavonia (slạ-vō′ni-ạ), div. of N. W. Yugoslavia, see **Croatia and Slavonia.**

Sleswick or **Slesvig**, see **Schleswig.**

Slide Mountain (slīd moun′tạn), highest of Catskills, S. E. N. Y., el. 4,204 ft.; # 42 N, 74:25 W.

Sligo (slī′gō), county, Connaught prov., N. W. Irish Free State, area 0.7, pop. 67, and its *, a spt. on Sligo Bay, pop. 12; # 54:15 N, 8:29 W. [pop. 29; # 42:40 N, 26:20 E.

Slivno (slēv′nọ) or **Sliven** (slē′ven), city, E. C. Bulgaria,

Slovakia (slọ-vak′i-ạ), prov., E. Cz.-S., area 18.9, pop. 3,331, * Bratislava (Pressburg); # 48:45 N, 20 E.: southern part absorbed into Hungary in 1938, remainder taken under protection of Germany in 1939.

Slovenia (slọ-vē′ni-ạ), former prov. of N. Yugoslavia, area 6.3, pop. 1,056; * Ljubljana; # 46 N, 15 E. [# 57 N, 13 E.

Småland (smâ′länd), S. E. low plateau section of Sweden,

Smethwick (smeтн′ik), suburb of Birmingham, S. W. C. Eng., pop. 78; # 52:30 N, 2 W.

Smichow (smē′chọf), a suburb of Praha, Bohemia, pop. 56; # 50:4 N, 14:24 E.

Smoky Mountains, Great (smō′ki), range, N. Car. and Tenn., highest 6,619 ft.; # 35:33 N, 83:40 W.

Smolensk (smo-lyensk′), prov., S. W. C. Russia, area 22, pop. 2,026, and its *, on Dnieper riv., pop. 57; univ.; # 54:50 N, 32:10 E.

Smyrna (smēr′nä), prov., S. W. Asiatic Turkey, pop. 425, and its *, a spt. on Ægean Sea, pop. ab. 150; # 38:25 N, 27:10 E.

Snake (snāk), riv., N. W. Wyo. to Columbia riv., len. 950 mi.; Shoshone Falls; # 40:15 N, 119:2 W.

Snoqualmie (snọ-kwol′mi), falls of Snoqualmie riv., W. C. Wash., height, 268 ft.; # ab. 47:30 N, 121:40 W.

Snowdon (snō′dọn), mt., N. W. Wales, highest in Wales and Eng., el. 3,560 ft.; # 53:5 N, 4:3 W.

Snow Mountains (snō), lofty range, W. Papua, summit, Mt. Carstensz, el. 15,969 ft.; # 4 S, 139 E.

Society Islands (sọ-sī′ẹ-ti), Fr. isls., S. Pacific oc., esp. Tahiti, area 0.7, pop. 9; # 16 to 18 S, 148 to 155 W.

Socotra (sọ-kō′trạ), isl., Br. protection, mouth of Gulf of Aden, Indian oc., area 1, pop. 12, * Tamarida; # 12:30 N, 50 E.

(variable) ḍ as d or j, ş as s or sh, ţ as t or ch, ʐ as z or zh; o, F. cloche; ü, F. menu; ċh, Sc. loch; ṅ, F. bonbon; ′, primary accent; ″, secondary accent; †, obsolete; <, from; +, and; =, equals. See also lists at beginning of book.

Södertälje (sė-dėr-tel′ye), a S. W. suburb of Stockholm, S. E. Sweden, pop. 16; # 59:12 N, 17:38 E.

Soerabaja (sö-rä-bī′ä), city, N. E. Java; best port; well fortified; pop. 192; # 7:15 S, 112:45 E.

Soerakarta (sö-rä-kär′tä) or **Surakarta,** city, E. Java, pop. 137; # 7:30 S, 110:45 E.

Soest (zōst), city, Westfalen (Westphalia), W. Ger., pop. 21; # 51:34 N, 8:6 E.

Sofia (sō-fē′ä), city, W. C. Bulgaria, its *, pop. 154; univ. # 42:40 N, 23:18 E.

Sogne (sog′ne), fjord, S. W. Norway, len. 115 mi.; # 61 N, 6 E.

Soissons (swä-sôn̓), city, N. E. Fr., on Aisne riv., pop. 14; battle, 1918; # 49:25 N, 3:15 E.

Sokoto (sō-kō′tō), prov., N. W. Nigeria, W. Africa; pop. ab. 8,000; # 13 N, 6 E.

Solent (sō′lẹnt), channel bet. Isle of Wight and mainland of Hampshire, S. Eng.; # 50:45 N, 1:25 W.

Soleure (so-lėr) or **Solothurn** (zō′lō-törn), city, * of Solothurn canton, N. W. Switz., pop. 13; # 47:13 N, 7:32 E.

Solingen (zō′ling-ẹn), an E. suburb of Düsseldorf, W. Ger., pop. 52; # 51:10 N, 7:4 E.

Solnhofen (zoln′hō-fẹn), vil., Bavaria, S. W. Ger.; lithographic stone; oldest fossil bird; # 48:55 N, 10:58 E.

Solomon (sol′ọ-mọn), isl. group, S. Pacific oc., N. E. of Aust., area 11, pop. ab. 150, * Bougainville; # 8 S, 159 E.

Solothurn (zō′lō-törn), canton, N. W. Switz., area 0.3, pop. 131, and its *, pop. 13; # 47:15 N, 7:30 E.

Solway Firth (sol′wä fėrth), indentation bet. N. W. Eng. and S. W. Scotland; len. 38 mi.; # 54:50 N, 3:30 W.

Somaliland (sō-mä′lẹ-land), a Br. protectorate on the Gulf of Aden, N. E. Africa, area 68, pop. 300, * Berbera, pop. 30; # 10 N, 47 E. — an Italian colony, ext. E. Africa, area 139, pop. 650, * Mogadishu; # 6 N, 46 E. — a Fr. colony in N. E. Africa, area 6, pop. 65, * Jibuti or Djibouti; # 12 N, 42 E.

Sombor (som′bôr), city, N. E. Yugoslavia, pop. 31; # 45:45 N, 19:8 E.

Somerset (sum′ėr-set) or **Somersetshire,** county, S. W. Eng., area 1.6, pop. 466, * Taunton; # 51:15 N, 3 W.

Somerville (sum′ėr-vil), a N. suburb of Boston, Mass., pop. 102; # 42:24 N, 71:3 W.

Somme (som), riv., N. E. Fr. to Atlantic oc., len. 140 mi.; # 50:10 N, 1:45 E. — dept., N. E. Fr., area 2.4, pop. 453, * Amiens, pop. 93; # 49:56 N, 2:15 E.

Sondrio (sôn′drē-ō), prov., Lombardy, N. Italy, area 1.2, pop. 131, and its *, pop. 10; # 46:10 N, 9:52 E.

Songka (song′kä′), riv., S. W. China to Gulf of Tonkin, len. 500 mi.; # 20:30 N, 106:15 E.

Sonneberg (zon′ė-berċh), dist., S. Thuringia, S. C. Ger., area 0.1, pop. 73, and its *, on Steinach riv., pop. 21; # 50:22 N, 11:11 E.

Sonora (sō-nō′rä), state, N. W. Mexico, area 77, pop. 275, * Hermosillo, pop. 20; # 29 N, 110 W.

Soo (sö), see **Sault Ste. Marie.**

Soochow (sō′chou′), city, E. C. China, near Shanghai, pop. est. 300; silks; # 31:16 N, 120:32 E.

Sorata (sō-rä′tä) or **Illampu,** mt., Bolivian Andes, N. of LaPaz, el. 21,836 ft.; # 15:55 S, 68:28 W.

Soria (sō′rē-ä), prov., N. E. C. Spain, area 4, pop. 148, and its *, pop. 7; # 41:45 N, 2:34 W.

Sorrento (sôr-ren′tō), *anc.* Surrentum, coastal city, S. Bay of Naples, Italy, pop. 7; cathedral and Greek and Roman antiquities; # 40:38 N, 14:22 E.

Sosnowiec or **Sosnoviets** (sōs-nō′vyets), city, S. W. Poland, pop. 86; # 50:18 N, 19:10 E.

Soudan, see **Sudan.**

Soufrière (sö-frē-âr′), volcano, St. Vincent, W. Indies, el. 3,000 ft., erupted 1902; # 13:50 N, 61:2 W. — **Grande,** active volcano, Guadeloupe, W. Indies, el. 4,869 ft.; # 16:20 N, 61:45 W.

Sound, The (sound), strait bet. Seeland, Denmark and Sweden, least width, 4 mi.; # 55:30 N, 12:45 E.

Souris (sö′ris), riv., S. E. Sask., N. C. N. Dak., to Assiniboine riv., Manitoba, len. ab. 400 mi.; # 49:40 N, 99:50 W.

South Africa, Union of (af′ri-kạ), Br. dominion, S. Africa, area 473, pop. 6,929 (white, 1,519), * Pretoria and Capetown; # 25 S, 25 E.

South African Republic, a former name of Transvaal prov.

South America (ạ-mer′i-kạ), continent S. E. of N. Am. area ab. 6,856, pop. ab. 90,000; # 10 S, 60 W.

Southampton (south-amp′tọn), county, S. C. Eng., area 1.4, pop. 910 and its *, a spt., pop. 165; # 50:55 N, 1:28 W. — isl., entrance to Hudson Bay, area ab. 17; # 64 N, 84 W.

South Australia (âs-trā′li-ạ), state, S. C. Australia, area 380, pop. 529, * Adelaide, pop. with suburbs, 279; # 30 S, 135 E.

South Bend (bend), city, N. C. Ind., pop. 101; automobiles; Notre Dame Univ.; # 41:40 N, 86:18 W.

South Bethlehem (beth′lẹ-ẹm), now part of Bethlehem, Pa.

Southbridge (south′brij), tn., S. C. Mass., pop. twp. 17; # 42:6 N, 72:3 W.

South Carolina (kar-ọ-lī′nạ), state S. E. U.S.A., bet. N. C. and Ga., area 31, pop. 1,900, * Columbia, pop. 62; chief city, Charleston, pop. 71; # 34 N, 81 W.

South China Sea, sea bet. Indo-China and Philippines and Borneo; # 12 N, 114 E.

South Dakota (dạ-kō′tạ), state, N. C. U.S.A., bet. N. D. and Neb., area 78, pop. 643, * Pierre, pop. 4; chief city, Sioux Falls, pop. 41; # 44 N, 100 W.

South Downs (dounz), range of hills, S. E. Eng.; # 50:55 N, 0:30 W.

South East Cape (ēst kāp), S. end of Tasmania; # 43:40 S, 147 E.

Southend-on-Sea (south-end′), spt. on Thames estuary, S. E. Eng., pop. 93; # 51:32 N, 0:42 E.

Southern Lines, R.R., Washington, D. C., to Fla. and La.; total mileage, 6,971.

Southern Pacific Lines, R.R., New Orleans to Calif., Utah, Br. Columbia; highest part, Transcontinental, 4,610 ft., Ore.-Calif., 8,247 ft.; completed 1883; total mileage 13,099.

Southern Rhodesia (rọ-dē′zhi-ạ), see **Rhodesia, South.**

South Georgia (jôr′jiạ), isl., S. Atlantic oc., E. of Cape Horn, area 1, pop. 1; Br. sealing station; # 54 S, 36:30 W.

South Hadley (had′li), tn., W. C. Mass., pop. 7; Mt. Holyoke College; # 42:15 N, 72:37 W.

South Holland (hol′ạnd), see **Holland, South.**

South Island, S. isl., New Zealand, area 58, pop. ab. 400; # 43 S, 170 E.

South Melbourne (mel′bọrn), a S. suburb of Melbourne, Vic., S. E. Australia, pop. 47; # 37:51 S, 145 E.

South Orange (or′ạnj), tn., N. E. New Jersey, pop. 14; Seton Hall College; # 40:45 N, 74:16 W.

South Platte (plat), riv., C. Colo. to Platte riv., len. ab. 350 mi.; # 41:9 N, 100:45 W.

South Pole, S. end of axis of earth's rotation; Amundsen (Nor.), Dec., 1911; Scott (Eng.), Jan., 1912.

Southport (south′pōrt), spt. city, 25 mi. N. of Liverpool, W. C. Eng., pop. 72; # 53:40 N, 3 W.

South Shields (shēldz), spt. city, Tyne mouth, N. E. Eng., pop. 125; # 55 N, 1:27 W.

South Vancouver (van-kö′vėr), a S. suburb of Vancouver, Br. Col., pop. 32; # 49:15 N, 123:8 W.

Southwark (suᴛн′ärk), a borough of London, S. of Thames riv., pop. 184; # 51:31 N, 0:4 W.

Southwell (south′wel), tn., Nottinghamshire, C. Eng., pop. 3; cathedral; # 53:4 N, 0:52 W.

Southwest Africa, formerly Ger. S. W. Africa, area 322, pop. 230, * Windhuk, pop. 15; mandate of U. of S. Africa; # 22 S, 18 E.

Soya (sō-yä′), or **La Pérouse,** strait bet. Yezo and Sakhalin (Karafuto) isls., Japan; # 45:40 N, 142 E.

Spain (spān), *Sp.* **España,** *anc.* Hispania, republic, S. W. Europe, area 194, pop. 20,000, * Madrid, pop. 814; # 40 N, 4 W.

Spalato (spä-lä′tō), *anc.* Spalatum, spt. city, C. Dalmatia, Yugoslavia, pop. 25; # 43:31 N, 16:26 E.

Spandau (shpän′dou), a W. div. of Berlin, Ger., pop. 110; # 52:32 N, 13:13 E.

Spanish Guinea, see **Guinea, Spanish.**

Spanish Morocco (mọ-rok′ō), N. Morocco, area ab. 18 (1/12), pop. 600; "sphere of influence"; # 35 N, 5 W.

Spanish Peninsula (pē-nin′sụ-lä), see **Iberia.**

Sparta (spär′tä), tn., S. C. Morea pen., S. Greece, pop. 4, * of anc. Laconia; # 37:7 N, 22:25 E.

Spartanburg (spär′tạn-bėrg), city, N. W. S. Car., pop. 32; Spartanburg, Converse and Wofford colleges; # 35 N, 81:50 W.

---

fat, fāte, fär, fȧll, ȧsk, fâre; net, mē, hėr; pin, pīne; not, nōte, mȯve, nôr; up, lūte, pṳll; oi, oil; ou, out; (lightened) aviạry, ẹlect, agọny, intọ, ụnite; (obscured) errạnt, oper̈ä, ardẹnt, actọr, natụre; ch, chip; g, go; th, thin; ᴛн, then; y, you;

Spencer (spen'ser), gulf, S. E. S. Australia, len. 200 mi.; # 34 S, 137 E.

Spey (spā), riv., N. C. Scotland to N. Sea, len. 110 mi.; # 57:40 N, 3:8 W.

Speyer (spī'er), *Eng.* often **Spires,** city on Rhine, * of Rhein-pfalz, S. W. Ger., pop. 25; # 49:20 N, 8:25 E.

Spezia (spet'sē-ä), prov., Liguria, N. W. Italy, area 0.3, pop. 209, and its *, a spt., pop. 88; naval station; #44:12 N, 9:45 E.

Spice Islands, see **Moluccas.**

Spiral Tunnels (spīr'ạl), tunnels on Canadian Pacific R.R. bet. Hector and Field, Br. Columbia, len. 3,255 and 2,921 ft.; # 51:24 N, 116:28 W.

Spires (spīrz), see **Speyer.**

Spithead (spit'hed), roadstead, S. of Eng., N. of Isle of Wight; # 50:46 N, 1:12 W.

Spitzbergen (spits-bėr'gẹn), group of isls., Arctic oc., N. of Norway, lat. 74 to 81, area 25, pop. ab. 1; Norwegian colony; coal; # 79 N, 20 E.

Split (split), see **Spalato.**

Spokane (spō-kan'), city, E. C. Wash., pop. 122; wheat flour; college; # 47:42 N, 117:28 W.

Spoleto (spō-lā'tō), *anc.* Spoletium, city, Perugia, C. Italy, pop. 26; #42:43 N, 12:43 E.

Sporades (spor'ạ-dēz), two groups of isls., S. Ægean Sea, N. on W. side, S. on E. side; # 39:5 N, 23:45 E.

Spree (shprā), riv., Saxony, S. Ger., through Berlin to Havel riv., len. 220 mi.; # 52:32 N, 13:13 E.

Springfield (spring'fēld), city, S. W. C. Mass., on Conn. riv., pop. 150; U. S. Armory; Y. M. C. A. college; #42:7 N, 72:35 W. — city, S. C. Illinois, state *, pop. 76; # 39:46 N, 89:38 W. — city, S. W. C. Mo., pop. 61; Drury College; # 37:15 N, 93:20 W. — city, S. W. C. Ohio, pop. 71; Wittenberg College; # 39:55 N, 83:47 W.

Srinagar (sri-nug'ur), city, * of Kashmir, ext. N. W. India on Jhelum riv., pop. 142; # 34:10 N, 74:45 W.

Staffa (staf'ạ), small isl., W. of Mull, Argyll, W. Scotland; Fingal's cave, len. 288 ft., height 117 ft.; # 56:26 N, 6:21 W.

Stafford (staf'ọrd), county, W. C. Eng., area 1.1, pop. 1,349, and its *, pop. 23; # 52:50 N, 2:12 W.

Staked Plain (stäkt plän), treeless plain, N. W. Texas; "Llano Estacado"; # 34 N, 102 W.

Stambul (stäm-bōl'), Turkish part of Constantinople.

Stamford (stam'fọrd), city, S. W. Conn., pop. 48; # 41:3 N, 73:33 W.

St. Andrews (an'dröz), see **Saint Andrews.**

Stanley (stan'li), falls, 7 cataracts of Congo riv., near Stanleyville, S. Africa; now circumvented by R.R.; # 0:30 S, 25:20 E. — pool, expansion of Congo riv., near Stanleyville; # 4:12 S, 15:22 E.

Stanovoi (stä-nō-voi'), mt. range, 1,000 mi. long, near Pacific coast of Siberia; highest ab. 7,000 ft.; # 60 N, 144 E.

Stara-Planina (stä'rä plä-nē'nä), Bulgarian name of Balkan Mts., S. Bulgaria; #43:20 N, 23 E.

Stara-Zagora (stä'rä zä'gō-rä), dept., C. Bulgaria, area 3, pop. 551, and its *, pop. 25; #42:55 N, 25:38 E.

Stargard (shtär'gärt), city, Pomerania, N. E. Ger., pop. 32; # 53:21 N, 15:3 E.

Stassfurt (shtäs'fúrt), city, Saxony prov., S. C. Prussia, pop. 20; potash; salt; chemicals; # 51:50 N, 11:35 E.

State College, tn., C. Pa., pop. 6; Penn. State College; #40:50 N, 77:52 W.

Staten Island (stat'n ī'lạnd), portion of New York, coextensive with Richmond borough, area 0.06; pop. 174; #40:35 N, 74:9 W.

Staubbach (stoub'äch), falls, N. W. of Jungfrau, C. Switz., height 870 ft.; # 46:35 N, 7:54 E.

Staunton (stăn'tọn), tn., N. W. C. Va., pop. 13; military acad.; # 38:8 N, 79:5 W.

Stavanger (stä-väng'ger), spt. city, ext. S. W. Norway, pop. 44; # 58:40 N, 5:40 E.

Stavropol (stäv'rō-pol-y'), prov., S. E. Russia, area 20, pop. 1,175, and its *, pop. 64; # 53:30 N, 49 E.

Steelton (stēl'tọn), tn., S. E. C. Pa., pop. 13; #40:16 N, 76:52 W.

Steglitz (shtä'glits), a S. div. of Berlin, Ger., pop. 154; # 52:28 N, 13:20 E.

Stendal (shten'däl), city, Sachsen, (Saxony) Prussia, pop. 30; # 52:38 N, 11:50 E.

Stepney (step'ni), a borough of London, Eng., pop. 249; # 51:31 N, 0:2 W.

Steppes (steps), semiarid, grassy plains as in S. E. Russia and American Great Plains; # 45 N, 65 E; 40 N, 103 W. — see **Kirghiz.**

Sterkrade (shterk'rä-dè); a N. suburb of Hamborn, Ruhr Valley, W. Ger., pop. 51; # 51:30 N, 6:50 E.

Stettin (shte-tēn'), city on Oder riv., * of Pommern, N. Ger., pop. 251; ship building; # 53:25 N, 14:35 E.

Stettiner Haff (shte-tē'nėr häf), coastal lake, N. Pommern, N. E. Ger., len. 60 mi.; # 53:45 N, 14:20 E.

Steubenville (stū'bẹn-vil), city, E. C. Ohio, on Ohio riv., pop. 38; # 40:25 N, 80:38 W.

Stevens Point (stē'vẹnz), tn., E. C. Wis., pop. 16; # 44:30 N, 89:32 W.

Stewart (stū'ạrt), S. isl. of New Zealand, area 0.7; # 47:7 S, 167:50 E.

Steyr (shtīr), city on Ems riv., N. C. Austria, pop. 22; # 48:2 N, 14:24 E.

Stillwater (stil'wå"tėr), tn., N. C. Okla., pop. 10; state A. and M. College; # 36:8 N, 97:4 W.

Stirling (stėr'ling), county, S. C. Scotland, area 0.5, pop. 158, and its *, pop. 21; # 56:5 N, 4 W. — falls, W. S. Island, New Zealand, height 500 ft.; # 46:16 S, 170 E.

Stockholm (stok'hōlm), spt. city, S. E. C. Sweden, its *, pop. 430, pop. with suburbs 684; univ.; # 59:16 N, 18 E.

Stockport (stok'pōrt), suburb of Manchester, W. C. Eng., pop. 126; # 3:24 N, 2:9 W.

Stockton (stok'tọn), city, C. Calif., pop. 55; College of the Pacific; # 37:58 N, 121:15 W.

Stockton-on-Tees (stok'tọn-on-tēz), city, Durham, N. E. Eng., pop. 67; # 54:35 N, 1:25 W.

Stoke Newington (stōk nū'ing-tọn), a N. W. borough of London, Eng., pop. 52; # 51:34 N, 0:4.

Stoke-on-Trent (stōk'on-trent'), city, W. C. Eng., pop. 276; pottery; # 53 N, 2:15 W.

Stolp (shtolp), city, Pommern, N. E. Ger., pop. 42; # 54:28 N, 17:3 E.

Stonehenge (stōn'henj), prehistoric ruin, Salisbury Plain, S. of Eng., slabs of rock 16–18 ft. high; # 51:11 N, 1:50 W.

Stourbridge (stour'brij), a W. suburb of Birmingham, S. W. C. Eng., pop. 18; # 52:27 N, 2:8 W.

Strait of Dover, see **Dover.**

Straits Settlements (sträts set'l-mẹnts), Br. colony, Malay pen., Singapore, Penang, Malacca, Cocos isl., area 1.6, pop. 929, * Singapore, pop. 350; # 3:30 N, 101 E.

Stralsund (shträl'sùnt), spt., Pommern, N. E. Ger., pop. 39; # 54:20 N, 13:5 E.

Strasbourg (sträs-bör'), city on Rhine, N. E. Fr., * of Bas-Rhin dept., pop. 181; cathedral; Univ. of Strasbourg; # 48:35 N, 7:45 E.

Stratford (strat'fọrd), an E. urban suburb of London, Eng.; # 51:34 N, 0:0. — city, S. W. Ontario, pop. 16; # 43:23 N, 81 W.

Stratford-on-Avon (strat'fọrd-on-ā'vọn), tn., Warwickshire, S. C. Eng., pop. 9; Shakspere's birthplace and burial-place; # 52:15 N, 1:45 W.

Straubing (shtrou'bing), city, Lower Bavaria, S. W. Ger., pop. 23; # 48:53 N, 12:35 E.

Strawberry Valley (strå'bėr"i val'i), irrigation proj., N. C. Utah, water carried in tunnel 19,000 ft. long through Wasatch Mts.; # 40 N, 111 W.

Streator (strē'tėr), city, N. E. C. Ill., pop. 15; # 41:6 N, 88:50 W.

Stretford (stret'fọrd), a S. W. suburb of Manchester, C. Eng., pop. 47; # 53:27 N, 2:19 W.

Stromboli (strom'bō-lē), active vol. on isl. N. of Strait of Messina, Italy; height 3,040 ft.; # 38:46 N, 15:12 E.

Struma (strö'mä), *anc.* Strymon, riv., W. Bulg., S. to Ægean sea, len. 200 mi.; # 40:55 N, 23:35 E.

Stuttgart (stut'gärt), city, * of Württemberg, S. W. Ger., pop. 337; #48:46 N, 9:13 E.

Styr (stēr), riv., Galicia and Poland to Pripet riv., len. 300 mi.; # 52 N, 26:22 E.

Styria (stir'i-ạ), prov., S. E. Austria, area 6.3, pop. 979; * Graz; # 47:20 N, 14:10 E.

(variable) ḍ as d or j, ṣ as s or sh, ṭ as t or ch, ẓ as z or zh; *o*, F. cloche; ü, F. menu; ċh, Sc. loch; ñ, F. bonbon; ', primary accent; ", secondary accent; †, obsolete; <, from; +, and; =, equals. See also lists at beginning of book.

Suakin (swä′kin), spt., Anglo-Egyptian Sudan on Red Sea, pop. 12; # 19 N, 37:15 E.

Subotica (sö′bō-ti-tsä), see **Szabadka.**

Sucre (sö′krä), city, S. W. C. Bolivia, pop. 30; supreme court and nominally the *; # 19 S, 65:20 W.

Sudan (sö-dän′), grassy region bet. Sahara and tropical jungle, N. Africa; # 17 N, 8 E. — a Fr. colony in W. Africa, area 648, pop. ab. 2,500, * Bamako, pop. 16; # 13 N, 5 W. — Anglo-Egyptian, see **Anglo-Egyptian Sudan.**

Sudeten (sö-de′ṭen) or **Sudetes**, mts. bet. Silesia and Bohemia; # 50:30 N, 16 E.

Suez (sö′ez or sö-ez′), sea level canal between Mediterranean and Red Seas, across isthmus connecting Africa and Asia, length 100 mi., depth now 36 ft.; cut 1859–1869 by De Lesseps; # 30:45 N, 32:18 E. — spt. city, S. end of canal at N. end of Gulf of Suez, pop. 31; # 29:58 N, 32:33 E.

Suffolk (suf′ọk), county, E. Mass., area .055, pop. 863 (1940), * Boston, pop. 771; # 42:20 N, 71:5 W. — **East,** county, S. E. Eng., area 0.9, pop. 291, * Ipswich, pop. 82; # 52:10 N, 1:20 E. — **West,** county, S. E. Eng., area 0.6, pop. 109; # 52:10 N, 0:40 E.

Sukhum (sù-köm′), dist., N. W. Georgian rep., area 2.5, pop. 175, and its *, a spt. on Black Sea, pop. 62; # 43 N, 41 E.

Sullys Hill (sul′iz), national park, Devils Lake, N. Dak.; wild fowl; # ab. 47:55 N, 98:50 W.

Sulu (sö′lö), numerous small isls., S. W. Philippines, area 1, pop. 173; # 6 N, 121 E. — sea bet. N. Borneo and Philippines, 8 N, 120 E.

Sumatra (sö-mä′trä), large isl., W. Dutch E. Indies, area 163, pop. 5,849; # 0:5 S, 102 E.

Sumbawa (söm-bä′wä), isl., Dutch E. Indies, 150 mi. E. of Java, area 5, pop. 246; vol. eruption, 1815; # 8:45 S, 118 E.

Summit (sum′it), tn., in N. E. New Jersey, pop. 16; # 40:42 N, 74:22 W.

Sumter (sum′ṭer), tn., E. C. S. Carolina, pop. 16; # 33:56 N, 80:19 W.

Sunbury (sun′bẹ-ri), city, E. C. Pa., pop. 15; # 40:52 N, 76:50 W.

Sunda (sun′dä), strait bet. Java and Sumatra, E. Indies, least width, 16 mi.; # 6 S, 106 E.

Sunderland (sun′dẽr-lạnd), spt. city near Newcastle, N. E. Eng., pop. 164; coal port; # 54:57 N, 1:27 W.

Sundsvall (sönds′väl), spt. city, E. C. Sweden, pop. 17; lumber; # 62:25 N, 17:5 E.

Sungari (sön-gä-rē′), riv., E. Mongolia and Manchuria to Amur riv., len. 800 mi.; # 47:50 N, 132:20 E.

Superior (sụ-pē′ri-ọr), largest of the Great Lakes, bet. U.S.A. and Canada, area 31.8, el. 602 ft., len. 400 mi., maximum depth 1,008 ft.; # 48 N, 88 W. — city, ext. N. W. Wis., adjacent to Duluth, Minn., pop. 35; lake port; # 46:42 N, 92:5 W.

Sura (sö-rà′), riv. S. C. Russia to Volga riv., len. ab. 500 mi.; # 56:10 N, 46 E.

Surabaya (sö-rä-bī′ä), see **Soerabaja.**

Surakarta (sö-rä-kär′tä), see **Soerakarta.**

Suram (sö-ram′), important pass and R.R. tunnel, Georgian republic, Transcaucasia; # ab. 42:2 N, 43:35 E.

Surat (sö-rät′, sö′rut), spt. city, N. of Bombay, W. India, pop. 117; # 21:10 N, 72:50 E.

Surinam (sö-ri-näm′), see **Guiana, Dutch.**

Surma (sùr′mä), riv., Assam, N. E. India to Barak riv., len. 560 mi.; # ab. 24:30 N, 91:15 E.

Surrentum (su-ren′tum), see **Sorrento.**

Surrey (sur′i), county, S. E. C. Eng., area 0.7, pop. 930, * Guildford; # 51:15 N, 0:25 W.

Susa (sö′sä), anc. city, * of Elam, Persia; # 32:14 N, 48:19 E. — spt., N. E. Tunis, pop. 25; # 36 N, 11 E.

Susquehanna (sus-kwẹ-han′ä), riv., S. C. New York, to Chesapeake Bay, len. 256 mi.; # 39:30 N, 76:5 W.

Sussex, East (sus′eks), county, S. E. Eng., area 0.8, pop. 532, * Lewes, pop. 12; # 51 N, 0:10 E.

Sussex, West, county, S. E. Eng., area 0.6, pop. 196; # 51 N, 30 W.

Sutherland (suᵀн′ẽr-lạnd), county, ext. N. C. Scotland, area 2, pop. 17, * Dornoch; # 51:10 N, 4:30 W. — falls, S. W. S. Isl., New Zealand, height 1,904 ft.; # 44:40 S, 167:40 E.

Sutlej (sut′lej) or **Ghara**, riv., Tibet to Indus riv., N. W. India, len. 900 mi.; # 29 N, 70:35 E.

Suva (sö′vä), spt., S. E. Viti Levu, * of Fiji, S. Pacific oc., pop. 6, with suburbs 13; # 18:8 S, 178:25 E.

Suvalkai (sö-väl′kï), city, N. Poland, claimed by Lithuania, pop. 32; # 54:5 N, 22:55 E.

Suwanee (sù-wä′nē), riv., S. C. Ga. and N. W. Fla. to Gulf of Mexico, len. 200 mi.; # 29:15 N, 83:5 W.

Sverige (svä′rē-ye), official name of Sweden.

Swabia (swä′bi-ạ), see **Schwaben.**

Swakopmund (swä′kōp-mùnd), spt., mandate of S. W. Africa, at mouth of Swakop riv., pop. 4; summer resort; # 22 S, 14:50 E.

Swansea (swon′sē), spt. city on Swansea Bay, S. Wales, pop. 162; tin-plate; coal; # 51:38 N, 3:58 W.

Swarthmore (swärth′mōr), a Pa. suburb of Philadelphia, pop. 4; Swarthmore College; # 39:50 N, 75:20 W.

Swatow (swä-tou′), spt. city, S. E. China, pop. est. 82; typhoon, Aug. 3, 1922; # 23:30 N, 116:45 E.

Swaziland (swä′zē-land), Br. protectorate, S. E. Africa, area 7, pop. 134; * Mbabane; # 26 S, 32 E.

Sweden (swē′ḍen), kingdom, E. Scandinavian pen., area 173, pop. 6,006, * Stockholm, pop. 430; # 63 N, 15 E.

Swindon (swin′dọn), city, 30 mi. E. of Bristol, S. Eng., pop. 56; # 51:31 N, 1:47 W.

Swinemünde (svē′nẽ-mün′dẽ), spt. on Baltic Sea, N. E. Ger., pop. 20; # 53:54 N, 14:16 E.

Swissvale (swis′väl), an E. suburb of Pittsburgh, S. W. Pa., pop. 16; # 40:25 N, 79:53 W.

Switzerland (swit′zẽr-lạnd), republic, W. C. Europe, area 16, pop. 3,880, * Berne, pop. 105; # 47 N, 8 E.

Sybaris (sib′ạ-ris), anc. city, S. Italy, destroyed 510 B.C.; # 39:45 N, 16:30 E.

Sydney (sid′ni), spt. city, S. E. Australia, * of New S. Wales, pop. 981 (with suburbs); splendid harbor; Univ. of Sydney; # 33:53 S, 151:12 E. — city, Cape Breton Isl., Nova Scotia, pop. 23, with **Sydney Mines**, pop. 31; # 46:20 N, 60:10 W.

Syedlets (syed′lyets), see **Siedlce.**

Syene (sī-ēn′), anc. name of Assuan, Egypt.

Syra (sē′rä), see **Syros.**

Syracuse (sir′ạ-kūs, -kūs′), city, C. New York, pop. 206; Syracuse Univ.; salt; # 43:4 N, 76:12 W. — see **Siracusa.**

Syr-Darja (sēr där′yä), see **Sir-Daria.**

Syria (sir′i-ạ), Fr. mandate, Near East, bet. Palestine and Turkey, area 60, pop. ab. 3,000, * Beirut; # 35 N, 38 E.

Syrian Desert (sir′i-ạn), desert, N. Arabia, bordering Syria; # 31 N, 40 E.

Syrian Saddle or **Gate,** broad pass, Euphrates Valley to Mediterranean Sea via Aleppo and Antioch; # 36:5 N, 37:20 E.

Syros (sī′ros), *anc.* Syra, isl., C. Cyclades, S. W. Ægean sea, area .03, pop. 32, and its port (also called Hermopolis), a free port; # 37:25 N, 25 E.

Syzran (siz-rän′y), city, S. E. Russia, on Volga riv., pop. 52; # 53:10 N, 48:33 E.

Szabadka (so′bod-ko) or **Subotica**, city, N. Yugoslavia, pop. 102; # 46:7 N, 19:40 E.

Szechwan (sä-chö-än′) or **Sze Chuan**, prov., S. W. C. China Proper, area 218, pop. est. 50,000, * Chengtu, pop. est. 450; # 30:30 N, 104 E.

Szeged (seg′ed) or **Szegdin**, city on Tisza riv., S. E. Hungary, pop. 119; univ.; # 46:15 N, 20:9 E.

Szombathely (sōm′bot-hel-y′), city, W. Hungary, pop. 35; cathedral; # 47:14 N, 16:36 E.

T

Taal (tä-äl′), lake, S. of Manila, Luzón, Philippines, and active vol. on isl. in same, el. 1,050 ft.; # 13:52 N, 120:55 E.

Tabasco (tä-bäs′kō), state, S. E. Mexico, area 10, pop. 178, * San Juan Bautista, pop. 10; # 18 N, 93 W.

Table Mountain (tä′b'l), flat topped mt. overlooking Cape Town, Union of S. Africa, el. 3,549 ft.; # 34 S, 18:20 E.

Tabor (tä′bôr), tn., S. C. Bohemia, pop. 13; # 49:25 N, 14:40 E. — mt., 6 mi. S. E. of Nazareth, Palestine; el. 1,843 ft.; # 32:42 N, 35:24 E.

Tabora (tä-bō′rä), tn., W. C. Tanganyika, E. Africa, pop. ab. 37; # 5 S, 32:50 E.

---

fat, fāte, fär, fȧll, ȧsk, fãre; net, mē, hẽr; pin, pīne; not, nōte, mŏve, nôr; up, lūte, pùll; oi, oil; ou, out; (lightened) aviạry, ẹlect, agọny, intọ, ụnite; (obscured) errạnt, operä, ardẹnt, actọr, natụre; ch, chip; g, go; th, thin; ᴛʜ, then; y, you;

Tabriz (tä-brēz′), city, N. W. Persia, pop. ab. 200, * of Azerbaijan prov.; #38:5 N, 46:10 E.

Tacna (täk′nä), dept., ext. S. Peru, area 5, held by Chile 1884–1929, restored to Peru 1929, * Tacna, pop. 14; #18 S, 70:20 W.

Tacoma (ta̤-kō′ma̤), city, W. C. Wash., on Puget Sound, pop. 109; College of Puget Sound; #47:15 N, 122:30 W. — pk., Cascades, W. C. Wash.; el. 14,408 ft. (according to Congressional action, the correct name of the peak often called Mt. Rainier); #46:52 N, 121:45 W.

Taconic (ta̤-kon′ik), low mt. range, N. E. New York, W. Mass. and Ver., summit 3,816 ft.; #42:20 N, 73:30 W.

Tacora (tä-kō′rä), vol. mt., ext. N. Chile, el. 19,736 ft.; #17:44 S, 69:49 W.

Tacuba (tä-kō′bä), a N. W. suburb of Mexico City, Mex., pop. 30; #19:35 N, 99:12 W.

Tacubaya (tä-kö-bä′yä), a S. W. suburb of Mexico City, Mex., pop. 36; National Observatory; #19:25 N, 99:12 W.

Tafilet (tä-fē-let′), oasis, S. Morocco, area 0.5, pop. ab. 100; #31 N, 4 W.

Taganrog (tä-gän-rog′), spt. on Gulf of Taganrog, Sea of Azov, S. Russia, pop. 70; #47:12 N, 38:55 E.

Tagus (tä′gus), *Sp.* **Tajo,** *Port.* **Tejo,** riv., C. Spain, across Portugal to Atlantic oc. at Lisboa, len. 566 mi.; #38:3 N, 9 W.

Tahiti (tä-hē′tē), beautiful isl., Society Isls., S. Pacific, area 0.6, pop. 7, * Papeete, pop. 5; Fr.; #17:40 S, 149:30 W.

Tahoe (tä′hō), lake, E. Calif.-W. Nev., area ab. 0.2; resort; el. 6,225 ft.; #39:1 N, 120 W.

Taichu (tī′chō′), inland city, N. W. Taiwan (Formosa), pop. 32; #24:15 N, 120:45 E.

Taihoku (ti-hō′kö), chief city and * of Taiwan (Formosa), pop. 180; #25 N, 121:30 E.

Tai-Hu (tī′hö′), lake, delta of Hwangho, W. of Shanghai, area 1; #31:15 N, 120 E.

Taiku (tī′kō′) or **Taikyu-fu,** inland city, S. E. Korea, pop. 55 (16 Japanese); #35:46 N, 128:32 E.

Taimyr (tī-mēr′), pen., ext. N. Asia, to 76 N; #74 N, 100 E.

Tainan (tī′nän′), treaty port, S. W. Taiwan (Formosa), pop. 77; #23 N, 120:4 E.

Taiping (tī′ping′), city, * of Perak, Federated Malay States, pop. 21; #4:55 N, 100:44 E.

Taiwan (tī-wän′) or **Formosa,** Japanese isl. near China, area 14, pop. 3,655; #23:30 N, 121 E.

Taiyuan (tī′yū-än), walled city, N. C. China Proper, * of Shansi prov., pop. est. 230; #37:45 N, 112:3 E.

Tajo (tä′HŌ), see **Tagus.**

Takamatsu (tä-kä-mät′sö), spt. city, N. E. Shikoku isl., Japan, pop. 72; #34:2 N, 134:2 E.

Takaoka (tä-kä-ō′kä), city, N. W. C. Honshu isl., Japan, pop. 43; #36:45 N, 137 E.

Takasaki (tä-kä-sä′kē), inland city, C. Honshu isl., Japan, pop. 36; #36:20 N, 139 E.

Takata (tä′kä-tä), city, N. C. Honshu isl., Japan, pop. 31; #37:10 N, 138:15 E.

Takla-makan (tä′klä-mä-kän′), desert, Tarim Basin, Chinese Turkestan; #39 N, 81 E.

Talca (täl′kä), prov., C. Chile, area 4, pop. 134, and its *, pop. 36; #35:20 S, 71:46 W.

Talcahuano (täl-kä-wä′nō), spt., N. Concepción, C. Chile, pop. 22; #36:40 S, 73:12 W.

Talien-wan (tä′li-en-wän′), see **Dairen.**

Tallahassee (tal-a̤-has′ē), tn., N. W. Florida, state *, pop. 16; state college; #30:30 N, 84:20 W.

Tallinn (täl′lin), formerly **Reval,** spt., Gulf of Finland, * of Estonia, pop. 130; #59:25 N, 24:45 E.

Tamaqua (ta̤-mä′kwa̤), tn., E. C. Pa., pop. 12; #40:46 N, 75:59 W.

Tamatave (tä-mä-täv′), chief port of Madagascar, pop. 12; #18:8 S, 49:22 E.

Tamaulipas (tä-mou-lē′päs), state, N. E. Mexico, area 31, pop. 288, * Ciudad Victoria, pop. 15; #24 N, 98 W.

Tambora (täm′bō-rä), vol., Sumbawa Isl., Dutch E. Indies, eruption, 1815; #8:12 S, 118:5 E.

Tambov (täm-bôf′), prov., S. C. Russia, area 26, pop. 3,400, and its *, on Oka riv., pop. 70; univ.; #52:5 N, 41:25 E.

Tammerfors (täm′ěr-fors), see **Tampere.**

Tampa (tam′pä), city, W. C. Florida, on Tampa Bay, len. 40 mi., pop. 108; #27:55 N, 82:30 W.

Tampere (täm′pe-rä), formerly **Tammerfors,** city, S. W. Finland, pop. 49; #61:28 N, 23:45 E.

Tampico (täm-pē′kō), spt. city, Tamaulipas, E. C. Mexico, pop. 68; petroleum; #22:11 N, 97:50 W.

Tana (tä′nä), riv., Br. E. Africa to Indian oc., len. ab. 500 mi.; #2:50 S, 40:30 E.

Tanagra (tan′a̤-grä), anc. tn., Bœotia, S. E. Greece; #ab. 38:20 N, 23:45 E.

Tanana (tä-nä-nä′), riv., S. E. Alaska to Yukon, len. ab. 700 mi.; #65:5 N, 152:25 W.

Tananarivo (tä-nä-nä-rē′vō) see **Antananarivo.**

Tanganyika (tän-gän-yē′kä), lake, C. Africa, bet. Belgian Congo and Tanganyika Ter., len. 400 mi., area 13, greatest depth 2,100 ft.; #7 S, 30 E. — Br. mandate, E. Africa, area 365, pop. 4,121, * Dar-es-Salaam, pop. 25; #6 S, 34 E.

Tangier (tan-jēr′), spt. city, N. W. Africa, near Strait of Gibraltar, pop. 62; internationalized; #35:46 N, 5:52 W.

Tanis (tä′nis), anc. city, Nile delta, Egypt; #30:58 N, 31:53 E.

Tanjore (tan-jōr′), city, Madras, S. E. India, pop. 60; #10:4 N, 79:1 E.

Tanta (tän′tä), city, Nile delta, N. Egypt, pop. 74: #30:50 N, 31 E.

Tapajos, Rio (tä-pä-zhōsh′), large S. trib. of Amazon riv., C. Brazil, len. 1,100 mi.; #2:15 S, 54:40 W.

Taranaki (tä-rä-nä′kē), prov., S. W. N. Island, New Zealand, area 4, pop. 62; #39:10 S, 174:10 E.

Taranto (tä-rän′tō), prov., Apulia, S. E. Italy, pop. 275, and its *, *anc.* Tarentum, a spt. on Gulf of Taranto, pop. 104; #40:28 N, 17:14 E.

Tarapacá (tä″rä-pä-kä′), prov., ext. N. Chile, area 21, pop. 113; nitrate; #20 S, 69:38 W.

Tarbagatai (tär-bä-gä-tī′), prov., ext. W. Mongolia; #46 N, 84 E.

Târgu Mures (tir′gú mö′resh), city in Romania.

Tarim (tä-rēm′), vast basin, E. Turkestan, #39:45 N, 83 E., and a riv. 1,000 mi. long, to Lop Nor; #39:45 N, 89:20 E.

Tarn (tärn), dept., S. C. Fr., area 2.2, pop. 296, * Albi, pop. 15; #43:52 N, 2:5 E.

Tarn-et-Garonne (tärn-ä-ga̤-rōn), dept., S. W. C. Fr., area 1.4, pop. 160, * Montauban, pop. 31; #44 N, 1:10 E.

Tarnopol (tär′no-pol-y′), city, S. E. Poland on Seret riv., pop. 31; #49:4 N, 25:25 E.

Tarnów (tär′nof), city, W. Galicia, S. W. Poland, pop. 37; #50:2 N, 21 E.

Tarragona (tär-rä-gō′nä), prov., Catalonia, N. E. Spain, area 2.5, pop. 363, and its *, a spt., pop. 28; #41:15 N, 1:1 E.

Tarsus (tär′sus), city, near Adana, S. C. Anatolia, pop. 26; #36:55 N, 34:50 E.

Tartar Republic (tär′tär), soviet republic, E. C. Russia, area 26, pop. 2,852, * Kazan, pop. 195; #ab. 55:45 N, 49:5 E.

Tartu (tär′tö), *Ger.* **Dorpat,** city, C. Estonia, pop. 50; univ.; #58:25 N, 26:45 E.

Tasavalta, Suomen (tä′sä-väl″tä, swô′men), official name of Finland.

Tashkent (täsh-kent′), city, * of Turkestan rep., Soviet Russia in Asia, pop. 201; #41:25 N, 69:1 E.

Tasman (täz′ma̤n), sea, part of Pacific oc. bet. Aust. and New Zealand; #38 S, 155 E. — bay, N. coast S. Isl., New Zealand; #40:55 S, 173:23 E.

Tasmania (taz-mä′ni-a̤), isl., S. E. of Australia, a State of the Commonwealth of Australia; area 26, pop. 227, * Hobart, pop. 52; #42 S, 147 E.

Tatar (tä-tär′), strait bet. Sakhalin-Karafuto and Siberia; #50 N, 142 E. — see **Tartar.**

Tateyama (tä-tä-yä′mä), vol., C. Honshu, Japan, el. 9,630 ft.; #36:32 N, 137:40 E.

Tátra, High (tä′trä), highest group of Carpathian Mts., E. Cz-S., el. 8,735 ft.; #49:1 N, 20 E.

Taunton (tän′ton, tân′tun), city, S. E. Mass., pop. 37; #41:52 N, 71:3 W. — city, W. C. Somerset, Eng., pop. 23; #51:2 N, 3:9 W.

Taurida (tä′rē-dä), former prov., S. Russia, see **Crimea.**

Taurus (tâ′rus), mt. range, S. W. Asia Minor, bordering Mediterranean Sea; summit, el. 11,483 ft.; #37 N, 34 E.

Tay (tä), riv., from Loch Tay to Firth of Tay, Perth, N. E. Scotland, len. 120 mi., Scotland's largest; #56:20 N, 3:28 W.

Taylor (tā′lọr), tn., N. E. Pa., pop. 9; # 41:24 N, 75:45 W.

Taz (täz), bay, N. side of Gulf of Ob, N. W. Siberia, and riv. entering, len. 300 mi.; # 68 N, 77:20 E.

Tees (tēz), riv., Westmorland, Eng., E. to N. Sea, len. 70 mi.; # 54:37 N, 1:15 W.

Tegucigalpa (tā-gö-sē-gäl′pä), city, * of Honduras, C. America, pop. 40; # 14:9 N, 87 W.

Teheran (teh-e-rän′) or **Tehran**, city, N. C. Persia, its *, pop. 220; # 35:50 N, 51:35 E.

Tehran (teh-rän′), see **Teheran**.

Tehri (teh-rē′), see **Garhwal**.

Tehuantepec (tā-wän-tā-pek′), gulf, isthmus (130 mi. wide) and tn., near narrowest portion of Mexico, pop. 16; # 16:2 N, 95:2 W.

Tejo (tā′zhọ), see **Tagus**.

Tel Aviv (tel ạ-vēv′), Jewish tn., near Jaffa, W. Palestine, pop. 140; # 32:2 N, 34:45 E.　　　　　　[# 35 N, 5 E.

Tell (tel), hill coastal region, N. Africa, esp. E. Atlas Mts.;

Tembuland (tem′bö-land), div. of Prov. of Cape of Good Hope, area 3, pop. 234, * Umtata; # 31:40 S, 28 E.

Temesvár (tem′esh-vär) or **Temisoara** (tā″mẹ-shọ-ä′rä) or **Timisoara** or **Timiswara**, city, ext. S. W. Romania, pop. 92; # 45:47 N, 21:13 E.　　　　　　[22:46 E.

Tempe (tem′pē), famous vale, Thessaly, E. Greece; #39:55 N,

Tempelhof (tem′pẹl-höf), a S. div. of Berlin, Ger., pop. 67; # 52:26 N, 13:23 E.

Temple (tem′pl), tn., C. Texas, pop. 15; # 31:4 N, 97: 20 W.

Temuco (tā-mö′kō), city, S. C. Chile, pop. 29, * of Cautin prov.; # 38:47 S, 72:45 W.

Tenedos (ten′ẹ-dos), Turkish isl., N. E. Ægean Sea, near Dardanelles, area .03; # 39:5 N, 26:5 E.

Tenerife (ten-èr-if′), largest of Canary Isls., off N. W. Africa, area 1, pop. 180, * Santa Cruz de, pop. 78; # 28:15 N, 16:3 W. — **Pico de**, vol., el. 12,190 ft.; # 28:15 N, 16:4 W.

Tengri, Khan (teng′grē, chän), peak Tian Shan mts., C. Asia, Tibet, el. 24,132 ft.; # 42:25 N, 80:20 E.

Tengri Nor (ten′grē nōr′), lofty lake, Tibetian Plateau, C. Asia, near Lhasa; el. 15,186 ft.; # 30:40 N, 90:30 E.

Tennessee (ten-ẹ-sē′), state, S. E. C. U.S.A., bordering Ky. and N. Car., area 42, pop. 2,916, * Nashville, pop. 167; largest city, Memphis, pop. 293; # 36 N, 86 W. — riv., E. Tenn. to the Ohio riv., len. 1,200 mi.; # 37:1 N, 88:3 W.

Tenos or **Tinos** (tē′nos), Greek isl., Cyclades, S. Ægean sea, area .08, pop. 12, and its spt.; # 37:32 N, 25:22 E.

Tepic (tā-pēk′), city, W. C. Mexico, * of ter. of Nayarit (formerly Tepic); pop. 15; # 21:25 N, 104:50 W.

Teplitz (tep′lits), city, N. Bohemia, Cz-S, pop. 29, with suburbs, 47; watering place; # 50:38 N, 13:50 E.

Teramo (tā′rä-mō), prov., Abruzzi, E. C. Italy, area 1, pop. 320, and its *, pop. 26; # 42:40 N, 13:45 E.

Terek (tye′rek), pass, bet. Russian and Chinese Turkestan; # 40:45 N, 74:3 E. — riv., Caucasus Mts. to Caspian sea, len. 400 mi.; # 43:48 N, 47:30 E.

Ternate (ter-nä′tä), isl., Dutch E. Indies, and its spt., the * of Ternate prov., pop. 7; # 0:50 N, 127:25 E.

Terni (ter′nē), city, Umbria, C. Italy, pop. comm. 33; near falls of Velino riv.; # 42:34 N, 12:37 E.

Terre Haute (ter′ẹ hōt), city, on Wabash riv., W. C. Ind., pop. 63; State Normal College; Rose Polytechnic Institute; coal; # 39:28 N, 87:25 W.

Teruel (tā-rö-el′), prov., E. C. Spain, area 5.7, pop. 249, and its *, pop. 10; # 40:23 N, 1:12 W.

Tessin (te-sēn′; *Fr.* te-saṅ), see **Ticino**.

Tetuán (tet-ö-än′), city, Spanish zone, N. Morocco, pop. 31; # 35:37 N, 5:22 W.

Teulada (tā-ö-lä′dä), cape, ext. S. Sardiniạ; # 38:52 N, 8:39 E.

Teverone (tā-vā-rō′nä), riv., Apennines, C. Italy to Tiber riv., near Rome; falls, 315 ft., near Tivoli; # ab. 42 N, 12:27 E.

Texarkana (teks-är-kan′ạ), city on Texas-Ark. boundary, pop. 29; # 33:23 N, 94:4 W.

Texas (tek′sạs), state, S. C. U.S.A., bordering Mexico, Gulf and Okla., area 266, pop. 6,415, * Austin, pop. 88; largest city, Houston, pop. 385; # 32 N, 100 W.

Thailand (tā′ē-land), official name for Siam.

Thames (temz, tämz), riv., S. W. Eng., E. through London to N. Sea, len. 160 mi.; # 51:30 N, 0:45 E.

Thanet (than′et), isl., N. E. tip of Kent, S. E. Eng., area .04.

Thar (tur) or **Indian Desert**, arid region, E. of mid Indus Valley, N. W. India; # 28 N, 72 E.

Thasos (thä′sos), Greek isl., ext. N. Ægean Sea, area 0.2, pop. 12; # 40:40 N, 24:38 E.

Thebes (thēbz), anc. city on Nile riv.; ruins; # 25:45 N, 32:38 E. — anc. city-kingdom, S. E. Greece; # 38:20 N, 23:18 E.

Theiss (tīs), see **Tisza**.

Thera (thē′rạ), see **Santorin**.

Therezina (tā-re-zē′nä), city, E. C. Brazil, * of Piauhy, pop. 58; # 5:40 S, 42:30 W.

Thermopylæ (thèr-mop′i-lē), pass, N. E. Greece; battle, 480 B.C.; # 38:46 N, 22:45 E.

Thessalonica (thes″ạ-lọ-nī′kä), anc. name of Salonika.

Thessaly (thes′ạ-li) and **Arta**, dept., N. C. Greece, pop. 491; # 39:45 N, 22:30 E.

Thian Shan (ti-än′ shän′), see **Tian Shan**.

Thibet, see **Tibet**.

Thorn (tōrn), see **Torun**.

Thoune, see **Thun**.

Thousand Islands (thou′sạnd ī′lạndz), group of ab. 1,500 isls., St. Lawrence riv., near Lake Ontario; resorts; # 44:15 N, 76:10 W.

Thrace (thrās), region bordering N. Ægean Sea; # 41:30 N, 27 E. — dept., ext. N. E. Greece, pop. 704; # 41 N, 25 E.

Three Rivers (thrē riv′ẹrz), city on St. Lawrence riv., S. Quebec, pop. 30; # 46:30 N, 72:25 W.

Thun or **Thoune** (tön), city, on Lake of Thun, C. Switz., pop. 14; # 46:45 N, 7:40 E.

Thurgau (tür′gou) or **Thurgovie**, canton, ext. N. E. Switz., area .04, pop. 136, * Frauenfeld; # 47:33 N, 9 E.

Thüringen (tü′ring-ẹn), *Eng.* **Thuringia**, state, S. C. Ger., area 4.5, pop. 1,625, * Weimar, pop. 41; # 50:50 N, 10:20 E; — see **Saxe**.

Thüringer Wald (tü′ring-èr vält), low mt. range, S. W. Ger., len. 75 mi., highest el. 3,400 ft.; # 50:40 N, 10:45 E.

Thursday Island (thèrz′dā ī′lạnd), isl. and port, Torres Strait, N. E. Australia; pop. 1; # 10:40 S, 142:10 E.

Tian Shan (tē-än′ shän′), mt. range, Turkestan, C. Asia, highest Khan Tengri, el. 24,132 ft.; # 42:30 N, 80 E.

Tiber (tī′bèr), *anc.* Tiberis, riv., Apennines, Tuscany, C. Italy, past Rome to Tyrrhenian Sea, len. 244 mi.; # 41:45 N, 12:15 E.

Tiberias (tī-bē′ri-ạs) or **Tubariya**, tn., W. coast of Sea of Galilee, pop. 7; # 32:47 N, 35:32 E.

Tibesti (tē-bes-tē′), N. part of Fr. Equatorial Africa, including Tibesti Mts. in C. Sahara; # 22 N, 16 E.

Tibet (ti-bet′, tib′et), lofty plateau, S. C. Asia; # 32 N, 90 E; a Chinese Outer Ter., area 463, pop. ab. 2,000, * Lhasa, pop. 20; # 32 N, 90 E.

Ticino (tē-chē′nō) or **Tessin**, canton, S. C. Switz., area 1, pop. 152, * Bellinzona; # 46:15 N, 8:35 E. —, *anc.* Ticinus, riv., S. E. Switz., to Po riv., near Pavia, It., len. 150 mi.; # 45:8 N, 9:16 E.

Ticonderoga (tī-kon-dẹ-rō′gä), vil. on Lake Champlain, N. E. New York, pop. 3; old fort; # 43:52 N, 73:28 W.

Tiehling (ti-e′ling′), city, S. Manchuria, pop. 33; # 42:20 N, 123:51 E.

Tien Shan, see **Tian Shan**.

Tientsin (tē-en′tsēn′), city, N. China, * of Chihli prov., pop. est. 800; # 39:10 N, 117:10 E.

Tiergarten (tēr′gär-tẹn), a W. C. div. of Berlin, Ger., pop. 277; # 52:31 N, 13:20 E.

Tierra del Fuego (tē-er′rä del fwä′gō), group of isls., S. end of S. America; # 54 S, 69 W. — ter., S. Argentina, the E. part of group, area 8, pop. 3; # 55 S, 67 W.

Tiffin (tif′in), tn., N. W. C. Ohio, pop. 16; Heidelberg College; # 41:9 N, 83:12 W.

Tiflis (tyẹf-lyēs′), officially **Tpilisi**, city, * of Transcaucasian and Georgian Soviets, pop. 347; univ.; # 41:40 N, 44: 50 E.

Tigré (tē-grā), prov., N. Ethiopia (Abyssinia), * Adowa; # 14 N, 38 E.

Tigris (tī′gris), riv., Armenia to Persian Gulf, len. 1,100 mi.; # 31 N, 46:45 E.

Tihwafu (tē-hwä-fö′), see **Urumtsi**.

Tilburg (til′bừrch), city, N. Brabant, S. C. Neth., pop. 68; # 51:35 N, 5:7 E.

Tilsit (til′sit), city, ext. N. E. Ger., on Memel riv., pop. 50; # 55:5 N, 21:30 E.

Timaru (tē′mä-rö), spt. city, E. C. S. Island, New Zealand, pop. 17; # 44:20 S, 171:5 E.

Timbuktu (tim-buk′tö), city of Fr. Sudan, W. Africa, pop. 7; # 16:50 N, 2:50 W.

Timisoara (tē′′mē-shō-ä′rä), see **Temesvár.**

Timor (tē-mōr′), isl., E. Indies, bet. Celebes and Australia, area 14, pop. 1,500; E. part is Portuguese, area 7, pop. 378, * Dilli; W. part is Dutch, area 6, pop. 1,147; # 9:15 S, 125 E.

Timorlaut (tē-mōr′lout), isl., S. of Papua, Dutch E. Indies, area 2, pop. 25; # 7:30 S, 131:30 E.

Timor Sea (tē-mōr′ sē), part of Indian oc. bet. Australia and Timor; # 12 S, 125 E.

Timpanogos (tim-pä-nō′gos), cave, a national monument, C. Utah, near American Fork; # 40:23 N, 111:50 W.

Tinnevelly (tin-e-vel′i), city, Madras, S. India, pop. 54; # 8:44 N, 77:44 E.

Tinos (tē′nōs), see **Tenos.**

Tippecanoe (tip′′ē-ka-nö′), riv., N. W. Ind., to Wabash riv., len. 200 mi.; # 40:30 N, 86:45 W.

Tipperary (tip-ė-rā′ri), county, Munster, S. C. Ireland, area 1.5, pop. 152, and a tn. therein, pop. 6; # 52:29 N, 8:9 W.

Tirach Mir (tē′ruch mēr), mt., highest of Hindu Kush, N. W. India, el. 25,420 ft.; # 36:25 N, 72 E.

Tirana (tē-rä′nä), tn., C. Albania, its *, pop. 12; # 41:20 N, 19:50 E.

Tirol (tir′ol; Ger. tē-rōl′), see **Tyrol.**

Tisza (tē′so) or **Theiss**, riv., Carpathian Mts., S. to Danube riv. at Belgrade, len. 800 mi.; # 45:10 N, 20:15 E.

Titicaca (tē-tē-kä′kä), lake bet. S. Peru and Bolivia, area 3, el. 12,508 ft.; highest large lake; # 16 S, 69 W.

Tivoli (tē′vō-lē), anc. Tiber, tn., 18 mi. E. N. E. Rome, Italy, pop. comm. 15; # 41:58 N, 12:48 E.

Tizi-n-Tamjurt (tē-zē-n-täm-zhūr), highest peak of Atlas Mts., N. W Africa, el. 14,764 ft.; # 30:50 N, 7:50 W.

Tizi Ouzou (tē-zē′ ö-zö′), city, Algeria, pop. 35; # 36:44 N, 4:5 E.

Tlaxcala (tläs-kä′lä), state, S. E. C. Mexico, area 2, pop. 179, and its *, pop. 3; # 19:20 N, 98:15 W.

Tlemcen (tlem-sen′), city, N. W. Algeria, pop. 43; # 34:51 N, 1:20 W.

Tobago (tō-bä′gō), isl., near Trinidad, Br. W. Indies; area 1, pop. 23; # 11:20 N, 60:40 W.

Tobata (tō-bä′tä), spt. city, S. Honshu, Japan, pop. 38; # 34:39 N, 136:50 E.

Tobol (to-bol′y′), riv., S. Ural Mts., N. E. to Irtysh riv., len. 800 mi.; # 57 N, 68 E.

Tobolsk (tō-bolsk′), former prov., W. C. Siberia, area 536, pop. 1,842, and its *, pop. 25; # 58:10 N, 68:20 E.

Tocantins (tō-kän-tēnz′), riv., E. Brazil, Goyaz, N. to Pará riv., len. 1,500 mi.; # 2 S, 49:15 W.

Tödi (te′dē), range of mts., E. C. Switz., and its highest pk., el. 11,887 ft.; # 46:50 N, 8:45 E.

Togoland (tō′gō-land), former Ger. possession, Equatorial Africa, now absorbed in Gold Coast and Dahomey, q.v.

Tokio, see **Tokyo.**

Tokushima (tō-kú-shē′mä), spt. city, N. E. Shikoku isl., Japan, pop. 75; # 34:5 N, 134:35 E.

Tokyo (tō′kē-ō), city, S. E. Honshu isl., * of Japan, pop. 1,095 (1925), with suburbs, pop. 5,164; earthquake and fire, Sept. 1, 1923; Imperial, Tokyo, Meiji and Waseda univs.; # 35:42 N, 139:46 E.

Toledo (tō-lē′dō), city, N. W. Ohio, W. end of Lake Erie, pop. 282; # 41:40 N, 83:32 W. — prov., Spain, area 6, pop. 451, and its *, pop. 26; cathedral; # 39:51 N, 4:1 W.

Tolima (tō-lē′mä), mt. pk., highest in Colombia, el. 18,320 ft.; # 4:45 N, 75:35 W. — dept., W. C. Colombia, area 10, pop. 329, * Ibagué; # 3 N, 75:30 W.

Toluca (tō-lö′kä), city, * of Mexico state, S. C. Mex., pop. 31; # 19:15 N, 99:45 W.

Tombigbee (tom-big′bē), riv., N. E. Miss. to Mobile Bay, len. 475 mi.; # 30:50 N, 88 W.

Tomini (tō-mē′nē), large gulf, N. E. Celebes, E. Indies; # 0:30 S, 121 E.

Tomsk (tomsk), prov., W. C. Siberia, area 159, pop. 1,086, and its *. on Tom riv., pop. 100; # 56:30 N, 85:10 E.

Tonawanda (ton-a-won′da), tn., N. W. New York, pop. 13; # 43:1 N, 78:53 W.

Tonga (tong′gä, tō′ngä), group of isls., S. W. Pacific, area 0.4, pop. 25, * Nukualofa; Br. Protectorate; # 20 S, 174:30 E.

Tongking (tong-king′), gulf, portion of S. China Sea, W. of Hainan; len. 300 mi.; # 20 N, 108 E. — see **Tonking.**

Tonk (tongk), native state of Rajputana, N. W. India, area 3, pop. 288, and its *. pop. 30; # 26:10 N, 76 E.

Tonking (ton-king′), N. E. part Fr. Indo-China, area 41, pop. 6,850, * Hanoi, pop. 74; # 21:30 N, 104:30 E.

Tonle Sap (ton′lä säp), lake, C. Cambodia, area 0.1 to 0.8 (wet season); rice; # 13 N, 104 E.

Tonopah (tō-nō-pä′), mining city, S. C. Nev., pop. 4; rich gold and silver mines; # 38:5 N, 117:15 W.

Tönsberg (tèns-bar′y′), spt., S. E. Norway, on Christiania fjord, pop. 13; # 59:16 N, 10:25 E.

Toowoomba (tö-wöm′ba), city, S. E. Queensland, Australia, pop. 21; # 27:35 S, 152:5 E.

Topeka (tō-pē′kä), city, E. C. Kansas, State *, pop. 68; Washburn College and State Normal; # 39:5 N, 95: 42 W.

Torino (tō-rē′nō), Eng. **Turin**, prov., Piedmont, N. Italy; area 4, pop. 1,253, and its *, anc. Taurasia, pop. 502; univ.; # 45:5 N, 7:40 E.

Torneå Elf (tōr′nē-ō), riv., boundary bet. N. Sweden and Finland, len. 300 mi.; # 65:50 N, 24 E.

Toronto (tō-ron′tō), city on Lake Ontario, S. E. Ontario, prov. *, pop. 631; Univ. of Toronto; McMasters Univ.; Victoria College; # 43:40 N, 79:25 W.

Torquay (tôr-kē′), watering place, S. Devon, S. W. Eng., pop. 30; # 50:29 N, 3:31 W.

Torrens (tor′enz), salt lake, S. Australia, len. 130 mi.; # 31 S, 138:5 E.

Torreón (tôr-rä-ōn′), tn., Coahuila, N. E. Mexico, pop. 40; # 25:40 N, 103:25 W.

Torres (tor′res), strait bet. N. E. Australia and Papua, width 90 mi.; # 9:30 S, 142 E.

Torrington (tor′ing-ton), city, N. W. Conn., pop. 27; # 41:51 N, 73:8 W.

Tortuga (tor-tö′gä), isl., N. of Haiti, to Haiti, West Indies, len. 25 mi.; # 20 N, 72:40 W. — coastal isl. of Venezuela; # 11 N, 65:25 W.

Torun (tö′rön), city, N. W. Poland, on Vistula riv., pop. 40; # 53 N, 18:20 E.

Tosa (tō′sä), waterfall, Gries Pass, Pennine Alps, N. Italy, height 470 ft.; # 46:24 N, 8:25 E.

Tottenham (tot′en-am), a N. urban suburb of London, Eng., pop. 140; # 51:36 N, 0:4 W.

Tottori (tōt′tō-rē), spt. city, W. Honshu isl., Japan, pop. 35; # 35:30 N, 134:12 E.

Toul (töl), tn., N. E. Fr., 10 mi. W. of Nancy, pop. 14; # 48:40 N, 5:50 E.

Toulon (tö-lôn), spt. city, S. E. Fr., 30 mi. E. of Marseille, pop. 106; naval station; # 43:5 N, 5:55 E.

Toulouse (tö-löz), city, S. Fr., * of Haute-Garonne dept., pop. 175; univ.; # 43:45 N, 1:25 E.

Touraine (tö-rän), anc. prov., W. C. Fr.; * Tours; # 47 N, 0:30 E.

Tourane (tö-rän) or **Turan**, chief port of Annam, E. Fr. Indo-China, pop. ab. 10; # 16 N, 108:5 E.

Tourcoing (tör-kwaṅ), city, ext. N. Fr., 12 mi. N. of Lille, pop. 79; # 50:45 N, 3:5 E.

Tournai (tör-nā), city, S. W. Belgium, pop. 36; near Lille, Fr.; # 50:35 N, 3:28 E.

Tours (tör), city on Loire riv., W. C. Fr., pop. 75; battle 732; # 47:20 N, 0:40 E.

Townsville (tounz′vil), spt. city, E. C. Queensland, Aust., pop. 21; # 19:15 S, 146:45 E.

Toyama (tō′yä-mä), city on Toyama Bay, N. C. Honshu isl., Japan, pop. 67; # 36:43 N, 137:12 E.

Toyohashi (tō′yō-hä′shē), spt. city, Ise Bay, S. Honshu isl., Japan, pop. 82; # 34:45 N, 137:20 E.

Trafalgar (traf-al-gär′, tra-fal′gar), cape, S. Spain, W. of Gibraltar; battle, Nelson, 1805; # 36:10 N, 6:3 W.

Tralee (tra-lē′), spt. city, on Tralee Bay, * of Kerry Co., ext. S. W. Ireland, pop. 10; # 52:18 N, 9:44 W.

Trani (trä′nē), spt. city, Apulia, S. E. Italy, pop. comm. 31; # 41:16 N, 16:26 E.

(variable) ḍ as d or j, ṣ as s or sh, ṭ as t or ch, ẓ as z or zh; o, F. cloche; ü, F. menu; ċh, Sc. loch; ṅ, F. bonbon; ′, primary accent; ″, secondary accent; †, obsolete; <, from; +, and; =, equals. See also lists at beginning of book.

Trans-Andine (trans), R.R. tunnel, Argentina-Chile, el. 10,486 ft., len. 5 mi.: opened 1910; # 32:50 S, 70:8 W.

Transbaikalia (trans-bī-kä′li-ạ), prov., Far E. Region, Soviet Siberia, area 238, pop. 972, * Chita; # 53 N, 114 E.

Transcaucasia (trans-kâ-kā′shiạ), Soviet republic, in and S. of Caucasus Mts., area 76, pop. 5,421, consists of Azerbaijan, Georgia, Armenia, * Tiflis, pop. 347; # 42 N, 45 E.

Trans-Jordania (trans-jôr-dā′ni-ạ) or **Kerak,** Br. protectorate, E. of Palestine, pop. ab. 300, * Amman; # 31 N, 36 E.

Transkei (trans-kī′), div. of prov. of Cape of Good Hope, area 2.5, pop. 198, * Butterworth; # 32:10 S, 28 E.

Transvaal (trans-väl′), prov., Union of S. Africa; area 110, pop. 2,088, * Pretoria, pop. 74; gold; # 24 S, 30 E.

Transylvania (tran-sil-vā′ni-ạ), prov., W. C. Romania, area 22.3, pop. 2,678; # 45:10 N, 23:30 E.

Transylvanian Alps (tran-sil-vā′ni-ạn alps), mt. range, S. W. Romania, S. continuation of Carpathians, summit Negoi, el. 8,369 ft.; # 45:20 N, 24 E.

Trapani (trä′pä-nē), prov., N. W. Sicily, area 1, pop. 409, and its *, anc. Drepanum, a spt., pop. 71; # 38:1 N, 12:29 E.

Trasimeno (trä-sē-mā′nō), lake, Perugia, C. Italy; # 43:10 N, 12:5 E.

Trás-os-Montes (träsh′ōsh-mon′tesh), prov., N. E. Portugal, area 4.2, pop. 406, * Bragança; # 41:35 N, 7 W.

Travancore (trav-ạn-kōr′), native state, S. India, area 7.6, pop. 4,006, * Trivandrum, pop. 73; # 10 N, 77 E.

Traverse City (trav′ẽrs), lake port, N. W. Mich., pop. 14; # 44:45 N, 85:35 W.

Traz, see **Trás-os-Montes.**

Trebbia (treb′bē-ä), riv., N. Apennines to Po riv., N. Italy, len. 75 mi.; battle, Hannibal, 218 B.C.; # 45 N, 9:37 E.

Trebizond (treb′i-zond), prov., N. W. Asiatic Turkey, area 17, pop. 1,122, and its *, a spt. on Black Sea, pop. 55; # 40:55 N, 39:50 E.

Trengganu (treng-gä′nō), a Br. protected state, E. coast Malay pen., area 6, pop. 154, * Kuala, pop. 12; # 5:17 N, 103:5 E.

Trent (trent), city, Tyrol, N. Italy, pop. 35; Council, 1545–63; # 46:3 N, 11:7 E. — riv., C. Eng., to the Humber, len. 125 mi.; # 53:42 N, 0:45 W.

Trentino (tren-tē′nō), region, ext. N. Italy, pop. 642, formerly Austrian, * Trento (Trent), pop. 35; # 46:5 N, 11:6 E.

Trento (tren′tō), see **Trent.**

Trenton (tren′tọn), city, C. New Jersey, state *, on Delaware riv., pop. 125; # 40:15 N, 74:42 W.

Treptow (träp′tō), a S. E. div. of Berlin, Ger., pop. 96; # 52:27 N, 13:30 E.

Treves (trēvz), see **Trier.**

Treviso (trä-vē′sō), prov., Venetia, N. E. Italy, area 1, pop. 548, and its *, pop. 50; # 45:40 N, 12:15 E.

Trichinopoly (trich-i-nop′ọ-li), city, S. E. India, on Cauvery riv., pop. 120; # 10:40 N, 78:45 E.

Trier (trēr), city on Moselle riv. near Luxemburg, S. W. Ger., pop. 58; # 49:45 N, 6:40 E.

Trieste (trē-es′tä), prov., Venezia Giulia, N. E. Italy, pop. 326, and its *, a spt., pop. 239; # 45:40 N, 13:46 E.

Trikkala (trē′kä-lä), nome, Thessaly, C. Greece, area 2.2, pop. 199, and its *, on Peneius riv., pop. 20; # 39:33 N, 21:42 E.

Trinidad (trin′i-dad; Sp. trē-nē-ᴛнäᴛн′), isl., near Venezuela, a Br. colony, area 2, pop. 456, * Port of Spain, pop. 64; asphalt; # 10:30 N, 61:15 W. — tn., S. E. Colo., pop. 13; # 37:15 N, 104:30 W. — spt. city, S. C. Cuba, pop. 44; # 21:55 N, 80 W.

Trinity (trin′i-ti), riv., N. Texas to Galveston Bay, len. 530 mi.; # 29:50 N, 94:45 W.

Tripoli (trip′ọ-li), spt. city, * of Tripolitanian portion of Libia Italiana, N. Africa, pop. 60; # 32:40 N, 13:25 E. — anc. Tarabulus, spt. city in Fr. mandate of Great Lebanon, Syria, pop. 30; # 34:26 N, 35:51 E.

Tripura (trē-pö′rä) or **Tippera,** native state of Bengal, N. E. India, area 4, pop. 304; # 23:30 N, 91 E.

Tristan da Cunha (tris-tän′ dä kön′yä), group, Br. isls., S. Atlantic oc., area .05: # 37:5 S, 12:10 W.

Trivandrum (trē-vun′drŭm), city, S. India, * of Travancore state, pop. 73; # 8:29 N, 76:59 E.

Trollhätta (trōl-het′ä), falls of the Göta riv., outlet of Lake Väner, height 108 ft.; # 58:16 N, 12:19 E.

Trollhättan (trōl-het′än), city, S. W. Sweden, pop. 17; # 58:16 N, 12:19 E.

Tromsö (trom′sẻ), prov., N. Norway, area 10, pop. 91, and its *, a spt. on Tromsö sound, pop. 10; fisheries; # 69:39 N, 18:57 E.

Trondhjem (tron′yem), spt. city, on Trondhjem fjord (len. 80 mi.), C. Norway, pop. 55; # 63:25 N, 10:25 E.

Tropics, The (trop′iks), zone bet. lat. 23½ N. and S. or bet. 30 N. and S.

Tropics of Cancer and Capricorn, lat. 23:27 N. and S.; farthest from equator that sun is ever overhead at noon.

Troppau (trop′pou), see **Opava.**

Trowbridge (trō′brij), tn., Wilts, S. W. Eng., pop. 12; # 51:19 N, 2:12 W.

Troy (troi), city, E. C. New York, pop. 70; men's collars; Rensselaer Polytech. Inst., Russell Sage College; # 42:46 N, 73:45 W. — ruins of anc. city, Asiatic side of Dardanelles; # 40 N, 26:15 E.

Troyes (trwä), city, N. E. C. Fr., * of Aube dept., pop. 55: # 48:20 N, 4:5 E.

Truckee (truk-ē′), pass across Sierra Nevada Mts., E. C. Calif., el. 7,017 ft.; # 39 N, 121 W.

Trujillo (trö-ᴴēl′yō), state in N. W. Venezuela, pop. 179, and its *, pop. 12; # 8:53 N, 70:16 W. — a city in N. W. Peru, pop. 25, * of Libertad; # 8:10 S, 79:5 W.

Truro (trö′rō), spt., S. W. Cornwall, S. W. Eng., pop. 11: mines; cathedral; # 50:15 N, 5:5 W. — tn., head of Bay of Fundy, Nova Scotia, pop. 8; Agricultural and Normal Colleges; # 45:25 N, 63:14 W.

Tsaritsyn (tsä-rē′tsin), city on Volga riv., S. Soviet Russia. pop. 81; # 48:45 N, 44:25 E.

Tsinan (tsē-nän′), spt. city, N. E. China, * of Shantung prov., pop. est. 400; # 36:55 N, 117:40 E.

Tsingtao (tsing-tou′), port, S. Shantung pen., China, pop. est. 60; # 36:10 N, 120:35 E.

Tsinling Shan (tsin-ling′ shän′), E-W. mt. range, W. C. China, highest ab. 13,000 ft.; # 34 N, 108 E.

Tsitsihar (tsēt-sē-här′), city, N. Manchuria, * of Heilung-Kiang prov., pop. 50; # 47:30 N, 124 E.

Tsu (tsö), city in Ise Bay, S. Honshu isl., Japan, pop. 53; # 34:42 N, 136:30 E.

Tsugaru (tsö-gä′rö), strait bet. Honshu and Hokkaido (Yezo) isls., Japan; # 41:30 N, 140:30 E.

Tsuruoka (tsö′rö-ō′kä), city, N. Honshu isl., Japan, pop. 32; # 38:41 N, 139:50 E.

Tsushima (tsö-shē′mä′), strait bet. Kyushiu and Tsu isls., Japan; # 34 N, 129:30 E.

Tuamotu (twä-mō′tō), group isls., often called The Low Archipelago, E. S. Pacific oc., area 0.3, pop. 4; Fr.; # 20 S, 140 W.

Tübingen (tü′bing-ẹn), city, S. C. Württemberg, S. W. Ger., pop. 21; univ.; # 48:32 N, 9:2 E.

Tucson (tö-son′), city, S. E. Ariz., pop. 37; State Univ.; # 32:15 N, 110:55 W.

Tucumán (tö-kö-män′), prov., N. W. Argentina, area 10, pop. 380, and its *, pop. 91; # 26:50 S, 65:20 W.

Tula (tö′lä), prov., W. C. Russia, area 12, pop. 1,800, and its *, pop. 137; # 54:20 N, 37:30 E.

Tulare (tö-lär′), lake, S. C. Calif., area fluctuating, sometimes 0.4; # 36 N, 119:45 W.

Tulsa (tul′sạ), city, N. E. Okla., pop. 142; petroleum center; Tulsa Univ.; # 36:10 N, 95:55 W.

Tumbes (töm′bās), prov. ext. N. W. Peru, area 2, pop. 9, and its *, a spt.; # 3:35 S, 80:27 W.

Tunbridge (tun′brij), or **Tunbridge Wells,** city, S. C. Kent, S. E. Eng., pop. 36; mineral wells; resort; # 51:8 N, 0:16 E.

Tungting (töng′ting′), lake, Hunan prov., S. C. China Proper, area 2, # 29:15 N, 112:45 E.

Tunguragua (tön-gö-rä′gwä), prov., Ecuador, area 2, pop. 127. — vol. therein, el. 16,690 ft.; # 1:28 S, 78:31 W.

Tunguska (tûn-gûs′kä), **Lower, Stony** and **Upper,** three long E. trib. of Yenisei riv., Siberia; Lower, # 64:14 N, 95 E; Stony, # 61, 90 E; Upper, # 58:5 N, 93 E.

Tunis (tū′nis), spt. city, * of Tunisia, N. Africa, pop. 172; # 36:40 N, 10 E.

Tunisia (tū-nish′i-ạ), Fr. protectorate, N. Africa, area 50, pop. 2,095, * Tunis, pop. 172; officially known as Afrikiya; # 35 N, 10 E.

---

fat, fāte, fär, fåll, åsk, fåre; net, mē, hẽr; pin, pīne; not, nōte, mȯve, nȯr; up, lūte, půll; oi, oil; ou, out; (lightened) aviạry, ẹlect, agọny, intọ, ūnite; (obscured) errạnt, operạ, ardẹnt, actọr, natūre; ch, chip; g, go; th, thin; ᴛн, then; y, you;

Tunja (tön'ʜä), tn., N. C. Colombia, pop. 10, * of Boyacá (Tunja) dept.; # 5:40 N, 73:40 W.

Tupungato (tö-pön-gä'tö), mt. pk., Andes, near Mt. Aconcagua, el. 20,286 ft.; # 33:18 S, 69:50 W.

Turfan (tör-fän'), basin, Chinese Turkestan, 427 ft. below sea level. — tn. therein, pop. 20; # 43:6 N, 89:24 E.

Turin (tū'rin), see **Torino.**

Turkestan (tör-ke-stän'), region, S. W. C. Asia, partly in Russia, China and Afghanistan; # 39 N, 80 E. — **Russian;** former Soviet, area 572, pop. 7,202, * Tashkent, pop. 201, see **Uzbek;** #45 N, 76 E. — **Chinese or E.,** lowland bet. Tian Shan Mts. and Tibet Plateau; # 39 N, 82 E.

Turkey (tėr'ki), republic, Asia Minor and ext. S. E. Europe, area 294, pop. 16,158, * Angora, pop. 123; # 39 N, 35 E.

Turku (tör'kö), formerly **Åbo** or **Obo,** spt. S. W. Finland, pop. 58; univ.; # 60:26 N, 22:18 E.

Turku-Pori (tör'kö pö'ri), formerly Björneborg, dept., S. W. Finland, area 8.4, pop. 503, * Pori, pop. 17; # 61:29 N, 21:50 E.

Turnhout (tėrn-hout'; *Fr.* tür-nöt), city, 25 mi. E. N. E. of Antwerp, Belgium, pop. 25; # 51:19 N, 4:57 E.

Turquino (tör-kē'nö), mt., ext. S. E. Cuba, highest in Cuba; el. 8,397 ft.; # 19:58 N, 76:46 W.

Tuscaloosa (tus-ka̤-lö'sä), city, N. W. C. Ala., pop. 27; State Univ.; # 33:10 N, 87:40 W.

Tuscan Isls.(tus'ka̤n), bet. Tuscany, Italy, and Corsica; Elba, Pianosa, Capraja and 3 smaller isls.; # 42:30 N, 10:30 E.

Tuscany (tus'ka̤-ni), dept., N. C. Italy, area 8.9, pop. 2,766, * Florence, pop. 254; # 43:25 N, 10:36 E.

Tusculum (tus'kṳ-lum), anc. tn., 12 mi. S. E. of Rome, Italy, # 41:50 N, 12:15 E.

Tuskegee (tus-kē'gē), tn., S. E. Ala., pop. 2; Tuskegee Institute (negro); # 32:23 N, 85:45 W.

Tutuila (tö-tö-ē'lä), largest isl. of Am. Samoa, S. Pacific, area .05, pop. 10; # 14:20 S, 170:45 W.

Tver (tvyär), prov., N. W. C. Russia, area 21, pop. 1,813, and its *, on upper Volga riv., pop. 65; # 56:50 N, 35:45 E.

Tweed (twēd), riv., S. Scotland to N. Sea, boundary bet. Eng. and Scotland, len. 90 mi.; # 55:48 N, 2:2 W.

Tweeddale (twēd'dāl), see **Peebles.**

Twickenham (twik'n-a̤m), city, Middlesex, on Thames riv., S. E. Eng., pop. 35; # 51:27 N, 0.20 W.

Twin Cities, see **Minneapolis** and **St. Paul.**

Twin Falls, falls of Snake riv., S. C. Idaho, height 180 ft. — tn., near-by, pop. 12; # 42:30 N, 114:25 W.

Tyler (tī'lėr), tn., N. E. Texas, pop. 28; # 32:19 N, 95:28 W.

Tyne (tīn), riv., Cumberland, Eng., E. to N. Sea, len. 70 mi.; # 55 N, 1:27 W.

Tynemouth (tīn'muth or tin'muth), spt. city, N. E. Eng., pop. 65; # 55:3 N, 1:28 W.

Tyre (tīr), modern **Sur,** spt., S. W. Syria; # 33:16 N, 35:12 E.

Tyrol (tir'ol), Alpine prov., W. Austria, area 4.9, pop. 315; # 47:15 N, 10:5 E.

Tyrone (ti-rōn'), county, W. C. N. Ireland, area 1.2, pop. 143, * Omagh; # 54:35 N, 7:10 W. — tn., C. Pa., pop. 9; # 40:41 N, 78:15 W.

Tyrrhenian (ti-rē'ni-a̤n), sea, part of Mediterranean bet. Italy and Sardinia-Corsica; # 40 N, 13 E.

U

Ubangi (ö-bäng'gē), riv., chief N. trib. of Congo riv., C. Africa, len. 700 mi.; # 0:30 S, 17:33 E.

Ubangi-Shari (ö-bäng'gē-shä'rē), colony of Fr. Equatorial Africa, area 208, pop. 605, * Bangui; # 7 N, 21 E.

Ucayali (ö-kī-ä'lē), riv., E. Peru, trib. of Amazon riv., len. 1,000 mi.; # 4:40 S, 73:50 W.

Udaipur (ö-dī-pör'), native state, Rajputana, N. W. India, area 13, pop. 1,380, and its *, pop. 35; # 24:35 N, 73:45 E.

Udine (ö'dē-nä), prov., Venetia, N. E. Italy, area 2.5, pop. 956, and its *, pop. 56; # 46:3 N, 13:14 E.

Ueda (ö-e-dä'), city, C. Honshu isl., Japan, pop. 33; # 36:26 N, 138:12 E.

Ufa (ö'fä), prov., E. C. Soviet Russia, area 27, pop. 2,000, and its *, the * of Bashkir rep., pop. 103; # 54:50 N, 55:55 E.

Uganda (ö-gän'dä), a Br. protectorate, Equatorial Africa, area 110, pop. est. 3,127, * Entebbe and; Kampala; # 2 N, 35 E.

Uinta (ū-in'ta̤), mt. range, N. E. Utah; summit, Gilbert Pk., el. 13,687 ft.; # 40:40 N, 110 W.

Uist (wēst), N. and S. isls. of Outer Hebrides, W. Scotland; # 57:35 N, 57:15 N, 7:20 W.

Ujiji (ö-jē'jē), tn., on Lake Tanganyika, Br. C. Africa; pop. 25; # 4:50 S, 29:50 E.

Uji-Yamada (ö'jē-yä'mä-dä), city, on Atsuta Bay, S. C. Honshu isl., Japan, pop. 45; # 34:28 N, 136:41 E.

Ujpest or **Uipest** (ö'y-pesht), a W. suburb of Budapest, pop. 56; # 47:34 N, 19:5 E.

Ukraine (ū'krän or ö-krän'), soviet republic, S. W. Russia, area 172, pop. 27,857, * Kharkov, pop. 284; # 49 N, 35 E.

Uleå(ö'le-â), lake and riv., W. C. Finland.

Uleåborg, see **Oulun.**

Uliasutai (öl"yä-sṳ-tī'), city, N. C. Mongolia; # 47:55 N, 96:50 E.

Ulm (ölm), city, on Danube riv., S. E. Württemberg, S. W. Ger., pop. 57; # 48:25 N, 10 E.

Ulster (ul'stėr), former prov., Ireland, area 8.5, now mostly N. Ireland State; see **Cavan, Donegal** and **Monaghan;** Irish Free State part, area 3, pop. 331; # 54:30 N, 7 W.

Umbria (um'bri-a̤), see **Perugia.**

Uncompahgre (un-kom-pä'gre), mt. pk., W. Colo., el. 14,280 ft. — riv. and pass near-by; # ab. 38 N, 107:44 W.

Ungava (ung-gä'va̤), bay, N. Labrador pen., N. Quebec. — formerly a dist. of Canada; # 59 N, 68 W.

Union City (ū'nyọn), city, in N. E. New Jersey, pop. 56; # 40:47 N, 74:2 W.

Union of South Africa, Br. dominion, S. Africa, area 472, pop. 9,590, * Pretoria and Capetown; # 28 S, 24 E.

Union Pacific System, R.R., Omaha to Pacific Coast, etc., highest point, el. 8,247 ft.; completed 1869; total mileage, 9,676.

Uniontown (ū'nyọn-toun), city, S. W. Pa., pop. 22; # 39:55 N, 79:45 W.

United Kingdom, Great Britain and N. Ireland, area 95, pop. 46,000, * London, pop. 7,616; # 54 N, 2 W.

United Provinces of Agra and Oudh, prov. of N. C. India, area 107, pop. 45,376, * Allahabad; chief city, Lucknow, pop. 241; # 28 N, 80 E.

United States of America, republic, S. C. N. America, area, main part, 3,027, outlying possessions, area 716; pop. main part, 131,669, outlying possessions, pop. 18,952; * Washington, D. C., pop. 663; chief city, New York, pop. 7,455; # 40 N, 99 W.

Unley (un'li), a suburb of Adelaide, S. Australia, pop. 34; # 34:57 S, 138:37 E.

Unterfranken (ŭn'tėr-fräng'ken), N. W. div. of Bayern (Bavaria), S. W. Ger., area 3.4, pop. 768, * Würzburg, pop. 88; # 50 N, 10 E.

Unterwalden (ŭn'tėr-väl-den), canton, Switz., see **Nidwalden** and **Obwalden;** # 46:53 N, 8:15 E.

Unzha (ön-zä'), navigable riv., E. C. Russia, S. to Volga riv., len. 400 mi.; # 57:20 N, 43 E.

Upolu (ö-pö-lö'), isl., W. Samoa, area 0.6, pop. 18; New Zealand mandate; # 13:55 S, 171:45 W.

Upper Austria, prov., E. Austria, area 4.6, pop. 876, *Linz, pop. 102; # 48 N, 14 E.

Upper Bavaria, see **Oberbayern.**

Upper Canada, former name of Ontario.

Upper Egypt, the Nile valley bet. 22 and 30 N.

Upper Palatinate (pa̤-lat'i-na̤t), see **Oberpfalz.**

Upper Senegal, see **Sudan.**

Upper Silesia (si-lē'shi-a̤), see **Oberschlesien.**

Uppsala (öp-sä'lä), prov., N. W. of Stockholm, Sweden, area 2, pop. 140, and its *, pop. 30; univ.; cathedral; # 59:52 N, 17:40 E.

Ur (ėr), city and dist., S. E. anc. Babylonia, on Euphrates riv.; # ab. 32 N, 45 E.

Ural (ū'ra̤l), mt. range, E. Russia, often considered boundary bet. Europe and Asia; highest, Mt. Telpos, el. 5,540 ft.; platinum; # 60 N, 59 E. — riv., S. E. Russia to Caspian sea, len. 1,000 mi.; # 47 N, 52 E.

Uralsk (ö-rälsk'), city on Ural riv., W. Steppes, pop. 58; # 51:15 N, 51:20 E.

Urbana (ėr-ban'a̤), tn., N. E. C. Ill., pop. 14; adjacent to Champaign; state univ.; # 40:8 N, 88:17 W.

(variable) d̨ as d or j, ṣ as s or sh, t̨ as t or ch, z̨ as z or zh; o, F. cloche; ü, F. menu; c̆h, Sc. loch; ṅ, F. bonbon; ', primary accent; ", secondary accent; †, obsolete; <, from; +, and; =, equals. See also lists at beginning of book.

Urbino (ör-bē′nō), city, Marche, C. Italy, pop. comm. 18; birthplace of Raphael; castle; univ.; # 43:43 N, 12:38 E.

Urfa (ur̄-fä′), prov., S. C. Asiatic Turkey, pop. 155 and its *, pop. 50; # 37:5 N, 38:42 E.

Urga (ur̄′gä), city, * of N. Mongolia, pop. ab. 30; # 48:35 N, 106:50 E. — or **Kulun,** a lake nearby; # 49 N, 117:45 E.

Uri (ō′ri), canton, E. Switz., area 0.4, pop. 24, * Altdorf; # 46:48 N, 8:40 E.

Urianhai (ō′ri-än-hä′ē), prov., ext. N. W. Mongolia; # 51:30 N, 96 E.

Urmia (ör-mē′ä), salt lake, N. W. Persia, area 2; # 38 N, 45:30 E. — city, on W. shore, pop. ab. 30; # 37:35 N, 45:5 E.

Uruguay (ū′ru̇-gwā), republic, S. E. S. America, area 72, pop. 2,093, * Montevideo, pop. 683; # 32 S, 55 W. — riv., trib. of Rio de la Plata, S. S. America, len. 931 mi.; # 34 S, 58:28 W.

Urumtsi (u̇-röm′tsē), city, N. C. Sinkiang prov., W. China; # 43:50 N, 87:40 E.

Usk (usk), riv., Brecknockshire, Wales, across Monmouth to Severn riv. at Newport, len. 70 mi.; # 51:35 N, 2:58 W. — town in C. Monmouth, pop. 2; # 51:43 N, 2:54 W.

Uskup (üs-küp′), see **Skoplje.**

Uspallata (ös-päl-yä′tä), pass in Andes bet. Argentina and Chile, el. 12,464 ft., now tunneled; see **Trans-Andine;** # 32:50 S, 70:8 W.

Utah (ū′tâ), state, N. W. U.S.A., bet. Colo. and Nev., area 85, pop. 550, * Salt Lake City, pop. 150; second city, Ogden, pop. 44; # 39 N, 112 W.

Utica (ū′ti-kạ), city, C. New York, on Mohawk riv., pop. 101; # 43:8 N, 75:12 W.

Utrecht (ū′trekt), prov., C. Neth., area 0.5, pop. 368, and its *, pop. 149; Univ. of Utrecht; # 52:7 N, 5:7 E.

Utsunomiya (öt″su̇-nō-mē′yä), inland city, C. Honshu isl., Japan, pop. 64; # 36:35 N, 139:55 E.

Uwajima (ö-wä-jē′mä), spt. city, W. Shikoku isl., Japan, pop. 39; # 33:13 N, 132:31 E.

Uyeda, see **Ueda.**

Uzbek (öz-bek′), Russian Socialist Soviet Republic, S. W. C. Asia, area 104, pop. 3,519; * Tashkent; consists of Bokhara and Khiva; # 40 N, 60 E.

V

Vaal (väl), riv., S. E. Transvaal, S. W. to Orange riv., S. Africa, len. 700 mi.; # 29 S, 24:50 E.

Vaasan (vä′sän), dept., S. W. Finland, area 15.8, pop. 557, and its *, formerly **Vasa,** pop. 24; # 63:8 N, 21:42 E.

Váh or **Waag** (väch), riv., N. E. Slovakia, Cz.-S., S. W. to Danube, len. 250 mi.; # 47:45 N, 18:10 E.

Valais (vá-lā) or **Wallis,** canton, S. W. Switz., area 2, pop. 128, * Sion; # 46:36 N, 6:30 E.

Valdai Hills (väl′dī), low plateau, W. C. Russia, source of Volga, Dwina and Volkhove rivs.; summit ab. 1,000 ft.; # 57:30 N, 33 E.

Valdivia (väl-dē′vē-ä), prov. of S. C. Chile, area 9, pop. 175, and its *, pop. 27; # 40 S, 73 W.

Valdosta (val-dos′tä), tn., S. C. Ga., pop. 16; # 30:50 N, 83:20 W.

Valence (vá-loṅs), city on Rhône riv., S. E. Fr., * of Drôme dept., pop. 29; # 44:58 N, 4:58 E.

Valencia (va-len′shi-ạ; *Sp.* vä-len′thyä), prov., S. E. Spain, area 4.1, pop. 932, and its *, pop. 256, a spt.; univ.; # 39:30 N, 0:25 W. — former prov., including also Alicante and Castellón; # 39:30 N, 0:30 W. — city, N. C. Venezuela, * of Carabobo, pop. 29; # 10:15 N, 68 W.

Valenciennes (vä-loṅ-syen′), city, N. Fr., 26 mi. S. E. of Lille, pop. 34; # 50:25 N, 3:30 E.

Valladolid (väl-yä-тнō-lēтн′), prov., N. C. Spain, area 3, pop. 278, and its *, pop. 79; univ.; # 41:35 N, 4:40 W.

Vallejo (väl-yā′нō), city, N. W. C. Calif., pop. 20; # 38:7 N, 122:15 W.

Valletta (vä-let′tä) or **Valetta,** ft. spt., Malta, Mediterranean Sea, pop. 61; # 35:55 N, 14:20 E.

Valley Forge (val′i fôrj′), village, Chester county, S. E. Pa.; # 40:7 N, 75:28 W.

Valona (vä-lō′nä), *anc.* Aulon, see **Avlona.**

Valparaiso (val-pạ-rī′sō, *Sp.* väl″pä-rä-ē′sō), prov., C. Chile, area 2, pop. 320, and its *, the chief seaport of Chile, pop.

193; univ.; # 33:1 S, 71:42 W. — (val-pạ-rā′zō), tn., N. W. Ind., pop. 9; Lutheran Univ.; # 41:29 N, 87:2 W.

Valtellina (väl-tel-lē′nä), region, N. Lombardy, Italy, Adda Valley; # 46:10 N, 10 E.

Van (vän), salt lake, E. Turkish Asia Minor, el. 5,909 ft., len. 80 mi.; # 38:30 N, 42:40 E. — prov., pop. 51, and a tn. on Lake Van, pop. 30; # 38:30 N, 43 E.

Vancouver (van-kö′vēr), spt. city, mainland, S. W. Br. Columbia, pop. 247, with suburbs, pop. 140; provincial univ.; # 49:15 N, 123:8 W. — tn., ext. S. W. Wash., pop. 19; # 45:37 N, 122:42 W. — isl., S. W. Br. Columbia, area 20, pop. ab. 60; 50 N, 126 W.

Vandergrift (van′dēr-grift), tn., N. W. Pa., pop. 11; # 41:40 N, 79:10 W.

Van Diemen's (van-dē′mẹnz), gulf, near Darwin, N. Australia, 12 S, 132 E.

Väner (ve′nēr), lake, S. W. Sweden, len. 100 mi., area 2.1, sometimes called **Vanern, Wener** or **Wenern;** # 59 N, 13 E.

Vannes (vån), spt., Brittany, N. W. Fr., pop. 16; # 47:40 N, 2:45 W.

Vanua Levu (vä-nö′ä lä′vö), second largest of Fiji isls., area 2, pop. ab. 30; # 16:55 S, 178:50 E.

Var (vär), dept., S. E. Fr., coast, area 2.3, pop. 323, * Draguignan; # 43:35 N, 7:10 E.

Varanger (vä-räng′gēr), gulf-like fjord, ext. N. E. Norway; # 70 N, 31 E.

Vardar (vär-där′), *anc.* Pæonia, riv., S. Yugoslavia, to Gulf of Salonika, len. 180 mi.; # 40:35 N, 22:45 E.

Varna (vär′nä), spt. city, N. E. Bulgaria, on Black Sea, pop. 51; # 43:13 N, 27:55 E.

Varshava (vär-shä′vä) or **Warsaw,** city, C. Poland, its *, pop. 936; # 52:15 N, 21 E.

Varta (vär′tä), Polish part of Warthe riv.

Vasa (vä′sä), see **Vaasan.**

Västerås (ves-tēr-ōs′) or **Vesteras,** dist., S. E. Sweden, area 23, pop. 190, and its *, pop. 30; # 59:36 N, 16:31 E.

Vatican City (vat′i-kạn), papal state (established 1929), within Rome, Italy, including the Vatican and St. Peter's, area .00017 (109 acres), pop. 1; # 41:54 N, 12:25 E.

Vätter (vet′tēr), lake, S. Sweden, len. 80 mi.; area 0.7; # 58:10 N, 14:30 E.   [* Avignon; # 43:56 N, 5:8 E.

Vaucluse (vō-klüz′), dept., S. E. Fr., area 1.4, pop. 246,

Vaud (vō) or **Waadt,** canton, ext. W. Switz., area 1, pop. 332, * Lausanne; # 46:36 N, 6:30 E.

Vecht (vecht), riv., N. W. Ger. to Zuider Zee, Neth., len. 100 mi.; # 52:38 N, 6:3 E.

Veglia (väl′yä) or **Krk,** isl., N. Dalmatia, Yugoslavia, len. 25 mi.; # 45:5 N, 14:35 E.   [12:25 E.

Veii (vē′yī), anc. city, just N. of Rome, Italy; # ab. 42 N,

Velbert (fel′bērt), city, Rheinland, W. Ger., pop. 27; # 51:21 N, 7:3 E.   [plains; # 25 S, 27 E.

Veld (velt), region, Transvaal, S. E. Africa, mostly grassy

Velino (vä-lē′nō), riv., C. Italy, Mt. Velino, el. 8,160 ft., to Nera riv., a trib. of Tiber, falls 190 and 300 ft.; # 42:9 N, 13:22 E.

Velzen or **Velsen** (vel′sẹn), city on Amsterdam ship canal, Neth., pop. 30; # 52:22 N, 4:40 E.

Vendée (voṅ-dā), dept., coast of W. C. Fr., area 2.7, pop. 397, * La-Roche-Sur-Yon; # 46:45 N, 1:20 W.

Vendôme (voṅ-dōm), tn., N. W. C. Fr., pop. 10; # 47:45 N, 1:8 E.

Vener, see **Väner.**

Venetia (ve-nē′shiạ), dept., N. E. Italy, area 9.5, pop. 4,200, * Venice, pop. 192; # 46 N, 12:30 E.

Venezia (vä-net′syä), *Eng.* **Venice.** prov., Venetia, N. E. Italy, area 1, pop. 519, and its *, pop. 192; tourist resort; a spt. at the head of Gulf of Venice; # 45:27 N, 12:20 E.

Venezia Giulia (jö′lyä), dept., ext. N. Italy, pop. 729; from Austria in 1919; # 46:30 N, 12:30 E.

Venezuela (ven-ẹ-zwē′lạ), republic, N. S. America, area 396, pop. 3,490, * Caracas, pop. 203; # 7 N, 65 W.

Venice (ven′is), seaside resort near Los Angeles, Calif., pop. 14; # 34 N, 118:28 W. — see **Venezia. — Gulf of,** N. part of Adriatic sea; # 45:20 N, 13 E.

Venlo (ven-lō′), city, Limburg, S. Neth., pop. 22; # 51:25 N, 6:10 E.

Ventspils (vent′spils) *formerly* **Windau,** spt. city, W. Latvia, pop. 15; # 57:24 N, 21:32 E.

Vera Cruz (vĕ′rä-krōz), state, E. Mexico, area 28, pop. 1,165, * Jalapa, pop. 8; #19 N, 96:30 W. — spt. city, S. E. Mex., pop. 68; chief Mexican port; #19:10 N, 96:10 W.

Vercelli (ver-chel′lē), city, Piedmont, N. W. Italy, pop. comm. 32; #45:20 N, 8:27 E.

Verde (vĕrd), cape, ext. W. Africa; #14:45 N, 17:20 W.

Verdun (ver-duṅ), city, N. E. Fr., on Meuse riv., pop. 22; battles, 1916; #49:10 N, 5:20 E. — city, a S. suburb of Montreal, S. E. Canada, pop. 25; #45:27 N, 73:32 W.

Verendrye (vĕ-rän-drē′), butte on Missouri riv., near Spanish, N. Dak.; a national monument; #ab. 48 N, 102·30 W.

Verkhoyansk (vyer-ko-yänsk′), low mt. range, E. Siberia; #63 N, 138 E. — gold-mining city, on Yana riv., N. of this range, pop. 0.4; coldest temperature, 92° F. below; #67:10 N, 134 E.

Vermilion (vĕr-mil′yọn), tn., S. E. S. Dak., pop. 3; State Univ.; #42:46 N, 96:56 W. — low mt. range, N. E. Minn.; iron ore; #48:10 N, 92:40 W.

Vermont (vĕr-mont′), state, N. E. U.S.A., bet. New York and New Hampshire, area 10, pop. 359, * Montpelier, pop. 8; chief city, Burlington, pop. 28; #44 N, 72:30 W.

Verona (vā-rō′nä), prov., Venetia, N. E. Italy, area 1.2, pop. 523, and its *, pop. 93; #45:27 N, 11 E.

Versailles (vĕr-sālz′, *Fr.* ver-sä-y′), city, N. Fr., 10 mi. W. of Paris, pop. 65; treaty, 1919; palace; #48:48 N, 2:8 E.

Verviers (ver-vyā), city, 11 mi. E. of Liége, E. Belgium, pop. 42; lead and zinc mines; woolens; #50:40 N, 5:50 E.

Vesuvius (vẹ-sū′vi-us), active vol., E. of Bay of Naples, Italy, el. 4,012 ft.; notable eruptions, 79 A.D. and 1906; #40:49 N, 14:26 E.

Vetter, see **Vätter.**

Vevey (ve-vā) or **Vivis,** city on Lake of Geneva, S. W. Switz., pop. 13; #46:30 N, 6:55 E.

Viborg (vē′borċh), see **Viipuri.**

Vicenza (vē-chent′zä), prov., Venetia, N. E. Italy, area 1, pop. 542, and its *, pop. 60; #45:30 N, 11:32 E.

Vichy (vē-shē, *Eng.* vish/i), tn., Allier riv., S. C. Fr.; hot springs resort; pop. 18; #46:8 N, 3:30 E.

Vicksburg (viks′bẽrg), city, S. W. Miss., on Mississippi riv., pop. 24; national military park; #32:20 N, 90:55 W.

Victoria (vik-tō′ri-ä), state, S. E. tip of Australia, area 88, pop. 1,637, * Melbourne, pop. 853 (with suburbs); #37 S, 145 E. — spt. city, S. Vancouver Isl., * of Br. Columbia, pop. 39; #48:27 N, 123:25 W. — city, usually called Hongkong, isl. of Hongkong, coast of S. China, pop. 350; #22:15 N, 114:10 E. — spt. city, S. E. Brazil, * of Espirito Santo, pop. ab. 10; #20:20 S, 40:20 W. — lake, Br. Equatorial Africa, area 32.1, largest lake in world aside from the Caspian Sea; outlet Nile riv.; #4 S, 33 E. — falls, Zambezi riv., Rhodesia, S. Africa, height 400 ft.; large volume; #17:56 S, 25:56 E. — falls, see **Iguassú.** — isl., N. of Canada, area ab. 9; #71 N, 110 W. — **Land, South,** part of Antarctica S. of Australia and New Zealand; 75 S, 160 E.

Vienna (vē-en′ä), city on Danube, * of Austria, pop. 1,866; univ.; #48:12 N, 16:22 E.

Vienne (vyen), dept., W. C. Fr., area 2.7, pop. 306, * Poitiers, pop. 41; #46:15 N, 0:30 E. — city on Rhône riv. near Lyon, S. E. C. Fr., pop. 25; #45:30 N, 4:55 E.

Vienne (Haute), see **Haute-Vienne.**

Viersen (fēr′zen), city, Rheinland, W. Ger., pop. 32; #51:16 N, 6:23 E.

Vigan (vē′gän), spt. city, N. W. Luzón, Philippine Isls., pop. 18; #17:30 N, 120:25 E.

Vigo (vē′gō), spt. city, Galicia, N. W. Spain, pop. 53; #42:12 N, 8:43 W.

Viipuri (vē′pụ-rē), formerly **Viborg,** dept., S. E. Finland, area 12, pop. 572, and its *, a spt., pop. 31; #60:40 N, 28:45 E.

Villa Rica (vēl′yä rē′kä), tn., S. C. Paraguay, pop. 26; #25:46 S, 56:25 W.

Villeurbanne (vēl-ür-bàn), a suburb of Lyon, S. E. C. Fr., pop. 56; #45:46 N, 4:53 E.

Vilnius (vēl′nẹ-ús) or **Vilna** (vēl′nä), city, former * of Lithuania, pop. 208; univ.; captured by Poland in 1920, returned to Lithuania by Russia in 1939; #54:40 N, 25:20 E.

Viña del Mar (vē′nyä del mär′), seacoast resort of C. Chile, pop. 35; #33:2 S, 71:40 W.

Vincennes (vin-senz′; *Fr.* vaṅ-sen), an E. suburb of Paris,

pop. 27; castle; #48:46 N, 2:27 E. — city, S. W. Ind., on Wabash riv., pop. 18; #38:40 N, 87:30 W.

Virginia (vẽr-jin′i-ä), state, S. E. C. U.S.A., bet. N. Car. and Md., area 43, pop. 2,678, * Richmond, pop. 193; second city, Norfolk, pop. 144; #37 N, 78 W. — tn., N. E. Minn., pop. 12; iron mining; #47:35 N, 92:30 W. — tn., W. C. Nev., pop. 1; silver mines on Comstock lode; #39:20 N, 119:38 W.

Virgin Islands (vẽr′jin), isls. E. of Porto Rico; Br., area .06, pop. 5; American, area 0.1, pop. 25; #18:25 N, 64:40 W.

Visayan (vē-sä′yän) or **Bisayan,** sea, C. Philippines, and small isls. in same; #11:30 N, 123:30 E.

Visby (vēs′bü) or **Wisby,** spt., Gottland Isl., S. E. Sweden, pop. 10; former center of Hanseatic League; #57:37 N, 18:19 E.

Viso (vē′sō), **Monte,** pk., highest of Cottian Alps, N. W. border of Piedmont, Italy, el. 12,605 ft.; #44:38 N, 7:5 E.

Vistula (vis′tụ-lä), *Ger.* **Weichsel,** riv., Carpathian Mts., past Warsaw, N. to Baltic Sea near Danzig, len. 650 mi.; #54:20 N, 18:55 E.

Vitebsk (vē-tyebsk′), prov., W. C. Russia, area 16, pop. 1,353, and its *, on Dvina riv., pop. 80; #55:15 N, 30:15 E.

Viti Levu (vē′tē lev′ŏ), largest of Fiji isls., S. Pacific, area 4, pop. 111, * Suva; #17:45 S, 178 E.

Vitim (vē-tyēm′), plateau, E. of Lake Baikal, and riv. to Lena riv., len. 1,000 mi.; #53:30 N, 113 E.

Vitoria (vē-tō′rē-ä), city, * Alava prov., N. Spain, pop. 35; #42:50 N, 2:45 W.

Vizagapatam (vē-zä″gạ-pạ-täm′), spt., N. E. Madras, S. E. India, pop. 45; #17:50 N, 83:20 E.

Vizcaya (vēth-kä′yä) or **Biscay,** prov., N. Spain, area 0.8, pop. 432, * Bilbao, pop. 120; #43:15 N, 3 W.

Vlaardingen (vlär′ding-ẹn), city, 10 mi. W. of Rotterdam, Neth., pop. 27; #51:54 N, 4:21 E.

Vladikavkaz (vlä′dẹ-kàv-käz′), city in Caucasus Mts., * of Mountain Soviet Republic, pop. 76; #43 N, 44:40 E.

Vladimir (vlä-dyē′mir), prov., C. Russia, area 15, pop. 1,288, and its *, pop. 23; cathedrals; #56:10 N, 40:20 E.

Vladivostok (vlä′dẹ-vos-tôk′), spt. on Sea of Japan, E. Siberia, pop. 95; #43:5 N, 131:50 E.

Vlissingen (vlis′ing-ẹn), see **Flushing.**

Vltava (vl′tä-vä) or **Moldau,** riv., S. Bohemia, to Elbe riv., len. 270 mi.; #50:50 N, 14:30 E.

Volga (vol′gä), riv., Valdai Hills, W. C. Russia, to Caspian Sea, len. 2,400 mi.; #45:55 N, 47:45 E.

Volhynia (vol-hin′i-ä), prov., Ukraine, S. W. Russia, area 12, pop. 1,405, * Zhitomir, pop. 87; #50:50 N, 26 E. — prov., E. Poland, area 12, pop. 1,434; #51 N, 26 E.

Vologda (vo′log-dä), city, N. E. Russia, pop. 47; #59:20 N, 39:40 E. — see **Zhiryan.**

Volos (vô′lōs), *anc.* Iolcus, spt. city on Gulf of Volos, E. C. Greece, pop. 30; #39:25 N, 23 E.

Volta (vol′tä), riv., S. to Gulf of Guinea from Upper Volta Dist., Fr. W. Africa; len. 670 mi.; #riv. 5:50 N, 0:50 E; dist. 13 N, 1 W.

Volterra (vol-ter′rä), city, Tuscany, N. W. C. Italy, pop. 6, comm. 16; Etruscan ruins; #43:25 N, 10:50 E.

Vorarlberg (fōr′ärl-berċh), prov., ext. W. Austria, area 1, pop. 140, * Bregenz; #47:13 N, 10 E.

Vöringfos (vẽ′ring-fos), cascade, head of Hardanger fjord, S. W. Norway, height 475 ft.; #60:25 N, 7:16 E.

Voronezh (vo-rô′nyesh), prov., S. C. Russia, area 25, pop. 3,063, and its *, on Don riv., pop. 93; univ.; #51:40 N, 39 E.

Vosges (vōzh), low mts., E. Fr.; #48:15 N, 7:10 E. — dept., ext. E. C. Fr., area 2.3, pop. 384, * Épinal, pop. 30; #48:12 N, 6:20 E.

Votiak (vo-tyäk′) or **Vyatka,** autonomous Soviet area, E. C. Russia, area 11, pop. 686, * Izhevsk; #58:38 N, 49:42 E.

Voyvodina (voi′vọ-dē′nä), prov. N. E. Yugoslavia, area 7.6, pop. 1,380; #ab. 46 N, 20 E.

Vuelta Abajo (vwel′tä ä-bä′Hō), region, 90 × 10 mi., W. Cuba; tobacco; #ab. 22:30 N, 83:30 W.

Vulcano (vŏl-kä′nō) or **Volcano,** isl. of Lipari group, Messina prov., Italy; active vol.; source of name volcano; #38:24 N, 14:27 E.

Vyatka (vē-ät′kä), city, E. C. Russia, pop. 44; #58:38 N, 49:42 E. — see **Votiak.**

(variable) ḍ as d or j, ṣ as s or sh, ṭ as t or ch, ẓ as z or zh; o, F. cloche; ü, F. menu; ċh, Sc. loch; ṅ, F. bonbon; ′, primary accent; ″, secondary accent; †, obsolete; <, from; +, and; =, equals. See also lists at beginning of book.

Vyernyi (vyer'nyǐ), cǐty, Russian Turkestan, pop. 42; # 43:1 N. 77 E.

Vyrnwy (vẽr'nö-ē), riv. and dam. N. C. Wales, height 136 ft., len. 1,350 ft., cost $3,000,000; greatest in Europe; # 52:47 N, 3:30 W.

W

Waadt (vät), see **Vaud.**

Waal (wäl), riv., the part of the Rhine riv. in Neth.; # 51:50 N, 4:55 E.

Wabash (wȧ'bash), riv., N. W. Ohio to Ohio riv., partly bet. Ill. and Ind., len. 550 mi.; # 37:50 N, 88 W. — tn., N. C. Ind., on Wabash riv., pop. 10; # 40:47 N, 85:50 W. — **Canal,** barge canal, Lake Erie to Ohio riv. at Evansville, Ind., via Wabash valley; important, 1832–57.

Waco (wā'kō), city, C. Texas, pop. 56; Baylor Univ.; # 31:30 N, 97:10 W.

Wadai (wä-dī), part of Fr. Equatorial Africa, area 170, pop. ab. 1,000; # 12:25 N, 19 E.

Wagga Wagga (wôg'ȧ wôg'ȧ), tn., S. E. C. New S. Wales, Australia, pop. 8; irrigation project; # 35:10 S, 147:25 E.

Waialeale (wī-ä-lȧ-ä'lȧ), mt. pk., isl. of Kauai, Hawaiian Isls., el. 5,030 ft.; rainiest station in world; average rainfall 476 inches per year; # 22:5 N, 159:30 W.

Waichow (wī'chou'), spt. city, Kwangtung prov., S. E. China; pop. est. 400; # 23:3 N, 114:35 E.

Wakamatsu (wä-kä-mät'sù), inland city, N. C. Honshu isl., Japan, pop. 50; # 37:31 N, 139:57 E. — city, N. Kyushiu isl., Japan, pop. 42; # 33:55 N, 130:47 E.

Wakayama (wä-kä-yä'mä), spt. city, S. W. Honshu isl., Japan, pop. 94; # 34:15 N, 135:10 E.

Wakefield (wāk'fēld), city, 10 mi. S. of Leeds, C. Eng., pop. 54; # 53:42 N, 1:29 W. — a N. suburb of Boston, E. Mass., pop. twp. 16; # 42:30 N, 71:5 W.

Walachia (wo-lā'ki-ȧ), div., S. W. Romania, area 29.8, pop. 7,904, * Bucharest, pop. 345; # 44:20 N, 25:45 E.

Wald (vält), an E. suburb of Düsseldorf, W. Ger., pop. 27; # 51:12 N, 7:3 E.

Waldeck (väl'dek), prov., Prussia, W. C. Ger., area 0.4, pop. 56, * Arolsen, pop. 3; # 51:20 N, 9:5 E.

Waldenburg (väl'den-bùrch), city, Silesia, S. E. Ger., pop. 44; # 50:46 N, 16:16 E.

Wales (wālz), div. of Br. Empire, W. Britain, area 7, pop. 2,207; # 52:30 N, 3:30 W.

Walfish (wol'fish), see **Walvis.**

Walker (wȧ'kẽr), lake, S. W. Nev., len. 28 mi.; # 38:40 N, 118:45 W. — riv., entering it, from Yosemite National Park, len. 120 mi. — mt. range, W. of lake; summits over 10,000 ft.; # 38:50 N, 118:50 W.

Wallachia, see **Walachia.**

Wallasey (wol'ȧ-si), a W. suburb of Liverpool, W. C. Eng., pop. 91; # 53:26 N, 3:4 W.

Walla Walla (wol'ȧ wol'ȧ), city, S. E. Wash., pop. 18; Whitman and Walla Walla colleges; # 46:3 N, 118:20 W.

Wallis (väl'lĭs), see **Valais.**

Wallsend (wâlz'end), suburb of Newcastle, N. E. Eng., pop. 45; # 55 N, 1:31 W.

Walnut Canyon (wȧl'nut kan'yọn), national monument near Flagstaff, Ariz.; cliff dwellings; # 35:5 N, 111:45 W.

Walsall (wȧl'sȧl), a N. suburb of Birmingham, S. W. C. Eng., pop. 100; # 52:36 N, 2 W.

Waltham (wol'thạm), city, E. C. Mass., pop. 40; watches; # 42:22 N, 71:15 W.

Walvis (wol'vĭs) or **Walfish,** bay, tn. and dist., S. W. Africa Mandate, area .4, pop. 1; # 23 S, 15 E.

Wandsbek (vänts'bek), an E. suburb of Hamburg, N. Ger., pop. 39; # 53:34 N, 10:5 E.

Wandsworth (wondz'wẽrth), a borough of London, Eng., pop. 329; # 51:28 N, 0:9 W.

Wanganui (wâng'ga-nö-ē̩), spt. city, S. W. N. Island, New Zealand, pop. 25; # 39:45 S, 175:2 E.

Wanhsien (wän-si-en'), city on Yangtse riv., C. China, pop. est. 100; # 30:52 N, 108:33 E.

Warminster (wâr'min-stẽr), tn., Wiltshɩre, Eng.

Warren (wor'en), city, N. E. Ohio, pop. 43; # 41:15 N, 80:52 W. — tn., N. W. Pa., pop. 15; # 41:48 N, 79:8 W.

Warrington (wor'ing-tọn), city bet. Lɩverpool and Manchester, W. C. Eng., pop. 79; # 53:23 N, 2:36 W.

Warsaw (wâr'sȧ), city, C. Poland, its *, pop. 936; univ.; # 52:15 N, 21 E.

Warszawa (vär-shä'vä), official name of Warsaw.

Warthe (vär'tè), *Pol.* **Varta,** riv., Poland, W. past Posen to Oder riv., len. 450 mi.; # 52:40 N, 14:40 E.

Warwick (wor'ĭk), county, S. E. Eng., area 0.9, pop. 1,390, and its *, pop. 12; # 52:21 N, 1:42 W.

Wasatch (wȧ-sach'), mt. range, C. N. Utah, highest Timpanogos, el. 11,957 ft.; # 41 N, 111:30 W.

Wash, The (wosh), baylike estuary, E. C. Eng., len. 22 mi.; # 53 N, 0:15 E.

Washington (wosh'ing-tọn), city, * of U.S.A., on Potomac riv. bet. Md. and Va., pop. 663, with suburbs, ab. 908; Catholic, Howard, Georgetown and George Washington univs.; # 38:52 N, 77 W. — state, N. W. U.S.A., bet. Br. Columbia and Ore., area 69, pop. 1,736, * Olympia, pop. 13; chief city, Seattle, pop. 368 (1940); # 47:30 N, 120 W. — city, S. W. Pa., pop. 26; Washington and Jefferson College; # 40:14 N, 80:18 W. — lake, just E. of Seattle, Wash., len. 20 mi.; # 47:37 N, 122:15 W.

Washington, Mount, pk., N. E. New Hampshire, White Mts., highest pk. in N. E. U.S.A., el. 6,293 ft.; # 44:15 N, 71:18 W.

Washita (wosh'i-tȧ) or **Ouachita,** riv., W. Ark. to Red riv., C. La., len. 550 mi.; # 31:10 N, 91:50 W.

Waterbury (wȧ'tẽr-ber-i), city, W. C. Conn., pop. 99; watches; # 41:32 N, 73:3 W.

Waterford (wȧ'tẽr-fọrd), county, Munster, S. E. Ireland, area 0.7, pop. 57; # 52:15 N, 7:7 W. — spt. city therein, on Waterford Haven, pop. 27; # 52:15 N, 7:5 W.

Waterloo (wȧ'tẽr-lö), vil., 10 mi. S. of Brussels, Belgium; battle, 1815; # 50:43 N, 4:23 E. — city, N. E. C. Iowa, pop. 52; # 42:30 N, 92:20 W.

Watertown (wȧ'tẽr-toun), city, N. W. New York, pop. 33; # 44 N, 75:55 W. — city, E. C. Mass., pop. 35 (twp.); # 42:22 N, 71:11 W. — tn., N. E. S. Dak., pop. 11; # 44:55 N, 97:5 W.

Waterville (wȧ'tẽr-vil), tn., S. C. Maine, pop. 17; Colby College; # 44:32 N, 69:35 W.

Watervliet (wȧ'tẽr-vlēt), city, E. C. New York, pop. 16; U. S. Arsenal and gun factory; # 42:46 N, 73:45 W.

Watling (wot'ling), isl., now called **San Salvador.**

Wattenscheid (vät'ẹn-shīt), an E. suburb of Essen, Ruhr, W. Ger., pop. 30; # 51:28 N, 7:7 E.

Waukegan (wȧ-kē'gạn), lake shore suburb of Chicago, Ill., pop. 34; # 42:25 N, 87:50 W.

Waukesha (wȧ'kē̩-shä), tn., S. E. Wis., pop. 19; Carroll College; # 43 N, 88:15 W.

Wausau (wȧ'sȧ), city, E. C. Wis., pop. 27; # 45 N, 89:38 W.

Waverley (wā'vẽr-li), a S. E. suburb of Sydney, New S. Wales, Australia, pop. 37; # 33:56 S, 151:16 E.

Waycross (wā'krôs), city, S. E. Ga., pop. 17; college; # 31:15 N, 82:25 W.

Wayne (wān), county, S. E. Mich., area 0.62, pop. ab. 2,016 (1940), * Detroit; # 42:15 N, 83:24 W.

Waynesboro (wānz'bur-ọ̄), tn., S. C. Pa., pop. 10; # 39:46 N, 77:32 W.

Weald (wēld), wooded district of Kent, Surrey and Essex Cos., S. E. Eng.; # 51:5 N, 0:10 E.

Weddell (wed'el), sea, wide gulf, Antarctica, S. of E. S. America; # 72:30 S, 40 W.

Wedding (ved'ing), a N. W. part of greater Berlin, Ger., pop. 347; # 52:32 N, 13:20 E.

Weehawken (wē-hȧ'kẹn), tn. on Hudson riv., N. E. New Jersey, opp. New York City, pop. 14; # 40:46 N, 74 W.

Weichsel (vīk'sẹl), see **Vistula.**

Weihaiwei (wā″hī-wā), city, leased to Br., Shantung prov., N. E. China, area 0.3, pop. 154; # 37:32 N, 122:5 E.

Wei Ho (wā' hō'), riv., N. E. China, mostly on delta of Hwangho; floods; # 39:5 N, 117:10 E. — riv., N. W. China, largest trib. of Hwangho, entering at Great Bend; # 34:45 N, 110:30 E.

Weihsien (wā-si-en'), city, Shantung prov., N. E. China, pop. est. 100; # 36:47 N, 119:10 E.

Weimar (vī'mär), dist., area 0.5, pop. 97, and city, * of Thuringia, S. C. Ger., pop. 46; # 51 N, 11:17 E.

Weinheim (vīn'hīm), city, N. Baden, S. W. Ger., pop. 15; # 49:33 N, 8:40 E.

---

fat, fāte, fär, fȧll, ȧsk, fãre; net, mē, hẽr; pin, pīne; not, nōte, möve, nôr; up, lūte, pùll; oi, oil; ou, out; (lightened) aviạry, ẹlect, agọny, intọ, ūnite; (obscured) errạnt, operạ̈, ardẹnt, actọr, natūre; ch, chɩp; g, go; th, thin; ʀʜ, then; y, you;

Weissensee (vī'sẹn-zā), a N. E. div. of Berlin, Ger., pop. 58; # 52:32 N, 13:28 E.

Weisshorn (vīs'hôrn), pk., Valais Alps, S. Switz., el. 14,803 ft.; # 46:6 N, 7:43 E.

Welland (wel'ạnd), tn., S. W. Ontario, pop. 9; # 43 N, 79:15 W. — **Canal**, ship canal, bet. Lakes Erie and Ontario, in Canada, len. 26 mi.; # 42:55 N, 79:15 W.

Wellesley (welz'li), tn. near Boston, E. C. Mass., pop. 15; Wellesley College; # 42:12 N, 71:20 W. — prov., part of Straits Settlements, area 0.3, pop. 130; # 5:20 N, 100:30 E.

Wellington (wel'ing-tọn), spt. city, * of New Zealand, S. end of N. Island, pop. 115; Victoria College; # 41:18 S, 174:47 E. — prov., New Zealand, area 11, pop. 249: # 41:18 S, 174:47 E.

Wells, Tunbridge, see **Tunbridge.**

Wemyss (wēmz), parish, Fifeshire, Scotland, pop. 25; castle; # 56:8 N, 3:5 W.

Wenatchee (wẹ-nach'ẹ), tn. on Columbia riv., C. Wash., pop. 12; apples; pears; # 47:25 N, 120:20 W.

Wenchow (wẹn'chou'), spt. city, S. E. C. China, pop. est. 125; # 28 N, 120:30 E.

Wenner (ven'ẹr), lake, see **Väner.**

Werdau (vār'dou), a W. suburb of Zwickau, C. Ger., pop. 21; # 50:44 N, 12:22 E.

Wernigerode (ver"nẹ-gẹ-rō'dẹ), city, Sachsen (Saxony), Prussia, pop. 21; # 51:50 N, 10:48 E.

Weser (vā'zẹr), riv., Thuringia Wald, S. W. Ger., N. to estuary of N. Sea, len. 300 mi.; upper portion called Werra riv.; # 53:30 N, 8:30 E.

Wessex (wes'eks), anc. kingdom, S. Eng.; # 51 N, 2 W.

West Allis (west al'is), a W. suburb of Milwaukee, Wis., pop. 36; # 43:2 N, 88 W.

West Bromwich (brum'ich), a N. W. suburb of Birmingham, C. Eng., pop. 78; # 52:31 N, 2 W.

West Chester (ches'tẹr), tn., S. E. Pa., pop. 13; # 39:58 N, 75:33 W.

Westchester, county, S. E. New York, area 0.45, pop. 574 (1940), * White Plains, pop. 40; chief city Yonkers, pop. 143; # 40:55 N, 73:50 W.

Western Australia (wes'tẹrn âs-trā'liạ), state, W. Aust., area 976, pop. 356, * Perth, pop. 64; # 25 S, 122 E.

Western Ghats (gâts), mt. range, W. margin of Deccan Plateau, S. India; # 15 N, 74:30 E.

Western Pacific Line, R.R., Salt Lake to San Francisco, via Feather River Canyon; completed 1909; highest point, 5,712 ft.

Westfalen (vest-fä'lẹn), *Eng.* **Westphalia**, prov., S. W. Prussia, N. W. Ger., area 7.8, pop. 4,827, * Düsseldorf, pop. 430; # 51:50 N, 8 E.

Westfield (-fēld), tn., S. W. Mass., pop. twp., 19; # 42:10 N, 72:47 W.

West Flanders, see **Flanders, West.**

West Ham (ham), an E. suburb of London, Eng., pop. 314; # 51:32 N, 0:1 E.

West Hartlepool (här'tl-pōl), spt., Tees Mouth, N. E. Eng., pop. 71; # 54:41 N, 1:15 W.

West Hoboken (hō'bō-kẹn), now part of Union City, a New Jersey suburb of New York City, pop. 40: # 40:45 N, 74:3 W.

West Indies (in'diz), isls. in Atlantic oc. bet. Fla. and S. America; see **Cuba, Haiti, Jamaica**, etc.; # 20 N, 70 W.

Westland, prov., W. S. Island, New Zealand, area 5, pop. 14; # 43:30 S, 170 E.

West Lothian (lō'ҭҺi-ạn), or **Linlithgow**, county, S. E. Scotland, area .01, pop. 82, * Linlithgow; # 55:58 N, 3:37 W.

Westminster (west'min-stẹr), a borough of London, Eng.. pop. 141; abbey; # 51:31 N, 0:7 W.

Westmorland (west'mọr-lạnd), county, N. W. Eng., area 0.8, pop. 66, * Appleby; # 54:28 N, 2:40 W.

Westmount (west'mount), city, S. Quebec, pop. 18; # 45:30 N, 73:35 W.

West New York, a New Jersey suburb of New York City, pop. 39; # 40:48 N, 74 W.

West Orange, city, N. E. New Jersey, pop. 26; # 40:47 N, 74:14 W.

West Palm Beach, city, S. E. Fla., pop. 34; # 26:40 N, 80:10 W.

Westphalia (-fä'li-ạ), see **Westfalen.**

West Point, tn., S. E. New York, on Hudson riv., pop. 1; U. S. Military Academy; # 41:25 N, 74 W.

West Riding (rīd'ing), administrative county, Yorkshire, N. C. Eng., area 2.8, pop. 3,182; # 53:50 N, 1:30 W.

West River, see **Si-kiang.**

West Springfield (spring'fēld), suburb of Springfield, Mass., pop. 17; # 42:7 N, 72:38 W.

West Virginia (vẹr-jin'i-ạ), state, E. C. U.S.A., bet. Va. and Ohio, area 24, pop. 1,902, * Charleston, pop. 68; chief city, Huntington, pop. 79; # 39 N, 81 W.

West Warwick (wor'ik), tn., E. C. Rhode Island, pop. 18 (twp.); # 41:45 N, 71:25 W.

Wetar (wet'är), isl., N. of Timor, E. Indies, area 2; # 7:50 S, 126:30 E.

Wetter (vet'ẹr), see **Vätter.**

Wetterhorn (vet'ẹr-hôrn), prominent pk., Bernese Alps, C. Switz., el. 12,150 ft.; # 46:38 N, 8:7 E.

Wexford (weks'fọrd), county, ext. S. E. Ireland, area 0.9, pop. 102, and its *, spt. town, on Wexford Harbor, pop. 11; # 52:15 N, 6:32 W.

Weymouth (wā'muth), tn., E. C. Mass., pop. 24 (twp.); # 42:15 N, 71 W.

Wheeling (hwē'ling), city, N. W. Va., on Ohio riv., pop. 61; # 40:4 N, 80:44 W.

Whitby (hwit'bi), spt. tn., mouth of Esk riv., York, Eng., pop. 13; abbey; # 54:30 N, 0:40 W.

White Horse, mt. pass, N. of Skagway, Alaska, el. 2,800 ft., and R.R. tn. at head of navigation of Yukon riv., N. W. Canada; # 60:40 N, 134:55 W.

White Mountains, mts., N. E. New Hampshire, highest in N. E. U.S.A.; summit, Mt. Washington, el. 6,293 ft.; # 44:15 N, 71:20 W.

White Nile (nīl), Nile riv., above junction of Blue Nile (Khartoum), Anglo-Egyptian Sudan; local name, Bahr el Abiad; # 15:30 N, 32:30 E.

White Plains (plānz), city, S. E. New York, pop. 40; # 41:3 N, 73:48 W.

White River, riv., N. W. Ark., to Mississippi riv., len. 800 mi.; # 34 N, 91:5 W. — riv., E. C. Ind., through Indianapolis to Wabash riv., len. ab. 200 mi.; # 38:25 N, 87:45 W. — riv., N. W. Neb. and S. W. S. Dak. to Missouri riv. through the Big Bad Lands, len. ab. 300 mi.; # 43:30 N, 99:20 W.

White Russia (rush'ạ), name loosely applied to a region of W. Russia. — Rep. Soviet Union, W. Russia, area 23, pop. 4,205, * Minsk; # 53:50 N, 27:35 E.

White Sea (sē), arm of Arctic oc., N. Russia, len. 500 mi.; # 66 N, 38 E.

Whiting (hwīt'ing), tn., N. W. Ind., pop. 10; petroleum refining; # 41:41 N, 87:29 W.

Whitney (hwit'ni), mt. pk., Sierra Nevadas, E. C. Calif., el. 14,501 ft.; highest in U. S. Proper; # 36:35 N, 118:20 W.

Wichita (wich'i-tâ), city, S. E. C. Kansas, pop. 115; Friends Univ., Fairmount College; # 37:45 N, 97:25 W. — low mts., S. W. Okla.; # 34:40 N, 98:40 W.

Wichita Falls, city, N. C. Texas, pop. 45; # 33:50 N, 98:30 W.

Wicklow (wik'lō), county, Leinster, E. C. Ireland, area 0.8, pop. 62; and its *, a spt. Wicklow Head, pop. 3; # 53 N, 6:4 W.

Wieliczka (vye-lyēch'kä), tn., 8 mi. S. E. Krakow, Poland, pop. 7; salt mines; # 50 N, 20:4 E.

Wien (vēn), Ger. form of Vienna, * of Austria.

Wiener Neustadt (vē'nẹr noi'shtät), city, E. C. Austria, * of Lower Austria, pop. 37; # 47:45 N, 16:30 E.

Wiesbaden (vēs'bä-dẹn), city, * Hessen-Nassau, 10 mi. N. of Mainz, S. Ger., pop. 105; resort; hot springs; # 50:7 N, 8:13 E.

Wiesdorf (vēs'dôrf), suburb of Düsseldorf, W. Ger., pop. 30; # ab. 51:14 N, 6:50 E.

Wigan (wig'ạn), city, almost bet. Liverpool and Manchester, W. C. Eng., pop. 92; coal; # 53:32 N, 2:37 W.

Wight, Isle of (wīt), isl., S. Eng., area 0.15, pop. 95; * Newport; # 50:40 N, 1:20 W.

Wigtown (wig'tọn), county, ext. S. W. Scotland, area 0.5, pop. 29, and its *, a spt. on Wigtown Bay; # 54:50 N, 4:15 W.

Wilhelmina (vil-hel-mē'nạ), mt. pk., Snow Mts., Papua, E. Indies, el. 15,680 ft.; # 4:10 S, 138:45 E.

Wilhelmshaven (vil'helms-hä"fẹn), spt. on Jade Bay, Hannover, N. W. Ger., pop. 25; # 53:33 N, 8:5 E.

(variable) ḍ as d or j, ş as s or sh, ţ as t or ch, ẓ as z or zh; o, F. cloche; ü, F. menu; ċh, Sc. loch; ṅ, F. bonbon; ', primary accent; ", secondary accent; †, obsolete; <, from; +, and; =, equals. See also lists at beginning of book.

Wilkes-Barre (wilks'bar-i), city, N. E. C. Pa., pop. 86; anthracite; ⋕41:16 N, 75:52 W.

Wilkinsburg (wil'kinz-bèrg), city, S. W. Pa., pop. 30; ⋕40:26 N, 79:54 W.

Willamette (wil-am'et), riv., W. Ore. through Portland to Columbia riv., len. 275 mi.; ⋕45:40 N, 122:45 W.

Willemstad (wil'ẹm-stät), spt., isl. of Curaçao, and * of Dutch W. Indies, pop. 17; ⋕12 N, 69 W.

Willesden (wilz'dẹn), a W. suburb of London, Eng., pop. 160; ⋕51:32 N, 0:14 W.

Williamsburg (wil'yạmz-bèrg), tn., S. E. Va., pop. 4; William and Mary College; ⋕37:15 N, 76:38 W.

Williamson (wil'yạm-sọn), mt. peak, S. E. Calif., el. 14,384 ft., near Mt. Whitney; ⋕36:39 N, 118:19 W.

Williamsport (wil'yạmz-pôrt), city, N. C. Pa., pop. 44; ⋕41:12 N, 77:1 W.

Williamstown (wil'yạmz-toun), tn., N. W. Mass., pop. 4; Williams College; ⋕42:43 N, 73:12 W.

Willimantic (wil-i-man'tik), tn., E. C. Conn., pop. 12; ⋕41:45 N, 72:12 W.

Willoughby (wil'ọ-bi), suburb of Sydney, New S. Wales, Australia, pop. 28; ⋕33:53 S, 151:12 E. — cape, S. Australia; ⋕35:51 S, 138:7 E.

Wills Creek Watergap, an important pass through Wills Mt., W. of Cumberland, W. Md.; Fort Cumberland; Cumberland National road; R.R.; ⋕39:37 N, 78:50 W.

Wilmersdorf (vil'mèrs-dôrf), a S. W. div. of Berlin, Ger., pop. 166; ⋕53:7 N, 13:55 E.

Wilmington (wil'ming-tọn), city, ext. N. Dela., pop. 113; near Philadelphia; ⋕39:42 N, 75:32 W. — city, S. E. N. Car., pop. 33; ⋕34:20 N, 77:55 W.

Wilno (vēl'nọ), see **Vilnius**.

Wilson (wil'sọn), tn., E. C. N. Car., pop. 19; ⋕35:44 N, 77:54 W. — dam across Tennessee riv., at Muscle Shoals, Ala., most massive masonry dam in world, len. 4,500 ft., height 96 ft.; ⋕34:50 N, 87:50 W. — mt. pk. near Los Angeles, S. W. Calif.; solar observatory; ⋕34:14 N, 118:4 W. — promontory, most S. point of Aust.; 39:20 S, 146:25 E.

Wiltshire (wilt'shir), county, S. C. Eng., area 1.3, pop. 292, * Salisbury; ⋕51:25 N, 2 W.

Wimbledon (wim'bl-dọn), a S. W. suburb of London, Eng., pop. 70; ⋕51:26 N, 0:13 W.

Winchester (win'ches-tèr), city, C. Hampshire, S. Eng., pop. 24; cathedral; ⋕51:2 N, 1:21 W.

Windau (vin'dou), see **Ventspils**.

Wind Cave (wind kāv), cave, near Hot Springs, Black Hills, S. W. S. Dak.; National Park, est. 1903; ⋕43:32 N, 103:40 W.

Windermere (win'dèr-mēr), tn., Westmorland Co., Eng., pop. 6; ⋕54:23 N, 2:55 W. — lake (largest in Eng.), bet. Westmorland and Lancashire; ⋕54:20 N, 2:57 W.

Windhuk or **Windhoek** (vint'hùk), city, * of S. W. Africa Mandate, pop. 15; ⋕22:15 S, 17:20 E.

Wind River (wind riv'èr), mt. range, W. C. Wyo., Gannett Pk. el. 13,785 ft.; Fremont Pk., el. 13,720 ft.; ⋕43 N, 109 W.

Windsor (win'zọr), tn., Berkshire, 15 mi. W. of London, pop. 13; ⋕51:28 N, 0:36 W. — city, S. Ontario, opp. Detroit, pop. 39; ⋕42:20 N, 83:2 W.

Windsor Castle (win'zọr), Berkshire, S. E. Eng.; chief residence of Br. sovereigns; covers 12 acres, has park of 1,500 acres; ⋕51:29 N, 0:36 W.

Windward (wind'wạrd), channel, strait bet. Cuba and Haiti; ⋕20 N, 74 W. — isls., S. Isls. of Lesser Antilles, W. Indies; ⋕13 N, 61 W.

Winfield (win'fēld), tn., S. E. C. Kan., pop. 10; S. W. College; ⋕37:12 N, 97:2 W.

Winnebago (win-ẹ-bā'gọ), lake, E. Wis., len. 30 mi.; ⋕44 N, 88:25 W.

Winnepesaukee (win″ẹ-pẹ-sâ'kẹ), lake, E. C. New Hampshire, len. 25 mi.; ⋕43:38 N, 71:20 W.

Winnipeg (win'i-peg), city, S. Manitoba, pop. 216, with suburbs, 230, prov. *; Univ. of Manitoba; ⋕49:50 N, 97:10 W. — lake, Manitoba, area 9, len. 270 mi.; ⋕53 N, 98 W. — riv., Lake of Woods to Lake Winnipeg, len. 275 mi.; ⋕50:45 N, 96:30 W.

Winnipegosis (win″i-pẹ-gọ'sis), lake, S. E. Manitoba, len. 250 mi., area 2; ⋕51:50 N, 100 W.

Winona (wi-nọ'nạ), city, S. E. Minn., on Mississippi riv.,

pop. 22; St. Teresa and State Teachers colleges; ⋕44 N, 91:45 W.

Winston-Salem (win'stọn-sā'lẹm), city, N. W. N. Car., pop. 80; Salem College; ⋕36:10 N, 80:10 W.

Winterthur (vin'tèr-tör), city, 15 mi. N. W. of Zurich, N. E. Switz., pop. 50; ⋕47:30 N, 8:45 E.

Winthrop (win'throp), tn., E. C. Mass., pop. 17 (twp.); ⋕42:22 N, 71 W.

Wisby (wiz'bi), see **Visby**.

Wisconsin (wis-kon'sin), state, N. E. C. U.S.A., bet. Lake Michigan and Mississippi riv., area 56, pop. 3,138, * Madison, pop. 67; chief city, Milwaukee, pop. 587; ⋕45 N, 90 W. — riv., N. Wis. to Mississippi riv., len. 500 mi.; ⋕43 N, 91:9 W.

Wismar (vis'mär), spt., on Baltic sea, Mecklenburg, N. Ger., pop. 26; ⋕53:50 N, 11:30 E.

Witten (vit'ẹn), city, Westfalen, W. Ger., pop. 45; ⋕51:26 N, 7:19 E.

Wittenberg (wit'ẹn-bèrg, vit'ẹn-berċh), city on Elbe riv., Saxony prov., Prussia, pop. 23; univ.; Reformation began 1517; ⋕51:50 N, 12:40 E.

Wittenberge (vit″ẹn-ber'gè), city, Brandenburg, N. C. Ger., pop. 26; ⋕53 N, 11:45 E.

Witwatersrand (wit-wä'tèrs-rand), ridge of gold-bearing gravels near Johannesburg, S. Africa; ⋕26 S, 27:30 E.

Woburn (wọ'bèrn), tn., E. C. Mass., pop. 20; ⋕42:31 N, 71:7 W.

Woking (wọ'king), city, Surrey, 24 mi. S. W. of London, Eng., pop. 25; cemetery; ⋕51:18 N, 0:33 W.

Wolfville (wùlf'vil), village, Bay of Fundy, Nova Scotia; Acadia Univ.; ⋕45:5 N, 64:21 W.

Wolverhampton (wùl-vèr-hamp'tọn), city, 20 mi. N. W. of Birmingham, S. W. C. Eng., pop. 107; ⋕52:37 N, 2:12 W.

Woodlawn (wùd'lân), a N. W. suburb of Pittsburgh, S. W. Pa., pop. 18; ⋕ab. 40:45 N, 80:15 W. — ward, a former S. suburb of Chicago, Ill.; ⋕41:48 N, 87:37 W.

Woods, Lake of the (wùdz), lake, on boundary bet. Minn., U.S.A., and Canada; contains most N. extension of U.S., lat. 49:25 N; ⋕49:30 N, 94:30 W.

Woods Hole, vil. on Buzzards Bay, S. E. Mass.; marine biological station; ⋕41:32 N, 70:38 W.

Woodstock (wùd'stok), tn., Oxfordshire, S. C. Eng., pop. 2; Blenheim Palace; ⋕51:51 N, 1:22 W. — tn., S. W. Ontario, pop. 10; ⋕43:10 N, 80:50 W.

Woolwich (wùl'ich), an E. borough of London, Eng., pop. 140; arsenal; ⋕51:29 N, 0:4 E.

Woonsocket (wọn-sok'et), city, N. E. Rhode Island, pop. 49; ⋕42 N, 71:30 W.

Wooster (wùs'tèr), tn., N. E. C. Ohio, pop. 12; Wooster College; ⋕40:48 N, 81:56 W.

Worcester (wùs'tèr), city, S. E. C. Mass., pop. 194; Clark Univ.; Holy Cross College; Worcester Polytech.; ⋕42:15 N, 71:50 W. — city, S. W. C. Eng., pop. 50; porcelain; ⋕52:12 N, 2:12 W.

Worcestershire (wùs'tèr-shèr), county, S. W. C. Eng., area 0.7, pop. 406, * Worcester, pop. 50; ⋕52:12 N, 2:12 W.

Worms (vörms, wèrmz), city on Rhine riv., Hessen, S. W. Ger., pop. 47; ⋕49:40 N, 8:18 E.

Wrangell (rang'gel), active volcano, S. E. Alaska, el. 14,005 ft.; ⋕56:30 N, 132:30 W. — isl., Arctic oc., N. W. of Bering Strait; ⋕71:15 N, 180 W.

Wrath (ràth), cape, ext. N. W. Scotland; ⋕58:35 N, 5 W.

Wrexham (reks'ạm), city, E. Denbigh, N. E. Wales, pop. 19; ⋕53:3 N, 3 W.

Wuchang (wö-chäng'), city, S. E. C. China, on Yangtse riv., * of Hupeh prov., pop. est. 500; ⋕30:31 N, 114:23 E.

Wuchow (wö-chö'), city on Si-kiang riv., S. China, pop. est. 75; ⋕23:30 N, 111:25 E.

Wuhu (wö'hö'), city on lower Yangtse riv., E. C. China, pop. est. 120; ⋕31:21 N, 118:30 E.

Wupper (vöp'pèr), riv., N. W. Ger., through Elberfeld-Barmen to Rhine riv. near Cologne, len. 65 mi.; industrial region; ⋕ab. 51:5 N, 6:40 E.

Württemberg (vür'tẹm-berċh), state, S. W. Ger., bet. Baden and Bayern, area 7.5, pop. 2,591, * Stuttgart, pop. 337; ⋕48:30 N, 8:35 E.

Würzburg (vürts'bùrċh), city on Main riv., N. W. Bayern (Bavaria), S. W. Ger., pop. 89; univ.; ⋕49:45 N, 9:55 E.

---

fat, fāte, fär, fåll, åsk, fåre; net, mē, hèr; pin, pīne; not, nōte, möve, nôr; up, lūte, pùll; oi, oil; ou, out; (lightened) aviạry, ẹlect, agọny, intọ, ụnite; (obscured) errạnt, operạ, ardẹnt, actọr, natụre; ch, chip; g, go; th, thin; ᴛн, then; y, you;

Wyandotte (wī'ạn-dot), city, S. E. Mich., pop. 31; # 42:12 N, 83:8 W.

Wyoming (wī-ō'ming), state, N. W. C. U.S.A., bet. Mont. and Colo., area 98, pop. 251, * Cheyenne, pop. 22; second city, Casper, pop. 18; # 43 N, 107 W. — mt. range, Wyo., # 42:30 N, 110:30 W. — valley, N. E. Pa., massacre 1778; # 42:50 N, 78:4 W.

X

Xanthe (zan'the) or **Xanthi**, tn., E. Macedonia, N. E. Greece, pop. 17; # 41:10 N, 24:52 E.

Xeros (ze'ros), see **Saros**.

Xingú (shĕn-gö'), riv., E. Brazil, entering mouths of Amazon, len. 1,100 mi.; # 1:50 S, 52 W.

Y

Yablonoi (yä-blo-noi'), mt. range, E. of Lake Baikal, Siberia; highest, ab. 8,000 ft.; # 53 N, 116 E.

Yahata or **Yawata** (yä'wä-tä), city, an E. suburb of Tokyo, S. Honshu isl., Japan, pop. 118; # 35:43 N, 139:55 E.

Yakima (yak'i-mạ), city, W. C. Wash., pop. 27; pears and apples; # 46:35 N, 120:30 W.

Yakutsk (yä-kōtsk'), soviet republic, N. E. Siberia, area 1,457, pop. 323, and its *, pop. 8; # 61:50 N, 129:55 E.

Yalmal (yäl-mäl'), pen., N. W. Siberia, len. 380 mi.; # 70 N, 69 E.

Yamada, see **Uji-Yamada**.

Yamagata (yä'mä-gä'tä), inland city, N. C. Honshu isl., Japan, pop. 56; # 38:14 N, 140:18 E.

Yana (yä'nạ), riv., Verkhoyansk Mts. to Arctic oc., len. 550 mi.; gold placers; # 71 N, 136 E.

Yanaon (yȧ-nȧ-ôň), Fr. city prov., mouth Godavari riv., S. E. India, pop. 5; # 16:45 N, 82:12 E.

Yangchau (yäng'chou'), city, S. Kiangsu prov., E. C. China, pop. est. 100; # 32:23 N, 119:30 E.

Yangtse-Kiang (yäng'tse-kē-äng'), riv., E. Tibet to E. China Sea, len. 3,000 mi.; navigable for 2,000 mi.; # 32 N, 120: 15 E.

Yanina or **Yannina** (yä'nē-nä), city, N. W. Greece, pop. 21; # 39:48 N, 20:54 E.

Yankton (yangk'tọn), tn. on Missouri riv., S. E. S. Dak., pop. 7; Yankton College; # 42:50 N, 97:21 W.

Yaoundé (yȧ-ön-dā), city, * of Fr. Mandate, Cameroon, W. Africa, pop. 30; # 3:51 N, 11:39 E.

Yap (yäp), isl., chief of Caroline isl., S. W. N. Pacific, pop. 7; Japanese Mandate; # 9:30 N, 138:10 E.

Yapurá (yä-pö-rä'), riv., S. E. Colombia and N. W. Brazil, trib. of Amazon riv., len. 1,750 mi.; # 3 S, 65 W.

Yarkand (yär-känd'), city, pop. 60, and riv., S. E. Chinese Turkestan; # 38:15 N, 77:30 E.

Yarmouth, Great (yär'muth), spt. city, Norfolk, E. Eng., pop. 57; fishing fleet; # 52:38 N, 1:45 E.

Yaroslavl (yä-ro-slä'vl) or **Yaroslav**, prov., C. Russia, area 6, pop. 1,300, and its *, on Volga riv., pop. 100; univ.; # 57:35 N, 39:50 E. — see **Jaroslaw**, Poland.

Yarrow (yar'ō), riv., Selkirkshire, S. E. Scot., to Tweed riv., len. 35 mi.; # 55:32 N, 2:50 W.

Yaunde (youn'de), see **Yaoundé**.

Yawata, see **Yahata**.

Yaxartes (yax-är'tes), riv., Tian Shan Mts., to Lake Aral, len. 1,400 mi.; # 46 N, 61 E.

Yazoo (ya'zō), riv., N. W. Miss. to Mississippi riv., len. 300 mi.; # 32:25 N, 91 W.

Yeddo or **Yedo** (yed'ō), see **Tokyo**.

Yeisk (yā'isk), city, Georgian Republic, pop. 48; # 46:40 N, 38:15 E.

Yekaterinodar (ye-kä"tye-rē-nō-där'), see **Ekaterinodar**.

Yekaterinoslav (ye-kä"tye-rē-nō-släf'), see **Ekaterinoslav**.

Yelets (ye-lyets') or **Elets**, city, Orel prov., S. C. Russia, pop. 57; # 52:45 N, 38:37 E.

Yellow (yel'ō) or **Hwangho**, riv., N. China and Tibet to Yellow Sea, len. ab. 2,300 mi.; # 37:50 N, 118:35 E. — sea, part of Pacific oc., bet. N. China and Korea; # 36 N, 123 E.

Yellow Springs (springz), tn., S. W. C. Ohio, pop. 2; Antioch College; # 39:48 N, 83:52 W.

Yellowstone (yel'ō-stōn), riv., N. W. Wyo., to Missouri riv., 1,100 mi.; # 47:55 N, 103:55 W. — lake, N. W. Wyo., len. 20 mi.; # 44:30 N, 110:20 W.

Yellowstone National Park, ext. N. W. Wyo., with a bit of Mont. and Idaho, area 3.3; geysers; hot springs; canyon; falls: Upper, height 110 ft., Lower, height 436 ft.; # 44:30 N, 110:30 W.

Yemen (yem'ẹn), kingdom, S. W. Arabia, area ab. 75, pop. ab. 5,500, * Sana, el. 7,260, pop. ab. 42; # 15 N, 44 E.

Yenchowfu (yen-chou-fö'), city, Shantung prov., E. China, pop. est. 50; # 35:45 N, 117 E.

Yenisei (yen-ē-sā'ē), riv., Sayan Mts., S. Siberia to Arctic oc., 2,500 mi.; # 70 N, 84 E.

Yeniseisk (yen-ē-sā'isk), prov., C. Siberia, area 982, pop. 1,193, and its *, pop. 8; # 58:15 N, 92 E.

Yenpingfu (yen-ping-fö'), city, C. Fukien prov., S. E. China, pop. est. 200; # 26:41 N, 118:12 E.

Yezd (yezd), prov., C. Persia, area 18, and its *, pop. ab. 45; # 32 N, 54:20 E.

Yezo (yez'ō), large N. isl. of Japan, area 30, pop. 1,134; also known as Hokkaido and Hokushii; # 43 N, 141 E.

Yguassu, see **Iguassú**.

Yingkow (ying-kou'), spt. city, mouth of Liao riv., port of Newchwang, S. Manchuria, pop. 60; # 40:43 N, 122:9 E.

Yokkaichi (yōk'kī-chē), coastal city, S. W. Honshu isl., Japan, pop. 40; # 35 N, 136:40 E.

Yokohama (yō-kō-hä'mạ), chief seaport of Japan, near Tokyo, pop. 406; temporarily reduced by earthquake, Sept. 1, 1923; # 35:27 N, 139:39 E.

Yokosuka (yō'kō-sö'kä), spt. city, Tokyo Bay, S. Honshu isl., Japan, pop. 102; # 35:17 N, 139:40 E.

Yonezawa (yō'ne-zä'wä), inland city, N. C. Honshu isl., Japan, pop. 45; # 37:56 N, 140:5 E.

Yonkers (yong'kẽrz), a N. suburb of New York City, on Hudson riv., pop. 143; # 40:56 N, 73:53 W.

Yonne (yon), riv. and dept., C. Fr., area 2.9, pop. 273, * Auxerre; # 48:25 N, 3 E.

York (yôrk), city, N. E. C. Eng., pop. 86; cathedral; # 53:50 N, 1:10 W. — tn., S. C. Pa., pop. 57; # 39:58 N, 76:45 W. — tn., S. E. Neb., pop. 5; York College; # 40:52 N, 97:35 W. — cape, ext. N. Australia; # 10:40 S, 142:30 E. — cape, S. W. N. Greenland; # 76 N, 64 W.

Yorkshire (yôrk'shir) or **York**, county, N. C. Eng., area 6, pop. 4,100; now divided into administrative counties of E., W. and N. Riding; # 54 N, 1:10 W.

Yorktown (yôrk'toun), tn., S. E. Va.; surrender of Cornwallis, Oct. 19, 1781; # 37:12 N, 76:30 W.

Yorubaland (yō'rú-bä-land"), S. W. part of Nigeria, former native kingdom; # 6 N, 5 E.

Yosemite National Park (yō-sem'i-tẹ), canyon, E. C. Calif., lofty waterfalls: Upper, 1,436 ft.; Middle, 626 ft.; Lower, 400 ft.; Merced Falls, 700 ft.; # 37:45 N, 119:30 W.

Youngstown (yungz'toun), city, E. Ohio, pop. 168; steel; # 41:5 N, 80:42 W.

Ypres (ē-pr), city, S. W. Belgium, pop. 15; many battles 1914–18; # 50:50 N, 2:50 E.

Ypsilanti (ip-si-lan'ti), tn., S. E. Mich., pop. 12; State Teachers College; # 42:15 N, 83:35 W.

Yssel, see **Ijssel**.

Yucatan (yö-kä-tän') pen., S. E. Mex.; # 18 N, 89 W. — state, N. Yucatan pen., Mex., area 16, pop. 358, * Mérida, pop. 62; # 20:30 N, 89 W. — **Channel of**, bet. Cuba and pen., width 125 mi.; # 22 N, 86 W.

Yugoslavia (yö'gō-slä'vi-ȧ) (formerly "Serb, Croat, and Slovene State"). kingdom, S. E. Europe, area 96, pop. 12,017, * Beograd (Belgrade), pop. 112; # 44 N, 20 E.

Yukon (yö'kon), riv., N. W. Canada across Alaska to Bering Sea, len. 2,050 mi.; # 62:50 N, 164 W. — ter., N. W. Canada, area 207, pop. 4, * Dawson, pop. 3; gold; # 63 N, 135 W.

Yuma (yö'mä), tn., S. W. Ariz., on Colorado riv., pop. 5; irrigation; # 32:40 N, 114:35 W.

Yungpingfu (yủng-ping-fö'), city, Chihli prov., N. China, pop. est. 200; # 39:53 N, 118:50 E.

Yunnan (yủn-nän'), prov., S. W. China, area 147, pop. est. 9,000, and its *, often called Yunnanfu, pop. 45; # 25 N, 102:38 E.

Yurev (yủr'yef) or **Dorpat**, now **Tartu**.

Yuzovka (yŏ-sof′kä), city, Donetz prov., Ukraine, S. W. Russia, pop. 49; # 48 N, 37:48 E.

Z

Zaandam (zän-däm′), a W. suburb of Amsterdam, Neth., pop. 30; # 52:27 N, 4:51 E.

Zabrsze, see **Hindenburg.**

Zacatecas (sä-kä-tä′käs), state, N. W. C. Mexico, area 24, pop. 379, and its *, pop. 26; # 22:45 N, 102:45 W.

Zagazig (zä-gä-zēg′), city, Nile delta, N. Egypt, pop. 42; # 30:35 N, 31:33 E.

Zágráb (zä′gräb) or **Agram,** city, on Sana riv., * of Croatia, N. W. Yugoslavia, pop. 108; univ.; # 45:48 N, 15:59 E.

Zahleh or **Zahle** (zä′le), tn. bet. Beirut and Damascus, Syria, pop. 13; # 33:50 N, 33:50 E.

Zambezi (zam-bē′zi), riv., S. E. Africa, len. ab. 1,600 mi., Angola to Indian oc.; Victoria Falls, # 18:30 S, 36 E.

Zamboanga (säm-bō-äng′gä), spt. city, ext. S. W. Mindanao isl., Philippines, pop. 31; # 7 N, 122:5 E.

Zamora (thä-mō′rä), prov., N. W. C. Spain, area 4.1, pop. 263, and its *, pop. 16; # 41:30 N, 5:46 W.

Zanesville (zānz′vil), city, S. E. Ohio, pop. 38; # 39:57 N, 82 W.

Zante (zän′te), anc. Zacynthos, Greek isl., W. of Morea pen., area 0.2, pop. 45, and its spt., pop. 11; # 37:45 N, 20: 45 E.

Zanzibar (zan-zi-bär′), a Br. protectorate off E. coast of Africa, comprising isl. of Zanzibar, area 0.6, five other isls., and a bit of mainland; total area 1, pop. 200, * Zanzibar, pop. 35; # 6 S, 39:20 E.

Zara (zä′rä), spt., Dalmatian coast, ext. E. Italy, pop. 17; # 44:7 N, 15:15 E.

Zaragoza (thä-rä-gō′thä) or **Saragossa,** prov., N. E. Spain, area 6.7, pop. 512, and its *, on Ebro riv., pop. 154; # 41:40 N, 0:51 W.

Zealand or **Zeeland** (zē′land), prov., mostly isls., S. W. Neth., area 0.7, pop. 249, * Vlissingen (Flushing), pop. 22; # 51:30 N, 3:45 E. — see **Seeland.**

Zeebrügge (zā′brŭg-ė), spt., N. W. Belgium, ship canal to Bruges; # 51:20 N, 3:11 E.

Zehlendorf (tsäl′ęn-dôrf), a S. W. div. of Berlin, Ger., pop. 43; # 52:27 N, 13:15 E.

Zeitz (tsīts), city, Sachsen, Prussia, pop. 34; # 51:3 N, 12:8 E.

Zerbst (tserpst), city, N. Anhalt State, C. Ger., pop. 19; # 51:55 N, 12:10 E.

Zermatt (tser-mät′), vil., S. Switz., near Matterhorn, pop. 2; resort; el. 5,315 ft.; # 46:1 N, 7:44 E.

Zhiryan (zhē′rę-ȧn) or **Vologda,** autonomous soviet, N. E. Russia, area 107, pop. 187, ** Korni and Ust-Slysolsk; # 61:30 N, 50 E.

Zhitomir (zhē-to′męr) or **Volhynia,** city, Ukraine, S. W. C. Russia, pop. 87; # 50:19 N, 28:40 E.

Zion (zī′ọn), national park, S. W. Utah; canyon and coloring; # 37:40 N, 113 W. — an anc. name of **Jerusalem,** Palestine.

Zittau (tsit′tou), city, E. Sachsen, S. Ger., pop. 38; # 50:52 N, 14:48 E.

Žižkov (zhish′kof), a manufacturing suburb of Praha, Bohemia, pop. 72; # ab. 50:5 N, 14:28 E.

Zoug, see **Zug.**

Zug (tsŭch), canton, W. C. Switz., area 0.1, pop. 32, and its * on Lake Zug, pop. 10; # 47:10 N, 8:32 E.

Zugspitze (tsŭch-shpit′sė), highest pk. in Ger. Alps, boundary of Bavaria, el. 9,722 ft.; # 47:25 N, 10:59 E.

Zuider Zee (zī′dèr zē), shallow gulf, N. C. Neth., len. 80 mi.; # 52:30 N, 5:30 E.

Zululand (zŏ′lŏ-land), part of Natal, E. prov. of Union of S. Africa; area 10, pop. 220; * Eshowe; # 28 S, 31 E.

Zungaria, see **Sungari.**

Zuñi (zŏ′nyē), mts., N. W. New Mexico; pueblos; # 35:15 N, 108:15 W.

Zurich (zŏ′rik), canton, N. C. Switz., area 0.7, pop. 539, and its *, pop. 207, on Lake Zurich, area .04; univ.; # 47:15 N, 8:45 E.

Zuyder Zee, see **Zuider Zee.**

Zweibrücken (tsvī′brŭk-ęn), tn., Palatinate, S. W. Ger., pop. 15; castle; # 49:17 N, 7:20 E.

Zwickau (tsvik′ou), div., W. Sachsen, S. Ger., area 1, pop. 795, and its *, pop. 80; # 50:44 N, 12:30 E.

Zwolle (zwol′ė), city, Overyssel, E. C. Neth., pop. 38; shipyards; # 52:33 N, 6:6 E.

Zyrian, see **Zhiryan.**

---

fat, fāte, fär, fåll, ȧsk, fāre; net, mē, hėr; pin, pīne; not, nōte, möve, nôr; up, lūte, půll; oi, oil; ou, out; (lightened) aviȧry, ęlect, agȯny, intọ, ŭnite; (obscured) errȧnt, operä, ardęnt, actọr, natụre; ch, chip; g, go; th, thin; ᴛʜ, then; y, you; (variable) ḍ as d or j, ş as s or sh, ṭ as t or ch, ẓ as z or zh; o, F. cloche; ü, F. menu; ċh, Sc. loch; ṅ, F. bonbon; ′, primary accent; ″, secondary accent; †, obsolete; <, from; +, and; =, equals. See also lists at beginning of book.

POPULATION OF PLACES IN THE UNITED STATES
WITH 5,000 OR MORE INHABITANTS IN 1940

Asterisk (*) indicates township or town.

ALABAMA				ARKANSAS		CALIFORNIA	
		Prichard	6,084				
		Selma	19,834	Arkadelphia	5,078	Alameda	36,256
Alexander City	6,640	Sheffield	7,933	Batesville	5,267	Albany	11,493
Andalusia	6,886	Sylacauga	6,269	Blytheville	10,652	Alhambra	38,935
Anniston	25,523	Talladega	9,298	Camden	8,975	Anaheim	11,031
Bessemer	22,826	Tarrant City	6,833	Conway	5,782	Antioch	5,106
Birmingham	267,583	Troy	7,055	El Dorado	15,858	Arcadia	9,122
Cullman	5,074	Tuscaloosa	27,493	Fayetteville	8,212	Azusa	5,209
Decatur	16,604	Tuscumbia	5,515	Forrest City	5,699	Bakersfield	29,252
Dothan	17,194			Fort Smith	36,584	Bell	11,264
Eufaula	6,269			Helena	8,546	Belvedere *	37,192
Fairfield	11,703	**ARIZONA**		Hope	7,475	Berkeley	85,547
Florence	15,043			Hot Springs	21,370	Beverly Hills	26,823
Gadsden	36,975	Bisbee	5,853	Jonesboro	11,729	Brawley	11,718
Greenville	5,075	Douglas	8,623	Little Rock	88,039	Burbank	34,337
Homewood	7,397	Flagstaff	5,080	Malvern	5,290	Burlingame	15,940
Huntsville	13,050	Globe	6,141	North Little Rock	21,137	Calexico	5,415
Jasper	6,847	Mesa	7,224	Paragould	7,079	Chico	9,287
Lanett	6,141	Nogales	5,135	Pine Bluff	21,290	Chula Vista	5,138
Mobile	78,720	Phoenix	65,414	Russellville	5,927	Coalinga	5,026
Montgomery	78,084	Prescott	6,018	Stuttgart	5,628	Colton	9,686
Opelika	8,487	Tucson	36,818	Texarkana	11,821	Compton	16,198
Phenix City	15,351	Yuma	5,325	Van Buren	5,422	Corona	8,764

Coronado	6,932	Stockton	54,714	Fort Pierce	8,040
Culver City	8,976	Torrance	9,950	Gainesville	13,757
Daly City	9,625	Tulare	8,259	Hollywood	6,239
El Centro	10,017	Upland	6,316	Jacksonville	173,065
El Cerrito	6,137	Vallejo	20,072	Key West	12,927
Eureka	17,055	Visalia	8,904	Lake City	5,836
Fresno	60,685	Watsonville	8,937	Lakeland	22,068
Fullerton	10,442	Whittier	16,115	Lake Wales	5,024
Gardena	5,909	Woodland	6,637	Lake Worth	7,408
Glendale	82,582			Marianna	5,079
Grass Valley	5,701	**COLORADO**		Miami	172,172
Hanford	8,234			Miami Beach	28,012
Hawthorne	8,263	Alamosa	5,613	Ocala	8,986
Hayward	6,736	Boulder	12,958	Orlando	36,736
Hermosa Beach	7,197	Canon City	6,690	Palatka	7,140
Huntington Park	28,648	Colorado Springs	36,789	Panama City	11,610
Inglewood	30,114	Denver	322,412	Pensacola	37,449
Lodi	11,079	Durango	5,887	Plant City	7,491
Long Beach	164,271	Englewood	9,680	River Junction	7,110
Los Angeles	1,504,277	Fort Collins	12,251	St. Augustine	12,090
Lynwood	10,982	Grand Junction	12,479	St. Petersburg	60,812
Madera	6,457	Greeley	15,995	Sanford	10,217
Manhattan Beach	6,398	La Junta	7,040	Sarasota	11,141
Martinez	7,381	Longmont	7,406	Tallahassee	16,240
Marysville	6,646	Loveland	6,145	Tampa	108,391
Maywood	10,731	Pueblo	52,162	West Palm Beach	33,693
Merced	10,135	Sterling	7,411	Winter Haven	6,199
Modesto	16,379	Trinidad	13,223		
Monrovia	12,807	Walsenburg	5,855	**GEORGIA**	
Montebello	8,016				
Monterey	10,084	**CONNECTICUT**		Albany	19,055
Monterey Park	8,531			Americus	9,281
Napa	7,740	Ansonia	19,210	Athens	20,650
National City	10,344	Bridgeport	147,121	Atlanta	302,288
Oakland	302,163	Bristol	30,167	Augusta	65,919
Ontario	14,197	Danbury	22,339	Bainbridge	6,352
Orange	7,901	Derby	10,287	Brunswick	15,035
Oxnard	8,519	East Hartford *	18,615	Carrollton	6,214
Pacific Grove	6,249	Hartford	166,267	Cartersville	6,141
Palo Alto	16,774	Meriden	39,494	Cedartown	9,025
Pasadena	81,864	Middletown	26,495	College Park	8,213
Petaluma	8,034	Naugatuck	15,388	Columbus	53,280
Piedmont	9,866	New Britain	68,685	Cordele	7,929
Pittsburg	9,520	New Haven	160,605	Dalton	10,448
Pomona	23,539	New London	30,456	Decatur	16,561
Porterville	6,270	Norwalk	39,849	Douglas	5,175
Redding	8,109	Norwich	23,652	Dublin	7,814
Redlands	14,324	Putnam	7,775	East Point	12,403
Redondo Beach	13,092	Rockville	7,572	Elberton	6,188
Redwood City	12,453	Shelton	10,971	Fitzgerald	7,388
Richmond	23,642	Southington	5,088	Gainesville	10,243
Riverside	34,696	Stamford	47,938	Griffin	13,222
Roseville	6,653	Stratford *	22,580	Hapeville	5,059
Sacramento	105,958	Torrington	26,988	La Grange	21,983
Salinas	11,586	Wallingford	11,425	Macon	57,865
San Anselmo	5,790	Waterbury	99,314	Marietta	8,667
San Bernardino	43,646	West Hartford *	33,776	Milledgeville	6,778
San Bruno	6,519	West Haven *	30,021	Moultrie	10,147
San Buenaventura		Willimantic	12,101	Newnan	7,182
(Ventura)	13,264	Winsted	7,674	Rome	26,282
San Diego	203,341			Savannah	95,996
San Fernando	9,094	**DELAWARE**		Statesboro	5,028
San Francisco	634,536			Thomaston	6,396
San Gabriel	11,867	Dover	5,517	Thomasville	12,683
San Jose	68,457	Wilmington	112,504	Tifton	5,228
San Leandro	14,601			Toccoa	5,494
San Luis Obispo	8,881	**DISTRICT OF**		Valdosta	15,595
San Marino	8,175	**COLUMBIA**		Waycross	16,763
San Mateo	19,403				
San Rafael	8,573	Washington	663,091	**IDAHO**	
Santa Ana	31,921				
Santa Barbara	34,958	**FLORIDA**		Boise City	26,130
Santa Clara	6,650			Burley	5,329
Santa Cruz	16,896	Bartow	6,158	Caldwell	7,272
Santa Maria	8,522	Bradenton	7,444	Coeur d'Alene	10,049
Santa Monica	53,500	Clearwater	10,136	Idaho Falls	15,024
Santa Paula	8,986	Coral Gables	8,294	Lewiston	10,548
Santa Rosa	12,605	Daytona Beach	22,584	Moscow	6,014
South Gate	26,945	De Land	7,041	Nampa	12,149
South Pasadena	14,356	Fort Lauderdale	17,996	Pocatello	18,133
South San Francisco	6,629	Fort Myers	10,604	Twin Falls	11,851

ILLINOIS	
Alton	31,255
Arlington Heights	5,668
Aurora	47,170
Batavia	5,101
Beardstown	6,505
Belleville	28,405
Bellwood	5,220
Belvidere	8,094
Benton	7,372
Berwyn	48,451
Bloomington	32,868
Blue Island	16,638
Brookfield	10,817
Cairo	14,407
Calumet City	13,241
Canton	11,577
Carbondale	8,550
Centralia	16,343
Champaign	23,302
Charleston	8,197
Chester	5,110
Chicago	3,396,808
Chicago Heights	22,461
Cicero	64,712
Clinton	6,331
Collinsville	9,767
Danville	36,919
Decatur	59,305
De Kalb	9,146
Des Plaines	9,518
Dixon	10,671
Downers Grove	9,526
Du Quoin	7,515
East Moline	12,359
East Peoria	6,806
East St. Louis	75,609
Edwardsville	8,008
Effingham	6,180
Elgin	38,333
Elmhurst	15,458
Elmwood Park	13,689
Evanston	65,389
Flora	5,474
Forest Park	14,840
Freeport	22,366
Galesburg	28,876
Glencoe	6,825
Glen Ellyn	8,055
Granite City	22,974
Harrisburg	11,453
Harvey	17,878
Herrin	9,352
Highland Park	14,476
Hinsdale	7,336
Hoopeston	5,381
Jacksonville	19,844
Johnston City	5,418
Joliet	42,365
Kankakee	22,241
Kewanee	16,901
La Grange	10,479
Lake Forest	6,885
La Salle	12,812
Lawrenceville	6,213
Lincoln	12,752
Litchfield	7,048
Lombard	7,075
Macomb	8,764
Madison	7,782
Marion	9,251
Mattoon	15,827
Maywood	26,648
Melrose Park	10,933
Metropolis	6,287
Moline	34,608
Monmouth	9,096
Morris	6,145
Mount Carmel	6,987
Mount Vernon	14,724

Murphysboro	8,976	Marion	26,767	Atchison	12,648	Monroe	28,309
Naperville	5,272	Martinsville	5,009	Chanute	10,142	Morgan City	6,969
Niles Center	7,172	Michigan City	26,476	Coffeyville	17,355	Natchitoches	6,812
Normal	6,983	Mishawaka	28,298	Concordia	6,255	New Iberia	13,747
North Chicago	8,465	Mount Vernon	5,638	Dodge City	8,487	New Orleans	494,537
Oak Park	66,015	Muncie	49,720	El Dorado	10,045	Opelousas	8,980
Olney	7,831	New Albany	25,414	Emporia	13,188	Plaquemine	5,049
Ottawa	16,005	New Castle	16,620	Fort Scott	10,557	Ruston	7,107
Pana	5,966	Noblesville	5,575	Garden City	6,285	Shreveport	98,167
Paris	9,281	Peru	12,432	Great Bend	9,044	Tallulah	5,712
Park Ridge	12,063	Plymouth	5,713	Hays	6,385	Thibodaux	5,851
Pekin	19,407	Portland	6,362	Hutchinson	30,013	West Monroe	8,560
Peoria	105,087	Princeton	7,786	Independence	11,565		
Peru	8,983	Richmond	35,147	Iola	7,244	**MAINE**	
Pontiac	9,585	Rushville	5,960	Junction City	8,507		
Princeton	5,224	Seymour	8,620	Kansas City	121,458	Auburn	19,817
Quincy	40,469	Shelbyville	10,791	Lawrence	14,390	Augusta	19,360
River Forest	9,487	South Bend	101,268	Leavenworth	19,220	Bangor	29,822
Riverside	7,935	Sullivan	5,077	McPherson	7,194	Bath	10,235
Rockford	84,637	Tell City	5,395	Manhattan	11,659	Belfast	5,540
Rock Island	42,775	Terre Haute	62,693	Newton	11,048	Biddeford	19,790
St. Charles	5,870	Tipton	5,101	Ottawa	10,193	Brewer	6,510
Salem	7,319	Valparaiso	8,736	Parsons	14,294	Brunswick	7,003
Springfield	75,503	Vincennes	18,228	Pittsburg	17,571	Calais	5,161
Spring Valley	5,010	Wabash	9,653	Pratt	6,591	Gardiner	6,044
Sterling	11,363	Warsaw	6,378	Salina	21,073	Lewiston	38,598
Streator	14,930	Washington	9,312	Topeka	67,833	Old Town	7,688
Summit	7,043	West Lafayette	6,270	Wellington	7,246	Portland	73,643
Taylorville	8,313	Whiting	10,307	Wichita	114,966	Presque Isle	5,456
Urbana	14,064	Winchester	5,303	Winfield	9,506	Rockland	8,899
Vandalia	5,288					Rumford Falls	8,447
Venice	5,454	**IOWA**		**KENTUCKY**		Saco	8,631
Villa Park	7,236					South Portland	15,781
Waukegan	34,241	Albia	5,157	Ashland	29,537	Waterville	16,688
West Frankfort	12,383	Ames	12,555	Bellevue	8,741	Westbrook	11,087
Wheaton	7,389	Atlantic	5,802	Bowling Green	14,585		
Wilmette	17,226	Boone	12,373	Corbin	7,893	**MARYLAND**	
Winnetka	12,430	Burlington	25,832	Covington	62,018		
Wood River	8,197	Carroll	5,389	Danville	6,734	Annapolis	13,069
Woodstock	6,123	Cedar Falls	9,349	Dayton	8,379	Baltimore	859,100
Zion	6,555	Cedar Rapids	62,120	Fort Thomas	11,034	Cambridge	10,102
		Centerville	8,413	Frankfort	11,492	Cumberland	39,483
		Chariton	5,754	Glasgow	5,815	Frederick	15,802
INDIANA		Charles City	8,681	Harlan	5,122	Frostburg	7,659
		Cherokee	7,469	Hazard	7,397	Hagerstown	32,491
Anderson	41,572	Clinton	26,270	Henderson	13,160	Hyattsville	6,575
Auburn	5,415	Council Bluffs	41,439	Hopkinsville	11,724	Salisbury	13,313
Bedford	12,514	Creston	8,033	Jenkins	9,428	Takoma Park	8,938
Bicknell	5,110	Davenport	66,039	Lexington	49,304		
Bloomington	20,870	Decorah	5,303	Louisville	319,077	**MASSACHUSETTS**	
Bluffton	5,417	Des Moines	159,819	Ludlow	6,185		
Brazil	8,126	Dubuque	43,892	Madisonville	8,209	Abington *	5,708
Clinton	7,092	Estherville	5,651	Mayfield	8,619	Adams *	12,608
Columbus	11,738	Fairfield	6,773	Maysville	6,572	Amesbury *	10,862
Connersville	12,898	Fort Dodge	22,904	Middlesborough	11,777	Amherst *	6,410
Crawfordsville	11,089	Fort Madison	14,063	Newport	30,631	Andover *	11,122
Decatur	5,861	Grinnell	5,210	Owensboro	30,245	Arlington *	40,013
East Chicago	54,637	Iowa City	17,182	Paducah	33,765	Athol *	11,180
Elkhart	33,434	Keokuk	15,076	Paris	6,697	Attleboro	22,071
Elwood	10,913	Knoxville	6,936	Princeton	5,389	Auburn *	6,629
Evansville	97,062	Le Mars	5,353	Richmond	7,335	Barnstable *	8,333
Fort Wayne	118,410	Marshalltown	19,240	Somerset	6,154	Belmont *	26,867
Frankfort	13,706	Mason City	27,080	Winchester	8,594	Beverly	25,537
Franklin	6,264	Muscatine	18,286			Boston	770,816
Gary	111,719	Newton	10,462	**LOUISIANA**		Braintree *	16,378
Goshen	11,375	Oelwein	7,801			Bridgewater *	8,902
Greensburg	6,065	Oskaloosa	11,024	Abbeville	6,672	Brockton	62,343
Hammond	70,184	Ottumwa	31,570	Alexandria	27,066	Brookline *	49,786
Hartford City	6,946	Perry	5,977	Bastrop	6,626	Cambridge	110,879
Hobart	7,166	Red Oak	5,763	Baton Rouge	34,719	Canton *	6,381
Huntington	13,903	Shenandoah	6,846	Bogalusa	14,604	Chelsea	41,259
Indianapolis	386,972	Sioux City	82,364	Bossier City	5,786	Chicopee	41,664
Jasper	5,041	Spencer	6,599	Crowley	9,523	Clinton *	12,440
Jeffersonville	11,493	Storm Lake	5,274	Eunice	5,242	Concord *	7,972
Kendallville	5,431	Washington	5,227	Gretna	10,879	Danvers *	14,179
Kokomo	33,795	Waterloo	51,743	Hammond	6,033	Dartmouth *	9,011
Lafayette	28,798	Webster City	6,738	Houma	9,052	Dedham *	15,508
La Porte	16,180			Jackson	5,384	Dracut *	7,339
Lebanon	6,529	**KANSAS**		Jennings	7,343	Easthampton *	10,316
Linton	6,263			Lafayette	19,210	Everett	46,784
Logansport	20,177	Abilene	5,671	Lake Charles	21,207	Fairhaven *	10,938
Madison	6,923	Arkansas City	12,752	Minden	6,677		

Fall River	115,428	Woburn	19,751	Wyandotte	30,618
Fitchburg	41,824	Worcester	193,694	Ypsilanti	12,121
Framingham *	23,214				
Franklin *	7,303	**MICHIGAN**		**MINNESOTA**	
Gardner	20,206				
Gloucester	24,046	Adrian	14,230	Albert Lea	12,200
Great Barrington *	5,824	Albion	8,345	Alexandria	5,051
Greenfield *	15,672	Alma	7,202	Anoka	6,426
Haverhill	46,752	Alpena	12,808	Austin	18,307
Hingham *	8,003	Ann Arbor	29,815	Bemidji	9,427
Holyoke	53,750	Battle Creek	43,453	Brainerd	12,071
Hudson *	8,042	Bay City	47,956	Chisholm	7,487
Ipswich *	6,348	Benton Harbor	16,668	Cloquet	7,304
Lawrence	84,323	Berkley	6,406	Columbia Heights	6,035
Leominster	22,226	Birmingham	11,196	Crookston	7,161
Lexington *	13,187	Cadillac	9,855	Detroit Lakes	5,015
Lowell	101,389	Charlotte	5,544	Duluth	101,065
Longmeadow *	5,790	Cheboygan	5,673	Edina	5,855
Ludlow *	8,181	Coldwater	7,343	Ely	5,970
Lynn	98,123	Dearborn	63,584	Eveleth	6,887
Malden	58,010	Detroit	1,623,452	Fairibault	14,527
Mansfield *	6,530	Dowagiac	5,007	Fairmont	6,988
Marblehead *	10,856	East Detroit	8,584	Fergus Falls	10,848
Marlborough *	15,154	East Lansing	5,839	Hastings	5,662
Maynard *	6,812	Ecorse	13,209	Hibbing	16,385
Medford	63,083	Escanaba	14,830	International Falls	5,626
Melrose	25,333	Ferndale	22,523	Little Falls	6,047
Methuen *	21,880	Flint	151,543	Mankato	15,654
Middleborough *	9,032	Grand Haven	8,799	Minneapolis	492,370
Milford *	15,388	Grand Rapids	164,292	Montevideo	5,220
Millbury *	6,983	Greenville	5,321	Moorhead	9,491
Milton *	18,708	Grosse Pointe	6,179	New Ulm	8,743
Montague *	7,582	Grosse Pointe Farms	7,217	Owatonna	8,694
Natick *	13,851	Grosse Pointe Park	12,646	Red Wing	9,962
Needham *	12,445	Hamtramck	49,839	Richfield	6,750
New Bedford	110,341	Hancock	5,554	Robbinsdale	6,018
Newburyport	13,916	Hastings	5,175	Rochester	26,312
Newton	69,873	Highland Park	50,810	St. Cloud	24,173
North Adams	22,213	Hillsdale	6,381	St. Louis Park	7,737
Northampton	24,794	Holland	14,616	St. Paul	287,736
North Andover *	7,524	Inkster	7,044	St. Peter	5,870
North Attleborough *	10,359	Ionia	6,392	South St. Paul	11,844
Northbridge *	10,242	Iron Mountain	11,080	Stillwater	7,013
Norwood *	15,383	Ironwood	13,369	Thief River Falls	6,019
Orange *	5,611	Ishpeming	9,491	Virginia	12,264
Palmer *	9,149	Jackson	49,656	West St. Paul	5,733
Peabody	21,711	Kalamazoo	54,097	Willmar	7,623
Pittsfield	49,684	Kingsford	5,771	Winona	22,490
Plymouth *	13,100	Lansing	78,753	Worthington	5,918
Quincy	75,810	Lapeer	5,365		
Randolph *	7,634	Lincoln Park	15,236	**MISSISSIPPI**	
Reading *	10,866	Ludington	8,701		
Revere	34,405	Manistee	8,694	Biloxi	17,475
Rockland *	8,087	Manistique	5,399	Brookhaven	6,232
Salem	41,213	Marquette	15,928	Canton	6,011
Saugus *	14,825	Marshall	5,253	Clarksdale	12,168
Somerset *	5,873	Menominee	10,230	Columbia	6,064
Somerville	102,177	Midland	10,329	Columbus	13,645
Southbridge *	16,825	Monroe	18,478	Corinth	7,818
South Hadley *	6,856	Mount Clemens	14,389	Greenville	20,892
Spencer *	6,641	Mount Pleasant	8,413	Greenwood	14,767
Springfield	149,554	Muskegon	47,697	Grenada	5,831
Stoneham *	10,765	Muskegon Heights	16,047	Gulfport	15,195
Stoughton *	8,632	Negaunee	6,813	Hattiesburg	21,026
Swampscott *	10,761	Niles	11,328	Jackson	62,107
Taunton	37,395	Owosso	14,424	Laurel	20,598
Uxbridge *	6,417	Petoskey	6,019	McComb	9,898
Wakefield *	16,223	Plymouth	5,360	Meridian	35,481
Walpole *	7,443	Pontiac	66,626	Natchez	15,296
Waltham	40,020	Port Huron	32,759	Pascagoula	5,900
Ware *	7,557	River Rouge	17,008	Picayune	5,129
Watertown *	35,427	Roseville	9,023	Tupelo	8,212
Webster *	13,186	Royal Oak	25,087	Vicksburg	24,460
Wellesley *	15,127	Saginaw	82,794	West Point	5,627
Westfield	18,793	St. Clair Shores	10,405	Yazoo City	7,258
West Springfield *	17,135	St. Joseph	8,963		
Weymouth *	23,868	Sault Ste. Marie	15,847	**MISSOURI**	
Whitman *	7,759	Sturgis	7,214	Boonville	6,089
Winchendon *	6,575	Three Rivers	6,710	Brookfield	6,174
Winchester *	15,081	Traverse City	14,455	Cape Girardeau	19,426
Winthrop *	16,768	Trenton	5,284	Carthage	10,585

Caruthersville	6,612
Charleston	5,182
Chillicothe	8,012
Clayton	13,069
Clinton	6,041
Columbia	18,399
De Soto	5,121
Ferguson	5,724
Flat River	5,401
Fulton	8,297
Hannibal	20,865
Independence	16,066
Jefferson City	24,268
Joplin	37,144
Kansas City	399,178
Kennett	6,335
Kirksville	10,080
Kirkwood	12,132
Lebanon	5,025
Lexington	5,341
Maplewood	12,875
Marshall	8,533
Maryville	5,700
Mexico	9,053
Moberly	12,920
Neosho	5,318
Nevada	8,181
Poplar Bluff	11,163
Richmond Heights	12,802
Rolla	5,141
St. Charles	10,803
St. Joseph	75,711
St. Louis	816,048
Sedalia	20,428
Sikeston	7,944
Springfield	61,238
Trenton	7,046
University City	33,023
Warrensburg	5,868
Washington	6,756
Webb City	7,033
Webster Groves	18,394

MONTANA

Anaconda	11,004
Billings	23,261
Bozeman	8,665
Butte	37,081
Great Falls	29,928
Havre	6,427
Helena	15,056
Kalispell	8,245
Lewistown	5,874
Livingston	6,642
Miles City	7,313
Missoula	18,449

NEBRASKA

Alliance	6,253
Beatrice	10,883
Columbus	7,632
Fairbury	6,304
Falls City	6,146
Fremont	11,862
Grand Island	19,130
Hastings	15,145
Kearney	9,643
Lincoln	81,984
McCook	6,212
Nebraska City	7,339
Norfolk	10,490
North Platte	12,429
Omaha	223,844
Scottsbluff	12,057
York	5,383

NEVADA

Las Vegas	8,422
Reno	21,317
Sparks	5,318

NEW HAMPSHIRE

Berlin	19,084
Claremont *	12,144
Concord	27,171
Derry *	5,400
Dover	14,990
Exeter *	5,398
Franklin	6,749
Keene	13,832
Laconia	13,484
Lebanon *	7,590
Manchester	77,685
Nashua	32,927
Newport *	5,304
Portsmouth	14,821
Rochester	12,012
Somersworth	6,136

NEW JERSEY

Asbury Park	14,617
Atlantic City	64,094
Audubon	8,906
Bayonne	79,198
Belleville	28,167
Bergenfield	10,275
Bloomfield	41,623
Bogota	7,346
Boonton	6,739
Bound Brook	7,616
Bridgeton	15,992
Burlington	10,905
Camden	117,536
Carlstadt	5,644
Carteret	11,976
Cliffside Park	16,892
Clifton	48,827
Collingswood	12,685
Cranford *	12,860
Dover	10,491
Dumont	7,556
Dunellen	5,360
East Orange	68,945
East Rutherford	7,268
Elizabeth	109,912
Englewood	18,966
Fair Lawn	9,017
Fairview	8,770
Fort Lee	9,468
Freehold	6,952
Garfield	28,044
Glen Ridge	7,331
Glen Rock	5,177
Gloucester City	13,692
Guttenberg	6,200
Hackensack	26,279
Haddonfield	9,742
Haddon Heights	5,555
Haledon	5,303
Hammonton	7,668
Harrison	14,171
Hasbrouck Heights	6,716
Hawthorne	12,610
Highland Park	9,002
Hillside *	18,556
Hoboken	50,115
Irvington	55,328
Jersey City	301,173
Kearny	39,467
Keyport	5,147
Leonia	5,763
Linden	24,115
Lodi	11,552
Long Branch	17,408
Lyndhurst *	17,454
Madison	7,944
Manville	6,065
Maplewood *	23,139
Metuchen	6,557

Millburn *	11,652
Millville	14,806
Montclair	39,807
Morristown	15,270
Neptune *	10,207
Newark	429,760
New Brunswick	33,180
Newton	5,533
North Arlington	9,904
North Bergen *	39,714
North Plainfield	10,586
Nutley	21,954
Orange	35,717
Palisades Park	8,141
Palmyra	5,178
Passaic	61,394
Paterson	139,656
Paulsboro	7,011
Pennsauken *	17,745
Penns Grove	6,488
Perth Amboy	41,242
Phillipsburg	18,314
Pitman	5,507
Plainfield	37,469
Pleasantville	11,050
Princeton	7,719
Prospect Park	5,714
Rahway	17,498
Red Bank	10,974
Ridgefield	5,271
Ridgefield Park	11,277
Ridgewood	14,948
Roselle	13,597
Roselle Park	9,661
Rutherford	15,466
Salem	8,618
Sayreville	8,186
Secaucus	9,754
Somerville	8,720
South Amboy	7,802
South Orange	13,742
South Plainfield	5,379
South River	10,714
Summit	16,165
Teaneck *	25,275
Tenafly	7,413
Totowa	5,130
Trenton	124,697
Union City	56,173
Union *	24,730
Ventnor City	7,905
Verona	8,957
Vineland	7,914
Wallington	8,981
Weehawken *	14,363
Westfield	18,458
West New York	39,439
West Orange	25,662
Westwood	5,388
Wildwood	5,150
Woodbridge *	27,191
Woodbury	8,306
Wood-Ridge	5,739

NEW MEXICO

Albuquerque	35,449
Carlsbad	7,116
Clovis	10,065
Gallup	7,041
Hobbs	10,619
Las Cruces	8,385
Las Vegas city	5,941
Las Vegas town	6,421
Portales	5,104
Raton	7,607
Roswell	13,482
Santa Fe	20,325
Silver City	5,044
Tucumcari	6,194

NEW YORK

Albany	130,577
Amityville	5,058
Amsterdam	33,329
Auburn	35,753
Batavia	17,267
Beacon	12,572
Binghamton	78,309
Bronxville	6,888
Buffalo	575,901
Canandaigua	8,321
Catskill	5,429
Cedarhurst	5,463
Cohoes	21,955
Corning	16,212
Cortland	15,881
Depew	6,084
Dobbs Ferry	5,883
Dunkirk	17,713
East Aurora	5,253
East Rochester	6,691
East Rockaway	5,610
Elmira	45,106
Endicott	17,702
Floral Park	12,950
Fredonia	5,738
Freeport	20,410
Fulton	13,362
Garden City	11,223
Geneva	15,555
Glen Cove	12,415
Glens Falls	18,836
Gloversville	23,329
Great Neck	6,167
Hamburg	5,467
Hastings-on-Hudson	7,057
Haverstraw	5,909
Hempstead	20,856
Herkimer	9,617
Hornell	15,649
Hudson	11,517
Hudson Falls	6,654
Ilion	8,927
Irondequoit *	23,376
Ithaca	19,730
Jamestown	42,638
Johnson City	18,039
Johnstown	10,666
Kenmore	18,612
Kingston	28,589
Lackawanna	24,058
Lancaster	7,236
Larchmont	5,970
Little Falls	10,163
Lockport	24,379
Long Beach	9,036
Lynbrook	14,557
Malone	8,743
Malverne	5,153
Mamaroneck	13,034
Massena	11,328
Mechanicville	7,449
Medina	5,871
Middletown	21,908
Mineola	10,064
Mount Kisco	5,941
Mount Vernon	67,362
Newark	9,646
Newburgh	31,883
New Rochelle	58,408
New York City	7,454,995
Bronx Borough	1,394,711
Brooklyn Borough	2,698,285
Manhattan	
Borough	1,889,924
Queens Borough	1,297,634
Richmond Borough	174,441
Niagara Falls	78,029
North Pelham	5,052
North Tarrytown	8,804

North Tonawanda	20,254
Norwich	8,694
Nyack	5,206
Ogdensburg	16,346
Olean	21,506
Oneida	10,291
Oneonta	11,731
Ossining	15,996
Oswego	22,062
Owego	5,068
Patchogue	7,181
Peekskill	17,311
Pelham Manor	5,302
Penn Yan	5,308
Plattsburgh	16,351
Port Chester	23,073
Port Jervis	9,749
Poughkeepsie	40,478
Rensselaer	10,768
Rochester	324,975
Rockville Centre	18,613
Rome	34,214
Rye	9,865
Salamanca	9,011
Saranac Lake	7,138
Saratoga Springs	13,705
Scarsdale	12,966
Schenectady	87,549
Scotia	7,960
Seneca Falls	6,452
Solvay	8,201
Syracuse	205,967
Tarrytown	6,874
Tonawanda	13,008
Troy	70,304
Tuckahoe	6,563
Tupper Lake	5,451
Utica	100,518
Valley Stream	16,679
Watertown	33,385
Watervliet	16,114
Waverly	5,450
Wellsville	5,942
White Plains	40,327
Williston Park	5,750
Yonkers	142,598

NORTH CAROLINA

Asheboro	6,981
Asheville	51,310
Burlington	12,198
Canton	5,037
Charlotte	100,899
Concord	15,572
Dunn	5,256
Durham	60,195
Elizabeth City	11,564
Fayetteville	17,428
Forest City	5,035
Gastonia	21,313
Goldsboro	17,274
Greensboro	59,319
Greenville	12,674
Hamlet	5,111
Henderson	7,647
Hendersonville	5,381
Hickory	13,487
High Point	38,495
Kings Mountain	6,547
Kinston	15,388
Laurinburg	5,685
Lenoir	7,598
Lexington	10,550
Lumberton	5,803
Monroe	6,475
Mooresville	6,682
Morganton	7,670
Mount Airy	6,286
New Bern	11,815
Newton	5,407

Raleigh	46,897	Kenton	7,593
Reidsville	10,387	Lakewood	69,160
Roanoke Rapids	8,545	Lancaster	21,940
Rocky Mount	25,568	Lima	44,711
Salisbury	19,037	Lockland	5,601
Shelby	14,037	Logan	6,177
Statesville	11,440	Lorain	44,125
Tarboro	7,148	Mansfield	37,154
Thomasville	11,041	Maple Heights	6,728
Washington	8,569	Marietta	14,543
Wilmington	33,407	Marion	30,817
Wilson	19,234	Martins Ferry	14,729
Winston-Salem	79,815	Massillon	26,644
		Miamisburg	5,544

NORTH DAKOTA

		Middletown	31,220
		Mingo Junction	5,192
Bismarck	15,496	Mount Vernon	10,122
Devils Lake	6,204	Nelsonville	5,368
Dickinson	5,839	Newark	31,487
Fargo	32,580	New Boston	6,024
Grand Forks	20,228	New Philadelphia	12,328
Jamestown	8,790	Niles	16,273
Mandan	6,685	North College Hill	5,231
Minot	16,577	Norwalk	8,211
Valley City	5,917	Norwood	34,010
Williston	5,790	Oakwood	7,652
		Painesville	12,235

OHIO

		Parma	16,365
		Piqua	16,049
Akron	244,791	Portsmouth	40,466
Alliance	22,405	Ravenna	8,538
Ashland	12,453	Reading	6,079
Ashtabula	21,405	Rocky River	8,291
Athens	7,696	St. Bernard	7,387
Barberton	24,028	St. Marys	5,532
Barnesville	5,002	Salem	12,301
Bedford	7,390	Sandusky	24,874
Bellaire	13,799	Shaker Heights	23,393
Bellefontaine	9,808	Shelby	6,643
Bellevue	6,127	Sidney	9,790
Berea	6,025	South Euclid	6,146
Bexley	8,705	Springfield	70,662
Bowling Green	7,190	Steubenville	37,651
Bryan	5,404	Struthers	11,739
Bucyrus	9,727	Tiffin	16,102
Cambridge	15,044	Toledo	282,349
Campbell	13,785	Toronto	7,426
Canton	108,401	Troy	9,697
Cheviot	9,043	Uhrichsville	6,435
Chillicothe	20,129	University Heights	5,981
Cincinnati	455,610	Upper Arlington	5,370
Circleville	7,982	Urbana	8,335
Cleveland	878,336	Van Wert	9,227
Cleveland Heights	54,992	Wadsworth	6,495
Columbus	306,087	Wapakoneta	5,225
Conneaut	9,355	Warren	42,837
Coshocton	11,509	Washington Court	
Cuyahoga Falls	20,546	House	9,402
Dayton	210,718	Wellston	5,537
Defiance	9,744	Wellsville	7,672
Delaware	8,944	Wilmington	5,971
Delphos	5,746	Wooster	11,543
Dover	9,691	Xenia	10,633
East Cleveland	39,495	Youngstown	167,720
East Liverpool	23,555	Zanesville	37,500
East Palestine	5,123		
Elyria	25,120		

OKLAHOMA

Euclid	17,866		
Findlay	20,228	Ada	15,143
Fostoria	13,453	Altus	8,593
Fremont	14,710	Alva	5,055
Galion	8,685	Anadarko	5,579
Gallipolis	7,832	Ardmore	16,886
Garfield Heights	16,989	Bartlesville	16,267
Girard	9,805	Blackwell	8,537
Grandview Heights	6,960	Bristow	6,050
Greenville	7,745	Chickasha	14,111
Hamilton	50,592	Clinton	6,736
Ironton	15,851	Cushing	7,703
Jackson	6,295	Duncan	9,207
Kent	8,581	Durant	10,027

Elk City	5,021	Carbondale	19,371
El Reno	10,078	Carlisle	13,984
Enid	28,081	Carnegie	12,663
Frederick	5,109	Centerville	6,317
Guthrie	10,018	Chambersburg	14,852
Henryetta	6,905	Charleroi	10,784
Hobart	5,177	Cheltenham *	19,082
Holdenville	6,632	Chester	59,285
Hugo	5,909	Clairton	16,381
Lawton	18,055	Clearfield	9,372
McAlester	12,401	Coaldale	6,163
Miami	8,345	Coatesville	14,006
Muskogee	32,332	Collingdale (Darby	
Norman	11,429	P.O.)	8,162
Oklahoma City	204,424	Columbia	11,547
Okmulgee	16,051	Connellsville	13,608
Pauls Valley	5,104	Conshohocken	10,776
Pawhuska	5,443	Coraopolis	11,086
Perry	5,045	Corry	6,935
Picher	5,848	Crafton	7,163
Ponca City	16,794	Danville	7,122
Sapulpa	12,249	Darby	10,334
Sand Springs	6,137	Dickson City	11,548
Seminole	11,547	Donora	13,180
Shawnee	22,053	Dormont	12,974
Stillwater	10,097	Du Bois	12,080
Tulsa	142,157	Dunmore	23,086
Vinita	5,685	Dupont	5,278
Wewoka	10,315	Duquesne	20,693
Woodward	5,406	Duryea	8,275
		Easton	33,589
		East Pittsburgh	6,079

OREGON

		East Stroudsburg	6,404
		Edwardsville	7,998
Albany	5,654	Ellwood City	12,329
Astoria	10,389	Emmaus	6,731
Baker	9,342	Ephrata	6,199
Bend	10,021	Erie	116,955
Corvallis	8,392	Etna	7,223
Eugene	20,838	Exeter	5,802
Grants Pass	6,028	Farrell	13,899
Klamath Falls	16,497	Ford City	5,795
La Grande	7,747	Forest Hills	5,248
Marshfield	5,259	Forty Fort	6,293
Medford	11,281	Frackville	8,035
Oregon City	6,124	Franklin	9,948
Pendleton	8,847	Freeland	6,593
Portland	305,394	Gettysburg	5,916
Salem	30,908	Glassport	8,748
The Dalles	6,266	Greensburg	16,743
		Greenville	8,149

PENNSYLVANIA

		Grove City	6,296
Abington *	20,857	Hanover	13,076
Aliquippa	27,023	Hanover *	16,439
Allentown	96,904	Harrisburg	83,893
Altoona	80,214	Harrison *	13,161
Ambridge	18,968	Haverford *	27,594
Archbald	8,296	Hazleton	38,009
Arnold	10,898	Hollidaysburg	5,910
Ashland	7,045	Homestead	19,041
Ashley	6,371	Honesdale	5,687
Avalon	6,155	Huntingdon	7,170
Bangor	5,687	Indiana	10,050
Beaver	5,641	Jeannette	16,220
Beaver Falls	17,098	Jenkintown	5,024
Bellefonte	5,304	Jersey Shore	5,432
Bellevue	10,488	Johnstown	66,668
Berwick	13,181	Kane	6,133
Bethlehem	58,490	Kingston	20,679
Blairsville	5,002	Kittanning	7,550
Blakely	8,106	Kulpmont	6,159
Bloomsburg	9,799	Lancaster	61,345
Brackenridge	6,400	Lansdale	9,316
Braddock	18,326	Lansdowne	10,837
Bradford	17,691	Lansford	8,710
Brentwood	7,552	Larksville	8,467
Bridgeport	5,904	Latrobe	11,111
Bristol	11,895	Lebanon	27,206
Brownsville	8,015	Lehighton	6,615
Butler	24,477	Lewistown	13,017
Canonsburg	12,599	Lock Haven	10,810

Lower Merion *	39,566
Luzerne	7,082
McAdoo	5,127
McKeesport	55,355
McKees Rocks	17,021
Mahanoy City	13,442
Meadville	18,919
Mechanicsburg	5,709
Media	5,351
Middletown	7,046
Midland	6,373
Millvale	7,811
Milton	8,313
Minersville	8,686
Monaca	7,061
Monessen	20,257
Monongahela City	8,825
Morrisville	5,493
Mount Carmel	17,780
Mount Lebanon *	19,571
Mount Oliver	6,981
Mount Pleasant	5,824
Munhall	13,900
Nanticoke	24,387
Nanty-Glo	6,217
Narberth	5,217
Nazareth	5,721
New Brighton	9,630
New Castle	47,638
New Kensington	24,055
Norristown	38,181
Northampton	9,622
North Braddock	15,679
Oakmont	6,260
Oil City	20,379
Old Forge	11,892
Olyphant	9,252
Palmerton	7,475
Palmyra	5,239
Philadelphia	1,931,334
Phoenixville	12,282
Pitcairn	6,310
Pittsburgh	671,659
Pittston	17,828
Plains *	15,621
Plymouth	15,507
Pottstown	20,194
Pottsville	24,530
Prospect Park	5,100
Punxsutawney	9,482
Quakertown	5,150
Rankin	7,470
Reading	110,568
Ridgway	6,253
Rochester	7,441
St. Clair	6,809
St. Marys	7,653
Sayre	7,569
Schuylkill Haven	6,518
Scottdale	6,493
Scranton	140,404
Sewickley	5,614
Shaler *	11,185
Shamokin	18,810
Sharon	25,622
Sharpsburg	8,202
Sharpsville	5,129
Shenandoah	19,790
Shippensburg	5,244
Somerset	5,430
South Williamsport	6,033
State College	6,226
Steelton	13,115
Stowe *	12,577
Stroudsburg	6,186
Summit Hill	5,406
Sunbury	15,462
Swissvale	15,919
Swoyerville	9,234
Tamaqua	12,486
Tarentum	9,846

Taylor	9,002
Throop	7,382
Titusville	8,126
Turtle Creek	9,805
Tyrone	8,845
Uniontown	21,819
Upper Darby *	56,883
Vandergrift	10,725
Warren	14,891
Washington	26,166
Waynesboro	10,231
West Chester	13,289
West Hazleton	7,523
West Pittston	7,943
West View	7,215
West York	5,590
Wilkes-Barre	86,236
Wilkinsburg	29,853
Williamsport	44,355
Wilmerding	5,662
Wilson	8,217
Windber	9,057
Winton	7,989
Yeadon	8,524
York	56,712

RHODE ISLAND

Barrington *	6,231
Bristol *	11,159
Burrillville *	8,185
Central Falls	25,248
Cranston	47,085
Cumberland *	10,625
East Providence *	32,165
Johnston *	10,672
Lincoln *	10,577
Newport	30,532
North Providence *	12,156
Pawtucket	75,797
Providence	253,504
Warren *	8,158
Warwick	28,757
Westerly *	11,199
West Warwick *	18,188
Woonsocket	49,303

SOUTH CAROLINA

Aiken	6,168
Anderson	19,424
Camden	5,747
Charleston	71,275
Chester	6,392
Clinton	5,704
Columbia	62,396
Conway	5,066
Darlington	6,236
Easley	5,183
Florence	16,054
Gaffney	7,636
Georgetown	5,559
Greenville	34,734
Greenwood	3,020
Hartsville	5,399
Laurens	6,894
Marion	5,746
Newberry	7,510
Orangeburg	10,521
Rock Hill	15,009
Spartanburg	32,249
Sumter	15,874
Union	8,478

SOUTH DAKOTA

Aberdeen	17,015
Brookings	5,346
Huron	10,843
Lead	7,520

Madison	5,018
Mitchell	10,633
Rapid City	13,844
Sioux Falls	40,832
Watertown	10,617
Yankton	6,798

TENNESSEE

Alcoa	5,131
Athens	6,930
Bristol	14,004
Chattanooga	128,163
Clarksville	11,831
Cleveland	11,351
Columbia	10,579
Dyersburg	10,034
Elizabethton	8,516
Greeneville	6,784
Harriman	5,620
Humboldt	5,160
Jackson	24,332
Johnson City	25,332
Kingsport	14,404
Knoxville	111,580
Lebanon	5,950
Maryville	5,609
Memphis	292,942
Morristown	8,050
Murfreesboro	9,495
Nashville	167,402
Paris	6,395
Pulaski	5,314
Shelbyville	6,537
Springfield	6,668
Union City	7,256

TEXAS

Abilene	26,612
Alamo Heights	5,700
Alice	7,792
Amarillo	51,686
Austin	87,930
Bay City	6,594
Beaumont	59,061
Beeville	6,789
Big Spring	12,604
Bonham	6,349
Borger	10,018
Brady	5,002
Breckenridge	5,826
Brenham	6,435
Brownsville	22,083
Brownwood	13,398
Bryan	11,842
Cameron	5,040
Childress	6,464
Cleburne	10,558
Coleman	6,054
Colorado	5,213
Corpus Christi	57,301
Corsicana	15,232
Crystal City	6,529
Cuero	5,474
Dallas	294,734
Del Rio	13,343
Denison	15,581
Denton	11,192
Eagle Pass	6,459
Edinburg	8,718
Electra	5,588
El Paso	96,810
Ennis	7,087
Fort Worth	177,662
Gainesville	9,651
Galveston	60,862
Goose Creek	6,929
Graham	5,175
Greenville	13,995
Harlingen	13,306

Henderson	6,437
Highland Park	10,288
Hillsboro	7,799
Houston	384,514
Huntsville	5,108
Jacksonville	7,213
Kerrville	5,572
Kilgore	6,708
Kingsville	7,782
Lamesa	6,038
Laredo	39,274
Lockhart	5,018
Longview	13,758
Lubbock	31,853
Lufkin	9,567
McAllen	11,877
McKinney	8,555
Marlin	6,542
Marshall	18,410
Mercedes	7,624
Mexia	6,410
Midland	9,352
Mineral Wells	6,303
Mission	5,982
Nacogdoches	7,538
Navasota	6,138
New Braunfels	6,976
Odessa	9,573
Orange	7,472
Palestine	12,144
Pampa	12,895
Paris	18,678
Plainview	8,263
Port Arthur	46,140
Robstown	6,780
Rusk	5,699
San Angelo	25,802
San Antonio	253,854
San Benito	9,501
San Marcos	6,006
Seguin	7,006
Sherman	17,156
Sulphur Springs	6,742
Sweetwater	10,367
Taylor	7,875
Temple	15,344
Terrell	10,481
Texarkana	17,019
Texas City	5,748
Tyler	28,279
University Park	14,458
Uvalde	6,679
Vernon	9,277
Victoria	11,566
Waco	55,982
Waxahachie	8,655
Weatherford	5,924
Weslaco	6,883
West University Place	9,221
Wichita Falls	45,112

UTAH

Brigham	5,641
Logan	11,868
Murray	5,740
Ogden	43,688
Price	5,214
Provo	18,071
Salt Lake City	149,934
South Salt Lake	5,701
Tooele	5,001

VERMONT

Barre	10,909
Bennington	7,628
Brattleboro	9,622
Burlington	27,686
Montpelier	8,006